Sports Collectors Digest
Voice for the Hobby
The hobby's oldest and largest publication

 2008 Standard Catalog of

Collectibles publication partner of Major League Baseball

BASEBALL CARDS

17th Edition

Edited by
Don Fluckinger
and the editors of Sports Collectors Digest® /Tuff Stuff®

"If you'll not settle for anything less than your best, you will be amazed at what you can accomplish."

—Vince Lombardi

©2007 Krause Publications

Published by

krause publications

An Imprint of F+W Publications

700 East State Street • Iola, WI 54990-0001
715-445-2214 • 888-457-2873
www.krausebooks.com

Our toll-free number to place an order or obtain
a free catalog is (800) 258-0929.

ISSN 1935-0546
ISBN-13: 978-0-89689-524-9
ISBN-10: 0-89689-524-6

Designed by: Stacy Bloch

Edited by: Justin Moen

Printed in the United States of America

FOREWORD

Thanks for purchasing the *2008 SCD Standard Catalog of Baseball Cards.* My former colleague Bob Lemke edited the first 16 editions of this book. He might have moved on to another position but I assure you that he's still present here in mind and spirit: Since I took this book over, I've leaned on Bob heavily. He's been an invaluable help in advising me and patiently answering a thousand "what would you do?" questions I've emailed him over the last year.

So for that, I say thanks, Bob. You're a gentlemen and a baseball card scholar.

You'd think that, except for the 2007 issues, there wouldn't be more major league baseball cards to catalog. Wrong! We've added more sets this year and reinstated the entire 1933 Goudey Sport Kings set. Collectors love to send me the mystery cards they've purchased from auction houses, online, or at flea markets and garage sales. Between Bob, the experts on hand at *SCD*, and my contacts in the hobby, I've run down the checklists and values for most of these "new vintage" sets readers have emailed.

Our acknowlegments section overflows with new names and old who added their piece to the catalog. I would like to single out in particular PSA president Joe Orlando, Barry Sloate and Rob Lifson of Robert Edward Auctions for going the extra mile in helping me track down information. Of course, there would be no book without the work of acquisitions editor Paul Kennedy and behind-the-scenes machinations of my editor Justin Moen, who by now knows more about databases than Bill Gates. Joe Clemens and Steve Bloedow of *Tuff Stuff* also did more pricing research than I would have imagined possible. Finally, Jack Doucette deserves a tip of the hat for bringing me to the card collecting hobby.

Lastly, I can't leave out former *SCD* editor Rocky Landsverk, who matched me to this project and convinced the Krause powers that be that I'd tend to Bob Lemke's legacy with the care it deserved. Hope I measured up. Thanks to all.

Enjoy the book and most of all, best of luck in your collecting pursuits. If you find a major-league player card that isn't here, by all means email me at tuffstuff@prospecthillpub.com and I'll start digging all over again.

— Don Fluckinger

ACKNOWLEDGMENTS

Hundreds of individuals have made countless valuable contributions that have been incorporated into the *Standard Catalog of Baseball Cards*. While all cannot be acknowledged, special appreciation is extended to the following principal contributors who have exhibited a special dedication by creating, revising or verifying listings and technical data, reviewing market valuations or providing cards to be illustrated.

Rob Adesso • Ken Agona • Gary Agostino • Lisa Albano • Dan Albaugh • Will Allison • Mark Anker • Ellis Anmuth • Steve Applebaum • Bill Atkinson

Rand Bailey • Bill Ballew • Andy Baran • Gary Bartolett • Judy Bartolett • Bob Bartosz • John Beisiegel • Karen Bell • Dr. Charles E. Belles • Dave Berman • Cathy Black • Jerry A. Blum • Ralph Blunt Jr. • Mike Bodner • Bill Bossert • Bob Bostoff • Brian Boston • Jim Boushley • Mike Boyd • John Brigandi • Scott Brockelman • Lou Brown • Dan Bruner • Greg Bussineau

Billy Caldwell • Len Caprisecca • Tony Carrafiell • Brian Cataquet • Lee Champion • Dwight Chapin • Lou Chericoni • Ryan Christoff • Jim Clarke • Shane Cohen • Rich Cole • Charles Conlon • Eric Cooper • Bill Cornell • Bryan Couling • Bob Crabill • Clyde Cripe • Al Cristafulli • Jim Cumpton • Robert Curtiss

Pete D'Luhosch • Tom Daniels • Stuart Dansinger • James Davis • Dick DeCourcy • Ken Degnan • Dan DeKing • Mike Del Gado • Bill Diebold • Larry Dluhy • Brett Domue • John Dorsey

Curtis Earl • Eric Eichelkraut • Mark Elliott • Shirley Eross • John B. Esch • Joe Esposito • Dan Even • Doak Ewing

Julian Fernandez • David Festberg • Robert Fisk • Jay Finglass • Nick Flaviano • Rick Fleury • Jeff Fritsch • Larry Fritsch

Gary Gagen • Richard Galasso • Tom Galic • Richard R. Gallagher • Chris Gallutia • Tony Galovich • Phillip Garrou • Gary Gatanis • Frank Giffune • Richard Gilkeson • Gerald J. Glasser • Philip Glazer • Keith David Goldfarb • Jack Goodman • Bill Goodwin • Dick Goddard • Howard Gordon • Mike Gordon • Sean Gottlieb • Bob Gray • Wayne Grove • Gerry Guenther • Don Guilbert • Tom Guilfoile

David Hall • Joel Hall • Walter Hall • Gary Hamilton • Tom Harbin • Don Harrison • Rich Hawksley • Herbert Hecht • Bill Henderson • Kathy Henry • Pete Henrici • Steve Hershkowitz • Bob Hicks • Gregg Hitesman • John Hoffman • Dennis Hollenbeck • Jack Horkan • Jim Horne • Brent Horton • Ron Hosmer • Marvin Huck • Brad Hudecek

Bob Ivanjack

Robert Jacobsen • David Jenkins • Donn Jennings • Scott Jensen • Andrew Jerome • Jim Johnston • Stewart Jones • Larry Jordan

Judy Kay • Allan Kaye • Michael Keedy • Frank Keetz • Mark Kemmerle • Rick Keplinger • John King • John Kitleson • Terry Knouse • Bob Koehler • David Kohler • A.F. Kokol • Dan Kravitz

Steve Lacasse • Lee Lasseigne • Mark K. Larson • William Lawrence • Scott Lawson • Richard Leech • Morley Leeking • Tom Leon • Don Lepore • Rod Lethbridge • Scott Letts • David Levin • Stuart Leviton • Howie Levy • Hal Lewis • Rob Lifson • Lew Lipset • Jeff Litteral • Dick Lloyd • Chuck Lobenthal • Leon Luckey

Mark Macrae • Paul Marchant • Robert Marek • Bob Marotto • Aart Martineau • Bob Marquette • Richard Masson • Bill Mastro • Ralph Maya • Dan McKee • Fred McKie • Tony McLaughlin • Don McPherson • John Mehlin • Bill Mendel • H. Dexter • Joe Merkel • Blake Meyer • Louis Middleton • Bob Miller • Jay Miller • Keith Mitchell • J.A. Monaco • Robert Montgomery • Joe Moreno • Brian Morris • Mike Mosier • Scott Mosley • Mike Mowrey • Peter Mudavin • Mark Murphy • David Musser

Frank Nagy • Steve Neimand • Roger Neufeldt • Tim Newcomb • Joe Newman • Bill Nicolls • Chuck Nobriga • Mark Nochta • Wayne Nochta

Bud Obermeyer • Jeff Obermeyer • Keith Olbermann

D.J. Panaia • Joe Pasternack • Marty Perry • Tom Pfirrman • Dan Piepenbrok • Stan Pietruska • Paul Pollard • Harvey Poris

Pat Quinn

Ed Ranson • Fred Rapaport • Steve Rice • Mike Rich • Bob Richardson • Al Richter • Gavin Riley • Ron Ritzler • Tom Reid • Bob Robles • Mike Rodell • Scott Roemer • Mike Rogers • Chris Ronan • Rocky Rosato • Alan Rosen • John Rumierz • Bob Rund • Moe Ryan

Len Samworth • Jon Sands • Kevin Savage • Stephen Schauer • Allan Schoenberger • Dave Schwartz • Robert Scott • Larry Serota • 707 Sports Cards • Jim Sexton • Corey Shanus • Max Silberman • Paul Sjolin • Barry Sloate • Joe Smith • Mark Soltan • John Spalding • Kevin Spears • Gene Speranza • Nigel Spill • Jerry Spillman • David Spivack • Don Steinbach • Dan Stickney • Larry Stone • Ken Stough • Al Strumpf • Doug Stultz • Jim Suckow • Rich Suen • Joe Szeremet

J.J. Teaparty • Erik Teller • Lee Temanson • K.J. Terplak • Mark Theotikos • Dick Tinsley • Gary Tkac • Bud Tompkins • Scott Torrey • Dan Tripper

Rich Unruh • Jack Urban • Glen Van Aken • Frank Van Damme

Geno Wager • Frank Wakefield • Pete Waldman • Eric Waller • Tony Walls • Gary Walter • Frank Ward • Adam Warshaw • Dave Weber • Ken Weimer • Jeff Weiss • Richard Weiss • Dale Weselowski • E.C. Wharton-Tigar • Charles Williamson • Jay Wolt • Frank Wozny • Bill Wright

Rhys Yeakley • Kit Young

Ted Zanidakis

2008 Standard Catalog of
Baseball Cards

HOW TO USE THIS CATALOG

This catalog has been uniquely designed to serve the needs of collectors and dealers at all levels from beginning to advanced. It provides a comprehensive guide to more than 140 years of baseball card issues, arranged so that even the most novice hobbyist can consult it with confidence and ease.

The following explanations summarize the general practices used in preparing this catalog's listings. However, because of specialized requirements which may vary from card set to card set, these must not be considered ironclad. Where these standards have been set aside, appropriate notations are usually incorporated.

ARRANGEMENT

The most important feature in identifying and pricing a baseball card is its set of origin. Therefore the main body of this catalog, covering cards issued from 1867-date, has been alphabetically arranged within specific eras of issue according to the name by which the set is most popularly known to collectors, or by which it can be most easily identified by a person examining a card.

Previous editions of this catalog relied heavily upon card set identification numbers originated in Jefferson Burdick's pioneering *American Card Catalog.* However, since that work was last updated over 40 years ago its numbering system has become arcane and is little used by the present generation of hobbyists. Where practical, sets which were listed in previous editions by their ACC designations have been reclassified alphabetically by a more readily identifiable signpost, such as manufacturer's name. Most of those sets continue to bear the ACC catalog number in the set heading and will be cross-referenced in the table of contents.

Among card issuers that produced sets for more than a single year, their sets are then listed chronologically, from earliest to most recent, again within specific eras.

Within each set, the cards are listed by their designated card number, or in the absence of card numbers, alphabetically according to the last name of the player pictured. Listing numbers found in parentheses indicate the number does not appear on the card. Certain cards which fall outside the parameters of the normal card numbering for a specific set may be found at the beginning or end of the listings for that set.

Listings are generally arranged in two major sections – major league and minor league issues.

MAJOR LEAGUE ISSUES

The main body of the book details major league baseball card issues from 1867 through the first half of 2007, divided into two sections: Vintage (1867-1980) and Modern (1981-date). In general, prior to about 1990, this will include issues that picture one or more baseball players, usually contemporary with their playing days, printed on paper or cardboard in a variety of shapes and sizes and given away as a premium with the purchase of another product or service. After 1990 or so the definition is broadened to remove the restriction of the card as an ancillary product and to include those printed on plastic, wood, metal, etc.

Included within each era's listings are related non-card collectibles featuring baseball players which do not fit under the definition previously given for baseball cards. These include many items on which players are depicted on materials other than paper or cardboard, such as pins, coins, silks, leathers, patches, felts, pennants, metallic ingots, statues, figurines, limited-edition artworks and others.

Also presented herein are foreign issues, one of the growth areas of the baseball card hobby in recent years. These encompass the various issues from countries outside of North America, particularly Latin America. Since the 1920s a variety of baseball cards, stamps and stickers have emanated from the Caribbean, South America and elsewhere chronicling the various winter baseball leagues that have flourished there, often stocked with former and future major league stars and, in the early years, providing the only contemporary cards of many U.S. and Latin Negro Leagues players.

Incorporated into the listings are some modern collectors' issues. There exists within the hobby a great body of cards known as "collectors' issues" (sometimes generically known as "broders") by virtue of their nature of having been produced solely for the hobby card market. These cards and sets are distinguished from "legitimate" issues in not having been created as a sales promotional item for another product or service – bubble gum, soda, snack cakes, dog food, cigarettes, gasoline, etc. This distinction, however, is no longer so easy to make since the early 1990s, when many baseball card issues by even the major national companies began to be sold without an accompanying product.

By their nature, and principally because the person issuing them was always free to print and distribute more of the same if they should ever attain any real value, collectors' issues were generally regarded by the hobby as having little or no premium value. Since the leagues and players' union began to enforce licensing restrictions in the early

1953 Topps Satchell Paige

2002 Upper Deck Ichiro Suzuki

1990s, the nature of collector's issues changed dramatically. The sets that were the work of an individual catering to the hobby market with an issue of relatively limited numbers and basic technology have given way to more sophisticated productions, often marketed to the general public, as well as the hobby.

The distinction between "collectors" and "legitimate" cards may be barely perceptible but is noted whenever possible. Generally, those collectors' emissions share some or all of these characteristics: 1) Prior to around 1990 they were not licensed by the players depicted, nor by their teams or leagues. 2) They were sold as complete sets rather than by pack or as singles. 3) The issue was marketed almost exclusively to the card collecting hobby audience through advertising in trade papers and public sporting press, and within the hobby's dealer network. 4) The cards were sold on a stand-alone basis, that is, not as a premium or adjunct to the sale of another product or service.

MINOR LEAGUE ISSUES (1867-1969)

Prior to 1970 virtually all minor league baseball cards were issued as single cards rather than as complete sets. Like contemporary major league cards they were usually intended as premiums given away with the purchase of goods and services.

The listings which follow offer individual card prices in three grades of preservation to allow accurate valuations of superstar and other special interest cards, along with cards that were short-printed or otherwise are scarce.

IDENTIFICATION

While most modern baseball cards are well identified on front, back or both, as to date and issue, such has not always been the case. In general, the back of the card is more useful in identifying the set of origin than the front. The issuer or sponsor's name will usually appear on the back since, after all, baseball cards were first produced as a promotional item to stimulate sales of other products. As often as not, that issuer's name is the name by which the set is known to collectors and under which it will be found listed in this catalog.

In some difficult cases, identifying a baseball card's general age, if not specific year of issue, can usually be accomplished by studying the biological or statistical information on the back of the card. The last year mentioned in either the biography or stats is usually the year which preceded the year of issue.

Over the years there have been many cards issued that bear no identification features at all with which to pinpoint the issuer. In such cases, they are cataloged by the names under which they are best known in the hobby. Many of the strip-card issues of the 1920s, for example, remain listed under the "W" catalog number where they were originally enumerated in the American Card Catalog.

It is the ultimate goal, through the use of cross listings and more detailed indexes, to allow a person holding a card in his hand to find the catalog listing for that card with the greatest ease.

PHOTOGRAPHS

Wherever possible a photograph of the front and (prior to 1981) back of at least one representative card from most of the sets listed in this catalog has been incorporated into the listings to assist identification. (Persons who can provide sample cards for photography purposes for those sets which are missing photos in this volume are encouraged to contact the editor.)

Photographs have been printed in reduced size. The actual size of cards in each set is usually given in the introductory text preceding its listing, unless the card is the current standard size (2.5" by 3.5").

DATING

The dating of baseball cards by year of issue on the front or back of the card itself is a relatively new phenomenon. In most cases, to accurately determine a date of issue for an unidentified

Sammy Sosa

1990 Upper Deck Sammy Sosa

1954 Fruiterie Saint Louis Tommy Lasorda

Come One... Come All

The PSA Set Registry

Much like the world of grading services, some collectible registries claim to service a particular niche within the hobby, leaving some collectors out in the cold.

At PSA, we service collectors with all types of interests. Whether you collect by year, by team or by player. Whether you collect sports or non-sports. Whether you collect modern or vintage, autographed or game-used, no other registry can provide the diversity that makes the PSA Set Registry$_{SM}$ the largest and most respected in the industry.

The staff at PSA recognizes that different collectors enjoy various types of collectibles.

No matter what you collect, we feel that every collector deserves a place to call their own, a place that they can showcase their collection no matter how big or small. It doesn't matter if your collection is worth $100 or $10,000,000, there is a place where dedicated collectors hang out.

That place is the PSA Set Registry, home to over 28,000 sets and growing.

For more information on how to get your prized collectibles graded by PSA or how to participate on the PSA Set Registry, please visit our website at www.psacard.com or call one of our representatives toll-free at (800) 325-1121.

The Foundation of All Great Collections

card, it must be studied for clues. As mentioned, the biography, career summary or statistics on the back of the card are the best way to pinpoint a year of issue. In most cases, the year of issue will be the year after the last season mentioned on the card.

Luckily for today's collector, earlier generations have done much of the research in determining year of issue for those cards that bear no clues. The painstaking task of matching the players' listed and/or pictured team against their career records often allowed an issue date to be determined.

In some cases, particular card sets were issued over a period of more than one calendar year, but since they are collected together as a single set, their specific year of issue is not important. Such sets will be listed with their complete known range of issue years.

There remain some early issues for which an exact year of issue cannot be reliably pinpointed. In those cases a "best guess" date or one in the middle of the possible range has been used to identify the issue; such cases are usually noted in the introductory text.

NUMBERING

While many baseball card issues as far back as the 1880s have featured card numbers assigned by the issuer to facilitate the collecting of a complete set, the practice has by no means been universal. Even today, not every set bears card numbers.

Logically, those baseball cards that were numbered by their manufacturer are presented in that numerical order within the listings of this catalog whenever possible. In a few cases, complete player checklists were obtained from earlier published sources that did not note card numbers, and so numbers have been arbitrarily assigned. Many other unnumbered issues have been assigned catalog numbers to facilitate their universal identification within the hobby, especially when buying and selling by mail. Among some issues for which the complete checklist remains unknown and for which new discoveries are still being reported, gaps have been left in the assigned numbering to facilitate future additions.

In all cases, numbers that have been assigned, or which otherwise do not appear on the card through error or by design, are shown in this catalog within parentheses. In virtually all cases, unless a more natural system suggested itself by the unique matter of a particular set, the assignment of numbers by the cataloging staff has been done by alphabetical arrangement of the players' last names or the card's principal title.

Significant collectible variations for any particular card are noted within the listings by the application of a suffix letter. In instances of variations, the suffix "a" is assigned to the variation which was created first, when it can be so identified.

NAMES

The identification of a player by full name on the front of his baseball card has been a common practice only since the 1920s. Prior to that, the player's last name and team were the usual information found on the card front.

As a general – though not universally applied – practice, the listings in this volume present the player's name exactly as it appears on the front of the card. If the player's full name only appears on the back, rather than on the front of the card, the listing may correspond to that designation.

A player's name checklisted in **bold italic** type indicates a rookie card as defined later in this introduction.

Cards that contain misspelled first or last names, or even wrong initials, will usually have included in their listings the incorrect information, with a correction accompanying in parentheses. This extends also to cases where the name on the card does not correspond to the player actually pictured.

In some cases, to facilitate efficient presentations, to maintain ease of use for the reader, or to allow for proper computer sorting of data, a player's name or card title may be listed other than as it actually appears on the card.

GRADING

It is necessary that some sort of card grading standard be used so that buyer and seller (especially when dealing through the Internet or by mail) may reach an informed agreement on the value of a card.

Pre-1981 cards are generally priced in the three grades of preservation in which those cards are most commonly encountered in the daily buying and selling in the hobby marketplace. They are listed in grades of Near Mint (NR MT), Excellent (EX) and Very Good (VG), reflecting the basic fact that few cards were able to survive for 25, 50 or even 100 years in close semblance to the condition of their issue.

The pricing of cards in these three conditions will allow readers to accurately price cards which fall in intermediate grades, such as EX-MT, or VG-EX.

Although grades below Very Good are not generally priced in this volume, close approximations of low-grade card values may be figured on the following formula: Good condition cards are valued at about 50% of VG price, with Fair cards about 50% of Good.

Cards in Poor condition have little or no market value except in the cases of the rarest and most expensive cards. In such cases, value has to be negotiated individually.

Modern (1981-date) issues, which have been preserved in top condition in considerable numbers, are listed only in the grade of Near Mint-to-Mint (NM/M). Earlier editions of this book priced such cards under the heading of Mint condition. However, the rise of independent grading services in the past decade and their use of the NM/M designation to describe the vast majority of new card specimens has influenced the marketplace to the extent that only a small percentage of cards, even fresh from the pack, can meet the strict standards for a true Mint example. The switch to a NM/M designation is part of the catalog's commitment to accurately reflect the current conditions of the card market.

As with older cards, values for lower-grade cards from 1981-date may be generally figured by using a figure of 75% of the NM/M price for Near Mint specimens, and 40% of the Mint price for Excellent cards.

For the benefit of the reader, we present herewith the grading guide which was originally formulated in 1981 by *Baseball Cards* magazine and *Sports Collectors Digest*, and has been continually refined since that time.

These grading definitions have been used in the pricing of cards in this book, but they are by no means a universally-accepted grading standard.

The potential buyer of a baseball card should keep that in mind when encountering cards of nominally the same grade, but at a price which differs widely from that quoted in this book.

Ultimately, the collector himself must formulate his own personal grading standards in deciding whether cards available for purchase meet the needs of his own collection.

No collector is required to adhere to the grading standards presented herewith – nor to any other published grading standards.

Mint (MT): A perfect card. Well-centered, with parallel borders that appear equal to the naked eye. Four sharp, square corners. No creases, edge dents, surface scratches, paper flaws, loss of luster, yellowing or fading, regardless of age. No imperfectly printed card – out of register, badly cut or ink flawed – or card stained by contact with gum, wax or other substances can be considered truly Mint even if new out of the pack. Generally, to be considered in Mint

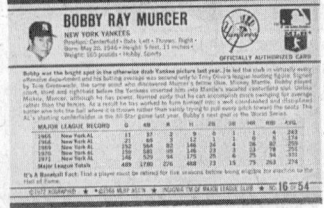

1972 Kellogg's Bobby Murcer (front and back)

condition, a card's borders must exist in a ratio of no greater than 60/40 side to side and top to bottom.

Near Mint/Mint (NM/M): A nearly perfect card. Well-centered, with at least three sharp, square corners. No creases, edge dents, surface scratches, paper flaws, loss of luster, yellowing or fading, regardless of age. No imperfectly printed card – out of register, badly cut or ink flawed – or card stained by contact with gum, wax or other substances can be considered Near Mint/ Mint, even if new out of the pack. Generally, to be considered in NM/M condition, a card's borders must exist in a ratio of no greater than 65/35 side to side and top to bottom.

Near Mint (NR MT): At first glance, a Near Mint card appears perfect; upon closer examination, however, a minor flaw will be discovered. On well-centered cards, at least two of the four corners must be perfectly sharp; the others showing a minor imperfection upon close inspection. A slightly off-center card with one or more borders being noticeably unequal – no worse than in a ratio of 70/30 S/S or T/B – would also fit this grade.

Excellent (EX): Corners are still fairly sharp with only moderate wear. Card borders may be off-center as much as 80/20. No creases. May have very minor gum, wax or product stains, front or back. Surfaces may show slight loss of luster from rubbing across other cards.

Very Good (VG): Show obvious handling. Corners rounded and/or perhaps showing minor creases. Other minor creases may be visible. Surfaces may exhibit loss of luster, but all printing is intact. May show major gum, wax or other packaging stains. No major creases, tape marks or extraneous markings or writing. All four borders visible, though the ratio may be as poor as 95/5. Exhibits honest wear.

Good (G): A well-worn card, but exhibits no intentional damage or abuse. May have major or multiple creases and/or corners rounded well beyond the border. A Good card will generally sell for about 50% the value of a card in Very Good condition.

Fair (F or Fr.): Shows excessive wear, along with damage or abuse. Will show all the wear characteristics of a Good card, along with such damage as thumb tack holes in or near margins, evidence of having been taped or pasted, perhaps small tears around the edges, or creases so heavy as to break the cardboard. Backs may show minor added pen or pencil writing, or be missing small bits of paper. Still, basically a complete card. A Fair card will generally sell for 50% the value of a Good specimen.

Poor (P): A card that has been tortured to death. Corners or other areas may be torn off. Card may have been trimmed, show holes from a paper punch or have been used for BB gun practice. Front may have extraneous pen or pencil writing, or other defacement. Major portions of front or back design may be missing. Not a pretty sight.

In addition to these terms, collectors may encounter intermediate grades, such as VG-EX or EX-MT. These cards usually have characteristics of both the lower and higher grades, and are generally priced midway between those two values.

1959 Topps Yogi Berra

2004 Donruss Jeff Bagwell

With the rise in popularity of third-party authentication/grading services since the mid-1990s, it must be stressed that the grades and corresponding values presented in this book are for "raw" cards – cards which have not been independently graded. Depending on the reputation of the certification firm, cards that have been graded and encased in plastic slabs may sell for a significant premium over the values found here. This is especially true of high-grade specimens of vintage cards that in certified grades of Near Mint/Mint, Mint or Gem Mint may bring multiples of "catalog" value. Even collector-grade vintage cards can command a premium when authenticated, graded and slabbed because potential buyers may feel more secure in such cards' authenticity and freedom from tampering.

ROOKIE CARDS

While the status (and automatic premium value) that a player's rookie card carries has fluctuated in recent years, and though the hobby still has not reached a universal definition of a rookie card, many significant vintage-era rookie cards are noted in this catalog's listings by the use of **_bold italic_** type. Conversely, many significant modern-era rookie cards are noted in this catalog's listings by the use of **RC** or **(RC)**. Beginning with products issued in 2006, cards with an **(RC)** logo indicate the featured player has a rookie card issued prior to that year. For purposes of this catalog, a player's rookie card is considered to be any card in a nationally distributed, licensed Major League base (non-insert) set from a major manufacturer in the first year in which that player appears on a card, regardless of whether that player has yet appeared in a Major League game or is technically a rookie according to MLB definition.

VALUATIONS

Values quoted in this book represent the current retail market at the time of compilation (Summer, 2007). The quoted values are the result of a unique system of evaluation and verification created by the catalog's editors. Utilizing specialized computer analysis and drawing upon recommendations provided through their daily involvement in the publication of the hobby's leading sport collectors' periodicals, as well as the input of consultants, dealers and collectors, each listing is, in the final analysis, the interpretation of that data by one or more of the editors.

It should be stressed, however, that this book is intended to serve only as an aid in evaluating cards; actual market conditions are constantly changing. This is especially true of the cards of current players, whose on-field performance during the course of a season can greatly affect the value of their cards – upwards or downwards. Because of the extremely volatile nature of new card prices

especially high-end issues, we have chosen not to include the very latest releases from the major companies, feeling it is better to have no listings at all for those cards than to have inaccurate values in print. For the same reasons, many 21st Century cards and sets are presented here without pricing. Extremely limited-production (or even unique) cards, often autographs and game-used equipment cards, may not be seen in the hobby market with enough frequency to establish realistic "book" values.

Because this volume is intended to reflect the national market, users will find regional price variances caused by demand differences. Cards of Astros slugger Jeff Bagwell will, for instance, often sell at prices greater than quoted herein at shops and shows in the Houston area. Conversely, his cards may be acquired at a discount from these valuations when purchased on the East or West Coast.

Publication of this book is not intended as a solicitation to buy or sell the listed cards by the editors, publisher or contributors.

Again, the values here are retail prices – what a collector can expect to pay when buying a card from a dealer. The wholesale price, that which a collector can expect to receive from a dealer when selling cards, will be significantly lower.

Many dealers operate on a 100 percent mark-up, generally paying about 50 percent of a card's retail value for cards that they are purchasing for inventory. On some high-demand cards, dealers will pay 100 percent or more of retail value, anticipating continued price increases. Conversely, for many low-demand cards, such as common (non-star) players' cards, dealers may pay as little as 10 percent or even less of retail with many base-brand cards of recent years having no resale value at all.

SET PRICES

Collectors may note that the complete set prices for newer issues quoted in these listings are usually significantly lower than the total of the value of the individual cards that comprise the set. This reflects two factors in the baseball card market. First, a seller is often willing to take a lower composite price for a complete set as a "volume discount" and to avoid carrying in inventory a large number of common-player or other lower-demand cards.

Second, to a degree, the value of common cards can be said to be inflated as a result of having a built-in overhead charge to justify the dealer's time in sorting cards, carrying them in stock and filling orders. This accounts for the fact that even brand new base-brand baseball cards, which cost the dealer around two cents each when bought in bulk, carry individual price tags of five cents or higher.

1971 Topps Steve Garvey

Some set prices shown, especially for vintage cards in top condition, are merely theoretical in that it is unlikely that a complete set exists in that condition. In general among older cards the range of conditions found in even the most painstakingly assembled complete set make the set values quoted useful only as a starting point for price negotiations.

ERRORS/VARIATIONS

It is often hard for the beginning collector to understand that an error on a baseball card, in and of itself, does not necessarily add premium value to that card. It is usually only when the correcting of an error in a subsequent printing creates a variation that premium value attaches to an error.

Minor errors, such as wrong stats or personal data, misspellings, inconsistencies, etc. – usually affecting the back of the card – are very common, especially in recent years. Unless a corrected variation was also printed, these errors are not noted in the listings of

2006 Upper Deck Rookie Foil Gold Val Majewski

2007 Topps Ryan Howard

this book because they are not generally perceived by collectors to have premium value.

On the other hand, major effort has been expended to include the most complete listings ever for collectible variation cards. Many scarce and valuable variations are included in these listings because they are widely collected and often have significant premium value.

In the boom years of the early 1990s, some card companies produced their basic sets at more than one printing facility. This frequently resulted in numerous minor variations in photo cropping and back data presentation. Combined with a general decline in quality control from the mid-1980s through the early 1990s, which allowed unprecedented numbers of uncorrected error cards to be released, this caused a general softening of collector interest in errors and variations. Despite the fact most of these modern variations have no premium value, they are listed here as a matter of record.

COUNTERFEITS/REPRINTS

As the value of baseball cards has risen in the past 25+ years, certain cards and sets have become too expensive for the average collector to obtain. This, along with changes in the technology of color printing, has given rise to increasing numbers of counterfeit and reprint cards.

While both terms describe essentially the same thing – a modern-day copy that attempts to duplicate as closely as possible an original baseball card – there are differences that are important to the collector.

Generally a counterfeit is made with the intention of deceiving somebody into believing it is genuine, and thus paying large amounts of money for it. The counterfeiter takes every pain to try to make his fakes look as authentic as possible.

A reprint, on the other hand, while it may have been made to look as close as possible to an original card, is made with the intention of allowing collectors to buy them as substitutes for cards they may never be otherwise able to afford. The big difference is that a reprint is generally marked as such, usually on the back of the card.

1941 Play Ball "Lefty" Grove

In other cases, like the Topps 1952 reprint set and later Archives issues, the replicas are printed in a size markedly different from the originals, or utilizing current technology that differs from that available in the past. Collectors should be aware, however, that unscrupulous persons will sometimes cut off or otherwise obliterate the distinguishing word – "Reprint," "Copy," – or modern copyright date on the back of a reprint card in an attempt to pass it as genuine.

A collector's best defense against reprints and counterfeits is to acquire a knowledge of the look and feel of genuine baseball cards of various eras and issues.

UNLISTED CARDS

Persons encountering cards which are not listed in this reference should not immediately infer that they have something rare and/or valuable. With hundreds of thousands of baseball cards issued over the past century and thousands more being issued each year, this catalog's comprehensiveness will always remain relative. This is especially true in the area of modern cards and sets released regionally, and the vast universe of foreign and collectors' issues for which coverage has only recently begun. Readers who have cards or sets that are not covered in this edition are invited to correspond with the editor for purposes of adding to the compilation work now in progress. A photocopy or scan of the card's front and back will assist in determining its status. **For questions relating to modern-era cards, contact: Joe Clemens, *Standard Catalog of Baseball Cards*, 700 E. State St., Iola, Wis. 54990; e-mail Joseph.Clemens@fwpubs.com. For questions relating to vintage era cards, contact: Don Fluckinger, *Prospect Hill Publishing*, 32 Montgomery Ave., Nashua, NH 03060-5008; email Don@tuffstuff@prospecthillpub.com.** Major contributions will be acknowledged in future editions.

NEW ISSUES

Because new baseball cards are being issued all the time, the cataloging of them remains an on-going challenge. The editors will attempt to keep abreast of new issues so that they may be added to future editions of this book. Readers are invited to submit news of new issues, especially limited-edition or regionally issued cards, to the editor at the address above.

Abbreviation Key

IS: Interleague Showdown

OPS: Overprinted "Promotional Sample"

ED: Expansion Draft

AS: All-Star

HL: Hit List

RC: Rookie Class

RC or (RC): Rookie Card

UPT: Unlimited Potential/Talent

SF: Star Factor

SP: Short Print

DT: Double Team

GLS: Gold Leaf Stars

CC: Curtain Calls

GLR: Gold Leaf Rookies

TP: Top Performers

FF: Future Foundation

DK: Diamond King

RR: Rated Rookie

DP: Double Print

IA: In Action

PC: Promo Card

SR: Star Rookie

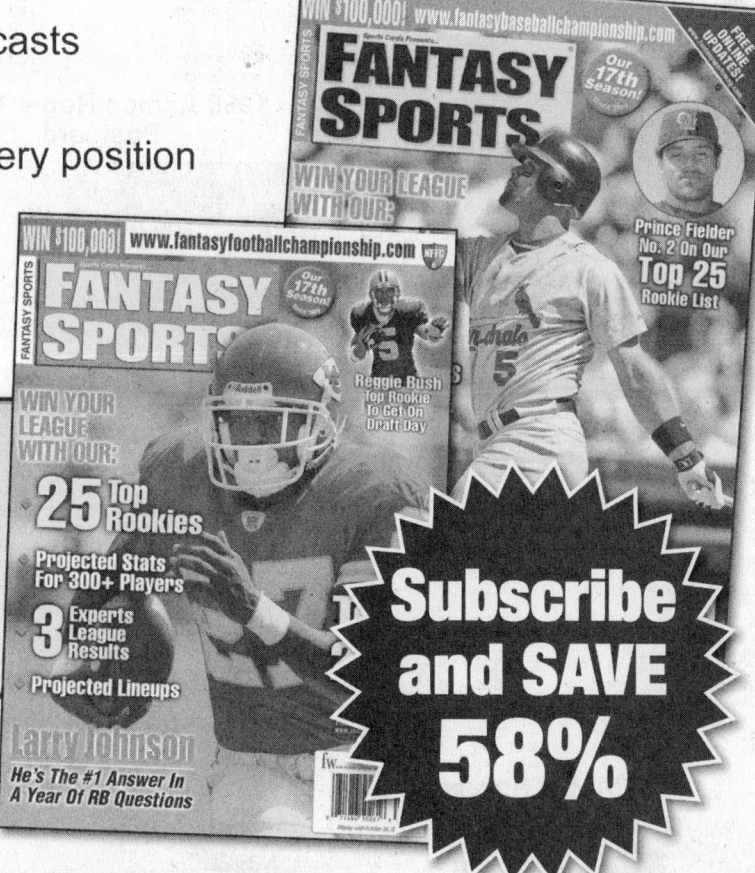

VINTAGE MAJOR LEAGUE CARDS (1869-1980)

The vast majority of cards and collectibles listed in this section were issued between 1869 and 1980 and feature major league players only. The term "card" is used rather loosely as in this context it is construed to include virtually any cardboard or paper product, of whatever size and/or shape, depicting baseball players and issued to stimulate the sales of another product or service.

A

1976 A & P Brewers

The Aaron and Yount cards from this regional issue support the set price. The set was issued by the A & P grocery chain. Oversize - 5-7/8" x 9" - cards (actually printed on semi-gloss paper) were given out at the stores in 1976 in series of four with the purchase of select weekly grocery specials. Players are pictured in tight capless portraits. Each photo has a black facsimile autograph; backs are blank. The unnumbered cards are checklisted here in alphabetical order.

		NM	EX	VG
Complete Set (16):		35.00	17.50	10.50
Common Player:		3.00	1.50	.90
(1)	Henry Aaron	20.00	10.00	6.00
(2)	Pete Broberg	3.00	1.50	.90
(3)	Jim Colborn	3.00	1.50	.90
(4)	Mike Hegan	3.00	1.50	.90
(5)	Tim Johnson	3.00	1.50	.90
(6)	Von Joshua	3.00	1.50	.90
(7)	Sixto Lezcano	3.00	1.50	.90
(8)	Don Money	3.00	1.50	.90
(9)	Charlie Moore	3.00	1.50	.90
(10)	Darrell Porter	3.00	1.50	.90
(11)	George Scott	3.00	1.50	.90
(12)	Bill Sharp	3.00	1.50	.90
(13)	Jim Slaton	3.00	1.50	.90
(14)	Bill Travers	3.00	1.50	.90
(15)	Robin Yount	10.00	5.00	3.00
(16)	County Stadium	3.00	1.50	.90

1976 A & P Royals

Identical in format to the Brewers' set issued around Milwaukee, these 5-7/8" x 9" photos picture players without their caps in posed portraits. The cards were given away four per week with the purchase of selected grocery item specials. Cards have a Players' Associa-

tion logo in the upper-left corner, and a black facsimile autograph on front. Backs are blank. The unnumbered cards are checklisted here alphabetically.

		NM	EX	VG
Complete Set (16):		40.00	20.00	12.00
Common Player:		3.00	1.50	.90
(1)	Doug Bird	3.00	1.50	.90
(2)	George Brett	20.00	10.00	6.00
(3)	Steve Busby	3.00	1.50	.90
(4)	Al Cowens	3.00	1.50	.90
(5)	Al Fitzmorris	3.00	1.50	.90
(6)	Dennis Leonard	3.00	1.50	.90
(7)	Buck Martinez	3.00	1.50	.90
(8)	John Mayberry	3.00	1.50	.90
(9)	Hal McRae	4.50	2.25	1.25
(10)	Amos Otis	4.50	2.25	1.25
(11)	Fred Patek	3.00	1.50	.90
(12)	Tom Poquette	3.00	1.50	.90
(13)	Mel Rojas	3.00	1.50	.90
(14)	Tony Solaita	3.00	1.50	.90
(15)	Paul Splittorff	3.00	1.50	.90
(16)	Jim Wohlford	3.00	1.50	.90

1968 Aamco Roger Maris Postcard

 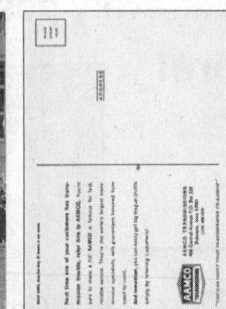

The cited date is approximate on this large-format (about 6" x 9") postcard. The borderless front has a color pose of the reigning home run king with the legend, "It's a real pennant winner!" The postcard format back is directed at auto service professionals, encouraging them to refer transmission problems to a local Aamco facility. A color Aamco logo is at bottom-left.

	NM	EX	VG
Roger Maris	150.00	75.00	45.00

1954 ABC Freight Postcard

So far only one player is known in this black-and-white glossy postcard issue. The front has a posed photo with facsimile autograph. The wide white border at bottom was likely to accomodate an authentic signature. The divided back carries in its upper-left corner the two-line message "You can't miss by playing ball with/ABC Freight Forwarding Corp." However, on the sole known specimen, that message has been obliterated by being overprinted with a decorative black design. Format is 3-1/2" x 5-7/16".

		NM	EX	VG
(1)	Ted Kluszewski/Btg	150.00	75.00	45.00
(2)	Ted Kluszewski/Fielding	150.00	75.00	45.00

1932 Abdulla Tobacco

Babe Ruth, Amerika

Along with several other contemporary ca— issues from Germany, Babe Ruth is the lone repre—sentative from American baseball in this series of 2(cards. Cards are 1-11/16" x 2-1/2" and feature sepi— tone photos on front, with the celebrity's name ar— nation printed in the white border at bottom. Back— are in German and include a card number.

		NM	EX	V
196	Babe Ruth	1,750	875.00	525.•

1949-1950 Acebo y Cia

These small (about 1-1/2" x 1-3/4") Cuban card— were issued in matchboxes, probably over more tha— one season, as some players are known in pho— variations. Fronts have a black-and-white or duoton— photo, bordered, with the player name in plain typ— Backs have player information presented in one — several different styles, or are blank-backed. It — likely this checklist, which includes a significant co— tingent of American players, is not complete.

		NM	EX	V
Common Player:		100.00	50.00	30.•
(1)	Bob Addis	100.00	50.00	30.•
(2)	Luis Aloma	100.00	50.00	30.•
(3)	Ferrel (Ferrell) Anderson	100.00	50.00	30.•
(4)	Bill Antonello	100.00	50.00	30.•
(5)	Mario Arencibia	100.00	50.00	30.•
(6)	Maurice Atwright	100.00	50.00	30.•
(7)	Wesley Bailey	100.00	50.00	30.•
(8)	Vic Barnhart	100.00	50.00	30.•
(9)	Carlos Blanco	100.00	50.00	30.•
(10)	Herberto Blanco	100.00	50.00	30.•
(11)	Adolfo Cabrera	100.00	50.00	30.•
(12)	Emilio Cabrera	100.00	50.00	30.•
(13)	Lorenzo "Chiquitin" Cabrera	100.00	50.00	30.•
(14)	Rafael Villa Cabrera	100.00	50.00	30.•
(15)	Samuel Calderone	100.00	50.00	30.•
(16)	Avelino Canizares	100.00	50.00	30.•
(17)	Clemente "Sungo" Carreras	100.00	50.00	30.•
(18)	Jack Cassini	100.00	50.00	30.•
(19)	Aristonico Cocorreoso	100.00	50.00	30.•
(20)	Carlos Colas	100.00	50.00	30.•
(21)	Kevin (Chuck) Connors	450.00	225.00	135.•
(22)	Sandalio "Potrellilo" Consuegra	125.00	62.00	37.•
(23)	Agustin Cordeiro	100.00	50.00	30.•
(24)	Reinaldo Cordeiro	100.00	50.00	30.•
(25)	Reinaldo Cordeiro	100.00	50.00	30.•

(26)	Alejandro Crespo	100.00	50.00	30.00
(27)	Raymond "Talua" Dandridge	500.00	250.00	150.00
(28)	Jose "Pipo" de la Noval	100.00	50.00	30.00
(29)	Carlos "Yiqui" De Souza	100.00	50.00	30.00
(30)	Mario Diaz	100.00	50.00	30.00
(31)	Lino Donoso	100.00	50.00	30.00
(32)	Claro Duany	100.00	50.00	30.00
(33)	Gumersindo Elba	100.00	50.00	30.00
(34)	Paul (Al) Epperly	100.00	50.00	30.00
(35)	Roberto "Tarzan" Estalella	125.00	65.00	35.00
(36)	Jose Ma. Fernandez	100.00	50.00	30.00
(37)	Jose Ma. Fernandez Jr.	100.00	50.00	30.00
(38)	Rodolfo Fernandez	100.00	50.00	30.00
(39)	Thomas Fine	100.00	50.00	30.00
(40)	Andres Fleitas	100.00	50.00	30.00
(41)	Pedro Formental	100.00	50.00	30.00
(42)	"Sojito" Gallardo	100.00	50.00	30.00
(43)	Chicuelo Garcia	100.00	50.00	30.00
(44)	Manuel "Cocaina" Garcia	150.00	75.00	45.00
(45)	Pablo Garcia	100.00	50.00	30.00
(46)	Silvio Garcia	100.00	50.00	30.00
(47)	Lloyd Gearhart (Reverse image.)	100.00	50.00	30.00
(48)	Lloyd Gearhart (Corrected)	100.00	50.00	30.00
(49)	(Al) Gerheauser	100.00	50.00	30.00
(50)	Albert Gionfrido (Gionfriddo)	125.00	65.00	35.00
(51)	Leonardo Goicochea	100.00	50.00	30.00
(52)	Enrique Gonzalez	100.00	50.00	30.00
(53)	Hiram Gonzalez	100.00	50.00	30.00
(54)	Miguel Angel Gonzalez	125.00	65.00	35.00
(55)	Fermin Guerra	100.00	50.00	30.00
(56)	Wes Hamner	100.00	50.00	30.00
(57)	Eugene Handley	100.00	50.00	30.00
(58)	Rollie Hemsley	100.00	50.00	30.00
(59)	Salvador Hernandez	100.00	50.00	30.00
(60)	Clarence Hicks	100.00	50.00	30.00
(61)	Manuel "Chino" Hidalgo	100.00	50.00	30.00
(62)	Bob Hooper	100.00	50.00	30.00
(63)	Amado Ibanez	100.00	50.00	30.00
(64)	Don Lenhardt	100.00	50.00	30.00
(65)	Vicente Lopez	100.00	50.00	30.00
(66)	Raul Lopez	100.00	50.00	30.00
(67)	"Tony" Lorenzo	100.00	50.00	30.00
(68)	Adolfo Luque	150.00	75.00	45.00
(69)	John Bill Maldovan	100.00	50.00	30.00
(70)	Max Manning	250.00	125.00	75.00
(71)	Conrado Marrero	125.00	65.00	35.00
(72)	Rogelio "Limonar" Martinez/ Pitching	100.00	50.00	30.00
(73)	Rogelio "Limonar" Martinez/ Portrait	100.00	50.00	30.00
(74)	Agapito Mayor	100.00	50.00	30.00
(75)	Lester McCrabb	100.00	50.00	30.00
(76)	Guillermo "Willy" Miranda	125.00	65.00	35.00
(77)	Rene Monteagudo	100.00	50.00	30.00
(78)	Julio "Jiqui" Moreno	100.00	50.00	30.00
(79)	Ernesto Morrilla	100.00	50.00	30.00
(80)	Howie Moss	100.00	50.00	30.00
(81)	Rafael Sam Noble	100.00	50.00	30.00
(82)	Regino Otero	100.00	50.00	30.00
(83)	Oliverio Ortiz	100.00	50.00	30.00
(84)	Roberto Ortiz/Btg	100.00	50.00	30.00
(85)	Roberto Ortiz/Portait	100.00	50.00	30.00
(86)	Pedro Pages	100.00	50.00	30.00
(87)	Leonard Pearson	250.00	125.00	75.00
(88)	Eddie Pellagrin (Pellagrini)	100.00	50.00	30.00
(89)	Conrado Perez	100.00	50.00	30.00
(90)	Damon Phillips	100.00	50.00	30.00
(91)	Jose "Pototo" Piloto	100.00	50.00	30.00
(92)	William Powell	100.00	50.00	30.00
(93)	Al Prendergast	100.00	50.00	30.00
(94)	Napoleon Reyes (Holding bat.)	100.00	50.00	30.00
(95)	Napoleon Reyes (No bat.)	100.00	50.00	30.00
(96)	Donald Richmond	100.00	50.00	30.00
(97)	Hector Rodriguez	100.00	50.00	30.00
(98)	Oscar Rodriguez	100.00	50.00	30.00
(99)	Julio Rojo	100.00	50.00	30.00
(100)	Octavio Rubert	100.00	50.00	30.00
(101)	Arturo Seijas	100.00	50.00	30.00
(102)	Raymond Shore (Arms crossed.)	100.00	50.00	30.00
(103)	Raymond Shore (Pose unrecorded.)	100.00	50.00	30.00
(104)	Ford Smith	100.00	50.00	30.00
(105)	Rene Solis	100.00	50.00	30.00
(106)	Roberto Fernandez Tapanes	100.00	50.00	30.00
(107)	Don Thompson	100.00	50.00	30.00
(108)	Gilberto Torres	100.00	50.00	30.00
(109)	Quincy Trouppe	150.00	75.00	45.00
(110)	Christian Van Cuyk	100.00	50.00	30.00
(111)	John Van Cuyk	100.00	50.00	30.00
(112)	Ben Wade	100.00	50.00	30.00
(113)	Archie Wilson	100.00	50.00	30.00
(114)	Edward Wright	100.00	50.00	30.00
(115)	Adrian Zabala	100.00	50.00	30.00

1970 Action Cartridge

This set of boxes with baseball players' pictures on them was issued by Action Films Inc. of Mountain View, Calif., in 1970-71. The boxes, measuring 2-5/8" x 6" x 1" deep, contained 8mm film cartridges of various professional athletes demonstrating playing tips. The movie series include 12 baseball players. Other sports represented were football, golf, tennis, hockey and skiing, a total of 40, in all. Boxes feature color player portraits inside an oval and include a facsimile autograph. The values listed are for complete boxes or player panels, without the movie cartridge.

		NM	EX	VG
Complete Set (12):		275.00	135.00	85.00
Common Player:		7.50	3.75	2.25
Box W/Cartridge: 2X				
Viewer:		60.00	30.00	20.00
1	Tom Seaver	40.00	20.00	12.00
2	Dave McNally	7.50	3.75	2.25
3	Bill Freehan	7.50	3.75	2.25
4	Willie McCovey	25.00	12.50	7.50
5	Glenn Beckett, Don Kessinger	7.50	3.75	2.25
6	Brooks Robinson	30.00	15.00	9.00
7	Hank Aaron	60.00	30.00	18.00
8	Reggie Jackson	45.00	22.50	13.50
9	Pete Rose	50.00	25.00	15.00
10	Lou Brock	25.00	12.50	7.50
11	Willie Davis	7.50	3.75	2.25
12	Rod Carew	25.00	12.50	7.50

1933-1934 Adams Hat Stores

In the early 1930s a men's haberdasher issued a series of colorized 8" x 10" portrait photos of baseball players and other celebrities dressed in suit-and-tie and wearing a hat. Above a facsimile autograph on front is a testimonial for Adams Hats. Backs are stamped, "Property of Adams Hat Stores, Inc." The location of the issuing store or stores in unknown. Only the ballplayers are listed here.

		NM	EX	VG
Complete Set (3):		1,750	875.00	525.00
Common Player:		600.00	300.00	180.00
(1)	Carl Hubbell	600.00	300.00	180.00
(2)	Lefty Gomez	600.00	300.00	180.00
(3)	John McGraw	600.00	300.00	180.00

1910 A Fan For A Fan

These cardboard novelties were produced by the American Tobacco Co. About 7-1/4 in diameter, the bursting baseball and portrait are printed in color with a facsimile autograph. The handle is about 5" long. The back is blank. The known fans are listed here alphabetically; the checklist is likely incomplete.

		NM	EX	VG
Complete Set (5):		30,000	16,000	9,750
Common Player:		2,400	1,200	725.00
(1)	Frank Baker	4,500	2,250	1,350
(2)	Hal Chase	3,600	1,800	1,100
(3)	Ty Cobb	15,000	7,500	4,500
(4)	Larry Doyle	2,400	1,200	725.00
(5)	Christy Mathewson	5,500	2,750	1,650

1939 African Tobacco

The unlikely venue of the "other" U.S.A. (Union of South Africa) is the provenance of this rare Babe Ruth card. The African Tobacco Company issued a set of 100 cards in a series titled "The World of Sport." The cards were issued in both a large (2-1/4" x 3-1/4") and small (1-3/4" x 2-1/2") format. Fronts have a black-and-white photo of Ruth, with a white border all around. Backs are printed in both English and Afrikaner.

		NM	EX	VG
34	Babe Ruth/Large	1,250	625.00	375.00
34	Babe Ruth/Small	1,250	625.00	375.00

1924-1925 Aguilitas Segundas

This set is known to collectors as Aguilitas Segundas for the top line of the ad on back. In reality, this second series cigarette card issue was issued several years before the Aguilitas first series counterpart. About 1-1/2" x 2-3/8", the cards have round black-and-white player portrait photos in a debossed rectangular area on glossy stock. Beneath the photo is a player name or nickname, with "BASE BALL" below. The ballplayers are a subset of a 900-card issue which included movie and stage stars, soccer players, boxers and other subjects. All baseball players are known within the numerical range of 841 through 899, though only four cards are known above #880, and none between #880-895. The known ballplayers comprise 44, many of whom were stars of the Negro Leagues, including several Hall of Famers and some who appear on no other career-contemporary cards. Cards are checklisted with the name as shown on the card, further identification, where necessary, is listed. parenthetically. Many surviving specimens show evidence of having been glued into an album which largely accounts for their survival in the area's hot, humid climate. Examples are rarely seen in condition approaching Excellent.

		NM	EX	VG
Common Player:		220.00	120.00	65.00
841	(Pablo "Champion") Mesa	220.00	120.00	65.00
842	A. (Armando) Marsans	250.00	125.00	75.00
843	C. (Cristobal) Torriente	7,500	2,250	1,350
844	Merito Acosta	220.00	120.00	65.00
845	Cheo Ramos	220.00	120.00	65.00
846	Joe (John Henry "Pop") Lloyd	5,000	2,750	1,650
847	(Herman Matias) Rios	220.00	120.00	65.00
848	(Lucas) Boada	220.00	120.00	65.00
849	(Jose) Mendez	6,000	1,750	1,000

		NM	EX	VG
850	(Valentin) Dreke	350.00	175.00	100.00
851	(Eugenio) Morin	220.00	120.00	65.00
852	Mayari (Esteban "Mayari" Montalvo)	250.00	125.00	75.00
853	(Valentin) Dreke	350.00	175.00	105.00
854	(Julio) Rojo	220.00	120.00	65.00
855	(Rafael) Almeida	250.00	125.00	75.00
856	(Emilio) Palmero	220.00	120.00	65.00
857	(Adolfo) Luque	800.00	250.00	150.00
858	(Isidro) Fabre	250.00	125.00	75.00
859	(Manuel) Cueto	220.00	120.00	65.00
860	Dibu (Pedro Dibut)	220.00	120.00	65.00
861	Cheo Ramos	220.00	120.00	65.00
862	(Jesse) Hubbard	750.00	375.00	225.00
863	Kakin (Gonzalez)	220.00	120.00	65.00
864	(Jose Maria) Fernandez	220.00	120.00	65.00
865	(Snake) Henry	450.00	225.00	135.00
866	Cruje (Ernie Krueger)	450.00	225.00	135.00
867	(Manuel) Parrado	220.00	120.00	65.00
868	(Chuck) Dressen	250.00	125.00	75.00
869	(Oscar) Charleston	10,000	3,500	2,150
870	Sam (John Henry "Pop") Lloyd	10,000	2,750	1,650
871	Mc. Key (Raleigh "Biz" Mackey)	6,000	2,250	1,350
872	P. (Eusebio "Papo") Gonzalez	220.00	120.00	65.00
873	(Clint) Thomas	600.00	300.00	180.00
874	(Dobie) Moore	600.00	300.00	180.00
875	(Frank) Duncan	600.00	300.00	180.00
876	O. (Oscar) Rodriguez	220.00	120.00	65.00
877	Lopito (Jose "Lopito" Lopez)	200.00	100.00	60.00
878	E. (Eustaquio "Bombin") Pedroso	1,000	500.00	300.00
879	(Dick) Lundy	6,000	1,375	825.00
880	Sirike (Valentin "Sirique" Gonzalez)	220.00	120.00	65.00
895	(Oscar) Tuero	220.00	120.00	65.00
897	(Alejandro) Oms	1,200	600.00	360.00
898	Peter (Jesse Petty)	250.00	125.00	75.00
899	(Danny) Clark	220.00	120.00	65.00

1926-1927 Aguilitas

Uniforms worn by some of the players indicate this set was produced after the related series known as "Segundas," or Second Series. The baseball players - all Cuban nationals - are among 100 athletes (including soccer players and boxers) in a 900-card multi-subject set issued in packs of Aguilitas cigarettes. The cards are printed in black-and-white on glossy stock. On front is a large square portrait or action pose. In the bottom border is "BASE-BALL" with the player name and position below. Names as shown on the cards are presneted in this checklist, with further identification as necessary provided parenthetically. Several of the cards are duplicated in the series with different card numbers. Like most contemporary Latin American issues, surviving examples are seldom found in high-grade and often with evidence of having been mounted in an album.

		NM	EX	VG
Common Player:		165.00	85.00	50.00
751	Cheo Hernandez	165.00	85.00	50.00
752	(Jose Maria) Fernandez	200.00	100.00	60.00
756	R. (Ricardo) Torres	165.00	85.00	50.00
759	Jacinto Calvo	165.00	85.00	50.00
761	E. (Emilio) Palmero	165.00	85.00	50.00
763	Champion (Pablo) Mesa	250.00	125.00	75.00
769	C. (Carlos) Zarza	165.00	85.00	50.00
771	Fernando Rios	165.00	85.00	50.00
772	J. (Joseito) Rodriguez	165.00	85.00	50.00
774	(Juanelo) Mirabal (Same as #824.)	250.00	125.00	75.00
776	L. (Lalo) Rodriguez	165.00	85.00	50.00
777	A. (Adolfo) Luque	350.00	175.00	100.00
778	Alejandro Oms	3,500	1,250	750.00
779	(Armando) Marsans (Same as #829.)	375.00	185.00	110.00
782a	A. (Alfredo) Cabrera	165.00	85.00	50.00
782b	Daniel Blanco (Same as #832.)	165.00	85.00	50.00
787	B. (Bartolo) Portuando	250.00	125.00	75.00
791	A. (Agustin) Navarro	165.00	85.00	50.00
796	R. (Raphael "Busta") Quintana	165.00	85.00	50.00
797	(Roberto) Puig (Same as #847.)	165.00	85.00	50.00
817	(Oscar) Levis	165.00	85.00	50.00
819	Raul Atan	165.00	85.00	50.00
821	(Jose) Pepin Perez	165.00	85.00	50.00
822	(Isidro) Fabre	200.00	100.00	60.00

		NM	EX	VG
823	(Bienvenido "Hooks") Jimenez	250.00	125.00	75.00
824	(Juanelo) Mirabal (Same as #774.)	250.00	125.00	75.00
825	Tomas Calvo	165.00	85.00	50.00
826	(Pelayo) Chacon	250.00	125.00	75.00
829	(Armando) Marsans (Same as #779.)	375.00	185.00	110.00
832	Daniel Blanco (Same as #782.)	165.00	85.00	50.00
836	(Valentin) Dreke	250.00	125.00	75.00
838	(Jose) Echarri	165.00	85.00	50.00
839	Miguel Angel (Gonzalez)	300.00	150.00	90.00
841	(Oscar) Estrada	300.00	150.00	90.00
846	Acostica (Jose Acosta)	300.00	150.00	90.00
847	(Roberto) Puig (Same as #797.)	165.00	85.00	50.00
849	(Cesar) Alvarez	165.00	85.00	50.00

1954 Alaga Syrup Willie Mays Postcard

The year of issue on this one-card set is approximate. In 3-1/4" x 5-1/2" format the black-and-white card has a borderless portrait on front with a facsimile autograph. Back has an ad for Alaga Syrup, along with standard postcard elements.

		NM	EX	VG
(1)	Willie Mays	300.00	150.00	90.00

1944-45 Albertype Hall of Fame Plaque Postcards - Type 1

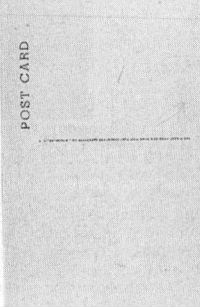

From 1944-1952 Albertype was the official producer of the Baseball Hall of Fame's postcards available for public sale. The 3-1/2" x 5-1/2" black-and-white cards depict the bronze plaque of each inductee. Fronts have a white border. Postcard-style backs have a bit of player data and identification of the specific producer. In the first type of Albertype plaque postcards, issued 1944-45, the line of type beneath the plaque photo has an abbreviation for New York. Later Albertypes spelled out the state name. The unnumbered cards are checklisted here alphabetically.

		NM	EX	VG
Complete Set (38):		800.00	400.00	240.00
Common Player:		20.00	10.00	6.00
(1)	G.C. Alexander	25.00	12.50	7.50
(2)	Adrian Anson	20.00	10.00	6.00
(3)	Roger Bresnahan	20.00	10.00	6.00
(4)	Dan Brouthers	20.00	10.00	6.00
(5)	Morgan Bulkeley	20.00	10.00	6.00
(6)	Alexander Cartwright	20.00	10.00	6.00
(7)	Henry Chadwick	20.00	10.00	6.00
(8)	Fred Clarke	20.00	10.00	6.00
(9)	Ty Cobb	40.00	20.00	12.00
(10)	Eddie Collins	20.00	10.00	6.00
(11)	Jimmy Collins	20.00	10.00	6.00
(12)	Charles A. Comiskey	20.00	10.00	6.00
(13)	Candy Cummings	20.00	10.00	6.00
(14)	Ed Delahanty	20.00	10.00	6.00
(15)	Hugh Duffy	20.00	10.00	6.00
(16)	Buck Ewing	20.00	10.00	6.00
(17)	Lou Gehrig	50.00	25.00	15.00
(18)	Rogers Hornsby	20.00	10.00	6.00
(19)	Hughie Jennings	20.00	10.00	6.00
(20)	Ban Johnson	20.00	10.00	6.00
(21)	Walter Johnson	30.00	15.00	9.00
(22)	Willie Keeler	20.00	10.00	6.00
(23)	King Kelly	20.00	10.00	6.00
(24)	Nap Lajoie	20.00	10.00	6.00
(25)	Kenesaw Landis	20.00	10.00	6.00
(26)	Connie Mack	20.00	10.00	6.00
(27)	Christy Mathewson	30.00	15.00	9.00
(28)	John McGraw	20.00	10.00	6.00
(29)	Jim O'Rourke	20.00	10.00	6.00
(30)	Chas. Radbourn	20.00	10.00	6.00
(31)	Wilbert Robinson	20.00	10.00	6.00
(32)	Babe Ruth	65.00	32.00	19.50
(33)	George Sisler	20.00	10.00	6.00
(34)	Al Spalding	20.00	10.00	6.00
(35)	Tris Speaker	20.00	10.00	6.00
(36)	Honus Wagner	30.00	15.00	9.00
(37)	George Wright	20.00	10.00	6.00
(38)	Cy Young	30.00	15.00	9.00

1946-52 Albertype Hall of Fame Plaque Postcards - Type 2

From 1944-1952 Albertype was the official producer of the Baseball Hall of Fame's postcards available for public sale. The 3-1/2" x 5-1/2" black-and-white cards depict the bronze plaque of each inductee. Fronts have a white border. Postcard-style backs have a bit of biographical data and identification of the specific issuer. In the second series of Albertype plaque postcards, issued 1946-52, the line of type beneath the plaque photo spells out the New York state name. The unnumbered cards are checklisted here alphabetically. Those cards found only in this series are noted with an asterisk. Because the Foxx and Ott cards were first issued in 1951, and the Paul Waner, Heilmann and 1864 Knickerboker Nine in 1952, they are scarcer than those issued earlier.

		NM	EX	VG
Complete Set (63):		1,325	675.00	425.00
Common Player:		20.00	10.00	6.00
(1)	G.C. Alexander	25.00	12.50	7.50
(2)	Adrian Anson	20.00	10.00	6.00
(3)	Roger Bresnahan	20.00	10.00	6.00
(4)	Dan Brouthers	20.00	10.00	6.00
(5)	Mordecai Brown (*)	25.00	12.50	7.50
(6)	Morgan Bulkeley	20.00	10.00	6.00
(7)	Jesse Burkett (*)	25.00	12.50	7.50
(8)	Alexander Cartwright	20.00	10.00	6.00
(9)	Henry Chadwick	20.00	10.00	6.00
(10)	Frank Chance (*)	25.00	12.50	7.50
(11)	Jack Chesbro (*)	25.00	12.50	7.50
(12)	Fred Clarke	20.00	10.00	6.00
(13)	Ty Cobb	40.00	20.00	12.00
(14)	Mickey Cochrane (*)	25.00	12.50	7.50
(15)	Eddie Collins	20.00	10.00	6.00
(16)	Jimmy Collins	20.00	10.00	6.00
(17)	Charles A. Comiskey	20.00	10.00	6.00
(18)	Candy Cummings	20.00	10.00	6.00
(19)	Ed Delahanty	20.00	10.00	6.00
(20)	Hugh Duffy	20.00	10.00	6.00
(21)	Johnny Evers (*)	25.00	12.50	7.50
(22)	Buck Ewing	20.00	10.00	6.00
(23)	James E. (Jimmy) Foxx (*)	45.00	22.00	13.50
(24)	Frankie Frisch (*)	25.00	12.50	7.50
(25)	Lou Gehrig	50.00	25.00	15.00
(26)	Charlie Gehringer (*)	25.00	12.50	7.5
(27)	Clark Griffith (*)	25.00	12.50	7.5
(28)	Lefty Grove (*)	25.00	12.50	7.5
(29)	Harry Heilmann (*)	40.00	20.00	12.0
(30)	Rogers Hornsby	20.00	10.00	6.0
(31)	Carl Hubbell (*)	25.00	12.50	7.5
(32)	Hughie Jennings	20.00	10.00	6.0
(33)	Ban Johnson	20.00	10.00	6.0
(34)	Walter Johnson	30.00	15.00	9.0
(35)	Willie Keeler	20.00	10.00	6.0
(36)	King Kelly	20.00	10.00	6.0
(37)	Nap Lajoie	20.00	10.00	6.0
(38)	Kenesaw Landis	20.00	10.00	6.0
(39)	Connie Mack	20.00	10.00	6.0
(40)	Christy Mathewson	30.00	15.00	9.0
(41)	Tommy McCarthy (*)	25.00	12.50	7.5
(62)	Joe McGinnity (*)	25.00	12.50	7.5
(43)	John McGraw	20.00	10.00	6.0

Captions:

A LUQUE (PICHER) — SERIE ARTISTICA CIGARROS "AGUILITAS" Obsequio a sus favorecedores No. 751

1954 Alaga Syrup Willie Mays Postcard — "Willie Mays says: I was raised on ALAGA Syrup."

JACK ROOSEVELT ROBINSON — BROOKLYN N.L. 1947 TO 1956

		NM	EX	VG
(44)	Kid Nichols (*)	25.00	12.50	7.50
(45)	Jim O'Rourke (*)	20.00	10.00	6.00
(46)	Mel Ott (*)	35.00	17.50	10.50
(47)	Herb Pennock (*)	25.00	12.50	7.50
(48)	Ed Plank (*)	25.00	12.50	7.50
(49)	Chas. Radbourn (*)	20.00	10.00	6.00
(50)	Wilbert Robinson	20.00	10.00	6.00
(51)	Babe Ruth	65.00	32.00	19.50
(52)	George Sisler	20.00	10.00	6.00
(53)	Al Spalding	20.00	10.00	6.00
(54)	Tris Speaker	20.00	10.00	6.00
(55)	Joe Tinker (*)	25.00	12.50	7.50
(56)	Pie Traynor (*)	25.00	12.50	7.50
(57)	Rube Waddell (*)	25.00	12.50	7.50
(58)	Honus Wagner	30.00	15.00	9.00
(59)	Ed Walsh (*)	25.00	12.50	7.50
(60)	Paul Waner (*)	35.00	17.50	10.50
(61)	George Wright	20.00	10.00	6.00
(62)	Cy Young	30.00	15.00	9.00
(63)	Knickerbocker Nine 1864	35.00	17.50	10.50

1970 Carl Aldana Orioles

Belanger

Little is known about the distribution or origin of this 12-card regional set, which was available in 1970 in the Baltimore area. Measuring 3-1/4" x 2-1/8", the unnumbered cards picture members of the Baltimore Orioles and include two poses of Brooks Robinson. The cards feature line drawings of the players surrounded by a plain border. The player's last name appears below the portrait sketch. The set was named after Carl Aldana, who supplied the artwork for the cards.

		NM	EX	VG
Complete Set (12):		125.00	65.00	40.00
Common Player:		12.00	6.00	3.50
(1)	Mark Belanger	12.00	6.00	3.50
(2)	Paul Blair	12.00	6.00	3.50
(3)	Mike Cuellar	12.00	6.00	3.50
(4)	Ellie Hendricks	12.00	6.00	3.50
(5)	Dave Johnson	12.00	6.00	3.50
(6)	Dave McNally	12.00	6.00	3.50
(7)	Jim Palmer	45.00	22.50	13.50
(8)	Boog Powell	25.00	12.50	7.50
(9)	Brooks Robinson (Diving - face showing.)	40.00	20.00	12.00
(10)	Brooks Robinson (Diving - back showing.)	40.00	20.00	12.00
(11)	Frank Robinson	60.00	30.00	18.00
(12)	Earl Weaver	15.00	7.50	4.50

1971 Carl Aldana

Lang

Devoid of any indication of when produced or by whom, this set of obscure players of the 1940s and 1950s was a collectors' issue from Carl Aldana circa 1971. The cards are blank-backed, about 2-1/8" x 2-/4". Fronts have a red background with an artwork player portrait in blue. The player's last name and card umber are in dark blue, his first name in white. For a ew of the players, this is their only known baseball card.

		NM	EX	VG
Complete Set (16):		125.00	60.00	37.50
Common Player:		10.00	5.00	3.00
	Wally Hood	10.00	5.00	3.00
	Jim Westlake	10.00	5.00	3.00
	Stan McWilliams	10.00	5.00	3.00
	Les Fleming	10.00	5.00	3.00
	John Ritchey	10.00	5.00	3.00
	Steve Nagy	10.00	5.00	3.00
	Ken Gables	10.00	5.00	3.00

		NM	EX	VG
8	Maurice Fisher	10.00	5.00	3.00
9	Don Lang	10.00	5.00	3.00
10	Harry Malmburg (Malmberg)	10.00	5.00	3.00
11	Jack Conway	10.00	5.00	3.00
12	Don White	10.00	5.00	3.00
13	Dick Lajeskie	10.00	5.00	3.00
14	Walt Judnich	10.00	5.00	3.00
15	Joe Kirrene	10.00	5.00	3.00
16	Ed Sauer	10.00	5.00	3.00

1940s Alerta Antonio Alcalde Premium Pictures

There are still gaps in the hobby's knowledge of this late-1940s/early-1950s Cuban issue. Evidently a premium used in a contest conducted by a newspaper or sports periodical, these pictures are printed on semi-gloss paper in an 8" x 11" format. Featured on front are black-and-white posed action or portrait photos. The team name and symbol are above and a portrait, presumably of Antonio, is at bottom. Pictures are highlighted by color graphics: blue for Almendares, green for Cienfuegos, red for Havana and orange for Marianao. Backs are blank, but are sometimes seen with a round rubber-stamped "Alerta" logo or red boxed "ANTONIO, ALCALDE." The unnumbered pictures are listed here alphabetically within team. The pictures include many American players and those who spent time in the major leagues.

		NM	EX	VG
Complete Set (70):		2,000	1,000	400.00
Common Player:		30.00	15.00	6.00
	ALMENDARES SCORPIONS			
(1)	Bill Antonello	35.00	17.50	7.00
(2)	Francisco Campos	35.00	17.50	7.00
(3)	Avelino Canizares	30.00	15.00	6.00
(4)	Yiqui De Souza	30.00	15.00	6.00
(5)	Rodolfo Fernandez	30.00	15.00	6.00
(6)	Andres Fleitas	30.00	15.00	6.00
(7)	Al Gionfriddo	35.00	17.50	7.00
(8)	Fermin Guerra	35.00	17.50	7.00
(9)	Bob Hooper	35.00	17.50	7.00
(10)	Vincente Lopez	30.00	15.00	6.00
(11)	Conrado Marrero	35.00	17.50	7.00
(12)	Agapito Mayor	30.00	15.00	6.00
(13)	Willy Miranda	35.00	17.50	7.00
(14)	Rene Monteagudo	35.00	17.50	7.00
(15)	Roberto Ortiz	35.00	17.50	7.00
(16)	Hector Rodriguez	35.00	17.50	7.00
(17)	Octavio Rubert	30.00	15.00	6.00
(18)	Rene Solis	30.00	15.00	6.00
	CIENFUEGOS ELEPHANTS			
(1)	Bob Addis	35.00	17.50	7.00
(2)	Sam Calderone	35.00	17.50	7.00
(3)	Jack Cassini	35.00	17.50	7.00
(4)	Alejandro Crespo	35.00	17.50	7.00
(5)	Paul (Al) Epperly	35.00	17.50	7.00
(6)	Thomas Fine	35.00	17.50	7.00
(7)	Pedro Formental (Formenthal)	30.00	15.00	6.00
(8)	Francisco Gallardo	30.00	15.00	6.00
(9)	Lloyd Gearhart	35.00	17.50	7.00
(10)	Leonardo Goicochea	30.00	15.00	6.00
(11)	Salvador Hernandez	35.00	17.50	7.00
(12)	Clarence (Buddy) Hicks	35.00	17.50	7.00
(13)	Max Manning	45.00	22.00	9.00
(14)	San (Ray) Noble	35.00	17.50	7.00
(15)	Regino Otero	35.00	17.50	7.00
(16)	Pedro Pages	30.00	15.00	6.00
(17)	Napoleon Reyes	35.00	17.50	7.00
(18)	Ernie Shore	35.00	17.50	7.00
(19)	Adrian Zabala	35.00	17.50	7.00
(1)	Ferrell Anderson	35.00	17.50	7.00
(2)	Wess Bailey	30.00	15.00	6.00
(3)	Vic Barnhart	35.00	17.50	7.00
(4)	Herberto Blanco	30.00	15.00	6.00
(5)	Emilio Cabrera	30.00	15.00	6.00
(6)	Pedro Formental (Formenthal)	30.00	15.00	6.00
(7)	Al Gerheauser	35.00	17.50	7.00
(8)	Miguel Angel Gonzalez	60.00	30.00	12.00
(9)	Chino Hidalgo	30.00	15.00	6.00
(10)	Jimmy Lenhart	30.00	15.00	6.00
(11)	Adolfo Luque	60.00	30.00	12.00
(12)	Max Manning	45.00	22.50	9.00
(13)	Julio Moreno	35.00	17.50	7.00
(14)	Lenox Pearson	45.00	22.50	9.00
(15)	Don Richmond	35.00	17.50	7.00
(16)	John Ford Smith	30.00	15.00	6.00
(17)	Don Thompson	35.00	17.50	7.00

		NM	EX	VG
(18)	Gilberto Torres	35.00	17.50	7.00
	MARIANAO TIGERS			
(1)	Mario Arencibia	30.00	15.00	6.00
(2)	Carlos Blanco	30.00	15.00	6.00
(3)	Chiquitin Cabbera	30.00	15.00	6.00
(4)	Sandalio Consuegra	35.00	17.50	7.00
(5)	Reinaldo Cordeiro	30.00	15.00	6.00
(6)	Talua (Ray) Dandridge	350.00	175.00	75.00
(7)	Mario Diaz	30.00	15.00	6.00
(8)	Claro Duany	35.00	17.50	7.00
(9)	Roberto Estalella	35.00	17.50	7.00
(10)	Chicuelo Garcia	30.00	15.00	6.00
(11)	Wesley Hamner	35.00	17.50	7.00
(12)	Rollie Hemsley	35.00	17.50	7.00
(13)	Amado Ibanez	30.00	15.00	6.00
(14)	Limonar (Rogelio) Martinez	35.00	17.50	7.00
(15)	Don Phillips	30.00	15.00	6.00
(16)	Bartholomew (Jim) Prendergast	35.00	17.50	7.00
(17)	John Trouppe	35.00	17.50	7.00

1904 Allegheny Card Co.

By definition the rarest card issue of the early 20th Century is this baseball game set featuring only National League players. It is thought that the sole known boxed set was produced as a prototype and never actually reached distribution. The issue contains 104 player cards and a "Ball Counter" card for each team. Cards are in playing-card format, about 2-1/2" x 3-1/2" with rounded corners. Backs are printed in red with baseball equipment pictured. Fronts are printed in blue with a circular player portrait at center. Team name is at top, with player's last name (occasionally with initials and occasionally misspelled) beneath. The unique boxed set was discovered in the late 1980s. It was sold at auction in 1991 for $26,400, and again in 1995 for $11,000, after which it was broken up for individual card sales. The checklist is presented here in alphabetical order. All cards appear to have been hand-cut.

		NM	EX	VG
Common Player:		1,500	750.00	450.00
(1)	Ed Abbaticchio	1,500	750.00	450.00
(2)	Harry Aubrey	1,500	750.00	450.00
(3)	Charlie Babb	1,500	750.00	450.00
(4)	George Barclay	1,500	750.00	450.00
(5)	Shad Barry	1,500	750.00	450.00
(6)	Bill Beagen (Bergen)	1,500	750.00	450.00
(7)	Ginger Beaumont	1,500	750.00	450.00
(8)	Jake Beckley	2,500	875.00	525.00
(9)	Frank Bowerman	1,500	750.00	450.00
(10)	Dave Brain	1,500	750.00	450.00
(11)	Kitty Bransfield	1,500	750.00	450.00
(12)	Roger Bresnahan	2,500	875.00	525.00
(13)	Mordecai Brown	2,500	875.00	525.00
(14)	George Browne	1,500	750.00	450.00
(15)	Al Buckenberger	1,500	750.00	450.00
(16)	Jimmy Burke	1,500	750.00	450.00
(17)	Fred Carisch	1,500	750.00	450.00
(18)	Pat Carney	1,500	750.00	450.00
(19)	Doc Casey	1,500	750.00	450.00
(20)	Frank Chance	3,000	875.00	525.00
(21)	Fred Clarke	2,500	875.00	525.00
(22)	Dick Cooley	1,500	750.00	450.00
(23)	Bill Dahlen	1,750	750.00	450.00
(24)	Tom Daly	1,500	750.00	450.00
(25)	Charlie Dexter	1,500	750.00	450.00
(26)	Johnny Dobbs	1,500	750.00	450.00
(27)	Mike Donlin	1,500	750.00	450.00
(28)	Patsy Donovan	1,500	750.00	450.00
(29)	Red Dooin	1,500	750.00	450.00
(30)	Klondike Douglas (Douglass)	1,500	750.00	450.00
(31)	Jack Doyle	1,500	750.00	450.00
(32)	Bill Duggleby	1,500	750.00	450.00
(33)	Jack Dunn	1,500	750.00	270.00
(34)	Johnny Evers	3,000	875.00	525.00
(35)	John Farrel (Farrell)	1,500	750.00	450.00
(36)	Tim Flood	1,500	750.00	450.00
(37)	Chick Fraser	1,500	750.00	450.00
(38)	Ned Garver	1,500	750.00	450.00
(39)	Doc Gessler	1,500	750.00	450.00
(40)	Billy Gilbert	1,500	750.00	450.00
(41)	Kid Gleason	2,500	750.00	450.00
(42)	Ed Greminger (Gremminger)	1,500	750.00	450.00
(43)	Jim Hackett	1,500	750.00	450.00
(44)	Noodles Hahn	1,500	750.00	450.00
(45)	Ed. Hanlon	2,500	875.00	525.00
(46)	Jack Harper	1,500	750.00	450.00
(47)	Rudy Hulswitt	1,500	750.00	450.00
(48)	Fred Jacklitsch	1,500	750.00	450.00
(49)	Davy Jones	1,500	750.00	450.00
(50)	Oscar Jones	1,500	750.00	450.00
(51)	Bill Keister	1,500	750.00	450.00

(52)	Joe Kelley	2,500	875.00	525.00
(53)	Brickyard Kennedy	1,500	750.00	450.00
(54)	Johnny Kling	1,500	750.00	450.00
(55)	Otto Kruger (Krueger)	1,500	750.00	450.00
(56)	Tommy Leach	1,500	750.00	450.00
(57)	Sam Leever	1,750	875.00	525.00
(58)	Bobby Lowe	1,500	750.00	450.00
(59)	Carl Lundgren	1,500	750.00	450.00
(60)	Christy Mathewson	8,000	2,000	1,200
(61)	Tom McCreery	1,500	750.00	450.00
(62)	Chappie McFarland	1,500	750.00	450.00
(63)	Dan McGann	1,500	750.00	450.00
(64)	Iron Man McGinnity	2,500	875.00	525.00
(65)	John McGraw	2,500	875.00	525.00
(66)	Jock Menefee	1,500	750.00	450.00
(67)	Sam Mertes	1,500	750.00	450.00
(68)	Fred Mitchell	1,500	750.00	450.00
(69)	Pat Moran	1,500	750.00	450.00
(70)	Ed Murphy	1,500	750.00	450.00
(71)	Jack O'Neill	1,500	750.00	450.00
(72)	Mike O'Neill	1,500	750.00	450.00
(73)	Heinie Peitz	1,500	750.00	450.00
(74)	Ed Phelps	1,500	750.00	450.00
(75)	Deacon Phillippe	1,500	750.00	450.00
(76)	Togie Pittinger	1,500	750.00	450.00
(77)	Ed Poole	1,500	750.00	450.00
(78)	Tommy Raub	1,500	750.00	450.00
(79)	Bill Reidy	1,500	750.00	450.00
(80)	Claude Ritchie	1,500	750.00	450.00
(81)	Lew Ritter	1,500	750.00	450.00
(82)	Frank Roth	1,500	750.00	450.00
(83)	Jack Ryan	1,500	750.00	450.00
(84)	Jimmy Scheckard (Sheckard)	1,500	750.00	450.00
(85)	Jimmy Sebring	7,500	2,000	1,200
(86)	Frank Selee	1,500	750.00	450.00
(87)	Cy Seymour	1,500	750.00	450.00
(88)	Harry Smith	1,500	750.00	450.00
(89)	Homer Smoot	1,500	750.00	450.00
(90)	Tully Sparks	1,500	750.00	450.00
(91)	Joe Stanley	1,500	750.00	450.00
(92)	Harry Steinfeldt	1,500	750.00	450.00
(93)	Sammy Strang	1,500	750.00	450.00
(94)	Jack Suthoff (Sutthoff)	1,500	750.00	450.00
(95)	Jack Taylor	1,500	750.00	450.00
(96)	Luther Taylor	1,750	875.00	525.00
(97)	Roy Thomas	1,500	750.00	450.00
(98)	Joe Tinker	1,750	875.00	525.00
(99)	Fred Tinney (Tenney)	1,500	750.00	450.00
(100)	Honus Wagner	10,000	2,000	1,200
(101)	Jack Warner	1,500	750.00	450.00
(102)	Jake Weimer	1,500	750.00	450.00
(103)	Vic Willis	1,750	875.00	525.00
(104)	Harry Wolverton	1,500	750.00	450.00
(105)	Boston Ball Counter	165.00	80.00	50.00
(106)	Brooklyn Ball Counter	165.00	80.00	50.00
(107)	Chicago Ball Counter	165.00	80.00	50.00
(108)	Cincinnati Ball Counter	165.00	80.00	50.00
(109)	New York Ball Counter	165.00	80.00	50.00
(110)	Philadelpia Ball Counter	165.00	80.00	50.00
(111)	Pittsburgh Ball Counter	165.00	80.00	50.00
(112)	St. Louis Ball Counter	165.00	80.00	50.00

1888 Allen & Ginter World's Champions (N28)

This 50-card set was titled "The World Champions" and includes 10 baseball players and 40 other sports personalities such as John L. Sullivan and Buffalo Bill Cody. The approximately 1-1/2" x 2-3/4" cards were inserted in boxes of Allen & Ginter cigarettes. The card fronts are color lithographs on white card stock, and are considered among the most attractive cards ever produced. All card backs have a complete checklist for this unnumbered set, which includes six eventual Hall of Famers.

		NM	EX	VG
Complete Set (10):		27,000	14,500	8,100
Common Player:		850.00	425.00	250.00
(1)	Adrian C. Anson	6,000	2,500	1,500
(2)	Chas. W. Bennett	1,000	425.00	250.00
(3)	R.L. Caruthers	1,000	425.00	250.00
(4)	John Clarkson	2,500	925.00	550.00
(5)	Charles Comiskey	3,000	1,300	760.00
(6)	Capt. John Glasscock	1,000	425.00	250.00
(7)	Timothy Keefe	2,500	875.00	500.00
(8)	Mike Kelly	4,000	1,500	900.00
(9)	Joseph Mulvey	1,000	425.00	250.00
(10)	John Ward	2,500	875.00	500.00

1888 Allen & Ginter World's Champions Album (A16)

By redeeming 50 of the coupons found in boxes of A&G cigarettes, a lithographed album could be obtained in which to house the 50 cards of The World's Champions, Series 1 (N28). About 6" x 8", the album features an ornately decorated cover reproducing the cards of the day's top athletes, John L. Sullivan and Monte Ward. The back cover is blank. Inside, secured by means of string ties at three places, are 12 dual-sided color pages on which to glue the cards in the series. The album had its own designation in the American Card Catalog, A16.

	NM	EX	VG
World's Champions Album (A16)	4,000	2,000	1,200

1888 Allen & Ginter World's Champions (N29)

Building on the success of its first series of tobacco cards, Allen & Ginter issued a second series of "World Champions" in 1888. Once again, 50 of these approximately 1-1/2" x 2-3/4" color cards were produced, in virtually the same format. Only six baseball players are included in this set. The most obvious difference from the first series cards is the absence of the Allen & Ginter name on the card fronts.

		NM	EX	VG
Complete Set (6):		8,500	4,250	2,500
Common Player:		950.00	360.00	280.00
(1)	Wm. Ewing	2,750	1,000	785.00
(2)	Jas. H. Fogarty	950.00	360.00	280.00
	(Middle initial actually G.)			
(3)	Charles H. Getzin (Getzien)	950.00	360.00	280.00
(4)	Geo. F. Miller	950.00	360.00	280.00
(5)	John Morrell (Morrill)	1,050	400.00	295.00
(6)	James Ryan	950.00	360.00	280.00

1888 Allen & Ginter World's Champions Album (A17)

By redeeming 50 of the coupons found in boxes of A&G cigarettes, a lithographed album could be obtained in which to house the 50 cards of The World's Champions, Series 2 (N29). About 6" x 8", the album features a handsomely decorated cover of a trumpeteer. The back cover is also in color with A&G's pipe-smoking man logo. Inside, secured by means of string ties at three places, are 12 dual-sided color pages on which to glue the cards in the series. The album had its own designation in the American Card Catalog, A16.

	NM	EX	VG
World's Champions Album (A17)	3,500	1,750	900.00

1888 Allen & Ginter World's Champions (N43)

Presumably issued in a larger-than-standard cigarette package, the 50 cards designated N43 in the "American Card Catalog" are enhanced versions of the Allen & Ginter World's Champions (N29) series of 1888. As with the N29 set, six of the athletes in N43 are baseball players. The larger cards measure about 3-1/4" x 2-7/8" compared to the 1-1/2" x 2-3/4" size of the N29s. The larger format allows for the use of baseball-related color lithography to the right and left of the central player portrait. Like the N29 cards, backs of the N43 A&Gs present the entire "Series Two" checklist along with advertising of the Richmond tobacco company. Only the baseball players are cataloged here.

		NM	EX	VG
Complete Set (6):		24,000	12,000	7,000
Common Player:		3,500	1,350	850.00
(1)	Wm. Ewing	6,500	2,500	1,550
(2)	Jas. H. Fogarty	3,500	1,350	850.00
	(Middle initial actually G.)			
(3)	Charles H. Getzin (Getzien)	3,500	1,350	850.00
(4)	Geo. F. Miller	3,500	1,350	850.00
(5)	John Morrell (Morrill)	3,500	1,575	975.00
(6)	James Ryan	3,500	1,350	850.00

1888 Allen & Ginter Girl Baseball Players (N48, N508)

The Pitcher

At least three different brands of cigarette advertising can be found on the several different styles of photographic cards depicting women in baseball uniforms. About 1-1/2" x 2-5/8", the cards picture models, rather than real ballplayers. The sepia-toned full-length photos are usually captioned with a position and a number and have a small square or other device advertising a particular brand. Some Dixie and Virginia Brights brand cards are known with advertising on back but most cards are blank-backed. As many as 36 different photos are thought to exist.

	NM	EX	V
Ad Backs: 2X			
Common Player	650.00	325.00	200.0

1946-1947 Almanaque Deportivo

Former and future Major Leaguers mix with Negro Leaguers and Caribbean stars in this issue. Apparently sold in sheets of four, well-cut example of these cards measure a nominal 1-7/8" x 2-1/2" and are printed in color on thin paper. Player identification is on the back of the card, usually with career notes and a large advertisement from one of many different sponsors. A colorful album was issued to house the set. Like all Cuban cards of the era, specimens surviving in grades of VG or better are scarce.

		NM	EX	VG
Complete Set (160):		6,000	3,000	1,800
Common Player:		35.00	17.50	10.00
Album:		400.00	200.00	120.00
A-1	Adolfo Luque	60.00	30.00	20.00
A-2	Tomas de la Cruz	35.00	17.50	10.00
A-3	Roberto Ortiz	45.00	22.50	13.50
A-4	Evelio Martinez	35.00	17.50	10.00
A-5	Jess Jessup	90.00	45.00	27.50
A-6	Santos Amaro	35.00	17.50	10.00
A-7	Rene Gonzalez	35.00	17.50	10.00
A-8	Buck O'Neil	625.00	310.00	185.00
A-9	J. (Lefty) Gaines	90.00	45.00	27.50
A-10	Max Lanier	45.00	22.50	13.50
A-11	George Hausmann	35.00	17.50	10.00
A-12	Avelino Canizares	35.00	17.50	10.00
A-13	Calampio Leon	35.00	17.50	10.00
A-14	Conrado Marrero	50.00	25.00	15.00
A-15	Alberto Leal	35.00	17.50	10.00
A-16	Lloyd Davenport	90.00	45.00	27.50
A-17	Teodoro Oxamendi	35.00	17.50	10.00
A-18	Santiago Ulrich	35.00	17.50	10.00
A-19	Lazaro Salazar	100.00	50.00	30.00
A-20	Cheo Ramos	35.00	17.50	10.00
A-21	Jorge Comellas	35.00	17.50	10.00
A-22	Agapito Mayor	35.00	17.50	10.00
A-23	Hector Rodriguez	45.00	22.50	13.50
A-24	Joe Williams	35.00	17.50	10.00
A-25	Andres Fleitas	35.00	17.50	10.00
C-1	Martin Dihigo	500.00	250.00	150.00
C-2	Alejandro Carrasquel	35.00	17.50	10.00
C-3	Adrian Zabala	35.00	17.50	10.00
C-4	Jimmy Roy	35.00	17.50	10.00
C-5	Napoleon Reyes	80.00	40.00	25.00
C-6	Stanislas Bread	35.00	17.50	10.00
C-7	Roland Gladu	35.00	17.50	10.00
C-8	Roy Zimmerman	35.00	17.50	10.00
C-9	Max Manning	125.00	62.50	37.50
C-10	Myron Hayworth	35.00	17.50	10.00
C-11	Pedro Miro	35.00	17.50	10.00
C-12	Jose Luis Colas	35.00	17.50	10.00
C-13	Conrado Perez	35.00	17.50	10.00
C-14	Luis Tiant Sr.	45.00	22.50	13.50
C-15	Ramon Heredia	35.00	17.50	10.00
C-16	Vinicio Garcia	35.00	17.50	10.00
C-17	(Walt) Nothe	35.00	17.50	10.00
C-18	Danny Gardella	35.00	17.50	10.00
C-19	Alejandro Crespo	60.00	30.00	20.00
C-20	Ray Noble	35.00	17.50	10.00
C-21	Pedro Pages	35.00	17.50	10.00
F-1	Napoleon y C. Blanco/Action	35.00	17.50	10.00
F-2	Chanquilon y H. Rodriguez/Action	35.00	17.50	10.00
F-3	Estalella y Fleitas/Action	35.00	17.50	10.00
F-4	Castano y Kimbro/Action	35.00	17.50	10.00
H-1	Miguel Angel Gonzalez	55.00	27.50	16.50
H-2	Pedro (Natilla) Jimenez	35.00	17.50	10.00
H-3	Fred Martin	35.00	17.50	10.00
H-4	James Lamarque	80.00	40.00	25.00
H-5	Salvador Hernandez	35.00	17.50	10.00
H-6	S. (Hank) Thompson	50.00	25.00	15.00
H-7	Antonio Ordenana	35.00	17.50	10.00
H-8	Manuel Garcia	35.00	17.50	10.00
H-9	Alberto Hernandez	35.00	17.50	10.00
H-10	Terry McDuffie	45.00	22.50	13.50
H-11	Louis Frank Klein	35.00	17.50	10.00
H-12	Herberto Blanco	35.00	17.50	10.00
H-13	H.(Henry) Kimbro	150.00	75.00	45.00
H-14	Rene Monteagudo	35.00	17.50	10.00
H-15	Lennox Pearson	100.00	50.00	30.00
H-16	Carlos Blanco	35.00	17.50	10.00
H-17	Pedro Formental	55.00	27.50	16.50
H-18	William Bell	35.00	17.50	10.00
H-19	Raul Navarro	35.00	17.50	10.00
H-20	Lazaro Medina	35.00	17.50	10.00
I-1	Julio Moreno	35.00	17.50	10.00
I-2	Daniel Parra	35.00	17.50	10.00
I-3	Rogelio Martinez	35.00	17.50	10.00
I-4	J. Antonio Zardon	35.00	17.50	10.00
I-5	Julian Acosta	35.00	17.50	10.00
I-6	Orlando Suarez	35.00	17.50	10.00
I-7	Manuel Hidalgo	35.00	17.50	10.00
I-8	Fermin Guerra	35.00	17.50	10.00
I-9	Regino Otero	35.00	17.50	10.00
I-10	Jorge Juan Torres	35.00	17.50	10.00
I-11	Valeriano Fano	35.00	17.50	10.00
I-12	Amado Ibanez	35.00	17.50	10.00
I-13	"Atares" Garcia	35.00	17.50	10.00
I-14	Armando Gallart	35.00	17.50	10.00

L-15	Perdo Dunabeitia	35.00	17.50	10.00
L-16	Oscar del Calvo	35.00	17.50	10.00
L-17	Johnny Davis	100.00	50.00	30.00
L-18	Emilio Cabrera	35.00	17.50	10.00
L-19	Lee Holleman	35.00	17.50	10.00
L-20	Antonio Napoles	35.00	17.50	10.00
L-21	Pedro Diaz	35.00	17.50	10.00
L-22	Lazaro Bernal	35.00	17.50	10.00
L-23	Hector Arago	35.00	17.50	10.00
L-24	Oscar Garmendia	35.00	17.50	10.00
L-25	Barney Serrell	90.00	45.00	27.50
L-26	Armando Marsans	55.00	27.50	16.50
L-27	Mario Diaz	35.00	17.50	10.00
L-28	Raymond Dandridge	350.00	175.00	105.00
L-29	Leon Tredway	35.00	17.50	10.00
L-30	Orestes Perera	35.00	17.50	10.00
L-31	Armando Vazquez	35.00	17.50	10.00
L-32	Cleveland Clark	50.00	25.00	15.00
L-33	Johnny Williams	90.00	45.00	27.50
L-34	Clarence Iott	35.00	17.50	10.00
L-35	Gilberto Torres	35.00	17.50	10.00
L-36	George Brown	35.00	17.50	10.00
L-37	Wayne Johnson	35.00	17.50	10.00
L-38	Miguel Angel Carmona	35.00	17.50	10.00
L-39	Leovigildo Xiques	35.00	17.50	10.00
L-40	Rafael Rivas	35.00	17.50	10.00
L-41	Joaquin Gutierrez	35.00	17.50	10.00
L-42	Miguel Lastra	35.00	17.50	10.00
L-43	Francisco Quicutis	35.00	17.50	10.00
L-44	Silvio Garcia	90.00	45.00	27.50
L-45	Angel Fleitas	35.00	17.50	10.00
L-46	Eddy Chandler	35.00	17.50	10.00
L-47	Gilberto Castillo	35.00	17.50	10.00
L-48	Isidoro Leon	35.00	17.50	10.00
L-49	Antonio Rodriguez	35.00	17.50	10.00
L-50	Laniel Hooker	90.00	45.00	27.50
L-51	Charles Perez	35.00	17.50	10.00
L-52	Ruben Garcia	35.00	17.50	10.00
L-53	Raquel Antunez	35.00	17.50	10.00
L-54	Claro Duany	45.00	22.50	13.50
L-55	Bucker (Booker) McDaniels	90.00	45.00	27.50
L-56	Francisco Jimenez	35.00	17.50	10.00
L-57	Luis Minsal	35.00	17.50	10.00
L-58	Rogelio Linares	35.00	17.50	10.00
L-59	Isasio Gonzalez	35.00	17.50	10.00
L-60	Manolo Parrado	35.00	17.50	10.00
L-61	Jose Maria Fernandez	35.00	17.50	10.00
L-62	Rogelio Valdes	35.00	17.50	10.00
L-63	R. Franco	35.00	17.50	10.00
L-64	J. Cedan	35.00	17.50	10.00
L-65	Jacinto Roque	35.00	17.50	10.00
L-66	Pablo Garcia	35.00	17.50	10.00
M-1	Pipo de la Noval	35.00	17.50	10.00
M-2	J. Valenzuela	35.00	17.50	10.00
M-3	Oliverio Ortiz	35.00	17.50	10.00
M-4	Antonio Castanos	35.00	17.50	10.00
M-5	Sandalio Consuegra	45.00	22.50	13.50
M-6	(Jim) Lindsey	35.00	17.50	10.00
M-7	Roberto Estalella	35.00	17.50	10.00
M-8	Lino Donoso	35.00	17.50	10.00
M-9	Paul Calvert	35.00	17.50	10.00
M-10	Gilberto Valdivia	35.00	17.50	10.00
M-11	Orestes Minoso	125.00	65.00	37.50
M-12	J. Cabrera	35.00	17.50	10.00
M-13	Manuel Godinez	35.00	17.50	10.00
M-14	Frank Casanovas	35.00	17.50	10.00
M-15	Roberto Avila	60.00	30.00	20.00
M-16	Pedro Orta	35.00	17.50	10.00
M-17	Feliciano Castro	35.00	17.50	10.00
M-18	Mario Arencibia	35.00	17.50	10.00
M-19	Antonio Diaz	35.00	17.50	10.00
M-20	Aristonico Correoso	35.00	17.50	10.00
M-21	Angel Gonzalez	35.00	17.50	10.00
M-22	Murray Franklin	35.00	17.50	10.00
M-23	Francisco Campos	35.00	17.50	10.00
M-24	Angel Castro	35.00	17.50	10.00

1910 All Star Base-Ball

This rare set was issued circa 1910 by candy maker J.H. Dockman & Son. The cards, measuring approximately 1-7/8" x 3-3/8", were printed on the front and back of boxes of candy sold as "All Star Base-Ball Package." There are two players on each box; one on front (with a thumbnail notch at top), the other on back. The cards consist of drawings that bear no resemblance to the player named. In fact, the artwork on these cards crudely reproduces the images from the T3 Turkey Red cabinet series, giving a different player's name to each of the borrowed images. Many are found which were cut from the box immediately below the "PACKAGE" line, while others were cut to the full size of the panel. Values shown here presume the latter format.

		NM	EX	VG
Complete Set (24):		45,000	22,500	10,000
Common Player:		1,700	825.00	460.00
(1)	Johnny Bates	1,700	825.00	460.00
(2)	Heinie Beckendorf	1,700	825.00	460.00
(3)	Joe Birmingham	1,700	825.00	460.00
(4)	Roger Bresnahan	2,400	1,200	720.00
(5)	Al Burch	1,700	825.00	460.00
(6)	Donie Bush	1,700	825.00	460.00
(7)	Frank Chance	2,400	1,200	720.00
(8)	Ty Cobb	4,000	2,000	1,200
(9)	Wid Conroy	1,700	825.00	460.00
(10)	Jack Coombs	1,700	825.00	460.00
(11)	George Gibson	1,700	825.00	460.00
(12)	Dick Hoblitzel	1,700	825.00	460.00
(13)	Johnny Kling	1,700	825.00	460.00
(14)	Frank LaPorte	1,700	825.00	460.00
(15)	Ed Lennox	1,700	825.00	460.00
(16)	Connie Mack	2,400	1,200	720.00
(17)	Christy Mathewson	4,065	2,030	1,250
(18)	Matty McIntyre	1,700	825.00	460.00
(19)	Al Schweitzer	1,700	825.00	460.00
(20)	Jimmy Sheckard	1,700	825.00	460.00
(21)	Bill Sweeney	1,700	825.00	460.00
(22)	Terry Turner	1,700	825.00	460.00
(23)	Hans Wagner	3,250	1,625	1,000
(24)	Harry Wolter	1,700	825.00	460.00

1950 All-Star Baseball "Pin-Ups"

This set of ten 7" diameter black-and-white player photos was issued in the form of a booklet, with the individual pictures perforated to be punched out. Each picture has a hole at the top for hanging. The front and back cover of the book are identical and picture Ted Williams, along with a list of the players inside. Backs of each player picture have how-to-tips for playing a specific position, hitting, base stealing, etc. Published by Garden City Publishing Co., Inc., the book carried a cover price of 50 cents. The unnumbered pictures are checklisted here alphabetically.

		NM	EX	VG
Complete Book:		1,250	625.00	375.00
Complete Set, Singles (10):		800.00	400.00	240.00
Common Player:		25.00	12.50	7.50
(1)	Joe DiMaggio	200.00	100.00	60.00
(2)	Jim Hegan	25.00	12.50	7.50
(3)	Gil Hodges	75.00	37.50	22.50
(4)	George Kell	35.00	17.50	10.00
(5)	Ralph Kiner	45.00	22.50	13.50
(6)	Stan Musial	100.00	50.00	30.00
(7)	Mel Parnell	25.00	12.50	7.50
(8)	Phil Rizzuto	75.00	37.50	22.50
(9)	Jackie Robinson	150.00	75.00	45.00
(10)	Ted Williams	150.00	75.00	45.00

1954 All-Star Photo Pack

The complete checklist for this series of 6" x 8-3/4" blank-back, black-and-white player photos is unknown. The method of distribution is also speculative, though it is most likely they were sold in photo packs at concession stands. Photos, mostly posed action shots, are bordered in white and have the player name in a white strip near the bottom.

		NM	EX	VG
Complete Set (24):		400.00	200.00	120.00
Common Player:		10.00	5.00	3.00
(1)	Bobby Avila	10.00	5.00	3.00
(2)	Ernie Banks	25.00	12.50	7.50
(3)	Larry "Yogi" Berra	25.00	12.50	7.50
(4)	Ray Boone	10.00	5.00	3.00
(5)	Roy Campanella	25.00	12.50	7.50
(6)	Alvin Dark	10.00	5.00	3.00
(7)	Mike Garcia	10.00	5.00	3.00
(8)	Al Kaline	20.00	10.00	6.00
(9)	Ralph Kiner	15.00	7.50	4.50
(10)	Ted Kluszewski	15.00	7.50	4.50
(11)	Harvey Kuenn	10.00	5.00	3.00
(12)	Mickey Mantle	90.00	45.00	27.50
(13)	Ed Mathews	20.00	10.00	6.00
(14)	Willie Mays	50.00	25.00	15.00
(15)	Orestes Minoso	12.50	6.25	3.75
(16)	Stan Musial	35.00	17.50	10.00
(17)	Don Newcombe	12.50	6.25	3.75
(18)	Allie Reynolds	12.50	6.25	3.75
(19)	Robin Roberts	15.00	7.50	4.50
(20)	Eddie Robinson	10.00	5.00	3.00
(21)	Jackie Robinson	45.00	22.50	13.50
(22)	Al Schoendienst	15.00	7.50	4.50
(23)	Duke Snider	20.00	10.00	6.00
(24)	Ted Williams	80.00	40.00	24.00

1949 All Stars Photo Pack

This set of "American and National League All Stars" player pictures is comprised of 6-1/4" x 9" black-and-white photos bordered in white with a simulated signature printed on front. Backs are blank. The set came in a red, black and white paper envelope with several of the pictures shown on front and red stars for decoration. The unnumbered pictures are listed here alphabetically.

		NM	EX	VG
Complete Set (20):		375.00	185.00	110.00
Common Player:		12.50	6.00	4.00
(1)	Luke Appling	17.50	9.00	5.00
(2)	Lou Boudreau	17.50	9.00	5.00
(3)	Dom DiMaggio	15.00	7.50	4.50
(4)	Joe DiMaggio	60.00	30.00	18.00
(5)	Bobby Doerr	17.50	9.00	5.00
(6)	Bob Feller	25.00	12.50	7.50
(7)	Joe Gordon	12.50	6.00	4.00
(8)	Tommy Henrich	12.50	6.00	4.00
(9)	George Kell	17.50	9.00	5.00
(10)	Ralph Kiner	17.50	9.00	5.00
(11)	Bob Lemon	17.50	9.00	5.00
(12)	Marty Marion	12.50	6.00	4.00
(13)	Stan Musial	35.00	17.50	10.00
(14)	Don Newcomb (Newcombe)	17.50	9.00	5.00
(15)	Pee Wee Reese	25.00	12.50	7.50
(16)	Phil Rizzuto	25.00	12.50	7.50
(17)	Jackie Robinson	45.00	22.50	13.50
(18)	Enos Slaughter	17.50	9.00	5.00
(19)	Vern Stephens	12.50	6.00	4.00
(20)	Ted Williams	45.00	22.50	13.50

1971 Allstate Insurance

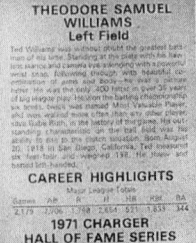

This four-card series was distributed as part of an internal sales promotion for Allstate Insurance. Graphic artist Ray Lending, an Allstate employee, created the 2-1/2" x 3-1/4" cards in duo-tone black and green on white. Card fronts show the players in batting stance, with the player name in one of the upper corners and the "Hall of Fame Series" logo printed across the bottom of the card. The card backs carry the player's full name and position, followed by a brief career summary, biography, and Career Highlights chart listing major league totals. "1971 Charger" and "Hall of Fame Series" are printed at the bottom of the card back. 8,000 sets were distributed.

		NM	EX	VG
Complete Set (4):		400.00	200.00	120.00
Common Player:		50.00	25.00	15.00
(1)	Ty Cobb	50.00	25.00	15.00
(2)	Stan Musial	50.00	25.00	15.00
(3)	Babe Ruth	200.00	100.00	60.00
(4)	Ted Williams	150.00	75.00	45.00

1894 Alpha Photo-Engraving Baltimore Orioles

The rarest baseball card set of the 1890s (each card is known in only a single example) is the Baltimore Orioles team set issued by The Alpha Photo-Engraving Co. of that city. The round-corner 2-3/8" x 3-7/16" cards feature black-and-white photos of the National League champions in formalwear. Last-name identification is in a strip below the photo and a white border surrounds both. On the red-and-white backs a large ad for the producer is at center, while small baseball batter figures are in each corner surrounded by a leafy background. The unnumbered cards are checklisted here alphabetically, though the list may not be complete; one glaring omission is Hall of Fame outfielder Willie Keeler. In early 2006 the set was sold and broken up. Each card was authenticated and graded by SGC, with grades ranging from Fair to Very Good.

		NM	EX	VG
Common Player:				15,000
(1)	Frank Bonner			15,000
(2)	Steve Brodie			15,000
(3)	Dan Brouthers			75,000
(4)	Duke Esper			15,000
(5)	Kid Gleason			15,000
(6)	Ned Hanlon			65,000
(7)	Bill Hawke			15,000
(8)	George Hemming			15,000
(9)	Hughie Jennings			65,000
(10)	Joe Kelley			125,000
(11)	John McGraw			125,000
(12)	Sadie McMahon			15,000
(13)	Heinie Reitz			15,000
(14)	Wilbert Robinson			65,000

1916 Altoona Tribune

This Pennsylvania daily newspaper was one of several regional advertisers to use this black-and-white, 1-5/8" x 3" 200-card set for promotional pur-

poses. The Altoona issue shares the checklist of the 1916 M101-4 Blank Backs. Type card and superstar collectors will pay a significant premium for a Tribune version of a specific card.

PREMIUM:
Common Player: 4-6X
Hall of Famer: 2-4X
(See 1916 M101-4 Blank Backs for checklist and base card values.)

1948 American Association Babe Ruth

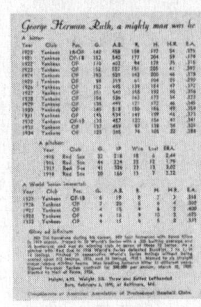

According to the credit line at bottom back (a version of the card is known without the credit line), this card was produced by the Midwestern AAA minor league known as the American Association. How or why it was distributed is unknown. From the inscriptions on back, it appears as if the card was issued shortly after Ruth's death in 1948. The black-and-white card measures 4" x 5-11/16".

	NM	EX	VG
Babe Ruth	200.00	100.00	60.00

1909-11 American Beauty Cigarettes

Two versions of the American Beauty Cigarettes advertising on the backs of T206 can be found; with and without a decorative border surrounding the typography, which is printed in green. All "350 Subjects" American Beauty cards originated from Factory No. 25 in Virginia. Because of the size of the original cigarette packaging in which they were a premium insert, American Beauty T206s may be a bit narrower than the standard 1-7/16". While the "350 Subjects" series is designated here as a 1910 issue, it is possible some cards were actually issued in 1909 or 1911. Among T205, AB backs may be found printed in either black or green, the latter somewhat scarcer.

PREMIUM:
T205: 2X
T206 350 Series: 1.5-2X
T206 460 Series: 2-2.5X
(See T205, T206 for checklists and base card values.
Note: Cards with American Beauty backs may be somewhat narrower than standard 1-7/16" due to smaller original cigarette packaging.)

1908 American Caramel (E91, Set A)

Issued by Philadelphia's American Caramel Co. 1908-1910, the E91 set of Base Ball Caramels has limited popularity with collectors because many of the color drawings show "generic" players rather than the named major leaguers; the same artwork was used to depict two or three different players. The player's name, position and team appear in the white border at bottom. The cards measure approximately 1-1/2" x 2-3/4" and were issued in three separate series. The

JAMES COLLINS
3 B., ATHLETICS (A. L.)

Base Ball Caramels.

THIS CARD IS ONE OF A SET OF THIRTY-THREE BASE BALL PLAYERS, CONSISTING OF NEW YORK, PHILADELPHIA AND CHICAGO BASE BALL TEAMS, ONE OF WHICH IS WRAPPED WITH EVERY BASE BALL CARAMEL.

ATHLETICS (A. L.)
Ralph O. Seybold s.s.
Reuben Oldring c. r.
Edward S. Plank p.
Daniel F. Murphy 2 p.
Harry Davis l b.
George E. Waddell p.
Fred. L. Hartsel r. f.
James Collins 3 b.
Simon Nicholls s.s.
Osee Schreckengost c.
Charles Bender p.

NEW YORK (N. L.)
Leslie H. Taylor p.
Fred Tenney 1 b.
J. T. Meyers c.
J. J. McGraw, Mgr.
Chris. Matthewson p.
Joseph McGinnity p.
J. B. Seymour o. f.
Daniel Shay 3 b.
Arthur Devlin b ss.
Michael Donlin r. f.
Roger Bresnahan c.

CHICAGO (N. L.)
John Evers 2 b.
Mordecai Brown p.
Frank Chance c.
James Scheckard c. f.
Joseph B. Tinker s. s.

Orvill Overall r. f.
John Kling c.
Edward Reulbach p.
James Slagle c. f.
Frank Shulte. r. f.

Manufactured only by the
AMERICAN CARAMEL CO.

can be differentiated by their backs, which checklist the cards. Set A lists the Athletics in the upper-left, the Giants at upper-right and the Cubs below. Set B lists the Cubs and Athletics on top with the Giants below, and Set C list Pittsburg and Washington on top with Boston below. A line indicating the cards were "Manufactured Only by the American Caramel Co." appears at the bottom.

		NM	EX	VG
	Complete Set (33):	10,000	4,000	2,500
	Common Player:	200.00	75.00	40.00
(1)	Charles Bender	425.00	175.00	100.00
(2)	Roger Bresnahan	425.00	175.00	100.00
(3)	Albert Bridwell	200.00	75.00	45.00
(4)	Mordecai Brown	425.00	175.00	100.00
(5)	Frank Chance	425.00	175.00	100.00
(6)	James Collins	425.00	175.00	100.00
(7)	Harry Davis	200.00	75.00	40.00
(8)	Arthur Devlin	200.00	75.00	40.00
(9)	Michael Donlin	200.00	75.00	40.00
(10)	John Evers	425.00	175.00	100.00
(11)	Frederick L. Hartsel	200.00	75.00	40.00
(12)	John Kling	200.00	75.00	40.00
(13)	Christopher Matthewson (Mathewson)	1,750	785.00	435.00
(14)	Joseph McGinnity	425.00	175.00	100.00
(15)	John J. McGraw	425.00	175.00	100.00
(16)	Daniel F. Murphy	200.00	75.00	40.00
(17)	Simon Nicholls	200.00	75.00	40.00
(18)	Reuben Oldring	200.00	75.00	40.00
(19)	Orvill Overall (Orval)	200.00	75.00	40.00
(20)	Edward S. Plank	750.00	325.00	185.00
(21)	Edward Reulbach	200.00	75.00	40.00
(22)	James Scheckard (Sheckard)	200.00	75.00	40.00
(23)	Osee Schreckengost (Ossee)	200.00	75.00	40.00
(24)	Ralph O. Seybold	200.00	75.00	40.00
(25)	J. Bentley Seymour	200.00	75.00	40.00
(26)	Daniel Shay	200.00	75.00	40.00
(27)	Frank Shulte (Schulte)	200.00	75.00	40.00
(28)	James Slagle	200.00	75.00	40.00
(29)	Harry Steinfeldt	200.00	75.00	40.00
(30)	Luther H. Taylor	400.00	160.00	100.00
(31)	Fred Tenney	200.00	75.00	40.00
(32)	Joseph B. Tinker	425.00	175.00	100.00
(33)	George Edward Waddell	425.00	175.00	100.00

1909 American Caramel (E91, Set B)

ATHLETICS

FRANK BAKER
3 B. ATHLETICS

Base Ball Caramels

THIS CARD IS ONE OF A SET OF THIRTY-THREE BASE BALL PLAYERS, PHILADELPHIA AND CHICAGO BASE BALL CLUBS, ONE OF WHICH IS WRAPPED WITH THIS BASE BALL CARAMEL.

Manufactured only by the
AMERICAN CARAMEL CO.

		NM	EX	VG
	Complete Set (33):	9,500	4,000	2,400
	Common Player:	200.00	75.00	40.00
(1)	James Archer	200.00	75.00	40.00
(2)	Frank Baker	425.00	175.00	100.00
(3)	John Barry	200.00	75.00	40.00
(4)	Charles Bender	425.00	175.00	100.00
(5)	Albert Bridwell	200.00	75.00	40.00
(6)	Mordecai Brown	425.00	175.00	100.00
(7)	Frank Chance	425.00	175.00	100.00
(8)	Edw. Collins	425.00	175.00	100.00
(9)	Harry Davis	200.00	75.00	40.00
(10)	Arthur Devlin	200.00	75.00	40.00
(11)	Michael Donlin	200.00	75.00	40.00
(12)	Larry Doyle	200.00	75.00	40.00

(13)	John Evers	425.00	175.00	100.00
(14)	Robt. Ganley	200.00	75.00	40.00
(15)	Frederick L. Hartsel	200.00	75.00	40.00
(16)	Arthur Hoffman (Hofman)	200.00	75.00	40.00
(17)	Harry Krause	200.00	75.00	40.00
(18)	Rich. W. Marquard	425.00	175.00	100.00
(19)	Christopher Matthewson (Mathewson)	1,100	450.00	275.00
(20)	John J. McGraw	425.00	175.00	100.00
(21)	J.T. Meyers	200.00	75.00	40.00
(22)	Dan Murphy	200.00	75.00	40.00
(23)	Jno. J. Murray	200.00	75.00	40.00
(24)	Orvill Overall (Orval)	200.00	75.00	40.00
(25)	Edward S. Plank	750.00	325.00	185.00
(26)	Edward Reulbach	200.00	75.00	40.00
(27)	James Scheckard (Sheckard)	200.00	75.00	40.00
(28)	J. Bentley Seymour	200.00	75.00	40.00
(29)	Harry Steinfeldt	200.00	75.00	40.00
(30)	Frank Shulte (Schulte)	200.00	75.00	40.00
(31)	Fred Tenney	200.00	75.00	40.00
(32)	Joseph B Tinker	425.00	175.00	100.00
(33)	Ira Thomas	200.00	75.00	40.00

1910 American Caramel (E91, Set C)

WM. SCHIPKE
Philadelphia (A. L.)

Base Ball Caramels

AMERICAN CARAMEL CO.

		NM	EX	VG
	Complete Set (33):	11,000	4,400	2,850
	Common Player:	200.00	75.00	40.00
(1)	W.J. Barbeau	200.00	75.00	40.00
(2)	Geo. Browne	200.00	75.00	40.00
(3)	Robt. Chech (Charles)	200.00	75.00	40.00
(4)	Fred Clarke	425.00	175.00	100.00
(5)	Wid Conroy	200.00	75.00	40.00
(6)	James Delehanty (Delahanty)	200.00	75.00	40.00
(7)	Jon A. Donohue (Donahue)	200.00	75.00	40.00
(8)	P. Donahue	200.00	75.00	40.00
(9)	Geo. Gibson	200.00	75.00	40.00
(10)	Robt. Groom	200.00	75.00	40.00
(11)	Harry Hooper	425.00	175.00	100.00
(12)	Tom Hughes	200.00	75.00	40.00
(13)	Walter Johnson	1,000	400.00	250.00
(14)	Edwin Karger	200.00	75.00	40.00
(15)	Tommy Leach	200.00	75.00	40.00
(16)	Sam'l Leever	200.00	75.00	40.00
(17)	Harry Lord	200.00	75.00	40.00
(18)	Geo. F. McBride	200.00	75.00	40.00
(19)	Ambr. McConnell	200.00	75.00	40.00
(20)	Clyde Milan	200.00	75.00	40.00
(21)	J.B. Miller	200.00	75.00	40.00
(22)	Harry Niles	200.00	75.00	40.00
(23)	Chas. Phillipi (Phillippe)	200.00	75.00	40.00
(24)	T.H. Speaker	650.00	275.00	125.00
(25)	Jacob Stahl	200.00	75.00	40.00
(26)	Chas. E. Street	200.00	75.00	40.00
(27)	Allen Storke	200.00	75.00	40.00
(28)	Robt. Unglaub	200.00	75.00	40.00
(29)	C. Wagner	200.00	75.00	40.00
(30)	Hans Wagner	2,900	1,250	575.00
(31)	Victor Willis	425.00	175.00	100.00
(32)	Owen Wilson	200.00	75.00	40.00
(33)	Jos. Wood	300.00	125.00	75.00

1909-11 American Caramel (E90-1)

Davis, 1b Phila. Amer.

BASE BALL SERIES
100 SUBJECTS
BASE BALL
CARAMELS
MFG BY
AMERICAN CARAMEL CO
PHILA, PA.

The E90-1 set was issued by the American Caramel Co. from 1909 through 1911, with the bulk of the set being produced in the first year. The cards, which nominally measure 1-1/2" x 2-3/4" (with the usual tolerances for original cutting variations), were issued with sticks of caramel candy. They are color renderings of photographs. Backs state that 100 subjects are included in the set though more actually do exist. There are several levels of scarcity in the set, those levels being mostly determined by the year the cards were issued. For the reader's convenience, the players' first names have been added in the checklist that follows. The complete set price includes all variations.

		NM	EX	VG
	Complete Set (120):	150,000.	75,000.	40,000
	Common Player:	250.00	115.00	65.00
(1)	Bill Bailey	250.00	115.00	65.00
(2)	Home Run Baker	925.00	425.00	240.00
(3)	Jack Barry	400.00	185.00	100.00
(4)	George Bell	250.00	115.00	65.00
(5)	Harry Bemis	1,200	550.00	310.00
(6)	Chief Bender	750.00	345.00	200.00
(7)	Bob Bescher	250.00	115.00	65.00
(8)	Cliff Blankenship	325.00	150.00	85.00
(9)	John Bliss	280.00	130.00	75.00
(10)	Bill Bradley	300.00	140.00	80.00
(11)	Kitty Bransfield ("P" on shirt.)	325.00	150.00	85.00
(12)	Kitty Bransfield (No "P.")	450.00	200.00	115.00
(13)	Roger Bresnahan	550.00	255.00	145.00
(14)	Al Bridwell	400.00	185.00	100.00
(15)	Buster Brown (Boston)	1,000	460.00	260.00
(16)	Mordecai Brown (Chicago)	685.00	315.00	180.00
(17)	Donie Bush	250.00	115.00	65.00
(18)	John Butler	350.00	160.00	90.00
(19)	Howie Camnitz	800.00	375.00	210.00
(20)	Frank Chance	925.00	425.00	240.00
(21)	Hal Chase	525.00	240.00	135.00
(22)	Fred Clarke (Philadelphia)	525.00	240.00	135.00
(23)	Fred Clarke (Pittsburgh)	2,625	1,200	675.00
(24)	Wally Clement	280.00	130.00	75.00
(25)	"Ty" Cobb	6,500	3,000	1,700
(26)	Eddie Collins	600.00	275.00	155.00
(27)	Sam Crawford	800.00	375.00	210.00
(28)	Frank Corridon	375.00	175.00	100.00
(29)	Lou Criger	425.00	200.00	110.00
(30)	George Davis	1,800	825.00	475.00
(31)	Harry Davis	250.00	115.00	65.00
(32)	Ray Demmitt	750.00	350.00	200.00
(33)	Mike Donlin	935.00	430.00	245.00
(34)	Wild Bill Donovan	250.00	115.00	65.00
(35)	Red Dooin	325.00	150.00	85.00
(36)	Patsy Dougherty	400.00	185.00	100.00
(37)	Hugh Duffy	4,000	1,850	1,000
(38)	Jimmy Dygert	325.00	150.00	85.00
(39)	Rube Ellis	250.00	115.00	65.00
(40)	Clyde Engle	425.00	200.00	110.00
(41)	Art Fromme	400.00	185.00	100.00
(42)	George Gibson (Back view.)	725.00	335.00	190.00
(43)	George Gibson (Front view.)	525.00	240.00	135.00
(44)	Peaches Graham	3,000	925.00	525.00
(45)	Eddie Grant	600.00	275.00	155.00
(46)	Dolly Gray	250.00	115.00	65.00
(47)	Bob Groom	375.00	175.00	100.00
(48)	Charley Hall	900.00	415.00	235.00
(49)	Roy Hartzell/Fielding	450.00	200.00	115.00
(50)	Roy Hartzell/Btg	750.00	345.00	200.00
(51)	Heinie Heitmuller	280.00	130.00	75.00
(52)	Harry Howell (Follow-through.)	650.00	300.00	175.00
(53)	Harry Howell (Wind-up.)	350.00	160.00	90.00
(54)	Tex Irwin (Erwin)	800.00	375.00	210.00
(55)	Frank Isbell	250.00	115.00	65.00
(56)	Joe Jackson	30,000	13,750	7,750
(57)	Hughie Jennings	575.00	265.00	150.00
(58)	Buck Jordon (Jordan)	250.00	115.00	65.00
(59)	Addie Joss/Portrait	750.00	350.00	200.00
(60)	Addie Joss/Pitching	2,500	700.00	400.00
(61)	Ed Karger	1,200	550.00	310.00
(62)	Willie Keeler/Portrait (Pink background.)	950.00	435.00	245.00
(63)	Willie Keeler/Portrait (Red background.)	1,900	875.00	500.00
(64)	Willie Keeler/Throwing	3,000	825.00	475.00
(65)	John Knight	500.00	230.00	130.00
(66)	Harry Krause	350.00	160.00	90.00
(67)	Nap Lajoie	1,500	700.00	400.00
(68)	Tommy Leach/Throwing	250.00	115.00	65.00
(69)	Tommy Leach/Btg	300.00	140.00	80.00
(70)	Sam Leever	250.00	115.00	65.00
(71)	Hans Lobert	1,250	575.00	325.00
(72)	Harry Lumley	325.00	150.00	85.00
(73)	Rube Marquard	875.00	400.00	225.00
(74)	Christy Matthewson (Mathewson)	3,750	1,725	975.00
(75)	Stuffy McInnes (McInnis)	250.00	115.00	65.00
(76)	Harry McIntyre	250.00	115.00	65.00
(77)	Larry McLean	5,000	1,600	910.00
(78)	George McQuillan	250.00	115.00	65.00
(79)	Dots Miller	400.00	185.00	100.00
(80)	Fred Mitchell (New York)	250.00	115.00	65.00
(81)	Mike Mitchell (Cincinnati)	12,000	5,525	3,125
(82)	George Mullin	300.00	140.00	80.00
(83)	Rebel Oakes	250.00	115.00	65.00
(84)	Paddy O'Connor	500.00	230.00	130.00
(85)	Charley O'Leary	280.00	130.00	75.00
(86)	Orval Overall	1,000	460.00	260.00
(87)	Jim Pastorius	500.00	230.00	130.00
(88)	Ed Phelps	450.00	200.00	115.00
(89)	Eddie Plank	1,700	780.00	440.00
(90)	Lew Richie	1,200	550.00	310.00
(91)	Germany Schaefer	250.00	115.00	65.00
(92)	Biff Schlitzer	430.00	200.00	110.00
(93)	Johnny Seigle (Siegle)	285.00	130.00	75.00
(94)	Dave Shean	3,500	1,600	910.00
(95)	Jimmy Sheckard	280.00	130.00	75.00
(96)	Tris Speaker	3,500	1,275	715.00

		NM	EX	VG
(97)	Jake Stahl	2,600	1,200	675.00
(98)	Oscar Stanage	325.00	150.00	85.00
(99)	George Stone (No hands visible.)	250.00	115.00	65.00
(100)	George Stone (Left hand visible.)	400.00	185.00	100.00
(101)	George Stovall	500.00	230.00	130.00
(102)	Ed Summers	400.00	185.00	100.00
(103)	Bill Sweeney (Boston)	4,000	1,600	900.00
(104)	Jeff Sweeney (New York)	500.00	230.00	130.00
(105)	Jesse Tannehill (Chicago A.L.)	250.00	115.00	65.00
(106)	Lee Tannehill (Chicago N.L.)	250.00	115.00	65.00
(107)	Fred Tenney	750.00	345.00	200.00
(108)	Ira Thomas (Philadelphia)	250.00	115.00	65.00
(109)	Roy Thomas (Boston)	375.00	175.00	95.00
(110)	Joe Tinker	650.00	300.00	175.00
(111)	Bob Unglaub	250.00	115.00	65.00
(112)	Jerry Upp	3,500	1,600	910.00
(113)	Honus Wagner/Btg	4,250	1,950	1,100
(114)	Honus Wagner/Throwing	4,250	1,950	1,100
(115)	Bobby Wallace	575.00	265.00	150.00
(116)	Ed Walsh	6,000	2,300	1,300
(117)	Vic Willis	800.00	375.00	210.00
(118)	Hooks Wiltse	280.00	130.00	75.00
(119)	Cy Young (Cleveland)	2,750	1,275	725.00
(120)	Cy Young (Boston)	4,000	1,850	1,000

1910 American Caramel Pirates (E90-2)

Closely related to the E90-1 American Caramel set, the E90-2 set consists of 11 cards featuring members of the 1909 champion Pittsburgh Pirates. The cards measure a nominal 1-1/2" x 2-5/8", though tolerances must be allowed for original cutting variations common to the era. They display a color lithograph on front set upon a solid color background of either red, green blue or pink. The player's name and "Pittsburg" appear in blue capital letters in the border beneath the portrait. The backs are identical to those in the E90-1 set, depicting a drawing of a ball, glove and crossed bats with the words "Base Ball Caramels" and a reference to "100 Subjects." The set includes Hall of Famers Honus Wagner and Fred Clarke.

		NM	EX	VG
Complete Set (11):		30,000	13,500	7,000
Common Player:		1,200	550.00	300.00
(1)	Babe Adams	1,200	550.00	300.00
(2)	Fred Clarke	2,000	900.00	500.00
(3)	George Gibson	1,200	550.00	300.00
(4)	Ham Hyatt	1,200	550.00	300.00
(5)	Tommy Leach	1,200	550.00	300.00
(6)	Sam Leever	1,200	550.00	300.00
(7)	Nick Maddox	1,200	550.00	300.00
(8)	Dots Miller	1,200	550.00	300.00
(9)	Deacon Phillippe	1,200	550.00	300.00
(10)	Honus Wagner	17,500	7,875	4,375
(11)	Owen Wilson	1,200	550.00	300.00

1910 American Caramel White Sox/Cubs (E90-3)

Similar in size (nominally 1-1/2" x 2-3/4", but with the usual tolerances for cutting variations on cards of the era) and style to the more popular E90-1 set, the E90-3 set was issued by the American Caramel Co. in 1910. The 20-card, color lithograph set includes 11 Chicago Cubs and nine White Sox. The fronts of the cards have a similar design to the E90-1 set, although different pictures were used. The backs can be differentiated by two major changes: The bottom of the card indicates the American Caramel Co. of "Chicago," rather than Philadelphia, and the top of the card contains the phrase "All The Star Players," rather than "100 Subjects."

		NM	EX	VG
Complete Set (20):		40,000	20,000	7,500
Common Player:		1,700	850.00	425.00
(1)	Jimmy Archer	1,700	850.00	425.00
(2)	Lena Blackburne	1,700	850.00	425.00
(3)	Mordecai Brown	3,000	1,500	750.00
(4)	Frank Chance	1,700	850.00	425.00
(5)	King Cole	1,700	850.00	425.00
(6)	Patsy Dougherty	1,700	850.00	425.00
(7)	Johnny Evers	3,000	1,500	750.00
(8)	Chick Gandil	4,500	2,250	1,125
(9)	Ed Hahn	1,700	850.00	425.00
(10a)	Solly Hofman	1,700	850.00	425.00
(10b)	Solly Hofman (Broken "m" in last name gives appearance of "Hofnlan." Discovery specimen graded SGC Good auctioned for $3,190 in 2006.)			
(11)	Orval Overall	1,700	850.00	425.00
(12)	Fred Payne	1,700	850.00	425.00
(13)	Billy Purtell	1,700	850.00	425.00
(14)	Wildfire Schulte	1,700	850.00	425.00
(15)	Jimmy Sheckard	1,700	850.00	425.00
(16)	Frank Smith	1,700	850.00	425.00
(17)	Harry Steinfeldt	1,700	850.00	425.00
(18a)	Joe Tinker (Blue background.)	3,000	1,500	750.00
(18b)	Joe Tinker (Green background.)	3,000	1,500	750.00
(19)	Ed Walsh	3,000	1,500	750.00
(20)	Rollie Zeider	1,700	850.00	425.00

1910 American Caramel Die-cuts (E125)

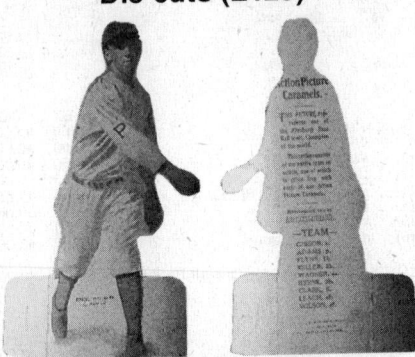

Issued circa 1910 by the American Caramel Co., this set of die-cut cards is so rare that it wasn't even known to exist until the late 1960s. Apparently inserted in boxes of caramels, these cards, which are die-cut figures of baseball players, vary in size but are all relatively large - some measuring 7" high and 4" wide. Players from the Athletics, Red Sox, Giants and Pirates are known with a team checklist appearing on the back. According to the checklists, the set would be complete at 41 cards (including two separate poses of Honus Wagner), but to date only about 20 different cards have been found. The set is designated as E125.

		NM	EX	VG
Common Player:		3,000	1,400	900.00
(1)	Babe Adams (Arms at sides.)	3,000	1,400	900.00
(2)	Red Ames/Throwing	3,000	1,400	900.00
(3)	Home Run Baker	5,000	2,250	1,500
(4)	Jack Barry/Fielding	3,000	1,400	900.00
(5)	Chief Bender	5,600	2,500	1,700
(6)	Al Bridwell/Fielding	3,000	1,400	900.00
(7)	Bobby Byrne/Throwing	3,000	1,400	900.00
(8)	Bill Carrigan/Catching	3,000	1,400	900.00
(9)	Ed Cicotte/Throwing	3,000	1,400	900.00
(10)	Fred Clark (Clarke)/Fielding	5,000	2,250	1,500
(11)	Eddie Collins	5,000	2,250	1,500
(12)	Harry Davis/Fielding	3,000	1,400	900.00
(13)	Art Devlin/Fielding	3,000	1,400	900.00
(14)	Josh Devore	3,000	1,400	900.00
(15)	Larry Doyle/Throwing	3,000	1,400	900.00
(16)	John Flynn/Running	3,000	1,400	900.00
(17)	George Gibson (Hands in glove.)	3,000	1,400	900.00
(18)	Topsy Hartzell (Hartsell)/Fielding	3,000	1,400	900.00
(19)	Harry Hooper/Throwing	5,000	2,250	1,500
(20)	Harry Krause	3,000	1,400	900.00
(21)	Tommy Leach/Fielding	3,000	1,400	900.00
(22)	Harry Lord/Throwing	3,000	1,400	900.00
(23)	Christy Mathewson (Wind-up.)	18,750	8,400	5,600
(24)	Amby McConnell/Fielding	3,000	1,400	900.00
(25)	Fred Merkle	3,000	1,400	900.00
(26)	Dots Miller/Throwing	3,000	1,400	900.00
(27)	Danny Murphy	3,000	1,400	900.00
(28)	Red Murray/Fielding	3,000	1,400	900.00
(29)	Harry Niles/Fielding	3,000	1,400	900.00
(30)	Rube Oldring	3,000	1,400	900.00
(31)	Eddie Plank/Throwing	18,750	8,400	5,600
(32)	Cy Seymour/Fielding	3,000	1,400	900.00
(33)	Tris Speaker/Batting	11,250	5,100	3,400
(34)	Tris Speaker/Fielding	11,250	5,100	3,400
(35)	Jake Stahl/Fielding	3,000	1,400	900.00
(36)	Ira Thomas	3,000	1,400	900.00
(37)	Heinie Wagner/Fielding	3,000	1,400	900.00
(38)	Honus Wagner/Batting	25,000	11,250	7,500
(39)	Honus Wagner/Throwing	25,000	11,250	7,500
(40)	Art Wilson	3,000	1,400	900.00
(41)	Owen Wilson/Throwing	3,000	1,400	900.00
(42)	Hooks Wiltse/Throwing	3,000	1,400	900.00

1915 American Caramel (E106)

This 48-card set, designated E106 by the American Card Catalog, was produced by the American Caramel Co., of York, Pa., in 1915 and includes players from the National, American and Federal Leagues. Cards measure 1-1/2" x 2-3/4". The set is related to the E90-1 and E92 sets, from which the artwork is taken, but this issue has a glossy coating on front, which makes the cards very susceptible to cracking.

		NM	EX	VG
Complete Set (48):		80,000	40,000	24,000
Common Player:		700.00	350.00	200.00
(1)	Jack Barry	700.00	350.00	200.00
(2)	Chief Bender (White hat.)	1,300	650.00	400.00
(3)	Chief Bender (Striped hat.)	1,300	650.00	400.00
(4)	Bob Bescher	700.00	350.00	200.00
(5)	Roger Bresnahan	1,300	650.00	400.00
(6)	Al Bridwell	700.00	350.00	200.00
(7)	Donie Bush	700.00	350.00	200.00
(8)	Hal Chase/Portrait	700.00	350.00	200.00
(9)	Hal Chase/Catching	700.00	350.00	200.00
(10)	Ty Cobb (W/bat, facing front.)	9,000	4,500	2,700
(11)	Ty Cobb/Btg (Facing to side.)	8,500	4,250	2,250
(12)	Eddie Collins	1,300	650.00	400.00
(13)	Sam Crawford	1,300	650.00	400.00
(14)	Ray Demmitt	700.00	350.00	200.00
(15)	Wild Bill Donovan	700.00	350.00	200.00
(16)	Red Dooin	700.00	350.00	200.00
(17)	Mickey Doolan	700.00	350.00	200.00
(18)	Larry Doyle	700.00	350.00	200.00
(19)	Clyde Engle	700.00	350.00	200.00
(20)	Johnny Evers	1,300	650.00	400.00
(21)	Art Fromme	700.00	350.00	200.00
(22)	George Gibson/Catching (Back view.)	700.00	350.00	200.00
(23)	George Gibson/Catching (Front view.)	700.00	350.00	200.00
(24)	Roy Hartzell	700.00	350.00	200.00
(25)	Fred Jacklitsch	700.00	350.00	200.00
(26)	Hugh Jennings	1,300	650.00	400.00
(27)	Otto Knabe	700.00	350.00	200.00
(28)	Nap Lajoie	1,300	650.00	400.00
(29)	Hans Lobert	700.00	350.00	200.00
(30)	Rube Marquard	1,300	650.00	400.00
(31)	Christy Matthewson (Mathewson)	4,450	2,200	1,330
(32)	John McGraw	1,300	650.00	400.00
(33)	George McQuillan	700.00	350.00	200.00
(34)	Dots Miller	700.00	350.00	200.00
(35)	Danny Murphy	700.00	350.00	200.00
(36)	Rebel Oakes	700.00	350.00	200.00
(37)	Eddie Plank	1,500	750.00	450.00
(38)	Germany Schaefer	700.00	350.00	200.00
(39)	Tris Speaker	1,800	900.00	550.00
(40)	Oscar Stanage	700.00	350.00	200.00
(41)	George Stovall	700.00	350.00	200.00
(42)	Jeff Sweeney	700.00	350.00	200.00
(43)	Joe Tinker/Portrait	1,300	650.00	400.00
(44)	Joe Tinker/Btg	1,300	650.00	400.00
(45)	Honus Wagner/Btg	13,040	6,250	3,750
(46)	Honus Wagner/Throwing	13,040	6,250	3,750
(47)	Hooks Wiltse	700.00	350.00	200.00
(48)	Heinie Zimmerman	700.00	350.00	200.00

1921 American Caramel Series of 80 (E121)

Issued circa 1921, the E121 Series of 80 is designated as such because of the card reverses which indicate the player pictured is just one of 80 baseb

JOHN GRANEY
UU. O. F.—Cleveland Americans

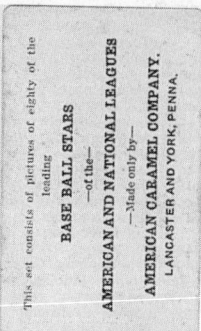

This set consists of pictures of eighty of the leading
BASE BALL STARS
of the
AMERICAN AND NATIONAL LEAGUES.
Made only by—
AMERICAN CARAMEL COMPANY.
LANCASTER and YORK, PENNA.

stars in the set. The figure of 80 supplied by the American Caramel Co. is incorrect as over 100 different pictures do exist. The unnumbered cards, which measure about 2" x 3-1/4", feature black and white photos. Two different backs exist for the Series of 80. The common back variation has the first line ending with the word "the," while the scarcer version ends with the word "eighty." The complete set price does not include the variations.

		NM	EX	VG
Complete Set (121):		52,500	21,500	10,000
Common Player:		150.00	60.00	30.00
(1)	G.C. Alexander (Arms above head.)	750.00	300.00	150.00
(2)	Grover Alexander (Right arm forward.)	1,500	600.00	300.00
(3)	Jim Bagby	150.00	60.00	30.00
(4a)	J. Franklin Baker	400.00	160.00	80.00
(4b)	Frank Baker	400.00	160.00	80.00
(5)	Dave Bancroft/Btg	400.00	160.00	80.00
(6)	Dave Bancroft/Leaping	400.00	160.00	80.00
(7)	Ping Bodie	150.00	60.00	30.00
(8)	George Burns	150.00	60.00	30.00
(9)	Geo. J. Burns	150.00	60.00	30.00
(10)	Owen Bush	150.00	60.00	30.00
(11)	Max Carey/Btg	400.00	160.00	80.00
(12)	Max Carey (Hands at hips.)	400.00	160.00	80.00
(13)	Cecil Causey	150.00	60.00	30.00
(14)	Ty Cobb/Throwing (Looking front.)	1,800	725.00	360.00
(15a)	Ty Cobb/Throwing (Looking right, Mgr. on front.)	1,800	725.00	360.00
(15b)	Ty Cobb/Throwing (Looking right, Manager on front.)	1,800	725.00	360.00
(16)	Eddie Collins	400.00	160.00	80.00
(17)	"Rip" Collins	150.00	60.00	30.00
(18)	Jake Daubert	150.00	60.00	30.00
(19)	George Dauss	150.00	60.00	30.00
(20)	Charles Deal (Dark uniform.)	150.00	60.00	30.00
(21)	Charles Deal (White uniform.)	150.00	60.00	30.00
(22)	William Doak	150.00	60.00	30.00
(23)	Bill Donovan	150.00	60.00	30.00
(24)	"Phil" Douglas	150.00	60.00	30.00
(25a)	Johnny Evers/Manager	400.00	160.00	80.00
(25b)	Johnny Evers/Manager	400.00	160.00	80.00
(26)	Urban Faber (Dark uniform.)	400.00	160.00	80.00
(27)	Urban Faber (White uniform.)	400.00	160.00	80.00
(28)	William Fewster (First name actually Wilson.)	150.00	60.00	30.00
(29)	Eddie Foster	150.00	60.00	30.00
(30)	Frank Frisch	400.00	160.00	80.00
(31)	W.L. Gardner	150.00	60.00	30.00
(32a)	Alexander Gaston (No position on front.)	150.00	60.00	30.00
(32b)	Alexander Gaston (Position on front.)	150.00	60.00	30.00
(33)	"Kid" Gleason	150.00	60.00	30.00
(34)	"Mike" Gonzalez	150.00	60.00	30.00
(35)	Hank Gowdy	150.00	60.00	30.00
(36)	John Graney	150.00	60.00	30.00
(37)	Tom Griffith	150.00	60.00	30.00
(38)	Heinie Groh	150.00	60.00	30.00
(39)	Harry Harper	150.00	60.00	30.00
(40)	Harry Heilman (Heilmann)	400.00	160.00	80.00
(41)	Walter Holke/Portrait	150.00	60.00	30.00
(42)	Walter Holke/Throwing	150.00	60.00	30.00
(43)	Charles Hollacher (Hollocher)	150.00	60.00	30.00
(44)	Harry Hooper	400.00	160.00	80.00
(45)	Rogers Hornsby	1,100	450.00	225.00
(46)	Waite Hoyt	400.00	160.00	80.00
(47)	Miller Huggins	400.00	160.00	80.00
(48)	Wm. C. Jacobson	150.00	60.00	30.00
(49)	Hugh Jennings	400.00	160.00	80.00
(50)	Walter Johnson/Throwing	1,350	550.00	275.00
(51)	Walter Johnson (Hands at chest.)	1,425	575.00	285.00
(52)	James Johnston	150.00	60.00	30.00
(53)	Joe Judge	150.00	60.00	30.00
(54)	George Kelly	400.00	160.00	80.00
(55)	Dick Kerr	150.00	60.00	30.00
(56)	P.J. Kilduff	150.00	60.00	30.00
(57a)	Bill Killifer (Incorrect name.)	150.00	60.00	30.00
(57b)	Bill Killefer (Correct name.)	150.00	60.00	30.00
(58)	John Lavan	150.00	60.00	30.00
(59)	"Nemo" Leibold	150.00	60.00	30.00
(60)	Duffy Lewis	150.00	60.00	30.00
(61)	Al. Mamaux	150.00	60.00	30.00
(62)	"Rabbit" Maranville	400.00	160.00	80.00
(63a)	Carl May (Mays)	200.00	80.00	40.00
(63b)	Carl Mays (Correct name.)	200.00	80.00	40.00
(64)	John McGraw	400.00	160.00	80.00

(65)	Jack McInnis	150.00	60.00	30.00
(66)	M.J. McNally	150.00	60.00	30.00
(67)	Emil Muesel (Photo is Lou DeVormer.)	150.00	60.00	30.00
(68)	R. Meusel	150.00	60.00	30.00
(69)	Clyde Milan	150.00	60.00	30.00
(70)	Elmer Miller	150.00	60.00	30.00
(71)	Otto Miller	150.00	60.00	30.00
(72)	Guy Morton	150.00	60.00	30.00
(73)	Eddie Murphy	150.00	60.00	30.00
(74)	"Hy" Myers	150.00	60.00	30.00
(75)	Arthur Nehf	150.00	60.00	30.00
(76)	Steve O'Neill	150.00	60.00	30.00
(77a)	Roger Peckinbaugh (Incorrect name.)	150.00	60.00	30.00
(77b)	Roger Peckinpaugh (Correct name.)	150.00	60.00	30.00
(78a)	Jeff Pfeffer (Brooklyn)	150.00	60.00	30.00
(78b)	Jeff Pfeffer (St. Louis)	150.00	60.00	30.00
(79)	Walter Pipp	250.00	100.00	50.00
(80)	Jack Quinn	150.00	60.00	30.00
(81)	John Rawlings	150.00	60.00	30.00
(82)	E.C. Rice	400.00	160.00	80.00
(83)	Eppa Rixey, Jr.	400.00	160.00	80.00
(84)	Robert Roth	150.00	60.00	30.00
(85a)	Ed. Roush (C.F.)	400.00	160.00	80.00
(85b)	Ed. Roush (L.F.)	400.00	160.00	80.00
(86a)	Babe Ruth	17,500	7,000	3,500
(86b)	"Babe" Ruth	17,500	7,000	3,500
(86c)	George Ruth	19,000	7,600	3,800
(87)	"Bill" Ryan	150.00	60.00	30.00
(88)	"Slim" Sallee (Glove showing.)	150.00	60.00	30.00
(89)	"Slim" Sallee (No glove showing.)	150.00	60.00	30.00
(90)	Ray Schalk	400.00	160.00	80.00
(91)	Walter Schang	150.00	60.00	30.00
(92a)	Fred Schupp (Name incorrect.)	150.00	60.00	30.00
(92b)	Ferd Schupp (Name correct.)	150.00	60.00	30.00
(93)	Everett Scott	150.00	60.00	30.00
(94)	Hank Severeid	150.00	60.00	30.00
(95)	Robert Shawkey	150.00	60.00	30.00
(96a)	Pat Shea	150.00	60.00	30.00
(96b)	"Pat" Shea	150.00	60.00	30.00
(97)	George Sisler/Btg	400.00	160.00	80.00
(98)	George Sisler/Throwing	400.00	160.00	80.00
(99)	Earl Smith	150.00	60.00	30.00
(100)	Frank Snyder	150.00	60.00	30.00
(101a)	Tris Speaker/Mgr.	800.00	325.00	160.00
(101b)	Tris Speaker/Mgr. (Large projection.)	800.00	325.00	160.00
(101c)	Tris Speaker/Mgr. (Small projection.)	800.00	325.00	160.00
(102)	Milton Stock	150.00	60.00	30.00
(103)	Amos Strunk	150.00	60.00	30.00
(104)	Zeb Terry	150.00	60.00	30.00
(105)	Chester Thomas	150.00	60.00	30.00
(106)	Fred Toney (Trees in background.)	150.00	60.00	30.00
(107)	Fred Toney (No trees.)	150.00	60.00	30.00
(108)	George Tyler	150.00	60.00	30.00
(109)	Jim Vaughn (Dark hat.)	150.00	60.00	30.00
(110)	Jim Vaughn (White hat.)	150.00	60.00	30.00
(111)	Bob Veach (Glove in air.)	150.00	60.00	30.00
(112)	Bob Veach (Arms crossed.)	150.00	60.00	30.00
(113)	Oscar Vitt	150.00	60.00	30.00
(114)	W. Wambsganss (Photo actually Fred Coumbe.)	150.00	60.00	30.00
(115)	Aaron Ward	150.00	60.00	30.00
(116)	Zach Wheat	400.00	160.00	80.00
(117)	George Whitted	150.00	60.00	30.00
(118)	Fred Williams	150.00	60.00	30.00
(119)	Ivy B. Wingo	150.00	60.00	30.00
(120)	Joe Wood	300.00	125.00	60.00
(121)	"Pep" Young	150.00	60.00	30.00

1922 American Caramel Series of 120 (E121)

ELMER SMITH
O. F.—Boston Americans

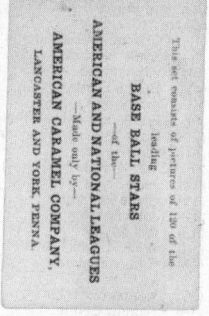

AMERICAN CARAMEL COMPANY,
LANCASTER AND YORK, PENNA.

AMERICAN AND NATIONAL LEAGUES.
Made only by—
BASE BALL STARS
of the
leading
This set consists of pictures of 120 of the

Produced by American Caramel Co. the E121 Series of 120 has back advertising that claims that the set contained 120 subjects. Identical in design to the E121 Series of 80 set except for the card backs, the black-and-white cards measure about 2" x 3-1/4". Numerous variations are found in the set, most involving a change in the player's name, team or position. The complete set price does not include variations.

		NM	EX	VG
Complete Set (127):		60,000	24,000	12,000
Common Player:		100.00	40.00	25.00
(1)	Chas. "Babe" Adams	150.00	60.00	30.00
(2)	G.C. Alexander	750.00	300.00	150.00

(3)	Jim Bagby	150.00	60.00	30.00
(4)	Dave Bancroft	400.00	160.00	80.00
(5)	Turner Barber	150.00	60.00	30.00
(6a)	Carlson Bigbee (Correct name Carson L. Bigbee.)	150.00	60.00	30.00
(6b)	Carlson L. Bigbee	150.00	60.00	30.00
(6c)	Corson L. Bigbee	150.00	60.00	30.00
(6d)	L. Bigbee	150.00	60.00	30.00
(7)	"Bullet Joe" Bush	150.00	60.00	30.00
(8)	Max Carey	400.00	160.00	80.00
(9)	Cecil Causey	150.00	60.00	30.00
(10)	Ty Cobb/Btg			
(11)	Ty Cobb/Throwing	2,500	1,000	500.00
(12)	Eddie Collins	2,250	900.00	450.00
(13)	A. Wilbur Cooper	150.00	60.00	30.00
(14)	Stanley Coveleskie (Coveleski)	400.00	160.00	80.00
(15)	Dave Danforth	150.00	60.00	30.00
(16)	Jake Daubert	150.00	60.00	30.00
(17)	George Dauss	150.00	60.00	30.00
(18)	Dixie Davis	150.00	60.00	30.00
(19)	Chas. A. Deal	150.00	60.00	30.00
(20)	Lou DeVormer	150.00	60.00	30.00
(21)	William Doak	150.00	60.00	30.00
(22)	Phil Douglas	150.00	60.00	30.00
(23)	Urban Faber	400.00	160.00	80.00
(24)	Bib Falk (Bibb)	150.00	60.00	30.00
(25)	Wm. Fewster (First name actually Wilson.)	150.00	60.00	30.00
(26)	Max Flack	150.00	60.00	30.00
(27)	Ira Falgstead (Flagstead)	150.00	60.00	30.00
(28)	Frank Frisch	400.00	160.00	80.00
(29)	W.L. Gardner	150.00	60.00	30.00
(30)	Alexander Gaston	150.00	60.00	30.00
(31)	E.P. Gharrity	150.00	60.00	30.00
(32)	George Gibson	150.00	60.00	30.00
(33)	Chas. "Whitey" Glazner	150.00	60.00	30.00
(34)	"Kid" Gleason	150.00	60.00	30.00
(35)	Hank Gowdy	150.00	60.00	30.00
(36)	John Graney	150.00	60.00	30.00
(37)	Tom Griffith	150.00	60.00	30.00
(38)	Chas. Grimm	150.00	60.00	30.00
(39)	Heine Groh	150.00	60.00	30.00
(40)	Jess Haines	400.00	160.00	80.00
(41)	Harry Harper	150.00	60.00	30.00
(42)	Harry Heilman/Fielding (Name incorrect.)	450.00	180.00	90.00
(43)	Harry Heilmann/Btg (Name correct.)	600.00	240.00	120.00
(44)	Clarence Hodge	150.00	60.00	30.00
(45)	Walter Holke/Portrait	150.00	60.00	30.00
(46)	Walter Holke/Throwing	150.00	60.00	30.00
(47)	Charles Hollocher	150.00	60.00	30.00
(48)	Harry Hooper	400.00	160.00	80.00
(49a)	Rogers Hornsby (2B.)	1,100	450.00	225.00
(49b)	Rogers Hornsby (O.F.)	1,100	450.00	225.00
(50)	Waite Hoyt	400.00	160.00	80.00
(51)	Miller Huggins	400.00	160.00	80.00
(52)	Walter Johnson	1,350	550.00	275.00
(53)	Joe Judge	150.00	60.00	30.00
(54)	George Kelly	400.00	160.00	80.00
(55)	Dick Kerr	150.00	60.00	30.00
(56)	P.J. Kilduff	150.00	60.00	30.00
(57)	Bill Killifer (Killefer)/Btg	150.00	60.00	30.00
(58)	Bill Killifer (Killefer)/Throwing	150.00	60.00	30.00
(59)	John Lavan	150.00	60.00	30.00
(60)	Walter Mails	150.00	60.00	30.00
(61)	"Rabbit" Maranville	400.00	160.00	80.00
(62)	Elwood Martin	150.00	60.00	30.00
(63)	Carl Mays	200.00	80.00	40.00
(64)	John J. McGraw	400.00	160.00	80.00
(65)	Jack McInnis	150.00	60.00	30.00
(66)	M.J. McNally	150.00	60.00	30.00
(67)	Emil Meusel (Photo actually Lou DeVormer.)	150.00	60.00	30.00
(68)	R. Meusel	150.00	60.00	30.00
(69)	Clyde Milan	150.00	60.00	30.00
(70)	Elmer Miller	150.00	60.00	30.00
(71)	Otto Miller	150.00	60.00	30.00
(72)	Johnny Mostil	150.00	60.00	30.00
(73)	Eddie Mulligan	150.00	60.00	30.00
(74a)	Hy Myers	150.00	60.00	30.00
(74b)	"Hy" Myers	150.00	60.00	30.00
(75)	Earl Neale	300.00	120.00	60.00
(76)	Arthur Nehf	150.00	60.00	30.00
(77)	Leslie Nunamaker	150.00	60.00	30.00
(78)	Joe Oeschger	150.00	60.00	30.00
(79)	Chas. O'Leary	150.00	60.00	30.00
(80)	Steve O'Neill	150.00	60.00	30.00
(81)	D.B. Pratt	150.00	60.00	30.00
(82a)	John Rawlings (2B.)	150.00	60.00	30.00
(82b)	John Rawlings (Utl.)	150.00	60.00	30.00
(83)	E.S. Rice (Initials actually E.C.)	400.00	160.00	80.00
(84)	Eppa J. Rixey	400.00	160.00	80.00
(85)	Eppa Rixey, Jr.	400.00	160.00	80.00
(86)	Wilbert Robinson	400.00	160.00	80.00
(87)	Tom Rogers	150.00	60.00	30.00
(88a)	Ed Rounnel (Rommel)	150.00	60.00	30.00
(88b)	Ed. Rommel	150.00	60.00	30.00
(89)	Ed Roush	400.00	160.00	80.00
(90)	"Muddy" Ruel	150.00	60.00	30.00
(91)	Walter Ruether	150.00	60.00	30.00
(92a)	Babe Ruth (Photo montage.)	10,000	4,000	2,000
(92b)	"Babe" Ruth (Photo montage.)	10,000	4,000	2,000
(93a)	Babe Ruth (Holding bird.)	10,000	4,000	2,000
(93b)	"Babe" Ruth (Holding bird.)	10,000	4,000	2,000
(94)	"Babe" Ruth (Holding ball.)	10,000	4,000	2,000
(95)	Bill Ryan	150.00	60.00	30.00
(96)	Ray Schalk/Catching	400.00	160.00	80.00
(97)	Ray Schalk/Btg	400.00	160.00	80.00
(98)	Wally Schang	150.00	60.00	30.00
(99)	Ferd Schupp	150.00	60.00	30.00
(100)	Everett Scott	150.00	60.00	30.00
(101)	Joe Sewell	400.00	160.00	80.00
(102)	Robert Shawkey	150.00	60.00	30.00
(103)	Pat Shea	150.00	60.00	30.00
(104)	Earl Sheely	150.00	60.00	30.00

(105)	Urban Schocker	150.00	60.00	30.00
(106)	George Sisler/Btg	400.00	160.00	80.00
(107)	George Sisler/Throwing	400.00	160.00	80.00
(108)	Earl Smith	150.00	60.00	30.00
(109)	Elmer Smith	150.00	60.00	30.00
(110)	Frank Snyder	150.00	60.00	30.00
(111)	Bill Southworth	150.00	60.00	30.00
(112a)	Tris Speaker (Large projection.)	600.00	240.00	120.00
(112b)	Tris Speaker (Small projection.)	600.00	240.00	120.00
(113a)	Milton Stock	150.00	60.00	30.00
(113b)	Milton J. Stock	150.00	60.00	30.00
(114)	Amos Strunk	150.00	60.00	30.00
(115)	Zeb Terry	150.00	60.00	30.00
(116)	Fred Toney	150.00	60.00	30.00
(117)	George Topocer (Toporcer)	150.00	60.00	30.00
(118)	Bob Veach	150.00	60.00	30.00
(119)	Oscar Vitt	150.00	60.00	30.00
(120)	Curtis Walker	150.00	60.00	30.00
(121)	W. Wambsganss (Photo actually Fred Coumbe.)	150.00	60.00	30.00
(122)	Aaron Ward	150.00	60.00	30.00
(123)	Zach Wheat	400.00	160.00	80.00
(124a)	George Whitted (Pittsburgh)	150.00	60.00	30.00
(124b)	George Whitted (Brooklyn)	150.00	60.00	30.00
(125)	Fred Williams	150.00	60.00	30.00
(126)	Ivy B. Wingo	150.00	60.00	30.00
(127)	Ross Young (Youngs)	400.00	160.00	80.00

1922 American Caramel Series of 80 (E122)

 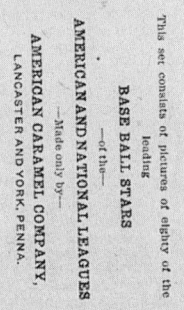

Known as E122 in the American Card Catalog, this set is actually a parallel of the E121 American Caramel set. The cards are nearly identical to E121's "Series of 80," except the player's name, position and team are printed inside a gray rectangle at the bottom of the card, and the photos have a more coarse appearance. At 2" x 3-1/4", the E122s are slightly shorter than E121s.

		NM	EX	VG
	Complete Set (81):	30,000	12,000	6,000
	Common Player:	100.00	40.00	25.00
(1)	Grover Alexander	750.00	300.00	150.00
(2)	Jim Bagby	150.00	60.00	30.00
(3)	J. Franklin Baker	400.00	160.00	80.00
(4)	Dave Bancroft	400.00	160.00	80.00
(5)	Ping Bodie	150.00	60.00	30.00
(6)	George Burns	150.00	60.00	30.00
(7)	Geo. J. Burns	150.00	60.00	30.00
(8)	Owen Bush	150.00	60.00	30.00
(9)	Max Carey	400.00	160.00	80.00
(10)	Cecil Causey	150.00	60.00	30.00
(11)	Ty Cobb	1,900	760.00	380.00
(12)	Eddie Collins	400.00	160.00	80.00
(13)	Jake Daubert	150.00	60.00	30.00
(14)	George Dauss	150.00	60.00	30.00
(15)	Charles Deal	150.00	60.00	30.00
(16)	William Doak	150.00	60.00	30.00
(17)	Bill Donovan	150.00	60.00	30.00
(18)	Johnny Evers	400.00	160.00	80.00
(19)	Urban Faber	400.00	160.00	80.00
(20)	Eddie Foster	150.00	60.00	30.00
(21)	W.L. Gardner	150.00	60.00	30.00
(22)	"Kid" Gleason	150.00	60.00	30.00
(23)	Hank Gowdy	150.00	60.00	30.00
(24)	John Graney	150.00	60.00	30.00
(25)	Tom Griffith	150.00	60.00	30.00
(26)	Sam Harris (Stan "Bucky")	400.00	160.00	80.00
(27)	Harry Heilman (Heilmann)	400.00	160.00	80.00
(28)	Walter Holke	150.00	60.00	30.00
(29)	Charles Hollacher (Hollocher)	150.00	60.00	30.00
(30)	Harry Hooper	400.00	160.00	80.00
(31)	Rogers Hornsby	600.00	240.00	120.00
(32)	Wm. C. Jacobson	150.00	60.00	30.00
(33)	Walter Johnson	1,100	450.00	225.00
(34)	James Johnston	150.00	60.00	30.00
(35)	Joe Judge	150.00	60.00	30.00
(36)	George Kelly	400.00	160.00	80.00
(37)	Dick Kerr	150.00	60.00	30.00
(38)	P.J. Kilduff	150.00	60.00	30.00
(39)	Bill Killefer	150.00	60.00	30.00
(40)	John Lavan	150.00	60.00	30.00
(41)	Duffy Lewis	150.00	60.00	30.00
(42)	Perry Lipe	150.00	60.00	30.00
(43)	Al. Mamaux	150.00	60.00	30.00
(44)	"Rabbit" Maranville	400.00	160.00	80.00
(45)	Carl May (Mays)	200.00	80.00	40.00
(46)	John McGraw	400.00	160.00	80.00
(47)	Jack McInnis	150.00	60.00	30.00

(48)	Clyde Milan	150.00	60.00	30.00
(49)	Otto Miller	150.00	60.00	30.00
(50)	Guy Morton	150.00	60.00	30.00
(51)	Eddie Murphy	150.00	60.00	30.00
(52)	"Hy" Myers	150.00	60.00	30.00
(53)	Steve O'Neill	150.00	60.00	30.00
(54)	Roger Peckinbaugh (Peckinpaugh)	150.00	60.00	30.00
(55)	Jeff Pfeffer	150.00	60.00	30.00
(56)	Walter Pipp	175.00	70.00	35.00
(57)	E.C. Rice	400.00	160.00	80.00
(58)	Eppa Rixey, Jr.	400.00	160.00	80.00
(59)	Babe Ruth	9,000	3,600	1,800
(60)	"Slim" Sallee	150.00	60.00	30.00
(61)	Ray Schalk	400.00	160.00	80.00
(62)	Walter Schang	150.00	60.00	30.00
(63a)	Fred Schupp (Name incorrect.)	150.00	60.00	30.00
(63b)	Ferd Schupp (Name correct.)	150.00	60.00	30.00
(64)	Everett Scott	150.00	60.00	30.00
(65)	Hank Severeid	150.00	60.00	30.00
(66)	George Sisler/Btg	400.00	160.00	80.00
(67)	George Sisler/Throwing	750.00	300.00	150.00
(68)	Tris Speaker	750.00	300.00	150.00
(69)	Milton Stock	150.00	60.00	30.00
(70)	Amos Strunk	150.00	60.00	30.00
(71)	Chester Thomas	150.00	60.00	30.00
(72)	George Tyler	150.00	60.00	30.00
(73)	Jim Vaughn	150.00	60.00	30.00
(74)	Bob Veach	150.00	60.00	30.00
(75)	Oscar Vitt	150.00	60.00	30.00
(76)	W. Wambsganss	150.00	60.00	30.00
(77)	Zach Wheat	400.00	160.00	80.00
(78)	Fred Williams	150.00	60.00	30.00
(79)	Ivy B. Wingo	150.00	60.00	30.00
(80)	Joe Wood	150.00	60.00	30.00
(81)	Pep Young	150.00	60.00	30.00

1922 American Caramel Series of 240 (E120)

One of the most popular sets of the 1920s candy cards, the 1922 E120s were produced by the American Caramel Co. and distributed with sticks of caramel candy. The unnumbered cards measure 2" x 3-1/2". Cards depicting players from the American League are printed in brown ink on thin cream cardboard; National Leaguers are printed in green on blue-green stock. Backs carry team checklists. Many of the E120 photos were used in other sets of the era. A pair of 11-1/2" x 10-1/2" albums, holding 120 each and stamped American or National League were also issued.

		NM	EX	VG
	Complete Set (240):	70,000	27,500	14,500
	Common Player:	110.00	50.00	30.00
	Album:	300.00	150.00	90.00
(1)	Charles (Babe) Adams	175.00	70.00	35.00
(2)	Eddie Ainsmith	175.00	70.00	35.00
(3)	Vic Aldridge	175.00	70.00	35.00
(4)	Grover C. Alexander	900.00	360.00	180.00
(5)	Jim Bagby	175.00	70.00	35.00
(6)	Frank (Home Run) Baker	500.00	200.00	100.00
(7)	Dave (Beauty) Bancroft	500.00	200.00	100.00
(8)	Walt Barbare	175.00	70.00	35.00
(9)	Turner Barber	175.00	70.00	35.00
(10)	Jess Barnes	175.00	70.00	35.00
(11)	Clyde Barnhart	175.00	70.00	35.00
(12)	John Bassler	175.00	70.00	35.00
(13)	Will Bayne	175.00	70.00	35.00
(14)	Walter (Huck) Betts	175.00	70.00	35.00
(15)	Carson Bigbee	175.00	70.00	35.00
(16)	Lu Blue	175.00	70.00	35.00
(17)	Norman Boeckel	400.00	160.00	80.00
(18)	Sammy Bohne	175.00	70.00	35.00
(19)	George Burns	175.00	70.00	35.00
(20)	George Burns	175.00	70.00	35.00
(21)	"Bullet Joe" Bush	175.00	70.00	35.00
(22)	Leon Cadore	175.00	70.00	35.00
(23)	Marty Callaghan	175.00	70.00	35.00
(24)	Frank Calloway (Callaway)	175.00	70.00	35.00
(25)	Max Carey	500.00	200.00	100.00
(26)	Jimmy Caveney	175.00	70.00	35.00
(27)	Virgil Cheeves	175.00	70.00	35.00
(28)	Vern Clemons	175.00	70.00	35.00
(29)	Ty Cob (Cobb)	3,500	1,400	700.00
(30)	Bert Cole	175.00	70.00	35.00
(31)	Eddie Collins	500.00	200.00	100.00
(32)	John (Shano) Collins	175.00	70.00	35.00
(33)	T.P. (Pat) Collins	175.00	70.00	35.00
(34)	Wilbur Cooper	175.00	70.00	35.00

(35)	Harry Courtney	175.00	70.00	35.00
(36)	Stanley Coveleskie (Coveleski)	500.00	200.00	100.00
(37)	Elmer Cox	175.00	70.00	35.00
(38)	Sam Crane	175.00	70.00	35.00
(39)	Walton Cruise	175.00	70.00	35.00
(40)	Bill Cunningham	175.00	70.00	35.00
(41)	George Cutshaw	175.00	70.00	35.00
(42)	Dave Danforth	175.00	70.00	35.00
(43)	Jake Daubert	175.00	70.00	35.00
(44)	George Dauss	175.00	70.00	35.00
(45)	Frank (Dixie) Davis	175.00	70.00	35.00
(46)	Hank DeBerry	175.00	70.00	35.00
(47)	Albert Devormer (Lou DeVormer)	175.00	70.00	35.00
(48)	Bill Doak	175.00	70.00	35.00
(49)	Pete Donohue	175.00	70.00	35.00
(50)	"Shufflin" Phil Douglas	175.00	70.00	35.00
(51)	Joe Dugan	175.00	70.00	35.00
(52)	Louis (Pat) Duncan	175.00	70.00	35.00
(53)	Jimmy Dykes	175.00	70.00	35.00
(54)	Howard Ehmke	175.00	70.00	35.00
(55)	Frank Ellerbe	175.00	70.00	35.00
(56)	Urban (Red) Faber	500.00	200.00	100.00
(57)	Bib Falk (Bibb)	175.00	70.00	35.00
(58)	Dana Fillingim	175.00	70.00	35.00
(59)	Max Flack	175.00	70.00	35.00
(60)	Ira Flagstead	175.00	70.00	35.00
(61)	Art Fletcher	175.00	70.00	35.00
(62)	Horace Ford	175.00	70.00	35.00
(63)	Jack Fournier	175.00	70.00	35.00
(64)	Frank Frisch	500.00	200.00	100.00
(65)	Ollie Fuhrman	175.00	70.00	35.00
(66)	Clarence Galloway	175.00	70.00	35.00
(67)	Larry Gardner	175.00	70.00	35.00
(68)	Walter Gerber	175.00	70.00	35.00
(69)	Ed Gharrity	175.00	70.00	35.00
(70)	John Gillespie	175.00	70.00	35.00
(71)	Chas. (Whitey) Glazner	175.00	70.00	35.00
(72)	Johnny Gooch	175.00	70.00	35.00
(73)	Leon Goslin	500.00	200.00	100.00
(74)	Hank Gowdy	175.00	70.00	35.00
(75)	John Graney	175.00	70.00	35.00
(76)	Tom Griffith	175.00	70.00	35.00
(77)	Burleigh Grimes	500.00	200.00	100.00
(78)	Oscar Ray Grimes	175.00	70.00	35.00
(79)	Charlie Grimm	175.00	70.00	35.00
(80)	Heinie Groh	175.00	70.00	35.00
(81)	Jesse Haines	500.00	200.00	100.00
(82)	Earl Hamilton	175.00	70.00	35.00
(83)	Gene (Bubbles) Hargrave	175.00	70.00	35.00
(84)	Bryan Harris (Harriss)	175.00	70.00	35.00
(85)	Joe Harris	175.00	70.00	35.00
(86)	Stanley Harris	500.00	200.00	100.00
(87)	Chas. (Dowdy) Hartnett	500.00	200.00	100.00
(88)	Bob Hasty	175.00	70.00	35.00
(89)	Joe Hauser	225.00	90.00	45.00
(90)	Clif Heathcote	175.00	70.00	35.00
(91)	Harry Heilmann	500.00	200.00	100.00
(92)	Walter (Butch) Henline	175.00	70.00	35.00
(93)	Clarence (Shovel) Hodge	175.00	70.00	35.00
(94)	Walter Holke	175.00	70.00	35.00
(95)	Charles Hollocher	175.00	70.00	35.00
(96)	Harry Hooper	500.00	200.00	100.00
(97)	Rogers Hornsby	900.00	360.00	180.00
(98)	Waite Hoyt	500.00	200.00	100.00
(99)	Wilbur Hubbell (Wilbert)	175.00	70.00	35.00
(100)	Bernard (Bud) Hungling	175.00	70.00	35.00
(101)	Will Jacobson	175.00	70.00	35.00
(102)	Charlie Jamieson	175.00	70.00	35.00
(103)	Ernie Johnson	175.00	70.00	35.00
(104)	Sylvester Johnson	175.00	70.00	35.00
(105)	Walter Johnson	1,600	650.00	325.00
(106)	Jimmy Johnston	175.00	70.00	35.00
(107)	W.R. (Doc) Johnston	175.00	70.00	35.00
(108)	"Deacon" Sam Jones	175.00	70.00	35.00
(109)	Bob Jones	175.00	70.00	35.00
(110)	Percy Jones	175.00	70.00	35.00
(111)	Joe Judge	175.00	70.00	35.00
(112)	Ben Karr	175.00	70.00	35.00
(113)	Johnny Kelleher	175.00	70.00	35.00
(114)	George Kelly	500.00	200.00	100.00
(115)	Lee King	175.00	70.00	35.00
(116)	Wm (Larry) Kopff (Kopf)	175.00	70.00	35.00
(117)	Marty Krug	175.00	70.00	35.00
(118)	Johnny Lavan	175.00	70.00	35.00
(119)	Nemo Leibold	175.00	70.00	35.00
(120)	Roy Leslie	175.00	70.00	35.00
(121)	George Leverette (Leverett)	175.00	70.00	35.00
(122)	Adolfo Luque	175.00	70.00	35.00
(123)	Walter Mails	175.00	70.00	35.00
(124)	Al Mamaux	175.00	70.00	35.00
(125)	"Rabbit" Maranville	500.00	200.00	100.00
(126)	Cliff Markle	175.00	70.00	35.00
(127)	Richard (Rube) Marquard	500.00	200.00	100.00
(128)	Carl Mays	200.00	80.00	40.00
(129)	Hervey McClellan (Harvey)	175.00	70.00	35.00
(130)	Austin McHenry	175.00	70.00	35.00
(131)	"Stuffy" McInnis	175.00	70.00	35.00
(132)	Martin McManus	175.00	70.00	35.00
(133)	Mike McNally	175.00	70.00	35.00
(134)	Hugh McQuillan	175.00	70.00	35.00
(135)	Lee Meadows	175.00	70.00	35.00
(136)	Mike Menosky	175.00	70.00	35.00
(137)	Bob (Dutch) Meusel	175.00	70.00	35.00
(138)	Emil (Irish) Meusel	175.00	70.00	35.00
(139)	Clyde Milan	175.00	70.00	35.00
(140)	Edmund (Bing) Miller	175.00	70.00	35.00
(141)	Elmer Miller	175.00	70.00	35.00
(142)	Lawrence (Hack) Miller	175.00	70.00	35.00
(143)	Clarence Mitchell	175.00	70.00	35.00
(144)	George Mogridge	175.00	70.00	35.00
(145)	Roy Moore	175.00	70.00	35.00
(146)	John L. Mokan	175.00	70.00	35.00
(147)	John Morrison	175.00	70.00	35.00
(148)	Johnny Mostil	175.00	70.00	35.00
(149)	Elmer Myers	175.00	70.00	35.00
(150)	Hy Myers	175.00	70.00	35.00

(151)	Roliene Naylor (Roleine)	175.00	70.00	35.00
(152)	Earl "Greasy" Neale	175.00	70.00	35.00
(153)	Art Nehf	175.00	70.00	35.00
(154)	Les Nunamaker	175.00	70.00	35.00
(155)	Joe Oeschger	175.00	70.00	35.00
(156)	Bob O'Farrell	175.00	70.00	35.00
(157)	Ivan Olson	175.00	70.00	35.00
(158)	George O'Neil	175.00	70.00	35.00
(159)	Steve O'Neill	175.00	70.00	35.00
(160)	Frank Parkinson	175.00	70.00	35.00
(161)	Roger Peckinpaugh	175.00	70.00	35.00
(162)	Herb Pennock	500.00	200.00	100.00
(163)	Ralph (Cy) Perkins	175.00	70.00	35.00
(164)	Will Pertica	175.00	70.00	35.00
(165)	Jack Peters	175.00	70.00	35.00
(166)	Tom Phillips	175.00	70.00	35.00
(167)	Val Picinich	175.00	70.00	35.00
(168)	Herman Pillette	175.00	70.00	35.00
(169)	Ralph Pinelli	175.00	70.00	35.00
(170)	Wallie Pipp	175.00	70.00	35.00
(171)	Clark Pittenger (Clarke)	175.00	70.00	35.00
(172)	Raymond Powell	175.00	70.00	35.00
(173)	Derrill Pratt	175.00	70.00	35.00
(174)	Jack Quinn	175.00	70.00	35.00
(175)	Joe (Goldie) Rapp	175.00	70.00	35.00
(176)	John Rawlings	175.00	70.00	35.00
(177)	Walter (Dutch) Reuther (Ruether)	175.00	70.00	35.00
(178)	Sam Rice	500.00	200.00	100.00
(179)	Emory Rigney	175.00	70.00	35.00
(180)	Jimmy Ring	175.00	70.00	35.00
(181)	Eppa Rixey	500.00	200.00	100.00
(182)	Charles Robertson	175.00	70.00	35.00
(183)	Ed Rommel	175.00	70.00	35.00
(184)	Eddie Roush	500.00	200.00	100.00
(185)	Harold (Muddy) Ruel (Herold)	175.00	70.00	35.00
(186)	Babe Ruth	15,000	6,000	3,000
(187)	Ray Schalk	500.00	200.00	100.00
(188)	Wallie Schang	175.00	70.00	35.00
(189)	Ray Schmandt	175.00	70.00	35.00
(190)	Walter Schmidt	175.00	70.00	35.00
(191)	Joe Schultz	175.00	70.00	35.00
(192)	Everett Scott	175.00	70.00	35.00
(193)	Henry Severeid	175.00	70.00	35.00
(194)	Joe Sewell	500.00	200.00	100.00
(195)	Howard Shanks	175.00	70.00	35.00
(196)	Bob Shawkey	175.00	70.00	35.00
(197)	Earl Sheely	175.00	70.00	35.00
(198)	Will Sherdel	175.00	70.00	35.00
(199)	Ralph Shinners	175.00	70.00	35.00
(200)	Urban Shocker	175.00	70.00	35.00
(201)	Charles (Chick) Shorten	175.00	70.00	35.00
(202)	George Sisler	500.00	200.00	100.00
(203)	Earl Smith (N.Y. Giants)	175.00	70.00	35.00
(204)	Earl Smith (Washington)	175.00	70.00	35.00
(205)	Elmer Smith	175.00	70.00	35.00
(206)	Jack Smith	175.00	70.00	35.00
(207)	Sherrod Smith	175.00	70.00	35.00
(208)	Colonel Snover	175.00	70.00	35.00
(209)	Frank Snyder	175.00	70.00	35.00
(210)	Al Sothoron	175.00	70.00	35.00
(211)	Bill Southworth	175.00	70.00	35.00
(212)	Tris Speaker	900.00	360.00	180.00
(213)	Arnold Statz	175.00	70.00	35.00
(214)	Milton Stock	175.00	70.00	35.00
(215)	Amos Strunk	175.00	70.00	35.00
(216)	Jim Tierney	175.00	70.00	35.00
(217)	John Tobin	175.00	70.00	35.00
(218)	Fred Toney	175.00	70.00	35.00
(219)	George Toporcer	175.00	70.00	35.00
(220)	Harold (Pie) Traynor	500.00	200.00	100.00
(221)	George Uhle	175.00	70.00	35.00
(222)	Elam Vangilder	175.00	70.00	35.00
(223)	Bob Veach	175.00	70.00	35.00
(224)	Clarence (Tillie) Walker	175.00	70.00	35.00
(225)	Curtis Walker	175.00	70.00	35.00
(226)	Al Walters	175.00	70.00	35.00
(227)	Bill Wambsganss	175.00	70.00	35.00
(228)	Aaron Ward	175.00	70.00	35.00
(229)	John Watson	175.00	70.00	35.00
(230)	Frank Welch	175.00	70.00	35.00
(231)	Zach Wheat	500.00	200.00	100.00
(232)	Fred (Cy) Williams	175.00	70.00	35.00
(233)	Kenneth Williams	175.00	70.00	35.00
(234)	Ivy Wingo	175.00	70.00	35.00
(235)	Joe Wood	400.00	160.00	80.00
(236)	Lawrence Woodall	175.00	70.00	35.00
(237)	Russell Wrightstone	175.00	70.00	35.00
(238)	Everett Yaryan	175.00	70.00	35.00
(239)	Ross Young (Youngs)	500.00	200.00	100.00
(240)	J.T. Zachary	175.00	70.00	35.00

1927 American Caramel Series of 60 (E126)

Issued in 1927 by the American Caramel Co., of Lancaster, Pa., this obscure 60-card set was one of the last of the caramel card issues. Measuring 2" x 3-1/4", the cards differ from most sets of the period because they are numbered. The back of each card includes an offer for an album to house the set which includes players from all 16 major league teams. The set has the American Card Catalog designation E126.

		NM	EX	VG
Complete Set (60):		36,500	14,500	7,250
Common Player:		125.00	55.00	30.00
1	John Gooch	200.00	80.00	40.00
2	Clyde L. Barnhart	200.00	80.00	40.00
3	Joe Busch (Bush)	200.00	80.00	40.00
4	Lee Meadows	200.00	80.00	40.00
5	E.T. Cox	200.00	80.00	40.00
6	"Red" Faber	600.00	240.00	120.00
7	Aaron Ward	200.00	80.00	40.00
8	Ray Schalk	600.00	240.00	120.00
9	"Specks" Toporcer ("Specs")	200.00	80.00	40.00
10	Bill Southworth	200.00	80.00	40.00
11	Allen Sothoron	200.00	80.00	40.00
12	Will Sherdel	200.00	80.00	40.00
13	Grover Alexander	1,000	400.00	200.00
14	Jack Quinn	200.00	80.00	40.00
15	C. Galloway	200.00	80.00	40.00
16	"Eddie" Collins	600.00	240.00	120.00
17	"Ty" Cobb	3,800	1,550	775.00
18	Percy Jones	200.00	80.00	40.00
19	Chas. Grimm	200.00	80.00	40.00
20	"Bennie" Karr	200.00	80.00	40.00
21	Charlie Jamieson	200.00	80.00	40.00
22	Sherrod Smith	200.00	80.00	40.00
23	Virgil Cheeves	200.00	80.00	40.00
24	James Ring	200.00	80.00	40.00
25	"Muddy" Ruel	200.00	80.00	40.00
26	Joe Judge	200.00	80.00	40.00
27	Tris Speaker	1,000	400.00	200.00
28	Walter Johnson	2,000	800.00	400.00
29	E.C. "Sam" Rice	600.00	240.00	120.00
30	Hank DeBerry	200.00	80.00	40.00
31	Walter Henline	200.00	80.00	40.00
32	Max Carey	600.00	240.00	120.00
33	Arnold J. Statz	200.00	80.00	40.00
34	Emil Meusel	200.00	80.00	40.00
35	T.P. "Pat" Collins	200.00	80.00	40.00
36	Urban Shocker	200.00	80.00	40.00
37	Bob Shawkey	200.00	80.00	40.00
38	"Babe" Ruth	15,000	6,000	3,000
39	Bob Meusel	200.00	80.00	40.00
40	Alex Ferguson	200.00	80.00	40.00
41	"Stuffy" McInnis	200.00	80.00	40.00
42	"Cy" Williams	200.00	80.00	40.00
43	Russel Wrightstone (Russell)	200.00	80.00	40.00
44	John Tobin	200.00	80.00	40.00
45	Wm. C. Jacobson	200.00	80.00	40.00
46	Bryan "Slim" Harriss	200.00	80.00	40.00
47	Elam Vangilder	200.00	80.00	40.00
48	Ken Williams	200.00	80.00	40.00
49	Geo. R. Sisler	800.00	325.00	160.00
50	Ed Brown	200.00	80.00	40.00
51	Jack Smith	200.00	80.00	40.00
52	Dave Bancroft	600.00	240.00	120.00
53	Larry Woodall	200.00	80.00	40.00
54	Lu Blue	200.00	80.00	40.00
55	Johnny Bassler	200.00	80.00	40.00
56	"Jakie" May	200.00	80.00	40.00
57	Horace Ford	200.00	80.00	40.00
58	"Curt" Walker	200.00	80.00	40.00
59	"Artie" Nehf	200.00	80.00	40.00
60	Geo. Kelly	600.00	240.00	120.00

1908 American League Pub. Co. Postcards

This set of black-and-white postcards was produced by the American League Publishing Co., Cleveland. The 3-1/2" x 5" cards have a large player posed-action photo against a white background and a smaller oval portrait photo in one of the top corners. A box at bottom contains some biographical data. The otherwise blank back has postcard indicia printed in black. The set carries an American Card Catalog designation of PC770. As might be expected, all but two of the players in the known checklist were contemporary members of the Cleveland ballclub.

		NM	EX	VG
Complete Set (16):		10,000	5,000	3,000
Common Player:		350.00	175.00	100.00
(1)	Harry Bay	350.00	175.00	100.00
(2)	Harry Bemis	350.00	175.00	100.00
(3)	Charles Berger	350.00	175.00	100.00
(4)	Joseph Birmingham	350.00	175.00	100.00
(5)	W. Bradley	350.00	175.00	100.00
(6)	Tyrus R. Cobb	2,500	1,250	750.00
(7)	Walter Clarkson	350.00	175.00	100.00
(8)	Elmer Flick	600.00	300.00	180.00
(9)	C.T. Hickman	350.00	175.00	100.00
(10)	William Hinchman	350.00	175.00	100.00
(11)	Addie Joss	750.00	375.00	225.00
(12)	Glen Liebhardt (Glenn)	350.00	175.00	100.00
(13)	Nap Lajoie	750.00	375.00	225.00
(14)	George Nill	350.00	175.00	100.00
(15)	George Perring	350.00	175.00	100.00
(16)	Honus Wagner	1,800	900.00	540.00

1950 American Nut & Chocolate Pennants (F150)

Although there is nothing on these small (1-7/8" x 4") felt pennants to identify the issuer, surviving ads show that the American Nut & Chocolate Co. of Boston sold them as a set of 22 for 50 cents. The pennants of American League players are printed in blue on white, while National Leaguers are printed in red on white. The pennants feature crude line-art drawings of the players at left, along with a facsimile autograph. A 10 percent variation in the size of the printing on the Elliott and Sain pennants has been noted, and may exist on others, as well. An approximately 17" x 7" version of the Ted Williams pennant is known and was available as a mail-in premium. Other players may also exist in that format. The checklist here is arranged alphabetically.

		NM	EX	VG
Complete Set (22):		1,800	900.00	550.00
Common Player:		65.00	32.50	20.00
(1)	Ewell Blackwell	65.00	32.50	20.00
(2)	Harry Brecheen	65.00	32.50	20.00
(3)	Phil Cavarretta	65.00	32.50	20.00
(4)	Bobby Doerr	100.00	50.00	30.00
(5)	Bob Elliott	65.00	32.50	20.00
(6)	Boo Ferriss	65.00	32.50	20.00
(7)	Joe Gordon	65.00	32.50	20.00
(8)	Tommy Holmes	65.00	32.50	20.00
(9)	Charles Keller	65.00	32.50	20.00
(10)	Ken Keltner	65.00	32.50	20.00
(11)	Ralph Kiner	100.00	50.00	30.00
(12)	Whitey Kurowski	65.00	32.50	20.00
(13)	Johnny Pesky	65.00	32.50	20.00
(14)	Pee Wee Reese	130.00	65.00	40.00
(15)	Phil Rizzuto	130.00	65.00	40.00
(16)	Johnny Sain	65.00	32.50	20.00
(17)	Enos Slaughter	100.00	50.00	30.00
(18)	Warren Spahn	100.00	50.00	30.00
(19)	Vern Stephens	65.00	32.50	20.00
(20)	Earl Torgeson	65.00	32.50	20.00
(21)	Dizzy Trout	65.00	32.50	20.00
(22)	Ted Williams	260.00	130.00	80.00
(22)	Ted Williams (17" x 7")	900.00	450.00	275.00

1968 American Oil Sweepstakes

Babe Ruth won fame as the greatest slugger in baseball history. He set many records including his 714 regular-season home runs which made him one of baseball's biggest attractions.

BABE RUTH

$1.00 ONE DOLLAR

Right side

One of several contemporary sweepstakes run by gas stations, this game required matching right- and left-side game pieces of the same athletic figure (or sporty auto) to win the stated prize. Naturally one side or the other was distributed in extremely limited quantities to avoid paying out too many prizes. Cards were given away in perforated pairs with a qualifying gasoline purchase. Uncut pairs carry a small premium over single cards. Data on which card halves were the rare part needed for redemption is incomplete and would have an effect on the collector value of surviving specimens. Individual game pieces measure 2-9/16" x 2-1/8" and are printed in color. Only the baseball players in the set are listed here.

		NM	EX	VG
(1a)	Mickey Mantle/Action (Left side, $10.)	40.00	20.00	12.00
(1b)	Mickey Mantle/Portrait (Right side, $10.)	30.00	15.00	9.00
(2a)	Willie Mays/Action (Left side, $10)	40.00	20.00	12.00
(2b)	Willie Mays/Portrait (Right side, $10)	25.00	12.50	7.50
(3a)	Babe Ruth/Action (Left side, $1)	40.00	20.00	12.00
(3b)	Babe Ruth/Portrait (Right side, $1)	25.00	12.50	7.50

1910 American Sports Candy and Jewelry

(See 1910 Orange Borders.)

1962 American Tract Society

A TIP FOR YOU

These full-color cards, which carry religious messages on the back, were issued in 1962 by the American Tract Society, an interdenominational, non-sectarian publisher of Christian literature in the United States since 1825. Known as "Tracards," the cards measure 2-3/4" x 3-1/2" and feature color photographs on the fronts. The set includes religious scenes along with photos of various celebrities and sports stars, including baseball players Felipe Alou, Bobby Richardson, Jerry Kindall and Al Worthington. (There are two poses each of Alou and Kindall.) The backs carry rather lengthy, first-person religious testimonials from the players. The cards are numbered on the back in the lower right corner.

		NM	EX	VG
	Complete Set (6):	70.00	35.00	20.00
	Common Player:	10.00	5.00	3.00
43	Bobby Richardson	25.00	12.50	7.50
51a	Jerry Kindall (Cleveland)	10.00	5.00	3.00
51b	Jerry Kindall (Minnesota)	10.00	5.00	3.00
52a	Felipe Alou/Kneeling	15.00	7.50	4.50
52b	Felipe Alou/Btg	15.00	7.50	4.50
66	Al Worthington	10.00	5.00	3.00

1973 John B. Anderson Former Greats

This set of postcard-sized black-and-white cards features the artwork of John B. Anderson, a New York collector. Each card includes a facsimile autograph on front; backs are blank. The unnumbered cards are checklisted here in alphabetical order.

		NM	EX	VG
	Complete Set (12):	30.00	15.00	9.00
	Common Player:	4.00	2.00	1.25
(1)	Ty Cobb	6.00	3.00	1.75
(2)	Mickey Cochrane	4.00	2.00	1.25
(3)	Roberto Clemente	10.00	5.00	3.00
(4)	Lou Gehrig	10.00	5.00	3.00
(5)	Frank Frisch	4.00	2.00	1.25
(6)	Gil Hodges	6.00	3.00	1.75
(7)	Rogers Hornsby	4.00	2.00	1.25
(8)	Connie Mack	6.00	3.00	1.75
(9)	Christy Mathewson	6.00	3.00	1.75
(10)	Jackie Robinson	10.00	5.00	3.00
(11)	Babe Ruth	10.00	5.00	3.00
(12)	Pie Traynor	4.00	2.00	1.25

1977 John B. Anderson Aaron-Mays

This set of postcard size, black-and-white drawings is a collectors issue. Cards are blank-backed.

		NM	EX	VG
	Complete Set (4):	5.00	2.50	1.50
	Common Card:	2.00	1.00	.60
(1)	Hank Aaron (Arm in air.)	2.00	1.00	.60
(2)	Hank Aaron/Portrait	2.00	1.00	.60
(3)	Willie Mays (Giants)	2.00	1.00	.60
(4)	Willie Mays (Mets)	2.00	1.00	.60

1977 John B. Anderson New York Teams

Joe DiMaggio

Stars and local favorites of the three New York teams of the 1940s and 1950s are featured in this set of collectors cards. The 3-1/2" x 5-1/2" blank-back, black-and-white cards feature artwork by John B. Anderson. The unnumbered cards are checklisted here in alphabetical order.

		NM	EX	VG
	Complete Set (24):	45.00	27.50	13.50
	Common Player:	4.00	2.00	1.25
(1)	Yogi Berra	6.00	3.00	1.75
(2)	Ralph Branca	4.00	2.00	1.25
(3)	Dolf Camilli	4.00	2.00	1.25
(4)	Roy Campanella	6.00	3.00	1.75
(5)	Jerry Coleman	4.00	2.00	1.25
(6)	Frank Crosetti	4.00	2.00	1.25
(7)	Bill Dickey	4.00	2.00	1.25
(8)	Joe DiMaggio	15.00	7.50	4.50
(9)	Sid Gordon	4.00	2.00	1.25
(10)	Babe Herman	4.00	2.00	1.25
(11)	Carl Hubbell	4.00	2.00	1.25
(12)	Billy Johnson	4.00	2.00	1.25
(13)	Ernie Lombardi	4.00	2.00	1.25
(14)	Willard Marshall	4.00	2.00	1.25
(15)	Willie Mays	10.00	5.00	3.00
(16)	Joe McCarthy	4.00	2.00	1.25
(17)	Joe Medwick	4.00	2.00	1.25
(18)	Joe Moore	4.00	2.00	1.25
(19)	Andy Pafko	4.00	2.00	1.25
(20)	Jackie Robinson	10.00	5.00	3.00
(21)	Red Ruffing	4.00	2.00	1.25
(22)	Bill Terry	4.00	2.00	1.25
(23)	Hoyt Wilhelm	4.00	2.00	1.25
(24)	Gene Woodling	4.00	2.00	1.25

1904 Anonymous Studio Cabinets

Collins

The origins of this series of cabinet photos are unknown, as is the full entent of the issue. It is known that the portraits are the uncredited work of Boston photographer Carl Horner. Sixteen pieces were sold in the 1991 Copeland Auction, though only the players listed here have been reliably checklisted. The cabinets measure about 5-3/8" x 6-7/8" and have black or dark gray borders. Some pieces are reported to have slate-blue blank backs. The player's last name is presented in the lower-left corner in black or white outline scrip. The unnumbered cards are checklisted here in alphabetical order.

		NM	EX	VG
	Common Player:	750.00	375.00	225.00
(1)	Jake Beckley	750.00	375.00	225.00
(2)	Roger Bresnahan	750.00	375.00	225.00
(3)	Jimmy Collins	750.00	375.00	225.00
(4)	Lave Cross	600.00	300.00	180.00
(5)	Hugh Duffy	600.00	300.00	180.00
(6)	Clark Griffith	750.00	375.00	225.00
(7)	Danny Hoffman	600.00	300.00	180.00
(8)	Connie Mack	750.00	375.00	225.00
(9)	Iron Man McGinity (McGinnity)	750.00	375.00	225.00
(10)	John McGraw	750.00	375.00	225.00
(11)	Matty McIntyre	600.00	300.00	180.00

1912 Anonymous T207

While most T207s are found with one of five different cigarette brands advertised on back, there is a less commonly encountered type with no such ad. They are known as Anonymous backs. Two types are known, one originating from Factory 3 in Louisiana and one from Virginia's Factory 25. The latter is much scarcer though commands little additional premium.

(See 1912 T207 for checklist and price guide.)

1925 Anonymous Postcards

Mgr. STANLEY HARRIS
Washington Senators

POST CARD

The date attributed is speculative based on the limited number of known subjects. These 3-1/4" x 5-1/2" cards have a square portrait photo at center in black-and-white. With the exception of Babe Ruth, all known subjects were managers in 1925. The subject is identified by name (in either all-caps or upper- and lower-case, team, and, sometimes, title "Mgr." At least two styles of undivided backs have been found, with an ornate "POST CARD" device at top and a stamp box. The cards are printed on low-grade cardboard. Collector uncertainty as to the origins of the cards and the potential supply has kept market prices down.

	NM	EX	VG
Common Player:	300.00	150.00	90.00
Tyrus Cobb	400.00	200.00	120.00
Mgr. Tyrus Cobb	400.00	200.00	120.00
Stanley Harris	200.00	100.00	60.00
Walter Johnson	300.00	150.00	90.00
John McGraw	200.00	100.00	60.00
"Bill" McKechnie	200.00	100.00	60.00
Wilbert Robinson	200.00	100.00	60.00
Babe Ruth	600.00	300.00	180.00

1940s-50s Anonymous Premium Photos

Harry Heilman

There is no indication on these 8" x 10" black-and-white photos as to who produced them or for what purpose. The blank-backed, white-bordered pictures have the player identified with a sometimes-misspelled script signature. It is not known if this checklist is complete.

		NM	EX	VG
	Complete Set (12):	300.00	150.00	90.00
	Common Player:	20.00	10.00	6.00
(1)	Ty Cobb	40.00	20.00	12.00
(2)	Dizzy Dean	25.00	12.50	7.50
(3)	Bob Feller	25.00	12.50	7.50
(4)	Lou Gehrig	40.00	20.00	12.00
(5)	Harry Heilman (Heilmann)	20.00	10.00	6.00
(6)	Roger (Rogers) Hornsby	25.00	12.50	7.50
(7)	Walter Johnson	25.00	12.50	7.50
(8)	Christy Mathewson	30.00	15.00	9.00
(9)	Bob Meusel	20.00	10.00	6.00
(10)	Irish Emil Meusel	20.00	10.00	6.00
(11)	Babe Ruth	50.00	25.00	15.00
(12)	Zack Wheat	20.00	10.00	6.00

1949-1950 Ansco Almendares Scorpions

This set of the Cuban Professional League champions of the 1949-50 season was sponsored by Ansco Cameras and Film, whose logo appears on front. Some cards have on back a rubber-stamp with the name of an Havana photo studio, which may have distributed the cards. The cards are actual black-and-white photos on glossy photo paper, measuring about 3" x 3-7/8". The Scorpions had many former and future major leaguers on their roster. Cards are listed alphabetically here.

		NM	EX	VG
	Complete Set (20):	3,250	1,625	975.00
	Common Player:	150.00	60.00	40.00
(1)	Bill Antonello	175.00	70.00	45.00
(2)	Zungo Cabrera	150.00	60.00	40.00
(3)	Tony Castanos	150.00	60.00	40.00
(4)	Avelino Canizares	150.00	60.00	40.00
(5)	Kevin (Chuck) Connors	450.00	180.00	110.00
(6)	Andres Fleitas	150.00	60.00	40.00
(7)	Al Gionfriddo	175.00	70.00	45.00
(8)	Fermin Guerra	150.00	60.00	40.00
(9)	Gene Handley	150.00	60.00	40.00
(10)	Bob Hooper	150.00	60.00	40.00
(11)	Vincente Lopez	150.00	60.00	40.00
(12)	Conrado Marrero	175.00	70.00	45.00
(13)	Agapito Mayor	150.00	60.00	40.00
(14)	Willie Miranda	175.00	70.00	45.00
(15)	Rene Monteagudo	150.00	60.00	40.00
(16)	Roberto Ortiz	150.00	60.00	40.00
(17)	Hector Rodriguez	150.00	60.00	40.00
(18)	Octavio Rubert	150.00	60.00	40.00
(19)	Rene Solis	150.00	60.00	40.00
(20)	Ed Wright	150.00	60.00	40.00

1961-62 Apple Fresh Milk Minnesota Twins

(See 1961, 1962 Cloverleaf Dairy Minnesota Twins.)

1971 Arco

In 1971, players from four major league teams in the east were featured in a set of facsimile autographed color photos in a gas station giveaway program. Following the promotion, leftover pictures were sold directly to collectors in the pages of the existing hobby media. The photos share an 8" x 10" format,

---

with virtually all of the players being pictured without caps. Red, white and blue stars flank the player name in the bottom border. Black-and-white backs have career summary and stats, personal data, team sponsor and union logos and an ad for frames for the pictures. The unnumbered photos are listed here alphabetically within team.

		NM	EX	VG
	Complete Set (49):	175.00	90.00	50.00
	Common Player:	3.00	1.50	.90
	RED SOX TEAM SET:	60.00	30.00	18.00
(1)	Luis Aparicio	10.00	5.00	3.00
(2)	Ken Brett	4.00	2.00	1.25
(3)	Billy Conigliaro	4.00	2.00	1.25
(4)	Ray Culp	4.00	2.00	1.25
(5)	Doug Griffin	4.00	2.00	1.25
(6)	Bob Montgomery	4.00	2.00	1.25
(7)	Gary Peters	4.00	2.00	1.25
(8)	George Scott	5.00	2.50	1.50
(9)	Sonny Siebert	4.00	2.00	1.25
(10)	Reggie Smith	5.00	2.50	1.50
(11)	Ken Tatum	4.00	2.00	1.25
(12)	Carl Yastrzemski	15.00	7.50	4.50
	YANKEES TEAM SET:	65.00	32.50	20.00
(1)	Jack Aker	6.00	3.00	1.75
(2)	Stan Bahnsen	6.00	3.00	1.75
(3)	Frank Baker	6.00	3.00	1.75
(4)	Danny Cater	6.00	3.00	1.75
(5)	Horace Clarke	6.00	3.00	1.75
(6)	John Ellis	6.00	3.00	1.75
(7)	Gene Michael	6.00	3.00	1.75
(8)	Thurman Munson	12.00	6.00	3.50
(9)	Bobby Murcer	7.50	3.75	2.25
(10)	Fritz Peterson	6.00	3.00	1.75
(11)	Mel Stottlemyre	6.00	3.00	1.75
(12)	Roy White	7.50	3.75	2.25
	PHILLIES TEAM SET:	40.00	20.00	12.00
(1)	Larry Bowa	3.00	1.50	.90
(2)	Jim Bunning	10.00	5.00	3.00
(3)	Roger Freed	3.00	1.50	.90
(4)	Terry Harmon	3.00	1.50	.90
(5)	Larry Hisle	3.00	1.50	.90
(6)	Joe Hoerner	3.00	1.50	.90
(7)	Deron Johnson	3.00	1.50	.90
(8)	Tim McCarver	5.00	2.50	1.50
(9)	Don Money	3.00	1.50	.90
(10)	Dick Selma	3.00	1.50	.90
(11)	Chris Short	3.00	1.50	.90
(12)	Tony Taylor	3.00	1.50	.90
(13)	Rick Wise	3.00	1.50	.90
	PIRATES TEAM SET:	65.00	32.50	20.00
(1)	Gene Alley	3.00	1.50	.90
(2)	Steve Blass	3.00	1.50	.90
(3)	Roberto Clemente	30.00	15.00	9.00
(4)	Dave Giusti	3.00	1.50	.90
(5)	Richie Hebner	3.00	1.50	.90
(6)	Bill Mazeroski	7.50	3.75	2.25
(7)	Bob Moose	3.00	1.50	.90
(8)	Al Oliver	4.50	2.25	1.25
(9)	Bob Robertson	3.00	1.50	.90
(10)	Manny Sanguillen	3.00	1.50	.90
(11)	Willie Stargell	7.50	3.75	2.25
(12)	Luke Walker	3.00	1.50	.90

1980-81 Argus Publishing Reggie Jackson

Some of the cars from Reggie Jackson's collection of hot rods and vintage vehicles were featured on a series of promotional cards issued by the publisher of Hot Rodding and Super Chevy magazines. The standard-size color cards have photos of Jackson with his cars on front, along with magazine and other logos. Backs have information on Jackson's cars. It was reported 10,000 of each were produced for distribution at automotive trade shows and a California drag strip.

		NM	EX	VG
	Complete Set (3):	40.00	20.00	12.00
(1)	1980 SEMA Show (Reggie Jackson) (1932 Ford highboy)	20.00	10.00	6.00
2	1981 SEMA (Reggie Jackson) (1932 Ford 5-window)	10.00	5.00	3.00
3	1981 Super Chevy Sunday (Reggie Jackson) (1955 Chevrolet)	10.00	5.00	3.00

1955 Armour Coins

In 1955, Armour inserted a plastic "coin" into packages of hot dogs. A raised profile of a ballplayer is on front along with the player's name and team. On

---

back, between a diamond diagram and crossed bats are name, team, position, birthplace and date, batting and throwing preference, and 1954 hitting or pitching record. The coins measure 1-1/2" in diameter and are unnumbered. They can be found in a variety of colors, some of which are much scarcer than others and elicit higher prices from Armour specialists who have studied their relative scarcities. Values shown are for coins in the most common colors (aqua, blue, green, orange and red). Each 1955 coin can be found in two different "bust tilts" in which the tip of the cap and back point of the bust point to distinctly different areas of the rim. These variations are too arcane for the average collector. The complete set price includes only the most common variations.

		NM	EX	VG
	Complete Set (24):	700.00	350.00	210.00
	Common Player:	15.00	6.00	3.75
(1a)	John "Johnny" Antonelli ("New York Giants" on back.)	80.00	40.00	25.00
(1b)	John "Johnny" Antonelli ("N.Y. Giants" on back.)	15.00	7.50	4.50
(2)	Larry "Yogi" Berra	25.00	12.50	7.50
(3)	Delmar "Del" Crandall	15.00	7.50	4.50
(4)	Lawrence "Larry" Doby	25.00	12.50	7.50
(5)	James "Jim" Finigan	15.00	7.50	4.50
(6)	Edward "Whitey" Ford	40.00	20.00	12.00
(7a)	James "Junior" Gilliam ("Bats L or R")	60.00	30.00	18.00
(7b)	James "Junior" Gilliam ("Bats L - R", thick lips, wide gap between "BROOKLYN" and "DODGERS.")	35.00	17.50	10.00
(7c)	James "Junior" Gilliam ("Bats L - R", thin lips, narrow gap between "BROOKLYN" and "DODGERS.")	45.00	22.50	13.50
(8)	Harvey "Kitten" Haddix	15.00	7.50	4.50
(9a)	Ranson "Randy" Jackson (Ranson) ("Infielder" on back.)	30.00	15.00	9.00
(9b)	Ranson "Randy" Jackson (Ranson) ("Infielder" on back)	50.00	25.00	15.00
(10a)	Jack "Jackie" Jensen ("Boston Reb Sox")	60.00	30.00	18.00
(10b)	Jack "Jackie" Jensen ("Boston Red Sox")	20.00	10.00	6.00
(11)	Theodore "Ted" Kluszewski	20.00	10.00	6.00
(12a)	Harvey E. Kuenn (widely spaced letters in name; last line on back is bats/throws)	30.00	15.00	9.00
(12b)	Harvey E. Kuenn (Widely spaced letters in name; last line on back is 1954 average.)	100.00	50.00	30.00
(12c)	Harvey E. Kuenn (Condensed letters in name; last line on back is 1954 average.)	70.00	35.00	20.00
(13a)	Charles "Mickey" Mantel (Incorrect spelling.)	115.00	55.00	35.00
(13b)	Charles "Mickey" Mantle (Corrected)("Bats L or R")	400.00	200.00	120.00
(13c)	Charles "Mickey" Mantle (Corrected)("bats L - R")	400.00	200.00	120.00
(14)	Donald "Don" Mueller/SP	30.00	15.00	9.00
(15)	Harold "Pee Wee" Reese	25.00	12.50	7.50
(16)	Allie P. Reynolds	15.00	7.50	4.50
(17)	Albert "Flip" Rosen	20.00	10.00	6.00
(18)	Curtis "Curt" Simmons	20.00	10.00	6.00
(19)	Edwin "Duke" Snider	100.00	50.00	30.00
(20)	Warren Spahn	40.00	20.00	12.00
(21)	Frank Thomas/SP	25.00	12.50	7.50
(22a)	Virgil "Fire" Trucks (WHITESOX)	25.00	12.50	7.50
(22b)	Virgil "Fire" Trucks (WHITE SOX)	50.00	25.00	15.00
(23)	Robert "Bob" Turley	25.00	12.50	7.50
(24)	James "Mickey" Vernon	15.00	7.50	4.50

1958 Armour S.F. Giants Tabs

1958 Armour S.F. Giants Tabs

In the Giants' first season on the West Coast, packages of Armour hot dogs in the Bay Area could be found with a small (about 2" x 1-5/8") lithographed tin player "tab" enclosed. In team colors of black, white and orange the tabs have black-and-white portraits at center, around which is a round, square or diamond shaped device bearing the team name and other graphic touches. At the sides are wings with baseballs or caps printed thereon. A 1/2" tab is at top with a slotted panel at bottom. The tab of one piece could be inserted into the slot of another to create a chain of these pieces, or the top tab could be folded over a shirt pocket to wear the item as a badge. The unnumbered pieces are checklisted here alphabetically. NM values quoted are for unbent pieces only.

		NM	EX	VG
Complete Set (10):		2,700	1,350	825.00
Common Player:		250.00	125.00	75.00
(1)	Johnny Antonelli	250.00	125.00	75.00
(2)	Curt Barclay	250.00	125.00	75.00
(3)	Ray Crone	250.00	125.00	75.00
(4)	Whitey Lockman	250.00	125.00	75.00
(5a)	Willie Mays (Portrait in circle.)	450.00	225.00	135.00
(5b)	Willie Mays (Portrait in diamond.)	450.00	225.00	135.00
(6)	Don Mueller	250.00	125.00	75.00
(7)	Danny O'Connell	250.00	125.00	75.00
(8)	Hank Sauer	250.00	125.00	75.00
(9)	Daryl Spencer	250.00	125.00	75.00
(10)	Bobby Thomson	250.00	125.00	75.00

1959 Armour Bacon K.C. Athletics

ROGER MARIS
Star Outfielder
K. C. Athletics

Not so much a baseball card set as a handful of related single-card issues used at player promotional appearances, a total of four cards are currently known of this issue. Measuring either 5-1/2" x 3-1/4" or 5-1/2" x 4", the horizontal-format cards are printed in black-and-white on paper stock and are blank-backed. A posed player photo appears at left, with an ad for Armour bacon at right. Cards were given out at player appearances at local supermarkets. To date, all known specimens have been found autographed and are priced as such.

		NM	EX	VG
Complete Set (4):		900.00	450.00	275.00
Common Player:		75.00	37.00	22.00
(1)	Harry Chiti	75.00	37.50	22.50
(2)	Whitey Herzog	90.00	45.00	27.50
(3)	Roger Maris (Photo to waist.)	600.00	300.00	180.00
(4)	Roger Maris (Hands on knees.)	600.00	300.00	180.00

1959 Armour Coins

After a three-year layoff, Armour again inserted plastic "coins" into its hot dog packages. The coins retained their 1-1/2" size but did not include as much detailed information as in 1955. Missing from the coins' backs is information such as birthplace and date, team, and batting and throwing preference. The fronts contain the player's name and, unlike 1955, only the team nickname is given. The set consists of 20 coins which come in a myriad of colors. Common colors are navy blue, royal blue, medium green, orange and red. Many other colors are known, many of them scarce and of extra value to Armour specialists. In 1959, Armour had a mail-in offer of 10 coins for $1, which accounts for half of the coins in the set being much more plentiful than the others.

		NM	EX	VG
Complete Set (20):		400.00	200.00	120.00
Common Player:		15.00	7.50	4.50
(1)	Hank Aaron	30.00	15.00	9.00
(2)	John Antonelli	15.00	7.50	4.50

		NM	EX	VG
(3)	Richie Ashburn	30.00	15.00	9.00
(4)	Ernie Banks	30.00	15.00	9.00
(5)	Don Blasingame	15.00	7.50	4.50
(6)	Bob Cerv	15.00	7.50	4.50
(7)	Del Crandall	15.00	7.50	4.50
(8)	Whitey Ford	25.00	12.50	7.50
(9)	Nellie Fox	20.00	10.00	6.00
(10)	Jackie Jensen	20.00	10.00	6.00
(11)	Harvey Kuenn	30.00	15.00	9.00
(12)	Frank Malzone	20.00	10.00	6.00
(13)	Johnny Podres	30.00	15.00	9.00
(14)	Frank Robinson	30.00	15.00	9.00
(15)	Roy Sievers	15.00	7.50	4.50
(16)	Bob Skinner	15.00	7.50	4.50
(17)	Frank Thomas	15.00	7.50	4.50
(18)	Gus Triandos	15.00	7.50	4.50
(19)	Bob Turley	20.00	10.00	6.00
(20)	Mickey Vernon	15.00	7.50	4.50

1960 Armour Coins

The 1960 Armour coin issue is identical in number and style to the 1959 set. The unnumbered coins, 1-1/2" in diameter, once again came in a variety of colors. Common colors for 1960 are pale blue, royal blue, red, red-orange, light green, dark green and yellow. Values shown are for common-colored pieces. Scarcer colors exist and may be of premium value to specialists. The Bud Daley coin is very scarce, although it is not known why. Theories for the scarcity center on broken molding equipment, contract disputes, or that the coin was only inserted in a test product that quickly proved to be unsuccessful. As in 1959, a mail-in offer for 10 free coins was made available by Armour. The complete set price includes only the most common variations. Many 1960 Armour coins are found with only partial rims on back (Mantle is particularly susceptible to this condition). Coins without full back rims can grade no higher than VG.

		NM	EX	VG
Complete Set (20):		1,100	550.00	325.00
Common Player:		12.50	6.25	3.75
(1a)	Hank Aaron (Braves)	25.00	12.50	7.50
(1b)	Hank Aaron (Milwaukee Braves)	40.00	20.00	12.00
(2)	Bob Allison	20.00	10.00	6.00
(3)	Ernie Banks	30.00	15.00	9.00
(4)	Ken Boyer	12.50	6.25	3.75
(5)	Rocky Colavito	35.00	17.50	10.50
(6)	Gene Conley	12.50	6.25	3.75
(7)	Del Crandall	12.50	6.25	3.75
(8)	Bud Daley	750.00	375.00	225.00
(9a)	Don Drysdale (L.A condensed)	35.00	17.50	10.50
(9b)	Don Drysdale (Space between L. and A.)	25.00	12.50	7.50
(10)	Whitey Ford	20.00	10.00	6.00
(11)	Nellie Fox	15.00	7.50	4.50
(12)	Al Kaline	20.00	10.00	6.00
(13a)	Frank Malzone (Red Sox)	12.50	6.25	3.75
(13b)	Frank Malzone (Boston Red Sox)	20.00	10.00	6.00
(14)	Mickey Mantle	75.00	37.50	22.50
(15)	Ed Mathews	20.00	10.00	6.00
(16)	Willie Mays	50.00	25.00	15.00
(17)	Vada Pinson	12.50	6.25	3.75
(18)	Dick Stuart	12.50	6.25	3.75
(19)	Gus Triandos	12.50	6.25	3.75
(20)	Early Wynn	12.50	6.25	3.75

1908 Art Post Card Co. Our Home Team

This set of team post cards presents players from five Midwestern teams in a foldout format. The cover of the accordian-fold novelty is in orange and green. A 3-1/2" x 5-1/2" postcard depicts a ballfield and various pieces of baseball equipment. Printed on a large baseball is "Our Home Team." Folded inside are a number of 2" x 2-1/4" panels with one or two player photos printed on each side. Each player is identified, though misspelled names are common.

		NM	EX	VG
Complete Set (5):		5,500	2,750	1,650
Common Team Card:		800.00	400.00	250.00
(1)	Chicago Cubs (Three Finger Brown, Frank Chance, Johnny Evers, Chick Fraser, Solly Hofman, Johnny Kling, Carl Lundgren, Pat Moran, Jake Pfeister, Ed Reulbach, Wildfire Schulte, Jimmy Sheckard, Jimmy Slagle, Harry Steinfeldt, Joe Tinker, Heinie Zimmerman)	1,200	600.00	360.00
(2)	Chicago White Sox (Nick Altrock, John Anderson, Jake Atz, George Davis, Jiggs Donohue (Donahue), Patsy Dougherty, Eddie Hahn, Frank Isbell, Fielder Jones, Frank Owen, George Rohe, Billy Sullivan, Lee Tannehill, Ed Walsh, Doc White)	1,850	925.00	550.00
(3)	Detroit Tigers (William Caughlin (Coughlin), Ty Cobb, Sam Crawford, Wild Bill Donovan, Red Downs, Hughie Jennings, Davy Jones, Red Killefer, Ed Killian, Matty McIntyre, George Mullin, Charley O'Leary, Fred Payne, Claude Rossman, Germany Schaefer, Boss Schmidt, George Suggs, Ed Summers, Ira Thomas, George Winter, Ed Willett)	2,000	1,000	600.00
(4)	St. Louis Browns (Bob Bailey, Bert Blue, Dode Criss, Bill Dinneen, Hobe Ferris, Bill Graham, Roy Hartzell, Danny Hoffman, Harry Howell, Charlie Jones, Tom Jones, Jimmy McAleer, Jack O'Connor, Barney Pelty, Jack Powell, Al Schweitzer, Tubby Spencer, George Stone, Rube Waddell, Bobby Wallace, Jimmy Williams, Joe Yeager)	950.00	475.00	285.00
(5)	St. Louis Cardinals	800.00	400.00	240.00

1953-55 Artvue Hall of Fame Plaque Postcards - Type 1

From 1953-1963, Artvue was the official producer of the Baseball Hall of Fame's postcards available for public sale. The 3-1/2" x 5-1/2" black-and-white cards depict the bronze plaque of each inductee. Fronts have a white border. Postcard-style backs have a bit of player data and identification of the specific producer. On Type 1 Artvue cards issued 1953-55, the bolt holes in the four corners of the plaque are open. The Type 2 Artvues have baseball bolts in each corner of the plaque. The unnumbered cards are checklisted here alphabetically.

		NM	EX	VG
Complete Set (79):		2,000	1,000	600.0
Common Player:		30.00	15.00	9.0
(1)	G.C. Alexander	30.00	15.00	9.0
(2)	Adrian Anson	30.00	15.00	9.0
(3)	Frank Baker	30.00	15.00	9.0
(4)	Ed Barrow	30.00	15.00	9.0
(5)	Chief Bender	30.00	15.00	9.0
(6)	Roger Bresnahan	30.00	15.00	9.0
(7)	Dan Brouthers	30.00	15.00	9.0
(8)	Mordecai Brown	30.00	15.00	9.0
(9)	Morgan Bulkeley	30.00	15.00	9.0
(10)	Jesse Burkett	30.00	15.00	9.0

		NM	EX	VG
(11)	Alexander Cartwright	30.00	15.00	9.00
(12)	Henry Chadwick	30.00	15.00	9.00
(13)	Frank Chance	30.00	15.00	9.00
(14)	Jack Chesbro	30.00	15.00	9.00
(15)	Fred Clarke	30.00	15.00	9.00
(16)	Ty Cobb	80.00	40.00	24.00
(17)	Mickey Cochrane	30.00	15.00	9.00
(18)	Eddie Collins	30.00	15.00	9.00
(19)	Jimmy Collins	30.00	15.00	9.00
(20)	Charles Comiskey	30.00	15.00	9.00
(21)	Tom Connolly	30.00	15.00	9.00
(22)	Candy Cummings	30.00	15.00	9.00
(23)	Dizzy Dean	30.00	15.00	9.00
(24)	Ed Delahanty	30.00	15.00	9.00
(25)	Bill Dickey	30.00	15.00	9.00
(26)	Joe DiMaggio	80.00	40.00	24.00
(27)	Hugh Duffy	30.00	15.00	9.00
(28)	Johnny Evers	30.00	15.00	9.00
(29)	Buck Ewing	30.00	15.00	9.00
(30)	Jimmie Foxx	30.00	15.00	9.00
(31)	Frankie Frisch	30.00	15.00	9.00
(32)	Lou Gehrig	90.00	45.00	27.50
(33)	Charlie Gehringer	30.00	15.00	9.00
(34)	Clark Griffith	30.00	15.00	9.00
(35)	Lefty Grove	30.00	15.00	9.00
(36)	Gabby Hartnett	30.00	15.00	9.00
(37)	Harry Heilmann	30.00	15.00	9.00
(38)	Rogers Hornsby	30.00	15.00	9.00
(39)	Carl Hubbell	30.00	15.00	9.00
(40)	Hughie Jennings	30.00	15.00	9.00
(41)	Ban Johnson	30.00	15.00	9.00
(42)	Walter Johnson	60.00	30.00	18.00
(43)	Willie Keeler	30.00	15.00	9.00
(44)	King Kelly	30.00	15.00	9.00
(45)	Bill Klem	30.00	15.00	9.00
(46)	Nap Lajoie	30.00	15.00	9.00
(47)	Kenesaw Landis	30.00	15.00	9.00
(48)	Ted Lyons	30.00	15.00	9.00
(49)	Connie Mack	30.00	15.00	9.00
(50)	Rabbit Maranville	30.00	15.00	9.00
(51)	Christy Mathewson	60.00	30.00	18.00
(52)	Tommy McCarthy	30.00	15.00	9.00
(53)	Joe McGinnity	30.00	15.00	9.00
(54)	John McGraw	30.00	15.00	9.00
(55)	Kid Nichols	30.00	15.00	9.00
(56)	Jim O'Rourke	30.00	15.00	9.00
(57)	Mel Ott	30.00	15.00	9.00
(58)	Herb Pennock	30.00	15.00	9.00
(59)	Ed Plank	30.00	15.00	9.00
(60)	Chas. Radbourn	30.00	15.00	9.00
(61)	Wilbert Robinson	30.00	15.00	9.00
(62)	Babe Ruth	120.00	60.00	35.00
(63)	Ray Schalk	30.00	15.00	9.00
(64)	Al Simmons	30.00	15.00	9.00
(65)	George Sisler	30.00	15.00	9.00
(66)	Al Spalding	30.00	15.00	9.00
(67)	Tris Speaker	30.00	15.00	9.00
(68)	Bill Terry	30.00	15.00	9.00
(69)	Joe Tinker	30.00	15.00	9.00
(70)	Pie Traynor	30.00	15.00	9.00
(71)	Dazzy Vance	30.00	15.00	9.00
(72)	Rube Waddell	30.00	15.00	9.00
(73)	Honus Wagner	60.00	30.00	18.00
(74)	Bobby Wallace	30.00	15.00	9.00
(75)	Ed Walsh	30.00	15.00	9.00
(76)	Paul Waner	30.00	15.00	9.00
(77)	George Wright	30.00	15.00	9.00
(78)	Harry Wright	30.00	15.00	9.00
(79)	Cy Young	60.00	30.00	18.00

1956-63 Artvue Hall of Fame Plaque Postcards - Type 2

From 1953-1963, Artvue was the official producer of the Baseball Hall of Fame's postcards available for public sale. The 3-1/2" x 5-1/2" black-and-white cards depict the bronze plaque of each inductee. Fronts have a white border. Postcard-style backs have a bit of player data and identification of the specific producer. On Type 2 Artvue cards, issued 1956-63, there are baseball bolts in each corner of the plaque. The unnumbered cards are checklisted here alphabetically. Players unique to Type 2 are noted with an asterisk.

		NM	EX	VG
Complete Set (94):		2,000	1,000	600.00
Common Player:		25.00	12.50	7.50
(1)	G.C. Alexander	25.00	12.50	7.50
(2)	Adrian Anson	25.00	12.50	7.50
(3)	Frank Baker	25.00	12.50	7.50

		NM	EX	VG
(4)	Ed Barrow	25.00	12.50	7.50
(5)	Chief Bender	25.00	12.50	7.50
(6)	Roger Bresnahan	25.00	12.50	7.50
(7)	Dan Brouthers	25.00	12.50	7.50
(8)	Mordecai Brown	25.00	12.50	7.50
(9)	Morgan Bulkeley	25.00	12.50	7.50
(10)	Jesse Burkett	25.00	12.50	7.50
(11)	Max Carey (*)	25.00	12.50	7.50
(12)	Alexander Cartwright	25.00	12.50	7.50
(13)	Henry Chadwick	25.00	12.50	7.50
(14)	Frank Chance	25.00	12.50	7.50
(15)	Jack Chesbro	25.00	12.50	7.50
(16)	Fred Clarke	25.00	12.50	7.50
(17)	John Clarkson (*)	25.00	12.50	7.50
(18)	Ty Cobb	60.00	30.00	18.00
(19)	Mickey Cochrane	25.00	12.50	7.50
(20)	Eddie Collins	25.00	12.50	7.50
(21)	Jimmy Collins	25.00	12.50	7.50
(22)	Charles Comiskey	25.00	12.50	7.50
(23)	Tom Connolly	25.00	12.50	7.50
(24)	Sam Crawford (*)	25.00	12.50	7.50
(25)	Joe Cronin (*)	25.00	12.50	7.50
(26)	Candy Cummings	25.00	12.50	7.50
(27)	Dizzy Dean	25.00	12.50	7.50
(28)	Ed Delahanty	25.00	12.50	7.50
(29)	Bill Dickey	25.00	12.50	7.50
(30)	Joe DiMaggio	80.00	40.00	24.00
(31)	Hugh Duffy	25.00	12.50	7.50
(32)	Johnny Evers	25.00	12.50	7.50
(33)	Buck Ewing	25.00	12.50	7.50
(34)	Bob Feller (*)	25.00	12.50	7.50
(35)	Elmer Flick (*)	25.00	12.50	7.50
(36)	Jimmie Foxx	25.00	12.50	7.50
(37)	Frank Frisch	25.00	12.50	7.50
(38)	Lou Gehrig	80.00	40.00	24.00
(39)	Charlie Gehringer	25.00	12.50	7.50
(40)	Hank Greenberg (*)	25.00	12.50	7.50
(41)	Clark Griffith	25.00	12.50	7.50
(42)	Lefty Grove	25.00	12.50	7.50
(43)	Billy Hamilton (*)	25.00	12.50	7.50
(44)	Gabby Hartnett	25.00	12.50	7.50
(45)	Harry Heilmann	25.00	12.50	7.50
(46)	Rogers Hornsby	25.00	12.50	7.50
(47)	Carl Hubbell	25.00	12.50	7.50
(48)	Hughie Jennings	25.00	12.50	7.50
(49)	Ban Johnson	25.00	12.50	7.50
(50)	Walter Johnson	40.00	20.00	12.00
(51)	Willie Keeler	25.00	12.50	7.50
(52)	King Kelly	25.00	12.50	7.50
(53)	Bill Klem	25.00	12.50	7.50
(54)	Nap Lajoie	25.00	12.50	7.50
(55)	Kenesaw Landis	25.00	12.50	7.50
(56)	Ted Lyons	25.00	12.50	7.50
(57)	Connie Mack	25.00	12.50	7.50
(58)	Rabbit Maranville	25.00	12.50	7.50
(59)	Christy Mathewson	40.00	20.00	12.00
(60)	Joe McCarthy (*)	25.00	12.50	7.50
(61)	Tommy McCarthy	25.00	12.50	7.50
(62)	Joe McGinnity	25.00	12.50	7.50
(63)	John McGraw	25.00	12.50	7.50
(64)	Bill McKechnie (*)	25.00	12.50	7.50
(65)	Kid Nichols	25.00	12.50	7.50
(66)	Jim O'Rourke	25.00	12.50	7.50
(67)	Mel Ott	25.00	12.50	7.50
(68)	Herb Pennock	25.00	12.50	7.50
(69)	Ed Plank	25.00	12.50	7.50
(70)	Charles Radbourn	25.00	12.50	7.50
(71)	Sam Rice (*)	25.00	12.50	7.50
(72)	Eppa Rixey (*)	25.00	12.50	7.50
(73)	Jackie Robinson (*)	40.00	20.00	12.00
(74)	Wilbert Robinson	25.00	12.50	7.50
(75)	Edd Roush (*)	25.00	12.50	7.50
(76)	Babe Ruth	120.00	60.00	35.00
(77)	Ray Schalk	25.00	12.50	7.50
(78)	Al Simmons	25.00	12.50	7.50
(79)	George Sisler	25.00	12.50	7.50
(80)	Albert Spalding	25.00	12.50	7.50
(81)	Tris Speaker	25.00	12.50	7.50
(82)	Bill Terry	25.00	12.50	7.50
(83)	Joe Tinker	25.00	12.50	7.50
(84)	Pie Traynor	25.00	12.50	7.50
(85)	Dazzy Vance	25.00	12.50	7.50
(86)	Rube Waddell	25.00	12.50	7.50
(87)	Honus Wagner	40.00	20.00	12.00
(88)	Bobby Wallace	25.00	12.50	7.50
(89)	Ed Walsh	25.00	12.50	7.50
(90)	Paul Waner	25.00	12.50	7.50
(91)	Zack Wheat (*)	25.00	12.50	7.50
(92)	George Wright	25.00	12.50	7.50
(93)	Harry Wright	25.00	12.50	7.50
(94)	Cy Young	40.00	20.00	12.00

1967 Ashland Oil Grand Slam Baseball

These baseball player folders were issued in conjunction with a sweepstakes conducted at Ashland gas stations. The cards were originally issued in the form of a sealed tri-fold. When opened to 7-1/2" x 2", a

black-and-white player photo is pictured at center. Back of the panel offers contest rules. The unnumbered panels are listed here in alphabetical order.

		NM	EX	VG
Complete Set (12):		375.00	185.00	110.00
Common Player:		20.00	10.00	6.00
(1)	Jim Bunning	30.00	15.00	9.00
(2)	Elston Howard	25.00	12.50	7.50
(3)	Al Kaline	50.00	25.00	15.00
(4)	Harmon Killebrew	30.00	15.00	9.00
(5)	Ed Kranepool	20.00	10.00	6.00
(6)	Jim Maloney/SP	75.00	37.00	22.00
(7)	Bill Mazeroski	30.00	15.00	9.00
(8)	Frank Robinson	40.00	20.00	12.00
(9)	Ron Santo	25.00	12.50	7.50
(10)	Joe Torre	25.00	12.50	7.50
(11)	Leon Wagner	20.00	10.00	6.00
(12)	Pete Ward	20.00	10.00	6.00

1895 Ashman Studio Cabinets

The date attributed is speculative and about at the midpoint of the sole known subject's tenure with the Baltimore Orioles of the National League. In typical cabinet format, about 4-1/2" x 6-1/2", the card features a sepia-toned portrait photo attached to a blank-back, cream-colored thick cardboard mount bearing the advertising at bottom of the Baltimore photographer's studio. It is unknown whether cabinets of any of McGraw's teammates or adversaries were also produced.

	NM	EX	VG
John McGraw	10,000	5,000	3,000

1933 Astra Margarine

One of several "foreign" Babe Ruth cards issued during his prime was included in a 112-card set produced as premiums for Astra margarine in Germany. Ruth is the only major league ballplayer in the issue. Cards are in full color, measuring 2-3/4" x 4-1/8". Backs of the unnumbered cards are printed in German. Three types of backs can be found on the Ruth card. Type 1, has the Astra name nearly centered. The Type 2 back has the brand name printed closer to the bottom of the card, with only four lines of type under it. Type 3 is a variation of Type 2 on which the appropriate page number (83) of the accompanying album is mentioned on the line immediately above "Handbuch des Sports" near the top. One card was given with the purchase of each 1/2 pound of margarine and the album could be ordered by mail. See also Sanella Margarine.

	NM	EX	VG
Type 1 Babe Ruth (Astra centered.)	1,500	750.00	450.00
Type 2 Babe Ruth (Astra at bottom.)	1,750	875.00	525.00
Type 3 Babe Ruth	3,500	1,750	1,000
(Astra at bottom w/83.)			

1978 Atlanta Nobis Center

In conjunction with a May 1978 card show to benefit the training/rehabilitation center supported by Hall of Fame linebacker Tommy Nobis, this collectors' set

felipe alou

OUTFIELD
THE BRAVES

Felipe Alou Led Braves in hits in 1966 and 1968. One of three brothers who came up through the Giants organization. A Brave from 1964 to 1969, hitting a career high .327 in 154 games for the 1966 Braves during their first Atlanta season.

was issued. Most of the players on the 2-1/2" x 3-1/2" cards are former stars of the Boston, Milwaukee or Atlanta Braves, though players from a few other teams and footballer Nobis are also included; several of the players appeared at the show as autograph guests. The cards are in the style of 1959 Topps, with black-and-white player photos in a circle at center and a light green background. The career summary on back is in black-and-white. The unnumbered cards are checklisted here in alphabetical order.

		NM	EX	VG
Complete Set (24):		25.00	12.50	7.50
Common Player:		1.50	.70	.45
(1)	Hank Aaron	6.00	3.00	1.75
(2)	Joe Adcock	1.50	.70	.45
(3)	Felipe Alou	1.50	.70	.45
(4)	Frank Bolling	1.50	.70	.45
(5)	Orlando Cepeda	2.00	1.00	.60
(6)	Ty Cline	1.50	.70	.45
(7)	Tony Cloninger	1.50	.70	.45
(8)	Del Crandall	1.50	.70	.45
(9)	Fred Haney	1.50	.70	.45
(10)	Pat Jarvis	1.50	.70	.45
(11)	Ernie Johnson	1.50	.70	.45
(12)	Ken Johnson	1.50	.70	.45
(13)	Denny Lemaster	1.50	.70	.45
(14)	Eddie Mathews	2.00	1.00	.60
(15)	Lee Maye	1.50	.70	.45
(16)	Denis Menke	1.50	.70	.45
(17)	Felix Millan	1.50	.70	.45
(18)	Johnny Mize	2.00	1.00	.60
(19)	Tommy Nobis	1.50	.70	.45
(20)	Gene Oliver	1.50	.70	.45
(21)	Johnny Sain	1.75	.90	.50
(22)	Warren Spahn	2.00	1.00	.60
(23)	Joe Torre	2.00	1.00	.60
(24)	Bob Turley	1.75	.90	.50

1968 Atlantic Oil Play Ball Game Cards

Collect with American League Player numbered 7 and WIN $10

PLAYER NUMBER

JOE PEPITONE
New York Yankees
American League

Because some of the cards were redeemable either alone or in combination for cash awards, and thus were issued in lesser quantities, completion of this game issue was difficult from day one. Fifty different players are known in the issue, along with a number of variations. The majority of the cards can be found with card backs either explaining the game rules or picturing a pitcher throwing to a batter. The cards were issued in two-card panels, designed to be separated into a pair of 2-1/2" x 3-1/2" cards. For lack of an MLB license, the color player photos at center have the uniform logos removed. Printed at top is the face value of the particular card, while the player's name, team and league are printed in the bottom border. A large player number is printed in a white circle at bottom-right. American Leaguers' cards are bordered in red, while the National League cards have blue borders.

		NM	EX	VG
Complete Set (Non-winners)(40):		350.00	175.00	100.00
Common Player:		6.00	3.00	1.50
Instant Winner Card:		30.00	15.00	9.00
AMERICAN LEAGUE				
1a	Tony Oliva	6.00	3.00	1.75
1b	Brooks Robinson	15.00	7.50	4.50
1c	Pete Ward	6.00	3.00	1.75
2a	Max Alvis	6.00	3.00	1.75
2b	Campy Campaneris	6.00	3.00	1.75
2c	Jim Fregosi	6.00	3.00	1.75
2d	Al Kaline	20.00	10.00	6.00
2e	Tom Tresh	6.00	3.00	1.75
3	Bill Freehan ($2,500 winner)	300.00	150.00	90.00

4	Tommy Davis ($100 winner)	100.00	50.00	30.00
5a	Norm Cash	7.50	3.75	2.25
5b	Frank Robinson	15.00	7.50	4.50
5c	Carl Yastrzemski	25.00	12.50	7.50
6a	Joe Pepitone	7.50	3.75	2.25
6b	Boog Powell	10.00	5.00	3.00
6c	George Scott	6.00	3.00	1.75
6d	Fred Valentine	6.00	3.00	1.75
7	Tom McCraw ($10 winner)	75.00	37.00	22.00
8	Andy Etchebarren ($5 winner)	50.00	25.00	15.00
9a	Dean Chance	6.00	3.00	1.75
9b	Joel Horlen	6.00	3.00	1.75
9c	Jim Lonborg	6.00	3.00	1.75
9d	Sam McDowell	6.00	3.00	1.75
10	Earl Wilson ($1 winner)	35.00	17.50	10.50
11	Jose Santiago	6.00	3.00	1.75
NATIONAL LEAGUE				
1a	Bob Aspromonte	6.00	3.00	1.75
1b	Lou Brock	12.00	6.00	3.50
1c	Johnny Callison	6.00	3.00	1.75
1d	Pete Rose	25.00	12.50	7.50
1e	Maury Wills	7.50	3.75	2.25
2	Tommie Agee ($2,500 winner)	300.00	150.00	90.00
3a	Felipe Alou	7.50	3.75	2.25
3b	Jim Hart	6.00	3.00	1.75
3c	Vada Pinson	7.50	3.75	2.25
4a	Hank Aaron	25.00	12.50	7.50
4b	Orlando Cepeda	10.00	5.00	3.00
4c	Willie McCovey	12.00	6.00	3.50
4d	Ron Santo	9.00	4.50	2.75
5	Ernie Banks ($100 winner)	450.00	225.00	135.00
6	Ron Fairly ($10 winner)	75.00	37.50	22.50
7a	Roberto Clemente	75.00	37.50	22.50
7b	Roger Maris	25.00	12.50	7.50
7c a	Ron Swoboda (Collect w/ N.L. #6, win $10.)	6.00	3.00	1.75
7c b	Ron Swoboda (Collect w/ N.L. #8, win $5.)	45.00	22.00	13.50
8	Billy Williams ($5 winner)	95.00	47.00	28.00
9a	Jim Bunning	9.00	4.50	2.75
9b	Bob Gibson	12.00	6.00	3.50
9c	Jim Maloney	6.00	3.00	1.75
9d	Mike McCormick	6.00	3.00	1.75
10	Milt Pappas	6.00	3.00	1.75
11	Claude Osteen ($1 winner)	35.00	17.50	10.00

1969 Atlantic-Richfield Boston Red Sox

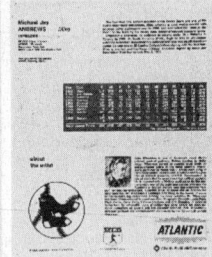

One of many larger-format (8" x 10") baseball premiums sponsored as gas station giveaways in the late 1960s and early 1970s was this set of Boston Red Sox player pictures by celebrity artist John Wheeldon sponsored by the Atlantic-Richfield Oil Co. Done in pastel colors, the pictures feature large portraits and smaller action pictures of the player against a bright background. A facsimile autograph is pencilled in beneath the pictures, and the player's name is printed in the white bottom border. Backs are printed in black-and-white and include biographical and career data, full major and minor league stats, a self-portrait and biography of the artist and the logos of the team, players' association and sponsor. The unnumbered pictures are checklisted here alphabetically.

		NM	EX	VG
Complete Set (12):		75.00	35.00	25.00
Common Player:		6.00	3.00	1.75
(1)	Mike Andrews	6.00	3.00	1.75
(2)	Tony Conigliaro	10.00	5.00	3.00
(3)	Ray Culp	6.00	3.00	1.75
(4)	Russ Gibson	6.00	3.00	1.75
(5)	Dalton Jones	6.00	3.00	1.75
(6)	Jim Lonborg	8.00	4.00	2.50
(7)	Sparky Lyle	8.00	4.00	2.50
(8)	Syd O'Brien	6.00	3.00	1.75
(9)	George Scott	8.00	4.00	2.50
(10)	Reggie Smith	8.00	4.00	2.50
(11)	Rico Petrocelli	8.00	4.00	2.50
(12)	Carl Yastrzemski	25.00	12.50	7.50

1962 Auravision Records

Similar in design and format to the 16-record set which was issued in 1964, this test issue can be differentiated by the stats on the back. On the 1962 record, Mantle is shown in a right-handed batting pose, as compared to a follow-through on the 1964 record. Where Gentile and Colavito are shown in the uniform of K.C. A's on the 1964 records, they are shown as a Tiger (Colavito) and Oriole (Gentile) on the earlier version. The set is checklisted here alphabetically.

		NM	EX	VG
Complete Set (8):		300.00	150.00	90.00
Common Player:		15.00	7.50	4.50
(1)	Ernie Banks	30.00	15.00	9.00
(2)	Rocky Colavito	25.00	12.50	7.50
(3)	Whitey Ford	30.00	15.00	9.00
(4)	Jim Gentile	15.00	7.50	4.50
(5)	Mickey Mantle	100.00	50.00	30.00
(6)	Roger Maris	35.00	17.50	10.50
(7)	Willie Mays	50.00	25.00	15.00
(8)	Warren Spahn	30.00	15.00	9.00

1964 Auravision Records

Never a candidate for the Billboard "Hot 100," this series of baseball picture records is popular with collectors due to the high-quality photos on front and back. On the grooved front side of the 6-3/4" x 6-3/4" plastic-laminated cardboard record is a color player photo with facsimile autograph, Sports Record trophy logo and 33-1/3 RPM notation. A color border surrounds the photo and is carried over to the unrecorded back side. There is another photo on back, along with a career summary and complete major and minor league stats and instructions for playing the record. In the bottom border is a copyright notice by Sports Champions Inc., and a notice that the Auravision Record is a product of Columbia Records. A hole at center of the record could be punched out for playing and the records featured a five-minute interview with the player by sportscaster Marty Glickman. The records were originally a mail-in premium available through an offer on Milk Dud candy boxes. Large quantities of the records made their way into the hobby as remainders. For early-1960s baseball items they remain reasonably priced today. The unnumbered records are checklisted here alphabetically. The Mays record is unaccountably much scarcer than the others.

		NM	EX	VG
Complete Set (16):		150.00	75.00	45.00
Common Player:		6.00	3.00	1.75
(1)	Bob Allison	6.00	3.00	1.75
(2)	Ernie Banks	9.00	4.50	2.75
(3)	Ken Boyer	6.00	3.00	1.75
(4)	Rocky Colavito	7.50	3.75	2.25
(5)	Don Drysdale	9.00	4.50	2.75
(6)	Whitey Ford	10.00	5.00	3.00
(7)	Jim Gentile	6.00	3.00	1.75
(8)	Al Kaline	10.00	5.00	3.00
(9)	Sandy Koufax	20.00	10.00	6.00
(10)	Mickey Mantle	25.00	12.50	7.50
(11)	Roger Maris	12.50	6.25	3.75
(12)	Willie Mays	75.00	37.50	22.50
(13)	Bill Mazeroski	9.00	4.50	2.75
(14)	Frank Robinson	9.00	4.50	2.75
(15)	Warren Spahn	9.00	4.50	2.75
(16)	Pete Ward	6.00	3.00	1.75

1945 Autographs Game

Politicians, movie stars and athletes are amon[g] the celebrities featured in this game from Leiste[r] Game Co. The 2-1/2" x 3-1/2" cards are printed in re[d] and black on white and were found in pairs. The celeb[...]

rity whose signature was reproduced on the card was seen in a photograph and top, while his paired partner was shown at bottom in an artist's depiction. Only two baseball players are included in the set.

	NM	EX	VG
Complete Boxed Set (55):	650.00	325.00	195.00
9A Joe DiMaggio, Babe Ruth (DiMaggio signature.)	75.00	37.50	22.50
9A Babe Ruth, Joe DiMaggio (Ruth signature.)	125.00	62.50	37.50

1949 Baas Cheri-Cola

Only five of these premium issues have ever been cataloged so it's unknown how many comprise a set. The 7-5/8" x 9-1/2" pictures feature black-and-white player photos on front, with the player's name printed in white script. On back, printed in red, is an ad for Baas Cheri-Cola Drink. The unnumbered pictures are checklisted in alphabetical order.

		NM	EX	VG
Common Player:		125.00	65.00	40.00
(1)	Bobby Doerr	150.00	75.00	45.00
(2)	Bob Feller	250.00	125.00	75.00
(3)	Ken Keltner	125.00	65.00	40.00
(4)	John Sain	125.00	65.00	40.00
(5)	Ted Williams	600.00	300.00	180.00

1930 Baguer Chocolate

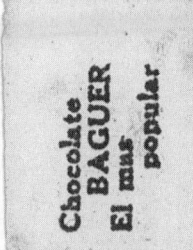

Babe Herman

This rare Cuban issue was apparently current between the start of the 1930 season and the redemption expiration date of Jan. 31, 1931. The set consists of 90 black-and-white player photos, about 5/8" x 7/8". The pictures have white borders and a white strip at the bottom of photo with some form of the player's name. Backs are printed in red, "Chocolate BAGUER El mas popular." An album was issued to collect the pictures and when full it could be exchanged for baseball equipment, toys or candy. The unnumbered cards are checklisted here in alphabetical order.

		NM	EX	VG
Complete Set (90):		5,500	3,750	2,200
Common Player:		30.00	20.00	12.00
Album:		75.00	52.00	30.00
(1)	George Bancroft (Dave)	65.00	45.00	25.00
(2)	Clyde Beck	30.00	20.00	12.00
(3)	Larry Benton	30.00	20.00	12.00
(4)	Max Bishop	30.00	20.00	12.00
(5)	Clarence Blair	30.00	20.00	12.00
(6)	Fred Blake	30.00	20.00	12.00
(7)	Mitchell Blake/SP	80.00	55.00	30.00
(8)	Joe Boley	30.00	20.00	12.00
(9)	Jim Bottomley	65.00	45.00	25.00
(10)	George Burns	30.00	20.00	12.00
(11)	Guy Bush	30.00	20.00	12.00
(12)	Mickey Cochrane	75.00	50.00	30.00
(13)	Eddie Collins	75.00	50.00	30.00
(14)	Kiki Cuyler	65.00	45.00	25.00
(15)	Jimmy Dikes (Dykes)	30.00	20.00	12.00
(16)	Leo Dixon	30.00	20.00	12.00
(17)	Pete Donohue	30.00	20.00	12.00
(18)	Taylor Douthit	30.00	20.00	12.00
(19)	George Earnshaw	30.00	20.00	12.00
(20)	R. Elliot (Jumbo Elliott)	30.00	20.00	12.00
(21)	Joe (Woody) English	30.00	20.00	12.00

(22)	Urban Faber	65.00	45.00	25.00
(23)	Lewis Fonseca	30.00	20.00	12.00
(24)	Jimmy Foxx	275.00	190.00	110.00
(25)	Walter French	30.00	20.00	12.00
(26)	Frankie Frisch	75.00	50.00	30.00
(27)	Lou Gehrig	600.00	420.00	240.00
(28)	Walter Gerber	30.00	20.00	12.00
(29)	Miguel A. Gonzalez	65.00	45.00	25.00
(30)	Goose Goslin	65.00	45.00	25.00
(31)	W. Grampp (Henry)	30.00	20.00	12.00
(32)	Burleigh Grimes	65.00	45.00	25.00
(33)	Charlie Grimm	30.00	20.00	12.00
(34)	Lefty Grove	75.00	50.00	30.00
(35)	Geo. Haas	30.00	20.00	12.00
(36)	(Bill) Hallahan	30.00	20.00	12.00
(37)	Stanley Harris	65.00	45.00	25.00
(38)	Geo. (Charles "Gabby") Hartnett	65.00	45.00	25.00
(39)	Cliff Heathcote	30.00	20.00	12.00
(40)	Babe Herman	30.00	20.00	12.00
(41)	Andy High	30.00	20.00	12.00
(42)	Rogers Hornsby	100.00	70.00	40.00
(43)	Dan Howley	30.00	20.00	12.00
(44)	Travis Jackson	65.00	45.00	25.00
(45)	Walter Johnson	250.00	175.00	100.00
(46)	Fred Lindstrom	65.00	45.00	25.00
(47)	Alfonso Lopez	75.00	50.00	30.00
(48)	Red Lucas	30.00	20.00	12.00
(49)	(Dolf) Luque	65.00	45.00	25.00
(50)	Pat Malone	30.00	20.00	12.00
(51)	Harry (Heinie) Manush	65.00	45.00	25.00
(52)	Fred Marberry	30.00	20.00	12.00
(53)	Joe McCarthy	65.00	45.00	25.00
(54)	J.J. McGraw	65.00	45.00	25.00
(55)	G. Mc. Millan (Norman McMillan)	30.00	20.00	12.00
(56)	Bing Miller	30.00	20.00	12.00
(57)	J. (Johnny) Moore	30.00	20.00	12.00
(58)	Buddy Myers (Myer)	30.00	20.00	12.00
(59)	Bob O'Farrell	30.00	20.00	12.00
(60)	Melvin Ott	75.00	50.00	30.00
(61)	Herb Pennock	65.00	45.00	25.00
(62)	Cy Perkins	30.00	20.00	12.00
(63)	Jack Quinn	30.00	20.00	12.00
(64)	Chas. Rhen (Rhem)	30.00	20.00	12.00
(65)	Harry Rice	30.00	20.00	12.00
(66)	Sam Rice	65.00	45.00	35.00
(67)	Lance Richbourg	30.00	20.00	12.00
(68)	W. (Wilbert) Robinson	65.00	45.00	25.00
(69)	Eddie Rommell (Rommel)	30.00	20.00	12.00
(70)	Charles Root	30.00	20.00	12.00
(71)	Muddy Ruel	30.00	20.00	12.00
(72)	Babe Ruth	900.00	630.00	360.00
(73)	Wally Schang	30.00	20.00	12.00
(74)	Bill Shores	30.00	20.00	12.00
(75)	Al Simmons	65.00	45.00	25.00
(76)	Geo. Sisler	75.00	50.00	30.00
(77)	Earl Smith	30.00	20.00	12.00
(78)	Riggs Stephenson	30.00	20.00	12.00
(79)	Joe (Walter "Lefty") Stewart	30.00	20.00	12.00
(80)	H. Summa	30.00	20.00	12.00
(81)	Bill Terry	65.00	45.00	25.00
(82)	Fresco Thompson	30.00	20.00	12.00
(83)	Charley Tolson	30.00	20.00	12.00
(84)	'Pie' Traynor	65.00	45.00	25.00
(85)	Dazzy Vance	65.00	45.00	25.00
(86)	Rube Walberg	30.00	20.00	12.00
(87)	'Hack' Wilson	65.00	45.00	25.00
(88)	Jimmy Wilson	30.00	20.00	12.00
(89)	Glenn Wright	30.00	20.00	12.00
(90)	Tom Zachary	30.00	20.00	12.00

1950s-70s Mel Bailey Player Postcards

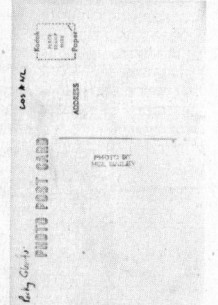

Photographer and hobbyist Mel Bailey was a prolific baseball photographer who produced many player postcards for their use in responding to fan requests for pictures and autographs. Several different formats of back design may be found. No checklist has been promulgated.

(Typical players $3-5; stars and Hall of Famers $10-30.)

1941 Ballantine Coasters

National League pitcher-catcher pairs are featured on this set of drink coasters issued by Ballantine Ale & Beer. The 4-1/2" diameter composition coasters are printed in black with orange, blue or red highlights. Fronts have line drawings of the batterymates and a few words about the previous or coming season. Backs have a Ballantine's ad. It is unknown whether there are more than these three coasters in the series.

		NM	EX	VG
Common Coaster:		35.00	17.50	10.00
(1)	Bob Klinger, Virgil Davis (Pirates)	35.00	17.50	10.00
(2a)	Lon Warneke, Gus Mancuso (Cardinals)("AT THE GAME IT'S . . ." above portraits.)	35.00	17.50	10.00
(2b)	Lon Warneke, Gus Mancuso (Cardinals)("At the Game it's" below portraits.)	35.00	17.50	10.00
(3)	Whit Wyatt, Mickey Owen (Dodgers)	35.00	17.50	10.00

1911 Baltimore News Newsboys Series

This scarce version of E94 carries on its back the notation, "Baltimore News Newsboy Series" and offers $1 to the first 35 boys completing the full set. Unlike the Close Candy Co. cards, the newspaper version is found only with the light blue background on front. The issue was designated M131 in the American Card Catalog.

		NM	EX	VG
Complete Set (30):		85,000	42,500	25,000
Common Player:		3,000	1,500	1,000
(1)	Jimmy Austin	3,000	1,500	1,000
(2)	Johnny Bates	3,000	1,500	1,000
(3)	Bob Bescher	3,000	1,500	1,000
(4)	Bobby Byrne	3,000	1,500	1,000
(5)	Frank Chance	7,500	3,750	2,250
(6)	Ed Cicotte	6,000	3,000	1,800
(7)	Ty Cobb	75,000	37,500	22,500
(8)	Sam Crawford	7,500	3,750	2,250
(9)	Harry Davis	3,000	1,500	1,000
(10)	Art Devlin	3,000	1,500	1,000
(11)	Josh Devore	3,000	1,500	1,000
(12)	Mickey Doolan	3,000	1,500	1,000
(13)	Patsy Dougherty	3,000	1,500	1,000
(14)	Johnny Evers	7,500	3,750	2,250
(15)	Eddie Grant	3,000	1,500	1,000
(16)	Hugh Jennings	7,500	3,750	2,250
(17)	Red Kleinow	3,000	1,500	1,000
(18)	Joe Lake	3,000	1,500	1,000
(19)	Nap Lajoie	9,000	4,500	2,700
(20)	Tommy Leach	3,000	1,500	1,000
(21)	Hans Lobert	3,000	1,500	1,000
(22)	Harry Lord	3,000	1,500	1,000
(23)	Sherry Magee	3,000	1,500	1,000
(24)	John McGraw	11,250	5,625	3,375
(25)	Earl Moore	3,000	1,500	1,000
(26)	Red Murray	3,000	1,500	1,000
(27)	Tris Speaker	13,500	6,750	4,050
(28)	Terry Turner	3,000	1,500	1,000
(29)	Honus Wagner	55,500	27,750	16,650
(30)	"Old" Cy. Young	22,500	11,250	6,750

1914 Baltimore News Terrapins

Players from both of Baltimore's professional baseball teams are included in this set of schedule cards from the local newspaper. That season fans could support the Orioles of the International League or the Terrapins of the Federal League. The newspaper's cards are 2-5/8" x 3-5/8", monochrome printed in either red or blue with a wide border. Players are pictured in full-length posed action photos with the backgrounds erased in favor of a few artificial shadows. The player name, position and league are shown on front. Backs have a schedule "AT HOME" and "ABROAD" of the appropriate team with an ad for the paper at top and a curious line at bottom which reads, "This Card is Given to," with space for a signature. The unnumbered cards are checklisted here in alphabetical order, though it is presumed the checklist is incomplete. Only the Federal Leaguers' cards are listed here; the Orioles will be found in the minor league section of this catalog. This scarce version of E94 carries on its back the notation, "Baltimore Newsboy Series." Unlike the Close Candy Co. cards, the newspaper version is found only with the light blue background on front.

		NM	EX	VG
(1)	Neal Ball	8,800	4,400	2,640
(2)	Mike Doolan	8,800	4,400	2,640
(3)	Happy Finneran	8,800	4,400	2,640
(4)	Fred Jacklitch (Jacklitsch)	8,800	4,400	2,640
(5)	Otto Knabe	8,800	4,400	2,640
(6)	Benny Meyers (Meyer)	8,800	4,400	2,640
(7)	Jack Quinn	8,800	4,400	2,640
(8)	Hack Simmons	8,800	4,400	2,640
(9)	Frank Smith	8,800	4,400	2,640
(10)	George Suggs	8,800	4,400	2,640
(11)	Harry (Swats) Swacina	8,800	4,400	2,640
(12)	Ducky Yount	8,800	4,400	2,640
(13)	Guy Zinn	8,800	4,400	2,640

1954 Baltimore Orioles Picture Pack

This appears to be a team-issued photo pack in the O's first season after moving from St. Louis. The black-and-white poses are 6" x 8" in format, bordered in white and blank-backed. Pictures have a facsimile autograph on front. At least three versions of the photo pack were issued over the course of the season to reflect roster changes. It is unknown whether this checklist is complete.

		NM	EX	VG
Complete Set (33):		600.00	300.00	180.00
Common Player:		20.00	10.00	6.00
(1)	Cal Abrams	20.00	10.00	6.00
(2)	Neil Berry	20.00	10.00	6.00
(3)	Vern Bickford	20.00	10.00	6.00
(4)	Jim Brideweser	20.00	10.00	6.00
(5)	Bob Chakales	20.00	10.00	6.00
(6)	Gil Coan	20.00	10.00	6.00
(7)	Joe Coleman	20.00	10.00	6.00
(8)	Clint Courtney	20.00	10.00	6.00
(9)	Chuck Diering	20.00	10.00	6.00
(10)	Jim Dyck	20.00	10.00	6.00
(11)	Howie Fox	20.00	10.00	6.00
(12)	Jim Fridley/Btg	20.00	10.00	6.00
(13)	Jim Fridley/Portrait	20.00	10.00	6.00
(14)	Jehosie Heard	25.00	12.50	7.50
(15)	Bill Hunter	20.00	10.00	6.00
(16)	Darrell Johnson	20.00	10.00	6.00
(17)	Dick Kokos	20.00	10.00	6.00
(18)	Lou Kretlow	20.00	10.00	6.00
(19)	Dick Kryhoski	20.00	10.00	6.00
(20)	Don Larsen	40.00	20.00	12.00
(21)	Don Lenhardt	20.00	10.00	6.00
(22)	Dick Littlefield	20.00	10.00	6.00
(23)	Sam Mele	20.00	10.00	6.00
(24)	Les Moss	20.00	10.00	6.00
(25)	Ray Murray	20.00	10.00	6.00
(26)	Billy O'Dell	20.00	10.00	6.00
(27)	Duane Pillette	20.00	10.00	6.00
(28)	Vern Stephens	20.00	10.00	6.00
(29)	Marlin Stuart	20.00	10.00	6.00
(30)	Bob Turley	40.00	20.00	12.00
(31)	Eddie Waitkus	20.00	10.00	6.00
(32)	Vic Wertz	25.00	12.50	7.50
(33)	Bob Young	20.00	10.00	6.00

1958 Baltimore Orioles Team Issue

CLIFFORD CONNIE JOHNSON (CONNIE)

These blank-backed, black-and-white cards are approximately postcard size at 3-1/4" x 5-1/2" and feature posed portraits of the players printed on semi-gloss cardboard. The unnumbered cards are checklisted here alphabetically.

		NM	EX	VG
Complete Set (16):		165.00	82.00	49.00
Common Player:		12.00	6.00	3.50
(1)	Bob Boyd	12.00	6.00	3.50
(2)	Harry Brecheen	12.00	6.00	3.50
(3)	Hal Brown	12.00	6.00	3.50
(4)	Jim Busby	12.00	6.00	3.50
(5)	Foster Castleman	12.00	6.00	3.50
(6)	Billy Gardner	12.00	6.00	3.50
(7)	Connie Johnson	12.00	6.00	3.50
(8)	Ken Lehman	12.00	6.00	3.50
(9)	Willie Miranda	12.00	6.00	3.50
(10)	Bob Nieman	12.00	6.00	3.50
(11)	Paul Richards	12.00	6.00	3.50
(12)	Brooks Robinson	36.00	18.00	11.00
(13)	Gus Triandos	12.00	6.00	3.50
(14)	Dick Williams	12.00	6.00	3.50
(15)	Gene Woodling	18.00	9.00	5.50
(16)	George Zuverink	12.00	6.00	3.50

1970 Baltimore Orioles Traffic Safety

DAVE JOHNSON
2ND BASE
Baltimore Orioles

YOU STEP OFF THE BAG

AT SECOND—
"YOU'RE OUT!"

YOU STEP OFF THE CURB

IN TRAFFIC—
"YOU'RE OUT!"

PLAY IT SAFE!

D.C. DEPARTMENT OF MOTOR VEHICLES OFFICE OF TRAFFIC SAFETY

Similar in concept and design to the much more common Washington Senators safety issue of the same year, the Orioles cards are printed on yellow paper in 2-1/2" x 3-7/8" format. Fronts have player photo, name, team and position; backs have a safety message and notice of sponsorship by the D.C. Department of Motor Vehicles Office of Traffic Safety.

		NM	EX	VG
Complete Set (10):		25.00	12.50	7.50
Common Player:		2.50	1.25	.75
(1)	Mark Bellanger (Belanger)	2.50	1.25	.75
(2)	Paul Blair	2.50	1.25	.75
(3)	Don Buford	2.50	1.25	.75
(4)	Mike Cuellar (Back in Spanish.)	4.00	2.00	1.25
(5)	Dave Johnson	2.50	1.25	.75
(6)	Dave McNally	2.50	1.25	.75
(7)	Boog Powell	5.00	2.50	1.50
(8)	Merv Rettenmund	2.50	1.25	.75
(9)	Brooks Robinson	10.00	5.00	3.00
(10)	Earl Weaver	3.50	1.75	1.00

1971 Bank of Montreal Rusty Staub

This 4" x 6" color card was issued by the Bank of Montreal, probably in conjunction with an autograph appearance by the popular Expos slugger. The front has a photo of the player working on his war club. The team and sponsor's logo are at top-right. On back are the player's stats.

	NM	EX	VG
Rusty Staub	32.50	16.00	10.00

1913 Tom Barker Game (WG6)

Nearly identical in format to "The National Game" card set, this issue features a different back design of a red-and-white line art representation of a batter.

FOUL FLY—
BATTER
WAGNER
PITTS.
TRIPLE PLAY

BARKER

Fronts of the round-cornered, 2-1/2" x 3-1/2" cards have a black-and-white player pose, or game action photo, along with two game scenarios used when playing the card game. There are nine action photos in the set. Player cards are checklisted here alphabetically. The set originally sold for 50 cents. The set was reprinted in the 1980s.

		NM	EX	VG
Complete Set (54):		6,155	2,760	1,530
Common Player:		48.00	24.00	15.00
Game Box:		78.00	36.00	18.00
(1)	Grover Alexander	360.00	162.00	90.00
(2)	Frank Baker	120.00	54.00	30.00
(3)	Chief Bender	120.00	54.00	30.00
(4)	Bob Bescher	48.00	24.00	15.00
(5)	Joe Birmingham	48.00	24.00	15.00
(6)	Roger Bresnahan	120.00	54.00	30.00
(7)	Nixey Callahan	48.00	24.00	15.00
(8)	Bill Carrigan	48.00	24.00	15.00
(9)	Frank Chance	120.00	54.00	30.00
(10)	Hal Chase	78.00	36.00	19.00
(11)	Fred Clarke	120.00	54.00	30.00
(12)	Ty Cobb	810.00	360.00	210.00
(13)	Sam Crawford	120.00	54.00	30.00
(14)	Jake Daubert	48.00	24.00	15.00
(15)	Red Dooin	48.00	24.00	15.00
(16)	Johnny Evers	120.00	54.00	30.00
(17)	Vean Gregg	48.00	24.00	15.00
(18)	Clark Griffith	120.00	54.00	30.00
(19)	Dick Hoblitzel	48.00	24.00	15.00
(20)	Miller Huggins	120.00	54.00	30.00
(21)	Joe Jackson	1,920	870.00	480.00
(22)	Hughie Jennings	120.00	54.00	30.00
(23)	Walter Johnson	420.00	180.00	110.00
(24)	Ed Konetchy	48.00	24.00	15.00
(25)	Nap Lajoie	120.00	54.00	30.00
(26)	Connie Mack	120.00	54.00	30.00
(27)	Rube Marquard	120.00	54.00	30.00
(28)	Christy Mathewson	420.00	180.00	110.00
(29)	John McGraw	120.00	54.00	30.00
(30)	Chief Meyers	48.00	24.00	15.00
(31)	Clyde Milan	48.00	24.00	15.00
(32)	Marty O'Toole	48.00	24.00	15.00
(33)	Nap Rucker	48.00	24.00	15.00
(34)	Tris Speaker	160.00	75.00	40.00
(35)	George Stallings	48.00	24.00	15.00
(36)	Bill Sweeney	48.00	24.00	15.00
(37)	Joe Tinker	120.00	54.00	30.00
(38)	Honus Wagner	720.00	330.00	180.00
(39)	Ed Walsh	120.00	54.00	30.00
(40)	Zach Wheat	120.00	54.00	30.00
(41)	Ivy Wingo	48.00	24.00	15.00
(42)	Joe Wood	72.00	33.00	18.00
(43)	Cy Young	420.00	180.00	100.00
(---)	Rules Card	48.00	24.00	15.00
(---)	Score Card	48.00	24.00	15.00
	ACTION PHOTO CARDS			
(A1)	Better swinging, looking forward	18.00	8.10	4.50
(A2)	Batter swinging, looking back	18.00	8.10	4.50
(A3)	Runner sliding, fielder at bag	18.00	8.10	4.50
(A4)	Runner sliding, umpire behind	48.00	24.00	15.00
(A5)	Runner sliding, hugging base	18.00	8.10	4.50
(A6)	Sliding play at plate, umpire at left	18.00	8.10	4.50
(A7)	Sliding play at plate, umpire at right	18.00	8.10	4.50
(A8)	Play at plate, runner standing	18.00	8.10	4.50
(A9)	Runner looking backwards	18.00	8.10	4.50

1974-80 Bob Bartosz Postcards

DAVEY JOHNSON

Through the last half of the 1970s, Bob Bartosz, who was a photographer covering the Phillies for a New Jersey daily newspaper, produced a series of player postcards. Most cards were produced at the request of the players for use in handling fan requests. Generally, no more than 500 cards of each player were ever produced. Most of the cards are in black-and-white with player name in a white stripe. Three cards were done in color. Size varies, but averages about 3-5/8" x 5-1/2". Back designs also vary, with most simply having Bartosz' credit line vertically at center. The unnumbered cards are checklisted here in alphabetical order.

		NM	EX	VG
Complete Set (32):				
Common Player:		3.00	1.50	.90
BLACK-AND-WHITE POSTCARDS				
(1)	Hank Aaron (16th career grand slam.)	7.50	3.75	2.25
(2)	Richie Ashburn (5th Delaware Valley Show)	3.00	1.50	.90
(3)	James Cool Papa Bell	3.00	1.50	.90
(4)	Bob Boone	4.00	2.00	1.25
(5)	Jimmie Crutchfield	3.00	1.50	.90
(6)	Barry Foote	3.00	1.50	.90
(7)	Steve Garvey	4.00	2.00	1.25
(8)	Tommy Hutton (Phillies)	3.00	1.50	.90
(9)	Tommy Hutton (Blue Jays)	3.00	1.50	.90
(10)	Dane Iorg	3.00	1.50	.90
(11)	Davey Johnson	3.00	1.50	.90
(12)	Jay Johnstone	3.00	1.50	.90
(13)	Dave Kingman (Stadium background.)	3.00	1.50	.90
(14)	Dave Kingman (Black background.)	3.00	1.50	.90
(15)	Greg Luzinski (Both feet show.)	3.00	1.50	.90
(16)	Greg Luzinski (Only left foot shows.)	3.00	1.50	.90
(17)	Jerry Martin (Phillies)	3.00	1.50	.90
(18)	Jerry Martin (Cubs)	3.00	1.50	.90
(19)	Tim McCarver	4.00	2.00	1.25
(20)	John Montefusco	3.00	1.50	.90
(21)	Jerry Mumphrey	3.00	1.50	.90
(22)	Phil Niekro	4.00	2.00	1.25
(23)	Robin Roberts (Hall of Fame induction.)	3.00	1.50	.90
(24)	Robin Roberts (4th Delaware Valley Show)	3.00	1.50	.90
(25)	Steve Swisher	3.00	1.50	.90
(26)	Tony Taylor (Uniform number visible.)	3.00	1.50	.90
(27)	Tony Taylor (Number is covered.)	3.00	1.50	.90
(28)	Tom Underwood	3.00	1.50	.90
(29)	Billy Williams (N.L. umpire.)	3.00	1.50	.90
(30)	1974 National League All-Stars	4.00	2.00	1.25
	COLOR POSTCARDS			
(1)	Greg Luzinski	7.50	3.75	2.25
(2)	Bill Madlock	7.50	3.75	2.25
(3)	Jason Thompson	6.00	3.00	1.75

1978 Bob Bartosz Baseball Postcards

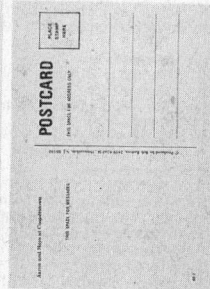

Newspaper photographer Bob Bartosz produced a book of postcards in 1978 combining player poses, action shots and stadium photos. Two dozen cards are printed in 4" x 5-1/2" black-and-white format and perforated on pages of four in the 8-1/2" x 11" book. Backs have standard postcard indicia and are numbered with a "BB" prefix and titled, all printing in black.

	NM	EX	VG
Complete Book (24):	30.00	15.00	9.00
Common Player:	1.50	.70	.45
25th anniversary of the 1950 Phillies (Group photo at old-timers game.)	1.50	.70	.45
Aaron and Mays at Cooperstown (Hank Aaron, Willie Mays)	4.00	2.00	1.25
Willie Mays	7.50	3.75	2.25
Aaron signing Autographs (Hank Aaron)	3.00	1.50	.90
Dizzy Dean (Old-timers action sequence.)	2.50	1.25	.70
Jack Russell Stadium, Clearwater, Fla.	1.50	.70	.45
Paddy Livingston	1.50	.70	.45
Bob Feller (Old-timers game.)	2.50	1.25	.70
Hall of Fame Game at Doubleday Field	1.50	.70	.45

		NM	EX	VG
10	Doubleday Field at Cooperstown, N.Y.	1.50	.70	.45
11	Three Rivers Stadium, Pittsburgh	1.50	.70	.45
12	Hall of Fame Game at Doubleday Field	1.50	.70	.45
13	Shibe Park from the air	1.50	.70	.45
14	Olympic Stadium, Montreal	1.50	.70	.45
15	A tree grows at home plate (Shibe Park - 1974)	1.50	.70	.45
16	The Bleachers, Wrigley Field	1.50	.70	.45
17	Another Home Run (Hank Aaron)	2.50	1.25	.70
18	Home Run King (Hank Aaron)	2.25	1.25	.70
19	Autograph Time - 1950 (Phillies signing balls)	1.50	.70	.45
20	The Champs (1976 Phillies)	1.50	.70	.45
21	Last Day - Shibe Park, 1977	1.50	.70	.45
22	Connie Mack Stadium, Philadelphia	1.50	.70	.45
23	Shibe Park	1.50	.70	.45
24	Shibe Park	1.50	.70	.45

1911 Baseball Bats

Issued circa 1911, cards in this rare 47-card issue were printed on the back panel of "Baseball Bats" penny candy. The cards themselves measure approximately 1-3/8" x 2-3/8" and feature a black-and-white player photo surrounded by an orange and white border. Player's name and team are printed in small, black capital letters near the bottom of the photo. Cards are blank-backed.

		NM	EX	VG
Complete Set (50):		40,000	20,000	12,000
Common Player:		550.00	275.00	165.00
(1)	Red Ames	550.00	275.00	165.00
(2)	Home Run Baker	1,100	550.00	330.00
(3)	Jack Barry	550.00	275.00	165.00
(4)	Ginger Beaumont	550.00	275.00	165.00
(5)	Chief Bender	1,100	550.00	330.00
(6)	Al Bridwell	550.00	275.00	165.00
(7)	Mordecai Brown	1,100	550.00	330.00
(8)	Bill Corrigan (Carrigan)	550.00	275.00	165.00
(9)	Frank Chance	1,100	550.00	330.00
(10)	Hal Chase	850.00	425.00	250.00
(11)	Ed Cicotte	925.00	460.00	275.00
(12)	Fred Clark (Clarke)	1,100	550.00	330.00
(13)	Ty Cobb	5,000	2,500	1,500
(14)	King Cole	550.00	275.00	165.00
(15)	Eddie Collins	1,100	550.00	330.00
(16)	Sam Crawford	1,100	550.00	330.00
(17)	Lou Criger	550.00	275.00	165.00
(18)	Harry Davis	550.00	275.00	165.00
(19)	Jim Delehanty	550.00	275.00	165.00
(20)	Art Devlin	550.00	275.00	165.00
(21)	Josh Devore	550.00	275.00	165.00
(22)	Wild Bill Donovan	550.00	275.00	165.00
(23)	Larry Doyle	550.00	275.00	165.00
(24)	Johnny Evers	1,100	550.00	330.00
(25)	John Flynn	550.00	275.00	165.00
(26)	George Gibson	550.00	275.00	165.00
(27)	Solly Hoffman (Hofman)	550.00	275.00	165.00
(28)	Walter Johnson	2,200	1,100	660.00
(29)	Johnny Kling	550.00	275.00	165.00
(30)	Nap Lajoie	1,100	550.00	330.00
(31)	Christy Mathewson	2,200	1,100	660.00
(32)	Matty McIntyre	550.00	275.00	165.00
(33)	Fred Merkle	550.00	275.00	165.00
(34)	Danny Murphy	550.00	275.00	165.00
(35)	Tom Needham	550.00	275.00	165.00
(36)	Harry Niles	550.00	275.00	165.00
(37)	Rube Oldring	550.00	275.00	165.00
(38)	Wildfire Schulte	550.00	275.00	165.00
(39)	Cy Seymour	550.00	275.00	165.00
(40)	Jimmy Sheckard	550.00	275.00	165.00
(41)	Tris Speaker	1,375	685.00	400.00
(42)	Oscar Stanage/Btg (Front view.)	550.00	275.00	165.00
(43)	Oscar Stanage/Btg (Side view.)	550.00	275.00	165.00
(44)	Ira Thomas	550.00	275.00	165.00
(45)	Joe Tinker	1,100	550.00	330.00
(46)	Heinie Wagner	550.00	275.00	165.00
(47)	Honus Wagner	4,500	2,250	1,350
(48)	Ed Walsh	1,100	550.00	330.00
(49)	Art Wilson	550.00	275.00	165.00
(50)	Owen Wilson	550.00	275.00	165.00

1887-1893 Baseball Currency

Because of their similarity in size (about 7-3/4" x 3-3/8"), design and color to then-circulating U.S. paper money, this form of advertising flyer was thought to catch the attention of the general public. The notes were printed in black-and-green (some 1889 Chicago notes are printed in black-and-red) on white. Fronts have at left a large oval portrait of the team's president or manager. At right on the Chicago and Detroit notes is a full-figure rendering of an unnamed Cap Anson. On the St. Louis notes, there is a picture of the Wilman Trophy indicative of the team's 1886 World's Championship. On the 1893 note, National League President N.E. Young is pictured at left, with a grouping of baseball equipment at right. In the center is a large ornate date with either "National Base Ball League" or "National / Base Ball Association" at top in gothic typography. Backs have black-and-white woodcuts of the team's players on a decorative green (or red) background. The notes were originally printed with large open spaces on front and back so that advertising messages could be overprinted by local merchants. The value of the notes can be affected by the location of a specific advertiser and/or the content of his message. Sports collectors compete with numismatists for examples of these advertising pieces.

	NM	EX	VG
1887 Chicago White Stockings (Front: Pres. A.G. Spalding. Back: Cap Anson, Mark Baldwin, John Clarkson, Tom Daily (Daly), Dell Darling, Silver Flint, Lou Hardie, Fred Pfeffer, Jimmy Ryan, Marty Sullivan, Billy Sunday, Ed Williamson.)	2,000	1,000	600.00
1887 Detroit Wolverines (Front: Manager Bill Watkins. Back: Lady Baldwin, Charlie Bennett, Fatty Briody, Dan Brouthers, Fred Dunlap, Charlie Ganzel, Ned Hanlon, Hardy Richardson, Jack Rowe, Sam Thompson, Stump Weidman (Wiedman), Deacon White.)	2,250	1,125	675.00
1887 St. Louis Browns (Front: Pres. Chris Von Der Ahe. Back: Jack Boyle, Doc Bushong, Bob Caruthers, Charlie Comiskey, Dave Foutz, Bill Gleason, Arlie Latham, Tip O'Neil (O'Neill), Yank Robinson, Curt Welch.)	3,500	1,750	1,050
1888 Chicago White Stockings (Front: Pres. A.G. Spalding. Back: Cap Anson, Mark Baldwin, John Clarkson, Tom Daily (Daly), Dell Darling, Silver Flint, Lou Hardie, Fred Pfeffer, Jimmy Ryan, Marty Sullivan, Billy Sunday, Ed Williamson.)	2,000	1,000	600.00
1888 Detroit Wolverines (Front: Manager Bill Watkins. Back: Lady Baldwin, Charlie Bennett, Fatty Briody, Dan Brouthers, Fred Dunlap, Charlie Ganzel, Ned Hanlon, Hardy Richardson, Jack Rowe, Sam Thompson, Stump Weidman (Wiedman), Deacon White.)	2,250	1,125	675.00
1889 Chicago White Stockings (Front: Pres. A.G. Spalding. Back: Cap Anson, Mark Baldwin, Tom Burns, Tom Daily (Daly), Dell Darling, Silver Flint, Bob Pettit, Fred Pfeffer, Jimmy Ryan, Marty Sullivan, George Van Haltren, Ed Williamson.)	2,000	1,000	600.00
1893 National League All-Stars (Front: Pres. N.E. Young. Back: Bob Allen, Cap Anson, Mark Baldwin, John Clarkson, Charles Comiskey, Dave Foutz, King Kelly, Billy Nash, Jim O'Rourke, Fred Pfeffer, George Van Haltren, John Ward.)(Value Undetermined)			

1979 Baseball Favorites "1953 Bowman"

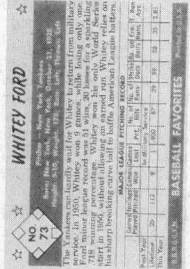

This collectors' series was designed to represent an extension of the 64-card 1953 Bowman black-and-white card issue. This series uses the same design on its 2-1/2" x 3-3/4" format. Fronts have a black-and-white player photo with no extraneous graphics. Backs are printed in red and black and offer career highlights, stats and biographical data, written as if in 1953. Many of the players in this collectors' edition originally appeared in Bowman's 1953 color series. Issue price was about $7.

		NM	EX	VG
Complete Set (16):		25.00	12.50	7.50
Common Player:		.75	.40	.25
65	Monte Irvin	.75	.40	.25
66	Early Wynn	.75	.40	.25
67	Robin Roberts	.75	.40	.25
68	Stan Musial	3.00	1.50	.90
69	Ernie Banks	1.50	.75	.45
70	Willie Mays	4.50	2.25	1.25
71	Yogi Berra	2.25	1.25	.70
72	Mickey Mantle	9.00	4.50	2.75
73	Whitey Ford	1.25	.60	.40
74	Bob Feller	.75	.40	.25
75	Ted Williams	4.50	2.25	1.25
76	Satchel Paige	3.00	1.50	.90
77	Jackie Robinson	3.00	1.50	.90
78	Ed Mathews	.75	.40	.25
79	Warren Spahn	.75	.40	.25
80	Ralph Kiner	.75	.40	.25

1964 Baseball Greats Postcard

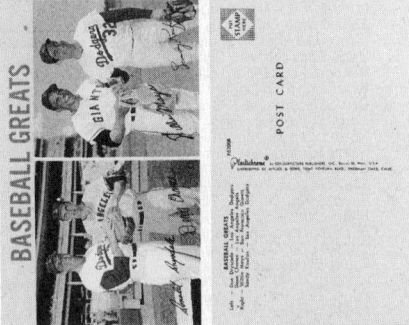

Four of California's star players are pictured on this standard-format (5-1/2" x 3-1/2") color postcard in a pair of two-player poses. Each player's facsimile autograph appears on front. Back is in typical postcard format with player identification, a stamp box and vertical center divider with publisher and distributor information. (See also Baseball Stars - Present and Future.)

	NM	EX	VG
Don Drysdale, Dean Chance, Willie Mays, Sandy Koufax	40.00	20.00	12.00

1910-57 Baseball Magazine Player Posters

Beginning shortly after its 1908 debut, Baseball Magazine produced a lengthy series of player posters which it offered as premiums to readers. Ranging in size from 9" x 12-1/4" to 9" x 20" (and a series of super-size 1957s), the posters feature poses of top players in sepia tones bordered in white. In the bottom border over the years appeared various formats of player identification, copyright information and promotion for the magazine. The unnumbered posters are listed here alphabetically by year. Some posters were reprinted over the years and there may exist pose variations as well as posters which have escaped this list. Names shown here may not coincide with the form in which they actually appear on the posters. Inaccuracies in, or incompleteness of, the checklist is the likely result of its having been compiled from ads appearing in the magazine.

		NM	EX	VG
1910				
(1)	Ty Cobb	350.00	175.00	105.00

		NM	EX	VG
(2)	Johnny Evers	150.00	75.00	45.00
(3)	Hughie Jennings	100.00	50.00	30.00
(4)	Honus Wagner	300.00	150.00	90.00
1912				
(1)	Babe Adams	60.00	30.00	18.00
(2)	Howie Camnitz	60.00	30.00	18.00
(3)	Frank Chance	125.00	62.00	37.00
(4)	Claude Hendrix	60.00	30.00	18.00
(5)	Marty O'Toole	60.00	30.00	18.00
(6)	Boston Red Sox Team	250.00	125.00	75.00
(7)	New York Giants Team	250.00	125.00	75.00
1913				
(1)	Jimmy Archer	60.00	30.00	18.00
(2)	Jack Barry	60.00	30.00	18.00
(3)	Joe Bush	60.00	30.00	18.00
(4)	Sam Crawford	100.00	50.00	30.00
(5)	Eddie Collins	125.00	62.00	37.00
(6)	Jake Daubert	60.00	30.00	18.00
(7)	Larry Doyle	60.00	30.00	18.00
(8)	Art Fletcher	60.00	30.00	18.00
(9)	Joe Jackson	1,000	500.00	300.00
(10)	Walter Johnson	250.00	125.00	75.00
(11)	Nap Lajoie	200.00	100.00	60.00
(12)	Connie Mack	100.00	50.00	30.00
(13)	Fritz Maisel	60.00	30.00	18.00
(14)	Rube Marquard	100.00	50.00	30.00
(15)	Christy Mathewson	250.00	125.00	75.00
(16)	John McGraw	125.00	62.00	37.00
(17)	Stuffy McInnis	60.00	30.00	18.00
(18)	"Chief" Meyers	60.00	30.00	18.00
(19)	Red Murray	60.00	30.00	18.00
(20)	Eddie Plank	125.00	62.00	37.00
(21)	"Nap" Rucker	60.00	30.00	18.00
(22)	Reb Russell	60.00	30.00	18.00
(23)	Tris Speaker	125.00	62.00	37.00
(24)	Ed Walsh	100.00	50.00	30.00
(25)	Smokey Joe Wood	75.00	37.00	22.00
(26)	Boston Braves Team	250.00	125.00	75.00
(27)	Philadelphia Athletics Team	250.00	125.00	75.00
1914				
(1)	Home Run Baker	100.00	50.00	30.00
(2)	Larry Cheney	60.00	30.00	18.00
(3)	Joe Connolly	60.00	30.00	18.00
(4)	Hank Gowdy	60.00	30.00	18.00
(5)	Bill James	60.00	30.00	18.00
(6)	Jimmy Lavender	60.00	30.00	18.00
(7)	Rabbit Maranville	100.00	50.00	30.00
(8)	Dick Rudolph	60.00	30.00	18.00
(9)	Wally Schang	60.00	30.00	18.00
(10)	Bob Shawkey	60.00	30.00	18.00
(11)	Jimmy Sheckard	60.00	30.00	18.00
(12)	Charles Schmidt	60.00	30.00	18.00
(13)	Wildfire Schulte	60.00	30.00	18.00
(14)	Lefty Tyler	60.00	30.00	18.00
(15)	Boston Braves Team	200.00	100.00	60.00
(16)	Chicago Cubs Team	200.00	100.00	60.00
(17)	Chicago Whales Team	250.00	125.00	75.00
(18)	Cincinnati Reds Team	200.00	100.00	60.00
(19)	Cleveland Indians Team	200.00	100.00	60.00
(20)	Detroit Tigers Team	200.00	100.00	60.00
(21)	New York Yankees Team	200.00	100.00	60.00
(22)	St. Louis Browns Team	200.00	100.00	60.00
(23)	Washington Senators Team	200.00	100.00	60.00
1915				
(1)	Grover Alexander	125.00	62.00	37.00
(2)	Chief Bender	100.00	50.00	30.00
(3)	Harry Hooper	100.00	50.00	30.00
(4)	Duffy Lewis	60.00	30.00	18.00
(5)	Tris Speaker	100.00	50.00	30.00
(6)	Boston Red Sox Team	200.00	100.00	60.00
(7)	Chicago White Sox Team	200.00	100.00	60.00
(8)	Philadelphia Athletics Team	200.00	100.00	60.00
(9)	Philadelphia Phillies Team	200.00	100.00	60.00
(10)	St. Louis Cardinals Team	200.00	100.00	60.00
1916				
(1)	Larry Gardner	50.00	25.00	15.00
(2)	Buck Herzog	50.00	25.00	15.00
(3)	Rogers Hornsby	75.00	37.00	22.00
(4)	Walter Johnson	160.00	80.00	48.00
(5)	Fielder Jones	50.00	25.00	15.00
(6)	Benny Kauff	50.00	25.00	15.00
(7)	Dave Robertson	50.00	25.00	15.00
(8)	Babe Ruth/Pitching	300.00	150.00	90.00
(9)	George Sisler	75.00	37.00	22.00
(10)	Zack Wheat	75.00	37.00	22.00
(11)	Boston Red Sox Team	150.00	75.00	45.00
(12)	Brooklyn Dodgers Team	100.00	50.00	30.00
(13)	Philadelphia Phillies Team	100.00	50.00	30.00
1917				
(1)	George Burns	50.00	25.00	15.00
(2)	Ed Cicotte	150.00	75.00	45.00
(3)	Art Fletcher	50.00	25.00	15.00
(4)	Red Faber	50.00	25.00	15.00
(5)	Happy Felsch	150.00	75.00	45.00
(6)	Ferd Schupp	50.00	25.00	15.00
(7)	Ray Schalk	50.00	25.00	15.00
(8)	Buck Weaver	150.00	75.00	45.00
(9)	Boston Red Sox Team	150.00	75.00	45.00
(10)	New York Giants Team	150.00	75.00	45.00
1918				
(1)	Home Run Baker	75.00	37.00	22.00
1919				
(1)	Ed Cicotte	75.00	37.00	22.00
(2)	Chicago White Sox Team	400.00	200.00	120.00
(3)	Cincinnati Reds Team	125.00	62.00	37.00
1920				
(1)	Jim Bagby	30.00	15.00	9.00
(2)	Dave Bancroft	45.00	22.00	13.50
(3)	Max Carey	45.00	22.00	13.50
(4)	Harry Coveleski	45.00	22.00	13.50
(5)	Hod Eller	30.00	15.00	9.00
(6)	Burleigh Grimes	45.00	22.00	13.50
(7)	Heinie Groh	30.00	15.00	9.00
(8)	Rogers Hornsby	45.00	22.00	13.50
(9)	Walter Johnson	75.00	37.00	22.00
(10)	Dick Kerr	30.00	15.00	9.00
(11)	Pat Moran	30.00	15.00	9.00
(12)	Duster Mails	30.00	15.00	9.00

		NM	EX	VG
(13)	Hy Myers	30.00	15.00	9.00
(14)	Steve O'Neill	30.00	15.00	9.00
(15)	Edd Roush	45.00	22.00	13.50
(16)	Dutch Ruether	30.00	15.00	9.00
(17)	Babe Ruth/Btg	700.00	350.00	210.00
	(No stands in background.)			
(18)	Ray Schalk	45.00	22.00	13.50
(19)	Earl Smith	30.00	15.00	9.00
(20)	Sherrod Smith	30.00	15.00	9.00
(21)	Tris Speaker	45.00	22.00	13.50
(22)	Hippo Vaughn	30.00	15.00	9.00
(23)	Bobby Veach	30.00	15.00	9.00
(24)	Bill Wambsganss	30.00	15.00	9.00
(25)	Brooklyn Dodgers Team	125.00	62.00	37.00
(26)	Cleveland Indians Team	125.00	62.00	37.00
1921				
(1)	Dave Bancroft	45.00	22.00	13.50
(2)	Wilbur Cooper	30.00	15.00	9.00
(3)	Phil Douglas	30.00	15.00	9.00
(4)	Frank Frisch	50.00	25.00	15.00
(5)	Harry Heilmann	45.00	22.00	13.50
(6)	Waite Hoyt	45.00	22.00	13.50
(7)	George Kelly	45.00	22.00	13.50
(8)	Carl Mays	45.00	22.00	13.50
(9)	Mike McNally	30.00	15.00	9.00
(10)	Irish Meusel	30.00	15.00	9.00
(11)	Bob Meusel	30.00	15.00	9.00
(12)	Art Nehf	30.00	15.00	9.00
(13)	Wally Schang	30.00	15.00	9.00
(14)	Walter Schmidt	30.00	15.00	9.00
(15)	Frank Snyder	30.00	15.00	9.00
(16)	Aaron Ward	30.00	15.00	9.00
(17)	Ross Youngs	45.00	22.00	13.50
(18)	New York Giants Team	100.00	50.00	30.00
(19)	New York Yankees Team	300.00	150.00	90.00
(20)	Pittsburgh Pirates Team	100.00	50.00	30.00
1922 - NONE				
1923				
(1)	New York Giants Team	90.00	45.00	27.00
(2)	New York Yankees Team	200.00	100.00	60.00
1924				
(1)	Johnny Bassler	30.00	15.00	9.00
(2)	Jim Bottomley	45.00	22.00	13.50
(3)	Kiki Cuyler	45.00	22.00	13.50
(4)	Joe Dugan	30.00	15.00	9.00
(5)	Bibb Falk	30.00	15.00	9.00
(6)	Jack Fournier	30.00	15.00	9.00
(7)	Goose Goslin	45.00	22.00	13.50
(8)	Sam Harris	30.00	15.00	9.00
(9)	Gabby Hartnett	45.00	22.00	13.50
(10)	Travis Jackson	45.00	22.00	13.50
(11)	Baby Doll Jacobson	30.00	15.00	9.00
(12)	Charlie Jamieson	30.00	15.00	9.00
(13)	Herb Pennock	45.00	22.00	13.50
(14)	Sam Rice	45.00	22.00	13.50
(15)	Eppa Rixey	45.00	22.00	13.50
(16)	Muddy Ruel	30.00	15.00	9.00
(17)	Hollis Thurston	30.00	15.00	9.00
(18)	Pie Traynor	45.00	22.00	13.50
(19)	Dazzy Vance	45.00	22.00	13.50
(20)	Kenny Williams	30.00	15.00	9.00
(21)	New York Giants Team	90.00	45.00	27.00
(22)	Washington Senators Team	90.00	45.00	27.00
1925				
(1)	Vic Aldridge	30.00	15.00	9.00
(2)	Mickey Cochrane	45.00	22.00	13.50
(3)	Ted Lyons	45.00	22.00	13.50
(4)	Eddie Rommel	30.00	15.00	9.00
(5)	Al Simmons	45.00	22.00	13.50
(6)	Glenn Wright	30.00	15.00	9.00
(7)	Pittsburgh Pirates Team	90.00	45.00	27.00
(8)	Washington Senators Team	90.00	45.00	27.00
1926				
(1)	Les Bell	30.00	15.00	9.00
(2)	George H. Burns	30.00	15.00	9.00
(3)	Hughie Critz	30.00	15.00	9.00
(4)	Henry (Lou) Gehrig/Portrait	250.00	125.00	75.00
(5)	Ray Kremer	30.00	15.00	9.00
(6)	Bob O'Farrell	30.00	15.00	9.00
(7)	Tommy Thevenow	30.00	15.00	9.00
(8)	George Uhle	30.00	15.00	9.00
(9)	Hack Wilson	45.00	22.00	13.50
(10)	New York Yankees Team	250.00	125.00	75.00
(11)	St. Louis Cardinals Team	90.00	45.00	27.00
1927				
(1)	Carmen Hill	30.00	15.00	9.00
(2)	Tony Lazzeri	45.00	22.00	13.50
(3)	Fred Lindstrom	45.00	22.00	13.50
(4)	Charlie Root	30.00	15.00	9.00
(5)	Lloyd Waner	45.00	22.00	13.50
(6)	Paul Waner	45.00	22.00	13.50
(7)	New York Yankees Team	200.00	100.00	60.00
(8)	Pittsburgh Pirates Team	90.00	45.00	27.00
1928				
(1)	Jimmie Foxx	60.00	30.00	18.00
1929				
(1)	Guy Bush	30.00	15.00	9.00
(2)	Lefty Grove	45.00	22.00	13.50
(3)	Chicago Cubs Team	125.00	62.00	37.00
(4)	Philadelphia Athletics Team	90.00	45.00	27.00
1930				
(1)	George Earnshaw	30.00	15.00	9.00
(2)	Wes Ferrell	30.00	15.00	9.00
(3)	Charley Gelbert	30.00	15.00	9.00
(4)	Babe Herman	30.00	15.00	9.00
(5)	Chuck Klein	45.00	22.00	13.50
(6)	Philadelphia Athletics Team	90.00	45.00	27.00
(7)	St. Louis Cardinals Team	90.00	45.00	27.00
1931				
(1)	Earl Averill	45.00	22.00	13.50
(2)	Ed Brandt	30.00	15.00	9.00
(3)	Ben Chapman	30.00	15.00	9.00
(4)	Joe Cronin	45.00	22.00	13.50
(5)	Bill Hallahan	30.00	15.00	9.00
(6)	Pepper Martin	40.00	20.00	12.00
1932 - NONE				
1933				
(1)	Dizzy Dean	75.00	37.00	22.00

(2)	Lou Gehrig/Btg	225.00	110.00	67.00
(3)	Carl Hubbell	60.00	30.00	18.00
(4)	Heinie Manush	45.00	22.00	13.50
(5)	Mel Ott	45.00	22.00	13.50
(6)	Babe Ruth/Btg (Stands in background.)	250.00	125.00	75.00
(7)	Hal Schumacher	30.00	15.00	9.00
(8)	Lon Warneke	30.00	15.00	9.00
(9)	New York Giants Team	90.00	45.00	27.00
(10)	Washington Senators Team	90.00	45.00	27.00

1934

(1)	Dick Bartell	30.00	15.00	9.00
(2)	Paul Dean	45.00	22.00	13.50
(3)	Lefty Gomez	45.00	22.00	13.50
(4)	Rogers Hornsby	45.00	22.00	13.50
(5)	Ducky Medwick	45.00	22.00	13.50
(6)	Van Lingle Mungo	30.00	15.00	9.00
(7)	Schoolboy Rowe	30.00	15.00	9.00
(8)	Arky Vaughan	45.00	22.00	13.50
(9)	Lloyd Waner	45.00	22.00	13.50
(10)	Paul Waner	45.00	22.00	13.50
(11)	Detroit Tigers Team	100.00	50.00	30.00

1935

(1)	Wally Berger	30.00	15.00	9.00
(2)	Ripper Collins	30.00	15.00	9.00
(3)	Charley Gehringer	45.00	22.00	13.50
(4)	Hank Greenberg	60.00	30.00	18.00
(5)	Mel Harder	30.00	15.00	9.00
(6)	Billy Herman	45.00	22.00	13.50
(7)	Buddy Myer	30.00	15.00	9.00
(8)	Al Simmons	45.00	22.00	13.50
(9)	Bill Terry	45.00	22.00	13.50
(10)	Joe Vosmik	30.00	15.00	9.00
(11)	Chicago Cubs Team	100.00	50.00	30.00
(12)	Detroit Tigers Team	90.00	45.00	27.00

1936

(1)	Luke Appling	45.00	22.00	13.50
(2)	Frank Demaree	30.00	15.00	9.00
(3)	Paul Derringer	30.00	15.00	9.00
(4)	Joe DiMaggio	80.00	40.00	24.00
(5)	Vern Kennedy	30.00	15.00	9.00
(6)	Ernie Lombardi	45.00	22.00	13.50
(7)	Joe Moore	30.00	15.00	9.00
(8)	Terry Moore	30.00	15.00	9.00
(9)	Moose Solters	30.00	15.00	9.00
(10)	Hal Trosky	30.00	15.00	9.00
(11)	Bill Werber	30.00	15.00	9.00
(12)	New York Giants Team	100.00	50.00	30.00
(13)	New York Yankees Team	200.00	100.00	60.00

1937

(1)	Cy Blanton	30.00	15.00	9.00
(2)	Dolph Camilli	30.00	15.00	9.00
(3)	Joe Cronin	45.00	22.00	13.50
(4)	Bill Dickey	50.00	25.00	15.00
(5)	Bob Feller	50.00	25.00	15.00
(6)	Stan Hack	30.00	15.00	9.00
(7)	Buddy Hassett	30.00	15.00	9.00
(8)	Bill Lee	30.00	15.00	9.00
(9)	Buddy Lewis	30.00	15.00	9.00
(10)	Johnny Mize	45.00	22.00	13.50
(11)	Jimmy Ripple	30.00	15.00	9.00
(12)	Charles Ruffing	45.00	22.00	13.50
(13)	Cecil Travis	30.00	15.00	9.00
(14)	Gee Walker	30.00	15.00	9.00

1938

(1)	Ethan Allen	30.00	15.00	9.00
(2)	Clay Bryant	30.00	15.00	9.00
(3)	Harland Clift	30.00	15.00	9.00
(4)	Frank Crosetti	35.00	17.50	10.50
(5)	Harry Danning	30.00	15.00	9.00
(6)	Bobby Doerr	45.00	22.00	13.50
(7)	Augie Galan	30.00	15.00	9.00
(8)	Ival Goodman	30.00	15.00	9.00
(9)	Joe Gordon	30.00	15.00	9.00
(10)	Tommy Henrich	35.00	17.50	10.50
(11)	Mike Kreevich	30.00	15.00	9.00
(12)	Frank McCormick	30.00	15.00	9.00
(13)	Babe Phelps	30.00	15.00	9.00
(14)	Johnny Rizzo	30.00	15.00	9.00
(15)	Red Rolfe	30.00	15.00	9.00
(16)	Johnny Vander Meer	35.00	17.50	10.50
(17)	Rudy York	30.00	15.00	9.00

1939

(1)	Morrie Arnovich	30.00	15.00	9.00
(2)	Jimmie Foxx	45.00	22.00	13.50
(3)	Luke Hamlin	30.00	15.00	9.00
(4)	Bob Johnson	35.00	17.50	10.50
(5)	Charlie Keller	35.00	17.50	10.50
(6)	Ken Keltner	35.00	17.50	10.50
(7)	Emil "Dutch" Leonard	30.00	15.00	9.00
(8)	Bobo Newsom	30.00	15.00	9.00
(9)	Don Padgett	30.00	15.00	9.00
(10)	Bucky Walters	30.00	15.00	9.00
(11)	Ted Williams	120.00	60.00	36.00

1940 (9-1/2" x 12")

(1)	George Case	20.00	10.00	6.00
(2)	Babe Dahlgren	20.00	10.00	6.00
(3)	Elbie Fletcher	20.00	10.00	6.00
(4)	Cookie Lavagetto	20.00	10.00	6.00
(5)	Barney McCosky	20.00	10.00	6.00
(6)	Bill McGee	20.00	10.00	6.00
(7)	Ducky Medwick	40.00	20.00	12.00
(8)	Eddie Miller	20.00	10.00	6.00
(9)	Hugh Mulcahy	20.00	10.00	6.00
(10)	Claude Passeau	20.00	10.00	6.00
(11)	Rip Radcliff	20.00	10.00	6.00
(12)	Jim Tabor	20.00	10.00	6.00
(13)	Eugene "Junior" Thompson	20.00	10.00	6.00
(14)	Mike Tresh	20.00	10.00	6.00
(15)	Roy Weatherly	20.00	10.00	6.00
(16)	Norm "Babe" Young	20.00	10.00	6.00

1941 (9-1/2" x 12")

(1)	Sam Chapman	20.00	10.00	6.00
(2)	Ty Cobb	60.00	30.00	18.00
(3)	Mort Cooper	20.00	10.00	6.00
(4)	Dom DiMaggio	40.00	20.00	12.00
(5)	Jeff Heath	20.00	10.00	6.00
(6)	Thornton Lee	20.00	10.00	6.00
(7)	Danny Litwhiler	20.00	10.00	6.00
(8)	Al Lopez	40.00	20.00	12.00
(9)	Christy Mathewson	60.00	30.00	18.00
(10)	Joe McCarthy	40.00	20.00	12.00
(11)	Bill Nicholson	20.00	10.00	6.00
(12)	Pete Reiser	20.00	10.00	6.00
(13)	Elmer Riddle	20.00	10.00	6.00
(14)	Phil Rizzuto	60.00	30.00	18.00
(15)	Johnny Rucker	20.00	10.00	6.00
(16)	Hans Wagner	60.00	30.00	18.00

1942 (9-1/2" x 12")

(1)	Jim Bagby	20.00	10.00	6.00
(2)	Ernie Bonham	20.00	10.00	6.00
(3)	Lou Boudreau	40.00	20.00	12.00
(4)	Tommy Bridges	20.00	10.00	6.00
(5)	Jimmy Brown	20.00	10.00	6.00
(6)	Dolph Camilli	20.00	10.00	6.00
(7)	Walker Cooper	20.00	10.00	6.00
(8)	Bob Elliott	20.00	10.00	6.00
(9)	Lou Gehrig/Btg	100.00	50.00	30.00
(10)	Tex Hughson	20.00	10.00	6.00
(11)	Eddie Joost	20.00	10.00	6.00
(12)	Don Kolloway	20.00	10.00	6.00
(13)	Phil Marchildon	20.00	10.00	6.00
(14)	Clyde McCullough	20.00	10.00	6.00
(15)	George McQuinn	20.00	10.00	6.00
(16)	Cliff Melton	20.00	10.00	6.00
(17)	Lou Novikoff	20.00	10.00	6.00
(18)	Mickey Owen	20.00	10.00	6.00
(19)	Pee Wee Reese	50.00	25.00	15.00
(20)	Stan Spence	20.00	10.00	6.00
(21)	Vern Stephens	20.00	10.00	6.00
(22)	Virgil Trucks	20.00	10.00	6.00
(23)	Fred "Dixie" Walker	20.00	10.00	6.00
(24)	Max West	20.00	10.00	6.00

1943 (9-1/2" x 12")

(1)	Hiram Bithorn	20.00	10.00	6.00
(2)	Spud Chandler	20.00	10.00	6.00
(3)	Al Javery	20.00	10.00	6.00
(4)	Bill Johnson	20.00	10.00	6.00
(5)	Kenesaw Landis	40.00	20.00	12.00
(6)	Tony Lupien	20.00	10.00	6.00
(7)	Marty Marion	25.00	12.50	7.50
(8)	Stan Musial	60.00	30.00	18.00
(9)	Bobo Newsom	20.00	10.00	6.00
(10)	Babe Ruth/Portrait	80.00	40.00	24.00
(11)	Rip Sewell	20.00	10.00	6.00
(12)	Joe Schultz	20.00	10.00	6.00
(13)	Dizzy Trout	20.00	10.00	6.00
(14)	Mickey Vernon	20.00	10.00	6.00
(15)	Dick Wakefield	20.00	10.00	6.00
(16)	Mickey Witek	20.00	10.00	6.00
(17)	Early Wynn	40.00	20.00	12.00
(18)	New York Yankees Team	90.00	45.00	27.00
(19)	St. Louis Cardinals Team	90.00	45.00	27.00

1944 (9-1/2" x 12")

(1)	Augie Galan	20.00	10.00	6.00
(2)	Johnny Hopp	20.00	10.00	6.00
(3)	Jack Kramer	20.00	10.00	6.00
(4)	Johnny Lindell	20.00	10.00	6.00
(5)	Ray Mueller	20.00	10.00	6.00
(6)	Hal Newhouser	40.00	20.00	12.00
(7)	Nelson Potter	20.00	10.00	6.00
(8)	Ray Sanders	20.00	10.00	6.00
(9)	"Snuffy" Stirnweiss	20.00	10.00	6.00
(10)	Jim Tobin	20.00	10.00	6.00
(11)	Thurman Tucker	20.00	10.00	6.00
(12)	Bill Voiselle	20.00	10.00	6.00
(13)	Ted Wilks	20.00	10.00	6.00
(14)	Detroit Tigers Team	90.00	45.00	27.00
(15)	St. Louis Browns Team	90.00	45.00	27.00
(16)	St. Louis Cardinals Team	90.00	45.00	27.00

1945 (9-1/2" x 12")

(1)	Phil Cavarretta	20.00	10.00	6.00
(2)	Russ Christopher	20.00	10.00	6.00
(3)	Tony Cuccinello	20.00	10.00	6.00
(4)	Boo Ferriss	20.00	10.00	6.00
(5)	Hal Gregg	20.00	10.00	6.00
(6)	Steve Gromek	20.00	10.00	6.00
(7)	Ducky Medwick	40.00	20.00	12.00
(8)	George Myatt	20.00	10.00	6.00
(9)	Frank Overmire	20.00	10.00	6.00
(10)	Andy Pafko	25.00	12.50	7.50
(11)	Red Schoendienst	40.00	20.00	12.00
(12)	Chicago Cubs Team	90.00	45.00	27.00
(13)	Detroit Tigers Team	75.00	37.00	22.00

1946

(1)	Joe Beggs	20.00	10.00	6.00
(2)	Johnny Berardino	25.00	12.50	7.50
(3)	Bill Bevens	20.00	10.00	6.00
(4)	Harry Brecheen	20.00	10.00	6.00
(5)	Mickey Harris	20.00	10.00	6.00
(6)	Kirby Higbe	20.00	10.00	6.00
(7)	Dave Koslo	20.00	10.00	6.00
(8)	Whitey Kurowski	20.00	10.00	6.00
(9)	Vic Lombardi	20.00	10.00	6.00
(10)	Phil Masi	20.00	10.00	6.00
(11)	Mike McCormick	20.00	10.00	6.00
(12)	Johnny Mize	40.00	20.00	12.00
(13)	Hal Newhouser	40.00	20.00	12.00
(14)	Johnny Pesky	20.00	10.00	6.00
(15)	Howie Pollett	20.00	10.00	6.00
(16)	Jerry Priddy	20.00	10.00	6.00
(17)	Aaron Robinson	20.00	10.00	6.00
(18)	Enos Slaughter	40.00	20.00	12.00
(19)	Eddie Stanky	20.00	10.00	6.00
(20)	Hal Wagner	20.00	10.00	6.00
(21)	Rudy York	20.00	10.00	6.00
(22)	Boston Red Sox Team	75.00	37.00	22.00
(23)	St. Louis Cardinals Team	75.00	37.00	22.00

1947

(1)	Ewell Blackwell	20.00	10.00	6.00
(2)	Ralph Branca	20.00	10.00	6.00
(3)	Billy Cox	20.00	10.00	6.00
(4)	Bob Dillinger	20.00	10.00	6.00
(5)	Joe Dobson	20.00	10.00	6.00
(6)	Joe Gordon	20.00	10.00	6.00
(7)	Hank Greenberg	45.00	22.00	13.50
(8)	Clint Hartung	20.00	10.00	6.00
(9)	Jim Hegan	20.00	10.00	6.00
(10)	Larry Jansen	20.00	10.00	6.00
(11)	George Kell	40.00	20.00	12.00
(12)	Ken Keltner	20.00	10.00	6.00
(13)	Ralph Kiner	40.00	20.00	12.00
(14)	Willard Marshall	20.00	10.00	6.00
(15)	Walt Masterson	20.00	10.00	6.00
(16)	"Red" Munger	20.00	10.00	6.00
(17)	Don Newcombe	25.00	12.50	7.50
(18)	Hal Newhouser	40.00	20.00	12.00
(19)	Joe Page	20.00	10.00	6.00
(20)	Babe Ruth/Portrait	100.00	50.00	30.00
(21)	Warren Spahn	40.00	20.00	12.00
(22)	Harry Taylor	20.00	10.00	6.00
(23)	Harry "The Hat" Walker	20.00	10.00	6.00
(24)	Brooklyn Dodgers Team	100.00	50.00	30.00
(25)	New York Yankees Team	150.00	75.00	45.00

1948

(1)	Richie Ashburn	40.00	20.00	12.00
(2)	Rex Barney	20.00	10.00	6.00
(3)	Gene Bearden	20.00	10.00	6.00
(4)	Lou Brissie	20.00	10.00	6.00
(5)	Alvin Dark	20.00	10.00	6.00
(6)	Larry Doby	40.00	20.00	12.00
(7)	Carl Furillo	25.00	12.50	7.50
(8)	Frank Gustine	20.00	10.00	6.00
(9)	Fred Hutchinson	20.00	10.00	6.00
(10)	Sheldon Jones	20.00	10.00	6.00
(11)	Bob Lemon	40.00	20.00	12.00
(12)	Hank Majeski	20.00	10.00	6.00
(13)	Barney McCosky	20.00	10.00	6.00
(14)	Mel Parnell	20.00	10.00	6.00
(15)	Carl Scheib	20.00	10.00	6.00
(16)	Al Zarilla	20.00	10.00	6.00
(17)	Boston Braves Team	75.00	37.00	22.00
(18)	Cleveland Indians Team	75.00	37.00	22.00

1949

(1)	Hoot Evers	20.00	10.00	6.00
(2)	Bob Feller	40.00	20.00	12.00
(3)	Billy Goodman	20.00	10.00	6.00
(4)	Sid Gordon	20.00	10.00	6.00
(5)	Gil Hodges	40.00	20.00	12.00
(6)	Art Houtteman	20.00	10.00	6.00
(7)	Dale Mitchell	20.00	10.00	6.00
(8)	Vic Raschi	20.00	10.00	6.00
(9)	Robin Roberts	40.00	20.00	12.00
(10)	Ray Scarborough	20.00	10.00	6.00
(11)	Duke Snider	50.00	25.00	15.00
(12)	Vic Wertz	20.00	10.00	6.00
(13)	Ted Williams	75.00	37.00	22.00
(14)	Brooklyn Dodgers Team	90.00	45.00	27.00
(15)	New York Yankees Team	90.00	45.00	27.00

1950

(1)	Hank Bauer	15.00	7.50	4.50
(2)	Yogi Berra	30.00	15.00	9.00
(3)	Walt Dropo	12.00	6.00	3.50
(4)	Del Ennis	12.00	6.00	3.50
(5)	Johnny Groth	12.00	6.00	3.50
(6)	Granny Hamner	12.00	6.00	3.50
(7)	Ted Kluszewski	15.00	7.50	4.50
(8)	Johnny Lipon	12.00	6.00	3.50
(9)	Hank Sauer	12.00	6.00	3.50
(10)	Earl Torgeson	12.00	6.00	3.50
(11)	New York Yankees Team	50.00	25.00	15.00
(12)	Philadelphia Phillies Team	35.00	17.50	10.50

1951

(1)	Grover Alexander	15.00	7.50	4.50
(2)	Chico Carrasquel	15.00	7.50	4.50
(3)	Bubba Church	12.00	6.00	3.50
(4)	Alvin Dark	12.00	6.00	3.50
(5)	Luke Easter	12.00	6.00	3.50
(6)	Carl Erskine	15.00	7.50	4.50
(7)	Ned Garver	12.00	6.00	3.50
(8)	Rogers Hornsby	15.00	7.50	4.50
(9)	Walter Johnson	25.00	12.50	7.50
(10)	Tony Lazzeri	15.00	7.50	4.50
(11)	Whitey Lockman	12.00	6.00	3.50
(12)	Ed Lopat	15.00	7.50	4.50
(13)	Sal Maglie	12.00	6.00	3.50
(14)	Willie Mays	150.00	75.00	45.00
(15)	Gil McDougald	20.00	10.00	6.00
(16)	Irv Noren	12.00	6.00	3.50
(17)	Eddie Robinson	12.00	6.00	3.50
(18)	Jackie Robinson	125.00	62.00	37.00
(19)	Red Rolfe	12.00	6.00	3.50
(20)	Tris Speaker	20.00	10.00	6.00
(21)	Eddie Stanky	12.00	6.00	3.50
(22)	Clyde Vollmer	12.00	6.00	3.50
(23)	Wes Westrum	12.00	6.00	3.50
(24)	Cy Young	25.00	12.50	7.50
(25)	New York Giants Team	40.00	20.00	12.00
(26)	New York Yankees Team	60.00	30.00	18.00

1952

(1)	Bobby Avila	12.00	6.00	3.50
(2)	Lou Boudreau	20.00	10.00	6.00
(3)	Jim Busby	12.00	6.00	3.50
(4)	Roy Campanella	30.00	15.00	9.00
(5)	Gil Coan	12.00	6.00	3.50
(6)	Walker Cooper	12.00	6.00	3.50
(7)	Al Corwin	12.00	6.00	3.50
(8)	Murry Dickson	12.00	6.00	3.50
(9)	Leo Durocher	20.00	10.00	6.00
(10)	Bob Elliott	12.00	6.00	3.50
(11)	Ferris Fain	12.00	6.00	3.50
(12)	Jimmie Foxx	20.00	10.00	6.00
(13)	Mike Garcia	12.00	6.00	3.50
(14)	Hank Greenberg	25.00	12.50	7.50
(15)	Solly Hemus	12.00	6.00	3.50
(16)	Monte Irvin	20.00	10.00	6.00
(17)	Sam Jethroe	12.00	6.00	3.50
(18)	Ellis Kinder	12.00	6.00	3.50
(19)	Dick Kryhoski	12.00	6.00	3.50
(20)	Clem Labine	15.00	7.50	4.50
(21)	Mickey Mantle	200.00	100.00	60.00
(22)	Connie Marrero	12.00	6.00	3.50
(23)	Cass Michaels	12.00	6.00	3.50
(24)	Minnie Minoso	15.00	7.50	4.50

(25)	Don Mueller	12.00	6.00	3.50
(26)	Mel Parnell	12.00	6.00	3.50
(27)	Allie Reynolds	15.00	7.50	4.50
(28)	"Preacher" Roe	15.00	7.50	4.50
(29)	Saul Rogovin	12.00	6.00	3.50
(30)	Al Rosen	15.00	7.50	4.50
(31)	Red Schoendienst	20.00	10.00	6.00
(32)	Andy Seminick	12.00	6.00	3.50
(33)	Bobby Shantz	12.00	6.00	3.50
(34)	Duke Snider	25.00	12.50	7.50
(35)	Gerry Staley	12.00	6.00	3.50
(36)	Gene Stephens	12.00	6.00	3.50
(37)	Max Surkont	12.00	6.00	3.50
(38)	Bobby Thomson	12.00	6.00	3.50
(39)	Elmer Valo	12.00	6.00	3.50
(40)	Eddie Waitkus	12.00	6.00	3.50
(41)	Gene Woodling	15.00	7.50	4.50
(42)	Eddie Yost	12.00	6.00	3.50
(43)	Gus Zernial	12.00	6.00	3.50
(44)	Brooklyn Dodgers Team	50.00	25.00	15.00
(45)	New York Yankees Team	75.00	37.00	22.00

1953

(1)	Joe Black	15.00	7.50	4.50
(2)	Billy Cox	12.00	6.00	3.50
(3)	Billy Loes	12.00	6.00	3.50
(4)	Billy Martin	15.00	7.50	4.50
(5)	Eddie Mathews	25.00	12.50	7.50
(6)	George Shuba	12.00	6.00	3.50
(7)	Hoyt Wilhelm	20.00	10.00	6.00

1954

(1)	Joe Adcock	12.00	6.00	3.50
(2)	Johnny Antonelli	12.00	6.00	3.50
(3)	Gus Bell	12.00	6.00	3.50
(4)	Jim Greengrass	12.00	6.00	3.50
(5)	Bob Grim	12.00	6.00	3.50
(6)	Frank House	12.00	6.00	3.50
(7)	Jackie Jensen	12.00	6.00	3.50
(8)	Al Kaline	25.00	12.50	7.50
(9)	Harvey Kuenn	15.00	7.50	4.50
(10)	Willie Miranda	12.00	6.00	3.50
(11)	Wally Moon	12.00	6.00	3.50
(12)	Ray Moore	12.00	6.00	3.50
(13)	Don Mossi	12.00	6.00	3.50
(14)	Stan Musial	30.00	15.00	9.00
(15)	Hal Naragon	12.00	6.00	3.50
(16)	Chet Nichols	12.00	6.00	3.50
(17)	Billy Pierce	12.00	6.00	3.50
(18)	Arnie Portocarrero	12.00	6.00	3.50
(19)	James "Dusty" Rhodes	12.00	6.00	3.50
(20)	Babe Ruth	50.00	25.00	15.00
(21)	Dean Stone	12.00	6.00	3.50
(22)	Bob Turley	15.00	7.50	4.50
(23)	Jim Wilson	12.00	6.00	3.50
(24)	New York Giants Team	50.00	25.00	15.00

1955

(1)	Gene Conley	12.00	6.00	3.50
(2)	Elston Howard	15.00	7.50	4.50
(3)	Hank Sauer	12.00	6.00	3.50

1956

(1)	Hank Bauer	15.00	7.50	4.50
(2)	Yogi Berra	25.00	12.50	7.50
(3)	Ray Boone	12.00	6.00	3.50
(4)	Ken Boyer	15.00	7.50	4.50
(5)	Tom Brewer	12.00	6.00	3.50
(6)	Bob Buhl	12.00	6.00	3.50
(7)	Nellie Fox	20.00	10.00	6.00
(8)	Bob Keegan	12.00	6.00	3.50
(9)	Don Larsen	15.00	7.50	4.50
(10)	Jim Lemon	12.00	6.00	3.50
(11)	Danny O'Connell	12.00	6.00	3.50
(12)	Jim Pendleton	12.00	6.00	3.50
(13)	Bob Rush	12.00	6.00	3.50
(14)	Roy Sievers	12.00	6.00	3.50
(15)	Gus Zernial	12.00	6.00	3.50

1957

(1)	Hank Aaron	30.00	15.00	9.00
(2)	Joe Adcock	12.00	6.00	3.50
(3)	Luis Arroyo	12.00	6.00	3.50
(4)	Ed Bailey	12.00	6.00	3.50
(5)	Ernie Banks	25.00	12.50	7.50
(6)	Roy Campanella	20.00	10.00	6.00
(7)	Billy Cox	12.00	6.00	3.50
(8)	Del Crandall	12.00	6.00	3.50
(9)	Whitey Ford	25.00	12.50	7.50
(10)	Bob Friend	12.00	6.00	3.50
(11)	Carl Furillo	15.00	7.50	4.50
(12)	Granny Hamner	12.00	6.00	3.50
(13)	Gil Hodges	15.00	7.50	4.50
(14)	Billy Hoeft	12.00	6.00	3.50
(15)	Walter Johnson	25.00	12.50	7.50
(16)	George Kell	20.00	10.00	6.00
(17)	Ted Kluszewski	20.00	10.00	6.00
(18)	Johnny Kucks	12.00	6.00	3.50
(19)	Harvey Kuenn	12.00	6.00	3.50
(20)	Clem Labine	12.00	6.00	3.50
(21)	Vern Law	12.00	6.00	3.50
(22)	Brooks Lawrence	12.00	6.00	3.50
(23)	Bob Lemon	20.00	10.00	6.00
(24)	Sherman Lollar	12.00	6.00	3.50
(25)	Billy Martin	15.00	7.50	4.50
(25)	Eddie Mathews	20.00	10.00	6.00
(26)	Charlie Maxwell	12.00	6.00	3.50
(27)	Willie Mays	60.00	30.00	18.00
(28)	Gil McDougald	15.00	7.50	4.50
(29)	Willie Miranda	12.00	6.00	3.50
(30)	Jimmy Piersall	12.00	6.00	3.50
(31)	Pee Wee Reese	25.00	12.50	7.50
(32)	"Rip" Repulski	12.00	6.00	3.50
(33)	Robin Roberts	20.00	10.00	6.00
(34)	Frank Robinson	30.00	15.00	9.00
(35)	Al Rosen	12.00	6.00	3.50
(36)	Babe Ruth	60.00	30.00	18.00
(37)	Herb Score	15.00	7.50	4.50
(38)	Enos Slaughter	20.00	10.00	6.00
(39)	Warren Spahn	20.00	10.00	6.00
(40)	Johnny Temple	12.00	6.00	3.50
(41)	Mickey Vernon	12.00	6.00	3.50

1957 (17-1/2" x 20")

(1)	Johnny Antonelli	30.00	15.00	9.00
(2)	Hank Bauer	45.00	22.00	13.50
(3)	Frank House	30.00	15.00	9.00
(4)	Jackie Jensen	35.00	17.50	10.00
(5)	Al Kaline	45.00	22.00	13.50
(6)	Bob Lemon	35.00	17.50	10.00
(7)	Chet Nichols	30.00	15.00	9.00
(8)	Al Rosen	30.00	15.00	9.00
(9)	Dean Stone	30.00	15.00	9.00
(10)	Bob Turley	35.00	17.50	10.00
(11)	Mickey Vernon	30.00	15.00	9.00

1915 Baseball Magazine Premium

A special "Park Edition" of the April "Baseball Magazine," produced for sale at major league ballparks, was published in 1915. The cover features a J.F. Kernan portrait of Walter Johnson. Bound inside was a Kernan portrait of Christy Mathewson, printed on heavy, slick paper designed to be removed for display.

	NM	EX	VG
Complete Magazine:	3,500	2,500	1,500
Christy Mathewson (Premium)	2,000	1,000	600.00

1913 Baseball Managers Scorecard/Fan

This novelty souvenir item was presumable made for sale or as a giveaway promotion which could be customized with sponsors' advertising on the back. The body of the fan is a heavy cardboard ovoid about 9-1/2" x 9". At center is a scorecard. Printed in color around the scoring section are colorful caricatures of each National and American League manager either in a costume representing the team nickname or holding a mascot, etc. The piece is stapled to a 6" wooden stick. Local advertising may or may not appear on the back.

	NM	EX	VG
Joe Birmingham, Nixey Callahan, Frank, Chance, Fred Clarke, Bill Dahlen, Red, Dooin, Jonny Evers, Clark Griffith,, Miller Huggins, Hughie Jennings, Connie, Mack, John McGraw, Jake Stahl, George, Stallings, George Stovall, Joe Tinker	1,150	575.00	345.00

1950 Baseball Player Charms

The date of issue for this novelty item is conjectural, based on known player selection. Packaged in plastic bubbles for sale in vending machines, these charms are found in several different shapes - rectangle, octagon, etc. - and colors of plastic. A black-and-white photo appears at center with a loop at top for hanging. Size also varies but is about 3/4" x 1-1/4". Players are not identified on the charm and there is no number. The checklist here is in alphabetical order, and likely not complete.

	NM	EX	VG
Common Player:	20.00	10.00	6.00
(1) Yogi Berra	45.00	22.00	13.50
(2) Ewell Blackwell	20.00	10.00	6.00
(3) Roy Campanella	45.00	22.00	13.50
(4) Joe DiMaggio	75.00	37.00	22.00
(5) Carl Erskine	20.00	10.00	6.00
(6) Bob Feller	25.00	12.50	7.50
(7) Carl Furillo	22.50	11.00	6.75
(8) Lou Gehrig	65.00	32.00	19.50
(9) Ralph Kiner	20.00	10.00	6.00
(10) Stan Musial	55.00	27.00	16.50
(11) Andy Pafko	20.00	10.00	6.00
(12) Pee Wee Reese	35.00	17.50	10.50
(13) Phil Rizzuto	30.00	15.00	9.00
(14) Jackie Robinson	65.00	32.00	19.50
(15) Babe Ruth	95.00	47.00	28.00
(16) Duke Snider	35.00	17.50	10.50
(17) Wally Westlake	20.00	10.00	6.00
(18) Ted Williams	60.00	30.00	18.00

1952 Baseball Player Doubleheader Charms

These vending machine prizes were probabl[y] issued in the early 1950s, though pinning down a date via player selection is imprecise. About 7/8" in diameter, these novelties have black-and-white player photos on front and back, with the player['s] name in script beneath his portrait. A clear plastic dome covers the photos and is wrapped with a looped band for hanging. The unnumbered charm[s] are listed here in alphabetical order.

	NM	EX	VG
Complete Set (31):	550.00	275.00	175.00
Common Player:	25.00	12.50	7.5
(1) Richie Ashburn, Phil Masi	30.00	15.00	9.0
(2) Hank Bauer, Johnny Pesky	25.00	12.50	7.5
(3) Yogi Berra, Duke Snider	45.00	22.00	13.5
(4) Ewell Blackwell, "Big" Jim Konstanty	25.00	12.50	7.5
(5) Lou Boudreau, Allie Reynolds	27.50	13.50	8.2
(6) Leland Brissie, Albert Schoendienst	27.50	13.50	8.2
(7) Roy Campanella, Bob Elliott	30.00	15.00	9.0
(8) Phil Cavarretta, Virgil Stallcup	25.00	12.50	7.5
(9) Sam Chapman, Larry Jansen	25.00	12.50	7.5
(10) Jerry Coleman, George Kell	27.50	13.50	8.2
(11) Billy Cox, Junior Thompson	25.00	12.50	7.5
(12) Walt Dropo, Myron McCormick	25.00	12.50	7.5
(13) Al Evans, Wes Westrum	25.00	12.50	7.5
(14) Walter Evers, Cliff Mapes	25.00	12.50	7.5
(15) Bob Feller, Phil Rizzuto	35.00	17.50	10.5
(16) Gordon Goldsberry, Stan Musial	30.00	15.00	9.0
(17) Clint Hartung, Don Kolloway	25.00	12.50	7.5
(18) Grady Hatton, Tommy Holmes	25.00	12.50	7.5
(19) Tommy Henrich, Ted Kluszewski	27.50	13.50	8.2
(20) Gene Hermanski, Hal Newhouser	25.00	12.50	7.5
(21) Art Houtteman, Jackie Robinson	45.00	22.00	13.5
(22) Sid Hudson, Andy Pafko	25.00	12.50	7.5
(23) Ed Kazak, Bob Lemon	27.50	13.50	8.2
(24) Ellis Kinder, Gus Zernial	25.00	12.50	7.5
(25) Ralph Kiner, Joe Page	27.50	13.50	8.2
(26) Ed Lopat, Paul Trout	25.00	12.50	7.5
(27) Don Newcombe, Vic Wertz	25.00	12.50	7.5
(28) Dave Philley, Aaron Robinson	25.00	12.50	7.5
(29) Vic Raschi, Enos Slaughter	27.50	13.50	8.2

(30)	Pee Wee Reese, Gene Woodling	30.00 15.00 9.00
(31)	George Tebbetts, Eddie Yost	25.00 12.50 7.50

1961 Baseball Player Key Chains

The maker of these postage-stamp size (1-1/8" x 1-1/2") black-and-white, blank-back "cards" is unknown. From the inclusion of numerous journeyman Pirates players in the set, it probably has a Pittsburgh origin. Possibly intended for sale at stadium souvenir counters, they were made to be inserted into clear plastic key chain novelties, and have a semi-gloss front surface. Unnumbered, they are checklisted here alphabetically.

		NM	EX	VG
Complete Set (69):		400.00	200.00	120.00
Common Player:		5.00	2.50	1.50
(1)	Hank Aaron	15.00	7.50	4.50
(2)	Bob Allison	5.00	2.50	1.50
(3)	George Altman	5.00	2.50	1.50
(4)	Luis Aparicio	7.50	3.75	2.25
(5)	Richie Ashburn	7.50	3.75	2.25
(6)	Ernie Banks	10.00	5.00	3.00
(7)	Earl Battey	5.00	2.50	1.50
(8)	Hank Bauer	6.00	3.00	1.75
(9)	Gus Bell	5.00	2.50	1.50
(10)	Yogi Berra	10.00	5.00	3.00
(11)	Ken Boyer	6.00	3.00	1.75
(12)	Lew Burdette	5.00	2.50	1.50
(13)	Smoky Burgess	5.00	2.50	1.50
(14)	Orlando Cepeda	7.50	3.75	2.25
(15)	Gino Cimoli	5.00	2.50	1.50
(16)	Roberto Clemente	20.00	10.00	6.00
(17)	Del Crandall	5.00	2.50	1.50
(18)	Dizzy Dean	9.00	4.50	2.75
(19)	Don Drysdale	7.50	3.75	2.25
(20)	Sam Esposito	5.00	2.50	1.50
(21)	Roy Face	5.00	2.50	1.50
(22)	Nelson Fox	7.50	3.75	2.25
(23)	Bob Friend	5.00	2.50	1.50
(24)	Lou Gehrig	12.50	6.25	3.75
(25)	Joe Gibbon	5.00	2.50	1.50
(26)	Jim Gilliam	6.00	3.00	1.75
(27)	Fred Green	5.00	2.50	1.50
(28)	Pumpsie Green	5.00	2.50	1.50
(29)	Dick Groat	6.00	3.00	1.75
(30)	Harvey Haddix	5.00	2.50	1.50
(31)	Don Hoak	5.00	2.50	1.50
(32)	Glen Hobbie	5.00	2.50	1.50
(33)	Frank Howard	6.00	3.00	1.75
(34)	Jackie Jensen	5.00	2.50	1.50
(35)	Sam Jones	5.00	2.50	1.50
(36)	Al Kaline	9.00	4.50	2.75
(37)	Harmon Killebrew	7.50	3.75	2.25
(38)	Harvey Kuenn	5.00	2.50	1.50
(39)	Norm Larker	5.00	2.50	1.50
(40)	Vernon Law	5.00	2.50	1.50
(41)	Mickey Mantle	30.00	15.00	9.00
(42)	Roger Maris	12.00	6.00	3.50
(43)	Eddie Mathews	7.50	3.75	2.25
(44)	Willie Mays	12.00	6.00	3.50
(45)	Bill Mazeroski	7.50	3.75	2.25
(46)	Willie McCovey	7.50	3.75	2.25
(47)	Lindy McDaniel	5.00	2.50	1.50
(48)	Roy McMillan	5.00	2.50	1.50
(49)	Minnie Minoso	6.00	3.00	1.75
(50)	Danny Murtaugh	5.00	2.50	1.50
(51)	Stan Musial	12.00	6.00	3.50
(52)	Rocky Nelson	5.00	2.50	1.50
(53)	Bob Oldis	5.00	2.50	1.50
(54)	Vada Pinson	6.00	3.00	1.75
(55)	Vic Power	5.00	2.50	1.50
(56)	Robin Roberts	7.50	3.75	2.25
(57)	Pete Runnels	5.00	2.50	1.50
(58)	Babe Ruth	20.00	10.00	6.00
(59)	Ron Santo	6.00	3.00	1.75
(60)	Dick Schofield	5.00	2.50	1.50
(61)	Bob Skinner	5.00	2.50	1.50
(62)	Hal Smith	5.00	2.50	1.50
(63)	Duke Snider	9.00	4.50	2.75
(64)	Warren Spahn	7.50	3.75	2.25
(65)	Dick Stuart	5.00	2.50	1.50
(66)	Willie Tasby	5.00	2.50	1.50
(67)	Tony Taylor	5.00	2.50	1.50
(68)	Bill Virdon	5.00	2.50	1.50
(69)	Ted Williams	17.50	9.00	5.00

1978 Baseball Player Patches

These card-size (about 2-1/2" x 3-1/4") cloth patches feature embroidered player portraits on a white background with a color border. Uniform logos are not present. The patches originally sold for $2.50 apiece from the Penn Emblem Co., Philadelphia, though the company's name is not found on the patches. The unnumbered patches are listed here in alphabetical order.

		NM	EX	VG
Complete Set (103):		350.00	175.00	100.00
Common Player:		3.00	1.50	.90
(1)	Buddy Bell	3.00	1.50	.90
(2)	Johnny Bench	10.00	5.00	3.00
(3)	Vida Blue	3.00	1.50	.90
(4)	Bobby Bonds	3.00	1.50	.90
(5)	Bob Boone	3.00	1.50	.90
(6)	Larry Bowa	3.00	1.50	.90
(7)	George Brett	12.00	6.00	3.50
(8)	Lou Brock	9.00	4.50	2.75
(9)	Rick Burleson	3.00	1.50	.90
(10)	Jeff Burroughs	3.00	1.50	.90
(11)	Bert Campaneris	3.00	1.50	.90
(12)	John Candelaria	3.00	1.50	.90
(13)	Rod Carew	9.00	4.50	2.75
(14)	Steve Carlton	9.00	4.50	2.75
(15)	Gary Carter	7.50	3.75	2.25
(16)	Dave Cash	3.00	1.50	.90
(17)	Cesar Cedeno	3.00	1.50	.90
(18)	Ron Cey	3.00	1.50	.90
(19)	Chris Chambliss	3.00	1.50	.90
(20)	Jack Clark	3.00	1.50	.90
(21)	Dave Concepcion	3.00	1.50	.90
(22)	Cecil Cooper	3.00	1.50	.90
(23)	Jose Cruz	3.00	1.50	.90
(24)	Andre Dawson	3.00	1.50	.90
(25)	Dan Driessen	3.00	1.50	.90
(26)	Rawly Eastwick	3.00	1.50	.90
(27)	Dwight Evans	3.00	1.50	.90
(28)	Mark Fidrych	4.50	2.25	1.25
(29)	Rollie Fingers	7.50	3.75	2.25
(30)	Carlton Fisk	9.00	4.50	2.75
(31)	George Foster	3.00	1.50	.90
(32)	Steve Garvey	6.00	3.00	1.75
(33)	Rich Gossage	3.00	1.50	.90
(34)	Bobby Grich	3.00	1.50	.90
(35)	Ross Grimsley	3.00	1.50	.90
(36)	Ron Guidry	3.00	1.50	.90
(37)	Mike Hargrove	3.00	1.50	.90
(38)	Keith Hernandez	3.00	1.50	.90
(39)	Larry Hisle	3.00	1.50	.90
(40)	Bob Horner	3.00	1.50	.90
(41)	Roy Howell	3.00	1.50	.90
(42)	"Catfish" Hunter	7.50	3.75	2.25
(43)	Reggie Jackson	12.00	6.00	3.50
(44)	Tommy John	4.00	2.00	1.25
(45)	Jim Kern	3.00	1.50	.90
(46)	Chet Lemon	3.00	1.50	.90
(47)	Davey Lopes	3.00	1.50	.90
(48)	Greg Luzinski	3.00	1.50	.90
(49)	Fred Lynn	3.00	1.50	.90
(50)	Garry Maddox	3.00	1.50	.90
(51)	Bill Madlock	3.00	1.50	.90
(52)	Jon Matlack	3.00	1.50	.90
(53)	John Mayberry	3.00	1.50	.90
(54)	Lee Mazzilli	3.00	1.50	.90
(55)	Rick Monday	3.00	1.50	.90
(56)	Don Money	3.00	1.50	.90
(57)	Willie Montanez	3.00	1.50	.90
(58)	John Montefusco	3.00	1.50	.90
(59)	Joe Morgan	9.00	4.50	2.75
(60)	Thurman Munson	7.50	3.75	2.25
(61)	Bobby Murcer	3.00	1.50	.90
(62)	Graig Nettles	3.00	1.50	.90
(63)	Phil Niekro	7.50	3.75	2.25
(64)	Al Oliver	3.00	1.50	.90
(65)	Amos Otis	3.00	1.50	.90
(66)	Jim Palmer	9.00	4.50	2.75
(67)	Dave Parker	3.00	1.50	.90
(68)	Fred Patek	3.00	1.50	.90
(69)	Tony Perez	7.50	3.75	2.25
(70)	Lou Piniella	4.00	2.00	1.25
(71)	Biff Pocoroba	3.00	1.50	.90
(72)	Darrell Porter	3.00	1.50	.90
(73)	Rick Reuschel	3.00	1.50	.90
(74)	Jim Rice	6.00	3.00	1.75
(75a)	Pete Rose (Red border.)	12.00	6.00	3.50
(75b)	Pete Rose (Blue border.)	12.00	6.00	3.50
(76)	Joe Rudi	3.00	1.50	.90
(77)	Rick Reuschel	3.00	1.50	.90
(78)	Nolan Ryan	15.00	7.50	4.50
(79)	Manny Sanguillen	3.00	1.50	.90
(80)	Mike Schmidt	12.00	6.00	3.50
(81)	George Scott	3.00	1.50	.90
(82)	Tom Seaver	9.00	4.50	2.75
(83)	Ted Simmons	3.00	1.50	.90
(84)	Reggie Smith	3.00	1.50	.90
(85)	Willie Stargell	9.00	4.50	2.75
(86)	Rennie Stennett	3.00	1.50	.90
(87)	Jim Sundberg	3.00	1.50	.90
(88)	Bruce Sutter	7.50	3.75	2.25
(89)	Frank Tanana	3.00	1.50	.90
(90)	Garry Templeton	3.00	1.50	.90
(91)	Gene Tenace	3.00	1.50	.90
(92)	Jason Thompson	3.00	1.50	.90
(93)	Luis Tiant	3.00	1.50	.90
(94)	Joe Torre	4.50	2.25	1.25
(95)	Ellis Valentine	3.00	1.50	.90
(96)	Bob Watson	3.00	1.50	.90
(97)	Frank White	3.00	1.50	.90
(98)	Lou Whitaker	3.00	1.50	.90
(99)	Bump Wills	3.00	1.50	.90
(100)	Dave Winfield	9.00	4.50	2.75
(101)	Butch Wynegar	3.00	1.50	.90
(102)	Carl Yastrzemski	12.00	6.00	3.50
(103)	Richie Zisk	3.00	1.50	.90

Fantasy Baseball Player Pencil Clips

This series of modern (circa late 1990s) pencil clips features old-time baseball stars. The pieces feature enameled round buttons in various sizes attached to a steel frame designed to be slipped over a pencil, ostensibly for use with a scorecard during a ball game. These are often sold on eBay and at flea markets by persons purporting them to be old.

NO COLLECTIBLE VALUE
Ty Cobb
Christy Mathewson
Satchel Paige
(St. Louis Browns)
Babe Ruth (Champions)
Honus Wagner
1959 World Series White Sox

1913 Baseball Player Stamps

The extent of this issue and the exact date and manner of its issue are not known. The large-format (about 1-13/16" x 2-1/2") stamps have color artwork of the players on a baseball diamond background. A solid colored frame with art deco detailing separates the picture from the white border. Backs are, of course, blank.

	NM	EX	VG
Chief Bender	200.00	100.00	60.00
Ty Cobb	1,750	875.00	525.00
Joe Jackson	2,250	1,125	675.00
Christy Mathewson	475.00	235.00	140.00
Tris Speaker	200.00	100.00	60.00

1892 Base Ball Scenes (N360)

The N360 American Card Catalog designation covers the several tobacco manufacturers who issued this type of card to advertise various brands.

Obviously, the cards do not picture actual ballplayers, but rather have on their fronts color lithographs of attractive women in baseball uniforms and in game action. Approximately 2-3/16" x 3-15/16" most cards have a tiny line of type at bottom carrying a Donaldson Bros., N.Y., copyright. Those cards issued to promote the Little Rhody Cut Plus brand have a script ad message on front and a monthly schedule of the 12-team National League on back. Advertising for the various brands of tobacco companies may be printed directly on the card back, on a paper label pasted over another ad or overprinted on a previously printed ad. Cards are known with these manufacturers and brands. S.W. Venable: Cockade, Gay Head, Helmet, Ideal and Pluck; G.F. Young & Bro.: Little Rhody, and M.T. Coffey. Nine different poses are known for the card fronts.

	NM	EX	VG
Common Card:	600.00	300.00	180.00

1913 Base Ball Series Notebooks

The issue date cited is conjectural, based on writing found in a surviving specimen of this child's notebook. The 8" x 10" notebook has on its cover a baseball diamond and bleachers drawing in white on a beige background. Printed above and below the artwork are full-color reproductions of five baseball cards from the Philadelphia Caramel issues of 1909 (E95) and 1910 (E96). The cover is printed on thinner stock the original cards and has no printing on the reverse side. This has led to cut copies of these cards being misidentified as proofs. Because similar blank-back, thin stock cards are known of other players, it is possible other notebook covers may exist.

	NM	EX	VG
Complete Notebook:			
Fred Clark (Clarke)(E96), Nap Lajoie (E96), Jake Pfeister (E96), Honus Wagner (E95), Ed Willetts (Willett)(E95)	750.00	375.00	225.00
OBSERVED SINGLES			
Harry Krause (E95)	100.00	40.00	20.00

1911 Baseball Scorecard Fan

This unusual player collectible is a combination fan and scorecard published circa 1911. The cardboard scorecard is about 10-1/2" x 9" and stapled to an approximately 11" long wooden handle. Printed in black-and-white, there are 16 player portraits at top, separated by a baseball. At center is the portrait of young lady and at bottom is a ball-in-mitt photo. The fans can be found with various local advertising overprinted on front or back: Barton's Barber Shop, Ira P. File Ice Cream and Confectionary, Maine's Bliss School of Business, Poole Pianos, Kemper phar-

macy, etc. The players are identified by last name and for lack of uniform details, specific identification of a few of them is speculative.

	NM	EX	VG
Germany Schaeffer (Schaefer), Bobby Wallace, Billy Sullivan, Hal Chase, George Moriarty, Harry Lord, Harry Davis, Nap Lajoie, Mickey Doolan, Clark Griffith, Bill Dahlen, Jeff Sweeney, Frank Chance, Art Devlin, Fred Clark (Clarke), Roger Bresnahan	1,200	600.00	360.00

1964 Baseball Stars - Present and Future Photocard

This large-format (11" x 8-1/2") color card features three group photos of top stars of the day. In addition to the photos, there are facsimile autographs of each player on the bright yellow background. Back is blank. (See also Baseball Greats Postcard.)

	NM	EX	VG
Sheet:	25.00	12.50	7.50
Dean Chance, Don Drysdale, Dick Farrell, Jim Fregosi, Sandy Koufax, Willie Mays, Joe Pepitone, Dick Radatz			

1912 Base Ball Stars Series

This set of blank-backed, black-and-white 6" x 9" pictures features the contestants of the 1912 World Series - the Red Sox and Giants. It is possible these pictures were sold at the ballparks during the Series. The checklist here is probably incomplete. The unnumbered pictures have been listed alphabetically within team.

	NM	EX	VG
Common Player:	450.00	225.00	135.00
BOSTON RED SOX			
(1) Hugh Bedient	450.00	225.00	135.00
(2) Joe Wood	480.00	240.00	145.00
N.Y. GIANTS			
(1) Rube Marquard	525.00	260.00	150.00
(2) Christy Mathewson	1,050	525.00	315.00
(3) Jeff Tesreau	450.00	225.00	135.00

1938 Baseball Tabs

The issuer and manner of distribution for these baseball tabs is unknown. About 3/4" diameter, with bendable wings at each side, the points of which could be stuck through fabric and thus attached to a cap or jacket, the tabs have black-and-white player portraits on a baseball-style background in one of several colors. Most of the player first names have parentheses around them. The team tabs have a large nickname at center and the city and league at bottom. The inclusion

of American Association teams argues for distribution in the upper Midwest. The unnumbered tabs are listed here in alphabetical order.

		NM	EX	VG
Complete Set (53):		3,000	1,500	900.00
Common Player:		50.00	25.00	15.50
Common Team:		50.00	25.00	15.00
(1)	Luke Appling	75.00	37.00	22.00
(2)	Earl Averill	75.00	37.00	22.00
(3)	Phil Cavarretta	50.00	25.00	15.00
(4)	Dizzy Dean	100.00	50.00	30.00
(5)	Paul Derringer	50.00	25.00	15.00
(6)	Bill Dickey	90.00	45.00	27.00
(7)	Joe DiMaggio	450.00	225.00	135.00
(8)	Bob Feller	75.00	37.00	22.00
(9)	Lou Fette	50.00	25.00	15.00
(10)	Jimmie Foxx	100.00	50.00	30.00
(11)	Lou Gehrig	375.00	185.00	110.00
(12)	Charley Gehringer	75.00	37.00	22.00
(13)	Lefty Gomez	75.00	37.00	22.00
(14)	Hank Greenberg	90.00	45.00	27.00
(15)	Lefty Grove	75.00	37.00	22.00
(16)	Mule Haas	50.00	25.00	15.00
(17)	Gabby Hartnett	75.00	37.00	22.00
(18)	Rollie Hemsley	50.00	25.00	15.00
(19)	Carl Hubbell	75.00	37.00	22.00
(20)	Chuck Klein	75.00	37.00	22.00
(21)	Red Kress	50.00	25.00	15.00
(22)	Push-Em-Up-Tony Lazzeri	75.00	37.00	22.00
(23)	Ted Lyons	75.00	37.00	22.00
(24)	Joe Medwick	75.00	37.00	22.00
(25)	Van Lingle Mungo	50.00	25.00	15.00
(26)	Rip Radcliff	50.00	25.00	15.00
(27)	Schoolboy Rowe	50.00	25.00	15.00
(28)	Al Simmons	75.00	37.00	22.00
(29)	Little Poison Waner	75.00	37.00	22.00
(30)	Athletics (Philadelphia)	50.00	25.00	15.00
(31)	Bees (Boston)	50.00	25.00	15.00
(32)	Blues (Kansas City)	50.00	25.00	15.00
(33)	Brewers (Milwaukee)	50.00	25.00	15.00
(34)	Browns (St. Louis)	50.00	25.00	15.00
(35)	Cardinals (St. Louis)	50.00	25.00	15.00
(36)	Colonels (Louisville)	50.00	25.00	15.00
(37)	Cubs (Chicago)	50.00	25.00	15.00
(38)	Dodgers (Brooklyn)	50.00	25.00	15.00
(39)	Giants (New York)	50.00	25.00	15.00
(40)	Indians (Cleveland)	50.00	25.00	15.00
(41)	Indians (Indianapolis)	50.00	25.00	15.00
(42)	Millers (Minneapolis)	50.00	25.00	15.00
(43)	Mud-Hens (Toledo)	50.00	25.00	15.00
(44)	Nationals (Washington)	50.00	25.00	15.00
(45)	Phillies (Philadelphia)	50.00	25.00	15.00
(46)	Pirates (Pittsburgh)	50.00	25.00	15.00
(47)	Red Birds (Columbus)	50.00	25.00	15.00
(48)	Reds (Cincinnati)	50.00	25.00	15.00
(49)	Red Sox (Boston)	50.00	25.00	15.00
(50)	Saints (St. Paul)	50.00	25.00	15.00
(51)	Tigers (Detroit)	50.00	25.00	15.00
(52)	White Sox (Chicago)	50.00	25.00	15.00
(53)	Yankees (New York)	65.00	32.00	19.50

1934-36 Batter-Up (R318)

National Chicle's 192-card "Batter-Up" set was issued over a three-year period. The blank-backed cards are die-cut, enabling collectors of the era to fold the top of the card over so that it could stand upright on its own support. The cards can be found in black-and-white or a variety of color tints. Card numbers 1-80 measure 2-3/8" x 3-1/4" in size, while the high-numbered cards (#81-192) measure 2-3/8" x 3" (1/4" smaller in height). The high-numbered cards are significantly more difficult to find than the lower numbers. The set's ACC designation is R318.

	NM	EX	VG
Complete Set (192):	25,000	10,000	5,000
Common Player (1-80):	95.00	40.00	20.00

	Common Player (81-192):	175.00	70.00	35.00
1	Wally Berger	175.00	60.00	30.00
2	Ed Brandt	95.00	40.00	20.00
3	Al Lopez	300.00	120.00	60.00
4	Dick Bartell	95.00	40.00	20.00
5	Carl Hubbell	300.00	120.00	60.00
6	Bill Terry	300.00	120.00	60.00
7	Pepper Martin	95.00	40.00	20.00
8	Jim Bottomley	300.00	120.00	60.00
9	Tommy Bridges	95.00	40.00	20.00
10	Rick Ferrell	300.00	120.00	60.00
11	Ray Benge	95.00	40.00	20.00
12	Wes Ferrell	95.00	40.00	20.00
13	Bill Cissell	95.00	40.00	20.00
14	Pie Traynor	300.00	120.00	60.00
15	Roy Mahaffey	95.00	40.00	20.00
16	Chick Hafey	300.00	120.00	60.00
17	Lloyd Waner	300.00	120.00	60.00
18	Jack Burns	95.00	40.00	20.00
19	Buddy Myer	95.00	40.00	20.00
20	Bob Johnson	95.00	40.00	20.00
21	Arky Vaughn (Vaughan)	300.00	120.00	60.00
22	Red Rolfe	95.00	40.00	20.00
23	Lefty Gomez	300.00	120.00	60.00
24	Earl Averill	300.00	120.00	60.00
25	Mickey Cochrane	300.00	120.00	60.00
26	Van Mungo	95.00	40.00	20.00
27	Mel Ott	425.00	175.00	85.00
28	Jimmie Foxx	550.00	225.00	110.00
29	Jimmy Dykes	95.00	40.00	20.00
30	Bill Dickey	300.00	120.00	60.00
31	Lefty Grove	300.00	120.00	60.00
32	Joe Cronin	300.00	120.00	60.00
33	Frankie Frisch	300.00	120.00	60.00
34	Al Simmons	300.00	120.00	60.00
35	Rogers Hornsby	475.00	190.00	95.00
36	Ted Lyons	300.00	120.00	60.00
37	Rabbit Maranville	300.00	120.00	60.00
38	Jimmie Wilson	95.00	40.00	20.00
39	Willie Kamm	95.00	40.00	20.00
40	Bill Hallahan	95.00	40.00	20.00
41	Gus Suhr	95.00	40.00	20.00
42	Charlie Gehringer	300.00	120.00	60.00
43	Joe Heving	95.00	40.00	20.00
44	Adam Comorosky	95.00	40.00	20.00
45	Tony Lazzeri	300.00	120.00	60.00
46	Sam Leslie	95.00	40.00	20.00
47	Bob Smith	95.00	40.00	20.00
48	Willis Hudlin	95.00	40.00	20.00
49	Carl Reynolds	95.00	40.00	20.00
50	Fred Schulte	95.00	40.00	20.00
51	Cookie Lavagetto	95.00	40.00	20.00
52	Hal Schumacher	95.00	40.00	20.00
53	Doc Cramer	95.00	40.00	20.00
54	Si Johnson	95.00	40.00	20.00
55	Ollie Bejma	95.00	40.00	20.00
56	Sammy Byrd	95.00	40.00	20.00
57	Hank Greenberg	425.00	175.00	85.00
58	Bill Knickerbocker	95.00	40.00	20.00
59	Billy Urbanski	95.00	40.00	20.00
60	Ed Morgan	95.00	40.00	20.00
61	Eric McNair	95.00	40.00	20.00
62	Ben Chapman	95.00	40.00	20.00
63	Roy Johnson	95.00	40.00	20.00
64	"Dizzy" Dean	625.00	250.00	125.00
65	Zeke Bonura	95.00	40.00	20.00
66	Firpo Marberry	95.00	40.00	20.00
67	Gus Mancuso	95.00	40.00	20.00
68	Joe Vosmik	95.00	40.00	20.00
69	Earl Grace	95.00	40.00	20.00
70	Tony Piet	95.00	40.00	20.00
71	Rollie Hemsley	95.00	40.00	20.00
72	Fred Fitzsimmons	95.00	40.00	20.00
73	Hack Wilson	300.00	120.00	60.00
74	Chick Fullis	95.00	40.00	20.00
75	Fred Frankhouse	95.00	40.00	20.00
76	Ethan Allen	95.00	40.00	20.00
77	Heinie Manush	300.00	120.00	60.00
78	Rip Collins	95.00	40.00	20.00
79	Tony Cuccinello	95.00	40.00	20.00
80	Joe Kuhel	125.00	50.00	25.00
81	Thomas Bridges	175.00	70.00	35.00
82	Clinton Brown	175.00	70.00	35.00
83	Albert Blanche	175.00	70.00	35.00
84	"Boze" Berger	175.00	70.00	35.00
85	Goose Goslin	425.00	175.00	85.00
86	Vernon Gomez	475.00	190.00	95.00
87	Joe Glen (Glenn)	175.00	70.00	35.00
88	Cy Blanton	175.00	70.00	35.00
89	Tom Carey	175.00	70.00	35.00
90	Ralph Birkhofer	175.00	70.00	35.00
91	Frank Gabler	175.00	70.00	35.00
92	Dick Coffman	175.00	70.00	35.00
93	Ollie Bejma	175.00	70.00	35.00
94	Leroy Earl Parmalee	175.00	70.00	35.00
95	Carl Reynolds	175.00	70.00	35.00
96	Ben Cantwell	175.00	70.00	35.00
97	Curtis Davis	175.00	70.00	35.00
98	Wallace Moses, Billy Webb	400.00	160.00	80.00
99	Ray Benge	175.00	70.00	35.00
100	"Pie" Traynor	425.00	175.00	85.00
101	Phil. Cavarretta	175.00	70.00	35.00
102	"Pep" Young	175.00	70.00	35.00
103	Willis Hudlin	175.00	70.00	35.00
104	Mickey Haslin	175.00	70.00	35.00
105	Oswald Bluege	175.00	70.00	35.00
106	Paul Andrews	175.00	70.00	35.00
107	Edward A. Brandt	175.00	70.00	35.00
108	Dan Taylor	175.00	70.00	35.00
109	Thornton T. Lee	175.00	70.00	35.00
110	Hal Schumacher	175.00	70.00	35.00
111	Minter Hayes, Ted Lyons	450.00	180.00	90.00
112	Odell Hale	175.00	70.00	35.00
113	Earl Averill	425.00	175.00	85.00
114	Italo Chelini	175.00	70.00	35.00
115	Ivy Andrews, Jim Bottomley	550.00	225.00	110.00
116	Bill Walker	175.00	70.00	35.00
117	Bill Dickey	600.00	250.00	125.00
118	Gerald Walker	175.00	70.00	35.00
119	Ted Lyons	425.00	175.00	85.00
120	Elden Auker (Eldon)	175.00	70.00	35.00
121	Wild Bill Hallahan	175.00	70.00	35.00
122	Freddy Lindstrom	425.00	175.00	85.00
123	Oral C. Hildebrand	175.00	70.00	35.00
124	Luke Appling	425.00	175.00	85.00
125	"Pepper" Martin	300.00	120.00	60.00
126	Rick Ferrell	425.00	175.00	85.00
127	Ival Goodman	175.00	70.00	35.00
128	Joe Kuhel	175.00	70.00	35.00
129	Ernest Lombardi	425.00	175.00	85.00
130	Charles Gehringer	425.00	175.00	85.00
131	Van L. Mungo	200.00	80.00	40.00
132	Larry French	175.00	70.00	35.00
133	"Buddy" Myer	175.00	70.00	35.00
134	Mel Harder	175.00	70.00	35.00
135	Augie Galan	175.00	70.00	35.00
136	"Gabby" Hartnett	425.00	175.00	85.00
137	Stan Hack	175.00	70.00	35.00
138	Billy Herman	425.00	175.00	85.00
139	Bill Jurges	175.00	70.00	35.00
140	Bill Lee	175.00	70.00	35.00
141	"Zeke" Bonura	175.00	70.00	35.00
142	Tony Piet	175.00	70.00	35.00
143	Paul Dean	275.00	110.00	55.00
144	Jimmy Foxx	725.00	300.00	150.00
145	Joe Medwick	425.00	175.00	85.00
146	Rip Collins	175.00	70.00	35.00
147	Melo Almada	175.00	70.00	35.00
148	Allan Cooke	175.00	70.00	35.00
149	Moe Berg	525.00	225.00	110.00
150	Adolph Camilli	175.00	70.00	35.00
151	Oscar Melillo	175.00	70.00	35.00
152	Bruce Campbell	175.00	70.00	35.00
153	Lefty Grove	525.00	225.00	110.00
154	John Murphy	175.00	70.00	35.00
155	Luke Sewell	175.00	70.00	35.00
156	Leo Durocher	425.00	175.00	85.00
157	Lloyd Waner	425.00	175.00	85.00
158	Guy Bush	175.00	70.00	35.00
159	Jimmy Dykes	175.00	70.00	35.00
160	Steve O'Neill	175.00	70.00	35.00
161	Gen. Crowder	175.00	70.00	35.00
162	Joe Cascarella	175.00	70.00	35.00
163	"Bud" Hafey	175.00	70.00	35.00
164	"Gilly" Campbell	175.00	70.00	35.00
165	Ray Hayworth	175.00	70.00	35.00
166	Frank Demaree	175.00	70.00	35.00
167	John Babich	175.00	70.00	35.00
168	Marvin Owen	175.00	70.00	35.00
169	Ralph Kress	175.00	70.00	35.00
170	"Mule" Haas	175.00	70.00	35.00
171	Frank Higgins	175.00	70.00	35.00
172	Walter Berger	175.00	70.00	35.00
173	Frank Frisch	425.00	175.00	85.00
174	Wess Ferrell (Wes)	175.00	70.00	35.00
175	Pete Fox	175.00	70.00	35.00
176	John Vergez	175.00	70.00	35.00
177	William Rogell	175.00	70.00	35.00
178	"Don" Brennan	175.00	70.00	35.00
179	James Bottomley	425.00	175.00	85.00
180	Travis Jackson	425.00	175.00	85.00
181	Robert Rolfe	175.00	70.00	35.00
182	Frank Crosetti	250.00	100.00	50.00
183	Joe Cronin	425.00	175.00	85.00
184	"Schoolboy" Rowe	200.00	80.00	40.00
185	"Chuck" Klein	425.00	175.00	85.00
186	Lon Warneke	175.00	70.00	35.00
187	Gus Suhr	175.00	70.00	35.00
188	Ben Chapman	175.00	70.00	35.00
189	Clint. Brown	200.00	80.00	40.00
190	Paul Derringer	200.00	80.00	40.00
191	John Burns	200.00	80.00	40.00
192	John Broaca	375.00	100.00	50.00

1958 Bazooka "My Favorite Team" Patches

These screen-printed felt patches were available via a mail-in offer found in Topps baseball cards. Approximately 5" in diameter, they were intended to be sewn on jackets, caps, etc.

		NM	EX	VG
	Complete Set (16):	450.00	225.00	135.00
	Common Patch:	30.00	15.00	9.00
(1)	Baltimore Orioles	30.00	15.00	9.00
(2)	Boston Red Sox	35.00	17.50	10.50
(3)	Chicago Cubs	45.00	22.00	13.50
(4)	Chicago White Sox	30.00	15.00	9.00
(5)	Cincinnati Reds	30.00	15.00	9.00
(6)	Cleveland Indians	30.00	15.00	9.00
(7)	Detroit Tigers	30.00	15.00	9.00
(8)	Kansas City A's	30.00	15.00	9.00
(9)	Los Angeles Dodgers	40.00	20.00	12.00
(10)	Milwaukee Braves	35.00	17.50	10.50
(11)	New York Yankees	50.00	25.00	15.00
(12)	Philadelphia Phillies	30.00	15.00	9.00
(13)	Pittsburgh Pirates	30.00	15.00	9.00
(14)	San Francisco Giants	40.00	20.00	12.00
(15)	St. Louis Cardinals	30.00	15.00	9.00
(16)	Washington Senators	35.00	17.50	10.50

1959 Bazooka

The 1959 Bazooka set, consisting of 23 full-color, unnumbered cards, was printed on boxes of one-cent Topps bubble gum. The blank-backed cards measure 2-13/16" x 4-15/16", when properly cut. Nine cards were first issued, with 14 being added to the set later. The nine more plentiful cards are #'s 1, 5, 8, 9, 14, 15, 16, 17 and 22. Complete boxes would command double the price shown.

		NM	EX	VG
	Complete Set (23):	8,500	4,250	2,500
	Common Player:	100.00	50.00	30.00
(1a)	Hank Aaron (Name in white.)	500.00	250.00	150.00
(1b)	Hank Aaron (Name in yellow.)	485.00	240.00	145.00
(2)	Richie Ashburn/SP	450.00	225.00	135.00
(3)	Ernie Banks/SP	500.00	250.00	150.00
(4)	Ken Boyer/SP	250.00	125.00	75.00
(5)	Orlando Cepeda	200.00	100.00	60.00
(6)	Bob Cerv/SP	250.00	125.00	75.00
(7)	Rocky Colavito/SP	450.00	225.00	135.00
(8)	Del Crandall	100.00	50.00	30.00
(9)	Jim Davenport	100.00	50.00	30.00
(10)	Don Drysdale/SP	485.00	240.00	145.00
(11)	Nellie Fox/SP	450.00	225.00	135.00
(12)	Jackie Jensen/SP	250.00	125.00	75.00
(13)	Harvey Kuenn/SP	250.00	125.00	75.00
(14)	Mickey Mantle	1,750	875.00	525.00
(15)	Willie Mays	500.00	250.00	150.00
(16)	Bill Mazeroski	225.00	110.00	65.00
(17)	Roy McMillan	100.00	50.00	30.00
(18)	Billy Pierce/SP	250.00	125.00	75.00
(19)	Roy Sievers/SP	250.00	125.00	75.00
(20)	Duke Snider/SP	750.00	375.00	225.00
(21)	Gus Triandos/SP	250.00	125.00	75.00
(22)	Bob Turley	200.00	100.00	60.00
(23)	Vic Wertz/SP	250.00	125.00	75.00

1959 Bazooka Pennants

These screen-printed felt pennants were available via a mail-in offer found in Topps baseball cards. Approximately 15" long and 5" wide, they have a "COPYRIGHT BAZOOKA" bar near the wide end.

		NM	EX	VG
	Complete Set (16):	600.00	300.00	180.00
	Common Team:	40.00	20.00	12.00
(1)	Baltimore Orioles	40.00	20.00	12.00
(2)	Boston Red Sox	40.00	20.00	12.00
(3)	Chicago Cubs	40.00	20.00	12.00
(4)	Chicago White Sox	45.00	22.50	13.50
(5)	Cincinnati Redlegs	40.00	20.00	12.00
(6)	Cleveland Indians	40.00	20.00	12.00
(7)	Detroit Tigers	40.00	20.00	12.00
(8)	Kansas City A's	40.00	20.00	12.00
(9)	Los Angeles Dodgers	45.00	22.50	13.50
(10)	Milwaukee Braves	40.00	20.00	12.00

		NM	EX	VG
(11)	New York Yankees	50.00	25.00	15.00
(12)	Philadelphia Phillies	40.00	20.00	12.00
(13)	Pittsburgh Pirates	40.00	20.00	12.00
(14)	San Francisco Giants	40.00	20.00	12.00
(15)	St. Louis Cardinals	40.00	20.00	12.00
(16)	Washington Senators	40.00	20.00	12.00

1960 Bazooka

ROCKY COLAVITO
CLEVELAND INDIANS   outfield
NO. 30 OF 36 CARDS

Three-card panels were printed on the bottoms of Bazooka bubble gum boxes in 1960. The blank-backed set is comprised of 36 cards with the card number located at the bottom of each full-color card. Individual cards measure 1-13/16" x 2-3/4"; the panels measure 2-3/4" x 5-1/2".

		NM	EX	VG
Complete Panel Set (12):		2,200	1,100	650.00
Complete Singles Set (36):		2,000	1,000	600.00
Common Player:		15.00	7.50	4.50
	Panel (1)	125.00	62.00	37.00
1	Ernie Banks	90.00	45.00	27.00
2	Bud Daley	15.00	7.50	4.50
3	Wally Moon	15.00	7.50	4.50
	Panel (2)	200.00	100.00	60.00
4	Hank Aaron	150.00	75.00	45.00
5	Milt Pappas	15.00	7.50	4.50
6	Dick Stuart	15.00	7.50	4.50
	Panel (3)	325.00	160.00	97.00
7	Roberto Clemente	200.00	100.00	60.00
8	Yogi Berra	90.00	45.00	27.00
9	Ken Boyer	25.00	12.50	7.50
	Panel (4)	100.00	50.00	30.00
10	Orlando Cepeda	50.00	25.00	15.00
11	Gus Triandos	15.00	7.50	4.50
12	Frank Malzone	15.00	7.50	4.50
	Panel (5)	200.00	100.00	60.00
13	Willie Mays	150.00	75.00	45.00
14	Camilo Pascual	15.00	7.50	4.50
15	Bob Cerv	15.00	7.50	4.50
	Panel (6)	125.00	62.00	37.00
16	Vic Power	15.00	7.50	4.50
17	Larry Sherry	15.00	7.50	4.50
18	Al Kaline	75.00	37.00	22.00
	Panel (7)	200.00	100.00	60.00
19	Warren Spahn	75.00	37.00	22.00
20	Harmon Killebrew	75.00	37.00	22.00
21	Jackie Jensen	25.00	12.50	7.50
	Panel (8)	175.00	87.00	52.00
22	Luis Aparicio	50.00	25.00	15.00
23	Gil Hodges	50.00	25.00	15.00
24	Richie Ashburn	50.00	25.00	15.00
	Panel (9)	125.00	62.00	37.00
25	Nellie Fox	50.00	25.00	15.00
26	Robin Roberts	50.00	25.00	15.00
27	Joe Cunningham	15.00	7.50	4.50
	Panel (10)	200.00	100.00	60.00
28	Early Wynn	50.00	25.00	15.00
29	Frank Robinson	75.00	37.00	22.00
30	Rocky Colavito	50.00	25.00	15.00
	Panel (11)	750.00	375.00	225.00
31	Mickey Mantle	500.00	250.00	150.00
32	Glen Hobbie	15.00	7.50	4.50
33	Roy McMillan	15.00	7.50	4.50
	Panel (12)	60.00	30.00	18.00
34	Harvey Kuenn	15.00	7.50	4.50
35	Johnny Antonelli	15.00	7.50	4.50
36	Del Crandall	15.00	7.50	4.50

1960 Bazooka Hot Iron Transfers

Team logo transfers were available via a mail-in offer found on cards inserted into packs of 1960 Topps. Varying in size and shape, but generally about 5" square, the transfers were packaged in a colorful envelope which provided instructions for ironing the logo to a t-shirt or other cloth surface. Unlike earlier Bazooka mail-in premiums, the gum is not named on the transfers. Values shown are for transfers without the envelope. Envelopes, which carried the name and logo of the team inside, are valued about the same as the transfer itself.

		NM	EX	VG
Complete Set (16):		300.00	150.00	90.00
Common Team:		20.00	10.00	6.00
Envelope: 1X				
(1)	Baltimore Orioles	20.00	10.00	6.00
(2)	Boston Red Sox	20.00	10.00	6.00
(3)	Chicago Cubs	20.00	10.00	6.00
(4)	Chicago White Sox	20.00	10.00	6.00
(5)	Cincinnati Redlegs	20.00	10.00	6.00
(6)	Cleveland Indians	20.00	10.00	6.00
(7)	Detroit Tigers	20.00	10.00	6.00
(8)	Kansas City A's	20.00	10.00	6.00
(9)	Los Angeles Dodgers	22.50	11.00	6.75
(10)	Milwaukee Braves	20.00	10.00	6.00
(11)	New York Yankees	25.00	12.50	7.50
(12)	Philadelphia Phillies	20.00	10.00	6.00
(13)	Pittsburgh Pirates	22.50	11.00	6.75
(14)	San Francisco Giants	20.00	10.00	6.00
(15)	St. Louis Cardinals	20.00	10.00	6.00
(16)	Washington Senators	20.00	10.00	6.00

1961 Bazooka

TED KLUSZEWSKI
LOS ANGELES ANGELS   1st base
NO. 18 OF 36 CARDS

Similar in design to the 1960 Bazooka set, the 1961 edition consists of 36 cards printed in panels of three on the bottom of Bazooka bubble gum boxes. The full-color cards, which measure 1-13/16" x 2-3/4" individually and 2-3/4" x 5-1/2" as panels, are numbered 1 through 36. The backs are blank.

		NM	EX	VG
Complete Set, Panels (12):		1,500	750.00	450.00
Complete Set, Singles (36):		1,200	600.00	350.00
Common Player:		12.00	6.00	3.50
	Panel (1)	750.00	375.00	225.00
1	Art Mahaffey	12.00	6.00	3.50
2	Mickey Mantle	650.00	325.00	200.00
3	Ron Santo	25.00	12.50	7.50
	Panel (2)	225.00	110.00	65.00
4	Bud Daley	12.00	6.00	3.50
5	Roger Maris	100.00	50.00	30.00
6	Eddie Yost	12.00	6.00	3.50
	Panel (3)	75.00	37.50	22.50
7	Minnie Minoso	15.00	7.50	4.50
8	Dick Groat	13.50	7.00	4.00
9	Frank Malzone	12.00	6.00	3.50
	Panel (4)	100.00	50.00	30.00
10	Dick Donovan	12.00	6.00	3.50
11	Ed Mathews	45.00	22.50	13.50
12	Jim Lemon	12.00	6.00	3.50
	Panel (5)	75.00	37.50	22.50
13	Chuck Estrada	12.00	6.00	3.50
14	Ken Boyer	15.00	7.50	4.50
15	Harvey Kuenn	12.00	6.00	3.50
	Panel (6)	100.00	50.00	30.00
16	Ernie Broglio	12.00	6.00	3.50
17	Rocky Colavito	25.00	12.50	7.50
18	Ted Kluszewski	25.00	12.50	7.50
	Panel (7)	250.00	125.00	75.00
19	Ernie Banks	100.00	50.00	30.00
20	Al Kaline	45.00	22.50	13.50
21	Ed Bailey	12.00	6.00	3.50
	Panel (8)	250.00	125.00	75.00
22	Jim Perry	12.00	6.00	3.50
23	Willie Mays	100.00	50.00	30.00
24	Bill Mazeroski	40.00	20.00	12.00
	Panel (9)	100.00	50.00	30.00
25	Gus Triandos	12.00	6.00	3.50
26	Don Drysdale	45.00	22.50	13.50
27	Frank Herrera	12.00	6.00	3.50
	Panel (10)	100.00	50.00	30.00
28	Earl Battey	12.00	6.00	3.50
29	Warren Spahn	45.00	22.50	13.50
30	Gene Woodling	12.00	6.00	3.50
	Panel (11)	100.00	50.00	30.00
31	Frank Robinson	45.00	22.50	13.50
32	Pete Runnels	12.00	6.00	3.50
33	Woodie Held	12.00	6.00	3.50
	Panel (12)	100.00	50.00	30.00

		NM	EX	VG
34	Norm Larker	12.00	6.00	3.50
35	Luis Aparicio	35.00	17.50	10.00
36	Bill Tuttle	12.00	6.00	3.50

1962 Bazooka

KEN BOYER
ST. LOUIS CARDINALS   3rd base

In 1962, Bazooka increased the size of its set to 45 full-color cards. The set is unnumbered and was printed in panels of three on the bottoms of bubble gum boxes. Individual cards measure 1-13/16" x 2-3/4" in size, with panels at 2-3/4" x 5-1/2". In the checklist that follows the cards have been numbered alphabetically, using the name of the player who appears on the left end of the panel. Panels (1), (11) and (15) were issued in much shorter supply and command a higher price.

		NM	EX	VG
Complete Set, Panels (15):		4,000	2,000	1,200
Complete Set, Singles (45):		3,750	1,850	1,100
Common Player:		12.50	6.25	3.75
	Panel (1)	850.00	425.00	255.00
(1)	Bob Allison	160.00	80.00	45.00
(2)	Ed Mathews	400.00	200.00	120.00
(3)	Vada Pinson	200.00	100.00	60.00
	Panel (2)	100.00	50.00	30.00
(4)	Earl Battey	12.50	6.25	3.75
(5)	Warren Spahn	45.00	22.50	13.50
(6)	Lee Thomas	12.50	6.25	3.75
	Panel (3)	75.00	40.00	25.00
(7)	Orlando Cepeda	30.00	15.00	9.00
(8)	Woodie Held	12.50	6.25	3.75
(9)	Bob Aspromonte	12.50	6.25	3.75
	Panel (4)	200.00	100.00	60.00
(10)	Dick Howser	12.50	6.25	3.75
(11)	Roberto Clemente	125.00	65.00	35.00
(12)	Al Kaline	45.00	22.50	13.50
	Panel (5)	125.00	65.00	35.00
(13)	Joey Jay	12.50	6.25	3.75
(14)	Roger Maris	85.00	42.50	25.00
(15)	Frank Howard	15.00	7.50	4.50
	Panel (6)	175.00	90.00	50.00
(16)	Sandy Koufax	125.00	65.00	35.00
(17)	Jim Gentile	12.50	6.25	3.75
(18)	Johnny Callison	12.50	6.25	3.75
	Panel (7)	50.00	25.00	15.00
(19)	Jim Landis	12.50	6.25	3.75
(20)	Ken Boyer	13.00	6.50	4.00
(21)	Chuck Schilling	12.50	6.25	3.75
	Panel (8)	575.00	285.00	175.00
(22)	Art Mahaffey	12.50	6.25	3.75
(23)	Mickey Mantle	500.00	250.00	150.00
(24)	Dick Stuart	13.50	6.75	4.00
	Panel (9)	100.00	50.00	30.00
(25)	Ken McBride	12.50	6.25	3.75
(26)	Frank Robinson	45.00	22.50	13.50
(27)	Gil Hodges	30.00	15.00	9.00
	Panel (10)	175.00	85.00	50.00
(28)	Milt Pappas	12.50	6.25	3.75
(29)	Hank Aaron	125.00	65.00	35.00
(30)	Luis Aparicio	30.00	15.00	9.00
	Panel (11)	900.00	450.00	275.00
(31)	Johnny Romano	160.00	80.00	50.00
(32)	Ernie Banks	500.00	250.00	150.00
(33)	Norm Siebern	160.00	80.00	50.00
	Panel (12)	75.00	35.00	25.00
(34)	Ron Santo	20.00	10.00	6.00
(35)	Norm Cash	15.00	7.50	4.50
(36)	Jimmy Piersall	15.00	7.50	4.50
	Panel (13)	175.00	85.00	50.00
(37)	Don Schwall	12.50	6.25	3.75
(38)	Willie Mays	125.00	65.00	35.00
(39)	Norm Larker	12.50	6.25	3.75
	Panel (14)	110.00	55.00	35.00
(40)	Bill White	12.50	6.25	3.75
(41)	Whitey Ford	50.00	25.00	15.00
(42)	Rocky Colavito	30.00	15.00	9.00
	Panel (15)	750.00	375.00	225.00
(43)	Don Zimmer	200.00	100.00	60.00
(44)	Harmon Killebrew	350.00	175.00	100.00
(45)	Gene Woodling	160.00	80.00	50.00

The Mint-Mint examples of vintage cards carry a significant premium over the Near Mint values shown here. This premium reflects limited availability of the highest-grade cards as well as demand for particular cards or sets in the best possible condition.

1963 Bazooka

The 1963 Bazooka issue reverted to a 12-panel, 36-card set, but saw a change in the size of the cards. Individual cards measure 1-9/16" x 2-1/2", while panels are 2-1/2" x 4-11/16". The card design was altered also, with the player's name, team and position situated in a white oval at the bottom of the card. The full-color, blank-backed set is numbered 1-36. The complete set was counterfeited circa 2002, with many cards sold in "FGA" certified slabs, depressing the value of cards not graded by a major certification company.

		NM	EX	VG
Complete Set, Panels (12):		1,750	875.00	525.00
Complete Set, Singles (36):		1,200	600.00	350.00
Common Player:		10.00	5.00	3.00
Panel (1)		450.00	225.00	135.00
1	Mickey Mantle (Batting righty.)	325.00	160.00	100.00
2	Bob Rodgers	10.00	5.00	3.00
3	Ernie Banks	60.00	30.00	18.00
Panel (2)		95.00	50.00	30.00
4	Norm Siebern	10.00	5.00	3.00
5	Warren Spahn/Portrait	35.00	17.50	10.00
6	Bill Mazeroski	25.00	12.50	7.50
Panel (3)		175.00	90.00	50.00
7	Harmon Killebrew/Btg	50.00	25.00	15.00
8	Dick Farrell/Portrait	10.00	5.00	3.00
9	Hank Aaron (Glove in front.)	90.00	45.00	27.50
Panel (4)		150.00	75.00	45.00
10	Dick Donovan	10.00	5.00	3.00
11	Jim Gentile/Btg	10.00	5.00	3.00
12	Willie Mays (Bat in front.)	100.00	50.00	30.00
Panel (5)		125.00	65.00	35.00
13	Camilo Pascual (Hands at waist.)	10.00	5.00	3.00
14	Roberto Clemente/Portrait	100.00	50.00	30.00
15	Johnny Callison (Pinstriped uniform.)	10.00	5.00	3.00
Panel (6)		150.00	75.00	45.00
16	Carl Yastrzemski/Kneeling	60.00	30.00	18.00
17	Don Drysdale	35.00	17.50	10.00
18	Johnny Romano/Portrait	10.00	5.00	3.00
Panel (7)		45.00	22.50	13.50
19	Al Jackson	10.00	5.00	3.00
20	Ralph Terry	10.00	5.00	3.00
21	Bill Monbouquette	10.00	5.00	3.00
Panel (8)		150.00	75.00	45.00
22	Orlando Cepeda	35.00	17.50	10.00
23	Stan Musial	75.00	40.00	25.00
24	Floyd Robinson (No pinstripes.)	10.00	5.00	3.00
Panel (9)		45.00	22.50	13.50
25	Chuck Hinton/Btg	10.00	5.00	3.00
26	Bob Purkey	10.00	5.00	3.00
27	Ken Hubbs	12.50	6.25	3.75
Panel (10)		75.00	40.00	25.00
28	Bill White	10.00	5.00	3.00
29	Ray Herbert	10.00	5.00	3.00
30	Brooks Robinson (Glove in front.)	40.00	20.00	12.00
Panel (11)		100.00	50.00	30.00
31	Frank Robinson/Btg	40.00	20.00	12.00
32	Lee Thomas	10.00	5.00	3.00
33	Rocky Colavito (Detroit)	30.00	15.00	9.00
Panel (12)		90.00	45.00	27.50
34	Al Kaline/Kneeling	45.00	22.50	13.50
35	Art Mahaffey	10.00	5.00	3.00
36	Tommy Davis (Follow-through.)	10.00	5.00	3.00

1963 Bazooka All-Time Greats

Consisting of 41 cards, the Bazooka All-Time Greats set was issued as inserts (5 per box) in boxes of Bazooka bubble gum. A black-and-white portrait photo of the player is placed inside a gold plaque within a white border. Card backs contain a brief biography of the player. The numbered cards measure 1-9/16" x 2-1/2". size. Cards can be found with silver fronts instead of gold; the silver are worth double the values listed.

		NM	EX	VG
Complete Set (41):		675.00	335.00	200.00
Common Player:		13.50	6.75	4.00
Silver: 2.5X				
1	Joe Tinker	13.50	6.75	4.00
2	Harry Heilmann	13.50	6.75	4.00
3	Jack Chesbro	13.50	6.75	4.00
4	Christy Mathewson	30.00	15.00	9.00
5	Herb Pennock	13.50	6.75	4.00
6	Cy Young	30.00	15.00	9.00
7	Ed Walsh	13.50	6.75	4.00
8	Nap Lajoie	13.50	6.75	4.00
9	Eddie Plank	13.50	6.75	4.00
10	Honus Wagner	35.00	17.50	10.00
11	Chief Bender	13.50	6.75	4.00
12	Walter Johnson	30.00	15.00	9.00
13	Three-Fingered Brown	13.50	6.75	4.00
14	Rabbit Maranville	13.50	6.75	4.00
15	Lou Gehrig	60.00	30.00	18.00
16	Ban Johnson	13.50	6.75	4.00
17	Babe Ruth	65.00	32.50	20.00
18	Connie Mack	13.50	6.75	4.00
19	Hank Greenberg	20.00	10.00	6.00
20	John McGraw	13.50	6.75	4.00
21	Johnny Evers	13.50	6.75	4.00
22	Al Simmons	13.50	6.75	4.00
23	Jimmy Collins	13.50	6.75	4.00
24	Tris Speaker	13.50	6.75	4.00
25	Frank Chance	13.50	6.75	4.00
26	Fred Clarke	13.50	6.75	4.00
27	Wilbert Robinson	13.50	6.75	4.00
28	Dazzy Vance	13.50	6.75	4.00
29	Grover Alexander	16.00	8.00	4.75
30	Kenesaw Landis	13.50	6.75	4.00
31	Willie Keeler	13.50	6.75	4.00
32	Rogers Hornsby	16.00	8.00	4.75
33	Hugh Duffy	13.50	6.75	4.00
34	Mickey Cochrane	13.50	6.75	4.00
35	Ty Cobb	60.00	30.00	18.00
36	Mel Ott	13.50	6.75	4.00
37	Clark Griffith	13.50	6.75	4.00
38	Ted Lyons	13.50	6.75	4.00
39	Cap Anson	13.50	6.75	4.00
40	Bill Dickey	13.50	6.75	4.00
41	Eddie Collins	13.50	6.75	4.00

1964 Bazooka

The 1964 Bazooka set is identical in design and size to the previous year's effort. However, different photographs were used from year to year. The 1964 set consists of 36 full-color, blank-backed cards numbered 1 through 36. Individual cards measure 1-9/16"

x 2-1/2"; three-card panels measure 2-1/2" x 4-11/16". Sheets of ten full-color baseball stamps were inserted in each box of bubble gum.

		NM	EX	VG
Complete Set, Panels (12):		1,400	700.00	425.00
Complete Set, Singles (36):		950.00	475.00	275.00
Common Player:		10.00	5.00	3.00
Panel (1)		225.00	110.00	70.00
1	Mickey Mantle (Bat on shoulder.)	200.00	100.00	60.00
2	Dick Groat	10.00	5.00	3.00
3	Steve Barber	10.00	5.00	3.00
Panel (2)		75.00	37.00	22.00
4	Ken McBride	10.00	5.00	3.00
5	Warren Spahn (Cap to waist.)	35.00	17.50	10.50
6	Bob Friend	10.00	5.00	3.00
Panel (3)		150.00	75.00	45.00
7	Harmon Killebrew/Portrait	35.00	17.50	10.50
8	Dick Farrell (Hands above head.)	10.00	5.00	3.00
9	Hank Aaron (Glove to left.)	75.00	37.50	22.50
Panel (4)		150.00	75.00	45.00
10	Rich Rollins	10.00	5.00	3.00
11	Jim Gentile/Portrait	10.00	5.00	3.00
12	Willie Mays (Looking to left.)	75.00	37.50	22.50
Panel (5)		150.00	75.00	45.00
13	Camilo Pascual (Follow-through.)	10.00	5.00	3.00
14	Roberto Clemente/Throwing	75.00	37.50	22.50
15	Johnny Callison/Btg (Screen showing)	10.00	5.00	3.00
Panel (6)		125.00	62.00	37.00
16	Carl Yastrzemski/Btg	40.00	20.00	12.00
17	Billy Williams/Kneeling	30.00	15.00	9.00
18	Johnny Romano/Btg	10.00	5.00	3.00
Panel (7)		65.00	32.50	20.00
19	Jim Maloney	10.00	5.00	3.00
20	Norm Cash	12.50	6.25	3.75
21	Willie McCovey	30.00	15.00	9.00
Panel (8)		40.00	20.00	12.00
22	Jim Fregosi/Btg	10.00	5.00	3.00
23	George Altman	10.00	5.00	3.00
24	Floyd Robinson (Pinstriped uniform.)	10.00	5.00	3.00
Panel (9)		40.00	20.00	12.00
25	Chuck Hinton/Portrait	10.00	5.00	3.00
26	Ron Hunt/Btg	10.00	5.00	3.00
27	Gary Peters/Pitching	10.00	5.00	3.00
Panel (10)		90.00	45.00	27.00
28	Dick Ellsworth	10.00	5.00	3.00
29	Elston Howard (w/ bat)	20.00	10.00	6.00
30	Brooks Robinson (Kneeling w/ glove.)	35.00	17.50	10.50
Panel (11)		175.00	87.00	52.00
31	Frank Robinson (Uniform number shows.)	35.00	17.50	10.50
32	Sandy Koufax (Glove in front.)	75.00	37.50	22.50
33	Rocky Colavito (Kansas City)	25.00	12.50	7.50
Panel (12)		90.00	45.00	27.00
34	Al Kaline (Holding two bats.)	40.00	20.00	12.00
35	Ken Boyer (Cap to waist.)	10.00	5.00	3.00
36	Tommy Davis/Btg	10.00	5.00	3.00

1964 Bazooka Stamps

Occasionally mislabeled "Topps Stamps," the 1964 Bazooka stamps were produced by Topps, but found only in boxes of Bazooka bubble gum. Issued in sheets of ten, 100 color stamps make up the set. Each stamp measures 1" x 1-1/2" in size. While the stamps are not individually numbered, the sheets are numbered one through ten. The stamps are commonly found as complete sheets of ten and are priced in that fashion in the checklist that follows.

		NM	EX	VG
Complete Sheet Set (10x10):		750.00	375.00	225.00
Common Sheet:		35.00	17.50	10.00
Common Stamp:		4.00	2.00	1.25
1	Max Alvis, Ed Charles, Dick Ellsworth, Jimmie Hall, Frank Malzone, Milt Pappas, Vada Pinson, Tony Taylor, Pete Ward, Bill White	35.00	17.50	10.50
2	Bob Aspromonte, Larry Jackson, Willie Mays, Al McBean, Bill Monbouquette, Bobby Richardson, Floyd Robinson, Frank Robinson, Norm Siebern, Don Zimmer	80.00	40.00	25.00

		NM	EX	VG
3	Ernie Banks, Roberto Clemente, Curt Flood, Jesse Gonder, Woody Held, Don Lock, Dave Nicholson, Joe Pepitone, Brooks Robinson, Carl Yastrzemski	120.00	60.00	35.00
4	Hank Aguirre, Jim Grant, Harmon Killebrew, Jim Maloney, Juan Marichal, Bill Mazeroski, Juan Pizarro, Boog Powell, Ed Roebuck, Ron Santo	85.00	45.00	25.00
5	Jim Bouton, Norm Cash, Orlando Cepeda, Tommy Harper, Chuck Hinton, Albie Pearson, Ron Perranoski, Dick Radatz, Johnny Romano, Carl Willey	45.00	25.00	15.00
6	Steve Barber, Jim Fregosi, Tony Gonzalez, Mickey Mantle, Jim O'Toole, Gary Peters, Rich Rollins, Warren Spahn, Dick Stuart, Joe Torre	165.00	80.00	50.00
7	Felipe Alou, George Altman, Ken Boyer, Rocky Colavito, Jim Davenport, Tommy Davis, Bill Freehan, Bob Friend, Ken Johnson, Billy Moran	40.00	20.00	12.00
8	Earl Battey, Ernie Broglio, Johnny Callison, Donn Clendenon, Don Drysdale, Jim Gentile, Elston Howard, Claude Osteen, Billy Williams, Hal Woodeshick	55.00	27.50	16.50
9	Hank Aaron, Jack Baldschun, Wayne Causey, Moe Drabowsky, Dick Groat, Frank Howard, Al Jackson, Jerry Lumpe, Ken McBride, Rusty Staub	65.00	32.50	19.50
10	Vic Davalillo, Dick Farrell, Ron Hunt, Al Kaline, Sandy Koufax, Eddie Mathews, Willie McCovey, Camilo Pascual, Lee Thomas	85.00	45.00	25.00

1965 Bazooka

MICKEY MANTLE
N. Y. Yankees OF
NO. 1 OF 36 CARDS

The 1965 Bazooka set is identical to the 1963 and 1964 sets. Different players were added each year and different photographs were used for those players being included again. Individual cards cut from the boxes measure 1-9/16" x 2-1/2". Complete three-card panels measure 2-1/2" x 4-11/16". Cards are again blank-backed.

		NM	EX	VG
	Complete Set, Panels (12):	1,300	650.00	400.00
	Complete Set, Singles (36):	900.00	450.00	275.00
	Common Player:	10.00	5.00	3.00
	Panel (1)	275.00	135.00	85.00
1	Mickey Mantle (Batting lefty.)	200.00	100.00	60.00
2	Larry Jackson	10.00	5.00	3.00
3	Chuck Hinton	10.00	5.00	3.00
	Panel (2)	40.00	20.00	12.00
4	Tony Oliva	12.50	6.25	3.75
5	Dean Chance	10.00	5.00	3.00
6	Jim O'Toole	10.00	5.00	3.00
	Panel (3)	125.00	65.00	35.00
7	Harmon Killebrew (Bat on shoulder.)	35.00	17.50	10.50
8	Pete Ward	10.00	5.00	3.00
9	Hank Aaron/Btg	75.00	37.50	22.50
	Panel (4)	125.00	62.00	37.00
10	Dick Radatz	10.00	5.00	3.00
11	Boog Powell	12.50	6.25	3.75
12	Willie Mays (Looking down.)	75.00	37.50	22.50
	Panel (5)	250.00	125.00	75.00
13	Bob Veale	10.00	5.00	3.00
14	Roberto Clemente/Btg	100.00	50.00	30.00
15	Johnny Callison/Btg (No screen in background.)	10.00	5.00	3.00
	Panel (6)	60.00	30.00	18.00
	Joe Torre	15.00	7.50	4.50
	Billy Williams/Btg	25.00	12.50	7.50
	Bob Chance	10.00	5.00	3.00
	Panel (7)	50.00	25.00	15.00
	Bob Aspromonte	10.00	5.00	3.00
	Joe Christopher	10.00	5.00	3.00
	Jim Bunning	25.00	12.50	7.50

		NM	EX	VG
	Panel (8)	75.00	37.50	22.50
22	Jim Fregosi	10.00	5.00	3.00
23	Bob Gibson	30.00	15.00	9.00
24	Juan Marichal	25.00	12.50	7.50
	Panel (9)	40.00	20.00	12.00
25	Dave Wickersham	10.00	5.00	3.00
26	Ron Hunt/Throwing	10.00	5.00	3.00
27	Gary Peters/Portrait	85.00	42.50	25.00
	Panel (10)	15.00	7.50	4.50
28	Ron Santo	12.50	6.25	3.75
29	Elston Howard (w/ glove)	35.00	17.50	10.50
30	Brooks Robinson/Portrait	200.00	100.00	60.00
	Panel (11)	35.00	17.50	10.50
31	Frank Robinson/Portrait	100.00	50.00	30.00
32	Sandy Koufax (Hands over head.)	20.00	10.00	6.00
33	Rocky Colavito (Cleveland)	75.00	37.00	22.00
	Panel (12)	35.00	17.50	10.50
34	Al Kaline/Portrait	10.00	5.00	3.00
35	Ken Boyer/Portrait	10.00	5.00	3.00
36	Tommy Davis/Fielding			

1966 Bazooka

JUAN MARICHAL
S. F. GIANTS P
NO. 10 OF 48 CARDS

The 1966 Bazooka set was increased to 48 cards. Printed in panels of three on the bottoms of boxes of bubble gum, the full-color cards are blank-backed and numbered. Individual cards measure 1-9/16" x 2-1/2"; panels measure 2-1/2" x 4-11/16". Most of those 1966 Bazooka cards which have the same player/number combination as 1967 share the same photo and are indistinguishable as singles or panels; year of issue for complete boxes can be distinguished by the small photo on front of Koufax (1966) or Mantle (1967).

		NM	EX	VG
	Complete Set, Panels (16):	2,200	1,100	650.00
	Complete Set, Singles (48):	1,500	750.00	450.00
	Common Player:	10.00	5.00	3.00
	Panel (1)	175.00	85.00	50.00
1	Sandy Koufax	100.00	50.00	30.00
2	Willie Horton	13.50	6.75	4.00
3	Frank Howard	13.50	6.75	4.00
	Panel (2)	60.00	30.00	18.00
4	Richie Allen	16.50	8.25	5.00
5	Mel Stottlemyre	10.00	5.00	3.00
6	Tony Conigliaro	20.00	10.00	6.00
	Panel (3)	400.00	200.00	120.00
7	Mickey Mantle	300.00	150.00	90.00
8	Leon Wagner	10.00	5.00	3.00
9	Ed Kranepool	10.00	5.00	3.00
	Panel (4)	120.00	60.00	36.00
10	Juan Marichal	35.00	17.50	10.00
11	Harmon Killebrew	50.00	25.00	15.00
12	Johnny Callison	10.00	5.00	3.00
	Panel (5)	100.00	50.00	30.00
13	Roy McMillan	10.00	5.00	3.00
14	Willie McCovey	40.00	20.00	12.00
15	Rocky Colavito	30.00	15.00	9.00
	Panel (6)	150.00	75.00	45.00
16	Willie Mays	80.00	40.00	24.00
17	Sam McDowell	10.00	5.00	3.00
18	Vern Law	10.00	5.00	3.00
	Panel (7)	80.00	40.00	24.00
19	Jim Fregosi	10.00	5.00	3.00
20	Ron Fairly	10.00	5.00	3.00
21	Bob Gibson	40.00	20.00	12.00
	Panel (8)	110.00	55.00	35.00
22	Carl Yastrzemski	60.00	30.00	18.00
23	Bill White	10.00	5.00	3.00
24	Bob Aspromonte	10.00	5.00	3.00
	Panel (9)	150.00	75.00	45.00
25	Dean Chance (California)	10.00	5.00	3.00
26	Roberto Clemente	100.00	50.00	30.00
27	Tony Cloninger	10.00	5.00	3.00
	Panel (10)	135.00	65.00	40.00
28	Curt Blefary	10.00	5.00	3.00
29	Milt Pappas	10.00	5.00	3.00
30	Hank Aaron	80.00	40.00	24.00
	Panel (11)	130.00	65.00	40.00
31	Jim Bunning	40.00	20.00	12.00
32	Frank Robinson/Portrait	50.00	25.00	15.00
33	Bill Skowron	13.50	6.75	4.00
	Panel (12)	100.00	50.00	30.00
34	Brooks Robinson	50.00	25.00	15.00
35	Jim Wynn	10.00	5.00	3.00
36	Joe Torre	17.50	8.75	5.25
	Panel (13)	225.00	110.00	65.00
37	Jim Grant	10.00	5.00	3.00
38	Pete Rose	135.00	65.00	40.00
39	Ron Santo	20.00	10.00	6.00

		NM	EX	VG
	Panel (14)	90.00	45.00	27.50
40	Tom Tresh	13.50	6.75	4.00
41	Tony Oliva	13.50	6.75	4.00
42	Don Drysdale	40.00	20.00	12.00
	Panel (15)	40.00	20.00	12.00
43	Pete Richert	10.00	5.00	3.00
44	Bert Campaneris	10.00	5.00	3.00
45	Jim Maloney	130.00	65.00	40.00
	Panel (16)	50.00	25.00	15.00
46	Al Kaline	10.00	5.00	3.00
47	Eddie Fisher	40.00	20.00	12.00
48	Billy Williams			

1967 Bazooka

The 1967 Bazooka set is identical in design to the sets of 1964-1966. Printed in panels of three on the bottoms of bubble gum boxes, the set is made up of 48 full-color, blank-backed, numbered cards. Individual cards measure 1-9/16" x 2-1/2"; complete panels measure 2-1/2" x 4-11/16". Most of those 1967 Bazooka cards which have the same player/number combination as 1966 share the same photo and are indistinguishable as singles or panels; complete boxes can be distinguished by the small photo on front of Koufax (1966) or Mantle (1967).

		NM	EX	VG
	Complete Set, Panels (18):	2,400	1,200	700.00
	Complete Set, Singles (48):	1,500	750.00	450.00
	Common Player:	10.00	5.00	3.00
	Panel (1)	40.00	20.00	12.00
1	Rick Reichardt	10.00	5.00	3.00
2	Tommie Agee	10.00	5.00	3.00
3	Frank Howard	12.50	6.25	3.75
	Panel (2)	55.00	27.50	16.50
4	Richie Allen	17.50	8.75	5.25
5	Mel Stottlemyre	12.50	6.25	3.75
6	Tony Conigliaro	12.50	6.25	3.75
	Panel (3)	600.00	300.00	180.00
7	Mickey Mantle	400.00	200.00	120.00
8	Leon Wagner	10.00	5.00	3.00
9	Gary Peters	10.00	5.00	3.00
	Panel (4)	150.00	75.00	45.00
10	Juan Marichal	50.00	25.00	15.00
11	Harmon Killebrew	60.00	30.00	18.00
12	Johnny Callison	10.00	5.00	3.00
	Panel (5)	135.00	65.00	40.00
13	Denny McLain	20.00	10.00	6.00
14	Willie McCovey	50.00	25.00	15.00
15	Rocky Colavito	30.00	15.00	9.00
	Panel (6)	150.00	75.00	45.00
16	Willie Mays	90.00	45.00	27.00
17	Sam McDowell	10.00	5.00	3.00
18	Jim Kaat	13.50	6.75	4.00
	Panel (7)	100.00	50.00	30.00
19	Jim Fregosi	10.00	5.00	3.00
20	Ron Fairly	10.00	5.00	3.00
21	Bob Gibson	50.00	25.00	15.00
	Panel (8)	120.00	60.00	36.00
22	Carl Yastrzemski	65.00	32.50	20.00
23	Bill White	10.00	5.00	3.00
24	Bob Aspromonte	10.00	5.00	3.00
	Panel (9)	175.00	85.00	50.00
25	Dean Chance (Minnesota)	10.00	5.00	3.00
26	Roberto Clemente	100.00	50.00	30.00
27	Tony Cloninger	10.00	5.00	3.00
	Panel (10)	150.00	75.00	45.00
28	Curt Blefary	10.00	5.00	3.00
29	Phil Regan	10.00	5.00	3.00
30	Hank Aaron	90.00	45.00	27.00
	Panel (11)	175.00	85.00	50.00
31	Jim Bunning	50.00	25.00	15.00
32	Frank Robinson/Btg	60.00	30.00	18.00
33	Ken Boyer	10.00	5.00	3.00
	Panel (12)	120.00	60.00	36.00
34	Brooks Robinson	60.00	30.00	18.00
35	Jim Wynn	10.00	5.00	3.00
36	Joe Torre	17.50	8.75	5.25
	Panel (13)	275.00	135.00	80.00
37	Tommy Davis	10.00	5.00	3.00
38	Pete Rose	150.00	75.00	45.00
39	Ron Santo	20.00	10.00	6.00
	Panel (14)	100.00	50.00	30.00
40	Tom Tresh	12.00	6.00	3.50
41	Tony Oliva	12.50	6.25	3.75
42	Don Drysdale	50.00	25.00	15.00
	Panel (15)	40.00	20.00	12.00
43	Pete Richert	10.00	5.00	3.00
44	Bert Campaneris	10.00	5.00	3.00
45	Jim Maloney	175.00	85.00	50.00
	Panel (16)	60.00	30.00	18.00
46	Al Kaline	10.00	5.00	3.00
47	Matty Alou	50.00	25.00	15.00
48	Billy Williams			

1968 Bazooka

The design of the 1968 Bazooka set is radically different from previous years. The player cards are sit...

ated on the sides of the boxes with the box back containing "Tipps From The Topps." Four unnumbered player cards, measuring 1-1/4" x 3-1/8", are featured on each box. The box back includes a small player photo plus illustrated tips on various aspects of the game of baseball. Boxes are numbered 1-15 on the top panels. There are 56 different player cards in the set, with four of the cards (Agee, Drysdale, Rose, Santo) being used twice to round out the set of 15 boxes.

		NM	EX	VG
Complete Box Set (15):		4,250	2,125	1,250
Complete Singles Set (60):		3,000	1,500	900.00
Common Player:		10.00	5.00	3.00
	Box 1 - Bunting	275.00	135.00	80.00
1	Maury Wills	15.00	7.50	4.50
(1)	Clete Boyer	15.00	7.50	4.50
(2)	Paul Casanova	10.00	5.00	3.00
(3)	Al Kaline	65.00	32.50	20.00
(4)	Tom Seaver	80.00	40.00	25.00
	Box 2 - Batting	250.00	125.00	75.00
2	Carl Yastrzemski	80.00	40.00	25.00
(5)	Matty Alou	10.00	5.00	3.00
(6)	Bill Freehan	10.00	5.00	3.00
(7)	Jim Hunter	45.00	22.50	13.50
(8)	Jim Lefebvre	10.00	5.00	3.00
	Box 3 - Stealing Bases	175.00	85.00	50.00
3	Bert Campaneris	10.00	5.00	3.00
(9)	Bobby Knoop	10.00	5.00	3.00
(13)	Tim McCarver	15.00	7.50	4.50
(11)	Frank Robinson	65.00	32.50	20.00
(12)	Bob Veale	10.00	5.00	3.00
	Box 4 - Sliding	100.00	50.00	30.00
4	Maury Wills	15.00	7.50	4.50
(13)	Joe Azcue	10.00	5.00	3.00
(14)	Tony Conigliaro	15.00	7.50	4.50
(15)	Ken Holtzman	10.00	5.00	3.00
(16)	Bill White	10.00	5.00	3.00
	Box 5 - The Double Play	315.00	155.00	95.00
5	Julian Javier	10.00	5.00	3.00
(17)	Hank Aaron	175.00	87.00	52.00
(18)	Juan Marichal	45.00	22.50	13.50
(19)	Joe Pepitone	17.50	9.00	5.00
(20)	Rico Petrocelli	15.00	7.50	4.50
	Box 6 - Playing 1st Base	375.00	185.00	110.00
6	Orlando Cepeda	50.00	25.00	15.00
(21)	Tommie Agee	10.00	5.00	3.00
(22a)	Don Drysdale (No period after "A" in team name.)	40.00	20.00	12.00
(22b)	Don Drysdale (Period after "A.")	40.00	20.00	12.00
(23)	Pete Rose	175.00	87.00	52.00
(24)	Ron Santo	17.50	9.00	5.00
	Box 7 - Playing 2nd Base	225.00	110.00	65.00
7	Bill Mazeroski	50.00	25.00	15.00
(25)	Jim Bunning	45.00	22.50	13.50
(26)	Frank Howard	15.00	7.50	4.50
(27)	John Roseboro	10.00	5.00	3.00
(28)	George Scott	10.00	5.00	3.00
	Box 8 - Playing 3rd Base	275.00	135.00	80.00
8	Brooks Robinson	65.00	32.50	20.00
(29)	Tony Gonzalez	10.00	5.00	3.00
(30)	Willie Horton	15.00	7.50	4.50
(31)	Harmon Killebrew	65.00	32.50	20.00
(32)	Jim McGlothlin	10.00	5.00	3.00
	Box 9 - Playing Shortstop	150.00	75.00	45.00
9	Jim Fregosi	10.00	5.00	3.00
(33)	Max Alvis	10.00	5.00	3.00
(34)	Bob Gibson	45.00	22.50	13.50
(35)	Tony Oliva	15.00	7.50	4.50
(36)	Vada Pinson	15.00	7.50	4.50
	Box 10 - Catching	160.00	80.00	45.00
10	Joe Torre	17.50	9.00	5.00
(37)	Dean Chance	10.00	5.00	3.00
(38)	Tommy Davis	10.00	5.00	3.00
(39)	Ferguson Jenkins	45.00	22.00	13.50
(40)	Rick Monday	10.00	5.00	3.00
	Box 11 - Pitching	850.00	425.00	255.00
11	Jim Lonborg	15.00	7.50	4.50
(41)	Curt Flood	15.00	7.50	4.50
(42)	Joel Horlen	10.00	5.00	3.00
(43)	Mickey Mantle	650.00	325.00	195.00
(44)	Jim Wynn	10.00	5.00	3.00
	Box 12 - Fielding the Pitcher's Position	375.00	185.00	110.00
12	Mike McCormick	10.00	5.00	3.00
(45)	Roberto Clemente	200.00	100.00	60.00
(46)	Al Downing	10.00	5.00	3.00
(47)	Don Mincher	10.00	5.00	3.00
(48)	Tony Perez	45.00	22.00	13.50

	Box 13 - Coaching	225.00	110.00	65.00
13	Frank Crosetti	15.00	7.50	4.50
(49)	Rod Carew	55.00	27.50	16.50
(50)	Willie McCovey	55.00	27.50	16.50
(51)	Ron Swoboda	10.00	5.00	3.00
(52)	Earl Wilson	10.00	5.00	3.00
	Box 14 - Playing the Outfield	250.00	125.00	75.00
14	Willie Mays	175.00	87.00	52.00
(53)	Richie Allen	15.00	7.50	4.50
(54)	Gary Peters	10.00	5.00	3.00
(55)	Rusty Staub	17.50	9.00	5.00
(56)	Billy Williams	50.00	25.00	15.00
	Box 15 - Base Running	375.00	185.00	110.00
15	Lou Brock	55.00	27.50	16.50
(57)	Tommie Agee	10.00	5.00	3.00
(58)	Don Drysdale	40.00	20.00	12.00
(59)	Pete Rose	175.00	87.00	52.00
(60)	Ron Santo	17.50	9.00	5.00

1969-70 Bazooka

Issued over a two-year span, the 1969-70 Bazooka set utilized the box bottom and sides. The bottom, entitled "Baseball Extra," features an historic event in baseball; the 3" x 6-1/4" panels are numbered 1-12. Two "All-Time Great" cards were located on each side of the box. These cards are not numbered and have no distinct borders; individual cards measure 1-1/4" x 3-1/8". The prices in the checklist that follows are for complete boxes only. Cards/panels cut from the boxes have a greatly reduced value - 25% of the complete box prices for all cut pieces.

		NM	EX	VG
Complete Set (12):		325.00	160.00	100.00
Common Box:		20.00	10.00	6.00
1	No-Hit Duel By Toney & Vaughn (Mordecai Brown, Ty Cobb, Willie Keeler, Eddie Plank)	30.00	15.00	9.00
2	Alexander Conquers Yanks (Rogers Hornsby, Ban Johnson, Walter Johnson, Al Simmons)	20.00	10.00	6.00
3	Yanks' Lazzeri Sets AL Record (Grover Alexander, Chief Bender, Christy Mathewson, Cy Young)	25.00	12.50	7.50
4	HR Almost Hit Out Of Stadium (Hugh Duffy, Lou Gehrig, Tris Speaker, Joe Tinker)	20.00	10.00	6.00
5	4 Consecutive Homers By Lou (Frank Chance, Mickey Cochrane, John McGraw, Babe Ruth)	35.00	17.50	10.00
6	No-Hit Game By Walter Johnson (Johnny Evers, Walter Johnson, John McGraw, Cy Young)	20.00	10.00	6.00
7	Twelve RBIs By Bottomley (Ty Cobb, Eddie Collins, Johnny Evers, Lou Gehrig)	35.00	17.50	10.00
8	Ty Ties Record (Mickey Cochrane, Eddie Collins, Mel Ott, Honus Wagner)	20.00	10.00	6.00
9	Babe Ruth Hits 3 HRs in Game (Cap Anson, Jack Chesbro, Al Simmons, Tris Speaker)	35.00	17.50	10.00
10	Calls Shot In Series Game (Nap Lajoie, Connie Mack, Rabbit Maranville, Ed Walsh)	35.00	17.50	10.00
11	Ruth's 60th HR Sets New Record (Frank Chance, Nap Lajoie, Mel Ott, Joe Tinker)	35.00	17.50	10.00
12	Double Shutout By Ed Reulbach (Rogers Hornsby, Rabbit Maranville, Christy Mathewson, Honus Wagner)	20.00	10.00	6.00

1971 Bazooka Numbered Set

The 1971 Bazooka numbered set is a proof set produced by the company after the unnumbered set was released. The set is comprised of 48 cards as opposed to the 36 cards which make up the unnumbered set. Issued in panels of three, the 12 cards not found in the unnumbered set are #1-3, 13-15, 34-36 and 43-45. All

other cards are identical to those found in the unnumbered set. The cards, which measure 2" x 2-5/8", contain full-color photos and are blank-backed.

		NM	EX	VG
Complete Panel Set (16):		1,300	655.00	400.00
Complete Singles Set (48):		950.00	475.00	275.00
Common Player:		7.50	3.75	2.25
	Panel (1)	100.00	50.00	30.00
1	Tim McCarver	12.50	6.25	3.75
2	Frank Robinson	35.00	17.50	10.00
3	Bill Mazeroski	30.00	15.00	9.00
	Panel (2)	100.00	50.00	30.00
4	Willie McCovey	30.00	15.00	9.00
5	Carl Yastrzemski	40.00	20.00	12.00
6	Clyde Wright	7.50	3.75	2.25
	Panel (3)	60.00	30.00	18.00
7	Jim Merritt	7.50	3.75	2.25
8	Luis Aparicio	25.00	12.50	7.50
9	Bobby Murcer	12.50	6.25	3.75
	Panel (4)	30.00	15.00	9.00
10	Rico Petrocelli	7.50	3.75	2.25
11	Sam McDowell	7.50	3.75	2.25
12	Cito Gaston	7.50	3.75	2.25
	Panel (5)	85.00	42.50	25.00
13	Ferguson Jenkins	25.00	12.50	7.50
14	Al Kaline	35.00	17.50	10.00
15	Ken Harrelson	7.50	3.75	2.25
	Panel (6)	115.00	55.00	35.00
16	Tommie Agee	7.50	3.75	2.25
17	Harmon Killebrew	35.00	17.50	10.00
18	Reggie Jackson	45.00	22.50	13.50
	Panel (7)	60.00	30.00	18.00
19	Juan Marichal	25.00	12.50	7.50
20	Frank Howard	10.00	5.00	3.00
21	Bill Melton	7.50	3.75	2.25
	Panel (8)	125.00	65.00	35.00
22	Brooks Robinson	35.00	17.50	10.00
23	Hank Aaron	60.00	30.00	18.00
24	Larry Dierker	7.50	3.75	2.25
	Panel (9)	60.00	30.00	18.00
25	Jim Fregosi	7.50	3.75	2.25
26	Billy Williams	30.00	15.00	9.00
27	Dave McNally	7.50	3.75	2.25
	Panel (10)	65.00	32.50	20.00
28	Rico Carty	7.50	3.75	2.25
29	Johnny Bench	35.00	17.50	10.00
30	Tommy Harper	7.50	3.75	2.25
	Panel (11)	110.00	55.00	30.00
31	Bert Campaneris	7.50	3.75	2.25
32	Pete Rose	50.00	25.00	15.00
33	Orlando Cepeda	25.00	12.50	7.50
	Panel (12)	65.00	32.50	20.00
34	Maury Wills	7.50	3.75	2.25
35	Tom Seaver	35.00	17.50	10.00
36	Tony Oliva	10.00	5.00	3.00
	Panel (13)	120.00	60.00	35.00
37	Bill Freehan	7.50	3.75	2.25
38	Roberto Clemente	75.00	37.50	22.50
39	Claude Osteen	7.50	3.75	2.25
	Panel (14)	65.00	32.50	20.00
40	Rusty Staub	12.50	6.25	3.75
41	Bob Gibson	30.00	15.00	9.00
42	Amos Otis	7.50	3.75	2.25
	Panel (15)	55.00	27.50	16.50
43	Jim Wynn	7.50	3.75	2.25
44	Richie Allen	20.00	10.00	6.00
45	Tony Conigliaro	15.00	7.50	4.50
	Panel (16)	110.00	55.00	35.00
46	Randy Hundley	7.50	3.75	2.25
47	Willie Mays	60.00	30.00	18.00
48	Jim Hunter	25.00	12.50	7.50

1971 Bazooka Unnumbered Set

This Bazooka set was issued in 1971, consisting of 36 full-color, blank-backed, unnumbered cards. Printed in panels of three on the bottoms of bubble gum boxes, individual cards measure 2" x 2-5/8"; complete panels measure 2-5/8" x 5-5/16". In the checklist that follows, the cards have been numbered by panel using the name of the player who appears on the left end of the panel.

	NM	EX	VG
Complete Panel Set (12):	700.00	350.00	210.00
Complete Singles Set (36):	600.00	300.00	180.00
Common Player:	5.00	2.50	1.50
Panel (1)	110.00	55.00	30.00
(1) Tommie Agee	5.00	2.50	1.50
(2) Harmon Killebrew	35.00	17.50	10.00
(3) Reggie Jackson	45.00	22.50	13.50
Panel (2)	110.00	55.00	30.00
(4) Bert Campaneris	5.00	2.50	1.50
(5) Pete Rose	50.00	25.00	15.00
(6) Orlando Cepeda	25.00	12.50	7.50
Panel (3)	65.00	32.50	20.00
(7) Rico Carty	5.00	2.50	1.50
(8) Johnny Bench	40.00	20.00	12.00
(9) Tommy Harper	5.00	2.50	1.50
Panel (4)	90.00	45.00	27.50
(10) Bill Freehan	5.00	2.50	1.50
(11) Roberto Clemente	60.00	30.00	18.00
(12) Claude Osteen	5.00	2.50	1.50
Panel (5)	55.00	27.50	16.50
(13) Jim Fregosi	5.00	2.50	1.50
(14) Billy Williams	30.00	15.00	9.00
(15) Dave McNally	5.00	2.50	1.50
Panel (6)	110.00	55.00	30.00
(16) Randy Hundley	5.00	2.50	1.50
(17) Willie Mays	50.00	25.00	15.00
(18) Jim Hunter	25.00	12.50	7.50
Panel (7)	55.00	27.50	16.50
(19) Juan Marichal	25.00	12.50	7.50
(20) Frank Howard	7.50	3.75	2.25
(21) Bill Melton	5.00	2.50	1.50
Panel (8)	100.00	50.00	30.00
(22) Willie McCovey	30.00	15.00	9.00
(23) Carl Yastrzemski	40.00	20.00	12.00
(24) Clyde Wright	5.00	2.50	1.50
Panel (9)	55.00	27.50	16.50
(25) Jim Merritt	5.00	2.50	1.50
(26) Luis Aparicio	25.00	12.50	7.50
(27) Bobby Murcer	9.00	4.50	2.75
Panel (10)	25.00	12.50	7.50
(28) Rico Petrocelli	5.00	2.50	1.50
(29) Sam McDowell	5.00	2.50	1.50
(30) Cito Gaston	5.00	2.50	1.50
Panel (11)	115.00	55.00	35.00
(31) Brooks Robinson	35.00	17.50	10.50
(32) Hank Aaron	50.00	25.00	15.00
(33) Larry Dierker	5.00	2.50	1.50
Panel (12)	60.00	30.00	18.00
(34) Rusty Staub	7.50	3.75	2.25
(35) Bob Gibson	30.00	15.00	9.00
(36) Amos Otis	7.50	3.75	2.25

1930 Becker Bros. Theatre

Only recently brought to light, the issue date attributed here is uncertain and may be clarified if and when additions to the checklist are made. About post-card size, the cards have sepia portraits of Philadelphia A's players on front, identified in the white border at bottom. Backs have advertising for the theatre, including a list of upcoming features.

	NM	EX	VG
Common Player:	150.00	75.00	45.00
(1) Max Bishop	150.00	75.00	45.00
(2) Mickey Cochrane	250.00	125.00	75.00
(3) Sammy Hale	150.00	75.00	45.00
(4) Jimmie Foxx	300.00	150.00	90.00
(5) Al Simmons	250.00	125.00	75.00

1958 Bell Brand Dodgers

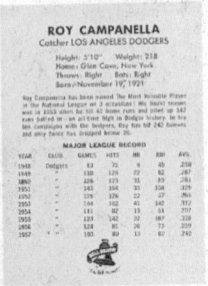

Celebrating the Dodgers first year of play in Los Angeles, Bell Brand inserted ten different unnumbered cards in their bags of potato chips and corn chips. The cards, which measure 3" x 4", have a sepia-colored photo inside a 1/4" green woodgrain border. The card backs feature statistical and biographical information and include the Bell Brand logo. Roy Campanella is included in the set despite a career-ending car wreck that prevented him from ever playing in Los Angeles.

	NM	EX	VG
Complete Set (10):	5,500	2,750	1,650
Common Player:	125.00	65.00	35.00
1 Roy Campanella	400.00	200.00	120.00
2 Gino Cimoli/SP	1,200	600.00	360.00
3 Don Drysdale	350.00	175.00	100.00
4 Junior Gilliam	125.00	65.00	35.00
5 Gil Hodges	350.00	175.00	105.00
6 Sandy Koufax	1,350	675.00	410.00
7 Johnny Podres/SP	600.00	300.00	180.00
8 Pee Wee Reese	400.00	200.00	120.00
9 Duke Snider	900.00	450.00	270.00
10 Don Zimmer	135.00	65.00	40.00

1958 Bell Brand Dodgers Ad Poster

Evidently a point-of-purchase in-store display to draw attention to its premiere offering of baseball cards, this 22" x 36" blank-back poster is, like the cards themselves, printed in green and sepia on white. The top pictures a super-size picture of Don Drysdale's card from the set.

	NM	EX	VG
Bell Brand Dodgers Ad Poster (Don Drysdale)	4,250	2,100	1,250

1960 Bell Brand Dodgers

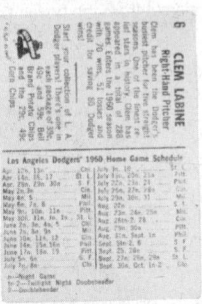

Bell Brand returned with a baseball card set in 1960 that was entirely different in style to their previous effort. The cards, which measure 2-1/2" x 3-1/2", feature beautiful, full-color photos. The backs carry a short player biography, the 1960 Dodgers home schedule, and the Bell Brand logo. Twenty different numbered cards were inserted in various size bags of potato chips and corn chips. Although sealed in cellophane, the cards were still subject to grease stains. Cards #'s 6, 12 and 18 are the scarcest in the set.

	NM	EX	VG
Complete Set (20):	1,500	750.00	450.00
Common Player:	45.00	22.50	13.50
1 Norm Larker	45.00	22.50	13.50
2 Duke Snider	150.00	75.00	45.00
3 Danny McDevitt	45.00	22.50	13.50
4 Jim Gilliam	50.00	25.00	15.00
5 Rip Repulski	45.00	22.50	13.50
6 Clem Labine/SP	90.00	45.00	27.50
7 John Roseboro	45.00	22.50	13.50
8 Carl Furillo	60.00	30.00	18.00
9 Sandy Koufax	300.00	150.00	90.00
10 Joe Pignatano	45.00	22.50	13.50
11 Chuck Essegian	45.00	22.50	13.50
12 John Klippstein/SP	150.00	75.00	45.00
13 Ed Roebuck	45.00	22.50	13.50
14 Don Demeter	45.00	22.50	13.50
15 Roger Craig	45.00	22.50	13.50
16 Stan Williams	45.00	22.50	13.50
17 Don Zimmer	60.00	30.00	18.00
18 Walter Alston/SP	100.00	50.00	30.00
19 Johnny Podres	60.00	30.00	18.00
20 Maury Wills	75.00	37.50	22.50

1961 Bell Brand Dodgers

The 1961 Bell Brand set is identical in format to the previous year, although printed on thinner stock. Cards can be distinguished from the 1960 set by the 1961 schedule on the backs. The cards, which mea-

NORM LARKER
INFIELDER L.A. DODGERS

sure 2-7/16" x 3-1/2", are numbered by the player's uniform number. Twenty different cards were inserted into various size potato chip and corn chip packages, each card being sealed in a cellophane wrapper.

	NM	EX	VG
Complete Set (20):	1,500	750.00	450.00
Common Player:	50.00	25.00	15.00
3 Willie Davis	60.00	30.00	18.00
4 Duke Snider	175.00	85.00	50.00
5 Norm Larker	50.00	25.00	15.00
8 John Roseboro	50.00	25.00	15.00
9 Wally Moon	50.00	25.00	15.00
11 Bob Lillis	50.00	25.00	15.00
12 Tom Davis	60.00	30.00	18.00
14 Gil Hodges	150.00	75.00	45.00
16 Don Demeter	50.00	25.00	15.00
19 Jim Gilliam	60.00	30.00	18.00
22 John Podres	60.00	30.00	18.00
24 Walter Alston	75.00	37.50	22.50
30 Maury Wills	110.00	55.00	30.00
32 Sandy Koufax	250.00	125.00	75.00
34 Norm Sherry	60.00	30.00	18.00
37 Ed Roebuck	50.00	25.00	15.00
38 Roger Craig	50.00	25.00	15.00
40 Stan Williams	50.00	25.00	15.00
43 Charlie Neal	50.00	25.00	15.00
51 Larry Sherry	60.00	30.00	18.00

1962 Bell Brand Dodgers

SANDY KOUFAX
PITCHER L.A. DODGERS

The 1962 Bell Brand set is identical in style to the previous two years and cards can be distinguished by the 1962 Dodgers schedule on the back. Each card measures 2-7/16" x 3-1/2" and is numbered by the player's uniform number. Printed on glossy stock, the 1962 set was less susceptible to grease stains.

	NM	EX	VG
Complete Set (20):	1,700	850.00	500.00
Common Player:	50.00	25.00	15.00
3 Willie Davis	50.00	25.00	15.00
4 Duke Snider	200.00	100.00	60.00
6 Ron Fairly	50.00	25.00	15.00
8 John Roseboro	50.00	25.00	15.00
9 Wally Moon	50.00	25.00	15.00
12 Tom Davis	50.00	25.00	15.00
16 Ron Perranoski	50.00	25.00	15.00
19 Jim Gilliam	55.00	27.50	16.50
20 Daryl Spencer	50.00	25.00	15.00
22 John Podres	55.00	27.50	16.50
24 Walter Alston	75.00	37.50	22.50
25 Frank Howard	55.00	27.50	16.50
30 Maury Wills	90.00	45.00	27.50
32 Sandy Koufax	250.00	125.00	75.00
34 Norm Sherry	60.00	30.00	18.00
37 Ed Roebuck	50.00	25.00	15.00
40 Stan Williams	50.00	25.00	15.00
51 Larry Sherry	60.00	30.00	18.00
53 Don Drysdale	125.00	65.00	35.00
56 Lee Walls	50.00	25.00	15.00

1962 Bell Brand Dodgers Ad Poster

This 8-1/2" x 11-1/2" color poster was distributed to retailers to solicit sales of Bell Brand items. The

The Mint-Mint examples of vintage cards carry a significant premium over the Near Mint values shown here. This premium reflects limited availability of the highest-grade cards as well as demand for particular cards or sets in the best possible condition.

Another three million Bell Brand Dodger Cards like these will score more **SALES** for you

!!!! All new in '62 !!!!

And here's the play from Bell Brand

sheet has actual size pictures of six of the cards from the set. On back is retailer information.

	NM	EX	VG
1962 Bell Brand Ad Poster (Koufax, Roseboro, Wills, Moon, Snider, Sherry)	900.00	450.00	275.00

1951 Berk Ross

Entitled "Hit Parade of Champions," the 1951 Berk Ross set features 72 stars of various sports. The cards, which measure 2-1/16" x 2-1/2" and have tinted color photographs, were issued in four boxes containing two-card panels. The issue is divided into four subsets with the first ten players of each series being baseball players. Only the baseball players are listed in the checklist that follows. Complete panels are valued 50 percent higher than the sum of the individual cards.

	NM	EX	VG
Complete Boxed Set (72):	2,100	1,100	650.00
Complete Baseball Set (40):	1,325	660.00	395.00
Common Player:	13.50	6.75	4.00
1-1 Al Rosen	16.00	8.00	5.00
1-2 Bob Lemon	20.00	10.00	6.00
1-3 Phil Rizzuto	50.00	25.00	15.00
1-4 Hank Bauer	16.00	8.00	5.00
1-5 Billy Johnson	13.50	6.75	4.00
1-6 Jerry Coleman	13.50	6.75	4.00
1-7 Johnny Mize	25.00	12.50	7.50
1-8 Dom DiMaggio	20.00	10.00	6.00
1-9 Richie Ashburn	30.00	15.00	9.00
1-10 Del Ennis	13.50	6.75	4.00
2-1 Stan Musial	150.00	75.00	45.00
2-2 Warren Spahn	25.00	12.50	7.50
2-3 Tommy Henrich	16.00	8.00	5.00
2-4 Larry "Yogi" Berra	100.00	50.00	30.00
2-5 Joe DiMaggio	300.00	150.00	90.00
2-6 Bobby Brown	13.50	6.75	4.00
2-7 Granville Hamner	13.50	6.75	4.00
2-8 Willie Jones	13.50	6.75	4.00
2-9 Stanley Lopata	13.50	6.75	4.00
2-10 Mike Goliat	13.50	6.75	4.00
3-1 Ralph Kiner	20.00	10.00	6.00
3-2 Billy Goodman	13.50	6.75	4.00
3-3 Allie Reynolds	16.00	8.00	5.00
3-4 Vic Raschi	16.00	8.00	5.00
3-5 Joe Page	13.50	6.75	4.00
3-6 Eddie Lopat	13.50	6.75	4.00
3-7 Andy Seminick	13.50	6.75	4.00
3-8 Dick Sisler	13.50	6.75	4.00
3-9 Eddie Waitkus	13.50	6.75	4.00
3-10 Ken Heintzelman	13.50	6.75	4.00
4-1 Gene Woodling	16.00	8.00	5.00
4-2 Cliff Mapes	13.50	6.75	4.00
4-3 Fred Sanford	13.50	6.75	4.00
4-4 Tommy Bryne	13.50	6.75	4.00
4-5 Eddie (Whitey) Ford	180.00	90.00	55.00
4-6 Jim Konstanty	13.50	6.75	4.00
4-7 Russ Meyer	13.50	6.75	4.00
4-8 Robin Roberts	20.00	10.00	6.00
4-9 Curt Simmons	13.50	6.75	4.00
4-10 Sam Jethroe	13.50	6.75	4.00

1952 Berk Ross

Although the card size is different (2" x 3"), the style of the fronts and backs of the 1952 Berk Ross set is similar to the previous year's effort. Seventy-two unnum-

HIT PARADE OF CHAMPIONS
Trade Mark Reg. U.S. Pat. Off.

MICKEY MANTLE

Outfielder, New York Yankees
Member of the N. Y. Yankees
World Champions

Born Commerce, Oklahoma
October 20, 1931

Height 5-10, Weight 175
Throws Right, Bats Left or Right
1951 Hit .267 in 96 Games

bered cards make up the set. Rizzuto is included twice in the set and the Blackwell and Fox cards have transposed backs. The cards were issued individually rather than as two-card panels like in 1951.

		NM	EX	VG
Complete Set (72):		5,000	2,500	1,500
Common Player:		25.00	12.50	7.50
(1)	Richie Ashburn	50.00	25.00	15.00
(2)	Hank Bauer	30.00	15.00	9.00
(3)	Larry "Yogi" Berra	175.00	85.00	50.00
(4)	Ewell Blackwell (Photo actually Nelson Fox.)	75.00	37.50	22.50
(5)	Bobby Brown	25.00	12.50	7.50
(6)	Jim Busby	25.00	12.50	7.50
(7)	Roy Campanella	140.00	70.00	40.00
(8)	Chico Carrasquel	25.00	12.50	7.50
(9)	Jerry Coleman	25.00	12.50	7.50
(10)	Joe Collins	25.00	12.50	7.50
(11)	Alvin Dark	25.00	12.50	7.50
(12)	Dom DiMaggio	35.00	17.50	10.00
(13)	Joe DiMaggio	400.00	200.00	120.00
(14)	Larry Doby	40.00	20.00	12.00
(15)	Bobby Doerr	40.00	20.00	12.00
(16)	Bob Elliot (Elliott)	25.00	12.50	7.50
(17)	Del Ennis	25.00	12.50	7.50
(18)	Ferris Fain	25.00	12.50	7.50
(19)	Bob Feller	100.00	50.00	30.00
(20)	Nelson Fox (Photo actually Ewell Blackwell.)	125.00	60.00	35.00
(21)	Ned Garver	25.00	12.50	7.50
(22)	Clint Hartung	25.00	12.50	7.50
(23)	Jim Hearn	25.00	12.50	7.50
(24)	Gil Hodges	75.00	37.50	22.50
(25)	Monte Irvin	40.00	20.00	12.00
(26)	Larry Jansen	25.00	12.50	7.50
(27)	George Kell	40.00	20.00	12.00
(28)	Sheldon Jones	25.00	12.50	7.50
(29)	Monte Kennedy	25.00	12.50	7.50
(30)	Ralph Kiner	40.00	20.00	12.00
(31)	Dave Koslo	25.00	12.50	7.50
(32)	Bob Kuzava	25.00	12.50	7.50
(33)	Bob Lemon	40.00	20.00	12.00
(34)	Whitey Lockman	25.00	12.50	7.50
(35)	Eddie Lopat	25.00	12.50	7.50
(36)	Sal Maglie	25.00	12.50	7.50
(37)	Mickey Mantle	2,100	1,050	650.00
(38)	Billy Martin	90.00	45.00	27.50
(39)	Willie Mays	500.00	250.00	150.00
(40)	Gil McDougal (McDougald)	30.00	15.00	9.00
(41)	Orestes Minoso	30.00	15.00	9.00
(42)	Johnny Mize	50.00	25.00	15.00
(43)	Tom Morgan	25.00	12.50	7.50
(44)	Don Mueller	25.00	12.50	7.50
(45)	Stan Musial	250.00	125.00	75.00
(46)	Don Newcombe	35.00	17.50	10.00
(47)	Ray Noble	25.00	12.50	7.50
(48)	Joe Ostrowski	25.00	12.50	7.50
(49)	Mel Parnell	25.00	12.50	7.50
(50)	Vic Raschi	25.00	12.50	7.50
(51)	Pee Wee Reese	125.00	65.00	35.00
(52)	Allie Reynolds	30.00	15.00	9.00
(53)	Bill Rigney	25.00	12.50	7.50
(54)	Phil Rizzuto/Bunting	90.00	45.00	27.00
(55)	Phil Rizzuto/Swinging	200.00	100.00	60.00
(56)	Robin Roberts	40.00	20.00	12.00
(57)	Eddie Robinson	25.00	12.50	7.50
(58)	Jackie Robinson	325.00	160.00	100.00
(59)	Elwin "Preacher" Roe	25.00	12.50	7.50
(60)	Johnny Sain	30.00	15.00	9.00
(61)	Albert "Red" Schoendienst	40.00	20.00	12.00
(62)	Duke Snider	140.00	70.00	40.00
(63)	George Spencer	25.00	12.50	7.50
(64)	Eddie Stanky	25.00	12.50	7.50
(65)	Henry Thompson	25.00	12.50	7.50
(66)	Bobby Thomson	30.00	15.00	9.00
(67)	Vic Wertz	25.00	12.50	7.50
(68)	Waldon Westlake	25.00	12.50	7.50
(69)	Wes Westrum	25.00	12.50	7.50
(70)	Ted Williams	450.00	225.00	135.00
(71)	Gene Woodling	30.00	15.00	9.00
(72)	Gus Zernial	25.00	12.50	7.50

1956 Big League Stars Statues

While the plastic statues in this set are virtually identical to the set issued in 1955 by Dairy Queen, the packaging of the Big League Stars statues on a card with all the usual elements of a baseball card makes them more collectible. The DQ versions of the statues are white, while the Big League versions are bronze colored. The statues measure about 3" tall and were

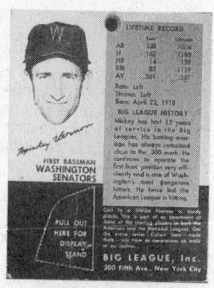

MICKEY VERNON
WASHINGTON SENATORS

FIRST BASEMAN
WASHINGTON SENATORS

BIG LEAGUE STARS • SERIES 3

PULL OUT HERE FOR DISPLAY STAND

BIG LEAGUE, Inc.
200 Fifth Ave. New York City

sold in a 4" x 5" cardboard and plastic blister pack for about 19 cents. Complete league sets were also sold in a large package. The singles package features the player's name in a large banner near the top with his team printed below and line drawings of ballplayers in action around the statue. Backs have a player portrait photo with facsimile autograph, position, team, previous year and career stats and a career summary. A perforated tab at bottom can be pulled out to make a stand for the display. Most packages are found with the hole at top punched out to allow for hanging on a hook. Besides singles, larger packages of nine National or American league statues were also sold in a window-box. The set is checklisted alphabetically.

		NM	EX	VG
Complete Set (18):		4,000	2,000	1,200
Common Player:		60.00	30.00	18.00
UNOPENED PACKAGED STATUES				
(1)	John Antonelli	125.00	65.00	35.00
(2)	Bob Avila	125.00	65.00	35.00
(3)	Yogi Berra	400.00	200.00	120.00
(4)	Roy Campanella	400.00	200.00	120.00
(5)	Larry Doby	175.00	85.00	50.00
(6)	Del Ennis	125.00	65.00	35.00
(7)	Jim Gilliam	150.00	75.00	45.00
(8)	Gil Hodges	400.00	200.00	120.00
(9)	Harvey Kuenn	125.00	65.00	35.00
(10)	Bob Lemon	150.00	75.00	45.00
(11)	Mickey Mantle	2,000	1,000	600.00
(12)	Ed Mathews	300.00	150.00	90.00
(13)	Minnie Minoso	125.00	65.00	35.00
(14)	Stan Musial	600.00	300.00	180.00
(15)	Pee Wee Reese	400.00	200.00	120.00
(16)	Al Rosen	125.00	65.00	35.00
(17)	Duke Snider	400.00	200.00	120.00
(18)	Mickey Vernon	125.00	65.00	35.00
STATUES				
(1)	John Antonelli	40.00	20.00	12.00
(2)	Bob Avila	40.00	20.00	12.00
(3)	Yogi Berra	150.00	75.00	45.00
(4)	Roy Campanella	150.00	75.00	45.00
(5)	Larry Doby	60.00	30.00	18.00
(6)	Del Ennis	40.00	20.00	12.00
(7)	Jim Gilliam	50.00	25.00	15.00
(8)	Gil Hodges	125.00	62.00	37.00
(9)	Harvey Kuenn	40.00	20.00	12.00
(10)	Bob Lemon	60.00	30.00	18.00
(11)	Mickey Mantle	300.00	150.00	90.00
(12)	Ed Mathews	100.00	50.00	30.00
(13)	Minnie Minoso	50.00	25.00	15.00
(14)	Stan Musial	200.00	100.00	60.00
(15)	Pee Wee Reese	150.00	75.00	45.00
(16)	Al Rosen	45.00	22.00	13.50
(17)	Duke Snider	150.00	75.00	45.00
(18)	Mickey Vernon	40.00	20.00	12.00
PACKAGE/CARD ONLY				
(1)	John Antonelli	50.00	25.00	15.00
(2)	Bob Avila	50.00	25.00	15.00
(3)	Yogi Berra	150.00	75.00	45.00
(4)	Roy Campanella	150.00	75.00	45.00
(5)	Larry Doby	75.00	37.50	22.00
(6)	Del Ennis	50.00	25.00	15.00
(7)	Jim Gilliam	65.00	32.50	20.00
(8)	Gil Hodges	100.00	50.00	30.00
(9)	Harvey Kuenn	50.00	25.00	15.00
(10)	Bob Lemon	75.00	37.50	22.00
(11)	Mickey Mantle	1,200	600.00	360.00
(12)	Ed Mathews	125.00	62.50	37.50
(13)	Minnie Minoso	75.00	37.50	22.00
(14)	Stan Musial	175.00	85.00	50.00
(15)	Pee Wee Reese	150.00	75.00	45.00
(16)	Al Rosen	50.00	25.00	15.00
(17)	Duke Snider	150.00	75.00	45.00
(18)	Mickey Vernon	50.00	25.00	15.00

1978 Big T/ Tastee Freeze Discs

One player from each major league team was selected for inclusion in this discs set distributed by Big T family restaurants and Tastee Freeze stands in

North Carolina, and possibly other parts of the country. The 3-3/8" diameter discs have a sepia-toned player portrait photo at center within a white diamond and surrounded by a brightly colored border with four colored stars at top. Licensed by the Players Association through Michael Schecter Associates, the photos have had uniform logos removed. Backs are printed in red, white and blue and have the sponsor's logos and a line of 1977 stats, along with a card number.

		NM	EX	VG
Complete Set (26):		30.00	15.00	9.00
Common Player:		2.00	1.00	.60
1	Buddy Bell	2.00	1.00	.60
2	Jim Palmer	8.00	4.00	2.50
3	Steve Garvey	5.00	2.50	1.50
4	Jeff Burroughs	2.00	1.00	.60
5	Greg Luzinski	2.00	1.00	.60
6	Lou Brock	8.00	4.00	2.50
7	Thurman Munson	5.00	2.50	1.50
8	Rod Carew	8.00	4.00	2.50
9	George Brett	20.00	10.00	6.00
10	Tom Seaver	15.00	7.50	4.50
11	Willie Stargell	8.00	4.00	2.50
12	Jerry Koosman	2.00	1.00	.60
13	Bill North	2.00	1.00	.60
14	Richie Zisk	2.00	1.00	.60
15	Bill Madlock	2.00	1.00	.60
16	Carl Yastrzemski	15.00	7.50	4.50
17	Dave Cash	2.00	1.00	.60
18	Bob Watson	2.00	1.00	.60
19	Dave Kingman	2.00	1.00	.60
20	Gene Tenace	2.00	1.00	.60
21	Ralph Garr	2.00	1.00	.60
22	Mark Fidrych	4.00	2.00	1.25
23	Frank Tanana	2.00	1.00	.60
24	Larry Hisle	2.00	1.00	.60
25	Bruce Bochte	2.00	1.00	.60
26	Bob Bailor	2.00	1.00	.60

1955-60 Bill and Bob Braves Postcards

One of the most popular and scarce of the 1950s color postcard series is the run of Milwaukee Braves known as "Bill and Bobs." While some of the cards do carry a photo credit acknowledging the pair, and a few add a Bradenton, Fla., (spring training home of the Braves) address, little else is known about the issuer. The cards themselves appear to have been purchased by the players to honor photo and autograph requests. Several of the cards carry facsimile autographs pre-printed on the front. The cards feature crisp full-color photos on their borderless fronts. Postcard backs have a variety of printing including card numbers, photo credits, a Kodachrome logo and player name. Some cards are found with some of those elements, some with none. There is some question whether Frank Torre's card is actually a Bill and Bob product, because it is 1/16" narrower than the standard 3-1/2" x 5-1/2" format of the other cards, features the player with a Pepsi bottle in his hand and is rubber-stamped on back with a Pepsi bottler's address. The Torre card is usually collected along with the rest of the set.

		NM	EX	VG
Complete Set (20):		4,600	2,300	1,350
Common Player:		100.00	50.00	30.00
(1)	Hank Aaron	1,200	600.00	360.00
(2)	Joe Adcock/Fielding	185.00	90.00	55.00
(3)	Joe Adcock (Bat on shoulder.)	185.00	90.00	55.00
(4)	Joe Adcock (Kneeling with two bats.)	145.00	75.00	45.00
(5)	Billy Bruton /Kneeling	185.00	90.00	55.00
(6)	Billy Bruton/Throwing	250.00	125.00	75.00
(7)	Bob Buhl	100.00	50.00	30.00
(8)	Lou Burdette	100.00	50.00	30.00
(9)	Gene Conley	100.00	50.00	30.00
(10)	Wes Covington/Kneeling (One bat.)	145.00	75.00	45.00
(11)	Wes Covington/Kneeling (Seven bats.)	145.00	75.00	45.00
(12)	Del Crandall/Kneeling (One bat.)	135.00	65.00	40.00
(13)	Del Crandall/Kneeling (Two bats.)	135.00	65.00	40.00
(14)	Chuck Dressen	145.00	75.00	45.00
(15)	Charlie Grimm	245.00	120.00	75.00
(16)	Fred Haney	235.00	115.00	70.00

(17)	Bob Keely	185.00	90.00	55.00
(18)	Eddie Mathews	400.00	200.00	120.00
(19)	Warren Spahn	500.00	250.00	150.00
(20)	Frank Torre	245.00	120.00	75.00

1923-24 Billiken

Apparently issued as a premium with its Billiken brand cigars, these cards were issued by Villaamil, Santalla y Ca. About 2" x 2-5/8", the cards have black-and-white posed photos surrounded with a white border. Below the picture the player's last name and team are presented in typewriter style. Among the scarcest and most popular of the pre-war Cuban issues, the set features many players from the Negro Leagues. Counterfeits are known.

		NM	EX	VG
Common Player:		800.00	325.00	160.00
	ALMENDARES			
(1)	Bernardo Baro	1,200	480.00	240.00
(2)	Manuel Cueto	900.00	360.00	180.00
(3)	Valentin Dreke	1,200	480.00	240.00
(4)	Isidro Fabre	900.00	360.00	180.00
(5)	Jose Maria Fernandez	800.00	325.00	160.00
(6)	Oscar Fuhr	1,200	480.00	240.00
(7)	Bienvenido "Hooks" Gimenez (Jimenez)	1,000	400.00	200.00
(8)	"Snake" Henry (Henry)	800.00	325.00	160.00
(9)	Ramon "Mike" Herrera	800.00	325.00	160.00
(10)	Jesse Hubbard	1,500	600.00	300.00
(11)	Armando Marsans	1,800	720.00	360.00
(12)	Jackie May (Jakie)	900.00	360.00	180.00
(13)	Eugenio Morin	800.00	325.00	160.00
(14)	Joseito Rodriguez	800.00	325.00	160.00
(15)	Nip Winters	2,000	800.00	400.00
	HABANA			
(16)	Eufemio Abreu	900.00	360.00	180.00
(17)	John Bischoff	800.00	325.00	160.00
(18)	Clark	800.00	325.00	160.00
(19)	Andy Cooper	5,000	2,000	1,000
(20)	Mack Eglefton (Eggleston)	1,300	520.00	260.00
(21)	Bienvenido "Hooks" Gimenez (Jimenez)	1,200	480.00	240.00
(22)	Marcelino Guerra	800.00	325.00	160.00
(23)	Oscar Levis	900.00	360.00	180.00
(24)	John Henry "Pop" Lloid (Lloyd)	15,000	6,000	3,000
(25)	Juanelo Mirabal	900.00	360.00	180.00
(26)	Bartolo Portuando (Portuondo)	1,200	480.00	240.00
(27)	Raphael "Busta" Quintana	800.00	325.00	160.00
(28)	Buster Ross	800.00	325.00	160.00
(29)	Clint Thomas	1,500	600.00	300.00
(30)	Edgar Westley (Wesley)	1,500	600.00	300.00
	MARIANAO			
(31)	Merito Acosta	800.00	325.00	160.00
(32)	Jose Acostica	800.00	325.00	160.00
(33)	D. Brown	800.00	325.00	160.00
(34)	E. Brown	800.00	325.00	160.00
(35)	Rogelio Crespo	800.00	325.00	160.00
(36)	Harry Deberry	800.00	325.00	160.00
(37)	Charlie Dressen	900.00	360.00	180.00
(38)	Freddie Fitzmann (Fitzsimmons)	800.00	325.00	160.00
(39)	Griffin	800.00	325.00	160.00
(40)	Ernie Krueger	800.00	325.00	160.00
(41)	Slim Love	800.00	325.00	160.00
(42)	Jose "Pepin" Perez	800.00	325.00	160.00
(43)	Rgal (Rigal)	800.00	325.00	160.00
(44)	Hank Sceiber (Schreiber)	800.00	325.00	160.00
(45)	Cristobal Torriente	15,000	6,000	3,000
	SANTA CLARA			
(46)	Oscar Charleston	15,000	6,000	3,000
(47)	Rube Currie	1,500	600.00	300.00
(48)	Pedro Dibut	900.00	360.00	180.00
(49)	Eddie Douglas (Douglass)	1,500	600.00	300.00
(50)	Frank Duncan	1,500	600.00	300.00
(51)	Oliver Marcell (Marcelle)	5,000	2,000	1,000
(52)	Mayari (Esteban Montalvo)	900.00	360.00	180.00
(53)	Jose Mendez	6,000	2,400	1,200
(54)	Augustin "Tinti" Molina	800.00	325.00	160.00
(55)	Dobie Moore	1,500	600.00	300.00
(56)	Alejandro Oms	2,000	800.00	400.00
(57)	Herman Rios	900.00	360.00	180.00
(58)	Julio Rojo	900.00	360.00	180.00
(59)	Red Ryan	1,200	480.00	240.00
(60)	Frank Wardfield (Warfield)	1,500	600.00	300.00

1916 Block and Kuhl Co.

Best known for its use as a promotional medium for The Sporting News, this 200-card set can be found with ads on the back for several local and regional businesses. Among them is the Block and Kuhl department store, Peoria, Ill. Type card and superstar collectors can expect to pay a significant

premium for individual cards with Block and Kuhl's advertising. The checklist is believed to generally parallel the 1916 M101-4 Blank Backs. Cards measures 1-5/8" x 3" and are printed in black-and-white.

(See 1916 M101-4 Blank Backs for checklist.)

1911 Blome's Chocolates (E94)

Advertising for Blome's Chocolates overprinted in purple on the back of these cards is one of several brands produced by George Close Candy Co. Type collectors will pay a premium of up to 5-7X for a Blome's version as opposed to the generic Close Candy version of the same player.

(See 1911 George Close Candy Co. for checklist and base card values.)

1933 Blue Bird Babe Ruth

A small hoard of the (a) cards appeared in the market in early 1994 making available a card which had previously been virtually unknown. Printed in black-and-white on thin card stock, the piece measures 3-7/8" x 5-7/8". The photo on front was used in modified form on several other early-1930s issues. The back offers balls and gloves available for redemption with soft drink bottle caps and cash. The discovery of the (b) version came in 1999.

		NM	EX	VG
(1a)	Babe Ruth (Batting follow-through, front view.)	2,000	1,000	600.00
(1b)	Babe Ruth (Batting follow-through, side view.)	3,500	1,750	1,00

1930 Blue Ribbon Malt Chicago Cubs

These player pictures were originally printed as part of a 40" x 12" advertising piece by Blue Ribbon Malt. However, if cut from the piece, there is no identification of the issuer. Individual black-and-white pictures have facsimile autographs on front and measure 3-1/2" high by 1-7/16" to 3" wide. The backs are blank. The unnumbered pictures are checklisted here in alphabetical order, with names as they appear on the photos.

		NM	EX	VG
	Complete Uncut Sheet:	500.00	250.00	150.00
	Complete Set, Singles (28):	335.00	165.00	100.00
	Common Player:	20.00	10.00	6.00
(1)	Clyde Beck	20.00	10.00	6.00
(2)	Lester Bell	20.00	10.00	6.00
(3)	Clarence Blair	20.00	10.00	6.00
(4)	Fred Blake	20.00	10.00	6.00
(5)	Jimmie Burke	20.00	10.00	6.00
(6)	Guy Bush	20.00	10.00	6.00
(7)	Hazen "Kiki" Cuyler	40.00	20.00	12.00
(8)	Woody English	20.00	10.00	6.00
(9)	Eddie Farrell	20.00	10.00	6.00
(10)	Charlie Grimm	20.00	10.00	6.00
(11)	Leo "Gabby" Hartnett	40.00	20.00	12.00
(12)	Clift Heathcote	20.00	10.00	6.00
(13)	Rogers Hornsby	65.00	32.00	19.50
(14)	George L. Kelly	40.00	20.00	12.00
(15)	Pierce "Pat" Malone	20.00	10.00	6.00
(16)	Joe McCarthy	20.00	10.00	6.00
(17)	Lynn Nelson	20.00	10.00	6.00
(18)	Bob Osborn	20.00	10.00	6.00
(19)	Jess Petty	20.00	10.00	6.00
(20)	Charlie Root	20.00	10.00	6.00
(21)	Ray Schalk	40.00	20.00	12.00
(22)	John Schulte	20.00	10.00	6.00
(23)	Al Shealy	20.00	10.00	6.00
(24)	Riggs Stephenson	20.00	10.00	6.00
(25)	Dan Taylor	20.00	10.00	6.00
(26)	Zack Taylor	20.00	10.00	6.00
(27)	Bud Teachout	20.00	10.00	6.00
(28)	Lewis "Hack" Wilson	60.00	30.00	18.00

1930 Blue Ribbon Malt Chicago White Sox

These player pictures were originally printed as part of a 40" x 12" advertising piece by Blue Ribbon Malt. However, if cut from the piece, there is no identification of the issuer. Individual black-and-white pictures have facsimile autographs on front and measure 3-1/2" high by 1-7/16" to 2-7/8" wide. The backs are blank. The unnumbered pictures are checklisted here in alphabetical order, with names as they appear on the photos.

		NM	EX	VG
	Complete Uncut Sheet:	1,000	500.00	300.00
	Complete Set (27):	400.00	200.00	120.00
	Common Player:	20.00	10.00	6.00
(1)	"Chick" Autry	20.00	10.00	6.00
(2)	"Red" Barnes	20.00	10.00	6.00
(3)	Moe Berg	60.00	30.00	18.00
(4)	Garland Braxton	20.00	10.00	6.00
(5)	Donie Bush	20.00	10.00	6.00
(6)	Pat Caraway	20.00	10.00	6.00
(7)	Bill Cissell	20.00	10.00	6.00
(8)	"Bud" Clancy	20.00	10.00	6.00
(9)	Clyde Crouse	20.00	10.00	6.00
(10)	U.C. Faber	50.00	25.00	15.00
(11)	Bob Fothergill	20.00	10.00	6.00
(12)	Frank J. "Dutch" Henry	20.00	10.00	6.00
(13)	Smead Jolley	20.00	10.00	6.00
(14)	Bill "Willie" Kamm	20.00	10.00	6.00
(15)	Bernard "Mike" Kelly	20.00	10.00	6.00
(16)	Johnny Kerr	20.00	10.00	6.00
(17)	Ted Lyons	50.00	25.00	15.00
(18)	Harold McKain	20.00	10.00	6.00
(19)	"Jim" Moore	20.00	10.00	6.00
(20)	"Greg" Mulleavy	20.00	10.00	6.00
(21)	Carl N. Reynolds	20.00	10.00	6.00
(22)	Blondy Ryan	20.00	10.00	6.00
(23)	"Benny" Tate	20.00	10.00	6.00
(24)	Tommy Thomas	20.00	10.00	6.00
(25)	Ed Walsh, Jr.	20.00	10.00	6.00
(26)	Johnny Watwood	20.00	10.00	6.00
(27)	Bob Weiland	20.00	10.00	6.00

1930 Blue Ribbon Malt Premiums

The manner of distribution for this series is unknown. And, while the name of the sponsor does not appear, the similarity to other Blue Ribbon Malt issues pinpoints their source. The premiums are a 5" x 7" black-and-white photo (sometimes, but not always, mounted on a heavy gray cardboard 6-1/4" x 8-3/4" backing). A facsimile autograph is on the photo. This incomplete checklist is presented alphabetically by team.

		NM	EX	VG
	Common Player:	225.00	110.00	65.00
	CHICAGO CUBS			
(1)	Clyde Beck	225.00	110.00	65.00
(2)	Lester Bell	225.00	110.00	65.00
(3)	Clarence Blair	225.00	110.00	65.00
(4)	Fred Blake	225.00	110.00	65.00
(5)	Jimmy Burke	225.00	110.00	65.00
(6)	Guy Bush	225.00	110.00	65.00
(7)	Hal Carlson	225.00	110.00	65.00
(8)	Hazen "Kiki" Cuyler	300.00	150.00	90.00
(9)	Woody English	225.00	110.00	65.00
(10)	Charlie Grimm	225.00	110.00	65.00
(11)	Leo "Gabby" Hartnett	300.00	150.00	90.00
(12)	Cliff Heathcote	225.00	110.00	65.00
(13)	Rogers Hornsby	400.00	200.00	120.00
(14)	Perce "Pat" Malone	225.00	110.00	65.00
(15)	Joe McCarthy	275.00	135.00	80.00
(16)	Malcolm Moss	225.00	110.00	65.00
(17)	Lynn Nelson	225.00	110.00	65.00
(18)	Bob Osborn	225.00	110.00	65.00
(19)	Charles Root	225.00	110.00	65.00
(20)	Ray Schalk	275.00	135.00	80.00
(21)	John Schulte	225.00	110.00	65.00
(22)	Al Shealy	225.00	110.00	65.00
(23)	Riggs Stephenson	225.00	110.00	65.00
(24)	Dan Taylor	225.00	110.00	65.00
(25)	Zack Taylor	225.00	110.00	65.00
(26)	Chas. J. Tolson	225.00	110.00	65.00
(27)	Hal Totten/Announcer	225.00	110.00	65.00
(28)	Lewis "Hack" Wilson	350.00	175.00	105.00
	CHICAGO WHITE SOX			
(1)	Donie Bush	225.00	110.00	65.00
(2)	Bill Cissell	225.00	110.00	65.00
(4)	Red Faber	275.00	135.00	85.00
(5)	Smead Jolley	225.00	110.00	65.00
(7)	Willie Kamm	225.00	110.00	65.00
(9)	Ted Lyons	275.00	135.00	85.00
(11)	Carl Reynolds	225.00	110.00	65.00
(13)	Art Shires	225.00	110.00	65.00
(15)	Tommy Thomas	225.00	110.00	65.00
(16)	Johnny Watwood	225.00	110.00	65.00

1931 Blue Ribbon Malt

Players of the Chicago Cubs and White Sox are featured in this series of 4-7/8" x 6-7/8" black-and-white photos. Each blank-backed photo is bordered in white with "Compliments of BLUE RIBBON MALT-America's Biggest Seller" printed in the bottom border and a facsimile autograph across the photo. It is likely players other than those listed here were also issued.

		NM	EX	VG
	Common Player:	90.00	45.00	27.00
(1)	Lu Blue	90.00	45.00	27.00
(2)	Lew Fonseca	90.00	45.00	27.00

		NM	EX	VG
(3)	Vic Frazier	90.00	45.00	27.00
(4)	John Kerr	90.00	45.00	27.00
(5)	Bob Smith	90.00	45.00	27.00
(6)	Billy Sullivan	90.00	45.00	27.00
(7)	Lewis "Hack" Wilson	125.00	62.00	37.00

1933 Blum's Baseball Bulletin Premiums

The year of issue presented is speculative, based on biographical information on the relatively few examples studied. This series of 9-1/2" x 13-5/8" (Small) or 11-1/2" x 13-3/4" (Large) black-and-white blank-back pictures was, according to a credit line beneath the bottom frame of baseballs, "Compiled by Fred J. Blum, Publisher, Blum's Baseball Bulletin." The checklist here is incomplete.

		NM	EX	VG
	Common Player:	200.00	100.00	60.00
(1)	Edward T. Collins/S	300.00	150.00	90.00
(2)	Jacob E. Daubert/S	200.00	100.00	60.00
(3)	William E. Donovan/L	200.00	100.00	60.00
(4)	John J. Evers/S	300.00	150.00	90.00
(5)	Henry K. Groh/L	200.00	100.00	60.00
(6)	Lefty Grove/L	400.00	200.00	120.00
(7)	Walter Johnson/S	500.00	250.00	150.00
(8)	Napoleon Lajoie/S	350.00	175.00	105.00
(9)	Walter J.V. Maranville/S	300.00	150.00	90.00
(10)	James (Wicky) McAvoy/L	200.00	100.00	60.00
(11)	Rochester 1911/L (Team composite.)	200.00	100.00	60.00
(12)	Tristam Speaker/S	400.00	200.00	120.00
(13)	George Toporcer/L	200.00	100.00	60.00

1961-1963 Bobbin' Head Dolls

Some of the top stars of the day were caricatured in the first generation of bobbin' head dolls. Additionally, Mantle and Maris were depicted in a pair of color 5" x 7" advertising photos depicting the home run heroes of 1961 holding their dolls. The players are pictured in belt-to-cap photos wearing road uniforms and posed in a stadium setting. Backs are blank.

	NM	EX	VG
Roberto Clemente (6-1/2" doll)	4,500	2,250	1,350
Roberto Clemente (Picture box.)	1,000	500.00	300.00

Mickey Mantle (Ad photo.)	325.00	160.00	95.00
Mickey Mantle (6-1/2" doll, round or square base.)	1,100	550.00	330.00
Mickey Mantle (Mini (4-1/2") doll.)	1,500	750.00	450.00
Mickey Mantle (Large or small picture box.)	750.00	375.00	225.00
Roger Maris (Ad photo.)	175.00	87.00	52.00
Roger Maris (6-1/2" doll)	450.00	225.00	135.00
Roger Maris (Mini (5-1/2") doll.)	650.00	325.00	195.00
Roger Maris (Large or small picture box.)	900.00	450.00	275.00
Willie Mays (White base, dark face, 6-1/2" doll.)	750.00	375.00	225.00
Willie Mays (White base, light face, 6-1/2" doll.)	475.00	235.00	140.00
Willie Mays (Gold base, 6-1/2" doll.)	2,250	1,125	675.00

1947 Bond Bread

Issued by "Homogenized" Bond Bread in 1947, this set consists of 48 unnumbered black-and-white cards, each measuring about 2-1/4" x 3-1/2" with rounded or square corners. Of the 48 cards, 44 are baseball players; four picture boxers. Borderless fronts have either portraits or posed action photos and the player's facsimile autograph or name in script. In the 1980s a large quantity of half the cards in the set (all with square corners) was uncovered in a New York warehouse. Sometime after 2000, the square-cornered cards were illegally reprinted, often sold in high-graded slabs from unknown grading companies. Those cards that were not known to be affected by the find/reprinting are indicated in the checklist here with an "SP." The issue was designated in the American Card Catalog as W571 / D305.

		NM	EX	VG
Complete Set (48):		1,600	800.00	475.00
Common Player:		15.00	7.50	4.50
(1)	Rex Barney/SP	20.00	10.00	6.00
(2)	Yogi Berra/SP	75.00	37.50	22.50
(3)	Ewell Blackwell	15.00	7.50	4.50
(4)	Lou Boudreau	20.00	10.00	6.00
(5)	Ralph Branca/SP	20.00	10.00	6.00
(6)	Harry Brecheen	15.00	7.50	4.50
(7)	Dom DiMaggio/SP	50.00	25.00	15.00
(8)	Joe DiMaggio/SP	275.00	135.00	85.00
(9)	Bobbie Doerr (Bobby)	20.00	10.00	6.00
(10)	Bruce Edwards/SP	20.00	10.00	6.00
(11)	Bob Elliott	15.00	7.50	4.50
(12)	Del Ennis	15.00	7.50	4.50
(13)	Bob Feller	25.00	12.50	7.50
(14)	Carl Furillo/SP	35.00	17.50	10.00
(15)	Cid Gordon (Sid)/SP	20.00	10.00	6.00
(16)	Joe Gordon	15.00	7.50	4.50
(17)	Joe Hatten/SP	20.00	10.00	6.00
(18)	Gil Hodges/SP	75.00	37.50	22.50
(19)	Tommy Holmes	15.00	7.50	4.50
(20)	Larry Janson (Jansen)/SP	20.00	10.00	6.00
(21)	Sheldon Jones/SP	20.00	10.00	6.00
(22)	Edwin Joost/SP	20.00	10.00	6.00
(23)	Charlie Keller/SP	20.00	10.00	6.00
(24)	Ken Keltner	15.00	7.50	4.50
(25)	Buddy Kerr/SP	20.00	10.00	6.00
(26)	Ralph Kiner	20.00	10.00	6.00
(27)	John Lindell/SP	20.00	10.00	6.00
(28)	Whitey Lockman/SP	20.00	10.00	6.00
(29)	Willard Marshall/SP	20.00	10.00	6.00
(30)	Johnny Mize	20.00	10.00	6.00
(31)	Stan Musial	60.00	30.00	18.00
(32)	Andy Pafko	15.00	7.50	4.50
(33)	Johnny Pesky	15.00	7.50	4.50
(34)	Pee Wee Reese/SP	125.00	65.00	35.00
(35)	Phil Rizzuto	30.00	15.00	9.00
(36)	Aaron Robinson	15.00	7.50	4.50
(37)	Jackie Robinson	90.00	45.00	27.50
(38)	John Sain	15.00	7.50	4.50
(39)	Enos Slaughter	20.00	10.00	6.00
(40)	Vern Stephens	15.00	7.50	4.50
(41)	George Tebbetts/SP	20.00	10.00	6.00
(42)	Bob Thomson/SP	25.00	12.50	7.50
(43)	Johnny Vandermeer (VanderMeer)/SP	20.00	10.00	6.00
(44)	Ted Williams	90.00	45.00	27.00
BOXERS				
(45)	Primo Carnera	15.00	7.50	4.50
(46)	Marcel Cerdan/SP	40.00	20.00	12.00
(47)	Jake LaMotta/SP	60.00	30.00	18.00
(48)	Joe Louis	30.00	15.00	9.00

1947 Bond Bread Exhibits

The manner of distribution of these variants of the "Bond Bread" (W571 / D305) baseball cards is believed to have been via penny arcade dispensers. About the same size as contemporary Exhibit Supply Co. cards (3-3/8" x 5-3/8"), these are printed in black-and-white and blank-backed. Over 75% of the baseball players known in the base Bond Bread set have been reported in this format, plus one player, Walker Cooper, not in the base set. The four W571 / D305 boxers have not yet been reported in this format.

		NM	EX	VG
Complete Set (33):		1,250	625.00	375.00
Common Player:		25.00	12.50	7.50
(1)	Rex Barney			
(2)	Yogi Berra			
(3)	Ewell Blackwell	25.00	12.50	7.50
(4)	Lou Boudreau	30.00	15.00	9.00
(5)	Ralph Branca			
(6)	Harry Brecheen	25.00	12.50	7.50
(--)	Walker Cooper	50.00	25.00	15.00
(7)	Dom DiMaggio	30.00	15.00	9.00
(8)	Joe DiMaggio	200.00	100.00	60.00
(9)	Bobbie Doerr (Bobby)	35.00	17.50	10.00
(10)	Bruce Edwards			
(11)	Bob Elliott	25.00	12.50	7.50
(12)	Del Ennis	25.00	12.50	7.50
(13)	Bob Feller	40.00	20.00	12.00
(14)	Carl Furillo	100.00	50.00	30.00
(15)	Cid Gordon (Sid)			
(16)	Joe Gordon	25.00	12.50	7.50
(17)	Joe Hatten			
(18)	Gil Hodges	90.00	45.00	27.50
(19)	Tommy Holmes	25.00	12.50	7.50
(20)	Larry Janson (Jansen)	25.00	12.50	7.50
(21)	Sheldon Jones	25.00	12.50	7.50
(22)	Edwin Joost	25.00	12.50	7.50
(23)	Charlie Keller			
(24)	Ken Keltner	25.00	12.50	7.50
(25)	Buddy Kerr	25.00	12.50	7.50
(26)	Ralph Kiner	30.00	15.00	9.00
(27)	John Lindell	25.00	12.50	7.50
(28)	Whitey Lockman	25.00	12.50	7.50
(29)	Willard Marshall			
(30)	Johnny Mize	30.00	15.00	9.00
(31)	Stan Musial	75.00	37.50	22.50
(32)	Andy Pafko	25.00	12.50	7.50
(33)	Johnny Pesky	25.00	12.50	7.50
(34)	Pee Wee Reese	100.00	50.00	30.00
(35)	Phil Rizzuto	50.00	25.00	15.00
(36)	Aaron Robinson	25.00	12.50	7.50
(37)	Jackie Robinson	175.00	90.00	55.00
(38)	John Sain	25.00	12.50	7.50
(39)	Enos Slaughter	30.00	15.00	9.00
(40)	Vern Stephens	25.00	12.50	7.50
(41)	George Tebbetts	25.00	12.50	7.50
(42)	Bob Thomson			
(43)	Johnny Vandermeer (VanderMeer)	25.00	12.50	7.50
(44)	Ted Williams	175.00	85.00	55.00

1947 Bond Bread Premiums

While there is no empirical evidence, it is believed these 6-5/8" x 9" black-and-white, blank-back player pictures are associated with the Bond Bread card issue, since they share the same photos and script names, right down to the misspellings. They were likely made available to bread buyers as some sort of premium. The checklist presented here is the same as that of the card issue. Though not all of the premium pictures have been confirmed, it is reasonable to presume their existence.

		NM	EX	VG
Common Player:		40.00	20.00	12.00
(1)	Rex Barney	40.00	20.00	12.00
(2)	Yogi Berra	150.00	75.00	45.00
(3)	Ewell Blackwell	40.00	20.00	12.00
(4)	Lou Boudreau	75.00	37.50	22.50
(5)	Ralph Branca	60.00	30.00	18.00
(6)	Harry Brecheen	40.00	20.00	12.00
(7)	Dom DiMaggio	60.00	30.00	18.00
(8)	Joe DiMaggio	600.00	300.00	180.00
(9)	Bobbie Doerr (Bobby)	60.00	30.00	18.00
(10)	Bruce Edwards	40.00	20.00	12.00
(11)	Bob Elliott	40.00	20.00	12.00
(12)	Del Ennis	50.00	25.00	15.00
(13)	Bob Feller	150.00	75.00	45.00

(14)	Carl Furillo	60.00	30.00	18.00
(15)	Cid Gordon (Sid)	40.00	20.00	12.00
(16)	Joe Gordon	40.00	20.00	12.00
(17)	Joe Hatten	40.00	20.00	12.00
(18)	Gil Hodges	100.00	50.00	30.00
(19)	Tommy Holmes	40.00	20.00	12.00
(20)	Larry Janson (Jansen)	40.00	20.00	12.00
(21)	Sheldon Jones	40.00	20.00	12.00
(22)	Edwin Joost	40.00	20.00	12.00
(23)	Charlie Keller	45.00	22.50	13.50
(24)	Ken Keltner	40.00	20.00	12.00
(25)	Buddy Kerr	40.00	20.00	12.00
(26)	Ralph Kiner	75.00	37.50	22.50
(27)	John Lindell	40.00	20.00	12.00
(28)	Whitey Lockman	40.00	20.00	12.00
(29)	Willard Marshall	40.00	20.00	12.00
(30)	Johnny Mize	75.00	37.50	22.50
(31)	Stan Musial	300.00	150.00	90.00
(32)	Andy Pafko	40.00	20.00	12.00
(33)	Johnny Pesky	40.00	20.00	12.00
(34)	Pee Wee Reese	150.00	75.00	45.00
(35)	Phil Rizzuto	150.00	75.00	45.00
(36)	Aaron Robinson	40.00	20.00	12.00
(37)	Jackie Robinson	1,000	500.00	300.00
(38)	John Sain	50.00	25.00	15.00
(39)	Enos Slaughter	75.00	37.50	22.50
(40)	Vern Stephens	40.00	20.00	12.00
(41)	George Tebbetts	40.00	20.00	12.00
(42)	Bob Thomson	60.00	30.00	18.00
(43)	Johnny Van Der Meer (VanderMeer)	40.00	20.00	12.00
(44)	Ted Williams	350.00	175.00	100.00
BOXERS				
(45)	Primo Carnera	45.00	22.50	13.50
(46)	Marcel Cerdan	40.00	20.00	12.00
(47)	Jake LaMotta	60.00	30.00	18.00
(48)	Joe Louis	75.00	37.50	22.50

1947 Bond Bread Perforated, Dual-Sided

The manner of distribtion for this variant of the "Bond Bread" (W571/D305) cards is unknown, although anecdotal evidence suggests a connection with Bar Nunn show stores. About the size of the commonly seen blank-backed baseball cards (2-1/4" x 3-1/2"), these differ in that they have two, three or four sides perforated, indicating they were issued in sheet form. Also, this group has, instead of a blank back, another picture. All but one of the pictures seen thus far are of Western movie stars. None are named on the cards, but they include John Wayne, Hopalong Cassidy, Gene Autry and Noah Berry. The only non-Western back seen is Michigan quarterback Bob Chappius, paired with Tommy Holmes. Thus far, none of the short-printed Bond Bread cards have been seen in this format. Assigned numbers correspond to the Bond Bread set.

		NM	EX	VG
Complete Set (24):		550.00	275.00	165.00
Common Card:				
(3)	Ewell Blackwell	15.00	7.50	4.50
(4)	Lou Boudreau	22.50	11.00	6.75
(6)	Harry Brecheen	15.00	7.50	4.50
(9)	Bobbie Doerr (Bobby)	22.50	11.00	6.75
(11)	Bob Elliott	15.00	7.50	4.50
(12)	Del Ennis	15.00	7.50	4.50
(13)	Bob Feller	25.00	12.50	7.50
(16)	Joe Gordon	15.00	7.50	4.50
(19)	Tommy Holmes	15.00	7.50	4.50
(24)	Ken Keltner	15.00	7.50	4.50
(26)	Ralph Kiner	22.50	11.00	6.75
(30)	Johnny Mize	22.50	11.00	6.75
(31)	Stan Musial	60.00	30.00	18.00
(32)	Andy Pafko	15.00	7.50	4.50
(33)	Johnny Pesky	15.00	7.50	4.50
(35)	Phil Rizzuto	30.00	15.00	9.00
(36)	Aaron Robinson	15.00	7.50	4.50
(37)	Jackie Robinson	110.00	55.00	35.00
(38)	John Sain	15.00	7.50	4.50
(39)	Enos Slaughter	22.50	11.00	6.75
(40)	Vern Stephens	15.00	7.50	4.50
(44)	Ted Williams	110.00	55.00	35.00
BOXERS				
(45)	Primo Carnera	15.00	7.50	4.50
(48)	Joe Louis	30.00	15.00	9.00

1947 Bond Bread Jackie Robinson

"MY FAVORITE AT 'HOME PLATE' IS THAT GOOD BOND BREAD. IT TASTES GRAND AND PACKS LOTS OF ENERGY!"

JACKIE'S RIGHT, FOLKS! SWITCH TO TODAY'S BOND BREAD. IT'S MADE WITH MORE OF EVERYTHING HONESTLY GOOD

The modern major leagues' first black player is featured in this set issued by Bond Bread in 1947. The cards, measuring 2-1/4" x 3-1/2", are black-and-white photos of Robinson in various action and portrait poses. The unnumbered cards bear three different backs advertising Bond Bread. Four cards use a horizontal format. Card #6 was issued in greater quantities and perhaps was a promotional card; its back is the only one containing a short biography of Robinson.

	NM	EX	VG
Complete Set (13):	9,500	4,750	2,850
Common Card:	750.00	375.00	225.00
(1) Jackie Robinson (Awaiting pitch.)	750.00	375.00	225.00
(2) Jackie Robinson/Btg (White shirt sleeves.)	750.00	375.00	225.00
(3) Jackie Robinson/Btg (No shirt sleeves.)	750.00	375.00	225.00
(4) Jackie Robinson/Leaping (Scoreboard in background.)	750.00	375.00	225.00
(5) Jackie Robinson/Leaping (No scoreboard.)	750.00	375.00	225.00
(6) Jackie Robinson/Portrait (Facsimile autograph.)	750.00	375.00	225.00
(7) Jackie Robinson/Portrait (Holding glove in air.)	750.00	375.00	225.00
(8) Jackie Robinson (Running down baseline.)	750.00	375.00	225.00
(9) Jackie Robinson (Running to catch ball.)	750.00	375.00	225.00
(10) Jackie Robinson/Sliding	750.00	375.00	225.00
(11) Jackie Robinson (Stretching for throw, ball in glove.)	750.00	375.00	225.00
(12) Jackie Robinson (Stretching for throw, no ball visible.)	750.00	375.00	225.00
(13) Jackie Robinson/Throwing	750.00	375.00	225.00

1912 Boston American Series Red Sox Postcards

TRIS SPEAKER
STAR OUTFIELDER AND CHAMPION
BATTER OF THE RED SOX
BOSTON AMERICAN SERIES

Star players from the World Champion Red Sox are featured in two sets of postcards issued by one of the city's daily newspapers. This set carries the notation "Boston American Series" at bottom right and is approximately 3-1/2" x 5-1/2". The cards are printed in sepia tones with a cream border. At bottom is the player name and position on two lines. Backs have typical postcard markings and a three-line notation, "PHOTOS OF / NOTED BALL PLAYERS / BOSTON SUNDAY AMERICAN SERIES."

	NM	EX	VG
Complete Set (6):	2,400	1,200	725.00
Common Player:	400.00	200.00	120.00
(1) Forrest Cady	400.00	200.00	120.00
(2) Hub Perdue	400.00	200.00	120.00
(3) Tris Speaker	550.00	275.00	165.00
(4) Jake Stahl	400.00	200.00	120.00
(5) Heinie Wagner	400.00	200.00	120.00
(6) Joe Wood	400.00	200.00	120.00

1936 Boston American Sport Stamps

BOSTON AMERICAN
S P O R T   S T A M P

H. LAVAGETTO, 3B, PIRATES

"Harry Lavagetto — Cookie joined the Pittsburgh Pirates at their spring training camp in 1934 . . . and immediately caught on at the keystone sack . . . such associates on that squad as Arky Vaughan and Gus Suhr have helped him to hold down his job . . . a hard and throws right-handed and is a very classy fielder . . . batted .280 last season . . . 22 years old . . . stands 5 feet 11½

Similar to several contemporary issues, the Sport Stamps were printed on the pages of the daily newspaper over the course of the season. About 2" x 3-1/2", depending on the length of the biography and how well they were cut off the paper, they are printed in black-and-white. A tightly cropped player portrait is centered on a 2" x 2-5/8" stamp design with the paper's name above and the player's name, position and team below. This checklist may not be complete. Two of the players (Castleman, R. Johnson) have the paper at top listed as "SUNDAY ADVERTISER." Many of the stamps were issued in pairs, and at least a couple of football players are known, as well as the listed baseball players.

	NM	EX	VG
Common Player:	12.00	6.00	3.50
(1) J. (John) Allen	12.00	6.00	3.50
(2) I. (Ivy) Andrews	12.00	6.00	3.50
(3) E. (Elden)(Eldon) Auker	12.00	6.00	3.50
(4) E. (Earl) Averill	20.00	10.00	6.00
(5) R. (Richard) Bartell	12.00	6.00	3.50
(6) R. (Roy) Bell	12.00	6.00	3.50
(7) .R. (Raymond) Benge	12.00	6.00	3.50
(8) M. (Morris) Berg	30.00	15.00	9.00
(9) Walter Berger	12.00	6.00	3.50
(10) C. (Charles) Berry	12.00	6.00	3.50
(11) (George) Blaeholder	12.00	6.00	3.50
(12) A. (Albert) Blanche	12.00	6.00	3.50
(13) D. (Darrell) Blanton	12.00	6.00	3.50
(14) O. (Oswald) Bleuge (Bluege)	12.00	6.00	3.50
(15) W. (William) Bolton	12.00	6.00	3.50
(16) H. (Henry) Bonura	12.00	6.00	3.50
(17) J. (James) Bottomley	20.00	10.00	6.00
(18) J. (Joseph) Bowman	12.00	6.00	3.50
(19) E. (Edward) Brandt	12.00	6.00	3.50
(20) C. (Clinton) Brown	12.00	6.00	3.50
(21) J. (John) Burnett	12.00	6.00	3.50
(22) G. (Guy) Bush	12.00	6.00	3.50
(23) A. (Albert) Butcher	12.00	6.00	3.50
(24) E. (Earl) Caldwell	12.00	6.00	3.50
(25) D. (Dolph) Camilli	12.00	6.00	3.50
(26) B. (Bruce) Campbell	12.00	6.00	3.50
(27) J. (Joseph) Cascarella	12.00	6.00	3.50
(28) C. (Clyde) Castleman	12.00	6.00	3.50
(29) P. (Philip) Cavarretta	12.00	6.00	3.50
(30) W. (William) Chapman	12.00	6.00	3.50
(31) L. (Louis) Chiozza	12.00	6.00	3.50
(32) H. (Harland) Clift	12.00	6.00	3.50
(33) G. (Gordon) Cochrane	25.00	12.50	7.50
(34) J. (James) Collins	12.00	6.00	3.50
(35) A. (Allen) Cooke	12.00	6.00	3.50
(36) J. (Joseph) Coscarart	12.00	6.00	3.50
(37) Roger Cramer	12.00	6.00	3.50
(38) J. (Joseph) Cronin	20.00	10.00	6.00
(39) F. (Frank) Crosetti	15.00	7.50	4.50
(40) A. (Alvin) Crowder	12.00	6.00	3.50
(41) A. (Anthony) Cuccinello	12.00	6.00	3.50
(42) H. (Hazen) Cuyler	20.00	10.00	6.00
(43) H. (Harry) Danning	12.00	6.00	3.50
(44) V. (Virgil) Davis	12.00	6.00	3.50
(45) J. (Jerome) Dean	35.00	17.50	10.50
(46) P. (Paul) Dean	16.00	8.00	4.75
(47) J. (Joseph) Demaree	12.00	6.00	3.50
(48) Paul Derringer	12.00	6.00	3.50
(49) G. (George) Dickey	12.00	6.00	3.50
(50) W. (William) Dickey	25.00	12.50	7.50
(51) L. (Leo) Durocher	20.00	10.00	6.00
(52) J. (James) Dykes	12.00	6.00	3.50
(53) G. (George) Earnshaw	12.00	6.00	3.50
(54) E. (Elmwood)(Elwood) English	12.00	6.00	3.50
(55) R. (Robert) Feller	25.00	12.50	7.50
(56) R. (Richard) Ferrell	20.00	10.00	6.00
(57) Wes Ferrell	12.00	6.00	3.50
(58) (Louis) Finney	12.00	6.00	3.50
(59) F. (Fred) Fitzsimmons	12.00	6.00	3.50
(60) Jimmy Foxx	30.00	15.00	9.00
(61) (Fred) Frankhouse	12.00	6.00	3.50
(62) L. (Lawrence) French	12.00	6.00	3.50
(63) (Frank) Frisch	20.00	10.00	6.00
(64) A. (August) Galan	12.00	6.00	3.50
(65) H. (Heny)(Henry) Gehrig	60.00	30.00	18.00
(66) C. (Charles) Gehringer	20.00	10.00	6.00
(67) (Charles) Gelbert	12.00	6.00	3.50
(68) A. (Angelo) Giuliani	12.00	6.00	3.50
(69) V. (Vernon) Gomez	20.00	10.00	6.00
(70) L. (Leon) Goslin	20.00	10.00	6.00
(71) R. (Robert) Grace	12.00	6.00	3.50
(72) C. (Charles) Grimm	12.00	6.00	3.50
(73) Robert Grove	25.00	12.50	7.50
(74) G. (George) Haas	12.00	6.00	3.50
(75) I. (Irving) Hadley	12.00	6.00	3.50
(76) M. (Melvin) Harder	12.00	6.00	3.50
(77) C. (Charles) Hartnett	20.00	10.00	6.00
(78) M. (Minter) Hayes	12.00	6.00	3.50
(79) R. (Ralston) Hemsley	12.00	6.00	3.50
(80) F. (Floyd) Herman	12.00	6.00	3.50
(81) (Michael) Higgins	12.00	6.00	3.50
(82) M. (Myril) Hoag	12.00	6.00	3.50
(83) E. (Elon) Hogsett	12.00	6.00	3.50
(84) R. (Rogers) Hornsby	25.00	12.50	7.50
(85) W. (Waite) Hoyt	20.00	10.00	6.00
(86) W. (Willis) Hudlin	12.00	6.00	3.50
(87) T. (Travis) Jackson	20.00	10.00	6.00
(88) R. (Robert) Johnson	12.00	6.00	3.50
(89) R. (Roy) Johnson	12.00	6.00	3.50
(90) B. (Baxter) Jordan	12.00	6.00	3.50
(91) W. (William) Jurgess (Jurges)	12.00	6.00	3.50
(92) (Lloyd) Kennedy	12.00	6.00	3.50
(93) C. (Charles) Klein	20.00	10.00	6.00
(94) (William) Knickerbocker	12.00	6.00	3.50
(95) J. (John) Knott	12.00	6.00	3.50
(96) M. (Mark) Koenig	12.00	6.00	3.50
(97) J. (Joseph) Kuhel	12.00	6.00	3.50
(98) L. (Lynford) Lary	12.00	6.00	3.50
(99) H. (Harry) Lavagetto	12.00	6.00	3.50
(100) A. (Anthony) Lazzeri	20.00	10.00	6.00
(101) W. (William) Lee	12.00	6.00	3.50
(102) H. (Henry) Leiber	12.00	6.00	3.50
(103) Wm. (William) Lewis	12.00	6.00	3.50
(104) E. (Edward) Linke	12.00	6.00	3.50
(105) E. (Ernest) Lombardi	20.00	10.00	6.00
(106) Al Lopez	20.00	10.00	6.00
(107) C. (Charles) Lucas	12.00	6.00	3.50
(108) T. (Theodore) Lyons	20.00	10.00	6.00
(109) Dan MacFayden	12.00	6.00	3.50
(110) P. (Percy)(Perce) Malone	12.00	6.00	3.50
(111) A. (Augustus) Mancuso	12.00	6.00	3.50
(112) (John) Martin	15.00	7.50	4.50
(113) J. (Joseph) Medwick	12.00	6.00	3.50
(114) E. (Edmund) Miller	12.00	6.00	3.50
(115) J. (John) Mize	20.00	10.00	6.00
(116) Gene Moore	12.00	6.00	3.50
(117) R. (Randolph) Moore	12.00	6.00	3.50
(118) V. (Van Lingle) Mungo	12.00	6.00	3.50
(119) C. (Charles) Myer	12.00	6.00	3.50
(120) A. (Alfred) Niemiec	12.00	6.00	3.50
(121) (Fred) Ostermueller	12.00	6.00	3.50
(122) M. (Melvin) Ott	25.00	12.50	7.50
(123) L. (LeRoy) Parmelee	12.00	6.00	3.50
(124) A. (Anthony) Piet	12.00	6.00	3.50
(125) A. (Alvin) Powell	12.00	6.00	3.50
(126) F. (Frank) Pytlak	12.00	6.00	3.50
(127) R. (Ray) Radcliff	12.00	6.00	3.50
(128) R. (Robert) Reis	12.00	6.00	3.50
(129) (Carl) Reynolds	12.00	6.00	3.50
(130) J. (John) Rhodes	12.00	6.00	3.50
(131) R. (Robert) Rolfe	12.00	6.00	3.50
(132) C. (Charles) Root	12.00	6.00	3.50
(133) L. (Lynwood) Rowe	12.00	6.00	3.50
(134) C. (Charles) Ruffing	20.00	10.00	6.00
(135) F. (Fred) Schulte	12.00	6.00	3.50
(136) H. (Harold) Schumacher	12.00	6.00	3.50
(137) J. (James) Sewell	12.00	6.00	3.50
(138) A. (Aloysius) Simmons	20.00	10.00	6.00
(139) J. (Julius) Soulters (Solters)	12.00	6.00	3.50
(140) G. (George) Stainback	12.00	6.00	3.50
(141) J. (Johnathan)(John) Stone	12.00	6.00	3.50
(142) J. (Joseph) Stripp	12.00	6.00	3.50
(143) W. (William) Terry	20.00	10.00	6.00
(144) T. (Thomas) Thevenow	12.00	6.00	3.50
(145) A. (Alphonse) Thomas	12.00	6.00	3.50
(146) C. (Cecil) Travis	12.00	6.00	3.50
(147) H. (Harold) Traynor	20.00	10.00	6.00
(148) H. (Harold) Trosky	12.00	6.00	3.50
(149) R. (Russell) Van Atta	12.00	6.00	3.50
(150) F. (Floyd) Vaughan	20.00	10.00	6.00
(151) J. (Joseph) Vosmik	12.00	6.00	3.50
(152) G. (Gerald) Walker	12.00	6.00	3.50
(153) W. (William) Walter	12.00	6.00	3.50
(154) L. (Lloyd) Waner	20.00	10.00	6.00
(155) P. (Paul) Waner	20.00	10.00	6.00
(156) L. (Lonnie) Warneke	12.00	6.00	3.50
(157) G. (George) Watkins	12.00	6.00	3.50
(158) J. (Joyner) White	12.00	6.00	3.50
(159) (Burgess) Whitehead	12.00	6.00	3.50
(160) (Earl) Whitehill	12.00	6.00	3.50
(161) A. (Arthur) Whitney	12.00	6.00	3.50
(162) J. (Jack) Wilson	12.00	6.00	3.50
(163) J. (James) Wilson	12.00	6.00	3.50

1912 Boston Daily American Souvenir Postcards

HEINIE WAGNER
CAPTAIN OF RED SOX.
Boston Daily American Souvenir

A second style of postcard issued by a local newspaper to honor the World Champions is labeled at bottom-left "Boston American Souvenir." The 3-1/2" x 5-1/2" cards are printed in black on a cream colored stock. The player name and position are printed inside the photo frame. In the bottom-right border is a union logo and the number "96." The back has standard postcard markings.

	NM	EX	VG
Common Player:	450.00	225.00	135.00
(1) Forrest Cady	450.00	225.00	135.00
(2) Ray Collins	450.00	225.00	135.00
(3) Rabbit Maranville	600.00	300.00	180.00
(4) Heinie Wagner	450.00	225.00	135.00
(5) Joe Wood	500.00	250.00	150.00

1912 Boston Garter

If it weren't for the checklist printed on the back of the few known specimens, the extent of this extremely rare issue would be unknown. Many of the cards mentioned on the back have yet to be seen. Issued by the George Frost Company of Boston, and packed one card per box of a dozen garters, the approximately 4" x 8-1/4" cards are printed in color lithography on the front, and black-and-white on the back. Fronts have a picture of the player standing near his locker or sitting in a chair, dressing in his uniform. The issuer's Boston-brand garter is prominently shown below the player's boxer shorts. A window in the background displays a cityscape or ballpark scene. There was a card issued for one player on each of the 16 major league teams of the day. Large-format (21-1/2" x 11-1/4") cardboard window display posters which reproduce pairs of the cards are sometimes seen in the hobby.

		NM	EX	VG
Common Player:		30,000	12,000	7,250
(1)	Bob Bescher	30,000	12,000	7,250
(2)	Roger Bresnahan	40,000	13,750	8,250
(3)	Frank Chance	40,000	15,000	9,000
(4)	Hal Chase	30,000	12,500	7,500
(5)	Fred Clarke	40,000	13,750	8,250
(6)	Eddie Collins	40,000	13,750	8,250
(7)	Charles Dooin	30,000	12,000	7,250
(8)	Hugh Jennings	40,000	13,750	8,250
(9)	Walter Johnson	60,000	17,500	10,500
(10)	Johnny Kling	30,000	12,000	7,250
(11)	Larry Lajoie	45,000	15,000	9,000
(12)	Frank LaPorte	30,000	12,000	7,250
(13)	Christy Mathewson	75,000	37,500	22,500
(14)	Nap Rucker	30,000	12,000	7,250
(15)	Tris Speaker	45,000	15,000	9,000
(16)	Ed Walsh	40,000	13,750	8,250

1914 Boston Garter - Color

 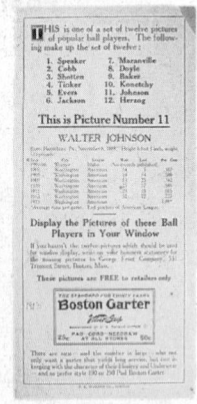

The second of what are presumed to have been three annual issue by the George Frost Co., Boston, contains 12 cards. The colorful lithograph fronts have a player picture in front of a ballpark diagram. A large Boston-brand garter appears at the bottom. Baseballs with the Boston Garter name appear in each upper corner. Black-and-white backs have a checklist for the set, career statistics for the player pictured and details on the cards' availability. Retailers received one card per box of dozen garters and could write to the company to complete the set. About 4" x 8-1/4", they were intended to be displayed in shop windows.

		NM	EX	VG
Common Player:		7,500	3,000	1,800
1	Tris Speaker	30,000	10,000	6,000
2	Ty Cobb	60,000	17,500	10,500
3	Burt Shotten (Shotton)	7,500	3,000	1,800
4	Joe Tinker	15,000	6,250	3,750
5	Johnny Evers	15,500	6,250	3,750
6	Joe Jackson	100,000	30,000	18,000

7	Rabbit Maranville	15,000	6,250	3,750
8	Larry Doyle	7,500	3,000	1,800
9	Frank Baker	15,000	6,250	3,750
10	Ed Konetchy	7,500	3,000	1,800
11	Walter Johnson	35,000	10,000	6,000
12	Buck Herzog	7,500	3,000	1,800

1914 Boston Garter - Sepia

The 1914 date attributed to this 10-card set may or may not be accurate. Since the company's other two known issues can be reliably dated and were produced using the color lithographic process, it is presumed that the use of photographs would have come later. Fronts of the approximately 3-3/4" x 6-1/4" cards feature a green duo-tone photo of the player. His last name appears in white script at the bottom, along with a baseball with the Boston Garter name. Backs have a checklist of the set and information on how retail store owners can send for additional cards to supplement those which were packaged one per box of a dozen garters.

		NM	EX	VG
Complete Set (10):		140,000	70,000	42,500
Common Player:		15,000	7,500	4,500
1	Christy Mathewson	35,000	20,000	12,500
2	Red Murray	7,500	3,750	2,250
3	Eddie Collins	15,000	7,500	4,500
4	Hugh Jennings	15,000	7,500	4,500
5	Hal Chase	12,000	6,000	3,600
6	Bob Bescher	7,500	3,750	2,250
7	Red Dooin	7,500	3,750	2,250
8	Larry Lajoie	15,000	7,500	4,500
9	Tris Speaker	20,000	10,000	6,000
10	Heinie Zimmerman	7,500	3,750	2,250

1909 Boston Herald Supplements

Members of the Red Sox and Braves were featured in this series of supplements in the Boston Sunday Herald. About 7-1/4" x 9-3/4", the blank-back, posed-action pictures are sepia toned. A black box at bottom has player identification, an issue date and a note to "See Story on Sporting Page." While the pictures themselves are numbered, this checklist, almost certainly incomplete, is arranged alphabetically. Some of the pictures show cross-town rivals on the same piece.

		NM	EX	VG
BOSTON BRAVES				
(1)	Chick Autry	200.00	100.00	60.00
(2)	Johnny Bates	200.00	100.00	60.00
(3)	Ginger Beaumont	200.00	100.00	60.00
(4)	Beals Becker	200.00	100.00	60.00
(5)	Frank Bowerman	200.00	100.00	60.00
(6)	Jack Coffey	200.00	100.00	60.00
(7)	Peaches Graham	200.00	100.00	60.00
(8)	Al Mattern	200.00	100.00	60.00
(9)	Harry Smith	200.00	100.00	60.00
(10)	Bill Sweeney	200.00	100.00	60.00
("Tom") Thomas H. Tuckey		200.00	100.00	60.00
BOSTON RED SOX				
(1)	Charlie Chech	200.00	100.00	60.00

(2)	Bill Carrigan	200.00	100.00	60.00
(3)	Pat Donahue	200.00	100.00	60.00
(4)	"Doc" (Harry H.) Gessler	200.00	100.00	60.00
(5)	Harry Hooper	300.00	150.00	90.00
(5)	Harry Lord	200.00	100.00	60.00
(6)	Amby McConnell	200.00	100.00	60.00
(7)	Harry Niles	200.00	100.00	60.00
(8)	Tris Speaker	400.00	200.00	120.00
BOSTON BRAVES/RED SOX				
(1)	Johnny Bates, Harry Hooper	150.00	75.00	45.00
(2)	Ginger Beaumont, Tris Speaker	150.00	75.00	45.00
(3)	Ed Cicotte, Tommy Tuckey	250.00	125.00	75.00
(4)	Bill Dahlen, Heinie Wagner	150.00	75.00	45.00
(5)	Doc Gessler, Frank Bowerman	150.00	75.00	45.00
(6)	Harry Lord, Unknown Brave	150.00	75.00	45.00
(7)	Amby McConnell, Jack Coffey	150.00	75.00	45.00
(8)	Harry Smith, Pat Donahue	150.00	75.00	45.00
(9)	Jake Stahl, Chick Autrey (Autry)	150.00	75.00	45.00

1908 Boston Oyster House Chicago Cubs

 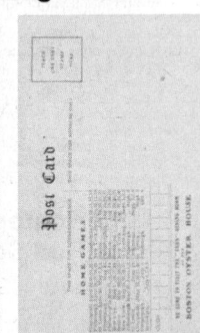

Located in Chicago, not Boston, this restaurant featured, according to its advertising, "The 'Cubs' Dining Room." In keeping with that theme, the business adopted as a promotion the set of Cubs/Teddy Bear postcards issued the previous year by Grignon, a local publisher. The restaurant version has on its back a 1908 Cubs home schedule and rudimentary scorecard, along with standard postcard markings.

	NM	EX	VG
Common Player:	500.00	250.00	150.00
Stars: 1X			

(See 1907 Grignon Chicago Cubs postcards for checklist and base values.)

1908 Boston Red Sox Foldout Postcard

At first glance this standard-size (about 5-1/2" x 3-1/2") postcard reveals on its front only portrait photos of the the owners and grounds of the Boston Red Sox, with a cotter-pinned baseball at left printed in red. Hidden behind the ball, however, is an accordian-folded strip of black-and-white player photos, printed front-to-back, in a size of about 1-1/8" x 1-3/4".

	NM	EX	VG
1908 Boston Red Sox	4,500	2,250	1,350

1910 Boston Red Sox Cabinets

Details are lacking on this high-quality photographic issue depicting the 1910 Red Sox. The sepia photos picture the players in full-length poses and are glued to cardboard mattes. There is no identification on the pieces, nor on the decorative paper folders in which they were apparently originally sold.

		NM	EX	VG
Common Player:		350.00	175.00	100.00
(1)	Hugh Bradley	350.00	175.00	100.00
(2)	Bill Carrigan	350.00	175.00	100.00
(3)	Ed Cicotte	1,000	500.00	300.00
(4)	Ray Collins	350.00	175.00	100.00
(5)	Clyde Engle	350.00	175.00	100.00
(6)	Larry Gardner	350.00	175.00	100.00
(7)	Charley Hall	350.00	175.00	100.00
(8)	Harry Hooper	750.00	375.00	225.00
(9)	Ben Hunt	350.00	175.00	100.00
(10)	Duffy Lewis	500.00	250.00	150.00
(11)	Tom Madden	350.00	175.00	100.00

(12)	Doc Moskiman	350.00 175.00 100.00
(13)	Harry Smith	350.00 175.00 100.00
(14)	Tris Speaker	1,000 500.00 300.00
(15)	Jake Stahl	350.00 175.00 100.00
(16)	Heinie Wagner	350.00 175.00 100.00

1912 Boston Red Sox Tattoos

This set of tattoos is similar to a number of other issues of the era, most of which were made in Germany. This issue features members of the World Champion Boston Red Sox. Approximately 1-3/8" x 1-3/4", the tattoos are printed in mirror-image in bright colors. Images are crude line art with no resemblance to the actual players. Players are identified at bottom by at least a last name. A position is designated in the background of the picture. These items were issued on a perforated sheet. "Collins" may represent retired Red Sox Jimmy Collins or 1912 pitcher Ray Collins. The unnumbered tattoos are listed here alphabetically, though the listing may not be complete.

		NM	EX	VG
Complete Set (13):		475.00	235.00	140.00
Common Player:		35.00	17.50	10.00
1)	Hugh Bedient	35.00	17.50	10.00
2)	Hick Cady	35.00	17.50	10.00
3)	Collins	35.00	17.50	10.00
4)	Clyde Engle	35.00	17.50	10.00
5)	Charley Hall	35.00	17.50	10.00
6)	Martin Krug	35.00	17.50	10.00
7)	Jerry McCarthy/Mascot	35.00	17.50	10.00
8)	Les Nunamaker	35.00	17.50	10.00
9)	Larry Pape	35.00	17.50	10.00
10)	Tris Speaker	125.00	65.00	35.00
11)	Jake Stahl	35.00	17.50	10.00
12)	Heinie Wagner	35.00	17.50	10.00
13)	Joe Wood	50.00	25.00	15.00

1940 Boston Red Sox Photo Pack

Approximately 6" x 9", these blank-back, black-and-white pictures depict the BoSox in (usually) neck-to-cap poses. The pictures are bordered in white and there is a facsimile autograph on each photo.

		NM	EX	VG
Complete Set (25):		300.00	150.00	75.00
Common Player:		8.00	4.00	2.50
1)	Jim Bagby	8.00	4.00	2.50
2)	Bill Butland	8.00	4.00	2.50
3)	Tom Carey	8.00	4.00	2.50
4)	Doc Cramer	8.00	4.00	2.50
5)	Joe Cronin	15.00	7.50	4.50
6)	Gene Desautels	8.00	4.00	2.50
7)	Emerson Dickman	8.00	4.00	2.50
8)	Dom DiMaggio	15.00	7.50	4.50
9)	Bobby Doerr	15.00	7.50	4.50
10)	Lou Finney	8.00	4.00	2.50
11)	Jimmie Foxx	35.00	17.50	10.00
12)	Denny Galehouse	8.00	4.00	2.50
13)	Joe Glenn	8.00	4.00	2.50
14)	Lefty Grove	30.00	15.00	9.00
15)	Mickey Harris	8.00	4.00	2.50
16)	Herbie Hash	8.00	4.00	2.50
17)	Joe Heving	8.00	4.00	2.50
18)	Leo Nonnenkamp	8.00	4.00	2.50
19)	Fritz Ostermueller	8.00	4.00	2.50
20)	Mickey Owen	8.00	4.00	2.50
21)	John Peacock	8.00	4.00	2.50
22)	Jim Tabor	8.00	4.00	2.50
23)	Charles Wagner	8.00	4.00	2.50
24)	Ted Williams	60.00	30.00	18.00
25)	Jack Wilson	8.00	4.00	2.50

1941 Boston Red Sox Photo Pack

Approximately 6" x 9", these blank-back, black-and-white pictures depict the BoSox in informal poses, most leaning on the dugout top step. The pictures are bordered in white and there is a facsimile autograph on each photo. It is possible this checklist (arranged alphabetically) is incomplete as other players may have been added to or deleted from the set to conform to roster changes during the season.

		NM	EX	VG
Complete Set (25):		200.00	100.00	60.00
Common Player:		8.00	4.00	2.50
1)	Paul Campbell			

(2)	Tom Carey	8.00	4.00	2.50
(3)	Joe Cronin	20.00	10.00	6.00
(4)	Emerson Dickman	8.00	4.00	2.50
(5)	Dom DiMaggio	15.00	7.50	4.50
(6)	Joe Dobson	8.00	4.00	2.50
(7)	Bobby Doerr	12.00	6.00	3.50
(8)	Lou Finney	8.00	4.00	2.50
(9)	Bill Fleming	8.00	4.00	2.50
(10)	Pete Fox	8.00	4.00	2.50
(11)	Jimmie Foxx	30.00	15.00	9.00
(12)	Lefty Grove	25.00	12.50	7.50
(13)	Mickey Harris	8.00	4.00	2.50
(14)	Tex Hughson	8.00	4.00	2.50
(15)	Earl Johnson	8.00	4.00	2.50
(16)	Lefty Judd	8.00	4.00	2.50
(17)	Dick Newsome	8.00	4.00	2.50
(18)	Skeeter Newsome	8.00	4.00	2.50
(19)	John Peacock	8.00	4.00	2.50
(20)	Frank Pytlak	8.00	4.00	2.50
(21)	Mike Ryba	8.00	4.00	2.50
(22)	Stan Spence	8.00	4.00	2.50
(23)	Jim Tabor	8.00	4.00	2.50
(24)	Charlie Wagner	8.00	4.00	2.50
(25)	Ted Williams	50.00	25.00	15.00
(26)	Jack Wilson	8.00	4.00	2.50

1942 Boston Red Sox Photo Pack

In a format of approximately 6-1/2" x 9", these team-issued player portraits are blank-backed, black-and-white with a white border. Most photos are chest-to-cap presentations and all have a facsimile autograph. Some of the players in the issue can be seen wearing the "HEALTH" patch which MLB adopted during World War II. This checklist may not be complete as it is possible some players were added or deleted from the set to reflect mid-season roster moves.

		NM	EX	VG
Complete Set (25):		275.00	135.00	85.00
Common Player:		10.00	5.00	3.00
(1)	Mace Brown	10.00	5.00	3.00
(2)	Bill Butland	10.00	5.00	3.00
(3)	Paul Campbell	10.00	5.00	3.00
(4)	Tom Carey	10.00	5.00	3.00
(5)	Ken Chase	10.00	5.00	3.00
(6)	Bill Conroy	10.00	5.00	3.00
(7)	Joe Cronin	20.00	10.00	6.00
(8)	Dom DiMaggio	20.00	10.00	6.00
(9)	Joe Dobson	10.00	5.00	3.00
(10)	Bobby Doerr	20.00	10.00	6.00
(11)	Lou Finney	10.00	5.00	3.00
(12)	Pete Fox	10.00	5.00	3.00
(13)	Jimmie Foxx	40.00	20.00	12.00
(14)	Tex Hughson	10.00	5.00	3.00
(15)	Oscar Judd	10.00	5.00	3.00
(16)	Tony Lupien	10.00	5.00	3.00
(17)	Dick Newsome	10.00	5.00	3.00
(18)	Skeeter Newsome	10.00	5.00	3.00
(19)	John Peacock	10.00	5.00	3.00
(20)	Johnny Pesky	10.00	5.00	3.00
(21)	Mike Ryba	10.00	5.00	3.00
(22)	Jim Tabor	10.00	5.00	3.00
(23)	Yank Terry	10.00	5.00	3.00
(24)	Charlie Wagner	10.00	5.00	3.00
(25)	Ted Williams	60.00	30.00	18.00

1943 Boston Red Sox Photo Pack

In a format of approximately 6-1/2" x 9", these team-issued player portraits are blank-backed, black-and-white with a white border. Most photos are chest-to-cap presentations and all have a facsimile autograph. Some of the players in the issue can be seen wearing the "HEALTH" patch which MLB adopted during World War II. This checklist may not be complete as it is possible some players were added or deleted from the set to reflect mid-season roster moves.

		NM	EX	VG
Complete Set (24):		125.00	65.00	40.00
Common Player:		8.00	4.00	2.50
(1)	Mace Brown	8.00	4.00	2.50
(2)	Ken Chase	8.00	4.00	2.50
(3)	Bill Conroy	8.00	4.00	2.50
(4)	Joe Cronin	15.00	7.50	4.50
(5)	Joe Dobson	8.00	4.00	2.50
(6)	Bobby Doerr	15.00	7.50	4.50
(7)	Pete Fox	8.00	4.00	2.50
(8)	Ford Garrison	8.00	4.00	2.50
(9)	Tex Hughson	8.00	4.00	2.50
(10)	Oscar Judd	8.00	4.00	2.50
(11)	Andy Karl	8.00	4.00	2.50
(12)	Eddie Lake	8.00	4.00	2.50
(13)	John Lazor	8.00	4.00	2.50
(14)	Lou Lupien	10.00	5.00	3.00
(15)	Tony Lupien	8.00	4.00	2.50
(16)	Dee Miles	8.00	4.00	2.50
(17)	Dick Newsome	8.00	4.00	2.50
(18)	Skeeter Newsome	8.00	4.00	2.50
(19)	Roy Partee	8.00	4.00	2.50
(20)	John Peacock	8.00	4.00	2.50
(21)	Mike Ryba	8.00	4.00	2.50
(22)	Al Simmons	15.00	7.50	4.50
(23)	Jim Tabor	8.00	4.00	2.50
(24)	Yank Terry	8.00	4.00	2.50

1946 Boston Red Sox Photo Pack

The American League champion Red Sox are featured in this team-issue photo pack. The player portraits are printed in black-and-white on heavy paper in 6-1/2" x 9" format. The photos have a white border and a facsimile autograph on front. Backs are blank. The unnumbered pictures are listed here in alphabetical order.

		NM	EX	VG
Complete Set (25):		225.00	110.00	65.00
Common Player:		6.00	3.00	1.75
(1)	Ernie Andres	6.00	3.00	1.75
(2)	Jim Bagby	6.00	3.00	1.75
(3)	Mace Brown	6.00	3.00	1.75
(4)	Joe Cronin	12.00	6.00	3.50
(5)	Leon Culbertson	6.00	3.00	1.75
(6)	Mel Deutsch	6.00	3.00	1.75
(7)	Dom DiMaggio	10.00	5.00	3.00
(8)	Joe Dobson	6.00	3.00	1.75
(9)	Bobby Doerr	12.00	6.00	3.50
(10)	Boo Ferriss	6.00	3.00	1.75
(11)	Mickey Harris	6.00	3.00	1.75
(12)	Randy Heflin	6.00	3.00	1.75
(13)	Tex Hughson	6.00	3.00	1.75
(14)	Earl Johnson	6.00	3.00	1.75
(15)	Ed McGah	6.00	3.00	1.75
(16)	George Metkovich	6.00	3.00	1.75
(17)	Roy Partee	6.00	3.00	1.75
(18)	Eddie Pellagrini	6.00	3.00	1.75
(19)	Johnny Pesky	7.50	3.75	2.25
(20)	Rip Russell	6.00	3.00	1.75
(21)	Mike Ryba	6.00	3.00	1.75
(22)	Charlie Wagner	6.00	3.00	1.75
(23)	Hal Wagner	6.00	3.00	1.75
(24)	Ted Williams	60.00	30.00	18.00
(25)	Rudy York	6.00	3.00	1.75

1947 Boston Red Sox Photo Pack

In the same 6-1/2" x 9" format which the team had used for its photo packs since 1942, this set of black-and-white, blank-back pictures features (usually) chest-to-cap portraits with white borders, a dark background and a facsimile autograph within the picture. Some of the photos were re-used from previous years' issues, or were re-issued in subsequent years. The unnumbered pictures are checklisted here in alphabetical order. This list may or may not be complete; it is possible other players' photos were added or deleted to reflect seasonal roster changes.

		NM	EX	VG
Complete Set (25):		200.00	100.00	60.00
Common Player:		6.00	3.00	1.75
(1)	Joe Cronin	15.00	7.50	4.50
(2)	Leon Culberson	6.00	3.00	1.75
(3)	Dom DiMaggio	12.50	6.25	3.75
(4)	Joseph Dobson	6.00	3.00	1.75
(5)	Bobby Doerr	15.00	7.50	4.50
(6)	Harry Dorish	6.00	3.00	1.75
(7)	Dave "Boo" Ferriss	6.00	3.00	1.75
(8)	Tommy Fine	6.00	3.00	1.75
(9)	Don Gutteridge	6.00	3.00	1.75
(10)	Mickey Harris	6.00	3.00	1.75
(11)	Tex Hughson	6.00	3.00	1.75
(12)	Earl Johnson	6.00	3.00	1.75
(13)	Bob Klinger	6.00	3.00	1.75
(14)	Sam Mele	6.00	3.00	1.75
(15)	Wally Moses	6.00	3.00	1.75
(16)	Johnny Murphy	6.00	3.00	1.75
(17)	Mel Parnell	6.00	3.00	1.75
(18)	Roy Partee	6.00	3.00	1.75
(19)	Eddie Pellagrini	6.00	3.00	1.75
(20)	Johnny Pesky	7.50	3.75	2.25
(21)	Rip Russell	6.00	3.00	1.75
(22)	Birdie Tebbetts	6.00	3.00	1.75
(23)	Ted Williams	60.00	30.00	18.00
(24)	Rudy York	6.00	3.00	1.75
(25)	Bill Zuber	6.00	3.00	1.75

1948 Boston Red Sox Photo Pack

In the same 6-1/2" x 9" format which the team had used for its photo packs since 1942, this set of black-and-white, blank-back pictures features (usually) chest-to-cap portraits with white borders, a dark background and a facsimile autograph within the picture. Some of the photos were re-used from previous years' issues, or were re-issued in subsequent years. The unnumbered pictures are checklisted here in alphabetical order. This list may or may not be complete; it is possible other players' photos were added or deleted to reflect seasonal roster changes.

		NM	EX	VG
Complete Set (25):		200.00	100.00	60.00
Common Player:		6.00	3.00	1.75
(1)	Matt Batts	6.00	3.00	1.75
(2)	Dom DiMaggio	15.00	7.50	4.50
(3)	Joseph Dobson	6.00	3.00	1.75
(4)	Bobby Doerr	15.00	7.50	4.50
(5)	Harry Dorish	6.00	3.00	1.75
(6)	Dave "Boo" Ferriss	6.00	3.00	1.75
(7)	Dennis Galehouse	6.00	3.00	1.75
(8)	Billy Goodman	6.00	3.00	1.75
(9)	Mickey Harris	6.00	3.00	1.75
(10)	Bill Hitchcock	6.00	3.00	1.75
(11)	Earl Johnson	6.00	3.00	1.75
(12)	Jake Jones	6.00	3.00	1.75
(13)	Ellis Kinder	6.00	3.00	1.75
(14)	Jack Kramer	6.00	3.00	1.75
(15)	Joe McCarthy	15.00	7.50	4.50
(16)	Maurice McDermott	6.00	3.00	1.75
(17)	Sam Mele	6.00	3.00	1.75
(18)	Wally Moses	6.00	3.00	1.75
(19)	Mel Parnell	6.00	3.00	1.75

		NM	EX	VG
(20)	Johnny Pesky	7.50	3.75	2.25
(21)	Stan Spence	6.00	3.00	1.75
(22)	Vern Stephens	6.00	3.00	1.75
(23)	Chuck Stobbs	6.00	3.00	1.75
(24)	Birdie Tebbetts	6.00	3.00	1.75
(25)	Ted Williams	60.00	30.00	18.00

1949 Boston Red Sox Photo Pack

In the same 6-1/2" x 9" format the team used for its photo packs since 1942, this set of black-and-white, blank-back pictures features (usually) chest-to-cap portraits with white borders, a dark background and a facsimile autographs within the picture. Some of the photos were re-used from previous years' issues, or were re-issued in subsequent years. The unnumbered pictures are checklisted here in alphabetical order.

		NM	EX	VG
Complete Set (25):		200.00	100.00	60.00
Common Player:		6.00	3.00	1.80
(1)	Matt Batts	6.00	3.00	1.80
(2)	Merrill Combs	6.00	3.00	1.80
(3)	Dom DiMaggio	15.00	7.50	4.50
(4)	Joe Dobson	6.00	3.00	1.80
(5)	Bobby Doerr	15.00	7.50	4.50
(6)	David "Boo" Ferris	6.00	3.00	1.80
(7)	Bill Goodman	6.00	3.00	1.80
(8)	Mickey Harris	6.00	3.00	1.80
(9)	Billy Hitchcock	6.00	3.00	1.80
(10)	Tex Hughson	6.00	3.00	1.80
(11)	Earl Johnson	6.00	3.00	1.80
(12)	Ellis Kinder	6.00	3.00	1.80
(13)	Jack Kramer	6.00	3.00	1.80
(14)	Joe McCarthy	15.00	7.50	4.50
(15)	Sam Mele	6.00	3.00	1.80
(16)	Tommy O'Brien	6.00	3.00	1.80
(17)	Mel Parnell	6.00	3.00	1.80
(18)	Johnny Pesky	6.00	3.00	1.80
(19)	Frank Quinn	6.00	3.00	1.80
(20)	Vern Stephens	6.00	3.00	1.80
(21)	Chuck Stobbs	6.00	3.00	1.80
(22)	Lou Stringer	6.00	3.00	1.80
(23)	Birdie Tebbetts	6.00	3.00	1.80
(24)	Ted Williams	60.00	30.00	18.00
(25)	Al Zarilla	6.00	3.00	1.80

1950 Boston Red Sox Photo Pack

In the same approximately 6-1/2" x 9" format which the team had used for its photo packs since the 1940s, this set of black-and-white, blank-back pictures features (usually) chest-to-cap portraits with white borders, a dark background and a facsimile autograph within the photo. Some of the photos were re-used from previous years' issues. The unnumbered pictures are checklisted here in alphabetical order. This list may or may not be complete; it is possible other players' photos were added or deleted to reflect seasonal roster changes.

	NM	EX	VG
Complete Set (25):	150.00	75.00	40.00

Common Player:		4.00	2.00	1.25
(1)	Matt Batts	4.00	2.00	1.25
(2)	Earle Combs	7.50	3.75	2.25
(3)	Dom DiMaggio	9.00	4.50	2.75
(4)	Joe Dobson	4.00	2.00	1.25
(5)	Bobby Doerr	9.00	4.50	2.75
(6)	Walt Dropo	12.00	6.00	3.50
(7)	Bill Goodman	4.00	2.00	1.25
(8)	Earl Johnson	4.00	2.00	1.25
(9)	Ken Keltner	4.00	2.00	1.25
(10)	Ellis Kinder	4.00	2.00	1.25
(11)	Walt Masterson	4.00	2.00	1.25
(12)	Joe McCarthy	9.00	4.50	2.75
(13)	Maurice McDermott	4.00	2.00	1.25
(14)	Al Papai	4.00	2.00	1.25
(15)	Mel Parnell	4.00	2.00	1.25
(16)	Johnny Pesky	4.00	2.00	1.25
(17)	Buddy Rosar	4.00	2.00	1.25
(18)	Charley Schanz	4.00	2.00	1.25
(19)	Vern Stephens	4.00	2.00	1.25
(20)	Chuck Stobbs	4.00	2.00	1.25
(21)	Lou Stringer	4.00	2.00	1.25
(22)	Birdie Tebbetts	4.00	2.00	1.25
(23)	Ted Williams	30.00	15.00	9.00
(24)	Tom Wright	4.00	2.00	1.25
(25)	Al Zarilla	4.00	2.00	1.25

1953 Boston Red Sox Photo Pack

In the same approximately 61/2" x 9" format which the team had used for its photo packs since the 1940s, this set of black-and-white, blank-back pictures features (usually) chest-to-cap portraits with white borders and a facsimile autograph within the photo. Some of the photos were re-used from previous years' issues. The unnumbered pictures are checklisted here in alphabetical order. This list may or may not be complete; it is possible other players' photos were added or deleted to reflect seasonal roster changes.

		NM	EX	VG
Complete Set (30):		120.00	60.00	35.00
Common Player:		4.00	2.00	1.2
(1)	Milt Bolling	4.00	2.00	1.2
(2)	Lou Boudreau	9.00	4.50	2.7
(3)	Harold Brown	4.00	2.00	1.2
(4)	Bill Consolo	4.00	2.00	1.2
(5)	Dom DiMaggio	15.00	7.50	4.5
(6)	Hoot Evers	4.00	2.00	1.2
(7)	Ben Flowers	4.00	2.00	1.2
(8)	Hershell Freeman	4.00	2.00	1.2
(9)	Dick Gernert	4.00	2.00	1.2
(10)	Bill Goodman	4.00	2.00	1.2
(11)	Marv Grissom	4.00	2.00	1.2
(12)	Ken Holcombe	4.00	2.00	1.2
(13)	Sid Hudson	4.00	2.00	1.2
(14)	George Kell	9.00	4.50	2.7
(15)	Bill Kennedy	4.00	2.00	1.2
(16)	Ellis Kinder	4.00	2.00	1.2
(17)	Ted Lepcio	4.00	2.00	1.2
(18)	Johnny Lipon	4.00	2.00	1.2
(19)	Maurice McDermott	4.00	2.00	1.2
(20)	John Merson	4.00	2.00	1.2
(21)	Gus Niarhos	4.00	2.00	1.2
(22)	Willard Nixon	4.00	2.00	1.2
(23)	Mel Parnell	4.00	2.00	1.2
(24)	Jim Piersall	6.00	3.00	1.7
(25)	Gene Stephens	4.00	2.00	1.2
(26)	Tommy Umphlett	4.00	2.00	1.2
(27)	Bill Werle	4.00	2.00	1.2
(28)	Sam White	4.00	2.00	1.2
(29)	Del Wilber	4.00	2.00	1.2
(30)	Al Zarilla	4.00	2.00	1.2

1954 Boston Red Sox Photo Pack

In the same approximately 6-1/2" x 9" format which the team had used for its photo packs since the 1940s, this set of black-and-white, blank-back pictures features (usually) chest-to-cap portraits with white borders and a facsimile autograph within the photo. Some of the photos were re-used from previous years' issues. The unnumbered pictures are checklisted here in alphabetical...

cal order. This list may or may not be complete; it is possible other players' photos were added or deleted to reflect seasonal roster changes. The set was sold in a red and white paper envelope.

		NM	EX	VG
Complete Set (30):		125.00	62.50	37.50
Common Player:		4.00	2.00	1.25
(1)	Harry Agganis	15.00	7.50	4.50
(2)	Milt Bolling	4.00	2.00	1.25
(3)	Lou Boudreau	9.00	4.50	2.75
(4)	Tom Brewer	4.00	2.00	1.25
(5)	Harold Brown	4.00	2.00	1.25
(6)	Truman Clevenger	4.00	2.00	1.25
(7)	Bill Consolo	4.00	2.00	1.25
(8)	Joe Dobson	4.00	2.00	1.25
(9)	Hoot Evers	4.00	2.00	1.25
(10)	Dick Gernert	4.00	2.00	1.25
(11)	Bill Goodman	4.00	2.00	1.25
(12)	Bill Henry	4.00	2.00	1.25
(13)	Tom Herrin	4.00	2.00	1.25
(14)	Sid Hudson	4.00	2.00	1.25
(15)	Jackie Jensen	6.00	3.00	1.75
(16)	George Kell	9.00	4.50	2.75
(17)	Leo Kiely	4.00	2.00	1.25
(18)	Ellis Kinder	4.00	2.00	1.25
(19)	Ted Lepcio	4.00	2.00	1.25
(20)	Charlie Maxwell	4.00	2.00	1.25
(21)	Willard Nixon	4.00	2.00	1.25
(22)	Karl Olsen	4.00	2.00	1.25
(23)	Mickey Owen	4.00	2.00	1.25
(24)	Mel Parnell	4.00	2.00	1.25
(25)	Jim Piersall	6.00	3.00	1.75
(26)	Frank Sullivan	4.00	2.00	1.25
(27)	Bill Werle	4.00	2.00	1.25
(28)	Sammy White	4.00	2.00	1.25
(29)	Ted Williams	30.00	15.00	9.00
(30)	Del Wilber	4.00	2.00	1.25

1957 Boston Red Sox Photo Pack

JIMMY PIERSALL

In approximately the same 5" x 7" black-and-white, blank-back format as the later Jay Publishing issues, this team issue is distinguished by the lack of a team name in the bottom border. Some of the photos were re-used in the following year's issue. Sets were originally sold in a manila envelope for 25 cents.

		NM	EX	VG
Complete Set (12):		45.00	22.00	13.50
Common Player:		3.00	1.50	.90
(1)	Tom Brewer	3.00	1.50	.90
(2)	Dick Gernert	3.00	1.50	.90
(3)	Mike Higgins	3.00	1.50	.90
(4)	Jackie Jensen	4.50	2.25	1.25
(5)	Frank Malzone	3.00	1.50	.90
(6)	Gene Mauch	4.50	2.25	1.25
(7)	Jimmy Piersall	4.50	2.25	1.25
(8)	Dave Sisler	3.00	1.50	.90
(9)	Frank Sullivan	3.00	1.50	.90
(10)	Mickey Vernon	3.00	1.50	.90
(11)	Sammy White	3.00	1.50	.90
(12)	Ted Williams	20.00	10.00	6.00

1958 Boston Red Sox Photo Pack

In approximately the same 5" x 7" black-and-white, blank-back format as the contemporary Jay Publishing issues, this team issue is distinguished by the lack of a team name in the bottom border. Some of the photos were re-used from the previous year's issue. Sets were originally sold in a manila envelope for 25 cents.

		NM	EX	VG
Complete Set (12):		45.00	22.00	13.50
Common Player:		3.00	1.50	.90
(1)	Ken Aspromonte	3.00	1.50	.90
(2)	Tom Brewer	3.00	1.50	.90
(3)	Mike Higgins	3.00	1.50	.90
(4)	Jack Jensen	4.50	2.25	1.25
(5)	Frank Malzone	3.00	1.50	.90
(6)	Will Nixon	3.00	1.50	.90
(7)	Jim Piersall	4.50	2.25	1.25
(8)	Pete Runnels	3.00	1.50	.90
(9)	Gene Stephens	3.00	1.50	.90
(10)	Frank Sullivan	3.00	1.50	.90
(11)	Sam White	3.00	1.50	.90
(12)	Ted Williams	20.00	10.00	6.00

1959 Boston Red Sox Photo Pack

In approximately the same 5" x 7" black-and-white, blank-back format as the contemporary Jay Publishing issues, this team issue is distinguished by the lack of a team name in the bottom border. Some of the photos were re-used from the previous years' issues. Sets were originally sold in a manila envelope for 25 cents.

		NM	EX	VG
Complete Set (12):		45.00	22.00	13.50
Common Player:		3.00	1.50	.90
(1)	Tom Brewer	3.00	1.50	.90
(2)	Don Buddin	3.00	1.50	.90
(3)	Dick Gernert	3.00	1.50	.90
(4)	Mike Higgins	3.00	1.50	.90
(5)	Jack Jensen	4.50	2.25	1.25
(6)	Frank Malzone	3.00	1.50	.90
(7)	Jim Piersall	4.50	2.25	1.25
(8)	Pete Runnels	3.00	1.50	.90
(9)	Gene Stephens	3.00	1.50	.90
(10)	Frank Sullivan	3.00	1.50	.90
(11)	Sam White	3.00	1.50	.90
(12)	Ted Williams	20.00	10.00	6.00

1960 Boston Red Sox Photo Pack

In approximately the same 5" x 7" black-and-white, blank-back format as the contemporary Jay Publishing issues, this team issue is distinguished by the lack of a team name in the bottom border. Some of the photos were re-used from the previous years' issues. Sets were originally sold in a manila envelope for 25 cents. The fact that more than 12 players are known indicates there were some changes in specific contents over the course of the season to reflect roster changes.

		NM	EX	VG
Complete Set (14):		50.00	25.00	15.00
Common Player:		3.00	1.50	.90
(1)	Tom Brewer	3.00	1.50	.90
(2)	Don Buddin	3.00	1.50	.90
(3)	Jerry Casale	3.00	1.50	.90
(4)	Ike Delock	3.00	1.50	.90
(5)	Pumpsie Green	3.00	1.50	.90
(6)	Bill Jurges	3.00	1.50	.90
(7)	Frank Malzone	3.00	1.50	.90
(8)	Pete Runnels	3.00	1.50	.90
(9)	Ed Sadowski	3.00	1.50	.90
(10)	Gene Stephens	3.00	1.50	.90
(11)	Willie Tasby	3.00	1.50	.90
(12)	Bobby Thomson	3.00	1.50	.90
(13)	Vic Wertz	3.00	1.50	.90
(14)	Ted Williams	20.00	10.00	6.00

1968 Boston Red Sox Team Issue

About 5-1/2" x 7-1/2", these black-and-white player pictures have posed photos, bordered in white, with a facsimile autograph. Backs are blank. The alphabetized checklist here is likely incomplete.

		NM	EX	VG
Complete Set (8):		15.00	7.50	4.50
Common Player:		2.00	1.00	.60
(1a)	Mike Andrews ("B" on cap.)	2.00	1.00	.60
(1b)	Mike Andrews (No "B.")	2.00	1.00	.60
(2)	Darrell Brandon	2.00	1.00	.60
(3)	Bobby Doerr	3.00	1.50	.90
(4)	Ken Harrelson	2.50	1.25	.70
(5)	Jim Lonborg	2.50	1.25	.70
(6)	Rico Petrocelli	3.00	1.50	.90
(7)	Reggie Smith	2.50	1.25	.70
(8)	Dick Williams	2.00	1.00	.60

1969 Boston Red Sox Team Issue

This team-issue photo pack features black-and-white portrait photos on a 4-1/4" x 7" blank-back format, similar to the team's 1971 issue. The player's name and team nickname are designated in the white border at top. The unnumbered cards are checklisted here in alphabetical order.

		NM	EX	VG
Complete Set (12):		60.00	30.00	15.00
Common Player:		4.00	2.00	1.25
(1)	Mike Andrews	4.00	2.00	1.25
(2)	Tony Conigliaro	9.00	4.50	2.75
(3)	Russ Gibson	4.00	2.00	1.25
(4)	Dalton Jones	4.00	2.00	1.25
(5)	Bill Landis	4.00	2.00	1.25
(6)	Jim Lonborg	5.00	2.50	1.50
(7)	Sparky Lyle	4.00	2.00	1.25
(8)	Rico Petrocelli	5.00	2.50	1.50
(9)	George Scott	5.00	2.50	1.50
(10)	Reggie Smith	4.00	2.00	1.25
(11)	Dick Williams	4.00	2.00	1.25
(12)	Carl Yastrzemski	15.00	7.50	4.50

1978 Boston Red Sox of the 1950s-1960s

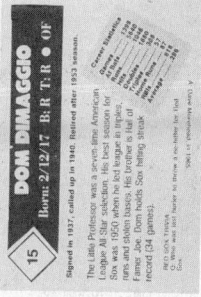

The date of actual issue, the name of the issuer and even the "official" title of this collectors' edition card set is currently unknown. The 2-1/2" x 3-1/2" cards are printed in black-and-white on front and backs. Fronts have the style of the 1953 Bowmans, with only a player photo and a white border. Backs are reminiscent of the 1955 Bowman, with player identification, career highlights, stats and a Red Sox trivia question. Cards #1-64 concentrate on the 1950s, cards #65-128 feature 1960s players.

		NM	EX	VG
Complete Set (128):		100.00	50.00	30.00
Common Player:		4.00	2.00	1.25
1	Harry Agganis	12.00	6.00	3.50
2	Ken Aspromonte	4.00	2.00	1.25
3	Bobby Avila	4.00	2.00	1.25
4	Frank Baumann	4.00	2.00	1.25
5	Lou Berberet	4.00	2.00	1.25
6	Milt Bolling	4.00	2.00	1.25
7	Lou Boudreau	6.00	3.00	1.75
8	Ted Bowsfield	4.00	2.00	1.25
9	Tom Brewer	4.00	2.00	1.25
10	Don Buddin	4.00	2.00	1.25
11	Jerry Casale	4.00	2.00	1.25
12	Billy Consolo	4.00	2.00	1.25
13	Pete Daley	4.00	2.00	1.25
14	Ike Delock	4.00	2.00	1.25
15	Dom DiMaggio	9.00	4.50	2.75
16	Bobby Doerr	6.00	3.00	1.75
17	Walt Dropo	5.00	2.50	1.50
18	Arnie Earley	4.00	2.00	1.25
19	Hoot Evers	4.00	2.00	1.25
20	Mike Fornieles	4.00	2.00	1.25
21	Gary Geiger	4.00	2.00	1.25
22	Don Gile	4.00	2.00	1.25
23	Joe Ginsberg	4.00	2.00	1.25
24	Billy Goodman	4.00	2.00	1.25
25	Pumpsie Green	4.00	2.00	1.25
26	Grady Hatton	4.00	2.00	1.25
27	Billy Herman	5.00	2.50	1.50
28	Jackie Jensen	5.00	2.50	1.50
29	George Kell	6.00	3.00	1.75
30	Marty Keough	4.00	2.00	1.25

31	Leo Kiely	4.00	2.00	1.25
32	Ellis Kinder	4.00	2.00	1.25
33	Billy Klaus	4.00	2.00	1.25
34	Don Lenhardt	4.00	2.00	1.25
35	Ted Lepcio	4.00	2.00	1.25
36	Frank Malzone	4.00	2.00	1.25
37	Gene Mauch	4.00	2.00	1.25
38	Maury McDermott	4.00	2.00	1.25
39	Bill Monbouquette	4.00	2.00	1.25
40	Chet Nichols	4.00	2.00	1.25
41	Willard Nixon	4.00	2.00	1.25
42	Jim Pagliaroni	4.00	2.00	1.25
43	Mel Parnell	4.00	2.00	1.25
44	Johnny Pesky	4.00	2.00	1.25
45	Jimmy Piersall	5.00	2.50	1.50
46	Bob Porterfield	4.00	2.00	1.25
47	Pete Runnels	4.00	2.00	1.25
48	Dave Sisler	4.00	2.00	1.25
49	Riverboat Smith	4.00	2.00	1.25
50	Gene Stephens	4.00	2.00	1.25
51	Vern Stephens	4.00	2.00	1.25
52	Chuck Stobbs	4.00	2.00	1.25
53	Dean Stone	4.00	2.00	1.25
54	Frank Sullivan	4.00	2.00	1.25
55	Haywood Sullivan	4.00	2.00	1.25
56	Birdie Tebbetts	4.00	2.00	1.25
57	Mickey Vernon	4.00	2.00	1.25
58	Vic Wertz	4.00	2.00	1.25
59	Sammy White	4.00	2.00	1.25
60	Ted Williams	20.00	10.00	6.00
61	Ted Wills	4.00	2.00	1.25
62	Earl Wilson	4.00	2.00	1.25
63	Al Zarilla	4.00	2.00	1.25
64	Norm Zauchin	4.00	2.00	1.25
65	Ted Williams, Carl Yastrzemski	12.00	6.00	3.50
66	Dick Williams, Carl Yastrzemski, Jim Lonborg, George Scott	10.00	5.00	3.00
67	Tony Conigliaro, Billy Conigliaro	9.00	4.50	2.75
68	Jerry Adair	4.00	2.00	1.25
69	Mike Andrews	4.00	2.00	1.25
70	Gary Bell	4.00	2.00	1.25
71	Dennis Bennett	4.00	2.00	1.25
72	Ed Bressoud	4.00	2.00	1.25
73	Ken Brett	4.00	2.00	1.25
74	Lu Clinton	4.00	2.00	1.25
75	Billy Conigliaro	5.00	2.50	1.50
76	Tony Conigliaro	6.00	3.00	1.75
77	Gene Conley	4.00	2.00	1.25
78	Ray Culp	4.00	2.00	1.25
79	Dick Ellsworth	4.00	2.00	1.25
80	Joe Foy	4.00	2.00	1.25
81	Russ Gibson	4.00	2.00	1.25
82	Jim Gosger	4.00	2.00	1.25
83	Lennie Green	4.00	2.00	1.25
84	Ken Harrelson	4.00	2.00	1.25
85	Tony Horton	4.00	2.00	1.25
86	Elston Howard	5.00	2.50	1.50
87	Dalton Jones	4.00	2.00	1.25
88	Eddie Kasko	4.00	2.00	1.25
89	Joe Lahoud	4.00	2.00	1.25
90	Jack Lamabe	4.00	2.00	1.25
91	Jim Lonborg	5.00	2.50	1.50
92	Sparky Lyle	5.00	2.50	1.50
93	Felix Mantilla	4.00	2.00	1.25
94	Roman Mejias	4.00	2.00	1.25
95	Don McMahon	4.00	2.00	1.25
96	Dave Morehead	4.00	2.00	1.25
97	Gerry Moses	4.00	2.00	1.25
98	Mike Nagy	4.00	2.00	1.25
99	Russ Nixon	4.00	2.00	1.25
100	Gene Oliver	4.00	2.00	1.25
101	Dan Osinski	4.00	2.00	1.25
102	Rico Petrocelli	5.00	2.50	1.50
103	Juan Pizarro	4.00	2.00	1.25
104	Dick Radatz	4.00	2.00	1.25
105	Vicente Romo	4.00	2.00	1.25
106	Mike Ryan	4.00	2.00	1.25
107	Jose Santiago	4.00	2.00	1.25
108	Chuck Schilling	4.00	2.00	1.25
109	Dick Schofield	4.00	2.00	1.25
110	Don Schwall	4.00	2.00	1.25
111	George Scott	4.00	2.00	1.25
112	Norm Siebern	4.00	2.00	1.25
113	Sonny Siebert	4.00	2.00	1.25
114	Reggie Smith	5.00	2.50	1.50
115	Bill Spanswick	4.00	2.00	1.25
116	Tracy Stallard	4.00	2.00	1.25
117	Lee Stange	4.00	2.00	1.25
118	Jerry Stephenson	4.00	2.00	1.25
119	Dick Stuart	4.00	2.00	1.25
120	Tom Sturdivant	4.00	2.00	1.25
121	Jose Tartabull	4.00	2.00	1.25
122	George Thomas	4.00	2.00	1.25
123	Lee Thomas	4.00	2.00	1.25
124	Bob Tillman	4.00	2.00	1.25
125	Gary Waslewski	4.00	2.00	1.25
126	Dick Williams	4.00	2.00	1.25
127	John Wyatt	4.00	2.00	1.25
128	Carl Yastrzemski	12.00	6.00	3.50

1979 Boston Red Sox Team Issue

The origins of this Boston Red Sox card set are unclear. It may have been a team issue. The wide white bottom border beneath the black-and-white photo on the 2-1/2" x 3-1/2" cards may have been intended for autographing. Backs have player personal data and complete major and minor league stats. The checklist here, listed alphabetically, may not be complete.

		NM	EX	VG
Complete Set (24):		50.00	25.00	15.00
Common Player:		3.00	1.50	.90
(1)	Gary Allenson	3.00	1.50	.90
(2)	Jack Brohamer	3.00	1.50	.90
(3)	Tom Burgmeier	3.00	1.50	.90
(4)	Rick Burleson	3.00	1.50	.90
(5)	Bill Campbell	3.00	1.50	.90
(6)	Dick Drago	3.00	1.50	.90
(7)	Dennis Eckersley	12.00	6.00	3.50
(8)	Dwight Evans	4.50	2.25	1.25
(9)	Carlton Fisk	15.00	7.50	4.50
(10)	Andy Hassler	3.00	1.50	.90
(11)	Butch Hobson	3.00	1.50	.90
(12)	Fred Lynn	7.50	3.75	2.25
(13)	Bob Montgomery	3.00	1.50	.90
(14)	Mike O'Berry	3.00	1.50	.90
(15)	Jerry Remy	3.00	1.50	.90
(16)	Steve Renko	3.00	1.50	.90
(17)	Jim Rice	7.50	3.75	2.25
(18)	George Scott	4.50	2.25	1.25
(19)	Bob Stanley	3.00	1.50	.90
(20)	Mike Torrez	3.00	1.50	.90
(21)	Larry Wolfe	3.00	1.50	.90
(22)	Jim Wright	3.00	1.50	.90
(23)	Carl Yastrzemski	20.00	10.00	6.00
(24)	Gary Hancock, Stan Papi (Two-sided.)	3.00	1.50	.90

1917 Boston Store

ED. KONETCHY
1st B.—Boston Nationals
04

BOYS
Who Want

Clothing — Waists
Hats — Shirts
Caps — Collars
Shoes — Neckwear
Hosiery — Handkerchiefs
Underwear — Gloves

AND

Sporting Goods of Every Sort will have varieties best here— and prices lowest.

Boston Store
STATE MADISON AND DEARBORN STS.

One of several regional advertisers to use this 200-card set as a promotional medium was this Chicago department store. While variations are known of cards #76, 90, 121, 146, and 190 in the Collins-McCarthy ad-back version of this set, it is unclear whether those variations also exist in the Boston Store issue. The American Card Catalog listed these 2" x 3-1/4" black-and-white cards as H801-8.

		NM	EX	VG
Complete Set (200):		80,000	40,000	24,000
Common Player:		150.00	75.00	45.00
1	Sam Agnew	150.00	75.00	45.00
2	Grover Alexander	800.00	400.00	240.00
3	W.S. Alexander (W.E.)	150.00	75.00	45.00
4	Leon Ames	150.00	75.00	45.00
5	Fred Anderson	150.00	75.00	45.00
6	Ed Appleton	150.00	75.00	45.00
7	Jimmy Archer	150.00	75.00	45.00
8	Jimmy Austin	150.00	75.00	45.00
9	Jim Bagby	150.00	75.00	45.00
10	H.D. Baird	150.00	75.00	45.00
11	J. Franklin Baker	500.00	250.00	150.00
12	Dave Bancroft	500.00	250.00	150.00
13	Jack Barry	150.00	75.00	45.00
14	Joe Benz	150.00	75.00	45.00
15	Al Betzel	150.00	75.00	45.00
16	Ping Bodie	150.00	75.00	45.00
17	Joe Boehling	150.00	75.00	45.00
18	Eddie Burns	150.00	75.00	45.00
19	George Burns	150.00	75.00	45.00
20	Geo. J. Burns	150.00	75.00	45.00
21	Joe Bush	150.00	75.00	45.00
22	Owen Bush	150.00	75.00	45.00
23	Bobby Byrne	150.00	75.00	45.00
24	Forrest Cady	150.00	75.00	45.00
25	Max Carey	500.00	250.00	150.00
26	Ray Chapman	200.00	100.00	60.00
27	Larry Cheney	150.00	75.00	45.00
28	Eddie Cicotte	900.00	450.00	275.00
29	Tom Clarke	150.00	75.00	45.00
30	Ty Cobb	4,250	2,125	1,275
31	Eddie Collins	500.00	250.00	150.00

32	"Shauno" Collins (Shano)	150.00	75.00	45.00
33	Fred Coumbe	150.00	75.00	45.00
34	Harry Coveleskie (Coveleski)	150.00	75.00	45.00
35	Gavvy Cravath	150.00	75.00	45.00
36	Sam Crawford	500.00	250.00	150.00
37	Geo. Cutshaw	150.00	75.00	45.00
38	Jake Daubert	150.00	75.00	45.00
39	Geo. Dauss	150.00	75.00	45.00
40	Charles Deal	150.00	75.00	45.00
41	"Wheezer" Dell	150.00	75.00	45.00
42	William Doak	150.00	75.00	45.00
43	Bill Donovan	150.00	75.00	45.00
44	Larry Doyle	150.00	75.00	45.00
45	Johnny Evers	500.00	250.00	150.00
46	Urban Faber	500.00	250.00	150.00
47	"Hap" Felsch	1,500	750.00	450.00
48	Bill Fischer	150.00	75.00	45.00
49	Ray Fisher	150.00	75.00	45.00
50	Art Fletcher	150.00	75.00	45.00
51	Eddie Foster	150.00	75.00	45.00
52	Jacques Fournier	150.00	75.00	45.00
53	Del Gainer (Gainor)	150.00	75.00	45.00
54	Bert Gallia	150.00	75.00	45.00
55	"Chic" Gandil (Chick)	450.00	225.00	135.00
56	Larry Gardner	150.00	75.00	45.00
57	Joe Gedeon	150.00	75.00	45.00
58	Gus Getz	150.00	75.00	45.00
59	Frank Gilhooley	150.00	75.00	45.00
60	Wm. Gleason	150.00	75.00	45.00
61	M.A. Gonzales (Gonzalez)	200.00	100.00	60.00
62	Hank Gowdy	150.00	75.00	45.00
63	John Graney	150.00	75.00	45.00
64	Tom Griffith	150.00	75.00	45.00
65	Heinie Groh	150.00	75.00	45.00
66	Bob Groom	150.00	75.00	45.00
67	Louis Guisto	150.00	75.00	45.00
68	Earl Hamilton	150.00	75.00	45.00
69	Harry Harper	150.00	75.00	45.00
70	Grover Hartley	150.00	75.00	45.00
71	Harry Heilmann	500.00	250.00	150.00
72	Claude Hendrix	150.00	75.00	45.00
73	Olaf Henriksen	150.00	75.00	45.00
74	John Henry	150.00	75.00	45.00
75	"Buck" Herzog	150.00	75.00	45.00
76a	Hugh High (White stockings, photo actually Claude Williams.)	400.00	200.00	120.00
76b	Hugh High (Black stockings, correct photo.)	200.00	100.00	60.00
77	Dick Hoblitzell	150.00	75.00	45.00
78	Walter Holke	150.00	75.00	45.00
79	Harry Hooper	500.00	250.00	150.00
80	Rogers Hornsby	750.00	375.00	225.00
81	Ivan Howard	150.00	75.00	45.00
82	Joe Jackson	12,500	6,250	3,750
83	Harold Janvrin	150.00	75.00	45.00
84	William James	150.00	75.00	45.00
85	C. Jamieson	150.00	75.00	45.00
86	Hugh Jennings	500.00	250.00	150.00
87	Walter Johnson	1,100	550.00	330.00
88	James Johnston	150.00	75.00	45.00
89	Fielder Jones	150.00	75.00	45.00
90a	Joe Judge (Bat on right shoulder, photo actually Ray Morgan.)	400.00	200.00	120.00
90b	Joe Judge (Bat on left shoulder, correct photo.)	200.00	100.00	60.00
91	Hans Lobert	150.00	75.00	45.00
92	Benny Kauff	150.00	75.00	45.00
93	Wm. Killefer Jr.	150.00	75.00	45.00
94	Ed. Konetchy	150.00	75.00	45.00
95	John Lavan	150.00	75.00	45.00
96	Jimmy Lavender	150.00	75.00	45.00
97	"Nemo" Leibold	150.00	75.00	45.00
98	H.B. Leonard	150.00	75.00	45.00
99	Duffy Lewis	150.00	75.00	45.00
100	Tom Long	150.00	75.00	45.00
101	Wm. Louden	150.00	75.00	45.00
102	Fred Luderus	150.00	75.00	45.00
103	Lee Magee	150.00	75.00	45.00
104	Sherwood Magee	150.00	75.00	45.00
105	Al Mamaux	150.00	75.00	45.00
106	Leslie Mann	150.00	75.00	45.00
107	"Rabbit" Maranville	500.00	250.00	150.00
108	Rube Marquard	500.00	250.00	150.00
109	Armando Marsans	240.00	120.00	72.00
110	J. Erskine Mayer	150.00	75.00	45.00
111	George McBride	150.00	75.00	45.00
112	Lew McCarty	150.00	75.00	45.00
113	John J. McGraw	500.00	250.00	150.00
114	Jack McInnis	150.00	75.00	45.00
115	Lee Meadows	150.00	75.00	45.00
116	Fred Merkle	150.00	75.00	45.00
117	"Chief" Meyers	150.00	75.00	45.00
118	Clyde Milan	150.00	75.00	45.00
119	Otto Miller	150.00	75.00	45.00
120	Clarence Mitchell	150.00	75.00	45.00
121a	Ray Morgan (Bat on left shoulder, photo actually Joe Judge.)	400.00	200.00	120.00
121b	Ray Morgan (Bat on right shoulder, correct photo.)	200.00	100.00	60.00
122	Guy Morton	150.00	75.00	45.00
123	"Mike" Mowrey	150.00	75.00	45.00
124	Elmer Myers	150.00	75.00	45.00
125	"Hy" Myers	150.00	75.00	45.00
126	A.E. Neale	300.00	150.00	90.00
127	Arthur Nehf	150.00	75.00	45.00
128	J.A. Niehoff	150.00	75.00	45.00
129	Steve O'Neill	150.00	75.00	45.00
130	"Dode" Paskert	150.00	75.00	45.00
131	Roger Peckinpaugh	200.00	100.00	60.00
132	"Pol" Perritt	150.00	75.00	45.00
133	"Jeff" Pfeffer	150.00	75.00	45.00
134	Walter Pipp	150.00	75.00	45.00
135	Derril Pratt (Derrill)	150.00	75.00	45.00
136	Bill Rariden	150.00	75.00	45.00
137	E.C. Rice	500.00	250.00	150.00

138	Wm. A. Ritter (Wm. H.)	150.00	75.00	45.00
139	Eppa Rixey	500.00	250.00	150.00
140	Davey Robertson	150.00	75.00	45.00
141	"Bob" Roth	150.00	75.00	45.00
142	Ed. Roush	500.00	250.00	150.00
143	Clarence Rowland	150.00	75.00	45.00
144	Dick Rudolph	150.00	75.00	45.00
145	William Rumler	150.00	75.00	45.00
146a	Reb Russell (Pitching follow-thru, photo actually Mellie Wolfgang.)	400.00	200.00	120.00
146b	Reb Russell (Hands at side, correct photo.)	200.00	100.00	60.00
147	"Babe" Ruth	25,000	12,500	7,500
148	Vic Saier	150.00	75.00	45.00
149	"Slim" Sallee	150.00	75.00	45.00
150	Ray Schalk	500.00	250.00	150.00
151	Walter Schang	150.00	75.00	45.00
152	Frank Schulte	150.00	75.00	45.00
153	Ferd Schupp	150.00	75.00	45.00
154	Everett Scott	150.00	75.00	45.00
155	Hank Severeid	150.00	75.00	45.00
156	Howard Shanks	150.00	75.00	45.00
157	Bob Shawkey	150.00	75.00	45.00
158	Jas. Sheckard	150.00	75.00	45.00
159	Ernie Shore	150.00	75.00	45.00
160	C.H. Shorten	150.00	75.00	45.00
161	Burt Shotton	150.00	75.00	45.00
162	Geo. Sisler	800.00	400.00	240.00
163	Elmer Smith	150.00	75.00	45.00
164	J. Carlisle Smith	150.00	75.00	45.00
165	Fred Snodgrass	150.00	75.00	45.00
166	Tris Speaker	750.00	375.00	225.00
167	Oscar Stanage	150.00	75.00	45.00
168	Charles Stengel	500.00	250.00	150.00
169	Milton Stock	150.00	75.00	45.00
170	Amos Strunk	150.00	75.00	45.00
171	"Zeb" Terry	150.00	75.00	45.00
172	"Jeff" Tesreau	150.00	75.00	45.00
173	Chester Thomas	150.00	75.00	45.00
174	Fred Toney	150.00	75.00	45.00
175	Terry Turner	150.00	75.00	45.00
176	George Tyler	150.00	75.00	45.00
177	Jim Vaughn	150.00	75.00	45.00
178	Bob Veach	150.00	75.00	45.00
179	Oscar Vitt	150.00	75.00	45.00
180	Hans Wagner	3,000	1,500	900.00
181	Clarence Walker	150.00	75.00	45.00
182	Jim Walsh	150.00	75.00	45.00
183	Al Walters	150.00	75.00	45.00
184	W. Wambsganss	150.00	75.00	45.00
185	Buck Weaver	1,200	600.00	350.00
186	Carl Weilman	150.00	75.00	45.00
187	Zack Wheat	500.00	250.00	150.00
188	Geo. Whitted	150.00	75.00	45.00
189	Joe Wilhoit	150.00	75.00	45.00
190a	Claude Williams (Black stockings, photo actually Hugh High.)	800.00	400.00	240.00
190b	Claude Williams (White stockings, correct photo.)	1,500	750.00	450.00
191	Fred Williams	150.00	75.00	45.00
192	Art Wilson	150.00	75.00	45.00
193	Lawton Witt	150.00	75.00	45.00
194	Joe Wood	200.00	100.00	60.00
195	William Wortman	150.00	75.00	45.00
196	Steve Yerkes	150.00	75.00	45.00
197	Earl Yingling	150.00	75.00	45.00
198	"Pep" Young (Photo actually Ralph Young.)	150.00	75.00	45.00
199	Rollie Zeider	150.00	75.00	45.00
200	Henry Zimmerman	150.00	75.00	45.00

1909 Boston Sunday Post Red Sox Stars

Members of the Boston American League team are presented in this series of Sunday supplements from one of the city's daily newspapers. Measuring about 8" × 10", and possibly having been issued in two-page spreads, the blank-back pieces combine artist's renderings of action photos with circular portraits about 2-3/8" in diameter, printed in sepia tones. At bottom is printed the player name, team, position and a caption for the picture, along with the newspaper's credit line. It is possible this checklist is incomplete since a few of the team's stars have yet to be reported.

		NM	EX	VG
	Common Player:	150.00	75.00	45.00
1)	Frank Arellanes	150.00	75.00	45.00
2)	William Carrigan	150.00	75.00	45.00
3)	Charles Chech	150.00	75.00	45.00
4)	Edward Cicotte	250.00	125.00	75.00
(5)	Harry Hooper	250.00	125.00	75.00
(6)	Harry Lord	150.00	75.00	45.00
(7)	Ambrose McConnell	150.00	75.00	45.00
(8)	Harry Niles	150.00	75.00	45.00
(9)	Tris Speaker	300.00	150.00	90.00
(10)	Edward Spencer	150.00	75.00	45.00
(11)	Garland Stahl	150.00	75.00	45.00
(12)	Harry Wolter	150.00	75.00	45.00

1972 Bowery Bank Joe DiMaggio

These cards were issued to promote the New York City bank's relationship with spokesman Joe DiMaggio. The 2-1/2" x 3-1/2" cards have a posed color photo on front. The back has a black-and-white portrait, biographical data, career highlights and stats on a pink background.

	NM	EX	VG
Joe DiMaggio	17.50	9.00	5.00

1948 Bowman

Bowman Gum Co.'s premiere set of 1948 was one of the first major issues of the post-war period. Forty-eight black-and-white cards comprise the set, with each card measuring 2-1/16" x 2-1/2". The card backs, printed in black ink on gray stock, include the card number and the player's name, team, position, and a short biography. Twelve cards (marked with an "SP") were printed in short supply when they were removed from the 36-card printing sheet to make room for the set's high numbers (#37-48).

		NM	EX	VG
	Complete Set (48):	10,000	5,000	3,000
	Common Player (1-36):	120.00	60.00	36.00
	Common Player (37-48):	120.00	60.00	36.00
1	Bob Elliott	300.00	120.00	36.00
2	Ewell Blackwell	280.00	140.00	80.00
3	Ralph Kiner	600.00	300.00	180.00
4	Johnny Mize	340.00	170.00	100.00
5	Bob Feller	900.00	440.00	260.00
6	Yogi Berra	2,000	1,000	500.00
7	Pete Reiser/SP	600.00	300.00	180.00
8	Phil Rizzuto/SP	1,100	540.00	320.00
9	Walker Cooper	120.00	60.00	36.00
10	Buddy Rosar	120.00	60.00	36.00
11	Johnny Lindell	120.00	60.00	36.00
12	Johnny Sain	280.00	140.00	80.00
13	Willard Marshall/SP	240.00	120.00	72.00
14	Allie Reynolds	260.00	130.00	80.00
15	Eddie Joost	120.00	60.00	36.00
16	Jack Lohrke/SP	240.00	120.00	72.00
17	Enos Slaughter	420.00	200.00	120.00
18	Warren Spahn	1,600	800.00	480.00
19	Tommy Henrich	240.00	120.00	72.00
20	Buddy Kerr/SP	240.00	120.00	72.00
21	Ferris Fain	160.00	80.00	48.00
22	Floyd (Bill) Bevens/SP	240.00	120.00	72.00
23	Larry Jansen	120.00	60.00	36.00
24	Emil (Dutch) Leonard/SP	240.00	120.00	72.00
25	Barney McCoskey (McCosky)	120.00	60.00	36.00
26	Frank Shea/SP	240.00	120.00	72.00
27	Sid Gordon	120.00	60.00	36.00
28	Emil Verban/SP	240.00	120.00	72.00
29	Joe Page/SP	500.00	260.00	140.00
30	Whitey Lockman/SP	300.00	150.00	90.00
31	Bill McCahan	120.00	60.00	36.00
32	Bill Rigney	120.00	60.00	36.00
33	Billy Johnson	120.00	60.00	36.00
34	Sheldon Jones/SP	240.00	120.00	72.00
35	Snuffy Stirnweiss	120.00	60.00	36.00
36	Stan Musial	3,000	1,500	900.00
37	Clint Hartung	240.00	120.00	72.00
38	Red Schoendienst	1,200	500.00	300.00
39	Augie Galan	240.00	120.00	72.00
40	Marty Marion	400.00	200.00	120.00
41	Rex Barney	340.00	170.00	100.00
42	Ray Poat	240.00	120.00	72.00
43	Bruce Edwards	320.00	160.00	96.00
44	Johnny Wyrostek	240.00	120.00	72.00
45	Hank Sauer	240.00	120.00	72.00
46	Herman Wehmeier	240.00	120.00	72.00
47	Bobby Thomson	560.00	280.00	160.00
48	Dave Koslo	640.00	160.00	90.00

1949 Bowman

In 1949, Bowman increased the size of its issue to 240 numbered cards. The 2-1/16" x 2-1/2" cards are black-and-white photos overprinted with team uniform colors on a background of various solid pastel colors. Beginning with card #109 in the set, Bowman added the players' names on the card fronts. Twelve cards (#4, 78, 83, 85, 88, 98, 109, 124, 127, 132 and 143), which were produced in the first four series of printings, were reprinted in the seventh series with either a card front or back modification. These variations are noted in the checklist. Cards #1-3 and 5-73 can be found with either white or gray backs. The complete set value shown here does not include the higher priced variation cards.

		NM	EX	VG
	Complete Set (240):	15,000	7,500	4,500
	Common Player (1-144):	20.00	10.00	6.00
	Common Player (145-240):	50.00	25.00	15.00
1	Vernon Bickford	200.00	15.00	9.00
2	"Whitey" Lockman	20.00	10.00	6.00
3	Bob Porterfield	20.00	10.00	6.00
4a	Jerry Priddy (No name on front.)	20.00	10.00	6.00
4b	Jerry Priddy (Name on front.)	60.00	30.00	18.00
5	Hank Sauer	20.00	10.00	6.00
6	Phil Cavarretta	20.00	10.00	6.00
7	Joe Dobson	20.00	10.00	6.00
8	Murry Dickson	20.00	10.00	6.00
9	Ferris Fain	20.00	10.00	6.00
10	Ted Gray	20.00	10.00	6.00
11	Lou Boudreau	60.00	30.00	18.00
12	Cass Michaels	20.00	10.00	6.00
13	Bob Chesnes	20.00	10.00	6.00
14	Curt Simmons	50.00	25.00	15.00
15	Ned Garver	30.00	15.00	9.00
16	Al Kozar	20.00	10.00	6.00
17	Earl Torgeson	20.00	10.00	6.00
18	Bobby Thomson	65.00	32.50	20.00
19	Bobby Brown	75.00	37.50	22.50
20	Gene Hermanski	20.00	10.00	6.00
21	Frank Baumholtz	20.00	10.00	6.00
22	Harry "P-Nuts" Lowrey	20.00	10.00	6.00
23	Bobby Doerr	60.00	30.00	18.00
24	Stan Musial	425.00	180.00	100.00
25	Carl Scheib	20.00	10.00	6.00
26	George Kell	65.00	32.50	20.00
27	Bob Feller	225.00	110.00	60.00
28	Don Kolloway	20.00	10.00	6.00
29	Ralph Kiner	95.00	47.50	27.50
30	Andy Seminick	20.00	10.00	6.00
31	Dick Kokos	20.00	10.00	6.00
32	Eddie Yost	20.00	10.00	6.00
33	Warren Spahn	135.00	65.00	40.00
34	Dave Koslo	20.00	10.00	6.00
35	Vic Raschi	100.00	50.00	30.00
36	Pee Wee Reese	165.00	85.00	50.00
37	John Wyrostek	20.00	10.00	6.00
38	Emil Verban	20.00	10.00	6.00
39	Bill Goodman	20.00	10.00	6.00
40	"Red" Munger	20.00	10.00	6.00
41	Lou Brissie	20.00	10.00	6.00
42	"Hoot" Evers	20.00	10.00	6.00
43	Dale Mitchell	20.00	10.00	6.00
44	Dave Philley	20.00	10.00	6.00
45	Wally Westlake	20.00	10.00	6.00
46	Robin Roberts	200.00	100.00	60.00
47	Johnny Sain	50.00	25.00	15.00
48	Willard Marshall	20.00	10.00	6.00
49	Frank Shea	30.00	15.00	9.00
50	Jackie Robinson	950.00	475.00	230.00
51	Herman Wehmeier	20.00	10.00	6.00
52	Johnny Schmitz	20.00	10.00	6.00
53	Jack Kramer	20.00	10.00	6.00
54	Marty Marion	35.00	17.50	10.00
55	Eddie Joost	20.00	10.00	6.00
56	Pat Mullin	20.00	10.00	6.00
57	Gene Bearden	20.00	10.00	6.00
58	Bob Elliott	20.00	10.00	6.00
59	Jack Lohrke	20.00	10.00	6.00
60	Yogi Berra	275.00	135.00	80.00
61	Rex Barney	25.00	12.50	7.50
62	Grady Hatton	20.00	10.00	6.00
63	Andy Pafko	20.00	10.00	6.00
64	Dom DiMaggio	75.00	37.50	22.50

#	Player	NM	EX	VG
65	Enos Slaughter	80.00	40.00	24.00
66	Elmer Valo	20.00	10.00	6.00
67	*Alvin Dark*	50.00	25.00	15.00
68	Sheldon Jones	20.00	10.00	6.00
69	Tommy Henrich	55.00	27.50	16.50
70	**Carl Furillo**	135.00	65.00	40.00
71	Vern Stephens	20.00	10.00	6.00
72	Tommy Holmes	20.00	10.00	6.00
73	Billy Cox	45.00	22.50	13.50
74	Tom McBride	20.00	10.00	6.00
75	Eddie Mayo	20.00	10.00	6.00
76	Bill Nicholson	20.00	10.00	6.00
77	Ernie Bonham	20.00	10.00	6.00
78a	Sam Zoldak (No name on front.)	20.00	10.00	6.00
78b	Sam Zoldak (Name on front.)	60.00	30.00	18.00
79	Ron Northey	20.00	10.00	6.00
80	Bill McCahan	20.00	10.00	6.00
81	Virgil "Red" Stallcup	20.00	10.00	6.00
82	Joe Page	35.00	17.50	10.00
83a	Bob Scheffing (No name on front.)	20.00	10.00	6.00
83b	Bob Scheffing (Name on front.)	60.00	30.00	18.00
84	***Roy Campanella***	625.00	310.00	185.00
85a	Johnny Mize (No name on front.)	85.00	42.50	25.00
85b	Johnny Mize (Name on front.)	120.00	60.00	36.00
86	Johnny Pesky	20.00	10.00	6.00
87	Randy Gumpert	20.00	10.00	6.00
88a	Bill Salkeld (No name on front.)	20.00	10.00	6.00
88b	Bill Salkeld (Name on front.)	60.00	30.00	18.00
89	Mizell Platt	20.00	10.00	6.00
90	Gil Coan	20.00	10.00	6.00
91	Dick Wakefield	20.00	10.00	6.00
92	Willie Jones	20.00	10.00	6.00
93	Ed Stevens	20.00	10.00	6.00
94	***Mickey Vernon***	30.00	15.00	9.00
95	Howie Pollett	20.00	10.00	6.00
96	Taft Wright	20.00	10.00	6.00
97	Danny Litwhiler	20.00	10.00	6.00
98a	Phil Rizzuto (No name on front.)	150.00	75.00	45.00
98b	Phil Rizzuto (Name on front.)	275.00	135.00	85.00
99	Frank Gustine	20.00	10.00	6.00
100	**Gil Hodges**	215.00	100.00	60.00
101	Sid Gordon	25.00	12.50	7.50
102	Stan Spence	20.00	10.00	6.00
103	Joe Tipton	20.00	10.00	6.00
104	**Ed Stanky**	35.00	17.50	10.00
105	Bill Kennedy	20.00	10.00	6.00
106	Jake Early	20.00	10.00	6.00
107	Eddie Lake	20.00	10.00	6.00
108	Ken Heintzelman	20.00	10.00	6.00
109a	Ed Fitz Gerald (Script name on back.)	20.00	10.00	6.00
109b	Ed Fitz Gerald (Printed name on back.)	60.00	30.00	18.00
110	***Early Wynn***	165.00	80.00	45.00
111	Red Schoendienst	80.00	40.00	24.00
112	Sam Chapman	20.00	10.00	6.00
113	Ray Lamanno	20.00	10.00	6.00
114	Allie Reynolds	65.00	32.50	20.00
115	Emil "Dutch" Leonard	20.00	10.00	6.00
116	Joe Hatten	20.00	10.00	6.00
117	Walker Cooper	20.00	10.00	6.00
118	Sam Mele	20.00	10.00	6.00
119	Floyd Baker	20.00	10.00	6.00
120	Cliff Fannin	20.00	10.00	6.00
121	Mark Christman	20.00	10.00	6.00
122	George Vico	20.00	10.00	6.00
123	Johnny Blatnick	20.00	10.00	6.00
124a	Danny Murtaugh (Script name on back.)	20.00	10.00	6.00
124b	Danny Murtaugh (Printed name on back.)	60.00	30.00	18.00
125	Ken Keltner	20.00	10.00	6.00
126a	Al Brazle (Script name on back.)	20.00	10.00	6.00
126b	Al Brazle (Printed name on back.)	60.00	30.00	18.00
127a	Henry Majeski (Script name on back.)	20.00	10.00	6.00
127b	Henry Majeski (Printed name on back.)	60.00	30.00	18.00
128	Johnny Vander Meer	35.00	17.50	10.00
129	Billy Johnson	30.00	15.00	9.00
130	Harry "The Hat" Walker	25.00	12.50	7.50
131	Paul Lehner	20.00	10.00	6.00
132a	Al Evans (Script name on back.)	20.00	10.00	6.00
132b	Al Evans (Printed name on back.)	60.00	30.00	18.00
133	Aaron Robinson	20.00	10.00	6.00
134	Hank Borowy	20.00	10.00	6.00
135	Stan Rojek	20.00	10.00	6.00
136	Hank Edwards	20.00	10.00	6.00
137	Ted Wilks	20.00	10.00	6.00
138	"Buddy" Rosar	20.00	10.00	6.00
139	Hank "Bow-Wow" Arft	20.00	10.00	6.00
140	Ray Scarborough	20.00	10.00	6.00
141	"Tony" Lupien	20.00	10.00	6.00
142	Eddie Waitkus	20.00	10.00	6.00
143a	Bob Dillinger (Script name on back.)	20.00	10.00	6.00
143b	Bob Dillinger (Printed name on back.)	60.00	30.00	18.00
144	Mickey Haefner	20.00	10.00	6.00
145	"Blix" Donnelly	50.00	25.00	15.00
146	Mike McCormick	55.00	27.50	16.50
147	Elmer Singleton	50.00	25.00	15.00
148	Bob Swift	50.00	25.00	15.00
149	Roy Partee	60.00	30.00	18.00
150	Allie Clark	50.00	25.00	15.00
151	Mickey Harris	50.00	25.00	15.00
152	Clarence Maddern	50.00	25.00	15.00
153	Phil Masi	50.00	25.00	15.00
154	Clint Hartung	50.00	25.00	15.00
155	Mickey Guerra	50.00	25.00	15.00
156	Al Zarilla	50.00	25.00	15.00
157	Walt Masterson	50.00	25.00	15.00
158	Harry Brecheen	50.00	25.00	15.00
159	Glen Moulder	50.00	25.00	15.00
160	Jim Blackburn	50.00	25.00	15.00
161	"Jocko" Thompson	50.00	25.00	15.00
162	**Preacher Roe**	200.00	100.00	60.00
163	Clyde McCullough	50.00	25.00	15.00
164	**Vic Wertz**	70.00	35.00	20.00
165	"Snuffy" Stirnweiss	60.00	30.00	18.00
166	Mike Tresh	50.00	25.00	15.00
167	Boris "Babe" Martin	50.00	25.00	15.00
168	Doyle Lade	50.00	25.00	15.00
169	Jeff Heath	50.00	25.00	15.00
170	Bill Rigney	50.00	25.00	15.00
171	Dick Fowler	50.00	25.00	15.00
172	Eddie Pellagrini	50.00	25.00	15.00
173	Eddie Stewart	50.00	25.00	15.00
174	**Terry Moore**	125.00	65.00	35.00
175	Luke Appling	175.00	85.00	50.00
176	Ken Raffensberger	50.00	25.00	15.00
177	Stan Lopata	50.00	25.00	15.00
178	Tommy Brown	55.00	27.50	16.50
179	Hugh Casey	55.00	27.50	16.50
180	Connie Berry	50.00	25.00	15.00
181	Gus Niarhos	50.00	25.00	15.00
182	Hal Peck	50.00	25.00	15.00
183	Lou Stringer	50.00	25.00	15.00
184	Bob Chipman	50.00	25.00	15.00
185	Pete Reiser	70.00	35.00	20.00
186	"Buddy" Kerr	50.00	25.00	15.00
187	Phil Marchildon	50.00	25.00	15.00
188	Karl Drews	50.00	25.00	15.00
189	Earl Wooten	50.00	25.00	15.00
190	***Jim Hearn***	60.00	30.00	18.00
191	Joe Haynes	50.00	25.00	15.00
192	Harry Gumbert	50.00	25.00	15.00
193	Ken Trinkle	50.00	25.00	15.00
194	Ralph Branca	95.00	47.50	27.50
195	Eddie Bockman	50.00	25.00	15.00
196	Fred Hutchinson	50.00	25.00	15.00
197	Johnny Lindell	60.00	30.00	18.00
198	Steve Gromek	50.00	25.00	15.00
199	"Tex" Hughson	50.00	25.00	15.00
200	Jess Dobernic	50.00	25.00	15.00
201	Sibby Sisti	50.00	25.00	15.00
202	Larry Jansen	50.00	25.00	15.00
203	Barney McCosky	50.00	25.00	15.00
204	Bob Savage	50.00	25.00	15.00
205	Dick Sisler	50.00	25.00	15.00
206	Bruce Edwards	55.00	27.50	16.50
207	Johnny Hopp	50.00	25.00	15.00
208	"Dizzy" Trout	50.00	25.00	15.00
209	Charlie Keller	85.00	42.50	25.00
210	Joe Gordon	50.00	25.00	15.00
211	Dave "Boo" Ferris	50.00	25.00	15.00
212	Ralph Hamner	50.00	25.00	15.00
213	Charles "Red" Barrett	50.00	25.00	15.00
214	***Richie Ashburn***	555.00	290.00	175.00
215	Kirby Higbe	50.00	25.00	15.00
216	"Schoolboy" Rowe	50.00	25.00	15.00
217	Marino Pieretti	50.00	25.00	15.00
218	Dick Kryhoski	50.00	25.00	15.00
219	***Virgil "Fire" Trucks***	60.00	30.00	18.00
220	Johnny McCarthy	50.00	25.00	15.00
221	Bob Muncrief	50.00	25.00	15.00
222	Alex Kellner	50.00	25.00	15.00
223	Bob Hofman	50.00	25.00	15.00
224	***Satchel Paige***	1,250	850.00	525.00
225	**Gerry Coleman**	100.00	50.00	30.00
226	***Duke Snider***	900.00	475.00	300.00
227	Fritz Ostermueller	50.00	25.00	15.00
228	Jackie Mayo	50.00	25.00	15.00
229	**Ed Lopat**	100.00	50.00	30.00
230	Augie Galan	50.00	25.00	15.00
231	Earl Johnson	50.00	25.00	15.00
232	George McQuinn	50.00	25.00	15.00
233	***Larry Doby***	375.00	185.00	110.00
234	"Rip" Sewell	50.00	25.00	15.00
235	Jim Russell	50.00	25.00	15.00
236	Fred Sanford	60.00	30.00	18.00
237	Monte Kennedy	50.00	25.00	15.00
238	**Bob Lemon**	265.00	130.00	80.00
239	Frank McCormick	50.00	25.00	15.00
240	Norm "Babe" Young (Photo actually Bobby Young.)	125.00	30.00	15.00

1950 Bowman

WALKER COOPER — Catcher—Boston Braves — Born—Atherton, Mo., Jan. 8, 1915 — Height: 6-3 — Weight: 210 — Throws: Right — Bats: Right. The quality of the 1950 Bowman Regular (Red) Tint, May 1946. Began 1949 with Giants who purchased him from Cards in 1946. After 42 games the Giants sold him to Reds. Finished season with .255 batting average, batted in 83 runs, in one game with 3 homers struck majors with Cards in 1940. No. 111 in the 1950 SERIES of BASEBALL Picture Cards. © 1950 Bowman Gum, Inc., Phila., Pa., U.S.A.

The quality of the 1950 Bowman issue showed a marked improvement over the company's previous efforts. The cards are color art reproductions of actual photographs and measure 2-1/16" x 2-1/2". Backs include the same type of information found in the previous year's issue but are designed in a horizontal format. Cards found in the first two series (#1-72) are the scarcer of the issue. The backs of the final

72 cards (#181-252) can be found with or without the copyright line at the bottom of the card, the "without" version being the less common.

#	Player	NM	EX	VG
Complete Set (252):		12,500	6,000	3,500
Common Player (1-72):		50.00	25.00	15.00
Common Player (73-252):		20.00	10.00	6.00
1	Mel Parnell	550.00	35.00	15.00
2	Vern Stephens	50.00	25.00	15.00
3	Dom DiMaggio	130.00	65.00	40.00
4	***Gus Zernial***	90.00	45.00	27.50
5	Bob Kuzava	50.00	25.00	15.00
6	Bob Feller	300.00	150.00	90.00
7	Jim Hegan	50.00	25.00	15.00
8	George Kell	125.00	65.00	35.00
9	Vic Wertz	50.00	25.00	15.00
10	Tommy Henrich	75.00	37.50	22.50
11	Phil Rizzuto	265.00	130.00	80.00
12	Joe Page	65.00	32.50	20.00
13	Ferris Fain	50.00	25.00	15.00
14	Alex Kellner	50.00	25.00	15.00
15	Al Kozar	50.00	25.00	15.00
16	***Roy Sievers***	90.00	45.00	27.50
17	Sid Hudson	50.00	25.00	15.00
18	Eddie Robinson	50.00	25.00	15.00
19	Warren Spahn	365.00	175.00	100.00
20	Bob Elliott	50.00	25.00	15.00
21	Pee Wee Reese	275.00	125.00	80.00
22	Jackie Robinson	900.00	400.00	225.00
23	***Don Newcombe***	175.00	85.00	50.00
24	Johnny Schmitz	50.00	25.00	15.00
25	Hank Sauer	50.00	25.00	15.00
26	Grady Hatton	50.00	25.00	15.00
27	Herman Wehmeier	50.00	25.00	15.00
28	Bobby Thomson	100.00	50.00	30.00
29	Ed Stanky	60.00	30.00	18.00
30	Eddie Waitkus	50.00	25.00	15.00
31	***Del Ennis***	80.00	40.00	24.00
32	Robin Roberts	225.00	110.00	65.00
33	Ralph Kiner	125.00	60.00	35.00
34	Murry Dickson	50.00	25.00	15.00
35	Enos Slaughter	125.00	60.00	35.00
36	Eddie Kazak	50.00	25.00	15.00
37	Luke Appling	100.00	50.00	30.00
38	Bill Wight	50.00	25.00	15.00
39	Larry Doby	175.00	85.00	50.00
40	Bob Lemon	125.00	60.00	35.00
41	"Hoot" Evers	50.00	25.00	15.00
42	Art Houtteman	50.00	25.00	15.00
43	Bobby Doerr	100.00	50.00	30.00
44	Joe Dobson	50.00	25.00	15.00
45	Al Zarilla	50.00	25.00	15.00
46	Yogi Berra	425.00	210.00	125.00
47	Jerry Coleman	60.00	30.00	18.00
48	Lou Brissie	50.00	25.00	15.00
49	Elmer Valo	50.00	25.00	15.00
50	Dick Kokos	50.00	25.00	15.00
51	Ned Garver	50.00	25.00	15.00
52	Sam Mele	50.00	25.00	15.00
53	Clyde Vollmer	50.00	25.00	15.00
54	Gil Coan	50.00	25.00	15.00
55	"Buddy" Kerr	50.00	25.00	15.00
56	***Del Crandell*** (Crandall)	55.00	27.50	16.50
57	Vernon Bickford	50.00	25.00	15.00
58	Carl Furillo	65.00	32.50	20.00
59	Ralph Branca	60.00	30.00	18.00
60	Andy Pafko	50.00	25.00	15.0
61	Bob Rush	50.00	25.00	15.0
62	Ted Kluszewski	150.00	75.00	45.00
63	Ewell Blackwell	50.00	25.00	15.0
64	Alvin Dark	50.00	25.00	15.0
65	Dave Koslo	50.00	25.00	15.0
66	Larry Jansen	50.00	25.00	15.0
67	Willie Jones	50.00	25.00	15.0
68	Curt Simmons	50.00	25.00	15.0
69	Wally Westlake	50.00	25.00	15.0
70	Bob Chesnes	50.00	25.00	15.0
71	Red Schoendienst	85.00	42.50	25.00
72	Howie Pollet	50.00	25.00	15.0
73	Willard Marshall	20.00	10.00	6.0
74	***Johnny Antonelli***	40.00	20.00	12.0
75	Roy Campanella	200.00	100.00	60.0
76	Rex Barney	25.00	12.50	7.5
77	Duke Snider	200.00	100.00	60.0
78	Mickey Owen	20.00	10.00	6.0
79	Johnny Vander Meer	25.00	12.50	7.5
80	Howard Fox	20.00	10.00	6.0
81	Ron Northey	20.00	10.00	6.0
82	"Whitey" Lockman	20.00	10.00	6.0
83	Sheldon Jones	20.00	10.00	6.0
84	Richie Ashburn	190.00	95.00	55.0
85	Ken Heintzelman	20.00	10.00	6.0
86	Stan Rojek	20.00	10.00	6.0
87	Bill Werle	20.00	10.00	6.0
88	Marty Marion	30.00	15.00	9.0
89	George Munger	20.00	10.00	6.0
90	Harry Brecheen	20.00	10.00	6.0
91	Cass Michaels	20.00	10.00	6.0
92	Hank Majeski	20.00	10.00	6.0
93	Gene Bearden	20.00	10.00	6.0
94	Lou Boudreau	70.00	35.00	20.0
95	Aaron Robinson	20.00	10.00	6.0
96	Virgil "Fire" Trucks	20.00	10.00	6.0
97	Maurice McDermott	20.00	10.00	6.0
98	Ted Williams	800.00	350.00	210.0
99	Billy Goodman	20.00	10.00	6.0
100	Vic Raschi	50.00	25.00	15.0
101	Bobby Brown	55.00	27.50	16.5
102	Billy Johnson	30.00	15.00	9.0
103	Eddie Joost	20.00	10.00	6.0
104	Sam Chapman	20.00	10.00	6.0
105	Bob Dillinger	20.00	10.00	6.0
106	Cliff Fannin	20.00	10.00	6.0
107	Sam Dente	20.00	10.00	6.0
108	Ray Scarborough	20.00	10.00	6.0
109	Sid Gordon	20.00	10.00	6.0

110	Tommy Holmes	20.00	10.00	6.00
111	Walker Cooper	20.00	10.00	6.00
112	Gil Hodges	125.00	60.00	35.00
113	Gene Hermanski	20.00	10.00	6.00
114	*Wayne Terwilliger*	25.00	12.50	7.50
115	Roy Smalley	20.00	10.00	6.00
116	Virgil "Red" Stallcup	20.00	10.00	6.00
117	Bill Rigney	20.00	10.00	6.00
118	Clint Hartung	20.00	10.00	6.00
119	Dick Sisler	20.00	10.00	6.00
120	Jocko Thompson	20.00	10.00	6.00
121	Andy Seminick	20.00	10.00	6.00
122	Johnny Hopp	20.00	10.00	6.00
123	Dino Restelli	20.00	10.00	6.00
124	Clyde McCullough	20.00	10.00	6.00
125	Del Rice	20.00	10.00	6.00
126	Al Brazle	20.00	10.00	6.00
127	Dave Philley	20.00	10.00	6.00
128	Phil Masi	20.00	10.00	6.00
129	Joe Gordon	20.00	10.00	6.00
130	Dale Mitchell	20.00	10.00	6.00
131	Steve Gromek	20.00	10.00	6.00
132	Mickey Vernon	20.00	10.00	6.00
133	Don Kolloway	20.00	10.00	6.00
134	"Dizzy" Trout	20.00	10.00	6.00
135	Pat Mullin	20.00	10.00	6.00
136	"Buddy" Rosar	20.00	10.00	6.00
137	Johnny Pesky	20.00	10.00	6.00
138	Allie Reynolds	60.00	30.00	18.00
139	Johnny Mize	65.00	32.50	20.00
140	Pete Suder	20.00	10.00	6.00
141	Joe Coleman	20.00	10.00	6.00
142	*Sherman Lollar*	25.00	12.50	7.50
143	Eddie Stewart	20.00	10.00	6.00
144	Al Evans	20.00	10.00	6.00
145	Jack Graham	20.00	10.00	6.00
146	Floyd Baker	20.00	10.00	6.00
147	*Mike Garcia*	30.00	15.00	9.00
148	Early Wynn	70.00	35.00	20.00
149	Bob Swift	20.00	10.00	6.00
150	George Vico	20.00	10.00	6.00
151	Fred Hutchinson	20.00	10.00	6.00
152	Ellis Kinder	20.00	10.00	6.00
153	Walt Masterson	20.00	10.00	6.00
154	Gus Niarhos	30.00	15.00	9.00
155	Frank "Spec" Shea	30.00	15.00	9.00
156	Fred Sanford	30.00	15.00	9.00
157	Mike Guerra	20.00	10.00	6.00
158	Paul Lehner	20.00	10.00	6.00
159	Joe Tipton	20.00	10.00	6.00
160	Mickey Harris	20.00	10.00	6.00
161	Sherry Robertson	20.00	10.00	6.00
162	Eddie Yost	20.00	10.00	6.00
163	Earl Torgeson	20.00	10.00	6.00
164	Sibby Sisti	20.00	10.00	6.00
165	Bruce Edwards	25.00	12.50	7.50
166	Joe Hatten	25.00	12.50	7.50
167	Preacher Roe	50.00	25.00	15.00
168	Bob Scheffing	20.00	10.00	6.00
169	Hank Edwards	20.00	10.00	6.00
170	Emil Leonard	20.00	10.00	6.00
171	Harry Gumbert	20.00	10.00	6.00
172	Harry Lowrey	20.00	10.00	6.00
173	Lloyd Merriman	20.00	10.00	6.00
174	*Henry Thompson*	30.00	15.00	9.00
175	Monte Kennedy	20.00	10.00	6.00
176	"Blix" Donnelly	20.00	10.00	6.00
177	Hank Borowy	20.00	10.00	6.00
178	Eddy Fitz Gerald	20.00	10.00	6.00
179	Charles Diering	20.00	10.00	6.00
180	Harry "The Hat" Walker	20.00	10.00	6.00
181	Marino Pieretti	20.00	10.00	6.00
182	Sam Zoldak	20.00	10.00	6.00
183	Mickey Haefner	20.00	10.00	6.00
184	Randy Gumpert	20.00	10.00	6.00
185	Howie Judson	20.00	10.00	6.00
186	Ken Keltner	20.00	10.00	6.00
187	Lou Stringer	20.00	10.00	6.00
188	Earl Johnson	20.00	10.00	6.00
189	Owen Friend	20.00	10.00	6.00
190	Ken Wood	20.00	10.00	6.00
191	Dick Starr	20.00	10.00	6.00
192	Bob Chipman	20.00	10.00	6.00
193	Pete Reiser	30.00	15.00	9.00
194	Billy Cox	35.00	17.50	10.00
195	Phil Cavarretta	20.00	10.00	6.00
196	Doyle Lade	20.00	10.00	6.00
197	Johnny Wyrostek	20.00	10.00	6.00
198	Danny Litwhiler	20.00	10.00	6.00
199	Jack Kramer	20.00	10.00	6.00
200	Kirby Higbe	20.00	10.00	6.00
201	Pete Castiglione	20.00	10.00	6.00
202	Cliff Chambers	20.00	10.00	6.00
203	Danny Murtaugh	20.00	10.00	6.00
204	Granny Hamner	20.00	10.00	6.00
205	Mike Goliat	20.00	10.00	6.00
206	Stan Lopata	20.00	10.00	6.00
207	Max Lanier	20.00	10.00	6.00
208	Jim Hearn	20.00	10.00	6.00
209	Johnny Lindell	20.00	10.00	6.00
210	Ted Gray	20.00	10.00	6.00
211	Charlie Keller	30.00	15.00	9.00
212	Gerry Priddy	20.00	10.00	6.00
213	Carl Scheib	20.00	10.00	6.00
214	Dick Fowler	20.00	10.00	6.00
215	Ed Lopat	50.00	25.00	15.00
216	Bob Porterfield	30.00	15.00	9.00
217	Casey Stengel	70.00	35.00	20.00
218	Cliff Mapes	20.00	10.00	6.00
219	*Hank Bauer*	70.00	35.00	20.00
220	Leo Durocher	60.00	30.00	18.00
221	Don Mueller	20.00	10.00	6.00
222	Bobby Morgan	25.00	12.50	7.50
223	Jimmy Russell	25.00	12.50	7.50
224	Jack Banta	25.00	12.50	7.50
225	Eddie Sawyer	20.00	10.00	6.00
226	*Jim Konstanty*	30.00	15.00	9.00
227	Bob Miller	20.00	10.00	6.00
228	Bill Nicholson	20.00	10.00	6.00
229	Frank Frisch	40.00	20.00	12.00
230	Bill Serena	20.00	10.00	6.00
231	Preston Ward	20.00	10.00	6.00
232	*Al Rosen*	55.00	27.50	16.50
233	Allie Clark	20.00	10.00	6.00
234	*Bobby Shantz*	45.00	22.50	13.50
235	Harold Gilbert	20.00	10.00	6.00
236	Bob Cain	20.00	10.00	6.00
237	Bill Salkeld	20.00	10.00	6.00
238	Nippy Jones	20.00	10.00	6.00
239	Bill Howerton	20.00	10.00	6.00
240	Eddie Lake	20.00	10.00	6.00
241	Neil Berry	20.00	10.00	6.00
242	Dick Kryhoski	20.00	10.00	6.00
243	Johnny Groth	20.00	10.00	6.00
244	Dale Coogan	20.00	10.00	6.00
245	Al Papai	20.00	10.00	6.00
246	*Walt Dropo*	35.00	17.50	10.00
247	*Irv Noren*	30.00	15.00	9.00
248	*Sam Jethroe*	40.00	20.00	12.00
249	"Snuffy" Stirnweiss	20.00	10.00	6.00
250	Ray Coleman	20.00	10.00	6.00
251	Les Moss	20.00	10.00	6.00
252	Billy DeMars	65.00	20.00	7.50

1951 Bowman

In 1951, Bowman increased the number of cards in its set for the third consecutive year when it issued 324 cards. The cards are, like 1950, color art reproductions of actual photographs but now measure 2-1/16" x 3-1/8" in size. The player's name is in a black strip on front. Several of the pictures are enlargements of the 1950 version. The high-numbered series (#253-324), which includes the rookie cards of Mantle and Mays, are the scarcest of the issue.

		NM	EX	VG
	Complete Set (324):	20,000	9,500	5,500
	Common Player (1-252):	17.50	9.00	5.00
	Common Player (253-324):	40.00	20.00	12.00
1	*Whitey Ford*	1,200	460.00	200.00
2	Yogi Berra	375.00	125.00	75.00
3	Robin Roberts	75.00	37.50	22.50
4	Del Ennis	17.50	9.00	5.00
5	Dale Mitchell	17.50	9.00	5.00
6	Don Newcombe	75.00	37.50	22.50
7	Gil Hodges	80.00	40.00	25.00
8	Paul Lehner	17.50	9.00	5.00
9	Sam Chapman	17.50	9.00	5.00
10	Red Schoendienst	75.00	37.50	22.50
11	"Red" Munger	17.50	9.00	5.00
12	Hank Majeski	17.50	9.00	5.00
13	Ed Stanky	20.00	10.00	6.00
14	Alvin Dark	17.50	9.00	5.00
15	Johnny Pesky	17.50	9.00	5.00
16	Maurice McDermott	17.50	9.00	5.00
17	Pete Castiglione	17.50	9.00	5.00
18	Gil Coan	17.50	9.00	5.00
19	Sid Gordon	17.50	9.00	5.00
20	Del Crandall	17.50	9.00	5.00
21	"Snuffy" Stirnweiss	17.50	9.00	5.00
22	Hank Sauer	17.50	9.00	5.00
23	"Hoot" Evers	17.50	9.00	5.00
24	Ewell Blackwell	17.50	9.00	5.00
25	Vic Raschi	40.00	20.00	12.00
26	Phil Rizzuto	145.00	70.00	40.00
27	Jim Konstanty	17.50	9.00	5.00
28	Eddie Waitkus	17.50	9.00	5.00
29	Allie Clark	17.50	9.00	5.00
30	Bob Feller	120.00	60.00	35.00
31	Roy Campanella	190.00	95.00	55.00
32	Duke Snider	200.00	100.00	60.00
33	Bob Hooper	17.50	9.00	5.00
34	Marty Marion	25.00	12.50	7.50
35	Al Zarilla	17.50	9.00	5.00
36	Joe Dobson	17.50	9.00	5.00
37	Whitey Lockman	17.50	9.00	5.00
38	Al Evans	17.50	9.00	5.00
39	Ray Scarborough	17.50	9.00	5.00
40	*Gus Bell*	30.00	15.00	9.00
41	Eddie Yost	17.50	9.00	5.00
42	Vern Bickford	17.50	9.00	5.00
43	Billy DeMars	17.50	9.00	5.00
44	Roy Smalley	17.50	9.00	5.00
45	Art Houtteman	17.50	9.00	5.00
46	George Kell	50.00	25.00	15.00
47	Grady Hatton	17.50	9.00	5.00
48	Ken Raffensberger	17.50	9.00	5.00
49	Jerry Coleman	20.00	10.00	6.00
50	Johnny Mize	50.00	25.00	15.00
51	Andy Seminick	17.50	9.00	5.00
52	Dick Sisler	17.50	9.00	5.00
53	Bob Lemon	50.00	25.00	15.00
54	*Ray Boone*	35.00	17.50	10.00
55	Gene Hermanski	20.00	10.00	6.00
56	Ralph Branca	50.00	25.00	15.00
57	Alex Kellner	17.50	9.00	5.00
58	Enos Slaughter	50.00	25.00	15.00
59	Randy Gumpert	17.50	9.00	5.00
60	"Chico" Carrasquel	20.00	10.00	6.00
61	Jim Hearn	17.50	9.00	5.00
62	Lou Boudreau	45.00	22.50	13.50
63	Bob Dillinger	17.50	9.00	5.00
64	Bill Werle	17.50	9.00	5.00
65	Mickey Vernon	17.50	9.00	5.00
66	Bob Elliott	17.50	9.00	5.00
67	Roy Sievers	17.50	9.00	5.00
68	Dick Kokos	17.50	9.00	5.00
69	Johnny Schmitz	17.50	9.00	5.00
70	Ron Northey	17.50	9.00	5.00
71	Jerry Priddy	17.50	9.00	5.00
72	Lloyd Merriman	17.50	9.00	5.00
73	Tommy Byrne	20.00	10.00	6.00
74	Billy Johnson	20.00	10.00	6.00
75	Russ Meyer	17.50	9.00	5.00
76	Stan Lopata	17.50	9.00	5.00
77	Mike Goliat	17.50	9.00	5.00
78	Early Wynn	60.00	30.00	18.00
79	Jim Hegan	17.50	9.00	5.00
80	Pee Wee Reese	125.00	65.00	35.00
81	Carl Furillo	55.00	27.50	16.50
82	Joe Tipton	17.50	9.00	5.00
83	Carl Scheib	17.50	9.00	5.00
84	Barney McCosky	17.50	9.00	5.00
85	Eddie Kazak	17.50	9.00	5.00
86	Harry Brecheen	17.50	9.00	5.00
87	Floyd Baker	17.50	9.00	5.00
88	Eddie Robinson	17.50	9.00	5.00
89	Henry Thompson	17.50	9.00	5.00
90	Dave Koslo	17.50	9.00	5.00
91	Clyde Vollmer	17.50	9.00	5.00
92	Vern Stephens	17.50	9.00	5.00
93	Danny O'Connell	17.50	9.00	5.00
94	Clyde McCullough	17.50	9.00	5.00
95	Sherry Robertson	17.50	9.00	5.00
96	Sandy Consuegra	17.50	9.00	5.00
97	Bob Kuzava	17.50	9.00	5.00
98	Willard Marshall	17.50	9.00	5.00
99	Earl Torgeson	17.50	9.00	5.00
100	Sherman Lollar	17.50	9.00	5.00
101	Owen Friend	17.50	9.00	5.00
102	Emil "Dutch" Leonard	17.50	9.00	5.00
103	Andy Pafko	17.50	9.00	5.00
104	Virgil "Fire" Trucks	17.50	9.00	5.00
105	Don Kolloway	17.50	9.00	5.00
106	Pat Mullin	17.50	9.00	5.00
107	Johnny Wyrostek	17.50	9.00	5.00
108	Virgil Stallcup	17.50	9.00	5.00
109	Allie Reynolds	45.00	22.50	13.50
110	Bobby Brown	30.00	15.00	9.00
111	Curt Simmons	17.50	9.00	5.00
112	Willie Jones	17.50	9.00	5.00
113	Bill "Swish" Nicholson	17.50	9.00	5.00
114	Sam Zoldak	17.50	9.00	5.00
115	Steve Gromek	17.50	9.00	5.00
116	Bruce Edwards	20.00	10.00	6.00
117	Eddie Miksis	20.00	10.00	6.00
118	Preacher Roe	60.00	30.00	18.00
119	Eddie Joost	17.50	9.00	5.00
120	Joe Coleman	17.50	9.00	5.00
121	Gerry Staley	17.50	9.00	5.00
122	*Joe Garagiola*	75.00	37.50	22.50
123	Howie Judson	17.50	9.00	5.00
124	Gus Niarhos	17.50	9.00	5.00
125	Bill Rigney	17.50	9.00	5.00
126	Bobby Thomson	50.00	25.00	15.00
127	*Sal Maglie*	75.00	37.50	22.50
128	Ellis Kinder	17.50	9.00	5.00
129	Matt Batts	17.50	9.00	5.00
130	Tom Saffell	17.50	9.00	5.00
131	Cliff Chambers	17.50	9.00	5.00
132	Cass Michaels	17.50	9.00	5.00
133	Sam Dente	17.50	9.00	5.00
134	Warren Spahn	135.00	65.00	40.00
135	Walker Cooper	17.50	9.00	5.00
136	Ray Coleman	17.50	9.00	5.00
137	Dick Starr	17.50	9.00	5.00
138	Phil Cavarretta	17.50	9.00	5.00
139	Doyle Lade	17.50	9.00	5.00
140	Eddie Lake	17.50	9.00	5.00
141	Fred Hutchinson	17.50	9.00	5.00
142	Aaron Robinson	17.50	9.00	5.00
143	Ted Kluszewski	60.00	30.00	18.00
144	Herman Wehmeier	17.50	9.00	5.00
145	Fred Sanford	17.50	9.00	5.00
146	Johnny Hopp	17.50	9.00	5.00
147	Ken Heintzelman	17.50	9.00	5.00
148	Granny Hamner	17.50	9.00	5.00
149	"Bubba" Church	17.50	9.00	5.00
150	Mike Garcia	17.50	9.00	5.00
151	Larry Doby	70.00	35.00	20.00
152	Cal Abrams	20.00	10.00	6.00
153	Rex Barney	20.00	10.00	6.00
154	Pete Suder	17.50	9.00	5.00
155	Lou Brissie	17.50	9.00	5.00
156	Del Rice	17.50	9.00	5.00
157	Al Brazle	17.50	9.00	5.00
158	Chuck Diering	17.50	9.00	5.00
159	Eddie Stewart	17.50	9.00	5.00
160	Phil Masi	17.50	9.00	5.00
161	Wes Westrum	17.50	9.00	5.00
162	Larry Jansen	17.50	9.00	5.00
163	Monte Kennedy	17.50	9.00	5.00
164	Bill Wight	17.50	9.00	5.00
165	Ted Williams	625.00	240.00	155.00
166	Stan Rojek	17.50	9.00	5.00
167	Murry Dickson	17.50	9.00	5.00
168	Sam Mele	17.50	9.00	5.00
169	Sid Hudson	17.50	9.00	5.00
170	Sibby Sisti	17.50	9.00	5.00
171	Buddy Kerr	17.50	9.00	5.00

172	Ned Garver	17.50	9.00	5.00
173	Hank Arft	17.50	9.00	5.00
174	Mickey Owen	17.50	9.00	5.00
175	Wayne Terwilliger	17.50	9.00	5.00
176	Vic Wertz	17.50	9.00	5.00
177	Charlie Keller	17.50	9.00	5.00
178	Ted Gray	17.50	9.00	5.00
179	Danny Litwhiler	17.50	9.00	5.00
180	Howie Fox	17.50	9.00	5.00
181	Casey Stengel	75.00	37.50	22.50
182	Tom Ferrick	20.00	10.00	6.00
183	Hank Bauer	35.00	17.50	10.00
184	Eddie Sawyer	17.50	9.00	5.00
185	Jimmy Bloodworth	17.50	9.00	5.00
186	Richie Ashburn	100.00	50.00	30.00
187	Al Rosen	35.00	17.50	10.00
188	*Roberto Avila*	25.00	12.50	7.50
189	Erv Palica	20.00	10.00	6.00
190	Joe Hatten	20.00	10.00	6.00
191	Billy Hitchcock	17.50	9.00	5.00
192	Hank Wyse	17.50	9.00	5.00
193	Ted Wilks	17.50	9.00	5.00
194	Harry "Peanuts" Lowrey	17.50	9.00	5.00
195	Paul Richards	20.00	10.00	6.00
196	*Bill Pierce*	32.50	16.00	10.00
197	Bob Cain	17.50	9.00	5.00
198	*Monte Irvin*	110.00	55.00	35.00
199	Sheldon Jones	17.50	9.00	5.00
200	Jack Kramer	17.50	9.00	5.00
201	Steve O'Neill	17.50	9.00	5.00
202	Mike Guerra	17.50	9.00	5.00
203	*Vernon Law*	40.00	20.00	12.00
204	Vic Lombardi	17.50	9.00	5.00
205	Mickey Grasso	17.50	9.00	5.00
206	Connie Marrero	17.50	9.00	5.00
207	Billy Southworth	17.50	9.00	5.00
208	"Blix" Donnelly	17.50	9.00	5.00
209	Ken Wood	17.50	9.00	5.00
210	Les Moss	17.50	9.00	5.00
211	Hal Jeffcoat	17.50	9.00	5.00
212	Bob Rush	17.50	9.00	5.00
213	Neil Berry	17.50	9.00	5.00
214	Bob Swift	17.50	9.00	5.00
215	Kent Peterson	17.50	9.00	5.00
216	Connie Ryan	17.50	9.00	5.00
217	Joe Page	27.50	13.50	8.00
218	Ed Lopat	32.50	16.00	10.00
219	*Gene Woodling*	40.00	20.00	12.00
220	Bob Miller	17.50	9.00	5.00
221	Dick Whitman	17.50	9.00	5.00
222	Thurman Tucker	17.50	9.00	5.00
223	Johnny Vander Meer	25.00	12.50	7.50
224	Billy Cox	27.50	13.50	8.00
225	*Dan Bankhead*	30.00	15.00	9.00
226	Jimmy Dykes	17.50	9.00	5.00
227	Bobby Shantz	20.00	10.00	6.00
228	*Cloyd Boyer*	17.50	9.00	5.00
229	Bill Howerton	17.50	9.00	5.00
230	Max Lanier	17.50	9.00	5.00
231	Luis Aloma	17.50	9.00	5.00
232	*Nellie Fox*	145.00	70.00	40.00
233	Leo Durocher	40.00	20.00	12.00
234	Clint Hartung	17.50	9.00	5.00
235	Jack Lohrke	17.50	9.00	5.00
236	"Buddy" Rosar	17.50	9.00	5.00
237	Billy Goodman	17.50	9.00	5.00
238	Pete Reiser	20.00	10.00	6.00
239	Bill MacDonald	17.50	9.00	5.00
240	Joe Haynes	17.50	9.00	5.00
241	Irv Noren	17.50	9.00	5.00
242	Sam Jethroe	17.50	9.00	5.00
243	Johnny Antonelli	17.50	9.00	5.00
244	Cliff Fannin	17.50	9.00	5.00
245	John Berardino	25.00	12.50	7.50
246	Bill Serena	17.50	9.00	5.00
247	Bob Ramazotti	17.50	9.00	5.00
248	*Johnny Klippstein*	17.50	9.00	5.00
249	Johnny Groth	17.50	9.00	5.00
250	Hank Borowy	17.50	9.00	5.00
251	Willard Ramsdell	17.50	9.00	5.00
252	"Dixie" Howell	17.50	9.00	5.00
253	*Mickey Mantle*	7,000	3,500	2,100
254	*Jackie Jensen*	85.00	40.00	25.00
255	Milo Candini	40.00	20.00	12.00
256	Ken Silvestri	40.00	20.00	12.00
257	Birdie Tebbetts	40.00	20.00	12.00
258	*Luke Easter*	45.00	22.50	13.50
259	Charlie Dressen	40.00	20.00	12.00
260	*Carl Erskine*	75.00	37.50	22.00
261	Wally Moses	40.00	20.00	12.00
262	Gus Zernial	40.00	20.00	12.00
263	Howie Pollet	40.00	20.00	12.00
264	Don Richmond	40.00	20.00	12.00
265	*Steve Bilko*	40.00	20.00	12.00
266	Harry Dorish	40.00	20.00	12.00
267	Ken Holcombe	40.00	20.00	12.00
268	Don Mueller	40.00	20.00	12.00
269	Ray Noble	40.00	20.00	12.00
270	Willard Nixon	40.00	20.00	12.00
271	Tommy Wright	40.00	20.00	12.00
272	Billy Meyer	40.00	20.00	12.00
273	Danny Murtaugh	40.00	20.00	12.00
274	George Metkovich	40.00	20.00	12.00
275	Bucky Harris	50.00	25.00	15.00
276	Frank Quinn	40.00	20.00	12.00
277	Roy Hartsfield	40.00	20.00	12.00
278	Norman Roy	40.00	20.00	12.00
279	Jim Delsing	40.00	20.00	12.00
280	Frank Overmire	40.00	20.00	12.00
281	Al Widmar	40.00	20.00	12.00
282	Frank Frisch	55.00	27.50	16.50
283	Walt Dubiel	40.00	20.00	12.00
284	Gene Bearden	40.00	20.00	12.00
285	Johnny Lipon	40.00	20.00	12.00
286	Bob Usher	40.00	20.00	12.00
287	Jim Blackburn	40.00	20.00	12.00
288	Bobby Adams	40.00	20.00	12.00
289	Cliff Mapes	50.00	25.00	15.00
290	Bill Dickey	85.00	42.50	25.00
291	Tommy Henrich	55.00	27.50	16.50
292	Eddie Pellagrini	40.00	20.00	12.00
293	Ken Johnson	40.00	20.00	12.00
294	Jocko Thompson	40.00	20.00	12.00
295	Al Lopez	70.00	35.00	20.00
296	Bob Kennedy	40.00	20.00	12.00
297	Dave Philley	40.00	20.00	12.00
298	Joe Astroth	40.00	20.00	12.00
299	Clyde King	50.00	25.00	15.00
300	Hal Rice	40.00	20.00	12.00
301	Tommy Glaviano	40.00	20.00	12.00
302	Jim Busby	40.00	20.00	12.00
303	Marv Rotblatt	40.00	20.00	12.00
304	Allen Gettel	40.00	20.00	12.00
305	*Willie Mays*	2,400	900.00	480.00
306	*Jim Piersall*	90.00	45.00	27.50
307	Walt Masterson	40.00	20.00	12.00
308	Ted Beard	40.00	20.00	12.00
309	Mel Queen	40.00	20.00	12.00
310	Erv Dusak	40.00	20.00	12.00
311	Mickey Harris	40.00	20.00	12.00
312	*Gene Mauch*	50.00	25.00	15.00
313	Ray Mueller	40.00	20.00	12.00
314	Johnny Sain	45.00	22.50	13.50
315	Zack Taylor	40.00	20.00	12.00
316	Duane Pillette	40.00	20.00	12.00
317	*Smoky Burgess*	60.00	30.00	18.00
318	Warren Hacker	40.00	20.00	12.00
319	Red Rolfe	40.00	20.00	12.00
320	Hal White	40.00	20.00	12.00
321	Earl Johnson	40.00	20.00	12.00
322	Luke Sewell	40.00	20.00	12.00
323	*Joe Adcock*	80.00	35.00	20.00
324	Johnny Pramesa	100.00	22.50	12.00

1952 Bowman

Bowman reverted to a 252-card set in 1952, but retained the card size (2-1/16" x 3-1/8") employed the preceding year. The cards, which are color art reproductions of actual photographs, feature a facsimile autograph on front.

		NM	EX	VG
	Complete Set (252):	10,000	5,000	3,000
	Common Player (1-216):	20.00	10.00	6.00
	Common Player (217-252):	40.00	20.00	12.00
1	Yogi Berra	525.00	160.00	65.00
2	Bobby Thomson	70.00	35.00	20.00
3	Fred Hutchinson	20.00	10.00	6.00
4	Robin Roberts	100.00	50.00	30.00
5	*Minnie Minoso*	90.00	45.00	27.50
6	Virgil "Red" Stallcup	20.00	10.00	6.00
7	Mike Garcia	20.00	10.00	6.00
8	Pee Wee Reese	95.00	47.50	27.50
9	Vern Stephens	20.00	10.00	6.00
10	Bob Hooper	20.00	10.00	6.00
11	Ralph Kiner	60.00	30.00	18.00
12	Max Surkont	20.00	10.00	6.00
13	Cliff Mapes	20.00	10.00	6.00
14	Cliff Chambers	20.00	10.00	6.00
15	Sam Mele	20.00	10.00	6.00
16	Omar Lown	20.00	10.00	6.00
17	Ed Lopat	55.00	27.50	16.50
18	Don Mueller	20.00	10.00	6.00
19	Bob Cain	20.00	10.00	6.00
20	Willie Jones	20.00	10.00	6.00
21	Nellie Fox	65.00	32.50	20.00
22	Willard Ramsdell	20.00	10.00	6.00
23	Bob Lemon	60.00	30.00	18.00
24	Carl Furillo	50.00	25.00	15.00
25	Maurice McDermott	20.00	10.00	6.00
26	Eddie Joost	20.00	10.00	6.00
27	Joe Garagiola	30.00	15.00	9.00
28	Roy Hartsfield	20.00	10.00	6.00
29	Ned Garver	20.00	10.00	6.00
30	Red Schoendienst	45.00	22.50	13.50
31	Eddie Yost	20.00	10.00	6.00
32	Eddie Miksis	20.00	10.00	6.00
33	*Gil McDougald*	60.00	30.00	18.00
34	Al Dark	20.00	10.00	6.00
35	Granny Hamner	20.00	10.00	6.00
36	Cass Michaels	20.00	10.00	6.00
37	Vic Raschi	30.00	15.00	9.00
38	Whitey Lockman	20.00	10.00	6.00
39	Vic Wertz	20.00	10.00	6.00
40	"Bubba" Church	20.00	10.00	6.00
41	"Chico" Carrasquel	20.00	10.00	6.00
42	Johnny Wyrostek	20.00	10.00	6.00
43	Bob Feller	120.00	60.00	35.00
44	Roy Campanella	160.00	80.00	50.00
45	Johnny Pesky	20.00	10.00	6.00
46	Carl Scheib	20.00	10.00	6.00
47	Pete Castiglione	20.00	10.00	6.00

48	Vernon Bickford	20.00	10.00	6.00
49	Jim Hearn	20.00	10.00	6.00
50	Gerry Staley	20.00	10.00	6.00
51	Gil Coan	20.00	10.00	6.00
52	Phil Rizzuto	125.00	65.00	35.00
53	Richie Ashburn	90.00	45.00	27.50
54	Billy Pierce	25.00	12.50	7.50
55	Ken Raffensberger	20.00	10.00	6.00
56	Clyde King	25.00	12.50	7.50
57	Clyde Vollmer	20.00	10.00	6.00
58	Hank Majeski	20.00	10.00	6.00
59	Murry Dickson	20.00	10.00	6.00
60	Sid Gordon	20.00	10.00	6.00
61	Tommy Byrne	20.00	10.00	6.00
62	Joe Presko	20.00	10.00	6.00
63	Irv Noren	20.00	10.00	6.00
64	Roy Smalley	20.00	10.00	6.00
65	Hank Bauer	50.00	25.00	15.00
66	Sal Maglie	25.00	12.50	7.50
67	Johnny Groth	20.00	10.00	6.00
68	Jim Busby	20.00	10.00	6.00
69	Joe Adcock	20.00	10.00	6.00
70	Carl Erskine	40.00	20.00	12.00
71	Vernon Law	20.00	10.00	6.00
72	Earl Torgeson	20.00	10.00	6.00
73	Jerry Coleman	30.00	15.00	9.00
74	Wes Westrum	20.00	10.00	6.00
75	George Kell	45.00	22.50	13.50
76	Del Ennis	20.00	10.00	6.00
77	Eddie Robinson	20.00	10.00	6.00
78	Lloyd Merriman	20.00	10.00	6.00
79	Lou Brissie	20.00	10.00	6.00
80	Gil Hodges	100.00	50.00	30.00
81	Billy Goodman	20.00	10.00	6.00
82	Gus Zernial	20.00	10.00	6.00
83	Howie Pollet	20.00	10.00	6.00
84	Sam Jethroe	20.00	10.00	6.00
85	Marty Marion	25.00	12.50	7.50
86	Cal Abrams	25.00	12.50	7.50
87	Mickey Vernon	20.00	10.00	6.00
88	Bruce Edwards	20.00	10.00	6.00
89	Billy Hitchcock	20.00	10.00	6.00
90	Larry Jansen	20.00	10.00	6.00
91	Don Kolloway	20.00	10.00	6.00
92	Eddie Waitkus	20.00	10.00	6.00
93	Paul Richards	20.00	10.00	6.00
94	Luke Sewell	20.00	10.00	6.00
95	Luke Easter	20.00	10.00	6.00
96	Ralph Branca	40.00	20.00	12.00
97	Willard Marshall	20.00	10.00	6.00
98	Jimmy Dykes	20.00	10.00	6.00
99	Clyde McCullough	20.00	10.00	6.00
100	Sibby Sisti	20.00	10.00	6.00
101	Mickey Mantle	1,450	650.00	365.00
102	Peanuts Lowrey	20.00	10.00	6.00
103	Joe Haynes	20.00	10.00	6.00
104	Hal Jeffcoat	20.00	10.00	6.00
105	Bobby Brown	35.00	17.50	10.00
106	Randy Gumpert	20.00	10.00	6.00
107	Del Rice	20.00	10.00	6.00
108	George Metkovich	20.00	10.00	6.00
109	Tom Morgan	30.00	15.00	9.00
110	Max Lanier	20.00	10.00	6.00
111	"Hoot" Evers	20.00	10.00	6.00
112	"Smoky" Burgess	20.00	10.00	6.00
113	Al Zarilla	20.00	10.00	6.00
114	Frank Hiller	20.00	10.00	6.00
115	Larry Doby	60.00	30.00	18.00
116	Duke Snider	200.00	100.00	60.00
117	Bill Wight	20.00	10.00	6.00
118	Ray Murray	20.00	10.00	6.00
119	Bill Howerton	20.00	10.00	6.00
120	Chet Nichols	20.00	10.00	6.00
121	Al Corwin	20.00	10.00	6.00
122	Billy Johnson	20.00	10.00	6.00
123	Sid Hudson	20.00	10.00	6.00
124	Birdie Tebbetts	20.00	10.00	6.00
125	Howie Fox	20.00	10.00	6.00
126	Phil Cavarretta	20.00	10.00	6.00
127	Dick Sisler	20.00	10.00	6.00
128	Don Newcombe	45.00	22.50	13.50
129	Gus Niarhos	20.00	10.00	6.00
130	Allie Clark	20.00	10.00	6.00
131	Bob Swift	20.00	10.00	6.00
132	Dave Cole	20.00	10.00	6.00
133	Dick Kryhoski	20.00	10.00	6.00
134	Al Brazle	20.00	10.00	6.00
135	Mickey Harris	20.00	10.00	6.00
136	Gene Hermanski	20.00	10.00	6.00
137	Stan Rojek	20.00	10.00	6.00
138	Ted Wilks	20.00	10.00	6.00
139	Jerry Priddy	20.00	10.00	6.00
140	Ray Scarborough	20.00	10.00	6.00
141	Hank Edwards	20.00	10.00	6.00
142	Early Wynn	45.00	22.50	13.50
143	Sandy Consuegra	20.00	10.00	6.00
144	Joe Hatten	20.00	10.00	6.00
145	Johnny Mize	80.00	40.00	24.00
146	Leo Durocher	45.00	22.50	13.50
147	Marlin Stuart	20.00	10.00	6.00
148	Ken Heintzelman	20.00	10.00	6.00
149	Howie Judson	20.00	10.00	6.00
150	Herman Wehmeier	20.00	10.00	6.00
151	Al Rosen	30.00	15.00	9.00
152	Billy Cox	40.00	20.00	12.00
153	Fred Hatfield	20.00	10.00	6.00
154	Ferris Fain	20.00	10.00	6.00
155	Billy Meyer	20.00	10.00	6.00
156	Warren Spahn	90.00	45.00	27.50
157	Jim Delsing	20.00	10.00	6.00
158	Bucky Harris	30.00	15.00	9.00
159	Dutch Leonard	20.00	10.00	6.00
160	Eddie Stanky	20.00	10.00	6.00
161	Jackie Jensen	45.00	22.50	13.50
162	Monte Irvin	55.00	27.50	16.50
163	Johnny Lipon	20.00	10.00	6.00
164	Connie Ryan	20.00	10.00	6.00
165	Saul Rogovin	20.00	10.00	6.00

		NM	EX	VG
66	Bobby Adams	20.00	10.00	6.00
67	Bob Avila	20.00	10.00	6.00
68	Preacher Roe	35.00	17.50	10.00
69	Walt Dropo	20.00	10.00	6.00
70	Joe Astroth	20.00	10.00	6.00
71	Mel Queen	20.00	10.00	6.00
72	Ebba St. Claire	20.00	10.00	6.00
73	Gene Bearden	20.00	10.00	6.00
74	Mickey Grasso	20.00	10.00	6.00
75	Ransom Jackson	20.00	10.00	6.00
76	Harry Brecheen	20.00	10.00	6.00
77	Gene Woodling	35.00	17.50	10.00
78	Dave Williams	20.00	10.00	6.00
79	Pete Suder	20.00	10.00	6.00
80	Eddie Fitz Gerald	20.00	10.00	6.00
81	Joe Collins	30.00	15.00	9.00
82	Dave Koslo	20.00	10.00	6.00
83	Pat Mullin	20.00	10.00	6.00
84	Curt Simmons	20.00	10.00	6.00
85	Eddie Stewart	20.00	10.00	6.00
86	Frank Smith	20.00	10.00	6.00
87	Jim Hegan	20.00	10.00	6.00
88	Charlie Dressen	30.00	15.00	9.00
89	Jim Piersall	30.00	15.00	9.00
90	Dick Fowler	20.00	10.00	6.00
91	*Bob Friend*	25.00	12.50	7.50
92	John Cusick	20.00	10.00	6.00
93	Bobby Young	20.00	10.00	6.00
94	Bob Porterfield	20.00	10.00	6.00
95	Frank Baumholtz	20.00	10.00	6.00
96	Stan Musial	335.00	160.00	85.00
97	*Charlie Silvera*	35.00	17.50	10.00
98	Chuck Diering	20.00	10.00	6.00
99	Ted Gray	20.00	10.00	6.00
200	Ken Silvestri	20.00	10.00	6.00
201	Ray Coleman	20.00	10.00	6.00
202	Harry Perkowski	20.00	10.00	6.00
203	Steve Gromek	20.00	10.00	6.00
204	Andy Pafko	20.00	10.00	6.00
205	Walt Masterson	20.00	10.00	6.00
206	Elmer Valo	20.00	10.00	6.00
207	George Strickland	20.00	10.00	6.00
208	Walker Cooper	20.00	10.00	6.00
209	Dick Littlefield	20.00	10.00	6.00
210	Archie Wilson	20.00	10.00	6.00
211	Paul Minner	20.00	10.00	6.00
212	Solly Hemus	20.00	10.00	6.00
213	Monte Kennedy	20.00	10.00	6.00
214	Ray Boone	20.00	10.00	6.00
215	Sheldon Jones	20.00	10.00	6.00
216	Matt Batts	20.00	10.00	6.00
217	Casey Stengel	125.00	60.00	35.00
218	Willie Mays	925.00	400.00	175.00
219	Neil Berry	40.00	20.00	12.00
220	Russ Meyer	40.00	20.00	12.00
221	Lou Kretlow	40.00	20.00	12.00
222	"Dixie" Howell	40.00	20.00	12.00
223	*Harry Simpson*	45.00	22.50	13.50
224	Johnny Schmitz	40.00	20.00	12.00
225	Del Wilber	40.00	20.00	12.00
226	Alex Kellner	40.00	20.00	12.00
227	Clyde Sukeforth	40.00	20.00	12.00
228	Bob Chipman	40.00	20.00	12.00
229	Hank Arft	40.00	20.00	12.00
230	Frank Shea	40.00	20.00	12.00
231	*Dee Fondy*	40.00	20.00	12.00
232	Enos Slaughter	95.00	47.50	27.50
233	Bob Kuzava	50.00	25.00	15.00
234	Fred Fitzsimmons	40.00	20.00	12.00
235	Steve Souchock	40.00	20.00	12.00
236	Tommy Brown	40.00	20.00	12.00
237	Sherman Lollar	40.00	20.00	12.00
238	*Roy McMillan*	40.00	20.00	12.00
239	Dale Mitchell	40.00	20.00	12.00
240	*Billy Loes*	45.00	22.50	13.50
241	Mel Parnell	40.00	20.00	12.00
242	Everett Kell	40.00	20.00	12.00
243	"Red" Munger	40.00	20.00	12.00
244	*Lew Burdette*	60.00	30.00	18.00
245	George Schmees	40.00	20.00	12.00
246	Jerry Snyder	40.00	20.00	12.00
247	John Pramesa	40.00	20.00	12.00
248a	Bill Werle (. after G and most of W missing.)	40.00	20.00	12.00
248b	Bill Werle (Full signature.)	40.00	20.00	12.00
249	Henry Thompson	40.00	20.00	12.00
250	Ike Delock	40.00	20.00	12.00
251	Jack Lohrke	40.00	20.00	12.00
252	Frank Crosetti	180.00	30.00	15.00

1952 Bowman Proofs

Coincident to Topps issue of its "Giant Size" baseball cards in 1952, Bowman began experimenting with up-sizing its card issues from the then-current 2-1/16"

x 3-1/8". A group of proof cards was produced using 12 players from the '52 Bowman set. The proofs are 2-1/2" x 3-3/4", overall about 45% larger than the issued '52s. Each proof is found in two types, black-and-white and color. Both have blank-backs except for hand-written notes with the player's name, team and card number in the '52 set. Many of the proofs feature slight differences from the issued versions, such as uniform changes, elimination of background elements or picture cropping. The color proofs include a facsimile autograph. A small group of these proof cards entered the hobby early in the 1980s when a former Bowman executive disposed of his hobby card files. The proofs are numbered according to their number within the 1952 Bowman set.

		NM	EX	VG
	Common Player, B/W:	300.00	150.00	90.00
	Common Player, Color:	450.00	225.00	135.00
1	Yogi Berra (b/w)	1,000	500.00	300.00
1	Yogi Berra (Color)	1,600	800.00	480.00
2	Bobby Thomson (b/w)	600.00	300.00	180.00
2	Bobby Thomson (Color)	1,000	500.00	300.00
3	Fred Hutchinson (b/w)	400.00	200.00	120.00
3	Fred Hutchinson (Color)	450.00	225.00	135.00
4	Robin Roberts (b/w)	725.00	360.00	215.00
4	Robin Roberts (Color)	1,200	600.00	360.00
10	Bob Hooper (b/w)	400.00	200.00	120.00
10	Bob Hooper (Color)	450.00	225.00	135.00
11	Ralph Kiner (b/w)	725.00	360.00	215.00
11	Ralph Kiner (Color)	1,200	600.00	360.00
12	Max Surkont (b/w)	400.00	200.00	120.00
12	Max Surkont (Color)	450.00	225.00	135.00
13	Cliff Mapes (b/w)	400.00	200.00	120.00
13	Cliff Mapes (Color)	450.00	225.00	135.00
14	Cliff Chambers (b/w)	400.00	200.00	120.00
14	Cliff Chambers (Color)	450.00	225.00	135.00
34	Alvin Dark (b/w)	400.00	200.00	120.00
34	Alvin Dark (Color)	450.00	225.00	135.00
39	Vic Wertz (b/w)	400.00	200.00	120.00
39	Vic Wertz (Color)	450.00	225.00	135.00
142	Early Wynn (b/w)	650.00	325.00	195.00
142	Early Wynn (Color)	1,200	600.00	360.00
176	Harry Brecheen (b/w)	400.00	200.00	120.00
176	Harry Brecheen (Color)	450.00	225.00	135.00

1953 Bowman

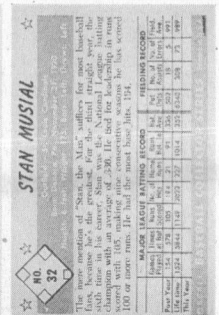

The first set of contemporary major league players featuring actual color photographs, the 160-card 1953 Bowman color set remains one of the most popular issues of the postwar era. The set is greatly appreciated for its uncluttered look; card fronts that contain no names, teams or facsimile autographs. Bowman increased the size of the cards to 2-1/2" x 3-3/4" to better compete with Topps' larger format. Bowman copied an idea from the 1952 Topps set and developed card backs that gave player career and previous-year statistics. The high-numbered cards (#113-160) are the scarcest of the set, with #113-128 being especially scarce.

		NM	EX	VG
	Complete Set (160):	16,000	7,500	4,250
	Common Player (1-112):	35.00	17.50	10.00
	Common Player (113-160):	90.00	45.00	25.00
1	Davey Williams	300.00	45.00	13.50
2	Vic Wertz	45.00	17.50	10.00
3	Sam Jethroe	35.00	17.50	10.00
4	Art Houtteman	35.00	17.50	10.00
5	Sid Gordon	35.00	17.50	10.00
6	Joe Ginsberg	35.00	17.50	10.00
7	Harry Chiti	35.00	17.50	10.00
8	Al Rosen	55.00	27.50	16.50
9	Phil Rizzuto	210.00	105.00	60.00
10	Richie Ashburn	110.00	55.00	35.00
11	Bobby Shantz	35.00	17.50	10.00
12	Carl Erskine	50.00	25.00	15.00
13	Gus Zernial	35.00	17.50	10.00
14	Billy Loes	55.00	27.50	16.50
15	Jim Busby	35.00	17.50	10.00
16	Bob Friend	35.00	17.50	10.00
17	Gerry Staley	35.00	17.50	10.00
18	Nellie Fox	90.00	45.00	25.00
19	Al Dark	35.00	17.50	10.00
20	Don Lenhardt	35.00	17.50	10.00
21	Joe Garagiola	50.00	25.00	15.00
22	Bob Porterfield	35.00	17.50	10.00
23	Herman Wehmeier	35.00	17.50	10.00
24	Jackie Jensen	45.00	22.50	13.50
25	"Hoot" Evers	35.00	17.50	10.00
26	Roy McMillan	35.00	17.50	10.00
27	Vic Raschi	70.00	35.00	20.00
28	"Smoky" Burgess	45.00	22.50	13.50
29	Roberto Avila	35.00	17.50	10.00
30	Phil Cavarretta	35.00	17.50	10.00
31	Jimmy Dykes	35.00	17.50	10.00
32	Stan Musial	465.00	160.00	90.00
33	Pee Wee Reese	550.00	275.00	165.00
34	Gil Coan	35.00	17.50	10.00
35	Maury McDermott	35.00	17.50	10.00
36	Minnie Minoso	85.00	42.50	25.00
37	Jim Wilson	35.00	17.50	10.00
38	Harry Byrd	35.00	17.50	10.00
39	Paul Richards	35.00	17.50	10.00
40	Larry Doby	145.00	75.00	45.00
41	Sammy White	35.00	17.50	10.00
42	Tommy Brown	35.00	17.50	10.00
43	Mike Garcia	35.00	17.50	10.00
44	Hank Bauer, Yogi Berra, Mickey Mantle	675.00	230.00	125.00
45	Walt Dropo	35.00	17.50	10.00
46	Roy Campanella	215.00	105.00	65.00
47	Ned Garver	35.00	17.50	10.00
48	Hank Sauer	35.00	17.50	10.00
49	Eddie Stanky	35.00	17.50	10.00
50	Lou Kretlow	35.00	17.50	10.00
51	Monte Irvin	55.00	27.50	16.50
52	Marty Marion	45.00	22.50	13.50
53	Del Rice	35.00	17.50	10.00
54	"Chico" Carrasquel	35.00	17.50	10.00
55	Leo Durocher	70.00	35.00	20.00
56	Bob Cain	35.00	17.50	10.00
57	Lou Boudreau	75.00	37.50	22.50
58	Willard Marshall	35.00	17.50	10.00
59	Mickey Mantle	1,200	525.00	290.00
60	Granny Hamner	35.00	17.50	10.00
61	George Kell	60.00	30.00	18.00
62	Ted Kluszewski	90.00	45.00	27.50
63	Gil McDougald	85.00	42.50	25.00
64	Curt Simmons	35.00	17.50	10.50
65	Robin Roberts	110.00	55.00	35.00
66	Mel Parnell	35.00	17.50	10.00
67	Mel Clark	35.00	17.50	10.00
68	Allie Reynolds	85.00	42.50	25.00
69	Charlie Grimm	35.00	17.50	10.00
70	Clint Courtney	35.00	17.50	10.00
71	Paul Minner	35.00	17.50	10.00
72	Ted Gray	35.00	17.50	10.00
73	Billy Pierce	40.00	20.00	12.00
74	Don Mueller	35.00	17.50	10.00
75	Saul Rogovin	35.00	17.50	10.00
76	Jim Hearn	35.00	17.50	10.00
77	Mickey Grasso	35.00	17.50	10.00
78	Carl Furillo	80.00	40.00	25.00
79	Ray Boone	35.00	17.50	10.00
80	Ralph Kiner	115.00	55.00	35.00
81	Enos Slaughter	145.00	70.00	45.00
82	Joe Astroth	35.00	17.50	10.00
83	Jack Daniels	35.00	17.50	10.00
84	Hank Bauer	80.00	40.00	25.00
85	Solly Hemus	35.00	17.50	10.00
86	Harry Simpson	35.00	17.50	10.00
87	Harry Perkowski	35.00	17.50	10.00
88	Joe Dobson	35.00	17.50	10.00
89	Sandalio Consuegra	35.00	17.50	10.00
90	Joe Nuxhall	35.00	17.50	10.00
91	Steve Souchock	35.00	17.50	10.00
92	Gil Hodges	190.00	95.00	55.00
93	Billy Martin, Phil Rizzuto	235.00	115.00	70.00
94	Bob Addis	35.00	17.50	10.00
95	Wally Moses	35.00	17.50	10.00
96	Sal Maglie	65.00	32.50	20.00
97	Eddie Mathews	275.00	135.00	80.00
98	Hector Rodriguez	35.00	17.50	10.00
99	Warren Spahn	280.00	140.00	85.00
100	Bill Wight	35.00	17.50	10.00
101	Red Schoendienst	95.00	47.50	27.50
102	Jim Hegan	35.00	17.50	10.00
103	Del Ennis	35.00	17.50	10.00
104	Luke Easter	35.00	17.50	10.00
105	Eddie Joost	35.00	17.50	10.00
106	Ken Raffensberger	35.00	17.50	10.00
107	Alex Kellner	35.00	17.50	10.00
108	Bobby Adams	35.00	17.50	10.00
109	Ken Wood	35.00	17.50	10.00
110	Bob Rush	35.00	17.50	10.00
111	Jim Dyck	35.00	17.50	10.00
112	Toby Atwell	35.00	17.50	10.00
113	Karl Drews	90.00	45.00	25.00
114	Bob Feller	525.00	230.00	125.00
115	Cloyd Boyer	90.00	45.00	25.00
116	Eddie Yost	90.00	45.00	25.00
117	Duke Snider	625.00	265.00	145.00
118	Billy Martin	425.00	210.00	125.00
119	Dale Mitchell	90.00	45.00	25.00
120	Marlin Stuart	90.00	45.00	25.00
121	Yogi Berra	600.00	300.00	180.00
122	Bill Serena	90.00	45.00	25.00
123	Johnny Lipon	90.00	45.00	25.00
124	Charlie Dressen	110.00	55.00	35.00
125	Fred Hatfield	90.00	45.00	25.00
126	Al Corwin	90.00	45.00	25.00
127	Dick Kryhoski	90.00	45.00	25.00
128	"Whitey" Lockman	90.00	45.00	25.00
129	Russ Meyer	95.00	47.50	27.50
130	Cass Michaels	90.00	45.00	25.00
131	Connie Ryan	90.00	45.00	25.00
132	Fred Hutchinson	90.00	45.00	25.00
133	Willie Jones	90.00	45.00	25.00
134	Johnny Pesky	90.00	45.00	25.00
135	Bobby Morgan	95.00	47.50	27.50
136	Jim Brideweser	100.00	50.00	30.00
137	Sam Dente	90.00	45.00	25.00
138	"Bubba" Church	90.00	45.00	25.00
139	Pete Runnels	90.00	45.00	25.00
140	Alpha Brazle	90.00	45.00	25.00
141	Frank "Spec" Shea	90.00	45.00	25.00
142	Larry Miggins	90.00	45.00	25.00
143	Al Lopez	115.00	55.00	35.00
144	Warren Hacker	90.00	45.00	25.00

		NM	EX	VG
145	George Shuba	125.00	60.00	35.00
146	Early Wynn	210.00	105.00	60.00
147	Clem Koshorek	90.00	45.00	25.00
148	Billy Goodman	90.00	45.00	25.00
149	Al Corwin	90.00	45.00	25.00
150	Carl Scheib	90.00	45.00	25.00
151	Joe Adcock	90.00	45.00	25.00
152	Clyde Vollmer	90.00	45.00	25.00
153	Whitey Ford	700.00	350.00	210.00
154	Omar "Turk" Lown	90.00	45.00	25.00
155	Allie Clark	90.00	45.00	25.00
156	Max Surkont	90.00	45.00	25.00
157	Sherman Lollar	90.00	45.00	25.00
158	Howard Fox	90.00	45.00	25.00
159	Mickey Vernon	95.00	47.50	27.50
	(Photo actually Floyd Baker.)			
160	Cal Abrams	425.00	50.00	27.50

1953 Bowman Black & White

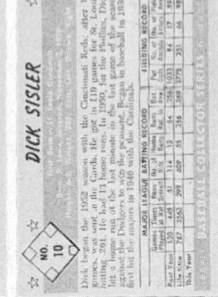

The 1953 Bowman black-and-white set is similar in all respects to the 1953 Bowman color cards, except that it lacks color. Sixty-four cards, which measure 2-1/2" x 3-3/4", comprise the set.

		NM	EX	VG
Complete Set (64):		4,500	2,125	1,275
Common Player:		55.00	25.00	15.00
1	Gus Bell	215.00	35.00	20.00
2	Willard Nixon	65.00	30.00	15.00
3	Bill Rigney	55.00	25.00	15.00
4	Pat Mullin	55.00	25.00	15.00
5	Dee Fondy	55.00	25.00	15.00
6	Ray Murray	55.00	25.00	15.00
7	Andy Seminick	55.00	25.00	15.00
8	Pete Suder	55.00	25.00	15.00
9	Walt Masterson	55.00	25.00	15.00
10	Dick Sisler	55.00	25.00	15.00
11	Dick Gernert	55.00	25.00	15.00
12	Randy Jackson	55.00	25.00	15.00
13	Joe Tipton	55.00	25.00	15.00
14	Bill Nicholson	55.00	25.00	15.00
15	Johnny Mize	100.00	50.00	30.00
16	Stu Miller	55.00	25.00	15.00
17	Virgil Trucks	55.00	25.00	15.00
18	Billy Hoeft	55.00	25.00	15.00
19	Paul LaPalme	55.00	25.00	15.00
20	Eddie Robinson	55.00	25.00	15.00
21	Clarence "Bud" Podbielan	55.00	25.00	15.00
22	Matt Batts	55.00	25.00	15.00
23	Wilmer Mizell	55.00	25.00	15.00
24	Del Wilber	55.00	25.00	15.00
25	Johnny Sain	100.00	50.00	30.00
26	Preacher Roe	90.00	45.00	25.00
27	Bob Lemon	130.00	65.00	35.00
28	Hoyt Wilhelm	140.00	70.00	40.00
29	Sid Hudson	55.00	25.00	15.00
30	Walker Cooper	55.00	25.00	15.00
31	Gene Woodling	100.00	50.00	30.00
32	Rocky Bridges	55.00	25.00	15.00
33	Bob Kuzava	55.00	25.00	15.00
34	Ebba St. Clair (St. Claire)	55.00	25.00	15.00
35	Johnny Wyrostek	55.00	25.00	15.00
36	Jim Piersall	90.00	45.00	25.00
37	Hal Jeffcoat	55.00	25.00	15.00
38	Dave Cole	55.00	25.00	15.00
39	Casey Stengel	600.00	225.00	115.00
40	Larry Jansen	55.00	25.00	15.00
41	Bob Ramazotti	55.00	25.00	15.00
42	Howie Judson	55.00	25.00	15.00
43a	Hal Bevan (Birth year 1950.)	55.00	25.00	15.00
43b	Hal Bevan (Birth year 1930.)	120.00	60.00	35.00
44	Jim Delsing	55.00	25.00	15.00
45	Irv Noren	100.00	50.00	30.00
46	Bucky Harris	100.00	50.00	35.00
47	Jack Lohrke	55.00	25.00	15.00
48	Steve Ridzik	55.00	25.00	15.00
49	Floyd Baker	55.00	25.00	15.00
50	Emil "Dutch" Leonard	55.00	25.00	15.00
51	Lew Burdette	75.00	35.00	20.00
52	Ralph Branca	100.00	50.00	30.00
53	Morris Martin	55.00	25.00	15.00
54	Bill Miller	55.00	25.00	15.00
55	Don Johnson	55.00	25.00	15.00
56	Roy Smalley	55.00	25.00	15.00
57	Andy Pafko	55.00	25.00	15.00
58	Jim Konstanty	55.00	25.00	15.00
59	Duane Pillette	55.00	25.00	15.00
60	Billy Cox	100.00	50.00	30.00
61	Tom Gorman	80.00	40.00	25.00
62	Keith Thomas	55.00	25.00	15.00
63	Steve Gromek	55.00	25.00	15.00
64	Andy Hansen	75.00	25.00	15.00

1953 Bowman Color Proofs

Four subjects are known to have survived in proof form created prior to the production of Bowman's landmark 1953 color card set. In the same 2-1/2" x 3-3/4" size as the issued cards, the proofs are blank-backed and lack the black frame line separating the picture from the white border. The Enos Slaughter card is otherwise identical to the issued version. The Spahn was changed to a different, more close-up picture for the issued card. The "Dodgers In Action" card was never issued, nor was the Ferris Fain card, probably due to Fain's trade from the A's to the White Sox prior to the 1953 season.

	NM	EX	VG
Complete Set (4):	4,800	2,400	1,450
Common Player:	750.00	375.00	225.00
(1) Dodgers In Action	2,200	1,100	660.00
(2) Ferris Fain	1,650	825.00	495.00
(3) Enos Slaughter	750.00	375.00	225.00
(4) Warren Spahn	1,800	900.00	540.00

1954 Bowman

Bowman's 1954 set consists of 224 full-color cards that measure 2-1/2" x 3-3/4". It is believed that contractual problems caused the withdrawal of card #66 (Ted Williams) from the set, creating one of the most sought-after scarcities of the postwar era. The Williams card was replaced by Jim Piersall (who is also #210) in subsequent print runs. The set contains over 40 variations, most involving statistical errors on the card backs that were corrected. On most cards neither variation carries a premium value as both varieties appear to have been printed in equal amounts. The complete set price that follows does not include all variations or #66 Williams.

		NM	EX	VG
Complete Set (224):		5,000	2,400	1,400
Common Player (1-128):		10.00	5.00	3.00
Common Player (129-224):		12.00	6.00	3.50
1	Phil Rizzuto	100.00	35.00	20.00
2	Jack Jensen	25.00	7.50	4.50
3	Marion Fricano	10.00	5.00	3.00
4	Bob Hooper	10.00	5.00	3.00
5	Billy Hunter	10.00	5.00	3.00
6	Nellie Fox	45.00	22.50	13.50
7	Walter Dropo	10.00	5.00	3.00
8	Jim Busby	10.00	5.00	3.00
9	Dave Williams	10.00	5.00	3.00
10	Carl Erskine	25.00	12.50	7.50
11	Sid Gordon	10.00	5.00	3.00
12a	Roy McMillan (551/1290 At Bat)	12.00	6.00	3.50
12b	Roy McMillan (557/1296 At Bat)	15.00	7.50	4.50
13	Paul Minner	10.00	5.00	3.00
14	Gerald Staley	10.00	5.00	3.00
15	Richie Ashburn	55.00	27.50	16.50
16	Jim Wilson	10.00	5.00	3.00
17	Tom Gorman	12.50	6.25	3.75
18	"Hoot" Evers	10.00	5.00	3.00
19	Bobby Shantz	10.00	5.00	3.00
20	Artie Houtteman	10.00	5.00	3.00
21	Vic Wertz	10.00	5.00	3.00
22a	Sam Mele (213/1661 Putouts)	12.00	6.00	3.50
22b	Sam Mele (217/1665 Putouts)	15.00	7.50	4.50
23	*Harvey Kuenn*	20.00	10.00	6.0
24	Bob Porterfield	10.00	5.00	3.0
25a	Wes Westrum (1.000/.987 Field Avg.)	12.00	6.00	3.5
25b	Wes Westrum (.982/.986 Field Avg.)	15.00	7.50	4.5
26a	Billy Cox (1.000/.960 Field Avg.)	15.00	7.50	4.5
26b	Billy Cox (.972/.960 Field Avg.)	20.00	10.00	6.0
27	Dick Cole	10.00	5.00	3.0
28a	Jim Greengrass (Birthplace Addison, N.J.)	20.00	10.00	6.0
28b	Jim Greengrass (Birthplace Addison, N.Y.)	12.00	6.00	3.5
29	Johnny Klippstein	10.00	5.00	3.0
30	Del Rice	10.00	5.00	3.0
31	"Smoky" Burgess	10.00	5.00	3.0
32	Del Crandall	10.00	5.00	3.0
33a	Vic Raschi (No trade line.)	27.50	13.50	8.2
33b	Vic Raschi (Traded line.)	50.00	25.00	15.0
34	Sammy White	10.00	5.00	3.0
35a	Eddie Joost (Quiz answer is 8)	12.00	6.00	3.5
35b	Eddie Joost (Quiz answer is 33.)	15.00	7.50	4.5
36	George Strickland	10.00	5.00	3.0
37	Dick Kokos	10.00	5.00	3.0
38a	Minnie Minoso (.895/.961 Field Avg.)	25.00	12.50	7.5
38b	Minnie Minoso (.963/.963 Field Avg.)	30.00	15.00	9.0
39	Ned Garver	10.00	5.00	3.0
40	Gil Coan	10.00	5.00	3.0
41a	Alvin Dark (.986/.960 Field Avg.)	12.00	6.00	3.5
41b	Alvin Dark (.968/.960 Field Avg.)	15.00	7.50	4.5
42	Billy Loes	15.00	7.50	4.5
43a	Bob Friend (20 shutouts in quiz question.)	12.00	6.00	3.5
43b	Bob Friend (16 shutouts in quiz question.)	15.00	7.50	4.5
44	Harry Perkowski	10.00	5.00	3.0
45	Ralph Kiner	35.00	17.50	10.0
46	"Rip" Repulski	10.00	5.00	3.0
47a	Granny Hamner (.970/.953 Field Avg.)	12.00	6.00	3.5
47b	Granny Hamner (.953/.951 Field Avg.)	15.00	7.50	4.5
48	Jack Dittmer	10.00	5.00	3.0
49	Harry Byrd	12.50	6.25	3.7
50	George Kell	30.00	15.00	9.0
51	Alex Kellner	10.00	5.00	3.0
52	Joe Ginsberg	10.00	5.00	3.0
53a	Don Lenhardt (.969/.984 Field Avg.)	12.00	6.00	3.5
53b	Don Lenhardt (.966/.983 Field Avg.)	15.00	7.50	4.5
54	"Chico" Carrasquel	10.00	5.00	3.0
55	Jim Delsing	10.00	5.00	3.0
56	Maurice McDermott	10.00	5.00	3.0
57	Hoyt Wilhelm	27.50	13.50	8.2
58	Pee Wee Reese	70.00	35.00	20.0
59	Bob Schultz	10.00	5.00	3.0
60	Fred Baczewski	10.00	5.00	3.0
61a	Eddie Miksis (.954/.962 Field Avg.)	12.00	6.00	3.5
61b	Eddie Miksis (.954/.961 Field Avg.)	15.00	7.50	4.5
62	Enos Slaughter	35.00	17.50	10.0
63	Earl Torgeson	10.00	5.00	3.0
64	Eddie Mathews	65.00	32.50	20.0
65	Mickey Mantle	900.00	350.00	215.0
66a	Ted Williams	2,100	975.00	500.0
66b	Jimmy Piersall	60.00	30.00	18.0
67a	Carl Scheib (.306 Pct. with two lines under bio.)	25.00	12.50	7.5
67b	Carl Scheib (.306 Pct. with one line under bio.)	12.00	6.00	3.5
67c	Carl Scheib (.300 Pct.)	15.00	7.50	4.5
68	Bob Avila	10.00	5.00	3.0
69	Clinton Courtney	10.00	5.00	3.0
70	Willard Marshall	10.00	5.00	3.0
71	Ted Gray	10.00	5.00	3.0
72	Ed Yost	10.00	5.00	3.0
73	Don Mueller	10.00	5.00	3.0
74	Jim Gilliam	35.00	17.50	10.0
75	Max Surkont	10.00	5.00	3.0
76	Joe Nuxhall	10.00	5.00	3.0
77	Bob Rush	10.00	5.00	3.0
78	Sal Yvars	10.00	5.00	3.0
79	Curt Simmons	10.00	5.00	3.0
80a	Johnny Logan (106 Runs)	12.00	6.00	3.5
80b	Johnny Logan (100 Runs)	15.00	7.50	4.5
81a	Jerry Coleman (1.000/.975 Field Avg.)	15.00	7.50	4.5
81b	Jerry Coleman (.952/.975 Field Avg.)	20.00	10.00	6.0
82a	Bill Goodman (.965/.986 Field Avg.)	12.00	6.00	3.5
82b	Bill Goodman (.972/.985 Field Avg.)	15.00	7.50	4.5
83	Ray Murray	10.00	5.00	3.0
84	Larry Doby	45.00	22.50	13.5
85a	Jim Dyck (.926/.956 Field Avg.)	12.00	6.00	3.5
85b	Jim Dyck (.947/.960 Field Avg.)	15.00	7.50	4.5
86	Harry Dorish	10.00	5.00	3.0
87	Don Lund	10.00	5.00	3.0
88	Tommy Umphlett	10.00	5.00	3.0
89	Willie Mays	390.00	125.00	75.0
90	Roy Campanella	105.00	50.00	30.0
91	Cal Abrams	10.00	5.00	3.0
92	Ken Raffensberger	10.00	5.00	3.0
93a	Bill Serena (.983/.966 Field Avg.)	12.00	6.00	3.5
93b	Bill Serena (.977/.966 Field Avg.)	15.00	7.50	4.5

		NM	EX	VG
94a	Solly Hemus (476/1343 Assists)	12.00	6.00	3.50
94b	Solly Hemus (477/1343 Assists)	15.00	7.50	4.50
95	Robin Roberts	40.00	20.00	12.00
96	Joe Adcock	10.00	5.00	3.00
97	Gil McDougald	20.00	10.00	6.00
98	Ellis Kinder	10.00	5.00	3.00
99a	Peter Suder (.985/.974 Field Avg.)	12.00	6.00	3.50
99b	Peter Suder (.978/.974 Field Avg.)	15.00	7.50	4.50
100	Mike Garcia	10.00	5.00	3.00
101	*Don Larsen*	40.00	20.00	12.00
102	Bill Pierce	10.00	5.00	3.00
103a	Stephen Souchock (144/1192 Putouts)	12.00	6.00	3.50
103b	Stephen Souchock (147/1195 Putouts)	15.00	7.50	4.50
104	Frank Spec Shea	10.00	5.00	3.00
105a	Sal Maglie (Quiz answer is 8)	20.00	10.00	6.00
105b	Sal Maglie (Quiz answer is 1904)	30.00	15.00	9.00
106	Clem Labine	20.00	10.00	6.00
107	Paul LaPalme	10.00	5.00	3.00
108	Bobby Adams	10.00	5.00	3.00
109	Roy Smalley	10.00	5.00	3.00
110	Red Schoendienst	30.00	15.00	9.00
111	Murry Dickson	10.00	5.00	3.00
112	Andy Pafko	10.00	5.00	3.00
113	Allie Reynolds	20.00	10.00	6.00
114	Willard Nixon	10.00	5.00	3.00
115	Don Bollweg	10.00	5.00	3.00
116	Luke Easter	10.00	5.00	3.00
117	Dick Kryhoski	10.00	5.00	3.00
118	Bob Boyd	10.00	5.00	3.00
119	Fred Hatfield	10.00	5.00	3.00
120	Mel Hoderlein	10.00	5.00	3.00
121	Ray Katt	10.00	5.00	3.00
122	Carl Furillo	30.00	15.00	9.00
123	Toby Atwell	10.00	5.00	3.00
124a	Gus Bell (15/27 Errors)	12.00	6.00	3.50
124b	Gus Bell (11/26 Errors)	15.00	7.50	4.50
125	Warren Hacker	10.00	5.00	3.00
126	Cliff Chambers	10.00	5.00	3.00
127	Del Ennis	10.00	5.00	3.00
128	Ebba St. Claire	10.00	5.00	3.00
129	Hank Bauer	35.00	17.50	10.00
130	Milt Bolling	12.00	6.00	3.50
131	Joe Astroth	12.00	6.00	3.50
132	Bob Feller	80.00	40.00	25.00
133	Duane Pillette	12.00	6.00	3.50
134	Luis Aloma	12.00	6.00	3.50
135	Johnny Pesky	12.00	6.00	3.50
136	Clyde Vollmer	12.00	6.00	3.50
137	Al Corwin	12.00	6.00	3.50
138a	Gil Hodges (.993/.991 Field Avg.)	70.00	35.00	20.00
138b	Gil Hodges (.992/.991 Field Avg.)	100.00	50.00	30.00
139a	Preston Ward (.961/.992 Field Avg.)	15.00	7.50	4.50
139b	Preston Ward (.990/.992 Field Avg.)	17.50	8.75	5.25
140a	Saul Rogovin (7-12 Won/Lost with 2 Strikeouts)	15.00	7.50	4.50
140b	Saul Rogovin (7-12 Won/Lost with 62 Strikeouts)	17.50	8.75	5.25
140c	Saul Rogovin (8-12 Won/Lost)	40.00	20.00	12.00
141	Joe Garagiola	30.00	15.00	9.00
142	Al Brazle	12.00	6.00	3.50
143	Willie Jones	12.00	6.00	3.50
144	*Ernie Johnson*	30.00	15.00	9.00
145a	Billy Martin	60.00	30.00	18.00
	(.985/.983 Field Avg.)			
145b	Billy Martin	70.00	35.00	20.00
	(.983/.982 Field Avg.)			
146	Dick Gernert	12.00	6.00	3.50
147	Joe DeMaestri	12.00	6.00	3.50
148	Dale Mitchell	12.00	6.00	3.50
149	Bob Young	12.00	6.00	3.50
150	Cass Michaels	12.00	6.00	3.50
151	Pat Mullin	12.00	6.00	3.50
152	Mickey Vernon	12.00	6.00	3.50
153a	"Whitey" Lockman (100/331 Assists)	15.00	7.50	4.50
153b	"Whitey" Lockman (102/333 Assists)	17.50	8.75	5.25
154	Don Newcombe	60.00	30.00	18.00
155	*Frank Thomas*	25.00	12.50	7.50
156a	Rocky Bridges (320/467 Assists)	15.00	7.50	4.50
156b	Rocky Bridges (328/475 Assists)	17.50	8.75	5.25
157	Omar Lown	12.00	6.00	3.50
158	Stu Miller	12.00	6.00	3.50
159	John Lindell	12.00	6.00	3.50
160	Danny O'Connell	12.00	6.00	3.50
161	Yogi Berra	110.00	55.00	35.00
162	Ted Lepcio	12.00	6.00	3.50
163a	Dave Philley (152 Games, no traded line.)	50.00	25.00	15.00
163b	Dave Philley (152 Games, traded line.)	22.50	11.00	6.75
163c	Dave Philley (157 Games, traded line.)	27.50	13.50	8.25
164	Early Wynn	45.00	22.50	13.50
165	Johnny Groth	12.00	6.00	3.50
166	Sandy Consuegra	12.00	6.00	3.50
167	Bill Hoeft	12.00	6.00	3.50
168	Edward Fitz Gerald	12.00	6.00	3.50
169	Larry Jansen	12.00	6.00	3.50
170	Duke Snider	125.00	60.00	35.00
171	Carlos Bernier	12.00	6.00	3.50
172	Andy Seminick	12.00	6.00	3.50
173	Dee Fondy	12.00	6.00	3.50
174a	Pete Castiglione (.966/.959 Field Avg.)	15.00	7.50	4.50

		NM	EX	VG
174b	Pete Castiglione (.970/.959 Field Avg.)	17.50	8.75	5.25
175	Mel Clark	12.00	6.00	3.50
176	Vernon Bickford	12.00	6.00	3.50
177	Whitey Ford	100.00	50.00	30.00
178	Del Wilber	12.00	6.00	3.50
179a	Morris Martin (44 ERA)	15.00	7.50	4.50
179b	Morris Martin (4.44 ERA)	17.50	8.75	5.25
180	Joe Tipton	12.00	6.00	3.50
181	Les Moss	12.00	6.00	3.50
182	Sherman Lollar	12.00	6.00	3.50
183	Matt Batts	12.00	6.00	3.50
184	Mickey Grasso	12.00	6.00	3.50
185a	*Daryl Spencer* (.941/.944 Field Avg.)	15.00	7.50	4.50
185b	*Daryl Spencer* (.933/.936 Field Avg.)	17.50	8.75	5.25
186	Russ Meyer	15.00	7.50	4.50
187	Vern Law	12.00	6.00	3.50
188	Frank Smith	12.00	6.00	3.50
189	Ransom Jackson	12.00	6.00	3.50
190	Joe Presko	12.00	6.00	3.50
191	Karl Drews	12.00	6.00	3.50
192	Lew Burdette	12.00	6.00	3.50
193	Eddie Robinson	15.00	7.50	4.50
194	Sid Hudson	12.00	6.00	3.50
195	Bob Cain	12.00	6.00	3.50
196	Bob Lemon	30.00	15.00	9.00
197	Lou Kretlow	12.00	6.00	3.50
198	Virgil Trucks	12.00	6.00	3.50
199	Steve Gromek	12.00	6.00	3.50
200	Connie Marrero	12.00	6.00	3.50
201	Bob Thomson	20.00	10.00	6.00
202	George Shuba	15.00	7.50	4.50
203	Vic Janowicz	25.00	12.50	7.50
204	Jack Collum	12.00	6.00	3.50
205	Hal Jeffcoat	12.00	6.00	3.50
206	Steve Bilko	12.00	6.00	3.50
207	Stan Lopata	12.00	6.00	3.50
208	Johnny Antonelli	12.00	6.00	3.50
209	Gene Woodling (Photo reversed.)	35.00	17.50	10.00
210	Jimmy Piersall	35.00	17.50	10.00
211	Jim Robertson	12.00	6.00	3.50
212a	Owen Friend (.964/.957 Field Avg.)	15.00	7.50	4.50
212b	Owen Friend (.967/.958 Field Avg.)	17.50	8.75	5.25
213	Dick Littlefield	12.00	6.00	3.50
214	Ferris Fain	12.00	6.00	3.50
215	Johnny Bucha	12.00	6.00	3.50
216a	Jerry Snyder (.988/.988 Field Avg.)	15.00	7.50	4.50
216b	Jerry Snyder (.968/.968 Field Avg.)	17.50	8.75	5.25
217a	Henry Thompson (.956/.951 Field Avg.)	15.00	7.50	4.50
217b	Henry Thompson (.958/.952 Field Avg.)	17.50	8.75	5.25
218	Preacher Roe	35.00	17.50	10.00
219	Hal Rice	12.00	6.00	3.50
220	Hobie Landrith	12.00	6.00	3.50
221	Frank Baumholtz	12.00	6.00	3.50
222	Memo Luna	15.00	7.50	4.50
223	Steve Ridzik	12.00	6.00	3.50
224	Billy Bruton	45.00	12.00	5.00

1955 Bowman

Bowman produced its final baseball card set as an independent card maker in 1955, a popular issue that has color player photographs placed inside a television set design. The set consists of 320 cards measuring 2-1/2" x 3-3/4". High-numbered cards (#225-320) appear to have replaced certain low-numbered cards on the press sheets and are scarcer. The high series includes 31 umpire cards.

		NM	EX	VG
	Complete Set (320):	7,000	3,500	2,000
	Common Player (1-224):	12.50	6.25	3.75
	Common Player (225-320):	25.00	12.50	7.50
1	Hoyt Wilhelm	65.00	30.00	18.00
2	Al Dark	15.00	7.50	4.50
3	Joe Coleman	12.50	6.25	3.75
4	Eddie Waitkus	12.50	6.25	3.75
5	Jim Robertson	12.50	6.25	3.75
6	Pete Suder	12.50	6.25	3.75
7	Gene Baker	12.50	6.25	3.75
8	Warren Hacker	12.50	6.25	3.75
9	Gil McDougald	25.00	12.50	7.50
10	Phil Rizzuto	60.00	30.00	18.00
11	Billy Bruton	12.50	6.25	3.75
12	Andy Pafko	12.50	6.25	3.75
13	Clyde Vollmer	12.50	6.25	3.75

		NM	EX	VG
14	Gus Keriazakos	12.50	6.25	3.75
15	*Frank Sullivan*	12.50	6.25	3.75
16	Jim Piersall	12.50	6.25	3.75
17	Del Ennis	12.50	6.25	3.75
18	Stan Lopata	12.50	6.25	3.75
19	Bobby Avila	12.50	6.25	3.75
20	Al Smith	12.50	6.25	3.75
21	Don Hoak	15.00	7.50	4.50
22	Roy Campanella	75.00	37.50	22.50
23	Al Kaline	80.00	40.00	24.00
24	Al Aber	12.50	6.25	3.75
25	Minnie Minoso	30.00	15.00	9.00
26	Virgil Trucks	12.50	6.25	3.75
27	Preston Ward	12.50	6.25	3.75
28	Dick Cole	12.50	6.25	3.75
29	Red Schoendienst	25.00	12.50	7.50
30	Bill Sarni	12.50	6.25	3.75
31	Johnny Temple	12.50	6.25	3.75
32	Wally Post	12.50	6.25	3.75
33	Nellie Fox	35.00	17.50	10.00
34	Clint Courtney	12.50	6.25	3.75
35	Bill Tuttle	12.50	6.25	3.75
36	Wayne Belardi	12.50	6.25	3.75
37	Pee Wee Reese	50.00	25.00	15.00
38	Early Wynn	25.00	12.50	7.50
39	Bob Darnell	15.00	7.50	4.50
40	Vic Wertz	12.50	6.25	3.75
41	Mel Clark	12.50	6.25	3.75
42	Bob Greenwood	12.50	6.25	3.75
43	Bob Buhl	12.50	6.25	3.75
44	Danny O'Connell	12.50	6.25	3.75
45	Tom Umphlett	12.50	6.25	3.75
46	Mickey Vernon	12.50	6.25	3.75
47	Sammy White	12.50	6.25	3.75
48a	Milt Bolling (Frank Bolling back.)	20.00	10.00	6.00
48b	Milt Bolling (Milt Bolling back.)	20.00	10.00	6.00
49	Jim Greengrass	12.50	6.25	3.75
50	Hobie Landrith	12.50	6.25	3.75
51	Elvin Tappe	12.50	6.25	3.75
52	Hal Rice	12.50	6.25	3.75
53	Alex Kellner	12.50	6.25	3.75
54	Don Bollweg	12.50	6.25	3.75
55	Cal Abrams	12.50	6.25	3.75
56	Billy Cox	12.50	6.25	3.75
57	Bob Friend	12.50	6.25	3.75
58	Frank Thomas	12.50	6.25	3.75
59	Whitey Ford	70.00	35.00	20.00
60	Enos Slaughter	30.00	15.00	9.00
61	Paul LaPalme	12.50	6.25	3.75
62	Royce Lint	12.50	6.25	3.75
63	Irv Noren	15.00	7.50	4.50
64	Curt Simmons	12.50	6.25	3.75
65	*Don Zimmer*	30.00	15.00	9.00
66	George Shuba	15.00	7.50	4.50
67	Don Larsen	30.00	15.00	9.00
68	*Elston Howard*	80.00	40.00	24.00
69	Bill Hunter	15.00	7.50	4.50
70	Lew Burdette	12.50	6.25	3.75
71	Dave Jolly	12.50	6.25	3.75
72	Chet Nichols	12.50	6.25	3.75
73	Eddie Yost	12.50	6.25	3.75
74	Jerry Snyder	12.50	6.25	3.75
75	Brooks Lawrence	12.50	6.25	3.75
76	Tom Poholsky	12.50	6.25	3.75
77	Jim McDonald	12.50	6.25	3.75
78	Gil Coan	12.50	6.25	3.75
79	Willie Miranda	12.50	6.25	3.75
80	Lou Limmer	12.50	6.25	3.75
81	Bob Morgan	12.50	6.25	3.75
82	Lee Walls	12.50	6.25	3.75
83	Max Surkont	12.50	6.25	3.75
84	George Freese	12.50	6.25	3.75
85	Cass Michaels	12.50	6.25	3.75
86	Ted Gray	12.50	6.25	3.75
87	Randy Jackson	12.50	6.25	3.75
88	Steve Bilko	12.50	6.25	3.75
89	Lou Boudreau	25.00	12.50	7.50
90	Art Ditmar	12.50	6.25	3.75
91	Dick Marlowe	12.50	6.25	3.75
92	George Zuverink	12.50	6.25	3.75
93	Andy Seminick	12.50	6.25	3.75
94	Hank Thompson	12.50	6.25	3.75
95	Sal Maglie	12.50	6.25	3.75
96	Ray Narleski	12.50	6.25	3.75
97	John Podres	30.00	15.00	9.00
98	Jim Gilliam	27.50	13.50	8.25
99	Jerry Coleman	15.00	7.50	4.50
100	Tom Morgan	15.00	7.50	4.50
101a	Don Johnson (Ernie Johnson (Braves) on front.)	60.00	30.00	18.00
101b	Don Johnson (Don Johnson (Orioles) on front.)	27.50	13.50	8.25
102	Bobby Thomson	17.50	8.75	5.25
103	Eddie Mathews	55.00	27.50	16.50
104	Bob Porterfield	12.50	6.25	3.75
105	Johnny Schmitz	12.50	6.25	3.75
106	Del Rice	12.50	6.25	3.75
107	Solly Hemus	12.50	6.25	3.75
108	Lou Kretlow	12.50	6.25	3.75
109	Vern Stephens	12.50	6.25	3.75
110	Bob Miller	12.50	6.25	3.75
111	Steve Ridzik	12.50	6.25	3.75
112	Granny Hamner	12.50	6.25	3.75
113	Bob Hall	12.50	6.25	3.75
114	Vic Janowicz	12.50	6.25	3.75
115	Roger Bowman	12.50	6.25	3.75
116	Sandy Consuegra	12.50	6.25	3.75
117	Johnny Groth	12.50	6.25	3.75
118	Bobby Adams	12.50	6.25	3.75
119	Joe Astroth	12.50	6.25	3.75
120	Ed Burtschy	12.50	6.25	3.75
121	Rufus Crawford	12.50	6.25	3.75
122	Al Corwin	12.50	6.25	3.75
123	Marv Grissom	12.50	6.25	3.75
124	Johnny Antonelli	12.50	6.25	3.75
125	Paul Giel	12.50	6.25	3.75
126	Billy Goodman	12.50	6.25	3.75

127	Hank Majeski	12.50	6.25	3.75
128	Mike Garcia	12.50	6.25	3.75
129	Hal Naragon	12.50	6.25	3.75
130	Richie Ashburn	50.00	25.00	15.00
131	Willard Marshall	12.50	6.25	3.75
132a	Harvey Kueen (Misspelled last name.)	25.00	12.50	7.50
132b	Harvey Kuenn (Corrected)	35.00	17.50	10.00
133	Charles King	12.50	6.25	3.75
134	Bob Feller	60.00	30.00	18.00
135	Lloyd Merriman	12.50	6.25	3.75
136	Rocky Bridges	12.50	6.25	3.75
137	Bob Talbot	12.50	6.25	3.75
138	Davey Williams	12.50	6.25	3.75
139	Billy & Bobby Shantz	15.00	7.50	4.50
140	Bobby Shantz	12.50	6.25	3.75
141	Wes Westrum	12.50	6.25	3.75
142	Rudy Regalado	12.50	6.25	3.75
143	Don Newcombe	25.00	12.50	7.50
144	Art Houtteman	12.50	6.25	3.75
145	Bob Nieman	12.50	6.25	3.75
146	Don Liddle	12.50	6.25	3.75
147	Sam Mele	12.50	6.25	3.75
148	Bob Chakales	12.50	6.25	3.75
149	Cloyd Boyer	12.50	6.25	3.75
150	Bill Klaus	12.50	6.25	3.75
151	Jim Brideweser	12.50	6.25	3.75
152	Johnny Klippstein	12.50	6.25	3.75
153	Eddie Robinson	15.00	7.50	4.50
154	*Frank Lary*	12.50	6.25	3.75
155	Gerry Staley	12.50	6.25	3.75
156	Jim Hughes	15.00	7.50	4.50
157a	Ernie Johnson (Don Johnson (Orioles) picture on front.)	15.00	7.50	4.50
157b	Ernie Johnson (Ernie Johnson (Braves) picture on front.)	30.00	15.00	9.00
158	Gil Hodges	40.00	20.00	12.00
159	Harry Byrd	12.50	6.25	3.75
160	Bill Skowron	40.00	20.00	12.00
161	Matt Batts	12.50	6.25	3.75
162	Charlie Maxwell	12.50	6.25	3.75
163	Sid Gordon	12.50	6.25	3.75
164	Toby Atwell	12.50	6.25	3.75
165	Maurice McDermott	12.50	6.25	3.75
166	Jim Busby	12.50	6.25	3.75
167	Bob Grim	15.00	7.50	4.50
168	Yogi Berra	100.00	50.00	30.00
169	Carl Furillo	27.50	13.50	8.25
170	Carl Erskine	25.00	12.50	7.50
171	Robin Roberts	32.50	16.00	10.00
172	Willie Jones	12.50	6.25	3.75
173	"Chico" Carrasquel	12.50	6.25	3.75
174	Sherman Lollar	12.50	6.25	3.75
175	Wilmer Shantz	12.50	6.25	3.75
176	Joe DeMaestri	12.50	6.25	3.75
177	Willard Nixon	12.50	6.25	3.75
178	Tom Brewer	12.50	6.25	3.75
179	Hank Aaron	200.00	70.00	40.00
180	Johnny Logan	12.50	6.25	3.75
181	Eddie Miksis	12.50	6.25	3.75
182	Bob Rush	12.50	6.25	3.75
183	Ray Katt	12.50	6.25	3.75
184	Willie Mays	180.00	85.00	45.00
185	Vic Raschi	12.50	6.25	3.75
186	Alex Grammas	12.50	6.25	3.75
187	Fred Hatfield	12.50	6.25	3.75
188	Ned Garver	12.50	6.25	3.75
189	Jack Collum	12.50	6.25	3.75
190	Fred Baczewski	12.50	6.25	3.75
191	Bob Lemon	30.00	15.00	9.00
192	George Strickland	12.50	6.25	3.75
193	Howie Judson	12.50	6.25	3.75
194	Joe Nuxhall	12.50	6.25	3.75
195a	Erv Palica (No traded line.)	30.00	15.00	9.00
195b	Erv Palica (Traded line.)	125.00	60.00	35.00
196	Russ Meyer	15.00	7.50	4.50
197	Ralph Kiner	35.00	17.50	10.00
198	Dave Pope	12.50	6.25	3.75
199	Vernon Law	12.50	6.25	3.75
200	Dick Littlefield	12.50	6.25	3.75
201	Allie Reynolds	25.00	12.50	7.50
202	Mickey Mantle	525.00	250.00	125.00
203	Steve Gromek	12.50	6.25	3.75
204a	Frank Bolling (Milt Bolling back.)	45.00	22.50	13.50
204b	Frank Bolling (Frank Bolling back.)	30.00	15.00	9.00
205	"Rip" Repulski	12.50	6.25	3.75
206	Ralph Beard	12.50	6.25	3.75
207	Frank Shea	12.50	6.25	3.75
208	Ed Fitz Gerald	12.50	6.25	3.75
209	"Smoky" Burgess	12.50	6.25	3.75
210	Earl Torgeson	12.50	6.25	3.75
211	John "Sonny" Dixon	12.50	6.25	3.75
212	Jack Dittmer	12.50	6.25	3.75
213	George Kell	30.00	15.00	9.00
214	Billy Pierce	12.50	6.25	3.75
215	Bob Kuzava	12.50	6.25	3.75
216	Preacher Roe	15.00	7.50	4.50
217	Del Crandall	12.50	6.25	3.75
218	Joe Adcock	12.50	6.25	3.75
219	"Whitey" Lockman	12.50	6.25	3.75
220	Jim Hearn	12.50	6.25	3.75
221	Hector "Skinny" Brown	12.50	6.25	3.75
222	Russ Kemmerer	12.50	6.25	3.75
223	Hal Jeffcoat	12.50	6.25	3.75
224	Dee Fondy	12.50	6.25	3.75
225	Paul Richards	25.00	12.50	7.50
226	W.F. McKinley/Umpire	30.00	15.00	9.00
227	Frank Baumholtz	25.00	12.50	7.50
228	John M. Phillips	25.00	12.50	7.50
229	Jim Brosnan	25.00	12.50	7.50
230	Al Brazle	25.00	12.50	7.50
231	Jim Konstanty	25.00	12.50	7.50
232	Birdie Tebbetts	25.00	12.50	7.50
233	Bill Serena	25.00	12.50	7.50
234	Dick Bartell	25.00	12.50	7.50

235	J.A. Paparella/Umpire	30.00	15.00	9.00
236	Murry Dickson	25.00	12.50	7.50
237	Johnny Wyrostek	25.00	12.50	7.50
238	Eddie Stanky	25.00	12.50	7.50
239	Edwin A. Rommel/Umpire	30.00	15.00	9.00
240	Billy Loes	25.00	12.50	7.50
241	John Pesky	25.00	12.50	7.50
242	Ernie Banks	240.00	100.00	70.00
243	Gus Bell	25.00	12.50	7.50
244	Duane Pillette	25.00	12.50	7.50
245	Bill Miller	25.00	12.50	7.50
246	Hank Bauer	45.00	22.50	13.50
247	Dutch Leonard	25.00	12.50	7.50
248	Harry Dorish	25.00	12.50	7.50
249	Billy Gardner	25.00	12.50	7.50
250	Larry Napp/Umpire	30.00	15.00	9.00
251	Stan Jok	25.00	12.50	7.50
252	Roy Smalley	25.00	12.50	7.50
253	Jim Wilson	25.00	12.50	7.50
254	Bennett Flowers	25.00	12.50	7.50
255	Pete Runnels	25.00	12.50	7.50
256	Owen Friend	25.00	12.50	7.50
257	Tom Alston	25.00	12.50	7.50
258	John W. Stevens/Umpire	30.00	15.00	9.00
259	*Don Mossi*	35.00	17.50	10.00
260	Edwin H. Hurley/Umpire	30.00	15.00	9.00
261	Walt Moryn	25.00	12.50	7.50
262	Jim Lemon	25.00	12.50	7.50
263	Eddie Joost	25.00	12.50	7.50
264	Bill Henry	25.00	12.50	7.50
265	Al Barlick/Umpire	75.00	37.50	22.50
266	Mike Fornieles	25.00	12.50	7.50
267	George Honochick/Umpire	50.00	25.00	15.00
268	Roy Lee Hawes	25.00	12.50	7.50
269	Joe Amalfitano	25.00	12.50	7.50
270	Chico Fernandez	25.00	12.50	7.50
271	Bob Hooper	25.00	12.50	7.50
272	John Flaherty/Umpire	30.00	15.00	9.00
273	"Bubba" Church	25.00	12.50	7.50
274	Jim Delsing	25.00	12.50	7.50
275	William T. Grieve/Umpire	30.00	15.00	9.00
276	Ike Delock	25.00	12.50	7.50
277	Ed Runge/Umpire	30.00	15.00	9.00
278	*Charles Neal*	35.00	17.50	10.00
279	Hank Soar/Umpire	30.00	15.00	9.00
280	Clyde McCullough	25.00	12.50	7.50
281	Charles Berry/Umpire	30.00	15.00	9.00
282	Phil Cavarretta	25.00	12.50	7.50
283	Nestor Chylak/Umpire	65.00	32.50	20.00
284	William A. Jackowski/Umpire	30.00	15.00	9.00
285	Walt Dropo	25.00	12.50	7.50
286	Frank Secory/Umpire	30.00	15.00	9.00
287	Ron Mrozinski	25.00	12.50	7.50
288	Dick Smith	25.00	12.50	7.50
289	Art Gore/Umpire	30.00	15.00	9.00
290	Hershell Freeman	25.00	12.50	7.50
291	Frank Dascoli/Umpire	30.00	15.00	9.00
292	Marv Blaylock	25.00	12.50	7.50
293	Thomas D. Gorman/Umpire	30.00	15.00	9.00
294	Wally Moses	25.00	12.50	7.50
295	Lee Ballanfant/Umpire	30.00	15.00	9.00
296	*Bill Virdon*	30.00	15.00	9.00
297	"Dusty" Boggess/Umpire	30.00	15.00	9.00
298	Charlie Grimm	25.00	12.50	7.50
299	Lonnie Warneke/Umpire	30.00	15.00	9.00
300	Tommy Byrne	30.00	15.00	9.00
301	William Engeln/Umpire	30.00	15.00	9.00
302	*Frank Malzone*	30.00	15.00	9.00
303	Jocko Conlan/Umpire	65.00	32.50	20.00
304	Harry Chiti	25.00	12.50	7.50
305	Frank Umont/Umpire	30.00	15.00	9.00
306	Bob Cerv	30.00	15.00	9.00
307	"Babe" Pinelli/Umpire	25.00	12.50	7.50
308	Al Lopez	35.00	17.50	10.00
309	Hal Dixon/Umpire	30.00	15.00	9.00
310	Ken Lehman	30.00	15.00	9.00
311	Larry Goetz/Umpire	30.00	15.00	9.00
312	Bill Wight	25.00	12.50	7.50
313	Augie Donatelli/Umpire	30.00	15.00	9.00
314	Dale Mitchell	25.00	12.50	7.50
315	Cal Hubbard/Umpire	60.00	30.00	18.00
316	Marion Fricano	25.00	12.50	7.50
317	Bill Summers/Umpire	30.00	15.00	9.00
318	Sid Hudson	25.00	12.50	7.50
319	Al Schroll	25.00	12.50	7.50
320	George Susce, Jr.	50.00	15.00	7.00

1956 Bowman Prototypes

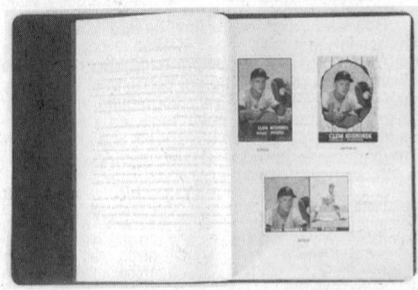

To gauge consumer demand for a 1956 baseball card set that it never issued, Bowman produced a "Baseball Card Preference Study" report. The report survives today in the form of a 24-page notebook that includes samples of the three designs apparently preferred by the pre-teen boys surveyed. All three cards are glued to one page of the report and all feature the photo of Pirates catcher Clem Koshorek

used in the 1953 Bowman set. It is believed only two of the reports survive.

(Sold for $10,440 in 5/05 auction.)

1963 George Brace All Time Chicago Cubs

The year of issue attributed here is only theoretical. The set consists of a window envelope which contains 18 5-1/4" x 7" black-and-white photos of former Cubs greats by famed Chicago baseball photographer George Brace. The blank-backed unnumbered pictures have player identification in the white border at bottom. They are checklisted here alphabetically.

		NM	EX	VG
Complete Set (18):		50.00	25.00	15.00
Common Player:		7.50	3.75	2.25
(1)	Grover Cleveland Alexander	10.00	5.00	3.00
(2)	Cap Anson	10.00	5.00	3.00
(3)	Three Finger Brown	9.00	4.50	2.75
(4)	Frank Chance	9.00	4.50	2.75
(5)	Johnny Evers	9.00	4.50	2.75
(6)	Charlie Grimm	7.50	3.75	2.25
(7)	Stan Hack	7.50	3.75	2.25
(8)	Gabby Hartnett	7.50	3.75	2.25
(9)	Billy Herman	7.50	3.75	2.25
(10)	Charlie Hollocher	7.50	3.75	2.25
(11)	Billy Jurges	7.50	3.75	2.25
(12)	Johnny Kling	7.50	3.75	2.25
(13)	Joe McCarthy	7.50	3.75	2.25
(14)	Ed Reulbach	7.50	3.75	2.25
(15)	Albert Spalding	7.50	3.75	2.25
(16)	Joe Tinker	9.00	4.50	2.75
(17)	Hippo Vaughn	7.50	3.75	2.25
(18)	Hack Wilson	9.00	4.50	2.75

1974 Bramac 1933 National League All-Stars

This early collectors issue features black-and-white photos of the premiere N.L. All-Star team in their distinctive dress uniforms. Cards are in a 2-1/2 x 3-1/4 format.

		NM	EX	VG
Complete Set (18):		30.00	15.00	9.00
Common Player:		6.00	3.00	1.75
1	Paul Waner	6.00	3.00	1.75
2	Woody English	6.00	3.00	1.75
3	Dick Bartell	6.00	3.00	1.75
4	Chuck Klein	6.00	3.00	1.75
5	Tony Cuccinello	6.00	3.00	1.75
6	Lefty O'Doul	6.00	3.00	1.75
7	Gabby Hartnett	6.00	3.00	1.75
8	Lon Warneke	6.00	3.00	1.75
9	Wally Berger	6.00	3.00	1.75
10	Chick Hafey	6.00	3.00	1.75
11	Frank Frisch	6.00	3.00	1.75
12	Carl Hubbell	6.00	3.00	1.75
13	Bill Hallahan	6.00	3.00	1.75
14	Hal Schumacher	6.00	3.00	1.75
15	Pie Traynor	6.00	3.00	1.75
16	Bill Terry	6.00	3.00	1.75
17	Pepper Martin	6.00	3.00	1.75
18	Jimmy Wilson	6.00	3.00	1.75

1908-11 H.H. Bregstone Browns/Cardinals Post Cards (PC743)

Among the rarest of the early 20th Century baseball player postcards are those of the St. Louis Browns and Cardinals from H.H. Bregstone, also

St. Louis. The 3-1/2" x 5-1/2" cards feature sepia player photos that are borderless at top and sides. At bottom is a box with the player's name, team, position, league and the issuer's address. Backs are standard postcard format. The unnumbered cards are checklisted here alphabetically within team. With a single exception (Gregory), all of the Browns players are from 1909, while the range of Cardinals spans the era 1908-1911.

	NM	EX	VG
Complete Set, Browns (22):	9,500	4,750	2,750
Complete Set, Cardinals (34):	18,000	9,000	5,500
Common Player:	500.00	250.00	150.00
ST. LOUIS BROWNS			
(1) Bill Bailey	500.00	250.00	150.00
(2) Lou Criger	500.00	250.00	150.00
(3) Dode Criss	500.00	250.00	150.00
(4) Bill Dineen	500.00	250.00	150.00
(5) Hobe Ferris	500.00	250.00	150.00
(6) Bill Graham	500.00	250.00	150.00
(7) B Gregory	500.00	250.00	150.00
(8) Art Griggs	500.00	250.00	150.00
(9) Roy Hartzell	500.00	250.00	150.00
(10) Danny Hoffman	500.00	250.00	150.00
(11) Harry Howell	500.00	250.00	150.00
(12) Tom Jones	500.00	250.00	150.00
(13) Jimmy McAleer	500.00	250.00	150.00
(14) Ham Patterson	500.00	250.00	150.00
(15) Barney Pelty	500.00	250.00	150.00
(16) Al Schweitzer	500.00	250.00	150.00
(17) Wib Smith	500.00	250.00	150.00
(18) Jim Stephens	500.00	250.00	150.00
(19) George Stone	500.00	250.00	150.00
(20) Rube Waddell	750.00	375.00	225.00
(21) Bobby Wallace	750.00	375.00	225.00
(22) Jimmy Williams	500.00	250.00	150.00
ST. LOUIS CARDINALS			
(1) Jap Barbeau	500.00	250.00	150.00
(2) Shad Barry	500.00	250.00	150.00
(3) Fred Beebe	500.00	250.00	150.00
(4) Frank Betcher	500.00	250.00	150.00
(5) Jack Bliss	500.00	250.00	150.00
(6) Roger Bresnahan	800.00	400.00	240.00
(7) Bobby Byrne	500.00	250.00	150.00
(8) Chappie Charles	500.00	250.00	150.00
(9) Frank Corridon	500.00	250.00	150.00
(10) Joe Delahanty	700.00	350.00	210.00
(11) Rube Ellis	500.00	250.00	150.00
(12) Steve Evans	500.00	250.00	150.00
(13) Art Fromme	500.00	250.00	150.00
(14) Rube Geyer	500.00	250.00	150.00
(15) Billy Gilbert	500.00	250.00	150.00
(16) Bob Harmon	500.00	250.00	150.00
(17) Irv Higginbotham	500.00	250.00	150.00
(18) Tom Higgins	500.00	250.00	150.00
(19) Art Hoelskoetter	500.00	250.00	150.00
(20) Miller Huggins	750.00	375.00	225.00
(21) Rudy Hulswitt	500.00	250.00	150.00
(22) Adam Johnson	500.00	250.00	150.00
(23) Ed Konetchy	500.00	250.00	150.00
(24) Johnny Lush	500.00	250.00	150.00
(25) Lee Magee	500.00	250.00	150.00
(26) Stoney McGlynn	500.00	250.00	150.00
(27) Rebel Oakes	500.00	250.00	150.00
(28) Bill O'Hara	500.00	250.00	150.00
(29) Patsy O'Rourke	500.00	250.00	150.00
(30) Ed Phelps	500.00	250.00	150.00
(31) Charlie Rhodes	500.00	250.00	150.00
(32) Elmer Rieger	500.00	250.00	150.00
(33) Slim Sallee	500.00	250.00	150.00
(34) Vic Willis	750.00	375.00	225.00

1903-1904 Breisch-Williams

Many veteran collectors now believe that Breisch-Williams Confectionary Co. of Oxford, Pa., was just one of several firms that used the black-and-white card issue cataloged as E107 as a premium. A relatively small percentage of E107s are found with a purple rubber-stamped "THE BREISCH- WILLIAMS CO" message diagonally on back. It is speculated the stamp may have been used to "cancel" cards there were returned in a prize redemption program. The overprinted cards currently carry a premium of 2-3X the value of blank-backed or "One of a ..." E107s. With only a single known exception, all Breisch-Williams stamped cards are of Type 1.

(See E107 Type 1 and Type 2 for checklist and base value information.)

1909-10 C.A. Briggs Co. (E97)

This card is one of a set of 30 BALL PLAYERS Cards, as follows :
AUSTIN, New York American
BRADLEY, Cleveland American
BIRMINGHAM, Cleveland American
BRANSFIELD, Philadelphia National
CARRIGAN, Boston American
CAMNITZ, Pittsburg National
DURHAM, New York National
DYGERT, Philadelphia American
DOOLAN, Philadelphia National
DEVORE, New York National
DAVIS, Philadelphia American
HEMPHILL, New York American
HEINCHMAN, Cleveland American
HARTSEL, Philadelphia American
KROH, Chicago National
KLINOW, New York American
KELLY, Boston National
KEELER, New York National
McINTYRE, Detroit American
McCONNELL, Boston American
MOORE, Philadelphia National
MULLIN, Detroit American
MURRAY, New York National
MEYERS, New York National
NICHOLS, Cleveland American
ROSSMAN, Detroit American
SULLIVAN, Chicago American
STEINFELDT, Cincinnati National
SCHLEI, New York National
CY. YOUNG, Cleveland American
C.A. BRIGGS CO., Lozenge Makers
Boston, Mass.

CY. YOUNG, Boston, Nat'l

Measuring approximately 1-1/2" x 2-3/4", this set is nearly identical to several other candy issues of the same period. Designated as E97 in the American Card Catalog, the set was issued in 1909-1910 by "C.A. Briggs Co., Lozenge Makers of Boston, Mass." The front of the card shows a tinted player photo, with the player's last name, position and team printed below. Backs are printed in brown and checklist the 30 players in the set alphabetically. The C.A. Briggs Co. name appears at the bottom. Black-and-white examples of this set have also been found on a thin paper stock with blank backs and are believed to be "proof cards." They are valued about 2-3X the figures shown here. Five variations are also found in the set. The more expensive variations are not included in the complete set price.

	NM	EX	VG
Complete Set (30):	60,000	24,000	12,000
Common Player:	2,500	1,000	500.00
Proofs: 2-3X			
(1) Jimmy Austin	2,500	1,000	500.00
(2) Joe Birmingham	2,500	1,000	500.00
(3) Bill Bradley	2,500	1,000	500.00
(4) Kitty Bransfield	2,500	1,000	500.00
(5) Howie Camnitz	2,500	1,000	500.00
(6) Bill Carrigan	2,500	1,000	500.00
(7) Harry Davis	2,500	1,000	500.00
(8) Josh Devore	2,500	1,000	500.00
(9a) Mickey Dolan (Doolan)	2,500	1,000	500.00
(9b) Mickey Doolan	2,500	1,000	500.00
(10) Bull Durham	2,500	1,000	500.00
(11) Jimmy Dygert	2,500	1,000	500.00
(12a) Topsy Hartsell (Hartsel)	2,500	1,000	500.00
(12b) Topsy Hartsel	2,500	1,000	500.00
(13) Bill Heinchman (Hinchman)	2,500	1,000	500.00
(14) Charlie Hemphill	2,500	1,000	500.00
(15) Wee Willie Keeler	8,000	3,200	1,600
(16) Joe Kelly (Kelley)	8,000	3,200	1,600
(17) Red Kleinow	2,500	1,000	500.00
(18) Rube Kroh	2,500	1,000	500.00
(19) Matty McIntyre	2,500	1,000	500.00
(20) Amby McConnell	2,500	1,000	500.00
(21) Chief Meyers	2,500	1,000	500.00
(22) Earl Moore	2,500	1,000	500.00
(23) George Mullin	2,500	1,000	500.00
(24) Red Murray	2,500	1,000	500.00
(25a) Simon Nichols (Nicholls) (Philadelphia)	4,000	1,600	800.00
(25b) Simon Nichols (Nicholls) (Cleveland)	2,500	1,000	500.00
(26) Claude Rossman	2,500	1,000	500.00
(27) Admiral Schlei	2,500	1,000	500.00
(28a) Harry Steinfeld (Name incorrect.)	3,200	1,300	650.00
(28b) Harry Steinfeldt (Name correct.)	4,400	1,800	900.00
(29a) Dennis Sullivan (Chicago)	2,500	1,000	500.00
(29b) Dennis Sullivan (Boston)	20,000	8,000	4,000
(30a) Cy. Young (Cleveland) (Picture actually Irv Young.)	15,000	6,000	3,000
(30b) Cy. Young (Boston) (Picture actually Irv Young.)	16,000	6,400	3,200

1933 C.A. Briggs Co. Babe Ruth

Stars in a variety of sports are featured in this series of candy issues. Card #24 has a drawing on front against a red background. The player bears more than a passing resemblance to Babe Ruth and on the back of the 2-3/8" x 2-7/8" card, along with a short history of baseball, Babe Ruth and his $52,000 contract for 1933 are mentioned. At bottom are details for redeeming a set of the 31 cards for baseball equipment or a pound of chocolates.

	NM	EX	VG
24 Baseball (Babe Ruth)	1,000	500.00	300.00

1953-54 Briggs Meats

The Briggs Meat set was issued over a two-year span (1953-54) and features 28 players from the Washington Senators and 12 from the New York teams. The set was issued in two-card panels on hot dog packages sold in the Washington, D.C. vicinity. The color cards, which are blank-backed and measure 2-1/4" x 3-1/2", are printed on waxed cardboard. Pictures of the New York players can also be found on cards in the 1954 Dan-Dee Potato Chips and 1953-1955 Stahl-Meyer Franks sets. There is a slight difference in style between the Senators cards and those of the New York players. The white panel beneath the photo of the Washington players includes a facsimile autograph plus a few biographical details about the player. The New York players' cards have only the player's name and facsimile signature in that panel. Several of the Senators cards command a premium for scarcity.

	NM	EX	VG
Complete Set (40):	35,000	17,500	7,000
Common Player:	900.00	450.00	180.00
(1) Hank Bauer	1,000	500.00	200.00
(2) James Busby	900.00	450.00	180.00
(3) Tommy Byrne	900.00	450.00	180.00
(4) Gil Coan	900.00	450.00	180.00
(5) John Dixon	900.00	450.00	180.00
(6) Carl Erskine	1,000	500.00	200.00
(7) Edward Fitzgerald (Fitz Gerald)	900.00	450.00	180.00
(8) Newton Grasso	900.00	450.00	180.00
(9) Melvin Hoderlein	900.00	450.00	180.00
(10) Gil Hodges	1,500	750.00	300.00
(11) Monte Irvin	1,000	500.00	200.00
(12) Jackie Jensen	950.00	475.00	190.00
(13) Whitey Lockman	900.00	450.00	180.00
(14) Mickey Mantle	7,500	3,750	1,500
(15) Conrado Marrero	900.00	450.00	180.00
(16) Walter Masterson	900.00	450.00	180.00
(17) Carmen Mauro	900.00	450.00	180.00
(18) Willie Mays	4,500	2,250	900.00
(19) Mickey McDermott	900.00	450.00	180.00
(20) Gil McDougald	1,000	500.00	200.00
(21) Julio Moreno	900.00	450.00	180.00
(22) Don Mueller	900.00	450.00	180.00
(23) Don Newcombe	1,000	500.00	200.00
(24) Robert Oldis	900.00	450.00	180.00
(25) Erwin Porterfield	900.00	450.00	180.00
(26) Phil Rizzuto	1,200	600.00	240.00
(27) James Runnels	900.00	450.00	180.00
(28) John Schmitz	900.00	450.00	180.00
(29) Angel Scull	900.00	450.00	180.00
(30) Frank Shea	900.00	450.00	180.00
(31) Albert Sima	900.00	450.00	180.00
(32) Duke Snider	1,800	900.00	360.00
(33) Charles Stobbs	900.00	450.00	180.00
(34) Willard Terwilliger	900.00	450.00	180.00
(35) Joe Tipton	900.00	450.00	180.00
(36) Thomas Umphlett	900.00	450.00	180.00
(37) Gene Verble	900.00	450.00	180.00
(38) James Vernon	900.00	450.00	180.00
(39) Clyde Vollmer	900.00	450.00	180.00
(40) Edward Yost	900.00	450.00	180.00

1947 Brillantina Sol de Oro Managers

The approximately 6" x 8" black-and-white pictures were issued in conjunction with a contest run by an Havana shampoo company. Fronts have photos of the managers of Cuba's four professional teams, bordered with white, with a facsimile autograph and message. A sponsor's credit line is in the bottom border. Backs have further promotional copy for the shampoo and rules of the contest.

	NM	EX	VG
Complete Set (4):	600.00	300.00	180.00
Common Player:	150.00	75.00	45.00
(1) Salvador Hernandez	150.00	75.00	45.00
(2) Adolfo Luque	250.00	125.00	75.00
(3) Napoleon Reyes	200.00	100.00	60.00
(4) Lazaro Salazar	150.00	75.00	45.00

1909-12 Broad Leaf Cigarettes

Cards with the Broad Leaf brand advertising on back can be found among the three most popular cigarette card issues circa 1910: T205 Gold Border, T206 White Border and T207 Brown Background. Two types are seen in T206, one that mentions "350 Subjects" and another, much rarer, that mentions "460 Subjects." Because some of the scarcer cards in T207 are often found with Broadleaf (as it was then spelled) backs, it is not practical to quote a value multiplier; premiums for such cards have already been factored into the prices under T207. In T205, Broad Leaf backs can be found printed in either black or brown-olive green.

PREMIUMS:
T205: 6X
T206 350 Subjects: 6-8X
T206 460 Subjects, Common: 50-60X
T206 460 Subjects, HoF: 15-25X
(See T205, T206, T207 for checklists.)

1974 Broder N.Y. Mets Tour of Japan

Veteran collector Ed Broder who was stationed with the U.S. Army in Japan, produced this collectors' issue chronicling the goodwill tour undertaken by the National League Champion N.Y. Mets. Nominally measuring about 1-7/8" x 3", cards have borderless black-and-white photos on front with no player identification or other graphics. Backs have player name, team and "1974 New York Mets Tour of Japan" in typewriter font along with a team logo. The unnumbered cards are checklisted here alphabetically.

	NM	EX	VG
Complete Set (20):	60.00	30.00	18.00
Common Player:	4.00	2.00	1.25
(1) Yogi Berra	20.00	10.00	6.00
(2) Wayne Garrett	8.00	4.00	2.50
(3) Ron Hodges	8.00	4.00	2.50
(4) Tsuneo Horiuchi	8.00	4.00	2.50
(5) Kazumasa Kono	4.00	2.00	1.25
(6) Jerry Koosman	8.00	4.00	2.50
(7) Ed Kranepool, John Milner, unidentified Japanese player, Joe Torre	4.00	2.00	1.25
(8) Jon Matlack	8.00	4.00	2.50
(9) Felix Millan	8.00	4.00	2.50
(10) John Milner	8.00	4.00	2.50
(11) Shigeo Nagashima	10.00	5.00	3.00
(12) Sadaharu Oh	15.00	7.50	4.50
(13) Tom Seaver	40.00	20.00	12.00
(14) Yososhi Sekimoto	4.00	2.00	1.25
(15) Tamio Suetsugu	4.00	2.00	1.25
(16) Kazumi Takahashi	4.00	2.00	1.25
(17) Yoshima Takahashi	4.00	2.00	1.25
(18) George Theodore	8.00	4.00	2.50
(19) Joe Torre, Kazuyoshi Yamamoto	15.00	7.50	4.50
(20) Kazuyoshi Yamamoto, Tetsuhara Kawakami	10.00	5.00	3.00

1975 Broder All-Time N.Y. Mets

Nolan Ryan 1966-71

Veteran collector Ed Broder produced this collectors' issue. Nominally measuring about 1-7/8" x 3-1/8", cards have borderless black-and-white photos on front. Some cards have the dates of their tenure with the team on front. The unnumbered cards are checklisted here alphabetically.

	NM	EX	VG
Complete Set (12):	45.00	22.50	13.50
Common Player:	4.00	2.00	1.25
(1) Yogi Berra	7.50	3.75	2.25
(2) Bud Harrelson	4.00	2.00	1.25
(3) Jim Hickman	4.00	2.00	1.25
(4) Al Jackson	4.00	2.00	1.25
(5) Cleon Jones	4.00	2.00	1.25
(6) Jerry Koosman	4.00	2.00	1.25
(7) Ed Kranepool	4.00	2.00	1.25
(8) Tug McGraw	4.00	2.00	1.25
(9) Nolan Ryan	15.00	7.50	4.50
(10) Tom Seaver	9.00	4.50	2.75
(11) Warren Spahn	6.00	3.00	1.75
(12) Casey Stengal (Stengel)	6.00	3.00	1.75

1975 Broder 1962 "Original" N.Y. Mets

Sherman Jones

Veteran collector Ed Broder produced this collectors' issue. Nominally measuring about 2" x 3", cards have borderless black-and-white photos on front with only the player name for identification. Backs are blank. The unnumbered cards are checklisted here alphabetically.

	NM	EX	VG
Complete Set (12):	50.00	25.00	15.00
Common Player:	5.00	2.50	1.50
(1) Richie Ashburn	10.00	5.00	3.00
(2) Gus Bell	5.00	2.50	1.50
(3) Roger Craig	5.00	2.50	1.50
(4) Gil Hodges	10.00	5.00	3.00
(5) Rogers Hornsby	7.50	3.75	2.25
(6) Sherman Jones	5.00	2.50	1.50
(7) Rod Kanehl	5.00	2.50	1.50
(8) Clem Labine	5.00	2.50	1.50
(9) Hobie Landrith	5.00	2.50	1.50
(10) R.G. Miller	5.00	2.50	1.50
(11) Wilmer Mizell	5.00	2.50	1.50
(12) Charley Neal	5.00	2.50	1.50
(13) Casey Stengal (Stengel)	7.50	3.75	2.25
(14) Frank Thomas	5.00	2.50	1.50
(15) Marv Throneberry	5.00	2.50	1.50

1975 Broder Major Leagues - The 1950's

Veteran collector Ed Broder produced this collectors' issue. Nominally measuring about 2" x 3", cards have borderless black-and-white photos on front with only the player name for identification. Backs are blank. The unnumbered cards are checklisted here alphabetically. The set is notable in that a number of familiar players are pictured with teams not seen on their Topps and Bowman cards. The set sold originally for $2.20.

	NM	EX	VG
Complete Set (28):	100.00	50.00	30.00
Common Player:	4.00	2.00	1.25
(1) Bobby Adams	4.00	2.00	1.25
(2) Richie Ashburn	6.50	3.25	2.00
(3) Ken Aspromonte	4.00	2.00	1.25
(4) Ray Boone	5.00	2.50	1.50
(5) Lou Boudreau	6.50	3.25	2.00
(6) Smoky Burgess	4.00	2.00	1.25
(7) Phil Cavaretta (Cavarretta)	4.00	2.00	1.25
(8) Gene Conley	4.00	2.00	1.25
(9) Del Crandell (Crandall)	4.00	2.00	1.25
(10) Bob Friend	4.00	2.00	1.25
(11) Harvey Haddix	4.00	2.00	1.25
(12) Fred Haney	4.00	2.00	1.25
(13) Ted Kluszewski	5.00	2.50	1.50
(14) Jim Konstanty	4.00	2.00	1.25
(15) Sandy Koufax	7.50	3.75	2.25
(16) Harvey Kuenn	4.00	2.00	1.25
(17) Bob Lemon	6.00	3.00	1.75
(18) Marty Marion	4.00	2.00	1.25
(19) Minnie Minoso	5.00	2.50	1.50
(20) Stan Musial	7.00	3.50	2.00
(21) Albie Pearson	4.00	2.00	1.25
(22) Paul Richards	4.00	2.00	1.25
(23) Hank Sauer	4.00	2.00	1.25
(24) Herb Score	4.00	2.00	1.25
(25) Bob Skinner	4.00	2.00	1.25
(26) Enos Slaughter	6.00	3.00	1.75
(27) Gus Triandos	4.00	2.00	1.25
(28) Gus Zernial	4.00	2.00	1.25

1975 Broder Major League Postcards

This series of 3-1/8" x 5-1/8", borderless, blank-back pictures was advertised as the first in a proposed series designed to accommodate player autographs. Only California Angels and Montreal Expos players are included. The cards are printed on thin cardboard and feature close-up portraits with the player name in black type.

	NM	EX	VG
Complete Set (9):	25.00	12.50	7.50
Common Player:	3.00	1.50	.90
(1) Tim Foli	3.00	1.50	.90
(2) Barry Foote	3.00	1.50	.90
(3) Mike Jorgensen	3.00	1.50	.90
(4) Larry Lintz	3.00	1.50	.90
(5) Dave McNally	3.00	1.50	.90
(6) Steve Rodgers (Rogers)	3.00	1.50	.90
(7) Nolan Ryan	10.00	5.00	3.00
(8) Bill Singer	3.00	1.50	.90
(9) Dick Williams	3.00	1.50	.90

1978 Broder Photocards

lloyd waner

This collectors' issue features late 1970s photos of some of the game's stars from the 1920s-1960s. Cards are printed in 3-1/2" x 5-1/2", blank-back, black-and-white format on thick grayback card stock. Cards were printed four to a sheet and often found on uncut sheets.

		NM	EX	VG
Complete Set (16):		40.00	20.00	12.00
Common Player:		3.00	1.50	.90
(1)	Walt Alston	3.00	1.50	.90
(2)	Luke Appling	3.00	1.50	.90
(3)	Ernie Banks	4.50	2.25	1.25
(4)	Yogi Berra	4.50	2.25	1.25
(5)	Bill Dickey	4.00	2.00	1.25
(6)	Bob Feller/Pitching	4.00	2.00	1.25
(7)	Bob Feller/Portrait	4.00	2.00	1.25
(8)	Billy Herman	3.00	1.50	.90
(9)	Bob Lemon	3.00	1.50	.90
(10)	Mickey Mantle	6.00	3.00	1.75
(11)	Willie Mays/Btg	5.00	2.50	1.50
(12)	Willie Mays/Portrait	5.00	2.50	1.50
(13)	Johnny Mize	3.00	1.50	.90
(14)	Pee Wee Reese	4.00	2.00	1.25
(15)	Allie Reynolds	3.00	1.50	.90
(16)	Brooks Robinson	4.00	2.00	1.25
(17)	Enos Slaughter	3.00	1.50	.90
(18)	Warren Spahn	3.00	1.50	.90
(19)	Lloyd Waner	3.00	1.50	.90
(20)	Ted Williams	5.00	2.50	1.50

1940 Brooklyn Dodgers Picture Pack

Rookie Pee Wee Reese appears in this team-issued set of black-and-white pictures. The 6" x 9" pictures have player portraits surrounded by a white border. A facsimile autograph appears on front. Backs are blank. The unnumbered pictures are checklisted here in alphabetical order. Because of roster changes, it is possible the specific makeup of the packs may have changed once or more over the course of the season. Some of the pictures were reused in subsequent years' offerings.

		NM	EX	VG
Complete Set (25):		150.00	75.00	45.00
Common Player:		8.00	4.00	2.50
(1)	Dolf Camilli	8.00	4.00	2.50
(2)	Tex Carleton	8.00	4.00	2.50
(3)	Hugh Casey	8.00	4.00	2.50
(4)	Pete Coscarart	8.00	4.00	2.50
(5)	Curt Davis	8.00	4.00	2.50
(6)	Leo Durocher	12.00	6.00	3.50
(7)	Fred Fitzsimmons	8.00	4.00	2.50
(8)	Herman Franks	8.00	4.00	2.50
(9)	Joe Gallagher	8.00	4.00	2.50
(10)	Charlie Gilbert	8.00	4.00	2.50
(11)	Luke Hamlin	8.00	4.00	2.50
(12)	Johnny Hudson	8.00	4.00	2.50
(13)	Newt Kimball	8.00	4.00	2.50
(14)	Cookie Lavagetto	8.00	4.00	2.50
(15)	Gus Mancuso	8.00	4.00	2.50
(16)	Joe Medwick	12.00	6.00	3.50
(17)	Van Lingle Mungo	10.00	5.00	3.00
(18)	Babe Phelps	8.00	4.00	2.50
(19)	Tot Pressnell	8.00	4.00	2.50
(20)	Pee Wee Reese	24.00	12.00	7.25
(21)	Vito Tamulis	8.00	4.00	2.50
(22)	Joe Vosmik	8.00	4.00	2.50
(23)	Dixie Walker	8.00	4.00	2.50
(24)	Jimmy Wasdell	8.00	4.00	2.50
(25)	Whitlow Wyatt	8.00	4.00	2.50

1941 Brooklyn Dodgers Picture Pack

This team-issued set of 6" x 9" black-and-white pictures has player portraits surrounded by a white border. A facsimile autograph appears on front. Backs are blank. The unnumbered pictures are checklisted here in alphabetical order. Because of roster changes, it is possible the specific makeup of the packs may have changed once or more over the course of the season and that there may have been players issued other than those listed here. Some of the pictures were reused the 1940 offering. Team-issued pictures of 1940-41 can be differentiated from later years by their ballpark backgrounds.

		NM	EX	VG
Complete Set (25):		185.00	95.00	55.00
Common Player:		10.00	5.00	3.00
(1)	Mace Brown	10.00	5.00	3.00
(2)	Dolph Camilli	10.00	5.00	3.00
(3)	Hugh Casey	10.00	5.00	3.00
(4)	Pete Coscarart	10.00	5.00	3.00
(5)	Curt Davis	10.00	5.00	3.00
(6)	Leo Durocher	15.00	7.50	4.50
(7)	Fred Fitzsimmons	10.00	5.00	3.00
(8)	Luke Hamlin	10.00	5.00	3.00
(9)	Billy Herman	15.00	7.50	4.50
(10)	Kirby Higbe	10.00	5.00	3.00
(11)	Newt Kimball	10.00	5.00	3.00
(12)	Harry "Cookie" Lavagetto	10.00	5.00	3.00
(13)	Joe Medwick	15.00	7.50	4.50
(14)	Mickey Owen	10.00	5.00	3.00
(15)	Babe Phelps	10.00	5.00	3.00
(16)	Pee Wee Reese	25.00	12.50	7.50
(17)	Pete Reiser	10.00	5.00	3.00
(18)	Lew Riggs	10.00	5.00	3.00
(19)	Bill Swift	10.00	5.00	3.00
(20)	Vito Tamulis	10.00	5.00	3.00
(21)	Joe Vosmik	10.00	5.00	3.00
(22)	Dixie Walker	10.00	5.00	3.00
(23)	Jimmy Wasdell	10.00	5.00	3.00
(24)	Kemp Wicker	10.00	5.00	3.00
(25)	Whit Wyatt	10.00	5.00	3.00

1942 Brooklyn Dodgers Picture Pack

This set of 6" x 9" black-and-white team-issued pictures features player portrait photos in a studio setting. The pictures have a white border all around, and there is a facsimile autograph on front. Backs are blank. The unnumbered pictures are checklisted here alphabetically. Pictures from the 1942 and 1943 photo packs are indistinguishable except for player selection.

		NM	EX	VG
Complete Set (25):		150.00	75.00	45.00
Common Player:		8.00	4.00	2.50
(1)	Johnny Allen	8.00	4.00	2.50
(2)	Frenchy Bordagaray	8.00	4.00	2.50
(3)	Dolf Camilli	8.00	4.00	2.50
(4)	Hugh Casey	8.00	4.00	2.50
(5)	Curt Davis	8.00	4.00	2.50
(6)	Leo Durocher	12.00	6.00	3.50
(7)	Larry French	8.00	4.00	2.50
(8)	Augie Galan	8.00	4.00	2.50
(9)	Ed Head	8.00	4.00	2.50
(10)	Billy Herman	12.00	6.00	3.50
(11)	Kirby Higbe	8.00	4.00	2.50
(12)	Alex Kampouris	8.00	4.00	2.50
(13)	Newt Kimball	8.00	4.00	2.50
(14)	Joe Medwick	12.00	6.00	3.50
(15)	Mickey Owen	8.00	4.00	2.50
(16)	Pee Wee Reese	16.00	8.00	4.75
(17)	Pete Reiser	10.00	5.00	3.00
(18)	Lew Riggs	8.00	4.00	2.50
(19)	Johnny Rizzo	8.00	4.00	2.50
(20)	Schoolboy Rowe	10.00	5.00	3.00
(21)	Billy Sullivan	8.00	4.00	2.50
(22)	Arky Vaughan	12.00	6.00	3.50
(23)	Dixie Walker	8.00	4.00	2.50
(24)	Les Webber	8.00	4.00	2.50
(25)	Whitlow Wyatt	8.00	4.00	2.50

1943 Brooklyn Dodgers Picture Pack

This set of 6" x 9" black-and-white team-issued pictures features player portrait photos in a studio setting. The pictures have a white border all around, and there is a facsimile autograph on front. Backs are blank. The unnumbered pictures are checklisted here alphabetically. Pictures from the 1942 and 1943 photo packs are indistinguishable except for player selection.

		NM	EX	VG
Complete Set (25):		150.00	75.00	45.00
Common Player:		8.00	4.00	2.50
(1)	Johnny Allen	8.00	4.00	2.50
(2)	Frenchy Bordagaray	8.00	4.00	2.50
(3)	Bob Bragan	10.00	5.00	3.00
(4)	Dolf Camilli	8.00	4.00	2.50
(5)	Johnny Cooney	8.00	4.00	2.50
(6)	John Corriden	8.00	4.00	2.50
(7)	Curt Davis	8.00	4.00	2.50
(8)	Leo Durocher	12.00	6.00	3.50
(9)	Fred Fitzsimmons	8.00	4.00	2.50
(10)	Augie Galan	8.00	4.00	2.50
(11)	Al Glossop	8.00	4.00	2.50
(12)	Ed Head	8.00	4.00	2.50
(13)	Billy Herman	12.00	6.00	3.50
(14)	Kirby Higbe	8.00	4.00	2.50
(15)	Max Macon	8.00	4.00	2.50
(16)	Joe Medwick	12.00	6.00	3.50
(17)	Rube Melton	8.00	4.00	2.50
(18)	Dee Moore	8.00	4.00	2.50
(19)	"Buck" Newsom	10.00	5.00	3.00
(20)	Mickey Owen	8.00	4.00	2.50
(21)	Arky Vaughan	12.00	6.00	3.50
(22)	Dixie Walker	8.00	4.00	2.50
(23)	Paul Waner	12.00	6.00	3.50
(24)	Les Webber	8.00	4.00	2.50
(25)	Whitlow Wyatt	8.00	4.00	2.50

1946 Brooklyn Dodgers Picture Pack

This team-issued set of player portrait pictures is in a blank-back 6-1/2" x 9" format. A facsimile autograph appears on front. Like many souvenir-stand photo packs of the era, it is possible the specific contents of this product may have changed during the course of the season as players joined and left the team.

		NM	EX	VG
Complete Set (25):		125.00	65.00	40.00
Common Player:		6.00	3.00	1.80
(1)	Andy Anderson	6.00	3.00	1.80
(2)	Henry Behrman	6.00	3.00	1.80
(3)	Ralph Branca	6.00	3.00	1.80
(4)	Hugh Casey	6.00	3.00	1.80
(5)	Leo Durocher	9.00	4.50	2.75
(6)	Carl Furillo	12.00	6.00	3.50
(7)	Augie Galan	6.00	3.00	1.80
(8)	Hal Gregg	6.00	3.00	1.80
(9)	Joe Hatten	6.00	3.00	1.80
(10)	Al Head	6.00	3.00	1.80
(11)	Art Herring	6.00	3.00	1.80
(12)	Billy Herman	9.00	4.50	2.75
(13)	Kirby Higbe	6.00	3.00	1.80
(14)	Gene Hermanski	6.00	3.00	1.80
(15)	Harry "Cookie" Lavagetto	6.00	3.00	1.80
(16)	Vic Lombardi	6.00	3.00	1.80

		NM	EX	VG
(17)	Pee Wee Reese	12.00	6.00	3.50
(18)	Pete Reiser	6.00	3.00	1.80
(19)	Stan Rojek	6.00	3.00	1.80
(20)	Mike Sandlock	6.00	3.00	1.80
(21)	Eddie Stanky	7.50	3.75	2.25
(22)	Ed Stevens	6.00	3.00	1.80
(23)	Dixie Walker	6.00	3.00	1.80
(24)	Les Webber	6.00	3.00	1.80
(25)	Dick Whitman	6.00	3.00	1.80

1947 Brooklyn Dodgers Picture Pack

This team-issued set of player portrait pictures is in a blank-back 6-1/2" x 9" format. A facsimile autograph appears on front. Like many souvenir-stand photo packs of the era, it is possible the specific contents of this product may have changed during the course of this season as players joined and left the team.

		NM	EX	VG
Complete Set (25):		350.00	175.00	105.00
Common Player:		9.00	4.50	2.75
(1)	Ray Blades	9.00	4.50	2.75
(2)	Bobby Bragan	9.00	4.50	2.75
(3)	Ralph Branca	9.00	4.50	2.75
(4)	Tommy Brown	9.00	4.50	2.75
(5)	Hugh Casey	9.00	4.50	2.75
(6)	Ed Chandler	20.00	10.00	6.00
(7)	Carl Furillo	9.00	4.50	2.75
(8)	Hal Gregg	9.00	4.50	2.75
(9)	Joe Hatten	9.00	4.50	2.75
(10)	Gene Hermanski	9.00	4.50	2.75
(11)	Gil Hodges	40.00	20.00	12.00
(12)	Spider Jorgensen	9.00	4.50	2.75
(13)	Clyde King	9.00	4.50	2.75
(14)	Vic Lombardi	9.00	4.50	2.75
(15)	Rube Melton	9.00	4.50	2.75
(16)	Eddie Miksis	9.00	4.50	2.75
(17)	Pee Wee Reese	30.00	15.00	9.00
(18)	Pete Reiser	9.00	4.50	2.75
(19)	Jackie Robinson	80.00	40.00	24.00
(20)	Stan Rojek	9.00	4.50	2.75
(21)	Burt Shotton	40.00	20.00	12.00
(22)	Duke Snider	12.50	6.25	3.75
(23)	Eddie Stanky	9.00	4.50	2.75
(24)	Harry Taylor	9.00	4.50	2.75
(25)	Dixie Walker	9.00	4.50	2.75

1948 Brooklyn Dodgers Picture Pack

This team-issued set of player portrait pictures is in a blank-back 6-1/2" x 9" format. A facsimile autograph appears on front. Like many souvenir-stand photo packs of the era, it is possible the specific contents of this product may have changed during the course of this season as players joined and left the team, and that pictures were re-used from year-to-year.

		NM	EX	VG
Complete Set (26):		300.00	150.00	95.00
Common Player:		8.00	4.00	2.50
(1)	Rex Barney	8.00	4.00	2.50

		NM	EX	VG
(2)	Ray Blades	8.00	4.00	2.50
(3)	Bobby Bragan	8.00	4.00	2.50
(4)	Ralph Branca	8.00	4.00	2.50
(5)	Tommy Brown	8.00	4.00	2.50
(6)	Hugh Casey	8.00	4.00	2.50
(7)	Billy Cox	8.00	4.00	2.50
(8)	Leo Durocher	15.00	7.50	4.50
(9)	Bruce Edwards	8.00	4.00	2.50
(10)	Carl Furillo	20.00	10.00	6.00
(11)	Joe Hatten	8.00	4.00	2.50
(12)	Gene Hermanski	8.00	4.00	2.50
(13)	Gil Hodges	30.00	15.00	9.00
(14)	Spider Jorgensen	8.00	4.00	2.50
(15)	Don Lund	8.00	4.00	2.50
(16)	Eddie Miksis	8.00	4.00	2.50
(17)	Jake Pitler	8.00	4.00	2.50
(18)	Pee Wee Reese	25.00	12.50	7.50
(19)	Pete Reiser	8.00	4.00	2.50
(20)	Jackie Robinson	65.00	32.00	19.50
(21)	Preacher Roe	12.00	6.00	3.50
(22)	Burt Shotton	8.00	4.00	2.50
(23)	Clyde Sukeforth	8.00	4.00	2.50
(24)	Harry Taylor	8.00	4.00	2.50
(25)	Arky Vaughan	15.00	7.50	4.50
(26)	Preston Ward	8.00	4.00	2.50

1949 Brooklyn Dodgers Picture Pack

This team-issued set of player portrait pictures is in a blank-back 6-1/2" x 9" format. A facsimile autograph appears on front. Like many souvenir-stand photo packs of the era, it is possible the specific contents of this product may have changed during the course of this season as players joined and left the team, and that pictures were re-used from year-to-year.

		NM	EX	VG
Complete Set (25):		575.00	300.00	160.00
Common Player:		8.00	5.00	3.00
(1)	Jack Banta	8.00	5.00	3.00
(2)	Rex Barney	8.00	5.00	3.00
(3)	Ralph Branca	12.50	6.25	3.75
(4)	Tommy Brown	8.00	5.00	3.00
(5)	Roy Campanella	200.00	100.00	60.00
(6)	Billy Cox	8.00	5.00	3.00
(7)	Bruce Edwards	8.00	5.00	3.00
(8)	Carl Furillo	20.00	10.00	6.00
(9)	Joe Hatten	8.00	5.00	3.00
(10)	Gene Hermanski	8.00	5.00	3.00
(11)	Gil Hodges	40.00	20.00	12.00
(12)	Johnny Hopp	8.00	5.00	3.00
(13)	Spider Jorgensen	8.00	5.00	3.00
(14)	Mike McCormick	8.00	5.00	3.00
(15)	Eddie Miksis	8.00	5.00	3.00
(16)	Don Newcombe	100.00	50.00	30.00
(17)	Erv Palica	8.00	5.00	3.00
(18)	Jake Pitler	8.00	5.00	3.00
(19)	Pee Wee Reese	50.00	25.00	15.00
(20)	Jackie Robinson	75.00	37.00	22.00
(21)	Preacher Roe	12.50	6.25	3.75
(22)	Burt Shotton	8.00	5.00	3.00
(23)	Duke Snider	50.00	25.00	15.00
(24)	Milt Stock	8.00	5.00	3.00
(25)	Clyde Sukeforth	8.00	5.00	3.00

1952 Brooklyn Dodgers Schedule Cards

These postcard-size black-and-white cards have popular Dodgers players on front and the 1952 season's schedule printed on back. Some cards have a postcard-style back on which the right side has space for an address. Others cards have ticket price infor-

mation in that space. How many different cards were issued is not known. Credit on the back is given to Lumitone Photoprint of New York.

	NM	EX	VG
Common Card:	225.00	110.00	67.00
Gil Hodges	400.00	200.00	120.00
Pee Wee Reese	400.00	200.00	120.00
Jackie Robinson	600.00	300.00	180.00
Duke Snider	400.00	200.00	120.00

1955 Brooklyn Dodgers Picture Pack

This set of approximately 5" x 7" blank-back, black-and-white pictures was a souvenir stand item at Ebbets Field. Player photos are chest-to-cap portraits surrounded by a white border with the player name at bottom in all-caps, followed by the team nickname in upper- and lower-case type. The unnumbered pictures are listed here alphabetically. The set was sold for 25 cents in a white paper envelope with "WORLD CHAMPION Dodgers" printed in blue.

		NM	EX	VG
Complete Set (12):		100.00	50.00	30.00
Common Player:		8.00	4.00	2.50
(1)	Walter Alston	8.00	4.00	2.50
(2)	Roy Campanella	20.00	10.00	6.00
(3)	Carl Erskine	8.00	4.00	2.50
(4)	Carl Furillo	10.00	5.00	3.00
(5)	Gil Hodges	16.00	8.00	4.75
(6)	Randy Jackson	8.00	4.00	2.50
(7)	Clem Labine	8.00	4.00	2.50
(8)	Don Newcombe	8.00	4.00	2.50
(9)	Johnny Podres	8.00	4.00	2.50
(10)	Peewee Reese	13.50	6.75	4.00
(11)	Jackie Robinson	24.00	12.00	7.25
(12)	Duke Snider	16.00	8.00	4.75

1956 Brooklyn Dodgers Picture Pack

DON DRYSDALE, Dodgers

This set of 5" x 7" blank-back, black-and-white pictures was a souvenir stand item at Ebbets Field. Player photos are surrounded by a white border with the player name at bottom in all-caps, followed by the team nickname in upper- and lower-case type. The unnumbered pictures are listed here alphabetically. The same photos were offered in a 50-piece Yankees-Dodgers "World Series Picture Portfolio."

		NM	EX	VG
Complete Set (25):		250.00	125.00	75.00
Common Player:		10.00	5.00	3.00
(1)	Walter Alston	12.50	6.25	3.75
(2)	Sandy Amoros	12.50	6.25	3.75
(3)	Joe Becker	10.00	5.00	3.00
(4)	Don Bessent	10.00	5.00	3.00
(5)	Roy Campanella	30.00	15.00	9.00
(6)	Roger Craig	10.00	5.00	3.00
(7)	Don Drysdale	25.00	12.50	7.50
(8)	Carl Erskine	12.50	6.25	3.75
(9)	Chico Fernandez	10.00	5.00	3.00
(10)	Carl Furillo	15.00	7.50	4.50
(11)	Jim Gilliam	15.00	7.50	4.50
(12)	Billy Herman	12.50	6.25	3.75
(13)	Gil Hodges	25.00	12.50	7.50
(14)	Randy Jackson	10.00	5.00	3.00
(15)	Sandy Koufax	35.00	17.50	10.50

		NM	EX	VG
(16)	Clem Labine	12.50	6.25	3.75
(17)	Sal Maglie	10.00	5.00	3.00
(18)	Charlie Neal	10.00	5.00	3.00
(19)	Don Newcombe	12.50	6.25	3.75
(20)	Jake Pitler	10.00	5.00	3.00
(21)	Peewee Reese	20.00	10.00	6.00
(22)	Jackie Robinson	35.00	17.50	10.50
(23)	Ed Roebuck	10.00	5.00	3.00
(24)	Duke Snider	25.00	12.50	7.50
(25)	Al Walker	10.00	5.00	3.00

1957 Brooklyn Dodgers Picture Pack

In their final year in Brooklyn, the Dodgers issued this souvenir-stand picture pack, offered for 25 cents. The pictures are 5" x 7", blank-back, black-and-white. Player portraits are surrounded by a white border with the player name at bottom in all-caps and "Dodgers" in upper- and lower-case type. The unnumbered pictures are listed here alphabetically.

		NM	EX	VG
Complete Set (12):		125.00	65.00	40.00
Common Player:		10.00	5.00	3.00
(1)	Walter Alston	15.00	7.50	4.50
(2)	Roy Campanella	25.00	12.50	7.50
(3)	Carl Furillo	15.00	7.50	4.50
(4)	Jim Gilliam	15.00	7.50	4.50
(5)	Gil Hodges	20.00	10.00	6.00
(6)	Randy Jackson	10.00	5.00	3.00
(7)	Clem Labine	10.00	5.00	3.00
(8)	Sal Maglie	10.00	5.00	3.00
(9)	Don Newcombe	12.50	6.25	3.75
(10)	Johnny Podres	15.00	7.50	4.50
(11)	Peewee Reese	20.00	10.00	6.00
(12)	Duke Snider	20.00	10.00	6.00

1953-55 Brown & Bigelow

Some of baseball's biggest stars, either as they appeared in the mid-1950s or as spirit images, instruct All-American boys in the skills of baseball on this series of cards. Produced by the St. Paul firm of Brown & Bigelow, the 2-1/4" x 3-1/2", round-cornered cards can be found either as playing cards or with schedules printed on the back. The cards could be customized by local sponsors in a panel at the bottom of the artwork. The Medcalf artwork is also seen on contemporary wall and desk calendars and other printed items.

		NM	EX	VG
	UNOPENED DECKS			
(1)	Ty Cobb	45.00	22.50	13.50
(2)	Lou Gehrig	50.00	25.00	15.00
(3)	Connie Mack	30.00	15.00	9.00
(4)	John McGraw	30.00	15.00	9.00
(5)	Babe Ruth	65.00	32.50	20.00
(6)	Honus Wagner	40.00	20.00	12.00
	SINGLE CARDS			
(1)	Ty Cobb	6.00	3.00	1.75
(2)	Lou Gehrig	8.00	4.00	2.50
(3)	Connie Mack	4.00	2.00	1.25
(4)	John McGraw	4.00	2.00	1.25
(5)	Babe Ruth	10.00	5.00	3.00
(6)	Honus Wagner	5.00	2.50	1.50

1911-14 Brunners Bread (D304)

(See 1911-1914 General Baking Co. for checklist and values.)

1910 Brush Detroit Tigers Postcards

The makers of this short-lived (1907-11) automobile evidently engaged members of the hometown team to endorse their product. The 3-1/2" x 5-3/8" black-and-white postcards have a bordered photo on front showing a Tigers player (in uniform or suit) with the auto. A few lines of petry about the player complete the design. Backs have typical postcard format. It is likely the checklist here is incomplete.

		NM	EX	VG
(1)	Ty Cobb	4,000	2,000	1,200
(2)	Hughie Jennings	1,500	750.00	450.00
(3)	Matty McIntyre	750.00	375.00	225.00
(4)	George Mullin	750.00	375.00	225.00
(5)	Charlie Schmidt	750.00	375.00	225.00

1979 Bubble Yum Toronto Blue Jays

 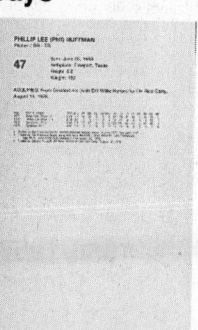

Members of the Toronto Blue Jays in the team's third season are featured in this set of 5-1/2" x 8-1/2" black-and-white player pictures. Fronts feature player portraits identified by their full name and position. In the wide bottom border are team and sponsor logos. Backs have player biographical data, major and minor league stats, acquisition information and career highlights. Cards are numbered by uniform number.

		NM	EX	VG
Complete Set (20):		65.00	32.50	20.00
Common Player:		4.00	2.00	1.25
1	Bob Bailor	4.00	2.00	1.25
4	Alfredo Griffin	4.00	2.00	1.25
7	Roy Hartsfield	4.00	2.00	1.25
9	Rick Cerone	4.00	2.00	1.25
10	John Mayberry	4.00	2.00	1.25
11	Luis Gomez	4.00	2.00	1.25
13	Roy Howell	4.00	2.00	1.25
18	Jim Clancy	4.00	2.00	1.25
19	Otto Velez	4.00	2.00	1.25
20	Al Woods	4.00	2.00	1.25
21	Rico Carty	4.00	2.00	1.25
22	Rick Bosetti	4.00	2.00	1.25
23	Dave Lemanczyk	4.00	2.00	1.25
24	Tom Underwood	4.00	2.00	1.25
31	Bobby Doerr	6.00	3.00	1.75
34	Jesse Jefferson	4.00	2.00	1.25
38	Balor Moore	4.00	2.00	1.25
44	Tom Buskey	4.00	2.00	1.25
46	Dave Freisleben	4.00	2.00	1.25
47	Phil Huffman	4.00	2.00	1.25

1976 Buckmans Discs

One of several regional sponsors of player disc sets in 1976 was Buckmans Ice Cream Village in Rochester, N.Y. The discs are 3-3/8" diameter with a black-and-white player portrait photo in the center of the baseball design. A line of red stars is above, while the left and right panels feature one of several bright colors. Produced by Michael Schecter Associates under license from the Major League Baseball Players Association, the player photos have had uniform and cap logos removed. Backs are printed in red and purple. The unnumbered checklist here is presented in alphabetical order.

		NM	EX	VG
Complete Set (70):		60.00	30.00	18.00
Common Player:		.75	.40	.25
(1)	Henry Aaron	6.00	3.00	1.75
(2)	Johnny Bench	3.50	1.75	1.00
(3)	Vida Blue	.75	.40	.25
(4)	Larry Bowa	.75	.40	.25
(5)	Lou Brock	2.50	1.25	.70
(6)	Jeff Burroughs	.75	.40	.25
(7)	John Candelaria	.75	.40	.25
(8)	Jose Cardenal	.75	.40	.25
(9)	Rod Carew	2.50	1.25	.70
(10)	Steve Carlton	2.50	1.25	.70
(11)	Dave Cash	.75	.40	.25
(12)	Cesar Cedeno	.75	.40	.25
(13)	Ron Cey	.75	.40	.25
(14)	Carlton Fisk	2.50	1.25	.70
(15)	Tito Fuentes	.75	.40	.25
(16)	Steve Garvey	2.00	1.00	.60
(17)	Ken Griffey	.75	.40	.25
(18)	Don Gullett	.75	.40	.25
(19)	Willie Horton	.75	.40	.25
(20)	Al Hrabosky	.75	.40	.25
(21)	Catfish Hunter	2.50	1.25	.70
(22)	Reggie Jackson (A's)	5.00	2.50	1.50
(23)	Randy Jones	.75	.40	.25
(24)	Jim Kaat	.75	.40	.25
(25)	Don Kessinger	.75	.40	.25
(26)	Dave Kingman	.75	.40	.25
(27)	Jerry Koosman	.75	.40	.25
(28)	Mickey Lolich	.75	.40	.25
(29)	Greg Luzinski	.75	.40	.25
(30)	Fred Lynn	.75	.40	.25
(31)	Bill Madlock	.75	.40	.25
(32)	Carlos May (White Sox)	.75	.40	.25
(33)	John Mayberry	.75	.40	.25
(34)	Bake McBride	.75	.40	.25
(35)	Doc Medich	.75	.40	.25
(36)	Andy Messersmith (Dodgers)	.75	.40	.25
(37)	Rick Monday	.75	.40	.25
(38)	John Montefusco	.75	.40	.25
(39)	Jerry Morales	.75	.40	.25
(40)	Joe Morgan	2.50	1.25	.70
(41)	Thurman Munson	2.50	1.25	.70
(42)	Bobby Murcer	.75	.40	.25
(43)	Al Oliver	.75	.40	.25
(44)	Jim Palmer	2.50	1.25	.70
(45)	Dave Parker	.75	.40	.25
(46)	Tony Perez	2.50	1.25	.70
(47)	Jerry Reuss	.75	.40	.25
(48)	Brooks Robinson	3.00	1.50	.90
(49)	Frank Robinson	3.00	1.50	.90
(50)	Steve Rogers	.75	.40	.25
(51)	Pete Rose	6.00	3.00	1.75
(52)	Nolan Ryan	20.00	10.00	6.00
(53)	Manny Sanguillen	.75	.40	.25
(54)	Mike Schmidt	5.00	2.50	1.50
(55)	Tom Seaver	3.00	1.50	.90
(56)	Ted Simmons	.75	.40	.25
(57)	Reggie Smith	.75	.40	.25
(58)	Willie Stargell	2.50	1.25	.70
(59)	Rusty Staub	.75	.40	.25
(60)	Rennie Stennett	.75	.40	.25
(61)	Don Sutton	2.50	1.25	.70
(62)	Andy Thornton (Cubs)	.75	.40	.25
(63)	Luis Tiant	.75	.40	.25
(64)	Joe Torre	1.50	.70	.45
(65)	Mike Tyson	.75	.40	.25
(66)	Bob Watson	.75	.40	.25
(67)	Wilbur Wood	.75	.40	.25
(68)	Jimmy Wynn	.75	.40	.25
(69)	Carl Yastrzemski	3.50	1.75	1.00
(70)	Richie Zisk	.75	.40	.25

1916 Bucyrus Brewing Co. (M101-4)

One of a dozen or so firms that utilized Felix Mendelsohn's baseball card issue as an advertising medium was this Ohio brewery. Unlike the other companies, however, Bucyrus did not issue individual cards, but only a 42" x 28" uncut sheet containing all 200 cards and labeled "1916 - BASEBALL'S HALL OF FAME - 1916." If cut from the sheet, the single cards would be indistinguishable from the blank-back version of M101-4.

	NM	EX	VG
Complete Uncut Sheet:	35,000	25,000	15,000

(See 1916 M101-4 Blank Backs for checklist.)

1950 Buitoni Macaroni Joe DiMaggio Pins

At least two styles of 1-1/2" diameter pinback buttons are known from the Yankee Clipper's association with a New York pasta company. One style has a black-and-white portrait photo at the center of a red-stiched baseball design. Printed in red at top is "JOE DiMAGGIO / TV CLUB." At bottom is the program sponsor's name. Another style has a photo of the player with a bat over his shoulder on a yellow background. "JOE DiMAGGIO CLUB" is at top, BUITONI/ FOODS CORP." at bottom, both in red. Each style was reproduced in 2-1/4" size early in the 21st Century; those replicas have no collectible value.

	NM	EX	VG
Joe DiMaggio/Portrait	500.00	250.00	150.00
Joe DiMaggio (w/bat)	1,200	600.00	360.00

1932 Bulgaria Sport Tobacco

Despite the name of the sponsoring issuer, this set of cards is a product of Germany. Only a single major league ballplayer is pictured among the 272 cards in the set: Babe Ruth, who shares a card with boxing great Max Schmeling in a photo taken in the U.S. The black-and-white cards in the set measure 1-5/8" x 2-3/8" and have backs printed in German, including a card number.

		NM	EX	VG
256	Babe Ruth, Max Schmeling	300.00	150.00	90.00

1952-1953 Burger Beer Cincinnati Reds

Whether or not they were a promotional issue of Burger Beer (they are not marked as to issuer),

advanced collectors of 1950s Reds memorabilia ascribe these 8" x 10-1/2" black-and-white photos to the long-time Reds sponsor because of their similarity to later Burger editions. The blank-back photos have portraits or posed action shots surrounded with white borders. In the wide bottom border is a C Reds logo, with the player name and (usually) position at right in all-capitals. The Clyde King picture, which can be reliably dated to 1953, his only season with the Reds, is a portrait drawing, rather than a photo, and has no position listed. The unnumbered pictures are listed here alphabetically and the checklist presented is likely incomplete.

		NM	EX	VG
Common Player:		30.00	15.00	9.00
(1)	Joe Adcock/Fielding	40.00	20.00	12.00
(2)	Bob Borkowski/Btg (Follow-through)	30.00	15.00	9.00
(3)	Grady Hatton/Portrait	30.00	15.00	9.00
(4)	Niles Jordan/Portrait	30.00	15.00	9.00
(5)	Clyde King (Portrait art.)	30.00	15.00	9.00
(7)	Willard Marshall/Btg (Follow-through)	30.00	15.00	9.00
(8)	Ed Pellagrini/Portrait	30.00	15.00	9.00
(9)	Bud Podbielan/Portrait	30.00	15.00	9.00
(10)	John Temple/Btg (Follow-through)	30.00	15.00	9.00

1955 Burger Beer Cincinnati Reds

The evidence attributing these 8-1/2" x 11" black-and-white player pictures to one of the team's radio sponsors, Burger Beer, is apocryphal, based largely on the format, which is similar to the company's 1956-64 promotional issues. This series has player portraits or poses bordered in white. In the bottom border, flanked by team logos are three lines of capital-letter typography with the player's name, position and team. Backs are blank. This checklist is likely not complete.

		NM	EX	VG
Common Player:		30.00	15.00	9.00
(1)	Gus Bell	30.00	15.00	9.00
(2)	Rocky Bridges	30.00	15.00	9.00
(3)	Jackie Collum	30.00	15.00	9.00
(4)	Art Fowler	30.00	15.00	9.00
(5)	Ray Jablonski	30.00	15.00	9.00
(6)	Johnny Klippstein	30.00	15.00	9.00
(7)	Ted Kluszewski	45.00	22.00	13.50
(8)	Roy McMillan	30.00	15.00	9.00
(9)	Rudy Minarcin	30.00	15.00	9.00
(10)	Joe Nuxhall	45.00	22.00	13.50
(11)	Wally Post	30.00	15.00	9.00
(12)	Gerry Staley	30.00	15.00	9.00
(13)	Birdie Tebbetts	30.00	15.00	9.00

1956-1957 Burger Beer Cincinnati Reds

GUS BELL

COURTESY OF SPARKLE * A FINE YEAR AFTER YEAR

The 1956 and 1957 series of 8-1/2" x 11" black-and-white player photos from one of the Reds' broadcast sponsors can be distinguished from later issues by the presence of an advertising slogan at the bottom of the otherwise blank black, "COURTESY OF BURGER - A FINER BEER YEAR AFTER YEAR." Players are identified on the bottom front border in large capital letters. Because at least one player is known in both portrait and posed action photos, poses other than portraits are indicated in parentheses.

		NM	EX	VG
Common Player:		30.00	15.00	9.00
(1)	Ed Bailey (Portrait to top button.)	30.00	15.00	9.00
(2)	Ed Bailey (Portrait to chest showing number.)	30.00	15.00	9.00
(3)	Gus Bell (Portrait to chest showing number.)	30.00	15.00	9.00
(4)	Joe Black	30.00	15.00	9.00
(5)	Smoky Burgess/Btg	35.00	17.50	10.50
(6)	George Crowe/Btg	30.00	15.00	9.00
(7)	Don Hoak	30.00	15.00	9.00
(8)	Waite Hoyt/Broadcaster	30.00	15.00	9.00
(9)	Ray Jablonski/Throwing	30.00	15.00	9.00
(10)	Hal Jeffcoat (Follow-through)	30.00	15.00	9.00
(11)	Ted Kluszewski/Btg	50.00	25.00	15.00
(12)	Ted Kluszewski (Portrait to top button.)	50.00	25.00	15.00
(13)	Brooks Lawrence (Follow-through.)	30.00	15.00	9.00
(14)	Roy McMillan/Btg	30.00	15.00	9.00
(15)	Roy McMillan/Fielding	30.00	15.00	9.00

		NM	EX	VG
(16)	Roy McMillan (Portrait to second button.)	30.00	15.00	9.00
(17)	Jackie Moran/Broadcaster	30.00	15.00	9.00
(18)	Joe Nuxhall	30.00	15.00	9.00
(19)	Wally Post	30.00	15.00	9.00
(20)	Frank Robinson/Fielding	150.00	75.00	45.00
(21)	Frank Robinson/Portrait (White cap.)	125.00	62.00	37.00
(22)	Birdie Tebbetts	30.00	15.00	9.00
(23)	Johnny Temple (Portrait to second button.)	30.00	15.00	9.00
(24)	Johnny Temple (Portrait to chest showing number.)	30.00	15.00	9.00
(25)	Johnny Temple (Ready to throw.)	30.00	15.00	9.00
(26)	Bob Thurman/Batting	30.00	15.00	9.00

1958-1959 Burger Beer Cincinnati Reds

THOMAS

The 1958-1959 series of 8-1/2" x 11" black-and-white player photos can be distinguished by the presence of an advertising slogan at the bottom of the otherwise blank black, "COURTESY OF SPARKLE * BREWED BURGER BEER / HAVE FUN - HAVE A BURGER." Players are identified by first and last name, or by last name only on the bottom front border in large capital letters. The team name may or may not appear, as well.

		NM	EX	VG
Common Player:		30.00	15.00	9.00
(1)	Ed. Bailey/Portrait	30.00	15.00	9.00
(2)	Gus Bell/Portrait (Dark cap.)	30.00	15.00	9.00
(4)	Waite Hoyt (At microphone.)	30.00	15.00	9.00
(6)	Jerry Lynch/Portrait	30.00	15.00	9.00
(7)	Roy McMillan/Portrait	30.00	15.00	9.00
(8)	(Don) Newcombe/Portrait	30.00	15.00	9.00
(9)	Joe Nuxhall (Follow-through.)	30.00	15.00	9.00
(11)	Vada Pinson/Portrait	45.00	22.00	13.50
(12)	Bob Purkey/Portrait	30.00	15.00	9.00
(13)	Frank Robinson/Btg (Dark cap.)	125.00	62.00	37.00
(14)	Frank Robinson/Fielding	125.00	62.00	37.00
(15)	Frank Robinson/Portrait (White cap.)	125.00	62.00	37.00
(16)	Manager Mayo Smith (Adjusting cap.)	30.00	15.00	9.00
(17)	John Temple/Portrait	30.00	15.00	9.00
(18)	Frank Thomas/Btg	30.00	15.00	9.00
(19)	(Frank) Thomas/Portrait	30.00	15.00	9.00

1960-64 Burger Beer Cincinnati Reds

VADA PINSON
(Cincinnati Reds)

The sponsor is not identified (except on 1959 issues which are marked on back, "COURTESY OF SPARKLE * BREWED BURGER BEER / HAVE FUN - HAVE A BURGER)", nor the year of issue published on these 8-1/2" x 11" player photos. Uniform and cap styles can give some idea of when the photos were taken. Photos are black-and-white portraits or action poses surrounded by white borders with the player and team names at bottom. Backs are blank. The unnumbered photos are listed here in alphabetical order. Some photos were re-issued year after year with only minor changes in cropping; these are not listed separately. This checklist will likely remain incomplete for some time. Gaps have been in the assigned numbering to accommodate future additions.

	NM	EX	VG
Common Player:			
(1) Ed Bailey/Portrait	15.00	7.50	4.50
(2) Ed. Bailey/Portrait	15.00	7.50	4.50
(3) Don Blasingame/Fielding	15.00	7.50	4.50
(4) Gus Bell/Btg	15.00	7.50	4.50
(5) Gus Bell (Fielding fly ball.)	15.00	7.50	4.50
(6) Gus Bell/Portrait	15.00	7.50	4.50
(7) Gordon Coleman (Bat behind cap.)	15.00	7.50	4.50
(8) Gordon Coleman (Bat behind shoulder.)	15.00	7.50	4.50
(9) Gordon Coleman/Fielding	15.00	7.50	4.50
(11) John Edwards/Portrait (Light tower in background.)	15.00	7.50	4.50
(12) John Edwards/Portrait (No tower.)	15.00	7.50	4.50
(13) Gene Freese/Fielding	15.00	7.50	4.50
(14) Jay Hook (Follow-through.)	15.00	7.50	4.50
(15) Waite Hoyt/Announcer (Portrait at microphone.)	15.00	7.50	4.50
(16) Waite Hoyt/Announcer (Portrait w/folder.)	15.00	7.50	4.50
(17) Fred Hutchinson/Portrait (C on vest.)	15.00	7.50	4.50
(18) Fred Hutchinson/Portrait (Half of "1" and "C.")	15.00	7.50	4.50
(19) Fred Hutchinson/Portrait (C Reds on vest.)	15.00	7.50	4.50
(20) Fred. Hutchinson (Only top of chest emblem shows.)	15.00	7.50	4.50
(22) Joey Jay (Follow-through.)	15.00	7.50	4.50
(23) Joey Jay/Portrait	15.00	7.50	4.50
(24) Eddie Kasko/Btg	15.00	7.50	4.50
(25) Eddie Kasko/Fielding	15.00	7.50	4.50
(26) Gene Kelly/Announcer	15.00	7.50	4.50
(27) Jerry Lynch/Btg	15.00	7.50	4.50
(28) Jim Maloney/Portrait	15.00	7.50	4.50
(29) Roy McMillan/Fielding	15.00	7.50	4.50
(31) Don Newcombe (Wind-up.)	20.00	10.00	6.00
(32) Joe Nuxhall (Follow-through, long-sleeve undershirt.)	15.00	7.50	4.50
(33) Joe Nuxhall (follow-through, short-sleeve undershirt)	15.00	7.50	4.50
(34) Jim O'Toole/Portrait	15.00	7.50	4.50
(35) Jim O'Toole (Windup.)	15.00	7.50	4.50
(36) Jim O'Toole (Follow-through.)	15.00	7.50	4.50
(37) Don Pavletich/Portrait	15.00	7.50	4.50
(38) Vada Pinson/Btg (No players in background.)	20.00	10.00	6.00
(39) Vada Pinson/Btg (Players in background.)	20.00	10.00	6.00
(40) Vada Pinson (Catching fly ball.)	20.00	10.00	6.00
(41) Vada Pinson (Hands on knees.)	20.00	10.00	6.00
(43) Wally Post/Btg	15.00	7.50	4.50
(44) Wally Post/Portrait	15.00	7.50	4.50
(45) Bob Purkey/Pitching (Right foot visible.)	15.00	7.50	4.50
(46) Bob Purkey/Pitching (Right foot not visible.)	15.00	7.50	4.50
(47) Bob Purkey/Portrait (Teeth don't show.)	15.00	7.50	4.50
(48) Bob Purkey/Portrait (Teeth show.)	15.00	7.50	4.50
(50) Frank Robinson/Btg (Dark cap.)	45.00	22.00	13.50
(51) Frank Robinson/Btg (White cap.)	45.00	22.00	13.50
(52) Frank Robinson (Fielding fly ball.)	45.00	22.00	13.50
(53) Frank Robinson/Portrait (Pinstripes, black background.)	45.00	22.00	13.50
(54) Frank Robinson/Portrait (Pinstripes, natural sky background.)	45.00	22.00	13.50
(55) Frankie Robinson (Head turned back to camera.)	45.00	22.00	13.50
(56) Pete Rose (Portrait to chest.)	200.00	100.00	60.00

1977 Burger Chef Funmeal Discs

The largest of the disc sets produced by Michael Schechter Associates is the 216-piece issue for the Burger Chef fast food restaurant chain. The discs were issued nine-per-team on a cardboard tray accompanying a 69-cent Funmeal for kids. The 2-3/8" discs could be punched out of the tray. They share the basic design of other MSA discs of the era. A black-and-white player photo is in the center of a baseball design. Because the discs were licensed only by the Players Association, the player photos have had cap logos airbrushed away. The left and right side panels are in one of several bright colors. Backs feature a Burger Chef cartoon character in color. The individual discs are unnumbered.

	NM	EX	VG
Complete Set, Trays (24):	100.00	50.00	30.00
Complete Set, Singles (216):	90.00	45.00	27.00
Common Player:	.75	.35	.20
1A Cincinnati Reds (Full tray.)	20.00	10.00	6.00
(1A1) Johnny Bench	4.50	2.25	1.25
(1A2) Dave Concepcion	.75	.35	.20
(1A3) Dan Driessen	.75	.35	.20
(1A4) George Foster	.75	.35	.20
(1A5) Cesar Geronimo	.75	.35	.20
(1A6) Ken Griffey	1.25	.60	.40
(1A7) Joe Morgan	3.50	1.75	1.00
(1A8) Gary Nolan	.75	.35	.20
(1A9) Pete Rose	7.50	3.75	2.25
2A St. Louis Cardinals (Full tray.)	10.00	5.00	3.00
(2A1) Lou Brock	3.50	1.75	1.00
(2A2) John Denny	.75	.35	.20
(2A3) Pete Falcone	.75	.35	.20
(2A4) Keith Hernandez	.75	.40	.25
(2A5) Al Hrabosky	.75	.35	.20
(2A6) Bake McBride	.75	.35	.20
(2A7) Ken Reitz	.75	.35	.20
(2A8) Ted Simmons	.75	.35	.20
(2A9) Mike Tyson	.75	.35	.20
3A Detroit Tigers (Full tray.)	8.00	4.00	2.50
(3A1) Mark Fidrych	1.50	.70	.45
(3A2) Bill Freehan	.75	.35	.20
(3A3) John Hiller	.75	.35	.20
(3A4) Willie Horton	.75	.35	.20
(3A5) Ron LeFlore	.75	.35	.20
(3A6) Ben Oglivie	.75	.35	.20
(3A7) Aurelio Rodriguez	.75	.35	.20
(3A8) Rusty Staub	1.25	.60	.40
(3A9) Jason Thompson	.75	.35	.20
4A Cleveland Indians (Full tray.)	8.00	4.00	2.50
(4A1) Buddy Bell	.75	.35	.20
(4A2) Frank Duffy	.75	.35	.20
(4A3) Dennis Eckersley	2.75	1.50	.80
(4A4) Ray Fosse	.75	.35	.20
(4A5) Wayne Garland	.75	.35	.20
(4A6) Duane Kuiper	.75	.35	.20
(4A7) Dave LaRoche	.75	.35	.20
(4A8) Rick Manning	.75	.35	.20
(4A9) Rick Waits	.75	.35	.20
5A Chicago White Sox (Full tray.)	8.00	4.00	2.50
(5A1) Jack Brohamer	.75	.35	.20
(5A2) Bucky Dent	1.00	.50	.30
(5A3) Ralph Garr	.75	.35	.20
(5A4) Bart Johnson	.75	.35	.20
(5A5) Lamar Johnson	.75	.35	.20
(5A6) Chet Lemon	.75	.35	.20
(5A7) Jorge Orta	.75	.35	.20
(5A8) Jim Spencer	.75	.35	.20
(5A9) Richie Zisk	.75	.35	.20
6A Chicago Cubs (Full tray.)	8.00	4.00	2.50
(6A1) Bill Bonham	.75	.35	.20
(6A2) Bill Buckner	1.25	.60	.40
(6A3) Ray Burris	.75	.35	.20
(6A4) Jose Cardenal	.75	.35	.20
(6A5) Bill Madlock	.75	.35	.20
(6A6) Jerry Morales	.75	.35	.20
(6A7) Rick Reuschel	.75	.35	.20
(6A8) Manny Trillo	.75	.35	.20
(6A9) Joe Wallis	.75	.35	.20
7A Minnesota Twins (Full tray.)	10.00	5.00	3.00
(7A1) Lyman Bostock	.75	.35	.20
(7A2) Rod Carew	3.50	1.75	1.00
(7A3) Mike Cubbage	.75	.35	.20
(7A4) Dan Ford	.75	.35	.20
(7A5) Dave Goltz	.75	.35	.20
(7A6) Larry Hisle	.75	.35	.20
(7A7) Tom Johnson	.75	.35	.20
(7A8) Bobby Randall	.75	.35	.20
(7A9) Butch Wynegar	.75	.35	.20
8A Houston Astros (Full tray.)	8.00	4.00	2.50
(8A1) Enos Cabell	.75	.35	.20
(8A2) Cesar Cedeno	.75	.35	.20
(8A3) Jose Cruz	.75	.35	.20
(8A4) Joe Ferguson	.75	.35	.20
(8A5) Ken Forsch	.75	.35	.20
(8A6) Roger Metzger	.75	.35	.20
(8A7) J.R. Richard	.75	.35	.20
(8A8) Leon Roberts	.75	.35	.20
(8A9) Bob Watson	.75	.35	.20
1B Baltimore Orioles (Full tray.)	15.00	7.50	4.50
(1B1) Mark Belanger	.75	.35	.20
(1B2) Paul Blair	.75	.35	.20
(1B3) Al Bumbry	.75	.35	.20
(1B4) Doug DeCinces	.75	.35	.20
(1B5) Ross Grimsley	.75	.35	.20
(1B6) Lee May	.75	.35	.20
(1B7) Jim Palmer	3.50	1.75	1.00
(1B8) Brooks Robinson	4.50	2.25	1.25
(1B9) Ken Singleton	.75	.35	.20
2B Boston Red Sox (Full tray.)	15.00	7.50	4.50
(2B1) Rick Burleson	.75	.35	.20
(2B2) Dwight Evans	.75	.40	.25
(2B3) Carlton Fisk	3.50	1.75	1.00
(2B4) Fergie Jenkins	2.75	1.50	.80
(2B5) Bill Lee	.75	.35	.20
(2B6) Fred Lynn	.75	.35	.20
(2B7) Jim Rice	1.50	.70	.45
(2B8) Luis Tiant	.75	.35	.20
(2B9) Carl Yastrzemski	4.50	2.25	1.25
3B Kansas City Royals (Full tray.)	13.50	6.75	4.00
(3B1) Doug Bird	.75	.35	.20
(3B2) George Brett	6.00	3.00	1.75
(3B3) Dennis Leonard	.75	.35	.20
(3B4) John Mayberry	.75	.35	.20
(3B5) Hal McRae	.75	.35	.20
(3B6) Amos Otis	.75	.35	.20
(3B7) Fred Patek	.75	.35	.20
(3B8) Tom Poquette	.75	.35	.20
(3B9) Paul Splittorff	.75	.35	.20
4B Milwaukee Brewers (Full tray.)	10.00	5.00	3.00
(4B1) Jerry Augustine	.75	.35	.20
(4B2) Sal Bando	.75	.35	.20

	NM	EX	VG
(4B3) Von Joshua	.75	.35	.20
(4B4) Sixto Lezcano	.75	.35	.20
(4B5) Charlie Moore	.75	.35	.20
(4B6) Ed Rodriguez	.75	.35	.20
(4B7) Jim Slaton	.75	.35	.20
(4B8) Bill Travers	.75	.35	.20
(4B9) Robin Yount	3.50	1.75	1.00
5B Texas Rangers (Full tray.)	10.00	5.00	3.00
(5B1) Juan Beniquez	.75	.35	.20
(5B2) Bert Blyleven	.75	.35	.20
(5B3) Bert Campaneris	.75	.35	.20
(5B4) Tom Grieve	.75	.35	.20
(5B5) Mike Hargrove	.75	.35	.20
(5B6) Toby Harrah	.75	.35	.20
(5B7) Gaylord Perry	2.75	1.50	.80
(5B8) Lenny Randle	.75	.35	.20
(5B9) Jim Sundberg	.75	.35	.20
6B Atlanta Braves (Full tray.)	8.00	4.00	2.50
(6B1) Jeff Burroughs	.75	.35	.20
(6B2) Darrel Chaney	.75	.35	.20
(6B3) Gary Matthews	.75	.35	.20
(6B4) Andy Messersmith	.75	.35	.20
(6B5) Willie Montanez	.75	.35	.20
(6B6) Phil Niekro	2.75	1.50	.80
(6B7) Tom Paciorek	.75	.35	.20
(6B8) Jerry Royster	.75	.35	.20
(6B9) Dick Ruthven	.75	.35	.20
7B Pittsburgh Pirates (Full tray.)	10.00	5.00	3.00
(7B1) John Candelaria	.75	.35	.20
(7B2) Duffy Dyer	.75	.35	.20
(7B3) Al Oliver	1.25	.60	.40
(7B4) Dave Parker	.75	.40	.25
(7B5) Jerry Reuss	.75	.35	.20
(7B6) Bill Robinson	.75	.35	.20
(7B7) Willie Stargell	3.50	1.75	1.00
(7B8) Rennie Stennett	.75	.35	.20
(7B9) Frank Taveras	.75	.35	.20
8B New York Yankees (Full tray.)	20.00	10.00	6.00
(8B1) Chris Chambliss	.75	.35	.20
(8B2) Don Gullett	.75	.35	.20
(8B3) Catfish Hunter	2.75	1.50	.80
(8B4) Reggie Jackson	5.00	2.50	1.50
(8B5) Thurman Munson	4.50	2.25	1.25
(8B6) Graig Nettles	.75	.35	.20
(8B7) Willie Randolph	.75	.35	.20
(8B8) Mickey Rivers	.75	.35	.20
(8B9) Roy White	.75	.35	.20
1C California Angels (Full tray.)	25.00	12.50	7.50
(1C1) Bobby Bonds	.75	.35	.20
(1C2) Dave Chalk	.75	.35	.20
(1C3) Bobby Grich	.75	.35	.20
(1C4) Paul Hartzell	.75	.35	.20
(1C5) Ron Jackson	.75	.35	.20
(1C6) Jerry Remy	.75	.35	.20
(1C7) Joe Rudi	.75	.35	.20
(1C8) Nolan Ryan	16.00	8.00	4.75
(1C9) Frank Tanana	.75	.35	.20
2C Oakland A's (Full tray.)	8.00	4.00	2.50
(2C1) Stan Bahnsen	.75	.35	.20
(2C2) Vida Blue	.75	.35	.20
(2C3) Phil Garner	.75	.35	.20
(2C4) Paul Lindblad	.75	.35	.20
(2C5) Mike Norris	.75	.35	.20
(2C6) Bill North	.75	.35	.20
(2C7) Manny Sanguillen	.75	.35	.20
(2C8) Mike Torrez	.75	.35	.20
(2C9) Claudell Washington	.75	.35	.20
3C Los Angeles Dodgers (Full tray.)	10.00	5.00	3.00
(3C1) Ron Cey	.75	.35	.20
(3C2) Steve Garvey	2.00	1.00	.60
(3C3) Davey Lopes	.75	.35	.20
(3C4) Rick Monday	.75	.35	.20
(3C5) Doug Rau	.75	.35	.20
(3C6) Rick Rhoden	.75	.35	.20
(3C7) Reggie Smith	.75	.35	.20
(3C8) Don Sutton	2.75	1.50	.80
(3C9) Steve Yeager	.75	.35	.20
4C Montreal Expos (Full tray.)	10.00	5.00	3.00
(4C1) Gary Carter	3.00	1.50	.90
(4C2) Dave Cash	.75	.35	.20
(4C3) Tim Foli	.75	.35	.20
(4C4) Barry Foote	.75	.35	.20
(4C5) Larry Parrish	.75	.35	.20
(4C6) Tony Perez	3.00	1.50	.90
(4C7) Steve Rogers	.75	.35	.20
(4C8) Del Unser	.75	.35	.20
(4C9) Ellis Valentine	.75	.35	.20
5C New York Mets (Full tray.)	13.50	6.75	4.00
(5C1) Bud Harrelson	.75	.35	.20
(5C2) Dave Kingman	1.00	.50	.30
(5C3) Jerry Koosman	.75	.35	.20
(5C4) Ed Kranepool	.75	.35	.20
(5C5) Skip Lockwood	.75	.35	.20
(5C6) Jon Matlack	.75	.35	.20
(5C7) Felix Millan	.75	.35	.20
(5C8) Tom Seaver	4.50	2.25	1.25
(5C9) John Stearns	.75	.35	.20
6C Philadelphia Phillies (Full tray.)	15.00	7.50	4.50
(6C1) Bob Boone	1.00	.50	.30
(6C2) Larry Bowa	.75	.35	.20
(6C3) Steve Carlton	3.50	1.75	1.00
(6C4) Jay Johnstone	.75	.35	.20
(6C5) Jim Kaat	1.25	.60	.40
(6C6) Greg Luzinski	.75	.40	.25
(6C7) Garry Maddox	.75	.35	.20
(6C8) Tug McGraw	1.25	.60	.40
(6C9) Mike Schmidt	6.00	3.00	1.75
7C San Diego Padres (Full tray.)	10.00	5.00	3.00
(7C1) Rollie Fingers	2.75	1.50	.80
(7C2) George Hendrick	.75	.35	.20
(7C3) Enzo Hernandez	.75	.35	.20
(7C4) Mike Ivie	.75	.35	.20
(7C5) Randy Jones	.75	.35	.20
(7C6) Butch Metzger	.75	.35	.20
(7C7) Dave Rader	.75	.35	.20
(7C8) Gene Tenace	.75	.35	.20
(7C9) Dave Winfield	3.50	1.75	1.00

		NM	EX	VG
8C	San Francisco Giants (Full tray.)	8.00	4.00	2.50
(8C1)	Jim Barr	.75	.35	.20
(8C2)	Willie Crawford	.75	.35	.20
(8C3)	Larry Herndon	.75	.35	.20
(8C4)	Randy Moffitt	.75	.35	.20
(8C5)	John Montefusco	.75	.35	.20
(8C6)	Bobby Murcer	.75	.35	.20
(8C7)	Marty Perez	.75	.35	.20
(8C8)	Chris Speier	.75	.35	.20
(8C9)	Gary Thomasson	.75	.35	.20

1977 Burger King Tigers

This series of color 8" x 10" player portraits was given away one per week at Detroit area Burger Kings. Backs are blank and there is no player identification on the front. The photos are checklisted here alphabetically.

		NM	EX	VG
Complete Set (4):		40.00	20.00	12.00
Common Player:		10.00	5.00	3.00
(1)	Mark Fidrych (Holding glove.)	15.00	7.50	4.50
(2)	Ron LeFlore (Black guy w/bat.)	10.00	5.00	3.00
(3)	Dave Rozema (Winding up.)	10.00	5.00	3.00
(4)	Mickey Stanley (White guy w/bat.)	10.00	5.00	3.00

1977 Burger King Yankees

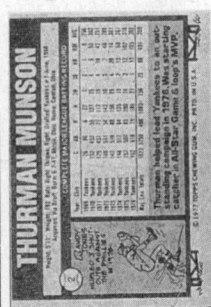

The first Topps-produced set for Burger King restaurants was issued in the New York area, featuring the A.L. champion Yankees. Twenty-two players plus an unnumbered checklist were issued at the beginning of the promotion with card #23 (Lou Piniella) being added to the set later. The "New York Post" reported production of the first 22 player cards at about 170,000 of each. The Piniella card was issued in limited quantities. Cards are 2-1/2" x 3-1/2" and have fronts identical to the regular 1977 Topps set except for numbers 2, 6, 7, 13, 14, 15, 17, 20 and 21. These cards feature different poses or major picture-cropping variations. It should be noted that very minor cropping variations between the regular Topps sets and the Burger King issues exist throughout the years the sets were produced.

		NM	EX	VG
Complete Set w/Piniella (24):		20.00	10.00	6.00
Complete Set no Piniella (23):		13.50	6.75	4.00
Common Player:		.25	.13	.08
1	Yankees Team (Billy Martin)	.75	.40	.25
2	Thurman Munson	5.00	2.50	1.50
3	Fran Healy	.25	.13	.08
4	Catfish Hunter	1.50	.70	.45
5	Ed Figueroa	.25	.13	.08
6	Don Gullett	.25	.13	.08
7	Mike Torrez	.25	.13	.08
8	Ken Holtzman	.25	.13	.08
9	Dick Tidrow	.25	.13	.08
10	Sparky Lyle	.40	.20	.12
11	Ron Guidry	.45	.25	.14
12	Chris Chambliss	.25	.13	.08
13	Willie Randolph	.45	.25	.14
14	Bucky Dent	.45	.25	.14
15	Graig Nettles	.60	.30	.20
16	Fred Stanley	.25	.13	.08
17	Reggie Jackson	5.00	2.50	1.50
18	Mickey Rivers	.25	.13	.08
19	Roy White	.40	.20	.12
20	Jim Wynn	.40	.20	.12
21	Paul Blair	.25	.13	.08
22	Carlos May	.25	.13	.08

		NM	EX	VG
23	Lou Piniella	15.00	7.50	4.50
---	Checklist	.05	.03	.02

1978 Burger King Astros

Burger King restaurants in the Houston area distributed a Topps-produced set showcasing the Astros. Cards are standard 2-1/2" x 3-1/2" and are numbered 1-22, plus and unnumbered checklist. Fronts are identical to the regular 1978 Topps set with the exception of card numbers 21, Dave Bergman, who appeared on a Rookie Outfielders cards in the '78 Topps set; and 22, Jesus Alou, who did not have a card in the regular issue. Although not noted in the following checklist, it should be remembered that very minor picture-cropping variations between the regular Topps issues and the 1977-1980 Burger King sets do exist.

		NM	EX	VG
Complete Set (23):		15.00	7.50	4.50
Common Player:		.75	.40	.25
1	Bill Virdon	.90	.45	.25
2	Joe Ferguson	.75	.40	.25
3	Ed Herrmann	.75	.40	.25
4	J.R. Richard	1.50	.70	.45
5	Joe Niekro	1.25	.60	.40
6	Floyd Bannister	.75	.40	.25
7	Joaquin Andujar	.75	.40	.25
8	Ken Forsch	.75	.40	.25
9	Mark Lemongello	.75	.40	.25
10	Joe Sambito	.75	.40	.25
11	Gene Pentz	.75	.40	.25
12	Bob Watson	.90	.45	.25
13	Julio Gonzalez	.75	.40	.25
14	Enos Cabell	.75	.40	.25
15	Roger Metzger	.75	.40	.25
16	Art Howe	.90	.45	.25
17	Jose Cruz	1.00	.50	.30
18	Cesar Cedeno	1.00	.50	.30
19	Terry Puhl	.75	.40	.25
20	Wilbur Howard	.75	.40	.25
21	Dave Bergman	.75	.40	.25
22	Jesus Alou	1.00	.50	.30
---	Checklist	.10	.05	.03

1978 Burger King Rangers

Issued by Burger King restaurants in the Dallas-Fort Worth area, this Topps-produced set features the Texas Rangers. Cards are standard 2-1/2" x 3-1/2" and identical in style to the regular 1978 Topps set with the following exceptions: #'s 5, 8, 10, 12, 17, 21 and 22. An unnumbered checklist card was included with the set.

		NM	EX	VG
Complete Set (23):		15.00	7.50	4.50
Common Player:		.75	.40	.25
1	Billy Hunter	.75	.40	.25
2	Jim Sundberg	.75	.40	.25
3	John Ellis	.75	.40	.25
4	Doyle Alexander	.75	.40	.25
5	Jon Matlack	.75	.40	.25
6	Dock Ellis	.75	.40	.25
7	George Medich	.75	.40	.25
8	Fergie Jenkins	6.00	3.00	1.75
9	Len Barker	.75	.40	.25
10	Reggie Cleveland	.75	.40	.25
11	Mike Hargrove	1.00	.50	.30
12	Bump Wills	1.00	.50	.30
13	Toby Harrah	1.00	.50	.30
14	Bert Campaneris	1.00	.50	.30
15	Sandy Alomar	1.00	.50	.30
16	Kurt Bevacqua	.75	.40	.25
17	Al Oliver	1.50	.70	.45
18	Juan Beniquez	.75	.40	.25

		NM	EX	VG
19	Claudell Washington	.75	.40	.25
20	Richie Zisk	.75	.40	.25
21	John Lowenstein	.75	.40	.25
22	Bobby Thompson	.75	.40	.25
---	Checklist	.10	.05	.03

1978 Burger King Tigers

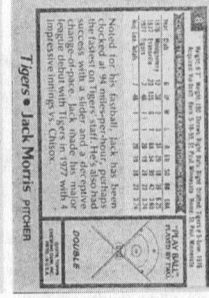

Rookie cards of Morris, Trammell and Whitaker make the Topps-produced 1978 Burger King Detroit Tigers issue the most popular of the BK sets. Twenty-two player cards and an unnumbered checklist make up the set which was issued in the Detroit area. Cards measure 2-1/2" x 3-1/2", and are identical to the regular 1978 Topps issue with the following exceptions: #'s 6, 7, 8, 13, 15 and 16. Numerous minor picture-cropping variations between the regular Topps issues and the Burger King sets appear from 1977-1980; these minor variations are not noted in the following checklist.

		NM	EX	VG
Complete Set (23):		25.00	12.50	7.50
Common Player:		.75	.40	.25
1	Ralph Houk	.90	.45	.25
2	Milt May	.75	.40	.25
3	John Wockenfuss	.75	.40	.25
4	Mark Fidrych	2.50	1.25	.70
5	Dave Rozema	.75	.40	.25
6	Jack Billingham	.75	.40	.25
7	Jim Slaton	.75	.40	.25
8	Jack Morris	3.00	1.50	.90
9	John Hiller	.75	.40	.25
10	Steve Foucault	.75	.40	.25
11	Milt Wilcox	.75	.40	.25
12	Jason Thompson	.75	.40	.25
13	Lou Whitaker	6.00	3.00	1.75
14	Aurelio Rodriguez	.75	.40	.25
15	Alan Trammell	10.00	5.00	3.00
16	Steve Dillard	.75	.40	.25
17	Phil Mankowski	.75	.40	.25
18	Steve Kemp	.75	.40	.25
19	Ron LeFlore	.90	.45	.25
20	Tim Corcoran	.75	.40	.25
21	Mickey Stanley	.75	.40	.25
22	Rusty Staub	.90	.45	.25
---	Checklist	.10	.05	.03

1978 Burger King Yankees

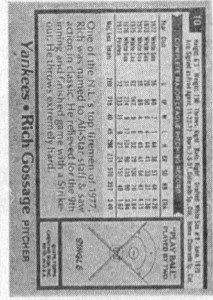

Produced by Topps for Burger King outlets in the New York area for the second year in a row, the 1978 Yankees set contains 22 cards plus an unnumbered checklist. The cards are numbered 1 through 22 and are the standard size of 2-1/2" x 3-1/2". The cards feature the same pictures found in the regular 1978 Topps set except for numbers 10, 11 and 16. Only those variations containing different poses or major picture-cropping differences are noted. Numerous minor picture-cropping variations, that are very insignificant in nature, exist between the regular Topps sets and the Burger King issues of 1977-1980.

		NM	EX	VG
Complete Set (23):		15.00	7.50	4.50
Common Player:		.50	.25	.15
1	Billy Martin	1.50	.70	.45
2	Thurman Munson	5.00	2.50	1.50
3	Cliff Johnson	.50	.25	.15
4	Ron Guidry	1.00	.50	.30
5	Ed Figueroa	.50	.25	.15
6	Dick Tidrow	.50	.25	.15
7	Catfish Hunter	2.00	1.00	.60
8	Don Gullett	.50	.25	.15

		NM	EX	VG
9	Sparky Lyle	1.00	.50	.30
10	Rich Gossage	1.50	.70	.45
11	Rawly Eastwick	.50	.25	.15
12	Chris Chambliss	.50	.25	.15
13	Willie Randolph	1.00	.50	.30
14	Graig Nettles	1.00	.50	.30
15	Bucky Dent	1.00	.50	.30
16	Jim Spencer	.50	.25	.15
17	Fred Stanley	.50	.25	.15
18	Lou Piniella	1.25	.60	.40
19	Roy White	1.00	.50	.30
20	Mickey Rivers	.50	.25	.15
21	Reggie Jackson	6.00	3.00	1.75
22	Paul Blair	.50	.25	.15
---	Checklist	.10	.05	.03

1979 Burger King Phillies

Twenty-two Phillies players are featured in the 1979 Burger King issue given out in the Philadelphia area. The Topps-produced set, measuring 2-1/2" x 3-1/2", also includes an unnumbered checklist. Cards are identical to the regular 1979 Topps set except #1, 11, 12, 13, 14, 17 and 22, which have different poses. Very minor picture-cropping variations between the regular Topps issues and the Burger King sets can be found throughout the four years the cards were produced, but only those variations featuring major changes are noted in the checklists.

		NM	EX	VG
Complete Set (23):		7.50	3.75	2.25
Common Player:		.25	.13	.08
1	Danny Ozark	.25	.13	.08
2	Bob Boone	.45	.25	.14
3	Tim McCarver	.50	.25	.15
4	Steve Carlton	1.50	.70	.45
5	Larry Christenson	.25	.13	.08
6	Dick Ruthven	.25	.13	.08
7	Ron Reed	.25	.13	.08
8	Randy Lerch	.25	.13	.08
9	Warren Brusstar	.25	.13	.08
10	Tug McGraw	.40	.20	.12
11	Nino Espinosa	.25	.13	.08
12	Doug Bird	.25	.13	.08
13	Pete Rose	3.00	1.50	.90
14	Manny Trillo	.25	.13	.08
15	Larry Bowa	.40	.20	.12
16	Mike Schmidt	3.00	1.50	.90
17	Pete Mackanin	.25	.13	.08
18	Jose Cardenal	.25	.13	.08
19	Greg Luzinski	.25	.13	.08
20	Garry Maddox	.25	.13	.08
21	Bake McBride	.25	.13	.08
22	Greg Gross	.25	.13	.08
---	Checklist	.08	.04	.02

1979 Burger King Yankees

The New York Yankees were featured in a Topps-produced Burger King set for the third consecutive year in 1979. Once again, 22 numbered player cards and an unnumbered checklist made up the set. Cards measure 2-1/2" x 3-1/2", and are identical to the 1979 Topps regular set except for #4, 8, 9 and 22 which included new poses. Numerous minor picture cropping variations between the regular Topps issue and the Burger King sets of 1977-1980 exist.

		NM	EX	VG
Complete Set (23):		7.50	3.75	2.25
Common Player:		.25	.13	.08
1	Yankees Team (Bob Lemon)	.75	.40	.25
2	Thurman Munson	2.50	1.25	.70
3	Cliff Johnson	.25	.13	.08

		NM	EX	VG
4	Ron Guidry	.60	.30	.20
5	Jay Johnstone	.40	.20	.12
6	Catfish Hunter	1.25	.60	.40
7	Jim Beattie	.25	.13	.08
8	Luis Tiant	.40	.20	.12
9	Tommy John	.75	.40	.25
10	Rich Gossage	.60	.30	.20
11	Ed Figueroa	.25	.13	.08
12	Chris Chambliss	.25	.13	.08
13	Willie Randolph	.40	.20	.12
14	Bucky Dent	.40	.20	.12
15	Graig Nettles	.40	.20	.12
16	Fred Stanley	.25	.13	.08
17	Jim Spencer	.25	.13	.08
18	Lou Piniella	.60	.30	.20
19	Roy White	.40	.20	.12
20	Mickey Rivers	.25	.13	.08
21	Reggie Jackson	4.00	2.00	1.25
22	Juan Beniquez	.25	.13	.08
---	Checklist	.06	.03	.02

1980 Burger King Phillies

Philadelphia-area Burger King outlets issued a 23-card set featuring the Phillies for the second in a row in 1980. The Topps-produced set, measuring 2-1/2" x 3-1/2", contains 22 player cards and an unnumbered checklist. Fronts are identical in design to the regular 1980 Topps sets with the following exceptions: #1, 3, 8, 14 and 22 feature new poses. Very minor picture-cropping variations between the regular Topps issues and the Burger King sets exist in all years. Those minor differences are not noted in the checklists. The 1980 Burger King sets were the first to include the Burger King logo on the card backs.

		NM	EX	VG
Complete Set (23):		6.00	3.00	1.75
Common Player:		.10	.05	.03
1	Dallas Green	.15	.08	.05
2	Bob Boone	.50	.25	.15
3	Keith Moreland	.25	.13	.08
4	Pete Rose	2.50	1.25	.70
5	Manny Trillo	.10	.05	.03
6	Mike Schmidt	2.50	1.25	.70
7	Larry Bowa	.20	.10	.06
8	John Vukovich	.10	.05	.03
9	Bake McBride	.10	.05	.03
10	Garry Maddox	.10	.05	.03
11	Greg Luzinski	.25	.13	.08
12	Greg Gross	.10	.05	.03
13	Del Unser	.10	.05	.03
14	Lonnie Smith	.40	.20	.12
15	Steve Carlton	1.00	.50	.30
16	Larry Christenson	.10	.05	.03
17	Nino Espinosa	.10	.05	.03
18	Randy Lerch	.10	.05	.03
19	Dick Ruthven	.10	.05	.03
20	Tug McGraw	.15	.08	.05
21	Ron Reed	.10	.05	.03
22	Kevin Saucier	.10	.05	.03
---	Checklist	.05	.03	.02

1980 Burger King Pitch, Hit & Run

In 1980, Burger King issued, in conjunction with its "Pitch, Hit & Run" promotion, a Topps-produced set featuring pitchers (card #s 1-11), hitters (#s 12-22), and base stealers (#s 23-33). Fronts, which carry the Burger King logo, are identical in design to the regular 1980 Topps set except for numbers 1, 4, 5, 7, 9, 10, 16, 17, 18, 22, 23, 27, 28, 29 and 30, which feature dif-

ferent poses. Cards measure 2-1/2" x 3-1/2" in size. An unnumbered checklist was included with the set.

		NM	EX	VG
Complete Set (34):		10.00	5.00	3.00
Common Player:		.10	.05	.03
1	Vida Blue	.10	.05	.03
2	Steve Carlton	1.00	.50	.30
3	Rollie Fingers	.65	.35	.20
4	Ron Guidry	.25	.13	.08
5	Jerry Koosman	.10	.05	.03
6	Phil Niekro	.65	.35	.20
7	Jim Palmer	1.00	.50	.30
8	J.R. Richard	.10	.05	.03
9	Nolan Ryan	4.00	2.00	1.25
10	Tom Seaver	1.00	.50	.30
11	Bruce Sutter	1.00	.50	.30
12	Don Baylor	.10	.05	.03
13	George Brett	2.00	1.00	.60
14	Rod Carew	1.00	.50	.30
15	George Foster	.10	.05	.03
16	Keith Hernandez	.10	.05	.03
17	Reggie Jackson	1.50	.70	.45
18	Fred Lynn	.10	.05	.03
19	Dave Parker	.10	.05	.03
20	Jim Rice	.30	.15	.09
21	Pete Rose	3.00	1.50	.90
22	Dave Winfield	1.00	.50	.30
23	Bobby Bonds	.10	.05	.03
24	Enos Cabell	.10	.05	.03
25	Cesar Cedeno	.10	.05	.03
26	Julio Cruz	.10	.05	.03
27	Ron LeFlore	.10	.05	.03
28	Dave Lopes	.10	.05	.03
29	Omar Moreno	.10	.05	.03
30	Joe Morgan	1.00	.50	.30
31	Bill North	.10	.05	.03
32	Frank Taveras	.10	.05	.03
33	Willie Wilson	.10	.05	.03
---	Checklist	.05	.03	.02

1916 Burgess-Nash Clothiers

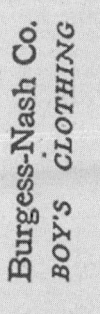

GAVVY CRAVATH R. F.—Philadelphia Nat'ls 34

This 200-card set can be found with ads on the back for several local and regional businesses. Among them is Burgess-Nash clothiers, from Omaha, Neb. Type card and superstar collectors can expect to pay a significant premium for cards with the Burgess-Nash advertising, compared to the generic M101-4 Blank Backs values. Cards measure about 1-5/8" x 3" and are printed in black-and-white.

PREMIUM: 2-3X
(See 1916 M101-4 Blank Backs for checklist.)

1935 George Burke Detroit Tigers Photo Stamps

This team set of black-and-white, 1-1/16" x 1-1/4" photo stamps was produced by baseball photographer George Burke. The set was printed on two sheets of 12 players each. Each stamp has the player's name, position abbreviation and city in black or white typography. The blank-backed ungummed stamps of the 1935 World's Champs are checklisted here in alphabetical order.

	NM	EX	VG
Complete Set (24):	325.00	160.00	95.00
Common Player:	10.00	5.00	3.00
(1) Elden Auker	10.00	5.00	3.00
(2) Del Baker	10.00	5.00	3.00
(3) Tom Bridges	10.00	5.00	3.00
(4) Herman Clifton	10.00	5.00	3.00
(5) Mickey Cochrane	30.00	15.00	9.00
(6) Alvin Crowder	10.00	5.00	3.00
(7) Ervin Fox	10.00	5.00	3.00
(8) Charles Gehringer	30.00	15.00	9.00
(9) Leon Goslin	30.00	15.00	9.00
(10) Henry Greenberg	45.00	22.50	13.50
(11) Raymond Hayworth	10.00	5.00	3.00
(12) Elon Hogsett	10.00	5.00	3.00
(13) Roxie Lawson	10.00	5.00	3.00
(14) Marvin Owen	10.00	5.00	3.00
(15) Ralph Perkins	10.00	5.00	3.00
(16) Frank Reiber	10.00	5.00	3.00
(17) Wm. Rogell	10.00	5.00	3.00
(18) Lynwood Rowe	12.50	6.25	3.75
(19) Henry Schuble	10.00	5.00	3.00
(20) Hugh Shelley	10.00	5.00	3.00
(21) Victor Sorrell	10.00	5.00	3.00
(22) Joseph Sullivan	10.00	5.00	3.00
(23) Gerald Walker	10.00	5.00	3.00
(24) Joyner White	10.00	5.00	3.00

1935-37 George Burke Postage Stamp Photos

These small (3/4" x 1") black-and-white stamps were produced by Chicago baseball portraitist George Burke for sale to individual players for use in answering fan mail. The stamps were not a big seller, though the checklist presented alphabetically here is surely incomplete. The unnumbered stamps, which are blank-backed, were not self-adhesive and were printed in sheets of at least six of the same player. Some of the photo-stamps have facsimile autographs, others do not.

	NM	EX	VG
Common Player:	10.00	5.00	3.00
Luke Appling	20.00	10.00	6.00
Jimmy Austin	10.00	5.00	3.00
Dick Bartell	10.00	5.00	3.00
Huck Betts	10.00	5.00	3.00
George Blaeholder	10.00	5.00	3.00
Jim Bottomley	20.00	10.00	6.00
Earl Browne	10.00	5.00	3.00
Irving Burns	10.00	5.00	3.00
Sam Byrd	10.00	5.00	3.00
Gilly Campbell	10.00	5.00	3.00
James (Tex) Carleton	10.00	5.00	3.00
Hugh Casey	10.00	5.00	3.00
James "Rip" Collins	10.00	5.00	3.00
Earle Combs	20.00	10.00	6.00
Adam Comorosky	10.00	5.00	3.00
Jocko Conlan	20.00	10.00	6.00
Kiki Cuyler	20.00	10.00	6.00
Paul Derringer	10.00	5.00	3.00
Jim DeShong	10.00	5.00	3.00
Bill Dickey	20.00	10.00	6.00
Bill Dietrich	10.00	5.00	3.00
Carl Doyle	10.00	5.00	3.00
Chuck Dressen	10.00	5.00	3.00
Jimmy Dykes	10.00	5.00	3.00
Hank Erickson	10.00	5.00	3.00
Wes Ferrell	10.00	5.00	3.00
Arthur Fletcher	10.00	5.00	3.00
Jimmie Foxx	40.00	20.00	12.00
(Facsimile autograph.)			
Jimmie Foxx (No autograph.)	40.00	20.00	12.00
Larry French	10.00	5.00	3.00
Benny Frey	10.00	5.00	3.00
Tony Freitas	10.00	5.00	3.00
Frankie Frisch	20.00	10.00	6.00
Ed Gharrity	10.00	5.00	3.00
Lefty Gomez	20.00	10.00	6.00
Charlie Grimm	10.00	5.00	3.00
Stan Hack	10.00	5.00	3.00
Chick Hafey	20.00	10.00	6.00
Mel Harder	10.00	5.00	3.00
Bucky Harris	20.00	10.00	6.00
Gabby Hartnett	20.00	10.00	6.00
Roy Henshaw	10.00	5.00	3.00
Babe Herman	15.00	7.50	4.50
Billy Herman	20.00	10.00	6.00
Leroy Herrmann	10.00	5.00	3.00
Myril Hoag	10.00	5.00	3.00
Al Hollingsworth	10.00	5.00	3.00
Carl Hubbell	30.00	15.00	9.00
Bob Johnson	10.00	5.00	3.00
Douglas Johnson	10.00	5.00	3.00
Si Johnson	10.00	5.00	3.00
George L. Kelly	20.00	10.00	6.00
Chuck Klein	20.00	10.00	6.00
Mark Koenig	10.00	5.00	3.00

	NM	EX	VG
Tony Lazzeri	30.00	15.00	9.00
Bill Lee	10.00	5.00	3.00
Dutch Leonard	10.00	5.00	3.00
Ernie Lombardi	20.00	10.00	6.00
Al Lopez	20.00	10.00	6.00
Adolfo Luque	15.00	7.50	4.50
Earle Mack	10.00	5.00	3.00
Roy Mahaffey	10.00	5.00	3.00
Gus Mancuso	10.00	5.00	3.00
Rabbit Maranville	20.00	10.00	6.00
Johnny Marcum	10.00	5.00	3.00
Joe McCarthy	20.00	10.00	6.00
Eric McNair	10.00	5.00	3.00
Van Lingle Mungo	10.00	5.00	3.00
Skeeter Newsome	10.00	5.00	3.00
Mel Ott	40.00	20.00	12.00
Claude Passeau	10.00	5.00	3.00
Monte Pearson	10.00	5.00	3.00
Raymond Pepper	10.00	5.00	3.00
Charlie Root	10.00	6.00	3.00
Red Ruffing	20.00	10.00	6.00
George Selkirk	10.00	5.00	3.00
Joe Sewell	20.00	10.00	6.00
Luke Sewell	10.00	5.00	3.00
Al Simmons	20.00	10.00	6.00
Casey Stengel	20.00	10.00	6.00
Riggs Stephenson	10.00	5.00	3.00
Alan Strange	10.00	5.00	3.00
Gus Suhr	10.00	5.00	3.00
Billy Sullivan	10.00	5.00	3.00
Dan Taylor	10.00	5.00	3.00
Fay Thomas	10.00	5.00	3.00
Hal Trosky	10.00	5.00	3.00
Honus Wagner	40.00	20.00	12.00
Rube Walberg	10.00	5.00	3.00
Paul Waner	20.00	10.00	6.00
Lon Warneke	10.00	5.00	3.00
Harold Warstler	10.00	5.00	3.00
Billy Webb	10.00	5.00	3.00
Whitlow Wyatt	10.00	5.00	3.00

1933 Butter Cream (R306)

 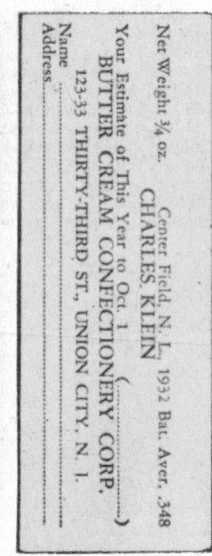

The 1933 Butter Cream set consists of unnumbered, black-and-white cards which measure 1-1/4" x 3-1/2". Backs feature a contest in which the collector was to estimate players' statistics by a specific date. Two different backs are known: 1) Estimate through Sept. 1 and no company address, and 2) Estimate through Oct. 1 with the Butter Cream address. The ACC designation for the set is R306.

	NM	EX	VG
Complete Set (30):	30,000	15,000	7,500
Common Player:	750.00	375.00	165.00
(1) Earl Averill	1,000	500.00	225.00
(2) Ed. Brandt	750.00	375.00	165.00
(3) Guy T. Bush	750.00	375.00	165.00
(4) Gordon Cochrane	1,000	500.00	225.00
(5) Joe Cronin	1,000	500.00	225.00
(6) George Earnshaw	750.00	375.00	165.00
(7) Wesley Ferrell	750.00	375.00	165.00
(8) "Jimmy" E. Foxx	2,000	1,000	440.00
(9) Frank C. Frisch	1,000	500.00	225.00
(10) Charles M. Gelbert	750.00	375.00	165.00
(11) "Lefty" Robert M. Grove	1,200	600.00	265.00
(12) Leo Charles Hartnett	1,000	500.00	225.00
(13) "Babe" Herman	750.00	375.00	165.00
(14) Charles Klein	1,000	500.00	220.00
(15) Ray Kremer	750.00	375.00	165.00
(16) Fred C. Linstrom (Lindstrom)	1,000	500.00	225.00
(17) Ted A. Lyons	1,000	500.00	225.00
(18) "Pepper" John L. Martin	900.00	450.00	200.00
(19) Robert O'Farrell	750.00	375.00	165.00
(20) Ed. A. Rommel	750.00	375.00	165.00
(21) Charles Root	750.00	375.00	165.00
(22) Harold "Muddy" Ruel (Herold)	750.00	375.00	165.00
(23) Babe Ruth	8,000	4,000	1,750
(24) "Al" Simmons	1,000	500.00	225.00
(25) "Bill" Terry	1,000	500.00	225.00
(26) George E. Uhle	750.00	375.00	165.00
(27) Lloyd J. Waner	1,000	500.00	225.00
(28) Paul G. Waner	1,000	500.00	225.00
(29) Hack Wilson	1,000	500.00	225.00
(30) Glen. Wright	750.00	375.00	165.00

1934 Butterfinger (R310)

Cards in this set were available as a premium with Butterfinger and other candy products. The unnumbered cards measure approximately 7-3/4" x 9-1/2" and can be found printed either on paper or heavy cardboard. The cardboard variety carry red advertising for Butterfinger and are valued about 4X the paper version. The black-and-white cards feature a player photo with facsimile autograph. Similar cards in a 6-1/2" x 8-1/2" format are a companion Canadian issue.

	NM	EX	VG
Complete Set (65):	6,500	3,250	2,000
Common Player:	60.00	30.00	18.00
Cardboard Ad Variety: 4X			
(1) Earl Averill	110.00	55.00	35.00
(2) Richard Bartell	60.00	30.00	18.00
(3) Larry Benton	60.00	30.00	18.00
(4) Walter Berger	60.00	30.00	18.00
(5) Jim Bottomley (Bottomley)	110.00	55.00	35.00
(6) Ralph Boyle	60.00	30.00	18.00
(7) Tex Carleton	60.00	30.00	18.00
(8) Owen T. Carroll	60.00	30.00	18.00
(9) Ben Chapman	60.00	30.00	18.00
(10) Gordon (Mickey) Cochrane	110.00	55.00	35.00
(11) James Collins	60.00	30.00	18.00
(12) Joe Cronin	110.00	55.00	35.00
(13) Alvin Crowder	60.00	30.00	18.00
(14) "Dizzy" Dean	240.00	120.00	75.00
(15) Paul Derringer	60.00	30.00	18.00
(16) William Dickey	125.00	62.00	37.00
(17) Leo Durocher	110.00	55.00	35.00
(18) George Earnshaw	60.00	30.00	18.00
(19) Richard Ferrell	110.00	55.00	35.00
(20) Lew Fonseca	60.00	30.00	18.00
(21a) Jimmy Fox (Name incorrect.)	225.00	110.00	70.00
(21b) Jimmy Foxx (Name correct.)	185.00	95.00	55.00
(22) Benny Frey	60.00	30.00	18.00
(23) Frankie Frisch	110.00	55.00	35.00
(24) Lou Gehrig	750.00	375.00	225.00
(25) Charles Gehringer	110.00	55.00	35.00
(26) Vernon Gomez	110.00	55.00	35.00
(27) Ray Grabowski	60.00	30.00	18.00
(28) Robert (Lefty) Grove	150.00	75.00	45.00
(29) George (Mule) Haas	60.00	30.00	18.00
(30) "Chick" Hafey	110.00	55.00	35.00
(31) Stanley Harris	110.00	55.00	35.00
(32) J. Francis Hogan	60.00	30.00	18.00
(33) Ed Holley	60.00	30.00	18.00
(34) Rogers Hornsby	150.00	75.00	45.00
(35) Waite Hoyt	110.00	55.00	35.00
(36) Walter Johnson	250.00	125.00	75.00
(37) Jim Jordan	60.00	30.00	18.00
(38) Joe Kuhel	60.00	30.00	18.00
(39) Hal Lee	60.00	30.00	18.00
(40) Gus Mancuso	60.00	30.00	18.00
(41) Henry Manush	110.00	55.00	35.00
(42) Fred Marberry	60.00	30.00	18.00
(43) Pepper Martin	85.00	45.00	25.00
(44) Oscar Melillo	60.00	30.00	18.00
(45) Johnny Moore	60.00	30.00	18.00
(46) Joe Morrissey	60.00	30.00	18.00
(47) Joe Mowrey	60.00	30.00	18.00
(48) Bob O'Farrell	60.00	30.00	18.00
(49) Melvin Ott	125.00	65.00	35.00
(50) Monte Pearson	60.00	30.00	18.00
(51) Carl Reynolds	60.00	30.00	18.00
(52) Charles Ruffing	110.00	55.00	35.00
(53) Babe Ruth	750.00	375.00	225.00
(54) John "Blondy" Ryan	60.00	30.00	18.00
(55) Al Simmons	110.00	55.00	35.00
(56) Al Spohrer	60.00	30.00	18.00
(57) Gus Suhr	60.00	30.00	18.00
(58) Steve Swetonic	60.00	30.00	18.00
(59) Dazzy Vance	110.00	55.00	35.00
(60) Joe Vosmik	60.00	30.00	18.00
(61) Lloyd Waner	110.00	55.00	35.00
(62) Paul Waner	110.00	55.00	35.00
(63) Sam West	60.00	30.00	18.00
(64) Earl Whitehill	60.00	30.00	18.00
(65) Jimmy Wilson	60.00	30.00	18.00

1934 Butterfinger - Canadian (V94)

Similar to the U.S. issue, though smaller in size at 6-1/2" x 8-1/2", these black-and-white paper cards include a number of players not found in the U.S. issue. Like the "regular" Butterfinger cards, each of the Canadian pieces includes a facsimile autograph on the front; backs are blank.

	NM	EX	VG
Complete Set (58):	4,500	2,250	1,350
Common Player:	50.00	25.00	15.00
(1) Earl Averill	100.00	50.00	30.00
(2) Larry Benton	50.00	25.00	15.00
(3) Jim Bottomly (Bottomley)	100.00	50.00	30.00
(4) Tom Bridges	50.00	25.00	15.00
(5) Bob Brown	50.00	25.00	15.00
(6) Owen T. Carroll	50.00	25.00	15.00
(7) Gordon (Mickey) Cochrane	100.00	50.00	30.00
(8) Roger Cramer	50.00	25.00	15.00
(9) Joe Cronin	100.00	50.00	30.00
(10) Alvin Crowder	50.00	25.00	15.00
(11) "Dizzy" Dean	185.00	95.00	55.00
(12) Edward Delker	50.00	25.00	15.00
(13) William Dickey	125.00	62.00	37.00
(14) Richard Ferrell	100.00	50.00	30.00
(15) Lew Fonseca	50.00	25.00	15.00
(16a) Jimmy Fox (Name incorrect.)	145.00	75.00	45.00
(16b) Jimmy Foxx (Name correct.)	145.00	75.00	45.00
(17) Chick Fullis	50.00	25.00	15.00
(18) Lou Gehrig	600.00	300.00	180.00
(19) Charles Gehringer	100.00	50.00	30.00
(20) Vernon Gomez	100.00	50.00	30.00
(21) Robert (Lefty) Grove	125.00	62.00	37.00
(22) George (Mule) Haas	50.00	25.00	15.00
(23) "Chick" Hafey	100.00	50.00	30.00
(24) Stanley Harris	100.00	50.00	30.00
(25) Frank Higgins	50.00	25.00	15.00
(26) J. Francis Hogan	50.00	25.00	15.00
(27) Ed Holley	50.00	25.00	15.00
(28) Waite Hoyt	100.00	50.00	30.00
(29) Jim Jordan	50.00	25.00	15.00
(30) Hal Lee	50.00	25.00	15.00
(31) Gus Mancuso	50.00	25.00	15.00
(32) Oscar Melillo	50.00	25.00	15.00
(33) Austin Moore	50.00	25.00	15.00
(34) Randy Moore	50.00	25.00	15.00
(35) Joe Morrissey	50.00	25.00	15.00
(36) Joe Mowrey	50.00	25.00	15.00
(37) Bobo Newsom	50.00	25.00	15.00
(38) Ernie Orsatti	50.00	25.00	15.00
(39) Carl Reynolds	50.00	25.00	15.00
(40) Walter Roettger	50.00	25.00	15.00
(41) Babe Ruth	650.00	325.00	200.00
(42) John "Blondy" Ryan	50.00	25.00	15.00
(43) John Salveson	50.00	25.00	15.00
(44) Al Simmons	100.00	50.00	30.00
(45) Al Smith	50.00	25.00	15.00
(46) Harold Smith	50.00	25.00	15.00
(47) Allyn Stout	50.00	25.00	15.00
(48) Fresco Thompson	50.00	25.00	15.00
(49) Art Veltman	50.00	25.00	15.00
(50) Johnny Vergez	50.00	25.00	15.00
(51) Gerald Walker	50.00	25.00	15.00
(52) Paul Waner	100.00	50.00	30.00
(53) Burgess Whitehead	50.00	25.00	15.00
(54) Earl Whitehill	50.00	25.00	15.00
(55) Robert Weiland	50.00	25.00	15.00
(56) Jimmy Wilson	50.00	25.00	15.00
(57) Bob Worthington	50.00	25.00	15.00
(58) Tom Zachary	50.00	25.00	15.00

1911-14 Butter Krust Bread (D304)

EAT
Butter Krust
BREAD
FRESH EVERY MORNING

FLEISCHMANN BAKERY
GENERAL BAKING COMPANY

THERE ARE 25 SUBJECTS
IN THIS SET.
ONE WRAPPED WITH EACH LOAF OF
BUTTER KRUST BREAD
G.B.C.   102

(See 1911-14 General Baking Co. for checklist and values.)

1914 B18 Blankets

These 5-1/4"-square flannels were issued in 1914 wrapped around several popular brands of tobacco. The flannels, whose American Card Catalog designation is B18, picked up the nickname blankets because many of them were sewn together to form bed covers or throws. Different color combinations on the flannels exist for all 10 teams included in the set. The complete set price includes only the lowest-priced variation for each of the 90 players.

	NM	EX	VG
Complete Set (90):	7,000	3,500	2,000
Complete Set W/Variations (202):	55,000	27,500	16,500
Common Player:	40.00	20.00	12.00
(1a) Babe Adams (Purple pennants.)	80.00	40.00	25.00
(1b) Babe Adams (Red pennants.)	130.00	65.00	40.00
(2a) Sam Agnew (Purple basepaths.)	80.00	40.00	25.00
(2b) Sam Agnew (Red basepaths.)	125.00	65.00	35.00
(3a) Eddie Ainsmith (Green pennants.)	40.00	20.00	12.00
(3b) Eddie Ainsmith (Brown pennants.)	40.00	20.00	12.00
(4a) Jimmy Austin (Purple basepaths.)	80.00	40.00	25.00
(4b) Jimmy Austin (Red basepaths.)	90.00	45.00	27.00
(5a) Del Baker (White infield.)	40.00	20.00	12.00
(5b) Del Baker (Brown infield.)	150.00	75.00	45.00
(5c) Del Baker (Red infield.)	1,650	825.00	495.00
(6a) Johnny Bassler (Purple pennants.)	90.00	45.00	27.00
(6b) Johnny Bassler (Yellow pennants.)	125.00	65.00	35.00
(7a) Paddy Bauman (Baumann) (White infield.)	40.00	20.00	12.00
(7b) Paddy Bauman (Baumann) (Brown infield.)	150.00	75.00	45.00
(7c) Paddy Bauman (Baumann) (Red infield.)	1,650	825.00	495.00
(8a) Luke Boone (Blue infield.)	40.00	20.00	12.00
(8b) Luke Boone (Green infield.)	40.00	20.00	12.00
(9a) George Burns (Brown basepaths.)	40.00	20.00	12.00
(9b) George Burns (Green basepaths.)	40.00	20.00	12.00
(10a) Tioga George Burns (White infield.)	40.00	20.00	12.00
(10b) Tioga George Burns (Brown infield.)	150.00	75.00	45.00
(10c) Tioga George Burns (Red infield.)	1,650	825.00	495.00
(11a) Max Carey (Purple pennants.)	150.00	75.00	45.00
(11b) Max Carey (Red pennants.)	175.00	85.00	55.00
(12a) Marty Cavanaugh (Kavanagh) (White infield.)	40.00	20.00	12.00
(12b) Marty Cavanaugh (Kavanagh) (Brown infield.)	150.00	75.00	45.00
(12c) Marty Cavanaugh (Kavanagh) (Red infield.)	1,650	825.00	495.00
(12d) Marty Kavanaugh (Kavanagh)	200.00	100.00	60.00
(13a) Frank Chance (Green infield.)	100.00	50.00	30.00
(13b) Frank Chance (Brown pennants, blue infield.)	100.00	50.00	30.00
(13c) Frank Chance (Yellow pennants, blue infield.)	450.00	225.00	135.00
(14a) Ray Chapman (Purple pennants.)	125.00	65.00	35.00
(14b) Ray Chapman (Yellow pennants.)	200.00	100.00	60.00
(15a) Ty Cobb (White infield.)	500.00	250.00	150.00
(15b) Ty Cobb (Brown infield.)	700.00	350.00	210.00
(15c) Ty Cobb (Red infield.)	15,000	7,500	4,500
(16a) King Cole (Blue infield.)	40.00	20.00	12.00
(16b) King Cole (Green infield.)	40.00	20.00	12.00
(17a) Joe Connolly (White infield.)	40.00	20.00	12.00
(17b) Joe Connolly (Brown infield.)	150.00	75.00	45.00
(17c) Joe Connolly (Red infield.)	1,650	825.00	495.00
(18a) Harry Coveleski (White infield.)	40.00	20.00	12.00
(18b) Harry Coveleski (Brown infield.)	150.00	75.00	45.00
(18c) Harry Coveleski (Red infield.)	1,650	825.00	495.00
(19a) George Cutshaw (Blue infield.)	40.00	20.00	12.00
(19b) George Cutshaw (Green infield.)	40.00	20.00	12.00
(20a) Jake Daubert (Blue infield.)	45.00	22.50	13.50
(20b) Jake Daubert (Green infield.)	45.00	22.50	13.50
(21a) Ray Demmitt (White infield.)	40.00	20.00	12.00
(21b) Ray Demmitt (Brown infield.)	150.00	75.00	45.00
(21c) Ray Demmitt (Red infield.)	1,650	825.00	495.00
(22a) Bill Doak (Purple pennants.)	80.00	40.00	24.00
(22b) Bill Doak (Yellow pennants.)	125.00	65.00	35.00
(23a) Cozy Dolan (Purple pennants.)	80.00	40.00	25.00
(23b) Cozy Dolan (Yellow pennants.)	150.00	75.00	45.00
(24a) Larry Doyle (Brown basepaths.)	45.00	22.50	13.50
(24b) Larry Doyle (Green basepaths.)	45.00	22.50	13.50
(25a) Art Fletcher (Brown basepaths.)	40.00	20.00	12.00
(25b) Art Fletcher (Green basepaths.)	40.00	20.00	12.00
(26a) Eddie Foster (Brown pennants.)	40.00	20.00	12.00
(26b) Eddie Foster (Green pennants.)	40.00	20.00	12.00
(27a) Del Gainor (White infield.)	50.00	25.00	15.00
(27b) Del Gainor (Brown infield.)	150.00	75.00	45.00
(28a) Chick Gandil (Brown pennants.)	100.00	50.00	30.00
(28b) Chick Gandil (Green pennants.)	125.00	65.00	35.00
(29a) George Gibson (Purple pennants.)	80.00	40.00	25.00
(29b) George Gibson (Red pennants.)	90.00	45.00	27.00
(30a) Hank Gowdy (White infield.)	40.00	20.00	12.00
(30b) Hank Gowdy (Brown infield.)	150.00	75.00	45.00
(30c) Hank Gowdy (Red infield.)	1,650	825.00	495.00
(31a) Jack Graney (Purple pennants.)	90.00	45.00	27.00
(31b) Jack Graney (Yellow pennants.)	125.00	65.00	35.00
(32a) Eddie Grant (Brown basepaths.)	40.00	20.00	12.00
(32b) Eddie Grant (Green basepaths.)	40.00	20.00	12.00
(33a) Tommy Griffith (White infield, green pennants.)	40.00	20.00	12.00
(33b) Tommy Griffith (White infield, red pennants.)	1,500	750.00	450.00
(33c) Tommy Griffith (Brown infield.)	125.00	65.00	35.00
(33d) Tommy Griffith (Red infield.)	1,650	825.00	495.00
(34a) Earl Hamilton (Purple basepaths.)	80.00	40.00	25.00
(34b) Earl Hamilton (Red basepaths.)	90.00	45.00	27.00
(35a) Roy Hartzell (Blue infield.)	40.00	20.00	12.00
(35b) Roy Hartzell (Green infield.)	40.00	20.00	12.00
(36a) Miller Huggins (Purple pennants.)	160.00	80.00	45.00
(36b) Miller Huggins (Yellow pennants.)	245.00	120.00	75.00
(37a) John Hummel (Blue infield.)	40.00	20.00	12.00
(37b) John Hummel (Green infield.)	40.00	20.00	12.00
(38a) Ham Hyatt (Purple pennants.)	80.00	40.00	24.00
(38b) Ham Hyatt (Red pennants.)	90.00	45.00	27.00
(39a) Joe Jackson (Purple pennants.)	1,350	675.00	400.00
(39b) Joe Jackson (Yellow pennants.)	1,100	550.00	330.00
(40a) Bill James (White infield.)	40.00	20.00	12.00
(40b) Bill James (Brown infield.)	160.00	80.00	50.00
(40c) Bill James (Red infield.)	1,650	825.00	495.00
(41a) Walter Johnson (Brown infield.)	300.00	150.00	90.00
(41b) Walter Johnson (Green infield.)	275.00	135.00	80.00
(42a) Ray Keating (Blue infield.)	40.00	20.00	12.00
(42b) Ray Keating (Green infield.)	40.00	20.00	12.00
(43a) Joe Kelley (Kelly) (Purple pennants.)	90.00	45.00	27.00
(43b) Joe Kelley (Kelly) (Red pennants.)	90.00	45.00	27.00
(44a) Ed Konetchy (Purple pennants.)	60.00	30.00	18.00
(44b) Ed Konetchy (Red pennants.)	90.00	45.00	27.00
(45a) Nemo Leibold (Purple pennants.)	75.00	37.50	22.00
(45b) Nemo Leibold (Yellow pennants.)	150.00	75.00	45.00
(46a) Fritz Maisel (Blue infield.)	40.00	20.00	12.00
(46b) Fritz Maisel (Green infield.)	40.00	20.00	12.00
(47a) Les Mann (White infield.)	40.00	20.00	12.00
(47b) Les Mann (Brown infield.)	150.00	75.00	45.00
(47c) Les Mann (Red infield.)	1,650	825.00	495.00
(48a) Rabbit Maranville (White infield.)	130.00	65.00	39.00
(48b) Rabbit Maranville (Brown infield.)	250.00	125.00	75.00
(48c) Rabbit Maranville (Red infield.)	3,000	1,500	900.00
(49a) Bill McAllister (McAllester) (Purple basepaths.)	80.00	40.00	25.00
(49b) Bill McAllister (McAllester) (Red basepaths.)	100.00	50.00	30.00
(50a) George McBride (Brown pennants.)	40.00	20.00	12.00
(50b) George McBride (Green pennants.)	40.00	20.00	12.00
(51a) Chief Meyers (Brown basepaths.)	40.00	20.00	12.00
(51b) Chief Meyers (Green basepaths.)	40.00	20.00	12.00
(52a) Clyde Milan (Brown infield.)	40.00	20.00	12.00
(52b) Clyde Milan (Green infield.)	40.00	20.00	12.00
(53a) J. Miller (Purple pennants.)	80.00	40.00	25.00
(53b) J. Miller (Yellow pennants.)	125.00	65.00	35.00
(54a) Otto Miller (Blue infield.)	40.00	20.00	12.00
(54b) Otto Miller (Green infield.)	40.00	20.00	12.00
(55a) Willie Mitchell (Purple pennants.)	80.00	40.00	25.00
(55b) Willie Mitchell (Yellow pennants.)	150.00	75.00	45.00
(56a) Danny Moeller (Brown pennants.)	40.00	20.00	12.00
(56b) Danny Moeller (Green pennants.)	40.00	20.00	12.00
(57a) Ray Morgan (Brown pennants.)	40.00	20.00	12.00
(57b) Ray Morgan (Green pennants.)	40.00	20.00	12.00
(58a) George Moriarty (White infield.)	40.00	20.00	12.00
(58b) George Moriarty (Brown infield.)	150.00	75.00	45.00

		NM	EX	VG
(58c)	George Moriarty (Red infield.)	1,650	825.00	495.00
(59a)	Mike Mowrey (Purple pennants.)	80.00	40.00	25.00
(59b)	Mike Mowrey (Red pennants.)	90.00	45.00	27.00
(60a)	Red Murray (Brown basepaths.)	40.00	20.00	12.00
(60b)	Red Murray (Green basepaths.)	40.00	20.00	12.00
(61a)	Ivy Olson (Purple pennants.)	80.00	40.00	25.00
(61b)	Ivy Olson (Yellow pennants.)	160.00	80.00	50.00
(62a)	Steve O'Neill (Purple pennants.)	75.00	37.50	22.00
(62b)	Steve O'Neill (Red pennants.)	150.00	75.00	45.00
(62c)	Steve O'Neill (Yellow pennants.)	150.00	75.00	45.00
(63a)	Marty O'Toole (Purple pennants.)	80.00	40.00	25.00
(63b)	Marty O'Toole (Red pennants.)	90.00	45.00	27.00
(64a)	Roger Peckinpaugh (Blue infield.)	45.00	22.50	13.50
(64b)	Roger Peckinpaugh (Green infield.)	45.00	22.50	13.50
(65a)	Hub Perdue (White infield.)	40.00	20.00	12.00
(65b)	Hub Perdue (Brown infield.)	150.00	75.00	45.00
(65c)	Hub Purdue (Red infield.)	1,650	825.00	495.00
(66a)	Del Pratt (Purple basepaths.)	80.00	40.00	25.00
(66b)	Del Pratt (Red basepaths.)	90.00	45.00	27.00
(67a)	Hank Robinson (Purple pennants.)	80.00	40.00	25.00
(67b)	Hank Robinson (Yellow pennants.)	130.00	65.00	40.00
(68a)	Nap Rucker (Blue infield.)	40.00	20.00	12.00
(68b)	Nap Rucker (Green infield.)	40.00	20.00	12.00
(69a)	Slim Sallee (Purple pennants.)	100.00	50.00	30.00
(69b)	Slim Sallee (Yellow pennants.)	150.00	75.00	45.00
(70a)	Howard Shanks (Brown pennants.)	40.00	20.00	12.00
(70b)	Howard Shanks (Green pennants.)	40.00	20.00	12.00
(70c)	Howard Shanks (White infield.)	40.00	20.00	12.00
(71a)	Burt Shotton (Purple basepaths.)	80.00	40.00	25.00
(71b)	Burt Shotton (Red basepaths.)	75.00	37.50	22.00
(72a)	Red Smith (Blue infield.)	40.00	20.00	12.00
(72b)	Red Smith (Green infield.)	40.00	20.00	12.00
(73a)	Fred Snodgrass (Brown basepaths.)	40.00	20.00	12.00
(73b)	Fred Snodgrass (Green basepaths.)	40.00	20.00	12.00
(74a)	Bill Steele (Purple pennants.)	80.00	40.00	24.00
(74b)	Bill Steele (Yellow pennants.)	150.00	75.00	45.00
(75a)	Casey Stengel (Blue infield.)	100.00	50.00	30.00
(75b)	Casey Stengel (Green infield.)	100.00	50.00	30.00
(76a)	Jeff Sweeney (Blue infield.)	40.00	20.00	12.00
(76b)	Jeff Sweeney (Green infield.)	40.00	20.00	12.00
(77a)	Jeff Tesreau (Brown basepaths.)	40.00	20.00	12.00
(77b)	Jeff Tesreau (Green basepaths.)	40.00	20.00	12.00
(78a)	Terry Turner (Purple pennants.)	80.00	40.00	25.00
(78b)	Terry Turner (Yellow pennants.)	150.00	75.00	45.00
(79a)	Lefty Tyler (White infield.)	40.00	20.00	12.00
(79b)	Lefty Tyler (Brown infield.)	150.00	75.00	45.00
(79c)	Lefty Tyler (Red infield.)	1,650	825.00	495.00
(80a)	Jim Viox (Purple pennants.)	80.00	40.00	25.00
(80b)	Jim Viox (Red pennants.)	90.00	45.00	27.00
(81a)	Bull Wagner (Blue infield.)	40.00	20.00	12.00
(81b)	Bull Wagner (Green infield.)	40.00	20.00	12.00
(82a)	Bobby Wallace (Purple basepaths.)	150.00	75.00	45.00
(82b)	Bobby Wallace (Red basepaths.)	150.00	75.00	45.00
(83a)	Dee Walsh (Purple basepaths.)	80.00	40.00	25.00
(83b)	Dee Walsh (Red basepaths.)	90.00	45.00	27.00
(84a)	Jimmy Walsh (Blue infield.)	40.00	20.00	12.00
(84b)	Jimmy Walsh (Green infield.)	40.00	20.00	12.00
(85a)	Bert Whaling (White infield.)	40.00	20.00	12.00
(85b)	Bert Whaling (Brown infield.)	150.00	75.00	45.00
(85c)	Bert Whaling (Red infield.)	1,650	825.00	495.00
(86a)	Zach Wheat (Blue infield.)	125.00	65.00	35.00
(86b)	Zach Wheat (Green infield.)	100.00	50.00	30.00
(87a)	Possum Whitted (Purple pennants.)	80.00	40.00	25.00
(87b)	Possum Whitted (Yellow pennants.)	125.00	65.00	35.00
(88a)	Gus Williams (Purple basepaths.)	80.00	40.00	25.00
(88b)	Gus Williams (Red basepaths.)	90.00	45.00	27.00
(89a)	Owen Wilson (Purple pennants.)	80.00	40.00	25.00
(89b)	Owen Wilson (Yellow pennants.)	150.00	75.00	45.00
(90a)	Hooks Wiltse (Brown basepaths.)	40.00	20.00	12.00
(90b)	Hooks Wiltse (Green basepaths.)	40.00	20.00	12.00

1937 BF-UNC Felt Pennants

Based on the known player-team combinations in this probably incomplete checklist, 1937 seems the most likely date of issue. The pennants measure

about 2-1/4" across the top and taper to a point at the end of their 5" length. About halfway down is a blue-and-white trapezoid with a player photo within a circle on a pinstriped background. The team name is printed in two lines at top. It is believed each player can be found with more than one base pennant color and team-name printing.

		NM	EX	VG
	Common Player:	150.00	75.00	45.00
(1)	Dizzy Dean	650.00	325.00	195.00
(2)	Bobby Feller	500.00	250.00	150.00
(3)	Hank Greenberg	500.00	250.00	150.00
(4)	Lefty Grove	450.00	225.00	135.00
(5)	Joe Moore	150.00	75.00	45.00
(6)	Wallace Moses	150.00	75.00	45.00
(7)	Lynwood Rowe	150.00	75.00	45.00
(7)	Joe Stripp	150.00	75.00	45.00
(8)	Floyd Vaughan	400.00	200.00	120.00

1916 BF2 Felt Pennants

Issued circa 1916, this unnumbered set consists of 97 felt pennants with a small black-and-white player photo glued to each. The triangular pennants measure approximately 2-7/8" across the top and taper to a length of about 5-3/4" long, while the photos are 1-3/4" x 1-1/4" and appear to be identical to photos used for M101-4/M101-5 issues of the same period. The pennants list the player's name and team. The pennants were given away as premiums with the purchase of 5-cent loaves of Ferguson Bakery bread in the Roxbury, Mass., area.

(See 1916 Ferguson Bakery Felt Pennants for checklist and values.)

1936-37 BF3 Felt Player/Team Pennants

The checklists for these series of felt pennants issued circa 1936-1938 are not complete, and new examples are still being reported. The pennants do not carry any manufacturer's name although packages found with various pieces attribute the issues to

Red Ball Sales, a gum company in Chicago, and Grandpa Brands Co., Cincinnati, another gum company. One pennant was given away with the purchase of a stick of gum, and at least one wrapper indicates large format (28" x 12") versions of the Red Ball pennants could be had in a redemption program. The pennants vary in size slightly but generally measure approximately 2-1/2" x 4-1/2" and were issued in various styles and colors. Most of the printing is white, although some pennants have been found with other colors of printing, and the same pennant is often found in more than one color combination. The pennants feature both individual players and teams, including some minor league clubs. The pennants were grouped together in the American Card Catalog under the designation of BF3. Advanced collectors have categorized the pennants into a number of basic design types, depending on what elements are included on the pennant. The unnumbered felts are listed alphabetically within type. Gaps have been left in the assigned numbers to accommodate future discoveries.

	NM	EX	VG
Common Pennant:	25.00	12.50	7.50

1936-37 Type 1 - Player Name and Silhouette

Generic silhouette figures in action poses are featured at the left end of this series of pennants. Player names at right can be found in a number of different typographic styles. Gaps have been left in the assigned numbering for future additions.

		NM	EX	VG
	Common Pennant:	60.00	30.00	18.00
(1)	Luke Appling/Btg	80.00	40.00	25.00
(2)	Earl Averill/Btg	80.00	40.00	25.00
(3)	Wally Berger/Fielding	60.00	30.00	18.00
(4)	Zeke Bonura/Fielding	60.00	30.00	18.00
(5)	Dolph Camilli/Fielding	60.00	30.00	18.00
(6)	Ben Chapman/Btg	60.00	30.00	18.00
(7)	Mickey Cochrane/Catching	90.00	45.00	27.00
(8)	Rip Collins/Btg	60.00	30.00	18.00
(9)	Joe Cronin/Btg	80.00	40.00	25.00
(10)	Kiki Cuyler/Running	80.00	40.00	25.00
(11)	Dizzy Dean/Pitching	135.00	65.00	40.00
(12)	Frank Demaree/Btg	60.00	30.00	18.00
(13)	Paul Derringer/Pitching	60.00	30.00	18.00
(14)	Bill Dickey/Catching	90.00	45.00	27.00
(15)	Jimmy Dykes/Fielding	60.00	30.00	18.00
(16)	Bob Feller/Pitching	110.00	55.00	35.00
(17)	Wes Ferrell/Btg	60.00	30.00	18.00
(19)	Jimmy Foxx	100.00	50.00	30.00
(20)	Larry French/Btg	60.00	30.00	18.00
(21)	Franky Frisch/Running	90.00	45.00	27.00
(23)	Lou Gehrig/Throwing	300.00	150.00	90.00
(24)	Charlie Gehringer/Running	90.00	45.00	27.00
(25)	Lefty Gomez/Pitching	80.00	40.00	25.00
(26)	Goose Goslin/Btg	80.00	40.00	25.00
(30)	Hank Greenberg/Fielding	110.00	55.00	35.00
(31)	Charley Grimm/Fielding	60.00	30.00	18.00
(33)	Lefty Grove/Pitching	90.00	45.00	27.00
(34)	Gabby Hartnett/Catching	80.00	40.00	25.00
(35)	Rollie Hemsley/Catching	60.00	30.00	18.00
(36)	Billy Herman/Fielding	80.00	40.00	25.00
(37)	Frank Higgins/Fielding	60.00	30.00	18.00
(38)	Rogers Hornsby/Btg	100.00	50.00	30.00
(39)	Carl Hubbell/Pitching	90.00	45.00	27.00
(40)	Chuck Klein/Throwing	80.00	40.00	25.00
(41)	Tony Lazzeri/Btg	80.00	40.00	25.00
(42)	Hank Leiber/Fielding	60.00	30.00	18.00
(43)	Ernie Lombardi/Catching	80.00	40.00	25.00
(44)	Al Lopez/Throwing	80.00	40.00	25.00
(45)	Gus Mancuso/Running	60.00	30.00	18.00
(46)	Heinie Manush/Btg	80.00	40.00	25.00
(47)	Pepper Martin/Btg	70.00	35.00	20.00
(48)	Joe McCarthy/Kneeling	80.00	40.00	25.00
(49)	Wally Moses/Running	60.00	30.00	18.00
(50)	Van Mungo/Standing	60.00	30.00	18.00
(52)	Mel Ott/Throwing	90.00	45.00	27.00
(53)	Schoolboy Rowe/Pitching	60.00	30.00	18.00
(54)	Babe Ruth/Btg	450.00	225.00	135.00
(55)	George Selkirk/Btg	60.00	30.00	18.00
(56)	Luke Sewell/Sliding	60.00	30.00	18.00
(57)	Joe Stripp/Btg	60.00	30.00	18.00
(58)	Pie Traynor/Btg	80.00	40.00	25.00
(59)	Hal Trosky/Fielding	60.00	30.00	18.00
(60)	Floyd Vaughan/Running (Script name.)	80.00	40.00	25.00
(61)	Floyd Vaughan/Running (Block name.)	80.00	40.00	25.00
(62)	Joe Vosmik/Running	60.00	30.00	18.00
(64)	Paul Waner/Btg	80.00	40.00	25.00
(65)	Lon Warneke/Pitching	60.00	30.00	18.00
(66)	Jimmy Wilson/Fielding	60.00	30.00	18.00

1936-37 Type 2 - Player's Name, Team Nickname, Figure

Team nicknames have been added at the spine of this style of pennant. As with Type 1, some players can be found in more than one pose and/or typography. Gaps have been left in the assigned numbering to accomodate future additions.

		NM	EX	VG
	Common Pennant:	60.00	30.00	18.00
(1)	Luke Appling/Btg (Block name.)	80.00	40.00	25.00
(2)	Luke Appling/Btg (Script name.)	80.00	40.00	25.00
(3)	Earl Averill/Fielding	80.00	40.00	25.00
(4)	Earl Averill/Running	80.00	40.00	24.00
(5)	Wally Berger/Throwing	60.00	30.00	18.00
(6)	Zeke Bonura/Btg	60.00	30.00	18.00
(7)	Dolph Camilli/Btg	60.00	30.00	18.00
(8)	Ben Chapman/Throwing	60.00	30.00	18.00
(9)	Mickey Cochrane/Throwing	90.00	45.00	27.00
(10)	Rip Collins/Btg	60.00	30.00	18.00
(11)	Joe Cronin/Throwing	80.00	40.00	25.00
(12)	Kiki Cuyler/Throwing	80.00	40.00	25.00
(13)	Dizzy Dean/Batting	110.00	55.00	35.00
(14)	Dizzy Dean/Throwing	110.00	55.00	35.00
(15)	Frank Demaree/Btg	60.00	30.00	18.00
(16)	Paul Derringer/Throwing	60.00	30.00	18.00
(17)	Bill Dickey/Throwing	110.00	55.00	35.00
(18)	Joe DiMaggio (Block letters through figure.)	260.00	130.00	80.00
(19)	Joe DiMaggio (Script)	260.00	130.00	80.00
(20)	Jimmy Dykes/Throwing	60.00	30.00	18.00
(21)	Bob Feller (Block letters.)	110.00	55.00	35.00
(22)	Bob Feller (Script)	110.00	55.00	35.00
(23)	Wes Ferrell/Throwing	60.00	30.00	18.00
(24)	Larry French/Btg	60.00	30.00	18.00
(25)	Frank Frisch/Fielding	90.00	45.00	27.00
(27)	Lou Gehrig/Btg (Block letters.)	300.00	150.00	90.00
(28)	Lou Gehrig/Btg (Script)	300.00	150.00	90.00
(29)	Lou Gehrig/Fielding	300.00	150.00	90.00
(31)	Lefty Gomez/Pitching	90.00	45.00	27.00
(32)	Goose Goslin/Btg	90.00	45.00	27.00
(33)	Hank Greenberg/Btg	110.00	55.00	35.00
(34)	Hank Greenberg/Throwing	110.00	55.00	35.00
(35)	Charlie Grimm/Fielding	60.00	30.00	18.00
(36)	Lefty Grove/Btg	90.00	45.00	27.00
(37)	Lefty Grove/Pitching	90.00	45.00	27.00
(38)	Gabby Hartnett/Btg	80.00	40.00	25.00
(39)	Gabby Hartnett/Catching	80.00	40.00	25.00
(40)	Billy Herman/Btg (Facing right, name over figure)	80.00	40.00	25.00
(41)	Billy Herman/Btg (Facing right, name through body)	80.00	40.00	25.00
(42)	Billy Herman/Btg (Facing left.)	80.00	40.00	25.00
(44)	Roger (Rogers) Hornsby/ Btg	100.00	50.00	30.00
(45)	Carl Hubbell/Pitching	90.00	45.00	27.00
(49)	Tony Lazzeri/Throwing	80.00	40.00	25.00
(50)	Hank Leiber/Btg	60.00	30.00	18.00
(52)	Ernie Lombardi/Btg	80.00	40.00	25.00
(54)	Gus Mancuso/Btg	60.00	30.00	18.00
(55)	Heinie Manush/Btg	80.00	40.00	25.00
(56)	Pepper Martin/Btg	75.00	37.50	22.00
(57)	Joe McCarthy/Btg	80.00	40.00	25.00
(58)	Joe Medwick/Btg	80.00	40.00	25.00
(59)	Van Lingle Mungo/Btg	60.00	30.00	18.00
(60)	Van Lingo Mungo (Lingle)/Btg	60.00	30.00	18.00
(64)	Schoolboy Rowe/Btg	60.00	30.00	18.00
(65)	Babe Ruth/Btg	450.00	225.00	135.00
(67)	George Selkirk/Btg	60.00	30.00	18.00
(68)	Luke Sewell/Btg	60.00	30.00	18.00
(69)	Joe Stripp/Btg	60.00	30.00	18.00
(70)	Bill Terry/Btg	80.00	40.00	25.00
(71)	Bill Terry/Fielding	80.00	40.00	25.00
(73)	Pie Traynor/Throwing	80.00	40.00	25.00
(74)	Hal Trosky/Btg	60.00	30.00	18.00
(75)	Floyd Vaughan/Btg	80.00	40.00	25.00
(76)	Joe Vosmik/Throwing	60.00	30.00	18.00
(77)	Paul Waner/Btg	80.00	40.00	25.00
(80)	Lon Warneke/Btg	60.00	30.00	18.00
(81)	Lon Warneke/Btg (Wind-up.)	60.00	30.00	18.00
(83)	Jimmy Wilson/Pitching	60.00	30.00	18.00

1936-37 Type 3 - Player's Name, Team Nickname

No player silhouettes are found on this series of pennants. The player name is at right, with his team's nickname at the spine. Despite the fact he left the team in 1934, Babe Ruth's pennant shows him with the Yankees. Gaps have been left in the assigned numbering to accomodate future additions.

		NM	EX	VG
	Common Pennant:	60.00	30.00	18.00
(1)	Luke Appling (Block letters.)	80.00	40.00	25.00
(2)	Luke Appling (Script)	80.00	40.00	25.00
(4)	Wally Berger	60.00	30.00	18.00
(6)	Zeke Bonura	60.00	30.00	18.00
(7)	Dolph Camilli	60.00	30.00	18.00
(9)	Ben Chapman	60.00	30.00	18.00
(10)	Mickey Cochrane	80.00	40.00	25.00
(11)	Rip Collins	60.00	30.00	18.00
(12)	Joe Cronin	80.00	40.00	25.00
(13)	Kiki Cuyler	80.00	40.00	25.00
(14)	Dizzy Dean	135.00	65.00	40.00
(15)	Frank Demaree	60.00	30.00	18.00
(16)	Paul Derringer	60.00	30.00	18.00
(17)	Bill Dickey	110.00	55.00	35.00
(18)	Joe DiMaggio (Script name.)	300.00	150.00	90.00
(19)	Jimmy Dykes	60.00	30.00	18.00
(20)	Bob Feller (Script name,)	110.00	55.00	35.00
(21)	Wes Ferrell	60.00	30.00	18.00
(22)	Jimmie Foxx	90.00	45.00	27.00
(23)	Larry French	60.00	30.00	18.00
(24)	Franky Frisch	80.00	40.00	25.00
(25)	Lou Gehrig (Script name.)	300.00	150.00	90.00
(26)	Charlie Gehringer	80.00	40.00	25.00
(28)	Lefty Gomez	80.00	40.00	25.00
(29)	Goose Goslin	80.00	40.00	24.00
(30)	Hank Greenberg	90.00	45.00	27.00
(31)	Charley Grimm	60.00	30.00	18.00
(32)	Lefty Grove	90.00	45.00	27.00
(33)	Gabby Hartnett	80.00	40.00	25.00
(35)	Rollie Hemsley	60.00	30.00	18.00
(36)	Billy Herman (Block letters.)	80.00	40.00	25.00
(37)	Billy Herman (Script)	80.00	40.00	25.00
(38)	Frank Higgins	60.00	30.00	18.00
(39)	Roger Hornsby (Rogers)	90.00	45.00	27.00
(40)	Carl Hubbell	80.00	40.00	25.00
(41)	Chuck Klein	80.00	40.00	25.00
(42)	Tony Lazzeri	80.00	40.00	25.00
(43)	Hank Leiber	60.00	30.00	18.00
(44)	Ernie Lombardi	80.00	40.00	25.00
(45)	Al Lopez	80.00	40.00	25.00
(46)	Gus Mancuso	60.00	30.00	18.00
(48)	Heinie Manush	80.00	40.00	25.00
(49)	Pepper Martin	70.00	35.00	20.00
(50)	Joe McCarthy	80.00	40.00	25.00
(51)	Joe Medwick	80.00	40.00	25.00
(52)	Wally Moses	60.00	30.00	18.00
(53)	Van Mungo	60.00	30.00	18.00
(54)	Mel Ott	80.00	40.00	25.00
(55)	Schoolboy Rowe	60.00	30.00	18.00
(56)	Babe Ruth	400.00	200.00	120.00
(57)	George Selkirk	60.00	30.00	18.00
(58)	Luke Sewell	60.00	30.00	18.00
(59)	Al Simmons	80.00	40.00	25.00
(60)	Joe Stripp	60.00	30.00	18.00
(61)	Bill Terry	80.00	40.00	25.00
(62)	Pie Traynor	80.00	40.00	25.00
(63)	Hal Trosky	60.00	30.00	18.00
(64)	Joe Vosmik	60.00	30.00	18.00
(65)	Floyd Vaughan	80.00	40.00	25.00
(66)	Paul Waner	80.00	40.00	25.00
(67)	Lon Warneke	60.00	30.00	18.00
(68)	Jimmy Wilson	60.00	30.00	18.00
(71)				

1936-37 Type 4 - Team Nickname and Silhouette Player

One of two closely related series of these collectible pennants, this type has a team nickname in combination with a silhouette figure of one or more baseball figures. Collectors should be aware that similar pennants, perhaps even sharing the same designs, were issued circa 1950 in boxes of candy from American Nut & Chocolate of Boston. The AN&C pennants should be distinguishable by their smaller size of approximately 4" x 1-7/8". Gaps in the assigned numbering have been left to accomodate future additions.

		NM	EX	VG
	Common Pennant:	40.00	20.00	12.00
(1)	Athletics/Fielder	40.00	20.00	12.00
(2)	Browns/Catcher	40.00	20.00	12.00
(3)	Cubs/Batter	40.00	20.00	12.00
(4)	Dodgers/Batter	40.00	20.00	12.00
(5)	Dodgers/Fielder	40.00	20.00	12.00
(7)	Giants (Sliding into base.)	40.00	20.00	12.00
(8)	Giants (Standing at base.)	40.00	20.00	12.00
(9)	Giants (Two players.)	40.00	20.00	12.00
(10)	Phillies/Pitcher	40.00	20.00	12.00
(12)	Reds/Batter	40.00	20.00	12.00
(13)	Reds/Catcher	40.00	20.00	12.00
(14)	Reds/Pitcher	40.00	20.00	12.00
(15)	Red Sox (Batter and catcher.)	40.00	20.00	12.00
(16)	White Sox (Batter left of team name.)	40.00	20.00	12.00
(17)	White Sox (Batter inside "W.")	40.00	20.00	12.00
(18)	White Sox/Catcher	40.00	20.00	12.00
(19)	White Sox (Profile)	40.00	20.00	12.00
(20)	White Sox/Pitcher	40.00	20.00	12.00
(21)	Yankees/Batter	40.00	20.00	12.00
(22)	Yankees/Fielder	40.00	20.00	12.00

1936-37 Type 5 - Team Nickname with Emblem

Closely related to the Type 4 style, these pennants combine a team nickname with a symbolic figure or depictions of baseball equipment. Collectors should be aware that similar pennants, perhaps even sharing the same designs, were issued circa 1950 in boxes of candy from American Nut & Chocolate of Boston. The AN&C pennants should be distinguishable by their smaller size of approximately 4" x 1-7/8". Gaps have been left in the numbering to accomodate future additions.

		NM	EX	VG
	Common Pennant:	40.00	20.00	12.00
(1)	Athletics (Elephant, no tusks.)	40.00	20.00	12.00
(2)	Athletics (Elephant, w/tusks.)	40.00	20.00	12.00
(3)	Athletics (Gothic script, w/bat, ball.)	40.00	20.00	12.00
(5)	Bees (Bee is crossbar of "B.")	40.00	20.00	12.00
(6)	Bees (Bee is loops of "B.")	40.00	20.00	12.00
(7)	Brooklyn (Crossed bats over "B.")	40.00	20.00	12.00
(9)	Browns/Ball	40.00	20.00	12.00
(10)	Browns/Bat	40.00	20.00	12.00
(11)	Browns (Bat is spine of "B", balls in loops.)	40.00	20.00	12.00
(12)	Cardinals/Bat	40.00	20.00	12.00
(13)	Cardinals (Cardinal inside "C", profile.)	40.00	20.00	12.00
(14)	Cardinals (Cardinal inside "C" front view.)	40.00	20.00	12.00
(15)	Cardinals (Four birds on "C.")	40.00	20.00	12.00
(16)	Cubs (Cub w/bat.)	40.00	20.00	12.00
(17)	Cubs (Cub's head.)	40.00	20.00	12.00
(18)	Cubs (Cub sitting in "C.")	40.00	20.00	12.00
(20)	Dodgers/Ball	40.00	20.00	12.00
(21)	Dodgers/Ball (Bat and glove.)	40.00	20.00	12.00
(22)	Dodgers (Trolley car.)	40.00	20.00	12.00
(23)	Giants (Crossed bats and ball.)	40.00	20.00	12.00
(25)	Indians (Indians)	40.00	20.00	12.00
(26)	Indians (Indian profile, nine feathers.)	40.00	20.00	12.00
(27)	Indians (Indian profile, headdress.)	40.00	20.00	12.00
(30)	Phillies (Liberty Bell.)	40.00	20.00	12.00
(32)	Pirates (Pirate, no knife.)	40.00	20.00	12.00
(33)	Pirates (Pirate w/knife.)	40.00	20.00	12.00
(34)	Pirates (Peg-legged pirate w/sword.)	40.00	20.00	12.00
(35)	Pirates (Skull and crossed bones.)	40.00	20.00	12.00
(36)	Reds (Man with stein.)	40.00	20.00	12.00
(37)	Reds (W/ball.)	40.00	20.00	12.00
(39)	Red Sox/Ball	40.00	20.00	12.00
(40)	Red Sox/Bat	40.00	20.00	12.00
(41)	Red Sox (Ball and bat.)	40.00	20.00	12.00
(42)	Red Sox/Stocking	40.00	20.00	12.00
(44)	Senators/Bat	40.00	20.00	12.00
(45)	Senators/Cap (Dome, "S" superimposed.)	40.00	20.00	12.00
(46)	Senators (Capital Dome, "S" to right.)	40.00	20.00	12.00
(47)	Senators (Man's profile in top hat.)	40.00	20.00	12.00
(48)	Sox (W/bat and ball.)	40.00	20.00	12.00
(49)	Tigers (Bat left, ball right.)	40.00	20.00	12.00
(50)	Tigers/Cap	40.00	20.00	12.00
(51)	Tigers (Prowling tiger.)	40.00	20.00	12.00
(52)	Tigers (Tiger head in circle.)	40.00	20.00	12.00
(53)	Tigers (Tiger head, no circle.)	40.00	20.00	12.00

Vintage cards in Good condition are valued at about 50% of the Very Good values shown here. Cards in Fair condition are valued at 25% or less of VG.

1936-37 Type 6 - Team Name Only

		NM	EX	VG
Common Pennant:		40.00	20.00	12.00
(1)	ATHLETICS	40.00	20.00	12.00
(2)	ATHLETICS (PHILA. on spine.)	40.00	20.00	12.00
(3)	BEES	40.00	20.00	12.00
(4)	BEES (BOSTON on spine.)	40.00	20.00	12.00
(5)	CARDINALS	40.00	20.00	12.00
(6)	CUBS	40.00	20.00	12.00
(7)	CUBS (CHICAGO on spine.)	40.00	20.00	12.00
(8)	DODGERS	40.00	20.00	12.00
(9)	DODGERS (BROOKLYN on spine.)	40.00	20.00	12.00
(10)	GIANTS	40.00	20.00	12.00
(11)	GIANTS (NEW YORK on spine.)	40.00	20.00	12.00
(12)	INDIANS	40.00	20.00	12.00
(13)	PHILLIES	40.00	20.00	12.00
(14)	PHILLIES (PHILLIES on spine.)	40.00	20.00	12.00
(15)	PIRATES	40.00	20.00	12.00
(16)	PIRATES (PITTSBURGH on spine.)	40.00	20.00	12.00
(17)	REDS	40.00	20.00	12.00
(18)	REDS (CINCINNATI on spine.)	40.00	20.00	12.00
(19)	SENATORS	40.00	20.00	12.00
(20)	WASH. SENATORS	40.00	20.00	12.00
(21)	SOX	40.00	20.00	12.00
(22)	TIGERS	40.00	20.00	12.00
(23)	WHITE SOX	40.00	20.00	12.00
(24)	YANKEES	40.00	20.00	12.00
(25)	YANKEES (NEW YORK on spine.)	40.00	20.00	12.00

1936 Type 7 - Player, Team W/Pennant, Cap, Ball, Etc.

This group of pennants is slightly longer, at about 5-1/4", than the majority of BF 3 pennants. It is believed that two players from each team will eventually be accounted for.

		NM	EX	VG
Common Pennant:		40.00	20.00	12.00
(1)	Luke Appling	55.00	27.00	16.50
(2)	Wally Berger	40.00	20.00	12.00
(3)	Dolph Camilli	40.00	20.00	12.00
(4)	Dizzy Dean	90.00	45.00	27.00
(5)	Frank Demaree	40.00	20.00	12.00
(6)	Joe DiMaggio	200.00	100.00	60.00
(7)	Jimmie Foxx	75.00	37.00	22.00
(8)	Lou Gehrig	200.00	100.00	60.00
(9)	Earl Grace	40.00	20.00	12.00
(10)	Hank Greenberg	75.00	37.00	22.00
(11)	Gabby Hartnett	55.00	27.00	16.50
(12)	Rollie Hemsley	40.00	20.00	12.00
(13)	Carl Hubbell	55.00	27.00	16.50
(14)	Bob Johnson	40.00	20.00	12.00
(15)	Ernie Lombardi	55.00	27.00	16.50
(16)	Al Lopez	55.00	27.00	16.50
(17)	Joe Medwick	55.00	27.00	16.50
(18)	Van Lingle Mungo	45.00	22.00	13.50
(19)	Billy Myers	40.00	20.00	12.00
(20)	Mel Ott	55.00	27.00	16.50
(21)	Frank Pytlak	40.00	20.00	12.00
(23)	Schoolboy Rowe	40.00	20.00	12.00
(25)	Hal Trosky	55.00	27.00	16.50
(28)	Arky Vaughan	55.00	27.00	16.50
(29)	Paul Waner	55.00	27.00	16.50
(30)	Earl Whitehill	40.00	20.00	12.00

1936-37 Type 8 - Misc. Designs

Pennants in this series are generally unique in their style and do not fit into any of the other categories.

		NM	EX	VG
Common Pennant:		60.00	30.00	18.00
(1)	Wes Ferrell ("RED SOX" reversed out of bat on spine.)	60.00	30.00	18.00
(2)	Larry French (Name, team, year on ball.)	60.00	30.00	18.00
(3)	Goose Goslin (Name above and below bat, "TIGERS" on bat.)	75.00	37.50	22.00
(4)	Charley Root (Name above and below bat, "CUBS" on bat.)	60.00	30.00	18.00
(5)	Billy Sullivan ("INDIANS" reversed out of bat on spine.)	60.00	30.00	18.00
(6)	CHAMPIONS/YANKEES/1936 (Team name in red triangle at center.)	100.00	50.00	30.00

1937 Type 9 - Player Name, 1937 On Ball, Team Name

Players from only four teams - Bees, Cardinals, Cubs and White Sox - are known in this style. The pennants have a large baseball at left with three panels containing the player's first name, last name and "1937." At right is the team nickname.

		NM	EX	VG
Common Pennant:		60.00	30.00	18.00
(1)	Luke Appling	80.00	40.00	25.00
(2)	Wally Berger	60.00	30.00	18.00
(3)	Zeke Bonura	60.00	30.00	18.00
(4)	Frenchy Bordagaray	60.00	30.00	18.00
(5)	Clint Brown	60.00	30.00	18.00
(6)	Clay Bryant	60.00	30.00	18.00
(7)	Guy Bush	60.00	30.00	18.00
(8)	Sugar Cain	60.00	30.00	18.00
(9)	Tex Carleton	60.00	30.00	18.00
(10)	Phil Cavaretta (Cavarretta)	60.00	30.00	18.00
(11)	Phil Cavaretta	60.00	30.00	18.00
(12)	Irving Cherry	60.00	30.00	18.00
(13)	Ripper Collins	60.00	30.00	18.00
(14)	Tony Cuccinello	60.00	30.00	18.00
(15)	Curt Davis	60.00	30.00	18.00
(16)	Dizzy Dean	135.00	65.00	40.00
(17)	Paul Dean	75.00	37.50	22.00
(18)	Frank Demaree	60.00	30.00	18.00
(19)	Bill Dietrich	60.00	30.00	18.00
(21)	Vinc DiMaggio (Vince)	75.00	37.50	22.00
(22)	Leo Durocher	80.00	40.00	25.00
(23)	Jimmy Dykes	60.00	30.00	18.00
(24)	Burt Fletcher	60.00	30.00	18.00
(25)	Wes Flowers	60.00	30.00	18.00
(26)	Vic Frasier	60.00	30.00	18.00
(27)	Larry French	60.00	30.00	18.00
(28)	Linus Frey	60.00	30.00	18.00
(29)	Frank Frisch	80.00	40.00	25.00
(30)	Augie Galan	60.00	30.00	18.00
(31)	Charlie Grimm	60.00	30.00	18.00
(32)	Geo. Haas	60.00	30.00	18.00
(33)	Stan Hack	70.00	35.00	21.00
(34)	Jessie Haines	80.00	40.00	25.00
(35)	Gabby Hartnett	80.00	40.00	25.00
(36)	Minter Hayes	60.00	30.00	18.00
(37)	Billy Herman	80.00	40.00	25.00
(38)	Walter Highbee (Kirby Higbe)	60.00	30.00	18.00
(39)	Roy Johnson	60.00	30.00	18.00
(41)	Baxter Jordan	60.00	30.00	18.00
(42)	Billy Jurges	60.00	30.00	18.00
(43)	Vernon Kennedy	60.00	30.00	18.00
(44)	Mike Kreevich	60.00	30.00	18.00
(45)	Bill Lee	60.00	30.00	18.00
(46)	Thorn Lee	60.00	30.00	18.00
(47)	Al Lopez	80.00	40.00	25.00
(48)	Andy Lotshaw	60.00	30.00	18.00
(49)	Ted Lyons	80.00	40.00	25.00
(50)	Dan MacFayden	60.00	30.00	18.00
(51)	Henry Majeski	70.00	35.00	20.00
(52)	Pepper Martin	60.00	30.00	18.00
(53)	Stuart Martin	60.00	30.00	18.00
(54)	Joe Marty	60.00	30.00	18.00
(55)	Tommy McBride	60.00	30.00	18.00
(56)	Bill McKechnie	80.00	40.00	25.00
(57)	Joe Medwick	80.00	40.00	25.00
(58)	Steve Mesner	60.00	30.00	18.00
(59)	Hank Meyer	60.00	30.00	18.00
(60)	Johnny Mize	80.00	40.00	25.00
(61)	Gene Moore	60.00	30.00	18.00
(62)	Terry Moore	60.00	30.00	18.00
(63)	Ken O'Dea	60.00	30.00	18.00
(64)	Brusie Ogrodowski	60.00	30.00	18.00
(65)	Tony Piet	60.00	30.00	18.00
(66)	Ray Radcliff	60.00	30.00	18.00
(67)	Bob Reis	60.00	30.00	18.00
(68)	Dunc Rigney	60.00	30.00	18.00
(69)	Les Rock	60.00	30.00	18.00
(70)	Chas. Root	60.00	30.00	18.00
(71)	Larry Rosenthal	60.00	30.00	18.00
(72)	Luke Sewell	60.00	30.00	18.00
(73)	Merv Shea	60.00	30.00	18.00
(74)	Tuck Stainback	60.00	30.00	18.00
(75)	Hank Steinbacher	60.00	30.00	18.00
(76)	Monty Stratton	70.00	35.00	20.00
(77)	Ken Sylvestri	60.00	30.00	18.00
(78)	Billie Urbanski	60.00	30.00	18.00
(79)	Fred Walker	60.00	30.00	18.00
(81)	Lon Warneke	60.00	30.00	18.00
(82)	Johnnie Whitehead	60.00	30.00	18.00
(83)				

1938 Type 10 - Player Name, 1938 On Ball, Team Name

Identical in format to the 1937 version, these pennants feature only members of the Detroit Tigers. The player's first name, last name and "1938" are stacked on the panels of a large baseball design at left, while "TIGERS" is at right.

		NM	EX	VG
Common Pennant:		60.00	30.00	18.00
(1)	Harry Eisenstat	60.00	30.00	18.00
(2)	Pete Fox	60.00	30.00	18.00
(3)	Vern Kennedy	60.00	30.00	18.00
(4)	Roxie Lawson	60.00	30.00	18.00
(5)	Tony Piet	60.00	30.00	18.00
(6)	Rudy York	60.00	30.00	18.00

1936-37 Type 11 - Minor League and Team

Minor league team nicknames and a league designation are combined with a player figure or symbol in this series. The checklist is believed complete with eight teams each from the Southern Association, International League and American Association.

		NM	EX	VG
Complete Set (24):		950.00	475.00	275.00
Common Pennant:		40.00	20.00	12.00
(1)	Barons - Southern	40.00	20.00	12.00
(2)	Bears - International	40.00	20.00	12.00
(3)	Bisons - International	40.00	20.00	12.00
(4)	Blues - Amer. Assn.	40.00	20.00	12.00
(5)	Brewers - Amer. Assn.	40.00	20.00	12.00
(6)	Chicks - Southern	40.00	20.00	12.00
(7)	Chiefs - International	40.00	20.00	12.00
(8)	Colonels - Amer. Assn.	40.00	20.00	12.00
(9)	Crackers - Sou'n. Ass'n.	40.00	20.00	12.00
(10)	Giants - International	40.00	20.00	12.00
(11)	Indians - Amer. Assn.	40.00	20.00	12.00
(12)	Lookouts - Sou'n. Ass'n.	40.00	20.00	12.00
(13)	Maple Leafs - International	40.00	20.00	12.00
(14)	Millers - Amer. Assn.	40.00	20.00	12.00
(15)	Mud Hens - Amer. Assn.	40.00	20.00	12.00
(16)	Orioles - International	40.00	20.00	12.00
(17)	Pelicans - Sou'n. Ass'n.	40.00	20.00	12.00
(18)	Red Birds - Amer. Assn.	40.00	20.00	12.00
(19)	Red Wings - Int'l	40.00	20.00	12.00
(20)	Royals - Int'l	40.00	20.00	12.00
(21)	Saints - Amer. Assn.	40.00	20.00	12.00
(22)	Smokies - Southern	40.00	20.00	12.00
(23)	Travelers - Sou'n. Ass'n.	40.00	20.00	12.00
(24)	Vols - Sou'n Ass'n.	40.00	20.00	12.00

1936-37 Type 12 - Jumbo Teams

According to advertising on the Red Ball Gum packaging with which most types of the Bf3 felt pennants were sold, jumbo size - about 28-1/2" x 11" -

versions of 16 team pennants could be had by redeeming 25 wrappers and 15 cents for each desired pennant. The large-format pennants are identical in design to some of the smaller pieces from Types 4, 5 and 8.

	NM	EX	VG
Complete Set (16):			
Common Pennant:	300.00	150.00	90.00
(1) Boston Bees	300.00	150.00	90.00
(2) Boston Red Sox	300.00	150.00	90.00
(3) Brooklyn Dodgers	300.00	150.00	90.00
(4) Chicago Cubs	300.00	150.00	90.00
(5) Chicago White Sox	300.00	150.00	90.00
(6) Cincinnati Reds	300.00	150.00	90.00
(7) Cleveland Indians	300.00	150.00	90.00
(8) Detroit Tigers	300.00	150.00	90.00
(9) New York Giants	300.00	150.00	90.00
(10) New York Yankees	400.00	200.00	120.00
(11) Philadelphia Athletics	300.00	150.00	90.00
(12) Philadelphia Phillies	300.00	150.00	90.00
(13) Pittsburgh Pirates	300.00	150.00	90.00
(14) St. Louis Browns	300.00	150.00	90.00
(15) St. Louis Cardinals	300.00	150.00	90.00
(16) Washington Senators	300.00	150.00	90.00

1937 BF104 Blankets

A throwback to the 1914 B18 blankets, little is known about these 3-1/2"-square felts. They were designated as BF104 in the American Card Catalog. The issuer and manner of distribution remain a mystery. Subjects are depicted in either portrait or action artwork. This checklist likely is not complete.

	NM	EX	VG
Common Player:	300.00	150.00	90.00
(1) Moe Berg	500.00	250.00	150.00
(2) Cy Blanton	300.00	150.00	90.00
(3) Earle Brucker	300.00	150.00	90.00
(4) Mickey Cochrane	600.00	300.00	180.00
(5) Joe Cronin	600.00	300.00	180.00
(6) Tony Cuccinello	300.00	150.00	90.00
(7) Dizzy Dean	1,200	600.00	360.00
(8) Frank Demaree	300.00	150.00	90.00
(9) Jimmie Foxx	900.00	450.00	275.00
(10) Larry French	300.00	150.00	90.00
(11) Frankie Frisch	600.00	300.00	180.00
(12) Hank Greenberg	1,000	500.00	300.00
(13) Gabby Hartnett	600.00	300.00	180.00
(14) Billy Herman	600.00	300.00	180.00
(15) Woody Jensen	300.00	150.00	90.00
(16) Billy Jurges	300.00	150.00	90.00
(17) Harry Kelly (Kelley)	300.00	150.00	90.00
(18) Thornton Lee	300.00	150.00	90.00
(19) Danny MacFayden	300.00	150.00	90.00
(20) Connie Mack	600.00	300.00	180.00
(21) Stu Martin	300.00	150.00	90.00
(22) Joe Medwick	600.00	300.00	180.00
(23) Ray Mueller	300.00	150.00	90.00
(24) L. Newsome	300.00	150.00	90.00
(25) Monty Stratton	405.00	200.00	120.00
(26) Pie Traynor	600.00	300.00	180.00
(27) Jim Turner	300.00	150.00	90.00
(28) Bill Werber	300.00	150.00	90.00
(29) Jack Wilson	300.00	150.00	90.00
(30) Rudy York	300.00	150.00	90.00

1909 Cabanas

In conjunction with a post-season visit by the A.L. Champion Detroit Tigers (who without Hall of Famer Ty Cobb and Sam Crawford won only four of 12 games from the locals), Cabanas brand cigarettes issued this set. About 1-1/2" x 2-1/4" the cards feature black-and-white portrait photos. Players from the Almendares team have a blue frame and some colorized blue details on their uniforms, Havana players

are in red, the Tigers are in gray. Printed on backs of the cards is (roughly translated) "The best way to form a valuable collection of baseball players of the Cuban clubs and the foreign visitors is to smoke Cabanas." It is unknown whether the checklists presented here alphabetically are complete.

	NM	EX	VG
Common Cuban Player:	600.00	300.00	175.00
Common Tigers Player:	900.00	450.00	275.00
ALMENDARES B.B.C.			
(1) Rafael Almeida	700.00	350.00	210.00
(2) Armando Cabanas	700.00	350.00	210.00
(3) Alfredo Cabrera	600.00	300.00	175.00
(4) Regino "Mamelo" Garcia	1,150	575.00	345.00
(5a) Heliodoro Hidalgo (C.F.)	1,150	575.00	345.00
(5b) Heliodoro Hidalgo (C.F. Jabuco)	1,150	575.00	345.00
(6) Armando Marsans	700.00	350.00	210.00
(7) Esteban Prats	600.00	300.00	175.00
(8) Carlos "Bebe" Royer	700.00	350.00	210.00
HABANA B.B.C.			
(1) Luis Bustamante	2,250	1,125	675.00
(2) Luis "Chico" Gonzalez	600.00	300.00	175.00
(3) Valentin "Sirique" Gonzalez	600.00	300.00	175.00
(4) Ricardo Hernandez	600.00	300.00	175.00
(5) Preston "Pete" Hill (Value Undetermined)			
(6) Angel D. Mesa	600.00	300.00	175.00
(7) Augustin "Tinti" Molina	700.00	350.00	210.00
(8) Carlos "Chino" Moran	600.00	300.00	175.00
(9) Luis "Mulo" Padron	3,500	1,750	1,050
(10) Elilio Palomino	600.00	300.00	175.00
(11) Pastor H. Pareda	600.00	300.00	180.00
(12) Agustin Parpetti	2,000	1,000	600.00
(13) Inocencio Perez	600.00	300.00	175.00
(14) Bruce Petway	7,500	3,750	2,250
(15) Gonzalo Sanchez	600.00	300.00	175.00
DETROIT TIGERS			
(1) C. Beckendorff (Beckendorf)	900.00	450.00	275.00
(2) Owen (Donie) Bush	900.00	450.00	275.00
(3) Hopke	900.00	450.00	275.00
(4) David Jones	900.00	450.00	275.00
(5) William Lelivelt	900.00	450.00	275.00
(6) Matty Mc. Intyre	900.00	450.00	275.00
(7) George Moriarty	900.00	450.00	275.00
(8) George Mullin	900.00	450.00	275.00
(9) Frank O'Laughlin/Umpire (O'Loughlin)	1,200	600.00	360.00
(10) Charles O'Leary	900.00	450.00	275.00
(11) Charles Schmidt	900.00	450.00	275.00
(12) Edgar Willetts (Willett)	900.00	450.00	275.00

1955 Cain's Jimmy Piersall

The date of issue is speculative for these promotional postcards. The borderless black-and-white photo on the front of the 3-1/2" x 5-1/2" cards shows the popular BoSox star in a fielding pose. A blue facsimile autograph is printed at top. The postcard-format back has a drawing of the product beneath an advertising message bearing Piersall's signature. Similar cards advertising Colonial Meats are also known.

	NM	EX	VG
Autographed:	125.00	65.00	35.00
Jimmy Piersall (Mayonnaise)	80.00	40.00	24.00
Jimmy Piersall (Potato chips.)	80.00	40.00	24.00
Jimmy Piersall (Riviera dressing.)	80.00	40.00	24.00

1965 California Angels Matchbook Covers

These 1-1/2" x 4-1/2" matchbooks can be found with the advertising of two different banks printed on them; both are products of the local Universal Match Corp., and are printed in black and gold on white on front, with the inside surface in black-and-white. The County National Bank version has the player portrait photo within a plain black frame. Inside, the CNB matchbooks have player identification and personal data and 1964 stats. There is also an offer to redeem 15 different players' matchbooks for two free game tickets. The Santa Ana Savings matchbooks have the same player information and ads for the bank and the Angels' radio station. The player photos on front of the Santa Ana matchbooks have a gold frame. Values shown are for complete but empty covers, with the striker surface intact. Complete matchbooks with matches bring about 2X the values quoted.

	NM	EX	VG
Complete Set (15):	120.00	60.00	35.00
Common Player:	10.00	5.00	3.00
(1) Dean Chance	12.50	6.25	3.75
(2) Lu Clinton	10.00	5.00	3.00
(3) Jim Fregosi	10.00	5.00	3.00
(4) Ed Kirkpatrick	10.00	5.00	3.00
(5) Bobby Knoop	10.00	5.00	3.00
(6) Barry Latman	10.00	5.00	3.00
(7) Bob Lee	10.00	5.00	3.00
(8) Ken McBride	10.00	5.00	3.00
(9) Fred Newman	10.00	5.00	3.00
(10) Jimmy Piersall	20.00	10.00	6.00
(11) Rick Reichardt	10.00	5.00	3.00
(12) Bill Rigney	10.00	5.00	3.00
(13) Bob Rodgers	10.00	5.00	3.00
(14) Tom Satriano	10.00	5.00	3.00
(15) Willie Smith	10.00	5.00	3.00

1976 California Pacific Bank

Whether these are a legitimate promotional issue or a made-for-collectors set is unknown. The cards may have been created for use at autograph appearances at a Fullerton, Calif., bank. About 3-5/8" x 5", though the size varies, the black-and-white blank-back cards have player photos on front (some of which are reproductions of team-issued photos) and a promotional message describing the bank's "Big League Service." Two poses of Steve Carlton are known.

	NM	EX	VG
Complete Set (7):	60.00	30.00	18.00
Common Player:	5.00	2.50	1.50

		NM	EX	VG
(1)	Steve Busby	5.00	2.50	1.50
(2)	Steve Carlton	15.00	7.50	4.50
(3)	Steve Carlton	15.00	7.50	4.50
(4)	Bill Russell	5.00	2.50	1.50
(5)	Mike Schmidt	20.00	10.00	6.00
(6)	Ted Simmons	5.00	2.50	1.50
(7)	Don Sutton	10.00	5.00	3.00

1950 Callahan Hall of Fame

KENESAW MOUNTAIN LANDIS

These cards, which feature artist Mario DeMarco's drawings of Hall of Famers, were produced from 1950 through 1956 and sold by the Baseball Hall of Fame in Cooperstown and at major league ballparks. The cards measure 1-3/4" x 2-1/2" and include a detailed player biography on the back. When introduced in 1950 the set included all members of the Hall of Fame up to that time, and then new cards were added each year as more players were elected. Therefore, cards of players appearing in all previous editions are more common than those players who appeared in just one or two years. When the set was discontinued in 1956 it consisted of 82 cards, which is now considered a complete set. The cards are not numbered and are listed here alphabetically. B.E. Callahan of Chicago, the publisher of "Who's Who in Baseball," produced the card set.

		NM	EX	VG
	Original 1950 Boxed Set (62):	500.00	250.00	150.00
	Complete Set (82):	1,900	950.00	575.00
	Common Player:	6.00	3.00	1.75
(1)	Grover Alexander	25.00	12.50	7.50
(2)	"Cap" Anson	15.00	7.50	4.50
(3)	J. Franklin "Home Run" Baker	150.00	75.00	45.00
(4)	Edward G. Barrow	35.00	17.50	10.00
(5a)	Charles "Chief" Bender (Bio ends "... immortal name for him.")	25.00	12.50	7.50
(5b)	Charles "Chief" Bender (Bio ends "... died in 1954.")	35.00	17.50	10.00
(6)	Roger Bresnahan	10.00	5.00	3.00
(7)	Dan Brouthers	15.00	7.50	4.50
(8)	Mordecai Brown	10.00	5.00	3.00
(9)	Morgan G. Bulkeley	10.00	5.00	3.00
(10)	Jesse Burkett	16.00	8.00	4.75
(11)	Alexander Cartwright	12.50	6.25	3.75
(12)	Henry Chadwick	12.00	6.00	3.50
(13)	Frank Chance	16.00	8.00	4.75
(14)	Albert B. Chandler	350.00	175.00	100.00
(15)	Jack Chesbro	7.50	3.75	2.25
(16)	Fred Clarke	10.00	5.00	3.00
(17)	Ty Cobb	50.00	25.00	15.00
(18a)	Mickey Cochran (Name incorrect.)	10.00	5.00	3.00
(18b)	Mickey Cochrane (Name correct.)	12.00	6.00	3.50
(19a)	Eddie Collins (Second paragraph of bio begins "Eddie had every ...")	9.00	4.50	2.75
(19b)	Eddie Collins (Second paragraph of bio begins "He was brilliant ...")	13.50	6.75	4.00
(20)	Jimmie Collins	12.50	6.25	3.75
(21)	Charles A. Comiskey	12.50	6.25	3.75
(22)	Tom Connolly	50.00	25.00	15.00
(23)	Candy Cummings	9.00	4.50	2.75
(24)	Dizzy Dean	45.00	22.50	13.50
(25)	Ed Delahanty	6.00	3.00	1.75
(26a)	Bill Dickey (First paragraph of bio ends "... He was right-handed all the way.")	30.00	15.00	9.00
(26b)	Bill Dickey (First paragraph of bio ends "... during his final year.")	35.00	17.50	10.50
(27)	Joe DiMaggio	180.00	90.00	54.00
(28)	Hugh Duffy	7.50	3.75	2.25
(29)	Johnny Evers	13.50	6.75	4.00
(30)	Buck Ewing	10.00	5.00	3.00
(31)	Jimmie Foxx	20.00	10.00	6.00
(32)	Frank Frisch	6.00	3.00	1.75
(33)	Lou Gehrig	85.00	42.50	25.00
(34a)	Charles Gehringer (White cap.)	9.00	4.50	2.75
(34b)	Charlie Gehringer (Dark cap.)	11.00	5.50	3.25
(35)	Clark Griffith	6.00	3.00	1.75
(36)	Lefty Grove	10.00	5.00	3.00
(37)	Leo "Gabby" Hartnett	40.00	20.00	12.00
(38)	Harry Heilmann	25.00	12.50	7.50
(39)	Rogers Hornsby	16.00	8.00	4.75
(40)	Carl Hubbell	12.00	6.00	3.50
(41)	Hughey Jennings	6.00	3.00	1.75
(42)	Ban Johnson	7.50	3.75	2.25
(43)	Walter Johnson	10.00	5.00	3.00
(44)	Willie Keeler	7.50	3.75	2.25
(45)	Mike Kelly	10.00	5.00	3.00
(46)	Bill Klem	65.00	32.50	20.00
(47)	Napoleon Lajoie	11.00	5.50	3.25
(48)	Kenesaw M. Landis	6.00	3.00	1.75
(49)	Ted Lyons	100.00	50.00	30.00
(50)	Connie Mack	12.00	6.00	3.50
(51)	Walter Maranville	20.00	10.00	6.00
(52)	Christy Mathewson	10.00	5.00	3.00
(53)	Tommy McCarthy	12.50	6.25	3.75
(54)	Joe McGinnity	6.00	3.00	1.75
(55)	John McGraw	10.00	5.00	3.00
(56)	Charles Nichols	16.00	8.00	4.75
(57)	Jim O'Rourke	9.00	4.50	2.75
(58)	Mel Ott	16.00	8.00	4.75
(59)	Herb Pennock	9.00	4.50	2.75
(60)	Eddie Plank	10.00	5.00	3.00
(61)	Charles Radbourne	10.00	5.00	3.00
(62)	Wilbert Robinson	6.00	3.00	1.75
(63)	Babe Ruth	90.00	45.00	27.50
(64)	Ray "Cracker" Schalk	30.00	15.00	9.00
(65)	Al Simmons	60.00	30.00	18.00
(66a)	George Sisler (Bio ends "Sisler today is ...")	13.50	6.75	4.00
(66b)	George Sisler (Bio ends "Sisler was chosen as ...")	9.00	4.50	2.75
(67)	A. G. Spalding	10.00	5.00	3.00
(68)	Tris Speaker	16.00	8.00	4.75
(69)	Bill Terry	30.00	15.00	9.00
(70)	Joe Tinker	10.00	5.00	3.00
(71)	"Pie" Traynor	10.00	5.00	3.00
(72)	Clarence A. "Dazzy" Vance	30.00	15.00	9.00
(73)	Rube Waddell	9.00	4.50	2.75
(74)	Hans Wagner	30.00	15.00	9.00
(75)	Bobby Wallace	13.50	6.75	4.00
(76)	Ed Walsh	10.00	5.00	3.00
(77a)	Paul Waner (Complete black frame line around picture.)	9.00	4.50	2.75
(77b)	Paul Waner (Bottom missing on black frame line around picture.)	40.00	20.00	12.00
(78)	George Wright	7.50	3.75	2.25
(79)	Harry Wright	20.00	10.00	6.00
(80)	Cy Young	12.50	6.25	3.75
(---)	Museum Exterior View (No date at top of list on back.)	35.00	17.50	10.00
(---)	Museum Exterior View (Date "1954" on top of list on back.)	60.00	30.00	18.00
(---)	Museum Interior View (Back copy ends, "... to all baseball men.")	30.00	15.00	9.00
(---)	Museum Interior View (Back copy ends "... playing days are concluded.")	13.50	6.75	4.00

1898 Cameo Pepsin Gum Pins

The first large set of baseball player pins is this issue from Whitehead & Hoag, advertising Cameo Pepsin Gum. The 1-1/4" pins have a sepia player portrait photo at center, with name and team at top left and right. It is very difficult to find pins with clear pictures as they tend to darken and fade with time. Pins were issued with a paper inset in back advertising the gum, but are often found with the paper missing. It is likely that there will be future additions to this checklist. The unnumbered pins are presented here in alphabetical order, with gaps in the numbering to accomodate future additions.

		NM	EX	VG
	Common Player:	950.00	475.00	285.00
(1)	John Anderson	950.00	475.00	285.00
(2)	Cap Anson	3,000	1,200	725.00
(3)	Jimmy Bannon	950.00	475.00	285.00
(4)	Billy Barnie	950.00	475.00	285.00
(5)	Marty Bergen	950.00	475.00	285.00
(6)	Beville (Indianapolis)	950.00	475.00	285.00
(7)	Louis Bierbauer	950.00	475.00	285.00
(8)	Frank Bowerman	950.00	475.00	285.00
(9)	Ted Breitenstein	950.00	475.00	285.00
(10)	Herbert Briggs	950.00	475.00	285.00
(11)	Richard Brown	950.00	475.00	285.00
(12)	Eddie Burk (Burke)	950.00	475.00	285.00
(13)	Jesse Burkett	3,000	1,200	725.00
(14)	William Clark (Clarke)	950.00	475.00	285.00
(15)	Jack Clements	950.00	475.00	285.00
(16)	Jimmy Collins	2,600	1,200	725.00
(17)	Tommy Corcoran	950.00	475.00	285.00
(18)	Corkman (Indianapolis)	950.00	475.00	285.00
(19)	Lave Cross	950.00	475.00	285.00
(20)	Nig Cuppy	950.00	475.00	285.00
(21)	Bill Dahlen	950.00	475.00	285.00
(22)	Bill Dammon (Dammann)	950.00	475.00	285.00
(23)	Dan Daub	950.00	475.00	285.00
(24)	George Decker	950.00	475.00	285.00
(25)	Ed Delahanty	3,000	1,250	750.00
(26)	Cozy Dolan	950.00	475.00	285.00
(27)	Tim Donahue	950.00	475.00	285.00
(28)	Patsy Donovan	950.00	475.00	285.00
(30)	Donnelly (Cedar Rapids)	950.00	475.00	285.00
(31)	Hugh Duffy	2,600	1,200	725.00
(32)	Jack Dunn	950.00	475.00	285.00
(33)	Bones Ely	950.00	475.00	285.00
(34)	Buck Ewing	2,600	1,200	725.00
(35)	Fields (Buffalo)	950.00	475.00	285.00
(36)	Tim Flood	950.00	475.00	285.00
(37)	Foreman (Indianapolis)	950.00	475.00	285.00
(38)	Charlie Ganzel	950.00	475.00	285.00
(39)	Jot Goar (Pittsburgh)	950.00	475.00	285.00
(40)	Jot Goar (Indianapolis)	950.00	475.00	285.00
(41)	Gray (Indianapolis)	950.00	475.00	285.00
(42)	Mike Griffin	950.00	475.00	285.00
(43)	Clark Griffith	2,400	1,200	725.00
(44)	Billy Hamilton	2,500	1,250	750.00
(45)	Bill Hart	950.00	475.00	285.00
(46)	Charles Hastings	950.00	475.00	285.00
(47)	Pink Hawley	950.00	475.00	285.00
(48)	B. Hill (Cedar Rapids)	950.00	475.00	285.00
(49)	Bill Hoffer	950.00	475.00	285.00
(51)	Bug Holliday	950.00	475.00	285.00
(52)	Horton (Baltimore)	950.00	475.00	285.00
(53)	Dummy Hoy	2,000	1,000	600.00
(54)	Jim Hughey	950.00	475.00	285.00
(55)	Charlie Irwin	950.00	475.00	285.00
(56)	Hughie Jennings	2,400	1,200	725.00
(57)	Willie Keeler	2,400	1,200	725.00
(58)	Kennedy (Cedar Rapids)	950.00	475.00	285.00
(59)	Frank Killen	950.00	475.00	285.00
(60)	Malachi Kittredge	950.00	475.00	285.00
(61)	Candy LaChance	950.00	475.00	285.00
(62)	Bill Lange	950.00	475.00	285.00
(63)	Herman Long	950.00	475.00	285.00
(64)	Bobby Lowe	950.00	475.00	285.00
(65)	Denny Lyons	950.00	475.00	285.00
(66)	Connie Mack	3,000	1,250	750.00
(67)	Willard Mains	950.00	475.00	285.00
(68)	Barry McCormick	950.00	475.00	285.00
(69)	Chippy McGarr	950.00	475.00	285.00
(70)	John McGraw	950.00	475.00	285.00
(71)	Sadie McMann (McMahon)	950.00	475.00	285.00
(72)	Bid McPhee	3,000	1,500	900.00
(73)	Bill Merritt	950.00	475.00	285.00
(74)	Dusty Miller	950.00	475.00	285.00
(75)	Motz (Indianapolis)	950.00	475.00	285.00
(76)	Kid Nichols	2,500	1,250	750.00
(77)	Jack O'Connor	950.00	475.00	285.00
(78)	John Pappaulan (Pappalau) (pitcher, not R.F.)	950.00	475.00	285.00
(79)	Heinie Peitz	950.00	475.00	285.00
(80)	Phillips (Indianapolis)	950.00	475.00	285.00
(81)	Arlie Pond	950.00	475.00	285.00
(82)	Jack Powell	950.00	475.00	285.00
(83)	Bill Reidy	950.00	475.00	285.00
(84)	Heinie Reitz	950.00	475.00	285.00
(85)	Billy Rhines	950.00	475.00	285.00
(86)	Claude Richie (Ritchey)	950.00	475.00	285.00
(87)	Rowe (Buffalo)	950.00	475.00	285.00
(88)	John Ryan	950.00	475.00	285.00
(89)	Pop Schreiver (Schriver)	950.00	475.00	285.00
(90)	Bill Shindle	950.00	475.00	285.00
(91)	Broadway Aleck Smith	950.00	475.00	285.00
(92)	Elmer Smith (Pittsburgh)	950.00	475.00	285.00
(93)	Germany Smith	950.00	475.00	285.00
(94)	Louis Sockalexis (Value Undetermined)			
(95)	Speer (Milwaukee)	950.00	475.00	285.00
(96)	Jake Stenzel	950.00	475.00	285.00
(97)	Joe Sugden	950.00	475.00	285.00
(98)	Jim Sullivan	950.00	475.00	285.00
(99)	Patsy Tebeau	950.00	475.00	285.00
(100)	Fred Tenney	950.00	475.00	285.00
(101)	Tucker (Boston)	950.00	475.00	285.00
(102)	Urquhart (Buffalo)	950.00	475.00	285.00
(103)	Farmer Vaughn	950.00	475.00	285.00
(104)	Bobby Wallace	2,400	1,200	725.00
(105)	Watkins (Indianapolis)	950.00	475.00	285.00
(106)	Weaver (Milwaukee)	950.00	475.00	285.00
(107)	Wood (Indianapolis)	950.00	475.00	285.00
(108)	Cy Young	4,000	2,000	1,200
(109)	Chief Zimmer	1,150	575.00	345.00
(110)	1897 Brooklyn Team	1,150	575.00	345.00
(111)	1897 Buffalo Team	1,150	575.00	345.00
(112)	1897 Indianapolis Team	1,150	575.00	345.00
(113)	1897 Pittsburgh Team	1,150	575.00	345.00
(114)	1897 Toronto Team	1,150	575.00	345.00

1958 Roy Campanella Career Summary Card

This card was probably produced to allow Campy to respond to fan mail following his career-ending auto wreck in 1957. The 3-1/8" x 5" card is printed in black-and-white on thin semi-gloss cardboard. Front has a portrait photo and facsimile autograph, with a white stripe at top and bottom. The back has a career statistical summary, apparently taken from a contemporary Baseball Register.

	NM	EX	VG
Roy Campanella	20.00	10.00	6.00

1974 Capital Publishing Co.

This ambitious collectors issue offered more than 100 cards of "old-timers" in an attractive 4-1/8" x 5-1/4" format. Card fronts have black-and-white photos with white borders all-around. Backs have player identification, biographical data and major league stats.

		NM	EX	VG
Complete Set (104):		200.00	100.00	60.00
Common Player:		6.00	3.00	1.75
1	Babe Ruth	15.00	7.50	4.50
2	Lou Gehrig	10.00	5.00	3.00
3	Ty Cobb	9.00	4.50	2.75
4	Jackie Robinson	7.50	3.75	2.25
5	Roger Connor	6.00	3.00	1.75
6	Harry Heilmann	6.00	3.00	1.75
7	Clark Griffith	6.00	3.00	1.75
8	Ed Walsh	6.00	3.00	1.75
9	Hugh Duffy	6.00	3.00	1.75
10	Russ Christopher	6.00	3.00	1.75
11	Snuffy Stirnweiss	6.00	3.00	1.75
12	Willie Keeler	6.00	3.00	1.75
13	Buck Ewing	6.00	3.00	1.75
14	Tony Lazzeri	6.00	3.00	1.75
15	King Kelly	6.00	3.00	1.75
16	Jimmy McAleer	6.00	3.00	1.75
17	Frank Chance	6.00	3.00	1.75
18	Sam Zoldak	6.00	3.00	1.75
19	Christy Mathewson	7.50	3.75	2.25
20	Eddie Collins	6.00	3.00	1.75
21	Cap Anson	6.00	3.00	1.75
22	Steve Evans	6.00	3.00	1.75
23	Mordecai Brown	6.00	3.00	1.75
24	Don Black	6.00	3.00	1.75
25	Home Run Baker	6.00	3.00	1.75
26	Jack Chesbro	6.00	3.00	1.75
27	Gil Hodges	6.00	3.00	1.75
28	Dan Brouthers	6.00	3.00	1.75
29	Don Hoak	6.00	3.00	1.75
30	Herb Pennock	6.00	3.00	1.75
31	Vern Stephens	6.00	3.00	1.75
32	Cy Young	7.50	3.75	2.25
33	Ed Cicotte	7.50	3.75	2.25
34	Sam Jones	6.00	3.00	1.75
35	Ed Waitkus	6.00	3.00	1.75
36	Roger Bresnahan	6.00	3.00	1.75
37	Fred Merkle	6.00	3.00	1.75
38	Ed Delehanty (Delahanty)	6.00	3.00	1.75
39	Tris Speaker	6.00	3.00	1.75
40	Fred Clarke	6.00	3.00	1.75
41	Johnny Evers	6.00	3.00	1.75
42	Mickey Cochrane	6.00	3.00	1.75
43	Nap Lajoie	6.00	3.00	1.75
44	Charles Comiskey	6.00	3.00	1.75
45	Sam Crawford	6.00	3.00	1.75
46	Ban Johnson	6.00	3.00	1.75
47	Ray Schalk	6.00	3.00	1.75
48	Pat Moran	6.00	3.00	1.75
49	Walt Judnich	6.00	3.00	1.75
50	Bill Killefer	6.00	3.00	1.75
51	Jimmie Foxx	6.00	3.00	1.75
52	Red Rolfe	6.00	3.00	1.75
53	Howie Pollett	6.00	3.00	1.75
54	Wally Pipp	6.00	3.00	1.75
55	Chief Bender	6.00	3.00	1.75
56	Connie Mack	6.00	3.00	1.75
57	Bump Hadley	6.00	3.00	1.75
58	Al Simmons	6.00	3.00	1.75
59	Hughie Jennings	6.00	3.00	1.75
60	Johnny Allen	6.00	3.00	1.75
61	Fred Snodgrass	6.00	3.00	1.75
62	Heinie Manush	6.00	3.00	1.75
63	Dazzy Vance	6.00	3.00	1.75
64	George Sisler	6.00	3.00	1.75
65	Jim Bottomley	6.00	3.00	1.75
66	Ray Chapman	6.00	3.00	1.75
67	Hal Chase	6.00	3.00	1.75
68	Jack Barry	6.00	3.00	1.75
69	George Burns	6.00	3.00	1.75
70	Jim Barrett	6.00	3.00	1.75
71	Grover Alexander	6.00	3.00	1.75
72	Elmer Flick	6.00	3.00	1.75
73	Jake Flowers	6.00	3.00	1.75
74	Al Orth	6.00	3.00	1.75
75	Cliff Aberson	6.00	3.00	1.75
76	Moe Berg	7.50	3.75	2.25
77	Bill Bradley	6.00	3.00	1.75
78	Max Bishop	6.00	3.00	1.75
79	Jimmy Austin	6.00	3.00	1.75
80	Beals Becker	6.00	3.00	1.75
81	Jack Clements	6.00	3.00	1.75
82	Cy Blanton	6.00	3.00	1.75
83	Garland Braxton	6.00	3.00	1.75
84	Red Ames	6.00	3.00	1.75
85	Hippo Vaughn	6.00	3.00	1.75
86	Ray Caldwell	6.00	3.00	1.75
87	Clint Brown	6.00	3.00	1.75
88	Joe Jackson	15.00	7.50	4.50
89	Pete Appleton	6.00	3.00	1.75
90	Ed Brandt	6.00	3.00	1.75
91	Walter Johnson	7.50	3.75	2.25
92	Dizzy Dean	6.00	3.00	1.75
93	Nick Altrock	6.00	3.00	1.75
94	Buck Weaver	7.50	3.75	2.25
95	George Blaeholder	6.00	3.00	1.75
96	Jim Bagby	6.00	3.00	1.75
97	Ted Blankenship	6.00	3.00	1.75
98	Babe Adams	6.00	3.00	1.75
99	Lefty Williams	7.50	3.75	2.25
100	Tommy Bridges	6.00	3.00	1.75
101	Rube Benton	6.00	3.00	1.75
102	Unknown	6.00	3.00	1.75
103	Max Butcher	6.00	3.00	1.75
104	Chick Gandil	7.50	3.75	2.25

1945-46 Caramelo Deportivo Cuban League

One of the better-known of Cuba's baseball card issues is the 100-card set issued by Caramelo Deportivo (Sporting Caramels) covering the 1945-46 Cuban winter league season. Printed in black-and-white on very thin 1-7/8" x 2-5/8" paper, the cards were intended to be pasted into an album issued for the purpose. Fronts have a card number, but no player identification; backs have the player's name, a few biographical and career details and an ad for the issuer, in as many as three different configurations. Many former and future Major Leaguers and stars of the U.S. Negro Leagues will be found on this checklist; sometimes providing the only cards issued contemporary with their playing careers.

		NM	EX	VG
Complete Set, No Reyes (99):		6,500	3,250	1,950
Common Player:		25.00	12.50	7.50
Album:		200.00	100.00	60.00
1	Caramelo Deportivo Title Card	7.50	3.75	2.25
2	Action scene	12.50	6.25	3.75
3	Amado Maestri/Umpire	25.00	12.50	7.50
4	Bernardino Rodriguez/Umpire	25.00	12.50	7.50
5	Quico Magrinat/Umpire	25.00	12.50	7.50
6	Cuco Conder/Announcer	25.00	12.50	7.50
7	Marianao Team Banner	10.00	5.00	3.00
8	Armando Marsans	75.00	37.50	22.00
9	Jose Fernandez	25.00	12.50	7.50
10	Jose Luis Colas	25.00	12.50	7.50
11	"Charlotio" Orta (Charolito)	25.00	12.50	7.50
12	Barney Serrell	50.00	25.00	15.00
13	Claro Duany	30.00	15.00	9.00
14	Antonio Castanos	25.00	12.50	7.50
15	Virgilio Arteaga	25.00	12.50	7.50
16	Gilberto Valdivia	25.00	12.50	7.50
17	Jugo Cabrera	25.00	12.50	7.50
18	Lazaro Salazar	75.00	37.50	22.00
19	Julio Moreno	25.00	12.50	7.50
20	Oliverio Ortiz	25.00	12.50	7.50
21	Lou Knerr	25.00	12.50	7.50
22	Francisco Campos	25.00	12.50	7.50
23	Red Adams	25.00	12.50	7.50
24	Sandalio Consuegra	25.00	12.50	7.50
25	Ray Dandridge	800.00	400.00	240.00
26	Booker McDaniels	40.00	20.00	12.00
27	Orestes Minoso	675.00	335.00	200.00
28	Daniel Parra	25.00	12.50	7.50
29	Roberto Estalella	25.00	12.50	7.50
30	Raymond Brown	2,150	1,100	650.00
31	Havana Team Banner	10.00	5.00	3.00
32	Miguel Gonzalez	40.00	20.00	12.00
33	Julio Rojo	25.00	12.50	7.50
34	Herberto Blanco	25.00	12.50	7.50
35	Pedro Formenthal	30.00	15.00	9.00
36	Rene Monteagudo	25.00	12.50	7.50
37	Carlos Blanco	25.00	12.50	7.50
38	Salvador Hernandez	25.00	12.50	7.50
39	Rogelio Linares	25.00	12.50	7.50
40	Antonio Ordenana	25.00	12.50	7.50
41	Pedro Jiminez	25.00	12.50	7.50
42	Charley Kaiser	25.00	12.50	7.50
43	Manuel "Cocaina" Garcia	80.00	40.00	24.00
44	Sagua Hernandez	25.00	12.50	7.50
45	Lou Klein	25.00	12.50	7.50
46	Manuel Hidalgo	25.00	12.50	7.50
47	Dick Sisler	35.00	17.50	10.00
48	Jim Rebel	25.00	12.50	7.50
49	Raul Navarro	25.00	12.50	7.50
50	Pedero Medina	25.00	12.50	7.50
51	Charlie (Terries) McDuffie	75.00	37.50	22.00
52	Fred Martin	25.00	12.50	7.50
53	Julian Acosta	25.00	12.50	7.50
54	Cienfuegos Team Banner	10.00	5.00	3.00
55	Adolfo Luque	125.00	62.00	37.00
56	Jose Ramos	25.00	12.50	7.50
57	Conrado Perez	25.00	12.50	7.50
58	Antonio Rodriguez	25.00	12.50	7.50
59	Alejandro Crespo	30.00	15.00	9.00
60	Roland Gladu	25.00	12.50	7.50
61	Pedro Pages	25.00	12.50	7.50
62	Silvio Garcia	80.00	40.00	24.00
63	Carlos Colas	25.00	12.50	7.50
64	Salvatore Maglie	125.00	60.00	35.00
65	Martin Dihigo	1,250	625.00	375.00
66	Luis Tiant Sr.	185.00	90.00	55.00
67	Jim Roy	25.00	12.50	7.50
68	Ramon Roger	25.00	12.50	7.50
69	Adrian Zabala	25.00	12.50	7.50
70	Armando Gallart	25.00	12.50	7.50
71	Jose Zardon	25.00	12.50	7.50
72	Ray Berres	25.00	12.50	7.50
73	Napoleon Reyes/SP	1,500	750.00	450.00
74	Jose Gomez	25.00	12.50	7.50
75	Loevigildo Xiques	25.00	12.50	7.50
76	Almendares Team Banner	10.00	5.00	3.00
77	Reinaldo Coreiro	25.00	12.50	7.50
78	Bartalo Portaundo (Bartolo Portuondo)	25.00	12.50	7.50
79	Jacinto Roque	25.00	12.50	7.50
80	Hector Arago	25.00	12.50	7.50
81	Gilberto Torres	30.00	15.00	9.00
82	Roberto Ortiz	30.00	15.00	9.00
83	Hector Rodriguez	25.00	12.50	7.50
84	Chifian Clark	40.00	20.00	12.00
85	Fermin Guerra	30.00	15.00	9.00
86	Jorge Comellas	25.00	12.50	7.50
87	Regino Otero	25.00	12.50	7.50
88	Tomas de la Cruz	30.00	15.00	9.00
89	Mario Diaz	25.00	12.50	7.50
90	Luis Aloma	25.00	12.50	7.50
91	Lloyd Davenport	40.00	20.00	12.00
92	Agapito Mayor	25.00	12.50	7.50
93	Ramon Bragana	100.00	50.00	30.00
94	Avelino Canizares	25.00	12.50	7.50
95	Santiago Ulrich	25.00	12.50	7.50
96	Beto Avila	50.00	25.00	15.00
97	Santos Amaro	30.00	15.00	9.00
98	Andres Fleitas	25.00	12.50	7.50
99	Limonar Martinez	25.00	12.50	7.50
100	Juan Montero	25.00	12.50	7.50

1946-47 Caramelo Deportivo Cuban League

Following its 100-card issue of the previous Cuban winter league season, this candy company issued a 185-card set for 1946-47. Besides more players, extra cards included banners, stadiums, managers, umpires and sportscasters. Printed on paper stock and intended to be pasted into an accompanying album, the cards measure about 1-7/8" x 2-1/2", though inconsistent cutting creates both over- and under-sized cards. Fronts have black-and-white player photos and a circle with a card number. Photos are often fuzzy or dark, indicative of their having been picked up from another source, such as a newspaper. Backs repeat the card number and have the player name at top, along with his Cuban League and, frequently, U.S. professional affiliation. Some 60 of the players in the set played in the segregated Negro Leagues of the era. A large ad for the candy and its sellers appear at bottom of the back. Because of the thin stock and placement in albums, these cards are usually found creased and/or with back damage.

		NM	EX	VG
Complete Set (185):		12,000	6,000	3,600
Common Player:		50.00	25.00	15.00
Album:		250.00	125.00	75.00
1	Introduction card	25.00	12.50	7.50
2	New El Cerro Stadium	25.00	12.50	7.50
3	Stadium La Tropical	25.00	12.50	7.50
4	Maestri, Bernardino and Magrinat (El Cerro umpires.)	50.00	25.00	15.00
5	La Tropical umpires (Atan, Lopez, Vidal and Morales)	50.00	25.00	15.00
6	Cuco Conde/Announcer	25.00	12.50	7.50
7	Cienfuegos Team Banner	25.00	12.50	7.50
8	Martin Dihigo	750.00	375.00	225.00
9a	Napoleon Reyes	60.00	30.00	18.00
9b	Napoleon Reyes	60.00	30.00	18.00

10	Adrian Zabala	50.00	25.00	15.00
11	Roland Gladu	50.00	25.00	15.00
12	Alejandro Crespo	100.00	50.00	30.00
13	Alejandro Carrasquel	50.00	25.00	15.00
14	Napoleon Heredia	50.00	25.00	15.00
15	Andres Mesa	50.00	25.00	15.00
16	Pedro Pages	50.00	25.00	15.00
17	Danny Gardella	50.00	25.00	15.00
18	Conrado Perez	50.00	25.00	15.00
19	Myron Hayworth	50.00	25.00	15.00
20	Pedro Miro	50.00	25.00	15.00
21	Guillermo Vargas	50.00	25.00	15.00
22	Hoot Gibson	50.00	25.00	15.00
23	Rafael Noble	55.00	27.50	16.50
24	Ramon Roger	50.00	25.00	15.00
25	Luis Arango	50.00	25.00	15.00
26	Roy Zimmerman	50.00	25.00	15.00
27	Luis Tiant Sr.	125.00	65.00	35.00
28	Jean Roy	55.00	27.50	16.50
29	Stanislov Bread	50.00	25.00	15.00
30	Walter Nothe	50.00	25.00	15.00
31	Vinicio Garcia	50.00	25.00	15.00
32	Dan (Max) Manning	200.00	100.00	60.00
33	Habana Lions Team Banner	25.00	12.50	7.50
34	Miguel A. Gonzalez	80.00	40.00	24.00
35	Pedro Formental	100.00	50.00	30.00
36	Ray Navarro	50.00	25.00	15.00
37	Pedro Jiminez	50.00	25.00	15.00
38	Rene Monteagudo	50.00	25.00	15.00
39	Salvador Hernandez	50.00	25.00	15.00
40	Hugh (Terris) Mc. Duffie	70.00	35.00	20.00
41	Herberto Blanco	50.00	25.00	15.00
42	Harry (Henry) Kimbro	130.00	65.00	40.00
43	Lloyd (Lennie) Pearson	180.00	90.00	55.00
44	W. Bell	55.00	27.50	16.50
45	Carlos Blanco	50.00	25.00	15.00
46	Hank Thompson	70.00	35.00	20.00
47	Manuel ("Cocaina") Garcia	150.00	75.00	45.00
48	Alberto Hernandez	50.00	25.00	15.00
49	Tony Ordenana	50.00	25.00	15.00
50	Lazaro Medina	50.00	25.00	15.00
51	Fred Martin	50.00	25.00	15.00
52	Eddie (Jim) Lamarque	150.00	75.00	45.00
53	Juan Montero	50.00	25.00	15.00
54	Lou Klein	50.00	25.00	15.00
55	Pablo Garcia	50.00	25.00	15.00
56	Julio Rojo	50.00	25.00	15.00
57	Almendares Team Banner	25.00	12.50	7.50
58	Adolfo Luque	90.00	45.00	27.50
59	Cheo Ramos	50.00	25.00	15.00
60	Avelino Canizares	50.00	25.00	15.00
61	George Hausmann	50.00	25.00	15.00
62	Homero Ariosa	50.00	25.00	15.00
63	Santos Amaro	50.00	25.00	15.00
64	Hank Robinson	60.00	30.00	18.00
65	Lazaro Salazar	200.00	100.00	60.00
66	Andres Fleitas	50.00	25.00	15.00
67	Hector Rodriguez	80.00	40.00	24.00
68	Jorge Comellas	50.00	25.00	15.00
69	Lloyd Davenport	130.00	65.00	40.00
70	Tomas de la Cruz	50.00	25.00	15.00
71a	Roberto Ortiz	80.00	40.00	24.00
71b	Roberto Ortiz	50.00	25.00	15.00
72	Jess (Gentry) Jessup	130.00	65.00	40.00
73	Agapito Mayor	50.00	25.00	15.00
74	William	50.00	25.00	15.00
75	Santiago Ullrich	50.00	25.00	15.00
76	Coty Leal	50.00	25.00	15.00
77	Max Lanier	55.00	27.50	16.50
78	Buck O'Neill	800.00	400.00	240.00
79	Mario Ariosa	50.00	25.00	15.00
80	Lefty Gaines	130.00	65.00	40.00
81	Marianao Team Banner	25.00	12.50	7.50
82	Armando Marsans	80.00	40.00	24.00
83	Antonio Castanos	50.00	25.00	15.00
84	Orestes Minoso	200.00	100.00	60.00
85	Murray Franklin	50.00	25.00	15.00
86	Roberto Estalella	50.00	25.00	15.00
87	A. Castro	50.00	25.00	15.00
88	Gilberto Valdivia	50.00	25.00	15.00
89	Baffeth (Lloyd "Pepper" Bassett)	130.00	65.00	40.00
90	Oliverio Ortiz	50.00	25.00	15.00
91	Francisco Campos	50.00	25.00	15.00
92	Sandalio Consuegra	65.00	32.50	20.00
93	Lorenzo Cabrera	50.00	25.00	15.00
94	Roberto Avila	80.00	40.00	24.00
95	Chanquilon Diaz	50.00	25.00	15.00
96	Pedro Orta	50.00	25.00	15.00
97	Cochihuila Valenzuela	50.00	25.00	15.00
98	Ramon Carneado	50.00	25.00	15.00
99	Aristonico Correoso	50.00	25.00	15.00
100	Daniel Doy	50.00	25.00	15.00
101	Joe Lindsay	50.00	25.00	15.00
102	Habana Reds Team Banner	25.00	12.50	7.50
103	Gilberto Torres	50.00	25.00	15.00
104	Oscar Rodriguez	50.00	25.00	15.00
105	Isidoro Leon	50.00	25.00	15.00
106	Julio Moreno	50.00	25.00	15.00
107	Chulungo del Monte	50.00	25.00	15.00
108	Len Hooker	100.00	50.00	30.00
109	Antonio Napoles	50.00	25.00	15.00
110	Orlando Suarez	50.00	25.00	15.00
111	Guillermo Monje	50.00	25.00	15.00
112	Isasio Gonzalez	50.00	25.00	15.00
113	Regino Otero	50.00	25.00	15.00
114	Angel Fleitas	50.00	25.00	15.00
115	Jorge Torres	50.00	25.00	15.00
116	Claro Duany	100.00	50.00	30.00
117	Charles Perez	50.00	25.00	15.00
118	Francisco Quicutis	50.00	25.00	15.00
119	Lazaro Bernal	50.00	25.00	15.00
120	Tommy Warren	50.00	25.00	15.00
121	Clarence Iott	55.00	27.00	16.50
122	P. Newcomb (Don Newcombe)	600.00	300.00	180.00
123	Gilberto Castillo	50.00	25.00	15.00
124	Matanzas Team Banner	25.00	12.50	7.50

125	Silvio Garcia	200.00	100.00	60.00
126	Bartolo Portuondo	50.00	25.00	15.00
127	Pedro Arango	50.00	25.00	15.00
128	Yuyo Acosta	50.00	25.00	15.00
129	Jose Cendan	50.00	25.00	15.00
130	Eddie Chandler	50.00	25.00	15.00
131	Rogelio Martinez	50.00	25.00	15.00
132	Atares Garcia	50.00	25.00	15.00
133	Manuel Godinez	50.00	25.00	15.00
134	John Williams	130.00	65.00	40.00
135	Emilio Cabrera	50.00	25.00	15.00
136	Barney Serrell	130.00	65.00	40.00
137	Armando Gallart	50.00	25.00	15.00
138	Ruben Garcia	50.00	25.00	15.00
139	Loevigildo Xiques	50.00	25.00	15.00
140	Chifian (Chiflan) Clark	130.00	65.00	40.00
141	Jacinto Roque	50.00	25.00	15.00
142	John (Johnny) Davis	150.00	75.00	45.00
143	Norman Wilson	50.00	25.00	15.00
144	Camaguey Team Banner	25.00	12.50	7.50
145	Antonio Rodriguez	50.00	25.00	15.00
146	Manuel Parrado	50.00	25.00	15.00
147	Leon Treadway	50.00	25.00	15.00
148	Amado Ibanez	50.00	25.00	15.00
149	Teodoro Oxamendi	50.00	25.00	15.00
150	Adolfo Cabrera	50.00	25.00	15.00
151	Oscar Garmendia	50.00	25.00	15.00
152	Hector Arago	50.00	25.00	15.00
153	Evelio Martinez	50.00	25.00	15.00
154	Raquel Antunez	50.00	25.00	15.00
155	Lino Donoso	50.00	25.00	15.00
156	Eliecer Alvarez	50.00	25.00	15.00
157	George Brown	50.00	25.00	15.00
158	Roberto Johnson	50.00	25.00	15.00
159	Rafael Franco	50.00	25.00	15.00
160	Miguel A. Carmona	50.00	25.00	15.00
161	Lilo Fano	50.00	25.00	15.00
162	Orestes Pereda	50.00	25.00	15.00
163	Pedro Diaz	50.00	25.00	15.00
164	Oriente Team Banner	25.00	12.50	7.50
165	Fermin Guerra	50.00	25.00	15.00
166	Jose M. Fernandez	50.00	25.00	15.00
167	Cando Lopez	50.00	25.00	15.00
168	Conrado Marrero	60.00	30.00	18.00
169	Oscar del Calvo	50.00	25.00	15.00
170	Booker McDaniels	150.00	75.00	45.00
171	Rafael Rivas	50.00	25.00	15.00
172	Daniel Parra	50.00	25.00	15.00
173	L. Holleman	50.00	25.00	15.00
174	Rogelio Valdes	50.00	25.00	15.00
175	Raymond Dandridge	950.00	475.00	285.00
176	Manuel Hidalgo	50.00	25.00	15.00
177	Miguel Lastra	50.00	25.00	15.00
178	Luis Minsal	50.00	25.00	15.00
179	Andres Vazquez	50.00	25.00	15.00
180	Jose A. Zardon	50.00	25.00	15.00
181	Jose Luis Colas	50.00	25.00	15.00
182	Rogelio Linares	50.00	25.00	15.00
183	Mario Diaz	50.00	25.00	15.00
184	R. Verdes	50.00	25.00	15.00
185	Indio Jiminez	50.00	25.00	15.00

1948-1949 Caramelos El Indio

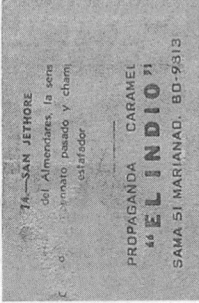

Perhaps the rarest of the late-1940s Cuban caramel cards is this issue picturing members of the island's four-team professional winter league. Measuring 1-5/8" x 2-7/16", the cards are printed in black-and-white on thick paper stock. Front photos are bordered in black with no player identification. On back at top is a card number and player name, along with a few words about the player. At bottom is an ad for the sponsor. Many American players, including Negro Leaguers, are included in the issue. The set is arranged alphabetically by team. An album was available in which to mount the cards. As with most contemporary Cuban issues, low-grade survivors are the norm, with Good condition being about the best seen, making the pricing here somewhat hypothetical.

		NM	EX	VG
Common Player:		200.00	100.00	60.00
Album:		300.00	150.00	90.00
1	Fermin Guerra	275.00	135.00	80.00
2	Rodolfo Fernandez	200.00	100.00	60.00
3	Reinaldo Cordeiro	200.00	100.00	60.00
4	Andres Fleitas	200.00	100.00	60.00
5	Tango Suarez	200.00	100.00	60.00
6	Ken Connors (Kevin "Chuck")	600.00	300.00	180.00
7	Rene Gonzalez	200.00	100.00	60.00
8	Jinny Bloodwrth (Jimmy Bloodworth)	275.00	135.00	80.00
9	Sojito Gallardo	200.00	100.00	60.00
10	Hector Rodriguez	275.00	135.00	80.00
11	Avelino Canizares	200.00	100.00	60.00

12	Gilberto Torres	200.00	100.00	60.00
13	Monte Yrving (Monte Irvin)	1,600	800.00	475.00
14	San Jethore (Sam Jethroe)	325.00	160.00	100.00
15	Al Gionfrido (Gionfriddo)	275.00	135.00	80.00
16	Santos Amaro	275.00	135.00	80.00
17	Hiram Gonzalez	200.00	100.00	60.00
18	Conrado Marrero	275.00	135.00	80.00
19	Jorge Comellas	200.00	100.00	60.00
20	Agapito Mayor	200.00	100.00	60.00
21	Octavio Rubert	200.00	100.00	60.00
22	Tata Solis	200.00	100.00	60.00
23	Morris Martin	275.00	135.00	80.00
24	Cyde (Clyde) King	275.00	135.00	80.00
25	Miguel Angel Gonzalez	325.00	160.00	100.00
26	Joseito Rodriguez	200.00	100.00	60.00
27	Sungo Carreras	200.00	100.00	60.00
28	Hank Anderson	275.00	135.00	80.00
29	Emilio Cabrera	200.00	100.00	60.00
30	Lennox Pearson	325.00	160.00	100.00
31	Herberto Blanco	200.00	100.00	60.00
32	Pablo Garcia	200.00	100.00	60.00
33	Chino Hidalgo	200.00	100.00	60.00
34	Amado Ibanez	200.00	100.00	60.00
35	Carlos Blanco	200.00	100.00	60.00
36	Henry Thompson	275.00	135.00	80.00
37	Henry Kimbro	275.00	135.00	80.00
38	Pedro Formental	275.00	135.00	80.00
39	Saguita Hernandez	200.00	100.00	60.00
40	Francisco Quicutis	200.00	100.00	60.00
41	George Stancer (Stanceu)	275.00	135.00	80.00
42	Jim Yockin (Yochim)	275.00	135.00	80.00
43	Tony Lorenzo	200.00	100.00	60.00
44	Rafael Rivas	200.00	100.00	60.00
45	Jose Cerdan	200.00	100.00	60.00
46	Cocaina Garcia	325.00	160.00	100.00
47	Bill Schuster	275.00	135.00	80.00
48	Oliverio Ortiz	200.00	100.00	60.00
49	Salvador Hernandez	200.00	100.00	60.00
50	Oscar Rodriguez	200.00	100.00	60.00
51	Julio Rojo	200.00	100.00	60.00
52	Ray Noble	250.00	125.00	75.00
53	Regino Otero	200.00	100.00	60.00
54	Peter Coscarat (Coscarart)	275.00	135.00	80.00
55	Jimmy Redmond	275.00	135.00	80.00
56	Mc. Quillan (Glenn McQuillen)	275.00	135.00	80.00
57	Stan Bread	275.00	135.00	80.00
58	Armando Gallart	200.00	100.00	60.00
59	Angel Fleitas	200.00	100.00	60.00
60	Pedro Pages	200.00	100.00	60.00
61	Alejandro Crespo	275.00	135.00	80.00
62	Jose Luis Colas	200.00	100.00	60.00
63	Conrado Perez	200.00	100.00	60.00
64	Coaker Triplett (Triplett)	275.00	135.00	80.00
65	Pedro Dunabeitia	200.00	100.00	60.00
66	Maik Sukont (Max Surkont)	275.00	135.00	80.00
67	Max Mamming (Manning)	525.00	260.00	150.00
68	Jom Mikan	275.00	135.00	80.00
69	Herman Bess (Besse)	275.00	135.00	80.00
70	Wito (Luis) Aloma	275.00	135.00	80.00
71	Raul Lopez	200.00	100.00	60.00
72	Silvio Garcia	300.00	150.00	90.00
73	Gilberto Torres	200.00	100.00	60.00
74	Pipo de la Noval	200.00	100.00	60.00
75	Jose Maria Fernandez	200.00	100.00	60.00
76	Vitico Munoz	200.00	100.00	60.00
77	Luis Suarez	200.00	100.00	60.00
78	Wilfredo Salas	200.00	100.00	60.00
79	Julio Moreno	200.00	100.00	60.00
80	Bill Harrington	275.00	135.00	80.00
81	Oreste (Minnie) Minoso	525.00	260.00	150.00
82	Clarence Hicks	275.00	135.00	80.00
83	Pedro Ballester	200.00	100.00	60.00
84	Jose Hawerton	200.00	100.00	60.00
85	Ramon Roger	200.00	100.00	60.00
86	M Arenciba	200.00	100.00	60.00
87	Louis Kahn	275.00	135.00	80.00
88	Mario Diaz	200.00	100.00	60.00
89	Chiquitin Cabrera	200.00	100.00	60.00
90	Beto Avila	200.00	100.00	60.00
91	Cisco Campos	200.00	100.00	60.00
92	Johnny Simmons	275.00	135.00	80.00
93	Claro Duany	275.00	135.00	80.00
94	Clyde (Dave) Barnhill	800.00	400.00	240.00
95	Clarence Beer	275.00	135.00	80.00
96	Joaquin Gutierrez	200.00	100.00	60.00

1955 Carling Beer Cleveland Indians

Apparently the first of a line of premium photos which extended into the early 1960s. Measuring 8-1/2" x 12" and printed in black-and-white on semi-gloss thin card stock, these photocards are blank-backed. The

1955 Carling photos are identifiable from the 1956 issue, with which they share a "DBL" prefix to the card number in the lower-right corner, by the phrase "Great Champions" appearing just under the player photo.

	NM	EX	VG
Complete Set (11):	750.00	375.00	225.00
Common Player:	60.00	30.00	18.00
96A Ralph Kiner	110.00	55.00	35.00
96Ba Larry Doby	100.00	50.00	30.00
96Bb Herb Score	75.00	37.50	22.50
96C Al Rosen	75.00	37.50	22.50
96D Mike Garcia	60.00	30.00	18.00
96E Early Wynn	90.00	45.00	27.50
96F Bob Feller	150.00	75.00	45.00
96G Jim Hegan	60.00	30.00	18.00
96H George Strickland	60.00	30.00	18.00
96K Bob Lemon	90.00	45.00	27.50
96L Art Houtteman	60.00	30.00	18.00

1956 Carling Beer Cleveland Indians

This set was sponsored by Carling Black Label Beer. The oversized (8-1/2" x 12") cards feature black-and-white posed photos with the player's name in a white strip and a Carling ad at the bottom of the card front. Backs are blank. Like the cards issued in 1955, the 1956 set carries a DBL 96 series indication in the lower-right corner and lists brewery locations as Cleveland, St. Louis and Belleville, Ill. Unlike the '55 photocards, however, the first line under the player photo on the 1956 issue is "Premium Quality." Cards numbered DBL 96I and DBL 96J are unknown.

	NM	EX	VG
Complete Set (10):	900.00	450.00	275.00
Common Player:	60.00	30.00	18.00
96A Al Smith	60.00	30.00	18.00
96B Herb Score	120.00	60.00	35.00
96C Al Rosen	90.00	45.00	27.50
96D Mike Garcia	60.00	30.00	18.00
96E Early Wynn	120.00	60.00	35.00
96F Bob Feller	200.00	100.00	60.00
96G Jim Hegan	60.00	30.00	18.00
96H George Strickland	60.00	30.00	18.00
96K Bob Lemon	120.00	60.00	35.00
96L Art Houtteman	60.00	30.00	18.00

1957 Carling Beer Cleveland Indians

The fact that Kerby Farrell managed the Indians only in 1957 pinpoints the year of issue for those Carling Beer photocards which carry a DBL 179 series number in the lower-right corner. Following the black-and-white, blank-backed 8-1/2" x 12" format of earlier issues, the 1957 Carlings list on the bottom line breweries at Cleveland; Frankenmuth, Mich.; Natick, Mass., and, Belleville, Ill. Cards numbered DBL 179I and DBL 179J are are currently unknown.

	NM	EX	VG
Complete Set (10):	900.00	450.00	275.00
Common Player:	60.00	30.00	18.00
179A Vic Wertz	60.00	30.00	18.00
179B Early Wynn	100.00	50.00	30.00
179C Herb Score	90.00	45.00	27.50
179D Bob Lemon	100.00	50.00	30.00

	NM	EX	VG
179E Ray Narleski	60.00	30.00	18.00
179F Jim Hegan	60.00	30.00	18.00
179G Bob Avila	60.00	30.00	18.00
179H Al Smith	60.00	30.00	18.00
179K Kerby Farrell	60.00	30.00	18.00
179L Rocky Colavito	300.00	150.00	90.00

1958 Carling Beer Cleveland Indians

Identical in format to earlier issues, the 1958 premium photos can be distinguished by the card number printed in the lower-right corner. Cards in the 1958 series have numbers which begin with a DBL 2 or DBL 217 prefix.

	NM	EX	VG
Complete Set (10):	725.00	360.00	215.00
Common Player:	60.00	30.00	18.00
2 Vic Wertz	60.00	30.00	18.00
217 Minnie Minoso	100.00	50.00	30.00
217B Gene Woodling	60.00	30.00	18.00
217C Russ Nixon	60.00	30.00	18.00
217D Bob Lemon	120.00	60.00	35.00
217E Bobby Bragan	60.00	30.00	18.00
217F Cal McLish	60.00	30.00	18.00
217G Rocky Colavito	150.00	75.00	45.00
217H Herb Score	100.00	50.00	30.00
217J Chico Carrasquel	60.00	30.00	18.00

1959 Carling Beer Cleveland Indians

The appearance of Billy Martin among Carling photocards labeled with a DBL 266 prefix fixes the year of issue to 1959, the fiery second baseman's only year with the Tribe. Once again the 8-1/2" x 12" black-and-white, blank-backed cards follow the format of previous issues. Breweries listed on the bottom of the 1959 Carlings are Cleveland; Atlanta; Frankenmuth, Mich.; Natick, Mass.; Belleville, Ill., and, Tacoma, Wash.

	NM	EX	VG
Complete Set (6):	600.00	300.00	180.00
Common Player:	75.00	37.50	22.50
266A Vic Power	75.00	37.50	22.50
266B Minnie Minoso	100.00	50.00	30.00
266C Herb Score	100.00	50.00	30.00
266D Rocky Colavito	150.00	75.00	45.00
266E Jimmy Piersall	100.00	50.00	30.00
266F Billy Martin	150.00	75.00	45.00

1961 Carling Beer Cleveland Indians

Totally different player selection and the use of an LB prefix to the number in the lower-right corner define the 1961 issue from Carling Beer. Otherwise the photocards share the same 8-1/2" x 12" black-and-white format with earlier issues. The blank-backed cards of the 1961 issue list only a single brewery, Cleveland, at the bottom of the ad portion of the issues. The checklist here is arranged alphabetically. Cards numbered LB 420I and LB420J are unknown.

	NM	EX	VG
Complete Set (10):	600.00	300.00	180.00
Common Player:	60.00	30.00	18.00
420A Jimmy Piersall	100.00	50.00	30.00

	NM	EX	VG
420B Willie Kirkland	60.00	30.00	18.00
420C Johnny Antonelli	60.00	30.00	18.00
420D John Romano	60.00	30.00	18.00
420E Woodie Held	60.00	30.00	18.00
420F Tito Francona	60.00	30.00	18.00
420G Jim Perry	90.00	45.00	27.50
420H Bubba Phillips	60.00	30.00	18.00
420K John Temple	60.00	30.00	18.00
420L Vic Power	60.00	30.00	18.00

1909-11 Carolina Brights

Among the last of the T206 cards printed, those with Carolina Brights advertising on back are scarce and command a significant premium. The advertising on back is printed in black.

PREMIUMS:
Common Player: 5-6X
Typical Hall of Famer: 3-4X
(See T206 for checklist and base card values.)

1976 Carousel Discs

One of several regional sponsors of player disc sets in 1976 was the Michigan snack bar chain, Carousel. The sponsor's discs are unique in that they do not have pre-printed backs, but rather have a black rubber-stamp on the otherwise blank back. To date more than 20 such stamps have been seen, reportedly from New Jersey to Alaska. The discs are 3-3/8" diameter with a black-and-white player portrait photo in the center of the baseball design. A line of red stars is above, while the left and right panels feature one of several bright colors. Produced by Michael Schecter Associates under license from the Major League Baseball Players Association, the player photos have had uniform and cap logos removed. The unnumbered checklist here is presented in alphabetical order.

		NM	EX	VG
Complete Set (70):		35.00	17.50	10.00
Common Player:		2.00	1.00	.60
(1)	Henry Aaron	12.50	6.25	3.75
(2)	Johnny Bench	7.50	3.75	2.25
(3)	Vida Blue	2.00	1.00	.60
(4)	Larry Bowa	2.00	1.00	.60
(5)	Lou Brock	5.00	2.50	1.50
(6)	Jeff Burroughs	2.00	1.00	.60
(7)	John Candelaria	2.00	1.00	.60
(8)	Jose Cardenal	2.00	1.00	.60
(9)	Rod Carew	5.00	2.50	1.50
(10)	Steve Carlton	5.00	2.50	1.50
(11)	Dave Cash	2.00	1.00	.60
(12)	Cesar Cedeno	2.00	1.00	.60
(13)	Ron Cey	2.00	1.00	.60
(14)	Carlton Fisk	5.00	2.50	1.50
(15)	Tito Fuentes	2.00	1.00	.60
(16)	Steve Garvey	3.50	1.75	1.00
(17)	Ken Griffey	2.00	1.00	.60
(18)	Don Gullett	2.00	1.00	.60
(19)	Willie Horton	2.00	1.00	.60
(20)	Al Hrabosky	2.00	1.00	.60
(21)	Catfish Hunter	5.00	2.50	1.50
(22a)	Reggie Jackson (A's)	7.50	3.75	2.25
(22b)	Reggie Jackson (Orioles)	10.00	5.00	3.00
(23)	Randy Jones	2.00	1.00	.60
(24)	Jim Kaat	2.00	1.00	.60
(25)	Don Kessinger	2.00	1.00	.60
(26)	Dave Kingman	1.75	.90	.50
(27)	Jerry Koosman	2.00	1.00	.60
(28)	Mickey Lolich	2.00	1.00	.60
(29)	Greg Luzinski	2.00	1.00	.60
(30)	Fred Lynn	2.00	1.00	.60
(31)	Bill Madlock	2.00	1.00	.60

(32a)	Carlos May (White Sox)	3.00	1.50	.90
(32b)	Carlos May (Yankees)	2.00	1.00	.60
(33)	John Mayberry	2.00	1.00	.60
(34)	Bake McBride	2.00	1.00	.60
(35)	Doc Medich	2.00	1.00	.60
(36a)	Andy Messersmith (Dodgers)	3.00	1.50	.90
(36b)	Andy Messersmith (Braves)	2.00	1.00	.60
(37)	Rick Monday	2.00	1.00	.60
(38)	John Montefusco	2.00	1.00	.60
(39)	Jerry Morales	2.00	1.00	.60
(40)	Joe Morgan	5.00	2.50	1.50
(41)	Thurman Munson	4.50	2.25	1.25
(42)	Bobby Murcer	2.00	1.00	.60
(43)	Al Oliver	2.00	1.00	.60
(44)	Jim Palmer	5.00	2.50	1.50
(45)	Dave Parker	2.00	1.00	.60
(46)	Tony Perez	5.00	2.50	1.50
(47)	Jerry Reuss	2.00	1.00	.60
(48)	Brooks Robinson	6.00	3.00	1.75
(49)	Frank Robinson	6.00	3.00	1.75
(50)	Steve Rogers	2.00	1.00	.60
(51)	Pete Rose	12.50	6.25	3.75
(52)	Nolan Ryan	15.00	7.50	4.50
(53)	Manny Sanguillen	2.00	1.00	.60
(54)	Mike Schmidt	12.00	6.00	3.50
(55)	Tom Seaver	5.00	2.50	1.50
(56)	Ted Simmons	2.00	1.00	.60
(57)	Reggie Smith	2.00	1.00	.60
(58)	Willie Stargell	5.00	2.50	1.50
(59)	Rusty Staub	1.75	.90	.50
(60)	Rennie Stennett	2.00	1.00	.60
(61)	Don Sutton	5.00	2.50	1.50
(62a)	Andy Thornton (Cubs)	3.00	1.50	.90
(62b)	Andy Thornton (Expos)	2.00	1.00	.60
(63)	Luis Tiant	2.00	1.00	.60
(64)	Joe Torre	3.00	1.50	.90
(65)	Mike Tyson	2.00	1.00	.60
(66)	Bob Watson	2.00	1.00	.60
(67)	Wilbur Wood	2.00	1.00	.60
(68)	Jimmy Wynn	2.00	1.00	.60
(69)	Carl Yastrzemski	6.00	3.00	1.75
(70)	Richie Zisk	2.00	1.00	.60

1973 Norm Cash Day Card

As part of the Tiger Stadium festivities on August 12, this 7" x 5" color card was given to fans. Besides an action photo of the feared slugger, his facsimile autograph appears.

	NM	EX	VG
Norm Cash	12.50	6.25	3.75

1939 Centennial of Baseball Stamps

Part of the pagentry surrounding the 1939 centennial of the fabled beginnings of baseball was this set of player and history stamps and an accompanying 36-page album. The single stamps measure about 1-5/8" x 2-1/8" and are blank-backed. Stamps #1-13 deal with the game's history; most feature artwork by famed baseball artist and former major league pitcher Al Demaree. Stamps #14-25 feature photos of the game's greats in tombstone frames surrounded by colorful borders.

	NM	EX	VG
Complete Set, w/Album (25):	1,000	500.00	300.00
Common Player:	50.00	25.00	15.00
Common Historical:	20.00	10.00	6.00
Uncut Stamp Sheet (25):	1,000	500.00	300.00
Album:	80.00	40.00	25.00

1	Abner Doubleday	50.00	25.00	15.00
2	1849 Knickerbockers	50.00	25.00	15.00
3	Ball/bat Standards	20.00	10.00	6.00
4	1858 Brooklyn vs. New York Series	50.00	25.00	15.00
5	1859 Amherst vs. Williams Series	20.00	10.00	6.00
6	Curve Ball (Arthur Cummings)	50.00	25.00	15.00
7	First Admission Fee	20.00	10.00	6.00
8	First Professional Players	50.00	25.00	15.00
9	First No-Hitter (George Bradley)	50.00	25.00	15.00
10	Morgan G. Bulkeley	50.00	25.00	15.00
11	First World's Champions	50.00	25.00	15.00
12	Byron Bancroft (Ban) Johnson	50.00	25.00	15.00
13	First Night Game	20.00	10.00	6.00
14	Grover Cleveland Alexander	60.00	30.00	18.00
15	Tyrus Raymond Cobb	150.00	75.00	45.00
16	Eddie Collins	50.00	25.00	15.00
17	Wee Willie Keeler	50.00	25.00	15.00
18	Walter Perry Johnson	75.00	37.50	22.50
19	Napoleon (Larry) Lajoie	50.00	25.00	15.00
20	Christy Mathewson	75.00	37.50	22.50
21	George Herman (Babe) Ruth	300.00	150.00	90.00
22	George Sisler	50.00	25.00	15.00
23	Tristam E. (Tris) Speaker	60.00	30.00	18.00
24	Honus Wagner	100.00	50.00	30.00
25	Denton T. (Cy) Young	75.00	37.50	22.50

1952 Central National Bank of Cleveland

The scope of this issue is undetermined. It is possible a player card was given as a premium for deposits in the bank's "Baseball Savings Club." The cards are about 6-3/4" x 4-3/4", printed in dark blue on cream-colored stock with a blank back. Titled "OFFICIAL 'PLAYER-HISTORY' CARD," it features an action pose, facsimile signature, personal data, career summary and complete stats.

	NM	EX	VG
Common Player:	100.00	50.00	30.00
Early Wynn	200.00	100.00	60.00

1929 Certified's Ice Cream Pins

Unless or until further players are seen in this series, the date of issue will have to remain uncertain. Apparently given away by Wrigley Field's ice cream concessionaire, these 1" diameter pin-backs feature player portraits and typography in sepia tones lithographed on a white background.

	NM	EX	VG
Complete Set (5):	2,600	1,300	775.00
Common Player:	450.00	225.00	135.00
(1)	Joe Bush	450.00	225.00	135.00
(2)	Kiki Cuyler	600.00	300.00	180.00
(3)	Rogers Hornsby	725.00	360.00	215.00
(4)	Riggs Stephenson	450.00	225.00	135.00
(5)	Hack Wilson	600.00	300.00	180.00

1964 Challenge the Yankees Game

The 50 player cards in this set were part of a boxed dice baseball game produced by Hassenfeld Bros. of Pawtucket, R.I. Cards are approximately 4" x 5-1/2" and blank-backed, featuring a small black-and-white photo, a facsimile autograph and a few biographical details and stats. Player selection is virtually the same for the games issued in 1964 and 1965,

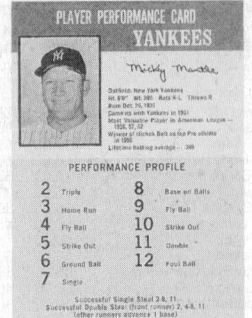

and the only way to distinguish cards from each year is to study the stats. Cards are unnumbered and are checklisted below in alphabetical order.

		NM	EX	VG
Complete Boxed Set:		1,200	600.00	350.00
Complete Card Set (50):		850.00	425.00	250.00
Common Player:		9.00	4.50	2.75
(1)	Hank Aaron	150.00	75.00	45.00
(2)	Yogi Berra	45.00	22.50	13.50
(3)	Johnny Blanchard	9.00	4.50	2.75
(4)	Jim Bouton	20.00	10.00	6.00
(5)	Clete Boyer	15.00	7.50	4.50
(6)	Marshall Bridges	9.00	4.50	2.75
(7)	Harry Bright	9.00	4.50	2.75
(8)	Tom Cheney	9.00	4.50	2.75
(9)	Del Crandall	9.00	4.50	2.75
(10)	Al Downing	9.00	4.50	2.75
(11)	Whitey Ford	40.00	20.00	12.00
(12)	Tito Francona	9.00	4.50	2.75
(13)	Jake Gibbs	9.00	4.50	2.75
(14)	Pedro Gonzalez	9.00	4.50	2.75
(15)	Dick Groat	9.00	4.50	2.75
(16)	Steve Hamilton	9.00	4.50	2.75
(17)	Elston Howard	20.00	10.00	6.00
(18)	Al Kaline	45.00	22.50	13.50
(19)	Tony Kubek	30.00	15.00	9.00
(20)	Phil Linz	9.00	4.50	2.75
(21)	Hector Lopez	9.00	4.50	2.75
(22)	Art Mahaffey	9.00	4.50	2.75
(23)	Frank Malzone	9.00	4.50	2.75
(24)	Mickey Mantle	250.00	125.00	75.00
(25)	Juan Marichal	30.00	15.00	9.00
(26)	Roger Maris	75.00	37.50	22.50
(27)	Eddie Mathews	30.00	15.00	9.00
(28)	Bill Mazeroski	30.00	15.00	9.00
(29)	Ken McBride	9.00	4.50	2.75
(30)	Willie McCovey	30.00	15.00	9.00
(31)	Tom Metcalf	9.00	4.50	2.75
(32)	Jim O'Toole	9.00	4.50	2.75
(33)	Milt Pappas	9.00	4.50	2.75
(34)	Joe Pepitone	15.00	7.50	4.50
(35)	Ron Perranoski	9.00	4.50	2.75
(36)	Johnny Podres	9.00	4.50	2.75
(37)	Dick Radatz	9.00	4.50	2.75
(38)	Hal Reniff	9.00	4.50	2.75
(39)	Bobby Richardson	30.00	15.00	9.00
(40)	Rich Rollins	9.00	4.50	2.75
(41)	Ron Santo	20.00	10.00	6.00
(42)	Moose Skowron	20.00	10.00	6.00
(43)	Duke Snider	30.00	15.00	9.00
(44)	Bill Stafford	9.00	4.50	2.75
(45)	Ralph Terry	9.00	4.50	2.75
(46)	Tom Tresh	15.00	7.50	4.50
(47)	Pete Ward	9.00	4.50	2.75
(48)	Carl Warwick	9.00	4.50	2.75
(49)	Stan Williams	9.00	4.50	2.75
(50)	Carl Yastrzemski	75.00	37.50	22.50

1965 Challenge the Yankees Game

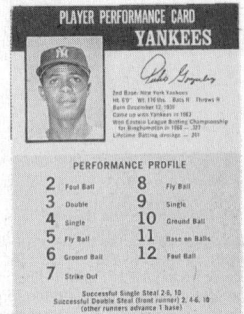

The player cards in this set were part of a boxed dice baseball game produced by Hassenfeld Bros. of Pawtucket, R.I. Cards are approximately 4" x 5-1/2" and blank-backed, featuring a small black-and-white photo, a facsimile autograph and a few biographical details and stats. Player selection is virtually the same for the games issued in 1964 and 1965, and the only way to distinguish cards from each year is to study the stats. Cards are unnumbered and are checklisted below in alphabetical order. The card of

Yankee pitcher Rollie Sheldon was apparently withdrawn following his May 3 trade to Kansas City and is scarcer than the rest of the set.

	NM	EX	VG
Complete Boxed Set:	1,500	750.00	450.00
Complete Card Set (50):	1,000	500.00	300.00
Common Player:	10.00	5.00	3.00
(1) Henry Aaron	125.00	62.00	37.00
(2) Johnny Blanchard	10.00	5.00	3.00
(3) Jim Bouton	12.50	6.25	3.75
(4) Clete Boyer	12.50	6.25	3.75
(5) Leon Carmel	10.00	5.00	3.00
(6) Joe Christopher	10.00	5.00	3.00
(7) Vic Davalillo	10.00	5.00	3.00
(8) Al Downing	10.00	5.00	3.00
(9) Whitey Ford	50.00	25.00	15.00
(10) Bill Freehan	10.00	5.00	3.00
(11) Jim Gentile	10.00	5.00	3.00
(12) Jake Gibbs	10.00	5.00	3.00
(13) Pedro Gonzalez	10.00	5.00	3.00
(14) Dick Groat	10.00	5.00	3.00
(15) Steve Hamilton	10.00	5.00	3.00
(16) Elston Howard	20.00	10.00	6.00
(17) Al Kaline	50.00	25.00	15.00
(18) Tony Kubek	25.00	12.50	7.50
(19) Phil Linz	10.00	5.00	3.00
(20) Don Lock	10.00	5.00	3.00
(21) Hector Lopez	10.00	5.00	3.00
(22) Art Mahaffey	10.00	5.00	3.00
(23) Frank Malzone	10.00	5.00	3.00
(24) Mickey Mantle	350.00	175.00	100.00
(25) Juan Marichal	40.00	20.00	12.00
(26) Roger Maris	90.00	45.00	27.00
(27) Eddie Mathews	50.00	25.00	15.00
(28) Bill Mazeroski	40.00	20.00	12.00
(29) Ken McBride	10.00	5.00	3.00
(30) Tim McCarver	15.00	7.50	4.50
(31) Willie McCovey	40.00	20.00	12.00
(32) Tom Metcalf	10.00	5.00	3.00
(33) Pete Mikkelsen	10.00	5.00	3.00
(34) Jim O'Toole	10.00	5.00	3.00
(35) Milt Pappas	10.00	5.00	3.00
(36) Joe Pepitone	12.50	6.25	3.75
(37) Ron Perranoski	10.00	5.00	3.00
(38) Johnny Podres	12.50	6.25	3.75
(39) Dick Radatz	10.00	5.00	3.00
(40) Pedro Ramos	10.00	5.00	3.00
(41) Hal Reniff	10.00	5.00	3.00
(42) Bobby Richardson	25.00	12.50	7.50
(43) Rich Rollins	10.00	5.00	3.00
(44) Ron Santo	20.00	10.00	6.00
(45) Rollie Sheldon/SP	75.00	37.00	22.00
(46) Bill Stafford	10.00	5.00	3.00
(47) Mel Stottlemyre	12.50	6.25	3.75
(48) Tom Tresh	12.50	6.25	3.75
(49) Pete Ward	10.00	5.00	3.00
(50) Carl Yaztrzemski	75.00	37.00	22.00

1947 Champ Hats Premiums

Dixie Walker says: "CHAMP HATS are sure winners in style and quality"

The attributed date is speculative, based on the limited known player selection. These 8" x 10" sepia photo cards have player pictures in uniform. In the wide bottom border is: "(Player Name) says:" and an ad message. Backs are blank.

	NM	EX	VG
Common Player:	250.00	125.00	75.00
(1) Mickey Vernon	250.00	125.00	75.00
(2) Dixie Walker	250.00	125.00	75.00

1957-1962 Charcoal Steak House Ted Kluszewski

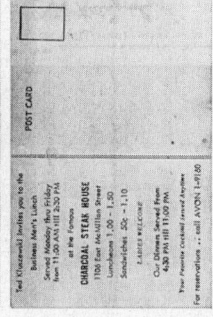

The true scope of this issue combined with the related Ted Kluszewski Steak House cards (see also) is not known. Based on cards showing Klu in Reds and Angels uniforms, it is possible examples may yet be seen in Pirates and White Sox uniforms. About 4" x 6", the black-and-white cards have a facsimile signature of Kluszewski on front. The back is in postcard style and advertises the Cincinnati restaurant he operated with Jack Stayin.

	NM	EX	VG
Ted Kluszewski (Angels)	75.00	40.00	25.00

1961 Chemstrand Iron-On Patches

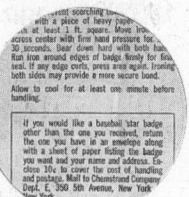

These colorful 2-1/2" diameter cloth patches were included with the purchase of a boy's sport shirt for a short period in 1961. The patches were issued in a cello package with instructions for ironing it onto the shirt. The package also offered the opportunity to trade the player patch for a different star.

	NM	EX	VG
Complete Set (9):	550.00	275.00	165.00
Common Player:	40.00	20.00	12.00
(1) Ernie Banks	75.00	37.50	22.00
(2) Yogi Berra	75.00	37.50	22.00
(3) Nellie Fox	60.00	30.00	18.00
(4) Dick Groat	40.00	20.00	12.00
(5) Al Kaline	60.00	30.00	18.00
(6) Harmon Killebrew	60.00	30.00	18.00
(7) Frank Malzone	40.00	20.00	12.00
(8) Willie Mays	115.00	55.00	35.00
(9) Warren Spahn	60.00	30.00	18.00

1976 Chevrolet Baseball Centennial Prints

In conjunction with the centennial of organized baseball, Chevrolet commissioned a set of paintings by artist Robert Thom which were reproduced in an 8-1/2" x 11" format and distributed by local auto dealers. Fronts carry the picture's title in the white border at bottom. Backs have a description of the picture on front.

	NM	EX	VG
Complete Set (4):	40.00	20.00	12.00
Common Print:	8.00	4.00	2.50
(1) The First Game/1876	8.00	4.00	2.50
(2) The Gashouse Gang (Pepper Martin, Bill Werber)	8.00	4.00	2.50
(3) The Mighty Babe (Babe Ruth)	15.00	7.50	4.50
(4) The Record Breaker (Hank Aaron)	12.50	6.25	3.75

1908 Chicago Cubs/ White Sox Postcards

The issuer of this postcard set is unknown. The only identification on the card is a dollar sign within a

shield which apears near the center on back, along with standard postcard indicia. Fronts of the 3-7/16" x 5-3/8" cards have black-and-white player photos on a gray background. A plain strip at bottom has the player's name on a top line; his position and team on a second line. The checklist presented here is probably not complete.

	NM	EX	VG
Complete Set, Cubs (11):	3,000	1,500	900.00
Complete Set, White Sox (9):	3,500	1,750	1,000
Common Player:	200.00	100.00	60.00
CUBS			
(1) Mordecai Brown	400.00	200.00	120.00
(2) Frank Chance	400.00	200.00	120.00
(3) Johnny Evers	400.00	200.00	120.00
(4) Solly Hoffman (Hofman)	200.00	100.00	60.00
(5) John Kling	200.00	100.00	60.00
(6) "Jack" Pfiester	200.00	100.00	60.00
(7) Edw. Reulbach	200.00	100.00	60.00
(8) James Sheckard	200.00	100.00	60.00
(9) Harry Steinfeldt	200.00	100.00	60.00
(10) Joe Tinker	400.00	200.00	120.00
(11) Chicago National League, Cubs. (Team photo)	500.00	250.00	150.00
WHITE SOX			
(1) "Nic" Altrock	400.00	200.00	120.00
(2) "Jakey" Atz	500.00	250.00	150.00
(3) Geo. Davis	600.00	300.00	180.00
(4) "Jiggs" Donahue	300.00	150.00	90.00
(5) "Pat" Dougherty	300.00	150.00	90.00
(6) "Eddie" Hahn	300.00	150.00	90.00
(7) Frank Isbell	300.00	150.00	90.00
(8) Fielder Jones	300.00	150.00	90.00
(9) "Ed" Walsh	650.00	325.00	195.00

1972 Chicago Cubs & Chicago White Sox Color Caricatures

Produced on 11" x 14" textured cardboard stock by Chi-Foursome Inc. in 1972, these caricatures were intended for sale at gas stations and supermarkets, but were never released at these locations. Only a small quantity was sold at Wrigley Field. It is believed that only about 3,000 of each player was produced. At least one known gas station advertisement display indicates 49 cents with $3 purchase of gasoline.

	NM	EX	VG
CUBS	10.00	5.00	3.00
Complete Set (15):	100.00	50.00	30.00
Common player:	10.00	5.00	3.00
Ernie Banks	20.00	10.00	6.00
Glenn Beckert	10.00	5.00	3.00
Fergie Jenkins	14.00	7.00	4.50
Don Kessinger	10.00	5.00	3.00
Milt Pappas	10.00	5.00	3.00
Joe Pepitone	10.00	5.00	3.00
Ron Santo	20.00	10.00	6.00
Billy Williams	10.00	5.00	3.00
WHITE SOX	10.00	5.00	3.00
Mike Andrews	10.00	5.00	3.00
Ed Herrmann	10.00	5.00	3.00
Pat Kelly	10.00	5.00	3.00
Carlos May	10.00	5.00	3.00
Bill Melton	14.00	7.00	4.50
Chuck Tanner	10.00	5.00	3.00
Wilbur Wood	14.00	7.00	4.50

1931 Chicago Cubs Picture Pack

In the second-year of team-issued photo packs during the 1930s-1940s was this set of 1931 Cubs. The 6-1/8" x 9-1/2" sepia-toned pictures have facsimile autographs across the front and a white border around. Backs are blank. Like all the team's other photo packs, it is possible the specific make-up of the 30 pictures in each set changed as personnel came and went during the season. A number of non-playing team personnel are also in the set.

		NM	EX	VG
	Complete Set (35):	450.00	225.00	135.00
	Common Player:	12.50	6.25	3.75
(1)	Ed Baecht	12.50	6.25	3.75
(2)	Clyde Beck	12.50	6.25	3.75
(3)	Les Bell	12.50	6.25	3.75
(4)	Clarence Blair	12.50	6.25	3.75
(5)	John F. Blake	12.50	6.25	3.75
(6)	Guy Bush	12.50	6.25	3.75
(7)	Kiki Cuyler	30.00	15.00	9.00
(8)	Woody English	12.50	6.25	3.75
(9)	Earl Grace	12.50	6.25	3.75
(10)	Charlie Grimm	15.00	7.50	4.50
(11)	Gabby Hartnett	30.00	15.00	9.00
(12)	Rollie Hemsley	12.50	6.25	3.75
(13)	Rogers Hornsby	60.00	30.00	18.00
(14)	Bill Jurges	12.50	6.25	3.75
(15)	Pat Malone	12.50	6.25	3.75
(16)	Jakie May	12.50	6.25	3.75
(17)	John Moore	12.50	6.25	3.75
(18)	Charley O'Leary	12.50	6.25	3.75
(19)	Charlie Root	15.00	7.50	4.50
(20)	Ray Schalk	30.00	15.00	9.00
(21)	Bob Smith	12.50	6.25	3.75
(22)	Riggs Stephenson	15.00	7.50	4.50
(23)	Les Sweetland	12.50	6.25	3.75
(24)	Dan Taylor	12.50	6.25	3.75
(25)	Zack Taylor	12.50	6.25	3.75
(26)	Bud Teachout	12.50	6.25	3.75
(27)	Lon Warneke	12.50	6.25	3.75
(28)	Hack Wilson	45.00	22.00	13.50
	Non-Playing Personnel			
(29)	Margaret Donahue	12.50	6.25	3.75
(30)	Bob Lewis	12.50	6.25	3.75
	(Traveling secretary.)			
(31)	Andy Lotshaw/Trainer	12.50	6.25	3.75
(32)	John Seys	12.50	6.25	3.75
(33)	William Veeck/President	45.00	22.00	13.50
(34)	W.M. Walker/VP	12.50	6.25	3.75
(35)	P.K. Wrigley	12.50	6.25	3.75
(36)	William Wrigley/Owner	17.50	8.75	5.25

1932 Chicago Cubs Picture Pack

This is one of many Cubs team issues of player pictures in the 1930s-1940s. The large format (6-1/8" x 9-1/4") set features action poses of the players in black-and-white on a black background. A bit of the ground at the players' feet is also included in the photo portion. A white facsimile autograph in the black background identifies the player. Backs are blank. The unnumbered pictures are checklisted here in alphabetical order. Some pictures of non-playing personnel were also issued.

		NM	EX	VG
	Complete Set (35):	325.00	165.00	100.00
	Common Player:	12.50	6.25	3.75
(1)	Guy Bush	12.50	6.25	3.75
(2)	Gilly Campbell	12.50	6.25	3.75
(3)	Red Corriden	12.50	6.25	3.75
(4)	Kiki Cuyler	25.00	12.50	7.50
(5)	Frank Demaree	12.50	6.25	3.75
(6)	Woody English	12.50	6.25	3.75
(7)	Burleigh Grimes	25.00	12.50	7.50
(8)	Charlie Grimm	12.50	6.25	3.75
(9)	Marv Gudat	12.50	6.25	3.75
(10)	Stan Hack	15.00	7.50	4.50
(11)	Gabby Hartnett	25.00	12.50	7.50
(12)	Rollie Hemsley	12.50	6.25	3.75
(13)	Billy Herman	25.00	12.50	7.50
(14)	LeRoy Herrman	12.50	6.25	3.75
(15)	Billy Jurges	12.50	6.25	3.75
(16)	Mark Koenig	12.50	6.25	3.75
(17)	Pat Malone	12.50	6.25	3.75
(18)	Jake May	12.50	6.25	3.75
(19)	Johnny Moore	12.50	6.25	3.75
(20)	Charley O'Leary	12.50	6.25	3.75
(21)	Lance Richbourg	12.50	6.25	3.75
(22)	Charlie Root	15.00	7.50	4.50
(23)	Bob Smith	12.50	6.25	3.75
(24)	Riggs Stephenson	15.00	7.50	4.50
(25)	Harry Taylor	12.50	6.25	3.75
(26)	Zack Taylor	12.50	6.25	3.75
(27)	Bud Tinning	12.50	6.25	3.75
(28)	Lon Warneke	12.50	6.25	3.75
	Non-playing Personnel			
(29)	Marge Donahue	12.50	6.25	3.75
(30)	Bob Lewis	12.50	6.25	3.75
	(Traveling secretary.)			
(31)	John Seys	12.50	6.25	3.75
(32)	Bill Veeck/President	25.00	12.50	7.50
(33)	W.M. Walker	12.50	6.25	3.75
(34)	Phil Wrigley	12.50	6.25	3.75
(35)	William Wrigley	12.50	6.25	3.75

1932 Chicago Cubs Team Issue

Because of its similarity in format to the team's picture pack issue of 1932, it is presumed this card set was also a team production. The blank-back cards are about 2-1/4" x 2-1/2" with player poses and a bit of ground underfoot set against a white background which has a facsimile autograph. This checklist is incomplete and arranged alphabetically.

	NM	EX	VG
Common Player:	300.00	150.00	90.00
Charlie Grimm	300.00	150.00	90.00
Marv Gudat	300.00	150.00	90.00
Stanley C. Hack	350.00	175.00	100.00
Rolly Hemsley	300.00	150.00	90.00
Jakie May	300.00	150.00	90.00
Bud Tinning	300.00	150.00	90.00

1933 Chicago Cubs Picture Pack

Likely a concession stand souvenir item, this large format (5-7/8" x 8-7/8") set features action poses of the players in black-and-white on a black background. A bit of the ground at the players' feet is also included in the photo portion. A white facsimile autograph in the black background identifies the player. Backs are blank. The unnumbered pictures are checklisted here in alphabetical order. Some pictures of non-playing personnel were included.

		NM	EX	VG
	Complete Set (30):	275.00	135.00	85.00
	Common Player:	12.50	6.25	3.75
(1)	Guy Bush	12.50	6.25	3.75
(2)	Gilly Campbell	12.50	6.25	3.75
(3)	John M. Corriden	12.50	6.25	3.75
(4)	Kiki Cuyler	25.00	12.50	7.50
(5)	J. Frank Demaree	12.50	6.25	3.75
(6)	Woody English	12.50	6.25	3.75
(7)	Burleigh A. Grimes	25.00	12.50	7.50
(8)	Charlie Grimm	12.50	6.25	3.75
(9)	Leo "Gabby" Hartnett	25.00	12.50	7.50
(10)	Harvey Hendrick	12.50	6.25	3.75
(11)	Roy Henshaw	12.50	6.25	3.75
(12)	Babe Herman	15.00	7.50	4.50
(13)	William Herman	25.00	12.50	7.50
(14)	William Jurges	12.50	6.25	3.75
(15)	Mark Koenig	12.50	6.25	3.75
(16)	Perce "Pat" Malone	12.50	6.25	3.75
(17)	Lynn Nelson	12.50	6.25	3.75
(18)	Charlie Root	15.00	7.50	4.50
(19)	John Schulte	12.50	6.25	3.75
(20)	Riggs Stephenson	15.00	7.50	4.50
(21)	Zack Taylor	12.50	6.25	3.75
(22)	Bud Tinning	12.50	6.25	3.75
(23)	L. Warneke	12.50	6.25	3.75
	Non-playing Personnel			
(24)	Margaret Donahue	12.50	6.25	3.75
(25)	Robert C. Lewis	12.50	6.25	3.75
	(Traveling secretary.)			
(26)	John O. Seys	12.50	6.25	3.75
(27)	William L. Veeck/President	25.00	12.50	7.50
(28)	W.M. Walker	12.50	6.25	3.75
(29)	Philip K. Wrigley	12.50	6.25	3.75
(30)	Wm. Wrigley	12.50	6.25	3.75

1936 Chicago Cubs Picture Pack

Nearly identical in format to the 1933 issue, these 5-7/8" x 8-7/8" pictures are printed in black-and-white on a black background with (usually) a white facsimile autograph. Backs are blank. The specific make-up of photo packs sold at Wrigley Field may have changed over the course of the season as players came and went. The unnumbered pictures are checklisted here in alphabetical order.

		NM	EX	VG
	Complete Set (34):	240.00	120.00	72.00
	Common Player:	9.00	4.50	2.75
(1)	Ethan Allen	9.00	4.50	2.75
(2)	Clay Bryant	9.00	4.50	2.75
(3)	Tex Carleton	9.00	4.50	2.75
(4)	Phil Cavarretta	12.00	6.00	3.50
(5)	John Corriden	9.00	4.50	2.75
(6)	Frank Demaree	9.00	4.50	2.75
(7)	Curt Davis	9.00	4.50	2.75
(8)	Woody English	9.00	4.50	2.75
(9)	Larry French	9.00	4.50	2.75
(10)	Augie Galan	9.00	4.50	2.75
(11)	Johnny Gill	9.00	4.50	2.75
(12)	Charlie Grimm	12.00	6.00	3.50
(13)	Stan Hack	12.00	6.00	3.50
(14)	Gabby Hartnett	18.00	9.00	5.50
(15)	Roy Henshaw	9.00	4.50	2.75
(16)	Billy Herman	18.00	9.00	5.50
(17)	Roy Johnson	9.00	4.50	2.75
(18)	Bill Jurges	9.00	4.50	2.75
(19)	Chuck Klein	18.00	9.00	5.50
(20)	Fabian Kowalik	9.00	4.50	2.75
(21)	Bill Lee	9.00	4.50	2.75
(22)	Gene Lillard	9.00	4.50	2.75
(23)	Ken O'Dea	9.00	4.50	2.75
(24)	Charlie Root	12.00	6.00	3.50
(25)	Clyde Shoun	9.00	4.50	2.75
(26)	Tuck Stainback	9.00	4.50	2.75
(27)	Walter Stephenson	9.00	4.50	2.75
(28)	Lon Warneke	9.00	4.50	2.75
	Non-playing personnel			
(29)	Margaret Donahue	9.00	4.50	2.75
(30)	Bob Lewis	9.00	4.50	2.75
	(Traveling secretary.)			
(31)	Andy Lotshaw/Trainer	9.00	4.50	2.75
(32)	John O. Seys	9.00	4.50	2.75
(33)	Charles Weber	9.00	4.50	2.75
(34)	Wrigley Field	18.00	9.00	5.50

1939 Chicago Cubs Picture Pack

The use of a textured paper stock for these 6-1/2" x 9" pictures helps identify the 1939 team issue. The pictures once again feature sepia portrait photos with a white border. A facsimile autograph is at bottom. Backs are blank. The specific make-up of photo packs sold at Wrigley Field may have changed over the course of the season as players came and went. The unnumbered pictures are checklisted here in alphabetical order.

		NM	EX	VG
	Complete Set (25):	225.00	115.00	65.00
	Common Player:	9.00	4.50	2.75
(1)	Dick Bartell	9.00	4.50	2.75
(2)	Clay Bryant	9.00	4.50	2.75
(3)	Phil Cavarretta	12.00	6.00	3.50
(4)	John Corriden	9.00	4.50	2.75
(5)	Dizzy Dean	40.00	20.00	12.00
(6)	Larry French	9.00	4.50	2.75
(7)	Augie Galan	9.00	4.50	2.75
(8)	Bob Garbark	9.00	4.50	2.75
(9)	Jim Gleeson	9.00	4.50	2.75
(10)	Stan Hack	12.00	6.00	3.50
(11)	Gabby Hartnett	20.00	10.00	6.00

		NM	EX	VG
(12)	Billy Herman	20.00	10.00	6.00
(13)	Roy Johnson	9.00	4.50	2.75
(14)	Bill Lee	9.00	4.50	2.75
(15)	Hank Leiber	9.00	4.50	2.75
(16)	Gene Lillard	9.00	4.50	2.75
(17)	Gus Mancuso	9.00	4.50	2.75
(18)	Bobby Mattick	9.00	4.50	2.75
(19)	Vance Page	9.00	4.50	2.75
(20)	Claude Passeau	9.00	4.50	2.75
(21)	Carl Reynolds	9.00	4.50	2.75
(22)	Charlie Root	12.00	6.00	3.50
(23)	Glenn "Rip" Russell	9.00	4.50	2.75
(24)	Jack Russell	9.00	4.50	2.75
(25)	Earl Whitehill	9.00	4.50	2.75

1940 Chicago Cubs Picture Pack

The 1940 team-issue is identical in format to the 1939s: 6-1/2" x 9", printed on rough-surfaced paper stock with black-and-white portraits surrounded by a wide border and a facsimile autograph on front. Study of the uniforms, however, may help differentiate the issue from 1939, as the 1940 uniforms have no stripe on the shoulders. It is possible that 1939 pictures continued to be issued in the 1940 photo packs and that specific make-up of the packs changed with the team's roster. The blank-back pictures are unnumbered and checklisted here in alphabetical order.

		NM	EX	VG
Complete Set (25):		80.00	40.00	24.00
Common Player:		9.00	4.50	2.75
(1)	Dick Bartell	9.00	4.50	2.75
(2)	Clay Bryant	9.00	4.50	2.75
(3)	Phil Cavarretta	12.00	6.00	3.50
(4)	John Corriden	9.00	4.50	2.75
(5)	Bob Collins	9.00	4.50	2.75
(6)	"Del" Dallessandro	9.00	4.50	2.75
(7)	Larry French	9.00	4.50	2.75
(8)	Augie Galan	9.00	4.50	2.75
(9)	Jim Gleeson	9.00	4.50	2.75
(10)	Stan Hack	12.00	6.00	3.50
(11)	Gabby Hartnett	20.00	10.00	6.00
(12)	Billy Herman	20.00	10.00	6.00
(13)	Roy Johnson	9.00	4.50	2.75
(14)	Bill Lee	9.00	4.50	2.75
(15)	Hank Leiber	9.00	4.50	2.75
(16)	Bobby Mattick	9.00	4.50	2.75
(17)	Jake Mooty	9.00	4.50	2.75
(18)	Bill Nicholson	9.00	4.50	2.75
(19)	Vance Page	9.00	4.50	2.75
(20)	Claude Passeau	9.00	4.50	2.75
(21)	Ken Raffensberger	9.00	4.50	2.75
(22)	Bill Rogell	9.00	4.50	2.75
(23)	Charlie Root	9.00	4.50	2.75
(24)	Rip Russell	9.00	4.50	2.75
(25)	Al Todd	9.00	4.50	2.75

1941 Chicago Cubs Picture Pack

A change of paper stock to a smooth finish helps differentiate the 1941 team-issue from previous years' offerings. Size remains at 6-1/2" x 9" with sepia player portraits surrounded by a white border and overprinted with a facsimile autograph. Backs are blank on these unnumbered photos. The pictures are listed here in alphabetical order.

		NM	EX	VG
Complete Set (25):		190.00	95.00	57.00
Common Player:		9.00	4.50	2.75
(1)	Phil Cavarretta	12.00	6.00	3.50
(2)	Dom Dallessandro	9.00	4.50	2.75
(3)	Paul Erickson	9.00	4.50	2.75
(4)	Larry French	9.00	4.50	2.75
(5)	Augie Galan	9.00	4.50	2.75
(6)	Greek George	9.00	4.50	2.75
(7)	Charlie Gilbert	9.00	4.50	2.75
(8)	Stan Hack	12.00	6.00	3.50
(9)	Johnny Hudson	9.00	4.50	2.75
(10)	Bill Lee	9.00	4.50	2.75
(11)	Hank Leiber	9.00	4.50	2.75
(12)	Clyde McCullough	9.00	4.50	2.75
(13)	Jake Mooty	9.00	4.50	2.75
(14)	Bill Myers	9.00	4.50	2.75
(15)	Bill Nicholson	9.00	4.50	2.75
(16)	Lou Novikoff	9.00	4.50	2.75
(17)	Vern Olsen	9.00	4.50	2.75
(18)	Vance Page	9.00	4.50	2.75

		NM	EX	VG
(19)	Claude Passeau	9.00	4.50	2.75
(20)	Tot Pressnell	9.00	4.50	2.75
(21)	Charlie Root	12.00	6.00	3.50
(22)	Bob Scheffing	9.00	4.50	2.75
(23)	Lou Stringer	9.00	4.50	2.75
(24)	Bob Sturgeon	9.00	4.50	2.75
(25)	Cubs Staff (Dizzy Dean, Charlie Grimm, Dick Spalding, Jimmie Wilson)	12.00	6.00	3.50

1942 Chicago Cubs Picture Pack

The relatively small number of photos in this team-issued set indicates it may have been issued as a supplement to update earlier photo packs with players who were new to the Cubs. In the same 6-1/2" x 9" format as previous issues, the 1942s is printed in sepia on a smooth-surfaced paper. A facsimile autograph graces the front and the portrait photo is surrounded by a border. Backs are blank and the pictures are not numbered. The checklist here is in alphabetical order.

		NM	EX	VG
Complete Set (24):		175.00	90.00	55.00
Common Player:		9.00	4.50	2.75
(1)	Hiram Bithorn	12.00	6.00	3.50
(2)	Phil Cavarretta	9.00	4.50	2.75
(3)	"Del" Dallasandro	9.00	4.50	2.75
(4)	Paul Erickson	9.00	4.50	2.75
(5)	Bill Fleming	9.00	4.50	2.75
(6)	Charlie Gilbert	9.00	4.50	2.75
(7)	Stan Hack	15.00	7.50	4.50
(8)	Ed Hanyzewski	9.00	4.50	2.75
(9)	Chico Hernandez	9.00	4.50	2.75
(10)	Bill Lee	9.00	4.50	2.75
(11)	Harry Lowrey	9.00	4.50	2.75
(12)	Clyde McCullough	9.00	4.50	2.75
(13)	Lennie Merullo	9.00	4.50	2.75
(14)	Jake Mooty	9.00	4.50	2.75
(15)	Bill Nicholson	9.00	4.50	2.75
(16)	Lou Novikoff	9.00	4.50	2.75
(17)	Vern Olsen	9.00	4.50	2.75
(18)	Claude Passeau	9.00	4.50	2.75
(19)	Tot Pressnell	9.00	4.50	2.75
(20)	Glen "Rip" Russell	9.00	4.50	2.75
(21)	Bob Scheffing	9.00	4.50	2.75
(22)	Johnny Schmitz	9.00	4.50	2.75
(23)	Lou Stringer	9.00	4.50	2.75
(24)	Bob Sturgeon	9.00	4.50	2.75
(25)	Kiki Cuyler, Dick Spalding, Jimmie Wilson	9.00	4.50	2.75
(26)	Jimmie Wilson, Dick Spalding, Charlie Grimm, Dizzy Dean	15.00	7.50	4.50

1943 Chicago Cubs Picture Pack

It is impossible to differentiate pictures from the 1943 issue from those of early years and of 1944, since many pictures were reused and the format is identical: 6-1/2" x 9", black-and-white portrait photos with facsimile autograph and white borders. Backs are blank and the photos are not numbered. They are checklisted here alphabetically.

	NM	EX	VG
Complete Set (25):	215.00	105.00	65.00

		NM	EX	VG
Common Player:		9.00	4.50	2.75
(1)	Dick Barrett	9.00	4.50	2.75
(2)	Heinz Becker	9.00	4.50	2.75
(3)	Hiram Bithorn	12.00	6.00	3.50
(4)	Phil Cavarretta	9.00	4.50	2.75
(5)	"Del" Dallasandro	9.00	4.50	2.75
(6)	Paul Derringer	9.00	4.50	2.75
(7)	Paul Erickson	9.00	4.50	2.75
(8)	Bill Fleming	9.00	4.50	2.75
(9)	Stan Hack	12.00	6.00	3.50
(10)	Ed Hanyzewski	9.00	4.50	2.75
(11)	Chico Hernandez	9.00	4.50	2.75
(12)	Bill Lee	9.00	4.50	2.75
(13)	Peanuts Lowrey	9.00	4.50	2.75
(14)	Stu Martin	9.00	4.50	2.75
(15)	Clyde McCullough	9.00	4.50	2.75
(16)	Len Merullo	9.00	4.50	2.75
(17)	Bill Nicholson	9.00	4.50	2.75
(18)	Lou Novikoff	9.00	4.50	2.75
(19)	Claude Passeau	9.00	4.50	2.75
(20)	Ray Prim	9.00	4.50	2.75
(21)	Eddie Stanky	12.00	6.00	3.50
(22)	Al Todd	9.00	4.50	2.75
(23)	Lon Warneke	9.00	4.50	2.75
(24)	Hank Wyse	9.00	4.50	2.75
(25)	Cubs Coaches (Kiki Cuyler, Dick Spalding, Jimmie Wilson)	9.00	4.50	2.75

1944 Chicago Cubs Picture Pack

A slight size reduction, to 6" x 8-1/2", helps identify the team's 1944 photo pack. The pictures feature black-and-white portrait photos with a white border. A facsimile autograph is at bottom. Backs are blank. The specific make-up of photo packs sold at Wrigley Field may have changed over the course of the season as players came and went. The unnumbered pictures are checklisted here in alphabetical order.

		NM	EX	VG
Complete Set (25):		215.00	105.00	65.00
Common Player:		9.00	4.50	2.75
(1)	Heinz Becker	9.00	4.50	2.75
(2)	John Burrows	9.00	4.50	2.75
(3)	Phil Cavarretta	12.00	6.00	3.50
(4)	"Del" Dallessandro	9.00	4.50	2.75
(5)	Paul Derringer	9.00	4.50	2.75
(6)	Roy Easterwood	9.00	4.50	2.75
(7)	Paul Erickson	9.00	4.50	2.75
(8)	Bill Fleming	9.00	4.50	2.75
(9)	Jimmie Foxx	30.00	15.00	9.00
(10)	Ival Goodman	9.00	4.50	2.75
(11)	Ed Hanyzewski	9.00	4.50	2.75
(12)	Billy Holm	9.00	4.50	2.75
(13)	Don Johnson	9.00	4.50	2.75
(14)	Garth Mann	9.00	4.50	2.75
(15)	Len Merullo	9.00	4.50	2.75
(16)	John Miklos	9.00	4.50	2.75
(17)	Bill Nicholson	9.00	4.50	2.75
(18)	Lou Novikoff	9.00	4.50	2.75
(19)	Andy Pafko	12.00	6.00	3.50
(20)	Ed Sauer	9.00	4.50	2.75
(21)	Bill Schuster	9.00	4.50	2.75
(22)	Eddie Stanky	12.00	6.00	3.50
(23)	Hy Vandenberg	9.00	4.50	2.75
(24)	Hank Wyse	9.00	4.50	2.75
(25)	Tony York	9.00	4.50	2.75

1924 Chicago Evening American Cubs/White Sox Pins

These 1-3/8" diameter pins were issued by the Chicago Evening American newspaper to promote its peach-colored sports section. Rather crude blue-and-white line drawings of the players are at center, within an orange peach with the player's name at bottom. Borders are either white or dark blue. The pins were produced by Greenduck Metal Stamping of Chicago.

	NM	EX	VG
Complete Set (12):	3,500	1,750	1,000
Common Player:	200.00	100.00	65.00
(1) Grover Alexander	750.00	375.00	225.00
(2) Eddie Collins	450.00	225.00	135.00
(3) "Red" Faber	350.00	175.00	105.00
(4) Ray Grimes	200.00	100.00	65.00
(5) Charlie Hollocher	200.00	100.00	65.00
(6) Harry Hooper	350.00	175.00	105.00
(7) Willie Kamm	200.00	100.00	65.00
(8) Bill Killefer	200.00	100.00	65.00
(9) Bob O'Farrell	200.00	100.00	65.00
(10) Charlie Robertson	200.00	100.00	65.00
(11) Ray Schalk	350.00	175.00	100.00
(12) Jigger Statz	200.00	100.00	65.00

1930 Chicago Evening American Pins

Members of the Cubs and White Sox are featured on this series of pins issued by one of the local daily newspapers. Player portraits are featured in black-and-white on a white background on these 1-1/4" celluloid pins. Above the picture is the player's position, last name and team; below is the sponsor's name. The unnumbered pins are listed here in alphabetical order within team.

	NM	EX	VG
Complete Set (20):	6,500	3,250	1,950
Common Player:	250.00	125.00	75.00
Chicago Cubs Team Set (11):	3,500	1,750	1,000
(1) Les Bell	250.00	125.00	75.00
(2) Guy Bush	250.00	125.00	75.00
(3) Kiki Cuyler	350.00	175.00	100.00
(4) Woody English	250.00	125.00	75.00
(5) Charlie Grimm	250.00	125.00	75.00
(6) Gabby Hartnett	350.00	175.00	100.00
(7) Rogers Hornsby	750.00	375.00	225.00
(8) Joe McCarthy	350.00	175.00	100.00
(9) Charlie Root	250.00	125.00	75.00
(10) Riggs Stephenson	250.00	125.00	75.00
(11) Hack Wilson	400.00	200.00	120.00
Chicago White Sox Team Set (9):	3,000	1,500	900.00
(1) Moe Berg	1,000	500.00	300.00
(2) Bill Cissel (Cissell)	250.00	125.00	75.00
(3) Red Faber	350.00	175.00	105.00
(4) Bill Hunnefield	250.00	125.00	75.00
(5) Smead Jolley	250.00	125.00	75.00
(6) Willie Kamm	250.00	125.00	75.00
(7) Jimmy Moore	250.00	125.00	75.00
(8) Carl Reynolds	250.00	125.00	75.00
(9) Art Shires	250.00	125.00	75.00

1930 Chicago Herald and Examiner Babe Ruth Premium

This premium picture with a black-and-white batting pose of Ruth was issued by a Chicago newspaper. Two sizes are known, approximately 8-1/2" x 11-1/2" and 5" x 7". The pictures are blank-back. The year attributed is speculative.

	NM	EX	VG
Babe Ruth/Large	1,350	625.00	400.00
Babe Ruth/Small	1,350	625.00	400.00

1976 Chicagoland Collectors Association Chicago Greats

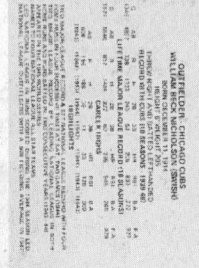

Chicago's Greats

Former stars of the Cubs and White Sox are featured in this collectors issue produced in conjunction with an early sports card and memorabilia show in Chicago. The 2-1/2" x 3-1/2" cards feature black-and-white action photos at center of most cards, with a portrait photo inset at top. Graphics around the front are in red. Backs have detailed career summaries. A starting team, manager and president for each of the Chicago teams is represented in the issue. Complete setes were originally sold for about $2 with uncut sheets sold for $6.

	NM	EX	VG
Complete Set (25):	15.00	7.50	4.50
Common Player:	2.00	1.00	.60
(1) Luke Appling	2.00	1.00	.60
(2) Ernie Banks	6.00	3.00	1.75
(3) Zeke Bonura	2.00	1.00	.60
(4) Phil Cavarretta	2.00	1.00	.60
(5) Jimmy Dykes	2.00	1.00	.60
(6) Red Faber, Ted Lyons	2.00	1.00	.60
(7) Nellie Fox	4.00	2.00	1.25
(8) Larry French	2.00	1.00	.60
(9) Charlie Grimm	2.00	1.00	.60
(10) Gabby Hartnett	2.00	1.00	.60
(11) Billy Herman	2.00	1.00	.60
(12) Mike Kreevich	2.00	1.00	.60
(13) Sherman Lollar	2.00	1.00	.60
(14) Al Lopez	2.00	1.00	.60
(15) Minnie Minoso	3.00	1.50	.90
(16) Wally Moses	2.00	1.00	.60
(17) Bill Nicholson	2.00	1.00	.60
(18) Claude Passeau	2.00	1.00	.60
(19) Billy Pierce	2.00	1.00	.60
(20) Ron Santo	2.00	1.00	.60
(21) Hank Sauer	2.00	1.00	.60
(22) Riggs Stephenson	2.00	1.00	.60
(23) Bill Veeck	2.00	1.00	.60
(24) P.K. Wrigley	2.00	1.00	.60
(25) Checklist	2.00	1.00	.60

1915 Chicago Tribune Supplements

As the 1915 baseball season opened, the Chicago Sunday Tribune ran supplements in its April 4 and April 11 editions featuring pictures of Chicago players. The black-and-white pictures are 8" x 11". Saier is pictured in uniform, the others are in street clothes. Printed in the white border beneath each photo is "Supplement to The Chicago Sunday Tribune, April 4 (or) 11, 1915." Each picture bears a facsimile autograph of the player and is blank-backed.

	NM	EX	VG
Complete Set (4):	400.00	200.00	120.00
Common Player:	50.00	25.00	15.00
(1) Roger Bresnahan (April 11)	100.00	50.00	30.00
(2) Eddie Collins (April 11)	100.00	50.00	30.00
(3) Vic Saier (April 11)	50.00	25.00	15.00
(4) Joe Tinker (April 4)	150.00	75.00	45.00

1917 Chicago White Sox Team Issue

This set of the World Champion White Sox (including several of the notorious Black Sox) was produced by Davis Printing Works in Chicago and apparently sold as a complete boxed set by the team. Individual cards measure about 1-11/16" x 2-3/4". Fronts feature

JOE JACKSON
LEFT FIELD

full-length black-and-white photos of the players on a light background with a white border. Player name and position are in black beneath the picture. Backs are blank. To date, only one set is known to exist. It sold at auction in 1991 for $45,100, again in 1997 for $46,000 and in 2001 for $50,330. The unnumbered cards are checklisted here alphabetically.

Complete Set (25):			
Value undetermined.			
(1) Joe Benz			
(2) Eddie Cicotte			
(3) Eddie Collins			
(4) Shano Collins			
(5) Charles Comiskey			
(6) Dave Danforth			
(7) Red Faber			
(8) Happy Felsch			
(9) Chick Gandil			
(10) Kid Gleason			
(11) Joe Jackson			
(12) Joe Jenkins			
(13) Ted Jourdan			
(14) Nemo Leibold			
(15) Byrd Lynn			
(16) Fred McMullin			
(17) Eddie Murphy			
(18) Swede Risberg			
(19) Pants Rowland			
(20) Reb Russell			
(21) Ray Schalk			
(22) James Scott			
(23) Buck Weaver			
(24) Lefty Williams			
(25) Mellie Wolfgang			

1940 Chicago White Sox Photo Pack

This set of souvenir photos was produced by Andy Lotshaw, who was a Cubs trainer. The 5-1/2" x 6-3/4" pictures have a sepia pose bordered in white, with a facsimile autograph. Backs are blank. The unnumbered pictures are checklisted here in alphabetical order.

	NM	EX	VG
Complete Set (25):	300.00	150.00	90.00
Common Player:	15.00	7.50	4.50
(1) Pete Appleton	15.00	7.50	4.50
(2) Luke Appling	30.00	15.00	9.00
(3) Clint Brown	15.00	7.50	4.50
(4) Bill Dietrich	15.00	7.50	4.50
(5) Jimmy Dykes	15.00	7.50	4.50
(6) Mule Haas	15.00	7.50	4.50
(7) Jack Hayes	15.00	7.50	4.50
(8) Bob Kennedy	15.00	7.50	4.50
(9) Jack Knott	15.00	7.50	4.50
(10) Mike Kreevich	15.00	7.50	4.50
(11) Joe Kuhel	15.00	7.50	4.50
(12) Thornton Lee	15.00	7.50	4.50
(13) Ted Lyons	25.00	12.50	7.50
(14) Eric McNair	15.00	7.50	4.50
(15) John Rigney	15.00	7.50	4.50
(16) Larry Rosenthal	15.00	7.50	4.50
(17) Ken Silvestri	15.00	7.50	4.50
(18) Eddie Smith	15.00	7.50	4.50
(19) J. Solters	15.00	7.50	4.50
(20) Monty Stratton	20.00	10.00	6.00
(21) Mike Tresh	15.00	7.50	4.50
(22) Tom Turner	15.00	7.50	4.50
(23) Skeeter Webb	20.00	10.00	6.00
(24) Ed Weiland	15.00	7.50	4.50
(25) Taft Wright	15.00	7.50	4.50

1948 Chicago White Sox Photo Pack

The last-place White Sox of 1948 are immortalized in this team-issued set of player photos. Individual players are pictured in a 6-1/2" x 9" portrait photo with a thin white border around. A facsimile autograph also appears on front. Backs are blank. A team photo was also included in the set. The photo pack was sold in a large white envelope with a red and blue team logo. The unnumbered pictures are checklisted here in alphabetical order.

		NM	EX	VG
Complete Set (30):		180.00	90.00	54.00
Common Player:		7.50	3.75	2.25
(1)	Luke Appling	18.00	9.00	5.50
(2)	Floyd Baker	7.50	3.75	2.25
(3)	Fred Bradley	7.50	3.75	2.25
(4)	Earl Caldwell	7.50	3.75	2.25
(5)	Red Faber	15.00	7.50	4.50
(6)	Bob Gillespie	7.50	3.75	2.25
(7)	Jim Goodwin	12.00	6.00	3.50
(8)	Orval Grove	7.50	3.75	2.25
(9)	Earl Harrist	7.50	3.75	2.25
(10)	Joe Haynes	7.50	3.75	2.25
(11)	Ralph Hodgin	7.50	3.75	2.25
(12)	Howie Judson	7.50	3.75	2.25
(13)	Bob Kennedy	7.50	3.75	2.25
(14)	Don Kolloway	7.50	3.75	2.25
(15)	Tony Lupien	7.50	3.75	2.25
(16)	Ted Lyons	15.00	7.50	4.50
(17)	Cass Michaels	7.50	3.75	2.25
(18)	Bing Miller	7.50	3.75	2.25
(19)	Buster Mills	7.50	3.75	2.25
(20)	Glen Moulder	7.50	3.75	2.25
(21)	Frank Papish	7.50	3.75	2.25
(22)	Ike Pearson	7.50	3.75	2.25
(23)	Dave Philley	7.50	3.75	2.25
(24)	Aaron Robinson	7.50	3.75	2.25
(25)	Mike Tresh	7.50	3.75	2.25
(26)	Jack Wallaesa	7.50	3.75	2.25
(27)	Ralph Weigel	7.50	3.75	2.25
(28)	Bill Wight	7.50	3.75	2.25
(29)	Taft Wright	7.50	3.75	2.25
(30)	Team picture	18.00	9.00	5.50

1960-64 Chicago White Sox Ticket Stubs

From 1960-64 tickets to White Sox home games at Comiskey Park were issued bearing player photos. Along with the photos on the backs of the 1-5/16" x 2-5/8" ticket stubs are career information and facsimile autographs. Photos were generally re-used from year to year and color variations, depending on the type of ticket, are known. Players from each year are listed here alphabetically.

		NM	EX	VG
Complete Set (113):		2,250	1,125	675.00
Common Player:		30.00	15.00	9.00
60-1	Luis Aparicio	75.00	37.00	22.00
60-2	Earl Battey	30.00	15.00	9.00
60-3	Frank Baumann	30.00	15.00	9.00
60-4	Dick Donovan	30.00	15.00	9.00
60-5	Nelson Fox	75.00	37.00	22.00
60-6	Gene Freese	30.00	15.00	9.00
60-7	Ted Kluszewski	60.00	30.00	18.00
60-8	Jim Landis	30.00	15.00	9.00
60-9	Barry Latman	30.00	15.00	9.00
60-10	Sherm Lollar	30.00	15.00	9.00
60-11	Al Lopez	45.00	22.00	13.50

		NM	EX	VG
60-12	Turk Lown	30.00	15.00	9.00
60-13	Orestes Minoso	50.00	25.00	15.00
60-14	Bill Pierce	30.00	15.00	9.00
60-15	Jim Rivera	30.00	15.00	9.00
60-16	Bob Shaw	30.00	15.00	9.00
60-17	Roy Sievers	30.00	15.00	9.00
60-18	Al Smith	30.00	15.00	9.00
60-19	Gerry Staley	30.00	15.00	9.00
60-20	Early Wynn	45.00	22.00	13.50
61-1	Luis Aparicio	75.00	37.00	22.00
61-2	Frank Baumann	30.00	15.00	9.00
61-3	Camilo Carreon	30.00	15.00	9.00
61-4	Sam Esposito	30.00	15.00	9.00
61-5	Nelson Fox	75.00	37.00	22.00
61-6	Billy Goodman	30.00	15.00	9.00
61-7	Jim Landis	30.00	15.00	9.00
61-8	Sherman Lollar	30.00	15.00	9.00
61-9	Al Lopez	45.00	22.00	13.50
61-10	J.C. Martin	30.00	15.00	9.00
61-11	Cal McLish	30.00	15.00	9.00
61-12	Orestes Minoso	50.00	25.00	15.00
61-13	Bill Pierce	30.00	15.00	9.00
61-14	Juan Pizarro	30.00	15.00	9.00
61-15	Bob Roselli	30.00	15.00	9.00
61-16	Herb Score	35.00	17.50	10.50
61-17	Bob Shaw	30.00	15.00	9.00
61-18	Roy Sievers	30.00	15.00	9.00
61-19	Al Smith	30.00	15.00	9.00
61-20	Gerry Staley	30.00	15.00	9.00
61-21	Early Wynn	45.00	22.00	13.50
62-1	Luis Aparicio	75.00	37.00	22.00
62-2	Frank Baumann	30.00	15.00	9.00
62-3	John Buzhardt	30.00	15.00	9.00
62-4	Camilo Carreon	30.00	15.00	9.00
62-5	Joe Cunningham	30.00	15.00	9.00
62-6	Bob Farley	30.00	15.00	9.00
62-7	Eddie Fisher	30.00	15.00	9.00
62-8	Nelson Fox	75.00	37.00	22.00
62-9	Jim Landis	30.00	15.00	9.00
62-10	Sherm Lollar	30.00	15.00	9.00
62-11	Al Lopez	45.00	22.00	13.50
62-12	Turk Lown	30.00	15.00	9.00
62-13	J.C. Martin	30.00	15.00	9.00
62-14	Cal McLish	30.00	15.00	9.00
62-15	Gary Peters	30.00	15.00	9.00
62-16	Juan Pizarro	30.00	15.00	9.00
62-17	Floyd Robinson	30.00	15.00	9.00
62-18	Bob Roselli	30.00	15.00	9.00
62-19	Herb Score	35.00	17.50	10.50
62-20	Al Smith	30.00	15.00	9.00
62-21	Charles Smith	30.00	15.00	9.00
62-22	Early Wynn	45.00	22.00	13.50
63-1	Frank Baumann	30.00	15.00	9.00
63-2	John Buzhardt	30.00	15.00	9.00
63-3	Camilo Carreon	30.00	15.00	9.00
63-4	Joe Cunningham	30.00	15.00	9.00
63-5	Dave DeBusschere	40.00	20.00	12.00
63-6	Eddie Fisher	30.00	15.00	9.00
63-7	Nelson Fox	75.00	37.00	22.00
63-8	Ron Hansen	30.00	15.00	9.00
63-9	Ray Herbert	30.00	15.00	9.00
63-10	Mike Hershberger	30.00	15.00	9.00
63-11	Joe Horlen	30.00	15.00	9.00
63-12	Grover Jones	30.00	15.00	9.00
63-13	Mike Joyce	30.00	15.00	9.00
63-14	Frank Kreutzer	30.00	15.00	9.00
63-15	Jim Landis	30.00	15.00	9.00
63-16	Sherman Lollar	30.00	15.00	9.00
63-17	Al Lopez	45.00	22.00	13.50
63-18	J.C. Martin	30.00	15.00	9.00
63-19	Charlie Maxwell	30.00	15.00	9.00
63-20	Dave Nicholson	30.00	15.00	9.00
63-21	Juan Pizarro	30.00	15.00	9.00
63-22	Floyd Robinson	30.00	15.00	9.00
63-23	Charley Smith	30.00	15.00	9.00
63-24	Pete Ward	30.00	15.00	9.00
63-25	Al Weis	30.00	15.00	9.00
63-26	Hoyt Wilhelm	45.00	22.00	13.50
63-27	Dom Zanni	30.00	15.00	9.00
64-1	Fritz Ackley	30.00	15.00	9.00
64-2	Frank Baumann	30.00	15.00	9.00
64-3	Don Buford	30.00	15.00	9.00
64-4	John Buzhardt	30.00	15.00	9.00
64-5	Camilo Carreon	30.00	15.00	9.00
64-6	Joe Cunningham	30.00	15.00	9.00
64-7	Dave DeBusschere	40.00	20.00	12.00
64-8	Eddie Fisher	30.00	15.00	9.00
64-9	Jim Golden	30.00	15.00	9.00
64-10	Ron Hansen	30.00	15.00	9.00
64-11	Ray Herbert	30.00	15.00	9.00
64-12	Mike Hershberger	30.00	15.00	9.00
64-13	Joe Horlen	30.00	15.00	9.00
64-14	Jim Landis	30.00	15.00	9.00
64-15	Al Lopez	45.00	22.00	13.50
64-16	J.C. Martin	30.00	15.00	9.00
64-17	Dave Nicholson	30.00	15.00	9.00
64-18	Gary Peters	30.00	15.00	9.00
64-19	Juan Pizarro	30.00	15.00	9.00
64-20	Floyd Robinson	30.00	15.00	9.00
64-21	Gene Stephens	30.00	15.00	9.00
64-22	Pete Ward	30.00	15.00	9.00
64-23	Al Weis	30.00	15.00	9.00
64-24	Hoyt Wilhelm	45.00	22.00	13.50

1899 Chickering Studio Boston Beaneaters Cabinets

These oversize (8-7/8" x 9-7/8") cabinet cards feature virtually every regular on the 1899 National League runners-up and this checklist may not be complete. The cards feature chest-up, capless sepia portraits of the players, glued to either black or gray cardboard mounts with the advertising of Boston's Elmer Chickering Studio in silver or gold leaf at bottom. Players are identified by first and last name in fancy black script at the bottom of the photo. Backs are blank.

		NM	EX	VG
Common Player:		2,000	650.00	425.00
(1)	Harvey Bailey	2,000	650.00	425.00
(2)	Martin Bergen	2,000	650.00	425.00
(3)	William Clarke	2,000	650.00	425.00
(4)	Jimmy Collins	5,000	1,800	1,075
(5)	Hugh Duffy	6,000	2,125	1,275
(6)	Billy Hamilton	5,000	2,000	1,200
(7)	Frank Killen	2,000	650.00	425.00
(8)	Ted Lewis	2,000	650.00	425.00
(9)	Herman Long	5,000	1,625	975.00
(10)	Bobby Lowe	2,000	750.00	450.00
(11)	Jouett Meekin	5,000	1,000	600.00
(12)	Charles Nichols	6,000	2,125	1,250
(13)	Fred Tenney	2,000	650.00	425.00

1956-1957 Chicle Peloteros

Napoleón Reyes, Manager

One of the few gumcard issues from Cuba, this set took a cue from American companies by skip-numbering the set to keep youngsters buying gum in search of cards that did not exist. The cards measure about 2" x 3". Fronts have color portrait photos bordered in white with the player name and card number in a colored strip below. Backs are in black-and-white with a few biographical notes and career highlights. The cards are printed on thick gray stock. A colorful album to house the cards was also produced.

		NM	EX	VG
Complete Set (40):		2,750	1,375	850.00
Common Player:		60.00	30.00	18.00
Album:		100.00	50.00	30.00
2	Emilio Cabrera	60.00	30.00	18.00
4	Conrado Marrero	100.00	50.00	30.00
5	Silvio Garcia	250.00	125.00	75.00
6	Russel (Russell) Nixon	75.00	37.50	22.50
7	Enrique Izquierdo	60.00	30.00	18.00
8	Lou Skinner	60.00	30.00	18.00
9	Robert Mc Kee	60.00	30.00	18.00
10	Gonzalo Naranjo	60.00	30.00	18.00
11	Trompoloco Rodriguez	60.00	30.00	18.00
12	Evelio Hernandez	60.00	30.00	18.00
26	Oscar Rodriguez	60.00	30.00	18.00
27	Jose (Cheo) Ramos	60.00	30.00	18.00
28	Napoleon Heredia	60.00	30.00	18.00
29	Camilo Pascual	150.00	75.00	45.00
30	Pedro Ramos	90.00	45.00	27.50
31	Rene Gutierrez	60.00	30.00	18.00
32	Julio (Jiqui) Moreno	65.00	32.50	20.00
33	Bud Daley	65.00	32.50	20.00
34	Dick Tomaneck (Tomanek)	60.00	30.00	18.00
35	Rafael Noble	65.00	32.50	20.00
50	Gilberto Torres	60.00	30.00	18.00
51	Salvador Hernandez	60.00	30.00	18.00
52	Pipo de la Noval	60.00	30.00	18.00
53	Juan Soler	60.00	30.00	18.00
54	Oscar Sierra	60.00	30.00	18.00
55	Billy Muffet (Muffett)	60.00	30.00	18.00
56	Robert Bluaylock (Blaylock)	60.00	30.00	18.00
57	Edwin Mayers	60.00	30.00	18.00
58	Vicente Amor	60.00	30.00	18.00
59	Raul Sanchez	60.00	30.00	18.00
75	Napoleon Reyes	90.00	45.00	27.50
76	Jose Maria Fernandez	90.00	45.00	27.50
77	Juan Izaguirre	60.00	30.00	18.00
79	Rene Friol	60.00	30.00	18.00
80	Asdrubal Baro	60.00	30.00	18.00
82	Juan Delis	60.00	30.00	18.00
83	Julio Becquer	60.00	30.00	18.00
84	Rodolfo Arias	60.00	30.00	18.00
86	Patricio Quintana	60.00	30.00	18.00
87	Aldo Salvent	60.00	30.00	18.00

1900 Chickering Studio Cabinets

The extent of this issue of standard-format (about 4-1/4" x 6-1/2") cabinets is unknown. Fronts have a studio pose with a decorative studio logo in the bottom border. Backs have a large ad for the renowned Boston photographer.

		NM	EX	VG
Common Player:				
(1)	Win Mercer	1,500	750.00	450.00
(2)	Kid Nichols	9,000	4,500	2,750

1977 Chilly Willee Discs

Virtually identical in format to the several locally sponsored disc sets of the previous year, these 3-3/8" diameter player discs were given away at participating frozen drink stands. Discs once again feature black-and-white player portrait photos in the center of a baseball design. The left and right panels are in one of several bright colors. Licensed by the Players' Association through Mike Schechter Associates, the player photos carry no uniform logos. Backs are printed in blue and red. The unnumbered discs are checklisted here alphabetically.

		NM	EX	VG
Complete Set (70):		65.00	32.50	20.00
Common Player:		1.00	.50	.30
(1)	Sal Bando	1.00	.50	.30
(2)	Buddy Bell	1.00	.50	.30
(3)	Johnny Bench	5.00	2.50	1.50
(4)	Larry Bowa	1.00	.50	.30
(5)	Steve Braun	1.00	.50	.30
(6)	George Brett	12.00	6.00	3.50
(7)	Lou Brock	5.00	2.50	1.50
(8)	Jeff Burroughs	1.00	.50	.30
(9)	Bert Campaneris	1.00	.50	.30
(10)	John Candelaria	1.00	.50	.30
(11)	Jose Cardenal	1.00	.50	.30
(12)	Rod Carew	5.00	2.50	1.50
(13)	Steve Carlton	5.00	2.50	1.50
(14)	Dave Cash	1.00	.50	.30
(15)	Cesar Cedeno	1.00	.50	.30
(16)	Ron Cey	1.00	.50	.30
(17)	Dave Concepcion	1.00	.50	.30
(18)	Dennis Eckersley	5.00	2.50	1.50
(19)	Mark Fidrych	2.50	1.25	.70
(20)	Rollie Fingers	4.00	2.00	1.25
(21)	Carlton Fisk	5.00	2.50	1.50
(22)	George Foster	1.00	.50	.30
(23)	Wayne Garland	1.00	.50	.30
(24)	Ralph Garr	1.00	.50	.30
(25)	Steve Garvey	2.00	1.00	.60
(26)	Cesar Geronimo	1.00	.50	.30
(27)	Bobby Grich	1.00	.50	.30
(28)	Ken Griffey Sr.	1.00	.50	.30
(29)	Don Gullett	1.00	.50	.30
(30)	Mike Hargrove	1.00	.50	.30
(31)	Al Hrabosky	1.00	.50	.30
(32)	Catfish Hunter	4.00	2.00	1.25
(33)	Reggie Jackson	10.00	5.00	3.00
(34)	Randy Jones	1.00	.50	.30
(35)	Dave Kingman	1.00	.50	.30
(36)	Jerry Koosman	1.00	.50	.30
(37)	Dave LaRoche	1.00	.50	.30
(38)	Greg Luzinski	1.00	.50	.30
(39)	Fred Lynn	1.00	.50	.30
(40)	Bill Madlock	1.00	.50	.30
(41)	Rick Manning	1.00	.50	.30
(42)	Jon Matlack	1.00	.50	.30
(43)	John Mayberry	1.00	.50	.30
(44)	Hal McRae	1.00	.50	.30
(45)	Andy Messersmith	1.00	.50	.30
(46)	Rick Monday	1.00	.50	.30
(47)	John Montefusco	1.00	.50	.30
(48)	Joe Morgan	5.00	2.50	1.50
(49)	Thurman Munson	4.00	2.00	1.25
(50)	Bobby Murcer	1.00	.50	.30
(51)	Bill North	1.00	.50	.30
(52)	Jim Palmer	5.00	2.50	1.50
(53)	Tony Perez	5.00	2.50	1.50
(54)	Jerry Reuss	1.00	.50	.30
(55)	Brooks Robinson	5.00	2.50	1.50
(56)	Pete Rose	10.00	5.00	3.00
(57)	Joe Rudi	1.00	.50	.30
(58)	Nolan Ryan	20.00	10.00	6.00
(59)	Manny Sanguillen	1.00	.50	.30
(60)	Mike Schmidt	12.00	6.00	3.50
(61)	Tom Seaver	5.00	2.50	1.50
(62)	Bill Singer	1.00	.50	.30
(63)	Willie Stargell	5.00	2.50	1.50
(64)	Rusty Staub	1.50	.70	.45
(65)	Luis Tiant	1.00	.50	.30
(66)	Bob Watson	1.00	.50	.30
(67)	Butch Wynegar	1.00	.50	.30
(68)	Carl Yastrzemski	5.00	2.50	1.50
(69)	Robin Yount	5.00	2.50	1.50
(70)	Richie Zisk	1.00	.50	.30

1929 Churchman's Cigarettes

Though he is identified nowhere on this English cigarette card, the home run swing of Babe Ruth on the front is unmistakable. The last of a set of 25 "Sports & Games in Many Lands" series, the approximately 2-5/8" x 1-3/8" cards have color artwork on the front and green-and-white backs. The back of the baseball card provides a short history of "The great national sport of the U.S.A."

		NM	EX	VG
25	Baseball, U.S.A. (Babe Ruth)	350.00	175.00	100.00

1963 Cincinnati Enquirer Reds' Scrapbook

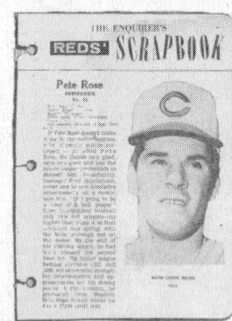

One of the city's newspapers carried this series that could be out of the newspaper and saved. The black-and-white clippings feature a player photo, stats, career notes and biographical data.

		NM	EX	VG
Complete Set (33):		150.00	75.00	45.00
Common Player:		3.00	1.50	.90
(1)	Don Blasingame	3.00	1.50	.90
(2)	Harry Bright	3.00	1.50	.90
(3)	Jim Brosnan	3.00	1.50	.90
(4)	Leo Cardenas	3.00	1.50	.90
(5)	Gerry Coleman	3.00	1.50	.90
(6)	John Edwards	3.00	1.50	.90
(7)	Sam Ellis	3.00	1.50	.90
(8)	Hank Foiles	3.00	1.50	.90
(9)	Gene Freese	3.00	1.50	.90
(10)	Jesse Gonder	3.00	1.50	.90
(11)	Tommy Harper	3.00	1.50	.90
(12)	Bill Henry	3.00	1.50	.90
(13)	Ken Hunt	3.00	1.50	.90
(14)	Fred Hutchinson	3.00	1.50	.90
(15)	Joey Jay	3.00	1.50	.90
(16)	Eddie Kasko	3.00	1.50	.90
(17)	Marty Keough	3.00	1.50	.90
(18)	Johnny Klippstein	3.00	1.50	.90
(19)	Jerry Lynch	3.00	1.50	.90
(20)	Jim Maloney	3.00	1.50	.90
(21)	Joe Nuxhall	4.50	2.25	1.25
(22)	Jim O'Toole	3.00	1.50	.90
(23)	Jim Owens	3.00	1.50	.90
(24)	Don Pavletich	3.00	1.50	.90
(25)	Vada Pinson	6.00	3.00	1.75
(26)	Wally Post	3.00	1.50	.90
(27)	Bob Purkey	3.00	1.50	.90
(28)	Frank Robinson	20.00	10.00	6.00
(29)	Pete Rose	90.00	45.00	27.00
(30)	Dave Sisler	3.00	1.50	.90
(31)	John Tsitouris	3.00	1.50	.90
(32)	Ken Walters	3.00	1.50	.90
(33)	Al Worthington	3.00	1.50	.90

1980 Cincinnati Enquirer Cincinnati Reds

 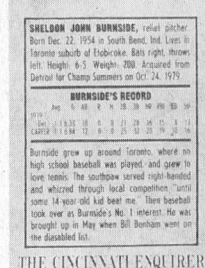

This set of paper "cards" was printed within the pages of the Cincinnati Enquirer newspaper. The 2-1/4" x 3" cards are printed in black-and-white (both front and back) on newsprint. Dotted lines show where the cards were to be cut. Fronts have a player photo and a drawing of Riverfront Stadium. The team logo is in an upper corner and player identification in a black band towards the bottom. Backs have biographical and career details along with stats. Cards are checklisted here according to the uniform numbers printed on front.

		NM	EX	VG
Complete Set (32):		100.00	50.00	30.00
Common Player:		3.00	1.50	.90
2	Russ Nixon	3.00	1.50	.90
3	John McNamara	3.00	1.50	.90
4	Harry Dunlop	3.00	1.50	.90
5	Johnny Bench	9.00	4.50	2.75
6	Bill Fischer	3.00	1.50	.90
7	Hector Cruz	3.00	1.50	.90
9	Vic Correll	3.00	1.50	.90
11	Ron Plaza	3.00	1.50	.90
12	Harry Spilman	3.00	1.50	.90
13	Dave Concepcion	3.00	1.50	.90
15	George Foster	3.00	1.50	.90
16	Ron Oester	3.00	1.50	.90
19	Don Werner	3.00	1.50	.90
20	Cesar Geronimo	3.00	1.50	.90
22	Dan Driessen	3.00	1.50	.90
23	Rick Auerbach	3.00	1.50	.90
25	Ray Knight	3.00	1.50	.90
26	Junior Kennedy	3.00	1.50	.90
28	Sam Mejias	3.00	1.50	.90
29	Dave Collins	3.00	1.50	.90
30	Ken Griffey	3.00	1.50	.90
31	Paul Moskau	3.00	1.50	.90
34	Sheldon Burnside	3.00	1.50	.90
35	Frank Pastore	3.00	1.50	.90
36	Mario Soto	3.00	1.50	.90
37	Dave Tomlin	3.00	1.50	.90
40	Doug Bair	3.00	1.50	.90
41	Tom Seaver	7.50	3.75	2.25
42	Bill Bonham	3.00	1.50	.90
44	Charlie Leibrandt	3.00	1.50	.90
47	Tom Hume	3.00	1.50	.90
51	Mike LaCoss	3.00	1.50	.90

1938 Cincinnati Post Reds

Over the course of several weeks during the summer of 1938, daily editions of the Cincinnati Post sports section carried a set of player portraits designed to be cut out and saved. The pieces measure 6" x 11" and feature a large photo with facsimile autograph, topped by a headline and carrying a short biography below. Everything is in black-and-white. The unnumbered series is checklisted here in alphabetical order.

		NM	EX	VG
Complete Set (25):		450.00	225.00	135.00
Common Player:		20.00	10.00	6.00
(1)	Wally Berger	30.00	15.00	9.00
(2)	Joe Cascarella	20.00	10.00	6.00
(3)	Harry Craft	20.00	10.00	6.00
(4)	Dusty Cooke	20.00	10.00	6.00
(5)	Peaches Davis	20.00	10.00	6.00
(6)	Paul Derringer	25.00	12.50	7.50
(7)	Linus (Junior) Frey	20.00	10.00	6.00
(8)	Lee Gamble	20.00	10.00	6.00
(9)	Ival Goodman	20.00	10.00	6.00
(10)	Hank Gowdy	20.00	10.00	6.00
(11)	Lee Grissom	20.00	10.00	6.00
(12)	Willard Hershberger	25.00	12.50	7.50
(13)	Don Lang	20.00	10.00	6.00
(14)	Ernie Lombardi	35.00	17.50	10.50
(15)	Buck McCormick	20.00	10.00	6.00
(16)	Bill McKechnie	35.00	17.50	10.50

(17)	Whitey Moore	20.00	10.00	6.00
(18)	Billy Myers	20.00	10.00	6.00
(19)	Clifford Richardson	20.00	10.00	6.00
(20)	Lewis Riggs	20.00	10.00	6.00
(21)	Edd Roush	35.00	17.50	10.50
(22)	Gene Schott	20.00	10.00	6.00
(23)	Johnny Vander Meer	30.00	15.00	9.00
(24)	Bucky Walter	20.00	10.00	6.00
(25)	James Weaver	20.00	10.00	6.00

1919-20 Cincinnati Reds Postcards

Two versions of each of the cards in this issue are known. Picturing members of the 1919 World Champions, the foils of the Black Sox scandal, these 3-1/2" x 5-1/2" cards have black-and-white player poses on front. In the white border at bottom (or occasionally, at top) are two lines of type. The top line has the player name and position. The second line can be found in two versions. One reads, "Cincinnati 'Reds' - Champions of National League 1919", the other, presumably a second printing following the World Series, reads, "Cincinnati 'Reds' World's Champions 1919." Backs are printed with standard postcard indicia. Some cards have been found with the advertising of Mt. Union Dairy on the back. The unnumbered cards are checklisted here in alphabetical order.

		NM	EX	VG
Complete Set (24):		3,000	1,500	900.00
Common Player:		150.00	75.00	45.00
(1)	Nick Allen	150.00	75.00	45.00
(2)	Rube Bressler	150.00	75.00	45.00
(3)	Jake Daubert	150.00	75.00	45.00
(4)	Pat Duncan	150.00	75.00	45.00
(5)	Hod Eller	150.00	75.00	45.00
(6)	Ray Fisher	150.00	75.00	45.00
(7)	Eddie Gerner	150.00	75.00	45.00
(8)	Heinie Groh	150.00	75.00	45.00
(9)	Larry Kopf	150.00	75.00	45.00
(10)	Adolfo Luque	175.00	85.00	50.00
(11)	Sherwood Magee	150.00	75.00	45.00
(12)	Roy Mitchell	150.00	75.00	45.00
(13)	Pat Moran	150.00	75.00	45.00
(14)	Greasy Neale	200.00	100.00	60.00
(15)	Bill Rariden	150.00	75.00	45.00
(16)	Morris Rath	150.00	75.00	45.00
(17)	Walter Reuther (Ruether)	150.00	75.00	45.00
(18)	Jimmy Ring	150.00	75.00	45.00
(19)	Eddie Roush	400.00	200.00	120.00
(20)	Harry Sallee	150.00	75.00	45.00
(21)	Hank Schreiber	150.00	75.00	45.00
(22)	Charles See	150.00	75.00	45.00
(23)	Jimmy Smith	150.00	75.00	45.00
(24)	Ivy Wingo	150.00	75.00	45.00

1938 Cincinnati Reds Team Issue

This set of 2" x 3" cards were sold as a boxed set at the ballpark. Fronts feature a black-and-white photo of the player with his name and position in a red strip beneath the picture. Backs have the player's name, position and a generally flattering description of the player's talents. The cards are not numbered. In the American Card Catalog, this issue was designated W711-1.

		NM	EX	VG
Complete Set (23):		1,000	500.00	300.00
Common Player:		40.00	20.00	12.00
(1)	Wally Berger ("... in a trade with the Giants in June.")	40.00	20.00	12.00
(2)	Joe Cascarella	40.00	20.00	12.00
(3)	Allen "Dusty" Cooke	40.00	20.00	12.00
(4)	Harry Craft	40.00	20.00	12.00
(5)	Ray "Peaches" Davis	40.00	20.00	12.00
(6)	Paul Derringer ("Won 22 games...this season.")	40.00	20.00	12.00
(7)	Linus Frey ("... only 25 now.")	40.00	20.00	12.00
(8)	Lee Gamble ("... Syracuse last year.")	40.00	20.00	12.00
(9)	Ival Goodman (No mention of 30 homers.)	40.00	20.00	12.00
(10)	Harry "Hank" Gowdy	40.00	20.00	12.00
(11)	Lee Grissom (No mention of 1938.)	40.00	20.00	12.00
(12)	Willard Hershberger	100.00	50.00	30.00

		NM	EX	VG
(13)	Ernie Lombardi (No mention of 1938 MVP.)	225.00	110.00	67.00
(14)	Frank McCormick	40.00	20.00	12.00
(15)	Bill McKechnie ("Last year he led ...")	200.00	100.00	60.00
(16)	Lloyd "Whitey" Moore ("... last year with Syracuse.")	40.00	20.00	12.00
(17)	Billy Myers ("... in his fourth year.")	40.00	20.00	12.00
(18)	Lee Riggs ("... in his fourth season ...")	40.00	20.00	12.00
(19)	Eddie Roush	200.00	100.00	60.00
(20)	Gene Schott	40.00	20.00	12.00
(21)	Johnny Vander Meer/Portrait	75.00	37.00	22.00
(22)	Wm. "Bucky" Walter ("... won 14 games ...")	40.00	20.00	12.00
(23)	Jim Weaver	40.00	20.00	12.00

1939 Cincinnati Reds Team Issue

An updating by one season of the team-issued 1938 W711-1 set, most of the players and poses on the 2" x 3" cards remained the same. A close study of the career summary on the card's back is necessary to determine which year of issue is at hand. The Livengood card is believed to have been withdrawn from distribution early and is scarce.

		NM	EX	VG
Complete Set (27):		1,250	625.00	375.00
Common Player:		40.00	20.00	12.00
(1)	Wally Berger ("... in a trade with the Giants in June, 1938.")	40.00	20.00	12.00
(2)	Nino Bongiovanni	40.00	20.00	12.00
(3)	Stanley "Frenchy" Bordagaray	40.00	20.00	12.00
(4)	Harry Craft	40.00	20.00	12.00
(5)	Ray "Peaches" Davis	40.00	20.00	12.00
(6)	Paul Derringer ("Won 21 games ... last year.")	45.00	22.00	13.50
(7)	Linus Frey ("... only 26 now.")	40.00	20.00	12.00
(8)	Lee Gamble ("... Syracuse in 1937.")	40.00	20.00	12.00
(9)	Ival Goodman (Mentions hitting 30 homers.)	40.00	20.00	12.00
(10)	Harry "Hank" Gowdy	40.00	20.00	12.00
(11)	Lee Grissom (Mentions 1938.)	40.00	20.00	12.00
(12)	Willard Hershberger	100.00	50.00	30.00
(13)	Eddie Joost	40.00	20.00	12.00
(14)	Wes Livengood	250.00	125.00	75.00
(15)	Ernie Lombardi (Mentions MVP of 1938.)	225.00	110.00	67.00
(16)	Frank McCormick	40.00	20.00	12.00
(17)	Bill McKechnie ("In 1937 he led ...")	200.00	100.00	60.00
(18)	Lloyd "Whitey" Moore ("... in 1937 with Syracuse.")	40.00	20.00	12.00
(19)	Billy Myers ("... in his fifth year ...")	40.00	20.00	12.00
(20)	Lee Riggs ("... in his fifth season...")	40.00	20.00	12.00
(21)	Les Scarsella	40.00	20.00	12.00
(22)	Eugene "Junior" Thompson	40.00	20.00	12.00
(23)	Johnny Vander Meer/Pitching	50.00	25.00	15.00
(24)	Wm. "Bucky" Walters ("Won 15 games ...")	40.00	20.00	12.00
(25)	Jim Weaver	40.00	20.00	12.00
(26)	Bill Werber	40.00	20.00	12.00
(27)	Jimmy Wilson	40.00	20.00	12.00

1940 Cincinnati Reds Team Issue

Another early Reds team issue, this set of black-and-white 2-1/8" x 2-5/8" cards is unnumbered and features player portrait photos on the front. Name, position, biographical information and five years' worth of stats are on the back. The Reds were World Champions in 1940 (defeating Detroit), and the set features several special World Series cards, making it one of the first to feature events as well as individuals. The set was listed in the American Card Catalog as W711-2.

		NM	EX	VG
Complete Set (35):		900.00	450.00	275.00
Common Player:		25.00	12.50	7.50
(1)	Morris Arnovich	25.00	12.50	7.50
(2)	William (Bill) Baker	25.00	12.50	7.50
(3)	Joseph Beggs	25.00	12.50	7.50
(4)	Harry Craft	25.00	12.50	7.50
(5)	Paul Derringer	25.00	12.50	7.50
(6)	Linus Frey	25.00	12.50	7.50
(7)	Ival Goodman	25.00	12.50	7.50
(8)	Harry (Hank) Gowdy	25.00	12.50	7.50
(9)	Witt Guise	25.00	12.50	7.50
(10)	Harry (Socko) Hartman	25.00	12.50	7.50
(11)	Willard Hershberger	35.00	17.50	10.50
(12)	John Hutchings	25.00	12.50	7.50
(13)	Edwin Joost	25.00	12.50	7.50
(14)	Ernie Lombardi	60.00	30.00	18.00
(15)	Frank McCormick	25.00	12.50	7.50
(16)	Myron McCormick	25.00	12.50	7.50
(17)	William Boyd McKechnie	60.00	30.00	18.00
(18)	Lloyd (Whitey) Moore	25.00	12.50	7.50
(19)	William (Bill) Myers	25.00	12.50	7.50
(20)	Lewis Riggs	25.00	12.50	7.50
(21)	Elmer Riddle	25.00	12.50	7.50
(22)	James A. Ripple	25.00	12.50	7.50
(23)	Milburn Shoffner	25.00	12.50	7.50
(24)	Eugene Thompson	25.00	12.50	7.50
(25)	James Turner	25.00	12.50	7.50
(26)	John Vander Meer	30.00	15.00	9.00
(27)	Wm. (Bucky) Walters	25.00	12.50	7.50
(28)	William (Bill) Werber	25.00	12.50	7.50
(29)	James Wilson	25.00	12.50	7.50
(30)	The Cincinnati Reds	25.00	12.50	7.50
(31)	The Cincinnati Reds World Champions	25.00	12.50	7.50
(32)	Tell the World About the Cincinnati Reds	25.00	12.50	7.50
(33)	Tell the World About the Cincinnati Reds Champions	25.00	12.50	7.50
(34)	Results 1940 World's Series	25.00	12.50	7.50
(35)	Debt. of Gratitude to Wm. Koeh Co.	25.00	12.50	7.50

1954-1955 Cincinnati Reds Postcards

The first team-issued Redlegs postcards of the modern era were produced during the 1954 and 1955 seasons for use by players in answering fan requests for pictures and autographs. The cards are 3-1/2" x 5-5/8", printed in black-and-white on non-glossy cardboard stock. Fronts have poses which are borderless at top and sides. At bottom is a 3/4" white strip which is either blank or which has the player and team name printed. Many cards are found with stamped facsimile. autographs, and/or authentically signed. Backs have a vertical line at center. At top-left is: "Cincinnati Baseball Club / Crosley Field / Cincinnati, Ohio." While there is no stamp box on the back, many of the cards have been postally used. The issue was listed in the "American Card Catalog" as PC746.

		NM	EX	VG
Common Player:		15.00	7.50	4.50
(1)	Bobby Adams/Fielding	15.00	7.50	4.50
(2)	Bobby Adams (Portrait to neck.)	15.00	7.50	4.50
(3)	Dr. Wayne Anderson/Trainer (Chest-up.)	30.00	15.00	9.00
(4)	Fred Baczewski (Ready to pitch.)	15.00	7.50	4.50
(5)	Ed Bailey (Batting to waist.)	15.00	7.50	4.50
(6)	Dick Bartell (Portrait to neck.)	15.00	7.50	4.50
(7)	Dick Bartell (Portrait to shoulders.)	15.00	7.50	4.50
(8)	Matt Batts (Batting follow-through.)	15.00	7.50	4.50
(9)	Gus Bell (Portrait to neck.)	15.00	7.50	4.50
(10)	Gus Bell (waist up, ready to hit.)	15.00	7.50	4.50

(11)	Joe Black (Standing in dugout.)	15.00	7.50	4.50
(12)	Bob Borkowski (Batting follow-through.)	15.00	7.50	4.50
(13)	Buzz Boyle/Scout (Chest-up in suit.)	40.00	20.00	12.00
(14)	Rocky Bridges (Portrait to neck.)	15.00	7.50	4.50
(15)	Smoky Burgess (Portrait to neck.)	15.00	7.50	4.50
(16)	Jackie Collum (Pitching follow-through.)	15.00	7.50	4.50
(17)	Jackie Collum (Portrait to neck.)	15.00	7.50	4.50
(18)	Powell Crosley, Jr./Portrait/President	15.00	7.50	4.50
(19)	Jimmy Dykes (Standing in dugout.)	15.00	7.50	4.50
(20)	Nino Escalera (Portrait to neck.)	15.00	7.50	4.50
(21)	Tom Ferrick (Portrait to neck.)	15.00	7.50	4.50
(22)	Art Fowler (hands over head)	15.00	7.50	4.50
(23)	Art Fowler (Portrait to neck.)	15.00	7.50	4.50
(24)	Hershell Freeman (Portrait to shoulders.)	15.00	7.50	4.50
(26)	Jim Greengrass (Waist-up, batting.)	15.00	7.50	4.50
(27)	Don Gross (Portrait to neck.)	15.00	7.50	4.50
(28)	Charley Harmon (Batting to belt.)	15.00	7.50	4.50
(29)	Ray Jablonski (Batting to belt.)	15.00	7.50	4.50
(30)	Howie Judson (Portrait to neck.)	15.00	7.50	4.50
(31)	Johnny Klippstein (Pitching follow-through.)	15.00	7.50	4.50
(32)	Ted Kluszewski/Btg (Cut out sleeves.)	30.00	15.00	9.00
(33)	Ted Kluszewski (Batting to belt.)	30.00	15.00	9.00
(34)	Ted Kluszewski (Batting follow-through, full length.)	30.00	15.00	9.00
(35)	Ted Kluszewski (Batting follow-through to waist.)	30.00	15.00	9.00
(36)	Ted Kluszewski (Batting follow-through, #18 on back.)	30.00	15.00	9.00
(37)	Ted Kluszewski (Stretching at 1B.)	30.00	15.00	9.00
(38)	Ted Kluszewski (Standing w/ four bats.)	30.00	15.00	9.00
(39)	Ted Kluszewski (Portrait to neck, looking right.)	30.00	15.00	9.00
(40)	Ted Kluszewski (Portrait to shoulders, leaning right.)	30.00	15.00	9.00
(41)	Hobie Landrith/Catching	15.00	7.50	4.50
(42)	Hobie Landrith (Pose to neck.)	15.00	7.50	4.50
(43)	William McKechnie, Jr./Portrait (Farm club supervisor.)	15.00	7.50	4.50
(44)	Roy McMillan (Portrait to neck.)	15.00	7.50	4.50
(45)	Roy McMillan (Ready to hit.)	15.00	7.50	4.50
(46)	Lloyd Merriman (Ready to hit.)	15.00	7.50	4.50
(47)	Rudy Minarcin (Portrait to neck.)	15.00	7.50	4.50
(48)	Rudy Minarcin (Portrait to shoulders, chain.)	15.00	7.50	4.50
(49)	Joe Nuxhall (Portrait to neck.)	15.00	7.50	4.50
(51)	Joe Nuxhall (Pitching follow-through.)	15.00	7.50	4.50
(52)	Stan Palys (Batting follow-through.)	15.00	7.50	4.50
(53)	Harry Perkowski (Portrait to neck.)	15.00	7.50	4.50
(54)	Bud Podbielan (Ready to pitch, belt visible.)	15.00	7.50	4.50
(55)	Bud Podbielan (Ready to pitch, no belt.)	15.00	7.50	4.50
(56)	Wally Post (Ready to hit to belt, fans in back.)	22.50	11.00	6.75
(57)	Wally Post (Ready to hit to hips.)	22.50	11.00	6.75
(58)	Wally Post (Batting follow-through, pole on left.)	22.50	11.00	6.75
(59)	Wally Post (Batting follow-through, no pole.)	22.50	11.00	6.75
(60)	Wally Post (Portrait to neck.)	22.50	11.00	6.75
(61)	Ken Raffensberger (Pitching wind-up.)	15.00	7.50	4.50
(62)	Steve Ridzik (Portrait to neck.)	15.00	7.50	4.50
(63)	Connie Ryan (Portrait to neck.)	15.00	7.50	4.50
(64)	Moe Savransky (Portrait to neck.)	15.00	7.50	4.50
(65)	Andy Seminick (Batting follow-through.)	15.00	7.50	4.50
(66)	Al Silvera (Portrait to shoulders.)	15.00	7.50	4.50
(67)	Frank Smith (Ready to pitch.)	15.00	7.50	4.50
(68)	Milt Smith (Portrait to shoulders.)	15.00	7.50	4.50
(69)	Gerry Staley (Ready to pitch.)	15.00	7.50	4.50
(70)	Birdie Tebbetts (Portrait to neck.)	15.00	7.50	4.50
(71)	Birdie Tebbetts (Portrait to shoulders.)	15.00	7.50	4.50
(72)	Johnny Temple (Portrait to neck, mouth closed.)	15.00	7.50	4.50
(73)	Johnny Temple (Portrait to neck, mouth open.)	15.00	7.50	4.50
(74)	Bob Thurman (Batting follow-through.)	15.00	7.50	4.50
(76)	Corky Valentine (Pitching follow-through.)	15.00	7.50	4.50
(77)	Herm Wehmeier (Portrait to neck.)	15.00	7.50	4.50
(78)	George Zuverink (Portrait to neck.)	15.00	7.50	4.50
(79)	Crosley Field	15.00	7.50	4.50

1956 Cincinnati Reds Postcards

TOM ACKER
Cincinnati Redlegs

After a number of years issuing printed postcards for players to answer fan mail, the team began a three-year run of glossy black-and-white photographic card sets in 1956. About 3-1/2" x 5-3/4", the cards usually feature portrait photos, though some action poses are also seen. The pictures are bordered in white with a 1" or so border at bottom with the player and team names. Differentiating the 1956s from similarly formatted issues in 1957-1958 is best done on back. The 1956 cards are divided-back with "Post Card" at top. At right, in the stamp box, is "Place Postage Stamp Here" and, at bottom, "This space for address." Cards are numbered here alphabetically, with gaps left in the assigned numbering for future additions.

		NM	EX	VG
	Complete Set (31):	350.00	175.00	105.00
	Common Player:	10.00	5.00	3.00
(1)	Tom Acker	10.00	5.00	3.00
(2)	Ed Bailey	10.00	5.00	3.00
(3)	Gus Bell	10.00	5.00	3.00
(4)	Joe Black	10.00	5.00	3.00
(5)	"Rocky" Bridges	10.00	5.00	3.00
(6)	"Smoky" Burgess	12.50	6.25	3.75
(7)	George Crowe	10.00	5.00	3.00
(8)	Jim Dyck	10.00	5.00	3.00
(9)	Jimmy Dykes	10.00	5.00	3.00
(11)	Bruce Edwards (Non-'56 back.)	10.00	5.00	3.00
(12)	Tom Ferrick	10.00	5.00	3.00
(13)	Joe Frazier	10.00	5.00	3.00
(14)	Hersh Freeman	10.00	5.00	3.00
(15)	Alex Grammas	10.00	5.00	3.00
(16)	Don Gross	10.00	5.00	3.00
(17)	Ray Jablonski	10.00	5.00	3.00
(18)	Larry Jansen	10.00	5.00	3.00
(19)	Hal Jeffcoat	10.00	5.00	3.00
(21)	Johnny Klippstein	10.00	5.00	3.00
(22)	Ted Kluszewski	20.00	10.00	6.00
(23)	Brooks Lawrence	10.00	5.00	3.00
(24)	Frank McCormick	10.00	5.00	3.00
(25)	Roy McMillan	10.00	5.00	3.00
(26)	Joe Nuxhall	12.50	6.25	3.75
(27)	Stan Palys ('56 back)	10.00	5.00	3.00
(28)	Stan Palys (Non-'56 back.)	10.00	5.00	3.00
(29)	Wally Post	10.00	5.00	3.00
(31)	Frank Robinson	75.00	37.00	22.00
(32)	"Birdie" Tebbetts	10.00	5.00	3.00
(33)	Johnny Temple	10.00	5.00	3.00
(34)	Bob Thurman	10.00	5.00	3.00

1957 Cincinnati Reds Picture Pack

FRANK ROBINSON, Redlegs

Similar in format to the Jay Publishing photo packs, this appears to be a team-issued souvenir item, with many of the pictures having been seen in other team-related contexts. The black-and-white, blank-backed pictures measure 5" x 7". They can be differentiated from contemporary Jay photos by the fact that only the team nickname, "Redlegs," appears, rather than city and team. Player names are in all-caps.

	NM	EX	VG
Complete Set (12):	45.00	22.50	13.50

	Common Player:	4.00	2.00	1.25
(1)	Ed Bailey	4.00	2.00	1.25
(2)	Gus Bell	4.00	2.00	1.25
(3)	Smoky Burgess	4.00	2.00	1.25
(4)	Hersh Freeman	4.00	2.00	1.25
(5)	Ted Kluszewski	7.50	3.75	2.25
(6)	Brooks Lawrence	4.00	2.00	1.25
(7)	Roy McMillan	4.00	2.00	1.25
(8)	Joe Nuxhall	4.00	2.00	1.25
(9)	Wally Post	4.00	2.00	1.25
(10)	Frank Robinson	15.00	7.50	4.50
(11)	Birdie Tebbetts	4.00	2.00	1.25
(12)	Johnny Temple	4.00	2.00	1.25

1957 Cincinnati Reds Postcards

JOHNNY KLIPPSTEIN
Cincinnati Redlegs

The second in a long run of glossy-front, black-and-white annual postcard issues, the 1957 can often be distinguished from the 1956 and 1958 cards by the appearance of players in sleeveless uniforms with dark undershirts. Even more distinguishing is that the 1957s, on back, have "PHOTO POST CARD" across the top, and lack the notice "This Space for Address" which appeared on the 1956 cards. The '57s can also be identified by "Divolite Peerless" which appears in the postage-stamp box. The 3-1/2" x 5-3/4" cards have white borders. At bottom is 1" white space with the player name and "Cincinnati Redlegs" and space for an autograph. The unnumbered cards are checklisted here in alphabetical order.

		NM	EX	VG
	Complete Set (34):	300.00	150.00	90.00
	Common Player:	9.00	4.50	2.75
(1)	Tom Acker	9.00	4.50	2.75
(2)	Ed Bailey	9.00	4.50	2.75
(3)	Gus Bell	9.00	4.50	2.75
(4)	"Rocky" Bridges	9.00	4.50	2.75
(5)	"Smoky" Burgess	11.00	5.50	3.25
(6)	George Crowe	9.00	4.50	2.75
(7)	Bobby Durnbaugh	9.00	4.50	2.75
(8)	Jimmy Dykes	9.00	4.50	2.75
(9)	Tom Ferrick	9.00	4.50	2.75
(10)	Art Fowler	9.00	4.50	2.75
(11)	Hersh Freeman	9.00	4.50	2.75
(12)	Alex Grammas	9.00	4.50	2.75
(13)	Don Gross	9.00	4.50	2.75
(14)	Warren Hacker	9.00	4.50	2.75
(15)	Bobby Henrich	9.00	4.50	2.75
(16)	Don Hoak	11.00	5.50	3.25
(17)	Hal Jeffcoat	9.00	4.50	2.75
(18)	Johnny Klippstein	9.00	4.50	2.75
(19)	Ted Kluszewski/Btg	18.00	9.00	5.50
(20)	Ted Kluszewski/Portrait	18.00	9.00	5.50
(21)	Brooks Lawrence	9.00	4.50	2.75
(22)	Jerry Lynch	9.00	4.50	2.75
(23)	Frank McCormick	9.00	4.50	2.75
(24)	Roy McMillan	9.00	4.50	2.75
(25)	Joe Nuxhall	9.00	4.50	2.75
(26)	Wally Post	9.00	4.50	2.75
(27)	Frank Robinson	45.00	22.00	13.50
(28)	Raul Sanchez	9.00	4.50	2.75
(29)	Art Schult	9.00	4.50	2.75
(30)	"Birdie" Tebbetts	9.00	4.50	2.75
(31)	Johnny Temple	9.00	4.50	2.75
(32)	Bob Thurman	9.00	4.50	2.75
(33)	Pete Whisenant/Btg	9.00	4.50	2.75
(34)	Pete Whisenant/Portrait	9.00	4.50	2.75

1958 Cincinnati Reds Postcards

WALT DROPO
Cincinnati Redlegs

Cards from the third of a long run of glossy-front, black-and-white annual postcard issues can be most often distinguished from similarly formatted 1956-57 cards by the appearance of players in white uniforms with white caps. Two back styles are known. One, like the 1957 issue, has a postage box with "Divolite Peerless" inside and one without the box, but with "Post Card" and "Actual Photograph." Both have a vertical dividing line. The 3-1/2" x 5-3/4" cards have white borders. At bottom is 1" white space with the player name and "Cincinnati Redlegs" and space for an autograph. The unnumbered cards are checklisted here in alphabetical order, though this list may not be complete as several stars are unknown in this style.

		NM	EX	VG
	Complete Set (30):	300.00	150.00	90.00
	Common Player:	9.00	4.50	2.75
(1)	Tom Acker	9.00	4.50	2.75
(2)	Dr. Wayne Anderson/Trainer	9.00	4.50	2.75
(3)	Ed Bailey	9.00	4.50	2.75
(4)	Steve Bilko	9.00	4.50	2.75
(5)	"Smoky" Burgess	11.00	5.50	3.25
(6)	George Crowe	9.00	4.50	2.75
(7)	Walt Dropo	9.00	4.50	2.75
(8)	Jimmie Dykes	9.00	4.50	2.75
(9)	Tom Ferrick	9.00	4.50	2.75
(10)	Dee Fondy	9.00	4.50	2.75
(11)	Alex Grammas	9.00	4.50	2.75
(12)	Harvey Haddix	9.00	4.50	2.75
(13)	Hal Jeffcoat	9.00	4.50	2.75
(14)	Alex Kellner	9.00	4.50	2.75
(15)	Johnny Klippstein	9.00	4.50	2.75
(16)	Turk Lown	9.00	4.50	2.75
(17)	Jerry Lynch	9.00	4.50	2.75
(18)	Roy McMillan	9.00	4.50	2.75
(19)	Ed Miksis/Pinstripes	9.00	4.50	2.75
(20)	Joe Nuxhall	10.00	5.00	3.00
(21)	Vada Pinson	15.00	7.50	4.50
(22)	Bob Purkey	9.00	4.50	2.75
(23)	Charley Rabe	9.00	4.50	2.75
(24)	John Riddle	9.00	4.50	2.75
(25)	Willard Schmidt	9.00	4.50	2.75
(26)	Manager "Birdie" Tebbetts (Portrait to neck.)	9.00	4.50	2.75
(27)	Manager "Birdie" Tebbetts/ Portrait (White background, #1 shows)	9.00	4.50	2.75
(28)	Johnny Temple	9.00	4.50	2.75
(29)	Bob Thurman	9.00	4.50	2.75
(30)	Pete Whisenant	9.00	4.50	2.75

1969 Citgo Coins

This 20-player set of small (about 1" in diameter) metal coins was issued by Citgo in 1969 to commemorate professional baseball's 100th anniversary. The brass-coated coins, susceptible to oxidation, display the player in a crude portrait with his name across the top. The backs honor the 100th anniversary of pro ball. The coins are unnumbered but are generally checklisted according to numbers that appear on a red, white and blue paper display folder that was available from Citgo by mail.

		NM	EX	VG
	Complete Set (20):	80.00	40.00	25.00
	Common Player:	2.00	1.00	.60
	Cardboard Display Folder:	30.00	15.00	9.00
	Unopened Pack:	12.00		
1	Denny McLain	2.50	1.25	.70
2	Dave McNally	2.00	1.00	.60
3	Jim Lonborg	2.00	1.00	.60
4	Harmon Killebrew	6.50	3.25	2.00
5	Mel Stottlemyre	2.00	1.00	.60
6	Willie Horton	2.00	1.00	.60
7	Jim Fregosi	2.00	1.00	.60
8	Rico Petrocelli	2.00	1.00	.60
9	Stan Bahnsen	2.00	1.00	.60
10	Frank Howard	2.50	1.25	.70
11	Joe Torre	2.50	1.25	.70
12	Jerry Koosman	2.00	1.00	.60
13	Ron Santo	3.50	1.75	1.00
14	Pete Rose	20.00	10.00	6.00
15	Rusty Staub	2.00	1.00	.60
16	Henry Aaron	20.00	10.00	6.00
17	Richie Allen	3.50	1.75	1.00
18	Ron Swoboda	2.00	1.00	.60
19	Willie McCovey	6.50	3.25	2.00
20	Jim Bunning	5.00	2.50	1.50

1969 Citgo New York Mets

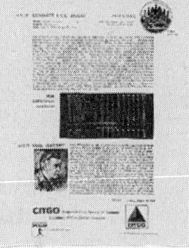

One of several regional issues in the Mets World Championship season of 1969, this set of 8" x 10" player portraits was sponsored by Citgo, whose gas stations distributed the pictures with fuel purchases. Fronts feature large portraits and smaller action pictures of the player, done in pastels, set against a bright pastel background. The paintings are the work of noted celebrity artist John Wheeldon. Beneath the pictures is a facsimile autograph. The player's name is printed in the bottom border. Backs are printed in black-and-white and include biography and career details, full major and minor league stats and a self-portrait and biography of the artist. Logos of the Mets, the Players' Association and the sponsor complete the back design. The unnumbered player pictures are checklisted here in alphabetical order.

		NM	EX	VG
	Complete Set (8):	65.00	32.00	19.50
	Common Player:	6.50	3.25	2.00
(1)	Tommie Agee	8.00	4.00	2.50
(2)	Ken Boswell	6.50	3.25	2.00
(3)	Gary Gentry	6.50	3.25	2.00
(4)	Jerry Grote	6.50	3.25	2.00
(5)	Cleon Jones	6.50	3.25	2.00
(6)	Jerry Koosman	8.00	4.00	2.50
(7)	Ed Kranepool	6.50	3.25	2.00
(8)	Tom Seaver	25.00	12.50	7.50

1975 Clark & Sons Baseball Favorites

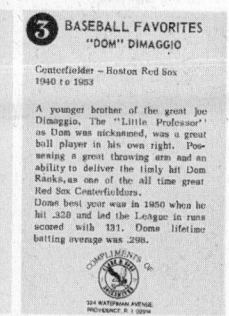

DOM DIMAGGIO

To commemorate the firm's 10 years in business and the Boston Red Sox first pennant since 1967, Clark & Sons Locksmiths of Rhode Island issued this set of Red Sox greats. Two versions were issued. The first has a "324 Waterman Avenue, Providence" address on back. A second printing corrected the errors to "324A Waterman Avenue, East Providence" and added a wavy line around the photo and name on front. Cards measure 2-1/2" x 3-5/8" and are printed in black-and-white.

		NM	EX	VG
	Complete Set (4):	12.50	6.25	3.75
	Common Player:	1.25	.60	.40
1	Bobby Doerr	2.00	1.00	.60
2	Ted Williams	10.00	5.00	3.00
3	Dom DiMaggio	2.50	1.25	.70
4	Johnny Pesky	1.25	.60	.40

1921 Clark's Bread

AL MAMAUX
P.—Brooklyn Nationals

CLARK'S BREAD

Try All Three Kinds of

FAMILY BREAD
AMERICAN MAID
KLEEN MAID

Pure, Clean and Wholesome

It is not known to what extent this set's checklist of base cards and possible variations parallels the contemporary blank-back 1921-1922 W575-1 strip cards. The cards measure about 2" x 3-1/4" and are printed in black-and-white. It is unknown into which region the bread cards might have been issued. Collectors have been known to pay a premium of 10X for this version.

	NM	EX	VG
Common Player:	600.00	300.00	180.00

(See 1921 American Caramel Series of 80 or 1922 W575-1 for checklists and base card values.)

1972 Classic Cards

The set depicts players from 1900-1909 in sepia-tone photos printed on thin, cream-colored card stock by the Flint, MI company not related to the 1990s card maker of the same name. The first series features sequentially numbered cards, the remainder marked only with a series number. Card size is 2-3/4" x 4-1/2" for the first series and 2-3/4" x 4-1/4" for the last three 30-card series.

		NM	EX	VG
	Complete Set (120):	50.00	25.00	10.00
	Common Player:	2.00	1.00	.60
1	Griffith, Cincinnati	2.00	1.00	.60
2	Johnson, Washington	2.00	1.00	.60
3	Ganley, Washington	2.00	1.00	.60
4	Tinker, Chicago	2.00	1.00	.60
5	Chance, Chicago	2.00	1.00	.60
6	Conroy, Washington	2.00	1.00	.60
7	Bresnahan, N.Y.	2.00	1.00	.60
8	Powell, Pittsburgh	2.00	1.00	.60
9	Pfeister, Chicago	2.00	1.00	.60
10	McCarthy, Boston	2.00	1.00	.60
11	McConnell, Boston	2.00	1.00	.60
12	Jennings, Detroit	2.00	1.00	.60
13	Lennox, Brooklyn	2.00	1.00	.60
14	McCormick, N.Y.	2.00	1.00	.60
15	Merkle, N.Y.	2.00	1.00	.60
16	Hoblitzell, Cincinnati	2.00	1.00	.60
17	Dahlen, Boston	2.00	1.00	.60
18	Chance, Chicago	2.00	1.00	.60
19	Ferguson, Boston	2.00	1.00	.60
20	Camnitz, Pittsburgh	2.00	1.00	.60
21	N.Y. (Neal Ball)	2.00	1.00	.60
22	Hemphill, N.Y.	2.00	1.00	.60
23	Baker, Philadelphia	2.00	1.00	.60
24	Mathewson, N.Y.	5.00	2.50	1.50
25	Burch, Brooklyn	2.00	1.00	.60
26	Grant, Philadelphia	2.00	1.00	.60
27	Ames, N.Y.	2.00	1.00	.60
28	Newton, N.Y.	2.00	1.00	.60
29	Moran, Chicago	2.00	1.00	.60
30	Lajoie, Cleveland	2.00	1.00	.60
(31)	Abstein, Pittsburgh	2.00	1.00	.60
(32)	Brown, Chicago	2.00	1.00	.60
(33)	Campbell, Cincinnati	2.00	1.00	.60
(34)	Cobb, Detroit	5.00	2.50	1.50
(35)	Crawford, Detroit	2.00	1.00	.60
(36)	Devlin, N.Y.	2.00	1.00	.60
(37)	Dooin, Philadelphia	2.00	1.00	.60
(38)	Dougherty, Chicago	2.00	1.00	.60
(39)	Downey, Cincinnati	2.00	1.00	.60
(40)	Doyle, New York	2.00	1.00	.60
(41)	Dunn, Brooklyn	2.00	1.00	.60
(42)	Durham, N.Y.	2.00	1.00	.60
(43)	Gibson, Pittsburgh	2.00	1.00	.60
(44)	Hartzel, Philadelphia	2.00	1.00	.60
(45)	Higginbotham, Chicago	2.00	1.00	.60
(46)	Hinchman	2.00	1.00	.60
(47)	Lajoie	2.00	1.00	.60
(48)	Mowery, Cincinnati	2.00	1.00	.60
(49)	Mullin, Detroit	2.00	1.00	.60
(50)	O'Hara, New York	2.00	1.00	.60
(51)	Overall, Chicago	2.00	1.00	.60
(52)	Perring, Cleveland	2.00	1.00	.60
(53)	Rossman, Detroit	2.00	1.00	.60
(54)	Schmidt, Detroit	2.00	1.00	.60
(55)	Steinfeldt, Chicago	2.00	1.00	.60
(56)	Stone, St. Louis	2.00	1.00	.60
(57)	Titus, Philadelphia	2.00	1.00	.60
(58)	Wagner, Pittsburgh	2.00	1.00	.60
(59)	Wamhow, N.Y.	2.00	1.00	.60
(60)	Wiltse, New York	2.00	1.00	.60
(61)	Barger, Brooklyn	2.00	1.00	.60
(62)	Bergen, Brooklyn	2.00	1.00	.60
(63)	Bowerman, Boston	2.00	1.00	.60
(64)	Bransfeld, Philadelphia	2.00	1.00	.60
(65)	Bresnahan, St. Louis	2.00	1.00	.60
(66)	Coakley, Chicago	2.00	1.00	.60
(67)	Donovan, Detroit	2.00	1.00	.60
(68)	Elberfeld, New York	2.00	1.00	.60
(69)	Evers, Chicago	2.00	1.00	.60
(70)	Fromme, Cincinnati	2.00	1.00	.60
(71)	Herzog, N.Y.	2.00	1.00	.60
(72)	Hummel, Cincinnati	2.00	1.00	.60
(73)	Jordan, Brooklyn	2.00	1.00	.60
(74)	Keeler, New York	2.00	1.00	.60
(75)	Lumley, Brooklyn	2.00	1.00	.60
(76)	Maddox, Pittsburgh	2.00	1.00	.60
(77)	McGinnity, New York	2.00	1.00	.60
(78)	McGraw, New York	2.00	1.00	.60
(79)	McIntyre, Brooklyn	2.00	1.00	.60
(80)	Moriarity, New York	2.00	1.00	.60
(81)	Pastorius, Brooklyn	2.00	1.00	.60
(82)	Purtell, Chicago	2.00	1.00	.60
(83)	Schulte, Chicago	2.00	1.00	.60
(84)	Sebring, Brooklyn	2.00	1.00	.60
(85)	Smith, Washington	2.00	1.00	.60
(86)	Speaker, Boston	5.00	2.50	1.50
(87)	Spencer, Boston	2.00	1.00	.60

		NM	EX	VG
(88)	Tuckey, Boston	2.00	1.00	.60
(89)	Vaughn, New York	2.00	1.00	.60
(90)	Wheat, Brooklyn	2.00	1.00	.60
(91)	Altizer, Chicago	2.00	1.00	.60
(92)	Bender, Philadelphia	2.00	1.00	.60
(93)	Cincinnati (Bob Ewing)	2.00	1.00	.60
(94)	Bresnahan, St. Louis	2.00	1.00	.60
(95)	Chappelle, Boston	2.00	1.00	.60
(96)	Chase, New York	2.00	1.00	.60
(97)	Daley, Cincinnati	2.00	1.00	.60
(98)	Davis, Chicago	2.00	1.00	.60
(99)	Delahanty, St. Louis	2.00	1.00	.60
(100)	Donohue, Washington	2.00	1.00	.60
(101)	Doyle, New York	2.00	1.00	.60
(102)	Ellis, St. Louis	2.00	1.00	.60
(103)	Graham, St. Louis	2.00	1.00	.60
(104)	Herzog, New York	2.00	1.00	.60
(105)	Hyatt, Pittsburgh	2.00	1.00	.60
(106)	Konetchy, St. Louis	2.00	1.00	.60
(107)	Lake, New York	2.00	1.00	.60
(108)	Lord, Boston	2.00	1.00	.60
(109)	New York (Luther Taylor)	2.00	1.00	.60
(110)	McLean, Cincinnati	2.00	1.00	.60
(111)	Needham, Chicago	2.00	1.00	.60
(112)	Pearce, Cincinnati	2.00	1.00	.60
(113)	Powell, Pittsburgh	2.00	1.00	.60
(114)	Purtell, Chicago	2.00	1.00	.60
(115)	Schreck, Philadelphia	2.00	1.00	.60
(116)	Storke, Pittsburgh	2.00	1.00	.60
(117)	Strunk, Philadelphia	2.00	1.00	.60
(118)	Summers, Detroit	2.00	1.00	.60
(119)	Thomas, Philadelphia	2.00	1.00	.60
(120)	Wagner, Boston	2.00	1.00	.60

1973 Roberto Clemente Memorial Postcard

This collectors' issue postcard was issued as a memorial. In standard 3-1/2" x 5-1/2" format with a postcard-style back, the black-and-white card has printed in the wide bottom border, the player's name, dates of his birth and death and, "In Memory OF A COURAGEOUS HUMAN BEING." On back is a credit line to Allied Printing.

	NM	EX	VG
Roberto Clemente	25.00	12.50	7.50

1913 Cleveland Indians Schedule Postcards

The extent to which the team may have used this type of postcard to announce forthcoming home series is unknown. It can be assumed other cards with other players featured were used during the course of the season. About 7" x 3-1/2", the card has

a portrait photo on the left end of its black-and-white front. On back, in red and black, are details of upcoming series and ticket outlet information.

	NM	EX	VG
Joe Birmingham	900.00	450.00	275.00
Ray Chapman	1,350	675.00	400.00
Jack Graney	900.00	450.00	275.00
Joe Jackson, Fred Clarke (Pirates exhibition game.)	2,500	1,250	750.00
Doc Johnston	900.00	450.00	275.00
Willie Mitchell	900.00	450.00	275.00

1947 Cleveland Indians Picture Pack

The first of several annual issues of player photo packs, the 1947 version offered "autographed photos" of all players on the team's roster as of July 1. All players were presented in studio quality portraits in 6" x 8-1/2" format, lithographed on heavy paper with a facsimile autograph. A thin white border surrounds the photo. Backs are blank. The photos were sold in sets for 50 cents. The unnumbered pictures are checklisted here alphabetically.

		NM	EX	VG
Complete Set (25):		100.00	50.00	30.00
Common Player:		3.00	1.50	.90
(1)	Don Black	4.00	2.00	1.25
(2)	Eddie Bockman	3.00	1.50	.90
(3)	Lou Boudreau	9.00	4.50	2.75
(4)	Jack Conway	3.00	1.50	.90
(5)	Larry Doby	25.00	12.50	7.50
(6)	Hank Edwards	3.00	1.50	.90
(7)	"Red" Embree	3.00	1.50	.90
(8)	Bob Feller	25.00	12.50	7.50
(9)	Les Fleming	3.00	1.50	.90
(10)	Allen Gettel	3.00	1.50	.90
(11)	Joe Gordon	3.00	1.50	.90
(12)	Steve Gromek	3.00	1.50	.90
(13)	Mel Harder	4.50	2.25	1.25
(14)	Jim Hegan	3.00	1.50	.90
(15)	Ken Keltner	4.50	2.25	1.25
(16)	Ed Klieman	3.00	1.50	.90
(17)	Bob Lemon	9.00	4.50	2.75
(18)	Al Lopez	9.00	4.50	2.75
(19)	George Metkovich	3.00	1.50	.90
(20)	Dale Mitchell	4.00	2.00	1.25
(21)	Hal Peck	3.00	1.50	.90
(22)	Eddie Robinson	3.00	1.50	.90
(23)	Hank Ruszkowski	3.00	1.50	.90
(24)	Pat Seerey	3.00	1.50	.90
(25)	Bryan Stephens	3.00	1.50	.90
(26)	Les Willis	3.00	1.50	.90

1947 Van Patrick Cleveland Indians Postcards

Fans could obtain these black-and-white postcard-size (3-1/2" x 5-1/2") photos of their favorite Indians players by writing to radio broadcaster Van Patrick. Backs do not have postcard markings, and carry a message from Patrick. The unnumbered cards are checklisted here alphabetically, though the listing may not be complete.

		NM	EX	VG
Common Player:		100.00	50.00	30.00
(1)	Don Black	100.00	50.00	30.00
(2)	Eddie Bockman	100.00	50.00	30.00
(3)	Lou Boudreau	200.00	100.00	60.00
(4)	Jack Conway	100.00	50.00	30.00
(5)	Hank Edwards	100.00	50.00	30.00
(6)	Red Embree	100.00	50.00	30.00
(7)	Bob Feller/Pitching	300.00	150.00	90.00
(8)	Bob Feller/Pitching (Leg in air.)	300.00	150.00	90.00
(9)	Les Fleming	100.00	50.00	30.00
(10)	Allen Gettel	100.00	50.00	30.00
(11)	Joe Gordon	125.00	62.00	37.00
(12)	Steve Gromek	100.00	50.00	30.00
(13)	Mel Harder	125.00	62.00	37.00
(14)	Jim Hegan	110.00	55.00	33.00
(15)	Ken Keltner	110.00	55.00	33.00
(16)	Ed Klieman	100.00	50.00	30.00
(17)	Bob Lemon	200.00	100.00	60.00
(18)	Al Lopez	200.00	100.00	60.00
(19)	George Metkovich	100.00	50.00	30.00
(20)	Dale Mitchell	100.00	50.00	30.00
(21)	Hal Peck	100.00	50.00	30.00
(22)	Eddie Robinson	100.00	50.00	30.00
(23)	Hank Ruszkowski	100.00	50.00	30.00
(24)	Pat Seerey	100.00	50.00	30.00
(25)	Bryan Stephens	100.00	50.00	30.00
(26)	Les Willis	100.00	50.00	30.00

1948-52 Cleveland Indians Pencil Clips

These celluloid and steel pencil clips were sold at the ballpark to be used on pencils given away with scorecards. The round button portion of the clip is about 3/4" in diameter, while the clip itself is a little over 1-1/2". Black-and-white player portraits are centered in a colored border with the team name at top and player name at bottom. While many of the same players and photos were used year after year, issue date of the clips can be determined by the border color. In 1951-1952, when blue borders were used, the year is distinguished by the presence (1951) or absence (1952) of a white union logo on back.

		NM	EX	VG
Common Player:		35.00	17.50	10.50
1948 (Black)				
(1)	Gene Bearden	35.00	17.50	10.50
(2)	John Berardino	40.00	20.00	12.00
(3)	Don Black	35.00	17.50	10.50
(4)	Lou Boudreau	45.00	22.00	13.50
(5)	Russ Christopher	35.00	17.50	10.50
(6)	Allie Clark	35.00	17.50	10.50
(7)	Larry Doby	60.00	30.00	18.00
(8)	Hank Edwards	35.00	17.50	10.50
(9)	Bob Feller	50.00	25.00	15.00
(10)	Al Gettel	35.00	17.50	10.50
(11)	Joe Gordon	35.00	17.50	10.50
(12)	Walt Judnich	35.00	17.50	10.50
(13)	Ken Keltner	35.00	17.50	10.50
(14)	Bob Lemon	45.00	22.00	13.50
(15)	Dale Mitchell	35.00	17.50	10.50
(16)	Bob Muncrief	35.00	17.50	10.50
(17)	Eddie Robinson	35.00	17.50	10.50
(18)	Pat Seerey	35.00	17.50	10.50
(19)	Joe Tipton	35.00	17.50	10.50
(20)	Thurman Tucker	35.00	17.50	10.50
1949 (Brown)				
(1)	Gene Bearden	35.00	17.50	10.50
(2)	Ray Boone	35.00	17.50	10.50
(3)	Lou Boudreau	45.00	22.00	13.50
(4)	Allie Clark	35.00	17.50	10.50
(5)	Larry Doby	55.00	27.00	16.50
(6)	Bob Feller	50.00	25.00	15.00
(7)	Mike Garcia	35.00	17.50	10.50
(8)	Joe Gordon	35.00	17.50	10.50
(9)	Steve Gromek	35.00	17.50	10.50
(10)	Jim Hegan	35.00	17.50	10.50
(11)	Ken Keltner	35.00	17.50	10.50
(12)	Bob Kennedy	35.00	17.50	10.50
(13)	Bob Lemon	45.00	22.00	13.50

		NM	EX	VG
(14)	Dale Mitchell	35.00	17.50	10.50
(15)	Satchel Paige	125.00	62.00	37.00
(16)	Mike Tresh	35.00	17.50	10.50
(17)	Bill Veeck	45.00	22.00	13.50
(18)	Mickey Vernon	35.00	17.50	10.50
(19)	Early Wynn	45.00	22.00	13.50
(20)	Sam Zoldak	35.00	17.50	10.50

1950 (White)

(1)	Bobby Avila	35.00	17.50	10.50
(2)	Al Benton	35.00	17.50	10.50
(3)	Ray Boone	35.00	17.50	10.50
(4)	Lou Boudreau	45.00	22.00	13.50
(5)	Larry Doby	55.00	27.00	16.50
(6)	Luke Easter	40.00	20.00	12.00
(7)	Bob Feller	50.00	25.00	15.00
(8)	Mike Garcia	40.00	20.00	12.00
(9)	Steve Gromek	35.00	17.50	10.50
(10)	Jim Hegan	35.00	17.50	10.50
(11)	Bob Kennedy	35.00	17.50	10.50
(12)	Bob Lemon	45.00	22.00	13.50
(13)	Dale Mitchell	35.00	17.50	10.50
(14)	Ray Murray	35.00	17.50	10.50
(15)	Al Rosen	40.00	20.00	12.00
(16)	Thurman Tucker	35.00	17.50	10.50
(17)	Dick Weik	35.00	17.50	10.50
(18)	Early Wynn	45.00	22.00	13.50

1950 (Blue w/union logo.)

(1)	Bobby Avila	35.00	17.50	10.50
(2)	Ray Boone	35.00	17.50	10.50
(3)	Larry Doby	55.00	27.00	16.50
(4)	Luke Easter	40.00	20.00	12.00
(5)	Bob Feller	50.00	25.00	15.00
(6)	Jim Hegan	35.00	17.50	10.50
(7)	Bob Kennedy	35.00	17.50	10.50
(8)	Bob Lemon	45.00	22.00	13.50
(9)	Al Lopez	45.00	22.00	13.50
(10)	Dale Mitchell	35.00	17.50	10.50
(11)	Al Rosen	40.00	20.00	12.00
(12)	Early Wynn	45.00	22.00	13.50

1952 (Blue, no logo.)

(1)	Bobby Avila	35.00	17.50	10.50
(2)	Lou Brissie	35.00	17.50	10.50
(3)	Bob Chakales	35.00	17.50	10.50
(4)	Merrill Combs	35.00	17.50	10.50
(5)	Larry Doby	55.00	27.00	16.50
(6)	Luke Easter	40.00	20.00	12.00
(7)	Bob Feller	50.00	25.00	15.00
(8)	Mike Garcia	40.00	20.00	12.00
(9)	Steve Gromek	35.00	17.50	10.50
(10)	Jim Hegan	35.00	17.50	10.50
(11)	Sam Jones	35.00	17.50	10.50
(12)	Bob Lemon	45.00	22.00	13.50
(13)	Barney McCosky	35.00	17.50	10.50
(14)	Dale Mitchell	35.00	17.50	10.50
(15)	Pete Reiser	35.00	17.50	10.50
(16)	Al Rosen	45.00	22.50	13.50
(17)	Harry Simpson	35.00	17.50	10.50
(18)	Birdie Tebbetts	35.00	17.50	10.50
(19)	Early Wynn	45.00	22.00	13.50

1948 Cleveland Indians Picture Pack

For its second year of production as a souvenir sales item, the Indians picture pack utilized the basic format of the previous year: black-and-white photos with a white border and facsimile autograph. Backs were again blank. The 1948 set can be differentiated from the 1947 issue by its size; at 6-1/2" x 9", the '48s are larger by a half-inch horizontally and vertically. The unmarked pictures are checklisted here in alphabetical order. The specific content of the packs may have changed over the course of the season with roster moves.

		NM	EX	VG
Complete Set (33):		300.00	150.00	90.00
Common Player:		6.00	3.00	1.75
(1)	Gene Bearden	6.00	3.00	1.75
(2)	Johnny Berardino	12.00	6.00	3.50
(3)	Don Black	7.50	3.75	2.25
(4)	Lou Boudreau	20.00	10.00	6.00
(5)	Russ Christopher	6.00	3.00	1.75
(6)	Allie Clark	6.00	3.00	1.75
(7)	Larry Doby	25.00	12.50	7.50
(8)	Hank Edwards	6.00	3.00	1.75
(9)	Bob Feller	25.00	12.50	7.50
(10)	Joe Gordon	6.00	3.00	1.75
(11)	Hank Greenberg/GM (In uniform.)	40.00	20.00	12.00
(12)	Hank Greenberg/GM (In civies.)	20.00	10.00	6.00
(13)	Steve Gromek	6.00	3.00	1.75
(14)	Mel Harder	6.00	3.00	1.75
(15)	Jim Hegan	6.00	3.00	1.75
(16)	Walt Judnich	6.00	3.00	1.75
(17)	Ken Keltner	6.00	3.00	1.75
(18)	Bob Kennedy	6.00	3.00	1.75
(19)	Ed Klieman	6.00	3.00	1.75
(20)	Bob Lemon	20.00	10.00	6.00
(21)	Al Lopez	20.00	10.00	6.00
(22)	Bill McKechnie	20.00	10.00	6.00
(23)	Dale Mitchell	6.00	3.00	1.75
(24)	Bob Muncrief	6.00	3.00	1.75
(25)	Satchel Paige	60.00	30.00	18.00
(26)	Hal Peck	6.00	3.00	1.75
(27)	Eddie Robinson	6.00	3.00	1.75
(28)	Muddy Ruel	6.00	3.00	1.75
(29)	Joe Tipton	6.00	3.00	1.75
(30)	Thurman Tucker	6.00	3.00	1.75
(31)	Bill Veeck/Owner	20.00	10.00	6.00
(32)	Sam Zoldak	6.00	3.00	1.75
(33)	Cleveland Municipal Stadium	9.00	4.50	2.75

1949 Cleveland Indians Display Photos

BOB FELLER - P. CLEVELAND INDIANS

Members of the Tribe are pictured (in the same poses found on their photo-pack issues) on these large-format (11" x 14") display photos, said to have been used for in-stadium promotions. It is possible there are others besides those checklisted here.

		NM	EX	VG
Complete Set (11):		650.00	325.00	200.00
Common Player:		40.00	20.00	12.00
(1)	Ray Boone	45.00	22.00	13.50
(2)	Larry Doby	100.00	50.00	30.00
(3)	Luke Easter	50.00	25.00	15.00
(4)	Bob Feller	125.00	62.00	37.00
(5)	Jim Hegan	40.00	20.00	12.00
(6)	Bob Kennedy	40.00	20.00	12.00
(7)	Bob Lemon	75.00	37.00	22.00
(8)	Al Lopez	75.00	37.00	22.00
(9)	Dale Mitchell	40.00	20.00	12.00
(10)	Al Rosen	50.00	25.00	15.00
(11)	Early Wynn	75.00	37.00	22.00

1949 Cleveland Indians Picture Pack - Action

Posed action photos are the focus of this team-issued picture pack. The black-and-white 6-1/2" x 9" photos feature white borders all around and a facsimile autograph on front. Backs are blank. The set was sold in a red and white paper envelope labeled "World Champion Cleveland Indians Autographed Action Photos." Backs are blank. The unnumbered pictures are checklisted here alphabetically. Unmarked reprints of this team-issue, complete with mailing envelope, were made in the late 1980s.

		NM	EX	VG
Complete Set (30):		175.00	90.00	55.00
Common Player:		4.00	2.00	1.25
(1)	Bob Avila	6.00	3.00	1.75
(2)	Gene Bearden	4.00	2.00	1.25
(3)	Al Benton	4.00	2.00	1.25
(4)	John Berardino	12.00	6.00	3.50
(5)	Ray Boone	6.00	3.00	1.75
(6)	Lou Boudreau	16.00	8.00	4.75
(7)	Allie Clark	4.00	2.00	1.25
(8)	Larry Doby	17.50	8.75	5.25
(9)	Bob Feller	20.00	10.00	6.00
(10)	Mike Garcia	6.00	3.00	1.75
(11)	Joe Gordon	4.00	2.00	1.25
(12)	Hank Greenberg/GM	12.00	6.00	3.50
(13)	Steve Gromek	4.00	2.00	1.25
(14)	Jim Hegan	4.00	2.00	1.25
(15)	Ken Keltner	4.00	2.00	1.25
(16)	Bob Kennedy	4.00	2.00	1.25
(17)	Bob Lemon	12.00	6.00	3.50
(18)	Dale Mitchell	4.00	2.00	1.25
(19)	Satchel Paige	40.00	20.00	12.00
(20)	Frank Papish	4.00	2.00	1.25
(21)	Hal Peck	4.00	2.00	1.25
(22)	Al Rosen	8.00	4.00	2.50
(23)	Mike Tresh	4.00	2.00	1.25
(24)	Thurman Tucker	4.00	2.00	1.25
(25)	Bill Veeck/Owner	12.00	6.00	3.50
(26)	Mickey Vernon	6.00	3.00	1.75
(27)	Early Wynn	12.00	6.00	3.50
(28)	Sam Zoldak	4.00	2.00	1.25
(29)	Indians Coaches (Mel Harder, Steve O'Neill, Bill McKechnie, Muddy Ruel, George Susce)	4.00	2.00	1.25
(30)	Municipal Stadium	6.00	3.00	1.75

1949 Cleveland Indians Picture Pack - Portraits

This set of player photos was produced by Big League Novelty Co., Cleveland, as credited on the paper envelope in which they were sold. The envelope has a crowned, big-nosed Indian caricature and mini-pictures of three of the players. The pictures are in a 6-1/2" x 9" blank-back format. They are black-and-white and virtually all depict the players in chest-to-cap portraits (many the same as previous and later years' issues) with a facsimile autograph. The unnumbered pictures are checklisted here alphabetically.

		NM	EX	VG
Complete Set (20):		75.00	40.00	25.00
Common Player:		3.00	1.50	.90
(1)	Bob Avila	4.50	2.25	1.25
(2)	Gene Bearden	3.00	1.50	.90
(3)	John Berardino	4.50	2.25	1.25
(4)	Lou Boudreau	7.50	3.75	2.25
(5)	Larry Doby	10.00	5.00	3.00
(6)	Bob Feller	12.50	6.25	3.75
(7)	Mike Garcia	4.50	2.25	1.25
(8)	Joe Gordon	3.00	1.50	.90
(9)	Steve Gromek	3.00	1.50	.90
(10)	Jim Hegan	3.00	1.50	.90
(11)	Ken Keltner	3.00	1.50	.90
(12)	Bob Kennedy	3.00	1.50	.90
(13)	Bob Lemon	5.00	2.50	1.50
(14)	Dale Mitchell	3.00	1.50	.90
(15)	Satchel Paige	30.00	15.00	9.00
(16)	Hal Peck	3.00	1.50	.90
(17)	Thurman Tucker	3.00	1.50	.90
(18)	Mickey Vernon	4.00	2.00	1.25
(19)	Early Wynn	5.00	2.50	1.50
(20)	Sam Zoldak	3.00	1.50	.90

1949 Cleveland Indians Sun Picture Camera

Lou Boudreau

These novelty cards are self-developing photo-prints sold by the team in packages of four that included negatives and pieces of photo-sensative paper which were used to make the 1-7/8" x 2" black-and-white blank-back pictures. Because existing negatives could be used to make many new prints, values for the prints themselves are low. Prices quoted here are for negative/print combinations.

	NM	EX	VG
Complete Set Negatives/ Prints (20):	3,000	1,500	900.00
Common Negative/Print:	125.00	65.00	35.00
(1) Gene Bearden	125.00	65.00	35.00
(2) Al Benton	125.00	65.00	35.00
(3) Ray Boone	125.00	65.00	35.00
(4) Lou Boudreau	200.00	100.00	60.00
(5) Allie Clark	125.00	65.00	35.50
(6) Larry Doby	250.00	125.00	75.00
(7) Bob Feller	250.00	125.00	75.00
(8) Mike Garcia	135.00	70.00	40.00
(9) Joe Gordon	125.00	65.00	35.00
(10) Steve Gromek	125.00	65.00	35.00
(11) Jim Hegan	125.00	65.00	35.00
(12) Ken Keltner	135.00	70.00	40.00
(13) Bob Kennedy	125.00	65.00	35.00
(14) Bob Lemon	200.00	100.00	60.00
(15) Dale Mitchell	125.00	65.00	35.00
(16) Hal Peck	125.00	65.00	35.00
(17) Satchel Paige	400.00	200.00	120.00
(18) Thurman Tucker	125.00	65.00	35.00
(19) Mickey Vernon	125.00	65.00	35.00
(20) Early Wynn	200.00	100.00	60.00

1950 Cleveland Indians Picture Pack

Similar in format to previous years' issues, these 6-1/2" x 9" black-and-white player poses have a white border and facsimile autograph on front. Backs are blank. The unnumbered photos are checklisted here alphabetically. It is possible the contents of specific picture packs changed over the course of the season to reflect roster moves.

	NM	EX	VG
Complete Set (27):	160.00	80.00	50.00
Common Player:	4.00	2.00	1.20
(1) Bobby Avila	5.00	2.50	1.50
(2) Gene Bearden	4.00	2.00	1.20
(3) Al Benton	4.00	2.00	1.20
(4) Ray Boone	5.00	2.50	1.50
(5) Lou Boudreau	12.00	6.00	3.50
(6) Allie Clark	4.00	2.00	1.20
(7) Larry Doby	17.50	8.75	5.25
(8) Luke Easter	6.00	3.00	1.75
(9) Bob Feller	20.00	10.00	6.00
(10) Jess Flores	4.00	2.00	1.20
(11) Mike Garcia	5.00	2.50	1.50
(12) Joe Gordon	4.00	2.00	1.20
(13) Hank Greenberg/GM	12.00	6.00	3.50
(14) Steve Gromek	4.00	2.00	1.20
(15) Jim Hegan	4.00	2.00	1.20
(16) Bob Kennedy	4.00	2.00	1.20
(17) Bob Lemon	12.00	6.00	3.50
(18) Dale Mitchell	4.00	2.00	1.20
(19) Ray Murray	4.00	2.00	1.20
(20) Chick Pieretti	4.00	2.00	1.20
(21) Al Rosen	6.00	3.00	1.75
(22) Dick Rozek	4.00	2.00	1.20
(23) Ellis Ryan/Owner	4.00	2.00	1.20
(24) Thurman Tucker	4.00	2.00	1.20
(25) Early Wynn	12.00	6.00	3.50
(26) Sam Zoldak	4.00	2.00	1.20
(27) Cleveland Municipal Stadium	8.00	4.00	2.50

1951 Cleveland Indians Picture Pack

While this set of Indians pictures shares the 6-1/2" x 9" format of the Tribe's other team issues of the era, it is unique in its use of a much glossier front surface. Pictures are, with the exception of the manager, game-action or posed-action in black-and-white, bordered in white and with a facsimile autograph. Backs are blank. It is unknown whether this checklist is complete or whether players were added or removed to reflect in-season roster changes.

	NM	EX	VG
Complete Set (26):	150.00	75.00	45.00
Common Player:	4.00	2.00	1.25
(1) Bob Avila	4.00	2.00	1.25
(2) Gene Bearden	4.00	2.00	1.25
(3) Ray Boone	6.00	3.00	1.75
(4) Lou Brissie	4.00	2.00	1.25
(5) Bob Chakales	4.00	2.00	1.25
(6) Sam Chapman	4.00	2.00	1.25
(7) Merrill Combs	4.00	2.00	1.25
(8) Larry Doby	15.00	7.50	4.50
(9) Luke Easter	6.00	3.00	1.75
(10) Red Fahr	4.00	2.00	1.25
(11) Bob Feller	20.00	10.00	6.00
(12) Mike Garcia	6.00	3.00	1.75
(13) Steve Gromek	4.00	2.00	1.25
(14) Jim Hegan	4.00	2.00	1.25
(15) Bob Kennedy	4.00	2.00	1.25
(16) Bob Lemon	12.50	6.25	3.75
(17) Al Lopez	12.50	6.25	3.75
(18) Milt Neilsen	4.00	2.00	1.25
(19) Al Rosen	8.00	4.00	2.50
(20) Dick Rozek	4.00	2.00	1.25
(21) Harry Simpson	4.00	2.00	1.25
(22) Snuffy Stirnweiss	4.00	2.00	1.25
(23) Birdie Tebbetts	4.00	2.00	1.25
(24) Johnny Vander Meer	6.00	3.00	1.75
(25) Early Wynn	12.50	6.25	3.75
(26) George Zuverink	4.00	2.00	1.25

1954 Cleveland Indians Picture Pack

Because many of the pictures found in the championship season picture pack are the same poses found in earlier issues, size can be used to differentiate the years of issue. For 1954, the pictures were down-sized slightly in height, to a 6" x 8-3/4" format, and printed on heavier paper than in previous years. Each of the portraits, poses and action photos are bordered in white and include a facsimile autograph. The unnumbered pictures are checklisted here alphabetically.

	NM	EX	VG
Complete Set (27):	125.00	65.00	40.00
Common Player:	4.00	2.00	1.25
(1) Bobby Avila	4.00	2.00	1.25
(2) Sam Dente	4.00	2.00	1.25
(3) Larry Doby	10.00	5.00	3.00
(4) Bob Feller	15.00	7.50	4.50
(5) Mike Garcia	4.00	2.00	1.25
(6) Bill Glynn	4.00	2.00	1.25
(7) Mike Hegan	4.00	2.00	1.25
(8) Bob Hooper	4.00	2.00	1.25
(9) Dave Hoskins	4.00	2.00	1.25
(10) Art Houtteman	4.00	2.00	1.25
(11) Bob Lemon	7.50	3.75	2.25
(12) Al Lopez	7.50	3.75	2.25
(13) Hank Majeski	4.00	2.00	1.25
(14) Dale Mitchell	4.00	2.00	1.25
(15) Don Mossi	6.00	3.00	1.75
(16) Hal Naragon	4.00	2.00	1.25
(17) Ray Narleski	4.00	2.00	1.25
(18) Hal Newhouser	7.50	3.75	2.25
(19) Dave Philley	4.00	2.00	1.25
(20) Dave Pope	4.00	2.00	1.25
(21) Rudy Regaldo	4.00	2.00	1.25

	NM	EX	VG
(22) Al Rosen	6.00	3.00	1.75
(23) Al Smith	4.00	2.00	1.25
(24) George Strickland	4.00	2.00	1.25
(25) Vic Wertz	4.00	2.00	1.25
(26) Wally Westlake	4.00	2.00	1.25
(27) Early Wynn	7.50	3.75	2.25

1955 Cleveland Indians Postcards

These team-issued black-and-white player post-cards can be distinguished from earlier and later issues by the uniformity of the photos. All pictures are head-and-shoulder portraits against a white background. Players are wearing caps with Chief Wahoo inside a "C." Some cards are found with a notation on back, "Pub. by Ed Wood, Forestville, Calif." Cards were sent out to fans by the team and/or player and are usually found with an autograph on front.

	NM	EX	VG
Complete Set (29):	400.00	200.00	120.00
Common Player:	12.00	6.00	3.50
(1) Bob Avila	15.00	7.50	4.50
(2) Tony Cuccinello	12.00	6.00	3.50
(3) Bud Daley	12.00	6.00	3.50
(4) Sam Dente	12.00	6.00	3.50
(5) Larry Doby	18.00	9.00	5.50
(6) Bob Feller	30.00	15.00	9.00
(7) Hank Foiles	12.00	6.00	3.50
(8) Mike Garcia	12.00	6.00	3.50
(9) Mel Harder	12.00	6.00	3.50
(10) Jim Hegan	12.00	6.00	3.50
(11) Art Houtteman	12.00	6.00	3.50
(12) Ralph Kiner	20.00	10.00	6.00
(13) Red Kress	12.00	6.00	3.50
(14) Ken Kuhn	12.00	6.00	3.50
(15) Bob Lemon	18.00	9.00	5.50
(16) Bill Lobe	12.00	6.00	3.50
(17) Dale Mitchell	12.00	6.00	3.50
(18) Don Mossi	12.00	6.00	3.50
(19) Hal Naragon	12.00	6.00	3.50
(20) Ray Narleski	12.00	6.00	3.50
(21) Dave Philley	12.00	6.00	3.50
(22) Al Rosen	15.00	7.50	4.50
(23) Herb Score	24.00	12.00	7.25
(24) Al Smith	12.00	6.00	3.50
(25) George Strickland	12.00	6.00	3.50
(26) Vic Wertz	12.00	6.00	3.50
(27) Wally Westlake	12.00	6.00	3.50
(28) Bill Wright	12.00	6.00	3.50
(29) Early Wynn	18.00	9.00	5.50

1956 Cleveland Indians Picture Pack

The Indians used a mix of styles in its souvenir picture pack for 1956. About 6-1/8" x 8-7/8", with white borders and blank backs, the pictures have a mix of portraits and posed action photos. Some pictures have a facsimile autograph while others have the players name in a white strip.

	NM	EX	VG
Complete Set (22):	90.00	45.00	27.50
Common Player:	4.00	2.00	1.25
(1) Earl Averill	4.00	2.00	1.25
(2) Bob Avila	4.00	2.00	1.25
(3) Jim Busby	4.00	2.00	1.25
(4) Chico Carrasquel	4.00	2.00	1.25
(5) Rocky Colavito	20.00	10.00	6.00
(6) Bob Feller	15.00	7.50	4.50
(7) Mike Garcia	4.00	2.00	1.25
(8) Jim Hegan	4.00	2.00	1.25
(9) Art Houtteman	4.00	2.00	1.25
(10) Bob Lemon	7.50	3.75	2.25
(11) Al Lopez	7.50	3.75	2.25
(12) Sam Mele	4.00	2.00	1.25
(13) Dale Mitchell	4.00	2.00	1.25
(14) Don Mossi	4.00	2.00	1.25
(15) Hal Naragon	4.00	2.00	1.25
(16) Ray Narleski	4.00	2.00	1.25
(17) Al Rosen	5.00	2.50	1.50
(18) Herb Score	7.50	3.75	2.25
(19) Al Smith	4.00	2.00	1.25
(20) George Strickland	4.00	2.00	1.25
(21) Gene Woodling	4.00	2.00	1.25
(22) Early Wynn	7.50	3.75	2.25

1884 Climax Poster

"Representatives of Professional Baseball in America" is the title of this sepia-toned lithograph produced by Lorillard tobacco as a premium for its Climax Red Tin Tag Plug chew. About 26" x 20", the poster depicts 16 top stars, managers and executives in street-clothed portraits on a background of ballplayers, equipment and ballparks.

	NM	EX	VG
1884 Climax Representatives of Baseball	25,000	12,500	7,500

1911 George Close Candy Co. (E94)

This 1911 issue is nearly identical to several contemporary candy and caramel sets. Issued by The George Close Co. of Cambridge, Mass., the approximately 1-1/2" x 2-3/4" cards feature color-tinted black-and-white player photos. Each card can be found with any of seven different background colors (blue, gold, green, olive, red, violet and yellow). Backs carry a set checklist. Eleven different back variations are known to exist. One variation contains just the checklist without any advertising, while ten other variations include overprinted backs advertising various candy products manufactured by Close. The set carries the ACC designation E94.

		NM	EX	VG
Complete Set (30):		90,000	45,000	27,500
Common Player:		1,500	750.00	450.00
Advertising Backs: 4-6X				
(1)	Jimmy Austin	1,500	750.00	450.00
(2)	Johnny Bates	1,500	750.00	450.00
(3)	Bob Bescher	1,500	750.00	450.00
(4)	Bobby Byrne	1,500	750.00	450.00
(5)	Frank Chance	2,100	1,050	630.00
(6)	Ed Cicotte	2,100	1,050	630.00
(7)	Ty Cobb	15,000	7,500	4,500
(8)	Sam Crawford	2,100	1,050	630.00
(9)	Harry Davis	1,500	750.00	450.00
(10)	Art Devlin	1,500	750.00	450.00
(11)	Josh Devore	1,500	750.00	450.00
(12)	Mickey Doolan	1,500	750.00	450.00
(13)	Patsy Dougherty	1,500	750.00	450.00
(14)	Johnny Evers	2,100	1,050	630.00
(15)	Eddie Grant	1,500	750.00	450.00
(16)	Hugh Jennings	2,100	1,050	630.00
(17)	Red Kleinow	1,500	750.00	450.00
(18)	Joe Lake	1,500	750.00	450.00
(19)	Nap Lajoie	2,400	1,200	725.00
(20)	Tommy Leach	1,500	750.00	450.00
(21)	Hans Lobert	1,500	750.00	450.00
(22)	Harry Lord	1,500	750.00	450.00
(23)	Sherry Magee	1,500	750.00	450.00
(24)	John McGraw	2,100	1,050	630.00
(25)	Earl Moore	1,500	750.00	450.00
(26)	Red Murray	1,500	750.00	450.00
(27)	Tris Speaker	3,250	1,625	975.00
(28)	Terry Turner	1,500	750.00	450.00
(29)	Honus Wagner	14,500	7,250	4,350
(30)	"Old" Cy Young	12,000	6,000	3,600

1961 Cloverleaf Dairy Minnesota Twins

These unnumbered cards picture members of the debut Minnesota Twins team. Measuring approximately 3-3/4" x 7-3/4", the cards were actually side panels from Cloverleaf (and Apple Fresh brand) Milk cartons. Complete cartons are valued at about twice the prices listed. The card includes a black-and-white player photo with name, position, personal data and year-by-year statistics appearing below. Green graphics highlight the panels. Some pictures were reissued in 1962 but can be differentiated from the 1961 set by the stats at bottom.

		NM	EX	VG
Complete Set (17):		1,125	550.00	335.00
Common Player:		75.00	37.00	22.00
(1)	Earl Battey	75.00	37.00	22.00
(2)	Reno Bertoia	75.00	37.00	22.00
(3)	Billy Gardner	75.00	37.00	22.00
(4)	Paul Giel	75.00	37.00	22.00
(5)	Lenny Green	75.00	37.00	22.00
(6)	Jim Kaat	80.00	40.00	24.00
(7)	Jack Kralick	75.00	37.00	22.00
(8)	Don Lee	75.00	37.00	22.00
(9)	Jim Lemon	75.00	37.00	22.00
(10)	Billy Martin	90.00	45.00	27.00
(11)	Don Mincher	75.00	37.00	22.00
(12)	Camilo Pascual	80.00	40.00	24.00
(13)	Pedro Ramos	75.00	37.00	22.00
(14)	Chuck Stobbs	75.00	37.00	22.00
(15)	Bill Tuttle	75.00	37.00	22.00
(16)	Jose Valdivielso	75.00	37.00	22.00
(17)	Zoilo Versalles	80.00	40.00	24.00

1962 Cloverleaf Dairy Minnesota Twins

These unnumbered cards picture members of the Minnesota Twins. Measuring approximately 3-3/4" x 7-3/4", the cards were actually side panels from Cloverleaf (and Apple Fresh brand) Milk cartons. Complete cartons are valued at about twice the prices listed. The card includes a black-and-white player photo with name, position, personal data and year-by-year statistics appearing below. Green graphics highlight the panels. Some pictures were reissued in 1962 but can be differentiated from the 1961 set by the stats at bottom.

		NM	EX	VG
Complete Set (24):		1,400	700.00	425.00
Common Player:		75.00	37.00	22.00
(1)	Bernie Allen	75.00	37.00	22.00
(2)	George Banks	75.00	37.00	22.00
(3)	Earl Battey	75.00	37.00	22.00
(4)	Joe Bonikowski	75.00	37.00	22.00
(5)	John Goryl	75.00	37.00	22.00
(6)	Lenny Green	75.00	37.00	22.00
(7)	Jim Kaat	80.00	40.00	24.00
(8)	Jack Kralick	75.00	37.00	22.00
(9)	Jim Lemon	75.00	37.00	22.00
(10)	Georges Maranda	75.00	37.00	22.00
(11)	Orlando Martinez	75.00	37.00	22.00
(12)	Don Mincher	75.00	37.00	22.00
(13)	Ray Moore	75.00	37.00	22.00
(14)	Hal Naragon	75.00	37.00	22.00
(15)	Camilo Pascual	80.00	40.00	24.00
(16)	Vic Power	80.00	40.00	24.00
(17)	Rich Rollins	75.00	37.00	22.00
(18)	Theodore Sadowski	75.00	37.00	22.00
(19)	Albert Stange	75.00	37.00	22.00
(20)	Dick Stigman	75.00	37.00	22.00
(21)	Bill Tuttle	75.00	37.00	22.00
(22)	Zoilo Versalles	80.00	40.00	24.00
(23)	Gerald Zimmerman	75.00	37.00	22.00
(24)	Manager and Coaches (Floyd Baker, Edward Fitz Gerald, Gordon Maltzberger, Sam Mele, George Strickland)	75.00	37.00	22.00

1912 Ty Cobb Postcard

There is no indication of a publisher on this card, nor that it is part of a multi-player series. In standard postcard format of 5-1/2" x 3-1/2", the card has a black-and-white photograph of a smiling Cobb and a caption in the bottom border, "TY COBB WORLDS'S GREATEST BALL PLAYER AND HIS FAVORITE BAT." The divided back has standard postcard markings.

	NM	EX	VG
Ty Cobb	3,500	1,750	1,000

1947 Coca-Cola All Time Sports Favorite

In 1947 Coke produced a series of 10 All Time Sports Favorite cardboard signs. On heavy cardboard with a framed look, the 13" x 15" signs have color artwork at center. In the bottom border are a few words about the athlete, along with a Coke bottle and round red logo. Only one baseball player appears in the series.

	NM	EX	VG
Ty Cobb	2,000	1,000	600.00

1952 Coca-Cola Playing Tips Test Cards

Apparently a regional issue to test the concept of baseball playing tips cards inserted into cartons of soda bottles, these test cards have a number of differences to the version which was more widely issued. The test cards feature a colorful drawing of the player with a bottle of Coke, along with his name in script and his team. Backs are printed in red on gray cardboard. Rizzuto's card has been seen with three different playing tips. Mays' card has a biography instead of a playing tip. The cards are irregularly shaped, measuring about 3-1/2" at their widest point, and about 7-1/2" in length.

		NM	EX	VG
Complete Set (3):		9,000	4,500	2,700
(1)	Willie Mays	5,000	2,500	1,500
(2)	Phil Rizzuto (Bunting tips.)	2,500	1,250	750.00
(3)	Phil Rizzuto (Pitching tips.)	2,500	1,250	750.00
(4)	Phil Rizzuto (SS fielding tips.)	2,500	1,250	750.00

1952 Coca-Cola Playing Tips

While more widely distributed than the three test cards, the 10-card set of playing tips cards is still scarce today. Issued in the metropolitan New York region, the cards include only players from the Yankees, Giants and Dodgers. Fronts feature color paintings of players in action, though the artwork bears little actual resemblance to the players named. The phrase "Coke is a natural" is in the background on pennants, panels, etc. The player's name, team and position are included in the picture. In the portion of the card meant to be inserted into the soda-bottle carton, the home schedule of the player's team for 1952 is presented. Printed in red on back are tips for playing the position of the pictured player. Cards are irregularly shaped, measuring about 3-1/2" at their widest point, and 7-1/2" in length. The unnumbered cards are checklisted here in alphabetical order.

	NM	EX	VG
Complete Set (10):	2,100	1,050	625.00
Common Player:	160.00	80.00	50.00
(1) Hank Bauer	275.00	135.00	82.00
(2) Carl Furillo	350.00	175.00	105.00
(3) Gil Hodges	450.00	225.00	135.00
(4) Ed Lopat	190.00	95.00	57.00
(5) Gil McDougald	250.00	125.00	75.00
(6) Don Mueller	150.00	75.00	45.00
(7) Pee Wee Reese	450.00	225.00	135.00
(8) Bobby Thomson (3B)	250.00	125.00	75.00
(9) Bobby Thomson/Hitting	350.00	175.00	105.00
(10) Wes Westrum	150.00	75.00	45.00

1953 Coca-Cola Signs

The attributed date is approximate, based on the uniforms in which the players are pictured. It is possible the series was issued over more than one year. The signs vary in size from about 10" x 12" to 12" x 15" and are made of cardboard. Some are die-cut to produce an irregular shape. Players are pictured in color artwork holding a bottle of Coke with one of several styles of Coca-Cola logo in the background.

	NM	EX	VG
Common Player:	750.00	375.00	225.00
(1) Bill Bruton	800.00	400.00	240.00
(2) Roy Campanella	2,500	1,250	750.00
(3) Larry Doby	1,500	750.00	450.00
(4) Monte Irvin	1,500	750.00	450.00
(5) Satchel Paige	4,000	2,000	1,200
(6) Phil Rizzuto	1,500	750.00	450.00

1967-68 Coca-Cola Bottle Caps

Over two seasons, bottles of Coke products (Coca-Cola, Fresca, Tab and Fanta) were sealed with caps bearing the pictures of major league ballplayers. The 1" diameter caps have a small baseball symbol on the top of the cap. Inside, protected by a clear plastic liner, is a black-and-white portrait photo of a player. (Most photos have cap insignia blacked out.) His team nickname is printed at top, his name at bottom and his position at right. To the left of the picture is an identification number, usually with a letter prefix. In areas with major league baseball teams, regional issues of the caps featured local players with a letter prefix to the number. Also released in those areas were American League or National League All-Star sets, with cap number preceded by an "A" or "N." In areas not served by major league teams, a 35-cap All-Star series with no prefix letter was issued. While most caps were identical in both years of issue, some player team changes, etc., were reflected in updated caps in 1968. Severe bending by bottle openers and rust are specific detriments to condition often found on these caps. Collectors usually save these caps without regard to which specific brand of soda appears on top, though obviously the Coca-Cola pieces are much more common. Cap-saver sheets

were available which, when filled, could be exchanged for a team set of photocards (see 1967 Dexter Press Premiums) or other prizes.

	NM	EX	VG
Complete Set (580):	4,000	2,000	1,200
Common Player:	5.00	2.50	1.50
Playing Tips (16):	3.00	1.50	.90
Sprite, Fresca, Tab + 10%			

MAJOR LEAGUE ALL-STARS

		NM	EX	VG
1	Richie Allen	7.50	3.75	2.25
2	Pete Rose	32.50	16.00	9.75
3	Brooks Robinson	25.00	12.50	7.50
4	Marcelino Lopez	5.00	2.50	1.50
5	Rusty Staub	5.00	2.50	1.50
6	Ron Santo	7.50	3.75	2.25
7	Jim Nash	5.00	2.50	1.50
8	Jim Fregosi	5.00	2.50	1.50
9	Paul Casanova	5.00	2.50	1.50
10	Willie Mays	45.00	22.50	13.50
11	Willie Stargell	15.00	7.50	4.50
12	Tony Oliva	7.50	3.75	2.25
13	Joe Pepitone	7.50	3.75	2.25
14	Juan Marichal	12.00	6.00	3.50
15	Jim Bunning	12.00	6.00	3.50
16	Claude Osteen	5.00	2.50	1.50
17	Carl Yastrzemski	25.00	12.50	7.50
18	Harmon Killebrew	25.00	12.50	7.50
19	Hank Aaron	45.00	22.50	13.50
20	Joe Torre	7.50	3.75	2.25
21	Ernie Banks	25.00	12.50	7.50
22	Al Kaline	25.00	12.50	7.50
23	Frank Robinson	25.00	12.50	7.50
24	Max Alvis	5.00	2.50	1.50
25	Elston Howard	7.50	3.75	2.25
26	Gaylord Perry	12.00	6.00	3.50
27	Bill Mazeroski	12.00	6.00	3.50
28	Ron Swoboda	5.00	2.50	1.50
29	Vada Pinson	7.50	3.75	2.25
30	Joe Morgan	25.00	12.50	7.50
31	Cleon Jones	5.00	2.50	1.50
32	Willie Horton	5.00	2.50	1.50
33	Leon Wagner	5.00	2.50	1.50
34	George Scott	5.00	2.50	1.50
35	Ed Charles	5.00	2.50	1.50

NATIONAL LEAGUE ALL-STARS

		NM	EX	VG
N19	Hank Aaron	40.00	20.00	12.00
N20	Jim Bunning	10.00	5.00	3.00
N21	Joe Torre	6.00	3.00	1.75
N22	Claude Osteen	5.00	2.50	1.50
N23	Ron Santo	6.00	3.00	1.75
N24	Joe Morgan	20.00	10.00	6.00
N25	Richie Allen	6.00	3.00	1.75
N26	Ron Swoboda	5.00	2.50	1.50
N27	Ernie Banks	20.00	10.00	6.00
N28	Bill Mazeroski	12.00	6.00	3.50
N29	Willie Stargell	12.00	6.00	3.50
N30	Pete Rose	25.00	12.50	7.50
N31	Gaylord Perry	10.00	5.00	3.00
N32	Rusty Staub	5.00	2.50	1.50
N33	Vada Pinson	6.00	3.00	1.75
N34	Juan Marichal	10.00	5.00	3.00
N35	Cleon Jones	5.00	2.50	1.50

AMERICAN LEAGUE ALL-STARS

		NM	EX	VG
A19	Al Kaline	20.00	10.00	6.00
A20	Frank Howard	5.00	2.50	1.50
A21	Brooks Robinson	20.00	10.00	6.00
A22	George Scott	5.00	2.50	1.50
A23	Willie Horton	5.00	2.50	1.50
A24	Jim Fregosi	5.00	2.50	1.50
A25	Ed Charles	5.00	2.50	1.50
A26	Harmon Killebrew	20.00	10.00	6.00
A27	Tony Oliva	6.00	3.00	1.75
A28	Joe Pepitone	6.00	3.00	1.75
A29	Elston Howard	6.00	3.00	1.75
A30	Jim Nash	5.00	2.50	1.50
A31	Marcelino Lopez	5.00	2.50	1.50
A32	Frank Robinson	20.00	10.00	6.00
A33	Leon Wagner	5.00	2.50	1.50
A34	Max Alvis	5.00	2.50	1.50
A35	Paul Casanova	5.00	2.50	1.50

PLAYING TIPS

		NM	EX	VG
19	SS fields ball . . .	3.00	1.50	.90
20	2b relays . . .	3.00	1.50	.90
21	1b completes DP	3.00	1.50	.90
22	Pitcher fields bunt . . .	3.00	1.50	.90
23	2b relays . . .	3.00	1.50	.90
24	1b complete DP	3.00	1.50	.90
25	CF makes catch . . .	3.00	1.50	.90
26	Catcher tags runner	3.00	1.50	.90

1967 ATLANTA BRAVES

		NM	EX	VG
B1	Gary Geiger	5.00	2.50	1.50
B2	Ty Cline	5.00	2.50	1.50
B3	Hank Aaron	45.00	22.50	13.50
B4	Gene Oliver	5.00	2.50	1.50
B5	Tony Cloninger	5.00	2.50	1.50
B6	Denis Menke	5.00	2.50	1.50
B7	Denny Lemaster	5.00	2.50	1.50
B8	Woody Woodward	5.00	2.50	1.50
B9	Joe Torre	7.50	3.75	2.25
B10	Ken Johnson	5.00	2.50	1.50
B11	Bob Bruce	5.00	2.50	1.50
B12	Felipe Alou	7.50	3.75	2.25
B13	Clete Boyer	5.00	2.50	1.50
B14	Wade Blasingame	5.00	2.50	1.50
B15	Don Schwall	5.00	2.50	1.50
B16	Dick Kelley	5.00	2.50	1.50
B17	Rico Carty	6.00	3.00	1.75
B18	Mack Jones	5.00	2.50	1.50

1968 ATLANTA BRAVES

		NM	EX	VG
B1	Cecil Upshaw	5.00	2.50	1.50
B2	Tito Francona	5.00	2.50	1.50
B3	Hank Aaron	40.00	20.00	12.00
B4	Pat Jarvis	5.00	2.50	1.50
B5	Tony Cloninger	5.00	2.50	1.50
B6	Phil Niekro	15.00	7.50	4.50
B7	Felix Millan	5.00	2.50	1.50
B8	Woody Woodward	5.00	2.50	1.50
B9	Joe Torre	7.50	3.75	2.25
B10	Ken Johnson	5.00	2.50	1.50
B11	Marty Martinez	5.00	2.50	1.50
B12	Felipe Alou	7.50	3.75	2.25
B13	Clete Boyer	5.00	2.50	1.50
B14	Sonny Jackson	5.00	2.50	1.50
B15	Deron Johnson	5.00	2.50	1.50
B16	Claude Raymond	5.00	2.50	1.50
B17	Rico Carty	6.00	3.00	1.75
B18	Mack Jones	5.00	2.50	1.50

1967 BALTIMORE ORIOLES

		NM	EX	VG
O1	Dave McNally	5.00	2.50	1.50
O2	Luis Aparicio	20.00	10.00	6.00
O3	Paul Blair	5.00	2.50	1.50
O4	Frank Robinson	25.00	12.50	7.50
O5	Jim Palmer	30.00	15.00	9.00
O6	Russ Snyder	5.00	2.50	1.50
O7	Stu Miller	5.00	2.50	1.50
O8	Dave Johnson	5.00	2.50	1.50
O9	Andy Etchebarren	5.00	2.50	1.50
O10	Brooks Robinson	25.00	12.50	7.50
O11	John Powell	12.00	6.00	3.50
O12	Sam Bowens	5.00	2.50	1.50
O13	Curt Blefary	5.00	2.50	1.50
O14	Ed Fisher	5.00	2.50	1.50
O15	Wally Bunker	5.00	2.50	1.50
O16	Moe Drabowsky	5.00	2.50	1.50
O17	Larry Haney	5.00	2.50	1.50
O18	Tom Phoebus	5.00	2.50	1.50

1968 BALTIMORE ORIOLES

		NM	EX	VG
O1	Dave McNally	5.00	2.50	1.50
O2	Jim Hardin	5.00	2.50	1.50
O3	Paul Blair	5.00	2.50	1.50
O4	Frank Robinson	25.00	12.50	7.50
O5	Bruce Howard	5.00	2.50	1.50
O6	John O'Donoghue	5.00	2.50	1.50
O7	Dave May	5.00	2.50	1.50
O8	Dave Johnson	5.00	2.50	1.50
O9	Andy Etchebarren	5.00	2.50	1.50
O10	Brooks Robinson	25.00	12.50	7.50
O11	John Powell	8.00	4.00	2.50
O12	Pete Richert	5.00	2.50	1.50
O13	Curt Blefary	5.00	2.50	1.50
O14	Mark Belanger	6.00	3.00	1.75
O15	Wally Bunker	5.00	2.50	1.50
O16	Don Buford	5.00	2.50	1.50
O17	Larry Haney	5.00	2.50	1.50
O18	Tom Phoebus	5.00	2.50	1.50

1967 BOSTON RED SOX

		NM	EX	VG
R1	Lee Stange	5.00	2.50	1.50
R2	Carl Yastrzemski	30.00	15.00	9.00
R3	Don Demeter	5.00	2.50	1.50
R4	Jose Santiago	5.00	2.50	1.50
R5	Darrell Brandon	5.00	2.50	1.50
R6	Joe Foy	5.00	2.50	1.50
R7	Don McMahon	5.00	2.50	1.50
R8	Dalton Jones	5.00	2.50	1.50
R9	Mike Ryan	5.00	2.50	1.50
R10	Bob Tillman	5.00	2.50	1.50
R11	Rico Petrocelli	6.00	3.00	1.75
R12	George Scott	5.00	2.50	1.50
R13	George Smith	5.00	2.50	1.50
R14	Dennis Bennett	5.00	2.50	1.50
R15	Hank Fischer	5.00	2.50	1.50
R16	Jim Lonborg	6.00	3.00	1.75
R17	Jose Tartabull	5.00	2.50	1.50
R18	George Thomas	5.00	2.50	1.50

1968 BOSTON RED SOX

		NM	EX	VG
R1	Lee Stange	5.00	2.50	1.50
R2	Gary Waslewski	5.00	2.50	1.50
R3	Gary Bell	5.00	2.50	1.50
R4	John Wyatt	5.00	2.50	1.50
R5	Darrell Brandon	5.00	2.50	1.50
R6	Joe Foy	5.00	2.50	1.50
R7	Ray Culp	5.00	2.50	1.50
R8	Dalton Jones	5.00	2.50	1.50
R9	Gene Oliver	5.00	2.50	1.50
R10	Jose Santiago	5.00	2.50	1.50
R11	Rico Petrocelli	6.00	3.00	1.75
R12	George Scott	5.00	2.50	1.50
R13	Mike Andrews	5.00	2.50	1.50
R14	Dick Ellsworth	5.00	2.50	1.50
R15	Norm Siebern	5.00	2.50	1.50
R16	Jim Lonborg	6.00	3.00	1.75
R17	Jerry Adair	5.00	2.50	1.50
R18	Elston Howard	5.00	2.50	1.50

1967 CALIFORNIA ANGELS

		NM	EX	VG
L19	Len Gabrielson	5.00	2.50	1.50
L20	Jackie Hernandez	5.00	2.50	1.50
L21	Paul Schaal	5.00	2.50	1.50
L22	Lew Burdette	5.00	2.50	1.50
L23	Jimmie Hall	5.00	2.50	1.50
L24	Fred Newman	5.00	2.50	1.50
L25	Don Mincher	5.00	2.50	1.50
L26	Bob Rodgers	5.00	2.50	1.50
L27	Jack Sanford	5.00	2.50	1.50
L28	Bobby Knoop	5.00	2.50	1.50
L29	Jose Cardenal	5.00	2.50	1.50
L30	Jim Fregosi	5.00	2.50	1.50
L31	George Brunet	5.00	2.50	1.50
L32	Marcelino Lopez	5.00	2.50	1.50
L33	Minnie Rojas	5.00	2.50	1.50
L34	Jay Johnstone	5.00	2.50	1.50
L35	Ed Kirkpatrick	5.00	2.50	1.50

1967 CHICAGO CUBS

		NM	EX	VG
C1	Ferguson Jenkins	15.00	7.50	4.50
C2	Ernie Banks	30.00	15.00	9.00
C3	Glenn Beckert	5.00	2.50	1.50
C4	Bob Hendley	5.00	2.50	1.50
C5	John Boccabella	5.00	2.50	1.50
C6	Ron Campbell	5.00	2.50	1.50
C7	Ray Culp	5.00	2.50	1.50
C8	Adolfo Phillips	5.00	2.50	1.50
C9	Don Bryant	5.00	2.50	1.50
C10	Randy Hundley	5.00	2.50	1.50
C11	Ron Santo	6.00	3.00	1.75
C12	Lee Thomas	5.00	2.50	1.50

C13	Billy Williams	25.00	12.50	7.50
C14	Ken Holtzman	5.00	2.50	1.50
C15	Cal Koonce	5.00	2.50	1.50
C16	Curt Simmons	5.00	2.50	1.50
C17	George Altman	5.00	2.50	1.50
C18	Bryon Browne	5.00	2.50	1.50

CHICAGO WHITE SOX

L1	Gary Peters	5.00	2.50	1.50
L2	Jerry Adair	5.00	2.50	1.50
L3	Al Weis	5.00	2.50	1.50
L4	Pete Ward	5.00	2.50	1.50
L5	Hoyt Wilhelm	15.00	7.50	4.50
L6	Don Buford	5.00	2.50	1.50
L7	John Buzhardt	5.00	2.50	1.50
L8	Wayne Causey	5.00	2.50	1.50
L9	Jerry McNertney	5.00	2.50	1.50
L10	Ron Hansen	5.00	2.50	1.50
L11	Tom McCraw	5.00	2.50	1.50
L12	Jim O'Toole	5.00	2.50	1.50
L13	Bill Skowron	6.00	3.00	1.75
L14	Joel Horlen	5.00	2.50	1.50
L15	Tommy John	12.00	6.00	3.50
L16	Bob Locker	5.00	2.50	1.50
L17	Ken Berry	5.00	2.50	1.50
L18	Tommie Agee	5.00	2.50	1.50

1967 CINCINNATI REDS

F1	Floyd Robinson	5.00	2.50	1.50
F2	Leo Cardenas	5.00	2.50	1.50
F3	Gordy Coleman	5.00	2.50	1.50
F4	Tommy Harper	5.00	2.50	1.50
F5	Tommy Helms	5.00	2.50	1.50
F6	Deron Johnson	5.00	2.50	1.50
F7	Jim Maloney	5.00	2.50	1.50
F8	Tony Perez	25.00	12.50	7.50
F9	Don Pavletich	5.00	2.50	1.50
F10	John Edwards	5.00	2.50	1.50
F11	Vada Pinson	7.50	3.75	2.25
F12	Chico Ruiz	5.00	2.50	1.50
F13	Pete Rose	40.00	20.00	12.00
F14	Bill McCool	5.00	2.50	1.50
F15	Joe Nuxhall	5.00	2.50	1.50
F16	Milt Pappas	5.00	2.50	1.50
F17	Art Shamsky	5.00	2.50	1.50
F18	Dick Simpson	5.00	2.50	1.50

1967 CLEVELAND INDIANS

I1	Luis Tiant	6.00	3.00	1.75
I2	Max Alvis	5.00	2.50	1.50
I3	Larry Brown	5.00	2.50	1.50
I4	Rocky Colavito	10.00	5.00	3.00
I5	John O'Donoghue	5.00	2.50	1.50
I6	Pedro Gonzalez	5.00	2.50	1.50
I7	Gary Bell	5.00	2.50	1.50
I8	Sonny Siebert	5.00	2.50	1.50
I9	Joe Azcue	5.00	2.50	1.50
I10	Lee Maye	5.00	2.50	1.50
I11	Chico Salmon	5.00	2.50	1.50
I12	Leon Wagner	5.00	2.50	1.50
I13	Fred Whitfield	5.00	2.50	1.50
I14	Jack Kralick	5.00	2.50	1.50
I15	Sam McDowell	6.00	3.00	1.75
I16	Dick Radatz	5.00	2.50	1.50
I17	Vic Davalillo	5.00	2.50	1.50
I18	Chuck Hinton	5.00	2.50	1.50

1968 CLEVELAND INDIANS

I1	Luis Tiant	6.00	3.00	1.75
I2	Max Alvis	5.00	2.50	1.50
I3	Larry Brown	5.00	2.50	1.50
I4	Tommy Harper	5.00	2.50	1.50
I5	Vern Fuller	5.00	2.50	1.50
I6	Jose Cardenal	5.00	2.50	1.50
I7	Dave Nelson	5.00	2.50	1.50
I8	Sonny Siebert	5.00	2.50	1.50
I9	Joe Azcue	5.00	2.50	1.50
I10	Lee Maye	5.00	2.50	1.50
I11	Chico Salmon	5.00	2.50	1.50
I12	Leon Wagner	5.00	2.50	1.50
I13	Eddie Fisher	5.00	2.50	1.50
I14	Stan Williams	5.00	2.50	1.50
I15	Sam McDowell	6.00	3.00	1.75
I16	Steve Hargan	5.00	2.50	1.50
I17	Vic Davalillo	5.00	2.50	1.50
I18	Duke Sims	5.00	2.50	1.50

1967 DETROIT TIGERS

T1	Larry Sherry	5.00	2.50	1.50
T2	Norm Cash	7.50	3.75	2.25
T3	Jerry Lumpe	5.00	2.50	1.50
T4	Dave Wickersham	5.00	2.50	1.50
T5	Joe Sparma	5.00	2.50	1.50
T6	Dick McAuliffe	5.00	2.50	1.50
T7	Fred Gladding	5.00	2.50	1.50
T8	Jim Northrup	5.00	2.50	1.50
T9	Bill Freehan	5.00	2.50	1.50
T10	Earl Wilson	5.00	2.50	1.50
T11	Dick Tracewski	5.00	2.50	1.50
T12	Don Wert	5.00	2.50	1.50
T13	Jake Wood	5.00	2.50	1.50
T14	Mickey Lolich	6.00	3.00	1.75
T15	Johnny Podres	5.00	2.50	1.50
T16	Bill Monbouquette	5.00	2.50	1.50
T17	Al Kaline	30.00	15.00	9.00
T18	Willie Horton	5.00	2.50	1.50

1968 DETROIT TIGERS

T1	Ray Oyler	5.00	2.50	1.50
T2	Norm Cash	7.50	3.75	2.25
T3	Mike Marshall	5.00	2.50	1.50
T4	Mickey Stanley	5.00	2.50	1.50
T5	Joe Sparma	5.00	2.50	1.50
T6	Dick McAuliffe	5.00	2.50	1.50
T7	Gates Brown	5.00	2.50	1.50
T8	Jim Northrup	5.00	2.50	1.50
T9	Bill Freehan	5.00	2.50	1.50
T10	Earl Wilson	5.00	2.50	1.50
T11	Dick Tracewski	5.00	2.50	1.50
T12	Don Wert	5.00	2.50	1.50
T13	Dennis Ribant	5.00	2.50	1.50
T14	Mickey Lolich	6.00	3.00	1.75
T15	Denny McLain	12.00	6.00	3.50
T16	Ed Mathews	25.00	12.50	7.50
T17	Al Kaline	30.00	15.00	9.00
T18	Willie Horton	5.00	2.50	1.50

1967 HOUSTON ASTROS

H1	Dave Giusti	5.00	2.50	1.50
H2	Bob Aspromonte	5.00	2.50	1.50
H3	Ron Davis	5.00	2.50	1.50
H4	Claude Raymond	5.00	2.50	1.50
H5	Barry Latman	5.00	2.50	1.50
H6	Chuck Harrison	5.00	2.50	1.50
H7	Bill Heath	5.00	2.50	1.50
H8	Sonny Jackson	5.00	2.50	1.50
H9	John Bateman	5.00	2.50	1.50
H10	Ron Brand	5.00	2.50	1.50
H11	Aaron Pointer	5.00	2.50	1.50
H12	Joe Morgan	25.00	12.50	7.50
H13	Rusty Staub	6.00	3.00	1.75
H14	Mike Cuellar	5.00	2.50	1.50
H15	Larry Dierker	5.00	2.50	1.50
H16	Dick Farrell	5.00	2.50	1.50
H17	Jim Landis	5.00	2.50	1.50
H18	Ed Mathews	25.00	12.50	7.50

1968 HOUSTON ASTROS

H1	Dave Giusti	5.00	2.50	1.50
H2	Bob Aspromonte	5.00	2.50	1.50
H3	Ron Davis	5.00	2.50	1.50
H4	Julio Gotay	5.00	2.50	1.50
H5	Fred Gladding	5.00	2.50	1.50
H6	Lee Thomas	5.00	2.50	1.50
H7	Wade Blasingame	5.00	2.50	1.50
H8	Denis Menke	5.00	2.50	1.50
H9	John Bateman	5.00	2.50	1.50
H10	Ron Brand	5.00	2.50	1.50
H11	Doug Rader	5.00	2.50	1.50
H12	Joe Morgan	25.00	12.50	7.50
H13	Rusty Staub	6.00	3.00	1.75
H14	Mike Cuellar	5.00	2.50	1.50
H15	Larry Dierker	5.00	2.50	1.50
H16	Denny Lemaster	5.00	2.50	1.50
H17	Jim Wynn	5.00	2.50	1.50
H18	Don Wilson	5.00	2.50	1.50

1967 KANSAS CTIY ATHLETICS

K1	Jim Nash	5.00	2.50	1.50
K2	Bert Campaneris	5.00	2.50	1.50
K3	Ed Charles	5.00	2.50	1.50
K4	Wes Stock	5.00	2.50	1.50
K5	John Odom	5.00	2.50	1.50
K6	Ossie Chavarria	5.00	2.50	1.50
K7	Jack Aker	5.00	2.50	1.50
K8	Dick Green	5.00	2.50	1.50
K9	Phil Roof	5.00	2.50	1.50
K10	Rene Lacheman	5.00	2.50	1.50
K11	Mike Hershberger	5.00	2.50	1.50
K12	Joe Nossek	5.00	2.50	1.50
K13	Roger Repoz	5.00	2.50	1.50
K14	Chuck Dobson	5.00	2.50	1.50
K15	Jim Hunter	15.00	7.50	4.50
K16	Lew Krausse	5.00	2.50	1.50
K17	Danny Cater	5.00	2.50	1.50
K18	Jim Gosger	5.00	2.50	1.50

1967 LOS ANGELES DODGERS

L1	Phil Regan	5.00	2.50	1.50
L2	Bob Bailey	5.00	2.50	1.50
L3	Ron Fairly	5.00	2.50	1.50
L4	Joe Moeller	5.00	2.50	1.50
L5	Don Sutton	15.00	7.50	4.50
L6	Ron Hunt	5.00	2.50	1.50
L7	Jim Brewer	5.00	2.50	1.50
L8	Lou Johnson	5.00	2.50	1.50
L9	John Roseboro	5.00	2.50	1.50
L10	Jeff Torborg	5.00	2.50	1.50
L11	John Kennedy	5.00	2.50	1.50
L12	Jim Lefebvre	5.00	2.50	1.50
L13	Wes Parker	5.00	2.50	1.50
L14	Bob Miller	5.00	2.50	1.50
L15	Claude Osteen	5.00	2.50	1.50
L16	Ron Perranoski	5.00	2.50	1.50
L17	Willie Davis	5.00	2.50	1.50
L18	Al Ferrara	5.00	2.50	1.50

1968 LOS ANGELES DODGERS

L1	Phil Regan	5.00	2.50	1.50
L2	Bob Bailey	5.00	2.50	1.50
L3	Ron Fairly	5.00	2.50	1.50
L4	Jim Brewer	5.00	2.50	1.50
L5	Don Sutton	15.00	7.50	4.50
L6	Tom Haller	5.00	2.50	1.50
L7	Rocky Colavito	12.00	6.00	3.50
L8	Jim Grant	5.00	2.50	1.50
L9	Jim Campanis	5.00	2.50	1.50
L10	Jeff Torborg	5.00	2.50	1.50
L11	Zoilo Versalles	6.00	3.00	1.75
L12	Jim Lefebvre	5.00	2.50	1.50
L13	Wes Parker	5.00	2.50	1.50
L14	Bill Singer	5.00	2.50	1.50
L15	Claude Osteen	5.00	2.50	1.50
L16	Len Gabrielson	5.00	2.50	1.50
L17	Willie Davis	5.00	2.50	1.50
L18	Al Ferrara	5.00	2.50	1.50

1967 MINNESOTA TWINS

M1	Ron Kline	5.00	2.50	1.50
M2	Bob Allison	6.00	3.00	1.75
M3	Earl Battey	5.00	2.50	1.50
M4	Jim Merritt	5.00	2.50	1.50
M5	Jim Perry	6.00	3.00	1.75
M6	Harmon Killebrew	25.00	12.50	7.50
M7	Dave Boswell	5.00	2.50	1.50
M8	Rich Rollins	5.00	2.50	1.50
M9	Jerry Zimmerman	5.00	2.50	1.50
M10	Al Worthington	5.00	2.50	1.50
M11	Cesar Tovar	5.00	2.50	1.50
M12	Sandy Valdespino	5.00	2.50	1.50
M13	Zoilo Versalles	6.00	3.00	1.75
M14	Dean Chance	6.00	3.00	1.75
M15	Jim Grant	5.00	2.50	1.50
M16	Jim Kaat	9.00	4.50	2.75
M17	Tony Oliva	10.00	5.00	3.00
M18	Andy Kosco	5.00	2.50	1.50

1968 MINNESOTA TWINS

M1	Rich Reese	5.00	2.50	1.50
M2	Bob Allison	6.00	3.00	1.75
M3	Ron Perranoski	5.00	2.50	1.50
M4	John Roseboro	5.00	2.50	1.50
M5	Jim Perry	6.00	3.00	1.75
M6	Harmon Killebrew	25.00	12.50	7.50
M7	Dave Boswell	5.00	2.50	1.50
M8	Rich Rollins	5.00	2.50	1.50
M9	Jerry Zimmerman	5.00	2.50	1.50
M10	Al Worthington	5.00	2.50	1.50
M11	Cesar Tovar	5.00	2.50	1.50
M12	Jim Merritt	5.00	2.50	1.50
M13	Bob Miller	5.00	2.50	1.50
M14	Dean Chance	6.00	3.00	1.75
M15	Ted Uhlaender	5.00	2.50	1.50
M16	Jim Kaat	9.00	4.50	2.75
M17	Tony Oliva	10.00	5.00	3.00
M18	Rod Carew	40.00	20.00	12.00

1967 NEW YORK METS

V19	Chuck Hiller	5.00	2.50	1.50
V20	Johnny Lewis	5.00	2.50	1.50
V21	Ed Kranepool	5.00	2.50	1.50
V22	Al Luplow	5.00	2.50	1.50
V23	Don Cardwell	5.00	2.50	1.50
V24	Cleon Jones	5.00	2.50	1.50
V25	Bob Shaw	5.00	2.50	1.50
V26	John Stephenson	5.00	2.50	1.50
V27	Ron Swoboda	5.00	2.50	1.50
V28	Ken Boyer	6.00	3.00	1.75
V29	Ed Bressoud	5.00	2.50	1.50
V30	Tommy Davis	5.00	2.50	1.50
V31	Roy McMillan	5.00	2.50	1.50
V32	Jack Fisher	5.00	2.50	1.50
V33	Tug McGraw	6.00	3.00	1.75
V34	Jerry Grote	5.00	2.50	1.50
V35	Jack Hamilton	5.00	2.50	1.50

1967 NEW YORK YANKEES

V1	Mel Stottlemyre	5.00	2.50	1.50
V2	Ruben Amaro	5.00	2.50	1.50
V3	Jake Gibbs	5.00	2.50	1.50
V4	Dooley Womack	5.00	2.50	1.50
V5	Fred Talbot	5.00	2.50	1.50
V6	Horace Clarke	5.00	2.50	1.50
V7	Jim Bouton	6.00	3.00	1.75
V8	Mickey Mantle	125.00	60.00	35.00
V9	Elston Howard	7.50	3.75	2.25
V10	Hal Reniff	5.00	2.50	1.50
V11	Charley Smith	5.00	2.50	1.50
V12	Bobby Murcer	6.00	3.00	1.75
V13	Joe Pepitone	6.00	3.00	1.75
V14	Al Downing	5.00	2.50	1.50
V15	Steve Hamilton	5.00	2.50	1.50
V16	Fritz Peterson	5.00	2.50	1.50
V17	Tom Tresh	6.00	3.00	1.75
V18	Roy White	6.00	3.00	1.75

1967 PHILADELPHIA PHILLIES

P1	Richie Allen	7.50	3.75	2.25
P2	Bob Wine	5.00	2.50	1.50
P3	Johnny Briggs	5.00	2.50	1.50
P4	John Callison	5.00	2.50	1.50
P5	Doug Clemens	5.00	2.50	1.50
P6	Dick Groat	5.00	2.50	1.50
P7	Dick Ellsworth	5.00	2.50	1.50
P8	Phil Linz	5.00	2.50	1.50
P9	Clay Dalrymple	5.00	2.50	1.50
P10	Bob Uecker	10.00	5.00	3.00
P11	Cookie Rojas	5.00	2.50	1.50
P12	Tony Taylor	5.00	2.50	1.50
P13	Bill White	5.00	2.50	1.50
P14	Larry Jackson	5.00	2.50	1.50
P15	Chris Short	5.00	2.50	1.50
P16	Jim Bunning	15.00	7.50	4.50
P17	Tony Gonzalez	5.00	2.50	1.50
P18	Don Lock	5.00	2.50	1.50

1967 PITTSBURGH PIRATES

E1	Al McBean	5.00	2.50	1.50
E2	Gene Alley	5.00	2.50	1.50
E3	Donn Clendenon	5.00	2.50	1.50
E4	Bob Veale	5.00	2.50	1.50
E5	Pete Mikkelsen	5.00	2.50	1.50
E6	Bill Mazeroski	20.00	10.00	6.00
E7	Steve Blass	5.00	2.50	1.50
E8	Manny Mota	5.00	2.50	1.50
E9	Jim Pagliaroni	5.00	2.50	1.50
E10	Jesse Gonder	5.00	2.50	1.50
E11	Jose Pagan	5.00	2.50	1.50
E12	Willie Stargell	25.00	12.50	7.50
E13	Maury Wills	9.00	4.50	2.75
E14	Elroy Face	5.00	2.50	1.50
E15	Woodie Fryman	5.00	2.50	1.50
E16	Vern Law	5.00	2.50	1.50
E17	Matty Alou	5.00	2.50	1.50
E18	Roberto Clemente	60.00	30.00	18.00

1967 SAN FRANCISCO GIANTS

G1	Bob Bolin	5.00	2.50	1.50
G2	Ollie Brown	5.00	2.50	1.50
G3	Jim Davenport	5.00	2.50	1.50
G4	Tito Fuentes	5.00	2.50	1.50
G5	Norm Siebern	5.00	2.50	1.50
G6	Jim Hart	5.00	2.50	1.50
G7	Juan Marichal	15.00	7.50	4.50
G8	Hal Lanier	5.00	2.50	1.50
G9	Tom Haller	5.00	2.50	1.50
G10	Bob Barton	5.00	2.50	1.50
G11	Willie McCovey	20.00	10.00	6.00
G12	Mike McCormick	5.00	2.50	1.50
G13	Frank Linzy	5.00	2.50	1.50
G14	Ray Sadecki	5.00	2.50	1.50
G15	Gaylord Perry	15.00	7.50	4.50
G16	Lindy McDaniel	5.00	2.50	1.50
G17	Willie Mays	60.00	30.00	18.00
G18	Jesus Alou	5.00	2.50	1.50

1968 SAN FRANCISCO GIANTS

G1	Bob Bolin	5.00	2.50	1.50
G2	Ollie Brown	5.00	2.50	1.50
G3	Jim Davenport	5.00	2.50	1.50
G4	Bob Barton	5.00	2.50	1.50
G5	Jack Hiatt	5.00	2.50	1.50
G6	Jim Hart	5.00	2.50	1.50

G7	Juan Marichal	15.00	7.50	4.50
G8	Hal Lanier	5.00	2.50	1.50
G9	Ron Hunt	5.00	2.50	1.50
G10	Ron Herbel	5.00	2.50	1.50
G11	Willie McCovey	20.00	10.00	6.00
G12	Mike McCormick	5.00	2.50	1.50
G13	Frank Linzy	5.00	2.50	1.50
G14	Ray Sadecki	5.00	2.50	1.50
G15	Gaylord Perry	15.00	7.50	4.50
G16	Lindy McDaniel	5.00	2.50	1.50
G17	Willie Mays	60.00	30.00	18.00
G18	Jesus Alou	5.00	2.50	1.50

1967 WASHINGTON SENATORS

S1	Bob Humphreys	5.00	2.50	1.50
S2	Bernie Allen	5.00	2.50	1.50
S3	Ed Brinkman	5.00	2.50	1.50
S4	Pete Richert	5.00	2.50	1.50
S5	Camilo Pascual	5.00	2.50	1.50
S6	Frank Howard	7.50	3.75	2.25
S7	Casey Cox	5.00	2.50	1.50
S8	Jim King	5.00	2.50	1.50
S9	Paul Casanova	5.00	2.50	1.50
S10	Dick Lines	5.00	2.50	1.50
S11	Dick Nen	5.00	2.50	1.50
S12	Ken McMullen	5.00	2.50	1.50
S13	Bob Saverine	5.00	2.50	1.50
S14	Jim Hannan	5.00	2.50	1.50
S15	Darold Knowles	5.00	2.50	1.50
S16	Phil Ortega	5.00	2.50	1.50
S17	Ken Harrelson	5.00	2.50	1.50
S18	Fred Valentine	5.00	2.50	1.50

1971 Coca-Cola Houston Astros

The constitution and distribution of these Coke premium pictures is unknown. Players are pictured in pastel drawings on the semi-gloss fronts of these 8" x 11" sheets. (The punch holes on the photographed card are not original.) A black facsimile autograph appears in the lower portion of the drawing and the player's name is printed in black in the white bottom border. Backs are printed in blue and red with a background photo of the Astrodome. Data on back includes biographical information, complete pro record and career summary. The unnumbered cards are checklisted here in alphabetical order; but this list is probably not complete.

		NM	EX	VG
Complete Set (12):		50.00	25.00	15.00
Common Player:		5.00	2.50	1.50
(1)	Jesus Alou	5.00	2.50	1.50
(2)	Wade Blasingame/SP	9.00	4.50	2.75
(3)	Cesar Cedeno	7.50	3.75	2.25
(4)	Larry Dierker	7.50	3.75	2.25
(5)	John Edwards	5.00	2.50	1.50
(6)	Denis Menke	5.00	2.50	1.50
(7)	Roger Metzger	5.00	2.50	1.50
(8)	Joe Morgan	15.00	7.50	4.50
(9)	Doug Rader	5.00	2.50	1.50
(10)	Bob Watson	5.00	2.50	1.50
(11)	Don Wilson	5.00	2.50	1.50
(12)	Jim Wynn/SP	12.00	6.00	3.50

1978 Coca-Cola/ WPLO Atlanta Braves

Co-sponsored by Coke and a local radio station, this set of Braves cards is rendered in blue-and-white line art portraits in a 3" x 4-1/4" format. A soda discount coupon was distributed with the set.

	NM	EX	VG
Complete Set (14):	30.00	15.00	9.00

Common Player:		3.00	1.50	.90
(1)	Barry Bonnell	3.00	1.50	.90
(2)	Jeff Burroughs	3.00	1.50	.90
(3)	Rick Camp	3.00	1.50	.90
(4)	Gene Garber	3.00	1.50	.90
(5)	Rod Gilbreath	3.00	1.50	.90
(6)	Bob Horner	4.50	2.25	1.25
(7)	Glenn Hubbard	3.00	1.50	.90
(8)	Gary Matthews	3.00	1.50	.90
(9)	Larry McWilliams	3.00	1.50	.90
(10)	Dale Murphy	9.00	4.50	2.75
(11)	Phil Niekro	5.00	2.50	1.50
(12)	Rowland Office	3.00	1.50	.90
(13)	Biff Pocoroba	3.00	1.50	.90
(14)	Jerry Royster	3.00	1.50	.90

1979 Coca-Cola/7-Eleven MVPs

The co-MVPs of the National League for 1979 are pictured on this 5" x 7" blank-back photo card. A red band at top identifies the player and the award. At bottom are Coke and 7-Eleven logos.

	NM	EX	VG
Keith Hernandez, Willie Stargell	6.00	3.00	1.80

1955 Coffee-Time Syrup Jimmy Piersall

 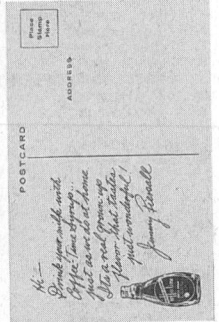

The date of issue is speculative for this promotional postcard. The borderless black-and-white photo on the front on this 3-1/2" x 5-1/2" card shows the popular BoSox star in a relaxed pose with right arm on knee. A blue facsimile autograph is printed at center. The postcard-format back has at left a product picture and an advertising message bearing Piersall's signature. Similar cards advertising Colonial Meats, Cain's and other products are also known, valued similarly.

	NM	EX	VG
Autographed: 2-3X	125.00	65.00	35.00
Jimmy Piersall	80.00	40.00	24.00

1909-1911 Colgan's Chips Stars of the Diamond (E254)

This unusual set of 1-1/2"-diameter round cards was issued over a three-year period by the Colgan Gum Co., Louisville, Ky. The cards were inserted in five-cent tins of Colgan's Mint Chips and Violet Chips brands of gum. The borderless cards feature a black-and-white player portrait on the front along with the player's last name, team and league. On more than a dozen cards, variations are known in the size of the photo and/or let-

tering on front. Since they cannot be identified without another card to compare with, they are noted here only with an asterisk. The card back identifies the set as "Stars of the Diamond" and carries advertising for Colgan's Gum. Some backs are seen with a line of type at the bottom stating, "208 IN PRESENT SERIES." Over 225 different players were pictured over the three-year period, but because of team changes and other notable variations, at least 289 different cards exist. This issue was catalogued as E254 in the American Card Catalog. A number of cards and variations which had been listed in earlier editions of this catalog have been eliminated for lack of proof of their existence. Gaps have been left in the assigned numbering to accommodate future additions. Persons with "Stars of the Diamond" players or variations that do no appear on this list should contact the editor.

		NM	EX	VG
Common Player:		75.00	35.00	20.00
Round Tin Package:		30.00	15.00	9.00
(1)	Ed Abbaticchio	75.00	35.00	20.00
(2)	Fred Abbott	75.00	35.00	20.00
(3a)	Bill Abstein (Pittsburg)	75.00	35.00	20.00
(3b)	Bill Abstein (Jersey City)	75.00	35.00	20.00
(4)	Babe Adams	75.00	35.00	20.00
(5)	Doc Adkins	75.00	35.00	20.00
(6a)	Dave Altizer (Cincinnati)	75.00	35.00	20.00
(6b)	Dave Altizer (Minneapolis)	75.00	35.00	20.00
(7)	Nick Altrock	95.00	50.00	30.00
(8)	Red Ames	75.00	35.00	20.00
(9a)	Jimmy Austin (New York)	75.00	35.00	20.00
(9b)	Jimmy Austin (St. Louis)	75.00	35.00	20.00
(10a)	Charlie Babb (Memphis)	75.00	35.00	20.00
(10b)	Charlie Babb (Norfolk)	75.00	35.00	20.00
(11)	Baerwald	75.00	35.00	20.00
(12)	Bill Bailey	75.00	35.00	20.00
(13)	Home Run Baker (*)	215.00	110.00	65.00
(14)	Jack Barry (*)	75.00	35.00	20.00
(15a)	Bill Bartley (Curved letters.)	75.00	35.00	20.00
(15b)	Bill Bartley (Horizontal letters.)	75.00	35.00	20.00
(16a)	Johnny Bates (Cincinnati)	75.00	35.00	20.00
(16b)	Johnny Bates (Philadelphia, black letters.)	75.00	35.00	20.00
(16c)	Johnny Bates (Philadelphia, white letters.)	75.00	35.00	20.00
(17)	Dick Bayless	75.00	35.00	20.00
(18a)	Ginger Beaumont (Boston)	75.00	35.00	20.00
(18b)	Ginger Beaumont (Chicago)	75.00	35.00	20.00
(18c)	Ginger Beaumont (St. Paul)	75.00	35.00	20.00
(19)	Beals Becker	75.00	35.00	20.00
(20)	George Bell	75.00	35.00	20.00
(21a)	Harry Bemis (Cleveland)	75.00	35.00	20.00
(21b)	Harry Bemis (Columbus)	75.00	35.00	20.00
(22a)	Heinie Berger (Cleveland)	75.00	35.00	20.00
(22b)	Heinie Berger (Columbus)	75.00	35.00	20.00
(23)	Beumiller	75.00	35.00	20.00
(24)	Joe Birmingham	75.00	35.00	20.00
(25)	Kitty Bransfield	75.00	35.00	20.00
(26)	Roger Bresnahan	215.00	110.00	65.00
(27)	Al Bridwell	75.00	35.00	20.00
(28)	Lew Brockett	75.00	35.00	20.00
(29)	Al Burch (*)	75.00	35.00	20.00
(30)	Burke	75.00	35.00	20.00
(31)	Donie Bush	75.00	35.00	20.00
(32)	Bill Byers	75.00	35.00	20.00
(33)	Howie Cammitz (Camnitz)	75.00	35.00	20.00
(34a)	Charlie Carr (Indianapolis)	75.00	35.00	20.00
(34b)	Charlie Carr (Utica)	75.00	35.00	20.00
(35)	Frank Chance	215.00	110.00	65.00
(36)	Hal Chase	150.00	80.00	40.00
(37)	Bill Clancy (Clancey)	75.00	35.00	20.00
(38a)	Fred Clarke (Pittsburg)	215.00	110.00	65.00
(38b)	Fred Clarke (Pittsburgh)	215.00	110.00	65.00
(39)	Tommy Clarke (Cincinnati)	75.00	35.00	20.00
(40)	Bill Clymer	75.00	35.00	20.00
(41)	Ty Cobb (*)	1,140	570.00	340.00
(42)	Eddie Collins	215.00	110.00	65.00
(43)	Bunk Congalton	75.00	35.00	20.00
(44)	Wid Conroy	75.00	35.00	20.00
(45)	Ernie Courtney	75.00	35.00	20.00
(46a)	Harry Coveleski (Cincinnati)	75.00	35.00	20.00
(46b)	Harry Coveleski (Chattanooga)	75.00	35.00	20.00
(47)	Doc Crandall	75.00	35.00	20.00
(48)	Gavvy Cravath	75.00	35.00	20.00
(49)	Dode Criss	75.00	35.00	20.00
(50a)	Jake Daubert (Memphis)	75.00	35.00	20.00
(50b)	Jake Daubert (Brooklyn)	75.00	35.00	20.00
(51)	Harry Davis (Philadelphia)	75.00	35.00	20.00
(52)	Davis (St. Paul)	75.00	35.00	20.00
(53)	Frank Delahanty	75.00	35.00	20.00
(54a)	Ray Demmett (Demmitt) (New York)	75.00	35.00	20.00
(54b)	Ray Demmett (Demmitt) (Montreal)	75.00	35.00	20.00
(55)	Art Devlin	75.00	35.00	20.00
(56)	Wild Bill Donovan	75.00	35.00	20.00
(57)	Mickey Doolin (Doolan)	75.00	35.00	20.00
(58)	Patsy Dougherty	75.00	35.00	20.00
(59)	Tom Downey	75.00	35.00	20.00
(60)	Larry Doyle	75.00	35.00	20.00
(61)	Jack Dunn	95.00	50.00	30.00
(62)	Dick Eagan (Egan)	75.00	35.00	20.00
(63a)	Kid Elberfield (Elberfeld) (Washington)	75.00	35.00	20.00
(63b)	Kid Elberfield (Elberfeld) (New York)	75.00	35.00	20.00
(64)	Rube Ellis	75.00	35.00	20.00
(65)	Clyde Engle (Boston)	75.00	35.00	20.00
(66)	Steve Evans (Horizontal letters.)	75.00	35.00	20.00
(67)	Johnny Evers	215.00	110.00	65.00
(68)	Cecil Ferguson	75.00	35.00	20.00
(69)	Hobe Ferris	75.00	35.00	20.00

No.	Player	NM	EX	VG
(70)	Field (*)	75.00	35.00	20.00
(71)	Fitzgerald	75.00	35.00	20.00
(72a)	Patsy Flaherty (Kansas City)	75.00	35.00	20.00
(72b)	Patsy Flaherty (Atlanta)	75.00	35.00	20.00
(73)	Jack Flater	75.00	35.00	20.00
(74a)	Elmer Flick (Cleveland)	215.00	110.00	65.00
(74b)	Elmer Flick (Toledo)	215.00	110.00	65.00
(75a)	James Freck (Frick, Baltimore)	90.00	45.00	30.00
(75b)	James Freck (Frick, Toronto)	75.00	35.00	20.00
(76)	Jerry Freeman (Photo actually Buck Freeman.)			
(77)	Art Fromme (*)	75.00	35.00	20.00
(78a)	Larry Gardner (Boston)	75.00	35.00	20.00
(78b)	Larry Gardner (New York)	75.00	35.00	20.00
(79)	Harry Gaspar	75.00	35.00	20.00
(80a)	Gus Getz (Boston)	75.00	35.00	20.00
(80b)	Gus Getz (Indianapolis)	75.00	35.00	20.00
(81)	George Gibson	75.00	35.00	20.00
(82a)	Moose Grimshaw (Toronto)	75.00	35.00	20.00
(82b)	Moose Grimshaw (Louisville)	75.00	35.00	20.00
(83)	Ed Hahn	75.00	35.00	20.00
(84)	John Halla (*)	75.00	35.00	20.00
(85)	Ed Hally (Holly)	75.00	35.00	20.00
(86)	Charlie Hanford	75.00	35.00	20.00
(87)	Topsy Hartsel	75.00	35.00	20.00
(88a)	Roy Hartzell (St. Louis)	75.00	35.00	20.00
(88b)	Roy Hartzell (New York)	75.00	35.00	20.00
(89)	Weldon Henley	75.00	35.00	20.00
(91)	Harry Hinchman	75.00	35.00	20.00
(92)	Solly Hofman	75.00	35.00	20.00
(93a)	Harry Hooper (Boston Na'l)	215.00	110.00	65.00
(93b)	Harry Hooper (Boston Am. L.)	240.00	120.00	75.00
(94)	Howard (*)	75.00	35.00	20.00
(95a)	Hughes (No name in uniform.)	75.00	35.00	20.00
(95b)	Hughes (Name and team name in uniform.)			
(96b)	Rudy Hulswitt (St. Louis)	75.00	35.00	20.00
(96c)	Rudy Hulswitt (Chattanooga)	75.00	35.00	20.00
(97)	John Hummel	75.00	35.00	20.00
(98)	George Hunter	75.00	35.00	20.00
(99)	Hugh Jennings	215.00	110.00	65.00
(100)	Davy Jones	75.00	35.00	20.00
(101)	Tom Jones	75.00	35.00	20.00
(102a)	Tim Jordan (Jordan, Brooklyn)	75.00	35.00	20.00
(102b)	Tim Jordan (Jordan, Atlanta)	75.00	35.00	20.00
(102c)	Tim Jordan (Jordan, Louisville)	75.00	35.00	20.00
(103)	Addie Joss	240.00	120.00	75.00
(104)	Al Kaiser	75.00	35.00	20.00
(105)	Joe Kelly (Kelley)	215.00	110.00	65.00
(106)	Bill Killefer (*)	75.00	35.00	20.00
(107a)	Ed Killian (Detroit)	75.00	35.00	20.00
(107b)	Ed Killian (Toronto)	75.00	35.00	20.00
(108)	Otto Knabe	75.00	35.00	20.00
(109)	Jack Knight	75.00	35.00	20.00
(111)	Ed Konetchy	75.00	35.00	20.00
(112)	Rube Kroh	75.00	35.00	20.00
(113)	James Lafitte	75.00	35.00	20.00
(114)	Lakoff	75.00	35.00	20.00
(115)	Frank Lange	75.00	35.00	20.00
(116a)	Frank LaPorte (St. Louis)	75.00	35.00	20.00
(116b)	Frank LaPorte (New York)	75.00	35.00	20.00
(117)	Tommy Leach	75.00	35.00	20.00
(118)	Bill Lelivelt	75.00	35.00	20.00
(119a)	Jack Lewis (Milwaukee)	75.00	35.00	20.00
(119b)	Jack Lewis (Indianapolis)	75.00	35.00	20.00
(120a)	Vive Lindaman (Boston)	75.00	35.00	20.00
(120b)	Vive Lindaman (Louisville)	75.00	35.00	20.00
(120c)	Vive Lindaman (Indianapolis)	75.00	35.00	20.00
(121)	Bris Lord	75.00	35.00	20.00
(122a)	Harry Lord (Boston)	75.00	35.00	20.00
(122b)	Harry Lord (Chicago)	75.00	35.00	20.00
(123)	Bill Ludwig (Milwaukee)	75.00	35.00	20.00
(124)	Nick Maddox	75.00	35.00	20.00
(125a)	Manser (Jersey City)	75.00	35.00	20.00
(125b)	Manser (Rochester)	75.00	35.00	20.00
(126)	Al Mattern	75.00	35.00	20.00
(127)	Bill Matthews	75.00	35.00	20.00
(128)	George McBride	75.00	35.00	20.00
(129)	McCarthy	75.00	35.00	20.00
(130)	McConnell	75.00	35.00	20.00
(131)	Moose McCormick	75.00	35.00	20.00
(132)	Dan McGann	75.00	35.00	20.00
(133)	Jim McGinley	75.00	35.00	20.00
(134)	Iron Man McGinnity	215.00	110.00	65.00
(135a)	Matty McIntyre (Detroit)	75.00	35.00	20.00
(135b)	Matty McIntyre (Chicago)	75.00	35.00	20.00
(136)	Larry McLean (*)(Three photo size variations known.)	75.00	35.00	20.00
(137)	Fred Merkle	75.00	35.00	20.00
(138a)	Merritt (Buffalo)	75.00	35.00	20.00
(138b)	Merritt (Jersey City)	75.00	35.00	20.00
(139)	Meyer (Newark)	75.00	35.00	20.00
(140)	Chief Meyers (New York)	75.00	35.00	20.00
(141)	Clyde Milan	75.00	35.00	20.00
(142)	Dots Miller	75.00	35.00	20.00
(143)	Mike Mitchell	75.00	35.00	20.00
(144)	Moran	75.00	35.00	20.00
(145a)	Bill Moriarty (Louisville)	75.00	35.00	20.00
(145b)	Bill Moriarty (Omaha)	75.00	35.00	20.00
(146)	George Moriarty	75.00	35.00	20.00
(147a)	George Mullen (Name incorrect.)			
(147b)	George Mullin (Name correct.)	75.00	35.00	20.00
(148a)	Simmy Murch (Chattanooga)	75.00	35.00	20.00
(148b)	Simmy Murch (Indianapolis)	75.00	35.00	20.00
(149)	Danny Murphy	75.00	35.00	20.00
(150a)	Red Murray (New York, white letters.)	75.00	35.00	12.00
(150b)	Red Murray (St. Paul)	75.00	35.00	20.00
(151)	Billy Nattress	75.00	35.00	20.00
(152a)	Red Nelson (St. Louis)	75.00	35.00	20.00
(152b)	Red Nelson (Toledo)	75.00	35.00	20.00
(153)	Rebel Oakes	75.00	35.00	20.00
(154)	Fred Odwell	75.00	35.00	20.00
(155a)	Al Orth (New York)	75.00	35.00	20.00
(155b)	Al Orth (Indianapolis)	75.00	35.00	20.00
(156)	Fred Osborn	75.00	35.00	20.00
(157)	Orval Overall	75.00	35.00	20.00
(158)	Owens	75.00	35.00	20.00
(159)	Fred Parent	75.00	35.00	20.00
(161a)	Dode Paskert (Cincinnati)	75.00	35.00	20.00
(161b)	Dode Paskert (Philadelphia)	75.00	35.00	20.00
(162)	Heinie Peitz	75.00	35.00	20.00
(163)	Bob Peterson	75.00	35.00	20.00
(164)	Jake Pfeister	75.00	35.00	20.00
(165)	Deacon Phillipe (Phillippe)	75.00	35.00	20.00
(166a)	Ollie Pickering (Louisville)	75.00	35.00	20.00
(166b)	Ollie Pickering (Minneapolis)	75.00	35.00	20.00
(166c)	Ollie Pickering (Omaha)	75.00	35.00	20.00
(167a)	Billy Purtell (Chicago)	75.00	35.00	20.00
(167b)	Billy Purtell (Boston)	75.00	35.00	20.00
(168)	Bugs Raymond	75.00	35.00	20.00
(169)	Pat Regan (Ragan)	75.00	35.00	20.00
(170)	Barney Reilly	75.00	35.00	20.00
(171)	Duke Reilly (Reilley)	75.00	35.00	20.00
(172)	Ed Reulbach	75.00	35.00	20.00
(173)	Claude Ritchey	75.00	35.00	20.00
(174)	Lou Ritter	75.00	35.00	20.00
(175)	Robinson	75.00	35.00	20.00
(176)	Rock	75.00	35.00	20.00
(177a)	Jack Rowan (Cincinnati)	75.00	35.00	20.00
(177b)	Jack Rowan (Philadelphia)	75.00	35.00	20.00
(178)	Nap Rucker	75.00	35.00	20.00
(179a)	Dick Rudolph (New York)	75.00	35.00	20.00
(179b)	Dick Rudolph (Toronto)	75.00	35.00	20.00
(180)	Jimmy Ryan	75.00	35.00	20.00
(181)	Slim Sallee	75.00	35.00	20.00
(182a)	Bill Schardt (Birmingham)	75.00	35.00	20.00
(182b)	Bill Schardt (Milwaukee)	75.00	35.00	20.00
(183)	Jimmy Scheckard (Sheckard)	75.00	35.00	20.00
(184a)	George Schirm (Birmingham)	75.00	35.00	20.00
(184b)	George Schirm (Buffalo)	75.00	35.00	20.00
(185)	Larry Schlafly	75.00	35.00	20.00
(186)	Wildfire Schulte	75.00	35.00	20.00
(187a)	James Seabaugh (Looking to left, photo actually Julius Weisman.)			
(187b)	James Seabaugh (Looking straight ahead, correct photo.)	75.00	35.00	20.00
(188)	Selby (*)	75.00	35.00	20.00
(189a)	Cy Seymour (New York)	75.00	35.00	20.00
(189b)	Cy Seymour (Baltimore)	75.00	35.00	20.00
(190)	Hosea Siner	75.00	35.00	20.00
(191)	G. Smith	75.00	35.00	20.00
(192a)	Sid Smith (Atlanta)	75.00	35.00	20.00
(192b)	Sid Smith (Buffalo)	75.00	35.00	20.00
(193)	Fred Snodgrass	75.00	35.00	20.00
(194a)	Bob Spade (Cincinnati)	75.00	35.00	20.00
(194b)	Bob Spade (Newark)	75.00	35.00	20.00
(195a)	Tully Sparks (Philadelphia)	75.00	35.00	20.00
(195b)	Tully Sparks (Richmond)	75.00	35.00	20.00
(196)	Tris Speaker (Boston Am.)	260.00	120.00	80.00
(197)	Tubby Spencer	75.00	35.00	20.00
(198)	Jake Stahl	75.00	35.00	20.00
(199)	John Stansberry (Stansbury)	75.00	35.00	20.00
(200)	Harry Steinfeldt (*)	75.00	35.00	20.00
(201)	George Stone	75.00	35.00	20.00
(202)	George Stovall	75.00	35.00	20.00
(203)	Gabby Street	75.00	35.00	20.00
(204a)	Sullivan (Louisville)	75.00	35.00	20.00
(204b)	Sullivan (Omaha)	75.00	35.00	20.00
(205a)	Ed Summers (No name in uniform.)			
(205b)	Ed Summers (White in uniform.)	75.00	35.00	20.00
(206)	Lee Tannehill	75.00	35.00	20.00
(207)	Taylor	75.00	35.00	20.00
(208)	Joe Tinker	215.00	110.00	65.00
(209)	John Titus	75.00	35.00	20.00
(210)	Terry Turner	75.00	35.00	20.00
(211a)	Bob Unglaub (Washington)	75.00	35.00	20.00
(211b)	Bob Unglaub (Lincoln)	75.00	35.00	20.00
(212a)	Rube Waddell (St. Louis)	215.00	110.00	65.00
(212b)	Rube Waddell (Minneapolis)	215.00	110.00	65.00
(212c)	Rube Waddell (Newark)	215.00	110.00	65.00
(213)	Honus Wagner (*)	1,140	570.00	340.00
(214)	Walker	75.00	35.00	20.00
(215)	Waller	75.00	35.00	20.00
(216)	Clarence Wauner (Wanner)	75.00	35.00	20.00
(217)	Julius Weisman (Name correct.)	75.00	35.00	20.00
(218)	Jack White (Buffalo)	75.00	35.00	20.00
(219)	Kirby White (Boston)	75.00	35.00	20.00
(220)	Julius Wiesman (Weisman)	75.00	35.00	20.00
(221)	Ed Willett	75.00	35.00	20.00
(222)	Otto Williams	75.00	35.00	20.00
(223)	Owen Wilson	75.00	35.00	20.00
(224)	Hooks Wiltse	75.00	35.00	20.00
(225a)	Orville Woodruff (Indianapolis)	75.00	35.00	20.00
(225b)	Orville Woodruff (Louisville)	75.00	35.00	20.00
(226)	Woods	75.00	35.00	20.00
(227)	Cy Young	570.00	280.00	170.00
(228)	Bill Zimmerman	75.00	35.00	20.00
(229)	Heinie Zimmerman	75.00	35.00	20.00

1912 Colgan's Chips Red Borders (E270)

This set, issued in 1912 by Colgan Gum Co., Louisville, Ky., is very similar to the 1909-11 Colgan's release. Measuring about 1-1/2" in diameter, the black-and-white player pictures were inserted in tins of Colgan's Mint and Violet Chips gum. They are differentiated from the earlier issues by their distinctive red borders and by the back of the cards, which advises collectors to "Send 25 Box Tops" for a photo of the "World's Pennant Winning Team." The issue is designated as the E270 Red Border set in the American Card Catalog. A Red Border card of Gavvy Cravath previous cataloged is now believed not to exist.

No.	Player	NM	EX	VG
	Complete Set (181):	50,000	25,000	14,400
	Common Player:	250.00	125.00	75.00
(1)	Ed Abbaticchio	250.00	125.00	75.00
(2)	Fred Abbott	250.00	125.00	75.00
(3)	Babe Adams	250.00	125.00	75.00
(4)	Doc Adkins	250.00	125.00	75.00
(5)	Red Ames	250.00	125.00	75.00
(6)	Charlie Babb	250.00	125.00	75.00
(7)	Bill Bailey	250.00	125.00	75.00
(8)	Home Run Baker	400.00	250.00	150.00
(9)	Jack Barry	250.00	125.00	75.00
(10)	Johnny Bates	250.00	125.00	75.00
(11)	Dick Bayless	250.00	125.00	75.00
(12)	Ginger Beaumont	250.00	125.00	75.00
(13)	Beals Becker	250.00	125.00	75.00
(14)	George Bell	250.00	125.00	75.00
(15)	Harry Bemis	250.00	125.00	75.00
(16)	Heinie Berger	250.00	125.00	75.00
(17)	Beumiller	250.00	125.00	75.00
(18)	Joe Birmingham	250.00	125.00	75.00
(19)	Kitty Bransfield	250.00	125.00	75.00
(20)	Roger Bresnahan	500.00	250.00	150.00
(21)	Lew Brockett	250.00	125.00	75.00
(22)	Al Burch	250.00	125.00	75.00
(23)	Donie Bush	250.00	125.00	75.00
(24)	Bill Byers	250.00	125.00	75.00
(25)	Howie Cammitz (Camnitz)	250.00	125.00	75.00
(26)	Charlie Carr	250.00	125.00	75.00
(27)	Frank Chance	500.00	250.00	150.00
(28)	Hal Chase	305.00	150.00	91.00
(29)	Fred Clarke (Pittsburg)	500.00	250.00	150.00
(30)	Tommy Clarke (Cincinnati)	250.00	125.00	75.00
(31)	Bill Clymer	250.00	125.00	75.00
(32)	Ty Cobb	3,750	1,875	1,125
(33)	Eddie Collins	500.00	250.00	150.00
(34)	Wid Conroy	250.00	125.00	75.00
(35)	Harry Coveleski	250.00	125.00	75.00
(37)	Dode Criss	250.00	125.00	75.00
(38)	Jake Daubert	250.00	125.00	75.00
(39)	Harry Davis (Philadelphia)	250.00	125.00	75.00
(40)	Davis (St. Paul)	250.00	125.00	75.00
(41)	Frank Delahanty	250.00	125.00	75.00
(42)	Ray Demmett (Demmitt)	250.00	125.00	75.00
(43)	Art Devlin	250.00	125.00	75.00
(44)	Wild Bill Donovan	250.00	125.00	75.00
(45)	Mickey Doolin (Doolan)	250.00	125.00	75.00
(46)	Patsy Dougherty	250.00	125.00	75.00
(47)	Tom Downey	250.00	125.00	75.00
(48)	Larry Doyle	250.00	125.00	75.00
(49)	Jack Dunn	250.00	125.00	75.00
(50)	Dick Eagan (Egan)	250.00	125.00	75.00
(51)	Kid Elberfield (Elberfeld)	250.00	125.00	75.00
(52)	Rube Ellis	250.00	125.00	75.00
(53)	Steve Evans	250.00	125.00	75.00
(54)	Johnny Evers	500.00	250.00	150.00
(55)	Cecil Ferguson	250.00	125.00	75.00
(56)	Hobe Ferris	250.00	125.00	75.00
(57)	Fisher	250.00	125.00	75.00
(58)	Fitzgerald	250.00	125.00	75.00
(59)	Elmer Flick	500.00	250.00	150.00
(60)	James Freck (Frick)	250.00	125.00	75.00
(61)	Art Fromme	250.00	125.00	75.00
(62)	Harry Gaspar	250.00	125.00	75.00
(63)	George Gibson	250.00	125.00	75.00
(64)	Moose Grimshaw	250.00	125.00	75.00
(65)	John Halla	250.00	125.00	75.00
(66)	Ed Hally (Holly)	250.00	125.00	75.00
(67)	Charlie Hanford	250.00	125.00	75.00
(68)	Topsy Hartsel	250.00	125.00	75.00
(69)	Roy Hartzell	250.00	125.00	75.00
(70)	Weldon Henley (Two sizes variations noted.)	250.00	125.00	75.00
(71)	Harry Hinchman	250.00	125.00	75.00
(72)	Solly Hofman	250.00	125.00	75.00
(73)	Harry Hooper	500.00	250.00	150.00
(74)	Howard	250.00	125.00	75.00
(75)	Hughes	250.00	125.00	75.00
(76)	Rudy Hulswitt	250.00	125.00	75.00
(77)	John Hummel	250.00	125.00	75.00
(78)	George Hunter	250.00	125.00	75.00
(79)	Hugh Jennings	500.00	250.00	150.00
(80)	Davy Jones	250.00	125.00	75.00
(81)	Tom Jones	250.00	125.00	75.00
(82)	Tim Jordan (Jordan)	250.00	125.00	75.00
(83)	Joe Kelly (Kelley)	500.00	250.00	150.00
(84)	Bill Killefer	250.00	125.00	75.00
(85)	Ed Killian	250.00	125.00	75.00
(86)	Otto Knabe	250.00	125.00	75.00
(87)	Jack Knight	250.00	125.00	75.00
(88)	Ed Konetchy	250.00	125.00	75.00
(89)	Rube Kroh	250.00	125.00	75.00
(90)	LaCrosse (Photo actually Bill Schardt.)	250.00	125.00	75.00
(91)	Frank LaPorte	250.00	125.00	75.00
(92)	Tommy Leach	250.00	125.00	75.00
(93)	Jack Lelivelt	250.00	125.00	75.00
(94)	Jack Lewis	250.00	125.00	75.00
(95)	Vive Lindaman	250.00	125.00	75.00
(96)	Bris Lord	250.00	125.00	75.00
(97)	Harry Lord	250.00	125.00	75.00
(98)	Bill Ludwig	250.00	125.00	75.00
(99)	Nick Maddox	250.00	125.00	75.00

	NM	EX	VG
(100) Manser	250.00	125.00	75.00
(101) Al Mattern	250.00	125.00	75.00
(102) George McBride	250.00	125.00	75.00
(103) McCarthy	250.00	125.00	75.00
(104) McConnell	250.00	125.00	75.00
(105) Moose McCormick	250.00	125.00	75.00
(106) Dan McGann	250.00	125.00	75.00
(107) Jim McGinley	250.00	125.00	75.00
(108) Iron Man McGinnity	500.00	250.00	150.00
(109) Matty McIntyre	250.00	125.00	75.00
(110) Larry McLean	250.00	125.00	75.00
(111) Fred Merkle	250.00	125.00	75.00
(112) Merritt	250.00	125.00	75.00
(113) Meyer (Newark)	250.00	125.00	75.00
(114) Chief Meyers	250.00	125.00	75.00
(115) Clyde Milan	250.00	125.00	75.00
(116) Dots Miller	250.00	125.00	75.00
(117) Mike Mitchell	250.00	125.00	75.00
(118) Bill Moriarty (Omaha)	250.00	125.00	75.00
(119) George Moriarty (Detroit)	250.00	125.00	75.00
(120) George Mullen (Mullin)	250.00	125.00	75.00
(121) Simmy Murch (Chattanooga)	250.00	125.00	75.00
(122) Simmy Murch (Indianapolis)	250.00	125.00	75.00
(123) Danny Murphy	250.00	125.00	75.00
(124) Red Murray	250.00	125.00	75.00
(125) Red Nelson	250.00	125.00	75.00
(126) Rebel Oakes	250.00	125.00	75.00
(127) Orval Overall	250.00	125.00	75.00
(128) Owens	250.00	125.00	75.00
(129) Fred Parent	250.00	125.00	75.00
(130) Dode Paskert	250.00	125.00	75.00
(131) Bob Peterson	250.00	125.00	75.00
(132) Jake Pfeister (Pfiester)	250.00	125.00	75.00
(133) Deacon Phillipe (Phillippe)	250.00	125.00	75.00
(134) Ollie Pickering	250.00	125.00	75.00
(135) Heinie Pietz (Peitz)	250.00	125.00	75.00
(136) Bugs Raymond	250.00	125.00	75.00
(137) Pat Regan (Ragan)	250.00	125.00	75.00
(138) Ed Reulbach	250.00	125.00	75.00
(139) Robinson	250.00	125.00	75.00
(140) Rock	250.00	125.00	75.00
(141) Jack Rowan	250.00	125.00	75.00
(142) Nap Rucker	250.00	125.00	75.00
(143) Dick Rudolph	250.00	125.00	75.00
(144) Slim Sallee	250.00	125.00	75.00
(145) Jimmy Scheckard (Sheckard)	250.00	125.00	75.00
(146) George Schirm	250.00	125.00	75.00
(147) Wildfire Schulte	250.00	125.00	75.00
(148) James Seabaugh	250.00	125.00	75.00
(149) Selby	250.00	125.00	75.00
(150) Cy Seymour	250.00	125.00	75.00
(151) Hosea Siner	250.00	125.00	75.00
(152) Sid Smith	250.00	125.00	75.00
(153) Fred Snodgrass	250.00	125.00	75.00
(154) Bob Spade	250.00	125.00	75.00
(155) Tully Sparks	250.00	125.00	75.00
(156) Tris Speaker	750.00	375.00	225.00
(157) Tubby Spencer	250.00	125.00	75.00
(158) John Stausberry (Stansbury)	250.00	125.00	75.00
(159) Harry Steinfeldt	250.00	125.00	75.00
(160) George Stone	250.00	125.00	75.00
(161) George Stovall	250.00	125.00	75.00
(162) Gabby Street	250.00	125.00	75.00
(163) Sullivan (Omaha)	250.00	125.00	75.00
(164) John Sullivan (Louisville)	250.00	125.00	75.00
(165) Ed Summers	250.00	125.00	75.00
(166) Joe Tinker	500.00	250.00	150.00
(167) John Titus	250.00	125.00	75.00
(168) Terry Turner	250.00	125.00	75.00
(169) Bob Unglaub	250.00	125.00	75.00
(170) Rube Waddell	500.00	250.00	150.00
(171) Walker	250.00	125.00	75.00
(172) Waller	250.00	125.00	75.00
(173) Kirby White (Boston)	250.00	125.00	75.00
(174) Jack White (Buffalo)	250.00	125.00	75.00
(175) Julius Wiesman (Weisman)	250.00	125.00	75.00
(176) Otto Williams	250.00	125.00	75.00
(177) Hooks Wiltse	250.00	125.00	75.00
(178) Orville Woodruff	250.00	125.00	75.00
(179) Woods	250.00	125.00	75.00
(180) Cy Young	1,560	780.00	470.00
(181) Bill Zimmerman	250.00	125.00	75.00
(182) Heinie Zimmerman	250.00	125.00	75.00

1912 Colgan's Chips Tin Tops

Except for the backs, these round black-and-white cards (about 1-1/2" diameter) are identical to the 1909-11 Colgan's Chips issue, and were inserted in tin cannisters of Colgan's Mint Chips and Violet Chips. The front features a portrait photo along with the player's last name, team and, where necessary, league. The back advises collectors to "Send 25 Tin Tops" and a two-cent stamp to receive a photo of the "World's Pennant Winning Team." The set carries the designation E270 in the American Card Catalog. Gaps have been left in the assigned numbering to allow integration of future discoveries.

	NM	EX	VG
Complete Set (214):	60,000	30,000	18,000

Common Player:	180.00	90.00	54.00
(1) Ed Abbaticchio	180.00	90.00	54.00
(2) Doc Adkins	180.00	90.00	54.00
(3) Joe Agler	180.00	90.00	54.00
(4) Eddie Ainsmith	180.00	90.00	54.00
(5) Whitey Alperman	180.00	90.00	54.00
(6) Red Ames (New York)	180.00	90.00	54.00
(7) Red Ames (Cincinnati)	180.00	90.00	54.00
(8) Jimmy Archer	180.00	90.00	54.00
(9) Tommy Atkins (Atlanta)	180.00	90.00	54.00
(10) Tommy Atkins (Ft. Wayne)	180.00	90.00	54.00
(11) Jake Atz (New Orleans)	180.00	90.00	54.00
(12) Jake Atz (Providence)	180.00	90.00	54.00
(13) Jimmy Austin	180.00	90.00	54.00
(14) Home Run Baker	360.00	180.00	110.00
(15) Johnny Bates	180.00	90.00	54.00
(16) Beck (Buffalo)	180.00	90.00	54.00
(17) Beebe	180.00	90.00	54.00
(18) Harry Bemis	180.00	90.00	54.00
(19) Bob Bescher	180.00	90.00	54.00
(20) Beumiller (Louisville)	180.00	90.00	54.00
(21) Joe Birmingham	180.00	90.00	54.00
(22) Roger Bresnahan	360.00	180.00	110.00
(23) Al Bridwell	180.00	90.00	54.00
(24) George Brown (Browne)	180.00	90.00	54.00
(26) Al Burch	180.00	90.00	54.00
(27) Burns	180.00	90.00	54.00
(28) Donie Bush	180.00	90.00	54.00
(29) Bobby Byrne	180.00	90.00	54.00
(30) Nixey Callahan	180.00	90.00	54.00
(31) Howie Camnitz	180.00	90.00	54.00
(32) Billy Campbell	180.00	90.00	54.00
(33) Charlie Carr	180.00	90.00	54.00
(34) Jay Cashion	180.00	90.00	54.00
(35) Frank Chance	360.00	180.00	110.00
(36) Hal Chase	220.00	110.00	65.00
(37) Ed Cicotte	270.00	135.00	80.00
(38) Clarke (Indianapolis)	180.00	90.00	54.00
(39) Fred Clarke (Pittsburg)	360.00	180.00	110.00
(40) Tommy Clarke (Cincinnati)	180.00	90.00	54.00
(41) Clemons	180.00	90.00	54.00
(42) Bill Clymer	180.00	90.00	54.00
(43) Ty Cobb	2,400	1,200	720.00
(44) Eddie Collins	360.00	180.00	110.00
(45) Bunk Congalton (Omaha)	180.00	90.00	54.00
(46) Bunk Congalton (Toledo)	180.00	90.00	54.00
(47) Cook	180.00	90.00	54.00
(48) Jack Coombs	180.00	90.00	54.00
(49) Corcoran	180.00	90.00	54.00
(50) Gavvy Cravath	180.00	90.00	54.00
(51) Sam Crawford	360.00	180.00	110.00
(52) Bill Dahlen	180.00	90.00	54.00
(53) Bert Daniels	180.00	90.00	54.00
(54) Jake Daubert	180.00	90.00	54.00
(55) Josh Devore (Cincinnati)	180.00	90.00	54.00
(56) Josh Devore (New York)	180.00	90.00	54.00
(57) Mike Donlin	180.00	90.00	54.00
(58) Wild Bill Donovan	180.00	90.00	54.00
(59) Red Dooin	180.00	90.00	54.00
(60) Mickey Doolan	180.00	90.00	54.00
(61) Larry Doyle	180.00	90.00	54.00
(62) Delos Drake	180.00	90.00	54.00
(63) Dick Egan	180.00	90.00	54.00
(64) Kid Elberfield (Elberfeld)	180.00	90.00	54.00
(65) Roy Ellam	180.00	90.00	54.00
(66) Elliott	180.00	90.00	54.00
(67) Rube Ellis	180.00	90.00	54.00
(68) Elwert	180.00	90.00	54.00
(69) Clyde Engle	180.00	90.00	54.00
(70) Jimmy Esmond	180.00	90.00	54.00
(71) Steve Evans	180.00	90.00	54.00
(72) Johnny Evers	360.00	180.00	110.00
(73) Hobe Ferris	180.00	90.00	54.00
(74) Russ Ford	180.00	90.00	54.00
(76) Ed Foster	180.00	90.00	54.00
(77) Friel	180.00	90.00	54.00
(78) John Frill	180.00	90.00	54.00
(79) Art Fromme	180.00	90.00	54.00
(80) Gus Getz (Newark)	180.00	90.00	54.00
(81) George Gibson	180.00	90.00	54.00
(82) Graham	180.00	90.00	54.00
(83) Eddie Grant (Cincinnati)	180.00	90.00	54.00
(84) Eddie Grant (New York)	180.00	90.00	54.00
(85) Grief	180.00	90.00	54.00
(86) Bob Groom	180.00	90.00	54.00
(87) Topsy Hartsel	180.00	90.00	54.00
(88) Roy Hartzell	180.00	90.00	54.00
(89) Harry Hinchman	180.00	90.00	54.00
(90) Dick Hoblitzell	180.00	90.00	54.00
(91) Happy Hogan (St. Louis)	180.00	90.00	54.00
(92) Happy Hogan (San Francisco)	180.00	90.00	54.00
(93) Harry Hooper	360.00	180.00	110.00
(94) Miller Huggins	360.00	180.00	110.00
(95) Hughes (Milwaukee)	180.00	90.00	54.00
(96) Hughes (Rochester)	180.00	90.00	54.00
(97) Rudy Hulswitt	180.00	90.00	54.00
(98) John Hummel	180.00	90.00	54.00
(99) George Hunter	180.00	90.00	54.00
(100) Shoeless Joe Jackson	20,000	4,800	2,880
(101) Jameson (Buffalo)	180.00	90.00	54.00
(102) Hugh Jennings	360.00	180.00	110.00
(103) Pete Johns	180.00	90.00	54.00
(104) Walter Johnson	780.00	390.00	235.00
(105) Davy Jones (Toledo)	180.00	90.00	54.00
(106) Tim Jordan	180.00	90.00	54.00
(107) Bob Keefe	180.00	90.00	54.00
(108) Wee Willie Keeler	360.00	180.00	110.00
(109) Joe Kelly (Kelley)	360.00	180.00	110.00
(110) Ed Killian	180.00	90.00	54.00
(111) Bill Killifer (Killefer)	180.00	90.00	54.00
(112) Johnny Kling (Boston)	180.00	90.00	54.00
(113) Klipfer	180.00	90.00	54.00
(114) Otto Knabe	180.00	90.00	54.00
(115) Jack Knight	180.00	90.00	54.00
(116) Ed Konetchy	180.00	90.00	54.00
(117) Paul Krichell	180.00	90.00	54.00
(118) James Lafitte	180.00	90.00	54.00
(119) Nap Lajoie	360.00	180.00	110.00

(120) Frank Lange	180.00	90.00	54.00
(121) Lee	180.00	90.00	54.00
(122) Jack Lewis	180.00	90.00	54.00
(123) Harry Lord	180.00	90.00	54.00
(124) Johnny Lush	180.00	90.00	54.00
(126) Madden	180.00	90.00	54.00
(127) Nick Maddox	180.00	90.00	54.00
(128) Sherry Magee	180.00	90.00	54.00
(129) Manser	180.00	90.00	54.00
(130) Frank Manusch (Manush) (New Orleans)	180.00	90.00	54.00
(131) Frank Manush (Toledo)	180.00	90.00	54.00
(132) Rube Marquard	360.00	180.00	110.00
(133) McAllister	180.00	90.00	54.00
(134) George McBride	180.00	90.00	54.00
(135) McCarthy (Newark)	180.00	90.00	54.00
(136) McCarthy (Toledo)	180.00	90.00	54.00
(137) McConnell	180.00	90.00	54.00
(138) Moose McCormick	180.00	90.00	54.00
(139) Larry McLean	180.00	90.00	54.00
(140) Fred Merkle	180.00	90.00	54.00
(141) Chief Meyers	180.00	90.00	54.00
(142) Clyde Milan	180.00	90.00	54.00
(143) Miller (Columbus)	180.00	90.00	54.00
(144) Dots Miller (Pittsburg)	180.00	90.00	54.00
(145) Clarence Mitchell	180.00	90.00	54.00
(146) Mike Mitchell	180.00	90.00	54.00
(147) Roy Mitchell	180.00	90.00	54.00
(148) Carlton Molesworth	180.00	90.00	54.00
(149) Herbie Moran	180.00	90.00	54.00
(150) George Moriarty	180.00	90.00	54.00
(151) George Mullen (Mullin)	180.00	90.00	54.00
(152) Danny Murphy	180.00	90.00	54.00
(153) Murray (Buffalo)	180.00	90.00	54.00
(154) Jim Murray	180.00	90.00	54.00
(155) Jake Northrop	180.00	90.00	54.00
(156) Rebel Oakes	180.00	90.00	54.00
(157) Rube Oldring	180.00	90.00	54.00
(158) Steve O'Neil (O'Neill)	180.00	90.00	54.00
(159) O'Rourke	180.00	90.00	54.00
(160) Owens (Minneapolis)	180.00	90.00	54.00
(161) Larry Pape	180.00	90.00	54.00
(162) Fred Parent	180.00	90.00	54.00
(163) Dode Paskert	180.00	90.00	54.00
(164) Heinie Peitz	180.00	90.00	54.00
(165) Perry	180.00	90.00	54.00
(166) Billy Purtell	180.00	90.00	54.00
(167) Bill Rariden	180.00	90.00	54.00
(168) Morrie Rath	180.00	90.00	54.00
(169) Bugs Raymond	180.00	90.00	54.00
(170) Ed Reulbach	180.00	90.00	54.00
(171) Nap Rucker	180.00	90.00	54.00
(172) Dick Rudolph	180.00	90.00	54.00
(173) Bud Ryan	180.00	90.00	54.00
(174) Slim Sallee	180.00	90.00	54.00
(176) Ray Schalk	180.00	90.00	54.00
(177) Jimmy Scheckard (Sheckard)	180.00	90.00	54.00
(178) Bob Shawkey	180.00	90.00	54.00
(179) Skeeter Shelton	180.00	90.00	54.00
(180) Burt Shotten (Shotton)	180.00	90.00	54.00
(181) Smith (Montreal)	180.00	90.00	54.00
(182) Sid Smith (Atlanta)	180.00	90.00	54.00
(183) Sid Smith (Newark)	180.00	90.00	54.00
(184) Fred Snodgrass	180.00	90.00	54.00
(185) Tris Speaker	540.00	270.00	160.00
(186) Jake Stahl	180.00	90.00	54.00
(187) John Stansberry (Stansbury)	180.00	90.00	54.00
(188) Amos Strunk	180.00	90.00	54.00
(189) Sullivan	180.00	90.00	54.00
(190) Harry Swacina	180.00	90.00	54.00
(191) Bill Sweeney	180.00	90.00	54.00
(192) Jeff Sweeney	180.00	90.00	54.00
(193) Lee Tannehill	180.00	90.00	54.00
(194) Dummy Taylor (Topeka)	300.00	150.00	90.00
(195) Jim Thorpe	12,000	3,900	2,340
(196) Joe Tinker	360.00	180.00	110.00
(197) John Titus (Boston)	180.00	90.00	54.00
(198) John Titus (Phiadelphia)	180.00	90.00	54.00
(199) Terry Turner	180.00	90.00	54.00
(201) Bob Unglaub	180.00	90.00	54.00
(202) Viebahn	180.00	90.00	54.00
(203) Rube Waddell	360.00	180.00	110.00
(204) Honus Wagner	2,500	750.00	450.00
(205) Bobby Wallace	360.00	180.00	110.00
(206) Ed Walsh	360.00	180.00	110.00
(207) Jack Warhop	180.00	90.00	54.00
(208) Harry Welchouce (Welchonce)	180.00	90.00	54.00
(209) Zach Wheat	360.00	180.00	110.00
(210) Kirb. White	180.00	90.00	54.00
(211) Kaiser Wilhelm	180.00	90.00	54.00
(212) Ed Willett	180.00	90.00	54.00
(213) Otto Williams	180.00	90.00	54.00
(214) Owen Wilson	180.00	90.00	54.00
(215) Hooks Wiltse	180.00	90.00	54.00
(216) Joe Wood	180.00	90.00	54.00
(217) Orville Woodruff	180.00	90.00	54.00
(218) Joe Yeager	180.00	90.00	54.00
(219) Bill Zimmerman	180.00	90.00	54.00
(220) Heinie Zimmerman	180.00	90.00	54.00

1909 "Colgan's Chips" Square Proofs

Though widely identified as being connected to the Colgan's Chips disc issues of 1909-1912, there is nothing to tie these square cards to the gum company except for the shared use of player photos. The squares measure about 1-3/8" x 1-3/4" and are blank-backed. Black-and-white player portrait photos have a last name and team identification beneath. Many, but not all, of the surviving specimens have paper and/or glue residue on back, leading to speculation they may have been part of an advertising piece. The extent of the checklist is unknown, with verified examples listed here.

COLLINS
Phila. Am. L.

	NM	EX	VG
Common Player:	250.00	120.00	80.00
(9) Red Ames	250.00	120.00	80.00
(12) Charlie Babb (Memphis)	250.00	120.00	80.00
(13) Baerwald (Memphis)	250.00	124.00	74.00
(15) Home Run Baker	600.00	300.00	180.00
(18) Johnny Bates	250.00	120.00	80.00
(20) Ginger Beaumont (Boston)	250.00	120.00	80.00
(21) Beals Becker	250.00	120.00	80.00
(29) Roger Bresnahan	600.00	300.00	180.00
(30) Al Bridwell	250.00	120.00	80.00
(31) Lew Brockett	250.00	124.00	74.00
(32) Al Burch	250.00	120.00	80.00
(34) Donie Bush	250.00	120.00	80.00
(36) Howie Camnitz	250.00	120.00	80.00
(38) Frank Chance	600.00	300.00	180.00
(41) Fred Clarke (Pittsburg)	600.00	300.00	180.00
(44) Ty Cobb	4,000	2,000	1,200
(45) Eddie Collins	600.00	300.00	180.00
(52) Dode Criss	250.00	120.00	80.00
(54) Jake Daubert (Memphis)	250.00	120.00	80.00
(55) Harry Davis (Philadelphia)	250.00	120.00	80.00
(58) Ray Demmett (Demmitt) (New York)	250.00	120.00	80.00
(69) Clyde Engle (New York)	250.00	120.00	80.00
(70) Steve Evans	250.00	120.00	80.00
(71) Johnny Evers	600.00	300.00	180.00
(83) Harry Gaspar	250.00	120.00	80.00
(84) Gus Getz (Boston)	250.00	120.00	80.00
(85) George Gibson	250.00	120.00	80.00
(96) Harry Hooper (Boston A.L.)	600.00	300.00	180.00
(103) Hugh Jennings	600.00	300.00	180.00
(107) Addie Joss	600.00	300.00	180.00
(114) Otto Knabe	250.00	120.00	80.00
(118) James Lafitte	250.00	120.00	80.00
(124) Bill Lelivelt	250.00	120.00	80.00
(129) Bill Ludwig (Milwaukee)	250.00	120.00	80.00
(131) Nick Maddox	250.00	120.00	80.00
(150) Dots Miller	250.00	120.00	80.00
(151) Mike Mitchell	250.00	120.00	80.00
(157) Danny Murphy	250.00	120.00	80.00
(170) Heinie Peitz	250.00	120.00	80.00
(190) Bill Schardt (Milwaukee)	250.00	120.00	80.00
(197) Cy Seymour (New York)	250.00	124.00	74.00
(201) Fred Snodgrass	250.00	120.00	80.00
(209) Bob Spade (Cincinnati)	250.00	120.00	80.00
(215) Bob Unglaub	250.00	120.00	80.00
(220) Rube Waddell (St. Louis)	600.00	300.00	180.00
(221) Honus Wagner (Pittsburg)	1,500	750.00	450.00
(231) Owen Wilson	250.00	120.00	80.00
(232) Hooks Wiltse	250.00	120.00	80.00
(234) Woods (Buffalo)	250.00	120.00	80.00

1917 Collins-McCarthy (E135)

This is one of the 200 pictures comprising
BASEBALL'S HALL of FAME
There are 199 others
Distributed by
Collins-McCarthy Candy Co.
SAN FRANCISCO : CAL.
"Just a little better"
Zee Nut and Candy Makers
Collins

CLAUDE HENDRIX
P.—Chicago Cubs
72

Produced by the Collins-McCarthy Candy Co. of San Francisco, the 200-card, black-and-white set represents the company's only venture into issuing non-Pacific Coast League players. The cards, numbered alphabetically, measure 2" x 3-1/4" and are printed on thin stock. Though the set is entitled "Baseball's Hall of Fame," many nondescript players appear in the issue. The complete set price does not include the more expensive variations. The same cards can be found with the advertising of other regional issuers on back, or blank-backed.

	NM	EX	VG
Complete Set (200):	70,000	35,000	21,000
Common Player:	150.00	75.00	45.00
1 Sam Agnew	150.00	75.00	45.00
2 Grover Alexander	600.00	300.00	180.00
3 W.S. Alexander (W.E.)	150.00	75.00	45.00
4 Leon Ames	150.00	75.00	45.00
5 Fred Anderson	150.00	75.00	45.00
6 Ed Appleton	150.00	75.00	45.00

7 Jimmy Archer	150.00	75.00	45.00
8 Jimmy Austin	150.00	75.00	45.00
9 Jim Bagby	150.00	75.00	45.00
10 H.D. Baird	150.00	75.00	45.00
11 J. Franklin Baker	350.00	175.00	100.00
12 Dave Bancroft	350.00	175.00	100.00
13 Jack Barry	150.00	75.00	45.00
14 Joe Benz	150.00	75.00	45.00
15 Al Betzel	150.00	75.00	45.00
16 Ping Bodie	150.00	75.00	45.00
17 Joe Boehling	150.00	75.00	45.00
18 Eddie Burns	150.00	75.00	45.00
19 George Burns	150.00	75.00	45.00
20 Geo. J. Burns	150.00	75.00	45.00
21 Joe Bush	150.00	75.00	45.00
22 Owen Bush	150.00	75.00	45.00
23 Bobby Byrne	150.00	75.00	45.00
24 Forrest Cady	150.00	75.00	45.00
25 Max Carey	350.00	175.00	100.00
26 Ray Chapman	175.00	85.00	50.00
27 Larry Cheney	150.00	75.00	45.00
28 Eddie Cicotte	450.00	225.00	135.00
29 Tom Clarke	150.00	75.00	45.00
30 Ty Cobb	4,500	2,250	1,350
31 Eddie Collins	350.00	175.00	100.00
32 "Shauno" Collins (Shano)	150.00	75.00	45.00
33 Fred Coumbe	150.00	75.00	45.00
34 Harry Coveleskie (Coveleski)	150.00	75.00	45.00
35 Gavvy Cravath	150.00	75.00	45.00
36 Sam Crawford	350.00	175.00	100.00
37 Geo. Cutshaw	150.00	75.00	45.00
38 Jake Daubert	150.00	75.00	45.00
39 Geo. Dauss	150.00	75.00	45.00
40 Charles Deal	150.00	75.00	45.00
41 "Wheezer" Dell	150.00	75.00	45.00
42 William Doak	150.00	75.00	45.00
43 Bill Donovan	150.00	75.00	45.00
44 Larry Doyle	150.00	75.00	45.00
45 Johnny Evers	350.00	175.00	100.00
46 Urban Faber	350.00	175.00	100.00
47 "Hap" Felsch	750.00	375.00	225.00
48 Bill Fischer	150.00	75.00	45.00
49 Ray Fisher	150.00	75.00	45.00
50 Art Fletcher	150.00	75.00	45.00
51 Eddie Foster	150.00	75.00	45.00
52 Jacques Fournier	150.00	75.00	45.00
53 Del Gainer (Gainor)	150.00	75.00	45.00
54 Bert Gallia	150.00	75.00	45.00
55 "Chic" Gandil (Chick)	450.00	225.00	135.00
56 Larry Gardner	150.00	75.00	45.00
57 Joe Gedeon	150.00	75.00	45.00
58 Gus Getz	150.00	75.00	45.00
59 Frank Gilhooley	150.00	75.00	45.00
60 Wm. Gleason	150.00	75.00	45.00
61 M.A. Gonzales (Gonzalez)	165.00	80.00	50.00
62 Hank Gowdy	150.00	75.00	45.00
63 John Graney	150.00	75.00	45.00
64 Tom Griffith	150.00	75.00	45.00
65 Heinie Groh	150.00	75.00	45.00
66 Bob Groom	150.00	75.00	45.00
67 Louis Guisto	150.00	75.00	45.00
68 Earl Hamilton	150.00	75.00	45.00
69 Harry Harper	150.00	75.00	45.00
70 Grover Hartley	150.00	75.00	45.00
71 Harry Heilmann	350.00	175.00	100.00
72 Claude Hendrix	150.00	75.00	45.00
73 Olaf Henriksen	150.00	75.00	45.00
74 John Henry	150.00	75.00	45.00
75 "Buck" Herzog	150.00	75.00	45.00
76a Hugh High (White stockings, photo actually Claude Williams.)	200.00	100.00	60.00
76b Hugh High (Black stockings, correct photo.)	175.00	85.00	50.00
77 Dick Hoblitzell	150.00	75.00	45.00
78 Walter Holke	150.00	75.00	45.00
79 Harry Hooper	350.00	175.00	100.00
80 Rogers Hornsby	650.00	325.00	195.00
81 Ivan Howard	150.00	75.00	45.00
82 Joe Jackson	16,500	8,500	5,000
83 Harold Janvrin	150.00	75.00	45.00
84 William James	150.00	75.00	45.00
85 C. Jamieson	150.00	75.00	45.00
86 Hugh Jennings	350.00	175.00	100.00
87 Walter Johnson	750.00	375.00	225.00
88 James Johnston	150.00	75.00	45.00
89 Fielder Jones	150.00	75.00	45.00
90a Joe Judge (Bat on right shoulder, photo actually Ray Morgan.)	200.00	100.00	60.00
90b Joe Judge (Bat on left shoulder, correct photo.)	175.00	85.00	50.00
91 Hans Lobert	150.00	75.00	45.00
92 Benny Kauff	150.00	75.00	45.00
93 Wm. Killefer Jr.	150.00	75.00	45.00
94 Ed. Konetchy	150.00	75.00	45.00
95 John Lavan	150.00	75.00	45.00
96 Jimmy Lavender	150.00	75.00	45.00
97 "Nemo" Leibold	150.00	75.00	45.00
98 H.B. Leonard	150.00	75.00	45.00
99 Duffy Lewis	150.00	75.00	45.00
100 Tom Long	150.00	75.00	45.00
101 Wm. Louden	150.00	75.00	45.00
102 Fred Luderus	150.00	75.00	45.00
103 Lee Magee	150.00	75.00	45.00
104 Sherwood Magee	150.00	75.00	45.00
105 Al Mamaux	150.00	75.00	45.00
106 Leslie Mann	150.00	75.00	45.00
107 "Rabbit" Maranville	350.00	175.00	100.00
108 Rube Marquard	350.00	175.00	100.00
109 Armando Marsans	165.00	80.00	50.00
110 J. Erskine Mayer	150.00	75.00	45.00
111 George McBride	150.00	75.00	45.00
112 Lew McCarty	150.00	75.00	45.00

113 John J. McGraw	350.00	175.00	100.00
114 Jack McInnis	150.00	75.00	45.00
115 Lee Meadows	150.00	75.00	45.00
116 Fred Merkle	150.00	75.00	45.00
117 "Chief" Meyers	150.00	75.00	45.00
118 Clyde Milan	150.00	75.00	45.00
119 Otto Miller	150.00	75.00	45.00
120 Clarence Mitchell	150.00	75.00	45.00
121a Ray Morgan (Bat on left shoulder, photo actually Joe Judge.)	200.00	100.00	60.00
121b Ray Morgan (Bat on right shoulder, correct photo.)	175.00	85.00	50.00
122 Guy Morton	150.00	75.00	45.00
123 "Mike" Mowrey	150.00	75.00	45.00
124 Elmer Myers	150.00	75.00	45.00
125 "Hy" Myers	150.00	75.00	45.00
126 A.E. Neale	165.00	80.00	50.00
127 Arthur Nehf	150.00	75.00	45.00
128 J.A. Niehoff	150.00	75.00	45.00
129 Steve O'Neill	150.00	75.00	45.00
130 "Dode" Paskert	150.00	75.00	45.00
131 Roger Peckinpaugh	150.00	75.00	45.00
132 "Pol" Perritt	150.00	75.00	45.00
133 "Jeff" Pfeffer	150.00	75.00	45.00
134 Walter Pipp	150.00	75.00	45.00
135 Derril Pratt (Derrill)	150.00	75.00	45.00
136 Bill Rariden	150.00	75.00	45.00
137 E.C. Rice	350.00	175.00	100.00
138 Wm. A. Ritter (Wm. H.)	150.00	75.00	45.00
139 Eppa Rixey	350.00	175.00	100.00
140 Davey Robertson	150.00	75.00	45.00
141 "Bob" Roth	150.00	75.00	45.00
142 Ed. Roush	350.00	175.00	100.00
143 Clarence Rowland	150.00	75.00	45.00
144 Dick Rudolph	150.00	75.00	45.00
145 William Rumler	150.00	75.00	45.00
146a Reb Russell (Pitching follow-thru, photo actually Mellie Wolfgang.)	200.00	100.00	60.00
146b Reb Russell (Hands at side, correct photo.)	175.00	85.00	50.00
147 "Babe" Ruth	12,500	6,250	3,750
148 Vic Saier	150.00	75.00	45.00
149 "Slim" Sallee	150.00	75.00	45.00
150 Ray Schalk	350.00	175.00	100.00
151 Walter Schang	150.00	75.00	45.00
152 Frank Schulte	150.00	75.00	45.00
153 Ferd Schupp	150.00	75.00	45.00
154 Everett Scott	150.00	75.00	45.00
155 Hank Severeid	150.00	75.00	45.00
156 Howard Shanks	150.00	75.00	45.00
157 Bob Shawkey	150.00	75.00	45.00
158 Jas. Sheckard	150.00	75.00	45.00
159 Ernie Shore	150.00	75.00	45.00
160 C.H. Shorten	150.00	75.00	45.00
161 Burt Shotton	150.00	75.00	45.00
162 Geo. Sisler	350.00	175.00	100.00
163 Elmer Smith	150.00	75.00	45.00
164 J. Carlisle Smith	150.00	75.00	45.00
165 Fred Snodgrass	150.00	75.00	45.00
166 Tris Speaker	650.00	325.00	195.00
167 Oscar Stanage	150.00	75.00	45.00
168 Charles Stengel	350.00	175.00	100.00
169 Milton Stock	150.00	75.00	45.00
170 Amos Strunk	150.00	75.00	45.00
171 "Zeb" Terry	150.00	75.00	45.00
172 "Jeff" Tesreau	150.00	75.00	45.00
173 Chester Thomas	150.00	75.00	45.00
174 Fred Toney	150.00	75.00	45.00
175 Terry Turner	150.00	75.00	45.00
176 George Tyler	150.00	75.00	45.00
177 Jim Vaughn	150.00	75.00	45.00
178 Bob Veach	150.00	75.00	45.00
179 Oscar Vitt	150.00	75.00	45.00
180 Hans Wagner	3,500	1,750	1,000
181 Clarence Walker	150.00	75.00	45.00
182 Jim Walsh	150.00	75.00	45.00
183 Al Walters	150.00	75.00	45.00
184 W. Wambsganss	150.00	75.00	45.00
185 Buck Weaver	1,000	500.00	300.00
186 Carl Weilman	150.00	75.00	45.00
187 Zack Wheat	350.00	175.00	100.00
188 Geo. Whitted	150.00	75.00	45.00
189 Joe Wilhoit	150.00	75.00	45.00
190a Claude Williams (Black stockings, photo actually Hugh High.)	600.00	300.00	180.00
190b Claude Williams (White stockings, correct photo.)	750.00	375.00	225.00
191 Fred Williams	150.00	75.00	45.00
192 Art Wilson	150.00	75.00	45.00
193 Lawton Witt	150.00	75.00	45.00
194 Joe Wood	150.00	75.00	45.00
195 William Wortman	150.00	75.00	45.00
196 Steve Yerkes	150.00	75.00	45.00
197 Earl Yingling	150.00	75.00	45.00
198 "Pep" (Ralph) Young	150.00	75.00	45.00
199 Rollie Zeider	150.00	75.00	45.00
200 Henry Zimmerman	150.00	75.00	45.00

1954 Colonial Meats Jimmy Piersall

These promotional postcards are known in at least two varieties. Each of the 3-1/2" x 5-1/2" cards shows the popular BoSox star in a portrait pose with facsimile autograph. The postcard-format back has at left a cartoon butcher and an advertising message bearing Piersall's signature. Similar cards advertising Cain's grocery products are also known.

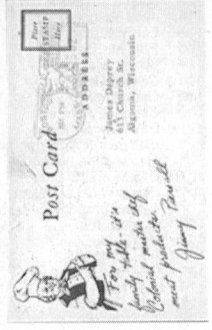

	NM	EX	VG
Autographed: 2-3X	125.00	65.00	35.00
(1) Jimmy Piersall (Chest-to-cap, back printed in black.)	80.00	40.00	24.00
(2) Jimmy Piersall (Waist-to-cap, back printed in black and blue.)	80.00	40.00	24.00

1888 Conly Cabinets

Contemporary, but much less numerous than, the Old Judge cabinet cards is this issue from a Boston photo studio. Carrying an April, 1888, copyright date, the 4-1/4" x 6-1/2" have sepia photos of the players in action poses. Backs have decorative advertising for the studio. The extent of the checklist is unknown.

	NM	EX	VG
John Clarkson (Ball in hands at chest.)	2,400	1,200	725.00
John Clarkson (Ball in hands at chest.)	2,400	1,200	725.00
John Clarkson (Right arm at back.)	2,400	1,200	725.00
John Clarkson (Right arm extended.)	2,400	1,200	725.00

1891 Conly Studio Cabinets

The extent of this issue from a Boston photo studio is unknown. The checklist begins here with three players from the Boston Reds American Associations champions. The 4-1/4" x 6-1/2" cards have a sepia portrait photo of the player in street clothes. Back has decorative advertising for the studio.

	NM	EX	VG
Common Player:	1,000	500.00	300.00
(1) Duke Farrell	1,000	500.00	300.00
(2) George Haddock	1,000	500.00	300.00
(3) Cub Stricker	1,000	500.00	300.00

1950s-70s L.L. Cook Milwaukee Braves/ Brewers Postcards

From a period of (roughly) 1956 through 1972 the L.L. Cook Co. of Milwaukee undertook the production of black-and-white photo postcards for various members of the local teams. Apparently printed to order to allow players and staff to respond to fan requests for pictures and autographs, the 3-1/2" x 5-1/2" cards have (usually) borderless poses on front. Postcard-style divided backs may or may not have a credit line vertically at center, and various versions of the standard postcard markings are seen. This checklist is likely incomplete.

	NM	EX	VG
Common Player:	30.00	15.00	9.00
(1) Hank Aaron	150.00	75.00	45.00
(2) Tommie Aaron	30.00	15.00	9.00
(3) Joe Adcock	40.00	20.00	12.00
(4) Ed Bailey	30.00	15.00	9.00
(5) Frank Bolling	30.00	15.00	9.00
(6) Bobby Bragan	30.00	15.00	9.00
(7) Ty Cline	30.00	15.00	9.00
(8) Wes Covington	30.00	15.00	9.00
(9) Ray Crone (White name on front.)	30.00	15.00	9.00
(10) Ray Crone (No name.)	30.00	15.00	9.00
(11) Fred Haney	30.00	15.00	9.00
(12) Ernie Johnson	30.00	15.00	9.00
(13) Ernie Johnson (Part of light tower shows.)	30.00	15.00	9.00
(14) Charlie Lau	30.00	15.00	9.00
(15) Mike Krsnich	30.00	15.00	9.00
(16) Roy McMillan	30.00	15.00	9.00
(17) Jerry McNertney (Brewers)	30.00	15.00	9.00
(18) Don Nottebart	30.00	15.00	9.00
(19) Phil Paine	30.00	15.00	9.00
(20) Ron Piche	30.00	15.00	9.00
(21) Juan Pizarro	30.00	15.00	9.00
(22) Bob Sadowski	30.00	15.00	9.00
(13) Red Schoendienst	50.00	25.00	15.00
(14) George Scott (Brewers)	30.00	15.00	9.00
(15) Bob Shaw	30.00	15.00	9.00
(16) Warren Spahn (Artwork portrait, white background.)	40.00	20.00	12.00
(17) Warren Spahn (Artwork portrait, yellow in background.)	40.00	20.00	12.00
(18) Warren Spahn (Eating with son.)	30.00	15.00	9.00
(19) Warren Spahn (Showing son new car.)	30.00	15.00	9.00
(20) Warren Spahn (In car, waving to family.)	30.00	15.00	9.00
(21) Al Spangler	30.00	15.00	9.00
(22) Frank Torre (Holding Pepsi.)	30.00	15.00	9.00
(23) Frank Torre (Holding Pepsi, facsimile autograph.)	30.00	15.00	9.00
(24) Frank Torre (Holding Pepsi, Brave patch shows.)	30.00	15.00	9.00
(25) Joe Torre/Kneeling	40.00	20.00	12.00
(26) Joe Torre/Portrait	40.00	20.00	12.00

1910 Coupon Cigarettes Type 1 (T213)

Though they feature the same pictures used in the contemporary T206 tobacco issue, Coupon Cigarette cards make up three distinct sets, produced between 1910 and 1919. Type 1 Coupon cards feature a mix of players from the National and American Leagues, and the Southern League. Nominally the traditional 1-7/16" x 2-1/8" cigarette-card size, fronts of the Coupons are identical to the more popular T206 series. Backs, however, clearly identify the cards as being a product of Coupon Cigarettes and allow the collector to easily differentiate among the three types. Type 1 cards, produced in 1910, carry a general advertisement for Coupon "Mild" Cigarettes, with no mention of price. Distribution of the Coupons was limited to the Louisiana area, making the set very difficult to checklist and even moreso to collect. Numerous variations further complicate the situation. It is quite possible the checklists here are incomplete and additions will surface in the future. Type 1 cards are considered the rarest of the Coupon issues, and, because they were printed on a thinner stock, they are especially difficult to find in top condition.

	NM	EX	VG
Complete Set (68):	30,000	15,000	8,500
Common Player:	300.00	140.00	85.00
(1) Harry Bay	300.00	140.00	85.00
(2) Beals Becker	300.00	140.00	85.00
(3) Chief Bender	850.00	425.00	250.00
(4) Bernhard	300.00	140.00	85.00
(5) Ted Breitenstein	300.00	140.00	85.00
(6) Bobby Byrne	300.00	140.00	85.00
(7) Billy Campbell	300.00	140.00	85.00
(8) Scoops Carey	850.00	425.00	250.00
(9) Frank Chance	850.00	425.00	250.00
(10) Chappy Charles	300.00	140.00	85.00
(11) Hal Chase/Portrait	425.00	210.00	125.00
(12) Hal Chase/Throwing	425.00	210.00	125.00
(13) Ty Cobb	7,750	3,875	2,325
(14) Bill Cranston	300.00	140.00	85.00
(15) Birdie Cree	300.00	140.00	85.00
(16) Wild Bill Donovan	300.00	140.00	85.00
(17) Mickey Doolan	300.00	140.00	85.00
(18) Jean Dubuc	300.00	140.00	85.00
(19) Joe Dunn	300.00	140.00	85.00
(20) Roy Ellam	300.00	140.00	85.00
(21) Clyde Engle	300.00	140.00	85.00
(22) Johnny Evers	850.00	425.00	250.00
(23) Art Fletcher	300.00	140.00	85.00
(24) Charlie Fritz	300.00	140.00	85.00
(25) Ed Greminger	300.00	140.00	85.00
(26) Bill Hart (Little Rock)	300.00	140.00	85.00
(27) Jimmy Hart (Montgomery)	300.00	140.00	85.00
(28) Topsy Hartsel	300.00	140.00	85.00
(29) Gordon Hickman	300.00	140.00	85.00
(30) Danny Hoffman	300.00	140.00	85.00
(31) Harry Howell	300.00	140.00	85.00
(32) Miller Huggins (Hands at mouth.)	850.00	425.00	250.00
(33) Miller Huggins/Portrait	850.00	425.00	250.00
(34) George Hunter	300.00	140.00	85.00
(35) A.O. "Dutch" Jordan	300.00	140.00	85.00
(36) Ed Killian	300.00	140.00	85.00
(37) Otto Knabe	300.00	140.00	85.00
(38) Frank LaPorte	300.00	140.00	85.00
(39) Ed Lennox	300.00	140.00	85.00
(40) Harry Lentz (Sentz)	300.00	140.00	85.00
(41) Rube Marquard	850.00	425.00	250.00
(42) Doc Marshall	300.00	140.00	85.00
(43) Christy Mathewson	2,150	1,100	650.00
(44) George McBride	300.00	140.00	85.00
(45) Pryor McElveen	300.00	140.00	85.00
(46) Matty McIntyre	300.00	140.00	85.00
(47) Mike Mitchell	300.00	140.00	85.00
(48) Carlton Molesworth	300.00	140.00	85.00
(49) Mike Mowrey	300.00	140.00	85.00
(50) Chief Myers (Meyers)/Btg	300.00	140.00	85.00
(51) Chief Myers (Meyers)/Fielding	300.00	140.00	85.00
(52) Dode Paskert	300.00	140.00	85.00
(53) Hub Perdue	300.00	140.00	85.00
(54) Arch Persons	300.00	140.00	85.00
(55) Ed Reagan	300.00	140.00	85.00
(56) Bob Rhoades (Rhoads)	300.00	140.00	85.00
(57) Ike Rockenfeld	300.00	140.00	85.00
(58) Claude Rossman	300.00	140.00	85.00
(59) Boss Schmidt	300.00	140.00	85.00
(60) Sid Smith	300.00	140.00	85.00
(61) Charlie Starr	300.00	140.00	85.00
(62) Gabby Street	300.00	140.00	85.00
(63) Ed Summers	300.00	140.00	85.00
(64) Jeff Sweeney	300.00	140.00	85.00
(65) Ira Thomas	300.00	140.00	85.00
(66) Woodie Thornton	300.00	140.00	85.00
(67) Ed Willett	300.00	140.00	85.00
(68) Owen Wilson	300.00	140.00	85.00

1914 Coupon Cigarettes Type 2 (T213)

Though they feature the same photos used in the contemporary T206 tobacco issue, Coupon Cigarette cards make up three distinct sets, produced between 1910 and 1919. Type 2 Coupons feature a mix of players from the three major leagues (National, American and Federal), and several minor leagues. The 1-7/16" x 2-5/8" Coupon fronts are virtually identical, except for the use of blue typography, to the more popular T206 series. Backs, however, clearly identify the cards as being a product of Coupon Cigarettes and allow the collector to easily differentiate among the three types. Type 2 cards, issued from

JOHNSON, Washington

MILD and SWEET
COUPON CIGARETTES
20 for 5 cents
MADE IN NEW ORLEANS
FACTORY No. 3. DIST. OF LA.

1914 to 1916, contain the words "MILD and SWEET" and "20 for 5 cents." Distribution of the Coupon cards was limited to the Louisiana area, making the set difficult to checklist and even moreso to collect. Numerous variations further complicate the situation. It is quite possible the checklists here are incomplete and additions will surface in the future. Although Type 2 cards are the most common, they were printed with a "glossy" coating, making them susceptible to cracking and creasing.

		NM	EX	VG
	Complete Set (188):	80,000	36,000	17,500
	Common Player:	275.00	125.00	60.00
(1)	Red Ames (Cincinnati)	275.00	125.00	60.00
(2)	Red Ames (St. Louis)	275.00	125.00	60.00
(3)	Home Run Baker (Phila. Amer.)	550.00	245.00	120.00
(4)	Home Run Baker (Philadelphia Amer.)	600.00	275.00	130.00
(5)	Home Run Baker (New York)	550.00	245.00	120.00
(6)	Cy Barger	275.00	125.00	60.00
(7)	Chief Bender (Trees in background, Philadelphia Amer.)	550.00	245.00	120.00
(8)	Chief Bender (Trees in background, Baltimore.)	550.00	245.00	120.00
(9)	Chief Bender (Trees in background, Philadelphia Nat.)	550.00	245.00	120.00
(10)	Chief Bender (No trees, Philadelphia Amer.)	550.00	245.00	120.00
(11)	Chief Bender (No trees, Baltimore)	550.00	245.00	120.00
(12)	Chief Bender (No trees, Philadelphia Natl.)	550.00	240.00	120.00
(13)	Bill Bradley	275.00	125.00	60.00
(14)	Roger Bresnahan (Chicago)	550.00	245.00	120.00
(15)	Roger Bresnahan (Toledo)	550.00	245.00	120.00
(16)	Al Bridwell (St. Louis)	275.00	125.00	60.00
(17)	Al Bridwell (Nashville)	275.00	125.00	60.00
(18)	Mordecai Brown (Chicago)	550.00	245.00	120.00
(19)	Mordecai Brown (St. Louis)	550.00	245.00	120.00
(20)	Bobby Byrne	275.00	125.00	60.00
(21)	Howie Camnitz (Arm at side.)	275.00	125.00	60.00
(22)	Howie Camnitz (Pittsburgh, hands above head.)	275.00	125.00	60.00
(23)	Howie Camnitz (Savannah, Hands above head.)	275.00	125.00	60.00
(24)	Billy Campbell	275.00	125.00	60.00
(25)	Frank Chance/Btg (New York)	550.00	245.00	120.00
(26)	Frank Chance/Bth (Los Angeles)	600.00	270.00	130.00
(27)	Frank Chance/Portrait (New York)	550.00	245.00	120.00
(28)	Frank Chance/Portrait (Los Angeles)	600.00	270.00	130.00
(29)	Bill Chapelle (Brooklyn, "R" on shirt/)	275.00	125.00	60.00
(30)	Larry Chapelle (Chappel) (Cleveland, no "R" on shirt, photo actually Bill Chapelle.)	275.00	125.00	60.00
(31)	Hal Chase (Chicago, holding trophy.)	365.00	165.00	80.00
(32)	Hal Chase (Buffalo, holding trophy.)	365.00	165.00	80.00
(33)	Hal Chase/Portrait (Chicago, blue background.)	365.00	165.00	80.00
(34)	Hal Chase/Portrait (Buffalo, blue background.)	365.00	165.00	80.00
(35)	Hal Chase/Throwing (Chicago)	365.00	165.00	80.00
(36)	Hal Chase/Throwing (Buffalo)	365.00	165.00	80.00
(37)	Ty Cobb/Portrait	7,250	3,250	1,600
(38)	Ty Cobb (Bat off shoulder.)	6,000	2,700	1,325
(39)	Eddie Collins (Philadelphia, "A" on shirt.)	600.00	270.00	130.00
(40)	Eddie Collins (Chicago, "A" on shirt.)	600.00	270.00	130.00
(41)	Eddie Collins (Chicago, no "A" on shirt.)	600.00	270.00	130.00
(42)	Doc Crandall (St. Louis Fed.)	275.00	125.00	60.00
(43)	Doc Crandall (St. Louis Amer.)	275.00	125.00	60.00
(44)	Sam Crawford	550.00	245.00	120.00
(45)	Birdie Cree	275.00	125.00	60.00
(46)	Harry Davis (Phila. Amer.)	275.00	125.00	60.00
(47)	Harry Davis (Philadelphia Amer.)	275.00	125.00	60.00
(48)	Ray Demmitt (Chicago Amer., New York uniform.)	275.00	125.00	60.00
(49)	Ray Demmitt (Chicago Amer., St. Louis uniform)	275.00	125.00	60.00
(50)	Josh Devore (Philadelphia)	275.00	125.00	60.00
(51)	Josh Devore (Chillicothe)	275.00	125.00	60.00
(52)	Mike Donlin (New York)	275.00	125.00	60.00
(53)	Mike Donlin (.300 batter 7 years.)	275.00	125.00	60.00
(54)	Wild Bill Donovan	275.00	125.00	60.00
(55)	Mickey Doolan/Btg (Baltimore)	275.00	125.00	60.00
(56)	Mickey Doolan/Btg (Chicago)	275.00	125.00	60.00
(57)	Mickey Doolan/Fielding (Baltimore)	275.00	125.00	60.00
(58)	Mickey Doolan/Fielding (Chicago)	275.00	125.00	60.00
(59)	Tom Downey	275.00	125.00	60.00
(60)	Larry Doyle/Btg	275.00	125.00	60.00
(61)	Larry Doyle/Portrait	275.00	125.00	60.00
(62)	Jean Dubuc	275.00	125.00	60.00
(63)	Jack Dunn (Picture is Joe Dunn.)	275.00	125.00	60.00
(64)	Kid Elberfield (Elberfeld) (Brooklyn)	275.00	125.00	60.00
(65)	Kid Elberfield (Elberfeld) (Chatanooga)	275.00	125.00	60.00
(66)	Steve Evans	275.00	125.00	60.00
(67)	Johnny Evers	550.00	245.00	120.00
(68)	Russ Ford	275.00	125.00	60.00
(69)	Art Fromme	275.00	125.00	60.00
(70)	Chick Gandil (Washington)	1,000	450.00	220.00
(71)	Chick Gandil (Cleveland)	550.00	245.00	120.00
(72)	Rube Geyer	275.00	125.00	60.00
(73)	Clark Griffith	550.00	245.00	120.00
(74)	Bob Groom	275.00	125.00	60.00
(75)	Buck Herzog ("B" on shirt.)	300.00	135.00	66.00
(76)	Buck Herzog (No "B" on shirt.)	400.00	180.00	88.00
(77)	Dick Hoblitzell (Cincinnati)	275.00	125.00	60.00
(78)	Dick Hoblitzell (Boston Nat.)	275.00	125.00	60.00
(79)	Dick Hoblitzell (Boston Amer.)	275.00	125.00	60.00
(80)	Solly Hofman	275.00	125.00	60.00
(81)	Solly Hofmann (Hofman)	275.00	125.00	60.00
(82)	Miller Huggins (Hands at mouth.)	550.00	245.00	120.00
(83)	Miller Huggins/Portrait	550.00	245.00	120.00
(84)	John Hummel (Brooklyn Nat.)	275.00	125.00	60.00
(85)	John Hummel (Brooklyn)	275.00	125.00	60.00
(86)	Hughie Jennings (Both hands showing.)	550.00	245.00	120.00
(87)	Hughie Jennings (One hand showing.)	550.00	245.00	120.00
(88)	Walter Johnson	2,500	1,125	550.00
(89)	Tim Jordan (Toronto)	275.00	125.00	60.00
(90)	Tim Jordan (Ft. Worth)	275.00	125.00	60.00
(91)	Joe Kelley (New York)	550.00	245.00	120.00
(92)	Joe Kelley (Toronto)	550.00	245.00	120.00
(93)	Otto Knabe	275.00	125.00	60.00
(94)	Ed Konetchy (Pittsburgh Nat.)	275.00	125.00	60.00
(95)	Ed Konetchy (Pittsburgh Fed.)	275.00	125.00	60.00
(96)	Ed Konetchy (Boston)	275.00	125.00	60.00
(97)	Harry Krause	275.00	125.00	60.00
(98)	Nap Lajoie (Phila. Amer.)	550.00	245.00	120.00
(99)	Nap Lajoie (Philadelphia Amer.)	550.00	245.00	120.00
(100)	Nap Lajoie (Cleveland)	550.00	245.00	120.00
(101)	Tommy Leach (Chicago)	275.00	125.00	60.00
(102)	Tommy Leach (Cincinnati)	275.00	125.00	60.00
(103)	Tommy Leach (Rochester)	275.00	125.00	60.00
(104)	Ed Lennox	275.00	125.00	60.00
(105)	Sherry Magee (Phila. Nat.)	275.00	125.00	60.00
(106)	Sherry Magee (Philadelphia Nat.)	275.00	125.00	60.00
(107)	Sherry Magee (Boston)	275.00	125.00	60.00
(108)	Rube Marquard (New York, pitching, "NY" on shirt.)	600.00	270.00	130.00
(109)	Rube Marquard (Brooklyn, pitching, no "NY" on shirt.)	550.00	245.00	120.00
(110)	Rube Marquard (New York, portrait, "NY" on shirt.)	550.00	245.00	120.00
(111)	Rube Marquard (Brooklyn, portrait, no "NY" on shirt.)	550.00	245.00	120.00
(112)	Christy Mathewson	3,000	1,350	660.00
(113)	John McGraw (Glove at side.)	550.00	245.00	120.00
(114)	John McGraw/Portrait	550.00	245.00	120.00
(115)	Larry McLean	275.00	125.00	60.00
(116)	George McQuillan (Pittsburgh)	275.00	125.00	60.00
(117)	George McQuillan (Phila. Nat.)	275.00	125.00	60.00
(118)	George McQuillan (Philadelphia Nat.)	275.00	125.00	60.00
(119)	Fred Merkle	275.00	125.00	60.00
(120)	Chief Meyers/Fielding (New York)	275.00	125.00	60.00
(121)	Chief Meyers/Fielding (Brooklyn)	275.00	125.00	60.00
(122)	Chief Meyers/Portrait (New York)	275.00	125.00	60.00
(123)	Chief Meyers/Portrait (Brooklyn)	275.00	125.00	60.00
(124)	Dots Miller	275.00	125.00	60.00
(125)	Mike Mitchell	275.00	125.00	60.00
(126)	Mike Mowrey (Pittsburgh Nat.)	275.00	125.00	60.00
(127)	Mike Mowrey (Pittsburgh Fed.)	275.00	125.00	60.00
(128)	Mike Mowrey (Brooklyn)	275.00	125.00	60.00
(129)	George Mullin (Indianapolis)	275.00	125.00	60.00
(130)	George Mullin (Newark)	275.00	125.00	60.00
(131)	Danny Murphy	275.00	125.00	60.00
(132)	Red Murray (New York)	275.00	125.00	60.00
(133)	Red Murray (Chicago)	275.00	125.00	60.00
(134)	Red Murray (Kansas City)	275.00	125.00	60.00
(135)	Tom Needham	275.00	125.00	60.00
(136)	Rebel Oakes	275.00	125.00	60.00
(137)	Rube Oldring (Phila. Amer.)	275.00	125.00	60.00
(138)	Rube Oldring (Philadelphia Amer.)	275.00	125.00	60.00
(139)	Dode Paskert (Phila. Nat.)	275.00	125.00	60.00
(140)	Dode Paskert (Philadelphia Nat.)	275.00	125.00	60.00
(141)	Billy Purtell	275.00	125.00	60.00
(142)	Jack Quinn (Baltimore)	275.00	125.00	60.00
(143)	Jack Quinn (Vernon)	275.00	125.00	60.00
(144)	Ed Reulbach (Brooklyn Nat.)	275.00	125.00	60.00
(145)	Ed Reulbach (Brooklyn Fed.)	275.00	125.00	60.00
(146)	Ed Reulbach (Pittsburgh)	275.00	125.00	60.00
(147)	Nap Rucker (Brooklyn)	275.00	125.00	60.00
(148)	Nap Rucker (Brooklyn Nat.)	275.00	125.00	60.00
(149)	Dick Rudolph	275.00	125.00	60.00
(150)	Germany Schaefer (Washington, "W" on shirt.)	275.00	125.00	60.00
(151)	Germany Schaefer (K.C. Fed., "W" on shirt.)	275.00	125.00	60.00
(152)	Germany Schaefer (New York, no "W" on shirt.)	275.00	125.00	60.00
(153)	Admiral Schlei/Btg	275.00	125.00	60.00
(154)	Admiral Schlei/Portrait	275.00	125.00	60.00
(155)	Boss Schmidt	275.00	125.00	60.00
(156)	Wildfire Schulte	275.00	125.00	60.00
(157)	Frank Smith	275.00	125.00	60.00
(158)	Tris Speaker	1,200	540.00	265.00
(159)	George Stovall	275.00	125.00	60.00
(160)	Gabby Street/Catching	275.00	125.00	60.00
(161)	Gabby Street/Portrait	275.00	125.00	60.00
(162)	Ed Summers	275.00	125.00	60.00
(163)	Bill Sweeney (Boston)	275.00	125.00	60.00
(164)	Bill Sweeney (Chicago)	275.00	125.00	60.00
(165)	Jeff Sweeney (New York)	275.00	125.00	60.00
(166)	Jeff Sweeney (Richmond)	275.00	125.00	60.00
(167)	Ira Thomas (Phila. Amer.)	275.00	125.00	60.00
(168)	Ira Thomas (Philadelphia Amer.)	275.00	125.00	60.00
(169)	Joe Tinker (Chicago Fed., bat off shoulder.)	550.00	245.00	120.00
(170)	Joe Tinker (Chicago Nat., bat off shoulder.)	550.00	245.00	120.00
(171)	Joe Tinker (Chicago Fed., bat off shoulder.)	550.00	245.00	120.00
(172)	Joe Tinker (Chicago Nat., bat off shoulder.)	550.00	245.00	120.00
(173)	Heinie Wagner	275.00	125.00	60.00
(174)	Jack Warhop (New York, "NY" on shirt.)	275.00	125.00	60.00
(175)	Jack Warhop (St. Louis, no "NY" on shirt.)	275.00	125.00	60.00
(176)	Zach Wheat (Brooklyn)	550.00	245.00	120.00
(177)	Zach Wheat (Brooklyn Nat.)	550.00	245.00	120.00
(178)	Kaiser Wilhelm	275.00	125.00	60.00
(179)	Ed Willett (St. Louis)	275.00	125.00	60.00
(180)	Ed Willett (Memphis)	275.00	125.00	60.00
(181)	Owen Wilson	275.00	125.00	60.00
(182)	Hooks Wiltse/Pitching (New York)	275.00	125.00	60.00
(183)	Hooks Wiltse/Pitching (Brooklyn)	275.00	125.00	60.00
(184)	Hooks Wiltse/Pitching (Jersey City)	275.00	125.00	60.00
(185)	Hooks Wiltse/Portrait (New York)	275.00	125.00	60.00
(186)	Hooks Wiltse/Portrait (Brooklyn)	275.00	125.00	60.00
(187)	Hooks Wiltse/Portrait (Jersey City)	275.00	125.00	60.00
(188)	Heinie Zimmerman	275.00	125.00	60.00

1919 Coupon Cigarettes Type 3 (T213)

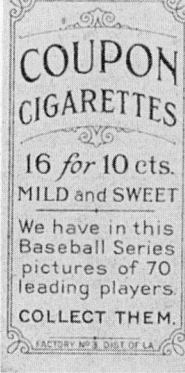

COBB, Detroit

COUPON CIGARETTES
16 for 10 cts.
MILD and SWEET
We have in this Baseball Series pictures of 70 leading players.
COLLECT THEM.
FACTORY No. 3. DIST. OF LA.

Though using the same photos seen in the contemporary T206 tobacco issue, Coupon Cigarette cards comprise three distinct sets produced between 1910 and 1919. Coupon cards feature a mix of players from the National and American Leagues, and several minor leagues. Slightly smaller than the usual cigarette-card format, Type 3 Coupons nominally measure 1-3/8" x 2-9/16", but are more prone to original size deviations than Type 1 or Type 2 Coupons. Except for the blue ink used in the player identification line, the fronts of the Coupon cards are virtually identical to the more popular T206 issue. Backs, however, clearly identify the cards as being a product of Coupon Cigarettes and allow the collector to easily differentiate among the three types. Type 3 cards, issued in 1919, advertise "16 for 10 cts." and mention "70 leading players." Distribution of the Coupon cards was limited to the Louisiana area, making the set difficult to checklist and even more difficult to collect. Numerous variations further complicate the situation. It is quite possible the checklists here are incomplete and additions will surface in the future. While most Type 3 Coupons mention on their backs, "FACTORY No. 3, DIST OF LA," some have been seen with that designation blacked out and an overprint applied citing "FACTORY No. 8, DIST OF LA."

		NM	EX	VG
Complete Set (70):		30,000	13,500	6,750
Common Player:		300.00	135.00	65.00
(1)	Red Ames	300.00	135.00	65.00
(2)	Home Run Baker	600.00	275.00	130.00
(3)	Chief Bender	600.00	275.00	130.00
	(No trees in background.)			
(4)	Chief Bender	600.00	275.00	130.00
	(Trees in background.)			
(5)	Roger Bresnahan	600.00	275.00	130.00
(6)	Al Bridwell	300.00	135.00	65.00
(7)	Miner Brown	600.00	275.00	130.00
(8)	Bobby Byrne	300.00	135.00	65.00
(9)	Frank Chance/Btg	600.00	275.00	130.00
(10)	Frank Chance/Portrait	600.00	275.00	130.00
(11)	Hal Chase (Holding trophy.)	450.00	200.00	100.00
(12)	Hal Chase/Portrait	450.00	200.00	100.00
(13)	Hal Chase/Throwing	450.00	200.00	100.00
(14)	Ty Cobb/Btg	3,750	1,675	825.00
(15)	Ty Cobb/Portrait	3,750	1,675	825.00
(16)	Eddie Collins	600.00	275.00	130.00
(17)	Sam Crawford	600.00	275.00	130.00
(18)	Harry Davis	300.00	135.00	65.00
(19)	Mike Donlin	300.00	135.00	65.00
(20)	Wild Bill Donovan	300.00	135.00	65.00
(21)	Mickey Doolan/Btg	300.00	135.00	65.00
(22)	Mickey Doolan/Fielding	300.00	135.00	65.00
(23)	Larry Doyle/Btg	300.00	135.00	65.00
(24)	Larry Doyle/Portrait	300.00	135.00	65.00
(25)	Jean Dubuc	300.00	135.00	65.00
(26)	Jack Dunn	300.00	135.00	65.00
(27)	Kid Elberfeld	300.00	135.00	65.00
(28)	Johnny Evers	600.00	275.00	130.00
(29)	Chick Gandil	550.00	250.00	125.00
(30)	Clark Griffith	600.00	275.00	130.00
(31)	Buck Herzog	300.00	135.00	65.00
(32)	Dick Hoblitzell	300.00	135.00	65.00
(33)	Miller Huggins	600.00	275.00	130.00
	(Hands at mouth.)			
(34)	Miller Huggins/Portrait	600.00	275.00	130.00
(35)	John Hummel	300.00	135.00	65.00
(36)	Hughie Jennings	600.00	275.00	130.00
	(Both hands showing.)			
(37)	Hughie Jennings	600.00	275.00	130.00
	(One hand showing.)			
(38)	Walter Johnson	900.00	400.00	200.00
(39)	Tim Jordan	300.00	135.00	65.00
(40)	Joe Kelley	600.00	275.00	130.00
(41)	Ed Konetchy	300.00	135.00	65.00
(42)	Larry Lajoie	600.00	275.00	130.00
(43)	Sherry Magee	300.00	135.00	65.00
(44)	Rube Marquard	600.00	275.00	130.00
(45)	Christy Mathewson	1,200	540.00	265.00
(47)	John McGraw (Glove at side.)	600.00	275.00	130.00
(48)	John McGraw/Portrait	600.00	275.00	130.00
(49)	George McQuillan	300.00	135.00	65.00
(50)	Fred Merkle	300.00	135.00	65.00
(51)	Dots Miller	300.00	135.00	65.00
(52)	Mike Mowrey	300.00	135.00	65.00
(53)	Chief Myers (Meyers)	300.00	135.00	65.00
	(Brooklyn)			
(54)	Chief Myers (Meyers)	300.00	135.00	65.00
	(New Haven)			
(55)	Dode Paskert	300.00	135.00	65.00
(56)	Jack Quinn	300.00	135.00	65.00
(57)	Ed Reulbach	300.00	135.00	65.00
(58)	Nap Rucker	300.00	135.00	65.00
(59)	Dick Rudolph	300.00	135.00	65.00
(60)	Herman Schaeffer (Schaefer)	300.00	135.00	65.00
(61)	Wildfire Schulte	300.00	135.00	65.00
(62)	Tris Speaker	750.00	335.00	165.00
(63)	Gabby Street/Catching	300.00	135.00	65.00
(64)	Gabby Street/Portrait	300.00	135.00	65.00
(65)	Jeff Sweeney	300.00	135.00	65.00
(66)	Ira Thomas	300.00	135.00	65.00
(67)	Joe Tinker	600.00	275.00	130.00
(68)	Zach Wheat	600.00	275.00	130.00
(69)	Geo. Wiltse	300.00	135.00	65.00
(70)	Heinie Zimmerman	300.00	135.00	65.00

1919 Coupon Cigarettes Type 3, Factory 8 Overprint

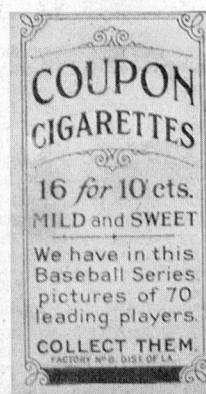

Of interest to specialty collectors is a variation of Type 3 Coupon cards on which the normal "FACTORY No. 3 . . ." line at bottom back has been blacked out and a "FACTORY No. 8 . . ." designation overprinted. The extent of the overprint checklist is unknown and at least one card (Cobb, bat off shoulder) is found as a Factory 8, but not yet verified to exist as a Factory 3 version.

	NM	EX	VG
Common Player:	600.00	300.00	180.00
Hall of Famers: 4-6X			
Chief Bender (No trees.)			
Ty Cobb (Bat off shoulder.)			
Eddie Collins			
Hughie Jennings			
(Both hands showing.)			
Rube Marquard			
John McGraw/Portrait			

1914 Cracker Jack (E145)

The 1914 Cracker Jack set, whose ACC designation is E145-1, is one of the most popular of the "E" card sets and features baseball stars from the American, National and Federal leagues. The 2-1/4" x 3" cards, are printed on thin stock and were inserted in boxes of Cracker Jack. The 1914 issue consists of 144 cards with tinted color photographs on a red background. Numbered backs feature a short biography plus an advertisement. The advertising on the low-numbered cards in the set indicates that 10 million cards were issued, while the high-numbered cards boast that 15 million were printed.

		NM	EX	VG
Complete Set (144):		375,000	115,000	45,000
Common Player:		850.00	260.00	100.00
1	Otto Knabe	2,000	325.00	125.00
2	Home Run Baker	2,350	775.00	350.00
3	Joe Tinker	2,350	775.00	350.00
4	Larry Doyle	850.00	260.00	100.00
5	Ward Miller	850.00	260.00	100.00
6	Eddie Plank	2,500	825.00	375.00
7	Eddie Collins	2,300	760.00	345.00
8	Rube Oldring	850.00	260.00	100.00
9	Artie Hoffman (Hofman)	850.00	260.00	100.00
10	Stuffy McInnis	850.00	260.00	100.00
11	George Stovall	850.00	260.00	100.00
12	Connie Mack	3,600	1,200	540.00
13	Art Wilson	850.00	260.00	100.00
14	Sam Crawford	2,300	760.00	345.00
15	Reb Russell	850.00	260.00	100.00
16	Howie Camnitz	850.00	260.00	100.00
17a	Roger Bresnahan	27,500	9,100	4,125
	(No number on back.)			
17b	Roger Bresnahan	2,300	760.00	345.00
	(Number on back.)			
18	Johnny Evers	2,300	760.00	345.00
19	Chief Bender	2,300	760.00	345.00
20	Cy Falkenberg	850.00	260.00	100.00
21	Heinie Zimmerman	850.00	260.00	100.00
22	Smokey Joe Wood	1,500	495.00	225.00
23	Charles Comiskey	2,300	760.00	345.00
24	George Mullen (Mullin)	850.00	260.00	100.00
25	Mike Simon	850.00	260.00	100.00
26	Jim Scott	850.00	260.00	100.00
27	Bill Carrigan	850.00	260.00	100.00
28	Jack Barry	850.00	260.00	100.00
29	Vean Gregg	850.00	260.00	100.00
30	Ty Cobb	30,000	10,000	4,500
31	Heinie Wagner	850.00	260.00	100.00
32	Mordecai Brown	2,300	760.00	345.00
33	Amos Strunk	850.00	260.00	100.00
34	Ira Thomas	850.00	260.00	100.00
35	Harry Hooper	2,300	760.00	345.00
36	Ed Walsh	2,300	760.00	345.00
37	Grover C. Alexander	9,000	2,975	1,350
38	Red Dooin	850.00	260.00	100.00
39	Chick Gandil	1,625	535.00	245.00
40	Jimmy Austin	850.00	260.00	100.00
41	Tommy Leach	850.00	260.00	100.00
42	Al Bridwell	850.00	260.00	100.00
43	Rube Marquard	3,900	1,300	585.00
44	Jeff Tesreau	850.00	260.00	100.00
45	Fred Luderus	850.00	260.00	100.00
46	Bob Groom	850.00	260.00	100.00
47	Josh Devore	850.00	260.00	100.00
48	Harry Lord	850.00	260.00	100.00
49	Dots Miller	850.00	260.00	100.00
50	John Hummell (Hummel)	850.00	260.00	100.00
51	Nap Rucker	850.00	260.00	100.00
52	Zach Wheat	2,300	760.00	345.00
53	Otto Miller	850.00	260.00	100.00
54	Marty O'Toole	850.00	260.00	100.00
55	Dick Hoblitzel (Hoblitzell)	850.00	260.00	100.00
56	Clyde Milan	850.00	260.00	100.00

		NM	EX	VG
57	Walter Johnson	8,500	2,800	1,275
58	Wally Schang	850.00	260.00	100.00
59	Doc Gessler	850.00	260.00	100.00
60	Rollie Zeider	850.00	260.00	100.00
61	Ray Schalk	2,300	760.00	345.00
62	Jay Cashion	850.00	260.00	100.00
63	Babe Adams	850.00	260.00	100.00
64	Jimmy Archer	850.00	260.00	100.00
65	Tris Speaker	7,200	2,400	1,080
66	Nap Lajoie	7,200	2,400	1,080
67	Doc Crandall	850.00	260.00	100.00
68	Honus Wagner	13,500	4,450	2,000
69	John McGraw	2,300	760.00	345.00
70	Fred Clarke	2,300	760.00	345.00
71	Chief Meyers	850.00	260.00	100.00
72	Joe Boehling	850.00	260.00	100.00
73	Max Carey	2,300	760.00	345.00
74	Frank Owens	850.00	260.00	100.00
75	Miller Huggins	2,300	760.00	345.00
76	Claude Hendrix	850.00	260.00	100.00
77	Hughie Jennings	2,300	760.00	345.00
78	Fred Merkle	850.00	260.00	100.00
79	Ping Bodie	850.00	260.00	100.00
80	Ed Reulbach	850.00	260.00	100.00
81	Jim Delehanty (Delahanty)	850.00	260.00	100.00
82	Gavvy Cravath	850.00	260.00	100.00
83	Russ Ford	850.00	260.00	100.00
84	Elmer Knetzer	850.00	260.00	100.00
85	Buck Herzog	850.00	260.00	100.00
86	Burt Shotten	850.00	260.00	100.00
87	Hick Cady	850.00	260.00	100.00
88	Christy Mathewson	120,000	40,000	18,000
89	Larry Cheney	850.00	260.00	100.00
90	Frank Smith	850.00	260.00	100.00
91	Roger Peckinpaugh	900.00	295.00	135.00
92	Al Demaree	850.00	260.00	100.00
93	Del Pratt	850.00	260.00	100.00
94	Eddie Cicotte	2,200	725.00	330.00
95	Ray Keating	850.00	260.00	100.00
96	Beals Becker	850.00	260.00	100.00
97	Rube Benton	850.00	260.00	100.00
98	Frank Laporte (LaPorte)	850.00	260.00	100.00
99	Frank Chance	9,000	3,000	1,350
100	Tom Seaton	850.00	260.00	100.00
101	Wildfire Schulte	850.00	260.00	100.00
102	Ray Fisher	850.00	260.00	100.00
103	Joe Jackson	45,000	15,000	7,500
104	Vic Saier	850.00	260.00	100.00
105	Jimmy Lavender	850.00	260.00	100.00
106	Joe Birmingham	850.00	260.00	100.00
107	Tom Downey	850.00	260.00	100.00
108	Sherry Magee	850.00	260.00	100.00
109	Fred Blanding	850.00	260.00	100.00
110	Bob Bescher	850.00	260.00	100.00
111	Nixey Callahan	850.00	260.00	100.00
112	Jeff Sweeney	850.00	260.00	100.00
113	George Suggs	850.00	260.00	100.00
114	George Moriarity (Moriarty)	850.00	260.00	100.00
115	Ad Brennan	850.00	260.00	100.00
116	Rollie Zeider	850.00	260.00	100.00
117	Ted Easterly	850.00	260.00	100.00
118	Ed Konetchy	850.00	260.00	100.00
119	George Perring	850.00	260.00	100.00
120	Mickey Doolan	850.00	260.00	100.00
121	Hub Perdue	850.00	260.00	100.00
122	Donie Bush	850.00	260.00	100.00
123	Slim Sallee	850.00	260.00	100.00
124	Earle Moore (Earl)	850.00	260.00	100.00
125	Bert Niehoff	850.00	260.00	100.00
126	Walter Blair	850.00	260.00	100.00
127	Butch Schmidt	850.00	260.00	100.00
128	Steve Evans	850.00	260.00	100.00
129	Ray Caldwell	850.00	260.00	100.00
130	Ivy Wingo	850.00	260.00	100.00
131	George Baumgardner	850.00	260.00	100.00
132	Les Nunamaker	850.00	260.00	100.00
133	Branch Rickey	2,300	760.00	345.00
134	Armando Marsans	900.00	295.00	135.00
135	Bill Killifer (Killefer)	850.00	260.00	100.00
136	Rabbit Maranville	2,750	900.00	410.00
137	Bill Rariden	850.00	260.00	100.00
138	Hank Gowdy	850.00	260.00	100.00
139	Rebel Oakes	850.00	260.00	100.00
140	Danny Murphy	850.00	260.00	100.00
141	Cy Barger	850.00	260.00	100.00
142	Gene Packard	850.00	260.00	100.00
143	Jake Daubert	850.00	260.00	100.00
144	Jimmy Walsh	2,000	350.00	110.00

1915 Cracker Jack (E145)

The 1915 Cracker Jack set (E145-2) is a reissue of the 1914 edition with some card additions and deletions, team designation changes, and new poses. A total of 176 cards comprise the set. Cards can be distinguished as either 1914 or 1915 by the advertising on the backs. The 1914 cards call the set complete at 144 pictures; the 1915 version notes 176 pictures.

Backs of 1915 Cracker Jack cards are printed upside-down in relation to the front. A complete set and an album were available from the company.

		NM	EX	VG
	Complete Set (176):	130,000	50,000	25,000
	Common Player (1-144):	300.00	110.00	65.00
	Common Player (145-176):	325.00	130.00	65.00
	Album:	750.00	375.00	225.00
1	Otto Knabe	1,400	475.00	125.00
2	Home Run Baker	1,100	450.00	225.00
3	Joe Tinker	1,100	450.00	225.00
4	Larry Doyle	300.00	110.00	65.00
5	Ward Miller	300.00	110.00	65.00
6	Eddie Plank	1,350	550.00	275.00
7	Eddie Collins	1,200	480.00	240.00
8	Rube Oldring	300.00	110.00	65.00
9	Artie Hoffman (Hofman)	300.00	110.00	65.00
10	Stuffy McInnis	300.00	110.00	65.00
11	George Stovall	300.00	110.00	65.00
12	Connie Mack	1,100	450.00	225.00
13	Art Wilson	300.00	110.00	65.00
14	Sam Crawford	1,100	450.00	225.00
15	Reb Russell	300.00	110.00	65.00
16	Howie Camnitz	300.00	110.00	65.00
17	Roger Bresnahan	1,100	450.00	225.00
18	Johnny Evers	1,100	450.00	225.00
19	Chief Bender	1,100	450.00	225.00
20	Cy Falkenberg	300.00	110.00	65.00
21	Heinie Zimmerman	300.00	110.00	65.00
22	Smokey Joe Wood	800.00	325.00	160.00
23	Charles Comiskey	1,100	450.00	225.00
24	George Mullen (Mullin)	300.00	110.00	65.00
25	Mike Simon	300.00	110.00	65.00
26	Jim Scott	300.00	110.00	65.00
27	Bill Carrigan	300.00	110.00	65.00
28	Jack Barry	300.00	110.00	65.00
29	Vean Gregg	300.00	110.00	65.00
30	Ty Cobb	11,500	4,600	2,300
31	Heinie Wagner	300.00	110.00	65.00
32	Mordecai Brown	1,250	500.00	250.00
33	Amos Strunk	300.00	110.00	65.00
34	Ira Thomas	300.00	110.00	65.00
35	Harry Hooper	1,100	450.00	225.00
36	Ed Walsh	1,100	450.00	225.00
37	Grover C. Alexander	3,250	1,300	650.00
38	Red Dooin	300.00	110.00	65.00
39	Chick Gandil	800.00	325.00	160.00
40	Jimmy Austin	300.00	110.00	65.00
41	Tommy Leach	300.00	110.00	65.00
42	Al Bridwell	300.00	110.00	65.00
43	Rube Marquard	1,100	450.00	225.00
44	Jeff Tesreau	300.00	110.00	65.00
45	Fred Luderus	300.00	110.00	65.00
46	Bob Groom	300.00	110.00	65.00
47	Josh Devore	300.00	110.00	65.00
48	Steve O'Neill	300.00	110.00	65.00
49	Dots Miller	300.00	110.00	65.00
50	John Hummell (Hummel)	300.00	110.00	65.00
51	Nap Rucker	300.00	110.00	65.00
52	Zach Wheat	1,100	450.00	225.00
53	Otto Miller	300.00	110.00	65.00
54	Marty O'Toole	300.00	110.00	65.00
55	Dick Hoblitzel (Hoblitzell)	300.00	110.00	65.00
56	Clyde Milan	300.00	110.00	65.00
57	Walter Johnson	5,000	2,000	1,000
58	Wally Schang	300.00	110.00	65.00
59	Doc Gessler	300.00	110.00	65.00
60	Oscar Dugey	300.00	110.00	65.00
61	Ray Schalk	1,100	450.00	225.00
62	Willie Mitchell	300.00	110.00	65.00
63	Babe Adams	300.00	110.00	65.00
64	Jimmy Archer	300.00	110.00	65.00
65	Tris Speaker	1,700	680.00	340.00
66	Nap Lajoie	1,550	625.00	310.00
67	Doc Crandall	300.00	110.00	65.00
68	Honus Wagner	9,000	3,600	1,800
69	John McGraw	1,100	450.00	225.00
70	Fred Clarke	1,100	450.00	225.00
71	Chief Meyers	300.00	110.00	65.00
72	Joe Boehling	300.00	110.00	65.00
73	Max Carey	1,100	450.00	225.00
74	Frank Owens	300.00	110.00	65.00
75	Miller Huggins	1,100	450.00	225.00
76	Claude Hendrix	300.00	110.00	65.00
77	Hughie Jennings	1,100	450.00	225.00
78	Fred Merkle	300.00	110.00	65.00
79	Ping Bodie	300.00	110.00	65.00
80	Ed Reulbach	300.00	110.00	65.00
81	Jim Delahanty (Delahanty)	300.00	110.00	65.00
82	Gavvy Cravath	300.00	110.00	65.00
83	Russ Ford	300.00	110.00	65.00
84	Elmer Knetzer	300.00	110.00	65.00
85	Buck Herzog	300.00	110.00	65.00
86	Burt Shotten	300.00	110.00	65.00
87	Hick Cady	300.00	110.00	65.00
88	Christy Mathewson	6,000	2,400	1,200
89	Larry Cheney	300.00	110.00	65.00
90	Frank Smith	300.00	110.00	65.00
91	Roger Peckinpaugh	350.00	140.00	70.00
92	Al Demaree	300.00	110.00	65.00
93	Del Pratt	300.00	110.00	65.00
94	Eddie Cicotte	1,000	400.00	200.00
95	Ray Keating	300.00	110.00	65.00
96	Beals Becker	300.00	110.00	65.00
97	Rube Benton	300.00	110.00	65.00
98	Frank Laporte (LaPorte)	300.00	110.00	65.00
99	Hal Chase	600.00	240.00	120.00
100	Tom Seaton	300.00	110.00	65.00
101	Wildfire Schulte	300.00	110.00	65.00
102	Ray Fisher	300.00	110.00	65.00
103	Joe Jackson	17,500	7,000	3,500
104	Vic Saier	300.00	110.00	65.00
105	Jimmy Lavender	300.00	110.00	65.00
106	Joe Birmingham	300.00	110.00	65.00
107	Tom Downey	300.00	110.00	65.00
108	Sherry Magee	300.00	110.00	65.00

109	Fred Blanding	300.00	110.00	65.00
110	Bob Bescher	300.00	110.00	65.00
111	Herbie Moran	300.00	110.00	65.00
112	Ed Sweeney	300.00	110.00	65.00
113	George Suggs	300.00	110.00	65.00
114	George Moriarity (Moriarty)	300.00	110.00	65.00
115	Ad Brennan	300.00	110.00	65.00
116	Rollie Zeider	300.00	110.00	65.00
117	Ted Easterly	300.00	110.00	65.00
118	Ed Konetchy	300.00	110.00	65.00
119	George Perring	300.00	110.00	65.00
120	Mickey Doolan	300.00	110.00	65.00
121	Hub Perdue	300.00	110.00	65.00
122	Donie Bush	300.00	110.00	65.00
123	Slim Sallee	300.00	110.00	65.00
124	Earle Moore (Earl)	300.00	110.00	65.00
125	Bert Niehoff	300.00	110.00	65.00
126	Walter Blair	300.00	110.00	65.00
127	Butch Schmidt	300.00	110.00	65.00
128	Steve Evans	300.00	110.00	65.00
129	Ray Caldwell	300.00	110.00	65.00
130	Ivy Wingo	300.00	110.00	65.00
131	George Baumgardner	300.00	110.00	65.00
132	Les Nunamaker	300.00	110.00	65.00
133	Branch Rickey	1,100	450.00	225.00
134	Armando Marsans	425.00	175.00	85.00
135	Bill Killifer (Killefer)	300.00	110.00	65.00
136	Rabbit Maranville	1,100	450.00	225.00
137	Bill Rariden	300.00	110.00	65.00
138	Hank Gowdy	300.00	110.00	65.00
139	Rebel Oakes	300.00	110.00	65.00
140	Danny Murphy	300.00	110.00	65.00
141	Cy Barger	300.00	110.00	65.00
142	Gene Packard	300.00	110.00	65.00
143	Jake Daubert	300.00	110.00	65.00
144	Jimmy Walsh	300.00	110.00	65.00
145	Ted Cather	325.00	130.00	65.00
146	Lefty Tyler	325.00	130.00	65.00
147	Lee Magee	325.00	130.00	65.00
148	Owen Wilson	325.00	130.00	65.00
149	Hal Janvrin	325.00	130.00	65.00
150	Doc Johnston	325.00	130.00	65.00
151	Possum Whitted	325.00	130.00	65.00
152	George McQuillen (McQuillan)	325.00	130.00	65.00
153	Bill James	325.00	130.00	65.00
154	Dick Rudolph	325.00	130.00	65.00
155	Joe Connolly	325.00	130.00	65.00
156	Jean Dubuc	325.00	130.00	65.00
157	George Kaiserling	325.00	130.00	65.00
158	Fritz Maisel	325.00	130.00	65.00
159	Heinie Groh	325.00	130.00	65.00
160	Benny Kauff	325.00	130.00	65.00
161	Edd Rousch (Roush)	1,250	500.00	250.00
162	George Stallings	325.00	130.00	65.00
163	Bert Whaling	325.00	130.00	65.00
164	Bob Shawkey	325.00	130.00	65.00
165	Eddie Murphy	325.00	130.00	65.00
166	Bullet Joe Bush	325.00	130.00	65.00
167	Clark Griffith	1,250	500.00	250.00
168	Vin Campbell	325.00	130.00	65.00
169	Ray Collins	325.00	130.00	65.00
170	Hans Lobert	325.00	130.00	65.00
171	Earl Hamilton	325.00	130.00	65.00
172	Erskine Mayer	450.00	180.00	90.00
173	Tilly Walker	325.00	130.00	65.00
174	Bobby Veach	325.00	130.00	65.00
175	Joe Benz	325.00	130.00	65.00
176	Hippo Vaughn	1,300	200.00	75.00

1930 Cracker Jack Pins (PR4)

Although no manufacturer is indicated on the pins themselves, this 25-player set was issued by Cracker Jack circa 1930. Each pin measures 13/16" in diameter and features a line drawing of a player portrait. The unnumbered pins are printed in blue and gray with backgrounds found in either yellow or gray.

		NM	EX	VG
	Complete Set (25):	1,600	800.00	475.00
	Common Player:	35.00	17.50	10.00
(1)	Charles Berry	35.00	17.50	10.00
(2)	Bill Cissell	35.00	17.50	10.00
(3)	KiKi Cuyler	60.00	30.00	18.00
(4)	Dizzy Dean	100.00	50.00	30.00
(5)	Wesley Ferrell	35.00	17.50	10.00
(6)	Frank Frisch	60.00	30.00	18.00
(7)	Lou Gehrig	250.00	125.00	75.00
(8)	Vernon Gomez	60.00	30.00	18.00
(9)	Goose Goslin	60.00	30.00	18.00
(10)	George Grantham	35.00	17.50	10.00
(11)	Charley Grimm	35.00	17.50	10.00
(12)	Lefty Grove	75.00	37.00	22.00
(13)	Gabby Hartnett	60.00	30.00	18.00
(14)	Travis Jackson	60.00	30.00	18.00
(15)	Tony Lazzeri	60.00	30.00	18.00
(16)	Ted Lyons	60.00	30.00	18.00
(17)	Rabbit Maranville	60.00	30.00	18.00
(18)	Carl Reynolds	35.00	17.50	10.00
(19)	Charles Ruffing	60.00	30.00	18.00
(20)	Al Simmons	60.00	30.00	18.00
(21)	Gus Suhr	35.00	17.50	10.00
(22)	Bill Terry	60.00	30.00	18.00
(23)	Dazzy Vance	60.00	30.00	18.00
(24)	Paul Waner	60.00	30.00	18.00
(25)	Lon Warneke	35.00	17.50	10.00

1979 Larry Crain Prints

"Baseball's Greatest Team," as voted during baseball's centennial, was featured on a set of 8-1/2" x 11" black-and-white prints by artist Larry Crain. Each print is signed and numbered by the artist. The set of 11 was originally sold for $25.

		NM	EX	VG
	Complete Set (11):	25.00	12.50	7.50
	Common Player:	3.00	1.50	.90
(1)	Yogi Berra	3.00	1.50	.90
(2)	Joe DiMaggio	5.00	2.50	1.50
(3)	Lou Gehrig	4.00	2.00	1.25
(4)	Rogers Hornsby	3.00	1.50	.90
(5)	Walter Johnson	3.00	1.50	.90
(6)	Willie Mays	4.00	2.00	1.25
(7)	Brooks Robinson	3.00	1.50	.90
(8)	Babe Ruth	5.00	2.50	1.50
(9)	Warren Spahn	3.00	1.50	.90
(10)	Casey Stengel	3.00	1.50	.90
(11)	Honus Wagner	3.00	1.50	.90

1976 Crane Potato Chips Discs

This unnumbered 70-card set of player discs was issued with Crane Potato Chips in 1976. The front of the discs are designed to look like a baseball with the player's black-and-white portrait in the center and vital data in side panels containing one of several bright colors. Discs measure 3-3/8" in diameter. This is the most common among several regionally issued sets sharing the same card fronts with different ads on back. The discs were produced by Michael Schechter Associates under license from the players' union. All uniform and cap logos have been deleted from the discs' photos. The unnumbered discs are checklisted here in alphabetical order. Several of the discs have team variations reflecting player moves. These are known only among the Crane discs and have not been verified in the issues of other advertisers.

		NM	EX	VG
	Complete Set (70):	25.00	12.50	7.50
	Common Player:	1.00	.50	.30
(1)	Henry Aaron	9.00	4.50	2.75
(2)	Johnny Bench	4.00	2.00	1.25
(3)	Vida Blue	1.00	.50	.30
(4)	Larry Bowa	1.00	.50	.30
(5)	Lou Brock	3.00	1.50	.90
(6)	Jeff Burroughs	1.00	.50	.30
(7)	John Candelaria	1.00	.50	.30
(8)	Jose Cardenal	1.00	.50	.30
(9)	Rod Carew	3.00	1.50	.90
(10)	Steve Carlton	3.00	1.50	.90
(11)	Dave Cash	1.00	.50	.30
(12)	Cesar Cedeno	1.00	.50	.30
(13)	Ron Cey	1.00	.50	.30
(14)	Carlton Fisk	3.00	1.50	.90
(15)	Tito Fuentes	1.00	.50	.30
(16)	Steve Garvey	2.00	1.00	.60
(17)	Ken Griffey	1.00	.50	.30
(18)	Don Gullett	1.00	.50	.30
(19)	Willie Horton	1.00	.50	.30
(20)	Al Hrabosky	1.00	.50	.30
(21)	Catfish Hunter	3.00	1.50	.90
(22a)	Reggie Jackson (A's)	6.00	3.00	1.75
(22b)	Reggie Jackson (Orioles)	15.00	7.50	4.50
(23)	Randy Jones	1.00	.50	.30
(24)	Jim Kaat	1.00	.50	.30
(25)	Don Kessinger	1.00	.50	.30
(26)	Dave Kingman	1.00	.50	.30
(27)	Jerry Koosman	1.00	.50	.30
(28)	Mickey Lolich	1.00	.50	.30
(29)	Greg Luzinski	1.00	.50	.30
(30)	Fred Lynn	1.00	.50	.30
(31)	Bill Madlock	1.00	.50	.30
(32a)	Carlos May (White Sox)	1.00	.50	.30
(32b)	Carlos May (Yankees)	1.00	.50	.30
(33)	John Mayberry	1.00	.50	.30
(34)	Bake McBride	1.00	.50	.30
(35)	Doc Medich	1.00	.50	.30
(36a)	Andy Messersmith (Dodgers)	1.00	.50	.30
(36b)	Andy Messersmith (Braves)	1.00	.50	.30
(37)	Rick Monday	1.00	.50	.30
(38)	John Montefusco	1.00	.50	.30
(39)	Jerry Morales	1.00	.50	.30

		NM	EX	VG
(40)	Joe Morgan	3.00	1.50	.90
(41)	Thurman Munson	3.00	1.50	.90
(42)	Bobby Murcer	1.00	.50	.30
(43)	Al Oliver	1.00	.50	.30
(44)	Jim Palmer	3.00	1.50	.90
(45)	Dave Parker	1.00	.50	.30
(46)	Tony Perez	3.00	1.50	.90
(47)	Jerry Reuss	1.00	.50	.30
(48)	Brooks Robinson	3.50	1.75	1.00
(49)	Frank Robinson	3.50	1.75	1.00
(50)	Steve Rogers	1.00	.50	.30
(51)	Pete Rose	8.00	4.00	2.50
(52)	Nolan Ryan	15.00	7.50	4.50
(53)	Manny Sanguillen	1.00	.50	.30
(54)	Mike Schmidt	6.00	3.00	1.75
(55)	Tom Seaver	4.00	2.00	1.25
(56)	Ted Simmons	1.00	.50	.30
(57)	Reggie Smith	1.00	.50	.30
(58)	Willie Stargell	3.00	1.50	.90
(59)	Rusty Staub	1.00	.50	.30
(60)	Rennie Stennett	1.00	.50	.30
(61)	Don Sutton	3.00	1.50	.90
(62a)	Andy Thornton (Cubs)	1.00	.50	.30
(62b)	Andy Thornton (Expos)	1.00	.50	.30
(63)	Luis Tiant	1.00	.50	.30
(64)	Joe Torre	2.00	1.00	.60
(65)	Mike Tyson	1.00	.50	.30
(66)	Bob Watson	1.00	.50	.30
(67)	Wilbur Wood	1.00	.50	.30
(68)	Jimmy Wynn	1.00	.50	.30
(69)	Carl Yastrzemski	4.00	2.00	1.25
(70)	Richie Zisk	1.00	.50	.30

1913 Cravats Felt Pennants

Little is known about this felt pennant issue, including the complete checklist. The name "Cravats" in the baseball above the player picture may represent the issuer, or describe the issue; the word "cravat" is an arcane term for a triangular piece of cloth. The pennants measure 4-1/8" across the top and are 9" long. Background colors are dark, with all printing in white. At center is a line art represntation of the player, with his name horizontally beneath and his team nickname vertically at bottom. At top is a bat and ball logo with the "Cravats" name. Most specimens are seen with a metal ring reinforcing the hole punched at top center. The known checklist points to 1913 as the most probable year of issue.

		NM	EX	VG
Common Player:		250.00	125.00	75.00
(1)	Eddie Ainsmith	250.00	125.00	75.00
(2)	"Home Run" Baker	450.00	225.00	135.00
(3)	Hugh Bedient	250.00	125.00	75.00
(4)	Ray Caldwell	250.00	125.00	75.00
(5)	Jack Coombs	250.00	125.00	75.00
(6)	C.S. Dooin	250.00	125.00	75.00
(7)	Lawrence Doyle	250.00	125.00	75.00
(8)	Ed Konetchy (Konetchy)	250.00	125.00	75.00
(9)	James Lavender	250.00	125.00	75.00
(10)	John J. McGraw	450.00	225.00	135.00
(11)	Stuffy McInnis (McInnis)	250.00	125.00	75.00
(12)	Christy Mathewson	1,150	575.00	345.00
(13)	J.T. (Chief) Meyer (Meyers)	250.00	125.00	75.00
(14)	Nap Rucker	250.00	125.00	75.00
(15)	Tris Speaker	600.00	300.00	180.00
(16)	Ed Sweeney	250.00	125.00	75.00
(17)	Jeff Tesreau	250.00	125.00	75.00
(18)	Ira Thomas	250.00	125.00	75.00
(19)	Joe Tinker	450.00	225.00	135.00
(20)	Ed Walsh	450.00	225.00	135.00

1922 Cream Nut/Goodie Bread

According to the advertising on back this set should comprise half of the known players from the generic W573 strip card issue. The black-and-white cards, about 2-1/16" x 3-3/8", share their format and player selection not only with W573, but also E120 American Caramel. Printed horizontally on the backs

is: "Ask Your Dealer for / CREAM NUT or GOODIE BREAD / and get / A BASE BALL STAR / 120 Different Subjects." The location of the issuing entity, the specific manner of distribution and the checklist are unknown as only a handful of this particular ad-back series have survived. Collectors will pay a premium for this version above the normal W573 blank-back.

(See 1922 W573)

1909 Croft's Candy (E92)

 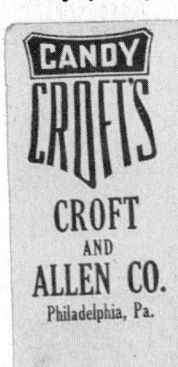

Because they share the format and pictures with several related issues (Croft's Cocoa, Dockman Gum, Nadja Caramels, etc.) this set shared the E92 designation in the American Card Catalog. It is more logical to present these sets as separate issues, based on the advertising which appears on back. Fronts of the 1-1/2" x 2-3/4" cards feature a color lithograph of the player. His last name, position and team are printed in black in the border below. Backs have a shield-shaped logo for Croft's Candy, a product of Croft & Allen Co., Philadelphia. Backs can be found printed in black, in blue (scarcer) or in red (extremely rare). Cards are unnumbered and the checklist is presented here alphabetically.

		NM	EX	VG
Complete Set (50):		125,000	50,000	25,000
Common Player:		1,065	425.00	220.00
Blue Back: 2-3X				
Red Back: Value Undeterminted				
(1)	Jack Barry	1,565	625.00	315.00
(2)	Harry Bemis	1,065	425.00	220.00
(3)	Chief Bender (Striped cap.)	4,065	1,625	815.00
(4)	Chief Bender (White cap.)	3,440	1,375	690.00
(5)	Bill Bergen	1,065	425.00	220.00
(6)	Bob Bescher	1,065	425.00	220.00
(7)	Al Bridwell	1,065	425.00	220.00
(8)	Doc Casey	1,065	425.00	220.00
(9)	Frank Chance	3,440	1,375	690.00
(10)	Hal Chase	2,000	815.00	405.00
(11)	Ty Cobb	18,750	7,500	3,750
(12)	Eddie Collins	3,750	1,500	750.00
(13)	Sam Crawford	2,815	1,125	565.00
(14)	Harry Davis	1,065	425.00	220.00
(15)	Art Devlin	1,065	425.00	220.00
(16)	Wild Bill Donovan	1,065	425.00	220.00
(17)	Red Dooin	1,500	600.00	300.00
(18)	Mickey Doolan	1,065	425.00	220.00
(19)	Patsy Dougherty	1,065	425.00	220.00
(20)	Larry Doyle/Throwing	1,065	425.00	220.00
(21)	Larry Doyle (With bat.)	1,065	425.00	220.00
(22)	Johnny Evers	3,440	1,375	690.00
(23)	George Gibson	1,065	425.00	220.00
(24)	Topsy Hartsel	1,065	425.00	220.00
(25)	Fred Jacklitsch	1,500	600.00	300.00
(26)	Hugh Jennings	2,815	1,125	565.00
(27)	Red Kleinow	1,065	425.00	220.00
(28)	Otto Knabe	1,250	500.00	250.00
(29)	Jack Knight	1,500	600.00	300.00
(30)	Nap Lajoie	4,065	1,625	815.00
(31)	Hans Lobert	1,065	425.00	220.00
(32)	Sherry Magee	1,065	425.00	220.00
(33)	Christy Matthewson (Mathewson)	9,690	3,875	1,940
(34)	John McGraw	2,815	1,125	565.00

1909 Croft's Cocoa (E92)

Like related issues once cataloged together as E92 (Croft's Candy, Dockman Gum, Nadja Caramels, etc.), these 1-1/2" x 2-3/4" cards feature a color player lithograph on front, which his name, position and team printed in the white border below. Backs have an ad for Crofts Swiss Milk Cocoa of Philadelphia. The checklist, presented here alphabetically, is identical to that of Croft's Candy.

		NM	EX	VG
Complete Set (50):		97,500	37,500	18,750
Common Player:		790.00	315.00	150.00
(1)	Jack Barry	1,200	490.00	240.00
(2)	Harry Bemis	790.00	315.00	150.00
(3)	Chief Bender (Striped hat.)	3,000	1,200	600.00
(4)	Chief Bender (White hat.)	1,800	720.00	360.00
(5)	Bill Bergen	790.00	315.00	150.00
(6)	Bob Bescher	790.00	315.00	150.00
(7)	Al Bridwell	790.00	315.00	150.00
(8)	Doc Casey	790.00	315.00	150.00
(9)	Frank Chance	1,650	660.00	330.00
(10)	Hal Chase	1,240	495.00	250.00
(11)	Ty Cobb	22,500	9,000	4,500
(12)	Eddie Collins	1,650	675.00	340.00
(13)	Sam Crawford	1,650	675.00	340.00
(14)	Harry Davis	790.00	315.00	150.00
(15)	Art Devlin	790.00	315.00	150.00
(16)	Wild Bill Donovan	790.00	315.00	150.00
(17)	Red Dooin	1,240	495.00	250.00
(18)	Mickey Doolan	790.00	315.00	150.00
(19)	Patsy Dougherty	790.00	315.00	150.00
(20)	Larry Doyle/Throwing	790.00	315.00	150.00
(21)	Larry Doyle (With bat.)	790.00	315.00	150.00
(22)	Johnny Evers	3,150	1,260	640.00
(23)	George Gibson	790.00	315.00	150.00
(24)	Topsy Hartsel	790.00	315.00	150.00
(25)	Fred Jacklitsch	1,240	495.00	250.00
(26)	Hugh Jennings	1,650	675.00	340.00
(27)	Red Kleinow	790.00	315.00	150.00
(28)	Otto Knabe	1,240	495.00	250.00
(29)	Jack Knight	1,240	495.00	250.00
(30)	Nap Lajoie	2,025	825.00	415.00
(31)	Hans Lobert	790.00	315.00	150.00
(32)	Sherry Magee	790.00	315.00	150.00
(33)	Christy Matthewson (Mathewson)	10,125	4,050	2,025
(34)	John McGraw	1,650	675.00	340.00
(35)	Larry McLean	790.00	315.00	150.00
(36)	Dots Miller/Btg	790.00	315.00	150.00
(37)	Dots Miller/Fielding	1,240	495.00	250.00
(38)	Danny Murphy	790.00	315.00	150.00
(39)	Bill O'Hara	790.00	315.00	150.00
(40)	Germany Schaefer	790.00	315.00	150.00
(41)	Admiral Schlei	790.00	315.00	150.00
(42)	Boss Schmidt	790.00	315.00	150.00
(43)	Johnny Seigle (Siegle)	1,015	405.00	205.00
(44)	Dave Shean	790.00	315.00	150.00
(45)	Boss Smith (Schmidt)	790.00	315.00	150.00
(46)	Joe Tinker	1,650	675.00	340.00
(47)	Honus Wagner/Btg	5,625	2,250	1,125
(48)	Honus Wagner/Throwing	5,625	2,250	1,125
(49)	Cy Young	5,250	2,100	1,050
(50)	Heinie Zimmerman	790.00	315.00	150.00

The "1909 Croft's Candy" checklist continues:

		NM	EX	VG
(35)	Larry McLean	1,065	425.00	220.00
(36)	Dots Miller/Btg	1,065	425.00	220.00
(37)	Dots Miller/Fielding	1,500	600.00	300.00
(38)	Danny Murphy	1,065	425.00	220.00
(39)	Bill O'Hara	4,065	425.00	220.00
(40)	Germany Schaefer	1,065	425.00	220.00
(41)	Admiral Schlei	1,065	425.00	220.00
(42)	Boss Schmidt	1,065	425.00	220.00
(43)	Johnny Seigle (Siegle)	1,065	425.00	220.00
(44)	Dave Shean	1,065	425.00	220.00
(45)	Boss Smith (Schmidt)	1,065	425.00	220.00
(46)	Joe Tinker	2,815	1,125	565.00
(47)	Honus Wagner/Btg	10,000	4,000	2,000
(48)	Honus Wagner/Throwing	15,000	6,000	3,000
(49)	Cy Young	8,125	3,250	1,625
(50)	Heinie Zimmerman	1,065	425.00	220.00

1969 Crown Brooks Robinson

The attributed date is speculative. This 3-9/16" x 5-11/16" card feaures a black-and-white portrait photo on front with the player name in blue scrip. A

BROOKS ROBINSON CHOOSES for ACTION!

blue panel at bottom has the gas company's logo and an ad slogan. On back is a black, red and white coupon offering a discount on a baseball. A blank panel at bottom was intended for use by individual service stations to print their name and address.

	NM	EX	VG
Brooks Robinson	150.00	75.00	45.00

1977-78 Cubic Corp. Sports Deck Playing Cards

Playing cards featuring pencil drawings of stars in various sports were produced on a limited basis in the late 1970s by Cubic Corp. of San Diego. The cards are standard bridge size (2-1/4" x 3-1/2") with rounded corners and feature the artwork of Al Landsman along with a facsimile autograph within a colored frame. Each deck has the same athlete on the back and sold for $1.60. There is no indication of the manufacturer on individual cards, it is only found on the box. It is believed most of the decks were only produced in limited sample quantities. Similar cards were produced for Pepsi and are listed thereunder. Only the baseball players are checklisted here, in alphabetical order.

		NM	EX	VG
(1)	Johnny Bench (Boxed deck.)	17.50	8.75	5.25
(1)	Johnny Bench (Single card.)	.50	.25	.15
(2)	Lou Gehrig (Boxed deck.)	25.00	12.50	7.50
(2)	Lou Gehrig (Single card.)	1.50	.70	.45
(3)	Catfish Hunter (Boxed deck.)	15.00	7.50	4.50
(3)	Catfish Hunter (Single card.)	.50	.25	.15
(4)	Randy Jones (Boxed deck.)	10.00	5.00	3.00
(4)	Randy Jones (Single card.)	.50	.25	.15
(5)	Mickey Mantle (Boxed deck.)	40.00	20.00	12.00
(5)	Mickey Mantle (Single card.)	4.00	2.00	1.25
(6)	Butch Metzger (Boxed deck.)	10.00	5.00	3.00
(6)	Butch Metzger (Single card.)	.50	.25	.15
(7)	Joe Morgan (Boxed deck.)	12.50	6.25	3.75
(7)	Joe Morgan (Single card.)	.50	.25	.15
(8)	Stan Musial (Boxed deck.)	25.00	12.50	7.50
(8)	Stan Musial (Single card.)	1.50	.70	.45
(9)	Jackie Robinson (Boxed deck.)	25.00	12.50	7.50
(9)	Jackie Robinson (Single card.)	1.50	.70	.45
(10)	Pete Rose (Boxed deck.)	35.00	17.50	10.00
(10)	Pete Rose (Single card.)	1.00	.50	.30
(11)	Babe Ruth (Boxed deck.)	30.00	15.00	9.00
(11)	Babe Ruth (Single card.)	3.00	1.50	.90
(12)	Tom Seaver (Boxed deck.)	30.00	15.00	9.00
(12)	Tom Seaver (Single card.)	1.00	.50	.30
(13)	Frank Tanana (Boxed deck.)	10.00	5.00	3.00
(13)	Frank Tanana (Single card.)	.50	.25	.15
(14)	Phillies logo/autographs (Boxed deck.)	10.00	5.00	3.00
(14)	Phillies logo/autographs (Single card.)	1.00	.50	.30

1911 Cullivan's Fireside Philadelphia A's (T208)

The 1911 T208 Firesides, an 18-card Philadelphia Athletics set issued by the Thomas Cullivan Tobacco Company of Syracuse, N.Y., is among the rarest of all 20th Century tobacco issues. Cullivan issued the set to commemorate the Athletics' 1910 Championship season, and, except for pitcher Jack Coombs, the

checklist includes nearly all key members of the club, including manager Connie Mack. The cards are the standard size for tobacco issues, about 1-1/2" x 2-5/8". The front of each card features a player portrait set against a colored background. The player's name and the word "Athletics" appear at the bottom, while "World's Champions 1910" is printed along the top. Backs advertise the set as the "Athletics Series" and advise that one card is included in each package of "Cullivan's Fireside Plain Scrap" tobacco. The same checklist was used for a similar Athletics set issued by Rochester Baking/Williams Baking (D359). Blank-backed versions are also known to exist.

		NM	EX	VG
Common Player:		11,250	5,625	3,375
(1)	Home Run Baker	25,000	12,500	7,500
(2)	Jack Barry	11,250	5,625	3,375
(3)	Chief Bender	25,000	12,500	7,500
(4)	Eddie Collins	25,000	12,500	7,500
(5)	Harry Davis	11,250	5,625	3,375
(6)	Jimmy Dygert	11,250	5,625	3,375
(7)	Topsy Hartsel	11,250	5,625	3,375
(8)	Harry Krause	11,250	5,625	3,375
(9)	Jack Lapp	11,250	5,625	3,375
(10)	Paddy Livingston	11,250	5,625	3,375
(11)	Bris Lord	11,250	5,625	3,375
(12)	Connie Mack	25,000	12,500	7,500
(13)	Cy Morgan	11,250	5,625	3,375
(14)	Danny Murphy	11,250	5,625	3,375
(15)	Rube Oldring	12,500	5,625	3,375
(16)	Eddie Plank	28,125	14,065	8,440
(17)	Amos Strunk	11,250	5,625	3,375
(18)	Ira Thomas	11,250	5,625	3,375

1964+ Curteichcolor Hall of Fame Plaque Postcards

(See Hall of Fame Yellow Plaque Postcards for checklist, price data.)

1909-12 Cycle Cigarettes

Cycle brand advertising found on the backs of T205, T206 and T207 cards generally indicates a slightly greater degree of scarcity than the most common back variations from those sets. While a value multiplier can generate a ballpark approximation of value for most cards from T205 and T206, it is not practical for T207s because all Cycle cards from that set are scarce and much of that scarcity has already been factored into the individual player prices quoted in the base T207 listings.

PREMIUMS:
T205: 1-1.5X
T206 350 Series: 1-1.5X
T206 460 Series: 2-3X
(See T205, T206, T207 for checklists and base card values.)

D

1959 Dad's Cookies Exhibits

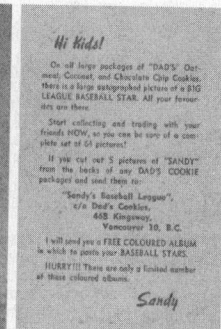

A Vancouver bakery that issued several type of hockey cards in later years created this set of baseball cards by overprinting the usually blank backs of the 64 cards in Exhibit Supply Co.'s 1959 issue. Cards measure 3-3/8" x 5-3/8" and are printed in reddish-gray-brown. The back indicates an album was available to house the set.

		NM	EX	VG
Complete Set (64):		3,000	1,500	900.00
Common Player:		35.00	17.50	10.00
(1)	Hank Aaron	200.00	100.00	60.00
(2)	Joe Adcock (Script name.)	35.00	17.50	10.00
(3)	Johnny Antonelli (Giants)	35.00	17.50	10.00
(4)	Luis Aparicio/Portrait	80.00	40.00	24.00
(5)	Richie Ashburn (Phillies)	100.00	50.00	30.00
(6)	Ed Bailey (With cap.)	35.00	17.50	10.00
(7)	Ernie Banks (Bat on shoulder, script name.)	150.00	75.00	45.00
(8)	Hank Bauer (N.Y. cap.)	50.00	25.00	15.00
(9)	Yogi Berra	150.00	75.00	45.00
(10)	Don Blasingame	35.00	17.50	10.00
(11)	Bill Bruton	35.00	17.50	10.00
(12)	Lew Burdette/Pitching (Side view.)	35.00	17.50	10.00
(13)	Chico Carrasquel/Portrait	35.00	17.50	10.00
(14)	Orlando Cepeda (To chest.)	80.00	40.00	24.00
(15)	Bob Cerv (A's cap.)	35.00	17.50	10.00
(16)	Delmar Crandall	35.00	17.50	10.00
(17)	Alvin Dark (Cubs)	35.00	17.50	10.00
(18)	Larry Doby	80.00	40.00	24.00
(19)	Dick Donovan (Sox cap.)	35.00	17.50	10.00
(20)	Don Drysdale/Portrait	90.00	45.00	27.00
(21)	Del Ennis	35.00	17.50	10.00
(22)	Whitey Ford/Pitching	125.00	62.00	37.00
(23)	Nelson Fox	80.00	40.00	24.00
(24)	Bob Friend	35.00	17.50	10.00
(25)	Billy Goodman/Btg	35.00	17.50	10.00
(26)	Whitey Herzog	35.00	17.50	10.00
(27)	Gil Hodges (LA on cap.)	75.00	37.50	22.00
(28)	Elston Howard	50.00	25.00	15.00
(29)	Jackie Jensen	50.00	25.00	15.00
(30)	Al Kaline (Portrait w/ two bats.)	100.00	50.00	30.00
(31)	Harmon Killebrew/Btg	100.00	50.00	30.00
(32)	Billy Klaus	35.00	17.50	10.00
(33)	Ted Kluzewski (Kluszewski) (Pirates uniform.)	60.00	30.00	18.00
(34)	Tony Kubek (Light background.)	60.00	30.00	18.00
(35)	Harvey Kuenn (D on cap.)	35.00	17.50	10.00
(36)	Don Larsen	35.00	17.50	10.00
(37)	Johnny Logan	35.00	17.50	10.00
(38)	Dale Long (C on cap.)	35.00	17.50	10.00
(39)	Mickey Mantle/Btg (No pinstripes, "c k" of "Mickey" separated.)	350.00	175.00	100.00
(40)	Eddie Mathews	100.00	50.00	30.00
(41)	Willie Mays/Portrait	200.00	100.00	60.00
(42)	Bill Mazeroski/Portrait	80.00	40.00	24.00
(43)	Lindy McDaniel	35.00	17.50	10.00
(44)	Gil McDougald	45.00	22.50	13.50
(45)	Orestes Minoso (C on cap.)	45.00	22.50	13.50
(46)	Stan Musial	175.00	87.00	52.00

		NM	EX	VG
(47)	Don Newcombe (Plain jacket.)	45.00	22.50	13.50
(48)	Andy Pafko (Yours truly.) (Plain uniform.)	35.00	17.50	10.00
(49)	Billy Pierce	35.00	17.50	10.00
(50)	Robin Roberts (Script name.)	80.00	40.00	24.00
(51)	Carl Sawatski (P on cap.)	35.00	17.50	10.00
(52)	Herb Score (C on cap.)	35.00	17.50	10.00
(53)	Roy Sievers/Portrait (W on cap, light background.)	35.00	17.50	10.00
(54)	Curt Simmons	35.00	17.50	10.00
(55)	Bill Skowron	50.00	25.00	15.00
(56)	Duke Snider (LA on cap.)	100.00	50.00	30.00
(57)	Warren Spahn (M on cap.)	100.00	50.00	30.00
(58)	Frankie Thomas (Photo actually Bob Skinner.)	50.00	25.00	15.00
(59)	Earl Torgeson (Plain uniform.)	35.00	17.50	10.00
(60)	Gus Triandos	35.00	17.50	10.00
(61)	Vic Wertz/Portrait	35.00	17.50	10.00
(62)	Ted Williams (Sincerely yours.) (#9 not showing.)	200.00	100.00	60.00
(63)	Gene Woodling (Script name.)	35.00	17.50	10.00
(64)	Gus Zernial (Script name.)	35.00	17.50	10.00

1972 Daily Juice Co.

This one-card "set" was regionally issued to Roberto Clemente Fan Club members. Large numbers of the cards found their way into the hobby, including in uncut sheet form. The cards feature a full-color front black-and-white back. The card measures the standard 2-1/2" in width but is somewhat longer, at 3-3/4". This unnumbered card remains about the least expensive baseball card that was issued during Clemente's lifetime.

		NM	EX	VG
	Uncut Sheet (30):	200.00	100.00	60.00
1	Roberto Clemente	15.00	7.50	4.50

1950s Dairy Council Curt Simmons Postcard

 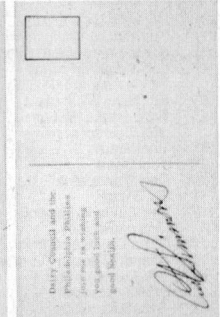

Issued by "The Dairy Council," probably locally, this black-and-white postcard features an action-pose photo of the star Phillies pitcher. There is a white facsimile autograph on front. Back of the 3-3/4" x 5-3/4" card has another facsimile autograph and the legend, "Dairy Council and the Philadelphia Phillies join me in wishing you good luck and good health."

	NM	EX	VG
Curt Simmons	60.00	30.00	18.00

1976 Dairy Isle Discs

One of several regional sponsors of player disc sets in 1976 was the upstate New York area chain, Dairy Isle. The discs are 3-3/8" diameter with a black-and-white

player portrait photo in the center of the baseball design. A line of red stars is above, while the left and right panels feature one of several bright colors. Produced by Michael Schecter Associates under license from the Major League Baseball Players Association, the player photos have had uniform and cap logos removed. Backs are printed in red and purple. The unnumbered checklist here is presented in alphabetical order.

		NM	EX	VG
	Complete Set (70):	45.00	22.50	13.50
	Common Player:	1.00	.50	.30
(1)	Henry Aaron	10.00	5.00	3.00
(2)	Johnny Bench	4.50	2.25	1.25
(3)	Vida Blue	1.00	.50	.30
(4)	Larry Bowa	1.00	.50	.30
(5)	Lou Brock	4.00	2.00	1.25
(6)	Jeff Burroughs	1.00	.50	.30
(7)	John Candelaria	1.00	.50	.30
(8)	Jose Cardenal	1.00	.50	.30
(9)	Rod Carew	4.00	2.00	1.25
(10)	Steve Carlton	4.00	2.00	1.25
(11)	Dave Cash	1.00	.50	.30
(12)	Cesar Cedeno	1.00	.50	.30
(13)	Ron Cey	1.00	.50	.30
(14)	Carlton Fisk	4.00	2.00	1.25
(15)	Tito Fuentes	1.00	.50	.30
(16)	Steve Garvey	3.00	1.50	.90
(17)	Ken Griffey	1.00	.50	.30
(18)	Don Gullett	1.00	.50	.30
(19)	Willie Horton	1.00	.50	.30
(20)	Al Hrabosky	1.00	.50	.30
(21)	Catfish Hunter	4.00	2.00	1.25
(22)	Reggie Jackson (A's)	6.00	3.00	1.75
(23)	Randy Jones	1.00	.50	.30
(24)	Jim Kaat	1.00	.50	.30
(25)	Don Kessinger	1.00	.50	.30
(26)	Dave Kingman	1.00	.50	.30
(27)	Jerry Koosman	1.00	.50	.30
(28)	Mickey Lolich	1.00	.50	.30
(29)	Greg Luzinski	1.00	.50	.30
(30)	Fred Lynn	1.00	.50	.30
(31)	Bill Madlock	1.00	.50	.30
(32)	Carlos May (White Sox)	1.00	.50	.30
(33)	John Mayberry	1.00	.50	.30
(34)	Bake McBride	1.00	.50	.30
(35)	Doc Medich	1.00	.50	.30
(36)	Andy Messersmith	1.00	.50	.30
(37)	Rick Monday	1.00	.50	.30
(38)	John Montefusco	1.00	.50	.30
(39)	Jerry Morales	1.00	.50	.30
(40)	Joe Morgan	4.00	2.00	1.25
(41)	Thurman Munson	3.00	1.50	.90
(42)	Bobby Murcer	1.00	.50	.30
(43)	Al Oliver	1.00	.50	.30
(44)	Jim Palmer	4.00	2.00	1.25
(45)	Dave Parker	1.00	.50	.30
(46)	Tony Perez	4.00	2.00	1.25
(47)	Jerry Reuss	1.00	.50	.30
(48)	Brooks Robinson	4.50	2.25	1.25
(49)	Frank Robinson	4.50	2.25	1.25
(50)	Steve Rogers	1.00	.50	.30
(51)	Pete Rose	10.00	5.00	3.00
(52)	Nolan Ryan	20.00	10.00	6.00
(53)	Manny Sanguillen	1.00	.50	.30
(54)	Mike Schmidt	6.00	3.00	1.75
(55)	Tom Seaver	4.50	2.25	1.25
(56)	Ted Simmons	1.00	.50	.30
(57)	Reggie Smith	1.00	.50	.30
(58)	Willie Stargell	4.00	2.00	1.25
(59)	Rusty Staub	1.25	.60	.40
(60)	Rennie Stennett	1.00	.50	.30
(61)	Don Sutton	4.00	2.00	1.25
(62)	Andy Thornton (Cubs)	1.00	.50	.30
(63)	Luis Tiant	1.00	.50	.30
(64)	Joe Torre	3.00	1.50	.90
(65)	Mike Tyson	1.00	.50	.30
(66)	Bob Watson	1.00	.50	.30
(67)	Wilbur Wood	1.00	.50	.30
(68)	Jimmy Wynn	1.00	.50	.30
(69)	Carl Yastrzemski	4.50	2.25	1.25
(70)	Richie Zisk	1.00	.50	.30

1977 Dairy Isle Discs

Virtually identical in format to the 1976 issue (substituting red and blue for the back ad in 1977, instead of the previous year's red and purple), these 3-3/8" diameter player discs were given away at Dairy Isle outlets. Discs once again feature black-and-white player portrait photos in the center of a baseball design. The left and right panels are in one of several bright colors. Licensed by the players' association through Mike Schechter Associates, the player photos carry no uniform logos. The unnumbered discs are checklisted here alphabetically.

		NM	EX	VG
	Complete Set (70):	30.00	15.00	9.00
	Common Player:	1.00	.50	.30
(1)	Sal Bando	1.00	.50	.30
(2)	Buddy Bell	1.00	.50	.30
(3)	Johnny Bench	4.50	2.25	1.25
(4)	Larry Bowa	1.00	.50	.30
(5)	Steve Braun	1.00	.50	.30
(6)	George Brett	10.00	5.00	3.00
(7)	Lou Brock	3.50	1.75	1.00
(8)	Jeff Burroughs	1.00	.50	.30
(9)	Bert Campaneris	1.00	.50	.30
(10)	John Candelaria	1.00	.50	.30
(11)	Jose Cardenal	1.00	.50	.30
(12)	Rod Carew	3.50	1.75	1.00
(13)	Steve Carlton	3.50	1.75	1.00
(14)	Dave Cash	1.00	.50	.30
(15)	Cesar Cedeno	1.00	.50	.30
(16)	Ron Cey	1.00	.50	.30
(17)	Dave Concepcion	1.00	.50	.30
(18)	Dennis Eckersley	3.50	1.75	1.00
(19)	Mark Fidrych	2.00	1.00	.60
(20)	Rollie Fingers	3.50	1.75	1.00
(21)	Carlton Fisk	3.50	1.75	1.00
(22)	George Foster	1.00	.50	.30
(23)	Wayne Garland	1.00	.50	.30
(24)	Ralph Garr	1.00	.50	.30
(25)	Steve Garvey	3.50	1.75	1.00
(26)	Cesar Geronimo	1.00	.50	.30
(27)	Bobby Grich	1.00	.50	.30
(28)	Ken Griffey	1.00	.50	.30
(29)	Don Gullett	1.00	.50	.30
(30)	Mike Hargrove	1.00	.50	.30
(31)	Al Hrabosky	1.00	.50	.30
(32)	Jim Hunter	3.50	1.75	1.00
(33)	Reggie Jackson	6.00	3.00	1.75
(34)	Randy Jones	1.00	.50	.30
(35)	Dave Kingman	1.00	.50	.30
(36)	Jerry Koosman	1.00	.50	.30
(37)	Dave LaRoche	1.00	.50	.30
(38)	Greg Luzinski	1.00	.50	.30
(39)	Fred Lynn	1.00	.50	.30
(40)	Bill Madlock	1.00	.50	.30
(41)	Rick Manning	1.00	.50	.30
(42)	Jon Matlack	1.00	.50	.30
(43)	John Mayberry	1.00	.50	.30
(44)	Hal McRae	1.00	.50	.30
(45)	Andy Messersmith	1.00	.50	.30
(46)	Rick Monday	1.00	.50	.30
(47)	John Montefusco	1.00	.50	.30
(48)	Joe Morgan	3.50	1.75	1.00
(49)	Thurman Munson	2.50	1.25	.70
(50)	Bobby Murcer	1.00	.50	.30
(51)	Bill North	1.00	.50	.30
(52)	Jim Palmer	3.50	1.75	1.00
(53)	Tony Perez	3.50	1.75	1.00
(54)	Jerry Reuss	1.00	.50	.30
(55)	Brooks Robinson	4.50	2.25	1.25
(56)	Pete Rose	10.00	5.00	3.00
(57)	Joe Rudi	1.00	.50	.30
(58)	Nolan Ryan	15.00	7.50	4.50
(59)	Manny Sanguillen	1.00	.50	.30
(60)	Mike Schmidt	6.00	3.00	1.75
(61)	Tom Seaver	4.50	2.25	1.25
(62)	Bill Singer	1.00	.50	.30
(63)	Willie Stargell	3.50	1.75	1.00
(64)	Rusty Staub	1.25	.60	.40
(65)	Luis Tiant	1.00	.50	.30
(66)	Bob Watson	1.00	.50	.30
(67)	Butch Wynegar	1.00	.50	.30
(68)	Carl Yastrzemski	4.50	2.25	1.25
(69)	Robin Yount	3.50	1.75	1.00
(70)	Richie Zisk	1.00	.50	.30

1956 Dairy Queen Stars Statues

This set is identical in composition and manufacture to the carded figures sold as Big League Stars (see listing). The DQ versions of the statues are white, while the Big League versions are bronze colored. The statues measure about 3" tall and were evidently sold or given away with a purchase at the chain of ice cream shops.

		NM	EX	VG
	Complete Set (18):	1,100	550.00	350.00
	Common Player:	40.00	20.00	12.00
(1)	John Antonelli	40.00	20.00	12.00
(2)	Bob Avila	40.00	20.00	12.00
(3)	Yogi Berra	100.00	50.00	30.00
(4)	Roy Campanella	100.00	50.00	30.00
(5)	Larry Doby	65.00	32.50	20.00
(6)	Del Ennis	40.00	20.00	12.00
(7)	Jim Gilliam	40.00	20.00	12.00
(8)	Gil Hodges	75.00	37.50	22.50
(9)	Harvey Kuenn	40.00	20.00	12.00
(10)	Bob Lemon	50.00	25.00	15.00
(11)	Mickey Mantle	325.00	160.00	100.00
(12)	Ed Mathews	75.00	37.50	22.50
(13)	Minnie Minoso	40.00	20.00	12.00

		NM	EX	VG
(14)	Stan Musial	160.00	80.00	50.00
(15)	Pee Wee Reese	100.00	50.00	30.00
(16)	Al Rosen	40.00	20.00	12.00
(17)	Duke Snider	100.00	50.00	30.00
(18)	Mickey Vernon	40.00	20.00	12.00

1954 Dan-Dee Potato Chips

Issued in bags of potato chips, the cards in this 29-card set are commonly found with grease stains despite their waxed surface. The unnumbered cards, which measure 2-1/2" x 3-5/8", feature color pictures. Backs have player statistical and biographical information. The set consists mostly of players from the Indians and Pirates. Photos of the Yankees players were also used for the Briggs Meats and Stahl-Meyer Franks sets.

		NM	EX	VG
Complete Set (29):		7,000	2,750	1,350
Common Player:		110.00	45.00	20.00
(1)	Bob Avila	110.00	45.00	20.00
(2)	Hank Bauer	135.00	55.00	25.00
(3)	Walker Cooper/SP	375.00	150.00	75.00
(4)	Larry Doby	140.00	55.00	25.00
(5)	Luke Easter	125.00	50.00	25.00
(6)	Bob Feller	350.00	140.00	70.00
(7)	Bob Friend	110.00	45.00	20.00
(8)	Mike Garcia	110.00	45.00	20.00
(9)	Sid Gordon	110.00	45.00	20.00
(10)	Jim Hegan	110.00	45.00	20.00
(11)	Gil Hodges	450.00	180.00	90.00
(12)	Art Houtteman	110.00	45.00	20.00
(13)	Monte Irvin	140.00	55.00	25.00
(14)	Paul LaPalm (LaPalme)	110.00	45.00	20.00
(15)	Bob Lemon	140.00	55.00	25.00
(16)	Al Lopez	140.00	55.00	25.00
(17)	Mickey Mantle	2,400	960.00	460.00
(18)	Dale Mitchell	110.00	45.00	20.00
(19)	Phil Rizzuto	250.00	100.00	50.00
(20)	Curtis Roberts	110.00	45.00	20.00
(21)	Al Rosen	125.00	50.00	25.00
(22)	Red Schoendienst	140.00	55.00	25.00
(23)	Paul Smith/SP	390.00	150.00	75.00
(24)	Duke Snider	300.00	120.00	60.00
(25)	George Strickland	110.00	45.00	20.00
(26)	Max Surkont	110.00	45.00	20.00
(27)	Frank Thomas/SP	200.00	80.00	40.00
(28)	Wally Westlake	110.00	45.00	20.00
(29)	Early Wynn	140.00	55.00	25.00

1977 Tom Daniels Burleigh Grimes

"OLD STUBBLEBEARD"

The career of Hall of Fame spitballer Burleigh Grimes is traced in this collectors' issue. The 2-1/2" x 3-1/2" cards have black-and-white photos from Grimes' collection, bordered in bright blue. A card title is in black in the bottom border. Backs are printed in black and blue on white and have a description of the front photo. One card in each set is authentically autographed by Grimes. Price at issue was $3.50; uncut sheets were also available.

		NM	EX	VG
Complete Set (16):		10.00	5.00	3.00
Common Card:		1.00	.50	.30
1	Dodger Manager 1937-38	1.00	.50	.30
2	"Lord Burleigh"	1.00	.50	.30
3	Last Spitballers	1.00	.50	.30
4	Grimes, Hornsby, McGraw, Roush	1.00	.50	.30
5	Winning Combination	1.00	.50	.30
6	World Champion	1.00	.50	.30
7	"Old Stubblebeard"	1.00	.50	.30

		NM	EX	VG
8	Grimes Meets McCarthy	1.00	.50	.30
9	Dodger Greats	1.00	.50	.30
10	"The Babe"	2.00	1.00	.60
11	Dodger Strategists	1.00	.50	.30
12	Bender and Grimes	1.00	.50	.30
13	Number '270'	1.00	.50	.30
14	The Origin	1.00	.50	.30
15	1964 HoF Inductees	1.00	.50	.30
16	"Lord Burleigh" 1977	1.00	.50	.30

1910 Darby Chocolates (E271)

The 1910 Darby Chocolates cards are among the rarest of all candy cards. The cards were printed on boxes of "Pennant" Chocolates, two players per box - one each on front and back. The cards feature black-and-white player action photos outlined with a thick dark shadow. The boxes are accented with orange or green graphics. Most of the known examples of this set were not found until 1982 when a group in fire-damaged condition was inadvisedly subjected to restoration. Values shown here are for cards in untampered-with state of preservation. Values for restored cards must be adjusted significantly downward. This checklist may or may not be complete.

		NM	EX	VG
Common Player:		12,000	6,000	3,500
(1)	Jimmy Archer	12,000	6,000	3,600
(2)	Chief Bender	16,000	8,000	4,800
(3)	Bob Bescher	12,000	6,000	3,600
(4)	Roger Bresnahan	16,000	8,000	4,800
(5)	Al Bridwell	12,000	6,000	3,600
(6)	Mordicai Brown (Mordecai)	16,000	8,000	4,800
(7)	"Eddie" Cicotte	13,500	6,750	4,000
(8)	Fred Clark (Clarke)	12,000	6,000	3,600
(9)	Ty. Cobb/Btg	30,000	15,000	9,000
(10)	"Ty" Cobb/Fielding	30,000	15,000	9,000
(11)	King Cole	12,000	6,000	3,600
(12)	E. Collins	16,000	8,000	4,800
(13)	Wid Conroy	12,000	6,000	3,600
(14)	"Sam" Crawford	16,000	8,000	4,800
(15)	Bill Dahlin (Dahlen)	12,000	6,000	3,600
(16)	Bill Donovan	12,000	6,000	3,600
(17)	"Pat" Dougherty	12,000	6,000	3,600
(18)	Kid Elberfeld	12,000	6,000	3,600
(19)	"Johnny" Evers	16,000	8,000	4,800
(20)	Charlie Herzog	12,000	6,000	3,600
(21)	Hughie Jennings	16,000	8,000	4,800
(22)	Walter Johnson	20,000	10,000	6,000
(23)	Ed Konetchy	12,000	6,000	3,600
(24)	Tommy Leach	12,000	6,000	3,600
(25)	Fred Luderous (Luderus)	12,000	6,000	3,600
(26)	"Mugsy" McGraw	16,000	8,000	4,800
(27)	"Mike" Mowery (Mowrey)	12,000	6,000	3,600
(28)	Jack Powell	12,000	6,000	3,600
(29)	Slim Sallee	12,000	6,000	3,600
(30)	James Scheckard (Sheckard)	12,000	6,000	3,600
(31)	Walter Snodgrass	12,000	6,000	3,600
(32)	"Tris" Speaker	17,500	8,750	5,250
(33)	Charlie Suggs	12,000	6,000	3,600
(34)	Fred Tenney	12,000	6,000	3,600
(35)	"Jim" Vaughn	12,000	6,000	3,600
(36)	"Hans" Wagner	40,000	13,750	8,250

1911 Harry Davis Day Postcard

HARRY DAVIS DAY
SHIBE PARK
WEDNESDAY, MAY 31st

In his final season with the Philadelphia Athletics, the star first baseman of the famed $100,000 Infield was honored with a "day" at Shibe Park. This standard-size black-and-white postcard was created to remind fans to attend the event. A pre-printed message on back over the facsimile signature of Connie Mack urges fans to "show our appreciation of what Captain Davis has done for baseball and the city of his birth."

	NM	EX	VG
Harry Davis	750.00	375.00	225.00

1970 Dayton Daily News Bubble-Gumless Cards

These "cards" are actually newspaper clippings which were issued on a daily basis during the baseball season by the Ohio newspaper. Labeled "Today's Hero," the clippings measure approximately 3-1/2" x 4" and are printed in black-and-white. At left is a portrait photo of the player, at right are personal data, stats and career highlights.

		NM	EX	VG
Complete Set (160):		2,000	1,000	600.00
Common Player:		9.00	4.50	2.75
1	Pete Rose	40.00	20.00	12.00
2	Johnny Bench	20.00	10.00	6.00
3	Maury Wills	12.00	6.00	3.50
4	Harmon Killebrew	20.00	10.00	6.00
5	Frank Robinson	20.00	10.00	6.00
6	Willie Mays	60.00	30.00	18.00
7	Hank Aaron	60.00	30.00	18.00
8	Tom Seaver	20.00	10.00	6.00
9	Sam McDowell	9.00	4.50	2.75
10	Rico Petrocelli	9.00	4.50	2.75
11a	Tony Perez (Dark cap.)	20.00	10.00	6.00
11b	Tony Perez (Light cap.)	20.00	10.00	6.00
12	Hoyt Wilhelm	15.00	7.50	4.50
13	Alex Johnson	9.00	4.50	2.75
14	Gary Nolan	9.00	4.50	2.75
15	Al Kaline	25.00	12.50	7.50
16	Bob Gibson	15.00	7.50	4.50
17	Larry Dierker	9.00	4.50	2.75
18	Ernie Banks	30.00	15.00	9.00
19	Lee May	9.00	4.50	2.75
20	Claude Osteen	9.00	4.50	2.75
21	Tony Horton	9.00	4.50	2.75
22	Mack Jones	9.00	4.50	2.75
23	Wally Bunker	9.00	4.50	2.75
24	Bill Hands	9.00	4.50	2.75
25	Bobby Tolan	9.00	4.50	2.75
26	Jim Wynn	9.00	4.50	2.75
27	Tom Haller	9.00	4.50	2.75
28	Carl Yastrzemski	25.00	12.50	7.50
29	Jim Merritt	9.00	4.50	2.75
30	Tony Oliva	12.00	6.00	3.50
31	Reggie Jackson	40.00	20.00	12.00
32	Bob Clemente	90.00	45.00	27.00
33	Tommy Helms	9.00	4.50	2.75
34	Boog Powell	12.00	6.00	3.50
35	Mickey Lolich	9.00	4.50	2.75
36	Frank Howard	12.00	6.00	3.50
37	Jim McGlothlin	9.00	4.50	2.75
38	Rusty Staub	12.00	6.00	3.50
39	Mel Stottlemyre	9.00	4.50	2.75
40	Rico Carty	9.00	4.50	2.75
41	Nate Colbert	9.00	4.50	2.75
42	Wayne Granger	9.00	4.50	2.75
43	Mike Hegan	9.00	4.50	2.75
44	Jerry Koosman	9.00	4.50	2.75
45	Jim Perry	9.00	4.50	2.75
46	Pat Corrales	9.00	4.50	2.75
47	Dick Bosman	9.00	4.50	2.75
48	Bert Campaneris	9.00	4.50	2.75
49	Larry Hisle	9.00	4.50	2.75
50	Bernie Carbo	9.00	4.50	2.75
51	Wilbur Wood	9.00	4.50	2.75
52	Dave McNally	9.00	4.50	2.75
53	Andy Messersmith	9.00	4.50	2.75
54	Jimmy Stewart	9.00	4.50	2.75
55	Luis Aparicio	15.00	7.50	4.50
56	Mike Cuellar	9.00	4.50	2.75
57	Bill Grabarkewitz	9.00	4.50	2.75
58	Dick Dietz	9.00	4.50	2.75
59	Dave Concepcion	9.00	4.50	2.75
60	Gary Gentry	9.00	4.50	2.75
61	Don Money	9.00	4.50	2.75
62	Rod Carew	20.00	10.00	6.00
63	Denis Menke	9.00	4.50	2.75
64	Hal McRae	9.00	4.50	2.75
65	Felipe Alou	9.00	4.50	2.75
66	Richie Hebner	9.00	4.50	2.75
67	Don Sutton	15.00	7.50	4.50
68	Wayne Simpson	9.00	4.50	2.75
69	Art Shamsky	9.00	4.50	2.75

		NM	EX	VG
70	Luis Tiant	9.00	4.50	2.75
71	Clay Carroll	9.00	4.50	2.75
72	Jim Hickman	9.00	4.50	2.75
73	Clarence Gaston	9.00	4.50	2.75
74	Angel Bravo	9.00	4.50	2.75
75	Jim Hunter	15.00	7.50	4.50
76	Lou Piniella	10.00	5.00	3.00
77	Jim Bunning	15.00	7.50	4.50
78	Don Gullett	9.00	4.50	2.75
79	Dan Cater	9.00	4.50	2.75
80	Richie Allen	13.50	6.75	4.00
81	Jim Bouton	10.00	5.00	3.00
82	Jim Palmer	15.00	7.50	4.50
83	Woody Woodward	9.00	4.50	2.75
84	Tom Agee	9.00	4.50	2.75
85	Carlos May	9.00	4.50	2.75
86	Ray Washburn	9.00	4.50	2.75
87	Denny McLain	10.00	5.00	3.00
88	Lou Brock	15.00	7.50	4.50
89	Ken Henderson	9.00	4.50	2.75
90	Roy White	9.00	4.50	2.75
91	Chris Cannizzaro	9.00	4.50	2.75
92	Willie Horton	9.00	4.50	2.75
93	Jose Cardenal	9.00	4.50	2.75
94	Jim Fregosi	9.00	4.50	2.75
95	Richie Hebner	9.00	4.50	2.75
96	Tony Conigliaro	10.00	5.00	3.00
97	Tony Cloninger	9.00	4.50	2.75
98	Mike Epstein	9.00	4.50	2.75
99	Ty Cline	9.00	4.50	2.75
100	Tommy Harper	9.00	4.50	2.75
101	Jose Azcue	9.00	4.50	2.75
102a	Glenn Beckert	9.00	4.50	2.75
102b	Ray Fosse	9.00	4.50	2.75
103	NOT ISSUED			
104	Gerry Moses	9.00	4.50	2.75
105	Bud Harrelson	9.00	4.50	2.75
106	Joe Torre	13.50	6.75	4.00
107	Dave Johnson	9.00	4.50	2.75
108	Don Kessinger	9.00	4.50	2.75
109	Bill Freehan	9.00	4.50	2.75
110	Sandy Alomar	9.00	4.50	2.75
111	Matty Alou	9.00	4.50	2.75
112	Joe Morgan	15.00	7.50	4.50
113	John Odom	9.00	4.50	2.75
114	Amos Otis	9.00	4.50	2.75
115	Jay Johnstone	9.00	4.50	2.75
116	Ron Perranoski	9.00	4.50	2.75
117	Manny Mota	9.00	4.50	2.75
118	Billy Conigliaro	9.00	4.50	2.75
119	Leo Cardenas	9.00	4.50	2.75
120	Rich Reese	9.00	4.50	2.75
121	Ron Santo	12.00	6.00	3.50
122	Gene Michael	9.00	4.50	2.75
123	Milt Pappas	9.00	4.50	2.75
124	Joe Pepitone	10.00	5.00	3.00
125	Jose Cardenal	9.00	4.50	2.75
126	Jim Northrup	9.00	4.50	2.75
127	Wes Parker	9.00	4.50	2.75
128	Fritz Peterson	9.00	4.50	2.75
129	Phil Regan	9.00	4.50	2.75
130	John Callison	9.00	4.50	2.75
131	Cookie Rojas	9.00	4.50	2.75
132	Claude Raymond	9.00	4.50	2.75
133	Darrel Chaney	9.00	4.50	2.75
134	Gary Peters	9.00	4.50	2.75
135	Del Unser	9.00	4.50	2.75
136	Joey Foy	9.00	4.50	2.75
137	Luke Walker	9.00	4.50	2.75
138	Bill Mazeroski	15.00	7.50	4.50
139	Tony Taylor	9.00	4.50	2.75
140	Leron Lee	9.00	4.50	2.75
141	Jesus Alou	9.00	4.50	2.75
142	Donn Clendenon	9.00	4.50	2.75
143	Merv Rettenmund	9.00	4.50	2.75
144	Bob Moose	9.00	4.50	2.75
145	Jim Kaat	10.00	5.00	3.00
146	Randy Hundley	9.00	4.50	2.75
147	Jim McAndrew	9.00	4.50	2.75
148	Manny Sanguillen	9.00	4.50	2.75
149	Bob Allison	9.00	4.50	2.75
150	Jim Maloney	9.00	4.50	2.75
151	Don Buford	9.00	4.50	2.75
152	Gene Alley	9.00	4.50	2.75
153	Cesar Tovar	9.00	4.50	2.75
154	Brooks Robinson	20.00	10.00	6.00
155	Milt Wilcox	9.00	4.50	2.75
156	Willie Stargell	20.00	10.00	6.00
157	Paul Blair	9.00	4.50	2.75
158	Andy Etchebarren	9.00	4.50	2.75
159	Mark Belanger	9.00	4.50	2.75
160	Elrod Hendricks	9.00	4.50	2.75

1973 Dean's Photo Service San Diego Padres

A true rookie-year issue for Dave Winfield is included in this set of 5-1/2" x 8-1/2" black-and-white, blank-backed player photos sponsored by Dean's Photo Service and given away by the team in five six-card series at various home games. Pictures have posed player portraits surrounded by a white border. Beneath are the name and position, with team and sponsor logos at bottom. The set is checklisted here alphabetically.

		NM	EX	VG
Complete Set (31):		80.00	40.00	24.00
Common Player:		4.00	2.00	1.25
(1)	Steve Arlin	4.00	2.00	1.25
(2)	Mike Caldwell	4.00	2.00	1.25
(3)	Dave Campbell	4.00	2.00	1.25
(4)	Nate Colbert	4.00	2.00	1.25
(5)	Mike Corkins	4.00	2.00	1.25
(6)	Pat Corrales	4.00	2.00	1.25
(7)	Jim Davenport	4.00	2.00	1.25
(8)	Dave Garcia	4.00	2.00	1.25
(9)	Clarence Gaston	4.00	2.00	1.25
(10)	Bill Greif	4.00	2.00	1.25
(11)	John Grubb	4.00	2.00	1.25
(12)	Enzo Hernandez	4.00	2.00	1.25
(13)	Randy Jones	4.00	2.00	1.25
(14)	Fred Kendall	4.00	2.00	1.25
(15)	Clay Kirby	4.00	2.00	1.25
(16)	Leron Lee	4.00	2.00	1.25
(17)	Dave Marshall	4.00	2.00	1.25
(18)	Don Mason	4.00	2.00	1.25
(19)	Jerry Morales	4.00	2.00	1.25
(20)	Ivan Murrell	4.00	2.00	1.25
(21)	Fred Norman	4.00	2.00	1.25
(22)	Johnny Podres	4.00	2.00	1.25
(23)	Dave Roberts	4.00	2.00	1.25
(24)	Vicente Romo	4.00	2.00	1.25
(25)	Gary Ross	4.00	2.00	1.25
(26)	Bob Skinner	4.00	2.00	1.25
(27)	Derrel Thomas	4.00	2.00	1.25
(28)	Rich Troedson	4.00	2.00	1.25
(29)	Whitey Wietelmann	4.00	2.00	1.25
(30)	Dave Winfield	25.00	12.50	7.50
(31)	Don Zimmer	5.00	2.50	1.50

1974 Dean's Photo Service San Diego Padres

This issue shares the same basic format as the years which preceded it and succeeded it. Fronts of the 5-1/2" x 8-1/2" cards have a large player portrait or pose at top, with the player's name and position below. In the wide white border at bottom are the team and sponsor's logos. Backs, for the first time, have a lengthy career summary, personal data and full professional stats. All printing is in black-and-white. The unnumbered cards are checklisted here alphabetically.

		NM	EX	VG
Complete Set (30):		70.00	35.00	21.00
Common Player:		4.00	2.00	1.25
(1)	Matty Alou	4.00	2.00	1.25
(2)	Bob Barton	4.00	2.00	1.25
(3)	Glenn Beckert	4.00	2.00	1.25
(4)	Jack Bloomfield	4.00	2.00	1.25
(5)	Nate Colbert	4.00	2.00	1.25
(6)	Mike Corkins	4.00	2.00	1.25
(7)	Jim Davenport	4.00	2.00	1.25
(8)	Dave Freisleben	4.00	2.00	1.25
(9)	Cito Gaston	4.00	2.00	1.25
(10)	Bill Greif	4.00	2.00	1.25
(11)	Johnny Grubb	4.00	2.00	1.25
(12)	Larry Hardy	4.00	2.00	1.25
(13)	Enzo Hernandez	4.00	2.00	1.25
(14)	Dave Hilton	4.00	2.00	1.25
(15)	Randy Jones	4.00	2.00	1.25
(16)	Fred Kendall	4.00	2.00	1.25
(17)	Gene Locklear	4.00	2.00	1.25
(18)	Willie McCovey	10.00	5.00	3.00
(19)	John McNamara	4.00	2.00	1.25
(20)	Rich Morales	4.00	2.00	1.25
(21)	Bill Posedel	4.00	2.00	1.25
(22)	Dave Roberts	4.00	2.00	1.25
(23)	Vicente Romo	4.00	2.00	1.25
(24)	Dan Spillner	4.00	2.00	1.25
(25)	Bob Tolan	4.00	2.00	1.25
(26)	Derrel Thomas	4.00	2.00	1.25
(27)	Rich Troedson	4.00	2.00	1.25
(28)	Whitey Wietelmann	4.00	2.00	1.25
(29)	Bernie Williams	4.00	2.00	1.25
(30)	Dave Winfield	15.00	7.50	4.50

1975 Dean's Photo Service San Diego Padres

 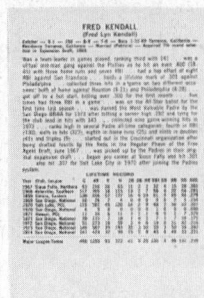

Player biographical data and stats continued on the backs of the cards in the 1975 series sponsored by Dean's. Once again the black-and-white pictures were in 5-1/2" x 8-1/2" format. Fronts have the player photo at top, with his name and position beneath. At bottom are the team and sponsor logos. The Padres logo consists of a cartoon character robed monk in various baseball poses. The pictures were given away at autograph nights during the season. The unnumbered photos are checklisted here in alphabetical order.

		NM	EX	VG
Complete Set (30):		60.00	30.00	18.00
Common Player:		4.00	2.00	1.25
(1)	Jim Davenport	4.00	2.00	1.25
(2)	Bob Davis	4.00	2.00	1.25
(3)	Rich Folkers	4.00	2.00	1.25
(4)	Alan Foster	4.00	2.00	1.25
(5)	Dave Freisleben	4.00	2.00	1.25
(6)	Danny Frisella	4.00	2.00	1.25
(7)	Tito Fuentes	4.00	2.00	1.25
(8)	Bill Greif	4.00	2.00	1.25
(9)	Johnny Grubb	4.00	2.00	1.25
(10)	Enzo Hernandez	4.00	2.00	1.25
(11)	Randy Hundley (Blank back.)	4.00	2.00	1.25
(12)	Mike Ivie	4.00	2.00	1.25
(13)	Jerry Johnson	4.00	2.00	1.25
(14)	Randy Jones	4.00	2.00	1.25
(15)	Fred Kendall	4.00	2.00	1.25
(16)	Ted Kubiak	4.00	2.00	1.25
(17)	Gene Locklear	4.00	2.00	1.25
(18)	Willie McCovey	10.00	5.00	3.00
(19)	Joe McIntosh	4.00	2.00	1.25
(20)	John McNamara	4.00	2.00	1.25
(21)	Tom Morgan	4.00	2.00	1.25
(22)	Dick Sharon	4.00	2.00	1.25
(23)	Dick Sisler	4.00	2.00	1.25
(24)	Dan Spillner	4.00	2.00	1.25
(25)	Brent Strom	4.00	2.00	1.25
(26)	Bobby Tolan	4.00	2.00	1.25
(27)	Dave Tomlin	4.00	2.00	1.25
(28)	Hector Torres (Blank back.)	4.00	2.00	1.25
(29)	Whitey Wietelmann	4.00	2.00	1.25
(30)	Dave Winfield	15.00	7.50	4.50

1976 Dean's Photo Service San Diego Padres

The last of four black-and-white team sets which were sponsored by Dean's was issued in 1976. The format was little different than previous years. Cards are 5-1/2" x 8-1/2" black-and-white. Fronts have a player portrait or pose surrounded by a white border. At bottom front are team and sponsor logos. Backs have personal data, a career summary and complete professional stats. The unnumbered cards are checklisted here in alphabetical order.

		NM	EX	VG
Complete Set (30):		60.00	30.00	18.00
Common Player:		4.00	2.00	1.25
(1)	Joe Amalfitano	4.00	2.00	1.25
(2)	Roger Craig	4.00	2.00	1.25
(3)	Bob Davis	4.00	2.00	1.25
(4)	Willie Davis	4.00	2.00	1.25
(5)	Rich Folkers	4.00	2.00	1.25
(6)	Alan Foster	4.00	2.00	1.25

(7)	Dave Freisleben	4.00	2.00	1.25
(8)	Tito Fuentes	4.00	2.00	1.25
(9)	John Grubb	4.00	2.00	1.25
(10)	Enzo Hernandez	4.00	2.00	1.25
(11)	Mike Ivie	4.00	2.00	1.25
(12)	Jerry Johnson	4.00	2.00	1.25
(13)	Randy Jones	4.00	2.00	1.25
(14)	Fred Kendall	4.00	2.00	1.25
(15)	Ted Kubiak	4.00	2.00	1.25
(16)	Willie McCovey	10.00	5.00	3.00
(17)	John McNamara	4.00	2.00	1.25
(18)	Luis Melendez	4.00	2.00	1.25
(19)	Butch Metzger	4.00	2.00	1.25
(20)	Doug Rader	4.00	2.00	1.25
(21)	Merv Rettenmund	4.00	2.00	1.25
(22)	Ken Reynolds	4.00	2.00	1.25
(23)	Dick Sisler	4.00	2.00	1.25
(24)	Dan Spillner	4.00	2.00	1.25
(25)	Brent Strom	4.00	2.00	1.25
(26)	Dave Tomlin	4.00	2.00	1.25
(27)	Hector Torres	4.00	2.00	1.25
(28)	Jerry Turner	4.00	2.00	1.25
(29)	Whitey Wietelmann	4.00	2.00	1.25
(30)	Dave Winfield	15.00	7.50	4.50

1938 Dizzy Dean's Service Station

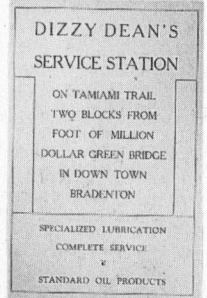

The date of issue of this one-card set is only a guess. The 4" x 6" black-and-white card advertises Dean's service station in Florida.

	NM	EX	VG
Dizzy Dean	350.00	175.00	100.00

1978 Dearborn Show

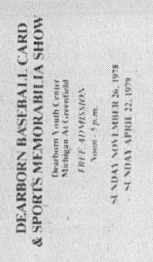

#13 NORM CASH

Former members of the Detroit Tigers, some of whom were scheduled to appear as autograph guests, are featured in this collectors' issue produced in conjunction with the 1978 Dearborn Baseball Card & Sports Memorabilia Show. The 2-5/8" x 3-5/8" cards have black-and-white player photos on front with the player name and card number in the white border at bottom. Backs, also in black-and-white, advertise the fall, 1978, and spring, 1979 shows.

		NM	EX	VG
	Complete Set (18):	60.00	30.00	18.00
	Common Player:	4.00	2.00	1.25
1	Rocky Colavito	15.00	7.50	4.50
2	Ervin Fox	4.00	2.00	1.25
3	Lynwood Rowe	4.00	2.00	1.25
4	Gerald Walker	4.00	2.00	1.25
5	Leon Goslin	4.00	2.00	1.25
6	Harvey Kuenn	6.00	3.00	1.75
7	Frank Howard	6.00	3.00	1.75
8	Woodie Fryman	4.00	2.00	1.25
9	Don Wert	4.00	2.00	1.25
10	Jim Perry	4.00	2.00	1.25
11	Mayo Smith	4.00	2.00	1.25
12	Al Kaline	20.00	10.00	6.00
13	Norm Cash	12.00	6.00	3.50
14	Mickey Cochrane	9.00	4.50	2.75
15	Fred Marberry	4.00	2.00	1.25
16	Bill Freehan	6.00	3.00	1.75
17	Charlie Gehringer	9.00	4.50	2.75
18	Jim Northrup	4.00	2.00	1.25

1980 Delacorte Press

As a promotion for its book, "Number 1," written by Billy Martin, Delacorte Press issued this card picturing Martin somewhat in the style of a 1978 Topps manager

card. The 3-1/2" x 2-1/2" card has a black-and-white photo of Martin as a Yankees manager, and a color photo as the A's manager. The front is bordered in red. Backs are printed in black, white and red with biographical details and promotional copy for the book.

		NM	EX	VG
1	Billy Martin	6.00	3.00	1.75

1971 Dell Today's Team Stamps

JACK DiLAURO

Pitcher — Bats right and left, throws right. Born 1943. Height 6-2. Weight 185. Relieved 42 times in 1970. Has good breaking ball and control. Good fielding pitcher who demonstrated ability to win three straight years in Triple-A ball. Originally signed by Tigers.

This issue was produced as a series of individual team (plus one All-Star) albums. The 8-1/2" x 10-7/8" booklets offer team and league histories and stats, photos of all-time team stars and two pages of 12 player stamps each. Each stamp is 1-7/8" x 2-15/16" and has a posed color photo and black facsimile autograph on front. Backs have the player name, biographical details and a few career highlights, along with an underprint of the team logo. The stamps are perforated for easy separation, though there are no spaces in the 12-page album for their housing once removed from the sheet. The team albums were sold individually (39 cents) as well as in six-team divisional sets ($2). The checklist is arranged alphabetically by team within league; individual stamps are unnumbered.

		NM	EX	VG
	Complete Set, Albums (25):	225.00	110.00	65.00
	Complete Set, Stamps (600):	175.00	90.00	50.00
	Common Player:	1.00	.50	.30
	Complete All-Star Album:	20.00	10.00	6.00
(1)	Hank Aaron	7.50	3.75	2.25
(2)	Luis Aparicio	2.50	1.25	.70
(3)	Ernie Banks	5.00	2.50	1.50
(4)	Johnny Bench	3.00	1.50	.90
(5)	Rico Carty	1.00	.50	.30
(6)	Roberto Clemente	10.00	5.00	3.00
(7)	Bob Gibson	2.50	1.25	.70
(8)	Willie Horton	1.00	.50	.30
(9)	Frank Howard	1.50	.70	.45
(10)	Reggie Jackson	6.00	3.00	1.75
(11)	Fergie Jenkins	1.50	.70	.45
(12)	Alex Johnson	1.00	.50	.30
(13)	Al Kaline	3.00	1.50	.90
(14)	Harmon Killebrew	3.00	1.50	.90
(15)	Willie Mays	7.50	3.75	2.25
(16)	Sam McDowell	1.00	.50	.30
(17)	Denny McLain	1.50	.70	.45
(18)	Boog Powell	1.50	.70	.45
(19)	Brooks Robinson	3.00	1.50	.90
(20)	Frank Robinson	3.00	1.50	.90
(21)	Pete Rose	7.50	3.75	2.25
(22)	Tom Seaver	3.00	1.50	.90
(23)	Rusty Staub	1.50	.70	.45
(24)	Carl Yastrzemski	3.00	1.50	.90
	Complete Atlanta Braves Album:	15.00	7.50	4.50
(1)	Hank Aaron	7.50	3.75	2.25
(2)	Tommie Aaron	1.00	.50	.30
(3)	Hank Allen	1.00	.50	.30
(4)	Clete Boyer	1.50	.70	.45
(5)	Oscar Brown	1.00	.50	.30
(6)	Rico Carty	1.00	.50	.30
(7)	Orlando Cepeda	2.50	1.25	.70
(8)	Bob Didier	1.00	.50	.30
(9)	Ralph Garr	1.00	.50	.30
(10)	Gil Garrido	1.00	.50	.30
(11)	Ron Herbel	1.00	.50	.30
(12)	Sonny Jackson	1.00	.50	.30
(13)	Pat Jarvis	1.00	.50	.30
(14)	Larry Jaster	1.00	.50	.30
(15)	Hal King	1.00	.50	.30

		NM	EX	VG
(16)	Mike Lum	1.00	.50	.30
(17)	Felix Millan	1.00	.50	.30
(18)	Jim Nash	1.00	.50	.30
(19)	Phil Niekro	2.00	1.00	.60
(20)	Bob Priddy	1.00	.50	.30
(21)	Ron Reed	1.00	.50	.30
(22)	George Stone	1.00	.50	.30
(23)	Cecil Upshaw	1.00	.50	.30
(24)	Hoyt Wilhelm	2.00	1.00	.60
	Complete Chicago Cubs Album:	15.00	7.50	4.50
(1)	Ernie Banks	5.00	2.50	1.50
(2)	Glenn Beckert	1.00	.50	.30
(3)	Danny Breeden	1.00	.50	.30
(4)	Johnny Callison	1.00	.50	.30
(5)	Jim Colborn	1.00	.50	.30
(6)	Joe Decker	1.00	.50	.30
(7)	Bill Hands	1.00	.50	.30
(8)	Jim Hickman	1.00	.50	.30
(9)	Ken Holtzman	1.00	.50	.30
(10)	Randy Hundley	1.00	.50	.30
(11)	Fergie Jenkins	2.00	1.00	.60
(12)	Don Kessinger	1.00	.50	.30
(13)	J.C. Martin	1.00	.50	.30
(14)	Bob Miller	1.00	.50	.30
(15)	Milt Pappas	1.00	.50	.30
(16)	Joe Pepitone	1.00	.50	.30
(17)	Juan Pizarro	1.00	.50	.30
(18)	Paul Popovich	1.00	.50	.30
(19)	Phil Regan	1.00	.50	.30
(20)	Roberto Rodriguez	1.00	.50	.30
(21)	Ken Rudolph	1.00	.50	.30
(22)	Ron Santo	1.50	.70	.45
(23)	Hector Torres	1.00	.50	.30
(24)	Billy Williams	2.50	1.25	.70
	Complete Cincinnati Reds Album:	20.00	10.00	6.00
(1)	Johnny Bench	3.00	1.50	.90
(2)	Angel Bravo	1.00	.50	.30
(3)	Bernie Carbo	1.00	.50	.30
(4)	Clay Carroll	1.00	.50	.30
(5)	Darrel Chaney	1.00	.50	.30
(6)	Ty Cline	1.00	.50	.30
(7)	Tony Cloninger	1.00	.50	.30
(8)	Dave Concepcion	1.00	.50	.30
(9)	Pat Corrales	1.00	.50	.30
(10)	Greg Garrett	1.00	.50	.30
(11)	Wayne Granger	1.00	.50	.30
(12)	Don Gullett	1.00	.50	.30
(13)	Tommy Helms	1.00	.50	.30
(14)	Lee May	1.00	.50	.30
(15)	Jim McGlothlin	1.00	.50	.30
(16)	Hal McRae	1.00	.50	.30
(17)	Jim Merritt	1.00	.50	.30
(18)	Gary Nolan	1.00	.50	.30
(19)	Tony Perez	2.50	1.25	.70
(20)	Pete Rose	7.50	3.75	2.25
(21)	Wayne Simpson	1.00	.50	.30
(22)	Jimmy Stewart	1.00	.50	.30
(23)	Bobby Tolan	1.00	.50	.30
(24)	Woody Woodward	1.00	.50	.30
	Complete Houston Astros Album:	10.00	5.00	3.00
(1)	Jesus Alou	1.00	.50	.30
(2)	Jack Billingham	1.00	.50	.30
(3)	Ron Cook	1.00	.50	.30
(4)	George Culver	1.00	.50	.30
(5)	Larry Dierker	1.00	.50	.30
(6)	Jack DiLauro	1.00	.50	.30
(7)	Johnny Edwards	1.00	.50	.30
(8)	Fred Gladding	1.00	.50	.30
(9)	Tom Griffin	1.00	.50	.30
(10)	Skip Guinn	1.00	.50	.30
(11)	Jack Hiatt	1.00	.50	.30
(12)	Denny Lemaster	1.00	.50	.30
(13)	Marty Martinez	1.00	.50	.30
(14)	John Mayberry	1.00	.50	.30
(15)	Denis Menke	1.00	.50	.30
(16)	Norm Miller	1.00	.50	.30
(17)	Joe Morgan	2.50	1.25	.70
(18)	Doug Rader	1.00	.50	.30
(19)	Jim Ray	1.00	.50	.30
(20)	Scipio Spinks	1.00	.50	.30
(21)	Bob Watkins	1.00	.50	.30
(22)	Bob Watson	1.00	.50	.30
(23)	Don Wilson	1.00	.50	.30
(24)	Jim Wynn	1.00	.50	.30
	Complete Los Angeles Dodgers Album:	12.50	6.25	3.75
(1)	Rich Allen	1.50	.70	.45
(2)	Jim Brewer	1.00	.50	.30
(3)	Bill Buckner	1.00	.50	.30
(4)	Willie Crawford	1.00	.50	.30
(5)	Willie Davis	1.00	.50	.30
(6)	Al Downing	1.00	.50	.30
(7)	Steve Garvey	6.00	3.00	1.75
(8)	Billy Grabarkewitz	1.00	.50	.30
(9)	Tom Haller	1.00	.50	.30
(10)	Jim Lefebvre	1.00	.50	.30
(11)	Pete Mikkelsen	1.00	.50	.30
(12)	Joe Moeller	1.00	.50	.30
(13)	Manny Mota	1.00	.50	.30
(14)	Claude Osteen	1.00	.50	.30
(15)	Wes Parker	1.00	.50	.30
(16)	Jose Pena	1.00	.50	.30
(17)	Bill Russell	1.00	.50	.30
(18)	Duke Sims	1.00	.50	.30
(19)	Bill Singer	1.00	.50	.30
(20)	Mike Strahler	1.00	.50	.30
(21)	Bill Sudakis	1.00	.50	.30
(22)	Don Sutton	2.00	1.00	.60
(23)	Jeff Torborg	1.00	.50	.30
(24)	Maury Wills	1.00	.50	.30
	Complete Montreal Expos Album:	10.00	5.00	3.00
(1)	Bob Bailey	1.00	.50	.30
(2)	John Bateman	1.00	.50	.30
(3)	John Boccabella	1.00	.50	.30

(4)	Ron Brand	1.00	.50	.30
(5)	Boots Day	1.00	.50	.30
(6)	Jim Fairey	1.00	.50	.30
(7)	Ron Fairly	1.00	.50	.30
(8)	Jim Gosger	1.00	.50	.30
(9)	Don Hahn	1.00	.50	.30
(10)	Ron Hunt	1.00	.50	.30
(11)	Mack Jones	1.00	.50	.30
(12)	Jose Laboy	1.00	.50	.30
(13)	Mike Marshall	1.00	.50	.30
(14)	Dan McGinn	1.00	.50	.30
(15)	Carl Morton	1.00	.50	.30
(16)	John O'Donoghue	1.00	.50	.30
(17)	Adolfo Phillips	1.00	.50	.30
(18)	Claude Raymond	1.00	.50	.30
(19)	Steve Renko	1.00	.50	.30
(20)	Marv Staehle	1.00	.50	.30
(21)	Rusty Staub	1.25	.60	.40
(22)	Bill Stoneman	1.00	.50	.30
(23)	Gary Sutherland	1.00	.50	.30
(24)	Bobby Wine	1.00	.50	.30
	Complete New York Mets Album:	25.00	12.50	7.50
(1)	Tommie Agee	1.00	.50	.30
(2)	Bob Aspromonte	1.00	.50	.30
(3)	Ken Boswell	1.00	.50	.30
(4)	Dean Chance	1.00	.50	.30
(5)	Donn Clendenon	1.00	.50	.30
(6)	Duffy Dyer	1.00	.50	.30
(7)	Dan Frisella	1.00	.50	.30
(8)	Wayne Garrett	1.00	.50	.30
(9)	Gary Gentry	1.00	.50	.30
(10)	Jerry Grote	1.00	.50	.30
(11)	Bud Harrelson	1.00	.50	.30
(12)	Cleon Jones	1.00	.50	.30
(13)	Jerry Koosman	1.00	.50	.30
(14)	Ed Kranepool	1.00	.50	.30
(15)	Dave Marshall	1.00	.50	.30
(16)	Jim McAndrew	1.00	.50	.30
(17)	Tug McGraw	1.00	.50	.30
(18)	Nolan Ryan	20.00	10.00	6.00
(19)	Ray Sadecki	1.00	.50	.30
(20)	Tom Seaver	3.00	1.50	.90
(21)	Art Shamsky	1.00	.50	.30
(22)	Ron Swoboda	1.00	.50	.30
(23)	Ron Taylor	1.00	.50	.30
(24)	Al Weis	1.00	.50	.30
	Complete Philadelphia Phillies Album:	10.00	5.00	3.00
(1)	Larry Bowa	1.00	.50	.30
(2)	Johnny Briggs	1.00	.50	.30
(3)	Bryon Browne	1.00	.50	.30
(4)	Jim Bunning	2.00	1.00	.60
(5)	Billy Champion	1.00	.50	.30
(6)	Mike Compton	1.00	.50	.30
(7)	Denny Doyle	1.00	.50	.30
(8)	Roger Freed	1.00	.50	.30
(9)	Woody Fryman	1.00	.50	.30
(10)	Oscar Gamble	1.00	.50	.30
(11)	Terry Harmon	1.00	.50	.30
(12)	Larry Hisle	1.00	.50	.30
(13)	Joe Hoerner	1.00	.50	.30
(14)	Deron Johnson	1.00	.50	.30
(15)	Barry Lersch	1.00	.50	.30
(16)	Tim McCarver	1.50	.70	.45
(17)	Don Money	1.00	.50	.30
(18)	Mike Ryan	1.00	.50	.30
(19)	Dick Selma	1.00	.50	.30
(20)	Chris Short	1.00	.50	.30
(21)	Ron Stone	1.00	.50	.30
(22)	Tony Taylor	1.00	.50	.30
(23)	Rick Wise	1.00	.50	.30
(24)	Billy Wilson	1.00	.50	.30
	Complete Pittsburgh Pirates Album:	30.00	15.00	9.00
(1)	Gene Alley	1.00	.50	.30
(2)	Steve Blass	1.00	.50	.30
(3)	Nelson Briles	1.00	.50	.30
(4)	Jim Campanis	1.00	.50	.30
(5)	Dave Cash	1.00	.50	.30
(6)	Roberto Clemente	10.00	5.00	3.00
(7)	Vic Davalillo	1.00	.50	.30
(8)	Dock Ellis	1.00	.50	.30
(9)	Jim Grant	1.00	.50	.30
(10)	Dave Giusti	1.00	.50	.30
(11)	Richie Hebner	1.00	.50	.30
(12)	Jackie Hernandez	1.00	.50	.30
(13)	Johnny Jeter	1.00	.50	.30
(14)	Lou Marone	1.00	.50	.30
(15)	Jose Martinez	1.00	.50	.30
(16)	Bill Mazeroski	2.50	1.25	.70
(17)	Bob Moose	1.00	.50	.30
(18)	Al Oliver	1.25	.60	.40
(19)	Jose Pagan	1.00	.50	.30
(20)	Bob Robertson	1.00	.50	.30
(21)	Manny Sanguillen	1.00	.50	.30
(22)	Willie Stargell	2.50	1.25	.70
(23)	Bob Veale	1.00	.50	.30
(24)	Luke Walker	1.00	.50	.30
	Complete San Diego Padres Album:	10.00	5.00	3.00
(1)	Jose Arcia	1.00	.50	.30
(2)	Bob Barton	1.00	.50	.30
(3)	Fred Beene	1.00	.50	.30
(4)	Ollie Brown	1.00	.50	.30
(5)	Dave Campbell	1.00	.50	.30
(6)	Chris Cannizzaro	1.00	.50	.30
(7)	Nate Colbert	1.00	.50	.30
(8)	Mike Corkins	1.00	.50	.30
(9)	Tommy Dean	1.00	.50	.30
(10)	Al Ferrara	1.00	.50	.30
(11)	Rod Gaspar	1.00	.50	.30
(12)	Cito Gaston	1.00	.50	.30
(13)	Enzo Hernandez	1.00	.50	.30
(14)	Clay Kirby	1.00	.50	.30
(15)	Don Mason	1.00	.50	.30
(16)	Ivan Murrell	1.00	.50	.30
(17)	Gerry Nyman	1.00	.50	.30

(18)	Tom Phoebus	1.00	.50	.30
(19)	Dave Roberts	1.00	.50	.30
(20)	Gary Ross	1.00	.50	.30
(21)	Al Santorini	1.00	.50	.30
(22)	Al Severinsen	1.00	.50	.30
(23)	Ron Slocum	1.00	.50	.30
(24)	Ed Spiezio	1.00	.50	.30
	Complete San Francisco Giants Album:	12.50	6.25	3.75
(1)	Bobby Bonds	1.25	.60	.40
(2)	Ron Bryant	1.00	.50	.30
(3)	Don Carrithers	1.00	.50	.30
(4)	John Cumberland	1.00	.50	.30
(5)	Mike Davison	1.00	.50	.30
(6)	Dick Dietz	1.00	.50	.30
(7)	Tito Fuentes	1.00	.50	.30
(8)	Russ Gibson	1.00	.50	.30
(9)	Jim Ray Hart	1.00	.50	.30
(10)	Bob Heise	1.00	.50	.30
(11)	Ken Henderson	1.00	.50	.30
(12)	Steve Huntz	1.00	.50	.30
(13)	Frank Johnson	1.00	.50	.30
(14)	Jerry Johnson	1.00	.50	.30
(15)	Hal Lanier	1.00	.50	.30
(16)	Juan Marichal	2.00	1.00	.60
(17)	Willie Mays	7.50	3.75	2.25
(18)	Willie McCovey	2.50	1.25	.70
(19)	Don McMahon	1.00	.50	.30
(20)	Jim Moyer	1.00	.50	.30
(21)	Gaylord Perry	2.00	1.00	.60
(22)	Frank Reberger	1.00	.50	.30
(23)	Rich Robertson	1.00	.50	.30
(24)	Bernie Williams	1.00	.50	.30
	Complete St. Louis Cardinals Album:	10.00	5.00	3.00
(1)	Matty Alou	1.00	.50	.30
(2)	Jim Beauchamp	1.00	.50	.30
(3)	Frank Bertaina	1.00	.50	.30
(4)	Lou Brock	2.50	1.25	.70
(5)	George Brunet	1.00	.50	.30
(6)	Jose Cardenal	1.00	.50	.30
(7)	Steve Carlton	2.50	1.25	.70
(8)	Moe Drabowsky	1.00	.50	.30
(9)	Bob Gibson	2.50	1.25	.70
(10)	Joe Hague	1.00	.50	.30
(11)	Julian Javier	1.00	.50	.30
(12)	Leron Lee	1.00	.50	.30
(13)	Frank Linzy	1.00	.50	.30
(14)	Dal Maxvill	1.00	.50	.30
(15)	Jerry McNertney	1.00	.50	.30
(16)	Fred Norman	1.00	.50	.30
(17)	Milt Ramirez	1.00	.50	.30
(18)	Dick Schofield	1.00	.50	.30
(19)	Mike Shannon	1.00	.50	.30
(20)	Ted Sizemore	1.00	.50	.30
(21)	Bob Stinson	1.00	.50	.30
(22)	Carl Taylor	1.00	.50	.30
(23)	Joe Torre	1.50	.70	.45
(24)	Mike Torrez	1.00	.50	.30
	Complete Baltimore Orioles Album:	15.00	7.50	4.50
(1)	Mark Belanger	1.00	.50	.30
(2)	Paul Blair	1.00	.50	.30
(3)	Don Buford	1.00	.50	.30
(4)	Terry Crowley	1.00	.50	.30
(5)	Mike Cuellar	1.00	.50	.30
(6)	Clay Dalrymple	1.00	.50	.30
(7)	Pat Dobson	1.00	.50	.30
(8)	Andy Etchebarren	1.00	.50	.30
(9)	Dick Hall	1.00	.50	.30
(10)	Jim Hardin	1.00	.50	.30
(11)	Elrod Hendricks	1.00	.50	.30
(12)	Grant Jackson	1.00	.50	.30
(13)	Dave Johnson	1.00	.50	.30
(14)	Dave Leonhard	1.00	.50	.30
(15)	Marcelino Lopez	1.00	.50	.30
(16)	Dave McNally	1.00	.50	.30
(17)	Curt Motton	1.00	.50	.30
(18)	Jim Palmer	2.00	1.00	.60
(19)	Boog Powell	1.00	.50	.30
(20)	Merv Rettenmund	1.00	.50	.30
(21)	Brooks Robinson	3.00	1.50	.90
(22)	Frank Robinson	3.00	1.50	.90
(23)	Pete Richert	1.00	.50	.30
(24)	Chico Salmon	1.00	.50	.30
	Complete Boston Red Sox Album:	15.00	7.50	4.50
(1)	Luis Aparicio	2.50	1.25	.70
(2)	Bobby Bolin	1.00	.50	.30
(3)	Ken Brett	1.00	.50	.30
(4)	Billy Conigliaro	1.00	.50	.30
(5)	Ray Culp	1.00	.50	.30
(6)	Mike Flore	1.00	.50	.30
(7)	John Kennedy	1.00	.50	.30
(8)	Cal Koonce	1.00	.50	.30
(9)	Joe Lahoud	1.00	.50	.30
(10)	Bill Lee	1.00	.50	.30
(11)	Jim Lonborg	1.00	.50	.30
(12)	Sparky Lyle	1.00	.50	.30
(13)	Mike Nagy	1.00	.50	.30
(14)	Don Pavletich	1.00	.50	.30
(15)	Gary Peters	1.00	.50	.30
(16)	Rico Petrocelli	1.00	.50	.30
(17)	Vicente Romo	1.00	.50	.30
(18)	Tom Satriano	1.00	.50	.30
(19)	George Scott	1.00	.50	.30
(20)	Sonny Siebert	1.00	.50	.30
(21)	Reggie Smith	1.00	.50	.30
(22)	Jarvis Tatum	1.00	.50	.30
(23)	Ken Tatum	1.00	.50	.30
(24)	Carl Yastrzemski	3.00	1.50	.90
	Complete California Angels Album:	10.00	5.00	3.00
(1)	Sandy Alomar	1.00	.50	.30
(2)	Joe Azcue	1.00	.50	.30
(3)	Ken Berry	1.00	.50	.30
(4)	Gene Brabender	1.00	.50	.30
(5)	Billy Cowan	1.00	.50	.30

(6)	Tony Conigliaro	1.50	.70	.45
(7)	Eddie Fisher	1.00	.50	.30
(8)	Jim Fregosi	1.00	.50	.30
(9)	Tony Gonzales (Gonzalez)	1.00	.50	.30
(10)	Alex Johnson	1.00	.50	.30
(11)	Fred Lasher	1.00	.50	.30
(12)	Jim Maloney	1.00	.50	.30
(13)	Rudy May	1.00	.50	.30
(14)	Ken McMullen	1.00	.50	.30
(15)	Andy Messersmith	1.00	.50	.30
(16)	Gerry Moses	1.00	.50	.30
(17)	Syd O'Brien	1.00	.50	.30
(18)	Mel Queen	1.00	.50	.30
(19)	Roger Repoz	1.00	.50	.30
(20)	Archie Reynolds	1.00	.50	.30
(21)	Chico Ruiz	1.00	.50	.30
(22)	Jim Spencer	1.00	.50	.30
(23)	Clyde Wright	1.00	.50	.30
(24)	Billy Wynne	1.00	.50	.30
	Complete Chicago White Sox Album:	10.00	5.00	3.00
(1)	Luis Alvarado	1.00	.50	.30
(2)	Mike Andrews	1.00	.50	.30
(3)	Tom Egan	1.00	.50	.30
(4)	Steve Hamilton	1.00	.50	.30
(5)	Ed Hermann	1.00	.50	.30
(6)	Joel Horlen	1.00	.50	.30
(7)	Tommy John	1.25	.60	.40
(8)	Bart Johnson	1.00	.50	.30
(9)	Jay Johnstone	1.00	.50	.30
(10)	Duane Josephson	1.00	.50	.30
(11)	Pat Kelly	1.00	.50	.30
(12)	Bobby Knoop	1.00	.50	.30
(13)	Carlos May	1.00	.50	.30
(14)	Lee Maye	1.00	.50	.30
(15)	Tom McGraw	1.00	.50	.30
(16)	Bill Melton	1.00	.50	.30
(17)	Rich Morales	1.00	.50	.30
(18)	Tom Murphy	1.00	.50	.30
(19)	Don O'Riley	1.00	.50	.30
(20)	Rick Reichardt	1.00	.50	.30
(21)	Bill Robinson	1.00	.50	.30
(22)	Bob Spence	1.00	.50	.30
(23)	Walt Williams	1.00	.50	.30
(24)	Wilbur Wood	1.00	.50	.30
	Complete Cleveland Indians Album:	10.00	5.00	3.00
(1)	Rick Austin	1.00	.50	.30
(2)	Buddy Bradford	1.00	.50	.30
(3)	Larry Brown	1.00	.50	.30
(4)	Lou Camilli	1.00	.50	.30
(5)	Vince Colbert	1.00	.50	.30
(6)	Ray Fosse	1.00	.50	.30
(7)	Alan Foster	1.00	.50	.30
(8)	Roy Foster	1.00	.50	.30
(9)	Rich Hand	1.00	.50	.30
(10)	Steve Hargan	1.00	.50	.30
(11)	Ken Harrelson	1.00	.50	.30
(12)	Jack Heidemann	1.00	.50	.30
(13)	Phil Hennigan	1.00	.50	.30
(14)	Dennis Higgins	1.00	.50	.30
(15)	Chuck Hinton	1.00	.50	.30
(16)	Tony Horton	1.00	.50	.30
(17)	Ray Lamb	1.00	.50	.30
(18)	Eddie Leon	1.00	.50	.30
(19)	Sam McDowell	1.00	.50	.30
(20)	Graig Nettles	1.25	.60	.40
(21)	Mike Paul	1.00	.50	.30
(22)	Vada Pinson	1.25	.60	.40
(23)	Ken Suarez	1.00	.50	.30
(24)	Ted Uhlaender	1.00	.50	.30
	Complete Detroit Tigers Album:	10.00	5.00	3.00
(1)	Ed Brinkman	1.00	.50	.30
(2)	Gates Brown	1.00	.50	.30
(3)	Ike Brown	1.00	.50	.30
(4)	Les Cain	1.00	.50	.30
(5)	Norm Cash	1.50	.70	.45
(6)	Joe Coleman	1.00	.50	.30
(7)	Bill Freehan	1.00	.50	.30
(8)	Cesar Gutierrez	1.00	.50	.30
(9)	John Hiller	1.00	.50	.30
(10)	Willie Horton	1.00	.50	.30
(11)	Dalton Jones	1.00	.50	.30
(12)	Al Kaline	3.00	1.50	.90
(13)	Mike Kilkenny	1.00	.50	.30
(14)	Mickey Lolich	1.00	.50	.30
(15)	Dick McAuliffe	1.00	.50	.30
(16)	Joe Niekro	1.00	.50	.30
(17)	Jim Northrup	1.00	.50	.30
(18)	Daryl Patterson	1.00	.50	.30
(19)	Jimmie Price	1.00	.50	.30
(20)	Bob Reed	1.00	.50	.30
(21)	Aurelio Rodriguez	1.00	.50	.30
(22)	Fred Scherman	1.00	.50	.30
(23)	Mickey Stanley	1.00	.50	.30
(24)	Tom Timmermann	1.00	.50	.30
	Complete Kansas City Royals Album:	10.00	5.00	3.00
(1)	Ted Abernathy	1.00	.50	.30
(2)	Wally Bunker	1.00	.50	.30
(3)	Tom Burgmeier	1.00	.50	.30
(4)	Bill Butler	1.00	.50	.30
(5)	Bruce Dal Canton	1.00	.50	.30
(6)	Dick Drago	1.00	.50	.30
(7)	Bobby Floyd	1.00	.50	.30
(8)	Gail Hopkins	1.00	.50	.30
(9)	Joe Keough	1.00	.50	.30
(10)	Ed Kirkpatrick	1.00	.50	.30
(11)	Tom Matchick	1.00	.50	.30
(12)	Jerry May	1.00	.50	.30
(13)	Aurelio Monteagudo	1.00	.50	.30
(14)	Dave Morehead	1.00	.50	.30
(15)	Bob Oliver	1.00	.50	.30
(16)	Amos Otis	1.00	.50	.30
(17)	Fred Patek	1.00	.50	.30
(18)	Lou Piniella	1.25	.60	.40
(19)	Cookie Rojas	1.00	.50	.30

(20)	Jim Rooker	1.00	.50	.30
(21)	Paul Schaal	1.00	.50	.30
(22)	Rich Severson	1.00	.50	.30
(23)	George Spriggs	1.00	.50	.30
(24)	Carl Taylor	1.00	.50	.30
	Complete Milwaukee	10.00	5.00	3.00
	Brewers Album:			
(1)	Dave Baldwin	1.00	.50	.30
(2)	Dick Ellsworth	1.00	.50	.30
(3)	John Gelnar	1.00	.50	.30
(4)	Tommy Harper	1.00	.50	.30
(5)	Mike Hegan	1.00	.50	.30
(6)	Bob Humphreys	1.00	.50	.30
(7)	Andy Kosco	1.00	.50	.30
(8)	Lew Krausse	1.00	.50	.30
(9)	Ted Kubiak	1.00	.50	.30
(10)	Skip Lockwood	1.00	.50	.30
(11)	Dave May	1.00	.50	.30
(12)	Bob Meyer	1.00	.50	.30
(13)	John Morris	1.00	.50	.30
(14)	Marty Pattin	1.00	.50	.30
(15)	Roberto Pena	1.00	.50	.30
(16)	Eduardo Rodriguez	1.00	.50	.30
(17)	Phil Roof	1.00	.50	.30
(18)	Ken Sanders	1.00	.50	.30
(19)	Ted Savage	1.00	.50	.30
(20)	Russ Snyder	1.00	.50	.30
(21)	Bob Tillman	1.00	.50	.30
(22)	Bill Voss	1.00	.50	.30
(23)	Danny Walton	1.00	.50	.30
(24)	Floyd Wicker	1.00	.50	.30
	Complete Minnesota	15.00	7.50	4.50
	Twins Album:			
(1)	Brant Alyea	1.00	.50	.30
(2)	Bert Blyleven	1.00	.50	.30
(3)	Dave Boswell	1.00	.50	.30
(4)	Leo Cardenas	1.00	.50	.30
(5)	Rod Carew	2.50	1.25	.70
(6)	Tom Hall	1.00	.50	.30
(7)	Jim Holt	1.00	.50	.30
(8)	Jim Kaat	1.00	.50	.30
(9)	Harmon Killebrew	2.50	1.25	.70
(10)	Charlie Manuel	1.00	.50	.30
(11)	George Mitterwald	1.00	.50	.30
(12)	Tony Oliva	1.25	.60	.40
(13)	Ron Perranoski	1.00	.50	.30
(14)	Jim Perry	1.00	.50	.30
(15)	Frank Quilici	1.00	.50	.30
(16)	Rich Reese	1.00	.50	.30
(17)	Rick Renick	1.00	.50	.30
(18)	Danny Thompson	1.00	.50	.30
(19)	Luis Tiant	1.00	.50	.30
(20)	Tom Tischinski	1.00	.50	.30
(21)	Cesar Tovar	1.00	.50	.30
(22)	Stan Williams	1.00	.50	.30
(23)	Dick Woodson	1.00	.50	.30
(24)	Bill Zepp	1.00	.50	.30
	Complete New York	15.00	7.50	4.50
	Yankees Album:			
(1)	Jack Aker	1.00	.50	.30
(2)	Stan Bahnsen	1.00	.50	.30
(3)	Curt Blefary	1.00	.50	.30
(4)	Bill Burbach	1.00	.50	.30
(5)	Danny Cater	1.00	.50	.30
(6)	Horace Clarke	1.00	.50	.30
(7)	John Ellis	1.00	.50	.30
(8)	Jake Gibbs	1.00	.50	.30
(9)	Ron Hansen	1.00	.50	.30
(10)	Mike Kekich	1.00	.50	.30
(11)	Jerry Kenney	1.00	.50	.30
(12)	Ron Klimkowski	1.00	.50	.30
(13)	Steve Kline	1.00	.50	.30
(14)	Mike McCormick	1.00	.50	.30
(15)	Lindy McDaniel	1.00	.50	.30
(16)	Gene Michael	1.00	.50	.30
(17)	Thurman Munson	1.50	.70	.45
(18)	Bobby Murcer	1.25	.60	.40
(19)	Fritz Peterson	1.00	.50	.30
(20)	Mel Stottlemyre	1.00	.50	.30
(21)	Pete Ward	1.00	.50	.30
(22)	Gary Waslewski	1.00	.50	.30
(23)	Roy White	1.00	.50	.30
(24)	Ron Woods	1.00	.50	.30
	Complete Oakland A's	15.00	7.50	4.50
	Album:			
(1)	Felipe Alou	1.00	.50	.30
(2)	Sal Bando	1.00	.50	.30
(3)	Vida Blue	1.00	.50	.30
(4)	Bert Campaneris	1.00	.50	.30
(5)	Ron Clark	1.00	.50	.30
(6)	Chuck Dobson	1.00	.50	.30
(7)	Dave Duncan	1.00	.50	.30
(8)	Frank Fernandez	1.00	.50	.30
(9)	Rollie Fingers	2.00	1.00	.60
(10)	Dick Green	1.00	.50	.30
(11)	Steve Hovley	1.00	.50	.30
(12)	Catfish Hunter	2.00	1.00	.60
(13)	Reggie Jackson	6.00	3.00	1.75
(14)	Marcel Lacheman	1.00	.50	.30
(15)	Paul Lindblad	1.00	.50	.30
(16)	Bob Locker	1.00	.50	.30
(17)	Don Mincher	1.00	.50	.30
(18)	Rick Monday	1.00	.50	.30
(19)	John Odom	1.00	.50	.30
(20)	Jim Roland	1.00	.50	.30
(21)	Joe Rudi	1.00	.50	.30
(22)	Diego Segui	1.00	.50	.30
(23)	Bob Stickels	1.00	.50	.30
(24)	Gene Tenace	1.00	.50	.30
	Complete Washington	12.50	6.25	3.75
	Senators Album:			
(1)	Bernie Allen	1.00	.50	.30
(2)	Dick Bosman	1.00	.50	.30
(3)	Jackie Brown	1.00	.50	.30
(4)	Paul Casanova	1.00	.50	.30
(5)	Casey Cox	1.00	.50	.30
(6)	Tim Cullen	1.00	.50	.30
(7)	Mike Epstein	1.00	.50	.30

(8)	Curt Flood	1.25	.60	.40
(9)	Joe Foy	1.00	.50	.30
(10)	Jim French	1.00	.50	.30
(11)	Bill Gogolewski	1.00	.50	.30
(12)	Tom Grieve	1.00	.50	.30
(13)	Joe Grzenda	1.00	.50	.30
(14)	Frank Howard	1.25	.60	.40
(15)	Joe Janeski	1.00	.50	.30
(16)	Darold Knowles	1.00	.50	.30
(17)	Elliott Maddox	1.00	.50	.30
(18)	Denny McLain	1.25	.60	.40
(19)	Dave Nelson	1.00	.50	.30
(20)	Horacio Pina	1.00	.50	.30
(21)	Jim Shellenback	1.00	.50	.30
(22)	Ed Stroud	1.00	.50	.30
(23)	Del Unser	1.00	.50	.30
(24)	Don Wert	1.00	.50	.30

1933 DeLong (R333)

HAROLD (PIE) TRAYNOR
PITTSBURGH PIRATES

The DeLong Co. of Boston was among the first to sell baseball cards with gum, issuing a set of 24 cards in 1933. DeLong cards measure about 1-15/16" x 2-15/16", with black-and-white player photos on a color background. The photos show the players in various action poses and positions them in the middle of a miniature stadium setting so that they appear to be giants. Most of the cards are vertically designed, but a few are horizontal. Backs were by Austen Lake, editor of the Boston Transcript, and contain tips to help youngsters become better ballplayers. The ACC designation for this set is R333.

		NM	EX	VG
	Complete Set (24):	30,000	8,000	4,000
	Common Player:	700.00	280.00	140.00
1	"Marty" McManus	1,260	280.00	140.00
2	Al Simmons	945.00	385.00	190.00
3	Oscar Melillo	700.00	280.00	140.00
4	William (Bill) Terry	945.00	385.00	190.00
5	Charlie Gehringer	945.00	385.00	190.00
6	Gordon (Mickey) Cochrane	945.00	385.00	190.00
7	Lou Gehrig	7,700	3,080	1,260
8	Hazen S. (Kiki) Cuyler	945.00	385.00	190.00
9	Bill Urbanski	700.00	280.00	140.00
10	Frank J. (Lefty) O'Doul	980.00	395.00	195.00
11	Freddie Lindstrom	945.00	385.00	190.00
12	Harold (Pie) Traynor	945.00	385.00	190.00
13	"Rabbit" Maranville	945.00	385.00	190.00
14	Vernon "Lefty" Gomez	945.00	385.00	190.00
15	Riggs Stephenson	700.00	280.00	140.00
16	Lon Warneke	700.00	280.00	140.00
17	Pepper Martin	700.00	280.00	140.00
18	Jimmy Dykes	700.00	280.00	140.00
19	Chick Hafey	945.00	385.00	190.00
20	Joe Vosmik	700.00	280.00	140.00
21	Jimmy Foxx (Jimmie)	1,260	505.00	250.00
22	Charles (Chuck) Klein	945.00	385.00	190.00
23	Robert (Lefty) Grove	1,540	595.00	300.00
24	"Goose" Goslin	945.00	385.00	190.00

1934 Al Demaree Die-Cuts (R304)

RUTH RF YANKEES
4

Among the rarest 1930s gum cards are those issued by Dietz Gum Co., a Chicago confectioner, in packages of "Ball Players in Action Chewing Gum." The cards are so rare that the complete checklist may never be known. The set was cataloged in the American Card Catalog. The cards feature photographic portraits of players set upon cartoon bodies drawn by former major league pitcher Demaree. The photo and artwork are generally in black-and-white, while the players on some teams have blue or red uniform details printed on. The cards can be folded to create a stand-up figure, but did not have a background to be cut or torn away, as is common with most die-cut baseball cards. Unfolded, the cards measure 6-1/2" long and from 1-5/8" to 1-3/4" wide, depending on pose.

		NM	EX	VG
	Common Player:	500.00	250.00	150.00
3	Earle Combs	825.00	410.00	245.00
4	Babe Ruth	12,500	6,250	3,750
5	Sam Byrd	600.00	300.00	180.00
6	Tony Lazzeri	825.00	410.00	245.00
7	Frank Crosetti	750.00	375.00	225.00
9	Lou Gehrig	12,000	6,000	3,600
10	Lefty Gomez	825.00	410.00	245.00
11	Mule Haas	500.00	250.00	150.00
12	Evar Swenson	500.00	250.00	150.00
13	Marv Shea	500.00	250.00	150.00
14	Al Simmons/Throwing	825.00	410.00	245.00
15	Jack Hayes	500.00	250.00	150.00
16	Al Simmons/Btg	825.00	410.00	245.00
17	Jimmy Dykes	500.00	250.00	150.00
18	Luke Appling	825.00	410.00	245.00
19	Ted Lyons	825.00	410.00	245.00
20	Red Kress	500.00	250.00	150.00
21	Gee Walker	500.00	250.00	150.00
22	Charlie Gehringer	825.00	410.00	245.00
23	Mickey Cochrane/Catching	825.00	410.00	245.00
24	Mickey Cochrane/Btg	825.00	410.00	245.00
25	Pete Fox	500.00	250.00	150.00
26	Firpo Marberry	500.00	250.00	150.00
28	Mickey Owen	500.00	250.00	150.00
35	Joe Vosmik	500.00	250.00	150.00
38	Harley Boss	500.00	250.00	150.00
41	Jack Burns	500.00	250.00	150.00
45	Ray Pepper	500.00	250.00	150.00
46	Bruce Campbell	500.00	250.00	150.00
48	Art Scharein	500.00	250.00	150.00
49	George Blaeholder	500.00	250.00	150.00
50	Rogers Hornsby	1,100	550.00	330.00
51	Eric McNair	500.00	250.00	150.00
54	Jimmie Foxx	1,250	625.00	375.00
56	Dib Williams	500.00	250.00	150.00
57	Lou Finney	500.00	250.00	150.00
61	Ossie Bluege	500.00	250.00	150.00
63	John Stone	500.00	250.00	150.00
64	Joe Cronin	825.00	410.00	245.00
66	Buddy Myer	500.00	250.00	150.00
67	Earl Whitehill	500.00	250.00	150.00
68	Fred Schulte	500.00	250.00	150.00
71	Ed Morgan	500.00	250.00	150.00
74	Carl Reynolds	500.00	250.00	150.00
76	Bill Cissell	500.00	250.00	150.00
77	Johnny Hodapp	500.00	250.00	150.00
78	Dusty Cooke	500.00	250.00	150.00
79	Lefty Grove	825.00	410.00	245.00
80	Max Bishop	500.00	250.00	150.00
81	Hughie Critz	500.00	250.00	150.00
82	Gus Mancuso	500.00	250.00	150.00
83	Kiddo Davis	500.00	250.00	150.00
84	Blondy Ryan	500.00	250.00	150.00
86	Travis Jackson	825.00	410.00	245.00
87	Mel Ott	1,100	550.00	330.00
89	Bill Terry	825.00	410.00	245.00
90	Carl Hubbell	1,100	550.00	330.00
91	Tony Cuccinello	500.00	250.00	150.00
92	Al Lopez	825.00	410.00	245.00
94	Johnny Frederick	500.00	250.00	150.00
96	Hack Wilson	850.00	425.00	255.00
97	Danny Taylor	500.00	250.00	150.00
98	Van Mungo	500.00	250.00	150.00
99	John Frederick	500.00	250.00	150.00
100	Sam Leslie	500.00	250.00	150.00
101	Sparky Adams	500.00	250.00	150.00
102a	Mark Koenig	500.00	250.00	150.00
102b	Ernie Lombardi	825.00	410.00	245.00
107	Syl Johnson	500.00	250.00	150.00
108	Jim Bottomley	825.00	410.00	245.00
110	Adam Comorosky	500.00	250.00	150.00
111	Dick Bartell	500.00	250.00	150.00
112	Harvey Hendrick	500.00	250.00	150.00
115	Don Hurst/Btg	500.00	250.00	150.00
117	Prince Oana	900.00	450.00	270.00
118	Ed Holley	500.00	250.00	150.00
120	Don Hurst/Throwing	500.00	250.00	150.00
121	Spud Davis	500.00	250.00	150.00
122	George Watkins	500.00	250.00	150.00
123	Frankie Frisch	825.00	410.00	245.00
124	Pepper Martin/Btg	500.00	250.00	150.00
125	Ripper Collins	500.00	250.00	150.00
126	Dizzy Dean	1,250	625.00	375.00
127	Pepper Martin/Fielding	500.00	250.00	150.00
128	Joe Medwick	825.00	410.00	245.00
129	Leo Durocher	825.00	410.00	245.00
130	Ernie Orsatti	500.00	250.00	150.00
132	Shanty Hogan	500.00	250.00	150.00
133a	Wes Shulmerich (Schulmerich)	500.00	250.00	150.00
133b	Randy Moore	500.00	250.00	150.00
135	Wally Berger	500.00	250.00	150.00
136	Pinky Whitney	500.00	250.00	150.00
137	Wally Berger	500.00	250.00	150.00
139	Rabbit Maranville	825.00	410.00	245.00
140	Ben Cantwell	500.00	250.00	150.00
141	Gus Suhr	500.00	250.00	150.00

		NM	EX	VG
142	Earl Grace	500.00	250.00	150.00
144	Arky Vaughan	825.00	410.00	245.00
145	Pie Traynor/Hitting	825.00	410.00	245.00
146	Tommy Thevenow	500.00	250.00	150.00
147	Lloyd Waner	825.00	410.00	245.00
148	Paul Waner	825.00	410.00	245.00
149	Pie Traynor/Throwing	825.00	410.00	245.00
151	Kiki Cuyler	825.00	410.00	245.00
152	Gabby Hartnett	825.00	410.00	245.00
153	Chuck Klein/Throwing	825.00	410.00	245.00
154	Chuck Klein	825.00	410.00	245.00
155	Bill Jurges	500.00	250.00	150.00
156	Woody English	500.00	250.00	150.00
158	Billy Herman	825.00	410.00	245.00
160	Charlie Grimm	500.00	250.00	150.00
161	Cy Rigler/Umpire	900.00	450.00	275.00
162	Bill Klem/Umpire	1,250	625.00	375.00
167	George Hildebrand/Umpire	500.00	250.00	150.00

(Observed specimens of cards below have had the tabs removed making it impossible to identify card numbers.)

		NM	EX	VG
----	Willie Kamm	500.00	250.00	150.00
----	Pinky Higgins	500.00	250.00	150.00
----	Bob Johnson	500.00	250.00	150.00
----	Roy Mahaffey	500.00	250.00	150.00
----	Buck Jordan	500.00	250.00	150.00

1950-51 Denia Puerto Rican League

JIM DAVIS

This issue was produced in conjunction with the 1950-51 Puerto Rican League winter season. Measurements vary slightly from a norm of about 1-3/4" x 2-1/8". Cards have colorized portrait photos with blank backs, probably intended to be glued into an album. Cards are unnumbered. This checklist is alphabetized, with gaps left for what is believed to be 57 uncataloged cards. Some of the players are veterans of the Negro Leagues and American major and minor leagues. Black-and-white reprints of the cards are known. A few cards have been found with a prize-redemption stamp on back.

		NM	EX	VG
Common Player:		125.00	65.00	40.00
(1)	Alberto Alberdeston	125.00	65.00	40.00
(2)	Jaime Almendro	125.00	65.00	40.00
(3)	Yiyo Alonso	125.00	65.00	40.00
(4)	Luis (Tite) Arroyo	150.00	75.00	45.00
(5)	Pedro J. Arroyo	125.00	65.00	40.00
(6)	Joe Atkins	150.00	75.00	45.00
(7)	Eugene Baker	200.00	100.00	60.00
(8)	Dan Bankhead	200.00	100.00	60.00
(9)	Sammy Bankhead	1,200	600.00	360.00
(10)	Ramon Bayron	125.00	65.00	40.00
(11)	Hiram Bithorn	200.00	100.00	60.00
(12)	Rafael Blasini	125.00	65.00	40.00
(13)	Bob Boyd	150.00	75.00	45.00
(14)	Roger Breard	125.00	65.00	40.00
(15)	Stan Breard	125.00	65.00	40.00
(16)	Barney Brown	1,000	500.00	300.00
(17)	Raymond Brown	2,000	1,000	600.00
(18)	Willard Brown	2,000	1,000	600.00
(19)	Jose A. Burgos	125.00	65.00	40.00
(20)	Joe Buzas	125.00	65.00	40.00
(21)	Luis R. Cabrera	125.00	65.00	40.00
(22)	Rafael Casanovas	125.00	65.00	40.00
(23)	N. Zurdo Castro	125.00	65.00	40.00
(24)	Perucho Cepeda	800.00	400.00	240.00
(25)	T. Gomez Checo	125.00	65.00	40.00
(26)	Al Cihoki (Cihocki)	125.00	65.00	40.00
(27)	Buster Clarkson	250.00	125.00	75.00
(28)	Francisco Coimbre	800.00	400.00	240.00
(29)	Eugene Collins	350.00	175.00	105.00
(30)	Monchile Concepcion	150.00	75.00	45.00
(31)	Charlie Corin	125.00	65.00	40.00
(32)	Herminio Cortfu	125.00	65.00	40.00
(33)	Johnny Cox	125.00	65.00	40.00
(34)	George Crowe	200.00	100.00	60.00
(35)	Jim Davis	125.00	65.00	40.00
(36)	Johnny Davis	450.00	225.00	135.00
(37)	Piper Davis	450.00	225.00	135.00
(38)	Leon Day	6,000	3,000	1,800
(39)	Ellis "Cot" Deal	150.00	75.00	45.00
(40)	Jack Dittmer	125.00	65.00	40.00
(41)	Verdes Drake	150.00	75.00	45.00
(42)	Saturnino Escalera	125.00	65.00	40.00
(43)	C. Guillaro Estrella	125.00	65.00	40.00
(44)	S. Federico	125.00	65.00	40.00
(45)	Dumbo Fernandez	125.00	65.00	40.00
(46)	Elias Frias	125.00	65.00	40.00

		NM	EX	VG
(47)	Les Fusselmann (Fusselman)	125.00	65.00	40.00
(48)	Felipe Garcia	125.00	65.00	40.00
(49)	(Carden) Gillenwater	125.00	65.00	40.00
(50)	Jim Gilliam	250.00	125.00	75.00
(51)	Ruben Gomez	200.00	100.00	60.00
(52)	Faelo Gonzalez	125.00	65.00	40.00
(53)	Gely Goyco	125.00	65.00	40.00
(54)	Jack Harshmann (Harshman)	125.00	65.00	40.00
(55)	Rudy Hernandez	125.00	65.00	40.00
(56)	Roy Hughes	125.00	65.00	40.00
(57)	Pachy Irizarry	125.00	65.00	40.00
(58)	Indian (Indio) Jiminez	125.00	65.00	40.00
(59)	Sam Jones	125.00	65.00	40.00
(60)	Walt Judnich	125.00	65.00	40.00
(61)	Russ Kearns	125.00	65.00	40.00
(62)	Billy Klaus	150.00	75.00	45.00
(63)	Jim Lamarque	350.00	175.00	105.00
(64)	Red Lynn	125.00	65.00	40.00
(65)	Bob Malloy	125.00	65.00	40.00
(66)	Clifford Mapes	125.00	65.00	40.00
(67)	Canena Marquez	450.00	225.00	135.00
(68)	Achin Matos	125.00	65.00	40.00
(69)	Benny Meyers	125.00	65.00	40.00
(70)	Henry Miller	150.00	75.00	45.00
(71)	Oscar Mir Flores	125.00	65.00	40.00
(72)	Jose E. Montalvo	125.00	65.00	40.00
(73)	Willie Morales	125.00	65.00	40.00
(74)	Gallego Munoz	125.00	65.00	40.00
(75)	Earl Naylor	125.00	65.00	40.00
(76)	Ernest Nevel	125.00	65.00	40.00
(77)	Don Nicholas	125.00	65.00	40.00
(78)	John O'Donnell	125.00	65.00	40.00
(79)	Guayuvin Olivo	150.00	75.00	45.00
(80)	Miguel Payano	125.00	65.00	40.00
(81)	Les Peden	125.00	65.00	40.00
(82)	Juan Perez	125.00	65.00	40.00
(83)	Palomo Perez	125.00	65.00	40.00
(84)	German Pizarro	125.00	65.00	40.00
(85)	Dave Pope	150.00	75.00	45.00
(86)	Milton Ralat	125.00	65.00	40.00
(87)	Enrique Reinoso	125.00	65.00	40.00
(88)	Roberto Rivera	125.00	65.00	40.00
(89)	Julio Rodriguez	125.00	65.00	40.00
(90)	Pedro Rodriguez	125.00	65.00	40.00
(91)	Domingo Rosello	125.00	65.00	40.00
(92)	Joe Rossi	125.00	65.00	40.00
(93)	Miguel Rueda	125.00	65.00	40.00
(94)	Ramon Salgado	125.00	65.00	40.00
(95)	Juan Sanchez	125.00	65.00	40.00
(96)	Carlos M. Santiago	125.00	65.00	40.00
(97)	Jose G. Santiago	125.00	65.00	40.00
(98)	V. Scarpatte	125.00	65.00	40.00
(99)	Jose Seda	125.00	65.00	40.00
(100)	Barney Serrell	350.00	175.00	105.00
(101)	Al Smith	200.00	100.00	60.00
(102)	Jose St. Clair	125.00	65.00	40.00
(103)	Tetelo Sterling	125.00	65.00	40.00
(104)	Russ Sullivan	125.00	65.00	40.00
(105)	Lonnie Summers	150.00	75.00	45.00
(106)	Jim Tabor	125.00	65.00	40.00
(107)	Bert Thiel	125.00	65.00	40.00
(108)	Valmy Thomas	125.00	65.00	40.00
(109)	Bob Thurman	350.00	175.00	105.00
(110)	Tiant Tineo	125.00	65.00	40.00
(111)	Gilberto Torres	125.00	65.00	40.00
(112)	Manuel Trabaux	125.00	65.00	40.00
(113)	Joe Tuminelli	125.00	65.00	40.00
(114)	Jose L. Velazquez	125.00	65.00	40.00
(115)	Ben Wade	150.00	75.00	45.00
(116)	Johnny Williams	250.00	125.00	75.00
(117)	Marvin Williams	150.00	75.00	45.00
(118)	Artie Wilson	450.00	225.00	135.00
(119)	Pedrin Zorrilla	125.00	65.00	40.00
(120)	Pito entrevista a Hornsby	300.00	150.00	90.00
(121)	El galardon del triunfo	125.00	65.00	40.00
(122)	Fanaticos de alta posicion	125.00	65.00	40.00
(123)	VOLO LA VERJA	125.00	65.00	40.00

1950-51 Denia Puerto Rican League - Action

115- Gilliam dió out a Casanovas

These 2-1/2" x 3-1/2" cards are part of a set of about 150 covering many different sports. The pictures are colorized photographs and the cards are blank-backed, intended to be glued into an album. The number of baseball subjects is not known. Confirmed subjects are listed here, with identified players listed parenthetically.

		NM	EX	VG
Common Card:		50.00	25.00	15.00
1	Tetelo tambien joronea. (Tetelo Vargas)	85.00	40.00	25.00
2	Taborn saca en home. (Earl Taborn)	50.00	25.00	15.00
3	Se la aguo la blanqueada.	50.00	25.00	15.00
4	R. Blasini se lesiona. (Rafael Blasini)	50.00	25.00	15.00
5	Atkins mofa, Polaco safe. (Joe Atkins)	50.00	25.00	15.00
6	CERCADO-	50.00	25.00	15.00
7	Pitcher se desliza - safe.	50.00	25.00	15.00
8	Fdo. Ramos tras homer (Fernando Ramos)	50.00	25.00	15.00
9	Wilson safe en terecera. (Artie Wilson)	65.00	30.00	20.00
10	Tiro malo - SAFE.	50.00	25.00	15.00
11	VILLODAS LO ESPERA - OUT. (Luis Villodas)	50.00	25.00	15.00
12	Perry da out a Gilliam - (Alonso Perry, Jim Gilliam)	85.00	40.00	25.00
13	Safe en primera -	50.00	25.00	15.00
14	Medina obsequia a Brown. (Medina Chapman, Willard Brown)	200.00	100.00	60.00
15	Tiro malo, Almendaro anota. (Jaime Almendro)	50.00	25.00	15.00
16	Ramos toco primero - OUT. (Fernando Ramos)	50.00	25.00	15.00
17	Brazo contra brazo -	50.00	25.00	15.00
18	Pedroso felicitado tras homer - (Fernando Pedroso)	50.00	25.00	15.00
19	QUE PASA, CEFO? (Cefo Conde)	50.00	25.00	15.00
20	Canena estafa home - (Canena Marquez)	65.00	30.00	20.00
21	Buen slide - SAFE.	50.00	25.00	15.00
22	Mucha vista, Powell. (Bill Powell)	50.00	25.00	15.00
23	OUT FORZADO.	50.00	25.00	15.00
24	Alomar out en home. (Guinea Alomar)	50.00	25.00	15.00
25	Regreso a base - SAFE.	50.00	25.00	15.00
26	Pitcher trata sorprender - SAFE.	50.00	25.00	15.00
27	LOS RECUERDA USTED?	50.00	25.00	15.00
28	Leo Thomas sale de juego. (Leo Thomas)	50.00	25.00	15.00
29	Atkins es felicitado por tribu. (Joe Atkins)	50.00	25.00	15.00
30	Trio campeonil cagueno (Manuel Hernandez, Quincy Trouppe, Chet Brewer)	135.00	65.00	40.00
31	Llegando y llegando -	50.00	25.00	15.00
32	El fotografoen accion -	50.00	25.00	15.00
33	El fotografo en accion	50.00	25.00	15.00
34	No me toques Arroyito - OUT. (Luis "Tite" Arroyo)	50.00	25.00	15.00
35	Taborn propina out. (Earl Taborn)	50.00	25.00	15.00
36	El Mucaro conecta homer - (Bob Thurman)	65.00	30.00	20.00
37	PANTALONES Y FALDAS. (Jose G. Santiago)	50.00	25.00	15.00
38	Buzas en la derrota. (Joe Buzas)	50.00	25.00	15.00
39	El Gran Jurado se reune. (Raymond Brown)	135.00	65.00	40.00
40	Canena se desliza - (Canena Marquez)	65.00	30.00	20.00
41	Que dijo el umpire?	50.00	25.00	15.00
42	Bernier sabe escurrirse - (Carlos Bernier)	50.00	25.00	15.00
43	Se la escapo, la bola - SAFE.	50.00	25.00	15.00
44	Squeeze play perfecto.	50.00	25.00	15.00
45	Cuidado, que la lleva!	50.00	25.00	15.00
46	Que el umpire diga -	50.00	25.00	15.00
47	Pepe Lucas boto la bola. (Pepe Lucas)	50.00	25.00	15.00
48	Gachito se apunta hit.	50.00	25.00	15.00
49	Peloteros o Luchadores?	50.00	25.00	15.00
50	Otoniel lo toca - OUT. (Otoniel Ortiz)	50.00	25.00	15.00
51	Premian a Jorge Rosas. (Jorge Rosas)	50.00	25.00	15.00
52	Markland dio homerun - (Jim Markland)	50.00	25.00	15.00
53	Blasini safe en primera. (Rafael Blasini)	50.00	25.00	15.00
54	Graham conecto homer - (Jack Graham)	50.00	25.00	15.00
55	Penalver se prepara - SAFE.	50.00	25.00	15.00
56	No quiere riesgos	50.00	25.00	15.00
57	Bin Torres esquiva - SAFE. (Bin Torres)	50.00	25.00	15.00
58	Mutua embestida- SAFE.	50.00	25.00	15.00
59	Lo sacaron a media base.	50.00	25.00	15.00
60	Llego transqueando.	50.00	25.00	15.00
61	Quedate quieto - dice el coach.	50.00	25.00	15.00
62	Buscando en vano su presa -	50.00	25.00	15.00
63	Besando la base?	50.00	25.00	15.00
64	Pescaron al Jueyito. (Jueyito Andrade)	50.00	25.00	15.00
65	Greco da tremendo toletazo.	50.00	25.00	15.00
66	Thomas catcher, Wallaesa al bate. (Valmy Thomas, Jack Wallaesa)	50.00	25.00	15.00
67	Trofeos de TRIPLE CAMPEON.	50.00	25.00	15.00
74	H. Reyes lanza, Sanchez Batea. (Herminio Reyes, Juan Sanchez)	50.00	25.00	15.00
77	Wilson apacigua a Bernier . . (Artie Wilson, Carlos Bernier)	85.00	40.00	25.00
78	Cogida de cuatro estrellas . . .	50.00	25.00	15.00
80	Davis out de Gachito - Wallaesa- . . (Johnny Davis, Jack Wallaesa)	50.00	25.00	15.00
81	Arroyo busca double-play. (Pedro J. Arroyo)	50.00	25.00	15.00
82	Ruben sale por lesion. (Ruben Gomez)	50.00	25.00	15.00

		NM	EX	VG
83	SAFE EN EL PLATO.	50.00	25.00	15.00
84	Buen esfuerzo, pero en vano . . .	50.00	25.00	15.00
85	ESTAS TRISTE, JONES? (Sam Jones)	50.00	25.00	15.00
87	Equipo ESTRELLAS NATIVAS	50.00	25.00	15.00
88	Arroyo batea, Scarpatte recibe (Pedro J. Arroyo, V. Scarpatte)	50.00	25.00	15.00
93	Cihoki recoge . . . out (Al Cihocki)	50.00	25.00	15.00
95	El arbitro pensativo . . . out.	50.00	25.00	15.00
97	Buena atrapada . . . del fotografo.	50.00	25.00	15.00
103	Villodas da hit. . . (Luis Villodas)	50.00	25.00	15.00
106	HIT EL BATAZO . . .	50.00	25.00	15.00
110	LO COGIERON LLEGANDO . . .	50.00	25.00	15.00
115	Gilliam dio out a Casanovas (Jim Gilliam, Rafael Casanovas)	85.00	40.00	25.00
124	Canena pone fuera a Bernier . . . (Canena Marquez, Carlos Bernier)	50.00	25.00	15.00
137	Terminado el swing . . .	50.00	25.00	15.00

1932 Charles Denby Cigars Cubs

This series of Chicago Cubs postcards was issued by the Fendrich Cigar Co., Evansville, Ind., to promote its Charles Denby brand in 1932. It is the last major tobacco-card issue produced before World War II. The cards are a standard postcard size (5-1/4" x 3-3/8") and feature a glossy black-and-white player photo with a facsimile autograph. In typical postcard style, the back of the card is divided in half, with a printed player profile on the left and room for the mailing address on the right. The back also includes an advertisement for Charles Denby Cigars, the mild five-cent cigar "for men who like to inhale." Eight players are known but more may exist.

		NM	EX	VG
Complete Set (8):		3,750	1,850	1,100
Common Player:		500.00	200.00	100.00
(1)	Hazen Cuyler	625.00	250.00	125.00
(2)	Elwood English	500.00	200.00	100.00
(3)	Charles J. Grimm	500.00	200.00	100.00
(4)	William Herman	750.00	300.00	150.00
(5)	Rogers Hornsby	1,000	400.00	200.00
(6)	William F. Jurges	500.00	200.00	100.00
(7)	Riggs Stephenson	500.00	200.00	100.00
(8)	Lonnie Warneke	500.00	200.00	100.00

1909 Derby Cigars N.Y. Giants

Although there is no advertising on these cards to indicate their origin, it is believed that this set was issued by Derby Cigars, a product of American Tobacco Co. A dozen different subjects, all New York Giants, have been found. The cards, many of which appear to be hand-cut measure about 1-3/4" x 2-3/4".

The cards feature an oval black-and-white player portrait on a red background. The player's name and position are in a white strip at bottom.

		NM	EX	VG
Complete Set (12):		40,000	16,000	8,000
Common Player:		3,250	1,300	650.00
(1)	Josh Devore	3,250	1,300	650.00
(2)	Larry Doyle	3,250	1,300	650.00
(3)	Art Fletcher	3,250	1,300	650.00
(4)	Buck Herzog	3,250	1,300	650.00
(5)	Rube Marquard	3,750	1,500	750.00
(6)	Christy Mathewson	7,500	3,000	1,500
(7)	Fred Merkle	3,250	1,300	650.00
(8)	Chief Meyers	3,250	1,300	650.00
(9)	Red Murray	3,250	1,300	650.00
(10)	John McGraw	3,500	1,400	700.00
(11)	Fred Snodgrass	3,250	1,300	650.00
(12)	Hooks Wiltse	3,250	1,300	650.00

1977 Detroit Caesars Discs

Virtually identical in format to the several locally sponsored disc sets of the previous year, these 3-3/8" diameter player discs were sponsored by a professional slow-pitch softball team. Discs once again feature black-and-white player portrait photos in the center of a baseball design. The left and right panels are in one of several bright colors. Licensed by the players' association through Mike Schechter Associates, the player photos carry no uniform logos. Backs are printed in green. The unnumbered discs are checklisted here alphabetically.

		NM	EX	VG
Complete Set (70):		125.00	65.00	35.00
Common Player:		2.50	1.25	.75
(1)	Sal Bando	2.50	1.25	.75
(2)	Buddy Bell	2.50	1.25	.75
(3)	Johnny Bench	6.00	3.00	1.75
(4)	Larry Bowa	2.50	1.25	.75
(5)	Steve Braun	2.50	1.25	.75
(6)	George Brett	15.00	7.50	4.50
(7)	Lou Brock	6.00	3.00	1.75
(8)	Jeff Burroughs	2.50	1.25	.75
(9)	Bert Campaneris	2.50	1.25	.75
(10)	John Candelaria	2.50	1.25	.75
(11)	Jose Cardenal	2.50	1.25	.75
(12)	Rod Carew	4.50	2.25	1.25
(13)	Steve Carlton	4.50	2.25	1.25
(14)	Dave Cash	2.50	1.25	.75
(15)	Cesar Cedeno	2.50	1.25	.75
(16)	Ron Cey	2.50	1.25	.75
(17)	Dave Concepcion	2.50	1.25	.75
(18)	Dennis Eckersley	3.00	1.50	.90
(19)	Mark Fidrych	5.00	2.50	1.50
(20)	Rollie Fingers	5.00	2.50	1.50
(21)	Carlton Fisk	6.00	3.00	1.75
(22)	George Foster	2.50	1.25	.75
(23)	Wayne Garland	2.50	1.25	.75
(24)	Ralph Garr	2.50	1.25	.75
(25)	Steve Garvey	4.00	2.00	1.25
(26)	Cesar Geronimo	2.50	1.25	.75
(27)	Bobby Grich	2.50	1.25	.75
(28)	Ken Griffey Sr.	2.50	1.25	.75
(29)	Don Gullett	2.50	1.25	.75
(30)	Mike Hargrove	2.50	1.25	.75
(31)	Al Hrabosky	2.50	1.25	.75
(32)	Jim Hunter	5.00	2.50	1.50
(33)	Reggie Jackson	9.00	4.50	2.75
(34)	Randy Jones	2.50	1.25	.75
(35)	Dave Kingman	3.50	1.75	1.00
(36)	Jerry Koosman	2.50	1.25	.75
(37)	Dave LaRoche	2.50	1.25	.75
(38)	Greg Luzinski	2.50	1.25	.75
(39)	Fred Lynn	2.50	1.25	.75
(40)	Bill Madlock	2.50	1.25	.75
(41)	Rick Manning	2.50	1.25	.75
(42)	Jon Matlock	2.50	1.25	.75
(43)	John Mayberry	2.50	1.25	.75
(44)	Hal McRae	2.50	1.25	.75
(45)	Andy Messersmith	2.50	1.25	.75
(46)	Rick Monday	2.50	1.25	.75
(47)	John Montefusco	2.50	1.25	.75
(48)	Joe Morgan	6.00	3.00	1.75
(49)	Thurman Munson	5.00	2.50	1.50
(50)	Bobby Murcer	2.50	1.25	.75
(51)	Bill North	2.50	1.25	.75
(52)	Jim Palmer	6.00	3.00	1.75
(53)	Tony Perez	5.00	2.50	1.50
(54)	Jerry Reuss	2.50	1.25	.75
(55)	Brooks Robinson	5.00	2.50	1.50
(56)	Pete Rose	15.00	7.50	4.50
(57)	Joe Rudi	2.50	1.25	.75
(58)	Nolan Ryan	30.00	15.00	9.00
(59)	Manny Sanguillen	2.50	1.25	.75
(60)	Mike Schmidt	15.00	7.50	4.50
(61)	Tom Seaver	7.50	3.75	2.25
(62)	Bill Singer	2.50	1.25	.75

---

(63)	Willie Stargell	6.00	3.00	1.75
(64)	Rusty Staub	3.50	1.75	1.00
(65)	Luis Tiant	2.50	1.25	.75
(66)	Bob Watson	2.50	1.25	.75
(67)	Butch Wynegar	2.50	1.25	.75
(68)	Carl Yastrzemski	7.50	3.75	2.25
(69)	Robin Yount	6.00	3.00	1.75
(70)	Richie Zisk	2.50	1.25	.75

1908 Detroit Free Press Tigers Postcards

Most of the stars of the 1907-09 American League Champion Detroit Tigers are found in this set of postcards issued by a local newspaper and reportedly sold at the stadium for $1 a set. The cards are 3-1/2" x 5-1/4", printed in black-and-white. Fronts have a border around the photo with the line, "Copyright by the Detroit Free Press, 1908" beneath the photo. At bottom is the player's last name in capital letters with his position in parentheses. Backs have standard postcard indicia. The unnumbered cards are checklisted here alphabetically. It is possible this list is not complete.

		NM	EX	VG
Complete Set (11):		4,000	2,000	1,200
Common Player:		400.00	200.00	120.00
(1)	Ty Cobb	950.00	475.00	285.00
(2)	Sam Crawford	400.00	200.00	120.00
(3)	Wild Bill Donovan	400.00	200.00	120.00
(4)	Hughie Jennings	400.00	200.00	120.00
(5)	Ed Killian	400.00	200.00	120.00
(6)	Matty McIntyre	400.00	200.00	120.00
(7)	George Mullen (Mullin)	400.00	200.00	120.00
(8)	Charley O'Leary	400.00	200.00	120.00
(9)	Boss Schmidt	400.00	200.00	120.00
(10)	Ed Summer (Summers)	400.00	200.00	120.00
(11)	Ed Willett	400.00	200.00	120.00

1934 Detroit Tigers Team Issue

This set of blank-back, postcard-sized black-and-white player photo cards is presumed to have been a team issue. Photos have white borders with the wider top border having three stripes. Player name and position are printed within the picture. The unnumbered cards are checklisted here alphabetically.

		NM	EX	VG
Complete Set (23):		1,200	600.00	350.00
Common Player:		60.00	30.00	18.00
(1)	Eldon Auker	60.00	30.00	18.00
(2)	Del Baker	60.00	30.00	18.00
(3)	Tommy Bridges	60.00	30.00	18.00
(4)	Mickey Cochrane	150.00	75.00	45.00
(5)	General Crowder	60.00	30.00	18.00
(6)	Frank Doljack	60.00	30.00	18.00
(7)	Carl Fischer	60.00	30.00	18.00
(8)	Pete Fox	60.00	30.00	18.00
(9)	Charlie Gehringer	150.00	75.00	45.00
(10)	Goose Goslin	150.00	75.00	45.00
(11)	"Hank" Greenberg	250.00	125.00	75.00
(12)	Luke Hamlin	60.00	30.00	18.00
(13)	Ray Hayworth	60.00	30.00	18.00
(14)	Elon Hogsett	60.00	30.00	18.00
(15)	Firpo Marberry	60.00	30.00	18.00
(16)	Marvin Owen	60.00	30.00	18.00
(17)	Cy Perkins	60.00	30.00	18.00
(18)	Billy Rogell	60.00	30.00	18.00

		NM	EX	VG
(19)	Schoolboy Rowe	60.00	30.00	18.00
(20)	Heinie Schuble	60.00	30.00	18.00
(21)	Vic Sorrell	60.00	30.00	18.00
(22)	Gee Walker	60.00	30.00	18.00
(23)	Jo-Jo White	60.00	30.00	18.00

1935 Detroit Free Press Tigers

Henry Greenberg

Colorized photos with brightly colored backgrounds and borders are featured in this series of newspaper pictures featuring the World Champion Detroit Tigers. About 9" x 11", the pictures are blank-backed. It is unclear whether these pictures were included with newspaper purchases or were sold as sets. The unnumbered pictures are checklisted here in alphabetical order. In the American Card Catalog, the set carried the designation M120.

		NM	EX	VG
Complete Set (21):		1,000	500.00	300.00
Common Player:		40.00	20.00	12.00
(1)	Eldon Auker	40.00	20.00	12.00
(2)	Del Baker	40.00	20.00	12.00
(3)	Tommy Bridges	40.00	20.00	12.00
(4)	Flea Clifton	40.00	20.00	12.00
(5)	Gordon Stanley (Mickey) Cochrane	100.00	50.00	30.00
(6)	Alvin Crowder	40.00	20.00	12.00
(7)	Frank Doljack	40.00	20.00	12.00
(8)	Carl Fischer	40.00	20.00	12.00
(9)	Pete Fox	40.00	20.00	12.00
(10)	Charles Gehringer	75.00	37.50	22.50
(11)	Goose Goslin	75.00	37.50	22.50
(12)	Henry Greenberg	125.00	65.00	35.00
(13)	Luke Hamlin	40.00	20.00	12.00
(14)	Ray Hayworth	40.00	20.00	12.00
(15)	Elon Hogsett	40.00	20.00	12.00
(16)	Joe Louis (boxer)	100.00	50.00	30.00
(17)	Firpo Marberry	40.00	20.00	12.00
(18)	Marvin Owen	40.00	20.00	12.00
(19)	Cy Perkins	40.00	20.00	12.00
(20)	Billy Rogell	40.00	20.00	12.00
(21)	Lynwood (Schoolboy) Rowe	45.00	22.50	13.50
(22)	Heinie Schuble	40.00	20.00	12.00
(23)	Vic Sorrell	40.00	20.00	12.00
(24)	Joe Sullivan	40.00	20.00	12.00
(25)	Jerry Walker	40.00	20.00	12.00
(26)	Jo-Jo White	40.00	20.00	12.00

1968 Detroit Free Press Bubblegumless Tiger Cards

DARYL Patterson
PITCHER

The World Champion Tigers are featured in this series of newspaper inserts published in August, 1968, by the "Detroit Magazine" rotogravure section of the Sunday "Detroit Free Press." The full-color fronts and the backs were printed on separate pages to allow them to be cut out and pasted on cardboard to make a baseball card. Backs are horizontally formatted and include a drawing of the player at left; biographical data and recent stats at right. Card elements measure 2-1/2" x 3-1/2". Values quoted are for front/back pairs. Unmatched fronts are priced at 45 percent of the prices shown; backs should be priced at 30 percent.

		NM	EX	VG
Complete Set, Uncut Pages:		250.00	125.00	75.00
Complete Set, Singles (28):		200.00	100.00	60.00
Common Player:		10.00	5.00	3.00
(1)	Gates Brown	10.00	5.00	3.00

		NM	EX	VG
(2)	Norm Cash	15.00	7.50	4.50
(3)	Tony Cuccinello	10.00	5.00	3.00
(4)	Pat Dobson	10.00	5.00	3.00
(5)	Bill Freehan	12.50	6.25	3.75
(6)	John Hiller	10.00	5.00	3.00
(7)	Willie Horton	10.00	5.00	3.00
(8)	Al Kaline	35.00	17.50	10.50
(9)	Fred Lasher	10.00	5.00	3.00
(10)	Mickey Lolich	15.00	7.50	4.50
(11)	Tom Matchick	10.00	5.00	3.00
(12)	Dick McAuliffe	10.00	5.00	3.00
(13)	Denny McLain	12.50	6.25	3.75
(14)	Don McMahon	10.00	5.00	3.00
(15)	Wally Moses	10.00	5.00	3.00
(16)	Jim Northrup	10.00	5.00	3.00
(17)	Ray Oyler	10.00	5.00	3.00
(18)	Daryl Patterson	10.00	5.00	3.00
(19)	Jim Price	10.00	5.00	3.00
(20)	Johnny Sain	10.00	5.00	3.00
(21)	Mayo Smith	10.00	5.00	3.00
(22)	Joe Sparma	10.00	5.00	3.00
(23)	Mickey Stanley	10.00	5.00	3.00
(24)	Dick Tracewski	10.00	5.00	3.00
(25)	Jon Warden	10.00	5.00	3.00
(26)	Don Wert	10.00	5.00	3.00
(27)	Earl Wilson	10.00	5.00	3.00
(28)	Jon Wyatt (John)	10.00	5.00	3.00

1978 Detroit Free Press Tigers

In its Sunday color magazine of April 16, 1978, the newspaper printed presumably authorized reproductions of all 1978 Topps cards which featured members of the Detroit Tigers. The magazine has a cover photo of Mark Fidrych. In the centerspread, reproduced in color, are pictures of the fronts of 20 Tigers cards. Two pages later the cards of three departed Tigers, five multi-player rookie cards and the team card are printed, also in full color. Three more pages have the backs of the cards, printed in black-and-white, rather than the orange-and-blue of genuine Topps cards. Instructions with the article invited readers to cut out the fronts and backs and paste them onto pieces of cardboard to make their own cards. Values shown are for complete front/back pairs.

		NM	EX	VG
Complete Magazine:		60.00	30.00	20.00
Complete Set, Singles (28):		30.00	15.00	9.00
Common Player:		3.00	1.50	.90
21	Steve Kemp	3.00	1.50	.90
45	Mark Fidrych	6.00	3.00	1.75
68	Steve Foucault	3.00	1.50	.90
94	Chuck Scrivener	3.00	1.50	.90
124	Dave Rozema	3.00	1.50	.90
151	Milt Wilcox	3.00	1.50	.90
176	Milt May	3.00	1.50	.90
232	Mickey Stanley	3.00	1.50	.90
258	John Hiller	3.00	1.50	.90
286	Ben Oglivie	3.00	1.50	.90
342	Aurelio Rodriguez	3.00	1.50	.90
370	Rusty Staub	6.00	3.00	1.75
385	Tito Fuentes	3.00	1.50	.90
404	Tigers Team Card (Color checklist back.)	6.00	3.00	1.75
456	Vern Ruhle	3.00	1.50	.90
480	Ron LeFlore	3.50	1.75	1.00
515	Tim Corcoran	3.00	1.50	.90
536	Roric Harrison	3.00	1.50	.90
559	Phil Mankowski	3.00	1.50	.90
607	Fernando Arroyo	3.00	1.50	.90
633	Tom Veryzer	3.00	1.50	.90
660	Jason Thompson	3.00	1.50	.90
684	Ralph Houk	3.50	1.75	1.00
701	Tom Hume, Larry Landreth, Steve McCatty, Bruce Taylor (Rookie Pitchers)	3.00	1.50	.90
703	Larry Andersen, Tim Jones, Mickey Mahler, Jack Morris (Rookie Pitchers)	7.50	3.75	2.25
704	Garth Iorg, Dave Oliver, Sam Perlozzo, Lou Whitaker (Rookie 2nd Basemen)	9.00	4.50	2.75
707	Mickey Klutts, Paul Molitor, Alan Trammell, U.L. Washington (Rookie Shortstops)	20.00	10.00	6.00
708	Bo Diaz, Dale Murphy, Lance Parrish, Ernie Whitt (Rookie Catchers)	10.00	5.00	3.00
723	Johnny Wockenfuss	3.00	1.50	.90

1964 Detroit Tigers Milk Bottle Caps

These small (1-5/16" diameter) cardboard milk bottle caps feature line drawings of the 1964 Tigers. The

VISIT TIGER STADIUM
Frank Lary
SEE THE TIGERS MORE IN '64

caps are printed in dark blue and orange on front and blank on back. The unnumbered caps are checklisted here in alphabetical order. A wire staple is found in most caps. The caps were reportedly produced for Twin Pines Dairy for use on bottles of chocolate milk.

		NM	EX	VG
Complete Set (14):		400.00	200.00	120.00
Common Player:		25.00	12.50	7.50
(1)	Hank Aguirre	25.00	12.50	7.50
(2)	Billy Bruton	25.00	12.50	7.50
(3)	Norman Cash	50.00	25.00	15.00
(4)	Don Demeter	25.00	12.50	7.50
(5)	Chuck Dressen	25.00	12.50	7.50
(6)	Bill Freehan	35.00	17.50	10.50
(7)	Al Kaline	150.00	75.00	45.00
(8)	Frank Lary	25.00	12.50	7.50
(9)	Jerry Lumpe	25.00	12.50	7.50
(10)	Dick McAuliffe	25.00	12.50	7.50
(11)	Bubba Phillips	25.00	12.50	7.50
(12)	Ed Rakow	25.00	12.50	7.50
(13)	Phil Regan	25.00	12.50	7.50
(14)	Dave Wickersham	25.00	12.50	7.50

1936 Detroit Times Sports Stamps

STAMPS
DETROIT TIMES
SPORT STAMP
CHARLEY GRIMM

Manager and first baseman for the National League champions, the Chicago Cubs . . . got his start as a pop vendor in St. Louis and ended up manager and vice president of the Chicago Cubs . . . Born St. Louis, Aug. 28, 1899 . . . followed Hornsby as manager and nine days after taking charge had the team in first place.

The date of issue listed is approximate and the actual period of issue may have spanned more than one year. Printed as part of the regular newspaper page, these feature items have a stamp-design photo element of about 2" x 2-1/2" atop a biographical and career summary. The list here is likely not complete.

		NM	EX	VG
Common Player:		12.00	6.00	3.50
(1)	Eldon Auker	12.00	6.00	3.50
(2)	Jack Burns	12.00	6.00	3.50
(3)	Mickey Cochrane (Dark cap.)	20.00	10.00	6.00
(4)	Mickey Cochrane (White cap.)	20.00	10.00	6.00
(5)	Dizzy Dean	25.00	12.50	7.50
(6)	Paul Dean	15.00	7.50	4.50
(7)	Wes Ferrell	15.00	7.50	4.50
(8)	Frank Frisch	20.00	10.00	6.00
(9)	Lou Gehrig	40.00	20.00	12.00
(10)	Charles Gehringer	20.00	10.00	6.00
(11)	Chas. Gehringer	20.00	10.00	6.00
(12)	Lefty Gomez	20.00	10.00	6.00
(13)	Charley Grimm	12.00	6.00	3.50
(14)	Van Lingle Mungo	12.00	6.00	3.50
(15)	Steve O'Neill	12.00	6.00	3.50
(16)	Babe Ruth	30.00	15.00	9.00
(17)	Al Simmons	20.00	10.00	6.00
(18)	Tris Speaker	25.00	12.50	7.50
(19)	Earl Whitehill	12.00	6.00	3.50

1966 Dexter Press California Angels

Less well-known than the New York firm's premium issues for Coca-Cola are Dexter Press' team issues. Sold for 50 cents in a cellophane bag with a colorful cardboard header the team issues are in the same basic design as the premium cards of 1967, but mea-

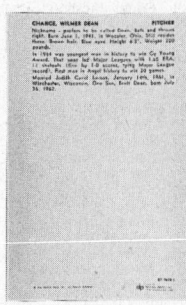

sure only 4" x 5-7/8". Though they were sold in sets of eight, more individual cards exist for the known teams, so it is evident there was some exchange of cards within the sets over the course of the sales period. Cards have color player poses with a black facsimile autograph at top and with or without a white border around. Backs are printed in blue with personal data and career highlights at top and copyright information at bottom. The cards are checklisted here alphabetically.

		NM	EX	VG
Complete Set (17):		100.00	50.00	30.00
Common Player:		10.00	5.00	3.00
(1)	Jose Cardenal	10.00	5.00	3.00
(2)	George Brunet	10.00	5.00	3.00
(3)	Dean Chance	12.00	6.00	3.50
(4)	Jim Fregosi	10.00	5.00	3.00
(5)	Ed Kirkpatrick	10.00	5.00	3.00
(6)	Bob Knoop	10.00	5.00	3.00
(7)	Bob Lee	10.00	5.00	3.00
(8)	Marcelino Lopez	10.00	5.00	3.00
(9)	Fred Newman	10.00	5.00	3.00
(10)	Albie Pearson	10.00	5.00	3.00
(11)	Jim Piersall	13.50	6.75	4.00
(12)	Rick Reichardt	10.00	5.00	3.00
(13)	Bob Rodgers	10.00	5.00	3.00
(14)	Paul Schaal	10.00	5.00	3.00
(15)	Norm Siebern	10.00	5.00	3.00
(16)	Willie Smith	10.00	5.00	3.00
(17)	Anaheim Stadium	10.00	5.00	3.00

1966 Dexter Press California Angels 8x10

The extent to which this larger format premium parallels the smaller set is currently unknown.

		NM	EX	VG
Common Player:		10.00	5.00	3.00
(1)	Dean Chance	15.00	7.50	4.50
(2)	Willie Smith	10.00	5.00	3.00

1966 Dexter Press California Angels Booklet

This souvenir-stand bound booklet offered pictures of the 1966 California Angels in two different sizes. Each 8-1/8" x 3-1/2" page features a pair of identical color photo cards. A postcard-size (3-1/2" x 5-1/2") portrait has a facsimile autograph of the player at top, attached by perforations to a 2-1/4" x 3-1/2" card, which in turn is perforated into the bound end of the book. Booklets originally sold for 50 cents. The unnumbered cards are checklisted here in alphabetical order.

		NM	EX	VG
Complete Booket:		150.00	75.00	45.00
Complete Set, Large (10):		60.00	30.00	18.00
Complete Set, Small (10):		40.00	20.00	12.00
Common Player, Large:		8.00	4.00	2.40
Common Player, Small:		6.00	3.00	1.80
Large Format (3-1/2" x 5-1/2")				
(1)	Jose Cardenal	8.00	4.00	2.50
(2)	Dean Chance	8.00	4.00	2.50
(3)	Jim Fregosi	8.00	4.00	2.50
(4)	Bob Knoop	8.00	4.00	2.50
(5)	Albie Pearson	8.00	4.00	2.50
(6)	Rick Reichardt	8.00	4.00	2.50
(7)	Bob Rodgers	8.00	4.00	2.50
(8)	Paul Schaal	8.00	4.00	2.50
(9)	Willie Smith	8.00	4.00	2.50
(10)	Anaheim Stadium	8.00	4.00	2.50
Small Format (2-1/4" x 3-1/2")				
(1)	Jose Cardenal	6.00	3.00	1.80
(2)	Dean Chance	6.00	3.00	1.80
(3)	Jim Fregosi	6.00	3.00	1.80
(4)	Bob Knoop	6.00	3.00	1.80
(5)	Albie Pearson	6.00	3.00	1.80
(6)	Rick Reichardt	6.00	3.00	1.80
(7)	Bob Rodgers	6.00	3.00	1.80
(8)	Paul Schaal	6.00	3.00	1.80
(9)	Willie Smith	6.00	3.00	1.80
(10)	Anaheim Stadium	6.00	3.00	1.80

1966-67 Dexter Press N.Y. Yankees

Less commonly encountered than the later Dexter Press/Coca-Cola premium issues are the team-set photocards produced by the New York firm. Cards were sold in bagged sets with a colorful cardboard header. Virtually identical in design to the 5-1/2" x 7" premium cards of 1967, the team-set pictures measure 4" x 5-7/8" with a white border around, and a black facsimile autograph at the top of, color player poses. Backs are printed in blue with a few biographical details at top and copyright information at bottom. The unnumbered cards are checklisted here in alphabetical order.

		NM	EX	VG
Complete Set (12):		200.00	100.00	60.00
Common Player:		15.00	7.50	4.50
(1)	Jim Bouton	17.50	8.75	5.25
(2)	Horace Clarke	15.00	7.50	4.50
(3)	Al Downing	15.00	7.50	4.50
(4)	Whitey Ford	20.00	10.00	6.00
(5)	Steve Hamilton	15.00	7.50	4.50
(6)	Elston Howard	17.50	8.75	5.25
(7)	Mickey Mantle	60.00	30.00	18.00
(8)	Joe Pepitone	17.50	8.75	5.25
(9)	Bill Robinson	15.00	7.50	4.50
(10)	Mel Stottlemyre	15.00	7.50	4.50
(11)	Tom Tresh	17.50	8.75	5.25
(12)	Steve Whitaker	15.00	7.50	4.50

1967 Dexter Press Premiums

Among the most attractive baseball collectibles issued during the 1960s were the cards produced by Dexter Press and issued in team sets as a premium by Coca-Cola. Eighteen of the 20 Major League teams participated in the promotion (only one California Angels player and no St. Louis Cardinals). The cards are in 5-1/2" x 7" glossy format. All of the color photos are waist-to-cap poses shot during spring training, and all cards feature a black facsimile autograph at the top of the photo. The cards have a 1/4" white border around the picture. Backs are printed in blue on white and include a few biographical details and career highlights. Nine of the 12 players in the All-Star issue can be differentiated from the same players' cards in the team sets by the lengthier biographies on back. The bios on the cards of Bunning, Mays and Santo are the same in both versions. While each of the cards has a number printed on back in the lower-right, they are checklisted here alphabetically within team. Sixteen of the Dexter Press premiums were issued in a smaller, borderless sticker set in 1983; it is an unauthorized collector issue.

		NM	EX	VG
Complete Set (229):		1,500	750.00	450.00
Common Player:		5.00	2.50	1.50
ALL-STARS				
(1)	Jim Bunning	7.50	3.75	2.25
(2)	Roberto Clemente	15.00	7.50	4.50
(3)	Willie Davis	5.00	2.50	1.50
(4)	Al Kaline	10.00	5.00	3.00
(5)	Harmon Killebrew	10.00	5.00	3.00
(6)	Willie Mays	12.50	6.25	3.75
(7)	Joe Pepitone	6.00	3.00	1.75
(8)	Brooks Robinson	10.00	5.00	3.00
(9)	Frank Robinson	10.00	5.00	3.00
(10)	Ron Santo	6.00	3.00	1.75
(11)	Joe Torre	6.00	3.00	1.75
(12)	Carl Yastrzemski	12.00	6.00	3.50
CALIFORNIA ANGELS				
(13)	Paul Schall	125.00	62.00	37.00
HOUSTON ASTROS				
(14)	Bob Aspromonte	5.00	2.50	1.50
(15)	John Bateman	5.00	2.50	1.50
(16)	Ron Davis	5.00	2.50	1.50
(17)	Larry Dierker	5.00	2.50	1.50
(18)	Dick Farrell	5.00	2.50	1.50
(19)	Dave Giusti	5.00	2.50	1.50
(20)	Chuck Harrison	5.00	2.50	1.50
(21)	Sonny Jackson	5.00	2.50	1.50
(22)	Jim Landis	5.00	2.50	1.50
(23)	Eddie Mathews	10.00	5.00	3.00
(24)	Joe Morgan	12.00	6.00	3.50
(25)	Rusty Staub	7.50	3.75	2.25
KANSAS CITY ATHLETICS				
(26)	Jack Aker	5.00	2.50	1.50
(27)	Campy Campaneris	5.00	2.50	1.50
(28)	Danny Cater	5.00	2.50	1.50
(29)	Ed Charles	5.00	2.50	1.50
(30)	Ossie Chavarria	5.00	2.50	1.50
(31)	Dick Green	5.00	2.50	1.50
(32)	Mike Hershberger	5.00	2.50	1.50
(33)	Lew Krausse	5.00	2.50	1.50
(34)	Jim Nash	5.00	2.50	1.50
(35)	Joe Nossek	5.00	2.50	1.50
(36)	Roger Repoz	5.00	2.50	1.50
(37)	Phil Roof	5.00	2.50	1.50
ATLANTA BRAVES				
(38)	Hank Aaron	25.00	12.50	7.50
(39)	Felipe Alou	6.00	3.00	1.75
(40)	Wade Blasingame	5.00	2.50	1.50
(41)	Clete Boyer	5.00	2.50	1.50
(42)	Bob Bruce	5.00	2.50	1.50
(43)	Ty Cline	5.00	2.50	1.50
(44)	Tony Cloninger	5.00	2.50	1.50
(45)	Ken Johnson	5.00	2.50	1.50
(46)	Dennis Menke	5.00	2.50	1.50
(47)	Gene Oliver	5.00	2.50	1.50
(48)	Joe Torre	7.50	3.75	2.25
(49)	Woody Woodward	5.00	2.50	1.50
CHICAGO CUBS				
(50)	George Altman	5.00	2.50	1.50
(51)	Ernie Banks	18.00	9.00	5.50
(52)	Glen Beckert (Glenn)	5.00	2.50	1.50
(53)	John Boccabella	5.00	2.50	1.50
(54)	Ray Culp	5.00	2.50	1.50
(55)	Ken Holtzman	5.00	2.50	1.50
(56)	Randy Hundley	5.00	2.50	1.50
(57)	Cal Koonce	5.00	2.50	1.50
(58)	Adolfo Phillips	5.00	2.50	1.50
(59)	Ron Santo	6.00	3.00	1.75
(60)	Lee Thomas	5.00	2.50	1.50
(61)	Billy Williams	10.00	5.00	3.00
LOS ANGELES DODGERS				
(62)	Bob Bailey	5.00	2.50	1.50
(63)	Willie Davis	5.00	2.50	1.50
(64)	Ron Fairly	5.00	2.50	1.50
(65)	Ron Hunt	5.00	2.50	1.50
(66)	Lou Johnson	5.00	2.50	1.50
(67)	John Kennedy	5.00	2.50	1.50
(68)	Jim Lefebvre	5.00	2.50	1.50
(69)	Claude Osteen	5.00	2.50	1.50
(70)	Wes Parker	5.00	2.50	1.50
(71)	Ron Perranoski	5.00	2.50	1.50
(72)	Phil Regan	5.00	2.50	1.50
(73)	Don Sutton	7.50	3.75	2.25
SAN FRANCISCO GIANTS				
(74)	Jesus Alou	5.00	2.50	1.50
(75)	Ollie Brown	5.00	2.50	1.50
(76)	Jim Davenport	5.00	2.50	1.50
(77)	Tito Fuentes	5.00	2.50	1.50
(78)	Tom Haller	5.00	2.50	1.50
(79)	Jim Hart	5.00	2.50	1.50
(80)	Hal Lanier	5.00	2.50	1.50
(81)	Willie Mays	15.00	7.50	4.50
(82)	Mike McCormick	5.00	2.50	1.50
(83)	Willie McCovey	12.00	6.00	3.50
(84)	Gaylord Perry	8.00	4.00	2.50
(85)	Norman Siebern	5.00	2.50	1.50
CLEVELAND INDIANS				
(86)	Max Alvis	5.00	2.50	1.50
(87)	Joe Azcue	5.00	2.50	1.50
(88)	Gary Bell	5.00	2.50	1.50
(89)	Larry Brown	5.00	2.50	1.50
(90)	Rocky Colavito	7.50	3.75	2.25
(91)	Vic Davalillo	5.00	2.50	1.50
(92)	Pedro Gonzalez	5.00	2.50	1.50
(93)	Chuck Hinton	5.00	2.50	1.50
(94)	Sam McDowell	6.00	3.00	1.75
(95)	Luis Tiant	6.00	3.00	1.75
(96)	Leon Wagner	5.00	2.50	1.50
(97)	Fred Whitfield	5.00	2.50	1.50
NEW YORK METS				
(98)	Ed Bressoud	5.00	2.50	1.50
(99)	Ken Boyer	7.00	3.50	2.00
(100)	Tommy Davis	6.00	3.00	1.75
(101)	Jack Fisher	5.00	2.50	1.50
(102)	Jerry Grote	5.00	2.50	1.50
(103)	Jack Hamilton	5.00	2.50	1.50
(104)	Cleon Jones	6.00	3.00	1.75
(105)	Ed Kranepool	5.00	2.50	1.50
(106)	Johnny Lewis	5.00	2.50	1.50
(107)	Bob Shaw	5.00	2.50	1.50
(108)	John Stephenson	5.00	2.50	1.50
(109)	Ron Swoboda	5.00	2.50	1.50
BALTIMORE ORIOLES				
(110)	Luis Aparicio	10.00	5.00	3.00
(111)	Curt Blefary	5.00	2.50	1.50
(112)	Wally Bunker	5.00	2.50	1.50
(113)	Andy Etchebarren	5.00	2.50	1.50
(114)	Eddie Fisher	5.00	2.50	1.50
(115)	Dave Johnson	5.00	2.50	1.50
(116)	Dave McNally	5.00	2.50	1.50

(8)	Paul Schaal	6.00	3.00	1.80
(9)	Willie Smith	6.00	3.00	1.80
(10)	Anaheim Stadium	6.00	3.00	1.80

		NM	EX	VG
(117)	Jim Palmer	10.00	5.00	3.00
(118)	John "Boog" Powell	8.00	4.00	2.50
(119)	Brooks Robinson	15.00	7.50	4.50
(120)	Frank Robinson	15.00	7.50	4.50
(121)	Russ Snyder	5.00	2.50	1.50
PHILADELPHIA PHILLIES				
(122)	Rich Allen	7.50	3.75	2.25
(123)	John Briggs	5.00	2.50	1.50
(124)	Jim Bunning	7.50	3.75	2.25
(125)	Johnny Callison	5.00	2.50	1.50
(126)	Clay Dalrymple	5.00	2.50	1.50
(127)	Dick Groat	5.00	2.50	1.50
(128)	Larry Jackson	5.00	2.50	1.50
(129)	Don Lock	5.00	2.50	1.50
(130)	Cookie Rojas	5.00	2.50	1.50
(131)	Chris Short	5.00	2.50	1.50
(132)	Tony Taylor	5.00	2.50	1.50
(133)	Bill White	5.00	2.50	1.50
PITTSBURGH PIRATES				
(134)	Gene Alley	5.00	2.50	1.50
(135)	Matty Alou	5.00	2.50	1.50
(136)	Roberto Clemente	45.00	22.00	13.50
(137)	Donn Clendenon	5.00	2.50	1.50
(138)	Woodie Fryman	5.00	2.50	1.50
(139)	Vern Law	5.00	2.50	1.50
(140)	Bill Mazeroski	10.00	5.00	3.00
(141)	Manny Mota	5.00	2.50	1.50
(142)	Jim Pagliaroni	5.00	2.50	1.50
(143)	Wilver Stargell	12.00	6.00	3.50
(144)	Bob Veale	5.00	2.50	1.50
(145)	Maury Wills	6.00	3.00	1.75
CINCINNATI REDS				
(146)	Leo Cardenas	5.00	2.50	1.50
(147)	Gordy Coleman	5.00	2.50	1.50
(148)	Johnny Edwards	5.00	2.50	1.50
(149)	Tommy Harper	5.00	2.50	1.50
(150)	Tommy Helms	5.00	2.50	1.50
(151)	Deron Johnson	5.00	2.50	1.50
(152)	Jim Maloney	5.00	2.50	1.50
(153)	Bill McCool	5.00	2.50	1.50
(154)	Milt Pappas	5.00	2.50	1.50
(155)	Vada Pinson	6.00	3.00	1.75
(156)	Pete Rose	30.00	15.00	9.00
(157)	Art Shamsky	5.00	2.50	1.50
BOSTON RED SOX				
(158)	Don Demeter	5.00	2.50	1.50
(159)	Bill Fischer	5.00	2.50	1.50
(160)	Joe Foy	5.00	2.50	1.50
(161)	Dalton Jones	5.00	2.50	1.50
(162)	Jim Lonborg	5.00	2.50	1.50
(163)	Rico Petrocelli	5.00	2.50	1.50
(164)	Jose Santiago	5.00	2.50	1.50
(165)	George Scott	5.00	2.50	1.50
(166)	George Smith	5.00	2.50	1.50
(167)	Jose Tartabull	5.00	2.50	1.50
(168)	Bob Tillman	5.00	2.50	1.50
(169)	Carl Yastrzemski	15.00	7.50	4.50
WASHINGTON SENATORS				
(170)	Bernie Allen	5.00	2.50	1.50
(171)	Ed Brinkman	5.00	2.50	1.50
(172)	Paul Casanova	5.00	2.50	1.50
(173)	Ken Harrelson	5.00	2.50	1.50
(174)	Frank Howard	6.00	3.00	1.75
(175)	Jim King	5.00	2.50	1.50
(176)	Ken McMullen	5.00	2.50	1.50
(177)	Dick Nen	5.00	2.50	1.50
(178)	Phil Ortega	5.00	2.50	1.50
(179)	Pete Richert	5.00	2.50	1.50
(180)	Bob Saverine	5.00	2.50	1.50
(181)	Fred Valentine	5.00	2.50	1.50
DETROIT TIGERS				
(182)	Norm Cash	6.00	3.00	1.75
(183)	Bill Freehan	5.00	2.50	1.50
(184)	Willie Horton	5.00	2.50	1.50
(185)	Al Kaline	12.00	6.00	3.50
(186)	Mickey Lolich	5.00	2.50	1.50
(187)	Jerry Lumpe	5.00	2.50	1.50
(188)	Dick McAuliffe	5.00	2.50	1.50
(189)	Johnny Podres	5.00	2.50	1.50
(190)	Joe Sparma	5.00	2.50	1.50
(191)	Dave Wickersham	5.00	2.50	1.50
(192)	Earl Wilson	5.00	2.50	1.50
(193)	Don Wert	5.00	2.50	1.50
MINNESOTA TWINS				
(194)	Bob Allison	5.00	2.50	1.50
(195)	Earl Battey	5.00	2.50	1.50
(196)	Dave Boswell	5.00	2.50	1.50
(197)	Dean Chance	5.00	2.50	1.50
(198)	Mudcat Grant	5.00	2.50	1.50
(199)	Harmon Killebrew	12.00	6.00	3.50
(200)	Jim Merritt	5.00	2.50	1.50
(201)	Tony Oliva	8.00	4.00	2.50
(202)	Rich Rollins	5.00	2.50	1.50
(203)	Ted Uhlaender	5.00	2.50	1.50
(204)	Sandy Valdespino	5.00	2.50	1.50
(205)	Zoilo Versalles	5.00	2.50	1.50
CHICAGO WHITE SOX				
(206)	Tommie Agee	5.00	2.50	1.50
(207)	Ken Berry	5.00	2.50	1.50
(208)	Don Buford	5.00	2.50	1.50
(209)	Ron Hansen	5.00	2.50	1.50
(210)	Joel Horlen	5.00	2.50	1.50
(211)	Tommy John	6.00	3.00	1.75
(212)	Bob Locker	5.00	2.50	1.50
(213)	Tommy McCraw	5.00	2.50	1.50
(214)	Jerry McNertney	5.00	2.50	1.50
(215)	Jim O'Toole	5.00	2.50	1.50
(216)	Bill "Moose" Skowron	7.00	3.50	2.00
(217)	Pete Ward	5.00	2.50	1.50
NEW YORK YANKEES				
(218)	Jim Bouton	6.00	3.00	1.75
(219)	Horace Clarke	5.00	2.50	1.50
(220)	Al Downing	5.00	2.50	1.50
(221)	Steve Hamilton	5.00	2.50	1.50
(222)	Elston Howard	7.50	3.75	2.25
(223)	Mickey Mantle	40.00	20.00	12.00
(224)	Joe Pepitone	6.00	3.00	1.75
(225)	Fritz Peterson	5.00	2.50	1.50
(226)	Charley Smith	5.00	2.50	1.50
(227)	Mel Stottlemyre	6.00	3.00	1.75
(228)	Tom Tresh	6.00	3.00	1.75
(229)	Roy White	6.00	3.00	1.75

1967 Dexter Press Team Posters

These 17" x 11" color posters reproduce the 12 cards (or on the Cubs sheet, three additional players) found in the 1967 Dexter Press premium team sets, in images about 2" x 3". The cards are pictured on a solid color background with color team logos. Printed on back are player identification and biographical information. Dexter Press copyright and credit lines are at bottom. It is not known whether other teams involved in the premium program can also be found in poster format.

	NM	EX	VG
California Angels	135.00	65.00	40.00
Chicago Cubs	180.00	90.00	55.00
Chicago White Sox	135.00	65.00	40.00
N.Y. Mets	180.00	90.00	55.00
N.Y. Yankees	300.00	150.00	90.00
Washington Senators	180.00	90.00	55.00

1968 Dexter Press Postcards

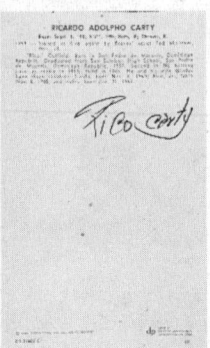

In its second year of printing premium cards for Coca-Cola, Dexter Press changed format and greatly reduced the number of participating teams and players. Only six teams were represented by 12-card sets, while an additional four teams had one or two players included. For 1968, Dexter Press produced its premiums in postcard (3-1/2" x 5-1/2") size. The cards featured borderless color player poses on front. Backs were printed in blue on white and included a facsimile autograph, biographical details and career highlights. Cards carry a Dexter Press serial number on back, but are checklisted here alphabetically within team.

		NM	EX	VG
Complete Set (77):		400.00	200.00	120.00
Common Player:		4.00	2.00	1.25
CALIFORNIA ANGELS				
(1)	Jim Fregosi	6.00	3.00	1.75
HOUSTON ASTROS				
(2)	Bob Aspromonte	4.00	2.00	1.25
(3)	John Bateman	4.00	2.00	1.25
(4)	Ron Brand	4.00	2.00	1.25
(5)	Mike Cuellar	4.00	2.00	1.25
(6)	Ron Davis	4.00	2.00	1.25
(7)	Dave Giusti	4.00	2.00	1.25
(8)	Julio Gotay	4.00	2.00	1.25
(9)	Denny Lemaster	4.00	2.00	1.25
(10)	Denis Menke	4.00	2.00	1.25
(11)	Joe Morgan	10.00	5.00	3.00
(12)	Rusty Staub	5.00	2.50	1.50
(13)	Jim Wynn	4.00	2.00	1.25
ATLANTA BRAVES				
(14)	Hank Aaron	15.00	7.50	4.50
(15)	Felipe Alou	5.00	2.50	1.50
(16)	Clete Boyer	4.00	2.00	1.25
(17)	Clay Carroll	4.00	2.00	1.25
(18)	Rico Carty	4.00	2.00	1.25
(19)	Tony Cloninger	4.00	2.00	1.25
(20)	Sonny Jackson	4.00	2.00	1.25
(21)	Ray Jarvis	4.00	2.00	1.25
(22)	Ken Johnson	4.00	2.00	1.25
(23)	Phil Niekro	8.00	4.00	2.50
(24)	Joe Torre	7.50	3.75	2.25
(25)	Woody Woodward	4.00	2.00	1.25
SAN FRANCISCO GIANTS				
(26)	Jesus Alou	4.00	2.00	1.25
(27)	Bob Bolin	4.00	2.00	1.25
(28)	Jim Davenport	4.00	2.00	1.25
(29)	Jim Hart	4.00	2.00	1.25
(30)	Jack Hiatt	4.00	2.00	1.25
(31)	Ron Hunt	4.00	2.00	1.25
(32)	Frank Linzy	4.00	2.00	1.25
(33)	Juan Marichal	9.00	4.50	2.75
(34)	Willie Mays	15.00	7.50	4.50
(35)	Mike McCormick	4.00	2.00	1.25
(36)	Gaylord Perry	8.00	4.00	2.50
(37)	Ray Sadecki	4.00	2.00	1.25
BALTIMORE ORIOLES				
(38)	Mark Belanger	4.00	2.00	1.25
(39)	Paul Blair	4.00	2.00	1.25
(40)	Curt Blefary	4.00	2.00	1.25
(41)	Don Buford	4.00	2.00	1.25
(42)	Moe Drabowsky	4.00	2.00	1.25
(43)	Andy Etchebarren	4.00	2.00	1.25
(44)	Dave Johnson	4.00	2.00	1.25
(45)	Dave McNally	4.00	2.00	1.25
(46)	Tom Phoebus	4.00	2.00	1.25
(47)	Boog Powell	5.00	2.50	1.50
(48)	Brooks Robinson	12.00	6.00	3.50
(49)	Frank Robinson	12.00	6.00	3.50
PHILADELPHIA PHILLIES				
(50)	Dick Allen	9.00	4.50	2.75
PITTSBURGH PIRATES				
(51)	Roberto Clemente	25.00	12.50	7.50
(52)	Bill Mazeroski	10.00	5.00	3.00
BOSTON RED SOX				
(53)	Jerry Adair	4.00	2.00	1.25
(54)	Mike Andrews	4.00	2.00	1.25
(55)	Gary Bell	4.00	2.00	1.25
(56)	Darrell Brandon	4.00	2.00	1.25
(57)	Dick Ellsworth	4.00	2.00	1.25
(58)	Joe Foy	4.00	2.00	1.25
(59)	Dalton Jones	4.00	2.00	1.25
(60)	Jim Lonborg	5.00	2.50	1.50
(61)	Dave Morehead	4.00	2.00	1.25
(62)	Rico Petrocelli	4.00	2.00	1.25
(63)	George Scott	4.00	2.00	1.25
(64)	John Wyatt	4.00	2.00	1.25
DETROIT TIGERS				
(65)	Bill Freehan	6.00	3.00	1.75
MINNESOTA TWINS				
(66)	Bob Allison	4.00	2.00	1.25
(67)	Dave Boswell	4.00	2.00	1.25
(68)	Rod Carew	10.00	5.00	3.00
(69)	Dean Chance	4.00	2.00	1.25
(70)	Jim Kaat	4.00	2.00	1.25
(71)	Harmon Killebrew	10.00	5.00	3.00
(72)	Russ Nixon	4.00	2.00	1.25
(73)	Tony Oliva	6.00	3.00	1.75
(74)	Rich Rollins	4.00	2.00	1.25
(75)	John Roseboro	4.00	2.00	1.25
(76)	Cesar Tovar	4.00	2.00	1.25
(77)	Ted Uhlaender	4.00	2.00	1.25

1979 Dexter Press Hall of Fame Plaque Postcards

(See Hall of Fame (Dexter Press) for checklist, value data.)

1960 Diamond Associates Postcards

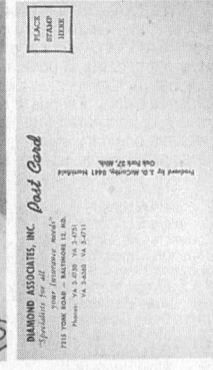

Based on the uniform style depicted on front, the actual year of issue for this card could be anywhere between 1958-1962. Produced by photographer J.D. McCarthy, apparently for the star catcher's off-season business, the 3-1/4" x 5-1/2" black-and-white card has a facsimile autograph on front. The postcard-style back has the address and phone numbers of the insurance company.

	NM	EX	VG
Gus Triandos	30.00	15.00	9.00

1940 Diamond Dust Punchboard Cards

FRANK McCORMICK

These paper cards are the consolation prizes from a popular gambling device of the Depression era, the punchboard. For five cents a customer could choose one of 624 holes on the punchboard and push a wood or metal punch through the paper on front, driving out the back a 1" x about 1-3/4" picture of a baseball player. Fifteen of the players were $1 winners and were produced in much shorter supply than the others; any which were redeemed would probably have been destroyed. The pictures are printed on ribbed paper to assist in fitting them into the board. They are pictures taken from the photos on contemporary "Salutation" Exhibit cards, though without uniform logos. They are printed in bright colors with the player name in a color bar at bottom. Backs are blank. The unnumbered cards are listed here in alphabetical order, with an asterisk indicating winners. The punchboard itself is highly collectible, with colorful baseball graphics and player pictures and names. Earlier and later versions of Diamond Dust punchboards are also known, but have not been checklisted.

		NM	EX	VG
	Complete Set (30):	850.00	425.00	250.00
	Common Player:	15.00	7.50	4.50
	Complete Unused Punchboard:	1,200	600.00	350.00
(1)	Luke Appling (*)	45.00	22.00	13.50
(2)	Earl Averill (*)	45.00	22.00	13.50
(3)	Adolf Camilli	15.00	7.50	4.50
(4)	Harland Clift (Harlond)	15.00	7.50	4.50
(5)	Joe Cronin (*)(Unconfirmed)	45.00	22.00	13.50
(6)	Tony Cuccinello	15.00	7.50	4.50
(7)	Dizzy Dean	35.00	17.50	10.50
(8)	Bill Dickey (*)	50.00	25.00	15.00
(9)	Joe DiMaggio (*)	125.00	62.00	37.00
(10)	Bob Feller	30.00	15.00	9.00
(11)	Jimmie Foxx (*)	45.00	22.00	13.50
(12)	Charlie Gehringer (*)	45.00	22.00	13.50
(13)	Lefty Gomez	25.00	12.50	7.50
(14)	Hank Greenberg	30.00	15.00	9.00
(15)	Lefty Grove	25.00	12.50	7.50
(16)	Gabby Hartnett	15.00	7.50	4.50
(17)	Carl Hubbell	25.00	12.50	7.50
(18)	Bob Johnson	15.00	7.50	4.50
(19)	Chuck Klein	25.00	12.50	7.50
(20)	Bill Lee	15.00	7.50	4.50
(21)	Ernie Lombardi (*)	45.00	22.00	13.50
(22)	Frank McCormick (*)	25.00	12.50	7.50
(23)	Joe Medwick	25.00	12.50	7.50
(24)	Johnny Mize (*)	45.00	22.00	13.50
(25)	Buck Newson (Newsom)	15.00	7.50	4.50
(26)	Mel Ott (*)	45.00	22.00	13.50
(27)	Johnny Rizzo (*)	25.00	12.50	7.50
(28)	Red Ruffing (*)(Unconfirmed)	45.00	22.00	13.50
(29)	Cecil Travis	15.00	7.50	4.50
(30)	Johnny Vander Meer	15.00	7.50	4.50
(31)	Arky Vaughan (*)	45.00	22.00	13.50
(32)	Lon Warneke	15.00	7.50	4.50
(33)	Rudy York (*)(Unconfirmed)	25.00	12.50	7.50

1979 Diamond Greats

SENATORS 1ST BASE

Roy Sievers
Diamond Greats 1979 # 75

	Life-	H	2B	HR	RBI	BA
Time	1703	292	318	1147	.267

Card collector, dealer and later Donruss photographer Jack Wallin produced this collectors' issue. Cards are in the 2-1/2" x 3-1/2" format, printed in black-and-white and blank-backed. Besides the player photo on front, there is identification and a line of career stats. Four 100-card series were issued. Series 1 concentrates on Yankees, Giants, Senators and Dodgers. Series 2 comprises the Cubs, White Sox, Cardinals and Browns. The third series features Braves, Red Sox, Reds and Indians. Series 4 concentrates on the Phillies, A's, Pirates and Tigers.

		NM	EX	VG
	Complete Set (400):	275.00	135.00	85.00
	Series 1 (1-100):	60.00	30.00	18.00
	Series 2 (101-200):	50.00	25.00	15.00
	Series 3 (201-300):	50.00	25.00	15.00
	Series 4 (301-400):	50.00	25.00	15.00
	Common Player:	2.00	1.00	.60
1	Joe DiMaggio	12.00	6.00	3.50
2	Ben Chapman	2.00	1.00	.60
3	Joe Dugan	2.00	1.00	.60
4	Bobby Shawkey	2.00	1.00	.60
5	Joe Sewell	2.00	1.00	.60
6	George Pipgras	2.00	1.00	.60
7	George Selkirk	2.00	1.00	.60
8	Babe Dahlgren	2.00	1.00	.60
9	Spud Chandler	2.00	1.00	.60
10	Duffy Lewis	2.00	1.00	.60
11	Lefty Gomez	3.00	1.50	.90
12	Atley Donald	2.00	1.00	.60
13	Whitey Witt	2.00	1.00	.60
14	Marius Russo	2.00	1.00	.60
15	Buddy Rosar	2.00	1.00	.60
16	Russ Van Atta	2.00	1.00	.60
17	Johnny Lindell	2.00	1.00	.60
18	Bobby Brown	2.00	1.00	.60
19	Tony Kubek	2.50	1.25	.70
20	Joe Beggs	2.00	1.00	.60
21	Don Larsen	2.50	1.25	.70
22	Andy Carey	2.00	1.00	.60
23	Johnny Kucks	2.00	1.00	.60
24	Elston Howard	2.50	1.25	.70
25	Roger Maris	4.00	2.00	1.25
26	Rube Marquard	2.50	1.25	.70
27	Sam Leslie	2.00	1.00	.60
28	Freddy Leach	2.00	1.00	.60
29	Fred Fitzsimmons	2.00	1.00	.60
30	Bill Terry	2.50	1.25	.70
31	Joe Moore	2.00	1.00	.60
32	Waite Hoyt	2.00	1.00	.60
33	Travis Jackson	2.00	1.00	.60
34	Gus Mancuso	2.00	1.00	.60
35	Carl Hubbell	3.00	1.50	.90
36	Bill Voiselle	2.00	1.00	.60
37	Hank Leiber	2.00	1.00	.60
38	Burgess Whitehead	2.00	1.00	.60
39	Johnny Mize	3.00	1.50	.90
40	Bill Lohrman	2.00	1.00	.60
41	Bill Rigney	2.00	1.00	.60
42	Cliff Melton	2.00	1.00	.60
43	Willard Marshall	2.00	1.00	.60
44	Wes Westrum	2.00	1.00	.60
45	Monte Irvin	3.00	1.50	.90
46	Marv Grissom	2.00	1.00	.60
47	Clyde Castleman	2.00	1.00	.60
48	Harry Gumbert	2.00	1.00	.60
49	Daryl Spencer	2.00	1.00	.60
50	Willie Mays	9.00	4.50	2.75
51	Sam West	2.00	1.00	.60
52	Fred Schulte	2.00	1.00	.60
53	Cecil Travis	2.00	1.00	.60
54	Tommy Thomas	2.00	1.00	.60
55	Dutch Leonard	2.00	1.00	.60
56	Jimmy Wasdell	2.00	1.00	.60
57	Doc Cramer	2.00	1.00	.60
58	Harland Clift (Harlond)	2.00	1.00	.60
59	Ken Chase	2.00	1.00	.60
60	Buddy Lewis	2.00	1.00	.60
61	Ossie Bluege	2.00	1.00	.60
62	Chuck Stobbs	2.00	1.00	.60
63	Jimmy DeShong	2.00	1.00	.60
64	Roger Wolff	2.00	1.00	.60
65	Luke Sewell	2.00	1.00	.60
66	Sid Hudson	2.00	1.00	.60
67	Jack Russell	2.00	1.00	.60
68	Walt Masterson	2.00	1.00	.60
69	George Myatt	2.00	1.00	.60
70	Monte Weaver	2.00	1.00	.60
71	Cliff Bolton	2.00	1.00	.60
72	Ray Scarborough	2.00	1.00	.60
73	Albie Pearson	2.00	1.00	.60
74	Gil Coan	2.00	1.00	.60
75	Roy Sievers	2.00	1.00	.60
76	Burleigh Grimes	2.00	1.00	.60
77	Charlie Hargreaves	2.00	1.00	.60
78	Babe Herman	2.00	1.00	.60
79	Fred Frankhouse	2.00	1.00	.60
80	Al Lopez	2.00	1.00	.60
81	Lonny Frey	2.00	1.00	.60
82	Dixie Walker	2.00	1.00	.60
83	Kirby Higbe	2.00	1.00	.60
84	Bobby Bragan	2.00	1.00	.60
85	Leo Durocher	2.00	1.00	.60
86	Woody English	2.00	1.00	.60
87	Preacher Roe	2.00	1.00	.60
88	Vic Lombardi	2.00	1.00	.60
89	Clyde Sukeforth	2.00	1.00	.60
90	Pee Wee Reese	5.00	2.50	1.50
91	Joe Hatten	2.00	1.00	.60
92	Gene Hermanski	2.00	1.00	.60
93	Ray Benge	2.00	1.00	.60
94	Duke Snider	5.00	2.50	1.50
95	Walter Alston	2.00	1.00	.60
96	Don Drysdale	3.00	1.50	.90
97	Andy Pafko	2.00	1.00	.60
98	Don Zimmer	2.00	1.00	.60
99	Carl Erskine	2.00	1.00	.60
100	Dick Williams	2.00	1.00	.60
101	Charlie Grimm	2.00	1.00	.60
102	Clarence Blair	2.00	1.00	.60
103	Johnny Moore	2.00	1.00	.60
104	Clay Bryant	2.00	1.00	.60
105	Billy Herman	2.00	1.00	.60
106	Hy Vandenberg	2.00	1.00	.60
107	Lennie Merullo	2.00	1.00	.60
108	Hank Wyse	2.00	1.00	.60
109	Dom Dallessandro	2.00	1.00	.60
110	Al Epperly	2.00	1.00	.60
111	Bill Nicholson	2.00	1.00	.60
112	Vern Olsen	2.00	1.00	.60
113	Johnny Schmitz	2.00	1.00	.60
114	Bob Scheffing	2.00	1.00	.60
115	Bob Rush	2.00	1.00	.60
116	Roy Smalley	2.00	1.00	.60
117	Ransom Jackson	2.00	1.00	.60
118	Cliff Chambers	2.00	1.00	.60
119	Harry Chiti	2.00	1.00	.60
120	Johnny Klippstein	2.00	1.00	.60
121	Gene Baker	2.00	1.00	.60
122	Walt Moryn	2.00	1.00	.60
123	Dick Littlefield	2.00	1.00	.60
124	Bob Speake	2.00	1.00	.60
125	Hank Sauer	2.00	1.00	.60
126	Monty Stratton	2.50	1.25	.70
127	Johnny Kerr	2.00	1.00	.60
128	Milt Gaston	2.00	1.00	.60
129	Eddie Smith	2.00	1.00	.60
130	Larry Rosenthal	2.00	1.00	.60
131	Orval Grove	2.00	1.00	.60
132	Johnny Hodapp	2.00	1.00	.60
133	Johnny Rigney	2.00	1.00	.60
134	Willie Kamm	2.00	1.00	.60
135	Ed Lopat	2.00	1.00	.60
136	Smead Jolley	2.00	1.00	.60
137	Ralph Hodgin	2.00	1.00	.60
138	Ollie Bejma	2.00	1.00	.60
139	Zeke Bonura	2.00	1.00	.60
140	Al Hollingsworth	2.00	1.00	.60
141	Thurman Tucker	2.00	1.00	.60
142	Cass Michaels	2.00	1.00	.60
143	Bill Wight	2.00	1.00	.60
144	Don Lenhardt	2.00	1.00	.60
145	Sammy Esposito	2.00	1.00	.60
146	Jack Harshman	2.00	1.00	.60
147	Turk Lown	2.00	1.00	.60
148	Jim Landis	2.00	1.00	.60
149	Bob Shaw	2.00	1.00	.60
150	Minnie Minoso	2.50	1.25	.70
151	Les Bell	2.00	1.00	.60
152	Taylor Douthit	2.00	1.00	.60
153	Jack Rothrock	2.00	1.00	.60
154	Terry Moore	2.00	1.00	.60
155	Max Lanier	2.00	1.00	.60
156	Don Gutteridge	2.00	1.00	.60
157	Stu Martin	2.00	1.00	.60
158	Stan Musial	5.00	2.50	1.50
159	Frank Crespi	2.00	1.00	.60
160	Johnny Hopp	2.00	1.00	.60
161	Ernie Koy	2.00	1.00	.60
162	Joe Garagiola	3.00	1.50	.90
163	Ed Kazak	2.00	1.00	.60
164	Joe Orengo	2.00	1.00	.60
165	Howie Krist	2.00	1.00	.60
166	Enos Slaughter	3.00	1.50	.90
167	Ray Sanders	2.00	1.00	.60
168	Walker Cooper	2.00	1.00	.60
169	Nippy Jones	2.00	1.00	.60
170	Dick Sisler	2.00	1.00	.60
171	Harvey Haddix	2.00	1.00	.60
172	Solly Hemus	2.00	1.00	.60
173	Ray Jablonski	2.00	1.00	.60
174	Alex Grammas	2.00	1.00	.60
175	Joe Cunningham	2.00	1.00	.60
176	Debs Garms	2.00	1.00	.60
177	Chief Hogsett	2.00	1.00	.60
178	Alan Strange	2.00	1.00	.60
179	Rick Ferrell	2.00	1.00	.60
180	Jack Kramer	2.00	1.00	.60
181	Jack Knott	2.00	1.00	.60
182	Bob Harris	2.00	1.00	.60
183	Billy Hitchcock	2.00	1.00	.60
184	Jim Walkup	2.00	1.00	.60
185	Roy Cullenbine	2.00	1.00	.60
186	Bob Muncrief	2.00	1.00	.60
187	Chet Laabs	2.00	1.00	.60
188	Vern Kennedy	2.00	1.00	.60
189	Bill Trotter	2.00	1.00	.60
190	Denny Galehouse	2.00	1.00	.60
191	Al Zarilla	2.00	1.00	.60
192	Hank Arft	2.00	1.00	.60
193	Nelson Potter	2.00	1.00	.60
194	Ray Coleman	2.00	1.00	.60
195	Bob Dillinger	2.00	1.00	.60
196	Dick Kokos	2.00	1.00	.60
197	Bob Cain	2.00	1.00	.60
198	Virgil Trucks	2.00	1.00	.60
199	Duane Pillette	2.00	1.00	.60
200	Bob Turley	2.00	1.00	.60
201	Wally Berger	2.00	1.00	.60
202	John Lanning	2.00	1.00	.60
203	Buck Jordan	2.00	1.00	.60
204	Jim Turner	2.00	1.00	.60
205	Johnny Cooney	2.00	1.00	.60
206	Hank Majeski	2.00	1.00	.60
207	Phil Masi	2.00	1.00	.60
208	Tony Cuccinello	2.00	1.00	.60
209	Whitey Wietelmann	2.00	1.00	.60
210	Lou Fette	2.00	1.00	.60
211	Vince DiMaggio	2.50	1.25	.70
212	Huck Betts	2.00	1.00	.60
213	Red Barrett	2.00	1.00	.60
214	Pinkey Whitney	2.00	1.00	.60
215	Tommy Holmes	2.00	1.00	.60

216	Ray Berres	2.00	1.00	.60
217	Mike Sandlock	2.00	1.00	.60
218	Max Macon	2.00	1.00	.60
219	Sibby Sisti	2.00	1.00	.60
220	Johnny Beazley	2.00	1.00	.60
221	Bill Posedel	2.00	1.00	.60
222	Connie Ryan	2.00	1.00	.60
223	Del Crandall	2.00	1.00	.60
224	Bob Addis	2.00	1.00	.60
225	Warren Spahn	3.00	1.50	.90
226	Johnny Pesky	2.00	1.00	.60
227	Dom DiMaggio	2.50	1.25	.70
228	Emerson Dickman	2.00	1.00	.60
229	Bobby Doerr	2.00	1.00	.60
230	Tony Lupien	2.00	1.00	.60
231	Roy Partee	2.00	1.00	.60
232	Stan Spence	2.00	1.00	.60
233	Jim Bagby	2.00	1.00	.60
234	Buster Mills	2.00	1.00	.60
235	Fabian Gaffke	2.00	1.00	.60
236	George Metkovich	2.00	1.00	.60
237	Tom McBride	2.00	1.00	.60
238	Charlie Wagner	2.00	1.00	.60
239	Eddie Pellagrini	2.00	1.00	.60
240	Harry Dorish	2.00	1.00	.60
241	Ike Delock	2.00	1.00	.60
242	Mel Parnell	2.00	1.00	.60
243	Matt Batts	2.00	1.00	.60
244	Gene Stephens	2.00	1.00	.60
245	Milt Bolling	2.00	1.00	.60
246	Charlie Maxwell	2.00	1.00	.60
247	Willard Nixon	2.00	1.00	.60
248	Sammy White	2.00	1.00	.60
249	Dick Gernert	2.00	1.00	.60
250	Rico Petrocelli	2.00	1.00	.60
251	Edd Roush	2.00	1.00	.60
252	Mark Koenig	2.00	1.00	.60
253	Jimmy Outlaw	2.00	1.00	.60
254	Ethan Allen	2.00	1.00	.60
255	Tony Freitas	2.00	1.00	.60
256	Frank McCormick	2.00	1.00	.60
257	Bucky Walters	2.00	1.00	.60
258	Harry Craft	2.00	1.00	.60
259	Nate Andrews	2.00	1.00	.60
260	Ed Lukon	2.00	1.00	.60
261	Elmer Riddle	2.00	1.00	.60
262	Lee Grissom	2.00	1.00	.60
263	Johnny Vander Meer	2.00	1.00	.60
264	Eddie Joost	2.00	1.00	.60
265	Kermit Wahl	2.00	1.00	.60
266	Ival Goodman	2.00	1.00	.60
267	Clyde Vollmer	2.00	1.00	.60
268	Grady Hatton	2.00	1.00	.60
269	Ted Kluszewski	3.00	1.50	.90
270	Johnny Pramesa	2.00	1.00	.60
271	Joe Black	2.50	1.25	.70
272	Roy McMillan	2.00	1.00	.60
273	Wally Post	2.00	1.00	.60
274	Joe Nuxhall	2.00	1.00	.60
275	Jerry Lynch	2.00	1.00	.60
276	Stan Coveleski	2.00	1.00	.60
277	Bill Wambsganss	2.00	1.00	.60
278	Bruce Campbell	2.00	1.00	.60
279	George Uhle	2.00	1.00	.60
280	Earl Averill	2.00	1.00	.60
281	Whit Wyatt	2.00	1.00	.60
282	Oscar Grimes	2.00	1.00	.60
283	Roy Weatherly	2.00	1.00	.60
284	Joe Dobson	2.00	1.00	.60
285	Bob Feller	3.00	1.50	.90
286	Jim Hegan	2.00	1.00	.60
287	Mel Harder	2.00	1.00	.60
288	Ken Keltner	2.00	1.00	.60
289	Red Embree	2.00	1.00	.60
290	Al Milnar	2.00	1.00	.60
291	Lou Boudreau	2.00	1.00	.60
292	Ed Klieman	2.00	1.00	.60
293	Steve Gromek	2.00	1.00	.60
294	George Strickland	2.00	1.00	.60
295	Gene Woodling	2.00	1.00	.60
296	Hank Edwards	2.00	1.00	.60
297	Don Mossi	2.00	1.00	.60
298	Eddie Robinson	2.00	1.00	.60
299	Sam Dente	2.00	1.00	.60
300	Herb Score	2.00	1.00	.60
301	Dolf Camilli	2.00	1.00	.60
302	Jack Warner	2.00	1.00	.60
303	Ike Pearson	2.00	1.00	.60
304	Johnny Peacock	2.00	1.00	.60
305	Gene Corbett	2.00	1.00	.60
306	Walt Millies	2.00	1.00	.60
307	Vance Dinges	2.00	1.00	.60
308	Joe Marty	2.00	1.00	.60
309	Hugh Mulcahey	2.00	1.00	.60
310	Boom Boom Beck	2.00	1.00	.60
311	Charley Schanz	2.00	1.00	.60
312	John Bolling	2.00	1.00	.60
313	Danny Litwhiler	2.00	1.00	.60
314	Emil Verban	2.00	1.00	.60
315	Andy Semenick	2.00	1.00	.60
316	John Antonelli	2.00	1.00	.60
317	Robin Roberts	3.00	1.50	.90
318	Richie Ashburn	3.00	1.50	.90
319	Curt Simmons	2.00	1.00	.60
320	Murry Dickson	2.00	1.00	.60
321	Jim Greengrass	2.00	1.00	.60
322	Gene Freese	2.00	1.00	.60
323	Bobby Morgan	2.00	1.00	.60
324	Don Demeter	2.00	1.00	.60
325	Eddie Sawyer	2.00	1.00	.60
326	Bob Johnson	2.00	1.00	.60
327	Ace Parker	3.00	1.50	.90
328	Joe Hauser	2.00	1.00	.60
329	Walt French	2.00	1.00	.60
330	Tom Ferrick	2.00	1.00	.60
331	Bill Werber	2.00	1.00	.60
332	Walt Masters	2.00	1.00	.60
333	Les McCrabb	2.00	1.00	.60

334	Ben McCoy	2.00	1.00	.60
335	Eric Tipton	2.00	1.00	.60
336	Al Rubeling	2.00	1.00	.60
337	Nick Etten	2.00	1.00	.60
338	Carl Scheib	2.00	1.00	.60
339	Dario Lodigiani	2.00	1.00	.60
340	Earle Brucker	2.00	1.00	.60
341	Al Brancato	2.00	1.00	.60
342	Lou Limmer	2.00	1.00	.60
343	Elmer Valo	2.00	1.00	.60
344	Bob Hooper	2.00	1.00	.60
345	Joe Astroth	2.00	1.00	.60
346	Pete Suder	2.00	1.00	.60
347	Dave Philley	2.00	1.00	.60
348	Gus Zernial	2.00	1.00	.60
349	Bobby Shantz	2.00	1.00	.60
350	Joe DeMaestri	2.00	1.00	.60
351	Fred Lindstrom	2.00	1.00	.60
352	Red Lucas	2.00	1.00	.60
353	Clyde Barnhart	2.00	1.00	.60
354	Nick Strincevich	2.00	1.00	.60
355	Lloyd Waner	2.00	1.00	.60
356	Guy Bush	2.00	1.00	.60
357	Joe Bowman	2.00	1.00	.60
358	Al Todd	2.00	1.00	.60
359	Mace Brown	2.00	1.00	.60
360	Larry French	2.00	1.00	.60
361	Elbie Fletcher	2.00	1.00	.60
362	Woody Jensen	2.00	1.00	.60
363	Rip Sewell	2.00	1.00	.60
364	Johnny Dickshot	2.00	1.00	.60
365	Pete Coscarart	2.00	1.00	.60
366	Bud Hafey	2.00	1.00	.60
367	Ken Heintzelman	2.00	1.00	.60
368	Wally Westlake	2.00	1.00	.60
369	Frank Gustine	2.00	1.00	.60
370	Smoky Burgess	2.00	1.00	.60
371	Dick Groat	2.00	1.00	.60
372	Vern Law	2.00	1.00	.60
373	Bob Skinner	2.00	1.00	.60
374	Don Cardwell	2.00	1.00	.60
375	Bob Friend	2.00	1.00	.60
376	Frank O'Rourke	2.00	1.00	.60
377	Birdie Tebbetts	2.00	1.00	.60
378	Charlie Gehringer	3.00	1.50	.90
379	Eldon Auker	2.00	1.00	.60
380	Tuck Stainback	2.00	1.00	.60
381	Chet Morgan	2.00	1.00	.60
382	Johnny Lipon	2.00	1.00	.60
383	Paul Richards	2.00	1.00	.60
384	Johnny Gorsica	2.00	1.00	.60
385	Ray Hayworth	2.00	1.00	.60
386	Jimmy Bloodworth	2.00	1.00	.60
387	Gene Desautels	2.00	1.00	.60
388	Jo Jo White	2.00	1.00	.60
389	Boots Poffenberger	2.00	1.00	.60
390	Barney McCosky	2.00	1.00	.60
391	Dick Wakefield	2.00	1.00	.60
392	Johnny Groth	2.00	1.00	.60
393	Steve Souchock	2.00	1.00	.60
394	George Vico	2.00	1.00	.60
395	Hal Newhouser	2.00	1.00	.60
396	Ray Herbert	2.00	1.00	.60
397	Jim Bunning	2.00	1.00	.60
398	Frank Lary	2.00	1.00	.60
399	Harvey Kuenn	2.00	1.00	.60
400	Eddie Mathews	3.00	1.50	.90

1911 Diamond Gum Pins (PE2)

The World's Champion Philadelphia A's are well represented and specially marked in this series of small 1" diameter pins. The sepia-toned center portion of the pin has a player portrait photo with his last name, team and league in white at left and right. Around that is a metallic blue border with a white inscription; either "World's Champions" on the A's players, or "Free with Diamond Gum" on the other players.

		NM	EX	VG
Complete Set (28):		30,000	15,000	9,000
Common Player:		500.00	250.00	150.00
(1)	Babe Adams	500.00	250.00	150.00
(2)	Home Run Baker	1,200	600.00	360.00
(3)	Chief Bender	1,200	600.00	360.00
(4)	Mordecai Brown	1,200	600.00	360.00
(5)	Donie Bush	500.00	250.00	150.00
(6)	Bill Carrigan	500.00	250.00	150.00
(7)	Frank Chance	1,200	600.00	360.00
(8)	Hal Chase	800.00	400.00	240.00
(9)	Ty Cobb	3,000	1,500	900.00
(10)	Eddie Collins	1,200	600.00	360.00
(11)	George Davis	500.00	250.00	150.00
(12)	Red Dooin	500.00	250.00	150.00
(13)	Larry Doyle	500.00	250.00	150.00
(14)	Johnny Evers	1,200	600.00	360.00
(15)	Miller Huggins	1,200	600.00	360.00
(16)	Hughie Jennings	1,200	600.00	360.00
(17)	Nap Lajoie	1,200	600.00	360.00
(18)	Harry Lord	500.00	250.00	150.00

(19)	Christy Mathewson	2,000	1,000	600.00
(20)	Dots Miller	500.00	250.00	150.00
(21)	George Mullen (Mullin)	500.00	250.00	150.00
(22)	Danny Murphy	500.00	250.00	150.00
(23)	Orval Overall	500.00	250.00	150.00
(24)	Eddie Plank	1,250	625.00	375.00
(25)	Hack Simmons	500.00	250.00	150.00
(26)	Ira Thomas	500.00	250.00	150.00
(27)	Joe Tinker	1,200	600.00	360.00
(28)	Honus Wagner	2,500	1,250	750.00
(29)	Cy Young	2,000	1,000	600.00

1934 Diamond Matchbooks - Silver Border

During much of the Great Depression, the hobby of matchbook collecting swept the country. Generally selling at two for a penny, the matchbooks began to feature photos and artwork to attract buyers. In the late 1930s, several series of sports subjects were issued by Diamond Match Co., of New York City. The first issue was a set of 200 baseball players known to collectors as "silver border" for the color of the photo frame on the approximately 1-1/2" x 4-1/8" (open) matchbooks. Player portrait or posed photos are printed in sepia on front, and can be found bordered in either red, green, blue or orange (though it is unclear whether all players can actually be found in the red version), theoretically creating an 800-piece color variation set. The player's name and team are printed on the "saddle" and there is a career summary on back, along with a design of glove, ball and bats. Matchbooks are commonly collected with the matches removed and the striker at back-bottom intact. Pieces without the striker are valued at 50 percent of these listed prices. Complete covers with matches bring a premium of 2-3X. The players are listed here alphabetically.

		NM	EX	VG
Complete Set (200):		4,500	2,250	1,350
Common Player:		20.00	10.00	6.00
(1)	Earl Adams	20.00	10.00	6.00
(2)	Ethan Allen	20.00	10.00	6.00
(3)	Eldon L. Auker	20.00	10.00	6.00
(4)	Delmar David Baker	20.00	10.00	6.00
(5)	Richard "Dick" Bartell	20.00	10.00	6.00
(6)	Walter Beck	20.00	10.00	6.00
(7)	Herman Bell	20.00	10.00	6.00
(8)	Ray Benge	20.00	10.00	6.00
(9)	Larry J. Benton	20.00	10.00	6.00
(10)	Louis W. Berger	20.00	10.00	6.00
(11)	Walter "Wally" Berger	20.00	10.00	6.00
(12)	Ray Berres	20.00	10.00	6.00
(13)	Charlie Berry	20.00	10.00	6.00
(14)	Walter M. "Huck" Betts	20.00	10.00	6.00
(15)	Ralph Birkofer	20.00	10.00	6.00
(16)	George F. Blaeholder	20.00	10.00	6.00
(17)	Jim Bottomley	40.00	20.00	12.00
(18a)	Ralph Boyle (Photo actually Virgil Davis, white cap.)	20.00	10.00	6.00
(18b)	Ralph Boyle (Correct photo, cark cap.)	20.00	10.00	6.00
(19)	Ed Brandt	20.00	10.00	6.00
(20)	Don Brennan	20.00	10.00	6.00
(21)	Irving (Jack) Burns	20.00	10.00	6.00
(22)	Guy "Joe" Bush	20.00	10.00	6.00
(23)	Adolph Camilli	20.00	10.00	6.00
(24)	Ben Cantwell	20.00	10.00	6.00
(25)	Tex Carleton	20.00	10.00	6.00
(26)	Owen Carroll	20.00	10.00	6.00
(27)	Louis Chiozza	20.00	10.00	6.00
(28)	Watson Clark	20.00	10.00	6.00
(29)	James A. Collins	20.00	10.00	6.00
(30)	Phil Collins	20.00	10.00	6.00
(31)	Edward J. Connolly	20.00	10.00	6.00
(32)	Raymond F. Coombs	20.00	10.00	6.00

		NM	EX	VG
(33)	Roger Cramer	20.00	10.00	6.00
(34)	Clifford Crawford	20.00	10.00	6.00
(35)	Hugh M. Critz	20.00	10.00	6.00
(36)	Alvin Crowder	20.00	10.00	6.00
(37)	Tony Cuccinello	20.00	10.00	6.00
(38)	Hazen "Kiki" Cuyler	40.00	20.00	12.00
(39)	Virgil Davis	20.00	10.00	6.00
(40)	Jerome "Dizzy" Dean	80.00	40.00	24.00
(41)	Paul Dean	35.00	17.50	10.50
(42)	Edward Delker	20.00	10.00	6.00
(43)	Paul Derringer	20.00	10.00	6.00
(44)	Eugene DeSautel	20.00	10.00	6.00
(45)	William J. Dietrich	20.00	10.00	6.00
(46)	Frank F. Doljack	20.00	10.00	6.00
(47)	Edward F. Durham	20.00	10.00	6.00
(48)	Leo Durocher	40.00	20.00	12.00
(49)	Jim Elliott	20.00	10.00	6.00
(50)	Charles D. English	20.00	10.00	6.00
(51)	Elwood G. English	20.00	10.00	6.00
(52)	Richard Ferrell	40.00	20.00	12.00
(53)	Wesley Ferrell (Existence Doubted)			
(54)	Charles W. Fischer	20.00	10.00	6.00
(55)	Freddy Fitzsimmons	20.00	10.00	6.00
(56)	Lew Fonseca	20.00	10.00	6.00
(57)	Fred Frankhouse	20.00	10.00	6.00
(58)	John Frederick	20.00	10.00	6.00
(59)	Benny Frey (Reds)	20.00	10.00	6.00
(60)	Linus Frey (Dodgers)	20.00	10.00	6.00
(61)	Frankie Frisch	45.00	22.00	13.50
(62)	Chick Fullis	20.00	10.00	6.00
(63)	August Galan	20.00	10.00	6.00
(64)	Milton Galatzer	120.00	60.00	36.00
(65)	Dennis W. Galehouse	20.00	10.00	6.00
(66)	Milton Gaston	20.00	10.00	6.00
(67)	Chas. Gehringer	45.00	22.00	13.50
(68)	Edward P. Gharrity	20.00	10.00	6.00
(69)	George Gibson	20.00	10.00	6.00
(70)	Isidore Goldstein	250.00	125.00	75.00
(71)	"Hank" Gowdy	20.00	10.00	6.00
(72)	Earl Grace	20.00	10.00	6.00
(73)	Chas. Grimm/Fielding	20.00	10.00	6.00
(74)	Chas. Grimm/Portrait	20.00	10.00	6.00
(75)	Frank T. Grube	20.00	10.00	6.00
(76)	Richard Gyselman	20.00	10.00	6.00
(77)	Stanley C. Hack	25.00	12.50	7.50
(78)	Irving Hadley	20.00	10.00	6.00
(79)	Charles "Chick" Hafey	40.00	20.00	12.00
(80)	Harold A. Haid	20.00	10.00	6.00
(81)	Jesse Haines	40.00	20.00	12.00
(82)	Odell A. Hale	20.00	10.00	6.00
(83)	Bill Hallahan	20.00	10.00	6.00
(84)	Luke D. Hamlin	20.00	10.00	6.00
(85)	Roy Hansen	20.00	10.00	6.00
(86)	Melvin Harder	20.00	10.00	6.00
(87)	William M. Harris	20.00	10.00	6.00
(88)	Gabby Hartnett	40.00	20.00	12.00
(89)	Harvey Hendrick	20.00	10.00	6.00
(90)	Floyd "Babe" Herman	25.00	12.50	7.50
(91)	William Herman	40.00	20.00	12.00
(92)	J. Francis Hogan	20.00	10.00	6.00
(93)	Elon Hogsett	20.00	10.00	6.00
(94)	Waite Hoyt	40.00	20.00	12.00
(95)	Carl Hubbell	50.00	25.00	15.00
(96)	Silas K. Johnson	20.00	10.00	6.00
(97)	Sylvester Johnson	20.00	10.00	6.00
(98)	Roy M. Joiner	20.00	10.00	6.00
(99)	Baxter Jordan	20.00	10.00	6.00
(100)	Arndt Jorgens	20.00	10.00	6.00
(101)	William F. Jurges	20.00	10.00	6.00
(102)	Vernon Kennedy	20.00	10.00	6.00
(103)	John F. Kerr	20.00	10.00	6.00
(104)	Charles "Chuck" Klein	40.00	20.00	12.00
(105)	Theodore Kleinhans	20.00	10.00	6.00
(106)	Bill Klem/Umpire	125.00	65.00	35.00
(107)	Robert G. Kline	20.00	10.00	6.00
(108)	William Knickerbocker	20.00	10.00	6.00
(109)	Jack H. Knott	20.00	10.00	6.00
(110)	Mark Koenig	20.00	10.00	6.00
(111)	William Lawrence	20.00	10.00	6.00
(112)	Thornton S. Lee	20.00	10.00	6.00
(113)	Wm. C. "Bill" Lee	20.00	10.00	6.00
(114)	Emil Leonard	20.00	10.00	6.00
(115)	Ernest Lombardi	40.00	20.00	12.00
(116)	Alfonso Lopez	40.00	20.00	12.00
(117)	Red Lucas	20.00	10.00	6.00
(118)	Ted Lyons	40.00	20.00	12.00
(119)	Daniel MacFayden	20.00	10.00	6.00
(120)	Ed. Majeski	20.00	10.00	6.00
(121)	Leroy Mahaffey	20.00	10.00	6.00
(122)	Pat Malone	20.00	10.00	6.00
(123)	Leo Mangum	20.00	10.00	6.00
(124)	Rabbit Maranville	40.00	20.00	12.00
(125)	Charles K. Marrow	20.00	10.00	6.00
(126)	William McKechnie	40.00	20.00	12.00
(127)	Justin McLaughlin	20.00	10.00	6.00
(128)	Marty McManus	20.00	10.00	6.00
(129)	Eric McNair	20.00	10.00	6.00
(130)	Joe Medwick	40.00	20.00	12.00
(131)	Jim Mooney	20.00	10.00	6.00
(132)	Joe Moore	20.00	10.00	6.00
(133)	Jim Moore	20.00	10.00	6.00
(134)	Randy Moore	20.00	10.00	6.00
(135)	Joe Morrissey	20.00	10.00	6.00
(136)	Joseph Mowrey	20.00	10.00	6.00
(137)	Fred W. Muller	20.00	10.00	6.00
(138)	Van Mungo	25.00	12.50	7.50
(139)	Glenn Myatt	20.00	10.00	6.00
(140a)	Lynn Nelson (Photo actually Eugene DeSautel, no "C" on cap.)			
(140b)	Lynn Nelson (Correct photo, "C" on cap.)	20.00	10.00	6.00
(141)	Henry Oana	60.00	30.00	18.00
(142)	Lefty O'Doul	35.00	17.50	10.50
(143)	Robert O'Farrell	20.00	10.00	6.00
(144)	Ernest Orsatti	20.00	10.00	6.00
(145)	Fritz R. Ostermueller	20.00	10.00	6.00
(146)	Melvin Ott	45.00	22.00	13.50
(147)	Roy Parmelee	20.00	10.00	6.00
(148)	Ralph Perkins	20.00	10.00	6.00
(149)	Frank Pytlak	20.00	10.00	6.00
(150)	Ernest C. Quigley/Umpire	45.00	22.00	13.50
(151)	George Rensa	20.00	10.00	6.00
(152)	Harry Rice	20.00	10.00	6.00
(153)	Walter Roettger	20.00	10.00	6.00
(154)	William G. Rogell	20.00	10.00	6.00
(155)	Edwin A. Rommel	20.00	10.00	6.00
(156)	Charlie Root	20.00	10.00	6.00
(157)	John Rothrock	20.00	10.00	6.00
(158)	Jack Russell	20.00	10.00	6.00
(159)	Blondy Ryan	20.00	10.00	6.00
(160)	Alexander (Al) Schacht	35.00	17.50	10.50
(161)	Wesley Schultmerick	20.00	10.00	6.00
(162)	Truett B. Sewell	20.00	10.00	6.00
(163)	Gordon Slade	20.00	10.00	6.00
(164)	Bob Smith	20.00	10.00	6.00
(165)	Julius J. Solters	20.00	10.00	6.00
(166)	Glenn Spencer	20.00	10.00	6.00
(167)	Al Spohrer	20.00	10.00	6.00
(168)	George Stainback	20.00	10.00	6.00
(169)	Albert "Dolly" Stark/Umpire	40.00	20.00	12.00
(170)	Casey Stengel	50.00	25.00	15.00
(171)	Riggs Stephenson	20.00	10.00	6.00
(172)	Walter C. Stewart	20.00	10.00	6.00
(173)	Lin Storti	20.00	10.00	6.00
(174)	Allyn (Fish Hook) Stout	20.00	10.00	6.00
(175)	Joe Stripp	20.00	10.00	6.00
(176)	Gus Suhr	20.00	10.00	6.00
(177)	Billy Sullivan, Jr.	20.00	10.00	6.00
(178)	Benny Tate	20.00	10.00	6.00
(179)	Danny Taylor	20.00	10.00	6.00
(180)	Tommy Thevenow	20.00	10.00	6.00
(181)	Bud Tinning	20.00	10.00	6.00
(182)	Cecil Travis	20.00	10.00	6.00
(183)	Forest F. Twogood	20.00	10.00	6.00
(184)	Bill Urbanski	20.00	10.00	6.00
(185)	Dazzy Vance	40.00	20.00	12.00
(186)	Arthur Veltman/SP	100.00	50.00	30.00
(187)	John L. Vergez	20.00	10.00	6.00
(188)	Gerald (Jerry) Walker	20.00	10.00	6.00
(189)	William H. Walker	20.00	10.00	6.00
(190)	Lloyd Waner	40.00	20.00	12.00
(191)	Paul Waner	40.00	20.00	12.00
(192)	Lon Warnecke	20.00	10.00	6.00
(193)	Harold B. Warstler	20.00	10.00	6.00
(194)	Bill Werber	20.00	10.00	6.00
(195)	Joyner White	20.00	10.00	6.00
(196)	Arthur Whitney	20.00	10.00	6.00
(197)	James Wilson	20.00	10.00	6.00
(198)	Lewis (Hack) Wilson	40.00	20.00	12.00
(199)	Ralph L. Winegarner	20.00	10.00	6.00
(200)	Thomas Zachary	20.00	10.00	6.00

1935 Diamond Matchbooks - Black Border

Only 24 players were issued in the 1935 Diamond Matchbook baseball series. Similar in design to the 1934 issue, these 1-1/2" x 4-1/8" matchbooks have sepia player portrait photos on front, framed in either red, green or blue. The overall borders of the cover are black. Backs of the 1935 issue feature a career summary overprinted on a silhouetted batting figure. The "saddle" has the player name and team superimposed on a baseball. These matchbooks are commonly collected with the matches removed and the striker at back-bottom intact. Pieces without the striker are valued at 50% of these listed prices. Complete covers with matches bring a premium of 2-3X. The players are listed here alphabetically.

		NM	EX	VG
Complete Set (24):		850.00	425.00	250.00
Common Player:		25.00	12.50	7.50
(1)	Ethan Allen/Red	25.00	12.50	7.50
(2)	Walter Berger/Red	25.00	12.50	7.50
(3)	Tommy Carey/Blue	25.00	12.50	7.50
(4)	Louis Chiozza/Blue	25.00	12.50	7.50
(5)	Jerome (Dizzy) Dean/Green	65.00	32.50	20.00
(6)	Frankie Frisch/Red	50.00	25.00	15.00
(7)	Charles Grimm/Blue	25.00	12.50	7.50
(8)	Charles Hafey/Red	40.00	20.00	12.00
(9)	J. Francis Hogan/Red	25.00	12.50	7.50
(10)	Carl Hubbell/Green	50.00	25.00	15.00
(11)	Charles Klein/Green	40.00	20.00	12.00
(12)	Ernest Lombardi/Blue	40.00	20.00	12.00
(13)	Alfonso Lopez/Blue	40.00	20.00	12.00
(14)	Rabbit Maranville/Green	40.00	20.00	12.00
(15)	Joe Moore/Red	25.00	12.50	7.50
(16)	Van Mungo/Green	25.00	12.50	7.50
(17)	Melvin (Mel) Ott/Blue	50.00	25.00	15.00
(18)	Gordon Slade/Green	25.00	12.50	7.50
(19)	Casey Stengel/Green	50.00	25.00	15.00
(20)	Tommy Thevenow/Red	25.00	12.50	7.50
(21)	Lloyd Waner/Red	40.00	20.00	12.00
(22)	Paul Waner/Green	50.00	25.00	15.00
(23)	Lon Warnecke/Blue	25.00	12.50	7.50
(24)	James Wilson/Blue	25.00	12.50	7.50

1935-36 Diamond Matchbooks

FRANKIE FRISCH
St. Louis "Cardinals"

By the career summaries on back of these covers it is evident this series was issued over a two-year period. Measuring about 1-1/2" x 4-1/8", the fronts have posed player photos printed in sepia. Borders can be found in red, green or blue, and it is believed that most, if not all, players, can be found in those three color varieties. Matchbooks in this series do not have the team name on back beneath the player name, as is the case on later series. Collectors generally prefer matchbooks to be complete with striker surface on bottom-back, though with matches removed. Values shown should be halved for covers without strikers. Complete with matches, covers will sell for a 2-3X premium over the values shown.

		NM	EX	VG
Complete Set (156):		3,500	1,750	1,000
Common Player:		20.00	10.00	6.00
(1)	Ethan Allen	20.00	10.00	6.00
(2)	Melo Almada	30.00	15.00	9.00
(3)	Eldon Auker	20.00	10.00	6.00
(4)	Dick Bartell	20.00	10.00	6.00
(5)	Aloysius Bejma	20.00	10.00	6.00
(6)	Ollie Bejma	20.00	10.00	6.00
(7)	Roy Chester Bell	20.00	10.00	6.00
(8)	Louis Berger	20.00	10.00	6.00
(9)	Walter Berger	20.00	10.00	6.00
(10)	Ralph Birkofer	20.00	10.00	6.00
(11)	Max Bishop	20.00	10.00	6.00
(12)	George Blaeholder	20.00	10.00	6.00
(13)	Henry (Zeke) Bonura	20.00	10.00	6.00
(14)	Jim Bottomley	35.00	17.50	10.50
(15)	Ed Brandt	20.00	10.00	6.00
(16)	Don Brennan	20.00	10.00	6.00
(17)	Lloyd Brown	20.00	10.00	6.00
(18)	Walter G. Brown	20.00	10.00	6.00
(19)	Claiborne Bryant	20.00	10.00	6.00
(20)	Jim Bucher	20.00	10.00	6.00
(21)	John Burnett	20.00	10.00	6.00
(22)	Irving Burns	20.00	10.00	6.00
(23)	Merritt Cain	20.00	10.00	6.00
(24)	Ben Cantwell	20.00	10.00	6.00
(25)	Tommy Carey	20.00	10.00	6.00
(26)	Tex Carleton	20.00	10.00	6.00
(27)	Joseph Cascarella	20.00	10.00	6.00
(28)	Thomas H. Casey	20.00	10.00	6.00
(29)	George Caster	20.00	10.00	6.00
(30)	Phil Cavarretta	20.00	10.00	6.00
(31)	Louis Chiozza	20.00	10.00	6.00
(32)	Edward Cihocki	20.00	10.00	6.00
(33)	Herman E. Clifton	20.00	10.00	6.00
(34)	Richard Coffman	20.00	10.00	6.00
(35)	Edward P. Coleman	20.00	10.00	6.00
(36)	James A. Collins	20.00	10.00	6.00

(37)	John Conlan	40.00	20.00	12.00
(38)	Roger Cramer	20.00	10.00	6.00
(39)	Hugh M. Critz	20.00	10.00	6.00
(40)	Alvin Crowder	20.00	10.00	6.00
(41)	Tony Cuccinello	20.00	10.00	6.00
(42)	Hazen "Kiki" Cuyler	35.00	17.50	10.50
(43)	Virgil Davis	20.00	10.00	6.00
(44)	Jerome Dean	75.00	37.00	22.00
(45)	Paul Derringer	20.00	10.00	6.00
(46)	James DeShong	20.00	10.00	6.00
(47)	William Dietrich	20.00	10.00	6.00
(48)	Leo Durocher	35.00	17.50	10.50
(49)	George Earnshaw	20.00	10.00	6.00
(50)	Elwood English	20.00	10.00	6.00
(51)	Louis Finney	20.00	10.00	6.00
(52)	Charles Fischer	20.00	10.00	6.00
(53)	Freddy Fitzsimmons	20.00	10.00	6.00
(54)	Benny Frey	20.00	10.00	6.00
(55)	Linus B. Frey	20.00	10.00	6.00
(56)	Frankie Frisch	40.00	20.00	12.00
(57)	August Galan	20.00	10.00	6.00
(58)	Milton Galatzer	20.00	10.00	6.00
(59)	Dennis Galehouse	20.00	10.00	6.00
(60)	Debs Garms	20.00	10.00	6.00
(61)	Angelo J. Giuliani	20.00	10.00	6.00
(62)	Earl Grace	20.00	10.00	6.00
(63)	Charles Grimm	20.00	10.00	6.00
(64)	Frank Grube	20.00	10.00	6.00
(65)	Stanley Hack	25.00	12.50	7.50
(66)	Irving "Bump" Hadley	20.00	10.00	6.00
(67)	Odell Hale	20.00	10.00	6.00
(68)	Bill Hallahan	20.00	10.00	6.00
(69)	Roy Hansen	20.00	10.00	6.00
(70)	Melvin Harder	20.00	10.00	6.00
(71)	Charles Hartnett	35.00	17.50	10.50
(72)	"Gabby" Hartnett	35.00	17.50	10.50
(73)	Clyde Hatter	20.00	10.00	6.00
(74)	Raymond Hayworth	20.00	10.00	6.00
(75)	Raymond Hayworth (W/chest protector.)	20.00	10.00	6.00
(76)	William Herman	35.00	17.50	10.50
(77)	Gordon Hinkle	20.00	10.00	6.00
(78)	George Hockette	20.00	10.00	6.00
(79)	James Holbrook	20.00	10.00	6.00
(80)	Alex Hooks	20.00	10.00	6.00
(81)	Waite Hoyt	35.00	17.50	10.50
(82)	Carl Hubbell	40.00	20.00	12.00
(83)	Roy M. Joiner	20.00	10.00	6.00
(84)	Sam Jones	20.00	10.00	6.00
(85)	Baxter Jordan	20.00	10.00	6.00
(86)	Arndt Jorgens	20.00	10.00	6.00
(87)	William F. Jurges	20.00	10.00	6.00
(88)	William Kamm	20.00	10.00	6.00
(89)	Vernon Kennedy	20.00	10.00	6.00
(90)	John Kerr	20.00	10.00	6.00
(91)	Charles Klein	40.00	20.00	12.00
(92)	Ted Kleinhans	20.00	10.00	6.00
(93)	Wm. Knickerbocker (Thighs-up.)	20.00	10.00	6.00
(94)	Wm. Knickerbocker (Waist-up.)	20.00	10.00	6.00
(95)	Jack Knott	20.00	10.00	6.00
(96)	Mark Koenig	20.00	10.00	6.00
(97)	Fabian L. Kowalik	20.00	10.00	6.00
(98)	Ralph Kress	20.00	10.00	6.00
(99)	Wm. C. "Bill" Lee	20.00	10.00	6.00
(100)	Louis Legett	20.00	10.00	6.00
(101)	Emil "Dutch" Leonard	20.00	10.00	6.00
(102)	Fred Lindstrom	35.00	17.50	10.50
(103)	Edward Linke (Pole in background.)	20.00	10.00	6.00
(104)	Edward Linke (No pole.)	20.00	10.00	6.00
(105)	Ernest Lombardi	35.00	17.50	10.50
(106)	Al Lopez	35.00	17.50	10.50
(107)	John Marcum	20.00	10.00	6.00
(108)	William McKechnie	35.00	17.50	10.50
(109)	Eric McNair	20.00	10.00	6.00
(110)	Joe Medwick	35.00	17.50	10.50
(111)	Oscar Melillo	20.00	10.00	6.00
(112)	John Michaels	20.00	10.00	6.00
(113)	Joe Moore	20.00	10.00	6.00
(114)	John Moore	20.00	10.00	6.00
(115)	Wallace Moses	20.00	10.00	6.00
(116)	Joseph Milligan	20.00	10.00	6.00
(117)	Van Mungo	25.00	12.50	7.50
(118)	Glenn Myatt	20.00	10.00	6.00
(119)	James O'Dea	20.00	10.00	6.00
(120)	Ernest Orsatti	20.00	10.00	6.00
(121)	Fred Ostermueller	20.00	10.00	6.00
(122)	Melvin "Mel" Ott	40.00	20.00	12.00
(123)	LeRoy Parmelee	20.00	10.00	6.00
(124)	Monte Pearson	20.00	10.00	6.00
(125)	Raymond Pepper	20.00	10.00	6.00
(126)	Raymond Phelps	20.00	10.00	6.00
(127)	George Pipgras	20.00	10.00	6.00
(128)	Frank Pytlak	20.00	10.00	6.00
(129)	Gordon Rhodes	20.00	10.00	6.00
(130)	Charlie Root	20.00	10.00	6.00
(131)	John Rothrock	20.00	10.00	6.00
(132)	Herold "Muddy" Ruel	20.00	10.00	6.00
(133)	Jack Saltzgaver	20.00	10.00	6.00
(134)	Fred Schulte	20.00	10.00	6.00
(135)	George Selkirk	20.00	10.00	6.00
(136)	Mervyn Shea	20.00	10.00	6.00
(137)	Al Spohrer	20.00	10.00	6.00
(138)	George Stainback	20.00	10.00	6.00
(139)	Casey Stengel	40.00	20.00	12.00
(140)	Walter Stephenson	20.00	10.00	6.00
(141)	Lee Stine	20.00	10.00	6.00
(142)	John Stone	20.00	10.00	6.00
(143)	Gus Suhr	20.00	10.00	6.00
(144)	Tommy Thevenow	20.00	10.00	6.00
(145)	Fay Thomas	20.00	10.00	6.00
(146)	Leslie Tietje	20.00	10.00	6.00
(147)	Bill Urbanski	20.00	10.00	6.00
(148)	William H. Walker	20.00	10.00	6.00
(149)	Lloyd Waner	40.00	20.00	12.00
(150)	Paul Waner	40.00	20.00	12.00

(151)	Lon Warnecke	20.00	10.00	6.00
(152)	Harold Warstler	20.00	10.00	6.00
(153)	Bill Werber	20.00	10.00	6.00
(154)	Vernon Wiltshere	20.00	10.00	6.00
(155)	James Wilson	20.00	10.00	6.00
(156)	Ralph Winegarner	20.00	10.00	6.00

1936 Diamond Matchbooks - Team on Back

This is the smallest series of baseball player matchbooks, with only 13 subjects, each found with borders of red, green or blue. Player poses on front are printed in sepia (except one variation of Grimm that is in black-and-white). This series can be differentiated from contemporary series by the appearance of the player's team name on back, beneath his name. Backs have a career summary. About 1-1/2" x 4-1/8", these matchbooks are commonly collected with the matches removed and the striker at back bottom intact. Pieces without the striker are valued at 50 percent of these listed prices. Complete covers with matches bring a premium of 2-3X. The players are listed here alphabetically.

		NM	EX	VG
Complete Set (13):		350.00	175.00	100.00
Common Player:		20.00	10.00	6.00
(1)	Tommy Carey	20.00	10.00	6.00
(2)	Tony Cuccinello	20.00	10.00	6.00
(3)	Freddy Fitzsimmons	20.00	10.00	6.00
(4)	Frank Frisch	45.00	22.00	13.50
(5a)	Charles Grimm (Home uniform, b/w.)	20.00	10.00	6.00
(5b)	Charlie Grimm (Home uniform, sepia.)	20.00	10.00	6.00
(6)	Charlie Grimm (Road uniform.)	20.00	10.00	6.00
(7)	Carl Hubbell	45.00	22.00	13.50
(8)	Baxter Jordan	20.00	10.00	6.00
(9)	Chuck Klein	45.00	22.00	13.50
(10)	Al Lopez	35.00	17.50	10.50
(11)	Joe Medwick	35.00	17.50	10.50
(12)	Van Lingle Mungo	25.00	12.50	7.50
(13)	Mel Ott	45.00	22.00	13.50

1936 Diamond Matchbooks - Chicago Cubs

This short series of baseball player matchbooks can each be found with borders of red, green or blue. Except for Dean, all photos are portraits, printed in sepia or black-and-white. Dean and Paul Waner are the only subjects in the set who were not members of the Chicago Cubs. This series can be differentiated from 1935-36 Diamond Matchbooks only by studying the career summary and stats on back. About 1-1/2" x 4-1/8", these matchbooks are commonly collected with the matches removed and the striker at back-bottom intact. Pieces without the striker are valued at 50 percent of these listed prices. Complete covers with matches bring a premium of 2-3X. The players are listed here alphabetically.

		NM	EX	VG
Complete Set (23):		350.00	175.00	100.00
Common Player:		12.50	6.25	3.75
(1)	Claiborne Bryant	12.50	6.25	3.75
(2)	Tex Carleton	12.50	6.25	3.75
(3)	Phil Cavarretta	12.50	6.25	3.75
(4)	James A. Collins	12.50	6.25	3.75
(5)	Curt Davis	12.50	6.25	3.75
(6)	Jerome "Dizzy" Dean	50.00	25.00	15.00
(7)	Frank Demaree	12.50	6.25	3.75
(8)	Larry French	12.50	6.25	3.75
(9)	Linus R. Frey	12.50	6.25	3.75
(10)	August Galan	12.50	6.25	3.75
(11)	Bob Garbark	12.50	6.25	3.75
(12)	Stanley Hack	15.00	7.50	4.50
(13)	Charles Hartnett	30.00	15.00	9.00
(14)	William Herman	30.00	15.00	9.00
(15)	William F. Jurges	12.50	6.25	3.75
(16)	William C. "Bill" Lee	12.50	6.25	3.75
(17)	Joe Marty	12.50	6.25	3.75
(18)	James K. O'Dea	12.50	6.25	3.75
(19)	LeRoy Parmelee	12.50	6.25	3.75
(20)	Charlie Root	12.50	6.25	3.75
(21)	Clyde Shoun	12.50	6.25	3.75
(22)	George Stainback	12.50	6.25	3.75
(23)	Paul Waner	40.00	20.00	12.00

1889 Diamond S Cigars Boston N.L.

(See 1889 Number 7 Cigars for checklist and value information.)

1934-36 Diamond Stars (R327)

Issued from 1934-36, the Diamond Stars set (ACC designation R327) consists of 108 cards. Produced by National Chicle, the cards measure 2-3/8" x 2-7/8" and are color art renderings of actual photographs on art deco backgrounds. The year of issue can usually be determined by the player's statistics found on the reverse of the card. Backs also feature either a player biography or a playing tip. Some cards can be found with either green or blue printing on the backs. The complete set price does not include the higher priced variations which make up the 170-card "master" set.

		NM	EX	VG
Complete Set (108):		22,500	9,000	4,000
Complete Set (170):		35,000	14,000	6,250
Common Player (1-84):		100.00	35.00	20.00
Common Player (85-96):		200.00	85.00	45.00
Common Player (97-108):		500.00	245.00	120.00
1a	"Lefty" Grove (1934 green back.)	5,040	770.00	245.00
1b	"Lefty" Grove (1935 green back.)	5,040	770.00	245.00
2a	Al Simmons (1934 green back.)	840.00	225.00	155.00

2b	Al Simmons (1935 green back.)	840.00	225.00	155.00
2c	Al Simmons (1936 blue back.)	910.00	365.00	180.00
3a	"Rabbit" Maranville (1934 green back.)	455.00	180.00	90.00
3b	"Rabbit" Maranville (1935 green back.)	455.00	180.00	90.00
4a	"Buddy" Myer (1934 green back.)	100.00	35.00	20.00
4b	"Buddy" Myer (1935 green back.)	100.00	35.00	20.00
4c	"Buddy" Myer (1936 blue back.)	105.00	45.00	20.00
5a	Tom Bridges (1934 green back.)	100.00	35.00	20.00
5b	Tom Bridges (1935 green back.)	100.00	35.00	20.00
5c	Tom Bridges (1936 blue back.)	105.00	45.00	20.00
6a	Max Bishop (1934 green back.)	100.00	35.00	20.00
6b	Max Bishop (1935 green back.)	100.00	35.00	20.00
7a	Lew Fonseca (1934 green back.)	100.00	35.00	20.00
7b	Lew Fonseca (1935 green back.)	100.00	35.00	20.00
8a	Joe Vosmik (1934 green back.)	100.00	35.00	20.00
8b	Joe Vosmik (1935 green back.)	100.00	35.00	20.00
8c	Joe Vosmik (1936 blue back.)	105.00	45.00	20.00
9a	"Mickey" Cochrane (1934 green back.)	455.00	180.00	90.00
9b	"Mickey" Cochrane (1935 green back.)	455.00	180.00	90.00
9c	"Mickey" Cochrane (1936 blue back.)	525.00	210.00	105.00
10a	Roy Mahaffey (1934 green back.)	100.00	35.00	20.00
10b	Roy Mahaffey (1935 green back.)	100.00	35.00	20.00
10c	Roy Mahaffey (1936 blue back.)	105.00	45.00	20.00
11a	Bill Dickey (1934 green back.)	525.00	210.00	105.00
11b	Bill Dickey (1935 green back.)	525.00	210.00	105.00
12a	Dixie Walker (1934 green back.)	100.00	35.00	20.00
12b	Dixie Walker (1935 green back.)	100.00	35.00	20.00
12c	Dixie Walker (1936 blue back.)	105.00	45.00	20.00
13a	George Blaeholder (1934 green back.)	100.00	35.00	20.00
13b	George Blaeholder (1935 green back.)	100.00	35.00	20.00
14a	Bill Terry (1934 green back.)	455.00	180.00	90.00
14b	Bill Terry (1935 green back.)	455.00	180.00	90.00
15a	Dick Bartell (1934 green back.)	100.00	35.00	20.00
15b	Dick Bartell (1935 green back.)	100.00	35.00	20.00
16a	Lloyd Waner (1934 green back.)	455.00	180.00	90.00
16b	Lloyd Waner (1935 green back.)	455.00	180.00	90.00
16c	Lloyd Waner (1936 blue back.)	560.00	225.00	115.00
17a	Frankie Frisch (1934 green back.)	455.00	180.00	90.00
17b	Frankie Frisch (1935 green back.)	455.00	180.00	90.00
18a	"Chick" Hafey (1934 green back.)	455.00	180.00	90.00
18b	"Chick" Hafey (1935 green back.)	455.00	180.00	90.00
19a	Van Mungo (1934 green back.)	315.00	125.00	65.00
19b	Van Mungo (1935 green back.)	315.00	125.00	65.00
20a	"Shanty" Hogan (1934 green back.)	100.00	35.00	20.00
20b	"Shanty" Hogan (1935 green back.)	100.00	35.00	20.00
21a	Johnny Vergez (1934 green back.)	100.00	35.00	20.00
21b	Johnny Vergez (1935 green back.)	100.00	35.00	20.00
22a	Jimmy Wilson (1934 green back.)	100.00	35.00	20.00
22b	Jimmy Wilson (1935 green back.)	100.00	35.00	20.00
22c	Jimmy Wilson (1936 blue back.)	105.00	45.00	20.00
23a	Bill Hallahan (1934 green back.)	100.00	35.00	20.00
23b	Bill Hallahan (1935 green back.)	100.00	35.00	20.00
24a	"Sparky" Adams (1934 green back.)	100.00	35.00	20.00
24b	"Sparky" Adams (1935 green back.)	100.00	35.00	20.00
25	Walter Berger	100.00	35.00	20.00
26a	"Pepper" Martin (1935 green back.)	160.00	65.00	30.00
26b	"Pepper" Martin (1936 blue back.)	175.00	70.00	35.00
27	"Pie" Traynor	200.00	85.00	45.00
28	"Al" Lopez	200.00	85.00	45.00
29	Robert Rolfe	100.00	35.00	20.00
30a	"Heinie" Manush	200.00	85.00	45.00
30b	"Heinie" Manush (1936 blue back.)	245.00	100.00	50.00
31a	"Kiki" Cuyler (1935 green back.)	200.00	85.00	45.00
31b	"Kiki" Cuyler (1936 blue back.)	245.00	100.00	50.00
32	Sam Rice	200.00	85.00	45.00
33	"Schoolboy" Rowe	125.00	50.00	20.00
34	Stanley Hack	125.00	50.00	20.00
35	Earle Averill	200.00	85.00	45.00
36a	Earnie Lombardi	560.00	225.00	115.00
36b	Ernie Lombardi	245.00	100.00	50.00
37	"Billie" Urbanski	100.00	35.00	20.00
38	Ben Chapman	100.00	35.00	20.00
39	Carl Hubbell	295.00	120.00	55.00
40	"Blondy" Ryan	100.00	35.00	20.00
41	Harvey Hendrick	100.00	35.00	20.00
42	Jimmy Dykes	100.00	35.00	20.00
43	Ted Lyons	200.00	85.00	45.00
44	Rogers Hornsby	525.00	210.00	105.00
45	"Jo Jo" White	100.00	35.00	20.00
46	"Red" Lucas	100.00	35.00	20.00
47	Cliff Bolton	100.00	35.00	20.00
48	"Rick" Ferrell	200.00	85.00	45.00
49	"Buck" Jordan	100.00	35.00	20.00
50	"Mel" Ott	310.00	120.00	55.00
51	John Whitehead	100.00	35.00	20.00
52	George Stainback	100.00	35.00	20.00
53	Oscar Melillo	100.00	35.00	20.00
54a	"Hank" Greenburg (Greenberg)	1,260	505.00	250.00
54b	"Hank" Greenberg	805.00	325.00	160.00
55	Tony Cuccinello	100.00	35.00	20.00
56	"Gus" Suhr	100.00	35.00	20.00
57	Cy Blanton	100.00	35.00	20.00
58	Glenn Myatt	100.00	35.00	20.00
59	Jim Bottomley	200.00	85.00	45.00
60	Charley "Red" Ruffing	200.00	85.00	45.00
61	"Billie" Werber	100.00	35.00	20.00
62	Fred M. Frankhouse	100.00	35.00	20.00
63	"Stonewall" Jackson	200.00	85.00	45.00
64	Jimmie Foxx	560.00	225.00	115.00
65	"Zeke" Bonura	100.00	35.00	20.00
66	"Ducky" Medwick	200.00	85.00	45.00
67	Marvin Owen	100.00	35.00	20.00
68	"Sam" Leslie	100.00	35.00	20.00
69	Earl Grace	100.00	35.00	20.00
70	"Hal" Trosky	100.00	35.00	20.00
71	"Ossie" Bluege	100.00	35.00	20.00
72	"Tony" Piet	100.00	35.00	20.00
73a	"Fritz" Ostermueller (1935 green back.)	100.00	35.00	20.00
73b	"Fritz" Ostermueller (1935 blue back.)	100.00	35.00	20.00
73c	"Fritz" Ostermueller (1936 blue back.)	105.00	45.00	20.00
74a	Tony Lazzeri (1935 green back.)	365.00	140.00	70.00
74b	Tony Lazzeri (1935 blue back.)	365.00	140.00	70.00
74c	Tony Lazzeri (1936 blue back.)	385.00	155.00	77.00
75a	Irving Burns (1935 green back.)	100.00	35.00	20.00
75b	Irving Burns (1935 green back.)	100.00	35.00	20.00
75c	Irving Burns (1936 blue back.)	105.00	45.00	20.00
76a	Bill Rogell (1935 green back.)	100.00	35.00	20.00
76b	Bill Rogell (1935 blue back.)	105.00	45.00	20.00
76c	Bill Rogell (1936 blue back.)	105.00	45.00	20.00
77a	Charlie Gehringer (1935 green back.)	350.00	140.00	70.00
77b	Charlie Gehringer (1935 green back.)	350.00	140.00	70.00
77c	Charlie Gehringer (1936 blue back.)	370.00	140.00	70.00
78a	Joe Kuhel (1935 green back.)	100.00	35.00	20.00
78b	Joe Kuhel (1935 blue back.)	100.00	35.00	20.00
78c	Joe Kuhel (1936 blue back.)	105.00	45.00	20.00
79a	Willis Hudlin (1935 green back.)	100.00	35.00	20.00
79b	Willis Hudlin (1935 blue back.)	100.00	35.00	20.00
79c	Willis Hudlin (1936 blue back.)	105.00	45.00	20.00
80a	Louis Chiozza (1935 green back.)	100.00	35.00	20.00
80b	Louis Chiozza (1935 blue back.)	100.00	35.00	20.00
80c	Louis Chiozza (1936 blue back.)	105.00	45.00	20.00
81a	Bill DeLancey (1935 green back)	100.00	35.00	20.00
81b	Bill DeLancey (1935 blue back.)	100.00	35.00	20.00
81c	Bill DeLancey (1936 blue back.)	105.00	45.00	20.00
82a	John Babich (1935 green back.)	100.00	35.00	20.00
82b	John Babich (1935 blue back.)	100.00	35.00	20.00
q2c	John Babich (1936 blue back.)	105.00	45.00	20.00
83a	Paul Waner (1935 green back.)	200.00	85.00	45.00
83b	Paul Waner (1935 blue back.)	200.00	85.00	45.00
83c	Paul Waner (1936 blue back.)	225.00	85.00	45.00
84a	Sam Byrd (1935 green back.)	100.00	35.00	20.00
84b	Sam Byrd (1935 blue back.)	100.00	35.00	20.00
84c	Sam Byrd (1936 blue back.)	105.00	45.00	20.00
85	Julius Solters	200.00	85.00	45.00
86	Frank Crosetti	350.00	140.00	70.00
87	Steve O'Neil (O'Neill)	200.00	85.00	45.00
88	Geo. Selkirk	200.00	85.00	45.00
89	Joe Stripp	200.00	85.00	45.00
90	Ray Hayworth	200.00	85.00	45.00
91	Bucky Harris	455.00	185.00	90.00
92	Ethan Allen	200.00	85.00	45.00
93	Alvin Crowder	200.00	85.00	45.00
94	Wes Ferrell	200.00	85.00	45.00
95	Luke Appling	455.00	185.00	90.00
96	Lew Riggs	200.00	85.00	45.00
97	"Al" Lopez	840.00	335.00	170.00
98	"Schoolboy" Rowe	500.00	245.00	120.00
99	"Pie" Traynor	805.00	325.00	160.00
100	Earle Averill (Earl)	805.00	325.00	160.00
101	Dick Bartell	500.00	245.00	120.00
102	Van Mungo	665.00	265.00	135.00
103	Bill Dickey	1,085	435.00	215.00
104	Robert Rolfe	500.00	245.00	120.00
105	"Ernie" Lombardi	840.00	335.00	170.00
106	"Red" Lucas	500.00	245.00	120.00
107	Stanley Hack	630.00	250.00	125.00
108	Walter Berger	1,120	280.00	135.00

1924 Diaz Cigarettes

Because they were printed in Cuba and feature only pitchers, the 1924 Diaz Cigarette cards are among the rarest and most intriguing of all tobacco issues. Produced in Havana for the Diaz brand, the black-and-white cards measure 1-3/4" x 2-1/2" and were printed on a semi-gloss stock. The player's name and position are listed at the bottom of the card, while his team and league appear at the top. According to the card backs, printed in Spanish, the set consists of 136 cards - all major league pitchers. But to date only the cards checklisted here have been discovered, and several of them never played in the major leagues.

	Common Player:	NM	EX	VG
1	Walter P. Johnson	5,250	2,200	1,100
2	Waite C. Hoyt	1,500	600.00	300.00
3	Grover C. Alexander	2,250	900.00	450.00
4	Thomas Sheehan	900.00	360.00	180.00
5	Pete Donohue	900.00	360.00	180.00
6	Herbert J. Pennock	1,350	550.00	275.00
7				
8	Carl Mays	1,100	450.00	225.00
9				
10	Allan S. Sothoron (Allen)	900.00	360.00	180.00
11	Wm. Piercy	900.00	360.00	180.00
12	Curtis Fullerton	900.00	360.00	180.00
13	Hollis Thurston	900.00	360.00	180.00
14	George Walberg	900.00	360.00	180.00
15	Fred Heimach	900.00	360.00	180.00
16	Sherrod M. Smith	900.00	360.00	180.00
17	Warren H. Ogden	900.00	360.00	180.00
18	Ernest P. Osborne (Earnest)	900.00	360.00	180.00
19	Walter H. Ruether	900.00	360.00	180.00
20	Burleigh A. Grimes	1,350	550.00	275.00
21	Joseph Genewich	900.00	360.00	180.00
22	Victor Aldridge	900.00	360.00	180.00
23	Arnold E. Stone	900.00	360.00	180.00
24	Lester C. Howe	900.00	360.00	180.00
25	George K. Murry (Murray)	900.00	360.00	180.00
26	Herman Pillette	900.00	360.00	180.00
27	John D. Couch	900.00	360.00	180.00
28	Tony C. Kaufmann	900.00	360.00	180.00
29	Frank (Jake) May	900.00	360.00	180.00
30	Howard J. Ehmke	900.00	360.00	180.00
31				
32				
33	Gorham V. Leverett	900.00	360.00	180.00
34	Bryan Harris	900.00	360.00	180.00
35	Paul F. Schreiber	900.00	360.00	180.00
36	Dewey Hinkle	900.00	360.00	180.00
37	Arthur C. Vance	1,350	550.00	275.00
38	Jesse J. Haines	1,350	550.00	275.00
39	Earl Hamilton	900.00	360.00	180.00
40	A. Wilbur Cooper	900.00	360.00	180.00
41	Thomas F. Long	900.00	360.00	180.00
42	Alex Ferguson	900.00	360.00	180.00
43	Chester Ross	900.00	360.00	180.00
44	John J. Quinn (Middle initial actually P.)	900.00	360.00	180.00
45	Ray C. Kolp	900.00	360.00	180.00
46	Arthur N. Nehf	900.00	360.00	180.00
47				
48				
49	Edwin A. Rommel	900.00	360.00	180.00
50	Theodore A. Lyons	1,350	550.00	275.00
51	Roy Meeker	900.00	360.00	180.00
52	John D. Stuart	900.00	360.00	180.00
53	Joseph Oeschger	900.00	360.00	180.00
54	Wayland Dean	900.00	360.00	180.00
55	Guy Morton	900.00	360.00	180.00
56	William L. Doak	900.00	360.00	180.00
57	Edward J. Pfeffer	900.00	360.00	180.00
58	Sam Gray	900.00	360.00	180.00
59				
60	Godfrey Brogan	900.00	360.00	180.00
61				
62	Howard E. Baldwin	900.00	360.00	180.00
63	Bert Lewis	900.00	360.00	180.00

		NM	EX	VG
64				
65	Dennis Burns	900.00	360.00	180.00
66	Roline C. Naylor (Roleine)	900.00	360.00	180.00
67	Walter H. Huntzinger	900.00	360.00	180.00
68	S. F. Baumgartner	900.00	360.00	180.00
69				
70	Clarence E. Mitchell	900.00	360.00	180.00
71				
72	Charles F. Clazner (Glazner)	900.00	360.00	180.00
73				
74				
75	Dennis J. Gearin	900.00	360.00	180.00
76	Jonathan T. Zachary	900.00	360.00	180.00
77				
78	Jess F. Winter (Jesse Winters)	900.00	360.00	180.00
79	Charles Ruffing	1,350	550.00	275.00
80	John W. Cooney	900.00	360.00	180.00
81	Leslie J. Bush (Middle initial A.)	900.00	360.00	180.00
82	William Harris	900.00	360.00	180.00
83	Joseph B. Shaute	900.00	360.00	180.00
84				
85	Eppa J. Rixey	1,350	550.00	275.00
86	William L. Sherdel	900.00	360.00	180.00
87	John C. Benton	900.00	360.00	180.00
88	Arthur R. Decatur	900.00	360.00	180.00
89	Harry G. Shriver	900.00	360.00	180.00
90	John D. Morrison	900.00	360.00	180.00
91	Walter M. Betts	900.00	360.00	180.00
92	Oscar Roettger	900.00	360.00	180.00
93				
94	Mike Cvengros	900.00	360.00	180.00
95	Leo L. Dickerman	900.00	360.00	180.00
96	Philip B. Weinart	2,400	960.00	480.00
97	Nicholas Dumovich	900.00	360.00	180.00
98				
99	Timothy A. McNamara	900.00	360.00	180.00
100	Allan Russell	900.00	360.00	180.00
101	Ted Blankenship	900.00	360.00	180.00
102	Howard E. Baldwin	900.00	360.00	180.00
103	Frank T. Davis	900.00	360.00	180.00
104	James C. Edwards	900.00	360.00	180.00
105	Hubert F. Pruett	900.00	360.00	180.00
106	Richard Rudolph	900.00	360.00	180.00
107				
108	Claude Jonnard	900.00	360.00	180.00
109				
110				
111	John M. Bentley (Initial actually N.)	900.00	360.00	180.00
112	Wilfred D. Ryan	900.00	360.00	180.00
113	George D. Metivier	900.00	360.00	180.00
114				
115	Sylvester Johnson	900.00	360.00	180.00
116	O.L. Fuhr	900.00	360.00	180.00
117				
118	Stanley Coveleski	1,350	550.00	275.00
119	Dave C. Danforth	900.00	360.00	180.00
120	Elam Van Gilder	900.00	360.00	180.00
121	Bert Cole	900.00	360.00	180.00
122	Kenneth E. Holoway (Holloway)	900.00	360.00	180.00
123	Charles Robertson	900.00	360.00	180.00
124				
125	George Dauss	900.00	360.00	180.00
126				
127				
128				
129	Phillip Bedgood	900.00	360.00	180.00
130	Fred Wingfield	900.00	360.00	180.00
131	George Mogridge	900.00	360.00	180.00
132	J. Martina	900.00	360.00	180.00
133	B.F. Speece	900.00	360.00	180.00
134	Harold Carlson	900.00	360.00	180.00
135	Wilbert W. Hubbell	900.00	360.00	180.00
136	Milton Gaston	900.00	360.00	180.00

(The following pitchers are known to have been included in the set, though their card numbers are unknown. They are listed here alphabetically, though the names may be different on the cards.)

		NM	EX	VG
---	Jess L. Barnes	900.00	360.00	180.00
---	Virgil E. Barnes	900.00	360.00	180.00
---	William Bayne	900.00	360.00	180.00
---	Lawrence J. Benton	900.00	360.00	180.00
---	Warren Collins (Rip)	900.00	360.00	180.00
---	Joubert Davenport (Lum)	900.00	360.00	180.00
---	Urban C. Faber	900.00	360.00	180.00
---	Robert K. Hasty	900.00	360.00	180.00
---	Frank J. Henry	900.00	360.00	180.00
---	Samuel P. Jones	900.00	360.00	180.00
---	Adolfo Luque	900.00	360.00	180.00
---	Fred Marberry	900.00	360.00	180.00
---	Richard W. Marquard	900.00	360.00	180.00
---	Walter H. McGrew (Slim)	900.00	360.00	180.00
---	Herbert McQuaid	900.00	360.00	180.00
---	Hugh A. McQuillan	900.00	360.00	180.00
---	Lee Meadows	900.00	360.00	180.00
---	Louis A. North	900.00	360.00	180.00
---	George W. Pipgras	900.00	360.00	180.00
---	James J. Ring	900.00	360.00	180.00
---	Robert Shawkey	900.00	360.00	180.00
---	Urban J. Shocker	900.00	360.00	180.00
---	George Uhle	900.00	360.00	180.00
---	John R. Watson	900.00	360.00	180.00
---	Ed L. Wells	900.00	360.00	180.00
---	Byron W. Yarrison	900.00	360.00	180.00
---	Paul V. Zahniser	900.00	360.00	180.00

1962 Dickson Orde & Co.

One of several English tobacco cards to include baseball among a series of world's sports, this card is of marginal interest to U.S. collectors because its color front pictures (from the back) a batter who could be Babe Ruth as part of a baseball scene on the front of the 2-5/8" x 1-3/8" card. The short description of baseball on the card's black-and-white back does

mention Ruth. The "Sports of the Countries" series comprises 25 cards.

		NM	EX	VG
11	America (Babe Ruth)	25.00	12.50	7.50

1980 Did You Know . . . ?

This collectors' edition was produced by artist Mel (?) Anderson. The blank-backed 3-1/4" x 6-3/8" cards have black-and-white drawings of ballplayers and a "Did You Know" trivia fact. The unnumbered cards are checklisted here alphabetically.

		NM	EX	VG
	Complete Set (30):	25.00	12.50	7.50
	Common Player:	2.00	1.00	.60
(1)	Richie Ashburn	4.00	2.00	1.25
(2)	Hank Bauer	2.50	1.25	.70
(3)	Ewell "The Whip" Blackwell	2.50	1.25	.70
(4)	Johnny Callison	2.00	1.00	.60
(5)	Roger "Doc" Cramer	2.00	1.00	.60
(6)	Harry Danning	2.00	1.00	.60
(7)	Ferris Fain	2.00	1.00	.60
(8)	Ned Garver	2.00	1.00	.60
(9)	Harvey Haddix	2.00	1.00	.60
(10)	Clint Hartung	2.00	1.00	.60
(11)	"Bobo" Holloman	2.00	1.00	.60
(12)	Ron Hunt	2.00	1.00	.60
(13)	Howard "Spud" Krist	2.00	1.00	.60
(14)	Emil "Dutch" Leonard	2.00	1.00	.60
(15)	Buddy Lewis	2.00	1.00	.60
(16)	Jerry Lynch	2.00	1.00	.60
(17)	Roy McMillan	2.00	1.00	.60
(18)	Johnny Mize	3.00	1.50	.90
(19)	Hugh Mulcahy	2.00	1.00	.60
(20)	Hal Newhouser	2.00	1.00	.60
(21)	Jim Perry	2.00	1.00	.60
(22)	Phil Rizzuto	4.00	2.00	1.25
(23)	Bobby Shantz	2.00	1.00	.60
(24)	Roy Sievers	2.00	1.00	.60
(25)	Nick Testa	3.00	1.50	.90
(26)	Cecil Travis	2.00	1.00	.60
(27)	Elmer "Valient" Valo	2.00	1.00	.60
(28)	Bill Werber	2.00	1.00	.60
(29)	Mickey Witek	2.00	1.00	.60
(30)	Hal Woodeshick	2.00	1.00	.60

1907-09 Dietsche Detroit Tigers Postcards (PC765-1)

Three apparent annual issues (1907-09) of the home team by Detroit postcard publisher A.C. Dietsche, these 3-1/2" x 5-1/2" black-and-white post-cards have most of the photographic background on front blackened out. The player's last name usually appears on the front. On back, along with the post-

card legalities are a short player biography and a dated copyright line. The postcards were sold in sets of 15 cards for 25 cents.

		NM	EX	VG
	Common Player:	150.00	60.00	30.00
Series 1 - 1907				
	Complete Set (16):	7,000	2,800	1,400
(1)	Tyrus R. Cobb/Btg	2,000	800.00	400.00
(2)	Tyrus R. Cobb/Fielding	3,000	1,200	600.00
(3)	William Coughlin	150.00	60.00	30.00
(4)	Samuel S. Crawford	325.00	130.00	65.00
(5)	William E. Donovan	150.00	60.00	30.00
(6)	Jerome W. Downs	150.00	60.00	30.00
(7)	Hughie A. Jennings	325.00	130.00	65.00
(8)	David Jones	150.00	60.00	30.00
(9)	Edward H. Killian	150.00	60.00	30.00
(10)	George J. Mullin	150.00	60.00	30.00
(11)	Charles O'Leary	150.00	60.00	30.00
(12)	Fred T. Payne	150.00	60.00	30.00
(13)	Claude Rossman	150.00	60.00	30.00
(14)	Herman W. Schaefer	150.00	60.00	30.00
(15)	Charles Schmidt	150.00	60.00	30.00
(16)	Edward Siever	150.00	60.00	30.00
Series 2 - 1908				
	Complete Set (22):	6,000	2,400	1,200
(1)	Henry Beckendorf	180.00	70.00	35.00
(2)	Owen Bush	180.00	70.00	35.00
(3)	Tyrus R. Cobb	2,500	1,000	500.00
(4)	William Coughlin	180.00	70.00	35.00
(5)	Sam Crawford	350.00	140.00	70.00
(6)	William E. Donovan	180.00	70.00	35.00
(7)	Jerome W. Downs	180.00	70.00	35.00
(8)	Hughie A. Jennings	350.00	140.00	70.00
(9)	Tom Jones	180.00	70.00	35.00
(10)	Edward H. Killian	180.00	70.00	35.00
(11)	Matthew McIntyre	180.00	70.00	35.00
(12)	George J. Moriarty	180.00	70.00	35.00
(13)	George J. Mullin	180.00	70.00	35.00
(14)	Charles O'Leary	180.00	70.00	35.00
(15)	Fred T. Payne	180.00	70.00	35.00
(16)	Germany Schaefer	180.00	70.00	35.00
(17)	Charles Schmidt	180.00	70.00	35.00
(18)	Oscar Stanage	180.00	70.00	35.00
(19)	Oren Edgar Summers	180.00	70.00	35.00
(20)	Ira Thomas	180.00	70.00	35.00
(21)	Edgar Willett	180.00	70.00	35.00
(22)	George Winter	180.00	70.00	35.00
Series 3 - 1909				
	Complete Set (4):	750.00	300.00	150.00
(1)	James Delehanty	200.00	80.00	40.00
(2)	Tom Jones	180.00	70.00	35.00
(3)	Ralph Works	180.00	70.00	35.00
(4)	Detroit Tigers Team	300.00	125.00	60.00

1907 Dietsche Chicago Cubs Postcards (PC765-2)

This series of early Cubs postcards was published by the same Detroit printer who issued Tigers postcard series from 1907-09. The Dietsche Cubs postcards are scarcer than the Tigers issues because they were only offered for sale in Detroit in conjunction with the 1907 World Series between the Tigers and Cubs, and few people bought the visiting team's cards. The 3-1/2" x 5-1/2" black-and-white cards have most of the photographic background blacked out on front. The player's last name may or may not appear on the front. Postcard style backs include a short career summary and a dated copyright line. The 15-card sets originally sold for 25 cents.

		NM	EX	VG
Complete Set (15):		5,500	2,200	1,100
Common Player:		340.00	135.00	65.00
(1)	Mordecai Brown	500.00	200.00	100.00
(2)	Frank L. Chance	500.00	200.00	100.00
(3)	John Evers	500.00	200.00	100.00
(4)	Arthur F. Hoffman (Hofman)	340.00	135.00	65.00
(5)	John Kling	340.00	135.00	65.00
(6)	Carl Lundgren	340.00	135.00	65.00
(7)	Patrick J. Moran	340.00	135.00	65.00
(8)	Orval Overall	340.00	135.00	65.00
(9)	John A. Pfeister	340.00	135.00	65.00
(10)	Edw. M. Ruelbach	340.00	135.00	65.00
(11)	Frank M. Schulte	340.00	135.00	65.00
(12)	James T. Sheckard	340.00	135.00	65.00
(13)	James Slagle	340.00	135.00	65.00
(14)	Harry Steinfeldt	340.00	135.00	65.00
(15)	Joseph B. Tinker	500.00	200.00	100.00

1907 Dietsche Posters

The images found on the Dietsche postcards were conglomerated on a pair of black-and-white cardboard posters. About 22" square, the posters are headlined: "FRANK CHANCE AND HIS 1907 PENNANT WINNERS" and "HUGHIE JENNINGS AND HIS GREA 1970 TIGERS."

	NM	EX	VG
1907 Chicago Cubs	1,000	500.00	300.00
1907 Detroit Tigers	1,000	500.00	300.00

1934 Dietz Gum Ball Players in Action

See 1934 Al Demaree Die-Cuts (R304).

1942 Joe DiMaggio Candy Box Card

With no maker's name visible, this crudely executed war-era card is believed to have been printed on a candy box. In a format of 2-7/16" x 3-3/16" it is printed in blue and orange on white, is perforated on the sides and blank-backed.

	NM	EX	VG
Joe DiMaggio	150.00	75.00	45.00

1950 Joe DiMaggio Oriental Tour Postcard

In the post-season of 1950, during the Korean War, Joe DiMaggio led a goodwill tour of the Orient, including stops to visit the troops and to baseball-related destinations in Japan. This Italian postcard shows DiMaggio and Lefty O'Doul in a colorized photo surrounded by Japanese schoolboy ballplayers. The postcard-style back describes the scene. The card measures about 6" x 4".

	NM	EX	VG
Joe DiMaggio	125.00	65.00	40.00

1951 Joe DiMaggio Baseball Shoes

This 2-1/2" x 3-1/2" card was included with DiMaggio brand baseball shoes. A hole punched in the upper-left corner allowed the card to be attached to the shoe strings. Front has an action pose of DiMaggio printed in black-and-white on a dark green background. A facsimile autograph is at center. At bottom is printed: "THE YANKEE CLIPPER." The back has another facsimile signature and the player's career highlights through the 1950 season.

	NM	EX	VG
Joe DiMaggio (Hang-tag card.)	140.00	70.00	40.00
Joe DiMaggio (Complete box, shoes, tag.)	650.00	325.00	200.00

1972-83 Dimanche/ Derniere Heure Photos

From 1972-74, and 1977-83, the Montreal magazine Dimanche / Derniere Heure (loosely translated, "Sunday / Latest Hour") issued color photos of Expos (and a few other) players. The 8-1/2" x 11" photos are printed on semi-gloss paper stock that is punched for a three-ring binder. Fronts have a large color photo with player data, stats and career highlights printed in black beneath - all in French. At left or top is usually the issue date in which the photo was included in the magazine. Backs are blank.

	NM	EX	VG
Common Player:	5.00	2.50	1.50
(Stars are valued up to $50.)			

1972 Dimanche/Derniere Heure Expos

		NM	EX	VG
Complete Set (37):		155.00	78.00	47.00
Common Player:		5.00	2.50	1.50
(1)	Bill Stoneman (April 9)	5.00	2.50	1.50
(2)	John Boccabella (April 16)	5.00	2.50	1.50
(3)	Gene Mauch (April 23)	5.00	2.50	1.50
(4)	Ron Hunt (April 30)	5.00	2.50	1.50
(5)	Steve Renko (May 7)	5.00	2.50	1.50
(6)	Boots Day (May 14)	5.00	2.50	1.50
(7)	Bob Bailey (May 21)	5.00	2.50	1.50
(8)	Ernie McAnally (May 28)	5.00	2.50	1.50
(9)	Ken Singleton (June 4)	5.00	2.50	1.50
(10)	Ron Fairly (June 11)	5.00	2.50	1.50
(11)	Ron Woods (June 18)	5.00	2.50	1.50
(12)	Mike Jorgensen (June 25)	5.00	2.50	1.50
(13)	Bobby Wine (July 2)	5.00	2.50	1.50
(14)	Mike Torrez (July 9)	5.00	2.50	1.50
(15)	Terry Humphrey (July 16)	5.00	2.50	1.50
(16)	Jim Fairey (July 23)	5.00	2.50	1.50
(17)	Tim Foli (July 30)	5.00	2.50	1.50
(18)	Clyde Mashore (Aug. 6)	5.00	2.50	1.50
(19)	Tim McCarver (Aug. 13)	9.00	4.50	2.75
(20)	Hector Torres (Aug. 20)	5.00	2.50	1.50
(21)	Tom Walker (Aug. 27)	5.00	2.50	1.50
(22)	Cal McLish (Sept. 3)	5.00	2.50	1.50
(23)	Balor Moore (Sept. 10)	5.00	2.50	1.50
(24)	John Strohmayer (Sept. 17)	5.00	2.50	1.50
(25)	Larry Doby (Sept. 24)	12.00	6.00	3.50
(26)	Hal Breeden (Oct. 1)	5.00	2.50	1.50
(27)	Mike Marshall (Oct. 8)	5.00	2.50	1.50

1973 Dimanche/Derniere Heure National Leaguers

		NM	EX	VG
Complete Set (16):		185.00	90.00	55.00
Common Player:		6.00	3.00	1.75
(1)	Roberto Clemente (April 15)	25.00	12.50	7.50
(2)	Coco Laboy (April 22)	6.00	3.00	1.75
(3)	Rusty Staub (April 29)	8.00	4.00	2.50
(4)	Johnny Bench (May 6)	12.50	6.25	3.75
(5)	Ferguson Jenkins (May 13)	9.00	4.50	2.75
(6)	Bob Gibson (May 20)	10.00	5.00	3.00
(7)	Hank Aaron (May 27)	20.00	10.00	6.00
(8)	Willie Montanez (June 3)	6.00	3.00	1.75
(9)	Willie McCovey (June 10)	10.00	5.00	3.00
(10)	Willie Davis (June 17)	6.00	3.00	1.75
(11)	Steve Carlton (June 24)	10.00	5.00	3.00
(12)	Willie Stargell (July 1)	10.00	5.00	3.00
(13)	Dave Bristol (July 8)	6.00	3.00	1.75
(14)	Larry Bowa (July 15)	6.00	3.00	1.75
(15)	Pete Rose (July 22)	20.00	10.00	6.00
(16)	Pepe Frias (July 29)	6.00	3.00	1.75

1974 Dimanche/Derniere Heure Expos

		NM	EX	VG
Complete Set (10):		40.00	20.00	12.00
Common Player:		5.00	2.50	1.50
(1)	Dennis Blair	5.00	2.50	1.50
(2)	Don Carrithers	5.00	2.50	1.50
(3)	Jim Cox	5.00	2.50	1.50
(4)	Willie Davis	5.00	2.50	1.50
(5)	Don Demola	5.00	2.50	1.50
(6)	Barry Foote	5.00	2.50	1.50
(7)	Larry Lintz	5.00	2.50	1.50
(8)	John Montague	5.00	2.50	1.50
(9)	Steve Rogers	5.00	2.50	1.50
(10)	Chuck Taylor	5.00	2.50	1.50

1977 Dimanche/Derniere Heure Expos

	NM	EX	VG
Complete Set (26):	125.00	62.00	37.00
Common Player:	5.00	2.50	1.50
(1) Steve Rogers (April 24)	5.00	2.50	1.50
(2) Tim Foli (May 1)	5.00	2.50	1.50
(3) Dick Williams (May 8)	5.00	2.50	1.50
(4) Larry Parrish (May 15)	5.00	2.50	1.50
(5) Jose Morales (May 22)	5.00	2.50	1.50
(6) Don Stanhouse (May 29)	5.00	2.50	1.50
(7) Gary Carter (June 5)	10.00	5.00	3.00
(8) Ellis Valentine (June 12)	5.00	2.50	1.50
(9) Dave Cash (June 19)	5.00	2.50	1.50
(10) Jackie Brown (June 26)	5.00	2.50	1.50
(11) Barry Foote (July 3)	5.00	2.50	1.50
(12) Dan Warthen (July 10)	5.00	2.50	1.50
(13) Tony Perez (July 17)	10.00	5.00	3.00
(14) Wayne Garrett (July 24)	5.00	2.50	1.50
(15) Bill Atkinson (July 31)	5.00	2.50	1.50
(16) Joe Kerrigan (Aug. 7)	5.00	2.50	1.50
(17) Mickey Vernon (Aug. 14)	5.00	2.50	1.50
(18) Jeff Terpko (Aug. 21)	5.00	2.50	1.50
(19) Andre Dawson (Aug. 28)	10.00	5.00	3.00
(20) Del Unser (Sept. 4)	5.00	2.50	1.50
(21) Stan Bahnsen (Sept. 11)	5.00	2.50	1.50
(22) Warren Cromartie (Sept. 18)	5.00	2.50	1.50
(23) Santo Alcala (Sept. 25)	5.00	2.50	1.50
(24) Wayne Twitchell (Oct. 2)	5.00	2.50	1.50
(25) Pepe Frias (Oct. 9)	5.00	2.50	1.50
(26) Sam Mejias (Oct. 16)	5.00	2.50	1.50

1978 Dimanche/Derniere Heure Expos

	NM	EX	VG
Complete Set (13):	62.00	31.00	18.50
Common Player:	5.00	2.50	1.50
(1) Ross Grimsley (May 7)	5.00	2.50	1.50
(2) Chris Speier (May 14)	5.00	2.50	1.50
(3) Norm Sherry (May 21)	5.00	2.50	1.50
(4) Hal Dues (May 28)	5.00	2.50	1.50
(5) Rudy May (June 4)	5.00	2.50	1.50
(6) Stan Papi (June 11)	5.00	2.50	1.50
(7) Darold Knowles (June 18)	5.00	2.50	1.50
(8) Bob Reece (June 25)	5.00	2.50	1.50
(9) Dan Schatzeder (July 2)	5.00	2.50	1.50
(10) Jim Brewer (July 9)	5.00	2.50	1.50
(11) Mike Garman (July 16)	5.00	2.50	1.50
(12) Woodie Fryman (July 23)	5.00	2.50	1.50
(13) Ed Hermann	5.00	2.50	1.50

1979 Dimanche/Derniere Heure Expos

	NM	EX	VG
Complete Set (8):	35.00	17.50	10.50
Common Player:	5.00	2.50	1.50
(1) Bill Lee (May 6)	5.00	2.50	1.50
(2) Elias Sosa (May 13)	5.00	2.50	1.50
(3) Tommy Hutton (May 20)	5.00	2.50	1.50
(4) Tony Solaita (May 27)	5.00	2.50	1.50
(5) Rodney Scott (June 3)	5.00	2.50	1.50
(6) Duffy Dyer (June 10)	5.00	2.50	1.50
(7) Jim Mason (June 17)	5.00	2.50	1.50
(8) Ken Macha (June 24)	5.00	2.50	1.50

1980 Dimanche/Derniere Heure Expos

	NM	EX	VG
Complete Set (23):	125.00	62.00	37.00
Common Player:	5.00	2.50	1.50
(1) Steve Rogers (April 20)	5.00	2.50	1.50
(2) Dick Williams (April 27)	5.00	2.50	1.50
(3) Bill Lee (May 4)	5.00	2.50	1.50
(4) Jerry White (May 11)	5.00	2.50	1.50
(5) Scott Sanderson (May 18)	5.00	2.50	1.50
(6) Ron LeFlore (May 25)	5.00	2.50	1.50
(7) Elias Sosa (June 1)	5.00	2.50	1.50
(8) Ellis Valentine (June 8)	5.00	2.50	1.50
(9) Rodney Scott (June 22)	5.00	2.50	1.50
(10) Woodie Fryman (June 29)	5.00	2.50	1.50
(11) Chris Speier (July 6)	5.00	2.50	1.50
(12) Warren Cromartie (July 13)	5.00	2.50	1.50
(13) Stan Bahnsen (July 20)	5.00	2.50	1.50
(14) Tommy Hutton (July 27)	5.00	2.50	1.50
(15) Bill Almon (Aug. 3)	5.00	2.50	1.50
(16) Fred Norman (Aug. 10)	5.00	2.50	1.50
(17) Andre Dawson (Aug. 17)	10.00	5.00	3.00
(18) John Tamargo (Aug. 24)	5.00	2.50	1.50
(19) Larry Parrish (Aug. 31)	5.00	2.50	1.50
(20) David Palmer (Sept. 7)	5.00	2.50	1.50
(21) Tony Bernazard (Sept. 14)	5.00	2.50	1.50
(22) Gary Carter (Sept. 21)	10.00	5.00	3.00
(23) Ken Macha (Sept. 28)	5.00	2.50	1.50

1888 Dixie Cigarettes Girl Baseball Players (N48)

(See 1888 Allen & Ginter Girl Baseball Players.)

1937 Dixie Lids

This unnumbered set of Dixie cup ice cream tops was issued in 1937 and consists of 24 different lids, although only six picture sports stars; four of whom are baseball players. The lids are found in two different sizes, either 2-11/16" in diameter or 2-5/16" in diameter. The 1937 Dixie lids have their "picture" side printed in black or dark red. The reverse carries the advertising of one of many local dairies which packaged the ice cream treats. The lids must have the small tab still intact to command top value.

	NM	EX	VG
Complete Set (4):	700.00	350.00	210.00
Common Player:	180.00	90.00	55.00
(1) Charles Gehringer	180.00	90.00	55.00
(2) Charles ("Gabby") Hartnett	180.00	90.00	55.00
(3) Carl Hubbell (Mouth closed.)	195.00	95.00	55.00
(4) Joe Medwick	180.00	90.00	55.00

1937 Dixie Lids Premiums

Issued as a premium offer in conjunction with the 1937 Dixie lids, this unnumbered set of color 8" x 10" pictures was printed on heavy paper and features the same subjects as the Dixie lids set. The 1937 Dixie premiums have a distinctive dark green band along the left margin containing the player's name. The back has smaller photos of the player in action with a large star at the top and a player write-up. The 1937 premiums are easily distinguished from the 1938 issue by the use of yellow ink for the names in the left border. A "My Scrapbook of Stars" album was issued in which to house the 24 sportd and movie stars issued in the series.

	NM	EX	VG
Complete Set (4):	500.00	250.00	150.00
Common Player:	150.00	75.00	45.00
Album:	300.00	150.00	90.00
(2) Charles Gehringer	150.00	75.00	45.00
(3) Charles (Gabby) Hartnett	150.00	75.00	45.00
(4) Carl Hubbell	175.00	87.00	52.00
(5) Joe (Ducky) Medwick	150.00	75.00	45.00

1938 Dixie Lids

Similar to its set of the previous year, the 1938 Dixie lids set is a 24-subject set that includes six sports stars - four of whom are baseball players. The lids are found in two sizes, either 2-11/16" in diameter or 2-5/16" in diameter. The 1938 Dixie Lids have their "picture" side printed in blue ink. The reverse carries advertising from one of many local dairies which packaged the ice cream cups. Dixie lids must have the small tab still intact to command top value.

	NM	EX	VG
Complete Set (4):	600.00	300.00	180.00
Common Player:	80.00	40.00	25.00
(1) Bob Feller	200.00	100.00	60.00
(2) Jimmie Foxx	200.00	100.00	60.00
(3) Carl Hubbell (Mouth open.)	175.00	85.00	50.00
(4) Wally Moses	80.00	40.00	25.00

1938 Dixie Lids Premiums

Issued in conjunction with the 1938 Dixie cup lids, this unnumbered set of 8" x 10" pictures contains the same subjects. A colored border surrounds the entire picture with the player's name in black at left. The back contains smaller photos of the player in action with his name in script at the top and a short write-up. A "My Scrapbook of Stars" album was issued in which to house the 24 sports and movie stars that comprise the complete series.

	NM	EX	VG
Complete Set (4):	425.00	210.00	125.00
Common Player:	62.00	31.00	18.50
Album:	300.00	150.00	90.00
(1) Bob Feller	125.00	62.00	37.00
(2) Jimmie Foxx	125.00	62.00	37.00
(3) Carl Hubbell	125.00	62.00	37.00
(4) Wally Moses	60.00	30.00	18.00

1952 Dixie Lids

After a 14-year break, another Dixie lid set, featuring 24 baseball players, appeared in 1952. The unnumbered lids are found in three sizes, the most common being 2-11/16" in diameter. Somewhat scarcer, and carrying a modest premium over the values listed, are lids in sizes of 2-1/4" or 3-3/16". All are printed with a blue tint on their "picture" side. The backs carry advertising from one of the many local or regional dairies which packaged the ice cream treats. The Dixie lids of the 1950s can be distinguished from earlier issues because the bottom of the photo is squared off to accommodate the player's name. Dixie lids must contain the small tab to command top value.

		NM	EX	VG
Complete Set (24):		5,500	2,750	1,650
Common Player:		200.00	100.00	60.00
(1)	Richie Ashburn	325.00	160.00	95.00
(2)	Tommy Byrne	200.00	100.00	60.00
(3)	Chico Carrasquel	200.00	100.00	60.00
(4)	Pete Castiglione	200.00	100.00	60.00
(5)	Walker Cooper	200.00	100.00	60.00
(6)	Billy Cox	225.00	110.00	65.00
(7)	Ferris Fain	200.00	100.00	60.00
(8)	Bobby Feller	350.00	175.00	100.00
(9)	Nelson Fox	325.00	160.00	95.00
(10)	Monte Irvin	275.00	135.00	80.00
(11)	Ralph Kiner	275.00	135.00	80.00
(12)	Cass Michaels	200.00	100.00	60.00
(13)	Don Mueller	200.00	100.00	60.00
(14)	Mel Parnell	200.00	100.00	60.00
(15)	Allie Reynolds	225.00	110.00	65.00
(16)	Preacher Roe	225.00	110.00	65.00
(17)	Connie Ryan	200.00	100.00	60.00
(18)	Hank Sauer	200.00	100.00	60.00
(19)	Al Schoendienst	275.00	135.00	80.00
(20)	Andy Seminick	200.00	100.00	60.00
(21)	Bobby Shantz	200.00	100.00	60.00
(22)	Enos Slaughter	275.00	135.00	80.00
(23)	Virgil Trucks	200.00	100.00	60.00
(24)	Gene Woodling	250.00	125.00	75.00

1952 Dixie Lids Premiums

This unnumbered set of 24 player photos was issued as a premium in conjunction with the 1952 Dixie cup lids and features the same subjects. The player's team and facsimile autograph appear along the bottom of the 8" x 10" blank-backed photo, which was printed on heavy paper. The 1952 Dixie premiums show the player's 1951 season statistics in the lower right corner.

		NM	EX	VG
Complete Set (24):		2,250	1,125	675.00
Common Player:		90.00	45.00	25.00
(1)	Richie Ashburn	225.00	110.00	65.00
(2)	Tommy Byrne	90.00	45.00	25.00
(3)	Chico Carrasquel	90.00	45.00	25.00
(4)	Pete Castiglione	90.00	45.00	25.00
(5)	Walker Cooper	90.00	45.00	25.00
(6)	Billy Cox	100.00	50.00	30.00
(7)	Ferris Fain	90.00	45.00	25.00
(8)	Bob Feller	225.00	110.00	65.00
(9)	Nelson Fox	200.00	100.00	60.00
(10)	Monte Irvin	125.00	60.00	35.00
(11)	Ralph Kiner	125.00	60.00	35.00
(12)	Cass Michaels	90.00	45.00	25.00
(13)	Don Mueller	90.00	45.00	25.00
(14)	Mel Parnell	90.00	45.00	25.00
(15)	Allie Reynolds	100.00	50.00	30.00
(16)	Preacher Roe	100.00	50.00	30.00
(17)	Connie Ryan	90.00	45.00	25.00
(18)	Hank Sauer	90.00	45.00	25.00
(19)	Al Schoendienst	125.00	60.00	35.00
(20)	Andy Seminick	90.00	45.00	25.00
(21)	Bobby Shantz	90.00	45.00	25.00
(22)	Enos Slaughter	125.00	60.00	35.00
(23)	Virgil Trucks	90.00	45.00	25.00
(24)	Gene Woodling	100.00	50.00	30.00

1953 Dixie Lids

The 1953 Dixie lids set again consists of 24 unnumbered players and is identical in design to the 1952 set. Lids are either 2-1/4" or 2-11/16" in diameter and must include the small tab to command top value. Backs of the lids may be found with advertising of many local or regional dairies which packaged the ice cream cups.

		NM	EX	VG
Complete Set (24):		4,000	2,000	1,200
Common Player:		120.00	60.00	35.00
(1)	Richie Ashburn	250.00	125.00	75.00
(2)	Chico Carrasquel	120.00	60.00	35.00
(3)	Billy Cox	130.00	65.00	40.00
(4)	Ferris Fain	120.00	60.00	35.00
(5)	Nelson Fox	200.00	100.00	60.00
(6a)	Sid Gordon (Boston)	240.00	120.00	70.00
(6b)	Sid Gordon (Milwaukee)	120.00	60.00	35.00
(7)	Warren Hacker	120.00	60.00	35.00
(8)	Monte Irvin	200.00	100.00	60.00
(9)	Jackie Jensen	180.00	90.00	55.00
(10a)	Ralph Kiner (Pittsburgh)	350.00	175.00	100.00
(10b)	Ralph Kiner (Chicago)	200.00	100.00	60.00
(11)	Ted Kluszewski	200.00	100.00	60.00
(12)	Bob Lemon	200.00	100.00	60.00
(13)	Don Mueller	120.00	60.00	35.00
(14)	Mel Parnell	120.00	60.00	35.00
(15)	Jerry Priddy	120.00	60.00	35.00
(16)	Allie Reynolds	130.00	65.00	40.00
(17)	Preacher Roe	130.00	65.00	40.00
(18)	Hank Sauer	120.00	60.00	35.00
(19)	Al Schoendienst	200.00	100.00	60.00
(20)	Bobby Shantz	120.00	60.00	35.00
(21)	Enos Slaughter	200.00	100.00	60.00
(22a)	Warren Spahn (Boston)	550.00	275.00	165.00
(22b)	Warren Spahn (Milwaukee)	500.00	250.00	150.00
(23a)	Virgil Trucks (Chicago)	250.00	125.00	75.00
(23b)	Virgil Trucks (St. Louis)	150.00	75.00	45.00
(24)	Gene Woodling	130.00	65.00	40.00

1953 Dixie Lids Premiums

This set of 8" x 10" photos was issued as a premium in conjunction with the 1953 Dixie lids set and includes the same subjects. A premium picture could be obtained in exchange for 12 lids. The player's team and facsimile autograph are at the bottom of the unnumbered, blank-backed photos. His 1952 season stats are shown in the lower right corner.

		NM	EX	VG
Complete Set (24):		3,000	1,500	900.00
Common Player:		100.00	50.00	30.00
(1)	Richie Ashburn	250.00	125.00	75.00
(2)	Chico Carrasquel	100.00	50.00	30.00
(3)	Billy Cox	120.00	60.00	35.00
(4)	Ferris Fain	100.00	50.00	30.00
(5)	Nelson Fox	200.00	100.00	60.00
(6)	Sid Gordon	100.00	50.00	30.00
(7)	Warren Hacker	100.00	50.00	30.00
(8)	Monte Irvin	180.00	90.00	55.00
(9)	Jack Jensen	120.00	60.00	35.00
(10)	Ralph Kiner	180.00	90.00	55.00
(11)	Ted Kluszewski	180.00	90.00	55.00
(12)	Bob Lemon	180.00	90.00	55.00
(13)	Don Mueller	100.00	50.00	30.00
(14)	Mel Parnell	100.00	50.00	30.00
(15)	Jerry Priddy	100.00	50.00	30.00
(16)	Allie Reynolds	120.00	60.00	35.00
(17)	Preacher Roe	120.00	60.00	35.00
(18)	Hank Sauer	100.00	50.00	30.00
(19)	Al Schoendienst	180.00	90.00	55.00
(20)	Bobby Shantz	120.00	60.00	35.00
(21)	Enos Slaughter	180.00	90.00	55.00
(22)	Warren Spahn	260.00	130.00	75.00
(23)	Virgil Trucks	100.00	50.00	30.00
(24)	Gene Woodling	120.00	60.00	35.00

1954 Dixie Lids

The 1954 Dixie lids set consists of 18 players. Each player is found in both a "left" and "right" version. The picture side features a black-and-white photo. The lids usually measure 2-11/16" in diameter, although two other sizes (2-1/4" and 3-3/16") also exist and are valued at a significant premium above the prices listed. The 1954 Dixie lids are similar to earlier issues, except they carry an offer for a "3-D Starviewer" around the outside edge. The small tabs must be attached to command top value. The lids are unnumbered. Backs can be found with advertising from many local or regional dairies which packaged the ice cream cups.

		NM	EX	VG
Complete Set (18):		2,000	1,000	600.00
Common Player:		120.00	60.00	35.00
2-1/4" or 3-3/16": 2-3X				
(1)	Richie Ashburn	250.00	125.00	75.00
(2)	Clint Courtney	120.00	60.00	35.00
(3)	Sid Gordon	120.00	60.00	35.00
(4)	Billy Hoeft	120.00	60.00	35.00
(5)	Monte Irvin	200.00	100.00	60.00
(6)	Jackie Jensen	130.00	65.00	40.00
(7)	Ralph Kiner	200.00	100.00	60.00
(8)	Ted Kluszewski	200.00	100.00	60.00
(9)	Gil McDougald	130.00	65.00	40.00
(10)	Minny Minoso	130.00	65.00	40.00
(11)	Danny O'Connell	120.00	60.00	35.00
(12)	Mel Parnell	120.00	60.00	35.00
(13)	Preacher Roe	130.00	65.00	40.00
(14)	Al Rosen	130.00	65.00	40.00
(15)	Al Schoendienst	200.00	100.00	60.00
(16)	Enos Slaughter	200.00	100.00	60.00
(17)	Gene Woodling	130.00	65.00	40.00
(18)	Gus Zernial	120.00	60.00	35.00

1909 Dockman & Sons Gum (E92)

Once cataloged as a part of the E92 compendium, the John Dockman & Sons Gum card issue differs from the Croft's Candy/Cocoa sets in that it has 10 fewer cards. Otherwise the format (1-1/2" x 2-3/4") and color litho player pictures are identical. Beneath the player picture on front is his last name, position and team. Backs, which describe the set as having 50 cards, are an ad for the gum company. Cards are checklisted here alphabetically.

		NM	EX	VG
Complete Set (40):		55,000	22,500	16,500
Common Player:		910.00	365.00	180.00
(1)	Harry Bemis	910.00	365.00	180.00
(2)	Chief Bender	1,620	660.00	330.00
(3)	Bill Bergen	910.00	365.00	180.00
(4)	Bob Bescher	910.00	365.00	180.00
(5)	Al Bridwell	910.00	365.00	180.00
(6)	Doc Casey	910.00	365.00	180.00
(7)	Frank Chance	1,800	720.00	360.00
(8)	Hal Chase	1,110	450.00	220.00
(9)	Sam Crawford	1,620	660.00	330.00
(10)	Harry Davis	910.00	365.00	180.00
(11)	Art Devlin	910.00	365.00	180.00
(12)	Wild Bill Donovan	910.00	365.00	180.00
(13)	Mickey Doolan	910.00	365.00	180.00
(14)	Patsy Dougherty	910.00	365.00	180.00
(15)	Larry Doyle/Throwing	910.00	365.00	180.00
(16)	Larry Doyle (with bat)	910.00	365.00	180.00
(17)	George Gibson	910.00	365.00	180.00
(18)	Topsy Hartsel	910.00	365.00	180.00
(19)	Hugh Jennings	1,620	660.00	330.00
(20)	Red Kleinow	910.00	365.00	180.00
(21)	Nap Lajoie	1,800	720.00	360.00
(22)	Hans Lobert	910.00	365.00	180.00
(23)	Sherry Magee	910.00	365.00	180.00
(24)	Christy Matthewson (Mathewson)	5,400	2,160	1,080
(25)	John McGraw	1,620	660.00	330.00
(26)	Larry McLean	910.00	365.00	180.00
(27)	Dots Miller	910.00	365.00	180.00
(28)	Danny Murphy	910.00	365.00	180.00
(29)	Bill O'Hara	910.00	365.00	180.00
(30)	Germany Schaefer	910.00	365.00	180.00
(31)	Admiral Schlei	910.00	365.00	180.00
(32)	Boss Schmidt	910.00	365.00	180.00
(33)	Johnny Seigle	910.00	365.00	180.00
(34)	Dave Shean	910.00	365.00	180.00
(35)	Boss Smith (Schmidt)	910.00	365.00	180.00
(36)	Joe Tinker	1,620	660.00	330.00

		NM	EX	VG
(37)	Honus Wagner/Btg	10,000	2,880	1,440
(38)	Honus Wagner/Throwing	10,000	2,880	1,440
(39)	Cy Young	4,200	1,680	840.00
(40)	Heinie Zimmerman	910.00	365.00	180.00

1969-1972 Dodge Postcards

1969 Dodge Polara 500

Bill's Best Catch of the Year... Dodge Fever

Bill Freehan Detroit All-Star Catcher

Between 1969-1972 Dodge issued a series of black-and-white promotional postcards featuring sports figures endorsing the car company's line-up. Player portrait photos on front are combined with a photo of one of the cars and some extraneous sales copy. Divided backs of the 5-1/2" x 3-1/2" cards have a couple sentences of career summary or highlights and a sales pitch. Only the baseball players are listed here, though stars from football, basketball, golf, hockey and racing were also included in the series.

		NM	EX	VG
	Common Player:	15.00	7.50	4.50
(1)	Lou Brock/1970	40.00	20.00	12.00
(2)	Lou Brock/1971	40.00	20.00	12.00
(3)	Bill Freehan/1969	30.00	15.00	9.00
(4)	Bill Freehan/1971	15.00	7.50	4.50
(5)	Bill Freehan/1972	15.00	7.50	4.50
(6)	Joe Garagiola/1970	20.00	10.00	6.00
(7)	Mickey Lolich/1969	15.00	7.50	4.50

1888-1889 Dogs Head Cabinets (N173)

DOGS HEAD & OLD JUDGE CIGARETTES Goodwin & Co. N.Y.

(See 1888-1889 Old Judge Cabinets.)

1950 Dominican Republic

151 Phill Rizzuto

Selection of known Major League players makes 1950 the best guess for year of issue of this Caribbean card set. Like many contemporary Latin issues, these were probably produced to be collected in an accompanying album. Printed on fragile paper in blue, red or green duo-tones, the cards measure about 1-5/8" x 2-3/8" and are blank-backed. The set may or may not be complete at 292, the highest number currently known. Players featured in the issue are drawn from the Dominican and Cuban winter leagues (including Negro Leagues and minor league players) as well as the majors. In the bottom border beneath the player photo is a card number and name. Names are frequently misspelled and this list may not have succeeded in correcting all of them, particularly the Latino players. It is hoped that gaps in the checklist will eventually be filled with confirmed specimens. Many of the photos on these cards appear to have been lifted - some even with the typography intact - from Bowman baseball cards of the era. Some, perhaps all, of the cards were printed in more than one color.

		NM	EX	VG
	Common Player:			
1	Guillermo Estrella			10.00
2	Benitez Redondo			10.00
3	Vidal Lopez			10.00
4	R. del Monte y C.			10.00
5				
6				
7	Juan Delfin Garcia			10.00
8	J. Raf. Carretero			10.00
9	J. Benjamin (Papo)			10.00
10				
11	Rufo E. Felix			10.00
12	Gallego Munoz			10.00
13	Julio A. Lara			10.00
14				
15				
16	Rafael Espada			10.00
17	Aladino Paez			10.00
18				
19	Pepe Lucas			10.00
20	Manolete Caceres			10.00
21	E.A. Lantigua			10.00
22	Olmedo Suarez			10.00
23	Chucho Ramos			10.00
24	Gullabin Olivo			10.00
25	Jose Luis Velazquez			10.00
26				
27	Felle Delgado			10.00
28				
29				
30	Alcibades Colon			10.00
31	Horacio Martinez			10.00
32	Ramon Burgos			10.00
33	Carlos A. Piallo			10.00
34	W.E. Springfield			10.00
35	Fiquito Suarez			10.00
36				
37				
38	Rafael Ortiz			10.00
39				
40				
41	Tetelo Vargas			10.00
42	Miguel Rueda			10.00
43	Hector Salazar			10.00
44				
45	Rafael Vargas			10.00
46				
47				
48				
49				
50	Gerard Thorne			10.00
51	Bienvenido Arias			10.00
52	Son Howell			15.00
53				
54				
55				
56				
57	P. Mateo (Richard)			10.00
58				
59				
60	Martin Dihigo			150.00
61				
62				
63				
64				
65	Octavio Blanco			10.00
66	Daniel Rodriguez			10.00
67				
68	Luis Villodas			10.00
69	Miguel Aracena			10.00
70	Amor Diaz			10.00
71	Juan B. Perdomo			10.00
72	Julio Martinez			10.00
73	Fernando Bueno			10.00
74	Rene Gutierrez			10.00
75	Israel Hernandez			10.00
76	Tomas Gomez Checo			10.00
77				
78	Miguel Tian Tineo			10.00
79	Rafael Valdez			10.00
80	Calampio Leon			10.00
81	Leonardo Coicochea			10.00
82	Herberto Blanco			10.00
83				
84	Rogelio Martinez			10.00
85				
86				
87	Silvio Garcia			10.00
88				
89	Napoleon Reyes			15.00
90				
91				
92				
93	Claro Duane (Duany)			10.00
94				
95				
96	Regino Otero			10.00
97	Avelino Canizares			10.00
98	Sandalio Consuegra			25.00
99	Roberto R. Topane			10.00
100	Jaok Cassin (Jack Cassini)			20.00
101	Jaime B. Prendesgart (Jim Prendergast)			20.00
102	Pablo Garcia			10.00
103				
104				
105				
106	Alejandro Crespo			20.00
107	Hiran Gonzalez			10.00
108	Rafael Noble			20.00
109				
110	Jose R. Lopez			10.00
111				
112				
113	Gilberto Torres			10.00
114				
115	Patato Pascual			10.00
116				
117				
118				
119	Gilberto Valdivia			10.00
120	Svdor. Hernandez			10.00
121				
122				
123				
124	Pedro Formental (Formenthal)			10.00
125				
126				
127				
128				
129				
130				
131				
132				
133				
134				
135	H. Wilson			25.00
136				
137				
138				
139	Carl Hubbell			35.00
140				
141				
142	Cocaina Garcia			10.00
143				
144				
145				
146				
147				
148				
149				
150				
151	Phill Rizzuto (Phil)			75.00
152	Bill Mc Cahan			20.00
153				
154	Allie Reynolds			55.00
155	Gill Coan (Gil)			20.00
156				
157	Mizell Platt			20.00
158				
159	Al S. "Red" (Schoendienst)			50.00
160	Jack Lorke (Lohrke)			20.00
161				
162				
163	Bill Nicholson			20.00
164	Sam Mele			20.00
165	Bob Schiffino (Scheffing)			20.00
166				
167				
168				
169	Harri Gumbert (Harry)			20.00
170				
171	Johnny Wyrostek			20.00
172				
173				
174				
175				
176				
177	Ken Keltner			25.00
178				
179	Harry Walker			25.00
180				
181				
182				
183				
184				
185	Sibby Sisti			20.00
186				
187	Eddie Waiticus (Waitkus)			25.00
188	Eddie Lake			20.00
189				
190	Hank Arft			20.00
191				
192				
193				
194	Walker Cooper			20.00
195	Al Brazle			20.00
196	Sam Champmann (Chapman)			20.00
197				
198	Doyle Lade			20.00
199				
200	Henry Eduards (Edwards)			20.00
201				
202				
203	N.Y. "Baby" (Norman "Babe" Young)			20.00
204				
205				
206	Bob Feller			75.00
207	Ralph Branca			35.00
208				
209				
210				
211	Larry (Yogi) Berra			75.00
212	Eddie Joost			20.00
213				
214				
215				
216				
217				
218				

219	Gil Hodges	55.00
220		
221		
222		
223	James, Vernon (Mickey)	25.00
224		
225		
226		
227		
228		
229		
230		
231		
232		
233		
234	Pete Raiser (Reiser)	30.00
235		
236	Bob Elliot	20.00
237		
238	Lou Boudreau	45.00
239	Danny Murtany	25.00
	(Photo is Joe Gordon.)	
240	Jakie Robinson (Jackie)	125.00
241		
242		
243	Tommy Henrick (Henrich)	25.00
244	Pee Wee Reese	55.00
245	Bobby Brower (Brown)	25.00
246		
247		
248	Enos Slaughter	35.00
249		
250		
251	Tommy Henrich	25.00
252	George Koslo (Dave)	20.00
253	Frank Gustino (Gustine)	20.00
254		
255		
256		
257	Bill Rigney	20.00
258		
259	Rex Barney	25.00
260		
261	Mark Christman	20.00
262	Whetey Lockman (Whitey)	20.00
263		
264	Ralph Kiner	55.00
265		
266	Cliff Fannin	20.00
267	Joe Page	25.00
268		
269		
270		
271	Johnny Sain	30.00
272		
273		
274		
275		
276		
277		
278		
279	Joe Dobson	20.00
280		
281	Carrol Lockman (Whitey)	20.00
282		
283	Monte Kennedy	20.00
284		
285		
286	Carlos Bernier	20.00
287		
288		
289	Buster Clarkson	20.00
290	Williard Brown (Willard)	25.00
291	Jim Rivera	25.00
292	Saturnino Escalera	20.00

1958 Dominican Republic

Felipe R. Alou.

The date of issue is speculative, based on the known winter ball career of the sole card known. The identity of the issuer and manner of distribution is unknown, though from their wide borders it is possible these were printed on some type of box or package and intended to be cut out and possibly placed into an album, as is customary with many Latin American baseball card issues. The cards are nominally about 2" x 2-1/2" and are printed in sepia on thin, blank-back cardboard. As with many issues of the era and area, these cards are found they are usually in wretched condition.

	NM	EX	VG
Felipe R. Alou			35.00

1959 Dominican Republic

The date of issue is speculative. The identity of the issuer and manner of distribution is unknown,

WALTER JAMES

though they appear to have been sold in strips or panels and intended to be separated and possibly placed into an album, as is customary with many Latin American baseball cards. The cards are nominally about 2-1/8" x 3-1/4" and printed in black or blue on thin, blank-back cardboard. As with many issues of the era and area, when these cards are found they are usually in wretched condition. These players certainly represent only a portion of the checklist.

	NM	EX	VG
Walter James			15.00
Osvaldo Virgil			25.00

1966 Dominican Republic

WILLY MCCOVY

The date of issue is speculative, based on the fact these cards "borrowed" their images from 1965 Topps cards. The identity of the issuer and manner of distribution is unknown, though from their wide borders it is possible these were printed on some type of box or package and intended to be cut out and possibly placed into an album, as is customary with many Latin American baseball card issues. The cards are nominally about 1-3/4" x 2-1/2" and are printed in red on thin, blank-back cardboard. As with many issues of the era and area, when these cards are found they are usually in wretched condition. These players probably represent only a portion of the checklist which may or may not comprise only Major League players.

		NM	EX	VG
(1)	Sandy Koufax			200.00
(2)	Juan Marichal			100.00
(3)	Willy Mays (Willie)			200.00
(4)	Willy McCovy (Willie McCovey)			45.00

1937 Donut Co. of American Thrilling Moments

The official title of this multi-subject card set is "Thrilling Moments in the Lives of Famous Americans." The cards, about 1-7/8" x 2-7/8", were printed

in groups of 18 on donut boxes. Each card is printed in black-and-white on a single background color. The cards themselves do not name the famous American depicted, but his biography is found in the album which was issued to house the set. Cards are blank-backed. There is only a single baseball playered in the 72-card set.

	NM	EX	VG
Beloved Baseball Idol of All Boys (Babe Ruth)	4,000	1,600	800.00

1953-55 Dormand Postcards

This mid-1950s issue features only selected players from the Yankees, Brooklyn Dodgers, White Sox and Philadelphia A's. Apparently produced on order by the players by Louis Dormand, a Long Island, N.Y., photographer, the cards were used to honor fan requests for photos and autographs. All cards have a facsimile autograph printed in front. Otherwise the fronts of these 3-1/2" x 5-1/2" postcards feature only sharp color photos with no border. Backs, printed in blue or green, feature a few player biographical and career details, one or two lines identifying the producer and usually product and series numbers. Most have a Kodachrome logo. Some cards do not have all of these elements and several are found blank-backed. The Gil Hodges card is considerably scarcer than the others in the set, with those of Jim Konstanty, Elston Howard, and Casey Stengel also seldom seen. Besides the standard-sized cards listed below, there are oversize versions of Rizzuto's and Mantle's cards. A variation of Johnny Sain's card shows his Arkansas Chevrolet dealership in a photo above the player's picture. The complete set price includes only the standard-size cards.

		NM	EX	VG
Common Player:		25.00	12.50	7.50
101a	Phil Rizzuto (Large autograph parallel to top.)	40.00	20.00	12.00
101b	Phil Rizzuto (Small autograph parallel to top.)	45.00	22.50	13.50
101c	Phil Rizzuto (Autograph angles downward.)	50.00	25.00	15.00
101d	Phil Rizzuto (9" x 12")	55.00	27.50	16.50
102	Yogi Berra	65.00	32.50	20.00
103	Ed Lopat	30.00	15.00	9.00
104	Hank Bauer (Small autograph.)	30.00	15.00	9.00
104	Hank Bauer (Large autograph.)	35.00	17.50	10.50
105	Joe Collins (Patch on sleeve, autograph at top.)	60.00	30.00	18.00
105	Joe Collins (Patch on sleeve, autograph at bottom.)	60.00	30.00	18.00
105	Joe Collins (No patch on sleeve.)	40.00	20.00	12.00
106	Ralph Houk	30.00	15.00	9.00
107	Bill Miller	27.50	13.50	8.25
108	Ray Scarborough	35.00	17.50	10.00
109	Allie Reynolds	25.00	12.50	7.50
110	Gil McDougald (Small autograph.)	25.00	12.50	7.50
110	Gil McDougald (Large autograph.)	25.00	12.50	7.50
111	Mickey Mantle (Bat on shoulder.)	100.00	50.00	30.00
111	Mickey Mantle (Batting stance, 3-1/2" x 5-1/2".)	75.00	37.50	22.50
111	Mickey Mantle (Bat on shoulder, 6" x 9".)	550.00	275.00	165.00
111	Mickey Mantle (Bat on shoulder, 9" x 12".)	1,200	600.00	360.00
112	Johnny Mize	90.00	45.00	27.50
113	Casey Stengel (Autograph at top.)	165.00	80.00	50.00
113	Casey Stengel (Autograph at bottom.)	165.00	80.00	50.00
114	Bobby Shantz (Autograph parallel to top.)	40.00	20.00	12.00
114	Bobby Shantz (Autograph angles downward.)	40.00	20.00	12.00
115	Whitey Ford	60.00	30.00	18.00
116	Johnny Sain (Beginning windup.)	35.00	17.50	10.00
116	Johnny Sain (Leg kick.)	25.00	12.50	7.50
116	Johnny Sain (With auto dealership ad.)	150.00	75.00	45.00
117	Jim McDonald	25.00	12.50	7.50
118	Gene Woodling	25.00	12.50	7.50

119	Charlie Silvera	30.00	15.00	9.00
120	Don Bollweg	25.00	12.50	7.50
121	Billy Pierce	30.00	15.00	9.00
122	Chico Carrasquel	25.00	12.50	7.50
123	Willie Miranda	25.00	12.50	7.50
124	Carl Erskine	65.00	32.50	20.00
125	Roy Campanella	150.00	75.00	45.00
126	Jerry Coleman	25.00	12.50	7.50
127	Pee Wee Reese	50.00	25.00	15.00
128	Carl Furillo	50.00	25.00	15.00
129	Gil Hodges	75.00	37.50	22.50
130	Billy Martin	30.00	15.00	9.00
131	NOT ISSUED			
132	Irv Noren	35.00	17.50	10.50
133	Enos Slaughter	65.00	32.50	20.00
134	Tom Gorman	25.00	12.50	7.50
135	Ed Robinson	35.00	17.50	10.00
136	Frank Crosetti	35.00	17.50	10.00
137	NOT ISSUED			
138	Jim Konstanty	150.00	75.00	45.00
139	Elston Howard	150.00	75.00	45.00
140	Bill Skowron	150.00	75.00	45.00

1941 Double Play (R330)

JOE DI MAGGIO
New York Yankees. Center fielder. Born Nov. 25, 1914. Bats right. Throws right. Height 6 ft. Weight 195 lbs. Batted .352. No. 63 Double Play

CHARLEY KELLER
New York Yankees. Left fielder. Born Sept. 12, 1916. Bats left. Throws right. Height 5 ft. 10 in. Wt. 190 lbs. Batted .286. No. 64 Double Play

Issued by Gum Products Inc., Cambridge, Mass., this set comprises 75 numbered cards with two consecutive numbers per card featuring 150 (130 different) players. The blank-backed cards measure about 3-1/8" x 2-1/2". Most feature sepia-toned portrait photos. Cards 81-82 through 99-100 have vertical "in action" photos of 40 of the players who also appear in portraits. The last 50 cards in the series are scarcer than the early numbers. Cards which have been cut in half to form single cards have little collector value.

		NM	EX	VG
Complete Set (75):		10,000	4,000	2,000
Common Player (1/2-99/100):		70.00	25.00	12.50
Common Player (101/102-149/150):		90.00	35.00	15.00
1-2	Larry French, Vance Page	90.00	30.00	15.00
3-4	Billy Herman, Stanley Hack	125.00	50.00	25.00
5-6	Linus Frey, John Vander Meer	75.00	30.00	15.00
7-8	Paul Derringer, Bucky Walters	70.00	25.00	12.50
9-10	Frank McCormick, Bill Werber	70.00	25.00	12.50
11-12	Jimmy Ripple, Ernie Lombardi	85.00	35.00	15.00
13-14	Alex Kampouris, John Wyatt	70.00	25.00	12.50
15-16	Mickey Owen, Paul Waner	110.00	45.00	20.00
17-18	Cookie Lavagetto, Harold Reiser	75.00	30.00	15.00
19-20	Jimmy Wasdell, Dolph Camilli	70.00	25.00	12.50
21-22	Dixie Walker, Ducky Medwick	110.00	45.00	20.00
23-24	Harold Reese, Kirby Higbe	600.00	240.00	120.00
25-26	Harry Danning, Cliff Melton	70.00	25.00	12.50
27-28	Harry Gumbert, Burgess Whitehead	70.00	25.00	12.50
29-30	Joe Orengo, Joe Moore	70.00	25.00	12.50
31-32	Mel Ott, Babe Young	200.00	80.00	40.00
33-34	Lee Handley, Arky Vaughan	110.00	45.00	20.00
35-36	Bob Klinger, Stanley Brown	70.00	25.00	12.50
37-38	Terry Moore, Gus Mancuso	70.00	25.00	12.50
39-40	Johnny Mize, Enos Slaughter	700.00	280.00	140.00
41-42	John Cooney, Sibby Sisti	70.00	25.00	12.50
43-44	Max West, Carvel Rowell	70.00	25.00	12.50
45-46	Danny Litwhiler, Merrill May	70.00	25.00	12.50
47-48	Frank Hayes, Al Brancato	70.00	25.00	12.50
49-50	Bob Johnson, Bill Nagel	70.00	25.00	12.50
51-52	Buck Newsom, Hank Greenberg	200.00	80.00	40.00
53-54	Barney McCosky, Charley Gehringer	140.00	55.00	25.00
55-56	Pinky Higgins, Dick Bartell	70.00	25.00	12.50
57-58	Ted Williams, Jim Tabor	650.00	260.00	130.00
59-60	Joe Cronin, Jimmy Foxx	275.00	110.00	55.00
61-62	Lefty Gomez, Phil Rizzuto	675.00	275.00	135.00
63-64	Joe DiMaggio, Charley Keller	750.00	300.00	150.00
65-66	Red Rolfe, Bill Dickey	125.00	50.00	25.00
67-68	Joe Gordon, Red Ruffing	120.00	45.00	20.00
69-70	Mike Tresh, Luke Appling	110.00	45.00	20.00
71-72	Moose Solters, John Rigney	70.00	25.00	12.50
73-74	Buddy Meyer, Ben Chapman (Myer)	70.00	25.00	12.50
75-76	Cecil Travis, George Case	70.00	25.00	12.50
77-78	Joe Krakauskas, Bob Feller	200.00	80.00	40.00
79-80	Ken Keltner, Hal Trosky	70.00	25.00	12.50
81-82	Ted Williams, Joe Cronin (In action.)	550.00	220.00	110.00
83-84	Joe Gordon, Charley Keller (in action)	90.00	35.00	15.00
85-86	Hank Greenberg, Red Ruffing (In action.)	225.00	90.00	45.00

87-88	Hal Trosky, George Case (In action.)	70.00	25.00	12.50
89-90	Mel Ott, Burgess Whitehead (In action.)	210.00	85.00	40.00
91-92	Harry Danning, Harry Gumbert (In action.)	70.00	25.00	12.50
93-94	Babe Young, Cliff Melton (In action.)	70.00	25.00	12.50
95-96	Jimmy Ripple, Bucky Walters (In action.)	70.00	25.00	12.50
97-98	Stanley Hack, Bob Klinger (In action.)	70.00	25.00	12.50
99-100	Johnny Mize, Dan Litwhiler (In action.)	135.00	55.00	25.00
101-102	Dom Dallessandro, Augie Galan	70.00	25.00	12.50
103-104	Bill Lee, Phil Cavarretta	90.00	35.00	15.00
105-106	Lefty Grove, Bobby Doerr	210.00	85.00	40.00
107-108	Frank Pytlak, Dom DiMaggio	115.00	45.00	20.00
109-110	Gerald Priddy, John Murphy	90.00	35.00	15.00
111-112	Tommy Henrich, Marius Russo	100.00	40.00	20.00
113-114	Frank Crosetti, John Sturm	100.00	40.00	20.00
115-116	Ival Goodman, Myron McCormick	90.00	35.00	15.00
117-118	Eddie Joost, Ernie Koy	90.00	35.00	15.00
119-120	Lloyd Waner, Hank Majeski	125.00	50.00	25.00
121-122	Buddy Hassett, Eugene Moore	90.00	35.00	15.00
123-124	Nick Etten, John Rizzo	90.00	35.00	15.00
125-126	Sam Chapman, Wally Moses	90.00	35.00	15.00
127-128	John Babich, Richard Siebert	90.00	35.00	15.00
129-130	Nelson Potter, Benny McCoy	90.00	25.00	15.00
131-132	Clarence Campbell, Louis Boudreau	125.00	50.00	25.00
133-134	Rolly Hemsley, Mel Harder	90.00	35.00	15.00
135-136	Gerald Walker, Joe Heving	90.00	35.00	15.00
137-138	John Rucker, Ace Adams	90.00	35.00	15.00
139-140	Morris Arnovich, Carl Hubbell	225.00	90.00	45.00
141-142	Lew Riggs, Leo Durocher	135.00	55.00	25.00
143-144	Fred Fitzsimmons, Joe Vosmik	90.00	35.00	15.00
145-146	Frank Crespi, Jim Brown	90.00	35.00	15.00
147-148	Don Heffner, Harland Clift (Harlond)	90.00	35.00	15.00
149-150	Debs Garms, Elbie Fletcher	90.00	35.00	15.00

1976 Douglas Cool Papa Bell

This collectors' issue was produced following the 1974 induction of James "Cool Papa" Bell into the Hall of Fame. Collector John Douglas collaborated with Bell to produce the set chronicling Bell's career (1922-46) in the Negro and Latin American pro leagues. Fronts have vintage sepia-toned photos of Bell surrounded by a yellow, green or orange woodgrain frame with a title plaque at bottom. Backs are in brown-and-white with a drawing of Bell at top and autobiographical material at center. A description of the photo and copyright data are at bottom. The unnumbered cards are checklisted here alphabetically by their titles.

		NM	EX	VG
Complete Set (13):		10.00	5.00	3.00
Common Card:		1.00	.50	.30
(1)	Amazing Speed	1.00	.50	.30
(2)	Brock Sets SB Record	1.00	.50	.30
(3)	Cool Papa	1.00	.50	.30
(4)	Cuba, 1928	1.00	.50	.30
(5)	Great Fielder, Too	1.00	.50	.30
(6)	HOF, Cooperstown	1.00	.50	.30
(7)	HOF Favorite	1.00	.50	.30
(8)	Induction Day, 1974	1.00	.50	.30
(9)	Monarchs' Manager	1.00	.50	.30
(10)	On Deck in Cuba	1.00	.50	.30
(11)	The Mexican Leagues	1.00	.50	.30
(12)	Touring Havana	1.00	.50	.30
(13)	With Josh Gibson	1.00	.50	.30

1977 Douglas Johnny Mize

In an effort to promote Johnny Mize for induction to the Hall of Fame, John Douglas created this collectors' issue. The Big Cat's career is traced on a series of 3-1/4" x 3-7/8" cards with black-and-white photos on a greenish-brown background. Black-and-white backs have a drawing of Mize at top with lengthy narrative below. The unnumbered cards are checklisted here by the title which appears on the front. Mize was selected for the Hall of Fame in 1981.

		NM	EX	VG
Complete Set (20):		9.00	4.50	2.75
Common Card:		1.00	.50	.30
(1)	Blattner, Gordon, Lombardi, Mize, Marshall	1.00	.50	.30
(2)	Call for Phillip Morris	1.00	.50	.30
(3)	Cardinal Slugger	1.00	.50	.30
(4)	Card's Big Stick	1.00	.50	.30
(5)	Early Photo - 1913	1.00	.50	.30
(6)	51 Homers, 1947	1.00	.50	.30
(7)	Home Run, 1952 Series	1.00	.50	.30
(8)	June 16, 1953	1.00	.50	.30
(9)	Louisville Poster - 1947	1.00	.50	.30
(10)	Mize, Happy Chandler, Bucky Harris	1.00	.50	.30
(11)	Mize, Reynolds, Johnson	1.00	.50	.30
(12)	N.L. Homer Champ 1948	1.00	.50	.30
(13)	Series MVP - 1952	1.00	.50	.30
(14)	St. Louis Star	1.00	.50	.30
(15)	The Navy - 1943	1.00	.50	.30
(16)	Vu-Master Slide	1.00	.50	.30
(17)	With Enos Slaughter	1.00	.50	.30
(18)	With Roy Rogers	1.00	.50	.30
(19)	With Terry Moore	1.00	.50	.30
(20)	Woodling, Raschi, Mize - 1952	1.00	.50	.30

1978 Dover Publications Great Players Postcards

This set of 32 collectors' issue postcards was originally issued in the form of an 8" x 11" booklet from which individual cards could be separated. The 3-7/8" x 5-1/2" cards are perforated on two sides, depending on their placement on a four-card page. Fronts have borderless sepia photos. Black-and-white backs have standard postcard indicia, copyright data, player identification and a brief career summary. The unnumbered cards are checklisted here alphabetically.

		NM	EX	VG
Complete Set, Booklet:		7.50	3.75	2.25
Complete Set, Singles (32):		7.50	3.75	2.25
Common Player:		.50	.25	.15
(1)	Grover Cleveland Alexander	.60	.30	.20
(2)	Chief Bender	.50	.25	.15
(3)	Roger Bresnahan	.50	.25	.15
(4)	Bullet Joe Bush	.50	.25	.15
(5)	Frank Chance	.50	.25	.15
(6)	Ty Cobb	1.25	.60	.40
(7)	Eddie Collins	.50	.25	.15
(8)	Stan Coveleski	.50	.25	.15
(9)	Sam Crawford	.50	.25	.15
(10)	Frankie Frisch	.50	.25	.15
(11)	Goose Goslin	.50	.25	.15
(12)	Harry Heilmann	.50	.25	.15
(13)	Rogers Hornsby	.75	.40	.25
(14)	Joe Jackson	4.00	2.00	1.25
(15)	Hughie Jennings	.50	.25	.15
(16)	Walter Johnson	1.00	.50	.30
(17)	Sad Sam Jones	.50	.25	.15
(18)	Rabbit Maranville	.50	.25	.15
(19)	Rube Marquard	.50	.25	.15
(20)	Christy Mathewson	1.00	.50	.30
(21)	John McGraw	.50	.25	.15

		NM	EX	VG
(22)	Herb Pennock	.50	.25	.15
(23)	Eddie Plank	.50	.25	.15
(24)	Edd Roush	.50	.25	.15
(25)	Babe Ruth	4.00	2.00	1.25
(26)	George Sisler	.50	.25	.15
(27)	Tris Speaker	.75	.40	.25
(28)	Casey Stengel	.50	.25	.15
(29)	Joe Tinker	.50	.25	.15
(30)	Pie Traynor	.50	.25	.15
(31)	Dazzy Vance	.50	.25	.15
(32)	Cy Young	.75	.40	.25

1925 Drake's

Among a series of 64 movie stars packaged with Drake's Cake in the mid-1920s was a card of Babe Ruth, who did some movie work for Universal Pictures at the time. The 2-7/16" x 4-3/16" black-and-white card has a portrait of Ruth on front, with his name, studio and card number in the bottom border. Backs have been seen with at least two styles of advertising, one for Drake's Cake and one for Yankee Cake.

		NM	EX	VG
61	Babe Ruth	3,750	1,875	1,125

1950 Drake's

 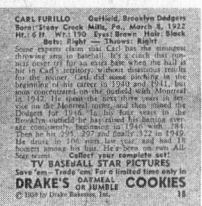

Entitled "TV Baseball Series," the 1950 Drake's Bakeries set pictures 36 different players on a television screen format. The cards, 2-1/2" x 2-1/2", contain black-and-white photos surrounded by a black border. Backs carry a player biography plus an advertisement advising collectors to look for the cards in packages of Oatmeal or Jumble cookies.

		NM	EX	VG
	Complete Set (36):	7,500	3,000	1,500
	Common Player:	150.00	60.00	30.00
1	Elwin "Preacher" Roe	250.00	100.00	50.00
2	Clint Hartung	150.00	60.00	30.00
3	Earl Torgeson	150.00	60.00	30.00
4	Leland "Lou" Brissie	150.00	60.00	30.00
5	Edwin "Duke" Snider	500.00	200.00	100.00
6	Roy Campanella	500.00	200.00	100.00
7	Sheldon "Available" Jones	150.00	60.00	30.00
8	Carroll "Whitey" Lockman	150.00	60.00	30.00
9	Bobby Thomson	175.00	70.00	35.00
10	Dick Sisler	150.00	60.00	30.00
11	Gil Hodges	300.00	120.00	60.00
12	Eddie Waitkus	150.00	60.00	30.00
13	Bobby Doerr	250.00	100.00	50.00
14	Warren Spahn	300.00	120.00	60.00
15	John "Buddy" Kerr	150.00	60.00	30.00
16	Sid Gordon	150.00	60.00	30.00
17	Willard Marshall	150.00	60.00	30.00
18	Carl Furillo	300.00	120.00	60.00
19	Harold "Pee Wee" Reese	400.00	160.00	80.00
20	Alvin Dark	150.00	60.00	30.00
21	Del Ennis	150.00	60.00	30.00
22	Eddie Stanky	150.00	60.00	30.00
23	Tommy "Old Reliable" Henrich	175.00	70.00	35.00
24	Larry "Yogi" Berra	500.00	200.00	100.00
25	Phil "Scooter" Rizzuto	500.00	200.00	100.00
26	Jerry Coleman	150.00	60.00	30.00
27	Joe Page	150.00	60.00	30.00
28	Allie Reynolds	175.00	70.00	35.00
29	Ray Scarborough	150.00	60.00	30.00
30	George "Birdie" Tebbetts	150.00	60.00	30.00
31	Maurice "Lefty" McDermott	150.00	60.00	30.00
32	Johnny Pesky	150.00	60.00	30.00
33	Dom "Little Professor" DiMaggio	190.00	75.00	35.00
34	Vern "Junior" Stephens	150.00	60.00	30.00
35	Bob Elliott	150.00	60.00	30.00
36	Enos "Country" Slaughter	325.00	130.00	65.00

1909-11 Drum Cigarettes

Other than Ty Cobb brand, Drum is the rarest of the various cigarette advertisements to be found on the backs of T206. Typography on the back is printed in a plum color. Multipliers shown are for "common" players; Hall of Fame players and other high-demand cards command a lesser premium relative to common-brand backs. Among T205 backs, Drum, printed in brown, ranks as the scarcest of the brands.

PREMIUMS
T205: 25X
T206: 40X
(See T205, T206 for checklists and base card values.)

1972 Don Drysdale's Restaurant Postcards

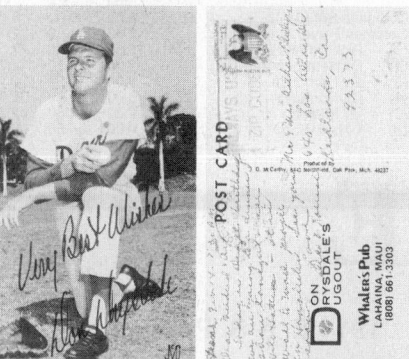

The date cited is taken from the postmark of an observed example. The actual span during which the cards were current is unknown. These versions of J.D. McCarthy postcards have on their 3-1/4" x 5-1/2" fronts a borderless black-and-white pose. The salutation and facsimile autograph are incuse printed in blue ink. Postcard style backs are known in three styles. One advertises Don Drysdale's Dugout in Santa Ana, Calif., another advertises his Club 53 in Kona, Hawaii, while a third advertizes Don Drysdale's Dugout and the Whaler's Pub on Maui.

	NM	EX	VG
Don Drysdale	16.00	8.00	4.75

1965 Dugan Bros. Casey Stengel

In celebration of the Ol' Perfesser's 75th birthday, the N.Y. Mets held a birthday party for him at Shea Stadium on July 25. This approximately 2-1/2" x 3-1/2" card was given to each of the 40,000+ fans in attendance, sponsored by Dugan Bros., a local bakery which also provided a birthday cake for the occasion. Unfortunately, Stengel was unable to attend the fete;

early that morning he broke his hip leaving a nightclub, ending his managerial career. The card is printed in blue on white. The back provides career highlights.

	NM	EX	VG
Casey Stengel	25.00	12.50	7.50

1888 Duke Talk of the Diamond (N135)

 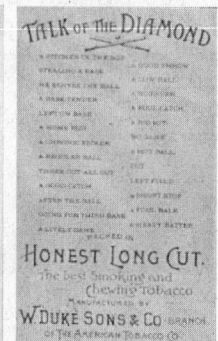

One of the more obscure 19th Century tobacco issues is a 25-card set issued by Honest Long Cut Tobacco in the late 1880's. Titled "Talk of the Diamond," the set features full-color cards measuring 4-1/8" x 2-1/2". Each card features a cartoon-like drawing illustrating a popular baseball term or expression. The left portion of the card pictures an unspecified player in a fielding position, and some of the artwork for that part of the set was borrowed from the more popular Buchner Gold Coin set (N284) issued about the same time. Because the "Talk of the Diamond" set does not feature individual players, it has never really captured the attention of baseball card collectors. It does, however, hold interest as a novelty item of the period. It carries an N135 American Card Catalog designation.

		NM	EX	VG
	Complete Set (25):	10,000	4,500	2,500
	Common Card:	385.00	155.00	75.00
(1)	A Base Tender	385.00	155.00	75.00
(2)	A Big Hit	385.00	155.00	75.00
(3)	A Chronic Kicker	385.00	155.00	75.00
(4)	A Foul Balk	385.00	155.00	75.00
(5)	A Foul Catch	385.00	155.00	75.00
(6)	A Good Catch	385.00	155.00	75.00
(7)	A Good Throw	385.00	155.00	75.00
(8)	A Heavy Batter	385.00	155.00	75.00
(9)	A Home Run	385.00	155.00	75.00
(10)	A Hot Ball	385.00	155.00	75.00
(11)	A Low Ball	385.00	155.00	75.00
(12)	A Pitcher in the Box	385.00	155.00	75.00
(13)	A Regular Ball	385.00	155.00	75.00
(14)	A Rounder	385.00	155.00	75.00
(15)	A Short Stop	385.00	155.00	75.00
(16)	After the Ball	385.00	155.00	75.00
(17)	Going for Third Base	385.00	155.00	75.00
(18)	He Serves the Ball	385.00	155.00	75.00
(19)	Left Field	385.00	155.00	75.00
(20)	Left on Base	385.00	155.00	75.00
(21)	Lively Game	385.00	155.00	75.00
(22)	No Game	385.00	155.00	75.00
(23)	Out	385.00	155.00	75.00
(24)	Stealing a Base	385.00	155.00	75.00
(25)	Three out-All out	385.00	155.00	75.00

1889 Duke's Terrors of America

Officially titled "The Terrors of America and their Doings," this set of tobacco inserts features color artwork of boys in all manners of activities, some mischievous. Several of the cards picture the lads playing sports, including baseball. The cards were issued in three sizes. The smallest measure 1-7/16" x 2-3/4" and have an ad on the checklist back for Duke's Cigarettes. A slightly larger 1-3/4" x 3-1/8"

version advertises Duke's Mixture. The largest features the card design on an ornate background and measures 2-1/2" x 4-3/16", advertising Honest Long Cut on back.

	NM	EX	VG
Duke's Cigarettes	80.00	40.00	24.00
Duke's Mixture	100.00	50.00	30.00
Honest Long Cut	200.00	100.00	60.00

1969 Dunkin' Donuts Chicago Cubs Bumper Stickers

This series of Cubs novelty collectibles was the first of two annual presentations. The stickers measure about 8" x 4" and have at their left end a photographic portrait of a player at one end of an artwork bat on a black background. At right is a baseball design with the sponsor's logo. A second version exists with "Cub Power" in place of the DD advertising. The unnumbered stickers are checklisted here alphabetically.

		NM	EX	VG
Complete Set (6):		350.00	175.00	100.00
Common Player:		30.00	15.00	9.00
(1)	Ernie Banks	125.00	65.00	35.00
(2)	Glenn Beckert	30.00	15.00	9.00
(3)	Randy Hundley	30.00	15.00	9.00
(4)	Don Kessinger	30.00	15.00	9.00
(5)	Ron Santo	60.00	30.00	18.00
(6)	Billy Williams	75.00	37.00	22.00

1970 Dunkin' Donuts Chicago Cubs Bumper Stickers

This series of Cubs novelty collectibles was the second of two annual presentations. The stickers measure about 8" x 4" and have at their left end a photographic portrait (without cap) of a player in a vaguely baseball-like design. In upper-left is a blue facsimile autograph. At right is "Cubs are no. 1," at bottom is a DD credit line. Basic color scheme of the graphics is red, white and blue. The unnumbered stickers are checklisted alphabetically.

		NM	EX	VG
Complete Set (6):		350.00	175.00	100.00
Common Player:		30.00	15.00	9.00
(1)	Ernie Banks	125.00	62.00	37.00
(2)	Glenn Beckert	30.00	15.00	9.00
(3)	Randy Hundley	30.00	15.00	9.00
(4)	Don Kessinger	30.00	15.00	9.00
(5)	Ron Santo	60.00	30.00	18.00
(6)	Billy Williams	75.00	37.00	22.00

1937 Dupont Cavalcade of America Premium

This 6" x 9" black-and-white card was distributed by NBC radio in conjunction with one of its weekly programs, which featured Babe Ruth on Sept. 29,

1937. The front has a bordered photo of Ruth in his classic batting follow-through. The back has information about the broadcast and details "The Babe's 54 Major League Records."

	NM	EX	VG
Babe Ruth	500.00	250.00	150.00

1972 Durochrome Chicago White Sox Decals

 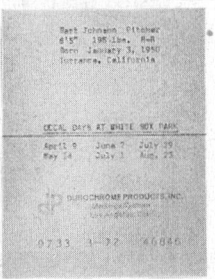

While they are technically stickers rather than decals, this set of six White Sox was given away during the course of half a dozen "Decal Days" at Comiskey Park, as listed on the peel-off back. The stickers measure 3-9/16" x 4-9/16" and feature posed action photos of the players in their vintage red-trimmed uniforms. Fronts have a facsimile autograph and, in the bottom border, the team name. Backs are printed in green and have a few vital statistics, an ad by the manufacturer and an enigmatic row of numbers at the bottom. The unnumbered stickers are checklisted here in alphabetical order.

		NM	EX	VG
Complete Set (6):		60.00	30.00	18.00
Common Player:		9.00	4.50	2.75
(1)	Richard Allen	25.00	12.50	7.50
(2)	Ed Hermann	9.00	4.50	2.75
(3)	Bart Johnson	9.00	4.50	2.75
(4)	Carlos May	9.00	4.50	2.75
(5)	Bill Melton	9.00	4.50	2.75
(6)	Wilbur Wood	9.00	4.50	2.75

E

1914 E. & S. Publishing Co.

Fewer than a dozen players have been reported from this issue. Front of the 5-1/2" x 3-3/4" postcards has a large portrait or action picture of the player at center, with a number of cartoons around. The printing is in blue ink. The back is done in ornate typography with copyright line, stamp box, etc. Other players may yet be discovered.

		NM	EX	VG
(1)	"Jimmie" Archer	300.00	150.00	90.00
(2)	Joe Benz	300.00	150.00	90.00
(3)	Ty Cobb	4,500	2,250	1,350
(4)	Miller Huggins	600.00	300.00	180.00
(5)	Joe Jackson	6,000	3,000	1,800
(6)	James Lavender	300.00	150.00	90.00
(7)	Christy Mathewson	2,500	1,250	750.00
(8)	"Tex" Russell	300.00	150.00	90.00
(9)	Frank Schulte	300.00	150.00	90.00
(10)	Jim Scott	300.00	150.00	90.00
(11)	Art Wilson	300.00	150.00	90.00

1940s Eagle Hall of Fame

The date of this issue can only be approximated, probably in the late 1940s. The 9-1/4" x 11-1/4" cards have high-gloss sepia photos on thick cardboard. A wood-look frame and identification plaques are pictured around the central photo. Backs are blank. The pictures were issued by the Carnegie (Pa.) Aerie of the Eagles, lodge #1134, according to the bottom "plaque." At top is "Eagle Hall of Fame." Presumably the four ballplayers and two boxers known were all members of that fraternal order. The unnumbered pieces are checklisted alphabetically.

		NM	EX	VG
Complete Set (6):		700.00	350.00	210.00
Common Player:		40.00	20.00	12.00
(1)	Bob Fitzsimmons/Boxer	40.00	20.00	12.00
(2)	Lefty Grove	150.00	75.00	45.00
(3)	Stan Musial	200.00	100.00	60.00
(4)	John Sullivan/Boxer	75.00	37.00	22.00
(5)	Honus Wagner	175.00	87.00	52.00
(6)	Cy Young	175.00	87.00	52.00

1979 Early Red Sox Favorites

This collectors' issue from Maine features players of the 1920s-1930s Red Sox. Cards are printed in black-and-white in a 2-5/8" x 3-3/4" format. Front photos are bordered in white and have identification of the players overprinted in black. Backs have a few stats, highlights or an explanation of the photo on front. Many cards feature more than one player.

		NM	EX	VG
Complete Set (24):		40.00	20.00	12.00
Common Player:		4.00	2.00	1.25
1	New Fenway Park	4.00	2.00	1.25
2	Mrs. Tom Yawkey and Mrs. Eddie Collins	4.00	2.00	1.25
3	Red Sox Outfielders - 1932 (Tom Oliver, Earl Webb, Jack Rothrock)	4.00	2.00	1.25
4	Red Sox Ace Pitchers (John Marcum, Wes Ferrell, Lefty Grove, Fritz Ostermueller)	4.00	2.00	1.25
5	John Gooch	4.00	2.00	1.25
6	Red Sox Recruits at Sarasota, Fla. (Joe Cronin)	4.00	2.00	1.25
7	Danny MacFayden	4.00	2.00	1.25
8	Dale Alexander	4.00	2.00	1.25
9	Robert (Fatsy) Fothergill	4.00	2.00	1.25
10	Red Sox Sunday Morning Workout	4.00	2.00	1.25
11	Jimmie Foxx (Siging ball for Mrs. Yawkey.)	6.00	3.00	1.75
12	Lefty Grove (Presented keys to new car.)	6.00	3.00	1.75
13	"Fireball" Lefty Grove	6.00	3.00	1.75
14	Praciticng Base Stealing (Jack Rothrock, Urban Pickering)	4.00	2.00	1.25
15	Tom Daly, Al Schacht, Herb Pennock	4.00	2.00	1.25
16	Eddie Collins, Heinie Manush	6.00	3.00	1.75
17	Tris Speaker	6.00	3.00	1.75
18	Home Run Star (Jimmie Foxx)	6.00	3.00	1.75
19	Smead Jolley	4.00	2.00	1.25
20	Hal Trosky, Jimmie Foxx	4.00	2.00	1.25
21	Herold "Muddy" Ruel, Wilcy "Fireman" Moore	4.00	2.00	1.25
22	Bob Quinn, Shano Collins	4.00	2.00	1.25
23	Tom Oliver	4.00	2.00	1.25
24	Joe Cronin, Herb Pennock, Buetter	4.00	2.00	1.25

1966 East Hills Pirates

JESSE GONDER [Catcher] =90

Stores in the East Hills Shopping Center, a large mall located in suburban Pittsburgh, distributed cards from this 25-card full-color set in 1966. The cards, which measure 3-1/4" x 4-1/4", are blank-backed and are numbered by the players' uniform numbers. The numbers appear in the lower right corners of the cards.

		NM	EX	VG
Complete Set (25):		50.00	25.00	15.00
Common Player:		2.50	1.25	.70
3	Harry Walker	2.50	1.25	.70
7	Bob Bailey	2.50	1.25	.70
8	Willie Stargell	10.00	5.00	3.00
9	Bill Mazeroski	10.00	5.00	3.00
10	Jim Pagliaroni	2.50	1.25	.70
11	Jose Pagan	2.50	1.25	.70
12	Jerry May	2.50	1.25	.70
14	Gene Alley	2.50	1.25	.70
15	Manny Mota	2.50	1.25	.70
16	Andy Rodgers	2.50	1.25	.70
17	Donn Clendenon	2.50	1.25	.70
18	Matty Alou	2.50	1.25	.70
19	Pete Mikkelsen	2.50	1.25	.70
20	Jesse Gonder	2.50	1.25	.70
21	Bob Clemente	30.00	15.00	9.00
22	Woody Fryman	2.50	1.25	.70
24	Jerry Lynch	2.50	1.25	.70
25	Tommie Sisk	2.50	1.25	.70
26	Roy Face	2.50	1.25	.70
28	Steve Blass	2.50	1.25	.70
32	Vernon Law	3.50	1.75	1.00
34	Al McBean	2.50	1.25	.70
39	Bob Veale	2.50	1.25	.70
43	Don Cardwell	2.50	1.25	.70
45	Gene Michael	2.50	1.25	.70

1933 Eclipse Import

No. 410
This is one of a series of 24 cards
JIMMY DYKES
Chicago White Sox
He is one of the few players who can play every position in the field but catch. A timely batter and dependable fielder, he hit .265 in over 150 games and played three infield positions in 1932. Played with Philadelphia Athletics for over 12 years, finally traded to White Sox this year. Dykes is 36 years old, about five feet nine inches tall and weighs 175 lbs.

Issued in 1933, this set was sold in eight-card strips. Numbered from 401 through 424, the cards measure 2-7/16" x 2-7/8". The design features a crude colored drawing of the player on the front. The back of the card displays the card number at the top followed by the player's name, team and a brief write-up. Card numbers 403, 413, and 414 are missing and probably correspond to the three unnumbered cards in the set. The set carries an American Card Catalog designation of R337.

		NM	EX	VG
Complete Set (24):		7,500	3,000	1,500
Common Player:		165.00	65.00	30.00
401	Johnny Vergez	165.00	65.00	30.00
402	Babe Ruth	1,200	480.00	240.00
403	Not Issued			
404	George Pipgras	165.00	65.00	30.00
405	Bill Terry	425.00	170.00	85.00
406	George Connally	165.00	65.00	30.00
407	Watson Clark	165.00	65.00	30.00
408	"Lefty" Grove	500.00	200.00	100.00
409	Henry Johnson	165.00	65.00	30.00
410	Jimmy Dykes	165.00	65.00	30.00
411	Henry Hine Schuble	165.00	65.00	30.00
412	Bucky Harris	425.00	170.00	85.00
413	Not Issued			
414	Not Issued			
415	Al Simmons	425.00	170.00	85.00
416	Henry "Heinie" Manush	425.00	170.00	85.00
417	Glen Myatt (Glenn)	165.00	65.00	30.00
418	Babe Herman	175.00	70.00	35.00
419	Frank Frisch	425.00	170.00	85.00
420	Tony Lazzeri	425.00	170.00	85.00
421	Paul Waner	425.00	170.00	85.00
422	Jimmy Wilson	165.00	65.00	30.00
423	Charles Grimm	165.00	65.00	30.00

424	Dick Bartell	165.00	65.00	30.00
----	Jimmy Fox (Jimmie Foxx)	600.00	240.00	120.00
----	Roy Johnson	165.00	65.00	30.00
----	Pie Traynor	425.00	170.00	85.00

1942 Editorial Bruguera Babe Ruth

BABE RUTH

The Babe is the only baseball player appearing is this 12-card series of "Figuras deportivas de fama mundial" (World famous sports figures) issued in Spain. The cards are blank-backed, about 4-3/4" x 3-1/2", with color artwork on front.

	NM	EX	VG
Babe Ruth	175.00	90.00	50.00

1930s Edwards, Ringer & Bigg Cigarettes

Though he is identified nowhere on this English cigarette card, the home run swing of Babe Ruth on the front is unmistakable. The last card in a set of 25 "Sports & Games in Many Lands" series, the approximately 2-5/8" x 1-3/8" cards have color artwork on the front and green-and-white backs. The back of the baseball card provides a short history of "The great national sport of the U.S.A." The card is nearly identical to the much more common 1929 Churchman's brand, except for the ads on back and the lack on the later card of the Churchman's name on top-right front.

		NM	EX	VG
25	Baseball, U.S.A. (Babe Ruth)	400.00	200.00	120.00

1909-11 El Principe de Gales Cigarettes

PREMIUMS:
Commons: 1-2X
Hall of Famers: 1-2X
(See T206 for checklist and base card values.)

1976 English's Chicken Baltimore Orioles Lids

It is uncertain whether the checklist presented here is complete. These 8-3/8" diameter fried chicken bucket lids are printed on heavy waxed cardboard in black-and-white. Cap logos have been airbrushed off. A few previous seasons' stats are printed to the left and right of the player photo.

		NM	EX	VG
Complete Set (4):		45.00	22.50	13.50
Common Player:		9.00	4.50	2.75
(1)	Mike Cuellar	9.00	4.50	1.75
(2)	Ken Holtzman	9.00	4.50	1.75
(3)	Lee May	9.00	4.50	1.75
(4)	Jim Palmer	20.00	10.00	6.00

1963-1973 Equitable Sports Hall of Fame

This series of black-and-white art prints was produced over more than a decade. About 8" x 11", the prints feature the artwork of Robert Riger or George Loh, reproduced from ads for the life insurance company. Nearly 95 pieces honoring athletes from many sports were produced. Only the baseball players are listed here.

		NM	EX	VG
Common Player:		6.00	3.00	1.80
(1)	Ernie Banks	7.50	3.75	2.25
(2)	Roy Campanella	7.50	3.75	2.25
(3)	Johnny Evers	6.00	3.00	1.80
(4)	Bob Feller	6.00	3.00	1.80
(5)	Lou Gehrig	10.00	5.00	3.00
(6)	Lefty Grove	6.00	3.00	1.80
(7)	Tommy Henrich	6.00	3.00	1.80
(8)	Carl Hubbell	6.00	3.00	1.80
(9)	Al Kaline	6.00	3.00	1.80
(10)	Jerry Koosman	6.00	3.00	1.80
(11)	Mickey Mantle	15.00	7.50	4.50
(12)	Eddie Mathews	6.00	3.00	1.80
(13)	Willie Mays	9.00	4.50	2.75
(14)	Stan Musial	9.00	4.50	2.75
(15)	Pee Wee Reese	6.00	3.00	1.80
(16)	Allie Reynolds	6.00	3.00	1.80
(17)	Robin Roberts	6.00	3.00	1.80
(18)	Brooks Robinson	6.00	3.00	1.80
(19)	Red Ruffing	6.00	3.00	1.80
(20)	Babe Ruth	12.50	6.25	3.75
(21)	Warren Spahn	6.00	3.00	1.80

1954 Esskay Hot Dogs Orioles

VINÍCIO "CHICO" GARCIA, Infielder
Born: December 13, 1926
Hometown: Mexico City, Mex.
Throws Right — Bats Right

Measuring 2-1/4" x 3-1/2", the 1954 Esskay Hot Dogs set features the Baltimore Orioles. The unnumbered color cards were issued in panels of two on packages of hot dogs and are usually found with grease stains. The cards have waxed fronts with blank backs on a white stock. Complete boxes of Esskay Hot Dogs are scarce and command a price of 2-3 times greater than the single card values.

		NM	EX	VG
Complete Set (34):		45,000	18,000	9,000
Common Player:		1,500	600.00	300.00
(1)	Neil Berry	1,500	600.00	300.00
(2)	Michael Blyzka	1,500	600.00	300.00
(3)	Harry Brecheen	1,500	600.00	300.00
(4)	Gil Coan	1,500	600.00	300.00
(5)	Joe Coleman	1,500	600.00	300.00
(6)	Clinton Courtney	1,500	600.00	300.00
(7)	Charles E. Diering	1,500	600.00	300.00
(8)	Jimmie Dykes	1,500	600.00	300.00
(9)	Frank J. Fanovich	1,500	600.00	300.00
(10)	Howard Fox	1,500	600.00	300.00
(11)	Jim Fridley	1,500	600.00	300.00
(12)	Vinicio "Chico" Garcia	1,500	600.00	300.00
(13)	Jehosie Heard	2,000	800.00	400.00
(14)	Darrell Johnson	1,500	600.00	300.00
(15)	Bob Kennedy	1,500	600.00	300.00
(16)	Dick Kokos	1,500	600.00	300.00
(17)	Dave Koslo	1,500	600.00	300.00
(18)	Lou Kretlow	1,500	600.00	300.00
(19)	Richard D. Kryhoski	1,500	600.00	300.00
(20)	Don Larsen	2,500	1,000	500.00
(21)	Donald E. Lenhardt	1,500	600.00	300.00
(22)	Richard Littlefield	1,500	600.00	300.00
(23)	Sam Mele	1,500	600.00	300.00
(24)	Les Moss	1,500	600.00	300.00
(25)	Ray L. Murray	1,500	600.00	300.00
(26a)	"Bobo" Newsom (No stadium lights in background.)	1,750	700.00	350.00
(26b)	"Bobo" Newson (Stadium lights in background.)	1,750	700.00	350.00
(27)	Tom Oliver	1,500	600.00	300.00
(28)	Duane Pillette	1,500	600.00	300.00
(29)	Francis M. Skaff	1,500	600.00	300.00
(30)	Marlin Stuart	1,500	600.00	300.00
(31)	Robert L. Turley	2,250	900.00	450.00
(32)	Eddie Waitkus	1,500	600.00	300.00
(33)	Vic Wertz	1,500	600.00	300.00
(34)	Robert G. Young	1,500	600.00	300.00

1955 Esskay Hot Dogs Orioles

For the second consecutive year, Esskay Meats placed baseball cards of Orioles players on their boxes of hot dogs. The unnumbered, color cards measure 2-1/4" x 3-1/2" and can be distinguished from the previous year by their unwaxed fronts and blank gray backs. Many of the same photos from 1954 were used with only minor picture-cropping differences. For 1955, only one player card per box was printed. The space which was occupied by the second player card in 1954 carried a prize redemption coupon on 1955 boxes.

		NM	EX	VG
Complete Set (26):		37,500	15,000	7,500
Common Player:		1,500	600.00	300.00
(1)	Cal Abrams	1,500	600.00	300.00
(2)	Robert S. Alexander	1,500	600.00	300.00
(3)	Harry Byrd	1,500	600.00	300.00
(4)	Gil Coan	1,500	600.00	300.00
(5)	Joseph P. Coleman	1,500	600.00	300.00
(6)	William R. Cox	1,500	600.00	300.00
(7)	Charles E. Diering	1,500	600.00	300.00
(8)	Walter A. Evers	1,500	600.00	300.00
(9)	Don Johnson	1,500	600.00	300.00
(10)	Robert D. Kennedy	1,500	600.00	300.00
(11)	Lou Kretlow	1,500	600.00	300.00
(12)	Robert L. Kuzava	1,500	600.00	300.00
(13)	Fred Marsh	1,500	600.00	300.00
(14)	Charles Maxwell	1,500	600.00	300.00
(15)	Jimmie McDonald	1,500	600.00	300.00
(16)	Bill Miller	1,500	600.00	300.00
(17)	Willy Miranda	1,500	600.00	300.00
(18)	Raymond L. Moore	1,500	600.00	300.00
(19)	John Lester Moss	1,500	600.00	300.00
(20)	"Bobo" Newsom	1,500	600.00	300.00
(21)	Duane Pillette	1,500	600.00	300.00
(22)	Edward S. Waitkus	1,500	600.00	300.00
(23)	Harold W. Smith	1,500	600.00	300.00
(24)	Gus Triandos	1,500	600.00	300.00

		NM	EX	VG
(25)	Eugene R. Woodling	1,750	700.00	350.00
(26)	Robert G. Young	1,500	600.00	300.00

1972 Esso Hispanic Coins

Little is known of these coins, except that they were distributed in Puerto Rico. Even the sponsor, Esso Oil Co., is not mentioned anywhere on the pieces. Made of aluminum and 1-1/4" in diameter, coin fronts have a portrait of the player with his name above. Backs are in Spanish and have the player's position, team, height, weight, date and place of birth. The coins of Tony Perez and, to a lesser extent, Rod Carew are scarcer than the others. A person receiving a Perez coin was able to exchange it for a full tank of gas. In 2006, a brass-finish Roberto Clemente coin was first reported, probably also a short-printed exchange coin.

		NM	EX	VG
Complete Set (13):		325.00	160.00	95.00
Common Player:		9.00	4.50	2.75
(1)	Luis Aparicio	15.00	7.50	4.50
(2)	Rod Carew	50.00	25.00	15.00
(3)	Rico Carty	9.00	4.50	2.75
(4)	Cesar Cedeno	9.00	4.50	2.75
(5)	Orlando Cepeda	15.00	7.50	4.50
(6)	Roberto Clemente	110.00	55.00	35.00
(7)	Mike Cuellar	9.00	4.50	2.75
(8)	Juan Marichal	15.00	7.50	4.50
(9)	Felix Millan	9.00	4.50	2.75
(10)	Guillermo Montanez	9.00	4.50	2.75
(11)	Tony Oliva	12.00	6.00	3.50
(12a)	Tany Perez (Tony)	75.00	37.50	22.50
(12b)	Tony Perez	75.00	37.50	22.50
(13)	Manny Sanguillen	9.00	4.50	2.75

1949 Eureka Sportstamps

The commissioner of baseball, president of the National League and 198 N.L. players are included in this issue. The stamps were issued on team sheets measuring 7-1/2" x 10", with individual stamps measuring 1-1/2" x 2". An album issued with the set provided short player biographies. The stamps feature colorized posed player action photos. At bottom is a yellow strip with the player's name, stamp number and copyright line. Stamps are numbered alphabetically within teams.

		NM	EX	VG
Complete Set (200):		900.00	450.00	275.00
Common Player:		5.00	2.50	1.50
Album w/mounted stamps:		400.00	200.00	120.00
Album:		75.00	37.50	22.00
1	Albert B. (Happy) Chandler	15.00	7.50	4.50
2	Ford Frick	5.00	2.50	1.50
3	Billy Southworth	5.00	2.50	1.50
4	Johnny Antonelli	5.00	2.50	1.50
5	Red Barrett	5.00	2.50	1.50
6	Clint Conatser	5.00	2.50	1.50
7	Alvin Dark	5.00	2.50	1.50
8	Bob Elliott	5.00	2.50	1.50
9	Glenn Elliott	5.00	2.50	1.50
10	Elbie Fletcher	5.00	2.50	1.50
11	Bob Hall	5.00	2.50	1.50
12	Jeff Heath	5.00	2.50	1.50
13	Bobby Hogue	5.00	2.50	1.50
14	Tommy Holmes	5.00	2.50	1.50
15	Al Lakeman	5.00	2.50	1.50
16	Phil Masi	5.00	2.50	1.50
17	Nelson Potter	5.00	2.50	1.50
18	Pete Reiser	10.00	5.00	3.00
19	Rick Rickert	5.00	2.50	1.50
20	Connie Ryan	5.00	2.50	1.50
21	Jim Russell	5.00	2.50	1.50
22	Johnny Sain	10.00	5.00	3.00
23	Bill Salkeld	5.00	2.50	1.50
24	Sibby Sisti	5.00	2.50	1.50
25	Warren Spahn	25.00	12.50	7.50
26	Eddie Stanky	5.00	2.50	1.50

27	Bill Voiselle	5.00	2.50	1.50
28	Bert Shotton	5.00	2.50	1.50
29	Jack Banta	5.00	2.50	1.50
30	Rex Barney	7.50	3.75	2.25
31	Ralph Branca	15.00	7.50	4.50
32	Tommy Brown	5.00	2.50	1.50
33	Roy Campanella	40.00	20.00	12.00
34	Billy Cox	7.50	3.75	2.25
35	Bruce Edwards	5.00	2.50	1.50
36	Carl Furillo	20.00	10.00	6.00
37	Joe Hatten	5.00	2.50	1.50
38	Gene Hermanski	5.00	2.50	1.50
39	Gil Hodges	25.00	12.50	7.50
40	Johnny Jorgensen	5.00	2.50	1.50
41	Lefty Martin	5.00	2.50	1.50
42	Mike McCormick	5.00	2.50	1.50
43	Eddie Miksis	5.00	2.50	1.50
44	Paul Minner	5.00	2.50	1.50
45	Sam Narron	10.00	5.00	3.00
46	Don Newcombe	20.00	10.00	6.00
47	Jake Pitler	5.00	2.50	1.50
48	Pee Wee Reese	35.00	17.50	10.50
49	Jackie Robinson	50.00	25.00	15.00
50	Duke Snider	40.00	20.00	12.00
51	Dick Whitman	5.00	2.50	1.50
52	Forrest Burgess	10.00	5.00	3.00
53	Phil Cavaretta	5.00	2.50	1.50
54	Bob Chipman	5.00	2.50	1.50
55	Walter Dubiel	5.00	2.50	1.50
56	Hank Edwards	5.00	2.50	1.50
57	Frankie Gustine	5.00	2.50	1.50
58	Hal Jeffcoat	5.00	2.50	1.50
59	Emil Kush	5.00	2.50	1.50
60	Doyle Lade	5.00	2.50	1.50
61	Dutch Leonard	5.00	2.50	1.50
62	Peanuts Lowrey	5.00	2.50	1.50
63	Gene Mauch	7.50	3.75	2.25
64	Cal McLish	5.00	2.50	1.50
65	Rube Novotney	5.00	2.50	1.50
66	Andy Pafko	5.00	2.50	1.50
67	Bob Ramozzotti	5.00	2.50	1.50
68	Herman Reich	5.00	2.50	1.50
69	Bob Rush	5.00	2.50	1.50
70	Johnny Schmitz	5.00	2.50	1.50
71	Bob Scheffing	5.00	2.50	1.50
72	Roy Smalley	5.00	2.50	1.50
73	Emil Verban	5.00	2.50	1.50
74	Al Walker	5.00	2.50	1.50
75	Harry Walker	5.00	2.50	1.50
76	Bucky Walters	5.00	2.50	1.50
77	Bob Adams	5.00	2.50	1.50
78	Ewell Blackwell	5.00	2.50	1.50
79	Jimmy Bloodworth	5.00	2.50	1.50
80	Walker Cooper	5.00	2.50	1.50
81	Tony Cuccinello	5.00	2.50	1.50
82	Jess Dobernic	5.00	2.50	1.50
83	Eddie Erautt	5.00	2.50	1.50
84	Frank Fanovich	5.00	2.50	1.50
85	Howie Fox	5.00	2.50	1.50
86	Grady Hatton	5.00	2.50	1.50
87	Homer Howell	5.00	2.50	1.50
88	Ted Kluszewski	20.00	10.00	6.00
89	Danny Litwhiler	5.00	2.50	1.50
90	Everett Lively	5.00	2.50	1.50
91	Lloyd Merriman	5.00	2.50	1.50
92	Phil Page	5.00	2.50	1.50
93	Kent Peterson	5.00	2.50	1.50
94	Ken Raffensberger	5.00	2.50	1.50
95	Luke Sewell	5.00	2.50	1.50
96	Virgil Stallcup	5.00	2.50	1.50
97	Johnny Vander Meer	10.00	5.00	3.00
98	Herman Wehmeier	5.00	2.50	1.50
99	Johnny Wyrostek	5.00	2.50	1.50
100	Benny Zientara	5.00	2.50	1.50
101	Leo Durocher	12.50	6.25	3.75
102	Hank Behrman	5.00	2.50	1.50
103	Augie Galan	5.00	2.50	1.50
104	Sid Gordon	5.00	2.50	1.50
105	Bert Haas	5.00	2.50	1.50
106	Andy Hansen	5.00	2.50	1.50
107	Clint Hartung	5.00	2.50	1.50
108	Kirby Higbe	5.00	2.50	1.50
109	George Hausman	5.00	2.50	1.50
110	Larry Jansen	5.00	2.50	1.50
111	Sheldon Jones	5.00	2.50	1.50
112	Monte Kennedy	5.00	2.50	1.50
113	Buddy Kerr	5.00	2.50	1.50
114	Dave Koslo	5.00	2.50	1.50
115	Joe Lafata	5.00	2.50	1.50
116	Whitey Lockman	5.00	2.50	1.50
117	Jack Lohrke	5.00	2.50	1.50
118	Willard Marshall	5.00	2.50	1.50
119	Bill Milne	5.00	2.50	1.50
120	Johnny Mize	15.00	7.50	4.50
121	Don Mueller	5.00	2.50	1.50
122	Ray Mueller	5.00	2.50	1.50
123	Bill Rigney	5.00	2.50	1.50
124	Bobby Thomson	7.50	3.75	2.25
125	Sam Webb	5.00	2.50	1.50
126	Wesley Westrum	5.00	2.50	1.50
127	Eddie Sawyer	5.00	2.50	1.50
128	Richie Ashburn	30.00	15.00	9.00
129	Benny Bengough	5.00	2.50	1.50
130	Charlie Bicknell	5.00	2.50	1.50
131	Buddy Blattner	5.00	2.50	1.50
132	Hank Borowy	5.00	2.50	1.50
133	Ralph Caballero	5.00	2.50	1.50
134	Blix Donnelly	5.00	2.50	1.50
135	Del Ennis	5.00	2.50	1.50
136	Granville Hamner	5.00	2.50	1.50
137	Ken Heintzelman	5.00	2.50	1.50
138	Stan Hollmig	5.00	2.50	1.50
139	Willie Jones	5.00	2.50	1.50
140	Jim Konstanty	5.00	2.50	1.50
141	Stan Lopata	5.00	2.50	1.50
142	Jackie Mayo	5.00	2.50	1.50
143	Bill Nicholson	5.00	2.50	1.50
144	Robin Roberts	60.00	30.00	18.00

		NM	EX	VG
145	Schoolboy Rowe	5.00	2.50	1.50
146	Andy Seminick	5.00	2.50	1.50
147	Ken Silvestri	5.00	2.50	1.50
148	Curt Simmons	5.00	2.50	1.50
149	Dick Sisler	5.00	2.50	1.50
150	Ken Trinkle	5.00	2.50	1.50
151	Eddie Waitkus	5.00	2.50	1.50
152	Bill Meyer	5.00	2.50	1.50
153	Monte Basgall	5.00	2.50	1.50
154	Eddie Bockman	5.00	2.50	1.50
155	Ernie Bonham	5.00	2.50	1.50
156	Hugh Casey	5.00	2.50	1.50
157	Pete Castiglione	5.00	2.50	1.50
158	Cliff Chambers	5.00	2.50	1.50
159	Murry Dickson	5.00	2.50	1.50
160	Ed Fitz Gerald	5.00	2.50	1.50
161	Les Fleming	5.00	2.50	1.50
162	Hal Gregg	5.00	2.50	1.50
163	Goldie Holt	5.00	2.50	1.50
164	Johnny Hopp	5.00	2.50	1.50
165	Ralph Kiner	20.00	10.00	6.00
166	Vic Lombardi	5.00	2.50	1.50
167	Clyde McCullough	5.00	2.50	1.50
168	Danny Murtaugh	5.00	2.50	1.50
169	Bill Posedel	5.00	2.50	1.50
170	Elmer Riddle	5.00	2.50	1.50
171	Stan Rojek	5.00	2.50	1.50
172	Rip Sewell	5.00	2.50	1.50
173	Eddie Stevens	5.00	2.50	1.50
174	Dixie Walker	5.00	2.50	1.50
175	Bill Werle	5.00	2.50	1.50
176	Wally Westlake	5.00	2.50	1.50
177	Eddie Dyer	5.00	2.50	1.50
178	Bill Baker	5.00	2.50	1.50
179	Al Brazle	5.00	2.50	1.50
180	Harry Brecheen	5.00	2.50	1.50
181	Chuck Diering	5.00	2.50	1.50
182	Joe Garagiola	13.50	6.75	4.00
183	Tom Galviano	5.00	2.50	1.50
184	Jim Hearn	5.00	2.50	1.50
185	Ken Johnson	5.00	2.50	1.50
186	Nippy Jones	5.00	2.50	1.50
187	Ed Kazak	5.00	2.50	1.50
188	Lou Klein	5.00	2.50	1.50
189	Marty Marion	5.00	2.50	1.50
190	George Munger	5.00	2.50	1.50
191	Stan Musial	45.00	22.00	13.50
192	Spike Nelson	5.00	2.50	1.50
193	Howie Pollet	5.00	2.50	1.50
194	Bill Reeder	5.00	2.50	1.50
195	Del Rice	5.00	2.50	1.50
196	Ed Sauer	5.00	2.50	1.50
197	Red Schoendienst	20.00	10.00	6.00
198	Enos Slaughter	20.00	10.00	6.00
199	Ted Wilks	5.00	2.50	1.50
200	Ray Yochim	5.00	2.50	1.50

1914 Evening Sun N.Y. Giants

The World's Champion 1913 N.Y. Giants are featured in this set of newspaper supplements titled, "Evening Sun's Gallery of Famous Baseball Players." It is believed the paper was published in Norwich, N.Y. Slightly larger than 9" x 12", the supplements feature black-and-white portraits by Lawrence Semon, who also produced a contemporary series of baseball postcards.

		NM	EX	VG
Complete Set (21):		7,000	3,500	2,100
Common Player:		200.00	100.00	60.00
(1)	George Burns	200.00	100.00	60.00
(2)	Doc Crandall	200.00	100.00	60.00
(3)	Al Demaree	200.00	100.00	60.00
(4)	Art Fletcher	200.00	100.00	60.00
(5)	Art Fromme	200.00	100.00	60.00
(6)	Grover Hartley	200.00	100.00	60.00
(7)	Buck Herzog	200.00	100.00	60.00
(8)	Rube Marquard	400.00	200.00	120.00
(9)	Christy Mathewson	1,200	600.00	360.00
(10)	Moose McCormick	200.00	100.00	60.00
(11)	John McGraw	400.00	200.00	120.00
(12)	Fred Merkle	200.00	100.00	60.00
(13)	Chief Meyers	200.00	100.00	60.00
(14)	Red Murray	200.00	100.00	60.00
(15)	Wilbert Robinson	400.00	200.00	120.00
(16)	Arthur Shafer	200.00	100.00	60.00
(17)	Fred Snodgrass	200.00	100.00	60.00
(18)	Jeff Tesreau	200.00	100.00	60.00
(19)	Jim Thorpe	1,750	875.00	525.00
(20)	Art Wilson	200.00	100.00	60.00
(21)	Hooks Wiltse	200.00	100.00	60.00

1916 Everybody's

Where "Everybody's" department store was located is unknown, but in 1916 they chose to use

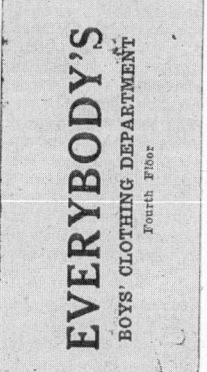

DICK RUDOLPH
P.—Boston Braves
149

EVERYBODY'S
BOYS' CLOTHING DEPARTMENT
Fourth Floor

baseball cards to promote their boy's wear department. The approximately 1-5/8" x 3" black-and-white cards share the format and checklist with the much more common M101-4 blank-back version and several other regional advertisers. Everybody's is one of the scarcest advertising backs to be found in this issue and the cards command a premium from type-card and superstar collectors.

Premium: 6-9X
(See 1916 M101-4 Blank Backs for checklist and base card values.)

1921 Exhibits

Geo.H.Babe Ruth
OUTFIELDER, NEW YORK, AM.L.

Ty.R.Cobb
OUTFIELDER, DETROIT, AM. L.

The Exhibit Supply Company of Chicago issued the first in a long series of postcard-size (3-3/8" x 5-3/8") baseball cards in 1921. The Exhibit cards were commonly sold in "penny arcade" vending machines. The 1921 series consists of 64 cards and includes four players from each of the 16 major league teams. The cards feature black-and-white photos with the player's name printed in a fancy script. The player's position and team appear below the name in small, hand-lettered capital letters. American League is designated as "AM.L.," which can help differentiate the 1921 series from future years. Some of the cards contain white borders while others do not. All have blank backs. There are various spelling errors in the picture legends.

		NM	EX	VG
Complete Set (64):		11,000	5,500	3,250
Common Player:		75.00	35.00	20.00
(1)	Chas. B. Adams	75.00	35.00	20.00
(2)	Grover C. Alexander	275.00	135.00	80.00
(3)	David Bancroft	175.00	85.00	50.00
(4)	Geo. J. Burns	75.00	35.00	20.00
(5)	Owen Bush	75.00	35.00	20.00
(6)	Max J. Carey	175.00	85.00	50.00
(7)	Ty R. Cobb	1,000	500.00	300.00
(8)	Eddie T. Collins	175.00	85.00	50.00
(9)	John Collins	75.00	35.00	20.00
(10)	Stanley Coveleskie (Coveleski)	200.00	100.00	60.00
(11)	Walton E. Cruise	75.00	35.00	20.00
(12)	Jacob E. Daubert	75.00	35.00	20.00
(13)	George Dauss	75.00	35.00	20.00
(14)	Charles A. Deal	75.00	35.00	20.00
(15)	Joe A. Dugan	75.00	35.00	20.00
(16)	James Dykes	75.00	35.00	20.00
(17)	U.C. "Red" Faber	175.00	85.00	50.00
(18)	J.F. Fournier	75.00	35.00	20.00
(19)	Frank F. Frisch	175.00	85.00	50.00
(20)	W.L. Gardner	75.00	35.00	20.00
(21)	H.M. "Hank" Gowdy	75.00	35.00	20.00
(22)	Burleigh A. Grimes	200.00	100.00	60.00
(23)	Heinie Groh	75.00	35.00	20.00
(24)	Jesse Haines	200.00	100.00	60.00
(25)	Sam Harris (Stanley)	200.00	100.00	60.00
(26)	Walter L. Holke	75.00	35.00	20.00
(27)	Charles J. Hollicher (Hollocher)	75.00	35.00	20.00
(28)	Rogers Hornsby	325.00	160.00	95.00
(29)	James H. Johnson (Johnston)	75.00	35.00	20.00
(30)	Walter P. Johnson	750.00	375.00	225.00
(31)	Sam P. Jones	75.00	35.00	20.00

		NM	EX	VG
(32)	Geo. L. Kelly	200.00	100.00	60.00
(33)	Dick Kerr	75.00	35.00	20.00
(34)	William L. Killifer (Killefer)	75.00	35.00	20.00
(35)	Ed Konetchy	75.00	35.00	20.00
(36)	John "Doc" Lavan	75.00	35.00	20.00
(37)	Walter J. Maranville	175.00	85.00	50.00
(38)	Carl W. Mays	75.00	35.00	20.00
(39)	J. "Stuffy" McInnis	75.00	35.00	20.00
(40)	Rollie C. Naylor	75.00	35.00	20.00
(41)	A. Earl Neale (Earle)	125.00	60.00	35.00
(42)	Ivan M. Olsen	75.00	35.00	20.00
(43)	S.F. "Steve" O'Neil (O'Neill)	75.00	35.00	20.00
(44)	Robert (Roger) Peckinpaugh	75.00	35.00	20.00
(45)	Ralph "Cy" Perkins	75.00	35.00	20.00
(46)	Raymond R. Powell	75.00	35.00	20.00
(47)	Joe "Goldie" Rapp	75.00	35.00	20.00
(48)	Edgar S. Rice	175.00	85.00	50.00
(49)	Jimmy Ring	75.00	35.00	20.00
(50)	Geo. H. "Babe" Ruth	2,750	1,375	825.00
(51)	Ray W. Schalk	175.00	85.00	50.00
(52)	Wallie Schang	75.00	35.00	20.00
(53)	Everett Scott	75.00	35.00	20.00
(54)	H.S. Shanks (Photo actually Wally Schang.)	75.00	35.00	20.00
(55)	Urban Shocker	75.00	35.00	20.00
(56)	Geo. H. Sisler	175.00	85.00	50.00
(57)	Tris Speaker	325.00	160.00	95.00
(58)	John Tobin	75.00	35.00	20.00
(59)	Robt. Veach	75.00	35.00	20.00
(60)	Zack D. Wheat	175.00	85.00	50.00
(61)	Geo. B. Whitted	75.00	35.00	20.00
(62)	Cy Williams	75.00	35.00	20.00
(63)	Kenneth R. Williams	75.00	35.00	20.00
(64)	Ivy B. Wingo	75.00	35.00	20.00

1922 Exhibits

Moses Yellowhorse
PITTSBURGH, N.L.

The Exhibit Supply Company continued the 3-3/8" x 5-3/8" format in 1922 but doubled the number of cards in the series to 128, including eight players from each team. All but nine of the players who appeared in the 1921 series are pictured in the 1922 set, along with 74 new players. The cards again display black-and-white photos with blank backs. Some photos have white borders. The player's name appears in script with the position and team below in small block capital letters. American League is designated as "A.L." Again, there are several spelling errors and incorrect player identifications. Only the 74 new additions are included in this checklist.

		NM	EX	VG
Complete Set (74):		7,500	3,750	2,250
Common Player:		85.00	40.00	25.00
(1)	Jim Bagby	85.00	40.00	25.00
(2)	J. Frank Baker	150.00	75.00	45.00
(3)	Walter Barbare	85.00	40.00	25.00
(4)	Turner Barber	85.00	40.00	25.00
(5)	John Bassler	85.00	40.00	25.00
(6)	Carlson L. Bigbee (Carson)	85.00	40.00	25.00
(7)	Sam Bohne	85.00	42.00	25.00
(8)	Geo. Burns	85.00	40.00	25.00
(9)	George Burns	85.00	40.00	25.00
(10)	Jeo Bush (Joe)	85.00	40.00	25.00
(11)	Leon Cadore	85.00	40.00	25.00
(12)	Jim Caveney	85.00	40.00	25.00
(13)	Wilbur Cooper	85.00	40.00	25.00
(14)	George Cutshaw	85.00	40.00	25.00
(15)	Dave Danforth	85.00	40.00	25.00
(16)	Bill Doak	85.00	40.00	25.00
(17)	Joe Dugan	85.00	40.00	25.00
(18)	Pat Duncan	85.00	40.00	25.00
(19)	Howard Emke (Ehmke)	85.00	40.00	25.00
(20)	Wm. Evans/Umpire	375.00	185.00	110.00
(21)	Bib Falk (Bibb)	85.00	40.00	25.00
(22)	Dana Fillingin (Fillingim)	85.00	40.00	25.00
(23)	Ira Flagstead	85.00	40.00	25.00
(24)	(Art) Fletcher	85.00	40.00	25.00
(25)	(Wally) Gerber	85.00	40.00	25.00
(26)	Ray Grimes	85.00	40.00	25.00
(27)	Harry Heilman (Heilmann)	150.00	75.00	45.00
(28)	George Hildebrand/Umpire	200.00	100.00	60.00
(29)	Wibur Hubbell (Wilbert)	85.00	40.00	25.00
(30)	Bill Jacobson	85.00	40.00	25.00
(31)	E.R. Johnson	85.00	40.00	25.00
(32)	Joe Judge	85.00	40.00	25.00
(33)	Bill Klem/Umpire	375.00	185.00	110.00
(34)	Harry Liebold (Leibold)	85.00	40.00	25.00
(35)	Walter Mails	85.00	40.00	25.00
(36)	Geo. Maisel	85.00	40.00	25.00

		NM	EX	VG
(37)	Lee Meadows	85.00	40.00	25.00
(38)	Clyde Milam (Milan)	85.00	40.00	25.00
(39)	Ed (Bing) Miller	85.00	40.00	25.00
(40)	Hack Miller	85.00	40.00	25.00
(41)	George Moriarty/Umpire	200.00	100.00	60.00
(42)	Robert Muesel (Meusel)	85.00	40.00	25.00
(43)	Harry Myers	85.00	40.00	25.00
(44)	Arthur Nehf	85.00	40.00	25.00
(45)	Joe Oeschger	85.00	40.00	25.00
(46)	Geo. O'Neil	85.00	40.00	25.00
(47)	Roger Peckinpaugh	85.00	40.00	25.00
(48)	Val Picinich	85.00	40.00	25.00
(49)	Bill Piercy	85.00	40.00	25.00
(50)	Derrill Pratt	85.00	40.00	25.00
(51)	Jack Quinn	85.00	40.00	25.00
(52)	Walter Reuther (Ruether)	85.00	40.00	25.00
(53)	Charles Rigler/Umpire	200.00	100.00	60.00
(54)	Eppa Rixey	150.00	75.00	45.00
(55)	Chas. Robertson	85.00	40.00	25.00
(56)	Everett Scott	85.00	40.00	25.00
(57)	Earl Sheely	85.00	40.00	25.00
(58)	Earl Smith/Portrait	85.00	40.00	25.00
(59)	Earl Smith/Standing (Photo actually Brad Kocher.)	85.00	40.00	25.00
(60)	Elmer Smith	85.00	40.00	25.00
(61)	Jack Smith (Photo actually Jimmy Smith.)	85.00	40.00	25.00
(62)	Sherrod Smith	85.00	40.00	25.00
(63)	Frank Snyder	85.00	40.00	25.00
(64)	Allan Sothoron (Allen)	85.00	40.00	25.00
(65)	Arnold Statz	85.00	40.00	25.00
(66)	Milton Stock	85.00	40.00	25.00
(67)	James Tierney	85.00	40.00	25.00
(68)	George Toporcer	85.00	40.00	25.00
(69)	Clarence (Tilly) Walker	85.00	40.00	25.00
(70)	Curtis Walker	85.00	40.00	25.00
(71)	Aaron Ward	85.00	40.00	25.00
(72)	Joe Wood	100.00	50.00	30.00
(73)	Moses Yellowhorse	300.00	150.00	90.00
(74)	Ross Young (Youngs)	150.00	75.00	45.00

1922 Eastern Exhibit Supply Co.

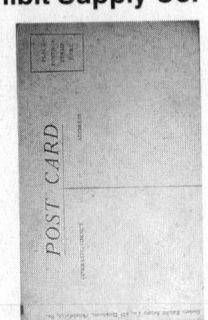

Postcard-style backs differentiate these cards from the more common Exhibit Supply Co., cards from Chicago. This 20-card series was produced by a Philadelphia company, although on some cards, the Eastern Exhibit copyright line on back has been blacked out and that of the Chicago company printed beneath it. The black-and-white cards measure 3-3/8" x 5-5/8".

		NM	EX	VG
Complete Set (20):		4,200	2,100	1,250
Common Player:		80.00	40.00	20.00
(1)	Grover Alexander	200.00	100.00	60.00
(2)	Dave Bancroft	125.00	65.00	35.00
(3)	Jesse Barnes	80.00	40.00	20.00
(4)	Joe Bush	80.00	40.00	20.00
(5)	Ty Cobb	750.00	375.00	225.00
(6)	Eddie Collins	125.00	65.00	35.00
(7)	Urban Faber	125.00	65.00	35.00
(8)	Clarence Galloway	80.00	40.00	20.00
(9)	Heinie Groh	125.00	65.00	35.00
(10)	Harry Heilmann	125.00	65.00	35.00
(11)	Charlie Hollocher	80.00	40.00	20.00
(12)	Rogers Hornsby	200.00	100.00	60.00
(13)	Walter Johnson	375.00	185.00	110.00
(14)	Eddie Rommel	80.00	40.00	20.00
(15)	Babe Ruth	1,550	775.00	465.00
(16)	Ray Schalk	125.00	65.00	35.00
(17)	Wallie Schang	80.00	40.00	20.00
(18)	Tris Speaker	200.00	100.00	60.00
(19)	Zach Wheat	125.00	65.00	35.00
(20)	Kenneth Williams	80.00	40.00	20.00

1923-24 Exhibits

The Exhibit cards for 1923 and 1924 are generally collected as a single 128-card series. The format remained basically the same as the previous year, 3-3/8" x 5-3/8", with black-and-white photos (some surrounded by a white border) and blank backs. The player's name is again shown in script with the position and team printed below in a small, square block-type style. Many of the same photos were used from previous years, although some are cropped differently, and some players have new team designations, team emblems removed, borders added or taken away, and other minor changes. Fifty-eight new cards are featured, including 38 players pictured for the first time in an Exhibit set. Only the 58 new cards are included in this checklist.

		NM	EX	VG
Complete Set (59):		20,000	10,000	6,000
Common Player:		225.00	110.00	65.00
(1)	Clyde Barnhart	225.00	110.00	65.00
(2)	Ray Blades	225.00	110.00	65.00
(3)	James Bottomley	400.00	200.00	120.00
(4)	George Burns	225.00	110.00	65.00
(5)	Dan Clark	225.00	110.00	65.00
(6)	Bill Doak	225.00	110.00	65.00
(7)	Joe Dugan	225.00	110.00	65.00
(8)	Howard J. Ehmke	225.00	110.00	65.00
(9)	Ira Flagstead	225.00	110.00	65.00
(10)	J.F. Fournier	225.00	110.00	65.00
(11)	Howard Freigan (Freigau)	225.00	110.00	65.00
(12)	C.E. Galloway	225.00	110.00	65.00
(13)	Joe Genewich	225.00	110.00	65.00
(14)	Mike Gonzales (Gonzalez)	275.00	135.00	82.00
(15)	H.M. "Hank" Gowdy	225.00	110.00	65.00
(16)	Charles Grimm	225.00	110.00	65.00
(17)	Heinie Groh	225.00	110.00	65.00
(18)	Chas. L. Harnett (Hartnett)	400.00	200.00	120.00
(19)	George Harper	225.00	110.00	65.00
(20)	Slim Harris (Harriss)	225.00	110.00	65.00
(21)	Clifton Heathcote	225.00	110.00	65.00
(22)	Andy High	225.00	110.00	65.00
(23)	Walter L. Holke	225.00	110.00	65.00
(24)	Charles D. Jamieson	225.00	110.00	65.00
(25)	Willie Kamm	225.00	110.00	65.00
(26)	Tony Kaufmann	225.00	110.00	65.00
(27)	Dudley Lee	225.00	110.00	65.00
(28)	Harry Liebold (Leibold)	225.00	110.00	65.00
(29)	Aldofo Luque	225.00	110.00	65.00
(30)	W.C. (Wid) Matthews	225.00	110.00	65.00
(31)	John J. McGraw	400.00	200.00	120.00
(32)	J. "Stuffy" McInnis	225.00	110.00	65.00
(33)	Johnny Morrison	225.00	110.00	65.00
(34)	John A. Mostil	225.00	110.00	65.00
(35)	J.F. O'Neill (Should be S.F.)	225.00	110.00	65.00
(36)	Ernest Padgett	225.00	110.00	65.00
(37)	Val Picinich	225.00	110.00	65.00
(38)	Bill Piercy	225.00	110.00	65.00
(39)	Herman Pillette	225.00	110.00	65.00
(40)	Wallie Pipp	275.00	135.00	82.00
(41)	Raymond R. Powell (Black background.)	225.00	110.00	65.00
(42)	Raymond R. Powell (Stands in background.)	225.00	110.00	65.00
(43)	Del. Pratt	225.00	110.00	65.00
(44)	E.E. Rigney	225.00	110.00	65.00
(45)	Eddie Rommel	225.00	110.00	65.00
(46)	Geo. H. "Babe" Ruth	7,500	3,750	2,250
(47)	Muddy Ruel	225.00	110.00	65.00
(48)	J.H. Sand	225.00	110.00	65.00
(49)	Henry Severeid	225.00	110.00	65.00
(50)	Joseph Sewell	400.00	200.00	120.00
(51)	Al. Simmons	450.00	225.00	135.00
(52)	R.E. Smith	225.00	110.00	65.00
(53)	Sherrod Smith	225.00	110.00	65.00
(54)	Casey Stengel	450.00	225.00	135.00
(55)	J.R. Stevenson (Stephenson)	225.00	110.00	65.00
(56)	James Tierney	225.00	110.00	65.00
(57)	Robt. Veach	225.00	110.00	65.00
(58)	L. Woodall	225.00	110.00	65.00
(59)	Russell G. Wrighstone	225.00	110.00	65.00

1925 Exhibits

The 1925 series of Exhibits contains 128 unnumbered cards, each measuring 3-3/8" x 5-3/8". The player's name (in all capital letters), position and team (along with a line reading "Made in U.S.A.") are printed in a small white box in a lower corner of the card. Most of the photos are vertical, however a few are horizontal. There are several misspellings in the set. Lou Gehrig's first baseball card appears in this issue. The cards are listed here in alphabetical order.

		NM	EX	VG
Complete Set (128):		32,500	16,000	9,750
Common Player:		125.00	65.00	35.00
(1)	Sparky Adams	125.00	65.00	35.00
(2)	Grover C. Alexander	300.00	150.00	90.00
(3)	David Bancroft	200.00	100.00	60.00
(4)	Jesse Barnes	125.00	65.00	35.00
(5)	John Bassler	125.00	65.00	35.00
(6)	Lester Bell	125.00	65.00	35.00
(7)	Lawrence Benton	125.00	65.00	35.00
(8)	Carson Bigbee	125.00	65.00	35.00
(9)	Max Bishop	125.00	65.00	35.00
(10)	Raymond Blates (Blades)	125.00	65.00	35.00
(11)	Oswald Bluege	125.00	65.00	35.00
(12)	James Bottomly (Bottomley)	200.00	100.00	60.00
(13)	Raymond Bressler	125.00	65.00	35.00
(14)	John Brooks	125.00	65.00	35.00
(15)	Maurice Burrus	125.00	65.00	35.00
(16)	Max Carey	200.00	100.00	60.00
(17)	Tyrus Cobb	1,100	550.00	330.00
(18)	Eddie Collins	200.00	100.00	60.00
(19)	Stanley Coveleski	200.00	100.00	60.00
(20)	Hugh M. Critz	125.00	65.00	35.00
(21)	Hazen Cuyler	225.00	110.00	65.00
(22)	George Dauss	125.00	65.00	35.00
(23)	I.M. Davis	125.00	65.00	35.00
(24)	John H. DeBerry	125.00	65.00	35.00
(25)	Art Decatur	125.00	65.00	35.00
(26)	Peter Donohue	125.00	65.00	35.00
(27)	Charles Dressen	125.00	65.00	35.00
(28)	James J. Dykes	125.00	65.00	35.00
(29)	Howard Ehmke	125.00	65.00	35.00
(30)	Bib Falk (Bibb)	125.00	65.00	35.00
(31)	Wilson Fewster	125.00	65.00	35.00
(32)	Max Flack	125.00	65.00	35.00
(33)	Ira Flagstead	125.00	65.00	35.00
(34)	Jacques F. Fournier	125.00	65.00	35.00
(35)	Howard Freigau	125.00	65.00	35.00
(36)	Frank Frisch	200.00	100.00	60.00
(37)	Henry L. Gehrig	12,000	6,000	3,600
(38)	Joseph Genewich	125.00	65.00	35.00
(39)	Walter Gerber	125.00	65.00	35.00
(40)	Frank Gibson	125.00	65.00	35.00
(41)	Leon Goslin	200.00	100.00	60.00
(42)	George Grantham	125.00	65.00	35.00
(43)	Samuel Gray	125.00	65.00	35.00
(44)	Burleigh A. Grimes	200.00	100.00	60.00
(45)	Charles Grimm	125.00	65.00	35.00
(46)	Heine Groh (Heinie)	125.00	65.00	35.00
(47)	Samuel Hale	125.00	65.00	35.00
(48)	George Harper	125.00	65.00	35.00
(49)	David Harris	125.00	65.00	35.00
(50)	Stanley Harris	200.00	100.00	60.00
(51)	Leo Hartnett	200.00	100.00	60.00
(52)	Nelson Hawks	125.00	65.00	35.00
(53)	Harry Heilmann	200.00	100.00	60.00
(54)	Walter Henline	125.00	65.00	35.00
(55)	Walter Holke	125.00	65.00	35.00
(56)	Harry Hooper	200.00	100.00	60.00
(57)	Rogers Hornsby	300.00	150.00	90.00
(58)	Wilbur Hubbell	125.00	65.00	35.00
(59)	Travis C. Jackson	200.00	100.00	60.00
(60)	William Jacobson	125.00	65.00	35.00
(61)	Charles Jamieson	125.00	65.00	35.00
(62)	James H. Johnson (Johnston)	125.00	65.00	35.00
(63)	Walter Johnson	400.00	200.00	120.00
(64)	Joseph Judge	125.00	65.00	35.00
(65)	Willie Kamm	125.00	65.00	35.00
(66)	Ray Kremer	125.00	65.00	35.00
(67)	Walter Lutzke	125.00	65.00	35.00
(68)	Walter Maranville	200.00	100.00	60.00
(69)	John ("Stuffy") McInnes (McInnis)	125.00	65.00	35.00
(70)	Martin McManus	125.00	65.00	35.00
(71)	Earl McNeely	125.00	65.00	35.00
(72)	Emil Meusel	125.00	65.00	35.00
(73)	Edmund (Bing) Miller	125.00	65.00	35.00
(74)	John Mokan	125.00	65.00	35.00
(75)	Clarence Mueller	125.00	65.00	35.00
(76)	Robert W. Muesel (Meusel)	125.00	65.00	35.00
(77)	Glenn Myatt	125.00	65.00	35.00
(78)	Arthur Nehf	125.00	65.00	35.00
(79)	George O'Neil	125.00	65.00	35.00
(80)	Frank O'Rourke	125.00	65.00	35.00
(81)	Ralph Perkins	125.00	65.00	35.00
(82)	Valentine Picinich	125.00	65.00	35.00
(83)	Walter C. Pipp	125.00	65.00	35.00
(84)	John Quinn	125.00	65.00	35.00
(85)	Emory Rigney	125.00	65.00	35.00
(86)	Eppa Rixey	200.00	100.00	60.00
(87)	Edwin Rommel	125.00	65.00	35.00
(88)	Ed (Edd) Roush	200.00	100.00	60.00
(89)	Harold Ruel (Herold)	125.00	65.00	35.00
(90)	Charles Ruffing	200.00	100.00	60.00
(91)	George H. "Babe" Ruth	1,700	850.00	510.00
(92)	John Sand	125.00	65.00	35.00
(93)	Henry Severid (Severeid)	125.00	65.00	35.00
(94)	Joseph Sewell	200.00	100.00	60.00
(95)	Ray Shalk (Schalk)	200.00	100.00	60.00
(96)	Walter H. Shang (Schang)	125.00	65.00	35.00
(97)	J.R. Shawkey	125.00	65.00	35.00
(98)	Earl Sheely	125.00	65.00	35.00
(99)	William Sherdell (Sherdel)	125.00	65.00	35.00
(100)	Urban J. Shocker	125.00	65.00	35.00
(101)	George Sissler (Sisler)	200.00	100.00	60.00
(102)	Earl Smith	125.00	65.00	35.00
(103)	Sherrod Smith	125.00	65.00	35.00
(104)	Frank Snyder	125.00	65.00	35.00
(105)	Wm. H. Southworth	125.00	65.00	35.00
(106)	Tristram Speaker	300.00	150.00	90.00
(107)	Milton J. Stock	125.00	65.00	35.00
(108)	Homer Summa	125.00	65.00	35.00

		NM	EX	VG
(109)	William Terry	225.00	110.00	65.00
(110)	Hollis Thurston	125.00	65.00	35.00
(111)	John Tobin	125.00	65.00	35.00
(112)	Philip Todt	125.00	65.00	35.00
(113)	George Torporcer (Toporcer)	125.00	65.00	35.00
(114)	Harold Traynor	200.00	100.00	60.00
(115)	A.C. "Dazzy" Vance	200.00	100.00	60.00
(116)	Robert Veach (Photo actually Ernest Vache.)	125.00	65.00	35.00
(117)	William Wambsganss	125.00	65.00	35.00
(118)	Aaron Ward	125.00	65.00	35.00
(119)	A.J. Weis	125.00	65.00	35.00
(120)	Frank Welch	125.00	65.00	35.00
(121)	Zack Wheat	200.00	100.00	60.00
(122)	Fred Williams	125.00	65.00	35.00
(123)	Kenneth Williams	125.00	65.00	35.00
(124)	Ernest Wingard	125.00	65.00	35.00
(125)	Ivy Wingo	125.00	65.00	35.00
(126)	Al Wings (Wingo)	125.00	65.00	35.00
(127)	Larry Woodall	125.00	65.00	35.00
(128)	Glen Wright (Glenn)	125.00	65.00	35.00

1925 Champions Babe Ruth Exhibit

This is part of a (presumably) 32-card multi-sport "World's Champions" issue and the only baseball player in the set. The 3-3/8" x 5-3/8" card is printed in black-and-white and has a blank back.

	NM	EX	VG
Babe Ruth	2,250	1,125	675.00

1926 Exhibits

The 1926 Exhibit cards are the same size (3-3/8" x 5-3/8") as previous Exhibit issues but are easily distinguished because of their blue-gray color. The set consists of 128 cards, 91 of which are identical to the photos in the 1925 series. The 37 new photos do not include the boxed caption used in 1925. The cards are unnumbered and are listed here alphabetically.

		NM	EX	VG
Complete Set (128):		22,500	11,250	6,750
Common Player:		125.00	60.00	35.00
(1)	Sparky Adams	125.00	60.00	35.00
(2)	David Bancroft	200.00	100.00	60.00
(3)	John Bassler	125.00	60.00	35.00
(4)	Lester Bell	125.00	60.00	35.00
(5)	John M. Bentley	125.00	60.00	35.00
(6)	Lawrence Benton	125.00	60.00	35.00
(7)	Carson Bigbee	125.00	60.00	35.00
(8)	George Bischoff (Team actually Boston A.L.)	125.00	60.00	35.00
(9)	Max Bishop	125.00	60.00	35.00
(10)	J. Fred Blake	125.00	60.00	35.00
(11)	Ted Blankenship	125.00	60.00	35.00
(12)	Raymond Blates (Blades)	125.00	60.00	35.00
(13)	Lucerne A. Blue (Luzerne)	125.00	60.00	35.00
(14)	Oswald Bluege	125.00	60.00	35.00
(15)	James Bottomly (Bottomley)	200.00	100.00	60.00
(16)	Raymond Bressler	125.00	60.00	35.00
(17)	Geo. H. Burns	125.00	60.00	35.00

		NM	EX	VG
(18)	Maurice Burrus	125.00	60.00	35.00
(19)	John Butler	125.00	60.00	35.00
(20)	Max Carey	200.00	100.00	60.00
(21)	Tyrus Cobb	1,400	700.00	425.00
(22)	Eddie Collins	200.00	100.00	60.00
(23)	Patrick T. Collins	125.00	60.00	35.00
(24)	Earl B. Combs (Earle)	225.00	110.00	65.00
(25)	James E. Cooney	125.00	60.00	35.00
(26)	Stanley Coveleski	200.00	100.00	60.00
(27)	Hugh M. Critz	125.00	60.00	35.00
(28)	Hazen Cuyler	200.00	100.00	60.00
(29)	George Dauss	125.00	60.00	35.00
(30)	Peter Donohue	125.00	60.00	35.00
(31)	Charles Dressen	125.00	60.00	35.00
(32)	James J. Dykes	125.00	60.00	35.00
(33)	Bib Falk (Bibb)	125.00	60.00	35.00
(34)	Edward S. Farrell	125.00	60.00	35.00
(35)	Wilson Fewster	125.00	60.00	35.00
(36)	Ira Flagstead	125.00	60.00	35.00
(37)	Howard Freigau	125.00	60.00	35.00
(38)	Bernard Friberg	125.00	60.00	35.00
(39)	Frank Frisch	200.00	100.00	60.00
(40)	Jacques F. Furnier (Fournier)	125.00	60.00	35.00
(41)	Joseph Galloway (Clarence) (Photo reversed.)	125.00	60.00	35.00
(42)	Henry L. Gehrig	2,350	1,175	725.00
(43)	Charles Gehringer	250.00	125.00	75.00
(44)	Joseph Genewich	125.00	60.00	35.00
(45)	Walter Gerber	125.00	60.00	35.00
(46)	Leon Goslin	200.00	100.00	60.00
(47)	George Grantham	125.00	60.00	35.00
(48)	Burleigh A. Grimes	200.00	100.00	60.00
(49)	Charles Grimm	125.00	60.00	35.00
(50)	Fred Haney	125.00	60.00	35.00
(51)	Wm. Hargrave	125.00	60.00	35.00
(52)	George Harper	125.00	60.00	35.00
(53)	Stanley Harris	200.00	100.00	60.00
(54)	Leo Hartnett	200.00	100.00	60.00
(55)	Joseph Hauser	125.00	60.00	35.00
(56)	C.E. Heathcote	125.00	60.00	35.00
(57)	Harry Heilmann	200.00	100.00	60.00
(58)	Walter Henline	125.00	60.00	35.00
(59)	Ramon Herrera	125.00	60.00	35.00
(60)	Andrew A. High	125.00	60.00	35.00
(61)	Rogers Hornsby	210.00	105.00	65.00
(62)	Clarence Huber	125.00	60.00	35.00
(63)	Wm. Hunnefield (Photo actually Tommy Thomas.)	125.00	60.00	35.00
(64)	William Jacobson	125.00	60.00	35.00
(65)	Walter Johnson	300.00	150.00	90.00
(66)	Joseph Judge	125.00	60.00	35.00
(67)	Willie Kamm	125.00	60.00	35.00
(68)	Ray Kremer	125.00	60.00	35.00
(69)	Anthony Lazzeri	250.00	125.00	75.00
(70)	Frederick Lindstrom	225.00	110.00	65.00
(71)	Walter Lutzke	125.00	60.00	35.00
(72)	John Makan (Mokan)	125.00	60.00	35.00
(73)	Walter Maranville	200.00	100.00	60.00
(74)	Martin McManus	125.00	60.00	35.00
(75)	Earl McNeely	125.00	60.00	35.00
(76)	Hugh A. McQuillan	125.00	60.00	35.00
(77)	Douglas McWeeny	125.00	60.00	35.00
(78)	Oscar Melillo	125.00	60.00	35.00
(79)	Edmund (Bind)(Bing) Miller	125.00	60.00	35.00
(80)	Clarence Mueller	125.00	60.00	35.00
(81)	Robert W. Muesel (Meusel)	125.00	60.00	35.00
(82)	Joseph W. Munson	125.00	60.00	35.00
(83)	Emil Musel (Meusel)	125.00	60.00	35.00
(84)	Glenn Myatt	125.00	60.00	35.00
(85)	Bernie F. Neis	125.00	60.00	35.00
(86)	Robert O'Farrell	125.00	60.00	35.00
(87)	George O'Neil	125.00	60.00	35.00
(88)	Frank O'Rourke	125.00	60.00	35.00
(89)	Ralph Perkins	125.00	60.00	35.00
(90)	Walter C. Pipp	135.00	65.00	40.00
(91)	Emory Rigney	125.00	60.00	35.00
(92)	James J. Ring	125.00	60.00	35.00
(93)	Eppa Rixey	200.00	100.00	60.00
(94)	Edwin Rommel	125.00	60.00	35.00
(95)	Ed. Roush	200.00	100.00	60.00
(96)	Harold Ruel (Herold)	125.00	60.00	35.00
(97)	Charles Ruffing	200.00	100.00	60.00
(98)	Geo. H. "Babe" Ruth	1,875	935.00	560.00
(99)	John Sand	125.00	60.00	35.00
(100)	Joseph Sewell	200.00	100.00	60.00
(101)	Ray Shalk (Schalk)	200.00	100.00	60.00
(102)	J.R. Shawkey	125.00	60.00	35.00
(103)	Earl Sheely	125.00	60.00	35.00
(104)	William Sherdell (Sherdel)	125.00	60.00	35.00
(105)	Urban J. Shocker	125.00	60.00	35.00
(106)	George Sissler (Sisler)	200.00	100.00	60.00
(107)	Earl Smith	125.00	60.00	35.00
(108)	Sherrod Smith	125.00	60.00	35.00
(109)	Frank Snyder	125.00	60.00	35.00
(110)	Tristram Speaker	210.00	105.00	65.00
(111)	Fred Spurgeon	125.00	60.00	35.00
(112)	Homer Summa	125.00	60.00	35.00
(113)	Edward Taylor	125.00	60.00	35.00
(114)	J. Taylor	125.00	60.00	35.00
(115)	William Terry	200.00	100.00	60.00
(116)	Hollis Thurston	125.00	60.00	35.00
(117)	Philip Todt	125.00	60.00	35.00
(118)	George Torporcer (Toporcer)	125.00	60.00	35.00
(119)	Harold Traynor	200.00	100.00	60.00
(120)	Wm. Wambsganss	125.00	60.00	35.00
(121)	John Warner	125.00	60.00	35.00
(122)	Zach Wheat	200.00	100.00	60.00
(123)	Kenneth Williams	125.00	60.00	35.00
(124)	Ernest Wingard	125.00	60.00	35.00
(125)	Fred Wingfield	125.00	60.00	35.00
(126)	Ivy Wingo	125.00	60.00	35.00
(127)	Glen Wright (Glenn)	125.00	60.00	35.00
(128)	Russell Wrightstone	125.00	60.00	35.00

1926-29 Postcard-Back Exhibits

Probably issued in the Philadelphia area, these cards can be found with plain backs, with postcard

backs including the legend: "This Side for Correspondence," and with postcard backs including the legend, "Not for use in Exhibit machines." Some printings also have the legend, "Made in U.S.A." added to the backs. The fronts are borderless photos which generally have the player's name, team and league designation printed in a hand-writing style; several variations in style have been noted. Five cards have typeset, rather than hand-written identification appearing in a white box: Cobb (Philadelphia), Frisch (N.Y.), Hornsby (Boston), Rouch (N.Y.) and Peckinpaugh (Cleveland), reflecting trades during the period of issue. Cards can be found printed in one of several different colors, and some or all players can be found in more than one color. Some subjects also appear with the photographic background removed. Cards size is about 3-3/8" x 5-3/8". The checklist below has been arranged alphabetically and is probably incomplete. Gaps have been left in the assigned numbers to accommodate future additions.

		NM	EX	VG
Common Player:		90.00	45.00	25.00
(1)	Virgie Barnes	90.00	45.00	25.00
(2)	Johnny Bassler	90.00	45.00	25.00
(3)	Sammy Bohne	200.00	100.00	60.00
(4)	Jim Bottomley	250.00	125.00	75.00
(5)	Ty Cobb (Detroit)	900.00	450.00	270.00
(6)	Ty Cobb (Athletics)	900.00	450.00	270.00
(7)	Mickey Cochrane	250.00	125.00	75.00
(8)	Urban Faber (Photo background.)	250.00	125.00	75.00
(9)	Urban Faber (Plain background.)	250.00	125.00	75.00
(10)	Jack Fournier	90.00	45.00	25.00
(11)	Jimmy Foxx	600.00	300.00	180.00
(12)	Frank Frisch (New York)	250.00	125.00	75.00
(13)	Frank Frisch (St. Louis)	275.00	135.00	80.00
(14)	Lou Gehrig/Btg (Photo background.)	2,000	1,000	600.00
(15)	Lou Gehrig/Btg (Plain background.)	2,000	1,000	600.00
(16)	Lou Gehrig/Portrait	2,000	1,000	600.00
(17)	Tom Griffith	90.00	45.00	25.00
(18)	Heinie Groh	90.00	45.00	25.00
(19)	Lefty Grove	500.00	250.00	150.00
(20)	George Haas	90.00	45.00	25.00
(21)	Stanley Harris	250.00	125.00	75.00
(22)	Charlie Hartnett (Photo background.)	250.00	125.00	75.00
(23)	Charlie Hartnett (Plain background.)	250.00	125.00	75.00
(24)	Harry Heilmann	250.00	125.00	75.00
(25)	Rogers Hornsby (St. Louis)	400.00	200.00	120.00
(26)	Rogers Hornsby (Boston)	600.00	300.00	180.00
(27)	Rogers Hornsby (Chicago)	400.00	200.00	120.00
(28)	Walter Johnson	600.00	300.00	180.00
(29)	Jimmy Johnston	90.00	45.00	25.00
(30)	Joe Judge	90.00	45.00	25.00
(31)	George Kelly	250.00	125.00	75.00
(32)	Chuck Klein	250.00	125.00	75.00
(33)	Hugh McQuillan	90.00	45.00	25.00
(34)	"Bob" Meusel	90.00	45.00	25.00
(35)	Bing Miller	90.00	45.00	25.00
(36)	Lefty O'Doul	150.00	75.00	45.00
(37)	Roger Peckinpaugh (Washington)	90.00	45.00	25.00
(38)	Roger Peckinpaugh (Cleveland)	90.00	45.00	25.00
(39)	Ralph Pinelli	90.00	45.00	25.00
(40)	Walter Pipp	125.00	60.00	35.00
(41)	Jimmy Ring	90.00	45.00	25.00
(42)	Eppa Rixey	250.00	125.00	75.00
(43)	Ed Rouch (Edd Roush) (Cincinnati)	250.00	125.00	75.00
(44)	Ed Rouch (Edd Roush) (New York)	250.00	125.00	75.00
(45)	Babe Ruth (Pose)	2,200	1,100	660.00
(46)	Babe Ruth (Batting follow-through.)	2,200	1,100	660.00
(47)	John Sand	90.00	45.00	25.00
(48)	Everett Scott	90.00	45.00	25.00
(49)	Al Simmons (View from side, "AM.L.")	250.00	125.00	75.00
(50)	Al Simmons (View from front, "A.L.")	250.00	125.00	75.00
(51)	George Sisler (Photo background.)	250.00	125.00	75.00
(52)	George Sisler (Plain background.)	250.00	125.00	75.00
(53)	Jack Smith	90.00	45.00	25.00
(54)	Tris Speaker (Photo background.)	350.00	175.00	100.00

		NM	EX	VG
(55)	Tris Speaker (Plain background.)	350.00	175.00	100.00
(56)	Phil Todt (Photo background.)	90.00	45.00	25.00
(57)	Phil Todt (Plain background.)	90.00	45.00	25.00
(58)	Specs Toporcer	90.00	45.00	25.00
(59)	Pie Traynor	250.00	125.00	75.00
(60)	Dazzy Vance	250.00	125.00	75.00
(61)	Rube Walberg	90.00	45.00	25.00
(62)	Paul Waner/Btg (Photo background.)	250.00	125.00	75.00
(63)	Paul Waner/Btg (Plain background.)	250.00	125.00	75.00
(64)	Paul Waner/Portrait	250.00	125.00	75.00
(65)	Zack Wheat	250.00	125.00	75.00
(66)	Cy Williams	90.00	45.00	25.00
(67)	Hack Wilson	250.00	125.00	75.00
(68)	Jimmy Wilson (Photo background.)	90.00	45.00	25.00
(69)	Jimmy Wilson (Plain background.)	90.00	45.00	25.00

1926-31 Postcard-Back Four-on-One Exhibits

In the same format as Exhibit Supply Co.'s Four-on-One series which debuted in 1929, this set differs in that players from different teams (or sports, or the entertainment world) are represented. The photos of most players are the same as those found on 1926-1929 Postcard-back Exhibits, though some team indications show that at least some of the cards could not have been printed prior to 1931. As with the single-player cards, examples have been found with blank backs, as well as postcard backs.

		NM	EX	VG
(1)	Lou Gehrig, Lefty Grove, Pete Donahue, Gordon Cochrane	2,200	1,100	650.00
(2)	Lefty O'Doul, Dazzy Vance, Hughey Critz, Art Shires	650.00	325.00	195.00
(3)	Eugene Criqui (boxer), Dave Shade (boxer), Joe Judge, Ty Cobb	3,000	1,500	900.00
(4)	Joe Judge, Ty Cobb, Charlie Chaplin (actor), Marie Prevost (actress)	2,500	1,250	750.00
(5)	Joe Judge, Paul Waner, Willie Kamm, Travis Jackson	750.00	375.00	225.00

1927 Exhibits

HAROLD TRAYNOR
PITTSBURG, N.L.

The Exhibit Supply Co. issued a set of 64 cards in 1927, each measuring 3-3/8" x 5-3/8". The set can be identified from earlier issues by its light green tint. The player's name and team appear in capital letters in one lower corner, while "Ex. Sup. Co., Chgo." and "Made in U.S.A." appear in the other. All 64 photos used in the 1927 set were borrowed from previous issues, but 13 players are listed with new teams. There are several misspellings and other labeling errors in the set. The unnumbered cards are listed here in alphabetical order.

		NM	EX	VG
Complete Set (64):		11,000	5,500	3,250
Common Player:		75.00	35.00	20.00
(1)	Sparky Adams	75.00	35.00	20.00
(2)	Grover C. Alexander	250.00	125.00	75.00
(3)	David Bancroft	150.00	75.00	45.00
(4)	John Bassler	75.00	35.00	20.00
(5)	John M. Bentley (Middle initial actually N.)	75.00	35.00	20.00
(6)	Fred Blankenship (Ted)	75.00	35.00	20.00
(7)	James Bottomly (Bottomley)	150.00	75.00	45.00
(8)	Raymond Bressler	75.00	35.00	20.00
(9)	Geo. H. Burns	75.00	35.00	20.00
(10)	John Buttler (Butler)	75.00	35.00	20.00
(11)	Tyrus Cobb	1,100	550.00	330.00
(12)	Eddie Collins	150.00	75.00	45.00
(13)	Hazen Cuyler	150.00	75.00	45.00
(14)	George Daus (Dauss)	75.00	35.00	20.00
(15)	A.R. Decatur	75.00	35.00	20.00
(16)	Wilson Fewster	75.00	35.00	20.00
(17)	Ira Flagstead	75.00	35.00	20.00
(18)	Henry L. Gehrig	1,200	600.00	360.00
(19)	Charles Gehringer	150.00	75.00	45.00
(20)	Joseph Genewich	75.00	35.00	20.00
(21)	Leon Goslin	150.00	75.00	45.00
(22)	Burleigh A. Grimes	150.00	75.00	45.00
(23)	Charles Grimm	75.00	35.00	20.00
(24)	Fred Haney	75.00	35.00	20.00
(25)	Wm. Hargrave	75.00	35.00	20.00
(26)	George Harper	75.00	35.00	20.00
(27)	Leo Hartnett	150.00	75.00	45.00
(28)	Clifton Heathcote	75.00	35.00	20.00
(29)	Harry Heilman (Heillmann)	150.00	75.00	45.00
(30)	Walter Henline	75.00	35.00	20.00
(31)	Andrew High	75.00	35.00	20.00
(32)	Rogers Hornsby	250.00	125.00	75.00
(33)	Wm. Hunnefield (Photo actually Tommy Thomas.)	75.00	35.00	20.00
(34)	Walter Johnson	650.00	325.00	195.00
(35)	Willie Kamm	75.00	35.00	20.00
(36)	Ray Kremer	75.00	35.00	20.00
(37)	Anthony Lazzeri	150.00	75.00	45.00
(38)	Fredrick Lindstrom (Frederick)	150.00	75.00	45.00
(39)	Walter Lutzke	75.00	35.00	20.00
(40)	John "Stuffy" McInnes (McInnis)	75.00	35.00	20.00
(41)	John Mokan	75.00	35.00	20.00
(42)	Robert W. Muesel (Meusel)	75.00	35.00	20.00
(43)	Glenn Myatt	75.00	35.00	20.00
(44)	Bernie Neis	75.00	35.00	20.00
(45)	Robert O'Farrell	75.00	35.00	20.00
(46)	Walter C. Pipp	100.00	50.00	30.00
(47)	Eppa Rixey	150.00	75.00	45.00
(48)	Harold Ruel (Herold)	75.00	35.00	20.00
(49)	Geo. H. "Babe" Ruth	2,100	1,100	630.00
(50)	Ray Schalk	150.00	75.00	45.00
(51)	George Sissler (Sisler)	150.00	75.00	45.00
(52)	Earl Smith	75.00	35.00	20.00
(53)	Wm. H. Southworth	75.00	35.00	20.00
(54)	Tristam Speaker (Tristram)	250.00	125.00	75.00
(55)	J. Taylor	75.00	35.00	20.00
(56)	Philip Todt	75.00	35.00	20.00
(57)	Harold Traynor	150.00	75.00	45.00
(58)	William Wambsganns (Wambsganss)	75.00	35.00	20.00
(59)	Zach Wheat	150.00	75.00	45.00
(60)	Kenneth Williams	75.00	35.00	20.00
(61)	Ernest Wingard	75.00	35.00	20.00
(62)	Fred Wingfield	75.00	35.00	20.00
(63)	Ivy Wingo	75.00	35.00	20.00
(64)	Russell Wrightstone	75.00	35.00	20.00

1928 Exhibits

FREDRICK LINDSTROM

The Exhibit Supply Co. switched to a blue tint for the photos in its 64-card set in 1928. There are 36 new photos in the set, including 24 new players. Four players from the previous year are shown with new teams and 24 of the cards are identical to the 1927 series, except for the color of the card. Cards are found with either blank backs or postcard backs. The photos are captioned in the same style as the 1927 set. The set again includes some misspelling and incorrect labels. The cards are unnumbered and are listed here in alphabetical order.

		NM	EX	VG
Complete Set (64):		9,500	4,750	2,750
Common Player:		80.00	40.00	20.00
(1)	Grover C. Alexander	400.00	200.00	120.00
(2)	David Bancroft	200.00	100.00	60.00
(3)	Virgil Barnes	80.00	40.00	20.00
(4)	Francis R. Blades	80.00	40.00	20.00
(5)	L.A. Blue	80.00	40.00	20.00
(6)	Edward W. Brown	80.00	40.00	20.00
(7)	Max G. Carey	200.00	100.00	60.00
(8)	Chalmer W. Cissell	80.00	40.00	20.00
(9)	Gordon S. Cochrane	200.00	100.00	60.00
(10)	Pat Collins	80.00	40.00	20.00
(11)	Hugh M. Critz	80.00	40.00	20.00
(12)	Howard Ehmke	80.00	40.00	20.00
(13)	E. English	80.00	40.00	20.00
(14)	Bib Falk (Bibb)	80.00	40.00	20.00
(15)	Ira Flagstead	80.00	40.00	20.00
(16)	Robert Fothergill	80.00	40.00	20.00
(17)	Frank Frisch	200.00	100.00	60.00
(18)	Lou Gehrig	1,200	600.00	360.00
(19)	Leon Goslin	200.00	100.00	60.00
(20)	Eugene Hargrave	80.00	40.00	20.00
(21)	Charles R. Hargraves (Hargreaves)	80.00	40.00	20.00
(22)	Stanley Harris	200.00	100.00	60.00
(23)	Bryan "Slim" Harriss	80.00	40.00	20.00
(24)	Leo Hartnett	200.00	100.00	60.00
(25)	Joseph Hauser	80.00	40.00	20.00
(26)	Fred Hoffman (Hofmann)	80.00	40.00	20.00
(27)	J. Francis Hogan	80.00	40.00	20.00
(28)	Rogers Hornsby	300.00	150.00	90.00
(29)	Chas. Jamieson	80.00	40.00	20.00
(30)	Sam Jones	*80.00	40.00	20.00
(31)	Ray Kremer	80.00	40.00	20.00
(32)	Fred Leach	80.00	40.00	20.00
(33)	Fredrick Lindstrom (Frederick)	200.00	100.00	60.00
(34)	Adolph Luque (Adolfo)	100.00	50.00	30.00
(35)	Theodore Lyons	200.00	100.00	60.00
(36)	Harry McCurdy	80.00	40.00	20.00
(37)	Glenn Myatt	80.00	40.00	20.00
(38)	John Ogden (Photo actually Warren Ogden.)	80.00	40.00	20.00
(39)	James Ring	80.00	40.00	20.00
(40)	A.C. Root (Should be C.H.)	80.00	40.00	20.00
(41)	Edd. Roush	200.00	100.00	60.00
(42)	Harold Ruel (Herold)	80.00	40.00	20.00
(43)	Geo. H. "Babe" Ruth	1,350	675.00	400.00
(44)	Henry Sand	80.00	40.00	20.00
(45)	Fred Schulte	80.00	40.00	20.00
(46)	Joseph Sewell	200.00	100.00	60.00
(47)	Walter Shang (Schang)	80.00	40.00	20.00
(48)	Urban J. Shocker	80.00	40.00	20.00
(49)	Al. Simmons	200.00	100.00	60.00
(50)	Earl Smith	80.00	40.00	20.00
(51)	Robert Smith	80.00	40.00	20.00
(52)	Jack Tavener	80.00	40.00	20.00
(53)	J. Taylor	80.00	40.00	20.00
(54)	Philip Todt	80.00	40.00	20.00
(55)	Geo. Uhle	80.00	40.00	20.00
(56)	Arthur "Dazzy" Vance	200.00	100.00	60.00
(57)	Paul Waner	200.00	100.00	60.00
(58)	Earl G. Whitehill (Middle intial actually O.)	80.00	40.00	20.00
(59)	Fred Williams	80.00	40.00	20.00
(60)	James Wilson	80.00	40.00	20.00
(61)	L.R. (Hack) Wilson	200.00	100.00	60.00
(62)	Lawrence Woodall	80.00	40.00	20.00
(63)	Glen Wright (Glenn)	80.00	40.00	20.00
(64)	William A. Zitzman (Zitzmann)	80.00	40.00	20.00

1929-30 Four-on-One Exhibits

Although the size of the card remained the same, the Exhibit Supply Co. of Chicago began putting four players' pictures on each card in 1929 - a practice that would continue for the next decade. Known as "four-on-one" cards, the players are identified by name and team at the bottom of the photos, which are separated by borders. The 32 cards in the 1929-30 series have postcard backs and were printed in a wide range of color combinations of black, brown and blue ink on blue, orange, green, red, white, and yellow backgrounds. Most of the backs are uncolored, however, cards with a black on red front have been seen with red backs, and cards with blue on yellow fronts have been seen with yellow backs. There are numerous spelling and caption errors in the set, and the player identified as Babe Herman is actually Jesse Petty.

		NM	EX	VG
Complete Set (32):		5,500	2,750	1,600
Common Card:		65.00	32.00	20.00
(1)	Earl J. Adams, R. Bartell, Earl Sheely, Harold Traynor	150.00	75.00	45.00
(2)	Dale Alexander, C. Gehringer, G.F. McManus (should be M.J.), H.F. Rice	150.00	75.00	45.00
(3)	Grover C. Alexander, James Bottomly (Bottomley), Frank Frisch, James Wilson	250.00	125.00	75.00
(4)	Martin G. Autrey (Autry), Alex Metzler, Carl Reynolds, Alphonse Thomas	65.00	32.50	20.00
(5)	Earl Averill, B.A. Falk, K. Holloway, L. Sewell	150.00	75.00	45.00
(6)	David Bancroft, Del L. Bisonette (Bissonette), John H. DeBerry, Floyd C. Herman (photo actually Jesse Petty)	150.00	75.00	45.00
(7)	C.E. Beck, Leo Hartnett, Rogers Hornsby, L.R. (Hack) Wilson	200.00	100.00	60.00
(8)	Ray Benge, Lester L. Sweetland, A.C. Whitney, Cy. Williams	65.00	32.50	20.00

		NM	EX	VG
(9)	Benny Bengough, Earl B. Coombs (Combs), Waite Hoyt, Anthony Lazzeri	200.00	100.00	60.00
(10)	L. Benton, Melvin Ott, Andrew Reese, William Terry	150.00	75.00	45.00
(11)	Max Bishop, James Dykes, Samuel Hale, Homer Summa	65.00	32.50	20.00
(12)	L.A. Blue, O. Melillo, F.O. Rourke (Frank O'Rourke), F. Schulte	65.00	32.50	20.00
(13)	Oswald Bluege, Leon Goslin, Joseph Judge, Harold Ruel (Herold)	150.00	75.00	45.00
(14)	Chalmer W. Cissell, John W. Clancy, Willie Kamm, John L. Kerr (Kerr's middle initial actually "F.")	65.00	32.50	20.00
(15)	Gordon S. Cochrane, Jimmy Foxx, Robert M. Grove, George Haas	250.00	125.00	75.00
(16)	Pat Collins, Joe Dugan, Edward Farrel (Farrell), George Sisler	150.00	75.00	45.00
(17)	H.M. Critz, G.L. Kelly, V.J. Picinich, W.C. Walker	150.00	75.00	45.00
(18)	Nick Cullop, D'Arcy Flowers, Harvey Hendrick, Arthur "Dazzy" Vance	150.00	75.00	45.00
(19)	Hazen Cuyler, E. English, C.J. Grimm, C.H. Root	150.00	75.00	45.00
(20)	Taylor Douthit, Chas. M. Gilbert (Gelbert), Chas. J. Hafey, Fred G. Haney	150.00	75.00	45.00
(21)	Leo Durocher, Henry L. Gehrig, Mark Koenig, Geo. H. "Babe" Ruth	1,400	700.00	400.00
(22)	L.A. Fonseca, Carl Lind, J. Sewell, J. Tavener	150.00	75.00	45.00
(23)	H.E. Ford, C.F. Lucas, C.A. Pittenger, E.V. Purdy	65.00	32.50	20.00
(24)	Bernard Friberg, Donald Hurst, Frank O'Doul, Fresco Thompson	65.00	32.50	20.00
(25)	S. Gray, R. Kress, H. Manush, W.H. Shang (Schang)	150.00	75.00	45.00
(26)	Charles R. Hargreaves, Ray Kremer, Lloyd Waner, Paul Waner	150.00	75.00	45.00
(27)	George Harper, Fred Maguire, Lance Richbourg, Robert Smith	65.00	32.50	20.00
(28)	Jack Hayes, Sam P. Jones, Chas. M. Myer, Sam Rice	150.00	75.00	45.00
(29)	Harry E. Heilman (Heilmann), C.N. Richardson, M.J. Shea, G.E. Uhle	150.00	75.00	45.00
(30)	J.A. Heving, R.R. Reeves (should be R.E.), J. Rothrock, C.H. Ruffing	150.00	75.00	45.00
(31)	J.F. Hogan, T.C. Jackson, Fred Lindstrom, J.D. Welsh	150.00	75.00	45.00
(32)	W.W. Regan, H. Rhyne, D. Taitt, P.J. Todt	65.00	32.50	20.00

1929 Exhibit "Star Picture Stamps"

This series of movie star Exhibit cards includes pictures of other celebrities who were featured in contemporary movies. Produced by Exhibit Supply Co. of Chicago, whose advertising appears on the postcard-style back, the 5-3/8" x 3-3/8" card has a red monochrome front which pictures the stars in the format of eight "Star Pictures Stamps." On this card, Ruth is pictured in the uniform he wore in the 1927 film "The Babe Comes Home."

	NM	EX	VG
Babe Ruth (w/Tom Mix, Charles Lindbergh, Charlie Chaplin, Jack Dempsey, Harold Lloyd, Douglas Fairbanks and Al Jolson)	750.00	375.00	225.00

1931-32 Four-on-One Exhibits

The 1931-1932 series issued by the Exhibit Co. again consisted of 32 cards, each picturing four players. The series can be differentiated from the previous year by the coupon backs, which list various premiums available (including kazoos, toy pistols and other prizes). The cards again were printed in various color combinations, including; black on green, blue on green, black on orange, black on red, blue on

white and black on yellow. There are numerous spelling and caption errors in the series. The Babe Herman/Jesse Petty error of the previous year was still not corrected, and the card of Rick Ferell not only misspells his name ("Farrel"), but also pictures the wrong player (Edward Farrell).

		NM	EX	VG
Complete Set (32):		5,500	2,750	1,600
Common Card:		90.00	45.00	27.00
(1)	Earl J. Adams, James Bottomly (Bottomley), Frank Frisch, James Wilson	150.00	75.00	45.00
(2)	Dale Alexander, C. Gehringer, G.F. McManus (should be M.J.), G.E. Uhle	150.00	75.00	45.00
(3)	L.L. Appling (should be L.B.), Chalmer W. Cissell, Willie Kamm, Ted Lyons	150.00	75.00	45.00
(4)	Buzz Arlett, Ray Benge, Chuck Klein, A.C. Whitney	150.00	75.00	45.00
(5)	Earl Averill, B.A. Falk, L.A. Fonseca, L. Sewell	150.00	75.00	45.00
(6)	Richard Bartell, Bernard Friberg, Donald Hurst, Harry McCurdy	90.00	45.00	27.00
(7)	Walter Berger, Fred Maguire, Lance Richbourg, Earl Sheely	90.00	45.00	27.00
(8)	Chas. Berry, Robt. Reeves, R.R. Reeves (should be R.E.), J. Rothrock	90.00	45.00	27.00
(9)	Del L. Bisonette (Bissonette), Floyd C. Herman (photo - J. Petty, Jack Quinn, Glenn Wright	90.00	45.00	27.00
(10)	L.A. Blue, Smead Jolley, Carl Reynolds, Henry Tate	90.00	45.00	27.00
(11)	O. Bluege, Joe Judge, Chas. M. Myer, Sam Rice	150.00	75.00	45.00
(12)	John Boley, James Dykes, E.J. Miller, Al. Simmons	150.00	75.00	45.00
(13)	Gordon S. Cochrane, Jimmy Foxx, Robert M. Grove, George Haas	325.00	160.00	95.00
(14)	Adam Comorosky, Gus Suhr, T.J. Thevenow, Harold Traynor	150.00	75.00	45.00
(15)	Earl B. Coombs (Combs), W. Dickey, Anthony Lazzeri, H. Pennock	225.00	110.00	65.00
(16)	H.M. Critz, J.F. Hogan, T.C. Jackson, Fred Lindstrom	150.00	75.00	45.00
(17)	Joe Cronin, H. Manush, F. Marberry, Roy Spencer	150.00	75.00	45.00
(18)	Nick Cullop, Les Durocher (Leo), Harry Heilmann, W.C. Walker	150.00	75.00	45.00
(19)	Hazen Cuyler, E. English, C.J. Grimm, C.H. Root	150.00	75.00	45.00
(20)	Taylor Douthit, Chas. M. Gilbert (Gelbert), Chas. J. Hafey, Bill Hallahan	90.00	45.00	27.00
(21)	Richard Farrel (Ferrell), S. Gray, R. Kress, W. Stewart (photo actually Ed Farrell)	90.00	45.00	27.00
(22)	W. Ferrell, J. Goldman, Hunnefield, Ed Morgan	90.00	45.00	27.00
(23)	Fred Fitzsimmons, Robert O'Farrell, Melvin Ott, William Terry	150.00	75.00	45.00
(24)	D'Arcy Flowers, Frank O'Doul, Fresco Thompson, Arthur "Dazzy" Vance	150.00	75.00	45.00
(25)	H.E. Ford (should be H.H.), Gooch, C.F. Lucas, W. Roettger	90.00	45.00	27.00
(26)	E. Funk, W. Hoyt, Mark Koenig, Wallie Schang	90.00	45.00	27.00
(27)	Henry L. Gehrig, Lyn Lary, James Reese (photo actually Andy Reese), Geo. H. "Babe" Ruth	1,150	575.00	345.00
(28)	George Grantham, Ray Kremer, Lloyd Waner, Paul Waner	150.00	75.00	45.00
(29)	Leon Goslin, O. Melillo, F.O. Rourke (Frank O'Rourke), F. Schulte	150.00	75.00	45.00
(30)	Leo Hartnett, Rogers Hornsby, J.R. Stevenson (Stephenson), L.R. (Hack) Wilson	200.00	100.00	60.00
(31)	D. MacFayden, H. Rhyne, Bill Sweeney, E.W. Webb	90.00	45.00	27.00
(32)	Walter Maranville, Randolph Moore, Alfred Spohrer, J.T. Zachary	150.00	75.00	45.00

1931-32 Babe Ruth Exhibit

The rarest Exhibit card to feature Babe Ruth, this circa 1931 issue has a photographic portrait of him in dress clothes, and is part of a 32-card movie stars series. Found in black-and-white or various color tints, this approximately 3-1/2" x 5-1/2" card has a facsimile autograph in white on front. It can be found with either a postcard-style back or a back offering premium merchandise.

	NM	EX	VG
Babe Ruth	900.00	450.00	270.00

1933 Four-on-One Exhibits

The 1933 series of four-on-one Exhibits consists of 16 cards with blank backs. Color combinations include: blue on green, black on orange, black on red, blue on white and black on yellow. Most have a plain, white back, although the black on yellow cards are also found with a yellow back. Most of the pictures used are reprinted from previous series, and there are some spelling and caption errors, including the Richard Ferrell/Edward Farrel mixup from the previous year. Al Lopez is shown as "Vincent" Lopez.

		NM	EX	VG
Complete Set (16):		4,000	2,000	1,200
Common Card:		85.00	40.00	25.00
(1)	Earl J. Adams, Frank Frisch, Chas. Gilbert (Gelbert), Bill Hallahan	150.00	75.00	45.00
(2)	Earl Averill, W. Ferrell, Ed Morgan, L. Sewell	150.00	75.00	45.00
(3)	Richard Bartell, Ray Benge, Donald Hurst, Chuck Klein	150.00	75.00	45.00
(4)	Walter Berger, Walter Maranville, Alfred Spohrer, J.T. Zachary	150.00	75.00	45.00
(5)	Charles Berry, L.A. Blue, Ted Lyons, Bob Seeds	150.00	75.00	45.00
(6)	Chas. Berry, D. MacFayden, H. Rhyne, E.W. Webb	85.00	40.00	25.00
(7)	Mickey Cochrane, Jimmy Foxx, Robert M. Grove, Al. Simmons	450.00	225.00	135.00
(8)	H.M. Critz, Fred Fitzsimmons, Fred Lindstrom, Robert O'Farrell	150.00	75.00	45.00
(9)	W. Dickey, Anthony Lazzeri, H. Pennock, George H. "Babe" Ruth	2,000	1,000	600.00
(10)	Taylor Douthit, George Grantham, Chas. J. Hafey, C.F. Lucas	150.00	75.00	45.00
(11)	E. English, C.J. Grimm, C.H. Root, J.R. Stevenson (Stephenson)	85.00	40.00	25.00
(12)	Richard Farrel (Farrell), Leon Goslin, S. Gray, O. Melillo (photo actually Ed Farrell)	150.00	75.00	45.00
(13)	C. Gehringer, "Muddy" Ruel, Jonathan Stone (first name - John, G.E. Uhle	150.00	75.00	45.00
(14)	Joseph Judge, H. Manush, F. Marberry, Roy Spencer	150.00	75.00	45.00
(15)	Vincent Lopez (Al), Frank O'Doul, Arthur "Dazzy" Vance, Glenn Wright	150.00	75.00	45.00
(16)	Gus Suhr, Tom J. Thevenow, Lloyd Waner, Paul Waner	150.00	75.00	45.00

1934 Four-on-One Exhibits

This 16-card series issued by the Exhibit Co. in 1934 is again blank-backed and continues the four-on-one format in a 3-3/8" x 5-3/8" size. The 1934 series can be differentiated from previous years by the more subdued colors of the cards, which include lighter shades of blue, brown, green and violet - all printed on white card stock. Many new photos were also used in the 1934 series. Of the 64 players included, 25 appear for the first time and another 16 were given new poses. Spelling was improved, but Al Lopez is still identified as "Vincent."

		NM	EX	VG
Complete Set (16):		2,750	1,350	825.00
Common Card:		75.00	35.00	20.00
(1)	Luke Appling, George Earnshaw, Al Simmons, Evar Swanson	125.00	60.00	35.00
(2)	Earl Averill, W. Ferrell, Willie Kamm, Frank Pytlak	125.00	60.00	35.00
(3)	Richard Bartell, Donald Hurst, Wesley Schulmerich, Jimmy Wilson	75.00	35.00	20.00
(4)	Walter Berger, Ed Brandt, Frank Hogan, Bill Urbanski	75.00	35.00	20.00
(5)	Jim Bottomley, Chas. J. Hafey, Botchi Lombardi, Tony Piet	125.00	60.00	35.00
(6)	Irving Burns, Irving Hadley, Rollie Hemsley, O. Melillo	75.00	35.00	20.00
(7)	Bill Cissell, Rick Ferrell, Lefty Grove, Roy Johnson	125.00	60.00	35.00
(8)	Mickey Cochrane, C. Gehringer, Goose Goslin, Fred Marberry	125.00	60.00	35.00
(9)	George Cramer (Roger), Jimmy Foxx, Frank Higgins, Slug Mahaffey	150.00	75.00	45.00
(10)	Joe Cronin, Alvin Crowder, Joe Kuhel, H. Manush	125.00	60.00	35.00
(11)	W. Dickey, Lou Gehrig, Vernon Gomez, Geo. H. "Babe" Ruth	1,400	700.00	425.00
(12)	E. English, C.J. Grimm, Chas. Klein, Lon Warneke	125.00	60.00	35.00
(13)	Frank Frisch, Bill Hallahan, Pepper Martin, John Rothrock	125.00	60.00	35.00
(14)	Carl Hubbell, Mel Ott, Blondy Ryan, Bill Terry	150.00	75.00	45.00
(15)	Leonard Koenecke, Sam Leslie, Vincent Lopez (Al), Glenn Wright	125.00	60.00	35.00
(16)	T.J. Thevenow, Pie Traynor, Lloyd Waner, Paul Waner	125.00	60.00	35.00

1935 Four-on-One Exhibits

Continuing with the same four-on-one format, the Exhibit Supply Co. issued another 16-card series in 1935. All cards were printed in a slate-blue color with a blank back. Seventeen of the players included in the 1935 series appear for the first time. While another 11 are shown with new poses. There are several spelling and caption errors. Babe Ruth appears in a regular Exhibit issue for the last time.

		NM	EX	VG
Complete Set (16):		4,000	2,000	1,200
Common Card:		75.00	35.00	20.00
(1)	Earl Averill, Mel Harder, Willie Kamm, Hal Trosky	125.00	60.00	35.00
(2)	Walter Berger, Ed Brandt, Frank Hogan, "Babe" Ruth	1,300	650.00	350.00
(3)	Henry Bonura, Jimmy Dykes, Ted Lyons, Al Simmons	125.00	60.00	35.00
(4)	Jimmy Bottomley, Paul Derringer, Chas. J. Hafey, Botchi Lombardi	125.00	60.00	35.00

		NM	EX	VG
(5)	Irving Burns, Rollie Hemsley, O. Melillo, L.N. Newson	75.00	35.00	20.00
(6)	Guy Bush, Pie Traynor, Floyd Vaughn (Vaughan), Paul Waner	125.00	60.00	35.00
(7)	Mickey Cochrane, C. Gehringer, Goose Goslin, Linwood Rowe (Lynwood)	125.00	60.00	35.00
(8)	Phil Collins, John "Blondy" Ryan, Geo. Watkins, Jimmy Wilson	75.00	35.00	20.00
(9)	George Cramer (Roger), Jimmy Foxx, Bob Johnson, Slug Mahaffey	150.00	75.00	45.00
(10)	Hughie Critz, Carl Hubbell, Mel Ott, Bill Terry	150.00	75.00	45.00
(11)	Joe Cronin, Rick Ferrell, Lefty Grove, Billy Werber	145.00	70.00	40.00
(12)	Tony Cuccinello, Vincent Lopez (Al), Van Mungo, Dan Taylor (photo actually George Puccinelli)	125.00	60.00	35.00
(13)	Jerome "Dizzy" Dean, Paul Dean, Frank Frisch, Pepper Martin	325.00	160.00	95.00
(14)	W. Dickey, Lou Gehrig, Vernon Gomez, Tony Lazzeri	900.00	450.00	275.00
(15)	C.J. Grimm, Gabby Hartnett, Chas. Klein, Lon Warneke	125.00	60.00	35.00
(16)	H. Manush, Buddy Meyer (Myer), Fred Schulte, Earl Whitehill	125.00	60.00	35.00

1936 Four-on-One Exhibits

The 1936 series of four-on-one cards again consisted of 16 cards in either green or slate blue with plain, blank backs. The series can be differentiated from the previous year's Exhibit cards by the line "PTD. IN U.S.A." at the bottom. Of the 64 players pictured, 16 appear for the first time and another nine are shown in new poses. The series is again marred by several spelling and caption errors.

		NM	EX	VG
Complete Set (16):		3,000	1,500	900.00
Common Card:		80.00	40.00	25.00
(1)	Paul Andrews, Harland Clift (Harlond), Rollie Hemsley, Sammy West	80.00	40.00	25.00
(2)	Luke Appling, Henry Bonura, Jimmy Dykes, Ted Lyons	100.00	50.00	30.00
(3)	Earl Averill, Mel Harder, Hal Trosky, Joe Vosmik	100.00	50.00	30.00
(4)	Walter Berger, Danny MacFayden, Bill Urbanski, Pinky Whitney	80.00	40.00	25.00
(5)	Charles Berry, Frank Higgins, Bob Johnson, Puccinelli	80.00	40.00	25.00
(6)	Ossie Bluege, Buddy Meyer (Myer), L.N. Newsom, Earl Whitehill	80.00	40.00	25.00
(7)	Stan. Bordagaray, Dutch Brandt, Fred Lindstrom, Van Mungo	100.00	50.00	30.00
(8)	Guy Bush, Pie Traynor, Floyd Vaughn (Vaughan), Paul Waner	100.00	50.00	30.00
(9)	Dolph Camilli, Curt Davis, Johnny Moore, Jimmy Wilson	80.00	40.00	25.00
(10)	Mickey Cochrane, C. Gehringer, Goose Goslin, Linwood Rowe (Lynwood)	100.00	50.00	30.00
(11)	Joe Cronin, Rick Ferrell, Jimmy Foxx, Lefty Grove	175.00	85.00	50.00
(12)	Jerome "Dizzy" Dean, Paul Dean, Frank Frisch, Joe "Ducky" Medwick	300.00	150.00	90.00
(13)	Paul Derringer, Babe Herman, Alex Kampouris, Botchi Lombardi	100.00	50.00	30.00
(14)	Augie Galan, Gabby Hartnett, Billy Herman, Lon Warneke	100.00	50.00	30.00
(15)	Lou Gehrig, Vernon Gomez, Tony Lazzeri, Red Ruffing	1,300	650.00	390.00
(16)	Carl Hubbell, Gus Mancuso, Mel Ott, Bill Terry	125.00	60.00	35.00

1937 Four-on-One Exhibits

The 1937 four-on-one Exhibit cards were printed in either green or bright blue. The backs are again blank. The 1937 cards are difficult to distinguish from the 1936 series, because both contain the "PTD. IN U.S.A." line along the bottom. Of the 64 photos, 47 are re-issues from previous series.

		NM	EX	VG
Complete Set (16):		2,750	1,350	825.00
Common Card:		60.00	30.00	18.00
(1)	Earl Averill, Bob Feller, Frank Pytlak, Hal Trosky	150.00	75.00	45.00
(2)	Luke Appling, Henry Bonura, Jimmy Dykes, Vernon Kennedy	125.00	60.00	35.00
(3)	Walter Berger, Alfonso Lopez, Danny MacFayden, Bill Urbanski	125.00	60.00	35.00
(4)	Cy Blanton, Gus Suhr, Floyd Vaughn (Vaughan), Paul Waner	125.00	60.00	35.00
(5)	Dolph Camilli, Johnny Moore, Wm. Walters, Pinky Whitney	60.00	30.00	18.00
(6)	Harland Clift (Harlond), Rollie Hemsley, Orval Hildebrand (Oral), Sammy West	60.00	30.00	18.00
(7)	Mickey Cochrane, C. Gehringer, Goose Goslin, Linwood Rowe (Lynwood)	125.00	60.00	35.00
(8)	Joe Cronin, Rick Ferrell, Jimmy Foxx, Lefty Grove	150.00	75.00	45.00
(9)	Jerome "Dizzy" Dean, Stuart Martin, Joe "Ducky" Medwick, Lon Warneke	175.00	85.00	50.00
(10)	Paul Derringer, Botchi Lombardi, Lew Riggs, Phil Weintraub	125.00	60.00	35.00
(11)	Joe DiMaggio, Lou Gehrig, Vernon Gomez, Tony Lazzeri	1,325	660.00	375.00
(12)	E. English, Johnny Moore, Van Mungo, Gordon Phelps	60.00	30.00	18.00
(13)	Augie Galan, Gabby Hartnett, Billy Herman, Bill Lee	125.00	60.00	35.00
(14)	Carl Hubbell, Sam Leslie, Gus. Mancuso, Mel Ott	125.00	60.00	35.00
(15)	Bob Johnson, Harry Kelly (Kelley), Wallace Moses, Billy Weber (Werber)	60.00	30.00	18.00
(16)	Joe Kuhel, Buddy Meyer (Myer), L.N. Newsom, Jonathan Stone (First name actually John.)	60.00	30.00	18.00

1938 Four-on-One Exhibits

The Exhibit Co. used its four-on-one format for the final time in 1938, issuing another 16-card series. The cards feature brown printing on white stock with the line "MADE IN U.S.A." appearing along the bottom. The backs are blank. Twelve players appeared for the first time and three others are shown in new poses. Again, there are several spelling and caption mistakes.

	NM	EX	VG
Complete Set (16):	3,250	1,600	975.00
Common Card:	83.00	41.00	25.00
(1) Luke Appling, Mike Kreevich, Ted Lyons, L. Sewell	125.00	60.00	35.00
(2) Morris Arnovich, Chas. Klein, Wm. Walters, Pinky Whitney	125.00	60.00	35.00
(3) Earl Averill, Bob Feller, Odell Hale, Hal Trosky	165.00	80.00	50.00
(4) Beau Bell, Harland Clift (Harlond), L.N. Newsom, Sammy West	80.00	40.00	25.00
(5) Cy Blanton, Gus Suhr, Floyd Vaughn (Vaughan), Paul Waner	125.00	60.00	35.00
(6) Tom Bridges, C. Gehringer, Hank Greenberg, Rudy York	125.00	60.00	35.00
(7) Dolph Camilli, Leo Durocher, Van Mungo, Gordon Phelps	125.00	60.00	35.00
(8) Joe Cronin, Jimmy Foxx, Lefty Grove, Joe Vosmik	165.00	80.00	50.00
(9) Tony Cuccinello, Vince DiMaggio, Roy Johnson, Danny MacFayden (Photo actually George Puccinelli.)	90.00	45.00	25.00
(10) Jerome "Dizzy" Dean, Augie Galan, Gabby Hartnett, Billy Herman	200.00	100.00	60.00
(11) Paul Derringer, Ival Goodman, Botchi Lombardi, Lew Riggs	125.00	60.00	35.00
(12) W. Dickey, Joe DiMaggio, Lou Gehrig, Vernon Gomez	1,375	685.00	400.00
(13) Rick Ferrell, W. Ferrell, Buddy Meyer (Myer), Jonathan Stone (First name actually John.)	125.00	60.00	35.00
(14) Carl Hubbell, Hank Leiber, Mel Ott, Jim Ripple	130.00	65.00	40.00
(15) Bob Johnson, Harry Kelly (Kelley), Wallace Moses, Billy Weber (Werber)	80.00	40.00	25.00
(16) Stuart Martin, Joe "Ducky" Medwick, Johnny Mize, Lon Warneke	125.00	60.00	35.00

1939-46 Salutation Exhibits

Referred to as "Exhibits" because they were issued by the Exhibit Supply Co. of Chicago, Ill., the bulk of this group was produced over an eight-year span, though production and sale of some players' cards continued well into the period of the 1947-66 Exhibits. These cards are frequently called "Salutations" because of the personalized greeting found on the card. The black-and-white cards, which measure 3-3/8" x 5-3/8", are unnumbered and blank-backed. Most Exhibits were sold through vending machines for a penny. The complete set price includes all variations.

	NM	EX	VG
Complete Set (83):	6,500	3,250	1,950
Common Player:	15.00	7.50	4.50
(1) Luke Appling ("Made In U.S.A." in left corner.)	20.00	10.00	6.00
(2) Luke Appling ("Made In U.S.A." in right corner.)	45.00	22.50	13.50
(3) Earl Averill	400.00	200.00	120.00
(4) Charles "Red" Barrett	20.00	10.00	6.00
(5) Henry "Hank" Borowy	15.00	7.50	4.50
(6) Lou Boudreau	25.00	12.50	7.50
(7) Adolf Camilli	30.00	15.00	9.00
(8) Phil Cavarretta	15.00	7.50	4.50
(9) Harland Clift (Harlond)	20.00	10.00	6.00
(10) Tony Cuccinello	40.00	20.00	12.00
(11) Dizzy Dean	140.00	70.00	45.00
(12) Paul Derringer	20.00	10.00	6.00
(13) Bill Dickey ("Made In U.S.A." in left corner.)	35.00	17.50	10.00
(14) Bill Dickey ("Made In U.S.A." in right corner.)	55.00	27.50	16.50
(15) Joe DiMaggio (Issued into the 1950s.)	150.00	75.00	45.00
(16) Bob Elliott	15.00	7.50	4.50
(17) Bob Feller/Portrait	120.00	60.00	35.00
(18) Bob Feller/Pitching	50.00	25.00	15.00
(19) Dave Ferriss	45.00	22.50	13.50
(20) Jimmy Foxx	75.00	37.50	22.50
(21) Lou Gehrig	1,750	875.00	525.00
(22) Charlie Gehringer	100.00	50.00	30.00

(23) Vernon Gomez	175.00	85.00	50.00
(24) Joe Gordon (Cleveland)	27.50	13.50	8.25
(25) Joe Gordon (New York)	15.00	7.50	4.50
(26) Hank Greenberg (Truly yours.)	35.00	17.50	10.00
(27) Hank Greenberg (Very truly yours.)	160.00	80.00	50.00
(28) Robert Grove	50.00	25.00	15.00
(29) Gabby Hartnett	175.00	85.00	50.00
(30) Buddy Hassett	20.00	10.00	6.00
(31) Jeff Heath (Large projection.)	25.00	12.50	7.50
(32) Jeff Heath (Small projection.)	25.00	12.50	7.50
(33) Kirby Higbe	20.00	10.00	6.00
(34) Tommy Holmes (Yours truly.)	15.00	7.50	4.50
(35) Tommy Holmes (Sincerely yours.)	130.00	65.00	40.00
(36) Carl Hubbell	40.00	20.00	12.00
(37) Bob Johnson	40.00	20.00	12.00
(38) Charles Keller ("MADE IN U.S.A." left corner.)	25.00	12.50	7.50
(39) Charles Keller ("MADE IN U.S.A." right corner.)	15.00	7.50	4.50
(40) Ken Keltner	25.00	12.50	7.50
(41) Chuck Klein	165.00	85.00	50.00
(42) Mike Kreevich	85.00	40.00	20.00
(43) Joe Kuhel	20.00	10.00	6.00
(44) Bill Lee	20.00	10.00	6.00
(45) Ernie Lombardi (Cordially)	325.00	160.00	95.00
(46) Ernie Lombardi (Cordially yours.)	20.00	10.00	6.00
(47) Martin Marion ("An Exhibit Card" in lower-left.)	20.00	10.00	6.00
(48) Marty Marion (No "An Exhibit Card.")	20.00	10.00	6.00
(49) Merrill May	25.00	12.50	7.50
(50) Frank McCormick ("Made In U.S.A." in left corner.)	30.00	15.00	9.00
(51) Frank McCormick ("Made In U.S.A." in right corner.)	15.00	7.50	4.50
(52) George McQuinn ("Made In U.S.A." in left corner.)	20.00	10.00	6.00
(53) George McQuinn ("Made In U.S.A." in right corner.)	15.00	7.50	4.50
(54) Joe Medwick	55.00	27.50	16.50
(55) Johnny Mize ("Made In U.S.A." in left corner.)	35.00	17.50	10.00
(56) Johnny Mize ("Made In U.S.A." in right corner.)	20.00	10.00	6.00
(57) Hugh Mulcahy	150.00	75.00	45.00
(58) Hal Newhouser	30.00	15.00	9.00
(59) Buck Newson (Newsom)	275.00	135.00	80.00
(60) Louis (Buck) Newsom	15.00	7.50	4.50
(61) Mel Ott ("Made In U.S.A." in left corner)	40.00	20.00	12.00
(62) Mel Ott ("Made In U.S.A." in right corner.)	25.00	12.50	7.50
(63) Andy Pafko ("C" on cap.)	20.00	10.00	6.00
(64) Andy Pafko (Plain cap.)	15.00	7.50	4.50
(65) Claude Passeau	15.00	7.50	4.50
(66) Howard Pollet ("Made In U.S.A." in left corner.)	20.00	10.00	6.00
(67) Howard Pollet ("Made In U.S.A." in right corner.)	15.00	7.50	4.50
(68) Pete Reiser ("Made In U.S.A." in left corner.)	45.00	22.50	13.50
(69) Pete Reiser ("Made In U.S.A." in right corner.)	20.00	10.00	6.00
(70) Johnny Rizzo	125.00	65.00	35.00
(71) Glenn Russell	75.00	37.50	22.00
(72) George Stirnweiss	20.00	10.00	6.00
(73) Cecil Travis	45.00	20.00	12.50
(74) Paul Trout	15.00	7.50	4.50
(75) Johnny Vander Meer	65.00	32.50	20.00
(76) Arky Vaughn (Vaughan)	22.50	11.00	6.75
(77) Fred "Dixie" Walker ("D" on cap.)	20.00	10.00	6.00
(78) Fred "Dixie" Walker ("D" blanked out.)	60.00	30.00	18.00
(79) "Bucky" Walters	15.00	7.50	4.50
(80) Lon Warneke	20.00	10.00	6.00
(81) Ted Williams (#9 shows.)	375.00	185.00	110.00
(82) Ted Williams (#9 not showing, issued at least through 1960.)	45.00	22.50	13.50
(83) Rudy York	20.00	10.00	6.00

1947-66 Exhibits

Jackie Robinson

Produced by the Exhibit Supply Co. of Chicago, these issues cover a span of 20 years. Each unnumbered, black-and-white card is printed on heavy card-

board measuring 3-3/8" x 5-3/8" and is blank-backed. The company issued new sets each year, with many players being repeated year after year. Other players appeared in only one or two years, thereby creating levels of scarcity. Many cards can be found with minor variations in the wording and placement of the credit line at bottom. Some pieces have been found printed on a semi-gloss paper stock, perhaps as proofs. Their value is 50 percent or less than the issued version.

	NM	EX	VG
Common Player:	9.00	4.50	2.75
(1) Hank Aaron	30.00	15.00	9.00
(2) Joe Adcock (Script signature.)	9.00	4.50	2.75
(3) Joe Adcock (Plain signature.)	10.00	5.00	3.00
(4) Max Alvis	30.00	15.00	9.00
(5) Johnny Antonelli (Braves)	9.00	4.50	2.75
(6) Johnny Antonelli (Giants)	10.00	5.00	3.00
(7) Luis Aparicio/Portrait	12.00	6.00	3.50
(8) Luis Aparicio/Btg	17.50	8.75	5.25
(9) Luke Appling	20.00	10.00	6.00
(10) Ritchie Ashburn (Phillies, first name incorrect.)	12.00	6.00	3.50
(11) Richie Ashburn (Phillies, first name correct.)	12.00	6.00	3.50
(12) Richie Ashburn (Cubs)	17.50	8.75	5.25
(13) Bob Aspromonte	9.00	4.50	2.75
(14) Toby Atwell	9.00	4.50	2.75
(15) Ed Bailey (With cap.)	10.00	5.00	3.00
(16) Ed Bailey (No cap.)	9.00	4.50	2.75
(17) Gene Baker	9.00	4.50	2.75
(18) Ernie Banks (Bat on shoulder, script signature.)	55.00	27.50	16.50
(19) Ernie Banks (Bat on shoulder, plain signature.)	17.50	8.75	5.25
(20) Ernie Banks/Portrait	30.00	15.00	9.00
(21) Steve Barber	9.00	4.50	2.75
(22) Earl Battey	10.00	5.00	3.00
(23) Matt Batts	9.00	4.50	2.75
(24) Hank Bauer (N.Y. cap.)	10.00	5.00	3.00
(25) Hank Bauer (Plain cap.)	12.00	6.00	3.50
(26) Frank Baumholtz	9.00	4.50	2.75
(27) Gene Bearden	9.00	4.50	2.75
(28) Joe Beggs	15.00	7.50	4.50
(29) Larry "Yogi" Berra	60.00	30.00	18.00
(30a) Yogi Berra ("MADE IN U.S.A." lower-right.)	35.00	17.50	10.00
(30b) Yogi Berra ("PRINTED IN U.S.A." lower-right.)	35.00	17.50	10.00
(31) Steve Bilko	10.00	5.00	3.00
(32) Ewell Blackwell/Pitching	10.00	5.00	3.00
(33) Ewell Blackwell/Portrait	9.00	4.50	2.75
(34) Don Blasingame (St. Louis cap.)	9.00	4.50	2.75
(35) Don Blasingame (Plain cap.)	17.50	8.75	5.25
(36) Ken Boyer	12.00	6.00	3.50
(37) Ralph Branca	12.00	6.00	3.50
(38) Jackie Brandt	40.00	20.00	12.00
(39) Harry Brecheen	9.00	4.50	2.75
(40) Tom Brewer	13.50	6.75	4.00
(41) Lou Brissie	10.00	5.00	3.00
(42) Bill Bruton	9.00	4.50	2.75
(43) Lew Burdette/Pitching (Side view.)	9.00	4.50	2.75
(44) Lew Burdette/Pitching (Front view.)	10.00	5.00	3.00
(45) Johnny Callison	12.50	6.25	3.75
(46) Roy Campanella	25.00	12.50	7.50
(47) Chico Carrasquel/Portrait	15.00	7.50	4.50
(48) Chico Carrasquel/Leaping	9.00	4.50	2.75
(49) George Case	13.50	6.75	4.00
(50) Hugh Casey	12.50	6.25	3.75
(51) Norm Cash	12.00	6.00	3.50
(52) Orlando Cepeda/Portrait	15.00	7.50	4.50
(53) Orlando Cepeda/Btg	15.00	7.50	4.50
(54) Bob Cerv (A's cap.)	12.00	6.00	3.50
(55) Bob Cerv (Plain cap.)	20.00	10.00	6.00
(56) Dean Chance	9.00	4.50	2.75
(57) Spud Chandler	15.00	7.50	4.50
(58) Tom Cheney	9.00	4.50	2.75
(59) Bubba Church	10.00	5.00	3.00
(60) Roberto Clemente	40.00	20.00	12.00
(61) Rocky Colavito/Portrait	35.00	17.50	10.00
(62) Rocky Colavito/Btg	25.00	12.50	7.50
(63) Choo Choo Coleman	12.00	6.00	3.50
(64) Gordy Coleman	30.00	15.00	9.00
(65) Jerry Coleman	10.00	5.00	3.00
(66) Mort Cooper	35.00	17.50	10.00
(67) Walker Cooper	9.00	4.50	2.75
(68) Roger Craig	12.00	6.00	3.50
(69) Delmar Crandall	9.00	4.50	2.75
(70) Joe Cunningham/Btg	40.00	20.00	12.00
(71) Joe Cunningham/Portrait	65.00	32.00	19.50
(72) Guy Curtwright (Curtright)	10.00	5.00	3.00
(73) Bud Daley	35.00	17.50	10.00
(74) Alvin Dark (Braves)	12.00	6.00	3.50
(75) Alvin Dark (Giants)	10.00	5.00	3.00
(76) Alvin Dark (Cubs)	12.00	6.00	3.50
(77) Murray Dickson (Murry)	25.00	12.50	7.50
(78) Bob Dillinger	12.00	6.00	3.50
(79) Dom DiMaggio	25.00	12.50	7.50
(80) Joe Dobson	30.00	15.00	9.00
(81a) Larry Doby (Bat on right border.)	40.00	20.00	12.00
(81b) Larry Doby (Bat well off right border.)	25.00	12.50	7.50
(82a) Bobby Doerr ("AN EXHIBIT CARD" lower-left.)	15.00	7.50	4.50
(82b) Bobby Doerr (No "AN EXHIBIT CARD.")	15.00	7.50	4.50
(83) Dick Donovan (Plain cap.)	12.00	6.00	3.50
(84) Dick Donovan (Sox cap.)	9.00	4.50	2.75
(85) Walter Dropo	9.00	4.50	2.75
(86) Don Drysdale (Glove at waist.)	20.00	10.00	6.00
(87) Don Drysdale/Portrait	35.00	17.50	10.00
(88) Luke Easter	15.00	7.50	4.50

		NM	EX	VG
(89)	Bruce Edwards	15.00	7.50	4.50
(90)	Del Ennis	15.00	7.50	4.50
(91)	Al Evans	10.00	5.00	3.00
(92)	Walter Evers	9.00	4.50	2.75
(93)	Ferris Fain/Fielding	12.00	6.00	3.50
(94)	Ferris Fain/Portrait	15.00	7.50	4.50
(95)	Dick Farrell	9.00	4.50	2.75
(96)	Ed "Whitey" Ford	30.00	15.00	9.00
(97)	Whitey Ford/Pitching	30.00	15.00	9.00
(98)	Whitey Ford/Portrait	175.00	85.00	50.00
(99)	Dick Fowler	12.50	6.25	3.75
(100)	Nelson Fox	25.00	12.50	7.50
(101)	Tito Francona	9.00	4.50	2.75
(102)	Bob Friend	9.00	4.50	2.75
(103)	Carl Furillo	25.00	12.50	7.50
(104)	Augie Galan	30.00	15.00	9.00
(105)	Jim Gentile	9.00	4.50	2.75
(106)	Tony Gonzalez	9.00	4.50	2.75
(107)	Billy Goodman/Leaping	17.50	8.75	5.25
(108)	Billy Goodman/Btg	12.00	6.00	3.50
(109)	Ted Greengrass (Jim)	9.00	4.50	2.75
(110)	Dick Groat	10.00	5.00	3.00
(111)	Steve Gromek	9.00	4.50	2.75
(112)	Johnny Groth	9.00	4.50	2.75
(113)	Orval Grove	15.00	7.50	4.50
(114)	Frank Gustine (Pirates uniform.)	20.00	10.00	6.00
(115)	Frank Gustine (Plain uniform.)	10.00	5.00	3.00
(116)	Berthold Haas	20.00	10.00	6.00
(117)	Grady Hatton	10.00	5.00	3.00
(118)	Jim Hegan	9.00	4.50	2.75
(119)	Tom Henrich	12.00	6.00	3.50
(120)	Ray Herbert	15.00	7.50	4.50
(121)	Gene Hermanski	10.00	5.00	3.00
(122)	Whitey Herzog	12.00	6.00	3.50
(123)	Kirby Higbe	30.00	15.00	9.00
(124)	Chuck Hinton	9.00	4.50	2.75
(125)	Don Hoak	15.00	7.50	4.50
(126)	Gil Hodges ("B" on cap.)	12.50	6.25	3.75
(127)	Gil Hodges ("LA" on cap.)	25.00	12.50	7.50
(128)	Johnny Hopp	13.50	6.75	4.00
(129)	Elston Howard	12.00	6.00	3.50
(130)	Frank Howard	15.00	7.50	4.50
(131)	Ken Hubbs	30.00	15.00	9.00
(132)	Tex Hughson	13.50	6.75	4.00
(133)	Fred Hutchinson	60.00	30.00	18.00
(134)	Monty Irvin (Monte)	12.00	6.00	3.50
(135)	Joey Jay	9.00	4.50	2.75
(136)	Jackie Jensen	45.00	22.50	13.50
(137)	Sam Jethroe	10.00	5.00	3.00
(138)	Bill Johnson	30.00	15.00	9.00
(139)	Walter Judnich	13.50	6.75	4.00
(140)	Al Kaline/Kneeling	25.00	12.50	7.50
(141)	Al Kaline (Portrait w/ two bats.)	17.50	8.75	5.25
(142)	George Kell	20.00	10.00	6.00
(143)	Charley Keller	12.50	6.25	3.75
(144)	Alex Kellner	9.00	4.50	2.75
(145)	Kenn (Ken) Keltner	10.00	5.00	3.00
(146)	Harmon Killebrew (With bat.)	50.00	25.00	15.00
(147)	Harmon Killebrew/Throwing	40.00	20.00	12.00
(148)	Harmon Killibrew (Killebrew)/Portrait	50.00	25.00	15.00
(149)	Ellis Kinder	9.00	4.50	2.75
(150)	Ralph Kiner	25.00	12.50	7.50
(151)	Billy Klaus	30.00	15.00	9.00
(152)	Ted Kluzewski (Kluszewski)/Btg	17.50	8.75	5.25
(153)	Ted Kluzewski (Kluszewski) (Pirates uniform.)	12.00	6.00	3.50
(154)	Ted Kluzewski (Kluszewski) (plain uniform.)	17.50	8.75	5.25
(155)	Don Kolloway	20.00	10.00	6.00
(156)	Jim Konstanty	10.00	5.00	3.00
(157)	Sandy Koufax	40.00	20.00	12.00
(158)	Ed Kranepool	55.00	27.50	16.50
(159)	Tony Kubek (Light background.)	16.00	8.00	4.75
(160)	Tony Kubek (Dark background.)	45.00	22.50	13.50
(161)	Harvey Kuenn ("D" on cap.)	30.00	15.00	9.00
(162)	Harvey Kuenn (Plain cap.)	16.00	8.00	4.75
(163)	Harvey Kuenn ("SF" on cap.)	15.00	7.50	4.50
(164)	Whitey Kurowski	30.00	15.00	9.00
(165)	Eddie Lake	12.00	6.00	3.50
(166)	Jim Landis	9.00	4.50	2.75
(167)	Don Larsen	10.00	5.00	3.00
(168)	Bob Lemon (Glove not visible.)	15.00	7.50	4.50
(169)	Bob Lemon (Glove partially visible.)	25.00	12.50	7.50
(170)	Buddy Lewis	25.00	12.50	7.50
(171)	Johnny Lindell	35.00	17.50	10.00
(172)	Phil Linz	25.00	12.50	7.50
(173)	Don Lock	25.00	12.50	7.50
(174)	Whitey Lockman	9.00	4.50	2.75
(175)	Johnny Logan	9.00	4.50	2.75
(176)	Dale Long ("P" on cap.)	9.00	4.50	2.75
(177)	Dale Long ("C" on cap.)	20.00	10.00	6.00
(178)	Ed Lopat	10.00	5.00	3.00
(179)	Harry Lowery (Name misspelled.)	10.00	5.00	3.00
(180)	Harry Lowrey (Name correct.)	10.00	5.00	3.00
(181)	Sal Maglie	9.00	4.50	2.75
(182)	Art Mahaffey	10.00	5.00	3.00
(183)	Hank Majeski	9.00	4.50	2.75
(184)	Frank Malzone	16.00	8.00	4.75
(185)	Mickey Mantle/Btg (Full-length.)	140.00	70.00	40.00
(186)	Mickey Mantle/Btg (Waist-up, "ck" in "Mickey" connected.)	120.00	60.00	35.00
(187)	Mickey Mantle/Btg (Waist-up, "c k" in "Mickey" connected.)	175.00	85.00	50.00
(188)	Mickey Mantle/Portrait	600.00	300.00	180.00
(189)	Martin Marion	20.00	10.00	6.00
(190)	Roger Maris	25.00	12.50	7.50
(191)	Willard Marshall	10.00	5.00	3.00
(192)	Eddie Matthews (Name incorrect.)	16.00	8.00	4.75
(193)	Eddie Mathews (Name correct.)	30.00	15.00	9.00
(194)	Ed Mayo	10.00	5.00	3.00
(195)	Willie Mays/Btg	45.00	22.50	13.50
(196)	Willie Mays/Btg	60.00	30.00	18.00
(197)	Bill Mazeroski/Portrait	16.00	8.00	4.75
(198)	Bill Mazeroski/Btg	16.00	8.00	4.75
(199)	Ken McBride	15.00	7.50	4.50
(200)	Barney McCaskey (McCosky)	13.50	6.75	4.00
(201)	Barney McCoskey (McCosky)	100.00	50.00	30.00
(202)	Lindy McDaniel	9.00	4.50	2.75
(203a)	Gil McDougald ("MADE IN U.S.A." lower-right.)	15.00	7.50	4.50
(203b)	Gil McDougald ("PRINTED IN U.S.A." lower-right.)	15.00	7.50	4.50
(204)	Albert Mele	30.00	15.00	9.00
(205)	Sam Mele	20.00	10.00	6.00
(206)	Orestes Minoso ("C" on cap.)	12.50	6.25	3.75
(207)	Orestes Minoso (Sox on cap.)	9.00	4.50	2.75
(208)	Dale Mitchell	9.00	4.50	2.75
(209)	Wally Moon	12.00	6.00	3.50
(210)	Don Mueller	10.00	5.00	3.00
(211)	Stan Musial/Kneeling	60.00	30.00	18.00
(212)	Stan Musial/Btg	70.00	35.00	20.00
(213)	Charley Neal	15.00	7.50	4.50
(214)	Don Newcombe (Shaking hands.)	25.00	12.50	7.50
(215)	Don Newcombe (Dodgers on jacket.)	9.00	4.50	2.75
(216)	Don Newcombe (Plain jacket.)	10.00	5.00	3.00
(217)	Hal Newhouser	35.00	17.50	10.00
(218)	Ron Northey	20.00	10.00	6.00
(219)	Bill O'Dell	9.00	4.50	2.75
(220)	Joe Page	20.00	10.00	6.00
(221)	Satchel Paige	90.00	45.00	25.00
(222)	Milt Pappas	9.00	4.50	2.75
(223)	Camilo Pascual	9.00	4.50	2.75
(224)	Albie Pearson	25.00	12.50	7.50
(225)	Johnny Pesky	9.00	4.50	2.75
(226)	Gary Peters	25.00	12.50	7.50
(227)	Dave Philley	9.00	4.50	2.75
(228)	Billy Pierce	9.00	4.50	2.75
(229)	Jimmy Piersall	15.00	7.50	4.50
(230)	Vada Pinson	12.50	6.25	3.75
(231)	Bob Porterfield	9.00	4.50	2.75
(232)	John "Boog" Powell	45.00	22.50	13.50
(233)	Vic Raschi	15.00	7.50	4.50
(234)	Harold "Peewee" Reese/Fielding (Ball partially visible.)	35.00	17.50	10.00
(235)	Harold "Peewee" Reese/Fielding (Ball not visible.)	25.00	12.50	7.50
(236)	Del Rice	12.50	6.25	3.75
(237)	Bobby Richardson	125.00	60.00	35.00
(238)	Phil Rizzuto	25.00	12.50	7.50
(239)	Robin Roberts (Script signature.)	14.50	7.25	4.25
(240)	Robin Roberts (Plain signature.)	25.00	12.50	7.50
(241)	Brooks Robinson	17.50	8.75	5.25
(242)	Eddie Robinson	9.00	4.50	2.75
(243)	Floyd Robinson	17.50	8.75	5.25
(244)	Frankie Robinson	60.00	30.00	18.00
(245)	Jackie Robinson	50.00	25.00	15.00
(246)	Preacher Roe	35.00	17.50	10.00
(247)	Bob Rogers (Rodgers)	30.00	15.00	9.00
(248)	Richard Rollins	25.00	12.50	7.50
(249)	Pete Runnels	13.50	6.75	4.00
(250)	John Sain	12.50	6.25	3.75
(251)	Ron Santo	25.00	12.50	7.50
(252)	Henry Sauer	10.00	5.00	3.00
(253)	Carl Sawatski ("M" on cap.)	9.00	4.50	2.75
(254)	Carl Sawatski ("P" on cap.)	9.00	4.50	2.75
(255)	Carl Sawatski (Plain cap.)	17.50	8.75	5.25
(256)	Johnny Schmitz	10.00	5.00	3.00
(257)	Red Schoendeinst (Schoendienst)/Fielding (Name in white.)	25.00	12.50	7.50
(258)	Red Schoendeinst (Schoendienst)/Fielding (Name in red-brown.)	30.00	15.00	9.00
(259)	Red Schoendinst (Schoendienst)/Btg	12.50	6.25	3.75
(260)	Herb Score ("C" on cap.)	15.00	7.50	4.50
(261)	Herb Score (Plain cap.)	17.50	8.75	5.25
(262)	Andy Seminick	9.00	4.50	2.75
(263)	Rip Sewell	20.00	10.00	6.00
(264)	Norm Siebern	9.00	4.50	2.75
(265)	Roy Sievers/Btg	15.00	7.50	4.50
(266)	Roy Sievers/Portrait ("W" on cap, light background.)	12.00	6.00	3.50
(267)	Roy Sievers/Portrait ("W" on cap, dark background.)	10.00	5.00	3.00
(268)	Roy Sievers/Portrait (Plain cap.)	20.00	10.00	6.00
(269)	Curt Simmons	10.00	5.00	3.00
(270)	Dick Sisler	10.00	5.00	3.00
(271)	Bill Skowron	12.50	6.25	3.75
(272)	Bill "Moose" Skowron	65.00	32.50	20.00
(273)	Enos Slaughter	20.00	10.00	6.00
(274)	Duke Snider ("B" on cap.)	22.50	11.00	6.75
(275)	Duke Snider ("LA" on cap.)	20.00	10.00	6.00
(276)	Warren Spahn ("B" on cap.)	20.00	10.00	6.00
(277)	Warren Spahn ("M" on cap.)	20.00	10.00	6.00
(278)	Stanley Spence	16.00	8.00	4.75
(279)	Ed Stanky (Plain uniform.)	17.50	8.75	5.25
(280)	Ed Stanky (Giants uniform.)	10.00	5.00	3.00
(281)	Vern Stephens/Btg	10.00	5.00	3.00
(282)	Vern Stephens/Portrait	10.00	5.00	3.00
(283)	Ed Stewart	10.00	5.00	3.00
(284)	Snuffy Stirnweiss	12.50	6.25	3.75
(285)	George "Birdie" Tebbetts	17.50	8.75	5.25
(286)	Frankie Thomas (Photo actually Bob Skinner.)	35.00	17.50	10.00
(287)	Frank Thomas/Portrait ("Best Wishes")	16.00	8.00	4.75
(288)	Lee Thomas	9.00	4.50	2.75
(289)	Bobby Thomson	25.00	12.50	7.50
(290)	Earl Torgeson (Braves uniform.)	9.00	4.50	2.75
(291)	Earl Torgeson (Plain uniform.)	10.00	5.00	3.00
(292)	Gus Triandos	12.00	6.00	3.50
(293)	Virgil Trucks	9.00	4.50	2.75
(294)	Johnny Vandermeer (VanderMeer)	25.00	12.50	7.50
(295)	Emil Verban	12.00	6.00	3.50
(296)	Mickey Vernon/Throwing	15.00	7.50	4.50
(297)	Mickey Vernon/Btg	9.00	4.50	2.75
(298)	Bill Voiselle	30.00	15.00	9.00
(299)	Leon Wagner	6.50	3.25	1.75
(300)	Eddie Waitkus/Throwing (hicago uniform.)	40.00	20.00	12.00
(301)	Eddie Waitkus/Throwing (Plain uniform.)	10.00	5.00	3.00
(302)	Eddie Waitkus/Portrait	15.00	7.50	4.50
(303)	Dick Wakefield	10.00	5.00	3.00
(304)	Harry Walker	40.00	20.00	12.00
(305)	Bucky Walters	20.00	10.00	6.00
(306)	Pete Ward	75.00	37.50	22.50
(307)	Herman Wehmeier	10.00	5.00	3.00
(308)	Vic Wertz/Btg	9.00	4.50	2.75
(309)	Vic Wertz/Portrait	9.00	4.50	2.75
(310)	Wally Westlake	10.00	5.00	3.00
(311)	Wes Westrum	17.50	8.75	5.25
(312)	Billy Williams	20.00	10.00	6.00
(313)	Maurice Wills	15.00	7.50	4.50
(314)	Gene Woodling (Script signature.)	9.00	4.50	2.75
(315)	Gene Woodling (Plain signature.)	12.00	6.00	3.50
(316)	Taffy Wright	10.00	5.00	3.00
(317)	Carl Yastrazemski (Yastrzemski)	200.00	100.00	60.00
(318)	Al Zarilla	12.50	6.25	3.75
(319)	Gus Zernial (Script signature.)	9.00	4.50	2.75
(320)	Gus Zernial (Plain signature.)	12.00	6.00	3.50
(321)	Braves Team/1948	50.00	25.00	15.00
(322)	Dodgers Team/1949	75.00	37.50	22.50
(323)	Dodgers Team/1952	65.00	32.50	20.00
(324)	Dodgers Team/1955	125.00	60.00	35.00
(325)	Dodgers Team/1956	60.00	30.00	18.00
(326)	Giants Team/1951	60.00	30.00	18.00
(327a)	Giants Team/1954 (Plain back.)	50.00	25.00	15.00
(328)	Indians Team/1948	55.00	27.50	16.50
(329)	Indians Team/1954	50.00	25.00	15.00
(330)	Phillies Team/1950	40.00	20.00	12.00
(331)	Yankees Team/1949	60.00	30.00	18.00
(332)	Yankees Team/1950	65.00	32.50	20.00
(333)	Yankees Team/1951	65.00	32.50	20.00
(334)	Yankees Team/1952	70.00	35.00	20.00
(335)	Yankees Team/1955	70.00	35.00	20.00
(336)	Yankees Team/1956	70.00	35.00	20.00

1948 Baseball's Great Hall of Fame Exhibits

Titled "Baseball's Great Hall of Fame," this 32-player set features black and white player photos against a gray background. The photos are accented by Greek columns on either side with brief player information printed at the bottom. The blank-backed cards are unnumbered and are listed here alphabetically. The cards measure 3-3/8" x 5-3/8". Collectors should be aware that 24 cards from this set were reprinted on whiter stock in 1974.

		NM	EX	VG
Complete Set (33):		500.00	250.00	150.00
Common Player:		7.50	3.75	2.25
(1)	Grover Cleveland Alexander	15.00	7.50	4.50
(2)	Roger Bresnahan	7.50	3.75	2.25
(3)	Frank Chance	7.50	3.75	2.25
(4)	Jack Chesbro	7.50	3.75	2.25
(5)	Fred Clarke	7.50	3.75	2.25
(6)	Ty Cobb	55.00	27.50	16.50
(7)	Mickey Cochrane	7.50	3.75	2.25
(8)	Eddie Collins	7.50	3.75	2.25
(9)	Hugh Duffy	7.50	3.75	2.25
(10)	Johnny Evers	7.50	3.75	2.25
(11)	Frankie Frisch	7.50	3.75	2.25
(12)	Lou Gehrig	35.00	17.50	10.00
(13)	Clark Griffith	7.50	3.75	2.25
(14)	Robert "Lefty" Grove	7.50	3.75	2.25

		NM	EX	VG
(15)	Rogers Hornsby	10.00	5.00	3.00
(16)	Carl Hubbell	7.50	3.75	2.25
(17)	Hughie Jennings	7.50	3.75	2.25
(18)	Walter Johnson	15.00	7.50	4.50
(19)	Willie Keeler	7.50	3.75	2.25
(20)	Napolean Lajoie	7.50	3.75	2.25
(21)	Connie Mack	7.50	3.75	2.25
(22)	Christy Matthewson (Mathewson)	20.00	10.00	6.00
(23)	John J. McGraw	7.50	3.75	2.25
(24)	Eddie Plank	7.50	3.75	2.25
(25)	Babe Ruth/Btg	60.00	30.00	18.00
(26)	Babe Ruth (Standing with bats.)	250.00	125.00	75.00
(27)	George Sisler	7.50	3.75	2.25
(28)	Tris Speaker	10.00	5.00	3.00
(29)	Joe Tinker	7.50	3.75	2.25
(30)	Rube Waddell	7.50	3.75	2.25
(31)	Honus Wagner	25.00	12.50	7.50
(32)	Ed Walsh	7.50	3.75	2.25
(33)	Cy Young	15.00	7.50	4.50

1953 Canadian Exhibits

This Canadian-issued set consists of 64 cards and includes both major leaguers and players from the Montreal Royals of the International League. The cards are slightly smaller than the U.S. exhibit cards, measuring 3-1/4" x 5-1/4", and are numbered. The blank-backed cards were printed on gray stock. Card numbers 1-32 have a green or red tint, while card numbers 33-64 have a blue or reddish-brown tint.

		NM	EX	VG
Complete Set (64):		1,750	875.00	525.00
Common Player (1-32):		15.00	7.50	4.50
Common Player (33-64):		9.00	4.50	2.75
1	Preacher Roe	20.00	10.00	6.00
2	Luke Easter	20.00	10.00	6.00
3	Gene Bearden	15.00	7.50	4.50
4	Chico Carrasquel	20.00	10.00	6.00
5	Vic Raschi	20.00	10.00	6.00
6	Monty (Monte) Irvin	30.00	15.00	9.00
7	Henry Sauer	15.00	7.50	4.50
8	Ralph Branca	20.00	10.00	6.00
9	Ed Stanky	20.00	10.00	6.00
10	Sam Jethroe	15.00	7.50	4.50
11	Larry Doby	30.00	15.00	9.00
12	Hal Newhouser	30.00	15.00	9.00
13	Gil Hodges	50.00	25.00	15.00
14	Harry Brecheen	15.00	7.50	4.50
15	Ed Lopat	20.00	10.00	6.00
16	Don Newcombe	25.00	12.50	7.50
17	Bob Feller	60.00	30.00	18.00
18	Tommy Holmes	15.00	7.50	4.50
19	Jackie Robinson	65.00	35.00	20.00
20	Roy Campanella	55.00	25.00	15.00
21	Harold "Peewee" Reese	50.00	25.00	15.00
22	Ralph Kiner	40.00	20.00	12.00
23	Dom DiMaggio	25.00	12.50	7.50
24	Bobby Doerr	30.00	15.00	9.00
25	Phil Rizzuto	50.00	25.00	15.00
26	Bob Elliott	15.00	7.50	4.50
27	Tom Henrich	20.00	10.00	6.00
28	Joe DiMaggio	200.00	100.00	60.00
29	Harry Lowery (Lowrey)	15.00	7.50	4.50
30	Ted Williams	75.00	37.50	22.50
31	Bob Lemon	40.00	20.00	12.00
32	Warren Spahn	50.00	25.00	15.00
33	Don Hoak	25.00	12.50	7.50
34	Bob Alexander	15.00	7.50	4.50
35	John Simmons	15.00	7.50	4.50
36	Steve Lembo	15.00	7.50	4.50
37	Norman Larker	20.00	10.00	6.00
38	Bob Ludwick	15.00	7.50	4.50
39	Walter Moryn	20.00	10.00	6.00
40	Charlie Thompson	15.00	7.50	4.50
41	Ed Roebuck	20.00	10.00	6.00
42	Russell Rose	15.00	7.50	4.50
43	Edmundo (Sandy) Amoros	25.00	12.50	7.50
44	Bob Milliken	15.00	7.50	4.50
45	Art Fabbro	15.00	7.50	4.50
46	Spook Jacobs	15.00	7.50	4.50
47	Carmen Mauro	15.00	7.50	4.50
48	Walter Fiala	15.00	7.50	4.50
49	Rocky Nelson	15.00	7.50	4.50
50	Tom La Sorda (Lasorda)	60.00	30.00	18.00
51	Ronnie Lee	15.00	7.50	4.50
52	Hampton Coleman	15.00	7.50	4.50
53	Frank Marchio	15.00	7.50	4.50
54	William Sampson	15.00	7.50	4.50
55	Gil Mills	15.00	7.50	4.50
56	Al Ronning	15.00	7.50	4.50
57	Stan Musial	75.00	37.50	22.50
58	Walker Cooper	9.00	4.50	2.75
59	Mickey Vernon	9.00	4.50	2.75
60	Del Ennis	9.00	4.50	2.75
61	Walter Alston	40.00	20.00	12.00
62	Dick Sisler	9.00	4.50	2.75
63	Billy Goodman	9.00	4.50	2.75
64	Alex Kellner	9.00	4.50	2.75

1955 Exhibits - Post Card Backs

For an unknkown purpose, the 64 Exhibit cards issued in 1955 (including many re-issued from earlier years) were produced in a very limited edition with a post card back, as opposed to the blank-back format usually found on the 3-3/8" x 5-3/8" cards.

		NM	EX	VG
Complete Set (64):		3,000	1,500	900.00
Common Player:		25.00	12.50	7.50
(1)	Joe Adcock	25.00	12.50	7.50
(2)	Ritchie (Richie) Ashburn	45.00	22.50	13.50
(3)	Toby Atwell	25.00	12.50	7.50
(4)	Gene Baker	25.00	12.50	7.50
(5)	Ernie Banks (Bat on shoulder, printed name.)	75.00	37.50	22.50
(6)	Matt Batts	25.00	12.50	7.50
(7)	Frank Baumholtz	25.00	12.50	7.50
(8)	Yogi Berra	125.00	65.00	35.00
(9)	Steve Bilko	25.00	12.50	7.50
(10)	Roy Campanella	60.00	30.00	18.00
(11)	Chico Carrasquel/Leaping	25.00	12.50	7.50
(12)	Alvin Dark (Giants)	25.00	12.50	7.50
(13)	Larry Doby	45.00	22.50	13.50
(14)	Walter Dropo	25.00	12.50	7.50
(15)	Del Ennis	25.00	12.50	7.50
(16)	Ferris Fain/Portrait	45.00	22.50	13.50
(17)	Bob Feller (Yours Truly)	100.00	50.00	30.00
(18)	Billy Goodman/Leaping	45.00	22.50	13.50
(19)	Ted (Jim) Greengrass	25.00	12.50	7.50
(20)	Steve Gromek	25.00	12.50	7.50
(21)	Johnny Groth	25.00	12.50	7.50
(22)	Jim Hegan	25.00	12.50	7.50
(23)	Gene Hermanski	25.00	12.50	7.50
(24)	Gil Hodges (B on cap.)	50.00	25.00	15.00
(25)	Monty (Monte) Irvin	45.00	22.50	13.50
(26)	Al Kaline/Kneeling	75.00	37.50	22.50
(27)	George Kell	45.00	22.50	13.50
(28)	Alex Kellner	25.00	12.50	7.50
(29)	Ted Kluszewski (Kluszewski)/Btg	60.00	30.00	18.00
(30)	Bob Lemon (Glove not showing.)	45.00	22.50	13.50
(31)	Whitey Lockman	25.00	12.50	7.50
(32)	Ed Lopat	30.00	15.00	9.00
(33)	Sal Maglie	25.00	12.50	7.50
(34)	Mickey Mantle/Btg (Waist-up.)	400.00	200.00	120.00
(35)	Ed Matthews (Mathews)	60.00	30.00	18.00
(36)	Willie Mays/Btg	200.00	100.00	60.00
(37)	Gil McDougald	30.00	15.00	9.00
(38)	Sam Mele	25.00	12.50	7.50
(39)	Orestes Minoso (C on cap.)	45.00	22.50	13.50
(40)	Dale Mitchell	25.00	12.50	7.50
(41)	Stan Musial/Kneeling	100.00	50.00	30.00
(42)	Andy Pafko (Yours truly.) (C on cap.)	25.00	12.50	7.50
(43)	Bob Porterfield	25.00	12.50	7.50
(44)	Vic Raschi	25.00	12.50	7.50
(45)	Harold "Peewee" Reese	60.00	30.00	18.00
(46)	Phil Rizzuto	60.00	30.00	18.00
(47)	Robin Roberts	45.00	22.50	13.50
(48)	Jackie Robinson	150.00	75.00	45.00
(49)	Henry Sauer	25.00	12.50	7.50
(50)	Johnny Schmitz	25.00	12.50	7.50
(51)	Red Schoendinst (Schoendienst)	45.00	22.50	13.50
(52)	Andy Seminick	25.00	12.50	7.50
(53)	Duke Snider (B on cap.)	60.00	30.00	18.00
(54)	Warren Spahn (B on cap.)	60.00	30.00	18.00
(55)	Vern Stephens/Portrait	25.00	12.50	7.50
(56)	Earl Torgeson (Braves uniform.)	25.00	12.50	7.50
(57)	Virgil Trucks	25.00	12.50	7.50
(58)	Mickey Vernon/Btg	25.00	12.50	7.50
(59)	Eddie Waitkus	25.00	12.50	7.50
(60)	Vic Wertz/Btg	25.00	12.50	7.50
(61)	Gene Woodling	25.00	12.50	7.50
(62)	Gus Zernial	25.00	12.50	7.50
(63)	Cleveland Indians 1954 American League Champions	150.00	75.00	45.00
(64)	New York Giants 1954 National League Champions	150.00	75.00	45.00

1959 Exhibits - Dad's Cookies

(See 1959 Dad's Cookies.)

1961 Exhibits - Wrigley Field

JOHN JOSEPH EVERS

Distributed at Chicago's Wrigley Field circa 1961, this 24-card set features members of the Baseball Hall of Fame. The cards measure 3-3/8" x 5-3/8" and include the player's full name along the bottom. They were printed on gray stock and have a postcard back. The set is unnumbered.

		NM	EX	VG
Complete Set (24):		750.00	375.00	225.00
Common Player:		10.00	5.00	3.00
(1)	Grover Cleveland Alexander	15.00	7.50	4.50
(2)	Adrian Constantine Anson	12.50	6.25	3.75
(3)	John Franklin Baker	10.00	5.00	3.00
(4)	Roger Phillip Bresnahan	10.00	5.00	3.00
(5)	Mordecai Peter Brown	10.00	5.00	3.00
(6)	Frank Leroy Chance	10.00	5.00	3.00
(7)	Tyrus Raymond Cobb	145.00	75.00	45.00
(8)	Edward Trowbridge Collins	10.00	5.00	3.00
(9)	James J. Collins	10.00	5.00	3.00
(10)	John Joseph Evers	10.00	5.00	3.00
(11)	Henry Louis Gehrig	145.00	75.00	45.00
(12)	Clark C. Griffith	10.00	5.00	3.00
(13)	Walter Perry Johnson	25.00	12.50	7.50
(14)	Anthony Michael Lazzeri	10.00	5.00	3.00
(15)	James Walter Vincent Maranville	10.00	5.00	3.00
(16)	Christopher Mathewson	30.00	15.00	9.00
(17)	John Joseph McGraw	10.00	5.00	3.00
(18)	Melvin Thomas Ott	10.00	5.00	3.00
(19)	Herbert Jeffries Pennock	10.00	5.00	3.00
(20)	George Herman Ruth	180.00	90.00	55.00
(21)	Aloysius Harry Simmons	10.00	5.00	3.00
(22)	Tristram Speaker	25.00	12.50	7.50
(23)	Joseph B. Tinker	10.00	5.00	3.00
(24)	John Peter Wagner	40.00	20.00	12.00

1962 Pittsburgh Exhibits

The attributed date is approximate since none is shown on the cards; nor is a credit line to the manufacturer. Player content suggests Pittsburgh was the center of distribution and veteran collectors report having received the cards in penny arcade vending machines at Kennywood Amusement Park near there. It has also been reported that the cards were given over the counter as prizes for getting a winning gumball from a machine. The 3-1/4" x 5-1/4" cards are printed in black-and-white, or red, black and white. They are usually blank-backed, but examples have been seen with apparent prize references printed on back. Most of the card "denominations" can be found with more than one subject. Besides the ballplayers listed here, the set contained TV and movie cowboys, rock-and-roll stars, boxers, wrestlers and cartoon characters.

		NM	EX	VG
Complete Set (81):		2,500	1,250	750.00
Common Player:		5.00	2.50	1.50
AC	Bill Mazeroski	25.00	12.50	7.50
2C	Whitey Ford	30.00	15.00	9.00
2C	Al Kaline	20.00	10.00	6.00
2C	Pirates logo cartoon	5.00	2.50	1.50
4C	Frank Robinson	20.00	10.00	6.00
4C	Babe Ruth	125.00	65.00	35.00
5C	Wilmer Mizell	5.00	2.50	1.50
5C	Mickey Mantle	175.00	85.00	50.00
5C	Honus Wagner	35.00	17.50	10.00
6C	Eddie Mathews	20.00	10.00	6.00
6C	Willie Mays	90.00	45.00	27.00
7C	Dodgers' "Bum" Cartoon Logo	5.00	2.50	1.50
7C	Eddie Mathews	20.00	10.00	6.00
7C	Willie Mays	90.00	45.00	27.00
8C	Walter Johnson	20.00	10.00	6.00
8C	Mickey Mantle	175.00	85.00	50.00
8C	Wilmer Mizell	5.00	2.50	1.50
9C	Hank Aaron	90.00	45.00	27.00
9C	Frank Robinson	20.00	10.00	6.00
10C	Lew Burdette	5.00	2.50	1.50
JC	Harvey Haddix	5.00	2.50	1.50
JC	Bill Mazeroski	25.00	12.50	7.50
JC	Al McBean	5.00	2.50	1.50
QC	Ty Cobb	60.00	30.00	18.00
QC	Whitey Ford	30.00	15.00	9.00
QC	Don Leppert	5.00	2.50	1.50
KC	Al Kaline	20.00	10.00	6.00
KC	Honus Wagner	35.00	17.50	10.00
AS	Lew Burdette	5.00	2.50	1.50
AS	Ty Cobb	60.00	30.00	18.00
2S	Smoky Burgess	5.00	2.50	1.50
3S	Don Hoak	5.00	2.50	1.50
4S	Roy Face	5.00	2.50	1.50
5S	Roberto Clemente	125.00	65.00	35.00
5S	Danny Murtaugh	5.00	2.50	1.50
6S	Christy Mathewson	25.00	12.50	7.50
6S	Dick Stuart	5.00	2.50	1.50
7S	Christy Mathewson	25.00	12.50	7.50
7S	Dick Stuart	5.00	2.50	1.50
8S	Danny Murtaugh	5.00	2.50	1.50
9S	Roy Face	5.00	2.50	1.50
10S	Don Hoak	5.00	2.50	1.50
JS	Smoky Burgess	5.00	2.50	1.50
QS	Walter Johnson	20.00	10.00	6.00
QS	Babe Ruth	125.00	65.00	35.00
KS	Hank Aaron	90.00	45.00	27.00
KS	Harvey Haddix	5.00	2.50	1.50
AH	Don Drysdale	20.00	10.00	6.00
AH	Ken Boyer	5.00	2.50	1.50
2H	Satchel Paige	60.00	30.00	18.00
3H	Rocky Colavito	20.00	10.00	6.00
4H	Stan Musial	50.00	25.00	15.00
4H	Bobby Richardson	15.00	7.50	4.50
5H	Ken Boyer	5.00	2.50	1.50
5H	Harmon Killebrew	20.00	10.00	6.00
6H	Luis Aparicio	20.00	10.00	6.00
6H	Ralph Kiner	20.00	10.00	6.00
7H	Sandy Koufax	75.00	37.50	22.00
8H	Warren Spahn	20.00	10.00	6.00
9H	Jimmy Piersall	5.00	2.50	1.50
10H	Yogi Berra	30.00	15.00	9.00
10H	Ralph Kiner	20.00	10.00	6.00
JH	Orlando Cepeda	20.00	10.00	6.00
JH	Ken Boyer	5.00	2.50	1.50
QH	Roger Maris	75.00	37.50	22.00
QH	Stan Musial	50.00	25.00	15.00
KH	Bob Purkey	5.00	2.50	1.50
AD	Don Drysdale	20.00	10.00	6.00
AD	Don Hoak	5.00	2.50	1.50
2D	Satchel Paige	60.00	30.00	18.00
6D	Luis Aparicio	20.00	10.00	6.00
6D	Ernie Banks	25.00	12.50	7.50
7D	Bill Virdon	5.00	2.50	1.50
7D	Sandy Koufax	75.00	37.50	22.00
8D	Bob Skinner	5.00	2.50	1.50
9D	Dick Groat	5.00	2.50	1.50
10D	Vernon Law	5.00	2.50	1.50
JD	Joe Adcock	5.00	2.50	1.50
JD	Orlando Cepeda	20.00	10.00	6.00
QD	Roger Maris	75.00	37.50	22.00
KD	Bob Friend	5.00	2.50	1.50

1962 Statistic Back Exhibits

In 1962, the Exhibit Supply Co. added career statistics to the yearly set they produced. The black-and-white, unnumbered cards measure 3-3/8" x 5-3/8". The statistics found on the back are printed in black or red.

		NM	EX	VG
Complete Set (32):		500.00	250.00	150.00
Common Player:		6.00	3.00	1.75
Red Backs: 1.5X				
(1)	Hank Aaron	35.00	17.50	10.00
(2)	Luis Aparicio	15.00	7.50	4.50
(3)	Ernie Banks	25.00	12.50	7.50
(4)	Larry "Yogi" Berra	25.00	12.50	7.50
(5)	Ken Boyer	7.50	3.75	2.25
(6)	Lew Burdette	6.00	3.00	1.75
(7)	Norm Cash	7.50	3.75	2.25
(8)	Orlando Cepeda	15.00	7.50	4.50
(9)	Roberto Clemente	50.00	25.00	15.00
(10)	Rocky Colavito	15.00	7.50	4.50
(11)	Ed "Whitey" Ford	17.50	8.75	5.25
(12)	Nelson Fox	15.00	7.50	4.50
(13)	Tito Francona	6.00	3.00	1.75
(14)	Jim Gentile	6.00	3.00	1.75
(15)	Dick Groat	6.00	3.00	1.75
(16)	Don Hoak	6.00	3.00	1.75
(17)	Al Kaline	17.50	8.75	5.25
(18)	Harmon Killebrew	17.50	8.75	5.25
(19)	Sandy Koufax	30.00	15.00	9.00
(20)	Jim Landis	6.00	3.00	1.75
(21)	Art Mahaffey	6.00	3.00	1.75
(22)	Frank Malzone	6.00	3.00	1.75
(23)	Mickey Mantle	100.00	50.00	30.00
(24)	Roger Maris	17.50	8.75	5.25
(25)	Eddie Mathews	17.50	8.75	5.25
(26)	Willie Mays	35.00	17.50	10.00
(27)	Wally Moon	6.00	3.00	1.75
(28)	Stan Musial	30.00	15.00	9.00
(29)	Milt Pappas	6.00	3.00	1.75
(30)	Vada Pinson	7.50	3.75	2.25
(31)	Norm Siebern	6.00	3.00	1.75
(32)	Warren Spahn	17.50	8.75	5.25

1963 Statistic Back Exhibits

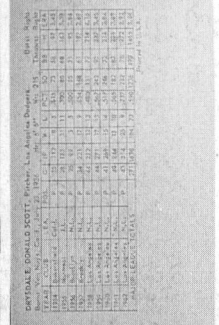

The Exhibit Supply Co. issued a 64-card set with career statistics on the backs of the cards in 1963. The unnumbered, black-and-white cards are printed on thick cardboard and measure 3-3/8" x 5-3/8" in size. The statistics on the back are only found printed in red.

		NM	EX	VG
Complete Set (64):		900.00	450.00	275.00
Common Player:		7.50	3.75	2.25
(1)	Hank Aaron	35.00	17.50	10.00
(2)	Luis Aparicio	15.00	7.50	4.50
(3)	Bob Aspromonte	7.50	3.75	2.25
(4)	Ernie Banks	25.00	12.50	7.50
(5)	Steve Barber	7.50	3.75	2.25
(6)	Earl Battey	7.50	3.75	2.25
(7)	Larry "Yogi" Berra	25.00	12.50	7.50
(8)	Ken Boyer	9.00	4.50	2.75
(9)	Lew Burdette	7.50	3.75	2.25
(10)	Johnny Callison	7.50	3.75	2.25
(11)	Norm Cash	9.00	4.50	2.75
(12)	Orlando Cepeda	15.00	7.50	4.50
(13)	Dean Chance	7.50	3.75	2.25
(14)	Tom Cheney	7.50	3.75	2.25
(15)	Roberto Clemente	40.00	20.00	12.00
(16)	Rocky Colavito	15.00	7.50	4.50
(17)	Choo Choo Coleman	7.50	3.75	2.25
(18)	Roger Craig	7.50	3.75	2.25
(19)	Joe Cunningham	7.50	3.75	2.25
(20)	Don Drysdale	15.00	7.50	4.50
(21)	Dick Farrell	7.50	3.75	2.25
(22)	Ed "Whitey" Ford	20.00	10.00	6.00
(23)	Nelson Fox	15.00	7.50	4.50
(24)	Tito Francona	7.50	3.75	2.25
(25)	Jim Gentile	7.50	3.75	2.25
(26)	Tony Gonzalez	7.50	3.75	2.25
(27)	Dick Groat	7.50	3.75	2.25
(28)	Ray Herbert	7.50	3.75	2.25
(29)	Chuck Hinton	7.50	3.75	2.25
(30)	Don Hoak	7.50	3.75	2.25
(31)	Frank Howard	9.00	4.50	2.75
(32)	Ken Hubbs	12.00	6.00	3.50
(33)	Joey Jay	7.50	3.75	2.25
(34)	Al Kaline	15.00	7.50	4.50
(35)	Harmon Killebrew	15.00	7.50	4.50
(36)	Sandy Koufax	30.00	15.00	9.00
(37)	Harvey Kuenn	7.50	3.75	2.25
(38)	Jim Landis	7.50	3.75	2.25
(39)	Art Mahaffey	7.50	3.75	2.25
(40)	Frank Malzone	7.50	3.75	2.25
(41)	Mickey Mantle	150.00	75.00	45.00
(42)	Roger Maris	15.00	7.50	4.50
(43)	Eddie Mathews	15.00	7.50	4.50
(44)	Willie Mays	35.00	17.50	10.00
(45)	Bill Mazeroski	15.00	7.50	4.50
(46)	Ken McBride	7.50	3.75	2.25
(47)	Wally Moon	7.50	3.75	2.25
(48)	Stan Musial	30.00	15.00	9.00
(49)	Charlie Neal	7.50	3.75	2.25
(50)	Bill O'Dell	7.50	3.75	2.25
(51)	Milt Pappas	7.50	3.75	2.25
(52)	Camilo Pascual	7.50	3.75	2.25
(53)	Jimmy Piersall	9.00	4.50	2.75
(54)	Vada Pinson	9.00	4.50	2.75
(55)	Brooks Robinson	20.00	10.00	6.00
(56)	Frankie Robinson	20.00	10.00	6.00
(57)	Pete Runnels	7.50	3.75	2.25
(58)	Ron Santo	9.00	4.50	2.75
(59)	Norm Siebern	7.50	3.75	2.25
(60)	Warren Spahn	20.00	10.00	6.00
(61)	Lee Thomas	7.50	3.75	2.25
(62)	Leon Wagner	7.50	3.75	2.25
(63)	Billy Williams	15.00	7.50	4.50
(64)	Maurice Wills	13.50	6.75	4.00

1974 Baseball's Great Hall of Fame Exhibits

Two dozen of the cards from the 1948 issue were reprinted in 1974 by the original publisher, Exhibit Supply Co., Chicago. The 1974 reissues are in the same 3-3/8" x 5-3/8" format as the originals, and in the same design. They are blank-backed and printed on a thinner, slicker cardboard stock than the 1948 cards. The reprints can be found printed in black, blue or brown. The unnumbered cards are checklisted here alphabetically.

		NM	EX	VG
Complete Set (24):		20.00	10.00	6.00
Common Player:		3.00	1.50	.90
(1)	Grover Cleveland Alexander	3.50	1.75	1.00
(2)	Roger Bresnahan	3.00	1.50	.90
(3)	Frank Chance	3.00	1.50	.90
(4)	Jack Chesbro	3.00	1.50	.90
(5)	Fred Clarke	3.00	1.50	.90
(6)	Ty Cobb	10.00	5.00	3.00
(7)	Mickey Cochrane	3.00	1.50	.90
(8)	Eddie Collins	3.00	1.50	.90
(9)	Johnny Evers	3.00	1.50	.90
(10)	Frankie Frisch	3.00	1.50	.90
(11)	Clark Griffith	3.00	1.50	.90
(12)	Robert "Lefty" Grove	3.00	1.50	.90
(13)	Rogers Hornsby	4.00	2.00	1.25
(14)	Hughie Jennings	3.00	1.50	.90
(15)	Walter Johnson	5.00	2.50	1.50
(16)	Connie Mack	3.00	1.50	.90
(17)	Christy Mathewson	5.00	2.50	1.50
(18)	John McGraw	3.00	1.50	.90
(19)	George Sisler	3.00	1.50	.90
(20)	Joe Tinker	3.00	1.50	.90
(21)	Rube Waddell	3.00	1.50	.90
(22)	Honus Wagner	6.00	3.00	1.75
(23)	Ed Walsh	3.00	1.50	.90
(24)	Cy Young	5.00	2.50	1.50

1977 Baseball's Great Hall of Fame Exhibits

A second set of "Baseball's Great Hall of Fame" exhibit cards was produced in 1977, most cards featuring more recent players than the 1948 issue. The cards were produced in the same 3-3/8" x 5-3/8" blank-back, black-and-white design as the 1948 cards, and are a genuine product of Exhibit Supply Co., Chicago. The new cards were printed on an extremely high grade of semi-gloss cardboard, in contrast to the earlier versions. Production was announced at 500,000 cards. The unnumbered cards are checklisted here alphabetically.

		NM	EX	VG
Complete Set (32):		35.00	17.50	10.00
Common Player:		2.00	1.00	.60
(1)	Luke Appling	2.00	1.00	.60
(2)	Ernie Banks	3.00	1.50	.90
(3)	Yogi Berra	3.00	1.50	.90
(4)	Roy Campanella	3.00	1.50	.90
(5)	Roberto Clemente	9.00	4.50	2.75
(6)	Alvin Dark	2.00	1.00	.60
(7)	Joe DiMaggio	9.00	4.50	2.75
(8)	Bob Feller	2.00	1.00	.60
(9)	Whitey Ford	2.00	1.00	.60
(10)	Jimmie Foxx	2.00	1.00	.60
(11)	Lou Gehrig	9.00	4.50	2.75
(12)	Charlie Gehringer	2.00	1.00	.60
(13)	Hank Greenberg	2.50	1.25	.70
(14)	Gabby Hartnett	2.00	1.00	.60

		NM	EX	VG
(15)	Carl Hubbell	2.00	1.00	.60
(16)	Al Kaline	2.00	1.00	.60
(17)	Mickey Mantle	15.00	7.50	4.50
(18)	Willie Mays	6.00	3.00	1.75
(19)	Johnny Mize	2.00	1.00	.60
(20)	Stan Musial	4.00	2.00	1.25
(21)	Mel Ott	2.00	1.00	.60
(22)	Satchel Paige	2.50	1.25	.70
(23)	Robin Roberts	2.00	1.00	.60
(24)	Jackie Robinson	6.00	3.00	1.75
(25)	Babe Ruth	12.00	6.00	3.50
(26)	Duke Snider	2.00	1.00	.60
(27)	Warren Spahn	2.00	1.00	.60
(28)	Tris Speaker	2.00	1.00	.60
(29)	Honus Wagner	3.00	1.50	.90
(30)	Ted Williams	6.00	3.00	1.75
(31)	Rudy York	2.00	1.00	.60
(32)	Cy Young	2.00	1.00	.60

1980 Exhibits

Following the purchase of the "remains" of the Exhibit Supply Co., by a collector in the late 1970s, this set of Exhibits was issued in 1980. The set utilized photos from earlier issues in the same 3-3/8" x 5-3/8" size. Each card carries a notation in white at the bottom, "An Exhibit Card 1980," to distinguish them from the older version. Sets could be purchased printed in sepia, red or blue, at $4.50 per set. A total of 5,000 sets were reported printed. The unnumbered cards are checklisted here alphabetically.

		NM	EX	VG
	Complete Set (32):	40.00	20.00	12.00
	Common Player:	2.00	1.00	.60
(1)	Johnny Antonelli	2.00	1.00	.60
(2)	Richie Ashburn	2.00	1.00	.60
(3)	Earl Averill	2.00	1.00	.60
(4)	Ernie Banks	4.00	2.00	1.25
(5)	Ewell Blackwell	2.00	1.00	.60
(6)	Lou Brock	2.00	1.00	.60
(7)	Dean Chance	2.00	1.00	.60
(8)	Roger Craig	2.00	1.00	.60
(9)	Lou Gehrig	20.00	10.00	6.00
(10)	Gil Hodges	2.00	1.00	.60
(11)	Jack Jensen	2.00	1.00	.60
(12)	Willie Keeler	2.00	1.00	.60
(13)	George Kell	2.00	1.00	.60
(14)	Alex Kellner	2.00	1.00	.60
(15)	Harmon Killebrew	2.00	1.00	.60
(16)	Dale Long	2.00	1.00	.60
(17)	Sal Maglie	2.00	1.00	.60
(18)	Roger Maris	4.00	2.00	1.25
(19)	Willie Mays	13.50	6.75	4.00
(20)	Minnie Minoso	2.00	1.00	.60
(21)	Stan Musial	10.00	5.00	3.00
(22)	Billy Pierce	2.00	1.00	.60
(23)	Jimmy Piersall	2.00	1.00	.60
(24)	Eddie Plank	2.00	1.00	.60
(25)	Pete Reiser	2.00	1.00	.60
(26)	Brooks Robinson	2.00	1.00	.60
(27)	Pete Runnels	2.00	1.00	.60
(28)	Herb Score	2.00	1.00	.60
(29)	Warren Spahn	2.00	1.00	.60
(30)	Billy Williams	2.00	1.00	.60
(31)	1948 Boston Braves Team	3.00	1.50	.90
(32)	1948 Cleveland Indians Team	3.00	1.50	.90

1980 Hall of Fame Exhibits

Following the purchase of the "remains" of the Exhibit Supply Co., by a collector in the late 1970s, this set of Exhibits was issued in 1980. The set utilizies photos from earlier issues in the same 3-3/8" x 5-3/8" size. Each card has a notation in white at the bottom, "An Exhibit Card 1980 Hall Of Fame," to distinguish them from the older version. Sets could be purchased printed in sepia, red or blue for $5. The unnumbered cards are checklisted here alphabetically.

		NM	EX	VG
	Complete Set (32):	25.00	12.50	7.50
	Common Player:	2.00	1.00	.60
(1)	Grover Cleveland Alexander	2.50	1.25	.70
(2)	Lou Boudreau	2.00	1.00	.60
(3)	Roger Bresnahan	2.00	1.00	.60
(4)	Roy Campanella	2.00	1.00	.60
(5)	Frank Chance	2.00	1.00	.60
(6)	Ty Cobb	5.00	2.50	1.50
(7)	Mickey Cochrane	2.00	1.00	.60
(8)	Dizzy Dean	2.50	1.25	.70
(9)	Joe DiMaggio	6.00	3.00	1.75
(10)	Bill Dickey	2.00	1.00	.60
(11)	Johnny Evers	2.00	1.00	.60
(12)	Jimmy Foxx	2.50	1.25	.70
(13)	Vernon Gomez	2.00	1.00	.60
(14)	Robert "Lefty" Grove	2.00	1.00	.60
(15)	Hank Greenberg	2.50	1.25	.70
(16)	Rogers Hornsby	2.00	1.00	.60
(17)	Carl Hubbell	2.00	1.00	.60
(18)	Hughie Jennings	2.00	1.00	.60
(19)	Walter Johnson	2.50	1.25	.70
(20)	Napoleon Lajoie	2.00	1.00	.60
(21)	Bob Lemon	2.00	1.00	.60
(22)	Mickey Mantle	12.00	6.00	3.50
(23)	Christy Mathewson	2.00	1.00	.60
(24)	Mel Ott	2.00	1.00	.60
(25)	Satchel Paige	2.50	1.25	.70
(26)	Jackie Robinson	4.00	2.00	1.25
(27)	Babe Ruth	9.00	4.50	2.75
(28)	Tris Speaker	2.00	1.00	.60
(29)	Joe Tinker	2.00	1.00	.60
(30)	Honus Wagner	3.00	1.50	.90
(31)	Ted Williams	4.00	2.00	1.25
(32)	Cy Young	2.50	1.25	.70

1990s Exhibit Card Unauthorized Reprints

Sometime during the 1990s (and possibly continuing today), unauthorized reprints of 16 popular Exhibit cards from the 1940s and 1950s were made. Besides printing anomalies on front resulting from re-screening genuine cards, the reprints are on the wrong weight (too thin) and color (too white on back) of cardboard. Collectors should use caution when purchasing any of the cards found in this group. Because the reprints are unauthorized, they have no collector value.

	Complete Set (16):
(1)	Hank Aaron
(2)	Yogi Berra
(3)	Roy Campanella
(4)	Whitey Ford/Pitching
(5)	Nelson Fox
(6)	Gil Hodges ("B"on cap.)
(7)	Mickey Mantle/Btg (Waist-up, "ck" in "Mickey" connected.)
(8)	Willie Mays/Btg
(9)	Stan Musial/Kneeling
(10)	Don Newcombe ("Dodgers" on jacket.)
(11)	Harold "Peewee" Reese (Ball partially visible.)
(12)	Duke Snider ("B" on cap.)
(13)	Warren Spahn ("B" on cap.)
(14)	Ted Williams (#9 not showing.)
(15)	1956 Brooklyn Dodgers
(16)	1956 N.Y. Yankees

1910 E-UNC Candy

Little is known about these 1910-era cards except that they appear to have been cut from a candy box. Printed in blue or red duo-tone and blank-backed, the cards measure about 2-3/4" per side. A 1-3/8" x 2-1/2" central image has a player photo with a diamond design around. Player identification is in a white strip at bottom.

		NM	EX	VG
	Common Player:	715.00	360.00	210.00
(1)	"Ty" Cobb	3,000	1,500	900.00
(2)	Eddie Collins	715.00	360.00	210.00
(3)	Johnny Evers	715.00	360.00	210.00
(4)	"Christy" Mathewson	1,425	715.00	430.00
(5)	"Honus" Wagner	1,800	900.00	540.00
(6)	"Cy" Young	1,425	715.00	430.00

1936 E-UNC Candy

These cards appear to be a secondary use of the center portions of the 1936 S and S Game cards, having the same player photos and data in a size which varies from about 1-3/4" to 1-7/8" wide and between 2-3/8" and 2-1/2" tall. These differ in that instead of the green backs found on most of the game cards, these have plain backs which are sometimes found with a rubber-stamped message to present the card for a free gift or candy bar. These stamps indicate the cards were used as a prize premium in an as yet unidentified candy company's promotion. With more than half of the S and S players known in this candy company version, it is not unreasonable to assume the checklists for both sets are the same.

		NM	EX	VG
	Complete Set (52):	3,000	1,500	900.00
	Common Player:	45.00	22.50	13.50
(1)	Luke Appling	90.00	45.00	25.00
(2)	Earl Averill	90.00	45.00	25.00
(3)	Zeke Bonura	45.00	22.50	13.50
(4)	Dolph Camilli	45.00	22.50	13.50
(5)	Ben Cantwell	45.00	22.50	13.50
(6)	Phil Cavaretta (Cavarretta)	45.00	22.50	13.50
(7)	Rip Collins	45.00	22.50	13.50
(8)	Joe Cronin	90.00	45.00	25.00
(9)	Frank Crosetti	60.00	30.00	18.00
(10)	Kiki Cuyler	90.00	45.00	25.00
(11)	Virgil Davis	45.00	22.50	13.50
(12)	Frank Demaree	45.00	22.50	13.50
(13)	Paul Derringer	45.00	22.50	13.50
(14)	Bill Dickey	120.00	60.00	35.00
(15)	Woody English	45.00	22.50	13.50
(16)	Fred Fitzsimmons	45.00	22.50	13.50
(17)	Richard Ferrell	90.00	45.00	25.00
(18)	Pete Fox	45.00	22.50	13.50
(19)	Jimmy Foxx	150.00	75.00	45.00
(20)	Larry French	45.00	22.50	13.50
(21)	Frank Frisch	100.00	50.00	30.00
(22)	August Galan	45.00	22.50	13.50
(23)	Chas. Gehringer	100.00	50.00	30.00
(24)	John Gill	45.00	22.50	13.50
(25)	Charles Grimm	45.00	22.50	13.50
(26)	Mule Haas	45.00	22.50	13.50
(27)	Stanley Hack	45.00	22.50	13.50
(28)	Bill Hallahan	45.00	22.50	13.50
(29)	Melvin Harder	45.00	22.50	13.50
(30)	Gabby Hartnett	90.00	45.00	25.00
(31)	Ray Hayworth	45.00	22.50	13.50
(32)	Ralston Hemsley	45.00	22.50	13.50
(33)	Bill Herman	90.00	45.00	25.00
(34)	Frank Higgins	45.00	22.50	13.50
(35)	Carl Hubbell	120.00	60.00	35.00
(36)	Bill Jurges	45.00	22.50	13.50
(37)	Vernon Kennedy	45.00	22.50	13.50
(38)	Chuck Klein	90.00	45.00	25.00
(39)	Mike Kreevich	45.00	22.50	13.50
(40)	Bill Lee	45.00	22.50	13.50
(41)	Jos. Medwick	90.00	45.00	25.00
(42)	Van Mungo	45.00	22.50	13.50
(43)	James O'Dea	45.00	22.50	13.50
(44)	Mel Ott	120.00	60.00	35.00
(45)	Rip Radcliff	45.00	22.50	13.50
(46)	Pie Traynor	90.00	45.00	25.00
(47)	Arky Vaughan (Vaughn)	90.00	45.00	25.00
(48)	Joe Vosmik	45.00	22.50	13.50

		NM	EX	VG
(49)	Lloyd Waner	90.00	45.00	25.00
(50)	Paul Waner	90.00	45.00	25.00
(51)	Lon Warneke	45.00	22.50	13.50
(52)	Floyd Young	45.00	22.50	13.50

1909-11 E90-1, E90-2, E90-3 American Caramel

(See 1909-11 American Caramel Co. for checklists, values.)

1908-09 E91 American Caramel Co.

(See 1908-09 American Caramel Co. for checklists, values.)

1909 E92 Nadja Caramels

(See 1909 Nadja Caramels.)

1910 E93 Standard Caramel Co.

(See 1910 Standard Caramel Co. for checklist, values.)

1911 E94

(See 1911 George Close Candy Co. for checklist and value data.)

1909 E95 Philadelphia Caramel

(See 1909 Philadelphia Caramel for checklist, price guide.)

1910 E96 Philadelphia Caramel

(See 1910 Philadelphia Caramel for checklist, values.)

1910 E98 "Set of 30"

This set of 30 subjects was issued in 1910 and is closely related to several other early candy issues. that are nearly identical. The cards measure 1-1/2" x 2-3/4" and feature color lithograph player pictures. The backs, printed in brown, contain a checklist of the set but no advertising or other information indicating the manufacturer. The set was designated E98 by the "American Card Catalog." While the cards are unnumbered, they are listed here according to the numbers on the back checklist. Some or all of the cards may be found with different colored backgrounds.

		NM	EX	VG
	Complete Set (30):	75,000	30,000	15,000
	Common Player:	1,500	480.00	240.00
(1)	Christy Matthewson (Mathewson)	7,500	3,000	1,500
(2)	John McGraw	2,500	860.00	430.00
(3)	Johnny Kling	1,500	480.00	240.00
(4)	Frank Chance	2,150	860.00	430.00
(5)	"Hans" Wagner	15,000	3,400	1,700
(6)	Fred Clarke	2,150	860.00	430.00
(7)	Roger Bresnahan	2,150	860.00	430.00
(8)	Hal Chase	2,000	800.00	400.00
(9)	Russ Ford	1,200	480.00	240.00
(10)	"Ty" Cobb	9,000	3,600	1,800
(11)	Hughey Jennings	2,150	860.00	430.00
(12)	Chief Bender	2,150	860.00	430.00
(13)	Ed Walsh	2,150	860.00	430.00
(14)	"Cy" Young (Picture actually Irv Young.)	9,000	3,000	1,500
(15)	Al Bridwell	1,500	480.00	240.00
(16)	Miner Brown	2,150	860.00	430.00
(17)	George Mullin	1,500	480.00	240.00
(18)	Chief Meyers	1,500	480.00	240.00
(19)	Hippo Vaughn	1,500	480.00	240.00
(20)	Red Dooin	1,500	480.00	300.00
(21)	Fred Tenny (Tenney)	1,500	480.00	240.00
(22)	Larry McLean	1,500	480.00	240.00
(23)	Nap Lajoie	5,000	2,500	1,000
(24)	Joe Tinker	2,150	860.00	430.00
(25)	Johnny Evers	2,150	860.00	430.00
(26)	Harry Davis	1,500	480.00	240.00
(27)	Eddie Collins	2,150	860.00	430.00
(28)	Bill Dahlen	1,500	480.00	240.00
(29)	"Connie" Mack	5,000	2,500	1,000
(30)	Jack Coombs	1,500	480.00	240.00

1909 E101 "Set of 50"

This 50-card set is closely related to the E92 issues by Nadja, Croft's, Dockman, etc. The fronts of the E101 cards are identical to the E92 set, but the back is "anonymous," containing no advertising or other information regarding the set's sponsor. The backs read simply "This card is one of a set of 50 Base Ball Players Prominent Members of National and American Leagues."

Vintage cards in Good condition are valued at about 50% of the Very Good values shown here. Cards in Fair condition are valued at 25% or less of VG.

Cobb, c.f. Detroit Am.

THIS CARD IS ONE OF A SET OF 50 Base Ball Players

PROMINENT MEMBERS OF NATIONAL AND AMERICAN LEAGUES,

		NM	EX	VG
	Complete Set (50):	75,000	30,000	15,000
	Common Player:	950.00	400.00	200.00
(1)	Jack Barry	950.00	400.00	200.00
(2)	Harry Bemis	950.00	400.00	200.00
(3)	Chief Bender (White hat.)	3,700	1,500	750.00
(4)	Chief Bender (Striped hat.)	4,200	1,700	850.00
(5)	Bill Bergen	950.00	400.00	200.00
(6)	Bob Bescher	950.00	400.00	200.00
(7)	Al Bridwell	1,500	600.00	300.00
(8)	Doc Casey	950.00	400.00	200.00
(9)	Frank Chance	3,700	1,500	750.00
(10)	Hal Chase	3,200	1,300	650.00
(11)	Ty Cobb	20,000	8,000	4,000
(12)	Eddie Collins	3,700	1,500	750.00
(13)	Sam Crawford	3,700	1,500	750.00
(14)	Harry Davis	1,500	600.00	300.00
(15)	Art Devlin	950.00	400.00	200.00
(16)	Wild Bill Donovan	950.00	400.00	200.00
(17)	Red Dooin	950.00	400.00	200.00
(18)	Mickey Doolan	950.00	400.00	200.00
(19)	Patsy Dougherty	950.00	400.00	200.00
(20)	Larry Doyle (With bat.)	950.00	400.00	200.00
(21)	Larry Doyle/Throwing	950.00	400.00	200.00
(22)	Johnny Evers	3,700	1,500	750.00
(23)	George Gibson	950.00	400.00	200.00
(24)	Topsy Hartsel	950.00	400.00	200.00
(25)	Fred Jacklitsch	950.00	400.00	200.00
(26)	Hugh Jennings	3,700	1,500	750.00
(27)	Red Kleinow	950.00	400.00	200.00
(28)	Otto Knabe	950.00	400.00	200.00
(29)	Jack Knight	950.00	400.00	200.00
(30)	Nap Lajoie	3,700	1,500	750.00
(31)	Hans Lobert	950.00	400.00	200.00
(32)	Sherry Magee	950.00	400.00	200.00
(33)	Christy Matthewson (Mathewson)	13,500	5,400	2,700
(34)	John McGraw	3,700	1,500	750.00
(35)	Larry McLean	950.00	400.00	200.00
(36)	Dots Miller/Btg	950.00	400.00	200.00
(37)	Dots Miller/Fielding	950.00	400.00	200.00
(38)	Danny Murphy	950.00	400.00	200.00
(39)	Bill O'Hara	950.00	400.00	200.00
(40)	Germany Schaefer	1,500	600.00	300.00
(41)	Admiral Schlei	950.00	400.00	200.00
(42)	Boss Schmidt	950.00	400.00	200.00
(43)	Johnny Seigle	1,500	600.00	300.00
(44)	Dave Shean	950.00	400.00	200.00
(45)	Boss Smith (Schmidt)	3,700	1,500	750.00
(46)	Joe Tinker	3,700	1,500	750.00
(47)	Honus Wagner/Btg	17,500	7,000	3,500
(48)	Honus Wagner/Throwing	17,500	7,000	3,500
(49)	Cy Young	12,500	5,000	2,500
(50)	Heinie Zimmerman	950.00	400.00	200.00

1909 E102 "Set of 25"

This Picture is one of a Set of Twenty-five BASE BALL PLAYERS, as follows:

COBB, Detroit.
EVERS, Chicago Nat.
DOYLE, New York Nat.
DOOIN, Phila. Nat.
COLLINS, Phila. Am.
LAJOIE, Cleveland.
MILLER, Pittsburg.
MAGEE, Phila. Nat.
TINKER, Chicago Nat.
SCHMIDT, Detroit.
LOBERT, Cincinnati.
WAGNER, Pittsburg.
MURPHY, Phila. Am.
BENDER, Phila. Am.
CRAWFORD, Detroit.
SCHAEFER, Washington.
MATTHEWSON, N. Y. Nat.
ZIMMERMAN, Chicago Nat.
CHASE, N. Y. Am.
BESCHER, Cincinnati.
SHEAN, Boston.
DOUGHERTY, Chicago Am.
DONOVAN, Detroit.
KLEINOW, New York Am.
KNABE, Philadelphia Nat.

Wagner, s.s. Pittsburg Nat'l

One of many similar early candy card sets, this set - designated as E102 in the American Card Catalog - was published no earlier than mid-1909. The producer of the set is unknown. Measuring approximately 1-1/2" x 2-3/4", the set is almost identical in design to the E101 set and other closely related issues. The set consists of 25 players, which are checklisted on the back of the card. Four of the players have been found in two variations, resulting in 29 different cards. Because there is no advertising on the cards, the set can best be identified by the words - "This Picture is one of a Set of Twenty-five Base Ball Players, as follows" - which appears on the back of each card.

		NM	EX	VG
	Complete Set (29):	55,000	22,000	11,000
	Common Player:	900.00	400.00	200.00
(1)	Chief Bender	1,500	600.00	300.00
(2)	Bob Bescher	900.00	400.00	200.00
(3)	Hal Chase	900.00	400.00	200.00
(4)	Ty Cobb	15,000	6,000	3,000
(5)	Eddie Collins	1,500	600.00	300.00
(6)	Sam Crawford	1,500	600.00	300.00
(7)	Wild Bill Donovan	900.00	400.00	200.00
(8)	Red Dooin	900.00	400.00	200.00
(9)	Patsy Dougherty	900.00	400.00	200.00
(10)	Larry Doyle/Btg	900.00	400.00	200.00
(11)	Larry Doyle/Throwing	900.00	400.00	200.00
(12)	Johnny Evers	1,500	600.00	300.00
(13)	Red Kleinow	900.00	400.00	200.00
(14)	Otto Knabe	900.00	400.00	200.00
(15)	Nap Lajoie	1,800	700.00	400.00
(16)	Hans Lobert	900.00	400.00	200.00
(17)	Sherry Magee	900.00	400.00	200.00
(18)	Christy Matthewson (Mathewson)	5,000	2,000	1,000
(19)	Dots Miller/Btg	900.00	400.00	200.00
(20)	Dots Miller/Fielding	1,650	650.00	325.00
(21)	Danny Murphy	900.00	400.00	200.00
(22)	Germany Schaefer	900.00	400.00	200.00
(23)	Boss Schmidt	900.00	400.00	200.00
(24)	Dave Shean	900.00	400.00	200.00
(25)	Boss Smith (Schmidt)	900.00	400.00	200.00
(26)	Joe Tinker	1,500	600.00	300.00
(27)	Honus Wagner/Btg	10,000	2,600	1,300
(28)	Honus Wagner/Throwing	10,000	2,600	1,300
(29)	Heinie Zimmerman	900.00	400.00	200.00

1910 E104 Nadja Caramels

(See 1910 Nadja Caramels.)

1915 E106 American Caramel Co.

(See 1915 American Caramel Co.)

1903-1904 E107 Type 1

W. GLEASON, 2 B, Phila., N

One of a hundred and fifty prominent Baseball players

Identified by the American Card Catalog as E107, this set is significant because it was one of the first major baseball card sets since the 1880s. It established the pattern for most of the tobacco and candy cards that followed over the next two decades. Measuring approximately 1-3/8" x 2-5/8", cards feature black-and-white player photos with the name, position and team in the bottom border. Most are found either with black back printing reading, "One of a hundred and fifty prominent Baseball players," or blank-backed, in about equal numbers. Also found are cards with a purple diagonal overprint stating "THE BREISCH-WILLIAMS CO." Type 1 consists of 147 known different players, plus 11 additional variations. The Type 2 cards are thicker than those of Type 1 and some (Keeler and Delehanty) cards have captions different from those found in Type 1. Values shown for EX and NM grades are mostly theoretical, as few cards are known in better than VG condition.

		NM	EX	VG
	Common Player:	10,200	4,100	2,000
	Breisch-Williams Overprint: 2-3X			
(1a)	John Anderson (St. Louis)	10,200	4,100	2,000
(1b)	John Anderson (New York)	10,200	4,100	2,000
(2)	Jimmy Barret (Barrett)	10,200	4,100	2,000
(3)	Ginger Beaumont	10,200	4,100	2,000
(4)	Fred Beck	10,200	4,100	2,000
(5)	Jake Beckley	30,000	15,000	9,000
(6)	Harry Bemis	10,200	4,100	2,000
(7)	Chief Bender	30,000	15,000	9,000
(8)	Bill Bernhard	10,200	4,100	2,000

(9)	Harry Bey (Bay)	10,200	4,100	2,000
(10)	Bill Bradley	10,200	4,100	2,000
(11)	Fritz Buelow	10,200	4,100	2,000
(12)	Nixey Callahan	10,200	4,100	2,000
(13)	Scoops Carey	10,200	4,100	2,000
(14)	Charley Carr	10,500	4,100	2,000
(15)	Bill Carrick	10,200	4,100	2,000
(16)	Doc Casey	10,500	4,100	2,000
(17)	Frank Chance	30,000	15,000	9,000
(18)	Jack Chesbro	30,000	15,000	9,000
(19)	Boileryard Clark (Clarke)	10,200	4,100	2,000
(20)	Fred Clarke	30,000	15,000	9,000
(21)	Jimmy Collins	30,000	15,000	9,000
(22)	Duff Cooley	10,200	4,100	2,000
(23)	Tommy Corcoran	10,200	4,100	2,000
(24)	Bill Coughlan (Coughlin)	10,200	4,100	2,000
(25)	Lou Criger	10,200	4,100	2,000
(26)	Lave Cross	10,200	4,100	2,000
(27)	Monte Cross	10,200	4,100	2,000
(28a)	Bill Dahlen (Brooklyn)	10,200	4,100	2,000
(28b)	Bill Dahlen (New York)	17,000	4,100	2,000
(29)	Tom Daly	10,200	4,100	2,000
(30)	George Davis	30,000	15,000	9,000
(31)	Harry Davis	10,200	4,100	2,000
(32)	Ed Delehanty (Delahanty)	30,000	15,000	9,000
(33)	Gene DeMont (DeMontreville)	10,200	4,100	2,000
(34a)	Pop Dillon (Detroit)	10,200	4,100	2,000
(34b)	Pop Dillon (Brooklyn)	16,200	8,100	4,800
(35)	Bill Dineen (Dinneen)	10,200	4,100	2,000
(36)	Red Donahue	10,200	4,100	2,000
(37)	Mike Donlin	10,200	4,100	2,000
(38)	Patsy Donovan	10,200	4,100	2,000
(39)	Patsy Dougherty (Photo actually Tom Hughes.)	10,200	4,100	2,000
(40)	Klondike Douglass	10,200	4,100	2,000
(41a)	Jack Doyle (Brooklyn)	10,200	4,100	2,000
(41b)	Jack Doyle (Philadelphia)	10,200	4,100	2,000
(42)	Lew Drill	10,200	4,100	2,000
(43)	Jack Dunn	10,200	4,100	2,000
(44a)	Kid Elberfield (Elberfeld) (Detroit)	10,200	4,100	2,000
(44b)	Kid Elberfield (Elberfeld) (No team designation.)	10,200	4,100	2,000
(45)	Duke Farrell	10,200	4,100	2,000
(46)	Hobe Ferris	10,200	4,100	2,000
(47)	Elmer Flick	30,000	15,000	9,000
(48)	Buck Freeman	10,200	4,100	2,000
(49)	Bill Freil (Friel)	10,200	4,100	2,000
(50)	Dave Fultz	10,200	4,100	2,000
(51)	Ned Garvin	10,200	4,100	2,000
(52)	Billy Gilbert	10,200	4,100	2,000
(53)	Harry Gleason	10,200	4,100	2,000
(54a)	Kid Gleason (New York)	10,200	4,100	2,000
(54b)	Kid Gleason (Philadelphia)	10,200	4,100	2,000
(55)	John Gochnauer (Gochnaur)	10,200	4,100	2,000
(56)	Danny Green	10,200	4,100	2,000
(57)	Noodles Hahn	10,200	4,100	2,000
(58)	Bill Hallman	10,200	4,100	2,000
(59)	Ned Hanlon	30,000	15,000	9,000
(60)	Dick Harley	10,200	4,100	2,000
(61)	Jack Harper	10,200	4,100	2,000
(62)	Topsy Hartsell (Hartsel)	10,200	4,100	2,000
(63)	Emmet Heidrick	10,200	4,100	2,000
(64)	Charlie Hemphill	10,200	4,100	2,000
(65)	Weldon Henley	10,200	4,100	2,000
(66)	Piano Legs Hickman	10,200	4,100	2,000
(67)	Harry Howell	10,200	4,100	2,000
(68)	Frank lasbel (Isbell)	10,200	4,100	2,000
(69)	Fred Jacklitzch (Jacklitsch)	10,200	4,100	2,000
(70)	Fielder Jones (Chicago)	10,200	4,100	2,000
(71)	Charlie Jones (Boston)	10,200	4,100	2,000
(72)	Addie Joss	30,000	15,000	9,000
(73)	Mike Kahoe	10,200	4,100	2,000
(74)	Wee Willie Keeler	30,000	15,000	9,000
(75)	Joe Kelley	30,000	15,000	9,000
(76)	Brickyard Kennedy	10,200	4,100	2,000
(77)	Frank Kitson	10,200	4,100	2,000
(78a)	Malachi Kittredge (Boston)	10,200	4,100	2,000
(78b)	Malachi Kittredge (Washington)	10,200	4,100	2,000
(79)	Candy LaChance	10,200	4,100	2,000
(80)	Nap Lajoie	30,000	15,000	9,000
(81)	Tommy Leach	10,200	4,100	2,000
(82a)	Watty Lee (Washington)	10,200	4,100	2,000
(82b)	Watty Lee (Pittsburg)	10,200	4,100	2,000
(83)	Sam Leever	10,200	4,100	2,000
(84)	Herman Long	10,200	4,100	2,000
(85a)	Billy Lush (Detroit)	10,200	4,100	2,000
(85b)	Billy Lush (Cleveland)	10,200	4,100	2,000
(86)	Christy Mathewson	78,000	39,000	24,000
(87)	Sport McAllister	10,200	4,100	2,000
(88)	Jack McCarthy	10,200	4,100	2,000
(89)	Barry McCormick	10,200	4,100	2,000
(90)	Ed McFarland (Chicago)	10,200	4,100	2,000
(91)	Herm McFarland (New York)	10,200	4,100	2,000
(92)	Joe McGinnity	30,000	15,000	9,000
(93)	John McGraw	30,000	15,000	9,000
(94a)	Deacon McGuire (Brooklyn)	10,200	4,100	2,100
(94b)	Deacon McGuire (New York)	17,000	4,100	2,000
(95)	Jock Menefee	10,200	4,100	2,000
(96)	Sam Mertes	10,200	4,100	2,000
(97)	Roscoe Miller (Picture actually George Mullin.)	10,200	4,100	2,000
(98)	Fred Mitchell	10,200	4,100	2,000
(99)	Earl Moore	10,200	4,100	2,000
(100)	Danny Murphy	10,200	4,100	2,000
(101)	Jack O'Connor	10,200	4,100	2,000
(102)	Al Orth	10,200	4,100	2,000
(103)	Dick Padden	10,200	4,100	2,000
(104)	Freddy Parent	10,200	4,100	2,000
(105)	Roy Patterson	10,200	4,100	2,000
(106)	Heinie Peitz	10,200	4,100	2,000
(107)	Deacon Phillipi (Phillippe)	10,200	4,100	2,000
(108)	Wiley Piatt	10,200	4,100	2,000
(109)	Ollie Pickering	10,200	4,100	2,000
(110)	Eddie Plank	78,000	39,000	24,000
(111a)	Ed Poole (Cincinnati)	10,200	4,100	2,000

(111b)	Ed Poole (Brooklyn)	10,200	4,100	2,000
(112a)	Jack Powell (St. Louis)	10,200	4,100	2,000
(112b)	Jack Powell (New York)	10,200	4,100	2,000
(113)	Mike Powers	10,200	4,100	2,000
(114)	Claude Ritchie (Ritchey)	10,200	4,100	2,000
(115)	Jimmy Ryan	10,200	4,100	2,000
(116)	Ossee Schreckengost	10,200	4,100	2,000
(117)	Kip Selbach	10,200	4,100	2,000
(118)	Socks Seybold	10,200	4,100	2,000
(119)	Jimmy Sheckard	10,200	4,100	2,000
(120)	Ed Siever	10,200	4,100	2,000
(121)	Harry Smith	10,200	4,100	2,000
(122)	Tully Sparks	10,200	4,100	2,000
(123)	Jake Stahl	10,200	4,100	2,000
(124)	Harry Steinfeldt	10,200	4,100	2,000
(125)	Sammy Strang	10,200	4,100	2,000
(126)	Willie Sudhoff	10,200	4,100	2,000
(127)	Joe Sugden	10,200	4,100	2,000
(128)	Billy Sullivan	10,200	4,100	2,000
(129)	Jack Taylor	10,200	4,100	2,000
(130)	Fred Tenney	10,200	4,100	2,000
(131)	Roy Thomas	10,200	4,100	2,000
(132a)	Jack Thoney (Cleveland)	10,200	4,100	2,000
(132b)	Jack Thoney (New York)	10,200	4,100	2,000
(133)	Jack Townsend	10,200	4,100	2,000
(134)	George Van Haltren	10,200	4,100	2,000
(135)	Rube Waddell	30,000	15,000	9,000
(136)	Honus Wagner	360,000	180,000	108,000
(137)	Bobby Wallace	30,000	15,000	9,000
(138)	Jack Warner	10,200	4,100	2,000
(139)	Jimmy Wiggs	10,200	4,100	2,000
(140)	Jimmy Williams	10,200	4,100	2,000
(141)	Vic Willis	30,000	15,000	9,000
(142)	Hooks Wiltse	10,200	4,100	2,000
(143)	George Winters (Winter)	10,200	4,100	2,000
(144)	Bob Wood	10,200	4,100	2,000
(145)	Joe Yeager	9,600	4,800	2,900
(146)	Cy Young	90,000	45,000	27,000
(147)	Chief Zimmer	10,200	4,100	2,000

1903-1904 E107 Type 2

DELAHANTY, Fielder, Wash.

Many of the Type 2 E107 cards seen to date do not measure the nominal 1-3/8" x 2-5/8" of the Type 1 cards, often having been cut more narrowly. Once thought to have been cut from an advertising piece, it now appears these were a regular production issue, as at least one specimen has been found with the purple diagonal overprint stating "THE BREISCH-WILLIAMS CO." Type 2 cards are printed on a thicker and more gray card stock than Type 1 and at least a few (Keeler and Delahanty) cards have captions different from those found in Type 1. NM values are principally theoretical as few cards in known in conditions better than EX.

		NM	EX	VG
Common Player:		9,000	3,600	1,800
(1)	Ed Delehanty (Delahanty)	50,000	20,000	10,000
(2)	Jack Doyle	9,000	3,600	1,800
(3)	Wee Willie Keeler	50,000	20,000	10,000
(4)	Nap Lajoie	50,000	20,000	10,000
(5)	Tommy Leach	9,000	3,600	1,800
(6)	Socks Seybold	9,000	3,600	1,800
(7)	Fred Tenney	9,000	3,600	1,800
(8)	Rube Waddell	50,000	20,000	10,000

1922 E120 American Caramel Series of 240

(See 1922 American Caramel Series of 240.)

1921-22 E121 American Caramel Series of 80/120

(See 1921 American Caramel Series of 80, Series of 120.)

1922 E122 American Caramel Series of 80

(See 1922 American Caramel Series of 80 for checklist, values.)

1910 E125 American Caramel Die-Cuts

(See 1910 American Caramel Die-Cuts for checklist, values.)

1927 E126 American Caramel Series of 60

(See 1927 American Caramel Series of 60.)

1927 E210 York Caramels

(See York Caramels.)

1921 E253 Oxford Confectionery

(See 1921 Oxford Confectionery.)

F

1961 F & M Bank Minnesota Twins Matchbook Covers

The star players on the inaugural Twins team are featured in this series of matchbook covers. The 1-1/2" x 4-7/16" matchbooks are printed in black, red and blue on white, and include a player portrait (players are shown wearing Washington Senators caps) and team logo on front. The sponsoring bank's picture and logo are on back. Inside the front cover are a few details about the player. Values shown are for complete but empty covers, with the striker surface intact. Complete matchbooks with matches bring about 2X the values quoted.

		NM	EX	VG
Complete Set (10):		70.00	35.00	20.00
Common Player:		7.50	3.75	2.25
(1)	Bob Allison	12.00	6.00	3.50
(2)	Earl Battey	9.00	4.50	2.75
(3)	Reno Bertoia	7.50	3.75	2.25
(4)	Billy Gardner	7.50	3.75	2.25
(5)	Lenny Green	7.50	3.75	2.25
(6)	Harmon Killebrew	20.00	10.00	6.00
(7)	Cookie Lavagetto	7.50	3.75	2.25
(8)	Jim Lemon	12.00	6.00	3.50
(9)	Camilo Pascual	12.00	6.00	3.50
(10)	Pedro Ramos	7.50	3.75	2.25

1962 F & M Bank Minnesota Twins Matchbook Covers

The '62 Twins are featured in this series of matchbook covers. The 1-1/2" x 4-7/16" matchbooks are printed in black, red and blue on white, and include a player portrait (new players who did not appear in the 1961 set are shown in Twins caps) and team logo on front. The sponsoring bank's picture and logo are on back. Inside the front cover are a few details about the player. Values shown are for complete but empty covers, with the striker surface intact. Complete matchbooks with matches bring about 2X the values quoted.

		NM	EX	VG
Complete Set (10):		75.00	37.00	22.00
Common Player:		7.50	3.75	2.25
(1)	Bob Allison	12.00	6.00	3.50
(2)	Earl Battey	9.00	4.50	2.75
(3)	Lenny Green	7.50	3.75	2.25
(4)	Jim Kaat	12.00	6.00	3.50
(5)	Harmon Killebrew	20.00	10.00	6.00
(6)	Jack Kralick	7.50	3.75	2.25
(7)	Jim Lemon	12.00	6.00	3.50
(8)	Camilo Pascual	12.00	6.00	3.50
(9)	Pedro Ramos	7.50	3.75	2.25
(10)	Zoilo Versalles	12.00	6.00	3.50

1966 Fairway Minnesota Twins

Color portraits of Twins favorites comprise this regional issue from a local grocery chain. The 8" x 10" glossy pictures have blue facsimile autographs on front and a white border. Black-and-white backs have a lengthy career summary, biographical data and full major and minor league stats. The unnumbered pictures are checklisted here in alphabetical order. There are no markings on the picture to identify the Fairway store.

		NM	EX	VG
Complete Set (17):		175.00	85.00	55.00
Common Player:		7.50	3.75	2.25
(1)	Bernie Allen	7.50	3.75	2.25
(2)	Bob Allison	13.50	6.75	4.00
(3)	Earl Battey	10.00	5.00	3.00
(4)	Jim Grant	7.50	3.75	2.25
(5)	Jimmie Hall	7.50	3.75	2.25
(6)	Jim Kaat	15.00	7.50	4.50
(7)	Harmon Killebrew	30.00	15.00	9.00
(8)	Jim Merritt	7.50	3.75	2.25
(9)	Don Mincher	7.50	3.75	2.25
(10)	Tony Oliva	15.00	7.50	4.50
(11)	Camilo Pascual	10.00	5.00	3.00
(12)	Jim Perry	10.00	5.00	3.00
(13)	Frank Quilici	7.50	3.75	2.25
(14)	Rich Rollins	7.50	3.75	2.25
(15)	Sandy Valdespino	7.50	3.75	2.25
(16)	Zoilo Versalles	13.50	6.75	4.00
(17)	Al Worthington	7.50	3.75	2.25

1964 Falstaff Beer

This 6" x 4" black-and-white postcard pictures the principal radio announcers for the CBS "Game of the Week" sponsored by the brewing company and was probably used to respond to fan requests for autographs. Facsimile signatures of the Hall of Famers are featured on front.

	NM	EX	VG
"Dizzy" Dean, "Pee Wee" Reese	20.00	10.00	6.00

1977 Family Fun Centers Padres

For 1977, Family Fun Centers, a chain of mini theme parks, took over sponsorship of the Padres annual issue of black-and-white player photos. The 5-1/2" x 8-1/2" photos have a large player pose at top-center, with his name and position below. In the bottom corners are team and sponsor logos. Backs have biographical data, complete stats and career highlights. Players are checklisted here alphabetically.

		NM	EX	VG
Complete Set (33):		90.00	45.00	27.50
Common Player:		4.50	2.25	1.25
(1)	Billy Almon	4.50	2.25	1.25
(2)	Joey Amalfitano	4.50	2.25	1.25
(3)	Tucker Ashford	4.50	2.25	1.25
(4)	Mike Champion	4.50	2.25	1.25
(5)	Roger Craig	4.50	2.25	1.25
(6)	Alvin Dark	4.50	2.25	1.25
(7)	Bob Davis	4.50	2.25	1.25
(8)	Rollie Fingers	12.50	6.25	3.75
(9)	Dave Freisleben	4.50	2.25	1.25
(10)	Tom Griffin	4.50	2.25	1.25
(11)	George Hendrick	4.50	2.25	1.25
(12)	Mike Ivie	4.50	2.25	1.25
(13)	Randy Jones	4.50	2.25	1.25
(14)	John McNamara	4.50	2.25	1.25
(15)	Bob Owchinko	4.50	2.25	1.25
(16)	Merv Rettenmund	4.50	2.25	1.25
(17)	Gene Richards	4.50	2.25	1.25
(18)	Dave Roberts	4.50	2.25	1.25
(19)	Jackie Robinson (Blank back.)	25.00	12.50	7.50
(20)	Rick Sawyer	4.50	2.25	1.25
(21)	Pat Scanlon	4.50	2.25	1.25
(22)	Bob Shirley	4.50	2.25	1.25
(23)	Bob Skinner	4.50	2.25	1.25
(24)	Dan Spillner	4.50	2.25	1.25
(25)	Gary Sutherland	4.50	2.25	1.25
(26)	Gene Tenace	4.50	2.25	1.25
(27)	Dave Tomlin	4.50	2.25	1.25
(28)	Jerry Turner	4.50	2.25	1.25
(29)	Bobby Valentine	4.50	2.25	1.25
(30)	Dave Wehrmeister	4.50	2.25	1.25
(31)	Whitey Wietelmann	4.50	2.25	1.25
(32)	Don Williams	4.50	2.25	1.25
(33)	Dave Winfield	15.00	7.50	4.50

1978 Family Fun Centers Angels

The players, manager and coaches of the '78 Angels are featured in this set of 3-1/2" x 5-1/2" sepia-tone cards. The unnumbered cards are checklisted alphabetically.

		NM	EX	VG
Complete Set (38):		90.00	45.00	25.00
Common Player:		2.50	1.25	.70
(1)	Don Aase	2.50	1.25	.70
(2)	Mike Barlow	2.50	1.25	.70
(3)	Don Baylor	3.50	1.75	1.00
(4)	Lyman Bostock	2.50	1.25	.70
(5)	Ken Brett	2.50	1.25	.70
(6)	Dave Chalk	2.50	1.25	.70
(7)	Bob Clear	2.50	1.25	.70
(8)	Brian Downing	2.50	1.25	.70
(9)	Ron Fairly	2.50	1.25	.70
(10)	Gil Flores	2.50	1.25	.70
(11)	Dave Frost	2.50	1.25	.70
(12)	Dave Garcia	2.50	1.25	.70
(13)	Bobby Grich	2.50	1.25	.70
(14)	Tom Griffin	2.50	1.25	.70
(15)	Marv Grissom	2.50	1.25	.70
(16)	Ike Hampton	2.50	1.25	.70
(17)	Paul Hartzell	2.50	1.25	.70
(18)	Terry Humphrey	2.50	1.25	.70
(19)	Ron Jackson	2.50	1.25	.70
(20)	Chris Knapp	2.50	1.25	.70
(21)	Ken Landreaux	2.50	1.25	.70
(22)	Carney Lansford	2.50	1.25	.70
(23)	Dave LaRoche	2.50	1.25	.70
(24)	John McNamara	2.50	1.25	.70
(25)	Dyar Miller	2.50	1.25	.70
(26)	Rick Miller	2.50	1.25	.70
(27)	Balor Moore	2.50	1.25	.70
(28)	Rance Mulliniks	2.50	1.25	.70
(29)	Floyd Rayford	2.50	1.25	.70
(30)	Jimmie Reese	4.00	2.00	1.25
(31)	Merv Rettenmund	2.50	1.25	.70
(32)	Joe Rudi	2.50	1.25	.70
(33)	Nolan Ryan	45.00	22.50	13.50
(34)	Bob Skinner	2.50	1.25	.70
(35)	Tony Solaita	2.50	1.25	.70
(36)	Frank Tanana	2.50	1.25	.70
(37)	Dickie Thon	2.50	1.25	.70
---	Header Card	.70	.35	.20

1978 Family Fun Centers Padres

In conjunction with the Padres' hosting of the 1978 All-Star Game, Family Fun Centers issued this set of cards covering the players, coaches, announcers and even the owner. The 3-1/2" x 5-1/2" cards have a plaque look with a 3" x 3-1/4" posed color photo set on a wood background. The player's name is in a gold box at bottom, with the team and sponsor's logos in between. Backs are in black-and-white with a player portrait photo and facsimile autograph at bottom, a few biographical details and career stats at top and an essay in the middle titled, "My Greatest Thrill in Baseball." A uniform number appears at top-left. The set is checklisted here in alphabetical order.

		NM	EX	VG
Complete Set (39):		75.00	37.50	22.50
Common Player:		3.00	1.50	.90
(1)	Bill Almon	3.00	1.50	.90
(2)	Tucker Ashford	3.00	1.50	.90
(3)	Chuck Baker	3.00	1.50	.90
(4)	Dave Campbell/Announcer	3.00	1.50	.90
(5)	Mike Champion	3.00	1.50	.90
(6)	Jerry Coleman/Announcer	3.00	1.50	.90
(7)	Roger Craig	3.00	1.50	.90
(8)	John D'Acquisto	3.00	1.50	.90
(9)	Bob Davis	3.00	1.50	.90
(10)	Chuck Estrada	3.00	1.50	.90
(11)	Rollie Fingers	9.00	4.50	2.75
(12)	Dave Freisleben	3.00	1.50	.90
(13)	Oscar Gamble	3.00	1.50	.90
(14)	Fernando Gonzalez	3.00	1.50	.90
(15)	Billy Herman	4.00	2.00	1.25
(16)	Randy Jones	3.00	1.50	.90
(17)	Ray Kroc/Owner	5.00	2.50	1.50
(18)	Mark Lee	3.00	1.50	.90
(19)	Mickey Lolich	3.00	1.50	.90
(20)	Bob Owchinko	3.00	1.50	.90
(21)	Broderick Perkins	3.00	1.50	.90
(22)	Gaylord Perry	9.00	4.50	2.75
(23)	Eric Rasmussen	3.00	1.50	.90
(24)	Don Reynolds	3.00	1.50	.90
(25)	Gene Richards	3.00	1.50	.90
(26)	Dave Roberts	3.00	1.50	.90
(27)	Phil Roof	3.00	1.50	.90
(28)	Bob Shirley	3.00	1.50	.90
(29)	Ozzie Smith	60.00	30.00	18.00
(30)	Dan Spillner	3.00	1.50	.90
(31)	Rick Sweet	3.00	1.50	.90
(32)	Gene Tenace	3.00	1.50	.90
(33)	Derrel Thomas	3.00	1.50	.90
(34)	Jerry Turner	3.00	1.50	.90
(35)	Dave Wehrmeister	3.00	1.50	.90
(36)	Whitey Wietelmann	3.00	1.50	.90
(37)	Don Williams	3.00	1.50	.90
(38)	Dave Winfield	15.00	7.50	4.50
(39)	All-Star Game	3.00	1.50	.90

1979 Family Fun Centers Padres

Each card features a posed color photo against a woodgrain border. Fronts have player identification, the Padres mascot and the logo of one of the sponsors - Family Fun Centers or Dean's Photo Service. Black-and-white backs have player personal data, major and minor league stats, a notation to "COLLECT ALL 36 CARDS" and a list of distribution dates. The 3-1/4" x 4-3/4" cards were issued in 12-1/2" x 9-1/2" perforated panels of six cards plus a coupon from each sponsor. Panels were given out one per month May through September at promotional games, making the set difficult to complete. Cards #25-30 have not been confirmed as issued.

		NM	EX	VG
Complete Set (30):		60.00	30.00	18.00
Common Player:		3.00	1.50	.90
1	Roger Craig	3.00	1.50	.90
2	John D'Acquisto	3.00	1.50	.90
3	Ozzie Smith	25.00	12.50	7.50
4	KGB Chicken	4.00	2.00	1.25
5	Gene Richards	3.00	1.50	.90
6	Jerry Turner	3.00	1.50	.90
7	Bob Owchinko	3.00	1.50	.90
8	Gene Tenace	3.00	1.50	.90
9	Whitey Wietelmann	3.00	1.50	.90
10	Bill Almon	3.00	1.50	.90
11	Dave Winfield	15.00	7.50	4.50
12	Mike Hargrove	3.00	1.50	.90
13	Fernando Gonzalez	3.00	1.50	.90
14	Barry Evans	3.00	1.50	.90
15	Steve Mura	3.00	1.50	.90
16	Chuck Estrada	3.00	1.50	.90
17	Bill Fahey	3.00	1.50	.90
18	Gaylord Perry	6.00	3.00	1.75
19	Dan Briggs	3.00	1.50	.90
20	Billy Herman	4.00	2.00	1.25
21	Mickey Lolich	3.00	1.50	.90
22	Broderick Perkins	3.00	1.50	.90
23	Fred Kendall	3.00	1.50	.90
24	Rollie Fingers	6.00	3.00	1.75
31	Bobby Tolan	3.00	1.50	.90
32	Doug Rader	3.00	1.50	.90
33	Dave Campbell	3.00	1.50	.90
34	Jay Johnstone	3.00	1.50	.90
35	Mark Lee	3.00	1.50	.90
36	Bob Shirley	3.00	1.50	.90

1980 Family Fun Centers Padres

Six Padres players or staff are featured on these 13" x 10" or 12-1/2" x 9-1/2" coupon sheets. At the right end of each glossy paper sheet is a group of coupons and advertising for the recreation centers, printed in black, yellow and green. At left are six photos. Each of the 3" x 4" photos has a color player pose. At either top or bottom, depending on placement on the sheet, is the player name in black, "FAMILY FUN CENTER" in green and a red building logo. Backs are blank and the sheets are not perforated.

	NM	EX	VG
Complete Set (7):	80.00	40.00	24.00
Common Sheet:	7.00	3.50	2.00

		NM	EX	VG
(1)	Kurt Bevacqua, Dave Cash, Paul Dade, Rollie Fingers, Don Williams, Dave Winfield	20.00	10.00	6.00
(2)	Ed Brinkman, Dave Edwards, Jack Krol, Luis Salazar, Craig Stimac, John Urrea	7.00	3.50	2.00
(3)	Jerry Coleman, John D'Acquisto, Bill Fahey, Randy Jones, Gene Richards, Ozzie Smith	30.00	15.00	9.00
(4)	Dave Campbell, Juan Eichelberger, Barry Evans, Bobby Tolan, Jerry Turner, Rick Wise	7.00	3.50	2.00
(5)	John Curtis, Al Heist, Gary Lucas, Willie Montanez, Aurelio Rodriguez, Gene Tenace	7.00	3.50	2.00
(6)	Eddie Doucette, Chuck Estrada, Tim Flannery, Eric Rasmussen, Bob Shirley, San Diego Chicken	10.00	5.00	3.00
(7)	Von Joshua, Fred Kendall, Dennis Kinney, Jerry Mumphrey, Steve Mura, Dick Phillips	7.00	3.50	2.00

1916 Famous and Barr Clothiers

The advertisement for this St. Louis clothier is among the most commonly found on the backs of this 200-player set that parallels the more common M101-5 Blank Backs issue. Famous and Barr was one of many regional advertisers to use the cards for local promotions. Premiums over the same cards in M101-5 Blank Backs are modest for most players, but can be substantial for the top stars. The cards are printed in black-and-white and measure 1-5/8" x 3".

		NM	EX	VG
Complete Set (200):		143,750	57,500	28,750
Common Player:		125.00	50.00	25.00
1	Babe Adams	190.00	65.00	25.00
2	Sam Agnew	125.00	50.00	25.00
3	Eddie Ainsmith	125.00	50.00	25.00
4	Grover Alexander	2,065	825.00	415.00
5	Leon Ames	125.00	50.00	25.00
6	Jimmy Archer	125.00	50.00	25.00
7	Jimmy Austin	125.00	50.00	25.00
8	J. Franklin Baker	720.00	290.00	145.00
9	Dave Bancroft	720.00	290.00	145.00
10	Jack Barry	125.00	50.00	25.00
11	Zinn Beck	125.00	50.00	25.00
12	Lute Boone	125.00	50.00	25.00
13	Joe Benz	125.00	50.00	25.00
14	Bob Bescher	125.00	50.00	25.00
15	Al Betzel	125.00	50.00	25.00
16	Roger Bresnahan	720.00	290.00	145.00
17	Eddie Burns	125.00	50.00	25.00
18	Geo. J. Burns	125.00	50.00	25.00
19	Joe Bush	125.00	50.00	25.00
20	Owen Bush	125.00	50.00	25.00
21	Art Butler	125.00	50.00	25.00
22	Bobbie Byrne	125.00	50.00	25.00
23a	Forrest Cady (May not exist.)			
23b	Mordecai Brown	720.00	290.00	145.00
24	Jimmy Callahan	125.00	50.00	25.00
25	Ray Caldwell	125.00	50.00	25.00
26	Max Carey	720.00	290.00	145.00
27	George Chalmers	125.00	50.00	25.00
28	Frank Chance	720.00	290.00	145.00
29	Ray Chapman	155.00	65.00	30.00
30	Larry Cheney	125.00	50.00	25.00
31	Eddie Cicotte	720.00	290.00	145.00
32	Tom Clarke	125.00	50.00	25.00
33	Eddie Collins	720.00	290.00	145.00
34	"Shauno" Collins	125.00	50.00	25.00
35	Charles Comisky (Comiskey)	720.00	290.00	145.00
36	Joe Connolly	125.00	50.00	25.00
37	Luther Cook	125.00	50.00	25.00
38	Jack Coombs	125.00	50.00	25.00
39	Dan Costello	125.00	50.00	25.00
40	Harry Coveleskie (Coveleski)	125.00	50.00	25.00
41	Gavvy Cravath	125.00	50.00	25.00
42	Sam Crawford	720.00	290.00	145.00
43	Jean Dale	125.00	50.00	25.00
44	Jake Daubert	125.00	50.00	25.00
45	Geo. A. Davis Jr.	125.00	50.00	25.00
46	Charles Deal	125.00	50.00	25.00
47	Al Demaree	125.00	50.00	25.00
48	William Doak	125.00	50.00	25.00
49	Bill Donovan	125.00	50.00	25.00
50	Charles Dooin	125.00	50.00	25.00
51	Mike Doolan	125.00	50.00	25.00
52	Larry Doyle	125.00	50.00	25.00
53	Jean Dubuc	125.00	50.00	25.00
54	Oscar Dugey	125.00	50.00	25.00
55	Johnny Evers	720.00	290.00	145.00
56	Urban Faber	720.00	290.00	145.00
57	"Hap" Felsch	1,000	400.00	200.00
58	Bill Fischer	125.00	50.00	25.00
59	Ray Fisher	125.00	50.00	25.00
60	Max Flack	125.00	50.00	25.00
61	Art Fletcher	125.00	50.00	25.00
62	Eddie Foster	125.00	50.00	25.00
63	Jacques Fournier	125.00	50.00	25.00
64	Del Gainer (Gainor)	125.00	50.00	25.00
65	Larry Gardner	125.00	50.00	25.00
66	Joe Gedeon	125.00	50.00	25.00
67	Gus Getz	125.00	50.00	25.00
68	Geo. Gibson	125.00	50.00	25.00
69	Wilbur Good	125.00	50.00	25.00
70	Hank Gowdy	125.00	50.00	25.00
71	John Graney	125.00	50.00	25.00
72	Tom Griffith	125.00	50.00	25.00
73	Heinie Groh	125.00	50.00	25.00
74	Earl Hamilton	125.00	50.00	25.00
75	Bob Harmon	125.00	50.00	25.00
76	Roy Hartzell	125.00	50.00	25.00
77	Claude Hendrix	125.00	50.00	25.00
78	Olaf Henriksen	125.00	50.00	25.00
79	John Henry	125.00	50.00	25.00
80	"Buck" Herzog	125.00	50.00	25.00
81	Hugh High	125.00	50.00	25.00
82	Dick Hoblitzell	125.00	50.00	25.00
83	Harry Hooper	720.00	290.00	145.00
84	Ivan Howard	125.00	50.00	25.00
85	Miller Huggins	720.00	290.00	145.00
86	Joe Jackson	25,000	10,000	5,000
87	William James	125.00	50.00	25.00
88	Harold Janvrin	125.00	50.00	25.00
89	Hugh Jennings	720.00	290.00	145.00
90	Walter Johnson	2,190	875.00	440.00
91	Fielder Jones	125.00	50.00	25.00
92	Bennie Kauff	125.00	50.00	25.00
93	Wm. Killefer Jr.	125.00	50.00	25.00
94	Ed. Konetchy	125.00	50.00	25.00
95	Napoleon Lajoie	720.00	290.00	145.00
96	Jack Lapp	125.00	50.00	25.00
97a	John Lavan (Correct spelling.)	125.00	50.00	25.00
97b	John Lavin (Incorrect spelling.)(May not exist.)			
98	Jimmy Lavender	125.00	50.00	25.00
99	"Nemo" Leibold	125.00	50.00	25.00
100	H.B. Leonard	125.00	50.00	25.00
101	Duffy Lewis	125.00	50.00	25.00
102	Hans Lobert	125.00	50.00	25.00
103	Tom Long	125.00	50.00	25.00
104	Fred Luderus	125.00	50.00	25.00
105	Connie Mack	720.00	290.00	145.00
106	Lee Magee	125.00	50.00	25.00
107	Al. Mamaux	125.00	50.00	25.00
108	Leslie Mann	125.00	50.00	25.00
109	"Rabbit" Maranville	720.00	290.00	145.00
110	Rube Marquard	720.00	290.00	145.00
111	Armando Marsans	155.00	65.00	30.00
112	J. Erskine Mayer	155.00	65.00	30.00
113	George McBride	125.00	50.00	25.00
114	John J. McGraw	720.00	290.00	145.00
115	Jack McInnis	125.00	50.00	25.00
116	Fred Merkle	125.00	50.00	25.00
117	Chief Meyers	125.00	50.00	25.00
118	Clyde Milan	125.00	50.00	25.00
119	Otto Miller	125.00	50.00	25.00
120	Willie Mitchel (Mitchell)	125.00	50.00	25.00
121	Fred Mollwitz	125.00	50.00	25.00
122	J. Herbert Moran	125.00	50.00	25.00
123	Pat Moran	125.00	50.00	25.00
124	Ray Morgan	125.00	50.00	25.00
125	Geo. Moriarty	125.00	50.00	25.00
126	Guy Morton	125.00	50.00	25.00
127	Ed. Murphy (Photo actually Danny Murphy.)	125.00	50.00	25.00
128	John Murray	125.00	50.00	25.00
129	"Hy" Myers	125.00	50.00	25.00
130	J.A. Niehoff	125.00	50.00	25.00
131	Leslie Nunamaker	125.00	50.00	25.00
132	Rube Oldring	125.00	50.00	25.00
133	Oliver O'Mara	125.00	50.00	25.00
134	Steve O'Neill	125.00	50.00	25.00
135	"Dode" Paskert	125.00	50.00	25.00
136	Roger Peckinpaugh (Photo actually Gavvy Cravath.)	125.00	50.00	25.00
137	E.J. Pfeffer (Photo actually Jeff Pfeffer.)	125.00	50.00	25.00
138	Geo. Pierce (Pearce)	125.00	50.00	25.00
139	Walter Pipp	125.00	50.00	25.00
140	Derril Pratt (Derrill)	125.00	50.00	25.00
141	Bill Rariden	125.00	50.00	25.00
142	Eppa Rixey	720.00	290.00	145.00
143	Davey Robertson	125.00	50.00	25.00
144	Wilbert Robinson	720.00	290.00	145.00
145	Bob Roth	125.00	50.00	25.00
146	Ed. Roush	720.00	290.00	145.00
147	Clarence Rowland	125.00	50.00	25.00
148	"Nap" Rucker	125.00	50.00	25.00
149	Dick Rudolph	125.00	50.00	25.00
150	Reb Russell	125.00	50.00	25.00
151	Babe Ruth	68,750	27,500	13,750
152	Vic Saier	125.00	50.00	25.00
153	"Slim" Sallee	125.00	50.00	25.00
154	"Germany" Schaefer	125.00	50.00	25.00
155	Ray Schalk	720.00	290.00	145.00
156	Walter Schang	125.00	50.00	25.00
157	Chas. Schmidt	125.00	50.00	25.00
158	Frank Schulte	125.00	50.00	25.00
159	Jim Scott	125.00	50.00	25.00

		NM	EX	VG
160	Everett Scott	125.00	50.00	25.00
161	Tom Seaton	125.00	50.00	25.00
162	Howard Shanks	125.00	50.00	25.00
163	Bob Shawkey (Photo actually Jack McInnis.)	125.00	50.00	25.00
164	Ernie Shore	125.00	50.00	25.00
165	Burt Shotton	125.00	50.00	25.00
166	George Sisler	720.00	290.00	145.00
167	J. Carlisle Smith	125.00	50.00	25.00
168	Fred Snodgrass	125.00	50.00	25.00
169	Geo. Stallings	125.00	50.00	25.00
170	Oscar Stanage (Photo actually Chas. Schmidt.)	125.00	50.00	25.00
171	Charles Stengel	815.00	325.00	165.00
172	Milton Stock	125.00	50.00	25.00
173	Amos Strunk (Photo actually Olaf Henriksen.)	125.00	50.00	25.00
174	Billy Sullivan	125.00	50.00	25.00
175	Chas. Tesreau	125.00	50.00	25.00
176	Jim Thorpe	13,750	5,500	2,750
177	Joe Tinker	720.00	290.00	145.00
178	Fred Toney	125.00	50.00	25.00
179	Terry Turner	125.00	50.00	25.00
180	Jim Vaughn	125.00	50.00	25.00
181	Bob Veach	125.00	50.00	25.00
182	James Voix	125.00	50.00	25.00
183	Oscar Vitt	125.00	50.00	25.00
184	Hans Wagner	5,000	1,065	530.00
185	Clarence Walker (Photo not Walker.)	125.00	50.00	25.00
186	Zach Wheat	720.00	290.00	145.00
187	Ed. Walsh	720.00	290.00	145.00
188	Buck Weaver	720.00	290.00	145.00
189	Carl Weilman	125.00	50.00	25.00
190	Geo. Whitted	125.00	50.00	25.00
191	Fred Williams	125.00	50.00	25.00
192	Art Wilson	125.00	50.00	25.00
193	J. Owen Wilson	125.00	50.00	25.00
194	Ivy Wingo	125.00	50.00	25.00
195	"Mel" Wolfgang	125.00	50.00	25.00
196	Joe Wood	220.00	90.00	45.00
197	Steve Yerkes	125.00	50.00	25.00
198	Rollie Zeider	125.00	50.00	25.00
199	Heiny Zimmerman	125.00	50.00	25.00
200	Ed. Zwilling	125.00	50.00	25.00

1906 Fan Craze - American League

One of the earliest 20th Century baseball card sets, this issue from the Fan Craze Co. of Cincinnati was designed as a deck of playing cards and was intended to be used as a baseball table game. Separate sets were issued for the National League, with backs printed in red, and the American League, which are blue-backed. Both sets feature black-and-white player portraits in an oval vignette with the player's name and team below. The top of the card indicates one of many various baseball plays, such as "Single," "Out at First," "Strike," "Stolen Base," etc. The unnumbered cards measure 2-1/2" x 3-1/2". An ad card identifies the set as "An Artistic Constellation of Great Stars." Sears sold the set for 48 cents, postpaid.

		NM	EX	VG
	Complete Set (51):	8,250	4,125	2,475
	Complete Boxed Set:	9,350	4,675	2,750
	Common Player:	90.00	45.00	25.00
(1)	Nick Altrock	110.00	55.00	35.00
(2)	Jim Barrett	90.00	45.00	25.00
(3)	Harry Bay	90.00	45.00	25.00
(4)	Albert Bender	330.00	165.00	100.00
(5)	Bill Bernhardt	90.00	45.00	25.00
(6)	W. Bradley	90.00	45.00	25.00
(7)	Jack Chesbro	330.00	165.00	100.00
(8)	Jimmy Collins	330.00	165.00	100.00
(9)	Sam Crawford	330.00	165.00	100.00
(10)	Lou Criger	90.00	45.00	25.00
(11)	Lave Cross	90.00	45.00	25.00
(12)	Monte Cross	90.00	45.00	25.00
(13)	Harry Davis	90.00	45.00	25.00
(14)	Bill Dinneen	90.00	45.00	25.00
(15)	Pat (Bill) Donovan	90.00	45.00	25.00
(16)	Pat Dougherty	90.00	45.00	25.00
(17)	Norman Elberfield (Elberfeld)	90.00	45.00	25.00
(18)	Hoke Ferris (Hobe)	90.00	45.00	25.00
(19)	Elmer Flick	330.00	165.00	100.00
(20)	Buck Freeman	90.00	45.00	25.00
(21)	Fred Glade	90.00	45.00	25.00
(22)	Clark Griffith	330.00	165.00	100.00
(23)	Charley Hickman	90.00	45.00	25.00
(24)	Wm. Holmes	90.00	45.00	25.00
(25)	Harry Howell	90.00	45.00	25.00
(26)	Frank Isbel (Isbell)	90.00	45.00	25.00

		NM	EX	VG
(27)	Albert Jacobson	90.00	45.00	25.00
(28)	Ban Johnson	330.00	165.00	100.00
(29)	Fielder Jones	90.00	45.00	25.00
(30)	Adrian Joss	330.00	165.00	100.00
(31)	Billy Keeler	330.00	165.00	100.00
(32)	Napoleon Lajoie	330.00	165.00	100.00
(33)	Connie Mack	330.00	165.00	100.00
(34)	Jimmy McAleer	90.00	45.00	25.00
(35)	Jim McGuire	90.00	45.00	25.00
(36)	Earl Moore	90.00	45.00	25.00
(37)	George Mullen (Mullin)	90.00	45.00	25.00
(38)	Billy Owen (Frank Owens)	90.00	45.00	25.00
(39)	Fred Parent	90.00	45.00	25.00
(40)	Case Patten	90.00	45.00	25.00
(41)	Ed Plank	550.00	275.00	165.00
(42)	Ossie Schreckengost	90.00	45.00	25.00
(43)	Jake Stahl	90.00	45.00	25.00
(44)	Fred (George) Stone	90.00	45.00	25.00
(45)	Wm. Sudhoff	90.00	45.00	25.00
(46)	Roy (Terry) Turner	90.00	45.00	25.00
(47)	G.E. Waddell	330.00	165.00	100.00
(48)	Bob Wallace	330.00	165.00	100.00
(49)	G. Harris White	90.00	45.00	25.00
(50)	Geo. Winters (Winter)	90.00	45.00	25.00
(51)	Cy Young	1,320	660.00	395.00

1906 Fan Craze - National League

Identical in size and format to the American League set of two years previous, this set of unnumbered cards was issued by the Fan Craze Co. of Cincinnati in 1906 and was designed like a deck of playing cards. The cards were intended to be used in playing a baseball table game. The National League cards are printed with red backs and black-and-white player photos on front. Sears sold the set for 48 cents postpaid.

		NM	EX	VG
	Complete Set (54):	11,000	5,500	3,300
	Complete Boxed Set:	17,600	8,800	5,225
	Common Player:	65.00	35.00	20.00
(1)	Leon Ames	65.00	35.00	20.00
(2)	Clarence Beaumont	65.00	35.00	20.00
(3)	Jake Beckley	330.00	165.00	100.00
(4)	Billy Bergen	65.00	35.00	20.00
(5)	Roger Bresnahan	330.00	165.00	100.00
(6)	George Brown (Browne)	65.00	35.00	20.00
(7)	Mordacai Brown	330.00	165.00	100.00
(8)	Jas. Casey	65.00	35.00	20.00
(9)	Frank Chance	330.00	165.00	100.00
(10)	Fred Clarke	330.00	165.00	100.00
(11)	Thos. Corcoran	65.00	35.00	20.00
(12)	Bill Dahlen	65.00	35.00	20.00
(13)	Mike Donlin	65.00	35.00	20.00
(14)	Charley Dooin	65.00	35.00	20.00
(15)	Mickey Doolin (Doolan)	65.00	35.00	20.00
(16)	Hugh Duffy	330.00	165.00	100.00
(17)	John E. Dunleavy	65.00	35.00	20.00
(18)	Bob Ewing	65.00	35.00	20.00
(19)	"Chick" Fraser	65.00	35.00	20.00
(20)	J. Edward (Edward H.) Hanlon	330.00	165.00	100.00
(21)	G.E. Howard	65.00	35.00	20.00
(22)	Miller Huggins	330.00	165.00	100.00
(23)	Joseph Kelley	330.00	165.00	100.00
(24)	John Kling	65.00	35.00	20.00
(25)	Tommy Leach	65.00	35.00	20.00
(26)	Harry Lumley	65.00	35.00	20.00
(27)	Carl Lundgren	65.00	35.00	20.00
(28)	Bill Maloney	65.00	35.00	20.00
(29)	Dan McGann	65.00	35.00	20.00
(30)	Joe McGinnity	330.00	165.00	100.00
(31)	John J. McGraw	330.00	165.00	100.00
(32)	Harry McIntire (McIntyre)	65.00	35.00	20.00
(33)	Charley Nichols	550.00	275.00	165.00
(34)	Mike O'Neil (O'Neill)	65.00	35.00	20.00
(35)	Orville (Orval) Overall	65.00	35.00	20.00
(36)	Frank Pfeffer	65.00	35.00	20.00
(37)	Deacon Phillippe	65.00	35.00	20.00
(38)	Charley Pittinger	65.00	35.00	20.00
(39)	Harry C. Pulliam	65.00	35.00	20.00
(40)	Claude Ritchey	65.00	35.00	20.00
(41)	Ed Ruelbach (Reulbach)	65.00	35.00	20.00
(42)	J. Bentley Seymour	65.00	35.00	20.00
(43)	Jim Sheckard	65.00	35.00	20.00
(44)	Jack Taylor	65.00	35.00	20.00
(45)	Luther H. Taylor	220.00	110.00	65.00
(46)	Fred Tenny (Tenney)	65.00	35.00	20.00
(47)	Harry Theilman (Jake Thielman)	65.00	35.00	20.00
(48)	Roy Thomas	65.00	35.00	20.00
(49)	Hans Wagner	5,000	2,065	1,240
(50)	Jake Weimer	65.00	35.00	20.00
(51)	Bob Wicker	65.00	35.00	20.00
(52)	Victor Willis	330.00	165.00	100.00
(53)	Lew (George "Hooks") Wiltsie	65.00	35.00	20.00
(54)	Irving Young	65.00	35.00	20.00

1922 Fans Cigarettes (T231)

 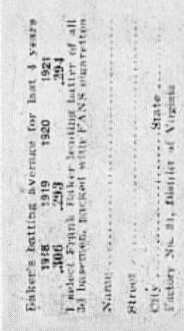

FRANK BAKER 61

More mystery surrounds this obscure set than any other tobacco issue. In fact, the only evidence of its existence until 1992 was a photocopy of a single card of Pittsburgh Pirates outfielder Carson Bigbee. Even the owner of the card is unknown. Cards measure approximately 2-1/2" x 1-1/2" and are black-and-white. Adding to the mystery is the number "85" which appears in the lower right corner on the front of the card, apparently indicating there were at least that many cards in the set. In 1992 card "61" was reported. Card backs displays the player's batting averages for each season from 1918 through 1921 and includes the line: "I select (name) leading batter of all (position), packed with FANS cigarettes." The statement is followed by blanks for a person to fill in his name and address, as if the card were some sort of "ballot." With only one specimen known of each, these are among the rarest baseball cards in the hobby. Their American Card Catalog designation is T231.

Values Undetermined
61 Frank Baker
85 Carson Bigbee

1939 Father & Son Shoes

Chuck Klein, outfielder, Phillies
Compliments Father & Son Shoes

This set features Phillies and A's players and was distributed in the Philadelphia area in 1939 by Father & Son Shoes stores. The unnumbered black and white cards measure 3" x 4". The player's name, position and team appear below the photo, along with the line "Compliments of Fathers & Son Shoes." The backs are blank. The checklist, arranged here alphabetically, may be incomplete.

		NM	EX	VG
	Complete Set (17):	5,000	2,500	1,500
	Common Player:	300.00	150.00	90.00
(1)	Morrie Arnovich	300.00	150.00	90.00
(2)	Earl Brucker	300.00	150.00	90.00
(3)	George Caster	300.00	150.00	90.00
(4)	Sam Chapman	300.00	150.00	90.00
(5)	Spud Davis	300.00	150.00	90.00
(6)	Joe Gantenbein	300.00	150.00	90.00
(7)	Bob Johnson	300.00	150.00	90.00
(8)	Chuck Klein	750.00	375.00	225.00
(9)	Herschel Martin	300.00	150.00	90.00
(10)	Merrill May	300.00	150.00	90.00
(11)	Wally Moses	300.00	150.00	90.00
(12)	Emmett Mueller	300.00	150.00	90.00
(13)	Hugh Mulcahy	300.00	150.00	90.00
(14)	Skeeter Newsome	300.00	150.00	90.00
(15)	Claude Passeau	300.00	150.00	90.00
(16)	George Scharien (Scharein)	300.00	150.00	90.00
(17)	Dick Siebert	300.00	150.00	90.00

1913 Fatima Team Cards (T200)

Issued by the Ligget & Myers Tobacco Co. in 1913 with Fatima brand cigarettes, the T200 set consists of eight National and eight American League team cards. The cards measure 2-5/8" x 4-3/4" and are glossy photographs on paper stock. Although it is unknown why, several of the cards are more difficult to obtain than others. The team cards feature 369 different players, managers and mascots. The card backs contain an offer for an enlarged copy (13" x

21") of a team card, minus the advertising on front, in exchange for 40 Fatima cigarette coupons.

		NM	EX	VG
Complete Set (16):		20,000	10,000	6,000
Common Card:		575.00	285.00	175.00
(1)	Boston Nationals	2,000	500.00	300.00
(2)	Brooklyn Nationals	950.00	475.00	285.00
(3)	Chicago Nationals	575.00	285.00	175.00
(4)	Cincinnati Nationals	700.00	350.00	210.00
(5)	New York Nationals	1,100	550.00	330.00
(6)	Philadelphia Nationals	575.00	285.00	175.00
(7)	Pittsburgh Nationals	750.00	375.00	225.00
(8)	St. Louis Nationals	1,750	875.00	525.00
(9)	Boston Americans	1,650	825.00	500.00
(10)	Chicago Americans	1,000	500.00	300.00
(11)	Cleveland Americans	1,900	950.00	575.00
(12)	Detroit Americans	3,750	1,875	1,125
(13)	New York Americans	2,250	1,125	675.00
(14)	Philadelphia Americans	650.00	325.00	200.00
(15)	St. Louis Americans	1,600	800.00	480.00
(16)	Washington Americans	2,100	1,050	625.00

1913 Fatima Premiums

DETROIT AMERICANS

Among the rarest of the tobacco cards are the large-format (21" x 13") versions of the T200 Fatima team photos which could be obtained by redeeming 40 coupons from cigarette packs. The premium-size team photos are virtually identical to the smaller cards, except they do not carry the Fatima advertising on the front. Because of their large size, the premiums are seldom seen in top grade. The complete set price is quoted as a hypothetical proposition only; none is known.

		NM	EX	VG
Common Card:		7,500	3,500	2,000
(1)	Boston Nationals	8,000	4,000	2,400
(2)	Brooklyn Nationals	8,000	4,000	2,400
(3)	Chicago Nationals	9,500	4,750	2,850
(4)	Cincinnati Nationals	7,500	3,500	2,000
(5)	New York Nationals	8,000	4,000	2,400
(6)	Philadelphia Nationals	7,500	3,500	2,000
(7)	Pittsburg Nationals	10,000	5,000	3,000
(8)	St. Louis Nationals	7,500	3,750	2,250
(9)	Boston Americans	12,500	6,250	3,750
(10)	Chicago Americans	8,000	4,000	2,400
(11)	Cleveland Americans	15,000	7,500	4,500
(12)	Detroit Americans	15,000	7,500	4,500
(13)	New York Americans	12,500	6,250	3,750
(14)	Philadelphia Americans	9,250	4,625	2,775
(15)	St. Louis Americans	9,000	4,500	2,700
(16)	Washington Americans	7,500	3,500	2,000

1913-1915 Fatima Posters

These blank-back, black-and-white (1913) or b/w with a color picture of a cigarette pack (1914-15) window posters were produced by Pictorial News Co. of New York for distribution by Fatima Cigarettes, whose advertising appears in the lower-right corner of the 12-1/2" x 19" pictures. To the left of the advertising are a couple of sentences about the player(s) pictured (usually in an an action pose). The pictures are numbered, but there is currently no idea as to the extent of the issue.

		NM	EX	VG
6	Frank Chance's New York Americans in Bermuda	1,200	600.00	360.00
15	Christy Mathewson	6,000	3,000	2,000
22	Ty Cobb	7,500	3,500	2,500
31	Pittsburgh Pirates Only Hope of West in National Race	1,000	500.00	300.00
33	Joe Jackson	4,500	2,250	1,350
35	Athletics' Star Pitchers the Giants Will Have to Beat (Chief Bender, Jack Coombs, Eddie Plank)	450.00	225.00	135.00
36	Cleveland Strong Second in the American League Race	650.00	325.00	200.00
43	Chicago Cubs Team	1,200	600.00	360.00
45	Plays that Made Baseball History (Various action photos.)	250.00	125.00	75.00
51	Walter Johnson	5,500	2,750	1,650
56	Opposing Pitchers in the Coming World's Series Battles (Christy Mathewson, Rube Marquard, Jeff Tesreau, Al Demaree, Chief Bender, Boardwalk Brown, Byron Houck, Eddie Plank)	650.00	325.00	195.00
105	Giants 'Clearing the Deck for Action' Down in Marlin (Mathewson, Snodgrass, Fletcher, etc.)	325.00	160.00	95.00
153	American League Pennant Winners Ready For the World's Series (1914 Philadelphia A's)	1,500	750.00	450.00
226	Ty Cobb, The Most Talked About Man in Big League Baseball	7,500	3,750	2,250
259	(1915 Philadelphia Phillies)	2,500	1,250	750.00
260	Red Sox Ready to do Battle for World's Championship (1915 Red Sox)	3,500	1,750	1,050

1914 Fatima (T222)

Unlike the typical 20th Century tobacco card issues, the T222 Fatima cards are glossy photographs on a thin paper stock and measure a larger 2-1/2" x 4-1/2". According to the back of the card, the set includes "100 photographs of famous Baseball Players, American Athletic Champions and Photoplay stars." The baseball portion of the set appears to be complete at 52. The set includes players from 13 of the 16 major league teams (no Red Sox, White Sox or Pirates). Most cards are seen with a small black number from 2-9 or 12-15 beneath the player's name. The same number can be found on up to seven cards. Cards with numbers 12-15 are considered short-prints and so designated in this alphabetical checklist.

		NM	EX	VG
Complete Set (52):		137,500	56,250	28,125
Common Player:		1,440	565.00	280.00
(1)	Grover Alexander	20,000	4,500	2,250
(2)	Jimmy Archer	1,440	565.00	280.00
(3)	Jimmy Austin/SP	3,440	1,375	690.00
(4)	Jack Barry	1,440	565.00	280.00
(5)	George Baumgardner/SP	3,440	1,375	690.00
(6)	Rube Benton	1,440	565.00	280.00
(7)	Roger Bresnahan	4,500	1,815	905.00
(8)	Boardwalk Brown	1,440	565.00	280.00
(9)	George Burns	1,440	565.00	280.00
(10)	Bullet Joe Bush	1,440	565.00	280.00
(11)	George Chalmers	1,440	565.00	280.00
(12)	Frank Chance	4,500	1,815	905.00
(13)	Al Demaree	1,440	565.00	280.00
(14)	Art Fletcher	1,440	565.00	280.00
(15)	Earl Hamilton/SP	3,440	1,375	690.00
(16)	John Henry/SP	3,440	1,375	690.00
(17)	Byron Houck	1,440	565.00	280.00
(18)	Miller Huggins	4,500	1,815	905.00
(19)	Hughie Jennings	4,500	1,815	905.00
(20)	Walter Johnson/SP	15,625	6,250	3,125
(21)	Ray Keating/SP	3,440	1,375	690.00
(22)	Jack Lapp	1,440	565.00	280.00
(23)	Tommy Leach	1,440	565.00	280.00
(24)	Nemo Leibold/SP	3,440	1,375	690.00
(25)	Jack Lelivelt/SP	3,440	1,375	690.00
(26)	Hans Lobert/SP	3,440	1,375	690.00
(27)	Lee Magee/SP	3,440	1,375	690.00
(28)	Sherry Magee/SP	3,440	1,375	690.00
(29)	Fritz Maisel	1,440	565.00	280.00
(30)	Rube Marquard	4,500	1,815	905.00
(31)	George McBride/SP	3,440	1,375	690.00
(32)	Stuffy McInnis	1,440	565.00	280.00
(33)	Larry McLean	1,440	565.00	280.00
(34)	Ray Morgan/SP	3,440	1,375	690.00
(35)	Eddie Murphy	1,440	565.00	280.00
(36)	Red Murray	1,440	565.00	280.00
(37)	Rube Oldring	1,440	565.00	280.00
(38)	Bill Orr	1,440	565.00	280.00
(39)	Hub Perdue	1,440	565.00	280.00
(40)	Art Phelan	1,440	565.00	280.00
(41)	Ed Reulbach	1,440	565.00	280.00
(42)	Vic Saier	1,140	565.00	280.00
(43)	Slim Sallee	1,440	565.00	280.00
(44)	Wally Schang	1,440	565.00	280.00
(45)	Wildfire Schulte/SP	3,440	1,375	690.00
(46)	J.C. "Red" Smith/SP	3,440	1,375	690.00
(47)	Amos Strunk	1,440	565.00	280.00
(48)	Bill Sweeney	1,440	565.00	280.00
(49)	Lefty Tyler	1,440	565.00	280.00
(50)	Ossie Vitt	1,440	565.00	280.00
(51)	Ivy Wingo	1,440	565.00	280.00
(52)	Heinie Zimmerman	1,440	565.00	280.00

1955 Felin's Franks

Because of the relatively few specimens in collectors' hands, it is believed this hot dog issue was never actually released. The 4" x 3-5/8" round-cornered panels have a red border front and back with a color player photo on the left side of the front. At right-front are the 1954 stats of a player different than that pictured. Each half of the front shares a large black number. According to the card back, hot dog buyers were supposed to match the pictures and stats of 30 different players to have a chance to win prizes.

		NM	EX	VG
Common Player:		1,250	625.00	375.00
1	Mayo Smith	1,250	625.00	375.00
2	Unknown (Probably coach Benny Bengough.)			
3	Wally Moses	1,250	625.00	375.00
4	Whit Wyatt	1,250	625.00	375.00
5	Maje McDonnell	1,250	625.00	375.00
6	Wiechec/Trainer	750.00	375.00	225.00
7	Murry Dickson	1,250	625.00	375.00
8	Earl Torgeson	1,250	625.00	375.00
9	Bobby Morgan	1,250	625.00	375.00
10	John Meyer	1,250	625.00	375.00
11	Bob Miller	1,250	625.00	375.00
12	Jim Owens	1,250	625.00	375.00
13	Steve Ridzik	1,250	625.00	375.00
14	Robin Roberts	2,000	1,000	600.00
15	Unknown (Probably Curt Simmons.)			
16	Herm Wehmeier	1,250	625.00	375.00
17	Smoky Burgess	1,250	625.00	375.00
18	Stan Lopata	1,250	625.00	375.00
19	Gus Niarhos	1,250	625.00	375.00
20	Floyd Baker	1,250	625.00	375.00
21	Marv Blaylock	1,250	625.00	375.00
22	Granny Hamner	1,250	625.00	375.00
23	Willie Jones	1,250	625.00	375.00
24	Unknown			
25	Unknown			
26	Richie Ashburn	2,250	1,125	675.00
27	Joe Lonnett	1,250	625.00	375.00
28	Mel Clark	1,250	625.00	375.00
29	Bob Greenwood	1,250	625.00	375.00
30	Unknown			

1913 Fenway Breweries/Tom Barker Game

Presumably distributed as a promotion for its Fenway brand of beer, a specially labeled boxed set of the Tom Barker baseball game cards was issued. Only the box, the Score Card and the card of Frank "Home Run" Baker are found bearing the red advertising overprint.

	NM	EX	VG
Complete Set (54):	6,000	3,000	1,800
Frank Baker	175.00	90.00	55.00
Score Card	40.00	20.00	12.00

1916 Ferguson Bakery (D381)

(See 1916 Fleischmann Bakery.)

1916 Ferguson Bakery Felt Pennants (BF2)

Issued circa 1916, this unnumbered set consists of 97 felt pennants with a small black-and-white player photo glued to each. The triangular pennants measure approximately 2-7/8" across the wide top and taper to a length of about 6". The photos are about 1-1/4" x 1-3/4" and appear to be identical to photos used for The Sporting News issues of the same period. The pennants list the player's name and team. The pennants were given away as premiums with the purchase of five-cent loaves of Ferguson Bakery bread in the Roxbury, Mass., area. It is believed that each player can be found on several different colors of background felt.

		NM	EX	VG
Complete Set (97):		27,500	13,500	8,250
Common Player:		175.00	85.00	50.00
(1)	Grover Alexander	600.00	300.00	180.00
(2)	Jimmy Archer	175.00	85.00	50.00
(3)	J. Franklin Baker	450.00	225.00	135.00
(4)	Dave Bancroft	450.00	225.00	135.00
(5)	Jack Barry	175.00	85.00	50.00
(6)	"Chief" Bender	450.00	225.00	135.00
(7)	Joe Benz	175.00	85.00	50.00
(8)	Mordecai Brown	450.00	225.00	135.00
(9)	Geo. J. Burns	175.00	85.00	50.00
(10)	"Donie" Bush	175.00	85.00	50.00
(11)	Forrest Cady	175.00	85.00	50.00
(12)	Max Carey	450.00	225.00	135.00
(13)	Ray Chapman	300.00	150.00	90.00
(14)	Ty Cobb	1,800	900.00	550.00
(15)	Eddie Collins	450.00	225.00	135.00
(16)	"Shauno" Collins	175.00	85.00	50.00
(17)	Charles Comiskey	450.00	225.00	135.00
(18)	Harry Coveleskie (Coveleski)	175.00	85.00	50.00
(19)	Gavvy Cravath	175.00	85.00	50.00
(20)	Sam Crawford	450.00	225.00	135.00
(21)	Jake Daubert	175.00	85.00	50.00
(22)	Josh Devore	175.00	85.00	50.00
(23)	Charles Dooin	175.00	85.00	50.00
(24)	Larry Doyle	175.00	85.00	50.00
(25)	Jean Dubuc	175.00	85.00	50.00
(26)	Johnny Evers	450.00	225.00	135.00
(27)	Urban Faber	450.00	225.00	135.00
(28)	Eddie Foster	175.00	85.00	50.00
(29)	Del Gainor (Gainor)	175.00	85.00	50.00
(30)	"Chic" Gandil	375.00	185.00	110.00
(31)	Joe Gedeon	175.00	85.00	50.00
(32)	Hank Gowdy	175.00	85.00	50.00

(33)	Earl Hamilton	175.00	85.00	50.00
(34)	Claude Hendrix	175.00	85.00	50.00
(35)	Buck Herzog	175.00	85.00	50.00
(36)	Harry Hooper	450.00	225.00	135.00
(37)	Miller Huggins	450.00	225.00	135.00
(38)	Joe Jackson	3,500	1,750	1,000
(39)	William James	175.00	85.00	50.00
(40)	Hugh Jennings	450.00	225.00	135.00
(41)	Walter Johnson	900.00	450.00	275.00
(42)	Fielder Jones	175.00	85.00	50.00
(43)	Joe Judge	175.00	85.00	50.00
(44)	Benny Kauff	175.00	85.00	50.00
(45)	Wm. Killefer	175.00	85.00	50.00
(46)	Napoleon Lajoie	450.00	225.00	135.00
(47)	Jack Lapp	175.00	85.00	50.00
(48)	John Lavan	175.00	85.00	50.00
(49)	Jimmy Lavender	175.00	85.00	50.00
(50)	"Dutch" Leonard	175.00	85.00	50.00
(51)	Duffy Lewis	175.00	85.00	50.00
(52)	Hans Lobert	175.00	85.00	50.00
(53)	Fred Luderus	175.00	85.00	50.00
(54)	Connie Mack	450.00	225.00	135.00
(55)	Sherwood Magee	175.00	85.00	50.00
(56)	Al Mamaux	175.00	85.00	50.00
(57)	"Rabbit" Maranville	450.00	225.00	135.00
(58)	Rube Marquard	450.00	225.00	135.00
(59)	George McBride	175.00	85.00	50.00
(60)	John J. McGraw	450.00	225.00	135.00
(61)	Jack McInnis	175.00	85.00	50.00
(62)	Fred Merkle	175.00	85.00	50.00
(63)	Chief Meyers	175.00	85.00	50.00
(64)	Clyde Milan	175.00	85.00	50.00
(65)	Otto Miller	175.00	85.00	50.00
(66)	Pat Moran	175.00	85.00	50.00
(67)	Ray Morgan	175.00	85.00	50.00
(68)	Guy Morton	175.00	85.00	50.00
(69)	Ed. Murphy	175.00	85.00	50.00
(70)	Rube Oldring	175.00	85.00	50.00
(71)	"Dode" Paskert	175.00	85.00	50.00
(72)	Walter Pipp	175.00	85.00	50.00
(73)	Clarence Rowland	175.00	85.00	50.00
(74)	"Nap" Rucker	175.00	85.00	50.00
(75)	Dick Rudolph	175.00	85.00	50.00
(76)	Reb Russell	175.00	85.00	50.00
(77)	Vic Saier	175.00	85.00	50.00
(78)	"Slim" Sallee	175.00	85.00	50.00
(79)	Ray Schalk	450.00	225.00	135.00
(80)	Walter Schang	175.00	85.00	50.00
(81)	Frank Schulte	175.00	85.00	50.00
(82)	Jim Scott	175.00	85.00	50.00
(83)	George Sisler	450.00	225.00	135.00
(84)	Geo. Stallings	175.00	85.00	50.00
(85)	Oscar Stanage	175.00	85.00	50.00
(86)	"Jeff" Tesreau	175.00	85.00	50.00
(87)	Joe Tinker	450.00	225.00	135.00
(88)	Geo. Tyler	175.00	85.00	50.00
(89)	Jim Vaughn	175.00	85.00	50.00
(90)	Bobby Veach	175.00	85.00	50.00
(91)	Hans Wagner	1,350	675.00	400.00
(92)	Ed. Walsh	450.00	225.00	135.00
(93)	Buck Weaver	750.00	375.00	225.00
(94)	Ivy Wingo	175.00	85.00	50.00
(95)	Joe Wood	350.00	175.00	100.00
(96)	"Pep" Young	175.00	85.00	50.00
(97)	Heiny Zimmerman	175.00	85.00	50.00

1916 Ferguson Bakery Photo Prize Pennants

As part of its baseball insert and premium program, the Roxbury, Mass., bakery issued this series of large (9" x 24") felt pennants bearing a black-and-white player photo (3" x 5"). The colorful pennants are decorated with baseball graphics and have player and team identification. The pennants were a

premium for redeeming 50 tickets from five-cent loaves of bread. Examples of the large-format pennants are so scarce only a handful of players are checklisted thus far.

		NM	EX	VG
Common Player:		9,000	4,500	2,750
(1)	Grover Alexander	15,000	7,500	4,500
(2)	Jack Barry	9,000	4,500	2,750
(3)	Ty Cobb	20,000	10,000	6,000
(4)	Bill Donovan	9,000	4,500	2,750
(5)	Miller Huggins	12,500	6,250	3,750
(6)	John McGraw	12,500	6,250	3,750

1957 Fine Arts Studio

The date of issue on this card is theoretical with no real evidence present on the piece. Published by Fine Arts Studio of Cleveland, the 3-1/2" x 5-1/2" card has a borderless color photo on front. Player identification is on back with standard postcard markings and credit lines to the publisher and printer (Dexter Press of New York).

	NM	EX	VG
75062 Richie Ashburn	100.00	50.00	30.00

1959 First Federal Savings Famous Senators Matchbooks

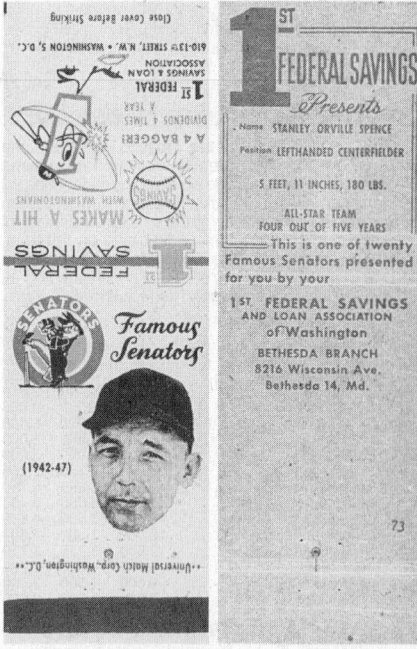

Star Senators of the 20th Century are featured in this series of matchbook covers. The 1-1/2" x 4-1/2" matchbooks include a black-and-white player portrait photo and team logo on front. The sponsoring bank's advertising is on back. Player identification and information are printed inside. Values shown are for complete but empty covers, with the striker surface intact. Complete matchbooks with matches bring about 2X the values quoted.

		NM	EX	VG
Complete Set (20):		325.00	160.00	95.00
Common Player:		15.00	7.50	4.50
(1)	Nick Altrock	15.00	7.50	4.50
(2)	Ossie Bluege	15.00	7.50	4.50
(3)	Joe Cronin	20.00	10.00	6.00
(4)	Alvin Crowder	15.00	7.50	4.50
(5)	Goose Goslin	20.00	10.00	6.00
(6)	Clark Griffith	20.00	10.00	6.00

		NM	EX	VG
(7)	Bucky Harris	20.00	10.00	6.00
(8)	Walter Johnson	45.00	22.00	13.50
(9)	Joe Judge	15.00	7.50	4.50
(10)	Harmon Killebrew	25.00	12.50	7.50
(11)	Joe Kuhel	15.00	7.50	4.50
(12)	Buddy Lewis	15.00	7.50	4.50
(13)	Clyde Milan	15.00	7.50	4.50
(14)	Buddy Myer	15.00	7.50	4.50
(15)	Roger Peckinpaugh	15.00	7.50	4.50
(16)	Sam Rice	20.00	10.00	6.00
(17)	Roy Sievers	15.00	7.50	4.50
(18)	Stanley Spence	15.00	7.50	4.50
(19)	Mickey Vernon	15.00	7.50	4.50
(20)	Samuel West	15.00	7.50	4.50

1953 First National Super Market Boston Red Sox

Four of the early 1950s Red Sox appear in this series issued by a Boston grocery chain. The cards may have been distributed in conjunction with players' in-store appearances. The cards measure 3-3/4" x 5" and are printed in black-and-white. A facsimile autograph appears on the front. Backs have the sponsor's advertising. The unnumbered cards are checklisted here alphabetically. See also 1953 Stop & Shop Boston Red Sox.

		NM	EX	VG
Complete Set (4):		2,500	1,250	750.00
Common Player:		750.00	375.00	225.00
(1)	Billy Goodman	750.00	375.00	225.00
(2)	Ellis Kinder	750.00	375.00	225.00
(3)	Mel Parnell	750.00	375.00	225.00
(4)	Sammy White	750.00	375.00	225.00

1951 Fischer's Bread Labels

This set of end-labels from loaves of bread consists of 32 player photos, each measuring approximately 2-3/4" square. The labels include the player's name, team and position, along with a few words about him. The bakery's slogan "Bread For Energy" appears in a dark band along the bottom. The set, which is unnumbered, was distributed in the Northeast.

		NM	EX	VG
Complete Set (32):		25,000	10,000	5,000
Common Player:		750.00	375.00	225.00
(1)	Vern Bickford	750.00	300.00	150.00
(2)	Ralph Branca	825.00	325.00	175.00
(3)	Harry Brecheen	750.00	300.00	150.00
(4)	"Chico" Carrasquel	750.00	300.00	150.00
(5)	Cliff Chambers	750.00	300.00	150.00
(6)	"Hoot" Evers	750.00	300.00	150.00
(7)	Ned Garver	750.00	300.00	150.00
(8)	Billy Goodman	750.00	300.00	150.00
(9)	Gil Hodges	1,350	550.00	275.00
(10)	Larry Jansen	750.00	300.00	150.00
(11)	Willie Jones	750.00	300.00	150.00
(12)	Eddie Joost	750.00	300.00	150.00
(13)	George Kell	1,250	500.00	250.00
(14)	Alex Kellner	750.00	300.00	150.00
(15)	Ted Kluszewski	1,200	480.00	240.00
(16)	Jim Konstanty	750.00	300.00	150.00
(17)	Bob Lemon	1,250	500.00	250.00
(18)	Cass Michaels	750.00	300.00	150.00
(19)	Johnny Mize	1,250	500.00	250.00
(20)	Irv Noren	750.00	300.00	150.00
(21)	Andy Pafko	750.00	300.00	150.00
(22)	Joe Page	750.00	300.00	150.00
(23)	Mel Parnell	750.00	300.00	150.00
(24)	Johnny Sain	825.00	330.00	165.00
(25)	"Red" Schoendienst	1,250	500.00	250.00
(26)	Roy Sievers	750.00	300.00	150.00
(27)	Roy Smalley	750.00	300.00	150.00
(28)	Herman Wehmeier	750.00	300.00	150.00

		NM	EX	VG
(29)	Bill Werle	750.00	300.00	150.00
(30)	Wes Westrum	750.00	300.00	150.00
(31)	Early Wynn	1,250	500.00	250.00
(32)	Gus Zernial	750.00	300.00	150.00

1970 Flavor-est Milk Milwaukee Brewers

Mike Hershberger

While purporting to be a dairy issue, this is actually a collectors' set produced by Illinois hobbyist Bob Solon. The cards picture members of the 1970 Brewers in their first year in Milwaukee. Posed action photos and portraits are printed in blue-and-white on a 2-3/8" x 4-1/4" format. The pictures are borderless at top and sides. At bottom is a white strip with the player name. Backs have a dairy ad. The unnumbered cards are checklisted here alphabetically. Ironically, this set was later reissued in a marked reprint.

		NM	EX	VG
Complete Set (24):		25.00	12.50	7.50
Common Player:		2.50	1.25	.70
(1)	Gene Brabender	2.50	1.25	.70
(2)	Dave Bristol	2.50	1.25	.70
(3)	Wayne Comer	2.50	1.25	.70
(4)	Cal Ermer	2.50	1.25	.70
(5)	Greg Goossen	2.50	1.25	.70
(6)	Tom Harper	3.50	1.75	1.00
(7)	Mike Hegan	3.50	1.75	1.00
(8)	Mike Hershberger	2.50	1.25	.70
(9)	Steve Hovley	2.50	1.25	.70
(10)	John Kennedy	2.50	1.25	.70
(11)	Lew Krausse	2.50	1.25	.70
(12)	Ted Kubiak	2.50	1.25	.70
(13)	Bob Locker	2.50	1.25	.70
(14)	Roy McMillan	2.50	1.25	.70
(15)	Jerry McNertney	2.50	1.25	.70
(16)	Bob Meyer	2.50	1.25	.70
(17)	John Morris	2.50	1.25	.70
(18)	John O'Donoghue	2.50	1.25	.70
(19)	Marty Pattin	2.50	1.25	.70
(20)	Rich Rollins	2.50	1.25	.70
(21)	Phil Roof	2.50	1.25	.70
(22)	Ted Savage	2.50	1.25	.70
(23)	Russ Snyder	2.50	1.25	.70
(24)	Dan Walton	3.50	1.75	1.00

1923 Fleer

Every Five - Cent Package of Fleer's Bobs and Fruit Hearts contains a picture of a famous person. Get the complete set of 120.

FRANK H. FLEER CORPORATION
Philadelphia

While only a few specimens are known to date, from the print on the back it can be presumed that all 60 of the baseball players from the blank-back strip card set cataloged as W515 were also issued with Fleer advertising on the verso. Several cards are also known with boxers, indicating another 60 cards of non-baseball athletes and other famous people were also produced. The 1-5/8" x 2-3/8" cards feature crude color line art of the player on front, with a black-and-white ad on back. The cards pre-date by more than a decade Fleer's "Cops and Robbers" set of 1935, and are some 35 years in advance of Fleer's first modern baseball issue.

	NM	EX	VG
Complete Set (60):	15,000	7,500	4,500
Common Player:	175.00	85.00	50.00

		NM	EX	VG
1	Bill Cunningham	175.00	85.00	50.00
2	Al Mamaux	175.00	85.00	50.00
3	"Babe" Ruth	1,325	660.00	400.00
4	Dave Bancroft	350.00	175.00	105.00
5	Ed Rommel	175.00	85.00	50.00
6	"Babe" Adams	175.00	85.00	50.00
7	Clarence Walker	175.00	85.00	50.00
8	Waite Hoyt	350.00	175.00	105.00
9	Bob Shawkey	175.00	85.00	50.00
10	"Ty" Cobb	1,000	500.00	300.00
11	George Sisler	350.00	175.00	105.00
12	Jack Bentley	175.00	85.00	50.00
13	Jim O'Connell	175.00	85.00	50.00
14	Frank Frisch	350.00	175.00	105.00
15	Frank Baker	350.00	175.00	105.00
16	Burleigh Grimes	350.00	175.00	105.00
17	Wally Schang	175.00	85.00	50.00
18	Harry Heilman (Heilmann)	350.00	175.00	105.00
19	Aaron Ward	175.00	85.00	50.00
20	Carl Mays	200.00	100.00	60.00
21	The Meusel Bros.	225.00	110.00	67.00
	(Bob Meusel, Irish Meusel)			
22	Arthur Nehf	175.00	85.00	50.00
23	Lee Meadows	175.00	85.00	50.00
24	"Casey" Stengel	375.00	185.00	110.00
25	Jack Scott	175.00	85.00	50.00
26	Kenneth Williams	175.00	85.00	50.00
27	Joe Bush	175.00	85.00	50.00
28	Tris Speaker	400.00	200.00	120.00
29	Ross Young (Youngs)	350.00	175.00	105.00
30	Joe Dugan	175.00	85.00	50.00
31	The Barnes Bros.	200.00	100.00	60.00
	(Jesse Barnes, Virgil Barnes)			
32	George Kelly	350.00	175.00	105.00
33	Hugh McQuillen (McQuillan)	175.00	85.00	50.00
34	Hugh Jennings	350.00	175.00	105.00
35	Tom Griffith	175.00	85.00	50.00
36	Miller Huggins	350.00	175.00	105.00
37	"Whitey" Witt	175.00	85.00	50.00
38	Walter Johnson	500.00	250.00	150.00
39	"Wally" Pipp	200.00	100.00	60.00
40	"Dutch" Reuther (Ruether)	175.00	85.00	50.00
41	Jim Johnston	175.00	85.00	50.00
42	Willie Kamm	175.00	85.00	50.00
43	Sam Jones	175.00	85.00	50.00
44	Frank Snyder	175.00	85.00	50.00
45	John McGraw	350.00	175.00	105.00
46	Everett Scott	175.00	85.00	50.00
47	"Babe" Ruth	1,325	660.00	400.00
48	Urban Shocker	175.00	85.00	50.00
49	Grover Alexander	400.00	200.00	120.00
50	"Rabbit" Maranville	350.00	175.00	105.00
51	Ray Schalk	350.00	175.00	105.00
52	"Heinie" Groh	175.00	85.00	50.00
53	Wilbert Robinson	350.00	175.00	105.00
54	George Burns	175.00	85.00	50.00
55	Rogers Hornsby	400.00	200.00	120.00
56	Zack Wheat	350.00	175.00	105.00
57	Eddie Roush	350.00	175.00	105.00
58	Eddie Collins	350.00	175.00	105.00
59	Charlie Hollocher	175.00	85.00	50.00
60	Red Faber	350.00	175.00	105.00

1959 Fleer Ted Williams

This 80-card 1959 Fleer set tells of the life of baseball great Ted Williams, from his childhood years up to 1958. The full-color cards measure 2-1/2" x 3-1/2" in size and make use of both horizontal and vertical formats. The card backs, all designed horizontally, contain a continuing biography of Williams. Card #68 was withdrawn from the set early in production and is scarce. Counterfeit cards of #68 have been produced and can be distinguished by a cross-hatch pattern which appears over the photo on the card fronts.

		NM	EX	VG
Complete Set (80):		2,100	1,000	500.00
Common Card:		12.50	6.25	3.75
Wax Pack (6):		550.00		
1	The Early Years	95.00	20.00	7.50
2	Ted's Idol (Babe Ruth)	65.00	32.50	20.00
3	Practice Makes Perfect	12.50	6.25	3.75
4	1934 - Ted Learns The Fine Points	12.50	6.25	3.75
5	Ted's Fame Spreads - 1935-36	12.50	6.25	3.75
6	Ted Turns Professional	20.00	10.00	6.00
7	1936 - From Mound To Plate	12.50	6.25	3.75
8	1937 - First Full Season	12.50	6.25	3.75
9	1937 - First Step To The Majors (With Eddie Collins.)	12.50	6.25	3.75
10	1938 - Gunning As A Pastime	12.50	6.25	3.75
11	1938 - First Spring Training (With Jimmie Foxx.)	30.00	15.00	9.00
12	1939 - Burning Up The Minors	20.00	10.00	6.00

13	1939 - Ted Shows He Will Stay	12.50	6.25	3.75
14	Outstanding Rookie of 1939	20.00	10.00	6.00
15	1940 - Williams Licks Sophomore Jinx	20.00	10.00	6.00
16	1941 - Williams' Greatest Year	12.50	6.25	3.75
17	1941 - How Ted Hit .400	30.00	15.00	9.00
18	1941 - All-Star Hero	12.50	6.25	3.75
19	1942 - Ted Wins Triple Crown	12.50	6.25	3.75
20	1942 - On To Naval Training	12.50	6.25	3.75
21	1943 - Honors For Williams	12.50	6.25	3.75
22	1944 - Ted Solos	12.50	6.25	3.75
23	1944 - Williams Wins His Wings	12.50	6.25	3.75
24	1945 - Sharpshooter	12.50	6.25	3.75
25	1945 - Ted Is Discharged	12.50	6.25	3.75
26	1946 - Off To A Flying Start	12.50	6.25	3.75
27	July 9, 1946 - One Man Show	12.50	6.25	3.75
28	July 14, 1946 - The Williams Shift	12.50	6.25	3.75
29	July 21, 1946, Ted Hits For The Cycle	20.00	10.00	6.00
30	1946 - Beating The Williams Shift	12.50	6.25	3.75
31	Oct. 1946 - Sox Lose The Series	12.50	6.25	3.75
32	1946 - Most Valuable Player	12.50	6.25	3.75
33	1947 - Another Triple Crown For Ted	12.50	6.25	3.75
34	1947 - Ted Sets Runs-Scored Record	12.50	6.25	3.75
35	1948 - The Sox Miss The Pennant	12.50	6.25	3.75
36	1948 - Banner Year For Ted	12.50	6.25	3.75
37	1949 - Sox Miss Out Again	12.50	6.25	3.75
38	1949 - Power Rampage	12.50	6.25	3.75
39	1950 - Great Start (with Joe Cronin and Eddie Collins)	12.50	6.25	3.75
40	July 11, 1950 - Ted Crashes Into Wall	12.50	6.25	3.75
41	1950 - Ted Recovers	12.50	6.25	3.75
42	1951 - Williams Slowed By Injury	12.50	6.25	3.75
43	1951 - Leads Outfielders In Double Play	12.50	6.25	3.75
44	1952 - Back To The Marines	12.50	6.25	3.75
45	1952 - Farewell To Baseball?	12.50	6.25	3.75
46	1952 - Ready For Combat	12.50	6.25	3.75
47	1953 - Ted Crash Lands Jet	12.50	6.25	3.75
48	July 14, 1953 - Ted Returns	12.50	6.25	3.75
49	1953 - Smash Return	12.50	6.25	3.75
50	March 1954 - Spring Injury	12.50	6.25	3.75
51	May 16, 1954 - Ted Is Patched Up	12.50	6.25	3.75
52	1954 - Ted's Comeback	12.50	6.25	3.75
53	1954 - Ted's Comeback Is A Sucess	12.50	6.25	3.75
54	Dec. 1954, Fisherman Ted Hooks a Big On	12.50	6.25	3.75
55	1955 - Ted Decides Retirement Is "No Go (With Joe Cronin.)	12.50	6.25	3.75
56	1955 - 2,000th Major League Hit	12.50	6.25	3.75
57	1956 - Ted Reaches 400th Homer	12.50	6.25	3.75
58	1957 - Williams Hits .388	12.50	6.25	3.75
59	1957 - Hot September For Ted	12.50	6.25	3.75
60	1957 - More Records For Ted	12.50	6.25	3.75
61	1957 - Outfielder Ted	12.50	6.25	3.75
62	1958 - 6th Batting Title For Ted	12.50	6.25	3.75
63	Ted's All-Star Record	35.00	17.50	10.00
64	1958 - Daughter And Famous Daddy	12.50	6.25	3.75
65	August 30, 1958	12.50	6.25	3.75
66	1958 - Powerhouse	12.50	6.25	3.75
67	Two Famous Fishermen (with Sam Snead)	20.00	10.00	6.00
68	Jan. 23, 1959 - Ted Signs For 1959	600.00	300.00	175.00
69	A Future Ted Williams?	12.50	6.25	3.75
70	Ted Williams & Jim Thorpe	30.00	15.00	9.00
71	Ted's Hitting Fundamentals #1	12.50	6.25	3.75
72	Ted's Hitting Fundamentals #2	12.50	6.25	3.75
73	Ted's Hitting Fundamentals #3	12.50	6.25	3.75
74	Here's How!	12.50	6.25	3.75
75	Williams' Value To Red Sox (with Babe Ruth, Eddie Collins)	30.00	15.00	9.00
76	Ted's Remarkable "On Base" Record	12.50	6.25	3.75
77	Ted Relaxes	12.50	6.25	3.75
78	Honors For Williams	12.50	6.25	3.75
79	Where Ted Stands	25.00	12.50	7.50
80	Ted's Goals For 1959	40.00	15.00	9.00

1960 Fleer Baseball Greats

The 1960 Fleer Baseball Greats set consists of 78 cards of the game's top players from the past, plus a card of Ted Williams, who was in his final major league season. The cards are standard size (2-1/2" x 3-1/2") and feature color photos inside blue, green, red or yellow borders. The card backs carry a short player biography plus career hitting or pitching statistics. Unissued cards with a Pepper Martin back (#80), but with another player pictured on the front, exist. All have been either cancelled with a slit cut out of the bottom, or show evidence of having been hand-cut from a sheet.

RABBIT MARANVILLE

		NM	EX	VG
	Complete Set (79):	850.00	425.00	250.00
	Common Player:	9.00	4.50	2.75
	Wax Pack:	550.00		
1	Nap Lajoie	22.50	7.50	4.00
2	Christy Mathewson	16.00	8.00	5.00
3	Babe Ruth	60.00	30.00	18.00
4	Carl Hubbell	9.00	4.50	2.75
5	Grover Cleveland Alexander	15.00	7.50	4.50
6	Walter Johnson	20.00	10.00	6.00
7	Chief Bender	9.00	4.50	2.75
8	Roger Bresnahan	9.00	4.50	2.75
9	Mordecai Brown	9.00	4.50	2.75
10	Tris Speaker	9.00	4.50	2.75
11	Arky Vaughan	9.00	4.50	2.75
12	Zack Wheat	9.00	4.50	2.75
13	George Sisler	9.00	4.50	2.75
14	Connie Mack	9.00	4.50	2.75
15	Clark Griffith	9.00	4.50	2.75
16	Lou Boudreau	9.00	4.50	2.75
17	Ernie Lombardi	9.00	4.50	2.75
18	Heinie Manush	9.00	4.50	2.75
19	Marty Marion	9.00	4.50	2.75
20	Eddie Collins	9.00	4.50	2.75
21	Rabbit Maranville	9.00	4.50	2.75
22	Joe Medwick	9.00	4.50	2.75
23	Ed Barrow	9.00	4.50	2.75
24	Mickey Cochrane	9.00	4.50	2.75
25	Jimmy Collins	9.00	4.50	2.75
26	Bob Feller	13.50	6.75	4.00
27	Luke Appling	9.00	4.50	2.75
28	Lou Gehrig	50.00	25.00	15.00
29	Gabby Hartnett	9.00	4.50	2.75
30	Chuck Klein	9.00	4.50	2.75
31	Tony Lazzeri	9.00	4.50	2.75
32	Al Simmons	9.00	4.50	2.75
33	Wilbert Robinson	9.00	4.50	2.75
34	Sam Rice	9.00	4.50	2.75
35	Herb Pennock	9.00	4.50	2.75
36	Mel Ott	9.00	4.50	2.75
37	Lefty O'Doul	9.00	4.50	2.75
38	Johnny Mize	9.00	4.50	2.75
39	Bing Miller	9.00	4.50	2.75
40	Joe Tinker	9.00	4.50	2.75
41	Frank Baker	9.00	4.50	2.75
42	Ty Cobb	30.00	15.00	9.00
43	Paul Derringer	9.00	4.50	2.75
44	Cap Anson	9.00	4.50	2.75
45	Jim Bottomley	9.00	4.50	2.75
46	Eddie Plank	9.00	4.50	2.75
47	Cy Young	16.00	8.00	5.00
48	Hack Wilson	9.00	4.50	2.75
49	Ed Walsh	9.00	4.50	2.75
50	Frank Chance	9.00	4.50	2.75
51	Dazzy Vance	9.00	4.50	2.75
52	Bill Terry	9.00	4.50	2.75
53	Jimmy Foxx	15.00	7.50	4.50
54	Lefty Gomez	9.00	4.50	2.75
55	Branch Rickey	9.00	4.50	2.75
56	Ray Schalk	9.00	4.50	2.75
57	Johnny Evers	9.00	4.50	2.75
58	Charlie Gehringer	9.00	4.50	2.75
59	Burleigh Grimes	9.00	4.50	2.75
60	Lefty Grove	9.00	4.50	2.75
61	Rube Waddell	9.00	4.50	2.75
62	Honus Wagner	15.00	7.50	4.50
63	Red Ruffing	9.00	4.50	2.75
64	Judge Landis	9.00	4.50	2.75
65	Harry Heilmann	9.00	4.50	2.75
66	John McGraw	9.00	4.50	2.75
67	Hughie Jennings	9.00	4.50	2.75
68	Hal Newhouser	9.00	4.50	2.75
69	Waite Hoyt	9.00	4.50	2.75
70	Bobo Newsom	9.00	4.50	2.75
71	Earl Averill	9.00	4.50	2.75
72	Ted Williams	50.00	25.00	15.00
73	Warren Giles	9.00	4.50	2.75
74	Ford Frick	9.00	4.50	2.75
75	Ki Ki Cuyler	9.00	4.50	2.75
76	Paul Waner	9.00	4.50	2.75
77	Pie Traynor	9.00	4.50	2.75
78	Lloyd Waner	9.00	4.50	2.75
79	Ralph Kiner	9.00	4.50	2.75
80	Pepper Martin (Unissued, slit-cancelled proof, Lefty Grove, Joe Tinker or Eddie Collins on front.)	2,000	800.00	400.00
80	Pepper Martin (Unissued hand-cut proof. Lefty Grove, Eddie Collins or Joe Tinker on front.)	2,750	1,350	825.00

1960-62 Fleer Team Logo Decals

These colorful team logo decals were pack inserts in Fleer's 1960-62 baseball card issues. The decals measure 2-1/4" x 3". Those issued in 1960 have a blue background on front. The 1961-62 decals have a white background on front. Backs have advertising for Fleer bubblegum and instructions on applying the decals. The 1961 decals have back printing in blue; the 1962s are in red.

	NM	EX	VG
Complete Set, 1960 (16):	100.00	50.00	30.00
Complete Set, 1961 (18):	100.00	50.00	30.00
Complete Set, 1962 (20):	250.00	125.00	75.00
1960 team decal, blue background.	9.00	4.50	2.75
1961 decal, white background, blue back.	4.50	2.25	1.25
1962 decal, white background, red back.	9.00	4.50	2.75

1961 Fleer Baseball Greats

FRED TONEY

In 1961, Fleer issued another set utilizing the Baseball Greats theme. The 154-card set was issued in two series and features a color (or colorized) player portrait against a colored background. The player's name is located in a pennant at bottom. Card backs feature orange and black on white stock and contain player biographical and statistical information. The cards measure 2-1/2" x 3-1/2" in size. Five-cent wax packs included five cards plus a team logo decal and sticker.

		NM	EX	VG
	Complete Set (154):	1,000	500.00	300.00
	Common Player:	6.00	3.00	1.75
	Wax Pack (5+1+1):	225.00		
1	Checklist (Frank Baker, Ty Cobb, Zach Wheat)	25.00	12.50	7.50
2	G.C. Alexander	7.50	3.75	2.25
3	Nick Altrock	6.00	3.00	1.75
4	Cap Anson	6.00	3.00	1.75
5	Earl Averill	6.00	3.00	1.75
6	Home Run Baker	6.00	3.00	1.75
7	Dave Bancroft	6.00	3.00	1.75
8	Chief Bender	6.00	3.00	1.75
9	Jim Bottomley	6.00	3.00	1.75
10	Roger Bresnahan	6.00	3.00	1.75
11	Mordecai Brown	6.00	3.00	1.75
12	Max Carey	6.00	3.00	1.75
13	Jack Chesbro	6.00	3.00	1.75
14	Ty Cobb	25.00	12.50	7.50
15	Mickey Cochrane	6.00	3.00	1.75
16	Eddie Collins	6.00	3.00	1.75
17	Earle Combs	6.00	3.00	1.75
18	Charles Comiskey	6.00	3.00	1.75
19	Ki Ki Cuyler	6.00	3.00	1.75
20	Paul Derringer	6.00	3.00	1.75
21	Howard Ehmke	6.00	3.00	1.75
22	Billy Evans	6.00	3.00	1.75
23	Johnny Evers	6.00	3.00	1.75
24	Red Faber	6.00	3.00	1.75
25	Bob Feller	10.00	5.00	3.00
26	Wes Ferrell	6.00	3.00	1.75
27	Lew Fonseca	6.00	3.00	1.75
28	Jimmy Foxx	7.50	3.75	2.25
29	Ford Frick	6.00	3.00	1.75
30	Frankie Frisch	6.00	3.00	1.75
31	Lou Gehrig	45.00	22.50	13.50
32	Charlie Gehringer	6.00	3.00	1.75
33	Warren Giles	6.00	3.00	1.75
34	Lefty Gomez	6.00	3.00	1.75
35	Goose Goslin	6.00	3.00	1.75
36	Clark Griffith	6.00	3.00	1.75
37	Burleigh Grimes	6.00	3.00	1.75
38	Lefty Grove	6.00	3.00	1.75
39	Chick Hafey	6.00	3.00	1.75
40	Jesse Haines	6.00	3.00	1.75
41	Gabby Hartnett	6.00	3.00	1.75
42	Harry Heilmann	6.00	3.00	1.75
43	Rogers Hornsby	6.00	3.00	1.75
44	Waite Hoyt	6.00	3.00	1.75

45	Carl Hubbell	6.00	3.00	1.75
46	Miller Huggins	6.00	3.00	1.75
47	Hughie Jennings	6.00	3.00	1.75
48	Ban Johnson	6.00	3.00	1.75
49	Walter Johnson	12.00	6.00	3.50
50	Ralph Kiner	6.00	3.00	1.75
51	Chuck Klein	6.00	3.00	1.75
52	Johnny Kling	6.00	3.00	1.75
53	Judge Landis	6.00	3.00	1.75
54	Tony Lazzeri	6.00	3.00	1.75
55	Ernie Lombardi	6.00	3.00	1.75
56	Dolf Luque	6.00	3.00	1.75
57	Heinie Manush	6.00	3.00	1.75
58	Marty Marion	6.00	3.00	1.75
59	Christy Mathewson	12.00	6.00	3.50
60	John McGraw	6.00	3.00	1.75
61	Joe Medwick	6.00	3.00	1.75
62	Bing Miller	6.00	3.00	1.75
63	Johnny Mize	6.00	3.00	1.75
64	Johnny Mostil	6.00	3.00	1.75
65	Art Nehf	6.00	3.00	1.75
66	Hal Newhouser	6.00	3.00	1.75
67	Bobo Newsom	6.00	3.00	1.75
68	Mel Ott	6.00	3.00	1.75
69	Allie Reynolds	6.00	3.00	1.75
70	Sam Rice	6.00	3.00	1.75
71	Eppa Rixey	6.00	3.00	1.75
72	Edd Roush	6.00	3.00	1.75
73	Schoolboy Rowe	6.00	3.00	1.75
74	Red Ruffing	6.00	3.00	1.75
75	Babe Ruth	65.00	32.50	20.00
76	Joe Sewell	6.00	3.00	1.75
77	Al Simmons	6.00	3.00	1.75
78	George Sisler	6.00	3.00	1.75
79	Tris Speaker	6.00	3.00	1.75
80	Fred Toney	6.00	3.00	1.75
81	Dazzy Vance	6.00	3.00	1.75
82	Jim Vaughn	6.00	3.00	1.75
83	Big Ed Walsh	6.00	3.00	1.75
84	Lloyd Waner	6.00	3.00	1.75
85	Paul Waner	6.00	3.00	1.75
86	Zach Wheat	6.00	3.00	1.75
87	Hack Wilson	6.00	3.00	1.75
88	Jimmy Wilson	6.00	3.00	1.75
89	Checklist (George Sisler, Pie Traynor)	20.00	10.00	6.00
90	Babe Adams	6.00	3.00	1.75
91	Dale Alexander	6.00	3.00	1.75
92	Jim Bagby	6.00	3.00	1.75
93	Ossie Bluege	6.00	3.00	1.75
94	Lou Boudreau	6.00	3.00	1.75
95	Tommy Bridges	6.00	3.00	1.75
96	Donnie Bush (Donie)	6.00	3.00	1.75
97	Dolph Camilli	6.00	3.00	1.75
98	Frank Chance	6.00	3.00	1.75
99	Jimmy Collins	6.00	3.00	1.75
100	Stanley Coveleskie (Coveleski)	6.00	3.00	1.75
101	Hughie Critz	6.00	3.00	1.75
102	General Crowder	6.00	3.00	1.75
103	Joe Dugan	6.00	3.00	1.75
104	Bibb Falk	6.00	3.00	1.75
105	Rick Ferrell	6.00	3.00	1.75
106	Art Fletcher	6.00	3.00	1.75
107	Dennis Galehouse	6.00	3.00	1.75
108	Chick Galloway	6.00	3.00	1.75
109	Mule Haas	6.00	3.00	1.75
110	Stan Hack	6.00	3.00	1.75
111	Bump Hadley	6.00	3.00	1.75
112	Billy Hamilton	6.00	3.00	1.75
113	Joe Hauser	6.00	3.00	1.75
114	Babe Herman	6.00	3.00	1.75
115	Travis Jackson	6.00	3.00	1.75
116	Eddie Joost	6.00	3.00	1.75
117	Addie Joss	6.00	3.00	1.75
118	Joe Judge	6.00	3.00	1.75
119	Joe Kuhel	6.00	3.00	1.75
120	Nap Lajoie	6.00	3.00	1.75
121	Dutch Leonard	6.00	3.00	1.75
122	Ted Lyons	6.00	3.00	1.75
123	Connie Mack	6.00	3.00	1.75
124	Rabbit Maranville	6.00	3.00	1.75
125	Fred Marberry	6.00	3.00	1.75
126	Iron Man McGinnity	6.00	3.00	1.75
127	Oscar Melillo	6.00	3.00	1.75
128	Ray Mueller	6.00	3.00	1.75
129	Kid Nichols	6.00	3.00	1.75
130	Lefty O'Doul	6.00	3.00	1.75
131	Bob O'Farrell	6.00	3.00	1.75
132	Roger Peckinpaugh	6.00	3.00	1.75
133	Herb Pennock	6.00	3.00	1.75
134	George Pipgras	6.00	3.00	1.75
135	Eddie Plank	6.00	3.00	1.75
136	Ray Schalk	6.00	3.00	1.75
137	Hal Schumacher	6.00	3.00	1.75
138	Luke Sewell	6.00	3.00	1.75
139	Bob Shawkey	6.00	3.00	1.75
140	Riggs Stephenson	6.00	3.00	1.75
141	Billy Sullivan	6.00	3.00	1.75
142	Bill Terry	6.00	3.00	1.75
143	Joe Tinker	6.00	3.00	1.75
144	Pie Traynor	6.00	3.00	1.75
145	George Uhle	6.00	3.00	1.75
146	Hal Troskey (Trosky)	6.00	3.00	1.75
147	Arky Vaughan	6.00	3.00	1.75
148	Johnny Vander Meer	6.00	3.00	1.75
149	Rube Waddell	6.00	3.00	1.75
150	Honus Wagner	25.00	12.50	7.50
151	Dixie Walker	6.00	3.00	1.75
152	Ted Williams	60.00	30.00	18.00
153	Cy Young	12.00	6.00	3.50
154	Ross Young (Youngs)	6.00	3.00	1.75

1961 Fleer World Champions Pennant Decals

The winner of each World Series from 1913-1960 is honored in this pack insert. The 3" x 1-1/4" decals

have a large red or blue pennant at center, with a team name or logo and the "WORLD CHAMPIONS" notation. The year of the Series win is at left on the pennant. The number of games won by each team is at top and bottom on right. Backs offer instructions for applying the decals.

		NM	EX	VG
	Complete Set (48):	300.00	150.00	90.00
	Common Decal:	6.00	3.00	1.75
(1)	1913 - A's	6.00	3.00	1.75
(2)	1914 - Braves	6.00	3.00	1.75
(3)	1915 - Red Sox	6.00	3.00	1.75
(4)	1916 - Red Sox	6.00	3.00	1.75
(5)	1917 - White Sox	6.00	3.00	1.75
(6)	1918 - Red Sox	6.00	3.00	1.75
(7)	1919 - Reds	9.00	4.50	2.75
(8)	1920 - Indians	6.00	3.00	1.75
(9)	1921 - Giants	6.00	3.00	1.75
(10)	1922 - Giants	6.00	3.00	1.75
(11)	1923 - Yankees	7.50	3.75	2.25
(12)	1924 - Senators	6.00	3.00	1.75
(13)	1925 - Yankees	7.50	3.75	2.25
(14)	1926 - Cardinals	6.00	3.00	1.75
(14)	1927 - Yankees	7.50	3.75	2.25
(14)	1928 - Yankees	7.50	3.75	2.25
(15)	1929 - A's	6.00	3.00	1.75
(16)	1930 - A's	6.00	3.00	1.75
(17)	1931 - Cardinals	6.00	3.00	1.75
(18)	1932 - Yankees	7.50	3.75	2.25
(19)	1933 - Giants	6.00	3.00	1.75
(20)	1934 - Cardinals	6.00	3.00	1.75
(21)	1935 - Tigers	6.00	3.00	1.75
(22)	1936 - Yankees	7.50	3.75	2.25
(23)	1937 - Yankees	7.50	3.75	2.25
(24)	1938 - Yankees	7.50	3.75	2.25
(25)	1939 - Yankees	7.50	3.75	2.25
(26)	1940 - Reds	6.00	3.00	1.75
(27)	1941 - Yankees	7.50	3.75	2.25
(28)	1942 - Cardinals	6.00	3.00	1.75
(29)	1943 - Yankees	7.50	3.75	2.25
(30)	1944 - Cardinals	6.00	3.00	1.75
(31)	1945 - Tigers	6.00	3.00	1.75
(32)	1946 - Cardinals	6.00	3.00	1.75
(33)	1947 - Yankees	7.50	3.75	2.25
(34)	1948 - Indians	6.00	3.00	1.75
(35)	1949 - Yankees	7.50	3.75	2.25
(36)	1950 - Yankees	7.50	3.75	2.25
(37)	1951 - Yankees	7.50	3.75	2.25
(38)	1952 - Yankees	7.50	3.75	2.25
(41)	1953 - Yankees	7.50	3.75	2.25
(42)	1954 - Giants	6.00	3.00	1.75
(43)	1955 - Dodgers	9.00	4.50	2.75
(44)	1956 - Yankees	7.50	3.75	2.25
(45)	1957 - Braves	7.50	3.75	2.25
(46)	1958 - Yankees	7.50	3.75	2.25
(47)	1959 - Dodgers	9.00	4.50	2.75
(48)	1960 - Pirates	9.00	4.50	2.75

1963 Fleer

A lawsuit by Topps stopped Fleer's 1963 set at one series of 66 cards. Issued with a cookie rather than gum, the set features color photos of current players. The card backs include statistical information for 1962 and career plus a brief player biography. The cards, which measure 2-1/2" x 3-1/2", are numbered 1-66. An unnumbered checklist was issued with the set and is included in the complete set price in the checklist that follows. The checklist and #46 Adcock are scarce.

		NM	EX	VG
	Complete Set (67):	1,500	750.00	450.00
	Common Player:	10.00	5.00	3.00
	Wax Pack:	1,000		
1	Steve Barber	40.00	10.00	5.00
2	Ron Hansen	10.00	5.00	3.00
3	Milt Pappas	10.00	5.00	3.00
4	Brooks Robinson	50.00	25.00	15.00
5	Willie Mays	90.00	45.00	27.50
6	Lou Clinton	10.00	5.00	3.00
7	Bill Monbouquette	10.00	5.00	3.00
8	Carl Yastrzemski	50.00	25.00	15.00
9	Ray Herbert	10.00	5.00	3.00
10	Jim Landis	10.00	5.00	3.00
11	Dick Donovan	10.00	5.00	3.00
12	Tito Francona	10.00	5.00	3.00
13	Jerry Kindall	10.00	5.00	3.00
14	Frank Lary	10.00	5.00	3.00
15	Dick Howser	10.00	5.00	3.00
16	Jerry Lumpe	10.00	5.00	3.00
17	Norm Siebern	10.00	5.00	3.00
18	Don Lee	10.00	5.00	3.00
19	Albie Pearson	10.00	5.00	3.00
20	Bob Rodgers	10.00	5.00	3.00
21	Leon Wagner	10.00	5.00	3.00
22	Jim Kaat	15.00	7.50	4.50
23	Vic Power	10.00	5.00	3.00
24	Rich Rollins	10.00	5.00	3.00
25	Bobby Richardson	17.50	9.00	5.00
26	Ralph Terry	10.00	5.00	3.00
27	Tom Cheney	10.00	5.00	3.00
28	Chuck Cottier	10.00	5.00	3.00
29	Jimmy Piersall	12.50	6.25	3.75
30	Dave Stenhouse	10.00	5.00	3.00
31	Glen Hobbie	10.00	5.00	3.00
32	Ron Santo	25.00	12.50	7.50
33	Gene Freese	10.00	5.00	3.00
34	Vada Pinson	12.50	6.25	3.75
35	Bob Purkey	10.00	5.00	3.00
36	Joe Amalfitano	10.00	5.00	3.00
37	Bob Aspromonte	10.00	5.00	3.00
38	Dick Farrell	10.00	5.00	3.00
39	Al Spangler	10.00	5.00	3.00
40	Tommy Davis	10.00	5.00	3.00
41	Don Drysdale	35.00	17.50	10.00
42	Sandy Koufax	100.00	50.00	30.00
43	*Maury Wills*	55.00	27.50	16.50
44	Frank Bolling	10.00	5.00	3.00
45	Warren Spahn	40.00	20.00	12.00
46	Joe Adcock/SP	80.00	40.00	24.00
47	Roger Craig	10.00	5.00	3.00
48	Al Jackson	10.00	5.00	3.00
49	Rod Kanehl	10.00	5.00	3.00
50	Ruben Amaro	10.00	5.00	3.00
51	John Callison	10.00	5.00	3.00
52	Clay Dalrymple	10.00	5.00	3.00
53	Don Demeter	10.00	5.00	3.00
54	Art Mahaffey	10.00	5.00	3.00
55	"Smoky" Burgess	10.00	5.00	3.00
56	Roberto Clemente	95.00	47.50	28.00
57	Elroy Face	10.00	5.00	3.00
58	Vernon Law	10.00	5.00	3.00
59	Bill Mazeroski	20.00	10.00	6.00
60	Ken Boyer	12.50	6.25	3.75
61	Bob Gibson	40.00	20.00	12.00
62	Gene Oliver	10.00	5.00	3.00
63	Bill White	13.50	6.75	4.00
64	Orlando Cepeda	22.50	11.00	6.75
65	Jimmy Davenport	10.00	5.00	3.00
66	Billy O'Dell	20.00	7.50	4.00
---	Checklist /SP	300.00	150.00	90.00

1966 Fleer All-Star Match Baseball

This seldom-seen issue was produced in the years when Fleer was locked out of the "regular" baseball card market. Standard 2-1/2" x 3-1/2" format cards are designed for playing a baseball match game. Backs have a portion of a black-and-white photo of Dodger pitcher Don Drysdale, which can be assembled in jigsaw puzzle fashion. Fronts are printed in red, blue, yellow and black, and numbered F1-F66. Because single cards have little collector appeal, the value of a set is considerably higher than the sum of the parts.

	NM	EX	VG
Complete Set (66):	400.00	200.00	120.00
Common Card:	6.00	3.00	1.75
Wax Pack:	200.00		
Don Drysdale			

1968-70 Fleer Major League Baseball Patches

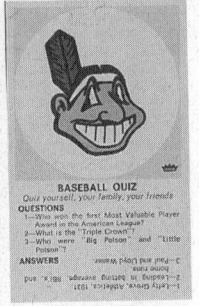

From 1968-70 Fleer sold bubblegum in wax packs which also included four team logo/quiz cards and half a dozen cloth patches, all for a dime. The 2-9/16" x 4-1/16" cards are blank-back and have on front a color team logo at top and three baseball trivia questions at bottom. The cloth patches are about 2-1/2" x 3-5/16" and are die-cut to allow the team logos and nameplates to be removed from the paper backing and stuck on jackets, etc.

		NM	EX	VG
Complete Set Logo Cards (24):		18.00	9.00	5.50
Common Logo Card:		1.50	.70	.45
Complete Set Cloth Patches (29):		35.00	17.50	10.00
Common Cloth Patch:		1.50	.75	.45
Wax Pack:		2.00		
Wax Box (24):		30.00		
LOGO/QUIZ CARDS				
(1)	Atlanta Braves	1.50	.70	.45
(2)	Baltimore Orioles	1.50	.70	.45
(3)	Boston Red Sox	1.50	.70	.45
(4)	California Angels	1.50	.70	.45
(5)	Chicago Cubs	1.50	.70	.45
(6)	Chicago White Sox	1.50	.70	.45
(7)	Cincinnati Reds	1.50	.70	.45
(8)	Cleveland Indians	1.50	.70	.45
(9)	Detroit Tigers	1.50	.70	.45
(10)	Houston Astros	1.50	.70	.45
(11)	Kansas City Royals	1.50	.70	.45
(12)	Los Angeles Dodgers	1.50	.70	.45
(13)	Minnesota Twins	1.50	.70	.45
(14)	Montreal Expos	2.50	1.25	.70
(15)	New York Mets	3.00	1.50	.90
(16)	New York Yankees	4.00	2.00	1.25
(17)	Oakland A's	2.50	1.25	.70
(18)	Philadelphia Phillies	1.50	.70	.45
(19)	Pittsburgh Pirates	1.50	.70	.45
(20)	San Diego Padres	2.50	1.25	.70
(21)	San Francisco Giants	1.50	.70	.45
(22)	Seattle Pilots	6.00	3.00	1.75
(23)	St. Louis Cardinals	1.50	.70	.45
(24)	Washington Senators	1.50	.70	.45
TEAM LOGO CLOTH PATCHES				
(1)	Atlanta Braves	1.50	.70	.45
(2)	Baltimore Orioles	1.50	.70	.45
(3)	Boston Red Sox	1.50	.70	.45
(4)	California Angels	1.50	.70	.45
(5)	Chicago Cubs	1.50	.70	.45
(6)	Chicago White Sox	1.50	.70	.45
(7)	Cincinnati Reds	1.50	.70	.45
(8)	Cleveland Indians (Indian head.)	1.50	.70	.45
(9)	Cleveland Indians (Batting Indian.)	1.50	.70	.45
(10)	Detroit Tigers	1.50	.70	.45
(11)	Houston Astros	1.50	.70	.45
(12)	Kansas City Royals	1.50	.70	.45
(13)	Los Angeles Dodgers	1.50	.70	.45
(14)	Milwaukee Brewers (M)	1.50	.70	.45
(15)	Milwaukee Brewers (Batting keg.)	1.50	.70	.45
(16)	Minnesota Twins	1.50	.70	.45
(17)	Montreal Expos	2.00	1.00	.60
(18)	New York Mets	2.00	1.00	.60
(19)	New York Yankees	3.00	1.50	.90
(20)	Oakland A's (Plain ball.)	2.00	1.00	.60
(21)	Oakland A's ("The SWINGIN'", white shoes, on ball.)	1.50	.70	.45
(22)	Philadelphia Phillies	1.50	.70	.45
(23)	Pittsburgh Pirates	1.50	.70	.45
(24)	San Diego Padres	2.00	1.00	.60
(25)	San Francisco Giants	1.50	.70	.45
(26)	Seattle Pilots	3.00	1.50	.90
(27)	St. Louis Cardinals	1.50	.70	.45
(28)	Washington Senators	1.50	.70	.45
(29)	Major League Baseball	1.50	.70	.45

1969 Fleer Cap Plaques

This set of novelty plaques features 3D impressions of each team's cap on thin plastic stock in a 3" x 4" format. Each cap plaque was sold in a wrapper with an easel backing board, surviving specimens of which are quite scarce.

Vintage cards in Good condition are valued at about 50% of the Very Good values shown here. Cards in Fair condition are valued at 25% or less of VG.

		NM	EX	VG
Complete Set (24):		1,200	600.00	350.00
Common Plaque:		45.00	22.50	13.50
Easel Backing Board:		22.00	11.00	6.50
Unopened Pack:		45.00		
(1)	Atlanta Braves	50.00	25.00	15.00
(2)	Baltimore Orioles	60.00	30.00	18.00
(3)	Boston Red Sox	50.00	25.00	15.00
(4)	California Angels	45.00	22.50	13.50
(5)	Chicago Cubs	60.00	30.00	18.00
(6)	Chicago White Sox	45.00	22.50	13.50
(7)	Cincinnati Reds	45.00	22.50	13.50
(8)	Cleveland Indians	45.00	22.50	13.50
(9)	Detroit Tigers	45.00	22.50	13.50
(10)	Houston Astros	45.00	22.50	13.50
(11)	Kansas City Royals	45.00	22.50	13.50
(12)	Los Angeles Dodgers	50.00	25.00	15.00
(13)	Minnesota Twins	45.00	22.50	13.50
(14)	Montreal Expos	45.00	22.50	13.50
(15)	New York Mets	75.00	37.50	22.50
(16)	New York Yankees	115.00	55.00	35.00
(17)	Oakland A's	60.00	30.00	18.00
(18)	Philadelphia Phillies	45.00	22.50	13.50
(19)	Pittsburgh Pirates	50.00	25.00	15.00
(20)	San Diego Padres	45.00	22.50	13.50
(21)	San Francisco Giants	45.00	22.50	13.50
(22)	Seattle Pilots	125.00	62.50	37.00
(23)	St. Louis Cardinals	50.00	25.00	15.00
(24)	Washington Senators	50.00	25.00	15.00

1970 Fleer Team Logo Decals

These colorful team logo decals were pack inserts in Fleer's 1970 World Series issue. The decals measure 2-7/16" x 2-3/4". Backs have instructions for applying the decals.

		NM	EX	VG
Complete Set (24):		90.00	45.00	27.50
Common Team:		7.50	3.75	2.25
(1)	Atlanta Braves	7.50	3.75	2.25
(2)	Baltimore Orioles	9.00	4.50	2.75
(3)	Boston Red Sox	7.50	3.75	2.25
(4)	California Angels	7.50	3.75	2.25
(5)	Chicago Cubs	7.50	3.75	2.25
(6)	Chicago White Sox	7.50	3.75	2.25
(7)	Cincinnati Reds	7.50	3.75	2.25
(8)	Cleveland Indians	7.50	3.75	2.25
(9)	Detroit Tigers	7.50	3.75	2.25
(10)	Houston Astros	7.50	3.75	2.25
(11)	Kansas City Royals	7.50	3.75	2.25
(12)	Los Angeles Dodgers	7.50	3.75	2.25
(13)	Milwaukee Brewers	7.50	3.75	2.25
(14)	Minnesota Twins	7.50	3.75	2.25
(15)	Montreal Expos	7.50	3.75	2.25
(16)	New York Mets	7.50	3.75	2.25
(17)	New York Yankees	9.00	4.50	2.75
(18)	Oakland A's	7.50	3.75	2.25
(19)	Philadelphia Phillies	7.50	3.75	2.25
(20)	Pittsburgh Pirates	9.00	4.50	2.75
(21)	San Diego Padres	7.50	3.75	2.25
(22)	San Francisco Giants	7.50	3.75	2.25
(23)	St. Louis Cardinals	7.50	3.75	2.25
(24)	Washington Senators	10.00	5.00	3.00

1970 Fleer World Series

Utilizing the artwork done by Robert Laughlin a few years earlier for a privately marketed set, Fleer offered the first of two World Series highlights sets in 1970. Cards have color front with light blue backs. No card was issued for the 1904 World Series because no Series was played. Cards are checklisted in chronological order.

		NM	EX	VG
Complete Set (66):		150.00	75.00	45.00
Common Card:		1.50	.70	.45
Wax Pack:		35.00		
1	1903 Red Sox/Pirates	2.50	1.25	.70
2	1905 Giants/A's (Christy Mathewson)	2.50	1.25	.70
3	1906 White Sox/Cubs	1.50	.70	.45
4	1907 Cubs/Tigers	1.50	.70	.45
5	1908 Cubs/Tigers (Tinker/Evers/Chance)	3.00	1.50	.90
6	1909 Pirates/Tigers (Honus Wagner/Ty Cobb)	7.50	3.75	2.25
7	1910 A's/Cubs (Chief Bender/Jack Coombs)	2.00	1.00	.60
8	1911 A's/Giants (John McGraw)	2.00	1.00	.60
9	1912 Red Sox/Giants	2.00	1.00	.60
10	1913 A's/Giants	1.50	.70	.45
11	1914 Braves/A's	2.00	1.00	.60
12	1915 Red Sox/Phillies (Babe Ruth)	5.00	2.50	1.50
13	1916 Red Sox/Dodgers (Babe Ruth)	5.00	2.50	1.50
14	1917 White Sox/Giants	1.50	.70	.45
15	1918 Red Sox/Cubs	1.50	.70	.45
16	1919 Reds/White Sox	3.00	1.50	.90
17	1920 Indians/Dodgers (Stan Coveleski)	2.00	1.00	.60
18	1921 Giants/Yankees (Kenesaw Landis)	2.00	1.00	.60
19	1922 Giants/Yankees (Heinie Groh)	2.00	1.00	.60
20	1923 Yankees/Giants (Babe Ruth)	7.50	3.75	2.25
21	1924 Senators/Giants (John McGraw)	2.50	1.25	.70
22	1925 Pirates/Senators (Walter Johnson)	3.00	1.50	.90
23	1926 Cardinals/Yankees (Grover Cleveland Alexander/Tony Lazzeri)	3.00	1.50	.90
24	1927 Yankees/Pirates	2.50	1.25	.70
25	1928 Yankees/Cardinals (Babe Ruth/Lou Gehrig)	7.50	3.75	2.25
26	1929 A's/Cubs	1.50	.70	.45
27	1930 A's/Cardinals	1.50	.70	.45
28	1931 Cardinals/A's (Pepper Martin)	2.00	1.00	.60
29	1932 Yankees/Cubs (Babe Ruth/Lou Gehrig)	7.50	3.75	2.25
30	1933 Giants/Senators (Mel Ott)	2.50	1.25	.70
31	1934 Cardinals/Tigers	1.50	.70	.45
32	1935 Tigers/Cubs (Charlie Gehringer/Tommy Bridges)	2.00	1.00	.60
33	1936 Yankees/Giants	2.00	1.00	.60
34	1937 Yankees/Giants (Carl Hubbell)	2.50	1.25	.70
35	1938 Yankees/Cubs (Lou Gehrig)	4.00	2.00	1.25
36	1939 Yankees/Reds	1.50	.70	.45
37	1940 Reds/Tigers (Mike McCormick)	1.50	.70	.45
38	1941 Yankees/Dodgers	2.00	1.00	.60
39	1942 Cardinals/Yankees	1.50	.70	.45
40	1943 Yankees/Cardinals	1.50	.70	.45
41	1944 Cardinals/Browns	2.00	1.00	.60
42	1945 Tigers/Cubs (Hank Greenberg)	2.50	1.25	.70
43	1946 Cardinals/Red Sox (Enos Slaughter)	2.00	1.00	.60
44	1947 Yankees/Dodgers (Al Gionfriddo)	2.00	1.00	.60
45	1948 Indians/Braves	1.50	.70	.45
46	1949 Yankees/Dodgers (Allie Reynolds/Preacher Roe)	2.00	1.00	.60
47	1950 Yankees/Phillies	2.00	1.00	.60
48	1951 Yankees/Giants	1.50	.70	.45
49	1952 Yankees/Dodgers (Johnny Mize/Duke Snider)	2.50	1.25	.70
50	1953 Yankees/Dodgers (Carl Erskine)	2.00	1.00	.60
51	1954 Giants/Indians (Johnny Antonelli)	1.50	.70	.45
52	1955 Dodgers/Yankees	2.00	1.00	.60
53	1956 Yankees/Dodgers	2.00	1.00	.60
54	1957 Braves/Yankees (Lew Burdette)	3.00	1.50	.90
55	1958 Yankees/Braves (Bob Turley)	1.50	.70	.45
56	1959 Dodgers/White Sox (Chuck Essegian)	2.00	1.00	.60
57	1960 Pirates/Yankees	2.00	1.00	.60
58	1961 Yankees/Reds (Whitey Ford)	2.00	1.00	.60
59	1962 Yankees/Giants	1.50	.70	.45

60	1963 Dodgers/Yankees (Bill Skowron)	1.50	.70	.45
61	1964 Cardinals/Yankees (Bobby Richardson)	2.00	1.00	.60
62	1965 Dodgers/Twins	2.00	1.00	.60
63	1966 Orioles/Dodgers	1.50	.70	.45
64	1967 Cardinals/Red Sox	1.50	.70	.45
65	1968 Tigers/Cardinals	2.00	1.00	.60
66	1969 Mets/Orioles	4.50	2.25	1.25

1971-80 Fleer World Series

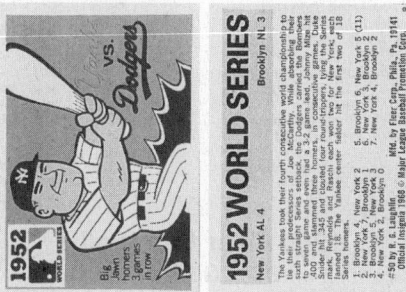

New artwork by Robert Laughlin is featured in the second of Fleer's World Series highlights sets. Fronts feature color art with backs printed in black. It appears as if the original set issued in 1971 was updated intermittently.

		NM	EX	VG
Complete Set (68):		135.00	65.00	40.00
Complete Set (75):		350.00	175.00	100.00
Common Card:		2.00	1.00	.60
Wax Pack:		30.00		
1	1903 Red Sox/Pirates (Cy Young)	6.00	3.00	1.75
2	1904 No World Series (John McGraw)	5.00	2.50	1.50
3	1905 Giants/A's (Christy Mathewson/Chief Bender)	5.00	2.50	1.50
4	1906 White Sox/Cubs	2.00	1.00	.60
5	1907 Cubs/Tigers	2.00	1.00	.60
6	1908 Cubs/Tigers (Ty Cobb)	5.00	2.50	1.50
7	1909 Pirates/Tigers	2.50	1.25	.70
8	1910 A's/Cubs (Eddie Collins)	2.50	1.25	.70
9	1911 A's/Giants (Home Run Baker)	2.50	1.25	.70
10	1912 Red Sox/Giants	2.00	1.00	.60
11	1913 A's/Giants (Christy Mathewson)	3.00	1.50	.90
12	1914 Braves/A's	2.00	1.00	.60
13	1915 Red Sox/Phillies (Grover Cleveland Alexander)	3.00	1.50	.90
14	1916 Red Sox/Dodgers (Jack Coombs)	2.00	1.00	.60
15	1917 White Sox/Giants (Red Faber)	2.50	1.25	.70
16	1918 Red Sox/Cubs (Babe Ruth)	6.00	3.00	1.75
17	1919 Reds/White Sox	4.00	2.00	1.25
18	1920 Indians/Dodgers (Elmer Smith)	2.50	1.25	.70
19	1921 Giants/Yankees (Waite Hoyt)	4.00	2.00	1.25
20	1922 Giants/Yankees (Art Nehf)	2.50	1.25	.70
21	1923 Giants/Yankees (Herb Pennock)	2.50	1.25	.70
22	1924 Senators/Giants (Walter Johnson)	4.00	2.00	1.25
23	1925 Pirates/Senators (Walter Johnson/Ki Ki Cuyler)	4.00	2.00	1.25
24	1926 Cardinals/Yankees (Rogers Hornsby)	4.00	2.00	1.25
25	1927 Yankees/Pirates	2.50	1.25	.70
26	1928 Yankees/Cardinals (Lou Gehrig)	5.00	2.50	1.50
27	1929 A's/Cubs (Howard Ehmke)	2.00	1.00	.60
28	1930 A's/Cardinals (Jimmie Foxx)	3.00	1.50	.90
29	1931 Cardinals/A's (Pepper Martin)	2.50	1.25	.70
30	1932 Yankees/Cubs (Babe Ruth)	6.00	3.00	1.75
31	1933 Giants/Senators (Carl Hubbell)	3.00	1.50	.90
32	1934 Cardinals/Tigers	2.00	1.00	.60
33	1935 Tigers/Cubs (Mickey Cochrane)	2.50	1.25	.70
34	1936 Yankees/Giants (Red Rolfe)	2.50	1.25	.70
35	1937 Yankees/Giants (Tony Lazerri)	4.00	2.00	1.25
36	1938 Yankees/Cubs	3.00	1.50	.90
37	1939 Yankees/Reds	3.00	1.50	.90
38	1940 Reds/Tigers (Mike McCormick)	2.00	1.00	.60
39	1941 Yankees/Dodgers (Charlie Keller)	2.50	1.25	.70
40	1942 Cardinals/Yankees (Whitey Kurowski/Johnny Beazley)	2.00	1.00	.60
41	1943 Yankees/Cardinals (Spud Chandler)	2.00	1.00	.60
42	1944 Cardinals/Browns (Mort Cooper)	2.50	1.25	.70

43	1945 Tigers/Cubs (Hank Greenberg)	3.00	1.50	.90
44	1946 Cardinals/Red Sox (Enos Slaughter)	2.50	1.25	.70
45	1947 Yankees/Dodgers (Johnny Lindell/Hugh Casey)	2.50	1.25	.70
46	1948 Indians/Braves	2.00	1.00	.60
47	1949 Yankees/Dodgers (Preacher Roe)	2.00	1.00	.60
48	1950 Yankees/Phillies (Allie Reynolds)	2.50	1.25	.70
49	1951 Yankees/Giants (Ed Lopat)	2.50	1.25	.70
50	1952 Yankees/Dodgers (Johnny Mize)	2.50	1.25	.70
51	1953 Yankees/Dodgers	2.50	1.25	.70
52	1954 Giants/Indians	2.00	1.00	.60
53	1955 Dodgers/Yankees (Duke Snider)	4.00	2.00	1.25
54	1956 Yankees/Dodgers	2.50	1.25	.70
55	1957 Braves/Yankees	2.50	1.25	.70
56	1958 Yankees/Braves (Hank Bauer)	2.50	1.25	.70
57	1959 Dodgers/White Sox (Duke Snider)	3.00	1.50	.90
58	1960 Pirates/Yankees (Bill Skowron/Bobby Richardson)	2.50	1.25	.70
59	1961 Yankees/Reds (Whitey Ford)	2.50	1.25	.70
60	1962 Yankees/Giants	2.00	1.00	.60
61	1963 Dodgers/Yankees	2.00	1.00	.60
62	1964 Cardinals/Yankees	2.50	1.25	.70
63	1965 Dodgers/Twins	2.50	1.25	.70
64	1966 Orioles/Dodgers	2.00	1.00	.60
65	1967 Cardinals/Red Sox	2.00	1.00	.60
66	1968 Tigers/Cardinals	2.50	1.25	.70
67	1969 Mets/Orioles	6.00	3.00	1.75
68	1970 Orioles/Reds	5.00	2.50	1.50
69	1971 Pirates/Orioles (Roberto Clemente)	35.00	17.50	10.00
70	1972 A's/Reds	15.00	7.50	4.50
71	1973 A's/Mets	15.00	7.50	4.50
(72)	1974 A's/Dodgers	50.00	25.00	15.00
(73)	1975 Reds/Red Sox	50.00	25.00	15.00
(74)	1976 Reds/Yankees	50.00	25.00	15.00
(75)	1977 Yankees/Dodgers	50.00	25.00	15.00

1972 Fleer Famous Feats

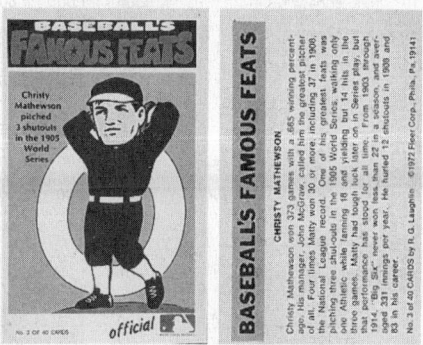

This 40-card set by sports artist R.G. Laughlin is oversized, 2-1/2" x 4". It features the pen and ink work of the artist, with several colors added to the front. The backs are printed in blue on white card stock. The Major League Baseball logo appears on the front of the card, one of the few Laughlin issues to do so. Selling price at issue was about $3.

		NM	EX	VG
Complete Set (40):		40.00	20.00	12.00
Common Player:		1.50	.75	.45
1	Joe McGinnity	2.00	1.00	.60
2	Rogers Hornsby	3.50	1.75	1.00
3	Christy Mathewson	4.00	2.00	1.25
4	Dazzy Vance	2.00	1.00	.60
5	Lou Gehrig	7.50	3.75	2.25
6	Jim Bottomley	2.00	1.00	.60
7	Johnny Evers	2.00	1.00	.60
8	Walter Johnson	4.00	2.00	1.25
9	Hack Wilson	2.00	1.00	.60
10	Wilbert Robinson	2.00	1.00	.60
11	Cy Young	3.50	1.75	1.00
12	Rudy York	1.50	.75	.45
13	Grover C. Alexander	2.00	1.00	.60
14	Fred Toney, Hippo Vaughn	1.50	.75	.45
15	Ty Cobb	7.50	3.75	2.25
16	Jimmie Foxx	3.50	1.75	1.00
17	Hub Leonard	1.50	.75	.45
18	Eddie Collins	2.00	1.00	.60
19	Joe Oeschger, Leon Cadore	1.50	.75	.45
20	Babe Ruth	9.00	4.50	2.75
21	Honus Wagner	4.00	2.00	1.25
22	Red Rolfe	1.50	.75	.45
23	Ed Walsh	2.00	1.00	.60
24	Paul Waner	2.00	1.00	.60
25	Mel Ott	2.50	1.25	.70
26	Eddie Plank	2.00	1.00	.60
27	Sam Crawford	2.00	1.00	.60
28	Napoleon Lajoie	2.00	1.00	.60
29	Ed Reulbach	1.50	.75	.45
30	Pinky Higgins	1.50	.75	.45
31	Bill Klem	2.00	1.00	.60
32	Tris Speaker	3.00	1.50	.90
33	Hank Gowdy	1.50	.75	.45
34	Lefty O'Doul	1.50	.75	.45

35	Lloyd Waner	2.00	1.00	.60
36	Chuck Klein	2.00	1.00	.60
37	Deacon Phillippe	1.50	.75	.45
38	Ed Delahanty	2.00	1.00	.60
39	Jack Chesbro	2.00	1.00	.60
40	Willie Keeler	2.00	1.00	.60

1973 Fleer Team Logo Decals

These colorful team logo decals were pack inserts in Fleer's "Wildest Days and Plays." The decals measure 4" x 2-11/16". Backs have instructions for applying the decals.

		NM	EX	VG
Complete Set (24):		110.00	55.00	33.00
Common Team:		9.00	4.50	2.75
(1)	Atlanta Braves	9.00	4.50	2.75
(2)	Baltimore Orioles	9.00	4.50	2.75
(3)	Boston Red Sox	9.00	4.50	2.75
(4)	California Angels	9.00	4.50	2.75
(5)	Chicago Cubs	9.00	4.50	2.75
(6)	Chicago White Sox	9.00	4.50	2.75
(7)	Cincinnati Reds	9.00	4.50	2.75
(8)	Cleveland Indians	9.00	4.50	2.75
(9)	Detroit Tigers	9.00	4.50	2.75
(10)	Houston Astros	9.00	4.50	2.75
(11)	Kansas City Royals	9.00	4.50	2.75
(12)	Los Angeles Dodgers	9.00	4.50	2.75
(13)	Milwaukee Brewers	9.00	4.50	2.75
(14)	Minnesota Twins	9.00	4.50	2.75
(15)	Montreal Expos	9.00	4.50	2.75
(16)	New York Mets	12.00	6.00	3.50
(17)	New York Yankees	10.00	5.00	3.00
(18)	Oakland A's	10.00	5.00	3.00
(19)	Philadelphia Phillies	9.00	4.50	2.75
(20)	Pittsburgh Pirates	11.00	5.50	3.25
(21)	San Diego Padres	9.00	4.50	2.75
(22)	San Francisco Giants	9.00	4.50	2.75
(23)	St. Louis Cardinals	9.00	4.50	2.75
(24)	Texas Rangers	12.00	6.00	3.50

1973 Fleer Team Signs

Each of the major league teams was represented in this issue of thick oversized (7-3/4" x 11-1/2") team logo signs. The blank-back signs have rounded corners and a grommeted hole at top-center for hanging. The unnumbered signs are checklisted here alphabetically.

		NM	EX	VG
Complete Set (24):		35.00	17.50	10.00
Common Team:		4.00	2.00	1.25
(1)	Atlanta Braves	4.00	2.00	1.25
(2)	Baltimore Orioles	4.00	2.00	1.25
(3)	Boston Red Sox	4.00	2.00	1.25
(4)	California Angels	4.00	2.00	1.25
(5)	Chicago Cubs	4.00	2.00	1.25
(6)	Chicago White Sox	4.00	2.00	1.25
(7)	Cincinnati Reds	5.00	2.50	1.50
(8)	Cleveland Indians	4.00	2.00	1.25
(9)	Detroit Tigers	4.00	2.00	1.25
(10)	Houston Astros	4.00	2.00	1.25
(11)	Kansas City Royals	4.00	2.00	1.25
(12)	Los Angeles Dodgers	4.00	2.00	1.25
(13)	Milwaukee Brewers	4.00	2.00	1.25
(14)	Minnesota Twins	4.00	2.00	1.25
(15)	Montreal Expos	4.00	2.00	1.25

(16)	New York Mets	5.00	2.50	1.50
(17)	New York Yankees	5.00	2.50	1.50
(18)	Oakland A's	5.00	2.50	1.50
(19)	Philadelphia Phillies	4.00	2.00	1.25
(20)	Pittsburgh Pirates	4.00	2.00	1.25
(21)	St. Louis Cardinals	4.00	2.00	1.25
(22)	San Francisco Giants	4.00	2.00	1.25
(23)	San Diego Padres	4.00	2.00	1.25
(24)	Texas Rangers	4.00	2.00	1.25

1973 Fleer Wildest Days and Plays

This 42-card set highlights unusual plays and happenings in baseball history, with the fronts featuring artwork by R.G. Laughlin. The cards are 2-1/2" x 4" and printed with color on the front and in red on the back. Original retail price was about $3.25.

		NM	EX	VG
Complete Set (42):		35.00	17.50	10.00
Common Player:		1.50	.70	.45
1	Cubs and Phillies Score 49 Runs in Game	1.50	.70	.45
2	Frank Chance Five HBP's in One Day	2.00	1.00	.60
3	Jim Thorpe Homered Into Three States	2.00	1.00	.60
4	Eddie Gaedel Midget in Majors	2.00	1.00	.60
5	Most Tied Game Ever	1.50	.70	.45
6	Seven Errors in One Inning	1.50	.70	.45
7	Four 20-Game Winners But No Pennant	1.50	.70	.45
8	Dummy Hoy Umpire Signals Strikes	2.00	1.00	.60
9	Fourteen Hits in One Inning	1.50	.70	.45
10	Yankees Not Shut Out for Two Years	1.50	.70	.45
11	Buck Weaver 17 Straight Fouls	2.00	1.00	.60
12	George Sisler Greatest Thrill	1.50	.70	.45
13	Wrong-Way Baserunner	1.50	.70	.45
14	Kiki Cuyler Sits Out Series	1.50	.70	.45
15	Grounder Climbed Wall	1.50	.70	.45
16	Gabby Street Washington Monument	1.50	.70	.45
17	Mel Ott Ejected Twice	2.00	1.00	.60
18	Shortest Pitching Career	1.50	.70	.45
19	Three Homers in One Inning	1.50	.70	.45
20	Bill Byron Singing Umpire	1.50	.70	.45
21	Fred Clarke Walking Steal of Home	1.50	.70	.45
22	Christy Mathewson 373rd Win Discovered	2.00	1.00	.60
23	Hitting Through the Unglaub Arc	1.50	.70	.45
24	Jim O'Rourke Catching at 52	1.50	.70	.45
25	Fired for Striking Out in Series	1.50	.70	.45
26	Eleven Run Inning on One Hit	1.50	.70	.45
27	58 Innings in 3 Days	1.50	.70	.45
28	Homer on Warm-up Pitch	1.50	.70	.45
29	Giants Win 26 Straight But Finish Fourth	1.50	.70	.45
30	Player Who Stole First Base	1.50	.70	.45
31	Ernie Shore Perfect Game in Relief	1.50	.70	.45
32	Greatest Comeback	1.50	.70	.45
33	All-Time Flash-in-the-Pan	1.50	.70	.45
34	Pruett Fanned Ruth 19 Out of 31	2.00	1.00	.60
35	Fixed Batting Race (Ty Cobb, Nap Lajoie)	2.00	1.00	.60
36	Wild Pitch Rebound Play	1.50	.70	.45
37	17 Straight Scoring Innings	1.50	.70	.45
38	Wildest Opening Day	1.50	.70	.45
39	Baseball's Strike One	1.50	.70	.45
40	Opening Day No-Hitter That Didn't Count	1.50	.70	.45
41	Jimmie Foxx 6 Straight Walks in One Game	2.00	1.00	.60
42	Entire Team Hit and Scored in Inning	1.50	.70	.45

1974 Fleer Baseball Firsts

This 42-card set from Fleer is titled "Baseball Firsts" and features several historical moments in baseball, as captured through the artwork of sports artist R.G. Laughlin. The cards are 2-1/2" x 4" and are

numbered on the back, which is gray card stock with black printing. The set is not licensed by Major League Baseball.

		NM	EX	VG
Complete Set (42):		80.00	40.00	25.00
Common Player:		2.00	1.00	.60
1	Slide	2.00	1.00	.60
2	Spring Training	2.00	1.00	.60
3	Bunt	2.00	1.00	.60
4	Catcher's Mask	2.00	1.00	.60
5	Four Straight Homers (Lou Gehrig)	10.00	5.00	3.00
6	Radio Broadcast	2.00	1.00	.60
7	Numbered Uniforms	2.00	1.00	.60
8	Shin Guards	2.00	1.00	.60
9	Players Association	2.00	1.00	.60
10	Knuckleball	2.00	1.00	.60
11	Player With Glasses	2.00	1.00	.60
12	Baseball Cards	12.00	6.00	3.50
13	Standardized Rules	2.00	1.00	.60
14	Grand Slam	2.00	1.00	.60
15	Player Fined	2.00	1.00	.60
16	Presidential Opener	2.00	1.00	.60
17	Player Transaction	2.00	1.00	.60
18	All-Star Game	2.00	1.00	.60
19	Scoreboard	2.00	1.00	.60
20	Cork-center Ball	2.00	1.00	.60
21	Scorekeeping	2.00	1.00	.60
22	Domed Stadium	2.00	1.00	.60
23	Batting Helmet	2.00	1.00	.60
24	Fatality	4.00	2.00	1.25
25	Unassisted Triple Play	2.00	1.00	.60
26	Home Run at Night	2.00	1.00	.60
27	Black Major Leaguer	4.00	2.00	1.25
28	Pinch Hitter	2.00	1.00	.60
29	Million Dollar World Series	2.00	1.00	.60
30	Tarpaulin	2.00	1.00	.60
31	Team Initials	2.00	1.00	.60
32	Pennant Playoff	2.00	1.00	.60
33	Glove	2.00	1.00	.60
34	Curve Ball	2.00	1.00	.60
35	Night Game	2.00	1.00	.60
36	Admission Charge	2.00	1.00	.60
37	Farm System	2.00	1.00	.60
38	Telecast	2.00	1.00	.60
39	Commissioner	2.00	1.00	.60
40	.400 Hitter	2.00	1.00	.60
41	World Series	2.00	1.00	.60
42	Player Into Service	2.00	1.00	.60

1975 Fleer Pioneers of Baseball

This 28-card set did not draw a great deal of interest in the hobby. The cards are slightly oversized (2-1/2" x 4") and feature sepia-toned photographs of old baseball players. The backs feature information about the player and the card number. A "Pioneers of Baseball" banner appears at the top of the card back. Each 10-cent pack included one card and one each cloth team pennant and patch, plus a stick of gum.

		NM	EX	VG
Complete Set (28):		20.00	10.00	6.00
Common Player:		1.50	.75	.45
Wax Pack:		6.00		
Wax Box (24):		65.00		
1	Cap Anson	1.50	.75	.45
2	Harry Wright	1.50	.75	.45

3	Buck Ewing	1.50	.75	.45
4	A.G. Spalding	1.50	.75	.45
5	Old Hoss Radbourn	1.50	.75	.45
6	Dan Brouthers	1.50	.75	.45
7	Roger Bresnahan	1.50	.75	.45
8	Mike Kelly	1.50	.75	.45
9	Ned Hanton	1.50	.75	.45
10	Ed Delahanty	1.50	.75	.45
11	Pud Galvin	1.50	.75	.45
12	Amos Rusie	1.50	.75	.45
13	Tommy McCarthy	1.50	.75	.45
14	Ty Cobb	6.00	3.00	1.75
15	John McGraw	1.50	.75	.45
16	Home Run Baker	1.50	.75	.45
17	Johnny Evers	1.50	.75	.45
18	Nap Lajoie	1.50	.75	.45
19	Cy Young	2.50	1.25	.70
20	Eddie Collins	1.50	.75	.45
21	John Glasscock	1.50	.75	.45
22	Hal Chase	1.50	.75	.45
23	Mordecai Brown	1.50	.75	.45
24	Jake Daubert	1.50	.75	.45
25	Mike Donlin	1.50	.75	.45
26	John Clarkson	1.50	.75	.45
27	Buck Herzog	1.50	.75	.45
28	Art Nehf	1.50	.75	.45

1980 Fleer Baseball's Famous Feats

Yet another incarnation of Robert Laughlin's "Baseball's Famous Feats" cartoon artwork is this 22-card issue, in standard 2-1/2" x 3-1/2" format. The player art is backed with team logo and pennant stickers, creating a huge variety of possible front/back combinations. The cards are licensed by Major League Baseball and numbered on the front.

		NM	EX	VG
Complete Set (22):		6.00	3.00	1.75
Common Player:		.75	.40	.25
1	Grover Cleveland Alexander	.75	.40	.25
2	Jimmy (Jimmie) Foxx	1.00	.50	.25
3	Ty Cobb	1.50	.70	.45
4	Walter Johnson	1.00	.50	.30
5	Hack Wilson	.75	.40	.25
6	Tris Speaker	1.00	.50	.30
7	Hank Gowdy	.75	.40	.25
8	Bill Klem	.75	.40	.25
9	Ed Reulbach	.75	.40	.25
10	Fred Toney, Hippo Vaughn	.75	.40	.25
11	Joe Oeschger, Leon Cadore	.75	.40	.25
12	Lloyd Waner	.75	.40	.25
13	Eddie Plank	.75	.40	.25
14	Deacon Phillippe	.75	.40	.25
15	Ed Dalahanty (Delahanty)	.75	.40	.25
16	Eddie Collins	.75	.40	.25
17	Jack Chesbro	.75	.40	.25
18	Red Rolfe	.75	.40	.25
19	Ed Walsh	.75	.40	.25
20	Honus Wagner	1.25	.60	.40
21	Nap Lajoie	.75	.40	.25
22	Cy Young	1.00	.50	.30

1980 Fleer World Series/ Team Logo Stickers

World Series cards similar to previous Fleer issues of the 1970s were issued in a new version in 1980. Wax packs containing five stickercards and a piece of bubblegum were offered for a nickel. Each card/sticker combination carried a World Series cartoon card from one of the Autumn Classics from 1940-1979. Unlike the earlier Fleer-Laughlin W.S.

cards, these are backed with a team-logo sticker, some of which bear the team's 1979 record, and some of which do not.

	NM	EX	VG
Complete Set (40):	50.00	25.00	15.00
Common Card:	1.50	.75	.45
Wax Pack (5):	4.00		
Wax Box (36):	80.00		
(1) 1940 Reds/Tigers (Mike McCormick)	1.50	.75	.45
(2) 1941 Yankees/Dodgers (Charlie Keller)	2.25	1.25	.75
(3) 1942 Cardinals/Yankees (Whitey Kurowski/Johnny Beazley)	2.25	1.25	.75
(4) 1943 Yankees/Cardinals (Spud Chandler)	2.25	1.25	.75
(5) 1944 Cardinals/Browns (Mort Cooper)	2.25	1.25	.75
(6) 1945 Tigers/Cubs (Hank Greenberg)	3.00	1.50	.90
(7) 1946 Cardinals/Red Sox (Enos Slaughter)	1.50	.75	.45
(8) 1947 Yankees/Dodgers (Johnny Lindell/Hugh Casey)	3.00	1.50	.90
(9) 1948 Indians/Braves	1.50	.75	.45
(10) 1949 Yankees/Dodgers (Preacher Roe)	3.00	1.50	.90
(11) 1950 Yankees/Phillies (Allie Reynolds)	3.00	1.50	.90
(12) 1951 Yankees/Giants (Ed Lopat)	3.00	1.50	.90
(13) 1952 Yankees/Dodgers (Johnny Mize)	4.00	2.00	1.25
(14) 1953 Yankees/Dodgers	4.00	2.00	1.25
(15) 1954 Giants/Indians	3.00	1.50	.90
(16) 1955 Dodgers/Yankees (Duke Snider)	4.50	2.25	1.25
(17) 1956 Yankees/Dodgers	4.00	2.00	1.25
(18) 1957 Braves/Yankees	4.00	2.00	1.25
(19) 1958 Yankees/Braves (Hank Bauer)	3.00	1.50	.90
(20) 1959 Dodgers/White Sox (Duke Snider)	3.00	1.50	.90
(21) 1960 Pirates/Yankees (Bill Skowron/Bobby Richardson)	4.50	2.25	1.25
(22) 1961 Yankees/Reds (Whitey Ford)	3.00	1.50	.90
(23) 1962 Yankees/Giants	3.00	1.50	.90
(24) 1963 Dodgers/Yankees	3.00	1.50	.90
(25) 1964 Cardinals/Yankees	3.00	1.50	.90
(26) 1965 Dodgers/Twins	1.50	.75	.45
(27) 1966 Orioles/Dodgers	1.50	.75	.45
(28) 1967 Cardinals/Red Sox	1.50	.75	.45
(29) 1968 Tigers/Cardinals	1.50	.75	.45
(30) 1969 Mets/Orioles	4.00	2.00	1.25
(31) 1970 Orioles/Reds	1.50	.75	.45
(32) 1971 Pirates/Orioles	1.50	.75	.45
(33) 1972 A's/Reds	1.50	.75	.45
(34) 1973 A's/Mets	1.50	.75	.45
(35) 1974 A's/Dodgers	1.50	.75	.45
(36) 1975 Reds/Red Sox	2.25	1.25	.75
(37) 1976 Reds/Yankees	1.50	.75	.45
(38) 1977 Yankees/Dodgers	2.25	1.25	.75
(39) 1978 Yankees/Dodgers	2.25	1.25	.75
(40) 1979 Pirates/Orioles	2.25	1.25	.75

1916 Fleischmann Bakery (D381)

B. W. KOCHER, Catcher
New York National

These cards were issued by a New York City bakery, presumably given away with the purchase of bread or other goods. The blank-back cards are printed in black-and-white in a 2-3/4" x 5-3/8" format. Fronts have player photos with the name, team and position in two lines beneath. Most cards have an Underwood & Underwood copyright notice on the picture. At bottom is a coupon that could be redeemed for an album to house the cards. Prices shown here are for cards without the coupon. Cards with coupon are valued at about the premium shown below. Cards are checklisted here in alphabetical order. Some cards can be found with differing sizes of the player's photo

and/or with wrong and corrected photos. A nearly identical issue was produced contemporarily by Ferguson Bread. The two can be distinguished by the two-line identification on front of the Fleischmann cards, and one-line identification on Fergusons.

	NM	EX	VG
Common Player:	390.00	190.00	115.00
With Coupon: 4-6X			
(1) Babe Adams	390.00	190.00	115.00
(2) Grover Alexander	720.00	290.00	155.00
(3) Walt E. Alexander	390.00	190.00	115.00
(4) Frank Allen	390.00	190.00	115.00
(5) Fred Anderson	390.00	190.00	115.00
(6) Dave Bancroft	540.00	215.00	110.00
(7) Jack Barry	390.00	190.00	115.00
(8a) Beals Becker (No uniform logo.)	390.00	190.00	115.00
(8b) Beals Becker (Partial uniform logo.)	390.00	190.00	115.00
(9) Eddie Burns	390.00	190.00	115.00
(10) George J. Burns	390.00	190.00	115.00
(11) Bobby Byrne	390.00	190.00	115.00
(12) Ray Caldwell	390.00	190.00	115.00
(13) James Callahan	390.00	190.00	115.00
(14) William Carrigan	390.00	190.00	115.00
(15) Larry Cheney	390.00	190.00	115.00
(16a) Tom Clark (No hand/glove.)	390.00	190.00	115.00
(16b) Tom Clark (Hand and glove show.)	390.00	190.00	115.00
(17) Ty Cobb	2,880	1,155	575.00
(18a) Ray W. Collins (Partial top button.)	390.00	190.00	115.00
(18b) Ray W. Collins (Full top button.)	390.00	190.00	115.00
(19) Jack Coombs	390.00	190.00	115.00
(20) A. Wilbur Cooper	390.00	190.00	115.00
(21) George Cutshaw	390.00	190.00	115.00
(22) Jake Daubert	390.00	190.00	115.00
(23) Wheezer Dell	390.00	190.00	115.00
(24) Bill Donovan	390.00	190.00	115.00
(25) Larry Doyle	390.00	190.00	115.00
(26) R.J. Egan	390.00	190.00	115.00
(27) Johnny Evers	540.00	215.00	110.00
(28) Ray Fisher	390.00	190.00	115.00
(29) Harry Gardner (Larry)	390.00	190.00	115.00
(30) Joe Gedeon	390.00	190.00	115.00
(31) Larry Gilbert	390.00	190.00	115.00
(32) Frank Gilhooley	390.00	190.00	115.00
(33) Hank Gowdy	390.00	190.00	115.00
(34) Sylvanus Gregg	390.00	190.00	115.00
(35) Tom Griffith	390.00	190.00	115.00
(36) Heinie Groh	390.00	190.00	115.00
(37) Bob Harmon	390.00	190.00	115.00
(38) Roy A. Hartzell	390.00	190.00	115.00
(39) Claude Hendrix	390.00	190.00	115.00
(40) Olaf Henriksen	390.00	190.00	115.00
(41) Buck Herzog	390.00	190.00	115.00
(42) Hugh High	390.00	190.00	115.00
(43) Dick Hoblitzell	390.00	190.00	115.00
(44) Herb Hunter	390.00	190.00	115.00
(45) Harold Janvrin	390.00	190.00	115.00
(46) Hugh Jennings	540.00	215.00	110.00
(47) John Johnston	390.00	190.00	115.00
(48) Erving Kantlehner	390.00	190.00	115.00
(49) Benny Kauff	390.00	190.00	115.00
(50a) Ray Keating (Error, striped cap, photo is Kocher.)	390.00	190.00	115.00
(50b) Ray Keating (Correct, "NY" on cap.)	390.00	190.00	115.00
(51) Wade Killefer	390.00	190.00	115.00
(52a) Elmer Knetzer (Error, no "B" on cap, photo is Konetchy.)	390.00	190.00	115.00
(52b) Elmer Knetzer (Correct, "B" on cap.)	390.00	190.00	115.00
(53a) B.W. Kocher (Error, "NY" on cap, photo is Keating.)	390.00	190.00	115.00
(53b) B.W. Kocher (Correct, striped cap.)	390.00	190.00	115.00
(54a) Ed. Konetchy (Error, "B" on cap, photo is Knetzer.)	390.00	190.00	115.00
(54b) Ed. Konetchy (Correct, no "B" on cap.)	390.00	190.00	115.00
(55) Fred Lauderous (Luderous)	390.00	190.00	115.00
(56) Dutch Leonard	390.00	190.00	115.00
(57) Duffy Lewis	390.00	190.00	115.00
(58) Slim Love	390.00	190.00	115.00
(59) Albert L. Mamaux	390.00	190.00	115.00
(60) Rabbit Maranville	540.00	215.00	110.00
(61) Rube Marquard	540.00	215.00	110.00
(62) Christy Mathewson	1,920	770.00	385.00
(63) Bill McKechnie	540.00	215.00	110.00
(64) Chief Meyer (Meyers)	390.00	190.00	115.00
(65) Otto Miller	390.00	190.00	115.00
(66) Fred Mollwitz	390.00	190.00	115.00
(67) Herbie Moran	390.00	190.00	115.00
(68) Mike Mowrey	390.00	190.00	115.00
(69) Dan Murphy	390.00	190.00	115.00
(70) Art Nehf	390.00	190.00	115.00
(71) Rube Oldring	390.00	190.00	115.00
(72) Oliver O'Mara	390.00	190.00	115.00
(73) Dode Paskert	390.00	190.00	115.00
(74) D.C. Pat Ragan	390.00	190.00	115.00
(75) William A. Rariden	390.00	190.00	115.00
(76) Davis Robertson	390.00	190.00	115.00
(77) Wm. Rodgers	390.00	190.00	115.00
(78) Edw. F. Rousch (Roush)	540.00	215.00	110.00
(79) Nap Rucker	390.00	190.00	115.00
(80) Dick Rudolph	390.00	190.00	115.00
(81) Wally Schang	390.00	190.00	115.00
(82) Rube Schauer	390.00	190.00	115.00
(83) Pete Schneider	390.00	190.00	115.00
(84) Ferd Schupp	390.00	190.00	115.00
(85) Ernie Shore	390.00	190.00	115.00
(86) Red Smith	390.00	190.00	115.00
(87) Fred Snodgrass	390.00	190.00	115.00
(88) Tris Speaker	660.00	265.00	130.00
(89) George Stallings	390.00	190.00	115.00
(90) Casey Stengel	575.00	230.00	115.00
(91) Sailor Stroud	390.00	190.00	115.00
(92) Amos Strunk	390.00	190.00	115.00
(93) Chas. (Jeff) Tesreau	390.00	190.00	115.00
(94a) Chester D. Thomas (One button shows.)	390.00	190.00	115.00
(94b) Chester D. Thomas (Two buttons.)	390.00	190.00	115.00
(95) Fred Toney	390.00	190.00	115.00
(96) Walt Tragesser	390.00	190.00	115.00
(97) Honus Wagner	5,000	960.00	480.00
(98) Carl Weilman	390.00	190.00	115.00
(99) Zack Wheat	540.00	215.00	110.00
(100) George Whitted	390.00	190.00	115.00
(101) Arthur Wilson	390.00	190.00	115.00
(102) Ivy Wingo	390.00	190.00	115.00
(103) Joe Wood	480.00	195.00	95.00

1940s Ford Babe Ruth Premium

The exact date of this premium photo's issue is unknown. The approximately 5" x 6-1/2" blank-back, black-and-white photo features Ruth in an oft-seen batting pose. In the wide white border at bottom is printed, "CONSULTANT / FORD MOTOR COMPANY / AMERICAN LEGION JUNIOR BASEBALL."

	NM	EX	VG
Babe Ruth	300.00	150.00	90.00

1961 Ford Pittsburgh Pirates Prints

The year after the team's dramatic World Series win over the Yankees, Pittsburgh area Ford dealers distributed a set of six player prints. The blank-back, 11-7/8 x 14-3/4" prints feature action drawings of the players by artist Robert Riger. Some of the prints are horizontal in format, some are vertical. A Ford Motor Co. copyright line appears in the lower-left corner and a line at bottom center identifies the player in the form of a title for the picture. The unnumbered prints are listed here in alphabetical order. The pictures were reprinted by an unauthorized party circa 1998.

	NM	EX	VG
Complete Set (6):	125.00	65.00	35.00
Common Player:	15.00	7.50	4.50
(1) BOB FRIEND COMES IN WITH THE FAST ONE (Bob Friend)	15.00	7.50	4.50
(2) CLEMENTE LINES ONE OVER SECOND (Roberto Clemente)	75.00	37.50	22.00
(3) GROAT CUTS DOWN A BRAVE STEAL (Dick Groat)	15.00	7.50	4.50
(4) HOAK HANDLES A HOT SHOT AT THIRD (Don Hoak)	15.00	7.50	4.50
(5) MAZ GETS THE BIG HIT (Bill Mazeroski)	30.00	15.00	9.00
(6) THE LAW (Vern Law)	15.00	7.50	4.50

1962 Ford Detroit Tigers Postcards

TERRY FOX, Pitcher
Detroit Tigers

Because baseball card collectors have to compete with auto memorabilia hobbyists for these scarce cards, they are among the most valuable postcard issues of the early 1960s. In 3-1/4" x 5-1/2" postcard format, the full-color cards feature photos taken on a golf course of players posed in front of various new Fords. White backs have a name, position and team, with a box for a stamp. Probably given out in conjunction with autograph appearances at car dealers (they are frequently found autographed), the set lacks some of the team's biggest stars (Al Kaline, Norm Cash), and includes coaches and even trainer Jack Homel. Probably because of lack of demand, the coaches' and trainer's cards are the scarcest to find today. The unnumbered cards are checklisted here alphabetically.

	NM	EX	VG
Complete Set (16):	1,425	710.00	425.00
Common Player:	60.00	30.00	18.00
(1) Hank Aguirre	90.00	45.00	27.50
(2) Steve Boros	120.00	60.00	35.00
(3) Dick Brown	90.00	45.00	27.50
(4) Jim Bunning	150.00	75.00	45.00
(5) Phil Cavaretta	135.00	65.00	40.00
(6) Rocky Colavito	185.00	90.00	55.00
(7) Terry Fox	60.00	30.00	18.00
(8) Purn Goldy	75.00	37.50	22.50
(9) Jack Homel	135.00	65.00	40.00
(10) Ron Kline	90.00	45.00	27.50
(11) Don Mossi	60.00	30.00	18.00
(12) George Myatt	120.00	60.00	35.00
(13) Ron Nischwitz	90.00	45.00	27.50
(14) Larry Osborne	60.00	30.00	18.00
(15) Phil Regan	90.00	45.00	27.50
(16) Mike Roarke	135.00	65.00	40.00

1938 Foto Fun

 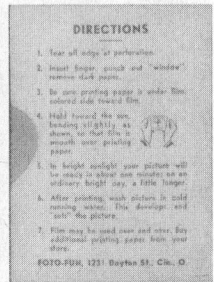

DIRECTIONS

An early attempt at a self-developing player photo-card (a technology that Topps used in the 1940s-50s) used a black-and-white negative and a piece of photo paper to create a blue-tint photo that could be placed in a gold cardboard frame. The back of the 2-3/4" x 3-5/8" frame is printed in brown and gives instructions for developing the photo. The checklist of the unnumbered cards, presented here alphabetically, may or may not be complete at 93.

	NM	EX	VG
Common Player:	160.00	80.00	45.00
(1) Luke Appling	375.00	185.00	110.00
(2) Morris Arnovich	160.00	80.00	45.00
(3) Eldon Auker	160.00	80.00	45.00
(4) Jim Bagby	160.00	80.00	45.00
(5) Red Barrett	160.00	80.00	45.00
(6) Roy Bell	160.00	80.00	45.00
(7) Wally Berger	160.00	80.00	45.00
(8) Oswald Bluege	160.00	80.00	45.00
(9) Frenchy Bordagaray	160.00	80.00	45.00
(10) Tom Bridges	160.00	80.00	45.00
(11) Dolf Camilli	160.00	80.00	45.00
(12) Ben Chapman	160.00	80.00	45.00
(13) Harland Clift (Harlond)	160.00	80.00	45.00
(14) Harry Craft	160.00	80.00	45.00
(15) Roger Cramer	160.00	80.00	45.00
(16) Joe Cronin	375.00	185.00	110.00
(17) Tony Cuccinello	160.00	80.00	45.00
(18) Kiki Cuyler	375.00	185.00	110.00

	NM	EX	VG
(19) Ellsworth Dahlgren	160.00	80.00	45.00
(20) Harry Danning	160.00	80.00	45.00
(21) Frank Demaree	160.00	80.00	45.00
(22) Gene Desautels	160.00	80.00	45.00
(23) Jim Deshong	160.00	80.00	45.00
(24) Bill Dickey	450.00	225.00	135.00
(25) Lou Fette	160.00	80.00	45.00
(26) Lou Finney	160.00	80.00	45.00
(27) Larry French	160.00	80.00	45.00
(28) Linus Frey	160.00	80.00	45.00
(29) Augie Galan	160.00	80.00	45.00
(30) Debs Garms	160.00	80.00	45.00
(31) Charles Gehringer	450.00	225.00	135.00
(32) Lefty Gomez	450.00	225.00	135.00
(33) Ival Goodman	160.00	80.00	45.00
(34) Lee Grissom	160.00	80.00	45.00
(35) Stan Hack	180.00	90.00	55.00
(36) Irving Hadley	160.00	80.00	45.00
(37) Rollie Hemsley	160.00	80.00	45.00
(38) Tommy Henrich	160.00	80.00	45.00
(39) Billy Herman	375.00	185.00	110.00
(40) Willard Hershberger	160.00	80.00	45.00
(41) Michael Higgins	160.00	80.00	45.00
(42) Oral Hildebrand	160.00	80.00	45.00
(43) Carl Hubbell	450.00	225.00	135.00
(44) Willis Hudlin	160.00	80.00	45.00
(45) Mike Kreevich	160.00	80.00	45.00
(46) Ralph Kress	160.00	80.00	45.00
(47) John Lanning	160.00	80.00	45.00
(48) Lyn Lary	160.00	80.00	45.00
(49) Cookie Lavagetto	160.00	80.00	45.00
(50) Thornton Lee	160.00	80.00	45.00
(51) Ernie Lombardi	375.00	185.00	110.00
(52) Al Lopez	375.00	185.00	110.00
(53) Ted Lyons	375.00	185.00	110.00
(54) Danny MacFayden	160.00	80.00	45.00
(55) Max Macon	160.00	80.00	45.00
(56) Pepper Martin	250.00	125.00	75.00
(57) Joe Marty	160.00	80.00	45.00
(58) Frank McCormick	160.00	80.00	45.00
(59) Bill McKechnie	375.00	185.00	110.00
(60) Joe Medwick	375.00	185.00	110.00
(61) Cliff Melton	160.00	80.00	45.00
(62) Charley Meyer (Myer)	160.00	80.00	45.00
(63) John Mize	450.00	225.00	135.00
(64) Terry Moore	180.00	90.00	55.00
(65) Whitey Moore	160.00	80.00	45.00
(66) Emmett Mueller	160.00	80.00	45.00
(67) Hugh Mulcahy	160.00	80.00	45.00
(68) Van L. Mungo	160.00	80.00	45.00
(69) Johnny Murphy	160.00	80.00	45.00
(70) Lynn Nelson	160.00	80.00	45.00
(71) Mel Ott	450.00	225.00	135.00
(72) Monte Pearson	160.00	80.00	45.00
(73) Bill Rogell	160.00	80.00	45.00
(74) George Selkirk	160.00	80.00	45.00
(75) Milt Shofner	160.00	80.00	45.00
(76) Al Simmons	375.00	185.00	110.00
(77) Clyde Shoun	160.00	80.00	45.00
(78) Gus Suhr	160.00	80.00	45.00
(79) Billy Sullivan	160.00	80.00	45.00
(80) Cecil Travis	160.00	80.00	45.00
(81) Pie Traynor	375.00	185.00	110.00
(82) Hal Trosky	160.00	80.00	45.00
(83) Jim Turner	160.00	80.00	45.00
(84) Johnny Vander Meer	160.00	80.00	45.00
(85) Oscar Vitt	160.00	80.00	45.00
(86) Gerald Walker	160.00	80.00	45.00
(87) Paul Waner	375.00	185.00	110.00
(88) Rabbit Warstler	160.00	80.00	45.00
(89) Bob Weiland	160.00	80.00	45.00
(90) Burgess Whitehead	160.00	80.00	45.00
(91) Earl Whitehill	160.00	80.00	45.00
(92) Rudy York	160.00	80.00	45.00
(93) Del Young	160.00	80.00	45.00

1887 Four Base Hits

NEW YORKS

Although the exact origin of this set is still in doubt, the Four Base Hits cards are among the rarest and most sought after of all 19th century tobacco issues. There is some speculation that the cards, measuring 2-1/4" x 3-7/8", were produced by Charles Gross & Co. because of their similarity to the Kalamazoo Bats issues, but there is also some evidence to support the theory that they were issued by August Beck & Co., producer of the Yum Yum set. The Four Base Hits cards feature sepia-toned photos with the player's name and position below the picture, and the words "Smoke Four Base Hits. Four For 10 Cents." along the bottom. The

card labeled "Daily" is a double error. The name should have been spelled "Daly," but the card actually pictures Billy Sunday. Many of the cards on this surely incomplete checklist are known to survive in only a single example; few in grades above VG.

	NM	EX	VG
Common Player:	25,000	15,000	
(1) John Clarkson	130,000	80,000	
(2) Tido Daily (Daly) (Photo is Billy Sunday.)	60,000	24,000	
(3) Pat Deasley	25,000	15,000	
(4) Mike Dorgan	25,000	15,000	
(5) Buck Ewing	115,000	80,000	
(6) Pete Gillespie	25,000	15,000	
(7) Frank Hankinson	25,000	15,000	
(8) King Kelly	150,000	120,000	
(9) Al Mays	25,000	15,000	
(10) Jim Mutrie	25,000	15,000	
(11) Chief Roseman	25,010	15,000	
(12) Marty Sullivan	25,000	15,000	
(13) Rip Van Haltren	25,000	15,000	
(14) John Ward	130,000	80,000	
(15) Mickey Welch	130,000	80,000	

1960s Nellie Fox Bowl Postcard

POST CARD

This specially marked version of a typical J.D. McCarthy postcard advertises on back the White Sox second baseman's bowling enterprise in Chambersburg, Pa. The card is black-and-white with a facsimile autograph on front.

	NM	EX	VG
Nellie Fox	35.00	17.50	10.50

1980 Franchise Babe Ruth

 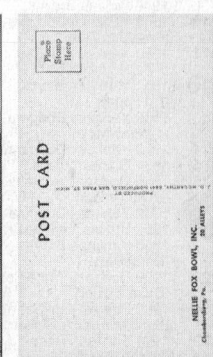

OUT OF ACTION—Babe Ruth gazes ruefully at the injured finger on his left hand. Babe tore the nail off when attempting a difficult catch in the outfield. With the Babe sidelined, the Yankees dropped five straight games.

7 © Copyright 1980 P.O. Box 506 BelAir, MD.

FRANCHISE
Collector's Edition-80 cards

The first in a series of collectors' issues relative to Maryland baseball, this 80-card set chronicles the life - on and off the field - of Babe Ruth. Fronts of the 2-1/2" x 3-1/2" cards have black-and-white photos surrounded by wide white borders. Backs are printed in red and black and include a caption and description of the front photo. At the time of issue, the set sold for about $8.

	NM	EX	VG
Complete Set (80):	35.00	17.50	10.00
Common Card:	1.00	.50	.30
1-80 Babe Ruth			

1961 Franklin Milk

While it is not part of the contemporary Cloverleaf Dairy milk carton Minnesota Twins issues, this carton is often collected alongside the others. Printed in red and blue, the portion of the milk carton advertising Harmon Killebrew's radio show measures about 4" x 4-1/2".

	NM	EX	VG
(1) Harmon Killebrew (Complete carton.)	1,600	800.00	480.00
(1) Harmon Killebrew (Cut panel.)	250.00	125.00	75.00

1964 Freihofer's Philadelphia Phillies

The attributed date is speculative, based on the players checklisted from this issue. These 8" x 10" pictures feature studio poses and are printed on heavy, non-glossy paper. A white border surrounds the photo, with the player name in typewriter-style all-caps at bottom. Backs are blank. Two styles of advertising have been seen imprinted on the pictures. Type 1 pictures have a bakery logo as part of the legend "ANOTHER FAVORITE / FROM FREIHOFER'S / that's who!" Type 2 pictures have a script inscription: "Best WISHES to a / Fellow Freihofer's Booster."

	NM	EX	VG
TYPE 1 (Logo)			
Ruben Amaro	50.00	25.00	15.00
Wes Covington	50.00	25.00	15.00
TYPE 2 (No logo.)			
Wes Covington	30.00	15.00	9.00

1963 French Bauer Reds Milk Caps

This regional set of cardboard milk bottle caps was issued in the Cincinnati area in 1963 and features 30 members of the Cincinnati Reds. The unnumbered, blank-backed discs are approximately 1-1/4" in diameter and feature rather crude drawings of the players with their names in script alongside the artwork and the words "Visit Beautiful Crosley Field/See The Reds in Action" along the outside. An album was issued to house the set. Some caps have been seen with incorrect picture/name combinations.

	NM	EX	VG
Complete Set (30):	1,300	650.00	400.00
Common Player:	25.00	12.50	7.50
Album:	100.00	50.00	30.00
(1) Don Blasingame	25.00	12.50	7.50
(2) Leo Cardenas	25.00	12.50	7.50
(3) Gordon Coleman	25.00	12.50	7.50
(4) Wm. O. DeWitt	25.00	12.50	7.50
(5) John Edwards	25.00	12.50	7.50
(6) Jesse Gonder	25.00	12.50	7.50
(7) Tommy Harper	25.00	12.50	7.50
(8) Bill Henry	25.00	12.50	7.50
(9) Fred Hutchinson	25.00	12.50	7.50
(10) Joey Jay	25.00	12.50	7.50
(11) Eddie Kasko	25.00	12.50	7.50
(12) Marty Keough	25.00	12.50	7.50
(13) Jim Maloney	25.00	12.50	7.50
(14) Joe Nuxhall	30.00	15.00	9.00
(15) Reggie Otero	25.00	12.50	7.50
(16) Jim O'Toole	25.00	12.50	7.50
(17) Jim Owens	25.00	12.50	7.50
(18) Vada Pinson	30.00	15.00	9.00
(19) Bob Purkey	25.00	12.50	7.50
(20) Frank Robinson	125.00	60.00	35.00
(21) Dr. Richard Rohde	25.00	12.50	7.50
(22) Pete Rose	500.00	250.00	150.00
(23) Ray Shore	25.00	12.50	7.50
(24) Dick Sisler	25.00	12.50	7.50
(25) Bob Skinner	25.00	12.50	7.50
(26) John Tsitorius	25.00	12.50	7.50

(27) Jim Turner	25.00	12.50	7.50
(28) Ken Walters	25.00	12.50	7.50
(29) Al Worthington	25.00	12.50	7.50
(30) Dom Zanni	25.00	12.50	7.50

1946 Friedman's Dodger Aces Postcard

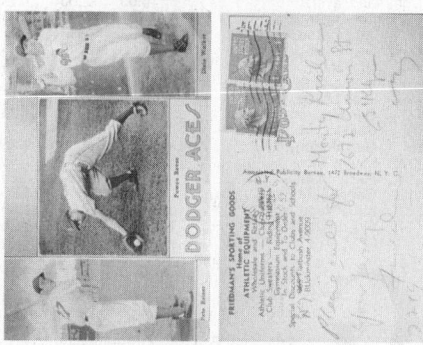

The date of issue is conjectural and could actually have been anytime in the 1940s until 1947, though the cards continued to be used at least into 1953 according to postally used examples. The 5-1/2" x 3-1/2" postcard has a linen finish on front and features color posed action photos of three Dodgers stars. Backs have information about the sporting goods store, a postage stamp box and a credit line to Associated Publicity Bureau.

	NM	EX	VG
Dodger Aces (Pete Reiser, Pewee (Pee Wee) Reese, Dixie Walker)	35.00	17.50	10.50

1960-61 Fritos Ticket Folders

Only a few players are known in this issue of folders which includes a "Jr. Guest Ticket" to selected Dodgers games. About 5-5/8" x 3", the folder has a black-and-white player portrait on front and is highlighted in red and yellow. When opened, the folder has advertising for Fritos corn chips (or other Firtos-Lay brands) and a Dodgers home schedule. Others may exist.

	NM	EX	VG
Common Player:	90.00	45.00	25.00
(1) Don Drysdale/1960 (Crispies advertising.)	250.00	125.00	75.00
(1) Don Drysdale/1961	200.00	100.00	60.00
(2) Gil Hodges/1960	200.00	100.00	60.00
(3) Frank Howard/1961	90.00	45.00	25.00
(4) Wally Moon/1960	150.00	75.00	45.00
(5) Charley Neal/1960	150.00	75.00	45.00

1977 Fritsch One-Year Winners

First printed in 1977, this collector's issue features players with brief, but often well-known, major league baseball careers. Because of the timing or duration of their playing days, few ever appeared on a major baseball card issue. The 2-1/2" x 3-1/2" cards have black-and-white photos on front, bordered in green, with the player name in white within a green strip at bottom. Backs are printed in black, red and white in similitude of the 1953 Bowman backs and contain personal data, stats and career highlights.

		NM	EX	VG
Complete Set (18):		12.00	6.00	3.50
Common Player:		1.00	.50	.30
1	Eddie Gaedel	5.00	2.50	1.50
2	Chuck Connors	3.00	1.50	.90
3	Joe Brovia	1.00	.50	.30
4	Ross Grimsley	1.00	.50	.30
5	Bob Thorpe	1.00	.50	.30
6	Pete Gray	5.00	2.50	1.50
7	Cy Buker	1.00	.50	.30
8	Ted Fritsch	2.00	1.00	.60
9	Ron Necciai	1.00	.50	.30
10	Nino Escalera	1.00	.50	.30
11	Bobo Holloman	1.00	.50	.30
12	Tony Roig	1.00	.50	.30
13	Paul Pettit	1.00	.50	.30
14	Paul Schramka	1.00	.50	.30
15	Hal Trosky	1.00	.50	.30
16	Floyd Wooldridge	1.00	.50	.30
17	Jim Westlake	1.00	.50	.30
18	Leon Brinkopf	1.00	.50	.30

1979 Fritsch One-Year Winners

PIDGE BROWNE

Players with short major-league careers, few of whom appeared on contemporary baseball cards, are featured in the second collectors' series of "One-Year Winners." The cards are numbered contiguously from the end of the 1977 issue and share a back format printed in red, white and black. Fronts of the 1979 issue have a white border and feature color player photos with a shadow box beneath carrying the name.

		NM	EX	VG
Complete Set (36):		40.00	20.00	12.00
Common Player:		3.00	1.50	.90
19	Daryl Robertson	3.00	1.50	.90
20	Gerry Schoen	3.00	1.50	.90
21	Jim Brenneman	3.00	1.50	.90
22	Pat House	3.00	1.50	.90
23	Ken Poulsen	3.00	1.50	.90
24	Arlo Brunsberg	3.00	1.50	.90
25	Jay Hankins	3.00	1.50	.90
26	Chuck Nieson	3.00	1.50	.90
27	Dick Joyce	3.00	1.50	.90
28	Jim Ellis	3.00	1.50	.90
29	John Duffie	3.00	1.50	.90
30	Vern Holtgrave	3.00	1.50	.90
31	Bill Bethea	3.00	1.50	.90
32	Joe Moock	3.00	1.50	.90
33	John Hoffman	3.00	1.50	.90
34	Jorge Rubio	3.00	1.50	.90
35	Fred Rath	3.00	1.50	.90
36	Jess Hickman	3.00	1.50	.90
37	Tom Fisher	3.00	1.50	.90
38	Dick Scott	3.00	1.50	.90
39	Jim Hibbs	3.00	1.50	.90
40	Paul Gilliford	3.00	1.50	.90
41	Bob Botz	3.00	1.50	.90
42	Jack Kubiszyn	3.00	1.50	.90
43	Rich Rusteck	3.00	1.50	.90
44	Roy Gleason	3.00	1.50	.90
45	Glenn Vaughn	3.00	1.50	.90
46	Bill Graham	3.00	1.50	.90
47	Dennis Musgraves	3.00	1.50	.90
48	Ron Henry	3.00	1.50	.90
49	Mike Jurewicz	3.00	1.50	.90
50	Pidge Browne	3.00	1.50	.90
51	Ron Keller	3.00	1.50	.90
52	Doug Gallagher	3.00	1.50	.90
53	Dave Thies	3.00	1.50	.90
54	Don Eaddy	3.00	1.50	.90

1928 Fro-joy (F52)

Capitalizing on the extreme popularity of Babe Ruth, these cards were given away with ice cream cones during the Aug. 6-11, 1928, "Fro-joy Cone Week." The 2-1/16" x 4" cards have black-and-white photos on front with a title and a few sentences explaining the photo. Backs contain advertising for Fro-joy Ice Cream and Cones. An uncut sheet along with a large-format action photo of Ruth was avail-

George Herman ("Babe") Ruth

"The Sultan of Swat," who holds the world's record for home-run hits in a single season with 60 circuit clouts during the regular playing season of 1927, topped by 2 more against Pittsburgh during the World's Series games last year.

Boys—Girls:

Fro-joy Ice Cream, in Fro-joy Cones, builds bone and strength. Eat one every day.

Chock-full of "YOUTH UNITS"

PICTURE NO. 1

This is the first in a series of six pictures of "Babe" Ruth being given free with Fro-joy Cones during the regular play-ing season of 1927, topped by 2 more against Pittsburgh during the World's Series games last year.

able in a mail-in redemption offer. Virtually all uncut sheets offered in the market today, and all color Fro-joy cards are modern counterfeits. Purchase of an uncut sheet without the original mailing envelope and/or premium picture is not advised. Cards graded by a major authentication firm carry a significant premium due to the prevalence of single-card counterfeits in the market.

		NM	EX	VG
	Complete Set (6):	3,250	1,625	975.00
	Uncut Sheet:	2,575	1,275	775.00
1	George Herman ("Babe") Ruth	750.00	375.00	225.00
2	Look Out, Mr. Pitcher!	500.00	250.00	150.00
3	Bang! The Babe Lines One Out!	500.00	250.00	150.00
4	When the "Babe" Comes Home	500.00	250.00	150.00
5	"Babe" Ruth's Grip!	200.00	100.00	60.00
6	Ruth is a Crack Fielder	500.00	250.00	150.00

1928 Fro-joy Premium Photo

This 8-1/2" x 10" photo of Babe Ruth was given away when a complete set of individual Fro-joy Babe Ruth cards was sent in for redemption. It is extremely scarce in its own right and is vital for verification of the authenticity of uncut Fro-joy card sheets. The premium photo is printed in blue in the debossed center area of a cream-colored card. A facsimile autograph of Ruth adorns the image.

	NM	EX	VG
Babe Ruth	1,200	600.00	360.00

1969 Fud's Photography Montreal Expos

Compliments of

JOSE LABOY

FUD'S PHOTOGRAPHY

This collectors' issue was produced by Bob Solon sometime after 1969. The 3-1/2" x 3" black-and-white horizontal cards have action photos of the

players with a white strip in the lower-right corner bearing the name. In the white border at top is "Compliments of," while the purported photo studio name is centered at bottom. Backs are blank. The unnumbered cards are checklisted here alphabetically.

		NM	EX	VG
	Complete Set (14):	40.00	20.00	12.00
	Common Player:	4.00	2.00	1.25
(1)	Bob Bailey	4.00	2.00	1.25
(2)	John Bateman	4.00	2.00	1.25
(3)	Don Bosch	4.00	2.00	1.25
(4)	Jim Grant	4.00	2.00	1.25
(5)	Mack Jones	4.00	2.00	1.25
(6)	Jose Laboy	4.00	2.00	1.25
(7)	Dan McGinn	4.00	2.00	1.25
(8)	Cal McLish	4.00	2.00	1.25
(9)	Carl Morton	4.00	2.00	1.25
(10)	Manny Mota	6.00	3.00	1.75
(11)	Rusty Staub	9.00	4.50	2.75
(12)	Gary Sutherland	4.00	2.00	1.25
(13)	Mike Wegener	4.00	2.00	1.25
(14)	Floyd Wicker	4.00	2.00	1.25

G

1888 G & B Chewing Gum (E223)

This set, issued with G&B Chewing Gum, is the first baseball card issued with candy or gum and the only 19th Century candy issue. The cards in the G&B set are small, measuring approximately 1-1/16" x 2-1/8", and nearly identical in format to the August Beck Yum Yum tobacco issue (N403). Many of the photos and pictures were shared between the sets. The player's name and position appear in thin capital letters below the photo, followed by either "National League" or "American League" (actually referring to the American Association) is indicated. Some of the "National League" cards also include the words "Chewing Gum" under the league designation. The set was assigned the ACC number E223. All of the action poses and some of the portraits are line drawings rather than photographs. Gaps have been left in the assigned numbering to accommodate future additions.

		NM	EX	VG
	Common Player:	10,000	4,000	2,500
(3)	Cap Anson/Btg	25,000	10,000	6,250
(4)	Cap Anson (Photo portrait.)	37,500	15,000	9,375
(7)	Lady Baldwin (Detroit) (Left arm extended.)	10,000	4,000	2,500
(9)	Mark Baldwin (Chicago) (Bat at side.)	10,000	4,000	2,500
(10)	Mark Baldwin (Chicago) (Photo portrait.)	31,250	12,500	7,815
(13)	Sam Barkley (Line portrait.)	10,000	4,000	2,500
(15)	Steve Brady (Photo portrait.)	31,250	12,500	7,815
(17)	Dan Brouthers (Pose unrecorded.)	31,250	12,500	7,815
(19)	Willard (California) Brown (Photo portrait.)	31,250	12,500	7,815
(20)	Willard (California) Brown (Line art.)	10,000	4,000	2,500
(23)	Charles Buffington (Buffinton) (Photo portrait.)	31,250	12,500	7,815
(25)	Tom Burns (Photo portrait.)	31,250	12,500	7,815
(27)	Doc Bushong (Line portrait.)	10,000	4,000	2,500
(29)	Bob Caruthers (Line portrait.)	10,000	4,000	2,500
(33)	John Clarkson (Photo portrait.)	37,500	15,000	9,375
(35)	John Coleman (Photo portrait.)	31,250	12,500	7,815
(37)	Charlie Comiskey (Photo portrait.)	18,750	7,500	4,690
(39)	Roger Connor/Btg	18,750	7,500	4,690
(40)	Roger Connor (Photo portrait.)	37,500	15,000	9,375
(43)	Con Daily (Photo portrait.)	31,250	12,500	7,815
(45)	Tom Deasley (Photo portrait.)	31,250	12,500	7,815
(47)	Jim Donahue (Photo portrait.)	31,250	12,500	7,815
(49)	Mike Dorgan (Photo portrait.)	31,250	12,500	7,815
(51)	Dude Esterbrook (Photo portrait.)	31,250	12,500	7,815
(53)	Buck Ewing (Photo portrait.)	37,500	15,000	9,375
(54)	Buck Ewing (With bat.)	18,750	7,500	4,690
(57)	Charlie Ferguson (Right arm head-high.)	10,000	4,000	2,500
(59)	Silver Flint (Line portrait.)	15,625	6,250	3,905
(61)	Pud Galvin (Ball in hands at front.)	18,750	7,500	4,690
(63)	Charlie Getzein (Getzien)/Throwing	10,000	4,000	2,500
(65)	Jack Glasscock (Line art.)	10,000	4,000	2,500
(67)	Will Gleason/Btg	10,000	4,000	2,500
(69)	Ed Greer (Photo portrait.)	31,250	12,500	7,815
(71)	Frank Hankinson (Photo portrait.)	31,250	12,500	7,815
(73)	Ned Hanlon/Btg	18,750	7,500	4,690
(75)	Pete Hotaling/Btg	15,625	6,250	3,905
(77)	Spud Johnson/Btg	10,000	4,000	2,500
(79)	Tim Keefe (Ball in hands above waist.)	18,750	7,500	4,690
(80)	Tim Keefe/Btg	18,750	7,500	4,690
(81)	Tim Keefe (Photo portrait.)	37,500	15,000	9,375
(83)	King Kelly/Btg	25,000	10,000	6,250
(84)	King Kelly (Photo, standing by urn.)	100,000	20,000	12,500
(87)	Gus Krock (Photo portrait.)	31,250	12,500	7,815
(89)	Arlie Latham (Line art.)	10,000	4,000	2,500
(91)	Connie Mack/Throwing	37,500	15,000	9,375
(93)	Kid Madden/Pitching	10,000	4,000	2,500
(95)	Al Mays (Photo portrait.)	31,250	12,500	7,815
(97)	Jumbo McGinnis (Line portrait.)	10,000	4,000	2,500
(99)	Doggie Miller (Leaning on bat.)	10,000	4,000	2,500
(101)	John Morrill (bat at side)	10,000	4,000	2,500
(103)	James Mutrie (Photo portrait.)	31,250	12,500	7,815
(105)	Hugh Nicoll (Nicol) (Line portrait.)	10,000	4,000	2,500
(107)	Tip O'Neill (Line portrait.)	10,000	4,000	2,500
(109)	Jim O'Rourke (Photo portrait.)	37,500	15,000	9,375
(111)	Dave Orr/Btg	10,000	4,000	2,500
(112)	Dave Orr (Photo portrait.)	31,250	12,500	7,815
(115)	Fred Pfeffer (Bat on shoulder.)	10,000	4,000	2,500
(117)	Henry Porter/Pitching	10,000	4,000	2,500
(119)	Al Reache (Reach) (Line portrait.)(Possibly unique; value undetermined.)			
(121)	Danny Richardson/Btg	10,000	4,000	2,500
(122)	Danny Richardson (Photo portrait.)	31,250	12,500	7,815
(125)	Yank Robinson (Line portrait.)	10,000	4,000	2,500
(127)	Chief Roseman (Photo portrait.)	31,250	12,500	7,815
(129)	Jimmy Ryan (Photo portrait.)	31,250	12,500	7,815
(130)	Jimmy Ryan/Throwing	10,000	4,000	2,500
(133)	Pop Smith (Photo portrait.)	31,250	12,500	7,815
(137)	Bill Sowders (Ball in hands at chest.)	10,000	4,000	2,500
(138)	Bill Sowders/Throwing	10,000	4,000	2,500
(139)	Albert Spaulding (Spalding) (Line portrait.) (Possibly unique; value undetermined.)			
(141)	Marty Sullivan (Line portrait.)	10,000	4,000	2,500
(143)	Billy Sunday/Fielding	15,620	6,250	3,905
(144)	Billy Sunday (Photo portrait.)	34,375	13,750	8,595
(145)	Ezra Sutton/Btg	10,000	4,000	2,500
(149)	Sam Thompson/Btg	18,750	7,500	4,690
(153)	Mike Tiernan/Btg	10,000	4,000	2,500
(154)	Mike Tiernan (Photo portrait.)	31,250	12,500	7,815
(157)	Larry Twitchell (Photo portrait.)	31,250	12,500	7,815
(159)	Rip Van Haltren (Photo portrait.)	31,250	12,500	7,815
(161)	Chris Von Der Ahe (Line portrait.)	10,000	4,000	2,500
(165)	John Ward (Photo portrait.)	37,500	15,000	9,375
(169)	Mickey Welch (Ball in hands above waist.)	18,750	7,500	4,690
(170)	Mickey Welch (Right arm extended forward.)	18,750	7,500	4,690
(171)	Mickey Welch (Photo portrait.)	37,500	15,000	9,375
(173)	Curt Welsh (Welch)	10,000	4,000	2,500
(177)	Jim Whitney	10,000	4,000	2,500
(181)	Pete Wood/Throwing	10,000	4,000	2,500

1966 H.F. Gardner Postcards

Baseball players (and track legend Jesse Owens) who were born in Alabama are featured in this issue credited on some of the cards' backs to a

Bessemer, Ala., firm, Scenic South Card Co. Fronts feature borderless color photos attributed to H.F. Gardner. The date given is somewhat arbitrary based on the mention of the Atlanta Braves on the back of a card. Cards are in standard 3-1/2" x 5-1/2" postcard size and format. A brief biography of the athletes appears on the back, along with the credits. A quantity of the Aarons and Williams cards were found in a warehouse in 1999, driving down their prices.

	NM	EX	VG
Complete Set (5):	15.00	7.50	4.50
Common Player:	3.00	1.50	.90
(1) Hank Aaron, Tommie Aaron	6.00	3.00	1.75
(2) Bill Bruton	3.50	1.75	1.00
(3) Lee Maye	3.50	1.75	1.00
(4) Jesse Owens	4.50	2.25	1.25
(5) Billy Williams	3.00	1.50	.90

1922 Gassler's American Maid Bread

JOE JUDGE
1st B.—Washington Americans

These 2" x 3-1/4" black-and-white cards are one of several versions of the W575-1 strip cards with custom-printed advertising on the backs. It is unknown whether each card in the W575-1 checklist can be found with the Gassler's back.

	NM	EX	VG
Common Player:	150.00	75.00	45.00
Stars: 4-6X			

(See W575-1 for checklist; Gassler values 3X-4X.)

1962 Gehl's Ice Cream

Issued only in the Milwaukee area to promote sales of Gold-Mine brand ice cream, the six cards in this black-and-white set all feature Roger Maris, who the previous year had broken Babe Ruth's season home run record. The 4" x 5" cards are blank backed and each has a facsimile autograph on front reading "To My / Gold Mine Pal / Roger Maris." The cards are unnumbered; a description of each is provided in the checklist.

	NM	EX	VG
Complete Set (6):	1,600	800.00	480.00
Common Card:	400.00	200.00	120.00
(1) Roger Maris (Bat on shoulder, close-up.)	400.00	200.00	120.00
(2) Roger Maris (Bat on shoulder, photo to waist.)	400.00	200.00	120.00
(3) Roger Maris (Batting stance.)	400.00	200.00	120.00
(4) Roger Maris ("Hitting My 61st," ballpark photo.)	325.00	160.00	100.00
(5) Roger Maris (Holding bat in hands.)	400.00	200.00	120.00
(6) Roger Maris (Portrait in warm-up jacket.)	400.00	200.00	120.00

1941 Lou Gehrig Memorial Ticket

On July 4, 1941, just a month after his death, the N.Y. Yankees scheduled special memorial ceremonies for the Iron Horse. Tickets for the event picture Gehrig and were issued in several colors and price ranges based on seat location. Most often found in stub form of about 3-3/8" x 2-1/2", full tickets are also occasionally seen, probably because a rainout on July 4 forced the ceremonies to the following Sunday.

	NM	EX	VG
Lou Gehrig (Ticket stub.)	1,300	650.00	390.00
Lou Gehrig (Full ticket.)	3,250	1,625	975.00

1911-14 General Baking Co. (D304)

MARTY O'TOOLE, PITTSBURG, NATL.

This issue by a bakery based in Buffalo, N.Y., is similar in design to contemporary tobacco and candy cards, but is larger in size, at 1-3/4" x 2-1/2". Fronts feature a color lithograph with the player's name and team below in capital letters. Some players who changed teams in 1913-14 are found with the team name obliterated at bottom by a black line. Five different back styles are known, listed here by the principal brand name: 1) Brunners, 2) Butter Krust, 3) General Baking Co., 4) Weber Bakery, 5) Martens Bakery. The complete set price does not include "no-team" variations. Modern counterfeits of the issue are widely seen in the hobby market.

	NM	EX	VG
Complete Set (25):	270,000	108,000	54,000
Common Player:	3,600	1,425	720.00
(1) J. Frank Baker	11,250	4,500	2,250
(2) Jack Barry	3,600	1,425	720.00
(3) George Bell	3,600	1,425	720.00
(4) Charles Bender	11,250	4,500	2,250
(5a) Frank Chance (Chicago)	11,250	4,500	2,250
(5b) Frank Chance (No team.)	15,000	6,000	3,000
(6a) Hal Chase (N.Y.)	4,500	2,100	900.00
(6b) Hal Chase (No team.)	5,400	2,400	1,200
(7) Ty Cobb	60,000	30,000	9,000
(8) Eddie Collins	11,250	4,500	2,250
(9a) Otis Crandall (N.Y.)	3,600	1,425	720.00
(9b) Otis Crandall (No team.)	5,250	2,250	1,050
(10) Sam Crawford	11,250	4,500	2,250
(11a) John Evers (Chicago)	11,250	4,500	2,250
(11b) John Evers (No team.)	15,000	6,000	3,000
(12) Arthur Fletcher	3,600	1,425	720.00
(13a) Charles Herzog (N.Y.)	3,600	1,425	720.00
(13b) Charles Herzog (No team.)	5,250	2,250	1,050
(14) M. (Billy) Kelly	3,600	1,425	720.00
(15) Napoleon Lajoie	15,000	6,750	3,750
(16) Rube Marquard	11,250	4,500	2,250
(17) Christy Mathewson	60,000	30,000	9,000
(18) Fred Merkle	3,600	1,425	720.00
(19) "Chief" Meyers	3,600	1,425	720.00
(20) Marty O'Toole	3,600	1,425	720.00
(21) Nap. Rucker	3,600	1,425	720.00
(22) Arthur Shafer	3,600	1,425	720.00
(23) Fred Tenny (Tenney)	6,000	2,550	1,350
(24) Honus Wagner	60,000	30,000	9,000
(25) Cy Young	52,500	24,000	7,500

1915 General Baking Co. (D303)

Issued in 1915 by the General Baking Co., these unnumbered cards measure 1-1/2" x 2-3/4". The player pictures and format of the cards is identical to the E106 set, but the D303 cards are easily identified by the advertisement for General Baking on the back.

COMPLIMENTS OF
GENERAL BAKING CO.
UNTIL SEPTEMBER 1ST
WRAPPED IN
STAR BREAD
FRENCH BREAD
LITTLE GENERAL BREAD

Cobb, c. f. Detroit Americans

	NM	EX	VG
Complete Set (51):	80,000	32,000	16,000
Common Player:	1,600	800.00	300.00
(1) Jack Barry	1,600	800.00	300.00
(2) Chief Bender (Blue background.)	3,000	1,700	800.00
(3) Chief Bender (Green background.)	3,000	1,750	800.00
(4) Bob Bescher (New York)	1,600	800.00	300.00
(5) Bob Bescher (St. Louis)	1,600	800.00	300.00
(6) Roger Bresnahan	3,000	1,750	800.00
(7) Al Bridwell	1,600	800.00	300.00
(8) Donie Bush	1,600	800.00	300.00
(9) Hal Chase/Catching	1,800	800.00	360.00
(10) Hal Chase/Portrait	1,800	900.00	360.00
(11) Ty Cobb/Btg	20,000	10,000	3,000
(12) Ty Cobb (Leaning on bat.)	30,000	15,000	5,000
(13) Eddie Collins	3,000	1,700	800.00
(14) Sam Crawford	3,000	1,700	800.00
(15) Ray Demmitt	1,600	800.00	300.00
(16) Wild Bill Donovan	1,600	800.00	300.00
(17) Red Dooin	1,600	800.00	300.00
(18) Mickey Doolan	1,600	800.00	300.00
(19) Larry Doyle	1,600	800.00	300.00
(20) Clyde Engle	1,600	800.00	300.00
(21) Johnny Evers	3,000	1,700	800.00
(22) Art Fromme	1,600	800.00	300.00
(23) George Gibson/Catching (Back view.)	1,600	800.00	300.00
(24) George Gibson/Catching (Front view.)	1,600	800.00	300.00
(25) Roy Hartzell	1,600	800.00	300.00
(26) Fred Jacklitsch	1,600	800.00	300.00
(27) Hugh Jennings	3,000	1,750	800.00
(28) Otto Knabe	1,600	800.00	300.00
(29) Nap Lajoie	4,000	2,000	1,000
(30) Hans Lobert	1,600	800.00	300.00
(31) Rube Marquard	1,500	850.00	400.00
(32) Christy Mathewson	6,000	3,500	1,250
(33) John McGraw	1,500	850.00	400.00
(34) George McQuillan	800.00	400.00	150.00
(35) Dots Miller	800.00	400.00	150.00
(36) Danny Murphy	800.00	400.00	150.00
(37) Rebel Oakes	800.00	400.00	150.00
(38) Eddie Plank (No position on front.)	1,500	850.00	400.00
(39) Eddie Plank (Position on front.)	4,000	2,500	1,000
(40) Germany Schaefer	800.00	400.00	150.00
(41) Boss Smith (Schmidt)	800.00	400.00	150.00
(42) Tris Speaker	2,200	1,200	600.00
(43) Oscar Stanage	800.00	400.00	150.00
(44) George Stovall	800.00	400.00	150.00
(45) Jeff Sweeney	800.00	400.00	150.00
(46) Joe Tinker/Btg	1,500	850.00	400.00
(47) Joe Tinker/Portrait	1,500	850.00	400.00
(48) Honus Wagner/Btg	10,000	5,000	1,500
(49) Honus Wagner/Throwing	15,000	7,500	2,500
(50) Hooks Wiltse	800.00	400.00	150.00
(51) Heinie Zimmerman	800.00	400.00	150.00

1908 General Photo Co. St. Louis Browns Postcards

RUBE WADDELL

The extent of this postcard issue by a hometown printer is unknown. It is likely other single-player postcards were issued. Approximately 3-1/2" x 5-1/2", the cards are black-and-white with a credit line on bottom: "Photo by General Photo Co., 610 Granite Bldg., St. Louis." On the team photo card, players are identified below the group photo.

		NM	EX	VG
(1)	"Rube" Waddell	500.00	250.00	150.00
(2)	St. Louis Browns - 1908	750.00	375.00	225.00

1948 Gentle's Bread Boston Braves

FOR ENERGY I PREFER

GENTLES

HOMSTYLE WHITE

WEIGHT 1 LB.

These 3" x 9" waxed-paper end labels were found on loaves of Gentle's bread. Printed in blue and red, the labels depict action poses of the National League Champion '48 Braves. A facsimile autograph appears with the photo. Backs are blank. The unnumbered labels are checklisted here alphabetically.

		NM	EX	VG
Complete Set (9):		3,000	1,500	900.00
Common Player:		400.00	200.00	120.00
(1)	Alvin Dark	450.00	225.00	135.00
(2)	Bob Elliott	400.00	200.00	120.00
(3)	Tommy Heath	400.00	200.00	120.00
(4)	Tommy Holmes	400.00	200.00	120.00
(5)	Phil Masi	400.00	200.00	120.00
(6)	John Sain	450.00	225.00	135.00
(7)	Warren Spahn	600.00	300.00	180.00
(8)	Eddie Stanky	450.00	225.00	135.00
(9)	Earl Torgeson	400.00	200.00	120.00

1956 Gentry Magazine Ty Cobb

In issue #20 of Gentry magazine, dated Fall, 1956, a feature article on card collecting was enhanced with the inclusion of an original Ty Cobb card tipped onto an interior page. Measuring about 4" x 2-1/4" and blank-backed, the color card is similar in design to the T205 tobacco card issue.

	NM	EX	VG
Complete Magazine:	125.00	65.00	40.00
Ty Cobb	90.00	45.00	27.00

1909-10 German Baseball Stamps

A marginal notation "Made in Germany" on one of the stamps in this series identifies its origins. Little else in known of them. The stamps measure about 1-3/8" to 1-1/2" by 1-3/4" to 1-7/8". They are printed in bright colors on a pink background with name and team in blue. Because of their European origins, there are many mistakes in player and team names. The crude pictures are not representative of the player named. Unnumbered stamps are listed here in alphabetical order. It is evident several different configurations of 35-stamp sheets must have been issued.

		NM	EX	VG
Complete Sheet (35):		1,150	575.00	345.00
Complete Set (41):		1,300	650.00	400.00
Common Player:		65.00	32.50	20.00
(1)	Ginger Beaumont	65.00	32.50	20.00
(2)	Frank Bowerman	65.00	32.50	20.00
(3)	Kitty Bransfield	65.00	32.50	20.00
(4)	Al Bridwell	65.00	32.50	20.00
(5a)	Roger Bresnahan (Light shirt.)	100.00	50.00	30.00
(5b)	Roger Bresnahan (Dark shirt.)	100.00	50.00	30.00
(6)	Bill Carrigan	65.00	32.50	20.00
(7)	Hal Chase	80.00	40.00	24.00
(8)	Eddie Collins	100.00	50.00	30.00
(9)	Harry Davis	65.00	32.50	20.00
(10)	Wild Bill Donovan	65.00	32.50	20.00
(11)	Larry Doyle	65.00	32.50	20.00
(12)	Jean Dubuc	65.00	32.50	20.00
(13)	Kid Elberfeld (Elberfeld)	65.00	32.50	20.00
(14)	Dick Hoblitzell	65.00	32.50	20.00
(15)	Solly Hoffman (Hofman)	65.00	32.50	20.00
(16)	Tim Jordan	65.00	32.50	20.00
(17)	Willie Keeler	100.00	50.00	30.00
(18)	Nap Lajoie	100.00	50.00	30.00
(19)	Tommy Leach	65.00	32.50	20.00
(20)	Christy Mathewson	325.00	160.00	100.00
(21)	Dots Miller	65.00	32.50	20.00
(22)	John McGraw	100.00	50.00	30.00
(23)	Eddie Plank	100.00	50.00	30.00
(24)	Jack Rowan	65.00	32.50	20.00
(25)	Nap Rucker	65.00	32.50	20.00
(26)	Shannon (Boston)	65.00	32.50	20.00
(27)	Frank Smith	65.00	32.50	20.00
(28)	Tris Speaker	120.00	60.00	35.00
(29)	Jake Stahl	65.00	32.50	20.00
(30)	Lee Tannehill	65.00	32.50	20.00
(31)	Fred Tenney	65.00	32.50	20.00
(32)	Ira Thomas	65.00	32.50	20.00
(33)	Joe Tinker	100.00	50.00	30.00
(34)	Honus Wagner	285.00	140.00	85.00
(35)	Jimmy Williams	65.00	32.50	20.00
(36)	Cy Young	165.00	85.00	50.00
(37)	baseball	15.00	7.50	4.50
(38)	bat	15.00	7.50	4.50
(39)	body protector	15.00	7.50	4.50
(40)	catcher's mask	15.00	7.50	4.50
(41)	crossed bats	15.00	7.50	4.50
(42)	glove	15.00	7.50	4.50

1923 German Baseball Transfers

With crude artwork lifted from the W515 strip card set, this issue of baseball player (and boxer) transfers was produced in Germany. Approximately 1-3/16" x 1-1/2", the stamps are printed in red on a green background. All of the design, except for the "MADE IN

GERMANY" notation in the white bottom margin, is in mirror-image, befitting their use as tattoos or transfers. Two of the baseball players are double-prints. The unnumbered stamps (baseball only) are checklisted here alphabetically.

		NM	EX	VG
Complete Baseball Set (13):		350.00	175.00	105.00
Complete Sheet (25):		400.00	200.00	120.00
Common Player:		40.00	20.00	12.00
(1)	Grover Alexander	45.00	22.00	13.50
(2)	Dave Bancroft	40.00	20.00	12.00
(3)	George (J.) Burns	30.00	15.00	9.00
(4)	"Ty" Cobb	100.00	50.00	30.00
(5)	Red Faber/DP	25.00	12.50	7.50
(6)	Arthur Nehf	30.00	15.00	9.00
(7)	"Babe" Ruth	200.00	100.00	60.00
(8)	Ray Schalk	40.00	20.00	12.00
(9)	Everett Scott	30.00	15.00	9.00
(10)	Bob Shawkey	30.00	15.00	9.00
(11)	Tris Speaker	45.00	22.00	13.50
(12)	"Casey" Stengel	45.00	22.00	13.50
(13)	Zack Wheat/DP	30.00	15.00	9.00

1922 Lou Gertenrich

One of the most attractive advertising backs of the 1920s is found on this version of the 1922 issue which is most often found with American Caramel ads on back. Gertenrich had a three-game major league career between 1901-1903, supporting his advertising claim of "The Baseball Player Candy Manufacturer." Probably originating in Chicago, these cards are 2" x 3-1/2" black-and-white. The set shares the checklist with the American Caramel Co. (E121) set of 120. Because of the scarcity and appeal of this regional issue, the Gertenrich versions carry a substantial premium for type-card and superstar collectors.

	NM	EX	VG
Common Player:	600.00	300.00	175.00
Stars: 3-4X			

(See 1922 American Caramel Series of 120 for checklist.)

1888 Gilbert & Bacon Cabinets

The known range of this cabinet card issue comprises mostly members of the 1888 Philadelphia Athletics and Phillies. The posed action photos on the approximately 4-1/4" x 6-1/2" cards are the same pictures seen on many of the players' Old Judge and Old Judge cabinet cards. The G&B cabinets have an embossed Goodwin & Co. copyright seal. An elaborate typescript Gilbert & Bacon studio logo is found in the bottom-left border, with the city named at right. Backs have an ornate studio logo.

		NM	EX	VG
Common Player:		2,500	1,000	600.00
(1)	Louis Bierbauer	2,500	1,000	600.00
(2)	Bill Blair	2,500	1,000	600.00
(3)	Charlie Ferguson (Ball in hands at chest.)	2,500	1,000	600.00
(4)	Charlie Ferguson/Btg	2,500	1,000	600.00
(5)	Charlie Ferguson/Throwing	2,500	1,000	600.00
(6)	Kid Gleason	2,500	1,000	600.00
(7)	John Henry	2,500	1,000	600.00
(8)	Henry Larkin	2,500	1,000	600.00
(9)	Denny Lyons	2,500	1,000	600.00

		NM	EX	VG
(11)	Deacon McGuire (Bat behind head.)	2,500	1,000	600.00
(12)	Deacon McGuire (Bat on shoulder)	2,500	1,000	600.00
(13)	Deacon McGuire/Fielding (Hands at waist.)	2,500	1,000	600.00
(14)	Deacon McGuire/Fielding (Hands head-high.)	2,500	1,000	600.00
(15)	Deacon McGuire/Throwing	2,500	1,000	600.00
(16)	George Pinkney (Bat at 45-degree angle.)	2,500	1,000	600.00
(17)	George Pinkney (Bat at 60-degree angle.)	2,500	1,000	600.00
(18)	George Pinkney (Bat nearly horizontal.)	2,500	1,000	600.00
(19)	George Pinkney (Fielding fly ball.)	2,500	1,000	600.00
(21)	George Pinkney (Fielding line drive.)	2,500	1,000	600.00
(22)	George Pinkney/Throwing	2,500	1,000	600.00
(23)	Ben Sanders (Ball in hands at chest.)	2,500	1,000	600.00
(24)	Ben Sanders/Btg	2,500	1,000	600.00
(25)	Ben Sanders (Fielding fly ball.)	2,500	1,000	600.00
(26)	Ben Sanders/Throwing	2,500	1,000	600.00
(27)	Harry Stovey	2,500	1,000	600.00
(28)	Michael Sullivan	2,500	1,000	600.00
(29)	Gus Weyhing	2,500	1,000	600.00
(31)	John Weyhing	2,500	1,000	600.00

1916 Gimbels

This version of the 1916 M101-5 and M101-4 Blank Backs can be found with three slightly different styles of typography on back.

	NM	EX	VG
Common Player:	130.00	65.00	40.00

Stars: 1-2X

(See 1916 M101-5 and M101-4 Blank Backs for checklists and base pricing.)

1953 Glendale Hot Dogs Tigers

Glendale Meats issued these unnumbered, full-color cards (2-5/8" x 3-3/4") in packages of hot dogs. Featuring only Detroit Tigers players, the card fronts contain a player picture with his name, a facsimile autograph, and the Tigers logo. Backs carry player statistical and biographical information plus an offer for a trip for two to the World Series. Collectors were advised to mail all the cards they had saved to Glendale Meats. The World Series trip plus 150 other prizes were to be given to the individuals sending in the most cards. As with most cards issued with food products, high-grade cards are tough to find because of the cards' susceptibilty to stains. The Houtteman card is extremely scarce.

		NM	EX	VG
Complete Set (28):		27,500	11,000	5,500
Common Player:		900.00	365.00	180.00
(1)	Matt Batts	900.00	365.00	180.00
(2)	Johnny Bucha	900.00	365.00	180.00
(3)	Frank Carswell	900.00	365.00	180.00
(4)	Jim Delsing	900.00	365.00	180.00
(5)	Walt Dropo	900.00	365.00	180.00
(6)	Hal Erickson	900.00	365.00	180.00
(7)	Paul Foytack	900.00	365.00	180.00
(8)	Owen Friend	900.00	365.00	180.00
(9)	Ned Garver	900.00	365.00	180.00
(10)	Joe Ginsberg	900.00	365.00	180.00
(11)	Ted Gray	900.00	365.00	180.00
(12)	Fred Hatfield	900.00	365.00	180.00
(13)	Ray Herbert	900.00	365.00	180.00
(14)	Bill Hitchcock	900.00	365.00	180.00
(15)	Bill Hoeft	900.00	365.00	180.00
(16)	Art Houtteman	5,000	2,000	1,000
(17)	Milt Jordan	900.00	365.00	180.00
(18)	Harvey Kuenn	1,200	480.00	240.00
(19)	Don Lund	900.00	365.00	180.00
(20)	Dave Madison	900.00	365.00	180.00
(21)	Dick Marlowe	900.00	365.00	180.00
(22)	Pat Mullin	900.00	365.00	180.00
(23)	Bob Nieman	900.00	365.00	180.00
(24)	Johnny Pesky	900.00	365.00	180.00
(25)	Jerry Priddy	900.00	365.00	180.00
(26)	Steve Souchock	900.00	365.00	180.00
(27)	Russ Sullivan	900.00	365.00	180.00
(28)	Bill Wight	1,100	450.00	225.00

1916 Globe Clothing Store (H801-9)

This 200-card set can be found with ads on the back for several local and regional businesses Among them is the Globe clothing store in St. Louis. Type card, team- and single-player collectors may pay a modest premium for individual cards with the Globe store's advertising over the parallel 1916 M101-4 Blank Backs values. This version carries an "American Card Catalog" designation of H801-9. Cards measure 1-5/8" x 3" and are printed in black-and-white.

	NM	EX	VG
Common Player:	225.00	110.00	65.00

Stars: 2-3X

(See 1916 M101-4 Blank Backs for checklist and base values.)

1969 Globe Imports Playing Cards

Largely ignored by collectors for more than 35 years, this issue has little to offer any but the most avid superstar collector. Printed in black-and-white on very thin white cardboard, either with blank backs, or with red-and-white checkerboard patterned backs, the cards measure 1-5/8" x 2-1/4". Muddy player action photos are at center of each card, with the player's name reversed out of a black strip at the bottom. It is likely this set was issued over a period of more than one year. The plain-back version was probably issued first, and has photos which include cap and jersey logos. The checked-back version seems to have been a later issue with many of the cards showing uniform logos airbrushed away. The photo quality of the checked-back cards is also much poorer than the plain-backs. A few players were substituted between the issues, and there may be more yet to be reported. The Babe Ruth AD card listed here is actually part of a multi-topic deck in similar format issued contemprarily with the baseball decks.

		NM	EX	VG
Complete Set (52+Joker):		20.00	10.00	6.00
Common Player:		.25	.15	.10
PLAIN BACK HEARTS				
2	Chris Short	.25	.15	.10
3	Tony Conigliaro	.75	.40	.25
4	Bill Freehan	.25	.15	.10
5	Willie McCovey	2.00	1.00	.60
6	Joel Horlen	.25	.15	.10
7	Ernie Banks	2.00	1.00	.60
8	Jim Wynn	.25	.15	.10
9	Brooks Robinson	2.00	1.00	.60
10	Orlando Cepeda	1.00	.50	.30
J	Al Kaline	2.00	1.00	.60
Q	Gene Alley	.25	.15	.10
K	Rusty Staub	.75	.40	.25
A	Willie Mays	4.00	2.00	1.25
CLUBS				
2	Reggie Smith	.25	.15	.10
3	Mike McCormick	.25	.15	.10
4	Tony Oliva	.50	.25	.15
5	Bud Harrelson	.25	.15	.10

		NM	EX	VG
6	Rick Reichardt	.25	.15	.10
7	Billy Williams	1.00	.50	.30
8	Pete Rose	6.00	3.00	1.75
9	Jim Maloney	.25	.15	.10
10	Tim McCarver	.75	.40	.25
J	Max Alvis	.25	.15	.10
Q	Ron Swoboda	.25	.15	.10
K	Johnny Callison	.25	.15	.10
A	Richie Allen	.75	.40	.25
DIAMONDS				
2	Paul Casanova	.25	.15	.10
3	Juan Marichal	1.00	.50	.30
4	Jim Fregosi	.25	.15	.10
5	Earl Wilson	.25	.15	.10
6	Tony Horton	.25	.15	.10
7	Harmon Killebrew	2.00	1.00	.60
8	Tom Seaver	3.00	1.50	.90
9	Curt Flood	.75	.40	.25
10	Frank Robinson	2.00	1.00	.60
J	Bob Aspromonte	.25	.15	.10
Q	Lou Brock	2.00	1.00	.60
K	Jim Lonborg	.25	.15	.10
A(a)	Bob Gibson	2.00	1.00	.60
A(b)	Babe Ruth	12.00	6.00	3.60
SPADES				
2	Cesar Tovar	.25	.15	.10
3	Rick Monday	.25	.15	.10
4	Richie Allen	.75	.40	.25
5	Mel Stottlemyre	.50	.25	.15
6	Tommy John	.75	.40	.25
7	Don Mincher	.25	.15	.10
8	Chico Cardenas	.25	.15	.10
9	Willie Davis	.25	.15	.10
10	Bert Campaneris	.25	.15	.10
J	Ron Santo	.75	.40	.25
Q	Al Ferrera	.25	.15	.10
K	Clete Boyer	.50	.25	.15
A(a)	Don Drysdale	3.00	1.50	.90
A(b)	Mickey Mantle	40.00	20.00	12.00
CHECKERBOARD BACK HEARTS				
2	Chris Short	.25	.15	.10
3	Tony Conigliaro	.75	.40	.25
4	Bill Freehan	.25	.15	.10
5	Willie McCovey	2.00	1.00	.60
6	Joel Horlen	.25	.15	.10
7	Ernie Banks	2.00	1.00	.60
8	Jim Wynn	.25	.15	.10
9	Brooks Robinson	2.00	1.00	.60
10	Orlando Cepeda	1.00	.50	.30
J	Al Kaline	2.00	1.00	.60
Q	Gene Alley	.25	.15	.10
K	Rusty Staub	.75	.40	.25
A	Willie Mays	6.00	3.00	1.75
CLUBS				
2	Reggie Smith	.25	.15	.10
3	Jerry Koosman	.25	.15	.10
4	Tony Oliva	.50	.25	.15
5	Bud Harrelson	.25	.15	.10
6	Rick Reichardt	.25	.15	.10
7	Billy Williams	1.00	.50	.30
8	Pete Rose	6.00	3.00	1.75
9	Jim Maloney	.25	.15	.10
10	Tim McCarver	.75	.40	.25
J	Max Alvis	.25	.15	.10
Q	Ron Swoboda	.25	.15	.10
K	Johnny Callison	.25	.15	.10
A	Richie Allen	.75	.40	.25
DIAMONDS				
2	Paul Casanova	.25	.15	.10
3	Juan Marichal	1.00	.50	.30
4	Jim Fregosi	.25	.15	.10
5	Earl Wilson	.25	.15	.10
6	Tony Horton	.25	.15	.10
7	Harmon Killebrew	2.00	1.00	.60
8	Tom Seaver	3.00	1.50	.90
9	Curt Flood	.75	.40	.25
10	Frank Robinson	2.00	1.00	.60
J	Bob Aspromonte	.25	.15	.10
Q	Lou Brock	2.00	1.00	.60
K	Jim Lonborg	.25	.15	.10
A	Bob Gibson	2.00	1.00	.60
SPADES				
2	Denny McLain	.50	.25	.15
3	Rick Monday	.25	.15	.10
4	Richie Allen	.75	.40	.25
5	Mel Stottlemyre	.50	.25	.15
6	Tommy John	.75	.40	.25
7	Don Mincher	.25	.15	.10
8	Chico Cardenas	.25	.15	.10
9	Willie Davis	.25	.15	.10
10	Bert Campaneris	.25	.15	.10
J	Ron Santo	.75	.40	.25
Q	Al Ferrera	.25	.15	.10
K	Clete Boyer	.50	.25	.15
A	Ken Harrelson	.25	.15	.10

1887 Gold Coin (Buchner) (N284)

Issued circa 1887, the N284 issue was produced by D. Buchner & Co. for its Gold Coin brand of chewing tobacco. Actually, the series was not comprised only of baseball players - actors, jockeys, firemen and policemen were also included. The cards, which measure 1-3/4" x 3", are color drawings. The set is not a popular one among collectors as the drawings do not in all cases represent the players designated on the cards. In most instances, players at a given position share the same drawing depicted on the card front. Three different card backs are found, all advising collectors to save the valuable chewing tobacco wrappers. Wrappers could be redeemed for various prizes.

KENNEDY, PITCHER, LACROSSE.

WE WILL PACK IN THE CELEBRATED Gold Coin Chewing Tobacco, THE PORTRAITS OF ALL THE LEADING BASEBALL PLAYERS IN THE COUNTRY, IN FULL UNIFORM. CONTINUE TO SAVE THE WRAPPERS under THEY ARE VALUABLE.

		NM	EX	VG
Complete Set (143):		160,000	80,000	50,000
Common Player:		800.00	400.00	200.00
(1)	Ed Andrews (Hands at neck.)	800.00	400.00	200.00
(2)	Ed Andrews (Hands waist high.)	800.00	400.00	200.00
(3)	Cap Anson (Hands outstretched.)	4,100	1,800	800.00
(4)	Cap Anson (Left hand on hip.)	5,300	2,400	1,100
(5)	Tug Arundel	800.00	400.00	200.00
(6)	Sam Barkley (Pittsburg)	800.00	400.00	200.00
(7)	Sam Barkley (St. Louis)	800.00	400.00	200.00
(8)	Charley Bassett	800.00	400.00	200.00
(9)	Charlie Bastian	800.00	400.00	200.00
(10)	Ed Beecher	800.00	400.00	200.00
(11)	Charlie Bennett	800.00	400.00	200.00
(12)	Henry Boyle	800.00	400.00	200.00
(13)	Dan Brouthers (Hands outstretched.)	3,100	1,400	600.00
(14)	Dan Brouthers (With bat.)	3,100	1,400	600.00
(15)	Tom Brown	800.00	400.00	200.00
(16)	Jack Burdock	800.00	400.00	200.00
(17)	Oyster Burns (Baltimore)	800.00	400.00	200.00
(18)	Tom Burns (Chicago)	800.00	400.00	200.00
(19)	Doc Bushong	800.00	400.00	200.00
(20)	John Cahill	800.00	400.00	200.00
(21)	Cliff Carroll (Washington)	800.00	400.00	200.00
(22)	Fred Carroll (Pittsburgh)	800.00	400.00	200.00
(23)	Bob Carruthers (Caruthers)	800.00	400.00	200.00
(24)	Dan Casey	800.00	400.00	200.00
(25)	John Clarkson (Ball at chest.)	2,800	1,250	600.00
(26)	John Clarkson (Arm oustretched.)	3,100	1,400	625.00
(27)	Jack Clements	800.00	400.00	200.00
(28)	John Coleman	800.00	400.00	200.00
(29)	Charles Comiskey	3,400	1,500	700.00
(30)	Roger Connor (Hands outstretched chest-level, "New York.")	2,800	1,250	600.00
(31)	Roger Connor (Hands oustretched face-level, "N.Y.")	3,100	1,400	625.00
(32)	John Corbett	800.00	400.00	200.00
(33)	Sam Craig (Crane)	800.00	400.00	200.00
(34)	Sam Crane	800.00	400.00	200.00
(35)	John Crowley	800.00	400.00	200.00
(36)	Ed Cushmann (Cushman)	800.00	400.00	200.00
(37)	Ed Dailey (Daily)	800.00	400.00	200.00
(38)	Con Daley (Daily)	800.00	400.00	200.00
(39)	Pat Deasley	800.00	400.00	200.00
(40)	Jerry Denny (Hands on knees.)	800.00	400.00	200.00
(41)	Jerry Denny (Hands on thighs.)	800.00	400.00	200.00
(42)	Jim Donnelly	800.00	400.00	200.00
(43)	Jim Donohue (Donahue)	800.00	400.00	200.00
(44)	Mike Dorgan/Right Field	800.00	400.00	200.00
(45)	Mike Dorgan/Batter	800.00	400.00	200.00
(46)	Fred Dunlap	800.00	400.00	200.00
(47)	Dude Esterbrook	800.00	400.00	200.00
(48)	Buck Ewing (Ready to tag.)	2,800	1,250	600.00
(49)	Buck Ewing (Hands at neck.)	3,100	1,400	625.00
(50)	Sid Farrar	800.00	400.00	200.00
(51)	Jack Farrell (Ready to tag.)	800.00	400.00	200.00
(52)	Jack Farrell (Hands at knees.)	800.00	400.00	200.00
(53)	Charlie Ferguson	800.00	400.00	200.00
(54)	Silver Flint	800.00	400.00	200.00
(55)	Jim Fogerty (Fogarty)	800.00	400.00	200.00
(56)	Tom Forster	800.00	400.00	200.00
(57)	Dave Foutz	800.00	400.00	200.00
(58)	Chris Fulmer	800.00	400.00	200.00
(59)	Joe Gerhardt	800.00	400.00	200.00
(60)	Charlie Getzein (Getzien)	800.00	400.00	200.00
(61)	Pete Gillespie/Left Field	800.00	400.00	200.00
(62)	Pete Gillespie/Batter	800.00	400.00	200.00
(63)	Barney Gilligan	800.00	400.00	200.00
(64)	Jack Glasscock (Fielding grounder.)	800.00	400.00	200.00
(65)	Jack Glasscock (Hands on knees.)	800.00	400.00	200.00
(66)	Will Gleason	800.00	400.00	200.00
(67)	George Gore	800.00	400.00	200.00
(68)	Frank Hankinson	800.00	400.00	200.00
(69)	Ned Hanlon	2,800	1,250	600.00
(70)	Jim Hart	800.00	400.00	200.00
(71)	Egyptian Healy	800.00	400.00	200.00
(72)	Paul Hines/Centre Field	800.00	400.00	200.00
(73)	Paul Hines/Batter	800.00	400.00	200.00
(74)	Joe Hornung	800.00	400.00	200.00
(75)	Arthur Irwin	800.00	400.00	200.00
(76)	Dick Johnston	800.00	400.00	200.00
(77)	Tim Keefe (Ball in hand.)	2,800	1,250	600.00
(78)	Tim Keefe (Ball out of hand.)	3,100	1,400	625.00
(79)	King Kelly/Right Field	3,400	1,500	700.00
(80)	King Kelly/Catcher	3,400	1,500	700.00
(81)	Ted Kennedy	800.00	400.00	200.00

(82)	Matt Kilroy	800.00	400.00	200.00
(83)	Arlie Latham	800.00	400.00	200.00
(84)	Jimmy Manning	800.00	400.00	200.00
(85)	Bill McClellan	800.00	400.00	200.00
(86)	Jim McCormick	800.00	400.00	200.00
(87)	Jack McGeachy	800.00	400.00	200.00
(88)	Jumbo McGinnis	800.00	400.00	200.00
(89)	George Meyers (Myers)	800.00	400.00	200.00
(90)	Doggie Miller	800.00	400.00	200.00
(91)	John Morrill (Hands outstretched.)	800.00	400.00	200.00
(92)	John Morrill (Hands at neck.)	800.00	400.00	200.00
(93)	Tom Morrissey (Morrissey)	800.00	400.00	200.00
(94)	Joe Mulvey (Hands on knees.)	800.00	400.00	200.00
(95)	Joe Mulvey (Hands above head.)	800.00	400.00	200.00
(96)	Al Myers	800.00	400.00	200.00
(97)	Candy Nelson	800.00	400.00	200.00
(98)	Hugh Nichol	800.00	400.00	200.00
(99)	Billy O'Brien	800.00	400.00	200.00
(100)	Tip O'Neil (O'Neill)	800.00	400.00	200.00
(101)	Orator Jim O'Rourke (Hands cupped.)	3,100	1,400	625.00
(102)	Orator Jim O'Rourke (Hands on thighs.)	3,100	1,400	625.00
(103)	Dave Orr	800.00	400.00	200.00
(104)	Jimmy Peoples	800.00	400.00	200.00
(105)	Fred Pfeffer	800.00	400.00	200.00
(106)	Bill Phillips	800.00	400.00	200.00
(107)	Mark Polhemus	800.00	400.00	200.00
(108)	Henry Porter	800.00	400.00	200.00
(109)	Blondie Purcell	800.00	400.00	200.00
(110)	Old Hoss Radbourn (Hands at chest.)	2,800	1,250	600.00
(111)	Old Hoss Radbourn (Hands above waist.)	3,100	1,400	625.00
(112)	Danny Richardson (New York, hands at knees.)	800.00	400.00	200.00
(113)	Danny Richardson (New York, foot on base.)	800.00	400.00	200.00
(114)	Hardy Richardson (Detroit, hands at right shoulder.)	800.00	400.00	200.00
(115)	Hardy Richardson (Detroit, right hand above head.)	800.00	400.00	200.00
(116)	Yank Robinson	800.00	400.00	200.00
(117)	George Rooks	800.00	400.00	200.00
(118)	Chief Rosemann (Roseman)	800.00	400.00	200.00
(119)	Jimmy Ryan	800.00	400.00	200.00
(120)	Emmett Seery (Hands at right shoulder.)	800.00	400.00	200.00
(121)	Emmett Seery (Hands outstretched.)	800.00	400.00	200.00
(122)	Otto Shomberg (Schomberg)	800.00	400.00	200.00
(123)	Pap Smith	800.00	400.00	200.00
(124)	Joe Strauss	800.00	400.00	200.00
(125)	Danny Sullivan (St. Louis)	800.00	400.00	200.00
(126)	Marty Sullivan (Chicago)	800.00	400.00	200.00
(127)	Billy Sunday	1,600	700.00	300.00
(128)	Ezra Sutton	800.00	400.00	200.00
(129)	Sam Thompson (Hand at belt.)	2,800	1,250	600.00
(130)	Sam Thompson (Hands chest high.)	3,100	1,400	625.00
(131)	Chris Von Der Ahe	2,800	1,250	600.00
(132)	John Ward (Felding grounder.)	2,800	1,250	600.00
(133)	John Ward (Hands by knee.)	3,100	1,400	625.00
(134)	John Ward (Hands on knees.)	3,100	1,400	625.00
(135)	Curt Welch	800.00	400.00	200.00
(136)	Deacon White	800.00	400.00	200.00
(137)	Art Whitney (Pittsburgh)	800.00	400.00	200.00
(138)	Jim Whitney (Washington)	800.00	400.00	200.00
(139)	Ned Williamson (Fielding grounder.)	800.00	400.00	200.00
(140)	Ned Williamson (Hands at chest.)	800.00	400.00	200.00
(141)	Medoc Wise	800.00	400.00	200.00
(142)	George Wood (Hands at right shoulder.)	800.00	400.00	200.00
(143)	George Wood (Stealing base.)	800.00	400.00	200.00

1961 Golden Press

Jerome Hanna Dean "Dizzy"

1930-1941 St. Louis, Chicago NL

During his first full five years in the major leagues, Dean won 120 games, for an average of 24 per year. In 1934 he reached his peak when he won 30 games, and lost only 7. That year Dizzy and his brother Paul each beat the Detroit Tigers twice to bring the World Series championship to St. Louis' Gas House Gang. Dean was the last major league pitcher to win 30 games. In the 1937 all-star game, a line drive hit Dean's toe and curtailed his brilliant pitching career.

Lifetime Record 13 yrs.

G	IP	W	PCT	SHO	SO
317	1966	150	.644	26	1155

Elected to Hall of Fame 1953

DIZZY DEAN pitcher

The 1961 Golden Press set features 33 players, all enshrined in the Baseball Hall of Fame. The full color cards measure 2-1/2" x 3-1/2" and came in a booklet with perforations so that they could be easily removed. Full books with the cards intact would command 50 percent over the set price in the checklist that follows. Card numbers 1-3 and 28-33 are slightly higher in price as they were located on the book's front and back covers, making them more susceptible to scuffing and wear. Cards in a larger (2-3/4" x 3-5/8"), apparently unperforated format are also known, though their method of distribution is unclear.

	NM	EX	VG
Complete Set (33):	100.00	50.00	30.00

		NM	EX	VG
Complete Set in Book:		175.00	85.00	50.00
Common Player:		3.00	1.50	.90
1	Mel Ott	3.00	1.50	.90
2	Grover Cleveland Alexander	5.00	2.50	1.50
3	Babe Ruth	40.00	20.00	12.00
4	Hank Greenberg	5.00	2.50	1.50
5	Bill Terry	3.00	1.50	.90
6	Carl Hubbell	3.00	1.50	.90
7	Rogers Hornsby	4.00	2.00	1.25
8	Dizzy Dean	5.00	2.50	1.50
9	Joe DiMaggio	20.00	10.00	6.00
10	Charlie Gehringer	3.00	1.50	.90
11	Gabby Hartnett	3.00	1.50	.90
12	Mickey Cochrane	3.00	1.50	.90
13	George Sisler	3.00	1.50	.90
14	Joe Cronin	3.00	1.50	.90
15	Pie Traynor	3.00	1.50	.90
16	Lou Gehrig	20.00	10.00	6.00
17	Lefty Grove	3.00	1.50	.90
18	Chief Bender	3.00	1.50	.90
19	Frankie Frisch	3.00	1.50	.90
20	Al Simmons	3.00	1.50	.90
21	Home Run Baker	3.00	1.50	.90
22	Jimmy Foxx	4.00	2.00	1.25
23	John McGraw	3.00	1.50	.90
24	Christy Mathewson	10.00	5.00	3.00
25	Ty Cobb	20.00	10.00	6.00
26	Dazzy Vance	3.00	1.50	.90
27	Bill Dickey	3.00	1.50	.90
28	Eddie Collins	3.00	1.50	.90
29	Walter Johnson	9.00	4.50	2.75
30	Tris Speaker	4.00	2.00	1.25
31	Nap Lajoie	3.00	1.50	.90
32	Honus Wagner	12.00	6.00	3.50
33	Cy Young	9.00	4.50	2.75

1955 Golden Stamp Books

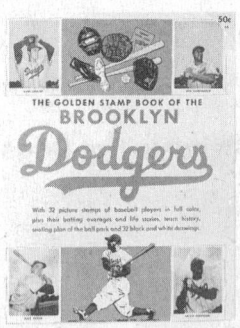

THE GOLDEN STAMP BOOK OF THE BROOKLYN Dodgers

The 1954 World Series contestants, Cleveland and the Giants, along with the popular Dodgers and Braves are featured in this set of stamp books. The 32-page albums measure about 8-1/2" x 11" and include drawings and write-ups for each of the 32 players and managers featured. Other pages of the album include team histories, stats, etc. Sheets of 16 color stamps each are bound into the front and back of the album. Individual stamps measure about 2" x 2-5/8" and are unnumbered. Values shown are for complete albums with the stamps not pasted in; albums with stamps affixed to the pages are worth about 50 percent. The players for each team are listed in the order in which they appear in the album.

		NM	EX	VG
Complete Set (4):		500.00	250.00	150.00
Common Stamp:		5.00	2.50	1.50
S-1	NEW YORK GIANTS ALBUM	125.00	65.00	35.00
(1)	1954 Team Photo	5.00	2.50	1.50
(2)	Leo Durocher	6.00	3.00	1.75
(3)	Johnny Antonelli	5.00	2.50	1.50
(4)	Sal Maglie	5.00	2.50	1.50
(5)	Ruben Gomez	5.00	2.50	1.50
(6)	Hoyt Wilhelm	6.00	3.00	1.75
(7)	Marv Grissom	5.00	2.50	1.50
(8)	Jim Hearn	5.00	2.50	1.50
(9)	Paul Giel	5.00	2.50	1.50
(10)	Al Corwin	5.00	2.50	1.50
(11)	George Spencer	5.00	2.50	1.50
(12)	Don Liddle	5.00	2.50	1.50
(13)	Windy McCall	5.00	2.50	1.50
(14)	Al Worthington	5.00	2.50	1.50
(15)	Wes Westrum	5.00	2.50	1.50
(16)	Whitey Lockman	5.00	2.50	1.50
(17)	Dave Williams	5.00	2.50	1.50
(18)	Hank Thompson	5.00	2.50	1.50
(19)	Alvin Dark	5.00	2.50	1.50
(20)	Monte Irvin	7.50	3.75	2.25
(21)	Willie Mays	50.00	25.00	15.00
(22)	Don Mueller	5.00	2.50	1.50
(23)	Dusty Rhodes	5.00	2.50	1.50
(24)	Ray Katt	5.00	2.50	1.50
(25)	Joe Amalfitano	5.00	2.50	1.50
(26)	Bill Gardner	5.00	2.50	1.50
(27)	Foster Castleman	5.00	2.50	1.50
(28)	Bobby Hofman	5.00	2.50	1.50
(29)	Bill Taylor	5.00	2.50	1.50
(30)	Manager and Coaches	5.00	2.50	1.50
(31)	Bobby Weinstein/Batboy	5.00	2.50	1.50
(32)	Polo Grounds	5.00	2.50	1.50
S-2	MILWAUKEE BRAVES ALBUM	125.00	65.00	35.00
(1)	1954 Team Photo	5.00	2.50	1.50
(2)	Charlie Grimm	5.00	2.50	1.50
(3)	Warren Spahn	7.50	3.75	2.25
(4)	Lew Burdette	5.00	2.50	1.50

(5)	Chet Nichols	5.00	2.50	1.50
(6)	Gene Conley	5.00	2.50	1.50
(7)	Bob Buhl	5.00	2.50	1.50
(8)	Jim Wilson	5.00	2.50	1.50
(9)	Dave Jolly	5.00	2.50	1.50
(10)	Ernie Johnson	5.00	2.50	1.50
(11)	Joey Jay	5.00	2.50	1.50
(12)	Dave Koslo	5.00	2.50	1.50
(13)	Charlie Gorin	5.00	2.50	1.50
(14)	Ray Crone	5.00	2.50	1.50
(15)	Del Crandall	5.00	2.50	1.50
(16)	Joe Adcock	5.00	2.50	1.50
(17)	Jack Dittmer	5.00	2.50	1.50
(18)	Eddie Mathews	15.00	7.50	4.50
(19)	Johnny Logan	5.00	2.50	1.50
(20)	Andy Pafko	5.00	2.50	1.50
(21)	Bill Bruton	5.00	2.50	1.50
(22)	Bobby Thomson	5.00	2.50	1.50
(23)	Charlie White	5.00	2.50	1.50
(24)	Danny O'Connell	5.00	2.50	1.50
(25)	Hank Aaron	50.00	25.00	15.00
(26)	Jim Pendleton	5.00	2.50	1.50
(27)	George Metkovich	5.00	2.50	1.50
(28)	Mel Roach	5.00	2.50	1.50
(29)	John Cooney	5.00	2.50	1.50
(30)	Bucky Walters	5.00	2.50	1.50
(31)	Charles Lacks/Trainer	5.00	2.50	1.50
(32)	Milwaukee County Stadium	5.00	2.50	1.50
S-3	BROOKLYN DODGERS ALBUM	200.00	100.00	60.00
(1)	Walter Alston	6.00	3.00	1.75
(2)	Don Newcombe	6.00	3.00	1.75
(3)	Carl Erskine	5.00	2.50	1.50
(4)	Johnny Podres	5.00	2.50	1.50
(5)	Billy Loes	5.00	2.50	1.50
(6)	Russ Meyer	5.00	2.50	1.50
(7)	Jim Hughes	5.00	2.50	1.50
(8)	Sandy Koufax	100.00	50.00	30.00
(9)	Joe Black	5.00	2.50	1.50
(10)	Karl Spooner	5.00	2.50	1.50
(11)	Clem Labine	5.00	2.50	1.50
(12)	Roy Campanella	15.00	7.50	4.50
(13)	Gil Hodges	12.00	6.00	3.50
(14)	Jim Gilliam	6.00	3.00	1.75
(15)	Jackie Robinson	50.00	25.00	15.00
(16)	Pee Wee Reese	15.00	7.50	4.50
(17)	Duke Snider	15.00	7.50	4.50
(18)	Carl Furillo	6.00	3.00	1.75
(19)	Sandy Amoros	5.00	2.50	1.50
(20)	Frank Kellert	5.00	2.50	1.50
(21)	Don Zimmer	6.00	3.00	1.75
(22)	Al Walker	5.00	2.50	1.50
(23)	Tommy Lasorda	7.50	3.75	2.25
(24)	Ed Roebuck	5.00	2.50	1.50
(25)	Don Hoak	5.00	2.50	1.50
(26)	George Shuba	5.00	2.50	1.50
(27)	Billy Herman	6.00	3.00	1.75
(28)	Jake Pitler	5.00	2.50	1.50
(29)	Joe Becker	5.00	2.50	1.50
(30)	Doc Wendler/Trainer, Carl Furillo	5.00	2.50	1.50
(31)	Charlie Di Giovanna/Batboy	5.00	2.50	1.50
(32)	Ebbets Field	5.00	2.50	1.50
S-4	CLEVELAND INDIANS ALBUM	100.00	50.00	30.00
(1)	Al Lopez	6.00	3.00	1.75
(2)	Bob Lemon	6.00	3.00	1.75
(3)	Early Wynn	6.00	3.00	1.75
(4)	Mike Garcia	5.00	2.50	1.50
(5)	Bob Feller	12.00	6.00	3.50
(6)	Art Houtteman	5.00	2.50	1.50
(7)	Herb Score	7.50	3.75	2.25
(8)	Don Mossi	7.50	3.75	2.25
(9)	Ray Narleski	5.00	2.50	1.50
(10)	Jim Hegan	5.00	2.50	1.50
(11)	Vic Wertz	5.00	2.50	1.50
(12)	Bobby Avila	5.00	2.50	1.50
(13)	George Strickland	5.00	2.50	1.50
(14)	Al Rosen	5.00	2.50	1.50
(15)	Larry Doby	6.00	3.00	1.75
(16)	Ralph Kiner	7.50	3.75	2.25
(17)	Al Smith	5.00	2.50	1.50
(18)	Wally Westlake	5.00	2.50	1.50
(19)	Hal Naragon	5.00	2.50	1.50
(20)	Hank Foiles	5.00	2.50	1.50
(21)	Hank Majeski	5.00	2.50	1.50
(22)	Bill Wight	5.00	2.50	1.50
(23)	Sam Dente	5.00	2.50	1.50
(24)	Dave Pope	5.00	2.50	1.50
(25)	Dave Philley	5.00	2.50	1.50
(26)	Dale Mitchell	5.00	2.50	1.50
(27)	Hank Greenberg/GM	10.00	5.00	3.00
(28)	Mel Harder	5.00	2.50	1.50
(29)	Ralph Kress	5.00	2.50	1.50
(30)	Tony Cuccinello	5.00	2.50	1.50
(31)	Bill Lobe	5.00	2.50	1.50
(32)	Cleveland Municipal Stadium	5.00	2.50	1.50

1934 Gold Medal Foods (R313A)

This set of unnumbered, blank-backed cards was issued by Gold Medal Foods (the Minneapolis parent company of Wheaties) to commemorate the 1934 World Series. The black-and-white cards measure 3-1/4" x 5-3/8". The checklist comprises six members each of the Detroit Tigers and St. Louis Cardinals, who were participants in the '34 World Series.

Vintage cards in Good condition are valued at about 50% of the Very Good values shown here. Cards in Fair condition are valued at 25% or less of VG.

		NM	EX	VG
Complete Set (12):		1,000	500.00	300.00
Common Player:		60.00	30.00	18.00
(1)	Tommy Bridges	60.00	30.00	18.00
(2)	Mickey Cochrane	90.00	45.00	27.50
(3)	Dizzy Dean	350.00	175.00	100.00
(4)	Paul Dean	75.00	37.50	22.50
(5)	Frank Frisch	90.00	45.00	27.50
(6)	"Goose" Goslin	90.00	45.00	27.50
(7)	William Hallahan	60.00	30.00	18.00
(8)	Fred Marberry	60.00	30.00	18.00
(9)	Johnny "Pepper" Martin	60.00	30.00	18.00
(10)	Joe Medwick	90.00	45.00	27.50
(11)	William Rogell	60.00	30.00	18.00
(12)	"Jo Jo" White	60.00	30.00	18.00

1930s Goodrich Tire Mickey Cochrane

Without postmarked examples for verification, the issue date of this promotional postcard can only be estimated. Front of the 5-1/4" x 3-1/4" postcard has line art of Cochrane and his endorsement for the company's tires. The card is printed in yellow, orange and black. The lower-right quadrant was likely left blank to allow local tire retailers to place their advertisement. Back of the card has a pre-printed one-cent stamp.

	NM	EX	VG
Mickey Cochrane	100.00	50.00	30.00

1888 Goodwin Champions (N162)

Issued in 1888 by New York's Goodwin & Co., the 50-card "Champions" set includes eight baseball players - seven from the National League and one from the American Association. The full-color cards, which measure 1-1/2" x 2-5/8", were inserted in packages of Old Judge and Gypsy Queen Cigarettes. A small ad for the cards lists all 50 subjects of the "Champions" set, which also included popular billiards players, bicyclists, marksmen, pugilists, run-

---

ners, wrestlers, college football stars, weightlifters, and Wild West star Buffalo Bill Cody. Four of the eight baseball players in the set (Anson, Kelly, Keefe and Brouthers) are Hall of Famers. The cards feature very attractive player portraits, making the "Champions" set among the most beautiful of all the 19th Century tobacco inserts. All cards can be found with or without a tiny line of type at the bottom of the back which reads, "Geo. S. Harris & Sons, Lith, Phila."

		NM	EX	VG
Complete Set (8):		40,000	15,500	7,000
Common Player:		3,500	1,450	650.00
Album:		7,500	3,750	2,250
(1)	Ed Andrews	3,500	1,450	650.00
(2)	Cap Anson	12,000	4,500	2,000
(3)	Dan Brouthers	5,000	2,125	950.00
(4)	Bob Caruthers	3,500	1,450	650.00
(5)	Fred Dunlap	3,500	1,450	650.00
(6)	Jack Glasscock	3,500	1,450	650.00
(7)	Tim Keefe	5,250	2,125	950.00
(8)	King Kelly	7,750	3,000	1,450

1889 Goodwin & Co. Baseball Album (A35)

As a mail-in redemption premium for 75 coupons from its Old Judge and Dog's Head cigarette brands, Goodwin offered this 12-page lithographed album. In an unusual 8-1/4" diameter format, the pages have a single hole punched at the side and are attached by a fancy tasseled cord allowing them to be fanned out for viewing. Front and back covers of the album depict a baseball, with the inside covers advertising the cigarettes, as does the sixth page of the album. The nine other pages depict in vivid color either single stars of the game or groups of four players, with an emphasis on the N.Y. Giants champions of 1888. Backs of the pages offer player stats for the previous season and schedules for various leagues for 1889. Because these albums are sometimes offered as single pages, they are priced as such here.

		NM	EX	VG
Complete Album:		20,000	10,000	6,000
(1)	Front cover	225.00	110.00	65.00
(2)	Mickey Welch, John Ward, Buck Ewing, Tim Keefe	1,100	550.00	330.00
(3)	Cap Anson	4,000	1,500	900.00
(4)	Jim O'Rourke, Danny Richardson, Roger Connor, George Gore	1,200	460.00	275.00
(5)	Mike "King" Kelly	3,000	1,500	900.00
(6)	Advertising	350.00	100.00	60.00
(7)	John Ward	2,125	1,050	635.00
(8)	Mike Slattery, Pat Murphy, Gil Hatfield, Ed Crane	750.00	375.00	225.00
(9)	Charles Comiskey	2,125	1,050	635.00
(10)	Willard Brown, Bill George, Elmer Foster, Michael Tiernan	850.00	425.00	255.00
(11)	Jim Mutrie, Lidell Titcomb, Art Whitney, Willie Breslin/ Mascot	875.00	435.00	260.00
(12)	Back cover	200.00	100.00	60.00

1933 Goudey (R319)

Goudey Gum Co.'s first baseball card issue was a 239-card effort in 1933. The cards are color art reproductions of either portrait or action photos. The numbered cards measure 2-3/8" x 2-7/8" and carry a short player biography on the reverse. Card #106 (Napoleon Lajoie) is listed in the set though it was not actually issued until 1934. The card is very scarce and is unique in that it carries a 1934 design front and a 1933 back. The Lajoie card is not included in the complete set prices quoted here. The ACC designation for the set is R319.

	NM	EX	VG
Complete Set (239):	110,000	37,500	19,500

Common Player (1-40):	250.00	85.00	45.00
Common Player (41-44):	165.00	55.00	30.00
Common Player (45-52):	200.00	70.00	35.00
Common Player (53-240):	165.00	55.00	30.00
1	Benny Bengough	5,500	435.00	90.00
2	Arthur (Dazzy) Vance	1,300	465.00	165.00
3	Hugh Critz	300.00	100.00	50.00
4	Henry "Heinie" Schuble	250.00	85.00	45.00
5	Floyd (Babe) Herman	500.00	175.00	90.00
6a	Jimmy Dykes (Age is 26 in bio.)	375.00	130.00	65.00
6b	Jimmy Dykes (Age is 36 in bio.)	375.00	130.00	65.00
7	Ted Lyons	925.00	325.00	165.00
8	Roy Johnson	250.00	85.00	45.00
9	Dave Harris	250.00	85.00	45.00
10	Glenn Myatt	250.00	85.00	45.00
11	Billy Rogell	250.00	85.00	45.00
12	George Pipgras	250.00	85.00	45.00
13	Lafayette Thompson	250.00	85.00	45.00
14	Henry Johnson	250.00	85.00	45.00
15	Victor Sorrell	250.00	85.00	45.00
16	George Blaeholder	250.00	85.00	45.00
17	Watson Clark	250.00	85.00	45.00
18	Herold (Muddy) Ruel	250.00	85.00	45.00
19	Bill Dickey	1,000	350.00	180.00
20	Bill Terry	925.00	325.00	165.00
21	Phil Collins	250.00	85.00	45.00
22	Harold (Pie) Traynor	925.00	325.00	165.00
23	Hazen (Ki-Ki) Cuyler	925.00	325.00	165.00
24	Horace Ford	250.00	85.00	45.00
25	Paul Waner	1,000	350.00	180.00
26	Chalmer Cissell	250.00	85.00	45.00
27	George Connally	250.00	85.00	45.00
28	Dick Bartell	250.00	85.00	45.00
29	Jimmy Foxx	2,400	840.00	430.00
30	Frank Hogan	250.00	85.00	45.00
31	Tony Lazzeri	925.00	325.00	165.00
32	John (Bud) Clancy	250.00	85.00	45.00
33	Ralph Kress	250.00	85.00	45.00
34	Bob O'Farrell	250.00	85.00	45.00
35	Al Simmons	925.00	325.00	165.00
36	Tommy Thevenow	250.00	85.00	45.00
37	Jimmy Wilson	250.00	85.00	45.00
38	Fred Brickell	250.00	85.00	45.00
39	Mark Koenig	250.00	85.00	45.00
40	Taylor Douthit	250.00	85.00	45.00
41	Gus Mancuso	165.00	55.00	30.00
42	Eddie Collins	475.00	165.00	85.00
43	Lew Fonseca	165.00	55.00	30.00
44	Jim Bottomley	415.00	145.00	75.00
45	Larry Benton	200.00	70.00	35.00
46	Ethan Allen	200.00	70.00	35.00
47	Henry (Heinie) Manush	600.00	210.00	110.00
48	Marty McManus	200.00	70.00	35.00
49	Frank Frisch	800.00	280.00	145.00
50	Ed Brandt	200.00	70.00	35.00
51	Charlie Grimm	200.00	70.00	35.00
52	Andy Cohen	225.00	80.00	40.00
53	George Herman (Babe) Ruth	11,350	3,600	1,825
54	Ray Kremer	165.00	55.00	30.00
55	Perce (Pat) Malone	165.00	55.00	30.00
56	Charlie Ruffing	415.00	145.00	75.00
57	Earl Clark	165.00	55.00	30.00
58	Frank (Lefty) O'Doul	250.00	85.00	45.00
59	Edmund (Bing) Miller	165.00	55.00	30.00
60	Waite Hoyt	415.00	145.00	75.00
61	Max Bishop	165.00	55.00	30.00
62	"Pepper" Martin	250.00	85.00	45.00
63	Joe Cronin	415.00	145.00	75.00
64	Burleigh Grimes	415.00	145.00	75.00
65	Milton Gaston	165.00	55.00	30.00
66	George Grantham	165.00	55.00	30.00
67	Guy Bush	165.00	55.00	30.00
68	Horace Lisenbee	165.00	55.00	30.00
69	Randy Moore	165.00	55.00	30.00
70	Floyd (Pete) Scott	165.00	55.00	30.00
71	Robert J. Burke	165.00	55.00	30.00
72	Owen Carroll	165.00	55.00	30.00
73	Jesse Haines	415.00	145.00	75.00
74	Eppa Rixey	415.00	145.00	75.00
75	Willie Kamm	165.00	55.00	30.00
76	Gordon (Mickey) Cochrane	475.00	165.00	85.00
77	Adam Comorosky	165.00	55.00	30.00
78	Jack Quinn	165.00	55.00	30.00
79	Urban (Red) Faber	415.00	145.00	75.00
80	Clyde Manion	165.00	55.00	30.00
81	Sam Jones	165.00	55.00	30.00
82	Dibrell Williams	165.00	55.00	30.00
83	Pete Jablonowski	165.00	55.00	30.00
84	Glenn Spencer	165.00	55.00	30.00
85	John Henry "Heinie" Sand	165.00	55.00	30.00
86	Phil Todt	165.00	55.00	30.00
87	Frank O'Rourke	165.00	55.00	30.00
88	Russell Rollings	165.00	55.00	30.00
89	Tris Speaker	550.00	190.00	95.00
90	Jess Petty	165.00	55.00	30.00
91	Tom Zachary	165.00	55.00	30.00
92	Lou Gehrig	3,200	1,475	700.00
93	John Welch	165.00	55.00	30.00
94	Bill Walker	165.00	55.00	30.00
95	Alvin Crowder	165.00	55.00	30.00
96	Willis Hudlin	165.00	55.00	30.00
97	Joe Morrissey	165.00	55.00	30.00
98	Walter Berger	165.00	55.00	30.00
99	Tony Cuccinello	165.00	55.00	30.00
100	George Uhle	165.00	55.00	30.00
101	Richard Coffman	165.00	55.00	30.00
102	Travis C. Jackson	415.00	145.00	75.00
103	Earl Combs (Earle)	415.00	145.00	75.00
104	Fred Marberry	165.00	55.00	30.00
105	Bernie Friberg	165.00	55.00	30.00
106	Napoleon (Larry) Lajoie	37,500	24,000	8,500
106p	Leo Durocher (Unique proof card.)			4,000
107	Henry (Heinie) Manush	415.00	145.00	75.00
108	Joe Kuhel	165.00	55.00	30.00
109	Joe Cronin	415.00	145.00	75.00

110	Leon (Goose) Goslin/Portrait	415.00	145.00	75.00
110p	Leon (Goose) Goslin (Proof card, batting - same as #168 - name in two lines on front.)	800.00	280.00	145.00
111	Monte Weaver	165.00	55.00	30.00
112	Fred Schulte	165.00	55.00	30.00
113	Oswald Bluege	165.00	55.00	30.00
114	Luke Sewell	165.00	55.00	30.00
115	Cliff Heathcote	165.00	55.00	30.00
116	Eddie Morgan	165.00	55.00	30.00
117	Walter (Rabbit) Maranville	415.00	145.00	75.00
118	Valentine J. (Val) Picinich	165.00	55.00	30.00
119	Rogers Hornsby	1,100	385.00	200.00
120	Carl Reynolds	165.00	55.00	30.00
121	Walter Stewart	165.00	55.00	30.00
122	Alvin Crowder	165.00	55.00	30.00
123	Jack Russell (Orange background, white cap.)	165.00	55.00	30.00
123(p a)	Jack Russell (Proof card, red background, dark cap - same as #167 - name in one line on front.)	400.00	140.00	70.00
123(p b)	Luke Sewell (Proof card, otherwise identical to #163.)	8,000	2,800	1,450
124	Earl Whitehill	165.00	55.00	30.00
125	Bill Terry	415.00	145.00	75.00
126	Joe Moore	165.00	55.00	30.00
127	Melvin Ott	725.00	250.00	125.00
128	Charles (Chuck) Klein	415.00	145.00	75.00
129	Harold Schumacher	165.00	55.00	30.00
130	Fred Fitzsimmons	165.00	55.00	30.00
131	Fred Frankhouse	165.00	55.00	30.00
132	Jim Elliott	165.00	55.00	30.00
133	Fred Lindstrom	415.00	145.00	75.00
134	Edgar (Sam) Rice	415.00	145.00	75.00
135	Elwood (Woody) English	165.00	55.00	30.00
136	Flint Rhem	165.00	55.00	30.00
137	Fred (Red) Lucas	165.00	55.00	30.00
138	Herb Pennock	415.00	145.00	75.00
139	Ben Cantwell	165.00	55.00	30.00
140	Irving (Bump) Hadley	165.00	55.00	30.00
141	Ray Benge	165.00	55.00	30.00
142	Paul Richards	165.00	55.00	30.00
143	Glenn Wright	165.00	55.00	30.00
144	George Herman (Babe) Ruth (Double-print; replaced card #106 on press sheet.)	6,500	2,575	1,175
145	George Walberg	165.00	55.00	30.00
146	Walter Stewart	165.00	55.00	30.00
147	Leo Durocher	415.00	145.00	75.00
148	Eddie Farrell	165.00	55.00	30.00
149	George Herman (Babe) Ruth	7,500	3,400	1,450
150	Ray Kolp	165.00	55.00	30.00
151	D'Arcy (Jake) Flowers	165.00	55.00	30.00
152	James (Zack) Taylor	165.00	55.00	30.00
153	Charles (Buddy) Myer	165.00	55.00	30.00
154	Jimmy Foxx	1,750	575.00	315.00
155	Joe Judge	165.00	55.00	30.00
156	Danny Macfayden (MacFayden)	165.00	55.00	30.00
157	Sam Byrd	165.00	55.00	30.00
158	Morris (Moe) Berg	665.00	235.00	135.00
159	Oswald Bluege	165.00	55.00	30.00
160	Lou Gehrig	4,000	1,200	625.00
161	Al Spohrer	165.00	55.00	30.00
162	Leo Mangum	165.00	55.00	30.00
163	Luke Sewell	165.00	55.00	30.00
164	Lloyd Waner	415.00	145.00	75.00
165	Joe Sewell	415.00	145.00	75.00
166	Sam West	165.00	55.00	30.00
167	Jack Russell (Name on two lines, see also #123p.)	165.00	55.00	30.00
168	Leon (Goose) Goslin (Name on one line, see also #110p.)	600.00	210.00	110.00
169	Al Thomas	165.00	55.00	30.00
170	Harry McCurdy	165.00	55.00	30.00
171	Charley Jamieson	165.00	55.00	30.00
172	Billy Hargrave	165.00	55.00	30.00
173	Roscoe Holm	165.00	55.00	30.00
174	Warren (Curley) Ogden	165.00	55.00	30.00
175	Dan Howley	165.00	55.00	30.00
176	John Ogden	165.00	55.00	30.00
177	Walter French	165.00	55.00	30.00
178	Jackie Warner	165.00	55.00	30.00
179	Fred Leach	165.00	55.00	30.00
180	Eddie Moore	165.00	55.00	30.00
181	George Herman (Babe) Ruth	7,000	3,200	1,350
182	Andy High	165.00	55.00	30.00
183	George Walberg	165.00	55.00	30.00
184	Charley Berry	165.00	55.00	30.00
185	Bob Smith	165.00	55.00	30.00
186	John Schulte	165.00	55.00	30.00
187	Henry (Heinie) Manush	415.00	145.00	75.00
188	Rogers Hornsby	1,200	425.00	215.00
189	Joe Cronin	415.00	145.00	75.00
190	Fred Schulte	165.00	55.00	30.00
191	Ben Chapman	165.00	55.00	30.00
192	Walter Brown	165.00	55.00	30.00
193	Lynford Lary	165.00	55.00	30.00
194	Earl Averill	415.00	145.00	75.00
195	Evar Swanson	165.00	55.00	30.00
196	Leroy Mahaffey	165.00	55.00	30.00
197	Richard (Rick) Ferrell	415.00	145.00	75.00
198	Irving (Jack) Burns	165.00	55.00	30.00
199	Tom Bridges	165.00	55.00	30.00
200	Bill Hallahan	165.00	55.00	30.00
201	Ernie Orsatti	165.00	55.00	30.00
202	Charles Leo (Gabby) Hartnett	415.00	145.00	75.00
203	Lonnie Warneke	165.00	55.00	30.00
204	Jackson Riggs Stephenson	165.00	55.00	30.00
205	Henry (Heinie) Meine	165.00	55.00	30.00
206	Gus Suhr	165.00	55.00	30.00
207	Melvin Ott	1,150	400.00	200.00
208	Byrne (Bernie) James	165.00	44.00	22.00
209	Adolfo Luque	200.00	70.00	36.00
210	Virgil Davis	165.00	55.00	30.00
211	Lewis (Hack) Wilson	650.00	225.00	115.00
212	Billy Urbanski	165.00	55.00	30.00

213	Earl Adams	165.00	55.00	30.00
214	John Kerr	165.00	55.00	30.00
215	Russell Van Atta	165.00	55.00	30.00
216	Vernon Gomez	415.00	145.00	75.00
217	Frank Crosetti	275.00	96.00	49.00
218	Wesley Ferrell	165.00	55.00	30.00
219	George (Mule) Haas	165.00	55.00	30.00
220	Robert (Lefty) Grove	775.00	275.00	140.00
221	Dale Alexander	165.00	55.00	30.00
222	Charley Gehringer	600.00	210.00	110.00
223	Jerome (Dizzy) Dean	1,200	425.00	215.00
224	Frank Demaree	165.00	55.00	30.00
225	Bill Jurges	165.00	55.00	30.00
226	Charley Root	165.00	55.00	30.00
227	Bill Herman	415.00	145.00	75.00
228	Tony Piet	165.00	55.00	30.00
229	Floyd Vaughan	415.00	145.00	75.00
230	Carl Hubbell	600.00	210.00	110.00
231	Joe Moore	165.00	55.00	30.00
232	Frank (Lefty) O'Doul	250.00	85.00	45.00
233	Johnny Vergez	165.00	55.00	30.00
234	Carl Hubbell	575.00	200.00	100.00
235	Fred Fitzsimmons	165.00	55.00	30.00
236	George Davis	165.00	55.00	30.00
237	Gus Mancuso	165.00	55.00	30.00
238	Hugh Critz	165.00	55.00	30.00
239	Leroy Parmelee	165.00	55.00	30.00
240	Harold Schumacher	350.00	75.00	35.00

1934 Goudey (R320)

The 1934 Goudey set contains 96 cards (2-3/8" x 2-7/8") that feature color art reproductions of player photographs. Card fronts have two different designs; one featuring a small portrait photo of Lou Gehrig with the the words "Lou Gehrig says..." inside a blue strip at the bottom, while the other design carries a red "Chuck Klein says..." strip and also has his photo. The card backs contain a short player biography that purports to have been written by Gehrig or Klein. The ACC designation for the set is R320. Albums, blue for N.L., magenta for A.L., were given away to the person who bought the last penny pack in each box of high-numbers or who mailed 50 wrappers to the gum company.

		NM	EX	VG
Complete Set (96):		30,000	11,000	5,250
Common Player (1-48):		120.00	45.00	20.00
Common Player (49-72):		160.00	55.00	25.00
Common Player (73-96):		260.00	90.00	45.00
Album:		500.00	250.00	150.00
1	Jimmy Foxx	3,000	600.00	210.00
2	Gordon (Mickey) Cochrane	425.00	175.00	85.00
3	Charlie Grimm	120.00	45.00	20.00
4	Elwood (Woody) English	120.00	45.00	20.00
5	Ed Brandt	120.00	45.00	20.00
6	Jerome (Dizzy) Dean	1,700	400.00	190.00
7	Leo Durocher	325.00	130.00	65.00
8	Tony Piet	120.00	45.00	20.00
9	Ben Chapman	120.00	45.00	20.00
10	Charles (Chuck) Klein	325.00	130.00	65.00
11	Paul Waner	325.00	130.00	65.00
12	Carl Hubbell	325.00	130.00	65.00
13	Frank Frisch	325.00	130.00	65.00
14	Willie Kamm	120.00	45.00	20.00
15	Alvin Crowder	120.00	45.00	20.00
16	Joe Kuhel	120.00	45.00	20.00
17	Hugh Critz	120.00	45.00	20.00
18	Henry (Heinie) Manush	325.00	130.00	65.00
19	Robert (Lefty) Grove	675.00	225.00	110.00
20	Frank Hogan	120.00	45.00	20.00
21	Bill Terry	325.00	130.00	65.00
22	Floyd Vaughan	325.00	130.00	65.00
23	Charley Gehringer	375.00	150.00	75.00
24	Ray Benge	120.00	45.00	20.00
25	Roger Cramer	120.00	45.00	20.00
26	Gerald Walker	120.00	45.00	20.00
27	Luke Appling	325.00	130.00	65.00
28	Ed. Coleman	120.00	45.00	20.00
29	Larry French	120.00	45.00	20.00
30	Julius Solters	120.00	45.00	20.00
31	Baxter Jordan	120.00	45.00	20.00
32	John (Blondy) Ryan	120.00	45.00	20.00
33	Frank (Don) Hurst	120.00	45.00	20.00
34	Charles (Chick) Hafey	325.00	130.00	65.00
35	Ernie Lombardi	325.00	130.00	65.00
36	Walter (Huck) Betts	120.00	45.00	20.00
37	Lou Gehrig	3,900	1,600	750.00
38	Oral Hildebrand	120.00	45.00	20.00
39	Fred Walker	120.00	45.00	20.00
40	John Stone	120.00	45.00	20.00
41	George Earnshaw	120.00	45.00	20.00
42	John Allen	120.00	45.00	20.00
43	Dick Porter	120.00	45.00	20.00
44	Tom Bridges	120.00	45.00	20.00
45	Oscar Melillo	120.00	45.00	20.00
46	Joe Stripp	120.00	45.00	20.00
47	John Frederick	120.00	45.00	20.00

48	James (Tex) Carleton	120.00	45.00	20.00
49	Sam Leslie	160.00	55.00	25.00
50	Walter Beck	160.00	55.00	25.00
51	Jim (Rip) Collins	160.00	55.00	25.00
52	Herman Bell	160.00	55.00	25.00
53	George Watkins	160.00	55.00	25.00
54	Wesley Schulmerich	160.00	55.00	25.00
55	Ed Holley	160.00	55.00	25.00
56	Mark Koenig	160.00	55.00	25.00
57	Bill Swift	160.00	55.00	25.00
58	Earl Grace	160.00	55.00	25.00
59	Joe Mowry	160.00	55.00	25.00
60	Lynn Nelson	160.00	55.00	25.00
61	Lou Gehrig	3,600	1,460	730.00
62	Henry Greenberg	1,350	550.00	275.00
63	Minter Hayes	160.00	55.00	25.00
64	Frank Grube	160.00	55.00	25.00
65	Cliff Bolton	160.00	55.00	25.00
66	Mel Harder	160.00	55.00	25.00
67	Bob Weiland	160.00	55.00	25.00
68	Bob Johnson	160.00	55.00	25.00
69	John Marcum	160.00	55.00	25.00
70	Ervin (Pete) Fox	160.00	55.00	25.00
71	Lyle Tinning	160.00	55.00	25.00
72	Arndt Jorgens	160.00	55.00	25.00
73	Ed Wells	260.00	90.00	45.00
74	Bob Boken	260.00	90.00	45.00
75	Bill Werber	260.00	90.00	45.00
76	Hal Trosky	260.00	90.00	45.00
77	Joe Vosmik	260.00	90.00	45.00
78	Frank (Pinkey) Higgins	260.00	90.00	45.00
79	Eddie Durham	260.00	90.00	45.00
80	Marty McManus	260.00	90.00	45.00
81	Bob Brown	260.00	90.00	45.00
82	Bill Hallahan	260.00	90.00	45.00
83	Jim Mooney	260.00	90.00	45.00
84	Paul Derringer	260.00	90.00	45.00
85	Adam Comorosky	260.00	90.00	45.00
86	Lloyd Johnson	260.00	90.00	45.00
87	George Darrow	260.00	90.00	45.00
88	Homer Peel	260.00	90.00	45.00
89	Linus Frey	260.00	90.00	45.00
90	Hazen (Ki-Ki) Cuyler	600.00	240.00	120.00
91	Dolph Camilli	275.00	95.00	45.00
92	Steve Larkin	275.00	95.00	45.00
93	Fred Ostermueller	275.00	95.00	45.00
94	Robert A. (Red) Rolfe	400.00	160.00	80.00
95	Myril Hoag	275.00	95.00	45.00
96	Jim DeShong	525.00	160.00	60.00

1934 Goudey Premiums (R309-1)

GEORGE HERMAN (BABE) RUTH

Consisting of just four unnumbered cards, this set of black-and-white photos was printed on heavy cardboard and issued as a premium by the Goudey Gum Co. in 1934. The cards measure 5-1/2" x 8-13/16" and are accented with a gold, picture-frame border and an easel on the back. Besides the game's greatest player, the set has team photos of the 1933 All-Star squads from each league and the World's Champion 1933 N.Y. Giants.

		NM	EX	VG
Complete Set (4):		3,250	1,625	975.00
Common Card:		600.00	300.00	180.00
(1)	American League All Stars	650.00	325.00	195.00
(2)	National League All Stars	600.00	300.00	180.00
(3)	"Worlds Champions 1933" (New York Giants)	750.00	375.00	225.00
(4)	George Herman (Babe) Ruth	1,250	625.00	375.00

1935 Goudey 4-in-1 (R321)

The 1935 Goudey set features color portraits of four players (usually) from the same team on each card. Thirty-six card fronts make up the set with 114 front/back combinations existing. The card backs form nine different puzzles: 1) Tigers Team, 2) Chuck Klein, 3) Frankie Frisch, 4) Mickey Cochrane, 5) Joe Cronin, 6) Jimmy Foxx, 7) Al Simmons, 8) Indians Team, and 9) Senators Team. The cards, which measure 2-3/8" x 2-7/8", have an ACC designation of R321. The numbering has been assigned for this checklist on the basis of alphabetical order of the players found on each card front.

PIET REDS · COMOROSKY REDS

BOTTOMLEY REDS ·

PICTURE 3 CARD F

		NM	EX	VG
Complete Set (36):		11,000	4,400	2,200
Common Card:		125.00	50.00	25.00
(1)	Sparky Adams, Jim Bottomley, Adam Comorosky, Tony Piet	300.00	120.00	60.00
(2)	Ethan Allen, Fred Brickell, Bubber Jonnard, Jimmie Wilson	125.00	30.00	15.00
(3)	Johnny Allen, Jimmie Deshong, Red Rolfe, Dixie Walker (DeShong)	125.00	30.00	15.00
(4)	Luke Appling, Jimmie Dykes, George Earnshaw, Luke Sewell	300.00	120.00	60.00
(5)	Earl Averill, Oral Hildebrand, Willie Kamm, Hal Trosky	300.00	120.00	60.00
(6)	Dick Bartell, Hughie Critz, Gus Mancuso, Mel Ott	300.00	120.00	60.00
(7)	Ray Benge, Fred Fitzsimmons, Mark Koenig, Tom Zachary	125.00	30.00	15.00
(8)	Larry Benton, Ben Cantwell, Flint Rhem, Al Spohrer	125.00	30.00	15.00
(9)	Charlie Berry, Bobby Burke, Red Kress, Dazzy Vance	300.00	120.00	60.00
(10)	Max Bishop, Bill Cissell, Joe Cronin, Carl Reynolds	300.00	120.00	60.00
(11)	George Blaeholder, Dick Coffman, Oscar Melillo, Sammy West	125.00	30.00	15.00
(12)	Cy Blanton, Babe Herman, Tom Padden, Gus Suhr	125.00	30.00	15.00
(13)	Zeke Bonura, Mule Haas, Jackie Hayes, Ted Lyons	300.00	120.00	60.00
(14)	Jim Bottomley, Adam Comorosky, Willis Hudlin, Glenn Myatt	300.00	120.00	60.00
(15)	Ed Brandt, Fred Frankhouse, Shanty Hogan, Gene Moore	125.00	50.00	25.00
(16)	Ed Brandt, Rabbit Maranville, Marty McManus, Babe Ruth	2,900	900.00	400.00
(17)	Tommy Bridges, Mickey Cochrane, Charlie Gehringer, Billy Rogell	350.00	140.00	70.00
(18)	Jack Burns, Frank Grube, Rollie Hemsley, Bob Weiland	125.00	30.00	15.00
(19)	Guy Bush, Waite Hoyt, Lloyd Waner, Paul Waner	350.00	140.00	70.00
(20)	Sammy Byrd, Danny MacFayden, Pepper Martin, Bob O'Farrell	125.00	30.00	15.00
(21a)	Gilly Campbell, Ival Goodman, Alex Kampouris, Billy Meyers (Myers) (No "Meyers.")	200.00	80.00	40.00
(21b)	Gilly Campbell, Ival Goodman, Alex Kampouris, Billy Meyers (Myers)	150.00	60.00	30.00
(22)	Tex Carleton, Dizzy Dean, Frankie Frisch, Ernie Orsatti	650.00	260.00	130.00
(23)	Watty Clark, Lonny Frey, Sam Leslie, Joe Stripp	125.00	30.00	15.00
(24)	Mickey Cochrane, Willie Kamm, Muddy Ruel, Al Simmons	350.00	140.00	70.00
(25)	Ed Coleman, Doc Cramer, Bob Johnson, Johnny Marcum	125.00	30.00	15.00
(26)	General Crowder, Goose Goslin, Firpo Marberry, Heinie Schuble	300.00	120.00	60.00
(27)	Kiki Cuyler, Woody English, Burleigh Grimes, Chuck Klein	350.00	140.00	70.00
(28)	Bill Dickey, Tony Lazzeri, Pat Malone, Red Ruffing	400.00	160.00	80.00
(29)	Rick Ferrell, Wes Ferrell, Fritz Ostermueller, Bill Werber	300.00	120.00	60.00
(30)	Pete Fox, Hank Greenberg, Schoolboy Rowe, Gee Walker	350.00	140.00	70.00
(31)	Jimmie Foxx, Pinky Higgins, Roy Mahaffey, Dib Williams	400.00	160.00	80.00
(32)	Bump Hadley, Lyn Lary, Heinie Manush, Monte Weaver	300.00	120.00	60.00
(33)	Mel Harder, Bill Knickerbocker, Lefty Stewart, Joe Vosmik	125.00	30.00	15.00
(34)	Travis Jackson, Gus Mancuso, Hal Schumacher, Bill Terry	300.00	120.00	60.00
(35)	Joe Kuhel, Buddy Meyer, John Stone, Earl Whitehill (Myer)	125.00	30.00	15.00
(36)	Red Lucas, Tommy Thevenow, Pie Traynor, Glenn Wright	300.00	120.00	60.00

1935 Goudey Puzzle-Backs

Each of the 36 card fronts in 1935 Goudey can be found with from two to four different backs that could be used to assemble a six-piece (single player) or 12-

JIMMY FOXX

piece (team photo or composite) puzzle. This listing checklists the different backs found with each front as well as the cards that comprise each of the nine puzzles. The numbers given for each puzzle piece correspond to the assigned numbers of the card fronts.

	Sparky Adams, Jim Bottomley, Adam Comorosky, Tony Piet
1H	Tigers, H
3F	Frisch, F
4F	Cochrane, F
5F	Cronin, F
	Ethan Allen, Fred Brickell, Bubber Jonnard, Jimmie Wilson
1E	Tigers, E
3C	Frisch, C
5C	Cronin, C
6C	Foxx, C
	Johnny Allen, Jimmie Deshong, Red Rolfe, Dixie Walker (DeShong)
8E	Indians, E
9E	Senators, E
	Luke Appling, Jimmie Dykes, George Earnshaw, Luke Sewell
1I	Tigers, I
2F	Klein, F
6F	Foxx, F
7F	Simmons, F
	Earl Averill, Oral Hildebrand, Willie Kamm, Hal Trosky
1L	Tigers, L
2E	Klein, E
6E	Foxx, E
7E	Simmons, E
	Dick Bartell, Hughie Critz, Gus Mancuso, Mel Ott
2A	Klein, A
4A	Cochrane, A
7A	Simmons, A
	Ray Benge, Fred Fitzsimmons, Mark Koenig, Tom Zachary
8A	Indians, A
9A	Senators, A
	Larry Benton, Ben Cantwell, Flint Rhem, Al Spohrer
8L	Indians, L
9L	Senators, L
	Charlie Berry, Bobby Burke, Red Kress, Dazzy Vance
2C	Klein, C
4C	Cochrane, C
7C	Simmons, C
	Max Bishop, Bill Cissell, Joe Cronin, Carl Reynolds
1G	Tigers, G
3E	Frisch, E
5E	Cronin, E
6E	Foxx, E
	George Blaeholder, Dick Coffman, Oscar Melillo, Sammy West
1F	Tigers, F
3D	Frisch, D
5D	Cronin, D
6D	Foxx, D
	Cy Blanton, Babe Herman, Tom Padden, Gus Suhr
8K	Indians, K
9K	Senators, K
	Zeke Bonura, Mule Haas, Jackie Hayes, Ted Lyons
8B	Indians, B
9B	Senators, B
	Jim Bottomley, Adam Comorosky, Willis Hudlin, Glenn Myatt
1K	Tigers, K
3B	Frisch, B
5B	Cronin, B
6B	Foxx, B
	Ed Brandt, Fred Frankhouse, Shanty Hogan, Gene Moore
2E	Klein, E
4E	Cochrane, E
7E	Simmons, E
	Ed Brandt, Rabbit Maranville, Marty McManus, Babe Ruth
1J	Tigers, J
3A	Frisch, A
4A	Cochrane, A
5A	Cronin, A
	Tommy Bridges, Mickey Cochrane, Charlie Gehringer, Billy Rogell
1D	Tigers, D
2D	Klein, D
6D	Foxx, D
7D	Simmons, D
	Jack Burns, Frank Grube, Rollie Hemsley, Bob Weiland
8C	Indians, C
9C	Senators, C
	Guy Bush, Waite Hoyt, Lloyd Waner, Paul Waner
1E	Tigers, E
3C	Frisch, C
4C	Cochrane, C
5C	Cronin, C

Sammy Byrd, Danny MacFayden, Pepper Martin,
Bob O'Farrell
2F   Klein, F
4F   Cochrane, F
7F   Simmons, F
Gilly Campbell, Ival Goodman, Alex Kampouris,
Billy Meyers (Myers)
8D   Indians, D
9D   Senators, D
Tex Carleton, Dizzy Dean, Frankie Frisch, Ernie Orsatti
1A   Tigers, A
2A   Klein, A
6A   Foxx, A
7A   Simmons, A
Watty Clark, Lonny Frey, Sam Leslie, Joe Stripp
1G   Tigers, G
3E   Frisch, E
4E   Cochrane, E
5E   Cronin, E
Mickey Cochrane, Willie Kamm, Muddy Ruel,
Al Simmons
1J   Tigers, J
3A   Frisch, A
5A   Cronin, A
6A   Foxx, A
Ed Coleman, Doc Cramer, Bob Johnson,
Johnny Marcum
8J   Indians, J
9J   Senators, J
General Crowder, Goose Goslin, Firpo Marberry,
Heinie Schuble
1H   Tigers, H
3F   Frisch, F
5F   Cronin, F
6F   Foxx, F
Kiki Cuyler, Woody English, Burleigh Grimes,
Chuck Klein
1F   Tigers, F
3D   Frisch, D
4D   Cochrane, D
5D   Cronin, D
Bill Dickey, Tony Lazzeri, Pat Malone, Red Ruffing
2D   Klein, D
4D   Cochrane, D
7D   Simmons, D
Rick Ferrell, Wes Ferrell, Fritz Ostermueller,
Bill Werber
8G   Indians, G
9G   Senators, G
Pete Fox, Hank Greenberg, Schoolboy Rowe,
Gee Walker
8F   Indians, F
9F   Senators, F
Jimmie Foxx, Pinky Higgins, Roy Mahaffey,
Dib Williams
1B   Tigers, B
2B   Klein, B
6B   Foxx, B
7B   Simmons, B
Bump Hadley, Lyn Lary, Heinie Manush,
Monte Weaver
1C   Tigers, C
2C   Klein, C
6C   Foxx, C
7C   Simmons, C
Mel Harder, Bill Knickerbocker, Lefty Stewart,
Joe Vosmik
8I   Indians, I
9I   Senators, I
Travis Jackson, Gus Mancuso, Hal Schumacher,
Bill Terry
1K   Tigers, K
3B   Frisch, B
4B   Cochrane, B
5B   Cronin, B
Joe Kuhel, Buddy Meyer, John Stone, Earl Whitehill
(Myer)
8H   Indians, H
9H   Senators, H
Red Lucas, Tommy Thevenow, Pie Traynor,
Glenn Wright
2B   Klein, B
4B   Cochrane, B
7B   Simmons, B

Picture 1, Detroit Tigers Team Photo

A (22)
B (31)
C (32)
D (17)
E (2)
E (19)
F (11)
F (27)
G (10)
G (23)
H (1)
H (26)
I (4)
J (16)
J (24)
K (14)
K (34)
L (5)

Picture 2, Chuck Klein

A (6)
A (22)
B (31)
B (36)
C (9)
C (32)
D (17)
D (28)
E (5)
E (15)
F (4)
F (20)

Picture 3, Frankie Frisch

A (16)

A (24)
B (14))
B (34)
C (2)
C (19)
D (11)
D (27)
E (10)
E (23)
F (1)
F (26)

Picture 4, Gordon (Mickey) Cochrane

A (6)
A (16)
B (34)
B (36)
C (9)
C (19)
D (27)
D (28)
E (15)
E (23)
F (1)
F (20)

Picture 5, Joe Cronin

A (16)
A (24)
B (14)
B (34)
C (2)
C (19)
D (11)
D (27)
E (10)
E (23)
F (1)
F (26)

Picture 6, Jimmy (Jimmie) Foxx

A (22)
A (24)
B (14)
B (31)
C (2)
C (32)
D (11)
D (17)
E (5)
E (10)
F (4)
F (26)

Picture 7, Al Simmons

A (6)
A (22)
B (31)
B (36)
C (9)
C (32)
D (17)
D (28)
E (5)
E (15)
F (4)
F (20)

Picture 8, Cleve. Indians Composite

A (7)
B (13)
C (18)
D (21)
E (3)
F (30)
G (34)
H (35)
I (32)
J (25)
K (12)
L (8)

Picture 9, Wash. Senators Composite

A (7)
B (13)
C (18)
D (21)
E (3)
F (30)
G (29)
H (35)
I (33)
J (25)
K (12)
L (8)

1935 Goudey Premiums (R309-2)

The black-and-white photos in this set were issued as a premium by retailers in exchange for coupons from 10 Goudey wrappers in 1935. The pictures measure 5-1/2" x 9" (or a bit longer), and are printed on thin, glossy paper. The unnumbered set includes three team collages and players, whose names are written in script in the "wide pen" style.

		NM	EX	VG
Complete Set (16):		5,000	2,500	1,500
Common Player:		275.00	135.00	82.00
(1)	Elden Auker	275.00	135.00	82.00
(2)	Johnny Babich	275.00	135.00	82.00
(3)	Dick Bartell	275.00	135.00	82.00
(4)	Lester R. Bell	275.00	135.00	82.00
(5)	Wally Berger	275.00	135.00	82.00
(6)	Mickey Cochrane	400.00	200.00	120.00
(7)	Ervin Fox, Leon "Goose" Goslin, Gerald Walker	325.00	160.00	97.00
(8)	Vernon Gomez	400.00	200.00	120.00
(9)	Hank Greenberg	500.00	250.00	150.00
(10)	Oscar Melillo	275.00	135.00	82.00
(11)	Mel Ott	400.00	200.00	120.00
(12)	Schoolboy Rowe	275.00	135.00	82.00
(13)	Vito Tamulis	275.00	135.00	82.00
(14)	Boston Red Sox	300.00	150.00	90.00
(15)	Cleveland Indians	300.00	150.00	90.00
(16)	Washington Senators	300.00	150.00	90.00

1936 Goudey (R322)

The 1936 Goudey set consists of black-and-white cards measuring 2-3/8" x 2-7/8". A facsimile autograph is positioned on the card fronts. Backs contain a brief player biography and were designed to be used to play a baseball game. Different game situations (out, single, double, etc.) are given on each card. Numerous front/back combinations exist in the set. The ACC designation for the set is R322.

		NM	EX	VG
Complete Set (25):		2,625	1,300	785.00
Common Player:		75.00	37.50	22.50
(1)	Walter Berger	75.00	37.50	22.50
(2)	Henry Bonura	75.00	37.50	22.50
(3)	Stan Bordagaray	75.00	37.50	22.50
(4)	Bill Brubaker	75.00	37.50	22.50
(5)	Dolf Camilli	75.00	37.50	22.50
(6)	Clydell Castleman	75.00	37.50	22.50
(7)	"Mickey" Cochrane	175.00	85.00	50.00
(8)	Joe Coscarart	75.00	37.50	22.50
(9)	Frank Crosetti	110.00	55.00	30.00
(10)	"Kiki" Cuyler	140.00	70.00	40.00
(11)	Paul Derringer	75.00	37.50	22.50
(12)	Jimmy Dykes	75.00	37.50	22.50
(13)	"Rick" Ferrell	140.00	70.00	40.00
(14)	"Lefty" Gomez	175.00	85.00	50.00
(15)	Hank Greenberg	275.00	135.00	80.00
(16)	"Bucky" Harris	140.00	70.00	40.00
(17)	"Rolly" Hemsley	75.00	37.50	22.50
(18)	Frank Higgins	75.00	37.50	22.50
(19)	Oral Hildebrand	75.00	37.50	22.50
(20)	"Chuck" Klein	140.00	70.00	40.00
(21)	"Pepper" Martin	110.00	55.00	30.00
(22)	"Buck" Newsom	75.00	37.50	22.50
(23)	Joe Vosmik	75.00	37.50	22.50
(24)	Paul Waner	140.00	70.00	40.00
(25)	Bill Werber	75.00	37.50	22.50

1936 Goudey "Wide Pen" Premiums (R314)

The premium cards originally listed in the American Card Catalog as R314 are known to generations of collectors as "Wide Pens" because of the distinctive, thick style of cursive printing used for the facsimile autographs. Current thinking is that the issue is actually comprised of several distinct types issued over the course of at least two years and sharing a basic 3-1/4" x 5-1/2" black-and-white unnumbered format. Dates attributed are speculative.

1936 Goudey "Wide Pen" Premiums - Type 1

These in-store premiums are known to collectors as "Wide Pens" because of the distinctive, thick style of cursive printing used for the facsimile autographs.

Al Simmons

Cards have a 3-1/4" x 5-1/2" black-and-white, unnumbered format. Type 1 cards have bordered photos with "LITHO IN U.S.A." in the bottom border.

		NM	EX	VG
Complete Set (120):		6,000	2,500	1,500
Common Player:		40.00	17.50	10.00
(1)	Ethan Allen/Kneeling	40.00	17.50	10.00
(2)	Earl Averill/Portrait	60.00	25.00	15.00
(3)	Dick Bartell/Portrait	40.00	17.50	10.00
(4)	Dick Bartell/Sliding	40.00	17.50	10.00
(5)	Walter Berger/Portrait	40.00	17.50	10.00
(6)	Geo. Blaeholder/Portrait	40.00	17.50	10.00
(7)	"Cy" Blanton/Portrait	40.00	17.50	10.00
(8)	"Cliff" Bolton/Portrait	40.00	17.50	10.00
(9)	Stan Bordagaray/Portrait	40.00	17.50	10.00
(10)	Tommy Bridges/Portrait	40.00	17.50	10.00
(11)	Bill Brubaker/Portrait	40.00	17.50	10.00
(12)	Sam Byrd/Portrait	40.00	17.50	10.00
(13)	Dolph Camilli/Portrait	40.00	17.50	10.00
(14)	Clydell Castleman/Pitching	40.00	17.50	10.00
(15)	Clydell Castleman/Portrait	40.00	17.50	10.00
(16)	"Phil" Cavaretta (Cavarretta)/Fielding	40.00	17.50	10.00
(17)	Ben Chapman, Bill Werber	50.00	20.00	15.00
(18)	"Mickey" Cochrane/Portrait	65.00	25.00	15.00
(19)	Earl Coombs (Earle Combs)/Btg	60.00	25.00	15.00
(20)	Joe Coscarart/Portrait	40.00	17.50	10.00
(21)	Joe Cronin/Kneeling	60.00	25.00	15.00
(22)	Frank Crosetti/Btg	45.00	20.00	12.00
(23)	Tony Cuccinello/Portrait	40.00	17.50	10.00
(24)	"Kiki" Cuyler/Portrait	60.00	25.00	15.00
(25)	Curt Davis/Pitching	40.00	17.50	10.00
(26)	Virgil Davis/Catching	40.00	17.50	10.00
(27)	Paul Derringer/Portrait	40.00	17.50	10.00
(28)	"Bill" Dickey/Catching	65.00	25.00	15.00
(29)	Joe DiMaggio, Joe McCarthy	575.00	240.00	150.00
(30)	Jimmy Dykes/Kneeling	40.00	17.50	10.00
(31)	"Rick" Ferrell/Catching	60.00	25.00	15.00
(32)	"Wes" Ferrell/Portrait	40.00	17.50	10.00
(33)	Rick Ferrell, Wes Ferrell	70.00	30.00	17.50
(34)	Lou Finney/Portrait	40.00	17.50	10.00
(35)	Ervin "Pete" Fox/Portrait	40.00	17.50	10.00
(36)	Tony Freitas/Portrait	40.00	17.50	10.00
(37)	Lonnie Frey/Btg	40.00	17.50	10.00
(38)	Frankie Frisch/Portrait	60.00	25.00	15.00
(39)	"Augie" Galan/Portrait	40.00	17.50	10.00
(40)	Charles Gehringer/Portrait	70.00	30.00	17.50
(41)	Charlie Gelbert/Portrait	40.00	17.50	10.00
(42)	"Lefty" Gomez/Portrait	70.00	30.00	17.50
(43)	"Goose" Goslin/Portrait	60.00	25.00	15.00
(44)	Earl Grace/Catching	40.00	17.50	10.00
(45)	Hank Greenberg/Portrait	175.00	75.00	45.00
(46)	"Mule" Haas/Btg	40.00	17.50	10.00
(47)	Odell Hale/Portrait	40.00	17.50	10.00
(48)	Bill Hallahan/Portrait	40.00	17.50	10.00
(49)	"Mel" Harder/Portrait	40.00	17.50	10.00
(50)	"Bucky" Harris/Portrait	60.00	25.00	15.00
(51)	"Gabby" Hartnett/Catching	60.00	25.00	15.00
(52)	Ray Hayworth/Catching	40.00	17.50	10.00
(53)	"Rolly" Hemsley/Catching	40.00	17.50	10.00
(54)	Babe Herman/Portrait	50.00	20.00	12.50
(55)	Frank Higgins/Portrait	40.00	17.50	10.00
(56)	Oral Hildebrand/Portrait	40.00	17.50	10.00
(57)	Myril Hoag/Portrait	40.00	17.50	10.00
(58)	Waite Hoyt/Pitching	60.00	25.00	15.00
(59)	Woody Jensen/Btg	40.00	17.50	10.00
(60)	Bob Johnson/Btg	40.00	17.50	10.00
(61)	"Buck" Jordan/Portrait	40.00	17.50	10.00
(62)	Alex Kampouris/Portrait	40.00	17.50	10.00
(63)	"Chuck" Klein/Portrait	60.00	25.00	15.00
(64)	Joe Kuhel/Portrait	40.00	17.50	10.00
(65)	Lyn Lary/Portrait	40.00	17.50	10.00
(66)	Harry Lavagetto/Portrait	40.00	17.50	10.00
(67)	Sam Leslie/Portrait	40.00	17.50	10.00
(68)	Freddie Lindstrom/Portrait	60.00	25.00	15.00
(69)	Ernie Lombardi/Throwing	60.00	25.00	15.00
(70)	"Al" Lopez/Throwing	60.00	25.00	15.00
(71)	Dan MacFayden/Portrait	40.00	17.50	10.00
(72)	John Marcum/Pitching	40.00	17.50	10.00
(73)	"Pepper" Martin/Portrait	50.00	20.00	12.50
(74)	Eric McNair/Portrait	40.00	17.50	10.00
(75)	"Ducky" Medwick/Kneeling	60.00	25.00	15.00
(76)	Gene Moore/Portrait	40.00	17.50	10.00
(77)	Randy Moore/Portrait	40.00	17.50	10.00
(78)	Terry Moore/Portrait	40.00	17.50	10.00
(79)	Edw. Moriarty/Portrait	40.00	17.50	10.00
(80)	"Wally" Moses/Portrait	40.00	17.50	10.00
(81)	"Buddy" Myer/Btg	40.00	17.50	10.00
(82)	"Buck" Newsom/Portrait	40.00	17.50	10.00

		NM	EX	VG
(83)	Steve O'Neill, Frank Pytlak	40.00	17.50	10.00
(84)	Fred Ostermueller/Portrait	40.00	17.50	10.00
(85)	Marvin Owen/Portrait	40.00	17.50	10.00
(86)	Tommy Padden/Portrait	40.00	17.50	10.00
(87)	Ray Pepper/Btg	40.00	17.50	10.00
(88)	Tony Piet/Portrait	40.00	17.50	10.00
(89)	"Rabbit" Pytlak/Throwing	40.00	17.50	10.00
(90)	"Rip" Radcliff/Portrait	40.00	17.50	10.00
(91)	Bobby Reis/Portrait	40.00	17.50	10.00
(92)	"Lew" Riggs/Fielding	40.00	17.50	10.00
(93)	Bill Rogell/Portrait	40.00	17.50	10.00
(94)	"Red" Rolfe/Portrait	40.00	17.50	10.00
(95)	"Schoolboy" Rowe/Portrait	45.00	20.00	12.00
(96)	Al Schacht/Portrait	50.00	20.00	12.50
(97)	"Luke" Sewell/Catching	40.00	17.50	10.00
(98)	Al Simmons/Portrait	60.00	25.00	15.00
(99)	John Stone/Portrait	40.00	17.50	10.00
(100)	Gus Suhr/Fielding	40.00	17.50	10.00
(101)	Joe Sullivan/Portrait	40.00	17.50	10.00
(102)	Bill Swift/Portrait	40.00	17.50	10.00
(103)	Vito Tamulis/Portrait	40.00	17.50	10.00
(104)	Dan Taylor/Portrait	40.00	17.50	10.00
(105)	Cecil Travis/Portrait	40.00	17.50	10.00
(106)	Hal Trosky/Portrait	40.00	17.50	10.00
(107)	"Bill" Urbanski/Portrait	40.00	17.50	10.00
(108)	Russ Van Atta/Portrait	40.00	17.50	10.00
(109)	"Arky" Vaughan/Portrait	60.00	25.00	15.00
(110)	Gerald Walker/Portrait	40.00	17.50	10.00
(111)	"Buck" Walter (Walters)/Portrait	40.00	17.50	10.00
(112a)	Lloyd Waner/Portrait (No "LITHO IN U.S.A.)	60.00	25.00	15.00
(112b)	Lloyd Waner/Portrait ("LITHO IN U.S.A.)	60.00	25.00	15.00
(113)	Paul Waner/Portrait	60.00	25.00	15.00
(114)	"Lon" Warneke/Portrait	40.00	17.50	10.00
(115)	"Rabbit" Warstler/Btg	40.00	17.50	10.00
(116)	Bill Werber/Portrait	40.00	17.50	10.00
(117)	"Jo Jo" White/Portrait	40.00	17.50	10.00
(118)	Burgess Whitehead/Portrait	40.00	17.50	10.00
(119)	John Whitehead/Portrait	40.00	17.50	10.00
(120)	Whitlow Wyatt/Portrait	40.00	17.50	10.00

1936 Goudey "Wide Pen" Premiums - Type 2

These 3-1/4" x 5-1/2" black-and-white, unnumbered cards are known as "Wide Pens" because of the distinctive cursive printing of the facsimile autographs. Type 2 and Type 3 cards share their photos. Type 2 cards have borders, but no "LITHO IN U.S.A." line. Some Type 2 cards also share their photos with Type 1, but have a different projection (size). Those are indicated parenthetically with an asterisk.

		NM	EX	VG
Complete Set (24):		1,800	850.00	500.00
Common Player:		60.00	27.50	15.00
(1)	Mel Almada/Kneeling	75.00	35.00	20.00
(2)	Lucius Appling/Portrait	90.00	40.00	22.50
(3)	Henry Bonura/Portrait	60.00	27.50	15.00
(4)	Ben Chapman, Bill Werber	80.00	35.00	20.00
(5)	Herman Clifton/Btg	60.00	27.50	15.00
(6)	Roger "Doc" Cramer/Portrait	60.00	27.50	15.00
(7)	Joe Cronin/Kneeling*	90.00	40.00	22.50
(8)	Jimmy Dykes/Kneeling*	60.00	27.50	15.00
(9)	Erwin "Pete" Fox (Ervin)/Portrait*	60.00	27.50	15.00
(10)	Jimmy Foxx/Portrait	175.00	80.00	45.00
(11)	Hank Greenberg/Portrait*	235.00	100.00	60.00
(12)	Oral Hildebrand/Portrait*	60.00	27.50	15.00
(13)	Alex Hooks/Fielding	60.00	27.50	15.00
(14)	Willis Hudlin/Throwing	60.00	27.50	15.00
(15)	Bill Knickerbocker/Portrait	60.00	27.50	15.00
(16)	Heine (Heinie) Manush/Portrait	90.00	40.00	22.50
(17)	Steve O'Neill/Portrait	60.00	27.50	15.00
(18)	Marvin Owen/Portrait*	60.00	27.50	15.00
(19)	Al Simmons (Bats on shoulder.)	90.00	40.00	22.50
(20)	Lem "Moose" Solters/Btg (First name actually Julius.)	60.00	27.50	15.00
(21)	Hal Trosky/Btg	60.00	27.50	15.00
(22)	Joe Vosmik/Btg	60.00	27.50	15.00
(23)	Joe Vosmik/Portrait	60.00	27.50	15.00
(24)	Earl Whitehill/Throwing	60.00	27.50	15.00

1936 Goudey "Wide Pen" Premiums - Type 3

Al Simmons

These 3-1/4" x 5-1/2" black-and-white, unnumbered cards are known as "Wide Pens" because of the distinctive cursive printing of the facsimile autographs. Type 2 and Type 3 cards share their photos. Type 3 cards are borderless and some also share their photos with Type 1, but have a different projection (size). Those are indicated parenthetically with an asterisk.

		NM	EX	VG
Complete Set (24):		1,800	850.00	500.00
Common Player:		60.00	27.50	15.00
(1)	Mel Almada/Kneeling	75.00	35.00	20.00
(2)	Lucius Appling/Portrait	90.00	40.00	22.50
(3)	Henry Bonura/Portrait	60.00	27.50	15.00
(4)	Ben Chapman, Bill Werber	80.00	35.00	20.00
(5)	Herman Clifton/Btg	60.00	27.50	15.00
(6)	Roger "Doc" Cramer/Portrait	60.00	27.50	15.00
(7)	Joe Cronin/Kneeling*	90.00	40.00	22.50
(8)	Jimmy Dykes/Kneeling*	60.00	27.50	15.00
(9)	Erwin "Pete" Fox (Ervin)/Portrait*	60.00	27.50	15.00
(10)	Jimmy Foxx/Portrait	175.00	80.00	45.00
(11)	Hank Greenberg/Portrait*	235.00	100.00	60.00
(12)	Oral Hildebrand/Portrait*	60.00	27.50	15.00
(13)	Alex Hooks/Fielding	60.00	27.50	15.00
(14)	Willis Hudlin/Throwing	60.00	27.50	15.00
(15)	Bill Knickerbocker/Portrait	60.00	27.50	15.00
(16)	Heine (Heinie) Manush/Portrait	90.00	40.00	22.50
(17)	Steve O'Neill/Portrait	60.00	27.50	15.00
(18)	Marvin Owen/Portrait*	60.00	27.50	15.00
(19)	Al Simmons (Bats on shoulder.)	90.00	40.00	22.50
(20)	Lem "Moose" Solters/Btg (First name actually Julius.)	60.00	27.50	15.00
(21)	Hal Trosky/Btg	60.00	27.50	15.00
(22)	Joe Vosmik/Btg	60.00	27.50	15.00
(23)	Joe Vosmik/Portrait	60.00	27.50	15.00
(24)	Earl Whitehill/Throwing	60.00	27.50	15.00

1937 Goudey "Wide Pen" Premiums - Type 4

Bobby Doerr

These premium cards are known to generations of collectors as "Wide Pens" because of the distinctive, thick style of cursive typography used for the facsimile autographs. They have a 3-1/4" x 5-1/2" black-and-white, unnumbered format. Type 4 cards are printed on a paper stock usually described as "creamy." They are bordered, but do not have a "LITHO IN U.S.A." line. Type 5 cards share the creamy paper stock of Type 4, and may have been part of the same issue, which would indicate Canadian origins. An asterisk after the pose indicates a photo shared with Type 1, though possibly of a larger or smaller projection.

		NM	EX	VG
Complete Set (36):		4,500	2,000	1,200
Common Player:		60.00	25.00	15.00
(1)	"Luke" Appling/Btg	90.00	40.00	22.50
(2)	Earl Averill/Portrait*	90.00	40.00	22.50
(3)	"Cy" Blanton/Pitching	60.00	25.00	15.00
(4)	"Zeke" Bonura/Btg	60.00	25.00	15.00
(5)	Tom Bridges/Throwing	60.00	25.00	15.00
(6)	Tommy Bridges/Portrait*	60.00	25.00	15.00
(7)	Mickey Cochrane/Portrait*	90.00	40.00	22.50
(8)	Joe Cronin/Kneeling*	90.00	40.00	22.50
(9)	"Joe" DiMaggio/Portrait	2,000	900.00	500.00
(10)	"Bobby" Doeer (Doerr)/Btg	90.00	40.00	22.50
(11)	Jimmy Dykes/Fielding	60.00	25.00	15.00
(12)	"Bob" Feller/Pitching	200.00	90.00	50.00
(13)	"Elbie" Fletcher/Fielding	60.00	25.00	15.00
(14)	Erwin "Pete" Fox (Ervin)/Portrait*	60.00	25.00	15.00
(15)	Pete Fox/Btg	60.00	25.00	15.00
(16)	"Gus" Galan/Btg	60.00	25.00	15.00
(17)	Charles Gehringer/Portrait*	90.00	40.00	22.50
(18)	Hank Greenberg/Portrait*	150.00	65.00	35.00
(19)	"Goose" Goslin/Portrait	90.00	40.00	22.50
(20)	Mel Harder/Portrait	60.00	25.00	15.00
(21)	"Gabby" Hartnett/Catching*	90.00	40.00	22.50
(22)	Ray Hayworth/Catching*	60.00	25.00	15.00
(23)	"Pinky" Higgins/Portrait	60.00	25.00	15.00
(24)	Carl Hubbell/Pitching	90.00	40.00	22.50
(25)	"Wally" Moses/Btg	60.00	25.00	15.00
(26)	Lou Newsom/Portrait	60.00	25.00	15.00
(27)	Marvin Owen/Portrait*	60.00	25.00	15.00

		NM	EX	VG
(28)	Bill Rogell/Portrait*	60.00	25.00	15.00
(29)	"Schoolboy" Rowe/Pitching	60.00	25.00	15.00
(30)	"Schoolboy" Rowe/Portrait*	60.00	25.00	15.00
(31)	Al Simmons/Portrait*	90.00	40.00	22.50
(32)	Julius Solters/Btg	60.00	25.00	15.00
(33)	"Hal" Trosky/Btg	60.00	25.00	15.00
(34)	Joe Vosmik/Kneeling	60.00	25.00	15.00
(35)	"Jo Jo" White/Portrait*	60.00	25.00	15.00
(36)	Johnnie Whitehead/Pitching	60.00	25.00	15.00

1937 Goudey "Wide Pen" Premiums - Type 5

These premium cards are known as "Wide Pens" because of the distinctive, thick style of cursive printing used for the facsimile autographs. they have a 3-1/4" x 5-1/2" black-and-white, unnumbered format. The photos are bordered, but do not have a "LITHO IN U.S.A." line. Type 5 cards are printed on a paper stock usually described as "creamy" and may have been part of the same issue as Type 4. Type 5 is comprised only of Toronto and Montreal (International League) players.

		NM	EX	VG
Complete Set (39):		3,500	1,600	900.00
Common Player:		90.00	40.00	25.00
(1)	Buddy Bates	90.00	40.00	25.00
(2)	Del Bisonette/Portrait	90.00	40.00	25.00
(3)	Lincoln Blakely	90.00	40.00	25.00
(4)	Isaac J. Boone	90.00	40.00	25.00
(5)	John H. Burnett/Btg	90.00	40.00	25.00
(6)	Leon Chagon	90.00	40.00	25.00
(7)	Gus Dugas/Portrait	90.00	40.00	25.00
(8)	Henry N. Erickson/Catching	90.00	40.00	25.00
(9)	Art Funk/Portrait	90.00	40.00	25.00
(10)	George Granger/Portrait	90.00	40.00	25.00
(11)	Thomas G. Heath	90.00	40.00	25.00
(12)	Phil Hensiek/Portrait	90.00	40.00	25.00
(13)	Leroy Herrmann/Throwing	90.00	40.00	25.00
(14)	Henry Johnson	90.00	40.00	25.00
(15)	Hal King/Portrait	90.00	40.00	25.00
(16)	Charles F. Lucas/Portrait	90.00	40.00	25.00
(17)	Edward S. Miller/Btg (Middle initial actually R.)	90.00	40.00	25.00
(18)	Jake F. Mooty/Pitching	90.00	40.00	25.00
(19)	Guy Moreau/Portrait (Street clothes.)	90.00	40.00	25.00
(20)	George Murray/Portrait	90.00	40.00	25.00
(21)	Glenn Myatt	90.00	40.00	25.00
(22)	Lauri Myllykangas	90.00	40.00	25.00
(23)	Francis J. Nicholas/Pitching	90.00	40.00	25.00
(24)	Bill O'Brien/Portrait (Street clothes.)	90.00	40.00	25.00
(25)	Thomas Oliver/Btg	90.00	40.00	25.00
(26)	James Pattison	90.00	40.00	25.00
(27)	Crip Polli/Portrait	90.00	40.00	25.00
(28)	Harlan Pool/Bats	90.00	40.00	25.00
(29)	Walter Purcey/Pitching	90.00	40.00	25.00
(30)	Bill Rhiel	90.00	40.00	25.00
(31)	Ben Sankey	90.00	40.00	25.00
(32)	Les Scarcella (Scarsella)/ Kneeling	90.00	40.00	25.00
(33)	Bob Seeds/Portrait	90.00	40.00	25.00
(34)	Frank Shaugnessy/Portrait	90.00	40.00	25.00
(35)	Harry Smythe/Portrait	90.00	40.00	25.00
(36)	Ben Tate/Portrait	90.00	40.00	25.00
(37)	Fresco Thompson/Portrait	90.00	40.00	25.00
(38)	Charles Wilson/Portrait	90.00	40.00	25.00
(39)	Francis Wistert/Pitching	90.00	40.00	25.00

1937 Goudey Knot Hole League

Though they do not picture or name any players, the fact these game cards were issued by Goudey makes them collectible for many hobbyists. While they carry a copyright date of 1935, the cards were not issued until 1937. About 2-3/8" x 2-7/8", and printed in red, white and blue, the cards were intended to be used to play a baseball game using the situations printed on the fronts. Despite advertising a series of 100 cards, only 24 were actually issued. The cards were designated R325 in the American Card Catalog.

		NM	EX	VG
Complete Set (24):		450.00	180.00	90.00
Common Card:		25.00	10.00	5.00
1	Double / Foul	25.00	10.00	5.00
2	Steals Home!!/Strike	25.00	10.00	5.00
3	Ball/Out	25.00	10.00	5.00
4	Strike/Ball	25.00	10.00	5.00
5	Strike/Wild Pitch	25.00	10.00	5.00
6	Ball/Out	25.00	10.00	5.00
7	Bunt - Scratch Hit!!/ Stolen Base!!	25.00	10.00	5.00
8	Hit by Pitched Ball/Out	25.00	10.00	5.00
9	Foul/Ball	25.00	10.00	5.00
10	Foul/Double!	25.00	10.00	5.00
11	Out/Ball	25.00	10.00	5.00
12	Foul/Force Out	25.00	10.00	5.00
13	Out/Single	25.00	10.00	5.00
14	Strike/Ball	25.00	10.00	5.00
15	Foul Tip/Strike!	25.00	10.00	5.00
16	Three Bagger/Out	25.00	10.00	5.00
17	Ball/Out	25.00	10.00	5.00
18	Out!!/Error!!!	25.00	10.00	5.00
19	Strike/Foul	25.00	10.00	5.00
20	Out/Double Play	25.00	10.00	5.00
21	!!Home Run!!/Ball	25.00	10.00	5.00
22	Out/Strike	25.00	10.00	5.00
23	Ball/Out	25.00	10.00	5.00
24	Lout!!/Error!!!	25.00	10.00	5.00

1937 Goudey Thum Movies

These 2" x 3" baseball novelty booklets create the illusion of baseball action in motion when the pages are rapidly flipped. The booklets are numbered on the top of the back page. Thum Movies were listed in the American Card Catalog as R342.

		NM	EX	VG
Complete Set (13):		1,750	875.00	525.00
Common Player:		70.00	35.00	20.00
1	John Irving Burns	70.00	35.00	20.00
2	Joe Vosmik	70.00	35.00	20.00
3	Mel Ott	225.00	110.00	65.00
4	Joe DiMaggio	525.00	260.00	155.00
5	Wally Moses	70.00	35.00	20.00
6	Van Lingle Mungo	70.00	35.00	20.00
7	Luke Appling	100.00	50.00	30.00
8	Bob Feller	225.00	110.00	65.00
9	Paul Derringer	70.00	35.00	20.00
10	Paul Waner	100.00	50.00	30.00
11	Joe Medwick	100.00	50.00	30.00
12	James Emory Foxx	225.00	110.00	65.00
13	Wally Berger	70.00	35.00	20.00

1938 Goudey (R323)

Sometimes referred to as the Goudey Heads-Up set, this issue begins numbering (#241) where the 1933 Goudey set left off. On the card fronts, a photo is used for the player's head with the body being a cartoon drawing. Twenty-four different players are pictured twice in the set. Cards #241-264 feature plain backgrounds on the fronts. Cards #265-288 contain the same basic design and photo but include small drawings and comments within the background. Backs have player statistical and biographical information. The ACC designation for the issue is R323.

		NM	EX	VG
Complete Set (48):		29,000	11,500	5,750
Common Player (241-264):		200.00	85.00	30.00
Common Player (265-288):		225.00	100.00	35.00
241	Charlie Gehringer	600.00	250.00	100.00
242	Ervin Fox	300.00	100.00	40.00
243	Joe Kuhel	200.00	85.00	30.00
244	Frank DeMaree	200.00	85.00	30.00
245	Frank Pytlak	200.00	85.00	30.00
246a	Ernie Lombardi (Red Sox)	675.00	270.00	135.00
246b	Ernie Lombardi (Reds followed by black baseball.)	425.00	200.00	85.00
246c	Ernie Lombardi (Reds)	350.00	140.00	70.00
247	Joe Vosmik	200.00	85.00	30.00
248	Dick Bartell	200.00	85.00	30.00
249	Jimmy Foxx	900.00	350.00	150.00
250	Joe DiMaggio	5,000	2,000	800.00
251	Bump Hadley	200.00	85.00	30.00
252	Zeke Bonura	200.00	85.00	30.00
253	Hank Greenberg	1,000	400.00	200.00
254	Van Lingle Mungo	400.00	100.00	40.00
255	Julius Solters	200.00	85.00	30.00
256	Vernon Kennedy	200.00	85.00	30.00
257	Al Lopez	425.00	200.00	85.00
258	Bobby Doerr	500.00	200.00	85.00
259	Bill Werber	200.00	85.00	30.00
260	Rudy York	200.00	85.00	30.00
261	Rip Radcliff	200.00	85.00	30.00
262	Joe Ducky Medwick	425.00	200.00	85.00
263	Marvin Owen	200.00	85.00	30.00
264	Bob Feller	2,000	700.00	300.00
265	Charlie Gehringer	600.00	200.00	100.00
266	Ervin Fox	225.00	100.00	35.00
267	Joe Kuhel	225.00	100.00	35.00
268	Frank DeMaree	225.00	100.00	35.00
269	Frank Pytlak	225.00	100.00	35.00
270	Ernie Lombardi	500.00	225.00	100.00
271	Joe Vosmik	225.00	100.00	35.00
272	Dick Bartell	225.00	100.00	35.00
273	Jimmy Foxx	1,200	500.00	200.00
274	Joe DiMaggio	6,500	2,800	1,000
275	Bump Hadley	225.00	100.00	35.00
276	Zeke Bonura	225.00	100.00	35.00
277	Hank Greenberg	1,200	500.00	250.00
278	Van Lingle Mungo	225.00	100.00	35.00
279	Julius Solters	225.00	100.00	35.00
280	Vernon Kennedy	225.00	100.00	35.00
281	Al Lopez	500.00	225.00	90.00
282	Bobby Doerr	550.00	250.00	100.00
283	Bill Werber	225.00	100.00	35.00
284	Rudy York	225.00	100.00	35.00
285	Rip Radcliff	225.00	100.00	35.00
286	Joe Ducky Medwick	500.00	225.00	90.00
287	Marvin Owen	225.00	100.00	35.00
288	Bob Feller	2,500	800.00	400.00

1938 Goudey Big League Baseball Movies

Probably issued in both 1937-38, according to the biographies on back, this set of "flip movies" was comprised of small (2" x 3") booklets whose pages produced a movie effect when flipped rapidly, similar to a penny arcade novelty popular at the time. There are 13 players in the set; each movie having two cleary labeled parts. The cover of the booklets identify the set as "Big League Baseball Movies." They carry the American Card Catalog designation R326.

		NM	EX	VG
Complete Set (26):		3,750	1,875	1,125
Common Player:		75.00	37.50	22.50
1a	John Irving Burns (Part 1)	75.00	37.50	22.50
1b	John Irving Burns (Part 2)	75.00	37.50	22.50
2a	Joe Vosmik (Part 1)	75.00	37.50	22.50
2b	Joe Vosmik (Part 2)	75.00	37.50	22.50
3a	Mel Ott (Part 1)	185.00	95.00	55.00
3b	Mel Ott (Part 2)	185.00	95.00	55.00
4a	Joe DiMaggio (Part 1, Joe DiMaggio cover photo.)	475.00	235.00	140.00
4aa	Joe DiMaggio (Part 1, Vince DiMaggio cover photo.)	375.00	185.00	110.00
4b	Joe DiMaggio (Part 2, Joe DiMaggio cover photo.)	475.00	235.00	140.00
4ba	Joe DiMaggio (Part 2, Vince DiMaggio cover photo.)	375.00	185.00	110.00
5a	Wally Moses (Part 1)	75.00	37.50	22.50
5b	Wally Moses (Part 2)	75.00	37.50	22.50
6a	Van Lingle Mungo (Part 1)	75.00	37.50	22.50
6b	Van Lingle Mungo (Part 2)	75.00	37.50	22.50
7a	Luke Appling (Part 1)	110.00	55.00	35.00
7b	Luke Appling (Part 2)	110.00	55.00	35.00
8a	Bob Feller (Part 1)	225.00	110.00	65.00
8b	Bob Feller (Part 2)	225.00	110.00	65.00
9a	Paul Derringer (Part 1)	75.00	37.50	22.50
9b	Paul Derringer (Part 2)	75.00	37.50	22.50
10a	Paul Waner (Part 1)	110.00	55.00	35.00
10b	Paul Waner (Part 2)	110.00	55.00	35.00
11a	Joe Medwick (Part 1)	110.00	55.00	35.00
11b	Joe Medwick (Part 2)	110.00	55.00	35.00
12a	James Emory Foxx (Part 1)	260.00	130.00	75.00
12b	James Emory Foxx (Part 2)	260.00	130.00	75.00
13a	Wally Berger (Part 1)	75.00	37.50	22.50
13b	Wally Berger (Part 2)	75.00	37.50	22.50

1939 Goudey Premiums (R303-A)

Although this unnumbered set of paper premiums has the name "Diamond Stars Gum" on the back, it is not related to National Chicle's Diamond Stars card sets. Rather, this 48-player set was a premium issued by the Goudey Gum Co. Each premium photo measures 4" x 6-3/16" and is printed in a brown-toned sepia.

The front of the photo includes a facsimile autograph, while the back contains drawings that illustrate various baseball tips. These pictures are soemtimes found with top and bottom border trimmed to a depth of 5-3/4" for distribution in Canada.

		NM	EX	VG
Complete Set (48):		6,000	2,400	1,200
Common Player:		75.00	30.00	15.00
(1)	Luke Appling	135.00	55.00	25.00
(2)	Earl Averill	135.00	55.00	25.00
(3)	Wally Berger	75.00	30.00	15.00
(4)	Darrell Blanton	75.00	30.00	15.00
(5)	Zeke Bonura	75.00	30.00	15.00
(6)	Mace Brown	75.00	30.00	15.00
(7)	George Case	75.00	30.00	15.00
(8)	Ben Chapman	75.00	30.00	15.00
(9)	Joe Cronin	135.00	55.00	25.00
(10)	Frank Crosetti	90.00	36.00	18.00
(11)	Paul Derringer	75.00	30.00	15.00
(12)	Bill Dickey	150.00	60.00	30.00
(13)	Joe DiMaggio	650.00	260.00	130.00
(14)	Bob Feller	225.00	90.00	45.00
(15)	Jimmy (Jimmie) Foxx	235.00	95.00	45.00
(16)	Charles Gehringer	135.00	55.00	25.00
(17)	Lefty Gomez	135.00	55.00	25.00
(18)	Ival Goodman	75.00	30.00	15.00
(19)	Joe Gordon	75.00	30.00	15.00
(20)	Hank Greenberg	175.00	70.00	35.00
(21)	Buddy Hassett	75.00	30.00	15.00
(22)	Jeff Heath	75.00	30.00	15.00
(23)	Tom Henrich	75.00	30.00	15.00
(24)	Billy Herman	135.00	54.00	27.00
(25)	Frank Higgins	75.00	30.00	15.00
(26)	Fred Hutchinson	75.00	30.00	15.00
(27)	Bob Johnson	75.00	30.00	15.00
(28)	Ken Keltner	75.00	30.00	15.00
(29)	Mike Kreevich	75.00	30.00	15.00
(30)	Ernie Lombardi	135.00	55.00	25.00
(31)	Gus Mancuso	75.00	30.00	15.00
(32)	Eric McNair	75.00	30.00	15.00
(33)	Van Mungo	75.00	30.00	15.00
(34)	Buck Newsom	75.00	30.00	15.00
(35)	Mel Ott	150.00	55.00	25.00
(36)	Marvin Owen	75.00	30.00	15.00
(37)	Frank Pytlak	75.00	30.00	15.00
(38)	Woodrow Rich	75.00	30.00	15.00
(39)	Charley Root	75.00	30.00	15.00
(40)	Al Simmons	135.00	55.00	25.00
(41)	James Tabor	75.00	30.00	15.00
(42)	Cecil Travis	75.00	30.00	15.00
(43)	Hal Trosky	75.00	30.00	15.00
(44)	Arky Vaughan	135.00	55.00	25.00
(45)	Joe Vosmik	75.00	30.00	15.00
(46)	Lon Warneke	75.00	30.00	15.00
(47)	Ted Williams	1,050	420.00	210.00
(48)	Rudy York	75.00	30.00	15.00

1939 Goudey Premiums (R303-B)

Although larger (4-3/4" x 7-1/4" to 7-3/8"), the photos in this 24-player set are identical to those in the R303-A issue of the same year, and the format of the set is unchanged. The set, designated as R303-B in the American Card Catalog, can be found in both black-and-white and sepia-toned, with backs printed in brown.

		NM	EX	VG
Complete Set (24):		2,500	1,000	500.00
Common Player:		60.00	24.00	12.00
(1)	Luke Appling	90.00	35.00	12.00
(2)	George Case	60.00	25.00	12.00

(3)	Ben Chapman	60.00	25.00	12.00
(4)	Joe Cronin	90.00	35.00	15.00
(5)	Bill Dickey	110.00	45.00	20.00
(6)	Joe DiMaggio	600.00	240.00	120.00
(7)	Bob Feller	150.00	60.00	30.00
(8)	Jimmy (Jimmie) Foxx	175.00	70.00	35.00
(9)	Lefty Gomez	90.00	35.00	15.00
(10)	Ival Goodman	60.00	25.00	12.00
(11)	Joe Gordon	60.00	25.00	12.00
(12)	Hank Greenberg	125.00	50.00	25.00
(13)	Jeff Heath	60.00	25.00	12.00
(14)	Billy Herman	90.00	35.00	15.00
(15)	Frank Higgins	60.00	25.00	12.00
(16)	Ken Keltner	60.00	25.00	12.00
(17)	Mike Kreevich	60.00	25.00	12.00
(18)	Ernie Lombardi	90.00	35.00	15.00
(19)	Gus Mancuso	60.00	25.00	12.00
(20)	Mel Ott	110.00	45.00	20.00
(21)	Al Simmons	90.00	35.00	15.00
(22)	Arky Vaughan	90.00	35.00	15.00
(23)	Joe Vosmik	60.00	25.00	12.00
(24)	Rudy York	60.00	25.00	12.00

1941 Goudey (R324)

Goudey Gum's last set was issued in 1941. The 2-3/8" x 2-7/8" (size approximate due to imprecise cutting) cards feature black-and-white photos set against blue, green, red or yellow backgrounds. The player's name, team and position plus the card number are supposed to be situated in a box at the bottom of the card. However, due to vagaries of cutting, some or all of the bottom printing might appear at the top of the card, greatly reducing its value. The card backs are blank. The ACC designation for the set is R324.

		NM	EX	VG
Complete Set (33):		8,500	3,400	1,700
Common Player:		200.00	80.00	40.00
1	Hugh Mulcahy	200.00	80.00	40.00
2	Harland Clift	200.00	80.00	40.00
3	Louis Chiozza	200.00	80.00	40.00
4	Warren (Buddy) Rosar	200.00	80.00	40.00
5	George McQuinn	200.00	80.00	40.00
6	Emerson Dickman	200.00	80.00	40.00
7	Wayne Ambler	200.00	80.00	40.00
8	Bob Muncrief	200.00	80.00	40.00
9	Bill Dietrich	200.00	80.00	40.00
10	Taft Wright	200.00	80.00	40.00
11	Don Heffner	200.00	80.00	40.00
12	Fritz Ostermueller	200.00	80.00	40.00
13	Frank Hayes	200.00	80.00	40.00
14	John (Jack) Kramer	200.00	80.00	40.00
15	Dario Lodigiani	200.00	80.00	40.00
16	George Case	200.00	80.00	40.00
17	Vito Tamulis	200.00	80.00	40.00
18	Whitlow Wyatt	200.00	80.00	40.00
19	Bill Posedel	200.00	80.00	40.00
20	Carl Hubbell	675.00	275.00	125.00
21	Harold Warstler/SP	375.00	150.00	75.00
22	Joe Sullivan/SP	375.00	150.00	75.00
23	Norman (Babe) Young/SP	375.00	150.00	75.00
24	Stanley Andrews/SP	375.00	150.00	75.00
25	Morris Arnovich/SP	600.00	240.00	120.00
26	Elburt Fletcher	200.00	80.00	40.00
27	Bill Crouch	200.00	80.00	40.00
28	Al Todd	200.00	80.00	40.00
29	Debs Garms	200.00	80.00	40.00
30	Jim Tobin	200.00	80.00	40.00
31	Chester Ross	200.00	80.00	40.00
32	George Coffman	200.00	80.00	40.00
33	Mel Ott	600.00	240.00	120.00

1955 Robert Gould All Stars Cards

One of three issues of miniature plastic player statues issued in the mid-Fifties was the All Stars series by Robert Gould Inc. of New York. The white plastic statues, which sold for about a quarter, came rubber-banded to a baseball card. The card measures 2-1/2" x 3-1/2" with a white border. A rather crude black-and-white line drawing of the player is set against a green background. There are a few biographical details and 1954 and lifetime stats. An "All Stars" logo is in an upper corner, while the card number is at lower-right. The cards are blank-backed. All cards have a pair of notches at the sides and two punch holes to hold the rubber band. Prices shown here are for the cards alone. A 2-5/8" x 3-5/8" album reproducing all 28 player cards was also issued.

		NM	EX	VG
Complete Set, Cards (28):		8,500	4,250	2,500
Common Player:		250.00	125.00	75.00
Album:		200.00	100.00	50.00
1	Willie Mays	1,100	550.00	325.00
2	Gus Zernial	250.00	125.00	75.00
3	Red Schoendienst	325.00	160.00	95.00
4	Chico Carrasquel	250.00	125.00	75.00
5	Jim Hegan	250.00	125.00	75.00
6	Curt Simmons	250.00	125.00	75.00
7	Bob Porterfield	250.00	125.00	75.00
8	Jim Busby	250.00	125.00	75.00
9	Don Mueller	250.00	125.00	75.00
10	Ted Kluszewski	275.00	135.00	80.00
11	Ray Boone	250.00	125.00	75.00
12	Smoky Burgess	250.00	125.00	75.00
13	Bob Rush	250.00	125.00	75.00
14	Early Wynn	300.00	150.00	90.00
15	Bill Bruton	250.00	125.00	75.00
16	Gus Bell	250.00	125.00	75.00
17	Jim Finigan	250.00	125.00	75.00
18	Granny Hamner	250.00	125.00	75.00
19	Hank Thompson	250.00	125.00	75.00
20	Joe Coleman	250.00	125.00	75.00
21	Don Newcombe	275.00	135.00	80.00
22	Richie Ashburn	325.00	160.00	95.00
23	Bobby Thomson	250.00	125.00	75.00
24	Sid Gordon	250.00	125.00	75.00
25	Gerry Coleman	250.00	125.00	75.00
26	Ernie Banks	850.00	425.00	255.00
27	Billy Pierce	250.00	125.00	75.00
28	Mel Parnell	250.00	125.00	75.00

1955 Robert Gould All-Stars Statues

One of three issues of miniature plastic player statues issued in the mid-Fifties was the All Stars series by Robert Gould Inc. of New York. The white plastic statues, which sold for about a quarter, came rubber-banded to a baseball card. Depending on pose, they vary in size from around 2" to 2-1/2". The figures have a round base with the player's name. Prices shown here are for the statues alone. The statues were also sold in seven-player boxed sets labeled "A" through "D."

		NM	EX	VG
Complete Set, Statues (28):		1,500	750.00	450.00
Common Player:		40.00	20.00	12.00
1	Willie Mays	300.00	150.00	90.00
2	Gus Zernial	40.00	20.00	12.00
3	Red Schoendienst	75.00	37.00	22.00
4	Chico Carrasquel	40.00	20.00	12.00
5	Jim Hegan	40.00	20.00	12.00
6	Curt Simmons	40.00	20.00	12.00
7	Bob Porterfield	40.00	20.00	12.00
8	Jim Busby	40.00	20.00	12.00
9	Don Mueller	40.00	20.00	12.00
10	Ted Kluszewski	50.00	25.00	15.00
11	Ray Boone	40.00	20.00	12.00
12	Smoky Burgess	40.00	20.00	12.00
13	Bob Rush	40.00	20.00	12.00
14	Early Wynn	60.00	30.00	18.00
15	Bill Bruton	40.00	20.00	12.00
16	Gus Bell	40.00	20.00	12.00
17	Jim Finigan	40.00	20.00	12.00
18	Granny Hamner	40.00	20.00	12.00
19	Hank Thompson	40.00	20.00	12.00
20	Joe Coleman	40.00	20.00	12.00
21	Don Newcombe	45.00	22.00	13.50
22	Richie Ashburn	75.00	37.00	22.00
23	Bobby Thomson	45.00	22.00	13.50
24	Sid Gordon	40.00	20.00	12.00

		NM	EX	VG
25	Gerry Coleman	40.00	20.00	12.00
26	Ernie Banks	240.00	120.00	72.00
27	Billy Pierce	40.00	20.00	12.00
28	Mel Parnell	40.00	20.00	12.00

1978 Grand Slam

26 Bill Terry — 1st base

Was the National League's last .400 hitter. Played all 14 years with the Giants, collecting 2193 hits and a lifetime batting average of .341. From 1927 through 1935 Bill's average never dipped below .320 with a high of .401 in 1930 with 254 hits. Was player-manager from 1932 through 1936. Collected over 200 hits in a season six times. Played in three World Series. Batting .295 in 16 games. Managed the Giants from 1937 through 1941. A member of the Baseball Hall of Fame, being inducted in 1954.

GRAND SLAM 1978

Bill Terry

This collectors' edition card set was produced by Jack Wallin. The black-and-white 2-1/4" x 3-1/4" cards have player poses or action photos on front, with the name in the white border at bottom. Backs have a career summary.

		NM	EX	VG
	Complete Set (200):	120.00	60.00	35.00
	Common Player:	2.00	1.00	.60
1	Leo Durocher	2.00	1.00	.60
2	Bob Lemon	2.00	1.00	.60
3	Earl Averill	2.00	1.00	.60
4	Dale Alexander	2.00	1.00	.60
5	Hank Greenberg	12.00	6.00	3.50
6	Waite Hoyt	2.00	1.00	.60
7	Al Lopez	2.00	1.00	.60
8	Lloyd Waner	2.00	1.00	.60
9	Bob Feller	2.00	1.00	.60
10	Guy Bush	2.00	1.00	.60
11	Stan Hack	2.00	1.00	.60
12	Zeke Bonura	2.00	1.00	.60
13	Wally Moses	2.00	1.00	.60
14	Fred Fitzsimmons	2.00	1.00	.60
15	Johnny Vander Meer	2.00	1.00	.60
16	Riggs Stephenson	2.00	1.00	.60
17	Bucky Walters	2.00	1.00	.60
18	Charlie Grimm	2.00	1.00	.60
19	Phil Cavarretta	2.00	1.00	.60
20	Wally Berger	2.00	1.00	.60
21	Joe Sewell	2.00	1.00	.60
22	Edd Roush	2.00	1.00	.60
23	Johnny Mize	2.00	1.00	.60
24	Bill Dickey	2.00	1.00	.60
25	Lou Boudreau	2.00	1.00	.60
26	Bill Terry	2.00	1.00	.60
27	Willie Kamm	2.00	1.00	.60
28	Charlie Gehringer	2.00	1.00	.60
29	Stan Coveleski	2.00	1.00	.60
30	Larry French	2.00	1.00	.60
31	George Kelly	2.00	1.00	.60
32	Terry Moore	2.00	1.00	.60
33	Billy Herman	2.00	1.00	.60
34	Babe Herman	2.00	1.00	.60
35	Carl Hubbell	2.00	1.00	.60
36	Buck Leonard	2.00	1.00	.60
37	Gus Suhr	2.00	1.00	.60
38	Burleigh Grimes	2.00	1.00	.60
39	Al Fonseca	2.00	1.00	.60
40	Travis Jackson	2.00	1.00	.60
41	Enos Slaughter	2.00	1.00	.60
42	Fred Lindstrom	2.00	1.00	.60
43	Rick Ferrell	2.00	1.00	.60
44	Cookie Lavagetto	2.00	1.00	.60
45	Stan Musial	12.00	6.00	3.50
46	Hal Trosky	2.00	1.00	.60
47	Hal Newhouser	2.00	1.00	.60
48	Paul Dean	2.00	1.00	.60
49	George Halas	6.00	3.00	1.75
50	Jocko Conlan	2.00	1.00	.60
51	Joe DiMaggio	30.00	15.00	9.00
52	Bobby Doerr	2.00	1.00	.60
53	Carl Reynolds	2.00	1.00	.60
54	Pete Reiser	2.00	1.00	.60
55	Frank McCormick	2.00	1.00	.60
56	Mel Harder	2.00	1.00	.60
57	George Uhle	2.00	1.00	.60
58	Doc Cramer	2.00	1.00	.60
59	Taylor Douthit	2.00	1.00	.60
60	Cecil Travis	2.00	1.00	.60
61	James Bell	2.00	1.00	.60
62	Charlie Keller	2.00	1.00	.60
63	Bill Hallahan	2.00	1.00	.60
64	Debs Garms	2.00	1.00	.60
65	Rube Marquard	2.00	1.00	.60
66	Rube Walberg	2.00	1.00	.60
67	Augie Galan	2.00	1.00	.60
68	George Pipgras	2.00	1.00	.60
69	Hal Schumacher	2.00	1.00	.60
70	Dolf Camilli	2.00	1.00	.60
71	Paul Richards	2.00	1.00	.60
72	Judy Johnson	2.00	1.00	.60
73	Frank Crosetti	2.00	1.00	.60
74	Harry Lowery	2.00	1.00	.60
75	Walter Alston	2.00	1.00	.60
76	Dutch Leonard	2.00	1.00	.60
77	Barney McCosky	2.00	1.00	.60
78	Joe Dobson	2.00	1.00	.60
79	Ted Lyons	2.00	1.00	.60
80	George Kell	2.00	1.00	.60
81	Johnny Pesky	2.00	1.00	.60
82	Hank Borowy	2.00	1.00	.60
83	Ewell Blackwell	2.00	1.00	.60
84	Pee Wee Reese	12.00	6.00	3.50
85	Monte Irvin	2.00	1.00	.60
86	Joe Moore	2.00	1.00	.60
87	Joe Wood	2.00	1.00	.60
88	Babe Dahlgren	2.00	1.00	.60
89	Bibb Falk	2.00	1.00	.60
90	Ed Lopat	2.00	1.00	.60
91	Rip Sewell	2.00	1.00	.60
92	Marty Marion	2.00	1.00	.60
93	Taft Wright	2.00	1.00	.60
94	Allie Reynolds	2.00	1.00	.60
95	Harry Walker	2.00	1.00	.60
96	Tex Hughson	2.00	1.00	.60
97	George Selkirk	2.00	1.00	.60
98	Dom DiMaggio	10.00	5.00	3.00
99	Walker Cooper	2.00	1.00	.60
100	Phil Rizzuto	10.00	5.00	3.00
101	Robin Roberts	2.00	1.00	.60
102	Joe Adcock	2.00	1.00	.60
103	Hank Bauer	2.00	1.00	.60
104	Frank Baumholtz	2.00	1.00	.60
105	Ray Boone	2.00	1.00	.60
106	Smoky Burgess	2.00	1.00	.60
107	Walt Dropo	2.00	1.00	.60
108	Alvin Dark	2.00	1.00	.60
109	Carl Erskine	2.00	1.00	.60
110	Dick Donovan	2.00	1.00	.60
111	Dee Fondy	2.00	1.00	.60
112	Mike Garcia	2.00	1.00	.60
113	Bob Friend	2.00	1.00	.60
114	Ned Garver	2.00	1.00	.60
115	Billy Goodman	2.00	1.00	.60
116	Larry Jansen	2.00	1.00	.60
117	Jackie Jensen	2.00	1.00	.60
118	John Antonelli	2.00	1.00	.60
119	Ted Kluszewski	2.00	1.00	.60
120	Harvey Kuenn	2.00	1.00	.60
121	Clem Labine	2.00	1.00	.60
122	Red Schoendienst	2.00	1.00	.60
123	Don Larsen	2.00	1.00	.60
124	Vern Law	2.00	1.00	.60
125	Charlie Maxwell	2.00	1.00	.60
126	Wally Moon	2.00	1.00	.60
127	Bob Nieman	2.00	1.00	.60
128	Don Newcombe	2.00	1.00	.60
129	Wally Post	2.00	1.00	.60
130	Johnny Podres	2.00	1.00	.60
131	Vic Raschi	2.00	1.00	.60
132	Dusty Rhodes	2.00	1.00	.60
133	Jim Rivera	2.00	1.00	.60
134	Pete Runnels	2.00	1.00	.60
135	Hank Sauer	2.00	1.00	.60
136	Roy Sievers	2.00	1.00	.60
137	Bobby Shantz	2.00	1.00	.60
138	Curt Simmons	2.00	1.00	.60
139	Bob Skinner	2.00	1.00	.60
140	Bill Skowron	2.00	1.00	.60
141	Warren Spahn	2.00	1.00	.60
142	Gerry Staley	2.00	1.00	.60
143	Frank Thomas	2.00	1.00	.60
144	Bobby Thomson	2.00	1.00	.60
145	Bob Turley	2.00	1.00	.60
146	Vic Wertz	2.00	1.00	.60
147	Bill Virdon	2.00	1.00	.60
148	Gene Woodling	2.00	1.00	.60
149	Eddie Yost	2.00	1.00	.60
150	Sandy Koufax	25.00	12.50	7.50
151	Lefty Gomez	2.00	1.00	.60
152	Al Rosen	2.00	1.00	.60
153	Vince DiMaggio	2.00	1.00	.60
154	Bill Nicholson	2.00	1.00	.60
155	Mark Koenig	2.00	1.00	.60
156	Max Lanier	2.00	1.00	.60
157	Ken Keltner	2.00	1.00	.60
158	Whit Wyatt	2.00	1.00	.60
159	Marv Owen	2.00	1.00	.60
160	Red Lucas	2.00	1.00	.60
161	Babe Phelps	2.00	1.00	.60
162	Pete Donohue	2.00	1.00	.60
163	Johnny Cooney	2.00	1.00	.60
164	Glenn Wright	2.00	1.00	.60
165	Willis Hudlin	2.00	1.00	.60
166	Tony Cuccinello	2.00	1.00	.60
167	Bill Bevens	2.00	1.00	.60
168	Dave Ferris	2.00	1.00	.60
169	Whitey Kurowski	2.00	1.00	.60
170	Buddy Hassett	2.00	1.00	.60
171	Ossie Bluege	2.00	1.00	.60
172	Hoot Evers	2.00	1.00	.60
173	Thornton Lee	2.00	1.00	.60
174	Virgil Davis	2.00	1.00	.60
175	Bob Shawkey	2.00	1.00	.60
176	Smead Jolley	2.00	1.00	.60
177	Andy High	2.00	1.00	.60
178	George McQuinn	2.00	1.00	.60
179	Mickey Vernon	2.00	1.00	.60
180	Birdie Tebbetts	2.00	1.00	.60
181	Jack Kramer	2.00	1.00	.60
182	Don Kolloway	2.00	1.00	.60
183	Claude Passeau	2.00	1.00	.60
184	Frank Shea	2.00	1.00	.60
185	Bob O'Farrell	2.00	1.00	.60
186	Bob Johnson	2.00	1.00	.60
187	Ival Goodman	2.00	1.00	.60
188	Mike Kreevich	2.00	1.00	.60
189	Joe Stripp	2.00	1.00	.60
190	Mickey Owen	2.00	1.00	.60
191	Hughie Critz	2.00	1.00	.60
192	Ethan Allen	2.00	1.00	.60
193	Billy Rogell	2.00	1.00	.60
194	Joe Kuhel	2.00	1.00	.60
195	Dale Mitchell	2.00	1.00	.60
196	Eldon Auker	2.00	1.00	.60
197	Johnny Beazley	2.00	1.00	.60
198	Spud Chandler	2.00	1.00	.60
199	Ralph Branca	2.00	1.00	.60
200	Joe Cronin	2.00	1.00	.60

1957-58 Graphics Arts Service Detroit Tigers Postcards

This series of Tigers postcards was issued over a two-year span by a Cincinnati printer. The 3-3/16" x 5-7/16" cards have a black-and-white borderless player photo on front with or without a facsimile autograph. Backs have standard postcard indicia, including the producer's name and address.

		NM	EX	VG
	Complete Set (22):	1,500	750.00	450.00
	Common Player:	60.00	30.00	18.00
(1)	Al Aber	60.00	30.00	18.00
(2)	Hank Aguirre	60.00	30.00	18.00
(3)	Reno Bertoia/Fielding	60.00	30.00	18.00
(4)	Reno Bertoia/Portrait	60.00	30.00	18.00
(5)	Frank Bolling	60.00	30.00	18.00
(6)	Jim Bunning	120.00	60.00	35.00
(7)	Jack Dittmer	60.00	30.00	18.00
(8)	Paul Foytack	60.00	30.00	18.00
(9)	Jim Hegan	60.00	30.00	18.00
(10)	Tommy Henrich	80.00	40.00	24.00
(11)	Billy Hoeft	60.00	30.00	18.00
(12)	Frank House	60.00	30.00	18.00
(13)	Al Kaline	180.00	90.00	55.00
(14)	Harvey Kuenn	80.00	40.00	24.00
(15)	Don Lee	60.00	30.00	18.00
(16)	Billy Martin	90.00	45.00	25.00
(17)	Tom Morgan	60.00	30.00	18.00
(18)	J.W. Porter	60.00	30.00	18.00
(19)	Ron Samford	60.00	30.00	18.00
(20)	Bob Shaw	60.00	30.00	18.00
(21)	Lou Sleater	60.00	30.00	18.00
(22)	Tim Thompson	60.00	30.00	18.00

1888 Gray Studio Cabinets

The posed action photos on the approximately 4-1/4" x 6-1/2" cards are the same pictures seen on many of the players' Old Judge and Old Judge cabinet cards. Gray cabinets are found with two fancy logotypes at lower-left. On one, the tail of the "y" underscores the "Gra," while on the other, fancy decorations bookend the studio name. The Boston address of the studio is at lower-right. Players are not identified on the cards, and the bacls are blank.

		NM	EX	VG
	Common Player:	1,250	625.00	375.00
(1)	Charlie Buffinton/Btg	1,250	625.00	375.00
(2)	Charlie Buffinton (Right arm forward.)	1,250	625.00	375.00
(3)	Dan Casey (Arms at sides.)	1,250	625.00	375.00
(4)	Dan Casey (Ball in hands at chest.)	1,250	625.00	375.00
(5)	Dan Casey (Left arm outstretched.)	1,250	625.00	375.00
(6)	Jack Clements/Btg	1,250	625.00	375.00
(7)	Jack Clements/Fielding (Hands chest-high.)	1,250	625.00	375.00
(8)	Jack Clements (Hands on knees.)	1,250	625.00	375.00
(12)	Ed Daily/Btg	1,250	625.00	375.00
(13)	Ed Daily (Holding ball in front of face.)	1,250	625.00	375.00

(14)	Ed Daily/Throwing	1,250	625.00	375.00
(16)	Sid Farrar (Arms crossed)	1,250	625.00	375.00
(17)	Sid Farrar (Fielding grounder.)	1,250	625.00	375.00
(18)	Sid Farrar (Fielding fly ball.)	1,250	625.00	375.00
(19)	Sid Farrar (Right hand on belt buckle.)	1,250	625.00	375.00
(21)	Charlie Ferguson (Ball in hands at chest.)	1,250	625.00	375.00
(22)	Charlie Ferguson/Btg	1,250	625.00	375.00
(23)	Charlie Ferguson (Tagging Tommy McCarthy.)	1,500	750.00	450.00
(24)	Charlie Ferguson/Throwing (Right arm back.)	1,250	625.00	375.00
(26)	Jim Fogarty/Btg	1,250	625.00	375.00
(27)	Jim Fogarty (Fielding grounder.)	1,250	625.00	375.00
(28)	Jim Fogarty/Fielding (Hands at neck.)	1,250	625.00	375.00
(29)	Jim Fogarty (Fielding on the run.)	1,250	625.00	375.00
(32)	Tom Gunning/Fielding (Hands at knees.)	1,250	625.00	375.00
(33)	Arthur Irwin/Btg	1,250	625.00	375.00
(34)	Arthur Irwin/Fielding (Hands chest-high.)	1,250	625.00	375.00
(35)	Arthur Irwin/Throwing	1,250	625.00	375.00
(39)	Tommy McCarthy/Btg	2,500	1,250	750.00
(40)	Tommy McCarthy/Fielding (Hands chest-high.)	2,500	1,250	750.00
(41)	Tommy McCarthy (Tagging baserunner.)	2,500	1,250	750.00
(42)	Tommy McCarthy/Throwing	2,500	1,250	750.00
(44)	Deacon McGuire/Btg	1,250	625.00	375.00
(45)	Deacon McGuire/Fielding (Hands chest-high.)	1,250	625.00	375.00
(48)	Joe Mulvey/Btg	1,250	625.00	375.00
(49)	Joe Mulvey/Fielding (Hands at waist.)	1,250	625.00	375.00
(50)	Joe Mulvey (Watching ball.)	1,250	625.00	375.00
(60)	George Wood/Btg	1,250	625.00	375.00
(61)	George Wood (Fielding fly ball.)	1,250	625.00	375.00
(62)	George Wood (Fielding grounder.)	1,250	625.00	375.00
(63)	George Wood/Throwing	1,250	625.00	375.00

1975-76 Great Plains Greats

This collectors' issue was issued in two series in conjunction with shows conducted by the Great Plains Sports Collectors Association. Cards are about 2-5/8" x 3-3/4". Fronts have black-and-white photos with heavy colored frames and white borders. Player name is overprinted on a diamond at bottom. Backs have a career summary and stats, and a sponsor's ad. The 1975 issue (#1-24) was sponsored by Sheraton Inns; the 1976 cards (#25-42) were sponsored by Nu-Sash Corp.

		NM	EX	VG
	Complete Set (43):	20.00	10.00	6.00
	Common Player:	1.00	.50	.30
1	Bob Feller	2.00	1.00	.60
2	Carl Hubbell	1.00	.50	.30
3	Jocko Conlan	1.00	.50	.30
4	Hal Trosky	1.00	.50	.30
5	Allie Reynolds	1.00	.50	.30
6	Burleigh Grimes	1.00	.50	.30
7	Jake Beckley	1.00	.50	.30
8	Al Simmons	1.00	.50	.30
9	Paul Waner	1.00	.50	.30
10	Chief Bender	1.00	.50	.30
11	Fred Clarke	1.00	.50	.30
12	Jim Bottomley	1.00	.50	.30
13	Dave Bancroft	1.00	.50	.30
14	Bing Miller	1.00	.50	.30
15	Walter Johnson	2.50	1.25	.70
16	Grover Alexander	2.50	1.25	.70
17	Bob Johnson	1.00	.50	.30
18	Roger Maris	2.50	1.25	.70
19	Ken Keltner	1.00	.50	.30
20	Red Faber	1.00	.50	.30
21	"Cool Papa" Bell	1.00	.50	.30
22	Yogi Berra	2.50	1.25	.70
23	Fred Lindstrom	1.00	.50	.30
24	Ray Schalk	1.00	.50	.30
	Checklist	.10	.05	.03
25	Lloyd Waner	1.00	.50	.30
26	Johnny Hopp	1.00	.50	.30
27	Mel Harder	1.00	.50	.30
28	Dutch Leonard	1.00	.50	.30
29	Bob O'Farrell	1.00	.50	.30
30	Cap Anson	1.00	.50	.30
31	Dazzy Vance	1.00	.50	.30
32	Red Schoendienst	1.00	.50	.30
33	George Pipgras	1.00	.50	.30

34	Harvey Kuenn	1.00	.50	.30
35	Red Ruffing	1.00	.50	.30
36	Roy Sievers	1.00	.50	.30
37	Ken Boyer	1.00	.50	.30
38	Al Smith	1.00	.50	.30
39	Casey Stengel	1.00	.50	.30
40	Bob Gibson	1.50	.70	.45
41	Mickey Mantle	10.00	5.00	3.00
42	Denny McLain	1.00	.50	.30

1908-1909 Greenfield's Chocolates Postcards

 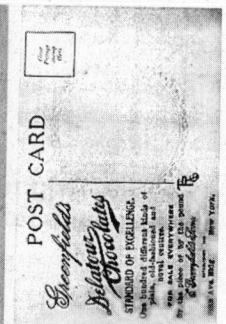

These special advertising versions of the Rose Company postcards were produced circa 1908-09. The 3-1/2" x 5-1/2" cards feature a black-and-white player portrait photo at center, surrounded by an embossed round gold frame. The player's surname and (usually) team are in a white panel under the photo. The background is green and includes crossed bats and a baseball, a diamond diagram and pictures of a fielder and batter. The postcard-format back is printed in black-and-white with a TRC logo at bottom-center. Printed at left in ornate typography is advertising for the New York confectioner. Two back styles are known apparently the result of the candy company's move from Fifth Ave. to Barclay St. (or vice versa) during the issuing period. It is unknown how many of the player postcards in the Rose Company series can be found with this advertising on back. While much rarer than Rose Co. cards without the advertising, the Greenfield's version currently carries only modest premium value, perhaps 10-20 percent higher than the regular version.

(See 1908-1909 Rose Company Postcards for checklist and base values.)

1916 Green-Joyce

Best known for its use as a promotional medium for The Sporting News, this 200-card set can be found with blank backs or with ads on the back for several local and regional businesses. Among them is Green-Joyce "Department of Sports," location unknown. Type-card and superstar collectors can expect to pay a premium for individual cards with Green-Joyce advertising as opposed to the more common M101-4 blank back values. Cards measure 1-5/8" x 3" and are printed in black-and-white.

PREMIUM: 3-4X
(See 1916 M101-4 Blank Backs for checklist and base values.)

1969 Greiner Tires Pittsburgh Pirates

One of the scarcer of the many Pirates regionals of the late 1960s is this eight-card issue. Printed on heavy paper in black-and-white, the 5-1/2" x 8-1/2" cards are blank-backed and unnumbered. They are checklisted here alphabetically. Some sources say the Matty Alou card is scarcer than the rest of the set.

Good Luck to Roberto Clemente and Pittsburgh Pirates from GREINER TIRE SERVICE
Route 30 West Phone 527-2811 Jeannette, Pa.

		NM	EX	VG
	Complete Set (8):	80.00	40.00	24.00
	Common Player:	4.50	2.25	1.25
(1)	Gene Alley	4.50	2.25	1.25
(2)	Matty Alou	30.00	15.00	9.00
(3)	Steve Blass	4.50	2.25	1.25
(4)	Roberto Clemente	30.00	15.00	9.00
(5)	Jerry May	4.50	2.25	1.25
(6)	Bill Mazeroski	12.50	6.25	3.75
(7)	Larry Shepard	4.50	2.25	1.25
(8)	Willie Stargell	12.50	6.25	3.75

1928 Greiners Bread

This set of about 1-3/8" x 2-1/2" black-and-white cards is a parallel of the strip card set cataloged as 1928 W502. The difference lies in advertising on the back of this version for an unidentified bakery's product.

		NM	EX	VG
	Complete Set (60):	8,500	3,500	1,750
	Common Player:	75.00	30.00	15.00
1	Burleigh Grimes	125.00	50.00	25.00
2	Walter Reuther (Ruether)	75.00	30.00	15.00
3	Joe Dugan	75.00	30.00	15.00
4	Red Faber	125.00	50.00	25.00
5	Gabby Hartnett	125.00	50.00	25.00
6	Babe Ruth	1,350	550.00	275.00
7	Bob Meusel	75.00	30.00	15.00
8	Herb Pennock	125.00	50.00	25.00
9	George Burns	75.00	30.00	15.00
10	Joe Sewell	125.00	50.00	25.00
11	George Uhle	75.00	30.00	15.00
12	Bob O'Farrell	75.00	30.00	15.00
13	Rogers Hornsby	150.00	60.00	30.00
14	"Pie" Traynor	125.00	50.00	25.00
15	Clarence Mitchell	75.00	30.00	15.00
16	Eppa Jepha Rixey	125.00	50.00	25.00
17	Carl Mays	90.00	35.00	18.00
18	Adolfo Luque	75.00	30.00	15.00
19	Dave Bancroft	125.00	50.00	25.00
20	George Kelly	125.00	50.00	25.00
21	Earl (Earle) Combs	125.00	50.00	25.00
22	Harry Heilmann	125.00	50.00	25.00
23	Ray W. Schalk	125.00	50.00	25.00
24	Johnny Mostil	75.00	30.00	15.00
25	Hack Wilson	125.00	50.00	25.00
26	Lou Gehrig	900.00	360.00	180.00
27	Ty Cobb	900.00	360.00	180.00
28	Tris Speaker	150.00	60.00	30.00
29	Tony Lazzeri	125.00	50.00	25.00
30	Waite Hoyt	125.00	50.00	25.00
31	Sherwood Smith	75.00	30.00	15.00
32	Max Carey	125.00	50.00	25.00
33	Eugene Hargrave	75.00	30.00	15.00
34	Miguel L. Gonzales (Miguel A. Gonzalez)	75.00	30.00	15.00
35	Joe Judge	75.00	30.00	15.00
36	E.C. (Sam) Rice	125.00	50.00	25.00
37	Earl Sheely	75.00	30.00	15.00
38	Sam Jones	75.00	30.00	15.00
39	Bib (Bibb) A. Falk	75.00	30.00	15.00
40	Willie Kamm	75.00	30.00	15.00
41	Stanley Harris	125.00	50.00	25.00
42	John J. McGraw	125.00	50.00	25.00
43	Artie Nehf	75.00	30.00	15.00
44	Grover Alexander	150.00	60.00	30.00
45	Paul Waner	125.00	50.00	25.00
46	William H. Terry	125.00	50.00	25.00
47	Glenn Wright	75.00	30.00	15.00
48	Earl Smith	75.00	30.00	15.00
49	Leon (Goose) Goslin	125.00	50.00	25.00
50	Frank Frisch	125.00	50.00	25.00
51	Joe Harris	75.00	30.00	15.00
52	Fred (Cy) Williams	75.00	30.00	15.00
53	Eddie Roush	125.00	50.00	25.00
54	George Sisler	125.00	50.00	25.00
55	Ed. Rommel	75.00	30.00	15.00
56	Rogers Peckinpaugh (Roger)	75.00	30.00	15.00
57	Stanley Coveleskie (Coveleski)	125.00	50.00	25.00
58	Lester Bell	75.00	30.00	15.00
59	L. Waner	125.00	50.00	25.00
60	John P. McInnis	75.00	30.00	15.00

1974 Greyhound Heroes on the Base Paths

The first of three annual baseball card folders honoring the stolen base leaders and runners-up in each league, this 20" x 9" five-panel sheet features six 4" x 3" cards printed in black-and-white with sepia graphics. Backs are printed in black, brown and white. Besides the cards, the folder contains information about the bus company's award, as well as major league stolen base records and base-stealing tips. Besides individual cards of the 1974 winner and runner-up in each league, the folder has cards picturing all winners and runners-up since 1965.

	NM	EX	VG
Complete Set, Folder:	10.00	5.00	3.00
Complete Set, Singles:	8.00	4.00	2.50
Common Player:	2.00	1.00	.60
(1) Lou Brock	4.00	2.00	1.25
(2) Rod Carew	4.00	2.00	1.25
(3) Davey Lopes	2.00	1.00	.60
(4) Bill North	2.00	1.00	.60
(5) A.L. Winners/Runners-Up	2.00	1.00	.60
(Don Buford, Bert Campaneris, Rod Carew, Tommy Harper, Dave Nelson, Bill North, Amos Otis, Fred Patek)			
(6) N.L. Winners/Runners-Up	2.00	1.00	.60
(Lou Brock, Jose Cardenal, Sonny Jackson, Davey Lopes, Joe Morgan, Bobby Tolan, Maury Wills)			

1975 Greyhound Heroes on the Base Paths

Six perforated 3-7/8" x 3" cards are featured on this folded five-panel 20" x 9" sheet honoring top base stealers in both leagues for the 1975 season. Four of the cards have each league's SB leader and runner-up in a black-and-white portrait photo with blue background. Backs are printed in black, blue and white and include major league stats. There are also two action photo cards with lists on the back of each year's winner and runner-up for the Greyhound Stolen Base Awards since 1965.

	NM	EX	VG
Complete Set, Folder:	7.00	3.50	2.00
Complete Set, Singles:	4.00	2.00	1.25
Common Player:	1.50	.70	.45
(1) Davey Lopes	1.50	.70	.45
(2) Davey Lopes/Action	1.50	.70	.45
(3) Joe Morgan	2.50	1.25	.70
(4) Bill North/Action	1.50	.70	.45
(5) Mickey Rivers	1.50	.70	.45
(6) Claudell Washington	1.50	.70	.45

1976 Greyhound Heroes on the Base Paths

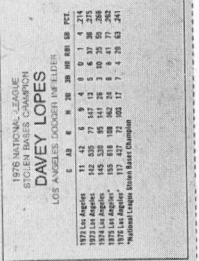

The last of three annual baseball card folders honoring the stolen base leaders and runners-up in each league, this 20" x 9" five-panel sheet features six 4" x 3" cards printed in black-and-white with sepia graphics. Backs are printed in black, brown and white. Besides the cards, the folder contains information about the bus company's award, as well as major league stolen base records and base-stealing tips. Besides individual cards of the 1974 winner and runner-up in each league, the folder includes two action-photo cards listing all winners and runners-up since 1965.

	NM	EX	VG
Complete Set, Folder:	6.00	3.00	1.75
Complete Set, Singles:	5.00	2.50	1.50
Common Player:	1.50	.70	.45
(1) Ronald Le Flore	1.50	.70	.45
(2) Davey Lopes	1.50	.70	.45
(3) Davey Lopes/Action	1.50	.70	.45
(4) Joe Morgan	3.00	1.50	.90
(5) Bill North	1.50	.70	.45
(6) Bill North/Action	1.50	.70	.45

1907 Grignon Chicago Cubs Postcards

The eventual 1907 World Champion Cubs are featured in this set of novelty postcards. Fronts of the 3-1/2" x 5-1/2" horizontal cards have a green background with white border. The central figure on each is a teddy bear in a baseball pose. In an upper corner is a black-and-white circular portrait of one of the Cubs, with identification below. A line of infield chatter - i.e., "This is a Cinch" - completes the design. Backs have standard postcard markings and some have been seen with advertising for local businesses. The unnumbered cards are checklisted here alphabetically.

	NM	EX	VG
Complete Set (16):	12,000	6,000	3,500
Common Player:	475.00	235.00	140.00
(1) Mordecai Brown	1,600	800.00	480.00
(2) Frank Chance	1,600	800.00	480.00
(3) John Evers	1,600	800.00	480.00
(4) Arthur Hofman	475.00	235.00	140.00
(5) John Kling	475.00	235.00	140.00
(6) Carl Lundgren	475.00	235.00	140.00
(7) Pat Moran	475.00	235.00	140.00
(8) Orvie Overall	475.00	235.00	140.00
(9) Jack Pfeister	475.00	235.00	140.00
(10) Ed Reulbach	475.00	235.00	140.00
(11) Frank Schulte	475.00	235.00	140.00
(12) James Sheckard	475.00	235.00	140.00
(13) James Slagle	475.00	235.00	140.00
(14) Harry Steinfeldt	475.00	235.00	140.00
(15) Jack Taylor	475.00	235.00	140.00
(16) Joe Tinker	1,600	800.00	480.00

"1959-60" Gulf Oil Corp.

These fantasy/fraud cards were first reported in the hobby in 1999, though the copyright line on back purports to date them from 1959-1960. Two types of cards were produced, one series of eight featuring line-art portraits, the other featuring re-screened photos taken from team photo packs and similar sources. Cards are 2-1/2" x 3-1/2" printed in black-and-white. The unnumbered cards are checklisted here alphabetically within series. Because the cards were illegally produced in violation of player rights and team copyrights, no collector value is attributed.

Complete Set (16):
Artwork Series

(1)	Ty Cobb
(2)	Bill Dickey
(3)	Joe DiMaggio
(4)	Lou Gehrig
(5)	Rogers Hornsby
(6)	Walter Johnson
(7)	Babe Ruth
(8)	Pie Traynor
	Photo Series
(1)	Don Drysdale
(2)	Bob Gibson
(3)	Sandy Koufax
(4)	Mickey Mantle
(5)	Roger Maris
(6)	Willie Mays
(7)	Willie McCovey
(8)	Stan Musial

1956 Gum Products Adventure

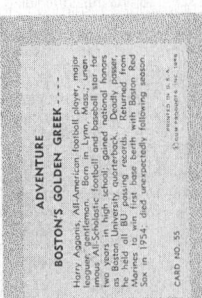

This series of 100 cards depicts all manner of action and adventure scenes, including several sports subjects, one of which is a baseball player. The card depicts Boston U. quarterback and Boston Red Sox prospect Harry Agganis, who died unexpectedly in 1955. The 3-1/2" x 2-1/2" horizontal card has a central portrait artwork of Agganis as a Red Sox, surrounded by other scenes from his personal and sporting life. The black-and-white back has a short biography.

		NM	EX	VG
55	Harry Agganis (Boston's Golden Greek)	25.00	12.50	7.50

1948 Gunther Beer Washington Senators Postcards

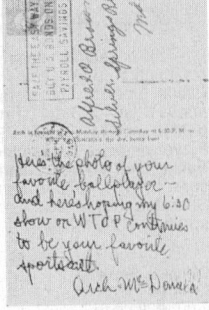

These postcards were apparently made available by writing to the radio voice of the Senators, Arch McDonald. A pre-printed message on the left side of the back urges the fan to keep listening to McDonald's program, sponsored by "Gunther's, the dry, beery beer." The black-and-white cards measure 3-1/2" x 5-1/2" and feature portrait photos of the Washington players. Most cards have two players side-by-side while manager Joe Kuhel has his own card. Player names are in heavy black letters across their chests. The cards are unnumbered and it is possible others will surface.

		NM	EX	VG
Complete Set (11):		3,000	1,500	900.00
Common Card:		285.00	140.00	85.00
(1)	Joe Kuhel	285.00	140.00	85.00
(2)	Gil Coan, Mickey Vernon	285.00	140.00	85.00
(3)	Al Evans, Scott Cary	285.00	140.00	85.00
(4)	Tom Ferrick, Harold Keller	285.00	140.00	85.00
(5)	Mickey Haefner, Forrest Thompson	285.00	140.00	85.00
(6)	Sid Hudson, Al Kozar	285.00	140.00	85.00
(7)	Walter Masterson, Rick Ferrell	325.00	160.00	95.00
(8)	Marino Pieretti, Leon Culberson	285.00	140.00	85.00
(9)	Sherrard Robertson, Eddie Lyons	285.00	140.00	85.00
(10)	Ray Scarborough, Kenneth McCreight	285.00	140.00	85.00
(11)	Early Wynn, Eddie Yost	400.00	200.00	120.00

1923-1924 Tomas Gutierrez

SANTA CLARA B. B. C.

Charleston - Outfielder

No. 46.

Cigarros Tomás Gutiérrez

La persona que nos entregue la colección completa de los clubs HABANA, MARIANAO, STA. CLARA y ALMENDARES, consistente en 85 postales del número 1 al 85 será gratificada con un lujoso Album con iguales postales ya impresas.

Cia. Cigarrera Diaz, S. A.
Finlay núm. 66
Antes Zanja-Habana.

The largest of the Cuban baseball card issues of the 1920s, this is also one of the scarcest and most popular. Printed in dark brown (some backs are in black) on sepia paper, the 1-5/8" x 2-3/8" cards were inserted into packs of Diaz cigarettes. Cards have portrait photos on front with team name at top and the player name (sometimes misspelled and sometimes a nickname) and position below. Backs, which can be found in three styles, have the card number and an offer for an album. It is the album offer which accounts for much of this issue's scarcity. The album was a hardcover, ornate book with pictures of each card pre-printed. It is believed that the album was available by turning in a complete set of the cards, which were not returned. Adding to the set's popularity is its inclusion of many Negro Leagues players including future Hall of Famers Oscar Charleston and Pop Lloyd. Following the checklist are the names of cards known to exist from their presence in the album, but whose number is unknown.

	NM	EX	VG
Complete Set (85): Value Undetermined			
Common Player:	350.00	140.00	70.00
Album:	4,500	2,250	1,350
SANTA CLARA			
1 Agustin "Tinti" Molina	350.00	140.00	70.00
2 Julio Rojo	450.00	180.00	90.00
3 Frank Duncan	1,750	700.00	350.00
4 Eustaquio "Bombin" Pedroso	2,250	900.00	450.00
5 Dave Brown	2,250	900.00	450.00
6 Pedro Dibut	450.00	180.00	90.00
7 Rube Currie	1,750	700.00	350.00
8 Jose Mendez	6,000	2,400	1,200
9 Esteban "Mayari" Montalvo	850.00	340.00	170.00
10 Frank Warfield	1,750	700.00	350.00
11 Oliver Marcelle	2,250	900.00	450.00
12 Dobie Moore	1,750	700.00	350.00
13 Herman Matias Rios	350.00	140.00	70.00
14 Oscar Charleston	20,000	8,000	4,000
15 Alejandro Oms	2,250	900.00	450.00
16 Pablo "Champion" Mesa	850.00	340.00	170.00
17 Bill Holland	2,250	900.00	450.00
18 Oscar "Heavy" Johnson	2,250	900.00	450.00
ALMENDARES			
19 Eugenio Morin	350.00	140.00	70.00
20 Snake Henry	350.00	140.00	70.00
21 Manuel Cueto	350.00	140.00	70.00
22 Jesse Hubbard	850.00	340.00	170.00
23 Kakin Gonzalez	350.00	140.00	70.00
24 Jose Maria Fernandez	350.00	140.00	70.00
25 Oscar Rodriguez	350.00	140.00	70.00
26 Lucas Boada	350.00	140.00	70.00
27 Eusebio "Papo" Gonzalez	350.00	140.00	70.00
28 Ramon "Paito" Herrera	350.00	140.00	70.00
29 Bernardo Baro	850.00	340.00	170.00
30 Armando Marsans	1,200	480.00	240.00
31 Isidro Fabre	850.00	340.00	170.00
32			
33 Valentin Dreke	850.00	340.00	170.00
34 Joseito Rodriguez	350.00	140.00	70.00
35 Jose "Cheo" Ramos	350.00	140.00	70.00
36 Willis "Pud" Flournoy	1,200	480.00	240.00
37 Oscar Tuero	350.00	140.00	70.00
38 Rafael Almeida	850.00	340.00	170.00
39 Almendares Pennant	350.00	140.00	70.00
--- Oscar Fuhr	350.00	140.00	70.00
MARIANAO			
40			
41 Don Brown	350.00	140.00	70.00
42			
43 (Ed) Morris	350.00	140.00	70.00
44 Ernie Krueger	350.00	140.00	70.00
45			
46 (Harry) McCurdy	350.00	140.00	70.00
47 Jose "Acostica" Acosta	350.00	140.00	70.00
48 Jacinto Calvo	350.00	140.00	70.00
49 (Eddie) Brown	350.00	140.00	70.00
50 (Rosy) Ryan	350.00	140.00	70.00
51 Rogelio Crespo	350.00	140.00	70.00
52 Hank Deberry	350.00	140.00	70.00
53 (Art) Phelan	350.00	140.00	70.00
54			
55 (Jimmy) Cooney	350.00	140.00	70.00
56a H. Scheiber (Hank Schreiber)/ Infielder	350.00	140.00	70.00
56b H. Scheiber (Hank Schreiber)/ Infielder	350.00	140.00	70.00
57			
58			

59				
---	Marianao Pennant	350.00	140.00	70.00
---	Merito Acosta	350.00	140.00	70.00
---	Otis Brannan	350.00	140.00	70.00
---	Charlie Dressen	450.00	180.00	90.00
---	Emilio Palmero	350.00	140.00	70.00
---	Jose "Pepin" Perez	350.00	140.00	70.00
---	Jess Petty	450.00	180.00	90.00
HAVANA				
60	Buster Ross	350.00	140.00	70.00
61	Juanelo Mirabal	350.00	140.00	70.00
62	Cristobal Torriente	17,500	7,000	3,500
63	John Henry "Pop" Lloyd	20,000	8,000	4,000
64	Oscar Levis	700.00	280.00	140.00
65	Pelayo Chacon	850.00	340.00	170.00
66	Eufemio Abreu	350.00	140.00	70.00
67	Mack Eggleston	850.00	340.00	170.00
68	(Tauca "Manzanillo") Campos	350.00	140.00	70.00
69	Raphael "Busta" Quintana	350.00	140.00	70.00
70	Merven "Red" Ryan	850.00	340.00	170.00
71	(Danny) Clark	350.00	140.00	70.00
72	Clint Thomas	1,000	400.00	200.00
73	Adolfo Luque	1,200	480.00	240.00
74	Marcelino Guerra	350.00	140.00	70.00
75	Bartolo Portuondo	850.00	340.00	170.00
76	Andy Cooper	6,000	2,400	1,200
77	(John) Bischoff	350.00	140.00	70.00
78	Edgar Wesley	1,750	700.00	350.00
79	Havana Pennant	350.00	140.00	70.00
---	Jacinto Calvo	300.00	120.00	60.00
---	Bienvenido "Hooks" Jimenez	250.00	100.00	50.00
MISCELLANEOUS				
80	Hector Magrinat/Umpire	350.00	140.00	70.00
81	Valentin "Sirique" Gonzalez/ Umpire	350.00	140.00	70.00
82	Slim Love (Marianao)	350.00	140.00	70.00
83	Cristobal Torriente (Marianao)	17,500	7,000	3,500
84				
85	Jakie May (Almendares)	450.00	180.00	90.00

1887 Gypsy Queen (N175)

GYPSY QUEEN

BROUTHERS, 1st B. Detroits.

CIGARETTES
GOODWIN & CO. N.Y.

The 1887 Gypsy Queen set is very closely related to the N172 Old Judge set and employs the same photos. Gypsy Queens are easily identified by the advertising along the top. A line near the bottom lists the player's name, position and team, followed by an 1887 copyright line and words "Cigarettes" and "Goodwin & Co. N.Y." Although the checklist is still considered incomplete, some 140 different poses have been discovered so far. Gypsy Queens were issued in two distinct sizes, the more common version measuring 1-1/2" x 2-1/2" (same as Old Judge) and a larger size measuring 2" x 3-1/2" which are considered extremely rare. The large Gypsy Queens are identical in format to the smaller size; the nine known examples are designated here.

	NM	EX	VG
Common Player:	3,000	1,500	905.00
(13) J. (Tug) Arundel/Fielding	3,000	1,500	905.00
(17) Mark Baldwin	3,000	1,500	905.00
(19 1) Sam Barkley/Fielding	3,000	1,500	905.00
(19 2) Sam Barkley (Tagging player.)	3,000	1,500	905.00
(19 3) Sam Barkley/Throwing	3,000	1,500	905.00
(35) Henry Boyle (Right arm outstretched.)	3,000	1,500	905.00
(43 1) Dan Brouthers (Looking at ball.)	7,500	3,750	2,250
(43 2) Dan Brouthers (Looking to right.)	7,500	3,750	2,250
(44 1) Tom Brown (Pittsburgh, bat at side.)	3,000	1,500	905.00
(44 2) Tom Brown/Catching (Pittsburgh)	3,000	1,500	905.00
(45L) Willard (California) Brown/ Throwing (N.Y., large)	18,750	9,375	5,625
(45 1) Willard (California) Brown/ Throwing (N.Y.)	3,000	1,500	905.00
(45 2) Willard (California) Brown (N.Y., wearing mask.)	3,440	1,720	1,030
(50) Charlie Buffington (Buffinton) (Bat at 45 degrees.)	3,000	1,500	905.00

	NM	EX	VG
(51) Ernie Burch/Fielding (Hands above head, outdoors.)	3,625	1,500	1,095
(53) Jack Burdock (Fielding grounder.)	3,625	1,500	1,095
(55) Watch Burnham	3,000	1,500	905.00
(59) Tom Burns	3,000	1,500	905.00
(60) Doc Bushong (Brown's Champions.)	5,315	2,655	1,595
(61) John (Patsy) Cahill	3,000	1,500	905.00
(68) Fred Carroll (Bat at side.)	3,000	1,500	905.00
(71) Bob Caruthers	3,000	1,500	905.00
(72 1) Dan Casey (Hands at chest.)	3,440	1,720	1,030
(72 2) Dan Casey (Left arm extended.)	3,000	1,500	905.00
(79 1) Jack Clements (Hands on knees.)	3,000	1,500	905.00
(79 2) Jack Clements (With bat.)	3,000	1,500	905.00
(83) John Coleman (Bat at side.)	3,000	1,500	905.00
(86) Charlie Comiskey	7,500	3,750	2,250
(88L) Roger Connor (Large, bat at 45 degrees.)	26,500	14,060	8,440
(88) Roger Connor (Hands on knees.)	7,500	3,750	2,250
(89) Dick Conway	3,000	1,500	905.00
(94) Larry Corcoran	3,000	1,500	905.00
(97 1) Sam Crane (Fielding grounder.)	3,000	1,500	905.00
(97 2) Sam Crane (With bat.)	3,000	1,500	905.00
(109) Ed Dailey	3,000	1,500	905.00
(113) Abner Dalrymple (Right arm cap-high.)	3,000	1,500	905.00
(117) Dell Darling	3,000	1,500	905.00
(121 1) Pat Dealey (Bat at side.)	3,000	1,500	905.00
(121 2) Pat Dealey (Bat on shoulder.)	3,000	1,500	905.00
(125L) Jerry Denny (Large, with bat.)	18,750	9,375	5,625
(125 1) Jerry Denny/Catching	3,000	1,500	905.00
(125 2) Jerry Denny (With bat.)	3,000	1,500	905.00
(130) Jim Donnelly (Bat at 45 degrees.)	3,000	1,500	905.00
(133) Mike Dorgan (Arms crossed.)	3,000	1,500	905.00
(149L) Buck Ewing (Large, catching fly ball.)	29,000	14,060	8,440
(149 1) Buck Ewing (Bat at 45 degrees.)	7,500	3,750	2,250
(149 2) Buck Ewing (Fielding fly ball.)	7,500	3,750	2,250
(149 3) Buck Ewing (Fielding ground ball.)	7,500	3,750	2,250
(156 1) Jack Farrell (Bat at side.)	3,000	1,500	905.00
(156 2) Jack Farrell (Bat in air.)	3,000	1,500	905.00
(156 3) Jack Farrell/Fielding	3,000	1,500	905.00
(156 4) Jack Farrell (Hands on thighs.)	3,000	1,500	905.00
(158 1) Charlie Ferguson (Hands at chest.)	3,625	1,500	1,095
(158 2) Charlie Ferguson (Right arm extended back.)	3,625	1,500	1,095
(158 3) Charlie Ferguson (Tagging player.)	3,000	1,500	905.00
(158 4) Charlie Ferguson (With bat.)	3,000	1,500	905.00
(161 1) Jocko Fields/Catching	3,000	1,500	905.00
(161 2) Jocko Fields (Tagging player.)	3,440	1,720	1,030
(161 3) Jocko Fields (With bat.)	3,000	1,500	905.00
(167 1) Jim Fogarty (Bat on shoulder.)	3,000	1,500	905.00
(167 2) Jim Fogarty (Fielding fly ball.)	3,000	1,500	905.00
(171) Dave Foutz (Brown's Champions.)	5,315	2,655	1,595
(178) John Gaffney (Bending to right.)	3,000	1,500	905.00
(171 1) Pud Galvin (Leaning on bat.)	7,500	3,750	2,250
(171 2) Pud Galvin (Without bat.)	7,500	3,750	2,250
(184 1) Emil Geiss (Hands above waist.)	3,000	1,500	905.00
(184 2) Emil Geiss (Right hand extended.)	3,000	1,500	905.00
(191 1) Pete Gillespie/Fielding	3,000	1,500	905.00
(191 2) Pete Gillespie (With bat.)	3,000	1,500	905.00
(192) Barney Gilligan	3,000	1,500	905.00
(194 1) Jack Glasscock (Hands on knees.)	3,000	1,500	905.00
(194 2) Jack Glasscock/Throwing	3,000	1,500	905.00
(194 3) Jack Glasscock (With bat.)	3,000	1,500	905.00
(195) Bill Gleason (Brown's Champions.)	5,315	2,655	1,595
(199 1) George Gore/Fielding	3,000	1,500	905.00
(199 2) George Gore (Hand at head level.)	3,000	1,500	905.00
(202) Ed Greer/Btg (Outdoors.)	4,690	2,345	1,405
(207 1) Tom Gunning (Stooping to catch low ball on left.)	3,000	1,500	905.00
(207 2) Tom Gunning/Bending (Hands by right knee.)	3,000	1,500	905.00
(215 1) Ned Hanlon/Catching	7,500	3,750	2,250
(215 2) Ned Hanlon (Bat at 45 degrees.)	7,500	3,750	2,250
(218 1) John Harkins (Hands above waist, outdoors.)	3,625	1,500	1,090
(218 2) John Harkins/Throwing (Outdoors)	4,690	2,345	1,405
(223) Egyptian Healey (Healy)/Btg	3,000	1,500	905.00
(232) Paul Hines (Hands at sides.)	3,000	1,500	905.00
(241) Joe Horning (Hornung) (Bat at 45 degrees.)	3,000	1,500	905.00
(244) Nat Hudson (Brown's Champions.)	5,315	2,655	1,595
(248 1) Arthur Irwin/Btg	3,000	1,500	905.00
(248 2) Arthur Irwin/Fielding (Hands below knees.)	3,000	1,500	905.00
(253 1) Dick Johnston/Catching	3,000	1,500	905.00
(253 2) Dick Johnston (With bat.)	3,000	1,500	905.00
(256L) Tim Keefe (Large, ball in hands at chest.)	30,000	15,000	9,000
(256 1) Tim Keefe (Ball in hands at chest.)	7,500	3,750	2,250
(256 2) Tim Keefe (Hands above waist, facing front.)	7,500	3,750	2,250
(256 3) Tim Keefe (Right hand extended at head level.)	7,500	7,500	2,250
(256 4) Tim Keefe (With bat.)	7,500	3,750	2,250

		NM	EX	VG
(261L)	King Kelly (Large, bat horizontal.)	29,000	14,060	8,440
(261 1)	King Kelly/Fielding (Hands chest-high.)	11,250	5,625	3,375
(261 2)	King Kelly/Portrait	11,250	5,625	3,375
(261 4)	King Kelly (With bat.)	10,625	5,315	3,190
(262)	Rudy Kemmler	3,000	1,500	905.00
(273 1)	Bill Krieg (Fielding thigh-high ball.)	3,000	1,500	905.00
(273 2)	Bill Krieg (With bat.)	3,000	1,500	905.00
(278)	Arlie Latham	3,000	1,500	905.00
(302 1)	Mike Mattimore (Hands above head.)	3,000	1,500	905.00
(302 2)	Mike Mattimore (Hands at neck.)	3,000	1,500	905.00
(302 3)	Mike Mattimore/Sliding	3,000	1,500	905.00
(307 1)	Tommy McCarthy/Catching	7,500	3,750	2,250
(307 2)	Tommy McCarthy/Sliding	7,500	3,750	2,250
(307 3)	Tommy McCarthy (With bat.)	7,500	3,750	2,250
(309)	Bill McClellan	3,000	1,500	905.00
(311 1)	Jim McCormick (Ball in hands at chest.)	3,000	1,500	905.00
(311 2)	Jim McCormick (Bat at 45 degrees.)	3,000	1,500	905.00
(316 1)	Jack McGeachy (Bat at 45 degrees.)	3,625	1,500	1,095
(316 2)	Jack McGeachy (Fielding ball over head.)	4,690	2,345	1,405
(318 1)	Deacon McGuire/Btg	3,000	1,500	905.00
(318 2)	Deacon McGuire/Catching	3,000	1,500	905.00
(321)	Alex McKinnon/Fielding (Hands waist-high.)	3,000	1,500	905.00
(326 1)	Jim McTamany (Bat on shoulder, outdoors.)	3,625	1,500	1,095
(326 2)	Jim McTamany/Fielding (Outdoors)	3,625	1,500	1,095
(330)	Doggie Miller	3,000	1,500	905.00
(336)	John Morrell (Morrill) (Hands on hips.)	3,440	1,720	1,030
(339)	Joe Mulvey (Fiedling ball at waist.)	3,000	1,500	905.00
(344 1)	Al Myers (Washington, bat vertical.)	3,000	1,500	905.00
(344 2)	Al Myers (Washington, hands on knees.)	3,000	1,500	905.00
(345 1)	George Myers (Indianapolis, stooping.)	3,000	1,500	905.00
(345 2)	George Myers (Indianapolis, with bat.)	3,000	1,500	905.00
(347)	Billy Nash/Portrait	3,000	1,500	905.00
(353)	Hugh Nicol (Brown's Champions.)	5,315	2,655	1,595
(358)	Jack O'Brien (Bat over shoulder, outdoors.)	3,000	1,500	905.00
(362 1)	Hank O'Day (Ball in hand.)	3,000	1,500	905.00
(362 2)	Hank O'Day (With bat.)	3,000	1,500	905.00
(365)	Tip O'Neill (Brown's Champions.)	5,315	2,655	1,595
(366)	Orator Jim O'Rourke/ Fielding	5,625	2,815	1,690
(367)	Tom O'Rourke (Bat at 45 degrees.)	3,000	1,500	905.00
(371)	Jimmy Peeples/Catching (Outdoors)	3,000	1,500	905.00
(374)	Fred Pfeffer/Throwing	3,000	1,500	905.00
(378)	George Pinkney (Pinckney)	3,000	1,500	905.00
(380)	Henry Porter/Throwing (Right hand cap-high, outdoors.)	3,625	1,500	1,095
(386)	Old Hoss Radbourn (With bat.)	7,500	3,750	2,250
(393L)	Danny Richardson (N.Y., large, bat at 45 degrees.)	22,000	10,940	6,565
(393 1)	Danny Richardson (N.Y., bat at 45 degrees.)	3,000	1,500	905.00
(393 2)	Danny Richardson (N.Y., moving to left, arms at sides.)	3,000	1,500	905.00
(394)	Hardy Richardson (Detroit)	3,000	1,500	905.00
(396)	John Roach/Btg	3,000	1,500	905.00
(399)	Yank Robinson (Brown's Champions.)	5,315	2,655	1,595
(403)	Jack Rowe (Bat at side.)	3,000	1,500	905.00
(405)	Jimmy Ryan (Ball in hands at chest.)	3,000	1,500	905.00
(415 1)	Emmett Seery (Arms folded.)	3,000	1,500	905.00
(415 2)	Emmett Seery (Ball in hands.)	3,000	1,500	905.00
(415 3)	Emmett Seery/Catching	3,000	1,500	905.00
(425)	George Shoch/Btg (W/umpire.)	3,000	1,500	905.00
(426)	Otto Shomberg (Schomberg) (Ball in hands at shoulder.)	3,000	1,500	905.00
(435)	Pop Smith	3,000	1,500	905.00
(446 1)	Bill Stemmyer (Stemmeyer) (Ball in hands at chest.)	3,000	1,500	905.00
(446 2)	Bill Stemmyer (Stemmeyer) (With bat.)	3,000	1,500	905.00
(459 1)	Ezra Sutton/Fielding	3,000	1,500	905.00
(459 2)	Ezra Sutton/Throwing	3,000	1,500	905.00
(459 3)	Ezra Sutton (With bat.)	3,000	1,500	905.00
(460)	Ed Swartwood (Kneeling to field, outdoors.)	4,690	2,345	1,405
(464)	Pop Tate/Fielding	3,000	1,500	905.00
(467)	William "Adonis" Terry	3,000	1,500	905.00
(468 1)	Sam Thompson (Arms folded.)	7,500	3,750	2,250
(468 2)	Sam Thompson (Bat at side.)	7,500	3,750	2,250
(468 3)	Sam Thompson (Swinging at ball.)	7,500	3,750	2,250
(469L)	Mike Tiernan (Large, fielding fly ball.)	18,750	9,375	5,625
(469)	Mike Tiernan (Fielding grounder.)	3,000	1,500	905.00
(472)	Steve Toole (With bat, outdoors.)	4,690	2,345	1,405
(480 1)	Larry Twitchell (Hands by chest.)	3,000	1,500	905.00
(480 2)	Larry Twitchell (Right hand extended.)	3,000	1,500	905.00

		NM	EX	VG
(489)	Chris Von Der Ahe	4,375	2,190	1,250
(491L)	John Ward/Throwing (Large)	29,000	14,060	8,440
(491)	John Ward	7,500	3,750	2,250
(493)	Bill Watkins/Portrait	3,000	1,500	905.00
(498)	Curt Welch	3,000	1,500	905.00
(511 1)	Art Whitney (Pittsburgh, bending.)	3,000	1,500	905.00
(511 2)	Art Whitney (Pittsburgh, with bat.)	3,000	1,500	905.00
(513)	Jim Whitney (Washington, throwing, r. hand waist-high.)	3,000	1,500	905.00
(515)	Ned Williamson/Throwing	3,625	1,500	1,095
(519)	Sam Wise	3,000	1,500	905.00
(521 1)	George Wood/Btg	3,000	1,500	905.00
(521 2)	George Wood/Throwing	3,000	1,500	905.00

H

1953 H-O Instant Oatmeal Records

Baseball playing tips from several star New York players are featured in this set of box-top premium records. For 25 cents and two oatmeal box tops, a set of three of the four records could be ordered by mail. The records are 4-3/4" in diameter and have a color player portrait with facsimile autograph on the back side, while the grooved recording side has an action pose in black-and-white.

		NM	EX	VG
Complete Set (4):		1,050	525.00	315.00
Common Player:		160.00	80.00	48.00
(1)	Roy Campanella	350.00	175.00	105.00
(2)	"Whitey" Lockman	175.00	87.00	52.00
(3)	Allie Reynolds	225.00	110.00	67.00
(4)	Duke Snider	350.00	175.00	105.00

1922 Haffner's Big-Tayto-Loaf Bread

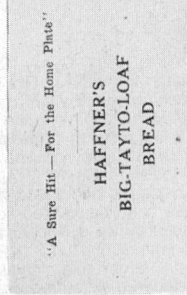

"A Sure Hit—For the Home Plate"

HAFFNER'S BIG-TAYTO-LOAF BREAD

WALTER JOHNSON
P.—Washington Americans

The bakery ad on the back is all that sets this issue apart from the blank-back W575-1 and several other versions with different sponsors named on back. The cards are 2" x 3-1/4" black-and-white. It is unknown whether each of the cards in the W575-1 checklist can be found in the Haffner's version.

PREMIUMS:
Common Players: 5-6X
Hall of Famers: 3-4X
(See W575-1 for checklist and card values.)

1951 Hage's Ice Cream Cleveland Indians

Similar in format to the Pacific Coast League cards produced by the dairy from 1949-51, these cards feature former members of the San Diego Padres, then a farm club of the Indians. Cards measure 2-5/8" x 3-1/8" and are printed in tones of sepia and green. Fronts have posed action photos similar to those found on contemporary Num Num and team photo pack pictures. A small white box on front has the player name and "CLEVELAND." There is a white border around the front photo. Backs are blank and unnumbered; the cards are presented here in alphabetical order.

		NM	EX	VG
Complete Set (6):		5,000	2,500	1,500
Common Player:		850.00	425.00	250.00
(1)	Ray Boone	850.00	425.00	250.00
(2)	Allie Clark	850.00	425.00	250.00
(3)	Jesse Flores	850.00	425.00	250.00
(4)	Al Olsen	850.00	425.00	250.00
(5)	Al Rosen	900.00	450.00	270.00
(6)	George Zuverink	850.00	425.00	250.00

1888 Joseph Hall Cabinets

BOSTON BALL CLUB, 1888.

These cabinet-sized (6-1/2" x 4-1/2") cards feature team photos taken by Joseph Hall, a well-known photographer of the day. Extremely rare, all have Hall's name beneath the photo and some include his Brooklyn address. The team is identified in large capital letters with the individual players identified in smaller type on both sides. Fourteen teams are known to date, but others may also exist, and Hall may have produced similar team cabinets in other years as well.

		NM	EX	VG
Common Team:		5,000	2,500	1,500
(1)	Athletic Ball Club/1888	10,000	5,000	3,000
(2)	Baltimore Ball Club/1888	14,000	7,000	4,200
(3)	Boston Ball Club/1888	15,000	7,500	4,500
(4)	Brooklyn Ball Club/1888	17,500	8,750	5,250
(5)	Chicago Ball Club/1888	35,000	17,500	10,000
(6)	Cincinnati Ball Club/1888	15,000	7,500	4,500
(7)	Cleveland Ball Club/1888	12,500	6,250	3,750
(8)	Detroit Ball Club/1888	16,000	8,000	4,800
(9)	Indianapolis Ball Club/1888	15,000	7,500	4,500
(10)	Kansas City Ball Club/1888	17,500	8,750	5,250
(11)	Louisville Ball Club/1888	12,500	6,250	3,750
(12)	New York Ball Club, League Champions/1889 (Wearing baseball uniforms.)	22,500	11,250	6,750
(13)	New York Ball Club, 1888 (Wearing tuxedos.)	18,500	9,250	5,550
(14)	St. Louis Baseball Club/1888	12,500	6,250	3,750
(15)	Washington Baseball Club/ 1888	40,000	20,000	12,000

1888 Joseph Hall Imperial Cabinets

Besides the standard-sized team-photo cabinet cards, super-sized versions of some (possibly all) teams were also available in a format known to collectors as an imperial cabinet. The large pictures use the same photos as the regular cabinets, enlarged to sizes as diverse as approximately 13" x 10" and 24" x 19" and mounted on heavy black or white backing boards. Printed on the mount in gold are the team name, date, player names and the Joseph Hall studio identification. Only those teams which have actually been observed in this format are listed here, with values generally set by their infrequent appearances in hobby auctions.

	NM	EX	VG
Cincinnati Ball Club/1888 (13" x 10")	12,500	6,250	3,750
St. Louis Ball Club/1888 (24" x 19")	12,500	6,250	3,750

1908 Hall's Studio N.Y. Giants Cabinets

Members of the N.Y. Giants are pictured in this series of approximately 4-1/2" x 6-1/2" cabinet photos from New York City photographer, Hall's Studio. The players are all identically posed bare-headed in white shirts buttoned at the collar. It is unknown whether this checklist is complete.

		NM	EX	VG
Common Player:		600.00	300.00	180.00
(1)	Al Bridwell	600.00	300.00	180.00
(2)	Doc Crandall	600.00	300.00	180.00
(3)	Larry Doyle	600.00	300.00	180.00
(4)	Buck Herzog	600.00	300.00	180.00
(5)	Rube Marquard	800.00	400.00	240.00
(6)	John McGraw	800.00	400.00	240.00
(7)	Fred Merkle	600.00	300.00	180.00

1939-43 Hall of Fame Sepia Postcards

The first Hall of Fame postcards were issued in two types between 1939-1943. They share an identical format and are differentiated by the typography on back, one set having been issued prior to the Hall of Fame's opening in June, 1939, and a later version issued after the opening. The 3-1/2" x 5-1/2" cards are similar in format to the later series printed in black-and-white and various colors, but this initial effort is printed in sepia on a cream-colored background. Most fronts picture the plaque of one of the 25 first inductees, with a wide bottom border to accomodate an autograph. Designated Type 1, this issue has a back caption which ends with, "National interest centers in the Centennial Celebration in 1939 at Cooperstown." The later version, Type 2, ends its description, "The National Base Ball Museum and Hall of Fame and Doubleday Field are maintained here as a Shrine to the national game." On both types, vertically at centers is a credit line "Pub. by National Base Ball Museum." At right are a stamp box and line for the mailing address. The unnumbered cards are listed here in alphabetical order within type.

		NM	EX	VG
Complete Set, Type 1 (35):		2,800	1,400	840.00
Complete Set, Type 2 (37):		3,250	1,625	975.00
Common Card:		60.00	30.00	18.00
TYPE 1				
(1)	G.C. Alexander	100.00	50.00	30.00
(2)	Adrian Anson	100.00	50.00	30.00
(3)	Morgan Bulkeley	100.00	50.00	30.00
(4)	Alexander Cartwright	100.00	50.00	30.00
(5)	Henry Chadwick	100.00	50.00	30.00
(6)	Ty Cobb	225.00	110.00	65.00
(7)	Eddie Collins	100.00	50.00	30.00
(8)	Chas. Comiskey	100.00	50.00	30.00
(9)	Candy Cummings	100.00	50.00	30.00
(10)	Buck Ewing	100.00	50.00	30.00
(11)	Ban Johnson	100.00	50.00	30.00
(12)	Walter Johnson	175.00	85.00	50.00
(13)	Willie Keeler	100.00	50.00	30.00
(14)	Napoleon Lajoie	100.00	50.00	30.00
(15)	Connie Mack	100.00	50.00	30.00
(16)	Christy Mathewson	175.00	85.00	50.00
(17)	John McGraw	100.00	50.00	30.00
(18)	Chas. Radbourne	100.00	50.00	30.00
(19)	Babe Ruth	450.00	225.00	135.00
(20)	George Sisler	100.00	50.00	30.00
(21)	Al Spalding	100.00	50.00	30.00
(22)	Tris Speaker	100.00	50.00	30.00
(23)	Honus Wagner	200.00	100.00	60.00
(24)	George Wright	100.00	50.00	30.00
(25)	Cy Young	150.00	75.00	45.00
(26)	The Abner Doubleday Baseball	50.00	25.00	15.00
(27)	Abner Doubleday, Major Gen'l	50.00	25.00	15.00
(28)	Doubleday Field in its Original State	50.00	25.00	15.00
(29)	Doubleday Field in 1938	50.00	25.00	15.00
(30)	Exhibition Game on Doubleday Field	50.00	25.00	15.00
(31)	Exterior - Ntl. Baseball Hall of Fame (no title on front)	50.00	25.00	15.00
(32)	Interior - Ntl. Baseball Museum	50.00	25.00	15.00
(33)	The Bust of Christy Mathewson	50.00	25.00	15.00
(34)	Entrance of the Hall of Fame	50.00	25.00	15.00
(35)	Ntl. Baseball Museum "Immortals"	50.00	25.00	15.00
TYPE 2				
(1)	G.C. Alexander	100.00	50.00	30.00
(2)	Adrian Anson	100.00	50.00	30.00
(3)	Morgan Bulkeley	100.00	50.00	30.00
(4)	Alexander Cartwright	100.00	50.00	30.00
(5)	Henry Chadwick	100.00	50.00	30.00
(6)	Ty Cobb	225.00	110.00	65.00
(7)	Eddie Collins	100.00	50.00	30.00
(8)	Charles Comiskey	100.00	50.00	30.00
(9)	Candy Cummings	100.00	50.00	30.00
(10)	Buck Ewing	100.00	50.00	30.00
(11)	Lou Gehrig	300.00	150.00	90.00
(12)	Rogers Hornsby	125.00	65.00	35.00
(13)	Ban Johnson	100.00	50.00	30.00
(14)	Walter Johnson	175.00	85.00	50.00
(15)	Willie Keeler	100.00	50.00	30.00
(16)	Napoleon Lajoie	100.00	50.00	30.00
(17)	Connie Mack	100.00	50.00	30.00
(18)	Christy Mathewson	175.00	85.00	50.00
(19)	John McGraw	100.00	50.00	30.00
(20)	Chas. Radbourne	100.00	50.00	30.00
(21)	Babe Ruth	450.00	225.00	135.00
(22)	George Sisler	100.00	50.00	30.00
(23)	Al Spalding	100.00	50.00	30.00
(24)	Tris Speaker	100.00	50.00	30.00
(25)	Honus Wagner	200.00	100.00	60.00
(26)	George Wright	100.00	50.00	30.00
(27)	Cy Young	150.00	75.00	45.00
(28)	The Abner Doubleday Baseball	50.00	25.00	15.00
(29)	Abner Doubleday, Major Gen'l	50.00	25.00	15.00
(30)	Doubleday Field in its Original State	50.00	25.00	15.00
(31)	Doubleday Field in 1938	50.00	25.00	15.00
(32)	Exhibition Game on Doubleday Field	50.00	25.00	15.00
(33)	Exterior - Ntl. Baseball Hall of Fame	50.00	25.00	15.00
(34)	Interior - Ntl. Baseball Hall of Fame	50.00	25.00	15.00
(35)	The Bust of Christy Mathewson	50.00	25.00	15.00
(36)	Entrance of the Hall of Fame	50.00	25.00	15.00
(37)	Ntl. Baseball Museum - "Immortals"	50.00	25.00	15.00

1944-63 Hall of Fame Black-and-White Plaque Postcards

(See listings cataloged under Albertype and Artvue.)

1939-63 Hall of Fame B/W Plaque Postcards - Autographed

Collecting Hall of Fame plaque postcards autographed by inductees has long been popular in the hobby. Obviously, completion of a set is impossible because many Hall of Famers have been inducted posthumously. Generally, the value of a genuinely autographed HoF plaque postcard is not so much dependent on star status of the player, but on the perception of how many such cards could have been autographed in his remaining lifetime. Players who died within months of their induction or who were uncooperative with autograph requests have cards that are far more valuable than many players of greater renown. While the majority of the players checklisted here could have signed both Albertye and Artvue cards, some players are possible only on the later

brand because their induction or death happened after 1952. Values quoted are for cards signed on the front. Cards signed on back can be worth 50 percent less.

	NM	EX	VG
Complete Set (55): Value Undetermined			
G.C. Alexander	1,250	1,125	935.00
Frank Baker	1,600	1,450	1,200
Ed Barrow	1,500	1,350	1,125
Chief Bender	550.00	500.00	410.00
Jesse Burkett	1,100	990.00	825.00
Max Carey	100.00	90.00	75.00
Fred Clarke	1,700	1,525	1,275
Ty Cobb	2,500	2,250	1,875
Mickey Cochrane	1,500	1,350	1,125
Eddie Collins	8,000	7,200	6,000
Tom Connolly	3,000	2,700	2,250
Sam Crawford	550.00	500.00	410.00
Joe Cronin	200.00	180.00	150.00
Dizzy Dean	325.00	290.00	245.00
Bill Dickey	150.00	135.00	110.00
Joe DiMaggio	550.00	500.00	410.00
Hugh Duffy	1,500	1,350	1,125
Johnny Evers	450.00	400.00	335.00
Bob Feller	35.00	30.00	25.00
Elmer Flick	500.00	450.00	375.00
Jimmie Foxx	4,000	3,600	3,000
Frankie Frisch	400.00	360.00	300.00
Lou Gehrig (Sepia only.)	2,000	1,800	1,500
Charlie Gehringer	60.00	55.00	45.00
Hank Greenberg	325.00	290.00	245.00
Clark Griffith	2,750	2,475	2,050
Lefty Grove	250.00	225.00	185.00
Gabby Hartnett	475.00	425.00	355.00
Rogers Hornsby	1,600	1,450	1,200
Carl Hubbell (Deduct 33% for post-stroke signature.)	65.00	58.00	49.00
Walter Johnson	1,400	1,250	1,050
Nap Lajoie	2,500	2,250	1,875
Ted Lyons	300.00	275.00	225.00
Connie Mack	1,450	1,300	1,100
Joe McCarthy	200.00	180.00	150.00
Bill McKechnie	900.00	810.00	675.00
Kid Nichols	3,500	3,150	2,625
Mel Ott	1,600	1,450	1,200
Sam Rice	175.00	155.00	130.00
Eppa Rixey (Possible but unlikely.)			
Jackie Robinson	2,250	2,025	1,675
Edd Roush	75.00	65.00	55.00
Babe Ruth (Value Undetermined)			
Ray Schalk	500.00	450.00	375.00
Al Simmons	1,750	1,575	1,300
George Sisler	500.00	450.00	375.00
Tris Speaker	1,500	1,350	1,125
Bill Terry	60.00	55.00	45.00
Joe Tinker	550.00	500.00	410.00
Pie Traynor	850.00	765.00	635.00
Dazzy Vance	1,700	1,525	1,275
Honus Wagner	2,800	2,525	2,100
Bobby Wallace	2,000	1,800	1,500
Ed Walsh	1,250	1,125	935.00
Paul Waner	1,550	1,400	1,150
Zack Wheat	650.00	585.00	485.00
Cy Young	2,400	2,150	1,800

1963 Hall of Fame Picture Pack

The attributed date is only approximate for this set of 5" x 7" black-and-white, blank-back pictures sold by the Hall of Fame. In the wide border beneath the player photo are identification, teams and years played, a few stats and induction year along with an HoF logo. Some of the same pictures were repeated in the later version of the issue.

		NM	EX	VG
Complete Set (24):		40.00	20.00	12.00
Common Player:		3.00	1.50	.90
(1)	Grover Alexander	4.00	2.00	1.25
(2)	Ty Cobb	6.00	3.00	1.75
(3)	Mickey Cochrane	3.00	1.50	.90
(4)	Eddie Collins	3.00	1.50	.90
(5)	Joe Cronin	3.00	1.50	.90
(6)	Bill Dickey	3.00	1.50	.90
(7)	Joe DiMaggio	7.50	3.75	2.25
(8)	Bob Feller	4.00	2.00	1.25
(9)	Frank Frisch	3.00	1.50	.90
(10)	Lou Gehrig	7.50	3.75	2.25
(11)	Rogers Hornsby	3.00	1.50	.90
(12)	Walter Johnson	4.00	2.00	1.25
(13)	Connie Mack	3.00	1.50	.90
(14)	Christy Mathewson	4.00	2.00	1.25
(15)	John McGraw	3.00	1.50	.90
(16)	Jackie Robinson	5.00	2.50	1.50
(17)	Babe Ruth	10.00	5.00	3.00
(18)	George Sisler	3.00	1.50	.90
(19)	Tris Speaker	3.00	1.50	.90
(20)	Bill Terry	3.00	1.50	.90
(21)	Pie Traynor	3.00	1.50	.90
(22)	Honus Wagner	4.00	2.00	1.25
(23)	Paul Waner	3.00	1.50	.90
(24)	Cy Young	4.00	2.00	1.25

1973 Hall of Fame Picture Pack

This set of 5" x 6-3/4" black-and-white player photos picture "Baseball's Greats Enshrined at Cooperstown, N.Y." Player career data is printed in the wide white border at bottom and there is a Hall of Fame logo at lower-left. The unnumbered pictures are listed here in alphabetical order.

		NM	EX	VG
	Complete Set (20):	20.00	10.00	6.00
	Common Player:	2.00	1.00	.60
(1)	Yogi Berra	3.00	1.50	.90
(2)	Roy Campanella	3.00	1.50	.90
(3)	Ty Cobb	4.00	2.00	1.25
(4)	Joe Cronin	2.50	1.25	.70
(5)	Dizzy Dean	3.00	1.50	.90
(6)	Joe DiMaggio	7.50	3.75	2.25
(7)	Bob Feller	3.00	1.50	.90
(8)	Lou Gehrig	7.50	3.75	2.25
(9)	Rogers Hornsby	3.00	1.50	.90
(10)	Sandy Koufax	5.00	2.50	1.50
(11)	Christy Mathewson	3.00	1.50	.90
(12)	Stan Musial	3.00	1.50	.90
(13)	Satchel Paige	3.00	1.50	.90
(14)	Jackie Robinson	5.00	2.50	1.50
(15)	Babe Ruth	10.00	5.00	3.00
(16)	Warren Spahn	2.50	1.25	.70
(17)	Casey Stengel	3.00	1.50	.90
(18)	Honus Wagner	3.00	1.50	.90
(19)	Ted Williams	5.00	2.50	1.50
(20)	Cy Young	3.00	1.50	.90

1979 Hall of Fame (Dexter Press) Plaque Postcards

This short-lived series, begun no later than 1979, features the Hall of Fame inductees' plaques on bright backgrounds of red, orange, blue and green. Because of the cards' color and finish, they are difficult to autograph.

		NM	EX	VG
	Complete Set (53):	350.00	175.00	105.00
	Common Player:	6.00	3.00	1.75
(1)	Grover Alexander	6.00	3.00	1.75
(2)	Lou Boudreau	6.00	3.00	1.75
(3)	Roy Campanella	10.00	5.00	3.00
(4)	Roberto Clemente	20.00	10.00	6.00
(5)	Ty Cobb	15.00	7.50	4.50
(6)	Stan Coveleski	6.00	3.00	1.75
(7)	Sam Crawford	6.00	3.00	1.75
(8)	Martin Dihigo	6.00	3.00	1.75
(9)	Joe DiMaggio	22.50	11.00	6.75
(10)	Billy Evans	6.00	3.00	1.75
(11)	Johnny Evers	6.00	3.00	1.75
(12)	Red Faber	6.00	3.00	1.75
(13)	Elmer Flick	6.00	3.00	1.75
(14)	Ford Frick	6.00	3.00	1.75
(15)	Frank Frisch	6.00	3.00	1.75
(16)	Pud Galvin	6.00	3.00	1.75
(17)	Lou Gehrig	20.00	10.00	6.00
(18)	Warren Giles	6.00	3.00	1.75
(19)	Will Harridge	6.00	3.00	1.75
(20)	Harry Heilmann	6.00	3.00	1.75
(21)	Harry Hooper	6.00	3.00	1.75
(22)	Waite Hoyt	6.00	3.00	1.75
(23)	Miller Huggins	6.00	3.00	1.75
(24)	Judy Johnson	6.00	3.00	1.75
(25)	Addie Joss	6.00	3.00	1.75
(26)	Tim Keefe	6.00	3.00	1.75
(27)	Willie Keeler	6.00	3.00	1.75
(28)	George Kelly	6.00	3.00	1.75
(29)	Sandy Koufax	15.00	7.50	4.50
(30)	Nap Lajoie	6.00	3.00	1.75
(31)	Pop Lloyd	6.00	3.00	1.75
(32)	Connie Mack	6.00	3.00	1.75
(33)	Larry MacPhail	6.00	3.00	1.75
(34)	Mickey Mantle	25.00	12.50	7.50
(35)	Heinie Manush	6.00	3.00	1.75
(36)	Eddie Mathews	6.00	3.00	1.75
(37)	Willie Mays	15.00	7.50	4.50
(38)	Ducky Medwick	6.00	3.00	1.75
(39)	Stan Musial	12.00	6.00	3.50
(40)	Herb Pennock	6.00	3.00	1.75
(41)	Edd Roush	6.00	3.00	1.75
(42)	Babe Ruth	25.00	12.50	7.50
(43)	Amos Rusie	6.00	3.00	1.75
(44)	Ray Schalk	6.00	3.00	1.75
(45)	Al Simmons	6.00	3.00	1.75
(46)	Albert Spalding	6.00	3.00	1.75
(47)	Joe Tinker	6.00	3.00	1.75
(48)	Pie Traynor	6.00	3.00	1.75
(49)	Dazzy Vance	6.00	3.00	1.75
(50)	Lloyd Waner	6.00	3.00	1.75
(51)	Ted Williams	20.00	10.00	6.00
(52)	Hack Wilson	6.00	3.00	1.75
(53)	Ross Youngs	6.00	3.00	1.75

1979 HoF (Dexter Press) Plaque Postcards - Autographed

		NM	EX	VG
(2)	Lou Boudreau	30.00	27.00	22.00
(3)	Roy Campanella			
	(Value Undetermined)			
(6)	Stan Coveleski	50.00	45.00	37.00
(9)	Joe DiMaggio	350.00	315.00	260.00
(22)	Waite Hoyt	100.00	90.00	75.00
(24)	Judy Johnson	65.00	60.00	50.00
(28)	George Kelly	75.00	65.00	55.00
(29)	Sandy Koufax	150.00	135.00	110.00
(34)	Mickey Mantle	400.00	360.00	300.00
(36)	Eddie Mathews	50.00	45.00	37.00
(37)	Willie Mays	50.00	45.00	37.00
(39)	Stan Musial	25.00	22.00	18.50
(41)	Edd Roush	50.00	45.00	37.00
(50)	Lloyd Waner	50.00	45.00	37.00
(51)	Ted Williams	300.00	270.00	225.00

1964-Date Hall of Fame Yellow Plaque Postcards

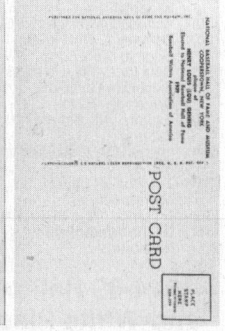

Since 1964 a number of related series of Hall of Fame Plaque Postcards have been produced by a pair of printers. The 3-1/2" x 5-1/2" postcards were first produced by Curteichcolor and, later, by Mike Roberts Color Productions. Like earlier HoF postcards, these series feature a color photo of an inductee's plaque on a yellow background. Black-and-white backs have a variety of player information, postcard indicia, copyright data and credit lines. Few hobbyists attmept to collect these by issuer, rather trying to assemble a complete set of each player regardless of who did the printing and when. Prior to 1977, single postcards sold for five cents at the HoF gift shop; in 1977 the price doubled to a dime, with complete sets (about 150) selling for $6. Today a complete set is available from the Hall of Fame for about $45, with singles at 25 cents apiece.

		NM	EX	VG
	Complete Set (256):	45.00	22.00	13.50
	Common Player:	.50	.25	.15
	Hank Aaron	.50	.25	.15
	Grover Alexander	.50	.25	.15
	Walter Alston	.50	.25	.15
	Sparky Anderson	.50	.25	.15
	Cap Anson	.50	.25	.15
	Luis Aparicio	.50	.25	.15
	Luke Appling	.50	.25	.15
	Richie Ashburn	.50	.25	.15
	Earl Averill	.50	.25	.15
	Frank Baker	.50	.25	.15
	Dave Bancroft	.50	.25	.15
	Ernie Banks	.50	.25	.15
	Al Barlick	.50	.25	.15
	Ed Barrow	.50	.25	.15
	Jake Beckley	.50	.25	.15
	Cool Papa Bell	.50	.25	.15
	Johnny Bench	.50	.25	.15
	Chief Bender	.50	.25	.15
	Yogi Berra	.50	.25	.15
	Wade Boggs	.50	.25	.15
	Jim Bottomley	.50	.25	.15
	Lou Boudreau	.50	.25	.15
	Roger Bresnahan	.50	.25	.15
	George Brett	.50	.25	.15
	Lou Brock	.50	.25	.15

	NM	EX	VG
Dan Brouthers	.50	.25	.15
Mordecai Brown	.50	.25	.15
Morgan Bulkeley	.50	.25	.15
Jim Bunning	.50	.25	.15
Jesse Burkett	.50	.25	.15
Roy Campanella	.50	.25	.15
Rod Carew	.50	.25	.15
Max Carey	.50	.25	.15
Steve Carlton	.50	.25	.15
Gary Carter	.50	.25	.15
Alexander Cartwright	.50	.25	.15
Orlando Cepeda	.50	.25	.15
Henry Chadwick	.50	.25	.15
Frank Chance	.50	.25	.15
A.B. (Happy) Chandler	.50	.25	.15
Oscar Charleston	.50	.25	.15
Jack Chesbro	.50	.25	.15
Nestor Chylak	.50	.25	.15
Fred Clarke	.50	.25	.15
John Clarkson	.50	.25	.15
Roberto Clemente	.50	.25	.15
Ty Cobb	.50	.25	.15
Mickey Cochrane	.50	.25	.15
Eddie Collins	.50	.25	.15
Jimmy Collins	.50	.25	.15
Earle Combs	.50	.25	.15
Charles Comiskey	.50	.25	.15
Jocko Conlan	.50	.25	.15
Tom Connolly	.50	.25	.15
Roger Connor	.50	.25	.15
Stan Coveleski	.50	.25	.15
Sam Crawford	.50	.25	.15
Joe Cronin	.50	.25	.15
Candy Cummings	.50	.25	.15
Kiki Cuyler	.50	.25	.15
Ray Dandridge	.50	.25	.15
George Davis	.50	.25	.15
Leon Day	.50	.25	.15
Dizzy Dean	.50	.25	.15
Ed Delahanty	.50	.25	.15
Bill Dickey	.50	.25	.15
Martin Dihigo	.50	.25	.15
Joe DiMaggio	.50	.25	.15
Larry Doby	.50	.25	.15
Bobby Doerr	.50	.25	.15
Don Drysdale	.50	.25	.15
Hugh Duffy	.50	.25	.15
Leo Durocher	.50	.25	.15
Dennis Eckersley	.50	.25	.15
Billy Evans	.50	.25	.15
Johnny Evers	.50	.25	.15
Buck Ewing	.50	.25	.15
Red Faber	.50	.25	.15
Bob Feller	.50	.25	.15
Rick Ferrell	.50	.25	.15
Rollie Fingers	.50	.25	.15
Carlton Fisk	.50	.25	.15
Elmer Flick	.50	.25	.15
Whitey Ford	.50	.25	.15
Bill Foster	.50	.25	.15
Rube Foster	.50	.25	.15
Nellie Fox	.50	.25	.15
Jimmie Foxx	.50	.25	.15
Ford Frick	.50	.25	.15
Frank Frisch	.50	.25	.15
Pud Galvin	.50	.25	.15
Lou Gehrig	.50	.25	.15
Charlie Gehringer	.50	.25	.15
Bob Gibson	.50	.25	.15
Josh Gibson	.50	.25	.15
Warren Giles	.50	.25	.15
Lefty Gomez	.50	.25	.15
Goose Goslin	.50	.25	.15
Hank Greenberg	.50	.25	.15
Clark Griffith	.50	.25	.15
Burleigh Grimes	.50	.25	.15
Lefty Grove	.50	.25	.15
Chick Hafey	.50	.25	.15
Jesse Haines	.50	.25	.15
Billy Hamilton	.50	.25	.15
Ned Hanlon	.50	.25	.15
Will Harridge	.50	.25	.15
Bucky Harris	.50	.25	.15
Gabby Hartnett	.50	.25	.15
Harry Heilmann	.50	.25	.15
Billy Herman	.50	.25	.15
Harry Hooper	.50	.25	.15
Rogers Hornsby	.50	.25	.15
Waite Hoyt	.50	.25	.15
Cal Hubbard	.50	.25	.15
Carl Hubbell	.50	.25	.15
Miller Huggins	.50	.25	.15
William Hulbert	.50	.25	.15
Catfish Hunter	.50	.25	.15
Monte Irvin	.50	.25	.15
Reggie Jackson	.50	.25	.15
Travis Jackson	.50	.25	.15
Fergie Jenkins	.50	.25	.15
Hughie Jennings	.50	.25	.15
Ban Johnson	.50	.25	.15
Judy Johnson	.50	.25	.15
Walter Johnson	.50	.25	.15
Addie Joss	.50	.25	.15
Al Kaline	.50	.25	.15
Tim Keefe	.50	.25	.15
Willie Keeler	.50	.25	.15
George Kell	.50	.25	.15
Joe Kelley	.50	.25	.15
George Kelly	.50	.25	.15
Mike "King" Kelly	.50	.25	.15
Harmon Killebrew	.50	.25	.15
Ralph Kiner	.50	.25	.15
Chuck Klein	.50	.25	.15
Bill Klem	.50	.25	.15
Sandy Koufax	.50	.25	.15
Nap Lajoie	.50	.25	.15
Kenesaw M. Landis	.50	.25	.15
Tommy Lasorda	.50	.25	.15

Tony Lazzeri	.50	.25	.15
Bob Lemon	.50	.25	.15
Buck Leonard	.50	.25	.15
Freddie Lindstrom	.50	.25	.15
Pop Lloyd	.50	.25	.15
Ernie Lombardi	.50	.25	.15
Al Lopez	.50	.25	.15
Ted Lyons	.50	.25	.15
Connie Mack	.50	.25	.15
Larry MacPhail	.50	.25	.15
Mickey Mantle	.50	.25	.15
Heinie Manush	.50	.25	.15
Rabbit Maranville	.50	.25	.15
Juan Marichal	.50	.25	.15
Rube Marquard	.50	.25	.15
Eddie Mathews	.50	.25	.15
Christy Mathewson	.50	.25	.15
Willie Mays	.50	.25	.15
Bill Mazeroski	.50	.25	.15
Joe McCarthy	.50	.25	.15
Tommy McCarthy	.50	.25	.15
Willie McCovey	.50	.25	.15
Joe McGinnity	.50	.25	.15
Bill McGowan	.50	.25	.15
John McGraw	.50	.25	.15
Bill McKechnie	.50	.25	.15
Lee MacPhail	.50	.25	.15
Bid McPhee	.50	.25	.15
Ducky Medwick	.50	.25	.15
Johnny Mize	.50	.25	.15
Paul Molitor	.50	.25	.15
Joe Morgan	.50	.25	.15
Eddie Murray	.50	.25	.15
Stan Musial	.50	.25	.15
Hal Newhouser	.50	.25	.15
Kid Nichols	.50	.25	.15
Phil Niekro	.50	.25	.15
Jim O'Rourke	.50	.25	.15
Mel Ott	.50	.25	.15
Satchel Paige	.50	.25	.15
Jim Palmer	.50	.25	.15
Herb Pennock	.50	.25	.15
Tony Perez	.50	.25	.15
Gaylord Perry	.50	.25	.15
Ed Plank	.50	.25	.15
Kirby Puckett	.50	.25	.15
Charles Radbourne	.50	.25	.15
Pee Wee Reese	.50	.25	.15
Sam Rice	.50	.25	.15
Branch Rickey	.50	.25	.15
Eppa Rixey	.50	.25	.15
Phil Rizzuto	.50	.25	.15
Robin Roberts	.50	.25	.15
Brooks Robinson	.50	.25	.15
Frank Robinson	.50	.25	.15
Jackie Robinson	.50	.25	.15
Wilbert Robinson	.50	.25	.15
Bullet Rogan	.50	.25	.15
Edd Roush	.50	.25	.15
Red Ruffing	.50	.25	.15
Amos Rusie	.50	.25	.15
Babe Ruth	.50	.25	.15
Nolan Ryan	.50	.25	.15
Ryne Sandberg	.50	.25	.15
Ray Schalk	.50	.25	.15
Mike Schmidt	.50	.25	.15
Red Schoendienst	.50	.25	.15
Tom Seaver	.50	.25	.15
Frank Selee	.50	.25	.15
Joe Sewell	.50	.25	.15
Al Simmons	.50	.25	.15
George Sisler	.50	.25	.15
Enos Slaughter	.50	.25	.15
Hilton Smith	.50	.25	.15
Ozzie Smith	.50	.25	.15
Duke Snider	.50	.25	.15
Warren Spahn	.50	.25	.15
Albert Spalding	.50	.25	.15
Tris Speaker	.50	.25	.15
Willie Stargell	.50	.25	.15
Turkey Stearnes	.50	.25	.15
Casey Stengel	.50	.25	.15
Don Sutton	.50	.25	.15
Bill Terry	.50	.25	.15
Sam Thompson	.50	.25	.15
Joe Tinker	.50	.25	.15
Paul Traynor	.50	.25	.15
Dazzy Vance	.50	.25	.15
Arky Vaughan	.50	.25	.15
Bill Veeck	.50	.25	.15
Rube Waddell	.50	.25	.15
Honus Wagner	.50	.25	.15
Bobby Wallace	.50	.25	.15
Ed Walsh	.50	.25	.15
Lloyd Waner	.50	.25	.15
Paul Waner	.50	.25	.15
Monte Ward	.50	.25	.15
Earl Weaver	.50	.25	.15
George Weiss	.50	.25	.15
Mickey Welch	.50	.25	.15
Willie Wells	.50	.25	.15
Zack Wheat	.50	.25	.15
Hoyt Wilhelm	.50	.25	.15
Billy Williams	.50	.25	.15
Joe Williams	.50	.25	.15
Ted Williams	.50	.25	.15
Vic Willis	.50	.25	.15
Hack Wilson	.50	.25	.15
Dave Winfield	.50	.25	.15
George Wright	.50	.25	.15
Harry Wright	.50	.25	.15
Early Wynn	.50	.25	.15
Carl Yastrzemski	.50	.25	.15
Tom Yawkey	.50	.25	.15
Cy Young	.50	.25	.15
Ross Youngs	.50	.25	.15
Robin Yount	.50	.25	.15

1964-Date Hall of Fame Yellow Plaque Postcards - Autographed

ROBERT WILLIAM ANDREW FELLER
CLEVELAND A.L. 1936 TO 1941
1945 TO 1956
PITCHED 3 NO-HIT GAMES IN A.L., 12 ONE-HIT
GAMES. SET MODERN STRIKEOUT RECORD
WITH 18 IN GAME, 348 FOR SEASON. LED
A.L. IN VICTORIES 6 (ONE TIE) SEASONS.
LIFE TIME RECORD: WON 266, LOST 162,
P.C. .621, E.R. AVERAGE 3.25, STRUCK OUT 2581.

NATIONAL BASEBALL HALL OF FAME & MUSEUM
Cooperstown, New York

This listing represents the Curteichcolor and Mike Roberts yellow Hall of Fame plaque postcards which are known to exist, or in a few cases are theoretically possible. Value of genuinely autographed HoF plaque postcards is not so much dependent on star status of the player, but on perception of how many such cards could exist given the time the player remained alive and in good health following his selection at Cooperstown. Players who died or were incapacitated shortly after induction may have more valuable autographed cards than currently living players of greater renown. Values quoted are for cards autographed on front; cards signed on the back can be worth 50 percent less.

	NM	EX	VG
Hank Aaron	55.00	45.00	35.00
Walter Alston	150.00	120.00	90.00
Sparky Anderson	55.00	45.00	35.00
Luis Aparicio	15.00	12.00	9.00
Luke Appling	20.00	16.00	12.00
Richie Ashburn	55.00	45.00	35.00
Earl Averill	50.00	40.00	30.00
Dave Bancroft	2,250	1,800	1,350
Ernie Banks	45.00	35.00	25.00
Al Barlick	15.00	12.00	9.00
Cool Papa Bell	50.00	40.00	30.00
Johnny Bench	45.00	36.00	27.00
Yogi Berra	25.00	20.00	15.00
Wade Boggs	50.00	40.00	30.00
Lou Boudreau	15.00	12.00	9.00
George Brett	125.00	100.00	75.00
Lou Brock	30.00	24.00	18.00
Jim Bunning	40.00	32.00	24.00
Roy Campanella			
(Value Undetermined)			
Rod Carew	50.00	40.00	30.00
Max Carey	60.00	50.00	35.00
Steve Carlton	35.00	30.00	20.00
Gary Carter	100.00	80.00	60.00
Orlando Cepeda	35.00	30.00	20.00
A.B. (Happy) Chandler	20.00	16.00	12.00
Earle Combs	300.00	240.00	180.00
Jocko Conlan	25.00	20.00	15.00
Stan Coveleski	30.00	24.00	18.00
"Stanislaus Kowalewski"	150.00	120.00	90.00
Sam Crawford	600.00	480.00	360.00
Joe Cronin	50.00	40.00	30.00
Ray Dandridge	15.00	12.00	9.00
Dizzy Dean	300.00	240.00	180.00
Bill Dickey	50.00	40.00	30.00
Joe DiMaggio	225.00	180.00	135.00
Larry Doby	90.00	70.00	55.00
Bobby Doerr	7.50	6.00	4.50
Don Drysdale	45.00	35.00	25.00
Dennis Eckersley	75.00	60.00	45.00
Red Faber	165.00	130.00	100.00
Bob Feller	7.50	6.00	4.50
Rick Ferrell	15.00	12.00	9.00
Rollie Fingers	20.00	16.00	12.00
Carlton Fisk	80.00	65.00	45.00
Elmer Flick	600.00	480.00	360.00
Whitey Ford	35.00	30.00	20.00
Jimmie Foxx	1,750	1,400	1,050
(Usually signed on back.)			
Ford Frick	225.00	180.00	135.00
Frank Frisch	300.00	240.00	180.00
Charlie Gehringer	30.00	24.00	18.00
Bob Gibson	30.00	24.00	18.00
Lefty Gomez	35.00	30.00	20.00
Goose Goslin	2,250	1,800	1,350
(Usually signed on back; value of such $750-1,000.)			
Hank Greenberg	175.00	140.00	100.00
Burleigh Grimes	35.00	30.00	20.00
Lefty Grove	160.00	130.00	95.00
Chick Hafey	725.00	580.00	435.00
Jesse Haines	125.00	100.00	75.00
Bucky Harris	325.00	260.00	195.00
Gabby Hartnett	725.00	580.00	435.00
Billy Herman	12.00	9.50	7.25
Harry Hooper	235.00	190.00	140.00
Waite Hoyt	40.00	32.00	24.00
Cal Hubbard	1,250	1,000	750.00
Carl Hubbell (Pre-stroke.)	40.00	32.00	24.00

Carl Hubbell (Post-stroke.)	25.00	20.00	15.00
Catfish Hunter	30.00	24.00	18.00
Monte Irvin	10.00	8.00	6.00
Reggie Jackson	75.00	60.00	45.00
Travis Jackson	30.00	24.00	18.00
Fergie Jenkins	15.00	12.00	9.00
Judy Johnson	30.00	24.00	18.00
Al Kaline	20.00	16.00	12.00
George Kell	7.50	6.00	4.50
George Kelly	40.00	32.00	24.00
Harmon Killebrew	25.00	20.00	15.00
Ralph Kiner	15.00	12.00	9.00
Sandy Koufax	125.00	100.00	75.00
Tommy Lasorda	100.00	80.00	60.00
Bob Lemon	12.00	9.50	7.25
Buck Leonard	15.00	12.00	9.00
(Post-stroke autographed cards worth 50%.)			
Freddie Lindstrom	75.00	60.00	45.00
Al Lopez	40.00	32.00	24.00
Ted Lyons	45.00	35.00	25.00
Lee MacPhail	35.00	28.00	21.00
Mickey Mantle	235.00	190.00	140.00
Heinie Manush	325.00	260.00	195.00
Juan Marichal	15.00	12.00	9.00
Rube Marquard	40.00	32.00	24.00
Eddie Mathews	25.00	20.00	15.00
Willie Mays	50.00	40.00	30.00
Bill Mazeroski	50.00	40.00	30.00
Joe McCarthy	80.00	65.00	45.00
Willie McCovey	35.00	28.00	21.00
Bill McKechnie			
(Possible, not likely.)			
Ducky Medwick	185.00	150.00	110.00
Johnny Mize	15.00	12.00	9.00
Paul Molitor	90.00	75.00	55.00
Joe Morgan	30.00	24.00	18.00
Eddie Murray	125.00	100.00	75.00
Stan Musial	25.00	20.00	15.00
Hal Newhouser	15.00	12.00	9.00
Phil Niekro	35.00	30.00	20.00
Satchel Paige	235.00	190.00	140.00
Jim Palmer	20.00	16.00	12.00
Tony Perez	50.00	40.00	30.00
Gaylord Perry	25.00	20.00	15.00
Kirby Puckett	125.00	100.00	75.00
Pee Wee Reese	45.00	35.00	25.00
Sam Rice	185.00	150.00	110.00
Phil Rizzuto	30.00	24.00	18.00
Robin Roberts	12.50	10.00	7.50
Brooks Robinson	12.50	10.00	7.50
Frank Robinson	25.00	20.00	15.00
Jackie Robinson	1,600	1,275	960.00
(Often signed on back; value of such $550.)			
Edd Roush	30.00	24.00	18.00
Red Ruffing	200.00	160.00	120.00
Nolan Ryan	65.00	50.00	40.00
Ryne Sandberg	60.00	45.00	35.00
Ray Schalk	450.00	360.00	270.00
Mike Schmidt	80.00	65.00	50.00
Red Schoendienst	30.00	24.00	18.00
Tom Seaver	40.00	32.00	24.00
Joe Sewell	15.00	12.00	9.00
George Sisler	200.00	160.00	120.00
Enos Slaughter	10.00	8.00	6.00
Ozzie Smith	95.00	75.00	55.00
Duke Snider	20.00	16.00	12.00
Warren Spahn	20.00	16.00	12.00
Willie Stargell	50.00	40.00	30.00
Casey Stengel	225.00	180.00	135.00
Bruce Sutter	60.00	45.00	35.00
Don Sutton	40.00	32.00	24.00
Bill Terry	25.00	20.00	15.00
Pie Traynor	850.00	680.00	510.00
Lloyd Waner	30.00	24.00	18.00
Paul Waner			
(Possible, not likely.)			
Earl Weaver	35.00	30.00	20.00
George Weiss			
(Possible, not likely.)			
Zack Wheat	450.00	360.00	270.00
Hoyt Wilhelm	15.00	12.00	9.00
Billy Williams	15.00	12.00	9.00
Ted Williams	200.00	160.00	120.00
Dave Winfield	100.00	80.00	60.00
Early Wynn	25.00	20.00	15.00
Carl Yastrzemski	55.00	45.00	35.00
Robin Yount	150.00	120.00	90.00

1973 Jack Hamilton's "The Pzazz" Postcard

JACK HAMILTON - PITCHER
Right Handed - 95 MPH

POST CARD

The date attributed is speculative, based on the not totally honest major league career summary printed on the back of this standard-size, black-and-white postcard. The front reproduces a J.D. McCarthy postcard of the pitcher in a New York Mets uniform. There is a white border all around and a facsimile autograph in blue. The back has a few career highlights and advertisement for Hamilton's "The Pzazz" restaurant in Branson, Mo.

	NM	EX	VG
Jack Hamilton	6.00	3.00	1.75

1961 Harmony Milk
Pittsburgh Pirates

The PIRATES train on HARMONY MILK

The attributed year of issue is approximate and subject to change if and when further players are added to the checklist. These premium photos are 8" x 10" in format, round-cornered with blank backs.

		NM	EX	VG
Common Player:		175.00	90.00	50.00
(1)	Roberto Clemente	600.00	300.00	180.00
(2)	Dick Groat	175.00	90.00	50.00
(3)	Don Hoak	175.00	90.00	50.00
(4)	Vern Law	175.00	90.00	50.00
(5)	Danny Murtaugh	175.00	90.00	50.00

1928 Harrington's Ice Cream

 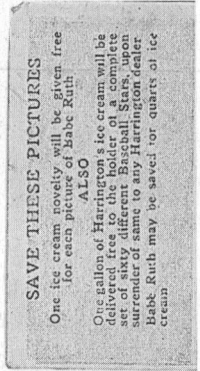

(11) GEORGE UHLE

SAVE THESE PICTURES

One ice cream novelty will be given free for each picture of Babe Ruth

ALSO

One gallon of Harrington's ice cream will be delivered free to the holder of a complete set of sixty different Baseball Stars, upon surrender of same to any Harrington dealer. Babe Ruth may be saved for quarts of ice cream.

Sharing the same format and checklist with several other (Tharp's, Yeungling's, Sweetman, etc.) contemporary ice cream sets this 60-card set includes all of the top stars of the day. Cards are printed in black-and-white on a 1-3/8" x 2-1/2" format. The player's name and card number appear either in a strip within the frame of the photo, or printed in the border beneath the photo. Card backs have a redemption offer that includes an ice cream bar in exchange for a Babe Ruth card, or a gallon of ice cream for a complete set of 60.

		NM	EX	VG
Complete Set (60):		20,000	8,000	4,000
Common Player:		90.00	35.00	20.00
1	Burleigh Grimes	350.00	140.00	70.00
2	Walter Reuther (Ruether)	90.00	35.00	20.00
3	Joe Dugan	90.00	35.00	20.00
4	Red Faber	350.00	140.00	70.00
5	Gabby Hartnett	350.00	140.00	70.00
6	Babe Ruth	5,000	2,000	1,000
7	Bob Meusel	90.00	35.00	20.00
8	Herb Pennock	350.00	140.00	70.00
9	George Burns	90.00	35.00	20.00
10	Joe Sewell	350.00	140.00	70.00
11	George Uhle	90.00	35.00	20.00
12	Bob O'Farrell	90.00	35.00	20.00
13	Rogers Hornsby	450.00	180.00	90.00
14	"Pie" Traynor	350.00	140.00	70.00
15	Clarence Mitchell	90.00	35.00	20.00
16	Eppa Jepha Rixey	350.00	140.00	70.00
17	Carl Mays	125.00	50.00	25.00
18	Adolfo Luque	100.00	40.00	20.00
19	Dave Bancroft	350.00	140.00	70.00
20	George Kelly	350.00	140.00	70.00
21	Earl (Earle) Combs	350.00	140.00	70.00
22	Harry Heilmann	350.00	140.00	70.00
23	Ray W. Schalk	350.00	140.00	70.00
24	Johnny Mostil	90.00	35.00	20.00
25	Hack Wilson	350.00	140.00	70.00
26	Lou Gehrig	6,000	1,400	700.00
27	Ty Cobb	1,500	600.00	300.00
28	Tris Speaker	450.00	180.00	90.00
29	Tony Lazzeri	350.00	140.00	70.00
30	Waite Hoyt	350.00	140.00	70.00
31	Sherwood Smith	90.00	35.00	20.00
32	Max Carey	350.00	140.00	70.00
33	Eugene Hargrave	90.00	35.00	20.00
34	Miguel L. Gonzalez (Middle initial A.)	100.00	40.00	20.00
35	Joe Judge	90.00	35.00	20.00
36	E.C. (Sam) Rice	350.00	140.00	70.00
37	Earl Sheely	90.00	35.00	20.00
38	Sam Jones	90.00	35.00	20.00
39	Bib (Bibb) A. Falk	90.00	35.00	20.00
40	Willie Kamm	90.00	35.00	20.00
41	Stanley Harris	350.00	140.00	70.00
42	John J. McGraw	350.00	140.00	70.00
43	Artie Nehf	90.00	35.00	20.00
44	Grover Alexander	450.00	180.00	90.00
45	Paul Waner	350.00	140.00	70.00
46	William H. Terry	350.00	140.00	70.00
47	Glenn Wright	90.00	35.00	20.00
48	Earl Smith	90.00	35.00	20.00
49	Leon (Goose) Goslin	350.00	140.00	70.00
50	Frank Frisch	350.00	140.00	70.00
51	Joe Harris	90.00	35.00	20.00
52	Fred (Cy) Williams	90.00	35.00	20.00
53	Eddie Roush	350.00	140.00	70.00
54	George Sisler	350.00	140.00	70.00
55	Ed. Rommel	90.00	35.00	20.00
56	Rogers Peckinpaugh (Roger)	90.00	35.00	20.00
57	Stanley Coveleskie (Coveleski)	350.00	140.00	70.00
58	Lester Bell	90.00	35.00	20.00
59	L. Waner	350.00	140.00	70.00
60	John P. McInnis	90.00	35.00	20.00

1930-1931 Harrison Studio
Homestead Grays Postcards

Whether the famed Negro League powerhouse team, the Homestead Grays, were in Little Rock, Ark., for spring training or on a barnstorming tour, they became the subjects of a series of postcards from the local photographer, Harrison Studio. The cards are in standard postcard format, featuring borderless black-and-white photographic poses. It is likely the checklist here is incomplete.

(1) Josh Gibson (Front/back autographed card sold at auction 4/06 for $81,200.)
(2) Ted Page
(3) Ambrose Reed
(4) Homestead Grays 1930 Team Photo
(5) Homestead Grays 1931 Team Photo

1911-12 Hassan Cigarettes

WYATT LEE

Prior to its sole sponsorship of the T202 Triplefolders set of 1912, Hassan was one of 10 American Tobacco Co. brands advertising on the backs of 1911 T205 Gold Borders. Two different factories on noted on these backs, No. 30 and No. 649, the former being slightly scarcer, though currently no more valuable. Hassan backs in T205 are printed in green and do not command any significant premium in the market.

(See T202, T205.)

1887 Hastings Cabinets

M.J. Kelly

From the Boston studio of G.H. Hastings, this standard-format (about 3-3/4" x 5-3/4") cabinet card depicts the 19th Century's most popular star in stylish street clothers. Printed beneath the portrait is a copyright line, player and team identification and the logo and address of the studio. Back is blank. It is unknown whether other ballplayers' portraits were produced, though it is likely.

	NM	EX	VG
M.J. Kelly	10,000	3,750	2,250

1952 Hawthorn-Mellody
Chicago White Sox Pins

This issue was sponsored by a local dairy. The 1-3/8" diameter pins have sepia lithographs of the players with "Club of Champs" printed above. A non-pictorial membership button is also part of the set. The unnumbered pins are listed here in alphabetical order.

		NM	EX	VG
Complete Set (11):		400.00	200.00	120.00
Common Player:		35.00	17.50	10.50
(1)	Ray Coleman	35.00	17.50	10.50
(2)	Sam Dente	35.00	17.50	10.50
(3)	Joe Dobson	35.00	17.50	10.50
(4)	Nelson Fox	80.00	40.00	24.00
(5)	Sherman Lollar	45.00	22.00	13.50
(6)	Bill Pierce	45.00	22.00	13.50
(7)	Eddie Robinson	35.00	17.50	10.50
(8)	Hector Rodriguez	35.00	17.50	10.50
(9)	Eddie Stewart	35.00	17.50	10.50
(10)	Al Zarilla	35.00	17.50	10.50
(11)	Member's pin	15.00	7.50	4.50

1959 R.H. Hayes Postcards

Whether there are any other player postcards distributed by R.H. Hayes of Kansas is unknown. Produced for Hayes by Dexter Press, which issued cards for Coke in later years, the 3-1/2" x 5-1/2" post-card has a borderless color photo on front with a fac-simile autograph at bottom. The postcard back has credit lines for Hayes and Dexter and a short biogra-phy of the player.

		NM	EX	VG
(1)	Hank Bauer	45.00	22.50	13.50

1911 Helmar Stamps (T332)

A collectible departure from the traditional tobacco cards of the period, Helmar Cigarettes in 1911 issued a series of small major league baseball player "stamps." The stamps, each measuring approximately 1-1/8" x 1-3/8", feature a black and white player por-trait surrounded by a colorful, ornate frame. The stamps were originally issued in a 2" x 2-1/2" glassine envelope which advertised the Helmar brand and pro-moted "Philately - the Popular European Rage." To date, 181 different player stamps have been found. The set includes as many as 50 different frame designs. The Helmar stamp set has been assigned a T332 designation by the American Card Catalog.

		NM	EX	VG
	Complete Set (180):	8,000	4,000	2,400
	Common Player:	50.00	25.00	15.00
(1)	Babe Adams	50.00	25.00	15.00
(2)	Red Ames	50.00	25.00	15.00
(3)	Jimmy Archer	50.00	25.00	15.00
(4)	Jimmy Austin	50.00	25.00	15.00
(5)	Home Run Baker	100.00	50.00	30.00
(6)	Neal Ball	50.00	25.00	15.00
(7)	Cy Barger	50.00	25.00	15.00
(8)	Jack Barry	50.00	25.00	15.00
(9)	Johnny Bates	50.00	25.00	15.00
(10)	Fred Beck	50.00	25.00	15.00
(11)	Beals Becker	50.00	25.00	15.00
(12)	George Bell	50.00	25.00	15.00
(13)	Chief Bender	100.00	50.00	30.00
(14)	Bob Bescher	50.00	25.00	15.00
(15)	Joe Birmingham	50.00	25.00	15.00
(16)	John Bliss	50.00	25.00	15.00
(17)	Bruno Block	50.00	25.00	15.00
(18)	Ping Bodie	50.00	25.00	15.00
(19)	Roger Bresnahan	100.00	50.00	30.00
(20)	Al Bridwell	50.00	25.00	15.00
(21)	Lew Brockett	50.00	25.00	15.00
(22)	Mordecai Brown	100.00	50.00	30.00
(23)	Bill Burns	50.00	25.00	15.00
(24)	Donie Bush	50.00	25.00	15.00
(25)	Bobby Byrne	50.00	25.00	15.00
(26)	Nixey Callahan	50.00	25.00	15.00
(27)	Howie Camnitz	50.00	25.00	15.00
(28)	Max Carey	100.00	50.00	30.00
(29)	Bill Carrigan	50.00	25.00	15.00
(30)	Frank Chance	100.00	50.00	30.00
(31)	Hal Chase	50.00	25.00	15.00
(32)	Ed Cicotte	80.00	40.00	24.00
(33)	Fred Clarke	100.00	50.00	30.00
(34)	Tommy Clarke	50.00	25.00	15.00
(35)	Ty Cobb	750.00	375.00	225.00
(36)	King Cole	50.00	25.00	15.00
(37)	Eddie Collins (Philadelphia)	100.00	50.00	30.00
(38)	Shano Collins (Chicago)	50.00	25.00	15.00
(39)	Wid Conroy	50.00	25.00	15.00
(40)	Doc Crandall	50.00	25.00	15.00
(41)	Sam Crawford	100.00	50.00	30.00
(42)	Birdie Cree	50.00	25.00	15.00
(43)	Bill Dahlen	50.00	25.00	15.00
(44)	Jake Daubert	50.00	25.00	15.00
(45)	Harry Davis	50.00	25.00	15.00
(46)	Jim Delahanty	50.00	25.00	15.00
(47)	Art Devlin	50.00	25.00	15.00
(48)	Josh Devore	50.00	25.00	15.00
(49)	Mike Donlin	50.00	25.00	15.00
(50)	Wild Bill Donovan	50.00	25.00	15.00
(51)	Red Dooin	50.00	25.00	15.00
(52)	Mickey Doolan	50.00	25.00	15.00
(53)	Patsy Dougherty	50.00	25.00	15.00
(54)	Tom Downey	50.00	25.00	15.00
(55)	Larry Doyle	50.00	25.00	15.00
(56)	Louis Drucke	50.00	25.00	15.00
(57)	Clyde Engle	50.00	25.00	15.00
(58)	Tex Erwin	50.00	25.00	15.00
(59)	Steve Evans	50.00	25.00	15.00
(60)	Johnny Evers	100.00	50.00	30.00
(61)	Jack Ferry	50.00	25.00	15.00
(62)	Ray Fisher	50.00	25.00	15.00
(63)	Art Fletcher	50.00	25.00	15.00
(64)	Russ Ford	50.00	25.00	15.00
(65)	Art Fromme	50.00	25.00	15.00
(66)	Earl Gardner	50.00	25.00	15.00
(67)	Harry Gaspar	50.00	25.00	15.00
(68)	George Gibson	50.00	25.00	15.00
(69)	Roy Golden	50.00	25.00	15.00
(70)	Hank Gowdy	50.00	25.00	15.00
(71)	Peaches Graham	50.00	25.00	15.00
(72)	Eddie Grant	50.00	25.00	15.00
(73)	Dolly Gray	50.00	25.00	15.00
(74)	Clark Griffith	100.00	50.00	30.00
(75)	Bob Groom	50.00	25.00	15.00
(76)	Bob Harmon	50.00	25.00	15.00
(77)	Grover Hartley	50.00	25.00	15.00
(78)	Arnold Hauser	50.00	25.00	15.00
(79)	Buck Herzog	50.00	25.00	15.00
(80)	Dick Hoblitzell	50.00	25.00	15.00
(81)	Solly Hoffman (Hofman)	50.00	25.00	15.00
(82)	Miller Huggins	100.00	50.00	30.00
(83)	Long Tom Hughes	50.00	25.00	15.00
(84)	John Hummel	50.00	25.00	15.00
(85)	Hughie Jennings	100.00	50.00	30.00
(86)	Walter Johnson	275.00	135.00	82.00
(87)	Davy Jones	50.00	25.00	15.00
(88)	Johnny Kling	50.00	25.00	15.00
(89)	Otto Knabe	50.00	25.00	15.00
(90)	Jack Knight	50.00	25.00	15.00
(91)	Ed Konetchy	50.00	25.00	15.00
(92)	Harry Krause	50.00	25.00	15.00
(93)	Nap Lajoie	100.00	50.00	30.00
(94)	Joe Lake	50.00	25.00	15.00
(95)	Frank LaPorte	50.00	25.00	15.00
(96)	Tommy Leach	50.00	25.00	15.00
(97)	Lefty Leifield	50.00	25.00	15.00
(98)	Ed Lennox	50.00	25.00	15.00
(99)	Paddy Livingston	50.00	25.00	15.00
(100)	Hans Lobert	50.00	25.00	15.00
(101)	Harry Lord	50.00	25.00	15.00
(102)	Fred Luderus	50.00	25.00	15.00
(103)	Sherry Magee	50.00	25.00	15.00
(104)	Rube Marquard	100.00	50.00	30.00
(105)	Christy Mathewson	300.00	150.00	90.00
(106)	Al Mattern	50.00	25.00	15.00
(107)	George McBride	50.00	25.00	15.00
(108)	Amby McConnell	50.00	25.00	15.00
(109)	John McGraw	100.00	50.00	30.00
(110)	Harry McIntire (McIntyre)	50.00	25.00	15.00
(111)	Matty McIntyre	50.00	25.00	15.00
(112)	Larry McLean	50.00	25.00	15.00
(113)	Fred Merkle	50.00	25.00	15.00
(114)	Chief Meyers	50.00	25.00	15.00
(115)	Clyde Milan	50.00	25.00	15.00
(116)	Dots Miller	50.00	25.00	15.00
(117)	Mike Mitchell	50.00	25.00	15.00
(118)	Earl Moore	50.00	25.00	15.00
(119)	Pat Moran	50.00	25.00	15.00
(120)	George Moriarty	50.00	25.00	15.00
(121)	Mike Mowrey	50.00	25.00	15.00
(122)	George Mullin	50.00	25.00	15.00
(123)	Danny Murphy	50.00	25.00	15.00
(124)	Red Murray	50.00	25.00	15.00
(125)	Tom Needham	50.00	25.00	15.00
(126)	Rebel Oakes	50.00	25.00	15.00
(127)	Rube Oldring	50.00	25.00	15.00
(128)	Marty O'Toole	50.00	25.00	15.00
(129)	Fred Parent	50.00	25.00	15.00
(130)	Dode Paskert	50.00	25.00	15.00
(131)	Barney Pelty	50.00	25.00	15.00
(132)	Eddie Phelps	50.00	25.00	15.00
(133)	Jack Powell	50.00	25.00	15.00
(134)	Jack Quinn	50.00	25.00	15.00
(135)	Ed Reulbach	50.00	25.00	15.00
(136)	Lew Richie	50.00	25.00	15.00
(137)	Reggie Richter	50.00	25.00	15.00
(138)	Jack Rowan	50.00	25.00	15.00
(139)	Nap Rucker	50.00	25.00	15.00
(140)	Slim Sallee	50.00	25.00	15.00
(141)	Doc Scanlan	50.00	25.00	15.00
(142)	Germany Schaefer	50.00	25.00	15.00
(143)	Boss Schmidt	50.00	25.00	15.00
(144)	Wildfire Schulte	50.00	25.00	15.00
(145)	Jim Scott	50.00	25.00	15.00
(146)	Tillie Shafer	50.00	25.00	15.00
(147)	Dave Shean	50.00	25.00	15.00
(148)	Jimmy Sheckard	50.00	25.00	15.00
(149)	Mike Simon	50.00	25.00	15.00
(150)	Fred Snodgrass	50.00	25.00	15.00
(151)	Tris Speaker	125.00	62.00	37.00
(152)	Oscar Stanage	50.00	25.00	15.00
(153)	Bill Steele	50.00	25.00	15.00
(154)	Harry Stovall	50.00	25.00	15.00
(155)	Gabby Street	50.00	25.00	15.00
(156)	George Suggs	50.00	25.00	15.00
(157)	Billy Sullivan	50.00	25.00	15.00
(158)	Bill Sweeney	50.00	25.00	15.00
(159)	Jeff Sweeney	50.00	25.00	15.00
(160)	Lee Tannehill	50.00	25.00	15.00
(161)	Ira Thomas	50.00	25.00	15.00
(162)	Joe Tinker	100.00	50.00	30.00
(163)	John Titus	50.00	25.00	15.00
(164)	Fred Toney	50.00	25.00	15.00
(165)	Terry Turner	50.00	25.00	15.00
(166)	Hippo Vaughn	50.00	25.00	15.00
(167)	Heinie Wagner	50.00	25.00	15.00
(168)	Bobby Wallace	100.00	50.00	30.00
(169)	Ed Walsh	100.00	50.00	30.00
(170)	Jack Warhop	50.00	25.00	15.00
(171)	Zach Wheat	100.00	50.00	30.00
(172)	Doc White	50.00	25.00	15.00
(173)	Ed Willett	50.00	25.00	15.00
(174)	Art Wilson (New York)	50.00	25.00	15.00
(175)	Owen Wilson (Pittsburgh)	50.00	25.00	15.00
(176)	Hooks Wiltse	50.00	25.00	15.00
(177)	Harry Wolter	50.00	25.00	15.00
(178)	Harry Wolverton	50.00	25.00	15.00
(179)	Cy Young	400.00	200.00	120.00
(180)	Irv Young	50.00	25.00	15.00

1910 Hermes Ice Cream Pirates Pins

The World's Champion Pittsburgh Pirates are featured on this colorful set of 1-1/4" pins. Sepia player portraits at center have a yellow border around with a blue banner at bottom and a skull and cross-bones. The players are not identified on the buttons, making them difficult to collect.

		NM	EX	VG
	Complete Set (12):	11,000	5,500	3,250
	Common Player:	450.00	225.00	135.00
(1)	Bill Abstein	450.00	225.00	135.00
(2)	Red Adams	450.00	225.00	135.00
(3)	Bobby Byrne	450.00	225.00	135.00
(4)	Howie Camnitz	450.00	225.00	135.00
(5)	Fred Clarke	450.00	225.00	135.00
(6)	George Gibson	450.00	225.00	135.00
(7)	Tommy Leach	450.00	225.00	135.00
(8)	Sam Leever	450.00	225.00	135.00
(9)	Dots Miller	450.00	225.00	135.00
(10)	Mike Simon	450.00	225.00	135.00
(11)	Honus Wagner	6,500	3,250	2,000
(12)	Owen Wilson	450.00	225.00	135.00

1916 Herpolsheimer Co.

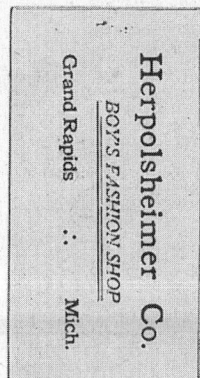

Advertising for a Michigan clothier is all that dif-ferentiates these cards from the more common Sporting News or blank-back M101-4 versions and those of other regional advertisers. The cards are black-and-white in 1-5/8" x 3" format. The Herpolshe-imer cards command a significant premium from type-card and superstar collectors.

PREMIUMS:
Common Players: 3-4X
Hall of Famers: 2-3X
  (See 1916 M101-4 Blank Backs for checklist and price guide.)

1921 Herpolsheimer's

Issued by a Grand Rapids, Michigan, department store that also produced a card set in 1916, this issue shares a basic format with the blank-backed strip-card set designated W575-1, though the known checklist of the Herpolsheimers includes cards that have not yet been verified in W575-1. It is also not known to what extent the variations listed among W575-1 are found among the Michigan store's ver-sion. The Herpolsheimer's cards differ from the strip cards in the inclusion of the advertising on the back and sometimes in photo and/or caption details. The 2-1/16" x 3-3/8" black-and-white cards are much scarcer than the strip-card version. The checklist presented here is incomplete. Gaps have been left in the assgned numbering to accomodate future additions. This set only game to the hobby's attention late in 2004 through a series of eBay auctions. Currently only a single example is known of each card. All known examples have a pencilled figure and dollar sign on back.

		NM	EX	VG
	Common Player:			450.00
(3)	Grover Alexander			1,100
(5)	J. Franklin Baker			750.00
(11)	Jim Bagby			450.00
(13)	Ping Bodie			450.00
(15)	George Burns			450.00
(16)	Geo. J. Burns			450.00
(18)	Owen Bush			450.00
(21)	Ty Cobb			4,000
(22)	Eddie Collins			750.00
(28)	George Dauss			450.00
(29)	Dave Davenport			450.00
(30)	Charles Deal			450.00
(33)	William Doak			450.00
(34)	Bill Donovan/Pitching			750.00
(39)	Urban Faber (Dark uniform.)			450.00
(45)	Art Fletcher			450.00
(47)	Jacques Fournier			450.00
(49)	W.L. Gardner			450.00
(52)	"Kid" Gleason			450.00
(54)	Hank Gowdy			450.00
(55)	John Graney (L.F.)			450.00
(57)	Tom Griffith			450.00
(67)	John Henry			450.00
(74)	Rogers Hornsby (2nd B.)			2,000
(79)	Hugh Jennings			450.00
(80)	Walter Johnson			4,500
(82)	James Johnston			450.00
(84)	Joe Judge/Btg			450.00
(89)	P.J. Kilduff			450.00
(93)	"Nemo" Leibold			450.00
(94)	Duffy Lewis			450.00
(95)	Al Mamaux			450.00
(96)	"Rabbit" Maranville			750.00
(101)	John McGraw (Manager)			750.00
(102)	Jack McInnis			450.00
(107)	Clyde Milan			450.00
(109)	Otto Miller			450.00
(112)	Guy Morton			450.00
(115)	Eddie Murphy			450.00
(116)	"Hy" Myers (C.F.)			450.00
(123)	Steve O'Neill			450.00
(124)	Roger Peckinbaugh (Peckinpaugh)			450.00
(125)	Jeff Pfeffer (Brooklyn)			450.00
(133)	E.C. Rice			750.00
(134)	Eppa Rixey, Jr.			750.00
(145)	Babe Ruth (R.F.)			10,000
(149)	"Slim" Sallee (Glove showing.)			450.00
(151)	Ray Schalk/Bunting			750.00
(153)	Walter Schang			450.00
(155)	Everett Scott (Boston)			1,250
(173)	Tris Speaker/Manager			750.00
(175)	Charles Stengel/Btg			750.00
(177)	Milton Stock			450.00
(178)	Amos Strunk (R.F.)			450.00
(181)	Zeb Terry (White uniform.)			450.00
(182)	Chester Thomas			450.00
(183)	Fred Toney (Both feet on ground.)			450.00
(186)	George Tyler			450.00
(187)	Jim Vaughn (Dark cap.)			450.00
(190)	Bob Veach (Arms folded.)			450.00
(191)	Oscar Vitt (3rd B.)			450.00
(193)	W. Wambsganss			450.00
(194)	Carl Weilman			450.00
(195)	Zach Wheat			750.00
(196)	George Whitted			450.00
(198)	Ivy B. Wingo			450.00
(200)	Joe Wood			675.00
(202)	"Pep" (Ralph) Young			450.00

1888 S.F. Hess (N338-2)

The most popular of the S.F. Hess & Co. issues, this 21-card set was issued in 1889 and pictures 16 players from the New York Giants, two New York Mets players, two from St. Louis and one from Detroit. The cards measure 2-3/4" x 1-1/2" and feature sepia-toned

photographs, most of which are enclosed in ovals with a dark background. The player's name is printed in capital letters just beneath the photo, and the S.F. Hess & Co. logo appears at the bottom (without using the Creole Cigarette brand name).

		NM	EX	VG
	Common Player:	7,200	3,600	2,160
(1)	Bill Brown	7,200	3,600	2,160
(2)	Roger Conner (Connor)	18,000	9,000	5,400
(3)	Ed Crane	7,200	3,600	2,160
(4)	Buck Ewing	18,000	9,000	5,400
(5)	Elmer Foster	7,200	3,600	2,160
(6)	Wm. George	7,200	3,600	2,160
(7)	Joe Gerhardt	7,200	3,600	2,160
(8)	Chas. Getzein (Getzien)	7,200	3,600	2,160
(9)	Geo. Gore	7,200	3,600	2,160
(10)	Gil Hatfield	7,200	3,600	2,160
(11)	Tim Keefe	18,000	9,000	5,400
(12)	Arlie Latham	7,200	3,600	2,160
(13)	Pat Murphy	7,200	3,600	2,160
(14)	Jim Mutrie	7,200	3,600	2,160
(15)	Dave Orr	7,200	3,600	2,160
(16)	Danny Richardson	7,200	3,600	2,160
(17)	Mike Slattery	7,200	3,600	2,160
(18)	Silent Mike Tiernan	7,200	3,600	2,160
(19)	Lidell Titcomb	7,200	3,600	2,160
(20)	Johnny Ward	18,000	9,000	5,400
(21)	Curt Welch	7,200	3,600	2,160
(22)	Mickey Welch	18,000	9,000	5,400
(23)	Arthur Whitney	7,200	3,600	2,160

1909-11 Hindu Cigarettes

Hindu backs are among the more difficult to find among the various cigarette-brand ads seen on T205 and T206 cards. T206s are usually found with the ad printed in brown ink. Much scarcer are those with the ad printed in red. Fewer than 50 T205s have ever been seen with the Hindu ad on back, printed in brown. Multipliers shown are for "common" player cards. Cards of Hall of Famers or other high-demand cards are usually figured by using a multiplier of about one-half those shown here.

PREMIUMS
T205: 15-20X
T206 Brown Commons: 8-10X
T206 Brown Hall of Famers: 5-7X
T206 Brown Southern Leaguers 3-4X
T206 Red Commons: 15X
T206 Red Hall of Famers: 10X
(See T205, T206 for checklists and base card values.)

1958 Hires Root Beer Test Set

Among the scarcest of the regional issues of the late 1950s is the eight-card test issue which preceded the Hires Root Beer set of 66 cards. The test cards differ from the regular issue in that they have sepia-toned, rather than color pictures, which are set against plain yellow or orange backgrounds (much like the 1958 Topps), instead of viewed through a knothole. Like the regular Hires cards, the 2-5/16" x 3-1/2" cards were issued with an attached wedge-shaped tab of like size. The tab offered membership in Hires' baseball fan club, and served to hold the card into the carton of bottled root beer with which it was given away.

	NM	EX	VG
Complete Set, W/Tab (8):	10,000	4,000	2,000
Common Player, W/Tab:	725.00	290.00	145.00
Complete Set, No Tab (8):	3,000	1,200	600.00

		NM	EX	VG
	Common Player, No Tab:	250.00	100.00	50.00
	WITH TAB			
(1)	Johnny Antonelli	725.00	290.00	145.00
(2)	Jim Busby	725.00	290.00	145.00
(3)	Chico Fernandez	725.00	290.00	145.00
(4)	Bob Friend	725.00	290.00	145.00
(5)	Vern Law	725.00	290.00	145.00
(6)	Stan Lopata	725.00	290.00	145.00
(7)	Willie Mays	5,000	2,000	1,000
(8)	Al Pilarcik	725.00	290.00	145.00
	NO TAB			
(1)	Johnny Antonelli	250.00	100.00	50.00
(2)	Jim Busby	250.00	100.00	50.00
(3)	Chico Fernandez	250.00	100.00	50.00
(4)	Bob Friend	250.00	100.00	50.00
(5)	Vern Law	250.00	100.00	50.00
(6)	Stan Lopata	250.00	100.00	50.00
(7)	Willie Mays	1,300	525.00	250.00
(8)	Al Pilarcik	250.00	100.00	50.00

1958 Hires Root Beer

Like most baseball cards issued with a tab in the 1950s, the Hires cards are extremely scarce today in their original form. The basic card was attached to a wedge-shaped tab that served the dual purpose of offering a fan club membership and of holding the card into the cardboard carton of soda bottles with which it was distributed. Measurements of the card vary somewhat, from about 2-3/8" to 2-5/8" wide and 3-3/8" to 3-5/8" tall (without tab). The tab extends for another 3-1/2". Numbering of the Hires set begins at 10 and goes through 76, with card #69 never issued, making a set complete at 66 cards.

		NM	EX	VG
	Complete Set, W/Tab (66):	5,250	2,650	1,550
	Common Player, W/Tab:	60.00	30.00	18.00
	Complete Set, No Tab (66):	3,250	1,600	975.00
	Common Player, No Tab:	35.00	17.50	10.00
	WITH TAB			
10	Richie Ashburn	165.00	80.00	50.00
11	Chico Carrasquel	60.00	30.00	18.00
12	Dave Philley	60.00	30.00	18.00
13	Don Newcombe	110.00	55.00	35.00
14	Wally Post	60.00	30.00	18.00
15	Rip Repulski	60.00	30.00	18.00
16	Chico Fernandez	60.00	30.00	18.00
17	Larry Doby	95.00	50.00	25.00
18	Hector Brown	60.00	30.00	18.00
19	Danny O'Connell	60.00	30.00	18.00
20	Granny Hamner	60.00	30.00	18.00
21	Dick Groat	60.00	30.00	18.00
22	Ray Narleski	60.00	30.00	18.00
23	Pee Wee Reese	165.00	85.00	50.00
24	Bob Friend	60.00	30.00	18.00
25	Willie Mays	500.00	250.00	150.00
26	Bob Nieman	60.00	30.00	18.00
27	Frank Thomas	60.00	30.00	18.00
28	Curt Simmons	60.00	30.00	18.00
29	Stan Lopata	60.00	30.00	18.00
30	Bob Skinner	60.00	30.00	18.00
31	Ron Kline	60.00	30.00	18.00
32	Willie Miranda	60.00	30.00	18.00
33	Bob Avila	60.00	30.00	18.00
34	Clem Labine	90.00	45.00	27.50
35	Ray Jablonski	60.00	30.00	18.00
36	Bill Mazeroski	110.00	55.00	35.00
37	Billy Gardner	60.00	30.00	18.00
38	Pete Runnels	60.00	30.00	18.00
39	Jack Sanford	60.00	30.00	18.00
40	Dave Sisler	60.00	30.00	18.00
41	Don Zimmer	90.00	45.00	27.00
42	Johnny Podres	90.00	45.00	27.50
43	Dick Farrell	60.00	30.00	18.00
44	Hank Aaron	425.00	210.00	125.00
45	Bill Virdon	60.00	30.00	18.00
46	Bobby Thomson	75.00	37.50	22.50
47	Willard Nixon	60.00	30.00	18.00
48	Billy Loes	60.00	30.00	18.00
49	Hank Sauer	60.00	30.00	18.00
50	Johnny Antonelli	60.00	30.00	18.00
51	Daryl Spencer	60.00	30.00	18.00
52	Ken Lehman	75.00	37.50	22.50
53	Sammy White	60.00	30.00	18.00

#	Player	NM	EX	VG
54	Charley Neal	75.00	37.50	22.50
55	Don Drysdale	165.00	80.00	50.00
56	Jack Jensen	65.00	32.50	20.00
57	Ray Katt	60.00	30.00	18.00
58	Franklin Sullivan	60.00	30.00	18.00
59	Roy Face	60.00	30.00	18.00
60	Willie Jones	60.00	30.00	18.00
61	Duke Snider/SP	250.00	125.00	75.00
62	Whitey Lockman	60.00	30.00	18.00
63	Gino Cimoli	75.00	37.00	22.50
64	Marv Grissom	60.00	30.00	18.00
65	Gene Baker	60.00	30.00	18.00
66	George Zuverink	60.00	30.00	18.00
67	Ted Kluszewski	135.00	70.00	40.00
68	Jim Busby	60.00	30.00	18.00
69	Not Issued			
70	Curt Barclay	60.00	30.00	18.00
71	Hank Foiles	60.00	30.00	18.00
72	Gene Stephens	60.00	30.00	18.00
73	Al Worthington	60.00	30.00	18.00
74	Al Walker	60.00	30.00	18.00
75	Bob Boyd	60.00	30.00	18.00
76	Al Pilarcik	60.00	30.00	18.00

NO TAB

#	Player	NM	EX	VG
10	Richie Ashburn	110.00	55.00	35.00
11	Chico Carrasquel	35.00	17.50	10.00
12	Dave Philley	35.00	17.50	10.00
13	Don Newcombe	65.00	32.50	20.00
14	Wally Post	35.00	17.50	10.00
15	Rip Repulski	35.00	17.50	10.00
16	Chico Fernandez	35.00	17.50	10.00
17	Larry Doby	75.00	37.50	22.50
18	Hector Brown	35.00	17.50	10.00
19	Danny O'Connell	35.00	17.50	10.00
20	Granny Hamner	35.00	17.50	10.00
21	Dick Groat	35.00	17.50	10.00
22	Ray Narleski	35.00	17.50	10.00
23	Pee Wee Reese	100.00	50.00	30.00
24	Bob Friend	35.00	17.50	10.00
25	Willie Mays	200.00	100.00	60.00
26	Bob Nieman	35.00	17.50	10.00
27	Frank Thomas	35.00	17.50	10.00
28	Curt Simmons	35.00	17.50	10.00
29	Stan Lopata	35.00	17.50	10.00
30	Bob Skinner	35.00	17.50	10.00
31	Ron Kline	35.00	17.50	10.00
32	Willie Miranda	35.00	17.50	10.00
33	Bob Avila	35.00	17.50	10.00
34	Clem Labine	45.00	22.50	13.50
35	Ray Jablonski	35.00	17.50	10.00
36	Bill Mazeroski	75.00	37.50	22.50
37	Billy Gardner	35.00	17.50	10.00
38	Pete Runnels	35.00	17.50	10.00
39	Jack Sanford	35.00	17.50	10.00
40	Dave Sisler	35.00	17.50	10.00
41	Don Zimmer	45.00	22.50	13.50
42	Johnny Podres	45.00	22.50	13.50
43	Dick Farrell	35.00	17.50	10.00
44	Hank Aaron	200.00	100.00	60.00
45	Bill Virdon	35.00	17.50	10.00
46	Bobby Thomson	45.00	22.50	13.50
47	Willard Nixon	35.00	17.50	10.00
48	Billy Loes	35.00	17.50	10.00
49	Hank Sauer	35.00	17.50	10.00
50	Johnny Antonelli	35.00	17.50	10.00
51	Daryl Spencer	35.00	17.50	10.00
52	Ken Lehman	40.00	20.00	12.00
53	Sammy White	35.00	17.50	10.00
54	Charley Neal	40.00	20.00	12.00
55	Don Drysdale	75.00	37.50	22.50
56	Jack Jensen	40.00	20.00	12.00
57	Ray Katt	35.00	17.50	10.00
58	Franklin Sullivan	35.00	17.50	10.00
59	Roy Face	35.00	17.50	10.00
60	Willie Jones	35.00	17.50	10.00
61	Duke Snider/SP	180.00	90.00	55.00
62	Whitey Lockman	35.00	17.50	10.00
63	Gino Cimoli	40.00	20.00	10.00
64	Marv Grissom	35.00	17.50	10.00
65	Gene Baker	35.00	17.50	10.00
66	George Zuverink	35.00	17.50	10.00
67	Ted Kluszewski	75.00	37.50	22.50
68	Jim Busby	35.00	17.50	10.00
69	NOT ISSUED			
70	Curt Barclay	35.00	17.50	10.00
71	Hank Foiles	35.00	17.50	10.00
72	Gene Stephens	35.00	17.50	10.00
73	Al Worthington	35.00	17.50	10.00
74	Al Walker	35.00	17.50	10.00
75	Bob Boyd	35.00	17.50	10.00
76	Al Pilarcik	35.00	17.50	10.00

1951-52 Hit Parade of Champions

(See 1951-52 Berk Ross.)

1977 Holiday Inn Discs

Virtually identical in format to the several locally sponsored disc sets of the previous year, these 3-3/8"
diameter player discs were given away five at a time with the purchase of a children's dinner at some 72 participating Holiday Inns in the Midwest. Discs once again feature black-and-white player portrait photos in the center of a baseball design. The left and right panels are in one of several bright colors. Licensed by the Players' Association through Mike Schechter Associates, the player photos carry no uniform logos. Backs are printed in green. The unnumbered discs are checklisted here alphabetically.

		NM	EX	VG
	Complete Set (70):	160.00	80.00	45.00
	Common Player:	2.00	1.00	.60
(1)	Sal Bando	2.00	1.00	.60
(2)	Buddy Bell	2.00	1.00	.60
(3)	Johnny Bench	6.00	3.00	1.75
(4)	Larry Bowa	2.00	1.00	.60
(5)	Steve Braun	2.00	1.00	.60
(6)	George Brett	20.00	10.00	6.00
(7)	Lou Brock	6.00	3.00	1.75
(8)	Jeff Burroughs	2.00	1.00	.60
(9)	Bert Campaneris	2.00	1.00	.60
(10)	John Candelaria	2.00	1.00	.60
(11)	Jose Cardenal	2.00	1.00	.60
(12)	Rod Carew	6.00	3.00	1.75
(13)	Steve Carlton	6.00	3.00	1.75
(14)	Dave Cash	2.00	1.00	.60
(15)	Cesar Cedeno	2.00	1.00	.60
(16)	Ron Cey	2.00	1.00	.60
(17)	Dave Concepcion	2.00	1.00	.60
(18)	Dennis Eckersley	5.00	2.50	1.50
(19)	Mark Fidrych	3.00	1.50	.90
(20)	Rollie Fingers	5.00	2.50	1.50
(21)	Carlton Fisk	6.00	3.00	1.75
(22)	George Foster	2.00	1.00	.60
(23)	Wayne Garland	2.00	1.00	.60
(24)	Ralph Garr	2.00	1.00	.60
(25)	Steve Garvey	4.00	2.00	1.25
(26)	Cesar Geronimo	2.00	1.00	.60
(27)	Bobby Grich	2.00	1.00	.60
(28)	Ken Griffey Sr.	2.50	1.25	.70
(29)	Don Gullett	2.00	1.00	.60
(30)	Mike Hargrove	2.00	1.00	.60
(31)	Al Hrabosky	2.00	1.00	.60
(32)	Jim Hunter	5.00	2.50	1.50
(33)	Reggie Jackson	10.00	5.00	3.00
(34)	Randy Jones	2.00	1.00	.60
(35a)	Dave Kingman (Mets)	2.50	1.25	.70
(35b)	Dave Kingman (Padres)	4.00	2.00	1.25
(36)	Jerry Koosman	2.00	1.00	.60
(37)	Dave LaRoche	2.00	1.00	.60
(38)	Greg Luzinski	2.00	1.00	.60
(39)	Fred Lynn	2.00	1.00	.60
(40)	Bill Madlock	2.00	1.00	.60
(41)	Rick Manning	2.00	1.00	.60
(42)	Jon Matlock	2.00	1.00	.60
(43)	John Mayberry	2.00	1.00	.60
(44)	Hal McRae	2.00	1.00	.60
(45)	Andy Messersmith	2.00	1.00	.60
(46)	Rick Monday	2.00	1.00	.60
(47)	John Montefusco	2.00	1.00	.60
(48)	Joe Morgan	6.00	3.00	1.75
(49)	Thurman Munson	4.00	2.00	1.25
(50)	Bobby Murcer	2.00	1.00	.60
(51)	Bill North	2.00	1.00	.60
(52)	Jim Palmer	6.00	3.00	1.75
(53)	Tony Perez	5.00	2.50	1.50
(54)	Jerry Reuss	2.00	1.00	.60
(55)	Brooks Robinson	6.00	3.00	1.75
(56)	Pete Rose	15.00	7.50	4.50
(57)	Joe Rudi	2.00	1.00	.60
(58)	Nolan Ryan	40.00	20.00	12.00
(59)	Manny Sanguillen	2.00	1.00	.60
(60)	Mike Schmidt	15.00	7.50	4.50
(61)	Tom Seaver	6.00	3.00	1.75
(62)	Bill Singer	2.00	1.00	.60
(63)	Willie Stargell	6.00	3.00	1.75
(64)	Rusty Staub	3.00	1.50	.90
(65)	Luis Tiant	2.00	1.00	.60
(66)	Bob Watson	2.00	1.00	.60
(67)	Butch Wynegar	2.00	1.00	.60
(68)	Carl Yastrzemski	7.50	3.75	2.25
(69)	Robin Yount	6.00	3.00	1.75
(70)	Richie Zisk	2.00	1.00	.60

1925 Holland World's Champions Washington Senators

The World's Champion Washington Senators were featured on a set issued in Winnipeg, Manitoba, of all places. The 1-1/2" x 3" cards have player portrait photos printed in blue on front. The black-printed back has a card number and details of a redemption offer of cards for ice cream. Like many such offers it appears as if card #16 was intentionally withheld or minimally distributed, making it very scarce today.

		NM	EX	VG
	Complete Set, No #16 (17):	17,500	8,750	5,250
	Common Player:	800.00	400.00	240.00
1	Ralph Miller	800.00	400.00	240.00
2	Earl McNeely	800.00	400.00	240.00
3	Allan Russell	800.00	400.00	240.00
4	Ernest Shirley	800.00	400.00	240.00
5	Sam Rice	1,200	600.00	360.00
6	Muddy Ruel	800.00	400.00	240.00
7	Ossie Bluege	800.00	400.00	240.00
8	Nemo Leibold	800.00	400.00	240.00
9	Paul Zahniser	800.00	400.00	240.00
10	Firpo Marberry	800.00	400.00	240.00
11	Warren Ogden	800.00	400.00	240.00
12	George Mogridge	800.00	400.00	240.00
13	Tom Zachary	800.00	400.00	240.00
14	Goose Goslin	1,200	600.00	360.00
15	Joe Judge	800.00	400.00	240.00
16	Roger Peckinpaugh	2,500	1,250	750.00
17	Bucky Harris	1,200	600.00	360.00
18	Walter Johnson	3,500	1,750	1,000

1916 Holmes to Homes Bread

Most often found with blank backs, this 200-card set can also be found with ads on the back for several local and regional businesses. Among them is Holmes to Homes Milk-Made Bread, location unknown. Type card collectors and superstar collectors can expect to pay a significant premium for individual cards with Holmes to Homes advertising. Cards measure 1-5/8" x 3" and are printed in black-and-white.

(See 1916 M101-5 Blank Backs for checklist and base value information.)

1921 Holsum Bread

Issued by the Weil Baking Co., New Orleans, which produced several sets in the 1910s, this issue shares a format, but not the checklist of the 1921 American Caramel Co. set known as E121, Series of 80, and the contemporary W575-1 blank-back strip cards. To what extent the base cards and known variations in those set are found among the Holsum version is unknown. The Holsum cards differ from E121 primarily in the advertising on the back and sometimes in photo and/or caption details. The approximately 2" x 3-1/4" black-and-white cards are much scarcer than the caramel version. The trial checklist presented here is incomplete.

		NM	EX	VG
	Common Player:	350.00	175.00	100.00
(4)	Jimmy Austin	350.00	175.00	100.00
(7)	Dave Bancroft	600.00	300.00	180.00
(13)	Jack Barry	350.00	175.00	100.00
(16)	Ping Bodie	350.00	175.00	100.00
(19)	George Burns	350.00	175.00	100.00

(26)	Ray Chapman	425.00	210.00	125.00
(28)	Eddie Cicotte	600.00	300.00	180.00
(37)	Geo. Cutshaw	350.00	175.00	100.00
(39)	Charles Deal (Dark uniform.)	350.00	175.00	100.00
(42)	Johnny Evers	600.00	300.00	180.00
(46)	Urban Faber (Dark uniform.)	600.00	300.00	180.00
(50)	Art Fletcher	350.00	175.00	100.00
(51)	Eddie Foster	350.00	175.00	100.00
(52)	Jacques Fournier	350.00	175.00	100.00
(80)	Rogers Hornsby	1,250	625.00	375.00
(85)	Joe Jackson (Value Undetermined)			
(88)	Walter Johnson (Hands at chest.)	2,000	1,000	600.00
(93)	Wm. Killefer Jr.	350.00	175.00	100.00
(95)	John Lavan	350.00	175.00	100.00
(97)	H.B. Leonard	350.00	175.00	100.00
(99)	Duffy Lewis	350.00	175.00	100.00
(105)	Al Mamaux	350.00	175.00	100.00
(107)	"Rabbit" Maranville	600.00	300.00	180.00
(116)	Otto Miller	350.00	175.00	100.00
(122)	Guy Morton	350.00	175.00	100.00
(124)	"Hy" Myers	350.00	175.00	100.00
(127)	Arthur Nehf	350.00	175.00	100.00
(129)	Steve O'Neill	350.00	175.00	100.00
(133)	Jeff Pfeffer	350.00	175.00	100.00
(136)	Bill Rariden	350.00	175.00	100.00
(153)	Walter Schang	350.00	175.00	100.00
(162)	Geo. Sisler	600.00	300.00	180.00
(164)	J. Carlisle Smith	350.00	175.00	100.00
(168)	Charles Stengel	600.00	300.00	180.00
(170)	Amos Strunk/Btg (Chicago Americans)	350.00	175.00	100.00
(171)	Amos Strunk (Arms at side, Chicago White Sox.)	350.00	175.00	100.00
(173)	Chester Thomas	350.00	175.00	100.00
(174)	Fred Toney	350.00	175.00	100.00
(175)	Jim Vaughn	350.00	175.00	100.00
(178)	Bob Veach	350.00	175.00	100.00
(184)	W. Wambsganss	350.00	175.00	100.00
(186)	Carl Weilman	350.00	175.00	100.00
(187)	Zack Wheat	600.00	300.00	180.00
(190)	Claude Williams (White stockings, correct photo.)	2,500	1,250	750.00
(202)	Pep Young	350.00	175.00	100.00

1959 Home Run Derby

GIL HODGES
LOS ANGELES DODGERS

This 20-card unnumbered set was produced by American Motors to publicize the Home Run Derby television program. The cards measure approximately 3-1/4" x 5-1/4" and feature black-and-white player photos on blank-backed white stock. The player name and team are printed beneath the photo. This set was reprinted (marked as such) in 1988 by Card Collectors' Co. of New York. An advertising poster is sometimes seen which is essentially an uncut sheet of the cards with a promotional message at bottom.

		NM	EX	VG
Complete Set (20):		10,000	5,000	3,000
Common Player:		175.00	85.00	50.00
Advertising Poster:		3,500	1,750	1,000
(1)	Hank Aaron	900.00	450.00	275.00
(2)	Bob Allison	175.00	85.00	50.00
(3)	Ernie Banks	700.00	350.00	210.00
(4)	Ken Boyer	200.00	100.00	60.00
(5)	Bob Cerv	175.00	85.00	50.00
(6)	Rocky Colavito	325.00	160.00	100.00
(7)	Gil Hodges	325.00	160.00	100.00
(8)	Jackie Jensen	175.00	85.00	50.00
(9)	Al Kaline	600.00	300.00	180.00
(10)	Harmon Killebrew	600.00	300.00	180.00
(11)	Jim Lemon	175.00	85.00	50.00
(12)	Mickey Mantle	2,250	1,125	675.00
(13)	Ed Mathews	550.00	275.00	165.00
(14)	Willie Mays	900.00	450.00	270.00
(15)	Wally Post	175.00	85.00	50.00
(16)	Frank Robinson	550.00	275.00	165.00
(17)	Mark Scott/Host	350.00	175.00	100.00
(18)	Duke Snider	600.00	300.00	180.00
(19)	Dick Stuart	175.00	85.00	50.00
(20)	Gus Triandos	175.00	85.00	50.00

1894 Honest (Duke) Cabinets (N142)

These color cabinet cards, which measure 6" x 9-1/2", were produced by W.H. Duke for its Honest

tobacco brand. The player name is centered at the bottom of the card front. The brand name "Honest" is located in the lower-left corner with the words "New York" in the lower-right corner. Three bicyclists are also part of the set.

		NM	EX	VG
Complete Set (4):		50,000	25,000	15,000
Common Player:		9,400	4,700	2,800
(1)	G.S. Davis	12,100	6,100	3,600
(2)	E.J. Delahanty	17,600	8,800	5,300
(3)	W.M. Nash	9,400	4,700	2,800
(4)	W. Robinson	18,400	9,200	5,500

1911-12 Honest Long Cut Tobacco

Advertising, printed in black, for Honest Long Cut tobacco is among the more commonly found on the backs of T205 Gold Border cards of 1911. The brand also advertised on the multi-sport T227 Series of Champions in 1912.

(See T205, T227 for checklists and values.)

1927 Honey Boy

GROVER ALEXANDER

The date of issue for this rare Canadian issue is conjectural. These black-and-white 1-5/8" x 2-3/8" cards were issued by the Purity Ice Cream Co. in Winnipeg, Canada, and were redeemable as a set of 21 for a brick of "Delicious Honey Boy Ice Cream." Besides the major leaguers in the set, there are also cards of local amateurs and semi-pros, including hockey Hall of Famer Steamer Maxwell and Chicago Blackhawks star Cecil Browne. The major leaguers are not identified by team, nor do their photos have team insignias present. When redeemed, cards were punch-cancelled. Values shown are for uncancelled cards; cards exhibiting the punch-holes would be worth about 50 percent of the indicated figures.

		NM	EX	VG
Complete Set (21):		24,000	12,000	7,500
Common (Major League) Player:		900.00	450.00	275.00
1	"Steamer" Maxwell (Arenas)	2,000	1,000	600.00

2	Cecil Browne (Dominion Express)	400.00	200.00	120.00
3	Carson McVey (Transcona)	400.00	200.00	120.00
4	Sam Perlman (Tigers)	400.00	200.00	120.00
5	"Snake" Siddle (Arenas)	400.00	200.00	120.00
6	Eddie Cass (Columbus)	400.00	200.00	120.00
7	Jimmy Bradley (Columbus)	400.00	200.00	120.00
8	Gordon Caslake (Dominion Express)	400.00	200.00	120.00
9	Ward McVey (Tigers)	400.00	200.00	120.00
10	"Tris" Speaker	1,800	900.00	540.00
11	George Sisler	1,500	750.00	450.00
12	E. Meusel	900.00	450.00	275.00
13	Ed. Roush	1,500	750.00	450.00
14	"Babe" Ruth	8,500	4,250	2,550
15	Harry Heilmann	1,500	750.00	450.00
16	Heinie Groh	900.00	450.00	275.00
17	Eddie Collins	1,500	750.00	450.00
18	Grover Alexander	1,650	825.00	495.00
19	Dave Bancroft	1,500	750.00	450.00
20	Frank Frisch	1,500	750.00	450.00
21	George Burns	900.00	450.00	275.00

1905-1909 Carl Horner Cabinets

Carl Horner was the premier baseball portraitist of the early 20th Century. From his Boston studio came the images of the day's stars and journeymen which live on today on some of the most popular baseball cards of the era - including the famed T206 Honus Wagner. Highly collectible in their own right are the cabinet photos produced by the studio. Because of rarity, values can be determined only on those rare occasions when an example comes onto the market. Because the body of his work was accomplished over a number of years, mounting style and other technical details of the generally 5-1/2" x 7" cabinets may vary. Because the players are not identified on the cabinet, identification can be a problem, though quite often a contemporary notation of the player's name can be found written on back.

	NM	EX	VG
Common Player:	1,000	500.00	300.00
Nick Altrock	2,500	1,250	750.00
Frank Arrelanes (Arellanes)	2,000	1,000	600.00
Frank Baker	3,500	1,750	1,050
Harry Barton	2,000	1,000	600.00
Jake Beckley	3,500	1,750	1,050
Frank Chance	3,500	1,750	1,050
Eddie Collins	3,500	1,750	1,050
Bill Dahlen	2,000	1,000	600.00
Frank Delahanty	2,250	1,125	675.00
Kid Elberfeld	2,000	1,000	600.00
Billy Gilbert	2,000	1,000	600.00
Danny Green	2,000	1,000	600.00
Walter Johnson	15,000	3,250	1,950
Addie Joss	4,000	2,000	1,200
Harry Krause	2,000	1,000	600.00
Rube Kroh	2,000	1,000	600.00
Bris Lord	2,000	1,000	600.00
Charlie Lush	2,000	1,000	600.00
Earl Moore	2,000	1,000	600.00
Harry Niles	2,000	1,000	600.00
Billy Sullivan	2,000	1,000	600.00
Joe Tinker	3,500	1,750	1,050
Honus Wagner	20,000	4,500	2,700
Victor Willis	3,500	1,750	1,050

1959 Hostess Bob Turley

BOB TURLEY
Now Pitching For
HOSTESS CAKES
Cup Cakes—Sno-Balls—Twinkies
Li'l Angels—Fruit Pies
Hostess Finer Pastries
Hostess Donuts and Donettes
and
WONDER BREAD
The bread that helps build
strong bodies 12 ways

The date attributed to this card is speculative. The 3-1/2" x 4-3/8" black-and-white card has an action pose of the Yankees pitcher on front surrounded by a white border. On back is a list of Hostess Cakes products.

	NM	EX	VG
Bob Turley	125.00	60.00	40.00

1975 Hostess

HANK AARON DESIGNATED HITTER Milwaukee BREWERS — RENNIE STENNETT INFIELD Pittsburgh PIRATES — RICO PETROCELLI INFIELD Boston RED SOX

The first of what would become five annual issues, the 1975 Hostess set consists of 50 three-card panels which formed the bottom of boxes of family-size snack cake products. Unlike many similar issues, the Hostess cards do not share common borders, so it was possible to cut them neatly and evenly from the box. Well-cut single cards measure 2-1/4" x 3-1/4", while a three-card panel measures 7-1/4" x 3-1/4". Because some of the panels were issued on packages of less popular snack cakes, they are somewhat scarcer today. Since the hobby was quite well-developed when the Hostess cards were first issued, there is no lack of complete panels. Even unused complete boxes are available today. Some of the photos in this issue also appear on Topps cards of the era.

		NM	EX	VG
	Complete Panel Set (50):	350.00	175.00	100.00
	Complete Set, Singles (150):	165.00	80.00	50.00
	Common Panel:	5.00	2.50	1.50
	Common Player:	1.00	.50	.30
	Panel (1)	5.00	2.50	1.50
1	Bobby Tolan	1.00	.50	.30
2	Cookie Rojas	1.00	.50	.30
3	Darrell Evans	1.25	.60	.40
	Panel (2)	10.00	5.00	3.00
4	Sal Bando	1.00	.50	.30
5	Joe Morgan	5.00	2.50	1.50
6	Mickey Lolich	1.25	.60	.40
	Panel (3)	10.00	5.00	3.00
7	Don Sutton	4.50	2.25	1.25
8	Bill Melton	1.00	.50	.30
9	Tim Foli	1.00	.50	.30
	Panel (4)	5.00	2.50	1.50
10	Joe Lahoud	1.00	.50	.30
11a	Bert Hooten (Incorrect spelling.)	1.50	.70	.45
11b	Burt Hooton (Corrected)	1.00	.50	.30
12	Paul Blair	1.00	.50	.30
	Panel (5)	5.00	2.50	1.50
13	Jim Barr	1.00	.50	.30
14	Toby Harrah	1.00	.50	.30
15	John Milner	1.00	.50	.30
	Panel (6)	5.00	2.50	1.50
16	Ken Holtzman	1.00	.50	.30
17	Cesar Cedeno	1.00	.50	.30
18	Dwight Evans	1.00	.50	.30
	Panel (7)	10.00	5.00	3.00
19	Willie McCovey	5.00	2.50	1.50
20	Tony Oliva	1.25	.60	.40
21	Manny Sanguillen	1.00	.50	.30
	Panel (8)	10.00	5.00	3.00
22	Mickey Rivers	1.00	.50	.30
23	Lou Brock	5.00	2.50	1.50
24	Graig Nettles	1.50	.70	.45
	Panel (9)	5.00	2.50	1.50
25	Jim Wynn	1.00	.50	.30
26	George Scott	1.00	.50	.30
27	Greg Luzinski	1.00	.50	.30
	Panel (10)	15.00	7.50	4.50
28	Bert Campaneris	1.00	.50	.30
29	Pete Rose	12.50	6.25	3.75
30	Buddy Bell	1.00	.50	.30
	Panel (11)	5.00	2.50	1.50
31	Gary Matthews	1.00	.50	.30
32	Fred Patek	1.00	.50	.30
33	Mike Lum	1.00	.50	.30
	Panel (12)	5.00	2.50	1.50
34	Ellie Rodriguez	1.00	.50	.30
35	Milt May	1.00	.50	.30
36	Willie Horton	1.00	.50	.30
	Panel (13)	10.00	5.00	3.00
37	Dave Winfield	5.00	2.50	1.50
38	Tom Grieve	1.00	.50	.30
39	Barry Foote	1.00	.50	.30
	Panel (14)	5.00	2.50	1.50
40	Joe Rudi	1.00	.50	.30
41	Bake McBride	1.00	.50	.30
42	Mike Cuellar	1.00	.50	.30
	Panel (15)	5.00	2.50	1.50
43	Garry Maddox	1.00	.50	.30
44	Carlos May	1.00	.50	.30
45	Bud Harrelson	1.00	.50	.30
	Panel (16)	10.00	5.00	3.00
46	Dave Chalk	1.00	.50	.30
47	Dave Concepcion	1.00	.50	.30
48	Carl Yastrzemski	7.50	3.75	2.25
	Panel (17)	10.00	5.00	3.00
49	Steve Garvey	3.00	1.50	.90
50	Amos Otis	1.00	.50	.30
51	Ricky Reuschel	1.00	.50	.30
	Panel (18)	10.00	5.00	3.00
52	Rollie Fingers	4.50	2.25	1.25
53	Bob Watson	1.00	.50	.30
54	John Ellis	1.00	.50	.30
	Panel (19)	10.00	5.00	3.00
55	Bob Bailey	1.00	.50	.30
56	Rod Carew	6.00	3.00	1.75
57	Richie Hebner	1.00	.50	.30
	Panel (20)	20.00	10.00	6.00
58	Nolan Ryan	15.00	7.50	4.50
59	Reggie Smith	1.00	.50	.30
60	Joe Coleman	1.00	.50	.30
	Panel (21)	10.00	5.00	3.00
61	Ron Cey	1.00	.50	.30
62	Darrell Porter	1.00	.50	.30
63	Steve Carlton	5.00	2.50	1.50
	Panel (22)	5.00	2.50	1.50
64	Gene Tenace	1.00	.50	.30
65	Jose Cardenal	1.00	.50	.30
66	Bill Lee	1.00	.50	.30
	Panel (23)	5.00	2.50	1.50
67	Davey Lopes	1.00	.50	.30
68	Wilbur Wood	1.00	.50	.30
69	Steve Renko	1.00	.50	.30
	Panel (24)	10.00	5.00	3.00
70	Joe Torre	3.00	1.50	.90
71	Ted Sizemore	1.00	.50	.30
72	Bobby Grich	1.00	.50	.30
	Panel (25)	12.50	6.25	3.75
73	Chris Speier	1.00	.50	.30
74	Bert Blyleven	1.25	.60	.40
75	Tom Seaver	6.00	3.00	1.75
	Panel (26)	5.00	2.50	1.50
76	Nate Colbert	1.00	.50	.30
77	Don Kessinger	1.00	.50	.30
78	George Medich	1.00	.50	.30
	Panel (27)	20.00	10.00	6.00
79	Andy Messersmith	1.00	.50	.30
80	Robin Yount	12.50	6.25	3.75
81	Al Oliver	1.25	.60	.40
	Panel (28)	15.00	7.50	4.50
82	Bill Singer	1.00	.50	.30
83	Johnny Bench	6.00	3.00	1.75
84	Gaylord Perry	4.50	2.25	1.25
	Panel (29)	5.00	2.50	1.50
85	Dave Kingman	1.00	.50	.30
86	Ed Herrmann	1.00	.50	.30
87	Ralph Garr	1.00	.50	.30
	Panel (30)	12.50	6.25	3.75
88	Reggie Jackson	7.50	3.75	2.25
89a	Doug Radar (Incorrect spelling.)	1.50	.70	.45
89b	Doug Rader (Corrected)	1.00	.50	.30
90	Elliott Maddox	1.00	.50	.30
	Panel (31)	5.00	2.50	1.50
91	Bill Russell	1.00	.50	.30
92	John Mayberry	1.00	.50	.30
93	Dave Cash	1.00	.50	.30
	Panel (32)	5.00	2.50	1.50
94	Jeff Burroughs	1.00	.50	.30
95	Ted Simmons	1.00	.50	.30
96	Joe Decker	1.00	.50	.30
	Panel (33)	10.00	5.00	3.00
97	Bill Buckner	1.25	.60	.40
98	Bobby Darwin	1.00	.50	.30
99	Phil Niekro	4.50	2.25	1.25
	Panel (34)	5.00	2.50	1.50
100	Mike Sundberg (Jim)	1.00	.50	.30
101	Greg Gross	1.00	.50	.30
102	Luis Tiant	1.00	.50	.30
	Panel (35)	5.00	2.50	1.50
103	Glenn Beckert	1.00	.50	.30
104	Hal McRae	1.00	.50	.30
105	Mike Jorgensen	1.00	.50	.30
	Panel (36)	5.00	2.50	1.50
106	Mike Hargrove	1.00	.50	.30
107	Don Gullett	1.00	.50	.30
108	Tito Fuentes	1.00	.50	.30
	Panel (37)	5.00	2.50	1.50
109	Johnny Grubb	1.00	.50	.30
110	Jim Kaat	1.25	.60	.40
111	Felix Millan	1.00	.50	.30
	Panel (38)	5.00	2.50	1.50
112	Don Money	1.00	.50	.30
113	Rick Monday	1.00	.50	.30
114	Dick Bosman	1.00	.50	.30
	Panel (39)	10.00	5.00	3.00
115	Roger Metzger	1.00	.50	.30
116	Fergie Jenkins	4.50	2.25	1.25
117	Dusty Baker	1.25	.60	.40
	Panel (40)	10.00	5.00	3.00
118	Billy Champion	1.00	.50	.30
119	Bob Gibson	5.00	2.50	1.50
120	Bill Freehan	1.00	.50	.30
	Panel (41)	5.00	2.50	1.50
121	Cesar Geronimo	1.00	.50	.30
122	Jorge Orta	1.00	.50	.30
123	Cleon Jones	1.00	.50	.30
	Panel (42)	10.00	5.00	3.00
124	Steve Busby	1.00	.50	.30
125a	Bill Madlock/Pitcher	1.50	.70	.45
125b	Bill Madlock/Infield	1.00	.50	.30
126	Jim Palmer	5.00	2.50	1.50
	Panel (43)	10.00	5.00	3.00
127	Tony Perez	5.00	2.50	1.50
128	Larry Hisle	1.00	.50	.30
129	Rusty Staub	1.25	.60	.40
	Panel (44)	20.00	10.00	6.00
130	Hank Aaron	13.50	6.75	4.00
131	Rennie Stennett	1.00	.50	.30
132	Rico Petrocelli	1.00	.50	.30
	Panel (45)	15.00	7.50	4.50
133	Mike Schmidt	12.50	6.25	3.75
134	Sparky Lyle	1.00	.50	.30
135	Willie Stargell	5.00	2.50	1.50
	Panel (46)	10.00	5.00	3.00
136	Ken Henderson	1.00	.50	.30
137	Willie Montanez	1.00	.50	.30
138	Thurman Munson	5.00	2.50	1.50
	Panel (47)	5.00	2.50	1.50
139	Richie Zisk	1.00	.50	.30
140	George Hendricks (Hendrick)	1.00	.50	.30
141	Bobby Murcer	1.50	.70	.45
	Panel (48)	15.00	7.50	4.50
142	Lee May	1.00	.50	.30
143	Carlton Fisk	5.00	2.50	1.50
144	Brooks Robinson	6.00	3.00	1.75
	Panel (49)	5.00	2.50	1.50
145	Bobby Bonds	1.25	.60	.40
146	Gary Sutherland	1.00	.50	.30
147	Oscar Gamble	1.00	.50	.30
	Panel (50)	10.00	5.00	3.00
148	Jim Hunter	4.50	2.25	1.25
149	Tug McGraw	1.25	.60	.40
150	Dave McNally	1.00	.50	.30

1975 Hostess Twinkies

HANK AARON DESIGNATED HITTER Milwaukee BREWERS

Believed to have been issued only in selected markets, and on a limited basis at that, the 1975 Hostess Twinkie set features 60 of the cards from the "regular" Hostess set of that year. The cards were issued one per pack with the popular snack cake. Cards #1-36 are a direct pick-up from the Hostess set, while the remaining 24 cards in the set were selected from the more popular names in the remainder of the Hostess issue - with an emphasis on West Coast players. Thus, after card #36, the '75 Twinkie cards are skip-numbered from 40-136. In identical 2-1/4" x 3-1/4" size, the Twinkie cards differ from the Hostess issue only in the presence of small black bars at top and bottom center of the back of the card. While cards actually issued with snack cakes are virtually always found with brown stains, enough unissued cards were leaked into the hobby to provide clean examples for those willing to search them out and pay the price.

		NM	EX	VG
	Complete Set (60):	800.00	325.00	80.00
	Common Player:	4.00	1.50	.40
1	Bobby Tolan	4.00	1.50	.40
2	Cookie Rojas	4.00	1.50	.40
3	Darrell Evans	4.00	1.50	.40
4	Sal Bando	4.00	1.50	.40
5	Joe Morgan	24.00	9.50	2.50
6	Mickey Lolich	6.00	2.50	.60
7	Don Sutton	20.00	8.00	2.00
8	Bill Melton	4.00	1.50	.40
9	Tim Foli	4.00	1.50	.40
10	Joe Lahoud	4.00	1.50	.40
11	Bert Hooten (Burt Hooton)	4.00	1.50	.40
12	Paul Blair	4.00	1.50	.40
13	Jim Barr	4.00	1.50	.40
14	Toby Harrah	4.00	1.50	.40
15	John Milner	4.00	1.50	.40
16	Ken Holtzman	4.00	1.50	.40
17	Cesar Cedeno	4.00	1.50	.40
18	Dwight Evans	4.00	1.50	.40
19	Willie McCovey	24.00	9.50	2.50
20	Tony Oliva	8.00	3.25	.80
21	Manny Sanguillen	4.00	1.50	.40
22	Mickey Rivers	4.00	1.50	.40
23	Lou Brock	24.00	9.50	2.50
24	Graig Nettles	6.00	2.50	.60
25	Jim Wynn	4.00	1.50	.40
26	George Scott	4.00	1.50	.40
27	Greg Luzinski	4.00	1.50	.40
28	Bert Campaneris	4.00	1.50	.40
29	Pete Rose	80.00	32.00	8.00
30	Buddy Bell	4.00	1.50	.40
31	Gary Matthews	4.00	1.50	.40
32	Fred Patek	4.00	1.50	.40
33	Mike Lum	4.00	1.50	.40
34	Ellie Rodriguez	4.00	1.50	.40
35	Milt May (Photo actually Lee May.)	4.00	1.50	.40
36	Willie Horton	4.00	1.50	.40
40	Joe Rudi	4.00	1.50	.40
43	Garry Maddox	4.00	1.50	.40
46	Dave Chalk	4.00	1.50	.40
49	Steve Garvey	15.00	6.00	1.50

#	Player	NM	EX	VG
52	Rollie Fingers	20.00	8.00	2.00
58	Nolan Ryan	100.00	40.00	10.00
61	Ron Cey	4.00	1.50	.40
64	Gene Tenace	4.00	1.50	.40
65	Jose Cardenal	4.00	1.50	.40
67	Dave Lopes	4.00	1.50	.40
68	Wilbur Wood	4.00	1.50	.40
73	Chris Speier	4.00	1.50	.40
77	Don Kessinger	4.00	1.50	.40
79	Andy Messersmith	4.00	1.50	.40
80	Robin Yount	40.00	16.00	.40
82	Bill Singer	4.00	1.50	.40
103	Glenn Beckert	4.00	1.50	.40
110	Jim Kaat	6.00	2.50	.60
112	Don Money	4.00	1.50	.40
113	Rick Monday	4.00	1.50	.40
122	Jorge Orta	4.00	1.50	.40
125	Bill Madlock	4.00	1.50	.40
130	Hank Aaron	75.00	30.00	7.50
136	Ken Henderson	4.00	1.50	.40

1976 Hostess

The second of five annual Hostess issues, the 1976 cards carried a "Bicentennial" color theme, with red, white and blue stripes at the bottom of the 2-1/4" x 3-1/4" cards. Like other Hostess issues, the cards were printed in panels of three as the bottom of family-size boxes of snack cake products. This leads to a degree of scarcity for some of the 150 cards in the set; those which were found on less-popular brands. A well-trimmed three-card panel measures 7-1/4" x 3-1/4". Some of the photos used in the 1976 Hostess set can also be found on Topps issues of the era. A "Hostess All-Star Team" album with spaces for 18 cards was available.

#	Player	NM	EX	VG
	Complete Panel Set (50):	300.00	150.00	90.00
	Complete Set, Singles (150):	250.00	125.00	75.00
	Common Panel:	5.00	2.50	1.50
	Common Player:	.75	.40	.25
	Album:	20.00	10.00	6.00
	Panel (1)	20.00	10.00	6.00
1	Fred Lynn	1.00	.50	.30
2	Joe Morgan	5.00	2.50	1.50
3	Phil Niekro	4.00	2.00	1.25
	Panel (2)	10.00	5.00	3.00
4	Gaylord Perry	4.00	2.00	1.25
5	Bob Watson	.75	.40	.25
6	Bill Freehan	.75	.40	.25
	Panel (3)	10.00	5.00	3.00
7	Lou Brock	5.00	2.50	1.50
8	Al Fitzmorris	.75	.40	.25
9	Rennie Stennett	.75	.40	.25
	Panel (4)	10.00	5.00	3.00
10	Tony Oliva	1.00	.50	.30
11	Robin Yount	5.00	2.50	1.50
12	Rick Manning	.75	.40	.25
	Panel (5)	7.00	3.50	2.00
13	Bobby Grich	.75	.40	.25
14	Terry Forster	.75	.40	.25
15	Dave Kingman	1.00	.50	.30
	Panel (6)	10.00	5.00	3.00
16	Thurman Munson	4.50	2.25	1.25
17	Rick Reuschel	.75	.40	.25
18	Bobby Bonds	1.00	.50	.30
	Panel (7)	10.00	5.00	3.00
19	Steve Garvey	3.50	1.75	1.00
20	Vida Blue	.75	.40	.25
21	Dave Rader	.75	.40	.25
	Panel (8)	10.00	5.00	3.00
22	Johnny Bench	5.00	2.50	1.50
23	Luis Tiant	.75	.40	.25
24	Darrell Evans	.75	.40	.25
	Panel (9)	7.00	3.50	2.00
25	Larry Dierker	.75	.40	.25
26	Willie Horton	.75	.40	.25
27	John Ellis	.75	.40	.25
	Panel (10)	7.00	3.50	2.00
28	Al Cowens	.75	.40	.25
29	Jerry Reuss	.75	.40	.25
30	Reggie Smith	.75	.40	.25
	Panel (11)	10.00	5.00	3.00
31	Bobby Darwin	.75	.40	.25
32	Fritz Peterson	.75	.40	.25
33	Rod Carew	5.00	2.50	1.50
	Panel (12)	20.00	10.00	6.00
34	Carlos May	.75	.40	.25
35	Tom Seaver	6.00	3.00	1.75
36	Brooks Robinson	6.00	3.00	1.75
	Panel (13)	7.00	3.50	2.00
37	Jose Cardenal	.75	.40	.25
38	Ron Blomberg	.75	.40	.25
39	Lee Stanton	.75	.40	.25
	Panel (14)	7.00	3.50	2.00
40	Dave Cash	.75	.40	.25
41	John Montefusco	.75	.40	.25
42	Bob Tolan	.75	.40	.25
	Panel (15)	7.00	3.50	2.00
43	Carl Morton	.75	.40	.25
44	Rick Burleson	.75	.40	.25
45	Don Gullett	.75	.40	.25
	Panel (16)	7.00	3.50	2.00
46	Vern Ruhle	.75	.40	.25
47	Cesar Cedeno	.75	.40	.25
48	Toby Harrah	.75	.40	.25
	Panel (17)	10.00	5.00	3.00
49	Willie Stargell	5.00	2.50	1.50
50	Al Hrabosky	.75	.40	.25
51	Amos Otis	.75	.40	.25
	Panel (18)	7.00	3.50	2.00
52	Bud Harrelson	.75	.40	.25
53	Jim Hughes	.75	.40	.25
54	George Scott	.75	.40	.25
	Panel (19)	10.00	5.00	3.00
55	Mike Vail	.75	.40	.25
56	Jim Palmer	5.00	2.50	1.50
57	Jorge Orta	.75	.40	.25
	Panel (20)	7.00	3.50	2.00
58	Chris Chambliss	.75	.40	.25
59	Dave Chalk	.75	.40	.25
60	Ray Burris	.75	.40	.25
	Panel (21)	10.00	5.00	3.00
61	Bert Campaneris	.75	.40	.25
62	Gary Carter	5.00	2.50	1.50
63a	Ron Cey	.75	.40	.25
63b	Ron Cey (Reversed negatives, unissued proof.)	35.00	17.50	10.50
	Panel (22)	27.50	13.50	8.25
64	Carlton Fisk	5.00	2.50	1.50
65	Marty Perez	.75	.40	.25
66	Pete Rose	12.00	6.00	3.50
	Panel (23)	7.00	3.50	2.00
67	Roger Metzger	.75	.40	.25
68	Jim Sundberg	.75	.40	.25
69	Ron LeFlore	.75	.40	.25
	Panel (24)	7.00	3.50	2.00
70	Ted Sizemore	.75	.40	.25
71	Steve Busby	.75	.40	.25
72	Manny Sanguillen	.75	.40	.25
	Panel (25)	10.00	5.00	3.00
73	Larry Hisle	.75	.40	.25
74	Pete Broberg	.75	.40	.25
75	Boog Powell	3.00	1.50	.90
	Panel (26)	8.00	4.00	2.50
76	Ken Singleton	.75	.40	.25
77	Rich Gossage	1.25	.60	.40
78	Jerry Grote	.75	.40	.25
	Panel (27)	35.00	17.50	10.50
79	Nolan Ryan	16.00	8.00	4.75
80	Rick Monday	.75	.40	.25
81	Graig Nettles	1.25	.60	.40
	Panel (28)	27.50	13.50	8.25
82	Chris Speier	.75	.40	.25
83	Dave Winfield	5.00	2.50	1.50
84	Mike Schmidt	7.50	3.75	2.25
	Panel (29)	10.00	5.00	3.00
85	Buzz Capra	.75	.40	.25
86	Tony Perez	5.00	2.50	1.50
87	Dwight Evans	.75	.40	.25
	Panel (30)	7.00	3.50	2.00
88	Mike Hargrove	.75	.40	.25
89	Joe Coleman	.75	.40	.25
90	Greg Gross	.75	.40	.25
	Panel (31)	7.00	3.50	2.00
91	John Mayberry	.75	.40	.25
92	John Candelaria	.75	.40	.25
93	Bake McBride	.75	.40	.25
	Panel (32)	20.00	10.00	6.00
94	Hank Aaron	12.00	6.00	3.50
95	Buddy Bell	.75	.40	.25
96	Steve Braun	.75	.40	.25
	Panel (33)	7.00	3.50	2.00
97	Jon Matlack	.75	.40	.25
98	Lee May	.75	.40	.25
99	Wilbur Wood	.75	.40	.25
	Panel (34)	7.00	3.50	2.00
100	Bill Madlock	.75	.40	.25
101	Frank Tanana	.75	.40	.25
102	Mickey Rivers	.75	.40	.25
	Panel (35)	10.00	5.00	3.00
103	Mike Ivie	.75	.40	.25
104	Rollie Fingers	4.00	2.00	1.25
105	Davey Lopes	.75	.40	.25
	Panel (36)	7.00	3.50	2.00
106	George Foster	.75	.40	.25
107	Denny Doyle	.75	.40	.25
108	Earl Williams	.75	.40	.25
	Panel (37)	7.00	3.50	2.00
109	Tom Veryzer	.75	.40	.25
110	J.R. Richard	.75	.40	.25
111	Jeff Burroughs	.75	.40	.25
	Panel (38)	17.50	8.75	5.25
112	Al Oliver	1.00	.50	.30
113	Ted Simmons	.75	.40	.25
114	George Brett	7.50	3.75	2.25
	Panel (39)	7.00	3.50	2.00
115	Frank Duffy	.75	.40	.25
116	Bert Blyleven	.75	.40	.25
117	Darrell Porter	.75	.40	.25
	Panel (40)	8.00	4.00	2.50
118	Don Baylor	1.00	.50	.30
119	Bucky Dent	.75	.40	.25
120	Felix Millan	.75	.40	.25
	Panel (41)	8.00	4.00	2.50
121a	Mike Cuellar	.75	.40	.25
121b	Andy Messersmith (Unissued proof.)	25.00	12.50	7.50
122	Gene Tenace	.75	.40	.25
123	Bobby Murcer	1.25	.60	.40
	Panel (42)	10.00	5.00	3.00
124	Willie McCovey	5.00	2.50	1.50
125	Greg Luzinski	.75	.40	.25
126	Larry Parrish	.75	.40	.25
	Panel (43)	8.00	4.00	2.50
127	Jim Rice	2.00	1.00	.60
128	Dave Concepcion	.75	.40	.25
129	Jim Wynn	.75	.40	.25
	Panel (44)	7.00	3.50	2.00
130	Tom Grieve	.75	.40	.25
131	Mike Cosgrove	.75	.40	.25
132	Dan Meyer	.75	.40	.25
	Panel (45)	7.00	3.50	2.00
133	Dave Parker	1.00	.50	.30
134	Don Kessinger	.75	.40	.25
135	Hal McRae	.75	.40	.25
	Panel (46)	13.50	6.75	4.00
136	Don Money	.75	.40	.25
137	Dennis Eckersley	5.00	2.50	1.50
138a	Fergie Jenkins	4.00	2.00	1.25
138b	Johnny Briggs (Unissued proof.)	25.00	12.50	7.50
	Panel (47)	10.00	5.00	3.00
139	Mike Torrez	.75	.40	.25
140	Jerry Morales	.75	.40	.25
141	Jim Hunter	4.00	2.00	1.25
	Panel (48)	7.00	3.50	2.00
142	Gary Matthews	.75	.40	.25
143	Randy Jones	.75	.40	.25
144	Mike Jorgensen	.75	.40	.25
	Panel (49)	17.50	8.75	5.25
145	Larry Bowa	.75	.40	.25
146	Reggie Jackson	7.50	3.75	2.25
147	Steve Yeager	.75	.40	.25
	Panel (50)	13.50	6.75	4.00
148	Dave May	.75	.40	.25
149	Carl Yastrzemski	6.00	3.00	1.75
150	Cesar Geronimo	.75	.40	.25

1976 Hostess Twinkies

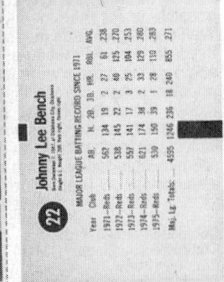

The 60 cards in this regionally issued (test markets only) set closely parallel the first 60 cards in the numerical sequence of the "regular" 1976 Hostess issue. The singular difference is the appearance on the back of a black band toward the center of the card at top and bottom. Also unlike the three-card panels of the regular Hostess issue, the 2-1/4" x 3-1/4" Twinkie cards were issued singly, as the cardboard stiffener for the cellophane-wrapped snack cakes. While cards actually issued with snack cakes are virtually always found with brown stains, enough unissued cards were leaked into the hobby to provide clean examples for those willing to search them out and pay the price.

#	Player	NM	EX	VG
	Complete Set (60):	500.00	200.00	50.00
	Common Player:	4.00	1.50	.40
1	Fred Lynn	4.00	1.50	.40
2	Joe Morgan	24.00	9.50	2.50
3	Phil Niekro	20.00	8.00	2.00
4	Gaylord Perry	20.00	8.00	2.00
5	Bob Watson	4.00	1.50	.40
6	Bill Freehan	4.00	1.50	.40
7	Lou Brock	24.00	9.50	2.50
8	Al Fitzmorris	4.00	1.50	.40
9	Rennie Stennett	4.00	1.50	.40
10	Tony Oliva	6.00	2.50	.60
11	Robin Yount	24.00	9.50	2.50
12	Rick Manning	4.00	1.50	.40
13	Bobby Grich	4.00	1.50	.40
14	Terry Forster	4.00	1.50	.40
15	Dave Kingman	5.00	2.00	.50
16	Thurman Munson	15.00	6.00	1.50
17	Rick Reuschel	4.00	1.50	.40
18	Bobby Bonds	4.00	1.50	.40
19	Steve Garvey	12.00	4.75	1.25
20	Vida Blue	4.00	1.50	.40
21	Dave Rader	4.00	1.50	.40
22	Johnny Bench	24.00	9.50	2.50
23	Luis Tiant	4.00	1.50	.40
24	Darrell Evans	4.00	1.50	.40
25	Larry Dierker	4.00	1.50	.40
26	Willie Horton	4.00	1.50	.40
27	John Ellis	4.00	1.50	.40
28	Al Cowens	4.00	1.50	.40
29	Jerry Reuss	4.00	1.50	.40
30	Reggie Smith	4.00	1.50	.40
31	Bobby Darwin	4.00	1.50	.40
32	Fritz Peterson	4.00	1.50	.40
33	Rod Carew	24.00	9.50	2.50
34	Carlos May	4.00	1.50	.40
35	Tom Seaver	30.00	12.00	3.00
36	Brooks Robinson	24.00	9.50	2.50
37	Jose Cardenal	4.00	1.50	.40
38	Ron Blomberg	4.00	1.50	.40

#	Player	NM	EX	VG
39	Lee Stanton	4.00	1.50	.40
40	Dave Cash	4.00	1.50	.40
41	John Montefusco	4.00	1.50	.40
42	Bob Tolan	4.00	1.50	.40
43	Carl Morton	4.00	1.50	.40
44	Rick Burleson	4.00	1.50	.40
45	Don Gullett	4.00	1.50	.40
46	Vern Ruhle	4.00	1.50	.40
47	Cesar Cedeno	4.00	1.50	.40
48	Toby Harrah	4.00	1.50	.40
49	Willie Stargell	24.00	9.50	2.50
50	Al Hrabosky	4.00	1.50	.40
51	Amos Otis	4.00	1.50	.40
52	Bud Harrelson	4.00	1.50	.40
53	Jim Hughes	4.00	1.50	.40
54	George Scott	4.00	1.50	.40
55	Mike Vail	4.00	1.50	.40
56	Jim Palmer	20.00	8.00	2.00
57	Jorge Orta	4.00	1.50	.40
58	Chris Chambliss	4.00	1.50	.40
59	Dave Chalk	4.00	1.50	.40
60	Ray Burris	4.00	1.50	.40

1976 Hostess Unissued Proofs

STEVE CARLTON
Philadelphia PHILLIES
PITCHER

To help prevent a recurrence of the errors which plagued Hostess' debut set in 1975, the company prepared proof sheets of the cards before they were printed onto the bottoms of snack cake boxes. Probably to have ready substitutes in case problems were found, or a card had to be withdrawn at the last minute, there were seven players printed in proof version that were never issued on boxes. In addition, changes to cards #61, 121 and 138 were made between the proof stage and issued versions (they are detailed in the 1976 Hostess listings). The proofs share the format and 2-1/4" x 3-1/4" size of the issued cards.

		NM	EX	VG
	Complete Set (9):	400.00	200.00	120.00
	Common Player:	40.00	20.00	12.00
151	Fergie Jenkins (Issued as #138.)	75.00	37.50	22.50
152	Mike Cuellar (Issued as #121.)	40.00	20.00	12.00
153	Tom Murphy	40.00	20.00	12.00
154	Dusty Baker	40.00	20.00	12.00
155	Barry Foote	40.00	20.00	12.00
156	Steve Carlton	100.00	50.00	30.00
157	Richie Zisk	40.00	20.00	12.00
158	Ken Holtzman	40.00	20.00	12.00
159	Cliff Johnson	40.00	20.00	12.00

1977 Hostess

PLAYER STATISTICS ON BACK OF EACH CARD

TOM SEAVER — New York METS PITCHER
PETE ROSE — Cincinnati REDS THIRD BASE
ROD CAREW — Minnesota TWINS FIRST BASE

The third of five consecutive annual issues, the 1977 Hostess cards retained the same card size - 2-1/4" x 3-1/4", set size - 150 cards, and mode of issue - three cards on a 7-1/4" x 3-1/4" panel, as the previous two efforts. Because they were issued as the bottom panel of snack cake boxes, and because some brands of

---

Hostess products were more popular than others, certain cards in the set are scarcer than others. A fold-out (to 8-1/2" x 22") All-Star Team album was available.

#	Player	NM	EX	VG
	Complete Panel Set (50):	250.00	125.00	75.00
	Complete Set, Singles (150):	200.00	100.00	60.00
	Common Panel:	4.00	2.00	1.25
	Common Player:	.75	.40	.25
	Album:	20.00	10.00	6.00
	Panel (1)	20.00	10.00	6.00
1	Jim Palmer	3.00	1.50	.90
2	Joe Morgan	3.00	1.50	.90
3a	Reggie Jackson	5.00	2.50	1.50
3b	Rod Carew (Unissued proof.)	20.00	10.00	6.00
	Panel (2)	25.00	12.50	7.50
4	Carl Yastrzemski	3.50	1.75	1.00
5	Thurman Munson	2.50	1.25	.70
6	Johnny Bench	3.50	1.75	1.00
	Panel (3)	30.00	15.00	9.00
7	Tom Seaver	3.00	1.50	.90
8	Pete Rose	7.50	3.75	2.25
9a	Rod Carew	3.00	1.50	.90
9b	Reggie Jackson (Unissued proof.)	75.00	37.00	22.00
	Panel (4)	4.00	2.00	1.25
10	Luis Tiant	.75	.40	.25
11	Phil Garner	.75	.40	.25
12	Sixto Lezcano	.75	.40	.25
	Panel (5)	4.00	2.00	1.25
13	Mike Torrez	.75	.40	.25
14	Davey Lopes	.75	.40	.25
15	Doug DeCinces	.75	.40	.25
	Panel (6)	4.00	2.00	1.25
16	Jim Spencer	.75	.40	.25
17	Hal McRae	.75	.40	.25
18	Mike Hargrove	.75	.40	.25
	Panel (7)	4.00	2.00	1.25
19	Willie Montanez	.75	.40	.25
20	Roger Metzger	.75	.40	.25
21	Dwight Evans	.75	.40	.25
	Panel (8)	5.00	2.50	1.50
22	Steve Rogers	.75	.40	.25
23	Jim Rice	1.25	.60	.40
24	Pete Falcone	.75	.40	.25
	Panel (9)	6.00	3.00	1.75
25	Greg Luzinski	.75	.40	.25
26	Randy Jones	.75	.40	.25
27	Willie Stargell	3.00	1.50	.90
	Panel (10)	5.00	2.50	1.50
28	John Hiller	.75	.40	.25
29	Bobby Murcer	.75	.40	.25
30	Rick Monday	.75	.40	.25
	Panel (11)	6.00	3.00	1.75
31	John Montefusco	.75	.40	.25
32	Lou Brock	3.00	1.50	.90
33	Bill North	.75	.40	.25
	Panel (12)	15.00	7.50	4.50
34	Robin Yount	3.00	1.50	.90
35	Steve Garvey	1.00	.50	.30
36	George Brett	5.00	2.50	1.50
	Panel (13)	4.00	2.00	1.25
37	Toby Harrah	.75	.40	.25
38	Jerry Royster	.75	.40	.25
39	Bob Watson	.75	.40	.25
	Panel (14)	5.00	2.50	1.50
40	George Foster	.75	.40	.25
41	Gary Carter	3.00	1.50	.90
42	John Denny	.75	.40	.25
	Panel (15)	20.00	10.00	6.00
43	Mike Schmidt	5.00	2.50	1.50
44	Dave Winfield	3.00	1.50	.90
45	Al Oliver	.90	.45	.25
	Panel (16)	4.00	2.00	1.25
46	Mark Fidrych	.75	.40	.25
47	Larry Herndon	.75	.40	.25
48	Dave Goltz	.75	.40	.25
	Panel (17)	4.00	2.00	1.25
49	Jerry Morales	.75	.40	.25
50	Ron LeFlore	.75	.40	.25
51	Fred Lynn	.75	.40	.25
	Panel (18)	4.00	2.00	1.25
52	Vida Blue	.75	.40	.25
53	Rick Manning	.75	.40	.25
54	Bill Buckner	.75	.40	.25
	Panel (19)	4.00	2.00	1.25
55	Lee May	.75	.40	.25
56	John Mayberry	.75	.40	.25
57	Darrel Chaney	.75	.40	.25
	Panel (20)	4.00	2.00	1.25
58	Cesar Cedeno	.75	.40	.25
59	Ken Griffey	.75	.40	.25
60	Dave Kingman	.75	.40	.25
	Panel (21)	4.00	2.00	1.25
61	Ted Simmons	.75	.40	.25
62	Larry Bowa	.75	.40	.25
63	Frank Tanana	.75	.40	.25
	Panel (22)	4.00	2.00	1.25
64	Jason Thompson	.75	.40	.25
65	Ken Brett	.75	.40	.25
66	Roy Smalley	.75	.40	.25
	Panel (23)	4.00	2.00	1.25
67	Ray Burris	.75	.40	.25
68	Rick Burleson	.75	.40	.25
69	Buddy Bell	.75	.40	.25
	Panel (24)	5.00	2.50	1.50
70	Don Sutton	2.50	1.25	.70
71	Mark Belanger	.75	.40	.25
72	Dennis Leonard	.75	.40	.25
	Panel (25)	5.00	2.50	1.50
73	Gaylord Perry	2.50	1.25	.70
74	Dick Ruthven	.75	.40	.25
75	Jose Cruz	.75	.40	.25
	Panel (26)	4.00	2.00	1.25
76	Cesar Geronimo	.75	.40	.25
77	Jerry Koosman	.75	.40	.25
78	Garry Templeton	.75	.40	.25

#	Player	NM	EX	VG
	Panel (27)	25.00	12.50	7.50
79	Jim Hunter	2.50	1.25	.70
80	John Candelaria	.75	.40	.25
81	Nolan Ryan	10.00	5.00	3.00
	Panel (28)	4.00	2.00	1.25
82	Rusty Staub	.90	.45	.25
83	Jim Barr	.75	.40	.25
84	Butch Wynegar	.75	.40	.25
	Panel (29)	4.00	2.00	1.25
85	Jose Cardenal	.75	.40	.25
86	Claudell Washington	.75	.40	.25
87	Bill Travers	.75	.40	.25
	Panel (30)	4.00	2.00	1.25
88	Rick Waits	.75	.40	.25
89	Ron Cey	.75	.40	.25
90	Al Bumbry	.75	.40	.25
	Panel (31)	4.00	2.00	1.25
91	Bucky Dent	.90	.45	.25
92	Amos Otis	.75	.40	.25
93	Tom Grieve	.75	.40	.25
	Panel (32)	4.00	2.00	1.25
94	Enos Cabell	.75	.40	.25
95	Dave Concepcion	.75	.40	.25
96	Felix Millan	.75	.40	.25
	Panel (33)	4.00	2.00	1.25
97	Bake McBride	.75	.40	.25
98	Chris Chambliss	.75	.40	.25
99	Butch Metzger	.75	.40	.25
	Panel (34)	4.00	2.00	1.25
100	Rennie Stennett	.75	.40	.25
101	Dave Roberts	.75	.40	.25
102	Lyman Bostock	.75	.40	.25
	Panel (35)	6.00	3.00	1.75
103	Rick Reuschel	.75	.40	.25
104	Carlton Fisk	3.00	1.50	.90
105	Jim Slaton	.75	.40	.25
	Panel (36)	5.00	2.50	1.50
106	Dennis Eckersley	2.50	1.25	.70
107	Ken Singleton	.75	.40	.25
108	Ralph Garr	.75	.40	.25
	Panel (37)	5.00	2.50	1.50
109	Freddie Patek	.75	.40	.25
110	Jim Sundberg	.75	.40	.25
111	Phil Niekro	2.50	1.25	.70
	Panel (38)	4.00	2.00	1.25
112	J.R. Richard	.75	.40	.25
113	Gary Nolan	.75	.40	.25
114	Jon Matlack	.75	.40	.25
	Panel (39)	7.50	3.75	2.25
115	Keith Hernandez	.75	.40	.25
116	Graig Nettles	.90	.45	.25
117	Steve Carlton	3.00	1.50	.90
	Panel (40)	4.00	2.00	1.25
118	Bill Madlock	.75	.40	.25
119	Jerry Reuss	.75	.40	.25
120	Aurelio Rodriguez	.75	.40	.25
	Panel (41)	4.00	2.00	1.25
121	Dan Ford	.75	.40	.25
122	Ray Fosse	.75	.40	.25
123	George Hendrick	.75	.40	.25
	Panel (42)	4.00	2.00	1.25
124	Alan Ashby	.75	.40	.25
125	Joe Lis	.75	.40	.25
126	Sal Bando	.75	.40	.25
	Panel (43)	5.00	2.50	1.50
127	Richie Zisk	.75	.40	.25
128	Rich Gossage	.75	.40	.25
129	Don Baylor	.75	.40	.25
	Panel (44)	4.00	2.00	1.25
130	Dave McKay	.75	.40	.25
131	Bobby Grich	.75	.40	.25
132	Dave Pagan	.75	.40	.25
	Panel (45)	4.00	2.00	1.25
133	Dave Cash	.75	.40	.25
134	Steve Braun	.75	.40	.25
135	Dan Meyer	.75	.40	.25
	Panel (46)	5.00	2.50	1.50
136	Bill Stein	.75	.40	.25
137	Rollie Fingers	2.50	1.25	.70
138	Brian Downing	.75	.40	.25
	Panel (47)	4.00	2.00	1.25
139	Bill Singer	.75	.40	.25
140	Doyle Alexander	.75	.40	.25
141	Gene Tenace	.75	.40	.25
	Panel (48)	4.00	2.00	1.25
142	Gary Matthews	.75	.40	.25
143	Don Gullett	.75	.40	.25
144	Wayne Garland	.75	.40	.25
	Panel (49)	4.00	2.00	1.25
145	Pete Broberg	.75	.40	.25
146	Joe Rudi	.75	.40	.25
147	Glenn Abbott	.75	.40	.25
	Panel (50)	4.00	2.00	1.25
148	George Scott	.75	.40	.25
149	Bert Campaneris	.75	.40	.25
150	Andy Messersmith	.75	.40	.25

1977 Hostess Twinkies

STEVE GARVEY
Los Angeles DODGERS
FIRST BASE

Steven Patrick Garvey

The 1977 Hostess Twinkie issue, at 150 different cards, is the largest of the single-panel Twinkie sets. It is also the most obscure. The cards, which measure 2-1/4" x 3-1/4" but are part of a larger panel, were found not only with Twinkies, but with Hostess Cupcakes as well. Cards #1-30 and 111-150 are Twinkies panels and #31-135 are Cupcakes panels. Complete Cupcakes panels are approximately 2-1/4" x 4-1/2" in size, while complete Twinkies panels measure 3-1/8" x 4-1/4" in size. The photos used in the set are identical to those in the 1977 Hostess three-card panel set. The main difference is the appearance of a black band at the center of the card back. While cards actually issued with snack cakes are virtually always found with brown stains, enough unissued cards were leaked into the hobby to provide clean examples for those willing to search them out and pay the price.

		NM	EX	VG
Complete Set (150):		725.00	300.00	75.00
Common Player:		4.00	1.50	.40
1	Jim Palmer	25.00	10.00	2.50
2	Joe Morgan	25.00	10.00	2.50
3	Reggie Jackson	40.00	16.00	4.00
4	Carl Yastrzemski	32.50	13.00	3.25
5	Thurman Munson	15.00	6.00	1.50
6	Johnny Bench	25.00	10.00	2.50
7	Tom Seaver	25.00	10.00	2.50
8	Pete Rose	65.00	26.00	6.50
9	Rod Carew	25.00	10.00	2.50
10	Luis Tiant	4.00	1.50	.40
11	Phil Garner	4.00	1.50	.40
12	Sixto Lezcano	4.00	1.50	.40
13	Mike Torrez	4.00	1.50	.40
14	Dave Lopes	4.00	1.50	.40
15	Doug DeCinces	4.00	1.50	.40
16	Jim Spencer	4.00	1.50	.40
17	Hal McRae	4.00	1.50	.40
18	Mike Hargrove	4.00	1.50	.40
19	Willie Montanez	4.00	1.50	.40
20	Roger Metzger	4.00	1.50	.40
21	Dwight Evans	4.00	1.50	.40
22	Steve Rogers	4.00	1.50	.40
23	Jim Rice	12.50	5.00	1.25
24	Pete Falcone	4.00	1.50	.40
25	Greg Luzinski	4.00	1.50	.40
26	Randy Jones	4.00	1.50	.40
27	Willie Stargell	25.00	10.00	2.50
28	John Hiller	4.00	1.50	.40
29	Bobby Murcer	4.00	1.50	.40
30	Rick Monday	4.00	1.50	.40
31	John Montefusco	4.00	1.50	.40
32	Lou Brock	25.00	10.00	2.50
33	Bill North	4.00	1.50	.40
34	Robin Yount	25.00	10.00	2.50
35	Steve Garvey	12.50	5.00	1.25
36	George Brett	40.00	16.00	4.00
37	Toby Harrah	4.00	1.50	.40
38	Jerry Royster	4.00	1.50	.40
39	Bob Watson	4.00	1.50	.40
40	George Foster	4.00	1.50	.40
41	Gary Carter	25.00	10.00	2.50
42	John Denny	4.00	1.50	.40
43	Mike Schmidt	40.00	16.00	4.00
44	Dave Winfield	25.00	10.00	2.50
45	Al Oliver	4.00	1.50	.40
46	Mark Fidrych	6.50	2.50	.60
47	Larry Herndon	4.00	1.50	.40
48	Dave Goltz	4.00	1.50	.40
49	Jerry Morales	4.00	1.50	.40
50	Ron LeFlore	4.00	1.50	.40
51	Fred Lynn	4.00	1.50	.40
52	Vida Blue	4.00	1.50	.40
53	Rick Manning	4.00	1.50	.40
54	Bill Buckner	4.00	1.50	.40
55	Lee May	4.00	1.50	.40
56	John Mayberry	4.00	1.50	.40
57	Darrel Chaney	4.00	1.50	.40
58	Cesar Cedeno	4.00	1.50	.40
59	Ken Griffey	4.00	1.50	.40
60	Dave Kingman	6.50	2.50	.60
61	Ted Simmons	4.00	1.50	.40
62	Larry Bowa	4.00	1.50	.40
63	Frank Tanana	4.00	1.50	.40
64	Jason Thompson	4.00	1.50	.40
65	Ken Brett	4.00	1.50	.40
66	Roy Smalley	4.00	1.50	.40
67	Ray Burris	4.00	1.50	.40
68	Rick Burleson	4.00	1.50	.40
69	Buddy Bell	4.00	1.50	.40
70	Don Sutton	20.00	8.00	2.00
71	Mark Belanger	4.00	1.50	.40
72	Dennis Leonard	4.00	1.50	.40
73	Gaylord Perry	20.00	8.00	2.00
74	Dick Ruthven	4.00	1.50	.40
75	Jose Cruz	4.00	1.50	.40
76	Cesar Geronimo	4.00	1.50	.40
77	Jerry Koosman	4.00	1.50	.40
78	Garry Templeton	4.00	1.50	.40
79	Catfish Hunter	20.00	8.00	2.00
80	John Candelaria	4.00	1.50	.40
81	Nolan Ryan	100.00	40.00	10.00
82	Rusty Staub	6.50	2.50	.60
83	Jim Barr	4.00	1.50	.40
84	Butch Wynegar	4.00	1.50	.40
85	Jose Cardenal	4.00	1.50	.40
86	Claudell Washington	4.00	1.50	.40
87	Bill Travers	4.00	1.50	.40
88	Rick Waits	4.00	1.50	.40
89	Ron Cey	4.00	1.50	.40
90	Al Bumbry	4.00	1.50	.40
91	Bucky Dent	4.00	1.50	.40
92	Amos Otis	4.00	1.50	.40
93	Tom Grieve	4.00	1.50	.40
94	Enos Cabell	4.00	1.50	.40
95	Dave Concepcion	4.00	1.50	.40
96	Felix Millan	4.00	1.50	.40
97	Bake McBride	4.00	1.50	.40
98	Chris Chambliss	4.00	1.50	.40
99	Butch Metzger	4.00	1.50	.40
100	Rennie Stennett	4.00	1.50	.40
101	Dave Roberts	4.00	1.50	.40
102	Lyman Bostock	4.00	1.50	.40
103	Rick Reuschel	4.00	1.50	.40
104	Carlton Fisk	25.00	10.00	2.50
105	Jim Slaton	4.00	1.50	.40
106	Dennis Eckersley	20.00	8.00	2.00
107	Ken Singleton	4.00	1.50	.40
108	Ralph Garr	4.00	1.50	.40
109	Freddie Patek	4.00	1.50	.40
110	Jim Sundberg	4.00	1.50	.40
111	Phil Niekro	20.00	8.00	2.00
112	J. R. Richard	4.00	1.50	.40
113	Gary Nolan	4.00	1.50	.40
114	Jon Matlack	4.00	1.50	.40
115	Keith Hernandez	4.00	1.50	.40
116	Graig Nettles	4.00	1.50	.40
117	Steve Carlton	25.00	10.00	2.50
118	Bill Madlock	4.00	1.50	.40
119	Jerry Reuss	4.00	1.50	.40
120	Aurelio Rodriguez	4.00	1.50	.40
121	Dan Ford	4.00	1.50	.40
122	Ray Fosse	4.00	1.50	.40
123	George Hendrick	4.00	1.50	.40
124	Alan Ashby	4.00	1.50	.40
125	Joe Lis	4.00	1.50	.40
126	Sal Bando	4.00	1.50	.40
127	Richie Zisk	4.00	1.50	.40
128	Rich Gossage	6.50	2.50	.60
129	Don Baylor	4.00	1.50	.40
130	Dave McKay	4.00	1.50	.40
131	Bob Grich	4.00	1.50	.40
132	Dave Pagan	4.00	1.50	.40
133	Dave Cash	4.00	1.50	.40
134	Steve Braun	4.00	1.50	.40
135	Dan Meyer	4.00	1.50	.40
136	Bill Stein	4.00	1.50	.40
137	Rollie Fingers	20.00	8.00	2.00
138	Brian Downing	4.00	1.50	.40
139	Bill Singer	4.00	1.50	.40
140	Doyle Alexander	4.00	1.50	.40
141	Gene Tenace	4.00	1.50	.40
142	Gary Matthews	4.00	1.50	.40
143	Don Gullett	4.00	1.50	.40
144	Wayne Garland	4.00	1.50	.40
145	Pete Broberg	4.00	1.50	.40
146	Joe Rudi	4.00	1.50	.40
147	Glenn Abbott	4.00	1.50	.40
148	George Scott	4.00	1.50	.40
149	Bert Campaneris	4.00	1.50	.40
150	Andy Messersmith	4.00	1.50	.40

1977 Hostess Unissued Proofs

The reason for the existence of these rare Hostess proofs is unknown, but there seems little doubt that they were never actually circulated; perhaps being held in reserve in case the cards actually printed on product boxes had to be replaced. The 10 cards were printed on a sheet in three-card panels, like the issued Hostess cards, plus a single of Briles. The proofs share the format of the issued cards, and the 2-1/4" x 3-1/4" size. Besides these "high number" proofs, there also exist numbering-variation proofs of cards #3, 9, 65 and 119 (see 1977 Hostess listings).

		NM	EX	VG
Complete Set (10):		400.00	200.00	120.00
Common Single:		40.00	20.00	12.00
151	Ed Kranepool	40.00	20.00	12.00
152	Ross Grimsley	40.00	20.00	12.00
153	Ken Brett	40.00	20.00	12.00
	(#65 in regular-issue set.)			
154	Rowland Office	40.00	20.00	12.00
155	Rick Wise	40.00	20.00	12.00
156	Paul Splittorff	40.00	20.00	12.00
157	Jerry Augustine	40.00	20.00	12.00
158	Ken Forsch	40.00	20.00	12.00
159	Jerry Reuss	40.00	20.00	12.00
160	Nelson Briles	40.00	20.00	12.00

1978 Hostess

Other than the design on the front of the card, there was little different about the 1978 Hostess cards from the three years' issues which had preceded it, or the one which followed. The 2-1/4" x 3-1/4" cards were printed in panels of three (7-1/4" x 3-1/4") as the bottom of family-sized boxes of snack cakes. The 1978 set was again complete at 150 cards. Like other years

of Hostess issues, there are scarcities within the 1978 set that are the result of those panels having been issued with less-popular brands of snack cakes.

		NM	EX	VG
Complete Panel Set (50):		275.00	135.00	80.00
Complete Set, Singles (150):		225.00	110.00	65.00
Common Panel:		6.00	3.00	1.75
Common Player:		.75	.40	.25
Album:		25.00	12.50	7.50
	Panel (1)	6.00	3.00	1.75
1	Butch Hobson	.75	.40	.25
2	George Foster	.75	.40	.25
3	Bob Forsch	.75	.40	.25
	Panel (2)	13.50	6.75	4.00
4	Tony Perez	4.00	2.00	1.25
5	Bruce Sutter	4.00	2.00	1.25
6	Hal McRae	.75	.40	.25
	Panel (3)	7.50	3.75	2.25
7	Tommy John	1.25	.60	.40
8	Greg Luzinski	.75	.40	.25
9	Enos Cabell	.75	.40	.25
	Panel (4)	10.00	5.00	3.00
10	Doug DeCinces	.75	.40	.25
11	Willie Stargell	4.50	2.25	1.25
12	Ed Halicki	.75	.40	.25
	Panel (5)	6.00	3.00	1.75
13	Larry Hisle	.75	.40	.25
14	Jim Slaton	.75	.40	.25
15	Buddy Bell	.75	.40	.25
	Panel (6)	6.00	3.00	1.75
16	Earl Williams	.75	.40	.25
17	Glenn Abbott	.75	.40	.25
18	Dan Ford	.75	.40	.25
	Panel (7)	6.00	3.00	1.75
19	Gary Matthews	.75	.40	.25
20	Eric Soderholm	.75	.40	.25
21	Bump Wills	.75	.40	.25
	Panel (8)	6.00	3.00	1.75
22	Keith Hernandez	.75	.40	.25
23	Dave Cash	.75	.40	.25
24	George Scott	.75	.40	.25
	Panel (9)	20.00	10.00	6.00
25	Ron Guidry	1.25	.60	.40
26	Dave Kingman	.75	.40	.25
27	George Brett	9.00	4.50	2.75
	Panel (10)	6.00	3.00	1.75
28	Bob Watson	.75	.40	.25
29	Bob Boone	.90	.45	.25
30	Reggie Smith	.75	.40	.25
	Panel (11)	45.00	22.00	13.50
31	Eddie Murray	18.50	9.25	5.50
32	Gary Lavelle	.75	.40	.25
33	Rennie Stennett	.75	.40	.25
	Panel (12)	6.00	3.00	1.75
34	Duane Kuiper	.75	.40	.25
35	Sixto Lezcano	.75	.40	.25
36	Dave Rozema	.75	.40	.25
	Panel (13)	6.00	3.00	1.75
37	Butch Wynegar	.75	.40	.25
38	Mitchell Page	.75	.40	.25
39	Bill Stein	.75	.40	.25
	Panel (14)	6.00	3.00	1.75
40	Elliott Maddox	.75	.40	.25
41	Mike Hargrove	.75	.40	.25
42	Bobby Bonds	.75	.40	.25
	Panel (15)	20.00	10.00	6.00
43	Garry Templeton	.75	.40	.25
44	Johnny Bench	4.50	2.25	1.25
45	Jim Rice	1.50	.70	.45
	Panel (16)	17.50	8.75	5.25
46	Bill Buckner	.75	.40	.25
47	Reggie Jackson	9.00	4.50	2.75
48	Freddie Patek	.75	.40	.25
	Panel (17)	10.00	5.00	3.00
49	Steve Carlton	4.50	2.25	1.25
50	Cesar Cedeno	.75	.40	.25
51	Steve Yeager	.75	.40	.25
	Panel (18)	6.00	3.00	1.75
52	Phil Garner	.75	.40	.25
53	Lee May	.75	.40	.25
54	Darrell Evans	.75	.40	.25
	Panel (19)	6.00	3.00	1.75
55	Steve Kemp	.75	.40	.25
56a	Dusty Baker	.90	.45	.25
56b	Andre Thornton	18.00	9.00	5.50
	(Unissued proof.)			
57	Ray Fosse	.75	.40	.25
	Panel (20)	6.00	3.00	1.75
58	Manny Sanguillen	.75	.40	.25
59	Tom Johnson	.75	.40	.25
60	Lee Stanton	.75	.40	.25

	Panel (21)	10.00	5.00	3.00
61	Jeff Burroughs	.75	.40	.25
62	Bobby Grich	.75	.40	.25
63	Dave Winfield	4.50	2.25	1.25
	Panel (22)	6.00	3.00	1.75
64	Dan Driessen	.75	.40	.25
65	Ted Simmons	.75	.40	.25
66	Jerry Remy	.75	.40	.25
	Panel (23)	6.00	3.00	1.75
67	Al Cowens	.75	.40	.25
68	Sparky Lyle	.75	.40	.25
69	Manny Trillo	.75	.40	.25
	Panel (24)	9.00	4.50	2.75
70	Don Sutton	4.00	2.00	1.25
71	Larry Bowa	.75	.40	.25
72	Jose Cruz	.75	.40	.25
	Panel (25)	10.00	5.00	3.00
73	Willie McCovey	4.50	2.25	1.25
74	Bert Blyleven	.75	.40	.25
75	Ken Singleton	.75	.40	.25
	Panel (26)	6.00	3.00	1.75
76	Bill North	.75	.40	.25
77	Jason Thompson	.75	.40	.25
78	Dennis Eckersley	4.00	2.00	1.25
	Panel (27)	6.00	3.00	1.75
79	Jim Sundberg	.75	.40	.25
80	Jerry Koosman	.75	.40	.25
81	Bruce Bochte	.75	.40	.25
	Panel (28)	45.00	22.00	13.50
82	George Hendrick	.75	.40	.25
83	Nolan Ryan	20.00	10.00	6.00
84	Roy Howell	.75	.40	.25
	Panel (29)	10.00	5.00	3.00
85	Butch Metzger	.75	.40	.25
86	George Medich	.75	.40	.25
87	Joe Morgan	4.50	2.25	1.25
	Panel (30)	6.00	3.00	1.75
88	Dennis Leonard	.75	.40	.25
89	Willie Randolph	.90	.45	.25
90	Bobby Murcer	.90	.45	.25
	Panel (31)	6.00	3.00	1.75
91	Rick Manning	.75	.40	.25
92	J.R. Richard	.75	.40	.25
93	Ron Cey	.75	.40	.25
	Panel (32)	6.00	3.00	1.75
94	Sal Bando	.75	.40	.25
95	Ron LeFlore	.75	.40	.25
96	Dave Goltz	.75	.40	.25
	Panel (33)	6.00	3.00	1.75
97	Dan Meyer	.75	.40	.25
98	Chris Chambliss	.75	.40	.25
99	Biff Pocoroba	.75	.40	.25
	Panel (34)	6.00	3.00	1.75
100	Oscar Gamble	.75	.40	.25
101	Frank Tanana	.75	.40	.25
102	Lenny Randle	.75	.40	.25
	Panel (35)	6.00	3.00	1.75
103	Tommy Hutton	.75	.40	.25
104	John Candelaria	.75	.40	.25
105	Jorge Orta	.75	.40	.25
	Panel (36)	6.00	3.00	1.75
106	Ken Reitz	.75	.40	.25
107	Bill Campbell	.75	.40	.25
108	Dave Concepcion	.75	.40	.25
	Panel (37)	6.00	3.00	1.75
109	Joe Ferguson	.75	.40	.25
110	Mickey Rivers	.75	.40	.25
111	Paul Splittorff	.75	.40	.25
	Panel (38)	20.00	10.00	6.00
112	Davey Lopes	.75	.40	.25
113	Mike Schmidt	9.00	4.50	2.75
114	Joe Rudi	.75	.40	.25
	Panel (39)	10.00	5.00	3.00
115	Milt May	.75	.40	.25
116	Jim Palmer	4.50	2.25	1.25
117	Bill Madlock	.75	.40	.25
	Panel (40)	6.00	3.00	1.75
118	Roy Smalley	.75	.40	.25
119	Cecil Cooper	.75	.40	.25
120	Rick Langford	.75	.40	.25
	Panel (41)	9.00	4.50	2.75
121	Ruppert Jones	.75	.40	.25
122	Phil Niekro	4.00	2.00	1.25
123	Toby Harrah	.75	.40	.25
	Panel (42)	6.00	3.00	1.75
124	Chet Lemon	.75	.40	.25
125	Gene Tenace	.75	.40	.25
126	Steve Henderson	.75	.40	.25
	Panel (43)	35.00	17.50	10.50
127	Mike Torrez	.75	.40	.25
128	Pete Rose	10.00	5.00	3.00
129	John Denny	.75	.40	.25
	Panel (44)	6.00	3.00	1.75
130	Darrell Porter	.75	.40	.25
131	Rick Reuschel	.75	.40	.25
132	Graig Nettles	.90	.45	.25
	Panel (45)	6.00	3.00	1.75
133	Garry Maddox	.75	.40	.25
134	Mike Flanagan	.75	.40	.25
135	Dave Parker	.75	.40	.25
	Panel (46)	10.00	5.00	3.00
136	Terry Whitfield	.75	.40	.25
137	Wayne Garland	.75	.40	.25
138	Robin Yount	4.50	2.25	1.25
	Panel (47)	20.00	10.00	6.00
139a	Gaylord Perry (San Diego)	4.00	2.00	1.25
139b	Gaylord Perry (Texas, unissued proof.)	30.00	15.00	9.00
140	Rod Carew	4.50	2.25	1.25
141	Wayne Gross	.75	.40	.25
	Panel (48)	9.00	4.50	2.75
142	Barry Bonnell	.75	.40	.25
143	Willie Montanez	.75	.40	.25
144	Rollie Fingers	4.00	2.00	1.25
	Panel (49)	35.00	17.50	10.50
145	Lyman Bostock	.75	.40	.25
146	Gary Carter	4.50	2.25	1.25
147	Ron Blomberg	.75	.40	.25
	Panel (50)	30.00	15.00	9.00
148	Bob Bailor	.75	.40	.25
149	Tom Seaver	5.00	2.50	1.50
150	Thurman Munson	4.00	2.00	1.25

1978 Hostess Unissued Proofs

Different versions of two of the issued cards (see 1978 Hostess #56, 139) plus 10 players who do not appear on the snack cake boxes constitute the proof set for '78 Hostess. The unissued proofs are identical in format to the cards actually issued and measure 2-1/4" x 3-1/4" at the dotted lines.

#	Player	NM	EX	VG
	Complete Set (10):	450.00	225.00	135.00
	Common Player:	50.00	25.00	15.00
151	Bill Robinson	50.00	25.00	15.00
152	Lou Piniella	75.00	37.50	22.50
153	Lamar Johnson	50.00	25.00	15.00
154	Mark Belanger	50.00	25.00	15.00
155	Ken Griffey	75.00	37.50	22.50
156	Ken Forsch	50.00	25.00	15.00
157	Ted Sizemore	50.00	25.00	15.00
158	Don Baylor	50.00	25.00	15.00
159	Dusty Baker	60.00	30.00	18.00
160	Al Oliver	75.00	37.50	22.50

1979 Hostess

The last of five consecutive annual issues, the 1979 Hostess set retained the 150-card set size, 2-1/4" x 3-1/4" single-card size and 7-1/4" x 3-1/4" three-card panel format from the previous years. The cards were printed as the bottom panel on family-size boxes of Hostess snack cakes. Some panels, which were printed on less-popular brands, are somewhat scarcer today than the rest of the set. Like all Hostess issues, because the hobby was in a well-developed state at the time of issue, the 1979s survive today in complete panels and complete unused boxes for collectors who like original packaging.

#	Player	NM	EX	VG
	Complete Panel Set (50):	250.00	125.00	75.00
	Complete Singles Set (150):	175.00	85.00	50.00
	Common Panel:	4.50	2.25	1.25
	Common Single Player:	.75	.40	.25
	Panel (1)	7.50	3.75	2.25
1	John Denny	.75	.40	.25
2a	Jim Rice ("d-of," unissued proof.)	15.00	7.50	4.50
2b	Jim Rice ("dh-of")	1.50	.70	.45
3	Doug Bair	.75	.40	.25
	Panel (2)	6.00	3.00	1.75
4	Darrell Porter	.75	.40	.25
5	Ross Grimsley	.75	.40	.25
6	Bobby Murcer	1.00	.50	.30
	Panel (3)	25.00	12.50	7.50
7	Lee Mazzilli	.75	.40	.25
8	Steve Garvey	1.50	.70	.45
9	Mike Schmidt	6.00	3.00	1.75
	Panel (4)	12.00	6.00	3.50
10	Terry Whitfield	.75	.40	.25
11	Jim Palmer	2.50	1.25	.70
12	Omar Moreno	.75	.40	.25
	Panel (5)	5.00	2.50	1.50
13	Duane Kuiper	.75	.40	.25
14	Mike Caldwell	.75	.40	.25
15	Steve Kemp	.75	.40	.25
	Panel (6)	5.00	2.50	1.50
16	Dave Goltz	.75	.40	.25
17	Mitchell Page	.75	.40	.25
18	Bill Stein	.75	.40	.25
	Panel (7)	5.00	2.50	1.50
19	Gene Tenace	.75	.40	.25
20	Jeff Burroughs	.75	.40	.25
21	Francisco Barrios	.75	.40	.25
	Panel (8)	7.50	3.75	2.25
22	Mike Torrez	.75	.40	.25
23	Ken Reitz	.75	.40	.25
24	Gary Carter	2.50	1.25	.70
	Panel (9)	9.00	4.50	2.75
25	Al Hrabosky	.75	.40	.25
26	Thurman Munson	1.50	.70	.45
27	Bill Buckner	.75	.40	.25
	Panel (10)	6.00	3.00	1.75
28	Ron Cey	.75	.40	.25
29	J.R. Richard	.75	.40	.25
30	Greg Luzinski	.75	.40	.25
	Panel (11)	5.00	2.50	1.50
31	Ed Ott	.75	.40	.25
32	Denny Martinez	.75	.40	.25
33	Darrell Evans	.75	.40	.25
	Panel (12)	5.00	2.50	1.50
34	Ron LeFlore	.75	.40	.25
35	Rick Waits	.75	.40	.25
36	Cecil Cooper	.75	.40	.25
	Panel (13)	15.00	7.50	4.50
37	Leon Roberts	.75	.40	.25
38a	Rod Carew (Large head.) (Bottom of collar trim does not show.)	3.00	1.50	.90
38b	Rod Carew (Small head.) (Bottom of collar trim shows.)	3.00	1.50	.90
39	John Henry Johnson	.75	.40	.25
	Panel (14)	5.00	2.50	1.50
40	Chet Lemon	.75	.40	.25
41	Craig Swan	.75	.40	.25
42	Gary Matthews	.75	.40	.25
	Panel (15)	5.00	2.50	1.50
43	Lamar Johnson	.75	.40	.25
44	Ted Simmons	.75	.40	.25
45	Ken Griffey	.75	.40	.25
	Panel (16)	6.00	3.00	1.75
46	Freddie Patek	.75	.40	.25
47	Frank Tanana	.75	.40	.25
48	Rich Gossage	1.00	.50	.30
	Panel (17)	5.00	2.50	1.50
49	Burt Hooton	.75	.40	.25
50	Ellis Valentine	.75	.40	.25
51	Ken Forsch	.75	.40	.25
	Panel (18)	6.00	3.00	1.75
52	Bob Knepper	.75	.40	.25
53	Dave Parker	.75	.40	.25
54	Doug DeCinces	.75	.40	.25
	Panel (19)	20.00	10.00	6.00
55	Robin Yount	3.00	1.50	.90
56	Rusty Staub	1.00	.50	.30
57	Gary Alexander	.75	.40	.25
	Panel (20)	5.00	2.50	1.50
58	Julio Cruz	.75	.40	.25
59	Matt Keough	.75	.40	.25
60	Roy Smalley	.75	.40	.25
	Panel (21)	15.00	7.50	4.50
61	Joe Morgan	3.00	1.50	.90
62	Phil Niekro	2.00	1.00	.60
63	Don Baylor	.75	.40	.25
	Panel (22)	20.00	10.00	6.00
64	Dwight Evans	.75	.40	.25
65	Tom Seaver	3.00	1.50	.90
66	George Hendrick	.75	.40	.25
	Panel (23)	25.00	12.50	7.50
67	Rick Reuschel	.75	.40	.25
68	George Brett	6.00	3.00	1.75
69	Lou Piniella	1.00	.50	.30
	Panel (24)	12.00	6.00	3.50
70	Enos Cabell	.75	.40	.25
71	Steve Carlton	2.50	1.25	.70
72	Reggie Smith	.75	.40	.25
	Panel (25)	5.00	2.50	1.50
73	Rick Dempsey	.75	.40	.25
74	Vida Blue	.75	.40	.25
75	Phil Garner	.75	.40	.25
	Panel (26)	5.00	2.50	1.50
76	Rick Manning	.75	.40	.25
77	Mark Fidrych	1.00	.50	.30
78	Mario Guerrero	.75	.40	.25
	Panel (27)	5.00	2.50	1.50
79	Bob Stinson	.75	.40	.25
80	Al Oliver	.75	.40	.25
81	Doug Flynn	.75	.40	.25
	Panel (28)	7.50	3.75	2.25
82	John Mayberry	.75	.40	.25
83	Gaylord Perry	2.00	1.00	.60
84	Joe Rudi	.75	.40	.25
	Panel (29)	5.00	2.50	1.50
85	Dave Concepcion	.75	.40	.25
86	John Candelaria	.75	.40	.25
87	Pete Vuckovich	.75	.40	.25
	Panel (30)	5.00	2.50	1.50
88	Ivan DeJesus	.75	.40	.25
89	Ron Guidry	.75	.40	.25
90	Hal McRae	.75	.40	.25
	Panel (31)	6.00	3.00	1.75
91	Cesar Cedeno	.75	.40	.25
92	Don Sutton	2.00	1.00	.60
93	Andre Thornton	.75	.40	.25
	Panel (32)	5.00	2.50	1.50
94	Roger Erickson	.75	.40	.25
95	Larry Hisle	.75	.40	.25
96	Jason Thompson	.75	.40	.25
	Panel (33)	5.00	2.50	1.50
97	Jim Sundberg	.75	.40	.25
98	Bob Horner	.75	.40	.25
99	Ruppert Jones	.75	.40	.25
	Panel (34)	60.00	30.00	18.00
100	Willie Montanez	.75	.40	.25
101	Nolan Ryan	12.00	6.00	3.50
102	Ozzie Smith	15.00	7.50	4.50
	Panel (35)	12.00	6.00	3.50
103	Eric Soderholm	.75	.40	.25
104	Willie Stargell	2.50	1.25	.70
105a	Bob Bailor (Photo reversed, unissued proof.)	.75	.40	.25
105b	Bob Bailor (Photo corrected.)	.75	.40	.25
	Panel (36)	12.50	6.25	3.75
106	Carlton Fisk	2.50	1.25	.70
107	George Foster	.75	.40	.25
108	Keith Hernandez	.75	.40	.25
	Panel (37)	5.00	2.50	1.50
109	Dennis Leonard	.75	.40	.25
110	Graig Nettles	1.00	.50	.30
111	Jose Cruz	.75	.40	.25
	Panel (38)	5.00	2.50	1.50
112	Bobby Grich	.75	.40	.25

No.	Player	NM	EX	VG
113	Bob Boone	.75	.40	.25
114	Davey Lopes	.75	.40	.25
	Panel (39)	15.00	7.50	4.50
115	Eddie Murray	3.00	1.50	.90
116	Jack Clark	.75	.40	.25
117	Lou Whitaker	.75	.40	.25
	Panel (40)	20.00	10.00	.25
118	Miguel Dilone	.75	.40	.25
119	Sal Bando	.75	.40	.25
120	Reggie Jackson	6.00	3.00	1.75
	Panel (41)	15.00	7.50	4.50
121	Dale Murphy	2.00	1.00	.60
122	Jon Matlack	.75	.40	.25
123	Bruce Bochte	.75	.40	.25
	Panel (42)	12.50	6.25	3.75
124	John Stearns	.75	.40	.25
125	Dave Winfield	3.00	1.50	.90
126	Jorge Orta	.75	.40	.25
	Panel (43)	25.00	12.50	7.50
127	Garry Templeton	.75	.40	.25
128	Johnny Bench	3.00	1.50	.90
129	Butch Hobson	.75	.40	.25
	Panel (44)	6.00	3.00	1.75
130	Bruce Sutter	2.50	1.25	.70
131	Bucky Dent	.75	.40	.25
132	Amos Otis	.75	.40	.25
	Panel (45)	5.00	2.50	1.50
133	Bert Blyleven	.75	.40	.25
134	Larry Bowa	.75	.40	.25
135	Ken Singleton	.75	.40	.25
	Panel (46)	5.00	2.50	1.50
136	Sixto Lezcano	.75	.40	.25
137	Roy Howell	.75	.40	.25
138	Bill Madlock	.75	.40	.25
	Panel (47)	5.00	2.50	1.50
139	Dave Revering	.75	.40	.25
140	Richie Zisk	.75	.40	.25
141	Butch Wynegar	.75	.40	.25
	Panel (48)	25.00	12.50	7.50
142	Alan Ashby	.75	.40	.25
143	Sparky Lyle	.75	.40	.25
144	Pete Rose	7.50	3.75	2.25
	Panel (49)	6.00	3.00	1.75
145	Dennis Eckersley	2.50	1.25	.70
146	Dave Kingman	.75	.40	.25
147	Buddy Bell	.75	.40	.25
	Panel (50)	5.00	2.50	1.50
148	Mike Hargrove	.75	.40	.25
149	Jerry Koosman	.75	.40	.25
150	Toby Harrah	.75	.40	.25

1979 Hostess Unissued Proofs

Identical in format to the 150 cards which were issued on boxes of Hostess snack cakes, these cards were possibly prepared in the event trades of players in the issued set required quick replacement. The reason these cards were never released is unknown. Cards measure 2-1/4" x 3-1/4" at the dotted-line borders. While some of the proofs are numbered on back, others have no card number.

		NM	EX	VG
Complete Set (17):		1,100	550.00	330.00
Common Player:		50.00	25.00	15.00
151	Dusty Baker	60.00	30.00	18.00
152	Mark Belanger	60.00	30.00	18.00
154	Al Cowens	50.00	25.00	15.00
155	Dan Driessen	50.00	25.00	15.00
157	Steve Henderson	50.00	25.00	15.00
159	Tommy John	75.00	37.50	22.50
160	Garry Maddox	50.00	25.00	15.00
(161)	Willie McCovey	250.00	125.00	75.00
(162)	Scott McGregor	50.00	25.00	15.00
(163)	Bill Nahorodny	50.00	25.00	15.00
(164)	Terry Puhl	50.00	25.00	15.00
(165)	Willie Randolph	50.00	25.00	15.00
(166)	Jim Slaton	50.00	25.00	15.00
(167)	Paul Splittorff	50.00	25.00	15.00
(168)	Frank Taveras	50.00	25.00	15.00
(169)	Alan Trammell	125.00	65.00	35.00
(170)	Bump Wills	50.00	25.00	15.00

1971 House of Jazz

Controversy has dogged this card set since the first reports of its existence in the early 1970s. The legitimacy of the issue has been questioned though certain hobby journalists traced the cards to a record store which supposedly gave them away with music purchases, along with similar cards depicting musicians. The 2-3/8" x 3-1/2" cards are printed in black-and-white with round corners. Backs of some, but not all, cards have a blue-and-white address sticker for "HOUSE OF JAZZ, LTD." The unnumbered cards are checklisted here in alphabetical order.

		NM	EX	VG
Complete Set (35):		200.00	100.00	60.00
Common Player:		5.00	2.50	1.50
(1)	John Antonelli	5.00	2.50	1.50
(2)	Richie Ashburn	6.00	3.00	1.75
(3)	Ernie Banks	6.50	3.25	2.00
(4)	Hank Bauer	5.00	2.50	1.50
(5)	Joe DiMaggio	15.00	7.50	4.50
(6)	Bobby Doerr	5.00	2.50	1.50
(7)	Herman Franks	5.00	2.50	1.50
(8)	Lou Gehrig	15.00	7.50	4.50
(9)	Granny Hamner	5.00	2.50	1.50
(10)	Al Kaline	6.50	3.25	2.00
(11)	Harmon Killebrew	6.00	3.00	1.75
(12)	Jim Konstanty	5.00	2.50	1.50
(13)	Bob Lemon	5.00	2.50	1.50
(14)	Ed Lopat	5.00	2.50	1.50
(15)	Stan Lopata	5.00	2.50	1.50
(16)	Peanuts Lowrey	5.00	2.50	1.50
(17)	Mickey Mantle	35.00	17.50	10.00
(18)	Phil Marchildon	5.00	2.50	1.50
(19)	Walt Masterson	5.00	2.50	1.50
(20)	Ed Mathews	6.00	3.00	1.75
(21)	Willie Mays	10.00	5.00	3.00
(22)	Don Newcombe	5.00	2.50	1.50
(23)	Joe Nuxhall	5.00	2.50	1.50
(24)	Satchel Paige	7.50	3.75	2.25
(25)	Roy Partee	5.00	2.50	1.50
(26)	Jackie Robinson	7.50	3.75	2.25
(27)	Babe Ruth	20.00	10.00	6.00
(28)	Carl Scheib	5.00	2.50	1.50
(29)	Bobby Shantz	5.00	2.50	1.50
(30)	Burt Shotton	5.00	2.50	1.50
(31)	Duke Snider	6.50	3.25	2.00
(32)	Warren Spahn	6.00	3.00	1.75
(33)	Johnny Temple	5.00	2.50	1.50
(34)	Ted Williams	10.00	5.00	3.00
(35)	Early Wynn	5.00	2.50	1.50

1962 Houston Colt .45s Booklets

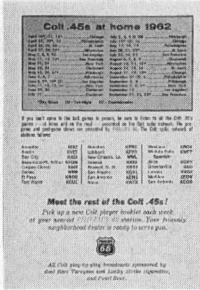

To introduce the members of the new Houston National League team, Phillips 66 gasoline sponsored (along with the team's cigarette and beer broadcast sponsors) this set of 24 player profile booklets given away one per week during the season. Fronts of the 16-page 5-3/8" x 7-7/16" booklets feature a blue and white action photo of the player on a bright orange background. Black and white graphics complete the design. The player's name appears in a Texas map outline. Backs have the 1962 Houston Colt .45s home-game schedule and details of the team's statewide radio network. Inside the booklet are a complete biography, stats and both posed and action photos of the players, along with families, teammates, etc. Because of player trades during the season, and lessened demand for some of the non-player booklets, some of the series are quite scarce. Each of the booklets can be found with different sponsors logos on front.

		NM	EX	VG
Complete Set (24):		240.00	120.00	72.00
Common Booklet:		15.00	7.50	4.50
(1)	Joe Amalfitano	15.00	7.50	4.50
(2)	Bob Aspromonte	15.00	7.50	4.50
(3)	Bob Bruce	15.00	7.50	4.50
(4)	Jim Campbell	18.00	9.00	5.50
(5)	Harry Craft	15.00	7.50	4.50
(6)	Dick Farrell	15.00	7.50	4.50
(7)	Dave Giusti	15.00	7.50	4.50
(8)	Jim Golden	15.00	7.50	4.50
(9)	J.C. Hartman	18.00	9.00	5.50
(10)	Ken Johnson	15.00	7.50	4.50
(11)	Norm Larker	15.00	7.50	4.50
(12)	Bob Lillis	15.00	7.50	4.50
(13)	Don McMahon	15.00	7.50	4.50
(14)	Roman Mejias	15.00	7.50	4.50
(15)	Jim Pendleton	18.00	9.00	5.50
(16)	Paul Richards (GM)	15.00	7.50	4.50
(17)	Bobby Shantz	30.00	15.00	9.00
(18)	Hal Smith	15.00	7.50	4.50
(19)	Al Spangler	15.00	7.50	4.50
(20)	Jim Umbricht	15.00	7.50	4.50
(21)	Carl Warwick	15.00	7.50	4.50
(22)	Hal Woodeshick	15.00	7.50	4.50
(23)	Coaches (James Adair, Bobby Bragan, Cot Deal, Luman Harris)	25.00	12.50	7.50
(24)	Announcers (Rene Cardenas, Orlando Diego, Gene Elston, Al Helfer, Lowell Passe, Guy Savage)	19.00	9.50	5.75

1967 Houston Astros Team Issue

This set of 12 player cards was issued by the Houston Astros, though the exact nature of the promotion is not known. Individual cards of 2-5/8" x 3-1/8" were printed on a perforated sheet about 9" x 10-1/2". Fronts have a posed color photo with a black facsimile autograph. Backs are printed in black on white with a yellow color block behind the player data and career notes. Full major and minor league stats are at bottom. The unnumbered cards are checklisted here in alphabetical order.

		NM	EX	VG
Complete Set, Sheet:		65.00	32.50	20.00
Complete Set, Singles (12):		65.00	32.50	20.00
Common Player:		8.00	4.00	2.50
(1)	Bob Aspromonte	8.00	4.00	2.50
(2)	John Bateman	8.00	4.00	2.50
(3)	Mike Cuellar	8.00	4.00	2.50
(4)	Larry Dierker	8.00	4.00	2.50
(5)	Dave Giusti	8.00	4.00	2.50
(6)	Grady Hatton	8.00	4.00	2.50
(7)	Bill Heath	8.00	4.00	2.50
(8)	Sonny Jackson	8.00	4.00	2.50
(9)	Ed Mathews	20.00	10.00	6.00
(10)	Joe Morgan	20.00	10.00	6.00
(11)	Rusty Staub	12.50	6.25	3.75
(12)	Jim Wynn	8.00	4.00	2.50

1953-1955 Howard Photo Service Postcards

Little is known about these postcards. Player and team combinations on the known pieces suggest a range of issue dates between 1953 and 1955. The 3-1/2" x 5-5/8" cards have a glossy black-and-white front photo. A rubber-stamp on the back attributes the card to "Howard Photo Service, N.Y.C." The specific pose on the second Turley card is not known. It is possible other cards may yet be discovered.

		NM	EX	VG
Common Player:		20.00	10.00	6.00
(1)	Ned Garver	20.00	10.00	6.00
(2)	Billy Hitchcock	20.00	10.00	6.00
(3)	Dave Madison	20.00	10.00	6.00
(4)	Willie Mays	165.00	85.00	50.00
(5)	Willie Mays	200.00	100.00	60.00
	(Seven-Up ad on back.)			
(6)	Bob Turley (Follow-through.)	30.00	15.00	9.00
(7)	Bob Turley (Wind-up.)	30.00	15.00	9.00

1976 HRT/RES 1942 Play Ball

TED WILLIAMS — Of
Boston Red Sox

This "phantom" continuation of the Play Ball series of 1939-41 was the creation of Ted Taylor and Bob Schmierer, whose initials appear in the copyright line on back. The 2-1/2" x 3-1/8" cards feature black-and-white photos on front and were printed on gray clay-content cardboard in a near replication of the stock found on the vintage Play Ball series. Backs were also done in style reminiscent of 1940s issues. Besides player data and career summaries, backs have a "1942 PLAY BALL - U.S.A." title line and either a "Buy War Bonds" or "'Keep Baseball Going' - FDR" slogan above the 1976 copyright line. The pair produced a number of other original and reprint issues in the 1970s. All of the others carry advertisements for their "Philly" card shows.

		NM	EX	VG
Complete Set (36):		30.00	15.00	9.00
Common Card:		1.00	.50	.30
1	Lou Gehrig	7.50	3.75	2.25
2	Joe DiMaggio	7.50	3.75	2.25
3	Phil Rizzuto	3.00	1.50	.90
4	Ted Williams	6.00	3.00	1.75
5	Charles Wagner	1.00	.50	.30
6	Thornton Lee	1.00	.50	.30
7	Taft Wright	1.00	.50	.30
8	Jeff Heath	1.00	.50	.30
9	Roy Mack	1.00	.50	.30
10	Pat Mullin	1.00	.50	.30
11	Al Benton	1.00	.50	.30
12	Bob Harris	1.00	.50	.30
13	Roy Cullenbine	1.00	.50	.30
14	Cecil Travis	1.00	.50	.30
15	Buck Newsom	1.00	.50	.30
16	Eddie Collins Jr.	1.00	.50	.30
17	Dick Siebert	1.00	.50	.30
18	Dee Miles	1.00	.50	.30
19	Pete Reiser	1.00	.50	.30
20	Dolph Camilli	1.00	.50	.30
21	Curt Davis	1.00	.50	.30
22	Spud Krist	1.00	.50	.30
23	Frank Crespi	1.00	.50	.30
24	Elmer Riddle	1.00	.50	.30
25	Bucky Walters	1.00	.50	.30
26	Vince DiMaggio	1.50	.70	.45
27	Max Butcher	1.00	.50	.30
28	Mel Ott	3.00	1.50	.90
29	Bob Carpenter	1.00	.50	.30
30	Claude Passeau	1.00	.50	.30
31	Dom Dallessandro	1.00	.50	.30
32	Casey Stengel	3.00	1.50	.90
33	Alva Javery	1.00	.50	.30
34	Hans Lobert	1.00	.50	.30
35	Nick Etten	1.00	.50	.30
36	John Podgajny	1.00	.50	.30

1976-77 HRT/RES 1947 Bowman

Advertised as "The Set That Never Was," this collectors' issue from Ted Taylor and Bob Schmierer used a 2-1/8" x 2-1/2" black-and-white format and gray cardboard stock to replicate the feel of the first post-WWII baseball cards. The set was issued in three series with advertising on back promoting the second (1976) and third (1977) annual EPSCC "Philly" shows. Series one (#1-49) was issued in 1976; series two (#50-81) and three (#82-113) were 1977 issues.

		NM	EX	VG
Complete Set (113):		90.00	45.00	27.50
Common Player:		1.00	.50	.30
1	Bobby Doerr	1.00	.50	.30
2	Stan Musial	3.00	1.50	.90
3	Babe Ruth	7.50	3.75	2.25
4	Joe DiMaggio	6.00	3.00	1.75
5	Andy Pafko	1.00	.50	.30
6	Johnny Pesky	1.00	.50	.30
7	Gil Hodges	1.50	.70	.45

		NM	EX	VG
8	Tommy Holmes	1.00	.50	.30
9	Ralph Kiner	1.00	.50	.30
10	Yogi Berra	2.00	1.00	.60
11	Bob Feller	1.50	.70	.45
12	Joe Gordon	1.00	.50	.30
13	Eddie Joost	1.00	.50	.30
14	Del Ennis	1.00	.50	.30
15	Johnny Mize	1.00	.50	.30
16	Pee Wee Reese	1.25	.60	.40
17	Jackie Robinson	4.00	2.00	1.25
18	Enos Slaughter	1.00	.50	.30
19	Vern Stephens	1.00	.50	.30
20	Bobby Thomson	1.00	.50	.30
21	Ted Williams	6.00	3.00	1.75
22	Bob Elliott	1.00	.50	.30
23	Mickey Vernon	1.00	.50	.30
24	Ewell Blackwell	1.00	.50	.30
25	Lou Boudreau	1.00	.50	.30
26	Ralph Branca	1.00	.50	.30
27	Harry Breechen (Brecheen)	1.00	.50	.30
28	Dom DiMaggio	1.00	.50	.30
29	Bruce Edwards	1.00	.50	.30
30	Sam Chapman	1.00	.50	.30
31	George Kell	1.00	.50	.30
32	Jack Kramer	1.00	.50	.30
33	Hal Newhouser	1.00	.50	.30
34	Charlie Keller	1.00	.50	.30
35	Ken Keltner	1.00	.50	.30
36	Hank Greenberg	1.25	.60	.40
37	Howie Pollet	1.00	.50	.30
38	Luke Appling	1.00	.50	.30
39	Pete Suder	1.00	.50	.30
40	Johnny Sain	1.00	.50	.30
41	Phil Cavaretta (Cavarretta)	1.00	.50	.30
42	Johnny Vander Meer	1.00	.50	.30
43	Mel Ott	1.00	.50	.30
44	Walker Cooper	1.00	.50	.30
45	Birdie Tebbetts	1.00	.50	.30
46	George Stirnweiss	1.00	.50	.30
47	Connie Mack	1.00	.50	.30
48	Jimmie Foxx	1.00	.50	.30
49	Checklist (Joe DiMaggio, Babe Ruth)	1.50	.70	.45
(50)	Honus Wagner T206 card (First series.)	1.00	.50	.30
51	Ted Taylor (First series.)	1.00	.50	.30
52	Bob Schmierer (First series.)	1.00	.50	.30
50	Schoolboy Rowe (Second series.)	1.00	.50	.30
51	Andy Seminick (Second series.)	1.00	.50	.30
52	Fred Walker (Second series.)	1.00	.50	.30
53	Virgil Trucks	1.00	.50	.30
54	Dizzy Trout	1.00	.50	.30
55	Walter Evers	1.00	.50	.30
56	Thurman Tucker	1.00	.50	.30
57	Fritz Ostermueller	1.00	.50	.30
58	Augie Galan	1.00	.50	.30
59	Norman Young	1.00	.50	.30
60	Skeeter Newsome	1.00	.50	.30
61	Jack Lohrke	1.00	.50	.30
62	Rudy York	1.00	.50	.30
63	Tex Hughson	1.00	.50	.30
64	Sam Mele	1.00	.50	.30
65	Fred Hutchinson	1.00	.50	.30
66	Don Black	1.00	.50	.30
67	Les Fleming	1.00	.50	.30
68	George McQuinn	1.00	.50	.30
69	Mike McCormick	1.00	.50	.30
70	Mickey Witek	1.00	.50	.30
71	Blix Donnelly	1.00	.50	.30
72	Elbie Fletcher	1.00	.50	.30
73	Hal Gregg	1.00	.50	.30
74	Dick Whitman	1.00	.50	.30
75	Johnny Neun	1.00	.50	.30
76	Doyle Lade	1.00	.50	.30
77	Ron Northey	1.00	.50	.30
78	Walker Cooper	1.00	.50	.30
79	Warren Spahn	1.00	.50	.30
80	Happy Chandler	1.00	.50	.30
81	Checklist (Connie Mack, Roy Mack, Connie Mack III)	1.00	.50	.30
82	Earle Mack	1.00	.50	.30
83	Buddy Rosar	1.00	.50	.30
84	Walt Judnich	1.00	.50	.30
85	Bob Kennedy	1.00	.50	.30
86	Mike Tresh	1.00	.50	.30
87	Sid Hudson	1.00	.50	.30
88	Eugene Thompson	1.00	.50	.30
89	Bill Nicholson	1.00	.50	.30
90	Stan Hack	1.00	.50	.30
91	Terry Moore	1.00	.50	.30
92	Ted Lyons	1.00	.50	.30
93	Barney McCosky	1.00	.50	.30
94	Stan Spence	1.00	.50	.30
95	Larry Jansen	1.00	.50	.30
96	Whitey Kurowski	1.00	.50	.30
97	Honus Wagner	1.50	.70	.45
98	Billy Herman	1.00	.50	.30
99	Jim Tabor	1.00	.50	.30
100	Phil Marchildon	1.00	.50	.30
101	Dave Ferriss	1.00	.50	.30
102	Al Zarilla	1.00	.50	.30
103	Bob Dillinger	1.00	.50	.30
104	Bob Lemon	1.00	.50	.30
105	Jim Hegan	1.00	.50	.30
106	Johnny Lindell	1.00	.50	.30
107	Willard Marshall	1.00	.50	.30
108	Walt Masterson	1.00	.50	.30
109	Carl Scheib	1.00	.50	.30
110	Bobby Brown	1.00	.50	.30
111	Cy Block	1.00	.50	.30
112	Sid Gordon	1.00	.50	.30
113	Checklist (Ty Cobb, Babe Ruth, Tris Speaker)	1.50	.70	.45

1977 HRT/RES Philadelphia 'Favorites'

ROBIN ROBERTS, Pitcher
Phillies, 1948-61

This collectors issue was produced by promoters Ted Taylor and Bob Schmierer to promote their third annual "Philly Show" in 1977. Printed in black-and-white on front and back, the 2-3/8" x 3-5/8" cards feature former Philadelphia A's and Phillies player photos on front, and an ad for the show on back. Cards were given away at area malls and sporting events to promote the show. Complete sets were originally sold for $2.75.

		NM	EX	VG
Complete Set (25):		30.00	15.00	9.00
Common Player:		2.00	1.00	.60
1	Connie Mack	2.00	1.00	.60
2	Larry Lajoie	2.50	1.25	.70
3	Eddie Collins	2.00	1.00	.60
4	Lefty Grove	2.50	1.25	.70
5	Al Simmons	2.00	1.00	.60
6	Jimmie Foxx	3.00	1.50	.90
7	Frank Baker	2.00	1.00	.60
8	Ferris Fain	2.00	1.00	.60
9	Jimmy Dykes	2.00	1.00	.60
10	Willie Jones	2.00	1.00	.60
11	Del Ennis	2.00	1.00	.60
12	Granny Hamner	2.00	1.00	.60
13	Andy Seminick	2.00	1.00	.60
14	Robin Roberts	4.00	2.00	1.25
15	Ed Delahanty	2.00	1.00	.60
16	Gavvy Cravath	2.00	1.00	.60
17	Cy Williams	2.00	1.00	.60
18	Chuck Klein	2.00	1.00	.60
19	Rich Ashburn	4.00	2.00	1.25
20	Bobby Shantz	2.00	1.00	.60
21	Gus Zernial	2.00	1.00	.60
22	Eddie Sawyer	2.00	1.00	.60
23	Grover Alexander	2.00	1.00	.60
24	Wally Moses	2.00	1.00	.60
25	Connie Mack Stadium	2.00	1.00	.60

1978 HRT/RES 1939 Father and Son Reprints

Wally Moses, outfielder, Phila. Athletics

Reprints of scarce 1939 Father and Son Shoes stores cards of local ballplayers (minus the original advertising on front) were created by Ted Taylor and Bob Schmierer to promote their fourth "Philly Show" in March, 1978. The 3" x 4" cards have black-and-white player photos on front. Backs carry an ad for the show and information about the reprints.

		NM	EX	VG
Complete Set (8):		7.50	3.75	2.25
Common Player:		1.00	.50	.30
(1)	Sam Chapman	1.00	.50	.30
(2)	Chuck Klein	1.50	.70	.45
(3)	Herschel Martin	1.00	.50	.30
(4)	Wally Moses	1.00	.50	.30
(5)	Hugh Mulcahy	1.00	.50	.30
(6)	Skeeter Newsome	1.00	.50	.30
(7)	George Scharien (Scharein)	1.00	.50	.30
(8)	Dick Siebert	1.00	.50	.30

1979 HRT/RES 1950 Phillies/ A's "Doubleheaders"

Though their names or initials do not appear on the cards, this collectors' set was issued by Ted Taylor and Bob Schmierer to promote the March and September, 1979, "Philly Shows," the sixth and seventh in the show's history. Borrowing from the format

Stan Lopata, Catcher   Eddie Waitkus, Infield

This card worth 25¢ off admission
6th Philadelphia
BASEBALL CARD SHOW
March 10 - 11, 1979
George Washington Motor Lodge
Willow Grove, Pa.

of the 1941 "Doubleheaders" bubblegum card issue, these 2-1/2" x 2-1/8" cards depict members of the 1950 Phillies "Whiz Kids" and the 1950 A's, the last team managed by Connie Mack. Fronts are printed in blue and white, backs in maroon and white. The dual-player cards feature various ads on back, while the managers' cards have a team narrative. The unnumbered cards are checklisted here alphabetically within team, by the last name of the player on the left.

		NM	EX	VG
Complete Set (30):		25.00	12.50	7.50
Common Card:		1.50	.70	.45
(1)	Joe Astroth, Dick Fowler	1.50	.70	.45
(2)	Sam Chapman, Lou Brissie	1.50	.70	.45
(3)	Bob Dillinger, Billy Hitchcock	1.50	.70	.45
(4)	Ben Guintini, Joe Tipton	1.50	.70	.45
(5)	Bob Hooper, Barney McCosky	1.50	.70	.45
(6)	Eddie Joost, Kermit Wahl	1.50	.70	.45
(7)	Ed Klieman, Mike Guerra	1.50	.70	.45
(8)	Paul Lehner, Ferris Fain	1.50	.70	.45
(9)	Connie Mack	1.50	.70	.45
(10)	Earle Mack, Mickey Cochrane	1.50	.70	.45
(11)	Wally Moses, Carl Scheib	1.50	.70	.45
(12)	Pete Suder, Alex Kellner	1.50	.70	.45
(13)	Elmer Valo, Bobby Shantz	1.50	.70	.45
(14)	Bob Wellman, Joe Coleman	1.50	.70	.45
(15)	Hank Wyse, Gene Markland	1.50	.70	.45
(16)	Johnny Blatnik, Ed Wright	1.50	.70	.45
(17)	Ralph Caballero, Bubba Church	1.50	.70	.45
(18)	Milo Candini, Hank Borowy	1.50	.70	.45
(19)	Blix Donnelly, Bill Nicholson	1.50	.70	.45
(20)	Del Ennis, Ken Heintzelman	1.50	.70	.45
(21)	Mike Goliat, Dick Whitman	1.50	.70	.45
(22)	Granny Hamner, Rich Ashburn	3.50	1.75	1.00
(23)	Willie Jones, Russ Meyer	1.50	.70	.45
(24)	Jim Konstanty, Ken Silvestri	1.50	.70	.45
(25)	Stan Lopata, Eddie Waitkus	1.50	.70	.45
(26)	Ed Sanicki, Robin Roberts	3.50	1.75	1.00
(27)	Eddie Sawyer	1.50	.70	.45
(28)	Andy Seminick, Ken Trinkle	1.50	.70	.45
(29)	Dick Sisler, Stan Hollmig/DP	1.50	.70	.45
(30)	Jocko Thompson, Curt Simmons	1.50	.70	.45

1957-1959 Hudepohl Beer Cincinnati Reds

These 8" x 10" black-and-white photos were distributed by Hudepohl Beer, although the brewery or brand is not mentioned on the pictures. They are identical in format to the team-issued publicity photos. The Hudepohl pictures differ from the team-issue in that the beer pictures have a semi-gloss finish and no printing on the back, while the team pictures have a glossy surface and a four-line warning on back not to use them for advertising purposes. The pictures have portrait or posed action photos, sometimes with the background removed. They are bordered in white with the player and team name at bottom. The type style is sans-serif for 1957 pictures, and serifed in 1959. Years of issue have been attributed according to corresponding team-issue photos and uniforms pictured. Because so many of the Hudepohl pictures are found autographed, it is possible they were distributed in conjunction with player promotional appearances. This checklist may well not be complete.

	NM	EX	VG
Common Player:	20.00	10.00	6.00
1957 (Redlegs, sans-serif.)			
Ed. Bailey/Btg	20.00	10.00	6.00
George Crowe/Btg	20.00	10.00	6.00
Ted Kluszewski/Btg	35.00	17.50	10.50
Brooks Lawrence (Follow-through.)	20.00	10.00	6.00
Roy McMillan/Btg	20.00	10.00	6.00
Joe Nuxhall (Follow-through.)	25.00	12.50	7.50

	NM	EX	VG
Manager "Birdie" Tebbetts/Portrait	20.00	10.00	6.00
1959 (Reds, serif.)			
Brooks Lawrence/Portrait	20.00	10.00	6.00

1960 Hudepohl Beer Cincinnati Reds

These 8" x 10" black-and-white photos were distributed by Hudepohl Beer, although the brewery or brand is not mentioned on the pictures. Similar in format to the team-issued publicity photos, the Hudepohl pictures differ in that they have a semi-gloss finish and no printing on the back, while the team pictures have a glossy surface and a four-line warning on back not to use them for advertising purposes. The pictures have portrait or posed action photos, sometimes with the background removed. They are bordered in white with the player and team name at bottom in a light sans-serif type. Years of issue have been attributed according to corresponding team-issue photos and uniforms pictured. Because so many of the Hudepohl pictures are found autographed, it is possible they were distributed in conjunction with player promotional appearances. This checklist may not be complete.

		NM	EX	VG
Common Player:		20.00	10.00	6.00
(1)	Ed. Bailey	20.00	10.00	6.00
(2)	Gus Bell	20.00	10.00	6.00
(3)	Jerry Lynch	20.00	10.00	6.00
(4)	Roy McMillan	20.00	10.00	6.00
(5)	Don Newcombe	20.00	10.00	6.00
(6)	Joe Nuxhall	25.00	12.50	7.50
(7)	Vada Pinson	30.00	15.00	9.00
(8)	Frank Robinson	85.00	42.00	25.00

1907 Geo. W. Hull Chicago White Sox Postcards

Members of the World Champion White Sox are featured on this single-team issue. Horizontal in format, the black-and-white cards measure about 5-1/2" x 3-1/2". All of the cards share a basic design of a player action posed photo at right, with his name, position, and "White Sox, World's Champions" in a white box beneath. The main part of the card pictures a clothesline full of white socks, each of which has a small round portrait photo of one of the players - 15 in all. In a larger portrait at lower-left is team owner Charles Comiskey. In the white border at top, each card has a witty statement such as "String of World-Beaters" and "Not Worn By Ladies, But Admired By Them." In the bottom border is, "Copyright 1907, Geo. W. Hull." Backs have been seen with a schedule of home games and with an ad from the Morrison Hotel and Boston Oyster House of Chicago.

		NM	EX	VG
Complete Set (16):		10,000	5,000	3,000
Common Player:		600.00	300.00	180.00
(1)	Nick Altrock	600.00	300.00	180.00
(2)	George Davis	950.00	475.00	285.00
(3)	Jiggs Donahue	600.00	300.00	180.00
(4)	Pat Dougherty	600.00	300.00	180.00
(5)	Eddie Hahn	600.00	300.00	180.00
(6)	Frank Isbell	600.00	300.00	180.00
(7)	Fielder Jones	600.00	300.00	180.00
(8)	Ed McFarland	600.00	300.00	180.00
(9)	Frank Owens	600.00	300.00	180.00
(10)	Roy Patterson	600.00	300.00	180.00
(11)	George Rohe	600.00	300.00	180.00
(12)	Frank Smith	600.00	300.00	180.00
(13)	Billy Sullivan	600.00	300.00	180.00
(14)	Lee Tannehill	600.00	300.00	180.00
(15)	Eddie Walsh	950.00	475.00	285.00
(16)	Doc White	600.00	300.00	180.00

1953 Hunter Wieners Cardinals

From the great era of the regionally issued hot dog cards in the mid-1950s, the 1953 Hunter wieners set of St. Louis Cardinals is among the rarest today. Originally issued in two-card panels, the cards are most often found as 2-1/4" x 3-1/4" singles today

when they can be found at all. The cards feature a light blue facsimile autograph printed over the stat box at the bottom. They are blank-backed.

		NM	EX	VG
Complete Set (26):		10,000	5,000	3,000
Common Player:		300.00	150.00	90.00
(1)	Steve Bilko	300.00	150.00	90.00
(2)	Cloyd Boyer	300.00	150.00	90.00
(3)	Al Brazle	300.00	150.00	90.00
(4)	Cliff Chambers	300.00	150.00	90.00
(5)	Michael Clark	300.00	150.00	90.00
(6)	Jack Crimian	300.00	150.00	90.00
(7)	Lester Fusselman	300.00	150.00	90.00
(8)	Harvey Haddix	325.00	160.00	100.00
(9)	Solly Hemus	300.00	150.00	90.00
(10)	Ray Jablonski	300.00	150.00	90.00
(11)	William Johnson	300.00	150.00	90.00
(12)	Harry Lowrey	300.00	150.00	90.00
(13)	Lawrence Miggins	300.00	150.00	90.00
(14)	Stuart Miller	300.00	150.00	90.00
(15)	Wilmer Mizell	300.00	150.00	90.00
(16)	Stanley Musial	3,000	1,500	900.00
(17)	Joseph Presko	300.00	150.00	90.00
(18)	Delbert Rice	300.00	150.00	90.00
(19)	Harold Rice	300.00	150.00	90.00
(20)	Willard Schmidt	300.00	150.00	90.00
(21)	Albert Schoendienst	650.00	325.00	195.00
(22)	Richard Sisler	300.00	150.00	90.00
(23)	Enos Slaughter	650.00	325.00	195.00
(24)	Gerald Staley	300.00	150.00	90.00
(25)	Edward Stanky	325.00	160.00	97.00
(26)	John Yuhas	300.00	150.00	90.00

1954 Hunter Wieners Cardinals

A nearly impossible set to complete today by virtue of the method of its issue, the 1954 Hunter hot dog set features what would traditionally be the front and back of a normal baseball card on two different cards. The "front," has a color photo with a box at bottom challenging the the collector to name the player and quote his stats. The "back" features cartoon Cardinals in action, and contains the answers. However, because both parts were printed on a single panel, and because most of the back (non-picture) portions of the panels were thrown away years ago, it is a formidable challenge to complete a '54 Hunter set today. There is no back printing on the 2-1/4" x 3-1/2" cards.

		NM	EX	VG
Complete Set (30):		9,000	4,500	2,700
Common Player:		250.00	125.00	75.00
(1)	Tom Alston	250.00	125.00	75.00
(2)	Steve Bilko	250.00	125.00	75.00
(3)	Al Brazle	250.00	125.00	75.00
(4)	Tom Burgess	250.00	125.00	75.00
(5)	Cot Deal	250.00	125.00	75.00
(6)	Alex Grammas	250.00	125.00	75.00
(7)	Harvey Haddix	250.00	125.00	75.00
(8)	Solly Hemus	250.00	125.00	75.00
(9)	Ray Jablonski	250.00	125.00	75.00
(10)	Royce Lint	250.00	125.00	75.00

		NM	EX	VG
(11)	Peanuts Lowrey	250.00	125.00	75.00
(12)	Memo Luna	250.00	125.00	75.00
(13)	Stu Miller	250.00	125.00	75.00
(14)	Stan Musial	2,000	1,000	600.00
(15)	Tom Poholsky	250.00	125.00	75.00
(16)	Bill Posedel	250.00	125.00	75.00
(17)	Joe Presko	250.00	125.00	75.00
(18)	Dick Rand	250.00	125.00	75.00
(19)	Vic Raschi	250.00	125.00	75.00
(20)	Rip Repulski	250.00	125.00	75.00
(21)	Del Rice	250.00	125.00	75.00
(22)	John Riddle	250.00	125.00	75.00
(23)	Mike Ryba	250.00	125.00	75.00
(24)	Red Schoendienst	500.00	250.00	150.00
(25)	Dick Schofield	275.00	135.00	82.00
(26)	Enos Slaughter	500.00	250.00	150.00
(27)	Gerry Staley	250.00	125.00	75.00
(28)	Ed Stanky	250.00	125.00	75.00
(29)	Ed Yuhas	250.00	125.00	75.00
(30)	Sal Yvars	250.00	125.00	75.00

1955 Hunter Wieners Cardinals

The 1955 team set of St. Louis Cardinals, included with packages of Hunter hot dogs, features the third format change in three years of issue. For 1955, the cards were printed in a tall, narrow (2" wide with the height tapering from 4-3/4" at left to 4-1/2" at right) format, two to a panel. The cards feature both a posed action photo and a portrait photo, along with a facsimile autograph and brief biographical data on the front. There is no back printing, as the cards were part of the wrapping for packages of hot dogs.

		NM	EX	VG
Complete Set (30):		11,000	5,500	3,250
Common Player:		250.00	125.00	75.00
(1)	Thomas Edison Alston	250.00	125.00	75.00
(2)	Kenton Lloyd Boyer	675.00	335.00	200.00
(3)	Harry Lewis Elliott	250.00	125.00	75.00
(4)	John Edward Faszholz	250.00	125.00	75.00
(5)	Joseph Filmore Frazier	250.00	125.00	75.00
(6)	Alexander Pete Grammas	250.00	125.00	75.00
(7)	Harvey Haddix	250.00	125.00	75.00
(8)	Solly Joseph Hemus	250.00	125.00	75.00
(9)	Lawrence Curtis Jackson	250.00	125.00	75.00
(10)	Tony R. Jacobs	250.00	125.00	75.00
(11)	Gordon Bassett Jones	250.00	125.00	75.00
(12)	Paul Edmore LaPalme	250.00	125.00	75.00
(13)	Brooks Ulysses Lawrence	250.00	125.00	75.00
(14)	Wallace Wade Moon	400.00	200.00	120.00
(15)	Stanley Frank Musial	2,700	1,350	810.00
(16)	Thomas George Poholsky	250.00	125.00	75.00
(17)	William John Posedel	250.00	125.00	75.00
(18)	Victor Angelo John Raschi	250.00	125.00	75.00
(19)	Eldon John Repulski	250.00	125.00	75.00
(20)	Delbert Rice	250.00	125.00	75.00
(21)	John Ludy Riddle	250.00	125.00	75.00
(22)	William F. Sarni	250.00	125.00	75.00
(23)	Albert Fred Schoendienst	550.00	275.00	165.00
(24)	Richard John Schofield (Actually John Richard.)	250.00	125.00	75.00
(25)	Frank Thomas Smith	250.00	125.00	75.00
(26)	Edward R. Stanky	275.00	135.00	82.00
(27)	Bobby Gene Tiefenauer	250.00	125.00	75.00
(28)	William Charles Virdon	400.00	200.00	120.00
(29)	Frederick E. Walker	250.00	125.00	75.00
(30)	Floyd Lewis Woolridge	250.00	125.00	75.00

1941 Huskies

This advertising card was issued by Huskies Whole Wheat Flakes cereal. In black-and-white, the card measures about 5-1/2" x 3-1/2". Facsimile autographs appear on the borderless front photo.

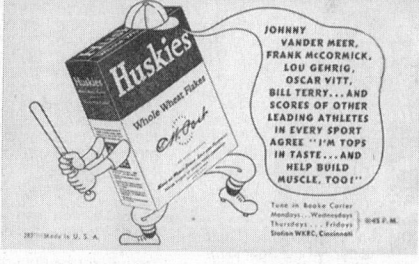

	NM	EX	VG
John Vander Meer, Frank McCormick	125.00	65.00	40.00

I

1976 Icee Drinks Reds

Issued in 1976 in the Cincinnati area by Icee Drinks, this 12-card set of semi-circular cards features members of the Reds. The cards measure approximately 2" in diameter with the bottom of the disc squared off. The cards were originally issued as soft drink lids. Fronts have a portrait photo in black-and-white, with uniform logos removed. Backs are blank. The cards are unnumbered. A 7" x 12" cap saver sheet was also available; it does not picture the players.

		NM	EX	VG
Complete Set (12):		60.00	30.00	18.00
Common Player:		2.00	1.00	.60
Saver Sheet:		27.00	13.50	8.00
(1)	Johnny Bench	10.00	5.00	3.00
(2)	Dave Concepcion	2.25	1.25	.70
(3)	Rawly Eastwick	2.00	1.00	.60
(4)	George Foster	2.25	1.25	.70
(5)	Cesar Geronimo	2.00	1.00	.60
(6)	Ken Griffey	2.50	1.25	.70
(7)	Don Gullett	2.00	1.00	.60
(8)	Will McEnaney	2.00	1.00	.60
(9)	Joe Morgan	6.00	3.00	1.75
(10)	Gary Nolan	2.00	1.00	.60
(11)	Tony Perez	4.00	2.00	1.25
(12)	Pete Rose	27.50	13.50	8.25

1963 I.D.L. Drug Store Pittsburgh Pirates

This set of 26 black-and-white cards was regionally distributed. The 4" x 5" semi-gloss cards are blank-backed and unnumbered. The checklist is arranged alphabetically. Johnny Logan's card is considered scarce and may have been pulled from distribution early.

		NM	EX	VG
Complete Set (27):		225.00	115.00	65.00
Common Player:		7.50	3.75	2.25
(1)	Bob Bailey	7.50	3.75	2.25
(2)	Forrest "Smoky" Burgess	7.50	3.75	2.25
(3)	Don Cardwell	7.50	3.75	2.25
(4)	Roberto Clemente	75.00	37.00	22.00
(5)	Donn Clendenon	10.00	5.00	3.00
(6)	Roy Face	7.50	3.75	2.25
(7)	Earl Francis	7.50	3.75	2.25
(8)	Bob Friend	7.50	3.75	2.25
(9)	Joe Gibbon	7.50	3.75	2.25
(10)	Julio Gotay	7.50	3.75	2.25
(11)	Harvey Haddix	7.50	3.75	2.25
(12)	Johnny Logan/SP	15.00	7.50	4.50
(13)	Bill Mazeroski	25.00	12.50	7.50
(14)	Al McBean	7.50	3.75	2.25
(15)	Danny Murtaugh	7.50	3.75	2.25
(16)	Sam Narron	7.50	3.75	2.25
(17)	Ron Northey	7.50	3.75	2.25
(18)	Frank Oceak	7.50	3.75	2.25
(19)	Jim Pagliaroni	7.50	3.75	2.25
(20)	Ted Savage	7.50	3.75	2.25
(21)	Dick Schofield	7.50	3.75	2.25
(22)	Bob Skinner/SP	15.00	7.50	4.50
(23)	Willie Stargell	25.00	12.50	7.50
(24)	Tom Sturdivant	7.50	3.75	2.25
(25)	Virgil "Fire" Trucks	7.50	3.75	2.25
(26)	Bob Veale	7.50	3.75	2.25
(27)	Bill Virdon	7.50	3.75	2.25

1916 Indianapolis Brewing Co.

Best known in blank-back form or with ads on back for The Sporting News, this 200-card set can be found with the imprint of several local and regional businesses. Among them is the Indianapolis Brewing Co. Type-card and superstar collectors can expect to pay a significant premium for individual cards with Indianapolis Brewing advertising. The checklist parallels that of the 1916 M101-4 Blank Backs. Cards measure 1-5/8" x 3" and are printed in black-and-white. The brewery originally advertised the set on its "Facts for Fans" booklet, at a cost of 25 cents.

		NM	EX	VG
Complete Set (200):		96,000	48,000	28,800
Common Player:		240.00	120.00	75.00
1	Babe Adams	360.00	120.00	75.00
2	Sam Agnew	240.00	120.00	75.00
3	Eddie Ainsmith	240.00	120.00	75.00
4	Grover Alexander	720.00	360.00	215.00
5	Leon Ames	240.00	120.00	75.00
6	Jimmy Archer	240.00	120.00	75.00
7	Jimmy Austin	240.00	120.00	75.00
8	H.D. Baird	240.00	120.00	75.00
9	J. Franklin Baker	540.00	270.00	160.00
10	Dave Bancroft	540.00	270.00	160.00
11	Jack Barry	240.00	120.00	75.00
12	Zinn Beck	240.00	120.00	75.00
13	"Chief" Bender	540.00	270.00	160.00
14	Joe Benz	240.00	120.00	75.00
15	Bob Bescher	240.00	120.00	75.00
16	Al Betzel	240.00	120.00	75.00
17	Mordecai Brown	540.00	270.00	160.00
18	Eddie Burns	240.00	120.00	75.00
19	George Burns	240.00	120.00	75.00
20	Geo. J. Burns	240.00	120.00	70.00
21	Joe Bush	240.00	120.00	75.00
22	"Donie" Bush	240.00	120.00	75.00
23	Art Butler	240.00	120.00	75.00
24	Bobbie Byrne	240.00	120.00	75.00
25	Forrest Cady	240.00	120.00	75.00
26	Jimmy Callahan	240.00	120.00	75.00
27	Ray Caldwell	240.00	120.00	75.00
28	Max Carey	540.00	270.00	160.00
29	George Chalmers	240.00	120.00	75.00
30	Ray Chapman	270.00	135.00	80.00
31	Larry Cheney	240.00	120.00	75.00
32	Eddie Cicotte	540.00	270.00	160.00
33	Tom Clarke	240.00	120.00	75.00
34	Eddie Collins	540.00	270.00	160.00

35	"Shauno" Collins	240.00	120.00	75.00
36	Charles Comiskey	540.00	270.00	160.00
37	Joe Connolly	240.00	120.00	75.00
38	Ty Cobb	3,600	1,800	1,080
39	Harry Coveleskie (Coveleski)	240.00	120.00	75.00
40	Gavvy Cravath	240.00	120.00	75.00
41	Sam Crawford	540.00	270.00	160.00
42	Jean Dale	240.00	120.00	75.00
43	Jake Daubert	240.00	120.00	75.00
44	Charles Deal	240.00	120.00	75.00
45	Al Demaree	240.00	120.00	75.00
46	Josh Devore	240.00	120.00	75.00
47	William Doak	240.00	120.00	75.00
48	Bill Donovan	240.00	120.00	75.00
49	Charles Dooin	240.00	120.00	75.00
50	Mike Doolan	240.00	120.00	75.00
51	Larry Doyle	240.00	120.00	75.00
52	Jean Dubuc	240.00	120.00	75.00
53	Oscar Dugey	240.00	120.00	75.00
54	Johnny Evers	540.00	270.00	160.00
55	Urban Faber	540.00	270.00	160.00
56	"Hap" Felsch	720.00	360.00	215.00
57	Bill Fischer	240.00	120.00	75.00
58	Ray Fisher	240.00	120.00	75.00
59	Max Flack	240.00	120.00	75.00
60	Art Fletcher	240.00	120.00	75.00
61	Eddie Foster	240.00	100.00	75.00
62	Jacques Fournier	240.00	120.00	75.00
63	Del Gainer (Gainor)	240.00	120.00	75.00
64	"Chic" Gandil	540.00	270.00	160.00
65	Larry Gardner	240.00	120.00	75.00
66	Joe Gedeon	240.00	120.00	75.00
67	Gus Getz	240.00	120.00	75.00
68	Geo. Gibson	240.00	120.00	75.00
69	Wilbur Good	240.00	120.00	75.00
70	Hank Gowdy	240.00	120.00	75.00
71	John Graney	240.00	120.00	75.00
72	Clark Griffith	540.00	270.00	160.00
73	Tom Griffith	240.00	120.00	75.00
74	Heinie Groh	240.00	120.00	75.00
75	Earl Hamilton	240.00	120.00	75.00
76	Bob Harmon	240.00	120.00	75.00
77	Roy Hartzell	240.00	120.00	75.00
78	Claude Hendrix	240.00	120.00	75.00
79	Olaf Henriksen	240.00	120.00	75.00
80	John Henry	240.00	120.00	75.00
81	"Buck" Herzog	240.00	120.00	75.00
82	Hugh High	240.00	120.00	75.00
83	Dick Hoblitzell	240.00	120.00	75.00
84	Harry Hooper	540.00	270.00	160.00
85	Ivan Howard	240.00	120.00	75.00
86	Miller Huggins	540.00	270.00	160.00
87	Joe Jackson	20,000	7,500	4,500
88	William James	240.00	120.00	75.00
89	Harold Janvrin	240.00	120.00	75.00
90	Hugh Jennings	540.00	270.00	160.00
91	Walter Johnson	1,800	900.00	540.00
92	Fielder Jones	240.00	120.00	75.00
93	Joe Judge	240.00	120.00	75.00
94	Bennie Kauff	240.00	120.00	75.00
95	Wm. Killefer Jr.	240.00	120.00	75.00
96	Ed. Konetchy	240.00	120.00	75.00
97	Napoleon Lajoie	600.00	300.00	180.00
98	Jack Lapp	240.00	120.00	75.00
99	John Lavan	240.00	120.00	75.00
100	Jimmy Lavender	240.00	120.00	75.00
101	"Nemo" Leibold	240.00	120.00	75.00
102	H.B. Leonard	240.00	120.00	75.00
103	Duffy Lewis	240.00	120.00	75.00
104	Hans Lobert	240.00	120.00	75.00
105	Tom Long	240.00	120.00	75.00
106	Fred Luderus	240.00	120.00	75.00
107	Connie Mack	540.00	270.00	160.00
108	Lee Magee	240.00	120.00	75.00
109	Sherwood Magee	240.00	120.00	75.00
110	Al. Mamaux	240.00	120.00	75.00
111	Leslie Mann	240.00	120.00	75.00
112	"Rabbit" Maranville	540.00	270.00	160.00
113	Rube Marquard	540.00	270.00	160.00
114	J. Erskine Mayer	360.00	180.00	110.00
115	George McBride	240.00	120.00	75.00
116	John J. McGraw	540.00	270.00	160.00
117	Jack McInnis	240.00	120.00	75.00
118	Fred Merkle	240.00	120.00	75.00
119	Chief Meyers	240.00	120.00	75.00
120	Clyde Milan	240.00	120.00	75.00
121	John Miller	240.00	120.00	75.00
122	Otto Miller	240.00	120.00	75.00
123	Willie Mitchell	240.00	120.00	75.00
124	Fred Mollwitz	240.00	120.00	75.00
125	Pat Moran	240.00	120.00	75.00
126	Ray Morgan	240.00	120.00	75.00
127	Geo. Moriarty	240.00	120.00	75.00
128	Guy Morton	240.00	120.00	75.00
129	Mike Mowrey	240.00	120.00	75.00
130	Ed. Murphy	240.00	120.00	75.00
131	"Hy" Myers	240.00	120.00	75.00
132	J.A. Niehoff	240.00	120.00	75.00
133	Rube Oldring	240.00	120.00	75.00
134	Oliver O'Mara	240.00	120.00	75.00
135	Steve O'Neill	240.00	120.00	75.00
136	"Dode" Paskert	240.00	120.00	75.00
137	Roger Peckinpaugh	240.00	120.00	75.00
138	Walter Pipp	240.00	120.00	75.00
139	Derril Pratt (Derrill)	240.00	120.00	75.00
140	Pat Ragan	240.00	120.00	75.00
141	Bill Rariden	240.00	120.00	75.00
142	Eppa Rixey	540.00	270.00	160.00
143	Davey Robertson	240.00	120.00	75.00
144	Wilbert Robinson	540.00	270.00	160.00
145	Bob Roth	240.00	120.00	75.00
146	Ed. Roush	540.00	270.00	160.00
147	Clarence Rowland	240.00	120.00	75.00
148	"Nap" Rucker	240.00	120.00	75.00
149	Dick Rudolph	240.00	120.00	75.00
150	Reb Russell	240.00	120.00	75.00
151	Babe Ruth	24,000	12,000	7,200
152	Vic Saier	240.00	120.00	75.00
153	"Slim" Sallee	240.00	120.00	75.00
154	Ray Schalk	540.00	270.00	160.00
155	Walter Schang	240.00	120.00	75.00
156	Frank Schulte	240.00	120.00	75.00
157	Everett Scott	240.00	120.00	75.00
158	Jim Scott	240.00	120.00	75.00
159	Tom Seaton	240.00	120.00	75.00
160	Howard Shanks	240.00	120.00	75.00
161	Bob Shawkey	240.00	120.00	75.00
162	Ernie Shore	240.00	120.00	75.00
163	Burt Shotton	240.00	120.00	75.00
164	Geo. Sisler	540.00	270.00	160.00
165	J. Carlisle Smith	240.00	120.00	75.00
166	Fred Snodgrass	240.00	120.00	75.00
167	Geo. Stallings	240.00	120.00	75.00
168	Oscar Stanage	240.00	120.00	75.00
169	Charles Stengel	540.00	270.00	160.00
170	Milton Stock	240.00	120.00	75.00
171	Amos Strunk	240.00	120.00	75.00
172	Billy Sullivan	240.00	120.00	75.00
173	"Jeff" Tesreau	240.00	120.00	75.00
174	Joe Tinker	540.00	270.00	160.00
175	Fred Toney	240.00	120.00	75.00
176	Terry Turner	240.00	120.00	75.00
177	George Tyler	240.00	120.00	75.00
178	Jim Vaughn	240.00	120.00	75.00
179	Bob Veach	240.00	120.00	75.00
180	James Viox	240.00	120.00	75.00
181	Oscar Vitt	240.00	120.00	75.00
182	Hans Wagner	5,000	1,200	720.00
183	Clarence Walker	240.00	120.00	75.00
184	Ed. Walsh	540.00	270.00	160.00
185	W. Wambsganss (Photo actually Fritz Coumbe.)	240.00	120.00	75.00
186	Buck Weaver	2,000	450.00	270.00
187	Carl Weilman	240.00	120.00	75.00
188	Zach Wheat	540.00	270.00	160.00
189	Geo. Whitted	240.00	120.00	75.00
190	Fred Williams	240.00	120.00	75.00
191	Art Wilson	240.00	120.00	75.00
192	J. Owen Wilson	240.00	120.00	75.00
193	Ivy Wingo	240.00	120.00	75.00
194	"Mel" Wolfgang	240.00	120.00	75.00
195	Joe Wood	360.00	180.00	110.00
196	Steve Yerkes	240.00	120.00	75.00
197	"Pep" Young	240.00	120.00	75.00
198	Rollie Zeider	240.00	120.00	75.00
199	Heiny Zimmerman	240.00	120.00	75.00
200	Ed. Zwilling	240.00	120.00	75.00

1923 Curtis Ireland Candy (E123)

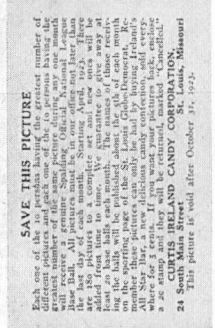

This set, identified in the ACC as E123, was issued in 1923 by the Curtis Ireland Candy Corp. of St. Louis and was distributed with Ireland's "All Star Bars." Except for the backs, the Ireland set is identical to the Willard Chocolate V100 set of the same year. Measuring 3-1/4" x 2-1/16", the cards feature sepia-toned photos with the player's name in script on the front. The backs advertise a contest which required the collector to mail in the cards in exchange for prizes, which probably explains their relative scarcity today.

#	Player	NM	EX	VG
	Complete Set (180):	125,000	50,000	30,000
	Common Player:	600.00	240.00	150.00
(1)	Chas. B Adams	600.00	240.00	150.00
(2)	Grover C. Alexander	1,000	400.00	250.00
(3)	J.P. Austin	600.00	240.00	150.00
(4)	J.C. Bagby	600.00	240.00	150.00
(5)	J. Franklin Baker	900.00	360.00	225.00
(6)	David J. Bancroft	900.00	360.00	225.00
(7)	Turner Barber	600.00	240.00	150.00
(8)	Jesse L. Barnes	600.00	240.00	150.00
(9)	J.C. Bassler	600.00	240.00	150.00
(10)	L.A. Blue	600.00	240.00	150.00
(11)	Norman D. Boeckel	600.00	240.00	150.00
(12)	F.L. Brazil (Brazill)	600.00	240.00	150.00
(13)	G.H. Burns	600.00	240.00	150.00
(14)	Geo. J. Burns	600.00	240.00	150.00
(15)	Leon Cadore	600.00	240.00	150.00
(16)	Max G. Carey	900.00	360.00	225.00
(17)	Harold G. Carlson	600.00	240.00	150.00
(18)	Lloyd R. Christenberry (Christenbury)	600.00	240.00	150.00
(19)	Vernon J. Clemons	600.00	240.00	150.00
(20)	T.R. Cobb	8,500	3,400	2,125
(21)	Bert Cole	600.00	240.00	150.00
(22)	John F. Collins	600.00	240.00	150.00
(23)	S. Coveleskie (Coveleski)	900.00	360.00	225.00
(24)	Walton E. Cruise	600.00	240.00	150.00
(25)	G.W. Cutshaw	600.00	240.00	150.00
(26)	Jacob E. Daubert	600.00	240.00	150.00
(27)	Geo. Dauss	600.00	240.00	150.00
(28)	F.T. Davis	600.00	240.00	150.00
(29)	Chas. A. Deal	600.00	240.00	150.00
(30)	William L. Doak	600.00	240.00	150.00
(31)	William E. Donovan	600.00	240.00	150.00
(32)	Hugh Duffy	900.00	360.00	225.00
(33)	J.A. Dugan	600.00	240.00	150.00
(34)	Louis B. Duncan	600.00	240.00	150.00
(35)	James Dykes	600.00	240.00	150.00
(36)	H.J. Ehmke	600.00	240.00	150.00
(37)	F.R. Ellerbe	600.00	240.00	150.00
(38)	E.G. Erickson	600.00	240.00	150.00
(39)	John J. Evers	900.00	360.00	225.00
(40)	U.C. Faber	900.00	360.00	225.00
(41)	B.A. Falk	600.00	240.00	150.00
(42)	Max Flack	600.00	240.00	150.00
(43)	Lee Fohl	600.00	240.00	150.00
(44)	Jacques F. Fournier	600.00	240.00	150.00
(45)	Frank F. Frisch	900.00	360.00	225.00
(46)	C.E. Galloway	600.00	240.00	150.00
(47)	W.C. Gardner	600.00	240.00	150.00
(48)	E.P. Gharrity	600.00	240.00	150.00
(49)	Geo. Gibson	600.00	240.00	150.00
(50)	Wm. Gleason	600.00	240.00	150.00
(51)	William Gleason	600.00	240.00	150.00
(52)	Henry M. Gowdy	600.00	240.00	150.00
(53)	I.M. Griffin	600.00	240.00	150.00
(54)	Thomas Griffith	600.00	240.00	150.00
(55)	Burleigh A. Grimes	900.00	360.00	225.00
(56)	Charles J. Grimm	600.00	240.00	150.00
(57)	Jesse J. Haines	900.00	360.00	225.00
(58)	S.R. Harris	900.00	360.00	225.00
(59)	W.B. Harris	600.00	240.00	150.00
(60)	R.K. Hasty	600.00	240.00	150.00
(61)	H.E. Heilman (Heilmann)	900.00	360.00	225.00
(62)	Walter J. Henline	600.00	240.00	150.00
(63)	Walter L. Holke	600.00	240.00	150.00
(64)	Charles J. Hollocher	600.00	240.00	150.00
(65)	H.B. Hooper	900.00	360.00	225.00
(66)	Rogers Hornsby	1,250	500.00	310.00
(67)	W.C. Hoyt	900.00	360.00	225.00
(68)	Miller Huggins	900.00	360.00	225.00
(69)	W.C. Jacobsen (Jacobson)	600.00	240.00	150.00
(70)	C.D. Jamieson	600.00	240.00	150.00
(71)	Ernest Johnson	600.00	240.00	150.00
(72)	W.P. Johnson	2,250	900.00	560.00
(73)	James H. Johnston	600.00	240.00	150.00
(74)	R.W. Jones	600.00	240.00	150.00
(75)	Samuel Pond Jones	600.00	240.00	150.00
(76)	J.I. Judge	600.00	240.00	150.00
(77)	James W. Keenan	600.00	240.00	150.00
(78)	Geo. L. Kelly	900.00	360.00	225.00
(79)	Peter J. Kilduff	600.00	240.00	150.00
(80)	William Killefer	600.00	240.00	150.00
(81)	Lee King	600.00	240.00	150.00
(82)	Ray Kolp	600.00	240.00	150.00
(83)	John Lavan	600.00	240.00	150.00
(84)	H.L. Leibold	600.00	240.00	150.00
(85)	Connie Mack	900.00	360.00	225.00
(86)	J.W. Mails	600.00	240.00	150.00
(87)	Walter J. Maranville	900.00	360.00	225.00
(88)	Richard W. Marquard	900.00	360.00	225.00
(89)	C.W. Mays	650.00	260.00	160.00
(90)	Geo. F. McBride	600.00	240.00	150.00
(91)	H.M. McClellan	600.00	240.00	150.00
(92)	John J. McGraw	900.00	360.00	225.00
(93)	Austin B. McHenry	600.00	240.00	150.00
(94)	J. McInnis	600.00	240.00	150.00
(95)	Douglas McWeeney (McWeeny)	600.00	240.00	150.00
(96)	M. Menosky	600.00	240.00	150.00
(97)	Emil F. Meusel	600.00	240.00	150.00
(98)	R. Meusel	600.00	240.00	150.00
(99)	Henry W. Meyers	600.00	240.00	150.00
(100)	J.C. Milan	600.00	240.00	150.00
(101)	John K. Miljus	600.00	240.00	150.00
(102)	Edmund J. Miller	600.00	240.00	150.00
(103)	Elmer Miller	600.00	240.00	150.00
(104)	Otto L. Miller	600.00	240.00	150.00
(105)	Fred Mitchell	600.00	240.00	150.00
(106)	Geo. Mogridge	600.00	240.00	150.00
(107)	Patrick J. Moran	600.00	240.00	150.00
(108)	John D. Morrison	600.00	240.00	150.00
(109)	J.A. Mostil	600.00	240.00	150.00
(110)	Clarence F. Mueller	600.00	240.00	150.00
(111)	A. Earle Neale	650.00	260.00	160.00
(112)	Joseph Oeschger	600.00	240.00	150.00
(113)	Robert J. O'Farrell	600.00	240.00	150.00
(114)	J.C. Oldham	600.00	240.00	150.00
(115)	I.M. Olson	600.00	240.00	150.00
(116)	Geo. M. O'Neil	600.00	240.00	150.00
(117)	S.F. O'Neill	600.00	240.00	150.00
(118)	Frank J. Parkinson	600.00	240.00	150.00
(119)	Geo. H. Paskert	600.00	240.00	150.00
(120)	R.T. Peckinpaugh	600.00	240.00	150.00
(121)	H.J. Pennock	900.00	360.00	225.00
(122)	Ralph Perkins	600.00	240.00	150.00
(123)	Edw. J. Pfeffer	600.00	240.00	150.00
(124)	W.C. Pipp	600.00	240.00	150.00
(125)	Charles Elmer Ponder	600.00	240.00	150.00
(126)	Raymond R. Powell	600.00	240.00	150.00
(127)	D.B. Pratt	600.00	240.00	150.00
(128)	Joseph Rapp	600.00	240.00	150.00
(129)	John H. Rawlings	600.00	240.00	150.00
(130)	E.S. Rice (Should be E.C.)	900.00	360.00	225.00
(131)	Branch Rickey	1,000	400.00	250.00
(132)	James J. Ring	600.00	240.00	150.00
(133)	Eppa J. Rixey	900.00	360.00	225.00
(134)	Davis A. Robertson	600.00	240.00	150.00
(135)	Edwin Rommel	600.00	240.00	150.00
(136)	Edd J. Roush	900.00	360.00	225.00
(137)	Harold Ruel (Herold)	600.00	240.00	150.00
(138)	Allen Russell	600.00	240.00	150.00
(139)	G.H. Ruth	12,500	5,000	3,125
(140)	Wilfred D. Ryan	600.00	240.00	150.00

(141)	Henry F. Sallee	600.00	240.00	150.00
(142)	W.H. Schang	600.00	240.00	150.00
(143)	Raymond H. Schmandt	600.00	240.00	150.00
(144)	Everett Scott	600.00	240.00	150.00
(145)	Henry Severeid	600.00	240.00	150.00
(146)	Jos. W. Sewell	900.00	360.00	225.00
(147)	Howard S. Shanks	600.00	240.00	150.00
(148)	E.H. Sheely	600.00	240.00	150.00
(149)	Ralph Shinners	600.00	240.00	150.00
(150)	U.J. Shocker	600.00	240.00	150.00
(151)	G.H. Sisler	900.00	360.00	225.00
(152)	Earl L. Smith	600.00	240.00	150.00
(153)	Earl S. Smith	600.00	240.00	150.00
(154)	Geo. A. Smith	600.00	240.00	150.00
(155)	J.W. Smith	600.00	240.00	150.00
(156)	Tris E. Speaker	1,350	540.00	335.00
(157)	Arnold Staatz	600.00	240.00	150.00
(158)	J.R. Stephenson	600.00	240.00	150.00
(159)	Milton J. Stock	600.00	240.00	150.00
(160)	John L. Sullivan	600.00	240.00	150.00
(161)	H.F. Tormahlen	600.00	240.00	150.00
(162)	Jas. A. Tierney	600.00	240.00	150.00
(163)	J.T. Tobin	600.00	240.00	150.00
(164)	Jas. L. Vaughn	600.00	240.00	150.00
(165)	R.H. Veach	600.00	240.00	150.00
(166)	C.W. Walker	600.00	240.00	150.00
(167)	A.L. Ward	600.00	240.00	150.00
(168)	Zack D. Wheat	900.00	360.00	225.00
(169)	George B. Whitted	600.00	240.00	150.00
(170)	Irvin K. Wilhelm	600.00	240.00	150.00
(171)	Roy H. Wilkinson	600.00	240.00	150.00
(172)	Fred C. Williams	600.00	240.00	150.00
(173)	K.R. Williams	600.00	240.00	150.00
(174)	Sam'l W. Wilson	600.00	240.00	150.00
(175)	Ivy B. Wingo	600.00	240.00	150.00
(176)	L.W. Witt	600.00	240.00	150.00
(177)	Joseph Wood	650.00	260.00	160.00
(178)	E. Yaryan	600.00	240.00	150.00
(179)	R.S. Young	600.00	240.00	150.00
(180)	Ross Young (Youngs)	900.00	360.00	225.00

1967 Irvindale Dairy Atlana Braves

the milk
of Athletes!

This quartet of Braves was printed in shades of deep red on the white background of a milk carton panel. Well-cut individual pieces measure 1-3/4" x 2-5/8" and are blank-backed.

		NM	EX	VG
Complete Set, Panel:		250.00	125.00	75.00
Complete Set, Singles:		175.00	85.00	45.00
Common Player:		40.00	20.00	12.00
(1)	Clete Boyer	40.00	20.00	12.00
(2)	Mack Jones	40.00	20.00	12.00
(3)	Denis Menke	40.00	20.00	12.00
(4)	Joe Torre	60.00	30.00	18.00

1976 Isaly's/Sweet William Discs

One of several regional sponsors of player disc sets in 1976 was the Pittsburgh area dairy store chain, Isaly's, and the Sweet William restaurants. The discs are 3-3/8" diameter with a black-and-white player portrait photo in the center of the baseball design. A line of red stars is above, while the left and right panels feature one of several bright colors. Produced by Michael Schecter Associates under license from the Major League Baseball Players Association,

the player photos have had uniform and cap logos removed. Backs are printed in red and purple. The unnumbered checklist here is presented in alphabetical order.

		NM	EX	VG
Complete Set (70):		15.00	7.50	4.50
Common Player:		.50	.25	.15
(1)	Henry Aaron	4.00	2.00	1.25
(2)	Johnny Bench	2.00	1.00	.60
(3)	Vida Blue	.50	.25	.15
(4)	Larry Bowa	.50	.25	.15
(5)	Lou Brock	2.00	1.00	.60
(6)	Jeff Burroughs	.50	.25	.15
(7)	John Candelaria	.50	.25	.15
(8)	Jose Cardenal	.50	.25	.15
(9)	Rod Carew	2.00	1.00	.60
(10)	Steve Carlton	2.00	1.00	.60
(11)	Dave Cash	.50	.25	.15
(12)	Cesar Cedeno	.50	.25	.15
(13)	Ron Cey	.50	.25	.15
(14)	Carlton Fisk	2.00	1.00	.60
(15)	Tito Fuentes	.50	.25	.15
(16)	Steve Garvey	1.50	.70	.45
(17)	Ken Griffey	.50	.25	.15
(18)	Don Gullett	.50	.25	.15
(19)	Willie Horton	.50	.25	.15
(20)	Al Hrabosky	.50	.25	.15
(21)	Catfish Hunter	2.00	1.00	.60
(22)	Reggie Jackson (A's)	3.00	1.50	.90
(23)	Randy Jones	.50	.25	.15
(24)	Jim Kaat	.50	.25	.15
(25)	Don Kessinger	.50	.25	.15
(26)	Dave Kingman	.50	.25	.15
(27)	Jerry Koosman	.50	.25	.15
(28)	Mickey Lolich	.50	.25	.15
(29)	Greg Luzinski	.50	.25	.15
(30)	Fred Lynn	.50	.25	.15
(31)	Bill Madlock	.50	.25	.15
(32)	Carlos May (White Sox)	.50	.25	.15
(33)	John Mayberry	.50	.25	.15
(34)	Bake McBride	.50	.25	.15
(35)	Doc Medich	.50	.25	.15
(36)	Andy Messersmith (Dodgers)	.50	.25	.15
(37)	Rick Monday	.50	.25	.15
(38)	John Montefusco	.50	.25	.15
(39)	Jerry Morales	.50	.25	.15
(40)	Joe Morgan	2.00	1.00	.60
(41)	Thurman Munson	2.00	1.00	.60
(42)	Bobby Murcer	.50	.25	.15
(43)	Al Oliver	.50	.25	.15
(44)	Jim Palmer	2.00	1.00	.60
(45)	Dave Parker	.50	.25	.15
(46)	Tony Perez	2.00	1.00	.60
(47)	Jerry Reuss	.50	.25	.15
(48)	Brooks Robinson	2.00	1.00	.60
(49)	Frank Robinson	2.00	1.00	.60
(50)	Steve Rogers	.50	.25	.15
(51)	Pete Rose	6.00	3.00	1.75
(52)	Nolan Ryan	12.00	6.00	3.50
(53)	Manny Sanguillen	.50	.25	.15
(54)	Mike Schmidt	3.00	1.50	.90
(55)	Tom Seaver	2.00	1.00	.60
(56)	Ted Simmons	.50	.25	.15
(57)	Reggie Smith	.50	.25	.15
(58)	Willie Stargell	2.00	1.00	.60
(59)	Rusty Staub	.75	.40	.25
(60)	Rennie Stennett	.50	.25	.15
(61)	Don Sutton	2.00	1.00	.60
(62)	Andy Thornton (Cubs)	.50	.25	.15
(63)	Luis Tiant	.50	.25	.15
(64)	Joe Torre	1.50	.70	.45
(65)	Mike Tyson	.50	.25	.15
(66)	Bob Watson	.50	.25	.15
(67)	Wilbur Wood	.50	.25	.15
(68)	Jimmy Wynn	.50	.25	.15
(69)	Carl Yastrzemski	2.50	1.25	.70
(70)	Richie Zisk	.50	.25	.15

1976 ISCA Hoosier Hot-Stove All-Stars

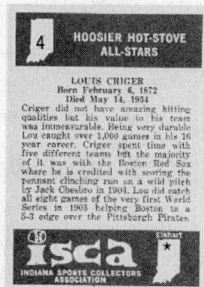

Famous native Hoosier ballplayers are featured in this collectors' issue from the Indiana Sports Collectors Assn. The 2-5/8" x 3-5/8" cards have black-and-white player photos on front framed in the state's outline. Red and blue graphics on a white background complete the design. Backs are in black and blue on white and include a career summary. A star on the state map at bottom indicates where the player was born.

		NM	EX	VG
Complete Set (26):		15.00	7.50	4.50
Common Player:		2.00	1.00	.60
1	Edd Roush	2.00	1.00	.60
2	Sam Thompson	2.00	1.00	.60

3	Chuck Klein	2.00	1.00	.60
4	Lou Criger	2.00	1.00	.60
5	Amos Rusie	2.00	1.00	.60
6	Billy Herman	2.00	1.00	.60
7	George Dauss	2.00	1.00	.60
8	Tom Thevenow	2.00	1.00	.60
9	Mordecai Brown	2.00	1.00	.60
10	Freddie Fitzsimmons	2.00	1.00	.60
11	Art Nehf	2.00	1.00	.60
12	Carl Erskine	3.00	1.50	.90
13	Don Larsen	3.00	1.50	.90
14	Gil Hodges	6.00	3.00	1.75
15	Pete Fox	2.00	1.00	.60
16	Butch Henline	2.00	1.00	.60
17	Doc Crandall	2.00	1.00	.60
18	Dizzy Trout	2.00	1.00	.60
19	Donie Bush	2.00	1.00	.60
20	Max Carey	2.00	1.00	.60
21	Eugene Hargrave, William Hargrave	2.00	1.00	.60
22	Sam Rice	2.00	1.00	.60
23	Babe Adams	2.00	1.00	.60
24	Cy Williams	2.00	1.00	.60
25	1913 Indianapolis Federal League Team	2.00	1.00	.60
26	Paul Frisz	2.00	1.00	.60

J

1912 J=K Candy

Originally printed on the front and back of candy boxes which advertised "100 Principal League Players," the extent of this series is currently unknown and the checklist presented here is almost certainly incomplete. The blank-back, black-and-white (some have a bit of color tinting) cards can be found in two sizes, 1-7/8" x 3-1/2" if printed on the box front, or 1-7/8" x 2-7/8" if printed on back. Player photos are framed with an ornate-cornered border. In a plaque at bottom, all in capital letters, are the player's name, position, team and league; the latter three designations are abbreviated. Gaps have been left in the assigned numbering to accommodate future discoveries.

		NM	EX	VG
Common Player:		2,000	1,000	600.00
(1)	Hugh Bedient	2,000	1,000	600.00
(2)	Hick Cady	2,000	1,000	600.00
(3)	Bill Carrigan	2,000	1,000	600.00
(4)	Hal Chase	2,500	1,250	750.00
(5)	Eddie Collins	3,000	1,500	900.00
(6)	Doc Crandall	2,000	1,000	600.00
(7)	Lou Criger	2,000	1,000	600.00
(8)	Harry Davis	2,000	1,000	600.00
(9)	Jim Delahanty	2,000	1,000	600.00
(10)	Art Devlin	2,000	1,000	600.00
(11)	Josh Devore	2,000	1,000	600.00
(12)	Larry Doyle	2,000	1,000	600.00
(13)	Larry Gardner	2,000	1,000	600.00
(14)	George Gibson	2,000	1,000	600.00
(15)	Charley Hall	2,000	1,000	600.00
(16)	Topsy Hartsel	2,000	1,000	600.00
(17)	Buck Herzog	2,000	1,000	600.00
(18)	Solly Hofman	2,000	1,000	600.00
(19)	Marty Krug	2,000	1,000	600.00
(20)	Duffy Lewis	2,000	1,000	600.00
(21)	Rube Marquard	3,000	1,500	900.00
(22)	Christy Mathewson	6,000	3,000	1,800
(23)	John McGraw	3,000	1,500	900.00
(24)	Red Murray	2,000	1,000	600.00
(25)	Harry Niles	2,000	1,000	600.00
(26)	Orval Overall	2,000	1,000	600.00
(27)	Larry Pape	2,000	1,000	600.00
(28)	Ed Reulbach	2,000	1,000	600.00
(29)	Cy Seymour	2,000	1,000	600.00
(30)	Jimmy Sheckard	2,000	1,000	600.00
(31)	Hack Simmons	2,000	1,000	600.00
(32)	Tris Speaker	4,800	2,400	1,450
(33)	Jake Stahl	2,000	1,000	600.00
(34)	Oscar Stanage	2,000	1,000	600.00
(35)	Harry Steinfeldt	2,000	1,000	600.00
(36)	Jeff Tesreau	2,000	1,000	600.00
(37)	Ira Thomas	2,000	1,000	600.00
(38)	Joe Tinker	3,000	1,500	900.00

		NM	EX	VG
(40)	Honus Wagner	12,000	6,000	3,600
(41)	Ed Walsh	3,000	1,500	900.00
(43)	Owen Wilson	2,000	1,000	600.00

1969 Jack In The Box California Angels

HOYT WILHELM
Pitcher
Career Record, 2.47 ERA

This regional issue was distributed a few cards per week at the chain's fast food restaurants. Blank-back cards are printed in black-and-white on thin white stock in a 1-15/16" x 3-1/2" format. The checklist for the unnumbered cards is presented here alphabetically.

		NM	EX	VG
Complete Set (13):		30.00	15.00	9.00
Common Player:		3.00	1.50	.90
(1)	Sandy Alomar	3.00	1.50	.90
(2)	Joe Azcue	3.00	1.50	.90
(3)	Jim Fregosi	3.50	1.75	1.00
(4)	Lou Johnson	3.00	1.50	.90
(5)	Jay Johnstone	6.00	3.00	1.75
(6)	Rudy May	3.00	1.50	.90
(7)	Jim McGlothlin	3.00	1.50	.90
(8)	Andy Messersmith	3.00	1.50	.90
(9)	Tom Murphy	3.00	1.50	.90
(10)	Rick Reichardt	3.00	1.50	.90
(11)	Aurelio Rodriguez	3.00	1.50	.90
(12)	Jim Spencer	3.00	1.50	.90
(13)	Hoyt Wilhelm	10.00	5.00	3.00

1971 Jack In The Box California Angels

Rudy May
CALIFORNIA ANGELS
P

Unlike the legitimate issue of 1969, this is an unauthorized collectors issue with no official connection to either the team of the fast food restaurant chain. The cards are printed in horizontal format on 4" x 2-1/2" manila paper in black ink. Fronts have a player portrait photo at left. Stacked at right are the player's name, team, position and Jack in the Box logo. Backs are blank. The set is checklisted here in alphabetical order.

		NM	EX	VG
Complete Set (10):		25.00	12.50	7.50
Common Player:		3.00	1.50	.90
(1)	Sandy Alomar	3.00	1.50	.90
(2)	Ken Berry	3.00	1.50	.90
(3)	Tony Conigliaro	15.00	7.50	4.50
(4)	Jim Fregosi	3.00	1.50	.90
(5)	Alex Johnson	3.00	1.50	.90
(6)	Rudy May	3.00	1.50	.90
(7)	Andy Messersmith	3.00	1.50	.90
(8)	"Lefty" Phillips	3.00	1.50	.90
(9)	Jim Spencer	3.00	1.50	.90
(10)	Clyde Wright	3.00	1.50	.90

1970 Jack in the Box Pittsburgh Pirates

Though this set is known within the hobby as the "Jack in the Box" Pirates, it bears no such advertising and has no actual connection to the restaurant chain; they are a collector's issue. The black-and-white

DAVE GIUSTI
Pittsburgh Pirates P
1969: 22g. 3-7 3.60

cards measure 2" x 3-1/2" and are blank-backed. Beneath the photo on front is the player identification and a few stats from the 1969 season.

		NM	EX	VG
Complete Set (12):		35.00	17.50	10.00
Common Player:		3.00	1.50	.90
(1)	Gene Alley	3.00	1.50	.90
(2)	Dave Cash	3.00	1.50	.90
(3)	Dock Ellis	3.00	1.50	.90
(4)	Dave Giusti	3.00	1.50	.90
(5)	Jerry May	3.00	1.50	.90
(6)	Bill Mazeroski	12.50	6.25	3.75
(7)	Al Oliver	6.00	3.00	1.75
(8)	Jose Pagan	3.00	1.50	.90
(9)	Fred Patek	3.00	1.50	.90
(10)	Bob Robertson	3.00	1.50	.90
(11)	Manny Sanguillen	4.50	2.25	1.25
(12)	Willie Stargell	12.50	6.25	3.75

1954 Bill Jacobellis N.Y. Giants

James (Dusty) Rhodes

In the Giants' championship season, New York photographer Bill Jacobellis produced this set of player/team pictures, probably to be sold at the Polo Grounds souvenir stands. The black-and-white pictures are blank-backed and measure about 8-1/4" x 10-1/2", printed on semi-gloss paper. The player name is centered in bold type in the white bottom border; at right is "Bill Jacobellis Photo." The unnumbered pictures are listed here in alphabetical order.

		NM	EX	VG
Complete Set (8):		110.00	55.00	32.50
Common Player:		12.50	6.25	3.75
(1)	John Antonelli	12.50	6.25	3.75
(2)	Alvin Dark	12.50	6.25	3.75
(3)	Ruben Gomez	12.50	6.25	3.75
(4)	Whitey Lockman	12.50	6.25	3.75
(5)	Willie Mays	60.00	30.00	18.00
(6)	Don Mueller	12.50	6.25	3.75
(7)	James (Dusty) Rhodes	12.50	6.25	3.75
(8)	N.Y. Giants of 1954	20.00	10.00	6.00

1968 Jamesway Trucking Co.

PETE ROSE
CINCINNATI REDS

Although it doesn't say so in the red logo which decorates this black-and-white card, Jamesway was a Southern Ohio trucking company. The 4" x 5-1/4" card

is blank-backed. The purpose for which the card was created and its manner of distribution is unknown.

	NM	EX	VG
Pete Rose	275.00	135.00	85.00

1958-1965 Jay Publishing Picture Packs

JOHN CALLISON, Philadelphia Phillies

The name "Picture Packs" has been used to describe this massive series of 5" x 7" black-and-white player photos issued by Jay Publishing's Big League Books division over the eight-year period from 1958 through 1965. The company also produced yearbooks for various major league teams during that period; many of the photos used in the yearbooks also appear in the Picture Packs. Picture Pack sets consist of 12 player/manager photos with name, city and team nickname in the bottom border. They were available by mail, at the ballparks and in stores. They were sold in either plain brown or white envelopes, or in clear plastic. Most were printed on a glossy, slick paper stock, although the quality of the paper may vary from team to team and year to year. The photos were issued anonymously, with no indication of the producer or year of issue. Two different types were issued, differentiated by the typeface used in the captions. Type 1 photos, issued from 1958 through 1961, were printed with a sans-serif style typeface, while Type 2 photos, issued from 1962 through 1965, used a serif typeface. Besides team sets there were a few special picture packs such as All-Stars, old-timers and World Series participants. Some years' team-set packs were updated (sometimes more than once) to reflect roster changes. Many pictures were reused from year to year.

	NM	EX	VG
Typical Team Set:	40.00	20.00	12.00
Common Player:	3.00	1.50	.90
Typical Hall of Famer:	10.00	5.00	3.00
Superstars:	20.00	10.00	6.00

1962 Jell-O

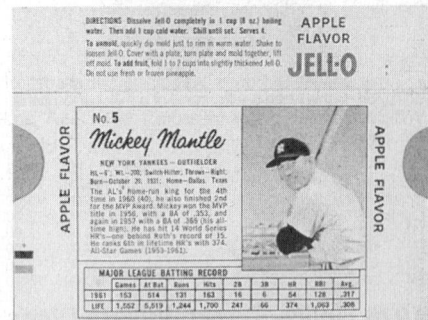

Virtually identical in content to the 1962 Post cereal cards, the '62 Jell-O set of 197 was only issued in the Midwest. Players and card numbers are identical in the two sets, except Brooks Robinson (#29), Ted Kluszewski (#82) and Smoky Burgess (#176) were not issued in the Jell-O version. The Jell-O cards are easy to distinguish from the Post of that year by the absence of the red oval Post logo and red or blue border around the stat box. Cards which have been neatly trimmed from the box on which they were printed will measure 3-1/2" x 2-1/2". Cards of some non-star players can be very scarce because they originally appeared on a limited number of boxes, or unpopular flavors or sizes.

		NM	EX	VG
Complete Set (197):		7,000	2,750	1,750
Common Player:		12.50	5.00	3.25
1	Bill Skowron	30.00	12.00	7.50
2	Bobby Richardson	500.00	200.00	125.00
3	Cletis Boyer	30.00	12.00	7.50
4	Tony Kubek	35.00	14.00	9.00
5	Mickey Mantle	350.00	140.00	90.00

		NM	EX	VG
6	Roger Maris	125.00	50.00	30.00
7	Yogi Berra	75.00	30.00	17.50
8	Elston Howard	30.00	12.00	7.50
9	Whitey Ford	60.00	25.00	15.00
10	Ralph Terry	25.00	10.00	6.25
11	John Blanchard	30.00	12.00	7.50
12	Luis Arroyo	15.00	6.00	3.75
13	Bill Stafford	30.00	12.00	7.50
14	Norm Cash	20.00	8.00	5.00
15	Jake Wood	12.50	5.00	3.25
16	Steve Boros	12.50	5.00	3.25
17	Chico Fernandez	12.50	5.00	3.25
18	Billy Bruton	12.50	5.00	3.25
19	Ken Aspromonte	12.50	5.00	3.25
20	Al Kaline	75.00	30.00	17.50
21	Dick Brown	12.50	5.00	3.25
22	Frank Lary	12.50	5.00	3.25
23	Don Mossi	12.50	5.00	3.25
24	Phil Regan	12.50	5.00	3.25
25	Charley Maxwell	12.50	5.00	3.25
26	Jim Bunning	30.00	12.00	7.50
27	Jim Gentile	12.50	5.00	3.25
28	Marv Breeding	12.50	5.00	3.25
29	Not issued			
30	Ron Hansen	12.50	5.00	3.25
31	Jackie Brandt	50.00	20.00	12.50
32	Dick Williams	12.50	5.00	3.25
33	Gus Triandos	12.50	5.00	3.25
34	Milt Pappas	12.50	5.00	3.25
35	Hoyt Wilhelm	30.00	12.00	7.50
36	Chuck Estrada	12.50	5.00	3.25
37	Vic Power	12.50	5.00	3.25
38	Johnny Temple	12.50	5.00	3.25
39	Bubba Phillips	30.00	12.00	7.50
40	Tito Francona	12.50	5.00	3.25
41	Willie Kirkland	12.50	5.00	3.25
42	John Romano	12.50	5.00	3.25
43	Jim Perry	15.00	6.00	3.75
44	Woodie Held	12.50	5.00	3.25
45	Chuck Essegian	12.50	5.00	3.25
46	Roy Sievers	15.00	6.00	3.75
47	Nellie Fox	40.00	16.00	10.00
48	Al Smith	15.00	6.00	3.75
49	Luis Aparicio	40.00	16.00	10.00
50	Jim Landis	12.50	5.00	3.25
51	Minnie Minoso	25.00	10.00	6.25
52	Andy Carey	30.00	12.00	7.50
53	Sherman Lollar	12.50	5.00	3.25
54	Bill Pierce	12.50	5.00	3.25
55	Early Wynn	50.00	20.00	12.50
56	Chuck Schilling	75.00	30.00	18.50
57	Pete Runnels	12.50	5.00	3.25
58	Frank Malzone	20.00	8.00	5.00
59	Don Buddin	15.00	6.00	3.75
60	Gary Geiger	15.00	6.00	3.75
61	Carl Yastrzemski	250.00	100.00	60.00
62	Jackie Jensen	60.00	24.00	15.00
63	Jim Pagliaroni	30.00	12.00	7.50
64	Don Schwall	12.50	5.00	3.25
65	Dale Long	12.50	5.00	3.25
66	Chuck Cottier	20.00	8.00	5.00
67	Billy Klaus	30.00	12.00	7.50
68	Coot Veal	12.50	5.00	3.25
69	Marty Keough	60.00	25.00	15.00
70	Willie Tasby	60.00	25.00	15.00
71	Gene Woodling	12.50	5.00	3.25
72	Gene Green	60.00	25.00	15.00
73	Dick Donovan	15.00	6.00	3.75
74	Steve Bilko	25.00	10.00	6.25
75	Rocky Bridges	30.00	12.00	7.50
76	Eddie Yost	15.00	6.00	3.75
77	Leon Wagner	15.00	6.00	3.75
78	Albie Pearson	15.00	6.00	3.75
79	Ken Hunt	20.00	8.00	5.00
80	Earl Averill	75.00	30.00	17.50
81	Ryne Duren	15.00	6.00	3.75
82	Not Issued			
83	Bob Allison	15.00	6.00	3.75
84	Billy Martin	20.00	8.00	5.00
85	Harmon Killebrew	75.00	30.00	17.50
86	Zoilo Versalles	15.00	6.00	3.75
87	Lennie Green	90.00	35.00	20.00
88	Bill Tuttle	60.00	25.00	15.00
89	Jim Lemon	60.00	25.00	15.00
90	Earl Battey	30.00	12.00	7.50
91	Camilo Pascual	25.00	10.00	6.25
92	Norm Siebern	12.50	5.00	3.25
93	Jerry Lumpe	12.50	5.00	3.25
94	Dick Howser	15.00	6.00	3.75
95	Gene Stephens	60.00	25.00	15.00
96	Leo Posada	15.00	6.00	3.75
97	Joe Pignatano	15.00	6.00	3.75
98	Jim Archer	15.00	6.00	3.75
99	Haywood Sullivan	30.00	12.00	7.50
100	Art Ditmar	12.50	5.00	3.25
101	Gil Hodges	100.00	40.00	25.00
102	Charlie Neal	15.00	6.00	3.75
103	Daryl Spencer	15.00	6.00	3.75
104	Maury Wills	30.00	12.00	7.50
105	Tommy Davis	30.00	12.00	7.50
106	Willie Davis	15.00	6.00	3.75
107	John Roseboro	60.00	25.00	15.00
108	John Podres	30.00	12.00	7.50
109	Sandy Koufax	100.00	40.00	25.00
110	Don Drysdale	125.00	50.00	30.00
111	Larry Sherry	90.00	35.00	20.00
112	Jim Gilliam	30.00	12.00	7.50
113	Norm Larker	60.00	25.00	15.00
114	Duke Snider	90.00	35.00	20.00
115	Stan Williams	60.00	25.00	15.00
116	Gordon Coleman	80.00	30.00	20.00
117	Don Blasingame	30.00	12.00	7.50
118	Gene Freese	50.00	20.00	12.50
119	Ed Kasko	60.00	25.00	15.00
120	Gus Bell	30.00	12.00	7.50
121	Vada Pinson	15.00	6.00	3.75
122	Frank Robinson	40.00	15.00	10.00
123	Bob Purkey	15.00	6.00	3.75
124	Joey Jay	15.00	6.00	3.75
125	Jim Brosnan	15.00	6.00	3.75
126	Jim O'Toole	15.00	6.00	3.75
127	Jerry Lynch	15.00	6.00	3.75
128	Wally Post	15.00	6.00	3.75
129	Ken Hunt	15.00	6.00	3.75
130	Jerry Zimmerman	15.00	6.00	3.75
131	Willie McCovey	60.00	25.00	15.00
132	Jose Pagan	30.00	12.00	7.50
133	Felipe Alou	15.00	6.00	3.75
134	Jim Davenport	15.00	6.00	3.75
135	Harvey Kuenn	15.00	6.00	3.75
136	Orlando Cepeda	50.00	20.00	12.50
137	Ed Bailey	15.00	6.00	3.75
138	Sam Jones	15.00	6.00	3.75
139	Mike McCormick	15.00	6.00	3.75
140	Juan Marichal	60.00	25.00	15.00
141	Jack Sanford	15.00	6.00	3.75
142	Willie Mays	125.00	50.00	30.00
143	Stu Miller	90.00	35.00	20.00
144	Joe Amalfitano	15.00	6.00	3.75
145	Joe Adcock	15.00	6.00	3.75
146	Frank Bolling	30.00	12.00	7.50
147	Ed Mathews	90.00	35.00	20.00
148	Roy McMillan	12.50	5.00	3.25
149	Hank Aaron	60.00	25.00	15.00
150	Gino Cimoli	30.00	12.00	7.50
151	Frank J. Thomas	12.50	5.00	3.25
152	Joe Torre	60.00	25.00	15.00
153	Lou Burdette	15.00	6.00	3.75
154	Bob Buhl	12.50	5.00	3.25
155	Carlton Willey	12.50	5.00	3.25
156	Lee Maye	50.00	20.00	12.50
157	Al Spangler	60.00	25.00	15.00
158	Bill White	90.00	35.00	20.00
159	Ken Boyer	75.00	30.00	17.50
160	Joe Cunningham	15.00	6.00	3.75
161	Carl Warwick	15.00	6.00	3.75
162	Carl Sawatski	75.00	30.00	17.50
163	Lindy McDaniel	12.50	5.00	3.25
164	Ernie Broglio	15.00	6.00	3.75
165	Larry Jackson	12.50	5.00	3.25
166	Curt Flood	25.00	10.00	6.25
167	Curt Simmons	60.00	25.00	15.00
168	Alex Grammas	30.00	12.00	7.50
169	Dick Stuart	15.00	6.00	3.75
170	Bill Mazeroski	60.00	25.00	15.00
171	Don Hoak	15.00	6.00	3.75
172	Dick Groat	15.00	6.00	3.75
173	Roberto Clemente	180.00	70.00	45.00
174	Bob Skinner	30.00	12.00	7.50
175	Bill Virdon	60.00	25.00	15.00
176	Not issued			
177	Elroy Face	15.00	6.00	3.75
178	Bob Friend	15.00	6.00	3.75
179	Vernon Law	30.00	12.00	7.50
180	Harvey Haddix	60.00	25.00	15.00
181	Hal Smith	30.00	12.00	7.50
182	Ed Bouchee	50.00	20.00	12.50
183	Don Zimmer	60.00	25.00	15.00
184	Ron Santo	35.00	15.00	9.00
185	Andre Rodgers	12.50	5.00	3.25
186	Richie Ashburn	50.00	20.00	12.50
187	George Altman	12.50	5.00	3.25
188	Ernie Banks	50.00	20.00	12.50
189	Sam Taylor	12.50	5.00	3.25
190	Don Elston	12.50	5.00	3.25
191	Jerry Kindall	50.00	20.00	12.50
192	Pancho Herrera	12.50	5.00	3.25
193	Tony Taylor	12.50	5.00	3.25
194	Ruben Amaro	30.00	12.00	7.50
195	Don Demeter	12.50	5.00	3.25
196	Bobby Gene Smith	60.00	25.00	15.00
197	Clay Dalrymple	12.50	5.00	3.25
198	Robin Roberts	60.00	25.00	15.00
199	Art Mahaffey	12.50	5.00	3.25
200	John Buzhardt	12.50	5.00	3.25

The high value of some non-star players' cards can be attributed to scarcity caused by the cards having originally been printed on unpopular flavors or sizes.

		NM	EX	VG
	Complete Set (200):	5,500	2,200	1,325
	Common Player:	7.50	3.00	2.00
1	Vic Power	15.00	6.00	3.50
2	Bernie Allen	65.00	25.00	15.00
3	Zoilo Versalles	65.00	25.00	15.00
4	Rich Rollins	7.50	3.00	2.00
5	Harmon Killebrew	50.00	20.00	12.50
6	Lenny Green	35.00	15.00	10.00
7	Bob Allison	15.00	6.00	3.50
8	Earl Battey	55.00	22.50	13.50
9	Camilo Pascual	10.00	4.00	2.50
10	Jim Kaat	60.00	25.00	15.00
11	Jack Kralick	7.50	3.00	2.00
12	Bill Skowron	65.00	25.00	15.00
13	Bobby Richardson	10.00	4.00	2.50
14	Cletis Boyer	7.50	3.00	2.00
15	Mickey Mantle	175.00	60.00	40.00
16	Roger Maris	40.00	15.00	10.00
17	Yogi Berra	30.00	12.00	7.50
18	Elston Howard	35.00	15.00	10.00
19	Whitey Ford	20.00	8.00	5.00
20	Ralph Terry	7.50	3.00	2.00
21	John Blanchard	30.00	12.00	7.50
22	Bill Stafford	25.00	10.00	6.00
23	Tom Tresh	7.50	3.00	2.00
24	Steve Bilko	7.50	3.00	2.00
25	Bill Moran	7.50	3.00	2.00
26	Joe Koppe	7.50	3.00	2.00
27	Felix Torres	7.50	3.00	2.00
28	Leon Wagner	10.00	4.00	2.50
29	Albie Pearson	7.50	3.00	2.00
30	Lee Thomas	7.50	3.00	2.00
31	Bob Rodgers	65.00	25.00	15.00
32	Dean Chance	7.50	3.00	2.00
33	Ken McBride	35.00	15.00	10.00
34	George Thomas	35.00	15.00	10.00
35	Joe Cunningham	60.00	25.00	15.00
36	Nelson Fox	12.50	5.00	3.00
37	Luis Aparicio	12.50	5.00	3.00
38	Al Smith	7.50	3.00	2.00
39	Floyd Robinson	7.50	3.00	2.00
40	Jim Landis	7.50	3.00	2.00
41	Charlie Maxwell	7.50	3.00	2.00
42	Sherman Lollar	15.00	6.00	3.50
43	Early Wynn	20.00	8.00	5.00
44	Juan Pizarro	75.00	30.00	17.50
45	Ray Herbert	50.00	20.00	12.50
46	Norm Cash	17.50	7.00	4.50
47	Steve Boros	35.00	15.00	10.00
48	Dick McAuliffe	7.50	3.00	2.00
49	Bill Bruton	15.00	6.00	3.75
50	Rocky Colavito	25.00	10.00	6.00
51	Al Kaline	30.00	12.00	7.50
52	Dick Brown	35.00	15.00	10.00
53	Jim Bunning	15.00	6.00	3.50
54	Hank Aguirre	7.50	3.00	2.00
55	Frank Lary	40.00	15.00	10.00
56	Don Mossi	40.00	15.00	10.00
57	Jim Gentile	7.50	3.00	2.00
58	Jackie Brandt	7.50	3.00	2.00
59	Brooks Robinson	30.00	12.00	7.50
60	Ron Hansen	7.50	3.00	2.00
61	Jerry Adair	175.00	70.00	45.00
62	John Powell	9.00	3.50	2.25
63	Russ Snyder	35.00	15.00	10.00
64	Steve Barber	7.50	3.00	2.00
65	Milt Pappas	40.00	15.00	10.00
66	Robin Roberts	10.00	4.00	2.50
67	Tito Francona	7.50	3.00	2.00
68	Jerry Kindall	35.00	15.00	10.00
69	Woodie Held	7.50	3.00	2.00
70	Bubba Phillips	7.50	3.00	2.00
71	Chuck Essegian	7.50	3.00	2.00
72	Willie Kirkland	35.00	15.00	10.00
73	Al Luplow	35.00	15.00	10.00
74	Ty Cline	75.00	30.00	17.50
75	Dick Donovan	7.50	3.00	2.00
76	John Romano	7.50	3.00	2.00
77	Pete Runnels	12.50	5.00	3.00
78	Ed Bressoud	100.00	40.00	25.00
79	Frank Malzone	7.50	3.00	2.00
80	Carl Yastrzemski	100.00	40.00	25.00
81	Gary Geiger	7.50	3.00	2.00
82	Lou Clinton	40.00	15.00	10.00
83	Earl Wilson	7.50	3.00	2.00
84	Bill Monbouquette	7.50	3.00	2.00
85	Norm Siebern	7.50	3.00	2.00
86	Jerry Lumpe	9.00	3.50	2.00
87	Manny Jimenez	9.00	3.50	2.25
88	Gino Cimoli	12.50	5.00	3.00
89	Ed Charles	75.00	30.00	17.50
90	Ed Rakow	7.50	3.00	2.00
91	Bob Del Greco	165.00	65.00	40.00
92	Haywood Sullivan	40.00	15.00	10.00
93	Chuck Hinton	7.50	3.00	2.00
94	Ken Retzer	35.00	15.00	10.00
95	Harry Bright	30.00	12.00	7.50
96	Bob Johnson	10.00	4.00	2.50
97	Dave Stenhouse	35.00	15.00	10.00
98	Chuck Cottier	7.50	3.00	2.00
99	Tom Cheney	9.00	3.50	2.00
100	Claude Osteen	75.00	30.00	17.50
101	Orlando Cepeda	15.00	6.00	3.50
102	Charley Hiller	35.00	15.00	10.00
103	Jose Pagan	35.00	15.00	10.00
104	Jim Davenport	7.50	3.00	2.00
105	Harvey Kuenn	7.50	3.00	2.00
106	Willie Mays	50.00	20.00	12.50
107	Felipe Alou	7.50	3.00	2.00
108	Tom Haller	35.00	15.00	10.00
109	Juan Marichal	25.00	10.00	6.00
110	Jack Sanford	12.50	5.00	3.00

1963 Jell-O

Like the other Post and Jell-O issues of the era, the '63 Jell-O set includes many scarce cards; primarily those which were printed as the backs of less popular brands and sizes of the gelatin dessert. Slightly smaller than the virtually identical Post cereal cards of the same year, the 200 cards in the Jell-O issue measure 3-3/8" x 2-1/2". The easiest way to distinguish 1963 Jell-O cards from Post cards is by the red line that separates the 1962 stats from the lifetime stats. On Post cards, the line extends almost all the way to the side borders, on the Jell-O cards, the line begins and ends much closer to the stats.

111	Bill O'Dell	7.50	3.00	2.00
112	Willie McCovey	100.00	40.00	25.00
113	Lee Walls	35.00	15.00	10.00
114	Jim Gilliam	60.00	25.00	15.00
115	Maury Wills	10.00	4.00	2.50
116	Ron Fairly	7.50	3.00	2.00
117	Tommy Davis	7.50	3.00	2.00
118	Duke Snider	20.00	8.00	5.00
119	Willie Davis	20.00	8.00	5.00
120	John Roseboro	7.50	3.00	2.00
121	Sandy Koufax	50.00	20.00	12.50
122	Stan Williams	30.00	12.00	7.50
123	Don Drysdale	12.50	5.00	3.00
124	Daryl Spencer	7.50	3.00	2.00
125	Gordy Coleman	7.50	3.00	2.00
126	Don Blasingame	50.00	20.00	12.50
127	Leo Cardenas	7.50	3.00	2.00
128	Eddie Kasko	80.00	35.00	20.00
129	Jerry Lynch	7.50	3.00	2.00
130	Vada Pinson	7.50	3.00	2.00
131	Frank Robinson	20.00	8.00	5.00
132	John Edwards	40.00	15.00	10.00
133	Joey Jay	7.50	3.00	2.00
134	Bob Purkey	7.50	3.00	2.00
135	Marty Keough	100.00	40.00	25.00
136	Jim O'Toole	40.00	15.00	10.00
137	Dick Stuart	7.50	3.00	2.00
138	Bill Mazeroski	12.50	5.00	3.00
139	Dick Groat	7.50	3.00	2.00
140	Don Hoak	7.50	3.00	2.00
141	Bob Skinner	12.50	5.00	3.00
142	Bill Virdon	7.50	3.00	2.00
143	Roberto Clemente	100.00	40.00	25.00
144	Smoky Burgess	7.50	3.00	2.00
145	Bob Friend	7.50	3.00	2.00
146	Al McBean	50.00	20.00	12.50
147	ElRoy Face	7.50	3.00	2.00
148	Joe Adcock	7.50	3.00	2.00
149	Frank Bolling	7.50	3.00	2.00
150	Roy McMillan	7.50	3.00	2.00
151	Eddie Mathews	12.50	5.00	3.00
152	Hank Aaron	50.00	20.00	12.50
153	Del Crandall	35.00	15.00	10.00
154	Bob Shaw	7.50	3.00	2.00
155	Lew Burdette	7.50	3.00	2.00
156	Joe Torre	50.00	20.00	12.50
157	Tony Cloninger	200.00	80.00	50.00
158	Bill White	7.50	3.00	2.00
159	Julian Javier	60.00	25.00	15.00
160	Ken Boyer	9.00	3.50	2.00
161	Julio Gotay	75.00	30.00	17.50
162	Curt Flood	25.00	10.00	6.00
163	Charlie James	65.00	25.00	15.00
164	Gene Oliver	50.00	20.00	12.50
165	Ernie Broglio	15.00	6.00	3.50
166	Bob Gibson	125.00	50.00	30.00
167	Lindy McDaniel	35.00	15.00	10.00
168	Ray Washburn	7.50	3.00	2.00
169	Ernie Banks	40.00	15.00	10.00
170	Ron Santo	15.00	6.00	3.50
171	George Altman	7.50	3.00	2.00
172	Billy Williams	100.00	40.00	25.00
173	Andre Rodgers	75.00	30.00	17.50
174	Ken Hubbs	15.00	6.00	3.75
175	Don Landrum	60.00	25.00	15.00
176	Dick Bertell	65.00	25.00	15.00
177	Roy Sievers	7.50	3.00	2.00
178	Tony Taylor	35.00	15.00	10.00
179	John Callison	7.50	3.00	2.00
180	Don Demeter	7.50	3.00	2.00
181	Tony Gonzalez	125.00	50.00	30.00
182	Wes Covington	50.00	20.00	12.50
183	Art Mahaffey	7.50	3.00	2.00
184	Clay Dalrymple	7.50	3.00	2.00
185	Al Spangler	7.50	3.00	2.00
186	Roman Mejias	7.50	3.00	2.00
187	Bob Aspromonte	250.00	100.00	60.00
188	Norm Larker	7.50	3.00	2.00
189	Johnny Temple	7.50	3.00	2.00
190	Carl Warwick	35.00	15.00	10.00
191	Bob Lillis	35.00	15.00	10.00
192	Dick Farrell	150.00	60.00	35.00
193	Gil Hodges	15.00	6.00	3.50
194	Marv Throneberry	7.50	3.00	2.00
195	Charlie Neal	75.00	30.00	17.50
196	Frank Thomas	25.00	10.00	6.00
197	Richie Ashburn	15.00	6.00	3.50
198	Felix Mantilla	60.00	25.00	15.00
199	Rod Kanehl	35.00	15.00	10.00
200	Roger Craig	75.00	30.00	17.50

1969 Jewel Food Chicago Cubs

This set of premium pictures was issued by the midwest regional home-delivery food service. The pic-tures are 6" x 9" color poses with white borders and blank backs. A facsimile autograph appears on front.

		NM	EX	VG
	Complete Set (20):	125.00	65.00	35.00
	Common Player:	6.00	3.00	1.80
(1)	Ted Abernathy	6.00	3.00	1.80
(2)	Hank Aguirre	6.00	3.00	1.80
(3)	Ernie Banks	30.00	15.00	9.00
(4)	Glenn Beckert	7.50	3.75	2.25
(5)	Bill Hands	6.00	3.00	1.80
(6)	Jim Hickman	6.00	3.00	1.80
(7)	Kenny Holtzman	6.00	3.00	1.75
(8)	Randy Hundley	7.50	3.75	2.25
(9)	Fergie Jenkins	12.50	6.25	3.75
(10)	Don Kessinger	7.50	3.75	2.25
(11)	Rich Nye	6.00	3.00	1.80
(12)	Paul Popovich	6.00	3.00	1.80
(13)	Jim Qualls	6.00	3.00	1.80
(14)	Phil Regan	6.00	3.00	1.80
(15)	Ron Santo	15.00	7.50	4.50
(16)	Dick Selma	6.00	3.00	1.80
(17)	Willie Smith	6.00	3.00	1.80
(18)	Al Spangler	6.00	3.00	1.80
(19)	Billy Williams	15.00	7.50	4.50
(20)	Don Young	6.00	3.00	1.80

1973 Jewel Food Baseball Photos

Jewel Food Stores, a midwestern grocery chain, issued three team sets of large-format baseball player photos in 1973. The 5-7/8" x 9" blank-back photos are full color and feature a facsimile autograph. Photos were sold in groups of four or five per week at five or ten cents per picture. There are 24 Milwaukee Brewers in the issue, and 16 each Chicago Cubs and Chicago White Sox. The unnumbered cards are alphabetized by team in the checklist below.

		NM	EX	VG
CHICAGO CUBS				
	Complete Set (16):	40.00	20.00	12.00
	Common Player:	4.00	2.00	1.25
(1)	Jack Aker	4.00	2.00	1.25
(2)	Glenn Beckert	5.00	2.50	1.50
(3)	Jose Cardenal	4.00	2.00	1.25
(4)	Carmen Fanzone	4.00	2.00	1.25
(5)	Burt Hooton	4.00	2.00	1.25
(6)	Fergie Jenkins	10.00	5.00	3.00
(7)	Don Kessinger	5.00	2.50	1.50
(8)	Jim Hickman	4.00	2.00	1.25
(9)	Randy Hundley	5.00	2.50	1.50
(10)	Bob Locker	4.00	2.00	1.25
(11)	Rick Monday	4.00	2.00	1.25
(12)	Milt Pappas	4.00	2.00	1.25
(13)	Rick Reuschel	4.00	2.00	1.25
(14)	Ken Rudolph	4.00	2.00	1.25
(15)	Ron Santo	10.00	5.00	3.00
(16)	Billy Williams	15.00	7.50	4.50
CHICAGO WHITE SOX				
	Complete Set (16):	30.00	15.00	9.00
	Common Player:	4.00	2.00	1.25
(17)	Dick Allen	7.50	3.75	2.25
(18)	Mike Andrews	4.00	2.00	1.25
(19)	Stan Bahnsen	4.00	2.00	1.25
(20)	Eddie Fisher	4.00	2.00	1.25
(21)	Terry Forster	4.00	2.00	1.25
(22)	Ken Henderson	4.00	2.00	1.25
(23)	Ed Hermann	4.00	2.00	1.25
(24)	John Jeter	4.00	2.00	1.25
(25)	Pat Kelly	4.00	2.00	1.25
(26)	Eddie Leon	4.00	2.00	1.25
(27)	Carlos May	4.00	2.00	1.25
(28)	Bill Melton	4.00	2.00	1.25
(29)	Tony Muser	4.00	2.00	1.25
(30)	Jorge Orta	4.00	2.00	1.25
(31)	Rick Reichardt	4.00	2.00	1.25
(32)	Wilbur Wood	4.00	2.00	1.25
MILWAUKEE BREWERS				
	Complete Set (25):	35.00	17.50	10.00
	Common Player:	4.00	2.00	1.25
(33)	Jerry Bell	4.00	2.00	1.25
(34)	John Briggs	4.00	2.00	1.25
(35)	Ollie Brown	4.00	2.00	1.25
(36)	Billy Champion	4.00	2.00	1.25
(37)	Jim Colborn	4.00	2.00	1.25
(38)	Bob Coluccio	4.00	2.00	1.25
(39)	John Felske	4.00	2.00	1.25
(40)	Pedro Garcia	4.00	2.00	1.25
(41)	Rob Gardner	4.00	2.00	1.25
(42)	Bob Heise	4.00	2.00	1.25
(43)	Tim Johnson	4.00	2.00	1.25
(44)	Joe Lahoud	4.00	2.00	1.25
(45)	Frank Linzy	4.00	2.00	1.25
(46)	Skip Lockwood	4.00	2.00	1.25
(47)	Dave May	4.00	2.00	1.25
(48)	Bob Mitchell	4.00	2.00	1.25
(49)	Don Money	4.00	2.00	1.25
(50)	Bill Parsons	4.00	2.00	1.25
(51)	Darrell Porter	4.00	2.00	1.25
(52)	Eduardo Rodriguez	4.00	2.00	1.25
(53)	Ellie Rodriguez	4.00	2.00	1.25
(54)	George Scott	5.00	2.50	1.50
(55)	Chris Short	4.00	2.00	1.25
(56)	Jim Slaton	4.00	2.00	1.25
(57)	John Vukovich	4.00	2.00	1.25

1977 Jewel Food Chicago Cubs/ White Sox

Once again in 1977 Jewel grocery stores in the Chicago area offered photos of local players with specific product purchases over a four-week period. The 5-7/8" x 9" color photos are printed on heavy paper. Fronts have player poses, a facsimile signature and the MLB Players Association logo in the upper-left corner. Backs are blank. The pictures are not numbered and are checklisted here alphabetically within team. It was reported 12,000 of each picture were produced.

		NM	EX	VG
	Complete Set, Cubs (16):	12.00	6.00	3.50
	Complete Set, White Sox (16):	12.00	6.00	3.50
	Common Player:	1.50	.70	.45
CHICAGO CUBS				
(1)	Larry Biittner	1.50	.70	.45
(2)	Bill Bonham	1.50	.70	.45
(3)	Bill Buckner	2.50	1.25	.70
(4)	Ray Burris	1.50	.70	.45
(5)	Jose Cardenal	1.50	.70	.45
(6)	Gene Clines	1.50	.70	.45
(7)	Ivan DeJesus	1.50	.70	.45
(8)	Willie Hernandez	1.50	.70	.45
(9)	Mike Krukow	1.50	.70	.45
(10)	George Mitterwald	1.50	.70	.45
(11)	Jerry Morales	1.50	.70	.45
(12)	Bobby Murcer	2.50	1.25	.70
(13)	Steve Ontiveros	1.50	.70	.45
(14)	Rick Reuschel	1.50	.70	.45
(15)	Bruce Sutter	3.50	1.75	1.00
(16)	Manny Trillo	1.50	.70	.45
CHICAGO WHITE SOX				
(1)	Alan Bannister	1.50	.70	.45
(2)	Francisco Barrios	1.50	.70	.45
(3)	Jim Essian	1.50	.70	.45
(4)	Oscar Gamble	1.50	.70	.45
(5)	Ralph Garr	1.50	.70	.45
(6)	Lamar Johnson	1.50	.70	.45
(7)	Chris Knapp	1.50	.70	.45
(8)	Ken Kravec	1.50	.70	.45
(9)	Lerrin LaGrow	1.50	.70	.45
(10)	Chet Lemon	1.50	.70	.45
(11)	Jorge Orta	1.50	.70	.45
(12)	Eric Soderholm	1.50	.70	.45
(13)	Jim Spencer	1.50	.70	.45
(14)	Steve Stone	2.50	1.25	.70
(15)	Wilbur Wood	1.50	.70	.45
(16)	Richie Zisk	1.50	.70	.45

1949 Jimmy Fund Boston Braves Die-Cuts

The reigning National League champions undertook the support of the Jimmy Fund, a Boston charity for children's cancer research, with a set of die-cut counter cards accompanying contributions boxes. Between about 6" and 8" at the base, and up to a foot tall, these heavy cardboard pieces feature sepia-toned player action photos in front of a large baseball on which is written, "THANK YOU! in behalf of 'JIMMY.'" with a facsimile signature below. Backs have a fold-out easel to stand the card up, and a notation that following the fund drive, the card should be given to the largest contributor at that location.

		NM	EX	VG
Complete Set (20):		15,000	7,500	4,500
Common Player:		750.00	375.00	225.00
(1)	Johnny Antonelli	750.00	375.00	225.00
(2)	Red Barrett	750.00	375.00	225.00
(3)	Vern Bickford	750.00	375.00	225.00
(4)	Clint Conatser	750.00	375.00	225.00
(5)	Al Dark	750.00	375.00	225.00
(6)	Bob Elliott	750.00	375.00	225.00
(7)	Glenn Elliott	750.00	375.00	225.00
(8)	Bobby Hogue	750.00	375.00	225.00
(9)	Tommy Holmes	750.00	.375.00	225.00
(10)	Pete Reiser	750.00	375.00	225.00
(11)	Marv Rickert	750.00	375.00	225.00
(12)	Jim Russell	750.00	375.00	225.00
(13)	Connie Ryan	750.00	375.00	225.00
(14)	Johnny Sain	850.00	425.00	255.00
(15)	Bill Salkeld	750.00	375.00	225.00
(16)	Sibby Sisti	750.00	375.00	225.00
(17)	Warren Spahn	1,200	600.00	360.00
(18)	Don Thompson	750.00	375.00	225.00
(19)	Earl Torgeson	750.00	375.00	225.00
(20)	Bill Voiselle	750.00	375.00	225.00

1978 JJH Reading Remembers

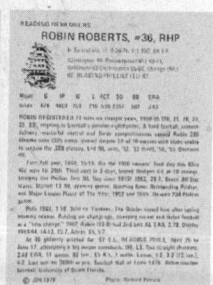

This collectors' issue was created to honor baseball players (and a few others) who were born, lived in or played in Berks County, Pa., particularly in Reading. The cards are 3" x 4" featuring borderless sepia photos on front. Most of the photos picture players in big league uniforms. Backs are in black-and-white and have career stats and summaries. A number of major leaguers who did not have cards contemporary with their careers are found in this set. Cards are numbered by uniform number. Production was reported as 1,000 sets.

		NM	EX	VG
Complete Set (23):		25.00	12.50	7.50
Common Player:		2.00	1.00	.60
1	Whitey Kurowski	2.00	1.00	.60
6	Carl Furillo	5.00	2.50	1.50
9	Roger Maris	10.00	5.00	3.00
12	Stan Wetzel	2.00	1.00	.60
17	Doug Clemens	2.00	1.00	.60
18	Randy Gumpert	2.00	1.00	.60
18	Ty Stofflet/Softball	2.00	1.00	.60
21	George Eyrich	2.00	1.00	.60
23	Vic Wertz	2.00	1.00	.60
24	Lenny Moore/Football	2.00	1.00	.60
25	Dick Gernert	2.00	1.00	.60
27	Herb Score	2.00	1.00	.60
27	Charlie Wagner	2.00	1.00	.60
28	Carl Mathias	2.00	1.00	.60
32	Jesse Levan	2.00	1.00	.60
34	Betz Klopp	2.00	1.00	.60
36	Robin Roberts	9.00	4.50	2.75
39	Bob Katz	2.00	1.00	.60
39	Harry Schaeffer	2.00	1.00	.60
40	Tommy Brown/Baseball/Football	1.50	.70	.45
46	Dom Dallessandro	2.00	1.00	.60
---	Lauer's Park	2.00	1.00	.60
---	John Updike/Author	2.00	1.00	.60

1950s J.J.K. Copyart Postcards

Issued from about 1950 through at least 1956, this series of glossy black-and-white player postcards appears to have been produced on order of the individual players to respond to fan requests for pictures and/or autographs. Fronts feature player poses bordered in white in about 3-1/2" x 5-1/2" format; most have facsimile autographs. Backs have typical postcard layout with a credit line to J.J.K. Copyart Photographers of New York City. Some players are known in more than one pose.

		NM	EX	VG
Common Player:		15.00	7.50	4.50
BOSTON/MILWAUKEE BRAVES				
(1)	Del Crandall	15.00	7.50	4.50
(2)	Tommy Holmes	15.00	7.50	4.50
(3)	Willard Marshall	15.00	7.50	4.50
(4)	Eddie Mathews	60.00	30.00	18.00
(5)	Eddie Mathews	60.00	30.00	18.00
(6)	Danny O'Connell	15.00	7.50	4.50
(7)	Sibby Sisti	15.00	7.50	4.50
(8)	Eddie Stanky	25.00	12.50	7.50
BROOKLYN DODGERS				
(1)	Jackie Robinson	200.00	100.00	60.00
NEW YORK GIANTS				
(1)	Johnny Antonelli	15.00	7.50	4.50
(2)	Johnny Antonelli	15.00	7.50	4.50
(3)	Sam Calderone	15.00	7.50	4.50
(4)	Jim Hearn	15.00	7.50	4.50
(5)	Jim Hearn	15.00	7.50	4.50
(6)	Larry Jansen	15.00	7.50	4.50
(7)	Whitey Lockman	15.00	7.50	4.50
(8)	Whitey Lockman	15.00	7.50	4.50
(9)	Don Mueller	15.00	7.50	4.50
(10)	Bill Rigney	15.00	7.50	4.50
(11)	Bill Rigney	15.00	7.50	4.50
(12)	Hank Sauer	15.00	7.50	4.50
(13)	Red Schoendienst	30.00	15.00	9.00
(14)	Daryl Spencer	15.00	7.50	4.50
(15)	Eddie Stanky	25.00	12.50	7.50
(16)	Wes Westrum	15.00	7.50	4.50
(17)	Wes Westrum	15.00	7.50	4.50
(18)	Hoyt Wilhelm	30.00	15.00	9.00
(19)	Al Worthington	15.00	7.50	4.50
PHILADELPHIA PHILLIES				
(1)	Del Ennis	15.00	7.50	4.50
(2)	Robin Roberts	30.00	15.00	9.00
(3)	Curt Simmons	15.00	7.50	4.50

1973 Johnny Pro Orioles

PUSH-OUT / STAND-UP PLAYER PHOTO SERIES

This regional set of large (4-1/4" x 7-1/4") die-cut cards was issued by Johnny Pro Enterprises Inc. of Baltimore and features only Orioles. The cards were designed to be punched out and folded to make baseball player figures that can stand up. The full-color die-cut figures appear against a green background. The cards are numbered according to the player's uniform number, which appears in a white box along with his name and position. The backs are blank. Three players (Robinson, Grich, and Palmer) appear in two poses each, and cards of Orlando Pena were not die-cut. Values listed are for complete cards not punched out. Cards originally sold for 15 cents apiece.

		NM	EX	VG
Complete Set (28):		135.00	65.00	40.00
Common Player:		3.00	1.50	.90
1	Al Bumbry	3.00	1.50	.90
2	Rich Coggins	3.00	1.50	.90
3a	Bobby Grich/Btg	5.00	2.50	1.50
3b	Bobby Grich/Fielding	5.00	2.50	1.50
4	Earl Weaver	6.00	3.00	1.75
5a	Brooks Robinson/Btg	25.00	12.50	7.50
5b	Brooks Robinson/Fielding	25.00	12.50	7.50
6	Paul Blair	4.00	2.00	1.25
7	Mark Belanger	4.00	2.00	1.25
8	Andy Etchebarren	3.00	1.50	.90
10	Elrod Hendricks	3.00	1.50	.90
11	Terry Crowley	3.00	1.50	.90
12	Tommy Davis	4.00	2.00	1.25
13	Doyle Alexander	3.00	1.50	.90
14	Merv Rettenmund	3.00	1.50	.90
15	Frank Baker	3.00	1.50	.90
19	Dave McNally	4.00	2.00	1.25
21	Larry Brown	3.00	1.50	.90
22a	Jim Palmer (Follow-thru.)	15.00	7.50	4.50
22b	Jim Palmer (Wind-up.)	15.00	7.50	4.50
23	Grant Jackson	3.00	1.50	.90
25	Don Baylor	6.00	3.00	1.75
26	Boog Powell	7.00	3.50	2.00
27	Orlando Pena	8.00	4.00	2.50
32	Earl Williams	3.00	1.50	.90
34	Bob Reynolds	3.00	1.50	.90
35	Mike Cuellar	5.00	2.50	1.50
39	Eddie Watt	3.00	1.50	.90

1974 Johnny Pro Phillies

LARRY BOWA
Infielder

Although slightly smaller (3-3/4" x 7-1/8") and featuring members of the Phillies, this set is very similar to the 1973 Johnny Pro Orioles set. The full-color die-cut player figures are set against a white background. Again, the set is numbered according to the player's uniform number. The values listed are for complete cards.

		NM	EX	VG
Complete Set (12):		150.00	75.00	45.00
Common Player:		3.00	1.50	.90
8	Bob Boone	7.50	3.75	2.25
10	Larry Bowa	7.50	3.75	2.25
16	Dave Cash	3.00	1.50	.90
19	Greg Luzinski	5.00	2.50	1.50
20	Mike Schmidt	100.00	50.00	30.00
22	Mike Anderson	3.00	1.50	.90
24	Bill Robinson	3.00	1.50	.90
25	Del Unser	3.00	1.50	.90
27	Willie Montanez	3.00	1.50	.90
32	Steve Carlton	25.00	12.50	7.50
37	Ron Schueler	3.00	1.50	.90
41	Jim Lonborg	3.00	1.50	.90

1922 Henry A. Johnson Wholesale Confectioner

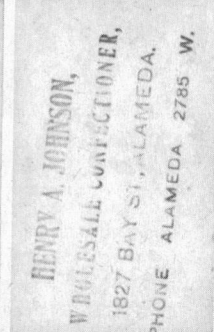

JOE JUDGE
1st B—Washington Americans

HENRY A. JOHNSON, WHOLESALE CONFECTIONER, 1827 BAY ST., ALAMEDA. PHONE ALAMEDA 2785 W.

To compete with other candy issues featuring baseball cards as premiums, Alameda, Calif., confectioner Henry A. Johnson purchased uncut sheets of the blank-back strip cards known as W575-1, overprinted their backs and packaged them with his Likem brand candy bars. The advertising on back gives the firm's name, address and telephone number. Collectors can expect to pay a premium of about 3X for this version. Only the type style shown here can definitely be traced to the 1920s. Other styles of typography are known to have been applied in the 1980s and later.

	NM	EX	VG
Common Player:	85.00	42.50	25.00
Stars: 2-3X			

(See W575-1 for checklist and base card values.)

1953 Johnston Cookies Braves

The first and most common of three annual issues, the '53 Johnstons were inserted into boxes of cookies on a regional basis. Complete sets were also available via a mail-in offer from the company, whose factory sits in the shadow of Milwaukee County Stadium. While at first glance appearing to be color photos, the pictures on the 25 cards in the set are actually well-done colorizations of black-and-white photos. Cards measure 2-9/16" x 3-5/8". Write-ups on the backs were "borrowed" from the Braves' 1953 yearbook.

		NM	EX	VG
	Complete Set (25):	500.00	250.00	150.00
	Common Player:	15.00	7.50	4.50
1	Charlie Grimm	15.00	7.50	4.50
2	John Antonelli	15.00	7.50	4.50
3	Vern Bickford	15.00	7.50	4.50
4	Bob Buhl	15.00	7.50	4.50
5	Lew Burdette	15.00	7.50	4.50
6	Dave Cole	15.00	7.50	4.50
7	Ernie Johnson	15.00	7.50	4.50
8	Dave Jolly	15.00	7.50	4.50
9	Don Liddle	15.00	7.50	4.50
10	Warren Spahn	150.00	75.00	45.00
11	Max Surkont	15.00	7.50	4.50
12	Jim Wilson	15.00	7.50	4.50
13	Sibby Sisti	15.00	7.50	4.50
14	Walker Cooper	15.00	7.50	4.50
15	Del Crandall	15.00	7.50	4.50
16	Ebba St. Claire	15.00	7.50	4.50
17	Joe Adcock	15.00	7.50	4.50
18	George Crowe	15.00	7.50	4.50
19	Jack Dittmer	15.00	7.50	4.50
20	Johnny Logan	15.00	7.50	4.50
21	Ed Mathews	150.00	75.00	45.00
22	Bill Bruton	15.00	7.50	4.50
23	Sid Gordon	15.00	7.50	4.50
24	Andy Pafko	15.00	7.50	4.50
25	Jim Pendleton	15.00	7.50	4.50

1954 Johnston Cookies Braves

In its second of three annual issues, Johnston's increased the number of cards in its 1954 Braves issue to 35, and switched to an unusual size, a narrow format, 2" x 3-7/8". Cards are listed here by uniform number. After his early-season injury (which gave Hank Aaron a chance to play regularly), Bobby Thomson's card was withdrawn, accounting for its scarcity and high value. Uncut sheets of 42 cards (including seven double-prints) in a size of about 12-1/2" x 27-3/4" are not uncommon. A 21-1/2" x 31" wall-hanging display poster with die-cuts into which cards could be inserted was available as a premium offer.

		NM	EX	VG
	Complete Set (35):	1,500	750.00	450.00
	Common Player:	20.00	10.00	6.00
	Uncut Sheet:	4,750	2,400	1,400
	Display Poster:	500.00	250.00	150.00
1	Del Crandall	20.00	10.00	6.00
3	Jim Pendleton	20.00	10.00	6.00
4	Danny O'Connell	20.00	10.00	6.00
5	Henry Aaron	750.00	375.00	225.00
6	Jack Dittmer	20.00	10.00	6.00
9	Joe Adcock	20.00	10.00	6.00
10	Robert Buhl	20.00	10.00	6.00
11	Phillip Paine (Phillips)/DP	20.00	10.00	6.00
12	Ben Johnson	20.00	10.00	6.00
13	Sibby Sisti	20.00	10.00	6.00
15	Charles Gorin	20.00	10.00	6.00
16	Chet Nichols	20.00	10.00	6.00
17	Dave Jolly/DP	20.00	10.00	6.00
19	Jim Wilson/DP	20.00	10.00	6.00
20	Ray Crone	20.00	10.00	6.00
21	Warren Spahn/DP	100.00	50.00	30.00
22	Gene Conley	20.00	10.00	6.00
23	Johnny Logan/DP	20.00	10.00	6.00
24	Charlie White	20.00	10.00	6.00
27	George Metkovich	20.00	10.00	6.00
28	John Cooney	20.00	10.00	6.00
29	Paul Burris	20.00	10.00	6.00
31	Wm. Walters/DP	20.00	10.00	6.00
32	Ernest T. Johnson	20.00	10.00	6.00
33	Lew Burdette	20.00	10.00	6.00
34	Bob Thomson/SP	165.00	80.00	50.00
35	Robert Keely	20.00	10.00	6.00
38	Billy Bruton	20.00	10.00	6.00
40	Charles Grimm	20.00	10.00	6.00
41	Ed Mathews	100.00	50.00	30.00
42	Sam Calderone/DP	20.00	10.00	6.00
47	Joey Jay	20.00	10.00	6.00
48	Andy Pafko	20.00	10.00	6.00
---	Dr. Charles Lacks/ Asst. Trainer	20.00	10.00	6.00
---	Joseph F. Taylor/ Asst. Trainer	20.00	10.00	6.00

1955 Johnston Cookies Braves

A third change in size and format was undertaken in the final year of Braves sets produced by Johnston's. The 35 cards in the 1955 set were issued in six fold-out panels of six cards each (Andy Pafko was double-printed). As in 1954, cards are numbered by uniform number, except those of the team equipment manager, trainer and road secretary (former Boston star Duffy Lewis). Single cards measure 2-7/8" x 4". Besides including panels in boxes of cookies, the '55 Johnstons could be ordered for 5¢ per panel by mail. The scarcest of the Johnston's issues, the 1955 set can be found today still in complete panels, or as single cards.

		NM	EX	VG
	Complete Folder Set (6):	1,250	625.00	375.00
	Complete Singles Set (35):	1,500	750.00	450.00
	Common Player:	30.00	20.00	12.00
	Common Folder:	200.00	100.00	60.00
1	Del Crandall	30.00	20.00	12.00
3	Jim Pendleton	30.00	20.00	12.00
4	Danny O'Connell	30.00	20.00	12.00
6	Jack Dittmer	30.00	20.00	12.00
9	Joe Adcock	30.00	20.00	12.00
10	Bob Buhl	30.00	20.00	12.00
11	Phil Paine	30.00	20.00	12.00
12	Ray Crone	30.00	20.00	12.00
15	Charlie Gorin	30.00	20.00	12.00
16	Dave Jolly	30.00	20.00	12.00
17	Chet Nichols	30.00	20.00	12.00
18	Chuck Tanner	30.00	20.00	12.00
19	Jim Wilson	30.00	20.00	12.00
20	Dave Koslo	30.00	20.00	12.00
21	Warren Spahn	100.00	50.00	30.00
22	Gene Conley	30.00	20.00	12.00
23	John Logan	30.00	20.00	12.00
24	Charlie White	30.00	20.00	12.00
28	Johnny Cooney	30.00	20.00	12.00
30	Roy Smalley	30.00	20.00	12.00
31	Bucky Walters	30.00	20.00	12.00
32	Ernie Johnson	30.00	20.00	12.00
33	Lew Burdette	30.00	20.00	12.00
34	Bobby Thomson	35.00	17.50	10.50
35	Bob Keely	30.00	20.00	12.00
38	Billy Bruton	30.00	20.00	12.00
39	George Crowe	30.00	20.00	12.00
40	Charlie Grimm	30.00	20.00	12.00
41	Eddie Mathews	100.00	50.00	30.00
44	Hank Aaron	450.00	225.00	135.00
47	Joe Jay	30.00	20.00	12.00
48	Andy Pakfo	30.00	20.00	12.00
----	Dr. Charles K. Lacks	30.00	20.00	12.00
---	Duffy Lewis	30.00	20.00	12.00
---	Joe Taylor	30.00	20.00	12.00
Series 1 Folder		475.00	240.00	140.00
	Hank Aaron, Lew Burdette, Del Crandall, Charlie Gorin, Bob Keely, Danny O'Connell			
Series 2 Folder		160.00	80.00	45.00
	Joe Adcock, Joe Jay, Dr. Charles K. Lacks, Chet Nichols, Andy Pafko, Charlie White			
Series 3 Folder		175.00	90.00	50.00
	Gene Conley, George Crowe, Jim Pendleton, Roy Smalley, Warren Spahn, Joe Taylor			
Series 4 Folder		160.00	80.00	45.00
	Billy Bruton, John Cooney, Dave Koslo, Johnny Logan, Andy Pafko			
Series 5 Folder		190.00	95.00	55.00
	Ray Crone, Ernie Johnson, Duffy Lewis, Eddie Mathews, Phil Paine, Chuck Tanner			
Series 6 Folder		160.00	80.00	45.00
	Bob Buhl, Jack Dittmer, Charlie Grimm, Bobby Thomson, Bucky Walters, Jim Wilson			

1976 Jerry Jonas Productions All Time Greats

This card set was produced only in prototype form with an estimated 50 of each printed. The cards were designed to introduce a baseball card promotion to team executives at their annual World Series meeting. The 2-3/4" x 3-3/4" cards have black-and-white player photos at center with colored borders reminiscent of the 1975 Topps cards. Backs are printed in black on blue and feature biographical data, career highlights and stats along with a credit line to Jerry Jones Productions. The proposed promotion was never adopted. The unnumbered cards are checklisted here in alphabetical order.

		NM	EX	VG
	Complete Set, Uncut Sheet:	450.00	225.00	135.00
	Complete Set, Singles (8):	450.00	225.00	135.00
	Common Player:	30.00	15.00	9.00
(1)	Grover Alexander	30.00	15.00	9.00
(2)	Rogers Hornsby	30.00	15.00	9.00
(3)	Sandy Koufax	150.00	75.00	45.00
(4)	Willie Mays	100.00	50.00	30.00
(5)	Stan Musial	50.00	25.00	15.00
(6)	Mel Ott	30.00	15.00	9.00
(7)	Robin Roberts	30.00	15.00	9.00
(8)	Honus Wagner	30.00	15.00	9.00

1911 Jones, Keyser & Arras Cabinets

Contemporary with the better-known Sporting Life, Turkey Red and Pinkerton cabinet photos, this series of baseball player cabinets was issued by the New York City studio of Jones, Keyser & Arras, whose address appears on the back of the card. The 4-1/2" x 7-1/4" cabinets have photos glued to stiff gray cardboard mounts. Both photo and mount are numbered within the known range of 301-349, making it likely there are 50 baseball players in the series. Most known subjects are from the three New York teams of the era. Photos carry at bottom a stylized J, K & A logo, a 1911 copyright and a number. That number is repeated in the bottom border of the mount, along with the player's last name and the team/league. Several photos are known which have been removed from the mount, making identification difficult.

		NM	EX	VG
Common Player:		2,400	1,200	720.00
301	Russ Ford	2,400	1,200	720.00
303	John Warhop	2,400	1,200	720.00
304	Bill Dahlen	2,400	1,200	720.00
306	Zack Wheat	4,000	2,000	1,200
307	Al Bridwell	2,400	1,200	720.00
308	Red Murray	2,400	1,200	720.00
310	Fred Snodgrass	2,400	1,200	720.00
311	Red Ames	2,400	1,200	720.00
312	Fred Merkle	2,400	1,200	720.00
313	Art Devlin	2,400	1,200	720.00
314	Hooks Wiltse	2,400	1,200	720.00
315	Josh Devore	2,400	120.00	720.00
316	Eddie Collins	4,000	2,000	1,200
317	Ed Reulbach	2,400	1,200	720.00
318	Jimmy Scheckard (Sheckard)	2,400	120.00	720.00
320	Frank Schulte	2,400	1,200	720.00
321	Solly Hofman	2,400	1,200	720.00
322	Bill Bergen	2,400	1,200	720.00
323	George Bell	2,400	1,200	720.00
324	Nap Rucker	2,400	120.00	720.00
325	Fred Clarke	4,000	2,000	1,200
326	Clark Griffith, Mgr.	4,000	2,000	1,200
327	Roger Bresnahan	4,000	2,000	1,200
328	Fred Tenney	2,400	1,200	720.00
329	Harry Lord	2,400	1,200	720.00
331	Walter Johnson	12,000	6,000	3,600
332	Nap Lajoie	4,000	2,000	1,200
333	Joe Tinker	4,000	2,000	1,200
334	Mordecai Brown	4,000	2,000	1,200
336	Jimmy Archer	2,400	1,200	720.00
338	Nixey Callahan	2,400	1,200	720.00
340	Hal Chase	3,500	1,750	1,050
341	Larry Doyle	2,400	1,200	720.00
342	Chief Meyers	2,400	1,200	720.00
343	Christy Mathewson	12,000	6,000	3,600
344	Bugs Raymond	2,400	1,200	720.00
345	John J. McGraw, Mgr.	4,000	2,000	1,200
346	Honus Wagner	15,000	7,500	4,500
347	Ty Cobb	25,000	12,500	7,500
348	Johnny Evers	4,000	2,000	1,200
349	Frank Chance	4,000	2,000	1,200

1863 Jordan & Co.

Because this card pictures a ballplayer on front with advertising on back, it has been described as the world's first baseball card. The 2-7/16" x 4-1/16" card doubled as a ticket to a benefit (to the players!) series of matches between New York and Brooklyn teams and all-stars at Hoboken, N.J., in Sept., 1863. The ticket cards were sold for 50 cents apiece, twice the cost of regular admission. According to surviving records, photos of four different players were used on the tickets.

(1)	William Crossley (Unknown)
(2)	William Hammond (12/04 auction, $19,364.)
(3)	Sam Wright (Unknown)
(4)	Harry Wright (Clipped-corners, 7/00 auction, $83,545.)

1931 Josetti Tobacco

This is one of several early 1930s German cigarette cards to picture Babe Ruth. In this case he is pictured on the 1-5/8" x 2-3/8" black-and-white card with American comedic actor Harold Lloyd. The card is part of a numbered set of 272 movie star cards. Backs are printed in German. The card can be found with Ruth's first name printed as George or as Babe.

Babe Ruth
Harold Lloyd

JOSETTI-FILMBILDER

		NM	EX	VG
151a	George Ruth, Harold Lloyd	450.00	225.00	135.00
151b	Babe Ruth, Harold Lloyd	450.00	225.00	135.00

1910 Ju-Ju Drums (E286)

Issued in 1910 with Ju Ju Drum Candy, this extremely rare set of circular baseball cards is very similar in design to the more common Colgan's Chips cards. About the size of a silver dollar (1-7/16" in diameter) the cards display a player photo on the front with the player's name and team printed below in a semi-circle design. The backs carry advertising for Ju-Ju Drums. The checklist contains 45 different players to date, but the issue - known as E286 in the American Card Catalog - is so rare that others are likely to exist.

		NM	EX	VG
Complete Set (45):		40,000	16,000	8,000
Common Player:		750.00	300.00	175.00
(1)	Eddie Ainsmith	750.00	300.00	175.00
(2)	Jimmy Austin	750.00	300.00	175.00
(3)	Chief Bender	1,500	600.00	360.00
(4)	Bob Bescher	750.00	300.00	175.00
(5)	Bruno Bloch (Block)	750.00	300.00	175.00
(6)	Frank Burke	750.00	300.00	175.00
(7)	Donie Bush	750.00	300.00	175.00
(8)	Frank Chance	1,500	600.00	360.00
(9)	Harry Cheek	750.00	300.00	175.00
(10)	Ed Cicotte	1,500	600.00	360.00
(11)	Ty Cobb	6,500	2,600	1,550
(12)	King Cole	750.00	300.00	175.00
(13)	Jack Coombs	750.00	300.00	175.00
(14)	Bill Dahlen	750.00	300.00	175.00
(15)	Bert Daniels	750.00	300.00	175.00
(16)	Harry Davis	750.00	300.00	175.00
(17)	Larry Doyle	750.00	300.00	175.00
(18)	Rube Ellis	750.00	300.00	175.00
(19)	Cecil Ferguson	750.00	300.00	175.00
(20)	Russ Ford	750.00	300.00	175.00
(21)	Bob Harnion (Harmon)	750.00	300.00	175.00
(22)	Ham Hyatt	750.00	300.00	175.00
(23)	Red Kellifer (Killifer)	750.00	300.00	175.00
(24)	Art Kruger (Krueger)	750.00	300.00	175.00
(25)	Tommy Leach	750.00	300.00	175.00
(26)	Harry Lumley	750.00	300.00	175.00
(27)	Christy Mathewson	3,500	1,400	840.00
(28)	John McGraw	1,500	600.00	360.00
(29)	Deacon McGuire	750.00	300.00	175.00
(30)	Chief Meyers	750.00	300.00	175.00
(31)	Otto Miller	750.00	300.00	175.00
(32)	Charlie Mullen	750.00	300.00	175.00
(33)	Tom Needham	750.00	300.00	175.00
(34)	Rube Oldring	750.00	300.00	175.00
(35)	Barney Pelty	750.00	300.00	175.00
(36)	Ed Reulbach	750.00	300.00	175.00
(37)	Jack Rowan	750.00	300.00	175.00
(38)	Dave Shean	750.00	300.00	175.00
(39)	Tris Speaker	2,000	800.00	480.00
(40)	Ed Sweeney	750.00	300.00	175.00
(41)	Honus Wagner	4,500	1,800	1,075
(42)	Jimmy Walsh	750.00	300.00	175.00
(43)	Kirby White	750.00	300.00	175.00
(44)	Ralph Works	750.00	300.00	175.00
(45)	Elmer Zacher	750.00	300.00	175.00

1893 Just So Tobacco

This set is so rare that only a dozen or so examples are known, although it is possible others remain to be reported. The set features only members of the Cleveland club, known then as the "Spiders." Measuring 2-1/2" x 3-7/8", these sepia-colored cards were printed on heavy paper. The player appears in a portrait photo with his name beneath and an ad for Just So Tobacco at bottom. The existence of this set wasn't even established until the 1960s, and for 15

years only two subjects were known. In 1981 and 1989 several more cards were discovered. To date only one or two copies of each of the known cards have turned up in collectors' hands, making it among the rarest of all baseball card issues.

		NM	EX	VG
Common Player:		25,000	17,500	
(1)	F.W. Boyd	25,000	17,500	
(2)	Burkette (Jesse Burkett) (Unique. Trimmed and restored. Value undetermined.)			
(3)	C.L. Childs ("Cupid")	25,000	17,500	
(4)	John Clarkson	30,000	18,000	
(5)	J.O. Connor (John O'Connor)	25,000	17,500	
(6)	G. Cuppy	25,000	17,500	
(7)	G.W. Davies	25,000	17,500	
(8)	C.M. Hastings	25,000	17,500	
(9)	E.J. McKean	25,000	17,500	
(10)	CAPt Tebeau ("Patsy")	25,000	17,500	
(11)	J.K. Virtue	25,000	17,500	
(12)	T.C. Williams	25,000	17,500	
(13)	D.T. Young (Cy)(Unique. Value undetermined.)			
(14)	C.L. Zimmer ("Chief")	25,000	17,500	

K

1950s Kabaya Caramel Babe Ruth

This card was part of a series produced by an Okayama, Japan candy company. The card measures about 1-1/2" x 2-1/8" with color artwork of Ruth on front. On back is Japanese script within the design of an open book.

	NM	EX	VG
Babe Ruth	1,200	600.00	350.00

1955 Kahn's Wieners Reds

Compliments of Kahn's Wieners
"THE WIENER THE WORLD AWAITED"

The first of what would become 15 successive years of baseball card issues by the Kahn's meat company of Cincinnati is also the rarest. The set consists of six Cincinnati Redlegs player cards, 3-1/4" x 4". Printed in black and white, with blank backs, the '55 Kahn's cards were distributed at a one-day promotional event at a Cincinnati amusement park, where the featured players were on hand to sign autographs. Like the other Kahn's issues through 1963, the '55 cards have a 1/2" white panel containing an advertising message below the player photo. These cards are sometimes found with this portion cut off, greatly reducing the value of the card.

		NM	EX	VG
Complete Set (6):		6,500	3,250	2,000
Common Player:		1,000	500.00	300.00
(1)	Gus Bell	1,250	625.00	375.00
(2)	Ted Kluszewski	1,450	725.00	435.00
(3)	Roy McMillan	1,000	500.00	300.00
(4)	Joe Nuxhall	1,000	500.00	300.00
(5)	Wally Post	1,000	500.00	300.00
(6)	Johnny Temple	1,000	500.00	300.00

1956 Kahn's Wieners Reds

Compliments of Kahn's Wieners
"THE WIENER THE WORLD AWAITED"

In 1956, Kahn's expanded its baseball card program to include 15 Redlegs players, and began issuing the cards one per pack in packages of hot dogs. Because the cards were packaged in direct contact with the meat, they are often found today in stained condition. In 3-1/4" x 4" format, black and white with blank backs, the '56 Kahn's cards can be distinguished from later issues by the presence of full stadium photographic backgrounds behind the player photos. Like all Kahn's issues, the 1956 set is unnumbered; the checklists are arranged alphabetically for convenience. The set features the first-ever baseball card of Hall of Famer Frank Robinson.

		NM	EX	VG
Complete Set (15):		3,250	1,625	1,000
Common Player:		150.00	75.00	45.00
(1)	Ed Bailey	150.00	75.00	45.00
(2)	Gus Bell	175.00	90.00	55.00
(3)	Joe Black	225.00	110.00	65.00
(4)	"Smoky" Burgess	200.00	100.00	60.00
(5)	Art Fowler	150.00	75.00	45.00
(6)	Hershell Freeman	150.00	75.00	45.00
(7)	Ray Jablonski	150.00	75.00	45.00
(8)	John Klippstein	150.00	75.00	45.00
(9)	Ted Kluszewski	365.00	180.00	110.00
(10)	Brooks Lawrence	150.00	75.00	45.00
(11)	Roy McMillan	150.00	75.00	45.00
(12)	Joe Nuxhall	150.00	75.00	45.00
(13)	Wally Post	150.00	75.00	45.00
(14)	Frank Robinson	1,000	500.00	300.00
(15)	Johnny Temple	150.00	75.00	45.00

1957 Kahn's Wieners

Compliments of Kahn's Wieners
"THE WIENER THE WORLD AWAITED"

In its third season of baseball card issue, Kahn's kept the basic 3-1/4" x 4" format, with black-and-white photos and blank backs. The issue was expanded to 28 players, all Pirates or Reds. The last of the blank-backed Kahn's sets until 1966, the 1957 Reds players can be distinguished from the 1956 issue by the general lack of background photo detail, in favor of a neutral light gray background. The Dick Groat card appears with two name variations, a facsimile autograph, "Richard Groat," and a printed "Dick Groat." Both Groat varieties are included in the complete set price.

		NM	EX	VG
Complete Set (29):		4,000	2,000	1,200
Common Player:		80.00	40.00	24.00
(1)	Tom Acker	80.00	40.00	24.00
(2)	Ed Bailey	80.00	40.00	24.00
(3)	Gus Bell	100.00	50.00	30.00
(4)	Smoky Burgess	100.00	50.00	30.00
(5)	Roberto Clemente	1,250	625.00	375.00
(6)	George Crowe	80.00	40.00	24.00
(7)	Elroy Face	80.00	40.00	24.00
(8)	Hershell Freeman	80.00	40.00	24.00
(9)	Robert Friend	80.00	40.00	24.00
(10a)	Dick Groat	190.00	95.00	55.00
(10b)	Richard Groat	190.00	95.00	55.00
(11)	Don Gross	80.00	40.00	24.00
(12)	Warren Hacker	80.00	40.00	24.00
(13)	Don Hoak	80.00	40.00	24.00
(14)	Hal Jeffcoat	80.00	40.00	24.00
(15)	Ron Kline	80.00	40.00	24.00
(16)	John Klippstein	80.00	40.00	24.00
(17)	Ted Kluszewski	225.00	110.00	65.00
(18)	Brooks Lawrence	80.00	40.00	24.00
(19)	Dale Long	80.00	40.00	24.00
(20)	Bill Mazeroski	325.00	160.00	95.00
(21)	Roy McMillan	80.00	40.00	24.00
(22)	Joe Nuxhall	80.00	40.00	24.00
(23)	Wally Post	80.00	40.00	24.00
(24)	Frank Robinson	300.00	150.00	90.00
(25)	Johnny Temple	80.00	40.00	24.00
(26)	Frank Thomas	80.00	40.00	24.00
(27)	Bob Thurman	80.00	40.00	24.00
(28)	Lee Walls	80.00	40.00	24.00

1958 Kahn's Wieners

Compliments of Kahn's Wieners
"THE WIENER THE WORLD AWAITED"

MY GREATEST THRILL IN BASEBALL
By GEORGE CROWE

Long-time Cincinnati favorite Wally Post became the only Philadelphia Phillies ballplayer to appear in the 15-year run of Kahn's issues when he was traded in 1958, but included as part of the otherwise exclusively Pirates-Reds set. Like previous years, the '58 Kahn's were 3-1/4" x 4", with black and white player photos. Unlike previous years, however, the cards had printing on the back, a story by the pictured player, titled "My Greatest Thrill in Baseball." Quite similar to the 1959 issue, the '58 Kahn's can be distinguished by the fact that the top line of the advertising panel at bottom has the word "Wieners" in 1958, but not in 1959. Several of the cards in the set appear to have been short-printed.

		NM	EX	VG
Complete Set (29):		4,500	2,250	1,350
Common Player:		100.00	50.00	30.00
(1)	Ed Bailey	100.00	50.00	30.00
(2)	Gene Baker	100.00	50.00	30.00
(3)	Gus Bell	110.00	55.00	35.00
(4)	Smoky Burgess	110.00	55.00	35.00
(5)	Roberto Clemente	900.00	450.00	275.00
(6)	George Crowe	100.00	50.00	30.00
(7)	Elroy Face	100.00	50.00	30.00
(8)	Henry Foiles	100.00	50.00	30.00
(9)	Dee Fondy	100.00	50.00	30.00
(10)	Robert Friend	100.00	50.00	30.00
(11)	Richard Groat	110.00	55.00	35.00
(12)	Harvey Haddix	100.00	50.00	30.00
(13)	Don Hoak	110.00	55.00	35.00
(14)	Hal Jeffcoat	110.00	55.00	35.00
(15)	Ronald L. Kline	110.00	55.00	35.00
(16)	Ted Kluszewski	200.00	100.00	60.00
(17)	Vernon Law	100.00	50.00	30.00
(18)	Brooks Lawrence	100.00	50.00	30.00
(19)	Bill Mazeroski	300.00	150.00	90.00
(20)	Roy McMillan	100.00	50.00	30.00
(21)	Joe Nuxhall	100.00	50.00	30.00
(22)	Wally Post	300.00	150.00	90.00
(23)	John Powers	100.00	50.00	30.00
(24)	Robert T. Purkey	100.00	50.00	30.00
(25)	Charles Rabe	300.00	150.00	90.00
(26)	Frank Robinson	600.00	300.00	180.00
(27)	Robert Skinner	100.00	50.00	30.00
(28)	Johnny Temple	100.00	50.00	30.00
(29)	Frank Thomas	300.00	150.00	90.00

1959 Kahn's Wieners

A third team was added to the Kahn's lineup in 1959, the Cleveland Indians joining the Pirates and Reds. Again printed in black-and-white in the 3-1/4" x 4" size, the 1959 Kahn's cards can be differentiated from the previous issue by the lack of the word "Wieners" on the top line of the advertising panel at bottom. Backs again featured a story written by the pictured player, such as "The Toughest Play I Had to Make," "My Most Difficult Moment in Baseball," etc. A number of the cards were short-printed.

THE TOUGHEST PLAY
I HAVE TO MAKE
by VADA PINSON

Compliments of Kahn's
"THE WIENER THE WORLD AWAITED"

		NM	EX	VG
Complete Set (38):		6,000	3,000	1,800
Common Player:		75.00	37.50	22.50
(1)	Ed Bailey	75.00	37.50	22.50
(2)	Gary Bell	75.00	37.50	22.50
(3)	Gus Bell	75.00	37.50	22.50
(4)	Richard Brodowski	500.00	250.00	150.00
(5)	Forrest Burgess	75.00	37.50	22.50
(6)	Roberto Clemente	850.00	425.00	255.00
(7)	Rocky Colavito	325.00	160.00	100.00
(8)	ElRoy Face	75.00	37.50	22.50
(9)	Robert Friend	75.00	37.50	22.50
(10)	Joe Gordon	75.00	37.50	22.50
(11)	Jim Grant	75.00	37.50	22.50
(12)	Richard M. Groat	90.00	45.00	27.00
(13)	Harvey Haddix	450.00	225.00	135.00
(14)	Woodie Held	450.00	225.00	135.00
(15)	Don Hoak	75.00	37.50	22.50
(16)	Ronald Kline	75.00	37.50	22.50
(17)	Ted Kluszewski	200.00	100.00	60.00
(18)	Vernon Law	75.00	37.50	22.50
(19)	Jerry Lynch	75.00	37.50	22.50
(20)	Billy Martin	115.00	55.00	35.00
(21)	Bill Mazeroski	250.00	125.00	75.00
(22)	Cal McLish	450.00	225.00	135.00
(23)	Roy McMillan	75.00	37.50	22.50
(24)	Minnie Minoso	80.00	40.00	24.00
(25)	Russell Nixon	75.00	37.50	22.50
(26)	Joe Nuxhall	75.00	37.50	22.50
(27)	Jim Perry	75.00	37.50	22.50
(28)	Vada Pinson	200.00	100.00	60.00
(29)	Vic Power	75.00	37.50	22.50
(30)	Robert Purkey	75.00	37.50	22.50
(31)	Frank Robinson	235.00	120.00	75.00
(32)	Herb Score	75.00	37.50	22.50
(33)	Robert Skinner	75.00	37.50	22.50
(34)	George Strickland	275.00	135.00	85.00
(35)	Richard L. Stuart	75.00	37.50	22.50
(36)	John Temple	75.00	37.50	22.50
(37)	Frank Thomas	75.00	37.50	22.50
(38)	George A. Witt	75.00	37.50	22.50

1960 Kahn's Wieners

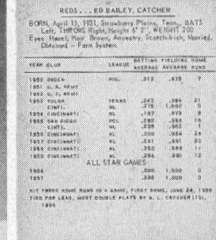

REDS . . . ED BAILEY, CATCHER
BORN, April 15, 1931, Strawberry Plains, Tenn.; BATS Left; THROWS Right; Height 6' 2"; WEIGHT 200

Ed Bailey

Compliments of Kahn's
"THE WIENER THE WORLD AWAITED"

Three more teams joined the Kahn's roster in 1960, the Chicago Cubs, Chicago White Sox and St. Louis Cardinals. Again 3-1/4" x 4" with black-and-white photos, the 1960 Kahn's cards featured for the first time player stats and personal data on the back, except Harvey Kuenn, which was issued with blank back, probably because of the lateness of his trade to the Indians.

		NM	EX	VG
Complete Set (42):		3,000	1,500	900.00
Common Player:		40.00	20.00	12.00
(1)	Ed Bailey	40.00	20.00	12.00
(2)	Gary Bell	40.00	20.00	12.00
(3)	Gus Bell	45.00	22.50	13.50
(4)	Forrest Burgess	45.00	22.50	13.50
(5)	Gino N. Cimoli	40.00	20.00	12.00
(6)	Roberto Clemente	725.00	360.00	215.00
(7)	ElRoy Face	40.00	20.00	12.00
(8)	Tito Francona	40.00	20.00	12.00
(9)	Robert Friend	40.00	20.00	12.00
(10)	Jim Grant	40.00	20.00	12.00
(11)	Richard Groat	40.00	20.00	12.00
(12)	Harvey Haddix	40.00	20.00	12.00
(13)	Woodie Held	40.00	20.00	12.00
(14)	Bill Henry	40.00	20.00	12.00
(15)	Don Hoak	40.00	20.00	12.00
(16)	Jay Hook	40.00	20.00	12.00
(17)	Eddie Kasko	40.00	20.00	12.00
(18)	Ronnie Kline	50.00	25.00	15.00
(19)	Ted Kluszewski	300.00	150.00	90.00
(20)	Harvey Kuenn	200.00	100.00	60.00
(21)	Vernon S. Law	45.00	22.50	13.50
(22)	Brooks Lawrence	40.00	20.00	12.00
(23)	Jerry Lynch	40.00	20.00	12.00
(24)	Billy Martin	90.00	45.00	27.00
(25)	Bill Mazeroski	150.00	75.00	45.00
(26)	Cal McLish	40.00	20.00	12.00
(27)	Roy McMillan	40.00	20.00	12.00

		NM	EX	VG
(28)	Don Newcombe	45.00	22.50	13.50
(29)	Russ Nixon	40.00	20.00	12.00
(30)	Joe Nuxhall	40.00	20.00	12.00
(31)	James J. O'Toole	40.00	20.00	12.00
(32)	Jim Perry	45.00	22.00	13.50
(33)	Vada Pinson	65.00	32.50	20.00
(34)	Vic Power	40.00	20.00	12.00
(35)	Robert T. Purkey	40.00	20.00	12.00
(36)	Frank Robinson	200.00	100.00	60.00
(37)	Herb Score	45.00	22.50	13.50
(38)	Robert R. Skinner	40.00	20.00	12.00
(39)	Richard L. Stuart	40.00	20.00	12.00
(40)	John Temple	40.00	20.00	12.00
(41)	Frank Thomas	50.00	25.00	15.00
(42)	Lee Walls	40.00	20.00	12.00

1961 Kahn's Wieners

After a single season, the Chicago and St. Louis teams dropped out of the Kahn's program, but the 1961 set was larger than ever, at 43 cards. The same basic format - 3-1/4" x 4" size, black-and-white photos and statistical information on the back - was retained. For the first time in '61, the meat company made complete sets of the Kahn's cards available to collectors via a mail-in offer. This makes the 1961 and later Kahn's cards considerably easier to obtain than the earlier issues.

		NM	EX	VG
Complete Set (43):		2,650	1,300	800.00
Common Player:		40.00	20.00	12.00
(1)	John A. Antonelli	40.00	20.00	12.00
(2)	Ed Bailey	40.00	20.00	12.00
(3)	Gary Bell	40.00	20.00	12.00
(4)	Gus Bell	45.00	22.00	13.50
(5)	James P. Brosnan	40.00	20.00	12.00
(6)	Forrest Burgess	45.00	22.00	13.50
(7)	Gino Cimoli	40.00	20.00	12.00
(8)	Roberto Clemente	825.00	410.00	245.00
(9)	Gordon Coleman	40.00	20.00	12.00
(10)	Jimmie Dykes	40.00	20.00	12.00
(11)	ElRoy Face	40.00	20.00	12.00
(12)	Tito Francona	40.00	20.00	12.00
(13)	Gene L. Freese	40.00	20.00	12.00
(14)	Robert Friend	40.00	20.00	12.00
(15)	Jim Grant	40.00	20.00	12.00
(16)	Richard M. Groat	40.00	20.00	12.00
(17)	Harvey Haddix	40.00	20.00	12.00
(18)	Woodie Held	40.00	20.00	12.00
(19)	Don Hoak	40.00	20.00	12.00
(20)	Jay Hook	40.00	20.00	12.00
(21)	Joe Jay	40.00	20.00	12.00
(22)	Eddie Kasko	40.00	20.00	12.00
(23)	Willie Kirkland	40.00	20.00	12.00
(24)	Vernon S. Law	40.00	20.00	12.00
(25)	Jerry Lynch	40.00	20.00	12.00
(26)	Jim Maloney	40.00	20.00	12.00
(27)	Bill Mazeroski	150.00	75.00	45.00
(28)	Wilmer D. Mizell	40.00	20.00	12.00
(29)	Glenn R. Nelson	40.00	20.00	12.00
(30)	James J. O'Toole	40.00	20.00	12.00
(31)	Jim Perry	40.00	20.00	12.00
(32)	John M. Phillips	40.00	20.00	12.00
(33)	Vada E. Pinson Jr.	55.00	27.00	16.50
(34)	Wally Post	40.00	20.00	12.00
(35)	Vic Power	40.00	20.00	12.00
(36)	Robert T. Purkey	40.00	20.00	12.00
(37)	Frank Robinson	250.00	125.00	75.00
(38)	John A. Romano Jr.	40.00	20.00	12.00
(39)	Dick Schofield	40.00	20.00	12.00
(40)	Robert Skinner	40.00	20.00	12.00
(41)	Hal Smith	40.00	20.00	12.00
(42)	Richard Stuart	40.00	20.00	12.00
(43)	John E. Temple	40.00	20.00	12.00

1962 Kahn's Wieners

Besides the familiar Reds, Pirates and Indians players in the 1962 Kahn's set, a fourth team was added, the Minnesota Twins, though the overall size of the set was decreased from the previous year, to 38 players in 1962. The cards retained the 3-1/4" x 4" black-and-white format of previous years. The '62 Kahn's set is awash in variations. Besides the photo and front design variations on the Bell, Purkey and Power cards, each Cleveland player can be found with two back variations, listing the team either as "Cleveland" or "Cleveland Indians." The complete set values listed below include all variations.

		NM	EX	VG
Complete Set (51):		2,250	1,125	675.00
Common Player:		15.00	7.50	4.50
(1a)	Gary Bell (Cleveland Indians back.)	100.00	50.00	30.00
(1b)	Gary Bell (Cleveland back.)	35.00	17.50	10.00
(2)	James P. Brosnan	15.00	7.50	4.50
(3)	Forrest Burgess	30.00	15.00	9.00
(4)	Leonardo Cardenas	15.00	7.50	4.50
(5)	Roberto Clemente	250.00	125.00	75.00
(6a)	Ty Cline (Cleveland Indians back.)	70.00	35.00	20.00
(6b)	Ty Cline (Cleveland back.)	30.00	15.00	9.00
(7)	Gordon Coleman	15.00	7.50	4.50
(8)	Dick Donovan	30.00	15.00	9.00
(9)	John Edwards	15.00	7.50	4.50
(10a)	Tito Francona (Cleveland Indians back.)	70.00	35.00	20.00
(10b)	Tito Francona (Cleveland back.)	30.00	15.00	9.00
(11)	Gene Freese	15.00	7.50	4.50
(12)	Robert B. Friend	20.00	10.00	6.00
(13)	Joe Gibbon	75.00	37.50	22.50
(14a)	Jim Grant (Cleveland Indians back.)	70.00	35.00	20.00
(14b)	Jim Grant (Cleveland back.)	30.00	15.00	9.00
(15)	Richard M. Groat	40.00	20.00	12.00
(16)	Harvey Haddix	15.00	7.50	4.50
(17a)	Woodie Held (Cleveland Indians back.)	70.00	35.00	20.00
(17b)	Woodie Held (Cleveland back.)	30.00	15.00	9.00
(18)	Bill Henry	15.00	7.50	4.50
(19)	Don Hoak	15.00	7.50	4.50
(20)	Ken Hunt	15.00	7.50	4.50
(21)	Joseph R. Jay	15.00	7.50	4.50
(22)	Eddie Kasko	15.00	7.50	4.50
(23a)	Willie Kirkland (Cleveland Indians back.)	70.00	35.00	20.00
(23b)	Willie Kirkland (Cleveland back.)	30.00	15.00	9.00
(24a)	Barry Latman (Cleveland Indians back.)	70.00	35.00	20.00
(24b)	Barry Latman (Cleveland back.)	30.00	15.00	9.00
(25)	Jerry Lynch	15.00	7.50	4.50
(26)	Jim Maloney	20.00	10.00	6.00
(27)	Bill Mazeroski	100.00	50.00	30.00
(28)	Jim O'Toole	15.00	7.50	4.50
(29a)	Jim Perry (Cleveland Indians back.)	70.00	35.00	20.00
(29b)	Jim Perry (Cleveland back.)	30.00	15.00	9.00
(30a)	John M. Phillips (Cleveland Indians back.)	70.00	35.00	20.00
(30b)	John M. Phillips (Cleveland back.)	30.00	15.00	9.00
(31)	Vada E. Pinson	30.00	15.00	9.00
(32)	Wally Post	15.00	7.50	4.50
(33a)	Vic Power (Cleveland Indians back.)	70.00	35.00	20.00
(33b)	Vic Power (Cleveland back.)	30.00	15.00	9.00
(33c)	Vic Power (Minnesota Twins back.)	150.00	75.00	45.00
(34a)	Robert T. Purkey (No autograph.)	150.00	75.00	45.00
(34b)	Robert T. Purkey (With autograph.)	35.00	17.50	10.00
(35)	Frank Robinson	100.00	50.00	30.00
(36a)	John Romano (Cleveland Indians back.)	70.00	35.00	20.00
(36b)	John Romano (Cleveland back.)	30.00	15.00	9.00
(37)	Dick Stuart	15.00	7.50	4.50
(38)	Bill Virdon	15.00	7.50	4.50

1963 Kahn's Wieners

In 1963, for the first time since Kahn's began issuing baseball cards in 1955, the design underwent a significant change, white borders were added to the top and sides of player photo. Also, the card size was changed to 3-3/16" x 4-1/4". Statistical and personal data continued to be printed on the card backs. Joining

traditional Reds, Pirates and Indians personnel in the 1963 set were a handful of New York Yankees and Dick Groat, in his new identity as a St. Louis Cardinal.

		NM	EX	VG
Complete Set (30):		2,000	1,000	600.00
Common Player:		50.00	25.00	15.50
(1)	Robert Bailey	50.00	25.00	15.50
(2)	Don Blasingame	50.00	25.00	15.50
(3)	Clete Boyer	90.00	45.00	27.00
(4)	Forrest Burgess	60.00	30.00	18.00
(5)	Leonardo Cardenas	50.00	25.00	15.50
(6)	Roberto Clemente	350.00	175.00	105.00
(7)	Don Clendennon (Donn Clendenon)	50.00	25.00	15.50
(8)	Gordon Coleman	50.00	25.00	15.50
(9)	John A. Edwards	50.00	25.00	15.50
(10)	Gene Freese	50.00	25.00	15.50
(11)	Robert B. Friend	50.00	25.00	15.00
(12)	Joe Gibbon	50.00	25.00	15.50
(13)	Dick Groat	90.00	45.00	27.00
(14)	Harvey Haddix	50.00	25.00	15.00
(15)	Elston Howard	100.00	50.00	30.00
(16)	Joey Jay	50.00	25.00	15.50
(17)	Eddie Kasko	50.00	25.00	15.50
(18)	Tony Kubek	100.00	50.00	30.00
(19)	Jerry Lynch	50.00	25.00	15.50
(20)	Jim Maloney	60.00	30.00	18.00
(21)	Bill Mazeroski	150.00	75.00	45.00
(22)	Joe Nuxhall	60.00	30.00	18.00
(23)	Jim O'Toole	50.00	25.00	15.50
(24)	Vada E. Pinson	90.00	45.00	27.00
(25)	Robert T. Purkey	50.00	25.00	15.50
(26)	Bob Richardson	100.00	50.00	30.00
(27)	Frank Robinson	200.00	100.00	60.00
(28)	Bill Stafford	60.00	30.00	18.00
(29)	Ralph W. Terry	60.00	30.00	18.00
(30)	Bill Virdon	60.00	30.00	18.00

1964 Kahn's Wieners

After nearly a decade of virtually identical card issues, the 1964 Kahn's issue was an abrupt change. In a new size, 3" x 3-1/2", the nearly square cards featured a borderless color photo. The only other design element on the front of the card was a facsimile autograph. The advertising slogan which had traditionally appeared on the front of the card was moved to the back, where it joined the player's stats and personal data. The teams in the 1964 issue once again reverted to the Reds, Pirates and Indians.

		NM	EX	VG
Complete Set (31):		1,150	600.00	350.00
Common Player:		20.00	10.00	6.00
(1)	Max Alvis	20.00	10.00	6.00
(2)	Bob Bailey	20.00	10.00	6.00
(3)	Leonardo Cardenas	20.00	10.00	6.00
(4)	Roberto Clemente	300.00	150.00	90.00
(5)	Donn A. Clendenon	20.00	10.00	6.00
(6)	Victor Davalillo	20.00	10.00	6.00
(7)	Dick Donovan	20.00	10.00	6.00
(8)	John A. Edwards	20.00	10.00	6.00
(9)	Robert Friend	20.00	10.00	6.00
(10)	Jim Grant	20.00	10.00	6.00
(11)	Tommy Harper	20.00	10.00	6.00
(12)	Woodie Held	20.00	10.00	6.00
(13)	Joey Jay	20.00	10.00	6.00
(14)	Jack Kralick	20.00	10.00	6.00
(15)	Jerry Lynch	20.00	10.00	6.00
(16)	Jim Maloney	20.00	10.00	6.00
(17)	Bill Mazeroski	75.00	37.50	22.00
(18)	Alvin McBean	20.00	10.00	6.00
(19)	Joe Nuxhall	20.00	10.00	6.00
(20)	Jim Pagliaroni	20.00	10.00	6.00
(21)	Vada E. Pinson Jr.	35.00	17.50	10.00
(22)	Robert T. Purkey	20.00	10.00	6.00
(23)	Pedro Ramos	20.00	10.00	6.00
(24)	Frank Robinson	75.00	37.50	22.50
(25)	John Romano	20.00	10.00	6.00
(26)	Pete Rose	250.00	125.00	75.00
(27)	John Tsitouris	20.00	10.00	6.00
(28)	Robert A. Veale Jr.	20.00	10.00	6.00
(29)	Bill Virdon	20.00	10.00	6.00
(30)	Leon Wagner	20.00	10.00	6.00
(31)	Fred Whitfield	20.00	10.00	6.00

1965 Kahn's Wieners

There was little change for the Kahn's issue in 1965 beyond the addition of Milwaukee Braves players to the Reds, Pirates and Indians traditionally included in the set. At 45 players, the 1965 issue was the largest of the Kahn's sets. Once again in 3" x 3-1/2" size, the 1965s retained the borderless color photo design of the previous season. A look at the stats on the back will confirm the year of issue, allowing differentiation between the 1964 and 1965 cards.

Compliments of Kahn's
"THE WIENER THE WORLD AWAITED"

		NM	EX	VG
	Complete Set (45):	1,250	625.00	400.00
	Common Player:	15.00	7.50	4.50
(1)	Hank Aaron	125.00	65.00	35.00
(2)	Max Alvis	15.00	7.50	4.50
(3)	Jose Azcue	15.00	7.50	4.50
(4)	Bob Bailey	15.00	7.50	4.50
(5)	Frank Bolling	15.00	7.50	4.50
(6)	Leonardo Cardenas	15.00	7.50	4.50
(7)	Rico Ricardo Carty	15.00	7.50	4.50
(8)	Donn A. Clendenon	15.00	7.50	4.50
(9)	Tony Cloninger	15.00	7.50	4.50
(10)	Gordon Coleman	15.00	7.50	4.50
(11)	Victor Davalillo	15.00	7.50	4.50
(12)	John A. Edwards	15.00	7.50	4.50
(13)	Sam Ellis	15.00	7.50	4.50
(14)	Robert Friend	15.00	7.50	4.50
(15)	Tommy Harper	15.00	7.50	4.50
(16)	Chuck Hinton	15.00	7.50	4.50
(17)	Dick Howser	15.00	7.50	4.50
(18)	Joey Jay	15.00	7.50	4.50
(19)	Deron Johnson	15.00	7.50	4.50
(20)	Jack Kralick	15.00	7.50	4.50
(21)	Denny Lemaster	15.00	7.50	4.50
(22)	Jerry Lynch	15.00	7.50	4.50
(23)	Jim Maloney	15.00	7.50	4.50
(24)	Lee Maye	15.00	7.50	4.50
(25)	Bill Mazeroski	60.00	30.00	18.00
(26)	Alvin McBean	15.00	7.50	4.50
(27)	Bill McCool	15.00	7.50	4.50
(28)	Sam McDowell	20.00	10.00	6.00
(29)	Donald McMahon	15.00	7.50	4.50
(30)	Denis Menke	15.00	7.50	4.50
(31)	Joe Nuxhall	15.00	7.50	4.50
(32)	Gene Oliver	15.00	7.50	4.50
(33)	Jim O'Toole	15.00	7.50	4.50
(34)	Jim Pagliaroni	15.00	7.50	4.50
(35)	Vada E. Pinson Jr.	25.00	12.50	7.50
(36)	Frank Robinson	100.00	50.00	30.00
(37)	Pete Rose	300.00	150.00	90.00
(38)	Willie Stargell	60.00	30.00	18.00
(39)	Ralph W. Terry	15.00	7.50	4.50
(40)	Luis Tiant	20.00	10.00	6.00
(41)	Joe Torre	25.00	12.50	7.50
(42)	John Tsitouris	15.00	7.50	4.50
(43)	Robert A. Veale Jr.	15.00	7.50	4.50
(44)	Bill Virdon	15.00	7.50	4.50
(45)	Leon Wagner	15.00	7.50	4.50

1966 Kahn's Wieners

BOB VEALE

The fourth new format in five years greeted collectors with the introduction of Kahn's 1966 issue. The design consists of a color photo bordered by white and yellow vertical stripes. The player's name is printed above the photo, and a facsimile autograph appears across the photo. As printed, the cards are 2-13/16" x 4-9/16" in size. The player photo area is about 2-13/16" x x 2-11/16", separated at top by a dotted line from an advertising panel with a red rose logo and the word "Kahn's" and by a dotted line at bottom from an irregularly shaped piece marked "CUT ALONG DOTTED LINES." Naturally, many of the cards are found today with the top and/or bottom portion cut off. Values listed here are for complete uncut cards; those without the ad portion and bottom panel are valued at 50 percent or less. Players from the Cincinnati Reds, Pittsburgh Pirates, Cleveland Indians and Atlanta Braves were included in the set. Since the cards are blank-backed, collectors must learn to differentiate player poses to determine year of issue for some cards.

	NM	EX	VG
Complete Set (32):	1,250	625.00	375.00

		NM	EX	VG
	Common Player:	15.00	7.50	4.50
(1)	Henry Aaron	200.00	100.00	60.00
(2)	Felipe Alou	20.00	10.00	6.00
(3)	Max Alvis	15.00	7.50	4.50
(4)	Robert Bailey	15.00	7.50	4.50
(5)	Wade Blasingame	15.00	7.50	4.50
(6)	Frank Bolling	15.00	7.50	4.50
(7)	Leo Cardenas	15.00	7.50	4.50
(8)	Roberto Clemente	400.00	200.00	120.00
(9)	Tony Cloninger	15.00	7.50	4.50
(10)	Vic Davalillo	15.00	7.50	4.50
(11)	John Edwards	15.00	7.50	4.50
(12)	Sam Ellis (White cap.)	15.00	7.50	4.50
(13)	Pedro Gonzalez	15.00	7.50	4.50
(14)	Tommy Harper	15.00	7.50	4.50
(15)	Deron Johnson	15.00	7.50	4.50
(16)	Mack Jones	15.00	7.50	4.50
(17)	Denny Lemaster	15.00	7.50	4.50
(18)	Jim Maloney (White cap.)	15.00	7.50	4.50
(19)	Bill Mazeroski	90.00	45.00	27.00
(20)	Bill McCool	15.00	7.50	4.50
(21)	Sam McDowell	25.00	12.50	7.50
(22)	Denis Menke	15.00	7.50	4.50
(23)	Joe Nuxhall	15.00	7.50	4.50
(24)	Jim Pagliaroni	15.00	7.50	4.50
(25)	Milt Pappas	15.00	7.50	4.50
(26)	Vada Pinson	25.00	12.50	7.50
(27)	Pete Rose (Right hand in glove.)	250.00	125.00	75.00
(28)	Sonny Siebert	15.00	7.50	4.50
(29)	Willie Stargell	90.00	45.00	27.00
(30)	Joe Torre	25.00	12.50	7.50
(31)	Bob Veale	15.00	7.50	4.50
(32)	Fred Whitfield	15.00	7.50	4.50

1967 Kahn's Wieners

PETE ROSE

Retaining the 1966 format, the '67 Kahn's set was expanded to 41 players by adding several New York Mets to the previous season's lineup of Reds, Pirates, Indians and Braves. Making this set especially challenging for collectors is the fact that some cards are found in a smaller size and/or with different colored stripes bordering the color player photo. On the majority of cards, the size remained about 2-13/16" x 4-9/16" (with ad at top and bottom panel; about 2-13/16" x 2-11/16" when cut on dotted lines). However, because of packing in different products, some cards can be found in 2-13/16" x 3-1/4" size (with ad; 2-13/16" x 2-1/8" without ad). The border stripe variations are listed below. Values quoted are for complete uncut cards; values drop by 50 percent or more for cards without the ad and/or bottom panels. All variation cards are included in the valuations given for the complete set.

		NM	EX	VG
	Complete Set (51):	1,800	900.00	550.00
	Common Player:	20.00	10.00	6.00
(1a)	Henry Aaron (Large size.)	125.00	65.00	35.00
(1b)	Henry Aaron (Small size.)	125.00	65.00	35.00
(2)	Gene Alley	20.00	10.00	6.00
(3)	Felipe Alou (Full-length, bat on shoulder.)	25.00	12.50	7.50
(4a)	Matty Alou (Yellow & white striped border.)	25.00	12.50	7.50
(4b)	Matty Alou (Red & white striped border.)	30.00	15.00	9.00
(5)	Max Alvis	20.00	10.00	6.00
(6a)	Ken Boyer (Yellow & white striped border.)	30.00	15.00	9.00
(6b)	Ken Boyer (Red, white & green striped border.)	35.00	17.50	10.00
(7)	Leo Cardenas	20.00	10.00	6.00
(8)	Rico Carty	20.00	10.00	6.00
(9)	Tony Cloninger	20.00	10.00	6.00
(10)	Tommy Davis	20.00	10.00	6.00
(11)	John Edwards	20.00	10.00	6.00
(12a)	Sam Ellis (Large size.) (Red cap.)	20.00	10.00	6.00
(12b)	Sam Ellis (Small size.) (Red cap.)	30.00	15.00	9.00
(13)	Jack Fisher	20.00	10.00	6.00
(14)	Steve Hargan	20.00	10.00	6.00
(15)	Tom Harper	20.00	10.00	6.00
(16a)	Tom Helms (Large size.)	20.00	10.00	6.00
(16b)	Tom Helms (Small size.)	35.00	17.50	10.00
(17)	Deron Johnson	20.00	10.00	6.00
(18)	Ken Johnson	20.00	10.00	6.00
(19)	Cleon Jones	20.00	10.00	6.00
(20a)	Ed Kranepool (Yellow & white striped border.)	20.00	10.00	6.00
(20b)	Ed Kranepool (Red & white striped border.)	30.00	15.00	9.00
(21a)	James Maloney (Yellow & white striped border.)	25.00	12.50	7.50
(21b)	James Maloney (Red & white striped border.)	30.00	15.00	9.00
(22)	Lee May	20.00	10.00	6.00
(23a)	Wm. Mazeroski (Large size.)	75.00	37.50	22.50
(23b)	Wm. Mazeroski (Small size.)	75.00	37.50	22.50
(24)	Wm. McCool	20.00	10.00	6.00
(25)	Sam McDowell (Blue sleeves.)	25.00	12.50	7.50
(26)	Dennis Menke (Denis)	20.00	10.00	6.00
(27)	Jim Pagliaroni	20.00	10.00	6.00
(28)	Don Pavletich	20.00	10.00	6.00
(29)	Tony Perez	60.00	30.00	18.00
(30)	Vada Pinson	30.00	15.00	9.00
(31)	Dennis Ribant	20.00	10.00	6.00
(32)	Pete Rose/Btg	275.00	135.00	85.00
(33)	Art Shamsky	20.00	10.00	6.00
(34)	Bob Shaw	20.00	10.00	6.00
(35)	Sonny Siebert	20.00	10.00	6.00
(36)	Wm. Stargell (First name actually Wilver.)	80.00	40.00	24.00
(37a)	Joe Torre (Large size.)	35.00	17.50	10.00
(37b)	Joe Torre (Small size.)	35.00	17.50	10.00
(38)	Bob Veale	20.00	10.00	6.00
(39)	Leon Wagner	20.00	10.00	6.00
(40a)	Fred Whitfield (Large size.)	20.00	10.00	6.00
(40b)	Fred Whitfield (Small size.)	20.00	10.00	6.00
(41)	Woody Woodward	20.00	10.00	6.00

1968 Kahn's Wieners

JOHN BENCH

The number of card size and stripe color variations increased with the 1968 Kahn's issue, though the basic card format was retained. Basic size is about 2-13/16" x 4-9/16" with top ad panel and bottom panel intact; 2-13/16" x 2-11/16" with ad and bottom panels cut off. Color photos are bordered by yellow and white vertical stripes. In addition to the basic issue, a number of the cards appear in a smaller, 2-13/16" x 3-1/4", size, while some appear with variations in the color of border stripes. One card, Maloney, can be found with a top portion advertising Blue Mountain brand meats, as well as Kahn's. The 1968 set features the largest number of teams represented in any Kahn's issue: Braves, Cubs, White Sox, Reds, Indians, Tigers, Mets and Pirates. Values quoted are for complete uncut cards, those without the ad and/or bottom panel are worth 50% or less. Complete set prices include all variations.

		NM	EX	VG
	Complete Set (56):	2,250	1,125	675.00
	Common Player:	20.00	10.00	6.00
(1a)	Hank Aaron (Large size.)	100.00	50.00	30.00
(1b)	Hank Aaron (Small size.)	125.00	62.00	37.00
(2)	Tommy Agee	20.00	10.00	6.00
(3a)	Gene Alley (Large size.)	20.00	10.00	6.00
(3b)	Gene Alley (Small size.)	30.00	15.00	9.00
(4)	Felipe Alou	25.00	12.50	7.50
(5a)	Matty Alou (Yellow striped border.)	25.00	12.50	7.50
(5b)	Matty Alou (Red striped border.)	25.00	12.50	7.50
(6a)	Max Alvis (Large size.)	20.00	10.00	6.00
(6b)	Max Alvis (Small size.)	30.00	15.00	9.00
(7)	Gerry Arrigo	20.00	10.00	6.00
(8)	John Bench	550.00	275.00	165.00
(9a)	Clete Boyer (Large size.)	20.00	10.00	6.00
(9b)	Clete Boyer (Small size.)	30.00	15.00	9.00
(10)	Larry Brown	20.00	10.00	6.00
(11a)	Leo Cardenas (Large size.)	20.00	10.00	6.00
(11b)	Leo Cardenas (Small size.)	30.00	15.00	9.00
(12a)	Bill Freehan (Large size.)	30.00	15.00	9.00
(12b)	Bill Freehan (Small size.)	30.00	15.00	9.00
(13)	Steve Hargan	20.00	10.00	6.00
(14)	Joel Horlen	20.00	10.00	6.00
(15)	Tony Horton	30.00	15.00	9.00
(16)	Willie Horton	25.00	12.50	7.50
(17)	Ferguson Jenkins	75.00	37.00	22.00
(18)	Deron Johnson	20.00	10.00	6.00
(19)	Mack Jones	20.00	10.00	6.00
(20)	Bob Lee	20.00	10.00	6.00
(21a)	Jim Maloney (Large size, rose logo.)	25.00	12.50	7.50
(21b)	Jim Maloney (Large size, Blue Mountain logo.)	60.00	30.00	18.00
(21c)	Jim Maloney (Small size, yellow & white striped border.)	30.00	15.00	9.00
(21d)	Jim Maloney (Small size, yellow, white & green striped border.)	30.00	15.00	9.00
(22a)	Lee May (Large size.)	25.00	12.50	7.50

		NM	EX	VG
(22b)	Lee May (Small size.)	30.00	15.00	9.00
(23a)	Wm. Mazeroski (Large size.)	50.00	25.00	15.00
(23b)	Wm. Mazeroski (Small size.)	65.00	32.50	20.00
(24)	Dick McAuliffe	20.00	10.00	6.00
(25)	Bill McCool	20.00	10.00	6.00
(26a)	Sam McDowell (Yellow striped border.)	25.00	12.50	7.50
(26b)	Sam McDowell (Red striped border.)	30.00	15.00	9.00
(27a)	Tony Perez (Yellow striped border.)	45.00	22.00	13.50
(27b)	Tony Perez (Red striped border.)	50.00	25.00	15.00
(28)	Gary Peters	20.00	10.00	6.00
(29a)	Vada Pinson (Large size.)	30.00	15.00	9.00
(29b)	Vada Pinson (Small size.)	30.00	15.00	9.00
(30)	Chico Ruiz	20.00	10.00	6.00
(31a)	Ron Santo (Yellow striped border.)	30.00	15.00	9.00
(31b)	Ron Santo (Red striped border.)	40.00	20.00	12.00
(32)	Art Shamsky	20.00	10.00	6.00
(33)	Luis Tiant (Arms above head.)	20.00	10.00	6.00
(34a)	Joe Torre (Large size.)	30.00	15.00	9.00
(34b)	Joe Torre (Small size.)	35.00	17.50	10.50
(35a)	Bob Veale (Large size.)	20.00	10.00	6.00
(35b)	Bob Veale (Small size.)	30.00	15.00	9.00
(36)	Leon Wagner	20.00	10.00	6.00
(37)	Billy Williams	75.00	37.00	22.00
(38)	Earl Wilson	20.00	10.00	6.00

1969 Kahn's Wieners

In its 15th consecutive year of baseball card issue, Kahn's continued the format adopted in 1966. The basic 22 players' cards were printed in about 2-13/16" x 4-9/16" size (with ad panel at top and bottom panel; 2-13/16" x 2-11/16" without panels) and are blanked-backed. Teams represented in the set are the Braves, Cubs, White Sox, Reds, Cardinals, Indians and Pirates. Cards feature a color photo and facsimile autograph bordered by yellow and white vertical stripes. At top is an ad panel consisting of the Kahn's red rose logo. However, because some cards were produced for inclusion in packages other than the standard hot dogs, a number of variations in card size and stripe color were created, as noted in the listings. The smaller size cards, 2-13/16" x 3-1/4" with top and bottom panels; 3/16" x 2-1/8" without panels, were created by more closely cropping the player photo at top and bottom. Values quoted are for complete uncut cards with both panels intact; deduct a minimum 50 percent for cards without the ad and/or bottom panel. Complete set values include all variations.

		NM	EX	VG
Complete Set (29):		1,200	600.00	375.00
Common Player:		25.00	12.50	7.50
(1a)	Hank Aaron (Large size.)	125.00	62.00	37.00
(1b)	Hank Aaron (Small size.)	140.00	70.00	42.00
(2)	Matty Alou	25.00	12.50	7.50
(3)	Max Alvis	25.00	12.50	7.50
(4)	Gerry Arrigo	25.00	12.50	7.50
(5)	Steve Blass	25.00	12.50	7.50
(6)	Clay Carroll (Follow-through.)	25.00	12.50	7.50
(7)	Tony Cloninger	25.00	12.50	7.50
(8)	George Culver	25.00	12.50	7.50
(9)	Joel Horlen (Follow-through.)	25.00	12.50	7.50
(10)	Tony Horton/Btg	35.00	17.50	10.50
(11)	Alex Johnson	25.00	12.50	7.50
(12a)	Jim Maloney (Large size.) (Arms at sides.)	30.00	15.00	9.00
(12b)	Jim Maloney (Small size.) (Arms at sides.)	35.00	17.50	10.50
(13a)	Lee May (Yellow striped border.)(Foot on bag.)	30.00	15.00	9.00
(13b)	Lee May (Red striped border.) (Foot on bag.)	35.00	17.50	10.50
(14a)	Bill Mazeroski (Yellow striped border.)	50.00	25.00	15.00
(14b)	Bill Mazeroski (Red striped border.)	55.00	27.00	16.50
(15a)	Sam McDowell (Yellow striped border.) (Right leg raised.)	30.00	15.00	9.00
(15b)	Sam McDowell (Red striped border.)(Right leg raised.)	35.00	17.50	10.50
(16a)	Tony Perez (Large size.) (Glove on base.)	60.00	30.00	18.00

(16b)	Tony Perez (Small size.) (Glove on base.)	75.00	37.50	22.50
(17)	Gary Peters (Follow-through.)	25.00	12.50	7.50
(18a)	Ron Santo (Yellow striped border.)	50.00	25.00	15.00
(18b)	Ron Santo (Red striped border.)	65.00	32.50	20.00
(19)	Luis Tiant (Arms at knees.)	25.00	12.50	7.50
(20)	Joe Torre	35.00	17.50	10.50
(21)	Bob Veale	25.00	12.50	7.50
(22)	Billy Williams (Bat behind head.)	80.00	40.00	24.00

1970s Kahn's Kielbasa Singles Carl Yastrzemski

The exact year or years of this label's issue are not known. The 4-7/8" x 3-1/8" cardboard package insert has a color portrait photo of baseball's most famous Polish player endorsing the polish sausage product.

	NM	EX	VG
Carl Yastrzemski	15.00	7.50	4.50

1887 Kalamazoo Bats (N690)

This set, issued circa 1887 by Charles Gross & Co. Phila., is one of the most difficult of all 19th Century tobacco issues. The cards measure a rather large 2-1/4" x 4" and feature a sepia-toned photograph on heavy cardboard. The player's name and team appear inside a white strip at the bottom of the photo, while a small ad for Kalamazoo Bats cigarettes is printed at the very bottom of the card. Some cards carry an 1887 copyright line, but there are indications that some of the cards date from 1886 or 1888. The unnumbered set pictures players from four teams - two from New York (Giants and Mets) and two from Philadelphia (Athletics and Phillies). A few of the cards picture more than one player, and some Philadelphia cards have been found with an ad on the back offering various prizes in exchange for saving the cards. The set has been assigned the American Card Catalog number N690. This checklist is likely not complete. Players from the New York teams are significantly rarer than those of the Philadelphia teams.

		NM	EX	VG
Common Player:		6,250	3,750	2,500
Advertising-back: 1.5X				
(1)	Ed Andrews	6,250	3,750	2,500
(2)	Charles Bastian, Lyons	7,000	4,200	2,800
(3)	Lou Bierbauer	7,000	4,200	2,800
(4)	Lou Bierbauer, Gallagher	7,000	4,200	2,800
(5)	Charles Buffinton (Buffinton)	6,250	3,750	2,500
(6)	Dan Casey	6,250	3,750	2,500
(7)	Jack Clements	7,000	4,200	2,800
(8)	Roger Connor (Three known.)	65,000	24,000	16,000
(9)	Larry Corcoran	7,500	4,500	3,000
(10)	Ed Cushman	17,500	10,500	7,000
(11)	Pat Deasley	17,500	10,500	7,000
(12)	Jim Devlin	6,250	3,750	2,500
(13)	Jim Donahue	17,500	10,500	7,000
(14)	Mike Dorgan	11,500	6,900	4,600
(15)	Dude Esterbrooke (Esterbrook.)	17,500	10,500	7,000
(16)	Buck Ewing (Possibly unique.)	85,000	27,000	18,000
(17)	Sid Farrar	6,250	3,750	2,500
(18)	Charlie Ferguson	6,250	3,750	2,500

(19)	Jim Fogarty	6,250	3,750	2,500
(20)	Jim Fogarty, Deacon McGuire	7,000	4,200	2,800
(21)	Elmer Foster	17,500	10,500	7,000
(22)	Whitey Gibson	7,000	4,200	2,800
(23)	Pete Gillespie	17,500	10,500	7,000
(24)	Tom Gunning	6,250	3,750	2,500
(25)	Arthur Irwin	6,250	3,750	2,500
(26)	Arthur Irwin, Al Maul	7,000	4,200	2,800
(27)	Tim Keefe	65,000	21,000	14,000
(28)	Henry Larkin	7,000	4,200	2,800
(29)	Henry Larkins (Larkin), Jocko Milligan	7,000	4,200	2,800
(30)	Jack Lynch	17,500	10,500	7,000
(31)	Denny Lyons (Athletics)	35,000	21,000	14,000
(32)	Harry Lyons (Phila.)	7,000	4,200	2,800
(33)	Harry Lyons (Phila.), Billy Taylor	7,000	4,200	2,800
(34)	Fred Mann	7,000	4,200	2,800
(35)	Charlie Mason	7,000	4,200	2,800
(36)	Bobby Mathews	7,000	4,200	2,800
(37)	Al Maul	6,250	3,750	2,500
(38)	Al Mays	17,500	10,500	7,000
(39)	Chippy McGan (McGarr)	7,000	4,200	2,800
(40)	Deacon McGuire (catching)	6,250	3,750	2,500
(41)	Deacon McGuire/Throwing	6,250	3,750	2,500
(42)	Tom McLaughlin	17,500	10,500	7,000
(43)	Jocko Milligan, Harry Stowe (Stovey)	7,000	4,200	2,800
(44)	Joseph Mulvey	6,250	3,750	2,500
(45)	Candy Nelson	17,500	10,500	7,000
(46)	Orator Jim O'Rourke (Possibly unique.)	75,000	21,000	14,000
(47)	Dave Orr	17,500	10,500	7,000
(48)	Tom Poorman	6,250	3,750	2,500
(49)	Danny Richardson	17,500	10,500	7,000
(50)	Wilbert Robinson	10,500	6,300	4,200
(51)	Wilbert Robinson, Fred Mann	10,500	6,300	4,200
(52)	Chief Roseman	17,500	10,500	7,000
(53)	Ed Seward (Possibly unique.)	14,000	8,400	5,600
(54)	Harry Stowe (Stovey) (Hands on hips.)	75,000	21,000	14,000
(55)	Harry Stowe (Stovey) (Hands outstretched.)	7,000	4,200	2,800
(56)	George Townsend	7,000	4,200	2,800
(57)	Jocko Milligan, George Townsend	7,900	4,750	3,150
(58)	John Ward (Possibly unique.)	100,000	28,500	19,000
(59)	Gus Weyhing	24,000	14,500	9,500
(60)	George Wood	6,250	3,750	2,500
(61)	Harry Wright	40,000	25,000	15,000

1887 Kalamazoo Bats Cabinets (N690-1)

This extremely rare issue of cabinet cards was issued as a premium by Charles Gross & Co. of Philadelphia, makers of the Kalamazoo Bats brand of cigarettes. Two distinct types have been found, both measuring 4-1/4" x 6-1/2". One variety displays the photo on a black mount with the words "Smoke Kalamazoo Bats" embossed in gold to the left. The other contains no advertising, although there is an oval embossment on the card, along with the words "Chas. Gross & Co." and an 1887 copyright line. These cards also have a distinctive pink color on the back of the cardboard mount. Because of the rarity of Kalamazoo Bats cabinets, and uncertainty as to completeness of this checklist, gaps have been left in the assigned numbering.

		NM	EX	VG
Common Player:		6,000	3,000	1,800
(1)	Ed Andrews	6,000	3,000	1,800
(2)	Charles Bastian, Daniel Casey, Billy Taylor			
(3)	Charles Bastian, Denny Lyons	6,000	3,000	1,800
(4)	Louis Bierbauer, Gallagher	6,000	3,000	1,800
(5)	Charles Buffington (Buffinton)	6,000	3,000	1,800
(6)	Daniel Casey	6,000	3,000	1,800
(7)	Jack Clements	6,000	3,000	1,800
(8)	Jim Devlin	6,000	3,000	1,800
(9)	Sid Farrar	6,000	3,000	1,800
(10)	Charlie Ferguson	6,000	3,000	1,800
(11)	Jim Fogarty	6,000	3,000	1,800
(12)	Whitey Gibson	6,000	3,000	1,800
(13)	Tom Gunning	6,000	3,000	1,800
(14)	Arthur Irwin	6,000	3,000	1,800

		NM	EX	VG
(15)	Arthur Irwin, Al Maul	6,000	3,000	1,800
(16)	Henry Larkins (Larkin), Jocko Milligan	6,000	3,000	1,800
(17)	Harry Lyons	6,000	3,000	1,800
(18)	Harry Lyons, Billy Taylor	6,000	3,000	1,800
(19)	Fred Mann	6,000	3,000	1,800
(20)	Fred Mann, Wilbert Robinson	10,000	3,000	1,800
(21)	Bobby Mathews	6,000	3,000	1,800
(22)	Al Maul	6,000	3,000	1,800
(23)	Chippy McCan (McGarr)	6,000	3,000	1,800
(24)	Deacon McGuire/Fielding	6,000	3,000	1,800
(25)	Deacon McGuire/Throwing	6,000	3,000	1,800
(26)	Jocko Milligan, Harry Stowe (Stovey)	6,000	3,000	1,800
(27)	Joseph Mulvey	6,000	3,000	1,800
(28)	Tom Poorman	6,000	3,000	1,800
(29)	Ed Seward	6,000	3,000	1,800
(30)	Harry Stowe (Stovey)	6,000	3,000	1,800
(31)	George Townsend	6,000	3,000	1,800
(32)	George Wood	6,000	3,000	1,800
(33)	Harry Wright	25,000	4,500	2,750
(35)	Athletic Club (Three known, $9,031 paid in 12/04 auction for Good example.)			
(36)	Boston B.B.C. (Believed unique, mount restored, brought $14,434 in 5/05 auction.)			
(37)	Detroit B.B.C. (Believed unique.)			
(38)	Philadelphia B.B.C. (Believed unique, VG, brought $9,935 in 12/04 auction.)			
(39)	Pittsburg B.B.C. (Believed unique, sold for $62,299 in Excellent in 12/05 auction.)			

1887 Kalamazoo Bats Team Cards (N693)

The team photos in this set were issued by Charles Gross & Co. of Philadelphia as a promotion for its Kalamazoo Bats brand of cigarettes. The cards, which are similar in design and size (about 4" x 2-1/4") to the related N690 series, are extremely rare. They feature a team photo with the caption in a white box at the bottom of the photo and an ad for Kalamazoo Bats to the left.

		NM	EX	VG
	Common Team:	9,000	3,250	1,975
(1)	Athletic Club	9,000	3,250	1,975
(2)	Baltimore B.B.C.	30,000	10,800	6,600
(3)	Boston B.B.C.	24,000	8,650	5,275
(4)	Detroit B.B.C.	12,000	4,325	2,650
(5)	Philadelphia B.B.C.	25,000	9,000	5,500
(6)	Pittsburg B.B.C.	30,000	3,250	1,975

1955 Kansas City Athletics Photo Pack

VIC POWER

In the first year following the team's move from Philadelphia to K.C., this set of player pictures was issued, probably sold as a souvenir stand item. The black-and-white photos are in an 8" x 10" format on heavy cardboard. Player poses or portraits are bordered in white with the player name in all-caps at bottom. Backs are blank. This checklist may be incomplete.

		NM	EX	VG
	Complete Set (29):	200.00	100.00	60.00
	Common Player:	9.00	4.50	2.75
(1)	Joe Astroth	9.00	4.50	2.75
(2)	Lou Boudreau	25.00	12.50	7.50
(3)	Cloyd Boyer	9.00	4.50	2.75
(4)	Art Ceccarelli	9.00	4.50	2.75
(5)	Harry Craft	9.00	4.50	2.75
(6)	Joe DeMaestri	9.00	4.50	2.75
(7)	Art Ditmar	9.00	4.50	2.75
(8)	Jim Finigan	9.00	4.50	2.75
(9)	Tom Gorman	9.00	4.50	2.75
(10)	Ray Herbert	9.00	4.50	2.75
(11)	Alex Kellner	9.00	4.50	2.75
(12)	Dick Kryhoski	9.00	4.50	2.75

		NM	EX	VG
(13)	Jack Littrell	9.00	4.50	2.75
(14)	Hector Lopez	9.00	4.50	2.75
(15)	Oscar Melillo	9.00	4.50	2.75
(16)	Arnie Portocarrero	9.00	4.50	2.75
(17)	Vic Power	15.00	7.50	4.50
(18)	Vic Raschi	12.00	6.00	3.50
(19)	Bill Renna	9.00	4.50	2.75
(20)	Johnny Sain	12.00	6.00	3.50
(21)	Bobby Shantz	12.00	6.00	3.50
(22)	Wilmer Shantz	9.00	4.50	2.75
(23)	Harry Simpson	15.00	7.50	4.50
(24)	Enos Slaughter	30.00	15.00	9.00
(25)	Lou Sleator	9.00	4.50	2.75
(26)	George Susce	9.00	4.50	2.75
(27)	Elmer Valo	9.00	4.50	2.75
(28)	Bill Wilson	9.00	4.50	2.75
(29)	Gus Zernial	15.00	7.50	4.50

1956-61 Kansas City Athletics Photocards

Issued over a period of several years these black-and-white photocards share an identical format. The cards are 3-1/4" x 5-1/2" with borderless poses and facsimile autographs on front. Backs are blank. The unnumbered cards are checklisted here in alphabetical order, though the list is surely not complete. Gaps have been left in the assigned numbering for future additions.

		NM	EX	VG
	Common Player:	15.00	7.50	4.50
(1)	Jim Archer	15.00	7.50	4.50
(2)	Mike Baxes	15.00	7.50	4.50
(3)	Zeke Bella	15.00	7.50	4.50
(4)	Lou Boudreau	30.00	15.00	9.00
(5)	Cletis Boyer	20.00	10.00	6.00
(6)	Wally Burnette	15.00	7.50	4.50
(7)	Chico Carrasquel	17.50	8.75	5.25
(8)	Bob Cerv	15.00	7.50	4.50
(9)	Harry Chiti	15.00	7.50	4.50
(10)	Harry Craft	15.00	7.50	4.50
(11)	Jack Crimian	15.00	7.50	4.50
(12)	Bud Daley	15.00	7.50	4.50
(13)	Bob Davis	15.00	7.50	4.50
(14)	Joe DeMaestri	15.00	7.50	4.50
(15)	Art Ditmar	15.00	7.50	4.50
(16)	Jim Ewell/Trainer	15.00	7.50	4.50
(17)	Jim Finigan	15.00	7.50	4.50
(18)	Hank Foiles	17.50	8.75	5.25
(19)	Ned Garver	15.00	7.50	4.50
(20)	Joe Ginsberg	15.00	7.50	4.50
(21)	Tom Gorman (Cap-to-knees.)	15.00	7.50	4.50
(22)	Tom Gorman/Pitching	15.00	7.50	4.50
(23)	Bob Grim	15.00	7.50	4.50
(24)	Johnny Groth	15.00	7.50	4.50
(25)	Kent Hadley	15.00	7.50	4.50
(26)	Ray Herbert	15.00	7.50	4.50
(27)	Troy Herriage	15.00	7.50	4.50
(28)	Whitey Herzog	20.00	10.00	6.00
(29)	Frank House	15.00	7.50	4.50
(32)	Alex Kellner	15.00	7.50	4.50
(33)	Lou Kretlow	15.00	7.50	4.50
(34)	Hec Lopez	15.00	7.50	4.50
(35)	Roger Maris	125.00	62.00	37.00
(36)	Oscar Melillo	15.00	7.50	4.50
(37)	Rance Pless	15.00	7.50	4.50
(38)	Vic Power	20.00	10.00	6.00
(39)	Jose Santiago	15.00	7.50	4.50
(40)	Bobby Shantz	25.00	12.50	7.50
(41)	Harry Simpson	17.50	8.75	5.25
(42)	Lou Skizas	15.00	7.50	4.50
(43)	Enos Slaughter	45.00	22.00	13.50
(44)	Hal Smith	15.00	7.50	4.50
(45)	George Susce	15.00	7.50	4.50
(46)	Wayne Terwilliger	15.00	7.50	4.50
(47)	Charles Thompson	15.00	7.50	4.50
(48)	Dick Tomanek	15.00	7.50	4.50
(49)	Bill Tuttle	15.00	7.50	4.50
(52)	Jack Urban	15.00	7.50	4.50
(53)	Preston Ward	15.00	7.50	4.50
(54)	Dick Williams	17.50	8.75	5.25
(55)	Gus Zernial/Btg	17.50	8.75	5.25
(56)	Gus Zernial/Fielding	17.50	8.75	5.25

1929 Kashin Publications (R316)

This set of 101 unnumbered cards was issued in 25-card boxed series, with cards measuring 3-1/2" x

4-1/2". The cards feature black-and-white photos with the player's name printed in script near the bottom of the photo. Team and league are designated at bottom in printed letters. The backs of the cards are blank. Four of the cards (Hadley, Haines, Siebold and Todt) are considered to be scarcer than the rest of the set. Some cards have been seen with "MADE IN U.S.A." in one of the picture's lower corners; their significance and value are undetermined.

		NM	EX	VG
	Complete Set (101):	9,500	4,750	2,750
	Common Player:	40.00	20.00	12.00
(1)	Dale Alexander	40.00	20.00	12.00
(2)	Ethan N. Allen	40.00	20.00	12.00
(3)	Larry Benton	40.00	20.00	12.00
(4)	Moe Berg	250.00	125.00	75.00
(5)	Max Bishop	40.00	20.00	12.00
(6)	Del Bissonette	40.00	20.00	12.00
(7)	Lucerne A. Blue	40.00	20.00	12.00
(8)	James Bottomley	100.00	50.00	30.00
(9)	Guy T. Bush	40.00	20.00	12.00
(10)	Harold G. Carlson	40.00	20.00	12.00
(11)	Owen Carroll	40.00	20.00	12.00
(12)	Chalmers W. Cissell (Chalmer)	40.00	20.00	12.00
(13)	Earl Combs	100.00	50.00	30.00
(14)	Hugh M. Critz	40.00	20.00	12.00
(15)	H.J. DeBerry	40.00	20.00	12.00
(16)	Pete Donohue	40.00	20.00	12.00
(17)	Taylor Douthit	40.00	20.00	12.00
(18)	Chas. W. Dressen	40.00	20.00	12.00
(19)	Jimmy Dykes	40.00	20.00	12.00
(20)	Howard Ehmke	40.00	20.00	12.00
(21)	Elwood English	40.00	20.00	12.00
(22)	Urban Faber	100.00	50.00	30.00
(23)	Fred Fitzsimmons	40.00	20.00	12.00
(24)	Lewis A. Fonseca	40.00	20.00	12.00
(25)	Horace H. Ford	40.00	20.00	12.00
(26)	Jimmy Foxx	235.00	115.00	70.00
(27)	Frank Frisch	100.00	50.00	30.00
(28)	Lou Gehrig	1,125	560.00	335.00
(29)	Charles Gehringer	100.00	50.00	30.00
(30)	Leon Goslin	100.00	50.00	30.00
(31)	George Grantham	40.00	20.00	12.00
(32)	Burleigh Grimes	100.00	50.00	30.00
(33)	Robert Grove	200.00	100.00	60.00
(34)	Bump Hadley	150.00	75.00	45.00
(35)	Charlie Hafey	100.00	50.00	30.00
(36)	Jesse J. Haines	250.00	125.00	75.00
(37)	Harvey Hendrick	40.00	20.00	12.00
(38)	Floyd C. Herman	40.00	20.00	12.00
(39)	Andy High	40.00	20.00	12.00
(40)	Urban J. Hodapp	40.00	20.00	12.00
(41)	Frank Hogan	40.00	20.00	12.00
(42)	Rogers Hornsby	175.00	85.00	50.00
(43)	Waite Hoyt	100.00	50.00	30.00
(44)	Willis Hudlin	40.00	20.00	12.00
(45)	Frank O. Hurst	40.00	20.00	12.00
(46)	Charlie Jamieson	40.00	20.00	12.00
(47)	Roy C. Johnson	40.00	20.00	12.00
(48)	Percy Jones	40.00	20.00	12.00
(49)	Sam Jones	40.00	20.00	12.00
(50)	Joseph Judge	40.00	20.00	12.00
(51)	Willie Kamm	40.00	20.00	12.00
(52)	Charles Klein	100.00	50.00	30.00
(53)	Mark Koenig	40.00	20.00	12.00
(54)	Ralph Kress	40.00	20.00	12.00
(55)	Fred M. Leach	40.00	20.00	12.00
(56)	Fred Lindstrom	100.00	50.00	30.00
(57)	Ad Liska	40.00	20.00	12.00
(58)	Fred Lucas (Red)	40.00	20.00	12.00
(59)	Fred Maguire	40.00	20.00	12.00
(60)	Perce L. Malone	40.00	20.00	12.00
(61)	Harry Manush (Henry)	100.00	50.00	30.00
(62)	Walter Maranville	100.00	50.00	30.00
(63)	Douglas McWeeney (McWeeny)	40.00	20.00	12.00
(64)	Oscar Melillo	40.00	20.00	12.00
(65)	Ed "Bing" Miller	40.00	20.00	12.00
(66)	Frank O'Doul	80.00	40.00	24.00
(67)	Melvin Ott	200.00	100.00	60.00
(68)	Herbert Pennock	100.00	50.00	30.00
(69)	William W. Regan	40.00	20.00	12.00
(70)	Harry F. Rice	40.00	20.00	12.00
(71)	Sam Rice	100.00	50.00	30.00
(72)	Lance Richbourgh (Richbourg)	40.00	20.00	12.00
(73)	Eddie Rommel	40.00	20.00	12.00
(74)	Chas. H. Root	40.00	20.00	12.00
(75)	Ed (Edd) Roush	100.00	50.00	30.00
(76)	Harold Ruel (Herold)	40.00	20.00	12.00
(77)	Charles Ruffing	125.00	65.00	35.00
(78)	Jack Russell	40.00	20.00	12.00
(79)	Babe Ruth	1,650	825.00	500.00

		NM	EX	VG
(80)	Fred Schulte	40.00	20.00	12.00
(81)	Harry Seibold	150.00	75.00	45.00
(82)	Joe Sewell	100.00	50.00	30.00
(83)	Luke Sewell	40.00	20.00	12.00
(84)	Art Shires	40.00	20.00	12.00
(85)	Al Simmons	100.00	50.00	30.00
(86)	Bob Smith	40.00	20.00	12.00
(87)	Riggs Stephenson	40.00	20.00	12.00
(88)	Wm. H. Terry	100.00	50.00	30.00
(89)	Alphonse Thomas	40.00	20.00	12.00
(90)	Lafayette F. Thompson	40.00	20.00	12.00
(91)	Phil Todt	150.00	75.00	45.00
(92)	Harold J. Traynor	100.00	50.00	30.00
(93)	Dazzy Vance	100.00	50.00	30.00
(94)	Lloyd Waner	100.00	50.00	30.00
(95)	Paul Waner	100.00	50.00	30.00
(96)	Jimmy Welsh	40.00	20.00	12.00
(97)	Earl Whitehill	40.00	20.00	12.00
(98)	A.C. Whitney	40.00	20.00	12.00
(99)	Claude Willoughby	40.00	20.00	12.00
(100)	Hack Wilson	200.00	100.00	60.00
(101)	Tom Zachary	40.00	20.00	12.00

1964 KDKA Pittsburgh Pirates Portraits

Issued prior to the radio/TV stations' much more common color player cards of 1968, this seldom-seen regional issue presents the 1964 Pittsburgh Pirates in a set of 28 large-format (8" x 11-7/8") schedule cards. The cards are printed in sepia tones on blank-backed cardboard. Fronts present a player pose and a '64 Pirates schedule. A redemption offer states that a pair of Bucs' tickets will be given in exchange for a complete set of the portraits, and the pictures will be returned, presumably cancelled in some fashion. The unnumbered cards are checklisted here alphabetically. While the cards advertise the Pirates' broadcasting partners, they were actually issued by Sweet Clean laundry as stiffeners for men's shirts that had been washed. The laundry's name is not mentioned anywhere on the cards.

		NM	EX	VG
Complete Set (28):		3,500	1,750	1,000
Common Player:		100.00	50.00	30.00
(1)	Gene Alley	100.00	50.00	30.00
(2)	Bob Bailey	100.00	50.00	30.00
(3)	Frank Bork	100.00	50.00	30.00
(4)	Smoky Burgess	100.00	50.00	30.00
(5)	Tom Butters	100.00	50.00	30.00
(6)	Don Cardwell	100.00	50.00	30.00
(7)	Roberto Clemente	600.00	300.00	180.00
(8)	Donn Clendenon	100.00	50.00	30.00
(9)	Elroy Face	100.00	50.00	30.00
(10)	Gene Freese	100.00	50.00	30.00
(11)	Bob Friend	100.00	50.00	30.00
(12)	Joe Gibbon	100.00	50.00	30.00
(13)	Julio Gotay	100.00	50.00	30.00
(14)	Rex Johnston	100.00	50.00	30.00
(15)	Vernon Law	100.00	50.00	30.00
(16)	Jerry Lynch	100.00	50.00	30.00
(17)	Bill Mazeroski	250.00	125.00	75.00
(18)	Al McBean	100.00	50.00	30.00
(19)	Orlando McFarlane	100.00	50.00	30.00
(20)	Manny Mota	100.00	50.00	30.00
(21)	Danny Murtaugh	100.00	50.00	30.00
(22)	Jim Pagliaroni	100.00	50.00	30.00
(23)	Dick Schofield	100.00	50.00	30.00
(24)	Don Schwall	100.00	50.00	30.00
(25)	Tommie Sisk	100.00	50.00	30.00
(26)	Willie Stargell	250.00	125.00	75.00
(27)	Bob Veale	100.00	50.00	30.00
(28)	Bill Virdon	100.00	50.00	30.00

1968 KDKA Pittsburgh Pirates

The most common of the many Pirates regional issues of the late 1960s, this 23-card set was sponsored by the Pirates' TV and radio flagship stations, KDKA in Pittsburgh. Cards measure 2-1/2" x 4" and feature at top front a color posed photo of the player, with no top or side borders. In the white panel beneath the photo are a facsimile autograph, the player's name, position and uniform number and the broadcasters' logo. Backs are printed in black on white and feature advertising for the radio and TV station. The checklist is presented here by uniform number.

Collect the Entire Series of Pirate Cards

Hear: Here: KDKA RADIO 1020

See: Here: KDKA-TV 2

PITTSBURGH PIRATES BASEBALL

Roberto Clemente
Outfielder
No. 21
KDKA

		NM	EX	VG
Complete Set (23):		125.00	65.00	35.00
Common Player:		5.00	2.50	1.50
7	Larry Shepard	5.00	2.50	1.50
8	Willie Stargell	15.00	7.50	4.50
9	Bill Mazeroski	15.00	7.50	4.50
10	Gary Kolb	5.00	2.50	1.50
11	Jose Pagan	5.00	2.50	1.50
12	Gerry May (Jerry)	5.00	2.50	1.50
14	Jim Bunning	10.00	5.00	3.00
15	Manny Mota	5.00	2.50	1.50
17	Donn Clendenon	5.00	2.50	1.50
18	Matty Alou	5.00	2.50	1.50
21	Roberto Clemente	40.00	20.00	12.00
22	Gene Alley	5.00	2.50	1.50
25	Tommy Sisk	5.00	2.50	1.50
26	Roy Face	5.00	2.50	1.50
27	Ron Kline	5.00	2.50	1.50
28	Steve Blass	5.00	2.50	1.50
29	Juan Pizarro	5.00	2.50	1.50
30	Maury Wills	6.50	3.25	2.00
34	Al McBean	5.00	2.50	1.50
35	Manny Sanguillen	5.00	2.50	1.50
38	Bob Moose	5.00	2.50	1.50
39	Bob Veale	5.00	2.50	1.50
40	Dave Wickersham	5.00	2.50	1.50

1922 Keating Candy Co.

WALTER PIPP
1st B.—New York Americans

JAMES P. KEATING CANDY
MANUFACTURER & DEALER
WHOLESALE ONLY
1125 11th ST.

To compete with other candy issues featuring baseball cards as premiums, Sacramento, Calif., wholesale candy merchant James P. Keating appears to have purchased uncut sheets of the blank-back strip cards known as W575-1, overprinted their backs and packaged them with his product. The advertising on back is rubber-stamped. The fact that examples are known that have been cancelled with a hole punch probably indicates there was some sort of prize redemption program attached to the issue. Collectors can expect to pay a premium of about 3X for this version.

	NM	EX	VG
Common Player:	85.00	45.00	25.00
Stars: 3X			

(See 1922 W575-1 for checklist and base card values.)

1971 Keds Kedcards

KEDKARD JOHNNY BENCH
BASEBALL

These (usually) 2-1/4" x 2-1/8" cards were printed on the side of Keds athletic shoe boxes. The cards have colorful drawings of various athletes, with dotted lines for cutting. Backs are blank.

		NM	EX	VG
Complete Panel Set (3):		150.00	75.00	45.00
Complete Set (10):		120.00	60.00	35.00
Common Player:		8.00	4.00	2.50
PANEL 1				
(1)	Dave Bing/Basketball	40.00	20.00	12.00
(2)	Clark Graebner/Tennis	8.00	4.00	2.50
(3)	Jim Maloney	10.00	5.00	3.00
(4)	Bubba Smith/Football	8.00	4.00	2.50
PANEL 2				
(5)	Johnny Bench	65.00	32.00	19.50
(6)	Willis Reed/Basketball	30.00	15.00	9.00
(7)	Bubba Smith/Football	10.00	5.00	3.00
(8)	Stan Smith/Tennis	8.00	4.00	2.50
PANEL 3				
(9)	Willis Reed/Basketball (5-1/4" x 3-1/2")	50.00	25.00	15.00
		15.00	7.50	4.50
(10)	Johnny Bench (5-1/4" x 3-1/2")	30.00	15.00	9.00

1937 Kellogg's Pep Sports Stamps

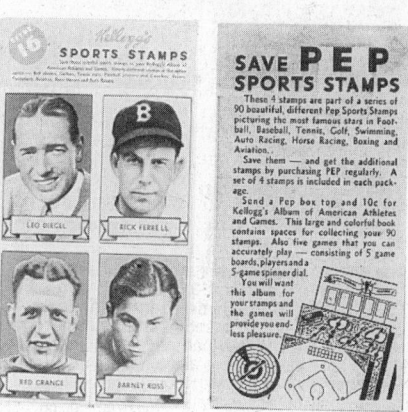

Kellogg's packaged a four-stamp panel of "Sports Stamps" in boxes of Pep cereal. While 24 panels comprise a complete set, six of the stamps were double-printed, creating a set of 90. Backs of the stamp panels gave details for ordering an album and game boards for playing with the stamps. The color-tinted stamps measure 1-1/8" x 2-3/4" individually, and 2-1/4" x 4-1/4" as a panel. Besides the ballplayers checklisted here, the Kellogg's/Pep stamps included football, tennis and golf players, swimmers, boxers, aviators and race horses. Baseball player stamps are listed here according to the number of the four-stamp panel on which they appeared. Prices for complete panels would be considerably higher, factoring in the other stamps on the sheet.

		NM	EX	VG
Complete Set (18):		900.00	450.00	275.00
Common Player:		60.00	30.00	18.00
Album:		300.00	150.00	100.00
1	Joe Medwick	60.00	30.00	18.00
3	Leo Durocher	60.00	30.00	18.00
5	Gabby Hartnett	60.00	30.00	18.00
6	Billy Herman	60.00	30.00	18.00
7	Luke Appling	60.00	30.00	18.00
8	Floyd Vaughan	60.00	30.00	18.00
9	Paul Waner	60.00	30.00	18.00
11	Bill Terry	60.00	30.00	18.00
12	George Selkirk	60.00	30.00	18.00
13	Walter Johnson	120.00	60.00	36.00
15	Lew Fonseca	60.00	30.00	18.00
16	Richard Ferrell	60.00	30.00	18.00
17	Johnny Evers	60.00	30.00	18.00
18	Sam West	60.00	30.00	18.00
19	Buddy Myer	60.00	30.00	18.00
20	Tris Speaker (Double print, also on Panel 23.)	60.00	30.00	18.00
21	Joe Tinker	60.00	30.00	18.00
22	Mordecai Brown	60.00	30.00	18.00
23	Tris Speaker (Double-print, also on Panel 20.)	60.00	30.00	18.00

1948 Kellogg's Corn Flakes Cuban Postcards

These advertising postcards were issued in Cuba. The approximately 3-1/2" x 5-3/8" black-and-white cards have a portrait photo on front. A small logo for the cereal appears in the lower-left corner, while a facsimile autograph is at lower-right. The back is in traditional postcard format, printed in English. This checklist is likely incomplete.

		NM	EX	VG
(1)	Tomas de la Cruz	400.00	200.00	120.00
(2)	Salvador Hernandez	400.00	200.00	120.00
(3)	Adolfo Luque	600.00	300.00	180.00
(4)	Roberto Ortiz	400.00	200.00	120.00
(5)	Napoleon Reyes	400.00	200.00	120.00
(6)	Lazaro Salazar	400.00	200.00	120.00

1948 Kellogg's Pep Celebrities

PHIL CAVARETTA

First baseman and outfielder, Chicago Cubs. National league batting champion and most valuable player in 1945. Joined Cubs at age of 17 and has lifetime batting average of .292. Bats and throws left-handed.

Get Complete Series with Kellogg's PEP

Five baseball players are included among the 18 athletes in this set of 1-3/8" x 1-5/8" cards. Fronts have player photos bordered in white. Backs have player name at top, a short career summary and a Kellogg's ad. The baseball players from the unnumbered set are listed here alphabetically.

		NM	EX	VG
Complete Set (5):		175.00	90.00	55.00
Common Player:		40.00	20.00	12.00
(1)	Phil Cavarretta	40.00	20.00	12.00
(2)	Orval Grove	40.00	20.00	12.00
(3)	Mike Tresh	40.00	20.00	12.00
(4)	Paul "Dizzy" Trout	40.00	20.00	12.00
(5)	Dick Wakefield	40.00	20.00	12.00

1970 Kellogg's

For 14 years in the 1970s and early 1980s, the Kellogg's cereal company provided Topps with virtually the only meaningful national competition in the baseball card market. Kellogg's kicked off its baseball card program in 1970 with a 75-player set of simulated 3-D cards. Single cards were available in selected brands of the company's cereal, while a mail-in program offered complete sets. The 3-D effect was achieved by the sandwiching of a clear color player photo between a purposely blurred stadium background scene and a layer of ribbed plastic. The relatively narrow dimension of the card, 2-1/4" x 3-1/2" and the nature of the plastic overlay seem to cause the cards to curl, often cracking the plastic layer, if not stored properly. Cards with major cracks in the plastic can be considered in Fair condition, at best.

		NM	EX	VG
Complete Set (75):		300.00	150.00	90.00
Common Player:		3.50	1.75	1.00
1	Ed Kranepool	3.50	1.75	1.00
2	Pete Rose	20.00	10.00	6.00
3	Cleon Jones	3.50	1.75	1.00
4	Willie McCovey	10.00	5.00	3.00
5	Mel Stottlemyre	3.50	1.75	1.00
6	Frank Howard	3.50	1.75	1.00
7	Tom Seaver	15.00	7.50	4.50
8	Don Sutton	10.00	5.00	3.00
9	Jim Wynn	3.50	1.75	1.00
10	Jim Maloney	3.50	1.75	1.00
11	Tommie Agee	3.50	1.75	1.00
12	Willie Mays	25.00	12.50	7.50
13	Juan Marichal	10.00	5.00	3.00
14	Dave McNally	3.50	1.75	1.00
15	Frank Robinson	15.00	7.50	4.50
16	Carlos May	3.50	1.75	1.00
17	Bill Singer	3.50	1.75	1.00
18	Rick Reichardt	3.50	1.75	1.00
19	Boog Powell	4.50	2.25	1.25
20	Gaylord Perry	10.00	5.00	3.00
21	Brooks Robinson	15.00	7.50	4.50
22	Luis Aparicio	10.00	5.00	3.00
23	Joel Horlen	3.50	1.75	1.00
24	Mike Epstein	3.50	1.75	1.00
25	Tom Haller	3.50	1.75	1.00
26	Willie Crawford	3.50	1.75	1.00
27	Roberto Clemente	35.00	17.50	10.00
28	Matty Alou	3.50	1.75	1.00
29	Willie Stargell	12.50	6.25	3.75
30	Tim Cullen	3.50	1.75	1.00
31	Randy Hundley	3.50	1.75	1.00
32	Reggie Jackson	20.00	10.00	6.00
33	Rich Allen	4.25	2.25	1.25
34	Tim McCarver	3.50	1.75	1.00
35	Ray Culp	3.50	1.75	1.00
36	Jim Fregosi	3.50	1.75	1.00
37	Billy Williams	12.50	6.25	3.75
38	Johnny Odom	3.50	1.75	1.00
39	Bert Campaneris	3.50	1.75	1.00
40	Ernie Banks	20.00	10.00	6.00
41	Chris Short	3.50	1.75	1.00
42	Ron Santo	6.00	3.00	1.75
43	Glenn Beckert	3.50	1.75	1.00
44	Lou Brock	12.50	6.25	3.75
45	Larry Hisle	3.50	1.75	1.00
46	Reggie Smith	3.50	1.75	1.00
47	Rod Carew	15.00	7.50	4.50
48	Curt Flood	3.50	1.75	1.00
49	Jim Lonborg	3.50	1.75	1.00
50	Sam McDowell	3.50	1.75	1.00
51	Sal Bando	3.50	1.75	1.00
52	Al Kaline	15.00	7.50	4.50
53	Gary Nolan	3.50	1.75	1.00
54	Rico Petrocelli	3.50	1.75	1.00
55	Ollie Brown	3.50	1.75	1.00
56	Luis Tiant	3.50	1.75	1.00
57	Bill Freehan	3.50	1.75	1.00
58	Johnny Bench	15.00	7.50	4.50
59	Joe Pepitone	3.50	1.75	1.00
60	Bobby Murcer	3.50	1.75	1.00
61	Harmon Killebrew	15.00	7.50	4.50
62	Don Wilson	3.50	1.75	1.00
63	Tony Oliva	3.50	1.75	1.00
64	Jim Perry	3.50	1.75	1.00
65	Mickey Lolich	3.50	1.75	1.00
66	Coco Laboy	3.50	1.75	1.00
67	Dean Chance	3.50	1.75	1.00
68	Ken Harrelson	3.50	1.75	1.00
69	Willie Horton	3.50	1.75	1.00
70	Wally Bunker	3.50	1.75	1.00
71a	Bob Gibson (1959 IP blank.)	12.50	6.25	3.75
71b	Bob Gibson (1959 IP 76)	12.50	6.25	3.75
72	Joe Morgan	12.50	6.25	3.75
73	Denny McLain	3.50	1.75	1.00
74	Tommy Harper	3.50	1.75	1.00
75	Don Mincher	3.50	1.75	1.00

1971 Kellogg's

The scarcest and most valuable of the Kellogg's editions, the 75-card 1971 set was the only one not offered by the company on a mail-in basis. The only way to complete it was to buy ... and buy and buy ... boxes of cereal. Kellogg's again used the simulated 3-D effect in the cards' design, with the same result being many of the 2-1/4" x 3-1/2" cards are found today with cracks resulting from the cards' curling. A number of scarcer back variations are checklisted below. In addition, all 75 cards can be found with and without the 1970 date before the "Xograph" copyright line on the back; though there is no difference in value.

		NM	EX	VG
Complete Set (75):		1,000	500.00	300.00
Common Player:		13.50	6.75	4.00
1a	Wayne Simpson (SO 120)	13.50	6.75	4.00
1b	Wayne Simpson (SO 119)	20.00	10.00	6.00
2	Tom Seaver	30.00	15.00	9.00
3a	Jim Perry (IP 2238)	13.50	6.75	4.00
3b	Jim Perry (IP 2239)	20.00	10.00	6.00
4a	Bob Robertson (RBI 94)	13.50	6.75	4.00
4b	Bob Robertson (RBI 95)	20.00	10.00	6.00
5	Roberto Clemente	70.00	35.00	20.00
6a	Gaylord Perry (IP 2014)	25.00	12.50	7.50
6b	Gaylord Perry (IP 2015)	30.00	15.00	9.00
7a	Felipe Alou (1970 Oakland NL)	20.00	10.00	6.00
7b	Felipe Alou (1970 Oakland AL)	25.00	12.50	7.50
8	Denis Menke	13.50	6.75	4.00
9a	Don Kessinger (Hits 849.)	13.50	6.75	4.00
9b	Don Kessinger (Hits 850.)	20.00	10.00	6.00
10	Willie Mays	45.00	22.00	13.50
11	Jim Hickman	13.50	6.75	4.00
12	Tony Oliva	17.50	8.75	5.25
13	Manny Sanguillen	13.50	6.75	4.00
14a	Frank Howard (1968 Washington NL)	30.00	15.00	9.00
14b	Frank Howard (1968 Washington AL)	20.00	10.00	6.00
15	Frank Robinson	30.00	15.00	9.00
16	Willie Davis	13.50	6.75	4.00
17	Lou Brock	25.00	12.50	7.50
18	Cesar Tovar	13.50	6.75	4.00
19	Luis Aparicio	25.00	12.50	7.50
20	Boog Powell	17.50	8.75	5.25
21a	Dick Selma (SO 584)	13.50	6.75	4.00
21b	Dick Selma (SO 587)	20.00	10.00	6.00
22	Danny Walton	13.50	6.75	4.00
23	Carl Morton	13.50	6.75	4.00
24a	Sonny Siebert (SO 1054)	13.50	6.75	4.00
24b	Sonny Siebert (SO 1055)	20.00	10.00	6.00
25	Jim Merritt	13.50	6.75	4.00
26a	Jose Cardenal (Hits 828)	13.50	6.75	4.00
26b	Jose Cardenal (Hits 829)	20.00	10.00	6.00
27	Don Mincher	13.50	6.75	4.00
28a	Clyde Wright (California state logo.)	13.50	6.75	4.00
28b	Clyde Wright (Angels crest logo.)	20.00	10.00	6.00
29	Les Cain	13.50	6.75	4.00
30	Danny Cater	13.50	6.75	4.00
31	Don Sutton	25.00	12.50	7.50
32	Chuck Dobson	13.50	6.75	4.00
33	Willie McCovey	25.00	12.50	7.50
34	Mike Epstein	13.50	6.75	4.00
35a	Paul Blair (Runs 386)	13.50	6.75	4.00
35b	Paul Blair (Runs 385)	20.00	10.00	6.00
36a	Gary Nolan (SO 577)	13.50	6.75	4.00
36b	Gary Nolan (SO 581)	20.00	10.00	6.00
37	Sam McDowell	13.50	6.75	4.00
38	Amos Otis	13.50	6.75	4.00
39a	Ray Fosse (RBI 69)	13.50	6.75	4.00
39b	Ray Fosse (RBI 70)	20.00	10.00	6.00
40	Mel Stottlemyre	13.50	6.75	4.00
41	Cito Gaston	13.50	6.75	4.00
42	Dick Dietz	13.50	6.75	4.00
43	Roy White	13.50	6.75	4.00
44	Al Kaline	30.00	15.00	9.00
45	Carlos May	13.50	6.75	4.00
46a	Tommie Agee (RBI 313)	13.50	6.75	4.00
46b	Tommie Agee (RBI 314)	20.00	10.00	6.00
47	Tommy Harper	13.50	6.75	4.00
48	Larry Dierker	13.50	6.75	4.00
49	Mike Cuellar	13.50	6.75	4.00
50	Ernie Banks	30.00	15.00	9.00
51	Bob Gibson	25.00	12.50	7.50
52	Reggie Smith	13.50	6.75	4.00
53a	Matty Alou (RBI 273)	13.50	6.75	4.00
53b	Matty Alou (RBI 274)	20.00	10.00	6.00
54a	Alex Johnson (California state logo.)	13.50	6.75	4.00
54b	Alex Johnson (Angels crest logo.)	20.00	10.00	6.00
55	Harmon Killebrew	30.00	15.00	9.00
56	Billy Grabarkewitz	13.50	6.75	4.00
57	Rich Allen	17.50	8.75	5.25
58	Tony Perez	25.00	12.50	7.50
59a	Dave McNally (SO 1065)	13.50	6.75	4.00
59b	Dave McNally (SO 1067)	20.00	10.00	6.00
60a	Jim Palmer (SO 564)	25.00	12.50	7.50
60b	Jim Palmer (SO 567)	30.00	15.00	9.00
61	Billy Williams	25.00	12.50	7.50
62	Joe Torre	20.00	10.00	6.00
63a	Jim Northrup (AB 2773)	13.50	6.75	4.00
63b	Jim Northrup (AB 2772)	20.00	10.00	6.00
64a	Jim Fregosi (Calif. state logo - Hits 1326.)	13.50	6.75	4.00
64b	Jim Fregosi (Calif. state logo - Hits 1327.)	20.00	10.00	6.00
64c	Jim Fregosi (Angels crest logo.)	20.00	10.00	6.00
65	Pete Rose	60.00	30.00	18.00
66a	Bud Harrelson (RBI 112)	13.50	6.75	4.00
66b	Bud Harrelson (RBI 113)	20.00	10.00	6.00
67	Tony Taylor	13.50	6.75	4.00
68	Willie Stargell	25.00	12.50	7.50
69	Tony Horton	25.00	12.50	7.50
70a	Claude Oseen (No number.)	25.00	12.50	7.50
70b	Claude Osteen (#70 on back.)	13.50	6.75	4.00
71	Glenn Beckert	13.50	6.75	4.00
72	Nate Colbert	13.50	6.75	4.00
73a	Rick Monday (AB 1705)	13.50	6.75	4.00
73b	Rick Monday (AB 1704)	20.00	10.00	6.00
74a	Tommy John (BB 444)	20.00	10.00	6.00
74b	Tommy John (BB 443)	25.00	12.50	7.50
75	Chris Short	13.50	6.75	4.00

1972 Kellogg's

For 1972, Kellogg's reduced both the number of cards in its set and the dimensions of each card, moving to a 2-1/8" x 3-1/4" size and fixing the set at 54 cards. Once again, the cards were produced to simulate a 3-D effect (see description for 1970 Kellogg's). The set was available via a mail-in offer. The checklist includes variations which resulted from

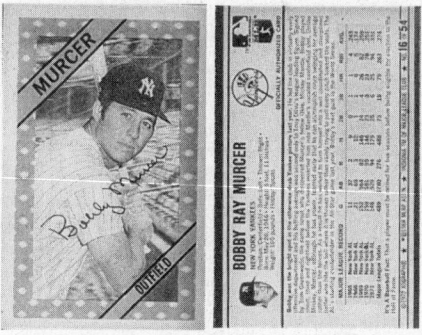

the correction of erroneous statistics on the backs of some cards. The complete set values quoted do not include the scarcer variations.

		NM	EX	VG
	Complete Set (54):	125.00	65.00	35.00
	Common Player:	1.00	.50	.30
1a	Tom Seaver (1970 ERA 2.85.)	10.00	5.00	3.00
1b	Tom Seaver (1970 ERA 2.81.)	7.50	3.75	2.25
2	Amos Otis	1.00	.50	.30
3a	Willie Davis (Runs 842)	2.00	1.00	.60
3b	Willie Davis (Runs 841)	1.25	.60	.40
4	Wilbur Wood	1.00	.50	.30
5	Bill Parsons	1.00	.50	.30
6	Pete Rose	15.00	7.50	4.50
7a	Willie McCovey (HR 360)	6.00	3.00	1.75
7b	Willie McCovey (HR 370)	5.00	2.50	1.50
8	Fergie Jenkins	3.50	1.75	1.00
9a	Vida Blue (ERA 2.35)	2.00	1.00	.60
9b	Vida Blue (ERA 2.31)	1.25	.60	.40
10	Joe Torre	2.50	1.25	.70
11	Merv Rettenmund	1.00	.50	.30
12	Bill Melton	1.00	.50	.30
13a	Jim Palmer (Games 170)	6.00	3.00	1.75
13b	Jim Palmer (Games 168)	4.50	2.25	1.25
14	Doug Rader	1.00	.50	.30
15a	Dave Roberts (...Seaver, the NL leader...)	2.00	1.00	.60
15b	Dave Roberts (...Seaver, the league leader...)	1.25	.60	.40
16	Bobby Murcer	1.25	.60	.40
17	Wes Parker	1.00	.50	.30
18a	Joe Coleman (BB 394)	2.00	1.00	.60
18b	Joe Coleman (BB 393)	1.25	.60	.40
19	Manny Sanguillen	1.00	.50	.30
20	Reggie Jackson	10.00	5.00	3.00
21	Ralph Garr	1.00	.50	.30
22	Jim "Catfish" Hunter	3.50	1.75	1.00
23	Rick Wise	1.00	.50	.30
24	Glenn Beckert	1.00	.50	.30
25	Tony Oliva	1.00	.50	.30
26a	Bob Gibson (SO 2577)	6.00	3.00	1.75
26b	Bob Gibson (SO 2578)	4.50	2.25	1.25
27a	Mike Cuellar (1971 ERA 3.80)	2.00	1.00	.60
27b	Mike Cuellar (1971 ERA 3.08)	1.25	.60	.40
28	Chris Speier	1.00	.50	.30
29a	Dave McNally (ERA 3.18)	2.00	1.00	.60
29b	Dave McNally (ERA 3.15)	1.25	.60	.40
30	Chico Cardenas	1.00	.50	.30
31a	Bill Freehan (AVG. .263)	2.00	1.00	.60
31b	Bill Freehan (AVG. .262)	1.25	.60	.40
32a	Bud Harrelson (Hits 634)	2.00	1.00	.60
32b	Bud Harrelson (Hits 624)	1.25	.60	.40
33a	Sam McDowell (...less than 200 innings...)	2.00	1.00	.60
33b	Sam McDowell (...less than 225 innings...)	1.25	.60	.40
34a	Claude Osteen (1971 ERA 3.25)	2.00	1.00	.60
34b	Claude Osteen (1971 ERA 3.51)	1.25	.60	.40
35	Reggie Smith	1.00	.50	.30
36	Sonny Siebert	1.00	.50	.30
37	Lee May	1.00	.50	.30
38	Mickey Lolich	1.00	.50	.30
39a	Cookie Rojas (2B 149)	2.00	1.00	.60
39b	Cookie Rojas (2B 150)	1.25	.60	.40
40	Dick Drago	1.00	.50	.30
41	Nate Colbert	1.00	.50	.30
42	Andy Messersmith	1.00	.50	.30
43a	Dave Johnson (AVG. .262)	2.00	1.00	.60
43b	Dave Johnson (AVG. .264)	1.25	.60	.40
44	Steve Blass	1.00	.50	.30
45	Bob Robertson	1.00	.50	.30
46a	Billy Williams (...missed only one last season...)	6.00	3.00	1.75
46b	Billy Williams (Phrase omitted.)	4.50	2.25	1.25
47	Juan Marichal	4.00	2.00	1.25
48	Lou Brock	4.00	2.00	1.25
49	Roberto Clemente	17.50	8.75	5.25
50	Mel Stottlemyre	1.00	.50	.30
51	Don Wilson	1.00	.50	.30
52a	Sal Bando (RBI 355)	2.00	1.00	.60
52b	Sal Bando (RBI 356)	1.25	.60	.40
53a	Willie Stargell (2B 197)	6.00	3.00	1.75
53b	Willie Stargell (2B 196)	4.50	2.25	1.25
54a	Willie Mays (RBI 1855)	15.00	7.50	4.50
54b	Willie Mays (RBI 1856)	12.00	6.00	3.50

1972 Kellogg's All-Time Baseball Greats

Kellogg's issued a second baseball card set in 1972, inserted into packages of breakfast rolls. The 2-1/4" x 3-1/2" cards also featured a simulated 3-D effect, but the 15 players in the set were "All-Time Baseball Greats," rather than current players. The set is virtually identical to a Rold Gold pretzel issue of 1970; the only difference being the 1972 copyright date on the back of the Kellog's cards, while the pretzel issue bears a 1970 date. The pretzel cards are considerably scarcer than the Kellogg's.

		NM	EX	VG
	Complete Set (15):	45.00	22.50	13.50
	Common Player:	2.50	1.25	.70
1	Walter Johnson	3.50	1.75	1.00
2	Rogers Hornsby	2.50	1.25	.70
3	John McGraw	2.50	1.25	.70
4	Mickey Cochrane	2.50	1.25	.70
5	George Sisler	2.50	1.25	.70
6	Babe Ruth (Portrait photo on back.)	15.00	7.50	4.50
7	Robert "Lefty" Grove	2.50	1.25	.70
8	Harold "Pie" Traynor	2.50	1.25	.70
9	Honus Wagner	5.00	2.50	1.50
10	Eddie Collins	2.50	1.25	.70
11	Tris Speaker	2.50	1.25	.70
12	Cy Young	3.50	1.75	1.00
13	Lou Gehrig	10.00	5.00	3.00
14	Babe Ruth (Action photo on back.)	15.00	7.50	4.50
15	Ty Cobb	10.00	5.00	3.00

1973 Kellogg's

The lone exception to Kellogg's long run of simulated 3-D effect cards came in 1973, when the cereal company's 54-card set was produced by "normal" printing methods. In 2-1/4" x 3-1/2" size, the design was otherwise quite compatible with the issues which preceded and succeeded it. Because it was available via a mail-in offer ($1.25 and two Raisin Bran boxtops), it is not as scarce as the earlier Kellogg's issues.

		NM	EX	VG
	Complete Set (54):	65.00	32.50	20.00
	Common Player:	.90	.45	.25
1	Amos Otis	.90	.45	.25
2	Ellie Rodriguez	.90	.45	.25
3	Mickey Lolich	.90	.45	.25
4	Tony Oliva	1.25	.60	.40
5	Don Sutton	3.50	1.75	1.00
6	Pete Rose	12.00	6.00	3.50
7	Steve Carlton	4.50	2.25	1.25
8	Bobby Bonds	.90	.45	.25
9	Wilbur Wood	.90	.45	.25
10	Billy Williams	4.50	2.25	1.25
11	Steve Blass	.90	.45	.25
12	Jon Matlack	.90	.45	.25
13	Cesar Cedeno	.90	.45	.25
14	Bob Gibson	4.50	2.25	1.25
15	Sparky Lyle	.90	.45	.25
16	Nolan Ryan	17.50	8.75	5.25
17	Jim Palmer	4.50	2.25	1.25
18	Ray Fosse	.90	.45	.25
19	Bobby Murcer	.90	.45	.25
20	Jim "Catfish" Hunter	3.50	1.75	1.00
21	Tug McGraw	.90	.45	.25
22	Reggie Jackson	9.00	4.50	2.75

23	Bill Stoneman	.90	.45	.25
24	Lou Piniella	.90	.45	.25
25	Willie Stargell	4.50	2.25	1.25
26	Dick Allen	2.50	1.25	.70
27	Carlton Fisk	4.50	2.25	1.25
28	Fergie Jenkins	3.50	1.75	1.00
29	Phil Niekro	3.50	1.75	1.00
30	Gary Nolan	.90	.45	.25
31	Joe Torre	2.50	1.25	.70
32	Bobby Tolan	.90	.45	.25
33	Nate Colbert	.90	.45	.25
34	Joe Morgan	4.50	2.25	1.25
35	Bert Blyleven	.90	.45	.25
36	Joe Rudi	.90	.45	.25
37	Ralph Garr	.90	.45	.25
38	Gaylord Perry	3.50	1.75	1.00
39	Bobby Grich	.90	.45	.25
40	Lou Brock	4.00	2.00	1.25
41	Pete Broberg	.90	.45	.25
42	Manny Sanguillen	.90	.45	.25
43	Willie Davis	.90	.45	.25
44	Dave Kingman	.90	.45	.25
45	Carlos May	.90	.45	.25
46	Tom Seaver	6.00	3.00	1.75
47	Mike Cuellar	.90	.45	.25
48	Joe Coleman	.90	.45	.25
49	Claude Osteen	.90	.45	.25
50	Steve Kline	.90	.45	.25
51	Rod Carew	4.50	2.25	1.25
52	Al Kaline	6.00	3.00	1.75
53	Larry Dierker	.90	.45	.25
54	Ron Santo	2.50	1.25	.70

1974 Kellogg's

For 1974, Kellogg's returned to the use of simulated 3-D for its 54-player baseball card issue (see 1970 Kellogg's listing for description). In 2-1/8" x 3-1/4" size, the cards were available as a complete set via a mail-in offer. The complete set price listed here does not include the more expensive variations.

		NM	EX	VG
	Complete Set (54):	65.00	32.50	20.00
	Common Player:	.90	.45	.25
1	Bob Gibson	3.50	1.75	1.00
2	Rick Monday	.90	.45	.25
3	Joe Coleman	.90	.45	.25
4	Bert Campaneris	.90	.45	.25
5	Carlton Fisk	4.00	2.00	1.25
6	Jim Palmer	3.50	1.75	1.00
7a	Ron Santo (Chicago Cubs)	2.25	1.25	.70
7b	Ron Santo (Chicago White Sox)	1.25	.60	.40
8	Nolan Ryan	16.00	8.00	4.75
9	Greg Luzinski	.90	.45	.25
10a	Buddy Bell (Runs 134)	2.25	1.25	.70
10b	Buddy Bell (Runs 135)	1.00	.50	.30
11	Bob Watson	.90	.45	.25
12	Bill Singer	.90	.45	.25
13	Dave May	.90	.45	.25
14	Jim Brewer	.90	.45	.25
15	Manny Sanguillen	.90	.45	.25
16	Jeff Burroughs	.90	.45	.25
17	Amos Otis	.90	.45	.25
18	Ed Goodson	.90	.45	.25
19	Nate Colbert	.90	.45	.25
20	Reggie Jackson	6.50	3.25	2.00
21	Ted Simmons	.90	.45	.25
22	Bobby Murcer	1.00	.50	.30
23	Willie Horton	1.00	.50	.30
24	Orlando Cepeda	3.50	1.75	1.00
25	Ron Hunt	.90	.45	.25
26	Wayne Twitchell	.90	.45	.25
27	Ron Fairly	.90	.45	.25
28	Johnny Bench	4.50	2.25	1.25
29	John Mayberry	.90	.45	.25
30	Rod Carew	4.00	2.00	1.25
31	Ken Holtzman	.90	.45	.25
32	Billy Williams	3.50	1.75	1.00
33	Dick Allen	1.50	.70	.45
34a	Wilbur Wood (SO 959)	1.50	.70	.45
34b	Wilbur Wood (SO 960)	1.00	.50	.30
35	Danny Thompson	.90	.45	.25
36	Joe Morgan	3.50	1.75	1.00
37	Willie Stargell	3.50	1.75	1.00
38	Pete Rose	10.00	5.00	3.00
39	Bobby Bonds	.90	.45	.25
40	Chris Speier	.90	.45	.25
41	Sparky Lyle	.90	.45	.25
42	Cookie Rojas	.90	.45	.25
43	Tommy Davis	.90	.45	.25
44	Jim "Catfish" Hunter	3.50	1.75	1.00
45	Willie Davis	.90	.45	.25
46	Bert Blyleven	.90	.45	.25

		NM	EX	VG
47	Pat Kelly	.90	.45	.25
48	Ken Singleton	.90	.45	.25
49	Manny Mota	.90	.45	.25
50	Dave Johnson	.90	.45	.25
51	Sal Bando	.90	.45	.25
52	Tom Seaver	4.50	2.25	1.25
53	Felix Millan	.90	.45	.25
54	Ron Blomberg	.90	.45	.25

1975 Kellogg's

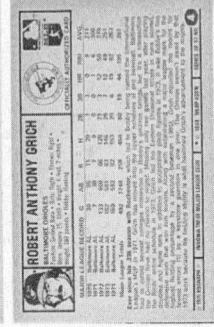

While the card size remained the same at 2-1/8" x 3-1/4", the size of the 1975 Kellogg's "3-D" set was increased by three, to 57 cards. Despite the fact cards could be obtained by a mail-in offer, as well as in cereal boxes, the '75 Kellogg's are noticeably scarcer than the company's other issues, with the exception of the 1971 set. Also helping to raise the value of the cards is the presence of an unusually large number of current and future Hall of Famers.

		NM	EX	VG
Complete Set (57):		175.00	90.00	55.00
Common Player:		2.00	1.00	.60
1	Roy White	2.00	1.00	.60
2	Ross Grimsley	2.00	1.00	.60
3	Reggie Smith	2.00	1.00	.60
4a	Bob Grich ("...1973 work..." in last line.)	3.00	1.50	.90
4b	Bob Grich (No "...1973 work...")	2.00	1.00	.60
5	Greg Gross	2.00	1.00	.60
6	Bob Watson	2.00	1.00	.60
7	Johnny Bench	10.00	5.00	3.00
8	Jeff Burroughs	2.00	1.00	.60
9	Elliott Maddox	2.00	1.00	.60
10	Jon Matlack	2.00	1.00	.60
11	Pete Rose	25.00	12.50	7.50
12	Leroy Stanton	2.00	1.00	.60
13	Bake McBride	2.00	1.00	.60
14	Jorge Orta	2.00	1.00	.60
15	Al Oliver	2.50	1.25	.70
16	John Briggs	2.00	1.00	.60
17	Steve Garvey	4.50	2.25	1.25
18	Brooks Robinson	10.00	5.00	3.00
19	John Hiller	2.00	1.00	.60
20	Lynn McGlothen	2.00	1.00	.60
21	Cleon Jones	2.00	1.00	.60
22	Fergie Jenkins	6.00	3.00	1.75
23	Bill North	2.00	1.00	.60
24	Steve Busby	2.00	1.00	.60
25	Richie Zisk	2.00	1.00	.60
26	Nolan Ryan	35.00	17.50	10.50
27	Joe Morgan	7.50	3.75	2.25
28	Joe Rudi	2.00	1.00	.60
29	Jose Cardenal	2.00	1.00	.60
30	Andy Messersmith	2.00	1.00	.60
31	Willie Montanez	2.00	1.00	.60
32	Bill Buckner	2.00	1.00	.60
33	Rod Carew	7.50	3.75	2.25
34	Lou Piniella	2.50	1.25	.70
35	Ralph Garr	2.00	1.00	.60
36	Mike Marshall	2.00	1.00	.60
37	Garry Maddox	2.00	1.00	.60
38	Dwight Evans	2.00	1.00	.60
39	Lou Brock	7.50	3.75	2.25
40	Ken Singleton	2.00	1.00	.60
41	Steve Braun	2.00	1.00	.60
42	Dick Allen	3.50	1.75	1.00
43	Johnny Grubb	2.00	1.00	.60
44a	Jim Hunter (Oakland)	9.00	4.50	2.75
44b	Jim Hunter (New York)	7.50	3.75	2.25
45	Gaylord Perry	6.00	3.00	1.75
46	George Hendrick	2.00	1.00	.60
47	Sparky Lyle	2.00	1.00	.60
48	Dave Cash	2.00	1.00	.60
49	Luis Tiant	2.00	1.00	.60
50	Cesar Geronimo	2.00	1.00	.60
51	Carl Yastrzemski	12.00	6.00	3.50
52	Ken Brett	2.00	1.00	.60
53	Hal McRae	2.00	1.00	.60
54	Reggie Jackson	15.00	7.50	4.50
55	Rollie Fingers	6.00	3.00	1.75
56	Mike Schmidt	15.00	7.50	4.50
57	Richie Hebner	2.00	1.00	.60

1976 Kellogg's

A sizeable list of corrected errors and other variation cards dots the checklist for the 57-card 1976 Kellogg's 3-D set. Again containing 57 cards, the first three cards in the set are found far less often than cards #4-57, indicating they were short-printed in relation to the rest of the set. The complete set values quoted below do not include the scarcer variation

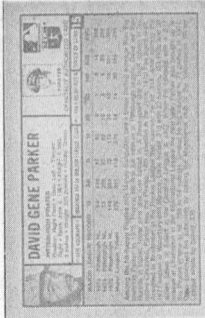

cards. Card size remained at 2-1/8" x 3-1/4". Cards #1-3 were significantly short-printed.

		NM	EX	VG
Complete Set (57):		70.00	35.00	20.00
Common Player:		1.25	.60	.40
1	Steve Hargan	10.00	5.00	3.00
2	Claudell Washington	10.00	5.00	3.00
3	Don Gullett	10.00	5.00	3.00
4	Randy Jones	1.25	.60	.40
5	Jim "Catfish" Hunter	3.50	1.75	1.00
6a	Clay Carroll (Cincinnati)	2.25	1.25	.70
6b	Clay Carroll (Chicago)	1.25	.60	.40
7	Joe Rudi	1.25	.60	.40
8	Reggie Jackson	9.00	4.50	2.75
9	Felix Millan	1.25	.60	.40
10	Jim Rice	2.00	1.00	.60
11	Bert Blyleven	1.25	.60	.40
12	Ken Singleton	1.25	.60	.40
13	Don Sutton	3.50	1.75	1.00
14	Joe Morgan	4.00	2.00	1.25
15	Dave Parker	1.50	.70	.45
16	Dave Cash	1.25	.60	.40
17	Ron LeFlore	1.25	.60	.40
18	Greg Luzinski	1.25	.60	.40
19	Dennis Eckersley	6.00	3.00	1.75
20	Bill Madlock	1.25	.60	.40
21	George Scott	1.25	.60	.40
22	Willie Stargell	4.00	2.00	1.25
23	Al Hrabosky	1.25	.60	.40
24	Carl Yastrzemski	7.50	3.75	2.25
25a	Jim Kaat (White Sox logo on back.)	3.00	1.50	.90
25b	Jim Kaat (Phillies logo on back.)	1.50	.70	.45
26	Marty Perez	1.25	.60	.40
27	Bob Watson	1.25	.60	.40
28	Eric Soderholm	1.25	.60	.40
29	Bill Lee	1.25	.60	.40
30a	Frank Tanana (1975 ERA 2.63)	2.00	1.00	.60
30b	Frank Tanana (1975 ERA 2.62)	1.25	.60	.40
31	Fred Lynn	1.50	.70	.45
32a	Tom Seaver (1967 PCT. 552)	7.50	3.75	2.25
32b	Tom Seaver (1967 Pct. .552)	6.00	3.00	1.75
33	Steve Busby	1.25	.60	.40
34	Gary Carter	4.00	2.00	1.25
35	Rick Wise	1.25	.60	.40
36	Johnny Bench	5.00	2.50	1.50
37	Jim Palmer	4.00	2.00	1.25
38	Bobby Murcer	1.50	.70	.45
39	Von Joshua	1.25	.60	.40
40	Lou Brock	4.00	2.00	1.25
41a	Mickey Rivers (Last line begins "In three...")	2.00	1.00	.60
41b	Mickey Rivers (Last line begins "The Yankees...")	1.25	.60	.40
42	Manny Sanguillen	1.25	.60	.40
43	Jerry Reuss	1.25	.60	.40
44	Ken Griffey	1.25	.60	.40
45a	Jorge Orta (AB 1616)	1.75	.90	.50
45b	Jorge Orta (AB 1615)	1.25	.60	.40
46	John Mayberry	1.25	.60	.40
47a	Vida Blue (2nd line reads "...pitched more innings ...")	2.25	1.25	.70
47b	Vida Blue (2nd line reads "...struck out more...")	1.25	.60	.40
48	Rod Carew	4.00	2.00	1.25
49a	Jon Matlack (1975 ER 87)	1.75	.90	.50
49b	Jon Matlack (1975 ER 86)	1.25	.60	.40
50	Boog Powell	2.25	1.25	.70
51a	Mike Hargrove (AB 935)	1.75	.90	.50
51b	Mike Hargrove (AB 934)	1.25	.60	.40
52a	Paul Lindblad (1975 ERA 2.72)	1.75	.90	.50
52b	Paul Lindblad (1975 ERA 2.73)	1.25	.60	.40
53	Thurman Munson	4.00	2.00	1.25
54	Steve Garvey	2.50	1.25	.70
55	Pete Rose	12.50	6.25	3.75
56a	Greg Gross (Games 302)	1.75	.90	.50
56b	Greg Gross (Games 334)	1.25	.60	.40
57	Ted Simmons	1.25	.60	.40

1977 Kellogg's

Other than another innovative card design to complement the simulated 3-D effect, there was little change in the 1977 Kellogg's issue. Set size remained at 57 cards, the set remained in the 2-1/8" x 3-1/4" format, and the cards were available either individually in boxes of cereal, or as a complete set via a mail-in box top offer. The 1977 set is the last in

which Kellogg's used a player portrait photo on the back of the card.

		NM	EX	VG
Complete Set (57):		60.00	30.00	18.00
Common Player:		.75	.40	.25
1	George Foster	.75	.40	.25
2	Bert Campaneris	.75	.40	.25
3	Fergie Jenkins	2.50	1.25	.70
4	Dock Ellis	.75	.40	.25
5	John Montefusco	.75	.40	.25
6	George Brett	12.50	6.25	3.75
7	John Candelaria	.75	.40	.25
8	Fred Norman	.75	.40	.25
9	Bill Travers	.75	.40	.25
10	Hal McRae	.75	.40	.25
11	Doug Rau	.75	.40	.25
12	Greg Luzinski	.75	.40	.25
13	Ralph Garr	.75	.40	.25
14	Steve Garvey	1.50	.70	.45
15	Rick Manning	.75	.40	.25
16a	Lyman Bostock (Back photo is N.Y. Yankee Dock Ellis)	7.50	3.75	2.25
16b	Lyman Bostock (correct back photo)	.75	.40	.25
17	Randy Jones	.75	.40	.25
18a	Ron Cey (58 homers in first sentence)	1.00	.50	.30
18b	Ron Cey (48 homers in first sentence.)	.75	.40	.25
19	Dave Parker	.75	.40	.25
20	Pete Rose	15.00	7.50	4.50
21a	Wayne Garland (Last line begins "Prior to...")	1.00	.50	.30
21b	Wayne Garland (Last line begins "There he...")	.75	.40	.25
22	Bill North	.75	.40	.25
23	Thurman Munson	4.50	2.25	1.25
24	Tom Poquette	.75	.40	.25
25	Ron LeFlore	.75	.40	.25
26	Mark Fidrych	1.00	.50	.30
27	Sixto Lezcano	.75	.40	.25
28	Dave Winfield	7.50	3.75	2.25
29	Jerry Koosman	.75	.40	.25
30	Mike Hargrove	.75	.40	.25
31	Willie Montanez	.75	.40	.25
32	Don Stanhouse	.75	.40	.25
33	Jay Johnstone	.75	.40	.25
34	Bake McBride	.75	.40	.25
35	Dave Kingman	.75	.40	.25
36	Freddie Patek	.75	.40	.25
37	Garry Maddox	.75	.40	.25
38a	Ken Reitz (Last line begins "The previous...")	1.00	.50	.30
38b	Ken Reitz (Last line begins "In late...")	.75	.40	.25
39	Bobby Grich	.75	.40	.25
40	Cesar Geronimo	.75	.40	.25
41	Jim Lonborg	.75	.40	.25
42	Ed Figueroa	.75	.40	.25
43	Bill Madlock	.75	.40	.25
44	Jerry Remy	.75	.40	.25
45	Frank Tanana	.75	.40	.25
46	Al Oliver	1.00	.50	.30
47	Charlie Hough	.75	.40	.25
48	Lou Piniella	1.00	.50	.30
49	Ken Griffey	.75	.40	.25
50	Jose Cruz	.75	.40	.25
51	Rollie Fingers	2.50	1.25	.70
52	Chris Chambliss	.75	.40	.25
53	Rod Carew	4.50	2.25	1.25
54	Andy Messersmith	.75	.40	.25
55	Mickey Rivers	.75	.40	.25
56	Butch Wynegar	.75	.40	.25
57	Steve Carlton	3.50	1.75	1.00

1978 Kellogg's

Besides the substitution of a Tony the Tiger drawing for a player portrait photo on the back of the card, the 1978 Kellogg's set offered no major changes from the previous few years issues. Cards were once again in the 2-1/8" x 3-1/4" format, with 57 cards comprising a complete set. Single cards were available in selected brands of the company's cereal, while complete sets could be obtained by a mail-in offer.

		NM	EX	VG
	Complete Set (57):	60.00	30.00	18.00
	Common Player:	.90	.45	.25
1	Steve Carlton	4.50	2.25	1.25
2	Bucky Dent	1.25	.60	.40
3	Mike Schmidt	13.50	6.75	4.00
4	Ken Griffey	.90	.45	.25
5	Al Cowens	.90	.45	.25
6	George Brett	13.50	6.75	4.00
7	Lou Brock	4.50	2.25	1.25
8	Rich Gossage	1.25	.60	.40
9	Tom Johnson	.90	.45	.25
10	George Foster	.90	.45	.25
11	Dave Winfield	4.50	2.25	1.25
12	Dan Meyer	.90	.45	.25
13	Chris Chambliss	.90	.45	.25
14	Paul Dade	.90	.45	.25
15	Jeff Burroughs	.90	.45	.25
16	Jose Cruz	.90	.45	.25
17	Mickey Rivers	.90	.45	.25
18	John Candelaria	.90	.45	.25
19	Ellis Valentine	.90	.45	.25
20	Hal McRae	.90	.45	.25
21	Dave Rozema	.90	.45	.25
22	Lenny Randle	.90	.45	.25
23	Willie McCovey	4.50	2.25	1.25
24	Ron Cey	.90	.45	.25
25	Eddie Murray	17.50	8.75	5.25
26	Larry Bowa	.90	.45	.25
27	Tom Seaver	5.00	2.50	1.50
28	Garry Maddox	.90	.45	.25
29	Rod Carew	4.50	2.25	1.25
30	Thurman Munson	4.50	2.25	1.25
31	Garry Templeton	.90	.45	.25
32	Eric Soderholm	.90	.45	.25
33	Greg Luzinski	.90	.45	.25
34	Reggie Smith	.90	.45	.25
35	Dave Goltz	.90	.45	.25
36	Tommy John	1.25	.60	.40
37	Ralph Garr	.90	.45	.25
38	Alan Bannister	.90	.45	.25
39	Bob Bailor	.90	.45	.25
40	Reggie Jackson	12.00	6.00	3.50
41	Cecil Cooper	.90	.45	.25
42	Burt Hooton	.90	.45	.25
43	Sparky Lyle	.90	.45	.25
44	Steve Ontiveros	.90	.45	.25
45	Rick Reuschel	.90	.45	.25
46	Lyman Bostock	.90	.45	.25
47	Mitchell Page	.90	.45	.25
48	Bruce Sutter	3.50	1.75	1.00
49	Jim Rice	2.50	1.25	.70
50	Bob Forsch	.90	.45	.25
51	Nolan Ryan	17.50	8.75	5.25
52	Dave Parker	.90	.45	.25
53	Bert Blyleven	.90	.45	.25
54	Frank Tanana	.90	.45	.25
55	Ken Singleton	.90	.45	.25
56	Mike Hargrove	.90	.45	.25
57	Don Sutton	3.50	1.75	1.00

1979 Kellogg's

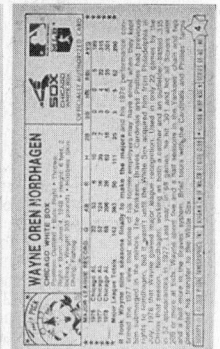

For its 1979 3-D issue, Kellogg's increased the size of the set to 60 cards, but reduced the width of the cards to 1-15/16". Depth stayed the same as in previous years, 3-1/4". The narrower card format seems to have compounded the problem of curling and subsequent cracking of the ribbed plastic surface which helps give the card a 3-D effect. Cards with major cracks can be graded no higher than VG. The complete set price in the checklist that follows does not include the scarcer variations. Numerous minor variations featuring copyright and trademark logos can be found in the set.

		NM	EX	VG
	Complete Set (60):	30.00	15.00	9.00
	Common Player:	.60	.30	.20
1	Bruce Sutter	2.50	1.25	.70
2	Ted Simmons	.60	.30	.20
3	Ross Grimsley	.60	.30	.20
4	Wayne Nordhagen	.60	.30	.20
5a	Jim Palmer (PCT .649)	3.00	1.50	.90

		NM	EX	VG
5b	Jim Palmer (PCT. .650)	3.00	1.50	.90
6	John Henry Johnson	.60	.30	.20
7	Jason Thompson	.60	.30	.20
8	Pat Zachry	.60	.30	.20
9	Dennis Eckersley	3.00	1.50	.90
10a	Paul Splittorff (IP 1665)	.60	.30	.20
10b	Paul Splittorff (IP 1666)	.60	.30	.20
11a	Ron Guidry (Hits 397)	.60	.30	.20
11b	Ron Guidry (Hits 396)	.60	.30	.20
12	Jeff Burroughs	.60	.30	.20
13	Rod Carew	3.00	1.50	.90
14a	Buddy Bell (No trade line in bio.)	1.00	.50	.30
14b	Buddy Bell (Trade line in bio.)	.60	.30	.20
15	Jim Rice	1.00	.50	.30
16	Garry Maddox	.60	.30	.20
17	Willie McCovey	3.00	1.50	.90
18	Steve Carlton	3.00	1.50	.90
19a	J. R. Richard (Stats begin with 1972.)	.60	.30	.20
19b	J. R. Richard (Stats begin with 1971.)	.60	.30	.20
20	Paul Molitor	3.00	1.50	.90
21a	Dave Parker (AVG. .281)	.60	.30	.20
21b	Dave Parker (AVG. .318)	.60	.30	.20
22a	Pete Rose (1978 3B 3)	7.50	3.75	2.25
22b	Pete Rose (1978 3B 33)	7.50	3.75	2.25
23a	Vida Blue (Runs 819)	.60	.30	.20
23b	Vida Blue (Runs 818)	.60	.30	.20
24	Richie Zisk	.60	.30	.20
25a	Darrell Porter (2B 101)	.60	.30	.20
25b	Darrell Porter (2B 111)	.60	.30	.20
26a	Dan Driessen (Games 642)	.60	.30	.20
26b	Dan Driessen (Games 742)	.60	.30	.20
27a	Geoff Zahn (1978 Minnesota)	.60	.30	.20
27b	Geoff Zahn (1978 Minnesota)	.60	.30	.20
28	Phil Niekro	2.50	1.25	.70
29	Tom Seaver	3.00	1.50	.90
30	Fred Lynn	.60	.30	.20
31	Bill Bonham	.60	.30	.20
32	George Foster	.60	.30	.20
33a	Terry Puhl (Last line of bio begins "Terry...")	.60	.30	.20
33b	Terry Puhl (Last line of bio begins "His...")	.60	.30	.20
34a	John Candelaria (Age is 24.)	.60	.30	.20
34b	John Candelaria (Age is 25.)	.60	.30	.20
35	Bob Knepper	.60	.30	.20
36	Freddie Patek	.60	.30	.20
37	Chris Chambliss	.60	.30	.20
38a	Bob Forsch (1977 Games 86.)	.60	.30	.20
38b	Bob Forsch (1977 Games 35.)	.60	.30	.20
39a	Ken Griffey (1978 AB 674)	.60	.30	.20
39b	Ken Griffey (1978 AB 614)	.60	.30	.20
40	Jack Clark	.60	.30	.20
41a	Dwight Evans (1978 Hits 13)	.60	.30	.20
41b	Dwight Evans (1978 Hits 123)	.60	.30	.20
42	Lee Mazzilli	.60	.30	.20
43	Mario Guerrero	.60	.30	.20
44	Larry Bowa	.60	.30	.20
45a	Carl Yastrzemski (Games 9930)	4.00	2.00	1.25
45b	Carl Yastrzemski (Games 9929)	4.00	2.00	1.25
46a	Reggie Jackson (1978 Games 162)	6.00	3.00	1.75
46b	Reggie Jackson (1978 Games 139)	6.00	3.00	1.75
47	Rick Reuschel	.60	.30	.20
48a	Mike Flanagan (1976 SO 57)	.60	.30	.20
48b	Mike Flanagan (1976 SO 56)	.60	.30	.20
49a	Gaylord Perry (1973 Hits 325)	2.50	1.25	.70
49b	Gaylord Perry (1973 Hits 315)	2.50	1.25	.70
50	George Brett	6.00	3.00	1.75
51a	Craig Reynolds (Last line of bio begins "He spent...")	.60	.30	.20
51b	Craig Reynolds (Last line of bio begins "In those...")	.60	.30	.20
52	Davey Lopes	.60	.30	.20
53a	Bill Almon (2B 31)	.60	.30	.20
53b	Bill Almon (2B 41)	.60	.30	.20
54	Roy Howell	.60	.30	.20
55	Frank Tanana	.60	.30	.20
56a	Doug Rau (1978 PCT. .577)	.60	.30	.20
56b	Doug Rau (1978 PCT. .625)	.60	.30	.20
57a	Rick Monday (1976 Runs 197)	.60	.30	.20
57b	Rick Monday (1976 Runs 107)	.60	.30	.20
58	Jon Matlack	.60	.30	.20
59a	Ron Jackson (Last line of bio begins "His best...")	.60	.30	.20
59b	Ron Jackson (Last line of bio begins "The Twins...")	.60	.30	.20
60	Jim Sundberg	.60	.30	.20

1980 Kellogg's

3-D SUPER STARS

The 1980 cereal company issue featured the narrowest format of any Kellogg's card, 1-7/8" x 3-1/4". For the second straight year, set size remained at 60 cards, available either singly in boxes of cereal, or as complete sets by a mail-in offer.

		NM	EX	VG
	Complete Set (60):	25.00	12.50	7.50
	Common Player:	.60	.30	.20
1	Ross Grimsley	.60	.30	.20
2	Mike Schmidt	4.00	2.00	1.25
3	Mike Flanagan	.60	.30	.20
4	Ron Guidry	.60	.30	.20
5	Bert Blyleven	.60	.30	.20
6	Dave Kingman	.60	.30	.20
7	Jeff Newman	.60	.30	.20
8	Steve Rogers	.60	.30	.20
9	George Brett	4.00	2.00	1.25
10	Bruce Sutter	2.00	1.00	.60
11	Gorman Thomas	.60	.30	.20
12	Darrell Porter	.60	.30	.20
13	Roy Smalley	.60	.30	.20
14	Steve Carlton	2.00	1.00	.60
15	Jim Palmer	2.00	1.00	.60
16	Bob Bailor	.60	.30	.20
17	Jason Thompson	.60	.30	.20
18	Graig Nettles	.60	.30	.20
19	Ron Cey	.60	.30	.20
20	Nolan Ryan	7.50	3.75	2.25
21	Ellis Valentine	.60	.30	.20
22	Larry Hisle	.60	.30	.20
23	Dave Parker	.60	.30	.20
24	Eddie Murray	2.00	1.00	.60
25	Willie Stargell	2.00	1.00	.60
26	Reggie Jackson	4.00	2.00	1.25
27	Carl Yastrzemski	2.50	1.25	.70
28	Andre Thornton	.60	.30	.20
29	Davey Lopes	.60	.30	.20
30	Ken Singleton	.60	.30	.20
31	Steve Garvey	1.00	.50	.30
32	Dave Winfield	2.00	1.00	.60
33	Steve Kemp	.60	.30	.20
34	Claudell Washington	.60	.30	.20
35	Pete Rose	6.00	3.00	1.75
36	Cesar Cedeno	.60	.30	.20
37	John Stearns	.60	.30	.20
38	Lee Mazzilli	.60	.30	.20
39	Larry Bowa	.60	.30	.20
40	Fred Lynn	.60	.30	.20
41	Carlton Fisk	2.00	1.00	.60
42	Vida Blue	.60	.30	.20
43	Keith Hernandez	.60	.30	.20
44	Jim Rice	1.00	.50	.30
45	Ted Simmons	.60	.30	.20
46	Chet Lemon	.60	.30	.20
47	Fergie Jenkins	2.00	1.00	.60
48	Gary Matthews	.60	.30	.20
49	Tom Seaver	2.50	1.25	.70
50	George Foster	.60	.30	.20
51	Phil Niekro	2.00	1.00	.60
52	Johnny Bench	2.50	1.25	.70
53	Buddy Bell	.60	.30	.20
54	Lance Parrish	.60	.30	.20
55	Joaquin Andujar	.60	.30	.20
56	Don Baylor	.60	.30	.20
57	Jack Clark	.60	.30	.20
58	J.R. Richard	.60	.30	.20
59	Bruce Bochte	.60	.30	.20
60	Rod Carew	2.00	1.00	.60

1969 Kelly's Potato Chips Pins

Consisting of 20 pins, each measuring approximately 1-3/16" in diameter, this set was issued by Kelly's Potato Chips in 1969 and has a heavy emphasis on St. Louis Cardinals. The pin has a black-and-white player photo in the center surrounded by either a red border (for A.L. players) or a blue border (for N.L. players) that displays the player's team and name at the top and bottom. "Kelly's" appears to the left while the word "Zip!" is printed to the right. The pins are unnumbered.

		NM	EX	VG
	Complete Set (20):	350.00	175.00	100.00
	Common Player:	5.00	2.50	1.50
(1)	Luis Aparicio	25.00	12.50	7.50
(2)	Ernie Banks	45.00	22.00	13.50
(3)	Glenn Beckert	5.00	2.50	1.50
(4)	Lou Brock	25.00	12.50	7.50
(5)	Curt Flood	5.00	2.50	1.50
(6)	Bob Gibson	25.00	12.50	7.50
(7)	Joel Horlen	5.00	2.50	1.50
(8)	Al Kaline	45.00	22.00	13.50
(9)	Don Kessinger	5.00	2.50	1.50

(10)	Mickey Lolich	5.00	2.50	1.50
(11)	Juan Marichal	25.00	12.50	7.50
(12)	Willie Mays	75.00	37.00	22.00
(13)	Tim McCarver	7.50	3.75	2.25
(14)	Denny McLain	6.00	3.00	1.75
(15)	Pete Rose	65.00	32.00	19.50
(16)	Ron Santo	7.50	3.75	2.25
(17)	Joe Torre	15.00	7.50	4.50
(18)	Pete Ward	5.00	2.50	1.50
(19)	Billy Williams	25.00	12.50	7.50
(20)	Carl Yastrzemski	60.00	30.00	.18.00

1887 W.S. Kimball Champions (N184)

Similar to sets issued by Allen & Ginter and Goodwin, the Kimball tobacco company of Rochester, N.Y., issued its own 50-card set of "Champions of Games and Sport" in 1887, and included four baseball players among the "billiardists, girl riders, tight-rope walkers" and other popular celebrities featured in the series. Measuring 1-1/2" x 2-3/4", the color lithograped artwork on the card features a posed portrait, which occupies the top three-fourths, and a drawing of the player in action at the bottom. The back of the card contains an ad for Kimball Cigarettes along with a list of the various sports and activities depicted in the set. The Kimball promotion also included an album to house the card set.

	NM	EX	VG
Complete Set (4):	5,000	2,000	1,500
Common Player:	1,000	400.00	300.00
Album:	3,750	1,500	900.00
(1) E.A. Burch	1,500	500.00	375.00
(2) Dell Darling	1,250	500.00	375.00
(3) Hardie Henderson	1,250	500.00	375.00
(4) James O'Neil (O'Neill)	1,250	500.00	375.00

1957-1959 Kiwanis Orioles Clinic

Details are lacking on this card which may or may not have been part of a series. Unless or until further players are checklisted, it is impossible to date the issue any more precisely. The front of the 2-7/8" x 3-1/4" card has a sepia photo that appears to have been copied from a team-issued postcard picture. On back is the Kiwanis International logo with "Compliments / of" above and "KIWANIS CLUB / OF / BALTIMORE CITY / KIWANIS - ORIOLE / BASEBALL CLINIC" below.

	NM	EX	VG
Bob Nieman	40.00	20.00	12.00

1955-1957 Ted Kluszewski Steak House

The true scope of this issue combined with the related Charcoal Steak House card (see also) is not known. Based on cards showing Klu in Reds and Angels uniforms, it is possible examples may yet be seen in Pirates and White Sox uniforms. Measuring about 3-1/2" x 5-1/2", the black-and-white cards have

a facsimile signature of Kluszewski on front. The back is postcard style and advertises the Cincinnati restaurant he operated with Jack Stayin.

	NM	EX	VG
Ted Kluszewski (Reds, fielding, white cap.)	75.00	37.50	22.50
Ted Kluszewski (Reds, portrait, dark cap.)	100.00	50.00	30.00

1930s Knickerbocker Beer Yankees Premium

Jacob Ruppert, who owned both the Yankees and the Knickerbocker Brewing Co., is pictured on this 10" x 8" black-and-white, blank-backed premium photo with a trio of his Italian stars. Facsimile autographs of all are printed on front.

	NM	EX	VG
Tony Lazzeri, Jacob Ruppert, Joe DiMaggio, Frank Crosetti	150.00	75.00	45.00

1921 Koester Bread N.Y. Giants/Yankees

The 1921 World Series was the first of many for the N.Y. Yankees, and it was the first "subway series," as their opponents were the Giants. This special card issue, a blank-backed version of the American Caramel Series of 120 (E121), featured the players, managers and coaches of each team. The 2" x about 3-1/4" cards feature black-and-white photos on front. They were distributed in October 1921 by E.H. Koester, a New York bakery. The unnumbered cards are checklisted here alphabetically within team. Several of the players in this issue do not appear in the contemporary American Caramel sets. A rarely seen album was issued to house the cards.

	NM	EX	VG
Complete Set (52):	45,000	22,500	13,500

Common Player:	500.00	250.00	150.00
Album:	800.00	400.00	240.00
N.Y. Giants Team Set:	19,000	9,500	5,700
(1) Dave Bancroft	1,500	750.00	450.00
(2) Jesse Barnes	500.00	250.00	150.00
(3) Howard Berry	500.00	250.00	150.00
(4) "Ed." Brown	500.00	250.00	150.00
(5) Jesse Burkett	1,875	940.00	565.00
(6) Geo. J. Burns	500.00	250.00	150.00
(7) Cecil Causey	500.00	250.00	150.00
(8) "Bill" Cunningham	500.00	250.00	150.00
(9) "Phil" Douglas	500.00	250.00	150.00
(10) Frank Frisch	1,500	750.00	450.00
(11) Alexander Gaston	500.00	250.00	150.00
(12) "Mike" Gonzalez	600.00	300.00	180.00
(13) Hugh Jennings	1,500	750.00	450.00
(14) George Kelly	1,500	750.00	450.00
(15) John McGraw	1,500	750.00	450.00
(16) Emil Meusel	500.00	250.00	150.00
(17) Arthur Nehf	500.00	250.00	150.00
(18) John Rawlings	500.00	250.00	150.00
(19) "Bill" Ryan	500.00	250.00	150.00
(20) "Slim" Sallee	500.00	250.00	150.00
(21) "Pat" Shea	500.00	250.00	150.00
(22) Earl Smith	500.00	250.00	150.00
(23) Frank Snyder	500.00	250.00	150.00
(24) Chas. Stengel	1,875	940.00	565.00
(25) Fred Toney	500.00	250.00	150.00
(26) Ross Young (Youngs)	1,875	940.00	565.00
N.Y. Yankees Team Set:	26,000	13,000	7,800
(1) Frank Baker	1,500	750.00	450.00
(2) "Rip" Collins	500.00	250.00	150.00
(3) Lou De Vormer	500.00	250.00	150.00
(4) Alex Ferguson	500.00	250.00	150.00
(5) William Fewster	500.00	250.00	150.00
(6) Harry Harper	500.00	250.00	150.00
(7) "Chicken" Hawks	500.00	250.00	150.00
(8) Fred Hoffmann (Hofmann)	500.00	250.00	150.00
(9) Waite Hoyt	1,500	750.00	450.00
(10) Miller Huggins	1,500	750.00	450.00
(11) Carl Mays	500.00	250.00	150.00
(12) M.J. McNally	500.00	250.00	150.00
(13) R. Meusel	500.00	250.00	150.00
(14) Elmer Miller	500.00	250.00	150.00
(15) John Mitchell	500.00	250.00	150.00
(16) Chas. O'Leary	500.00	250.00	150.00
(17) Roger Peckinpaugh	500.00	250.00	150.00
(18) William Piercy	500.00	250.00	150.00
(19) Walter Pipp	500.00	250.00	150.00
(20) Jack Quinn	500.00	250.00	150.00
(21) Tom Rogers	500.00	250.00	150.00
(22) Robert Roth	500.00	250.00	150.00
(23) George Ruth	15,000	7,500	4,500
(24) Walter Schang	500.00	250.00	150.00
(25) Robert Shawkey	500.00	250.00	150.00
(26) Aaron Ward	500.00	250.00	150.00

1911-16 Kotton Tobacco

The T216 baseball card set, issued with several brands by the People's Tobacco Co., is the last of the Louisiana cigarette sets and the most confusing. Issued over a period of several years between 1911 and 1916, the set employs the same pictures as several contemporary caramel and bakery sets. Cards measure a nominal 1-1/2" x 2-5/8", though reasonable allowance must be made for original cutting variances. Positive identification can be made by the back of the cards. The Peoples Tobacco cards carry advertising for one of three brands of cigarettes: Kotton, Mino or Virginia Extra. The Kotton brand is the most common, with cards found in two types; one has a glossy front finish, while a second scarcer type is printed on a thin paper. The thin paper cards command an additional 15% premium. The glossy-front cards can be found with either of two ad styles on back: "KOTTON / TOBACCO" (Factory No. 11) or "KOTTON / CIGARETTES" (Factory No. 4). The cards include players from the American, National and Federal Leagues. The complete set price includes only the least expensive of each variation.

	NM	EX	VG
Common Player:	1,000	500.00	300.00
(1) Jack Barry/Btg	1,000	500.00	300.00
(2) Jack Barry/Fielding	1,000	500.00	300.00
(3) Harry Bemis	1,000	500.00	300.00
(4a) Chief Bender (Philadelphia, striped cap.)	1,800	900.00	550.00

		NM	EX	VG
(4b)	Chief Bender (Baltimore, striped cap.)	1,800	900.00	550.00
(5a)	Chief Bender (Philadelphia, white cap.)	1,800	900.00	550.00
(5b)	Chief Bender (Baltimore, white cap.)	1,800	900.00	550.00
(6)	Bill Bergen	1,000	500.00	300.00
(7a)	Bob Bescher (Cincinnati)	1,000	500.00	300.00
(7b)	Bob Bescher (St. Louis)	1,000	500.00	300.00
(8)	Roger Bresnahan	1,800	900.00	550.00
(9)	Al Bridwell/Btg	1,000	500.00	300.00
(10a)	Al Bridwell/Sliding (New York)	1,000	500.00	300.00
(10b)	Al Bridwell/Sliding (St. Louis)	1,000	500.00	300.00
(11)	Donie Bush	1,000	500.00	300.00
(12)	Doc Casey	1,000	500.00	300.00
(13)	Frank Chance	1,800	900.00	550.00
(14a)	Hal Chase/Fielding (New York)	1,000	500.00	300.00
(14b)	Hal Chase/Fielding (Buffalo)	1,800	900.00	550.00
(15)	Hal Chase/Portrait	1,400	700.00	400.00
(16a)	Ty Cobb/Standing (Detroit Am.)	24,000	12,000	7,200
(16b)	Ty Cobb/Standing (Detroit Am.)	21,000	10,500	6,300
(17)	Ty Cobb/Btg (Detroit Am.)	24,000	12,000	7,200
(18a)	Eddie Collins (Phila. Am.)	1,800	900.00	550.00
(18b)	Eddie Collins (Phila. Amer.)	1,800	900.00	550.00
(19)	Eddie Collins (Chicago)	1,800	900.00	550.00
(20a)	Sam Crawford (Small print.)	1,800	900.00	550.00
(20b)	Sam Crawford (Large print.)	1,800	900.00	550.00
(21)	Harry Davis	1,000	500.00	300.00
(22)	Ray Demmitt	1,000	500.00	300.00
(23)	Art Devlin	1,000	500.00	300.00
(24a)	Wild Bill Donovan (Detroit)	1,000	500.00	300.00
(24b)	Wild Bill Donovan (New York)	1,000	500.00	300.00
(25a)	Red Dooin (Philadelphia)	1,000	500.00	300.00
(25b)	Red Dooin (Cincinnati)	1,000	500.00	300.00
(26a)	Mickey Doolan (Philadelphia)	1,000	500.00	300.00
(26b)	Mickey Doolan (Baltimore)	1,000	500.00	300.00
(27)	Patsy Dougherty	1,000	500.00	300.00
(28a)	Larry Doyle, Larry Doyle (N.Y. Nat'l, batting)	1,000	500.00	300.00
(28b)	Larry Doyle/Btg (New York Nat'l)	1,000	500.00	300.00
(29)	Larry Doyle/Throwing	1,000	500.00	300.00
(30)	Clyde Engle	1,000	500.00	300.00
(31a)	Johnny Evers (Chicago)	1,800	900.00	550.00
(31b)	Johnny Evers (Boston)	1,800	900.00	550.00
(32)	Art Fromme	1,000	500.00	300.00
(33a)	George Gibson (Pittsburg Nat'l, back view.)	1,000	500.00	300.00
(33b)	George Gibson (Pittsburgh Nat'l., back view.)	1,000	500.00	300.00
(34a)	George Gibson (Pittsburg Nat'l, front view.)	1,000	500.00	300.00
(34b)	George Gibson (Pittsburgh Nat'l., front view.)	1,000	500.00	300.00
(35a)	Topsy Hartsel (Phila. Am.)	1,000	500.00	300.00
(35b)	Topsy Hartsel (Phila. Amer.)	1,000	500.00	300.00
(36)	Roy Hartzell/Btg	1,000	500.00	300.00
(37)	Roy Hartzell/Catching	1,000	500.00	300.00
(38a)	Fred Jacklitsch (Philadelphia)	1,000	500.00	300.00
(38b)	Fred Jacklitsch (Baltimore)	1,000	500.00	300.00
(39a)	Hughie Jennings (Orange background.)	1,800	900.00	550.00
(39b)	Hughie Jennings (Red background.)	1,800	900.00	550.00
(40)	Red Kleinow	1,000	500.00	300.00
(41a)	Otto Knabe (Philadelphia)	1,000	500.00	300.00
(41b)	Otto Knabe (Baltimore)	1,000	500.00	300.00
(42)	Jack Knight	1,000	500.00	300.00
(43a)	Nap Lajoie (Philadelphia, fielding)	1,800	900.00	550.00
(43b)	Nap Lajoie/Fielding (Cleveland)	1,800	900.00	550.00
(44)	Nap Lajoie/Portrait	1,800	900.00	550.00
(45a)	Hans Lobert (Cincinnati)	1,000	500.00	300.00
(45b)	Hans Lobert (New York)	1,000	500.00	300.00
(46)	Sherry Magee	1,000	500.00	300.00
(47)	Rube Marquard	1,800	900.00	550.00
(48a)	Christy Matthewson (Mathewson) (large print.)	5,400	2,700	1,600
(48b)	Christy Matthewson (Mathewson) (Small print.)	5,400	2,700	1,600
(49a)	John McGraw (Large print.)	1,800	900.00	550.00
(49b)	John McGraw (Small print.)	1,800	900.00	550.00
(50)	Larry McLean	1,000	500.00	300.00
(51)	George McQuillan	1,000	500.00	300.00
(52)	Dots Miller/Btg	1,000	500.00	300.00
(53a)	Dots Miller/Fielding (Pittsburg)	1,000	500.00	300.00
(53b)	Dots Miller/Fielding (St. Louis)	1,000	500.00	300.00
(54a)	Danny Murphy (Philadelphia)	1,000	500.00	300.00
(54b)	Danny Murphy (Brooklyn)	1,000	500.00	300.00
(55)	Rebel Oakes	1,000	500.00	300.00
(56)	Bill O'Hara	1,000	500.00	300.00
(57)	Eddie Plank	2,400	1,200	700.00
(58a)	Germany Schaefer (Washington)	1,000	500.00	300.00
(58b)	Germany Schaefer (Newark)	1,000	500.00	300.00
(59)	Admiral Schlei	1,000	500.00	300.00
(60)	Boss Schmidt	1,000	500.00	300.00
(61)	Johnny Seigle	1,000	500.00	300.00
(62)	Dave Shean	1,000	500.00	300.00
(63)	Boss Smith (Schmidt)	1,000	500.00	300.00
(64)	Tris Speaker	2,400	1,200	700.00
(65)	Oscar Stanage	1,000	500.00	300.00
(66)	George Stovall	1,000	500.00	300.00
(67)	Jeff Sweeney	1,000	500.00	300.00
(68a)	Joe Tinker/Btg (Chicago Nat'l)	1,800	900.00	550.00
(68b)	Joe Tinker/Btg (Chicago Feds)	2,400	1,200	700.00
(69)	Joe Tinker/Portrait	1,800	900.00	550.00

		NM	EX	VG
(70a)	Honus Wagner/Btg (S.S.)	18,000	9,000	5,400
(70b)	Honus Wagner/Btg (2b.)	18,000	9,000	5,400
(71a)	Honus Wagner/Throwing (S.S.)	18,000	9,000	5,400
(71b)	Honus Wagner/Throwing (2b.)	18,000	9,000	5,400
(72)	Hooks Wiltse	1,000	500.00	300.00
(73)	Cy Young	4,200	2,100	1,300
(74a)	Heinie Zimmerman (2b.)	1,000	500.00	300.00
(74b)	Heinie Zimmerman (3b.)	1,000	500.00	300.00

1964 Sandy Koufax's Tropicana Postcard

In the early 1960s, Dodgers pitcher Sandy Koufax owned the Tropicana Motor Hotel in Hollywood. Among the collectible souvenirs of that venture are a pair of color postcards picturing the player overlooking the pool. The original version pictures Koufax in civilian clothes. A later version uses the same photo, but has a Dodgers uniform crudely drawn on Koufax' photo.

	NM	EX	VG
Sandy Koufax/Civilian	175.00	90.00	50.00
Sandy Koufax/Uniform	150.00	75.00	45.00

1907 Krieg & Co. Chicago Cubs Base Ball Mail Card

Distributed by a shoe retailers' supply firm, this foldout black-and-white postcard features the World Champion Cubs. About 5-1/4" x 3-1/2" closed, the foldout opens to reveal portrait photos of 16 of the players, two per post-card size panel. Manager Frank Chance and the team president each have their own panel. The back cover of the mailer has a composite photo of the team, with a 1907 National League schedule on its flip side.

	NM	EX	VG
1907 Chicago Cubs Foldout	2,000	1,000	600.00

1976 Kroger Cincinnati Reds

These 5-7/8" x 9" color photos were grocery store giveaways. Blank-backed and unnumbered, they are checklisted here alphabetically. Because the photos were licensed only by the players' union, and not Major League Baseball, photos do not show uniform logos.

		NM	EX	VG
Complete Set (16):		45.00	22.50	13.50
Common Player:		3.00	1.50	.90
(1)	Ed Armbrister	3.00	1.50	.90
(2)	Bob Bailey	3.00	1.50	.90
(3)	Johnny Bench	15.00	7.50	4.50
(4)	Jack Billingham	3.00	1.50	.90
(5)	Dave Concepcion	3.00	1.50	.90
(6)	Dan Driessen	3.00	1.50	.90
(7)	Rawly Eastwick	3.00	1.50	.90
(8)	George Foster	3.50	1.75	1.00
(9)	Cesar Geronimo	3.00	1.50	.90
(10)	Ken Griffey	3.00	1.50	.90
(11)	Don Gullett	3.00	1.50	.90
(12)	Joe Morgan	12.50	6.25	3.75
(13)	Gary Nolan	3.00	1.50	.90
(14)	Fred Norman	3.00	1.50	.90
(15)	Tony Perez	7.50	3.75	2.25
(16)	Pete Rose	24.00	12.00	7.25

1977 Kurland Tom Seaver

These large-format (4-3/16" x 5-1/2") black-and-white cards appear to have been produced in conjunction with promotional appearances by Seaver for Kurland Cadillac-Oldsmobile, a metropolitan New York auto dealer. Most of the cards seen are autographed by Seaver. The back is blank.

		NM	EX	VG
Complete Set (2):		150.00	75.00	45.00
Common Card:		75.00	37.00	22.00
(1)	Tom Seaver (N.Y. Mets)	75.00	37.00	22.00
(2)	Tom Seaver (Cincinnati Reds)	75.00	37.00	22.00

1926 Kut Outs Giants/ Yankees Die-Cuts

These black-and-white, blank-back, die-cut cards were sold as complete sets for 10 cents per team. The size varies with the pose depicted, but the cards are generally about 2" wide and 4-1/2" tall. The player's name is printed at the bottom of his photo. The unnumbered cards are checklisted here in alphabetical order by team. The issue is very similar to the Middy Bread Cardinals/Browns cards of 1927.

		NM	EX	VG
Complete Set (20):		14,500	5,800	2,900
Common Player:		350.00	140.00	70.00
	N.Y. Giants Team Set:	4,500	1,800	900.00
(1)	Ed Farrell	350.00	140.00	70.00
(2)	Frank Frisch	600.00	240.00	120.00
(3)	George Kelly	600.00	240.00	120.00
(4)	Freddie Lindstrom	600.00	240.00	120.00
(5)	John McGraw	600.00	240.00	120.00
(6)	Emil Meusel	350.00	140.00	70.00
(7)	John Scott	350.00	140.00	70.00
(8)	Frank Snyder	350.00	140.00	70.00
(9)	Billy Southworth	350.00	140.00	70.00
(10)	Ross Young (Youngs)	600.00	240.00	120.00
	N.Y. Yankees Team Set:	10,000	4,000	2,000
(11)	Pat Collins	350.00	140.00	70.00
(12)	Earle Combs	600.00	240.00	120.00
(13)	Joe Dugan	350.00	140.00	70.00
(14)	Lou Gehrig	2,500	1,000	500.00
(15)	Miller Huggins	600.00	240.00	120.00
(16)	Mark Koenig	350.00	140.00	70.00
(17)	Tony Lazzeri	600.00	240.00	120.00
(18)	Bob Meusel	350.00	140.00	70.00
(19)	Herb Pennock	600.00	240.00	120.00
(20)	Babe Ruth	5,000	2,000	1,000

1912 La Azora Cigars

These postcard-size (about 3-3/8" x 5-3/8") ad cards were issued by a Detroit cigar maker. Both cards feature of their front a borderless sepia photo of Ty

Cobb, though he is not named. The backs differ somewhat in format and content, but basically provide the Tigers' home and road schedules for the season.

		NM	EX	VG
Complete Set (2):		5,000	2,500	1,500
(1)	Ty Cobb/Fielding (Home schedule.)	3,000	1,500	900.00
(2)	Ty Cobb/Sliding (Road schedule.)	3,000	1,500	900.00

1958-60 L.A. Dodgers Premium Pictures

Apparently issued over a period of years from 1958 through at least 1960, these black-and-white, 8-1/2" x 11" premium pictures were sold as a set through Dodgers souvenir outlets, though the make-up of a set changed with the comings and goings of players. The blank-backed pictures feature on front a pencil portrait of the player, with his name printed towards the bottom. The signature of sports artist Nicholas Volpe also appears on front. The unnumbered pictures are checklisted here alphabetically.

		NM	EX	VG
Complete Set (16):		300.00	150.00	90.00
Common Player:		15.00	7.50	4.50
(1)	Walter Alston	17.50	8.75	5.25
(2)	Roy Campanella	30.00	15.00	9.00
(3)	Gino Cimoli	15.00	7.50	4.50
(4)	Don Drysdale	30.00	15.00	9.00
(5)	Carl Erskine	15.00	7.50	4.50
(6)	Carl Furillo	20.00	10.00	6.00
(7)	Jim Gilliam	17.50	8.75	5.25
(8)	Gil Hodges	30.00	15.00	9.00
(9)	Clem Labine	15.00	7.50	4.50
(10)	Wally Moon	15.00	7.50	4.50
(11)	Don Newcombe	17.50	8.75	5.25
(12)	Johnny Podres	17.50	8.75	5.25
(13)	Pee Wee Reese	30.00	15.00	9.00
(14)	Rip Repulski	15.00	7.50	4.50
(15)	Vin Scully, Jerry Doggett/ Announcers	15.00	7.50	4.50
(16)	Duke Snider	30.00	15.00	9.00

1959 L.A. Dodgers Postcards

In the team's second year in California, the Dodgers began production of an on-going set of color player postcards. Cards were usually sold in 10-card packs in stadium souvenir stands. The makeup of the packs sold varied as players came and went and cards were issued or withdrawn. When supplies of any player's cards were exhausted, he would be included in the current printing. Various photographers and printers were responsible for the issue over the years, but all utilized a similar format of 3-1/2" x 5-1/2" glossy borderless fronts and postcard style backs. The initial effort in 1959 has no player identification on the front. Backs are printed in brown, including player ID, birthdate and place, copyright date and credits to Mirro Krome and Crocker Co. Cards are numbered as shown here, but with an "LA-D-" prefix. The set was also available in the form of an accordian-foldout.

		NM	EX	VG
Complete Set (12):		400.00	200.00	125.00
Common Player:		30.00	15.00	9.00
901	Duke Snider	40.00	20.00	12.00
902	Gil Hodges	35.00	17.50	10.00
903	Johnny Podres	30.00	15.00	9.00
904	Carl Furillo	30.00	15.00	9.00
905	Don Drysdale	40.00	20.00	12.00
906	Sandy Koufax	75.00	37.50	22.50
907	Jim Gilliam	30.00	15.00	9.00
908	Don Zimmer	30.00	15.00	9.00
909	Charlie Neal	30.00	15.00	9.00
910	Norm Larker (Photo actually Joe Pignatano.)	30.00	15.00	9.00
911	Clem Labine (Photo actually Stan Williams.)	30.00	15.00	9.00
912	John Roseboro	30.00	15.00	9.00

1960 L.A. Dodgers Postcards

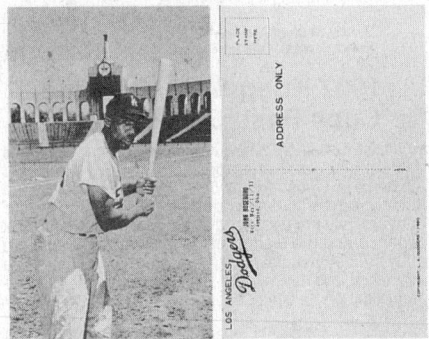

Like many baseball souvenirs, this set of team-issued postcards was "Made in Japan." The 3-1/2" x 5-1/2" cards share the basic format of the 1959 premiere issue with borderless color poses on front and postcard-style back. Backs are printed in blue with player ID and copyright date, but the cards are unnumbered. They are checklisted here alphabetically. The Carl Furillo card is scarce because it was withdrawn when he retired after playing only eight games in 1960.

		NM	EX	VG
Complete Set (12):		250.00	125.00	75.00
Common Player:		12.50	6.25	3.75
(1)	Walt Alston	12.50	6.25	3.75
(2)	Roger Craig	12.50	6.25	3.75
(3)	Don Drysdale	15.00	7.50	4.50
(4)	Carl Furillo	75.00	37.00	22.00
(5)	Gil Hodges	15.00	7.50	4.50
(6)	Sandy Koufax	60.00	30.00	18.00
(7)	Wally Moon	12.50	6.25	3.75
(8)	Charlie Neal	12.50	6.25	3.75
(9)	Johnny Podres	12.50	6.25	3.75
(10)	John Roseboro	12.50	6.25	3.75
(11)	Larry Sherry	12.50	6.25	3.75
(12)	Duke Snider	15.00	7.50	4.50

1962 L.A. Dodgers Pins

The attributed date is speculative based on available checklist information. This series of, presum-

ably, stadium souvenir pinback buttons is in an unusually large 3-1/2" format. The pins have black-and-white photos on a white or light blue background. Two styles of name presentation are known, those with names in a white strip at the bottom of the pin and those with the names overprinted on the photo and more towards the center.

	NM	EX	VG
Common Player:	75.00	37.50	22.00
NAME IN STRIP			
Don Drysdale	60.00	30.00	18.00
Duke Snider	125.00	62.00	37.00
NAME OVERPRINTED			
Gil Hodges	95.00	47.00	28.00
Sandy Koufax	500.00	250.00	150.00
Maury Wills	75.00	37.50	22.00

1963 L.A. Dodgers Pin-Ups

Borrowing on the concept of the 1938 Goudey Heads-up cards, this set was sold, probably at the stadium souvenir stands, in a white envelope labeled "Los Angeles Dodgers Pin-Ups." The cards feature large full-color head-and-cap photos set atop cartoon ballplayers' bodies. Cards are printed on 7-1/4" x 8-1/2" semi-gloss cardboard with blank backs. The player's name appears in black on the front, along with the instructions, "Push out character carefully. Take scissors and trim white around player's head." Each figure was die-cut to allow its easy removal from the background.

		NM	EX	VG
Complete Set (10):		75.00	35.00	25.00
Common Player:		6.00	3.00	1.75
(1)	Tommy Davis	7.50	3.75	2.25
(2)	Willie Davis	7.50	3.75	2.25
(3)	Don Drysdale	10.00	5.00	3.00
(4)	Ron Fairly	6.00	3.00	1.75
(5)	Frank Howard	7.50	3.75	2.25
(6)	Sandy Koufax	25.00	12.50	7.50
(7)	Joe Moeller	6.00	3.00	1.75
(8)	Ron Perranoski	6.00	3.00	1.75
(9)	John Roseboro	6.00	3.00	1.75
(10)	Maury Wills	7.50	3.75	2.25

1965 L.A. Dodgers Motion Pins

These "flasher" pins were issued in conjunction with the Dodgers' World Series appearance and ultimate victory in 1965. The 2-1/2" diameter pins feature player portraits on a seamed blue background resembling a baseball. When the angle of view is changed, the player's name and team logo and the starbursts pop in and out of sight.

	NM	EX	VG
Don Drysdale	15.00	7.50	4.50
Sandy Koufax	25.00	12.50	7.50
Dodgers logo - "Our Champs"	15.00	7.50	4.50

1979 L.A. Dodgers

Presumed to be a collectors' issue due to lack of sponsors or licensors logos, this set features the top players of the '79 Dodgers. Fronts of the 2-1/2" x 3-3/8" cards are borderless color photos. Backs are printed in blue and white with career highlights and personal data. Cards are checklisted here in alphabetical order.

GO DODGER BLUE!

Los Angeles Dodgers Baseball Star

STEVE GARVEY
UNIFORM #6   THROWS—R
                 BATS—R
1ST BASE

Steve's father is a bus driver in Florida who has chauffeured the Dodgers on many trips in the spring . . . Steve served as bat boy for the Dodgers and made many of those trips as a youngster . . . He graduated with a B.S. degree in 1971 from Michigan State University. . . Inducted in Florida Sports Hall of Fame in 1976.

	NM	EX	VG
Complete Set (15):	15.00	7.50	4.50
Common Player:	2.00	1.00	.60
(1) Dusty Baker	3.00	1.50	.90
(2) Ron Cey	2.00	1.00	.60
(3) Terry Forster	2.00	1.00	.60
(4) Steve Garvey	4.00	2.00	1.25
(5) Burt Hooton	2.00	1.00	.60
(6) Charlie Hough	2.00	1.00	.60
(7) Tommy Lasorda	3.00	1.50	.90
(8) Dave Lopes	2.00	1.00	.60
(9) Rick Monday	2.00	1.00	.60
(10) Manny Mota	2.00	1.00	.60
(11) Doug Rau	2.00	1.00	.60
(12) Bill Russell	2.00	1.00	.60
(13) Reggie Smith	2.00	1.00	.60
(14) Don Sutton	4.00	2.00	1.25
(15) Steve Yeager	2.00	1.00	.60

1980 L.A. Dodgers Police

TIPS FROM THE DODGERS

FOUL:
A batted ball that lands outside the fair boundaries is ruled a foul by the umpire.

The boundaries for citizens are called laws. If you don't know what a law allows you to do, ask a police officer. He'll be glad to explain what's fair or FOUL.

STEVE GARVEY
No. 6 – Infielder
Bats – Right   Height – 5'10"
Throws – Right   Weight – 190

Dodgers

Producers of one of the most popular police and safety sets in the hobby, the Dodgers began this successful promotion in 1980. The 2-13/16" x 4-1/8" cards feature full-color photos on front, along with brief personal statistics. Backs include "Tips from the Dodgers" along with the team and LAPD logos. Cards are numbered by player uniform number, with an unnumbered team card also included in the set.

		NM	EX	VG
Complete Set (30):		6.00	3.00	1.75
Common Player:		.50	.25	.15
5	Johnny Oates	.50	.25	.15
6	Steve Garvey	2.00	1.00	.60
7	Steve Yeager	.50	.25	.15
8	Reggie Smith	.50	.25	.15
9	Gary Thomasson	.50	.25	.15
10	Ron Cey	.60	.30	.20
12	Dusty Baker	.60	.30	.20
13	Joe Ferguson	.50	.25	.15
15	Davey Lopes	.50	.25	.15
16	Rick Monday	.50	.25	.15
18	Bill Russell	.50	.25	.15
20	Don Sutton	2.00	1.00	.60
21	Jay Johnstone	.50	.25	.15
23	Teddy Martinez	.50	.25	.15
27	Joe Beckwith	.50	.25	.15
28	Pedro Guerrero	.50	.25	.15
29	Don Stanhouse	.50	.25	.15
30	Derrel Thomas	.50	.25	.15
31	Doug Rau	.50	.25	.15
34	Ken Brett	.50	.25	.15
35	Bob Welch	.50	.25	.15
37	Robert Castillo	.50	.25	.15
38	Dave Goltz	.50	.25	.15
41	Jerry Reuss	.50	.25	.15
43	Rick Sutcliffe	.60	.30	.20
44	Mickey Hatcher	.50	.25	.15
46	Burt Hooton	.50	.25	.15
49	Charlie Hough	.50	.25	.15
51	Terry Forster	.50	.25	.15
---	Team Photo	.50	.25	.15

1913 Napoleon Lajoie Game

Although individual cards are not marked, these cards were produced as part of a Parker Brothers baseball board game called "The National American Baseball Game." Each of the approximately 2-3/8" x 3-1/4", round-cornered cards has a borderless photo on front picturing the Hall of Famer at bat. Backs have a chart of various baseball plays used in the game. Cards can be found with the Lajoie photo tinted either blue or red, the latter being somewhat scarcer.

Out on Strikes	2
Fly Out	2
Three Base Hit	4
One Base Hit	2
Home Run	1
Infield Hit—Out Home	6
Triple Play	
Out—Sacrifice Fly	7

	NM	EX	VG
Complete Game Set:	1,500	750.00	450.00
SINGLE CARD			
Napoleon Lajoie (Blue)	25.00	12.50	7.50
Napoleon Lajoie (Red)	45.00	22.50	13.50

1960 Lake To Lake Dairy Braves

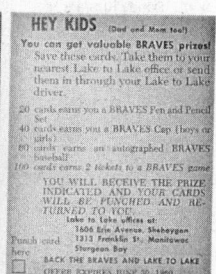

RED SCHOENDIENST
Second Base

HEY KIDS (Dad and Mom too!)
You can get valuable BRAVES prizes! Save these cards. Take them to your nearest Lake to Lake office or send them in through your Lake to Lake driver.

20 cards earns you a BRAVES Pen and Pencil Set
40 cards earns you a BRAVES Cap (boys or girls)
80 cards earns an autographed BRAVES baseball
100 cards earns 2 tickets to a BRAVES game

YOU WILL RECEIVE THE PRIZE INDICATED AND YOUR CARDS WILL BE PUNCHED AND RETURNED TO YOU
Lake to Lake offices at
1600 Erie Avenue, Sheboygan
1312 Franklin St., Manitowoc
Sturgeon Bay
Punch card here
BACK THE BRAVES AND LAKE TO LAKE
OFFER EXPIRES JUNE 30, 1960

This 28-card set of unnumbered 2-1/2" x 3-1/4" cards offers a special challenge for the condition-conscious collector. Originally issued by being stapled to milk cartons, the cards were redeemable for prizes ranging from pen and pencil sets to Braves tickets. When sent in for redemption, the cards had a hole punched in the corner. Naturally, collectors most desire cards without the staple or punch holes. Cards are printed in blue ink on front, red ink on back. Because he was traded in May, and his card withdrawn, the Ray Boone card is scarce; the Billy Bruton card is unaccountably scarcer still.

		NM	EX	VG
Complete Set (28):		2,250	1,125	650.00
Common Player:		35.00	17.50	10.00
(1)	Henry Aaron	500.00	250.00	150.00
(2)	Joe Adcock	35.00	17.50	10.00
(3)	Ray Boone	250.00	125.00	75.00
(4)	Bill Bruton	500.00	250.00	150.00
(5)	Bob Buhl	35.00	17.50	10.00
(6)	Lou Burdette	35.00	17.50	10.00
(7)	Chuck Cottier	35.00	17.50	10.00
(8)	Wes Covington	35.00	17.50	10.00
(9)	Del Crandall	35.00	17.50	10.00
(10)	Charlie Dressen	35.00	17.50	10.00
(11)	Bob Giggie	35.00	17.50	10.00
(12)	Joey Jay	35.00	17.50	10.00
(13)	Johnny Logan	35.00	17.50	10.00
(14)	Felix Mantilla	35.00	17.50	10.00
(15)	Lee Maye	35.00	17.50	10.00
(16)	Don McMahon	35.00	17.50	10.00
(17)	George Myatt	35.00	17.50	10.00
(18)	Andy Pafko	35.00	17.50	10.00
(19)	Juan Pizarro	35.00	17.50	10.00
(20)	Mel Roach	35.00	17.50	10.00
(21)	Bob Rush	35.00	17.50	10.00
(22)	Bob Scheffing	35.00	17.50	10.00
(23)	Red Schoendienst	75.00	37.50	22.50
(24)	Warren Spahn	150.00	75.00	45.00
(25)	Al Spangler	35.00	17.50	10.00
(26)	Frank Torre	35.00	17.50	10.00
(27)	Carl Willey	35.00	17.50	10.00
(28)	Whitlow Wyatt	35.00	17.50	10.00

1923-24 La Moda

Colección
LA MODA
Cigarros Ovalados
Esta hermosa colección
de fotografías consta de
todos los Sports Nacionales.
Villamil, Santalla y Ca.

This is appears to be a parallel to the more frequently encountered Cuban cigar cards advertising the Billiken brand. Specialists feel that the La Moda ("The Fashion") branded cards survive at a rate about one per 10 Billikens, though demand is not such that prices follow such a ratio.

	NM	EX	VG
Common Player:	1,000	400.00	200.00
Stars: 2X			

(See 1923-24 Billiken for checklist and base card values.)

1970 La Pizza Royale Expos

La Pizza Royale

RUSTY STAUB
Voltigeur

This colorful collectors' issue features only Montreal Expos. Each of the 2-1/2" x 5" cards can be found printed in red, yellow, blue of green duo-tones. "La Pizza Royale" is printed in white above the player photo. Below the photo is the player's name and, in French, his position. Backs are blank and the cards are unnumbered. The checklist is presented here alphabetically. The La Pizza Royale cards are a fantasy issue produced by a collector for sale within the hobby.

		NM	EX	VG
Complete Set (14):		20.00	10.00	6.00
Common Player:		2.00	1.00	.60
(1)	Bob Bailey	2.00	1.00	.60
(2)	John Boccabella	2.00	1.00	.60
(3)	Ron Fairly	3.00	1.50	.90
(4)	Jim Gosger	2.00	1.00	.60
(5)	Coco Laboy	2.00	1.00	.60
(6)	Gene Mauch	3.00	1.50	.90
(7)	Rich Nye	2.00	1.00	.60
(8)	John O'Donoghue	2.00	1.00	.60
(9)	Adolfo Phillips	2.00	1.00	.60
(10)	Howie Reed	2.00	1.00	.60
(11)	Marv Staehle	2.00	1.00	.60
(12)	Rusty Staub	4.50	2.25	1.25
(13)	Gary Sutherland	2.00	1.00	.60
(14)	Bobby Wine	2.00	1.00	.60

1967 Laughlin World Series

A'S vs. GIANTS
1911
McGRAW'S GORGEOUS "JINX SUITS"
PHILADELPHIA AL 4
NEW YORK NL 2

Apparently a prototype set for subsequent offerings by the sports artist R.G. Laughlin that were produced by Fleer, this set of 64 cards was printed in black-and-white with the cartoon line drawings for which Laughlin was noted. The cards are an odd size, 2-3/4" x 3-1/2", like so many of the Laughlin/Fleer issues of the period. The text on the back is printed in red and offer details of the World Series from that year.

		NM	EX	VG
Complete Set (64):		450.00	225.00	135.00
Common Card:		9.00	4.50	2.75
1	1903 Red Sox/Pirates	9.00	4.50	2.75
2	1905 Giants/A's (Christy Mathewson)	20.00	10.00	6.00
3	1906 White Sox/Cubs	9.00	4.50	2.75
4	1907 Cubs/Tigers	9.00	4.50	2.75
5	1908 Cubs/Tigers (Joe Tinker, Evers, Frank Chance)	20.00	10.00	6.00

		NM	EX	VG
6	1909 Pirates/Tigers (Honus Wagner, Ty Cobb)	30.00	15.00	9.00
7	1910 A's/Cubs	9.00	4.50	2.75
8	1911 A's/Giants (John McGraw)	9.00	4.50	2.75
9	1912 Red Sox/Giants	9.00	4.50	2.75
10	1913 A's/Giants	9.00	4.50	2.75
11	1914 Braves/A's	9.00	4.50	2.75
12	1915 Red Sox/Phillies (Babe Ruth)	35.00	17.50	10.00
13	1916 White Sox/Dodgers (Babe Ruth)	35.00	17.50	10.00
14	1917 White Sox/Giants	9.00	4.50	2.75
15	1918 Red Sox/Cubs	9.00	4.50	2.75
16	1919 Reds/White Sox	35.00	17.50	10.00
17	1920 Indians/Dodgers (Bill Wambsganss)	9.00	4.50	2.75
18	1921 Giants/Yankees (Waite Hoyt)	9.00	4.50	2.75
19	1922 Giants/Yankees (Frank Frisch, Heinie Groh)	9.00	4.50	2.75
20	1923 Yankees/Giants (Babe Ruth)	35.00	17.50	10.00
21	1924 Senators/Giants (Walter Johnson)	15.00	7.50	4.50
22	1925 Pirates/Senators (Walter Johnson)	15.00	7.50	4.50
23	1926 Cardinals/Yankees (Grover Alexander, Anthony Lazzeri)	15.00	7.50	4.50
24	1927 Yankees/Pirates	9.00	4.50	2.75
25	1928 Yankees/Cardinals (Babe Ruth, Lou Gehrig)	35.00	17.50	10.00
26	1929 A's/Cubs	9.00	4.50	2.75
27	1930 A's/Cardinals	9.00	4.50	2.75
28	1931 Cardinals/A's (Pepper Martin)	9.00	4.50	2.75
29	1932 Yankees/Cubs (Babe Ruth)	35.00	17.50	10.00
30	1933 Giants/Senators (Mel Ott)	12.50	6.25	3.75
31	1934 Cardinals/Tigers (Dizzy Dean, Paul Dean)	20.00	10.00	6.00
32	1935 Tigers/Cubs	9.00	4.50	2.75
33	1936 Yankees/Giants	9.00	4.50	2.75
34a	1937 Yankees/Giants (Carl Hubbell) (#11 on uniform.)	12.50	6.25	3.75
34b	1937 Yankees/Giants (Carl Hubbell) (#14 on uniform.)	12.50	6.25	3.75
35	1938 Yankees/Cubs	9.00	4.50	2.75
36	1939 Yankees/Reds (Joe DiMaggio)	30.00	15.00	9.00
37	1940 Reds/Tigers	9.00	4.50	2.75
38	1941 Yankees/Dodgers (Mickey Owen)	9.00	4.50	2.75
39	1942 Cardinals/Yankees	9.00	4.50	2.75
40	1943 Yankees/Cardinals (Joe McCarthy)	9.00	4.50	2.75
41	1944 Cardinals/Browns	9.00	4.50	2.75
42	1945 Tigers/Cubs (Hank Greenberg)	15.00	7.50	4.50
43	1946 Cardinals/Red Sox (Enos Slaughter)	9.00	4.50	2.75
44	1947 Yankees/Dodgers (Al Gionfriddo)	9.00	4.50	2.75
45	1948 Indians/Braves (Bob Feller)	12.50	6.25	3.75
46	1949 Yankees/Dodgers (Allie Reynolds, Preacher Roe)	20.00	10.00	6.00
47	1950 Yankees/Phillies	9.00	4.50	2.75
48	1951 Yankees/Giants	9.00	4.50	2.75
49	1952 Yankees/Dodgers (Johnny Mize, Duke Snider)	20.00	10.00	6.00
50	1953 Yankees/Dodgers (Casey Stengel)	20.00	10.00	6.00
51	1954 Giants/Indians (Dusty Rhodes)	9.00	4.50	2.75
52	1955 Dodgers/Yankees (Johnny Podres)	20.00	10.00	6.00
53	1956 Yankees/Dodgers (Don Larsen)	25.00	12.50	7.50
54	1957 Braves/Yankees (Lew Burdette)	9.00	4.50	2.75
55	1958 Yankees/Braves (Hank Bauer)	9.00	4.50	2.75
56	1959 Dodgers/White Sox (Larry Sherry)	9.00	4.50	2.75
57	1960 Pirates/Yankees	25.00	12.50	7.50
58	1961 Yankees/Reds (Whitey Ford)	20.00	10.00	6.00
59	1962 Yankees/Giants	9.00	4.50	2.75
60	1963 Dodgers/Yankees (Sandy Koufax)	20.00	10.00	6.00
61	1964 Cardinals/Yankees (Mickey Mantle)	35.00	17.50	10.00
62	1965 Dodgers/Twins (Sandy Koufax)	9.00	4.50	2.75
63	1966 Orioles/Dodgers	9.00	4.50	2.75
64	1967 Cardinals/Red Sox (Bob Gibson)	9.00	4.50	2.75

1972 Laughlin Great Feats

Sports artist R.G. Laughlin created this set of 50 numbered cards and one unnumbered title card highlighting top performances by stars over the years. The cards depict the player in pen and ink, with one variation of the set adding flesh tones to the players. One variation of the set has red borders, the other (with the flesh tones) blue. The cards are blank backed and numbered on the front with a brief caption. Cards measure about 2-9/16" x 3-9/16". Sets originally sold for about $3.

Great Feats 5

St. Lo.
257

George Sisler made 257 hits in 1920

		NM	EX	VG
Complete Set, Red (51):		45.00	22.50	13.50
Complete Set, Blue (51):		60.00	30.00	18.00
Common Player (Red):		1.50	.70	.45
Common Player (Blue): 1.5-2X				
1	Joe DiMaggio	12.00	6.00	3.50
2	Walter Johnson	4.50	2.25	1.25
3	Rudy York	1.50	.70	.45
4	Sandy Koufax	9.00	4.50	2.75
5	George Sisler	1.50	.70	.45
6	Iron Man McGinnity	1.50	.70	.45
7	Johnny VanderMeer	1.50	.70	.45
8	Lou Gehrig	12.00	6.00	3.50
9	Max Carey	1.50	.70	.45
10	Ed Delahanty	1.50	.70	.45
11	Pinky Higgins	1.50	.70	.45
12	Jack Chesbro	1.50	.70	.45
13	Jim Bottomley	1.50	.70	.45
14	Rube Marquard	1.50	.70	.45
15	Rogers Hornsby	1.50	.70	.45
16	Lefty Grove	1.50	.70	.45
17	Johnny Mize	1.50	.70	.45
18	Lefty Gomez	1.50	.70	.45
19	Jimmie Fox (Foxx)	1.50	.70	.45
20	Casey Stengel	1.50	.70	.45
21	Dazzy Vance	1.50	.70	.45
22	Jerry Lynch	1.50	.70	.45
23	Hughie Jennings	1.50	.70	.45
24	Stan Musial	4.50	2.25	1.25
25	Christy Mathewson	4.50	2.25	1.25
26	Elroy Face	1.50	.70	.45
27	Hack Wilson	1.50	.70	.45
28	Smoky Burgess	1.50	.70	.45
29	Cy Young	3.00	1.50	.90
30	Wilbert Robinson	1.50	.70	.45
31	Wee Willie Keeler	1.50	.70	.45
32	Babe Ruth	15.00	7.50	4.50
33	Mickey Mantle	15.00	7.50	4.50
34	Hub Leonard	1.50	.70	.45
35	Ty Cobb	7.50	3.75	2.25
36	Carl Hubbell	1.50	.70	.45
37	Joe Oeschger, Leon Cadore	1.50	.70	.45
38	Don Drysdale	1.50	.70	.45
39	Fred Toney, Hippo Vaughn	1.50	.70	.45
40	Joe Sewell	1.50	.70	.45
41	Grover Cleveland Alexander	1.50	.70	.45
42	Joe Adcock	1.50	.70	.45
43	Eddie Collins	1.50	.70	.45
44	Bob Feller	2.00	1.00	.60
45	Don Larsen	2.00	1.00	.60
46	Dave Philley	1.50	.70	.45
47	Bill Fischer	1.50	.70	.45
48	Dale Long	1.50	.70	.45
49	Bill Wambsganss	1.50	.70	.45
50	Roger Maris	4.50	2.25	1.25
---	Title Card	1.50	.70	.45

1973 Laughlin Super Stand-Ups

Babe

A dozen Hall of Famers are featured in this collectors' issue of stand-up figures. Printed in color on heavy cardboard, each is die-cut around the player action picture with typical measurements being 7" x 11". The stand-ups are much scarcer than most of the artist's other baseball issues. They are listed here alphabetically. The stand-ups originally retailed for $3.50 apiece.

	NM	EX	VG
Complete Set (13):	7,500	3,750	2,250
Common Player:	300.00	150.00	90.00
(1) Hank Aaron	650.00	325.00	195.00
(2) Johnny Bench	450.00	225.00	135.00
(3) Roberto Clemente	750.00	375.00	225.00
(4) Joe DiMaggio	750.00	375.00	225.00
(5) Lou Gehrig	750.00	375.00	225.00
(6) Gil Hodges	450.00	225.00	135.00
(7) Sandy Koufax	750.00	375.00	225.00
(8) Mickey Mantle	1,500	750.00	450.00
(9) Willie Mays	650.00	325.00	195.00
(10) Stan Musial	500.00	250.00	150.00
(11) Babe Ruth	1,200	600.00	360.00
(12) Tom Seaver	450.00	225.00	135.00
(13) Ted Williams	650.00	325.00	195.00

1974 Laughlin All-Star Games

ALL STAR GAMES

63
1963 Game
Municipal Stadium, Cleve. After four years, the All-Star game returned to one meeting. Mays drove in 2, walked, stole two bases, scored 2 and contributed great catch. Bunning had his 4th hitless AS stint. AL reliever Radatz K'd 5.
NL—0 1 2 0 1 0 0 1 0—5
AL—0 1 2 0 0 0 0 0 0—3
WP:Jackson LP:Bunning
© 1974 R.G. Laughlin

1963 NL 5 - AL 3

Five strikeouts for "The Monster"

With pen and ink drawings by R.G. Laughlin on the fronts, this set (40 cards) features one card from each year of the game from 1933 to 1973. The 2-3/4" x 3-3/8" cards show a player in black ink in front of a light blue background with a glossy finish, with red printing for the title of the set and the year. The backs are printed in blue, with the year of the All-Star Game serving as the card number. Issue price was $3.50.

		NM	EX	VG
Complete Set (40):		60.00	30.00	18.00
Common Player:		3.00	1.50	.90
33	Babe's Homer (Babe Ruth)	25.00	12.50	7.50
34a	Hub Fans Five (Carl Hubbell) (Uniform #11.)	4.50	2.25	1.25
34b	Hub Fans Five (Carl Hubbell) (Uniform #14.)	4.50	2.25	1.25
35	Foxx Smashes HR (Jimmie Foxx)	4.50	2.25	1.25
36	Ol' Diz Fogs 'Em (Dizzy Dean)	4.50	2.25	1.25
37	Four Hits for Ducky (Ducky Medwick)	3.00	1.50	.90
38	No-Hit Vandy (John VanderMeer)	3.00	1.50	.90
39	DiMaggio Homers (Joe DiMaggio)	20.00	10.00	6.00
40	West's 3-Run Shot (Max West)	3.00	1.50	.90
41	Vaughan Busts Two (Arky Vaughan)	3.00	1.50	.90
42	York's 2-Run Smash (Rudy York)	3.00	1.50	.90
43	Doerr's 3-Run Blast (Bobby Doerr)	3.00	1.50	.90
44	Cavarretta Reaches (Phil Cavarretta)	3.00	1.50	.90
46	Field Day for Ted (Ted Williams)	15.00	7.50	4.50
47	Big Cat Plants One (Johnny Mize)	3.00	1.50	.90
48	Raschi Pitches (Vic Raschi)	3.00	1.50	.90
49	Jackie Scores (Jackie Robinson)	12.00	6.00	3.50
50	Schoendienst Breaks (Red Schoendienst)	3.00	1.50	.90
51	Kiner Homers (Ralph Kiner)	3.00	1.50	.90
52	Sauer's Shot (Hank Sauer)	3.00	1.50	.90
53	Slaughter Hustles (Enos Slaughter)	3.00	1.50	.90
54	Rosen Hits (Al Rosen)	3.00	1.50	.90
55	Stan the Man's HR (Stan Musial)	7.50	3.75	2.25
56	Boyer Super (Ken Boyer)	3.00	1.50	.90
57	Kaline's Hits (Al Kaline)	4.50	2.25	1.25
58	Nellie Gets Two (Nellie Fox)	3.00	1.50	.90
59	Robbie Perfect (Frank Robinson)	4.50	2.25	1.25
60	Willie 3-for-4 (Willie Mays)	12.00	6.00	3.50
61	Bunning Hitless (Jim Bunning)	3.00	1.50	.90
62	Roberto Perfect (Roberto Clemente)	15.00	7.50	4.50
63	Monster Strikeouts (Dick Radatz)	3.00	1.50	.90
64	Callison's Homer (Johnny Callison)	3.00	1.50	.90
65	Stargell's Big Day (Willie Stargell)	3.00	1.50	.90
66	Brooks Gets Triple (Brooks Robinson)	4.50	2.25	1.25
67	Fergie Fans Six (Fergie Jenkins)	3.00	1.50	.90
68	Tom Terrific (Tom Seaver)	5.00	2.50	1.50
69	Stretch Belts Two (Willie McCovey)	3.00	1.50	.90
70	Yaz' Four Hits (Carl Yastrzemski)	4.50	2.25	1.25

		NM	EX	VG
71	Reggie Unloads (Reggie Jackson)	6.00	3.00	1.75
72	Henry Hammers (Hank Aaron)	12.00	6.00	3.50
73	Bonds Perfect (Bobby Bonds)	3.00	1.50	.90

1974 Laughlin Old-Time Black Stars

This set of slightly oversized cards (2-5/8" x 3-1/2") features drawings by R.G. Laughlin. The artwork is printed in brown and a light tan; backs are printed in brown on white stock. The set features many of the greatest players from the Negro Leagues. The cards carry no copyright date and no mention of the prolific Laughlin, but the simple line drawings are obviously his work, and a subsequent issue four years later by Laughlin removes any doubt. Original retail price at time of issue was about $3.25.

		NM	EX	VG
Complete Set (36):		60.00	30.00	18.00
Common Player:		2.00	1.00	.60
1	Smokey Joe Williams	5.00	2.50	1.50
2	Rap Dixon	2.00	1.00	.60
3	Oliver Marcelle	2.00	1.00	.60
4	Bingo DeMoss	4.00	2.00	1.25
5	Willie Foster	2.50	1.25	.70
6	John Beckwith	2.00	1.00	.60
7	Floyd (Jelly) Gardner	2.00	1.00	.60
8	Josh Gibson	10.00	5.00	3.00
9	Jose Mendez	5.00	2.50	1.50
10	Pete Hill	5.00	2.50	1.50
11	Buck Leonard	5.00	2.50	1.50
12	Jud Wilson	5.00	2.50	1.50
13	Willie Wells	5.00	2.50	1.50
14	Jimmie Lyons	2.00	1.00	.60
15	Satchel Paige	10.00	5.00	3.00
16	Louis Santop	5.00	2.50	1.50
17	Frank Grant	7.50	3.75	2.25
18	Christobel Torrienti	5.00	2.50	1.50
19	Bullet Rogan	4.00	2.00	1.25
20	Dave Malarcher	2.50	1.25	.70
21	Spot Poles	2.00	1.00	.60
22	Home Run Johnson	2.50	1.25	.70
23	Charlie Grant	4.00	2.00	1.25
24	Cool Papa Bell	5.00	2.50	1.50
25	Cannonball Dick Redding	2.00	1.00	.60
26	Ray Dandridge	5.00	2.50	1.50
27	Biz Mackey	7.50	3.75	2.25
28	Fats Jenkins	2.00	1.00	.60
29	Martin Dihigo	5.00	2.50	1.50
30	Mule Suttles	5.00	2.50	1.50
31	Bill Monroe	2.00	1.00	.60
32	Dan McClellan	2.00	1.00	.60
33	Pop Lloyd	5.00	2.50	1.50
34	Oscar Charleston	5.00	2.50	1.50
35	Andrew "Rube" Foster	5.00	2.50	1.50
36	William (Judy) Johnson	5.00	2.50	1.50

1974 Laughlin Sportslang

Featuring the cartoon artwork of R.G. Laughlin, this 41-card set features 40 cards (plus one unnumbered title card) detailing the history and derivation of slang terms from several sports. The cards are 2-3/4" x 3-1/4", with red and blue printing on the front and red on the back. The cards are numbered on the back.

		NM	EX	VG
Complete Set (41):		80.00	40.00	24.00
Common Card:		3.00	1.50	.80
1	Bull Pen	3.00	1.50	.80
2	Charley Horse	3.00	1.50	.80
3	Derby	3.00	1.50	.80
4	Anchor Man	3.00	1.50	.80
5	Mascot	3.00	1.50	.80
6	Annie Oakley	3.00	1.50	.80
7	Taxi Squad	3.00	1.50	.80
8	Dukes	3.00	1.50	.80
9	Rookie	3.00	1.50	.80
10	Jinx	3.00	1.50	.80
11	Dark Horse	3.00	1.50	.80
12	Hat Trick	3.00	1.50	.80
13	Bell Wether	3.00	1.50	.80
14	Love	3.00	1.50	.80
15	Red Dog	3.00	1.50	.80
16	Barnstorm	3.00	1.50	.80
17	Bull's Eye	3.00	1.50	.80
18	Rabbit Punch	3.00	1.50	.80
19	The Upper Hand	3.00	1.50	.80
20	Handi Cap	3.00	1.50	.80
21	Marathon	3.00	1.50	.80
22	Southpaw	3.00	1.50	.80
23	Boner	3.00	1.50	.80
24	Gridiron	3.00	1.50	.80
25	Fan	3.00	1.50	.80
26	Moxie	3.00	1.50	.80
27	Birdie	3.00	1.50	.80
28	Sulky	3.00	1.50	.80
29	Dribble	3.00	1.50	.80
30	Donnybrook	3.00	1.50	.80
31	The Real McCoy	3.00	1.50	.80
32	Even Stephen	3.00	1.50	.80
33	Chinese Homer	3.00	1.50	.80
34	English	3.00	1.50	.80
35	Garrison Finish	3.00	1.50	.80
36	Foot in the Bucket	3.00	1.50	.80
37	Steeple Chase	3.00	1.50	.80
38	Long Shot	3.00	1.50	.80
39	Nip and Tuck	3.00	1.50	.80
40	Battery	3.00	1.50	.80
----	Header Card	3.00	1.50	.80

1975 Laughlin Batty Baseball

This 25-card set depicts one humorous nickname for each of 24 Major League teams, plus one unnumbered title card. The cards are approximately standard size at 2-1/2" x 3-1/2", with simple black and white cartoon drawings on the front with orange backgrounds. The backs are blank and the cards are numbered on front.

		NM	EX	VG
Complete Set (25):		60.00	30.00	18.00
Common Card:		3.00	1.50	.90
1	Oakland Daze	3.00	1.50	.90
2	Boston Wet Sox	3.00	1.50	.90
3	Cincinnati Dreads	3.00	1.50	.90
4	Chicago Wide Sox	3.00	1.50	.90
5	Milwaukee Boozers	3.00	1.50	.90
6	Philadelphia Fillies	3.00	1.50	.90
7	Cleveland Engines	3.00	1.50	.90
8	New York Mitts	3.00	1.50	.90
9	Texas Ranchers	3.00	1.50	.90
10	San Francisco Gents	3.00	1.50	.90
11	Houston Disastros	3.00	1.50	.90
12	Chicago Clubs	3.00	1.50	.90
13	Minnesota Wins	3.00	1.50	.90
14	St. Louis Gardeners	3.00	1.50	.90
15	New York Yankers	3.00	1.50	.90
16	California Angles	3.00	1.50	.90
17	Pittsburg Irates	3.00	1.50	.90
18	Los Angeles Smoggers	3.00	1.50	.90
19	Baltimore Oreos	3.00	1.50	.90
20	Montreal Expose	3.00	1.50	.90
21	San Diego Parties	3.00	1.50	.90
22	Detroit Taggers	3.00	1.50	.90
23	Kansas City Broils	3.00	1.50	.90
24	Atlanta Briefs	3.00	1.50	.90
----	Header Card	3.00	1.50	.90

1976 Laughlin Diamond Jubilee

This set of 32 oversized cards (2-3/4" x 4") features Laughlin's drawings of baseball stars highlighting specific events or records. The fronts are printed in black and blue over a red background; the backs are numbered and printed in blue with information about the specific event. Sets originally sold for $3.50.

		NM	EX	VG
Complete Set (32):		90.00	45.00	25.00
Common Player:		2.00	1.00	.60
1	Nolan Ryan	30.00	15.00	9.00
2	Ernie Banks	4.50	2.25	1.25
3	Mickey Lolich	2.00	1.00	.60
4	Sandy Koufax	9.00	4.50	2.75
5	Frank Robinson	3.00	1.50	.90
6	Bill Mazeroski	3.00	1.50	.90
7	Catfish Hunter	2.00	1.00	.60
8	Hank Aaron	9.00	4.50	2.75
9	Carl Yastrzemski	3.00	1.50	.90
10	Jim Bunning	2.00	1.00	.60
11	Brooks Robinson	3.00	1.50	.90
12	John VanderMeer	2.00	1.00	.60
13	Harmon Killebrew	3.00	1.50	.90
14	Lou Brock	2.50	1.25	.70
15	Steve Busby	2.00	1.00	.60
16	Nate Colbert	2.00	1.00	.60
17	Don Larsen	2.50	1.25	.70
18	Willie Mays	9.00	4.50	2.75
19	David Clyde	2.00	1.00	.60
20	Mack Jones	2.00	1.00	.60
21	Mike Hegan	2.00	1.00	.60
22	Jerry Koosman	2.00	1.00	.60
23	Early Wynn	2.50	1.25	.70
24	Nellie Fox	2.50	1.25	.70
25	Joe DiMaggio	15.00	7.50	4.50
26	Jackie Robinson	12.00	6.00	3.50
27	Ted Williams	12.00	6.00	3.50
28	Lou Gehrig	12.00	6.00	3.50
29	Bobby Thomson	2.50	1.25	.70
30	Roger Maris	7.50	3.75	2.25
31	Harvey Haddix	2.00	1.00	.60
32	Babe Ruth	20.00	10.00	6.00

1976 Laughlin Indianapolis Clowns

Founder Syd Pollock

Syd Pollock organized the Miami Ethiopian Clowns in 1929. His concept was to create a black club that not only could play pro ball but add laughs and showmanship to the game. The Clowns preceded the Harlem Globetrotters by a year. The national semi-pro champions turned pro in 1942, becoming the Cincinnati Clowns and later the Indianapolis Clowns, as they won numerous Negro AL titles. Also a Braves scout, Pollock retired from traveling baseball in 1964, turning the team over to Ed Hamman. Syd passed away in 1968.

In a departure from the style of most Laughlin issues, this 42-card set does not use his artwork but rather black and white photos framed by a light blue border. The cards are oversized at 2-5/8" x 4-1/4", with red printing on front and back. The cards are numbered on the front.

		NM	EX	VG
Complete Set (42):		30.00	15.00	9.00
Common Player:		.60	.30	.20
1	Ed Hamman (Ed the Clown)	1.00	.50	.30
2	Dero Austin	.60	.30	.20
3	James Williams (Natureboy)	.60	.30	.20
4	Sam Brison (Birmingham)	.60	.30	.20
5	Richard King (King Tut)	.60	.30	.20
6	Syd Pollock (Founder)	.60	.30	.20
7	Natanial (Lefty) Small	.60	.30	.20
8	Grant Greene (Double Duty)	.60	.30	.20
9	Nancy Miller (Lady Umpire)	.60	.30	.20
10	Billy Vaughn	.60	.30	.20
11	Sam Brison (Putout for Sam)	.60	.30	.20
12	Ed Hamman	.60	.30	.20
13	Dero Austin (Home Delivery)	.60	.30	.20
14	Steve (Nub) Anderson	.60	.30	.20
15	Joe Cherry	.60	.30	.20
16	Reece (Goose) Tatum	3.00	1.50	.90
17	James Williams (Natureboy)	.60	.30	.20
18	Byron Purnell	.60	.30	.20
19	Bat Boy	.60	.30	.20
20	Spec BeBop	.60	.30	.20
21	Satchel Paige	5.00	2.50	1.50
22	Prince Jo Henry	.60	.30	.20
23	Ed Hamman, Syd Pollock	.60	.30	.20
24	Paul Casanova	.60	.30	.20
25	Steve (Nub) Anderson (Nub Singles)	.60	.30	.20
26	Comiskey Park	.60	.30	.20
27	Toni Stone (Second basewoman)	1.50	.70	.45
28	Dero Austin (Small target)	.60	.30	.20
29	Calling Dr. Kildare (Sam Brison, Natureboy Williams)	.60	.30	.20
30	Oscar Charleston	2.00	1.00	.60
31	Richard King (King Tut)	.60	.30	.20

		NM	EX	VG
32	Ed and Prospects (Ed Hamman, Joe Cherry, Hal King)	.60	.30	.20
33	Team bus	.60	.30	.20
34	Hank Aaron	6.00	3.00	1.75
35	The Greta Yogi	1.50	.70	.45
36	W.H. (Chauff) Wilson	.60	.30	.20
37	Doin' Their Thing (Sam Brison, Sonny Jackson)	.60	.30	.20
38	Billy Vaughn (The hard way.)	.60	.30	.20
39	James Williams (18 the easy way.)	.60	.30	.20
40	Casey & Ed (Ed Hamman, Casey Stengel)	1.25	.60	.40
---	Header Card	.60	.30	.20
---	Baseball Laff Book	.60	.30	.20

1978 Laughlin Long Ago Black Stars

In what appears very much like a second series save for slight title alteration, sports artist R.G. Laughlin produced this 36-card set in a format very similar to his 1974 issue highlighting Negro League stars. This set is printed in dark and light green on a non-glossy front, with printing on the back in black. Most of the more widely known Negro League stars appeared in the 1974 issue.

		NM	EX	VG
	Complete Set (36):	60.00	30.00	18.00
	Common Player:	1.50	.70	.45
1	Ted Trent	1.50	.70	.45
2	Larry Brown	1.50	.70	.45
3	Newt Allen	3.00	1.50	.90
4	Norman Stearns	4.50	2.25	1.25
5	Leon Day	6.00	3.00	1.75
6	Dick Lundy	1.50	.70	.45
7	Bruce Petway	1.50	.70	.45
8	Bill Drake	1.50	.70	.45
9	Chaney White	1.50	.70	.45
10	Webster McDonald	2.50	1.25	.70
11	Tommy Butts	1.50	.70	.45
12	Ben Taylor	4.50	2.25	1.25
13	James (Joe) Greene	1.50	.70	.45
14	Dick Seay	1.50	.70	.45
15	Sammy Hughes	1.50	.70	.45
16	Ted Page	3.00	1.50	.90
17	Willie Cornelius	1.50	.70	.45
18	Pat Patterson	1.50	.70	.45
19	Frank Wickware	1.50	.70	.45
20	Albert Haywood	1.50	.70	.45
21	Bill Holland	1.50	.70	.45
22	Sol White	4.50	2.25	1.25
23	Chet Brewer	3.00	1.50	.90
24	Crush Holloway	1.50	.70	.45
25	George Johnson	1.50	.70	.45
26	George Scales	1.50	.70	.45
27	Dave Brown	1.50	.70	.45
28	John Donaldson	1.50	.70	.45
29	William Johnson	3.00	1.50	.90
30	Bill Yancey	3.00	1.50	.90
31	Sam Bankhead	4.00	2.00	1.25
32	Leroy Matlock	1.50	.70	.45
33	Quincy Troupe	2.50	1.25	.70
34	Hilton Smith	3.00	1.50	.90
35	Jim Crutchfield	3.00	1.50	.90
36	Ted Radcliffe	4.00	2.00	1.25

1980 Laughlin Famous Feats

A set of 40 cards, this Famous Feats set by sports artist R.G. Laughlin carries a subtitle as the Second Series, apparently a reference to a 1972 issue of the same name by Laughlin that was produced by Fleer. Unlike many of the odd sized Laughlin issues, this one is the standard 2-1/2" x 3-1/2", with full color used with the artist's pen and ink drawings on the front. The cards are numbered on the front and the backs are blank.

		NM	EX	VG
	Complete Set (40):	15.00	7.50	4.50
	Common Player:	.75	.35	.20
1	Honus Wagner	2.50	1.25	.70
2	Herb Pennock	.75	.35	.20
3	Al Simmons	.75	.35	.20
4	Hack Wilson	.75	.35	.20
5	Dizzy Dean	1.50	.70	.45
6	Chuck Klein	.75	.35	.20
7	Nellie Fox	.75	.40	.25
8	Lefty Grove	.75	.35	.20
9	George Sisler	.75	.35	.20
10	Lou Gehrig	3.50	1.75	1.00
11	Rube Waddell	.75	.35	.20
12	Max Carey	.75	.35	.20
13	Thurman Munson	2.00	1.00	.60
14	Mel Ott	.75	.35	.20
15	Doc White	.75	.35	.20
16	Babe Ruth	6.00	3.00	1.75
17	Schoolboy Rowe	.75	.35	.20
18	Jackie Robinson	3.50	1.75	1.00
19	Joe Medwick	.75	.35	.20
20	Casey Stengel	.75	.35	.20
21	Roberto Clemente	4.50	2.25	1.25
22	Christy Mathewson	1.50	.70	.45
23	Jimmie Foxx	1.25	.60	.40
24	Joe Jackson	6.00	3.00	1.75
25	Walter Johnson	1.50	.70	.45
26	Tony Lazzeri	.75	.35	.20
27	Hugh Casey	.75	.35	.20
28	Ty Cobb	3.50	1.75	1.00
29	Stuffy McInnis	.75	.35	.20
30	Cy Young	1.25	.60	.40
31	Lefty O'Doul	.75	.35	.20
32	Eddie Collins	.75	.35	.20
33	Joe McCarty	.75	.35	.20
34	Ed Walsh	.75	.35	.20
35	George Burns	.75	.35	.20
36	Walt Dropo	.75	.35	.20
37	Connie Mack	.75	.35	.20
38	Babe Adams	.75	.35	.20
39	Rogers Hornsby	1.00	.50	.30
40	Grover C. Alexander	.75	.35	.20

1980 Laughlin 300/400/500

This unusual set features a combination of the line drawings of R.G. Laughlin and a photo head shot of the player depicted. The cards are actually square, 3-1/4" x 3-1/4", with a background in color depicting a baseball diamond. The set is based on 300 wins, batting .400 or better and 500 homers, with a total of 30 cards in the blank backed set. The cards are numbered on the front.

		NM	EX	VG
	Complete Set (30):	25.00	12.50	7.50
	Common Player:	1.50	.75	.45
1	Header card	1.50	.75	.45
2	Babe Ruth	10.00	5.00	3.00
3	Walter Johnson	3.00	1.50	.90
4	Ty Cobb	6.00	3.00	1.75
5	Christy Mathewson	3.00	1.50	.90
6	Ted Williams	4.00	2.00	1.25
7	Bill Terry	1.50	.75	.45
8	Grover C. Alexander	1.50	.75	.45
9	Napoleon Lajoie	1.50	.75	.45
10	Willie Mays	4.00	2.00	1.25
11	Cy Young	3.00	1.50	.90
12	Mel Ott	1.50	.75	.45
13	Joe Jackson	10.00	5.00	3.00
14	Harmon Killebrew	1.50	.75	.45
15	Warren Spahn	1.50	.75	.45
16	Hank Aaron	4.00	2.00	1.25
17	Rogers Hornsby	1.50	.75	.45
18	Mickey Mantle	10.00	5.00	3.00
19	Lefty Grove	1.50	.75	.45
20	Ted Williams	4.00	2.00	1.25
21	Jimmie Fox	1.50	.75	.45
22	Eddie Plank	1.50	.75	.45
23	Frank Robinson	1.50	.75	.45
24	George Sisler	1.50	.75	.45
25	Eddie Mathews	1.50	.75	.45
26	Early Wynn	1.50	.75	.45
27	Ernie Banks	1.50	.75	.45
28	Harry Heilmann	1.50	.75	.45
29	Lou Gehrig	7.50	3.75	2.25
30	Willie McCovey	1.50	.75	.45

1929 Leader Novelty Candy Co.

Though unmarked as such, these cards are believed to have been an insert in boxes of Leader Novelty Candy, or at least were so advertised in the famous Copeland Collection auction of 1991. They are one of two "mini" versions of the R316 Kashin Publications cards (see also W553), though it is not known whether the entire 101-card Kashin set was so paralleled. While sizes seem to vary significantly, nominal measurements for this version are about 1-3/4" x 2-5/8". Cards have been seen in duotones of red, sepia, purple and green. They are unnumbered and blank-backed. This checklist is known to be incomplete. Gaps have been left in the assigned numbering to accommodate additions.

		NM	EX	VG
	Common Player:	75.00	37.50	22.50
(7)	Lucerne A. Blue	75.00	37.00	22.00
(8)	James Bottomley	150.00	75.00	45.00
(13)	Earl (Earle) Combs	150.00	75.00	45.00
(26)	Jimmy Foxx	250.00	125.00	75.00
(27)	Frank Frisch	150.00	75.00	45.00
(33)	Robert Grove	175.00	87.00	52.00
(42)	Rogers Hornsby	200.00	100.00	60.00
(45)	Sam Jones	75.00	37.50	22.50
(50)	Joseph Judge	75.00	37.50	22.50
(52)	Charles Klein	150.00	75.00	45.00
(62)	Walter Maranville	150.00	75.00	45.00
(65)	Ed "Bing" Miller	75.00	37.00	22.00
(66)	Frank O'Doul	100.00	50.00	30.00
(67)	Melvin Ott	175.00	87.00	52.00
(74)	Eddie Rommel	75.00	37.00	22.00
(85)	Al Simmons	150.00	75.00	45.00
(92)	Harold J. Traynor	150.00	75.00	45.00
(93)	Dazzy Vance	150.00	75.00	45.00
(95)	Paul Waner	150.00	75.00	45.00
(100)	Hack Wilson	175.00	87.00	52.00

1922 Leader Theatre

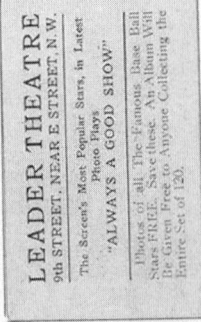

This issue by a Washington, D.C. moviehouse is a version of the W573 and W575-1 strip card sets on which at least two forms of customized advertising were printed on the card backs. The ads state that 120 cards (paralleling W573 and/or W575-1) were originally issued in this version. An album was also offered.

	NM	EX	VG
Common Player:	500.00	250.00	150.00

(See 1922 W573 and W575-1 for checklists and base card values. Add 5X premium for non-commons.)

1949 Leaf

The first color baseball cards of the post-World War II era were the 98-card, 2-3/8" x 2-7/8", set produced by Chicago's Leaf Gum Co. for issue in 1949. One of the toughest post-war sets to complete, exactly half of the issue - 49 cards - are significantly harder to find than the others. Probably intended to confound bubblegum buyers of the day, the set is skip-numbered between 1-168. Card backs contain offers of felt pennants, an album for the cards or 5-1/2" x 7-1/2" premium photos of Hall of Famers. While some cards carry a 1948 copyright date on

	NM	EX	VG
143 Dick Sisler/SP	900.00	360.00	180.00
144 Bob Dillinger/SP	900.00	360.00	180.00
146 Harold Reiser/SP	1,000	400.00	200.00
149 Henry Majeski/SP	900.00	360.00	180.00
153 Floyd Baker/SP	900.00	360.00	180.00
158 *Harry Brecheen*/SP	900.00	360.00	180.00
159 Mizell Platt	125.00	45.00	22.50
160 Bob Scheffing/SP	900.00	360.00	180.00
161 *Vernon Stephens*/SP	1,000	400.00	200.00
163 *Freddy Hutchinson*/SP	1,000	400.00	200.00
165 *Dale Mitchell*/SP	1,000	400.00	200.00
168 Phil Cavaretta/SP	900.00	360.00	180.00

1949 Leaf Premiums

These blank-back, sepia photos were available with the purchase of 1948 Leaf baseball cards. Measuring 5-5/8" x 7-1/4", the pictures have a facsimile autograph and a black box labeled "BASEBALL'S IMMORTALS" at bottom containing a short biography. The unnumbered pictures are checklisted alphabetically.

	NM	EX	VG
Complete Set (9):	6,000	3,000	1,800
Common Player:	400.00	200.00	120.00
(1) Grover Alexander	450.00	225.00	135.00
(2) Mickey Cochrane	400.00	200.00	120.00
(3) Lou Gehrig	1,200	600.00	360.00
(4) Walter Johnson	450.00	225.00	135.00
(5) Christy Mathewson	525.00	260.00	155.00
(6) John McGraw	400.00	200.00	120.00
(7) Babe Ruth	1,200	600.00	360.00
(Dark background, text boxes.)			
(8) Babe Ruth	1,200	600.00	360.00
(Light background, no text.)			
(9) Ed Walsh	400.00	200.00	120.00

1960 Leaf Pre-Production

Evidently produced prior to final approval for the design of the 1960 Leaf set, these cards all feature much larger player photos than the issued versions. Generally the issued cards have cap-to-waist photos while the pre-production cards have to cap-to-chin shots. Backs of the pre-production cards are virtually identical to the regular cards. The pre-production cards were never publically issued and show evidence of having been hand-cut. The cards of Donovan and Jay appear to be more common than the others.

	NM	EX	VG
Complete Set (8):	15,000	7,500	4,500
Common Player:	1,500	750.00	450.00
1 Luis Aparicio	4,500	2,250	1,350
12 Ken Boyer	2,150	1,075	645.00
17 Walt Moryn	1,250	625.00	375.00
23 Joey Jay	1,250	625.00	375.00
35 Jim Coates	2,250	1,125	675.00
58 Hal Smith	1,950	975.00	585.00
61 Vic Rehm	1,500	750.00	450.00
72 Dick Donovan	1,250	625.00	375.00

1960 Leaf

While known to the hobby as "Leaf" cards, this set of 144 carries the copyright of Sports Novelties Inc., Chicago. The 2-1/2" x 3-1/2" cards feature black-and-white player portrait photos, with plain background. Cards were sold in nickel wax packs with a marble, rather than a piece of bubble gum. The second half of the set, #73-144, are quite scarce. Card #25, Jim Grant, is found in two versions, with his

back, it is now believed the issue was not released until 1949. The complete set price does not include the higher value in the variation pairs.

	NM	EX	VG
Complete Set (98):	85,000	35,000	17,500
Common Player:	125.00	45.00	22.50
Common Short-print:	900.00	360.00	180.00
Album:	900.00	450.00	275.00
1 Joe DiMaggio	3,000	725.00	400.00
3 Babe Ruth	3,300	1,650	1,000
4 *Stan Musial*	1,700	850.00	510.00
5 *Virgil Trucks*/SP	1,150	460.00	230.00
8 *Satchel Paige*/SP	17,500	7,000	3,500
10 Paul Trout	125.00	45.00	22.50
11 Phil Rizzuto	325.00	130.00	65.00
13 Casimer Michaels/SP	900.00	360.00	180.00
14 Billy Johnson	125.00	45.00	22.50
17 Frank Overmire	125.00	45.00	22.50
19 John Wyrostek/SP	900.00	360.00	180.00
20 *Hank Sauer*/SP	1,000	400.00	200.00
22 Al Evans	125.00	45.00	22.50
26 Sam Chapman	125.00	45.00	22.50
27 Mickey Harris	125.00	45.00	22.50
28 *Jim Hegan*	125.00	45.00	22.50
29 Elmer Valo	125.00	45.00	22.50
30 *Bill Goodman*/SP	900.00	360.00	180.00
31 Lou Brissie	125.00	45.00	22.50
32 *Warren Spahn*	450.00	180.00	90.00
33 Harry Lowrey/SP	900.00	360.00	180.00
36 Al Zarilla/SP	900.00	360.00	180.00
38 *Ted Kluszewski*	300.00	120.00	60.00
39 Ewell Blackwell	130.00	50.00	25.00
42a Kent Peterson (Red cap.)	1,100	440.00	220.00
42b Kent Peterson (Black cap.)	125.00	45.00	22.50
43 Eddie Stevens/SP	900.00	360.00	180.00
45 Ken Keltner/SP	900.00	360.00	180.00
46 Johnny Mize	300.00	120.00	60.00
47 George Vico	125.00	45.00	22.50
48 Johnny Schmitz/SP	900.00	360.00	180.00
49 *Del Ennis*	130.00	50.00	25.00
50 Dick Wakefield	125.00	45.00	22.50
51 *Alvin Dark*/SP	1,750	700.00	350.00
53 John Vandermeer (Vander Meer)	225.00	90.00	45.00
54 Bobby Adams/SP	900.00	360.00	180.00
55 Tommy Henrich/SP	2,000	800.00	400.00
56 *Larry Jensen*	130.00	50.00	25.00
57 Bob McCall	125.00	45.00	22.50
59 Luke Appling	200.00	80.00	40.00
61 Jake Early	125.00	45.00	22.50
62 Eddie Joost/SP	900.00	360.00	180.00
63 Barney McCosky/SP	900.00	360.00	180.00
65 Bob Elliot (Elliott)	125.00	45.00	22.50
66 Orval Grove/SP	900.00	360.00	180.00
68 Ed Miller/SP	900.00	360.00	180.00
70 Honus Wagner	500.00	200.00	100.00
72 Hank Edwards	125.00	45.00	22.50
73 Pat Seerey	125.00	45.00	22.50
75 Dom DiMaggio/SP	1,400	560.00	280.00
76 Ted Williams	2,600	1,300	780.00
77 Roy Smalley	125.00	45.00	22.50
78 Walter Evers/SP	900.00	360.00	180.00
79 *Jackie Robinson*	1,800	550.00	325.00
81 George Kurowski/SP	900.00	360.00	180.00
82 Johnny Lindell	125.00	45.00	22.50
83 Bobby Doerr	225.00	90.00	45.00
84 Sid Hudson	125.00	45.00	22.50
q5 Dave Philley/SP	900.00	360.00	180.00
86 Ralph Weigel	125.00	45.00	22.50
88 Frank Gustine/SP	900.00	360.00	180.00
91 *Ralph Kiner*	175.00	70.00	35.00
93 Bob Feller/SP	3,250	1,300	650.00
95 George Stirnweiss	125.00	45.00	22.50
97 *Martin Marion*	150.00	60.00	30.00
98 Hal Newhouser/SP	1,800	725.00	360.00
102a Gene Hermansk (Incorrect spelling.)	2,750	1,100	550.00
102b Gene Hermanski (Correct spelling.)	135.00	55.00	25.00
104 Edward Stewart/SP	900.00	360.00	180.00
106 Lou Boudreau	200.00	80.00	40.00
108 Matthew Batts/SP	900.00	360.00	180.00
111 Gerald Priddy	125.00	45.00	22.50
113 Emil Leonard/SP	900.00	360.00	180.00
117 Joe Gordon	125.00	45.00	22.50
120 *George Kell*/SP	1,100	440.00	220.00
121 *John Pesky*/SP	1,000	400.00	200.00
123 Clifford Fannin/SP	900.00	360.00	180.00
125 *Andy Pafko*	160.00	65.00	30.00
127 Enos Slaughter/SP	1,750	700.00	350.00
128 Warren Rosar	125.00	45.00	22.50
129 Kirby Higbe/SP	900.00	360.00	180.00
131 Sid Gordon/SP	900.00	360.00	180.00
133 Tommy Holmes/SP	1,000	400.00	200.00
136a Cliff Aberson (Full sleeve.)	125.00	50.00	25.00
136b Cliff Aberson (Short sleeve.)	175.00	70.00	35.00
137 Harry Walker/SP	900.00	360.00	180.00
138 *Larry Doby*/SP	3,000	1,200	600.00
139 Johnny Hopp	125.00	45.00	22.50
142 *Danny Murtaugh*/SP	1,000	400.00	200.00

own picture (black cap) and with a photo of Brooks Lawrence (white cap). Three back variations of Hal Smith card #58 are also known. Complete set prices do not include variations. In the late 1990s, a large group of high-number (Series 2) boxes - in excess of 4,000 cards - was added to the surviving supply.

	NM	EX	VG
Complete Set (144):	2,000	1,000	500.00
Common Player (1-72):	9.00	4.50	2.75
Common Player (73-144):	12.00	6.00	3.50
Wax Pack, Series 1 (5):	120.00		
Wax Box, Series 1 (24):	2,400		
Wax Pack, Series 2 (5):	190.00		
Wax Box, Series 2 (24):	3,250		
1 Luis Aparicio	55.00	15.00	9.00
2 Woody Held	9.00	4.50	2.75
3 Frank Lary	9.00	4.50	2.75
4 Camilo Pascual	9.00	4.50	2.75
5 Frank Herrera	9.00	4.50	2.75
6 Felipe Alou	8.00	4.00	2.50
7 Bennie Daniels	9.00	4.50	2.75
8 Roger Craig	9.00	4.50	2.75
9 Eddie Kasko	9.00	4.50	2.75
10 Bob Grim	9.00	4.50	2.75
11 Jim Busby	9.00	4.50	2.75
12 Ken Boyer	17.50	8.75	5.25
13 Bob Boyd	9.00	4.50	2.75
14 Sam Jones	9.00	4.50	2.75
15 Larry Jackson	9.00	4.50	2.75
16 Roy Face	9.00	4.50	2.75
17 Walt Moryn	9.00	4.50	2.75
18 Jim Gilliam	8.00	4.00	2.50
19 Don Newcombe	8.00	4.00	2.50
20 Glen Hobbie	9.00	4.50	2.75
21 Pedro Ramos	9.00	4.50	2.75
22 Ryne Duren	8.00	4.00	2.50
23 Joe Jay	9.00	4.50	2.75
24 Lou Berberet	9.00	4.50	2.75
25a Jim Grant (White cap, photo actually Brooks Lawrence.)	15.00	7.50	4.50
25b Jim Grant (Dark cap, correct photo.)	22.50	11.00	6.75
26 Tom Borland	9.00	4.50	2.75
27 Brooks Robinson	25.00	12.50	7.50
28 Jerry Adair	9.00	4.50	2.75
29 Ron Jackson	9.00	4.50	2.75
30 George Strickland	9.00	4.50	2.75
31 Rocky Bridges	9.00	4.50	2.75
32 Bill Tuttle	9.00	4.50	2.75
33 Ken Hunt	9.00	4.50	2.75
34 Hal Griggs	9.00	4.50	2.75
35 Jim Coates	9.00	4.50	2.75
36 Brooks Lawrence	9.00	4.50	2.75
37 Duke Snider	30.00	15.00	9.00
38 Al Spangler	9.00	4.50	2.75
39 Jim Owens	9.00	4.50	2.75
40 Bill Virdon	9.00	4.50	2.75
41 Ernie Broglio	9.00	4.50	2.75
42 Andre Rodgers	9.00	4.50	2.75
43 Julio Becquer	9.00	4.50	2.75
44 Tony Taylor	9.00	4.50	2.75
45 Jerry Lynch	9.00	4.50	2.75
46 Clete Boyer	8.00	4.00	2.50
47 Jerry Lumpe	9.00	4.50	2.75
48 Charlie Maxwell	9.00	4.50	2.75
49 Jim Perry	9.00	4.50	2.75
50 Danny McDevitt	9.00	4.50	2.75
51 Juan Pizarro	9.00	4.50	2.75
52 *Dallas Green*	20.00	10.00	6.00
53 Bob Friend	9.00	4.50	2.75
54 Jack Sanford	9.00	4.50	2.75
55 Jim Rivera	9.00	4.50	2.75
56 Ted Wills	9.00	4.50	2.75
57 Milt Pappas	9.00	4.50	2.75
58a Hal Smith (Team & position on back.)	9.00	4.50	2.75
58b Hal Smith (Team blackened out on back.)	750.00	375.00	225.00
58c Hal Smith (Team missing on back.)	75.00	37.50	22.50
59 Bob Avila	9.00	4.50	2.75
60 Clem Labine	9.00	4.50	2.75
61 Vic Rehm	9.00	4.50	2.75
62 John Gabler	9.00	4.50	2.75
63 John Tsitouris	9.00	4.50	2.75
64 Dave Sisler	9.00	4.50	2.75
65 Vic Power	9.00	4.50	2.75
66 Earl Battey	9.00	4.50	2.75
67 Bob Purkey	9.00	4.50	2.75
68 Moe Drabowsky	9.00	4.50	2.75
69 Hoyt Wilhelm	15.00	7.50	4.50
70 Humberto Robinson	9.00	4.50	2.75
71 Whitey Herzog	9.00	4.50	2.75
72 Dick Donovan	9.00	4.50	2.75
73 Gordon Jones	12.00	6.00	3.50
74 Joe Hicks	12.00	6.00	3.50

75	*Ray Culp*	12.00	6.00	3.50
76	Dick Drott	12.00	6.00	3.50
77	Bob Duliba	12.00	6.00	3.50
78	Art Ditmar	12.00	6.00	3.50
79	Steve Korcheck	12.00	6.00	3.50
80	Henry Mason	12.00	6.00	3.50
81	Harry Simpson	12.00	6.00	3.50
82	Gene Green	12.00	6.00	3.50
83	Bob Shaw	12.00	6.00	3.50
84	Howard Reed	12.00	6.00	3.50
85	Dick Stigman	12.00	6.00	3.50
86	Rip Repulski	12.00	6.00	3.50
87	Seth Morehead	12.00	6.00	3.50
88	Camilo Carreon	12.00	6.00	3.50
89	John Blanchard	17.50	8.75	5.25
90	Billy Hoeft	12.00	6.00	3.50
91	Fred Hopke	12.00	6.00	3.50
92	Joe Martin	12.00	6.00	3.50
93	Wally Shannon	12.00	6.00	3.50
94	Baseball's Two Hal Smiths	50.00	25.00	15.00
95	Al Schroll	12.00	6.00	3.50
96	John Kucks	12.00	6.00	3.50
97	Tom Morgan	12.00	6.00	3.50
98	Willie Jones	12.00	6.00	3.50
99	Marshall Renfroe	12.00	6.00	3.50
100	Willie Tasby	12.00	6.00	3.50
101	Irv Noren	12.00	6.00	3.50
102	Russ Snyder	12.00	6.00	3.50
103	Bob Turley	17.50	8.75	5.25
104	Jim Woods	12.00	6.00	3.50
105	Ronnie Kline	12.00	6.00	3.50
106	Steve Bilko	12.00	6.00	3.50
107	Elmer Valo	12.00	6.00	3.50
108	Tom McAvoy	12.00	6.00	3.50
109	Stan Williams	12.00	6.00	3.50
110	Earl Averill	12.00	6.00	3.50
111	Lee Walls	12.00	6.00	3.50
112	Paul Richards	12.00	6.00	3.50
113	Ed Sadowski	12.00	6.00	3.50
114	Stover McIlwain (Photo actually Jim McAnany.)	17.50	8.75	5.25
115	Chuck Tanner (Photo actually Ken Kuhn.)	17.50	8.75	5.25
116	Lou Klimchock	12.00	6.00	3.50
117	Neil Chrisley	12.00	6.00	3.50
118	Johnny Callison	12.00	6.00	3.50
119	Hal Smith	12.00	6.00	3.50
120	Carl Sawatski	12.00	6.00	3.50
121	Frank Leja	12.00	6.00	3.50
122	Earl Torgeson	12.00	6.00	3.50
123	Art Schult	12.00	6.00	3.50
124	Jim Brosnan	12.00	6.00	3.50
125	Sparky Anderson	60.00	30.00	18.00
126	Joe Pignatano	12.00	6.00	3.50
127	Rocky Nelson	12.00	6.00	3.50
128	Orlando Cepeda	45.00	22.50	13.50
129	Daryl Spencer	12.00	6.00	3.50
130	Ralph Lumenti	12.00	6.00	3.50
131	Sam Taylor	12.00	6.00	3.50
132	Harry Brecheen	12.00	6.00	3.50
133	Johnny Groth	12.00	6.00	3.50
134	Wayne Terwilliger	12.00	6.00	3.50
135	Kent Hadley	12.00	6.00	3.50
136	Faye Throneberry	12.00	6.00	3.50
137	Jack Meyer	12.00	6.00	3.50
138	*Chuck Cottier*	12.00	6.00	3.50
139	Joe DeMaestri	12.00	6.00	3.50
140	Gene Freese	12.00	6.00	3.50
141	Curt Flood	30.00	15.00	9.00
142	Gino Cimoli	12.00	6.00	3.50
143	Clay Dalrymple	12.00	6.00	3.50
144	Jim Bunning	50.00	25.00	15.00

1923 Lections

EMIL MEUSEL
New York Giants

This series of cards was virtually unknown in the hobby until 1997 when 28 cards turned up in Albany, N.Y. The cards measure about 4" x 2-1/2" with rounded corners and are printed on very thick cardboard. At left front is an oval black-and-white player photo with name and team below. At right is green or orange art of a baseball game with the issuer's logo and trademark information. It is unknown with what, if any, product these cards were issued; a candy premium seems the most likely source. Most of the cards seen so far are in grades from Fair-Good, though a few are known in Ex-Mt.

		NM	EX	VG
Complete Set (10):		30,000	15,000	9,000
Common Player:		2,000	1,000	600.00
(1)	Frank Chance	3,500	1,750	1,050
(2)	Howard Ehmke	2,000	1,000	600.00
(3)	Frank Frisch	3,500	1,750	1,050
(4)	Roger (Rogers) Hornsby	5,000	2,500	1,500
(5)	Charles Jamieson	2,000	1,000	600.00
(6)	"Bob" Meusel	2,000	1,000	600.00

(7)	Emil Meusel	2,000	1,000	600.00
(8)	"Babe" Ruth	9,000	4,500	2,700
(9)	Charles Schmidt	2,000	1,000	600.00
(10)	"Bob" Shawkey	2,000	1,000	600.00

1975 Lee's Sweets

Baseball Greats

A series of 68 cards, of baseball's greatest players. Baseball is America's greatest game, a way of life. Most every child has at one time played baseball, and most every child has their favorite ballplayer.

Baseball is played in almost every corner of the world, by both young and old. These cards represent some of the greatest ballplayers that ever lived.

Lee's Sweets
Camp Hill, Ala.

Professing to be an issue of 68 cards of "Baseball Greats," this collectors' issue first appeared about 1975. Only four players are known. Fronts of the 2-1/2" x 3-3/16" cards have crudely printed black-and-white player photos. Backs describe the series and give the Lee's Sweets address as Camp Hill, Ala.

		NM	EX	VG
Complete Set (4):		25.00	12.50	7.50
Common Player:		6.00	3.00	1.75
(1)	Ty Cobb	6.00	3.00	1.75
(2)	Joe DiMaggio	6.00	3.00	1.75
(3)	Lou Gehrig	6.00	3.00	1.75
(4)	Babe Ruth	12.00	6.00	3.50

1909-11 Lenox Cigarettes

Many collectors rank the Lenox back as the third rarest among T206, behind only Ty Cobb and Drum. Lenox cards can be found with the back printing in either black or brown.

PREMIUMS
Black, Common Players: 12-15X
Black, Hall of Famers: 8-10X
Brown, Common Players: 75-100X
Brown, Hall of Famers: 40-60X
(See T206 for checklist and base card values.)

1969 Lincoln-Mercury Sports Panel Postcards

Various celebrity spokesmen on the Lincoln-Mercury Sports Panel can be found on a series of color postcards. In standard 5-1/2" x 3-1/2" format, cards have borderless color photos on front of the spokesman standing with one of the company's new cars; a facsimile autograph also appears. Divided backs identify the player and the automobile.

	NM	EX	VG
Al Kaline	80.00	40.00	25.00

1906 Lincoln Publishing Philadelphia A's

AMERICAN LEAGUE CHAMPIONS
1905 1906
GEORGE EDWARD WADDELL
ATHLETIC BASE BALL TEAM

Members of the American League Champions (says so right at the top) Philadelphia A's, decked out in their Sunday-best, are featured in this set of black-and-white postcards. The portraits are framed in fancy graphics which include a baseball, the dates 1905 and 1906 and the player's name in a banner beneath the photo. At bottom is a box with "ATHLETIC BASE BALL TEAM." Back of the approximately 3-1/2" x 5-1/2" cards has a box at upper-left enclosing "POST CARD." The unnumbered cards are listed here alphabetically.

		NM	EX	VG
Complete Set (20):		10,000	5,000	3,000
Common Player:		300.00	150.00	90.00
(1)	Chief Bender	1,500	750.00	450.00
(2)	Andy Coakley	300.00	150.00	90.00
(3)	Lave Cross	300.00	150.00	90.00
(4)	Monte Cross	300.00	150.00	90.00
(5)	Harry Davis	300.00	150.00	90.00
(6)	Jimmy Dygert	300.00	150.00	90.00
(7)	Topsy Hartsel	300.00	150.00	90.00
(8)	Weldon Henley	300.00	150.00	90.00
(9)	Danny Hoffman	300.00	150.00	90.00
(10)	John Knight	300.00	150.00	90.00
(11)	Bris Lord	300.00	150.00	90.00
(12)	Connie Mack	1,500	750.00	450.00
(13)	Danny Murphy	300.00	150.00	90.00
(14)	Joe Myers	300.00	150.00	90.00
(15)	Rube Oldring	300.00	150.00	90.00
(16)	Eddie Plank	2,000	1,000	600.00
(17)	Mike Powers	300.00	150.00	90.00
(18)	Ossee Schreckengost	300.00	150.00	90.00
(19)	Ralph Seybold	300.00	150.00	90.00
(20)	Rube Waddell	1,500	750.00	450.00

1975 Linnett MLB All-Stars

This series of pencil-portrait prints was done by sports artist Charles Linnett of Walpole, Mass. The black-and-white prints are on 8-1/2" x 11" textured paper, featuring a facsimile autograph of the player. Because the portraits are licensed only by the Players' Association, the players are pictured capless with no uniform logos visible. Backs are blank. The 1975 pictures differ from the 1976 issue in that they include a printed player name, besides the facsimile autograph. At least some of the portraits were given away in a ballpark "Portrait Day" promotion at Fenway Park, sponsored by Grant City (W.T. Grant Co.) department stores. A coupon accompanying the SGA portraits offered a discount on a package of three pictures, apparently the standard retail offering that carried a $1.19 price tag. This rudimentary checklist is certainly incomplete.

		NM	EX	VG
Common Player:		6.00	3.00	1.75
(25)	Fred Lynn	9.00	4.50	2.75
(50)	Tom Seaver	9.00	4.50	2.75
(75)	Carl Yastrzemski	12.00	6.00	3.50

1976 Linnett Portraits

This series of pencil-portrait prints was done by sports artist Charles Linnett of Walpole, Mass., and includes baseball, football, hockey, NBA and Harlem Globetrotters players (only baseball listed here). The black-and-white prints are on 8-1/2" x 11" textured paper, featuring a facsimile autograph of the player. Because the portraits are licensed only by the Players' Association, the players are pictured capless with no uniform logos visible. Backs are blank. The portraits originally sold for 50 cents apiece by mail.

		NM	EX	VG
Complete Baseball Set (176):		300.00	150.00	90.00
Common Player:		2.50	1.25	.75
(1)	Hank Aaron	10.00	5.00	3.00
(2)	Dick Allen	4.00	2.00	1.25
(3)	Matty Alou	2.50	1.25	.75
(4)	Mike Anderson	2.50	1.25	.75
(5)	Luis Aparicio	5.00	2.50	1.50
(6)	Sal Bando	2.50	1.25	.75
(7)	Mark Belanger	2.50	1.25	.70
(8)	Buddy Bell	2.50	1.25	.75
(9)	Johnny Bench	6.00	3.00	1.75
(10)	Jim Bibby	2.50	1.25	.75
(11)	Paul Blair	2.50	1.25	.75
(12)	Bert Blyleven	3.00	1.50	.90
(13)	Ron Blomberg	2.50	1.25	.75
(14)	Bob Bolin	2.50	1.25	.75
(15)	Bill Bonham	2.50	1.25	.75
(16)	Pedro Borbon	2.50	1.25	.75
(17)	Bob Boone	3.00	1.50	.90
(18)	Larry Bowa	2.50	1.25	.75
(19)	Steve Braun	2.50	1.25	.75
(20)	Ken Brett	2.50	1.25	.75
(21)	John Briggs	2.50	1.25	.75
(22)	Lou Brock	5.00	2.50	1.50
(23)	Jack Brohamer	2.50	1.25	.75
(24)	Steve Brye	2.50	1.25	.75
(25)	Bill Buckner	2.50	1.25	.70
(26)	Jeff Burroughs	2.50	1.25	.75
(27)	Steve Busby	2.50	1.25	.75
(28)	Bert Campaneris	2.50	1.25	.75
(29)	Bernie Carbo	2.50	1.25	.75
(30)	Jose Cardenal	2.50	1.25	.75
(31)	Steve Carlton	5.00	2.50	1.50
(32)	Rod Carew	5.00	2.50	1.50
(33)	Dave Cash	2.50	1.25	.75
(34)	Norm Cash	3.00	1.50	.90
(35)	Danny Cater	2.50	1.25	.75
(36)	Cesar Cedeno	2.50	1.25	.75
(37)	Orlando Cepeda	5.00	2.50	1.50
(38)	Ron Cey	2.50	1.25	.70
(39)	Chris Chambliss	2.50	1.25	.75
(40)	David Clyde	2.50	1.25	.75
(41)	Rich Coggins	2.50	1.25	.75
(42)	Jim Colborn	2.50	1.25	.75
(43)	Dave Concepcion	3.00	1.50	.90
(44)	Willie Crawford	2.50	1.25	.75
(45)	John Curtis	2.50	1.25	.75
(46)	Bobby Darwin	2.50	1.25	.75
(47)	Dan Driessen	2.50	1.25	.75
(48)	Duffy Dyer	2.50	1.25	.75
(49)	John Ellis	2.50	1.25	.75
(50)	Darrell Evans	2.50	1.25	.70
(51)	Dwight Evans	2.50	1.25	.70
(52)	Joe Ferguson	2.50	1.25	.75
(53)	Rollie Fingers	4.00	2.00	1.25
(54)	Carlton Fisk	5.00	2.50	1.50
(55)	Bill Freehan	2.50	1.25	.75
(56)	Jim Fregosi	2.50	1.25	.75
(57)	Oscar Gamble	2.50	1.25	.75
(58)	Pedro Garcia	2.50	1.25	.75
(59)	Ralph Garr	2.50	1.25	.75
(60)	Wayne Garrett	2.50	1.25	.75
(61)	Steve Garvey	2.50	1.25	.70
(62)	Cesar Geronimo	2.50	1.25	.75
(63)	Bob Gibson	5.00	2.50	1.50
(64)	Dave Giusti	2.50	1.25	.75
(65)	Bobby Grich	2.50	1.25	.75
(66)	Doug Griffin	2.50	1.25	.75
(67)	Mario Guerrero	2.50	1.25	.75
(68)	Don Gullett	2.50	1.25	.75
(69)	Tommy Harper	2.50	1.25	.75
(70)	Toby Harrah	2.50	1.25	.75
(71)	Bud Harrelson	2.50	1.25	.75
(72)	Vic Harris	2.50	1.25	.75
(73)	Richie Hebner	2.50	1.25	.75
(74)	George Hendrick	2.50	1.25	.75
(75)	Ed Hermann	2.50	1.25	.75
(76)	John Hiller	2.50	1.25	.75
(77)	Willie Horton	2.50	1.25	.75
(78)	Jim Hunter	4.00	2.00	1.25
(79)	Tommy Hutton	2.50	1.25	.75
(80)	Reggie Jackson	7.50	3.75	2.25
(81)	Fergie Jenkins	4.00	2.00	1.25
(82)	Dave Johnson	2.50	1.25	.75
(83)	Cleon Jones	2.50	1.25	.75
(84)	Al Kaline	6.00	3.00	1.75
(85)	John Kennedy	2.50	1.25	.75
(86)	Steve Kline	2.50	1.25	.75
(87)	Jerry Koosman	2.50	1.25	.75
(88)	Bill Lee	2.50	1.25	.75
(89)	Eddie Leon	2.50	1.25	.75
(90)	Bob Locker	2.50	1.25	.75
(91)	Mickey Lolich	3.00	1.50	.90
(92)	Jim Lonborg	2.50	1.25	.75
(93)	Davey Lopes	2.50	1.25	.75
(94)	Mike Lum	2.50	1.25	.75
(95)	Greg Luzinski	2.50	1.25	.75
(96)	Sparky Lyle	2.50	1.25	.75
(97)	Teddy Martinez	2.50	1.25	.75
(98)	Jon Matlack	2.50	1.25	.75
(99)	Dave May	2.50	1.25	.75
(100)	John Mayberry	2.50	1.25	.75
(101)	Willie Mays	10.00	5.00	3.00
(102)	Jim McAndrew	2.50	1.25	.75
(103)	Dick McAuliffe	2.50	1.25	.75
(104)	Sam McDowell	2.50	1.25	.70
(105)	Lynn McGlothen	2.50	1.25	.70
(106)	Tug McGraw	2.50	1.25	.70
(107)	Hal McRae	2.50	1.25	.75
(108)	Bill Melton	2.50	1.25	.75
(109)	Andy Messersmith	2.50	1.25	.75
(110)	Gene Michael	2.50	1.25	.75
(111)	Felix Millan	2.50	1.25	.75
(112)	Rick Miller	2.50	1.25	.75
(113)	John Milner	2.50	1.25	.75
(114)	Rick Monday	2.50	1.25	.75
(115)	Don Money	2.50	1.25	.75
(116)	Bob Montgomery	2.50	1.25	.75
(117)	Joe Morgan	5.00	2.50	1.50
(118)	Carl Morton	2.50	1.25	.75
(119)	Thurman Munson	4.00	2.00	1.25
(120)	Bobby Murcer	2.50	1.25	.75
(121)	Graig Nettles	3.00	1.50	.90
(122)	Jim Northrup	2.50	1.25	.75
(123)	Ben Oglivie	2.50	1.25	.75
(124)	Al Oliver	3.00	1.50	.90
(125)	Bob Oliver	2.50	1.25	.75
(126)	Jorge Orta	2.50	1.25	.75
(127)	Amos Otis	2.50	1.25	.75
(128)	Jim Palmer	5.00	2.50	1.50
(129)	Harry Parker	2.50	1.25	.75
(130)	Fred Patek	2.50	1.25	.75
(131)	Marty Pattin	2.50	1.25	.75
(132)	Tony Perez	4.00	2.00	1.25
(133)	Gaylord Perry	4.00	2.00	1.25
(134)	Jim Perry	2.50	1.25	.75
(135)	Rico Petrocelli	2.50	1.25	.75
(136)	Rick Reichardt	2.50	1.25	.75
(137)	Ken Reitz	2.50	1.25	.75
(138)	Jerry Reuss	2.50	1.25	.75
(139)	Bill Robinson	2.50	1.25	.75
(140)	Brooks Robinson	5.00	2.50	1.50
(141)	Frank Robinson	5.00	2.50	1.50
(142)	Cookie Rojas	2.50	1.25	.75
(143)	Pete Rose	9.00	4.50	2.75
(144)	Bill Russell	2.50	1.25	.75
(145)	Nolan Ryan	15.00	7.50	4.50
(146)	Manny Sanguillen	2.50	1.25	.75
(147)	George Scott	2.50	1.25	.75
(148)	Mike Schmidt	7.50	3.75	2.25
(149)	Tom Seaver	6.00	3.00	1.75
(150)	Sonny Siebert	2.50	1.25	.75
(151)	Ted Simmons	2.50	1.25	.75
(152)	Bill Singer	2.50	1.25	.75
(153)	Reggie Smith	2.50	1.25	.75
(154)	Chris Speier	2.50	1.25	.75
(155)	Charlie Spikes	2.50	1.25	.75
(156)	Paul Splittorff	2.50	1.25	.75
(157)	Mickey Stanley	2.50	1.25	.75
(158)	Lee Stanton	2.50	1.25	.75
(159)	Willie Stargell	5.00	2.50	1.50
(160)	Rusty Staub	3.00	1.50	.90
(161)	Rennie Stennett	2.50	1.25	.75
(162)	Steve Stone	3.00	1.50	.90
(163)	Mel Stottlemyre	2.50	1.25	.75
(164)	Don Sutton	4.00	2.00	1.25
(165)	George Theodore	2.50	1.25	.75
(166)	Danny Thompson	2.50	1.25	.75
(167)	Luis Tiant	3.00	1.50	.90
(168)	Joe Torre	3.50	1.75	1.00
(169)	Bobby Valentine	2.50	1.25	.75
(170)	Bob Veale	2.50	1.25	.75
(171)	Billy Williams	5.00	2.50	1.50
(172)	Wilbur Wood	2.50	1.25	.75
(173)	Jim Wynn	2.50	1.25	.75
(174)	Carl Yastrzemski	6.00	3.00	1.75
(175)	Robin Yount	5.00	2.50	1.50
(175)	Richie Zisk	2.50	1.25	.75

1976 Linnett Superstars

This frequently encountered set of 36 cards has enjoyed little collector interest since its issue in 1976. Officially known as "Pee-Wee Superstars," the cards measure 4" x 5-5/8". Player portraits by artist Charles Linnett are rendered in black-and-white pencil and set against a pale yellow background. Players are shown without caps or uniforms (most appear to be wearing white T-shirts). According to the logos at top the set was fully licensed by both the players' association and Major League Baseball, and team logos do appear in the lower-left corner. A facsimile autograph in red or purple appears on each card. Front borders are bright purple, red, green, dark brown or white. Card backs feature either a photo of an antique auto or a drawing of an historic sailing ship. Each of the 12 different back designs appears on one card from each team set. The

Linnetts were sold in panels of six perforated cards. An offer on the back of each card makes 8 x 10" premium portraits of each player available for 95 cents. The premium pictures have about the same value as the cards. Inexplicably, the cards are numbered from 90-125. Only the World's Champion Cincinnati Reds, A.L. Champion Boston Red Sox and N.L. runner-up Dodgers are represented in the issue.

		NM	EX	VG
Complete Panel Set (6):		15.00	7.50	4.50
Complete Singles Set (36):		15.00	7.50	4.50
Common Player:		.60	.30	.20
Panel 1		7.50	3.75	2.25
90	Don Gullett	.60	.30	.20
91	Johnny Bench	2.50	1.25	.70
92	Tony Perez	1.25	.60	.40
93	Mike Lum	.60	.30	.20
94	Ken Griffey	.60	.30	.20
95	George Foster	.60	.30	.20
Panel 2		9.00	4.50	2.75
96	Joe Morgan	2.50	1.25	.70
97	Pete Rose	6.00	3.00	1.75
98	Dave Concepcion	.60	.30	.20
99	Cesar Geronimo	.60	.30	.20
100	Dan Driessen	.60	.30	.20
101	Pedro Borbon	.60	.30	.20
Panel 3		7.50	3.75	2.25
102	Carl Yastrzemski	2.50	1.25	.70
103	Fred Lynn	.60	.30	.20
104	Dwight Evans	.60	.30	.20
105	Ferguson Jenkins	1.25	.60	.40
106	Rico Petrocelli	.60	.30	.20
107	Denny Doyle	.60	.30	.20
Panel 4		6.00	3.00	1.75
108	Luis Tiant	.60	.30	.20
109	Carlton Fisk	2.50	1.25	.70
110	Rick Burleson	.60	.30	.20
111	Bill Lee	.60	.30	.20
112	Rick Wise	.60	.30	.20
113	Jim Rice	1.00	.50	.30
Panel 5		6.00	3.00	1.75
114	Davey Lopes	.60	.30	.20
115	Steve Garvey	1.25	.60	.40
116	Bill Russell	.60	.30	.20
117	Ron Cey	.60	.30	.20
118	Steve Yaeger	.60	.30	.20
119	Doug Rau	.60	.30	.20
Panel 6		6.00	3.00	1.75
120	Don Sutton	1.75	.90	.50
121	Joe Ferguson	.60	.30	.20
122	Mike Marshall	.60	.30	.20
123	Bill Buckner	.60	.30	.20
124	Rick Rhoden	.60	.30	.20
125	Ted Sizemore	.60	.30	.20

1923 Little Wonder Picture Series

Some versions of the W515-2 strip cards are found with part of a line of type in the top border that reads "THE LITTLE WONDER PICTURE SERIES" and includes a Underwood (U&U) logo.

(See W515-2)

1887 Lone Jack St. Louis Browns (N370)

The Lone Jack set is among the rarest of all 19th Century tobacco issues. Issued by the Lone Jack Cigarette Co. of Lynchburg, Va., the set consists of 13 subjects, all members of the American Association champion St. Louis Browns. Photos for the set are enlarged versions of those used in the more popular N172 Old Judge series. Cards in the set measure 2-1/2" x 1-1/2" and carry an ad for Lone Jack Cigarettes along the bottom of the front. The set features the Browns' starting lineup for 1886 along with their two top pitchers, backup catcher and owner, Chris Von Der Ahe.

		NM	EX	VG
Common Player:		11,000	6,500	4,500
(1)	Doc Bushong	11,000	6,500	4,500
(2)	Parisian Bob Caruthers	11,000	6,500	4,500
(3)	Charles Commiskey (Comiskey)	40,000	12,000	8,000
(4)	Dave Foutz	11,000	6,500	4,500
(5)	Will Gleason	11,000	6,500	4,500
(6)	Nat Hudson	11,000	6,500	4,500
(7)	Rudy Kimler (Kemmler)	11,000	6,500	4,500
(8)	Arlie Latham	11,000	6,500	4,500
(9)	Little Nick Nicol	11,000	6,500	4,500
(10)	Tip O'Neil (O'Neill)	11,000	6,500	4,500
(11)	Yank Robinson	11,000	6,500	4,500
(12)	Chris Von Der Ahe	15,000	9,000	6,000
(13)	Curt Welsh (Welch)	11,000	6,500	4,500

1886 Lorillard Team Cards

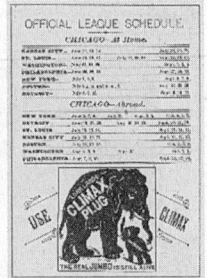

Issued in 1886 by Lorillard Tobacco Co., these 4" x 5-1/2" cards were issued for the Chicago, Detroit and New York baseball clubs. Each card carries the team's schedule (starting with June) on one side and features 11 player portraits enclosed in circles on the other. Each side has advertising for one of Lorillard's tobacco brands - Climax, Rebecca, etc.

		NM	EX	VG
Complete Set (4):		45,000	22,500	13,500
Common Team:		7,500	3,750	2,200
(1)	Chicago League Base Ball Club	13,500	6,750	4,050
(2)	Detroit League Base Ball Club	12,000	6,000	3,600
(3)	New York League Base Ball Club	10,000	5,000	3,000
(4)	Philadelphia League Base Ball Club	7,500	3,750	2,250

1949 Lummis Peanut Butter Phillies

This 12-card regional set featuring the Phillies was issued in the Philadelphia area by Lummis Peanut Butter in 1949. The cards measure 3-1/4" x 4-1/4" and are unnumbered. The fronts feature an action photo with a facsimile autograph, while the backs advertise a game ticket promotion by Lummis Peanut Butter. The same photos and checklist were also used for a regional sticker set issued by Sealtest Dairy the same year.

		NM	EX	VG
Complete Set (12):		22,500	11,250	6,750
Common Player:		1,350	675.00	400.00
(1)	Rich Ashburn	4,500	2,250	1,350
(2)	Hank Borowy	1,350	675.00	400.00
(3)	Del Ennis	1,500	750.00	450.00
(4)	Granny Hamner	1,350	675.00	400.00
(5)	Puddinhead Jones	1,350	675.00	400.00
(6)	Russ Meyer	1,350	675.00	400.00
(7)	Bill Nicholson	1,350	675.00	400.00
(8)	Robin Roberts	4,500	2,250	1,350
(9)	"Schoolboy" Rowe	1,350	675.00	400.00
(10)	Andy Seminick	1,350	675.00	400.00
(11)	Curt Simmons	1,500	750.00	450.00
(12)	Eddie Waitkus	1,350	675.00	400.00

1910 Luxello Cigars A's/Phillies Pins (P13)

Players from the two Philadelphia teams are pictured in this series of 7/8" black-and-white pins. The player's last name, team and position are printed below the photo; the Luxello Cigar name at top. On left and right are a horseshoe with monogram inside.

		NM	EX	VG
Complete Set (21):		17,500	8,750	5,250
Common Player:		750.00	375.00	225.00
	Philadelphia Athletics			
(1)	Franklin Baker	1,500	750.00	450.00
(2)	Jack Barry	750.00	375.00	225.00
(3)	Eddie Collins	1,500	750.00	450.00
(4)	John W. Coombs	750.00	375.00	225.00
(5)	Harry Davis	750.00	375.00	225.00
(6)	James Dygert	750.00	375.00	225.00
(7)	Heinie Heitmuller	750.00	375.00	225.00
(8)	Harry Krause	750.00	375.00	225.00
(9)	Paddy Livingston	750.00	375.00	225.00
(10)	Danny Murphy	750.00	375.00	225.00
(11)	Ed Plank	1,500	750.00	450.00
	Philadelphia Phillies			
(12)	John W. Bates	750.00	375.00	225.00
(13)	Chas. S. Dooin	750.00	375.00	225.00
(14)	Mike Doolan	750.00	375.00	225.00
(15)	Eddie Grant	750.00	375.00	225.00
(16)	Otto Knabe	750.00	375.00	225.00
(17)	Geo. McQuillan	750.00	375.00	225.00
(18)	Earl Moore	750.00	375.00	225.00
(19)	Lew Moren	750.00	375.00	225.00
(20)	Tully Sparks	750.00	375.00	225.00
(21)	John Titus	750.00	375.00	225.00

1912 L1 Leathers

One of the more unusual baseball collectibles of the tobacco era, the L1 "Leathers" were issued by Helmar Tobacco Co. in 1912 as a premium with its "Turkish Trophies" brand of cigarettes. The set featured 25 of the top baseball players and shared a checklist with the closely-related S81 "Silks," which were another part of the same promotion. The "Leathers," advertised as being 10" x 12", featured

drawings of baseball players on horsehide-shaped pieces of leather. The drawings were based on the pictures used for the popular T3 Turkey Red series issued a year earlier. Twenty of the 25 players in the "Leathers" set are from the T3 set. Five pitchers (Rube Marquard, Rube Benton, Marty O'Toole, Grover Alexander and Russ Ford) not pictured in T3 were added to the "Leathers" set, and the Frank Baker error was corrected. According to the promotion, each "Leather" was available in exchange for 50 Helmar coupons. In addition to the 25 baseball stars, the "Leathers" set also included more than 100 other subjects, including female athletes and bathing beauties, famous generals, Indian chiefs, actresses, national flags, college mascots and others.

		NM	EX	VG
Common Player:		3,000	1,500	900.00
86	Rube Marquard	7,500	3,750	2,250
87	Marty O'Toole	3,000	1,500	900.00
88	Rube Benton	3,000	1,500	900.00
89	Grover Alexander	8,500	4,250	2,550
90	Russ Ford	3,000	1,500	900.00
91	John McGraw	7,500	3,750	2,250
92	Nap Rucker	3,000	1,500	900.00
93	Mike Mitchell	3,000	1,500	900.00
94	Chief Bender	7,500	3,750	2,250
95	Home Run Baker	7,500	3,750	2,250
96	Nap Lajoie	7,500	3,750	2,250
97	Joe Tinker	7,500	3,750	2,250
98	Sherry Magee	3,000	1,500	900.00
99	Howie Camnitz	3,000	1,500	900.00
100	Eddie Collins	7,500	3,750	2,250
101	Red Dooin	3,000	1,500	900.00
102	Ty Cobb	45,000	22,500	13,500
103	Hugh Jennings	7,500	3,750	2,250
104	Roger Bresnahan	7,000	3,500	2,100
105	Jake Stahl	3,000	1,500	900.00
106	Tris Speaker	8,500	4,250	2,550
107	Ed Walsh	7,000	3,500	2,100
108	Christy Mathewson	15,000	7,500	4,500
109	Johnny Evers	7,000	3,500	2,100
110	Walter Johnson	15,000	7,500	4,500

M

1947 Mabley & Carew Cincinnati Reds

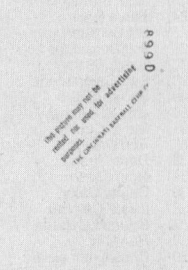

Pictures of Reds players and staff were given away and sold by the boys' shop of the Cincinnati department store. The black-and-white glossy photos measure 3-5/8" x 5-1/16" and have a white border. Backs have a rubber-stamped alpha-numeric identifier and the notice: "This picture may not be rented nor used for advertising purposes. The Cincinnati Baseball Club." The players are not named on the pictures. Small groups of pictures were apparently given away in a tan-and-orange paper folder measuring about 3-7/8" x 5-1/4". The folder pictures the store, has a team roster and schedule and a coupon for purchasing addtional photos at a relatively hefty 10 cents apiece. The pictures are listed here alphabetically.

		NM	EX	VG
Complete Set (28):		850.00	425.00	250.00
Common Player:		30.00	15.00	9.00
Folder:		60.00	30.00	18.00
(1)	Bob Adams	30.00	15.00	9.00
(2)	Frank Baumholtz	30.00	15.00	9.00
(3)	Ewell Blackwell	40.00	20.00	12.00
(4)	Ed Erautt	30.00	15.00	9.00
(5)	Augie Galan	30.00	15.00	9.00
(6)	Harry Gumbert	30.00	15.00	9.00
(7)	Bert Haas	30.00	15.00	9.00
(8)	Grady Hatton	30.00	15.00	9.00
(9)	John Hetki	30.00	15.00	9.00
(10)	George Kelly	30.00	15.00	9.00
(11)	Ray Lamanno	30.00	15.00	9.00
(12)	Everett Lively	30.00	15.00	9.00
(13)	Ed Lukon	30.00	15.00	9.00
(14)	Eddie Miller	30.00	15.00	9.00
(15)	Ray Mueller	30.00	15.00	9.00
(16)	John Neun	30.00	15.00	9.00
(17)	Phil Page	30.00	15.00	9.00
(18)	Kent Peterson	30.00	15.00	9.00

		NM	EX	VG
(19)	Hugh Poland	30.00	15.00	9.00
(20)	Ken Raffensberger	30.00	15.00	9.00
(21)	Elmer Riddle	30.00	15.00	9.00
(22)	Tom Tatum	30.00	15.00	9.00
(23)	Johnny Vander Meer	40.00	20.00	12.00
(24)	Clyde Vollmer	30.00	15.00	9.00
(25)	Kermit Wahl	30.00	15.00	9.00
(26)	Bucky Walters	30.00	15.00	9.00
(27)	Babe Young	30.00	15.00	9.00
(28)	Ben Zientara	30.00	15.00	9.00

1950s-70s MacGregor Advisory Staff Photos

MacGregor "THE CHOICE OF THOSE WHO PLAY THE GAME"

Advisory staff photos were a promotional item which debuted in the early 1950s, flourished in the Sixties and died in the early 1970s. Generally 8" x 10" (sometimes a little larger), these black-and-white (a few later were color) glossy photos picture players who had contracted with a major baseball equipment company to endorse and use their product. Usually the product - most often a glove - was prominently displayed in the photo. The pictures were often displayed in the windows of sporting goods stores or the walls of sports departments and were sometimes made available to customers. Because the companies tended to stick with players over the years, some photos were reissued, sometimes with and sometimes without a change of team, pose or typography. All MacGregor staff photos of the era are checklisted here in alphabetical order. Team designation and pose description is given for each known picture. The photos are checklisted here in alphabetical order. It is unlikely this list is complete. Several arrangements of typography in the bottom border are seen and some photos have a facsimile autograph.

	NM	EX	VG
Common Player:	15.00	7.50	4.50
Hank Aaron/Btg/Color (Atlanta)	25.00	12.50	7.50
Richie Ashburn (Cubs, full-length, hands on knees.)	25.00	12.50	7.50
Richie Ashburn (Phillies, full-length, hands on knees.)	40.00	20.00	12.00
Gus Bell/Kneeling (Reds)	15.00	7.50	4.50
Ed Bouchee (Phillies, upper body.)	15.00	7.50	4.50
Ed Brinkman (Senators, upper body.)	15.00	7.50	4.50
Roberto Clemente (Full-length.)	125.00	65.00	35.00
Del Crandall (Braves, catching crouch in gear, large.)	15.00	7.50	4.50
Del Crandall (Braves, catching crouch in gear, small.)	15.00	7.50	4.50
Del Crandall (Braves, catching crouch, no gear.)	15.00	7.50	4.50
Del Crandall (Braves, kneeling, glove on knee.)	15.00	7.50	4.50
Al Downing (Dodgers, glove at waist.)	15.00	7.50	4.50
Al Downing (Yankees, upper body.)	15.00	7.50	4.50
Ron Hansen/Fielding (White Sox)	15.00	7.50	4.50
Tommy Helms (Reds, full-length.)	15.00	7.50	4.50
Randy Hundley (Cubs, upper body.)	15.00	7.50	4.50
Jackie Jensen (Red Sox, chest-up.)	15.00	7.50	4.50
Jack Jensen (Red Sox, full-length, batting.)	15.00	7.50	4.50
Jack Jensen (Red Sox, full-length, hands on knees.)	15.00	7.50	4.50
Ralph Kiner (Cubs, hands on knees.)	30.00	15.00	9.00
Ralph Kiner (Pirates, full-length.)	25.00	12.50	7.50
Ted Kluszewski/Btg (Reds)	25.00	12.50	7.50
Ted Kluszewski/Fielding (White Sox)	25.00	12.50	7.50
Ted Kluszewski/Portrait (Reds)	35.00	17.50	10.00
Johnny Kucks/Pitching (Yankees)	15.00	7.50	4.50
Willie Mays (Giants, full-length.)	90.00	45.00	27.00
Bill Mazeroski/Btg (Pirates)	30.00	15.00	9.00

	NM	EX	VG
Mike McCormick (Giants, follow-through.)	15.00	7.50	4.50
Gil McDougald/Throwing (Yankees)	15.00	7.50	4.50
Gil McDougald (Yankees, upper-body portrait.)	15.00	7.50	4.50
Tony Oliva/Btg (Twins)	15.00	7.50	4.50
Tony Oliva (Twins, upper body.)	15.00	7.50	4.50
Claude Osteen/Pitching (Dodgers)	15.00	7.50	4.50
Claude Osteen/Portrait (Dodgers)	15.00	7.50	4.50
Juan Pizzaro (White Sox, follow-through.)	15.00	7.50	4.50
Robin Roberts/Portrait (Phillies)	25.00	12.50	7.50
Robin Roberts (Phillies, follow-through.)	25.00	12.50	7.50
Frank Robinson/Portrait (Orioles)	25.00	12.50	7.50
Pete Ros/Kneeling (Reds)	35.00	17.50	10.00
Pete Rose (Reds, leading off, color.)	65.00	32.50	20.00
Pete Rose (Reds, chest-to-cap portrait.)	35.00	17.50	10.00
Al Schoendienst/Kneeling (Cardinals)	25.00	12.50	7.50
Warren Spahn (Boston Braves, follow-through.)	25.00	12.50	7.50
Daryl Spencer (Cardinals, fielding grounder.)	15.00	7.50	4.50
Don Sutton (Dodgers, color, ready to pitch.)	20.00	10.00	6.00
Frank Torre (Braves, ready to throw.)	15.00	7.50	4.50

1960 MacGregor

MacGregor BASEBALL ADVISORY STAFF OF CHAMPIONS

The MacGregor Sporting Goods Co. was one of the pioneers in celebrity marketing, creating an advisory staff in 1960 to promote its products. The 25-card set features black-and-white photography of several stars and lesser lights, and even a couple of managers. The cards are 3-3/4" x 5" with a thin white border and the words "MacGregor Baseball Advisory Staff of Champions" on the bottom panel. The cards are not numbered and are blank-backed, and include a facsimile autograph in white on the front photo. The checklist is arranged here alphabetically.

		NM	EX	VG
Complete Set (25):		700.00	350.00	210.00
Common Player:		15.00	7.50	4.50
1	Hank Aaron	110.00	55.00	35.00
2	Richie Ashburn	35.00	17.50	10.00
3	Gus Bell	15.00	7.50	4.50
4	Lou Berberet	15.00	7.50	4.50
5	Jerry Casale	15.00	7.50	4.50
6	Del Crandall	15.00	7.50	4.50
7	Art Ditmar	15.00	7.50	4.50
8	Gene Freese	15.00	7.50	4.50
9	James Gilliam	17.50	8.75	5.25
10	Ted Kluszewski	35.00	17.50	10.00
11	Jim Landis	15.00	7.50	4.50
12	Al Lopez	30.00	15.00	9.00
13	Willie Mays	110.00	55.00	35.00
14	Bill Mazeroski	35.00	17.50	10.00
15	Mike McCormick	15.00	7.50	4.50
16	Gil McDougald	15.00	7.50	4.50
17	Russ Nixon	15.00	7.50	4.50
18	Bill Rigney	15.00	7.50	4.50
19	Robin Roberts	35.00	17.50	10.00
20	Frank Robinson	45.00	22.50	13.50
21	John Roseboro	15.00	7.50	4.50
22	Red Schoendienst	35.00	17.50	10.00
23	Bill Skowron	20.00	10.00	6.00
24	Daryl Spencer	15.00	7.50	4.50
25	Johnny Temple	15.00	7.50	4.50

1960-70s MacGregor Pete Rose

Besides the several series of card issues and Advisory Staff photos issued over the years, MacGregor produced a number of special Pete Rose cards to promote its relationship with one of baseball's top stars of the 1960s and 1970s. All cards in this listing are in black-and-white with blank backs. The 1965-66 cards are 3-1/2" x 5". The later cards are 5" x 7-1/4" to 7-1/2".

PETE ROSE, Member of the MacGregor Advisory Staff

		NM	EX	VG
1965	Pete Rose (Full-length photo, crouching w/glove.)	200.00	100.00	60.00
1966	Pete Rose (Half-length photo, crouching w/glove.)	200.00	100.00	60.00
1969	Pete Rose (Portrait to chest.)	100.00	50.00	30.00
1970	Pete Rose/Fielding (White background.)	75.00	37.50	22.00
1973	Pete Rose/Portrait	75.00	37.50	22.00
1974	Pete Rose (Portrait to waist, w/glove.)	75.00	37.50	22.00

1965 MacGregor

WILLIE MAYS
MEMBER OF THE MacGregor BRUNSWICK
ADVISORY STAFF

The 1965 MacGregor set is similar to earlier issues, with only a slight change in dimension to 3-1/2" x 5-1/8" and reduced in size to only 10 players. The cards are blank-backed and unnumbered and have a glossy finish. They are checklisted here alphabetically.

		NM	EX	VG
Complete Set (10):		375.00	185.00	110.00
Common Player:		10.00	5.00	3.00
(1)	Roberto Clemente	150.00	75.00	45.00
(2)	Al Downing	10.00	5.00	3.00
(3)	Johnny Edwards	10.00	5.00	3.00
(4)	Ron Hansen	10.00	5.00	3.00
(5)	Deron Johnson	10.00	5.00	3.00
(6)	Willie Mays	135.00	65.00	40.00
(7)	Tony Oliva	15.00	7.50	4.50
(8)	Claude Osteen	10.00	5.00	3.00
(9)	Bobby Richardson	15.00	7.50	4.50
(10)	Zoilo Versalles	10.00	5.00	3.00

1970s MacGregor Advisory Staff Photos

Henry Aaron Member of the MacGregor Advisory Staff

This advisory staff photo series was among the last in a line of promotional items which debuted in the early 1950s, flourished in the Sixties and died in the 1970s. While earlier advisory staff photos were generally 8" x 10", this later series of black-and-white glossy photos is in a 5" x 7" format. They picture players who had contracted with MacGregor to endorse and use its product. The pictures were often displayed in the windows of sporting goods stores or the walls of sports departments and were sometimes made available to customers. Because the companies tended to stick with players over the years, some photos were reissued, sometimes with a change of team, pose or typography. Known MacGregor staff photos of the era are checklisted here in alphabetical order. Team designation and pose description is given for each picture. It is unlikely this list is complete. Gaps have been left in the assigned numbering to accommodate future additions.

		NM	EX	VG
Common Player:		15.00	7.50	4.50
(1)	Hank Aaron	40.00	20.00	12.00
	(Braves, chest-to-cap.)			
(2)	Rod Carew	25.00	12.50	7.50
	(Twins, chest-to-cap.)			
(3)	Rod Carew	25.00	12.50	7.50
	(Twins, chin-to-cap.)			
(5)	George Foster	15.00	7.50	4.50
	(Reds, chest-to-cap.)			
(8)	Lee May	15.00	7.50	4.50
	(Orioles, chest-to-cap.)			
(10)	Joe Morgan	25.00	12.50	7.50
	(Reds, neck-to-cap.)			
(11)	Joe Morgan	25.00	12.50	7.50
	(Reds, waist-to-cap.)			
(12)	Thurman Munson	27.50	13.50	8.25
	(Yankees, neck-to-cap.)			
(15)	Tony Perez	25.00	12.50	7.50
	(Reds, neck-to-cap.)			
(16)	Tony Perez	25.00	12.50	7.50
	(Expos, chest-to-cap.)			
(20)	Don Sutton	20.00	10.00	6.00
	(Dodgers, chest-to-cap.)			
(21)	Don Sutton	20.00	10.00	6.00
	(Dodgers, neck-to-cap.)			

1975 MacGregor Advisory Staff Poster

This 19-1/2" x 26" color poster features Pete Rose in a game-action photo, leading off at first base. Two lines of type, "Winners Play MacGregor" and "The Greatest Name In Sports" are centered above the picture. Back is blank.

	NM	EX	VG
Pete Rose	50.00	25.00	15.00

1886 MacIntire Studio Cabinets

The number of baseball players who found themselves in front of the lens at the MacIntire photography studio in Philadelphia is unknown, but all those thus far seen were members of the 1886 Philadelphia National League team. In standard cabinet-card format of about 3-3/4" x 5-3/4", the pieces feature a cream-colored mount with a sepia photo.

		NM	EX	VG
Common Player:		4,500	3,000	2,000
(1)	Tony Cusick	4,500	3,000	2,000
(2)	Edward Dailey	4,500	3,000	2,000
(3)	Jack Farrell	4,500	3,000	2,000
(4)	Charlie Ganzel	4,500	3,000	2,000
(5)	Deacon McGuire	4,500	3,000	2,000
(6)	Cannonball Titcomb	4,500	3,000	2,000
(7)	Harry Wright	10,000	4,500	2,800
	(Facing his right.)			
(8)	Harry Wright	10,000	4,500	2,800
	(Pose unrecorded.)			
(9)	Team Photo	6,500	4,500	2,800

1951 Connie Mack Book

Connie Mack

In conjunction with the publication of Connie Mack's book "My 66 Years in the Big Leagues," a folder of cards titled, "Four Mighty Heroes" was also issued. The folder contained a quartet of black-and-white player cards. Fronts feature a player photo against a white background. Backs have a bit of player career data and an ad for Mack's book. Cards measure 2-1/4" x 3-1/2".

		NM	EX	VG
Complete Set (4):		1,900	950.00	575.00
Common Player:		275.00	135.00	80.00
Book:		60.00	30.00	18.00
(1)	Connie Mack	275.00	135.00	80.00
(2)	Christy Mathewson	400.00	200.00	120.00
(3)	Babe Ruth	1,000	500.00	300.00
(4)	Rube Waddell	275.00	135.00	80.00

1924 Walter Mails Card Game (WG7)

This set of playing cards features 56 subjects. Card backs are printed in either red or blue, featuring player and umpire figures in each corner. At center is the picture of a pitcher with the name of the game's creator beneath. Walter Mails was a major league pitcher between 1915-26. Fronts feature a black-and-white player photo with a facsimile autograph. Printed beneath are the player's name, position and team. At bottom is the designation of a play used in the card game. Both major and minor league players are included in the set. Cards are round-cornered and measure 2-5/16" x 3-1/2". The unnumbered cards are checklisted here alphabetically. It appears as if the blue-back set was issued first and in lesser quantities than those with red backs. Many variations of player personal data between the two colors of backs are reported.

		NM	EX	VG
Complete Set (56):		12,000	6,000	3,500
Common Player, Major Leaguer:		250.00	100.00	60.00
Common Player, Minor Leaguer:		200.00	80.00	50.00
Rules Card:		50.00	20.00	10.00
(1)	Russell "Buzz" Arlett	200.00	80.00	50.00
(2)	J.C. "Jim" Bagby	200.00	80.00	50.00
(3)	Dave "Beauty" Bancroft	500.00	200.00	125.00
(4)	Johnny Basseler (Bassler)	250.00	100.00	60.00
(5)	Jack Bentley	250.00	100.00	60.00
(6)	J.C. "Rube" Benton	250.00	100.00	60.00
(7)	Geo. Burns	250.00	100.00	60.00
(8)	"Bullet Joe" Bush	250.00	100.00	60.00
(9)	Harold P. Chavezo	200.00	80.00	50.00
(10)	Hugh Critz	200.00	80.00	50.00
(11)	"Jake" E. Daubert	250.00	100.00	60.00
(12)	Wheezer Dell	200.00	80.00	50.00
(13)	Joe Dugan	250.00	100.00	60.00
(14)	Pat Duncan	250.00	100.00	60.00
(15)	Howard J. Ehmke	250.00	100.00	60.00
(16)	Lewis Fonseca	250.00	100.00	60.00
(17)	Ray French	250.00	100.00	60.00
(18)	Ed Gharity (Gharrity)	250.00	100.00	60.00
(19)	Heinie Groh	250.00	100.00	60.00
(20)	George N. Groves	250.00	100.00	60.00
(21)	E.F. "Red" Hargrave	250.00	100.00	60.00
(22)	Elmer Jacobs	250.00	100.00	60.00
(23)	Walter Johnson	1,200	480.00	300.00
(24)	WM. "Duke" Kenworthy	250.00	100.00	60.00
(25)	Harry Krause	200.00	80.00	50.00
(26)	Ray Kremer	250.00	100.00	60.00
(27)	Walter Mails	250.00	100.00	60.00
(28)	Walter "Rabbitt" Maranville	500.00	200.00	125.00
(29)	John "Stuffy" McInnis	250.00	100.00	60.00
(30)	Marty McManus	250.00	100.00	60.00
(31)	Bob Meusel	250.00	100.00	60.00
(32)	Hack Miller	250.00	100.00	60.00
(33)	Pat J. Moran	250.00	100.00	60.00
(34)	Guy Morton	250.00	100.00	60.00
(35)	Johnny Mostil	250.00	100.00	60.00
(36)	Rod Murphy	200.00	80.00	50.00
(37)	Jimmy O'Connell	250.00	100.00	60.00
(38)	Steve O'Neil	250.00	100.00	60.00
(39)	Joe Oeschger	250.00	100.00	60.00
(40)	Roger Peckinpaugh	250.00	100.00	60.00
(41)	Ralph "Babe" Pinelli	250.00	100.00	60.00
(42)	Wally Pipp	250.00	100.00	60.00
(43)	Elmer Ponder	200.00	80.00	50.00
(44)	Sam Rice	500.00	200.00	125.00
(45)	Edwin Rommell (Rommel)	250.00	100.00	60.00
(46)	Walter Schmidt	250.00	100.00	60.00
(47)	Wilford Shupes	200.00	80.00	50.00
(48)	Joe Sewell	500.00	200.00	125.00
(49)	Pat Shea	200.00	80.00	50.00
(50)	W. "Paddy" Siglin	200.00	80.00	50.00
(51)	Geo. H. Sisler	500.00	200.00	125.00
(52)	William "Bill" Skiff	200.00	80.00	50.00
(53)	J. Smith	250.00	100.00	60.00
(54)	Harry "Suds" Sutherland	200.00	80.00	50.00
(55)	James A. Tierney	250.00	100.00	60.00
(56)	Geo. Uhle	250.00	100.00	60.00

1921-1930 Major League Ball Die-Cuts

COBB.
Center Field.
Batting Order 3
Detroit.
American League

These die-cut, blank-back player cards were issued over the period 1921-30 for use with a board game called, "Major League Ball - The Indoor Baseball Game Supreme," from The National Game Makers of Washington, D.C. Measuring about 2-1/2" to 2-3/4" tall x 1" to 1-1/4" wide, the cards were originally printed on a sheet of 14 from which they were punched out to play the game. The cards were issued in team sets with on-field roster changes reflected in the player cards over the years. Individual cards are generic, liberally sharing the same poses and portraits with identification possible only by changes to the uniform and the player ID printed in the box below the figure. That player data changed from year to year and the only way to determine exact year of issue is when the player card is found with a complete team set, often in a small pre-printed manila envelope. It is unknown whether all teams were issued in all years. According to information found with the game, stickers could be purchased each year to update the game's figures with new player identification. Beginning in at least 1925 player cards were numbered at bottom within team set.

	NM	EX	VG
Typical Team Set:	300.00	150.00	90.00
Common Player:	50.00	25.00	15.00
Typical Hall of Famer:	75.00	37.50	22.50
Ty Cobb	150.00	75.00	45.00
Lou Gehrig	200.00	100.00	60.00
Walter Johnson	125.00	65.00	40.00
Babe Ruth	350.00	175.00	100.00

1969 Major League Baseball Photostamps

This set of 216 player stamps, sponsored by the Major League Baseball Players Association (not authorized by MLB, thus the lack of team uniform insignia) was issued in professional baseball's centennial year of 1969 and was sold in 18 different uncut sheets, with 12 stamps on each sheet. Each individual stamp measured 2" x 3-1/4". There were nine sheets picturing National League players and nine picturing American Leaguers. The full-color stamps display facsimilie autographs on the fronts. The backs carry instructions to moisten the stamps and place them in a special album that was also available. Many sheets of these stamps were uncovered by a dealer in the early 1980s and they were available at inexpensive prices.

	NM	EX	VG
Complete Sheet Set (18):	60.00	30.00	18.00
Complete Singles Set (216):	60.00	30.00	18.00
A.L. Album and Sheets:	25.00	12.50	7.50
N.L. Album and Sheets:	35.00	17.50	10.00
Common Sheet:	3.50	1.75	1.00
Common Player:	.50	.25	.15
Sheet A.L. 1	3.75	2.00	1.00
(1) Don Buford	.50	.25	.15
(2) Mike Andrews	.50	.25	.15
(3) Max Alvis	.50	.25	.15
(4) Bill Freehan	.50	.25	.15
(5) Horace Clarke	.50	.25	.15
(6) Bernie Allen	.50	.25	.15
(7) Jim Fregosi	.50	.25	.15
(8) Joe Horlen	.50	.25	.15
(9) Jerry Adair	.50	.25	.15
(10) Harmon Killebrew	3.00	1.50	.90
(11) Johnny Odom	.50	.25	.15
(12) Steve Barber	.50	.25	.15
Sheet A.L. 2	2.50	1.25	.75
(13) Tom Harper	.50	.25	.15
(14) Boog Powell	1.00	.50	.30
(15) Jose Santiago	.50	.25	.15
(16) Sonny Siebert	.50	.25	.15
(17) Mickey Lolich	.75	.40	.25
(18) Tom Tresh	.75	.40	.25
(19) Camilo Pascual	.50	.25	.15
(20) Bob Rodgers	.50	.25	.15
(21) Pete Ward	.50	.25	.15
(22) Dave Morehead	.50	.25	.15
(23) John Roseboro	.50	.25	.15
(24) Bert Campaneris	.50	.25	.15
Sheet A.L. 3	3.75	2.00	1.00
(25) Danny Cater	.50	.25	.15
(26) Rich Rollins	.50	.25	.15
(27) Brooks Robinson	3.00	1.50	.90
(28) Rico Petrocelli	.50	.25	.15
(29) Larry Brown	.50	.25	.15
(30) Norm Cash	.75	.40	.25
(31) Jake Gibbs	.50	.25	.15
(32) Mike Epstein	.50	.25	.15
(33) George Brunet	.50	.25	.15
(34) Tom McCraw	.50	.25	.15
(35) Steve Whitaker	.50	.25	.15
(36) Bob Allison	.50	.25	.15
Sheet A.L. 4	2.50	1.25	.75
(37) Jim Kaat	.65	.35	.20
(38) Sal Bando	.50	.25	.15
(39) Ray Oyler	.50	.25	.15
(40) Dave McNally	.50	.25	.15
(41) George Scott	.50	.25	.15
(42) Joe Azcue	.50	.25	.15
(43) Jim Northrup	.50	.25	.15
(44) Fritz Peterson	.50	.25	.15
(45) Paul Casanova	.50	.25	.15
(46) Roger Repoz	.50	.25	.15
(47) Tommy John	.75	.40	.25
(48) Moe Drabowsky	.50	.25	.15
Sheet A.L. 5	2.50	1.25	.75
(49) Ed Kirkpatrick	.50	.25	.15
(50) Dean Chance	.50	.25	.15
(51) Mike Hershberger	.50	.25	.15
(52) Jack Aker	.50	.25	.15
(53) Andy Etchebarren	.50	.25	.15
(54) Ray Culp	.50	.25	.15
(55) Luis Tiant	.65	.35	.20
(56) Willie Horton	.50	.25	.15
(57) Roy White	.50	.25	.15
(58) Ken McMullen	.50	.25	.15
(59) Rick Reichardt	.50	.25	.15
(60) Luis Aparicio	3.00	1.50	.90
Sheet A.L. 6	2.50	1.25	.75
(61) Ken Berry	.50	.25	.15
(62) Wally Bunker	.50	.25	.15
(63) Tony Oliva	1.00	.50	.30
(64) Rick Monday	.50	.25	.15
(65) Chico Salmon	.50	.25	.15
(66) Paul Blair	.50	.25	.15
(67) Jim Lonborg	.50	.25	.15
(68) Zoilo Versalles	.50	.25	.15
(69) Denny McLain	.75	.40	.25
(70) Mel Stottlemyre	.50	.25	.15
(71) Joe Coleman	.50	.25	.15
(72) Bob Knoop	.50	.25	.15
Sheet A.L. 7	2.50	1.25	.75
(73) Chuck Hinton	.50	.25	.15
(74) Duane Josephson	.50	.25	.15
(75) Roger Nelson	.50	.25	.15
(76) Ted Uhlaender	.50	.25	.15
(77) John Donaldson	.50	.25	.15
(78) Tommy Davis	.50	.25	.15
(79) Frank Robinson	3.00	1.50	.90
(80) Dick Ellsworth	.50	.25	.15
(81) Sam McDowell	.50	.25	.15
(82) Dick McAuliffe	.50	.25	.15
(83) Bill Robinson	.50	.25	.15
(84) Frank Howard	.75	.40	.25
Sheet A.L. 8	5.00	2.50	1.50
(85) Ed Brinkman	.50	.25	.15
(86) Vic Davalillo	.50	.25	.15
(87) Gary Peters	.50	.25	.15
(88) Joe Foy	.50	.25	.15
(89) Rod Carew	3.00	1.50	.90
(90) Jim "Catfish" Hunter	2.00	1.00	.60
(91) Gary Bell	.50	.25	.15
(92) Dave Johnson	.50	.25	.15
(93) Ken Harrelson	.50	.25	.15
(94) Tony Horton	.50	.25	.15
(95) Al Kaline	3.00	1.50	.90
(96) Steve Hamilton	.50	.25	.15
Sheet A.L. 9	2.50	1.25	.75
(97) Joseph Pepitone	.75	.40	.25
(98) Ed Stroud	.50	.25	.15
(99) Jim McGlothlin	.50	.25	.15
(100) Wilbur Wood	.50	.25	.15
(101) Paul Schaal	.50	.25	.15
(102) Cesar Tovar	.50	.25	.15
(103) Jim Nash	.50	.25	.15
(104) Don Mincher	.50	.25	.15
(105) Thomas Phoebus	.50	.25	.15
(106) Reggie Smith	.50	.25	.15
(107) Jose Cardenal	.50	.25	.15
(108) Mickey Stanley	.50	.25	.15
Sheet N.L. 1	5.00	2.50	1.50
(109) Billy Williams	2.00	1.00	.60
(110) Mack Jones	.50	.25	.15
(111) Tom Seaver	3.00	1.50	.90
(112) Rich Allen	1.50	.70	.45
(113) Bob Veale	.50	.25	.15
(114) Curt Flood	.65	.35	.20
(115) Pat Jarvis	.50	.25	.15
(116) Jim Merritt	.50	.25	.15
(117) Joe Morgan	2.50	1.25	.70
(118) Tom Haller	.50	.25	.15
(119) Larry Stahl	.50	.25	.15
(120) Willie McCovey	2.50	1.25	.70
Sheet N.L. 2	6.00	3.00	1.75
(121) Ron Hunt	.50	.25	.15
(122) Ernie Banks	3.00	1.50	.90
(123) Jim Fairey	.50	.25	.15
(124) Tommy Agee	.50	.25	.15
(125) Cookie Rojas	.50	.25	.15
(126) Mateo Alou	.50	.25	.15
(127) Mike Shannon	.50	.25	.15
(128) Milt Pappas	.50	.25	.15
(129) Johnny Bench	3.00	1.50	.90
(130) Larry Dierker	.50	.25	.15
(131) Willie Davis	.50	.25	.15
(132) Tony Gonzalez	.50	.25	.15
Sheet N.L. 3	3.75	2.00	1.00
(133) Dick Selma	.50	.25	.15
(134) Jim Ray Hart	.50	.25	.15
(135) Phil Regan	.50	.25	.15
(136) Manny Mota	.50	.25	.15
(137) Cleon Jones	.50	.25	.15
(138) Rick Wise	.50	.25	.15
(139) Willie Stargell	2.50	1.25	.70
(140) Robert Gibson	2.50	1.25	.70
(141) Rico Carty	.50	.25	.15
(142) Gary Nolan	.50	.25	.15
(143) Doug Rader	.50	.25	.15
(144) Wes Parker	.50	.25	.15
Sheet N.L. 4	2.50	1.25	.75
(145) Bill Singer	.50	.25	.15
(146) Bill McCool	.50	.25	.15
(147) Juan Marichal	2.00	1.00	.60
(148) Randy Hundley	.50	.25	.15
(149) "Mudcat" Grant	.50	.25	.15
(150) Ed Kranepool	.50	.25	.15
(151) Tony Taylor	.50	.25	.15
(152) Gene Alley	.50	.25	.15
(153) Dal Maxvill	.50	.25	.15
(154) Felipe Alou	.65	.35	.20
(155) Jim Maloney	.50	.25	.15
(156) Jesus Alou	.50	.25	.15
Sheet N.L. 5	8.00	4.00	2.50
(157) Curt Blefary	.50	.25	.15
(158) Ron Fairly	.50	.25	.15
(159) Dick Kelley	.50	.25	.15
(160) Frank Linzy	.50	.25	.15
(161) Fergie Jenkins	2.00	1.00	.60
(162) Maury Wills	.75	.40	.25
(163) Jerry Grote	.50	.25	.15
(164) Chris Short	.50	.25	.15
(165) Jim Bunning	2.00	1.00	.60
(166) Nelson Briles	.50	.25	.15
(167) Orlando Cepeda	2.50	1.25	.70
(168) Pete Rose	8.00	4.00	2.50
Sheet N.L. 6	3.00	1.50	.90
(169) Tony Cloninger	.50	.25	.15
(170) Jim Wynn	.50	.25	.15
(171) Jim Lefebvre	.50	.25	.15
(172) Ron Davis	.50	.25	.15
(173) Mike McCormick	.50	.25	.15
(174) Ron Santo	.75	.40	.25
(175) Ty Cline	.50	.25	.15
(176) Jerry Koosman	.50	.25	.15
(177) Mike Ryan	.50	.25	.15
(178) Jerry May	.50	.25	.15
(179) Tim McCarver	.75	.40	.25
(180) Phil Niekro	2.00	1.00	.60
Sheet N.L. 7	15.00	7.50	4.50
(181) Hank Aaron	5.00	2.50	1.50
(182) Tommy Helms	.50	.25	.15
(183) Denis Menke	.50	.25	.15
(184) Don Sutton	2.00	1.00	.60
(185) Al Ferrera	.50	.25	.15
(186) Willie Mays	5.00	2.50	1.50
(187) Bill Hands	.50	.25	.15
(188) Rusty Staub	.70	.35	.20
(189) Bud Harrelson	.50	.25	.15
(190) Johnny Callison	.50	.25	.15
(191) Roberto Clemente	8.00	4.00	2.50
(192) Julian Javier	.50	.25	.15
Sheet N.L. 8	2.50	1.25	.75
(193) Joe Torre	1.25	.60	.40
(194) Bob Aspromonte	.50	.25	.15
(195) Lee May	.50	.25	.15
(196) Don Wilson	.50	.25	.15
(197) Claude Osteen	.50	.25	.15
(198) Ed Spiezio	.50	.25	.15
(199) Hal Lanier	.50	.25	.15
(200) Glenn Beckert	.50	.25	.15
(201) Bob Bailey	.50	.25	.15
(202) Ron Swoboda	.50	.25	.15
(203) John Briggs	.50	.25	.15
(204) Bill Mazeroski	2.50	1.25	.70
Sheet N.L. 9	3.75	2.00	1.00
(205) Tommie Sisk	.50	.25	.15
(206) Lou Brock	2.50	1.25	.70
(207) Felix Millan	.50	.25	.15
(208) Tony Perez	2.00	1.00	.60
(209) John Edwards	.50	.25	.15
(210) Len Gabrielson	.50	.25	.15
(211) Ollie Brown	.50	.25	.15
(212) Gaylord Perry	2.00	1.00	.60
(213) Don Kessinger	.50	.25	.15
(214) John Bateman	.50	.25	.15
(215) Ed Charles	.50	.25	.15
(216) Woodie Fryman	.50	.25	.15

1969 Major League Baseball Player Pins

ROBERTO CLEMENTE
PITTSBURGH PIRATES

Black-and-white or color player portraits (noted parenthetically) are featured in the center of a red, white and blue design on these 3-1/2" diameter pins. The existing checklist, which may be incomplete, shows a mix of contemporary and retired players. The celluloid pinback buttons were sold at concession stands around the Major Leagues. Production continued at least into 1970, based on some observed player/team combinations.

	NM	EX	VG
Common Player:	40.00	20.00	12.00
(1) Tommie Agee (b/w)	20.00	10.00	6.00
(2) Mike Andrews (b/w)	20.00	10.00	6.00
(3) Mike Andrews (Color)	20.00	10.00	6.00
(4) Luis Aparicio (b/w)	25.00	12.50	7.50
(5) Ernie Banks (b/w)	60.00	30.00	18.00
(6) Ernie Banks (b/w, 2-1/2")	60.00	30.00	18.00
(7) Ernie Banks (Color)	60.00	30.00	18.00
(8) Glenn Beckert (b/w)	20.00	10.00	6.00
(9) Curt Blefary (b/w)	20.00	10.00	6.00
(11) Ken Boswell (b/w)	20.00	10.00	6.00
(12) Lou Brock (b/w)	30.00	15.00	9.00
(13) Orlando Cepeda (b/w)	25.00	12.50	7.50
(14) Ed Charles (b/w)	20.00	10.00	6.00
(15) Horace Clarke (b/w)	20.00	10.00	6.00
(16) Roberto Clemente (b/w)	75.00	37.00	22.00
(17) Donn Clendenon (b/w)	20.00	10.00	6.00
(18) Billy Conigliaro (b/w)	20.00	10.00	6.00
(19) Tony Conigliaro (b/w)	25.00	12.50	7.50
(20) Tony Conigliaro (Color)	25.00	12.50	7.50
(22) Ray Culp (Color)	20.00	10.00	6.00
(23) Joe DiMaggio (b/w)	50.00	25.00	15.00
(24) Don Drysdale (b/w)	30.00	15.00	9.00
(25) Frank Fernandez (Color)	20.00	10.00	6.00
(26) Curt Flood (b/w)	20.00	10.00	6.00
(27) Lou Gehrig (b/w)	50.00	25.00	15.00
(28) Bob Gibson (b/w)	30.00	15.00	9.00
(29) Jim Hickman (b/w)	20.00	10.00	6.00
(31) Frank Howard (b/w)	22.50	11.00	6.75
(32) Randy Hundley (b/w)	20.00	10.00	6.00
(33) Reggie Jackson (Color)	60.00	30.00	18.00
(34) Ferguson Jenkins (b/w)	30.00	15.00	9.00
(35) Dalton Jones (b/w)	20.00	10.00	6.00
(36) Al Kaline (b/w)	60.00	30.00	18.00
(37) Don Kessinger (b/w)	20.00	10.00	6.00
(38) Harmon Killebrew (b/w)	30.00	15.00	9.00
(39) Jerry Koosman (Color)	20.00	10.00	6.00
(41) Jim Lonborg (b/w)	20.00	10.00	6.00
(42) Mickey Mantle (b/w)	100.00	50.00	30.00
(43) Carlos May (b/w)	20.00	10.00	6.00
(44) Willie McCovey (b/w)	25.00	12.50	7.50
(45) Denny McLain (b/w)	22.50	11.00	6.75
(46) Gene Michael (b/w)	20.00	10.00	6.00
(47) Bobby Murcer (Color)	22.50	11.00	6.75
(48) Joe Pepitone (b/w)	25.00	12.50	7.50
(49) Rico Petrocelli (b/w)	20.00	10.00	6.00
(51) Rico Petrocelli (Color)	20.00	10.00	6.00
(52) Pete Rose (b/w)	75.00	37.00	22.00
(53) Babe Ruth (b/w)	50.00	25.00	15.00
(54) Ron Santo (b/w)	22.50	11.00	6.75
(56) Ron Santo (Color)	22.50	11.00	6.75
(57) George Scott (b/w)	20.00	10.00	6.00
(58) Tom Seaver (b/w)	45.00	22.00	13.50
(59) Tom Seaver (Color)	45.00	22.00	13.50
(60) Reggie Smith (b/w)	20.00	10.00	6.00
(61) Reggie Smith (Color)	20.00	10.00	6.00
(62) Mel Stottlemyre (Color)	20.00	10.00	6.00
(63) Joe Torre (b/w)	22.50	11.00	6.75
(64) Tom Tresh (Color)	20.00	10.00	6.00
(65) Pete Ward (b/w)	20.00	10.00	6.00
(66) Roy White (b/w)	20.00	10.00	6.00
(67) Billy Williams (b/w)	25.00	12.50	7.50
(68) Carl Yastrzemski (b/w)	60.00	30.00	18.00
(69) Carl Yastrzemski (Color)	60.00	30.00	18.00

1969 Major League Baseball Players Assn. Pins

Issued by the Major League Baseball Players Association in 1969, this unnumbered set consists of 60 pins - 30 players from the N.L. and 30 from the A.L. Each pin measures approximately 7/8" in diameter and features a black-and-white player photo. A.L. players are surrounded by a red border, while N.L. players are framed in blue. The player's name and team appear at the top and bottom. Also along the bottom is a line reading "1969 MLBPA MFG. R.R. Winona, MINN."

		NM	EX	VG
Complete Set (60):		250.00	125.00	75.00
Common Player:		6.00	3.00	1.75
(1)	Hank Aaron	30.00	15.00	9.00
(2)	Richie Allen	10.00	5.00	3.00
(3)	Felipe Alou	7.50	3.75	2.25
(4)	Max Alvis	6.00	3.00	1.75
(5)	Luis Aparicio	12.50	6.25	3.75
(6)	Ernie Banks	15.00	7.50	4.50
(7)	Johnny Bench	15.00	7.50	4.50
(8)	Lou Brock	15.00	7.50	4.50
(9)	George Brunet	6.00	3.00	1.75
(10)	Johnny Callison	6.00	3.00	1.75
(11)	Rod Carew	15.00	7.50	4.50
(12)	Orlando Cepeda	12.50	6.25	3.75
(13)	Dean Chance	6.00	3.00	1.75
(14)	Roberto Clemente	40.00	20.00	12.00
(15)	Willie Davis	6.00	3.00	1.75
(16)	Don Drysdale	15.00	7.50	4.50
(17)	Ron Fairly	6.00	3.00	1.75
(18)	Curt Flood	6.00	3.00	1.75
(19)	Bill Freehan	6.00	3.00	1.75
(20)	Jim Fregosi	6.00	3.00	1.75
(21)	Bob Gibson	15.00	7.50	4.50
(22)	Ken Harrelson	6.00	3.00	1.75
(23)	Bud Harrelson	6.00	3.00	1.75
(24)	Jim Ray Hart	6.00	3.00	1.75
(25)	Tommy Helms	6.00	3.00	1.75
(26)	Joe Horlen	6.00	3.00	1.75
(27)	Tony Horton	7.50	3.75	2.25
(28)	Willie Horton	6.00	3.00	1.75
(29)	Frank Howard	7.50	3.75	2.25
(30)	Al Kaline	15.00	7.50	4.50
(31)	Don Kessinger	6.00	3.00	1.75
(32)	Harmon Killebrew	15.00	7.50	4.50
(33)	Jerry Koosman	6.00	3.00	1.75
(34)	Mickey Lolich	6.00	3.00	1.75
(35)	Jim Lonborg	6.00	3.00	1.75
(36)	Jim Maloney	6.00	3.00	1.75
(37)	Juan Marichal	12.50	6.25	3.75
(38)	Willie Mays	30.00	15.00	9.00
(39)	Tim McCarver	7.50	3.75	2.25
(40)	Willie McCovey	15.00	7.50	4.50
(41)	Sam McDowell	6.00	3.00	1.75
(42)	Denny McLain	7.50	3.75	2.25
(43)	Rick Monday	6.00	3.00	1.75
(44)	Tony Oliva	7.50	3.75	2.25
(45)	Joe Pepitone	7.50	3.75	2.25
(46)	Boog Powell	7.50	3.75	2.25
(47)	Rick Reichardt	6.00	3.00	1.75
(48)	Pete Richert	6.00	3.00	1.75
(49)	Brooks Robinson	15.00	7.50	4.50
(50)	Frank Robinson	15.00	7.50	4.50
(51)	Pete Rose	25.00	12.50	7.50
(52)	Ron Santo	9.00	4.50	2.75
(53)	Mel Stottlemyre	6.00	3.00	1.75
(54)	Ron Swoboda	6.00	3.00	1.75
(55)	Luis Tiant	6.00	3.00	1.75
(56)	Joe Torre	9.00	4.50	2.75
(57)	Pete Ward	6.00	3.00	1.75
(58)	Billy Williams	12.50	6.25	3.75
(59)	Jim Wynn	6.00	3.00	1.75
(60)	Carl Yastrzemski	15.00	7.50	4.50

1983 "1969" MLBPA Pins

Virtually identical in format to the 60-pin 1969 MLBPA issue, these pins were probably not issued prior to 1983 and despite what is printed thereon, are not a licensed issue of the players' association. The 7/8" diameter pins have a black-and-white player portrait photo on a white background at center. The photo is bordered in red or blue with the player name at top and team at bottom in white. A copyright line on back reads, "1969 MLBPA MFG IN U.S.A." Latter-day pins can be distinguished from the 1969s by the absence of mention of Winona, Minn., on the replicas.

Complete Set (36):
(1)	Hank Aaron
(2)	Bob Allison
(3)	Yogi Berra
(4)	Roy Campanella
(5)	Norm Cash
(6)	Orlando Cepeda
(7)	Roberto Clemente
(8)	Joe DiMaggio
(9)	Bobby Doerr
(10)	Don Drysdale
(11)	Bob Feller
(12)	Whitey Ford
(13)	Nellie Fox
(14)	Frank Howard
(15)	Jim "Catfish" Hunter
(16)	Al Kaline
(17)	Sandy Koufax
(18)	Mickey Mantle
(19)	Juan Marichal
(20)	Eddie Mathews
(21)	Willie Mays
(22)	Willie McCovey
(23)	Stan Musial
(24)	Tony Oliva
(25)	Satchel Paige
(26)	Phil Rizzuto
(27)	Robin Roberts
(28)	Brooks Robinson
(29)	Jackie Robinson
(30)	Ron Santo
(31)	Duke Snider
(32)	Warren Spahn
(33)	Bill Skowron
(34)	Billy Williams
(35)	Ted Williams
(36)	Maury Wills

1970 Major League Baseball Photostamps

BILL MELTON

For a second year, ballplayer "stamps" were sold in conjunction with team albums. Approximately 1-7/8" x 3", the pieces are printed on glossy paper in full color with a white border and facsimile autograph. Backs, which are not gummed, have gluing instructions and the players name at bottom. The 1970 issue can be differentiated from the 1969 issue in that they have uniform insignia present on the photos whereas the 1969 stamps do not. The unnumbered stamps are checklisted here alphabetically within team.

		NM	EX	VG
Complete Set (288):		200.00	100.00	60.00
Common Player:		1.00	.50	.30
ATLANTA BRAVES				
(1)	Hank Aaron	15.00	7.50	4.50
(2)	Bob Aspromonte	1.00	.50	.30
(3)	Rico Carty	1.00	.50	.30
(4)	Orlando Cepeda	6.00	3.00	1.75
(5)	Bob Didier	1.00	.50	.30
(6)	Tony Gonzalez	1.00	.50	.30
(7)	Pat Jarvis	1.00	.50	.30
(8)	Felix Millan	1.00	.50	.30
(9)	Jim Nash	1.00	.50	.30
(10)	Phil Niekro	4.00	2.00	1.25
(11)	Milt Pappas	1.00	.50	.30
(12)	Ron Reed	1.00	.50	.30
BALTIMORE ORIOLES				
(1)	Mark Belanger	1.00	.50	.30
(2)	Paul Blair	1.00	.50	.30
(3)	Don Buford	1.00	.50	.30
(4)	Mike Cuellar	1.00	.50	.30
(5)	Andy Etchebarren	1.00	.50	.30
(6)	Dave Johnson	1.00	.50	.30
(7)	Dave McNally	1.00	.50	.30
(8)	Tom Phoebus	1.00	.50	.30
(9)	Boog Powell	2.00	1.00	.60
(10)	Brooks Robinson	6.00	3.00	1.75
(11)	Frank Robinson	6.00	3.00	1.75
(12)	Chico Salmon	1.00	.50	.30
BOSTON RED SOX				
(1)	Mike Andrews	1.00	.50	.30
(2)	Ray Culp	1.00	.50	.30
(3)	Jim Lonborg	1.00	.50	.30
(4)	Sparky Lyle	1.00	.50	.30
(5)	Gary Peters	1.00	.50	.30
(6)	Rico Petrocelli	1.00	.50	.30
(7)	Vicente Romo	1.00	.50	.30
(8)	Tom Satriano	1.00	.50	.30
(9)	George Scott	1.00	.50	.30
(10)	Sonny Seibert	1.00	.50	.30
(11)	Reggie Smith	1.00	.50	.30
(12)	Carl Yastrzemski	6.00	3.00	1.75
CALIFORNIA ANGELS				
(1)	Sandy Alomar	1.00	.50	.30
(2)	Jose Azcue	1.00	.50	.30
(3)	Tom Egan	1.00	.50	.30
(4)	Jim Fregosi	1.00	.50	.30
(5)	Alex Johnson	1.00	.50	.30
(6)	Jay Johnstone	1.00	.50	.30
(7)	Rudy May	1.00	.50	.30
(8)	Andy Messersmith	1.00	.50	.30
(9)	Rick Reichardt	1.00	.50	.30
(10)	Roger Repoz	1.00	.50	.30
(11)	Aurelio Rodriguez	1.00	.50	.30
(12)	Ken Tatum	1.00	.50	.30
CHICAGO CUBS				
(1)	Ernie Banks	7.50	3.75	2.25
(2)	Glenn Beckert	1.00	.50	.30
(3)	Johnny Callison	1.00	.50	.30
(4)	Bill Hands	1.00	.50	.30
(5)	Randy Hundley	1.00	.50	.30
(6)	Ken Holtzman	1.00	.50	.30
(7)	Fergie Jenkins	4.00	2.00	1.25
(8)	Don Kessinger	1.00	.50	.30
(9)	Phil Regan	1.00	.50	.30
(10)	Ron Santo	2.00	1.00	.60
(11)	Dick Selma	1.00	.50	.30
(12)	Billy Williams	5.00	2.50	1.50
CHICAGO WHITE SOX				
(1)	Luis Aparicio	5.00	2.50	1.50
(2)	Ken Berry	1.00	.50	.30
(3)	Buddy Bradford	1.00	.50	.30
(4)	Ron Hansen	1.00	.50	.30
(5)	Joel Horlen	1.00	.50	.30
(6)	Tommy John	1.50	.70	.45
(7)	Duane Josephson	1.00	.50	.30
(8)	Bobby Knoop	1.00	.50	.30
(9)	Tom McCraw	1.00	.50	.30
(10)	Bill Melton	1.00	.50	.30
(11)	Walt Williams	1.00	.50	.30
(12)	Wilbur Wood	1.00	.50	.30
CINCINNATI REDS				
(1)	Johnny Bench	7.50	3.75	2.25
(2)	Tony Cloninger	1.00	.50	.30
(3)	Wayne Granger	1.00	.50	.30
(4)	Tommy Helms	1.00	.50	.30
(5)	Jim Maloney	1.00	.50	.30
(6)	Lee May	1.00	.50	.30
(7)	Jim McGlothlin	1.00	.50	.30
(8)	Jim Merritt	1.00	.50	.30
(9)	Gary Nolan	1.00	.50	.30
(10)	Tony Perez	5.00	2.50	1.50
(11)	Pete Rose	12.50	6.25	3.75
(12)	Bobby Tolan	1.00	.50	.30
CLEVELAND INDIANS				
(1)	Max Alvis	1.00	.50	.30
(2)	Larry Brown	1.00	.50	.30
(3)	Dean Chance	1.00	.50	.30
(4)	Dick Ellsworth	1.00	.50	.30
(5)	Vern Fuller	1.00	.50	.30
(6)	Ken Harrelson	1.00	.50	.30
(7)	Chuck Hinton	1.00	.50	.30
(8)	Tony Horton	1.00	.50	.30
(9)	Sam McDowell	1.00	.50	.30
(10)	Vada Pinson	1.50	.70	.45
(11)	Duke Sims	1.00	.50	.30
(12)	Ted Uhlaender	1.00	.50	.30
DETROIT TIGERS				
(1)	Norm Cash	1.50	.70	.45
(2)	Bill Freehan	1.00	.50	.30
(3)	Willie Horton	1.00	.50	.30
(4)	Al Kaline	7.50	3.75	2.25
(5)	Mike Kilkenny	1.00	.50	.30
(6)	Mickey Lolich	1.00	.50	.30
(7)	Dick McAuliffe	1.00	.50	.30
(8)	Denny McLain	1.50	.70	.45
(9)	Jim Northrup	1.00	.50	.30
(10)	Mickey Stanley	1.00	.50	.30
(11)	Tom Tresh	1.00	.50	.30
(12)	Earl Wilson	1.00	.50	.30
HOUSTON ASTROS				
(1)	Jesus Alou	1.00	.50	.30
(2)	Tommy Davis	1.00	.50	.30
(3)	Larry Dierker	1.00	.50	.30
(4)	Johnny Edwards	1.00	.50	.30
(5)	Fred Gladding	1.00	.50	.30
(6)	Denver Lemaster	1.00	.50	.30
(7)	Denis Menke	1.00	.50	.30
(8)	Joe Morgan	6.00	3.00	1.75
(9)	Joe Pepitone	1.50	.70	.45
(10)	Doug Rader	1.00	.50	.30
(11)	Don Wilson	1.00	.50	.30
(12)	Jim Wynn	1.00	.50	.30
KANSAS CITY ROYALS				
(1)	Jerry Adair	1.00	.50	.30
(2)	Wally Bunker	1.00	.50	.30
(3)	Bill Butler	1.00	.50	.30
(4)	Moe Drabowsky	1.00	.50	.30

		NM	EX	VG
(5)	Jackie Hernandez	1.00	.50	.30
(6)	Pat Kelly	1.00	.50	.30
(7)	Ed Kirkpatrick	1.00	.50	.30
(8)	Dave Morehead	1.00	.50	.30
(9)	Roger Nelson	1.00	.50	.30
(10)	Bob Oliver	1.00	.50	.30
(11)	Lou Piniella	1.50	.70	.45
(12)	Paul Schaal	1.00	.50	.30

LOS ANGELES DODGERS

(1)	Willie Davis	1.00	.50	.30
(2)	Len Gabrielson	1.00	.50	.30
(3)	Tom Haller	1.00	.50	.30
(4)	Jim Lefebvre	1.00	.50	.30
(5)	Manny Mota	1.00	.50	.30
(6)	Claude Osteen	1.00	.50	.30
(7)	Wes Parker	1.00	.50	.30
(8)	Bill Russell	1.00	.50	.30
(9)	Bill Singer	1.00	.50	.30
(10)	Ted Sizemore	1.00	.50	.30
(11)	Don Sutton	4.00	2.00	1.25
(12)	Maury Wills	1.00	.50	.30

MINNESOTA TWINS

(1)	Bob Allison	1.00	.50	.30
(2)	Dave Boswell	1.00	.50	.30
(3)	Leo Cardenas	1.00	.50	.30
(4)	Rod Carew	6.00	3.00	1.75
(5)	Jim Kaat	1.50	.70	.45
(6)	Harmon Killebrew	6.00	3.00	1.75
(7)	Tony Oliva	1.50	.70	.45
(8)	Jim Perry	1.00	.50	.30
(9)	Ron Perranoski	1.00	.50	.30
(10)	Rich Reese	1.00	.50	.30
(11)	Luis Tiant	1.00	.50	.30
(12)	Cesar Tovar	1.00	.50	.30

MONTREAL EXPOS

(1)	John Bateman	1.00	.50	.30
(2)	Bob Bailey	1.00	.50	.30
(3)	Ron Brand	1.00	.50	.30
(4)	Ty Cline	1.00	.50	.30
(5)	Ron Fairly	1.00	.50	.30
(6)	Mack Jones	1.00	.50	.30
(7)	Jose Laboy	1.00	.50	.30
(8)	Claude Raymond	1.00	.50	.30
(9)	Joe Sparma	1.00	.50	.30
(10)	Rusty Staub	1.50	.70	.45
(11)	Bill Stoneman	1.00	.50	.30
(12)	Bobby Wine	1.00	.50	.30

NEW YORK METS

(1)	Tommie Agee	1.00	.50	.30
(2)	Donn Clendenon	1.00	.50	.30
(3)	Joe Foy	1.00	.50	.30
(4)	Jerry Grote	1.00	.50	.30
(5)	Bud Harrelson	1.00	.50	.30
(6)	Cleon Jones	1.00	.50	.30
(7)	Jerry Koosman	1.00	.50	.30
(8)	Ed Kranepool	1.00	.50	.30
(9)	Nolan Ryan	25.00	12.50	7.50
(10)	Tom Seaver	6.00	3.00	1.75
(11)	Ron Swoboda	1.00	.50	.30
(12)	Al Weis	1.00	.50	.30

NEW YORK YANKEES

(1)	Jack Aker	1.00	.50	.30
(2)	Curt Blefary	1.00	.50	.30
(3)	Danny Cater	1.00	.50	.30
(4)	Horace Clarke	1.00	.50	.30
(5)	Jake Gibbs	1.00	.50	.30
(6)	Steve Hamilton	1.00	.50	.30
(7)	Bobby Murcer	1.50	.70	.45
(8)	Fritz Peterson	1.00	.50	.30
(9)	Bill Robinson	1.00	.50	.30
(10)	Mel Stottlemyre	1.00	.50	.30
(11)	Pete Ward	1.00	.50	.30
(12)	Roy White	1.50	.70	.45

OAKLAND A's

(1)	Felipe Alou	1.50	.70	.45
(2)	Sal Bando	1.00	.50	.30
(3)	Bert Campaneris	1.00	.50	.30
(4)	Chuck Dobson	1.00	.50	.30
(5)	Tito Francona	1.00	.50	.30
(6)	Dick Green	1.00	.50	.30
(7)	Catfish Hunter	4.00	2.00	1.25
(8)	Reggie Jackson	10.00	5.00	3.00
(9)	Don Mincher	1.00	.50	.30
(10)	Rick Monday	1.00	.50	.30
(11)	John Odom	1.00	.50	.30
(12)	Ray Oyler	1.00	.50	.30

PHILADELPHIA PHILLIES

(1)	Johnny Briggs	1.00	.50	.30
(2)	Jim Bunning	4.00	2.00	1.25
(3)	Curt Flood	1.50	.70	.45
(4)	Woodie Fryman	1.00	.50	.30
(5)	Larry Hisle	1.00	.50	.30
(6)	Joe Hoerner	1.00	.50	.30
(7)	Grant Jackson	1.00	.50	.30
(8)	Tim McCarver	1.50	.70	.45
(9)	Mike Ryan	1.00	.50	.30
(10)	Chris Short	1.00	.50	.30
(11)	Tony Taylor	1.00	.50	.30
(12)	Rick Wise	1.00	.50	.30

PITTSBURGH PIRATES

(1)	Gene Alley	1.00	.50	.30
(2)	Matty Alou	1.00	.50	.30
(3)	Roberto Clemente	20.00	10.00	6.00
(4)	Ron Davis	1.00	.50	.30
(5)	Richie Hebner	1.00	.50	.30
(6)	Jerry May	1.00	.50	.30
(7)	Bill Mazeroski	6.00	3.00	1.75
(8)	Bob Moose	1.00	.50	.30
(9)	Al Oliver	1.50	.70	.45
(10)	Manny Sanguillen	1.00	.50	.30
(11)	Willie Stargell	5.00	2.50	1.50
(12)	Bob Veale	1.00	.50	.30

SAN DIEGO PADRES

(1)	Ollie Brown	1.00	.50	.30
(2)	Dave Campbell	1.00	.50	.30
(3)	Nate Colbert	1.00	.50	.30
(4)	Pat Dobson	1.00	.50	.30
(5)	Al Ferrara	1.00	.50	.30

(6)	Dick Kelley	1.00	.50	.30
(7)	Clay Kirby	1.00	.50	.30
(8)	Bill McCool	1.00	.50	.30
(9)	Frank Reberger	1.00	.50	.30
(10)	Tommie Sisk	1.00	.50	.30
(11)	Ed Spiezio	1.00	.50	.30
(12)	Larry Stahl	1.00	.50	.30

SAN FRANCISCO GIANTS

(1)	Bobby Bonds	1.50	.70	.45
(2)	Jim Davenport	1.00	.50	.30
(3)	Dick Dietz	1.00	.50	.30
(4)	Jim Ray Hart	1.00	.50	.30
(5)	Ron Hunt	1.00	.50	.30
(6)	Hal Lanier	1.00	.50	.30
(7)	Frank Linzy	1.00	.50	.30
(8)	Juan Marichal	5.00	2.50	1.50
(9)	Willie Mays	15.00	7.50	4.50
(10)	Mike McCormick	1.00	.50	.30
(11)	Willie McCovey	6.00	3.00	1.75
(12)	Gaylord Perry	4.00	2.00	1.25

SEATTLE PILOTS

(1)	Steve Barber	1.00	.50	.30
(2)	Bobby Bolin	1.00	.50	.30
(3)	George Brunet	1.00	.50	.30
(4)	Wayne Comer	1.00	.50	.30
(5)	John Donaldson	1.00	.50	.30
(6)	Tommy Harper	1.00	.50	.30
(7)	Mike Hegan	1.00	.50	.30
(8)	Mike Hershberger	1.00	.50	.30
(9)	Steve Hovley	1.00	.50	.30
(10)	Bob Locker	1.00	.50	.30
(11)	Gerry McNertney	1.00	.50	.30
(12)	Rich Rollins	1.00	.50	.30

ST. LOUIS CARDINALS

(1)	Richie Allen	2.50	1.25	.70
(2)	Nelson Briles	1.00	.50	.30
(3)	Lou Brock	6.00	3.00	1.75
(4)	Jose Cardenal	1.00	.50	.30
(5)	Steve Carlton	6.00	3.00	1.75
(6)	Vic Davalillo	1.00	.50	.30
(7)	Bob Gibson	6.00	3.00	1.75
(8)	Julian Javier	1.00	.50	.30
(9)	Dal Maxvill	1.00	.50	.30
(10)	Cookie Rojas	1.00	.50	.30
(11)	Mike Shannon	1.00	.50	.30
(12)	Joe Torre	3.00	1.50	.90

WASHINGTON SENATORS

(1)	Bernie Allen	1.00	.50	.30
(2)	Dick Bosman	1.00	.50	.30
(3)	Ed Brinkman	1.00	.50	.30
(4)	Paul Casanova	1.00	.50	.30
(5)	Joe Coleman	1.00	.50	.30
(6)	Mike Epstein	1.00	.50	.30
(7)	Frank Howard	1.50	.70	.45
(8)	Ken McMullen	1.00	.50	.30
(9)	John Roseboro	1.00	.50	.30
(10)	Ed Stroud	1.00	.50	.30
(11)	Del Unser	1.00	.50	.30
(12)	Zoilo Versalles	1.00	.50	.30

1910 Makaroff Cigarettes World Series Postcard

The text on this postcard indicates it may have been given out at World Series games in Philadelphia and Chicago. Two versions are known, one with Connie Mack's portrait at left and the Athletics score listed first, and one with Frank Chance's portrait at left and the Cubs score listed first. On the black-and-white address side are photographic portraits of the A's and Cubs managers with appropriate team pennants. Below is scripted, "Saw the world's championship game to-day." Beneath that are lines to record the score. The front of the card is printed in black, white and red and has a picture of a smoking cigarette and a two-headed Russian eagle logo. At center is this "Dictum. / Think big, talk little, love much, laugh easily, / work hard, give freely, pay cash and be kind - / it is enough! Do these and you may smoke without / danger to your immortal soul."

	NM	EX	VG
Frank Chance, Connie Mack	350.00	175.00	100.00
Connie Mack, Frank Chance	350.00	175.00	100.00

1916 Mall Theatre

Best known for its use as a promotional medium for The Sporting News, this 200-card set can be found with ads on the back for several local and regional businesses. Among them is the Mall Theatre, location unknown. Type-card and superstar collectors can expect to pay a significant premium for individual cards with this advertising over generic 1916 M101-4 Blank Backs values. Cards measure 1-5/8" x 3" and are printed in black-and-white.

PREMIUM: 2-3X
(See 1916 M101-4 Blank Backs for checklist and base card values.)

1926-1927 Mallorquina Caramels

These tiny (about 3/4" x 1-1/8") cards were distributed with Mallorquina brandcaramels in Cuba. The black-and-white images are printed on hard photographic paper stock. The bordered portrait photos on front have a box at bottom with player identification and card number. Backs are printed in dark blue with the wording "LA MALLORQUINA / CARAMELOS / PELOTEROS" and a few graphic flourishes. The set's first 17 cards feature professional players, including a number of Negro Leagues stars. The last 83 cards in the set are Cuban amateurs. While there was probably some sort of album issued to house the set, none has been reported to date. Because the card of Hall of Famer Willie Foster is his only known career-contemporary issue, and that of Martin Dihigo is his earliest known, "book" values have not been assigned.

	Common Player:	NM	EX	VG
	Common Player:	200.00	100.00	60.00
1	Adolfo Luque	750.00	375.00	225.00
2	Alfredo Cabrera	250.00	125.00	75.00
3	George Scales	350.00	175.00	105.00
4	Jose Maria Fernandez	250.00	125.00	75.00
5	Oliver Marcelle	3,000	1,500	900.00
6	Oscar Rodriguez	200.00	100.00	60.00
7	Martin Dihigo (Value Undetermined)			
8	Cheo Ramos	250.00	125.00	75.00
9	Pop Lloyd	4,500	2,250	1,350
10	Joe Olivares	200.00	100.00	60.00
11	Brujo Rosell	200.00	100.00	60.00
12	Willie Foster (Value Undetermined)			
13	Cho Cho Correa	250.00	125.00	75.00
14	Larry Brown	350.00	175.00	105.00
15	Oscar Levis	250.00	125.00	75.00
16	Raul Alvarez	250.00	125.00	75.00
17	Juan Eckelson	250.00	125.00	75.00
18	Quesada	200.00	100.00	60.00
19	J. Rosado	200.00	100.00	60.00
20	A. Unanuo	200.00	100.00	60.00
21	A. Echavarria	200.00	100.00	60.00
22	C. Beltran	200.00	100.00	60.00
23	J. Beltran	200.00	100.00	60.00
24	G. Orama	200.00	100.00	60.00
25	E. Carrillo	200.00	100.00	60.00
26	A. Casuso	200.00	100.00	60.00
27	A. Consuegra	200.00	100.00	60.00
28	R. Gallardo	200.00	100.00	60.00

29	M. Sotolongo	200.00	100.00	60.00
30	M. Llano	200.00	100.00	60.00
31	H. Rocamora	200.00	100.00	60.00
32	Calvo	200.00	100.00	60.00
33	R. Inclan	200.00	100.00	60.00
34	Mendizabal	200.00	100.00	60.00
35	H. Alonso	200.00	100.00	60.00
36	C. Leonard	200.00	100.00	60.00
37	Cap Cordova	200.00	100.00	60.00
38	Cordova	200.00	100.00	60.00
39	Sarasua	200.00	100.00	60.00
40	E. Cubillas	200.00	100.00	60.00
41	B. Wilryc	200.00	100.00	60.00
42	Morera	200.00	100.00	60.00
43	C. Fernandez	200.00	100.00	60.00
44	Milian	200.00	100.00	60.00
45	P. Espinosa	200.00	100.00	60.00
46	Macia	200.00	100.00	60.00
47	J. Lagueruela	200.00	100.00	60.00
48	Bernal	200.00	100.00	60.00
49	J.A. Ruiz	200.00	100.00	60.00
50	Unknown			
51	J. Gayoso	200.00	100.00	60.00
52	Castro	200.00	100.00	60.00
53	C. Hernandez	200.00	100.00	60.00
54	Reynolds	200.00	100.00	60.00
55	M. Rodriguez	200.00	100.00	60.00
56	P. Flores	200.00	100.00	60.00
57	A. Collazo	200.00	100.00	60.00
58	R. Gonzalez	200.00	100.00	60.00
59	A. Casas	200.00	100.00	60.00
60	Barcena	200.00	100.00	60.00
61	Quesada	200.00	100.00	60.00
62	Riquerin	200.00	100.00	60.00
63	Carbonere	200.00	100.00	60.00
64	Vega	200.00	100.00	60.00
65	Rodriguez	200.00	100.00	60.00
66	A. Castillo	200.00	100.00	60.00
67	Y. Balleste	200.00	100.00	60.00
68	Fernandez	200.00	100.00	60.00
69	Garros	200.00	100.00	60.00
70	Cabada	200.00	100.00	60.00
71	R.P. Fernandez	200.00	100.00	60.00
72	R. Cejas	200.00	100.00	60.00
73	Gros	200.00	100.00	60.00
74	Mendez	200.00	100.00	60.00
75	M. Sotolongo	200.00	100.00	60.00
76	E. Vela	200.00	100.00	60.00
77	A. Vela	200.00	100.00	60.00
78	F. Pinera	200.00	100.00	60.00
79	M. Valdes	200.00	100.00	60.00
80	L. Romero	200.00	100.00	60.00
81	A. Febles	200.00	100.00	60.00
82	Lugo	200.00	100.00	60.00
83	Polo Calvo	200.00	100.00	60.00
84	Silvio O. Farrill	200.00	100.00	60.00
85	Zalazar	200.00	100.00	60.00
86	Tapia	200.00	100.00	60.00
87	Hernandez	200.00	100.00	60.00
88	Manrrara	200.00	100.00	60.00
89	J. Deschapelle	200.00	100.00	60.00
90	Arguelles	200.00	100.00	60.00
91	E. Arechaede	200.00	100.00	60.00
92	E. Quintanal	200.00	100.00	60.00
93	M. Valdes	200.00	100.00	60.00
94	J. Martinez	200.00	100.00	60.00
95	R. Martinez	200.00	100.00	60.00
96	F. Gali	200.00	100.00	60.00
97	A. Martinez	200.00	100.00	60.00
98	G. Hernandez	200.00	100.00	60.00
99	A. Fernandez	200.00	100.00	60.00
100	Armando Figarola	200.00	100.00	60.00

1961 Manny's Baseball Land 8x10s

In 1961, Manny's Baseball Land issued 18 10-piece 8" x 10" printed black-and-white photo packs, arranged by team. Manny's was a next-door neighbor of Yankee Stadium and the nation's largest purveyor of baseball souvenirs. These photo sets were sold for $1.50 per team. The blank-back photos were printed on semigloss paper. Portraits or posed action photos were surrounded by a white border which contains the player's name in all caps at bottom. The unnumbered pictures are checklisted here alphabetically by and within team.

		NM	EX	VG
Complete Set (180):		2,500	1,250	750.00
Common Player:		10.00	5.00	3.00

BALTIMORE ORIOLES

(1)	Jackie Brandt	10.00	5.00	3.00
(2)	Marv Breeding	10.00	5.00	3.00
(3)	Chuck Estrada	10.00	5.00	3.00
(4)	Jack Fisher	10.00	5.00	3.00
(5)	Jim Gentile	10.00	5.00	3.00
(6)	Ron Hansen	10.00	5.00	3.00
(7)	Milt Pappas	10.00	5.00	3.00
(8)	Brooks Robinson	30.00	15.00	9.00
(9)	Gus Triandos	10.00	5.00	3.00
(10)	Jerry Walker	10.00	5.00	3.00

BOSTON RED SOX

(11)	Tom Brewer	10.00	5.00	3.00
(12)	Don Buddin	10.00	5.00	3.00
(13)	Gene Conley	10.00	5.00	3.00
(14)	Mike Fornieles	10.00	5.00	3.00
(15)	Gary Geiger	10.00	5.00	3.00
(16)	Pumpsie Green	10.00	5.00	3.00
(17)	Jackie Jensen	15.00	7.50	4.50
(18)	Frank Malzone	10.00	5.00	3.00
(19)	Pete Runnels	10.00	5.00	3.00
(20)	Vic Wertz	10.00	5.00	3.00

CHICAGO CUBS

(21)	George Altman	10.00	5.00	3.00
(22)	Bob Anderson	10.00	5.00	3.00
(23)	Richie Ashburn	30.00	15.00	9.00
(24)	Ernie Banks	35.00	17.50	10.00
(25)	Don Cardwell	10.00	5.00	3.00
(26)	Moe Drabowsky	10.00	5.00	3.00
(27)	Don Elston	10.00	5.00	3.00
(28)	Jerry Kindall	10.00	5.00	3.00
(29)	Ron Santo	15.00	7.50	4.50
(30)	Bob Will	10.00	5.00	3.00

CHICAGO WHITE SOX

(31)	Luis Aparicio	25.00	12.50	7.50
(32)	Frank Baumann	10.00	5.00	3.00
(33)	Sam Esposito	10.00	5.00	3.00
(34)	Nellie Fox	30.00	15.00	9.00
(35)	Jim Landis	10.00	5.00	3.00
(36)	Sherman Lollar	10.00	5.00	3.00
(37)	Minnie Minoso	20.00	10.00	6.00
(38)	Billy Pierce	10.00	5.00	3.00
(39)	Bob Shaw	10.00	5.00	3.00
(40)	Early Wynn	25.00	12.50	7.50

CINCINNATI REDLEGS

(41)	Ed Bailey	10.00	5.00	3.00
(42)	Gus Bell	10.00	5.00	3.00
(43)	Gordon Coleman	10.00	5.00	3.00
(44)	Bill Henry	10.00	5.00	3.00
(45)	Jerry Lynch	10.00	5.00	3.00
(46)	Claude Osteen	10.00	5.00	3.00
(47)	Vada Pinson	12.50	6.25	3.75
(48)	Wally Post	10.00	5.00	3.00
(49)	Bob Purkey	10.00	5.00	3.00
(50)	Frank Robinson	35.00	17.50	10.00

CLEVELAND INDIANS

(51)	Mike de la Hoz	10.00	5.00	3.00
(52)	Tito Francona	10.00	5.00	3.00
(53)	Woody Held	10.00	5.00	3.00
(54)	Barry Latman	10.00	5.00	3.00
(55)	Jim Perry	10.00	5.00	3.00
(56)	Bubba Phillips	10.00	5.00	3.00
(57)	Jim Piersall	12.50	6.25	3.75
(58)	Vic Power	10.00	5.00	3.00
(59)	John Romano	10.00	5.00	3.00
(60)	Johnny Temple	10.00	5.00	3.00

DETROIT TIGERS

(61)	Hank Aguirre	10.00	5.00	3.00
(62)	Billy Bruton	10.00	5.00	3.00
(63)	Jim Bunning	25.00	12.50	7.50
(64)	Norm Cash	20.00	10.00	6.00
(65)	Rocky Colavito	25.00	12.50	7.50
(66)	Chico Fernandez	10.00	5.00	3.00
(67)	Paul Foytack	10.00	5.00	3.00
(68)	Al Kaline	35.00	17.50	10.00
(69)	Frank Lary	10.00	5.00	3.00
(70)	Don Mossi	10.00	5.00	3.00

KANSAS CITY ATHLETICS

(71)	Hank Bauer	10.00	5.00	3.00
(72)	Andy Carey	10.00	5.00	3.00
(73)	Leo "Bud" Daley	10.00	5.00	3.00
(74)	Ray Herbert	10.00	5.00	3.00
(75)	John Kucks	10.00	5.00	3.00
(76)	Jerry Lumpe	10.00	5.00	3.00
(77)	Norm Siebern	10.00	5.00	3.00
(78)	Haywood Sullivan	10.00	5.00	3.00
(79)	Marv Throneberry	10.00	5.00	3.00
(80)	Dick Williams	10.00	5.00	3.00

LOS ANGELES ANGELS

(81)	Ken Aspromonte	10.00	5.00	3.00
(82)	Steve Bilko	10.00	5.00	3.00
(83)	Bob Cerv	10.00	5.00	3.00
(84)	Ned Garver	10.00	5.00	3.00
(85)	Ken Hunt	10.00	5.00	3.00
(86)	Ted Kluszewski	25.00	12.50	7.50
(87)	Jim McAnany	10.00	5.00	3.00
(88)	Duke Maas	10.00	5.00	3.00
(89)	Albie Pearson	10.00	5.00	3.00
(90)	Eddie Yost	10.00	5.00	3.00

LOS ANGELES DODGERS

(91)	Don Drysdale	30.00	15.00	9.00
(92)	Jim Gilliam	12.50	6.25	3.75
(93)	Frank Howard	12.50	6.25	3.75
(94)	Sandy Koufax	50.00	25.00	15.00
(95)	Norm Larker	10.00	5.00	3.00
(96)	Wally Moon	10.00	5.00	3.00
(97)	Charles Neal	10.00	5.00	3.00
(98)	Johnny Podres	12.50	6.25	3.75
(99)	Larry Sherry	10.00	5.00	3.00
(100)	Maury Wills	12.50	6.25	3.75

MILWAUKEE BRAVES

(101)	Hank Aaron	50.00	25.00	15.00
(102)	Joe Adcock	10.00	5.00	3.00
(103)	Frank Bolling	10.00	5.00	3.00
(104)	Bob Buhl	10.00	5.00	3.00
(105)	Lew Burdette	10.00	5.00	3.00
(106)	Del Crandall	10.00	5.00	3.00
(107)	Ed Mathews	35.00	17.50	10.00
(108)	Roy McMillan	10.00	5.00	3.00
(109)	Warren Spahn	35.00	17.50	10.00
(110)	Al Spangler	10.00	5.00	3.00

MINNESOTA TWINS

(111)	Bob Allison	10.00	5.00	3.00
(112)	Earl Battey	10.00	5.00	3.00
(113)	Reno Bertola (Bertoia)	10.00	5.00	3.00
(114)	Billy Consolo	10.00	5.00	3.00
(115)	Billy Gardner	10.00	5.00	3.00
(116)	Harmon Killebrew	35.00	17.50	10.00
(117)	Jim Lemon	10.00	5.00	3.00
(118)	Camilo Pascual	10.00	5.00	3.00
(119)	Pedro Ramos	10.00	5.00	3.00
(120)	Chuck Stobbs	10.00	5.00	3.00

NEW YORK YANKEES

(121)	Larry "Yogi" Berra	35.00	17.50	10.00
(122)	John Blanchard	10.00	5.00	3.00
(123)	Ed "Whitey" Ford	35.00	17.50	10.00
(124)	Elston Howard	15.00	7.50	4.50
(125)	Tony Kubek	15.00	7.50	4.50
(126)	Mickey Mantle	65.00	32.50	20.00
(127)	Roger Maris	40.00	20.00	12.00
(128)	Bobby Richardson	15.00	7.50	4.50
(129)	Bill Skowron	15.00	7.50	4.50
(130)	Bob Turley	10.00	5.00	3.00

PHILADELPHIA PHILLIES

(131)	John Callison	10.00	5.00	3.00
(132)	Dick Farrell	10.00	5.00	3.00
(133)	Pancho Herrera	10.00	5.00	3.00
(134)	Joe Koppe	10.00	5.00	3.00
(135)	Art Mahaffey	10.00	5.00	3.00
(136)	Gene Mauch	10.00	5.00	3.00
(137)	Jim Owens	10.00	5.00	3.00
(138)	Robin Roberts	30.00	15.00	9.00
(139)	Frank Sullivan	10.00	5.00	3.00
(140)	Tony Taylor	10.00	5.00	3.00

PITTSBURGH PIRATES

(141)	Roberto Clemente	60.00	30.00	18.00
(142)	Roy Face	10.00	5.00	3.00
(143)	Bob Friend	10.00	5.00	3.00
(144)	Dick Groat	10.00	5.00	3.00
(145)	Harvey Haddix	10.00	5.00	3.00
(146)	Don Hoak	10.00	5.00	3.00
(147)	Vern Law	10.00	5.00	3.00
(148)	Bill Mazeroski	30.00	15.00	9.00
(149)	Wilmer Mizell	10.00	5.00	3.00
(150)	Bill Virdon	10.00	5.00	3.00

SAN FRANCISCO GIANTS

(151)	Felipe Alou	12.50	6.25	3.75
(152)	Orlando Cepeda	30.00	15.00	9.00
(153)	Sam Jones	10.00	5.00	3.00
(154)	Harvey Kuenn	10.00	5.00	3.00
(155)	Willie Mays	50.00	25.00	15.00
(156)	Mike McCormick	10.00	5.00	3.00
(157)	Willie McCovey	30.00	15.00	9.00
(158)	Stu Miller	10.00	5.00	3.00
(159)	Billy O'Dell	10.00	5.00	3.00
(160)	Jack Sanford	10.00	5.00	3.00

ST. LOUIS CARDINALS

(161)	Ernie Broglio	10.00	5.00	3.00
(162)	Ken Boyer	12.50	6.25	3.75
(163)	Joe Cunningham	10.00	5.00	3.00
(164)	Alex Grammas	10.00	5.00	3.00
(165)	Larry Jackson	10.00	5.00	3.00
(166)	Julian Javier	10.00	5.00	3.00
(167)	Lindy McDaniel	10.00	5.00	3.00
(168)	Stan Musial	45.00	22.50	13.50
(169)	Hal Smith	10.00	5.00	3.00
(170)	Daryl Spencer	10.00	5.00	3.00

WASHINGTON SENATORS

(171)	Pete Daley	10.00	5.00	3.00
(172)	Dick Donovan	10.00	5.00	3.00
(173)	Bob Johnson	10.00	5.00	3.00
(174)	Marty Keough	10.00	5.00	3.00
(175)	Billy Klaus	10.00	5.00	3.00
(176)	Dale Long	10.00	5.00	3.00
(177)	Carl Mathias	10.00	5.00	3.00
(178)	Willie Tasby	10.00	5.00	3.00
(179)	Mickey Vernon	10.00	5.00	3.00
(180)	Gene Woodling	10.00	5.00	3.00

1959 Mickey Mantle's Holiday Inn Postcard

The attributed date is speculative. Much rarer than the more common pose of Mantle in civvies in his Joplin, Mo. motel's lounge, this approximately 3-1/2" x 5-1/2" card features two color poses of the Mick in Yankees uniform on its front. The postcard-style back is printed in blue and gives motel information and features.

	NM	EX	VG
Mickey Mantle	100.00	50.00	30.00

1962 Mickey Mantle's Holiday Inn Postcard

This color postcard pictures Mantle in civilian clothes. On the back of the standard-size (about 3-1/2" x 5-1/2") card it says the Mick is "pictured in the

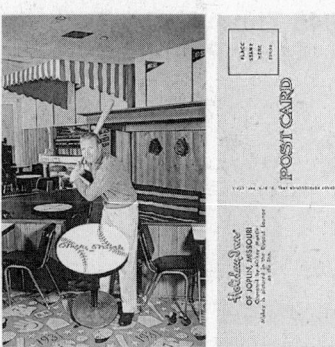

Dugout Lounge at the Inn." The "Inn" is the Joplin, Mo., Holiday Inn which Mantle owned. This was one of the more popular, and thus more common, of the souvenirs issued in conjunction with Mantle's motel.

	NM	EX	VG
Mickey Mantle	30.00	15.00	9.00

1962 Mickey Mantle's Holiday Inn Premium Photo

Probably issued in 1962, though not dated, this 8" x 10" photo pictures the M&M Boys in the lounge of Mantle's motel. Back is blank.

	NM	EX	VG
Mickey Mantle, Roger Maris	600.00	300.00	180.00

1963 Mickey Mantle Hospital Postcard

 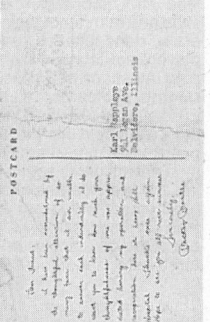

With a broken foot in 1963 following hard on a knee injury the previous season, Mantle spent considerable time in the hospital. To assist in answering a mountain of goodwill messages from fans, he had these postcards created. On front of the 3-1/2" x 5-1/2" card is a glossy black-and-white batting-pose photo. The back is printed in blue with a "Dear Friend" message thanking the fan for "the thoughtful attention" and ending optimistically, "Hope to see you all next season," above his facsimile autograph.

	NM	EX	VG
Mickey Mantle	450.00	225.00	135.00

1923 Maple Crispette (V117)

Issued by a Montreal candy company, these small (1-3/8" x 2-1/4") black-and-white cards were redeemable for baseball equipment, accounting for their scarcity today. Card #15, Stengel, was only discovered in 1992 and was obviously short-printed by the issuer to avoid giving away many bats, balls and gloves. Only a single specimen of the Stengel card is currently known; it is not included in the complete set prices.

		NM	EX	VG
Complete Set, no Stengel (29):		27,000	10,800	6,720
Common Player:		420.00	170.00	110.00
1	Jesse Barnes	420.00	170.00	110.00
2	Harold Traynor	720.00	290.00	180.00
3	Ray Schalk	720.00	290.00	180.00
4	Eddie Collins	720.00	290.00	180.00
5	Lee Fohl	420.00	170.00	110.00
6	Howard Summa	420.00	170.00	110.00
7	Waite Hoyt	720.00	290.00	180.00
8	Babe Ruth	8,700	3,600	1,920
9	Cozy Dolan	420.00	170.00	110.00
10	Johnny Bassler	420.00	170.00	110.00
11	George Dauss	420.00	170.00	110.00
12	Joe Sewell	720.00	290.00	180.00
13	Syl Johnson	420.00	170.00	110.00
14a	Wingo	420.00	170.00	110.00
14b	Ivy Wingo	420.00	170.00	110.00
15	Casey Stengel	18,000	9,000	4,500
16	Arnold Statz	420.00	170.00	110.00
17	Emil Meusel	420.00	170.00	110.00
18	Bill Jacobson	420.00	170.00	11.00
19	Jim Bottomley	720.00	290.00	180.00
20	Sam Bohne	540.00	215.00	130.00
21	Bucky Harris	720.00	290.00	180.00
22	Ty Cobb	3,000	1,200	750.00
23	Roger Peckinpaugh	420.00	170.00	110.00
24	Muddy Ruel	420.00	170.00	110.00
25	Bill McKechnie	720.00	290.00	180.00
26	Riggs Stephenson	420.00	170.00	110.00
27	Herb Pennock	720.00	290.00	180.00
28	Edd Roush	720.00	290.00	180.00
29	Bill Wambsganss	420.00	170.00	110.00
30	Walter Johnson	2,400	960.00	600.00

1962 Roger Maris Action Baseball Game

 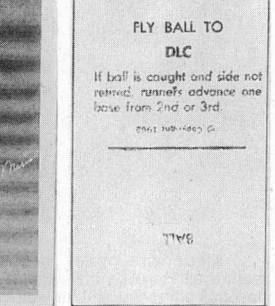

Baseball's new home run king was featured in this board game by Pressman Toy Co. Besides the colorful metal game board and other pieces, the set contains 88 playing cards. Each 2-1/4" x 3-1/2" card has a black-and-white photo on front of Maris in a batting pose, along with a white facsimile autograph. Backs have two possible game action plays printed, along with a copyright line.

	NM	EX	VG
Complete Game:	150.00	75.00	45.00
Single Card:	15.00	7.50	4.50
Roger Maris			

1913-14 Martens Bakery

(See 1911-14 General Baking Co. (D304))

1955 Mascot Dog Food

The date of issue shown is approximate. It is likely other players' cards exist, since the back mentions eight stars printed on the label, presumably of the dog food can. In black-and-white, the 3-1/2" x 5-1/2" card has on front a glossy action pose with a facsimile autograph personalized, "To My Mascot" and the player name and position printed in black in the bottom border. The back has an ad for a fan club offering an autographed 8x10, membership card and pin and set of eight postcards for a quarter and a label.

		NM	EX	VG
(1)	Robin Roberts	450.00	225.00	135.00

1971 Mattel Instant Replay Records

These 2-3/8" diameter plastic records were produced in conjunction with a hand-held, battery-operated record player. Paper inserts featured illustrations of players in baseball, football and basketball, as well as various racing vehicles and airplanes. The audio recounts career highlights of the depicted player. Additional records were sold in sets of four.

		NM	EX	VG
Complete Set (12):		250.00	125.00	75.00
Common Player:		10.00	5.00	3.00
(1)	Hank Aaron	30.00	15.00	9.00
(2)	Ernie Banks	15.00	7.50	4.50
(3)	Roberto Clemente	50.00	25.00	15.00
(4)	Al Kaline	15.00	7.50	4.50
(5)	Sandy Koufax	40.00	20.00	12.00
(6)	Roger Maris	15.00	7.50	4.50
(7)	Willie Mays	12.00	6.00	3.50
	(Plays one side only; came with record player purchase.)			
(8)	Willie McCovey	12.00	6.00	3.50
(9)	Tony Oliva	10.00	5.00	3.00
(10)	Frank Robinson	13.50	6.75	4.00
(11)	Tom Seaver	15.00	7.50	4.50
(12)	Willie Stargell	12.00	6.00	3.50

1895 Mayo's Cut Plug (N300)

These 1-5/8" x 2-7/8" cards were issued by the Mayo Tobacco Works of Richmond, Va. There are 48

cards in the set, with 40 different players pictured. Twenty-eight of the players are pictured in uniform and 12 are shown in street clothes. Eight players appear both ways. Eight of the uniformed players also appear in two variations, creating the 48-card total. Card fronts are black-and-white or sepia portraits on black cardboard, with a Mayo's Cut Plug ad at the bottom of each card. Cards have a blank black back and are unnumbered.

		NM	EX	VG
	Complete Set (48):	240,000	120,000	72,000
	Common Player:	2,200	880.00	440.00
(1)	Charlie Abbey	2,200	880.00	440.00
(2)	Cap Anson	19,200	7,680	3,840
(3)	Jimmy Bannon	2,200	880.00	440.00
(4a)	Dan Brouthers (Baltimore on shirt.)	10,800	4,320	2,160
(4b)	Dan Brouthers (Louisville on shirt.)	12,000	4,800	2,400
(5)	Ed Cartwright	2,200	880.00	440.00
(6)	John Clarkson	7,200	2,880	1,440
(7)	Tommy Corcoran	2,200	880.00	440.00
(8)	Lave Cross	2,200	880.00	440.00
(9)	Bill Dahlen	2,700	1,080	540.00
(10)	Tom Daly	2,200	880.00	440.00
(11)	E.J. Delehanty (Delahanty)	14,400	5,760	2,880
(12)	Hugh Duffy	7,200	2,880	1,440
(13a)	Buck Ewing (Cleveland on shirt.)	12,000	4,800	2,400
(13b)	Buck Ewing (Cincinnati on shirt.)	9,000	3,600	1,800
(14)	Dave Foutz	2,200	880.00	440.00
(15)	Charlie Ganzel	2,200	880.00	440.00
(16a)	Jack Glasscock (Pittsburg on shirt.)	2,700	1,080	540.00
(16b)	Jack Glasscock (Louisville on shirt.)	2,200	880.00	440.00
(17)	Mike Griffin	2,200	880.00	440.00
(18a)	George Haddock (No team on shirt.)	3,000	1,200	600.00
(18b)	George Haddock (Philadelphia on shirt.)	2,200	880.00	440.00
(19)	Bill Hallman	2,200	880.00	440.00
(20)	Billy Hamilton	7,200	2,880	1,440
(21)	Bill Joyce	2,200	880.00	440.00
(22)	Brickyard Kennedy	2,200	880.00	440.00
(23a)	Tom Kinslow (No team on shirt.)	3,000	1,200	600.00
(23b)	Tom Kinslow (Pittsburg on shirt.)	2,200	880.00	440.00
(24)	Arlie Latham	2,200	880.00	440.00
(25)	Herman Long	2,200	880.00	440.00
(26)	Tom Lovett	2,200	880.00	440.00
(27)	Bobby Lowe	2,200	880.00	440.00
(28)	Tommy McCarthy	7,200	2,880	1,440
(29)	Yale Murphy	2,200	880.00	440.00
(30)	Billy Nash	2,200	880.00	440.00
(31)	Kid Nichols	12,000	4,800	2,400
(32a)	Fred Pfeffer (2nd Base)	2,200	880.00	440.00
(32b)	Fred Pfeffer (Retired)	2,200	880.00	440.00
(33)	Wilbert Robinson	7,200	2,880	1,440
(34a)	Amos Russie (Incorrect spelling.)	15,000	6,000	3,000
(34b)	Amos Rusie (Correct)	10,800	4,320	2,160
(35)	Jimmy Ryan	2,200	880.00	440.00
(36)	Bill Shindle	2,200	880.00	440.00
(37)	Germany Smith	2,200	880.00	440.00
(38)	Otis Stocksdale (Stockdale)	2,200	880.00	440.00
(39)	Tommy Tucker	2,200	880.00	440.00
(40a)	Monte Ward (2nd Base)	10,800	4,320	2,160
(40b)	Monte Ward (Retired)	9,000	3,600	1,800

1896 Mayo's Die-Cut Game Cards (N301)

BATMAN N.Y.

Mayo Tobacco Works of Richmond, Va., issued an innovative, if not very popular, series of die-cut baseball player figures in 1896. These tiny (1-1/2" long by just 3/16" wide) cardboard figures were inserted in packages of Mayo's Cut Plug Tobacco and were designed to be used as part of a baseball board game. A "grandstand, base and teetotum" were available free by mail to complete the game pieces. Twenty-eight different die-cut figures were available, representing 26 unspecified New York and

Boston players along with two umpires. The players are shown in various action poses - either running, batting, pitching or fielding. The backs carry an ad for Mayo's Tobacco. The players shown do not relate to any actual members of the New York or Boston clubs, diminishing the popularity of this issue, which has an American Card Catalog designation of N301.

		NM	EX	VG
	Complete Set (28):	4,000	1,600	800.00
	Common Player:	150.00	60.00	30.00
(1a)	Pitcher (Boston)	150.00	60.00	30.00
(1b)	Pitcher (New York)	150.00	60.00	30.00
(2a)	1st Baseman (Boston)	150.00	60.00	30.00
(2b)	1st Baseman (New York)	150.00	60.00	30.00
(3a)	2nd Baseman (Boston)	150.00	60.00	30.00
(3b)	2nd Baseman (New York)	150.00	60.00	30.00
(4a)	3rd Baseman (Boston)	150.00	60.00	30.00
(4b)	3rd Baseman (New York)	150.00	60.00	30.00
(5a)	Right Fielder (Boston)	150.00	60.00	30.00
(5b)	Right Fielder (New York)	150.00	60.00	30.00
(6a)	Center Fielder (Boston)	150.00	60.00	30.00
(6b)	Center Fielder (New York)	150.00	60.00	30.00
(7a)	Left Fielder (Boston)	150.00	60.00	30.00
(7b)	Left Fielder (New York)	150.00	60.00	30.00
(8a)	Short Stop (Boston)	150.00	60.00	30.00
(8b)	Short Stop (New York)	150.00	60.00	30.00
(9a)	Catcher (Boston)	150.00	60.00	30.00
(9b)	Catcher (New York)	150.00	60.00	30.00
(10a)	Batman (Boston)	150.00	60.00	30.00
(10b)	Batman (New York)	150.00	60.00	30.00
(11a)	Runner (Boston, standing upright.)	150.00	60.00	30.00
(11b)	Runner (New York, standing upright.)	150.00	60.00	30.00
(12a)	Runner (Boston, bent slightly forward.)	150.00	60.00	30.00
(12b)	Runner (New York, bent slightly forward.)	150.00	60.00	30.00
(13a)	Runner (Boston, bent well forward.)	150.00	60.00	30.00
(13b)	Runner (New York, bent well forward.)	150.00	60.00	30.00
(14)	Umpire (Facing front.)	150.00	60.00	30.00
(15)	Field Umpire (Rrear view.)	150.00	60.00	30.00

1900 Mayo's Baseball Comics (T203)

"A Star Catcher"

UP TO DATE BASE BALL COMICS 25 DIFFERENT DESIGNS MAKE A COLLECTION

MAYO'S CUT PLUG IS ALWAYS GOOD for SMOKE and CHEW 5¢

As their name implies, the T203 Baseball Comics feature cartoon-like drawings that illustrate various baseball phrases and terminology. Issued with Winner Cut Plug and Mayo Cut Plug tobacco products, the complete set consists of 25 different comics, each measuring approximately 2-1/16" x 3-1/8". Because they do not picture individual players, these cards have never attracted much of a following among serious baseball card collectors. They do, however, hold some interest as a novelty item of the period.

		NM	EX	VG
	Complete Set (25):	3,000	1,500	650.00
	Common Card:	150.00	75.00	30.00
(1)	"A Crack Outfielder"	150.00	75.00	30.00
(2)	"A Fancy Twirler"	150.00	75.00	30.00
(3)	"A Fine Slide"	150.00	75.00	30.00
(4)	"A Fowl Bawl"	150.00	75.00	30.00
(5)	"A Great Game"	150.00	75.00	30.00
(6)	"A Home Run"	150.00	75.00	30.00
(7)	"An All Star Battery"	150.00	75.00	30.00
(8)	"A Short Stop"	150.00	75.00	30.00
(9)	"A Star Catcher"	150.00	75.00	30.00
(10)	"A White Wash"	150.00	75.00	30.00
(11)	"A Tie Game"	150.00	75.00	30.00
(12)	"A Two Bagger"	150.00	75.00	30.00
(13)	"A Wild Pitch"	150.00	75.00	30.00
(14)	"Caught Napping"	150.00	75.00	30.00
(15)	"On To The Curves"	150.00	75.00	30.00
(16)	"Out"	150.00	75.00	30.00
(17)	"Put Out On 1st"	150.00	75.00	30.00
(18)	"Right Over The Plate"	150.00	75.00	30.00
(19)	"Rooting For The Home Team"	150.00	75.00	30.00
(20)	"Stealing A Base"	150.00	75.00	30.00
(21)	"Stealing Home"	150.00	75.00	30.00
(22)	"Strike One"	150.00	75.00	30.00
(23)	"The Bleacher"	150.00	75.00	30.00
(24)	"The Naps"	150.00	75.00	30.00
(25)	"The Red Sox"	150.00	75.00	30.00

1948 Thom McAn Bob Feller Premium

This black-and-white 8" x 10" premium picture has on front a posed action photo and facsimile autograph. On back is a 25-question baseball quiz and advertising for the shoe store chain, along with a copyright for Melville Shoe Co.

	NM	EX	VG
Bob Feller	150.00	75.00	45.00

1950s-80s J.D. McCarthy Player Postcards

From the 1950s into the 1980s, Detroit area photographer J.D. McCarthy produced black-and-white postcards to order for hundreds of ballplayers to use in answering fan mail requests for pictures and autographs. Sizes and formats differed through the years, but most are about standard postcard size (3-1/2" x 5-1/2") with borderless poses on front. Some cards have a white strip with printed name on front, others have a facsimile autograph, while others have no identification at all. Some card fronts carry his stylized JcMD monogram. Backs, likewise, differ in the style and manner of their markings. Printing was generally done on thin, semi-gloss cardboard. Many players are found in more than one pose, or in cropping variations of a pose. Many players continued to re-order postcards long after their careers were over. Following McCarthy's death, archives of his negatives were sold into the hobby, making it theoretically possible for many cards to be reproduced in perpetuity. That mitigates against many of these cards attaining any great degree of collectible value, though they are popular with team and single-player collectors. Postally-used cards which carry a dated postmark are of the greatest value. Many cards, as the one pictured here, are autographed.

	NM	EX	VG
Common Player:	3.00	1.50	.90

1970 McDonald's Brewers

the original milwaukee brewers, 1970

McDonald's welcomed the American League Brewers to Milwaukee in 1970 by issuing a set of six baseball card panels. Five of the panels picture five players and a team logo, while the sixth panel contains six players, resulting in 31 different players. The panels measure 9" x 9-1/2" and feature full-color paintings of the players. Each sheet displays the heading, "The original Milwaukee Brewers, 1970." The cards are numbered by uniform number and the backs are blank. Although distributed by McDonald's, their name does not appear on the cards.

		NM	EX	VG
Complete Sheet Set (6):		15.00	7.50	4.50
Complete Singles Set (32):		15.00	7.50	4.50
Common Player:		.50	.25	.15
1	Ted Kubiak	.50	.25	.15
2	Ted Savage	.50	.25	.15
3	Dave Bristol	.50	.25	.15
5	Phil Roof	.50	.25	.15
6	Mike Hershberger	.50	.25	.15
7	Russ Snyder	.50	.25	.15
8	Mike Hegan	.50	.25	.15
9	Rich Rollins	.50	.25	.15
10	Max Alvis	.50	.25	.15
11	John Kennedy	.50	.25	.15
12	Dan Walton	.50	.25	.15
15	Jerry McNertney	.50	.25	.15
18	Wes Stock	.50	.25	.15
20	Wayne Comer	.50	.25	.15
21	Tommy Harper	.50	.25	.15
23	Bob Locker	.50	.25	.15
24	Lew Krausse	.50	.25	.15
25	John Gelnar	.50	.25	.15
26	Roy McMillan	.50	.25	.15
27	Cal Ermer	.50	.25	.15
28	Sandy Valdespino	.50	.25	.15
30	Jackie Moore	.50	.25	.15
32	Gene Brabender	.50	.25	.15
33	Marty Pattin	.50	.25	.15
34	Greg Goossen	.50	.25	.15
35	John Morris	.50	.25	.15
36	Steve Hovley	.50	.25	.15
38	Bob Meyer	.50	.25	.15
39	Bob Bolin	.50	.25	.15
43	John O'Donoghue	.50	.25	.15
49	George Lauzerique	.50	.25	.15
---	Logo Card	.50	.25	.15

1974 McDonald's Gene Michael

GENE "THE STICK" MICHAEL
Gene "The Stick" Michael

Though there is no advertising or logo on this one-card "set," this black-and-white card of "The Stick" in his last year as a Yankee was distributed by a Staten Island McDonald's restaurant during an autograph appearance. The card measures 2-5/8" x 4-3/8" and is blank-backed.

	NM	EX	VG
Gene "The Stick" Michael	25.00	12.50	7.50

1974 McDonald's Padres Discs

Envisioned as part of a line of sports promotional sets, this concept died following the test with San Diego area McDonalds. At the July 30, 1974, game, Padres fans were given a hinged plastic baseball con-

taining five Padres player photo discs plus a disc with the team's schedule and a Ronald McDonald disc which listed the dates on which the remaining eight player cards would be distributed at area McDonalds. Only 60,000 of the "starter set" discs were made, while 180,000 of each of the other player discs were printed. The 2-3/8" diameter discs feature a color photo on front and player stats on back. The promotion was the work of Photo Sports, Inc., of Los Angeles.

		NM	EX	VG
Complete Set (15):		25.00	12.50	7.50
Common Player:		1.00	.50	.30
(1)	Matty Alou	1.00	.50	.30
(2)	Glenn Beckert	3.00	1.50	.90
(3)	Nate Colbert	1.00	.50	.30
(4)	Bill Grief	1.00	.50	.30
(5)	John Grubb	1.00	.50	.30
(6)	Enzo Hernandez	3.00	1.50	.90
(7)	Randy Jones	3.00	1.50	.90
(8)	Fred Kendall	3.00	1.50	.90
(9)	Willie McCovey	6.00	3.00	1.75
(10)	John McNamara	3.00	1.50	.90
(11)	Dave Roberts	1.00	.50	.30
(12)	Bobby Tolan	1.00	.50	.30
(13)	Dave Winfield	15.00	7.50	4.50
(14)	Padres Home Game Schedule	1.50	.70	.45
(15)	Ronald McDonald	1.50	.70	.45

1978 McDonald's Boston Red Sox

Reportedly because of a production problem, distribtution of these cards was limited to a few Boston-area McDonald's restaurants for a very limited time. The blank-back, approximately 3-1/2" x 6" color cards have borderless portraits on front with the player's facsimile autograph. The cards were reportedly distributed in Treasure Chest meals for kids under 12.

		NM	EX	VG
Complete Set (6):		450.00	225.00	135.00
Common Player:		35.00	17.50	10.00
(1)	Rick Burleson	35.00	17.50	10.00
(2)	Carlton Fisk	125.00	60.00	35.00
(3)	Fred Lynn	75.00	37.50	22.50
(4)	Jim Rice	100.00	50.00	30.00
(5)	Luis Tiant	50.00	25.00	15.00
(6)	Carl Yastrzemski	150.00	75.00	45.00

1950-1952 Bill McGowan's School for Umpires

BILL McGOWAN'S SCHOOL for UMPIRES

Over a period of at least three years in the early 1950s, Hall of Fame American League umpire Bill McGowan issued a series of black-and-white postcards to promote his umpires' school in Florida. The 3-1/2" x 5-1/2" cards have bordered or borderless photos on front, some of which bear the imprint of Grogan Photo, Danville, Ill.

		NM	EX	VG
(1)	Bill McGowan's Umpire School Cocoa - 1950 - Florida (students on bleachers)	60.00	30.00	20.00
(2)	Bill McGowman's Umpire School - 1950 - Florida (students standing on field)	60.00	30.00	20.00
(3)	Bill McGowan/1951	500.00	250.00	150.00
(4)	Donatelli Instructs (Augie Donatelli)/1952	65.00	32.50	20.00
(5)	Guglielmo Instructs (Augie Guglielmo)/1952	65.00	32.50	20.00

1970s-80s Doug McWilliams Postcards

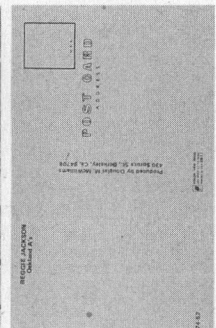

For more than two decades, California photographer Doug McWilliams (who also worked for Topps for 23 years) produced a series of black-and-white and color postcards for individual use by ballplayers, mostly members of the Oakland A's. Almost uniformly, the 3-1/2" x 5-1/2" cards have no graphics on front (a few have facsimile autographs), just a player pose or portrait. Backs have standard postcard markings, player identification, and McWilliams' credit lines. Backs carry a two-digit year of issue prefix to the card number. Postcards are printed in black-and-white unless noted.

	NM	EX	VG
Common Player:	3.00	1.50	.90
(See individual years for checklists and values.)			

1970 Doug McWilliams Postcards

		NM	EX	VG
1	Jim Roland	1.00	.50	.30
2a	Mudcat Grant, Mudcat Grant	1.50	.75	.45
2b	Mudcat Grant	1.50	.75	.45
3	Reggie Jackson (Color - only 50 produced.)	150.00	75.00	45.00
4	Darrell Osteen	1.00	.50	.30
5a	Tom Hafey (First printing.)	1.00	.50	.30
5b	Tom Hafey (Second printing.)	1.00	.50	.30
6	Chick Hafey	1.50	.75	.45

1970 Doug McWilliams Collectors' Issue Postcards

This set of black-and-white player postcards was produced by S.F. are photographer Doug McWilliams as a custom order for an Eastern collector. Fewer than 50 sets were reportedly produced. The 3-1/2" x 5-1/2" cards have glossy photographic fronts and standard postcard backs with player identification. The unnumbered cards are checklisted here in alphabetical order.

		NM	EX	VG
Complete Set (22):		400.00	200.00	125.00
Common Player:		20.00	10.00	6.00
(1)	Jerry Adair	20.00	10.00	6.00
(2)	Brant Alyea	20.00	10.00	6.00
(3)	Brant Alyea	20.00	10.00	6.00
(4)	Dwain Anderson	20.00	10.00	6.00
(5)	Curt Blefary	20.00	10.00	6.00
(6)	Bill Daniels	20.00	10.00	6.00
(7)	Mike Epstein	22.50	11.00	6.75
(8)	Adrian Garrett	20.00	10.00	6.00
(9)	Frank Fernandez	20.00	10.00	6.00
(10)	Mike Hegan	20.00	10.00	6.00
(11)	George Hendrick	20.00	10.00	6.00
(12)	Reggie Jackson	125.00	62.00	37.00
(13)	Reggie Jackson	125.00	62.00	37.00
(14)	Ron Klimkowski	20.00	10.00	6.00
(15)	Darold Knowles	20.00	10.00	6.00
(16)	Jerry Lumpe	20.00	10.00	6.00
(17)	Angel Mangual	20.00	10.00	6.00
(18)	Denny McLain	30.00	15.00	9.00
(19)	Denny McLain	30.00	15.00	9.00
(20)	Irv Noren	20.00	10.00	6.00
(21)	Ramon Webster	20.00	10.00	6.00
(22)	Dick Williams	20.00	10.00	6.00

1970 Doug McWilliams Oakland A's Postcards

These 3-1/2" x 5-1/2" black-and-white player postcards were produced by San Francisco photographer

Doug McWilliams for sale by Sports Cards for Collectors, a forerunner of TCMA. Each card can be found either with or without borders on front, the latter having a slightly enlarged image. Player identification is on back. The unnumbered cards are checklisted here alphabetically. Fewer than 50 sets were reported produced.

		NM	EX	VG
Complete Set (42):		400.00	200.00	125.00
Common Player:		15.00	7.50	4.50
(1)	Felipe Alou	20.00	10.00	6.00
(2)	Sal Bando	20.00	10.00	6.00
(3)	Vida Blue	25.00	12.50	7.50
(4)	Bobby Brooks	15.00	7.50	4.50
(5)	Bert Campaneris	25.00	12.50	7.50
(6)	"Babe" Dahlgren	15.00	7.50	4.50
(7)	Tommy Davis	17.50	8.75	5.25
(8)	Chuck Dobson	15.00	7.50	4.50
(9)	John Donaldson	15.00	7.50	4.50
(10)	Al Downing	15.00	7.50	4.50
(11)	Jim Driscoll	15.00	7.50	4.50
(12)	Dave Duncan	15.00	7.50	4.50
(13)	Frank Fernandez	15.00	7.50	4.50
(14)	Rollie Fingers	45.00	22.00	13.50
(15)	Tito Francona	15.00	7.50	4.50
(16)	Jim Grant	20.00	10.00	6.00
(17)	Dick Green	15.00	7.50	4.50
(18)	Larry Haney	15.00	7.50	4.50
(19)	Bobby Hofman	15.00	7.50	4.50
(20)	Steve Hovley	15.00	7.50	4.50
(21)	Jim Hunter	45.00	22.00	13.50
(22)	Reggie Jackson	125.00	62.00	37.00
(23)	Dave Johnson	15.00	7.50	4.50
(24)	Marcel Lacheman	15.00	7.50	4.50
(25)	Tony LaRussa	40.00	20.00	12.00
(26)	Paul Lindblad	15.00	7.50	4.50
(27)	Bob Locker	15.00	7.50	4.50
(28)	John McNamara	15.00	7.50	4.50
(29)	Don Mincher	15.00	7.50	4.50
(30)	Rick Monday	15.00	7.50	4.50
(31)	"Blue Moon" Odom	17.50	8.75	5.25
(32)	Darrell Osteen	15.00	7.50	4.50
(33)	Ray Oyler	15.00	7.50	4.50
(34)	Roberto Pena	15.00	7.50	4.50
(35)	Bill Posedel	15.00	7.50	4.50
(36)	Roberto Rodriguez	15.00	7.50	4.50
(37)	Jim Roland	15.00	7.50	4.50
(38)	Joe Rudi	20.00	10.00	6.00
(39)	Diego Segui	15.00	7.50	4.50
(40)	Jose Tartabull	15.00	7.50	4.50
(41)	Gene Tenace	15.00	7.50	4.50
(42)	Dooley Womack	15.00	7.50	4.50

1971 Doug McWilliams Postcards

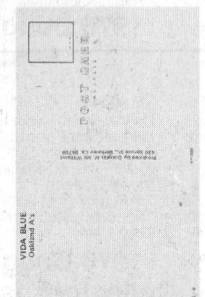

		NM	EX	VG
7	Larry Brown	3.00	1.50	.90
8a	Vida Blue (Color - first printing - KV3321.)	6.00	3.00	1.75
8b	Vida Blue (Color - second printing - KV3509.)	6.00	3.00	1.75
8c	Vida Blue (Color - third printing - KV4403.)	6.00	3.00	1.75
9	Dave Duncan	3.00	1.50	.90
10	George Hendrick (Color)	9.00	4.50	2.75
11	Mudcat Grant	3.00	1.50	.90
12	Mudcat Grant	3.00	1.50	.90

1972 Doug McWilliams Postcards

		NM	EX	VG
13	John Odom (Color)	6.00	3.00	1.75
14	Reggie Jackson (Color)	20.00	10.00	6.00

		NM	EX	VG
15	Sal Bando (Color)	6.00	3.00	1.75
16	Dan Cater	3.00	1.50	.90
17	Bob Locker	3.00	1.50	.90
18a	Joe Rudi (Equal edges to player.)	3.00	1.50	.90
18b	Joe Rudi (Bat close at bottom.)	3.00	1.50	.90
18c	Joe Rudi (Hand close to edge.)	3.00	1.50	.90
19	Larry Brown	3.00	1.50	.90
20a	Dick Green (First printing - glossy.)	3.00	1.50	.90
20b	Dick Green (Second printing - glossy, more contrast.)	3.00	1.50	.90
20c	Dick Green (Third printing - matte.)	3.00	1.50	.90
21	Vida Blue (Color)	6.00	3.00	1.75
22a	Joe Horlen (First printing - bright.)	3.00	1.50	.90
22b	Joe Horlen (Second printing - dark.)	3.00	1.50	.90
23	Gene Tenace (Color)	6.00	3.00	1.75
24a	Ted Kubiak (Glossy)	3.00	1.50	.90
24b	Ted Kubiak (Matte)	3.00	1.50	.90
A	Emeryville Ball Park	3.00	1.50	.90
B	Oakland Coliseum	3.00	1.50	.90

1973 Doug McWilliams Postcards

		NM	EX	VG
25	Rene Lachemann	3.00	1.50	.90
26	Tom Greive	3.00	1.50	.90
27	John Odom (Color)	6.00	3.00	1.75
28a	Rollie Fingers (First printing.)	9.00	4.50	2.75
28b	Rollie Fingers (Second printing - thinner stock.)	9.00	4.50	2.75
29	Jim Hunter (Color)	9.00	4.50	2.75
30	Ray Fosse (Color)	6.00	3.00	1.75
31	Charley Pride (Color)	15.00	7.50	4.50
32	Charley Pride (Color)	15.00	7.50	4.50
33	Bill North	3.00	1.50	.90
34	Damasco Blanco	3.00	1.50	.90
35	Paul Lindblad	3.00	1.50	.90
36	Rollie Fingers (Color)	9.00	4.50	2.75
37	Horacio Pina	3.00	1.50	.90
38	Bert Campaneris (Color)	7.50	3.75	2.25
39	Jim Holt (Color)	6.00	3.00	1.75
40	Sal Bando (Color)	6.00	3.00	1.75
41	Joe Rudi (Color)	6.00	3.00	1.75
42	Dick Williams (Color)	6.00	3.00	1.75
43	Jesus Alou	3.00	1.50	.90
44	Joe Niekro	3.75	2.00	1.25
45	Johnny Oates	3.00	1.50	.90

1974 Doug McWilliams Postcards

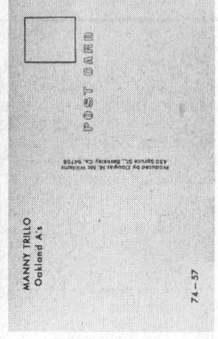

		NM	EX	VG
46a	Ray Fosse (Color - first printing - w/signature.)	6.00	3.00	1.75
46b	Ray Fosse (Color - second printing - no signature.)	6.00	3.00	1.75
46c	Ray Fosse (Color - third printing - no sig., very green grass.)	6.00	3.00	1.75
47	Jesus Alou	3.00	1.50	.90
48	John Summers	3.00	1.50	.90
49	Dal Maxvill	3.00	1.50	.90
50	Joe Rudi (Color)	6.00	3.00	1.75
51	Sal Bando (Color)	6.00	3.00	1.75
52	Reggie Jackson (Color)	20.00	10.00	6.00
53	Ted Kubiak (Color)	6.00	3.00	1.75
54	Dave Hamilton	3.00	1.50	.90
55	Gene Tenace (Color)	6.00	3.00	1.75
56a	Bob Locker (First printing - back foot near edge.)	3.00	1.50	.90
56b	Bob Locker (Second printing - foot 3/4" from edge.)	3.00	1.50	.90
57	Manny Trillo	3.00	1.50	.90

1975 Doug McWilliams Postcards

		NM	EX	VG
58a	Dan Godby (First printing.)	3.00	1.50	.90
58b	Dan Godby (Second printing - blank back.)	3.00	1.50	.90
58c	Dan Godby (Third printing - flat contrast.)	3.00	1.50	.90
59	Bob Locker	3.00	1.50	.90
60	Rollie Fingers (Color)	9.00	4.50	2.75
61	Glenn Abbott	3.00	1.50	.90
62	Jim Todd	3.00	1.50	.90

		NM	EX	VG
63	Phil Garner	3.00	1.50	.90
64	Paul Lindblad	3.00	1.50	.90
65	Bill North (Color)	6.00	3.00	1.75
66	Dick Sisler	3.00	1.50	.90
67	Angel Mangual	3.00	1.50	.90
68	Claudell Washington	3.00	1.50	.90

1976 Doug McWilliams Postcards

		NM	EX	VG
69	Oakland Coliseum (Color)	6.00	3.00	1.75
70	Sal Bando (Color)	6.00	3.00	1.75
71	Mike Torrez (Color)	6.00	3.00	1.75
72	Joe Lonnett	3.00	1.50	.90
73	Chuck Tanner	3.00	1.50	.90
74	Tommy Sandt	3.00	1.50	.90
75	Dick Bosman (Color)	6.00	3.00	1.75
76	Bert Campaneris (Color)	6.00	3.00	1.75
77	Ken Brett	6.00	3.00	1.75
78	Jim Todd (Color)	6.00	3.00	1.75
79	Jeff Newman	3.00	1.50	.90
80	John McCall	3.00	1.50	.90

1977 Doug McWilliams Postcards

		NM	EX	VG
81	Don Baylor (Color)	9.00	4.50	2.75
82	Lee Stange	3.00	1.50	.90
83	Rob Picciolo	3.00	1.50	.90
84	Jack Mc Keon (Color)	6.00	3.00	1.75
85	Rollie Fingers (Color)	9.00	4.50	2.75
86	Manny Sanguillen	3.00	1.50	.90
87	Tony Armas	3.00	1.50	.90
88	Jim Tyrone	3.00	1.50	.90
89	Wayne Gross	3.00	1.50	.90
90	Rick Langford	3.00	1.50	.90
91	Rich Gossage	3.00	1.50	.90
92	Phil Garner (Color)	6.00	3.00	1.75
93	Del Alston	3.00	1.50	.90
94	Bert Blyleven (Color)	7.50	3.75	2.25
95	Willie McCovey (Color)	9.00	4.50	2.75
96	Ken Brett (Color)	6.00	3.00	1.75
97	Doyle Alexander (Color)	6.00	3.00	1.75

1978 Doug McWilliams Postcards

		NM	EX	VG
98	Rene Lacheman	3.00	1.50	.90
99	Del Alston	3.00	1.50	.90
100	Lee Stange (Color)	6.00	3.00	1.75
101	Taylor Duncan	3.00	1.50	.90
102	Matt Keough	3.00	1.50	.90
103	Bruce Robinson	3.00	1.50	.90
104	Sal Bando (Color)	6.00	3.00	1.75

1979 Doug McWilliams Postcards

		NM	EX	VG
105	Alan Wirth	3.00	1.50	.90
106	Mike Edwards	3.00	1.50	.90
107	Craig Minetto	3.00	1.50	.90
108	Mike Morgan	3.00	1.50	.90
109	Brian Kingman	3.00	1.50	.90

1980 Doug McWilliams Postcards

		NM	EX	VG
110	Jim Essian	3.00	1.50	.90
111a	Willie McCovey (Color - first printing - no signature.)	9.00	4.50	2.75
111b	Willie McCovey (Color - second printing - w/signature, stamp at top.)	9.00	4.50	2.75
111c	Willie McCovey (Color - third printing - w/sig., stamp at bottom.)	9.00	4.50	2.75
112a	Willie McCovey (Color - first printing - no signature.)	9.00	4.50	2.75
112b	Willie McCovey (Color - second printing - w/signature.)	9.00	4.50	2.75

1964 Meadowgold Dairy

MICKEY MANTLE SANDY KOUFAX

WILLIE MAYS BILL MAZEROSKI

Four of the mid-Sixties' biggest stars appear as a panel on this milk carton issue. The four-player portion measures about 3-3/4" x 4-1/4" and is printed in shades of blue on the white background. Individual cards measure about 1-1/8" x 2-1/16" and are, of course, blank-backed. In 1998, a complete milk carton was sold at auction for $2,475.

		NM	EX	VG
Complete Set, Panel:		600.00	300.00	180.00
Complete Set, Singles (4):		475.00	250.00	150.00
Common Player:		60.00	30.00	18.00
(1)	Sandy Koufax	85.00	42.00	25.00
(2)	Mickey Mantle	260.00	130.00	78.00
(3)	Willie Mays	80.00	40.00	24.00
(4)	Bill Mazeroski	60.00	30.00	18.00

1911 Mecca Cigarettes

(See 1911 T201 Double Folders.)

1937 Joe "Ducky" Medwick

Little is known about these cards featuring the perennial All-Star of the Gashouse Gang. Both styles are in a round-cornered playing card format, about 2-1/4" x 3-1/2". Fronts have black-and-white artwork of Medwick swinging a bat against a large baseball. The background is black-and-orange with a facsimile autograph at bottom. Most cards are found with some sort of card-game baseball scenario on back, while another type has a black-and-white photo of Medwick signing autographs amid a gaggle of children. His name and the date appear at bottom. It is not known whether the two types of cards were distributed together.

	NM	EX	VG
Joe "Ducky" Medwick (Game card.)	45.00	22.50	13.50
Joe "Ducky" Medwick (Photo back.)	90.00	45.00	25.00

1910 Mello-Mint (E105)

Issued circa 1910 by Smith's Mello-Mint, "The Texas Gum," this set of 50 cards shares the same checklist and artwork as the better known E101 set. Mello-Mint cards are slightly smaller, measuring approximately 1-3/8" x 2-5/8", and are printed on thin paper, making them difficult to find in top condition. Also contributing to condition problems is the fact that many cards were folded vertically to fit the packaging. The backs contain advertising, printed in green, for Mello-Mint Gum. The set carries an ACC designation of E105. Two finds of multiple examples of about eight cards in the 1980s can mislead collectors into thinking the rest of the cards in the set are more common than is actually the case. The cards most heavily over-represented in those finds are indicated with an asterisk.

		NM	EX	VG
Complete Set (50):		170,000	65,000	30,000
Common Player:		1,200	480.00	240.00
(1)	Jack Barry	2,800	1,120	560.00
(2)	Harry Bemis	2,800	1,120	560.00
(3)	Chief Bender (White hat.)	5,600	2,240	1,120
(4)	Chief Bender (Striped hat.)	5,600	2,240	1,120
(5)	Bill Bergen	2,800	1,120	560.00

(6)	Bob Bescher (*)	1,200	480.00	240.00
(7)	Al Bridwell	2,800	1,120	560.00
(8)	Doc Casey (*)	1,200	480.00	240.00
(9)	Frank Chance	6,300	2,520	1,260
(10)	Hal Chase	3,990	1,610	805.00
(11)	Ty Cobb	11,200	4,480	2,240
(12)	Eddie Collins	6,300	2,520	1,260
(13)	Sam Crawford	6,300	2,520	1,260
(14)	Harry Davis	2,800	1,120	560.00
(15)	Art Devlin	2,800	1,120	560.00
(16)	Wild Bill Donovan	2,800	1,120	560.00
(17)	Red Dooin	2,800	1,120	560.00
(18)	Mickey Doolan	2,800	1,120	560.00
(19)	Patsy Dougherty	2,800	1,120	560.00
(20)	Larry Doyle (With bat.)	2,800	1,120	560.00
(21)	Larry Doyle/Throwing	2,800	1,120	560.00
(22)	Johnny Evers	6,300	2,520	1,260
(23)	George Gibson	2,800	1,120	560.00
(24)	Topsy Hartsel (*)	1,200	480.00	240.00
(25)	Fred Jacklitsch	2,800	1,120	560.00
(26)	Hugh Jennings	6,300	2,520	1,260
(27)	Red Kleinow	2,800	1,120	560.00
(28)	Otto Knabe	2,800	1,120	560.00
(29)	Jack Knight (*)	1,200	480.00	240.00
(30)	Nap Lajoie (*)	4,410	1,750	885.00
(31)	Hans Lobert	2,800	1,120	560.00
(32)	Sherry Magee	2,800	1,120	560.00
(33)	Christy Matthewson (Mathewson)	9,800	3,920	1,960
(34)	John McGraw	6,300	2,520	1,260
(35)	Larry McLean	2,800	1,120	560.00
(36)	Dots Miller/Btg	2,800	1,260	560.00
(37)	Dots Miller/Fielding	2,800	1,120	560.00
(38)	Danny Murphy (*)	1,200	480.00	240.00
(39)	Bill O'Hara	2,800	1,120	560.00
(40)	Germany Schaefer	2,800	1,120	560.00
(41)	Admiral Schlei	2,800	1,120	560.00
(42)	Boss Schmidt	2,800	1,120	560.00
(43)	Johnny Seigle	2,800	1,120	560.00
(44)	Dave Shean (*)	1,200	480.00	240.00
(45)	Boss Smith (Schmidt)	2,800	1,120	560.00
(46)	Joe Tinker	6,300	2,520	1,260
(47)	Honus Wagner/Btg	10,500	4,200	2,100
(48)	Honus Wagner/Throwing	10,500	4,200	2,100
(49)	Cy Young (*)	8,400	3,360	1,680
(50)	Heinie Zimmerman	2,800	1,120	560.00

1916 Felix Mendelsohn

This Chicago printing and publishing firm was the originator of the card set often found bearing the advertising of The Sporting News on back, or less frequently with ads from other concerns. Mendelsohn is not mentioned on the cards, which are blank-backed. Fronts of the 1-5/8" x 3" black-and-white cards have a player photo, name, position abbreviation, team and card number. The first version of the set, designated M101-5 in the ACC, was prepared in advance of the 1916 season and offered in ads in The Sporting News for $1, or a framed uncut sheet for $2.50. An updated version, designated M101-4 in the American Card Catalog, was released later in the summer.

(See 1916 M101-4 and M101-5 Blank Backs and 1917 M-UNC.)

1917 Felix Mendelsohn (M101-UNC)

These 2-1/4" x 4" blank-back, black-and-white cards may have been prototypes for a "Hall of Fame" card set advertised early in 1917 by Felix Mendelsohn in The Sporting News. A set of 200 was offered for $1, but may not have actually been produced. Each example of this set is believed to be unique.

(1) Walter Johnson (Value Undetermined)
(2) Christy Mathewson (Value Undetermined)
(3) Ray Schalk (Brought $1,464 in 4/05 auction, in Excellent condition.)

1917-1920 Felix Mendelsohn

Gandil
1st. B. Chicago White Sox.

This set of glossy black-and-white player photos was produced by Chicago publisher Felix Mendelsohn, whose initials appear beneath the copyright logo. The photos measure about 4-3/8" x 6-3/8" and feature action poses of the player whose name, position and team appear at the bottom of the borderless pictures. Four of the players in the checklist appear with two different teams, indicating the photos were issued over a period of several seasons. The set was offered in ads in The Sporting News at $5 for 100 pictures. This checklist may not be complete. Gaps have been left in the assigned numbering to accommodate future additions.

		NM	EX	VG
Complete Set (119):		40,000	20,000	12,000
Common Player:		125.00	60.00	35.00
(1)	Grover C. Alexander (Philadelphia)	600.00	300.00	180.00
(2)	Grover C. Alexander (Chicago)	600.00	300.00	180.00
(3)	Jim Bagby	125.00	60.00	35.00
(4)	Doug Baird	125.00	60.00	35.00
(5)	Franklin Baker	300.00	150.00	90.00
(6)	Dave Bancroft	300.00	150.00	90.00
(7)	Jack Barry	125.00	60.00	35.00
(8)	Johnny Bates	125.00	60.00	35.00
(9)	Carson Bigbee	125.00	60.00	35.00
(10)	"Ping" Bodie	125.00	60.00	35.00
(11)	George Burns	125.00	60.00	35.00
(12)	Joe Bush	125.00	60.00	35.00
(13)	Owen Bush	125.00	60.00	35.00
(14)	Ray Caldwell	125.00	60.00	35.00
(15)	Max Carey	300.00	150.00	90.00
(16)	Ray Chapman	150.00	75.00	45.00
(17)	Hal Chase	250.00	125.00	75.00
(18)	Eddie Cicotte	300.00	150.00	90.00
(19)	Ty Cobb	3,500	1,750	1,050
(20)	Eddie Collins	300.00	150.00	90.00
(21)	Harry Coveleskie (Coveleski)	125.00	60.00	35.00
(22)	"Gavvy" Cravath	125.00	60.00	35.00
(23)	Sam Crawford	300.00	150.00	90.00
(24)	Walton Cruise	125.00	60.00	35.00
(26)	George Cutshaw	125.00	60.00	35.00
(27)	Jake Daubert	125.00	60.00	35.00
(28)	George Dauss	125.00	60.00	35.00
(29)	Dave Davenport	125.00	60.00	35.00
(30)	Bill Doak	125.00	60.00	35.00
(31)	Larry Doyle	125.00	60.00	35.00
(32)	George Dumont	125.00	60.00	35.00
(33)	Howard Ehmke	125.00	60.00	35.00
(34)	Urban Faber	300.00	150.00	90.00
(35)	Happy Felsch	600.00	300.00	180.00
(36)	Art Fletcher	125.00	60.00	35.00
(37)	Del Gainer (Gainor)	125.00	60.00	35.00
(38)	Chick Gandil	300.00	150.00	90.00
(39)	Larry Gardner	125.00	60.00	35.00
(40)	Mike Gonzales (Gonzalez)	125.00	60.00	35.00
(41)	Jack Graney	125.00	60.00	35.00
(42)	Heinie Groh	125.00	60.00	35.00
(43)	Earl Hamilton	125.00	60.00	35.00
(44)	Harry Heilmann	300.00	150.00	90.00
(45)	Buck Herzog	125.00	60.00	35.00
(46)	Hugh High (New York, photo actually Bob Shawkey.)	125.00	60.00	35.00
(47)	Hugh High (Detroit, correct photo.)	125.00	60.00	35.00
(48)	Bill Hinchman	125.00	60.00	35.00
(49)	Dick Hoblitzell	125.00	60.00	35.00
(51)	Walter Holke (New York)	125.00	60.00	35.00
(52)	Walter Holke (Boston)	125.00	60.00	35.00
(53)	Harry Hooper	300.00	150.00	90.00
(54)	Rogers Hornsby	400.00	200.00	120.00
(55)	Joe Jackson	5,000	2,500	1,500
(56)	Bill Jacobson	125.00	60.00	35.00
(57)	Walter Johnson	900.00	450.00	270.00

(58)	Sam Jones	125.00	60.00	35.00
(59)	Joe Judge	125.00	60.00	35.00
(60)	Benny Kauff	125.00	60.00	35.00
(61)	Bill Killefer	125.00	60.00	35.00
(62)	Ed Konetchy (Boston)	125.00	60.00	35.00
(63)	Ed Konetchy (Brooklyn)	125.00	60.00	35.00
(64)	Nemo Leibold	125.00	60.00	35.00
(65)	Duffy Lewis	125.00	60.00	35.00
(66)	Fred Luderas (Luderus)	125.00	60.00	35.00
(67)	Fred Luderus	125.00	60.00	35.00
(68)	Al Mamaux	125.00	60.00	35.00
(69)	Les Mann	125.00	60.00	35.00
(70)	"Rabbit" Maranville	300.00	150.00	90.00
(71)	Armando Marsans	125.00	60.00	35.00
(72)	John McGraw	300.00	150.00	90.00
(73)	Stuffy McInnis	125.00	60.00	35.00
(74)	Lee Meadows	125.00	60.00	35.00
(76)	Fred Merkle	125.00	60.00	35.00
(77)	Clyde Milan	125.00	60.00	35.00
(78)	Otto Miller	125.00	60.00	35.00
(79)	Guy Morton	125.00	60.00	35.00
(80)	Hy Myers	125.00	60.00	35.00
(81)	Greasy Neale	150.00	75.00	45.00
(82)	Dode Paskert	125.00	60.00	35.00
(83)	Roger Peckinpaugh	125.00	60.00	35.00
(84)	Jeff Pfeffer	125.00	60.00	35.00
(85)	Walter Pipp	125.00	60.00	35.00
(86)	Bill Rariden	125.00	60.00	35.00
(87)	Johnny Rawlings	125.00	60.00	35.00
(88)	Sam Rice	300.00	150.00	90.00
(89)	Dave Robertson	125.00	60.00	35.00
(90)	Bob Roth	125.00	60.00	35.00
(91)	Ed Roush	300.00	150.00	90.00
(92)	Dick Rudolph	125.00	60.00	35.00
(93)	Babe Ruth (Red Sox)	4,500	2,250	1,350
(94)	Babe Ruth (New York)	5,000	2,500	1,500
(95)	Vic Saier	125.00	60.00	35.00
(96)	Ray Schalk	300.00	150.00	90.00
(97)	Hank Severeid	125.00	60.00	35.00
(98)	Ernie Shore	125.00	60.00	35.00
(99)	Burt Shotton	125.00	60.00	35.00
(101)	George Sisler	300.00	150.00	90.00
(102)	Jack Smith	125.00	60.00	35.00
(103)	Frank Snyder	125.00	60.00	35.00
(104)	Tris Speaker	400.00	200.00	120.00
(105)	Oscar Stanage	125.00	60.00	35.00
(106)	Casey Stengel	300.00	150.00	90.00
(107)	Amos Strunk	125.00	60.00	35.00
(108)	Jeff Tesreau	125.00	60.00	35.00
(109)	Fred Toney	125.00	60.00	35.00
(110)	Terry Turner	125.00	60.00	35.00
(111)	Jim Vaughn	125.00	60.00	35.00
(112)	Bobby Veach	125.00	60.00	35.00
(113)	Oscar Vitt	125.00	60.00	35.00
(114)	"Honus" Wagner	3,000	1,500	900.00
(115)	Tilly Walker	125.00	60.00	35.00
(116)	Bill Wambsganss	125.00	60.00	35.00
(117)	"Buck" Weaver	600.00	300.00	180.00
(118)	Zack Wheat	300.00	150.00	90.00
(119)	George Whitted	125.00	60.00	35.00
(120)	Cy Williams	125.00	60.00	35.00
(121)	Ivy Wingo	125.00	60.00	35.00
(122)	Pep ("Pep" Young)	125.00	60.00	35.00
(123)	Heinie Zimmerman	125.00	60.00	35.00

1975 Clarence Mengler Baseball's Best

Hank Aaron

This collectors' issue art set holds the distinction of being one of the first whose distribution was halted by the Major League Baseball Players Association for lack of a license to depict current players. Produced as an autograph medium by Illinois collector Clarence Mengler, the 5" x 3" blank-back cards have portraits drawn by Keith Peterson. Of the original production of 200 sets, fewer than half were sold before the union intervened with threatened legal action. Because of a spelling error, the Ralph Garr card was withdrawn early. Hal McRae's card, also misspelled, was not withdrawn. Originally sold in five series, the unnumbered cards are checklisted alphabetically within series.

		NM	EX	VG
Complete Set (125):		150.00	75.00	45.00
Common Player:		1.00	.50	.30
SERIES A				
(1)	Sal Bando	1.00	.50	.30
(2)	Johnny Bench	4.00	2.00	1.25
(3)	Jack Billingham	1.00	.50	.30
(4)	Paul Blair	1.00	.50	.30
(5)	Bert Blyleven	1.00	.70	.45
(6)	Lou Brock	2.50	1.25	.70
(7)	Jeff Burroughs	1.00	.50	.30
(8)	Nate Colbert	1.00	.50	.30
(9)	Carlton Fisk	2.50	1.25	.70
(10)	Bob Gibson	2.50	1.25	.70
(11)	Ferguson Jenkins	2.00	1.00	.60

(12)	Bob Johnson	1.00	.50	.30
(13)	Dave McNally	1.00	.50	.30
(14)	Bobby Murcer	1.50	.70	.45
(15)	Tony Muser	1.00	.50	.30
(16)	Phil Niekro	2.00	1.00	.60
(17)	Brooks Robinson	3.00	1.50	.90
(18)	Frank Robinson	3.00	1.50	.90
(19)	Nolan Ryan	12.00	6.00	3.50
(20)	Mike Schmidt	6.00	3.00	1.75
(21)	Willie Stargell	2.50	1.25	.70
(22)	Andre Thornton	1.00	.50	.30
(23)	Bobby Tolan	1.00	.50	.30
(24)	Jim Wynn	1.00	.50	.30
(25)	Richie Zisk	1.00	.50	.30
SERIES B				
(26)	Hank Aaron	9.00	4.50	2.75
(27)	Larry Bowa	1.00	.50	.30
(28)	Steve Carlton	2.50	1.25	.70
(29)	Cesar Cedeno	1.00	.50	.30
(30)	Jim Colborn	1.00	.50	.30
(31)	Tim Foli	1.00	.50	.30
(32)	Steve Garvey	1.50	.70	.45
(33)	Bud Harrelson	1.00	.50	.30
(34)	Willie Horton	1.00	.50	.30
(35)	Jim Hunter	2.00	1.00	.60
(36)	Reggie Jackson	6.00	3.00	1.75
(37)	Billy Martin	1.50	.70	.45
(38)	Bake McBride	1.00	.50	.30
(39)	Andy Messersmith	1.00	.50	.30
(40)	Rick Monday	1.00	.50	.30
(41)	Joe Morgan	2.50	1.25	.70
(42)	Tony Oliva	1.50	.70	.45
(43)	Amos Otis	1.00	.50	.30
(44)	Gaylord Perry	2.00	1.00	.60
(45)	Tom Seaver	5.00	2.50	1.50
(46)	Ken Singleton	1.00	.50	.30
(47)	Chris Speier	1.00	.50	.30
(48)	Gene Tenace	1.00	.50	.30
(49)	Del Unser	1.00	.50	.30
(50)	Carl Yastrzemski	5.00	2.50	1.50
SERIES C				
(51)	Steve Busby	1.00	.50	.30
(52)	Jose Cardenal	1.00	.50	.30
(53)	Rod Carew	2.50	1.25	.70
(54)	Ron Cey	1.00	.50	.30
(55)	Willie Davis	1.00	.50	.30
(56)	Barry Foote	1.00	.50	.30
(57)	Ken Holtzman	1.00	.50	.30
(58)	Davey Lopes	1.00	.50	.30
(59)	Greg Luzinski	1.00	.50	.30
(60)	Sparky Lyle	1.00	.50	.30
(61)	Dave May	1.00	.50	.30
(62)	Lee May	1.00	.50	.30
(63)	Doc Medich	1.00	.50	.30
(64)	Bill Melton	1.00	.50	.30
(65)	Randy Moffitt	1.00	.50	.30
(66)	Don Money	1.00	.50	.30
(67)	Al Oliver	1.50	.70	.45
(68)	George Scott	1.00	.50	.30
(69)	Ted Simmons	1.00	.50	.30
(70)	Charlie Spikes	1.00	.50	.30
(71)	Rusty Staub	1.25	.60	.40
(72)	Jim Sundberg	1.00	.50	.30
(73)	Bob Watson	1.00	.50	.30
(74)	Dick Williams	1.00	.50	.30
(75)	Dave Winfield	2.50	1.25	.70
SERIES D				
(76)	Vida Blue	1.00	.50	.30
(77)	Bobby Bonds	1.00	.50	.30
(78)	Jerry Coleman	1.00	.50	.30
(79)	Bob Coluccio	1.00	.50	.30
(80)	Joe Decker	1.00	.50	.30
(81)	Darrell Evans	1.00	.50	.30
(82)	Ralph Gaar (Garr)/SP	4.00	2.00	1.25
(83)	Richie Hebner	1.00	.50	.30
(84)	Ken Henderson	1.00	.50	.30
(85)	Bill Madlock	1.00	.50	.30
(86)	Jon Matlack	1.00	.50	.30
(87)	Carlos May	1.00	.50	.30
(88)	John Mayberry	1.00	.50	.30
(89)	Willie McCovey	2.50	1.25	.70
(90)	Lynn McGlothen	1.00	.50	.30
(91)	Tug McGraw	1.00	.50	.30
(92)	Roger Metzger	1.00	.50	.30
(93)	Jim Palmer	2.00	1.00	.60
(94)	Rico Petrocelli	1.00	.50	.30
(95)	Ellie Rodriguez	1.00	.50	.30
(96)	Steve Rogers	1.00	.50	.30
(97)	Pete Rose	9.00	4.50	2.75
(98)	Bill Singer	1.00	.50	.30
(99)	Don Sutton	2.00	1.00	.60
(100)	Billy Williams	2.50	1.25	.70
SERIES E				
(101)	Mark Belanger	1.00	.50	.30
(102)	Buddy Bell	1.00	.50	.30
(103)	Jim Bibby	1.00	.50	.30
(104)	Bob Boone	1.00	.50	.30
(105)	Ken Brett	1.00	.50	.30
(106)	Ron Bryant	1.00	.50	.30
(107)	Bill Buckner	1.00	.50	.30
(108)	Buzz Capra	1.00	.50	.30
(109)	Dave Concepcion	1.00	.50	.30
(110)	Rollie Fingers	2.00	1.00	.60
(111)	Bill Freehan	1.00	.50	.30
(112)	Bobby Grich	1.00	.50	.30
(113)	Fred Kendall	1.00	.50	.30
(114)	Don Kessinger	1.00	.50	.30
(115)	Hal McRae (McRae)	1.00	.50	.30
(116)	Thurman Munson	2.50	1.25	.70
(117)	Fred Patek	1.00	.50	.30
(118)	Doug Rader	1.00	.50	.30
(119)	A. (Aurelio) Rodriguez	1.00	.50	.30
(120)	Manny Sanguillen	1.00	.50	.30
(121)	Reggie Smith	1.00	.50	.30
(122)	Danny Thompson	1.00	.50	.30
(123)	Luis Tiant	1.00	.50	.30
(124)	Joe Torre	1.50	.70	.45
(125)	Wilbur Wood	1.00	.50	.30

1953-54 Marshall Merrell Milwaukee Braves Portfolio

One of several portfolios of Milwaukee Braves artwork produced during the team's first few years, this issue of 8" x 10" black-and-white lithographs was sold at County Stadium for 25 cents apiece. The player checklist here is believed to be complete, but it is possible other poses may be reported. The cards are blank-backed and unnumbered; the checklist here has been arranged alphabetically.

		NM	EX	VG
Complete Set (25):		900.00	450.00	275.00
Common Player:		25.00	12.50	7.50
(1)	Henry Aaron	200.00	100.00	60.00
(2)	Joe Adcock	25.00	12.50	7.50
(3)	Johnny Antonelli	25.00	12.50	7.50
(4)	Billy Bruton	25.00	12.50	7.50
(5)	Bob Buhl	25.00	12.50	7.50
(6)	Lou Burdette (Follow-through.)	25.00	12.50	7.50
(7)	Lew Burdette (Wind-up.)	25.00	12.50	7.50
(8)	Gene Conley	25.00	12.50	7.50
(9)	Del Crandall	25.00	12.50	7.50
(10)	Jack Dittmer	25.00	12.50	7.50
(11)	Sid Gordon/Btg	25.00	12.50	7.50
(12)	Sid Gordon/Standing	25.00	12.50	7.50
(13)	Charlie Grimm (Tomahawk on jersey.)	25.00	12.50	7.50
(14)	Charlie Grimm (No tomahawk.)	25.00	12.50	7.50
(15)	Don Liddle	25.00	12.50	7.50
(16)	Johnny Logan	25.00	12.50	7.50
(17)	Ed Mathews/Btg	75.00	37.50	22.50
(18)	Ed Mathews/Standing	75.00	37.50	22.50
(19)	Danny O'Connell	25.00	12.50	7.50
(20)	Andy Pafko	25.00	12.50	7.50
(21)	Jim Pendleton	25.00	12.50	7.50
(22)	Warren Spahn	75.00	37.50	22.50
(23)	Max Surkont	25.00	12.50	7.50
(24)	Bobby Thomson	45.00	22.50	13.50
(25)	Jim Wilson	25.00	12.50	7.50

1979 Metallic Creations Signature Miniatures

This collectors' issue was created by combining an approximately 3-1/2" tall pewter statue with a 3-5/8" x 5" baseball card. The statues were released in pewter at about $10 apiece and silver-plate at $20. The black-bordered cards feature color portraits in front of a pair of sepia action pictures. The artwork was by J. Payette. Fronts also feature a facsimile autograph. Backs have basic player personal data and career stats. It was reported that 5,000 of each card were printed, though most were never issued due to failure of the venture. The remaining cards and statues were sold into the hobby as remainders. It is unclear whether a Munson card exists, although the Munson statue and the Ryan card have been confirmed.

		NM	EX	VG
Complete Set, Cards (20):		240.00	120.00	70.00
Common Card:		7.50	3.75	2.25
Complete Set, Pewter Statues (20):		200.00	100.00	60.00
Common Statue:		7.50	3.75	2.25
Silver-plate Statues: 2X				
(1)	Hank Aaron (Card)	12.50	6.25	3.75
(1)	Hank Aaron (Statue)	12.50	6.25	3.75
(2)	Rod Carew (Card)	7.50	3.75	2.25
(2)	Rod Carew (Statue)	7.50	3.75	2.25
(3)	Cesar Cedeno (Card)	7.50	3.75	2.25
(4)	Ty Cobb (Card)	15.00	7.50	4.50
(4)	Ty Cobb (Statue)	12.50	6.25	3.75
(5)	Steve Garvey (Card)	15.00	7.50	4.50
(5)	Steve Garvey (Statue)	15.00	7.50	4.50

		NM	EX	VG
(6)	Lou Gehrig (Card)	15.00	7.50	4.50
(6)	Lou Gehrig (Statue)	15.00	7.50	4.50
(7)	Ron Guidry (Card)	7.50	3.75	2.25
(7)	Ron Guidry (Statue)	7.50	3.75	2.25
(8)	Rogers Hornsby (Card)	7.50	3.75	2.25
(8)	Rogers Hornsby (Statue)	7.50	3.75	2.25
(9)	Walter Johnson (Card)	10.00	5.00	3.00
(9)	Walter Johnson (Statue)	10.00	5.00	3.00
(10)	Ralph Kiner (Card)	7.50	3.75	2.25
(10)	Ralph Kiner (Statue)	7.50	3.75	2.25
(11)	Sandy Koufax (Card)	20.00	10.00	6.00
(11)	Sandy Koufax (Statue)	20.00	10.00	6.00
(12)	Davey Lopes (Card)	7.50	3.75	2.25
(12)	Davey Lopes (Statue)	7.50	3.75	2.25
(13)	Christy Mathewson (Card)	10.00	5.00	3.00
(13)	Christy Mathewson (Statue)	10.00	5.00	3.00
(14)	Willie Mays (Card)	15.00	7.50	4.50
(14)	Willie Mays (Statue)	15.00	7.50	4.50
(15)	Willie McCovey (Card)	10.00	5.00	3.00
(15)	Willie McCovey (Statue)	10.00	5.00	3.00
(16)	Thurman Munson (Statue)	10.00	5.00	3.00
(17)	Mel Ott (Card)	7.50	3.75	2.25
(17)	Mel Ott (Statue)	7.50	3.75	2.25
(18)	Babe Ruth (Card)	12.50	6.25	3.75
(18)	Babe Ruth (Statue)	12.50	6.25	3.75
(19)	Nolan Ryan (Card)	30.00	15.00	9.00
(20)	Tris Speaker (Card)	7.50	3.75	2.25
(20)	Tris Speaker (Statue)	7.50	3.75	2.25
(21)	Honus Wagner (Card)	10.00	5.00	3.00
(21)	Honus Wagner (Statue)	10.00	5.00	3.00

1938-39 Metropolitan Clothing Cincinnati Reds Postcards

(See 1937-39 Orcajo Cincinnati Reds postcards for checklist, values.)

1968 Metropolitan Museum of Art Burdick Collection

The date of issue is approximate for this set promoting New York's Metropolitan Museum of Art as the repository for the Jefferson Burdick collection, once the world's premier accumulation of trading cards. Burdick, author of the once-standard "American Card Catalog" donated his collection to the Met. The 2-3/4" x 3-5/8" black-and-white glossy card fronts reproduce 1928 R315 cards of major leaguers and earlier Zeenuts cards of minor leaguers. Backs have a few words about the museum and a "Printed in Western Germany" line. The unnumbered cards are checklisted here in alphabetical order.

		NM	EX	VG
Complete Set (8):		125.00	65.00	35.00
Common Player:		10.00	5.00	3.00
(1)	Max Bishop	10.00	5.00	3.00
(2)	Lou Gehrig	40.00	20.00	12.00
(3)	Carl Hubbell	15.00	7.50	4.50
(4)	Art Kores	10.00	5.00	3.00
(5)	Bill Leard	10.00	5.00	3.00
(6)	Babe Ruth	50.00	25.00	15.00
(7)	Dazzy Vance	10.00	5.00	3.00
(8)	Elmer Zacher	10.00	5.00	3.00

1931 Metropolitan Studio St. Louis Cardinals

Members of the St. Louis Cardinals are featured in this 30-card set. The cards were printed on heavy paper and feature sepia-toned photos. The player's name appears along the bottom white border below the photo. The cards measure 6-1/4" x 9-1/2" and are not numbered. Most cards feature the logo of Metropolitan Studio in a bottom corner, while others have "Sid Whiting St. Louis MO," and a few have no sponsor's credit.

		NM	EX	VG
Complete Set (30):		1,800	810.00	450.00
Common Player:		45.00	20.00	12.00
(1)	Earl "Sparky" Adams	45.00	20.00	12.00
(2)	Ray Blades	45.00	20.00	12.00
(3)	James Bottomley	95.00	45.00	25.00
(4)	Sam Breadon	45.00	20.00	12.00
(5)	James "Rip" Collins	45.00	20.00	12.00
(6)	Dizzy Dean	225.00	100.00	55.00
(7)	Paul Derringer	45.00	20.00	12.00
(8)	Jake Flowers	45.00	20.00	12.00
(9)	Frank Frisch	95.00	45.00	25.00
(10)	Charles Gelbert	45.00	20.00	12.00
(11)	Miguel Gonzales (Gonzalez)	80.00	35.00	20.00
(12)	Burleigh Grimes	95.00	45.00	25.00
(13)	Charles "Chick" Hafey	95.00	45.00	25.00
(14)	William Hallahan	45.00	20.00	12.00
(15)	Jesse Haines	95.00	45.00	25.00
(16)	Andrew High	45.00	20.00	12.00
(17)	Sylvester Johnson	45.00	20.00	12.00
(18)	Tony Kaufmann	45.00	20.00	12.00
(19)	James Lindsey	45.00	20.00	12.00
(20)	Gus Mancuso	45.00	20.00	12.00
(21)	John Leonard "Pepper" Martin	80.00	35.00	20.00
(22)	Ernest Orsatti	45.00	20.00	12.00
(23)	Charles Flint Rhem	45.00	20.00	12.00
(24)	Branch Rickey	125.00	55.00	35.00
(25)	Walter Roettger	45.00	20.00	12.00
(26)	Allyn Stout	45.00	20.00	12.00
(27)	"Gabby" Street	45.00	20.00	12.00
(28)	Clyde Wares	45.00	20.00	12.00
(29)	George Watkins	45.00	20.00	12.00
(30)	James Wilson	45.00	20.00	12.00

1979 Michigan Sports Collectors

Former Detroit Tigers, along with several baseball writers and announcers, including some who were appearing as autograph guests were featured in this collectors set issued in conjunction with the 1979 Troy, Mich. show. Cards are 3-1/2" x 5-1/16" black-and-white. Backs have personal data and a career summary of the pictured player, along with mention of the show. The unnumbered cards are checklisted here alphabetically.

		NM	EX	VG
Complete Set (20):		20.00	10.00	6.00
Common Player:		3.00	1.50	.90
(1)	Gates Brown	3.00	1.50	.90
(2)	Norm Cash	5.00	2.50	1.50
(3)	Al Cicotte	3.00	1.50	.90
(4)	Roy Cullenbine	3.00	1.50	.90
(5)	Gene Desautels	3.00	1.50	.90
(6)	Hoot Evers	3.00	1.50	.90
(7)	Joe Falls	3.00	1.50	.90
(8)	Joe Ginsberg	3.00	1.50	.90
(9)	Ernie Harwell	3.00	1.50	.90

(10)	Ray Herbert	3.00	1.50	.90
(11)	John Hiller	3.00	1.50	.90
(12)	Billy Hoeft	3.00	1.50	.90
(13)	Ralph Houk	4.00	2.00	1.25
(14)	Cliff Kachline	3.00	1.50	.90
(15)	George Kell	5.00	2.50	1.50
(16)	Ron LeFlore	4.00	2.00	1.25
(17)	Barney McCosky	3.00	1.50	.90
(18)	Jim Northrup	3.00	1.50	.90
(19)	Dick Radatz	3.00	1.50	.90
(20)	Tom Timmermann	3.00	1.50	.90

1940 Michigan Sportservice Detroit Tigers

Apparently a team issue sent to persons who wrote the team or players for photos, these blank-back cards measure 4-1/8" x 6-1/4" and are printed in black-and-white. A facsimile autograph is printed over the central portrait, which is surrounded by a border of baseballs. A few career notes are printed under the photo. At bottom-left is a union printing label. At bottom-right is printed, "Copyrighted 1939, Michigan Sportservice, Inc. Unauthorized Reproduction Prohibited." The unnumbered cards are checklisted here alphabetically.

		NM	EX	VG
Complete Set (21):		5,400	2,700	1,650
Common Player:		300.00	150.00	90.00
(1)	Earl Averill	350.00	175.00	105.00
(2)	Dick Bartell	300.00	150.00	90.00
(3)	Roy "Beau" Bell	300.00	150.00	90.00
(4)	Al Benton	300.00	150.00	90.00
(5)	Tommy Bridges	300.00	150.00	90.00
(6)	Frank Croucher	300.00	150.00	90.00
(7)	Pete Fox	300.00	150.00	90.00
(8)	Charlie Gehringer	400.00	200.00	120.00
(9)	Hank Greenberg	550.00	275.00	165.00
(10)	John Gorsica	300.00	150.00	90.00
(11)	Pinky Higgins	300.00	150.00	90.00
(12)	Fred Hutchinson	300.00	150.00	90.00
(13)	Ralph "Red" Kress	300.00	150.00	90.00
(14)	Barney McCosky	300.00	150.00	90.00
(15)	Archie R. McKain	300.00	150.00	90.00
(16)	Hal Newhouser	350.00	175.00	105.00
(17)	Louis "Buck" Newsom	300.00	150.00	90.00
(18)	Schoolboy Rowe	300.00	150.00	90.00
(19)	Birdie Tebbetts	300.00	150.00	90.00
(20)	Dizzy Trout	300.00	150.00	90.00
(21)	Rudy York	300.00	150.00	90.00

1975 Mid-Atlantic Sports Collectors Assn.

This "Baseball Royalty" collectors' set was issued in conjunction with the 1975 convention of the Mid-Atlantic Sports Collectors Association in Pikesville, Md. The blank-backed, 2-1/2" x 4-3/4" cards are printed in red and blue on white with player photos in blue. Each of the players in the set has a name or nickname pertaining to royalty. The unnumbered cards are checklisted here in alphabetical order.

		NM	EX	VG
Complete Set (8):		20.00	10.00	6.00
Common Player:		3.00	1.50	.90
(1)	Paul (Duke) Derringer	3.00	1.50	.90
(2)	Elroy (Baron of the Bullpen) Face	3.00	1.50	.90
(3)	Rogers (Rajah) Hornsby	5.00	2.50	1.50
(4)	(King) Carl Hubbell	4.00	2.00	1.25
(5)	Charley (King Kong) Keller	3.00	1.50	.90
(6)	Babe (Sultan of Swat) Ruth	10.00	5.00	3.00
(7)	(Prince) Hal Schumacher	3.00	1.50	.90
(8)	Edwin (Duke) Snider	7.50	3.75	2.25

1927 Middy Bread Browns/ Cardinals Die-Cuts

St. Louis Cardinals and St. Louis Browns players comprise this set. Black-and-white, blank-backed and unnumbered, the cards are known only in die-cut form, and vary in size according to the player pose, with a typical card measuring 2-1/4" x 4" or so. The checklist, arranged alphabetically, consists of 22 players from each team, but may be subject to future additions. Similar to the previous year's issue of Kut Outs Yankees and Giants die-cut cards, this issue features posed action photos with the backgrounds cut away and the player and team name printed at the bottom of the photo. Unlike the earlier New York issue, however, these cards carry an advertisement at bottom for Midday Bread, and were presumably issued in the St. Louis area, though the exact method of their distribution is unknown. Cards are blank-backed and unnumbered. As with all die-cut cards, various appendages and bat ends were easily torn off and cards with such defects suffer severe loss of value.

		NM	EX	VG
Complete Set (44):		13,500	6,750	4,250
Common Player:		300.00	120.00	60.00
St. Louis Browns				
(1)	Spencer Adams	450.00	180.00	90.00
(2)	Win Ballou	300.00	120.00	60.00
(3)	Walter Beck	300.00	120.00	60.00
(4)	Herschel Bennett	300.00	120.00	60.00
(5)	Stewart Bolen	300.00	120.00	60.00
(6)	Leo Dixon	300.00	120.00	60.00
(7)	Chester Falk	300.00	120.00	60.00
(8)	Milton Gaston	300.00	120.00	60.00
(9)	Walter Gerber	300.00	120.00	60.00
(10)	Sam Jones	300.00	120.00	60.00
(11)	Oscar Melillo	300.00	120.00	60.00
(12)	Bing Miller	300.00	120.00	60.00
(13)	Otis Miller	300.00	120.00	60.00
(14)	Billie Mullen	300.00	120.00	60.00
(15)	Ernie Nevers	600.00	240.00	120.00
(16)	Steve O'Neill	300.00	120.00	60.00
(17)	Harry Rice	300.00	120.00	60.00
(18)	George Sisler	500.00	200.00	100.00
(19)	Walter Stewart	300.00	120.00	60.00
(20)	Elam VanGilder	300.00	120.00	60.00
(21)	Ken Williams	300.00	120.00	60.00
(22)	Ernie Wingard	300.00	120.00	60.00
St. Louis Cardinals				
(1)	Grover Alexander	600.00	240.00	120.00
(2)	Herman Bell	300.00	120.00	60.00
(3)	Lester Bell	300.00	120.00	60.00
(4)	Ray Blades	300.00	120.00	60.00
(5)	Jim Bottomley	500.00	200.00	100.00
(6)	Danny Clark	300.00	120.00	60.00
(7)	Taylor Douthit	300.00	120.00	60.00
(8)	Frank Frisch	500.00	200.00	100.00
(9)	Chick Hafey	500.00	200.00	100.00

		NM	EX	VG
(10)	Jesse Haines	500.00	200.00	100.00
(11)	Vic Keen	300.00	120.00	60.00
(12)	Carlise Littlejohn	300.00	120.00	60.00
(13)	Bob McGraw	300.00	120.00	60.00
(14)	Bob O'Farrell	300.00	120.00	60.00
(15)	Art Reinhardt	300.00	120.00	60.00
(16)	Jimmy Ring	300.00	120.00	60.00
(17)	Walter Roettger	300.00	120.00	60.00
(18)	Robert Schang	300.00	120.00	60.00
(19)	Willie Sherdel	300.00	120.00	60.00
(20)	Billy Southworth	300.00	120.00	60.00
(21)	Tommy Thevenow	300.00	120.00	60.00
(22)	George Toporcer	300.00	120.00	60.00

1976 Midwest Sports Collectors Convention

7th Annual Midwest
Sport Collectors Convention
July 16, 17, 18, 1976
Troy-Hilton, Michigan

This collectors' issue was produced in conjunction with the 7th annual convention of the Midwest Sports Collectors in Troy, Mich. Former members of the Detroit Tigers, with an emphasis on the 1930s, are featured on the black-and-white, 2-3/8" x 2-7/8" cards. Players are depicted in portrait and action drawings, with personal data and career highlights added in either written or comic form. Backs advertise the show. The unnumbered cards are checklisted here in alphabetical order.

		NM	EX	VG
Complete Set (23):		15.00	7.50	4.50
Common Player:		3.00	1.50	.90
(1)	Eldon Auker	3.00	1.50	.90
(2)	Tommy Bridges	3.00	1.50	.90
(3)	Flea Clifton	3.00	1.50	.90
(4)	Mickey Cochrane	7.50	3.75	2.25
(5)	General Crowder	3.00	1.50	.90
(6)	Frank Doljack	3.00	1.50	.90
(7)	Carl Fischer	3.00	1.50	.90
(8)	Pete Fox	3.00	1.50	.90
(9)	Charlie Gehringer	6.00	3.00	1.75
(10)	Goose Goslin	4.50	2.25	1.25
(11)	Hank Greenberg	9.00	4.50	2.75
(12)	Luke Hamlin	3.00	1.50	.90
(13)	Ray Hayworth	3.00	1.50	.90
(14)	Chief Hogsett	3.00	1.50	.90
(15)	Firpo Marberry	3.00	1.50	.90
(16)	Marvin Owen	3.00	1.50	.90
(17)	Cy Perkins	3.00	1.50	.90
(18)	Bill Rogell	3.00	1.50	.90
(19)	Schoolboy Rowe	3.00	1.50	.90
(20)	Heinie Schuble	3.00	1.50	.90
(21)	Vic Sorrell	3.00	1.50	.90
(22)	Gee Walker	3.00	1.50	.90
(23)	Jo Jo White	3.00	1.50	.90

1980 Midwest Sports Collectors Convention

Reprints of a number of the player postcards of J.D. McCarthy were produced in conjunction with the 1980 Detroit show. The blank-backed, black-and-white postcards are 3-1/4" x 5-1/2" and all feature former Detroit Tigers. The unnumbered cards are checklisted here alphabetically.

		NM	EX	VG
Complete Set (11):		7.50	3.75	2.25
Common Player:		1.00	.50	.30
(1)	Bob Anderson	1.00	.50	.30

		NM	EX	VG
(2)	Babe Birrer	1.00	.50	.30
(3)	Frank Bolling	1.00	.50	.30
(4)	Jim Bunning	2.00	1.00	.60
(5)	Al Cicotte	1.00	.50	.30
(6)	Paul Foytack	1.00	.50	.30
(7)	Joe Ginsberg	1.00	.50	.30
(8)	Steve Gromek	1.00	.50	.30
(9)	Art Houtteman	1.00	.50	.30
(10)	Al Kaline	5.00	2.50	1.50
(11)	Harvey Kuenn	2.00	1.00	.60

1971 Milk Duds

These cards were issued on the backs of five-cent packages of Milk Duds candy. Most collectors prefer complete boxes, rather than cut-out cards, which measure approximately 1-13/16" x 2-5/8" when trimmed tightly. Values quoted below are for complete boxes. Cut cards will bring 50-75 percent of the quoted values. The set includes 37 National League and 32 American League players. Card numbers appear on the box flap, with each number from 1 through 24 being shared by three different players. A suffix (a, b and c) has been added for the collector's convenience. Harmon Killebrew, Brooks Robinson and Pete Rose were double-printed.

		NM	EX	VG
Complete Set, Boxes:		1,000	500.00	300.00
Complete Set, Singles (72):		500.00	250.00	150.00
Common Player:		10.00	5.00	3.00
1a	Frank Howard	12.00	6.00	3.50
1b	Fritz Peterson	10.00	5.00	3.00
1c	Pete Rose	55.00	27.50	16.50
2a	Johnny Bench	15.00	7.50	4.50
2b	Rico Carty	10.00	5.00	3.00
2c	Pete Rose	55.00	27.50	16.50
3a	Ken Holtzman	10.00	5.00	3.00
3b	Willie Mays	50.00	25.00	15.00
3c	Cesar Tovar	10.00	5.00	3.00
4a	Willie Davis	10.00	5.00	3.00
4b	Harmon Killebrew	15.00	7.50	4.50
4c	Felix Millan	10.00	5.00	3.00
5a	Billy Grabarkewitz	10.00	5.00	3.00
5b	Andy Messersmith	10.00	5.00	3.00
5c	Thurman Munson	45.00	22.50	13.50
6a	Luis Aparicio	13.50	6.75	4.00
6b	Lou Brock	13.50	6.75	4.00
6c	Bill Melton	10.00	5.00	3.00
7a	Ray Culp	10.00	5.00	3.00
7b	Willie McCovey	20.00	10.00	6.00
7c	Luke Walker	10.00	5.00	3.00
8a	Roberto Clemente	115.00	55.00	35.00
8b	Jim Merritt	10.00	5.00	3.00
8c	Claud Osteen (Claude)	10.00	5.00	3.00
9a	Stan Bahnsen	10.00	5.00	3.00
9b	Sam McDowell	10.00	5.00	3.00
9c	Billy Williams	15.00	7.50	4.50
10a	Jim Hickman	10.00	5.00	3.00
10b	Dave McNally	10.00	5.00	3.00
10c	Tony Perez	20.00	10.00	6.00
11a	Hank Aaron	40.00	20.00	12.00
11b	Glen Beckert (Glenn)	10.00	5.00	3.00
11c	Ray Fosse	10.00	5.00	3.00
12a	Alex Johnson	10.00	5.00	3.00
12b	Gaylord Perry	13.50	6.75	4.00
12c	Wayne Simpson	10.00	5.00	3.00
13a	Dave Johnson	10.00	5.00	3.00
13b	George Scott	10.00	5.00	3.00
13c	Tom Seaver	25.00	12.50	7.50
14a	Bill Freehan	10.00	5.00	3.00
14b	Bud Harrelson	10.00	5.00	3.00
14c	Manny Sanguillen	10.00	5.00	3.00
15a	Bob Gibson	15.00	7.50	4.50
15b	Rusty Staub	12.00	6.00	3.50
15c	Roy White	10.00	5.00	3.00
16a	Jim Fregosi	10.00	5.00	3.00
16b	Catfish Hunter	13.50	6.75	4.00
16c	Mel Stottlemyer (Stottlemyre)	10.00	5.00	3.00
17a	Tommy Harper	10.00	5.00	3.00
17b	Frank Robinson	20.00	10.00	6.00
17c	Reggie Smith	10.00	5.00	3.00
18a	Orlando Cepeda	20.00	10.00	6.00
18b	Rico Petrocelli	10.00	5.00	3.00
18c	Brooks Robinson	20.00	10.00	6.00
19a	Tony Oliva	12.00	6.00	3.50
19b	Milt Pappas	10.00	5.00	3.00

		NM	EX	VG
19c	Bobby Tolan	10.00	5.00	3.00
20a	Ernie Banks	30.00	15.00	9.00
20b	Don Kessinger	10.00	5.00	3.00
20c	Joe Torre	12.00	6.00	3.50
21a	Fergie Jenkins	13.50	6.75	4.00
21b	Jim Palmer	15.00	7.50	4.50
21c	Ron Santo	12.00	6.00	3.50
22a	Randy Hundley	10.00	5.00	3.00
22b	Dennis Menke (Denis)	10.00	5.00	3.00
22c	Boog Powell	12.00	6.00	3.50
23a	Dick Dietz	10.00	5.00	3.00
23b	Tommy John	10.00	5.00	3.00
23c	Brooks Robinson	20.00	10.00	6.00
24a	Danny Cater	10.00	5.00	3.00
24b	Harmon Killebrew	15.00	7.50	4.50
24c	Jim Perry	12.00	6.00	3.50

1933 George C. Miller (R300)

Jimmy Dykes, Infield

George C. Miller & Co. of Boston, Mass., issued a 32-card set in 1933. The set, which received limited distribution, consists of 16 National League and 16 American League players. The cards are color art reproductions of actual photographs and measure 2-3/8" x 2-7/8". Two distinct variations can be found for each card in the set. Type 1 cards have the names "Fox" and "Klien" misspelled on the back, while Type 2 cards have them correctly as "Foxx" and "Klein." Collectors were advised on the card backs to collect all 32 cards and return them for prizes. (Ivy Andrews' card was short-printed to avoid giving out too many prizes.) The cancelled cards were returned to the collector with the prize. Two forms of cancellation were used; one involved the complete trimming of the bottom one-quarter of the card, the other a diamond-shaped series of punch holes. Cancelled cards have a significantly decreased value.

		NM	EX	VG
	Complete Set (32):	65,000	30,000	16,000
	Common Player:	1,200	550.00	300.00
(1)	Dale Alexander	1,200	550.00	300.00
(2)	"Ivy" Paul Andrews	5,500	2,475	1,375
	Cut-cancelled: 1150.00			
	Punch-cancelled: 2,400			
(3)	Earl Averill	2,500	1,125	625.00
(4)	Dick Bartell	1,200	550.00	300.00
(5)	Walter Berger	1,200	550.00	300.00
(6)	Jim Bottomley	2,500	1,125	625.00
(7)	Joe Cronin	2,500	1,125	625.00
(8)	Jerome "Dizzy" Dean	3,000	1,350	750.00
(9)	William Dickey	2,500	1,125	625.00
(10)	Jimmy Dykes	1,200	550.00	300.00
(11)	Wesley Ferrell	1,200	550.00	300.00
(12)	Jimmy Foxx	3,500	1,575	875.00
(13)	Frank Frisch	2,500	1,125	625.00
(14)	Charlie Gehringer	2,500	1,125	625.00
(15)	Leon "Goose" Goslin	2,500	1,125	625.00
(16)	Charlie Grimm	1,200	550.00	300.00
(17)	Bob "Lefty" Grove	3,000	1,350	750.00
(18)	Charles "Chick" Hafey	2,500	1,125	625.00
(19)	Ray Hayworth	1,200	550.00	300.00
(20)	Charles "Chuck" Klein	2,500	1,125	625.00
(21)	Walter "Rabbit" Maranville	2,500	1,125	625.00
(22)	Oscar Melillo	1,200	550.00	300.00
(23)	Frank "Lefty" O'Doul	2,000	900.00	500.00
(24)	Melvin Ott	2,750	1,225	685.00
(25)	Carl Reynolds	1,200	550.00	300.00
(26)	Charles Ruffing	2,500	1,125	625.00
(27)	Al Simmons	2,500	1,125	625.00
(28)	Joe Stripp	1,200	550.00	300.00
(29)	Bill Terry	2,500	1,125	625.00
(30)	Lloyd Waner	2,500	1,125	625.00
(31)	Paul Waner	2,500	1,125	625.00
(32)	Lonnie Warneke	1,200	550.00	300.00

1969 Milton Bradley

TOMMY JOHN

The first of three sets issued by Milton Bradley over a four-year period, these cards were part of a baseball board game. The unnumbered cards measure 2" x 3" and have a white border surrounding the black-and-white player photo. The player's name appears above the photo in upper case letters. There are no team designations and the photos are airbrushed to eliminate team logos. Backs display biographical data along the top followed by a list of various game situations used in playing the board game. The cards have square corners. The 1969 and 1972 game cards are virtually identical in format. They can be differentiated by looking on the back at any numeral "1" in a line of red type. If the "1" does not have a base, it is a 1969 card; if there is a base, the card is a 1972. Besides individual player cards, there was a non-photographic team cards for each of the contemporary 24 Major League teams.

		NM	EX	VG
	Complete Boxed Set:	400.00	200.00	120.00
	Complete Set (296):	150.00	75.00	45.00
	Common Player:	.50	.25	.15
	Team Card:	2.00	1.00	.60
(1)	Hank Aaron	30.00	15.00	9.00
(2)	Ted Abernathy	.50	.25	.15
(3)	Jerry Adair	.50	.25	.15
(4)	Tommy Agee	.50	.25	.15
(5)	Bernie Allen	.50	.25	.15
(6)	Hank Allen	.50	.25	.15
(7)	Richie Allen	5.00	2.50	1.50
(8)	Gene Alley	.50	.25	.15
(9)	Bob Allison	.50	.25	.15
(10)	Felipe Alou	1.00	.50	.30
(11)	Jesus Alou	.50	.25	.15
(12)	Matty Alou	.50	.25	.15
(13)	Max Alvis	.50	.25	.15
(14)	Mike Andrews	.50	.25	.15
(15)	Luis Aparicio	10.00	5.00	3.00
(16)	Jose Arcia	.50	.25	.15
(17)	Bob Aspromonte	.50	.25	.15
(18)	Joe Azcue	.50	.25	.15
(19)	Ernie Banks	20.00	10.00	6.00
(20)	Steve Barber	.50	.25	.15
(21)	John Bateman	.50	.25	.15
(22)	Glen Beckert (Glenn)	.50	.25	.15
(23)	Gary Bell	.50	.25	.15
(24)	John Bench	15.00	7.50	4.50
(25)	Ken Berry	.50	.25	.15
(26)	Frank Bertaina	.50	.25	.15
(27)	Paul Blair	.50	.25	.15
(28)	Wade Blasingame	.50	.25	.15
(29)	Curt Blefary	.50	.25	.15
(30)	John Boccabella	.50	.25	.15
(31)	Bobby Lee Bonds	1.00	.50	.30
(32)	Sam Bowens	.50	.25	.15
(33)	Ken Boyer	1.00	.50	.30
(34)	Charles Bradford	.50	.25	.15
(35)	Darrell Brandon	.50	.25	.15
(36)	Jim Brewer	.50	.25	.15
(37)	John Briggs	.50	.25	.15
(38)	Nelson Briles	.50	.25	.15
(39)	Ed Brinkman	.50	.25	.15
(40)	Lou Brock	10.00	5.00	3.00
(41)	Gates Brown	.50	.25	.15
(42)	Larry Brown	.50	.25	.15
(43)	George Brunet	.50	.25	.15
(44)	Jerry Buchek	.50	.25	.15
(45)	Don Buford	.50	.25	.15
(46)	Jim Bunning	7.50	3.75	2.25
(47)	Johnny Callison	.50	.25	.15
(48)	Campy Campaneris	.50	.25	.15
(49)	Jose Cardenal	.50	.25	.15
(50)	Leo Cardenas	.50	.25	.15
(51)	Don Cardwell	.50	.25	.15
(52)	Rod Carew	12.50	6.25	3.75
(53)	Paul Casanova	.50	.25	.15
(54)	Norm Cash	1.50	.70	.45
(55)	Danny Cater	.50	.25	.15
(56)	Orlando Cepeda	10.00	5.00	3.00
(57)	Dean Chance	.50	.25	.15
(58)	Ed Charles	.50	.25	.15
(59)	Horace Clarke	.50	.25	.15
(60)	Roberto Clemente	45.00	22.00	13.50
(61)	Donn Clendenon	.50	.25	.15
(62)	Ty Cline	.50	.25	.15
(63)	Nate Colbert	.50	.25	.15
(64)	Joe Coleman	.50	.25	.15
(65)	Bob Cox	.50	.25	.15
(66)	Mike Cuellar	.50	.25	.15
(67)	Ray Culp	.50	.25	.15
(68)	Clay Dalrymple	.50	.25	.15
(69)	Vic Davalillo	.50	.25	.15
(70)	Jim Davenport	.50	.25	.15
(71)	Ron Davis	.50	.25	.15
(72)	Tommy Davis	.50	.25	.15
(73)	Willie Davis	.50	.25	.15
(74)	Chuck Dobson	.50	.25	.15
(75)	John Donaldson	.50	.25	.15
(76)	Al Downing	.50	.25	.15
(77)	Moe Drabowsky	.50	.25	.15
(78)	Dick Ellsworth	.50	.25	.15
(79)	Mike Epstein	.50	.25	.15
(80)	Andy Etchebarren	.50	.25	.15
(81)	Ron Fairly	.50	.25	.15
(82)	Dick Farrell	.50	.25	.15
(83)	Curt Flood	1.00	.50	.30
(84)	Joe Foy	.50	.25	.15
(85)	Tito Francona	.50	.25	.15
(86)	Bill Freehan	.75	.40	.25
(87)	Jim Fregosi	.50	.25	.15
(88)	Woodie Fryman	.50	.25	.15
(89)	Len Gabrielson	.50	.25	.15
(90)	Cito Gaston	.50	.25	.15
(91)	Jake Gibbs	.50	.25	.15
(92)	Russ Gibson	.50	.25	.15
(93)	Dave Giusti	.50	.25	.15
(94)	Tony Gonzalez	.50	.25	.15
(95)	Jim Gosger	.50	.25	.15
(96)	Julio Gotay	.50	.25	.15
(97)	Dick Green	.50	.25	.15
(98)	Jerry Grote	.50	.25	.15
(99)	Jimmie Hall	.50	.25	.15
(100)	Tom Haller	.50	.25	.15
(101)	Steve Hamilton	.50	.25	.15
(102)	Ron Hansen	.50	.25	.15
(103)	Jim Hardin	.50	.25	.15
(104)	Tommy Harper	.50	.25	.15
(105)	Bud Harrelson	.50	.25	.15
(106)	Ken Harrelson	.50	.25	.15
(107)	Jim Hart	.50	.25	.15
(108)	Woodie Held	.50	.25	.15
(109)	Tommy Helms	.50	.25	.15
(110)	Elrod Hendricks	.50	.25	.15
(111)	Mike Hershberger	.50	.25	.15
(112)	Jack Hiatt	.50	.25	.15
(113)	Jim Hickman	.50	.25	.15
(114)	John Hiller	.50	.25	.15
(115)	Chuck Hinton	.50	.25	.15
(116)	Ken Holtzman	.50	.25	.15
(117)	Joel Horlen	.50	.25	.15
(118)	Tony Horton	.50	.25	.15
(119)	Willie Horton	.50	.25	.15
(120)	Frank Howard	1.00	.50	.30
(121)	Dick Howser	.50	.25	.15
(122)	Randy Hundley	.50	.25	.15
(123)	Ron Hunt	.50	.25	.15
(124)	Catfish Hunter	7.50	3.75	2.25
(125)	Al Jackson	.50	.25	.15
(126)	Larry Jackson	.50	.25	.15
(127)	Reggie Jackson	30.00	15.00	9.00
(128)	Sonny Jackson	.50	.25	.15
(129)	Pat Jarvis	.50	.25	.15
(130)	Julian Javier	.50	.25	.15
(131)	Ferguson Jenkins	7.50	3.75	2.25
(132)	Manny Jimenez	.50	.25	.15
(133)	Tommy John	1.00	.50	.30
(134)	Bob Johnson	.50	.25	.15
(135)	Dave Johnson	.50	.25	.15
(136)	Deron Johnson	.50	.25	.15
(137)	Lou Johnson	.50	.25	.15
(138)	Jay Johnstone	.50	.25	.15
(139)	Cleon Jones	.50	.25	.15
(140)	Dalton Jones	.50	.25	.15
(141)	Duane Josephson	.50	.25	.15
(142)	Jim Kaat	1.50	.70	.45
(143)	Al Kaline	15.00	7.50	4.50
(144)	Don Kessinger	.50	.25	.15
(145)	Harmon Killebrew	12.50	6.25	3.75
(146)	Harold King	.50	.25	.15
(147)	Ed Kirkpatrick	.50	.25	.15
(148)	Fred Klages	.50	.25	.15
(149)	Ron Kline	.50	.25	.15
(150)	Bobby Knoop	.50	.25	.15
(151)	Gary Kolb	.50	.25	.15
(152)	Andy Kosco	.50	.25	.15
(153)	Ed Kranepool	.50	.25	.15
(154)	Lew Krausse	.50	.25	.15
(155)	Harold Lanier	.50	.25	.15
(156)	Jim Lefebvre	.50	.25	.15
(157)	Denny Lemaster	.50	.25	.15
(158)	Dave Leonhard	.50	.25	.15
(159)	Don Lock	.50	.25	.15
(160)	Mickey Lolich	1.50	.70	.45
(161)	Jim Lonborg	.75	.40	.25
(162)	Mike Lum	.50	.25	.15
(163)	Al Lyle	.50	.25	.15
(164)	Jim Maloney	.50	.25	.15
(165)	Juan Marichal	8.00	4.00	2.50
(166)	J.C. Martin	.50	.25	.15
(167)	Marty Martinez	.50	.25	.15
(168)	Tom Matchick	.50	.25	.15
(169)	Ed Mathews	12.50	6.25	3.75
(170)	Dal Maxvill	.50	.25	.15
(171)	Jerry May	.50	.25	.15
(172)	Lee May	.50	.25	.15
(173)	Lee Maye	.50	.25	.15
(174)	Willie Mays	30.00	15.00	9.00
(175)	Bill Mazeroski	12.50	6.25	3.75
(176)	Richard McAuliffe	.50	.25	.15
(177)	Al McBean	.50	.25	.15
(178)	Tim McCarver	.75	.40	.25
(179)	Bill McCool	.50	.25	.15
(180)	Mike McCormick	.50	.25	.15
(181)	Willie McCovey	12.50	6.25	3.75
(182)	Tom McCraw	.50	.25	.15
(183)	Lindy McDaniel	.50	.25	.15
(184)	Sam McDowell	.75	.40	.25
(185)	Orlando McFarlane	.50	.25	.15
(186)	Jim McGlothlin	.50	.25	.15
(187)	Denny McLain	1.25	.60	.40
(188)	Ken McMullen	.50	.25	.15
(189)	Dave McNally	.50	.25	.15
(190)	Gerry McNertney	.50	.25	.15
(191)	Dennis Menke (Denis)	.50	.25	.15
(192)	Felix Millan	.50	.25	.15
(193)	Don Mincher	.50	.25	.15
(194)	Rick Monday	.50	.25	.15
(195)	Joe Morgan	10.00	5.00	3.00
(196)	Bubba Morton	.50	.25	.15
(197)	Manny Mota	.50	.25	.15
(198)	Jim Nash	.50	.25	.15
(199)	Dave Nelson	.50	.25	.15
(200)	Dick Nen	.50	.25	.15
(201)	Phil Niekro	7.50	3.75	2.25
(202)	Jim Northrup	.50	.25	.15
(203)	Richard Nye	.50	.25	.15
(204)	Johnny Odom	.50	.25	.15
(205)	Tony Oliva	1.00	.50	.30
(206)	Gene Oliver	.50	.25	.15
(207)	Phil Ortega	.50	.25	.15
(208)	Claude Osteen	.50	.25	.15
(209)	Ray Oyler	.50	.25	.15

		NM	EX	VG
(210)	Jose Pagan	.50	.25	.15
(211)	Jim Pagliaroni	.50	.25	.15
(212)	Milt Pappas	.50	.25	.15
(213)	Wes Parker	.50	.25	.15
(214)	Camilo Pascual	.50	.25	.15
(215)	Don Pavletich	.50	.25	.15
(216)	Joe Pepitone	.50	.25	.15
(217)	Tony Perez	10.00	5.00	3.00
(218)	Gaylord Perry	7.50	3.75	2.25
(219)	Jim Perry	.50	.25	.15
(220)	Gary Peters	.50	.25	.15
(221)	Rico Petrocelli	.50	.25	.15
(222)	Adolfo Phillips	.50	.25	.15
(223)	Tom Phoebus	.50	.25	.15
(224)	Vada Pinson	2.00	1.00	.60
(225)	Boog Powell	2.00	1.00	.60
(226)	Frank Quilici	.50	.25	.15
(227)	Doug Rader	.50	.25	.15
(228)	Rich Reese	.50	.25	.15
(229)	Phil Regan	.50	.25	.15
(230)	Rick Reichardt	.50	.25	.15
(231)	Rick Renick	.50	.25	.15
(232)	Roger Repoz	.50	.25	.15
(233)	Dave Ricketts	.50	.25	.15
(234)	Bill Robinson	.50	.25	.15
(235)	Brooks Robinson	15.00	7.50	4.50
(236)	Frank Robinson	15.00	7.50	4.50
(237)	Bob Rodgers	.50	.25	.15
(238)	Cookie Rojas	.50	.25	.15
(239)	Rich Rollins	.50	.25	.15
(240)	Phil Roof	.50	.25	.15
(241)	Pete Rose	30.00	15.00	9.00
(242)	John Roseboro	.50	.25	.15
(243)	Chico Ruiz	.50	.25	.15
(244)	Ray Sadecki	.50	.25	.15
(245)	Chico Salmon	.50	.25	.15
(246)	Jose Santiago	.50	.25	.15
(247)	Ron Santo	2.50	1.25	.70
(248)	Tom Satriano	.50	.25	.15
(249)	Paul Schaal	.50	.25	.15
(250)	Tom Seaver	15.00	7.50	4.50
(251)	Art Shamsky	.50	.25	.15
(252)	Mike Shannon	.50	.25	.15
(253)	Chris Short	.50	.25	.15
(254)	Dick Simpson	.50	.25	.15
(255)	Duke Sims	.50	.25	.15
(256)	Reggie Smith	.50	.25	.15
(257)	Willie Smith	.50	.25	.15
(258)	Russ Snyder	.50	.25	.15
(259)	Al Spangler	.50	.25	.15
(260)	Larry Stahl	.50	.25	.15
(261)	Lee Stange	.50	.25	.15
(262)	Mickey Stanley	.50	.25	.15
(263)	Willie Stargell	10.00	5.00	3.00
(264)	Rusty Staub	1.00	.50	.30
(265)	Mel Stottlemyre	.50	.25	.15
(266)	Ed Stroud	.50	.25	.15
(267)	Don Sutton	7.50	3.75	2.25
(268)	Ron Swoboda	.50	.25	.15
(269)	Jose Tartabull	.50	.25	.15
(270)	Tony Taylor	.50	.25	.15
(271)	Luis Tiant	1.00	.50	.30
(272)	Bob Tillman	.50	.25	.15
(273)	Bobby Tolan	.50	.25	.15
(274)	Jeff Torborg	.50	.25	.15
(275)	Joe Torre	2.50	1.25	.70
(276)	Cesar Tovar	.50	.25	.15
(277)	Dick Tracewski	.50	.25	.15
(278)	Tom Tresh	.75	.40	.25
(279)	Ted Uhlaender	.50	.25	.15
(280)	Del Unser	.50	.25	.15
(281)	Hilario Valdespino	.50	.25	.15
(282)	Fred Valentine	.50	.25	.15
(283)	Bob Veale	.50	.25	.15
(284)	Zoilo Versalles	.50	.25	.15
(285)	Pete Ward	.50	.25	.15
(286)	Al Weis	.50	.25	.15
(287)	Don Wert	.50	.25	.15
(288)	Bill White	.50	.25	.15
(289)	Roy White	.50	.25	.15
(290)	Fred Whitfield	.50	.25	.15
(291)	Hoyt Wilhelm	7.50	3.75	2.25
(292)	Billy Williams	10.00	5.00	3.00
(293)	Maury Wills	.75	.40	.25
(294)	Earl Wilson	.50	.25	.15
(295)	Wilbur Wood	.50	.25	.15
(296)	Jerry Zimmerman	.50	.25	.15

1970 Milton Bradley

3	CATCHER
4	1ST BASEMAN
5	LEFT FIELDER
6	2ND BASEMAN
8	3RD BASEMAN
9	SHORTSTOP
10	CENTER FIELDER
11	RIGHT FIELDER
12	PITCHER

TONY TAYLOR
IF 12/19/35 5-9 TR BR

Except for the slightly larger (2-3/8" x 3-1/2") size, the format of the 1970 Milton Bradley set is similar to the 1969 Milton Bradley issue. Again designed for use with a baseball board game, the unnumbered black-and-white cards have rounded corners and wide white borders. The player's name appears in capital letters beneath the photo with his position, birthdate, height and batting and throwing preference on a line below. The back of the card shows the player's name along the top followed by a list of possible game situations used in playing the board game. There are no team designations on the cards and all team insignias have been airbrushed from the photos.

		NM	EX	VG
Complete Boxed Set:		175.00	85.00	45.00
Complete Card Set (28):		120.00	55.00	30.00
Common Player:		1.50	.70	.45
(1)	Hank Aaron	15.00	7.50	4.50
(2)	Ernie Banks	10.00	5.00	3.00
(3)	Lou Brock	7.50	3.75	2.25
(4)	Rod Carew	9.00	4.50	2.75
(5)	Roberto Clemente	15.00	7.50	4.50
(6)	Tommy Davis	1.50	.70	.45
(7)	Bill Freehan	1.50	.70	.45
(8)	Jim Fregosi	1.50	.70	.45
(9)	Tom Haller	1.50	.70	.45
(10)	Frank Howard	2.00	1.00	.60
(11)	Reggie Jackson	10.00	5.00	3.00
(12)	Harmon Killebrew	9.00	4.50	2.75
(13)	Mickey S. Lolich	1.50	.70	.45
(14)	Juan Marichal	6.00	3.00	1.75
(15)	Willie Mays	15.00	7.50	4.50
(16)	Willie McCovey	7.50	3.75	2.25
(17)	Sam McDowell	1.50	.70	.45
(18)	Dennis Menke (Denis)	1.50	.70	.45
(19)	Don Mincher	1.50	.70	.45
(20)	Phil Niekro	6.00	3.00	1.75
(21)	Rico Petrocelli	1.50	.70	.45
(22)	Boog Powell	2.00	1.00	.60
(23)	Frank Robinson	9.00	4.50	2.75
(24)	Pete Rose	15.00	7.50	4.50
(25)	Ron Santo	3.00	1.50	.90
(26)	Tom Seaver	9.00	4.50	2.75
(27)	Mel Stottlemyre	1.50	.70	.45
(28)	Tony Taylor	1.50	.70	.45

1972 Milton Bradley

The 1972 Milton Bradley set was again designed for use with a baseball table game. The 1972 cards are similar to the 1969 and 1970 issues. The unnumbered black-and-white cards measure 2" x 3" and display the player's name along the top of the card. Again, all team insignias have been eliminated by airbrushing, and there are no team designations indicated. Backs carry the player's name and personal data followed by a list of possible game situations used in playing the game. To differentiate a 1972 card from a 1969, look on back for a line of red type which contains the numeral "1." If the digit has a base, the card is a '72; if there is no base to the red "1," it is a 1969. Besides individual player cards, non-photographic team cards were issued for each of the contemporary 24 Major League teams.

		NM	EX	VG
Complete Boxed Set:		400.00	200.00	120.00
Complete Card Set (378):		350.00	175.00	110.00
Common Player:		.50	.25	.15
Team Card:		2.00	1.00	.60
(1)	Hank Aaron	25.00	12.50	7.50
(2)	Tommie Aaron	.50	.25	.15
(3)	Ted Abernathy	.50	.25	.15
(4)	Jerry Adair	.50	.25	.15
(5)	Tommy Agee	.50	.25	.15
(6)	Bernie Allen	.50	.25	.15
(7)	Hank Allen	.50	.25	.15
(8)	Richie Allen	1.50	.70	.45
(9)	Gene Alley	.50	.25	.15
(10)	Bob Allison	.50	.25	.15
(11)	Sandy Alomar	.50	.25	.15
(12)	Felipe Alou	.75	.40	.25
(13)	Jesus Alou	.50	.25	.15
(14)	Matty Alou	.50	.25	.15
(15)	Max Alvis	.50	.25	.15
(16)	Brant Alyea	.50	.25	.15
(17)	Mike Andrews	.50	.25	.15
(18)	Luis Aparicio	9.00	4.50	2.75
(19)	Jose Arcia	.50	.25	.15
(20)	Gerald Arrigo	.50	.25	.15
(21)	Bob Aspromonte	.50	.25	.15
(22)	Joe Azcue	.50	.25	.15
(23)	Robert Bailey	.50	.25	.15
(24)	Sal Bando	.50	.25	.15
(25)	Ernie Banks	17.50	8.75	5.25
(26)	Steve Barber	.50	.25	.15
(27)	Robert Barton	.50	.25	.15
(28)	John Bateman	.50	.25	.15
(29)	Glen Beckert (Glenn)	.50	.25	.15
(30)	John Bench	12.50	6.25	3.75
(31)	Ken Berry	.50	.25	.15
(32)	Frank Bertaina	.50	.25	.15
(33)	Paul Blair	.50	.25	.15
(34)	Stephen Blass	.50	.25	.15
(35)	Curt Blefary	.50	.25	.15
(36)	Bobby Bolin	.50	.25	.15
(37)	Bobby Lee Bonds	1.00	.50	.30
(38)	Donald Bosch	.50	.25	.15
(39)	Richard Bosman	.50	.25	.15
(40)	Dave Boswell	.50	.25	.15
(41)	Kenneth Boswell	.50	.25	.15
(42)	Cletis Boyer	.50	.25	.15
(43)	Ken Boyer	1.25	.60	.40
(44)	Charles Bradford	.50	.25	.15
(45)	Ronald Brand	.50	.25	.15
(46)	Ken Brett	.50	.25	.15
(47)	Jim Brewer	.50	.25	.15
(48)	John Briggs	.50	.25	.15
(49)	Nelson Briles	.50	.25	.15
(50)	Ed Brinkman	.50	.25	.15
(51)	James Britton	.50	.25	.15
(52)	Lou Brock	9.00	4.50	2.75
(53)	Gates Brown	.50	.25	.15
(54)	Larry Brown	.50	.25	.15
(55)	Ollie Brown	.50	.25	.15
(56)	George Brunet	.50	.25	.15
(57)	Don Buford	.50	.25	.15
(58)	Wallace Bunker	.50	.25	.15
(59)	Jim Bunning	6.00	3.00	1.75
(60)	William Butler	.50	.25	.15
(61)	Johnny Callison	.50	.25	.15
(62)	Campy Campaneris	.50	.25	.15
(63)	Jose Cardenal	.50	.25	.15
(64)	Leo Cardenas	.50	.25	.15
(65)	Don Cardwell	.50	.25	.15
(66)	Rod Carew	9.00	4.50	2.75
(67)	Cisco Carlos	.50	.25	.15
(68)	Steve Carlton	9.00	4.50	2.75
(69)	Clay Carroll	.50	.25	.15
(70)	Paul Casanova	.50	.25	.15
(71)	Norm Cash	1.50	.70	.45
(72)	Danny Cater	.50	.25	.15
(73)	Orlando Cepeda	9.00	4.50	2.75
(74)	Dean Chance	.50	.25	.15
(75)	Horace Clarke	.50	.25	.15
(76)	Roberto Clemente	30.00	15.00	9.00
(77)	Donn Clendenon	.50	.25	.15
(78)	Ty Cline	.50	.25	.15
(79)	Nate Colbert	.50	.25	.15
(80)	Joe Coleman	.50	.25	.15
(81)	William Conigliaro	.75	.40	.25
(82)	Casey Cox	.50	.25	.15
(83)	Mike Cuellar	.50	.25	.15
(84)	Ray Culp	.50	.25	.15
(85)	George Culver	.50	.25	.15
(86)	Vic Davalillo	.50	.25	.15
(87)	Jim Davenport	.50	.25	.15
(88)	Tommy Davis	.50	.25	.15
(89)	Willie Davis	.50	.25	.15
(90)	Larry Dierker	.50	.25	.15
(91)	Richard Dietz	.50	.25	.15
(92)	Chuck Dobson	.50	.25	.15
(93)	Pat Dobson	.50	.25	.15
(94)	John Donaldson	.50	.25	.15
(95)	Al Downing	.50	.25	.15
(96)	Moe Drabowsky	.50	.25	.15
(97)	John Edwards	.50	.25	.15
(98)	Thomas Egan	.50	.25	.15
(99)	Dick Ellsworth	.50	.25	.15
(100)	Mike Epstein	.50	.25	.15
(101)	Andy Etchebarren	.50	.25	.15
(102)	Ron Fairly	.50	.25	.15
(103)	Frank Fernandez	.50	.25	.15
(104)	Alfred Ferrara	.50	.25	.15
(105)	Michael Fiore	.50	.25	.15
(106)	Curt Flood	1.00	.50	.30
(107)	Vern Fuller	.50	.25	.15
(108)	Joe Foy	.50	.25	.15
(109)	Tito Francona	.50	.25	.15
(110)	Bill Freehan	.50	.25	.15
(111)	Jim Fregosi	.50	.25	.15
(112)	Woodie Fryman	.50	.25	.15
(113)	Len Gabrielson	.50	.25	.15
(114)	Philip Gagliano	.50	.25	.15
(115)	Cito Gaston	.50	.25	.15
(116)	Jake Gibbs	.50	.25	.15
(117)	Russ Gibson	.50	.25	.15
(118)	Dave Giusti	.50	.25	.15
(119)	Fred Gladding	.50	.25	.15
(120)	Tony Gonzalez	.50	.25	.15
(121)	Jim Gosger	.50	.25	.15
(122)	James Grant	.50	.25	.15
(123)	Thomas Griffin	.50	.25	.15
(124)	Dick Green	.50	.25	.15
(125)	Jerry Grote	.50	.25	.15
(126)	Tom Hall	.50	.25	.15
(127)	Tom Haller	.50	.25	.15
(128)	Steve Hamilton	.50	.25	.15
(129)	William Hands	.50	.25	.15
(130)	James Hannan	.50	.25	.15
(131)	Ron Hansen	.50	.25	.15
(132)	Jim Hardin	.50	.25	.15
(133)	Steve Hargan	.50	.25	.15
(134)	Tommy Harper	.50	.25	.15
(135)	Bud Harrelson	.50	.25	.15
(136)	Ken Harrelson	.50	.25	.15
(137)	Jim Hart	.50	.25	.15
(138)	Rich Hebner	.50	.25	.15
(139)	Michael Hedlund	.50	.25	.15
(140)	Tommy Helms	.50	.25	.15
(141)	Elrod Hendricks	.50	.25	.15
(142)	Ronald Herbel	.50	.25	.15
(143)	Jack Hernandez	.50	.25	.15

(144)	Mike Hershberger	.50	.25	.15
(145)	Jack Hiatt	.50	.25	.15
(146)	Jim Hickman	.50	.25	.15
(147)	Dennis Higgins	.50	.25	.15
(148)	John Hiller	.50	.25	.15
(149)	Chuck Hinton	.50	.25	.15
(150)	Larry Hisle	.50	.25	.15
(151)	Ken Holtzman	.50	.25	.15
(152)	Joel Horlen	.50	.25	.15
(153)	Tony Horton	.50	.25	.15
(154)	Willie Horton	.50	.25	.15
(155)	Frank Howard	.75	.40	.25
(156)	Robert Humphreys	.50	.25	.15
(157)	Randy Hundley	.50	.25	.15
(158)	Ron Hunt	.50	.25	.15
(159)	Catfish Hunter	6.00	3.00	1.75
(160)	Grant Jackson	.50	.25	.15
(161)	Reggie Jackson	15.00	7.50	4.50
(162)	Sonny Jackson	.50	.25	.15
(163)	Pat Jarvis	.50	.25	.15
(164)	Larry Jaster	.50	.25	.15
(165)	Julian Javier	.50	.25	.15
(166)	Ferguson Jenkins	6.00	3.00	1.75
(167)	Tommy John	1.00	.50	.30
(168)	Alexander Johnson	.50	.25	.15
(169)	Bob Johnson	.50	.25	.15
(170)	Dave Johnson	.50	.25	.15
(171)	Deron Johnson	.50	.25	.15
(172)	Jay Johnstone	.50	.25	.15
(173)	Cleon Jones	.50	.25	.15
(174)	Dalton Jones	.50	.25	.15
(175)	Mack Jones	.50	.25	.15
(176)	Richard Joseph	.50	.25	.15
(177)	Duane Josephson	.50	.25	.15
(178)	Jim Kaat	2.00	1.00	.60
(179)	Al Kaline	12.50	6.25	3.75
(180)	Richard Kelley	.50	.25	.15
(181)	Harold Kelly	.50	.25	.15
(182)	Gerald Kenney	.50	.25	.15
(183)	Don Kessinger	.50	.25	.15
(184)	Harmon Killebrew	9.00	4.50	2.75
(185)	Ed Kirkpatrick	.50	.25	.15
(186)	Bobby Knoop	.50	.25	.15
(187)	Calvin Koonce	.50	.25	.15
(188)	Jerry Koosman	.50	.25	.15
(189)	Andy Kosco	.50	.25	.15
(190)	Ed Kranepool	.50	.25	.15
(191)	Ted Kubiak	.50	.25	.15
(192)	Jose Laboy	.50	.25	.15
(193)	Joseph Lahoud	.50	.25	.15
(194)	William Landis	.50	.25	.15
(195)	Harold Lanier	.50	.25	.15
(196)	Fred Lasher	.50	.25	.15
(197)	John Lazar	.50	.25	.15
(198)	Jim Lefebvre	.50	.25	.15
(199)	Denny Lemaster	.50	.25	.15
(200)	Dave Leonhard	.50	.25	.15
(201)	Frank Linzy	.50	.25	.15
(202)	Mickey Lolich	.50	.25	.15
(203)	Jim Lonborg	.50	.25	.15
(204)	Mike Lum	.50	.25	.15
(205)	Al Lyle	.50	.25	.15
(206)	Jim Maloney	.50	.25	.15
(207)	Juan Marichal	7.50	3.75	2.25
(208)	David Marshall	.50	.25	.15
(209)	J.C. Martin	.50	.25	.15
(210)	Marty Martinez	.50	.25	.15
(211)	Tom Matchick	.50	.25	.15
(212)	Dal Maxvill	.50	.25	.15
(213)	Carlos May	.50	.25	.15
(214)	Jerry May	.50	.25	.15
(215)	Lee May	.50	.25	.15
(216)	Lee Maye	.50	.25	.15
(217)	Willie Mays	25.00	12.50	7.50
(218)	Bill Mazeroski	9.00	4.50	2.75
(219)	Richard McAuliffe	.50	.25	.15
(220)	Al McBean	.50	.25	.15
(221)	Tim McCarver	.75	.40	.25
(222)	Bill McCool	.50	.25	.15
(223)	Mike McCormick	.50	.25	.15
(224)	Willie McCovey	9.00	4.50	2.75
(225)	Tom McCraw	.50	.25	.15
(226)	Lindy McDaniel	.50	.25	.15
(227)	Sam McDowell	.50	.25	.15
(228)	Leon McFadden	.50	.25	.15
(229)	Daniel McGinn	.50	.25	.15
(230)	Jim McGlothlin	.50	.25	.15
(231)	Fred McGraw	.50	.25	.15
(232)	Denny McLain	.75	.40	.25
(233)	Ken McMullen	.50	.25	.15
(234)	Dave McNally	.50	.25	.15
(235)	Gerry McNertney	.50	.25	.15
(236)	William Melton	.50	.25	.15
(237)	Dennis Menke (Denis)	.50	.25	.15
(238)	John Messersmith	.50	.25	.15
(239)	Felix Millan	.50	.25	.15
(240)	Norman Miller	.50	.25	.15
(241)	Don Mincher	.50	.25	.15
(242)	Rick Monday	.50	.25	.15
(243)	Donald Money	.50	.25	.15
(244)	Barry Moore	.50	.25	.15
(245)	Bob Moose	.50	.25	.15
(246)	David Morehead	.50	.25	.15
(247)	Joe Morgan	9.00	4.50	2.75
(248)	Curt Motton	.50	.25	.15
(249)	Manny Mota	.50	.25	.15
(250)	Bob Murcer	.50	.25	.15
(251)	Thomas Murphy	.50	.25	.15
(252)	Ivan Murrell	.50	.25	.15
(253)	Jim Nash	.50	.25	.15
(254)	Joe Niekro	1.25	.60	.40
(255)	Phil Niekro	6.00	3.00	1.75
(256)	Gary Nolan	.50	.25	.15
(257)	Jim Northrup	.50	.25	.15
(258)	Richard Nye	.50	.25	.15
(259)	Johnny Odom	.50	.25	.15
(260)	John O'Donaghue	.50	.25	.15
(261)	Tony Oliva	1.00	.50	.30

(262)	Al Oliver	1.00	.50	.30
(263)	Robert Oliver	.50	.25	.15
(264)	Claude Osteen	.50	.25	.15
(265)	Ray Oyler	.50	.25	.15
(266)	Jose Pagan	.50	.25	.15
(267)	Jim Palmer	9.00	4.50	2.75
(268)	Milt Pappas	.50	.25	.15
(269)	Wes Parker	.50	.25	.15
(270)	Fred Patek	.50	.25	.15
(271)	Mike Paul	.50	.25	.15
(272)	Joe Pepitone	.50	.25	.15
(273)	Tony Perez	7.50	3.75	2.25
(274)	Gaylord Perry	6.00	3.00	1.75
(275)	Jim Perry	.50	.25	.15
(276)	Gary Peters	.50	.25	.15
(277)	Rico Petrocelli	.50	.25	.15
(278)	Tom Phoebus	.50	.25	.15
(279)	Lou Piniella	1.00	.50	.30
(280)	Vada Pinson	1.50	.70	.45
(281)	Boog Powell	1.50	.70	.45
(282)	Jim Price	.50	.25	.15
(283)	Frank Quilici	.50	.25	.15
(284)	Doug Rader	.50	.25	.15
(285)	Ron Reed	.50	.25	.15
(286)	Rich Reese	.50	.25	.15
(287)	Phil Regan	.50	.25	.15
(288)	Rick Reichardt	.50	.25	.15
(289)	Rick Renick	.50	.25	.15
(290)	Roger Repoz	.50	.25	.15
(291)	Mervin Rettenmund	.50	.25	.15
(292)	Dave Ricketts	.50	.25	.15
(293)	Juan Rios	.50	.25	.15
(294)	Bill Robinson	.50	.25	.15
(295)	Brooks Robinson	12.50	6.25	3.75
(296)	Frank Robinson	12.50	6.25	3.75
(297)	Aurelio Rodriguez	.50	.25	.15
(298)	Ellie Rodriguez	.50	.25	.15
(299)	Cookie Rojas	.50	.25	.15
(300)	Rich Rollins	.50	.25	.15
(301)	Vicente Romo	.50	.25	.15
(302)	Phil Roof	.50	.25	.15
(303)	Pete Rose	25.00	12.50	7.50
(304)	John Roseboro	.50	.25	.15
(305)	Chico Ruiz	.50	.25	.15
(306)	Mike Ryan	.50	.25	.15
(307)	Ray Sadecki	.50	.25	.15
(308)	Chico Salmon	.50	.25	.15
(309)	Manuel Sanguillen	.50	.25	.15
(310)	Ron Santo	3.00	1.50	.90
(311)	Tom Satriano	.50	.25	.15
(312)	Theodore Savage	.50	.25	.15
(313)	Paul Schaal	.50	.25	.15
(314)	Dick Schofield	.50	.25	.15
(315)	George Scott	.50	.25	.15
(316)	Tom Seaver	12.50	6.25	3.75
(317)	Art Shamsky	.50	.25	.15
(318)	Mike Shannon	.50	.25	.15
(319)	Chris Short	.50	.25	.15
(320)	Sonny Siebert	.50	.25	.15
(321)	Duke Sims	.50	.25	.15
(322)	William Singer	.50	.25	.15
(323)	Reggie Smith	.50	.25	.15
(324)	Willie Smith	.50	.25	.15
(325)	Russ Snyder	.50	.25	.15
(326)	Al Spangler	.50	.25	.15
(327)	James Spencer	.50	.25	.15
(328)	Ed Spiezio	.50	.25	.15
(329)	Larry Stahl	.50	.25	.15
(330)	Lee Stange	.50	.25	.15
(331)	Mickey Stanley	.50	.25	.15
(332)	Willie Stargell	9.00	4.50	2.75
(333)	Rusty Staub	2.00	1.00	.60
(334)	James Stewart	.50	.25	.15
(335)	George Stone	.50	.25	.15
(336)	William Stoneman	.50	.25	.15
(337)	Mel Stottlemyre	.50	.25	.15
(338)	Ed Stroud	.50	.25	.15
(339)	Ken Suarez	.50	.25	.15
(340)	Gary Sutherland	.50	.25	.15
(341)	Don Sutton	6.00	3.00	1.75
(342)	Ron Swoboda	.50	.25	.15
(343)	Fred Talbot	.50	.25	.15
(344)	Jose Tartabull	.50	.25	.15
(345)	Kenneth Tatum	.50	.25	.15
(346)	Tony Taylor	.50	.25	.15
(347)	Luis Tiant	.75	.40	.25
(348)	Bob Tillman	.50	.25	.15
(349)	Bobby Tolan	.50	.25	.15
(350)	Jeff Torborg	.50	.25	.15
(351)	Joe Torre	3.00	1.50	.90
(352)	Cesar Tovar	.50	.25	.15
(353)	Tom Tresh	.75	.40	.25
(354)	Ted Uhlaender	.50	.25	.15
(355)	Del Unser	.50	.25	.15
(356)	Bob Veale	.50	.25	.15
(357)	Zoilo Versalles	.50	.25	.15
(358)	Luke Walker	.50	.25	.15
(359)	Pete Ward	.50	.25	.15
(360)	Eddie Watt	.50	.25	.15
(361)	Ramon Webster	.50	.25	.15
(362)	Al Weis	.50	.25	.15
(363)	Don Wert	.50	.25	.15
(364)	Bill White	.50	.25	.15
(365)	Roy White	.50	.25	.15
(366)	Hoyt Wilhelm	6.00	3.00	1.75
(367)	Billy Williams	9.00	4.50	2.75
(368)	Walter Williams	.50	.25	.15
(369)	Maury Wills	.75	.40	.25
(370)	Don Wilson	.50	.25	.15
(371)	Earl Wilson	.50	.25	.15
(372)	Robert Wine	.50	.25	.15
(373)	Richard Wise	.50	.25	.15
(374)	Wilbur Wood	.50	.25	.15
(375)	William Woodward	.50	.25	.15
(376)	Clyde Wright	.50	.25	.15
(377)	James Wynn	.50	.25	.15
(378)	Jerry Zimmerman	.50	.25	.15

1957 Milwaukee Braves Picture Pack

HENRY AARON, Outfielder

Prior to the Jay Publishing Co. photo packs which dominated the market from 1958-62, the Braves issued this souvenir stand picture pack of 5" x 7" black-and-white, blank-back, player pictures. In the wide bottom border player names are printed in all-caps with the position indicated in upper- and lower-case letters. The unnumbered pictures are listed here in alphabetical order.

		NM	EX	VG
Complete Set (12):		100.00	50.00	30.00
Common Player:		7.50	3.75	2.25
(1)	Hank Aaron	30.00	15.00	9.00
(2)	Joe Adcock	7.50	3.75	2.25
(3)	Lew Burdette	7.50	3.75	2.25
(4)	Wes Covington	7.50	3.75	2.25
(5)	Del Crandall	7.50	3.75	2.25
(6)	Bob Hazle	7.50	3.75	2.25
(7)	Johnny Logan	7.50	3.75	2.25
(8)	Edwin Mathews	12.50	6.25	3.75
(9)	Don McMahon	7.50	3.75	2.25
(10)	Andy Pafko	7.50	3.75	2.25
(11)	Red Schoendienst	10.00	5.00	3.00
(12)	Warren Spahn	12.50	6.25	3.75

1965 Milwaukee Braves Picture Pack

HANK AARON, Braves

These 4-7/8" x 7-1/8" blank-back, black-and-white pictures were sold in groups of 12 in a white paper window envelope and possibly also as a complete set of 24. Besides the slight size difference, the team-issued pictures differ from the contemporary Jay Publishing pictures in that the city name is not included in the typography in the bottom border.

		NM	EX	VG
Complete Set (24):		75.00	37.50	22.50
Common Player:		3.00	1.50	.90
(1)	Hank Aaron	15.00	7.50	4.50
(2)	Sandy Alomar	3.00	1.50	.90
(3)	Felipe Alou	3.00	1.50	.90
(4)	Wade Blasingame	3.00	1.50	.90
(5)	Frank Bolling	3.00	1.50	.90
(6)	Bobby Bragan	3.00	1.50	.90
(7)	Rico Carty	3.00	1.50	.90
(8)	Ty Cline	3.00	1.50	.90
(9)	Tony Cloninger	3.00	1.50	.90
(10)	Mike de la Hoz	3.00	1.50	.90
(11)	Hank Fischer	3.00	1.50	.90
(12)	Mack Jones	3.00	1.50	.90
(13)	Gary Kolb	3.00	1.50	.90
(14)	Denny LeMaster	3.00	1.50	.90
(15)	Eddie Mathews	6.00	3.00	1.75
(16)	Lee Maye	3.00	1.50	.90
(17)	Denis Menke	3.00	1.50	.90
(18)	Billy O'Dell	3.00	1.50	.90
(19)	Gene Oliver	3.00	1.50	.90
(20)	Chi Chi Olivo	3.00	1.50	.90
(21)	Dan Osinki (Osinski)	3.00	1.50	.90
(22)	Bob Sadowski	3.00	1.50	.90
(23)	Bobby Tiefenauer	3.00	1.50	.90
(24)	Joe Torre	4.50	2.25	1.25

1980 Milwaukee Brewers/ Pepsi Fan Club

Star Milwaukee infielder Sal Bando is featured on this 2-1/2" x 3-1/2" membership card in a blue-bordered action pose. The back is printed in blue on white with both the team and soda logo.

	NM	EX	VG
Sal Bando	6.00	3.00	1.80

1912 Miner's Extra Series of Champions (T227)

 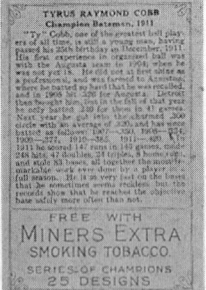

(See 1912 T227 Series of Champions for checklist, price guide.)

1977 Minneapolis Star Twins Scrapbook

Between July 4-August 12, the Star printed one player "Scrapbook" picture each day in the sports section. While sizes vary somewhat, most are about 4-3/16" x 10-3/16". Enclosed in a dotted-line border are a player portrait photo, facsimile autograph, position, uniform number, team logo, career highlights and full stats. Because they are printed on newsprint, the pictures are subject to rapid deterioration.

	NM	EX	VG
Complete Set (36):	100.00	50.00	30.00

Common Player:	4.00	2.00	1.25
7/4	Rod Carew	12.00	6.00	3.50
7/5	Geoff Zahn	4.00	2.00	1.25
7/6	Luis Gomez	4.00	2.00	1.25
7/7	Glenn Adams	4.00	2.00	1.25
7/8	Lyman Bostock	6.00	3.00	1.75
7/9	Bob Gorinski	4.00	2.00	1.25
7/11	Butch Wynegar	4.00	2.00	1.25
7/12	Rob Wilfong	4.00	2.00	1.25
7/13	Dave Goltz	4.00	2.00	1.25
7/14	Bill Butler	4.00	2.00	1.25
7/15	Bob Randall	4.00	2.00	1.25
7/16	Jeff Holly	4.00	2.00	1.25
7/18	Gene Mauch	4.00	2.00	1.25
7/19	Walt Terrell	4.00	2.00	1.25
7/20	Rich Chiles	4.00	2.00	1.25
7/21	Paul Thormodsgard	4.00	2.00	1.25
7/22	Dave Johnson	4.00	2.00	1.25
7/23	Mike Cubbage	4.00	2.00	1.25
7/25	Larry Hisle	4.00	2.00	1.25
7/26	Don McMahon	4.00	2.00	1.25
7/27	Glenn Borgmann	4.00	2.00	1.25
7/28	Craig Kusick	4.00	2.00	1.25
7/29	Ron Schueler	4.00	2.00	1.25
7/30	Karl Kuehl	4.00	2.00	1.25
8/1	Roy Smalley	4.00	2.00	1.25
8/2	Tony Oliva	7.50	3.75	2.25
8/3	Jerry Zimmerman	4.00	2.00	1.25
8/4	Dan Ford	4.00	2.00	1.25
8/5	Don Carrithers	4.00	2.00	1.25
8/6	Tom Johnson	4.00	2.00	1.25
8/8	Pete Redfern	4.00	2.00	1.25
8/9	Tom Burgmeier	4.00	2.00	1.25
8/10	Bud Bulling	4.00	2.00	1.25
8/11	Gary Serum	4.00	2.00	1.25
8/12	Calvin Griffith	4.00	2.00	1.25

1977-78 Minnesota Twins Team Issue

 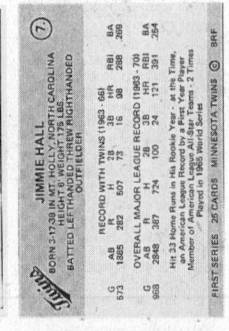

Produced by collector Barry Fritz, and sold by the team through its normal concession outlets, this set consists of two 25-card series. Cards 1-25 were issued in 1977; cards 26-50 in 1978. Measuring 2-5/8" x 3-3/4", card fronts feature quality color player poses with no other graphics. Backs are in black-and-white and have all player data, stats with the Twins and overall major league numbers, plus career highlights. Besides being sold as sets, the cards were also offered in uncut sheet form.

		NM	EX	VG
Complete Set (50):		35.00	17.50	10.00
Common Player:		1.00	.50	.30
1	Bob Allison	1.00	.50	.30
2	Earl Battey	1.00	.50	.30
3	Dave Boswell	1.00	.50	.30
4	Dean Chance	1.25	.60	.40
5	Jim Grant	1.25	.60	.40
6	Calvin Griffith	1.25	.60	.40
7	Jimmie Hall	1.00	.50	.30
8	Harmon Killebrew	6.00	3.00	1.75
9	Jim Lemon	1.00	.50	.30
10	Billy Martin	3.00	1.50	.90
11	Gene Mauch	1.00	.50	.30
12	Sam Mele	1.00	.50	.30
13	Metropolitan Stadium	1.50	.70	.45
14	Don Mincher	1.00	.50	.30
15	Tony Oliva	3.00	1.50	.90
16	Camilo Pascual	1.00	.50	.30
17	Jim Perry	1.25	.60	.40
18	Frank Quilici	1.00	.50	.30
19	Rich Reese	1.00	.50	.30
20	Bill Rigney	1.00	.50	.30
21	Cesar Tovar	1.00	.50	.30
22	Zoilo Versalles	1.00	.50	.30
23	Al Worthington	1.00	.50	.30
24	Jerry Zimmerman	1.00	.50	.30
25	Checklist/Souvenir List	1.00	.50	.30
26	Bernie Allen	1.00	.50	.30
27	Leo Cardenas	1.00	.50	.30
28	Ray Corbin	1.00	.50	.30
29	Joe Decker	1.00	.50	.30
30	Johnny Goryl	1.00	.50	.30
31	Tom Hall	1.00	.50	.30
32	Bill Hands	1.00	.50	.30
33	Jim Holt	1.00	.50	.30
34	Randy Hundley	1.00	.50	.30
35	Jerry Kindall	1.00	.50	.30
36	Johnny Klippstein	1.00	.50	.30
37	Jack Kralick	1.00	.50	.30
38	Jim Merritt	1.00	.50	.30
39	Joe Nossek	1.00	.50	.30
40	Ron Perranoski	1.00	.50	.30
41	Bill Pleis	1.00	.50	.30
42	Rick Renick	1.00	.50	.30
43	Jim Roland	1.00	.50	.30
44	Lee Stange	1.00	.50	.30
45	Dick Stigman	1.00	.50	.30
46	Danny Thompson	1.00	.50	.30
47	Ted Uhlaender	1.00	.50	.30
48	Sandy Valdespino	1.00	.50	.30
49	Dick Woodson	1.00	.50	.30
50	Checklist #26-50	1.00	.50	.30

1911-16 Mino Cigarettes (T216)

The T216 baseball card set, issued by several brands of the Peoples Tobacco Co., is the last of the Louisiana cigarette sets and the most confusing. Apparently issued over a period of several years between 1911 and 1916, the set employs the same pictures as several contemporary caramel and bakery sets. Positive identification can be made by the back of the cards. The Peoples Tobacco cards carry advertising for one of three brands of cigarettes: Kotton, Mino or Virginia Extra. The Kotton brand is the most common, while the Virginia Extra and Mino backs command a premium. T216 cards are found in two types; one has a glossy front finish, while a second scarcer type is printed on a thin paper. The thin paper cards command an additional 15 percent premium. The cards represent players from the American, National and Federal Leagues. Cards measure a nominal 1-1/2" x 2-5/8", though reasonable allowance for variance must be made on consideration of original standards for cutting.

		NM	EX	VG
Common Player:		1,920	870.00	480.00
(1)	Jack Barry/Btg	1,920	870.00	480.00
(2)	Jack Barry/Fielding	1,920	870.00	480.00
(3)	Harry Bemis	1,920	870.00	480.00
(4a)	Chief Bender (Philadelphia, striped cap.)	4,200	1,890	1,050
(4b)	Chief Bender (Baltimore, striped cap.)	4,200	1,890	1,050
(5a)	Chief Bender (Philadelphia, white cap.)	4,200	1,890	1,050
(5b)	Chief Bender (Baltimore, white cap.)	4,200	1,890	1,050
(6)	Bill Bergen	1,920	870.00	480.00
(7a)	Bob Bescher (Cincinnati)	1,920	870.00	480.00
(7b)	Bob Bescher (St. Louis)	1,920	870.00	480.00
(8)	Roger Bresnahan	4,200	1,890	1,050
(9)	Al Bridwell/Btg	1,920	870.00	480.00
(10a)	Al Bridwell/Sliding (New York)	1,920	870.00	480.00
(10b)	Al Bridwell/Sliding (St. Louis)	1,920	870.00	480.00
(11)	Donie Bush	1,920	870.00	480.00
(12)	Doc Casey	1,920	870.00	480.00
(13)	Frank Chance	4,200	1,890	1,050
(14a)	Hal Chase/Fielding (New York)	1,920	870.00	480.00
(14b)	Hal Chase/Fielding (Buffalo)	1,920	870.00	480.00
(15)	Hal Chase/Portrait	1,920	870.00	480.00
(16a)	Ty Cobb/Standing (Detroit Am.)	36,000	16,200	9,000
(16b)	Ty Cobb/Standing (Detroit Americans)	36,000	16,200	9,000
(17)	Ty Cobb/Btg (Detroit Americans)	36,000	16,200	9,000
(18a)	Eddie Collins (Phila. Am.)	4,200	1,890	1,050
(18b)	Eddie Collins (Phila. Am.)	4,200	1,890	1,050
(19)	Eddie Collins (Chicago)	4,200	1,890	1,050
(20a)	Sam Crawford (Small print.)	4,200	1,890	1,050
(20b)	Sam Crawford (Large print.)	4,200	1,890	1,050
(21)	Harry Davis	1,920	870.00	480.00
(22)	Ray Demmitt	1,920	870.00	480.00
(23)	Art Devlin	1,920	870.00	480.00
(24a)	Wild Bill Donovan (Detroit)	1,920	870.00	480.00
(24b)	Wild Bill Donovan (New York)	1,920	870.00	480.00
(25a)	Red Dooin (Philadelphia)	1,920	870.00	480.00
(25b)	Red Dooin (Cincinnati)	1,920	870.00	480.00
(26a)	Mickey Doolan (Philadelphia)	1,920	870.00	480.00
(26b)	Mickey Doolan (Baltimore)	1,920	870.00	480.00
(27)	Patsy Dougherty	1,920	870.00	480.00
(28a)	Larry Doyle (N.Y. Nat'l,) (w/bat)	1,920	870.00	480.00
(28b)	Larry Doyle (New York Nat'l) (w/bat)	1,920	870.00	480.00
(29)	Larry Doyle/Throwing	1,920	870.00	480.00
(30)	Clyde Engle	1,920	870.00	480.00

(31a)	Johnny Evers (Chicago)	4,200	1,890	1,050
(31b)	Johnny Evers (Boston)	4,200	1,890	1,050
(32)	Art Fromme	1,920	870.00	480.00
(33a)	George Gibson (Pittsburg Nat'l, back view.)		870.00	480.00
(33b)	George Gibson (Pittsburgh Nat'l., back view.)	1,920	870.00	480.00
(34a)	George Gibson (Pittsburg Nat'l, front view.)	1,920	870.00	480.00
(34b)	George Gibson (Pittsburgh Nat'l., front view.)	1,920	870.00	480.00
(35a)	Topsy Hartsel (Phila. Am.)	1,920	870.00	480.00
(35b)	Topsy Hartsel (Phila. Amer.)	1,920	870.00	480.00
(36)	Roy Hartzell/Btg	1,920	870.00	480.00
(37)	Roy Hartzell/Catching	1,920	870.00	480.00
(38a)	Fred Jacklitsch (Philadelphia)	1,920	870.00	480.00
(38b)	Fred Jacklitsch (Baltimore)	1,920	870.00	480.00
(39a)	Hughie Jennings (Orange background.)	4,200	1,890	1,050
(39b)	Hughie Jennings (Red background.)	4,200	1,890	1,050
(40)	Red Kleinow	1,920	870.00	480.00
(41a)	Otto Knabe (Philadelphia)	1,920	870.00	480.00
(41b)	Otto Knabe (Baltimore)	1,920	870.00	480.00
(42)	Jack Knight	1,920	870.00	480.00
(43a)	Nap Lajoie/Fielding (Philadelphia)	4,800	2,160	1,200
(43b)	Nap Lajoie/Fielding (Cleveland)	4,800	2,160	1,200
(44)	Nap Lajoie/Portrait	4,800	2,160	1,200
(45a)	Hans Lobert (Cincinnati)	1,920	870.00	480.00
(45b)	Hans Lobert (New York)	1,920	870.00	480.00
(46)	Sherry Magee	1,920	870.00	480.00
(47)	Rube Marquard	4,200	1,890	1,050
(48a)	Christy Matthewson (Mathewson) (Large print.)	18,000	8,100	4,500
(48b)	Christy Matthewson (Mathewson) (Small print.)	18,000	8,100	4,550
(49a)	John McGraw (Large print.)	4,200	1,890	1,050
(49b)	John McGraw (small print.)	4,200	1,890	1,050
(50)	Larry McLean	1,920	870.00	480.00
(51)	George McQuillan	1,920	870.00	480.00
(52)	Dots Miller/Btg	1,920	870.00	480.00
(53a)	Dots Miller/Fielding (Pittsburg)	1,920	870.00	480.00
(53b)	Dots Miller/Fielding (St. Louis)	1,920	870.00	480.00
(54a)	Danny Murphy (Philadelphia)	1,920	870.00	480.00
(54b)	Danny Murphy (Brooklyn)	1,920	870.00	480.00
(55)	Rebel Oakes	1,920	870.00	480.00
(56)	Bill O'Hara	1,920	870.00	480.00
(57)	Eddie Plank	5,400	2,430	1,350
(58a)	Germany Schaefer (Washington)	1,920	870.00	480.00
(58b)	Germany Schaefer (Newark)	1,920	870.00	480.00
(59)	Admiral Schlei	1,920	870.00	480.00
(60)	Boss Schmidt	1,920	870.00	480.00
(61)	Johnny Seigle	1,920	870.00	480.00
(62)	Dave Shean	1,920	870.00	480.00
(63)	Boss Smith (Schmidt)	1,920	870.00	480.00
(64)	Tris Speaker	7,800	3,510	1,950
(65)	Oscar Stanage	1,920	870.00	480.00
(66)	George Stovall	1,920	870.00	480.00
(67)	Jeff Sweeney	1,920	870.00	480.00
(68a)	Joe Tinker/Btg (Chicago Nat'l)	4,200	1,890	1,050
(68b)	Joe Tinker/Btg (Chicago Feds)	4,200	1,890	1,050
(69)	Joe Tinker/Portrait	4,200	1,890	1,050
(70a)	Honus Wagner (S.S.)	30,000	13,500	7,500
(70b)	Honus Wagner/Btg (2b)	30,000	13,500	7,500
(71a)	Honus Wagner/Throwing (S.S.)	30,000	13,500	7,500
(71b)	Honus Wagner Throwing (2b.)	30,000	13,500	7,500
(72)	Hooks Wiltse	1,920	870.00	480.00
(73)	Cy Young	15,000	6,750	3,750
(74a)	Heinie Zimmerman (2b.)	1,920	870.00	480.00
(74b)	Heinie Zimmerman (3b.)	1,920	870.00	480.00

1962 Molinari's Restaurant Frank Malzone

This black-and-white J.D. McCarthy postcard of the former Red Sox infielder was given to patrons of an Oneonta, N.Y., restaurant in which Malzone was a partner with his brother-in-law. The card measures 3-1/4" x 5-1/2" and has a facsimile autograph on front. A similar promotional postcard is listed under Ticoa Tires.

	NM	EX	VG
Frank Malzone	15.00	7.50	4.50

1911 Monarch Typewriter Philadelphia A's

These black-and-white postcards (about 3-1/2" x 5") depict the World Champion 1910 Philadelphia A's. Fronts have posed player photos with a black pin stripe and white borders. The player's name and position are printed in the bottom border. "Compliments of THE MONARCH TYPEWRITER COMPANY" appears in the top border. Backs are rather standard postcard fare, but include data about the World Series between 1903-1910.

	NM	EX	VG
Complete Set (6):	8,000	4,000	2,400
Common Player:	1,150	575.00	350.00
(1) John J. Barry	1,150	575.00	350.00
(2) Chief Bender	1,650	825.00	500.00
(3) Eddie Collins	1,650	825.00	500.00
(4) Rube Oldring	1,150	575.00	350.00
(5) Eddie Plank	1,650	825.00	500.00
(6) Ira Thomas	1,150	575.00	350.00

1970 Montreal Expos Player Pins

Produced by "Best in Sports" for sale in the Montreal area for 35¢ apiece, these 1-3/4" diameter pinbacks feature action poses of the players set against a white background. The player's name at top is in black.

	NM	EX	VG
Complete Set (16):	350.00	175.00	100.00
Common Player:	25.00	12.50	7.50
(1) John Bateman	25.00	12.50	7.50
(2) Ron Brand	25.00	12.50	7.50
(3) Ron Fairly	25.00	12.50	7.50
(4) Mack Jones	25.00	12.50	7.50
(5) Coco Laboy	25.00	12.50	7.50
(6) Gene Mauch	25.00	12.50	7.50
(7) Dan McGinn	25.00	12.50	7.50
(8) Adolfo Phillips	25.00	12.50	7.50
(9) Claude Raymond	25.00	12.50	7.50
(10) Steve Renko	25.00	12.50	7.50
(11) Marv Staehle	25.00	12.50	7.50
(12) Rusty Staub	40.00	20.00	12.00
(13) Bill Stoneman	25.00	12.50	7.50
(14) Gary Sutherland	25.00	12.50	7.50
(15) Bobby Wine	25.00	12.50	7.50
(16) Expos Team Logo	10.00	5.00	3.00

1972-76 Montreal Expos Matchbook Covers

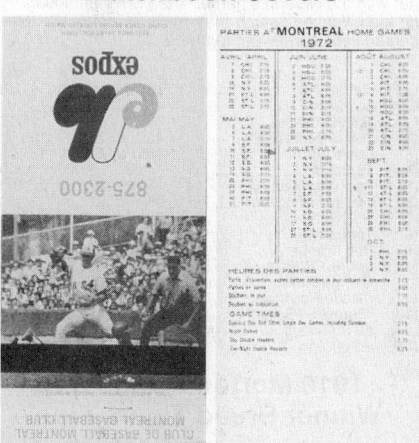

In 1972, 1973 and 1976, the Eddy Match Co., Montreal, issued series of seven matchbook covers featuring action photos. Fronts have a red, white and blue team logo on a white background. Backs have a bluetone action photo with the match-striking surface across the lower portion. The player in the photo is not identified on the matchbook. Inside of the 2-1/8" x 4-3/8" cover, printed in blue, is the team home schedule for that season. The unnumbered matchbook covers are checklisted here alphabetically by year. Values shown are for empty matchbooks; full matchbooks would be valued at 2-3X.

	NM	EX	VG
Complete Set (21):	40.00	20.00	12.00
Common Player:	4.00	2.00	1.25

1972				
(1)	Boots Day	4.00	2.00	1.25
(2)	Ron Fairly	4.00	2.00	1.25
(3)	Ron Hunt	4.00	2.00	1.25
(4)	Steve Renko	4.00	2.00	1.25
(5)	Rusty Staub	6.00	3.00	1.75
(6)	Bobby Wine	4.00	2.00	1.25
(7)	Hunt's 50th HBP (Scoreboard)	4.00	2.00	1.25
1973				
(1)	Tim Foli	4.00	2.00	1.25
(2)	Ron Hunt	4.00	2.00	1.25
(3)	Mike Jorgensen	4.00	2.00	1.25
(4)	Gene Mauch	4.00	2.00	1.25
(5)	Balor Moore	4.00	2.00	1.25
(6)	Ken Singleton	4.00	2.00	1.25
(7)	Bill Stoneman	4.00	2.00	1.25
1976				
(1)	Barry Foote	4.00	2.00	1.25
(2)	Mike Jorgensen	4.00	2.00	1.25
(3)	Pete Mackanin	4.00	2.00	1.25
(4)	Dale Murray	4.00	2.00	1.25
(5)	Larry Parrish	4.00	2.00	1.25
(6)	Steve Rogers	4.00	2.00	1.25
(7)	Dan Warthen	4.00	2.00	1.25

1916 Morehouse Baking Co.

While this 200-card set is most often found with blank backs or with the advertising of "The Sporting News" on the back, a number of scarcer regional advertisers also can be found. This Massachusetts baker inserted the cards into bread loaves and offered a redemption program. Since cards are known that correspond to both versions of the parent M101 Blank Backs, it not known whether the bakery's version parallels M101-4 and M101-5 or is a hybrid of the two.

PREMIUM: 2X
(See 1916 M101-4 and M101-5 Blank Backs for checklist and price guide.)

1907 Morgan Stationery "Red Belt" Postcards

Only one player is individually identified in this series of postcards, though the identities of others has been discovered over the years. The 3-1/2" x 5-1/2" cards have colorized player and group photos on front with a title printed in white in the lower-left corner. Some photos were taken at the Reds ballpark, then known as the Palace of Fans. Cards include pictures of Reds and Pirates of the National League, and Toledo of the minors. Many of the players have bright red belts, thus the set's nickname. Postcard backs have a credit line: "The Morgan Stationery Co., Cincinnati, O., Publishers." The unnumbered cards are checklisted here alphabetically by title.

	NM	EX	VG
Complete Set (12):	3,250	1,625	950.00
Common Card:	275.00	135.00	80.00
(1) After A High One	275.00	135.00	80.00
(2) A Home Run	275.00	135.00	80.00

		NM	EX	VG
(3)	Hit & Run	275.00	135.00	80.00
(4)	In Consultation	275.00	135.00	80.00
(5)	It's All in the Game - "Noise" (Pat Moran)	275.00	135.00	80.00
(6)	Huggins Second Baseman Par Excellence (Miller Huggins) (Stadium background.)	325.00	160.00	95.00
(7)	Huggins Second Baseman Par Excellance (Miller Huggins) (Low buildings in background.)	325.00	160.00	95.00
(8)	Opening of the Season 1907	275.00	135.00	80.00
(9)	Out to the Long Green	275.00	135.00	80.00
(10)	Practise (Practice) Makes Perfect (Sam Leever)	275.00	135.00	80.00
(11)	Safe	275.00	135.00	80.00
(12)	Use Two If Necessary (Hans Lobert)	275.00	135.00	80.00

1959 Morrell Meats Dodgers

This set of Los Angeles Dodgers was the first issue of a three-year run for the Southern California meat company. The 12 cards in this 2-1/2" x 3-1/2" set are unnumbered and feature full-frame, unbordered color photos. Card backs feature a company ad and list only the player's name, birthdate and birthplace. Two errors exist in the set; the cards naming Clem Labine and Norm Larker show photos of Stan Williams and Joe Pignatano, respectively.

		NM	EX	VG
Complete Set (12):		3,500	1,750	1,000
Common Player:		100.00	50.00	30.00
(1)	Don Drysdale	200.00	100.00	60.00
(2)	Carl Furillo	150.00	75.00	45.00
(3)	Jim Gilliam	125.00	60.00	35.00
(4)	Gil Hodges	200.00	100.00	60.00
(5)	Sandy Koufax	2,000	1,000	600.00
(6)	Clem Labine (Photo actually Stan Williams.)	100.00	50.00	30.00
(7)	Norm Larker (Photo actually Joe Pignatano.)	100.00	50.00	30.00
(8)	Charlie Neal	100.00	50.00	30.00
(9)	Johnny Podres	125.00	60.00	35.00
(10)	John Roseboro	100.00	50.00	30.00
(11)	Duke Snider	200.00	100.00	60.00
(12)	Don Zimmer	125.00	60.00	35.00

1960 Morrell Meats Dodgers

This 12-card set is the same 2-1/2" x 3-1/2" size as the 1959 set, and again features unbordered color card fronts. Five of the players included are new to the Morrell's sets. Card backs in 1960 list player statistics and brief personal data on each player. Cards of Gil Hodges, Carl Furillo and Duke Snider are apparently scarcer than others in the set.

		NM	EX	VG
Complete Set (12):		2,200	1,100	650.00
Common Player:		80.00	40.00	24.00
(1)	Walt Alston	90.00	45.00	27.50
(2)	Roger Craig	80.00	40.00	24.00
(3)	Don Drysdale	120.00	60.00	35.00
(4)	Carl Furillo	225.00	110.00	65.00
(5)	Gil Hodges	400.00	200.00	120.00
(6)	Sandy Koufax	500.00	250.00	150.00
(7)	Wally Moon	80.00	40.00	24.00
(8)	Charlie Neal	80.00	40.00	24.00
(9)	Johnny Podres	80.00	40.00	24.00
(10)	John Roseboro	80.00	40.00	24.00
(11)	Larry Sherry	80.00	40.00	24.00
(12)	Duke Snider	450.00	225.00	135.00

1961 Morrell Meats Dodgers

 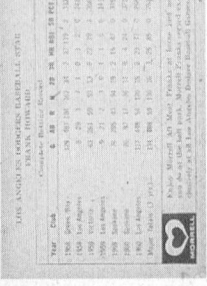

The Morrell set shrunk to just six cards in 1961, with a format almost identical to the 1960 cards. Card fronts are again full-color, unbordered photos. Player statistics appear on the backs. The unnumbered cards measure a slightly smaller 2-1/4" x 3-1/4", and comparison of statistical information can also distinguish the cards from the 1960 version.

		NM	EX	VG
Complete Set (6):		900.00	450.00	275.00
Common Player:		90.00	45.00	27.50
(1)	Tommy Davis	90.00	45.00	27.50
(2)	Don Drysdale	120.00	60.00	36.00
(3)	Frank Howard	90.00	45.00	27.50
(4)	Sandy Koufax	450.00	225.00	135.00
(5)	Norm Larker	90.00	45.00	27.50
(6)	Maury Wills	90.00	45.00	27.00

1910 Morton's Buster Brown Bread Tigers Pins (PD2)

Dating of these two issues is arbitrary, since there is no indication on the pins of vintage. Both sets feature members of the Detroit Tigers, American League champions of 1907-09. The Buster Brown Bread pins measure 1-1/4" in diameter and have a small black-and-white player portrait photo surrounded by a yellow border. Artwork to the left depicts Buster Brown with a tiger holding a blue banner with the Morton's name. The player photos carry no identification, which may make the checklist presented here somewhat tentative.

		NM	EX	VG
Complete Set (15):		10,000	5,000	3,000
Common Player:		450.00	225.00	135.00
(1)	Jimmy Archer	450.00	225.00	135.00
(2)	Heinie Beckendorf	450.00	225.00	135.00
(3)	Donie Bush	450.00	225.00	135.00
(4)	Ty Cobb	4,000	2,000	1,200
(5)	Sam Crawford	750.00	375.00	225.00
(6)	Wild Bill Donovan	450.00	225.00	135.00
(7)	Hughie Jennings	750.00	375.00	225.00
(8)	Tom Jones	450.00	225.00	135.00
(9)	Red Killefer	450.00	225.00	135.00
(10)	George Moriarty	450.00	225.00	135.00
(11)	George Mullin	450.00	225.00	135.00
(12)	Claude Rossman	450.00	225.00	135.00
(13)	"Germany" Schaefer	450.00	225.00	135.00
(14)	Ed Summers	450.00	225.00	135.00
(15)	Ed Willett	450.00	225.00	135.00

1910 Morton's Pennant Winner Bread Tigers Pins

The American League champion Detroit Tigers (1907-1909) are featured on this set of pins advertising — appropriately — Pennant Winner Bread. The 1-1/4" pins have black-and-white player photos surrounded by a yellow border. A Detroit banner with tiger head superimposed is at bottom. The players are not identified anywhere on the pins, which may make this checklist somewhat arbitrary.

		NM	EX	VG
Complete Set (16):		12,000	6,000	3,500
Common Player:		500.00	250.00	150.00
(1)	Jimmy Archer	500.00	250.00	150.00
(2)	Heinie Beckendorf	500.00	250.00	150.00
(3)	Donie Bush	500.00	250.00	150.00
(4)	Ty Cobb	4,000	2,000	1,200
(5)	Sam Crawford	750.00	375.00	225.00
(6)	Wild Bill Donovan	500.00	250.00	150.00
(7)	Hughie Jennings	750.00	375.00	225.00
(8)	Davy Jones	500.00	250.00	150.00
(9)	Matty McIntyre	500.00	250.00	150.00
(10)	George Moriarty	500.00	250.00	150.00
(11)	George Mullin	500.00	250.00	150.00
(12)	Claude Rossman	500.00	250.00	150.00
(13)	Herman Schaeffer (Schaefer)	500.00	250.00	150.00
(14)	Charles Schmidt	500.00	250.00	150.00
(15)	Ed Summers	500.00	250.00	150.00
(16)	Ed Willett	500.00	250.00	150.00

1916 Mothers' Bread (D303)

Apparently issued in 1916 by the New Orleans branch of the General Baking Co., these unnumbered cards measure 1-1/2" x 2-3/4". The player pictures and format of the cards are identical to the 1915 American Caramel (E106) and 1914 General Baking Co. (D303) sets, but this issue carries an advertisement for Mothers' Bread on back. This version is much scarcer than the General Baking or American Caramel types. It is known that at least one player appears in this set who is not found in E106/D303 and many players are found with team, league and postion changes. The checklist here is incomplete and additions are welcome. Gaps have been left in the assigned numbering for future additions.

		NM	EX	VG
Common Player:		2,500	1,500	900.00
(1)	Chief Bender (Brooklyn Nat'l.)	6,000	2,700	1,500
(2)	Bob Bescher (St. Louis Nat'l)	2,500	1,500	900.00
(3)	Rube Bressler (Phila. Am.)	2,500	1,500	900.00
(4)	Donie Bush (Detroit American)	2,500	1,500	900.00
(5)	Hal Chase/Portrait (Cincinnati Nat'l)	3,900	1,750	950.00
(6)	Bill Donovan	2,500	1,500	900.00
(7)	Larry Doyle (N.Y. Nat'l)	2,500	1,500	900.00
(8)	Happy Felsch (Chicago Am.) (Picture actually Ray Demmitt.)	7,500	3,375	1,875
(9)	George Gibson	2,500	1,500	900.00
(11)	Roy Hartzell	2,500	1,500	900.00
(15)	Nap Lajoie (Phila. Americans)	6,000	2,700	1,500
(16)	Hans Lobert (New York Nat'l)	2,500	1,500	900.00
(17)	William Louden (Cincinnati Nat'l)(picture is Otto Knabe)	2,500	1,500	900.00
(20)	Rube Marquard (Brooklyn Nat'l)	6,000	2,700	1,500
(21)	Christy Matthewson (Mathewson)	12,500	5,625	3,125
(22)	Billy Meyer (Phila. Am.) (Picture is Fred Jacklitsch.)	2,500	1,500	900.00
(24)	Ray Morgan (Washington Am.)(picture is Mike Doolan.)	2,500	1,500	900.00
(26)	Eddie Plank (St. Louis Am.)	10,000	4,500	2,500
(28)	Tris Speaker (Cleveland Am.)	7,500	3,375	1,875
(30)	Joe Tinker/Portrait (Mgr. Chicago Am.)	6,000	2,700	1,500
(33)	Honus Wagner/Btg	15,000	6,750	3,750
(35)	Buck Weaver/Btg (Picture is Joe Tinker.)	5,000	2,250	1,250

1919 Mother's Bread

Essentially a version of the W514 strip cards with an advertisement on the back, the Mother's Bread cards are much scarcer than the blank-backs with which they share a checklist. The cards are 1-1/2" x 2-1/2" with color drawings of the players on front, along with name, position, team, league and card number.

(See 1919 W514 for checklist; cards valued at 2.5X-3X W514 version.)

1955 Motorola Bob Feller Premium Photo

Dating of this promotional photo is approximate, based on the uniform details. The 8" x 10" glossy black-and-white photo features a facsimile autograph. Feller is described on the picture as "CONSULTANT ON YOUTH ACTIVITIES" for Motorola, Inc. The picture is blank-backed and its method of distribution is unknown.

	NM	EX	VG
Bob Feller	60.00	30.00	18.00

1976 Motorola

This set of (mostly) Hall of Famers was issued in conjunction with the annual convention of Motorola electronics dealers. Cards were issued singly in a wax wrapper with a piece of bubblegum. Sepia player photos are featured in an oval at center. Player identification and a career highlight are in the white frame around the photo. A sales message appears in a white box at bottom. Overall borders are rust colored. Backs have information about various Motorola products.

	NM	EX	VG
Complete Set (11):	25.00	12.50	7.50
Common Player:	2.50	1.25	.70
1 Honus Wagner	4.00	2.00	1.25
2 Nap Lajoie	2.50	1.25	.70
3 Ty Cobb	7.50	3.75	2.25
4 William Wambsganss	2.50	1.25	.70
5 Three Finger Brown	2.50	1.25	.70
6 Ray Schalk	2.50	1.25	.70
7 Frank Frisch	2.50	1.25	.70
8 Pud Galvin	2.50	1.25	.70
9 Babe Ruth	15.00	7.50	4.50
10 Grover Cleveland Alexander	3.00	1.50	.90
11 Frank L. Chance	2.50	1.25	.70

1943 M.P. & Co. (R302-1)

One of the few baseball card sets issued during World War II, this set of unnumbered cards, measuring approximately 2-5/8" x 2-1/4" was produced in two major types and at least five subtypes. The cards feature crude color drawings that have little resemblance to the player named. They were originally produced in strips and sold inexpensively in candy stores. The backs contain brief player write-ups. One major type has the player's full name, team and position on back. The second type has only the player's first and last name and position on back; no team. Variations in ink color and wording of the biographies on back are also seen. M.P. & Co. stands for Michael Pressner and Co., a New York City novelty and carnival supply firm.

	NM	EX	VG
Complete Set (24):	1,750	625.00	275.00
Common Player:	40.00	15.00	5.00
(1) Ernie Bonham	40.00	15.00	5.00
(2) Lou Boudreau	60.00	20.00	10.00
(3) Dolph Camilli	40.00	15.00	5.00
(4) Mort Cooper	40.00	15.00	5.00
(5) Walker Cooper	40.00	15.00	5.00
(6) Joe Cronin	60.00	20.00	10.00
(7) Hank Danning	40.00	15.00	5.00
(8) Bill Dickey	75.00	25.00	10.00
(9) Joe DiMaggio	300.00	100.00	45.00
(10) Bobby Feller	100.00	35.00	15.00
(11) Jimmy Foxx	75.00	25.00	10.00
(12) Hank Greenberg	100.00	35.00	15.00
(13) Stan Hack	40.00	15.00	5.00
(14) Tom Henrich	40.00	15.00	5.00
(15) Carl Hubbell	60.00	20.00	10.00
(16) Joe Medwick	60.00	20.00	10.00
(17) John Mize	60.00	20.00	10.00
(18) Lou Novikoff	40.00	15.00	5.00
(19) Mel Ott	60.00	20.00	10.00
(20) Pee Wee Reese	75.00	25.00	10.00
(21) Pete Reiser	40.00	15.00	5.00
(22) Charlie Ruffing	60.00	20.00	10.00
(23) Johnny VanderMeer	40.00	15.00	5.00
(24) Ted Williams	250.00	85.00	35.00

1949 M.P. & Co. (R302-2)

This set appears to be a re-issue of M.P. & Co.'s 1943 cards with several different players (although reusing the same pictures as the '43s). The cards, which measure about 2-11/16" x 2-1/4", feature crude drawings of generic baseball players which have little resemblance to the player named. Most backs include card number and player information. The numbering sequence begins with card 100. Numbers 104, 118, and 120 are unknown, while three of the cards are unnumbered. The set is assigned the American Card Catalog number R302-2.

	NM	EX	VG
Complete Set (25):	1,750	575.00	275.00
Common Player:	45.00	16.00	7.00
100 Lou Boudreau	60.00	20.00	9.00
101 Ted Williams	250.00	85.00	35.00
102 Buddy Kerr	45.00	16.00	7.00
103 Bobby Feller	75.00	25.00	10.00
104 Unknown			
105 Joe DiMaggio	325.00	115.00	50.00
106 Pee Wee Reese	75.00	25.00	10.00
107 Ferris Fain	45.00	16.00	7.00
108 Andy Pafko	45.00	16.00	7.00
109 Del Ennis	45.00	16.00	7.00
110 Ralph Kiner	60.00	20.00	9.00
111 Nippy Jones	45.00	16.00	7.00
112 Del Rice	45.00	16.00	7.00
113 Hank Sauer	45.00	16.00	7.00
114 Gil Coan	45.00	16.00	7.00
115 Eddie Joost	45.00	16.00	7.00
116 Alvin Dark	45.00	16.00	7.00
117 Larry Berra	75.00	25.00	10.00
118 Unknown			
119 Bob Lemon	60.00	20.00	9.00
120 Unknown			
121 Johnny Pesky	45.00	16.00	7.00
122 Johnny Sain	45.00	16.00	7.00
123 Hoot Evers	45.00	16.00	7.00
124 Larry Doby	60.00	20.00	9.00
---- Jimmy Foxx	100.00	35.00	15.00
---- Tom Henrich	45.00	16.00	7.00
---- Al Kozar	45.00	16.00	7.00

1948-49 M.P. & Co. Photoprints

One of several 1930s-1940s kits for do-it-yourself production of photos, this issue was produced in New York City by the novelty firm M.P. & Co. A complete outfit consists of a film negative and a piece of light-sensitive paper for producing the photo. The negative and resulting print measure about 2" x 2-1/4". The issue includes 13 subjects, mostly non-sport, but including Babe Ruth.

	NM	EX	VG
Babe Ruth (Negative)	300.00	150.00	90.00
Babe Ruth (Print)	75.00	37.50	22.00

1976 Mr. Softee Iron-Ons

Anecdotal evidence connects these iron-on transfers with the Mr. Softee dairy chain. About 4-1/2" x 6" inches, the color transfers have a player portrait on a baseball background, very similar in format to the 1978 Royal Crown Cola iron-ons. Like the RC pieces, the pictures have team logos removed from caps. The Mr. Softees include the team nickname beneath the player picture, along with a players association logo and an undated Quaker copyright line. The extent of the checklist is unknown.

	NM	EX	VG
Common Player:	4.00	2.00	1.25
(1) George Brett	10.00	5.00	3.00
(2) Jim Hunter	6.00	3.00	1.75
(3) Randy Jones	4.00	2.00	1.25
(4) Dave Kingman	5.00	2.50	1.50
(5) Jerry Koosman	4.00	2.00	1.25
(6) Fred Lynn	5.00	2.50	1.50
(7) Joe Morgan	6.00	3.00	1.75
(8) Thurman Munson	10.00	5.00	3.00
(9) Amos Otis	4.00	2.00	1.25
(10) Bill Russell	4.00	2.00	1.25
(11) Nolan Ryan	12.00	6.00	3.60
(12) Mike Schmidt	10.00	5.00	3.00

1977 Mrs. Carter's Bread Sports Illustrated Covers

This two-sport set was issued by Mrs. Carter's Bread. Fronts of the 3-1/2" x 4-3/4" cards reproduce SI covers in full color, surrounded by a white border. Backs have a special offer for SI subscriptions, and are printed in black and blue on white. Despite the higher card numbers, it does not appear any more than five were ever issued.

	NM	EX	VG
Complete Set (5):	35.00	17.50	10.00
Common Card:	3.00	1.50	.90
(1) George Brett	25.00	12.50	7.50
(2) George Foster	4.00	2.00	1.25
(3) Bump Wills	4.00	2.00	1.25
(4) Oakland Wins a Big One (Football)	4.00	2.00	1.25
(5) Michigan is No. 1 (Football)	6.00	3.00	1.75

1921 Mrs. Sherlock's Bread Pins

The date of issue for these pins is uncertain. The 7/8" diameter pins feature black-and-white player photos with a red border. The player's last name and team are printed beneath the photo; above is "Mrs. Sherlock's Home Made Bread." The set is one of several sponsored by the Toledo bakery. The Babe Ruth pin was reproduced circa 1999 in 1-3/4" size; it has no collectible value.

	NM	EX	VG
Complete Set (10):	4,750	2,400	1,400
Common Player:	100.00	50.00	30.00
(1) Grover Alexander	350.00	175.00	100.00
(2) Ty Cobb	850.00	425.00	255.00
(3) Rogers Hornsby	375.00	185.00	110.00
(4) Walter Johnson	375.00	185.00	110.00
(5) Rabbit Maranville	300.00	150.00	90.00
(6) Pat Moran	100.00	50.00	30.00
(7) "Babe" Ruth	1,100	550.00	330.00
(8) George Sisler	300.00	150.00	90.00
(9) Tris Speaker	375.00	185.00	110.00
(10) Honus Wagner	700.00	350.00	210.00

1975-96 MSA

(See listings under Michael Schechter Associates.)

1916 M101-5 Blank Backs

JIM THORPE
R. F.—New York Giants
176

The Chicago printing and publishing firm of Felix Mendelsohn was the originator of this card set, which is often found bearing advertising on back of several business from around the country. Mendelsohn is not mentioned on the cards, which are blank-backed. Fronts of the 1-5/8" x 3" black-and-white cards have a player photo, name, position abbreviation, team and card number. The set was prepared in advance of the 1916 season and offered in ads in The Sporting News for $1, or a framed uncut sheet for $2.50. The blank-backs are the most common version of M101-5. There were at least two printings of the set, creating several variations to correct errors or replace players.

	NM	EX	VG
Complete Set (200):	82,500	41,250	24,200
Common Player:	90.00	45.00	30.00
1 Babe Adams	100.00	35.00	20.00
2 Sam Agnew	90.00	45.00	30.00
3 Eddie Ainsmith	90.00	45.00	30.00
4 Grover Alexander	550.00	275.00	165.00
5 Leon Ames	90.00	45.00	30.00
6 Jimmy Archer	90.00	45.00	30.00
7 Jimmy Austin	90.00	45.00	30.00
8 J. Franklin Baker	360.00	175.00	105.00
9 Dave Bancroft	360.00	175.00	105.00
10 Jack Barry	90.00	45.00	30.00
11 Zinn Beck	90.00	45.00	30.00
12a Beals Becker	275.00	135.00	80.00
12b Lute Boone	90.00	45.00	30.00
13 Joe Benz	90.00	45.00	30.00
14 Bob Bescher	90.00	45.00	30.00
15 Al Betzel	90.00	45.00	30.00
16 Roger Bresnahan	360.00	175.00	105.00
17 Eddie Burns	90.00	45.00	30.00
18 Geo. J. Burns	90.00	45.00	30.00
19 Joe Bush	90.00	45.00	30.00
20 Owen Bush	90.00	45.00	30.00
21 Art Butler	90.00	45.00	30.00
22 Bobbie Byrne	90.00	45.00	30.00
23a Forrest Cady	330.00	165.00	100.00
23b Mordecai Brown	360.00	175.00	105.00
24 Jimmy Callahan	90.00	45.00	30.00
25 Ray Caldwell	90.00	45.00	30.00
26 Max Carey	360.00	175.00	105.00
27 George Chalmers	90.00	45.00	30.00
28 Frank Chance	360.00	175.00	105.00
29 Ray Chapman	110.00	55.00	35.00
30 Larry Cheney	90.00	45.00	30.00
31 Eddie Cicotte	360.00	175.00	105.00
32 Tom Clarke	90.00	45.00	30.00
33 Eddie Collins	360.00	175.00	105.00
34 "Shauno" Collins	90.00	45.00	30.00
35 Charles Comisky (Comiskey)	360.00	175.00	105.00
36 Joe Connolly	90.00	45.00	30.00
37 Luther Cook	90.00	45.00	30.00
38 Jack Coombs	90.00	45.00	30.00
39 Dan Costello	90.00	45.00	30.00
40 Harry Coveleskie (Coveleski)	90.00	45.00	30.00
41 Gavvy Cravath	90.00	45.00	30.00
42 Sam Crawford	360.00	175.00	105.00
43 Jean Dale	90.00	45.00	30.00
44 Jake Daubert	90.00	45.00	30.00
45 Geo. A. Davis Jr.	90.00	45.00	30.00
46 Charles Deal	90.00	45.00	30.00
47 Al Demaree	90.00	45.00	30.00
48 William Doak	90.00	45.00	30.00
49 Bill Donovan	90.00	45.00	30.00
50 Charles Dooin	90.00	45.00	30.00
51 Mike Doolan	90.00	45.00	30.00
52 Larry Doyle	90.00	45.00	30.00
53 Jean Dubuc	90.00	45.00	30.00
54 Oscar Dugey	90.00	45.00	30.00
55 Johnny Evers	360.00	175.00	105.00
56 Urban Faber	360.00	175.00	105.00
57 "Hap" Felsch	2,000	415.00	250.00
58 Bill Fischer	90.00	45.00	30.00
59 Ray Fisher	90.00	45.00	30.00
60 Max Flack	90.00	45.00	30.00
61 Art Fletcher	90.00	45.00	30.00
62 Eddie Foster	90.00	45.00	30.00
63 Jacques Fournier	90.00	45.00	30.00
64 Del Gainer (Gainor)	90.00	45.00	30.00
65 Larry Gardner	90.00	45.00	30.00
66 Joe Gedeon	90.00	45.00	30.00
67 Gus Getz	90.00	45.00	30.00
68 Geo. Gibson	90.00	45.00	30.00
69 Wilbur Good	90.00	45.00	30.00
70 Hank Gowdy	90.00	45.00	30.00
71 John Graney	90.00	45.00	30.00
72 Tom Griffith	90.00	45.00	30.00
73 Heinie Groh	90.00	45.00	30.00
74 Earl Hamilton	90.00	45.00	30.00
75 Bob Harmon	90.00	45.00	30.00
76 Roy Hartzell	90.00	45.00	30.00
77 Claude Hendrix	90.00	45.00	30.00
78 Olaf Henriksen	90.00	45.00	30.00
79 John Henry	90.00	45.00	30.00
80 "Buck" Herzog	90.00	45.00	30.00
81 Hugh High	90.00	45.00	30.00
82 Dick Hoblitzell	90.00	45.00	30.00
83 Harry Hooper	360.00	175.00	105.00
84 Ivan Howard	90.00	45.00	30.00
85 Miller Huggins	360.00	175.00	105.00
86 Joe Jackson	15,000	4,950	2,970
87 William James	90.00	45.00	30.00
88 Harold Janvrin	90.00	45.00	30.00
89 Hugh Jennings	360.00	175.00	105.00
90 Walter Johnson	1,500	550.00	330.00
91 Fielder Jones	90.00	45.00	30.00
92 Bennie Kauff	90.00	45.00	30.00
93 Wm. Killefer Jr.	90.00	45.00	30.00
94 Ed. Konetchy	90.00	45.00	30.00
95 Napoleon Lajoie	360.00	175.00	105.00
96 Jack Lapp	90.00	45.00	30.00
97a John Lavan (Correct spelling.)	90.00	45.00	30.00
97b John Lavin (Incorrect spelling.)	90.00	45.00	30.00
98 Jimmy Lavender	90.00	45.00	30.00
99 "Nemo" Leibold	90.00	45.00	30.00
100 H.B. Leonard	90.00	45.00	30.00
101 Duffy Lewis	90.00	45.00	30.00
102 Hans Lobert	90.00	45.00	30.00
103 Tom Long	90.00	45.00	30.00
104 Fred Luderus	90.00	45.00	30.00
105 Connie Mack	360.00	175.00	105.00
106 Lee Magee	90.00	45.00	30.00
107 Al. Mamaux	90.00	45.00	30.00
108 Leslie Mann	90.00	45.00	30.00
109 "Rabbit" Maranville	360.00	175.00	105.00
110 Rube Marquard	360.00	175.00	105.00
111 Armando Marsans	100.00	50.00	30.00
112 J. Erskine Mayer	90.00	45.00	30.00
113 George McBride	90.00	45.00	30.00
114 John J. McGraw	360.00	175.00	105.00
115 Jack McInnis	90.00	45.00	30.00
116 Fred Merkle	90.00	45.00	30.00
117 Chief Meyers	90.00	45.00	30.00
118 Clyde Milan	90.00	45.00	30.00
119 Otto Miller	90.00	45.00	30.00
120 Willie Mitchel (Mitchell)	90.00	45.00	30.00
121 Fred Mollwitz	90.00	45.00	30.00
122 J. Herbert Moran	90.00	45.00	30.00
123 Pat Moran	90.00	45.00	30.00
124 Ray Morgan	90.00	45.00	30.00
125 Geo. Moriarty	90.00	45.00	30.00
126 Guy Morton	90.00	45.00	30.00
127 Ed. Murphy (Photo actually Danny Murphy.)	90.00	45.00	30.00
128 John Murray	90.00	45.00	30.00
129 "Hy" Myers	90.00	45.00	30.00
130 J.A. Niehoff	90.00	45.00	30.00
131 Leslie Nunamaker	90.00	45.00	30.00
132 Rube Oldring	90.00	45.00	30.00
133 Oliver O'Mara	90.00	45.00	30.00
134 Steve O'Neill	90.00	45.00	30.00
135 "Dode" Paskert	90.00	45.00	30.00
136 Roger Peckinpaugh (Photo actually Gavvy Cravath.)	90.00	45.00	30.00
137 E.J. Pfeffer (Photo actually Jeff Pfeffer.)	90.00	45.00	30.00
138 Geo. Pierce (Pearce)	90.00	45.00	30.00
139 Walter Pipp	90.00	45.00	30.00
140 Derril Pratt (Derrill)	90.00	45.00	30.00
141 Bill Rariden	90.00	45.00	30.00
142 Eppa Rixey	360.00	175.00	105.00
143 Davey Robertson	90.00	45.00	30.00
144 Wilbert Robinson	360.00	175.00	105.00
145 Bob Roth	90.00	45.00	30.00
146 Ed. Roush	360.00	175.00	105.00
147 Clarence Rowland	90.00	45.00	30.00
148 "Nap" Rucker	90.00	45.00	30.00
149 Dick Rudolph	90.00	45.00	30.00
150 Reb Russell	90.00	45.00	30.00
151 Babe Ruth	30,000	13,750	8,250
152 Vic Saier	90.00	45.00	30.00
153 "Slim" Sallee	90.00	45.00	30.00
154 "Germany" Schaefer	90.00	45.00	30.00
155 Ray Schalk	360.00	175.00	105.00
156 Walter Schang	90.00	45.00	30.00
157 Chas. Schmidt	90.00	45.00	30.00
158 Frank Schulte	90.00	45.00	30.00
159 Jim Scott	90.00	45.00	30.00
160 Everett Scott	90.00	45.00	30.00
161 Tom Seaton	90.00	45.00	30.00
162 Howard Shanks	90.00	45.00	30.00
163 Bob Shawkey (Photo actually Jack McInnis.)	90.00	45.00	30.00
164 Ernie Shore	90.00	45.00	30.00
165 Burt Shotton	90.00	45.00	30.00
166 George Sisler	360.00	175.00	105.00
167 J. Carlisle Smith	90.00	45.00	30.00
168 Fred Snodgrass	90.00	45.00	30.00
169 Geo. Stallings	90.00	45.00	30.00
170 Oscar Stanage (Photo actually Chas. Schmidt.)	90.00	45.00	30.00
171 Charles Stengel	360.00	175.00	105.00
172 Milton Stock	90.00	45.00	30.00
173 Amos Strunk (Photo actually Olaf Henriksen.)	90.00	45.00	30.00
174 Billy Sullivan	90.00	45.00	30.00
175 Chas. Tesreau	90.00	45.00	30.00
176 Jim Thorpe	19,250	9,625	5,775
177 Joe Tinker	360.00	175.00	105.00
178 Fred Toney	90.00	45.00	30.00
179 Terry Turner	90.00	45.00	30.00
180 Jim Vaughn	90.00	45.00	30.00
181 Bob Veach	90.00	45.00	30.00
182 James Viox	90.00	45.00	30.00
183 Oscar Vitt	90.00	45.00	30.00
184 Hans Wagner	3,000	660.00	395.00
185 Clarence Walker (Photo not Walker.)	90.00	45.00	30.00
186a Bobby Wallace	5,500	2,750	1,650
186b Zach Wheat	360.00	175.00	105.00
187 Ed. Walsh	360.00	175.00	105.00
188 Buck Weaver	2,000	360.00	215.00
189 Carl Weilman	90.00	45.00	30.00
190 Geo. Whitted	90.00	45.00	30.00
191 Fred Williams	90.00	45.00	30.00
192 Art Wilson	90.00	45.00	30.00
193 J. Owen Wilson	90.00	45.00	30.00
194 Ivy Wingo	90.00	45.00	30.00
195 "Mel" Wolfgang	90.00	45.00	30.00
196 Joe Wood	500.00	110.00	65.00
197 Steve Yerkes	90.00	45.00	30.00
198 Rollie Zeider	90.00	45.00	30.00
199 Heiny Zimmerman	90.00	45.00	30.00
200 Ed. Zwilling	90.00	45.00	30.00

1916 M101-4 Blank Backs

JOE JACKSON
L. F.—Chicago White Sox
57

The "update" version of this set is nearly identical to the earlier cards. The 200 black-and-white cards once again are printed with player photo, name, position, team and card number on front and blank backs. This version appears to have been sold directly to consumers by the manufacturer, Felix Mendelsohn of Chicago. The same cards can be found with advertising on back from several businesses around the country. Most of the players included on the 1-5/8" x

3" cards also appear in the prior edition. Despite being labeled in the American Card Catalog as M101-4, this version was issued after the M101-5 version, with the first advertising appearing in August 1916. The complete set price does not include variations.

		NM	EX	VG
	Complete Set (200):	45,000	22,500	13,500
	Common Player:	60.00	30.00	18.00
1	Babe Adams	75.00	30.00	18.00
2	Sam Agnew	60.00	30.00	18.00
3	Eddie Ainsmith	60.00	30.00	18.00
4	Grover Alexander	375.00	185.00	110.00
5	Leon Ames	60.00	30.00	18.00
6	Jimmy Archer	60.00	30.00	18.00
7	Jimmy Austin	60.00	30.00	18.00
8	H.D. Baird	60.00	30.00	18.00
9	J. Franklin Baker	300.00	150.00	90.00
10	Dave Bancroft	300.00	150.00	90.00
11	Jack Barry	60.00	30.00	18.00
12	Zinn Beck	60.00	30.00	18.00
13	"Chief" Bender	300.00	150.00	90.00
14	Joe Benz	60.00	30.00	18.00
15	Bob Bescher	60.00	30.00	18.00
16	Al Betzel	60.00	30.00	18.00
17	Mordecai Brown	300.00	150.00	90.00
18	Eddie Burns	60.00	30.00	18.00
19	George Burns	60.00	30.00	18.00
20	Geo. J. Burns	60.00	30.00	18.00
21	Joe Bush	60.00	30.00	18.00
22	"Donie" Bush	60.00	30.00	18.00
23	Art Butler	60.00	30.00	18.00
24	Bobbie Byrne	60.00	30.00	18.00
25	Forrest Cady	60.00	30.00	18.00
26	Jimmy Callahan	60.00	30.00	18.00
27	Ray Caldwell	60.00	30.00	18.00
28	Max Carey	300.00	150.00	90.00
29	George Chalmers	60.00	30.00	18.00
30	Ray Chapman	90.00	45.00	25.00
31	Larry Cheney	60.00	30.00	18.00
32	Eddie Cicotte	300.00	150.00	90.00
33	Tom Clarke	60.00	30.00	18.00
34	Eddie Collins	300.00	150.00	90.00
35	"Shauno" Collins	60.00	30.00	18.00
36	Charles Comiskey	300.00	150.00	90.00
37	Joe Connolly	60.00	30.00	18.00
38	Ty Cobb	2,500	1,250	750.00
39	Harry Coveleskie (Coveleski)	60.00	30.00	18.00
40	Gavvy Cravath	60.00	30.00	18.00
41	Sam Crawford	300.00	150.00	90.00
42	Jean Dale	60.00	30.00	18.00
43	Jake Daubert	60.00	30.00	18.00
44	Charles Deal	60.00	30.00	18.00
45	Al Demaree	60.00	30.00	18.00
46	Josh Devore	60.00	30.00	18.00
47	William Doak	60.00	30.00	18.00
48	Bill Donovan	60.00	30.00	18.00
49	Charles Dooin	60.00	30.00	18.00
50	Mike Doolan	60.00	30.00	18.00
51	Larry Doyle	60.00	30.00	18.00
52	Jean Dubuc	60.00	30.00	18.00
53	Oscar Dugey	60.00	30.00	18.00
54	Johnny Evers	300.00	150.00	90.00
55	Urban Faber	300.00	150.00	90.00
56	"Hap" Felsch	2,000	375.00	225.00
57	Bill Fischer	60.00	30.00	18.00
58	Ray Fisher	60.00	30.00	18.00
59	Max Flack	60.00	30.00	18.00
60	Art Fletcher	60.00	30.00	18.00
61	Eddie Foster	60.00	30.00	18.00
62	Jacques Fournier	60.00	30.00	18.00
63	Del Gainer (Gainor)	60.00	30.00	18.00
64	"Chic" Gandil	500.00	250.00	150.00
65	Larry Gardner	60.00	30.00	18.00
66	Joe Gedeon	60.00	30.00	18.00
67	Gus Getz	60.00	30.00	18.00
68	Geo. Gibson	60.00	30.00	18.00
69	Wilbur Good	60.00	30.00	18.00
70	Hank Gowdy	60.00	30.00	18.00
71	John Graney	60.00	30.00	18.00
72	Clark Griffith	300.00	150.00	90.00
73	Tom Griffith	60.00	30.00	18.00
74	Heinie Groh	60.00	30.00	18.00
75	Earl Hamilton	60.00	30.00	18.00
76	Bob Harmon	60.00	30.00	18.00
77	Roy Hartzell	60.00	30.00	18.00
78	Claude Hendrix	60.00	30.00	18.00
79	Olaf Henriksen	60.00	30.00	18.00
80	John Henry	60.00	30.00	18.00
81	"Buck" Herzog	60.00	30.00	18.00
82	Hugh High	60.00	30.00	18.00
83	Dick Hoblitzell	60.00	30.00	18.00
84	Harry Hooper	300.00	150.00	90.00
85	Ivan Howard	60.00	30.00	18.00
86	Miller Huggins	300.00	150.00	90.00
87	Joe Jackson	15,000	4,000	2,400
88	William James	60.00	30.00	18.00
89	Harold Janvrin	60.00	30.00	18.00
90	Hugh Jennings	300.00	150.00	90.00
91	Walter Johnson	800.00	400.00	240.00
92	Fielder Jones	60.00	30.00	18.00
93	Joe Judge	60.00	30.00	18.00
94	Bennie Kauff	60.00	30.00	18.00
95	Wm. Killefer Jr.	60.00	30.00	18.00
96	Ed. Konetchy	60.00	30.00	18.00
97	Napoleon Lajoie	375.00	185.00	110.00
98	Jack Lapp	60.00	30.00	18.00
99	John Lavan	60.00	30.00	18.00
100	Jimmy Lavender	60.00	30.00	18.00
101	"Nemo" Leibold	60.00	30.00	18.00
102	H.B. Leonard	60.00	30.00	18.00
103	Duffy Lewis	60.00	30.00	18.00
104	Hans Lobert	60.00	30.00	18.00
105	Tom Long	60.00	30.00	18.00
106	Fred Luderus	60.00	30.00	18.00
107	Connie Mack	300.00	150.00	90.00
108	Lee Magee	60.00	30.00	18.00
109	Sherwood Magee	60.00	30.00	18.00
110	Al. Mamaux	60.00	30.00	18.00
111	Leslie Mann	60.00	30.00	18.00
112	"Rabbit" Maranville	300.00	150.00	90.00
113	Rube Marquard	300.00	150.00	90.00
114	J. Erskine Mayer	125.00	65.00	35.00
115	George McBride	60.00	30.00	18.00
116	John J. McGraw	300.00	150.00	90.00
117	Jack McInnis	60.00	30.00	18.00
118	Fred Merkle	60.00	30.00	18.00
119	Chief Meyers	60.00	30.00	18.00
120	Clyde Milan	60.00	30.00	18.00
121	John Miller	60.00	30.00	18.00
122	Otto Miller	60.00	30.00	18.00
123	Willie Mitchell	60.00	30.00	18.00
124	Fred Mollwitz	60.00	30.00	18.00
125	Pat Moran	60.00	30.00	18.00
126	Ray Morgan	60.00	30.00	18.00
127	Geo. Moriarty	60.00	30.00	18.00
128	Guy Morton	60.00	30.00	18.00
129	Mike Mowrey	60.00	30.00	18.00
130	Ed. Murphy	60.00	30.00	18.00
131	"Hy" Myers	60.00	30.00	18.00
132	J.A. Niehoff	60.00	30.00	18.00
133	Rube Oldring	60.00	30.00	18.00
134	Oliver O'Mara	60.00	30.00	18.00
135	Steve O'Neill	60.00	30.00	18.00
136	"Dode" Paskert	60.00	30.00	18.00
137	Roger Peckinpaugh	60.00	30.00	18.00
138	Walter Pipp	75.00	37.50	22.50
139	Derril Pratt (Derrill)	60.00	30.00	18.00
140	Pat Ragan	60.00	30.00	18.00
141	Bill Rariden	60.00	30.00	18.00
142	Eppa Rixey	300.00	150.00	90.00
143	Davey Robertson	60.00	30.00	18.00
144	Wilbert Robinson	300.00	150.00	90.00
145	Bob Roth	60.00	30.00	18.00
146	Ed. Roush	300.00	150.00	90.00
147	Clarence Rowland	60.00	30.00	18.00
148	"Nap" Rucker	60.00	30.00	18.00
149	Dick Rudolph	60.00	30.00	18.00
150	Reb Russell	60.00	30.00	18.00
151	Babe Ruth	15,000	7,500	4,500
152	Vic Saier	60.00	30.00	18.00
153	"Slim" Sallee	60.00	30.00	18.00
154	Ray Schalk	300.00	150.00	90.00
155	Walter Schang	60.00	30.00	18.00
156	Frank Schulte	60.00	30.00	18.00
157	Everett Scott	60.00	30.00	18.00
158	Jim Scott	60.00	30.00	18.00
159	Tom Seaton	60.00	30.00	18.00
160	Howard Shanks	60.00	30.00	18.00
161	Bob Shawkey	60.00	30.00	18.00
162	Ernie Shore	60.00	30.00	18.00
163	Burt Shotton	60.00	30.00	18.00
164	Geo. Sisler	300.00	150.00	90.00
165	J. Carlisle Smith	60.00	30.00	18.00
166	Fred Snodgrass	60.00	30.00	18.00
167	Geo. Stallings	60.00	30.00	18.00
168a	Oscar Stanage/Catching	60.00	30.00	24.00
168b	Oscar Stanage (Portrait to thighs.)	750.00	375.00	225.00
169	Charles Stengel	375.00	185.00	110.00
170	Milton Stock	60.00	30.00	18.00
171	Amos Strunk	60.00	30.00	18.00
172	Billy Sullivan	60.00	30.00	18.00
173	"Jeff" Tesreau	60.00	30.00	18.00
174	Joe Tinker	300.00	150.00	90.00
175	Fred Toney	60.00	30.00	18.00
176	Terry Turner	60.00	30.00	18.00
177	George Tyler	60.00	30.00	18.00
178	Jim Vaughn	60.00	30.00	18.00
179	Bob Veach	60.00	30.00	18.00
180	James Viox	60.00	30.00	18.00
181	Oscar Vitt	60.00	30.00	18.00
182	Hans Wagner	1,200	600.00	360.00
183	Clarence Walker	60.00	30.00	18.00
184	Ed. Walsh	300.00	150.00	90.00
185	W. Wambsganss (Photo actually Fritz Coumbe.)	60.00	30.00	18.00
186	Buck Weaver	600.00	300.00	180.00
187	Carl Weilman	60.00	30.00	18.00
188	Zach Wheat	300.00	150.00	90.00
189	Geo. Whitted	60.00	30.00	18.00
190	Fred Williams	60.00	30.00	18.00
191	Art Wilson	60.00	30.00	18.00
192	J. Owen Wilson	60.00	30.00	18.00
193	Ivy Wingo	60.00	30.00	18.00
194	"Mel" Wolfgang	60.00	30.00	18.00
195	Joe Wood	175.00	85.00	50.00
196	Steve Yerkes	60.00	30.00	18.00
197	"Pep" Young	60.00	30.00	18.00
198	Rollie Zeider	60.00	30.00	18.00
199	Heiny Zimmerman	60.00	30.00	18.00
200	Ed. Zwilling	60.00	30.00	18.00

Frank Robinson—OF
Baltimore Orioles

was issued in three series of eight cards each. No team insignias are visible on any of the cards. Packages described the cards as "Mini Posters."

		NM	EX	VG
	Complete Set (24):	475.00	240.00	140.00
	Common Player:	8.00	4.00	2.50
(1)	Hank Aaron	45.00	22.50	13.50
(2)	Richie Allen	12.50	6.25	3.75
(3)	Lou Brock	20.00	10.00	6.00
(4)	Paul Casanova	8.00	4.00	2.50
(5)	Roberto Clemente	95.00	47.50	28.00
(6)	Al Ferrara	8.00	4.00	2.50
(7)	Bill Freehan	8.00	4.00	2.50
(8)	Jim Fregosi	8.00	4.00	2.50
(9)	Bob Gibson	20.00	10.00	6.00
(10)	Tony Horton	8.00	4.00	2.50
(11)	Tommy John	8.00	4.00	2.50
(12)	Al Kaline	25.00	12.50	7.50
(13)	Jim Lonborg	8.00	4.00	2.50
(14)	Juan Marichal	20.00	10.00	6.00
(15)	Willie Mays	45.00	22.50	13.50
(16)	Rick Monday	8.00	4.00	2.50
(17)	Tony Oliva	8.00	4.00	2.50
(18)	Brooks Robinson	25.00	12.50	7.50
(19)	Frank Robinson	25.00	12.50	7.50
(20)	Pete Rose	35.00	17.50	10.00
(21)	Ron Santo	12.50	6.25	3.75
(22)	Tom Seaver	25.00	12.50	7.50
(23)	Rusty Staub	8.00	4.00	2.50
(24)	Mel Stottlemyre	8.00	4.00	2.50

1923-1924 Nacionales Cigarros

The baseball players in this mid-Twenties Cuban issue are part of a larger set which included boxers, actresses, actors, nudes, soccer players and others. The cards measure about 1-5/8" x 2-1/4" and have a distinctive wide black border on front. Backs identify the issue. An album was issued to house the set. The cards are printed on thin cardboard with a glossy finish.

		NM	EX	VG
	Complete Baseball Set (40):	60,000	24,000	12,000
	Common Player:	500.00	200.00	100.00
21	Rafael Almeida	1,500	600.00	300.00
22	Isidro Fabre	1,125	450.00	225.00
23	Eugenio Morin	500.00	200.00	100.00
24	Oscar Rodriguez	500.00	200.00	100.00
25	Joseito Rodriguez	500.00	200.00	100.00
26	Papo Gonzalez	500.00	200.00	100.00
27	Gutierrez	500.00	200.00	100.00
28	Valentin Dreke (Photo actually Lucas Boada.)	1,125	450.00	225.00
29	Jose Maria Fernandez	750.00	300.00	150.00
30	(Cheo) Ramos	500.00	200.00	100.00
31	Paito (Ramon Herrera)	500.00	200.00	100.00
32	Bernardo Baro	1,125	450.00	225.00
33	Manuel Cueto	750.00	300.00	150.00
34	(Oscar) Tuero	500.00	200.00	100.00
35	Kakin Gonzalez	500.00	200.00	100.00
36	Armando Marsans	1,500	600.00	300.00
37	Andy Cooper	9,000	3,600	1,800
38	Dolf Luque	2,500	1,000	500.00
39	Marcelino Guerra	500.00	200.00	100.00
40	Manzanillo (Tatic Campos)	500.00	200.00	100.00
41	Oscar Levis	750.00	300.00	150.00
42	Eufemio Abreu	500.00	200.00	100.00

1969 Nabisco Team Flakes

This set of cards is seen in two different sizes: 1-15/16" x 3" and 1-3/4" x 2-15/16". This is explained by the varying widths of the card borders on the backs of Nabisco cereal packages. Cards are action color photos bordered in yellow. Twenty-four of the top players in the game are included in the set, which

43	Cristobal Torriente	12,000	4,800	2,400
44	Juanelo Mirabal	750.00	300.00	150.00
45	Merito Acosta	500.00	200.00	100.00
46	Jose Acostica (Acosta)	500.00	200.00	100.00
47	Rogelio Crespo	500.00	200.00	100.00
48	(Jacinto) Calvo	750.00	300.00	150.00
49	(Emilio) Palmero	750.00	300.00	150.00
50	Jose Mendez	9,000	3,600	1,800
51	Alejandro Oms	3,750	1,500	750.00
52	Pedro Dibut	750.00	300.00	150.00
53	Strike (Valentin "Sirique" Gonzalez)	500.00	200.00	100.00
54	Magrinat (Hector Magrinut)	500.00	200.00	100.00
55	Raphael Quintana	500.00	200.00	100.00
56	Bienvenido Jimenez	750.00	300.00	150.00
57	Bartolo Portuondo (Portuondo)	1,500	600.00	300.00
58	(Pelayo) Chacon	1,500	600.00	300.00
59	Riant (Red Ryan)	1,500	600.00	300.00
60	Perico El Mano/Mascot	500.00	200.00	100.00

1909 Nadja Caramels (E92)

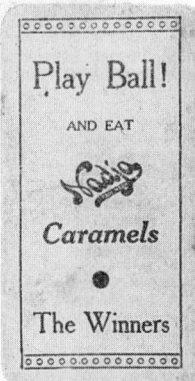

Tinker, s.s. Chicago Nat'l

One of several 1909-10 issues produced for Nadja Caramels, this set can be distinguished by the players in the checklist (alphabetized here) and the type beneath the color player lithograph. In this set, the player's last name is in upper and lower-case letters, and his position is given, along with the team. Backs of these 1-1/2" x 2-3/4" cards are identical to later Nadja issues, featuring an ad for the candy brand. Cataloged (along with the cards of Croft's Candy/Cocoa and Dockman Gum) as E92 in the "American Card Catalog," the Nadja set checklist differs from those issues in that it is larger and contains a group of St. Louis players not found in the other sets. Nadja was a brand name of the Blake-Wenneker Candy Co. of St. Louis.

		NM	EX	VG
Complete Set (62):		55,000	27,500	17,500
Common Player:		550.00	220.00	110.00
(1)	Bill Bailey	550.00	220.00	110.00
(2)	Jack Barry	550.00	220.00	110.00
(3)	Harry Bemis	550.00	220.00	110.00
(4)	Chief Bender (Striped cap.)	1,000	460.00	300.00
(5)	Chief Bender (White cap.)	1,000	460.00	300.00
(6)	Bill Bergen	550.00	220.00	110.00
(7)	Bob Bescher	550.00	220.00	110.00
(8)	Roger Bresnahan	1,000	460.00	300.00
(9)	Al Bridwell	550.00	220.00	110.00
(10)	Doc Casey	550.00	220.00	110.00
(11)	Frank Chance	1,000	460.00	300.00
(12)	Hal Chase	800.00	350.00	250.00
(13)	Ty Cobb	7,500	3,400	2,250
(14)	Eddie Collins	1,000	460.00	300.00
(15)	Sam Crawford	1,000	460.00	300.00
(16)	Harry Davis	550.00	220.00	110.00
(17)	Art Devlin	550.00	220.00	110.00
(18)	Bill Donovan	550.00	220.00	110.00
(19)	Red Dooin	550.00	220.00	110.00
(20)	Mickey Doolan	550.00	220.00	110.00
(21)	Patsy Dougherty	550.00	220.00	110.00
(22)	Larry Doyle/Throwing	550.00	220.00	110.00
(23)	Larry Doyle (With bat.)	550.00	220.00	110.00
(24)	Rube Ellis	550.00	220.00	110.00
(25)	Johnny Evers	1,000	460.00	300.00
(26)	George Gibson	550.00	220.00	110.00
(27)	Topsy Hartsel	550.00	220.00	110.00
(28)	Roy Hartzell/Btg	550.00	220.00	110.00
(29)	Roy Hartzell/Fielding	550.00	220.00	110.00
(30)	Harry Howell (Ready to pitch.)	550.00	220.00	110.00
(31)	Harry Howell (Follow-through.)	550.00	220.00	110.00
(32)	Fred Jacklitsch	550.00	220.00	110.00
(33)	Hugh Jennings	1,000	460.00	300.00
(34)	Red Kleinow	550.00	220.00	110.00
(35)	Otto Knabe	550.00	220.00	110.00
(36)	Jack Knight	550.00	220.00	110.00
(37)	Nap Lajoie	1,000	460.00	300.00
(38)	Hans Lobert	550.00	220.00	110.00
(39)	Sherry Magee	550.00	220.00	110.00
(40)	Christy Matthewson (Mathewson)	3,900	1,750	1,200
(41)	John McGraw	1,000	460.00	300.00
(42)	Larry McLean	550.00	220.00	110.00
(43)	Dots Miller/Btg	550.00	220.00	110.00
(44)	Dots Miller/Fielding	550.00	220.00	110.00
(45)	Danny Murphy	550.00	220.00	110.00
(46)	Rebel Oakes	550.00	220.00	110.00

(47)	Bill O'Hara	550.00	220.00	110.00
(48)	Eddie Phelps	550.00	220.00	110.00
(49)	Germany Schaefer	550.00	220.00	110.00
(50)	Admiral Schlei	550.00	220.00	110.00
(51)	Boss Schmidt	550.00	220.00	110.00
(52)	Johnny Seigle (Siegle)	550.00	220.00	110.00
(53)	Dave Shean	550.00	220.00	110.00
(54)	Boss Smith (Schmidt)	550.00	220.00	110.00
(55)	George Stone (Blue background.)	550.00	220.00	110.00
(56)	George Stone (Green background.)	550.00	220.00	110.00
(57)	Joe Tinker	1,000	460.00	300.00
(58)	Honus Wagner/Btg	6,000	2,700	1,800
(59)	Honus Wagner/Throwing	7,200	3,250	2,200
(60)	Bobby Wallace	1,000	460.00	300.00
(61)	Cy Young	2,500	1,150	750.00
(62)	Heinie Zimmerman	550.00	220.00	110.00

1910 Nadja Caramels Philadelphia Athletics (E104-1)

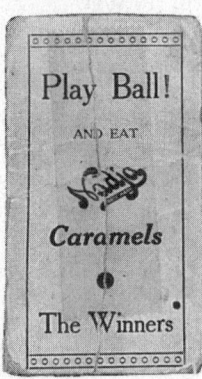

BENDER, ATHLETIC

The 18 Philadelphia Athletics players in this set, can each be found in three different variations. Each of the approximately 1-1/2" x 2-3/4" cards can be found with a plain portrait lithograph on front, and either a blank back or a back containing a Nadja ad. Each player can also be found with a black overprint on front, comprised of a white elephant figure on the uniform and the notation "World's Champions 1910" above. The overprinted cards are known only with blank backs, and are somewhat scarcer than the plain cards of either type. Nadja-back cards should be valued about the same as the overprinted type.

		NM	EX	VG
Complete Set, No O/P, Blank Back (18):		22,000	10,000	6,600
Complete Set, With O/P or Ad Back:		27,500	13,300	8,000
Common Player:		850.00	375.00	250.00
(1a)	Home Run Baker	1,750	800.00	500.00
(1b)	Home Run Baker ("World's Champions")	3,000	1,500	750.00
(2a)	Jack Barry	1,000	450.00	300.00
(2b)	Jack Barry ("World's Champions")	1,800	900.00	450.00
(3a)	Chief Bender	1,750	800.00	500.00
(3b)	Chief Bender ("World's Champions")	3,000	1,500	750.00
(4a)	Eddie Collins	1,750	800.00	500.00
(4b)	Eddie Collins ("World's Champions")	3,000	1,500	750.00
(5a)	Harry Davis	1,000	450.00	300.00
(5b)	Harry Davis ("World's Champions")	1,800	900.00	450.00
(6a)	Jimmy Dygert	1,000	450.00	300.00
(6b)	Jimmy Dygert ("World's Champions")	1,800	900.00	450.00
(7a)	Topsy Hartsel	1,000	450.00	300.00
(7b)	Topsy Hartel ("World's Champions")	1,800	900.00	450.00
(8a)	Harry Krause	1,000	450.00	300.00
(8b)	Harry Krause ("World's Champions")	1,800	900.00	450.00
(9a)	Jack Lapp	1,000	450.00	300.00
(9b)	Jack Lapp ("World's Champions")	1,800	900.00	450.00
(10a)	Paddy Livingstone (Livingston)	1,000	450.00	300.00
(10b)	Paddy Livingstone (Livingston) ("World's Champions")	1,800	900.00	450.00
(11a)	Bris Lord	1,000	450.00	300.00
(11b)	Bris Lord ("World's Champions")	1,800	900.00	450.00
(12a)	Connie Mack	1,750	800.00	500.00
(12b)	Connie Mack ("World's Champions")	4,000	2,000	1,000
(13a)	Cy Morgan	1,000	450.00	300.00
(13b)	Cy Morgan ("World's Champions")	1,800	900.00	450.00
(14a)	Danny Murphy	1,000	450.00	300.00
(14b)	Danny Murphy ("World's Champions")	1,800	900.00	450.00
(15a)	Rube Oldring	1,000	450.00	300.00
(15b)	Rube Oldring ("World's Champions")	1,800	900.00	450.00
(16a)	Eddie Plank	2,700	1,200	800.00
(16b)	Eddie Plank ("World's Champions")	5,000	2,500	1,250
(17a)	Amos Strunk	1,000	450.00	300.00
(17b)	Amos Strunk ("World's Champions")	1,800	900.00	450.00
(18a)	Ira Thomas	1,000	450.00	300.00
(18b)	Ira Thomas ("World's Champions")	1,800	900.00	450.00

1910 Nadja Caramels Pittsburgh Pirates (E104-2)

WAGNER, PITTSBURG

Similar to the contemporary American Caramel issue, this set of 1-1/2" x 2-3/4" cards features portrait color lithographs of the 1909 World's Champion Pittsburgh (spelled "Pittsburg") Pirates. Each card was issued with both blank back and with a back bearing a Nadja ad. The Nadja-backed cards are scarcer but command little premium.

		NM	EX	VG
Complete Set (11):		21,000	10,000	7,000
Common Player:		800.00	400.00	200.00
Ad Back: 1.25X				
(1)	Babe Adams	800.00	400.00	200.00
(2)	Fred Clarke	1,800	800.00	550.00
(3)	George Gibson	800.00	400.00	200.00
(4)	Ham Hyatt	800.00	400.00	200.00
(5)	Tommy Leach	800.00	400.00	200.00
(6)	Sam Leever	800.00	400.00	200.00
(7)	Nick Maddox	800.00	400.00	200.00
(8)	Dots Miller	800.00	400.00	200.00
(9)	Deacon Phillippe	800.00	400.00	200.00
(10)	Honus Wagner	12,000	5,400	3,600
(11)	Owen Wilson	800.00	400.00	200.00

1910 Nadja Caramels (E104-3)

MOORE, PHILADELPHIA

The cards in this issue can each be found with or without a Nadja ad on back; the latter being somewhat scarcer and carrying a premium over the values shown. These 1-1/2" x 2-3/4" cards can be distinguished from the 1909 issue by the line of type beneath the player portrait. On the 1910 cards, the player's last name is in all blue capital letters and there is no position designation given. This checklist is likely incomplete.

		NM	EX	VG
Common Player:		1,400	700.00	400.00
Ad Back: 1.25X				
(1)	Bill Abstein	1,400	700.00	400.00
(2)	Red Ames	1,400	700.00	400.00
(3)	Johnny Bates	1,400	700.00	400.00
(4)	Kitty Bransfield	1,400	700.00	400.00
(5)	Al Bridwell	1,400	700.00	400.00
(6)	Hal Chase	1,900	900.00	600.00
(7)	Doc Crandall	1,400	700.00	400.00
(8)	Sam Crawford	2,400	1,100	700.00
(9)	Jim Delehanty (Delahanty)	1,400	700.00	400.00
(10)	Art Devlin	1,400	700.00	400.00
(11)	Red Dooin	1,400	700.00	400.00
(12)	Mickey Doolan	1,400	700.00	400.00

		NM	EX	VG
(13)	Larry Doyle	1,400	700.00	400.00
(14)	Eddie Grant	1,400	700.00	400.00
(15)	Fred Jacklitsch	1,400	700.00	400.00
(16)	Hugh Jennings	2,400	1,100	700.00
(17)	Davy Jones	1,400	700.00	400.00
(18)	Tom Jones	1,400	700.00	400.00
(19)	Otto Knabe	1,400	700.00	400.00
(201	Sherry Magee	1,400	700.00	400.00
(21)	John McGraw	2,400	1,100	700.00
(22)	Matty McIntyre	1,400	700.00	400.00
(23)	Earl Moore	1,400	700.00	400.00
(24)	Pat Moren (Moran)	1,400	700.00	400.00
(25)	George Moriarity	1,400	700.00	400.00
(26)	George Mullin	1,400	700.00	400.00
(27)	Red Murray	1,400	700.00	400.00
(28)	Simon Nicholls	1,400	700.00	400.00
(29)	Charley O'Leary	1,400	700.00	400.00
(30)	Admiral Schlei	1,400	700.00	400.00
(31)	Boss Schmidt	1,400	700.00	400.00
(32)	Cy Seymore (Seymour)	1,400	700.00	400.00
(33)	Tully Sparks	1,400	700.00	400.00
(34)	Ed Summers	1,400	700.00	400.00
(35)	Ed Willetts (Willett)	1,400	700.00	400.00
(36)	Vic Willis	2,400	1,100	700.00
(37)	Hooks Wiltse	1,400	700.00	400.00

1912 Napoleon Little Cigars

While this cigarette brand advertising on the backs of T207 cards is less commonly encountered than Recruit, collectors do not attach a commensurate premium to them, largely because each of the players can be found with more common back ads.

PREMIUM: 2X
(See T207 for checklist and base card values.)

1963 Nassau County Boy Scouts

According to the text on the back, six cards were issued in this set. The other subjects are unknown, and may not feature any additional baseball players. The standard-size cards are printed in blue-and-white, both front and back, including a duo-tone photo of Snider in his only season with the Mets.

		NM	EX	VG
(1)	Duke Snider	150.00	75.00	45.00

1974 Nassau Tuberculosis and Respiratory Disease Assn.

The date attributed to these cards is arbitrary. The black-and-white 2-1/2" x 3-1/2" cards have a photo of the Yankees pitcher on front and a career summary on back, along with an anti-smoking message.

	NM	EX	VG
Whitey Ford (Facing his right.)	45.00	22.50	13.50
Whitey Ford (Follow-through.)	45.00	22.50	13.50

1921-23 National Caramel (E220)

Issued circa 1921 to 1923, this 120-card set is sometimes confused with contemporary American Caramel issues, but is easy to identify because of the words "Made only by National Caramel Company" on the back. With due consideration to normal cutting variances on cards of this era and type, E220s measure about 2" x 3-1/4" and feature black-and-white photos with the player's name, position and team at the bottom. In addition to the line indicating the manufacturer, the backs read "This set consists of pictures of 120 of the leading Base Ball Stars of the American and National Leagues". There are 115 different players included in the set, with five players shown on two cards each. About half of the photos in the set are identical to those used in various American Caramel sets, leading to some confusion regarding the three sets.

		NM	EX	VG
Complete Set (120):		27,500	13,500	8,250
Common Player:		100.00	50.00	30.00
(1)	Charles "Babe" Adams	100.00	50.00	30.00
(2)	G.C. Alexander	400.00	200.00	120.00
(3)	James Austin	100.00	50.00	30.00
(4)	Jim Bagbyk (Bagby)	100.00	50.00	30.00
(5)	Franklin "Home Run" Baker	300.00	150.00	90.00
(6)	Dave Bancroft	300.00	150.00	90.00
(7)	Turner Barber	100.00	50.00	30.00
(8)	George Burns (Cincinnati)	100.00	50.00	30.00
(9)	George Burns (Cleveland)	100.00	50.00	30.00
(10)	Joe Bush	100.00	50.00	30.00
(11)	Leon Cadore	100.00	50.00	30.00
(12)	Max Carey	300.00	150.00	90.00
(13)	Ty Cobb	1,750	875.00	525.00
(14)	Eddie Collins	300.00	150.00	90.00
(15)	John Collins	100.00	50.00	30.00
(16)	Wilbur Cooper	100.00	50.00	30.00
(17)	S. Coveleskie (Coveleski)	300.00	150.00	90.00
(18)	Walton Cruise	100.00	50.00	30.00
(19)	Wm. Cunningham	100.00	50.00	30.00
(20)	George Cutshaw	100.00	50.00	30.00
(21)	Jake Daubert	100.00	50.00	30.00
(22)	Chas. A. Deal	100.00	50.00	30.00
(23)	Bill Doak	100.00	50.00	30.00
(24)	Joe Dugan	100.00	50.00	30.00
(25)	Jimmy Dykes/Btg	100.00	50.00	30.00
(26)	Jimmy Dykes/Fielding	100.00	50.00	30.00
(27)	"Red" Faber	300.00	150.00	90.00
(28)	"Chick" Fewster	100.00	50.00	30.00
(29)	Wilson Fewster	100.00	50.00	30.00
(30)	Ira Flagstead	100.00	50.00	30.00
(31)	Arthur Fletcher	100.00	50.00	30.00
(32)	Frank Frisch	300.00	150.00	90.00
(33)	Larry Gardner	100.00	50.00	30.00
(34)	Walter Gerber	100.00	50.00	30.00
(35)	Charles Glazner	100.00	50.00	30.00
(36)	Hank Gowdy	100.00	50.00	30.00
(37)	J.C. Graney (Should be J.G.)	100.00	50.00	30.00
(38)	Tommy Griffith	100.00	50.00	30.00
(39)	Charles Grimm	100.00	50.00	30.00
(40)	Heinie Groh	100.00	50.00	30.00
(41)	Byron Harris	100.00	50.00	30.00
(42)	Sam Harris (Bucky)	300.00	150.00	90.00
(43)	Harry Heilman (Heilmann)	300.00	150.00	90.00
(44)	Claude Hendrix	100.00	50.00	30.00
(45)	Walter Henline	100.00	50.00	30.00
(46)	Chas. Hollocher	100.00	50.00	30.00
(47)	Harry Hooper	300.00	150.00	90.00
(48)	Rogers Hornsby	400.00	200.00	120.00
(49)	Waite Hoyt	300.00	150.00	90.00
(50)	Wilbert Hubbell	100.00	50.00	30.00
(51)	Wm. Jacobson	100.00	50.00	30.00
(52)	Walter Johnson	850.00	425.00	255.00
(53)	Jimmy Johnston	100.00	50.00	30.00
(54)	Joe Judge	100.00	50.00	30.00
(55)	Geo. "Bingo" Kelly	300.00	150.00	90.00
(56)	Dick Kerr	100.00	50.00	30.00
(57)	Pete Kilduff/Bending	100.00	50.00	30.00
(58)	Pete Kilduff/Leaping	100.00	50.00	30.00
(59)	Larry Kopf	100.00	50.00	30.00
(60)	H.B. Leonard	100.00	50.00	30.00
(61)	Harry Liebold (Leibold)	100.00	50.00	30.00
(62)	Walter "Buster" Mails ("Duster")	100.00	50.00	30.00
(63)	Walter "Rabbit" Maranville	300.00	150.00	90.00
(64)	Carl Mays	100.00	50.00	30.00
(65)	Lee Meadows	100.00	50.00	30.00
(66)	Bob Meusel	100.00	50.00	30.00
(67)	Emil Meusel	100.00	50.00	30.00
(68)	J.C. Milan	100.00	50.00	30.00
(69)	Earl Neale	125.00	60.00	35.00
(70)	Robert Nehf (Arthur)	100.00	50.00	30.00
(71)	Bernie Neis	100.00	50.00	30.00
(72)	Joe Oeschger	100.00	50.00	30.00
(73)	Robert O'Farrell	100.00	50.00	30.00
(74)	Ivan Olson	100.00	50.00	30.00
(75)	Steve O'Neill	100.00	50.00	30.00
(76)	Geo. Paskert	100.00	50.00	30.00
(77)	Roger Peckinpaugh	100.00	50.00	30.00
(78)	Herb Pennock	300.00	150.00	90.00
(79)	Ralph "Cy" Perkins	100.00	50.00	30.00
(80)	Scott Perry (Photo actually Ed Rommel.)	100.00	50.00	30.00
(81)	Jeff Pfeffer	100.00	50.00	30.00
(82)	V.J. Picinich	100.00	50.00	30.00
(83)	Walter Pipp	115.00	55.00	35.00
(84)	Derrill Pratt	100.00	50.00	30.00
(85)	Goldie Rapp	100.00	50.00	30.00
(86)	Edgar Rice	300.00	150.00	90.00
(87)	Jimmy Ring	100.00	50.00	30.00
(88)	Eddie Rousch (Roush)	300.00	150.00	90.00
(89)	Babe Ruth	8,000	4,000	2,400
(90)	Raymond Schmandt	100.00	50.00	30.00
(91)	Everett Scott	100.00	50.00	30.00
(92)	Joe Sewell	300.00	150.00	90.00
(93)	Wally Shang (Schang)	100.00	50.00	30.00
(94)	Maurice Shannon	100.00	50.00	30.00
(95)	Bob Shawkey	100.00	50.00	30.00
(96)	Urban Shocker	100.00	50.00	30.00
(97)	George Sisler	300.00	150.00	90.00
(98)	Earl Smith	100.00	50.00	30.00
(99)	John Smith	100.00	50.00	30.00
(100)	Sherrod Smith	100.00	50.00	30.00
(101)	Frank Snyder/Crouching	100.00	50.00	30.00
(102)	Frank Snyder/Standing	100.00	50.00	30.00
(103)	Tris Speaker	400.00	200.00	120.00
(104)	Vernon Spencer	100.00	50.00	30.00
(105)	Chas. "Casey" Stengle (Stengel)	350.00	175.00	100.00
(106)	Milton Stock/Btg	100.00	50.00	30.00
(107)	Milton Stock/Fielding	100.00	50.00	30.00
(108)	James Vaughn	100.00	50.00	30.00
(109)	Robert Veach	100.00	50.00	30.00
(110)	Wm. Wambsgauss (Wambsganss)	100.00	50.00	30.00
(111)	Aaron Ward	100.00	50.00	30.00
(112)	Zach Wheat	300.00	150.00	90.00
(113)	George Whitted/Btg	100.00	50.00	30.00
(114)	George Whitted/Fielding	100.00	50.00	30.00
(115)	Fred C. Williams	100.00	50.00	30.00
(116)	Arthur Wilson	100.00	50.00	30.00
(117)	Ivy Wingo	100.00	50.00	30.00
(118)	Lawton Witt	100.00	50.00	30.00
(119)	"Pep" Young (Photo actually Ralph Young.)	100.00	50.00	30.00
(120)	Ross Young (Youngs)	300.00	150.00	90.00

1936 National Chicle "Fine Pens" (R313)

Issued in 1936 by the National Chicle Co., this set consists of 120 cards, measuring 3-1/4" x 5-3/8". The black-and-white cards are blank-backed and unnumbered. Although issued by National Chicle, the name of the company does not appear on the cards. The set includes individual player portraits with facsimilie autographs, multi-player cards and action photos. The cards, known in the hobby as "Fine Pen" because of the thin style of writing used for the facsimilie autographs, were originally available as an in-store premium.

		NM	EX	VG
Complete Set (120):		6,500	3,250	1,950
Common Player:		40.00	20.00	12.00
(1)	Melo Almada	45.00	22.50	13.50
(2)	Nick Altrock, Al Schacht	40.00	20.00	12.00
(3)	Paul Andrews	40.00	20.00	12.00
(4)	Elden Auker (Eldon)	40.00	20.00	12.00
(5)	Earl Averill	75.00	37.50	22.50
(6)	John Babich, James Bucher	40.00	20.00	12.00
(7)	Jim Becher (Bucher)	40.00	20.00	12.00

		NM	EX	VG
(8)	Moe Berg	150.00	75.00	45.00
(9)	Walter Berger	40.00	20.00	12.00
(10)	Charles Berry	40.00	20.00	12.00
(11)	Ralph Birkhofer (Birkofer)	40.00	20.00	12.00
(12)	Cy Blanton	40.00	20.00	12.00
(13)	O. Bluege	40.00	20.00	12.00
(14)	Cliff Bolton	40.00	20.00	12.00
(15)	Zeke Bonura	40.00	20.00	12.00
(16)	Stan Bordagaray, George Earnshaw	40.00	20.00	12.00
(17)	Jim Bottomley, Charley Gelbert	50.00	25.00	15.00
(18)	Thos. Bridges	40.00	20.00	12.00
(19)	Sam Byrd	40.00	20.00	12.00
(20)	Dolph Camilli	40.00	20.00	12.00
(21)	Dolph Camilli, Billy Jurges	40.00	20.00	12.00
(22)	Bruce Campbell	40.00	20.00	12.00
(23)	Walter "Kit" Carson	40.00	20.00	12.00
(24)	Ben Chapman	40.00	20.00	12.00
(25)	Harlond Clift, Luke Sewell	40.00	20.00	12.00
(26)	Mickey Cochrane, Jimmy Fox (Foxx), Al Simmons	90.00	45.00	27.50
(27)	"Rip" Collins	40.00	20.00	12.00
(28)	Joe Cronin	75.00	37.50	22.50
(29)	Frank Crossetti (Crosetti)	40.00	20.00	12.00
(30)	Frank Crosetti, Jimmy Dykes	40.00	20.00	12.00
(31)	Kiki Cuyler, Gabby Hartnett	85.00	40.00	25.00
(32)	Paul Derringer	40.00	20.00	12.00
(33)	Bill Dickey, Hank Greenberg	90.00	45.00	27.50
(34)	Bill Dietrich	40.00	20.00	12.00
(35)	Joe DiMaggio, Hank Erickson	750.00	375.00	225.00
(36)	Carl Doyle	40.00	20.00	12.00
(37)	Charles Dressen, Bill Myers	40.00	20.00	12.00
(38)	Jimmie Dykes	40.00	20.00	12.00
(39)	Rick Ferrell, Wess Ferrell (Wes)	75.00	37.50	22.50
(40)	Pete Fox	40.00	20.00	12.00
(41)	Frankie Frisch	75.00	37.50	22.50
(42)	Milton Galatzer	40.00	20.00	12.00
(43)	Chas. Gehringer	75.00	37.50	22.50
(44)	Charley Gelbert	40.00	20.00	12.00
(45)	Joe Glenn	40.00	20.00	12.00
(46)	Jose Gomez	40.00	20.00	12.00
(47)	Lefty Gomez, Red Ruffing	90.00	45.00	27.50
(48)	Vernon Gomez	75.00	37.50	22.50
(49)	Leon Goslin	75.00	37.50	22.50
(50)	Hank Gowdy	40.00	20.00	12.00
(51)	"Hank" Greenberg	90.00	45.00	27.50
(52)	"Lefty" Grove	90.00	45.00	27.50
(53)	Stan Hack	40.00	20.00	12.00
(54)	Odell Hale	40.00	20.00	12.00
(55)	Wild Bill Hallahan	40.00	20.00	12.00
(56)	Mel Harder	40.00	20.00	12.00
(57)	Stanley Bucky Harriss (Harris)	75.00	37.50	22.50
(58)	Gabby Hartnett, Rip Radcliff	40.00	20.00	12.00
(59)	Gabby Hartnett, L. Waner	45.00	22.50	13.50
(60)	Gabby Hartnett, Lon Warnecke (Warneke)	40.00	20.00	12.00
(61)	Buddy Hassett	40.00	20.00	12.00
(62)	Babe Herman	40.00	20.00	12.00
(63)	Frank Higgins	40.00	20.00	12.00
(64)	Oral C. Hildebrand	40.00	20.00	12.00
(65)	Myril Hoag	40.00	20.00	12.00
(66)	Rogers Hornsby	90.00	45.00	27.50
(67)	Waite Hoyt	75.00	37.50	22.50
(68)	Willis G. Hudlin	40.00	20.00	12.00
(69)	"Woody" Jensen	40.00	20.00	12.00
(70)	Woody Jenson (Jensen)	40.00	20.00	12.00
(71)	William Knickerbocker	40.00	20.00	12.00
(72)	Joseph Kuhel	40.00	20.00	12.00
(73)	Cookie Lavagetto	40.00	20.00	12.00
(74)	Thornton Lee	40.00	20.00	12.00
(75)	Ernie Lombardi	75.00	37.50	22.50
(76)	Red Lucas	40.00	20.00	12.00
(77)	Connie Mack, John McGraw	75.00	37.50	22.50
(78)	Pepper Martin	40.00	20.00	12.00
(79)	George McQuinn	40.00	20.00	12.00
(80)	George McQuinn, Lee Stine	40.00	20.00	12.00
(81)	Joe Medwick	75.00	37.50	22.50
(82)	Oscar Melillo	40.00	20.00	12.00
(83)	"Buddy" Meyer (Myer)	40.00	20.00	12.00
(84)	Randy Moore	40.00	20.00	12.00
(85)	T. Moore, Jimmie Wilson	40.00	20.00	12.00
(86)	Wallace Moses	40.00	20.00	12.00
(87)	V. Mungo	40.00	20.00	12.00
(88)	Lamar Newsom (Newsome)	40.00	20.00	12.00
(89)	Lewis "Buck" Newsom (Louis)	40.00	20.00	12.00
(90)	Steve O'Neill	40.00	20.00	12.00
(91)	Tommie Padden	40.00	20.00	12.00
(92)	E. Babe Philips (Phelps)	40.00	20.00	12.00
(93)	Bill Rogel (Rogell)	40.00	20.00	12.00
(94)	Lynn "Schoolboy" Rowe	40.00	20.00	12.00
(95)	Luke Sewell	40.00	20.00	12.00
(96)	Al Simmons	75.00	37.50	22.50
(97)	Casey Stengel	80.00	40.00	24.00
(98)	Bill Swift	40.00	20.00	12.00
(99)	Cecil Travis	40.00	20.00	12.00
(100)	"Pie" Traynor	75.00	37.50	22.50
(101)	William Urbansky (Urbanski)	40.00	20.00	12.00
(102)	Arky Vaughn (Vaughan)	75.00	37.50	22.50
(103)	Joe Vosmik	40.00	20.00	12.00
(104)	Honus Wagner	135.00	65.00	40.00
(105)	Rube Walberg	40.00	20.00	12.00
(106)	Bill Walker	40.00	20.00	12.00
(107)	Gerald Walker	40.00	20.00	12.00
(108)	L. Waner, P. Waner, Big Jim Weaver	75.00	37.50	22.50
(109)	George Washington	40.00	20.00	12.00
(110)	Bill Werber	40.00	20.00	12.00
(111)	Sam West	40.00	20.00	12.00
(112)	Pinkey Whitney	40.00	20.00	12.00
(113)	Vernon Wiltshere (Wilshere)	40.00	20.00	12.00
(114)	"Pep" Young	40.00	20.00	12.00
(115)	Chicago White Sox 1936	40.00	20.00	12.00
(116)	Fence Busters	40.00	20.00	12.00
(117)	Talking It Over (Leo Durocher)	40.00	20.00	12.00
(118)	There She Goes! Chicago City Series	40.00	20.00	12.00

		NM	EX	VG
(119)	Ump Says No - Cleveland vs. Detroit	40.00	20.00	12.00
(120)	World Series 1935 (Phil Cavarretta, Goose Goslin, Lon Warneke)	40.00	20.00	12.00

1936 National Chicle Rabbit Maranville 'How To'

Issued by National Chicle in 1936, this 20-card set was a paper issue distributed with Batter-Up Gum. Unfolded, each paper measured 3-5/8" x 6". The numbered set featured a series of baseball tips from Rabbit Maranville and are illustrated with line drawings. American Card Catalog designation was R344.

		NM	EX	VG
Complete Set (20):		700.00	350.00	210.00
Common Card:		35.00	17.50	10.00
1	How to Pitch the Out Shoot	35.00	17.50	10.00
2	How to Throw the In Shoot	35.00	17.50	10.00
3	How to Pitch the Drop	35.00	17.50	10.00
4	How to Pitch the Floater	35.00	17.50	10.00
5	How to Run Bases	35.00	17.50	10.00
6	How to Slide	35.00	17.50	10.00
7	How to Catch Flies	35.00	17.50	10.00
8	How to Field Grounders	35.00	17.50	10.00
9	How to Tag A Man Out	35.00	17.50	10.00
10	How to Cover A Base	35.00	17.50	10.00
11	How to Bat	35.00	17.50	10.00
12	How to Steal Bases	35.00	17.50	10.00
13	How to Bunt	35.00	17.50	10.00
14	How to Coach Base Runner	35.00	17.50	10.00
15	How to Catch Behind the Bat	35.00	17.50	10.00
16	How to Throw to Bases	35.00	17.50	10.00
17	How to Signal	35.00	17.50	10.00
18	How to Umpire Balls and Strikes	35.00	17.50	10.00
19	How to Umpire Bases	35.00	17.50	10.00
20	How to Lay Out a Ball Field	35.00	17.50	10.00

1898-99 National Copper Plate Co. Portraits

Besides supplying The Sporting News with the player portrait supplements issued during 1899-1900, this Grand Rapids, Mich., firm also sold nearly identical pieces in portfolios of 50 in a hard-cover, string-bound book. Approximately 10" x 13", the pictures feature the players at the turn of the century in formal portrait poses; some are in uniform, some in civilian clothes. The pictures are vignetted on a white background with the player's full name, team and year of issue printed at bottom. At lower-left on most, but not all, of the pictures is National Copper Plate's credit line. Backs have a player biographies in elaborate scrollwork frames.

		NM	EX	VG
Complete Set (50):		50,000	25,000	15,000
Common Player:		900.00	360.00	180.00
(1)	M.F. Amole (M.G. "Doc")	900.00	360.00	180.00
(2)	A.C. Anson	2,000	800.00	400.00
(3)	Robert Becker	900.00	360.00	180.00
(4)	Martin Bergen	900.00	360.00	180.00
(5)	James A. Collins	1,750	700.00	350.00
(6)	Joe Corbett	900.00	360.00	180.00
(7)	Louis Criger	900.00	360.00	180.00
(8)	Lave Cross	900.00	360.00	180.00
(9)	Montford Cross	900.00	360.00	180.00
(10)	Eugene DeMontreville	900.00	360.00	180.00
(11)	Charles Dexter	900.00	360.00	180.00
(12)	P.J. Donovan	900.00	360.00	180.00
(13)	Thomas Dowd	900.00	360.00	180.00

		NM	EX	VG
(14)	John J. Doyle	900.00	360.00	180.00
(15)	Hugh Duffy	1,500	600.00	300.00
(16)	Frank Dwyer	900.00	360.00	180.00
(17)	Fred Ely ("Bones")	900.00	360.00	180.00
(18)	A.F. Esterquest	900.00	360.00	180.00
(19)	Wm. Ewing	1,500	600.00	300.00
(20)	Elmer Flick	1,500	600.00	300.00
(21)	Daniel Friend	900.00	360.00	180.00
(22)	George F. Gilpatrick (Gillpatrick)	900.00	360.00	180.00
(23)	J.M. Goar	900.00	360.00	180.00
(24)	Michael Griffin	900.00	360.00	180.00
(25)	Clark C. Griffith	1,500	600.00	300.00
(26)	William Hill	900.00	360.00	180.00
(27)	Dummy Hoy	1,750	700.00	350.00
(28)	James Hughes	900.00	360.00	180.00
(29)	William Joyce	900.00	360.00	180.00
(30)	William Keeler	1,500	600.00	300.00
(31)	Joseph J. Kelley	1,500	600.00	300.00
(32)	William Kennedy	900.00	360.00	180.00
(33)	William Lange	900.00	360.00	180.00
(34)	John J. McGraw	1,500	600.00	300.00
(35)	W.B. Mercer (George B. "Win")	900.00	360.00	180.00
(36)	Charles A. Nichols	1,750	700.00	350.00
(37)	Jerry Nops	900.00	360.00	180.00
(38)	John O'Connor	900.00	360.00	180.00
(39)	Richard Padden	900.00	360.00	180.00
(40)	Wilbert Robinson	1,500	600.00	300.00
(41)	William Shindle	900.00	360.00	180.00
(42)	Charles Stahl	900.00	360.00	180.00
(43)	E.F. Stein	900.00	360.00	180.00
(44)	S.L. Thompson	1,750	700.00	350.00
(45)	John Wagner	2,400	960.00	480.00
(46)	R.J. Wallace	1,500	600.00	300.00
(47)	Victor Willis	1,500	600.00	300.00
(48)	Parke Wilson	900.00	360.00	180.00
(49)	George Yeager	900.00	360.00	180.00
(50)	C.L. Zimmer	900.00	360.00	180.00

1913 National Game (WG5)

The patent date on the ornate red-and-white backs identify this as a 1913 issue. Fronts of the 2-1/2" x 3-1/2" cards have a black-and-white photo and a pair of baseball play scenarios used to play the card game. Corners are rounded. The set contains 43 identified player cards, a group of nine action photos in which the players are not identified and two header cards. The unnumbered cards are checklisted in alphabetical order. This set carries the ACC designation of WG5.

		NM	EX	VG
Complete Set (54):		6,000	3,000	1,800
Common Player:		55.00	30.00	20.00
Action Photo Card:		16.50	8.25	5.00
(1)	Grover Alexander	300.00	100.00	60.00
(2)	Frank Baker	150.00	50.00	30.00
(3)	Chief Bender	150.00	50.00	30.00
(4)	Bob Bescher	55.00	30.00	20.00
(5)	Joe Birmingham	55.00	30.00	20.00
(6)	Roger Bresnahan	150.00	50.00	30.00
(7)	Nixey Callahan	55.00	30.00	20.00
(8)	Frank Chance	150.00	50.00	30.00
(9)	Hal Chase	75.00	37.50	22.50
(10)	Fred Clarke	150.00	50.00	30.00
(11)	Ty Cobb	1,000	300.00	180.00
(12)	Sam Crawford	150.00	50.00	30.00
(13)	Bill Dahlen	55.00	30.00	20.00
(14)	Jake Daubert	55.00	30.00	20.00
(15)	Red Dooin	55.00	30.00	20.00
(16)	Johnny Evers	150.00	50.00	30.00
(17)	Vean Gregg	55.00	30.00	20.00
(18)	Clark Griffith	150.00	50.00	30.00
(19)	Dick Hoblitzel	55.00	30.00	20.00
(20)	Miller Huggins	150.00	50.00	30.00
(21)	Joe Jackson	3,500	800.00	480.00
(22)	Hughie Jennings	150.00	50.00	30.00
(23)	Walter Johnson	500.00	125.00	75.00
(24)	Ed Konetchy	55.00	30.00	20.00
(25)	Nap Lajoie	150.00	50.00	30.00
(26)	Connie Mack	150.00	50.00	30.00
(27)	Rube Marquard	150.00	50.00	30.00
(28)	Christy Mathewson	500.00	125.00	75.00
(29)	John McGraw	150.00	50.00	30.00
(30)	Larry McLean	55.00	30.00	20.00
(31)	Clyde Milan	55.00	30.00	20.00
(32)	Marty O'Toole	55.00	30.00	20.00
(33)	Nap Rucker	55.00	30.00	20.00
(34)	Tris Speaker	200.00	75.00	45.00
(35)	Jake Stahl	55.00	30.00	20.00
(36)	George Stallings	55.00	30.00	20.00
(37)	George Stovall	55.00	30.00	20.00
(38)	Bill Sweeney	55.00	30.00	20.00
(39)	Joe Tinker	150.00	50.00	30.00
(40)	Honus Wagner	1,000	200.00	120.00

		NM	EX	VG
(41)	Ed Walsh	150.00	50.00	30.00
(42)	Joe Wood	55.00	30.00	20.00
(43)	Cy Young	500.00	125.00	75.00
(---)	Rules Card	55.00	30.00	20.00
(---)	Score Card	55.00	30.00	20.00
(1A)	Batter swinging, looking forward.	15.00	7.50	4.50
(2A)	Batter swinging, looking back.	15.00	7.50	4.50
(3A)	Runner sliding, fielder at bag.	15.00	7.50	4.50
(4A)	Runner sliding, umpire behind. (Some collectors believe the player in the picture is Ty Cobb and are willing to pay a premium for this card.)	75.00	37.50	22.50
(5A)	Runner sliding, hugging base.	15.00	7.50	4.50
(6A)	Sliding play at plate, umpire at left.	15.00	7.50	4.50
(7A)	Sliding play at plate, umpire at right.	15.00	7.50	4.50
(8A)	Play at plate, runner standing.	15.00	7.50	4.50
(9A)	Runner looking backwards.	15.00	7.50	4.50

1952 National Tea Labels

Another set of bread end-labels, this checklist now comprises 44 players, although there is speculation that others remain to be cataloged. The unnumbered labels measure approximately 2-3/4" x 2-11/16" and are sometimes referred to as "Red Borders" because of their wide, red margins. The player's name and team are printed alongside his photo, and the slogan "Eat More Bread for Health" also appears on some labels.

		NM	EX	VG
Complete Set (44):		10,000	5,000	3,000
Common Player:		200.00	100.00	60.00
(1)	Gene Bearden	200.00	100.00	60.00
(2)	Yogi Berra	450.00	225.00	135.00
(3)	Lou Brissie	200.00	100.00	60.00
(4)	Sam Chapman	200.00	100.00	60.00
(5)	Chuck Diering	200.00	100.00	60.00
(6)	Dom DiMaggio	250.00	125.00	75.00
(7)	Bruce Edwards	200.00	100.00	60.00
(8)	Del Ennis	200.00	100.00	60.00
(9)	Ferris Fain	200.00	100.00	60.00
(10)	Bob Feller	375.00	185.00	110.00
(11)	Howie Fox	200.00	100.00	60.00
(12)	Sid Gordon	200.00	100.00	60.00
(13)	John Groth	200.00	100.00	60.00
(14)	Granny Hamner	200.00	100.00	60.00
(15)	Jim Hegan	200.00	100.00	60.00
(16)	Sheldon Jones	200.00	100.00	60.00
(17)	Howie Judson	200.00	100.00	60.00
(18)	Sherman Lollar	200.00	100.00	60.00
(19)	Clarence Marshall	200.00	100.00	60.00
(20)	Don Mueller	200.00	100.00	60.00
(21)	Danny Murtaugh	200.00	100.00	60.00
(22)	Dave Philley	200.00	100.00	60.00
(23)	Jerry Priddy	200.00	100.00	60.00
(24)	Bill Rigney	200.00	100.00	60.00
(25)	Robin Roberts	350.00	175.00	100.00
(26)	Eddie Robinson	200.00	100.00	60.00
(27)	Preacher Roe	225.00	110.00	65.00
(28)	Stan Rojek	200.00	100.00	60.00
(29)	Al Rosen	225.00	110.00	65.00
(30)	Bob Rush	200.00	100.00	60.00
(31)	Hank Sauer	200.00	100.00	60.00
(32)	Johnny Schmitz	200.00	100.00	60.00
(33)	Enos Slaughter	350.00	175.00	100.00
(34)	Duke Snider	400.00	200.00	120.00
(35)	Warren Spahn	375.00	185.00	110.00
(36)	Gerry Staley	200.00	100.00	60.00
(37)	Virgil Stallcup	200.00	100.00	60.00
(38)	George Stirnweiss	200.00	100.00	60.00
(39)	Earl Torgeson	200.00	100.00	60.00
(40)	Dizzy Trout	200.00	100.00	60.00
(41)	Mickey Vernon	200.00	100.00	60.00
(42)	Wally Westlake	200.00	100.00	60.00
(43)	Johnny Wyrostek	200.00	100.00	60.00
(44)	Eddie Yost	200.00	100.00	60.00

1922 Neilson's Chocolate Type 1 (V61)

This set is closely related to the popular 1922 American Caramels (E120). The 120-card set was issued in Canada by Neilson's Chocolate Bars and carries the American Card Catalog designation V61. The front of the approximately 2" x 3-1/2" black-and-white cards has oval posed action photos with a decorative border. In the bottom border is the player name, position and team. Backs contain an ad for Neilson's Chocolates. Two types of cards exist. Type 1 is printed on heavy paper (similar to E120), has a

card number in the lower-left corner and features Old English typography of the sponsor's name on back. Type 2 is printed on cardboard, has no card numbers and has no Old English typography on back.

		NM	EX	VG
Complete Set (120):		27,500	11,000	5,500
Common Player:		115.00	45.00	22.50
1	George Burns	115.00	45.00	22.50
2	John Tobin	115.00	45.00	22.50
3	J.T. Zachary	115.00	45.00	22.50
4	"Bullet" Joe Bush	115.00	45.00	22.50
5	Lu Blue	115.00	45.00	22.50
6	Clarence (Tillie) Walker	115.00	45.00	22.50
7	Carl Mays	115.00	45.00	22.50
8	Leon Goslin	300.00	120.00	60.00
9	Ed Rommel	115.00	45.00	22.50
10	Charles Robertson	115.00	45.00	22.50
11	Ralph (Cy) Perkins	115.00	45.00	22.50
12	Joe Sewell	300.00	120.00	60.00
13	Harry Hooper	300.00	120.00	60.00
14	Urban (Red) Faber	300.00	120.00	60.00
15	Bib Falk (Bibb)	115.00	45.00	22.50
16	George Uhle	115.00	45.00	22.50
17	Emory Rigney	115.00	45.00	22.50
18	George Dauss	115.00	45.00	22.50
19	Herman Pillette	115.00	45.00	22.50
20	Wallie Schang	115.00	45.00	22.50
21	Lawrence Woodall	115.00	45.00	22.50
22	Steve O'Neill	115.00	45.00	22.50
23	Edmund (Bing) Miller	115.00	45.00	22.50
24	Sylvester Johnson	115.00	45.00	22.50
25	Henry Severeid	115.00	45.00	22.50
26	Dave Danforth	115.00	45.00	22.50
27	Harry Heilmann	300.00	120.00	60.00
28	Bert Cole	115.00	45.00	22.50
29	Eddie Collins	300.00	120.00	60.00
30	Ty Cobb	3,500	1,400	700.00
31	Bill Wambsganss	115.00	45.00	22.50
32	George Sisler	300.00	120.00	60.00
33	Bob Veach	115.00	45.00	22.50
34	Earl Sheely	115.00	45.00	22.50
35	T.P. (Pat) Collins	115.00	45.00	22.50
36	Frank (Dixie) Davis	115.00	45.00	22.50
37	Babe Ruth	6,000	2,400	1,200
38	Bryan Harris	115.00	45.00	22.50
39	Bob Shawkey	115.00	45.00	22.50
40	Urban Shocker	115.00	45.00	22.50
41	Martin McManus	115.00	45.00	22.50
42	Clark Pittenger	115.00	45.00	22.50
43	"Deacon" Sam Jones	115.00	45.00	22.50
44	Waite Hoyt	300.00	120.00	60.00
45	Johnny Mostil	115.00	45.00	22.50
46	Mike Menosky	115.00	45.00	22.50
47	Walter Johnson	600.00	240.00	120.00
48	Wallie Pipp (Wally)	115.00	45.00	22.50
49	Walter Gerber	115.00	45.00	22.50
50	Ed Gharrity	115.00	45.00	22.50
51	Frank Ellerbe	115.00	45.00	22.50
52	Kenneth Williams	115.00	45.00	22.50
53	Joe Hauser	175.00	70.00	35.00
54	Carson Bigbee	115.00	45.00	22.50
55	Emil (Irish) Meusel	115.00	45.00	22.50
56	Milton Stock	115.00	45.00	22.50
57	Wilbur Cooper	115.00	45.00	22.50
58	Tom Griffith	115.00	45.00	22.50
59	Walter (Butch) Henline	115.00	45.00	22.50
60	Gene (Bubbles) Hargrave	115.00	45.00	22.50
61	Russell Wrightstone	115.00	45.00	22.50
62	Frank Frisch	300.00	120.00	60.00
63	Frank Parkinson	115.00	45.00	22.50
64	Walter (Dutch) Reuther (Ruether)	115.00	45.00	22.50
65	Bill Doak	115.00	45.00	22.50
66	Marty Callaghan	115.00	45.00	22.50
67	Sammy Bohne	175.00	70.00	35.00
68	Earl Hamilton	115.00	45.00	22.50
69	Grover C. Alexander	325.00	130.00	65.00
70	George Burns	115.00	45.00	22.50
71	Max Carey	300.00	120.00	60.00
72	Adolfo Luque	145.00	58.00	29.00
73	Dave (Beauty) Bancroft	300.00	120.00	60.00
74	Vic Aldridge	115.00	45.00	22.50
75	Jack Smith	115.00	45.00	22.50
76	Bob O'Farrell	115.00	45.00	22.50
77	Pete Donohue	115.00	45.00	22.50
78	Ralph Pinelli	115.00	45.00	22.50
79	Eddie Roush	300.00	120.00	60.00
80	Norman Boeckel	115.00	45.00	22.50
81	Rogers Hornsby	400.00	160.00	80.00
82	George Toporcer	115.00	45.00	22.50
83	Ivy Wingo	115.00	45.00	22.50
84	Virgil Cheeves	115.00	45.00	22.50
85	Vern Clemons	115.00	45.00	22.50
86	Lawrence (Hack) Miller	115.00	45.00	22.50

		NM	EX	VG
87	Johnny Kelleher	115.00	45.00	22.50
88	Heinie Groh	115.00	45.00	22.50
89	Burleigh Grimes	300.00	120.00	60.00
90	"Rabbit" Maranville	300.00	120.00	60.00
91	Charles (Babe) Adams	115.00	45.00	22.50
92	Lee King	115.00	45.00	22.50
93	Art Nehf	115.00	45.00	22.50
94	Frank Snyder	115.00	45.00	22.50
95	Raymond Powell	115.00	45.00	22.50
96	Wilbur Hubbell	115.00	45.00	22.50
97	Leon Cadore	115.00	45.00	22.50
98	Joe Oeschger	115.00	45.00	22.50
99	Jake Daubert	115.00	45.00	22.50
100	Will Sherdel	115.00	45.00	22.50
101	Hank DeBerry	115.00	45.00	22.50
102	Johnny Lavan	115.00	45.00	22.50
103	Jesse Haines	300.00	120.00	60.00
104	Joe (Goldie) Rapp	115.00	45.00	22.50
105	Oscar Ray Grimes	115.00	45.00	22.50
106	Ross Young (Youngs)	300.00	120.00	60.00
107	Art Fletcher	115.00	45.00	22.50
108	Clyde Barnhart	115.00	45.00	22.50
109	Louis (Pat) Duncan	115.00	45.00	22.50
110	Charlie Hollocher	115.00	45.00	22.50
111	Horace Ford	115.00	45.00	22.50
112	Bill Cunningham	115.00	45.00	22.50
113	Walter Schmidt	115.00	45.00	22.50
114	Joe Schultz	115.00	45.00	22.50
115	John Morrison	115.00	45.00	22.50
116	Jimmy Caveney	115.00	45.00	22.50
117	Zach Wheat	300.00	120.00	60.00
118	Fred (Cy) Williams	115.00	45.00	22.50
119	George Kelly	300.00	120.00	60.00
120	Jimmy Ring	115.00	45.00	22.50

1922 Neilson's Chocolate Type 2 (V61)

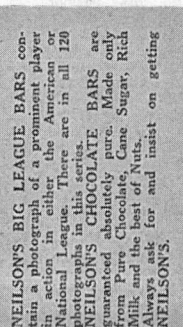

This set is closely related to the popular 1922 American Caramels (E120). The 120-card set was issued in Canada by Neilson's Chocolate Bars and carries the American Card Catalog designation V61. The front of the approximately 2" x 3-1/2" black-and-white cards has oval posed action photos with a decorative border. In the bottom border is the player name, position and team. Backs contain and ad for Neilson's Chocolates. Two types of cards exist. Type 1 is printed on heavy paper (similar to E120), has a card number in the lower-left corner and features Old English typography of the sponsor's name on back. Type 2 is printed on cardboard, has no card numbers and has no Old English typography on back.

		NM	EX	VG
Complete Set (120):		42,500	17,000	8,500
Common Player:		200.00	85.00	40.00
(1)	Charles (Babe) Adams	200.00	85.00	40.00
(2)	Vic Aldridge	200.00	85.00	40.00
(3)	Grover C. Alexander	750.00	300.00	150.00
(4)	Dave (Beauty) Bancroft	450.00	180.00	90.00
(5)	Clyde Barnhart	200.00	85.00	40.00
(6)	Carson Bigbee	200.00	85.00	40.00
(7)	Lu Blue	200.00	85.00	40.00
(8)	Norman Boeckel	200.00	85.00	40.00
(9)	Sammy Bohne	250.00	100.00	50.00
(10)	George Burns (Boston)	200.00	85.00	40.00
(11)	George Burns (Cincinnati)	200.00	85.00	40.00
(12)	"Bullet" Joe Bush	200.00	85.00	40.00
(13)	Leon Cadore	200.00	85.00	40.00
(14)	Marty Callaghan	200.00	85.00	40.00
(15)	Max Carey	450.00	180.00	90.00
(16)	Jimmy Caveney	200.00	85.00	40.00
(17)	Virgil Cheeves	200.00	85.00	40.00
(18)	Vern Clemons	200.00	85.00	40.00
(19)	Ty Cobb	5,500	2,200	1,100
(20)	Bert Cole	200.00	85.00	40.00
(21)	Eddie Collins	450.00	180.00	90.00
(22)	T.P. (Pat) Collins	200.00	85.00	40.00
(23)	Wilbur Cooper	200.00	85.00	40.00
(24)	Bill Cunningham	200.00	85.00	40.00
(25)	Dave Danforth	200.00	85.00	40.00
(26)	Jake Daubert	200.00	85.00	40.00
(27)	George Dauss	200.00	85.00	40.00
(28)	Frank (Dixie) Davis	200.00	85.00	40.00
(29)	Hank DeBerry	200.00	85.00	40.00
(30)	Bill Doak	200.00	85.00	40.00
(31)	Pete Donohue	200.00	85.00	40.00
(32)	Louis (Pat) Duncan	200.00	85.00	40.00
(33)	Frank Ellerbe	200.00	85.00	40.00
(34)	Urban (Red) Faber	450.00	180.00	90.00
(35)	Bib (Bibb) Falk	200.00	85.00	40.00
(36)	Art Fletcher	200.00	85.00	40.00

(37)	Horace Ford	200.00	85.00	40.00
(38)	Frank Frisch	450.00	180.00	90.00
(39)	Walter Gerber	200.00	85.00	40.00
(40)	Ed Gharrity	450.00	180.00	90.00
(41)	Leon Goslin	450.00	180.00	90.00
(42)	Tom Griffith	450.00	180.00	90.00
(43)	Burleigh Grimes	200.00	85.00	40.00
(44)	Oscar Ray Grimes	200.00	85.00	40.00
(45)	Heinie Groh	450.00	180.00	90.00
(46)	Jesse Haines	450.00	180.00	90.00
(47)	Earl Hamilton	200.00	85.00	40.00
(48)	Gene (Bubbles) Hargrave	200.00	85.00	40.00
(49)	Bryan Harris	200.00	85.00	40.00
(50)	Joe Hauser	350.00	140.00	70.00
(51)	Harry Heilmann	450.00	180.00	90.00
(52)	Walter (Butch) Henline	200.00	85.00	40.00
(53)	Charlie Hollocher	200.00	85.00	40.00
(54)	Harry Hooper	450.00	180.00	90.00
(55)	Rogers Hornsby	550.00	220.00	110.00
(56)	Waite Hoyt	450.00	180.00	90.00
(57)	Wilbert Hubbell	200.00	85.00	40.00
(58)	Sylvester Johnson	200.00	85.00	40.00
(59)	Walter Johnson	800.00	320.00	160.00
(60)	"Deacon" Sam Jones	200.00	85.00	40.00
(61)	Johnny Kelleher	200.00	85.00	40.00
(62)	George Kelly	450.00	180.00	90.00
(63)	Lee King	200.00	85.00	40.00
(64)	Johnny Lavan	200.00	85.00	40.00
(65)	Adolfo Luque	250.00	100.00	50.00
(66)	"Rabbit" Maranville	450.00	180.00	90.00
(67)	Carl Mays	200.00	85.00	40.00
(68)	Martin McManus	200.00	85.00	40.00
(69)	Mike Menosky	200.00	85.00	40.00
(70)	Emil (Irish) Meusel	200.00	85.00	40.00
(71)	Edmund (Bing) Miller	200.00	85.00	40.00
(72)	Lawrence (Hack) Miller	200.00	85.00	40.00
(73)	John Morrison	200.00	85.00	40.00
(74)	Johnny Mostil	200.00	85.00	40.00
(75)	Art Nehf	200.00	85.00	40.00
(76)	Joe Oeschger	200.00	85.00	40.00
(77)	Bob O'Farrell	200.00	85.00	40.00
(78)	Steve O'Neill	200.00	85.00	40.00
(79)	Frank Parkinson	200.00	85.00	40.00
(80)	Ralph (Cy) Perkins	200.00	85.00	40.00
(81)	Herman Pillette	200.00	85.00	40.00
(82)	Ralph Pinelli	200.00	85.00	40.00
(83)	Wallie (Wally) Pipp	200.00	85.00	40.00
(84)	Clark Pittinger	200.00	85.00	40.00
(85)	Raymond Powell	200.00	85.00	40.00
(86)	Joe (Goldie) Rapp	200.00	85.00	40.00
(87)	Walter (Dutch) Reuther	200.00	85.00	40.00
(88)	Emory Rigney	200.00	85.00	40.00
(89)	Jimmy Ring	200.00	85.00	40.00
(90)	Charles Robertson	200.00	85.00	40.00
(91)	Ed Rommel	200.00	85.00	40.00
(92)	Eddie Roush	450.00	180.00	90.00
(93)	Babe Ruth	7,500	3,000	1,500
(94)	Wallie (Wally) Schang	200.00	85.00	40.00
(95)	Walter Schmidt	200.00	85.00	40.00
(96)	Joe Schultz	200.00	85.00	40.00
(97)	Hank Severeid	200.00	85.00	40.00
(98)	Joe Sewell	450.00	180.00	90.00
(99)	Bob Shawkey	200.00	85.00	40.00
(100)	Earl Sheely	200.00	85.00	40.00
(101)	Will Sherdel	200.00	85.00	40.00
(102)	Urban Shocker	200.00	85.00	40.00
(103)	George Sisler	450.00	180.00	90.00
(104)	Jack Smith	200.00	85.00	40.00
(105)	Frank Snyder	200.00	85.00	40.00
(106)	Milton Stock	200.00	85.00	40.00
(107)	John Tobin	200.00	85.00	40.00
(108)	George Torporcer	200.00	85.00	40.00
(109)	George Uhle	200.00	85.00	40.00
(110)	Bob Veach	200.00	85.00	40.00
(111)	Clarence (Tillie) Walker	200.00	85.00	40.00
(112)	Bill Wambsganss	200.00	85.00	40.00
(113)	Zach Wheat	450.00	180.00	90.00
(114)	Fred (Cy) Williams	200.00	85.00	40.00
(115)	Kenneth Williams	200.00	85.00	40.00
(116)	Ivy Wingo	200.00	85.00	40.00
(117)	Lawrence Woodall	200.00	85.00	40.00
(118)	Russell Wrightstone	200.00	85.00	40.00
(119)	Ross Young (Youngs)	450.00	180.00	90.00
(120)	J.T. Zachary	200.00	85.00	40.00

1923 "Neilson's Chocolates"

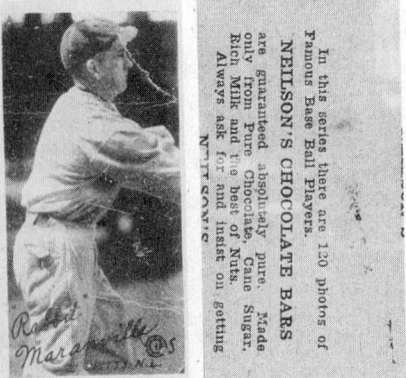

This issue, purporting to come from the Canadian candy maker which had produced a 1922 set, was first reported in 1996. The cards appear to be genuine W572 strip cards which have had a Neilson's ad over-printed on the back many years later in an apparent effort to defraud collectors. These altered W572s would have to be significantly downgraded to adjust for the defacing. It can be expected that any card that appears in W572 can be found with the Neilson's back, but the "discovery" contained only 47 different players.

(See W572 for checklist.)

1959 Neptune Sardines Jimmy Piersall

Like the earlier advertising postcards he did for various Cain's food products, this 3-1/2" x 5-1/2" black-and-white postcard carries the endorsement of the popular Indians outfielder for Neptune brand sardines. The front has a borderless photo of the player in a batting pose with a facsimile autograph at top. The back has standard postcard indicia along with the ad message and a product picture.

	NM	EX	VG
Jimmy Piersall	50.00	25.00	15.00

1976-81 New England Sports Collectors

From the period 1976-81, the New England Sports Collectors club issued a series of postcard-size (3-1/2" x 5-1/4") black-and-white card promoting their annual shows in Nashua, N.H. No card was issued in 1978.

		NM	EX	VG
Complete Set (5):		30.00	15.00	9.00
Common Player:		6.00	3.00	1.75
1	Joe DiMaggio/1976	8.00	4.00	2.50
2	Jackie Robinson/1977	6.00	3.00	1.75
3	Ted Williams/1979	7.00	3.50	2.00
4	Vince DiMaggio, Joe DiMaggio, Dom DiMaggio/1980	6.00	3.00	1.75
5	Mickey Mantle/1981	9.00	4.50	2.75

1895 Newsboy Cabinets (N566)

Issued in the 1890s by the National Tobacco Works, this massive cabinet card set was distributed as a premium with the Newsboy tobacco brand. Although the set contained over 500 popular actresses, athletes, politicians and other celebrities of the day, only about a dozen cards of baseball players have been found. The cards measure 4-1/4" x 6-1/2" and feature sepia-toned photographs mounted on a backing that usually has "Newsboy New York" printed at bottom. Each portrait photograph is numbered and a few of the photos are round. The ballplayers in the set are mostly members of the 1894 New York Giants with a couple of Brooklyn players. There are two known poses of John Ward. Cards have been seen with advertising on the back for Keystone cigars and Red Indian tobacco.

	NM	EX	VG
Common Player:	6,000	3,000	1,800

174	W.H. Murphy	6,000	3,000	1,800
175	Amos Rusie	15,000	4,500	2,750
176	Michael Tiernan	6,000	3,000	1,800
177	E.D. Burke	6,000	3,000	1,800
178	J.J. Doyle	6,000	3,000	1,800
179	W.B. Fuller	6,000	3,000	1,800
180	George Van Haltren	6,000	3,000	1,800
181	Dave Foutz	6,000	3,000	1,800
182	Jouett Meekin	6,000	3,000	1,800
183	Michael Griffin	6,000	3,000	1,800
201	W.H. (Dad) Clark (Clarke)	6,000	3,000	1,800
202	Parke Wilson	6,000	3,000	1,800
586	John Ward (Arms folded.)	9,250	4,625	2,775
587	John Ward (Bat at side.)	8,000	4,000	2,400

1886 New York Baseball Club (H812)

This rare 19th Century baseball issue can be classified under the general category of "trade" cards, a popular advertising vehicle of the period. The cards measure 3" x 4-3/4" and feature blue line-drawing portraits of members of the "New York Base Ball Club," which is printed along the top. As was common with this type of trade card, the bottom was left blank to accomodate various messages. The known examples of this set carry ads for local tobacco merchants and other businesses. The portraits are all based on the photographs used in the 1886 Old Judge set. The cards, which have been assigned an ACC designation of H812, are printed on thin paper rather than cardboard.

	NM	EX	VG
Complete Set (8):	70,000	31,000	17,000
Common Player:	6,000	2,700	1,200
(1) T. Dealsey	6,000	2,700	1,200
(2) M. Dorgan	6,000	2,700	1,200
(3) T. Esterbrook	6,000	2,700	1,200
(4) W. Ewing	13,500	6,750	4,000
(5) J. Gerhardt	6,000	2,700	1,200
(6) J. O'Rourke	13,500	6,750	4,000
(7) D. Richardson	6,000	2,700	1,200
(8) M. Welch	13,500	6,750	4,000

1969 N.Y. Boy Scouts

Cards featuring N.Y. Mets and Yankees players were used as a recruitment incentive in 1969. Cards are 2-1/2" x 3-1/2" and printed in black-and-white on thin cardboard. It is unknown, but likely, that players other than those checklisted here were also issued.

	NM	EX	VG
Common Player:	140.00	70.00	40.00
(1) Tommy Agee	175.00	85.00	50.00
(2) Bud Harrelson	175.00	85.00	50.00
(3) Cleon Jones	175.00	85.00	50.00
(4) Bobby Murcer	260.00	130.00	75.00
(5) Art Shamsky	140.00	70.00	40.00
(6) Tom Seaver	700.00	350.00	210.00
(7) Mel Stottlemyre	260.00	130.00	75.00
(8) Ron Swoboda	175.00	85.00	50.00

1879-80 N.Y. Clipper Woodcuts

The N.Y. Clipper was a weekly newspaper devoted to theater and sports (primarily baseball) coverage in New York City between 1853-1923. Like many contemporary papers, the Clipper featured woodcut engravings in its pages in a time before photographic reproduction of pictures was feasible. Between April, 1879, and November 1880, the paper printed a series of baseball player portraits. The early pieces were titled "The Clipper Prize Winners." and numbered. All of the woodcuts are about 4-1/2" x 5-3/4" in size featuring portraits within ornate frames with identification and biographical details below. Collectors prefer the woodcuts to be neatly trimmed from the newspaper page, with the biography at bottom intact. Because of the rarity of surviving examples, catalog values are undetermined. Many of these early stars of the game appear on no other contemprary cards or memorabilia issues.

1879
1 M.C. Dorgan (4/12)
2 H.F. McCormick (4/19)
3 Stephen A. Libby (4/26)
4 Roscoe C. Barnes (5/3)
5 David W. Force (5/10)
6 Herman Doescher (Dosher) (5/17)
7a Joseph Hornung (5/24)
7b William H. McGunnigle (5/31)
9 Harding Richardson (6/7)
(10) James L. White (7/14)
(11) Levi S. Meyerle (6/21)
(12) Joe Start (6/28)
(13) T.H. Murnam (Murnane) (7/5)
(14) Thomas York (7/12)
(15) Fred Dunlap (7/19)
(16) A.J. Leonard (7/26)
(17) J. Lee Richmond (8/2)
(18) Charles N. Snyder (8/9)
(19) John Cassidy (8/16)
(20) Charles Fulmer (8/23)
(21) Thomas Poorman (8/30)
(22) John Ward (9/6)
(23) Larry Corcoran (9/13)
(24) Douglas Allison (9/20)
(25) John J. Farrow (9/27)
(26) E.N. Williamson (10/4)
(27) George Wright (10/11)
(28) John J. Burdock (10/18)
(29) James O'Rourke (10/25)
(30) Philip Baker (11/1)
(31) Samuel W. Trott (11/8)
(32) John Lynch (11/15)
(33) A.G. Spalding (11/22)
(34) John C. Chapman (11/29)
(35) Paul A. Hines (12/6)
(36) Frank C. Bancroft (12/13)
(37) John T. O'Conner (12/20)
(38) Andrew J. Piercy (12/27)

1880
(39) Harold M. McClure (1/3)
(40) J.H. Gifford (1/24)
(41) Sam Wright (5/15)
(42) T.J. Keefe (5/22)
(43) M.J. Kelly (5/29)
(44) John Troy (6/5)
(45) Joe Quest (6/12)
(46) Alonzo Knight (6/19)
(47) Charles E. Mason (6/26)
(48) F.E. Goldsmith (7/3)
(49) R.E. McKelvy (7/10)
(50) Wm. McLean (umpire)(7/17)
(51) C.A. McVey (7/24)
(52) John Manning (7/31)
(53) Harry D. Stovey (8/7)
(54) George A. Wood (8/14)
(55) Robert T. Mathews (8/21)
(56) D. Brouthers (8/28)
(57) C.M. Smith (9/4)
(58) James L. Clinton (9/11)
(59) A.J. Bushong (9/18)
(60) William J. Sweeney (9/25)
(61) Roger Connor (10/2)
(62) William Hawes (10/9)
(63) Frank S. Flint (10/16)
(64) William L. Haug (10/23)
(65) M. Welch (10/30)
(66) Aaron B. Clapp (11/6)
(67) John J. Smith (11/13)
(68) George Creamer (11/20)

1905 N.Y. Giants Scorecard Postcard

Two versions, black-and-white and color, of this standard size (about 5-1/2" x 3-1/2") postcard were apparently available for several years as it is copyrighted 1905 but postally used examples from years later are often seen. The card has a black background with large cut-out letters "GIANTS" at center featuring action poses of six players. A grid at bottom allows by-inning scores of a game to be posted before mailing. The undivided back has an embellished double-ruled stamp box and a large ornate "Post Card" at top-center.

	NM	EX	VG
Black-and-white:	300.00	150.00	90.00
Color:	400.00	200.00	125.00

Frank Bowerman, Red Ames, Sam Mertes, Christy Mathewson, Iron Man McGinnity, Luther Taylor

1932 N.Y. Giants Schedule Postcards

These postcard-size (3-1/2" x 5-1/2") black-and-white cards have an action pose on front with the player's identification and previous season's stats. At bottom is information about ladies' days, directions to the Polo Grounds and an offer to receive a free picture of a favorite player. The divided back has the team's 1932 schedule at left and space for addressing at right. There is also a credit line to Minden Press. The Carl Hubbell card is far more common than all others and can be found on either a thick or thin card stock that is unlike the stock on which the other players are found.

	NM	EX	VG
Common Player:	300.00	150.00	90.00
(1) Ethan Allen	300.00	150.00	90.00
(2) Herman Bell	300.00	150.00	90.00
(3) Hugh Critz	300.00	150.00	90.00
(4) Freddie Fitzsimmons	300.00	150.00	90.00
(5) Chick Fullis	300.00	150.00	90.00
(6) Sam Gibson	300.00	150.00	90.00
(7) Fran Healey (Healy)	300.00	150.00	90.00
(8) Frank Hogan	300.00	150.00	90.00
(9a) Carl Hubbell (Thin stock.)	100.00	50.00	30.00
(9b) Carl Hubbell (Thick stock.)	450.00	225.00	135.00
(10) Travis Jackson	450.00	225.00	135.00
(11) Len Koenecke	300.00	150.00	90.00
(12) Sam Leslie	300.00	150.00	90.00
(13) Freddy Lindstrom	450.00	225.00	135.00
(14) Dolf Luque	325.00	160.00	97.00
(15) Clarence Mitchell	300.00	150.00	90.00
(16) Jim Mooney	300.00	150.00	90.00
(17) Bob O'Farrell	300.00	150.00	90.00
(18) Mel Ott	600.00	300.00	180.00
(19) Roy Parmelee	300.00	150.00	90.00
(20) Bill Terry	450.00	225.00	135.00
(21) Johnny Vergez	300.00	150.00	90.00
(22) Bill Walker	300.00	150.00	90.00

1948 N.Y. Giants Photo Pack

This set of player photos was sold at Polo Grounds souvenir stands. Pictures have player portraits in a 6-1/2" x 9" format. The black-and-white photos are blank-backed and have facsimile autographs printed near the bottom on front. A white border surrounds the front. The unnumbered photos are

checklisted here in alphabetical order. It is possible the specific lineup of the packs changed over the course of the season to reflect roster moves.

	NM	EX	VG
Complete Set (27):	200.00	100.00	60.00
Common Player:	5.00	2.50	1.50
(1) Jack Conway	5.00	2.50	1.50
(2) Walker Cooper	5.00	2.50	1.50
(3) Leo Durocher	9.00	4.50	2.75
(4) Sid Gordon	7.50	3.75	2.25
(5) Andy Hansen	5.00	2.50	1.50
(6) Clint Hartung	5.00	2.50	1.50
(7) Larry Jansen	5.00	2.50	1.50
(8) Sheldon Jones	5.00	2.50	1.50
(9) Monte Kennedy	5.00	2.50	1.50
(10) Buddy Kerr	5.00	2.50	1.50
(11) Dave Koslo	5.00	2.50	1.50
(12) Thornton Lee	5.00	2.50	1.50
(13) Mickey Livingston	5.00	2.50	1.50
(14) Whitey Lockman	5.00	2.50	1.50
(15) Jack Lohrke	5.00	2.50	1.50
(16) Willard Marshall	5.00	2.50	1.50
(17) Johnnie McCarthy	5.00	2.50	1.50
(18) Earl McGowan	7.50	3.75	2.25
(19) Johnny Mize	12.50	6.25	3.75
(20) Bobo Newsom	5.00	2.50	1.50
(21) Mel Ott	25.00	12.50	7.50
(22) Ray Poat	5.00	2.50	1.50
(23) Bobby Rhawn	5.00	2.50	1.50
(24) Bill Rigney	5.00	2.50	1.50
(25) Bobby Thomson	10.00	5.00	3.00
(26) Ken Trinkle	5.00	2.50	1.50
(27) Wesley N. Westrum	5.00	2.50	1.50

1949 N.Y. Giants Photo Pack

This set of player photos was sold at Polo Grounds souvenir stands. Pictures have player portraits in a 6-1/2" x 9" format. The black-and-white photos are blank-backed and have facsimile autographs printed near the bottom on front. A white border surrounds the front. The unnumbered photos are checklisted here in alphabetical order.

	NM	EX	VG
Complete Set (25):	200.00	100.00	60.00
Common Player:	5.00	2.50	1.50
(1) Hank Behrman	5.00	2.50	1.50
(2) Walker Cooper	5.00	2.50	1.50
(3) Leo Durocher	9.00	4.50	2.75
(4) Fred Fitzsimmons	5.00	2.50	1.50
(5) Frank Frisch	12.50	6.25	3.75
(6) Augie Galan	5.00	2.50	1.50
(7) Sid Gordon	7.50	3.75	2.25
(8) Bert Haas	5.00	2.50	1.50
(9) Andy Hansen	5.00	2.50	1.50
(10) Clint Hartung	5.00	2.50	1.50
(11) Bob Hofman	5.00	2.50	1.50
(12) Larry Jansen	5.00	2.50	1.50
(13) Sheldon Jones	5.00	2.50	1.50
(14) Monte Kennedy	5.00	2.50	1.50
(15) Buddy Kerr	5.00	2.50	1.50
(16) Dave Koslo	5.00	2.50	1.50
(17) Mickey Livingston	5.00	2.50	1.50
(18) Whitey Lockman	5.00	2.50	1.50
(19) Willard Marshall	5.00	2.50	1.50
(20) Johnny Mize	12.50	6.25	3.75
(21) Don Mueller	5.00	2.50	1.50
(22) Ray Poat	5.00	2.50	1.50
(23) Bobby Rhawn	5.00	2.50	1.50
(24) Bill Rigney	5.00	2.50	1.50
(25) Bobby Thomson	10.00	5.00	3.00

1954 N.Y. Journal-American

Issued during the Golden Age of baseball in New York City, this 59-card set features only players from the Giants, Yankees and Dodgers. The 2" x 4" cards were issued at newsstands with the purchase of the now-extinct newspaper. Card fronts have promotional copy and a contest serial number in addition to the player's name. Cards are printed in black-and-white on colored stock and unnumbered. Backs feature team schedules. It has been theorized that a 60th card should exist, probably a Brooklyn Dodger. Each card can be found with the word "OFFERS" printed in either red or black, depending on the contest number at bottom. Numbers beginning with "0" have the word in black. Numbers 100000-150000 have the word in red or black, and numbers over 150000 have the word in red.

DODGERS AT HOME
1954

April 15	Pittsburgh
April 17, 18*	New York
April 21 (N), 12	Philadelphia
May 11 (N), 12	Milwaukee
May 14 (N), 15	St. Louis
May 16* (2)	Cincinnati
May 18 (N), 19	Chicago
May 21 (N), 22, 23* (2), 24 (N)	Pittsburgh
May 25, 26 (N), 27	Philadelphia
June 15 (N), 16 (N), 17	Milwaukee
June 18 (N), 19, 20* (2)	Chicago
June 22, 23 (N), 24	Cincinnati
June 25 (N), 26, 27*	St. Louis
July 6 (N), 7 (N), 8	New York
July 9 (N), 10, 11* (2)	Philadelphia
July 22, 23 (N), 25	Chicago
July 30 (N), 31, Aug. 1*, 2	Milwaukee
Aug. 3 (N), 4 (N), 5	St. Louis
Aug. 6 (N), 7, 8*	Cincinnati
Aug. 13 (N), 14, 15*	New York
Aug. 20 (N), 21, 22*	Philadelphia
Sept. 6* (2)	Pittsburgh
Sept. 8 (N), 9	St. Louis
Sept. 10 (N), 11	Milwaukee
Sept. 12* (2)	Chicago
Sept. 14 (N), 15, 16	Cincinnati
Sept. 20 (N), 21	New York
Sept. 24, 25, 26*	Pittsburgh

*Sunday, Holiday   (N) Night Game
(2) Double Header

		NM	EX	VG
Complete Set (59):		4,750	2,400	1,400
Common Player:		20.00	10.00	6.00
(1)	Johnny Antonelli	40.00	20.00	12.00
(2)	Hank Bauer	45.00	22.50	13.50
(3)	Yogi Berra	125.00	65.00	35.00
(4)	Joe Black	65.00	32.50	20.00
(5)	Harry Byrd	40.00	20.00	12.00
(6)	Roy Campanella	200.00	100.00	60.00
(7)	Andy Carey	40.00	20.00	12.00
(8)	Jerry Coleman	40.00	20.00	12.00
(9)	Joe Collins	40.00	20.00	12.00
(10)	Billy Cox	65.00	32.50	20.00
(11)	Al Dark	40.00	20.00	12.00
(12)	Carl Erskine	65.00	32.50	20.00
(13)	Whitey Ford	125.00	65.00	35.00
(14)	Carl Furillo	90.00	45.00	27.50
(15)	Junior Gilliam	90.00	45.00	27.50
(16)	Ruben Gomez	40.00	20.00	12.00
(17)	Marv Grissom	40.00	20.00	12.00
(18)	Jim Hearn	40.00	20.00	12.00
(19)	Gil Hodges	125.00	65.00	35.00
(20)	Bobby Hofman	40.00	20.00	12.00
(21)	Jim Hughes	65.00	32.50	20.00
(22)	Monte Irvin	90.00	45.00	27.50
(23)	Larry Jansen	40.00	20.00	12.00
(24)	Ray Katt	40.00	20.00	12.00
(25)	Steve Kraly	40.00	20.00	12.00
(26)	Bob Kuzava	40.00	20.00	12.00
(27)	Clem Labine	65.00	32.50	20.00
(28)	Frank Leja	40.00	20.00	12.00
(29)	Don Liddle	40.00	20.00	12.00
(30)	Whitey Lockman	65.00	32.50	20.00
(31)	Billy Loes	40.00	20.00	12.00
(32)	Eddie Lopat	40.00	20.00	12.00
(33)	Sal Maglie	65.00	32.50	20.00
(34)	Mickey Mantle	650.00	325.00	200.00
(35)	Willie Mays	375.00	185.00	110.00
(36)	Gil McDougald	45.00	22.50	13.50
(37)	Russ Meyer	65.00	32.50	20.00
(38)	Bill Miller	40.00	20.00	12.00
(39)	Tom Morgan	40.00	20.00	12.00
(40)	Don Mueller	40.00	20.00	12.00
(41)	Don Newcombe	75.00	37.50	22.50
(42)	Irv Noren	40.00	20.00	12.00
(43)	Erv Palica	65.00	32.50	20.00
(44)	Pee Wee Reese	130.00	65.00	40.00
(45)	Allie Reynolds	40.00	20.00	12.00
(46)	Dusty Rhodes	40.00	20.00	12.00
(47)	Phil Rizzuto	125.00	65.00	35.00
(48)	Ed Robinson	40.00	20.00	12.00
(49)	Jackie Robinson	235.00	115.00	70.00
(50)	Preacher Roe	65.00	32.50	20.00
(51)	George Shuba	65.00	32.50	20.00
(52)	Duke Snider	200.00	100.00	60.00
(53)	Hank Thompson	40.00	20.00	12.00
(54)	Wes Westrum	40.00	20.00	12.00
(55)	Hoyt Wilhelm	110.00	55.00	32.50
(56)	Davey Williams	40.00	20.00	12.00
(57)	Dick Williams	65.00	32.50	20.00
(58)	Gene Woodling	45.00	22.50	13.50
(59)	Al Worthington	40.00	20.00	12.00

1969 N.Y. News Mets Portfolio of Stars

To commemorate the N.Y. Mets miracle season of 1969, one of the city's daily newspapers, The

News, issued a portfolio of player portraits done by editorial cartoonist Bruce Stark. The 9" x 12" pencil drawings are printed on heavy textured paper and were sold as a set in a folder labeled, "The 1969 Mets / A Portfolio of Stars." The black-and-white drawings are on a white background. A facsimile player autograph is printed at lower-left. At lower-right is the signature of the artist, Stark, along with the paper's logo and a union label. The blank-backed, unnumbered pieces are checklisted here alphabetically.

		NM	EX	VG
Complete Set (20):		225.00	110.00	70.00
Common Player:		7.50	3.75	2.25
(1)	Tommie Agee	7.50	3.75	2.25
(2)	Ken Boswell	7.50	3.75	2.25
(3)	Don Cardwell	7.50	3.75	2.25
(4)	Donn Clendenon	10.00	5.00	3.00
(5)	Wayne Garrett	7.50	3.75	2.25
(6)	Gary Gentry	7.50	3.75	2.25
(7)	Jerry Grote	7.50	3.75	2.25
(8)	Bud Harrelson	10.00	5.00	3.00
(9)	Gil Hodges	20.00	10.00	6.00
(10)	Cleon Jones	7.50	3.75	2.25
(11)	Jerry Koosman	7.50	3.75	2.25
(12)	Ed Kranepool	7.50	3.75	2.25
(13)	Jim McAndrew	7.50	3.75	2.25
(14)	Tug McGraw	10.00	5.00	3.00
(15)	Nolan Ryan	150.00	75.00	45.00
(16)	Tom Seaver	40.00	20.00	12.00
(17)	Art Shamsky	7.50	3.75	2.25
(18)	Ron Swoboda	7.50	3.75	2.25
(19)	Ron Taylor	7.50	3.75	2.25
(20)	Al Weis	7.50	3.75	2.25

1973 N.Y. News Mets/ Yankees Caricatures

Between June 17 and August 26, the Sunday color comics section of the N.Y. News carried a centerspread picturing one Mets and one Yankees player as caricatured by artist Bruce Stark. Each player picture is printed on newsprint in approximately 10-1/2" x 14-1/2", the pictures have a page of comics or other matter on their backs. Values shown are for single pages. Intact pairs or complete comics section would command a premium.

		NM	EX	VG
Complete Set (22):		200.00	100.00	60.00
Common Player:		6.00	3.00	1.75
	METS			
(1)	Yogi Berra (6/17)	17.50	8.75	5.25
(2)	Tom Seaver (6/24)	15.00	7.50	4.50
(3)	John Milner (7/1)	6.00	3.00	1.75
(4)	Felix Millan (7/8)	6.00	3.00	1.75
(5)	Bud Harrelson (7/15)	6.00	3.00	1.75
(6)	Jim Fregosi (7/22)	6.00	3.00	1.75
(7)	Jerry Grote (7/29)	6.00	3.00	1.75
(8)	Cleon Jones (8/5)	6.00	3.00	1.75
(9)	Willie Mays (8/12)	25.00	12.50	7.50
(10)	Rusty Staub (8/19)	9.00	4.50	2.75
(11)	Tug McGraw (8/26)	7.50	3.75	2.25
	YANKEES			
(12)	Ralph Houk (6/17)	7.50	3.75	2.25
(13)	Mel Stottlemyre (6/24)	7.50	3.75	2.25
(14)	Ron Blomberg (7/1)	6.00	3.00	1.75
(15)	Horace Clarke (7/8)	6.00	3.00	1.75
(16)	Gene Michael (7/15)	6.00	3.00	1.75
(17)	Graig Nettles (7/22)	7.50	3.75	2.25
(18)	Thurman Munson (7/29)	15.00	7.50	4.50
(19)	Roy White (8/5)	9.00	4.50	2.75
(20)	Bobby Murcer (8/12)	9.00	4.50	2.75
(21)	Matty Alou (8/19)	6.00	3.00	1.75
(22)	Sparky Lyle (8/26)	9.00	4.50	2.75

1916 N.Y. World Leaders in Baseball

This set of large-format (about 9" x 4") sepia-tone cards was issued to demonstrate the dominance of the World in New York City's newspaper wars. Each card has a portrait photo of a New York player. Most of the card is devoted to stats to boost the paper's claim as the "Pennant Winner in Advertising and Circulation." A note at left identifies the series as "'Leaders in Baseball' Series II." It is not known whether this checklist is complete.

		NM	EX	VG
Common Player:		600.00	300.00	180.00
(1)	Home Run Baker	750.00	375.00	225.00
(2)	Jake Daubert	600.00	300.00	180.00
(3)	Buck Herzog	600.00	300.00	180.00
(4)	Dave Robertson	600.00	300.00	180.00

1944 N.Y. Yankees Stamps

One of the few paper collectibles issued during World War II, this set includes several players who do not appear on any other contemporary baseball card issue. The 1-3/4" x 2-3/8" stamps were issued on a single sheet with an album marking the Yankees 1943 World Series win. Stamps are in full color with the player's name in white on a red strip at bottom. The unnumbered stamps are checklisted here alphabetically. An album, about 6-1/2" x 3-1/2", was issued to display the stamps.

		NM	EX	VG
Complete Set (30):		100.00	50.00	30.00
Common Player:		12.00	6.00	3.50
Uncut Sheet:		145.00	75.00	45.00
Album:		40.00	20.00	12.00
(1)	Ernie Bonham	12.00	6.00	3.50
(2)	Hank Borowy	12.00	6.00	3.50
(3)	Marvin Breuer	12.00	6.00	3.50
(4)	Tommy Byrne	12.00	6.00	3.50
(5)	Spud Chandler	15.00	7.50	4.50
(6)	Earl Combs (Earle)	25.00	12.50	7.50
(7)	Frank Crosetti	20.00	10.00	6.00
(8)	Bill Dickey	35.00	17.50	10.50
(9)	Atley Donald	12.00	6.00	3.50
(10)	Nick Etten	12.00	6.00	3.50
(11)	Art Fletcher	12.00	6.00	3.50
(12)	Joe Gordon	15.00	7.50	4.50
(13)	Oscar Grimes	12.00	6.00	3.50
(14)	Rollie Hemsley	12.00	6.00	3.50
(15)	Bill Johnson	12.00	6.00	3.50
(16)	Charlie Keller	15.00	7.50	4.50
(17)	John Lindell	15.00	7.50	4.50
(18)	Joe McCarthy	25.00	12.50	7.50
(19)	Bud Metheny	12.00	6.00	3.50
(20)	Johnny Murphy	12.00	6.00	3.50
(21)	Pat O'Daugherty	12.00	6.00	3.50
(22)	Marius Russo	12.00	6.00	3.50
(23)	John Schulte	12.00	6.00	3.50
(24)	Ken Sears	12.00	6.00	3.50
(25)	Tuck Stainback	12.00	6.00	3.50
(26)	George Stirnweiss	12.00	6.00	3.50
(27)	Jim Turner	12.00	6.00	3.50
(28)	Roy Weatherly	12.00	6.00	3.50
(29)	Charley Wensloff	12.00	6.00	3.50
(30)	Bill Zuber	12.00	6.00	3.50

1947-50 N.Y. Yankees Picture Pack

These team-issued sets offered fans at the souvenir stand more than two dozen pictures of the players and staff. The 6-1/2" x 9" pictures are in black-and-white with a white border and a facsimile autograph. Backs are blank. Players repeated over the years were represented by the same picture. The

unnumbered pictures are listed in aphabetical order by year of issue.

Common Player:	NM	EX	VG
Complete 1947 Set (25):	4.00	2.00	1.25
	100.00	50.00	30.00
(1) Yogi Berra	20.00	10.00	6.00
(2) Bill Bevens	4.00	2.00	1.25
(3) Bobby Brown	4.00	2.00	1.25
(4) Spud Chandler	4.00	2.00	1.25
(5) Frank Colman	4.00	2.00	1.25
(6) John Corriden	4.00	2.00	1.25
(7) Frank Crosetti	5.00	2.50	1.50
(8) Joe DiMaggio	40.00	20.00	12.00
(9) Chuck Dressen	4.00	2.00	1.25
(10) Randy Gumpert	4.00	2.00	1.25
(11) Bucky Harris	5.00	2.50	1.50
(12) Tommy Henrich	4.00	2.00	1.25
(13) Ralph Houk	5.00	2.50	1.50
(14) Don Johnson	4.00	2.00	1.25
(15) Bill Johnson	4.00	2.00	1.25
(16) Charlie Keller	5.00	2.50	1.50
(17) John Lindell	4.00	2.00	1.25
(18) George McQuinn	4.00	2.00	1.25
(19) Joe Page	4.00	2.00	1.25
(20) Allie Reynolds	5.00	2.50	1.50
(21) Phil Rizzuto	12.50	6.25	3.75
(22) Aaron Robinson	4.00	2.00	1.25
(23) Frank Shea	4.00	2.00	1.25
(24) Ken Silvestri	4.00	2.00	1.25
(25) George Stirnweiss	4.00	2.00	1.25
Complete 1948 Set (26):	100.00	50.00	30.00
(1) Yogi Berra	20.00	10.00	6.00
(2) Bobby Brown	4.00	2.00	1.25
(3) Red Corriden	4.00	2.00	1.25
(4) Frank Crosetti	5.00	2.50	1.50
(5) Joe DiMaggio	40.00	20.00	12.00
(6) Chuck Dressen	4.00	2.00	1.25
(7) Karl Drews	4.00	2.00	1.25
(8) Red Embree	4.00	2.00	1.25
(9) Randy Gumpert	4.00	2.00	1.25
(10) Bucky Harris	5.00	2.50	1.50
(11) Tommy Henrich	4.00	2.00	1.25
(12) Frank Hiller	4.00	2.00	1.25
(13) Bill Johnson	4.00	2.00	1.25
(14) Charlie Keller	5.00	2.50	1.50
(15) John Lindell	4.00	2.00	1.25
(16) Eddie Lopat	5.00	2.50	1.50
(17) Cliff Mapes	4.00	2.00	1.25
(18) George McQuinn	4.00	2.00	1.25
(19) Gus Niarhos	4.00	2.00	1.25
(20) George McQuinn	4.00	2.00	1.25
(21) Joe Page	4.00	2.00	1.25
(22) Vic Raschi	5.00	2.50	1.50
(23) Allie Reynolds	5.00	2.50	1.50
(24) Phil Rizzuto	12.50	6.25	3.75
(25) Frank Shea	4.00	2.00	1.25
(26) Snuffy Stirnweiss	4.00	2.00	1.25
Complete 1949 Set (25):	100.00	50.00	30.00
(1) Mel Allen	8.00	4.00	2.50
(2) Larry Berra	20.00	10.00	6.00
(3) Bobby Brown	4.00	2.00	1.25
(4) Tommy Byrne	4.00	2.00	1.25
(5) Jerry Coleman	4.00	2.00	1.25
(6) Frank Crosetti	5.00	2.50	1.50
(7) Bill Dickey	10.00	5.00	3.00
(8) Joe DiMaggio	40.00	20.00	12.00
(9) Tommy Henrich	4.00	2.00	1.25
(10) Bill Johnson	4.00	2.00	1.25
(11) Charlie Keller	5.00	2.50	1.50
(12) John Lindell	4.00	2.00	1.25
(13) Ed Lopat	5.00	2.50	1.50
(14) Gus Niarhos	4.00	2.00	1.25
(15) Joe Page	4.00	2.00	1.25
(16) Bob Porterfield	4.00	2.00	1.25
(17) Vic Raschi	4.00	2.00	1.25
(18) Allie Reynolds	5.00	2.50	1.50
(19) Phil Rizzuto	12.50	6.25	3.75
(20) Fred Sanford	4.00	2.00	1.25
(21) Frank Shea	4.00	2.00	1.25
(22) Casey Stengel	15.00	7.50	4.50
(23) George Stirnweiss	4.00	2.00	1.25
(24) Jim Turner	4.00	2.00	1.25
(25) Gene Woodling	5.00	2.50	1.50
Complete 1950 Set (25):	100.00	50.00	30.00
(1) Mel Allen	8.00	4.00	2.50
(2) Hank Bauer	5.00	2.50	1.50
(3) Larry Berra	20.00	10.00	6.00
(4) Bobby Brown	4.00	2.00	1.25
(5) Tommy Byrne	4.00	2.00	1.25
(6) Jerry Coleman	4.00	2.00	1.25
(7) Frank Crosetti	5.00	2.50	1.50
(8) Bill Dickey	10.00	5.00	3.00
(9) Joe DiMaggio	40.00	20.00	12.00
(10) Tommy Henrich	4.00	2.00	1.25
(11) Jack Jensen	7.50	3.75	2.25
(12) Bill Johnson	4.00	2.00	1.25
(13) Ed Lopat	5.00	2.50	1.50
(14) Cliff Mapes	4.00	2.00	1.25
(15) Joe Page	4.00	2.00	1.25
(16) Bob Porterfield	4.00	2.00	1.25
(17) Vic Raschi	5.00	2.50	1.50
(18) Allie Reynolds	5.00	2.50	1.50
(19) Phil Rizzuto	12.50	6.25	3.75
(20) Fred Sanford	4.00	2.00	1.25
(21) Charlie Silvera	5.00	2.50	1.50
(22) Casey Stengel	15.00	7.50	4.50
(23) George Stirnweiss	4.00	2.00	1.25
(24) Jim Turner	4.00	2.00	1.25
(25) Gene Woodling	5.00	2.50	1.50

1955-1957 N.Y. Yankees Picture Pack

The checklist for this set of 5" x 7" black-and-white, blank-back pictures does not allow pinpointing

its year of issue more closely. Similar in format to the later Jay Publishing photo packs, this issue differs in that only the team name (in upper- and lower-case letters), and not the city, is presented along with the player name (all-caps) in the identification line in the bottom border. The set was sold for 25 cents in a manila envelope. The unnumbered pictures are listed here alphabetically.

	NM	EX	VG
Complete Set (12):	75.00	37.50	22.50
Common Player:	4.00	2.00	1.25
(1) Hank Bauer	5.00	2.50	1.50
(2) Yogi Berra	7.50	3.75	2.25
(3) Tommy Byrne	4.00	2.00	1.25
(4) Andy Carey	4.00	2.00	1.25
(5) Joe Collins	4.00	2.00	1.25
(6) Whitey Ford	7.50	3.75	2.25
(7) Elston Howard	5.00	2.50	1.50
(8) Mickey Mantle	35.00	17.50	10.00
(9) Billy Martin	5.00	2.50	1.50
(10) Gil McDougald	4.00	2.00	1.25
(11) Casey Stengel	7.50	3.75	2.25
(12) Bob Turley	4.00	2.00	1.25

1956 N.Y. Yankees "Action Pictures"

This set of 8" x 10" black-and-white pictures was sold for 75 cents in a paper envelope marked "12 ACTION / PICTURES." The white bordered pictures have facsimile autographs or printed names on front and are blank-backed.

	NM	EX	VG
Complete Set (12):	125.00	65.00	49.00
Common Player:	6.00	3.00	1.75
(1) Hank Bauer	7.50	3.75	2.25
(2) Yogi Berra	15.00	7.50	4.50
(3) Andy Carey	6.00	3.00	1.75
(4) Joe Collins	6.00	3.00	1.75
(5) Whitey Ford	15.00	7.50	4.50
(6) Elston Howard	9.00	4.50	2.75
(7) Mickey Mantle	75.00	37.00	22.00
(8) Billy Martin	9.00	4.50	2.75
(9) Gil McDougald	7.50	3.75	2.25
(10) Phil Rizzuto	15.00	7.50	4.50
(11) Bill Skowron	9.00	4.50	2.75
(12) Bob Turley	7.50	3.75	2.25

1956 N.Y. Yankees Picture Pack

This set was issued, probably for sale at Yankee Stadium souvenir stands, in 1956, though some of the photos date as far back as 1951, and a few appear to have been taken during the 1955 World Series at Ebbets Field. Printed in black-and-white on semi-gloss paper, the pictures measure about 6" x 8-7/8". There is a 1/4" white border around the photo and a white strip at the bottom of each photo with the player's name. Backs are blank. The pictures are checklisted here in alphabetical order, but the list may not be complete. Some of the photos are familiar from their use on baseball cards, including the 1951 Bowman Mantle.

	NM	EX	VG
Complete Set (22):	275.00	135.00	80.00
Common Player:	8.00	4.00	2.50
(1) Hank Bauer	10.00	5.00	3.00
(2) Larry "Yogi" Berra	20.00	10.00	6.00
(3) Tommy Byrne	8.00	4.00	2.50
(4) Andy Carey	8.00	4.00	2.50
(5) Bob Cerv	8.00	4.00	2.50
(6) Gerry Coleman	8.00	4.00	2.50

(7) Joe Collins	8.00	4.00	2.50
(8) Ed "Whitey" Ford	20.00	10.00	6.00
(9) Bob Grim	8.00	4.00	2.50
(10) Elston Howard	10.00	5.00	3.00
(11) Johnny Kucks	8.00	4.00	2.50
(12) Don Larsen	12.50	6.25	3.75
(13) Jerry Lumpe	8.00	4.00	2.50
(14) Mickey Mantle	130.00	65.00	39.00
(15) Billy Martin	15.00	7.50	4.50
(16) Mickey McDermott	8.00	4.00	2.50
(17) Gil McDougald	10.00	5.00	3.00
(18) Tom Morgan	8.00	4.00	2.50
(19) Irv Noren	8.00	4.00	2.50
(20) Charlie Silvera	8.00	4.00	2.50
(21) Bill Skowron	10.00	5.00	3.00
(22) Bob Turley	10.00	5.00	3.00

1957 N.Y. Yankees Picture Pack

Nominally 8" x 10", the actual size on these blank-back, black-and-white pictures varies from about 7-1/2" to 8" wide by 9-7/8" x 10-1/8" tall. The player poses are surrounded with a white border. The player name is printed within the picture. Some of the photos used considerably pre-date the period of issue.

	NM	EX	VG
Complete Set (12):	125.00	65.00	40.00
Common Player:	10.00	5.00	3.00
(1) Hank Bauer	12.50	6.25	3.75
(2) Larry Berra	20.00	10.00	6.00
(3) Andy Carey	10.00	5.00	3.00
(4) Whitey Ford	20.00	10.00	6.00
(5) Elston Howard	12.50	6.25	3.75
(6) Tony Kubek	15.00	7.50	4.50
(7) Don Larsen	12.50	6.25	3.75
(8) Mickey Mantle	60.00	30.00	18.00
(9) Gil McDougald	12.50	6.25	3.75
(10) Bill Skowron	12.50	6.25	3.75
(11) Bob Turley	12.50	6.25	3.75
(12) Frank Crosetti, Bill Dickey, Casey Stengel, Jim Turner	10.00	5.00	3.00

1960 N.Y. Yankees "Action Pictures"

This set of 8" x 10" black-and-white pictures was sold for 75 cents in a paper envelope marked "12 ACTION / PICTURES." The white bordered pictures have facsimile autographs or printed names on front and are blank-backed.

	NM	EX	VG
Complete Set (12):	200.00	100.00	60.00
Common Player:	10.00	5.00	3.00
(1) Larry Berra	20.00	10.00	6.00
(2) Art Ditmar	10.00	5.00	3.00
(3) Whitey Ford	20.00	10.00	6.00
(4) Elston Howard	12.50	6.25	3.75
(5) Tony Kubek	15.00	7.50	4.50
(6) Hector Lopez	10.00	5.00	3.00
(7) Mickey Mantle	60.00	30.00	18.00
(8) Roger Maris	35.00	17.50	10.50
(9) Bobby Richardson	12.50	6.25	3.75
(10) Bill Skowron	12.50	6.25	3.75
(11) Casey Stengel	15.00	7.50	4.50
(12) Bob Turley	12.50	6.25	3.75

1970 N.Y. Yankees Clinic Schedule Postcards

This series of postcards was issued in conjunction with a series of baseball clinics which the Yankees put on for youngsters prior to selected home games. Fronts of the 3-1/2" x 5-1/2" glossy color cards have player portraits with a facsimile autograph in a white panel at bottom. Backs have player identification and career highlights, a schedule of the clinic days and credit line for Howard Photo Service. White and Murcer cards are scarce because of rainouts on their scheduled clinic appearance days. Cards are checklisted here in alphabetical order.

		NM	EX	VG
Complete Set (13):		130.00	65.00	40.00
Common Player:		3.00	1.50	.90
(1)	Stan Bahnsen	3.00	1.50	.90
(2)	Curt Blefary	3.00	1.50	.90
(3)	Danny Cater	3.00	1.50	.90
(4)	Horace Clarke	3.00	1.50	.90
(5)	Joe DiMaggio, Mickey Mantle	25.00	12.50	7.50
(6)	John Ellis	3.00	1.50	.90
(7)	Jerry Kenney	3.00	1.50	.90
(8)	Gene Michael	3.00	1.50	.90
(9)	Thurman Munson	30.00	15.00	9.00
(10)	Bobby Murcer	15.00	7.50	4.50
(11)	Fritz Peterson	3.00	1.50	.90
(12)	Mel Stottlemyre	4.50	2.25	1.25
(13)	Roy White	35.00	17.50	10.50

1971 N.Y. Yankees Clinic Schedule Postcards

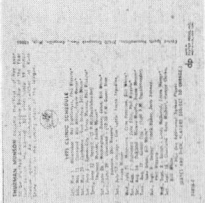

These postcards were issued in conjunction with a series of baseball clinics which the Yankees put on for youngsters prior to selected home games. Fronts of the 3-1/2" x 5-1/2" glossy color cards have player portraits with a facsimile autograph in a white panel at bottom. Backs are printed in blue, have player identification and career highlights and a schedule of the clinic days. Cards are checklisted here in alphabetical order.

		NM	EX	VG
Complete Set (16):		90.00	45.00	27.00
Common Player:		3.00	1.50	.90
(1)	Felipe Alou, Jim Lyttle	3.00	1.50	.90
(2)	Stan Bahnsen	3.00	1.50	.90
(3)	Frank Baker, Jerry Kenney	3.00	1.50	.90
(4)	Curt Blefary	3.00	1.50	.90
(5)	Danny Cater	3.00	1.50	.90
(6)	Horace Clarke, Gene Michael	3.00	1.50	.90
(7)	John Ellis	3.00	1.50	.90
(8)	Jake Gibbs	3.00	1.50	.90
(9)	Ralph Houk	3.00	1.50	.90
(10)	Mickey Mantle	30.00	15.00	9.00
(11)	Lindy McDaniel	3.00	1.50	.90
(12)	Thurman Munson	15.00	7.50	4.50
(13)	Bobby Murcer	4.50	2.25	1.25
(14)	Fritz Peterson	3.00	1.50	.90
(15)	Mel Stottlemyre	3.00	1.50	.90
(16)	Roy White	3.00	1.50	.90

1972 N.Y. Yankees Schedule Cards

The origins and distribution of these cards is unclear. They may have been a collector issue. The 2-1/4" x 3-1/2" cards are printed in blue and sepia. Fronts have player photos with a facsimile autograph

in the white border at bottom, between a pair of team insignia. Backs have the team schedule. The unnumbered cards are listed here alphabetically.

		NM	EX	VG
Complete Set (8):		350.00	175.00	100.00
Common Player:		30.00	15.00	9.00
(1)	Felipe Alou	35.00	17.50	10.50
(2)	Ron Blomberg	30.00	15.00	9.00
(3)	Thurman Munson	225.00	110.00	67.00
(4)	Bobby Murcer	35.00	17.50	10.50
(5)	Mel Stottlemyre	30.00	15.00	9.00
(6)	Ron Swoboda	30.00	15.00	9.00
(7)	Roy White	35.00	17.50	10.50
(8)	Frank Messer, Phil Rizzuto, Bill White/Announcers	30.00	15.00	9.00

1909 Niagara Baking Co.

This is a version of the set known as E101 "Set of 50" which has been rubber-stamped on back with an advertisement for Niagara Baking Co., of Lockport, N.Y. It is unclear whether all 50 cards in E101 can be found with the overprint. Because of the ease with which this regional variation could be faked, collectors must exercise extreme caution. Collectors can expect to pay a considerable premium over E101 prices for this version, especially for common players.

Values Undetermined
(See 1909 E101 for checklist.)

1953 Northland Bread Labels

This bread end-label set consists of 32 players - two from each major league team. The unnumbered black and white labels measure approximately 2-11/16" square and include the slogan "Bread for Energy" along the top. An album to house the labels was also part of the promotion.

		NM	EX	VG
Complete Set (32):		8,250	4,250	2,500
Common Player:		200.00	100.00	60.00
(1)	Cal Abrams	200.00	100.00	60.00
(2)	Richie Ashburn	400.00	200.00	120.00
(3)	Gus Bell	200.00	100.00	60.00
(4)	Jim Busby	200.00	100.00	60.00
(5)	Clint Courtney	200.00	100.00	60.00
(6)	Billy Cox	200.00	100.00	60.00
(7)	Jim Dyck	200.00	100.00	60.00
(8)	Nellie Fox	400.00	200.00	120.00
(9)	Sid Gordon	200.00	100.00	60.00
(10)	Warren Hacker	200.00	100.00	60.00
(11)	Jim Hearn	200.00	100.00	60.00
(12)	Fred Hutchinson	200.00	100.00	60.00
(13)	Monte Irvin	400.00	200.00	120.00
(14)	Jackie Jensen	225.00	110.00	65.00
(15)	Ted Kluszewski	350.00	175.00	100.00
(16)	Bob Lemon	400.00	200.00	120.00
(17)	Maury McDermott	200.00	100.00	60.00
(18)	Minny Minoso	350.00	175.00	105.00
(19)	Johnny Mize	400.00	200.00	120.00
(20)	Mel Parnell	200.00	100.00	60.00
(21)	Howie Pollet	200.00	100.00	60.00
(22)	Jerry Priddy	200.00	100.00	60.00
(23)	Allie Reynolds	200.00	100.00	60.00
(24)	Preacher Roe	250.00	125.00	75.00
(25)	Al Rosen	225.00	110.00	65.00
(26)	Connie Ryan	200.00	100.00	60.00

(27a)	Hank Sauer (Bread for Energy at top.)	200.00	100.00	60.00
(27b)	Hank Sauer (Top Taste at top.)	375.00	185.00	110.00
(28)	Red Schoendienst	400.00	200.00	120.00
(29)	Bobby Shantz	200.00	100.00	60.00
(30)	Enos Slaughter	400.00	200.00	120.00
(31)	Warren Spahn	400.00	200.00	120.00
(32)	Gus Zernial	200.00	100.00	60.00

1978 North Shore Dodge Cecil Cooper

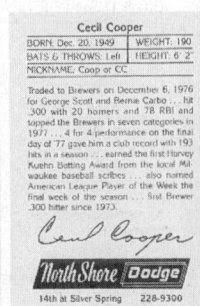

As part of his work as promotional spokesman for a local auto dealership, popular Brewers first baseman Cecil Cooper appears on a one-card set which was given to fans and collectors during public appearances. The card is printed in black-and-white in standard 2-1/2" x 3-1/2" size and is often found with a genuine autograph on the front.

	NM	EX	VG
Cecil Cooper	6.00	3.00	1.75
Cecil Cooper/Auto.	15.00	7.50	4.50

1980 Nostalgic Enterprises 1903 N.Y. Highlanders

New York City's first team in the American League, the 1903 Highlanders, are featured in this collectors' issue. Fronts of the 2-1/2" x 3-1/2" cards have black-and-white portrait photos with ornate graphics, highlighted in yellow, and a white border. Backs have season and lifetime stats, player data and an extensive career summary. The unnumbered cards are checklisted here in alphabetical order. Sets originally sold for about $2.50.

		NM	EX	VG
Complete Set (17):		15.00	7.50	4.50
Common Player:		2.00	1.00	.60
(1)	Monte Beville	2.50	1.25	.70
(2)	Jack Chesbro	2.00	1.00	.60
(3)	Wid Conroy	2.00	1.00	.60
(4)	Lefty Davis	2.00	1.00	.60
(5)	John Deering	2.50	1.25	.70
(6)	Kid Elberfeld	2.00	1.00	.60
(7)	Dave Fultz	2.00	1.00	.60
(8)	John Ganzel	2.00	1.00	.60
(9)	Clark Griffith	2.00	1.00	.60
(10)	Harry Howell	2.00	1.00	.60
(11)	Willie Keeler	2.00	1.00	.60
(12)	Herm McFarland	2.00	1.00	.60
(13)	Jack O'Connor	2.00	1.00	.60
(14)	Jesse Tannehill	2.00	1.00	.60
(15)	Jimmy Williams	2.00	1.00	.60
(16)	Jack Zalusky	2.50	1.25	.70
(17)	Header Card/Checklist	2.00	1.00	.60

1907-09 Novelty Cutlery Postcards (PC805)

An ornately bordered black-and-white or sepia portrait or action pose of the day's great players identifies these postcards from a Canton, Ohio, knife company. Cards measure the standard 3-1/2" x 5-1/2" size with postcard indicia on the back. The sponsor is identified in a tiny line of type beneath the lower-right corner of the player photo.

WALTER JOHNSTON

		NM	EX	VG
Complete Set (26):		60,000	30,000	18,000
Common Player:		1,400	560.00	280.00
(1)	Roger Bresnahan	1,800	720.00	360.00
(2)	Al Bridwell	1,400	560.00	280.00
(3)	Three Finger Brown	1,800	720.00	360.00
(4)	Frank Chance	1,800	720.00	360.00
(5)	Hal Chase	1,600	640.00	320.00
(6)	Ty Cobb	9,000	3,600	1,800
(7)	Eddie Collins	1,800	720.00	360.00
(8)	Sam Crawford	1,800	720.00	360.00
(9)	Art Devlin	1,400	560.00	280.00
(10)	Red Dooin	1,400	560.00	280.00
(11)	Elmer Flick	1,800	720.00	360.00
(12)	Sam Frock	1,400	560.00	280.00
(13)	George Gibson	1,400	560.00	280.00
(14)	Solly Hofman	1,400	560.00	280.00
(15)	Walter Johnston (Johnson)	3,000	1,200	600.00
(16)	Nap Lajoie	1,800	720.00	360.00
(17)	Bris Lord	1,400	560.00	280.00
(18)	Christy Mathewson	3,000	1,200	600.00
(19)	Orval Overall	1,400	560.00	280.00
(20)	Eddie Plank	1,800	720.00	360.00
(21)	Tris Speaker	2,500	1,000	500.00
(22)	Gabby Street	1,400	560.00	280.00
(23)	Honus Wagner	6,000	2,400	1,200
(24)	Ed Walsh	1,800	720.00	360.00
(25)	Ty Cobb, Honus Wagner	6,500	2,600	1,300
(26)	Johnny Evers, Germany Schaefer	1,600	640.00	320.00

1960 Nu-Card Baseball Hi-Lites

These large, 3-1/4" x 5-3/8" cards are printed in a mock newspaper format, with a headline, picture and story describing one of baseball's greatest moments. Cards #1-18 can be found either printed entirely in black, or in red-and-black, like the rest of the set. Each card is numbered in the upper-left corner. Backs offer a quiz question and answer.

		NM	EX	VG
Complete Set (72):		500.00	250.00	150.00
Common Player:		6.00	3.00	1.75
1	Babe Hits 3 Homers In A Series Game	40.00	20.00	12.00
2	Podres Pitching Wins Series	9.00	4.50	2.75
3	Bevans Pitches No Hitter, Almost	6.00	3.00	1.75
4	Box Score Devised By Reporter	6.00	3.00	1.75
5	VanderMeer Pitches 2 No Hitters	6.00	3.00	1.75
6	Indians Take Bums	6.00	3.00	1.75
7	DiMag Comes Thru	25.00	12.50	7.50
8	Mathewson Pitches 3 W.S. Shutouts	7.50	3.75	2.25
9	Haddix Pitches 12 Perfect Innings	6.00	3.00	1.75
10	Thomson's Homer Sinks Dodgers	9.00	4.50	2.75
11	Hubbell Strikes Out 5 A.L. Stars	6.00	3.00	1.75
12	Pickoff Ends Series (Marty Marion)	6.00	3.00	1.75
13	Cards Take Series From Yanks (Grover Cleveland Alexander)	6.00	3.00	1.75
14	Dizzy And Daffy Win Series	10.00	5.00	3.00
15	Owen Drops 3rd Strike	6.00	3.00	1.75
16	Ruth Calls His Shot	40.00	20.00	12.00
17	Merkle Pulls Boner	6.00	3.00	1.75
18	Larsen Hurls Perfect World Series Game	10.00	5.00	3.00
19	Bean Ball Ends Career of Mickey Cochrane	6.00	3.00	1.75
20	Banks Belts 47 Homers, Earns MVP Honors	6.00	3.00	1.75
21	Stan Musial Hits 5 Homers In 1 Day	12.50	6.25	3.75
22	Mickey Mantle Hits Longest Homer	60.00	30.00	18.00
23	Sievers Captures Home Run Title	6.00	3.00	1.75
24	Gehrig Consecutive Game Record Ends	25.00	12.50	7.50
25	Red Schoendienst Key Player In Victory	6.00	3.00	1.75
26	Midget Pinch-Hits For St. Louis Browns (Eddie Gaedel)	10.00	5.00	3.00
27	Willie Mays Makes Greatest Catch	25.00	12.50	7.50
28	Homer By Berra Puts Yanks In 1st Place	6.00	3.00	1.75
29	Campy National League's MVP	6.00	3.00	1.75
30	Bob Turley Hurls Yanks To Championship	6.00	3.00	1.75
31	Dodgers Take Series From Sox In Six	6.00	3.00	1.75
32	Furillo Hero As Dodgers Beat Chicago	6.00	3.00	1.75
33	Adcock Gets Four Homers And A Double	6.00	3.00	1.75
34	Dickey Chosen All Star Catcher	6.00	3.00	1.75
35	Burdette Beats Yanks In 3 Series Games	6.00	3.00	1.75
36	Umpires Clear White Sox Bench	6.00	3.00	1.75
37	Reese Honored As Greatest Dodger S.S.	7.50	3.75	2.25
38	Joe DiMaggio Hits In 56 Straight Games	30.00	15.00	9.00
39	Ted Williams Hits .406 For Season	25.00	12.50	7.50
40	Johnson Pitches 56 Scoreless Innings	6.00	3.00	1.75
41	Hodges Hits 4 Home Runs In Nite Game	6.00	3.00	1.75
42	Greenberg Returns To Tigers From Army	10.00	5.00	3.00
43	Ty Cobb Named Best Player Of All Time	15.00	7.50	4.50
44	Robin Roberts Wins 28 Games	6.00	3.00	1.75
45	Rizzuto's 2 Runs Save 1st Place	6.00	3.00	1.75
46	Tigers Beat Out Senators For Pennant (Hal Newhouser)	6.00	3.00	1.75
47	Babe Ruth Hits 60th Home Run	40.00	20.00	12.00
48	Cy Young Honored	6.00	3.00	1.75
49	Killebrew Starts Spring Training	6.00	3.00	1.75
50	Mantle Hits Longest Homer At Stadium	60.00	30.00	18.00
51	Braves Take Pennant (Hank Aaron)	6.00	3.00	1.75
52	Ted Williams Hero Of All Star Game	30.00	15.00	9.00
53	Robinson Saves Dodgers For Playoffs (Jackie Robinson)	12.50	6.25	3.75
54	Snodgrass Muffs A Fly Ball	6.00	3.00	1.75
55	Snider Belts 2 Homers	6.00	3.00	1.75
56	New York Giants Win 26 Straight Games (Christy Mathewson)	6.00	3.00	1.75
57	Ted Kluszewski Stars In 1st Game Win	6.00	3.00	1.75
58	Ott Walks 5 Times In A Single Game (Mel Ott)	6.00	3.00	1.75
59	Harvey Kuenn Takes Batting Title	6.00	3.00	1.75
60	Bob Feller Hurls 3rd No-Hitter Of Career	6.00	3.00	1.75
61	Yanks Champs Again! (Casey Stengel)	6.00	3.00	1.75
62	Aaron's Bat Beats Yankees In Series	10.00	5.00	3.00
63	Warren Spahn Beats Yanks in World Series	6.00	3.00	1.75
64	Ump's Wrong Call Helps Dodgers	6.00	3.00	1.75
65	Kaline Hits 3 Homers, 2 In Same Inning	6.00	3.00	1.75
66	Bob Allison Named A.L. Rookie of Year	6.00	3.00	1.75
67	McCovey Blasts Way Into Giant Lineup	6.00	3.00	1.75
68	Colavito Hits Four Homers In One Game	10.00	5.00	3.00
69	Erskine Sets Strike Out Record In W.S.	6.00	3.00	1.75
70	Sal Maglie Pitches No-Hit Game	6.00	3.00	1.75
71	Early Wynn Victory Crushes Yanks	6.00	3.00	1.75
72	Nellie Fox American League's M.V.P.	6.00	3.00	1.75

1961 Nu-Card Baseball Scoops

Very similar in style to their set of the year before, the Nu-Card Baseball Scoops were issued in a smaller 2-1/2" x 3-1/2" size, but still featured the mock newspaper card front. This 80-card set is num-

bered from 401 to 480, with numbers shown on both the card front and back. These cards, which commemorate great moments in individual players' careers, included only the headline and black and white photo on the fronts, with the descriptive story on the card backs. Cards are again printed in red and black. It appears the set may have been counterfeited, though when is not known. These cards can be determined by examining the card photo for unusual blurring and fuzziness.

		NM	EX	VG
Complete Set (80):		400.00	200.00	120.00
Common Player:		3.00	1.50	.90
Wax Pack (7):		100.00		
401	Gentile Powers Birds Into 1st	6.00	3.00	1.75
402	Warren Spahn Hurls No-Hitter, Whiffs 15	5.00	2.50	1.50
403	Mazeroski's Homer Wins Series For Bucs	10.00	5.00	3.00
404	Willie Mays' 3 Triples Paces Giants	15.00	7.50	4.50
405	Woodie Held Slugs 2 Homers, 6 RBIs	3.00	1.50	.90
406	Vern Law Winner Of Cy Young Award	3.00	1.50	.90
407	Runnels Makes 9 Hits in Twin-Bill	3.00	1.50	.90
408	Braves' Lew Burdette Wins No-Hitter	3.00	1.50	.90
409	Dick Stuart Hits 3 Homers, Single	3.00	1.50	.90
410	Don Cardwell Of Cubs Pitches No-Hit Game	3.00	1.50	.90
411	Camilo Pascual Strikes Out 15 Bosox	3.00	1.50	.90
412	Eddie Mathews Blasts 300th Big League HR	3.00	1.50	.90
413	Groat, NL Bat King, Named Loop's MVP	3.00	1.50	.90
414	AL Votes To Expand To 10 Teams (Gene Autry)	3.00	1.50	.90
415	Bobby Richardson Sets Series Mark	3.00	1.50	.90
416	Maris Nips Mantle For AL MVP Award	10.00	5.00	3.00
417	Merkle Pulls Boner	3.00	1.50	.90
418	Larsen Hurls Perfect World Series Game	5.00	2.50	1.50
419	Bean Ball Ends Career Of Mickey Cochrane	3.00	1.50	.90
420	Banks Belts 47 Homers, Earns MVP Award	6.00	3.00	1.75
421	Stan Musial Hits 5 Homers In 1 Day	9.00	4.50	2.75
422	Mickey Mantle Hits Longest Homer	35.00	17.50	10.50
423	Sievers Captures Home Run Title	3.00	1.50	.90
424	Gehrig Consecutive Game Record Ends	15.00	7.50	4.50
425	Red Schoendienst Key Player In Victory	3.00	1.50	.90
426	Midget Pinch-Hits For St. Louis Browns (Eddie Gaedel)	5.00	2.50	1.50
427	Willie Mays Makes Greatest Catch	20.00	10.00	6.00
428	Robinson Saves Dodgers For Playoffs	9.00	4.50	2.75
429	Campy Most Valuable Player	3.00	1.50	.90
430	Turley Hurls Yanks To Championship	3.00	1.50	.90
431	Dodgers Take Series From Sox In Six (Larry Sherry)	3.00	1.50	.90
432	Furillo Hero In 3rd World Series Game	3.00	1.50	.90
433	Adcock Gets Four Homers, Double	3.00	1.50	.90
434	Dickey Chosen All Star Catcher	3.00	1.50	.90
435	Burdette Beats Yanks In 3 Series Games	3.00	1.50	.90
436	Umpires Clear White Sox Bench	3.00	1.50	.90
437	Reese Honored As Greatest Dodgers S.S.	3.00	1.50	.90
438	Joe DiMaggio Hits In 56 Straight Games	20.00	10.00	6.00
439	Ted Williams Hits .406 For Season	20.00	10.00	6.00
440	Johnson Pitches 56 Scoreless Innings	3.00	1.50	.90
441	Hodges Hits 4 Home Runs In Nite Game	3.00	1.50	.90
442	Greenberg Returns To Tigers From Army	3.00	1.50	.90

		NM	EX	VG
443	Ty Cobb Named Best Player Of All Time	10.00	5.00	3.00
444	Robin Roberts Wins 28 Games	3.00	1.50	.90
445	Rizzuto's 2 Runs Save 1st Place	3.00	1.50	.90
446	Tigers Beat Out Senators For Pennant (Hal Newhouser)	3.00	1.50	.90
447	Babe Ruth Hits 60th Home Run	20.00	10.00	6.00
448	Cy Young Honored	4.50	2.25	1.25
449	Killebrew Starts Spring Training	3.00	1.50	.90
450	Mantle Hits Longest Homer At Stadium	35.00	17.50	10.50
451	Braves Take Pennant	3.00	1.50	.90
452	Ted Williams Hero Of All Star Game	20.00	10.00	6.00
453	Homer By Berra Puts Yanks In 1st Place	3.00	1.50	.90
454	Snodgrass Muffs A Fly Ball	3.00	1.50	.90
455	Babe Hits 3 Homers In A Series Game	25.00	12.50	7.50
456	New York Wins 26 Straight Games	3.00	1.50	.90
457	Ted Kluszewski Stars In 1st Series Win	3.00	1.50	.90
458	Ott Walks 5 Times In A Single Game	3.00	1.50	.90
459	Harvey Kuenn Takes Batting Title	3.00	1.50	.90
460	Bob Feller Hurls 3rd No-Hitter Of Career	3.00	1.50	.90
461	Yanks Champs Again! (Casey Stengel)	3.00	1.50	.90
462	Aaron's Bat Beats Yankees In Series	10.00	5.00	3.00
463	Warren Spahn Beats Yanks In World Series	3.00	1.50	.90
464	Ump's Wrong Call Helps Dodgers	3.00	1.50	.90
465	Kaline Hits 3 Homers, 2 In Same Inning	3.00	1.50	.90
466	Bob Allison Named A.L. Rookie Of Year	3.00	1.50	.90
467	DiMag Comes Thru	20.00	10.00	6.00
468	Colavito Hits Four Homers In One Game	3.50	1.75	1.00
469	Erskine Sets Strike Out Record In W.S.	3.00	1.50	.90
470	Sal Maglie Pitches No-Hit Game	3.00	1.50	.90
471	Early Wynn Victory Crushes Yanks	3.00	1.50	.90
472	Nellie Fox American League's MVP	3.00	1.50	.90
473	Pickoff Ends Series (Marty Marion)	3.00	1.50	.90
474	Podres Pitching Wins Series	3.00	1.50	.90
475	Owen Drops 3rd Strike	3.00	1.50	.90
476	Dizzy And Daffy Win Series	9.00	4.50	2.75
477	Mathewson Pitches 3 W.S. Shutouts	10.00	5.00	3.00
478	Haddix Pitches 12 Perfect Innings	3.00	1.50	.90
479	Hubbell Strike Out 5 A.L. Stars	3.00	1.50	.90
480	Homer Sinks Dodgers (Bobby Thomson)	6.00	3.00	1.75

1889 Number 7 Cigars (N526)

Three versions of this set picturing Boston Beaneaters (N.L.) players were issued in 1889. Number 7 and Diamond S cigars are the most commonly encountered advertising printed on the cards' backs. Cards with "C.S. White & Co." at top front are also known. The cards measure approximately 3-1/8" x 4-1/2" and feature black-and-white portrait drawings of the players with their name printed below in capital letters along with the team name. Backs carry ads for either Number 7 Cigars, a product of H.W.S. & Co. Howard W. Spurr & Co.), or Diamond S Cigars, advertised as the "Best 10 cent Cigar in America."

		NM	EX	VG
Complete Set (15):		20,000	8,000	4,000
Common Player:		1,100	450.00	225.00
(1)	C.W. Bennett	1,100	450.00	225.00
(2)	Dennis Brouthers	2,500	800.00	400.00
(3)	T.T. Brown	1,100	450.00	225.00
(4)	John G. Clarkson	2,500	800.00	400.00
(5)	C.W. Ganzel	1,100	450.00	225.00
(6)	James A. Hart	1,100	450.00	225.00
(7)	R.F. Johnston	1,100	450.00	225.00
(8)	M.J. Kelly	3,500	1,000	500.00

		NM	EX	VG
(9)	M.J. Madden	1,100	450.00	225.00
(10)	Wm. Nash	1,100	450.00	225.00
(11)	Jos. Quinn	1,100	450.00	225.00
(12)	Chas. Radbourn	2,500	800.00	400.00
(13)	J.B. Ray (Should be I.B.)	1,100	450.00	225.00
(14)	Hardie Richardson	1,100	450.00	225.00
(15)	Wm. Sowders	1,100	450.00	225.00

1949-1950 Num Num Cleveland Indians

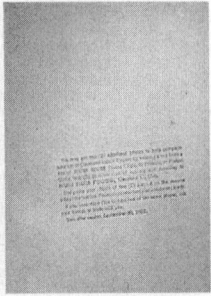

The 6-1/2" x 9" photopack pictures sold at Municipal Stadium in 1949 did double duty when they were also used as a premium for Num Num snack foods. A rubber-stamped notice on the back of the black-and-white photos offered two pictures for 10 cents and a box top, while encouraging trading. The pictures generally feature posed action shots with a facsimile autograph and white border. Backs are blank except for the rubber stamping. The unnumbered cards are checklisted here alphabetically.

		NM	EX	VG
Complete Set (34):		1,850	925.00	550.00
Common Player:		35.00	17.50	10.00
(1)	Bob Avila	35.00	17.50	10.00
(2)	Gene Bearden	35.00	17.50	10.00
(3)	Al Benton	35.00	17.50	10.00
(4)	John Berardino	45.00	22.50	13.50
(5)	Ray Boone	35.00	17.50	10.00
(6)	Lou Boudreau	65.00	30.00	15.00
(7)	Allie Clark	35.00	17.50	10.00
(8)	Larry Doby	65.00	30.00	15.00
(9)	Luke Easter	35.00	17.50	10.00
(10)	Bob Feller	125.00	60.00	30.00
(11)	Jess Flores	35.00	17.50	10.00
(12)	Mike Garcia	35.00	17.50	10.00
(13)	Joe Gordon	35.00	17.50	10.00
(14)	Hank Greenberg	125.00	65.00	35.00
(15)	Steve Gromek	35.00	17.50	10.00
(16)	Jim Hegan	35.00	17.50	10.00
(17)	Ken Keltner	35.00	17.50	10.00
(18)	Bob Kennedy	35.00	17.50	10.00
(19)	Bob Lemon	65.00	30.00	15.00
(20)	Dale Mitchell	35.00	17.50	10.00
(21)	Ray Murray	35.00	17.50	10.00
(22)	Satchell Paige	200.00	90.00	50.00
(23)	Frank Papish	35.00	17.50	10.00
(24)	Hal Peck	35.00	17.50	10.00
(25)	Chick Pieretti	35.00	17.50	10.00
(26)	Al Rosen	45.00	22.50	13.50
(27)	Dick Rozek (Glove out front.)	35.00	17.50	10.00
(28)	Dick Rozek (Glove under leg.)	35.00	17.50	10.00
(29)	Mike Tresh	35.00	17.50	10.00
(30)	Thurman Tucker	35.00	17.50	10.00
(31)	Bill Veeck	65.00	30.00	15.00
(32)	Mickey Vernon	35.00	17.50	10.00
(33)	Early Wynn	65.00	30.00	15.00
(34)	Sam Zoldak	35.00	17.50	10.00
(35)	Coaches (George Susce, Herold Ruel, Bill McKechnie, Steve O'Neill, Mel Harder)	35.00	17.50	10.00
(36)	Municipal Stadium	35.00	17.50	10.00

1952 Num Num Cleveland Indians

Distributed with packages of Num Num potato chips, pretzels and other snack foods, this black-and-white set, like the 1950 issue, was also issued in a slightly different format directly by the team. The Num Num cards have a 1" tab at the bottom which could

be redeemed, when a complete set was collected, for an autographed baseball. The team-issued version of the cards was printed without the tabs. Also like the 1950 Num Nums, Bob Kennedy's card is unaccountably scarce in the 1952 set. The '52 cards measure 3-1/2" x 5-1/2" including the tab, which has the card number on front, along with redemption details. Backs, also printed in black-and-white, repeat the card number in the upper-left corner. There is significant player biographical information and some 1951 season highlights. Cards with no tabs are worth about 1/3 less than the values quoted.

		NM	EX	VG
Complete Set, With Tabs (20):		5,750	2,300	1,150
Common Player, With Tab:		125.00	50.00	25.00
Complete Set, No Tabs (20):		3,250	1,300	650.00
Common Player, No Tab:		110.00	45.00	22.50
WITH TABS				
1	Lou Brissie	150.00	60.00	30.00
2	Jim Hegan	150.00	60.00	30.00
3	Birdie Tebbetts	150.00	60.00	30.00
4	Bob Lemon	300.00	120.00	60.00
5	Bob Feller	900.00	360.00	180.00
6	Early Wynn	300.00	120.00	60.00
7	Mike Garcia	150.00	60.00	30.00
8	Steve Gromek	150.00	60.00	30.00
9	Bob Chakales	150.00	60.00	30.00
10	Al Rosen	175.00	70.00	35.00
11	Dick Rozek	150.00	60.00	30.00
12	Luke Easter	175.00	70.00	35.00
13	Ray Boone	150.00	60.00	30.00
14	Bobby Avila	150.00	60.00	30.00
15	Dale Mitchell	150.00	60.00	30.00
16	Bob Kennedy/SP	1,600	640.00	320.00
17	Harry Simpson	150.00	60.00	30.00
18	Larry Doby	300.00	120.00	60.00
19	Sam Jones	150.00	60.00	30.00
20	Al Lopez	300.00	120.00	60.00
NO TABS				
1	Lou Brissie	100.00	40.00	20.00
2	Jim Hegan	100.00	40.00	20.00
3	Birdie Tebbetts	100.00	40.00	20.00
4	Bob Lemon	200.00	80.00	40.00
5	Bob Feller	600.00	240.00	120.00
6	Early Wynn	200.00	80.00	40.00
7	Mike Garcia	100.00	40.00	20.00
8	Steve Gromek	100.00	40.00	20.00
9	Bob Chakales	100.00	40.00	20.00
10	Al Rosen	125.00	50.00	25.00
11	Dick Rozek	100.00	40.00	20.00
12	Luke Easter	125.00	50.00	25.00
13	Ray Boone	100.00	40.00	20.00
14	Bobby Avila	100.00	40.00	20.00
15	Dale Mitchell	100.00	40.00	20.00
16	Bob Kennedy/SP	1,250	500.00	250.00
17	Harry Simpson	100.00	40.00	20.00
18	Larry Doby	200.00	80.00	40.00
19	Sam Jones	100.00	40.00	20.00
20	Al Lopez	200.00	80.00	40.00

1937 O-Pee-Chee

Kind of a combination of 1934 Goudeys and 1934-36 Batter Ups, the '37 OPC "Baseball Stars" set features black-and-white action photos against a stylized ballpark. About halfway up the 2-5/8" x 2-15/16" cards, the background was die-cut to allow it to be folded back to create a stand-up card. Backs are printed in English and French. The 40 cards in "Series A" are all American Leaguers, leading to speculation that a Series B of National League players was to have been issued at a later date. The set carries the American Card Catalog designation of V300.

		NM	EX	VG
Complete Set (40):		17,500	8,750	5,250
Common Player:		275.00	135.00	85.00
101	John Lewis	275.00	135.00	85.00
102	"Jack" Hayes	275.00	135.00	85.00
103	Earl Averill	400.00	200.00	120.00
104	Harland Clift (Harland)	275.00	135.00	85.00
105	"Beau" Bell	275.00	135.00	85.00
106	Jimmy Foxx (Jimmie)	1,050	525.00	315.00
107	Hank Greenberg	1,325	660.00	400.00
108	George Selkirk	275.00	135.00	85.00
109	Wally Moses	275.00	135.00	85.00
110	"Gerry" Walker	275.00	135.00	85.00

		NM	EX	VG
111	"Goose" Goslin	400.00	200.00	120.00
112	Charlie Gehringer	425.00	210.00	125.00
113	Hal Trosky	275.00	135.00	85.00
114	"Buddy" Myer	275.00	135.00	85.00
115	Luke Appling	400.00	200.00	120.00
116	"Zeke" Bonura	275.00	135.00	85.00
117	Tony Lazzeri	425.00	210.00	125.00
118	Joe DiMaggio	4,100	2,050	1,225
119	Bill Dickey	600.00	300.00	180.00
120	Bob Feller	1,600	800.00	480.00
121	Harry Kelley	275.00	135.00	85.00
122	Johnny Allen	275.00	135.00	85.00
123	Bob Johnson	275.00	135.00	85.00
124	Joe Cronin	400.00	200.00	120.00
125	"Rip" Radcliff	275.00	135.00	85.00
126	Cecil Travis	275.00	135.00	85.00
127	Joe Kuhel	275.00	135.00	85.00
128	Odell Hale	275.00	135.00	85.00
129	Sam West	275.00	135.00	85.00
130	Ben Chapman	275.00	135.00	85.00
131	Monte Pearson	275.00	135.00	85.00
132	"Rick" Ferrell	400.00	200.00	120.00
133	Tommy Bridges	275.00	135.00	85.00
134	"Schoolboy" Rowe	275.00	135.00	85.00
135	Vernon Kennedy	275.00	135.00	85.00
136	"Red" Ruffing	400.00	200.00	120.00
137	"Lefty" Grove	500.00	250.00	150.00
138	Wes Farrell	275.00	135.00	85.00
139	"Buck" Newsom	275.00	135.00	85.00
140	Rogers Hornsby	750.00	375.00	225.00

1960 O-Pee-Chee Tattoos

Though much scarcer than the contemporary Topps version, this Canadian specialty bubblegum issue does not currently enjoy any price premium. The OPC type is identifiable by its imprint on the outside of the wrapper.

(See 1960 Topps Tattoos for description, checklist and price guide.)

1965 O-Pee-Chee

 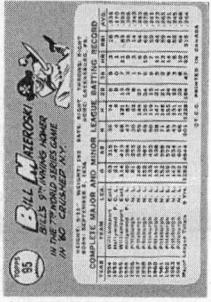

Identical in design to the 1965 Topps set, the Canadian-issued 1965 O-Pee-Chee set was printed on gray stock and consists of 283 cards, each measuring the standard 2-1/2" x 3-1/2". The words "Printed in Canada" appear along the bottom of the back of the cards. The checklist for '65 OPC parallels the first 283 cards in 1965 Topps.

	NM	EX	VG
Complete Set (283):	3,150	1,575	950.00
Common Player (1-196):	3.00	1.50	9.00
Common Player (197-283):	6.00	3.00	1.80
Stars: 2-3X Topps			

(See 1965 Topps #1-283 for checklist and star card values.)

1966 O-Pee-Chee

 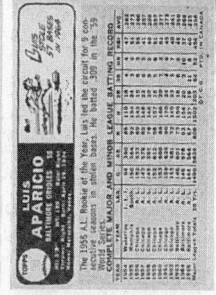

Utilizing the same design as the 1966 Topps set, the 1966 O-Pee-Chee set consists of 196 cards, measuring 2-1/2" x 3-1/2". The words "Ptd. in Canada" appear along the bottom on the back of the cards. The '66 OPC checklist parallels the first 196 cards in the Topps version.

	NM	EX	VG
Complete Set (196):	1,600	800.00	475.00
Common Player (1-196):	2.50	1.25	.75
Stars: 2-3X Topps			

(See 1966 Topps #1-196 for checklist and base star card values.)

1967 O-Pee-Chee

 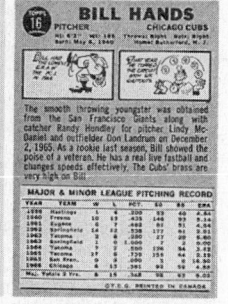

Cards in the 196-card Canadian set are nearly identical in design to the 1967 Topps set, except the words "Printed in Canada" are found on the back in the lower-right corner. Cards measure 2-1/2" x 3-1/2". The '67 OPC set parallels the first 196 cards on the Topps checklist, including "corrected" versions of the checklists and McCormick card.

	NM	EX	VG
Complete Set (196):	1,100	550.00	330.00
Common Player (1-109):	2.00	1.00	.60
Common Player (110-196):	2.50	1.25	.75
Stars: 2-3X Topps			

(See 1967 Topps #1-196 for checklist and base star card values.)

1968 O-Pee-Chee

The O-Pee-Chee set for 1968 again consists of 196 cards, in the standard 2-1/2" x 3-1/2". The design is identical to the 1968 Topps set, except the color of the backs is slightly different and the words "Prd. in Canada" appear in the lower-right corner of the back. The checklist parallels the first 196 cards in '68 Topps, though only the "b" versions of the checklists and name-color variations are found in OPC.

	NM	EX	VG
Complete Set (196):	2,000	1,000	600.00
Common Player:	2.00	1.00	.60
Stars: 2-3X Topps			

(See 1968 Topps #1-196 for checklist and base star card values.)

177	Mets Rookies (Jerry Koosman, Nolan Ryan)	825.00	410.00	245.00

1968 O-Pee-Chee Posters

The 5" x 7" "All Star Pin-ups" were inserts to 1968 OPC wax packs, but are virtually identical to the Topps version issued in 1967. The OPC posters have a small "Ptd. in Canada" line at bottom. They feature a full color picture with the player's name, position and team in a circle in the lower-right corner on front. The numbered set consists of 32 players (generally big names). Because the large paper pin-ups had to be folded several times to fit into the wax packs, they are almost never found in technical Mint or NM condition.

	NM	EX	VG
Complete Set (32):	300.00	150.00	90.00

1969 O-Pee-Chee

		Common Player:	3.00	1.50	.90
1	Brooks Robinson		12.00	6.00	3.50
2	Bert Campaneris		3.00	1.50	.90
3	Carl Yastrzemski		12.00	6.00	3.50
4	Roberto Clemente		25.00	12.50	7.50
5	Cleon Jones		3.00	1.50	.90
6	Don Drysdale		12.00	6.00	3.50
7	Orlando Cepeda		9.00	4.50	2.75
8	Hank Aaron		25.00	12.50	7.50
9	Tommie Agee		6.00	3.00	1.75
10	Boog Powell		4.50	2.25	1.25
11	Mickey Mantle		40.00	20.00	12.00
12	Chico Cardenas		3.00	1.50	.90
13	John Callison		3.00	1.50	.90
14	Frank Howard		3.75	2.00	1.25
15	Willie Mays		25.00	12.50	7.50
16	Sam McDowell		4.50	2.25	1.25
17	Al Kaline		12.00	6.00	3.50
18	Juan Marichal		9.00	4.50	2.75
19	Denny McLain		4.50	2.25	1.25
20	Matty Alou		3.00	1.50	.90
21	Felipe Alou		4.50	2.25	1.25
22	Joe Pepitone		4.50	2.25	1.25
23	Leon Wagner		3.00	1.50	.90
24	Bobby Knoop		3.00	1.50	.90
25	Tony Oliva		4.50	2.25	1.25
26	Joe Torre		4.50	2.25	1.25
27	Ron Santo		6.00	3.00	1.75
28	Willie McCovey		12.00	6.00	3.50
29	Frank Robinson		12.00	6.00	3.50
30	Ron Hunt		3.00	1.50	.90
31	Harmon Killebrew		12.00	6.00	3.50
32	Joe Morgan		12.00	6.00	3.50

1969 O-Pee-Chee

 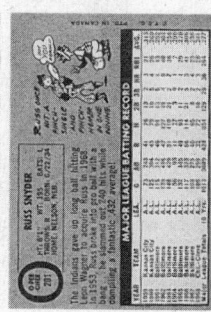

O-Pee-Chee increased the number of cards in its 1969 set to 218, maintaining the standard 2-1/2" x 3-1/2" size. The card design is identical to the 1969 Topps set, except for the appearance of an OPC logo on back, a slightly different color on the back and the words "Ptd. in Canada," which appear along the bottom. The checklist for '69 OPC parallels the Topps version, but includes only the later-printed "b" versions of the variation cards. This was the first year for the N.L. expansion Montreal Expos, and the Canadian versions of their cards generally sell for a modest premium.

	NM	EX	VG
Complete Set (218):	775.00	375.00	225.00
Common Player:	2.50	1.25	.75
Stars: 1-2X Topps			
Expos: 1.5X Topps			

(See 1969 Topps #1-218 for checklist and base star card values.)

1969 O-Pee-Chee Deckle

Very similar in design to the Topps Deckle Edge set of the same year, the 1969 O-Pee-Chee set consists of 24 (rather than Topps' 33) unnumbered black-and-white cards. The Canadian version measures 2-1/8" x 3-1/8", slightly smaller than the Topps set, but features the same "deckle cut" borders. The OPC set is blank-backed and has the facsimile autographs in black ink, rather than blue.

	NM	EX	VG
Complete Set (24):	160.00	80.00	45.00
Common Player:	2.50	1.25	.75
(1) Rich Allen	3.00	1.50	.90

		NM	EX	VG
(2)	Luis Aparicio	7.50	3.75	2.25
(3)	Rodney Carew	12.50	6.25	3.75
(4)	Roberto Clemente	30.00	15.00	9.00
(5)	Curt Flood	2.50	1.25	.75
(6)	Bill Freehan	2.50	1.25	.75
(7)	Robert Gibson	7.50	3.75	2.25
(8)	Ken Harrelson	2.50	1.25	.75
(9)	Tommy Helms	2.50	1.25	.75
(10)	Tom Haller	2.50	1.25	.75
(11)	Willie Horton	2.50	1.25	.70
(12)	Frank Howard	2.50	1.25	.75
(13)	Willie McCovey	10.00	5.00	3.00
(14)	Denny McLain	2.50	1.25	.75
(15)	Juan Marichal	7.50	3.75	2.25
(16)	Willie Mays	25.00	12.50	7.50
(17)	John "Boog" Powell	3.00	1.50	.90
(18)	Brooks Robinson	12.50	6.25	3.75
(19)	Ronald Santo	3.00	1.50	.90
(20)	Rusty Staub	3.00	1.50	.90
(21)	Mel Stottlemyre	2.50	1.25	.75
(22)	Luis Tiant	2.50	1.25	.75
(23)	Maurie Wills	2.50	1.25	.75
(24)	Carl Yastrzemski	12.50	6.25	3.75

1970 O-Pee-Chee

The 1970 O-Pee-Chee set, identical in design to the 1970 Topps set, expanded to 546 cards, measuring 2-1/2" x 3-1/2". The Canadian-issued O-Pee-Chee set is easy to distinguish because the backs are printed in both French and English and include the words "Printed in Canada." The '70 OPC checklist parallels the Topps versions. Besides the star cards generally bringing a premium over the Topps version due to scarcity, collectors pay a modest premium for OPC cards of Expos players.

	NM	EX	VG
Complete Set (546):	1,750	875.00	525.00
Common Player (1-459):	1.50	.75	.45
Common Player (460-546):	2.50	1.25	.75
Stars: 1-2X Topps			
Expos: 1.5X Topps			

(See 1970 Topps #1-546 for checklist and base card values.)

1971 O-Pee-Chee

For 1971 O-Pee-Chee increased the number of cards in its set to 752, the same as the 1971 Topps set, which shares the same black-bordered design. The backs of the OPC are printed in yellow, rather than green, in a slightly different format and (except card numbers 524-752) are printed in both French and English. The words "Printed in Canada" appear on the back. Fourteen of the OPC cards have different photos from their corresponding Topps' cards or list the player with a different team. The '71 OPC checklist parallels the Topps version. Because of relative scarcity, superstars in the OPC command a premium, as do cards of the "local" Expos players.

	NM	EX	VG
Complete Set (752):	3,000	1,500	900.00
Common Player (1-523):	2.75	1.50	.80
Common Player (524-643):	4.50	2.25	1.25
Common Player (644-752):	6.50	3.25	2.00
Stars: 1-2X Topps			
Expos: 1.5X Topps			

(See 1971 Topps for checklist and base card values.)

1972 O-Pee-Chee

Identical in design to the Topps cards of the same year, the Canadian-issued 1972 O-Pee-Chee set

 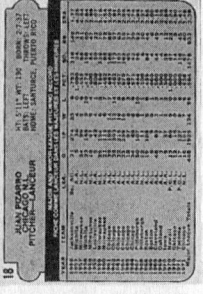

numbers 525 cards, measuring 2-1/2" x 3-1/2". The backs state "Printed in Canada" and are written in both French and English. The O-Pee-Chee card of Gil Hodges notes the Mets' manager's death. The '72 OPC set parallels the first 525 cards on the '72 Topps checklist, though without any of the scarcer "a" variations. Because of relative scarcity, superstars in the OPC brand bring a premium over Topps cards, while increased demand for Expos players causes their cards to bring a similar modest premium.

	NM	EX	VG
Complete Set (525):	875.00	425.00	250.00
Common Player (1-263):	.60	.30	.20
Common Player (264-394):	.90	.45	.25
Common Player (395-525):	1.00	.50	.30
Stars: 1-2X Topps			
Expos: 1.5X Topps			

(See 1972 Topps #1-525 for checklist and base card values.)

1973 O-Pee-Chee

The 1973 Canadian-issued O-Pee-Chee set numbers 660 cards and is identical in design and checklist (including only the later-printed "b" variations) to the 1973 Topps set. The backs of the OPC cards are written in both French and English and contain the line "Printed in Canada" along the bottom. The cards measure 2-1/2" x 3-1/2". Unlike the '73 Topps set, which was issued in series of increasing scarcity throughout the summer, the '73 OPC cards were issued in a single series, with cards #529-660 being somewhat short-printed. OPC star cards generally sell for more than the Topps version due to relative scarcity, while Expos players in OPC rate a similar premium due to increased "local" demand.

	NM	EX	VG
Complete Set (660):	500.00	250.00	150.00
Common Player (1-528):	.75	.35	.20
Common Player (529-660):	1.25	.60	.40
Stars: 1.5X Topps			
Wax Pack (10):	55.00		
Wax Box (36):	1,900		

(See 1973 Topps for checklist and base card values.)

1973 O-Pee-Chee Team Checklists

 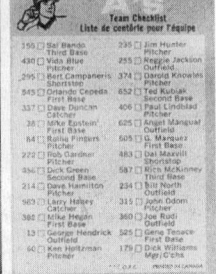

Similar to the 1973 Topps team checklist cards, this set was produced in Canada. The set consists of 24 unnumbered cards (2-1/2" x 3-1/2") with blue borders. The card fronts contain facsimile autographs of players from the same team. The backs contain team checklists of players found in the 1973 O-Pee-Chee regular issue set. The card backs contain the French

translation for Team Checklist plus a copyright line "O.P.C. Printed in Canada."

		NM	EX	VG
Complete Set (24):		40.00	20.00	12.00
Common Card:		3.00	1.50	.90
(1)	Atlanta Braves	3.00	1.50	.90
(2)	Baltimore Orioles	3.00	1.50	.90
(3)	Boston Red Sox	3.00	1.50	.90
(4)	California Angels	3.00	1.50	.90
(5)	Chicago Cubs	3.00	1.50	.90
(6)	Chicago White Sox	3.00	1.50	.90
(7)	Cincinnati Reds	4.00	2.00	1.25
(8)	Cleveland Indians	3.00	1.50	.90
(9)	Detroit Tigers	4.00	2.00	1.25
(10)	Houston Astros	3.00	1.50	.90
(11)	Kansas City Royals	3.00	1.50	.90
(12)	Los Angeles Dodgers	3.00	1.50	.90
(13)	Milwaukee Brewers	3.00	1.50	.90
(14)	Minnesota Twins	3.00	1.50	.90
(15)	Montreal Expos	6.00	3.00	1.75
(16)	New York Mets	4.00	2.00	1.25
(17)	New York Yankees	3.00	1.50	.90
(18)	Oakland A's	4.50	2.25	1.25
(19)	Philadelphia Phillies	3.00	1.50	.90
(20)	Pittsburgh Pirates	3.00	1.50	.90
(21)	St. Louis Cardinals	3.00	1.50	.90
(22)	San Diego Padres	3.00	1.50	.90
(23)	San Francisco Giants	3.00	1.50	.90
(24)	Texas Rangers	3.00	1.50	.90

1974 O-Pee-Chee

 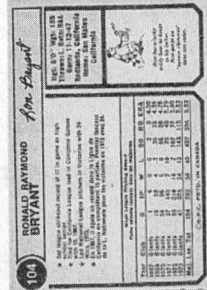

Again numbering 660 cards, the 1974 O-Pee-Chee set borrows its design and, except for 10 of the cards, shares its checklist with the Topps set of the same year. The cards measure the standard 2-1/2" x 3-1/2" and the backs are printed in both French and English and state "Printed in Canada." Because the OPC cards were printed later than Topps, there are no "Washington, Nat'l. League" variations in the Canadian set. Superstar cards and Expos players in OPC command a modest premium over the Topps version due to relative scarcity and increased local demand. Those OPC cards which differ from Topps are listed below, with the Topps version of each card number shown parenthetically.

		NM	EX	VG
Complete Set (660):		950.00	475.00	275.00
Common Player:		.50	.25	.15
Stars/Expos: 1.5X Topps				
Wax Pack (8):		65.00		
Wax Box (36):		2,150		
3	Aaron Special 1958-1959 (Aaron Special 1958-1961)	7.00	3.50	2.00
4	Aaron Special 1960-1961 (Aaron Special 1962-1965)	7.00	3.50	2.00
5	Aaron Special 1962-1963 (Aaron Special 1966-1969)	7.00	3.50	2.00
6	Aaron Special 1964-1965 (Aaron Special 1970-1973)	7.00	3.50	2.00
7	Aaron Special 1966-1967 (Jim Hunter)	7.00	3.50	2.00
8	Aaron Special 1968-1969 (George Theodore)	7.00	3.50	2.00
9	Aaron Special 1970-1973 (Mickey Lolich)	7.00	3.50	2.00
99	George Theodore (Brewers mgr./coaches)	1.50	.70	.45
166	Mickey Lolich (Royals mgr./coaches)	2.00	1.00	.60
196	Jim Hunter (Jim Fregosi)	7.50	3.75	2.25

(See 1974 Topps for checklist and base card values.)

1974 O-Pee-Chee Team Checklists

 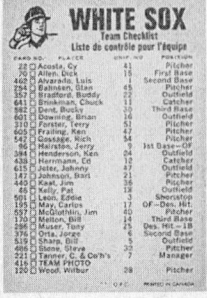

The 1974 O-Pee-Chee Team Checklists set is nearly identical to its Topps counterpart of the same year. Twenty-four unnumbered cards that measure 2-1/2" x 3-1/2" make up the set. The card fronts contain facsimile autographs while the backs carry a team checklist of players found in the regular issue O-Pee-Chee set of 1974. The cards have red borders and can be differentiated from the U.S. version by the "O.P.C. Printed in Canada" line on the back.

		NM	EX	VG
Complete Set (24):		25.00	12.50	7.50
Common Checklist:		1.50	.70	.40
(1)	Atlanta Braves	1.50	.70	.45
(2)	Baltimore Orioles	1.50	.70	.45
(3)	Boston Red Sox	1.50	.70	.45
(4)	California Angels	1.50	.70	.45
(5)	Chicago Cubs	1.50	.70	.45
(6)	Chicago White Sox	1.50	.70	.45
(7)	Cincinnati Reds	1.50	.70	.45
(8)	Cleveland Indians	1.50	.70	.45
(9)	Detroit Tigers	1.50	.70	.45
(10)	Houston Astros	1.50	.70	.45
(11)	Kansas City Royals	1.50	.70	.45
(12)	Los Angeles Dodgers	1.50	.70	.45
(13)	Milwaukee Brewers	1.50	.70	.45
(14)	Minnesota Twins	1.50	.70	.45
(15)	Montreal Expos	3.00	1.50	.90
(16)	New York Mets	1.50	.70	.45
(17)	New York Yankees	1.50	.70	.45
(18)	Oakland A's	1.50	.70	.45
(19)	Philadelphia Phillies	1.50	.70	.45
(20)	Pittsburgh Pirates	1.50	.70	.45
(21)	St. Louis Cardinals	1.50	.70	.45
(22)	San Diego Padres	1.50	.70	.45
(23)	San Francisco Giants	1.50	.70	.45
(24)	Texas Rangers	1.50	.70	.45

1975 O-Pee-Chee

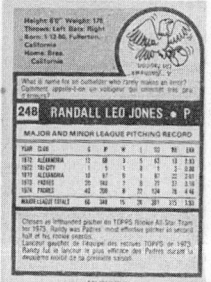

The 1975 O-Pee-Chee set was again complete at 660 cards, each measuring 2-1/2" x 3-1/2", and using the same design as the 1975 Topps set. The backs of the O-Pee-Chee cards are written in both French and English and state that the cards were printed in Canada. The checklist for OPC and Topps are identical in '75. Because they are relatively scarcer, OPC superstars sell for a premium over Topps. Expos players also enjoy a premium due to increased local demand.

	NM	EX	VG
Complete Set (660):	625.00	325.00	200.00
Common Player:	.45	.25	.15
Stars: 2X Topps			
Expos: 1.5X Topps			
Wax Pack (8):	30.00		
Wax Box (48):	1,200		
(See 1975 Topps for checklist and base card values.)			

1976 O-Pee-Chee

Identical in design to, and sharing a checklist with, the 1976 Topps set, the Canadian-issued 1976 O-Pee-Chees comprise 660 cards, each 2-1/2" x 3-1/2". The backs are printed in both French and English and state "Ptd. in Canada." Stars and Expos players enjoy a modest premium over the Topps versions due to relative scarcity and increased local demand.

	NM	EX	VG
Complete Set (660):	700.00	350.00	210.00
Common Player:	.20	.10	.05
Stars/Expos 2X Topps			

	NM	EX	VG
Wax Pack (8):	30.00		
Wax Box (48):	750.00		
(See 1976 Topps for checklist and base card values.)			

1977 O-Pee-Chee

The 1977 O-Pee-Chee set represents a change in philosophy for the Canadian company. The design of the set is still identical to the Topps set of the same year, but the number of cards was reduced to 264 with more emphasis on players from the two Canadian teams. The backs are printed in both French and English and state "O-Pee-Chee Printed in Canada." About 1/3 of the photos in the OPC set differ from the corresponding Topps cards either with entirely different photos, airbrushed uniform changes, the removal of All-Star and Rookie Team designations, or significant photo cropping variations. Cards measure the standard 2-1/2" x 3-1/2".

		NM	EX	VG
Complete Set (264):		125.00	65.00	40.00
Common Player:		.25	.13	.08
Wax Pack (8):		12.00		
Wax Box (48):		285.00		
1	Batting Leaders (George Brett, Bill Madlock)	4.00	2.00	1.25
2	Home Run Leaders (Graig Nettles, Mike Schmidt)	2.75	1.50	.80
3	Runs Batted In Leaders (George Foster, Lee May)	.25	.13	.08
4	Stolen Base Leaders (Dave Lopes, Bill North)	.25	.13	.08
5	Victory Leaders (Randy Jones, Jim Palmer)	1.00	.50	.30
6	Strikeout Leaders (Nolan Ryan, Tom Seaver)	12.50	6.25	3.75
7	Earned Run Avg. Leaders (John Denny, Mark Fidrych)	.25	.13	.08
8	Leading Firemen (Bill Campbell, Rawly Eastwick)	.25	.13	.08
9	Mike Jorgensen	.25	.13	.08
10	Jim Hunter	4.00	2.00	1.25
11	Ken Griffey	.25	.13	.08
12	Bill Campbell	.25	.13	.08
13	Otto Velez	.25	.13	.08
14	Milt May	.25	.13	.08
15	Dennis Eckersley	4.00	2.00	1.25
16	John Mayberry	.25	.13	.08
17	Larry Bowa	.25	.13	.08
18	Don Carrithers	.25	.13	.08
19	Ken Singleton	.25	.13	.08
20	Bill Stein	.25	.13	.08
21	Ken Brett	.25	.13	.08
22	Gary Woods	.25	.13	.08
23	Steve Swisher	.25	.13	.08
24	Don Sutton	4.00	2.00	1.25
25	Willie Stargell	4.00	2.00	1.25
26	Jerry Koosman	.25	.13	.08
27	Del Unser	.25	.13	.08
28	Bob Grich	.25	.13	.08
29	Jim Slaton	.25	.13	.08
30	Thurman Munson	4.00	2.00	1.25
31	Dan Driessen	.25	.13	.08
32	Tom Bruno (Not in Topps.)	.25	.13	.08
33	Larry Hisle	.25	.13	.08
34	Phil Garner	.25	.13	.08
35	Mike Hargrove	.25	.13	.08
36	Jackie Brown	.25	.13	.08
37	Carl Yastrzemski	7.50	3.75	2.25
38	Dave Roberts	.25	.13	.08
39	Ray Fosse	.25	.13	.08
40	Dave McKay	.25	.13	.08
41	Paul Splittorff	.25	.13	.08
42	Garry Maddox	.25	.13	.08
43	Phil Niekro	4.00	2.00	1.25
44	Roger Metzger	.25	.13	.08
45	Gary Carter	7.50	3.75	2.25
46	Jim Spencer	.25	.13	.08
47	Ross Grimsley	.25	.13	.08
48	Bob Bailor	.25	.13	.08
49	Chris Chambliss	.25	.13	.08
50	Will McEnaney	.25	.13	.08
51	Lou Brock	4.50	2.25	1.25
52	Rollie Fingers	4.00	2.00	1.25
53	Chris Speier	.25	.13	.08
54	Bombo Rivera	.25	.13	.08
55	Pete Broberg	.25	.13	.08
56	Bill Madlock	.25	.13	.08
57	Rick Rhoden	.25	.13	.08
58	Blue Jay Coaches (Don Leppert, Bob Miller, Jackie Moore, Harry Warner)	.50	.25	.15
59	John Candelaria	.25	.13	.08
60	Ed Kranepool	.25	.13	.08
61	Dave LaRoche	.25	.13	.08

62	Jim Rice	.75	.40	.25
63	Don Stanhouse	.25	.13	.08
64	Jason Thompson	.25	.13	.08
65	Nolan Ryan	25.00	12.50	7.50
66	Tom Poquette	.25	.13	.08
67	Leon Hooten	.25	.13	.08
68	Bob Boone	.25	.13	.08
69	Mickey Rivers	.25	.13	.08
70	Gary Nolan	.25	.13	.08
71	Sixto Lezcano	.25	.13	.08
72	Larry Parrish	.25	.13	.08
73	Dave Goltz	.25	.13	.08
74	Bert Campaneris	.25	.13	.08
75	Vida Blue	.25	.13	.08
76	Rick Cerone	.25	.13	.08
77	Ralph Garr	.25	.13	.08
78	Ken Forsch	.25	.13	.08
79	Willie Montanez	.25	.13	.08
80	Jim Palmer	4.50	2.25	1.25
81	Jerry White	.25	.13	.08
82	Gene Tenace	.25	.13	.08
83	Bobby Murcer	.25	.13	.08
84	Garry Templeton	.25	.13	.08
85	Bill Singer	.25	.13	.08
86	Buddy Bell	.25	.13	.08
87	Luis Tiant	.25	.13	.08
88	Rusty Staub	.25	.13	.08
89	Sparky Lyle	.25	.13	.08
90	Jose Morales	.25	.13	.08
91	Dennis Leonard	.25	.13	.08
92	Tommy Smith	.25	.13	.08
93	Steve Carlton	5.50	2.75	1.75
94	John Scott	.25	.13	.08
95	Bill Bonham	.25	.13	.08
96	Dave Lopes	.25	.13	.08
97	Jerry Reuss	.25	.13	.08
98	Dave Kingman	.35	.20	.11
99	Dan Warthen	.25	.13	.08
100	Johnny Bench	7.50	3.75	2.25
101	Bert Blyleven	.25	.13	.08
102	Cecil Cooper	.25	.13	.08
103	Mike Willis	.25	.13	.08
104	Dan Ford	.25	.13	.08
105	Frank Tanana	.25	.13	.08
106	Bill North	.25	.13	.08
107	Joe Ferguson	.25	.13	.08
108	Dick Williams	.25	.13	.08
109	John Denny	.25	.13	.08
110	Willie Randolph	.25	.13	.08
111	Reggie Cleveland	.25	.13	.08
112	Doug Howard	.25	.13	.08
113	Randy Jones	.25	.13	.08
114	Rico Carty	.25	.13	.08
115	Mark Fidrych	2.75	1.50	.80
116	Darrell Porter	.25	.13	.08
117	Wayne Garrett	.25	.13	.08
118	Greg Luzinski	.25	.13	.08
119	Jim Barr	.25	.13	.08
120	George Foster	.25	.13	.08
121	Phil Roof	.25	.13	.08
122	Bucky Dent	.25	.13	.08
123	Steve Braun	.25	.13	.08
124	Checklist 1-132	.40	.20	.12
125	Lee May	.25	.13	.08
126	Woodie Fryman	.25	.13	.08
127	Jose Cardenal	.25	.13	.08
128	Doug Rau	.25	.13	.08
129	Rennie Stennett	.25	.13	.08
130	Pete Vuckovich	.25	.13	.08
131	Cesar Cedeno	.25	.13	.08
132	Jon Matlack	.25	.13	.08
133	Don Baylor	.30	.15	.09
134	Darrel Chaney	.25	.13	.08
135	Tony Perez	4.00	2.00	1.25
136	Aurelio Rodriguez	.25	.13	.08
137	Carlton Fisk	4.00	2.00	1.25
138	Wayne Garland	.25	.13	.08
139	Dave Hilton	.25	.13	.08
140	Rawly Eastwick	.25	.13	.08
141	Amos Otis	.25	.13	.08
142	Tug McGraw	.25	.13	.08
143	Rod Carew	5.50	2.75	1.75
144	Mike Torrez	.25	.13	.08
145	Sal Bando	.25	.13	.08
146	Dock Ellis	.25	.13	.08
147	Jose Cruz	.25	.13	.08
148	Alan Ashby	.25	.13	.08
149	Gaylord Perry	4.00	2.00	1.25
150	Keith Hernandez	.25	.13	.08
151	Dave Pagan	.25	.13	.08
152	Richie Zisk	.25	.13	.08
153	Steve Rogers	.25	.13	.08
154	Mark Belanger	.25	.13	.08
155	Andy Messersmith	.25	.13	.08
156	Dave Winfield	6.00	3.00	1.75
157	Chuck Hartenstein	.25	.13	.08
158	Manny Trillo	.25	.13	.08
159	Steve Yeager	.25	.13	.08
160	Cesar Geronimo	.25	.13	.08
161	Jim Rooker	.25	.13	.08
162	Tim Foli	.25	.13	.08
163	Fred Lynn	.25	.13	.08
164	Ed Figueroa	.25	.13	.08
165	Johnny Grubb	.25	.13	.08
166	Pedro Garcia	.25	.13	.08
167	Ron LeFlore	.25	.13	.08
168	Rich Hebner	.25	.13	.08
169	Larry Herndon	.25	.13	.08
170	George Brett	15.00	7.50	4.50
171	Joe Kerrigan	.25	.13	.08
172	Bud Harrelson	.25	.13	.08
173	Bobby Bonds	.25	.13	.08
174	Bill Travers	.25	.13	.08
175	John Lowenstein	.25	.13	.08
176	Butch Wynegar	.25	.13	.08
177	Pete Falcone	.25	.13	.08
178	Claudell Washington	.25	.13	.08
179	Checklist 133-264	.40	.20	.12

		NM	EX	VG
180	Dave Cash	.25	.13	.08
181	Fred Norman	.25	.13	.08
182	Roy White	.25	.13	.08
183	Marty Perez	.25	.13	.08
184	Jesse Jefferson	.25	.13	.08
185	Jim Sundberg	.25	.13	.08
186	Dan Meyer	.25	.13	.08
187	Fergie Jenkins	6.00	3.00	1.75
188	Tom Veryzer	.25	.13	.08
189	Dennis Blair	.25	.13	.08
190	Rick Manning	.25	.13	.08
191	Doug Bird	.25	.13	.08
192	Al Bumbry	.25	.13	.08
193	Dave Roberts	.25	.13	.08
194	Larry Christenson	.25	.13	.08
195	Chet Lemon	.25	.13	.08
196	Ted Simmons	.25	.13	.08
197	Ray Burris	.25	.13	.08
198	Expos Coaches (Jim Brewer, Billy Gardner, Mickey Vernon, Ozzie Virgil)	.25	.13	.08
199	Ron Cey	.25	.13	.08
200	Reggie Jackson	12.50	6.25	3.75
201	Pat Zachry	.25	.13	.08
202	Doug Ault	.25	.13	.08
203	Al Oliver	.25	.13	.08
204	Robin Yount	5.50	2.75	1.75
205	Tom Seaver	7.50	3.75	2.25
206	Joe Rudi	.25	.13	.08
207	Barry Foote	.25	.13	.08
208	Toby Harrah	.25	.13	.08
209	Jeff Burroughs	.25	.13	.08
210	George Scott	.25	.13	.08
211	Jim Mason	.25	.13	.08
212	Vern Ruhle	.25	.13	.08
213	Fred Kendall	.25	.13	.08
214	Rick Reuschel	.25	.13	.08
215	Hal McRae	.25	.13	.08
216	Chip Lang	.25	.13	.08
217	Graig Nettles	.30	.15	.09
218	George Hendrick	.25	.13	.08
219	Glenn Abbott	.25	.13	.08
220	Joe Morgan	4.50	2.25	1.25
221	Sam Ewing	.25	.13	.08
222	George Medich	.25	.13	.08
223	Reggie Smith	.25	.13	.08
224	Dave Hamilton	.25	.13	.08
225	Pepe Frias	.25	.13	.08
226	Jay Johnstone	.25	.13	.08
227	J.R. Richard	.25	.13	.08
228	Doug DeCinces	.25	.13	.08
229	Dave Lemanczyk	.25	.13	.08
230	Rick Monday	.25	.13	.08
231	Manny Sanguillen	.25	.13	.08
232	John Montefusco	.25	.13	.08
233	Duane Kuiper	.25	.13	.08
234	Ellis Valentine	.25	.13	.08
235	Dick Tidrow	.25	.13	.08
236	Ben Oglivie	.25	.13	.08
237	Rick Burleson	.25	.13	.08
238	Roy Hartsfield	.25	.13	.08
239	Lyman Bostock	.25	.13	.08
240	Pete Rose	13.50	6.75	4.00
241	Mike Ivie	.25	.13	.08
242	Dave Parker	.35	.20	.11
243	Bill Greif	.25	.13	.08
244	Freddie Patek	.25	.13	.08
245	Mike Schmidt	15.00	7.50	4.50
246	Brian Downing	.25	.13	.08
247	Steve Hargan	.25	.13	.08
248	Dave Collins	.25	.13	.08
249	Felix Millan	.25	.13	.08
250	Don Gullett	.25	.13	.08
251	Jerry Royster	.25	.13	.08
252	Earl Williams	.25	.13	.08
253	Frank Duffy	.25	.13	.08
254	Tippy Martinez	.25	.13	.08
255	Steve Garvey	2.75	1.50	.80
256	Alvis Woods	.25	.13	.08
257	John Hiller	.25	.13	.08
258	Dave Concepcion	.25	.13	.08
259	Dwight Evans	.25	.13	.08
260	Pete MacKanin	.25	.13	.08
261	George Brett (Record Breaker)	5.00	2.50	1.50
262	Minnie Minoso (Record Breaker)	.25	.13	.08
263	Jose Morales (Record Breaker)	.25	.13	.08
264	Nolan Ryan (Record Breaker)	12.50	6.25	3.75

1978 O-Pee-Chee

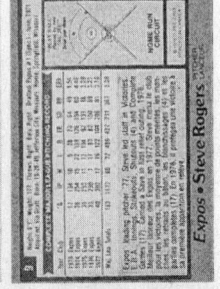

STEVE ROGERS

The 1978 O-Pee-Chee set was further reduced to 242 cards and again had heavy representation from the two Canadian teams. The cards measure the stan-dard 2-1/2" x 3-1/2" and the backs are printed in both French and English. The cards use the same design as the 1978 Topps set. Some of the cards contain an extra line on the front indicating a team change.

		NM	EX	VG
	Complete Set (242):	120.00	60.00	35.00
	Common Player:	.25	.13	.08
	Wax Pack (10):	8.00		
	Wax Box (36):	200.00		
1	Batting Leaders (Rod Carew, Dave Parker)	.75	.40	.25
2	Home Run Leaders (George Foster, Jim Rice)	.25	.13	.08
3	Runs Batted In Leaders (George Foster, Larry Hisle)	.25	.13	.08
4	Stolen Base Leaders (Freddie Patek, Frank Taveras)	.25	.13	.08
5	Victory Leaders (Steve Carlton, Dave Goltz, Dennis Leonard, Jim Palmer)	.45	.25	.14
6	Strikeout Leaders (Phil Niekro, Nolan Ryan)	1.50	.70	.45
7	Earned Run Avg. Ldrs. (John Candelaria, Frank Tanana)	.25	.13	.08
8	Leading Firemen (Bill Campbell, Rollie Fingers)	.45	.25	.14
9	Steve Rogers	.25	.13	.08
10	Graig Nettles	.25	.13	.08
11	Doug Capilla	.25	.13	.08
12	George Scott	.25	.13	.08
13	Gary Woods	.25	.13	.08
14	Tom Veryzer	.25	.13	.08
15	Wayne Garland	.25	.13	.08
16	Amos Otis	.25	.13	.08
17	Larry Christenson	.25	.13	.08
18	Dave Cash	.25	.13	.08
19	Jim Barr	.25	.13	.08
20	Ruppert Jones	.25	.13	.08
21	Eric Soderholm	.25	.13	.08
22	Jesse Jefferson	.25	.13	.08
23	Jerry Morales	.25	.13	.08
24	Doug Rau	.25	.13	.08
25	Rennie Stennett	.25	.13	.08
26	Lee Mazzilli	.25	.13	.08
27	Dick Williams	.25	.13	.08
28	Joe Rudi	.25	.13	.08
29	Robin Yount	2.00	1.00	.60
30	Don Gullett	.25	.13	.08
31	Roy Howell	.25	.13	.08
32	Cesar Geronimo	.25	.13	.08
33	Rick Langford	.25	.13	.08
34	Dan Ford	.25	.13	.08
35	Gene Tenace	.25	.13	.08
36	Santo Alcala	.25	.13	.08
37	Rick Burleson	.25	.13	.08
38	Dave Rozema	.25	.13	.08
39	Duane Kulper	.25	.13	.08
40	Ron Fairly	.25	.13	.08
41	Dennis Leonard	.25	.13	.08
42	Greg Luzinski	.25	.13	.08
43	Willie Montanez	.25	.13	.08
44	Enos Cabell	.25	.13	.08
45	Ellis Valentine	.25	.13	.08
46	Steve Stone	.25	.13	.08
47	Lee May	.25	.13	.08
48	Roy White	.25	.13	.08
49	Jerry Garvin	.25	.13	.08
50	Johnny Bench	2.00	1.00	.60
51	Garry Templeton	.25	.13	.08
52	Doyle Alexander	.25	.13	.08
53	Steve Henderson	.25	.13	.08
54	Stan Bahnsen	.25	.13	.08
55	Dan Meyer	.25	.13	.08
56	Rick Reuschel	.25	.13	.08
57	Reggie Smith	.25	.13	.08
58	Blue Jays Team	.50	.25	.15
59	John Montefusco	.25	.13	.08
60	Dave Parker	.25	.13	.08
61	Jim Bibby	.25	.13	.08
62	Fred Lynn	.25	.13	.08
63	Jose Morales	.25	.13	.08
64	Aurelio Rodriguez	.25	.13	.08
65	Frank Tanana	.25	.13	.08
66	Darrell Porter	.25	.13	.08
67	Otto Velez	.25	.13	.08
68	Larry Bowa	.25	.13	.08
69	Jim Hunter	1.50	.70	.45
70	George Foster	.25	.13	.08
71	Cecil Cooper	.25	.13	.08
72	Gary Alexander	.25	.13	.08
73	Paul Thormodsgard	.25	.13	.08
74	Toby Harrah	.25	.13	.08
75	Mitchell Page	.25	.13	.08
76	Alan Ashby	.25	.13	.08
77	Jorge Orta	.25	.13	.08
78	Dave Winfield	3.00	1.50	.90
79	Andy Messersmith	.25	.13	.08
80	Ken Singleton	.25	.13	.08
81	Will McEnaney	.25	.13	.08
82	Lou Piniella	.25	.13	.08
83	Bob Forsch	.25	.13	.08
84	Dan Driessen	.25	.13	.08
85	Dave Lemanczyk	.25	.13	.08
86	Paul Dade	.25	.13	.08
87	Bill Campbell	.25	.13	.08
88	Ron LeFlore	.25	.13	.08
89	Bill Madlock	.25	.13	.08
90	Tony Perez	.25	.13	.08
91	Freddie Patek	.25	.13	.08
92	Glenn Abbott	.25	.13	.08
93	Garry Maddox	.25	.13	.08
94	Steve Staggs	.25	.13	.08
95	Bobby Murcer	.25	.13	.08
96	Don Sutton	1.50	.70	.45
97	Al Oliver	.25	.13	.08
98	Jon Matlack	.25	.13	.08
99	Sam Mejias	.25	.13	.08
100	Pete Rose	6.00	3.00	1.75
101	Randy Jones	.25	.13	.08
102	Sixto Lezcano	.25	.13	.08
103	Jim Clancy	.25	.13	.08
104	Butch Wynegar	.25	.13	.08
105	Nolan Ryan	15.00	7.50	4.50
106	Wayne Gross	.25	.13	.08
107	Bob Watson	.25	.13	.08
108	Joe Kerrigan	.25	.13	.08
109	Keith Hernandez	.25	.13	.08
110	Reggie Jackson	5.00	2.50	1.50
111	Denny Doyle	.25	.13	.08
112	Sam Ewing	.25	.13	.08
113	Bert Blyleven	.25	.13	.08
114	Andre Thornton	.25	.13	.08
115	Milt May	.25	.13	.08
116	Jim Colborn	.25	.13	.08
117	Warren Cromartie	.25	.13	.08
118	Ted Sizemore	.25	.13	.08
119	Checklist 1-121	.35	.20	.11
120	Tom Seaver	2.50	1.25	.70
121	Luis Gomez	.25	.13	.08
122	Jim Spencer	.25	.13	.08
123	Leroy Stanton	.25	.13	.08
124	Luis Tiant	.25	.13	.08
125	Mark Belanger	.25	.13	.08
126	Jackie Brown	.25	.13	.08
127	Bill Buckner	.25	.13	.08
128	Bill Robinson	.25	.13	.08
129	Rick Cerone	.25	.13	.08
130	Ron Cey	.25	.13	.08
131	Jose Cruz	.25	.13	.08
132	Len Randle	.25	.13	.08
133	Bob Grich	.25	.13	.08
134	Jeff Burroughs	.25	.13	.08
135	Gary Carter	6.00	3.00	1.75
136	Milt Wilcox	.25	.13	.08
137	Carl Yastrzemski	2.50	1.25	.70
138	Dennis Eckersley	1.50	.70	.45
139	Tim Nordbrook	.25	.13	.08
140	Ken Griffey	.25	.13	.08
141	Bob Boone	.25	.13	.08
142	Dave Goltz	.25	.13	.08
143	Al Cowens	.25	.13	.08
144	Bill Atkinson	.25	.13	.08
145	Chris Chambliss	.25	.13	.08
146	Jim Slaton	.25	.13	.08
147	Bill Stein	.25	.13	.08
148	Bob Bailor	.25	.13	.08
149	J.R. Richard	.25	.13	.08
150	Ted Simmons	.25	.13	.08
151	Rick Manning	.25	.13	.08
152	Lerrin LaGrow	.25	.13	.08
153	Larry Parrish	.25	.13	.08
154	Eddie Murray	15.00	7.50	4.50
155	Phil Niekro	1.50	.70	.45
156	Bake McBride	.25	.13	.08
157	Pete Vuckovich	.25	.13	.08
158	Ivan DeJesus	.25	.13	.08
159	Rick Rhoden	.25	.13	.08
160	Joe Morgan	2.00	1.00	.60
161	Ed Ott	.25	.13	.08
162	Don Stanhouse	.25	.13	.08
163	Jim Rice	.50	.25	.15
164	Bucky Dent	.25	.13	.08
165	Jim Kern	.25	.13	.08
166	Doug Rader	.25	.13	.08
167	Steve Kemp	.25	.13	.08
168	John Mayberry	.25	.13	.08
169	Tim Foli	.25	.13	.08
170	Steve Carlton	2.00	1.00	.60
171	Pepe Frias	.25	.13	.08
172	Pat Zachry	.25	.13	.08
173	Don Baylor	.25	.13	.08
174	Sal Bando	.25	.13	.08
175	Alvis Woods	.25	.13	.08
176	Mike Hargrove	.25	.13	.08
177	Vida Blue	.25	.13	.08
178	George Hendrick	.25	.13	.08
179	Jim Palmer	2.00	1.00	.60
180	Andre Dawson	10.00	5.00	3.00
181	Paul Moskau	.25	.13	.08
182	Mickey Rivers	.25	.13	.08
183	Checklist 122-242	.35	.20	.11
184	Jerry Johnson	.25	.13	.08
185	Willie McCovey	2.00	1.00	.60
186	Enrique Romo	.25	.13	.08
187	Butch Hobson	.25	.13	.08
188	Rusty Staub	.45	.25	.14
189	Wayne Twitchell	.25	.13	.08
190	Steve Garvey	1.00	.50	.30
191	Rick Waits	.25	.13	.08
192	Doug DeCinces	.25	.13	.08
193	Tom Murphy	.25	.13	.08
194	Rich Hebner	.25	.13	.08
195	Ralph Garr	.25	.13	.08
196	Bruce Sutter	1.50	.70	.45
197	Tom Poquette	.25	.13	.08
198	Wayne Garrett	.25	.13	.08
199	Pedro Borbon	.25	.13	.08
200	Thurman Munson	2.00	1.00	.60
201	Rollie Fingers	1.50	.70	.45
202	Doug Ault	.25	.13	.08
203	Phil Garner	.25	.13	.08
204	Lou Brock	2.00	1.00	.60
205	Ed Kranepool	.25	.13	.08
206	Bobby Bonds	.25	.13	.08
207	Expos Team	.25	.13	.08
208	Bump Wills	.25	.13	.08
209	Gary Matthews	.25	.13	.08
210	Carlton Fisk	2.00	1.00	.60
211	Jeff Byrd	.25	.13	.08
212	Jason Thompson	.25	.13	.08
213	Larvell Blanks	.25	.13	.08
214	Sparky Lyle	.25	.13	.08
215	George Brett	6.00	3.00	1.75
216	Del Unser	.25	.13	.08

217	Manny Trillo	.25	.13	.08
218	Roy Hartsfield	.25	.13	.08
219	Carlos Lopez	.25	.13	.08
220	Dave Concepcion	.25	.13	.08
221	John Candelaria	.25	.13	.08
222	Dave Lopes	.25	.13	.08
223	Tim Blackwell	.25	.13	.08
224	Chet Lemon	.25	.13	.08
225	Mike Schmidt	6.00	3.00	1.75
226	Cesar Cedeno	.25	.13	.08
227	Mike Willis	.25	.13	.08
228	Willie Randolph	.25	.13	.08
229	Doug Bair	.25	.13	.08
230	Rod Carew	2.00	1.00	.60
231	Mike Flanagan	.25	.13	.08
232	Chris Speier	.25	.13	.08
233	Don Aase	.25	.13	.08
234	Buddy Bell	.25	.13	.08
235	Mark Fidrych	.30	.15	.09
236	Lou Brock (Record Breaker)	.75	.40	.25
237	Sparky Lyle (Record Breaker)	.25	.13	.08
238	Willie McCovey (Record Breaker)	.45	.25	.14
239	Brooks Robinson (Record Breaker)	.90	.45	.25
240	Pete Rose (Record Breaker)	2.00	1.00	.60
241	Nolan Ryan (Record Breaker)	10.00	5.00	3.00
242	Reggie Jackson (Record Breaker)	1.50	.70	.45

1979 O-Pee-Chee

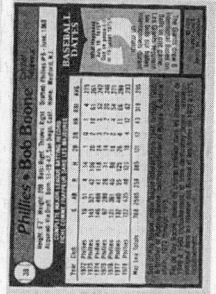

The 1979 O-Pee-Chee cards are nearly identical in design to the Topps set of the same year, but display the O-Pee-Chee logo inside the baseball in the lower-left corner of the front. The number of cards in the set was increased to 374, each measuring 2-1/2" x 3-1/2".

		NM	EX	VG
	Complete Set (374):	80.00	40.00	24.00
	Common Player:	.25	.13	.08
	Wax Pack (10):	10.00		
	Wax Box (36):	175.00		
1	Lee May	.25	.13	.08
2	Dick Drago	.25	.13	.08
3	Paul Dade	.25	.13	.08
4	Ross Grimsley	.25	.13	.08
5	Joe Morgan	2.00	1.00	.60
6	Kevin Kobel	.25	.13	.08
7	Terry Forster	.25	.13	.08
8	Paul Molitor	12.00	6.00	3.50
9	Steve Carlton	2.00	1.00	.60
10	Dave Goltz	.25	.13	.08
11	Dave Winfield	3.00	1.50	.90
12	Dave Rozema	.25	.13	.08
13	Ed Figueroa	.25	.13	.08
14	Alan Ashby	.25	.13	.08
15	Dale Murphy	2.50	1.25	.70
16	Dennis Eckersley	1.50	.70	.45
17	Ron Blomberg	.25	.13	.08
18	Wayne Twitchell	.25	.13	.08
19	Al Hrabosky	.25	.13	.08
20	Fred Norman	.25	.13	.08
21	Steve Garvey	1.00	.50	.30
22	Willie Stargell	2.00	1.00	.60
23	John Hale	.25	.13	.08
24	Mickey Rivers	.25	.13	.08
25	Jack Brohamer	.25	.13	.08
26	Tom Underwood	.25	.13	.08
27	Mark Belanger	.25	.13	.08
28	Elliott Maddox	.25	.13	.08
29	John Candelaria	.25	.13	.08
30	Shane Rawley	.25	.13	.08
31	Steve Yeager	.25	.13	.08
32	Warren Cromartie	.25	.13	.08
33	Jason Thompson	.25	.13	.08
34	Roger Erickson	.25	.13	.08
35	Gary Matthews	.25	.13	.08
36	Pete Falcone	.25	.13	.08
37	Dick Tidrow	.25	.13	.08
38	Bob Boone	.25	.13	.08
39	Jim Bibby	.25	.13	.08
40	Len Barker	.25	.13	.08
41	Robin Yount	2.00	1.00	.60
42	Sam Mejias	.25	.13	.08
43	Ray Burris	.25	.13	.08
44	Tom Seaver	2.50	1.25	.70
45	Roy Howell	.25	.13	.08
46	Jim Todd	.25	.13	.08
47	Frank Duffy	.25	.13	.08
48	Joel Youngblood	.25	.13	.08
49	Vida Blue	.25	.13	.08
50	Cliff Johnson	.25	.13	.08
51	Nolan Ryan	15.00	7.50	4.50
52	Ozzie Smith	20.00	10.00	6.00

53	Jim Sundberg	.25	.13	.08
54	Mike Paxton	.25	.13	.08
55	Lou Whitaker	1.00	.50	.30
56	Dan Schatzeder	.25	.13	.08
57	Rick Burleson	.25	.13	.08
58	Doug Bair	.25	.13	.08
59	Ted Martinez	.25	.13	.08
60	Bob Watson	.25	.13	.08
61	Jim Clancy	.25	.13	.08
62	Rowland Office	.25	.13	.08
63	Bobby Murcer	.25	.13	.08
64	Don Gullett	.25	.13	.08
65	Tom Paciorek	.25	.13	.08
66	Rick Rhoden	.25	.13	.08
67	Duane Kuiper	.25	.13	.08
68	Bruce Boisclair	.25	.13	.08
69	Manny Sarmiento	.25	.13	.08
70	Wayne Cage	.25	.13	.08
71	John Hiller	.25	.13	.08
72	Rick Cerone	.25	.13	.08
73	Dwight Evans	.25	.13	.08
74	Buddy Solomon	.25	.13	.08
75	Roy White	.25	.13	.08
76	Mike Flanagan	.25	.13	.08
77	Tom Johnson	.25	.13	.08
78	Glenn Burke	.25	.13	.08
79	Frank Taveras	.25	.13	.08
80	Don Sutton	1.50	.70	.45
81	Leon Roberts	.25	.13	.08
82	George Hendrick	.25	.13	.08
83	Aurelio Rodriguez	.25	.13	.08
84	Ron Reed	.25	.13	.08
85	Alvis Woods	.25	.13	.08
86	Jim Beattie	.25	.13	.08
87	Larry Hisle	.25	.13	.08
88	Mike Garman	.25	.13	.08
89	Tim Johnson	.25	.13	.08
90	Paul Splittorff	.25	.13	.08
91	Darrel Chaney	.25	.13	.08
92	Mike Torrez	.25	.13	.08
93	Eric Soderholm	.25	.13	.08
94	Ron Cey	.25	.13	.08
95	Randy Jones	.25	.13	.08
96	Bill Madlock	.25	.13	.08
97	Steve Kemp	.25	.13	.08
98	Bob Apodaca	.25	.13	.08
99	Johnny Grubb	.25	.13	.08
100	Larry Milbourne	.25	.13	.08
101	Johnny Bench	2.00	1.00	.60
102	Dave Lemanczyk	.25	.13	.08
103	Reggie Cleveland	.25	.13	.08
104	Larry Bowa	.25	.13	.08
105	Denny Martinez	1.00	.50	.30
106	Bill Travers	.25	.13	.08
107	Willie McCovey	2.00	1.00	.60
108	Wilbur Wood	.25	.13	.08
109	Dennis Leonard	.25	.13	.08
110	Roy Smalley	.25	.13	.08
111	Cesar Geronimo	.25	.13	.08
112	Jesse Jefferson	.25	.13	.08
113	Dave Revering	.25	.13	.08
114	Rich Gossage	.30	.15	.09
115	Steve Stone	.25	.13	.08
116	Doug Flynn	.25	.13	.08
117	Bob Forsch	.25	.13	.08
118	Paul Mitchell	.25	.13	.08
119	Toby Harrah	.25	.13	.08
120	Steve Rogers	.25	.13	.08
121	Checklist 1-125	.25	.13	.08
122	Balor Moore	.25	.13	.08
123	Rick Reuschel	.25	.13	.08
124	Jeff Burroughs	.25	.13	.08
125	Willie Randolph	.25	.13	.08
126	Bob Stinson	.25	.13	.08
127	Rick Wise	.25	.13	.08
128	Luis Gomez	.25	.13	.08
129	Tommy John	.25	.13	.08
130	Richie Zisk	.25	.13	.08
131	Mario Guerrero	.25	.13	.08
132	Oscar Gamble	.25	.13	.08
133	Don Money	.25	.13	.08
134	Joe Rudi	.25	.13	.08
135	Woodie Fryman	.25	.13	.08
136	Butch Hobson	.25	.13	.08
137	Jim Colborn	.25	.13	.08
138	Tom Grieve	.25	.13	.08
139	Andy Messersmith	.25	.13	.08
140	Andre Thornton	.25	.13	.08
141	Kevin Kravec	.25	.13	.08
142	Bobby Bonds	.25	.13	.08
143	Jose Cruz	.25	.13	.08
144	Dave Lopes	.25	.13	.08
145	Jerry Garvin	.25	.13	.08
146	Pepe Frias	.25	.13	.08
147	Mitchell Page	.25	.13	.08
148	Ted Sizemore	.25	.13	.08
149	Rich Gale	.25	.13	.08
150	Steve Ontiveros	.25	.13	.08
151	Rod Carew	2.00	1.00	.60
152	Lary Sorensen	.25	.13	.08
153	Willie Montanez	.25	.13	.08
154	Floyd Bannister	.25	.13	.08
155	Bert Blyleven	.25	.13	.08
156	Ralph Garr	.25	.13	.08
157	Thurman Munson	1.00	.50	.30
158	Bob Robertson	.25	.13	.08
159	Jon Matlack	.25	.13	.08
160	Carl Yastrzemski	2.50	1.25	.70
161	Gaylord Perry	1.50	.70	.45
162	Mike Tyson	.25	.13	.08
163	Cecil Cooper	.25	.13	.08
164	Pedro Borbon	.25	.13	.08
165	Art Howe	.25	.13	.08
166	Joe Coleman	.25	.13	.08
167	George Brett	6.00	3.00	1.75
168	Gary Alexander	.25	.13	.08
169	Chet Lemon	.25	.13	.08
170	Craig Swan	.25	.13	.08

171	Chris Chambliss	.25	.13	.08
172	John Montague	.25	.13	.08
173	Ron Jackson	.25	.13	.08
174	Jim Palmer	2.00	1.00	.60
175	Willie Upshaw	.75	.40	.25
176	Tug McGraw	.25	.13	.08
177	Bill Buckner	.25	.13	.08
178	Doug Rau	.25	.13	.08
179	Andre Dawson	3.50	1.75	1.00
180	Jim Wright	.25	.13	.08
181	Garry Templeton	.25	.13	.08
182	Bill Bonham	.25	.13	.08
183	Lee Mazzilli	.25	.13	.08
184	Alan Trammell	2.00	1.00	.60
185	Amos Otis	.25	.13	.08
186	Tom Dixon	.25	.13	.08
187	Mike Cubbage	.25	.13	.08
188	Sparky Lyle	.25	.13	.08
189	Juan Bernhardt	.25	.13	.08
190	Bump Wills	.25	.13	.08
191	Dave Kingman	.25	.13	.08
192	Lamar Johnson	.25	.13	.08
193	Lance Rautzhan	.25	.13	.08
194	Ed Herrmann	.25	.13	.08
195	Bill Campbell	.25	.13	.08
196	Gorman Thomas	.25	.13	.08
197	Paul Moskau	.25	.13	.08
198	Dale Murray	.25	.13	.08
199	John Mayberry	.25	.13	.08
200	Phil Garner	.25	.13	.08
201	Dan Ford	.25	.13	.08
202	Gary Thomasson	.25	.13	.08
203	Rollie Fingers	1.50	.70	.45
204	Al Oliver	.25	.13	.08
205	Doug Ault	.25	.13	.08
206	Scott McGregor	.25	.13	.08
207	Dave Cash	.25	.13	.08
208	Bill Plummer	.25	.13	.08
209	Ivan DeJesus	.25	.13	.08
210	Jim Rice	.75	.40	.25
211	Ray Knight	.25	.13	.08
212	Paul Hartzell	.25	.13	.08
213	Tim Foli	.25	.13	.08
214	Butch Wynegar	.25	.13	.08
215	Darrell Evans	.25	.13	.08
216	Ken Griffey	.25	.13	.08
217	Doug DeCinces	.25	.13	.08
218	Ruppert Jones	.25	.13	.08
219	Bob Montgomery	.25	.13	.08
220	Rick Manning	.25	.13	.08
221	Chris Speier	.25	.13	.08
222	Bobby Valentine	.25	.13	.08
223	Dave Parker	.25	.13	.08
224	Larry Biittner	.25	.13	.08
225	Ken Clay	.25	.13	.08
226	Gene Tenace	.25	.13	.08
227	Frank White	.25	.13	.08
228	Rusty Staub	.35	.20	.11
229	Lee Lacy	.25	.13	.08
230	Doyle Alexander	.25	.13	.08
231	Bruce Bochte	.25	.13	.08
232	Steve Henderson	.25	.13	.08
233	Jim Lonborg	.25	.13	.08
234	Dave Concepcion	.25	.13	.08
235	Jerry Morales	.25	.13	.08
236	Len Randle	.25	.13	.08
237	Bill Lee	.25	.13	.08
238	Bruce Sutter	1.50	.70	.45
239	Jim Essian	.25	.13	.08
240	Graig Nettles	.25	.13	.08
241	Otto Velez	.25	.13	.08
242	Checklist 126-250	.25	.13	.08
243	Reggie Smith	.25	.13	.08
244	Stan Bahnsen	.25	.13	.08
245	Garry Maddox	.25	.13	.08
246	Joaquin Andujar	.25	.13	.08
247	Dan Driessen	.25	.13	.08
248	Bob Grich	.25	.13	.08
249	Fred Lynn	.25	.13	.08
250	Skip Lockwood	.25	.13	.08
251	Craig Reynolds	.25	.13	.08
252	Willie Horton	.25	.13	.08
253	Rick Waits	.25	.13	.08
254	Bucky Dent	.25	.13	.08
255	Bob Knepper	.25	.13	.08
256	Miguel Dilone	.25	.13	.08
257	Bob Owchinko	.25	.13	.08
258	Al Cowens	.25	.13	.08
259	Bob Bailor	.25	.13	.08
260	Larry Christenson	.25	.13	.08
261	Tony Perez	1.50	.70	.45
262	Blue Jays Team	.25	.13	.08
263	Glenn Abbott	.25	.13	.08
264	Ron Guidry	.50	.25	.15
265	Ed Kranepool	.25	.13	.08
266	Charlie Hough	.25	.13	.08
267	Ted Simmons	.25	.13	.08
268	Jack Clark	.25	.13	.08
269	Enos Cabell	.25	.13	.08
270	Gary Carter	6.00	3.00	1.75
271	Sam Ewing	.25	.13	.08
272	Tom Burgmeier	.25	.13	.08
273	Freddie Patek	.25	.13	.08
274	Frank Tanana	.25	.13	.08
275	Leroy Stanton	.25	.13	.08
276	Ken Forsch	.25	.13	.08
277	Ellis Valentine	.25	.13	.08
278	Greg Luzinski	.25	.13	.08
279	Rick Bosetti	.25	.13	.08
280	John Stearns	.25	.13	.08
281	Enrique Romo	.25	.13	.08
282	Bob Bailey	.25	.13	.08
283	Sal Bando	.25	.13	.08
284	Matt Keough	.25	.13	.08
285	Biff Pocoroba	.25	.13	.08
286	Mike Lum	.25	.13	.08
287	Jay Johnstone	.25	.13	.08
288	John Montefusco	.25	.13	.08

		NM	EX	VG
	Complete Set (374):	110.00	55.00	32.50
	Common Player:	.15	.08	.05
	Wax Pack (10):	10.00		
	Wax Box (36):	290.00		

289	Ed Ott	.25	.13	.08
290	Dusty Baker	.25	.13	.08
291	Rico Carty	.25	.13	.08
292	Nino Espinosa	.25	.13	.08
293	Rich Hebner	.25	.13	.08
294	Cesar Cedeno	.25	.13	.08
295	Darrell Porter	.25	.13	.08
296	Rod Gilbreath	.25	.13	.08
297	Jim Kern	.25	.13	.08
298	Claudell Washington	.25	.13	.08
299	Luis Tiant	.25	.13	.08
300	Mike Parrott	.25	.13	.08
301	Pete Broberg	.25	.13	.08
302	Greg Gross	.25	.13	.08
303	Darold Knowles	.25	.13	.08
304	Paul Blair	.25	.13	.08
305	Julio Cruz	.25	.13	.08
306	Hal McRae	.25	.13	.08
307	Ken Reitz	.25	.13	.08
308	Tom Murphy	.25	.13	.08
309	Terry Whitfield	.25	.13	.08
310	J.R. Richard	.25	.13	.08
311	Mike Hargrove	.25	.13	.08
312	Rick Dempsey	.25	.13	.08
313	Phil Niekro	1.50	.70	.45
314	Bob Stanley	.25	.13	.08
315	Jim Spencer	.25	.13	.08
316	George Foster	.25	.13	.08
317	Dave LaRoche	.25	.13	.08
318	Rudy May	.25	.13	.08
319	Jeff Newman	.25	.13	.08
320	Rick Monday	.25	.13	.08
321	Omar Moreno	.25	.13	.08
322	Dave McKay	.25	.13	.08
323	Mike Schmidt	6.00	3.00	1.75
324	Ken Singleton	.25	.13	.08
325	Jerry Remy	.25	.13	.08
326	Bert Campaneris	.25	.13	.08
327	Pat Zachry	.25	.13	.08
328	Larry Herndon	.25	.13	.08
329	Mark Fidrych	.25	.13	.08
330	Del Unser	.25	.13	.08
331	Gene Garber	.25	.13	.08
332	Bake McBride	.25	.13	.08
333	Jorge Orta	.25	.13	.08
334	Don Kirkwood	.25	.13	.08
335	Don Baylor	.25	.13	.08
336	Bill Robinson	.25	.13	.08
337	Manny Trillo	.25	.13	.08
338	Eddie Murray	3.00	1.50	.90
339	Tom Hausman	.25	.13	.08
340	George Scott	.25	.13	.08
341	Rick Sweet	.25	.13	.08
342	Lou Piniella	.25	.13	.08
343	Pete Rose	15.00	7.50	4.50
344	Stan Papi	.25	.13	.08
345	Jerry Koosman	.25	.13	.08
346	Hosken Powell	.25	.13	.08
347	George Medich	.25	.13	.08
348	Ron LeFlore	.75	.40	.25
349	Expos Team	.25	.13	.08
350	Lou Brock	2.00	1.00	.60
351	Bill North	.25	.13	.08
352	Jim Hunter	1.50	.70	.45
353	Checklist 251-374	.25	.13	.08
354	Ed Halicki	.25	.13	.08
355	Tom Hutton	.25	.13	.08
356	Mike Caldwell	.25	.13	.08
357	Larry Parrish	.25	.13	.08
358	Geoff Zahn	.25	.13	.08
359	Derrel Thomas	.25	.13	.08
360	Carlton Fisk	2.00	1.00	.60
361	John Henry Johnson	.25	.13	.08
362	Dave Chalk	.25	.13	.08
363	Dan Meyer	.25	.13	.08
364	Sixto Lezcano	.25	.13	.08
365	Rennie Stennett	.25	.13	.08
366	Mike Willis	.25	.13	.08
367	Buddy Bell	.25	.13	.08
368	Mickey Stanley	.25	.13	.08
369	Dave Rader	.25	.13	.08
370	Burt Hooton	.25	.13	.08
371	Keith Hernandez	.25	.13	.08
372	Bill Stein	.25	.13	.08
373	Hal Dues	.25	.13	.08
374	Reggie Jackson	3.00	1.50	.90

1980 O-Pee-Chee

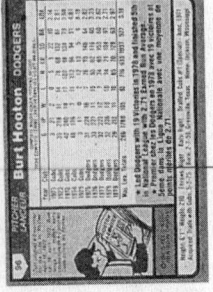

The 1980 Canadian-issued O-Pee-Chee set was again complete at 374 cards, which measure 2-1/2" x 3-1/2" and share the same design as the 1980 Topps set. The OPC cards are printed on a white stock, rather than the traditional gray stock used by Topps, and their backs are written in both French and English. Some of the cards include an extra line on the front indicating a new team designation.

		NM	EX	VG
1	Craig Swan	.15	.08	.05
2	Denny Martinez	.15	.08	.05
3	Dave Cash	.15	.08	.05
4	Bruce Sutter	1.50	.70	.45
5	Ron Jackson	.15	.08	.05
6	Balor Moore	.15	.08	.05
7	Dan Ford	.15	.08	.05
8	Pat Putnam	.15	.08	.05
9	Derrel Thomas	.15	.08	.05
10	Jim Slaton	.15	.08	.05
11	Lee Mazzilli	.15	.08	.05
12	Del Unser	.15	.08	.05
13	Mark Wagner	.15	.08	.05
14	Vida Blue	.15	.08	.05
15	Jay Johnstone	.15	.08	.05
16	Julio Cruz	.15	.08	.05
17	Tony Scott	.15	.08	.05
18	Jeff Newman	.15	.08	.05
19	Luis Tiant	.15	.08	.05
20	Carlton Fisk	1.50	.70	.45
21	Dave Palmer	.15	.08	.05
22	Bombo Rivera	.15	.08	.05
23	Bill Fahey	.15	.08	.05
24	Frank White	.15	.08	.05
25	Rico Carty	.15	.08	.05
26	Bill Bonham	.15	.08	.05
27	Rick Miller	.15	.08	.05
28	J.R. Richard	.15	.08	.05
29	Joe Ferguson	.15	.08	.05
30	Bill Madlock	.15	.08	.05
31	Pete Vuckovich	.15	.08	.05
32	Doug Flynn	.15	.08	.05
33	Bucky Dent	.15	.08	.05
34	Mike Ivie	.15	.08	.05
35	Bob Stanley	.15	.08	.05
36	Al Bumbry	.15	.08	.05
37	Gary Carter	5.00	2.50	1.50
38	John Milner	.15	.08	.05
39	Sid Monge	.15	.08	.05
40	Bill Russell	.15	.08	.05
41	John Stearns	.15	.08	.05
42	Dave Stieb	1.25	.60	.40
43	Ruppert Jones	.15	.08	.05
44	Bob Owchinko	.15	.08	.05
45	Ron LeFlore	.15	.08	.05
46	Ted Sizemore	.15	.08	.05
47	Ted Simmons	.15	.08	.05
48	Pepe Frias	.15	.08	.05
49	Ken Landreaux	.15	.08	.05
50	Manny Trillo	.15	.08	.05
51	Rick Dempsey	.15	.08	.05
52	Cecil Cooper	.15	.08	.05
53	Bill Lee	.15	.08	.05
54	Victor Cruz	.15	.08	.05
55	Johnny Bench	1.50	.70	.45
56	Rich Dauer	.15	.08	.05
57	Frank Tanana	.15	.08	.05
58	Francisco Barrios	.15	.08	.05
59	Bob Horner	.30	.15	.09
60	Fred Lynn	.15	.08	.05
61	Bob Knepper	.15	.08	.05
62	Sparky Lyle	.15	.08	.05
63	Larry Cox	.15	.08	.05
64	Dock Ellis	.15	.08	.05
65	Phil Garner	.15	.08	.05
66	Greg Luzinski	.25	.13	.08
67	Checklist 1-125	.15	.08	.05
68	Dave Lemanczyk	.15	.08	.05
69	Tony Perez	1.50	.70	.45
70	Gary Thomasson	.15	.08	.05
71	Craig Reynolds	.15	.08	.05
72	Amos Otis	.15	.08	.05
73	Biff Pocoroba	.15	.08	.05
74	Matt Keough	.15	.08	.05
75	Bill Buckner	.15	.08	.05
76	John Castino	.15	.08	.05
77	Rich Gossage	.25	.13	.08
78	Gary Alexander	.15	.08	.05
79	Phil Huffman	.15	.08	.05
80	Bruce Bochte	.15	.08	.05
81	Darrell Evans	.15	.08	.05
82	Terry Puhl	.15	.08	.05
83	Jason Thompson	.15	.08	.05
84	Lary Sorensen	.15	.08	.05
85	Jerry Remy	.15	.08	.05
86	Tony Brizzolara	.15	.08	.05
87	Willie Wilson	.15	.08	.05
88	Eddie Murray	3.00	1.50	.90
89	Larry Christenson	.15	.08	.05
90	Bob Randall	.15	.08	.05
91	Greg Pryor	.15	.08	.05
92	Glenn Abbott	.15	.08	.05
93	Jack Clark	.15	.08	.05
94	Rick Waits	.15	.08	.05
95	Luis Gomez	.15	.08	.05
96	Burt Hooton	.15	.08	.05
97	John Henry Johnson	.15	.08	.05
98	Ray Knight	.15	.08	.05
99	Rick Reuschel	.15	.08	.05
100	Champ Summers	.15	.08	.05
101	Ron Davis	.15	.08	.05
102	Warren Cromartie	.15	.08	.05
103	Ken Reitz	.15	.08	.05
104	Hal McRae	.15	.08	.05
105	Alan Ashby	.15	.08	.05
106	Kevin Kobel	.15	.08	.05
107	Buddy Bell	.15	.08	.05
108	Dave Goltz	.15	.08	.05
109	John Montefusco	.15	.08	.05
110	Lance Parrish	.65	.30	.20
111	Mike LaCoss	.15	.08	.05
112	Jim Rice	.30	.15	.09

		NM	EX	VG
113	Steve Carlton	1.50	.70	.45
114	Sixto Lezcano	.15	.08	.05
115	Ed Halicki	.15	.08	.05
116	Jose Morales	.15	.08	.05
117	Dave Concepcion	.15	.08	.05
118	Joe Cannon	.15	.08	.05
119	Willie Montanez	.15	.08	.05
120	Lou Piniella	.15	.08	.05
121	Bill Stein	.15	.08	.05
122	Dave Winfield	3.00	1.50	.90
123	Alan Trammell	.30	.15	.09
124	Andre Dawson	4.00	2.00	1.25
125	Marc Hill	.15	.08	.05
126	Don Aase	.15	.08	.05
127	Dave Kingman	.15	.08	.05
128	Checklist 126-250	.25	.13	.08
129	Dennis Lamp	.15	.08	.05
130	Phil Niekro	1.00	.50	.30
131	Tim Foli	.15	.08	.05
132	Jim Clancy	.15	.08	.05
133	Bill Atkinson	.15	.08	.05
134	Paul Dade	.15	.08	.05
135	Dusty Baker	.15	.08	.05
136	Al Oliver	.15	.08	.05
137	Dave Chalk	.15	.08	.05
138	Bill Robinson	.15	.08	.05
139	Robin Yount	1.50	.70	.45
140	Dan Schatzeder	.15	.08	.05
141	Mike Schmidt	5.00	2.50	1.50
142	Ralph Garr	.15	.08	.05
143	Dale Murphy	1.00	.50	.30
144	Jerry Koosman	.15	.08	.05
145	Tom Veryzer	.15	.08	.05
146	Rick Bosetti	.15	.08	.05
147	Jim Spencer	.15	.08	.05
148	Gaylord Perry	1.00	.50	.30
149	Paul Blair	.15	.08	.05
150	Don Baylor	.15	.08	.05
151	Dave Rozema	.15	.08	.05
152	Steve Garvey	.50	.25	.15
153	Elias Sosa	.15	.08	.05
154	Larry Gura	.15	.08	.05
155	Tim Johnson	.15	.08	.05
156	Steve Henderson	.15	.08	.05
157	Ron Guidry	.20	.10	.06
158	Mike Edwards	.15	.08	.05
159	Butch Wynegar	.15	.08	.05
160	Randy Jones	.15	.08	.05
161	Denny Walling	.15	.08	.05
162	Mike Hargrove	.15	.08	.05
163	Dave Parker	.15	.08	.05
164	Roger Metzger	.15	.08	.05
165	Johnny Grubb	.15	.08	.05
166	Steve Kemp	.15	.08	.05
167	Bob Lacey	.15	.08	.05
168	Chris Speier	.15	.08	.05
169	Dennis Eckersley	1.00	.50	.30
170	Keith Hernandez	.15	.08	.05
171	Claudell Washington	.15	.08	.05
172	Tom Underwood	.15	.08	.05
173	Dan Driessen	.15	.08	.05
174	Al Cowens	.15	.08	.05
175	Rich Hebner	.15	.08	.05
176	Willie McCovey	1.50	.70	.45
177	Carney Lansford	.15	.08	.05
178	Ken Singleton	.15	.08	.05
179	Jim Essian	.15	.08	.05
180	Mike Vail	.15	.08	.05
181	Randy Lerch	.15	.08	.05
182	Larry Parrish	.15	.08	.05
183	Checklist 251-374	.25	.13	.08
184	George Hendrick	.15	.08	.05
185	Bob Davis	.15	.08	.05
186	Gary Matthews	.15	.08	.05
187	Lou Whitaker	.15	.08	.05
188	Darrell Porter	.15	.08	.05
189	Wayne Gross	.15	.08	.05
190	Bobby Murcer	.15	.08	.05
191	Willie Aikens	.15	.08	.05
192	Jim Kern	.15	.08	.05
193	Cesar Cedeno	.15	.08	.05
194	Joel Youngblood	.15	.08	.05
195	Ross Grimsley	.15	.08	.05
196	Jerry Mumphrey	.15	.08	.05
197	Kevin Bell	.15	.08	.05
198	Garry Maddox	.15	.08	.05
199	Dave Freisleben	.15	.08	.05
200	Ed Ott	.15	.08	.05
201	Enos Cabell	.15	.08	.05
202	Pete LaCock	.15	.08	.05
203	Fergie Jenkins	1.50	.70	.45
204	Milt Wilcox	.15	.08	.05
205	Ozzie Smith	5.00	2.50	1.50
206	Ellis Valentine	.15	.08	.05
207	Dan Meyer	.15	.08	.05
208	Barry Foote	.15	.08	.05
209	George Foster	.15	.08	.05
210	Dwight Evans	.15	.08	.05
211	Paul Molitor	5.00	2.50	1.50
212	Tony Solaita	.15	.08	.05
213	Bill North	.15	.08	.05
214	Paul Splittorff	.15	.08	.05
215	Bobby Bonds	.15	.08	.05
216	Butch Hobson	.15	.08	.05
217	Mark Belanger	.15	.08	.05
218	Grant Jackson	.15	.08	.05
219	Tom Hutton	.15	.08	.05
220	Pat Zachry	.15	.08	.05
221	Duane Kuiper	.15	.08	.05
222	Larry Hisle	.15	.08	.05
223	Mike Krukow	.15	.08	.05
224	Johnnie LeMaster	.15	.08	.05
225	Billy Almon	.15	.08	.05
226	Joe Niekro	.15	.08	.05
227	Dave Revering	.15	.08	.05
228	Don Sutton	1.00	.50	.30
229	John Hiller	.15	.08	.05
230	Alvis Woods	.15	.08	.05

231	Mark Fidrych	.15	.08	.05
232	Duffy Dyer	.15	.08	.05
233	Nino Espinosa	.15	.08	.05
234	Doug Bair	.15	.08	.05
235	George Brett	5.00	2.50	1.50
236	Mike Torrez	.15	.08	.05
237	Frank Taveras	.15	.08	.05
238	Bert Blyleven	.15	.08	.05
239	Willie Randolph	.15	.08	.05
240	Mike Sadek	.15	.08	.05
241	Jerry Royster	.15	.08	.05
242	John Denny	.15	.08	.05
243	Rick Monday	.15	.08	.05
244	Jesse Jefferson	.15	.08	.05
245	Aurelio Rodriguez	.15	.08	.05
246	Bob Boone	.15	.08	.05
247	Cesar Geronimo	.15	.08	.05
248	Bob Shirley	.15	.08	.05
249	Expos Team	.25	.13	.08
250	Bob Watson	.15	.08	.05
251	Mickey Rivers	.15	.08	.05
252	Mike Tyson	.15	.08	.05
253	Wayne Nordhagen	.15	.08	.05
254	Roy Howell	.15	.08	.05
255	Lee May	.15	.08	.05
256	Jerry Martin	.15	.08	.05
257	Bake McBride	.15	.08	.05
258	Silvio Martinez	.15	.08	.05
259	Jim Mason	.15	.08	.05
260	Tom Seaver	2.00	1.00	.60
261	Rick Wortham	.15	.08	.05
262	Mike Cubbage	.15	.08	.05
263	Gene Garber	.15	.08	.05
264	Bert Campaneris	.15	.08	.05
265	Tom Buskey	.15	.08	.05
266	Leon Roberts	.15	.08	.05
267	Ron Cey	.15	.08	.05
268	Steve Ontiveros	.15	.08	.05
269	Mike Caldwell	.15	.08	.05
270	Nelson Norman	.15	.08	.05
271	Steve Rogers	.15	.08	.05
272	Jim Morrison	.15	.08	.05
273	Clint Hurdle	.15	.08	.05
274	Dale Murray	.15	.08	.05
275	Jim Barr	.15	.08	.05
276	Jim Sundberg	.15	.08	.05
277	Willie Horton	.15	.08	.05
278	Andre Thornton	.15	.08	.05
279	Bob Forsch	.15	.08	.05
280	Joe Strain	.15	.08	.05
281	Rudy May	.15	.08	.05
282	Pete Rose	9.00	4.50	2.75
283	Jeff Burroughs	.15	.08	.05
284	Rick Langford	.15	.08	.05
285	Ken Griffey	.15	.08	.05
286	Bill Nahorodny	.15	.08	.05
287	Art Howe	.15	.08	.05
288	Ed Figueroa	.15	.08	.05
289	Joe Rudi	.15	.08	.05
290	Alfredo Griffin	.15	.08	.05
291	Dave Lopes	.15	.08	.05
292	Rick Manning	.15	.08	.05
293	Dennis Leonard	.15	.08	.05
294	Bud Harrelson	.15	.08	.05
295	Skip Lockwood	.15	.08	.05
296	Roy Smalley	.15	.08	.05
297	Kent Tekulve	.15	.08	.05
298	Scot Thompson	.15	.08	.05
299	Ken Kravec	.15	.08	.05
300	Blue Jays Team	.25	.13	.08
301	Scott Sanderson	.15	.08	.05
302	Charlie Moore	.15	.08	.05
303	Nolan Ryan	20.00	10.00	6.00
304	Bob Bailor	.15	.08	.05
305	Bob Stinson	.15	.08	.05
306	Al Hrabosky	.15	.08	.05
307	Mitchell Page	.15	.08	.05
308	Garry Templeton	.15	.08	.05
309	Chet Lemon	.15	.08	.05
310	Jim Palmer	1.50	.70	.45
311	Rick Cerone	.15	.08	.05
312	Jon Matlack	.15	.08	.05
313	Don Money	.15	.08	.05
314	Reggie Jackson	5.00	2.50	1.50
315	Brian Downing	.15	.08	.05
316	Woodie Fryman	.15	.08	.05
317	Alan Bannister	.15	.08	.05
318	Ron Reed	.15	.08	.05
319	Willie Stargell	1.50	.70	.45
320	Jerry Garvin	.15	.08	.05
321	Cliff Johnson	.15	.08	.05
322	Doug DeCinces	.15	.08	.05
323	Gene Richards	.15	.08	.05
324	Joaquin Andujar	.15	.08	.05
325	Richie Zisk	.15	.08	.05
326	Bob Grich	.15	.08	.05
327	Gorman Thomas	.15	.08	.05
328	Chris Chambliss	.15	.08	.05
329	Blue Jays Future Stars (Butch Edge, Pat Kelly, Ted Wilborn)	.25	.13	.08
330	Larry Bowa	.15	.08	.05
331	Barry Bonnell	.15	.08	.05
332	John Candelaria	.15	.08	.05
333	Toby Harrah	.15	.08	.05
334	Larry Biittner	.15	.08	.05
335	Mike Flanagan	.15	.08	.05
336	Ed Kranepool	.15	.08	.05
337	Ken Forsch	.15	.08	.05
338	John Mayberry	.15	.08	.05
339	Rick Burleson	.15	.08	.05
340	Milt May	.15	.08	.05
341	Roy White	.15	.08	.05
342	Joe Morgan	1.50	.70	.45
343	Rollie Fingers	1.00	.50	.30
344	Mario Mendoza	.15	.08	.05
345	Stan Bahnsen	.15	.08	.05
346	Tug McGraw	.15	.08	.05

347	Rusty Staub	.15	.08	.05
348	Tommy John	.15	.08	.05
349	Ivan DeJesus	.15	.08	.05
350	Reggie Smith	.15	.08	.05
351	Expos Future Stars (Tony Bernazard, Randy Miller, John Tamargo)	.40	.20	.12
352	Floyd Bannister	.15	.08	.05
353	Rod Carew	1.50	.70	.45
354	Otto Velez	.15	.08	.05
355	Gene Tenace	.15	.08	.05
356	Freddie Patek	.15	.08	.05
357	Elliott Maddox	.15	.08	.05
358	Pat Underwood	.15	.08	.05
359	Graig Nettles	.15	.08	.05
360	Rodney Scott	.15	.08	.05
361	Terry Whitfield	.15	.08	.05
362	Fred Norman	.15	.08	.05
363	Sal Bando	.15	.08	.05
364	Greg Gross	.15	.08	.05
365	Carl Yastrzemski	2.00	1.00	.60
366	Paul Hartzell	.15	.08	.05
367	Jose Cruz	.15	.08	.05
368	Shane Rawley	.15	.08	.05
369	Jerry White	.15	.08	.05
370	Rick Wise	.15	.08	.05
371	Steve Yeager	.15	.08	.05
372	Omar Moreno	.15	.08	.05
373	Bump Wills	.15	.08	.05
374	Craig Kusick	.15	.08	.05

1969 Oakland A's (Andersen)

5. Joe DiMaggio—coach

OAKLAND A's

Though they are sometimes identified as an issue of Jack in the Box restaurants, there is no identifier of that nature on these cards. In fact, they are a collectors' fantasy issue sold only within the hobby by Boston photographer Mike Andersen. The blank-back black-and-white cards measure 2-1/8" x 3-5/8". Beneath the portrait photo on front is the player's name, position and uniform number. The team name is in gothic script at bottom. Cards are checklisted here by uniform number.

		NM	EX	VG
Complete Set (21):		80.00	40.00	24.00
Common Player:		2.50	1.25	.75
1	Dick Green	2.50	1.25	.75
2	Danny Cater	2.50	1.25	.75
3	Mike Hershberger	2.50	1.25	.75
4	Phil Roof	2.50	1.25	.75
5	Joe DiMaggio/Coach	30.00	15.00	9.00
6	Sal Bando	2.50	1.25	.75
7	Rick Monday	2.50	1.25	.75
9a	Bert Campaneris	5.00	2.50	1.50
9b	Reggie Jackson	45.00	22.00	13.50
13	Blue Moon Odom	3.50	1.75	1.00
17	Jim Pagliaroni	2.50	1.25	.75
19	Bert Campaneris	2.50	1.25	.75
20	Lew Krausse	2.50	1.25	.75
24	Joe Nossek	2.50	1.25	.75
25	Paul Lindblad	2.50	1.25	.75
27	Catfish Hunter	7.50	3.75	2.25
29	Chuck Dobson	2.50	1.25	.75
30	Jim Nash	2.50	1.25	.75
31	Ramon Webster	2.50	1.25	.75
35	Tom Reynolds	2.50	1.25	.75
42	Hank Bauer	2.50	1.25	.70

1969 Oakland A's (Broder)

Reggie Jackson

OAKLAND A's

A second issue of black-and-white collector cards featuring the 1969 A's was produced by West Coast collector/dealer Ed Broder. In larger (2-3/4" x 4") format the Broder issue is considerably scarcer than that produced by Mike Andersen. Availability of the Broders was advertised at 100 sets. The blank-back Broder cards have the player name in the wide white border beneath the photo. At bottom the city name is in gothic script with the A's logo on a base-ball flying out of a stadium. The unnumbered cards are checklisted here alphabetically.

		NM	EX	VG
Complete Set (14):		65.00	32.50	20.00
Common Player:		2.00	1.00	.60
(1)	Sal Bando	2.00	1.00	.60
(2)	Hank Bauer	2.00	1.00	.60
(3)	Bert Campaneris	3.00	1.50	.90
(4)	Dan Cater	2.00	1.00	.60
(5)	Joe DiMaggio	15.00	7.50	4.50
(6)	Chuck Dobson	2.00	1.00	.60
(7)	Dick Green	2.00	1.00	.60
(8)	Mike Hershberger	2.00	1.00	.60
(9)	Jim Hunter	8.00	4.00	2.50
(10)	Reggie Jackson	25.00	12.50	7.50
(11)	Bob Johnson	2.00	1.00	.60
(12)	Rick Monday	2.00	1.00	.60
(13)	Johnny Moon Odom	4.00	2.00	1.25
(14)	Phil Roof	2.00	1.00	.60

1970 Oakland A's (Andersen)

45 - ROBERTO RODRIQUEZ

Oakland A's

Boston baseball photographer Mike Andersen produced a second collectors' issue of Oakland A's cards in 1970. Nearly identical in format to his 1969 issue, the '70 team set measures 2-1/4" x 3-5/8" with black-and-white player poses at center. Uniform number, name and team are in the bottom border. Backs are blank. Cards are checklisted here by uniform number.

		NM	EX	VG
Complete Set (24):		30.00	15.00	9.00
Common Player:		1.50	.75	.45
1	Dick Green	1.50	.75	.45
6	Sal Bando	1.50	.75	.45
7	Rick Monday	1.50	.75	.45
8	Felipe Alou	2.00	1.00	.60
9	Reggie Jackson	15.00	7.50	4.50
10	Dave Duncan	1.50	.75	.45
11	John McNamera (McNamara)	1.50	.75	.45
12	Larry Haney	1.50	.75	.45
13	Blue Moon Odom	2.00	1.00	.60
17	Roberto Pena	1.50	.75	.45
19	Bert Campaneris	2.00	1.00	.60
24	Diego Segui	1.50	.75	.45
25	Paul Lindblad	1.50	.75	.45
27	Catfish Hunter	4.00	2.00	1.25
28	Mudcat Grant	1.50	.75	.45
29	Chuck Dobson	1.50	.75	.45
30	Don Mincher	1.50	.75	.45
31	Jose Tartabull	1.50	.75	.45
33	Jim Roland	1.50	.75	.45
34	Rollie Fingers	4.00	2.00	1.25
36	Tito Francona	1.50	.75	.45
38	Al Downing	1.50	.75	.45
39	Frank Fernandez	1.50	.75	.45
45	Roberto Rodriguez	1.50	.75	.45

1968 Official Major League Players Baseball Marbles

Produced by Creative Creations Inc., though not so identified on the marbles themselves, these approximately 3/4" hard plastic marbles have a player portrait photo (with cap logos removed) on one side and a facsimile autograph on the other, with "JAPAN" beneath. The marbles were issued in series of 20 on colorful cardboard packaging which pictures each player in the series. While the packaging says "Collect All 24 Series" only 120 marbles were actually issued. Suggested retail price at issue was $1.49 per series.

	NM	EX	VG
Complete Set (115):	675.00	325.00	200.00
Common Player:	4.00	2.00	1.25
(1) Hank Aaron	40.00	20.00	12.00
(2) Tommie Aaron	4.00	2.00	1.25
(3) Tommy Agee	4.00	2.00	1.25
(4) Richie Allen	7.00	3.50	2.00
(5) Gene Alley	4.00	2.00	1.25
(6) Bob Allison	4.00	2.00	1.25
(7) Felipe Alou	5.00	2.50	1.50
(8) Jesus Alou	4.00	2.00	1.25
(9) Matty Alou	4.00	2.00	1.25
(10) Max Alvis	4.00	2.00	1.25
(11) Mike Andrews	4.00	2.00	1.25
(12) Luis Aparicio	12.50	6.25	3.75
(13) Bob Aspromonte	4.00	2.00	1.25
(14) Stan Bahnsen	4.00	2.00	1.25
(15) Bob Bailey	4.00	2.00	1.25
(16) Ernie Banks	25.00	12.50	7.50
(17) Glenn Beckert	4.00	2.00	1.25
(18) Gary Bell	4.00	2.00	1.25
(19) Johnny Bench	30.00	15.00	9.00
(20) Ken Berry	4.00	2.00	1.25
(21) Paul Blair	4.00	2.00	1.25
(22) Bob Bolin	4.00	2.00	1.25
(23) Dave Boswell	4.00	2.00	1.25
(24) Nelson Briles	4.00	2.00	1.25
(25) Lou Brock	12.50	6.25	3.75
(26) Wally Bunker	4.00	2.00	1.25
(27) Johnny Callison	4.00	2.00	1.25
(28) Norm Cash	5.00	2.50	1.50
(29) Orlando Cepeda	12.50	6.25	3.75
(30) Dean Chance	4.00	2.00	1.25
(31) Roberto Clemente	50.00	25.00	15.00
(32) Donn Clendenon	4.00	2.00	1.25
(33) Tony Cloninger	4.00	2.00	1.25
(34) Tommy Davis	4.00	2.00	1.25
(35) Al Downing	4.00	2.00	1.25
(36) Curt Flood	4.00	2.00	1.25
(37) Bill Freehan	4.00	2.00	1.25
(38) Jim Fregosi	4.00	2.00	1.25
(39) Bob Gibson	12.50	6.25	3.75
(40) Jim "Mudcat" Grant	4.00	2.00	1.25
(41) Jerry Grote	4.00	2.00	1.25
(42) Jimmie Hall	4.00	2.00	1.25
(43) Tom Haller	4.00	2.00	1.25
(44) Ron Hansen	4.00	2.00	1.25
(45) Steve Hargan	4.00	2.00	1.25
(46) Ken Harrelson	4.00	2.00	1.25
(47) Jim Hart	4.00	2.00	1.25
(48) Jimmie Holt	4.00	2.00	1.25
(49) Joe Horlen	4.00	2.00	1.25
(50) Willie Horton	4.00	2.00	1.25
(51) Frank Howard	5.00	2.50	1.50
(52) Dick Hughes	4.00	2.00	1.25
(53) Randy Hundley	4.00	2.00	1.25
(54) Ron Hunt	4.00	2.00	1.25
(55) Jim "Catfish" Hunter	12.50	6.25	3.75
(56) Pat Jarvis	4.00	2.00	1.25
(57) Julian Javier	4.00	2.00	1.25
(58) Tommy John	6.00	3.00	1.75
(59) Deron Johnson	4.00	2.00	1.25
(60) Mack Jones	4.00	2.00	1.25
(61) Jim Kaat	5.00	2.50	1.50
(62) Al Kaline	20.00	10.00	6.00
(63) Don Kessinger	4.00	2.00	1.25
(64) Harmon Killebrew	20.00	10.00	6.00
(65) Jerry Koosman	4.00	2.00	1.25
(66) Jim Lefebvre	4.00	2.00	1.25
(67) Mickey Lolich	4.00	2.00	1.25
(68) Jim Lonborg	4.00	2.00	1.25
(69) Juan Marichal	12.50	6.25	3.75
(70) Roger Maris	30.00	15.00	9.00
(71) Ed Mathews	20.00	10.00	6.00
(72) Jerry May	4.00	2.00	1.25
(73) Willie Mays	40.00	20.00	12.00
(74) Dick McAuliffe	4.00	2.00	1.25
(75) Tim McCarver	5.00	2.50	1.50
(76) Willie McCovey	12.50	6.25	3.75
(77) Sam McDowell	4.00	2.00	1.25
(78) Denny McLain	5.00	2.50	1.50
(79) Dave McNally	4.00	2.00	1.25
(80) Denis Menke	4.00	2.00	1.25
(81) Jim Merritt	4.00	2.00	1.25
(82) Bob Miller	4.00	2.00	1.25
(83) Rick Monday	4.00	2.00	1.25
(84) Joe Morgan	12.50	6.25	3.75
(85) Gary Nolan	4.00	2.00	1.25
(86) Jim Northrup	4.00	2.00	1.25
(87) Rich Nye	4.00	2.00	1.25
(88) Tony Oliva	5.00	2.50	1.50
(89) Milt Pappas	4.00	2.00	1.25
(90) Camilo Pascual	4.00	2.00	1.25
(91) Joe Pepitone	5.00	2.50	1.50
(92) Tony Perez	12.50	6.25	

	NM	EX	VG
(93) Jim Perry	4.00	2.00	1.25
(94) Gary Peters	4.00	2.00	1.25
(95) Fritz Peterson	4.00	2.00	1.25
(96) Rico Petrocelli	4.00	2.00	1.25
(97) Vada Pinson	5.00	2.50	1.50
(98) Boog Powell	5.00	2.50	1.50
(99) Rick Reichardt	4.00	2.00	1.25
(100) Brooks Robinson	15.00	7.50	4.50
(101) Frank Robinson	15.00	7.50	4.50
(102) Pete Rose	40.00	20.00	12.00
(103) Chico Salmon	4.00	2.00	1.25
(104) Ron Santo	5.00	2.50	1.50
(105) George Scott	4.00	2.00	1.25
(106) Tom Seaver	15.00	7.50	4.50
(107) Dick Selma	4.00	2.00	1.25
(108) Mike Shannon	4.00	2.00	1.25
(109) Joe Sparma	4.00	2.00	1.25
(110) Willie Stargell	12.50	6.25	3.75
(111) Mel Stottlemyre	4.00	2.00	1.25
(113) Luis Tiant	4.00	2.00	1.25
(114) Cesar Tovar	4.00	2.00	1.25
(115) Tom Tresh	4.50	2.25	1.25
(116) Pete Ward	4.00	2.00	1.25
(117) Billy Williams	12.50	6.25	3.75
(118) Maury Wills	4.00	2.00	1.25
(119) Earl Wilson	4.00	2.00	1.25
(120) Dooley Womack	4.00	2.00	1.25

1974 Oh Henry! Henry Aaron Premium Photo

This 8" x 10" black-and-white photo was prepared as a premium for Oh Henry! candy. It features a full-length pose of Aaron and has a facsimile inscribed autographed on front.

	NM	EX	VG
Henry Aaron	20.00	10.00	6.00

1959 Oklahoma Today Major Leaguers

 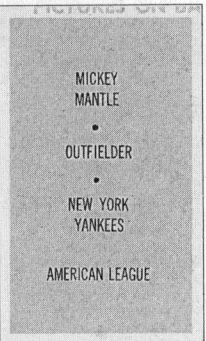

Contemporary and former ballplayers from the Sooner State were featured in this "card set" which was printed on the back cover of the Summer, 1959, issue of "Oklahoma Today" magazine. If cut from the cover, the cards measure about 1-11/16" x 2-3/4". Fronts have black-and-white photos on green, gold or aqua backgrounds. A white strip at bottom has the player name in red. Gray backs have the player name, position, team and league. The unnumbered cards are checklisted here in alphabetical order.

	NM	EX	VG
Complete Magazine:	1,350	675.00	400.00
Complete Set, Singles (20):	1,350	675.00	400.00
Common Player:	45.00	22.50	13.50
(1) Jerry Adair	45.00	22.00	13.50
(2) Harry Brecheen	45.00	22.00	13.50
(3) Johnny Callison	45.00	22.00	13.50
(4) Alvin Dark	45.00	22.50	13.50
(5) "Dizzy" Dean	60.00	30.00	18.00
(6) Paul Dean	45.00	22.00	13.50
(7) Don Demeter	45.00	22.50	13.50
(8) Carl Hubbell	50.00	25.00	15.00
(9) Mickey Mantle	500.00	250.00	150.00
(10) "Pepper" Martin	45.00	22.00	13.50
(11) Lindy McDaniel	45.00	22.50	13.50
(12) Von McDaniel	45.00	22.50	13.50
(13) Cal McLish	45.00	22.50	13.50
(14) Dale Mitchel (Mitchell)	45.00	22.50	13.50

	NM	EX	VG
(15) Allie Reynolds	45.00	22.00	13.50
(16) Warren Spahn	45.00	22.00	13.50
(17) Tom Sturdivant	45.00	22.50	13.50
(18) Jerry Walker	45.00	22.50	13.50
(19) Lloyd Waner	45.00	22.00	13.50
(20) Paul Waner	45.00	22.00	13.50

1948 Old Gold Jackie Robinson

These postcard-size (3-1/2" x 5-1/2") advertising pieces picture Jackie Robinson and a pack of Old Gold cigarettes on their black-and-white fronts, along with an endorsement from the player and his facsimile autograph. Each back has a different presentation of biography and career summary.

	NM	EX	VG
Jackie Robinson/Fielding	400.00	200.00	120.00
Jackie Robinson (In dugout.)	200.00	100.00	60.00

1886 Old Judge New York Giants (N167)

Produced in 1886, the rare N167 Old Judge tobacco cards were the first to be issued by New York's Goodwin & Co., the parent firm of Old Judge Cigarettes. The 1-1/2" x 2-1/2" sepia-toned cards were printed on thin paper and featured only members of the New York National League club. Twelve subjects are known to exist, five of whom are Hall of Famers. The front of each card lists the player's name, position and team and has the words "Old Judge" at the top. The backs contain another ad for the Old Judge brand and also include a line noting that the player poses were "copied from photo by J. Wood, 208 Bowery, N.Y."

	NM	EX	VG
Common Player:	40,000	20,000	12,000
(1) Roger Connor	90,000	45,000	27,000
(2) Larry Corcoran	40,000	20,000	12,000
(3) Mike Dorgan	40,000	20,000	12,000
(4) Dude Esterbrook	40,000	20,000	12,000
(5) Buck Ewing	90,000	45,000	27,000
(6) Joe Gerhardt	40,000	20,000	12,000
(7) Pete Gillespie	40,000	20,000	12,000
(8) Tim Keefe	90,000	45,000	27,000
(9) Orator Jim O'Rourke	90,000	45,000	27,000
(10) Danny Richardson	40,000	20,000	12,000
(11) John Ward	90,000	45,000	27,000
(12) Mickey Welsh (Welch)	90,000	45,000	27,000

1887-1890 Old Judge (N172)

This is one of the most fascinating of all card sets, being not only one of the first, but also the largest ever. The number of cards issued may never be finally determined. These cards were issued by the Goodwin & Co. tobacco firm in their Old Judge and, to a lesser extent, Gypsy Queen cigarettes. Players from more than 40 major and minor league teams are pictured on the nominally 1-7/16" x 2-1/2" cards (actual size varies), with some 500 different players known to exist. Up to 20 different pose, team and caption variations exist for some players. Cards were issued both with and without dates, numbered and unnumbered, and with both script and machine-printed identification. Known variations number over 3,500. The cards themselves are black-and-white (many now toned sepia or even pink) photographs pasted onto thick cardboard. They are blank-backed. Values shown here are for the most common examples of a specific player's cards, unless otherwise indicated. Demand for various photo, team, league, etc., variations can significantly affect value and, because of the relatively "thin" nature of the market for Old Judge cards, is subject to rapid fluctuations as collectors enter and leave the arena. These listings are presented alphabetically. Few Old Judge cards were issued with the player's first name, or even initial. Where verifiable, the first names have been added to these listings in the form most often encountered at the time of issue. Misspellings were common among the issue. Cases in which all of a player's cards were incorrectly spelled are listed by the misspelling, with the correct spelling in parentheses following. In cases where the name was sometimes spelled correctly, and sometimes not, the incorrect spellings are provided thus: "(Also: ...)". For each player, the number of different photo/team combinations known is indicated. Minor changes in the player identification caption, such as addition of an initial, presence or absence of period or comma, abbreviation of position, or spelling of team name, are not included in the number of cards listed. Team designations for each player are listed, where known. Pose/designation variations which have historically attracted increased collector interest are specified. These include such subsets as the Brown's Champions and Mets "spotted tie" portrait cards of 1887, the Player's League designations of 1890 and some other popularly collected subsets, such as the dual-player cards. Cards which depict and name both players are listed here under each player's name and are numbered with a "DP" prefix. League designations found in the listings include: AA - American Association; NL - National League; PL - Player's League; WA - Western Association. Gaps have been left in the assigned numbering to accommodate future additions.

		NM	EX	VG
Common Card:		600.00	275.00	150.00
(1)	Gus Albert (Alberts) 7			
1 (a)	(Cleveland)	600.00	275.00	150.00
1 (b)	(Milwaukee)	600.00	275.00	150.00
(2)	Charles Alcott 6			
2 (a)	(Mansfield)	600.00	275.00	150.00
2 (b)	(St. Louis Whites WA)	850.00	380.00	210.00
(3)	Daniel Alexander 4			
3 (a)	(Des Moines)	800.00	360.00	200.00
(4)	Bob Allen 7			
4 (a)	(Philadelphia NL)	600.00	275.00	150.00
4 (a)	(Pittsburgh)	600.00	275.00	150.00
(5)	Myron Allen 6			
5 (a)	(Kansas City)	600.00	275.00	150.00
(6)	Billy Alvord 3			
6 (a)	(Des Moines)	600.00	275.00	150.00
6 (b)	(Toledo)	850.00	380.00	210.00
(7)	Varney Anderson 3			
7 (a)	(St. Paul)	10,000	275.00	150.00
(8)	Ed Andrews 6			
8 (a)	(Philadelphia NL)	600.00	275.00	150.00
DP 1	(being tagged by Buster Hoover)	800.00	360.00	200.00
(9)	Wally Andrews 3			
9 (a)	(Omaha)	750.00	335.00	185.00
(10)	Bill Annis 4			
10 (a)	(Omaha)	775.00	350.00	200.00
10 (b)	(Worcester)	600.00	275.00	150.00

		NM	EX	VG
(11)	Cap Anson See Hall of Fame Section Following			
(12)	Joe Ardner 4			
12 (a)	(Kansas City)	600.00	275.00	150.00
12 (b)	(St. Joseph)	1,000	450.00	250.00
(13)	Tug Arundel 5			
13 (a)	(Indianapolis)	600.00	275.00	150.00
(14)	Jersey Bakley (Bakely) 5			
14 (a)	(Cleveland)	750.00	335.00	185.00
(15)	Kid Baldwin 5			
15 (a)	(Cincinnati)	600.00	275.00	150.00
(16)	Lady Baldwin 4			
16 (a)	(Detroit)	1,900	850.00	475.00
(17)	Mark Baldwin 10			
17 (a)	(Chicago NL)	750.00	335.00	185.00
17 (b)	(Chicago NL)/Portrait	1,200	540.00	300.00
17 (c)	(Chicago PL)	1,800	800.00	450.00
17 (d)	(Columbus)	600.00	275.00	150.00
(18)	Jim Banning 5			
18 (a)	(Washington)	600.00	275.00	150.00
(19)	Sam Barkley 8			
19 (a)	(Kansas City)	850.00	380.00	210.00
19 (b)	(Pittsburgh)	800.00	360.00	200.00
DP 6	(Watching Jocko Fields field.)	1,100	500.00	275.00
DP 7	(Tagged by Jocko Fields.)	1,100	500.00	275.00
(20)	John Barnes (Also: Barns) 2			
20 (a)	(St. Paul)	1,200	540.00	300.00
(21)	Billy Barnie 1			
21 (a)	(Baltimore)	850.00	380.00	210.00
(22)	Charley Bassett 3			
22 (a)	(Indianapolis)	600.00	275.00	150.00
22 (b)	(New York NL)	600.00	275.00	150.00
(23)	Charlie Bastian 6			
23 (a)	(Chicago NL)	600.00	275.00	150.00
23 (b)	(Chicago PL)	2,160	975.00	550.00
23 (c)	(Philadelphia NL)	600.00	275.00	150.00
DP 2	(Being tagged by Pop Schriver.)	1,000	450.00	250.00
(24)	Ed Beatin (Also: Beattin) 3			
24 (a)	(Cleveland)	600.00	275.00	150.00
(25)	Jake Beckley See Hall of Fame Section Following			
(26)	Stephen Behel 1			
26 (a)	(New York AA "dotted tie.")	16,500	7,425	4,125
(27)	Charlie Bennett 1			
27 (a)	(Boston NL)	600.00	275.00	150.00
(28)	Lou Bierbauer (Also: Bierbaur) 5			
28 (a)	(Philadelphia AA)	900.00	400.00	225.00
DP 3	(Tagging Bob Gamble.)	1,400	630.00	350.00
(29)	Bill Bishop 4			
29 (a)	(Pittsburgh)	600.00	275.00	150.00
29 (b)	(Syracuse)	600.00	275.00	150.00
(30)	Bill Blair 5			
30 (a)	(Hamilton)	900.00	400.00	225.00
30 (b)	(Philadelphia AA)	600.00	275.00	150.00
(31)	Ned Bligh 6			
31 (a)	(Columbus)	600.00	275.00	150.00
(32)	Walter Bogart 5			
32 (a)	(Indianapolis)	600.00	275.00	150.00
(33)	Boyce 4			
33 (a)	(Washington) (Never played for Wash.)	800.00	360.00	200.00
(34)	Boyd 2			
34 (a)	(Chicago Maroons WA)	1,750	785.00	435.00
(35)	Henry Boyle 6			
35 (a)	(Indianapolis)	650.00	290.00	160.00
35 (b)	(New York NL) (Never played for N.Y.)	600.00	275.00	150.00
(36)	Jack Boyle 6			
36 (a)	(Chicago PL)	4,800	2,160	1,200
36 (b)	(St. Louis AA)	700.00	315.00	175.00
(37)	George Bradley 5			
37 (a)	(Sioux City)	600.00	275.00	150.00
(38)	Nick Bradley 4			
38 (a)	(Kansas City)	600.00	275.00	150.00
38 (b)	(Worcester)	600.00	275.00	150.00
(39)	Steve Brady 1			
39 (a)	(New York AA "dotted tie.")	2,250	1,015	565.00
(40)	E.L. Breckenridge 1			
40 (a)	(Sacramento)(Value Undetermined)			
	Willie Breslin - See Mascot			
(41)	Timothy Brosnan (Also: Brosman) 8			
41 (a)	(Minneapolis)	600.00	275.00	150.00
41 (b)	(Sioux City)	600.00	275.00	150.00

		NM	EX	VG
(42)	Cal Broughton 5			
42 (a)	(St. Paul)	600.00	275.00	150.00
(43)	Dan Brouthers See Hall of Fame Section Following			
(44)	Tom Brown 7			
44 (a)	(Boston NL)	600.00	275.00	150.00
44 (b)	(Boston PL)	2,160	960.00	550.00
44 (c)	(Pittsburgh)	600.00	275.00	150.00
(45)	Willard (California) Brown 6			
45 1	(New York NL)	600.00	275.00	150.00
45 1	(New York PL)	1,800	800.00	450.00
(46)	Pete Browning 5			
46 (a)	(Louisville)	4,750	2,125	1,175
(47)	Charlie Brynan (Also: Bryn) 6			
47 (a)	(Chicago NL)	650.00	290.00	160.00
47 (b)	(Des Moines)	700.00	315.00	175.00
(48)	Al Buckenberger 2			
48 (a)	(Columbus)	600.00	275.00	150.00
(49)	Dick Buckley 7			
49 (a)	(Indianapolis)	600.00	275.00	150.00
49 (b)	(New York NL)	600.00	275.00	150.00
(50)	Charlie Buffinton (Also: Buffington) 4			
50 (a)	(Philadelphia NL)	600.00	275.00	150.00
50 (b)	(Philadelphia PL)	2,160	960.00	550.00
(51)	Ernie Burch 8			
51 (a)	(Brooklyn)	2,000	900.00	500.00
51 (b)	(St. Louis Whites WA)	600.00	275.00	150.00
(52)	Bill Burdick 4			
52 (a)	(Indianapolis)	600.00	275.00	150.00
52 (b)	(Omaha)	750.00	335.00	185.00
(53)	Jack Burdock 5			
53 (a)	(Boston NL)	1,100	495.00	275.00
(54)	Bob Burks (Burk) 3			
54 (a)	(Sioux City)	800.00	360.00	200.00
(55)	Watch Burnham 1			
55 (a)	(Indianapolis)	700.00	315.00	175.00
(56)	Jim Burns 8			
56 (a)	(Kansas City)	750.00	335.00	185.00
56 (b)	(Omaha)	600.00	275.00	150.00
(58)	Oyster Burns 5			
58 (a)	(Baltimore)	600.00	275.00	150.00
58 (b)	(Brooklyn)	750.00	335.00	185.00
DP 22	(being tagged by Sam Trott)	1,000	450.00	250.00
(59)	Tom Burns (Also: "E. Burns") 4			
59 (a)	(Chicago NL)	600.00	275.00	150.00
(60)	Doc Bushong 6			
60 (a)	(Brooklyn)	750.00	335.00	185.00
60 2	(St. Louis AA "Brown's Champions")	800.00	360.00	200.00
(61)	John (Patsy) Cahill 2			
61 (a)	(Indianapolis)	600.00	275.00	150.00
(62)	Count Campau 7			
62 (a)	(Detroit)	600.00	275.00	150.00
62 (b)	(Kansas City)	600.00	275.00	150.00
(63)	Jimmy Canavan 3			
63 (a)	(Omaha)	600.00	275.00	150.00
(64)	Bart Cantz (Also: McCantz) 5			
64 (a)	(Baltimore)	600.00	275.00	150.00
64 (b)	(St. Louis Whites WA)	600.00	275.00	150.00
(65)	Jack Carney 5			
65 (a)	(Washington)	600.00	275.00	150.00
(66)	Hick Carpenter 5			
66 (a)	(Cincinnati)	625.00	280.00	155.00
66 (b)	(tagging player)	1,250	560.00	310.00
(67)	Cliff Carroll 2			
67 (a)	(Washington)	600.00	275.00	150.00
(68)	Fred Carroll 3			
68 (a)	(Pittsburgh)	600.00	275.00	150.00
(69)	Scrappy Carroll 8			
69 (a)	(Chicago NL)	600.00	275.00	150.00
69 (b)	(St. Paul)	600.00	275.00	150.00
(70)	Ed Cartwright 5			
70 (a)	(Kansas City)	600.00	275.00	150.00
70 (b)	(St. Joseph)	600.00	275.00	150.00
(71)	Bob Caruthers 7			
71 (a)	(Brooklyn)	650.00	290.00	160.00
71 (b)	(St. Louis AA "Brown's Champions")	1,500	675.00	375.00
(72)	Dan Casey 3			
72 (a)	(Philadelphia NL)	600.00	275.00	150.00
(73)	Elton Chamberlain 6			
73 (a)	(St. Louis)	600.00	275.00	150.00
(74)	Cupid Childs 5			
74 (a)	(Philadelphia NL)	1,000	450.00	250.00

74 (b)	(Syracuse)	800.00	360.00	200.00

Chreve - See Shreve

(75)	Bob Clark 6			
75 (a)	(Brooklyn)	600.00	275.00	150.00
DP 4	(tagging Mickey Hughes)	2,000	900.00	500.00

(76)	Spider Clark 4			
76 (a)	(Washington)	650.00	290.00	160.00

(77)	Dad Clarke (Also: Clark) 11			
77 (a)	(Chicago NL)	600.00	275.00	150.00
77 (b)	(Omaha)	750.00	335.00	185.00

(78)   John Clarkson
See Hall of Fame Section Following

(79)	Jack Clements 3			
79 (a)	(Philadelphia NL)	600.00	275.00	150.00

(80)	Elmer Cleveland 6			
80 (a)	(New York NL)	600.00	275.00	150.00

(81)	Monk Cline 5			
81 (a)	(Sioux City)	600.00	275.00	150.00

(82)	Mike Cody 4			
82 (a)	(Des Moines)	800.00	360.00	200.00

(83)	John Coleman 5			
83 (a)	(Pittsburgh)	600.00	275.00	150.00

(84)	Bill Collins 13			
84 (a)	(Lowell)	600.00	275.00	150.00
84 (b)	(Newark)	725.00	325.00	180.00
84 (c)	(New York)	775.00	350.00	200.00
	(Never played for N.Y.)			

(85)	Hub Collins 6			
85 (a)	(Brooklyn)	600.00	275.00	150.00
85 (b)	(Louisville)	850.00	380.00	210.00

(86)   Charlie Comiskey
(Also: Commiskey)
86 (a) See Hall of Fame Section Following

(87)	Pete Connell 2			
87 (a)	(Des Moines, 3B, dark uniform)	625.00	280.00	155.00
87 (b)	(Des Moines, 1B, light uniform. Photo actually P.J. O'Connell.)	600.00	275.00	150.00

(88)   Roger Connor
(Also: Conner)
See Hall of Fame Section Following

(89)	Dick Conway 6			
89 (a)	(Boston NL)	900.00	405.00	225.00
89 (b)	(Worcester)	600.00	275.00	150.00

(90)	Jim Conway 5			
90 (a)	(Kansas City)	700.00	315.00	175.00

(91)	Pete Conway 10			
91 (a)	(Detroit)	700.00	315.00	175.00
91 (b)	(Pittsburgh)	600.00	275.00	150.00
91 (c)	(Indianapolis)	600.00	275.00	150.00

(92)	Paul Cook 4			
92 (a)	(Louisville)	600.00	275.00	150.00

(93)	Jimmy Cooney 5			
93 (a)	(Chicago NL)	600.00	275.00	150.00
93 (b)	(Omaha)	750.00	335.00	185.00

(94)	Larry Corcoran 4			
94 (a)	(Indianapolis)	750.00	335.00	185.00
94 (b)	(London)	750.00	335.00	185.00

(95)	Pop Corkhill 7			
95 (a)	(Brooklyn)	600.00	275.00	150.00
95 (b)	(Cincinnati)	700.00	315.00	175.00

(96)	Cannonball Crane 7			
96 (a)	(New York NL)	600.00	275.00	150.00
96 (b)	(New York PL)	2,160	975.00	550.00

(97)	Sam Crane 3			
97 (a)	(Washington)	600.00	275.00	150.00

(98)	Jack Crogan (Croghan) 5			
98 (a)	(Chicago Maroons WA)	1,750	785.00	435.00

(99)	John Crooks 7			
99 (a)	(Omaha)	750.00	335.00	185.00
99 (b)	(St. Louis Whites WA)	600.00	275.00	150.00

(100)	Lave Cross 6			
100 (a)	(Louisville)	600.00	275.00	150.00
100 (b)	(Philadelphia AA)	800.00	360.00	200.00
100 (c)	(Philadelphia PL)	2,160	975.00	550.00

(101)	William Crossley 5			
101 (a)	(Milwaukee)	650.00	290.00	160.00

(102)	Joe Crotty 5			
102 (a)	(New York AA "dotted tie.")	2,250	1,000	560.00
102 (b)	(Sioux City)	600.00	275.00	150.00

(103)	Billy Crowell 9			
103 (a)	(Cleveland)	600.00	275.00	150.00
103 (b)	(St. Joseph)	600.00	275.00	150.00

(104)	Jim Cudworth 4			
104 (a)	(Worcester)	600.00	275.00	150.00
(105)	Bert Cunningham 6			

105 (a)	(Baltimore)	750.00	335.00	185.00
105 (b)	(Philadelphia PL)	2,160	975.00	550.00

(106)	Tacks Curtis 5			
106 (a)	(St. Joseph)	800.00	360.00	200.00

(107)	Ed Cushman 3			
107 (a)	(New York AA "dotted tie")	2,250	1,015	565.00
107 (b)	(New York AA)	2,000	275.00	150.00
107 (c)	(Toledo)	1,500	675.00	375.00

(108)	Tony Cusick 2			
108 (a)	(Milwaukee)	5,000	275.00	150.00

(109)   Edward Dailey
(Also: Daley) 7

109 (a)	(Columbus)	600.00	275.00	150.00
109 (b)	(Philadelphia NL)	600.00	275.00	150.00
109 (c)	(Washington)	600.00	275.00	150.00

(110)	Vincent Dailey 1			
110 (a)	(Oakland) (SGC-graded Poor auctioned for $101,100 12/05.)			

(111)	Bill Daley 2			
111 (a)	(Boston NL)	650.00	290.00	160.00
111 (b)	(Boston PL)	1,920	865.00	480.00

(112)	Con Daley (Daily) 9			
112 (a)	(Boston NL)	600.00	275.00	150.00
112 (b)	(No name, team, etc.)	2,250	1,000	560.00
112 (c)	(Indianapolis)	600.00	275.00	150.00

(113)	Abner Dalrymple 7			
113 (a)	(Denver)	925.00	415.00	230.00
113 (b)	(Pittsburgh)	700.00	315.00	175.00

(114)	Sun Daly 5			
114 (a)	(Minneapolis)	775.00	350.00	195.00

(115)	Tom Daly 7			
115 (a)	(Chicago NL)	700.00	315.00	175.00
115 (b)	(Chicago NL)/Portrait	1,200	540.00	300.00
115 (c)	(Cleveland)	600.00	275.00	150.00
	(Never played with Cleveland.)			

(116)	Law Daniels 5			
116 (a)	(Kansas City)	600.00	275.00	150.00

(117)	Dell Darling 6			
117 (a)	(Chicago NL)	600.00	275.00	150.00
117 (b)	(portrait)	1,200	540.00	300.00
117 (c)	(Chicago PL)	2,160	975.00	550.00

(118)	William Darnbrough 2			
118 (a)	(Denver)	750.00	335.00	185.00

(119)	D.J. Davin 2			
119 (a)	(Milwaukee)	5,000	275.00	150.00

(120)	Jumbo Davis 5			
120 (a)	(Kansas City)	600.00	275.00	150.00

(121)	Pat Dealey (Also: Dealy) 6			
121 (a)	(Washington)	675.00	300.00	175.00

(122)	Tom Deasley 20			
122 (a)	(New York NL)	600.00	275.00	150.00
122 (b)	(Washington)	600.00	275.00	150.00

(123)	Harry Decker 5			
123 (a)	(Philadelphia NL)	650.00	290.00	160.00

(124)   Ed Delahanty
See Hall of Fame Section Following

(125)	Jerry Denny 4			
125 (a)	(Indianapolis)	600.00	275.00	150.00
125 (b)	(New York NL)	600.00	275.00	150.00

(126)	Jim Devlin (Also: Delvin) 5			
126 (a)	(St. Louis AA)	600.00	275.00	150.00

(127)	Tom Dolan 5			
127 (a)	(Denver)	600.00	275.00	150.00
127 (b)	(St. Louis AA)	600.00	275.00	150.00

(128)	Jack Donahue 1			
128 (a)	(San Francisco) (SGC-certified Poor, $52,240, 12/04 auction.)			

(129)   Jim Donahue
(Also: Donohue) 7

129 (a)	(New York AA "dotted tie.")	2,250	1,015	565.00
129 (b)	(Kansas City)	600.00	275.00	150.00

(130)	Jim Donnelly 3			
130 (a)	(Washington)	750.00	335.00	185.00

(131)	Charlie Dooley 1			
131 (a)	(Oakland) (SGC-certified Poor, $52,240, 12/04 auction.)			

(132)	John Doran 2			
132 (a)	(Omaha)	800.00	360.00	200.00

(133)	Mike Dorgan 17			
133 (a)	(New York NL)	600.00	275.00	150.00
	Sliding	950.00	430.00	225.00

(134)	Con Doyle 1			
134 (a)	(San Francisco) (Value Undetermined)			

(135)	Charlie Duffe (Duffee) 5			
135 (a)	(St. Louis AA)	750.00	335.00	185.00

(136)   Hugh Duffy
See Hall of Fame Section Following

(137)	Dan Dugdale 7			
137 (a)	(Chicago Maroons WA)	900.00	400.00	225.00
137 (b)	(Minneapolis)	750.00	335.00	185.00

(138)	Martin Duke 5			
138 (a)	(Minneapolis)	600.00	275.00	150.00

(139)	Fred Dunlap 9			
139 (b)	(Pittsburgh)	725.00	325.00	180.00

(140)	J.E. Dunn 5			
140 (a)	(Chicago Maroons WA)	2,100	945.00	525.00

(141)	Jesse Duryea 4			
141 (a)	(Cincinnati)	700.00	315.00	175.00
141 (b)	(St. Paul)	600.00	275.00	150.00

(142)	Frank Dwyer 5			
142 (a)	(Chicago NL)	600.00	275.00	150.00
142 (b)	(Chicago Maroons WA)	2,100	945.00	525.00

(143)	Billy Earle (Also: Earl) 4			
143 (a)	(Cincinnati)	600.00	275.00	150.00
143 (b)	(St. Paul)	600.00	275.00	150.00

(144)	Hi Ebright 2			
144 (a)	(Washington)	600.00	275.00	150.00

(145)	Red Ehret 4			
145 (a)	(Louisville)	600.00	275.00	150.00

Eidner - See Weidner

(146)	R. Emmerke 5			
146 (a)	(Des Moines)	700.00	315.00	175.00

(147)	Dude Esterbrook 11			
147 (a)	(Indianapolis)	600.00	275.00	150.00
147 (b)	(Louisville)	600.00	275.00	150.00
147 (c)	(New York AA)	1,125	500.00	280.00
147 (d)	(New York NL)	600.00	275.00	150.00

(148)	Henry Esterday (Easterday) 6			
148 (a)	(Columbus)	600.00	275.00	150.00
148 (b)	(Kansas City)	600.00	275.00	150.00

(149)   Buck Ewing
See Hall of Fame Section Following

(150)	John Ewing 4			
150 (a)	(Louisville)	700.00	315.00	175.00

(151)	Jay Faatz 3			
151 (a)	(Cleveland)	700.00	315.00	175.00

(152)	Bill Fagan 5			
152 (a)	(Denver)	750.00	335.00	185.00
152 (b)	(Kansas City)	650.00	290.00	160.00

(153)	Bill Farmer 7			
153 (a)	(Pittsburgh)	600.00	275.00	150.00
153 (b)	(St. Paul)	750.00	335.00	185.00

(154)	Sid Farrar (Also: Farrer, Faraer) 8			
154 (a)	(Philadelphia NL)	600.00	275.00	150.00
154 (b)	(Philadelphia PL)	2,160	975.00	550.00

(155)	Duke Farrell (Also: Farrel) 5			
155 (a)	(Chicago NL)	600.00	275.00	150.00
155 (b)	(Chicago PL)	2,160	975.00	550.00

(156)	Jack Farrell 12			
156 (a)	(Baltimore)	600.00	275.00	150.00
156 (b)	(Washington)	600.00	275.00	150.00
156 (c)	(Washington)	775.00	350.00	200.00
	(Tagging Paul Hines.)			

(157)	Frank Fennelly 5			
157 (a)	(Cincinnati)	600.00	275.00	150.00
157 (b)	(Philadelphia AA)	600.00	275.00	150.00

(158)	Charlie Ferguson 4			
158 (a)	(Philadelphia NL)	600.00	275.00	150.00

(159)	Alex Ferson 5			
159 (a)	(Washington)	750.00	335.00	185.00

(160)	Wallace Fessenden 4			
160 1	(Umpire)	1,600	720.00	400.00

(161)	Jocko Fields (Also: Field) 6			
161 (a)	(Pittsburgh)	600.00	275.00	150.00
DP 6	(Fielding, Sam Barkley looking on.)	1,100	500.00	275.00
DP 7	(Tagging Sam Barkley.)	1,100	495.00	275.00

(162)	Fischer 2			
162 (a)	(Chicago Maroons WA)	22,500	10,000	5,625

(163)	Thomas Flanigan (Flanagan) 4			
163 (a)	(Cleveland)	800.00	360.00	200.00
	(Never played for Cleveland)			
163 (b)	(Sioux City)	600.00	275.00	150.00

(164)	Silver Flint 5			
164 (a)	(Chicago NL)	900.00	400.00	225.00

(165)	Thomas Flood 5			
165 (a)	(St. Joseph)	600.00	275.00	150.00

(166)	Jocko Flynn 2			
166 (a)	(Omaha) (Two known.)	10,000		

(167)	Jim Fogarty (Also: Fogerty) 5			
167 (a)	(Philadelphia NL)	600.00	275.00	150.00

(168)	Frank Foreman 6			
168 (a)	(Baltimore)	600.00	275.00	150.00

168 (b)(Cincinnati) — 1,100 500.00 275.00

(169) Tom Forster
(Also: "F.W. Foster") 3
169 (a)(Hartford) — 600.00 275.00 150.00
169 (b)(Milwaukee) — 750.00 335.00 185.00
169 (c)(New York AA "dotted tie") — 2,250 1,015 565.00

(170) Elmer Foster 7
170 (a)(New York AA "dotted tie.") — 4,125 1,840 1,030
170 (b)(New York NL) — 600.00 275.00 150.00
170 (c)(Minneapolis) — 600.00 275.00 150.00

(171) Dave Foutz 5
171 (a)(Brooklyn) — 800.00 360.00 200.00
171 (b)(St. Louis AA "Brown's Champions") — 1,350 600.00 335.00

(172) Julie Freeman 5
172 (a)(Milwaukee) — 750.00 335.00 185.00

(173) Will Fry 4
173 (a)(St. Joseph) — 750.00 335.00 185.00

(174) Frank Fudger 1
174 (a)(Oakland) (Value Undetermined)

(175) Shorty Fuller 5
175 (a)(St. Louis AA) — 750.00 335.00 185.00

(176) William Fuller 5
176 (a)(Milwaukee) — 800.00 360.00 200.00

(177) Chris Fulmer (Also: Fullmer) 6
177 (a)(Baltimore) — 600.00 275.00 150.00
DP 8 (Tagging Tom Tucker.) — 1,750 785.00 435.00

(178) John Gaffney 1
178 (a)(Washington) — 775.00 350.00 195.00
DP 21 (Behind George Shoch.) — 1,000 450.00 250.00

(179) Pud Galvin
See Hall of Fame Section Following

(180) Bob Gamble 3
180 (a)(Philadelphia AA) — 600.00 275.00 150.00
DP 3 (Being tagged by Lou Bierbaur.) (Bierbauer) — 1,400 630.00 350.00

(181) Charlie Ganzel (Also: Gauzel) 5
181 (a)(Boston) — 600.00 275.00 150.00
181 (b)(Detroit) — 600.00 275.00 150.00

(182) Gid Gardner 5
182 (a)(Philadelphia NL) — 600.00 275.00 150.00
182 (b)(Washington) — 900.00 405.00 225.00
DP 9 (Tagging Miah Murray.) — 2,500 1,125 625.00

(183) Hank Gastreich (Gastright) 5
183 (a)(Columbus) — 600.00 275.00 150.00

(184) Emil Geiss 6
184 (a)(Chicago NL) — 600.00 275.00 150.00

(185) Frank Genins (Also: Genius) 5
185 (a)(Sioux City) — 650.00 290.00 160.00

(186) Bill George 5
186 (a)(New York NL) — 700.00 315.00 175.00

(187) Joe Gerhardt 4
187 (a)(Jersey City) — 600.00 275.00 150.00
187 (b)(New York NL) — 1,200 540.00 300.00

(188) Charlie Getzein (Getzien) 6
188 (a)(Detroit) — 600.00 275.00 150.00
188 (b)(Indianapolis) — 600.00 275.00 150.00

(189) Whitey Gibson 1
189 (a)(Philadelphia AA, two known.) (2003 auction) — 10,000 3,300

(190) Bob Gilks 6
190 (a)(Cleveland) — 700.00 315.00 175.00

(191) Pete Gillespie 5
191 (a)(New York NL) — 750.00 335.00 185.00

(192) Barney Gilligan 3
192 (a)(Detroit) — 600.00 275.00 150.00
192 (b)(Washington) — 625.00 280.00 155.00

(193) Frank Gilmore 5
193 (a)(Washington) — 900.00 405.00 225.00

(194) Jack Glasscock (Also: Glassock, Glass, Cock) 5
194 (a)(Indianapolis) — 675.00 305.00 170.00
194 (b)(New York NL) — 600.00 275.00 150.00

(195) Bill Gleason 5
195 (a)(Louisville) — 600.00 275.00 150.00
195 (b)(Philadelphia AA) — 600.00 275.00 150.00
195 (c)(St. Louis AA "Brown's Champions") — 1,750 785.00 435.00
DP 23 (w/ Curt Welch) — 2,000 900.00 500.00

(196) Kid Gleason 5
196 (a)(Philadelphia NL) — 600.00 275.00 150.00

(197) Ed Glenn 5
197 (a)(Sioux City) — 750.00 335.00 185.00

(198) Mike Goodfellow 9
198 (a)(Cleveland) — 800.00 360.00 200.00
198 (b)(Detroit) — 725.00 325.00 180.00

(199) George Gore 10

199 (a)(New York NL) — 900.00 405.00 225.00
199 (b)(New York PL) — 2,160 975.00 550.00

(200) Frank Graves 6
200 (a)(Minneapolis) — 600.00 275.00 150.00

(201) Bill Greenwood 8
201 (a)(Baltimore) — 1,100 495.00 275.00
201 (b)(Columbus) — 700.00 315.00 175.00

(202) Ed Greer 3
202 (a)(Brooklyn) — 750.00 335.00 185.00
DP 10 (Catching, Hardie Henderson batting.) — 1,000 450.00 250.00

(203) Mike Griffin 6
203 (a)(Baltimore) — 1,000 450.00 250.00
203 (b)(Philadelphia PL) — 2,160 975.00 550.00

(204) Clark Griffith
See Hall of Fame Section Following

(205) Henry Gruber 4
205 (a)(Cleveland) — 600.00 275.00 150.00

(206) Ad Gumbert 5
206 (a)(Chicago NL) — 600.00 275.00 150.00
206 (b)(Boston PL) — 2,160 975.00 550.00

(207) Tom Gunning 4
207 (a)(Philadelphia AA) — 600.00 275.00 150.00
207 (b)(Philadelphia NL) — 600.00 275.00 150.00

(208) Joe Gunson 4
208 (a)(Kansas City) — 650.00 290.00 160.00

(209) George Haddock 5
209 (a)(Washington) — 600.00 275.00 150.00

(210) Frank Hafner 5
210 (a)(Kansas City) — 650.00 290.00 160.00

(211) Willie Hahn/Mascot
211 (a)(Chicago NL) — 750.00 335.00 185.00
DP 24 (w/ Ned Williamson) — 3,500 1,575 875.00

Halliday - See Holliday

(212) Bill Hallman 6
212 (a)(Philadelphia NL) — 750.00 335.00 185.00
212 (b)(Philadelphia PL) — 2,160 975.00 550.00

(213) Billy Hamilton
See Hall of Fame Section Following

(214) Frank Hankinson 1
214 (a)(New York AA "dotted tie.") — 18,000 8,100 4,500

(215) Ned Hanlon 6
See Hall of Fame Section Following

Hannon - See Shannon

(216) Bill Hanrahan 9
216 (a)(Chicago Maroons WA) — 900.00 400.00 225.00
216 (b)(Minneapolis) — 600.00 275.00 150.00

(217) Al Hapeman 1
217 (a)(Sacramento) (Value Undetermined)

(218) John Harkins (Also: Harkens) 9
218 (a)(Baltimore) — 700.00 315.00 175.00
218 (b)(Brooklyn) — 600.00 275.00 150.00

(219) Bill Hart 5
219 (a)(Cincinnati) (Never played for Cincinnati.) — 600.00 275.00 150.00
219 (b)(Des Moines) — 750.00 335.00 185.00

(220) Bill Hasamdear (Hassamaer) 3
220 (a)(Kansas City) — 700.00 315.00 175.00

(221) Gil Hatfield 5
221 (a)(New York NL) — 700.00 315.00 175.00
221 (b)(New York PL) — 2,160 975.00 550.00

(222) Bill Hawes (Also Howes) 5
222 (a)(Minneapolis) — 700.00 315.00 175.00
222 (b)(St. Paul) — 775.00 350.00 195.00

(223) John J. "Egyptian" Healey (Healy) 5
223 (a)(Indianapolis) — 650.00 290.00 160.00
223 (b)(Washington) — 800.00 360.00 200.00
223 (c)(Washington, portrait, w/ moustache, no cap, possibly unique.) — 30,000 13,500 7,500

(224) John C. "Jack" Healy (Also: Healey) 8
224 (a)(Denver) — 925.00 415.00 230.00
224 (b)(Omaha) — 750.00 335.00 185.00

(225) Guy Hecker 5
225 (a)(Louisville) — 1,900 850.00 475.00

(226) Tony Hellman 5
226 (a)(Sioux City) — 700.00 315.00 175.00

(227) Hardie Henderson 13
227 (a)(Brooklyn) — 600.00 275.00 150.00
227 (b)(Pittsburgh) — 600.00 275.00 150.00
DP 10 (Batting, Ed Greer catching.) — 1,000 450.00 250.00
DP 11 (Tagging Jimmy Peoples.) — 1,400 630.00 350.00

(228) Moxie Hengle 10
228 (a)(Chicago Maroons WA) — 1,250 560.00 310.00
228 (b)(Minneapolis) — 800.00 360.00 200.00

(229) John Henry 5
229 (a)(Philadelphia) (Never actually played for Philadelphia.) — 600.00 275.00 150.00

(230) Ed Herr 7
230 (a)(Milwaukee) — 800.00 360.00 200.00
230 (b)(St. Louis Whites WA) — 600.00 275.00 150.00

(231) Hunkey Hines 4
231 (a)(St. Louis Whites WA) — 1,200 540.00 300.00

(232) Paul Hines 7
232 (a)(Indianapolis) — 800.00 360.00 200.00
232 (b)(Washington) — 750.00 335.00 185.00

(233) Frank Hoffman 4
233 (a)(Denver) — 850.00 380.00 210.00

(234) Eddie Hogan 5
234 (a)(Cleveland) — 675.00 300.00 175.00

(235) Bill Holbert 10
235 (a)(Brooklyn) — 900.00 400.00 225.00
235 (b)(Jersey City) — 900.00 400.00 225.00
235 (c)(New York AA "dotted tie") — 7,125 3,190 1,765
235 (d)(New York AA) — 600.00 275.00 150.00

(236) Bug Holliday (Also: Halliday) 7
236 (a)(Cincinnati) — 600.00 275.00 150.00
236 (b)(Des Moines) — 600.00 275.00 150.00

(238) Buster Hoover 3
238 (a)(Philadelphia) — 600.00 275.00 150.00
238 (b)(Toronto) (Never played for Phila. in N172 era.) — 675.00 300.00 175.00
DP 1 (Hoover tagging Ed Andrews.) — 1,000 450.00 250.00

(239) Charlie Hoover 7
239 (a)(Chicago) (Never played for Chicago.) — 600.00 275.00 150.00
239 (b)(Kansas City) — 700.00 315.00 175.00

(240) Jack Horner (Also: Hodner) 6
240 (a)(Milwaukee) — 600.00 275.00 150.00
240 (b)(New Haven) — 600.00 275.00 150.00
240 (c)(Photo actually E.H. Warner) — 600.00 275.00 150.00
DP 5 (w/ Ed Warner) — 1,000 450.00 250.00

(241) Joe Hornung (Also: Horning) 6
241 (a)(Baltimore) — 600.00 275.00 150.00
241 (b)(Boston) — 750.00 335.00 185.00
241 (c)(New York NL) — 600.00 275.00 150.00

(242) Pete Hotaling (Also: Hotoling) 4
242 (a)(Cleveland) — 600.00 275.00 150.00

Howes - See Hawes

(243) Dummy Hoy 5
243 (a)(Washington) — 7,500 3,375 1,875

(244) Nat Hudson 6
244 (a)(St. Louis AA "Brown's Champions") — 1,450 650.00 360.00
244 (b)(St. Louis AA) — 600.00 275.00 150.00

(245) Mickey Hughes 7
245 (a)(Brooklyn) — 600.00 275.00 150.00
DP 4 (being tagged by Bob Clark) — 2,000 900.00 500.00

(246) Al Hungler 4
246 (a)(Sioux City) — 700.00 315.00 175.00

(247) Bill Hutchinson 4
247 (a)(Chicago NL) — 1,200 540.00 300.00

(248) Arthur Irwin 13
248 (a)(Boston PL) — 960.00 435.00 240.00
248 (b)(Philadelphia NL) (Portrait, cap off.) — 775.00 350.00 195.00
— 2,000 900.00 500.00
248 (c)(Washington) — 600.00 275.00 150.00

(249) John Irwin 5
249 (a)(Washington) — 600.00 275.00 150.00
249 (b)(Wilkes-Barre) — 775.00 350.00 195.00

(250) A.C. Jantzen 5
250 (a)(Minneapolis) — 700.00 315.00 175.00

(251) Frederick Jevne 5
251 (a)(Minneapolis) — 725.00 325.00 180.00

(252) Spud Johnson 6
252 (a)(Columbus) — 600.00 275.00 150.00
252 (b)(Kansas City) — 800.00 360.00 200.00

(253) Dick Johnston 7
253 (a)(Boston NL) — 650.00 290.00 160.00
253 (b)(Boston PL) — 2,160 975.00 550.00

(254) W.T. Jordan 5
254 (a)(Minneapolis) — 800.00 360.00 200.00

(255) Heinie Kappell (Kappel) 8
255 (a)(Cincinnati) — 600.00 275.00 150.00
255 (b)(Columbus) — 600.00 275.00 150.00

(256) Tim (Also: Jim) Keefe, (Also: Keef, Keefep)
See Hall of Fame Section Following

(257) George Keefe 5
257 (a)(Washington) — 600.00 275.00 150.00

(258) Jim Keenan 5

258 (a)(Cincinnati) — 600.00 275.00 150.00

(259) Charlie Kelly 5
259 (a)(Philadelphia AA) — 1,600 720.00 400.00

(260) Honest John Kelly 4
260 (a)(Louisville) — 600.00 275.00 150.00
260 (b)(umpire WA) — 1,550 695.00 385.00
DP 14 (w/ Jim Powell) — 1,000 450.00 250.00

(261) King Kelly
See Hall of Fame Section Following

(262) Rudy Kemmler (Also: Kemler) 2
262 (a)(St. Louis AA "Brown's Champions") — 1,150 515.00 285.00
262 (b)(St. Paul) — 600.00 275.00 150.00

(263) Ted Kennedy 9
263 (a)(Des Moines) — 750.00 335.00 185.00
263 (b)(Omaha) — 1,000 450.00 250.00

(264) J.J. Kenyon 7
264 (a)(Des Moines) — 600.00 275.00 150.00
264 (b)(St. Louis Whites WA) — 675.00 305.00 170.00

(265) John Kerins 6
265 (a)(Louisville) — 750.00 335.00 185.00

(266) Matt Kilroy 7
266 (a)(Baltimore) — 1,200 540.00 300.00
266 (b)(Boston PL) — 2,160 975.00 550.00

(267) Silver King 3
267 (a)(Chicago PL) — 2,160 975.00 550.00
267 (b)(St. Louis AA) — 600.00 275.00 150.00

(268) Gus Kloff (Klopf) 7
268 (a)(Minneapolis) — 600.00 275.00 150.00
268 (b)(St. Joseph) — 600.00 275.00 150.00
DP 15 (w/ Bill Krieg) — 1,000 450.00 250.00

(269) Billy Klusman 7
269 (a)(Denver) — 950.00 425.00 235.00
269 (b)(Milwaukee) — 600.00 275.00 150.00

(270) Phil Knell 5
270 (a)(St. Joseph) — 700.00 315.00 175.00

(271) Ed Knouff 5
271 (a)(St. Louis AA) — 700.00 315.00 175.00

(272) Charles Kremmeyer (Krehmeyer) 1
272 (a)(Sacramento)(SGC-certified Fair, $50,233 12/04 auction.)

(273) Bill Krieg (Also: Kreig) 14
273 (a)(Minneapolis) — 675.00 300.00 175.00
273 (b)(St. Joseph) — 650.00 290.00 160.00
273 (c)(Washington) — 600.00 275.00 150.00
DP 15 (w/ Gus Kloff)(Klopf) — 1,000 450.00 250.00

(274) Gus Krock 5
274 (a)(Chicago NL) — 600.00 275.00 150.00

(275) Willie Kuehne (Also: Kuchne) 5
275 (a)(Pittsburgh) — 600.00 275.00 150.00

(276) Fred Lange 5
276 (a)(Chicago Maroons WA) — 1,750 785.00 435.00

(277) Henry Larkin 4
277 (a)(Philadelphia AA) — 600.00 275.00 150.00

(278) Arlie Latham 7
278 (a)(St. Louis AA "Brown's Champions") — 1,300 585.00 325.00
278 (b)(St. Louis AA) — 625.00 280.00 155.00
278 (c)(Chicago PL) — 2,160 975.00 550.00

(279) Chuck Lauer 4
279 (a)(Pittsburgh) — 600.00 275.00 150.00

(280) John Leighton 5
280 (a)(Omaha) — 750.00 335.00 185.00

(281) Levy 1
281 (a)(San Francisco)(Value Undetermined)

(282) Tom Loftus 2
282 (a)(Cleveland) — 600.00 275.00 150.00
282 (b)(St. Louis Whites WA) — 600.00 275.00 150.00

(283) Danny Long 1
283 (a)(Oakland)(Value Undetermined)

(284) Herman Long 7
284 (a)(Chicago Maroons WA) — 2,700 1,225 675.00
284 (b)(Kansas City) — 800.00 360.00 200.00

(285) Tom Lovett 6
285 (a)(Brooklyn) — 800.00 360.00 200.00
285 (b)(Omaha) — 750.00 335.00 185.00

(286) Bobby Lowe 6
286 (a)(Milwaukee) — 950.00 425.00 235.00
DP 18 (About to be tagged by Pat Pettee.) — 1,200 540.00 300.00

(287) Jack Lynch 5
287 (a)(New York AA "dotted tie.") — 2,250 1,015 565.00
287 (b)(New York AA) — 600.00 275.00 150.00

(288) Denny Lyons 4
288 (a)(Philadelphia AA) — 600.00 275.00 150.00

(289) Harry Lyons 6

(289) (a)(St. Louis AA) — 600.00 275.00 150.00
289 (b)(Jersey City) — 600.00 275.00 150.00

(290) Connie Mack 3
See Hall of Fame Section Following

(291) Reddy Mack 6
291 (a)(Baltimore) — 700.00 315.00 175.00
291 (b)(Louisville) — 600.00 275.00 150.00

(292) Jimmy Macullar 7
292 (a)(Des Moines) — 1,200 540.00 300.00
292 (b)(Milwaukee) — 600.00 275.00 150.00

(293) Kid Madden 9
293 (a)(Boston NL) — 600.00 275.00 150.00
293 (b)(Boston NL)/Portrait — 2,500 1,125 625.00
293 (c)(Boston PL) — 2,160 975.00 550.00

(294) Danny Mahoney 1
294 (a)(St. Joseph) — 2,200 990.00 550.00

(295) Willard Maines (Mains) 5
295 (a)(St. Paul) — 600.00 275.00 150.00

(296) Fred Mann 5
296 (a)(Hartford) — 600.00 275.00 150.00
296 (b)(St. Louis AA) — 600.00 275.00 150.00
(Never played for St. Louis.)

(297) Jimmy Manning 6
297 (a)(Kansas City) — 750.00 335.00 185.00

(298) Lefty Marr 7
298 (a)(Cincinnati) — 600.00 275.00 150.00
298 (b)(Columbus) — 675.00 305.00 170.00

(299) Mascot (Willie Breslin 1)
299 (a)New York NL (Caption reads "New York Mascot.") — 1,600 725.00 400.00

(300) Leech Maskrey 5
300 (a)(Des Moines) — 600.00 275.00 150.00
300 (b)(Milwaukee) — 600.00 275.00 150.00
300 (c)(Photo actually Jimmy Macullar.) — 600.00 275.00 150.00

Massitt - See Messitt

(301) Bobby Mathews 3
301 (a)(Philadelphia AA) — 800.00 360.00 200.00

(302) Mike Mattimore (Also: Mattemore) 19
302 (a)(New York NL) — 700.00 315.00 175.00
302 (b)(Philadelphia AA) — 625.00 280.00 155.00

(303) Al Maul 7
303 (a)(Pittsburgh) — 600.00 275.00 150.00

(304) Al Mays 5
304 (a)(New York AA "dotted tie.") — 2,250 1,015 565.00
304 (b)(Columbus) — 600.00 275.00 150.00

(305) Jimmy McAleer 4
305 (a)(Cleveland) — 600.00 275.00 150.00

(306) John McCarthy (McCarty) 3
306 (a)(Kansas City) — 800.00 360.00 200.00

(307) Tommy McCarthy
See Hall of Fame Section Following

(308) Jim McCauley 3
308 (a)(Chicago Maroons WA) — 1,750 785.00 435.00

(309) Bill McClellan (Also: McClennan) 3
309 (a)(Brooklyn) — 600.00 275.00 150.00
309 (b)(Denver) — 1,200 540.00 300.00

(310) Jim McCormack 4
310 (a)(St. Louis Whites WA) — 600.00 275.00 150.00

(311) Jim McCormick 10
311 (a)(Chicago) — 1,200 540.00 300.00
311 (b)(portrait) — 4,000 1,800 1,000
311 (c)(Pittsburgh) — 750.00 335.00 185.00

(312) McCreachery 1
312 (a)(Indianapolis)(Value Undetermined)
(Nobody named McCreachery ever managed Indianapolis. Photo actually Deacon White.)

(313) Tom McCullum (McCallum) 4
313 (a)(Minneapolis) — 600.00 275.00 150.00

(314) Jim McDonald 1
314 (a)(Oakland)(Value Undetermined)

(315) Chippy McGarr 5
315 (a)(Kansas City) — 600.00 275.00 150.00
315 (b)(St. Louis AA) — 600.00 275.00 150.00
315 (c)(St. Louis AA, batting, umpire behind.) — 775.00 350.00 195.00

(316) Jack McGeachy 4
316 (a)(Indianapolis) — 750.00 335.00 185.00

(317) John McGlone 7
317 (a)(Cleveland) — 600.00 275.00 150.00
317 (b)(Detroit) — 600.00 275.00 150.00

(318) Deacon McGuire 5
318 (a)(Philadelphia NL) — 650.00 290.00 160.00
318 (b)(Toronto) — 725.00 325.00 180.00

(319) Bill McGunnigle 1
319 (a)(Brooklyn) — 1,500 675.00 375.00

(320) Ed McKean 5
320 (a)(Cleveland) — 600.00 275.00 150.00

(321) Alex McKinnon 4
321 (a)(Pittsburgh) — 600.00 275.00 150.00

(322) Tom McLaughlin 1
322 (a)(New York AA "dotted tie.") — 5,250 2,365 1,315

(323) Bid McPhee
See Hall of Fame Section Following

(324) Jack McQuaid 1
324 (a)(Umpire) — 2,000 900.00 500.00

(325) James McQuaid 3
325 (a)(Denver) — 1,500 675.00 375.00

(326) Jim McTamany (Also: McTammany) 6
326 (a)(Brooklyn) — 1,500 675.00 375.00
326 (b)(Columbus) — 1,500 675.00 375.00
326 (c)(Kansas City) — 1,500 675.00 375.00

(327) George McVey 9
327 (a)(Denver) — 600.00 275.00 150.00
327 (b)(Milwaukee) — 600.00 275.00 150.00
327 (c)(St. Joseph) — 650.00 290.00 160.00

(328) Pete Meegan 1
328 (a)(San Francisco)(Value Undetermined)

(329) John Messitt (Also: Massitt, Wassitt) 3
329 (a)(Omaha) — 1,150 515.00 285.00

Micholson - See Nicholson

(330) Doggie Miller 5
330 (a)(Pittsburgh) — 600.00 275.00 150.00

(331) Joe Miller 3
331 (a)(Minneapolis) — 600.00 275.00 150.00
331 (b)(Omaha) — 650.00 290.00 160.00

(332) Jocko Milligan 6
332 (a)(Philadelphia PL) — 2,160 975.00 550.00
332 (b)(St. Louis AA) — 600.00 275.00 150.00

(333) E.L. Mills 5
333 (a)(Milwaukee) — 600.00 275.00 150.00

(334) Daniel Minnehan (Minahan) 4
334 (a)(Minneapolis) — 600.00 275.00 150.00

(335) Sam Moffet 3
335 (a)(Indianapolis) — 600.00 275.00 150.00

(336) John Morrill (Also: Morrell) 4
336 (a)(Boston NL) — 1,100 495.00 275.00
336 (b)(Boston NL)/Portrait — 1,750 785.00 435.00
336 (c)(Washington) — 900.00 405.00 225.00

(337) Ed Morris 6
337 (a)(Pittsburgh) — 600.00 275.00 150.00

(338) Tony Mullane 7
338 (a)(Cincinnati) — 1,375 622.00 350.00

(339) Joe Mulvey 4
339 (a)(Philadelphia NL) — 600.00 275.00 150.00
339 (b)(Philadelphia PL) — 2,160 975.00 550.00

(340) Pat Murphy 3
340 (a)(New York NL) — 600.00 275.00 150.00

(341) P.L. Murphy 5
341 (a)(St. Paul) — 600.00 275.00 150.00

(342) Miah Murray 5
342 (a)(Washington) — 600.00 275.00 150.00
DP 9 (Being tagged by Gid Gardner.) — 2,500 1,125 625.00

(343) Jim Mutrie 3
343 (a)(New York NL) — 1,750 785.00 435.00

(344) Al Myers 6
344 (a)(Philadelphia NL) — 600.00 275.00 150.00
344 (b)(Washington) — 675.00 300.00 175.00

(345) George Myers 3
345 (a)(Indianapolis) — 600.00 275.00 150.00

(346) Tom Nagle 6
346 (a)(Chicago NL) — 600.00 275.00 150.00
346 (b)(Omaha) — 675.00 305.00 170.00

(347) Billy Nash 7
347 (a)(Boston NL) — 800.00 360.00 200.00
347 (b)(tagging (unnamed) Old Hoss Radbourn) — 2,400 1,075 600.00
347 (c)(Boston PL) — 2,160 975.00 550.00

(348) Jack Nelson 1
348 (a)(New York AA "dotted tie.") — 5,250 2,365 1,315

(349) Kid Nichols
See Hall of Fame Section Following

(350) Samuel Nichols (Nichol) 4
350 (a)(Pittsburgh) — 600.00 275.00 150.00

(351) J.W. Nicholson 6
351 (a)(Chicago Maroons WA) — 1,750 785.00 435.00

(352) Parson Nicholson (Also: Micholson) 7

352 (a)(Cleveland) 600.00 275.00 150.00
    (Never played for Cleveland)
352 (b)(St. Louis Whites WA) 600.00 275.00 150.00

(353) Hugh Nicol (Also: Nicoll) 8
353 (a)(St. Louis AA "Brown's 800.00 360.00 200.00
    Champions")
353 (b)(Cincinnati) 725.00 325.00 180.00
DP 16 (Side by side w/ John Reilly.) 2,000 900.00 500.00
DP 17 (Facing John Reilly.) 2,200 990.00 550.00

(354) Frederick Nyce 4
354 (a)(Burlington) 600.00 275.00 150.00
354 (b)(St. Louis Whites WA) 600.00 275.00 150.00

(355) Doc Oberlander 8
355 (a)(Cleveland) 600.00 275.00 150.00
355 (b)(Syracuse) 600.00 275.00 150.00

(356) Billy O'Brien 5
356 (a)(Washington) 800.00 360.00 200.00

(357) Darby O'Brien 5
357 (a)("Brooklyns" or "Bk'ns.") 600.00 275.00 150.00

(358) Jack O'Brien 8
358 (a)(Baltimore) 600.00 275.00 150.00
358 (b)("Brooklyn") 600.00 275.00 150.00
358 (c)("mini photo") 5,000 2,250 1,250

(359) John O'Brien 4
359 (a)(Cleveland) 800.00 360.00 200.00

(360) P.J. O'Connell 5
360 (a)(Des Moines) 650.00 290.00 160.00
360 (b)(Omaha) 700.00 315.00 175.00

(361) Jack O'Connor 8
361 (a)(Cincinnati) 600.00 275.00 150.00
361 (b)(Columbus) 600.00 275.00 150.00

(362) Hank O'Day 3
362 (a)(Washington) 700.00 315.00 175.00

(363) Harry O'Day 1
363 (a)(Sacramento)(Value Undetermined)

(364) Norris O'Neill 1
364 (a)(Oakland)(Value Undetermined)

(365) Tip O'Neill (Also: O'Neil) 11
365 (a)(Chicago PL) 2,160 975.00 550.00
365 (b)(St. Louis AA "Brown's 1,500 675.00 375.00
    Champions")
365 (c)(St. Louis AA) 600.00 275.00 150.00
365 (d)(Photo actually Bill White.) 850.00 380.00 210.00
    (W/moustache, stooping to
    field grounder.)

(366) Orator Jim O'Rourke
    See Hall of Fame Section Following

(367) Tom O'Rourke
    (Also: Rourke) 8
367 (a)(Boston NL) 750.00 335.00 185.00
367 (b)(Jersey City) 600.00 275.00 150.00

(368) Dave Orr 10
368 (a)(Brooklyn) 800.00 360.00 200.00
368 (b)(Columbus) 850.00 380.00 210.00
368 (c)(New York AA "dotted tie") 10,500 4,725 2,625
368 (d)(New York AA) 600.00 275.00 150.00

(369) Charlie Parsons 4
369 (a)(Minneapolis) 600.00 275.00 150.00

(370) Owen Patton 8
370 (a)(Des Moines) 600.00 275.00 150.00
370 (b)(Minneapolis) 750.00 335.00 185.00

(371) Jimmy Peeples (Peoples) 4
371 (a)(Brooklyn) 600.00 275.00 150.00
371 (b)(Columbus) 700.00 315.00 175.00
DP 11 (Being tagged by Hardie 1,400 630.00 350.00
    Henderson.)

(372) Hip Perrier 1
372 (a)(San Francisco)(Value Undetermined)

(373) Pat Pettee 4
373 (a)(London) 600.00 275.00 150.00
373 (b)(Milwaukee) 600.00 275.00 150.00
DP 18 (About to tag Bobby Lowe.) 1,200 540.00 300.00

(374) Fred Pfeffer 5
374 (a)(Chicago NL) 950.00 425.00 235.00

(375) Dick Phelan 5
375 (a)(Des Moines) 600.00 275.00 150.00

(376) Bill Phillips 7
376 (a)(Brooklyn, large photo.) 1,200 540.00 300.00
376 (b)(Brooklyn, mini photo.) 4,500 2,025 1,125
376 (c)(Kansas City) 700.00 315.00 175.00

(377) John Pickett 12
377 (a)(Kansas City) 600.00 270.00 150.00
377 (b)(Philadelphia PL) 720.00 330.00 180.00
377 (c)(St. Paul) 600.00 275.00 150.00

(378) George Pinkney (Pinckney) 5
378 (a)(Brooklyn) 600.00 275.00 150.00

(379) Tom Poorman
    (Also: Poor Man, Porrman) 7
379 (a)(Milwaukee) 700.00 315.00 175.00
379 (b)(Philadelphia AA) 600.00 275.00 150.00
(380) Henry Porter 7

---

380 (a)(Brooklyn) 1,300 585.00 325.00
380 (b)(Kansas City) 975.00 440.00 245.00

(381) Jim Powell 5
381 (a)(Sioux City) 800.00 360.00 200.00
DP 14 (W/Honest John Kelly.) 1,400 630.00 350.00

(382) Thomas Powers (Power) 1
382 (a)(San Francisco)(Value Undetermined)

(383) Blondie Purcell 7
383 (b)(Baltimore) 600.00 275.00 150.00
383 (b)(Philadelphia AA) 600.00 275.00 150.00

(384) Tom Quinn 5
384 (a)(Baltimore) 775.00 350.00 200.00

(385) Joe Quinn 3
385 (a)(Boston NL) 1,200 540.00 300.00
385 (b)(Des Moines) 600.00 275.00 150.00

(386) Old Hoss Radbourn
    See Hall of Fame Section Following

(387) Paul Radford 8
387 (a)(Brooklyn) 600.00 275.00 150.00
387 (b)(Cleveland) 600.00 275.00 150.00

(388) Tom Ramsey 3
388 (a)(Louisville) 900.00 405.00 225.00

(389) Rehse 5
389 (a)(Minneapolis) 700.00 315.00 175.00

(390) Charlie Reilly (Also: Riley) 4
390 (a)(St. Paul) 600.00 275.00 150.00

(391) Long John Reilly 3
391 (a)(Cincinnati) 900.00 400.00 225.00
DP 16 (side by side w/ Hugh Nicol) 2,000 900.00 500.00
DP 17 (facing Hugh Nicol) 2,250 1,000 560.00

(392) Charlie Reynolds 4
392 (a)(Kansas City) 700.00 315.00 175.00

(393) Danny Richardson
    (Also: Richards) 5
393 (a)(New York NL) 600.00 275.00 150.00
393 (b)(New York PL) 2,160 975.00 550.00
DP 12 (being tagged by Tim Keefe) 2,250 1,000 560.00
DP 13 (Sliding, Tim Keefe fielding 2,250 1,000 560.00
    ball.)

(394) Hardy Richardson 5
394 (a)(Boston NL) 600.00 275.00 150.00
394 (b)(Detroit) 600.00 275.00 150.00

(395) Charlie Ripslager
    (Reipschlager) 1
395 (a)(New York AA "dotted tie.") 6,000 2,700 1,500

(396) John Roach 6
396 (a)(New York NL) 675.00 300.00 175.00

(397) M.C. Robinson 6
397 (a)(Minneapolis) 600.00 275.00 150.00

(398) Wilbert Robinson
    See Hall of Fame Section Following

(399) Yank Robinson 6
399 (a)(St. Louis AA "Brown's 1,200 540.00 300.00
    Champions")
399 (b)(St. Louis AA) 600.00 275.00 150.00

(400) George Rooks 6
400 (a)(Chicago Maroons WA) 900.00 400.00 225.00
400 (b)(Detroit) 600.00 275.00 150.00
    (Never played for Detroit.)

(401) Chief Roseman 1
401 (a)(New York AA "dotted tie.") 5,250 2,350 1,300

Rourke - See Tom O'Rourke

(402) Dave Rowe 8
402 (a)(Denver) 1,400 630.00 350.00
402 (b)(Kansas City, portrait) 5,500 2,475 1,375
402 (c)(Kansas City) 900.00 400.00 225.00

(403) Jack Rowe 3
403 (a)(Detroit) 775.00 350.00 195.00

(404) Amos Rusie (Also: Russie)
    See Hall of Fame Section Following

(405) Jimmy Ryan 8
405 (a)(Chicago NL) 600.00 275.00 150.00
405 (b)(Chicago PL) 2,160 975.00 550.00
405 (c)(Philadelphia) 600.00 275.00 150.00
    (Never player for Phila.)

(406) Harry Sage 6
406 (a)(Des Moines) 600.00 275.00 150.00
406 (b)(Toledo) 1,525 685.00 380.00
DP 19 (w/ Bill Van Dyke) 1,000 450.00 250.00
    (Des Moines)
DP 20 (w/ Bill Van Dyke)(Toledo) 1,000 450.00 250.00

(407) Ben Sanders 5
407 (a)(Philadelphia NL) 600.00 275.00 150.00
407 (b)(Philadelphia PL) 2,160 975.00 550.00

(408) Frank Scheibeck 4
408 (a)(Detroit) 750.00 335.00 185.00

(409) Al Schellhase 5
409 (a)(St. Joseph) 800.00 360.00 200.00

---

(410) Bill Schenkel
    (Also: Schenkle) 4
410 (a)(Milwaukee) 600.00 275.00 150.00

(411) L. Schildknecht 4
411 (a)(Des Moines) 600.00 275.00 150.00
411 (b)(Milwaukee) 600.00 275.00 150.00

(412) Gus Schmelz 2
412 (a)(Cincinnati) 1,500 675.00 375.00

Schoch - See Shoch

(413) Jumbo Schoeneck 8
413 (a)(Chicago Maroons WA) 2,200 990.00 550.00
413 (b)(Indianapolis) 600.00 275.00 150.00

(414) Pop Schriver 5
414 (a)(Philadelphia NL) 600.00 275.00 150.00
DP 2 (Tagging Charlie Bastian.) 1,000 450.00 250.00

Schwartwood - See Swartwood

(415) Emmett Seery 4
415 (a)(Indianapolis) 600.00 275.00 150.00

(416) Billy Serad 5
416 (a)(Cincinnati) 600.00 275.00 150.00
416 (b)(Toronto) 750.00 335.00 185.00

(417) Ed Seward 3
417 (a)(Philadelphia AA) 600.00 275.00 150.00

(418) Orator Shafer (Shaffer) 4
418 (a)(Des Moines) 600.00 275.00 150.00

(419) Taylor Shafer (Shaffer) 3
419 (a)(St. Louis Whites WA) 600.00 275.00 150.00
419 (b)(St. Paul) 600.00 275.00 150.00

(420) Daniel Shannon
    (Also: Hannon) 6
420 (a)(Louisville) 600.00 275.00 150.00
420 (b)(Omaha) 700.00 315.00 175.00
420 (c)(Philadelphia PL) 2,160 975.00 550.00

(421) Bill Sharsig 1
421 (a)(Philadelphia AA) 600.00 275.00 150.00

(422) John Shaw 5
422 (a)(Minneapolis) 600.00 275.00 150.00

(423) Samuel Shaw 4
423 (a)(Baltimore) 900.00 405.00 225.00
423 (b)(Newark) 1,000 450.00 250.00

(424) Bill Shindle (Also: Shindel) 7
424 (a)(Baltimore) 750.00 335.00 185.00
424 (b)(Philadelphia PL) 2,640 1,190 660.00
    ("PL" not on card.)

(425) George Shoch
    (Also: Schoch) 4
425 (a)(Washington) 600.00 275.00 150.00
DP 21 (batting, John Gaffney 1,000 450.00 250.00
    behind)

(426) Otto Shomberg (Schomberg) 3
426 (a)(Indianapolis) 600.00 275.00 150.00

(427) Lev Shreve 7
427 (a)(Indianapolis) 700.00 315.00 175.00

(428) Ed Silch 8
428 (a)(Brooklyn) 600.00 275.00 150.00
428 (b)(Denver) 725.00 325.00 180.00

(429) Mike Slattery 6
429 (a)(New York NL) 600.00 275.00 150.00
429 (b)(New York PL) 2,160 975.00 550.00

(430) Elmer Smith 5
430 (a)(Cincinnati) 600.00 275.00 150.00

(431) Fred Smith 5
431 (a)(Des Moines) 600.00 275.00 150.00

(432) Germany (Geo.) Smith 5
432 (a)(Brooklyn) 600.00 275.00 150.00

(433) Nick Smith 5
433 (a)(St. Joseph) 650.00 290.00 160.00

(434) Phenomenal Smith 10
434 (a)(Baltimore) 675.00 300.00 175.00
434 (b)(Baltimore, portrait.) 8,500 3,825 2,125
    (No team designation.)
434 (c)(Philadelphia AA) 1,100 495.00 275.00

(435) Pop Smith 5
435 (a)(Boston NL) 675.00 305.00 170.00
435 (b)(Pittsburgh) 600.00 275.00 150.00

(436) Skyrocket (Sam) Smith 4
436 (a)(Louisville) 600.00 275.00 150.00

(437) Pete Somers 5
437 (a)(St. Louis AA) 600.00 275.00 150.00
    (Never played for St. Louis.)

(438) Joe Sommer
    (Also: Sommers) 5
438 (a)(Baltimore) 900.00 400.00 225.00

(439) Pete Sommers 7
439 (a)(Chicago NL) 600.00 275.00 150.00
439 (b)(New York NL) 600.00 275.00 150.00
(440) Bill Sowders 7

440 (a)(Boston NL)	600.00	275.00	150.00
(441) John Sowders 4			
441 (a)(Kansas City)	650.00	290.00	160.00
441 (b)(St. Paul)	600.00	275.00	150.00
(442) Charlie Sprague 9			
442 (a)(Chicago NL)	600.00	275.00	150.00
442 (b)(Chicago Maroons WA)	900.00	400.00	225.00
442 (c)(Cleveland)	675.00	300.00	175.00
(443) Ed Sproat 5			
443 (a)(St. Louis Whites WA)	850.00	380.00	210.00
(444) Harry Staley (Also: Stoley) 7			
444 (a)(Pittsburgh)	600.00	275.00	150.00
444 (b)(St. Louis Whites WA)	675.00	305.00	170.00
(445) Dan Stearns (Also: Tearns) 4			
445 (a)(Des Moines)	600.00	275.00	150.00
445 (b)(Kansas City)	750.00	335.00	185.00
(446) Bill Stemmeyer			
(Also: Stemmyer) 6			
446 (a)(Boston NL)	600.00	275.00	150.00
446 (b)(Cleveland)	900.00	405.00	225.00
(447) B.F. Stephens 3			
447 (a)(Milwaukee)	600.00	275.00	150.00
(448) John Sterling 4			
448 (a)(Minneapolis)	600.00	275.00	150.00
(449) Len Stockwell 1			
449 (a)(San Francisco)(Value Determined)			
Stoley - See Staley			
(450) Harry Stovey 9			
450 (a)(Boston PL)	2,160	975.00	550.00
450 (b)(Philadelphia AA)	1,400	630.00	350.00
(451) Scott Stratton 5			
451 (a)(Louisville)	600.00	275.00	150.00
(452) Joe Strauss (Also: Straus) 8			
452 (a)(Milwaukee)	600.00	275.00	150.00
452 (b)(Omaha)	725.00	325.00	180.00
(453) Cub Stricker 3			
453 (a)(Cleveland)	600.00	275.00	150.00
(454) Marty Sullivan 7			
454 (a)(Chicago NL)	600.00	275.00	150.00
454 (b)(Indianapolis)	600.00	275.00	150.00
(455) Mike Sullivan 3			
455 (a)(Philadelphia AA)	600.00	275.00	150.00
(457) Billy Sunday 10			
457 (a)(Chicago NL)	1,750	785.00	435.00
457 (b)(Pittsburgh)	1,500	675.00	375.00
(458) Sy Sutcliffe 5			
458 (a)(Cleveland)	800.00	360.00	200.00
(459) Ezra Sutton 8			
459 (a)(Boston NL)	600.00	275.00	150.00
459 (b)(Milwaukee)	625.00	280.00	155.00
(460) Ed Swartwood			
(Also: Schwartwood) 7			
460 (a)(Brooklyn)	600.00	275.00	150.00
460 (b)(Des Moines)	600.00	275.00	150.00
460 (c)(Hamilton)	725.00	325.00	180.00
(461) Park Swartzel 6			
461 (a)(Kansas City)	600.00	275.00	150.00
(462) Pete Sweeney (Also: Sweeny) 5			
462 (a)(Washington)	900.00	400.00	225.00
(463) Louis Sylvester 1			
463 (a)(Sacramento)(Value Undetermined)			
(464) Pop Tate 6			
464 (a)(Baltimore)	600.00	275.00	150.00
464 (b)(Boston NL)	600.00	275.00	150.00
(465) Patsy (Oliver) Tebeau 8			
465 (a)(Chicago NL)	600.00	275.00	150.00
465 (b)(Cleveland)	700.00	315.00	175.00
Tearns - See Stearns			
(466) John Tener 5			
466 (a)(Chicago NL)	1,250	560.00	310.00
(467) Adonis Terry 5			
467 (a)(Brooklyn)	600.00	275.00	150.00
(468) Sam Thompson			
See Hall of Fame Section Following			
(469) Mike Tiernan 6			
469 (a)(New York NL)	600.00	275.00	150.00
(470) Cannonball Titcomb 5			
470 (a)(New York NL)	600.00	275.00	150.00
(471) Phil Tomney 4			
471 (a)(Louisville)	600.00	275.00	150.00
(472) Steve Toole 7			
472 (a)(Brooklyn)	750.00	335.00	185.00
472 (b)(Kansas City)	600.00	275.00	150.00
472 (c)(Rochester)	675.00	305.00	170.00
(473) George Townsend 3			

473 (a)(Philadelphia AA)	600.00	275.00	150.00
(474) Bill Traffley 4			
474 (a)(Des Moines)	600.00	275.00	150.00
(475) George Treadway			
(Also: Tredway) 6			
475 (a)(Denver)	675.00	305.00	170.00
475 (b)(St. Paul)	675.00	305.00	170.00
(476) Sam Trott 10			
476 (a)(Baltimore)	600.00	275.00	150.00
476 (b)(Newark)	600.00	275.00	150.00
DP 22 (tagging Oyster Burns)	1,000	450.00	250.00
(477) Tommy Tucker 5			
477 (a)(Baltimore)	1,200	540.00	300.00
DP 8 (Being tagged by Chris Fulmer.)	1,750	785.00	435.00
(478) A.M. Tuckerman 5			
478 (a)(St. Paul)	600.00	275.00	150.00
(479) George Turner 5			
479 (a)(Minneapolis)	600.00	275.00	150.00
(480) Larry Twitchell 6			
480 (a)(Cleveland)	600.00	275.00	150.00
480 (b)(Detroit)	600.00	275.00	150.00
(481) Jim Tyng 3			
481 (a)(Philadelphia NL)	600.00	275.00	150.00
(482) Bill Van Dyke 3			
482 (a)(Des Moines)	600.00	275.00	150.00
482 (b)(Toledo)	600.00	275.00	150.00
DP 19 (w/ Harry Sage)(Des Moines)	1,000	450.00	250.00
DP 20 (w/ Harry Sage)(Toledo)	1,000	450.00	250.00
(483) George Van Haltren 4			
483 (a)(Chicago NL)	1,300	585.00	325.00
(484) Farmer Vaughn 7			
484 (a)(Louisville)	600.00	275.00	150.00
484 (b)(New York PL)	2,160	975.00	550.00
(485) Peek-A-Boo Veach 4			
485 (a)(Sacramento)(Value Undetermined)			
485 (b)(St. Paul)	600.00	275.00	150.00
(486) Leon Viau 5			
486 (a)(Cincinnati)	675.00	300.00	170.00
(487) Bill Vinton 4			
487 (a)(Minneapolis)	700.00	315.00	175.00
(488) Joe Visner 5			
488 (a)(Brooklyn)	600.00	275.00	150.00
(489) Chris Von Der Ahe 1			
489 (a)(St. Louis AA "Brown's Champions")	3,250	1,450	810.00
(490) Reddy Walsh 5			
490 (a)(Omaha)	750.00	335.00	185.00
(491) John Ward			
See Hall of Fame Section Following			
(492) Ed Warner 2			
492 (a)(Milwaukee)	600.00	275.00	150.00
DP 5 (w/ Jack Horner)	1,000	450.00	250.00
Wassitt - See Messitt			
(493) Bill Watkins 2			
493 (a)(Detroit)	600.00	275.00	150.00
493 (b)(Kansas City)	800.00	360.00	200.00
(494) Farmer Weaver 4			
494 (a)(Louisville)	1,600	720.00	400.00
(495) Charlie Weber 5			
495 (a)(Sioux City)	800.00	360.00	200.00
(496) Stump Weidman (Wiedman) 4			
496 (a)(Detroit)	600.00	275.00	150.00
(497) Wild Bill Weidner (Widner) 5			
497 (a)(Columbus)	800.00	360.00	200.00
(498) Curt Welch (Also: Welsh) 7			
498 (a)(St. Louis AA "Brown's Champions")	1,500	675.00	375.00
498 (b)(Philadelphia AA)	700.00	315.00	175.00
DP 23 (w/ Bill Gleason)	2,000	900.00	500.00
(499) Mickey Welch (Also: Welsh)			
See Hall of Fame Section Following			
(500) Jake Wells 2			
500 (a)(Kansas City)	1,150	515.00	285.00
(501) Frank Wells 1			
501 (a)(Milwaukee)	750.00	335.00	185.00
(502) Joe Werrick 5			
502 (a)(Louisville)	600.00	275.00	150.00
502 (b)(St. Paul)	850.00	380.00	210.00
(503) Buck West 5			
503 (a)(Cleveland)	750.00	335.00	185.00
(504) Gus Weyhing 3			
504 (a)(Philadelphia AA)	700.00	315.00	175.00
(505) John Weyhing 4			
505 (a)(Columbus)	600.00	275.00	150.00

505 (b)(Philadelphia AA)	950.00	425.00	235.00
(Never played for Phila.)			
(506) Bobby Wheelock 9			
506 (a)(Boston NL)	600.00	275.00	150.00
506 (b)(Detroit)	600.00	275.00	150.00
(Never played for Detroit)			
506 (c)(Photo actually Con Daily)	600.00	275.00	150.00
(508) Pat Whitaker (Also: Whitacre) 7			
508 (a)(Baltimore)	600.00	275.00	150.00
508 (b)(Philadelphia AA)	600.00	275.00	150.00
(Never played for Philadelphia)			
(509) Bill White 5			
509 (a)(Louisville)	600.00	275.00	150.00
(510) Deacon White 10			
510 (a)(Detroit)	1,350	600.00	335.00
510 (b)(Pittsburgh)	600.00	275.00	150.00
(511) Art Whitney 7			
511 (a)(New York NL)	600.00	275.00	150.00
511 (b)(New York PL)	2,160	975.00	550.00
511 (c)(Pittsburgh)	600.00	275.00	150.00
511 (d)(w/dog)	2,400	1,075	600.00
(512) G. Whitney 5			
512 (a)(St. Joseph)	750.00	335.00	185.00
(513) Jim Whitney 4			
513 (a)(Indianapolis)	600.00	275.00	150.00
513 (b)(Washington)	650.00	290.00	160.00
E. Williams, W. Williams - See Ned Williamson			
(514) Jimmy Williams 2			
514 (a)(Cleveland)	900.00	400.00	225.00
(515) Ned Williamson 8			
515 (a)(Chicago NL)	1,200	540.00	300.00
515 (c)(In dress clothes.)	4,500	2,025	1,125
515 (c)(Chicago PL)	2,400	1,080	600.00
DP 24 (w/ Willie Hahn/Mascot)	3,500	1,575	875.00
(516) Tit Willis 5			
516 (a)(Omaha)	700.00	315.00	175.00
(517) Walt Wilmot 8			
517 (a)(Chicago NL)	600.00	275.00	150.00
517 (b)(Washington)	650.00	290.00	160.00
(518) George Winkleman			
(Winkelman) 4			
518 (a)(Hartford)	2,000	335.00	185.00
518 (b)(Minneapolis)	2,000	335.00	185.00
(519) Sam Wise 5			
519 (a)(Boston NL)	900.00	400.00	225.00
519 (b)(Washington)	600.00	275.00	150.00
(520) Chicken Wolf 5			
520 (a)(Louisville)	650.00	290.00	160.00
(521) George Wood 5 (L.F.)			
521 (a)(Philadelphia NL)	600.00	275.00	150.00
521 (b)(Philadelphia PL)	2,160	975.00	550.00
(522) Pete Wood 5 (P)			
522 (a)(Philadelphia NL)	775.00	350.00	195.00
(523) Harry Wright			
See Hall of Fame Section Following			
(524) Chief Zimmer 4			
524 (a)(Cleveland)	625.00	280.00	155.00
(525) Frank Zinn 3			
525 (a)(Philadelphia AA)	600.00	275.00	150.00

1887-1890 Old Judge Hall of Famers Pose Variations

Because of the popularity of collecting Old Judge cards of Hall of Famers, and the sometimes widely varying market values of different poses for those players, this appendix lists each known pose and/or caption variation. These listings disregard the presence, absence or placement of Old Judge advertising within the photo area. Caption variations consider only those machine-printed captions outside of the photo area.

		NM	EX	VG
(11)	Cap Anson			
11 (a)	Street Clothes			
	(A.C. ANSON, Chicagoes)	10,200	4,600	2,550
	(Chicago's)	10,200	4,600	2,550
	(ANSON, CAPT., Chicagos (N L))	15,000	6,750	3,750
11 (b)	In Uniform.			
	(Chicago N L)	250,000	43,200	24,000
(25)	Jake Beckley			
25 (a)	Pittsburgh			
	(Batting, "O" just visible on jersey, Pittsburghs.)	5,400	2,430	1,350
	(Batting, "O" just visible on jersey, Pittsburgs.)	5,400	2,425	1,350
	(Fielding, ball knee-high, "BECKLEY, 1st B., Pittsburghs.)	5,400	2,430	1,350
	(fielding, hands neck-high, Pittsburgh)	5,400	2,430	1,350
	(Fielding, hands neck-high, "J. BECKLEY, 1st B., Pittsburghs.")	7,800	3,500	1,950
	(Fielding, hands neck-high, Pittsburgs.)	5,400	2,430	1,350
25 (b)	St. Louis Whites			
	(Batting, "O" just visible on jersey.)	7,800	3,500	1,950
	(Batting, "TLO" visible on jersey.)	7,800	3,500	1,950
	(Fielding, ball knee-high, "J. BECKLEY, 1st B., St. Louis Whites.")	10,200	4,600	2,550
	(Fielding, hands neck-high, "J. BECKLEY.")	6,000	2,700	1,500
(43)	Dan Brouthers			
43 (a)	Boston, N.L.			
	(Bat at ready, looking to right, "1st B., Bostons.")	3,600	1,620	900.00
	(Fielding, Brouthers on front, Bostons.)	3,120	1,400	780.00
43 (b)	Boston, P.L.			
	(Pose unrecorded.)	7,200	3,240	1,800
43 (c)	Detroit			
	(Bat at ready, looking down at ball.)	4,800	2,160	1,200
	(Bat at ready, looking to right, "1st B., Detroits.")	4,500	2,000	1,125
	(Fielding, "BROUTHERS, 1st B. Detroits.")	5,100	2,280	1,260
	(Fielding, "D. BROUTHERS.")	4,800	2,160	1,200
(78)	John Clarkson			
78 (a)	Boston			
	(Batting, Bostons)	2,280	1,025	570.00
	(Right arm forward, left hand on thigh, Boston.)	2,280	1,025	570.00
	(Right arm forward, left hand on thigh, "P., Bostons.")	2,280	1,025	570.00
	(Right arm back, left hand clear of thigh, "P., Bostons.")	3,300	1,470	825.00
	(Right hand hip-high, Bostons.)	1,620	725.00	400.00
78 (b)	Chicago			
	(Ball in hands at chest, "P. Chicago.")	3,000	1,350	750.00
	(Batting, "P. Chicago.")	3,600	1,620	900.00
	(Fielding, hands head-high, "P. Chicago.")	3,600	1,620	900.00
	(Right arm forward, left hand on thigh, "P. Chicago.")	4,080	1,830	1,020
	(Right arm back, left hand clear of thigh, "P. Chicago.")	3,000	1,350	750.00
	(Right arm back, left hand on thigh, "P. Chicago.")	3,000	1,350	750.00
	(Right hand hip-high, "P. Chicago.")	3,000	1,350	750.00
(86)	Charlie Comiskey			
86 (a)	St. Louis Browns			
	("Brown's Champions")	7,620	3,420	1,890
86 (b)	St. Louis Browns			
	(Arms folded.)	5,100	2,300	1,275
	(Batting, "COMISKEY, Capt. St. Louis Browns.)	6,720	3,030	1,680
	(Fielding, hands head-high, "CHAS. COMISKEY, 1st B., Capt. St. Louis Browns.)	5,100	2,280	1,260
	(Fielding, hands shoulder-high, "COMISKEY., Capt. St. Louis.")	5,100	2,280	1,260
	(Fielding, hands shoulder-high, "C. COMMISKEY, 1st B., St. L. B's.")	4,800	2,160	1,200
	(Sliding, "CHAS. COMISKEY, 1st B., Capt. St. Louis Brown.")	4,800	2,160	1,200
	(Sliding, "COMISKEY, Capt. St. Louis.")	4,800	2,160	1,200
86 (c)	Chicago, P.L.			
	(Arms folded, "COMMISKEY, 1st B., Chicagos.")	24,000	10,800	6,000
(88)	Roger Connor			
88 (a)	New York, N.L.			
	(Batter's box on floor, script name.)	6,900	3,100	1,700
	(Bat on shoulder, name in script.)	6,900	3,100	1,700
	(Bat on shoulder, N Y's.)	5,100	2,400	1,200

		NM	EX	VG
	(Fielding, "B. CONNOR", New Yorks.)	5,100	2,400	1,200
	(Fielding, hands at waist, "CONNER, 1st B., New Yorks.")	5,100	2,400	1,200
	(Hands on knees, name in script.)	6,900	3,100	1,700
	(Hands on knees, New York.)	4,800	2,160	1,200
	(Hands on knees, New Yorks.)	4,800	2,160	1,200
	(Hands on knees, N Y's.)	4,800	2,160	1,200
(124)	Ed Delahanty			
124 (a)	Philadelphia			
	(Bat on right shoulder, "2d B., Phila.")	22,200	10,000	5,550
	(Bat on right shoulder, "2d B., Phila's.)	22,200	10,000	5,550
	(Bat nearly horizontal, "2d B., Phila.")	22,200	10,000	5,550
	(Fielding grounder, Phila)	19,200	8,640	4,800
	(Fielding, hands at waist, "2d B., Phila.")	16,800	7,560	4,200
	(Fielding, hands at waist, Phila's)	16,800	7,560	4,200
	(Throwing, "2d B., Phila.")	23,400	10,530	5,850
	(Throwing, Phila's)	23,400	10,530	5,850
(136)	Hugh Duffy			
136 (a)	Chicago, N.L.			
	(Batting, S.S. Chicago)	3,600	1,620	900.00
	(Batting, "H. DUFFY, S.S., Chicagos.")	3,600	1,625	900.00
	(Batting, "DUFFY, S.S., Chicago's.")	3,600	1,620	900.00
	(Fielding grounder, "H. DUFFY, S.S., Chicago.")	3,600	1,620	900.00
	(Fielding grounder, Chicagos.)	3,600	1,620	900.00
	(Fielding, hands chin-high, right heel behind left leg, Chicago.)	3,600	1,620	900.00
	(Fielding, hands chin-high, right heel behind left leg, Chicagos.)	3,600	1,620	900.00
	(Fielding, hands chin-high, right heel behind left leg, Chicago's.)	3,600	1,620	900.00
	(Fielding, hands neck-high, feet apart, Chicago.)	3,600	1,620	900.00
	(Throwing, right hand head-high, Chicago.)	3,600	1,620	900.00
	(Throwing, right hand head-high, Chicago's.)	3,600	1,620	900.00
136 (b)	Chicago, P.L.			
	(Pose unrecorded.)(Value Undetermined)			
(149)	Buck Ewing			
149 (a)	New York, N.L.			
	(Bat at 45 degrees, New Yorks.)	3,300	1,475	825.00
	(Bat at 45 degrees, N Y's)	3,300	1,470	825.00
	(Bat in hand at side, New Yorks.)	3,300	1,470	825.00
	(Bat nearly horizontal, Capt. New Yorks.)	3,300	1,470	825.00
	(Bat nearly horizontal, Captain, New Yorks.)	3,300	1,470	825.00
	(Fielding grounder, "BUCK EWING, Capt., New Yorks.")	3,300	1,470	825.00
	(Fielding grounder, "EWING, C., New Yorks.")	3,300	1,470	825.00
	(Fielding, hands head-high, New Yorks.)	3,300	1,470	825.00
	(Fielding, hands head-high, N Y's.)	3,300	1,470	825.00
	(Hands on knees, C. New Yorks.)	3,600	1,620	900.00
	(Hands on knees, Captain, New Yorks.)	3,600	1,620	900.00
	(Hands on knees, Capt. N Y's.)	3,600	1,620	900.00
	(Running to left, C., New Yorks.)	3,600	1,620	900.00
	(Running to left, Captain, New Yorks.)	3,600	1,620	900.00
	(Sliding, C., New York.)	3,600	1,620	900.00
	(Sliding, C., New Yorks.)	3,600	1,620	900.00
	(Sliding, Capt., New Yorks.)	3,600	1,620	900.00
	(Throwing, right arm forward, C., New Yorks.)	4,200	1,900	1,050
	(Throwing, right arm forward, Captain, New Yorks.)	4,200	1,900	1,050
	(Throwing, right hand waist-high at side, "EWING, Captain, New Yorks.")	4,800	2,160	1,200
149 (b)	New York, P.L.			
	(Hands on knees, C. New York (PL).)	7,800	3,500	1,950
149 (c)	With mascot Willie Breslin			
	("EWING & MASCOT, New Yorks.")	9,000	4,050	2,250
	(N. Y's)	9,000	4,050	2,250
149 (c)	"EWING, MASCOT New York P L" (A Fair-Good example sold at auction 5/05 for $7,475.)			
(179)	Pud Galvin			
179 (a)	Pittsburgh			
	(Arms at sides, P. Pittsburg.)	5,400	2,430	1,350
	(Arms at sides, P. Pittsburgh.)	5,400	2,430	1,350
	(arms at sides, P. Pittsburgh.)	5,400	2,430	1,350
	(Arms at sides, Pitcher.)	5,400	2,430	1,350
	(Ball in hands above waist, P.)	4,500	2,000	1,125
	(Ball in hands above waist, Pitcher.)	4,500	2,000	1,125
	(Bat at ready, P.)	4,500	2,000	1,125
	(Bat at ready, Pitcher.)	4,500	2,000	1,125

		NM	EX	VG
	(Bat in hand at side, "GALVIN, P. Pittsburg.")	8,700	3,900	2,160
	(Bat in hand at side, "GALVIN, Pitcher Pittsburg.")	8,750	3,900	2,160
	(Bat in hand at side "GALVIN, P., Pittsburgs.")	8,700	3,900	2,160
	(Bat in hand at side, "J. GALVIN, P., Pittsburghs.")	8,700	3,900	2,160
	(Bat in hand at side, "JIM GALVIN.")	8,700	3,900	2,160
(204)	Clark Griffith			
204 (a)	Milwaukee			
	(Ball in hands at chest.)	5,100	2,280	1,260
	(Batting, looking at ball.)	5,100	2,300	1,275
	(Batting, looking at camera, Milwaukee.)	5,100	2,280	1,260
	(Batting, looking at camera, Milwaukees.)	6,000	2,700	1,500
	(Pitching, hands at neck, Milwaukees.)	5,400	2,430	1,350
	(Pitching, right hand head-high, Milwaukees.)	5,100	2,280	1,260
(213)	Billy Hamilton			
213 (a)	Kansas City			
	(Batting, looking at camera, Kansas Citys)	3,900	1,750	975.00
	(Batting, looking up at ball, "L.F. KANSAS CITYS.")	3,900	1,740	975.00
	(Batting, looking up at ball, K.Cs.)	3,900	1,740	975.00
	(Fielding grounder.)	3,900	1,740	975.00
	(Fielding, hands above waist, "L.F. Kansas Citys.")	3,900	1,740	975.00
	(Fielding, hands neck-high, "L.F. Kansas Citys.")	3,900	1,740	975.00
213 (b)	Philadelphia, N.L.			
	(Fielding, hands above waist, Philadelphia N.L.)	2,880	1,300	720.00
	(Fielding, hands neck-high, Philadelphia N.L.)	2,880	1,300	720.00
(215)	Ned Hanlon			
215 (a)	Boston			
	(Never played for Boston)			
	(Bat in hand at sides, Bostons.)	3,600	1,620	900.00
215 (b)	Detroit			
	(Bat in hand at side, C.F. Detroits.)	3,600	1,620	900.00
	(Batting, Detroits)	3,600	1,620	900.00
	(Bielding, Detroits)	3,600	1,620	900.00
215 (c)	Pittsburgh			
	(Batting, Pittsburgs)	3,900	1,620	975.00
	(Bielding, C.F., Pittsburghs)	3,900	1,620	975.00
(256)	Tim Keefe			
256 (a)	New York, N.L.			
	(Ball in hands, front view, "KEEFE, P., New Yorks.")	3,360	1,500	840.00
	(Ball in hands, front view, TIM KEEFE, P. N.Y's.")	3,360	1,500	840.00
	(ball in hands, side view, "JIM KEEFE", New Yorks.)	3,360	1,500	840.00
	(Ball in hands, side view, "TIM KEEFE", New Yorks.)	3,360	1,500	840.00
	(Ball in hands, side view, "TIM KEEFE, P. N.Y's.")	3,360	1,500	840.00
	(Bat nearly horizontal, "KEEFE, P., New Yorks.")	3,360	1,500	840.00
	(Bat nearly horizontal, "TIM KEEF", New Yorks.)	3,360	1,500	840.00
	(Bat nearly horizontal, "TIM KEEFE", New Yorks.)	3,360	1,500	840.00
	(Bat nearly horizontal, "TIM KEEFE", N. Y'.)	3,360	1,500	840.00
	(Bat nearly vertical, "TIM KEEFE, P. N.Y's.")	3,360	1,500	840.00
	(Pitching, right hand at back, "JIM KEEFE", New Yorks.)	3,600	1,620	900.00
	(Pitching, right hand at back, "TIM KEEF", New Yorks.)	3,600	1,620	900.00
	(Pitching, right hand at back, "TIM KEEFE", New Yorks.)	3,600	1,620	900.00
	(Pitching, right hand at back, "TIM KEEFE", N. Y's.)	3,600	1,620	900.00
	(Pitching, right hand head-high, "KEEFE P., New Yorks.)	3,600	1,620	900.00
	(Pitching, right hand head-high, "TIM KEEFE, P. N.Y's.")	3,600	1,620	900.00
	(Pitching, right hand waist-high, "KEEFE, P., New Yorks.")	2,880	1,300	720.00
	(Pitching, right hand waist-high, "TIM KEEFE, P. N.Y's.")	2,880	1,300	720.00
256 (b)	New York, P.L.			
	(Pose unrecorded.)(Value Undetermined)			
DP 12	Tagging Danny Richardson			
	("KEEFE, P., New Yorks.")	2,700	1,225	675.00
	("Keefe & Richardson")	2,700	1,200	675.00
	("Keefe and Richardson Stealing 2d, N.Y's")	2,700	1,200	675.00
DP 13	Fielding Ball, Danny Richardson Sliding			
	("Keefe and Richardson Stealing 2d, N.Y's.")	3,600	1,620	900.00
(261)	King Kelly			
261 (a)	Chicago			
	(Bat at 45 degrees, left-handed, "$10,000 KELLY" Chicago on jersey.)	7,500	3,375	1,875
	(Portrait, bare head, "$10,000 KELLY", Chicago on jersey.)	9,300	3,970	2,300
	(Portrait in cap, "$10,000 KELLY", Chicago on jersey.)	7,800	3,500	1,950
261 (b)	Boston, N.L.			

(Bat at 45 degrees, "$10,000 KELLY.")	7,200	3,240	1,800
(Bat at 45 degrees, no position, Boston.)	6,000	2,700	1,500
(Bat at 45 degrees, "Kelly, C., Boston.")	4,800	2,160	1,200
(Bat at 45 degrees, "Kelly, C., Bostons.")	4,800	2,160	1,200
(Bat horizontal, "$10,000 KELLY.")	6,000	2,700	1,500
(Bat in left hand at side, "$10,000 KELLY.")	6,000	2,700	1,500
(Bat on right shoulder, "$10,000 KELLY.")	7,200	3,240	1,800
(Fielding, hands chest-high, "$10,000 KELLY.")	6,000	2,700	1,500
(Fielding, hands head-high, "$10,000 KELLY.")	6,000	2,700	1,500
(Portrait, bare head, "$10,000 KELLY," Boston on jersey.)	11,400	5,130	2,850

261 (c) Boston, P.L.
(Bat at 45 degrees, no position, Boston (PL).) (Value Undetermined)			

(290) Connie Mack
290 (a) Washington
(Batting, C)	10,800	4,860	2,700
(Batting, Catcher)	10,800	4,860	2,700
(Stooping, hands on knees, C. Washington.)	10,800	4,860	2,700
(Stooping, hands on knees, Catcher.)	10,800	4,860	2,700
(Throwing, C.)	10,800	4,860	2,700
(Throwing, Catcher, "C. MACK.")	10,800	4,860	2,700
(Throwing, Catcher, "MACK.")	10,800	4,860	2,700

(307) Tommy McCarthy
307 (a) Philadelphia, N.L.
(Batting, indoor background, "2d B. Phila.")	4,200	1,900	1,050
(Batting, indoor background, "McCARTHY, Second Base, Philadelphia.")	4,200	1,900	1,050
(Fielding, hands chest-high, "McCARTHY, 2d B. Phila.")	5,400	2,430	1,350
(Fielding, hands chest-high, Philadelphia.)	5,400	2,430	1,350
(Sliding, indoor background, 2d B. Phila.)	4,800	2,160	1,200
(Sliding, Philadelphia.)	4,800	2,160	1,200
(Tagging player, Phila)	4,200	1,900	1,050
(Tagging player, Philadelphia)	4,200	1,900	1,050
(Throwing, 2d B. Phila.)	4,200	1,900	1,050
(Throwing, Philadelphia)	4,200	1,900	1,050

307 (b) St. Louis Browns
(Batting, indoor background, St. Louis Browns.)	3,300	1,470	825.00
(Batting, outdoor background, St. Louis.)	3,300	1,470	825.00
(Batting, outdoor background, St. Louis Browns.)	3,300	1,470	825.00
(Fielding, hands chest-high, 2d B. St. Louis.)	3,300	1,470	825.00
(Fielding, hands chest-high, C.F.)	3,300	1,470	825.00
(Fielding, hands head-high, "TOMMY CARTHY", St. Louis Brown.)	3,300	1,470	825.00
(Fielding, hands head-high, "TOMMY McCARTHY", St. Louis Brown.)	3,300	1,470	825.00
(Fielding, hands head-high, "cCARTHY, C. F. St. Louis Brown.")	3,300	1,470	825.00
(Fielding, hands head-high, "TOMMY McCARTHY" St. Louis Browns.)	3,300	1,470	825.00
(Fielding, hands head-high, "T. McCARTHY, C.F., St. Louis Browns.")	3,300	1,470	825.00
(Sliding, indoor background, "McCARTHY, 2d B. St. Louis.")	3,300	1,470	825.00
(Sliding, indoor background, C.F., St. Louis.)	3,300	1,470	825.00
(Sliding, outdoor background, St. Louis.)	3,300	1,470	825.00
(Sliding, outdoor background, C.F. St. Louis Browns.)	3,300	1,470	825.00
(Tagging player, 2d B.)	3,300	1,470	825.00
(Tagging player, C.F.)	3,300	1,470	825.00
(Throwing, "T. McCARTHY", St. Louis.)	3,600	1,620	900.00
(Throwing, "T. McCARTHY", St. Louis Browns.)	3,600	1,620	900.00
(Throwing, "McCARTHY", St. Louis Browns.)	3,600	1,620	900.00
(Throwing, "McCARTHY, C.F., St. Louis.")	3,600	1,620	900.00

(323) Bid McPhee
323 (a) Cincinnati
(Batting, looking at ball, "McPHEE.")	30,000	13,500	7,500
(Batting, looking at ball, "JOHN McPHEE.")	30,000	13,500	7,500
(Batting, looking at camera, Cincinnati.)	30,000	13,500	7,500
(Batting, looking at camera, Cincinnati (NL).)	30,000	13,500	7,500
(Batting, looking at camera, Cincinnatti.)	30,000	13,500	7,500
(Fielding, hands ankle-high, "McPHEE, 2d B., Cincinnati.")	30,000	13,500	7,500
(Fielding, hands ankle-high, "JOHN McPHEE, 2d B., Cincinnatis.")	30,000	13,500	7,500

(Fielding, hands head-high, "McPHEE, 2d B., Cincinnati.")	30,000	13,500	7,500
(Fielding, hands head-high, "JOHN McPHEE, 2d B. Cincinnati.")	30,000	13,500	7,500
(Fielding, hands head-high, "McPHEE, 2d B., Cincinnatis.")	30,000	13,500	7,500
(Fielding, hands head-high, Cincinnatti.)	30,000	13,500	7,500
(Throwing, Cincinnati)	30,000	13,500	7,500
(Throwing, Cincinnatti)	30,000	13,500	7,500

(349) Kid Nichols
349 (a) Omaha
(Batting, looking at ball, Omaha.)	9,000	4,050	2,250
(Batting, looking at camera, Omaha.)	9,000	4,050	2,250
(Batting, looking at camera, "NICHOLS, P., Omahas.")	9,000	4,050	2,250
(Pitching, hands at chest, Omaha.)	9,000	4,050	2,250
(Pitching, right hand behind back, Omaha.)	9,600	4,320	2,400
(Pitching, right hand behind back, "NICHOLS, P., Omahas.")	9,600	4,320	2,400
(Pitching, right hand forward, P., Omaha.)	9,600	4,320	2,400
(Pitching, right hand forward, P., Omahas.)	9,600	4,320	2,400

(366) Orator Jim O'Rourke
366 (a) New York, N.L.
(Bat in hand at side, C., New Yorks.)	6,000	2,700	1,500
(Bat in hand at side, 3d B., New Yorks.)	6,000	2,700	1,500
(Bat in hand at side, 3d B. N.Y's.)	6,000	2,700	1,500
(Bat in hand at side, 3d B., N. Y's.)	6,000	2,700	1,500
(Batting, 3d B., New Yorks.)	6,000	2,700	1,500
(Batting, 3d B., N. Y's.)	6,000	2,700	1,500
(Fielding, "JIM O'ROURKE, 3d B. N. Y's.)	4,200	1,900	1,050
(Throwing, 3d B., N. Y's.)	4,800	2,160	1,200

(386) Old Hoss Radbourn
386 (a) Boston, N.L.
(Bat on shoulder, P., Boston.)	3,900	1,740	975.00
(Bat on shoulder, P., Bostons.)	3,900	1,750	975.00
(Bat on shoulder, Pitcher, Boston.)	3,900	1,740	975.00
(Bat on shoulder, Pitcher, Bostons.)	3,900	1,740	975.00
(Hands at waist, no space visible between hands and belt, P.)	3,600	1,620	900.00
(Hands at waist, no space visible between hands and belt, Pitcher.)	3,600	1,620	900.00
(Hands at waist, white uniform visible between hands and belt, P.)	4,800	2,160	1,200
(Hands at waist, white uniform visible between hands and belt, Pitcher.)	4,800	2,160	1,200
(Hands on hips, P.)	10,800	4,860	2,700
(Hands on hips, Pitcher.)	10,800	4,860	2,700
(Portrait, P., Boston.)	9,600	4,320	2,400
(Portrait, Pitcher, Boston.)	9,900	4,440	2,430
(Tagging Billy Nash, P., Boston.)	5,400	2,430	1,350
(Tagging Billy Nash, Pitcher.)	5,400	2,430	1,350

386 (b) Boston, P.L.
(hands on hips, Pitcher, Boston (PL).) (Vlaue Undetermined)			

(398) Wilbert Robinson
398 (a) Philadelphia Athletics
(Batting)	4,800	2,150	1,200
(Fielding, hands above head, C. Athletics.)	4,800	2,160	1,200
(Fielding, hands above head, C., Athletics.)	4,800	2,160	1,200
(Fielding, hands neck-high, C. Athletics.)	4,800	2,160	1,200
(Fielding, hands thigh-high.)	4,800	2,160	1,200
(Throwing)	4,800	2,160	1,200

(404) Amos Rusie
404 (a) Indianapolis
(Batting, P., Indianapolis)	4,200	1,900	1,050
(Pitching, hands at neck)	4,200	1,900	1,050
(Pitching, right hand forward chin-high.)	4,200	1,900	1,050
(Pitching, right hand head-high to side, "RUSIE, P., Indianapolis.)	6,000	2,700	1,500
(Pitching, right hand head-high to side, "RUSSIE.")	6,000	2,700	1,500
(Ball in right hand, thigh-high "P., Indianapolis.)	6,300	2,820	1,560

404 (b) New York, N.L.
(Pitching, hands at neck, New Yorks (NL).)	24,000	10,800	6,000
(Pitching, right hand forward chin-high, New Yorks (NL).)	24,000	10,800	6,000

(468) Sam Thompson
468 (a) Detroit
(Arms folded, R.F. Detroits.)	3,300	1,475	825.00
(Bat at 45 degrees, Detroits.)	3,900	1,740	975.00
(Bat in hand at side, Detroits.)	4,200	1,900	1,050
(Batting, ball above head, Detroits.)	3,000	1,350	750.00

(Batting, ball chest-high, R.F. Detroits.)	3,000	1,350	750.00

468 (b) Philadelphia, N.L.
(Arms folded, Phil'a (NL).)	2,640	1,190	660.00
(Bat in hand at side, Philadelphia.)	2,640	1,190	660.00
(Bat in hand at side, R.F., Philadelphias.)	2,640	1,190	660.00
(Bat in hand at side, Phila's.)	2,640	1,190	660.00

(491) John Ward
491 (a) New York, N.L.
(Batting, New Yorks)	2,880	1,300	720.00
(Batting, "Capt. JOHN WARD, S.S. N Y's.")	2,880	1,300	720.00
(Cap in hand at side, "Capt. JOHN WARD.")	4,200	1,900	1,050
(Cap in hand at side, "J. WARD, S.S., New Yorks.")	4,200	1,900	1,050
(Cap in hand at side, "JOHN WARD.")	4,200	1,900	1,050
(Hands behind back, New Yorks.)	3,000	1,350	750.00
(Hands behind back, "Capt. JOHN WARD, S.S. N Y's.")	3,000	1,350	750.00
(Hands on hips, "J.M. WARD, S.S. New Yorks.")	4,500	2,000	1,125
(Hands on hips, "Capt. JOHN WARD, S.S. N. Y's.")	6,600	2,970	1,650
(Portrait, "Capt. JOHN WARD.")	5,400	2,430	1,350
(Portrait, "J. WARD, S.S., New Yorks.")	5,400	2,430	1,350
(Portrait, "J.M. WARD, S.S., New Yorks.")	5,400	2,430	1,350
(Sliding, left hand raised, "Capt. JOHN WARD, S.S. N Y's.")	2,640	1,190	660.00
(Sliding, left hand raised, "J.M. WARD, S.S., New Yorks.")	2,640	1,190	660.00
(Sliding, left hand raised, "WARD.")	2,640	1,190	660.00
(Sliding, right hand raised, New Yorks.)	3,000	1,350	750.00
(Sliding, right hand raised, "Capt. JOHN WARD, S.S. N Y's.")	3,000	1,350	750.00
(Throwing, left profile, New Yorks)	4,200	1,900	1,050
(Throwing, left profile, "Capt. JOHN WARD, S.S. N. Y's.")	4,200	1,900	1,050
(Throwing, right profile, "Capt. JOHN WARD, S.S. N. Y's.")	4,200	1,900	1,050
(Throwing, right profile, "JOHN WARD.")	4,200	1,900	1,050

(499) Mickey Welch
499 (a) New York, N.L.
(Ball in hands above waist, "SMILING MICKEY.")	5,400	2,425	1,350
(Ball in hands above waist, "WELSH.")	5,400	2,430	1,350
(Right arm extended forward, "SMILING MICKEY.")	5,400	2,430	1,350
(Right hand at right thigh, "WELCH", New Yorks.)	5,400	2,430	1,350
(Right hand at right thigh, "WELCH", New Yorks (NL).)	5,400	2,430	1,350
(Right hand at right thigh, "WELSH", New Yorks.)	5,400	2,430	1,350
(Right hand head-high, "WELCH", New York.)	5,400	2,430	1,350
(Right hand head-high, "WELCH", N.Y's.)	5,400	2,430	1,350
(Right hand head-high, "WELSH", New York.)	5,400	2,430	1,350

(523) Harry Wright
523 (a) Philadelphia, N.L.
(Portrait, looking to his right, beard clear of right side of collar, "HARRY WRIGHT, Man'g. Philas.")	18,000	8,100	4,500
(Portrait, looking to his right, beard just over right side of collar, "Mgr., Phila. (NL).")	18,000	8,100	4,500
(Portrait, looking to his right, beard just over right side of collar, "Man'g. Phila.")	18,000	8,100	4,500
(Portrait, looking to his right, beard just over right side of collar, "Mgr. Phila's.")	18,000	8,100	4,500
(Portrait, looking to his left, "Man'g. Phila.")	18,000	8,100	4,500
(Portrait, looking to his left, "Man'g. Philas.")	18,000	8,100	4,500
(Portrait, looking to his left, Phila (NL).)	19,200	8,640	4,800
(Portrait, looking to his left, "Mgr. Phila's.")	18,000	8,100	5,400

1888-1889 Old Judge Cabinets (N173)

These cabinet cards were issued by Goodwin & Co. in 1888-89 as a premium available by exchanging coupons found in Old Judge or Dogs Head brand cigarettes. The cabinet cards consist of 3-3/4" x 5-3/4" photographs affixed to a cardboard backing that measures approximately 4-1/4" x 6-1/2". The mounting is usually pale yellow with gold-leaf trimmings, but backings have also been found in red, blue or black. An ad for Old Judge Cigarettes appears along the bottom of the cabinet. Cabinets obtained by exchanging coupons from Dogs Head cigarettes include an ad for both Old Judge

OLD JUDGE CIGARETTES Goodwin & Co., New York.

and Dogs Head, and are scarcer. According to an advertising sheet, cabinets were available of "every prominent player in the National League, Western League and American Association." There will continue to be additions to this checklist. This list includes all confirmed photo and team variations; minor differences in spelling of team name, position abbreviations or punctuation are not recorded, except in the case of Hall of Famers. Several Old Judge cabinets are not known to exist in the standard N172 format.

	NM	EX	VG
Common Player:	1,750	1,050	750.00
Black or Colored Mount: 2X			
Unlisted Dogs Head: 2-3X			
(4) Bob Allen			
4 (a) Pittsburgh, hands clasped at waist	1,750	1,050	750.00
4 (b) Pittsburgh, batting, Dogs Head	4,200	2,520	1,800
(7) Varney Anderson			
7 (a) Pitching, right hand head-high	1,750	1,050	750.00
(8) Ed Andrews			
8 (a) Philadelphia, both hands shoulder-high	1,750	1,050	750.00
8 (b) Philadelphia, one hand above head	1,750	1,050	750.00
DP 1 being tagged by Buster Hoover	3,000	1,800	1,300
(9) Wally Andrews			
9 (a) Omaha, hands shoulder-high	1,750	1,050	750.00
(11) Cap Anson			
11 (a) Portrait	16,200	9,720	6,960
11 (b) Portrait, Dogs Head	36,000	21,600	15,000
(15) Kid Baldwin			
15 (a) Ball in right hand, head-high	1,750	1,050	750.00
(16) Lady Baldwin			
16 (a) Detroit, pitching, left hand head-high	1,750	1,050	750.00
(17) Mark Baldwin			
17 (a) Chicago, batting, heels together	1,750	1,050	750.00
17 (b) Chicago, pitching, right hand above head	1,750	1,050	750.00
17 (c) Chicago, pitching, right hand waist-high	1,750	1,050	750.00
(20) John Barnes			
20 (a) portrait	1,750	1,050	750.00
(21) Billy Barnie			
21 (a) portrait	2,400	1,440	1,035
(22) Charley Bassett			
22 (a) Indianapolis, bat at ready	1,750	1,050	750.00
(23) Charlie Bastian			
23 (a) Chicago, bat over shoulder	1,750	1,050	750.00
23 (b) Chicago, fielding, hands chest-high	1,750	1,050	750.00
23 (c) Philadelphia, stooping to field low ball	1,750	1,050	750.00
DP 2 Philadelphia, tagging Pop Schriver	3,000	1,800	1,300
(24) Ed Beatin			
24 (a) pitching, right arm forward	1,750	1,050	750.00
(27) Charlie Bennett			
27 (a) Batting	1,750	1,050	750.00
27 (b) Batting, Dogs Head	4,200	2,520	1,800
(28) Lou Bierbauer			
28 (a) Fielding grounder	1,750	1,050	750.00
28 (b) Fielding, hands chest-high	2,700	1,620	1,160
28 (c) Throwing	3,000	1,800	1,320
(31) Ned Bligh			
31 (a) Fielding, hands head-high	1,750	1,050	750.00
(32) Bogart			
32 (a) Fielding, hands chest-high	1,750	1,050	750.00
(35) Henry Boyle			

35 (a) Indianapolis, pitch., right arm extended	1,750	1,050	750.00
(36) Jack Boyle			
36 (a) St. Louis, bat at side	1,750	1,050	750.00
36 (b) St. Louis, bat at ready	1,750	1,050	750.00
36 (c) St. Louis, catching, hands knee-high	1,750	1,050	750.00
(37) George Bradley			
37 (a) Sioux City, fielding, looking up at ball	1,750	1,050	750.00
(43) Dan Brouthers			
43 (a) Boston, batting	4,500	2,700	1,925
43 (b) Boston, batting, Dogs Head	7,800	4,680	3,360
43 (c) Boston, fielding, hands at waist	4,500	2,700	1,920
43 (d) Boston, throwing, horizontal format	4,800	2,880	2,070
43 (e) Detroit, batting	4,500	2,700	1,920
(44) Tom Brown			
44 (a) Boston, bat at ready	1,750	1,050	750.00
44 (b) Boston, fielding	1,750	1,050	750.00
(45) Willard (California) Brown			
45 (a) New York, bat at side	1,750	1,050	750.00
45 (b) New York, throwing, mask in left hand	1,750	1,050	750.00
(46) Pete Browning			
46 (a) Batting, feet together	3,600	2,160	1,560
(47) Charlie Brynan			
47 (a) Chicago, pitching, right arm neck-high	1,750	1,050	750.00
47 (b) Des Moines, pitching, right arm forward	1,750	1,050	750.00
(48) Al Buckenberger			
48 (a) Portrait, looking right	1,750	1,050	750.00
(49) Dick Buckley			
49 (a) Indianapolis, fielding, hands chest-high	1,750	1,050	750.00
(50) Charlie Buffinton			
50 (a) Fielding, hands chest-high	1,750	1,050	750.00
50 (b) Pitch., right hand above head, Dogs Head	7,200	4,320	3,090
(52) Jack Burdock			
52 (a) Fielding grounder	1,750	1,050	750.00
(56) Jim Burns			
56 (a) Kansas City, fielding grounder	1,750	1,050	750.00
(58) Oyster Burns			
58 (a) Brooklyn, bat at ready vertically	1,750	1,050	750.00
58 (b) Brooklyn, throwing, right hand head-high	1,750	1,050	750.00
(59) Tom Burns			
59 (a) Chicago, bat at side	1,750	1,050	750.00
59 (a) Chicago, bat at ready	1,750	1,050	750.00
59 (b) Chicago, fielding	1,750	1,050	750.00
59 (c) Chicago, tagging player	2,280	1,380	980.00
(60) Doc Bushong			
60 (a) Stooping, hands waist-high	1,750	1,050	750.00
60 (b) Throwing	3,000	1,800	1,300
(63) Jimmy Canavan			
63 (a) Batting	1,750	1,050	750.00
(66) Hick Carpenter			
66 (a) Batting	1,750	1,050	750.00
(68) Fred Carroll			
68 (a) Pittsburgh, throwing	1,750	1,050	750.00
(69) Scrappy Carroll			
69 (a) St. Paul, fielding, hands chest-high	2,700	1,620	1,160
(70) Ed Cartwright			
70 (a) St. Joseph, throwing	1,750	1,050	750.00
(71) Bob Caruthers			
71 (a) Batting, feet apart	1,750	1,050	750.00
71 (b) Holding ball in left hand, neck-high	5,700	3,420	2,400
(72) Daniel Casey			
72 (a) Pitching, left hand shoulder-high	1,750	1,050	750.00
(73) Elton Chamberlain			
73 (a) Batting, looking at camera	1,750	1,050	750.00
73 (b) Pitching, hands chest-high	1,750	1,050	750.00
73 (c) Pitching, right hand head-high	1,750	1,050	750.00
(74) Cupid Childs			
74 (a) fielding	1,750	1,050	750.00
(75) Bob Clark			
75 (a) Brooklyn, fielding, hands shoulder-high	1,750	1,050	750.00
75 (b) Brooklyn, throwing	1,750	1,050	750.00
DP 4 Brooklyn, tagging Mickey Hughes	5,400	3,240	2,300
DP 4 Brooklyn, tagging M. Hughes, Dogs Head	6,600	3,960	2,850
Clark, Chicago - See Dad Clarke			

(76) Spider Clark			
76 (a) Washington, pose unrecorded	1,750	1,050	750.00
(77) Dad Clark (Clarke)			
77 (a) Chicago, right arm extended forward	1,750	1,050	750.00
77 (b) Omaha, batting	1,750	1,050	750.00
(78) John Clarkson			
78 (a) Boston, batting	4,200	2,520	1,800
78 (b) Boston, right arm forward, left on thigh	5,700	3,420	2,460
78 (c) Boston, pitching, right arm back	4,200	2,520	1,800
78 (d) Boston, pitching, arm back, Dogs Head	8,400	5,040	3,600
(79) Jack Clements			
79 (a) Batting	1,750	1,050	750.00
79 (b) Fielding	2,580	1,560	1,100
79 (c) Hands on knees	1,750	1,050	750.00
(80) Elmer Cleveland			
80 (a) Pose unrecorded	1,750	1,050	750.00
(81) Monk Cline			
81 (a) Bat nearly vertical	1,750	1,050	750.00
(83) John Coleman			
83 (a) Ball in hands at waist	1,750	1,050	750.00
83 (b) Bat in hands below waist	1,750	1,050	750.00
(85) Hub Collins			
85 (a) Brooklyn, batting	1,750	1,050	750.00
85 (b) Brooklyn, fielding, hands chest-high	1,750	1,050	750.00
(86) Charlie Comiskey			
86 (a) Arms folded	6,000	3,600	2,580
86 (b) Fielding, hands neck-high, ball visible	6,000	3,600	2,580
86 (c) Fielding, hands shoulder-high, no ball	9,000	5,400	3,870
86 (d) Sliding	11,400	6,840	4,890
(88) Roger Connor			
88 (a) Batting, home plate, batter's boxes on floor	9,000	5,400	3,870
88 (b) Batting, outdoors scene on backdrop	7,800	4,800	3,360
88 (c) Fielding, hands at waist	6,000	3,600	2,580
88 (d) Hands on knees	6,000	3,600	2,580
(89) Dick Conway			
90 (a) Boston, bat in hand at side	3,600	2,160	1,560
(90) Jim Conway			
90 (a) Kansas City, pitching, left ear visible	1,750	1,050	750.00
90 (b) K.C., pitching, left ear not visible	1,750	1,050	750.00
(91) Pete Conway			
91 (a) Detroit, pitching, right hand extended	1,750	1,050	750.00
(92) Paul Cook			
92 (a) Fielding in mask	1,750	1,050	750.00
92 (b) Tagging baserunner	1,750	1,050	750.00
(93) Jimmy Cooney			
93 (a) Batting, Omaha, Dogs Head	4,200	2,520	1,800
(95) Pop Corkhill			
95 (a) Brooklyn, batting	1,750	1,050	750.00
95 (b) Brooklyn, fielding, hands neck-high	1,750	1,050	750.00
(96) Cannonball Crane			
96 (a) New York, pitching, right hand head-high	1,750	1,050	750.00
(99) John Crooks			
99 (a) Omaha, pose unrecorded	1,750	1,050	750.00
(100) Lave Cross			
100 (a) Louisville, hands on thighs	1,750	1,050	750.00
(105) Bert Cunningham			
105 (a) Both arms waist level	1,750	1,050	750.00
(109) Edward Dailey			
109 (a) Columbus, pitching, right hand head-high	1,750	1,050	750.00
109 (b) Washington, pitch., right hand head-high	1,750	1,050	750.00
(111) Bill Daley			
111 (a) Boston, pitching, hands above waist	1,750	1,050	750.00
(112) Con Daley (Daily)			
112 (a) Indianapolis, right hand on hip	1,750	1,050	750.00
(113) Abner Dalrymple			
113 (a) Pittsburgh, hands on hips, feet apart	1,750	1,050	750.00
(114) Sun Daly			
114 (a) Minneapolis, fielding, hands chest-high	1,750	1,050	750.00
(115) Tom Daly			
115 (a) Chicago, fielding, hands chest-high	1,750	1,050	750.00
115 (b) Chicago, hands on knees	1,750	1,050	750.00
115 (c) Washington, fielding, hands chest-high	1,750	1,050	750.00

Card	Description			
(117) Dell Darling				
117 (a)	Fielding, hands waist-high	1,750	1,050	750.00
(118) William Darnbrough				
118 (a)	Pitching	1,750	1,050	750.00
(123) Harry Decker				
123 (a)	Bat nearly horizontal	1,750	1,050	750.00
(124) Ed Delehanty				
124 (a)	Bat by shoulder	25,000	4,320	3,100
124 (b)	Bat horizontal	7,200	4,320	3,100
124 (c)	Fielding	18,000	10,800	7,740
(125) Jerry Denny				
125 (a)	Indianapolis, batting	1,750	1,050	750.00
125 (b)	Indianapolis, fielding	1,750	1,050	750.00
(126) Jim Devlin				
126 (a)	Pitching, left hand shoulder-high	1,750	1,050	750.00
126 (b)	Sliding	1,750	1,050	750.00
(130) Jim Donnelly				
130 (a)	Batting	1,750	1,050	750.00
(133) Mike Dorgan				
133 (a)	Sliding, horizontal format	2,700	1,620	1,160
(135) Charlie Duffe (Duffee)				
135 (a)	Batting	1,750	1,050	750.00
135 (b)	Fielding, bending to left	1,750	1,050	750.00
135 (c)	Fielding grounder	1,750	1,050	750.00
135 (d)	Fielding, standing upright	1,750	1,050	750.00
(136) Hugh Duffy				
136 (a)	Batting	3,900	2,340	1,680
136 (b)	Fielding, hands chin-high	3,900	2,340	1,680
136 (c)	Fielding grounder	4,800	2,880	2,070
(138) Martin Duke				
138 (a)	Ball in hands, chest-high	3,000	1,800	1,300
(139) Fred Dunlap				
139 (a)	Arms at side	1,750	1,050	750.00
139 (b)	Holding ball aloft	1,750	1,050	750.00
139 (c)	Holding ball aloft, Dogs Head	3,600	2,160	1,560
(141) Jesse Duryea				
141 (a)	Batting	1,750	1,050	750.00
(142) Frank Dwyer				
142 (a)	Bat at side	3,000	1,800	1,300
142 (b)	Bat in air	1,750	1,050	750.00
142 (c)	Fielding	1,750	1,050	750.00
(143) Billy Earle				
143 (a)	Cincinnati, fielding, hands over head	1,750	1,050	750.00
(145) Red Ehret				
145 (a)	Batting	1,750	1,050	750.00
(147) Dude Esterbrook				
147 (a)	Indianapolis, fielding grounder	1,750	1,050	750.00
147 (b)	Indianapolis, fielding, hands chest-high	1,750	1,050	750.00
(149) Buck Ewing				
149 (a)	New York, bat at side	4,800	2,880	2,070
149 (b)	New York, bat in air	4,800	2,880	2,070
149 (c)	New York, fielding, hands head-high	4,800	2,880	2,070
149 (d)	New York, hands on knees	4,800	2,880	2,070
149 (e)	New York, throwing, right arm extended forward	7,200	4,320	3,100
149 (f)	New York, with mascot Willie Breslin	18,000	10,800	7,740
149 (g)	New York, w/ mascot, Dogs Head	21,000	12,600	9,030
(150) John Ewing				
150 (a)	Louisville, bat almost vertical	1,750	1,050	750.00
(151) Jay Faatz				
151 (a)	Throwing	1,750	1,050	750.00
(152) Bill Farmer				
152 (a)	Pittsburgh, hands on knees	1,750	1,050	750.00
(154) Sid Farrar				
154 (a)	Fielding grounder	1,750	1,050	750.00
154 (b)	Fielding, hands head-high	1,750	1,050	750.00
(155) Duke Farrell				
155 (a)	Chicago, fielding grounder	1,750	1,050	750.00
155 (b)	Chicago, hands on knees	1,750	1,050	750.00
(157) Frank Fennelly				
157 (a)	Cincinnati, fielding grounder	1,750	1,050	750.00
(158) Charlie Ferguson				
158 (a)	Pitching, hands at chest	1,750	1,050	750.00
(159) Alex Ferson				
159 (a)	Pitching, hands neck-high, looking front	1,750	1,050	750.00
(161) Jocko Fields				
161 (a)	Hands on thighs	1,750	1,050	750.00
(164) Silver Flint				
164 (a)	Batting	1,750	1,050	750.00
164 (b)	Catching, with mask, hands waist-high	2,400	1,440	1,035
(167) Jim Fogarty				
167 (a)	Batting	1,750	1,050	750.00
167 (b)	Fielding, hands neck-high	1,750	1,050	750.00
167 (c)	Running to left	1,750	1,050	750.00
167 (d)	Sliding	1,750	1,050	750.00
(168) Frank Foreman				
168 (a)	Baltimore, ball in hands by right thigh	2,700	1,620	1,160
(170) Elmer Foster				
170 (a)	Minneapolis, batting	1,750	1,050	750.00
170 (b)	New York, fielding	1,750	1,050	750.00
(171) Dave Foutz				
171 (a)	Bat at 45 degrees	1,750	1,050	750.00
171 (b)	Throwing	1,750	1,050	750.00
(175) Shorty Fuller				
175 (a)	St. Louis, fielding	1,750	1,050	750.00
175 (b)	St. Louis, hands on knees	1,750	1,050	750.00
175 (c)	St. Louis, swinging bat	1,750	1,050	750.00
(177) Chris Fulmer				
DP 8	Tagging Tom Tucker, Dogs Head	5,400	3,240	2,300
(179) Pud Galvin				
179 (a)	Batting	3,600	2,150	1,550
(181) Charlie Ganzel				
181 (a)	Boston, batting	1,750	1,050	750.00
181 (b)	Boston, fielding, hands shoulder-high	3,000	1,800	1,300
181 (c)	Boston, fielding, hands thigh-high	1,750	1,050	750.00
(182) Gid Gardner				
182 (a)	Philadelphia, fielding low ball	1,750	1,050	750.00
(183) Hank Gastreich				
183 (a)	Pitching, left hand by thigh	1,750	1,050	750.00
(185) Frank Genins				
185 (a)	Batting, looking at ball	1,750	1,050	750.00
185 (b)	Batting, looking at camera	1,750	1,050	750.00
(186) Bill George				
186 (a)	Bat at side	1,750	1,050	750.00
(188) Charlie Getzein (Getzien)				
188 (a)	Pitching, hands above waist	1,750	1,050	750.00
(190) Bobby Gilks				
190 (a)	Batting	1,750	1,050	750.00
(192) Barney Gilligan				
192 (a)	Washington, fielding	1,750	1,050	750.00
(193) Frank Gilmore				
193 (a)	Pitching, hands neck-high	1,750	1,050	750.00
(194) Jack Glasscock				
194 (a)	Indianapolis, bat at side, Dogs Head	4,200	2,520	1,800
194 (b)	Indianapolis, hands on knees	1,750	1,050	750.00
194 (c)	Indianapolis, throwing	1,750	1,050	750.00
(195) Bill Gleason				
195 (a)	Louisville, batting	1,750	1,050	750.00
195 (b)	Louisville, stooping, hands clasped	1,750	1,050	750.00
DP 23	With Curt Welch	2,700	1,620	1,160
(196) Kid Gleason				
196 (a)	Philadelphia, fielding grounder	2,700	1,620	1,160
196 (b)	Philadelphia, ball in hands at chin	2,700	1,620	1,160
(197) Ed Glenn				
197 (a)	Fielding, hands neck-high	1,750	1,050	750.00
(199) George Gore				
199 (a)	Bat nearly horizontal	1,750	1,050	750.00
199 (b)	Bat at ready over left shoulder	1,750	1,050	750.00
199 (c)	Fielding grounder	1,750	1,050	750.00
(205) Henry Gruber				
205 (a)	Pitching, right hand chin-high	1,750	1,050	750.00
(206) Ad Gumbert				
206 (a)	Pitching, right hand eye-high	2,520	1,500	1,085
206 (b)	Pitching, right hand waist-high	1,750	1,050	750.00
(207) Tom Gunning				
207 (a)	Bending forward, hands by right knee	1,750	1,050	750.00
(208) Joe Gunson				
208 (a)	Wearing jacket	1,750	1,050	750.00
(212) Bill Hallman				
212 (a)	leaning left to catch ball chest-high	1,750	1,050	750.00
(213) Billy Hamilton				
213 (a)	Kansas City, batting	7,200	4,320	3,100
213 (b)	Kansas City, fielding, hands neck-high	7,200	4,320	3,100
213 (c)	Kansas City, fielding grounder	7,200	4,320	3,100
(215) Ned Hanlon				
215 (a)	Detroit, batting	3,600	2,160	1,560
215 (b)	Pittsburgh, fielding	3,900	2,340	1,680
(216) Bill Hanrahan				
216 (a)	Bat at side	1,750	1,050	750.00
(221) Gil Hatfield				
221 (a)	Bat at waist	1,750	1,050	750.00
221 (b)	Bat over shoulder	1,750	1,050	750.00
221 (c)	Fielding, hands chest-high	1,750	1,050	750.00
(223) Egyptian Healey (Healy)				
223 (a)	Indianapolis, pitching, hands at chest	1,750	1,050	750.00
(227) Hardie Henderson				
227 (a)	Brooklyn, outdoors, throwing, right hand head-high	2,400	1,440	1,035
(228) Moxie Hengle				
228 (a)	Minneapolis, hands on knees	1,750	1,050	750.00
(229) John Henry				
229 (a)	Throwing, right hand neck-high	1,750	1,050	750.00
(231) Hunkey Hines				
231 (a)	St. Louis Whites, fielding	1,750	1,050	750.00
(232) Paul Hines				
232 (a)	Washington, arms at side	1,750	1,050	750.00
(233) Frank Hoffman				
233 (a)	Pitching, right hand head-high	1,750	1,050	750.00
(235) Bill Holbert				
235 (a)	Throwing	1,750	1,050	750.00
(236) Bug Holliday				
236 (a)	Cincinnati, arms at side	1,750	1,050	750.00
236 (b)	Cincinnati, ball in hands at shoulder	1,750	1,050	750.00
(238) Buster Hoover				
238 (a)	Philadelphia, fielding, hands head-high	1,750	1,050	750.00
DP 1	Being tagged by Ed Andrews	3,000	1,800	1,300
(239) Charlie Hoover				
239 (a)	Chicago, fielding grounder (Never played for Chicago)	1,750	1,050	750.00
239 (b)	Kansas City, pose unrecorded	1,750	1,050	750.00
(241) Joe Hornung				
241 (a)	Boston, batting	1,750	1,050	750.00
(243) Dummy Hoy				
243 (a)	Fielding grounder	5,400	3,240	2,300
(244) Nat Hudson				
244 (a)	Ball in hands waist-high	1,750	1,050	750.00
244 (b)	Pitching, right hand head-high	1,750	1,050	750.00
244 (c)	pitching, right hand waist-high	1,750	1,050	750.00
(245) Mickey Hughes				
245 (a)	Holding ball at chest	1,750	1,050	750.00
245 (b)	Holding ball at side	1,750	1,050	750.00
245 (c)	Right hand extended	1,750	1,050	750.00
DP 4	Being tagged by Bob Clark	4,500	2,700	1,920
(247) Bill Hutchinson				
247 (a)	Ball in hand, right heel hidden	1,750	1,050	750.00
247 (b)	Ball in hand, right heel visible	1,750	1,050	750.00
247 (c)	Batting	1,750	1,050	750.00
(248) Arthur Irwin				
248 (a)	Philadelphia, fielding, hands chest-high	1,750	1,050	750.00
248 (b)	Phila., throwing, right hand head-high	1,750	1,050	750.00
(249) John Irwin				
249 (a)	Washington, hands on knees	1,750	1,050	750.00
249 (b)	Washington, throwing	1,750	1,050	750.00
(250) A.C. Jantzen				
250 (a)	Batting, looking at camera	1,750	1,050	750.00
(252) Spud Johnson				
252 (a)	Columbus, pose unrecorded	1,750	1,050	750.00
(253) Dick Johnston				
253 (a)	Batting, looking at ball	1,750	1,050	750.00
253 (b)	Hands on hips	1,750	1,050	750.00
(256) Tim Keefe				
256 (a)	Bat nearly horizontal, Old Judge	3,600	2,160	1,560
256 (b)	Bat nearly horizontal, Dogs Head	15,000	9,000	6,450
256 (c)	Ball in hands at chest	3,000	1,800	1,300
256 (d)	Pitching, right hand head-high	3,600	2,160	1,560
256 (e)	Pitching, right hand waist-high	3,600	2,160	1,560
(259) Charlie Kelly				
259 (a)	Philadelphia, fielding, hands head-high	1,750	1,050	750.00
(261) King Kelly				
261 (a)	"Kelly, Boston.", bat at 45-degree angle	7,200	4,320	3,100
261 (b)	"Kelly, Boston.", bat at 45-degree angle, Dogs Head	9,600	5,760	4,140
261 (c)	"Mike Kelly, C, Bostons", bat at 45-degree angle	7,200	4,320	3,100
261 (d)	"Kelly, Capt.", bat at 45-degree angle	7,200	4,320	3,100
(262) Rudy Kemmler				

262 (a)Fielding, hands chest-high | 1,750 | 1,050 | 750.00

(263) Ted Kennedy
263 (a)Omaha, pose unrecorded | 1,750 | 1,050 | 750.00

(264) J.J. Kenyon
264 (a)Des Moines, right hand in glove, head-high | 1,750 | 1,050 | 750.00

(265) John Kerins
265 (a)Hands on thighs | 1,750 | 1,050 | 750.00

(266) Matt Kilroy
266 (a)Pitching, hands waist-high to left | 1,750 | 1,050 | 750.00

(267) Silver King
267 (a)St. Louis, pitching, hands chest-high | 1,750 | 1,050 | 750.00
267 (b)St. Louis, pitching, hands chin-high | 1,750 | 1,050 | 750.00

(269) Billy Klusman
269 (a)Fielding grounder | 1,750 | 1,050 | 750.00

(274) Gus Krock
274 (a)Ball in hands above waist | 1,750 | 1,050 | 750.00
274 (b)Batting | 1,750 | 1,050 | 750.00
274 (c)Pitching, right hand chin-high | 1,750 | 1,050 | 750.00

(275) Willie Kuehne
275 (a)fielding grounder | 1,750 | 1,050 | 750.00

(277) Henry Larkin
277 (a)Fielding, hands thigh-high | 1,750 | 1,050 | 750.00
277 (b)Right hand shoulder-high | 1,750 | 1,050 | 750.00

(278) Arlie Latham
278 (a)Batting | 1,750 | 1,050 | 750.00
278 (b)Throwing | 3,300 | 1,980 | 1,400

(279) Chuck Lauer
279 (a)Fielding, hands chest-high | 1,750 | 1,050 | 750.00

(280) John Leighton
280 (a)Batting | 1,750 | 1,050 | 750.00
280 (b)Fielding | 1,750 | 1,050 | 750.00

(284) Herman Long
284 (a)Kansas City, bat at side | 1,750 | 1,050 | 750.00
284 (b)Kansas City, fielding, hands chest-high | 1,750 | 1,050 | 750.00

(285) Tom Lovett
285 (a)Brooklyn, bat on shoulder | 1,750 | 1,050 | 750.00
285 (b)Brooklyn, pitching, hands over head | 1,750 | 1,050 | 750.00
285 (c)Brooklyn, right hand extended | 1,750 | 1,050 | 750.00

(288) Denny Lyons
288 (a)Philadelphia AA, bat at ready | 1,750 | 1,050 | 750.00
288 (b)Phila. AA, fielding, left hand over head | 1,750 | 1,050 | 750.00

(289) Harry Lyons
289 (a)St. Louis, at first base | 1,750 | 1,050 | 750.00

(290) Connie Mack
290 (a)Washington, batting | 25,000 | 9,000 | 6,450
290 (b)Washington, squatting, hands on knees | 25,000 | 10,800 | 7,740

(292) Jimmy Macullar
292 (a)Des Moines, fielding, hands head-high | 1,750 | 1,050 | 750.00

(293) Kid Madden
293 (a)Ball in hand over head | 1,750 | 1,050 | 750.00
293 (b)Ball in hands, neck-high | 1,750 | 1,050 | 750.00
293 (c)Ball in left hand, eye-high | 1,750 | 1,050 | 750.00

(297) Jimmy Manning
297 (a)Bat at side | 1,750 | 1,050 | 750.00
297 (b)Fielding grounder | 1,750 | 1,050 | 750.00

(298) Lefty Marr
298 (a)Columbus, left hand neck-high | 1,750 | 1,050 | 750.00

(299) Mascot (Willie Breslin)
299 (a)New York | 3,300 | 1,980 | 1,400

(300) Leech Maskrey
300 (a)Des Moines, ball in hands chin-high | 1,750 | 1,050 | 750.00

(302) Mike Mattimore
302 (a)Phila. AA, sliding, left hand raised | 1,750 | 1,050 | 750.00

(303) Al Maul
303 (a)Pitching, hands at chest | 1,750 | 1,050 | 750.00

(304) Al Mays
304 (a)Pitching, hands chest-high | 1,750 | 1,050 | 750.00

(305) Jimmy McAleer
305 (a)Batting, looking at ball | 1,750 | 1,050 | 750.00

(307) Tommy McCarthy
307 (a)St. Louis, batting, indoors | 4,200 | 2,520 | 1,800
307 (b)St. Louis, right hand head-high, indoors | 4,200 | 2,520 | 1,800
307 (c)Tagging player | 5,520 | 3,300 | 2,370

(318) Deacon McGuire

318 (a)Phila., fielding, hands shoulder-high | 1,750 | 1,050 | 750.00

(319) Bill McGunnigle
319 (a)Looking to right | 1,750 | 1,050 | 750.00

(320) Ed McKean
320 (a)Batting, looking at camera | 1,750 | 1,050 | 750.00
320 (b)Fielding, hands over head | 1,750 | 1,050 | 750.00

(325) James McQuaid
325 (a)Fielding, hands near chin | 1,750 | 1,050 | 750.00

(330) Doggie Miller
330 (a)Pittsburgh, ball in hands, Dogs Head | 6,600 | 3,960 | 2,850
330 (b)Pittsburgh, bat at side | 1,750 | 1,050 | 750.00
330 (c)Fielding, hands chest-high | 1,750 | 1,050 | 750.00

(331) Joe Miller
331 (a)Minneapolis, bat at side
331 (b)Minneapolis, fielding | 1,750 | 1,050 | 750.00

(332) Jocko Milligan
332 (a)Bat at side | 1,750 | 1,050 | 750.00
332 (b)Bat in air | 1,750 | 1,050 | 750.00
332 (c)Fielding | 1,750 | 1,050 | 750.00
332 (d)Throwing | 1,750 | 1,050 | 750.00

(334) Daniel Minnehan (Minahan)
334 (a)Batting, looking at camera | 1,750 | 1,050 | 750.00

(335) Sam Moffet
335 (a)Pose unrecorded | 1,750 | 1,050 | 750.00

(336) John Morrill
336 (a)Boston, batting | 1,750 | 1,050 | 750.00

(338) Tony Mullane
338 (a)Ball in hands above waist | 3,300 | 1,980 | 1,400

(339) Joe Mulvey
339 (a)batting | 1,750 | 1,050 | 750.00
339 (b)Fielding | 1,750 | 1,050 | 750.00

(340) Pat Murphy
340 (a)New York, fielding, hands chin-high | 1,750 | 1,050 | 750.00

(341) P.L. Murphy
341 (a)St. Paul, batting | 2,400 | 1,450 | 1,025

(342) Miah Murray
342 (a)On knee, hands at shoulder | 1,750 | 1,050 | 750.00

(343) Jim Mutrie
343 (a)Seated | 1,750 | 1,050 | 750.00
343 (b)Standing | 1,750 | 1,050 | 750.00

(344) Al Myers
344 (a)Wash., right hand at side, left at back | 1,750 | 1,050 | 750.00

(345) George Myers
345 (a)Indianpolis, batting | 1,750 | 1,050 | 750.00

(346) Tom Nagle
346 (a)Omaha, batting | 1,750 | 1,050 | 750.00
346 (b)Fielding, Dogs Head | 7,200 | 4,320 | 3,100

(347) Billy Nash
347 (a)Hands on knees | 2,700 | 1,620 | 1,160
347 (b)Throwing | 1,750 | 1,050 | 750.00

(349) Kid Nichols
349 (a)Omaha, batting, looking at ball | 5,100 | 3,060 | 2,200
349 (b)Omaha, pitching, right hand forward | 5,100 | 3,060 | 2,200

(353) Hugh Nicol
DP 16 Side by side with Reilly, "Long & Short" | 2,700 | 1,620 | 1,160

(357) Darby O'Brien
357 (a)Brooklyn, batting, looking at camera | 1,750 | 1,050 | 750.00

(359) John O'Brien
359 (a)Cleveland, batting | 1,750 | 1,050 | 750.00
359 (b)Cleveland, pose unrecorded, Dogs Head | 5,700 | 3,420 | 2,460

(361) Jack O'Connor
361 (a)Columbus, throwing | 1,750 | 1,050 | 750.00

(362) Hank O'Day
362 (a)Ball in right hand, head-high | 1,750 | 1,050 | 750.00

(365) Tip O'Neill
365 (a)Bat held horizontally | 1,750 | 1,050 | 750.00
365 (b)Bat over shoulder | 1,750 | 1,050 | 750.00
365 (c)Fielding grounder | 1,750 | 1,050 | 750.00
365 (d)Throwing | 3,480 | 2,100 | 1,500

(366) Orator Jim O'Rourke
366 (a)New York, bat in hand at side | 4,800 | 2,880 | 2,070
366 (b)New York, batting | 5,700 | 3,420 | 2,460
366 (c)New York, throwing, hand head-high | 4,200 | 2,520 | 1,800

(367) Tom O'Rourke
367 (a)Boston, fielding, hands thigh-high | 2,700 | 1,620 | 1,160

(368) Dave Orr
368 (a)Columbus, bat at ready, nearly vertical | 1,750 | 1,050 | 750.00

(374) Fred Pfeffer
374 (a)Batting, looking at ball | 1,750 | 1,050 | 750.00
374 (b)Tagging player | 2,280 | 1,380 | 980.00
374 (c)Throwing, right-hand neck-high | 1,750 | 1,050 | 750.00

(375) Dick Phelan
375 (a)Batting, looking at ball | 1,750 | 1,050 | 750.00

(377) Jack Pickett
377 (a)St. Paul, bat over shoulder | 1,750 | 1,050 | 750.00
377 (b)St. Paul, fielding grounder | 1,750 | 1,050 | 750.00
377 (c)St. Paul, throwing, right hand head-high | 1,750 | 1,050 | 750.00

(378) George Pinkney
378 (a)Bat in air, nearly vertical | 1,750 | 1,050 | 750.00
378 (b)Bat over shoulder | 1,750 | 1,050 | 750.00
DP 25 (w/ Steve Toole) | 5,400 | 3,240 | 2,300

(381) Jim Powell
381 (a)Batting, looking at camera | 1,750 | 1,050 | 750.00

(383) Blondie Purcell
383 (a)Throwing | 1,750 | 1,050 | 750.00

(385) Joe Quinn
385 (a)Ball in hands by chin | 1,750 | 1,050 | 750.00
385 (b)Ready to run | 1,750 | 1,050 | 750.00

(386) Old Hoss Radbourn
386 (a)Hands at waist, Dogs Head | 7,800 | 4,680 | 3,360
386 (b)Hands on hips, bat on left | 3,600 | 2,160 | 1,560
386 (c)Tagging player | 4,200 | 2,520 | 1,800

(388) Tom Ramsey
388 (a)Bat at ready, nearly vertical | 1,750 | 1,050 | 750.00
388 (b)Bat over right shoulder, Dogs Head | 4,800 | 2,880 | 2,070

(390) Charlie Reilly
390 (a)St. Paul, throwing | 1,750 | 1,050 | 750.00

(391) Long John Reilly
391 (a)Cincinnati, fielding | 1,750 | 1,050 | 750.00
DP 16 Side by side w/Nicol, "Long & Short" | 2,700 | 1,620 | 1,160

(393) Danny Richardson
393 (a)New York, moving left, arms at side | 1,750 | 1,050 | 750.00
393 (b)New York, throwing | 1,750 | 1,050 | 750.00

(394) Hardy Richardson
394 (a)Boston, bat over shoulder | 1,750 | 1,050 | 750.00
394 (b)Detroit, bat over shoulder | 1,750 | 1,050 | 750.00
394 (c)Boston, fielding, hands head-high | 1,750 | 1,050 | 750.00

(398) Wilbert Robinson
398 (a)Philadelphia AA, batting | 4,500 | 2,700 | 1,980
398 (b)Phila. AA, catching, hands neck-high | 4,500 | 2,700 | 1,980
398 (c)Philadelphia AA, throwing | 4,500 | 2,700 | 1,980

(399) Yank Robinson
399 (a)St. Louis, batting | 2,520 | 1,500 | 1,085
399 (b)St. Louis, fielding grounder | 2,520 | 1,500 | 1,085
399 (c)St. Louis, hands at chest | 2,520 | 1,500 | 1,085

(402) Dave Rowe
402 (a)Kansas City, fielding, Dogs Head | 4,200 | 2,520 | 1,800

(403) Jack Rowe
403 (a)Detroit, batting, looking at camera | 1,750 | 1,050 | 750.00
403 (b)Detroit, bat on shoulder, looking at ball | 1,750 | 1,050 | 750.00

(404) Amos Rusie
404 (a)Indianapolis, ball in right hand, thigh-high | 9,000 | 5,400 | 3,900

(405) Jimmy Ryan
405 (a)Bat at side | 2,520 | 1,500 | 1,085
405 (b)Batting | 2,700 | 1,620 | 1,160
405 (c)Stooping for knee-high catch | 2,520 | 1,500 | 1,085
405 (d)Throwing, left hand head-high | 2,520 | 1,500 | 1,085

(407) Ben Sanders
407 (a)Batting | 1,750 | 1,050 | 750.00
407 (b)Fielding | 1,750 | 1,050 | 750.00
407 (c)Right hand head-high | 1,750 | 1,050 | 750.00

(408) Frank Scheibeck
408 (a)Fielding, hand over head | 1,750 | 1,050 | 750.00

(412) Gus Schmelz
412 (a)portrait | 1,750 | 1,050 | 750.00

(413) Jumbo Schoeneck
413 (a)fielding, hands chin-high | 1,750 | 1,050 | 750.00

(414) Pop Schriver
414 (a)Fielding, hands ankle-high | 1,750 | 1,050 | 750.00
414 (b)Hands cupped chest-high | 1,750 | 1,050 | 750.00
DP 2 Being tagged by Charlie Bastian | 3,000 | 1,800 | 1,300

(415) Emmett Seery
415 (a)Arms folded | 1,750 | 1,050 | 750.00

(417) Ed Seward
417 (a)Ball in hands neck-high | 1,750 | 1,050 | 750.00

(420) Daniel Shannon
420 (a)Louisville, leaning to tag player | 1,750 | 1,050 | 750.00

(421) Bill Sharsig
421 (a)Full length in bowler hat | 1,750 | 1,050 | 750.00

(425) George Shoch
425 (a)Fielding grounder | 1,750 | 1,050 | 750.00

(426) Otto Shomberg (Schomberg)
426 (a)Fielding, hands head-high | 1,750 | 1,050 | 750.00

(427) Lev Shreve
427 (a)Right hand eye-high, looking at camera | 1,750 | 1,050 | 750.00

(429) Mike Slattery
429 (a)Fielding, hands chest-high | 1,750 | 1,050 | 750.00

(430) Elmer Smith
(431) Germany Smith
431 (a)Cincinnati, pitching, left hand head-high, looking at camera | 1,750 | 1,050 | 750.00
431 (a)Brooklyn, batting, looking at ball | 1,750 | 1,050 | 750.00
431 (b)Brooklyn, hands on knees | 1,750 | 1,050 | 750.00
431 (c)Brooklyn, right hand head-high | 1,750 | 1,050 | 750.00

(435) Pop Smith
435 (a)Boston, batting | 1,750 | 1,050 | 750.00
435 (b)Pittsburgh, batting | 1,750 | 1,050 | 750.00
435 (c)Hands on knees | 1,750 | 1,050 | 750.00

(439) Pete Sommers
439 (a)portrait | 2,700 | 1,620 | 1,160

(440) Bill Sowders
440 (a)Boston, pitching, hands at throat | 1,750 | 1,050 | 750.00
440 (b)Boston, pitching, right hand cap-high, left hand waist-high | 2,400 | 1,440 | 1,035

(442) Charlie Sprague
442 (a)Chicago, left hand at back head-high | 1,750 | 1,050 | 750.00
442 (b)Cleveland, left hand at back head-high | 1,750 | 1,050 | 750.00

(444) Harry Staley
444 (a)Pitching, right hand chest-high | 1,750 | 1,050 | 750.00

(445) Dan Stearns
445 (a)Kansas City, fielding, hands neck-high | 3,000 | 1,800 | 1,300

(450) Harry Stovey
450 (a)Bat at ready by head | 2,700 | 1,620 | 1,160
450 (b)Fielding, hands chest-high, Dogs Head | 14,400 | 8,640 | 6,180
450 (c)Hands on knees | 1,750 | 1,050 | 750.00

(451) Scott Stratton
451 (a)Batting | 1,750 | 1,050 | 750.00

(452) Joe Straus (Strauss)
452 (a)Milwaukee, kneeling, looking to right | 1,750 | 1,050 | 750.00
452 (b)Omaha, throwing | 1,750 | 1,050 | 750.00

(453) Cub Stricker
453 (a)Fielding, hands over head | 1,750 | 1,050 | 750.00

(454) Marty Sullivan
454 (a)Chicago, batting, looking at ball | 1,750 | 1,050 | 750.00
454 (b)Indianapolis, hands chest-high | 1,750 | 1,050 | 750.00

(457) Billy Sunday
457 (a)Pittsburgh, bat at side | 4,200 | 2,520 | 1,800
457 (b)Pittsburgh, batting | 6,000 | 3,600 | 2,580
457 (c)Pittsburgh, fielding, hands thigh-high | 4,200 | 2,520 | 1,800

(459) Ezra Sutton
459 (a)Batting, looking down at ball | 1,750 | 1,050 | 750.00
459 (b)Fielding, hands shoulder-high | 1,750 | 1,050 | 750.00

(461) Park Swartzel
461 (a)Arms at side | 1,750 | 1,050 | 750.00

(464) Pop Tate
464 (a)Boston, batting | 1,750 | 1,050 | 750.00

(465) Patsy Tebeau
465 (a)Chicago, fielding grounder | 1,750 | 1,050 | 750.00

(466) John Tener
466 (a)Ball in right hand chin-high | 3,000 | 1,800 | 1,300
466 (b)Batting | 3,000 | 1,800 | 1,300

(467) Adonis Terry
467 (a)Arms extended horizontally | 1,750 | 1,050 | 750.00
467 (b)Bat on shoulder | 1,750 | 1,050 | 750.00

(468) Sam Thompson
468 (a)Detroit, bat ready at 45 degree angle | 7,800 | 4,680 | 3,360
468 (b)Philadelphia, batting, ball above head | 7,800 | 4,680 | 3,360

(469) Mike Tiernan
469 (a)Batting | 1,750 | 1,050 | 750.00
469 (b)Sliding | 2,700 | 1,620 | 1,160
469 (c)Throwing, left hand chin-high | 1,750 | 1,050 | 750.00

(470) Cannonball Titcomb
470 (a)Pitching, hands chin-high | 1,750 | 1,050 | 750.00

(471) Phil Tomney

---

(471) (a)Fielding, hands over head | 1,750 | 1,050 | 750.00

(472) Steve Toole
DP 25 (W/George Pinkney (Pinckney)) | 5,400 | 3,240 | 2,300

(473) George Townsend
473 (a)Bat at ready by head | 1,750 | 1,050 | 750.00
473 (b)Fielding, hands chest-high | 1,750 | 1,050 | 750.00

(474) Bill Traffley
474 (a)Hands on thighs | 1,750 | 1,050 | 750.00

(477) Tommy Tucker
477 (a)Ball in hands at chest | 1,750 | 1,050 | 750.00
DP 8   Being tagged by Chris Fulmer | 5,400 | 3,240 | 2,300

(479) George Turner
479 (a)Fielding, hands head-high | 1,750 | 1,050 | 750.00

(480) Larry Twitchell
480 (a)Cleveland, pitching, hands at chest | 1,750 | 1,050 | 750.00
480 (b)Detroit, pitching, hands at chest | 1,750 | 1,050 | 750.00

(481) Jim Tyng
481 (a)Pitching | 1,750 | 1,050 | 750.00

(483) George Van Haltren
483 (a)Batting | 3,600 | 2,160 | 1,560
483 (b)Ball in hands at waist | 3,600 | 2,160 | 1,560
482 (c)Right hand at thigh | 3,600 | 2,160 | 1,560

(484) Farmer Vaughn
484 (a)Bat at ready, looking at camera | 1,750 | 1,050 | 750.00

(488) Joe Visner
488 (a)Arms at side | 1,750 | 1,050 | 750.00
488 (b)Batting | 1,750 | 1,050 | 750.00
488 (c)Throwing | 1,750 | 1,050 | 750.00

(490) Reddy Walsh
490 (a)Batting | 1,750 | 1,050 | 750.00

(491) John Ward
491 (a)Hands behind back | 4,800 | 2,880 | 2,070
491 (b)Hands on hips | 8,400 | 5,040 | 3,600
491 (c)Portrait in dress clothes)(Value Undetermined
491 (d)Sliding, left arm in air | 4,800 | 2,880 | 2,070
491 (e)Throwing, right profile | 4,800 | 2,880 | 2,070
491 (f) Cap in right hand at side | 4,800 | 2,880 | 2,070
491 (g)Cap in right hand at side, Dogs Head | 7,200 | 4,320 | 3,100

(493) Bill Watkins
493 (a)Detroit, portrait | 1,750 | 1,050 | 750.00
493 (b)Kansas City, portrait | 1,750 | 1,050 | 750.00

(494) Farmer Weaver
494 (a)Fielding, left hand over head | 1,750 | 1,050 | 750.00

(496) Stump Weidman (Wiedman)
496 (a)New York, batting | 1,750 | 1,050 | 750.00

(497) Wild Bill Weidner (Widner)
497 (a)Batting | 1,750 | 1,050 | 750.00

(498) Curt Welch
498 (a)Philadelphia AA, fielding grounder | 1,750 | 1,050 | 750.00
DP 23 with Will Gleason | 2,700 | 1,620 | 1,160

(499) Mickey Welch
499 (a)N.Y., pitching, right arm extended forward, name incorrect (Welsh) | 3,600 | 2,160 | 1,560
499 (b)N.Y., pitching, right arm extended forward, name correct | 3,600 | 2,160 | 1,560
499 (c)N.Y., pitching, right arm behind head, Dogs Head | 18,000 | 10,800 | 7,740

(504) A.C. (Gus) Weyhing
504 (a)Philadelphia AA, right hand chest-high | 1,750 | 1,050 | 750.00

(505) John Weyhing
505 (a)Philadelphia AA, left hand chest-high (Never played for Philadelphia) | 1,750 | 1,050 | 750.00

(510) Deacon White
510 (a)Detroit, hands above head | 1,750 | 1,050 | 750.00
510 (b)looking down at ball | 1,750 | 1,050 | 750.00

(511) Art Whitney
511 (a)New York, with dog | 15,000 | 9,000 | 6,450
511 (b)New York, fielding, hands thigh-high | 1,750 | 1,050 | 750.00
511 (c)Pittsburgh, fielding, hands thigh-high | 1,750 | 1,050 | 750.00

(512) G. Whitney
512 (a)St. Joseph, batting, looking at ball | 1,750 | 1,050 | 750.00

(513) Jim Whitney
513 (a)Wash., pitching, right hand waist-high | 1,750 | 1,050 | 750.00

(515) Ned Williamson
515 (a)arms folded | 1,750 | 1,050 | 750.00
515 (b)batting, looking at ball | 1,750 | 1,050 | 750.00
515 (c)Fielding | 1,750 | 1,050 | 750.00
515 (d)Throwing | 1,750 | 1,050 | 750.00

(516) Tit Willis

---

516 (a)Pitching, arms head-high | 1,750 | 1,050 | 750.00

(517) Walt Wilmot
517 (a)Washington, fielding, hands at chest | 1,750 | 1,050 | 750.00

(519) Sam Wise
519 (a)Boston, bat at side | 1,750 | 1,050 | 750.00
519 (b)Boston, hands on knees | 2,400 | 1,440 | 1,035

(520) Chicken Wolf
520 (a)Bat at ready, team name visible on shirt | 1,750 | 1,050 | 750.00

(521) George Wood (L.F.)
521 (a)Both hands neck-high | 1,750 | 1,050 | 750.00
521 (b)Right hand head-high | 1,750 | 1,050 | 750.00

(522) Pete Wood (P.)
522 (a)Bat on shoulder | 1,750 | 1,050 | 750.00

(523) Harry Wright
523 (a)Portrait, looking to his left | 24,000 | 14,400 | 10,350

(524) Chief Zimmer
524 (a)Fielding, hands at chest | 1,750 | 1,050 | 750.00
524 (b)Throwing | 1,750 | 1,050 | 750.00

1965 Old London Coins

These 1-1/2" diameter metal coins were included in Old London snack food packages. The 40 coins in this set feature two players from each of the major leagues' 20 teams, except St. Louis (3) and the New York Mets (1). Coin fronts have color photos and player names, while the silver-colored backs give a brief biography. An Old London logo is also displayed on each coin back. Space Magic Ltd. produced the coins. This is the same company which produced similar sets for Topps in 1964 and 1971.

		NM	EX	VG
	Complete Set (40):	475.00	240.00	140.00
	Common Player:	3.00	1.50	.90
(1)	Henry Aaron	35.00	17.50	10.50
(2)	Richie Allen	7.50	3.75	2.25
(3)	Bob Allison	3.00	1.50	.90
(4)	Ernie Banks	25.00	12.50	7.50
(5)	Ken Boyer	4.50	2.25	1.25
(6)	Jim Bunning	15.00	7.50	4.50
(7)	Orlando Cepeda	12.50	6.25	3.75
(8)	Dean Chance	3.00	1.50	.90
(9)	Rocky Colavito	10.00	5.00	3.00
(10)	Vic Davalillo	3.00	1.50	.90
(11)	Tommy Davis	3.00	1.50	.90
(12)	Ron Fairly	3.00	1.50	.90
(13)	Dick Farrell	3.00	1.50	.90
(14)	Jim Fregosi	3.00	1.50	.90
(15)	Bob Friend	3.00	1.50	.90
(16)	Dick Groat	3.00	1.50	.90
(17)	Ron Hunt	3.00	1.50	.90
(18)	Chuck Hinton	3.00	1.50	.90
(19)	Ken Johnson	3.00	1.50	.90
(20)	Al Kaline	20.00	10.00	6.00
(21)	Harmon Killebrew	20.00	10.00	6.00
(22)	Don Lock	3.00	1.50	.90
(23)	Mickey Mantle	100.00	50.00	30.00
(24)	Roger Maris	30.00	15.00	9.00
(25)	Willie Mays	35.00	17.50	10.50
(26)	Bill Mazeroski	12.50	6.25	3.75
(27)	Gary Peters	3.00	1.50	.90
(28)	Vada Pinson	3.50	1.75	1.00
(29)	Boog Powell	4.50	2.25	1.25
(30)	Dick Radatz	3.00	1.50	.90
(31)	Brooks Robinson	20.00	10.00	6.00
(32)	Frank Robinson	20.00	10.00	6.00
(33)	Tracy Stallard	3.00	1.50	.90
(34)	Joe Torre	7.50	3.75	2.25
(35)	Leon Wagner	3.00	1.50	.90
(36)	Pete Ward	3.00	1.50	.90
(37)	Dave Wickersham	3.00	1.50	.90
(38)	Billy Williams	15.00	7.50	4.50
(39)	John Wyatt	3.00	1.50	.90
(40)	Carl Yastrzemski	25.00	12.50	7.50

1909-11 Old Mill Cigarettes

T206 cards bearing the Old Mill advertising are, with a major exception, among the most common of the set's back variations. Two styles of Old Mill T206 backs are found. One, which appears on cards of major league players and minor leaguers other than those from the Southern leagues, mentions a "BASE BALL / SUBJECTS / LARGE ASSORTMENT." The other specifies the four Southern leagues from which the players depicted originate. In recent years advanced T206 specialists have become aware of a brown-ink version of the Southern leagues back, much rarer than the black-ink version usually found on both types of Old Mill backs. All of the confirmed brown-ink cards appear to have been hand-cut from a sheet, leading to speculation as to whether they represent an actual issued variation or were salvaged from a scrapped printing. Contemporary with the T206 issues, Old Mill also produced a lengthy series of red-bordered minor league player cards in 1910. Those are listed in the minor league section of this book.

PREMIUMS
Common: 1.25X
Stars/So. Leagues: 1X
Brown-ink So. Leagues: 10X
(See S74, T3, T206.)

1910 Old Put Cigar

This is a version of the anonymous E98 "Set of 30" on which an advertisement for "OLD PUT / 5 ct. CIGAR" has been rubber-stamped in purple. Because of the ease with which these could be faked, collectors must exercise extreme caution.

		NM	EX	VG
Common Player:		3,750	1,875	1,125
(1)	Christy Matthewson (Mathewson)	12,000	6,000	3,600
(2)	John McGraw	3,000	1,500	900.00
(3)	Johnny Kling	3,750	1,875	1,025
(4)	Frank Chance	3,000	1,500	900.00
(5)	Hans Wagner	13,500	6,750	4,050
(6)	Fred Clarke	3,000	1,500	900.00
(7)	Roger Bresnahan	3,000	1,500	900.00
(8)	Hal Chase	6,000	3,000	1,800
(9)	Russ Ford	3,750	1,875	1,025
(10)	"Ty" Cobb	16,500	8,250	4,950
(11)	Hughey Jennings	3,000	1,500	900.00
(12)	Chief Bender	3,000	1,500	900.00
(13)	Ed Walsh	3,000	1,500	900.00
(14)	Cy Young	12,000	6,000	3,600
(15)	Al Bridwell	3,750	1,875	1,025
(16)	Miner Brown	3,000	1,500	900.00
(17)	George Mullin	3,750	1,875	1,025
(18)	Chief Meyers	3,750	1,875	1,025
(19)	Hippo Vaughn	3,750	1,875	1,025
(20)	Red Dooin	3,750	1,875	1,025
(21)	Fred Tenny (Tenney)	3,750	1,875	1,025
(22)	Larry McLean	3,750	1,875	1,025
(23)	Nap Lajoie	3,000	1,500	900.00
(24)	Joe Tinker	3,000	1,500	900.00
(25)	Johnny Evers	3,000	1,500	900.00
(26)	Harry Davis	3,750	1,875	1,025
(27)	Eddie Collins	3,000	1,500	900.00
(28)	Bill Dahlen	3,750	1,875	1,025
(29)	Connie Mack	3,000	1,500	900.00
(30)	Jack Coombs	3,750	1,875	1,025

1951 Olmes Studio Postcards

This line of Philadelphia player postcards (all but one from the A's) was produced by a local photographer, probably for player use in satisfying fans' autograph requests. The 3-1/2" x 5-1/2" cards have a glossy black-and-white player photo on front. Backs have only standard postcard indicia and the Olmes credit line.

Other players may remain to be checklisted. The unnumbered cards are listed here alphabetically.

		NM	EX	VG
Common Player:		75.00	37.50	22.50
(1)	Sam Chapman	75.00	37.50	22.50
(2)	Ferris Fain (Ready to hit, on grass.)	100.00	50.00	30.00
(3)	Ferris Fain/Btg (Choking up.)	100.00	50.00	30.00
(4)	Ferris Fain/Btg (Follow-through.)	100.00	50.00	30.00
(5)	Ferris Fain/Kneeling	100.00	50.00	30.00
(6)	Dick Fowler	75.00	37.50	22.50
(7)	Bob Hooper	75.00	37.50	22.50
(8)	Skeeter Kell	75.00	37.00	22.50
(9)	Paul Lehner	75.00	37.50	22.50
(10)	Lou Limmer	75.00	37.50	22.50
(11)	Barney McCosky	75.00	37.50	22.50
(12)	Robin Roberts	275.00	135.00	80.00
(13)	Carl Scheib	75.00	37.50	22.50
(14)	Bobby Shantz	75.00	37.50	22.50
(15)	Joe Tipton	75.00	37.50	22.50
(16)	Gus Zernial/Btg	100.00	50.00	30.00
(17)	Gus Zernial/Kneeling	100.00	50.00	30.00

1979 Open Pantry/ Lake to Lake MACC

To benefit Milwaukee Athletes Against Childhood Cancer the Open Pantry convenience stores in Wisconsin teamed with Lake to Lake Dairy to produce this card set. Red, white and black fronts of the 5" x 6" cards have a player photo, facsimile autograph and team logo. Backs are printed in red with a message from the player about the MACC fund. Besides members of the Milwaukee Brewers listed here, the set features Green Bay Packers and Milwaukee Bucks players. The unnumbered cards are checklisted here alphabetically.

		NM	EX	VG
Complete Set (12):		10.00	5.00	3.00
Common (Baseball) Player:		2.00	1.00	.60
(1)	Jerry Augustine	3.00	1.50	.90
(2)	Sal Bando	3.00	1.50	.90
(3)	Cecil Cooper	4.00	2.00	1.25
(4)	Larry Hisle	3.00	1.50	.90
(5)	Lary Sorensen	3.00	1.50	.90

1910 "Orange Borders"

Known in the hobby as "Orange Borders", these 1-1/2" x 2-7/16" cards were issued in 1910 and were printed on candy boxes that displayed the words "American Sports and Candy and Jewelry." The end flaps indicate the producers as the "Geo. Davis Co., Inc." and the "P.R. Warren Co., Warrenville Lowell, Mass." According to the box, the complete set includes "144 leading ballplayers," but to date just over two dozen different subjects are known. When found today, these black and white photos are often surrounded by orange borders which, in reality, were part of the candy box. Similar in format to the "Baseball Bats" cards, Orange Borders have player names which are hand-lettered, rather than typeset. Gaps have been left in the assigned numbering to accomodate future additions to the checklist.

		NM	EX	VG
Common Player:		960.00	390.00	190.00
(1)	Bill Bergen	960.00	390.00	190.00
(2)	Bill Bradley	960.00	390.00	190.00
(3)	Bill Carrigan	960.00	390.00	190.00
(4)	Hal Chase	1,140	455.00	230.00
(5)	Fred Clark (Clarke)	1,440	575.00	290.00
(6)	Ty Cobb	12,000	4,800	2,400
(7)	Sam Crawford	1,440	575.00	290.00
(8)	Lou Criger	960.00	390.00	190.00
(9)	Harry Davis	960.00	390.00	190.00
(11)	Art Devlin	960.00	390.00	190.00
(12)	Mickey Doolan	960.00	390.00	190.00
(13)	George Gibson	960.00	390.00	190.00
(14)	Addie Joss	1,560	625.00	315.00
(15)	Nap Lajoie	1,440	575.00	290.00
(16)	Frank LaPorte	960.00	390.00	190.00
(17)	Harry Lord	960.00	390.00	190.00
(18)	Christy Mathewson	5,400	2,160	1,080
(19)	Amby McConnell	960.00	390.00	190.00
(21)	John McGraw	1,440	575.00	290.00
(22)	Dots Miller	960.00	390.00	190.00
(23)	George Mullin	960.00	390.00	190.00
(24)	Eddie Plank	1,440	575.00	290.00
(25)	Tris Speaker	1,680	675.00	335.00
(26)	Jake Stahl	960.00	390.00	190.00
(27)	Honus Wagner/Btg	9,000	3,600	1,800
(28)	Honus Wagner/Portrait	9,000	3,600	1,800
(29)	Jack Warhop	960.00	390.00	190.00
(31)	American League Champions, 1909 (Detroit)	2,400	960.00	480.00
(32)	National League Champions, 1909 (Pittsburgh)	2,400	960.00	480.00

1976 Orbaker's Discs

One of several regional sponsors of player disc sets in 1976 was the Orbaker's restaurant chain. The discs are 3-3/8" diameter with a black-and-white player portrait photo in the center of the baseball design. A line of red stars is above, while the left and right panels feature one of several bright colors. Produced by Michael Schecter Associates under license from the Major League Baseball Players Association, the player photos have had uniform and cap logos removed. Backs are printed in red and purple. The unnumbered checklist here is presented in alphabetical order.

		NM	EX	VG
Complete Set (70):		50.00	25.00	15.00
Common Player:		1.00	.50	.30
(1)	Henry Aaron	20.00	10.00	6.00
(2)	Johnny Bench	6.00	3.00	1.75
(3)	Vida Blue	1.00	.50	.30
(4)	Larry Bowa	1.00	.50	.30
(5)	Lou Brock	4.00	2.00	1.25
(6)	Jeff Burroughs	1.00	.50	.30
(7)	John Candelaria	1.00	.50	.30
(8)	Jose Cardenal	1.00	.50	.30
(9)	Rod Carew	4.00	2.00	1.25
(10)	Steve Carlton	4.00	2.00	1.25
(11)	Dave Cash	1.00	.50	.30
(12)	Cesar Cedeno	1.00	.50	.30
(13)	Ron Cey	1.00	.50	.30
(14)	Carlton Fisk	4.00	2.00	1.25
(15)	Tito Fuentes	1.00	.50	.30
(16)	Steve Garvey	2.00	1.00	.60
(17)	Ken Griffey	1.00	.50	.30
(18)	Don Gullett	1.00	.50	.30
(19)	Willie Horton	1.00	.50	.30
(20)	Al Hrabosky	1.00	.50	.30
(21)	Catfish Hunter	3.00	1.50	.90
(22)	Reggie Jackson (A's)	12.00	6.00	3.50
(23)	Randy Jones	1.00	.50	.30
(24)	Jim Kaat	1.00	.50	.30
(25)	Don Kessinger	1.00	.50	.30
(26)	Dave Kingman	1.00	.50	.30
(27)	Jerry Koosman	1.00	.50	.30
(28)	Mickey Lolich	1.00	.50	.30
(29)	Greg Luzinski	1.00	.50	.30
(30)	Fred Lynn	1.00	.50	.30
(31)	Bill Madlock	1.00	.50	.30

		NM	EX	VG
(32)	Carlos May	1.00	.50	.30
(33)	John Mayberry	1.00	.50	.30
(34)	Bake McBride	1.00	.50	.30
(35)	Doc Medich	1.00	.50	.30
(36)	Andy Messersmith	1.00	.50	.30
(37)	Rick Monday	1.00	.50	.30
(38)	John Montefusco	1.00	.50	.30
(39)	Jerry Morales	1.00	.50	.30
(40)	Joe Morgan	4.00	2.00	1.25
(41)	Thurman Munson	3.00	1.50	.90
(42)	Bobby Murcer	1.00	.50	.30
(43)	Al Oliver	1.00	.50	.30
(44)	Jim Palmer	4.00	2.00	1.25
(45)	Dave Parker	1.00	.50	.30
(46)	Tony Perez	3.00	1.50	.90
(47)	Jerry Reuss	1.00	.50	.30
(48)	Brooks Robinson	6.00	3.00	1.75
(49)	Frank Robinson	6.00	3.00	1.75
(50)	Steve Rogers	1.00	.50	.30
(51)	Pete Rose	17.50	8.75	5.25
(52)	Nolan Ryan	25.00	12.50	7.50
(53)	Manny Sanguillen	1.00	.50	.30
(54)	Mike Schmidt	15.00	7.50	4.50
(55)	Tom Seaver	6.00	3.00	1.75
(56)	Ted Simmons	1.00	.50	.30
(57)	Reggie Smith	1.00	.50	.30
(58)	Willie Stargell	4.00	2.00	1.25
(59)	Rusty Staub	1.50	.70	.45
(60)	Rennie Stennett	1.00	.50	.30
(61)	Don Sutton	3.00	1.50	.90
(62)	Andy Thornton	1.00	.50	.30
(63)	Luis Tiant	1.00	.50	.30
(64)	Joe Torre	1.00	.50	.30
(65)	Mike Tyson	1.00	.50	.30
(66)	Bob Watson	1.00	.50	.30
(67)	Wilbur Wood	1.00	.50	.30
(68)	Jimmy Wynn	1.00	.50	.30
(69)	Carl Yastrzemski	6.00	3.00	1.75
(70)	Richie Zisk	1.00	.50	.30

1932 Orbit Gum Pins - Numbered (PR2)

Issued circa 1932, this skip-numbered set of small (13/16" diameter) pins was produced by Orbit Gum and carries the Amerian Card Catalog designation of PR2. A color player lithograph is set against a green background with the player's name and team printed on a strip of yellow below. The pin number is at the very bottom; pins after #40 are skip-numbered.

		NM	EX	VG
	Complete Set (53):	2,500	1,250	750.00
	Common Player:	30.00	15.00	9.00
1	Ivy Andrews	30.00	15.00	9.00
2	Carl Reynolds	30.00	15.00	9.00
3	Riggs Stephenson	30.00	15.00	9.00
4	Lon Warneke	30.00	15.00	9.00
5	Frank Grube	30.00	15.00	9.00
6	"Kiki" Cuyler	60.00	30.00	18.00
7	Marty McManus	30.00	15.00	9.00
8	Lefty Clark	30.00	15.00	9.00
9	George Blaeholder	30.00	15.00	9.00
10	Willie Kamm	30.00	15.00	9.00
11	Jimmy Dykes	30.00	15.00	9.00
12	Earl Averill	60.00	30.00	18.00
13	Pat Malone	30.00	15.00	9.00
14	Dizzy Dean	200.00	100.00	60.00
15	Dick Bartell	30.00	15.00	9.00
16	Guy Bush	30.00	15.00	9.00
17	Bud Tinning	30.00	15.00	9.00
18	Jimmy Foxx	150.00	75.00	45.00
19	Mule Haas	30.00	15.00	9.00
20	Lew Fonseca	30.00	15.00	9.00
21	Pepper Martin	40.00	20.00	12.00
22	Phil Collins	30.00	15.00	9.00
23	Bill Cissell	30.00	15.00	9.00
24	Bump Hadley	30.00	15.00	9.00
25	Smead Jolley	30.00	15.00	9.00
26	Burleigh Grimes	60.00	30.00	18.00
27	Dale Alexander	30.00	15.00	9.00
28	Mickey Cochrane	60.00	30.00	18.00
29	Mel Harder	30.00	15.00	9.00
30	Mark Koenig	30.00	15.00	9.00
31a	Lefty O'Doul (Dodgers)	50.00	25.00	15.00
31b	Lefty O'Doul (Giants)	90.00	45.00	27.00
32a	Woody English (With bat.)	30.00	15.00	9.00
32b	Woody English (Without bat.)	80.00	40.00	24.00
33a	Billy Jurges (With bat.)	30.00	15.00	9.00
33b	Billy Jurges (Without bat.)	80.00	40.00	24.00
34	Bruce Campbell	30.00	15.00	9.00
35	Joe Vosmik	30.00	15.00	9.00
36	Dick Porter	30.00	15.00	9.00
37	Charlie Grimm	30.00	15.00	9.00
38	George Earnshaw	30.00	15.00	9.00
39	Al Simmons	60.00	30.00	18.00
40	Red Lucas	30.00	15.00	9.00
51	Wally Berger	30.00	15.00	9.00
55	Jim Levey	30.00	15.00	9.00
58	Ernie Lombardi	60.00	30.00	18.00
64	Jack Burns	30.00	15.00	9.00
67	Billy Herman	60.00	30.00	18.00
72	Bill Hallahan	30.00	15.00	9.00
92	Don Brennan	30.00	15.00	9.00
96	Sam Byrd	30.00	15.00	9.00
99	Ben Chapman	30.00	15.00	9.00
103	John Allen	30.00	15.00	9.00
107	Tony Lazzeri	60.00	30.00	18.00
111	Earl Combs (Earle)	60.00	30.00	18.00
116	Joe Sewell	60.00	30.00	18.00
120	Vernon Gomez	60.00	30.00	18.00

1932 Orbit Gum Pins - Unnumbered (PR3)

This set, issued by Orbit Gum circa 1932, has the American Card Catalog designation PR3. The pins are identical to the PR2 set, except they are unnumbered.

		NM	EX	VG
	Complete Set (60):	3,750	1,850	1,100
	Common Player:	60.00	30.00	18.00
(1)	Dale Alexander	60.00	30.00	18.00
(2)	Ivy Andrews	60.00	30.00	18.00
(3)	Earl Averill	100.00	50.00	30.00
(4)	Dick Bartell	60.00	30.00	18.00
(5)	Wally Berger	60.00	30.00	18.00
(6)	George Blaeholder	60.00	30.00	18.00
(7)	Jack Burns	60.00	30.00	18.00
(8)	Guy Bush	60.00	30.00	18.00
(9)	Bruce Campbell	60.00	30.00	18.00
(10)	Bill Cissell	60.00	30.00	18.00
(11)	Lefty Clark	60.00	30.00	18.00
(12)	Mickey Cochrane	100.00	50.00	30.00
(13)	Phil Collins	60.00	30.00	18.00
(14)	"Kiki" Cuyler	100.00	50.00	30.00
(15)	Dizzy Dean	175.00	87.00	52.00
(16)	Jimmy Dykes	60.00	30.00	18.00
(17)	George Earnshaw	60.00	30.00	18.00
(18)	Woody English	60.00	30.00	18.00
(19)	Lew Fonseca	60.00	30.00	18.00
(20)	Jimmy (Jimmie) Foxx	175.00	87.00	52.00
(21)	Burleigh Grimes	100.00	50.00	30.00
(22)	Charlie Grimm	60.00	30.00	18.00
(23)	Lefty Grove	100.00	50.00	30.00
(24)	Frank Grube	60.00	30.00	18.00
(25)	Mule Haas	60.00	30.00	18.00
(26)	Bump Hadley	60.00	30.00	18.00
(27)	Chick Hafey	100.00	50.00	30.00
(28)	Jesse Haines	100.00	50.00	30.00
(29)	Bill Hallahan	60.00	30.00	18.00
(30)	Mel Harder	60.00	30.00	18.00
(31)	Gabby Hartnett	100.00	50.00	30.00
(32)	Babe Herman	65.00	32.00	19.50
(33)	Billy Herman	100.00	50.00	30.00
(34)	Rogers Hornsby	135.00	67.00	40.00
(35)	Roy Johnson	60.00	30.00	18.00
(36)	Smead Jolley	60.00	30.00	18.00
(37)	Billy Jurges	60.00	30.00	18.00
(38)	Willie Kamm	60.00	30.00	18.00
(39)	Mark Koenig	60.00	30.00	18.00
(40)	Jim Levey	60.00	30.00	18.00
(41)	Ernie Lombardi	100.00	50.00	30.00
(42)	Red Lucas	60.00	30.00	18.00
(43)	Ted Lyons	100.00	50.00	30.00
(44)	Connie Mack	100.00	50.00	30.00
(45)	Pat Malone	60.00	30.00	18.00
(46)	Pepper Martin	75.00	37.00	22.00
(47)	Marty McManus	60.00	30.00	18.00
(48)	Lefty O'Doul	80.00	40.00	24.00
(49)	Dick Porter	60.00	30.00	18.00
(50)	Carl Reynolds	60.00	30.00	18.00
(51)	Charlie Root	60.00	30.00	18.00
(52)	Bob Seeds	60.00	30.00	18.00
(53)	Al Simmons	100.00	50.00	30.00
(54)	Riggs Stephenson	60.00	30.00	18.00
(55)	Bud Tinning	60.00	30.00	18.00
(56)	Joe Vosmik	60.00	30.00	18.00
(57)	Rube Walberg	60.00	30.00	18.00
(58)	Paul Waner	100.00	50.00	30.00
(59)	Lon Warneke	60.00	30.00	18.00
(60)	Pinky Whitney	60.00	30.00	18.00

1937-39 Orcajo Cincinnati Reds Postcards (PC786)

Orcajo, a Dayton, Ohio, photo firm, issued a series of Reds player postcards (plus, inexplicably, Joe DiMaggio) from 1937-39. Besides those found with just the issuer's imprint on the back, some or all of the players' cards can be found with the advertising on front of the Val Decker Packing Co., a meat

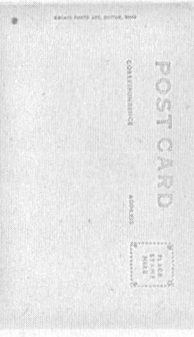

dealer, Metropolitan Clothing Co., and an inset photo of WHIO radio announcer Si Burick (the latter are the 1937 cards and have no Orcajo imprint on back, utilizing different photos than the 1938-39 cards). The 3-1/2" x 5-1/2" cards have glossy black-and-white player poses on front with the player's name over-printed. Backs have standard postcard indicia. A number of spelling errors and several variations exist. The unnumbered cards are checklisted here alphabetically; those with ads for the meat company, men's store or radio station are appropriately noted.

		NM	EX	VG
	Complete Set (37):	3,775	1,700	945.00
	Common Player:	100.00	45.00	25.00
(1)	Wally Berger	100.00	45.00	25.00
(2)	Bongiovanni (First name Nino.)	100.00	45.00	25.00
(3)	Frenchy Bordagaray	100.00	45.00	25.00
(4)	Joe Cascarella, Gene Schott (Val Decker only.)	100.00	45.00	25.00
(5)	Allan Cooke (Allen) (Val Decker only.)	100.00	45.00	25.00
(6)	Harry Craft (Also Val Decker.)	100.00	45.00	25.00
(7)	Kiki Cuyler (WHIO only.)	160.00	72.00	40.00
(8)	Ray Davis	100.00	45.00	25.00
(9)	Virgil Davis (Val Decker only.)	100.00	45.00	25.00
(10)	Paul Derringer (Also Val Decker.)	100.00	45.00	25.00
(11)	Joe DiMaggio	825.00	370.00	205.00
(12a)	Linus Frey (Also Val Decker.) (No right foot, large caption.)	100.00	45.00	25.00
(12b)	Linus Frey (Also Val Decker.) (Right foot shows, small caption.)	100.00	45.00	25.00
(13)	Lee Gamble	100.00	45.00	25.00
(14)	Ivan Goodman (Ival) (Also Val Decker.)	100.00	45.00	25.00
(15)	Hank Gowdy	100.00	45.00	25.00
(16)	Lee Grissom	100.00	45.00	25.00
(17a)	Willard Hershberger (Hershberger, name in white.)(Also Val Decker.)	100.00	45.00	25.00
(17b)	Willard Hershberger (Name in black.)	100.00	45.00	25.00
(18a)	Al Hollingsworth	100.00	45.00	25.00
(18b)	Al Hollingsworth (WHIO)	100.00	45.00	25.00
(18c)	Al Hollingsworth (Val Decker)	100.00	45.00	25.00
(19)	Hank Johnson	100.00	45.00	25.00
(20)	Edwin Joost	100.00	45.00	25.00
(21a)	Ernie Lombardi (Plain letters.) (Also Val Decker, Metro.)	160.00	72.00	40.00
(21b)	Ernie Lombardi (Fancy letters.) (Also Val Decker, Metro.)	160.00	72.00	40.00
(22)	Frank McCormick (Also Val Decker, Metro.)	100.00	45.00	25.00
(23)	Bill McKecknie (McKechnie)	145.00	65.00	36.00
(24)	Billy Meyers (Myers) (Also Val Decker.)	100.00	45.00	25.00
(25a)	Whitey Moore (Photo actually Bucky Walters.)	100.00	45.00	25.00
(25b)	Whitey Moore (Correct photo.)	100.00	45.00	25.00
(26)	Lew Riggs	100.00	45.00	25.00
(27)	Edd Roush (Val Decker only.)	145.00	65.00	36.00
(28a)	Leo Scarsella (Les)	160.00	72.00	40.00
(28b)	Les Scarcella (WHIO)	100.00	45.00	25.00
(29)	Gene Schott (Val Decker)	100.00	45.00	25.00
(30)	Milburn Shoffner	100.00	45.00	25.00
(31)	Junior Thompson	100.00	45.00	25.00
(32a)	Johnny VanderMeer/Throwing (Also Metro, Val Decker.)	175.00	79.00	44.00
(32b)	Johnny VanderMeer/Fielding (Also Metro.)	175.00	79.00	44.00
(33)	Bucky Walters	100.00	45.00	25.00
(34)	Bill Werber	100.00	45.00	25.00
(35)	Dick West	100.00	45.00	25.00
(36)	Jimmie Wilson	100.00	45.00	25.00
(37)	Cincinnati Reds Composite Team Card	100.00	45.00	25.00

1933 Oriental Theatre

To advertise its movie schedule for the week of June 17-23, as well as a Father's Day prize drawing, the Oriental Theatre (location unknown) printed its message on the back of a 1929 Kashin Publications (R316) card or cards. The extent to which this over-printing was undertaken is unknown.

	NM	EX	VG
Ed "Bing" Miller	125.00	62.50	37.50

1912 A.F. Orr Louis Sockalexis Photocard

This 3-1/2" x 5-1/2" sepia photocard carries the copyright of A.F. Orr of Old Town, Maine, hometown of the original Cleveland Indian. At the time of the card's issue, the fallen diamond star was operating a ferry and probably commissioned this image for sale to tourists.

	NM	EX	VG
Louis Sockalexis	2,000	1,000	600.00

1963 Otto Milk

The attributed issue date of this commemorative milk carton is approximate. A 4" x 8" panel on the front of the milk carton has a picture and history of Honus Wagner printed in red and blue. Wagner is the only ballplayer in the milk carton series honoring Western Pennsylvania celebrities.

		NM	EX	VG
(1)	Honus Wagner (Complete carton.)	250.00	125.00	75.00
(1)	Honus Wagner (Cut panel.)	60.00	30.00	18.00

1938 Our National Game Pins

This unnumbered 30-pin set issued circa 1938 carries the American Card Catalog designation of PM8. The pins, which measure 7/8" in diameter, have a bendable "tab" rather than a pin back. The player photo is printed in blue-and-white. The player's name and team are printed at bottom. The pins were originally sold on a square of cardboard decorated with stars and stripes and imprinted "OUR NATIONAL GAME" above the pin, and "A BASEBALL HERO" below. A large number of the pins, complete with their cardboard backing, were found in a hoard in Oklahoma in the early 1990s.

		NM	EX	VG
Complete Set (30):		1,200	600.00	350.00
Common Player:		20.00	10.00	6.00
(1)	Wally Berger	20.00	10.00	6.00
(2)	Lou Chiozza	20.00	10.00	6.00
(3)	Joe Cronin	40.00	20.00	12.00
(4)	Frank Crosetti	25.00	12.50	7.50
(5)	Jerome (Dizzy) Dean	75.00	37.00	22.00
(6)	Frank DeMaree (Demaree)	20.00	10.00	6.00
(7)	Joe DiMaggio	100.00	50.00	30.00
(8)	Bob Feller	65.00	32.00	19.50
(9)	Jimmy Foxx (Jimmie)	75.00	37.00	22.00
(10)	Lou Gehrig	100.00	50.00	30.00
(11)	Charles Gehringer	50.00	25.00	15.00
(12)	Lefty Gomez	40.00	20.00	12.00
(13)	Hank Greenberg	65.00	32.00	19.50
(14)	Irving (Bump) Hadley	20.00	10.00	6.00
(15)	Leo Hartnett	40.00	20.00	12.00
(16)	Carl Hubbell	50.00	25.00	15.00
(17)	John (Buddy) Lewis	20.00	10.00	6.00
(18)	Gus Mancuso	20.00	10.00	6.00
(19)	Joe McCarthy	40.00	20.00	12.00
(20)	Joe Medwick	40.00	20.00	12.00
(21)	Joe Moore	20.00	10.00	6.00
(22)	Mel Ott	50.00	25.00	15.00
(23)	Jake Powell	20.00	10.00	6.00
(24)	Jimmy Ripple	20.00	10.00	6.00
(25)	Red Ruffing	40.00	20.00	12.00
(26)	Hal Schumacher	20.00	10.00	6.00
(27)	George Selkirk	20.00	10.00	6.00
(28)	"Al" Simmons	40.00	20.00	12.00
(29)	Bill Terry	40.00	20.00	12.00
(30)	Harold Trosky	20.00	10.00	6.00

1936 Overland Candy Co. (R301)

Used as wrappers for a piece of penny candy, these 5" x 5-1/4" waxed papers are usually found with resultant folds and creases, though unfolded examples are known. Printed in dark blue, the top of the wrapper features a line drawing portrait of the player, his formal name and nickname, team, position and career summary. The unnumbered wrappers are checklisted here alphabetically.

		NM	EX	VG
Complete Set (57):		45,000	20,000	9,000
Common Player:		650.00	300.00	130.00
(1)	Melo (Mel) Almada	650.00	300.00	130.00
(2)	Lucius B. (Luke) Appling	900.00	400.00	180.00
(3)	Howard Earl Averill	900.00	400.00	180.00
(4)	Walter Antone (Wally) Berger	650.00	300.00	130.00
(5)	Henry John (Zeke) Bonura	650.00	300.00	130.00
(6)	Philip Joseph (Phil) Cavarretta	650.00	300.00	130.00
(7)	William Ben (Chappy) Chapman	650.00	300.00	130.00
(8)	Harland Clift (first name Harland)	650.00	300.00	130.00
(9a)	John Walter (Johnny) Cooney (Bees)	650.00	300.00	130.00
(9b)	John Walter (Johnny) Cooney (Dodgers)	650.00	300.00	130.00
(10)	Harry Danning	650.00	300.00	130.00
(11)	William N. (Bill) Dickey (middle initial is N)	950.00	425.00	190.00
(12a)	William J. (Bill) Dietrich (Athletics)	650.00	300.00	130.00
(12b)	William J. (Bill) Dietrich (White Sox)	650.00	300.00	130.00
(13)	Joseph (Deadpan Joe) DiMaggio	3,000	1,350	600.00
(14)	Wesley Cheek Ferrell	650.00	300.00	130.00
(15)	James Emory (Jimmie) Foxx	1,200	540.00	240.00
(16)	Henry Louis (Lou) Gehrig	3,150	1,425	630.00
(17)	Charles Leonard (Charley) Gehringer	900.00	400.00	180.00
(18)	Jose Luis (Chile) Gomez	650.00	300.00	130.00
(19)	Vernon (Lefty) Gomez	900.00	400.00	180.00
(20)	Joe Gordon	650.00	300.00	130.00
(21)	Henry (Hank) Greenberg	1,200	540.00	240.00
(22)	Robert Moses (Lefty) Grove	950.00	425.00	190.00
(23)	George W. (Mule) Haas	650.00	300.00	130.00
(24)	Ralston Burdett (Rollie) Hemsley	650.00	300.00	130.00
(25)	Michael Francis (Pinky) Higgins (Middle name Franklin.)	650.00	300.00	130.00
(26)	Oral Clyde (Hildy) Hildebrand	650.00	300.00	130.00
(27)	Robert Lee (Cherokee) Johnson	650.00	300.00	130.00
(28)	Baxter Byerly (Buck) Jordan	650.00	300.00	130.00
(29)	Ken Keltner	650.00	300.00	130.00
(30)	Fabian Kowalik	650.00	300.00	130.00
(31)	Harry A. Lavagetto	650.00	300.00	130.00
(32)	Anthony Michael (Poosh 'em Up) Lazzeri	900.00	400.00	180.00
(33)	Samuel A. Leslie	650.00	300.00	130.00
(34)	Dan (Slug) Lithwhiler (last name Litwhiler)	650.00	300.00	130.00
(35)	Theodore A. (Ted) Lyons	900.00	400.00	180.00
(36)	George McQuinn	650.00	300.00	130.00
(37)	John Robert (Skippy) Mize	900.00	400.00	180.00
(38)	Charles Solomon (Buddy) Myer	650.00	300.00	130.00
(39)	Louis Norman (Buck) Newsom	650.00	300.00	130.00
(40)	Raymond Pepper	650.00	300.00	130.00
(41)	Frank A. (Pity) Pytlak	650.00	300.00	130.00
(42)	Raymond Allen (Rip) Radcliff	650.00	300.00	130.00
(43)	Peter (Pete) Reiser (Correct name Harold Patrick)	650.00	300.00	130.00
(44)	Carl Nettles (Sheeps) Reynolds	650.00	300.00	130.00
(45)	Robert Abial (Red) Rolfe	650.00	300.00	130.00
(46)	Lynwood Thomas (Schoolboy) Rowe	650.00	300.00	130.00
(47)	Aloysius Harry (Al) Simmons	900.00	400.00	180.00
(48)	Cecil Howard Travis (middle name is Howell)	650.00	300.00	130.00
(49)	Harold Arthus (Hal) Trosky	650.00	300.00	130.00
(50)	Joseph Franklin (Joe) Vosmik	650.00	300.00	130.00
(51)	Harold Burton (Rabbit) Warstler	650.00	300.00	130.00
(52)	William M. (Bill) Werber	650.00	300.00	130.00
(53)	Max West	650.00	300.00	130.00
(54)	Samuel F. (Sam) West	650.00	300.00	130.00
(55)	Whitlow (Whit) Wyatt	650.00	300.00	130.00

1921 Oxford Confectionery (E253)

Issued in 1921 by Oxford Confectionery of Oxford, Pa., this 20-card set was printed on thin paper and distributed with caramels. Each card measures 1-5/8" x 2-3/4" and features a black-and-white player photo with the player's name and team printed in a white band along the bottom. The back carries a checklist of the players in the set, 14 of whom are now in the Hall of Fame. The set is designated as E253 in the ACC.

		NM	EX	VG
Complete Set (20):		35,000	15,750	7,000
Common Player:		1,000	450.00	200.00
(1)	Grover Alexander	1,800	810.00	360.00
(2)	Dave Bancroft	1,200	540.00	240.00
(3)	Max Carey	1,200	540.00	240.00
(4)	Ty Cobb	6,000	2,700	1,200
(5)	Eddie Collins	1,200	540.00	240.00
(6)	Frankie Frisch	1,200	540.00	240.00
(7)	Burleigh Grimes	1,200	540.00	240.00
(8)	"Bill" Holke (Walter)	1,000	450.00	200.00
(9)	Rogers Hornsby	1,800	810.00	360.00
(10)	Walter Johnson	3,000	1,350	600.00
(11)	Lee Meadows	1,000	450.00	200.00
(12)	Cy Perkins	1,000	450.00	200.00
(13)	Derrill Pratt	1,000	450.00	200.00
(14)	Ed Rousch (Roush)	1,200	540.00	240.00
(15)	"Babe" Ruth	12,000	5,400	2,400
(16)	Ray Schalk	1,200	540.00	240.00
(17)	George Sisler	1,200	540.00	240.00
(18)	Tris Speaker	1,800	810.00	360.00
(19)	Cy Williams	1,000	450.00	200.00
(20)	Whitey Witt	1,000	450.00	200.00

Checklists showing are card numbers in parentheses
( ) indicates the numbers do not appear on the cards.

P

1958 Packard-Bell

Issued by the "world's largest seller of TVs, radios and hi-fis", this set was distributed in California and features members of the newly arrived Los Angeles Dodgers and San Francisco Giants. The 3-1/2" x 5-1/2" black-and-white cards are unnumbered, checklisted here alphabetically.

		NM	EX	VG
	Complete Set (7):	1,500	750.00	450.00
	Common Player:	100.00	50.00	30.00
(1)	Walter Alston	125.00	65.00	35.00
(2)	John A. Antonelli	100.00	50.00	30.00
(3)	Jim Gilliam	125.00	65.00	35.00
(4)	Gil Hodges	200.00	100.00	60.00
(5)	Willie Mays	800.00	400.00	240.00
(6)	Bill Rigney	100.00	50.00	30.00
(7)	Hank Sauer	100.00	50.00	30.00

1978 Papa Gino's Discs

This promotion was largely confined to the Boston area, as 25 of the 40 players represented are Red Sox, the other 15 are all from American League teams. The 3-3/8" discs were given away with the purchase of soft drinks at the restaurant chain. Fronts have player portraits at center with name in the dark blue border at top and team below. Photos have the uniform logos airbrushed away because the discs were licensed only by the players' union, not MLB. Backs retain the color scheme with player data, previous season's stats, uniform and card numbers, sponsor's ad, etc.

		NM	EX	VG
	Complete Set (40):	20.00	10.00	6.00
	Common Player:	2.00	1.00	.60
1	Allen Ripley	2.00	1.00	.60
2	Jerry Remy	2.00	1.00	.60
3	Jack Brohamer	2.00	1.00	.60
4	Butch Hobson	2.00	1.00	.60
5	Dennis Eckersley	3.50	1.75	1.00
6	Sam Bowen	2.00	1.00	.60
7	Rick Burleson	2.00	1.00	.60
8	Carl Yastrzemski	5.00	2.50	1.50
9	Bill Lee	2.00	1.00	.60
10	Bob Montgomery	2.00	1.00	.60
11	Dick Drago	2.00	1.00	.60
12	Bob Stanley	2.00	1.00	.60
13	Fred Kendall	2.00	1.00	.60
14	Jim Rice	3.00	1.50	.90
15	George Scott	2.00	1.00	.60
16	Tom Burgmeier	2.00	1.00	.60
17	Frank Duffy	2.00	1.00	.60
18	Jim Wright	2.00	1.00	.60
19	Fred Lynn	2.00	1.00	.60
20	Bob Bailey	2.00	1.00	.60
21	Mike Torrez	2.00	1.00	.60
22	Bill Campbell	2.00	1.00	.60
23	Luis Tiant	2.00	1.00	.60
24	Dwight Evans	2.00	1.00	.60
25	Carlton Fisk	4.00	2.00	1.25
26	Reggie Jackson	5.00	2.50	1.50
27	Thurman Munson	3.50	1.75	1.00
28	Ron Guidry	2.00	1.00	.60
29	Bruce Bochte	2.00	1.00	.60
30	Richie Zisk	2.00	1.00	.60
31	Jim Palmer	4.00	2.00	1.25
32	Mark Fidrych	2.50	1.25	.70
33	Frank Tanana	2.00	1.00	.60
34	Buddy Bell	2.00	1.00	.60
35	Rod Carew	4.00	2.00	1.25
36	George Brett	7.50	3.75	2.25
37	Ralph Garr	2.00	1.00	.60
38	Larry Hisle	2.00	1.00	.60
39	Mitchell Page	2.00	1.00	.60
40	John Mayberry	2.00	1.00	.60

1974 Bob Parker 2nd Best

Star players who came in second, often to lesser-known players, in various statistical categories between 1899-1955 are featured in this collectors issue from Bob Parker. The blank-backed, black-and-white cards measure an unusual 3" x 8" and feature the story of the 1-2 finish in cartoon form. The unnumbered cards are listed here in chronological order.

		NM	EX	VG
	Complete Set (25):	55.00	25.00	15.00
	Common Player:	3.00	1.50	.90
(1)	Jesse Burkett, Ed Delahanty/ 1899	3.00	1.50	.90
(2)	Hans Wagner, Cy Seymour/ 1905	4.00	2.00	1.25
(3)	Gavvy Cravath, Jake Daubert/ 1913	3.00	1.50	.90
(4)	Joe Jackson, Ty Cobb/1913	10.00	5.00	3.00
(5)	Eddie Collins, Ty Cobb/1914	4.00	2.00	1.25
(6)	Babe Ruth, Heinie Manush/ 1926	7.50	3.75	2.25
(7)	Chick Hafey, Jim Bottomley, Hack Wilson/1928	3.00	1.50	.90
(8)	Paul Waner, Rogers Hornsby/1928	3.00	1.50	.90
(9)	Babe Herman, Lefty O'Doul/ 1929	3.00	1.50	.90
(10)	Al Simmons, Lew Fonseca/ 1929	3.00	1.50	.90
(11)	Lou Gehrig, Babe Ruth/1930	10.00	5.00	3.00
(12)	Babe Herman, Bill Terry/1930	3.00	1.50	.90
(13)	Chuck Klein, Hack Wilson/ 1930	3.00	1.50	.90
(14)	Jim Bottomley, Bill Terry, Chick Hafey/1931	3.00	1.50	.90
(15)	Jimmy (Jimmie) Foxx, Dale Alexander/1932	3.00	1.50	.90
(16)	Spud Davis, Chuck Klein/ 1933	3.00	1.50	.90
(17)	Heinie Manush, Jimmy Foxx/ 1933	3.00	1.50	.90
(18)	Mel Ott, Wally Berger/1935	3.00	1.50	.90
(19)	Joe Vosmik, Buddy Myer/ 1935	3.00	1.50	.90
(20)	Blimp Phelps, Paul Waner/ 1936	3.00	1.50	.90
(21)	Bobby Doerr, Lou Boudreau/ 1944	3.00	1.50	.90
(22)	Stan Musial, Dixie Walker/1944	4.00	2.00	1.25
(23)	George Kell, Billy Goodman/1950	3.00	1.50	.90
(24)	Al Rosen, Mickey Vernon/1953	3.00	1.50	.90
(25)	Vic Power, Al Kaline/1955	3.00	1.50	.90

1976 Bob Parker More Baseball Cartoons

This collectors' issue showcased the pen and ink artwork of Ohio cartoonist Bob Parker on cards featuring current and former ballplayers from the great to

the obscure. Cards are in 3-1/2" x 5" format with black-and-white fronts and blank backs.

		NM	EX	VG
	Complete Set (24)	65.00	32.50	20.00
	Common Card:	3.00	1.50	.90
1	Hank Aaron, Babe Ruth (All-Time HR Specialists./)	7.50	3.75	2.25
2	Ernie Banks	4.00	2.00	1.25
3	Rod Carew	3.00	1.50	.90
4	Joe DiMaggio	15.00	7.50	4.50
5	Doug Flynn	3.00	1.50	.90
6	Mike Garcia	3.00	1.50	.90
7	Steve Garvey, Greg Luzinski (All-Stars)	3.00	1.50	.90
8	Lou Gehrig	15.00	7.50	4.50
9	Chuck Klein, Hack Wilson (Hall of Famers?)	3.00	1.50	.90
10	Don Larsen	3.00	1.50	.90
11	Fred Lynn	3.00	1.50	.90
12	Roy Majtyka	3.00	1.50	.90
13	Pepper Martin	3.00	1.50	.90
14	Christy Mathewson	5.00	2.50	1.50
15	Cal McVey	3.00	1.50	.90
16	Tony Perez	3.00	1.50	.90
17	Lou Gehrig, Babe Ruth (Great Moments)	15.00	7.50	4.50
18	Everett Scott	3.00	1.50	.90
19	Bobby Thomson	3.00	1.50	.90
20	Ted Williams/1939	7.50	3.75	2.25
21	Ted Williams (Great Moments)	7.50	3.75	2.25
22	Bill Madlock	3.00	1.50	.90
23	Henry Chadwick, Buck Ewing, Albert Spalding, Honus Wagner (Hall of Famers)	3.00	1.50	.90
---	Checklist	3.00	1.50	.90

1977 Bob Parker Cincinnati Reds

In the late 1970s, Ohio cartoonist Bob Parker drew a series of Reds feature cartoons for the weekly "Reds Alert." Later, he assembled two groups of those cartoons into collectors' issue card sets. The cards are black-and-white with blank backs. Fronts have portraits and/or action main drawings, usually with some cartoon figures included to draw attention to the player's career highlights. Size is 3-1/2" x 5". The unnumbered series is listed in alphabetical order.

		NM	EX	VG
	Complete Set (48):	110.00	55.00	32.50
	Common Player:	3.00	1.50	.90
	UNNUMBERED SERIES (24)	55.00	25.00	15.00
(1)	Sparky Anderson	4.00	2.00	1.25
(2)	Wally Berger	3.00	1.50	.90
(3)	Pedro Borbon	3.00	1.50	.90
(4)	Rube Bressler	3.00	1.50	.90
(5)	Gordy Coleman	3.00	1.50	.90
(6)	Dave Concepcion	3.00	1.50	.90
(7)	Harry Craft	3.00	1.50	.90
(8)	Hugh Critz	3.00	1.50	.90
(9)	Dan Driessen	3.00	1.50	.90
(10)	Pat Duncan	3.00	1.50	.90
(11)	Lonnie Frey	3.00	1.50	.90
(12)	Ival Goodman	3.00	1.50	.90
(13)	Heinie Groh	3.00	1.50	.90
(14)	Noodles Hahn	3.00	1.50	.90
(15)	Mike Lum	3.00	1.50	.90
(16)	Bill McKechnie	3.00	1.50	.90
(17)	Pat Moran	3.00	1.50	.90
(18)	Billy Myers	3.00	1.50	.90

		NM	EX	VG
(19)	Gary Nolan	3.00	1.50	.90
(20)	Fred Norman	3.00	1.50	.90
(21)	Jim O'Toole	3.00	1.50	.90
(22)	Vada Pinson	4.00	2.00	1.25
(23)	Bucky Walters	3.00	1.50	.90
(24)	Checklist	3.00	1.50	.90
	NUMBERED SERIES (24):	60.00	30.00	18.00
1	Ted Kluszewski	6.00	3.00	1.75
2	Johnny Bench	10.00	5.00	3.00
3	Jim Maloney	3.00	1.50	.90
4	Bubbles Hargrave	3.00	1.50	.90
5	Don Gullett	3.00	1.50	.90
6	Joe Nuxhall	4.00	2.00	1.25
7	Edd Roush	3.00	1.50	.90
8	Wally Post	3.00	1.50	.90
9	George Wright	3.00	1.50	.90
10	George Foster	3.00	1.50	.90
11	Pete Rose	15.00	7.50	4.50
12	Red Lucas	3.00	1.50	.90
13	Joe Morgan	4.00	2.00	1.25
14	Eppa Rixey	3.00	1.50	.90
15	Bill Werber	3.00	1.50	.90
16	Frank Robinson	6.00	3.00	1.75
17	Dolf Luque	4.00	2.00	1.25
18	Paul Derringer	3.00	1.50	.90
19	Frank McCormick	3.00	1.50	.90
20	Ken Griffey	3.00	1.50	.90
21	Jack Billingham	3.00	1.50	.90
22	Larry Kopf	3.00	1.50	.90
23	Ernie Lombardi	3.00	1.50	.90
24	Johnny Vander Meer	3.00	1.50	.90

1977-81 Bob Parker Hall of Fame

This is one of many collectors issues produced in the mid to late 1970s by midwestern sports artist Bob Parker. The 3-3/8" x 5-1/2" cards are printed in sepia on tan cardboard; they are blank-backed. Fronts have a portrait drawing of the player, with career highlights in cartoon form. Three series were issued: #1-54 in 1977; #55-77 in 1980 and #78-100 in 1981. A header card was issued with each series.

		NM	EX	VG
	Complete Set (103):	125.00	65.00	35.00
	Common Player:	3.00	1.50	.90
	First Series Set (55):	50.00	25.00	15.00
---	First Series Header	1.00	.50	.30
1	Grover Alexander	3.00	1.50	.90
2	Cap Anson	3.00	1.50	.90
3	Luke Appling	3.00	1.50	.90
4	Ernie Banks	4.00	2.00	1.25
5	Chief Bender	3.00	1.50	.90
6	Jim Bottomley	3.00	1.50	.90
7	Dan Brouthers	3.00	1.50	.90
8	Morgan Bulkeley	3.00	1.50	.90
9	Roy Campanella	7.50	3.75	2.25
10	Alexander Cartwright	3.00	1.50	.90
11	Henry Chadwick	3.00	1.50	.90
12	John Clarkson	3.00	1.50	.90
13	Ty Cobb	10.00	5.00	3.00
14	Eddie Collins	3.00	1.50	.90
16	Charles Comiskey	3.00	1.50	.90
17	Sam Crawford	3.00	1.50	.90
18	Dizzy Dean	4.00	2.00	1.25
19	Joe DiMaggio	16.00	8.00	4.75
20	Buck Ewing	3.00	1.50	.90
21	Bob Feller	4.00	2.00	1.25
22	Lou Gehrig	16.00	8.00	4.75
23	Goose Goslin	3.00	1.50	.90
24	Burleigh Grimes	3.00	1.50	.90
25	Chick Hafey	3.00	1.50	.90
26	Rogers Hornsby	3.00	1.50	.90
27	Carl Hubbell	3.00	1.50	.90
28	Miller Huggins	3.00	1.50	.90
29	Tim Keefe	3.00	1.50	.90
30	Mike Kelly	3.00	1.50	.90
31	Nap Lajoie	3.00	1.50	.90
32	Freddie Lindstrom	3.00	1.50	.90
33	Connie Mack	3.00	1.50	.90
34	Mickey Mantle	25.00	12.50	7.50
35	Heinie Manush	3.00	1.50	.90
36	Joe McGinnity	3.00	1.50	.90
37	John McGraw	3.00	1.50	.90
38	Ed Plank	3.00	1.50	.90
39	Eppa Rixey	3.00	1.50	.90
40	Jackie Robinson	12.00	6.00	3.50
41	Edd Roush	3.00	1.50	.90
42	Babe Ruth	20.00	10.00	6.00
43	Al Simmons	3.00	1.50	.90
44	Al Spalding	3.00	1.50	.90

		NM	EX	VG
45	Tris Speaker	3.00	1.50	.90
46	Casey Stengel	3.00	1.50	.90
47	Bill Terry	3.00	1.50	.90
48	Rube Waddell	3.00	1.50	.90
49	Honus Wagner	5.00	2.50	1.50
50	Paul Waner	3.00	1.50	.90
51	John Montgomery Ward	3.00	1.50	.90
52	Ted Williams	10.00	5.00	3.00
53	George Wright	3.00	1.50	.90
54	Harry Wright	3.00	1.50	.90
	Second Series Set (24):	40.00	20.00	12.00
---	Second Series Header	1.00	.50	.30
55	Mordecai Brown	3.00	1.50	.90
56	Frank Chance	3.00	1.50	.90
57	Candy Cummings	3.00	1.50	.90
58	Frank Frisch	3.00	1.50	.90
59	Gabby Hartnett	3.00	1.50	.90
60	Billy Herman	3.00	1.50	.90
61	Waite Hoyt	3.00	1.50	.90
62	Walter Johnson	5.00	2.50	1.50
63	Kenesaw Landis	3.00	1.50	.90
64	Rube Marquard	3.00	1.50	.90
65	Christy Mathewson	6.00	3.00	1.75
66	Eddie Mathews	3.00	1.50	.90
67	Willie Mays	10.00	5.00	3.00
68	Bill McKechnie	3.00	1.50	.90
69	Stan Musial	7.50	3.75	2.25
70	Mel Ott	3.00	1.50	.90
71	Satchel Paige	7.50	3.75	2.25
72	Robin Roberts	3.00	1.50	.90
73	George Sisler	3.00	1.50	.90
74	Warren Spahn	3.00	1.50	.90
75	Joe Tinker	3.00	1.50	.90
76	Dazzy Vance	3.00	1.50	.90
77	Cy Young	6.00	3.00	1.75
	Third Series Set (24):	40.00	20.00	12.00
---	Third Series Header	1.00	.50	.30
78	Home Run Baker	3.00	1.50	.90
79	Yogi Berra	4.00	2.00	1.25
80	Max Carey	3.00	1.50	.90
81	Roberto Clemente	16.00	8.00	4.75
82	Mickey Cochrane	3.00	1.50	.90
83	Roger Connor	3.00	1.50	.90
84	Joe Cronin	3.00	1.50	.90
85	Kiki Cuyler	3.00	1.50	.90
86	Johnny Evers	3.00	1.50	.90
87	Jimmie Foxx	3.00	1.50	.90
88	Charlie Gehringer	3.00	1.50	.90
89	Lefty Gomez	3.00	1.50	.90
90	Jesse Haines	3.00	1.50	.90
91	Will Harridge	3.00	1.50	.90
92	Monte Irvin	3.00	1.50	.90
93	Addie Joss	3.00	1.50	.90
94	Al Kaline	3.00	1.50	.90
95	Sandy Koufax	10.00	5.00	3.00
96	Rabbit Maranville	3.00	1.50	.90
97	Jim O'Rourke	3.00	1.50	.90
98	Wilbert Robinson	3.00	1.50	.90
99	Pie Traynor	3.00	1.50	.90
100	Zack Wheat	3.00	1.50	.90

1968-70 Partridge Meats Reds

is unknown. The cards were produced in conjunction with Reds' autograph appearances at Kroger food stores in the Cincinnati area. Players' service with the Reds indicates this set was issued over a period of several years. Similar cards are known for other Cincinnati pro sports teams. The 1968 cards measure 4" x 5" and feature a black-and-white player photo set against a borderless white background. The player's name and team and the word "Likes" are printed in black, the ad for the issuing meat company at bottom is printed in red. Cards have a blank back. The 1969-70 cards are in the same format but in 3-3/4" x 5-1/2" format. The unnumbered cards are checklisted here in alphabetical order.

		NM	EX	VG
	Complete Set (11):	500.00	250.00	150.00
	Common Player:	20.00	10.00	6.00
(1)	Ted Abernathy	40.00	20.00	12.00
(2)	John Bench	50.00	25.00	15.00
(3)	Jimmy Bragan	20.00	10.00	6.00
(4)	Dave Bristol	40.00	20.00	12.00
(5)	Tommy Helms	40.00	20.00	12.00
(6)	Gary Nolan	20.00	10.00	6.00
(7)	Milt Pappas	40.00	20.00	12.00
(8)	Don Pavletich	40.00	20.00	12.00
(9)	Mel Queen	40.00	20.00	12.00
(10)	Pete Rose	150.00	75.00	45.00
(11)	Jim Stewart	40.00	20.00	12.00

1972 Partridge Meats Reds

Similar in format to the meat company's 1968-70 issue, these later cards are in a slightly different size

Lee May / Cincinnati / PHOTO COURTESY OF / Partridge meats

- 3-3/4" x 5-1/2". The ad on the '72 cards reads "Photo courtesy of Partridge Meats."

		NM	EX	VG
	Complete Set (7):	225.00	110.00	65.00
	Common Player:	30.00	15.00	9.00
(1)	Don Gullett	30.00	15.00	9.00
(2)	Lee May	30.00	15.00	9.00
(3)	Denis Menke	30.00	15.00	9.00
(4)	Jim Merritt	30.00	15.00	9.00
(5)	Gary Nolan	30.00	15.00	9.00
(6)	Tony Perez	60.00	30.00	18.00
(7)	Bob Tolan	30.00	15.00	9.00

1922 Wm. Paterson

25 BABE RUTH / New York Americans / Wm. Paterson, Limited / Brantford, Canada

Believed to have been a Canadian candy premium, this 50-card set of 2" x 3-1/4" cards features portrait or posed action photos with wide white borders. Beneath the photo is a card number, player name, team, and in two lines, "Wm. Paterson, Limited / Brantford, Canada." Backs are blank. Two distinct types are seen, black-and-white and sepia, though the reason for the variations is unknown.

		NM	EX	VG
	Complete Set (50):	60,000	24,000	12,000
	Common Player:	475.00	200.00	100.00
1	Eddie Roush	1,000	400.00	200.00
2	Rube Marquard	1,000	400.00	200.00
3	Del Gainor	475.00	200.00	100.00
4	George Sisler	1,000	400.00	200.00
5	Joe Bush	475.00	200.00	100.00
6	Joe Oeschger	475.00	200.00	100.00
7	Willie Kamm	475.00	200.00	100.00
8	John Watson	475.00	200.00	100.00
9	Dolf Luque	550.00	225.00	110.00
10	Miller Huggins	1,000	400.00	200.00
11	Wally Schang	475.00	200.00	100.00
12	Bob Shawkey	475.00	200.00	100.00
13	Tris Speaker	1,750	700.00	350.00
14	Hugh McQuillan	475.00	200.00	100.00
15	"Long George" Kelly	1,000	400.00	200.00
16	Ray Schalk	1,000	400.00	200.00
17	Sam Jones	475.00	200.00	100.00
18	Grover Alexander	1,750	700.00	350.00
19	Bob Meusel	475.00	200.00	100.00
20	"Irish" Emil Meusel	475.00	200.00	100.00
21	Rogers Hornsby	1,750	700.00	350.00
22	Harry Heilmann	1,000	400.00	200.00
23	Heinie Groh	475.00	200.00	100.00
24	Frank Frisch	1,000	400.00	200.00
25	Babe Ruth	15,000	6,000	3,000
26	Jack Bentley	475.00	200.00	100.00
27	Everett Scott	475.00	200.00	100.00
28	Max Carey	1,000	400.00	200.00
29	Chick Fewster	475.00	200.00	100.00
30	Cy Williams	475.00	200.00	100.00
31	Burleigh Grimes	1,000	400.00	200.00
32	Waite Hoyt	1,000	400.00	200.00
33	Frank Snyder	475.00	200.00	100.00
34	Clyde Milan	475.00	200.00	100.00
35	Eddie Collins	1,000	400.00	200.00
36	Travis Jackson	1,000	400.00	200.00
37	Ken Williams	475.00	200.00	100.00
38	Dave Bancroft	1,000	400.00	200.00
39	Mike McNally	475.00	200.00	100.00

40	John McGraw	1,000	400.00	200.00
41	Art Nehf	475.00	200.00	100.00
42	"Rabbit" Maranville	1,000	400.00	200.00
43	Charlie Grimm	475.00	200.00	100.00
44	Joe Judge	475.00	200.00	100.00
45	Wally Pipp	475.00	200.00	100.00
46	Ty Cobb	10,000	4,000	2,000
47	Walter Johnson	3,000	1,200	600.00
48	Jake Daubert	475.00	200.00	100.00
49	Zack Wheat	1,000	400.00	200.00
50	Herb Pennock	1,000	400.00	200.00

1921 Pathe Freres Phonograph Co.

 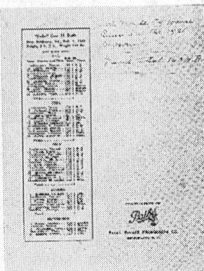

One of the rarest early-1920s Babe Ruth items is this premium photo issued by Pathe Freres Phonograph Co. of Brooklyn. Ruth is pictured bare-headed in a pinstriped uniform on the front of this approximately 7" x 9-1/4" card, printed in green and gray tones with a white border. A photo credit to White Studios of New York is given on the front and there is a facsimile autograph at bottom front. The black-and-white back has a listing of Ruth's 1920 homers in a box at left, and a Pathe ad at bottom-right.

	NM	EX	VG
Babe Ruth	3,500	1,750	1,050

1910 PC796 Sepia Postcards

 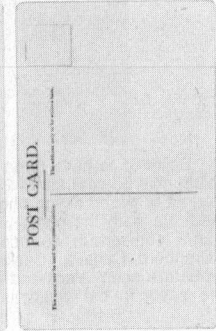

The manufacturer of these sepia-toned 3-1/2" x 5-1/2" postcards is unknown, but most of the photos utilized are familiar from other card issues of the era. Fronts have the player name at bottom in fancy capital letters. Backs have a standard divided postcard indicia. The set was given the PC796 designation in the "American Card Catalog." The unnumbered cards are checklisted here alphabetically.

		NM	EX	VG
Complete Set (25):		22,500	9,000	4,500
Common Player:		300.00	120.00	60.00
(1)	Roger Bresnahan	600.00	240.00	120.00
(2)	Al Bridwell	300.00	120.00	60.00
(3)	Mordecai Brown	600.00	240.00	120.00
(4)	Frank Chance	600.00	240.00	120.00
(5)	Hal Chase	450.00	180.00	90.00
(6)	Ty Cobb	4,250	1,700	850.00
(7)	Ty Cobb, Hanus Wagner	3,750	1,500	750.00
(8)	Eddie Collins	600.00	240.00	120.00
(9)	Sam Crawford	600.00	240.00	120.00
(10)	Art Devlin	300.00	120.00	60.00
(11)	Red Dooin	300.00	120.00	60.00
(12)	Johnny Evers, Germany Schaefer	400.00	160.00	80.00
(13)	Sam Frock	300.00	120.00	60.00
(14)	George Gibson	300.00	120.00	60.00
(15)	Artie Hoffman (Hofman)	300.00	120.00	60.00
(16)	Walter Johnson	1,200	480.00	240.00
(17)	Nap Lajoie	600.00	240.00	120.00
(18)	Harry Lord	300.00	120.00	60.00
(19)	Christy Mathewson	2,000	800.00	400.00
(20)	Orval Overall	300.00	120.00	60.00
(21)	Eddie Plank	600.00	240.00	120.00
(22)	Tris Speaker	750.00	300.00	150.00
(23)	Gabby Street	300.00	120.00	60.00
(24)	Honus Wagner	3,000	1,200	600.00
(25)	Ed Walsh	600.00	240.00	120.00

1869 Peck & Snyder Cincinnati Red Stockings - Small

Many consider this to be the first true baseball card in that it was produced in large quantities (relative to the cabinets and carte de visites of the era) and offered to firms wishing to place their advertising on the back. The 3-15/16" x 2-3/8" card features a sepia team photo on front of baseball's first real professional team, including Hall of Famers George and Harry Wright. The Peck & Snyder ad back is the most commonly found, but others are known, including a back which lists only the team's line-up.

	NM	EX	VG
Cincinnati Red Stocking Team	30,000	14,000	8,500

1869 Peck & Snyder Cincinnati Red Stockings - Large

Many consider this to be the first true baseball card in that it was produced in large quantities (relative to the cabinets and carte de visites of the era) and offered to firms wishing to place their advertising on the back. The 4-3/16" x 3-5/16" card features a sepia team photo on front of baseball's first real professional team, including Hall of Famers George and Harry Wright. In this larger format, the players are identified on front with the team name in ornate black or red (slightly scarcer) type at bottom. Backs have been seen with ads for New York "Sportsman's "Emporium" along with a caricature of a bearded ballplayer, and for "The New York City Base Ball & Skate Emporium," with a large illsutration of an ice skate.

	NM	EX	VG
Cincinnati Red Stocking Team	25,000	12,000	8,250

1870 Peck & Snyder Chicago White Stockings

Using popular baseball teams of the day as an advertising medium, this approximately 4" x 2-3/4" black-and-white card pictures and identifies on front the 1870 Chicago White Stockings of pre-National Association days. On back is an ad for Peck & Snyder of New York City.

Chicago White Stockings	NM	EX	VG
	10,000	5,000	3,000

1870 Peck & Snyder New York Mutuals

Using popular baseball teams of the day as an advertising medium, this apporoximately 4" x 2-3/4" black-and-white card pictures and identifies on front the 1870 New York Mutuals of pre-National Association days. On back is a cartoon ad for Peck & Snyder of New York City.

New York Mutuals	NM	EX	VG
James Creighton	75,000	37,500	22,500

1870 Peck & Snyder Philadelphia Athletics

A composite photo of the players in street clothes is featured on this promotional card for the New York City sporting goods dealer whose advertising appears on back.

Philadelphia Athletics
(Sold for $2,780 in 10/01 auction in Poor condition.)

1963 Pepsi-Cola Colt .45's

This issue was distributed regionally in Texas in bottled six-packs of Pepsi. The cards were issued on 2-3/8" x 9-1/8" panels. A 2-3/8" x 3-3/4" card was printed on each panel, which also included promos for Pepsi and the Colt .45's, as well as a team schedule. Card fronts are black-and-white posed action photos with blue and red trim. Backs offer player statistics and career highlights. The John Bateman card was apparently never distributed publicly and is among the rarest baseball cards of the 1960s. The unnumbered cards are checklisted here alphabetically. Values shown are for complete panels with top and bottom tabs; those without are valued about 25 percent.

		NM	EX	VG
Complete Set (15):		800.00	400.00	240.00
Common Player:		10.00	5.00	3.00
(1)	Bob Aspromonte	10.00	5.00	3.00
(2)	John Bateman/SP	2,500	1,250	750.00
(3)	Bob Bruce	10.00	5.00	3.00
(4)	Jim Campbell	10.00	5.00	3.00
(5)	Dick Farrell	10.00	5.00	3.00
(6)	Ernie Fazio	10.00	5.00	3.00
(7)	Carroll Hardy	10.00	5.00	3.00
(8)	J.C. Hartman	10.00	5.00	3.00
(9)	Ken Johnson	10.00	5.00	3.00
(10)	Bob Lillis/SP	375.00	185.00	110.00
(11)	Don McMahon	10.00	5.00	3.00
(12)	Pete Runnels	10.00	5.00	3.00
(13)	Al Spangler	10.00	5.00	3.00
(14)	Rusty Staub	35.00	17.50	10.00
(15)	Johnny Temple	10.00	5.00	3.00
(16)	Carl Warwick/SP	300.00	150.00	90.00

1977 Pepsi-Cola Baseball Stars

An Ohio regional promotion (the checklist is extra heavy with Indians and Reds players), large numbers of these cards found their way into hobby dealers' hands. Designed to be inserted into cartons of soda, the cards have a 3-3/8" diameter central disc attached with perforations to a baseball glove design. A tab beneath the glove contains the checklist (the card discs themselves are unnumbered) and a coupon on back for ordering a player t-shirt, the offer for which is made on the back of the player disc. The players' association logo appears on front, but the producer, Mike Schechter Associates, did not seek licensing by Major League Baseball, with the result that uniform logos have been removed from the black-and-white player photos. Prices shown are for complete glove/disc/tab cards. Values for unattached player discs would be no more than one-half of those shown. The discs of Reggie Jackson and Mike Schmidt can be found with either orange, green, purple, light blue or sky blue side panels; the other player discs are known in only one color each.

		NM	EX	VG
Complete Set (72):		35.00	17.50	10.00
W/Color Variations (80):		75.00	37.50	22.50
Common Player:		1.00	.50	.30
1	Robin Yount	4.00	2.00	1.25
2	Rod Carew	4.00	2.00	1.25
3	Butch Wynegar	1.00	.50	.30
4	Manny Sanguillen	1.00	.50	.30
5	Mike Hargrove	1.00	.50	.30
6	Larvel (Larvell) Blanks	1.00	.50	.30
7	Jim Kern	1.00	.50	.30
8	Pat Dobson	1.00	.50	.30
9	Rico Carty	1.00	.50	.30
10	John Grubb	1.00	.50	.30
11	Buddy Bell	1.00	.50	.30
12	Rick Manning	1.00	.50	.30
13	Dennis Eckersley	4.00	2.00	1.25
14	Wayne Garland	1.00	.50	.30
15	Dave LaRoche	1.00	.50	.30
16	Rick Waits	1.00	.50	.30
17	Ray Fosse	1.00	.50	.30
18	Frank Duffy	1.00	.50	.30
19	Duane Kuiper	1.00	.50	.30
20	Jim Palmer	4.00	2.00	1.25
21	Fred Lynn	1.00	.50	.30
22	Carlton Fisk	4.00	2.00	1.25
23	Carl Yastrzemski	6.00	3.00	1.75
24	Nolan Ryan	17.50	8.75	5.25
25	Bobby Grich	1.00	.50	.30
26	Ralph Garr	1.00	.50	.30
27	Richie Zisk	1.00	.50	.30
28	Ron LeFlore	1.00	.50	.30
29	Rusty Staub	1.00	.50	.30
30	Mark Fidrych	1.50	.70	.45
31	Willie Horton	1.00	.50	.30
32	George Brett	10.00	5.00	3.00
33	Amos Otis	1.00	.50	.30
34a	Reggie Jackson (Green)	7.50	3.75	2.25
34b	Reggie Jackson (Light blue)	7.50	3.75	2.25
34c	Reggie Jackson (Orange)	7.50	3.75	2.25
34d	Reggie Jackson (Purple)	7.50	3.75	2.25
34e	Reggie Jackson (Sky Blue)	7.50	3.75	2.25
35	Don Gullett	1.00	.50	.30
36	Thurman Munson	3.00	1.50	.90
37	Al Hrabosky	1.00	.50	.30
38	Mike Tyson	1.00	.50	.30
39	Gene Tenace	1.00	.50	.30
40	George Hendrick	1.00	.50	.30
41	Chris Speier	1.00	.50	.30
42	John Montefusco	1.00	.50	.30
43	Pete Rose	10.00	5.00	3.00
44	Johnny Bench	5.00	2.50	1.50
45	Dan Driessen	1.00	.50	.30
46	Joe Morgan	4.00	2.00	1.25
47	Dave Concepcion	1.00	.50	.30
48	George Foster	1.00	.50	.30
49	Cesar Geronimo	1.00	.50	.30
50	Ken Griffey	1.00	.50	.30
51	Gary Nolan	1.00	.50	.30
52	Santo Alcala	1.00	.50	.30
53	Jack Billingham	1.00	.50	.30
54	Pedro Borbon	1.00	.50	.30
55	Rawly Eastwick	1.00	.50	.30
56	Fred Norman	1.00	.50	.30
57	Pat Zachary (Zachry)	1.00	.50	.30
58	Jeff Burroughs	1.00	.50	.30
59	Manny Trillo	1.00	.50	.30
60	Bob Watson	1.00	.50	.30
61	Steve Garvey	1.50	.70	.45
62	Don Sutton	4.00	2.00	1.25
63	John Candelaria	1.00	.50	.30
64	Willie Stargell	4.00	2.00	1.25
65	Jerry Reuss	1.00	.50	.30
66	Dave Cash	1.00	.50	.30
67	Tom Seaver	5.00	2.50	1.50
68	Jon Matlock	1.00	.50	.30
69	Dave Kingman	1.00	.50	.30
70a	Mike Schmidt (Green)	7.50	3.75	2.25
70b	Mike Schmidt (Light Blue)	7.50	3.75	2.25
70c	Mike Schmidt (Orange)	7.50	3.75	2.25
70d	Mike Schmidt (Purple)	7.50	3.75	2.25
70e	Mike Schmidt (Sky Blue)	7.50	3.75	2.25
71	Jay Johnstone	1.00	.50	.30
72	Greg Luzinski	1.00	.50	.30

1977 Pepsi-Cola Cincinnati Reds Playing Cards

Similar to a multi-sport series produced by Cubic Corp. (see also), these playing cards sets feature on back the pencil drawings of Al Landsman. Each boxed deck featured one Reds star player within a red border. Also on each card back are a facsimile autograph and Pepsi logo. Cards are standard bridge size (2-1/4" x 3-1/2") with rounded corners. Decks were available by sending in 250 16-oz. Pepsi cap liners or a combination of cash and cap liners.

		NM	EX	VG
(1)	Johnny Bench (Boxed deck.)	35.00	17.50	10.00
(1)	Johnny Bench (Single card.)	1.50	.70	.45
(2)	Joe Morgan (Boxed deck.)	20.00	10.00	6.00
(2)	Joe Morgan (Single card.)	1.00	.50	.30
(3)	Pete Rose (Boxed deck.)	55.00	27.50	16.50
(3)	Pete Rose (Single card.)	4.00	2.00	1.25

1978 Pepsi-Cola Superstars

In its second year of producing carton-stuffer baseball cards, Cincinnati area Pepsi bottlers issued a 40-card set featuring 25 Reds players and 15 other major league stars. The entire carton insert measure 2-1/8" x 9-1/2". Besides the baseball card at top, there is a checklist and mail-in offer for playing cards featuring Johnny Bench, Joe Morgan and Pete Rose. The card element at the top measure 2-1/8" x 2-1/2". A player portrait, with uniform logos airbrushed off, is featured in black-and-white in a white star on a red background.

The Major League Baseball Player's Association logo appears in dark blue in the upper-left. Printed in black below are the player's name, team, position, birthdate and place and a few 1977 stats. In back, printed in red, white and blue, is part of the offer for the playing cards. Large quantities of this set found their way into hobby hands and they remain common today.

		NM	EX	VG
Complete Set (40):		30.00	15.00	9.00
Common Player:		.75	.35	.20
(1)	Sparky Anderson	2.00	1.00	.60
(2)	Rick Auerbach	.75	.35	.20
(3)	Doug Bair	.75	.35	.20
(4)	Buddy Bell	.75	.35	.20
(5)	Johnny Bench	4.00	2.00	1.25
(6)	Bill Bonham	.75	.35	.20
(7)	Pedro Borbon	.75	.35	.20
(8)	Larry Bowa	.75	.35	.20
(9)	George Brett	7.50	3.75	2.25
(10)	Jeff Burroughs	.75	.35	.20
(11)	Rod Carew	3.00	1.50	.90
(12)	Dave Collins	.75	.35	.20
(13)	Dave Concepcion	.75	.35	.20
(14)	Dan Driessen	.75	.35	.20
(15)	George Foster	.75	.35	.20
(16)	Steve Garvey	1.50	.70	.45
(17)	Cesar Geronimo	.75	.35	.20
(18)	Ken Griffey	.75	.35	.20
(19)	Ken Henderson	.75	.35	.20
(20)	Tom Hume	.75	.35	.20
(21)	Reggie Jackson	7.50	3.75	2.25
(22)	Junior Kennedy	.75	.35	.20
(23)	Dave Kingman	.75	.40	.25
(24)	Ray Knight	.75	.35	.20
(25)	Jerry Koosman	.75	.35	.20
(26)	Mike Lum	.75	.35	.20
(27)	Bill Madlock	.75	.35	.20
(28)	Joe Morgan	3.00	1.50	.90
(29)	Paul Moskau	.75	.35	.20
(30)	Fred Norman	.75	.35	.20
(31)	Jim Palmer	3.00	1.50	.90
(32)	Pete Rose	10.00	5.00	3.00
(33)	Nolan Ryan	12.50	6.25	3.75
(34)	Manny Sarmiento	.75	.35	.20
(35)	Tom Seaver	4.00	2.00	1.25
(36)	Ted Simmons	.75	.35	.20
(37)	Dave Tomlin	.75	.35	.20
(38)	Don Werner	.75	.35	.20
(39)	Carl Yastrzemski	4.00	2.00	1.25
(40)	Richie Zisk	.75	.35	.20

1980 Pepsi-Cola All-Stars Prototypes

These prototype cards were prepared by Topps and Mike Schechter Associates for a proposed Pepsi promotion. Three sets of the cards were given to Pepsi officials for consideration but only two were returned when the deal fell through. The third sheet was cut up and sold into the hobby. The Pepsi cards share the format of Topps' regular 1980 issue, although Pepsi logos have been added on front and back, name and banner colors changed on front and a position circle added. In 2005 a number of the individual cards were offered on eBay by Topps.

		NM	EX	VG
Common Player:		250.00	125.00	75.00
1	Rod Carew	1,000	500.00	300.00
2	Paul Molitor	1,000	500.00	300.00
3	George Brett	1,500	750.00	450.00
4	Robin Yount	1,000	500.00	300.00
5	Reggie Jackson	1,500	750.00	450.00
6	Fred Lynn	250.00	125.00	75.00
7	Ken Landreaux	250.00	125.00	75.00
8	Jim Sundberg	250.00	125.00	75.00
9	Ron Guidry (One known, other two cut from sheets and destroyed; negatives reversed.)	1,450	725.00	435.00
10	Jim Palmer	1,000	500.00	300.00
11	Goose Gossage	250.00	125.00	75.00
12	Keith Hernandez	250.00	125.00	75.00
13	Dave Lopes	250.00	125.00	75.00
14	Mike Schmidt	1,500	750.00	450.00
15	Garry Templeton	250.00	125.00	75.00
16	Dave Parker	250.00	125.00	75.00
17	George Foster	250.00	125.00	75.00
18	Dave Winfield	1,000	500.00	300.00
19	Ted Simmons	250.00	125.00	75.00
20	Steve Carlton	1,000	500.00	300.00
21	J.R. Richard	400.00	200.00	120.00
22	Bruce Sutter	1,000	500.00	300.00

1966 Gaylord Perry Insurance

GAYLORD PERRY
All Insurance Needs
P. O. Box 112
Williamston, N. C. 27892
Phone 792-6101

The attributed date is arbitrary, near the middle of his stay with the S.F. Giants in whose uniform he is pictured on this approximately 3-1/2" x 5-1/2", blank-backed, black-and-white "business" card for his insurance agency.

	NM	EX	VG
Gaylord Perry	40.00	20.00	12.00

1971 Pete Rose & Johnny Bench Lincoln-Mercury Postcards

This series of promotional postcards was issued in 1970-71 in conjunction with a Dayton, Ohio, Lincoln-Mercury auto dealership owned by Reds teammates Rose and Bench. Fronts of the 5-1/2" x 3-1/2" postcards feature color photos of new cars. Black-and-white backs have portraits of the players, a description of the auto, the address of the dealership and a credit line for the postcard's printer. Besides those listed here, other auto fronts may exist.

		NM	EX	VG
Common Card:		25.00	12.50	7.50
(1)	Johnny Bench, Pete Rose (1971 Lincoln Continental Sedan)	25.00	12.50	7.50
(2)	Johnny Bench, Pete Rose (1971 Mercury Cougar Convertible)	25.00	12.50	7.50
(3)	Johnny Bench, Pete Rose (1971 Mercury Montego)	25.00	12.50	7.50

1972 Pete Rose & Johnny Bench Lincoln-Mercury Postcards

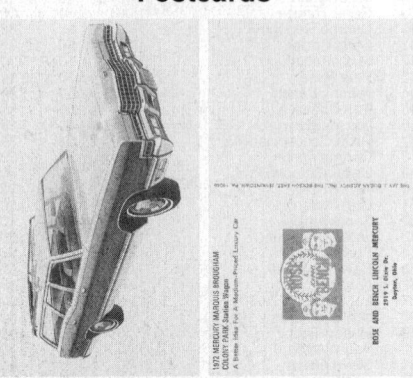

This series of promotional postcards was issued in 1971-72 in conjunction with a Dayton, Ohio, Lincoln-Mercury auto dealership owned by Reds teammates Rose and Bench. Fronts of the 5-1/2" x 3-1/2" postcards feature color photos of new cars. Black, white and backs have portraits of the players, a description of the auto, the address of the dealership and a credit line for the postcard's printer. Besides those listed here, other auto fronts may exist.

		NM	EX	VG
(1)	Pete Rose, Johnny Bench (1972 Mercury Marquis Brougham Colony Park Station Wagon)	25.00	12.50	7.50

1961 Peters Meats Twins

This set, featuring the first-year 1961 Minnesota Twins, is in a large, 4-5/8" x 3-1/2", format. Cards are on thick cardboard and heavily waxed, as they were used as partial packaging for the company's meat products. Card fronts feature full-color photos, team and Peters logos, and biographical information. The cards are blank-backed. Prices shown are for cards with the surrounding packaging panel. Cut cards are worth about 50-75% of the prices shown.

		NM	EX	VG
Complete Set, Panels (26):		1,600	800.00	475.00
Complete Set, Cards (26):		1,500	750.00	450.00
Common Player, Panel:		80.00	40.00	24.00
Common Player, Card:		50.00	25.00	15.00
1	Zoilo Versalles	160.00	80.00	48.00
2	Eddie Lopat	80.00	40.00	24.00
3	Pedro Ramos	160.00	80.00	48.00
4	Charles "Chuck" Stobbs	80.00	40.00	24.00
5	Don Mincher	80.00	40.00	24.00
6	Jack Kralick	80.00	40.00	24.00
7	Jim Kaat	125.00	65.00	35.00
8	Hal Naragon	80.00	40.00	24.00
9	Don Lee	80.00	40.00	24.00
10	Harry "Cookie" Lavagetto	80.00	40.00	24.00
11	Tom "Pete" Whisenant	80.00	40.00	24.00
12	Elmer Valo	80.00	40.00	24.00
13	Ray Moore	80.00	40.00	24.00
14	Billy Gardner	80.00	40.00	24.00
15	Lenny Green	80.00	40.00	24.00
16	Sam Mele	80.00	40.00	24.00
17	Jim Lemon	80.00	40.00	24.00
18	Harmon "Killer" Killebrew	400.00	200.00	120.00
19	Paul Giel	80.00	40.00	24.00
20	Reno Bertoia	80.00	40.00	24.00
21	Clyde McCullough	80.00	40.00	24.00
22	Earl Battey	80.00	40.00	24.00
23	Camilo Pascual	160.00	80.00	48.00
24	Dan Dobbek	80.00	40.00	24.00
25	Joe "Valvy" Valdivielso	80.00	40.00	24.00
26	Billy Consolo	80.00	40.00	24.00

1938-53 Philadelphia A's Team-Issue Photos

For a decade and a half the Philadelphia A's issued souvenir sets of black-and-white player photos. All are in a 7" x 10" format but the size of picture, the use of posed action and portrait photos and the type style of the name printed in the bottom border differ among the years. In many cases, pictures were re-issued year after year making it impossible 50 years later to reconstruct the composition of any particular year's issue. The unnumbered pictures are check-listed here alphabetically. Multiple player listings are the result of known pose variations. Gaps have been left in the assigned numbering for future additions.

		NM	EX	VG
Common Player:		12.00	6.00	3.50
(1)	Joe Astroth	12.00	6.00	3.50
(2)	Loren Babe	12.00	6.00	3.50
(3)	Johnny Babich	12.00	6.00	3.50
(4)	Bill Beckman	12.00	6.00	3.50
(5)	Joe Berry	12.00	6.00	3.50
(6)	Herman Besse	12.00	6.00	3.50
(7)	Hal Bevan	12.00	6.00	3.50
(8)	Henry Biasatti	12.00	6.00	3.50
(9)	Don Black	12.00	6.00	3.50
(10)	Lena Blackburne	12.00	6.00	3.50
(11)	Buddy Blair	12.00	6.00	3.50
(12)	Don Bollweg	12.00	6.00	3.50
(13)	Al Brancato	12.00	6.00	3.50
(14)	Lou Brissie	12.00	6.00	3.50
(15)	Earle Brucker	12.00	6.00	3.50
(16)	Earle Brucker	12.00	6.00	3.50
(17)	Earle Brucker	12.00	6.00	3.50
(18)	William Burgo	15.00	7.50	4.50
(19)	Joe Burns	12.00	6.00	3.50
(20)	Ed Burtschy	12.00	6.00	3.50
(21)	Edgar Busch	12.00	6.00	3.50
(22)	Harry Byrd	12.00	6.00	3.50
(23)	Fred Caligiuri	18.00	9.00	5.50
(24)	George Caster	12.00	6.00	3.50
(25)	Jim Castiglia	12.00	6.00	3.50
(27)	Sam Chapman	12.00	6.00	3.50
(28)	Sam Chapman	12.00	6.00	3.50
(29)	Sam Chapman	12.00	6.00	3.50
(30)	Russ Christopher	12.00	6.00	3.50
(31)	Joe Coleman	12.00	6.00	3.50
(32)	Eddie Collins Jr.	15.00	7.50	4.50
(33)	Lawrence Davis	12.00	6.00	3.50
(34)	Tom Davis	12.00	6.00	3.50
(35)	Chubby Dean	12.00	6.00	3.50
(36)	Joe DeMaestri	12.00	6.00	3.50
(37)	Russ Derry	12.00	6.00	3.50
(38)	Gene Desautels	12.00	6.00	3.50
(39)	Art Ditmar	12.00	6.00	3.50
(40)	Jimmy Dykes	12.00	6.00	3.50
(41)	Bob Estalella	12.00	6.00	3.50
(42)	Nick Etten	12.00	6.00	3.50
(43)	Ferris Fain	18.00	9.00	5.50
(44)	Tom Ferrick	12.00	6.00	3.50
(45)	Jim Finigan	12.00	6.00	3.50
(46)	Lewis Flick	12.00	6.00	3.50
(47)	Jesse Flores	12.00	6.00	3.50
(48)	Richard Fowler	12.00	6.00	3.50
(49)	Nelson Fox	30.00	15.00	9.00
(51)	Marion Fricano	12.00	6.00	3.50
(52)	Joe Gantenbein	12.00	6.00	3.50
(53)	Ford Garrison	12.00	6.00	3.50
(54)	Mike Guerra	12.00	6.00	3.50
(55)	Irv Hadley	12.00	6.00	3.50
(56)	Irv Hall	12.00	6.00	3.50
(57)	Luke Hamlin	12.00	6.00	3.50
(58)	Gene Handley	12.00	6.00	3.50
(59)	Bob Harris	12.00	6.00	3.50
(60)	Charlie Harris	12.00	6.00	3.50
(61)	Luman C. Harris (Full-length.)	12.00	6.00	3.50
(62)	Luman Harris	12.00	6.00	3.50
(63)	Frank Hayes	12.00	6.00	3.50
(64)	Bob Johnson	15.00	7.50	4.50

(65)	Bob Johnson	15.00	7.50	4.50
(66)	Eddie Joost	12.00	6.00	3.50
(67)	David Keefe	12.00	6.00	3.50
(68)	George Kell	20.00	10.00	6.00
(69)	Everett Kell	15.00	7.50	4.50
(70)	Alex Kellner	12.00	6.00	3.50
(71)	Alex Kellner	12.00	6.00	3.50
(72)	Lou Klein	12.00	6.00	3.50
(73)	Bill Knickerbocker	12.00	6.00	3.50
(74)	Jack Knott	12.00	6.00	3.50
(75)	Mike Kreevich	12.00	6.00	3.50
(76)	John Kucab	12.00	6.00	3.50
(77)	Paul Lehner	12.00	6.00	3.50
(78)	Bill Lillard	12.00	6.00	3.50
(79)	Lou Limmer	12.00	6.00	3.50
(80)	Lou Limmer	12.00	6.00	3.50
(81)	Dario Lodigiani	12.00	6.00	3.50
(82)	Connie Mack	20.00	10.00	6.00
(83)	Connie Mack	20.00	10.00	6.00
(84)	Connie Mack	20.00	10.00	6.00
(85)	Connie Mack	20.00	10.00	6.00
(86)	Earle Mack	15.00	7.50	4.50
(87)	Earle Mack	15.00	7.50	4.50
(88)	Felix Mackiewicz	12.00	6.00	3.50
(89)	Hank Majeski	12.00	6.00	3.50
(90)	Hank Majeski	12.00	6.00	3.50
(91)	Phil Marchildon	12.00	6.00	3.50
(92)	Phil Marchildon	12.00	6.00	3.50
(93)	Phil Marchildon	12.00	6.00	3.50
(94)	Morris Martin	12.00	6.00	3.50
(95)	Barney McCosky	12.00	6.00	3.50
(96)	Bennie McCoy	12.00	6.00	3.50
(97)	Les McCrabb	12.00	6.00	3.50
(98)	Bill McGhee	18.00	9.00	5.50
(99)	George McQuinn	12.00	6.00	3.50
(101)	Charlie Metro	12.00	6.00	3.50
(102)	Cass Michaels	12.00	6.00	3.50
(103)	Dee Miles	12.00	6.00	3.50
(104)	Wally Moses	12.00	6.00	3.50
(105)	Wally Moses	12.00	6.00	3.50
(106)	Ray Murray	12.00	6.00	3.50
(107)	Bill Nagel	12.00	6.00	3.50
(108)	Bobo Newsom	12.00	6.00	3.50
(109)	Skeeter Newsome	12.00	6.00	3.50
(110)	Hal Peck	12.00	6.00	3.50
(111)	Dave Philley	12.00	6.00	3.50
(112)	Cotton Pippen	12.00	6.00	3.50
(113)	Arnie Portocarrero	12.00	6.00	3.50
(114)	Nelson Potter	12.00	6.00	3.50
(115)	Vic Power	15.00	7.50	4.50
(116)	Jim Pruett	12.00	6.00	3.50
(117)	Bill Renna	12.00	6.00	3.50
(118)	Al Robertson	12.00	6.00	3.50
(119)	Ed Robinson	12.00	6.00	3.50
(120)	Buddy Rosar	12.00	6.00	3.50
(121)	Buddy Rosar	12.00	6.00	3.50
(122)	Al Rubeling	12.00	6.00	3.50
(123)	Joseph Rullo	18.00	9.00	5.50
(124)	Carl Scheib	12.00	6.00	3.50
(125)	Bill Shantz	15.00	7.50	4.50
(126)	Bob Shantz	18.00	9.00	5.50
(127)	Newman Shirley	12.00	6.00	3.50
(128)	Dick Siebert (Thigh-to-cap.)	12.00	6.00	3.50
(129)	Dick Siebert	12.00	6.00	3.50
(130)	Al Simmons	25.00	12.50	7.50
(131)	Al Simmons	25.00	12.50	7.50
(132)	Tuck Stainback	12.00	6.00	3.50
(133)	Pete Suder (waist-to-cap.)	12.00	6.00	3.50
(134)	Pete Suder	12.00	6.00	3.50
(135)	Bob Swift	12.00	6.00	3.50
(136)	Keith Thomas	12.00	6.00	3.50
(137)	Eric Tipton	12.00	6.00	3.50
(138)	Bob Trice	12.00	6.00	3.50
(139)	Elmer Valo (Portrait to waist.)	12.00	6.00	3.50
(140)	Elmer Valo	12.00	6.00	3.50
(141)	Ozzie Van Brabant	18.00	9.00	5.50
(142)	Porter Vaughan	12.00	6.00	3.50
(143)	Harold Wagner	12.00	6.00	3.50
(144)	Harold Wagner	12.00	6.00	3.50
(145)	Jack Wallaesa	12.00	6.00	3.50
(146)	Johnny Welaj	12.00	6.00	3.50
(147)	Elwood Wheaton	15.00	7.50	4.50
(148)	Don White	12.00	6.00	3.50
(149)	Jo Jo White	12.00	6.00	3.50
(151)	Roger Wolff	12.00	6.00	3.50
(152)	Tom Wright	12.00	6.00	3.50
(153)	Gus Zernial	17.50	8.75	5.25
(154)	1938 A's Team	30.00	15.00	9.00
(155)	1939 A's Team	30.00	15.00	9.00
(156)	1940 A's Team	30.00	15.00	9.00
(157)	1941 A's Team	30.00	15.00	9.00
(158)	1942 A's Team	30.00	15.00	9.00
(159)	1943 A's Team	30.00	15.00	9.00
(160)	1944 A's Team	30.00	15.00	9.00
(161)	1945 A's Team	30.00	15.00	9.00
(162)	1946 A's Team	24.00	12.00	7.25
(163)	1948 A's Team	24.00	12.00	7.25
(164)	1949 A's Team	24.00	12.00	7.25
(165)	Shibe Park	30.00	15.00	9.00

1954 Philadelphia A's Stickers

The issuer of this novelty set and the exact scope of its checklist are currently unknown. The pieces are printed in black-and-white on 4-1/2" x 8-1/4" gummed-back paper. Instructions on front say, "(Moisten back. Paste on Cardboard and cut out.)" Only the player name is printed beneath the photo.

Values shown are a national average. Some teams and players enjoy regional popularity that may affect market prices.

JOE ASTROTH

		NM	EX	VG
Common Player:		25.00	12.50	7.50
(1)	Joe Astroth	25.00	12.50	7.50
(2)	Marion Fricano	25.00	12.50	7.50
(3)	Forrest Jacobs	25.00	12.50	7.50
(4)	Eddie Joost	25.00	12.50	7.50
(5)	Morrie Martin	25.00	12.50	7.50
(6)	Vic Power	35.00	17.50	10.50
(7)	Jim Robertson	25.00	12.50	7.50
(8)	Bob Shantz	35.00	17.50	10.50
(9)	Pete Suder	25.00	12.50	7.50
(10)	Bob Trice	25.00	12.50	7.50

1952 Philadelphia A's/ Phillies Player Pins

Only players on the Philadelphia A's and Phillies are found in this series of player pinbacks. The 1-3/4" diameter celluloid pins have black-and-white player portraits on front. The player name is printed in block letters across his shoulders, while the team name is printed in script across the chest. It is possible other player pins may exist. The unnumbered pieces are checklisted here in alphabetical order.

		NM	EX	VG
Common Player:		150.00	75.00	45.00
	Philadelphia Athletics			
(1)	Ferris Fain	200.00	100.00	60.00
(2)	Bobby Shantz	200.00	100.00	60.00
(3)	Gus Zernial	200.00	100.00	60.00
	Philadelphia Phillies			
(1)	Richie Ashburn	300.00	150.00	90.00
(2)	Del Ennis	150.00	75.00	45.00
(3)	Granny Hamner	150.00	75.00	45.00
(4)	Willie Jones	150.00	75.00	45.00
(5)	Jim Konstanty	150.00	75.00	45.00
(6)	Robin Roberts	300.00	150.00	90.00
(7)	Andy Seminick	150.00	75.00	45.00
(8)	Curt Simmons	150.00	75.00	45.00
(9)	Eddie Waitkus	150.00	75.00	45.00

1948 Philadelphia Bulletin Stand-Ups

These player pictures were printed in the "Fun Book" color section of the Sunday paper. The full-body pose cutouts carry facsimile autographs and were printed four per week on a page of about 9-1/2" x 14". While the individual pictures vary in size according to the pose, most are about 3" to 4" x 6-1/2" to 7". The player pictures are in black-and-white with a blue background and red base. They were

intended to be cut out around the heavy black line, pasted to cardboard and folded at their base to create a stand-up figure. Values shown here are for well trimmed pieces without evidence of mounting. Complete pages carry a premium somewhat greater than the sum of the players present. While the totality of the Phillies issue appears to be known, only 22 of the A's players have been recorded thus far, and the date(s) of their issue are unconfirmed.

		NM	EX	VG
Common Player:		15.00	7.50	4.50
	PHILADELPHIA PHILLIES			
	July 25	90.00	45.00	27.00
(1)	Don Padgett	15.00	7.50	4.50
(2)	Schoolboy Rowe	15.00	7.50	4.50
(3)	Andy Seminick	15.00	7.50	4.50
(4)	Curt Simmons	20.00	10.00	6.00
	August 1	225.00	110.00	67.00
(5)	Richie Ashburn	150.00	75.00	45.00
(6)	Johnny Blatnik	15.00	7.50	4.50
(7)	Del Ennis	20.00	10.00	6.00
(8)	Harry Walker	15.00	7.50	4.50
	August 8	75.00	37.00	22.00
(9)	Bert Haas	15.00	7.50	4.50
(10)	Granny Hamner	15.00	7.50	4.50
(11)	Eddie Miller	15.00	7.50	4.50
(12)	Dick Sisler	15.00	7.50	4.50
	August 15	200.00	100.00	60.00
(13)	Ralph Caballero	15.00	7.50	4.50
(14)	Ed Heusser	15.00	7.50	4.50
(15)	Robin Roberts	125.00	62.00	37.00
(16)	Emil Verban	15.00	7.50	4.50
	August 22	75.00	37.00	22.00
(17)	Blix Donnelly	15.00	7.50	4.50
(18)	Walt Dubiel	15.00	7.50	4.50
(19)	Ken Heintzelman	15.00	7.50	4.50
(20)	"Dutch" Leonard	15.00	7.50	4.50
	August 29	75.00	37.00	22.00
(21)	Charlie Bicknell	15.00	7.50	4.50
(22)	Al Lakeman	15.00	7.50	4.50
(23)	Sam Nahem	15.00	7.50	4.50
(24)	Bama Rowell	15.00	7.50	4.50
	PHILADELPHIA A'S			
	June 13	75.00	37.00	22.00
(1)	Ferris Fain	15.00	7.50	4.50
(2)	Eddie Joost	15.00	7.50	4.50
(3)	Hank Majeski	15.00	7.50	4.50
(4)	Pete Suder	15.00	7.50	4.50
(5)	Lou Brissie	15.00	7.50	4.50
(6)	Sam Chapman	15.00	7.50	4.50
(7)	Ray Coleman	15.00	7.50	4.50
(8)	Billy DeMears	15.00	7.50	4.50
(9)	Dick Fowler	15.00	7.50	4.50
(10)	Herman Franks	15.00	7.50	4.50
(11)	Charlie Harris	15.00	7.50	4.50
(12)	Mike Guerra	15.00	7.50	4.50
(13)	Phil Marchildon	15.00	7.50	4.50
(14)	Bill McCahan	15.00	7.50	4.50
(15)	Barney McCosky	15.00	7.50	4.50
(16)	Buddy Rosar	15.00	7.50	4.50
(17)	Bob Savage	15.00	7.50	4.50
(18)	Carl Scheib	15.00	7.50	4.50
(19)	Elmer Valo	15.00	7.50	4.50
(20)	Skeeter Webb	15.00	7.50	4.50
(21)	Don White	15.00	7.50	4.50
(22)	Rudy York	15.00	7.50	4.50

1949 Philadelphia Bulletin A's/ Phillies

Each Sunday between May 22 and July 24, 1949, the "Fun Book" rotogravure section of the Bulletin included a page of (usually) six baseball "cards" of the hometeam A's and Phillies which could be cut out and pasted to cardboard. The left side (front) of each card has a sepia portrait of the player, while a colored box at right (back) has biographical and career information. Uncut and unfolded, each card measures about 4-1/2" x 3-5/8". If cut out and pasted onto cardboard, the created cards would measure about 2-1/4" x 3-5/8". Complete pages measure about 9-1/2" x 13-3/8". Values shown are for single "cards" which have been cut off the page, but not pasted onto a backing.

		NM	EX	VG
Complete Set (59):		1,600	800.00	480.00
Common Player:		25.00	12.50	7.50
MAY 22				
(1)	Richie Ashburn	265.00	130.00	79.00
(2)	Granny Hamner	25.00	12.50	7.50
(3)	Eddie Joost	25.00	12.50	7.50
(4)	Bill Nicholson	25.00	12.50	7.50
(5)	Buddy Rosar	25.00	12.50	7.50
(6)	Pete Suder	25.00	12.50	7.50
MAY 29				
(7)	Hank Borowy	25.00	12.50	7.50
(8)	Del Ennis	35.00	17.50	10.50
(9)	Ferris Fain	35.00	17.50	10.50
(10)	Phil Marchildon	25.00	12.50	7.50
(11)	Wally Moses	25.00	12.50	7.50
(12)	Eddie Waitkus	25.00	12.50	7.50
JUNE 5				
(13)	Dick Fowler	25.00	12.50	7.50
(14)	Willie Jones	25.00	12.50	7.50
(15)	Stan Lopata	25.00	12.50	7.50
(16)	Hank Majeski	25.00	12.50	7.50
(17)	Schoolboy Rowe	25.00	12.50	7.50
(18)	Elmer Valo	25.00	12.50	7.50
JUNE 12				
(19)	Joe Coleman	25.00	12.50	7.50
(20)	Charley Harris	25.00	12.50	7.50
(21)	Russ Meyer	25.00	12.50	7.50
(22)	Eddie Miller	25.00	12.50	7.50
(23)	Robin Roberts	265.00	130.00	79.00
(24)	Taft Wright	25.00	12.50	7.50
JUNE 19				
(25)	Lou Brissie	25.00	12.50	7.50
(26)	Ralph Caballero	25.00	12.50	7.50
(27)	Sam Chapman	25.00	12.50	7.50
(28)	Fermin (Mike) Guerra	25.00	12.50	7.50
(29)	Jim Konstanty	35.00	17.50	10.50
(30)	Curt Simmons	35.00	17.50	10.50
JUNE 26				
(31)	Charles Bicknell	25.00	12.50	7.50
(32)	Ken Heintzelman	25.00	12.50	7.50
(33)	Alex Kellner	25.00	12.50	7.50
(34)	Barney McCosky	25.00	12.50	7.50
(35)	Bobby Shantz	35.00	17.50	10.50
(36)	Ken Trinkle	25.00	12.50	7.50
JULY 3				
(37)	Blix Donnelly	25.00	12.50	7.50
(38)	Bill McCahan	25.00	12.50	7.50
(39)	Carl Scheib	25.00	12.50	7.50
(40)	Andy Seminick	25.00	12.50	7.50
(41)	Dick Sisler	25.00	12.50	7.50
(42)	Don White	25.00	12.50	7.50
JULY 10				
(43)	Joe Astroth	25.00	12.50	7.50
(44)	Henry Biasetti	25.00	12.50	7.50
(45)	Buddy Blattner	25.00	12.50	7.50
(46)	Thomas O. Davis	25.00	12.50	7.50
(47)	Stan Hollmig	25.00	12.50	7.50
(48)	Jackie Mayo	25.00	12.50	7.50
JULY 17				
(49)	Benny Bengough	25.00	12.50	7.50
(50)	Earle Brucker	25.00	12.50	7.50
(51)	Dusty Cooke	25.00	12.50	7.50
(52)	Jimmy Dykes	25.00	12.50	7.50
(53)	Cy Perkins	25.00	12.50	7.50
(54)	Al Simmons	40.00	20.00	12.00
JULY 24				
(55)	Nellie Fox	265.00	130.00	79.00
(56)	Connie Mack	200.00	100.00	60.00
(57)	Earle Mack	25.00	12.50	7.50
(58)	Eddie Sawyer	25.00	12.50	7.50
(59)	Ken Silvestri	25.00	12.50	7.50

1950 Philadelphia Bulletin Pin-Ups

This series of 8" x 10" black-and-white portraits of Phillies players, coaches, and manager was produced in two versions. A (mostly) numbered newsprint version was issued one per day in the paper,

between September 13-30. A premium version, printed on heavy paper with a semi-gloss finish and blank back, was made available to fans for a nickel at the newspaper's office or a dime by mail. Each of the pictures is a cap-less portrait with facsimile autograph on front. A number of players in the premium version were not issued in the newsprint style.

		NM	EX	VG
Complete Set (26):		900.00	450.00	275.00
Common Player:		40.00	20.00	12.00
(1)	Rich Ashburn	75.00	37.00	22.00
(2)	Jimmy Bloodworth	40.00	20.00	12.00
(3)	Ralph Caballero	40.00	20.00	12.00
(4)	Milo Candini	40.00	20.00	12.00
(5)	Emory Church	40.00	20.00	12.00
(6)	Sylvester (Blix) Donnelly	40.00	20.00	12.00
(7)	Del Ennis	50.00	25.00	15.00
(8)	Mike Goliat	40.00	20.00	12.00
(9)	Gran Hamner	40.00	20.00	12.00
(10)	Ken Heintzelman	40.00	20.00	12.00
(11)	Stan Hollmig	40.00	20.00	12.00
(12)	Ken Johnson	40.00	20.00	12.00
(13)	Willie Jones	40.00	20.00	12.00
(14)	Jim Konstanty	40.00	20.00	12.00
(15)	Stan Lopata	40.00	20.00	12.00
(16)	Russ Meyer	40.00	20.00	12.00
(17)	Bob Miller	40.00	20.00	12.00
(18)	Bill Nicholson	40.00	20.00	12.00
(19)	Robin Roberts	65.00	32.00	19.50
(20)	Eddie Sawyer	40.00	20.00	12.00
(21)	Andy Seminick	40.00	20.00	12.00
(22)	Ken Silvestri	40.00	20.00	12.00
(23)	Curtis T. Simmons	50.00	25.00	15.00
(24)	Dick Sisler	40.00	20.00	12.00
(25)	Eddie Waitkus	40.00	20.00	12.00
(26)	Dick Whitman	40.00	20.00	12.00

1964 Philadelphia Bulletin Phillies Album (Paper)

This series of newspaper features was the basis for the more often-encountered mail-in premiums. About 5-1/2" x 9", these pieces were printed in black-and-white in the sports section of the daily paper. The artwork is by staff artist Jim Porter. While the newspaper pieces are numbered, they are checklisted here in alphabetical order due to uncertainty about the original issue sequence.

		NM	EX	VG
Complete Set (27):		400.00	200.00	120.00
Common Player:		15.00	7.50	4.50
(1)	Richie Allen	40.00	20.00	12.00
(2)	Ruben Amaro	15.00	7.50	4.50
(3)	Jack Baldschun	15.00	7.50	4.50
(4)	Dennis Bennett	15.00	7.50	4.50
(5)	John Boozer	15.00	7.50	4.50
(6)	Johnny Briggs	15.00	7.50	4.50
(7)	Jim Bunning	50.00	25.00	15.00
(8)	Johnny Callison	15.00	7.50	4.50
(9)	Danny Cater	15.00	7.50	4.50
(10)	Wes Covington	15.00	7.50	4.50
(11)	Ray Culp	15.00	7.50	4.50
(12)	Clay Dalrymple	15.00	7.50	4.50
(13)	Tony Gonzalez	15.00	7.50	4.50
(14)	John Herrnstein	15.00	7.50	4.50
(15)	Alex Johnson	15.00	7.50	4.50
(16)	Art Mahaffey	15.00	7.50	4.50
(17)	Gene Mauch	15.00	7.50	4.50
(18)	Vic Power	15.00	7.50	4.50
(19)	Ed Roebuck	15.00	7.50	4.50
(20)	Cookie Rojas	15.00	7.50	4.50
(21)	Bobby Shantz	15.00	7.50	4.50
(22)	Chris Short	15.00	7.50	4.50
(23)	Tony Taylor	15.00	7.50	4.50
(24)	Frank Thomas	15.00	7.50	4.50
(25)	Gus Triandos	15.00	7.50	4.50
(26)	Bobby Wine	15.00	7.50	4.50
(27)	Rick Wise	15.00	7.50	4.50

1964 Philadelphia Bulletin Phillies Album

Color artwork by Jim Ponter is featured in this series of newspaper inserts. Portrait and action figures are combined on a blank-backed 8" x 10" format, along with

a facsimile autograph. The unnumbered pictures are checklisted here alphabetically, two varieties of Jim Bunning's picture have been reported.

		NM	EX	VG
Complete Set (28):		550.00	275.00	175.00
Common Player:		20.00	10.00	6.00
(1)	Richie Allen	60.00	30.00	18.00
(2)	Ruben Amaro	20.00	10.00	6.00
(3)	Jack Baldschun	20.00	10.00	6.00
(4)	Dennis Bennett	20.00	10.00	6.00
(5)	John Boozer	20.00	10.00	6.00
(6)	Johnny Briggs	20.00	10.00	6.00
(7)	Jim Bunning/Pitching	75.00	37.00	22.00
(8)	Jim Bunning/Portrait	60.00	30.00	18.00
(9)	Johnny Callison	20.00	10.00	6.00
(10)	Danny Cater	20.00	10.00	6.00
(11)	Wes Covington	20.00	10.00	6.00
(12)	Ray Culp	20.00	10.00	6.00
(13)	Clay Dalrymple	20.00	10.00	6.00
(14)	Tony Gonzalez	20.00	10.00	6.00
(15)	John Herrnstein	20.00	10.00	6.00
(16)	Alex Johnson	20.00	10.00	6.00
(17)	Art Mahaffey	20.00	10.00	6.00
(18)	Gene Mauch	20.00	10.00	6.00
(19)	Vic Power	20.00	10.00	6.00
(20)	Ed Roebuck	20.00	10.00	6.00
(21)	Cookie Rojas	20.00	10.00	6.00
(22)	Bobby Shantz	20.00	10.00	6.00
(23)	Chris Short	20.00	10.00	6.00
(24)	Tony Taylor	20.00	10.00	6.00
(25)	Frank Thomas	20.00	10.00	6.00
(26)	Gus Triandos	20.00	10.00	6.00
(27)	Bobby Wine	20.00	10.00	6.00
(28)	Rick Wise	20.00	10.00	6.00

1909 Philadelphia Caramel (E95)

Similar in style to several other early candy and caramel cards, the set designated as E95 by the American Card Catalog is a 25-card issue produced by the Philadelphia Caramel Co., Camden, N.J., in 1909. The cards measure approximately 1-1/2" x 2-5/8" and contain a full-color player drawing. The back, which differentiates the set from other similar issues, checklists the 25 players in black ink and displays the Philadelphia Caramel Co. name at the bottom. Blank-back cards printed on thinner stock exist; these are not proofs, but were cut off a "Base Ball Series" notebook cover, they are valued about 25-50% of a corresponding regular-issue card.

		NM	EX	VG
Complete Set (25):		50,000	20,000	10,000
Common Player:		850.00	350.00	165.00
1	Honus Wagner	13,000	5,200	2,600
2	Nick Maddox	850.00	350.00	165.00
3	Fred Merkle	850.00	350.00	165.00
4	Cy Morgan	850.00	350.00	165.00
5	Chief Bender	1,950	780.00	390.00
6	Harry Krause	850.00	350.00	165.00
7	Art Devlin	850.00	350.00	165.00
8	Matty McIntyre	850.00	350.00	165.00
9	Ty Cobb	15,600	5,200	2,600
10	Ed Willetts (Willett)	850.00	350.00	165.00
11	Sam Crawford	1,950	780.00	360.00
12	Christy Matthewson (Mathewson)	9,750	2,600	1,300
13	Hooks Wiltse	850.00	350.00	165.00
14	Larry Doyle	850.00	350.00	165.00
15	Tommy Leach	850.00	350.00	165.00

		NM	EX	VG
16	Harry Lord	850.00	350.00	165.00
17	Ed Cicotte	2,730	780.00	470.00
18	Bill Carrigan	850.00	350.00	165.00
19	Vic Willis	1,950	780.00	360.00
20	Johnny Evers	1,950	780.00	360.00
21	Frank Chance	1,950	780.00	360.00
22	Solly Hoffman (Hofman)	850.00	350.00	165.00
23	Eddie Plank	3,120	1,170	650.00
24	Eddie Collins	1,950	780.00	360.00
25	Ed Reulbach	850.00	350.00	165.00

1910 Philadelphia Caramel (E96)

This set of 30 subjects, known by the ACC designation E96, was issued in 1910 by the Philadelphia Caramel Co. The approximately 1-1/2" x 2-5/8" size and front design remained the same, but the two issues can be identified by the backs. The backs of E96 cards are printed in red and carry a checklist of 30 players. There is also a line at the bottom advising "Previous series 25, making total issue 55 cards." Just below that appears "Philadelphia Caramel Co./Camden, N.J." Blank-back cards printed on thinner stock are not proofs, but rather were cut off a "Base Ball Series" notebook cover. They are valued about 25-50 percent of a corresponding regular-issue card.

		NM	EX	VG
Complete Set (30):		38,500	15,500	9,500
Common Player:		1,100	400.00	200.00
1	Harry Davis	1,100	400.00	200.00
2	Connie Mack	2,200	900.00	500.00
3	Ira Thomas	1,100	400.00	200.00
4	Home Run Baker	2,000	800.00	400.00
5	Red Dooin	1,100	400.00	200.00
6	George McQuillan	1,100	400.00	200.00
7	Ed Konetchy	1,100	400.00	200.00
8	Ed Karger	1,100	400.00	200.00
9	Mike Mowrey	1,100	400.00	200.00
10	Red Murray	1,100	400.00	200.00
11	Nap Lajoie	2,700	1,100	500.00
12	Claude Rossman	1,100	400.00	200.00
13	Nap Rucker	1,100	400.00	200.00
14	Hugh Jennings	2,000	800.00	400.00
15	Wild Bill Donovan	1,100	400.00	200.00
16	Jim Delahanty	1,100	400.00	200.00
17	George Mullin	1,100	400.00	200.00
18	Frank Arrelanes (Arellanes)	1,100	400.00	200.00
19	Tubby Spencer	1,100	400.00	200.00
20	Johnny Kling	1,100	400.00	200.00
21	Jack Pfister (Pfiester)	1,100	400.00	200.00
22	Mordecai Brown	2,000	800.00	400.00
23	Joe Tinker	2,000	800.00	400.00
24	Fred Clark (Clarke)	2,000	800.00	400.00
25	George Gibson	1,100	400.00	200.00
26	Babe Adams	1,100	400.00	200.00
27	Red Ames	1,100	400.00	200.00
28	Rube Marquard	2,000	800.00	400.00
29	Buck Herzog	1,100	400.00	200.00
30	Chief Myers (Meyers)	1,100	400.00	200.00

1913 Philadelphia Caramel Proofs

The attribution of these cards to Philadelphia Caramel is speculative, since no advertising is found on their blank backs. The three known pieces, however, have pictures and color identical to the players' cards in the 1910 E96 Philadelphia Caramel issue. These proofs differ only in the team designations. Nominally 1-1/2" x 2-5/8", the known examples were hand-cut from a sheet and are, at present, each unique. The Kling card was offered at auction in 2003 without meeting a $500 reserve.

Frank Chance (New York, A.L.)
Harry Davis (Cleveland)
Johnny Kling (Boston, A.L.)

1913 Philadelphia Evening Telegraph Postcards

The attributed date of issue is speculative, about midway through Phillies manager Red Dooin's tenure. Issued by one of the city's daily newspapers, these 3-1/2" x 5-1/2" black-and-white postcards picture the managers of the Phils and A's in large portrait photos. The postcard-style back has ornate typography and embellishments.

		NM	EX	VG
Complete Set (2):		1,100	550.00	325.00
Common Card:		500.00	250.00	150.00
(1)	Charles Dooin	500.00	250.00	150.00
(2)	Connie Mack	650.00	325.00	200.00

1913 Philadelphia Evening Times Supplements

The checklist comprised almost entirely of Connie Mack's A's and John McGraw's Giants suggests this series of newspaper supplements was issued around World Series time. The blank-backed, sepia-toned pictures have posed action photos, are printed on light cardboard stock and measure about 7-1/2" x 9-1/2". This checklist may be incomplete.

		NM	EX	VG
Common Player:		200.00	100.00	60.00
(1)	Home Run Baker	400.00	200.00	120.00
(2)	Jack Barry	200.00	100.00	60.00
(3)	Chief Bender	400.00	200.00	120.00
(4)	George Burns	200.00	100.00	60.00
(5)	Ty Cobb	1,200	600.00	360.00
(6)	Eddie Collins	400.00	200.00	120.00
(7)	Al Demaree	200.00	100.00	60.00
(8)	Larry Doyle	200.00	100.00	60.00
(9)	Walter Johnson	800.00	400.00	240.00
(10)	Rube Marquard	400.00	200.00	120.00
(11)	Christy Mathewson	800.00	400.00	240.00
(12)	Stuffy McInnis	200.00	100.00	60.00
(13)	Chief Meyers	200.00	100.00	60.00
(14)	Rube Oldring	200.00	100.00	60.00
(15)	Eddie Plank	400.00	200.00	120.00
(16)	Jeff Tesreau	200.00	100.00	60.00

1950 Philadelphia Inquirer Fightin' Phillies

As the Whiz Kids battled to a National League pennant the "Philadelphia Inquirer" instituted a set of cut-out baseball cards in the Sunday rotogravure editions during September. The 4-7/8" x 6-7/8" cards have colored portrait photos surrounded with a white border. A facsimile autograph is printed across the chest. In the bottom border are the player's formal name, position, career summary and the line, "Inquirer Fightin' Phillies Album." Backs have whatever articles or ads were on the next page. The unnumbered cards are printed here in alphabetical order.

		NM	EX	VG
Complete Set (24):		350.00	175.00	105.00
Common Player:		15.00	7.50	4.50
(1)	Richie Ashburn	35.00	17.50	10.50
(2)	James Henry Bloodworth	15.00	7.50	4.50
(3)	Ralph Joseph Caballero	15.00	7.50	4.50
(4)	Milo Candini	15.00	7.50	4.50
(5)	Emory Church	15.00	7.50	4.50
(6)	Sylvester Urban Donnelly	15.00	7.50	4.50
(7)	Delmer Ennis	15.00	7.50	4.50
(8)	Mike Mitchel Goliat (Mitchell)	15.00	7.50	4.50
(9)	Granville Wilbur Hamner	15.00	7.50	4.50
(10)	Kenneth Alphonse Heintzelman	15.00	7.50	4.50
(11)	Stanley Ernst Hollmig	15.00	7.50	4.50
(12)	Kenneth W. Johnson	15.00	7.50	4.50
(13)	Willie Edward Jones	15.00	7.50	4.50
(14)	Stanley Edward Lopata	15.00	7.50	4.50
(15)	Russell Charles Meyer	15.00	7.50	4.50
(16)	Robert Miller	15.00	7.50	4.50
(17)	William Beck Nicholson	15.00	7.50	4.50
(18)	Robin Evan Roberts	35.00	17.50	10.50
(19)	Andrew Wasal Seminick	15.00	7.50	4.50
(20)	Kenneth Joseph Silvestri	15.00	7.50	4.50
(21)	Curtis Thomas Simmons	15.00	7.50	4.50
(22)	Richard Alan Sisler	15.00	7.50	4.50
(23)	Edward Stephen Waitkus	15.00	7.50	4.50
(24)	Dick Whitman	15.00	7.50	4.50

1954 Philadelphia Inquirer Album of Baseball Stars

A series of four baseball players from each of Philadelphia's teams appeared on a pair of pages in the Colorama color rotogravure section of the Sunday. Philadelphia Inquirer. Each picture is about 6-3/4" x 9-3/4" and was separated from the other three on its "ALBUM OF SPORTS" page by a black dotted line, indicative of an intention for them to be cut out and saved. Under the portrait is a brief career summary. Backs have other newspaper content as printed each Sunday.

		NM	EX	VG
Complete Set (8):		75.00	37.50	22.50
Common Player:		8.00	4.00	2.50
JULY 25				
(1)	Richie Ashburn	25.00	12.50	7.50
(2)	Jim Finigan	8.00	4.00	2.50
(3)	Gran Hamner	8.00	4.00	2.50
(4)	Bill Shantz	8.00	4.00	2.50
SEPT. 12				

		NM	EX	VG
(1)	Smoky Burgess	10.00	5.00	3.00
(2)	Arnold Portocarrero	8.00	4.00	2.50
(3)	Robin Roberts	16.00	8.00	4.75
(4)	Curt Simmons	10.00	5.00	3.00

1943 Philadelphia Phillies Photo Pack

Like many teams in that era, the Phillies issued souvenir photo packs for sale at the stadium and by mail-order. This team issue is in a 6" x 8-1/2", blank-back, black-and-white format. The player picture is bordered in white with the player name in all-caps in the bottom border. From the large number of players known, it is evident that the composition of the photo packs was changed from time to time as the team roster changed. It is possible this checklist is not complete. The unnumbered pictures have been listed here alphabetically.

		NM	EX	VG
Complete Set (40):		300.00	150.00	90.00
Common Player:		8.00	4.00	2.50
(1)	Buster Adams	8.00	4.00	2.50
(2)	Walter Beck	8.00	4.00	2.50
(3)	Stan Benjamin	8.00	4.00	2.50
(4)	Cy Blanton	8.00	4.00	2.50
(5)	Bobby Bragan	8.00	4.00	2.50
(6)	Charlie Brewster	8.00	4.00	2.50
(7)	Paul Busby	8.00	4.00	2.50
(8)	Ben Culp	8.00	4.00	2.50
(9)	Babe Dahlgren	8.00	4.00	2.50
(10)	Lloyd Dietz	8.00	4.00	2.50
(11)	Nick Etten	8.00	4.00	2.50
(12)	George Eyrich	8.00	4.00	2.50
(13)	Charlie Fuchs	8.00	4.00	2.50
(14)	Al Glossop	8.00	4.00	2.50
(15)	Al Gerheauser	8.00	4.00	2.50
(16)	"Bucky" Harris	12.00	6.00	3.50
(17)	Frank Hoerst	8.00	4.00	2.50
(18)	Si Johnson	8.00	4.00	2.50
(19)	Chuck Klein	15.00	7.50	4.50
(20)	Ernie Koy	8.00	4.00	2.50
(21)	Tex Kraus	8.00	4.00	2.50
(22)	Danny Litwhiler	8.00	4.00	2.50
(23)	Mickey Livingston	8.00	4.00	2.50
(24)	Hans Lobert	8.00	4.00	2.50
(25)	Henry Marnie	8.00	4.00	2.50
(26)	Merrill May	8.00	4.00	2.50
(27)	Rube Melton	8.00	4.00	2.50
(28)	Danny Murtaugh	10.00	5.00	3.00
(29)	Sam Nahem	8.00	4.00	2.50
(30)	Earl Naylor	8.00	4.00	2.50
(31)	Ron Northey	8.00	4.00	2.50
(32)	Tommy Padden	8.00	4.00	2.50
(33)	Ike Pearson	8.00	4.00	2.50
(34)	Johnny Podgajny	8.00	4.00	2.50
(35)	Schoolboy Rowe	10.00	5.00	3.00
(36)	Glen Stewart	8.00	4.00	2.50
(37)	Coaker Triplett	8.00	4.00	2.50
(38)	Lloyd Waner	15.00	7.50	4.50
(39)	Ben Warren	8.00	4.00	2.50
(40)	Jimmy Wasdell	8.00	4.00	2.50

1958 Philadelphia Phillies Picture Pack

This set of 5" x 7" blank-backed, black-and-white player pictures was most likely issued in 1958, though it is also possible the set was issued in 1957 (or both). This team-issue set differs from the contemporary Jay Publishing picture packs in that it does not have the city name in the identication line, only the player name in all-caps and "Phillies." The unnumbered pictures are listed here alphabetically.

		NM	EX	VG
Complete Set (12):		75.00	40.00	22.50
Common Player:		7.50	3.75	2.25
(1)	Harry Anderson	7.50	3.75	2.25
(2)	Richie Ashburn	15.00	7.50	4.50
(3)	Bob Bowman	7.50	3.75	2.25
(4)	Turk Farrell	7.50	3.75	2.25
(5)	Chico Fernandez	7.50	3.75	2.25
(6)	Granny Hamner	7.50	3.75	2.25
(7)	Stan Lopata	7.50	3.75	2.25
(8)	Rip Repulski	7.50	3.75	2.25
(9)	Robin Roberts	15.00	7.50	4.50
(10)	Jack Sanford	7.50	3.75	2.25
(11)	Curt Simmons	7.50	3.75	2.25
(12)	Mayo Smith	7.50	3.75	2.25

1958-60 Philadelphia Phillies Team Issue

Thus far 22 different cards have been discovered in this format; it is likely the checklist here is not yet complete. Like many teams, the Phillies issued these cards to players and staff to honor fan requests for photos and autographs. The cards are 3-1/4" x 5-1/2" and have black-and-white portrait photos with white borders. Backs are blank. The unnumbered cards are listed here alphabetically.

		NM	EX	VG
Common Player:		6.00	3.00	1.75
(1)	Harry Anderson	6.00	3.00	1.75
(2)	Richie Ashburn	12.00	6.00	3.50
(3)	Ed Bouchee	6.00	3.00	1.75
(4)	Smoky Burgess	7.50	3.75	2.25
(5)	Johnny Callison	8.00	4.00	2.50
(6)	Jim Coker	6.00	3.00	1.75
(7)	Clay Dalrymple	6.00	3.00	1.75
(8)	Del Ennis	7.50	3.75	2.25
(9)	Tony Gonzalez	6.00	3.00	1.75
(10)	Granny Hamner	6.00	3.00	1.75
(11)	Willie Jones	6.00	3.00	1.75
(12)	Stan Lopata	6.00	3.00	1.75
(13)	Art Mahaffey	6.00	3.00	1.75
(14)	Gene Mauch	6.00	3.00	1.75
(15)	Bob Morgan	6.00	3.00	1.75
(16)	Wally Post	6.00	3.00	1.75
(17)	Robin Roberts	12.00	6.00	3.50
(18)	Eddie Sawyer	6.00	3.00	1.75
(19)	Andy Seminick	6.00	3.00	1.50
(20)	Ray Semproch	6.00	3.00	1.75
(21)	Chris Short	6.00	3.00	1.75
(22)	Curt Simmons	8.00	4.00	2.50
(23)	Earl Torgeson	6.00	3.00	1.75

1964 Philadelphia Phillies Player Pins

Only four players are checklisted in this series, but it is expected more will be added in the future. These pinbacks are 2-3/16" in diameter and have black-and-white player portraits on front, on a white background. The player's name is printed at bottom in block letters.

		NM	EX	VG
Common Player:		45.00	22.50	13.50
(1)	Dick Allen	90.00	45.00	27.50
(2)	Jim Bunning	90.00	45.00	27.50
(3)	Chris Short	45.00	22.50	13.50
(4)	Roy Sievers	45.00	22.50	13.50

1965 Go! Phillies Go! Pins

These large (3-1/2" diameter) pinback buttons feature a dozen members of the '65 Phils. Player portraits are on a white background and have had the cap and pinstripes colored in red. At top, the title is printed in red and blue. The facsimile autograph at bottom is printed in blue.

		NM	EX	VG
Complete Set (12):		750.00	375.00	225.00
Common Player:		50.00	25.00	15.00
(1)	Rich Allen	100.00	50.00	30.00
(2)	Ruben Amaro	50.00	25.00	15.00
(3)	Bo Belinsky	65.00	32.50	20.00
(4)	Jim Bunning	100.00	50.00	30.00
(5)	Johnny Callison	65.00	32.50	20.00
(6)	Wes Covington	50.00	25.00	15.00
(7)	Ray Culp	50.00	25.00	15.00
(8)	Cookie Rojas	50.00	25.00	15.00
(9)	Chris Short	50.00	25.00	15.00
(10)	Dick Stuart	50.00	25.00	15.00
(11)	Tony Taylor	50.00	25.00	15.00
(12)	Bobby Wine	50.00	25.00	15.00

1965 Philadelphia Phillies Tiles

These decorative heavy ceramic tiles feature color portraits and facsimile autographs on a white background. In 6" x 6" format the tiles were made in England, but decorated in the U.S. They appear to have been originally issued with cork backing and some have been seen with a hangar attached on back.

		NM	EX	VG
Complete Set (12):		600.00	300.00	180.00
Common Player:		40.00	20.00	12.00
(1)	Richie Allen	100.00	50.00	30.00
(2)	Bo Belinsky	60.00	30.00	18.00
(3)	Jim Bunning	125.00	65.00	35.00
(4)	Johnny Callison	60.00	30.00	18.00
(5)	Wes Covington	40.00	20.00	12.00
(6)	Clay Dalrymple	40.00	20.00	12.00
(7)	Gene Mauch	40.00	20.00	12.00
(8)	Cookie Rojas	40.00	20.00	12.00
(9)	Tony Taylor	40.00	20.00	12.00
(10)	Chris Short	40.00	20.00	12.00
(11)	Dick Stuart	40.00	20.00	12.00
(12)	Bobby Wine	40.00	20.00	12.00

1967 Philadelphia Phillies Safe Driving

The honor of producing the only safety set of the 1960s goes to the Phillies for this traffic safety set. Measuring 2-3/4" x 4-1/2", the cards have a black-and-white front featuring the standard publicity photo of the player, with a facsimile autograph superimposed. Backs are printed in blue and include a few career and biographical details, along with the player's uniform number, by which the set is checklisted here. At bottom is a circle and shield design with the safety message.

		NM	EX	VG
Complete Set (13):		95.00	47.00	28.00
Common Player:		8.00	4.00	2.50
4	Gene Mauch	8.00	4.00	2.50
6	Johnny Callison	10.00	5.00	3.00
10	Bill White	10.00	5.00	3.00
11	Clay Dalrymple	8.00	4.00	2.50
12	Johnny Briggs	8.00	4.00	2.50
14	Jim Bunning	20.00	10.00	6.00
15	Dick Allen	18.00	9.00	5.50
16	Cookie Rojas	8.00	4.00	2.50
24	Dick Groat	10.00	5.00	3.00
25	Tony Gonzalez	8.00	4.00	2.50
37	Dick Ellsworth	8.00	4.00	2.50
41	Chris Short	8.00	4.00	2.50
46	Larry Jackson	8.00	4.00	2.50

1975 Philadelphia Phillies Photocards

JOE HOERNER

These 3-1/4" x 5-1/2" blank-back, black-and-white cards feature player portrait photos with only the player name in the white border at bottom. Fronts have a semi-gloss finish. It is likely the checklist, presented here alphabetically, is incomplete.

		NM	EX	VG
Common Player:		3.00	1.50	.90
(1)	Tom Hilgendorf	3.00	1.50	.90
(2)	Terry Harmon	3.00	1.50	.90
(3)	Joe Hoerner	3.00	1.50	.90
(4)	Tommy Hutton	3.00	1.50	.90
(5)	Jim Lonborg	4.00	2.00	1.25
(6)	John Oates	3.00	1.50	.90

1961 Phillies Cigar Mickey Mantle

This 6-1/2" x 9" blank-back color photo card of Mickey Mantle was part of a redemption program for Phillies cigars. For $3.39 and 20 cigar bands, a person could receive a Mickey Mantle model baseball glove and this "autographed" (facsimile) photo.

	NM	EX	VG
Mickey Mantle	125.00	62.50	37.50

1912 Photo Art Shop Boston Red Sox

Two postcards are currently known to have been produced, according to the legend on the back, by The Photo Art Shop of Swampscott, Mass. The standard-size (about 3-1/2" x 5-1/2") cards are printed in black-and-white. A vertically formatted card shows opposing World Series aces Joe Wood and Walter Johnson. A horizontal team-photo card has each player's last name printed over his picture and

describes the team as "Champions of the American League." The Red Sox went on to defeat the Giants in the World Series.

	NM	EX	VG
Joe Wood, Walter Johnson	1,800	900.00	540.00
1912 Boston Red Sox	900.00	450.00	275.00

1964 Photo Linen Emblems

The attributed date of issue is only approximate. About 3-1/2" x 4-1/2", these sew-on patches feature black-and-white photos with an embroidered red border. The patches were sold in a cello-wrapped package. The checklist presented here in alphabetical order is not complete.

		NM	EX	VG
Complete Set (10):		625.00	300.00	180.00
Common Player:		30.00	15.00	9.00
(1)	Yogi Berra	50.00	25.00	15.00
(2)	Clete Boyer	30.00	15.00	9.00
(3)	Elston Howard	30.00	15.00	9.00
(4)	Sandy Koufax	175.00	87.00	52.00
(5)	Tony Kubek	30.00	15.00	9.00
(6)	Mickey Mantle	250.00	125.00	75.00
(7)	Roger Maris	90.00	45.00	27.00
(8)	Joe Pepitone	30.00	15.00	9.00
(9)	Bobby Richardson	30.00	15.00	9.00
(10)	Tom Tresh	30.00	15.00	9.00

1972 Photo Sports Co. L.A. Dodgers

This is the first known issue of a sports novelty marketed by Photo Sports Co., Los Angeles. The company is best known to collectors for its 1974 McDonald's promotional "Foto Balls" with player discs. The Dodgers set is similar in concept with a hinged plastic baseball which opens to reveal player discs. A "keyhole" punched at the bottom of the discs keeps them in place within the ball. The Dodgers never rolled out the project and surviving sets are extremely rare. Discs are 2-5/8" diameter with borderless color photos on front. Backs have player stats and the team logo. The unnumbered discs are checklisted here in alphabetical order.

		NM	EX	VG
Complete Set (ball and discs):		300.00	150.00	90.00
Common Player:		16.00	8.00	4.75
(1)	Red Adams	16.00	8.00	4.75
(2)	Walt Alston	35.00	17.50	10.50
(3)	Willie Crawford	16.00	8.00	4.75
(4)	Willie Davis	24.00	12.00	7.25
(5)	Al Downing	16.00	8.00	4.75
(6)	Jim Gilliam	24.00	12.00	7.25
(7)	Bill Grabarkewitz	16.00	8.00	4.75
(8)	Jim Lefebvre	16.00	8.00	4.75
(9)	Pete Mikkelsen	16.00	8.00	4.75
(10)	Manny Mota	18.00	9.00	5.50
(11)	Claude Osteen	16.00	8.00	4.75
(12)	Wes Parker	16.00	8.00	4.75
(13)	Duke Sims	16.00	8.00	4.75
(14)	Bill Singer	16.00	8.00	4.75
(15)	Bill Sudakis	16.00	8.00	4.75
(16)	Don Sutton	30.00	15.00	9.00
(17)	Bob Valentine	18.00	9.00	5.50
(18)	Maury Wills	22.00	11.00	6.50

1953 Pictsweet Milwaukee Braves

STAR CATCHER
OF THE MILWAUKEE BRAVES
WALKER COOPER

This black-and-white mini-poster (8-1/2" x 11-1/4") depicts a player holding a package of frozen vegetables. They were probably intended for grocery store window or aisle display. Backs are blank. It's unknown how many players are in the set. See also, Top Taste Bread.

		NM	EX	VG
Common Player:		150.00	75.00	45.00
(1)	"Bullet Bill" Bruton	150.00	75.00	45.00
(2)	Walker Cooper	150.00	75.00	45.00
(3)	Sid Gordon	150.00	75.00	45.00
(4)	Charlie Grimm	150.00	75.00	45.00
(5)	Sibby Sisti	150.00	75.00	45.00
(6)	Max Surkont	150.00	75.00	45.00

1970 Pictures of Champions Baltimore Orioles

12
DAVE MAY

Pictures of Champions

Issued in 1970 in the Baltimore area, this 16-card set pictures members of the Baltimore Orioles. The 2-1/8" x 2-3/4" cards feature black and white player photos on orange card stock. The method of distribution is unknown.

		NM	EX	VG
Complete Set (16):		80.00	40.00	25.00
Common Player:		2.00	1.00	.60
4	Earl Weaver	7.50	3.75	2.25
5	Brooks Robinson	25.00	12.50	7.50
7	Mark Belanger	2.00	1.00	.60
8	Andy Etchebarren	2.00	1.00	.60
9	Don Buford	2.00	1.00	.60
10	Ellie Hendricks	2.00	1.00	.60
12	Dave May	2.00	1.00	.60
15	Dave Johnson	2.00	1.00	.60
16	Dave McNally	2.00	1.00	.60
20	Frank Robinson	20.00	10.00	6.00
22	Jim Palmer	20.00	10.00	6.00
24	Pete Richert	2.00	1.00	.60
29	Dick Hall	2.00	1.00	.60
35	Mike Cuellar	2.00	1.00	.60
39	Eddie Watt	2.00	1.00	.60
40	Dave Leonhard	2.00	1.00	.60

1909-11 Piedmont Cigarettes

In both T205 and T206, Piedmont is the brand found most often on the cards' backs. In T205, Piedmonts backs are printed in blue with either Factory 25 and 42 designation, the latter of which is much scarcer but commands little premium, more due to collector indifference than relative scarcity. In T206, the familiar blue Piedmont logo is found in all three series. In the "150 Subjects" and "350 Subjects" series, only Factory 25 (Va.) is seen. In the "350-460 Subjects" series, both

Factory 25 and Factory 42 (N.C.) are seen. The latter is much scarcer and commands a premium over the more common Factory 25 version.

FACTORY 42 OVERPRINTS
PREMIUM:
Common Players: 5-7X
Hall of Famers: 2X
(See T205, T206)

1914 Piedmont Art Stamps (T330-2)

This series of "Piedmont Art Stamps" looks like a fragile version of the more popular T205 Gold Border tobacco cards of 1911, employing the same basic design on front. The Piedmont stamps measure 1-1/2" x 2-5/8". Though the backs advertise "100 designs," more than 110 different players are known. And, because some of the players are pictured in two separate poses, there are actually 118 different stamps known, with new discoveries still being made. All but three of the subjects in the Piedmont set were taken from the T205 set; the exceptions being Joe Wood, Walt Blair and Bill Killifer. Because of their fragile composition, and since they are stamps that were frequently stuck to album pages, examples of Piedmont Art Stamps in Near Mint or better condition are very scarce. The back of the stamps offered a "handsome" album in exchange for 25 Piedmont coupons. The set has an American Card Catalog designation of T330-2. Gaps have been left in the assigned numbering to accommodate future additions.

		NM	EX	VG
Common Player:		150.00	60.00	30.00
(1)	Leon K. Ames	150.00	60.00	30.00
(2)	Jimmy Archer	150.00	60.00	30.00
(3)	Jimmy Austin	150.00	60.00	30.00
(4)	Home Run Baker	450.00	180.00	90.00
(5)	Cy Barger (Full "B" on cap.)	150.00	60.00	30.00
(6)	Cy Barger (Partial "B" on cap.)	150.00	60.00	30.00
(7)	Jack Barry	150.00	60.00	30.00
(8)	Johnny Bates	150.00	60.00	30.00
(9)	Fred Beck	150.00	60.00	30.00
(10)	Beals Becker	150.00	60.00	30.00
(11)	Chief Bender	450.00	180.00	90.00
(12)	Bob Bescher	150.00	60.00	30.00
(13)	Joe Birmingham	150.00	60.00	30.00
(14)	Walt Blair	150.00	60.00	30.00
(15)	Roger Bresnahan	450.00	180.00	90.00
(16)	Al Bridwell	150.00	60.00	30.00
(17)	Mordecai Brown	450.00	180.00	90.00
(18)	Bobby Byrne	150.00	60.00	30.00
(19)	Howie Camnitz	150.00	60.00	30.00
(20)	Bill Carrigan	150.00	60.00	30.00
(21)	Frank Chance	450.00	180.00	90.00
(22)	Hal Chase ("Chase" on front.)	250.00	100.00	50.00
(23)	Hal Chase ("Hal Chase" on front.)	300.00	120.00	60.00
(24)	Ed Cicotte	375.00	150.00	75.00
(25)	Fred Clarke	450.00	180.00	90.00
(26)	Ty Cobb	5,500	2,200	1,100
(27)	Eddie Collins (Mouth closed.)	450.00	180.00	90.00
(28)	Eddie Collins (Mouth open.)	450.00	180.00	90.00
(29)	Otis "Doc" Crandall	150.00	60.00	30.00
(30)	Bill Dahlen	150.00	60.00	30.00
(31)	Jake Daubert	150.00	60.00	30.00
(32)	Jim Delahanty	150.00	60.00	30.00
(33)	Josh Devore	150.00	60.00	30.00
(34)	Red Dooin	150.00	60.00	30.00
(35)	Mickey Doolan	150.00	60.00	30.00
(36)	Tom Downey	150.00	60.00	30.00
(37)	Larry Doyle	150.00	60.00	30.00
(38)	Dick Egan	150.00	60.00	30.00
(39)	Kid Elberfield (Elberfeld)	150.00	60.00	30.00
(40)	Clyde Engle	150.00	60.00	30.00
(41)	Louis Evans	150.00	60.00	30.00
(42)	Johnny Evers	450.00	180.00	90.00
(43)	Ray Fisher	150.00	60.00	30.00
(44)	Art Fletcher	150.00	60.00	30.00
(45)	Russ Ford (Dark cap.)	150.00	60.00	30.00
(46)	Russ Ford (White cap.)	150.00	60.00	30.00
(47)	Art Fromme	150.00	60.00	30.00
(48)	George Gibson	150.00	60.00	30.00
(49)	William Goode (Wilbur Good)	150.00	60.00	30.00
(51)	Eddie Grant	225.00	90.00	45.00
(52)	Clark Griiifith	450.00	180.00	90.00
(53)	Bob Groom	150.00	60.00	30.00
(54)	Bob Harmon	150.00	60.00	30.00
(55)	Arnold Hauser	150.00	60.00	30.00
(56)	Buck Herzog	150.00	60.00	30.00
(57)	Dick Hoblitzell	150.00	60.00	30.00
(58)	Miller Huggins	450.00	180.00	90.00
(59)	John Hummel	150.00	60.00	30.00
(60)	Hughie Jennings	450.00	180.00	90.00
(61)	Walter Johnson	750.00	300.00	150.00
(62)	Davy Jones	150.00	60.00	30.00
(63)	Bill Killifer (Killefer)	150.00	60.00	30.00
(64)	Jack Knight	150.00	60.00	30.00
(65)	Ed Konetchy	150.00	60.00	30.00
(66)	Frank LaPorte	150.00	60.00	30.00
(67)	Thomas Leach	150.00	60.00	30.00
(68)	Edgar Lennox	150.00	60.00	30.00
(69)	Hans Lobert	150.00	60.00	30.00
(70)	Harry Lord	150.00	60.00	30.00
(71)	Sherry Magee	150.00	60.00	30.00
(72)	Rube Marquard	450.00	180.00	90.00
(73)	Christy Mathewson	1,250	500.00	250.00
(74)	George McBride	150.00	60.00	30.00
(76)	J.J. McGraw	450.00	180.00	90.00
(77)	Larry McLean	150.00	60.00	30.00
(78)	Fred Merkle	150.00	60.00	30.00
(79)	Chief Meyers	150.00	60.00	30.00
(80)	Clyde Milan	150.00	60.00	30.00
(81)	Dots Miller	150.00	60.00	30.00
(82)	Mike Mitchell	150.00	60.00	30.00
(83)	Pat Moran	150.00	60.00	30.00
(84)	George Moriarity (Moriarty)	150.00	60.00	30.00
(85)	George Mullin	150.00	60.00	30.00
(86)	Danny Murphy	150.00	60.00	30.00
(87)	Jack "Red" Murray	150.00	60.00	30.00
(88)	Tom Needham	150.00	60.00	30.00
(89)	Rebel Oakes	150.00	60.00	30.00
(90)	Rube Oldring	150.00	60.00	30.00
(91)	Fred Parent	150.00	60.00	30.00
(92)	Dode Paskert	150.00	60.00	30.00
(93)	Jack Quinn	150.00	60.00	30.00
(94)	Ed Reulbach	150.00	60.00	30.00
(95)	Lewis Ritchie	150.00	60.00	30.00
(96)	Jack Rowan	150.00	60.00	30.00
(97)	Nap Rucker	150.00	60.00	30.00
(98)	Germany Schaefer	150.00	60.00	30.00
(99)	Wildfire Schulte	150.00	60.00	30.00
(101)	Jim Scott	150.00	60.00	30.00
(102)	Fred Snodgrass	150.00	60.00	30.00
(103)	Tris Speaker	600.00	240.00	120.00
(104)	Oscar Stamage (Stanage)	150.00	60.00	30.00
(105)	George Stovall	150.00	60.00	30.00
(106)	George Suggs	150.00	60.00	30.00
(107)	Jeff Sweeney	150.00	60.00	30.00
(108)	Ira Thomas	150.00	60.00	30.00
(109)	Joe Tinker	450.00	180.00	90.00
(110)	Terry Turner	150.00	60.00	30.00
(111)	Hippo Vaughn	150.00	60.00	30.00
(112)	Heinie Wagner	150.00	60.00	30.00
(113)	Bobby Wallace (No cap.)	450.00	180.00	90.00
(114)	Bobby Wallace (With cap.)	450.00	180.00	90.00
(115)	Ed Walsh	450.00	180.00	90.00
(116)	Zach Wheat	450.00	180.00	90.00
(117)	Irwin "Kaiser" Wilhelm	150.00	60.00	30.00
(118)	Ed Willett	150.00	60.00	30.00
(119)	Owen Wilson	150.00	60.00	30.00
(120)	Hooks Wiltse	150.00	60.00	30.00
(121)	Joe Wood	150.00	60.00	30.00

1939 Piel's Beer Coasters

New York Giants manager Bill Terry was the only baseball player among a trio of local celebrities endoring the beer brand in this series of approximately 4" diameter bar coasters. The printing is in black-and-red.

	NM	EX	VG
Bill Terry	30.00	15.00	9.00

1913-1915 Pinkerton Score/Photo/Post Cards

The picture portions of the T5 Pinkerton cabinets have also been seen in other formats, in printed rather than photographic presentation. The most desirable of these have backs printed for use as baseball scorecards. These measure a nominal 3-1/2" x 5-1/2", give or take 1/4". They are believed to have been printed some years after the cabinet cards. It is unknown to what extent the checklist of T5 can be found in this format. Postcard-style backs have also been seen for some Pinkerton pictures, as well as blank-backed versions; they are considerably discounted from the scorecard type. Confirmed examples are listed here.

		NM	EX	VG
Common Player:		250.00	125.00	75.00
	SCORECARD BACKS			
153	Hughie Jennings	500.00	250.00	150.00
159	Ty Cobb	2,500	1,250	750.00
203	King Cole	250.00	125.00	75.00
205	Heinie Zimmerman	250.00	125.00	75.00
206	Wildfire Schulte	250.00	125.00	75.00
208	Joe Tinker	500.00	250.00	150.00
251	Christy Mathewson	1,500	750.00	450.00
252	Fred Merkle	250.00	125.00	75.00
260	Larry Doyle	250.00	125.00	75.00
420	R.C. Hoblitzell	250.00	125.00	75.00
424	Mike Mitchell	250.00	125.00	75.00
505	Connie Mack	500.00	250.00	150.00
511	Eddie Collins	500.00	250.00	150.00
512	Frank Baker	500.00	250.00	150.00
872	Hans Wagner	800.00	400.00	240.00
	POSTCARD OR BLANK BACKS			
159	Ty Cobb	1,500	750.00	450.00
203	King Cole	150.00	75.00	45.00
206	Frank Schulte	150.00	75.00	45.00
208	Joe Tinker	250.00	125.00	75.00
251	Christy Mathewson	350.00	175.00	105.00
260	Larry Doyle	150.00	75.00	45.00
264	Chief Myers (Meyers)	150.00	75.00	45.00
419	Clark Griffith	250.00	125.00	75.00
424	Mike Mitchell	150.00	75.00	45.00
501	Chas. Bender	250.00	125.00	75.00
511	Eddie Collins	250.00	125.00	75.00
512	Frank Baker	250.00	125.00	75.00
627	Napoleon Lajoie	250.00	125.00	75.00
855	Fred Clarke	250.00	125.00	75.00
865	Babe Adams	150.00	75.00	45.00
872	Hans Wagner	600.00	300.00	180.00

1912 Pirate Cigarettes (T215)

This set can be considerd a British version of the T215 Red Cross Type 1 set. Distributed by Pirate brand cigarettes of Bristol and London, England, the fronts of the cards are identical to the Red Cross cards, but the green backs carry advertising for Pirate Cigarettes. It is believed that the Pirate cards were printed for distribution to U.S. servicemen in the South Seas. There is reason to believe the "standard"

tobacco card length of 2-5/8" (width 1-7/16") may not be universally applicable to the Pirate cards, possibly because of packaging considerations.

		NM	EX	VG
Common Player:		11,000	5,500	3,300
(1)	Red Ames	11,000	5,500	3,300
(2)	Home Run Baker	16,000	8,000	4,800
(3)	Neal Ball	11,000	5,500	3,300
(4)	Chief Bender	16,000	8,000	4,800
(5)	Al Bridwell	11,000	5,500	3,300
(6)	Bobby Byrne	11,000	5,500	3,300
(7)	Howie Camnitz	11,000	5,500	3,300
(8)	Frank Chance	9,800	4,900	2,950
(9)	Hal Chase	14,500	7,250	4,350
(10)	Eddie Collins	16,000	8,000	4,800
(11)	Doc Crandall	11,000	5,500	3,300
(12)	Sam Crawford	16,000	8,000	4,800
(13)	Birdie Cree	11,000	5,500	3,300
(14)	Harry Davis	11,000	5,500	3,300
(15)	Josh Devore	11,000	5,500	3,300
(16)	Mike Donlin	11,000	5,500	3,300
(17)	Mickey Doolan/Btg	11,000	5,500	3,300
(18)	Mickey Doolan/Fielding	11,000	5,500	3,300
(19)	Patsy Dougherty	11,000	5,500	3,300
(20)	Larry Doyle/Btg	11,000	5,500	3,300
(21)	Larry Doyle/Portrait	11,000	5,500	3,300
(22)	Jean Dubuc	11,000	5,500	3,300
(23)	Kid Elberfeld	11,000	5,500	3,300
(24)	Steve Evans	11,000	5,500	3,300
(25)	Johnny Evers	16,000	8,000	4,800
(26)	Russ Ford	11,000	5,500	3,300
(27)	Art Fromme	11,000	5,500	3,300
(28)	Clark Griffith	16,000	8,000	4,800
(29)	Bob Groom	11,000	5,500	3,300
(30)	Topsy Hartsel	11,000	5,500	3,300
(31)	Buck Herzog	11,000	5,500	3,300
(32)	Dick Hoblitzell	11,000	5,500	3,300
(33)	Solly Hofman	11,000	5,500	3,300
(34)	Del Howard	11,000	5,500	3,300
(35)	Miller Huggins (Hands at mouth.)	16,000	8,000	4,800
(36)	Miller Huggins/Portrait	16,000	8,000	4,800
(37)	John Hummel	11,000	5,500	3,300
(38)	Hughie Jennings (Both hands showing.)	16,000	8,000	4,800
(39)	Hughie Jennings (One hand showing.)	16,000	8,000	4,800
(40)	Walter Johnson	35,000	17,500	10,500
(41)	Joe Kelley	16,000	8,000	4,800
(42)	Ed Konetchy	11,000	5,500	3,300
(43)	Harry Krause	11,000	5,500	3,300
(44)	Nap Lajoie	16,000	8,000	4,800
(45)	Joe Lake	11,000	5,500	3,300
(46)	Lefty Leifield	11,000	5,500	3,300
(47)	Harry Lord	11,000	5,500	3,300
(48)	Sherry Magee	11,000	5,500	3,300
(49)	Rube Marquard/Pitching	16,000	8,000	4,800
(50)	Rube Marquard/Portrait	16,000	8,000	4,800
(51)	Joe McGinnity	16,000	8,000	4,800
(52)	John McGraw (Glove at side.)	16,000	8,000	4,800
(53)	John McGraw/Portrait	16,000	8,000	4,800
(54)	Harry McIntyre (Chicago)	11,000	5,500	3,300
(55)	Harry McIntyre (Brooklyn & Chicago)	11,000	5,500	3,300
(56)	Larry McLean	11,000	5,500	3,300
(57)	Fred Merkle	11,000	5,500	3,300
(58)	Chief Meyers	11,000	5,500	3,300
(59)	Mike Mitchell	11,000	5,500	3,300
(60)	Mike Mowrey	11,000	5,500	3,300
(61)	George Mullin	11,000	5,500	3,300
(62)	Danny Murphy	11,000	5,500	3,300
(63)	Red Murray	11,000	5,500	3,300
(64)	Rebel Oakes	11,000	5,500	3,300
(65)	Rube Oldring	11,000	5,500	3,300
(66)	Charley O'Leary	11,000	5,500	3,300
(67)	Dode Paskert	11,000	5,500	3,300
(68)	Barney Pelty	11,000	5,500	3,300
(69)	Billy Purtell	11,000	5,500	3,300
(70)	Jack Quinn	11,000	5,500	3,300
(71)	Ed Reulbach	11,000	5,500	3,300
(72)	Nap Rucker	11,000	5,500	3,300
(73)	Germany Schaefer	11,000	5,500	3,300
(74)	Wildfire Schulte	11,000	5,500	3,300
(75)	Jimmy Sheckard	11,000	5,500	3,300
(76)	Frank Smith	11,000	5,500	3,300
(77)	Tris Speaker	18,000	9,000	5,400
(78)	Jake Stahl	11,000	5,500	3,300
(79)	Harry Steinfeldt	11,000	5,500	3,300
(80)	Gabby Street	11,000	5,500	3,300
(81)	Ed Summers	11,000	5,500	3,300
(82)	Jeff Sweeney	11,000	5,500	3,300
(83)	Lee Tannehill	11,000	5,500	3,300
(84)	Ira Thomas	11,000	5,500	3,300
(85)	Joe Tinker	16,000	8,000	4,800
(86)	Heinie Wagner	11,000	5,500	3,300
(87)	Jack Warhop	11,000	5,500	3,300
(88)	Zack Wheat	16,000	8,000	4,800
(89)	Ed Willetts (Willett)	11,000	5,500	3,300
(90)	Owen Wilson	11,000	5,500	3,300
(91)	Hooks Wiltse/Pitching	11,000	5,500	3,300
(92)	Hooks Wiltse/Portrait	11,000	5,500	3,300

1910 Pittsburgh Gazette Times Honus Wagner Postcard

Describing him as "The Worlds' Greatest Base Ball Player," the local newspaper published this black-and-white standard size, typically marked, photographic postcard picturing the Flying Dutchman and landmarks from his Carnegie, Pa., hometown.

	NM	EX	VG
Honus Wagner	650.00	325.00	200.00

1904 Pittsburg Leader Honus Wagner Schedule

This 3-3/4" x 1-3/4" celluloid pocket schedule for the 1904 Pirates features on its front a black-and-white photographic portrait of the "KING OF BALL PLAYERS," Honus Wagner. Much of the remainder of the front and back printing is in regal purple typography.

	NM	EX	VG
Honus Wagner	3,500	1,750	1,100

1908 Pittsburgh Pirates Vignette Postcards

It has been reliably reported that 15 postcards and an album were produced for this souvenir issue sold at Pittsburgh's Exhibition Field. Only Pirates are pictured in this series of black-and-white standard-format postcards published locally by J.B. Coyle. Cards have an irregularly shaped posed photo of the player at center with his last name (or nickname), position and "PGH-08" crudely printed in white. Divided postcard backs have a stamp box and publisher's credit line. The incomplete checklist presented here is alphabetically arranged. Later editions of the American Card Catalog listed this set as PC800.

		NM	EX	VG
Common Player:		250.00	125.00	75.00
(1)	Abby (Ed Abbaticchio)	250.00	125.00	75.00
(2)	Howie Camnitz	250.00	125.00	75.00
(3)	Fred Clarke	350.00	175.00	105.00
(4)	George Gibson	250.00	125.00	75.00
(5)	Tommy Leach	250.00	125.00	75.00
(6)	Dan Moeller	250.00	125.00	75.00
(10)	Allen Storke	250.00	125.00	75.00
(14)	Honus Wagner	1,000	500.00	300.00
(15)	Owen Wilson	250.00	125.00	75.00

1909 Pittsburgh Pirates Extension Postcard

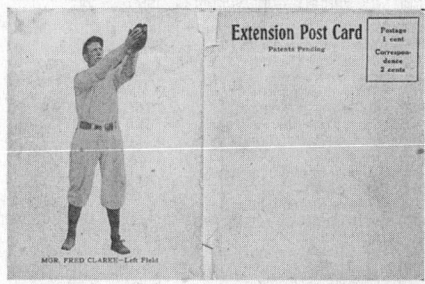

One of many novelty souvenirs commemorating the Bucs' World Championship season of 1909 was this uniquely formatted postcard. Picturing manager Fred Clarke on front, the 3-1/4" x 5-1/2" postcard opens up accordian fashion to a length of 14", revealing small action photos of 17 players each on a white background and identified by last name and position.

	NM	EX	VG
1909 Pittsburgh Pirates	3,000	1,500	900.00

1950-60s Pittsburgh Pirates Postcards

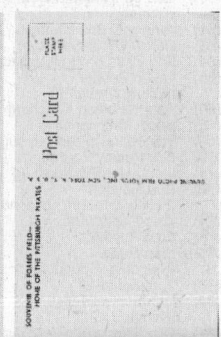

This listing encompasses the issues of several different postcard publishers who supplied black-and-white cards to the players for use in answering fan mail. Several different types of card stock are found, both matte and glossy. Some cards have postcard markings on back, others do not, especially those picturing players in the 1960s style sleeveless style uniforms. Because it is likely other players and poses will be reported, a description of each pose is included.

		NM	EX	VG
Common Player:		15.00	7.50	4.50
(1)	Gair Allie (Ready to hit.)	15.00	7.50	4.50
(2)	Toby Atwell (Squatting w/glove.)	15.00	7.50	4.50
(3)	Tony Bartirome (Stretching at 1B.)	15.00	7.50	4.50
(4)	Carlos Bernier/Btg	15.00	7.50	4.50
(5)	Ron Blackburn/Pitching (Left leg up.)	15.00	7.50	4.50
(6)	Ron Brand (Kneeling w/glove.)	15.00	7.50	4.50
(7)	Jim Bunning/Pitching (To letters.)	25.00	12.50	7.50
(8)	Don (Swede) Carlson/ Pitching (By wall.)	15.00	7.50	4.50
(9)	Pete Castiglione (Ready to hit,)	15.00	7.50	4.50
(10)	Pete Castiglione (Kneeling w/bat.)	15.00	7.50	4.50
(12)	Cliff Chambers/Pitching (Leg up.)	15.00	7.50	4.50
(13)	Bob Chesnes (Follow-through.)	15.00	7.50	4.50
(14)	Roberto Clemente (Kneeling w/bat.)	125.00	65.00	35.00
(15)	Dick Cole/Fielding	15.00	7.50	4.50
(16)	Dale Coogan (Ready to hit.)	15.00	7.50	4.50
(18)	Bobby Del Greco (Batting follow-through.)	15.00	7.50	4.50
(20)	Elroy Face (Follow-through, cloth cap, sleeves,)	17.50	8.75	5.25
(21)	Elroy Face (Follow-through, cloth cap, no sleeves.)	17.50	8.75	5.25
(22)	Elroy Face (Follow-through, helmet, sleeves,)	17.50	8.75	5.25
(23)	Elroy Face (Follow-through, helmet, no sleeves.)	17.50	8.75	5.25
(24)	Hank Foiles/Squatting	15.00	7.50	4.50
(25)	Gene Freese (Ready to hit.)	15.00	7.50	4.50
(26)	Bob Friend (Follow-through.)	15.00	7.50	4.50
(27)	Bob Friend/Pitching (Leg up.)	15.00	7.50	4.50
(28)	Bob Friend (Standing in dugout.)	15.00	7.50	4.50
(29)	Dick Groat (Ready to hit.)	17.50	8.75	5.25
(30)	Fred Haney (Arms folded.)	15.00	7.50	4.50
(31)	John Hetki (Follow-through.)	15.00	7.50	4.50

		NM	EX	VG
(32)	Johnny Hopp (Stretching at 1B.)	15.00	7.50	4.50
(34)	Ralph Kiner/Btg (Two decks.)	25.00	12.50	7.50
(35)	Nellie King (Follow-through.)	15.00	7.50	4.50
(36)	Ron Kline (Follow-through.)	15.00	7.50	4.50
(37)	Ron Kline/Pitching (Leg up.)	15.00	7.50	4.50
(38)	Ted Kluszewski (Kneeling with bat.)	20.00	10.00	6.00
(39)	Ted Kluszewski (Pose to chest.)	20.00	10.00	6.00
(41)	Nick Koback/Kneeling	15.00	7.50	4.50
(42)	Clem Koshorek/Fielding	15.00	7.50	4.50
(43)	Danny Kravitz (Ready to hit.)	15.00	7.50	4.50
(44)	Vern Law (Follow-through, bleachers.)	17.50	8.75	5.25
(45)	Vern Law (Follow-through, trees.)	17.50	8.75	5.25
(46)	Vern Law (Follow-through, right foot cut off.)	17.50	8.75	5.25
(47)	Vern Law/Kneeling	17.50	8.75	5.25
(48)	Vern Law/Pitching (Leg up.)	17.50	8.75	5.25
(49)	Lenny Levy/Catching	15.00	7.50	4.50
(50)	Lenny Levy (Standing in dugout.)	15.00	7.50	4.50
(51)	Dale Long/Btg	15.00	7.50	4.50
(52)	Dale Long (Kneeling w/bat.)	15.00	7.50	4.50
(53)	Jerry Lynch/Btg (Sleeves)	15.00	7.50	4.50
(54)	Jerry Lynch/Btg (No sleeves.)	15.00	7.50	4.50
(55)	Bill MacDonald/Pitching (Leg up.)	15.00	7.50	4.50
(56)	Bill Mazeroski/Fielding (Ball in glove, horizontal.)	25.00	12.50	7.50
(57)	Bill Mazeroski/Fielding (Ball in hand.)	25.00	12.50	7.50
(58)	Danny Murtaugh/Fielding	15.00	7.50	4.50
(59)	Danny Murtaugh/Portrait (Helmet)	15.00	7.50	4.50
(60)	George "Red" Munger/ Pitching	15.00	7.50	4.50
(61)	Johnny O'Brien/Jumping	15.00	7.50	4.50
(63)	Danny O'Connell/Btg	15.00	7.50	4.50
(64)	Bob Oldis (Portrait to belt.)	15.00	7.50	4.50
(65)	Laurin Pepper (Follow-through.)	15.00	7.50	4.50
(66)	Pete Peterson./Catching	15.00	7.50	4.50
(68)	Buddy Pritchard/Btg	15.00	7.50	4.50
(69)	Bob Purkey (Follow-through.)	15.00	7.50	4.50
(70)	Bob Purkey/Portrait	15.00	7.50	4.50
(71)	Mel Queen/Pitching (Leg up.)	15.00	7.50	4.50
(72)	Curt Raydon (Follow-through, horizontal.)	15.00	7.50	4.50
(74)	Dino Restelli/Btg	15.00	7.50	4.50
(75)	Stan Rojek/Btg	15.00	7.50	4.50
(76)	Stan Rojek (Standing in dugout.)	15.00	7.50	4.50
(78)	Tom Saffell/Btg	15.00	7.50	4.50
(80)	Don Schwall/Pitching (No cap.)	15.00	7.50	4.50
(81)	Bob Skinner/Btg	15.00	7.50	4.50
(82)	Bob Smith (Follow-through.)	15.00	7.50	4.50
(83)	Paul Smith/Btg	15.00	7.50	4.50
(84)	Art Swanson (Hands on hips.)	15.00	7.50	4.50
(86)	Frank Thomas/Btg (Cap)	17.50	8.75	5.25
(87)	Frank Thomas/Btg (Helmet)	17.50	8.75	5.25
(90)	Bill Virdon/Btg (Matte)	17.50	8.75	5.25
(91)	Bill Virdon/Btg (Glossy)	17.50	8.75	5.25
(92)	Bill Virdon/Kneeling	17.50	8.75	5.25
(93)	Harry Walker/Portrait	15.00	7.50	4.50
(94)	Lee Walls/Btg (Glove in pocket.)	15.00	7.50	4.50
(95)	Lee Walls/Btg (Trees)	15.00	7.50	4.50
(96)	Jim Walsh (Follow-through, horizontal.)	15.00	7.50	4.50
(97)	Preston Ward/Btg (#44 in background.)	15.00	7.50	4.50
(98)	Preston Ward/Btg (No #44)	15.00	7.50	4.50
(99)	Fred Waters/Pitching (Leg up.)	15.00	7.50	4.50
(100)	Bill Werle/Pitching	15.00	7.50	4.50

1950 Pittsburgh Pirates Photo Pack

The player photos in this picture pack that was sold at Forbes Field measure 6-1/2" x 9" and are printed in black-and-white on heavy, blank-backed paper. A facsimile "autograph" is printed on front of each picture, though all were written in the same hand. Several of the photos from this set were the basis for the color paintings found on 1951 Bowman cards. The unnumbered pictures are checklisted here alphabetically.

	NM	EX	VG
Complete Set (26):	250.00	125.00	75.00

Common Player:	12.00	6.00	3.50
(1)	Ted Beard	12.00	6.00	3.50
(2)	Gus Bell	20.00	10.00	6.00
(3)	Pete Castiglione	12.00	6.00	3.50
(4)	Cliff Chambers	12.00	6.00	3.50
(5)	Dale Coogan	12.00	6.00	3.50
(6)	Murry Dickson	12.00	6.00	3.50
(7)	Bob Dillinger	12.00	6.00	3.50
(8)	Froilan Fernandez	12.00	6.00	3.50
(9)	Johnny Hopp	12.00	6.00	3.50
(10)	Ralph Kiner	30.00	15.00	9.00
(11)	Vernon Law	20.00	10.00	6.00
(12)	Vic Lombardi	12.00	6.00	3.50
(13)	Bill MacDonald	12.00	6.00	3.50
(14)	Clyde McCullough	12.00	6.00	3.50
(15)	Bill Meyer	12.00	6.00	3.50
(16)	Ray Mueller	12.00	6.00	3.50
(17)	Danny Murtaugh	12.00	6.00	3.50
(18)	Jack Phillips	12.00	6.00	3.50
(19)	Mel Queen	12.00	6.00	3.50
(20)	Stan Rojek	12.00	6.00	3.50
(21)	Henry Schenz	12.00	6.00	3.50
(22)	George Strickland	12.00	6.00	3.50
(23)	Earl Turner	12.00	6.00	3.50
(24)	Jim Walsh	12.00	6.00	3.50
(25)	Bill Werle	12.00	6.00	3.50
(26)	Wally Westlake	12.00	6.00	3.50

1967 Pittsburgh Pirates Autograph Cards

A souvenir stand item introduced by the Pirates in 1967 was a series of color player cards bearing facsimile autographs. The 3-1/4" x 4-1/4" cards identify the player with a line of type beneath the photo giving name, position and uniform number. Backs are blank. The cards are checklisted here in alphabetical order.

		NM	EX	VG
Complete Set (24):		100.00	50.00	30.00
Common Player:		4.00	2.00	1.25
	SERIES A			
(1)	Gene Alley	4.00	2.00	1.25
(2)	Steve Blass	4.00	2.00	1.25
(3)	Roberto Clemente	35.00	17.50	10.00
(4)	Donn Clendenon	5.00	2.50	1.50
(5)	Roy Face	5.00	2.50	1.50
(6)	Jesse Gonder	4.00	2.00	1.25
(7)	Jerry May	4.00	2.00	1.25
(8)	Manny Mota	5.00	2.50	1.50
(9)	Jose Pagan	4.00	2.00	1.25
(10)	Dennis Ribant	4.00	2.00	1.25
(11)	Tommie Sisk	4.00	2.00	1.25
(12)	Bob Veale	4.00	2.00	1.25
	SERIES B			
(13)	Matty Alou	4.00	2.00	1.25
(14)	Woody Fryman	4.00	2.00	1.25
(15)	Vernon Law	5.00	2.50	1.50
(16)	Bill Mazeroski	17.50	8.75	5.25
(17)	Al McBean	4.00	2.00	1.25
(18)	Pete Mikkelsen	4.00	2.00	1.25
(19)	Jim Pagliaroni	4.00	2.00	1.25
(20)	Juan Pizarro	4.00	2.00	1.25
(21)	Andy Rodgers	4.00	2.00	1.25
(22)	Willie Stargell	15.00	7.50	4.50
(23)	Harry Walker	4.00	2.00	1.25
(24)	Maury Wills	6.50	3.25	2.00

1968 Pittsburgh Pirates Autograph Cards

These team-issued autograph cards were sold in packages at Forbes Field. The 3-1/4" x 4-1/4" cards feature a color player photo and facsimile autograph. They are blank-backed. Cards were issued in Series A and Series B, with header cards in each series providing a checklist. Cards are listed here by series according to the uniform number found on the card.

		NM	EX	VG
Complete Set (26):		45.00	22.00	13.50
Common Player:		2.00	1.00	.60
	SERIES A			
7	Larry Shepard	2.00	1.00	.60
11	Jose Pagan	2.00	1.00	.60
12	Jerry May	2.00	1.00	.60
14	Jim Bunning	7.50	3.75	2.25
15	Manny Mota	2.00	1.00	.60
17	Donn Clendenon	3.00	1.50	.90
21	Roberto Clemente	15.00	7.50	4.50
22	Gene Alley	2.00	1.00	.60
25	Tommie Sisk	2.00	1.00	.60
26	Roy Face	2.00	1.00	.60
28	Steve Blass	2.00	1.00	.60
39	Bob Veale	2.00	1.00	.60
--	Checklist Card, Series A	2.00	1.00	.60
	SERIES B			
8	Willie Stargell	8.00	4.00	2.50
9	Bill Mazeroski	9.00	4.50	2.75
10	Gary Kolb	2.00	1.00	.60
18	Matty Alou	2.50	1.25	.70
27	Ronnie Kline	2.00	1.00	.60
29	Juan Pizzaro	2.00	1.00	.60
30	Maury Wills	4.00	2.00	1.25
34	Al McBean	2.00	1.00	.60
35	Manny Sanguillen	2.00	1.00	.60
38	Bob Moose	2.00	1.00	.60
40	Dave Wickersham	2.00	1.00	.60
--	Jim Shellenback	2.00	1.00	.60
--	Checklist card, Series B	2.00	1.00	.60

1969 Pittsburgh Pirates Autograph Cards

Sold in Series A with a blue header card/checklist and Series B with a pink header card/checklist, these team-issue autograph cards were available at Forbes Field. Identical in format to the previous year's issue, the 3-1/4" x 4-1/4" cards are blank-backed and feature a color player photo on front with a facsimile autograph in the wide white bottom border. Cards are checklisted here by series and uniform number (found on card fronts) within series.

		NM	EX	VG
Complete Set:		50.00	25.00	15.00
Common Player:		2.00	1.00	.60
	Series A			
2	Fred Patek	2.00	1.00	.60
4	Larry Shepard	2.00	1.00	.60
8	Willie Stargell	6.00	3.00	1.75
9	Bill Mazeroski	9.00	4.50	2.75
10	Gary Kolb	2.00	1.00	.60
23	Luke Walker	2.00	1.00	.60
28	Steve Blass	2.00	1.00	.60
29	Al Oliver	4.00	2.00	1.25
35	Manny Sanguillen	2.50	1.25	.70
38	Bob Moose	2.00	1.00	.60
39	Bob Veale	2.00	1.00	.60
42	Chuck Hartenstein	2.00	1.00	.60
	Series B			
7	Bill Virdon	2.50	1.25	.70
11	Jose Pagan	2.00	1.00	.60
12	Jerry May	2.00	1.00	.60
14	Jim Bunning	7.50	3.75	2.25
18	Matty Alou	2.50	1.25	.70
20	Richie Hebner	3.00	1.50	.90
21	Roberto Clemente	15.00	7.50	4.50
22	Gene Alley	2.00	1.00	.60
32	Vernon Law	2.50	1.25	.70
36	Carl Taylor	2.00	1.00	.60
40	Dock Ellis	2.50	1.25	.70
43	Bruce Dal Canton	2.00	1.00	.60

1970 Pittsburgh Pirates (Andersen)

Boston baseball photographer Mike Andersen is believed to have produced this collectors' issue of Pirates cards. Nearly identical in format to his 1969-70 Oakland A's issues, the '70 Pirates measures 2-1/4" x 3-5/8" with black-and-white player poses at center.

Player identification and 1969 stats are in the bottom border. Backs are blank. Cards are checklisted here alphabetically.

		NM	EX	VG
Complete Set (12):		40.00	20.00	12.00
Common Player:		2.00	1.00	.60
(1)	Gene Alley	2.00	1.00	.60
(2)	Dave Cash	2.00	1.00	.60
(3)	Dock Ellis	2.00	1.00	.60
(4)	Dave Giusti	2.00	1.00	.60
(5)	Jerry May	2.00	1.00	.60
(6)	Bill Mazeroski	12.00	6.00	3.50
(7)	Al Oliver	4.00	2.00	1.25
(8)	Jose Pagan	2.00	1.00	.60
(9)	Fred Patek	2.00	1.00	.60
(10)	Bob Robertson	2.00	1.00	.60
(11)	Manny Sanguillen	2.00	1.00	.60
(12)	Willie Stargell	12.00	6.00	3.50

1970 Pittsburgh Pirates Autograph Cards

Retaining the 3-1/4" x 4-1/4" format from previous years, these team-issued autograph cards can be distinguished from the 1968-69 issues by the Three Rivers Stadium photo background on each card. The Pirates moved from Forbes Field in June, 1970. The set is checklisted here by uniform number without regard to Series A and B.

		NM	EX	VG
Complete Set (25):		90.00	45.00	27.50
Common Player:		3.00	1.50	.80
2	Fred Patek	3.00	1.50	.80
5	Dave Ricketts	3.00	1.50	.80
8	Willie Stargell	12.00	6.00	3.50
8	Bill Mazeroski	12.00	6.00	3.50
10	Richie Hebner	3.00	1.50	.90
11	Jose Pagan	3.00	1.50	.80
12	Jerry May	3.00	1.50	.80
16	Al Oliver	5.00	2.50	1.50
17	Dock Ellis	3.00	1.50	.80
18	Matty Alou	3.00	1.50	.80
19	Joe Gibbon	3.00	1.50	.80
21	Roberto Clemente	25.00	12.50	7.50
22	Gene Alley	3.00	1.50	.80
22	Orlando Pena	3.00	1.50	.80
23	Luke Walker	3.00	1.50	.80
25	John Jeter	3.00	1.50	.80
25	Bob Robertson	3.00	1.50	.80
30	Dave Cash	3.00	1.50	.80
31	Dave Giusti	3.00	1.50	.80
35	Manny Sanguillen	3.00	1.50	.90
36	Dick Calpaert (Colpaert)	3.00	1.50	.80
38	Bob Moose	3.00	1.50	.80
39	Bob Veale	3.00	1.50	.80
40	Danny Murtaugh	3.00	1.50	.80
50	Jim Nelson	3.00	1.50	.80

1971 Pittsburgh Pirates Autograph Cards

The '71 team-issued Pirates autograph cards are distinguished by the appearance of mustard-yellow caps on the players' portraits. Otherwise the blank-back 3-1/4" x 4-1/2" photocards are identical in format to those of earlier seasons. Players are checklisted here alphabetically within series.

	NM	EX	VG
Complete Set (20):	45.00	22.50	13.50

		NM	EX	VG
Common Player:		2.00	1.00	.60
Series A				
(1)	Gene Alley	2.00	1.00	.60
(2)	Nelson Briles	2.00	1.00	.60
(3)	Dave Cash	2.00	1.00	.60
(4)	Dock Ellis	2.00	1.00	.60
(5)	Mudcat Grant	2.50	1.25	.70
(6)	Bill Mazeroski	9.00	4.50	2.75
(7)	Jim Nelson	2.00	1.00	.60
(8)	Al Oliver	4.00	2.00	1.25
(9)	Manny Sanguillen	2.50	1.25	.70
(10)	Luke Walker	2.00	1.00	.60
Series B				
(11)	Steve Blass	2.00	1.00	.60
(12)	Bob Clemente	15.00	7.50	4.50
(13)	Dave Giusti	2.00	1.00	.60
(14)	Richie Hebner	2.50	1.25	.70
(15)	Bob Johnson	2.00	1.00	.60
(16)	Bob Moose	2.00	1.00	.60
(17)	Jose Pagan	2.00	1.00	.60
(18)	Bob Robertson	2.00	1.00	.60
(19)	Willie Stargell	8.00	4.00	2.50
(20)	Bob Veale	2.00	1.00	.60

1973 Pittsburgh Post-Gazette Pirates

This set of Pirates pictures was printed on newspaper stock one per day in the sports section of the daily paper. The black-bordered black-and-white photos are 5-1/4" x 9-1/4". At top is "'73 Pirate Album" and a short career summary. At bottom are 1972 and career stats. The first six pictures are unnumbered, the others are numbered alphabetically.

		NM	EX	VG
Complete Set (25):		125.00	60.00	35.00
Common Player:		6.00	3.00	1.75
	Gene Alley	6.00	3.00	1.75
	Steve Blass	6.00	3.00	1.75
	Nellie Briles	6.00	3.00	1.75
	Dave Cash	6.00	3.00	1.75
	Roberto Clemente	40.00	20.00	12.00
	Gene Clines	6.00	3.00	1.75
6	Vic Davalillo	6.00	3.00	1.75
7	Dock Ellis	6.00	3.00	1.75
8	Dave Giusti	6.00	3.00	1.75
9	Richie Hebner	6.00	3.00	1.75
10	Jackie Hernandez	6.00	3.00	1.75
11	Ramon Hernandez	6.00	3.00	1.75
12	Bob Johnson	6.00	3.00	1.75
13	Bruce Kison	6.00	3.00	1.75
14	Milt May	6.00	3.00	1.75
15	Bob Miller	6.00	3.00	1.75
16	Bob Moose	6.00	3.00	1.75
17	Al Oliver	7.50	3.75	2.25
18	Bob Robertson	6.00	3.00	1.75
19	Charlie Sands	6.00	3.00	1.75
20	Manny Sanguillen	6.00	3.00	1.75
21	Willie Stargell	12.00	6.00	3.50
22	Rennie Stennett	6.00	3.00	1.75
23	Luke Walker	6.00	3.00	1.75
24	Bill Virdon	7.50	3.75	2.25

1972 Pittsburgh Press "Buc-A-Day" Pirates

Through the month of March, 1972, the daily Pittsburgh Press carried a "Buc-A-Day" feature highlighting members of the team. The feature was intended to be cut out of the paper and saved. Individual pieces measure 3-3/8" wide and vary in length from 9-1/4" to 11-1/16" depending on the length of the biographical information provided. Each player is

pictured in a black-and-white photo in street clothes. Some are pictured with golf clubs, fishing poles, with their children, etc. Because of the nature of their distribution and their fragile nature, complete sets are very scarce.

		NM	EX	VG
Complete Set (25):		100.00	50.00	30.00
Common Player:		2.50	1.25	.70
1	Willie Stargell	7.50	3.75	2.25
2	Steve Blass	2.50	1.25	.70
3	Al Oliver	3.00	1.50	.90
4	Bob Moose	2.50	1.25	.70
5	Dave Cash	2.50	1.25	.70
6	Bill Mazeroski	7.50	3.75	2.25
7	Bob Johnson	2.50	1.25	.70
8	Nellie Briles	2.50	1.25	.70
9	Manny Sanguillen	3.00	1.50	.90
10	Vic Davalillo	2.50	1.25	.70
11	Dave Giusti	2.50	1.25	.70
12	Luke Walker	2.50	1.25	.70
13	Gene Clines	2.50	1.25	.70
14	Milt May	2.50	1.25	.70
15	Bob Robertson	2.50	1.25	.70
16	Roberto Clemente	15.00	7.50	4.50
17	Gene Alley	2.50	1.25	.70
18	Bruce Kison	2.50	1.25	.70
19	Jose Pagan	2.50	1.25	.70
20	Dock Ellis	2.50	1.25	.70
21	Richie Hebner	2.50	1.25	.70
22	Bob Miller	2.50	1.25	.70
23	Jackie Hernandez	2.50	1.25	.70
24	Rennie Stennett	2.50	1.25	.70
25	Bob Veale	2.50	1.25	.70

1948 Pittsburgh Provision & Packing Co.

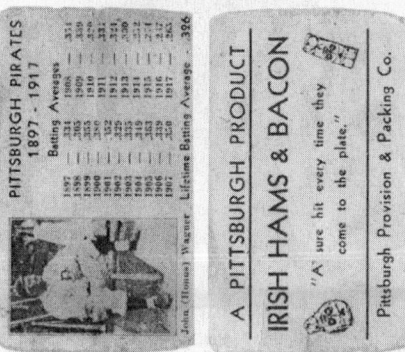

The attributed date is totally arbitrary, based on the photo shown. Also unknown are the scope of the issue and its manner of distribution. Hobby history would suggest the card was created to promote Wagner's ties to the meat company as a spokesman, or perhaps the card was created for Wagner to distribute at appearances on behalf of the packing company. The black-and-white cards measures about 4" x 2-1/2" and is printed on rather thin cardboard. It is not known whether similar cards exist for other players.

	NM	EX	VG
Honus Wagner	400.00	200.00	120.00

1936 Pittsburgh Sun-Telegraph Sport Stamps

Similar to several contemporary issues, the Sport Stamps were printed in a single edition of the daily newspaper. Thirteen players were printed for each of the 16 Major League teams. About 2" x 3", depending on the length of the biography and how well they were cut off the paper, they are printed in black-and-white. A tightly cropped player portrait is centered on a 1-3/4" x 2-1/4" stamp design with the paper's name above and the player's name, position and team below. This checklist is incomplete.

		NM	EX	VG
Complete Set (208):		12.00	6.00	3.50
Common Player:				
(1)	Ralph Birkofer	12.00	6.00	3.50
(2)	Cy Blanton	12.00	6.00	3.50
(3)	Bill Brubaker	12.00	6.00	3.50
(4)	Guy Bush	12.00	6.00	3.50
(5)	Ty Cobb	25.00	12.50	7.50
(6)	Jerome "Dizzy" Dean	25.00	12.50	7.50
(7)	Joe DiMaggio	75.00	37.00	22.00
(8)	Hank Greenberg	25.00	12.50	7.50
(9)	Waite Hoyt	20.00	10.00	6.00
(10)	Carl Hubbell	20.00	10.00	6.00
(11)	Woody Jensen	12.00	6.00	3.50
(12)	Red Lucas	12.00	6.00	3.50
(13)	Joe Medwick	20.00	10.00	6.00
(13)	Tommy Padden	12.00	6.00	3.50
(14)	Casey Stengel	20.00	10.00	6.00
(15)	Clarence Strass	12.00	6.00	3.50
(16)	Gus Suhr	12.00	6.00	3.50
(17)	Bill Swift	12.00	6.00	3.50
(18)	John Tising	12.00	6.00	3.50
(19)	Al Todd	12.00	6.00	3.50
(20)	Pie Traynor	20.00	10.00	6.00
(21)	Honus Wagner	25.00	12.50	7.50
(22)	Lloyd Waner	20.00	10.00	6.00
(23)	Paul Waner	20.00	10.00	6.00
(24)	Jim Weaver	12.00	6.00	3.50
(25)	Floyd Young	12.00	6.00	3.50

1954 Plankinton Milwaukee Braves Playing Tips

This set of "How to Play Better Baseball" poster booklets was apparently distributed in packages of hot dogs on a regional basis. Folded, the booklet measures 2-7/8" x 4-3/8" and has a black-and-white player portrait photo with a red background. When opened, the booklet forms an 11" x 17" poster offering big league tips from Braves players. The tips are well illustrated with many photos. There is a booklet for each position as well as one for right- and left-handed pitchers, a coach and even a team trainer.

		NM	EX	VG
Complete Set (12):		800.00	400.00	240.00
Common Player:		75.00	37.50	22.50
1	Joe Adcock	90.00	45.00	27.50
2	Danny O'Connell	75.00	37.50	22.50
3	Eddie Mathews	150.00	75.00	45.00
4	Johnny Logan	75.00	37.50	22.50
5	Bobby Thomson	90.00	45.00	27.50
6	Bill Bruton	75.00	37.50	22.50
7	Andy Pafko	75.00	37.50	22.50
8	Del Crandall	75.00	37.50	22.50
9	Warren Spahn	150.00	75.00	45.00
10	Gene Conley	75.00	37.50	22.50
11	Charlie Grimm	75.00	37.50	22.50
12	Joe Taylor	75.00	37.50	22.50

1939 Play Ball Samples

Each of the first 115 cards in the 1939 Play Ball set can be found with red overprinting on the back indicating sample card status. The overprint reads: "FREE / SAMPLE CARD / GET YOUR PICTURES OF / LEADING BASEBALL PLAYERS. / THREE PICTURE CARDS PACKED / IN EACH PACKAGE OF / "PLAY BALL

AMERICA" / BUBBLE GUM. / AT YOUR CANDY STORE / 1c." Collectors will pay a small premium for a type card of a common player. Sample cards of most star players sell for about double the price of the regular-issue cards, while DiMaggio and Williams samples sell for about the same price as their regular-issue cards.

		NM	EX	VG
Common Player:		35.00	17.50	10.00
26	Joe DiMaggio	1,300	650.00	390.00
92	Ted Williams	1,400	700.00	420.00

1939 Play Ball (R334)

With the issue of this card set by Gum Inc., a new era of baseball cards was born. Although the cards are black-and-white, the photos on front are of better quality than previously seen, and the 2-1/2" x 3-1/8" size was larger than virtually all of the tobacco and caramel cards of the early 20th Century. Card backs feature full player names, "Joseph Paul DiMaggio" instead of "Joe DiMaggio" and extensive biographies. Players are listed here by their most commonly used name. There are 161 cards in the set; card #126 was never issued. The complete set price does not include all back variations found in the low-numbered series. Many of the cards between #2-115 (indicated with an asterisk) can be found with the player name either in all capital letters, or in both upper- and lower-case letters. Minor differences in typography, along with variations in details of the biographical data, or within the wording of the career summary may be found on these cards that exist in two versions. No premium currently attaches to either version, though the cards with name in upper- and lower-case are somewhat scarcer.

		NM	EX	VG
Complete Set (161):		10,000	4,750	2,750
Common Player (1-115):		25.00	12.50	7.50
Common Player (116-162):		55.00	27.50	16.50
1	Jake Powell	135.00	15.00	7.50
2	Lee Grissom	25.00	12.50	7.50
3	Red Ruffing (*)	100.00	50.00	30.00
4	Eldon Auker (*)	25.00	12.50	7.50
5	Luke Sewell (*)	25.00	12.50	7.50
6	Leo Durocher (*)	100.00	50.00	30.00
7	Bobby Doerr (*)	100.00	50.00	30.00
8	Cotton Pippen	25.00	12.50	7.50
9	Jim Tobin (*)	25.00	12.50	7.50
10	Jimmie DeShong	25.00	12.50	7.50
11	Johnny Rizzo	25.00	12.50	7.50
12	Hersh Martin	25.00	12.50	7.50
13	Luke Hamlin (*)	25.00	12.50	7.50
14	Jim Tabor (*)	25.00	12.50	7.50
15	Paul Derringer (*)	25.00	12.50	7.50
16	Johnny Peacock	25.00	12.50	7.50
17	Emerson Dickman	25.00	12.50	7.50
18	Harry Danning (*)	25.00	12.50	7.50
19	Paul Dean	50.00	25.00	15.00
20	Joe Heving	25.00	12.50	7.50
21	Dutch Leonard (*)	25.00	12.50	7.50
22	Bucky Walters (*)	25.00	12.50	7.50
23	Burgess Whitehead	25.00	12.50	7.50
24	Dick Coffman (*)	25.00	12.50	7.50
25	George Selkirk (*)	25.00	12.50	7.50
26	Joe DiMaggio (*)	1,400	575.00	300.00
27	Fritz Ostermueller (*)	25.00	12.50	7.50
28	Syl Johnson	25.00	12.50	7.50
29	Jack Wilson (*)	25.00	12.50	7.50
30	Bill Dickey (*)	175.00	85.00	55.00
31	Sammy West (*)	25.00	12.50	7.50
32	Bob Seeds	25.00	12.50	7.50
33	Del Young	25.00	12.50	7.50
34	Frank Demaree (*)	25.00	12.50	7.50
35	Bill Jurges (*)	25.00	12.50	7.50
36	Frank McCormick (*)	25.00	12.50	7.50
37	Spud Davis	25.00	12.50	7.50
38	Billy Myers (*)	25.00	12.50	7.50
39	Rick Ferrell (*)	100.00	50.00	30.00
40	Jim Bagby Jr.	25.00	12.50	7.50
41	Lon Warneke (*)	25.00	12.50	7.50
42	Arndt Jorgens	25.00	12.50	7.50
43	Mel Almada	35.00	17.50	10.00
44	Don Heffner	25.00	12.50	7.50
45	Pinky May (*)	25.00	12.50	7.50
46	Morrie Arnovich (*)	40.00	20.00	12.00
47	Buddy Lewis (*)	25.00	12.50	7.50
48	Lefty Gomez (*)	100.00	50.00	30.00
49	Eddie Miller	25.00	12.50	7.50
50	Charlie Gehringer (*)	110.00	55.00	35.00
51	Mel Ott (*)	135.00	65.00	40.00
52	Tommy Henrich (*)	60.00	30.00	18.00
53	Carl Hubbell (*)	125.00	65.00	35.00
54	Harry Gumbert (*)	25.00	12.50	7.50
55	Arky Vaughan (*)	100.00	50.00	30.00

56	Hank Greenberg (*)	250.00	125.00	75.00
57	Buddy Hassett (*)	25.00	12.50	7.50
58	Lou Chiozza	25.00	12.50	7.50
59	Ken Chase	25.00	12.50	7.50
60	Schoolboy Rowe (*)	25.00	12.50	7.50
61	Tony Cuccinello (*)	25.00	12.50	7.50
62	Tom Carey	25.00	12.50	7.50
63	Heinie Mueller	25.00	12.50	7.50
64	Wally Moses (*)	25.00	12.50	7.50
65	Harry Craft (*)	25.00	12.50	7.50
66	Jimmy Ripple	25.00	12.50	7.50
67	Eddie Joost	25.00	12.50	7.50
68	Fred Sington	25.00	12.50	7.50
69	Elbie Fletcher	25.00	12.50	7.50
70	Fred Frankhouse	25.00	12.50	7.50
71	Monte Pearson (*)	25.00	12.50	7.50
72	Debs Garms (*)	25.00	12.50	7.50
73	Hal Schumacher (*)	25.00	12.50	7.50
74	Cookie Lavagetto (*)	25.00	12.50	7.50
75	Frenchy Bordagaray (*)	25.00	12.50	7.50
76	Goody Rosen	40.00	20.00	12.00
77	Lew Riggs	25.00	12.50	7.50
78	Moose Solters (*)	25.00	12.50	7.50
79	Joe Moore (*)	25.00	12.50	7.50
80	Pete Fox (*)	25.00	12.50	7.50
81	Babe Dahlgren (*)	25.00	12.50	7.50
82	Chuck Klein (*)	100.00	50.00	30.00
83	Gus Suhr (*)	25.00	12.50	7.50
84	Skeeter Newsome	25.00	12.50	7.50
85	Johnny Cooney (*)	25.00	12.50	7.50
86	Dolph Camilli (*)	25.00	12.50	7.50
87	Milt Shoffner	25.00	12.50	7.50
88	Charlie Keller	35.00	17.50	10.00
89	Lloyd Waner (*)	100.00	50.00	30.00
90	Bob Klinger (*)	25.00	12.50	7.50
91	Jack Knott (*)	25.00	12.50	7.50
92	Ted Williams (*)	2,100	1,000	500.00
93	Charley Gelbert (*)	25.00	12.50	7.50
94	Heinie Manush	100.00	50.00	30.00
95	Whit Wyatt (*)	25.00	12.50	7.50
96	Babe Phelps (*)	25.00	12.50	7.50
97	Bob Johnson (*)	25.00	12.50	7.50
98	Pinky Whitney (*)	25.00	12.50	7.50
99	Wally Berger (*)	25.00	12.50	7.50
100	Buddy Myer (*)	25.00	12.50	7.50
101	Doc Cramer (*)	25.00	12.50	7.50
102	Pep Young (*)	25.00	12.50	7.50
103	Moe Berg	140.00	75.00	45.00
104	Tommy Bridges (*)	25.00	12.50	7.50
105	Eric McNair (*)	25.00	12.50	7.50
106	Dolly Stark	50.00	25.00	15.00
107	Joe Vosmik	25.00	12.50	7.50
108	Frankie Hayes (*)	25.00	12.50	7.50
109	Myril Hoag (*)	25.00	12.50	7.50
110	Freddie Fitzsimmons	25.00	12.50	7.50
111	Van Lingle Mungo (*)	35.00	17.50	10.00
112	Paul Waner (*)	100.00	50.00	30.00
113	Al Schacht	50.00	25.00	15.00
114	Cecil Travis (*)	25.00	12.50	7.50
115	Red Kress (*)	25.00	12.50	7.50
116	Gene Desautels	55.00	27.50	16.50
117	Wayne Ambler	55.00	27.50	16.50
118	Lynn Nelson	55.00	27.50	16.50
119	Will Hershberger	55.00	27.50	16.50
120	Rabbit Warstler	55.00	27.50	16.50
121	Bill Posedel	55.00	27.50	16.50
122	George McQuinn	55.00	27.50	16.50
123	Peaches Davis	55.00	27.50	16.50
124	Jumbo Brown	55.00	27.50	16.50
125	Cliff Melton	55.00	27.50	16.50
126	Not issued			
127	Gil Brack	55.00	27.50	16.50
128	Joe Bowman	55.00	27.50	16.50
129	Bill Swift	55.00	27.50	16.50
130	Bill Brubaker	55.00	27.50	16.50
131	Mort Cooper	55.00	27.50	16.50
132	Jimmy Brown	55.00	27.50	16.50
133	Lynn Myers	55.00	27.50	16.50
134	Tot Pressnell	55.00	27.50	16.50
135	Mickey Owen	55.00	27.50	16.50
136	Roy Bell	55.00	27.50	16.50
137	Pete Appleton	55.00	27.50	16.50
138	George Case	55.00	27.50	16.50
139	Vito Tamulis	55.00	27.50	16.50
140	Ray Hayworth	55.00	27.50	16.50
141	Pete Coscarart	55.00	27.50	16.50
142	Ira Hutchinson	55.00	27.50	16.50
143	Earl Averill	225.00	110.00	65.00
144	Zeke Bonura	55.00	27.50	16.50
145	Hugh Mulcahy	55.00	27.50	16.50
146	Tom Sunkel	55.00	27.50	16.50
147	George Coffman	55.00	27.50	16.50
148	Bill Trotter	55.00	27.50	16.50
149	Max West	55.00	27.50	16.50
150	Jim Walkup	55.00	27.50	16.50
151	Hugh Casey	55.00	27.50	16.50
152	Roy Weatherly	55.00	27.50	16.50
153	Dizzy Trout	55.00	27.50	16.50
154	Johnny Hudson	55.00	27.50	16.50
155	Jimmy Outlaw	55.00	27.50	16.50
156	Ray Berres	55.00	27.50	16.50
157	Don Padgett	55.00	27.50	16.50
158	Bud Thomas	55.00	27.50	16.50
159	Red Evans	55.00	27.50	16.50
160	Gene Moore Jr.	55.00	27.50	16.50
161	Lonny Frey	60.00	32.50	16.50
162	Whitey Moore	200.00	30.00	17.50

1940 Play Ball (R335)

Following the success of its initial effort in 1939, Gum Inc. issued a bigger and better set in 1940. The 240 black-and-white cards are once again in 2-1/2" x 3-1/8" size, but the front photos are enclosed by a frame with the player's name. Backs again offer extensive biographies and are dated. A number of

"JOE MARTY"

216. JOSEPH ANTON MARTY — Outfielder, Philadelphia Phillies

former stars were issued along with contemporary players, and many Hall of Famers are included. The final 60 cards of the set are more difficult to obtain.

No	Player	NM	EX	VG
	Complete Set (240):	22,500	11,000	6,500
	Common Player (1-180):	35.00	17.50	10.00
	Common Player (181-240):	60.00	30.00	18.00
1	Joe DiMaggio	3,000	1,100	675.00
2	"Art" Jorgens	35.00	17.50	10.00
3	"Babe" Dahlgren	35.00	17.50	10.00
4	"Tommy" Henrich	60.00	30.00	18.00
5	"Monte" Pearson	35.00	17.50	10.00
6	"Lefty" Gomez	130.00	65.00	40.00
7	"Bill" Dickey	160.00	80.00	45.00
8	"Twinkletoes" Selkirk	35.00	17.50	10.00
9	"Charley" Keller	35.00	17.50	10.00
10	"Red" Ruffing	130.00	65.00	40.00
11	"Jake" Powell	35.00	17.50	10.00
12	"Johnny" Schulte	35.00	17.50	10.00
13	"Jack" Knott	35.00	17.50	10.00
14	"Rabbit" McNair	35.00	17.50	10.00
15	George Case	35.00	17.50	10.00
16	Cecil Travis	35.00	17.50	10.00
17	"Buddy" Myer	35.00	17.50	10.00
18	"Charley" Gelbert	35.00	17.50	10.00
19	Ken Chase	35.00	17.50	10.00
20	"Buddy" Lewis	35.00	17.50	10.00
21	"Rick" Ferrell	130.00	65.00	40.00
22	"Sammy" West	35.00	17.50	10.00
23	"Dutch" Leonard	35.00	17.50	10.00
24	Frank "Blimp" Hayes	35.00	17.50	10.00
25	"Cherokee" Bob Johnson	35.00	17.50	10.00
26	"Wally" Moses	35.00	17.50	10.00
27	"Ted" Williams	1,950	550.00	280.00
28	"Gene" Desautels	35.00	17.50	10.00
29	"Doc" Cramer	35.00	17.50	10.00
30	"Moe" Berg	160.00	80.00	45.00
31	Jack Wilson	35.00	17.50	10.00
32	"Jim" Bagby	35.00	17.50	10.00
33	"Fritz" Ostermueller	35.00	17.50	10.00
34	John Peacock	35.00	17.50	10.00
35	"Joe" Heving	35.00	17.50	10.00
36	"Jim" Tabor	35.00	17.50	10.00
37	Emerson Dickman	35.00	17.50	10.00
38	"Bobby" Doerr	130.00	65.00	40.00
39	"Tom" Carey	35.00	17.50	10.00
40	"Hank" Greenberg	450.00	225.00	135.00
41	"Charley" Gehringer	180.00	90.00	55.00
42	"Bud" Thomas	35.00	17.50	10.00
43	Pete Fox	35.00	17.50	10.00
44	"Dizzy" Trout	35.00	17.50	10.00
45	"Red" Kress	35.00	17.50	10.00
46	Earl Averill	130.00	65.00	40.00
47	"Old Os" Vitt	35.00	17.50	10.00
48	"Luke" Sewell	35.00	17.50	10.00
49	"Stormy Weather" Weatherly	35.00	17.50	10.00
50	"Hal" Trosky	35.00	17.50	10.00
51	"Don" Heffner	35.00	17.50	10.00
52	Myril Hoag	35.00	17.50	10.00
53	"Mac" McQuinn	35.00	17.50	10.00
54	"Bill" Trotter	35.00	17.50	10.00
55	"Slick" Coffman	35.00	17.50	10.00
56	"Eddie" Miller	35.00	17.50	10.00
57	Max West	35.00	17.50	10.00
58	"Bill" Posedel	35.00	17.50	10.00
59	"Rabbit" Warstler	35.00	17.50	10.00
60	John Cooney	35.00	17.50	10.00
61	"Tony" Cuccinello	35.00	17.50	10.00
62	"Buddy" Hassett	35.00	17.50	10.00
63	"Pete" Cascarart (Coscarart)	35.00	17.50	10.00
64	"Van" Mungo	40.00	20.00	12.00
65	"Fitz" Fitzsimmons	35.00	17.50	10.00
66	"Babe" Phelps	35.00	17.50	10.00
67	"Whit" Wyatt	35.00	17.50	10.00
68	"Dolph" Camilli	35.00	17.50	10.00
69	"Cookie" Lavagetto	35.00	17.50	10.00
70	"Hot Potato" Hamlin	35.00	17.50	10.00
71	Mel Almada	40.00	20.00	12.00
72	"Chuck" Dressen	35.00	17.50	10.00
73	"Bucky" Walters	35.00	17.50	10.00
74	"Duke" Derringer	35.00	17.50	10.00
75	"Buck" McCormick	35.00	17.50	10.00
76	"Lonny" Frey	35.00	17.50	10.00
77	"Bill" Hershberger	60.00	30.00	18.00
78	"Lew" Riggs	35.00	17.50	10.00
79	"Wildfire" Craft	35.00	17.50	10.00
80	"Bill" Myers	35.00	17.50	10.00
81	"Wally" Berger	35.00	17.50	10.00
82	"Hank" Gowdy	35.00	17.50	10.00
83	"Clif" Melton (Cliff)	35.00	17.50	10.00
84	"Jo-Jo" Moore	35.00	17.50	10.00
85	"Hal" Schumacher	35.00	17.50	10.00
86	Harry Gumbert	35.00	17.50	10.00
87	Carl Hubbell	160.00	80.00	45.00
88	"Mel" Ott	225.00	110.00	65.00
89	"Bill" Jurges	35.00	17.50	10.00
90	Frank Demaree	35.00	17.50	10.00
91	Bob "Suitcase" Seeds	35.00	17.50	10.00
92	"Whitey" Whitehead	35.00	17.50	10.00
93	Harry "The Horse" Danning	35.00	17.50	10.00
94	"Gus" Suhr	35.00	17.50	10.00
95	"Mul" Mulcahy	35.00	17.50	10.00
96	"Heinie" Mueller	35.00	17.50	10.00
97	"Morry" Arnovich	35.00	17.50	10.00
98	"Pinky" May	35.00	17.50	10.00
99	"Syl" Johnson	35.00	17.50	10.00
100	"Hersh" Martin	35.00	17.50	10.00
101	"Del" Young	35.00	17.50	10.00
102	"Chuck" Klein	130.00	65.00	40.00
103	"Elbie" Fletcher	35.00	17.50	10.00
104	"Big Poison" Waner	130.00	65.00	40.00
105	"Little Poison" Waner	130.00	65.00	40.00
106	"Pep" Young	35.00	17.50	10.00
107	"Arky" Vaughan	130.00	65.00	40.00
108	"Johnny" Rizzo	35.00	17.50	10.00
109	Don Padgett	35.00	17.50	10.00
110	"Tom" Sunkel	35.00	17.50	10.00
111	"Mickey" Owen	35.00	17.50	10.00
112	"Jimmy" Brown	35.00	17.50	10.00
113	"Mort" Cooper	35.00	17.50	10.00
114	"Lon" Warneke	35.00	17.50	10.00
115	"Mike" Gonzales (Gonzalez)	40.00	20.00	12.00
116	"Al" Schacht	60.00	30.00	18.00
117	"Dolly" Stark	75.00	37.50	22.50
118	"Schoolboy" Hoyt	130.00	65.00	40.00
119	"Ol Pete" Alexander	130.00	65.00	40.00
120	Walter "Big Train" Johnson	275.00	135.00	80.00
121	Atley Donald	35.00	17.50	10.00
122	"Sandy" Sundra	35.00	17.50	10.00
123	"Hildy" Hildebrand	35.00	17.50	10.00
124	"Colonel" Combs	120.00	60.00	35.00
125	"Art" Fletcher	35.00	17.50	10.00
126	"Jake" Solters	35.00	17.50	10.00
127	"Muddy" Ruel	35.00	17.50	10.00
128	"Pete" Appleton	35.00	17.50	10.00
129	"Bucky" Harris	120.00	60.00	35.00
130	"Deerfoot" Milan	35.00	17.50	10.00
131	"Zeke" Bonura	35.00	17.50	10.00
132	Connie Mack	120.00	60.00	35.00
133	"Jimmie" Foxx	300.00	150.00	90.00
134	"Joe" Cronin	130.00	65.00	40.00
135	"Line Drive" Nelson	35.00	17.50	10.00
136	"Cotton" Pippen	35.00	17.50	10.00
137	"Bing" Miller	35.00	17.50	10.00
138	"Beau" Bell	35.00	17.50	10.00
139	Elden Auker (Eldon)	35.00	17.50	10.00
140	"Dick" Coffman	35.00	17.50	10.00
141	"Casey" Stengel	175.00	85.00	50.00
142	"Highpockets" Kelly	120.00	60.00	35.00
143	"Gene" Moore	35.00	17.50	10.00
144	"Joe" Vosmik	35.00	17.50	10.00
145	"Vito" Tamulis	35.00	17.50	10.00
146	"Tot" Pressnell	35.00	17.50	10.00
147	"Johnny" Hudson	35.00	17.50	10.00
148	"Hugh" Casey	35.00	17.50	10.00
149	"Pinky" Shoffner	35.00	17.50	10.00
150	"Whitey" Moore	35.00	17.50	10.00
151	Edwin Joost	35.00	17.50	10.00
152	Jimmy Wilson	35.00	17.50	10.00
153	"Bill" McKechnie	120.00	60.00	35.00
154	"Jumbo" Brown	35.00	17.50	10.00
155	"Ray" Hayworth	35.00	17.50	10.00
156	"Daffy" Dean	65.00	32.50	20.00
157	"Lou" Chiozza	35.00	17.50	10.00
158	"Stonewall" Jackson	120.00	60.00	35.00
159	"Pancho" Snyder	35.00	17.50	10.00
160	"Hans" Lobert	35.00	17.50	10.00
161	"Debs" Garms	35.00	17.50	10.00
162	Joe Bowman	35.00	17.50	10.00
163	"Spud" Davis	35.00	17.50	10.00
164	"Ray" Berres	35.00	17.50	10.00
165	"Bob" Klinger	35.00	17.50	10.00
166	"Bill" Brubaker	35.00	17.50	10.00
167	"Frankie" Frisch	130.00	65.00	40.00
168	"Honus" Wagner	300.00	150.00	90.00
169	"Gabby" Street	35.00	17.50	10.00
170	"Tris" Speaker	135.00	70.00	40.00
171	Harry Heilmann	120.00	60.00	35.00
172	"Chief" Bender	120.00	60.00	35.00
173	"Larry" Lajoie	120.00	60.00	35.00
174	"Johnny" Evers	120.00	60.00	35.00
175	"Christy" Mathewson	250.00	125.00	75.00
176	"Heinie" Manush	130.00	65.00	40.00
177	Frank "Homerun" Baker	120.00	60.00	35.00
178	Max Carey	120.00	60.00	35.00
179	George Sisler	120.00	60.00	35.00
180	"Mickey" Cochrane	130.00	65.00	40.00
181	"Spud" Chandler	60.00	30.00	18.00
182	"Knick" Knickerbocker	60.00	30.00	18.00
183	Marvin Breuer	60.00	30.00	18.00
184	"Mule" Haas	60.00	30.00	18.00
185	"Joe" Kuhel	60.00	30.00	18.00
186	Taft Wright	60.00	30.00	18.00
187	"Jimmy" Dykes	60.00	30.00	18.00
188	"Joe" Krakauskas	60.00	30.00	18.00
189	"Jim" Bloodworth	60.00	30.00	18.00
190	"Charley" Berry	60.00	30.00	18.00
191	John Babich	60.00	30.00	18.00
192	"Dick" Siebert	60.00	30.00	18.00
193	"Chubby" Dean	60.00	30.00	18.00
194	Sam Chapman	60.00	30.00	18.00
195	"Dee" Miles	60.00	30.00	18.00
196	"Nonny" Nonnenkamp	60.00	30.00	18.00
197	"Lou" Finney	60.00	30.00	18.00
198	"Denny" Galehouse	60.00	30.00	18.00
199	"Pinky" Higgins	60.00	30.00	18.00
200	"Soupy" Campbell	60.00	30.00	18.00
201	Barney McCosky	60.00	30.00	18.00
202	Al Milnar	60.00	30.00	18.00
203	"Bad News" Hale	60.00	30.00	18.00
204	Harry Eisenstat	75.00	37.50	22.50
205	"Rollie" Hemsley	60.00	30.00	18.00
206	"Chet" Laabs	60.00	30.00	18.00
207	"Gus" Mancuso	60.00	30.00	18.00
208	Lee Gamble	60.00	30.00	18.00
209	"Hy" Vandenberg	60.00	30.00	18.00
210	"Bill" Lohrman	60.00	30.00	18.00
211	"Pop" Joiner	60.00	30.00	18.00
212	"Babe" Young	60.00	30.00	18.00
213	John Rucker	60.00	30.00	18.00
214	"Ken" O'Dea	60.00	30.00	18.00
215	"Johnnie" McCarthy	60.00	30.00	18.00
216	"Joe" Marty	60.00	30.00	18.00
217	Walter Beck	60.00	30.00	18.00
218	"Wally" Millies	60.00	30.00	18.00
219	Russ Bauers	60.00	30.00	18.00
220	Mace Brown	60.00	30.00	18.00
221	Lee Handley	60.00	30.00	18.00
222	"Max" Butcher	60.00	30.00	18.00
223	Hugh "Ee-Yah" Jennings	140.00	70.00	40.00
224	"Pie" Traynor	140.00	70.00	40.00
225	"Shoeless Joe" Jackson	2,900	1,250	700.00
226	Harry Hooper	140.00	70.00	40.00
227	"Pop" Haines	140.00	70.00	40.00
228	"Charley" Grimm	60.00	30.00	18.00
229	"Buck" Herzog	60.00	30.00	18.00
230	"Red" Faber	140.00	70.00	40.00
231	"Dolf" Luque	75.00	37.50	22.50
232	"Goose" Goslin	140.00	70.00	40.00
233	"Moose" Earnshaw	60.00	30.00	18.00
234	Frank "Husk" Chance	140.00	70.00	40.00
235	John J. McGraw	140.00	70.00	40.00
236	"Sunny Jim" Bottomley	140.00	70.00	40.00
237	"Wee Willie" Keeler	140.00	70.00	40.00
238	"Poosh 'Em Up Tony" Lazzeri	175.00	85.00	50.00
239	George Uhle	60.00	30.00	18.00
240	"Bill" Atwood	120.00	40.00	20.00

1940 Play Ball Colorized Proofs

"VAN" MUNGO — 64. VAN LINGLE MUNGO — Pitcher, Brooklyn Dodgers

Probably created as part of the process which resulted in the introduction of color cards in 1941, these 1940 Play Balls have very muted color tones. It is unknown how many other players' cards from 1940 PB were created or survive in this form. The Mungo and Dean cards, authenticated and graded Excellent by SGC, sold in a 12/04 auction for $2,221.

No	Player
64	"Van" Mungo
76	"Lonny" Frey
90	Frank Demaree
141	"Casey" Stengel
156	"Daffy" Dean

1941 Play Ball (R336)

"TED" WILLIAMS — 14. THEODORE SAMUEL WILLIAMS — Outfielder, Boston Red Sox

While the backs are quite similar to the black-and-white cards Gum Inc. issued in 1940, the card fronts in the 1941 set are printed in color. Many of the card photos, however, are just colorized versions of the player's 1940 card. The cards are still in the 2-1/2" x 3-1/8" size, but only 72 cards are included in the set. Card numbers 49-72 are rarer than the lower-numbered cards. The cards were printed in sheets of 12, and can still be found that way. Cards #1-48 can be found with or without the 1941 copyright date at lower-left; cards 49-72 are not found with the 1941 date. Some believe this indicates that a revised (no copyright) version of the low numbers and all of the high numbers were issued in 1942.

No	Player	NM	EX	VG
	Complete Set (72):	15,000	7,500	4,500
	Common Player (1-48):	75.00	37.50	22.50
	Common Player (49-72):	100.00	50.00	30.00
1	"Eddie" Miller	340.00	60.00	25.00
2	Max West	110.00	37.50	22.50
3	"Bucky" Walters	75.00	37.50	22.50
4	"Duke" Derringer	75.00	37.50	22.50
5	"Buck" McCormick	75.00	37.50	22.50
6	Carl Hubbell	260.00	130.00	75.00
7	"The Horse" Danning	75.00	37.50	22.50
8	"Mel" Ott	340.00	170.00	100.00
9	"Pinky" May	75.00	37.50	22.50

10	"Arky" Vaughan	190.00	95.00	55.00
11	Debs Garms	75.00	37.50	22.50
12	"Jimmy" Brown	75.00	37.50	22.50
13	"Jimmie" Foxx	500.00	250.00	150.00
14	"Ted" Williams	2,200	1,000	400.00
15	"Joe" Cronin	190.00	95.00	55.00
16	"Hal" Trosky	75.00	37.50	22.50
17	"Stormy" Weatherly	75.00	37.50	22.50
18	"Hank" Greenberg	500.00	250.00	150.00
19	"Charley" Gehringer	250.00	125.00	75.00
20	"Red" Ruffing	190.00	95.00	55.00
21	"Charlie" Keller	150.00	75.00	45.00
22	"Indian Bob" Johnson	75.00	37.50	22.50
23	"Mac" McQuinn	75.00	37.50	22.50
24	"Dutch" Leonard	75.00	37.50	22.50
25	"Gene" Moore	75.00	37.50	22.50
26	Harry "Gunboat" Gumbert	75.00	37.50	22.50
27	"Babe" Young	75.00	37.50	22.50
28	"Joe" Marty	75.00	37.50	22.50
29	Jack Wilson	75.00	37.50	22.50
30	"Lou" Finney	75.00	37.50	22.50
31	"Joe" Kuhel	75.00	37.50	22.50
32	Taft Wright	75.00	37.50	22.50
33	"Happy" Milnar	75.00	37.50	22.50
34	"Rollie" Hemsley	75.00	37.50	22.50
35	"Pinky" Higgins	75.00	37.50	22.50
36	Barney McCosky	75.00	37.50	22.50
37	"Soupy" Campbell	75.00	37.50	22.50
38	Atley Donald	75.00	37.50	22.50
39	"Tommy" Henrich	150.00	75.00	45.00
40	"Johnny" Babich	75.00	37.50	22.50
41	Frank "Blimp" Hayes	75.00	37.50	22.50
42	"Wally" Moses	75.00	37.50	22.50
43	Albert "Bronk" Brancato	75.00	37.50	22.50
44	Sam Chapman	75.00	37.50	22.50
45	Elden Auker (Eldon)	75.00	37.50	22.50
46	"Sid" Hudson	75.00	37.50	22.50
47	"Buddy" Lewis	75.00	37.50	22.50
48	Cecil Travis	75.00	37.50	22.50
49	"Babe" Dahlgren	100.00	50.00	30.00
50	"Johnny" Cooney	100.00	50.00	30.00
51	"Dolph" Camilli	100.00	50.00	30.00
52	Kirby Higbe	100.00	50.00	30.00
53	Luke "Hot Potato" Hamlin	100.00	50.00	30.00
54	"Pee Wee" Reese	600.00	300.00	180.00
55	"Whit" Wyatt	100.00	50.00	30.00
56	"Vandy" Vander Meer	100.00	50.00	30.00
57	"Moe" Arnovich	125.00	65.00	35.00
58	"Frank" Demaree	100.00	50.00	30.00
59	"Bill" Jurges	100.00	50.00	30.00
60	"Chuck" Klein	300.00	150.00	90.00
61	"Vince" DiMaggio	300.00	150.00	90.00
62	"Elbie" Fletcher	100.00	50.00	30.00
63	"Dom" DiMaggio	400.00	200.00	120.00
64	"Bobby" Doerr	300.00	150.00	90.00
65	"Tommy" Bridges	100.00	50.00	30.00
66	Harland Clift (Harland)	100.00	50.00	30.00
67	"Walt" Judnich	100.00	50.00	30.00
68	"Jack" Knott	100.00	50.00	30.00
69	George Case	100.00	50.00	30.00
70	"Bill" Dickey	350.00	175.00	100.00
71	"Joe" DiMaggio	3,000	1,300	700.00
72	"Lefty" Gomez	425.00	180.00	60.00

1941 Play Ball Paper Version

As cardboard became a critical commodity during the months prior to the United States' entry into WWII, Play Ball experimented by issuing a version of the first 24 cards in the 1941 set on paper sheets of 12, comprising the color-printed layer of the regular cards and the backs. These paper versions, understandably, did not stand up to handling as well as the cardboard cards and survivors are much scarcer today.

		NM	EX	VG
Complete Set (24):		10,000	5,000	3,000
Common Player:		160.00	55.00	30.00
Complete Sheet 1-12:		3,000	700.00	325.00
Complete Sheet 13-24:		7,000	3,500	2,100
1	Eddie Miller	160.00	55.00	30.00
2	Max West	160.00	55.00	30.00
3	Bucky Walters	160.00	55.00	30.00
4	"Duke" Derringer	160.00	55.00	30.00
5	"Buck" McCormick	160.00	55.00	30.00
6	Carl Hubbell	600.00	210.00	120.00
7	"The Horse" Danning	160.00	55.00	30.00
8	Mel Ott	650.00	225.00	130.00
9	"Pinky" May	160.00	55.00	30.00
10	"Arky" Vaughan	400.00	140.00	80.00
11	Debs Garms	160.00	55.00	30.00
12	"Jimmy" Brown	160.00	55.00	30.00
13	Jimmie Foxx	1,100	385.00	220.00
14	Ted Williams	3,200	1,125	640.00

15	Joe Cronin	400.00	140.00	80.00
16	Hal Trosky	160.00	55.00	30.00
17	Roy Weatherly	160.00	55.00	30.00
18	Hank Greenberg	1,100	385.00	220.00
19	Charley Gehringer	600.00	210.00	120.00
20	"Red" Ruffing	400.00	140.00	80.00
21	Charlie Keller	180.00	65.00	35.00
22	Bob Johnson	160.00	55.00	30.00
23	"Mac" McQuinn	160.00	55.00	30.00
24	Dutch Leonard	160.00	55.00	30.00

1976 Playboy Press Who Was Harry Steinfeldt?

(Babe Ruth)

This 12-card set was issued in 1976 by Playboy Press to promote author Bert Randolph Sugar's book "Who Was Harry Steinfeldt? & Other Baseball Trivia Questions." (Steinfeldt was the third baseman in the Cubs' famous infield that featured Hall of Famers Tinker, Evers and Chance). The black and white cards measure the standard 2-1/2" x 3-1/2" with a player photo on the front and a trivia question and ad for the book on the back.

		NM	EX	VG
Complete Set (12):		150.00	75.00	45.00
Common Player:		9.00	4.50	2.75
(1)	Frankie Baumholtz	9.00	4.50	2.75
(2)	Jim Bouton	12.00	6.00	3.50
(3)	Tony Conigliaro	9.00	4.50	2.75
(4)	Don Drysdale	17.50	8.75	5.25
(5)	Hank Greenberg	15.00	7.50	4.50
(6)	Walter Johnson	25.00	12.50	7.50
(7)	Billy Loes	9.00	4.50	2.75
(8)	Johnny Mize	15.00	7.50	4.50
(9)	Frank "Lefty" O'Doul	12.00	6.00	3.50
(10)	Babe Ruth	50.00	25.00	15.00
(11)	Johnny Sain	12.00	6.00	3.50
(12)	Jim Thorpe	40.00	20.00	12.00

1947 Pleetwood Slacks Jackie Robinson

The date of issue cited is conjectural. This card, about 5" x 8", depicts Jackie Robinson in a coat and tie in a black-and-white photo on front, along with a facsimile autograph. In a strip at bottom is his name and an endorsement for "Pleetwood Slacks." The back is blank. The card was probably used as an autograph vehicle for personal appearances by Robinson at clothing stores.

	NM	EX	VG
Jackie Robinson	600.00	300.00	180.00

1910-12 Plow Boy Tobacco

Plowboy Tobacco, a product of the Spaulding & Merrick Co., issued a set of cabinet-size cards in the Chicago area featuring members of the Cubs and White Sox. From the checklist, it appears the bulk of the set was originally issued in 1910 with a few additional cards appearing over the next several years. Measuring approximately 5-3/4" x 8", the Plow Boys feature sepia-toned player photos in poses not found on other tobacco issues. The player's name appears in the lower-left corner, while the team name appears in the lower-right. Two different backs are known.

 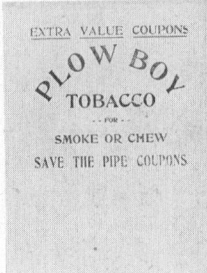

One consists of a simple advertisement for Plow Boy Tobacco, while a second, more difficult, variety includes a list of premiums available in exchange for coupons. The set is among the rarest of all 20th Century tobacco issues.

		NM	EX	VG
Common Player:		3,650	1,450	725.00
Premium Back: 1.5X				
(1)	Jimmy Archer	3,650	1,450	725.00
(2)	Ginger Beaumont	3,650	1,450	725.00
(3)	Lena Blackburne	3,650	1,450	725.00
(4)	Bruno Block	3,650	1,450	725.00
(5)	Ping Bodie	3,650	1,450	725.00
(6)	Mordecai Brown	5,500	2,200	1,100
(7)	Al Carson	3,650	1,450	725.00
(8)	Frank Chance	5,500	2,200	1,100
(9)	Ed Cicotte	5,250	2,100	1,050
(10)	King Cole	3,650	1,450	725.00
(11)	Shano Collins	3,650	1,450	725.00
(12)	George Davis	5,500	2,200	1,100
(13)	Patsy Dougherty	3,650	1,450	725.00
(14)	Johnny Evers	5,500	2,200	1,100
(15)	Chick Gandel (Gandil)	5,250	2,100	1,050
(16)	Ed Hahn	3,650	1,450	725.00
(17)	Solly Hoffman (Hofman)	3,650	1,450	725.00
(18)	Del Howard	3,650	1,450	725.00
(19)	Bill Jones	3,650	1,450	725.00
(20)	Johnny Kling	3,650	1,450	725.00
(21)	Rube Kroh	3,650	1,450	725.00
(22)	Frank Lange	3,650	1,450	725.00
(23)	Fred Luderus	3,650	1,450	725.00
(24)	Harry McIntyre (McIntire)	3,650	1,450	725.00
(25)	Ward Miller	3,650	1,450	725.00
(26)	Charlie Mullen	3,650	1,450	725.00
(27)	Tom Needham	3,650	1,450	725.00
(28)	Fred Olmstead	3,650	1,450	725.00
(29)	Orval Overall	3,650	1,450	725.00
(30)	Fred Parent	3,650	1,450	725.00
(31)	Fred Payne	3,650	1,450	725.00
(32)	Francis "Big Jeff" Pfeffer	3,650	1,450	725.00
(33)	Jake Pfeister	3,650	1,450	725.00
(34)	Billy Purtell	3,650	1,450	725.00
(35)	Ed Reulbach	3,650	1,450	725.00
(36)	Lew Richie	3,650	1,450	725.00
(37)	Jimmy Scheckard (Sheckard)	3,650	1,450	725.00
(38)	Wildfire Schulte	3,650	1,450	725.00
(39a)	Jim Scot (Name incorrect.)	3,650	1,450	725.00
(39b)	Jim Scott (Name correct.)	3,650	1,450	725.00
(40)	Frank Smith	3,650	1,450	725.00
(41)	Harry Steinfeldt	3,650	1,450	725.00
(42)	Billy Sullivan	3,650	1,450	725.00
(43)	Lee Tannehill	3,650	1,450	725.00
(44)	Joe Tinker	5,500	2,200	1,100
(45)	Ed Walsh	5,500	2,200	1,100
(46)	Doc White	3,650	1,450	725.00
(47)	Irv Young	3,650	1,450	725.00
(48)	Rollie Zeider	3,650	1,450	725.00
(49)	Heinie Zimmerman	3,650	1,450	725.00

1912 Plow's Candy (E300)

An extremely rare candy issue, cards in this 1912 set measure 3" x 4" and feature sepia-toned photos surrounded by a wide border. The player's name and team appear in the border below the photo, while the words "Plow's Candy Collection" appear at the top. The backs are blank. Not even known to exist until the late 1960s, this set has been assigned the designation of E300 and additions to the checklist continue to appear every few years.

	NM	EX	VG
Common Player:	3,000	1,500	900.00

		NM	EX	VG
(1)	Babe Adams	3,000	1,500	900.00
(2)	Home Run Baker	4,800	2,400	1,440
(3)	Cy Barger	3,000	1,500	900.00
(4)	Jack Barry	3,000	1,150	900.00
(5)	Johnny Bates	3,000	1,500	900.00
(7)	Joe Benz	3,000	1,150	900.00
(8)	Bill Berger (Bergen)	3,000	1,500	900.00
(9)	Roger Bresnahan	4,800	2,400	1,440
(10)	Mordecai Brown	4,800	2,400	1,440
(11)	Donie Bush	3,000	1,500	900.00
(12)	Bobby Byrne	3,000	1,500	900.00
(13)	Nixey Callahan	3,000	1,500	900.00
(14)	Hal Chase	4,500	2,250	1,350
(15)	Fred Clarke	4,800	2,400	1,440
(16)	Ty Cobb	40,000	16,500	9,900
(17)	King Cole	3,000	1,500	900.00
(18)	Eddie Collins	4,800	2,400	1,440
(19)	Jack Coombs	3,000	1,500	900.00
(20)	Bill Dahlen	3,000	1,500	900.00
(21)	Bert Daniels	3,000	1,500	900.00
(22)	Harry Davis	3,000	1,500	900.00
(23)	Jim Delehanty	3,000	1,500	900.00
(24)	Josh Devore	3,000	1,500	900.00
(25)	Wild Bill Donovan	3,000	1,500	900.00
(26)	Red Dooin	3,000	1,500	900.00
(27)	Larry Doyle	3,000	1,500	900.00
(28)	Johnny Evers	4,800	2,400	1,440
(29)	Russ Ford	3,000	1,500	900.00
(30)	Del Gainor	3,000	1,500	900.00
(31)	Vean Gregg	3,000	1,500	900.00
(32)	Bob Harmon	3,000	1,500	900.00
(33)	Arnold Hauser	3,000	1,500	900.00
(34)	Dick Hoblitzelle (Hoblitzell)	3,000	1,500	900.00
(35)	Solly Hofman	3,000	1,500	900.00
(36)	Miller Huggins	4,800	2,400	1,440
(37)	John Hummel	3,000	1,500	900.00
(38)	Walter Johnson	7,200	3,600	2,160
(39)	Johnny Kling	3,000	1,500	900.00
(41)	Nap Lajoie	5,400	2,700	1,620
(42)	Jack Lapp	3,000	1,500	900.00
(43)	Fred Luderus	3,000	1,500	900.00
(44)	Sherry Magee	3,000	1,500	900.00
(45)	Rube Marquard	4,800	2,400	1,440
(46)	Christy Mathewson	25,000	4,500	2,700
(47)	Stuffy McInnes (McInnis)	3,000	1,500	900.00
(48)	Larry McLean	3,000	1,500	900.00
(49)	Fred Merkle	3,000	1,500	900.00
(50)	Cy Morgan	3,000	1,500	900.00
(51)	George Moriarty	3,000	1,500	900.00
(52)	Mike Mowrey	3,000	1,500	900.00
(53)	Chief Myers (Meyers)	3,000	1,500	900.00
(54)	Rube Oldring	3,000	1,500	900.00
(55)	Marty O'Toole	3,000	1,500	900.00
(56)	Eddie Plank	5,400	2,700	1,620
(57)	Nap Rucker	3,000	1,500	900.00
(58)	Slim Sallee	3,000	1,500	900.00
(59)	Boss Schmidt	3,000	1,500	900.00
(60)	Jimmy Sheckard	3,000	1,500	900.00
(61)	Tris Speaker	5,400	2,700	1,620
(62)	Billy Sullivan	3,000	1,500	900.00
(63)	Ira Thomas	3,000	1,500	900.00
(64)	Joe Tinker	4,800	2,400	1,440
(65)	John Titus	3,000	1,500	900.00
(66)	Hippo Vaughan (Vaughn)	3,000	1,500	900.00
(67)	Honus Wagner	50,000	15,000	9,000
(68)	Ed Walsh	4,800	2,400	1,440
(69)	Bob Williams	3,000	1,500	900.00

1915 PM1 Ornate-Frame Pins

Little is known about these tiny (approximately 1-1/16" x 1") pins, such as who issued them, when and how they were distributed and how many are in the set. The pins feature a sepia-tone player photo surrounded by an ornate gilded metal frame. The player's name is usually printed in a black strip at the bottom of the photo. The pins were originally sold for 19 cents. Gaps have been left in the assigned numbering for future additions to the checklist.

		NM	EX	VG
Common Pin:		450.00	225.00	125.00
(1a)	Jimmy Archer	450.00	225.00	125.00
(1b)	Jimmy Archer (No name.)	575.00	285.00	175.00
(2)	Frank Baker	1,100	550.00	330.00
(3)	Jack Barry	450.00	225.00	135.00
(4)	Chief Bender (No name.)	1,100	550.00	330.00
(5)	Frank Chance	1,100	550.00	330.00
(6)	Ty Cobb	5,500	2,750	1,650
(7)	Jake Daubert	450.00	225.00	135.00
(8)	Al Demaree	450.00	225.00	125.00
(9a)	Johnny Evers (Name only.)	1,100	550.00	330.00
(9b)	Johnny Evers (Name and city.)	1,100	550.00	330.00
(10)	Rube Foster	450.00	225.00	125.00
(11)	Dick Hoblitzell	450.00	225.00	125.00
(12)	Walter Johnson	2,000	1,000	600.00
(13)	Benny Kauff	450.00	225.00	125.00
(14)	Johnny Kling (No name.)	450.00	225.00	135.00
(15)	Ed Konetchy	450.00	225.00	125.00
(16)	Nap Lajoie	1,100	550.00	330.00
(17)	Sherry Magee	450.00	225.00	135.00
(18)	Rube Marquard	1,100	550.00	330.00
(19)	Christy Mathewson	2,500	1,250	750.00
(21)	John McGraw	1,100	550.00	330.00
(22)	Ed Reulbach	450.00	225.00	135.00
(23)	Eppa Rixey	1,100	550.00	330.00
(24)	Babe Ruth	15,000	7,500	4,500
(25)	Tris Speaker/Btg (Facing forward.)	1,100	550.00	330.00
(26)	Tris Speaker/Btg (Side view.)	1,100	550.00	330.00
(27)	Jeff Tesreau	450.00	225.00	135.00
(28)	Joe Tinker	1,100	550.00	330.00
(29)	Honus Wagner	2,750	1,350	825.00

1928 PM6 Baseball Player Pins

The method of distribution for these small (3/8" diameter) pin-backs is unknown, but it has been reported they were given away in cereal boxes. The black-and-white photographic pins have the player name in a black arc at bottom. The extent of the checklist is unknown.

		NM	EX	VG
Common Player:		375.00	185.00	110.00
(1)	Grover Alexander	450.00	225.00	135.00
(2)	Ty Cobb	900.00	450.00	275.00
(3)	Bucky Harris	350.00	175.00	100.00
(4)	Rogers Hornsby	550.00	275.00	165.00
(5)	Walter Johnson	600.00	300.00	180.00
(6)	Babe Ruth	1,200	600.00	360.00
(7)	Geo. Sisler	350.00	175.00	100.00
(8)	Tris Speaker	450.00	225.00	135.00

1940 PM10 Baseball Player Pins

This was the first of two issues that share a nearly identical format. The 1-3/4" celluloid pin-back buttons feature a black-and-white player photo surrounded by a white border. The player's name is in black capital letters at bottom, and his team nickname in the same type size and style at top. These pins were originally sold at ballparks and other souvenir outlets. The checklist, arranged here in alphabetical order, is not complete.

	NM	EX	VG
Common Player:	30.00	15.00	9.00
Dick Bartell	30.00	15.00	9.00
Dolph Camilli	30.00	15.00	9.00
Bill Dickey	50.00	25.00	15.00
Joe DiMaggio	275.00	135.00	85.00
Lou Gehrig	700.00	350.00	210.00
Lou Gehrig (Black border, "NEVER FORGOTTEN" at top.)	650.00	325.00	195.00
Lefty Gomez	50.00	25.00	15.00
Carl Hubbell	100.00	50.00	30.00
Cliff Melton	30.00	15.00	9.00
Pete Reiser	30.00	15.00	9.00
Dixie Walker	30.00	15.00	9.00
Whitlow Wyatt	30.00	15.00	9.00

1951 PM10 Baseball Player Pins

This was the second of two issues that share a nearly identical format. The 1-3/4" celluloid pin-back buttons feature a black-and-white player photo surrounded by a white border. The player's name is in black capital letters at bottom, and full team name in the same type size and style at top. These pins were originally sold at ballparks and other souvenir outlets. The checklist, arranged here in alphabetical order, is likely not complete. Note that the woeful Pittsburgh Pirates represent more than half the known players in this issue.

	NM	EX	VG
Common Player:	50.00	25.00	15.00
Luke Easter	75.00	37.50	22.50
Ned Garver	50.00	25.00	15.00
Monte Irvin	100.00	50.00	30.00
Ralph Kiner	100.00	50.00	30.00
Bob Lemon	100.00	50.00	30.00
Willie Mays	175.00	87.00	52.00
Clyde McCullouhg (McCullough)	50.00	25.00	15.00
Billy Meyer	50.00	25.00	15.00
Danny Murtaugh	50.00	25.00	15.00
Don Newcombe	50.00	25.00	15.00
Saul Rogovin	50.00	25.00	15.00
Stan Rojek	50.00	25.00	15.00
Hank Thompson	50.00	25.00	15.00
Bill Werle	50.00	25.00	15.00

1950s-60s PM10 Baseball Player Pins - Name at Bottom

Issued over a period of years in a variety of styles, these celluloid pinback buttons have in common their approximately 1-3/4" diameter and the appearance of the player name at bottom. Black-and-white player portrait photos are found on a variety of backgrounds. In this checklist, the color of the background is listed, where known, immediately after the team name (where known). Other distinguishing characteristics may also be noted. The pins were usually originally sold with a red, white and blue swallow-tailed silk pennant attached and a brass chain with a baseball, bat or glove charms, or similar plastic toys. Values shown are for pins alone. The checklist here is incomplete.

	NM	EX	VG
Common Player:	20.00	10.00	6.00
Hank Aaron (Blue, script name, team above.)	100.00	50.00	30.00
Sandy Amoros (Brooklyn, blue.)	60.00	30.00	18.00
Harry Anderson (Phillies, white.)	125.00	65.00	35.00
John Antonelli (NY cap, "floating head.")	20.00	10.00	6.00
John Antonelli (SF cap, ring around photo.)	20.00	10.00	6.00
Luis Aparicio (White Sox, white.)	75.00	37.00	22.00
Ernest Banks (Cubs, white, no cap logo.)	475.00	235.00	140.00
Bo Belinsky (Phillies, white.)	40.00	20.00	12.00
Gus Bell (White)	20.00	10.00	6.00

Gus Bell ("CINCINNATI REDLEGS" beneath name.)	100.00	50.00	30.00
Larry Berra (White)	90.00	45.00	27.00
Larry Berra (Blue)	100.00	50.00	30.00
Yogi Berra	80.00	40.00	24.00
Joe Black (Brooklyn, photo.)	40.00	20.00	12.00
Joe Black (Brooklyn, white, facing front.)	40.00	20.00	12.00
Joe Black (Brooklyn, white, facing his left.)	25.00	12.50	7.50
Don Bollweg (A's, photo.)	20.00	10.00	6.00
Lou Boudreau (Photo, script name.)	60.00	30.00	18.00
Lou Boudreau (Red Sox, white.)	50.00	25.00	15.00
Jackie Brandt (Orioles, photo.)	40.00	20.00	12.00
Eddie Bressoud	20.00	10.00	6.00
Bill Bruton (Braves, white.)	100.00	50.00	30.00
Jim Bunning (Phillies)	40.00	20.00	12.00
Roy Campanella (Brooklyn, blue.)	90.00	45.00	27.50
Roy Campanella (Brooklyn, yellow.)	80.00	40.00	24.00
Roy Campanella (Brooklyn, white, cap backwards.)	75.00	37.50	22.50
Roy Campanella (Brooklyn, white, name across photo.)	60.00	30.00	18.00
Roy Campanella (Brooklyn, white, name under photo.)	60.00	30.00	18.00
Roy Campanella (Brooklyn, white, name in strip.)	100.00	50.00	30.00
Roy Campanella (Brooklyn, white circle border, team at top.)	250.00	125.00	75.00
Chico Carrasquel (Name in script, team at top.)	50.00	25.00	15.00
Phil Cavarretta (Cubs, script name, stars above.)	150.00	75.00	45.00
Orlando Cepeda (Gray)	30.00	15.00	9.00
Orlando Cepeda (S.F., name in strip, photo.)	30.00	15.00	9.00
Gerry Coleman (Dark)	40.00	20.00	12.00
Gerry Coleman (Light)	40.00	20.00	12.00
Tony Conigliaro (Red Sox, gray.)	40.00	20.00	12.00
Morton Cooper (Cardinals, white/black background.)	40.00	20.00	12.00
Billy Cox (Brooklyn, white, neck-to-cap.)	95.00	47.50	28.00
Billy Cox (Brooklyn, white, chest-to-cap.)	60.00	30.00	18.00
Alvin Dark (NY cap, "floating head.")	20.00	10.00	6.00
Jerome (Dizzy) Dean (Black)	90.00	45.00	27.50
Dom DiMaggio (White)	40.00	20.00	12.00
Dom DiMaggio (Dark)	40.00	20.00	12.00
Joe DiMaggio (Black)	475.00	235.00	140.00
Joe DiMaggio (Dark blue, name beyond shoulders.)	250.00	125.00	75.00
Joe DiMaggio (Light blue, name within shoulders.)	150.00	75.00	45.00
Joe DiMaggio (Light blue, name "ear to ear" - modern fantasy, no collectible value.)			
Joe DiMaggio (Green border.)	325.00	160.00	100.00
Joe DiMaggio (White, name in strip.)	200.00	100.00	60.00
Joe DiMaggio (White, name not in strip.)	215.00	100.00	65.00
Joe DiMaggio (Yellow, "YANKEES" under name.)	350.00	175.00	100.00
Larry Doby (Dark)	60.00	30.00	18.00
Larry Doby (Indians, white)	90.00	45.00	27.50
Carl Erskine (Brooklyn, white.)	75.00	37.50	22.50
Bob Feller (Indians, white.)	80.00	40.00	24.00
Bob Feller (Brown, name in script.)	325.00	160.00	100.00
Whitey Ford	80.00	40.00	24.00
Whitey Ford (White, name in strip, 3-1/2".)	200.00	100.00	60.00
Nelson Fox (White Sox, fox figures at top.)	350.00	175.00	100.00
Carl Furillo (Brooklyn, blue.)	75.00	37.50	22.50
Carl Furillo (Brooklyn, gray.)	65.00	32.50	20.00
Carl Furillo (Brooklyn, photo, dark sleeves.)	100.00	50.00	30.00
Carl Furillo (Brooklyn, photo, no sleeves.)	115.00	60.00	35.00
Ned Garver (Browns, white, belly-to-cap.)	30.00	15.00	9.00
Ned Garver (Browns, white, chest-to-cap.)	30.00	15.00	9.00
Junior Gilliam (Brooklyn, white.)	100.00	50.00	30.00
Junior Gilliam (Broklyn, photo.)	100.00	50.00	30.00
Ruben Gomez (SF cap, ring around photo.)	30.00	15.00	9.00
Billy Goodman (White)	100.00	50.00	30.00
Ron Hansen (Orioles, photo.)	40.00	20.00	12.00
Gabby Hartnett (Cubs, black.)	40.00	20.00	12.00
Mike Hegan (Indians, white border, script name.)	450.00	225.00	135.00
Tom Henrich (Gray)	40.00	20.00	12.00
Mike Higgins (Red Sox, dark.)	45.00	22.50	13.50
Gil Hodges (Brooklyn, blue.)	100.00	50.00	30.00
Gil Hodges (Brooklyn, red/orange.)	50.00	25.00	15.00
Gil Hodges (Brooklyn, photo.)	40.00	20.00	12.00
Gil Hodges (Brooklyn, white, name across photo.)	60.00	30.00	18.00
Gil Hodges (Brooklyn, white, name in strip.)	200.00	100.00	60.00
Gil Hodges (Brooklyn, white, name under photo.)	40.00	20.00	12.00
Gil Hodges (Mets, 3-1/2", name in strip.)	150.00	75.00	45.00
Roger Hornsby (Rogers) (Browns, white circle border.)	150.00	75.00	45.00
Monte Irvin (Giants, dark.)	80.00	40.00	24.00
Ransom Jackson (Cubs, stars above.)	150.00	75.00	45.00
Forrest "Spook" Jacobs (Gray)	20.00	10.00	6.00
Forrest "Spook" Jacobs (A's, photo.)	20.00	10.00	6.00
Jackie Jensen (Dark)	50.00	25.00	15.00
Jackie Jensen (White)	50.00	25.00	15.00
Ed Joost (A's, photo.)	20.00	10.00	6.00
Harmon Killebrew ("W" on cap, photo.)	375.00	185.00	110.00
Ralph Kiner (Color, facsimile autograph.)	40.00	20.00	12.00
Ralph Kiner (Cubs, hearts above.)	600.00	300.00	180.00
Ted Kluszewski (Dark, name overprinted horizontally.)	200.00	100.00	60.00
Ted Kluszewski (Reds, white, name in strip.)	40.00	20.00	12.00
Ed Kranepool (White)	50.00	25.00	15.00
Big Bill Lee (Cubs, black/gray.)	20.00	10.00	6.00
Bob Lemon (Light)	40.00	20.00	12.00
Whitey Lockman (NY cap, gray.)	25.00	12.50	7.50
Peanuts Lowrey (Cardinals, white.)	25.00	12.50	7.50
Sal Maglie (Brooklyn, photo.)	50.00	25.00	15.00
Frank Malzone	40.00	20.00	12.00
Mickey Mantle (White, batting to waist, name from elbow to armpit.)	275.00	135.00	80.00
Mickey Mantle (White, batting to waist, name from wrist to shoulder.)	300.00	150.00	90.00
Mickey Mantle (Blue, batting, left hand not visible, 1-3/4".)	350.00	175.00	100.00
Mickey Mantle (Baseball background, name in strip.)	200.00	100.00	60.00
Mickey Mantle (Blue, name in strip.) (Modern replicas are commonly encountered.)	250.00	125.00	75.00
Mickey Mantle (Blue, name in strip, looking over left shoulder, 3-1/2".)	150.00	75.00	45.00
Mickey Mantle (Yellow, name in strip, looking over left shoulder, 3-1/2".)	300.00	150.00	90.00
Mickey Mantle (White, portrait.)	300.00	150.00	90.00
Mickey Mantle (Blue, portrait, 3-1/2".)	1,750	875.00	525.00
Juan Marichal (SF cap, uncentered black border.)	60.00	30.00	18.00
Marty Marion (Browns, white circle border.)	300.00	150.00	90.00
Roger Maris (Blue, bat behind head, name in white strip, 3-1/2".)	100.00	50.00	30.00
Roger Maris (White, looking over shoulder, no cap insignia.)	125.00	65.00	35.00
Roger Maris (Orange, bat behind head, 3-1/2".)	100.00	50.00	30.00
Roger Maris (Yellow, bat behind head, 1-3/4".)	75.00	37.50	22.50
Roger Maris (Yellow, blue or purple, bat behind head, 2-1/4" - modern replica, no collectible value.)			
Roger Maris (Yellow, bat behind head, 3-1/2".)	100.00	50.00	30.00
Willie Mays (S.F. Giants, gray.)	325.00	160.00	97.00
Willie Mays (Photo, N.Y. cap.)	300.00	150.00	90.00
Willie Mays (photo, grass background, S.F. cap.)	300.00	150.00	90.00
Willie Mays (photo, stadium background, S.F. cap.)	300.00	150.00	90.00
Willie Mays (White, N.Y. cap.)	230.00	115.00	70.00
Willie Mays (White, S.F. cap.)	150.00	75.00	45.00
Willie McCovey (Bats on shoulder, no cap logo.)	200.00	100.00	60.00
Willie McCovey (SF cap, name in ear-to-ear white stripe.)	40.00	20.00	12.00
Gil McDougald (Yankees, gray.)	45.00	22.50	13.50
"Vinegar Bend" Mizell (Cardinals, white.)	30.00	15.00	9.00
Bill Monbouquette	40.00	20.00	12.00
Don Mueller (White, "floating head.")	40.00	20.00	12.00
Bobby Murcer (White)	30.00	15.00	9.00
Stan Musial (Cardinals, white, MUSIAL at bottom, "STAN" THE MAN at top.)	125.00	65.00	40.00
Stan Musial (Cardinals, white, piping shows.)	100.00	50.00	30.00
Stan Musial (Cardinals, white, no piping.)	100.00	50.00	30.00
Stan Musial (White, team name above photo, facsimile autograph.) (Modern replica exists in 2-3/16" size; no collectible value.)	100.00	50.00	30.00
Stan Musial (Yellow)	125.00	65.00	35.00
Don Newcombe (Brooklyn, blue.)	450.00	225.00	135.00
Don Newcombe (Brooklyn, white, name in strip.)	30.00	15.00	9.00
Don Newcombe (Brooklyn, white, name under photo.)	30.00	20.00	12.00
Don Newcombe (Brooklyn, white circle border, team at top.)	60.00	30.00	18.00
Don Newcombe (Yellow)	50.00	25.00	15.00
Dan O'Connell (SF cap, ring around photo.)	40.00	20.00	12.00
Andy Pafko (Brooklyn, black.)	30.00	15.00	9.00
Joe Page (White)	50.00	25.00	15.00
Leroy (Satchel) Paige (White)	175.00	85.00	50.00
Mel Parnell (Red Sox, white.)	45.00	22.50	13.50
Joe Pepitone (White)	30.00	15.00	9.00
Johnny Pesky (Red Sox, white.)	100.00	50.00	30.00
Billy Pierce (Name in serif type.)	40.00	20.00	12.00
Jimmy Piersall (Light)	50.00	25.00	15.00
Johnny Podres (Brooklyn, white.)	45.00	22.00	13.50
Wally Post ("CINCINNATI REDLEGS" beneath name.)	50.00	25.00	15.00
Vic Power (A's, photo.)	25.00	12.50	7.50
Dick Radatz (Red Sox, gray.)	30.00	15.00	9.00
Vic Raschi (Yankees, white.)	60.00	30.00	18.00
PeeWee Reese (Brooklyn, gray, name in strip.)	200.00	100.00	60.00
"Pee Wee" Reese (Brooklyn, gray, name across photo.)	60.00	30.00	18.00
"Pee Wee" Reese (Brooklyn, white, large photo.)	125.00	65.00	35.00
"Pee Wee" Reese (Brooklyn, white, small photo.)	100.00	50.00	30.00
"Pee Wee" Reese (Brooklyn, photo, name in strip.)	60.00	30.00	18.00
Bill Rigney (NY cap, dark background.)	20.00	10.00	6.00
Phil Rizzuto (White)	80.00	40.00	24.00
Robin Roberts (Phillies, photo.)	50.00	25.00	15.00
Frank Robinson ("Cincinnati Redlegs" at bottom.)	250.00	125.00	75.00
Jackie Robinson (Brooklyn, blue.)	300.00	150.00	90.00
Jackie Robinson (Brooklyn, yellow.)	190.00	95.00	55.00
Jackie Robinson (Brooklyn, white, chest-to-cap.)	200.00	100.00	60.00
Jackie Robinson (Brooklyn, white, neck-to-cap.)	250.00	125.00	75.00
Jackie Robinson (Brooklyn, white, name across bottom, facing his left.)	200.00	100.00	60.00
Jackie Robinson (Brooklyn, gray, name across photo, facing his left.)	200.00	100.00	60.00
Jackie Robinson (Brooklyn, white, name in strip, cap logo not visible.)	600.00	300.00	180.00
Jackie Robinson (Brooklyn, photo.)	275.00	135.00	80.00
Preacher Roe (Brooklyn, wind-up pose.)	90.00	45.00	27.50
Al Rosen (Light background.)	40.00	20.00	12.00
Charles Herbert Ruffing (Yankees, gray.)	40.00	20.00	12.00
Pete Runnels	40.00	20.00	12.00
Ron Santo (Cubs, white.)	40.00	20.00	12.00
Hank Sauer (Cubs, script name, stars above.)	150.00	75.00	45.00
Chuck Schilling	40.00	20.00	12.00
George Scott (White, "floating head.")	20.00	10.00	6.00
Bobby Shantz (A's, white.)	30.00	15.00	9.00
Frank Shea (Yankees, gray.)	50.00	25.00	15.00
Harry Simpson (Indians, white, team name at top, script name at bottom.)	650.00	325.00	195.00
Enos Slaughter (Cardinals, white.)	50.00	25.00	15.00
Enos Slaughter (Cardinals, black.)	50.00	25.00	15.00
Roy Smalley (Cubs, script name, stars above.)	150.00	75.00	45.00
Duke Snider (Brooklyn, white.)	80.00	40.00	24.00
Duke Snider (Brooklyn, blue.)	65.00	35.00	20.00
Duke Snider (Brooklyn, blue, 3-1/2".)	200.00	100.00	60.00
Duke Snider (Brooklyn, gray.)	75.00	37.50	22.50
Duke Snider (Brooklyn, photo.)	150.00	75.00	45.00
Gerald Staley (Cardinals, white.)	20.00	10.00	6.00
Bobby Thomson (NY cap, white, uniform shows.)	40.00	20.00	12.00
Bobby Thomson (NY cap, white, "floating head.")	30.00	15.00	9.00
Gus Triandos (Orioles, photo.)	40.00	20.00	12.00
Robt. Lee Trice (A's, photo.)	25.00	12.50	7.50
Sam White (Red Sox, white.)	30.00	15.00	9.00
James Hoyt Wilhelm (Orioles)	200.00	100.00	60.00
Ted Williams (Name beneath bust, white.)	200.00	100.00	60.00
Ted Williams (Name in strip, black.)	450.00	225.00	135.00
Ted Williams (Name in strip, white.)	400.00	200.00	120.00
Ted Williams (Name in strip, photo, belt-up.)	90.00	45.00	27.50
Ted Williams (Name in strip, photo, close-up.)	100.00	50.00	30.00
Carl Yastrzemski	100.00	50.00	30.00

1950s-60s PM10 Baseball Player Pins - Name at Top

This series of baseball player pins is similar to contemporary issues in its 1-3/4" (unless otherwise noted) black-and-white celluloid format, but differs in that the player name appears at top. Players known in the series indicate the buttons were issued over a period of several years, probably for sale in stadium concession stands and other souvenir outlets. The alphabetical checklist here is not complete.

Common Player:	NM	EX	VG
Felipe Alou (Script name.)	60.00	30.00	18.00
Luis Arroyo	40.00	20.00	12.00
Hank Bauer	20.00	10.00	6.00
Yogi Berra	60.00	30.00	18.00
Johnny Blanchard	135.00	67.00	40.00
Cletis Boyer	60.00	30.00	18.00
Roy Campanella (2-1/4")	75.00	37.00	22.00
Andy Carey	450.00	225.00	135.00
(2", Yankees, white.)	125.00	65.00	37.50
Joe Collins	60.00	30.00	18.00
Del Crandall (2-1/8")	40.00	20.00	12.00
Whitey Ford (2")	150.00	75.00	45.00
Whitey Ford (3-1/2" diameter)	400.00	200.00	120.00
Carl Furillo	75.00	37.00	22.00
(2", Brooklyn, white.)			
Junior Gilliam	75.00	37.00	22.00
Ruben Gomez	40.00	20.00	12.00
Ken Harrelson	50.00	25.00	15.00
(Red Sox, white)			
Don Hoak (Brooklyn, white)	60.00	30.00	18.00
Elston Howard	75.00	37.00	22.00
Jackie Jensen	75.00	37.00	22.00
(Red Sox, white)			
Clem Labine	60.00	30.00	18.00
(Brooklyn, white)			
Billy Loes	130.00	65.00	40.00
(2", Brooklyn, white)			
Ed Lopat	60.00	30.00	18.00
Hector Lopez	40.00	20.00	12.00
Frank Malzone	50.00	25.00	15.00
(Red Sox, white)			
Mickey Mantle (1-5/8")	500.00	250.00	150.00
Mickey Mantle (2-1/4")	300.00	150.00	90.00
Roger Maris (2", yellow)	150.00	75.00	45.00
Roger Maris (2-1/4", white)	3.00	1.00	1.00
Billy Martin	75.00	37.00	22.00
Willie Mays (2-1/4", white)	450.00	225.00	135.00
Gil McDougald	100.00	50.00	30.00
(2", Yankees, white)			
Bill Monbouquette	50.00	25.00	15.00
(Red Sox, white)			
Walt Moryn	250.00	125.00	75.00
(1-1/2", Brooklyn, white)			
Don Newcombe	125.00	62.00	37.00
(2", Brooklyn, white)			
Irv Noren	60.00	30.00	18.00
Johnny Podres	60.00	30.00	18.00
(2", Brooklyn, white)			
Allie Reynolds	60.00	30.00	18.00
Jackie Robinson	1,600	800.00	475.00
(2-1/16", Brooklyn, white)			
Preacher Roe	60.00	30.00	18.00
(Brooklyn, white)			
Pete Runnels	50.00	25.00	15.00
(Red Sox, white)			
Chuck Schilling	50.00	25.00	15.00
(Red Sox, white)			
Bill Skowron	60.00	30.00	18.00
Enos Slaughter	60.00	30.00	18.00
Duke Snider	135.00	67.00	40.00
Warren Spahn	120.00	60.00	36.00
Don Thompson	200.00	100.00	60.00
(2", Brooklyn, white)			
Bob Turley	60.00	30.00	18.00
Ted Williams	80.00	40.00	25.00
(1-3/4", name in strip at top, team in strip at bottom.)			
Gene Woodling	60.00	30.00	18.00
Carl Yastrzemski	200.00	100.00	60.00
Don Zimmer (Brooklyn, white)	75.00	37.50	22.50

1956 PM15 Yellow Basepath Pins

These pins were issued circa 1956; the sponsor of this 32-pin set is not indicated. The set, which has

been assigned the American Card Catalog designation PM15, is commonly called "Yellow Basepaths" because of the design of the pin, which features a black-and-white player photo set inside a green infield with yellow basepaths. The unnumbered pins measure 7/8" in diameter.

		NM	EX	VG
Complete Set (32):		4,500	2,250	1,350
Common Player:		85.00	40.00	25.00
(1)	Hank Aaron	400.00	200.00	120.00
(2)	Joe Adcock	85.00	40.00	25.00
(3)	Luis Aparicio	140.00	70.00	40.00
(4)	Richie Ashburn	150.00	75.00	45.00
(5)	Gene Baker	85.00	40.00	25.00
(6)	Ernie Banks	225.00	110.00	65.00
(7)	Yogi Berra	245.00	120.00	75.00
(8)	Bill Bruton	85.00	40.00	25.00
(9)	Larry Doby	140.00	70.00	40.00
(10)	Bob Friend	85.00	40.00	25.00
(11)	Nellie Fox	140.00	70.00	40.00
(12)	Ted Greengrass (Jim)	85.00	40.00	25.00
(13)	Steve Gromek	85.00	40.00	25.00
(14)	Johnny Groth	85.00	40.00	25.00
(15)	Gil Hodges	200.00	100.00	60.00
(16)	Al Kaline	150.00	75.00	45.00
(17)	Ted Kluzewski (Kluszewski)	140.00	70.00	40.00
(18)	Johnny Logan	85.00	40.00	25.00
(19)	Dale Long	85.00	40.00	25.00
(20)	Mickey Mantle	600.00	300.00	180.00
(21)	Ed Matthews (Mathews)	150.00	75.00	45.00
(22)	Minnie Minoso	100.00	50.00	30.00
(23)	Stan Musial	350.00	175.00	100.00
(24)	Don Newcombe	140.00	70.00	40.00
(25)	Bob Porterfield	85.00	40.00	25.00
(26)	Pee Wee Reese	200.00	100.00	60.00
(27)	Robin Roberts	140.00	70.00	40.00
(28)	Red Schoendienst	140.00	70.00	40.00
(29)	Duke Snider	225.00	110.00	65.00
(30)	Vern Stephens	85.00	40.00	25.00
(31)	Gene Woodling	100.00	50.00	30.00
(32)	Gus Zernial	85.00	40.00	25.00

1909-11 Polar Bear Tobacco

The most distinctive advertising-back found on 1909-11 T206 is that of Polar Bear with its dark blue background and white topography. A more conventional style of ad was used on 1911 T205 cards, also printed in blue. Because the cards were packaged loose among the tobacco leaves in Polar Bear pouches, stains on surviving cards are frequently seen. Polar Bear is among the most common brands found in both series.

PREMIUMS:
T205: 1X
T206: 1-1.5X
(See T205, T206 for checklists and card values.)

1889 Police Gazette Cabinets

Issued in the late 1880s through early 1890s as a premium by Police Gazette, a popular newspaper of the day, these cabinet cards are very rare. The 4-1/4" x 6-1/2" cards consist of sepia-toned photographs mounted on cardboard of various colors. Only about

two dozen players are currently known. Some photographs correspond to those used in the S.F. Hess card series and many players are depicted in suit and tie, rather than baseball uniform. Each card displays the name of the player beneath his portrait, along with the signature of "Richard K. Fox" and a line identifying him as "Editor and Proprietor / Police Gazette / Franklin Square, New York."

Common Player:	NM	EX	VG
Hick Carpenter	20,000	10,000	6,000
Fred Carroll	20,000	10,000	6,000
Bob Clark	20,000	10,000	6,000
John Coleman	20,000	10,000	6,000
Roger Conner (Connor)	25,000	12,500	7,500
Pete Conway	20,000	10,000	6,000
John Corkhill	20,000	10,000	6,000
Jerry Denny	20,000	10,000	6,000
Jas. A. Donohue (Donahue)	20,000	10,000	6,000
Buck Ewing	25,000	12,500	7,500
Bob Ferguson	20,000	10,000	6,000
Jocko Fields	20,000	10,000	6,000
Elmer Foster	20,000	10,000	6,000
Charlie Getzein (Getzien)	20,000	10,000	6,000
Pebbly Jack Glasscock	20,000	10,000	6,000
Bill Gleason	20,000	10,000	6,000
George Gore	20,000	10,000	6,000
Tim Keefe	25,000	12,500	7,500
Gus Krock	20,000	10,000	6,000
A.J. Maul	20,000	10,000	6,000
Ed Morris	20,000	10,000	6,000
Tip O'Neil (O'Neill)	20,000	10,000	6,000
N. (Fred) Pfeffer	20,000	10,000	6,000
Danny Richardson	20,000	10,000	6,000
A.B. Sanders	20,000	10,000	6,000
Charley (Pop) Smith	20,000	10,000	6,000
Elmer Smith	20,000	10,000	6,000
Harry Staley	20,000	10,000	6,000
William Swett (San Francisco)	25,000	12,500	7,500
George Tebeau	20,000	10,000	6,000
John Tener	22,500	11,250	6,750
Billy Terry (Adonis)	20,000	10,000	6,000
Sam Thompson	25,000	12,500	7,500
Curt Welch	20,000	10,000	6,000
Wheeler C. Wikoff (Wykoff)	20,000	10,000	6,000
(Pres. American Association)			

1895 Police Gazette Supplement

The 12 captains of the National League's teams, collectively termed "Our Baseball Heroes," are pictured in sepia lithographic portraits surrounding a colorful baseball action scene on this supplement issued with the June 1 edition of the men's newspaper. Overall the supplement measures about 21-1/2" x 15-1/2" and is the most impressive of the baseball items issued by the paper prior to the turn of the 20th Century.

	NM	EX	VG
Supplement:	15,000	7,000	4,000
Cap Anson			
Jack Boyle			
Ed Cartwright			
George Davis			
Buck Ewing			
Jack Glasscock			
Mike Griffin			
Connie Mack			
Doggie Miller			
Billy Nash			
Patsy Tebeau			
Wilbert Robinson			

1901-1917 Police Gazette Supplements

Each issue of the weekly men's magazine included a large-format (about 11-1/4" x 16-1/4") blank-backed, black-and-white supplement. In keeping with the publication's editorial focus at the time, the pictures featured baseball players, boxers, other athletes, actresses and female models. The photos appear in a frame design and measure about 8-1/2" x 12-1/2". The supplements are designated as such by a line of type at top or bottom that names the publication, issue number and issue date. The subject is identified in capital letters beneath the photo and there are a few lines of information at bottom. The magazine sometimes printed the same pictures in nearly identical format within its regular pages. These can be differentiated from the supplements in that they are on pink paper, have advertising or other editorial material on back and are not marked as supplements. Such pages do not enjoy the same popularity and value as the supplements. In this possibly incomplete checklist, the card number shown is the issue number in which the supplement was inserted. The player name or title may not always exactly correspond to that printed on the piece. Because of their large size, the supplements are often found trimmed to remove evidence of corner creases and edge damage. This checklist includes only the baseball subjects.

		NM	EX	VG
Common Player:		100.00	50.00	30.00
1901				
	George Davis (Issue date unknown.)	200.00	100.00	60.00
1251	Christy Mathewson	2,000	1,000	600.00
1903				
1351	Roy Thomas	100.00	50.00	30.00
1353	Red Dooin	100.00	50.00	30.00
1357	Tommy Leach	100.00	50.00	30.00
1359	John McGraw	200.00	100.00	60.00
1361	Cy Seymour	100.00	50.00	30.00
1363	Joe McGinnity	200.00	100.00	60.00
1365	Jack Cronin	100.00	50.00	30.00
1904				
1400	Dan McGann	100.00	50.00	30.00
1403	Red Ames	100.00	50.00	30.00
1407	Jack Warner	100.00	50.00	30.00
1411	Frank Bowerman	100.00	50.00	30.00
1413	Roger Bresnahan	200.00	100.00	60.00
1905				
1450	Joe McGinnity	200.00	100.00	60.00
1451	Napoleon Lajoie	250.00	125.00	75.00
1452	Hans Wagner	1,250	625.00	375.00
1453	Malachi Kittredge	100.00	50.00	30.00
1457	Jack Chesbro	200.00	100.00	60.00
1459	Roger Bresnahan	200.00	100.00	60.00
1461	1905 Pittsburg Team	900.00	450.00	275.00
1463	Willie Keeler	200.00	100.00	60.00
1465	Sam Mertes	100.00	50.00	30.00
1466	Dave Fultz	100.00	50.00	30.00
1467	Carlisle University Team	150.00	75.00	45.00
1468	Bill Hogg	100.00	50.00	30.00
1906				
1502	Aleck Smith	100.00	50.00	30.00
1504	Jack Kleinow	100.00	50.00	30.00
1505	Rube Waddell	200.00	100.00	60.00
1507	Clark Griffith	200.00	100.00	60.00
1510	Nap Shea	100.00	50.00	30.00
1516	Jimmy Casey	100.00	50.00	30.00
1518	Hal Chase	200.00	100.00	60.00
1907				
1548	Harry Davis	100.00	50.00	30.00
1549	Mike Powers	100.00	50.00	30.00
1551	Willie Keeler, Jack Kleinow	150.00	75.00	45.00
1554	Eddie Plank	250.00	125.00	75.00
1557	George Moriarty	100.00	50.00	30.00
1559	Bill Dahlen	100.00	50.00	30.00
1562	Cecil Ferguson	100.00	50.00	30.00
1564	Sammy Strang	100.00	50.00	30.00
1567	Hal Chase, Charlie Armbruster	150.00	75.00	45.00
1571	Mordecai Brown	200.00	100.00	60.00
1572	Danny Hoffman	100.00	50.00	30.00
1908				
1607	Harry Bay	100.00	50.00	30.00
1613	Harry Lunn	100.00	50.00	30.00
1615	Charley Hemphill	100.00	50.00	30.00
1909				
1655	Buck Herzog	100.00	50.00	30.00
1657	Al Bridwell	100.00	50.00	30.00
1660	Hans Lobert	100.00	50.00	30.00
1663	Bugs Raymond	100.00	50.00	30.00
1664	Harry Coveleski	100.00	50.00	30.00
1665	Chief Meyers	100.00	50.00	30.00
1667	Orval Overall	100.00	50.00	30.00
1673	Al Burch	100.00	50.00	30.00
1674	Mike Donlin	100.00	50.00	30.00
1676	Del Howard	100.00	50.00	30.00
1678	Dick Morris (Amateur)	100.00	50.00	30.00
1910				
1716	Jack Warhop	100.00	50.00	30.00

1717	George Mullen (Mullin)	100.00	50.00	30.00
1720	Russ Ford	100.00	50.00	30.00
1721	Owen Bush	100.00	50.00	30.00
1722	Sherry Magee	100.00	50.00	30.00
1724	Jack Dalton	100.00	50.00	30.00
1726	Bert Daniels	100.00	50.00	30.00
1727	Birdie Cree	100.00	50.00	30.00
1729	Josh Devore	100.00	50.00	30.00
1730	Louis Drucke	100.00	50.00	30.00
1911				
1771	Christy Mathewson	750.00	375.00	225.00
1779	Arthur Wilson	100.00	50.00	30.00
1782	Hans Wagner, Roger Bresnahan	750.00	375.00	225.00
1791	Home Run Baker	200.00	100.00	60.00
1912				
1812	Zach Wheat	200.00	100.00	60.00
1814	Rube Marquard	200.00	100.00	60.00
1821	Tex Erwin	100.00	50.00	30.00
1823	Heinie Zimmerman	100.00	50.00	30.00
1825	Jake Stahl	100.00	50.00	30.00
1913				
1856	Frank Chance	200.00	100.00	60.00
1861	Joe Wood	125.00	62.50	37.50
1867	Jim Thorpe	3,000	1,500	900.00
1872	Jake Daubert	100.00	50.00	30.00
1877	Nap Rucker	100.00	50.00	30.00
1883	Joe Jackson	2,000	1,000	600.00
1888	Walter Johnson	750.00	375.00	225.00
1914				
1920	Ty Cobb	1,500	750.00	450.00
1926	Sam Crawford	200.00	100.00	60.00
1932	Dave Robertson	100.00	50.00	30.00
1938	Fritz Maisel	100.00	50.00	30.00
1942	Boston N.L. Team	200.00	100.00	60.00
1943	Philadelphia A.L. Team	200.00	100.00	60.00
1915				
1961	Ray Caldwell	100.00	50.00	30.00
1966	Rabbit Maranville	200.00	100.00	60.00
1970	Sherry Magee	100.00	50.00	30.00
1975	Hans Lobert	100.00	50.00	30.00
1982	Eddie Collins	200.00	100.00	60.00
1985	Dick Hoblitzell	100.00	50.00	30.00
1989	Grover Alexander	500.00	250.00	150.00
1916				
2011	Larry Doyle	100.00	50.00	30.00
2018	Fred Luderus	100.00	50.00	30.00
2020	Jimmy Archer	100.00	50.00	30.00
2023	Dick Rudolph	100.00	50.00	30.00
2026	Benny Kauff	100.00	50.00	30.00
2029	Sam Crawford	200.00	100.00	60.00
2035	Nick Cullop	100.00	50.00	30.00
2040	Clarence Mitchell	100.00	50.00	30.00
2042	George Sisler	200.00	100.00	60.00
2046	Pol Perritt	100.00	50.00	30.00
1917				
2064	Ping Bodie	100.00	50.00	30.00
2070	Benny Kauff	100.00	50.00	30.00
2074	Hans Lobert	100.00	50.00	30.00
2078	Harry Coveleskie (Coveleski)	100.00	50.00	30.00
2081	Jack Coombs	100.00	50.00	30.00

1914 Polo Grounds Game (WG4)

Called the "Polo Grounds Game" for the green-and-white photo of that stadium on each card's back, this set was officially issued as "All Star Card Base Ball" by The Card Baseball Co. of Norfolk, Va. Fronts of the round-cornered 2-1/2" x 3-1/2" cards have a black-and-white player photo and a baseball play scenario that is used to play the game. The set as issued includes 30 different players cards and 24 duplicate cards on which different game plays are displayed. The unnumbered cards are checklisted here alphabetically.

		NM	EX	VG
Complete Boxed Set (54):		6,650	3,325	2,000
Complete Set (30):		3,000	1,500	900.00
Common Player:		40.00	20.00	12.00
(1)	Jimmy Archer	40.00	20.00	12.00
(2)	Frank Baker	125.00	50.00	30.00
(3)	Frank Chance	125.00	50.00	30.00
(4)	Larry Cheney	40.00	20.00	12.00
(5)	Ty Cobb	1,000	275.00	165.00
(6)	Eddie Collins	100.00	50.00	30.00
(7)	Larry Doyle	40.00	20.00	12.00
(8)	Art Fletcher	40.00	20.00	12.00
(9)	Claude Hendrix	40.00	20.00	12.00
(10)	Joe Jackson	1,500	385.00	230.00
(11)	Hughie Jennings	125.00	50.00	30.00
(12)	Nap Lajoie	125.00	50.00	30.00
(13)	Jimmy Lavender	40.00	20.00	12.00
(14)	Fritz Maisel	40.00	20.00	12.00
(15)	Rabbit Maranville	125.00	50.00	30.00
(16)	Rube Marquard	125.00	50.00	30.00
(17)	Matty (Christy Mathewson)	500.00	100.00	60.00
(18)	John McGraw	125.00	50.00	30.00
(19)	Stuffy McInnis	40.00	20.00	12.00
(20)	Chief Meyers	40.00	20.00	12.00
(21)	Red Murray	40.00	20.00	12.00
(22)	Ed Plank	150.00	50.00	30.00
(23)	Nap Rucker	40.00	20.00	12.00
(24)	Reb Russell	40.00	20.00	12.00
(25)	Wildfire Schulte	40.00	20.00	12.00
(26)	Jim Scott	40.00	20.00	12.00
(27)	Tris Speaker	175.00	62.00	37.00
(28)	Honus Wagner	750.00	175.00	105.00
(29)	Ed Walsh	125.00	50.00	30.00
(30)	Joe Wood	100.00	50.00	18.00

1915 Postaco Stamps

A small find of these early stamps in complete sheets of 12 in the mid-1990s made the issue collectible, rather than impossibly rare. Individual stamps are 1-3/4" x 2-1/8" and feature black-and-white player portraits set against a bright background of either yellow or red-orange. The player name, position (in most cases), team and league are designated at the bottom of the picture. In the black frame between the picture and the perforated white border is a copyright symbol and "Postaco." Backs are, of course, blank. Stamps are checklisted here in alphabetical order within color group.

		NM	EX	VG
Complete Set, Sheets (3):		3,000	1,500	900.00
Complete Set, Singles (36):		2,500	1,250	750.00
Common Player:		30.00	15.00	9.00
Red-Orange Background				
(1)	Home Run Baker	100.00	50.00	30.00
(2)	Chief Bender	100.00	50.00	30.00
(3)	George Burns	40.00	20.00	12.00
(4)	John Evers	100.00	50.00	30.00
(5)	Max Flack	40.00	20.00	12.00
(6)	Hank Gawdy (Gowdy)	40.00	20.00	12.00
(7)	Claude Ray Hendrix	40.00	20.00	12.00
(8)	Walter Johnson	200.00	100.00	60.00
(9)	Nap Lajoie	100.00	50.00	30.00
(10)	Hans Lobert	40.00	20.00	12.00
(11)	Sherwood Magee	40.00	20.00	12.00
(12)	Rabbit Maranville	100.00	50.00	30.00
(13)	Christy Mathewson	250.00	125.00	75.00
(14)	George McBride	40.00	20.00	12.00
(15)	John McGraw	100.00	50.00	30.00
(16)	Fred Merkle	40.00	20.00	12.00
(17)	Jack Miller	40.00	20.00	12.00
(18)	Emiliano Palmero	40.00	20.00	12.00
(19)	Pol Perritt	40.00	20.00	12.00
(20)	Derrill Pratt	40.00	20.00	12.00
(21)	Richard Rudolph	40.00	20.00	12.00
(22)	Butch Schmidt	40.00	20.00	12.00
(23)	Joe Tinker	100.00	50.00	30.00
(24)	Honus Wagner	300.00	150.00	90.00
Yellow Background				
(25)	G.C. Alexander	100.00	50.00	30.00
(26)	J.P. Archer	30.00	15.00	9.00
(27)	Ty Cobb	300.00	150.00	90.00
(28)	Eugene Cocreham	30.00	15.00	9.00
(29)	E.S. Cottrell	30.00	15.00	9.00
(30)	Josh Devore	30.00	15.00	9.00
(31)	A. Hartzell (Roy)	30.00	15.00	9.00
(32)	Wm. H. James (Middle initial actually L.)	30.00	15.00	9.00
(33)	Connie Mack	75.00	37.50	22.50
(34)	M. McHale	30.00	15.00	9.00
(35)	Geo. T. Stallings	30.00	15.00	9.00
(36)	Ed. Sweeney	30.00	15.00	9.00

1930 Post Cereal Famous North Americans

The year of issue is unconfirmed. Mathewson is the only baseball player from a group of cereal-box cards printed in panels of four and featuring presidents, generals, Indian chiefs, explorers, etc. The front is printed in red and blue, the back is blank. The card measures about 2-5/8" x 3-1/2".

CHRISTY MATHEWSON (1880-1925)—Greatest of all baseball pitchers.

Christy Mathewson

	NM	EX	VG
	600.00	300.00	180.00

1960 Post Cereal

These cards were issued on the backs of Grape Nuts Flakes cereal and measure an oversized 7" x 8-3/4". The nine cards in the set include five baseball players two football (Frank Gifford and John Unitas) and two basketball players (Bob Cousy and Bob Pettit). The full-color photos are bordered by a wood frame design. The cards covered the entire back of the cereal box and are blank backed. Card fronts include the player's name, team and a facsimile autograph. A panel on the side of the box has biographical information.

		NM	EX	VG
Common Player:		400.00	200.00	120.00
(1)	Don Drysdale	400.00	200.00	120.00
(2)	Al Kaline	400.00	200.00	120.00
(3)	Harmon Killebrew	400.00	200.00	120.00
(4)	Ed Mathews	400.00	200.00	120.00
(5)	Mickey Mantle	2,500	1,250	750.00

1961 Post Cereal

Two hundred different players are included in this set, but with variations the number of different cards exceeds 350. Cards were issued singly and in various panel configurations on the backs of cereal boxes, as well as on thinner stock in 10-card team sheets available from Post via a mail-in offer. Because of placement on less popular sizes and brands of cereal, or because they were issued only on box backs or company sheets, some cards were issued in significantly smaller quantities, making their prices much higher than other comparable players in the set. Well-cut individual cards measure about 3-1/2" x 2-1/2". All cards are numbered in the upper-left corner. Card fronts have full-color portrait photos of the player, along with biographical information and 1960 and career statistics. Backs are blank. The complete set price includes only the most common variation of each player.

		NM	EX	VG
Complete Set (200):		1,600	650.00	375.00
Common Player:		4.00	2.00	1.25
1a	Yogi Berra (Box)	40.00	16.00	10.00
1b	Yogi Berra (Company)	25.00	10.00	6.00
2a	Elston Howard (Box)	7.50	3.00	2.00
2b	Elston Howard (Company)	7.50	3.00	2.00
3a	Bill Skowron (Box)	7.50	3.00	2.00
3b	Bill Skowron (Company)	7.50	3.00	2.00

4a	Mickey Mantle (Box)	160.00	65.00	40.00
4b	Mickey Mantle (Company)	110.00	45.00	25.00
5	Bob Turley (Company)	40.00	16.00	10.00
6a	Whitey Ford (Box)	20.00	8.00	5.00
6b	Whitey Ford (Company)	12.50	5.00	3.00
7a	Roger Maris (Box)	35.00	15.00	9.00
7b	Roger Maris (Company)	35.00	15.00	9.00
8a	Bobby Richardson (Box)	15.00	6.00	4.00
8b	Bobby Richardson (Company)	10.00	4.00	2.50
9a	Tony Kubek (Box)	25.00	10.00	6.25
9b	Tony Kubek (Company)	35.00	15.00	9.00
10	Gil McDougald (Box)	60.00	25.00	15.00
11	Cletis Boyer (Box)	6.00	2.50	1.50
12a	Hector Lopez (Box)	12.50	5.00	3.00
12b	Hector Lopez (Company)	7.50	3.00	2.00
13	Bob Cerv (Box)	4.00	1.50	1.00
14	Ryne Duren (Box)	4.00	1.50	1.00
15	Bobby Shantz (Box)	4.00	1.50	1.00
16	Art Ditmar (Box)	4.00	1.50	1.00
17	Jim Coates (Box)	4.00	1.50	1.00
18	John Blanchard (Box)	4.00	1.50	1.00
19a	Luis Aparicio (Box)	7.50	3.00	2.00
19b	Luis Aparicio (Company)	15.00	6.00	4.00
20a	Nelson Fox (Box)	22.50	9.00	5.75
20b	Nelson Fox (Company)	20.00	8.00	5.00
21a	Bill Pierce (Box)	20.00	8.00	5.00
21b	Bill Pierce (Company)	9.00	3.50	2.25
22a	Early Wynn (Box)	17.50	7.00	4.50
22b	Early Wynn (Company)	25.00	10.00	6.25
23	Bob Shaw (Box)	125.00	50.00	30.00
24a	Al Smith (Box)	20.00	8.00	5.00
24b	Al Smith (Company)	17.50	7.00	4.50
25a	Minnie Minoso (Box)	15.00	6.00	4.00
25b	Minnie Minoso (Company)	10.00	4.00	2.50
26a	Roy Sievers (Box)	4.00	1.50	1.00
26b	Roy Sievers (Company)	7.50	3.00	2.00
27a	Jim Landis (Box)	15.00	6.00	3.75
27b	Jim Landis (Company)	7.50	3.00	2.00
28a	Sherman Lollar (Box)	4.00	1.50	1.00
28b	Sherman Lollar (Company)	7.50	3.00	2.00
29	Gerry Staley (Box)	4.00	1.50	1.00
30a	Gene Freese (Box, White Sox.)	4.00	1.50	1.00
30b	Gene Freese (Company, Reds.)	9.00	3.50	2.25
31	Ted Kluszewski (Box)	15.00	6.00	4.00
32	Turk Lown (Box)	4.00	1.50	1.00
33a	Jim Rivera (Box)	4.00	1.50	1.00
33b	Jim Rivera (Company)	7.50	3.00	2.00
34	Frank Baumann (Box)	4.00	1.50	1.00
35a	Al Kaline (Box)	25.00	10.00	6.25
35b	Al Kaline (Company)	30.00	12.00	7.50
36a	Rocky Colavito (Box)	30.00	12.00	7.50
36b	Rocky Colavito (Company)	22.50	9.00	5.75
37a	Charley Maxwell (Box)	20.00	8.00	5.00
37b	Charley Maxwell (Company)	15.00	6.00	3.75
38a	Frank Lary (Box)	4.00	1.50	1.00
38b	Frank Lary (Company)	9.00	3.50	2.00
39a	Jim Bunning (Box)	20.00	8.00	5.00
39b	Jim Bunning (Company)	15.00	6.00	4.00
40a	Norm Cash (Box)	4.00	1.50	1.00
40b	Norm Cash (Company)	12.50	5.00	3.00
41a	Frank Bolling (box, Tigers)	15.00	6.00	3.75
41b	Frank Bolling (Company, Braves.)	9.00	3.50	2.00
42a	Don Mossi (Box)	10.00	4.00	2.50
42b	Don Mossi (Company)	9.00	3.50	2.00
43a	Lou Berberet (Box)	10.00	4.00	2.50
43b	Lou Berberet (Company)	9.00	3.50	2.00
44	Dave Sisler (Box)	4.00	1.50	1.00
45	Ed Yost (Box)	4.00	1.50	1.00
46	Pete Burnside (Box)	4.00	1.50	1.00
47a	Pete Runnels (Box)	20.00	8.00	5.00
47b	Pete Runnels (Company)	17.50	7.00	4.50
48a	Frank Malzone (Box)	12.50	5.00	3.00
48b	Frank Malzone (Company)	7.50	3.00	2.00
49a	Vic Wertz (Box)	15.00	6.00	3.75
49b	Vic Wertz (Company)	20.00	8.00	5.00
50a	Tom Brewer (Box)	4.00	1.50	1.00
50b	Tom Brewer (Company)	7.50	3.00	2.00
51a	Willie Tasby (Box, no sold line.)	7.50	3.00	2.00
51b	Willie Tasby (Company, sold line.)	15.00	6.00	4.00
52a	Russ Nixon (Box)	4.00	1.50	1.00
52b	Russ Nixon (Company)	7.50	3.00	2.00
53a	Don Buddin (Box)	4.00	1.50	1.00
53b	Don Buddin (Company)	7.50	3.00	2.00
54a	Bill Monbouquette (Box)	4.00	1.50	1.00
54b	Bill Monbouquette (Company)	7.50	3.00	2.00
55a	Frank Sullivan (Box, Red Sox.)	4.00	1.50	1.00
55b	Frank Sullivan (Company, Phillies.)	25.00	10.00	6.25
56a	Haywood Sullivan (Box)	4.00	1.50	1.00
56b	Haywood Sullivan (Company)	7.50	3.00	2.00
57a	Harvey Kuenn (Box, Indians.)	25.00	10.00	6.25
57b	Harvey Kuenn (Company, Giants.)	9.00	3.50	2.00
58a	Gary Bell (Box)	7.50	3.00	2.00
58b	Gary Bell (Company)	7.50	3.00	2.00
59a	Jim Perry (Box)	4.00	1.50	1.00
59b	Jim Perry (Company)	7.50	3.00	2.00
60a	Jim Grant (Box)	4.00	1.50	1.00
60b	Jim Grant (Company)	20.00	8.00	5.00
61a	Johnny Temple (Box)	4.00	1.50	1.00
61b	Johnny Temple (Company)	7.50	3.00	2.00
62a	Paul Foytack (Box)	4.00	1.50	1.00
62b	Paul Foytack (Company)	7.50	3.00	2.00
63a	Vic Power (Box)	15.00	6.00	3.75
63b	Vic Power (Company)	7.50	3.00	2.00
64a	Tito Francona (Box)	4.00	1.50	1.00
64b	Tito Francona (Company)	7.50	3.00	2.00
65a	Ken Aspromonte (Box, no sold line.)	9.00	3.50	2.00

65b	Ken Aspromonte (Company, sold line.)	9.00	3.50	2.00
66	Bob Wilson (Box)	4.00	1.50	1.00
67a	John Romano (Box)	4.00	1.50	1.00
67b	John Romano (Company)	7.50	3.00	2.00
68a	Jim Gentile (Box)	4.00	1.50	1.00
68b	Jim Gentile (Company)	9.00	3.50	2.00
69a	Gus Triandos (Box)	4.00	1.50	1.00
69b	Gus Triandos (Company)	9.00	3.50	2.00
70	Gene Woodling (Box)	30.00	12.00	7.50
71a	Milt Pappas (Box)	4.00	1.50	1.00
71b	Milt Pappas (Company)	17.50	7.00	4.50
72a	Ron Hansen (Box)	4.00	1.50	1.00
72b	Ron Hansen (Company)	9.00	3.50	2.00
73	Chuck Estrada (Company)	110.00	45.00	27.50
74a	Steve Barber (Box)	12.00	4.75	3.00
74b	Steve Barber (Company)	9.00	3.50	2.00
75a	Brooks Robinson (Box)	35.00	15.00	9.00
75b	Brooks Robinson (Company)	35.00	15.00	9.00
76a	Jackie Brandt (Box)	4.00	1.50	1.00
76b	Jackie Brandt (Company)	9.00	3.50	2.00
77a	Marv Breeding (Box)	4.00	1.50	1.00
77b	Marv Breedding (Company)	9.00	3.50	2.00
78	Hal Brown (Box)	4.00	1.50	1.00
79	Billy Klaus (Box)	4.00	1.50	1.00
80a	Hoyt Wilhelm (Box)	7.50	3.00	2.00
80b	Hoyt Wilhelm (Company)	12.50	5.00	3.00
81a	Jerry Lumpe (Box)	9.00	3.50	2.00
81b	Jerry Lumpe (Company)	7.50	3.00	2.00
82a	Norm Siebern (Box)	4.00	1.50	1.00
82b	Norm Siebern (Company)	7.50	3.00	2.00
83a	Bud Daley (Box)	15.00	6.00	4.00
83b	Bud Daley (Company)	25.00	10.00	6.25
84a	Bill Tuttle (Box)	4.00	1.50	1.00
84b	Bill Tuttle (Company)	7.50	3.00	2.00
85a	Marv Throneberry (Box)	4.00	1.50	1.00
85b	Marv Throneberry (Company)	7.50	3.00	2.00
86a	Dick Williams (Box)	15.00	6.00	3.75
86b	Dick Williams (Company)	7.50	3.00	2.00
87a	Ray Herbert (Box)	4.00	1.50	1.00
87b	Ray Herbert (Company)	7.50	3.00	2.00
88a	Whitey Herzog (Box)	4.00	1.50	1.00
88b	Whitey Herzog (Company)	7.50	3.00	2.00
89a	Ken Hamlin (Box, no sold line.)	4.00	1.50	1.00
89b	Ken Hamlin (Company, sold line.)	9.00	3.50	2.00
90a	Hank Bauer (Box)	15.00	6.00	3.75
90b	Hank Bauer (Company)	9.00	3.50	2.00
91a	Bob Allison (Box, Minneapolis.)	9.00	3.50	2.00
91b	Bob Allison (Company, Minnesota.)	20.00	8.00	5.00
92a	Harmon Killebrew (Box, Minneapolis.)	50.00	20.00	12.50
92b	Harmon Killebrew (Company, Minnesota.)	60.00	24.00	15.00
93a	Jim Lemon (Box, Minneapolis.)	65.00	25.00	15.00
93b	Jim Lemon (Company, Minnesota.)	30.00	12.00	7.50
94	Chuck Stobbs (Company)	150.00	60.00	35.00
95a	Reno Bertoia (Box, Minneapolis.)	4.00	1.50	1.00
95b	Reno Bertoia (Company, Minnesota.)	20.00	8.00	5.00
96a	Billy Gardner (Box, Minneapolis.)	4.00	1.50	1.00
96b	Billy Gardner (Company, Minnesota.)	20.00	8.00	5.00
97a	Earl Battey (Box, Minneapolis.)	6.00	2.50	1.50
97b	Earl Battey (Company, Minnesota.)	20.00	8.00	5.00
98a	Pedro Ramos (Box, Minneapolis.)	4.00	1.50	1.00
98b	Pedro Ramos (Company, Minnesota.)	20.00	8.00	5.00
99a	Camilio Pascual (Camilo) (Box, Minneapolis.)	4.00	1.50	1.00
99b	Camilio Pascual (Camilo) (Company, Minnesota.)	20.00	8.00	5.00
100a	Billy Consolo (Box, Minneapolis.)	4.00	1.50	1.00
100b	Billy Consolo (Company, Minnesota.)	22.50	9.00	5.75
101a	Warren Spahn (Box)	35.00	14.00	9.00
101b	Warren Spahn (Company)	25.00	10.00	6.00
102a	Lew Burdette (Box)	4.00	1.50	1.00
102b	Lew Burdette (Company)	7.50	3.00	2.00
103a	Bob Buhl (Box)	4.00	1.50	1.00
103b	Bob Buhl (Company)	12.50	5.00	3.25
104a	Joe Adcock (Box)	12.50	5.00	3.25
104b	Joe Adcock (Company)	7.50	3.00	2.00
105a	John Logan (Box)	6.00	2.50	1.50
105b	John Logan (Company)	15.00	6.00	4.00
106	Ed Mathews (Company)	40.00	16.00	10.00
107a	Hank Aaron (Box)	30.00	12.00	7.50
107b	Hank Aaron (Company)	30.00	12.00	7.50
108a	Wes Covington (Box)	4.00	1.50	1.00
108b	Wes Covington (Company)	7.50	3.00	2.00
109a	Bill Bruton (Box, Braves.)	25.00	10.00	6.25
109b	Bill Bruton (Company, Tigers.)	12.50	5.00	3.00
110a	Del Crandall (Box)	6.00	2.50	1.50
110b	Del Crandall (Company)	7.50	3.00	2.00
111	Red Schoendienst (Box)	12.50	5.00	3.00
112	Juan Pizarro (Box)	4.00	1.50	1.00
113	Chuck Cottier (Box)	15.00	6.00	4.00
114	Al Spangler (Box)	4.00	1.50	1.00
115a	Dick Farrell (Box)	25.00	10.00	6.25
115b	Dick Farrell (Company)	7.50	3.00	2.00
116a	Jim Owens (Box)	15.00	6.00	3.75
116b	Jim Owens (Company)	7.50	3.00	2.00
117a	Robin Roberts (Box)	12.50	5.00	3.00
117b	Robin Roberts (Company)	12.50	5.00	3.00
118a	Tony Taylor (Box)	4.00	1.50	1.00
118b	Tony Taylor (Company)	7.50	3.00	2.00

		NM	EX	VG
119a	Lee Walls (Box)	4.00	1.50	1.00
119b	Lee Walls (Company)	7.50	3.00	2.00
120a	Tony Curry (Box)	4.00	1.50	1.00
120b	Tony Curry (Company)	7.50	3.00	2.00
121a	Pancho Herrera (Box)	4.00	1.50	1.00
121b	Pancho Herrera (Company)	7.50	3.00	2.00
122a	Ken Walters (Box)	4.00	1.50	1.00
122b	Ken Walters (Company)	7.50	3.00	2.00
123a	John Callison (Box)	4.00	1.50	1.00
123b	John Callison (Company)	7.50	3.00	2.00
124a	Gene Conley (Box, Phillies.)	4.00	1.50	1.00
124b	Gene Conley (Company, Red Sox.)	20.00	8.00	5.00
125a	Bob Friend (Box)	5.00	2.00	1.25
125b	Bob Friend (Company)	7.50	3.00	2.00
126a	Vernon Law (Box)	5.00	2.00	1.25
126b	Vernon Law (Company)	7.50	3.00	2.00
127a	Dick Stuart (Box)	4.00	1.50	1.00
127b	Dick Stuart (Company)	7.50	3.00	2.00
128a	Bill Mazeroski (Box)	20.00	8.00	5.00
128b	Bill Mazeroski (Company)	12.50	5.00	3.00
129a	Dick Groat (Box)	4.00	1.50	1.00
129b	Dick Groat (Company)	10.00	4.00	2.50
130a	Don Hoak (Box)	4.00	1.50	1.00
130b	Don Hoak (Company)	7.50	3.00	2.00
131a	Bob Skinner (Box)	4.00	1.50	1.00
131b	Bob Skinner (Company)	7.50	3.00	2.00
132a	Bob Clemente (Box)	50.00	20.00	12.50
132b	Bob Clemente (Company)	70.00	28.00	17.50
133	Roy Face (Box)	15.00	6.00	4.00
134	Harvey Haddix (Box)	10.00	4.00	2.50
135	Bill Virdon (Box)	40.00	16.00	10.00
136a	Gino Cimoli (Box)	4.00	1.50	1.00
136b	Gino Cimoli (Company)	7.50	3.00	2.00
137	Rocky Nelson (Box)	6.00	2.50	1.50
138a	Smoky Burgess (Box)	4.00	1.50	1.00
138b	Smoky Burgess (Company)	7.50	3.00	2.00
139	Hal Smith (Box)	6.00	2.50	1.50
140	Wilmer Mizell (Box)	12.00	4.75	3.00
141a	Mike McCormick (Box)	4.00	1.50	1.00
141b	Mike McCormick (Company)	7.50	3.00	2.00
142a	John Antonelli (Box, Giants.)	4.00	1.50	1.00
142b	John Antonelli (Company, Indians.)	9.00	3.50	2.00
143a	Sam Jones (Box)	5.00	2.00	1.25
143b	Sam Jones (Company)	7.50	3.00	2.00
144a	Orlando Cepeda (Box)	22.50	9.00	5.75
144b	Orlando Cepeda (Company)	12.50	5.00	3.00
145a	Willie Mays (Box)	55.00	22.50	13.50
145b	Willie Mays (Company)	45.00	18.00	10.00
146a	Willie Kirkland (Box, Giants.)	60.00	24.00	15.00
146b	Willie Kirkland (Company, Indians.)	25.00	10.00	6.25
147a	Willie McCovey (Box)	20.00	8.00	5.00
147b	Willie McCovey (Company)	25.00	10.00	6.00
148a	Don Blasingame (Box)	4.00	1.50	1.00
148b	Don Blasingame (Company)	7.50	3.00	2.00
149a	Jim Davenport (Box)	4.00	1.50	1.00
149b	Jim Davenport (Company)	7.50	3.00	2.00
150a	Hobie Landrith (Box)	4.00	1.50	1.00
150b	Hobie Landrith (Company)	7.50	3.00	2.00
151	Bob Schmidt (Box)	9.00	3.50	2.00
152a	Ed Bressoud (Box)	4.00	1.50	1.00
152b	Ed Bressoud (Company)	7.50	3.00	2.00
153a	Andre Rodgers (Box, no traded line.)	9.00	3.50	2.00
153b	Andre Rodgers (Box, traded line.)	4.00	1.50	1.00
154	Jack Sanford (Box)	20.00	8.00	5.00
155	Billy O'Dell (Box)	4.00	1.50	1.00
156a	Norm Larker (Box)	7.50	3.00	2.00
156b	Norm Larker (Company)	7.50	3.00	2.00
157a	Charlie Neal (Box)	4.00	1.50	1.00
157b	Charlie Neal (Company)	7.50	3.00	2.00
158a	Jim Gilliam (Box)	7.50	3.00	2.00
158b	Jim Gilliam (Company)	7.50	3.00	2.00
159a	Wally Moon (Box)	20.00	8.00	5.00
159b	Wally Moon (Company)	12.00	4.75	3.00
160a	Don Drysdale (Box)	20.00	8.00	5.00
160b	Don Drysdale (Company)	20.00	8.00	5.00
161a	Larry Sherry (Box)	4.00	1.50	1.00
161b	Larry Sherry (Company)	7.50	3.00	2.00
162	Stan Williams (Box)	7.50	3.00	2.00
163	Mel Roach (Box)	55.00	22.50	13.50
164a	Maury Wills (Box)	20.00	8.00	5.00
164b	Maury Wills (Company)	35.00	14.00	9.00
165	Tom Davis (Box)	4.00	1.50	1.00
166a	John Roseboro (Box)	4.00	1.50	1.00
166b	John Roseboro (Company)	7.50	3.00	2.00
167a	Duke Snider (Box)	15.00	6.00	3.75
167b	Duke Snider (Company)	20.00	8.00	5.00
168a	Gil Hodges (Box)	7.50	3.00	2.00
168b	Gil Hodges (Company)	12.50	5.00	3.00
169	John Podres (Box)	4.00	1.50	1.00
170	Ed Roebuck (Box)	4.00	1.50	1.00
171a	Ken Boyer (Box)	15.00	6.00	3.75
171b	Ken Boyer (Company)	7.50	3.00	2.00
172a	Joe Cunningham (Box)	12.50	5.00	3.00
172b	Joe Cunningham (Company)	9.00	3.50	2.00
173a	Daryl Spencer (Box)	4.00	1.50	1.00
173b	Daryl Spencer (Company)	7.50	3.00	2.00
174a	Larry Jackson (Box)	12.50	5.00	3.00
174b	Larry Jackson (Company)	7.50	3.00	2.00
175a	Lindy McDaniel (Box)	7.50	3.00	2.00
175b	Lindy McDaniel (Company)	7.50	3.00	2.00
176a	Bill White (Box)	4.00	1.50	1.00
176b	Bill White (Company)	7.50	3.00	2.00
177a	Alex Grammas (Box)	20.00	8.00	5.00
177b	Alex Grammas (Company)	7.50	3.00	2.00
178a	Curt Flood (Box)	4.00	1.50	1.00
178b	Curt Flood (Company)	12.50	5.00	3.00
179a	Ernie Broglio (Box)	4.00	1.50	1.00
179b	Ernie Broglio (Company)	8.00	3.25	2.00
180a	Hal Smith (Box)	8.00	3.25	2.00
180b	Hal Smith (Company)	12.50	5.00	3.00
181a	Vada Pinson (Box)	20.00	8.00	5.00
181b	Vada Pinson (Company)	7.50	3.00	2.00
182a	Frank Robinson (Box)	30.00	12.00	7.50

		NM	EX	VG
182b	Frank Robinson (Company)	35.00	15.00	9.00
183	Roy McMillan (Box)	100.00	40.00	25.00
184a	Bob Purkey (Box)	4.00	1.50	1.00
184b	Bob Purkey (Company)	7.50	3.00	2.00
185a	Ed Kasko (Box)	7.50	3.00	2.00
185b	Ed Kasko (Company)	7.50	3.00	2.00
186a	Gus Bell (Box)	4.00	1.50	1.00
186b	Gus Bell (Company)	7.50	3.00	2.00
187a	Jerry Lynch (Box)	4.00	1.50	1.00
187b	Jerry Lynch (Company)	7.50	3.00	2.00
188a	Ed Bailey (Box)	4.00	1.50	1.00
188b	Ed Bailey (Company)	7.50	3.00	2.00
189a	Jim O'Toole (Box)	4.00	1.50	1.00
189b	Jim O'Toole (Company)	7.50	3.00	2.00
190a	Billy Martin (Box, no sold line.)	6.00	2.50	1.50
190b	Billy Martin (Company, sold line.)	12.50	5.00	3.00
191a	Ernie Banks (Box)	35.00	15.00	9.00
191b	Ernie Banks (Company)	20.00	8.00	5.00
192a	Richie Ashburn (Box)	12.50	5.00	3.00
192b	Richie Ashburn (Company)	22.50	9.00	5.75
193a	Frank Thomas (Box)	100.00	40.00	25.00
193b	Frank Thomas (Company)	40.00	16.00	10.00
194a	Don Cardwell (Box)	6.00	2.50	1.50
194b	Don Cardwell (Company)	7.50	3.00	2.00
195a	George Altman (Box)	15.00	6.00	3.75
195b	George Altman (Company)	7.50	3.00	2.00
196a	Ron Santo (Box)	6.00	2.50	1.50
196b	Ron Santo (Company)	30.00	12.00	7.50
197a	Glen Hobbie (Box)	4.00	1.50	1.00
197b	Glen Hobbie (Company)	7.50	3.00	2.00
198a	Sam Taylor (Box)	4.00	1.50	1.00
198b	Sam Taylor (Company)	7.50	3.00	2.00
199a	Jerry Kindall (Box)	8.00	3.25	2.00
199b	Jerry Kindall (Company)	7.50	3.00	2.00
200a	Don Elston (Box)	12.00	4.75	3.00
200b	Don Elston (Company)	7.50	3.00	2.00

1961 Post Cereal Company Sheets

Via a mail-in offer, sheets of 10 cards from each team could be ordered from the cereal company. Known to collectors as "company" cards, the sheets were issued in a perforated format on cardboard that is somewhat thinner than box-back cards. Sheet cards have perforations on one, two, or three sides, depending on their original placement on the sheet. Because of player movements between the time the box-back cards and sheet cards were printed, some cards are only found on the mail-in sheets, while others could not be obtained via the mail-in offer, and some are shown on the sheets of the "wrong" team.

		NM	EX	VG
	Complete Set (16):	5,250	2,625	1,575
	Common Team:	300.00	150.00	90.00
(1)	Baltimore Orioles	300.00	150.00	90.00
(2)	Boston Red Sox	300.00	150.00	90.00
(3)	Chicago Cubs	300.00	150.00	90.00
(4)	Chicago White Sox	300.00	150.00	90.00
(5)	Cincinnati Reds	300.00	150.00	90.00
(6)	Cleveland Indians	300.00	150.00	90.00
(7)	Detroit Tigers	300.00	150.00	90.00
(8)	Kansas City Athletics	300.00	150.00	90.00
(9)	Los Angeles Dodgers	375.00	185.00	110.00
(10)	Milwaukee Braves	375.00	185.00	110.00
(11)	Minnesota Twins	475.00	235.00	140.00
(12)	New York Yankees	600.00	300.00	180.00
(13)	Philadelphia Phillies	300.00	150.00	90.00
(14)	Pittsburgh Pirates	375.00	185.00	110.00
(15)	San Francisco Giants	375.00	185.00	110.00
(16)	St. Louis Cardinals	300.00	150.00	90.00

1961 Post Cereal Display Pinwheel

Designed for use in grocery stores to promote sales of Post cereal with baseball cards on the back, this display features double-sided, oversize (about 8-1/2" x 6") examples of nine of the cards arranged in a circle. At center was a cardboard cutout of a youngster and accommodation for an electric motor.

	NM	EX	VG
Complete Display:	6,500	3,750	2,000

Ken Boyer, Lew Burdette, Roy Face, Whitey Ford, Nellie Fox, Jim Gentile, Jim Lemon, Willie Mays, Pete Runnels

1962 Post Cereal

Like the 1961 Post set, there are 200 players pictured in this set of 3-1/2" x 2-1/2" cards. Differences include a Post logo on the card fronts and the player's name in script lettering. Cards are again blank backed and were issued in panels of five to seven cards on cereal boxes. American League players are numbered 1-100 and National League players 101-200. With variations there are 210 cards known. Some of the '62 cards, usually those printed on the backs of less popular brands or sizes, were issued in smaller quantities and sell for more than players of star caliber. The cards of Mickey Mantle and Roger Maris were reproduced in a special two-card panel for a Life magazine insert. The card stock for this insert is slightly thinner, with white margins. The 1962 Post Canadian and Jell-O sets have virtually the same checklist as this set. The complete set price does not include the scarcer variations. The #5 Mickey Mantle card has been extensively counterfeited in recent years by pasting a reproduction of the Life magazine promo card (no lines in the stats area) to a piece of blank cardboard. All genuine cereal-box Mantle cards have a grid of lines in the stats area.

		NM	EX	VG
	Complete Set (200):	2,100	850.00	525.00
	Common Player:	4.00	1.50	1.00
	April 13 Life magazine w/ad panel:	90.00	50.00	30.00
1	Bill Skowron	10.00	4.00	2.50
2	Bobby Richardson	12.50	5.00	3.00
3	Cletis Boyer	7.50	3.00	2.00
4	Tony Kubek	9.00	3.50	2.00
5a	Mickey Mantle (From box, no printing on back.)	100.00	40.00	25.00
5b	Mickey Mantle (From ad, printing on back.)	60.00	25.00	15.00
6a	Roger Maris (From box, no printing on back.)	35.00	14.00	9.00
6b	Roger Maris (From ad, printing on back.)	30.00	12.00	7.50
7	Yogi Berra	27.50	11.00	7.00
8	Elston Howard	20.00	8.00	5.00
9	Whitey Ford	22.50	9.00	6.00
10	Ralph Terry	10.00	4.00	2.50
11	John Blanchard	4.00	1.50	1.00
12	Luis Arroyo	20.00	8.00	5.00
13	Bill Stafford	4.00	1.50	1.00
14a	Norm Cash (Throws: Right)	30.00	12.00	7.50
14b	Norm Cash (Throws: Left)	10.00	4.00	2.50
15	Jake Wood	7.50	3.00	2.00
16	Steve Boros	10.00	4.00	2.50
17	Chico Fernandez	4.00	1.50	1.00
18	Bill Bruton	4.00	1.50	1.00
19	Rocky Colavito	16.00	6.50	4.00
20	Al Kaline	20.00	8.00	5.00
21	Dick Brown	4.00	1.50	1.00
22	Frank Lary	4.00	1.50	1.00
23	Don Mossi	4.00	1.50	1.00
24	Phil Regan	4.00	1.50	1.00
25	Charley Maxwell	7.50	3.00	2.00
26	Jim Bunning	30.00	12.00	7.50
27a	Jim Gentile (Home: Baltimore)	4.00	1.50	1.00
27b	Jim Gentile (Home: San Lorenzo)	6.00	2.50	1.00
28	Marv Breeding	4.00	1.50	1.00
29	Brooks Robinson	17.50	7.00	4.50
30	Ron Hansen	4.00	1.50	1.00
31	Jackie Brandt	4.00	1.50	1.00
32	Dick Williams	4.00	1.50	1.00
33	Gus Triandos	4.00	1.50	1.00
34	Milt Pappas	7.50	3.00	2.00
35	Hoyt Wilhelm	15.00	6.00	3.50
36	Chuck Estrada	12.50	5.00	3.00
37	Vic Power	4.00	1.50	1.00
38	Johnny Temple	4.00	1.50	1.00
39	Bubba Phillips	4.00	1.50	1.00
40	Tito Francona	9.00	3.50	2.00
41	Willie Kirkland	4.00	1.50	1.00
42	John Romano	4.00	1.50	1.00
43	Jim Perry	4.00	1.50	1.00
44	Woodie Held	4.00	1.50	1.00
45	Chuck Essegian	4.00	1.50	1.00
46	Roy Sievers	4.00	1.50	1.00
47	Nellie Fox	7.50	3.00	2.00
48	Al Smith	4.00	1.50	1.00
49	Luis Aparicio	12.50	5.00	3.25
50	Jim Landis	7.50	3.00	2.00

51	Minnie Minoso	10.00	4.00	2.50
52	Andy Carey	7.50	3.00	2.00
53	Sherman Lollar	4.00	1.50	1.00
54	Bill Pierce	7.50	3.00	2.00
55	Early Wynn	50.00	20.00	12.50
56	Chuck Schilling	7.50	3.00	2.00
57	Pete Runnels	15.00	6.00	3.75
58	Frank Malzone	4.00	1.50	1.00
59	Don Buddin	4.00	1.50	1.00
60	Gary Geiger	25.00	10.00	6.25
61	Carl Yastrzemski	60.00	25.00	15.00
62	Jackie Jensen	7.50	3.00	2.00
63	Jim Pagliaroni	4.00	1.50	1.00
64	Don Schwall	4.00	1.50	1.00
65	Dale Long	4.00	1.50	1.00
66	Chuck Cottier	4.00	1.50	1.00
67	Billy Klaus	9.00	3.50	2.00
68	Coot Veal	9.00	3.50	2.00
69	Marty Keough	55.00	22.50	13.50
70	Willie Tasby	9.00	3.50	2.00
71	Gene Woodling	4.00	1.50	1.00
72	Gene Green	4.00	1.50	1.00
73	Dick Donovan	4.00	1.50	1.00
74	Steve Bilko	4.00	1.50	1.00
75	Rocky Bridges	4.00	1.50	1.00
76	Eddie Yost	4.00	1.50	1.00
77	Leon Wagner	4.00	1.50	1.00
78	Albie Pearson	7.50	3.00	2.00
79	Ken Hunt	4.00	1.50	1.00
80	Earl Averill	4.00	1.50	1.00
81	Ryne Duren	4.00	1.50	1.00
82	Ted Kluszewski	6.00	2.50	1.50
83	Bob Allison	90.00	35.00	20.00
84	Billy Martin	9.00	3.50	2.00
85	Harmon Killebrew	40.00	16.00	10.00
86	Zoilo Versalles	20.00	8.00	5.00
87	Lenny Green	10.00	4.00	2.50
88	Bill Tuttle	4.00	1.50	1.00
89	Jim Lemon	4.00	1.50	1.00
90	Earl Battey	4.00	1.50	1.00
91	Camilo Pascual	4.00	1.50	1.00
92	Norm Siebern	60.00	24.00	15.00
93	Jerry Lumpe	4.00	1.50	1.00
94	Dick Howser	4.00	1.50	1.00
95a	Gene Stephens (Born: Jan. 5)	4.00	1.50	1.00
95b	Gene Stephens (Born: Jan. 20)	20.00	8.00	5.00
96	Leo Posada	4.00	1.50	1.00
97	Joe Pignatano	7.50	3.00	2.00
98	Jim Archer	4.00	1.50	1.00
99	Haywood Sullivan	4.00	1.50	1.00
100	Art Ditmar	6.00	2.50	1.50
101	Gil Hodges	80.00	32.50	20.00
102	Charlie Neal	4.00	1.50	1.00
103	Daryl Spencer	25.00	10.00	6.00
104	Maury Wills	4.00	1.50	1.00
105	Tommy Davis	4.00	1.50	1.00
106	Willie Davis	4.00	1.50	1.00
107	John Roseboro	7.50	3.00	2.00
108	John Podres	4.00	1.50	1.00
109a	Sandy Koufax (Blue lines around stats.)	450.00	180.00	110.00
109b	Sandy Koufax (Red lines around stats.)	40.00	16.00	10.00
110	Don Drysdale	20.00	8.00	5.00
111	Larry Sherry	4.00	1.50	1.00
112	Jim Gilliam	7.50	3.00	2.00
113	Norm Larker	80.00	32.50	20.00
114	Duke Snider	20.00	8.00	5.00
115	Stan Williams	4.00	1.50	1.00
116	Gordy Coleman	75.00	30.00	18.50
117	Don Blasingame	12.50	5.00	3.00
118	Gene Freese	4.00	1.50	1.00
119	Ed Kasko	4.00	1.50	1.00
120	Gus Bell	4.00	1.50	1.00
121	Vada Pinson	7.50	3.00	2.00
122	Frank Robinson	50.00	20.00	12.50
123	Bob Purkey	4.00	1.50	1.00
124a	Joey Jay (Blue lines around stats.)	225.00	90.00	55.00
124b	Joey Jay (Red lines around stats.)	6.00	2.50	1.50
125	Jim Brosnan	35.00	14.00	9.00
126	Jim O'Toole	4.00	1.50	1.00
127	Jerry Lynch	65.00	25.00	15.00
128	Wally Post	4.00	1.50	1.00
129	Ken Hunt	4.00	1.50	1.00
130	Jerry Zimmerman	4.00	1.50	1.00
131	Willie McCovey	75.00	30.00	18.50
132	Jose Pagan	4.00	1.50	1.00
133	Felipe Alou	4.00	1.50	1.00
134	Jim Davenport	4.00	1.50	1.00
135	Harvey Kuenn	4.00	1.50	1.00
136	Orlando Cepeda	15.00	6.00	3.75
137	Ed Bailey	4.00	1.50	1.00
138	Sam Jones	4.00	1.50	1.00
139	Mike McCormick	4.00	1.50	1.00
140	Juan Marichal	80.00	32.00	20.00
141	Jack Sanford	4.00	1.50	1.00
142	Willie Mays	55.00	22.50	13.50
143	Stu Miller (Photo actually Chuck Hiller.)	5.00	2.00	1.25
144	Joe Amalfitano	35.00	14.00	9.00
145a	Joe Adock (Name incorrect.)	115.00	45.00	30.00
145b	Joe Adcock (Name correct.)	4.00	1.50	1.00
146	Frank Bolling	4.00	1.50	1.00
147	Ed Mathews	17.50	7.00	4.50
148	Roy McMillan	4.00	1.50	1.00
149	Hank Aaron	35.00	14.00	9.00
150	Gino Cimoli	4.00	1.50	1.00
151	Frank Thomas	4.00	1.50	1.00
152	Joe Torre	25.00	10.00	6.25
153	Lou Burdette	4.00	1.50	1.00
154	Bob Buhl	10.00	4.00	2.50
155	Carlton Willey	20.00	8.00	5.00
156	Lee Maye	20.00	8.00	5.00
157	Al Spangler	7.50	3.00	2.00

158	Bill White	45.00	18.00	10.00
159	Ken Boyer	6.00	2.50	1.50
160	Joe Cunningham	4.00	1.50	1.00
161	Carl Warwick	4.00	1.50	1.00
162	Carl Sawatski	4.00	1.50	1.00
163	Lindy McDaniel	4.00	1.50	1.00
164	Ernie Broglio	4.00	1.50	1.00
165	Larry Jackson	4.00	1.50	1.00
166	Curt Flood	4.00	1.50	1.00
167	Curt Simmons	4.00	1.50	1.00
168	Alex Grammas	4.00	1.50	1.00
169	Dick Stuart	10.00	4.00	2.50
170	Bill Mazeroski	20.00	8.00	5.00
171	Don Hoak	20.00	8.00	5.00
172	Dick Groat	4.00	1.50	1.00
173a	Roberto Clemente (Blue lines around stats.)	400.00	160.00	100.00
173b	Roberto Clemente (Red lines around stats.)	45.00	18.00	11.00
174	Bob Skinner	4.00	1.50	1.00
175	Bill Virdon	4.00	1.50	1.00
176	Smoky Burgess	9.00	3.50	2.25
177	Elroy Face	4.00	1.50	1.00
178	Bob Friend	4.00	1.50	1.00
179	Vernon Law	4.00	1.50	1.00
180	Harvey Haddix	4.00	1.50	1.00
181	Hal Smith	7.50	3.00	2.00
182	Ed Bouchee	4.00	1.50	1.00
183	Don Zimmer	4.00	1.50	1.00
184	Ron Santo	7.50	3.00	2.00
185	Andre Rodgers	4.00	1.50	1.00
186	Richie Ashburn	12.50	5.00	3.00
187a	George Altman (Last line is "...1955.")	6.00	2.50	1.50
187b	George Altman (Last line is "...1955.")	7.50	3.00	2.00
188	Ernie Banks	17.50	7.00	4.50
189	Sam Taylor	25.00	10.00	6.25
190	Don Elston	7.50	3.00	2.00
191	Jerry Kindall	4.00	1.50	1.00
192	Pancho Herrera	4.00	1.50	1.00
193	Tony Taylor	4.00	1.50	1.00
194	Ruben Amaro	9.00	3.50	2.00
195	Don Demeter	4.00	1.50	1.00
196	Bobby Gene Smith	4.00	1.50	1.00
197	Clay Dalrymple	4.00	1.50	1.00
198	Robin Roberts	10.00	4.00	2.50
199	Art Mahaffey	4.00	1.50	1.00
200	John Buzhardt	4.00	1.50	1.00

1962 Post Cereal - Canadian

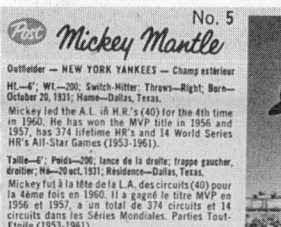

This Post set is scarce due to the much more limited distribution in Canada. Most cards were printed on the back of the cereal boxes and contain a full-color player photo with biography and statistics given in both French and English. Card backs are blank. Cards measure 3-1/2" x 2-1/2". This 200-card set is very similar to the Post Cereal cards printed in the United States. The Post logo appears at the upper-left corner in the Canadian issue. Several cards are scarce because of limited distribution and there are two Whitey Ford cards, the corrected version being the most scarce. The complete set price does not include the scarcer variations. Certain cereal brands had the cards packaged inside the box on perforated panels, and will be found with perforated edges on one side or other.

		NM	EX	VG
	Complete Set (200):	5,000	2,005	1,250
	Common Player:	8.00	3.25	2.00
1	Bill Skowron	35.00	15.00	9.00
2	Bobby Richardson	12.00	4.75	3.00
3	Cletis Boyer	10.00	4.00	2.50
4	Tony Kubek	12.00	4.75	3.00
5a	Mickey Mantle (Stats list 153 hits.)	215.00	85.00	55.00
5b	Mickey Mantle (163 hits; first line of bio ends: "4th time in.")	120.00	50.00	30.00
5c	Mickey Mantle (163 hits; first line of bio ends: "4th time.")	125.00	50.00	30.00
6a	Roger Maris (First line of French bio has large "P" in "Pour les circuits.")	65.00	25.00	15.00
6b	Roger Maris (French text reads, "Residence." Small "p" in "pour.")	55.00	22.50	13.50
6c	Roger Maris (French text reads, "a", not "Residence." Small "p" in "pour.")	55.00	22.50	13.50
7	Yogi Berra	40.00	16.00	10.00
8	Elston Howard	12.00	4.75	3.00

9a	Whitey Ford (Dodgers)	55.00	22.50	13.50
9b	Whitey Ford (Yankees)	80.00	32.00	20.00
10	Ralph Terry	95.00	38.00	24.00
11	John Blanchard	8.00	3.25	2.00
12	Luis Arroyo	8.00	3.25	2.00
13	Bill Stafford	8.00	3.25	2.00
14	Norm Cash	10.00	4.00	2.50
15	Jake Wood	8.00	3.25	2.00
16	Steve Boros	8.00	3.25	2.00
17	Chico Fernandez	8.00	3.25	2.00
18	Bill Bruton	8.00	3.25	2.00
19a	Rocky Colavito (Script name large.)	17.50	7.00	4.50
19b	Rocky Colavito (Script name small.)	17.50	7.00	4.50
20	Al Kaline	85.00	35.00	20.00
21	Dick Brown	12.00	4.75	3.00
22a	Frank Lary ("Residence-Northport, Alabama.")	17.50	7.00	4.50
22b	Frank Lary ("A Northport, Alabama.")	65.00	25.00	15.00
23	Don Mossi	8.00	3.25	2.00
24	Phil Regan	8.00	3.25	2.00
25	Charley Maxwell	8.00	3.25	2.00
26	Jim Bunning	25.00	10.00	6.25
27a	Jim Gentile (French bio begins "Le 8 mai, Jim ...")	13.50	5.50	3.50
27b	Jim Gentile (Begins, "Le 8 mai 1961, Jim ...")	13.50	5.50	3.50
28	Marv Breeding	17.50	7.00	4.50
29	Brooks Robinson	50.00	20.00	12.50
30	Ron Hansen	8.00	3.25	2.00
31	Jackie Brandt	8.00	3.25	2.00
32	Dick Williams	55.00	22.50	13.50
33	Gus Triandos	10.00	4.00	2.50
34	Milt Pappas	10.00	4.00	2.50
35	Hoyt Wilhelm	95.00	38.00	24.00
36	Chuck Estrada	8.00	3.25	2.00
37	Vic Power	8.00	3.25	2.00
38	Johnny Temple	8.00	3.25	2.00
39	Bubba Phillips	55.00	22.50	13.50
40	Tito Francona	55.00	22.50	13.50
41	Willie Kirkland	13.50	5.50	3.50
42	John Romano	13.50	5.50	3.50
43	Jim Perry	10.00	4.00	2.50
44	Woodie Held	8.00	3.25	2.00
45	Chuck Essegian	8.00	3.25	2.00
46	Roy Sievers	40.00	16.00	10.00
47	Nellie Fox	25.00	10.00	6.25
48	Al Smith	8.00	3.25	2.00
49	Luis Aparicio	100.00	40.00	25.00
50	Jim Landis	13.50	5.50	3.50
51	Minnie Minoso	55.00	22.50	13.50
52	Andy Carey	12.00	4.75	3.00
53	Sherman Lollar	8.00	3.25	2.00
54	Bill Pierce	10.00	4.00	2.50
55	Early Wynn	30.00	12.00	7.50
56	Chuck Schilling	10.00	4.00	2.50
57	Pete Runnels	10.00	4.00	2.50
58	Frank Malzone	8.00	3.25	2.00
59	Don Buddin	12.00	4.75	3.00
60	Gary Geiger	8.00	3.25	2.00
61	Carl Yastrzemski	60.00	25.00	15.00
62	Jackie Jensen	40.00	16.00	10.00
63	Jim Pagliaroni	8.00	3.25	2.00
64	Don Schwall	25.00	10.00	6.25
65	Dale Long	20.00	8.00	5.00
66	Chuck Cottier	8.00	3.25	2.00
67	Billy Klaus	8.00	3.25	2.00
68	Coot Veal	8.00	3.25	2.00
69	Marty Keough	8.00	3.25	2.00
70	Willie Tasby	125.00	50.00	30.00
71	Gene Woodling (Photo reversed.)	10.00	4.00	2.50
72	Gene Green	12.00	4.75	3.00
73	Dick Donovan	8.00	3.25	2.00
74	Steve Bilko	13.50	5.50	3.50
75	Rocky Bridges	12.00	4.75	3.00
76	Eddie Yost	8.00	3.25	2.00
77	Leon Wagner	65.00	25.00	15.00
78	Albie Pearson	13.50	5.50	3.50
79	Ken Hunt	8.00	3.25	2.00
80	Earl Averill	8.00	3.25	2.00
81	Ryne Duren	10.00	4.00	2.50
82	Ted Kluszewski	30.00	12.00	7.50
83	Bob Allison	13.50	5.50	3.50
84	Billy Martin	17.50	7.00	4.50
85	Harmon Killebrew	125.00	50.00	30.00
86	Zoilo Versalles	8.00	3.25	2.00
87	Lenny Green	95.00	38.00	24.00
88	Bill Tuttle	8.00	3.25	2.00
89	Jim Lemon	8.00	3.25	2.00
90	Earl Battey	13.50	5.50	3.50
91	Camilo Pascual	10.00	4.00	2.50
92	Norm Siebern	8.00	3.25	2.00
93	Jerry Lumpe	8.00	3.25	2.00
94	Dick Howser	80.00	32.00	20.00
95	Gene Stephens	8.00	3.25	2.00
96	Leo Posada	8.00	3.25	2.00
97	Joe Pignatano	8.00	3.25	2.00
98	Jim Archer	8.00	3.25	2.00
99	Haywood Sullivan	125.00	50.00	30.00
100	Art Ditmar	25.00	10.00	6.25
101	Gil Hodges	35.00	15.00	9.00
102	Charlie Neal	8.00	3.25	2.00
103	Daryl Spencer	8.00	3.25	2.00
104	Maury Wills	17.50	7.00	4.50
105	Tommy Davis	55.00	22.50	13.50
106	Willie Davis	12.00	4.75	3.00
107	John Rosboro (Roseboro)	10.00	4.00	2.50
108	John Podres	10.00	4.00	2.50
109	Sandy Koufax	80.00	32.00	20.00
110	Don Drysdale	35.00	15.00	9.00
111	Larry Sherry	55.00	22.50	13.50
112	Jim Gilliam	55.00	22.50	13.50
113	Norm Larker	8.00	3.25	2.00
114	Duke Snider	30.00	12.00	7.50
115	Stan Williams	13.50	5.50	3.50

116	Gordy Coleman	8.00	3.25	2.00
117	Don Blasingame	160.00	65.00	40.00
118	Gene Freese	40.00	16.00	10.00
119	Ed Kasko	13.50	5.50	3.50
120	Gus Bell	8.00	3.25	2.00
121	Vada Pinson	10.00	4.00	2.50
122	Frank Robinson	50.00	20.00	12.50
123	Bob Purkey	55.00	22.50	13.50
124	Joey Jay	8.00	3.25	2.00
125	Jim Brosnan	17.50	7.00	4.50
126	Jim O'Toole	8.00	3.25	2.00
127	Jerry Lynch	15.00	6.00	3.75
128	Wally Post	135.00	55.00	35.00
129	Ken Hunt	8.00	3.25	2.00
130	Jerry Zimmerman	8.00	3.25	2.00
131	Willie McCovey	40.00	16.00	10.00
132	Jose Pagan	12.00	4.75	3.00
133	Felipe Alou	10.00	4.00	2.50
134	Jim Davenport	8.00	3.25	2.00
135	Harvey Kuenn	10.00	4.00	2.50
136	Orlando Cepeda	25.00	10.00	6.25
137	Ed Bailey	75.00	30.00	18.50
138	Sam Jones	55.00	22.50	13.50
139	Mike McCormick	8.00	3.25	2.00
140	Juan Marichal	35.00	15.00	9.00
141	Jack Sanford	8.00	3.25	2.00
142a	Willie Mays (Big head.)	80.00	32.00	20.00
142b	Willie Mays (Small head.)	60.00	24.00	15.00
143	Stu Miller	8.00	3.25	2.00
144	Joe Amalfitano	100.00	40.00	25.00
145	Joe Adcock	13.50	5.50	3.50
146	Frank Bolling	13.50	5.50	3.50
147	Ed Mathews	30.00	12.00	7.50
148	Roy McMillan	24.00	9.50	6.00
149a	Hank Aaron (Script name large.)	80.00	32.00	20.00
149b	Hank Aaron (Script name small.)	60.00	24.00	15.00
150	Gino Cimoli	8.00	3.25	2.00
151	Frank Thomas	8.00	3.25	2.00
152	Joe Torre	25.00	10.00	6.25
153	Lou Burdette	25.00	10.00	6.25
154	Bob Buhl	10.00	4.00	2.50
155	Carlton Willey	12.00	4.75	3.00
156	Lee Maye	8.00	3.25	2.00
157	Al Spangler	8.00	3.25	2.00
158	Bill White	10.00	4.00	2.50
159	Ken Boyer	40.00	16.00	10.00
160	Joe Cunningham	8.00	3.25	2.00
161	Carl Warwick	55.00	22.50	13.50
162	Carl Sawatski	8.00	3.25	2.00
163	Lindy McDaniel	8.00	3.25	2.00
164	Ernie Broglio	8.00	3.25	2.00
165	Larry Jackson	8.00	3.25	2.00
166	Curt Flood	25.00	10.00	6.25
167	Curt Simmons	17.50	7.00	4.50
168	Alex Grammas	8.00	3.25	2.00
169	Dick Stuart	25.00	10.00	6.25
170	Bill Mazeroski	40.00	16.00	10.00
171	Don Hoak	8.00	3.25	2.00
172	Dick Groat	17.50	7.00	4.50
173	Roberto Clemente	100.00	40.00	25.00
174	Bob Skinner	8.00	3.25	2.00
175	Bill Virdon	10.00	4.00	2.50
176	Smoky Burgess	40.00	16.00	10.00
177	Elroy Face	17.50	7.00	4.50
178	Bob Friend	10.00	4.00	2.50
179	Vernon Law	10.00	4.00	2.50
180	Harvey Haddix	10.00	4.00	2.50
181	Hal Smith	85.00	35.00	20.00
182	Ed Bouchee	100.00	40.00	25.00
183	Don Zimmer	10.00	4.00	2.50
184	Ron Santo	13.50	5.50	3.50
185	Andre Rogers (Rodgers)	8.00	3.25	2.00
186	Richie Ashburn	30.00	12.00	7.50
187	George Altman	8.00	3.25	2.00
188	Ernie Banks	40.00	16.00	10.00
189	Sam Taylor	30.00	12.00	7.50
190	Don Elston	8.00	3.25	2.00
191	Jerry Kindall	8.00	3.25	2.00
192	Pancho Herrera	8.00	3.25	2.00
193	Tony Taylor	8.00	3.25	2.00
194	Ruben Amaro	8.00	3.25	2.00
195	Don Demeter	55.00	22.50	13.50
196	Bobby Gene Smith	8.00	3.25	2.00
197	Clay Dalrymple	8.00	3.25	2.00
198	Robin Roberts	45.00	18.00	11.00
199	Art Mahaffey	8.00	3.25	2.00
200	John Buzhardt	10.00	4.00	2.50

1963 Post Cereal

Another 200-player, 3-1/2" x 2-1/2" set that, with variations, totals more than 205 cards. Numerous color variations also exist due to the different cereal boxes on which the cards were printed. More than any of the other 1960s Post baseball issues, the set is rife with short-prints and other scarcities which make it more difficult to complete than earlier years' sets. The 1963 Post cards are almost identical to the '63 Jell-O set, which is a slight 1/4" narrower. Cards are blank-backed, with a color player photo, biographies and statistics on the numbered card fronts. No Post logo appears on the '63 cards. The complete set price does not include the scarcer variations. An album to hold the cards was given away at grocery stores in a display featuring Mickey Mantle.

		NM	EX	VG
	Complete Set (200):	4,500	1,800	1,000
	Common Player:	5.00	2.00	1.25
1	Vic Power	6.00	2.50	1.50
2	Bernie Allen	6.00	2.50	1.50
3	Zoilo Versalles	7.50	3.00	2.00
4	Rich Rollins	5.00	2.00	1.25
5	Harmon Killebrew	25.00	10.00	6.00
6	Lenny Green	35.00	15.00	9.00
7	Bob Allison	9.00	3.50	2.00
8	Earl Battey	12.50	5.00	3.00
9	Camilo Pascual	15.00	6.00	3.50
10a	Jim Kaat (Light pole in background.)	15.00	6.00	3.50
10b	Jim Kaat (no light pole)	10.00	4.00	2.50
11	Jack Kralick	7.50	3.00	2.00
12	Bill Skowron	15.00	6.00	3.50
13	Bobby Richardson	15.00	6.00	3.50
14	Cletis Boyer	6.00	2.50	1.50
15	Mickey Mantle	300.00	120.00	75.00
16	Roger Maris	115.00	45.00	30.00
17	Yogi Berra	30.00	12.00	7.50
18	Elston Howard	13.50	5.50	3.50
19	Whitey Ford	15.00	6.00	3.50
20	Ralph Terry	6.00	2.50	1.50
21	John Blanchard	10.00	4.00	2.50
22	Bill Stafford	5.00	2.00	1.25
23	Tom Tresh	9.00	3.50	2.00
24	Steve Bilko	15.00	6.00	3.50
25	Bill Moran	5.00	2.00	1.25
26a	Joe Koppe (1962 Avg. is .277.)	17.50	7.00	4.50
26b	Joe Koppe (1962 Avg. is .227.)	35.00	15.00	9.00
27	Felix Torres	7.50	3.00	2.00
28a	Leon Wagner (Lifetime Avg. is .278.)	15.00	6.00	3.50
28b	Leon Wagner (Lifetime Avg. is .272.)	25.00	10.00	6.00
29	Albie Pearson	5.00	2.00	1.25
30	Lee Thomas (Photo actually George Thomas.)	75.00	30.00	18.50
31	Bob Rodgers	5.00	2.00	1.25
32	Dean Chance	5.00	2.00	1.25
33	Ken McBride	7.50	3.00	2.00
34	George Thomas (Photo actually Lee Thomas.)	9.00	3.50	2.00
35	Joe Cunningham	5.00	2.00	1.25
36a	Nelson Fox (No bat showing.)	30.00	12.00	7.50
36b	Nelson Fox (Part of bat showing.)	25.00	10.00	6.00
37	Luis Aparicio	15.00	6.00	3.75
38	Al Smith	50.00	20.00	12.50
39	Floyd Robinson	100.00	40.00	25.00
40	Jim Landis	5.00	2.00	1.25
41	Charlie Maxwell	5.00	2.00	1.25
42	Sherman Lollar	5.00	2.00	1.25
43	Early Wynn	9.00	3.50	2.00
44	Juan Pizarro	5.00	2.00	1.25
45	Ray Herbert	5.00	2.00	1.25
46	Norm Cash	25.00	10.00	6.25
47	Steve Boros	5.00	2.00	1.25
48	Dick McAuliffe	35.00	15.00	9.00
49	Bill Bruton	12.50	5.00	3.00
50	Rocky Colavito	25.00	10.00	6.25
51	Al Kaline	25.00	10.00	6.25
52	Dick Brown	5.00	2.00	1.25
53	Jim Bunning	100.00	40.00	25.00
54	Hank Aguirre	5.00	2.00	1.25
55	Frank Lary	5.00	2.00	1.25
56	Don Mossi	7.50	3.00	2.00
57	Jim Gentile	9.00	3.50	2.00
58	Jackie Brandt	7.50	3.00	2.00
59	Brooks Robinson	25.00	10.00	6.00
60	Ron Hansen	5.00	2.00	1.25
61	Jerry Adair	130.00	50.00	30.00
62	John (Boog) Powell	15.00	6.00	3.75
63	Russ Snyder	5.00	2.00	1.25
64	Steve Barber	7.50	3.00	2.00
65	Milt Pappas	5.00	2.00	1.25
66	Robin Roberts	10.00	4.00	2.50
67	Tito Francona	5.00	2.00	1.25
68	Jerry Kindall	12.50	5.00	3.00
69	Woodie Held	5.00	2.00	1.25
70	Bubba Phillips	25.00	10.00	6.00
71	Chuck Essegian	5.00	2.00	1.25
72	Willie Kirkland	5.00	2.00	1.25
73	Al Luplow	5.00	2.00	1.25
74	Ty Cline	5.00	2.00	1.25
75	Dick Donovan	5.00	2.00	1.25
76	John Romano	5.00	2.00	1.25
77	Pete Runnels	6.00	2.50	1.50
78	Ed Bressoud	5.00	2.00	1.25
79	Frank Malzone	10.00	4.00	2.50
80	Carl Yastrzemski	250.00	100.00	62.00
81	Gary Geiger	5.00	2.00	1.25
82	Lou Clinton	5.00	2.00	1.25
83	Earl Wilson	7.50	3.00	2.00
84	Bill Monbouquette	5.00	2.00	1.25
85	Norm Siebern	5.00	2.00	1.25
86	Jerry Lumpe	100.00	40.00	25.00
87	Manny Jimenez	150.00	60.00	37.50
88	Gino Cimoli	9.00	3.50	2.00

89	Ed Charles	5.00	2.00	1.25
90	Ed Rakow	5.00	2.00	1.25
91	Bob Del Greco	5.00	2.00	1.25
92	Haywood Sullivan	5.00	2.00	1.25
93	Chuck Hinton	5.00	2.00	1.25
94	Ken Retzer	12.50	5.00	3.00
95	Harry Bright	5.00	2.00	1.25
96	Bob Johnson	7.50	3.00	2.00
97	Dave Stenhouse	20.00	8.00	5.00
98	Chuck Cottier	25.00	10.00	6.25
99	Tom Cheney	7.50	3.00	2.00
100	Claude Osteen	35.00	15.00	9.00
101	Orlando Cepeda	7.50	3.00	2.00
102	Charley Hiller	7.50	3.00	2.00
103	Jose Pagan	5.00	2.00	1.25
104	Jim Davenport	5.00	2.00	1.25
105	Harvey Kuenn	15.00	6.00	3.50
106	Willie Mays	40.00	16.00	10.00
107	Felipe Alou	7.50	3.00	2.00
108	Tom Haller	100.00	40.00	25.00
109	Juan Marichal	10.00	4.00	2.50
110	Jack Sanford	5.00	2.00	1.25
111	Bill O'Dell	5.00	2.00	1.25
112	Willie McCovey	12.50	5.00	3.00
113	Lee Walls	10.00	4.00	2.50
114	Jim Gilliam	15.00	6.00	3.50
115	Maury Wills	17.50	7.00	4.50
116	Ron Fairly	5.00	2.00	1.25
117	Tommy Davis	5.00	2.00	1.25
118	Duke Snider	25.00	10.00	6.25
119	Willie Davis	225.00	90.00	55.00
120	John Roseboro	5.00	2.00	1.25
121	Sandy Koufax	50.00	20.00	12.50
122	Stan Williams	9.00	3.50	2.00
123	Don Drysdale	20.00	8.00	5.00
124a	Daryl Spencer (No arm showing.)	7.50	3.00	2.00
124b	Daryl Spencer (Part of arm showing.)	15.00	6.00	3.50
125	Gordy Coleman	7.50	3.00	2.00
126	Don Blasingame	5.00	2.00	1.25
127	Leo Cardenas	5.00	2.00	1.25
128	Eddie Kasko	200.00	80.00	50.00
129	Jerry Lynch	35.00	15.00	9.75
130	Vada Pinson	15.00	6.00	3.50
131a	Frank Robinson (No stripes on cap.)	30.00	12.00	7.50
131b	Frank Robinson (Stripes on cap.)	75.00	30.00	17.50
132	John Edwards	15.00	6.00	3.50
133	Joey Jay	5.00	2.00	1.25
134	Bob Purkey	5.00	2.00	1.25
135	Marty Keough	15.00	6.00	3.50
136	Jim O'Toole	5.00	2.00	1.25
137	Dick Stuart	7.50	3.00	2.00
138	Bill Mazeroski	12.50	5.00	3.00
139	Dick Groat	6.00	2.50	1.50
140	Don Hoak	25.00	10.00	6.00
141	Bob Skinner	25.00	10.00	6.25
142	Bill Virdon	5.00	2.00	1.25
143	Roberto Clemente	60.00	24.00	15.00
144	Smoky Burgess	15.00	6.00	3.50
145	Bob Friend	5.00	2.00	1.25
146	Al McBean	5.00	2.00	1.25
147	El Roy Face (Elroy)	20.00	8.00	5.00
148	Joe Adcock	13.50	5.50	3.50
149	Frank Bolling	5.00	2.00	1.25
150	Roy McMillan	7.50	3.00	2.00
151	Eddie Mathews	22.50	9.00	5.75
152	Hank Aaron	50.00	20.00	12.50
153	Del Crandall	25.00	10.00	6.25
154a	Bob Shaw (Third sentence has "In 1959" twice.)	10.00	4.00	2.50
154b	Bob Shaw (Third sentence has "In 1959" once.)	9.00	3.50	2.00
155	Lew Burdette	20.00	8.00	5.00
156	Joe Torre	7.50	3.00	2.00
157	Tony Cloninger	5.00	2.00	1.25
158a	Bill White (Ht. 6')	6.00	2.50	1.50
158b	Bill White (Ht. 6'0")	6.00	2.50	1.50
159	Julian Javier	5.00	2.00	1.25
160	Ken Boyer	7.50	3.00	2.00
161	Julio Gotay	5.00	2.00	1.25
162	Curt Flood	100.00	40.00	25.00
163	Charlie James	9.00	3.50	2.00
164	Gene Oliver	5.00	2.00	1.25
165	Ernie Broglio	15.00	6.00	3.50
166	Bob Gibson	45.00	18.00	11.00
167a	Lindy McDaniel (Asterisk before trade line.)	10.00	4.00	2.50
167b	Lindy McDaniel (No asterisk before trade line.)	12.50	5.00	3.25
168	Ray Washburn	5.00	2.00	1.25
169	Ernie Banks	17.50	7.00	4.50
170	Ron Santo	25.00	10.00	6.25
171	George Altman	7.50	3.00	2.00
172	Billy Williams	95.00	35.00	25.00
173	Andre Rodgers	10.00	4.00	2.50
174	Ken Hubbs	25.00	10.00	6.00
175	Don Landrum	5.00	2.00	1.25
176	Dick Bertell	20.00	8.00	5.00
177	Roy Sievers	7.50	3.00	2.00
178	Tony Taylor	12.50	5.00	3.50
179	John Callison	5.00	2.00	1.25
180	Don Demeter	5.00	2.00	1.25
181	Tony Gonzalez	25.00	10.00	6.25
182	Wes Covington	35.00	15.00	9.00
183	Art Mahaffey	5.00	2.00	1.25
184	Clay Dalrymple	7.50	3.00	2.00
185	Al Spangler	6.00	2.50	1.50
186	Roman Mejias	7.50	3.00	2.00
187	Bob Aspromonte	475.00	190.00	120.00
188	Norm Larker	25.00	10.00	6.00
189	Johnny Temple	7.50	3.00	2.00
190	Carl Warwick	15.00	6.00	3.50
191	Bob Lillis	9.00	3.50	2.00
192	Dick Farrell	5.00	2.00	1.25
193	Gil Hodges	15.00	6.00	3.50

		NM	EX	VG
194	Marv Throneberry	7.50	3.00	2.00
195	Charlie Neal	30.00	12.00	7.50
196	Frank Thomas	235.00	95.00	60.00
197	Richie Ashburn	35.00	15.00	9.00
198	Felix Mantilla	10.00	4.00	2.50
199	Rod Kanehl	60.00	25.00	15.00
200	Roger Craig	10.00	4.00	2.50

1963 Post/Jell-O Album

The baseball history and other printed matter in this 26-page 8-1/2" x 11" album seems to point to 1963 as the issue date, though 1962 would not be impossible. Each major league team has a page on which the box-back cards from Post cereals and Jell-O could be pasted. The front cover is printed in red-and-white while the interior pages are in black-and-white.

	NM	EX	VG
Post/Jell-O Album	90.00	45.00	25.00

1978 Post Cereal Steve Garvey Baseball Tips

These 7-1/8" x 2-5/8" cut-out panels bordered in red "baseball" stitching were printed on the backs of 15-oz. (#1-6) and 20-oz. (#7-12) packages of Post Raisin Brand cereal. The panels have a green background with black-and-white artwork of a generic player illustrating the tip and a color portrait of Garvey.

		NM	EX	VG
Complete Set (12):		30.00	15.00	9.00
Common Panel:		3.00	1.50	.90
1	The Batting Stance	3.00	1.50	.90
2	Bunting	3.00	1.50	.90
3	Rounding First Base	3.00	1.50	.90
4	The Grip in Throwing	3.00	1.50	.90
5	Fielding a Pop-Up	3.00	1.50	.90
6	Proper Fielding Stances	3.00	1.50	.90
7	On-Deck Observation	3.00	1.50	.90
8	Sliding	3.00	1.50	.90
9	Hitting to the Opposite Field	3.00	1.50	.90
10	Throwing From the Outfield	3.00	1.50	.90
11	Mental Preparation for Each Play	3.00	1.50	.90
12	Total Conditioning	3.00	1.50	.90

1978 Post-Intelligencer 1969 Pilot Profiles

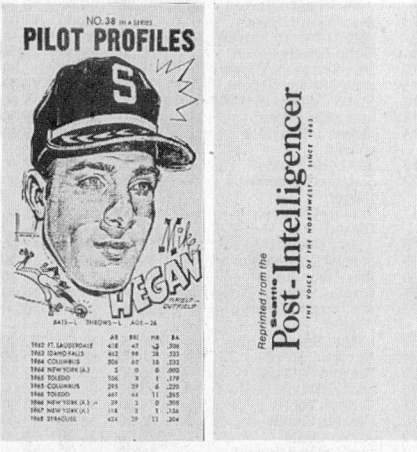

This series of cards of the one-year American League team states on its back they are reprinted from the Seattle Post-Intelligencer newspaper. The 2-3/8" x 5" cards are printed in black-and-white on

semi-gloss cardboard. Fronts feature a pencil caricature of the player and include major and minor league stats. A card number is at top. Backs have the newspaper's ad. The cards were a collectors' issue produced by long-time minor league card maker Frank Caruso, with the paper's permission. The cartoons originally ran in a 3" x 6-3/8" format within the pages of the newspaper and are themselves highly collectible, with values about 2X-3X those of the reprints listed here. Reprint sets were originally sold for $6.

		NM	EX	VG
Complete Set (39):		100.00	50.00	30.00
Common Player:		4.00	3.00	1.50
1	Don Mincher	4.00	3.00	1.50
2	Tommy Harper	5.00	2.50	1.50
3	Ray Oyler	4.00	3.00	1.50
4	Jerry McNertney	4.00	3.00	1.50
5	Not issued	4.00	3.00	1.50
6	Tommy Davis	5.00	2.50	1.50
7	Gary Bell	4.00	3.00	1.50
8	Chico Salmon	4.00	3.00	1.50
9	Jack Aker	4.00	3.00	1.50
10	Rich Rollins	4.00	3.00	1.50
11	Diego Segui	4.00	3.00	1.50
12	Steve Barber	5.00	2.50	1.50
13	Wayne Comer	4.00	3.00	1.50
14	John Kennedy	4.00	3.00	1.50
15	Buzz Stephen	4.00	3.00	1.50
16	Jim Gosger	4.00	3.00	1.50
17	Mike Ferraro	4.00	3.00	1.50
18	Marty Pattin	4.00	3.00	1.50
19	Gerry Schoen	4.00	3.00	1.50
20	Steve Hovely	4.00	3.00	1.50
21	Frank Crosetti	5.00	2.50	1.50
22	Charles Bates	4.00	3.00	1.50
23	Jose Vidal	4.00	3.00	1.50
24	Bob Richmond	4.00	3.00	1.50
25	Lou Piniella	6.00	3.00	1.75
26	John Miklos	4.00	3.00	1.50
27	John Morris	4.00	3.00	1.50
28	Larry Haney	4.00	3.00	1.50
29	Mike Marshall	5.00	2.50	1.50
30	Marv Staehle	4.00	3.00	1.50
31	Gus Gil	4.00	3.00	1.50
32	Sal Maglie	5.00	2.50	1.50
33	Ron Plaza	4.00	3.00	1.50
34	Ed O'Brien	4.00	3.00	1.50
35	Jim Bouton	6.00	3.00	1.75
36	Bill Stafford	4.00	3.00	1.50
37	Darrell Brandon	4.00	3.00	1.50
38	Mike Hegan	4.00	3.00	1.50
39	Dick Baney	4.00	3.00	1.50

1910 Doc Powers Day Postcard

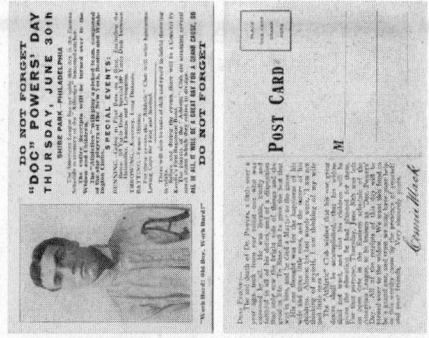

To announce to fans the forthcoming "'Doc' Powers' Day" benefit game, the Philadelphia A's produced this standard-sized (about 5-1/2" x 3-1/2") black-and-white postcard. Front has a photo of the late A's catcher and information about the special events to be held June 30. On back is a message over the facsimile autograph of Connie Mack asking fans to remember the widow and children of their fallen star.

	NM	EX	VG
Doc Powers	750.00	375.00	225.00

1975 Praeger Publishers Ty Cobb

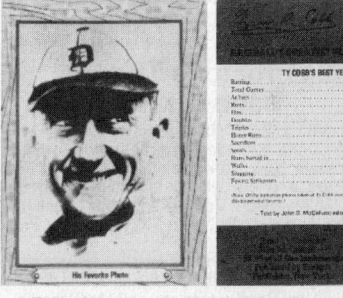

This set was produced by Washington state collector Stephen Mitchell in conjunction with Praeger Publishers of New York to promote the book "Ty

Cobb" by John McCallum. Slightly larger than the current 2-1/2" x 3-1/2" standard, the cards featured black-and-white photos on front surrounded by a woodgrain-effect frame and with a plaque at bottom bearing the card title. Backs have an excerpt from the book, an ad for the book and a facsimile autograph. Cards are numbered in a baseball at upper-right. Sets originally sold for $3.25.

		NM	EX	VG
Complete Set (20):		25.00	12.50	7.50
Common Card:		2.00	1.00	.60
1	Ty Breaks In	3.00	1.50	.90
2	Four Inches of the Plate	2.00	1.00	.60
3	Slashing into Third	2.00	1.00	.60
4	Inking Another Contract	2.00	1.00	.60
5	Captain Tyrus R. Cobb	2.00	1.00	.60
6	Ty with "The Big Train" (With Walter Johnson.)	4.00	2.00	1.25
7	The End of an Era (With Babe Ruth.)	6.00	3.00	1.75
8	All-Time Centerfielder	2.00	1.00	.60
9	Ty Could "Walk 'em down"	2.00	1.00	.60
10	Menacing Batsman	2.00	1.00	.60
11	With Brother Paul	2.00	1.00	.60
12	Thomas Edison, Cobb Fan	3.00	1.50	.90
13	Ty Tangles with Muggsy McGraw	2.50	1.25	.70
14	Author McCallum with Cy Young	2.00	1.00	.60
15	Speaker - DiMaggio - Cobb	5.00	2.50	1.50
16	Ted Gets a Lesson (With Ted Williams.)	5.00	2.50	1.50
17	Five for Five!	2.00	1.00	.60
18	"I have but one regret ..."	2.00	1.00	.60
19	Excellence: The Cobb Standard	2.00	1.00	.60
20	His Favorite Photo	3.00	1.50	.90

1954 Preferred Products Milwaukee Braves

Sold as a 12-piece set in an envelope marked "Braves Team Autographed Portraits," this portfolio was one of several issued in the team's early years in Milwaukee. The artwork is apparently by Scott Douglas, whose copyright appears on the outer envelope. The same pictures can be found on Preferred Product felt patches and t-shirts. These 8" x 10" portraits are printed in sepia on cream-colored heavy textured paper and feature facsimile autographs. Backs are blank. The unnumbered portraits are checklisted here alphabetically.

		NM	EX	VG
Complete Set (12):		300.00	150.00	90.00
Common Player:		25.00	12.50	7.50
(1)	Joe Adcock	25.00	12.50	7.50
(2)	Bill Bruton	25.00	12.50	7.50
(3)	Bob Buhl	25.00	12.50	7.50
(4)	Lew Burdette	25.00	12.50	7.50
(5)	Del Crandall	25.00	12.50	7.50
(6)	Johnny Logan	25.00	12.50	7.50
(7)	Ed Mathews	40.00	20.00	12.00
(8)	Danny O'Connell	25.00	12.50	7.50
(9)	Andy Pafko	25.00	12.50	7.50
(10)	Jim Pendleton	25.00	12.50	7.50
(11)	Warren Spahn	40.00	20.00	12.00
(12)	Bob Thomson	25.00	12.50	7.50

1954 Preferred Products Milwaukee Braves Patches

While they are not so identified, the use of the same portraits and facsimile autographs found on the company's player pictures pinpoint this as a Preferred Products issue, as does a paper tag enclosed in the cellophane wrapper in which the patch was sold. The patches are of heavy felt, with blue or sepia pictures and red "stitching" on the baseball background. At 4-7/8" in diameter, they were intended to be sewn to jackets, etc. While only a handful of players have been confirmed to date, it is possible, even likely, that all 12 of the players from the picture set were also issued in this format.

		NM	EX	VG
Common Player:		175.00	85.00	50.00
(1)	Joe Adcock	175.00	85.00	50.00
(2)	Bill Bruton	175.00	85.00	50.00
(3)	Lew Burdette	175.00	85.00	50.00
(5)	Del Crandall	175.00	85.00	50.00
(6)	Johnny Logan	175.00	85.00	50.00
(7)	Eddie Mathews	125.00	65.00	35.00
(8)	Danny O'Connell	175.00	85.00	50.00
(9)	Andy Pafko	175.00	85.00	50.00
(11)	Warren Spahn	125.00	65.00	35.00

1957-60 Preferred Products Milwaukee Braves

CARL SAWATSKI

Similar in format to the company's 1954 issue, these 8" x 10" portraits are printed in sepia on cream-colored heavy textured paper with player names printed beneath. Backs are blank. The unnumbered portraits are checklisted here alphabetically, but the list may not be complete.

		NM	EX	VG
Common Player:		25.00	12.50	7.50
(1)	Hank Aaron	100.00	50.00	30.00
(2)	Joe Adcock	25.00	12.50	7.50
(3)	Bill Bruton	25.00	12.50	7.50
(4)	Lew Burdette	25.00	12.50	7.50
(5)	Wes Covington	25.00	12.50	7.50
(6)	Johnny Logan	25.00	12.50	7.50
(7)	Carl Sawatski	25.00	12.50	7.50
(8)	Red Schoendienst	35.00	17.50	10.50
(9)	Frank Torre	25.00	12.50	7.50

1950 Prest-O-lite

The attributed date of issue is approximate for this multi-sport promotional postcard issue. Besides the two baseball players, football stars Doak Walker and Leon Hart also exist. The black-and-white, approximately 3-1/2" x 5-1/2" cards on front have a borderless action pose with a salutation and facsimile autograph. The postcard-style divided back has a pre-printed message over the player's facsimile autograph, asking the recipient to view ads for the battery manufacturer in various magazines.

	NM	EX	VG
Tommy Henrich	200.00	100.00	60.00
Ted Williams	400.00	200.00	120.00

1914 Pritchard Publishing Giants/Yankees Stamps

These colorful large-format (about 1-7/8" x 2-5/8") stamps are copyrighted 1914 by Pritchard Publishing Co., New York. All players are N.Y. Giants or Yankees. A similar issue of Yale baseball players is listed in the minor league section. The unnumbered stamps are listed alphabetically by team.

		NM	EX	VG
Common Player:		200.00	100.00	60.00
	N.Y. GIANTS			
(1)	Bob Bescher	200.00	100.00	60.00
(2)	George Burns	200.00	100.00	60.00
(3)	Josh Devore	200.00	100.00	60.00
(4)	Larry Doyle	200.00	100.00	60.00
(5)	Art Fletcher	200.00	100.00	60.00
(6)	Christy Mathewson	900.00	450.00	270.00
(7)	Fred Merkle	200.00	100.00	60.00
(8)	Chief Meyers	200.00	100.00	60.00
(9)	Red Murray	200.00	100.00	60.00
(10)	Fred Snodgrass	200.00	100.00	60.00
	N.Y. YANKEES			
(1)	Ray Caldwell	200.00	100.00	60.00
(2)	Les Channell	200.00	100.00	60.00
(3)	Roy Hartzell	200.00	100.00	60.00
(4)	Bill Holden	200.00	100.00	60.00
(5)	Fritz Maisel	200.00	100.00	60.00
(6)	Roger Peckinpaugh	200.00	100.00	60.00
(7)	Jeff Sweeney	200.00	100.00	60.00
(8)	Jimmy Walsh	200.00	100.00	60.00
(9)	Harry Williams	200.00	100.00	60.00

1956 Prize Frankies Cleveland Indians

VIC WERTZ - 10

ANY PERSON who collects a complete set of these pictures is entitled to TWO BOX SEATS for a future Indian game. One FREE picture is in each package of PRIZE BRAND FRANKIES. There are 24 different pictures. A complete set is 24 different pictures.

★

Complete sets should be sent to John Liber & Co., R.D. #3, Alliance, Ohio. Your tickets and this card will be mailed to you.

Though the back of the cards says 24 Indians' cards were issued, only one player has ever been seen - and precious few of him. The 2-1/4" x 3-3/8" cards have a black-and-white photo on front with the player's name and number in black in the white border at bottom. Backs have an Indian logo and instructions to redeem complete sets of the cards for a pair of box seats. It is unlikely this alone accounts for the scarcity of the cards. More likely this card was made as a prototype for a promotion that never materialized.

		NM	EX	VG
10	Vic Wertz	600.00	300.00	180.00

1924 Proctor's Theatre Babe Ruth

This 1-5/8" x 2-7/8" black-and-white card was issued to promote a vaudeville appearance by Babe Ruth in upstate New York during November 1924. The front has a photo with a facsimile autograph inscribed, "To My Mount Vernon Admirers." Back has details of his appearance.

Vintage cards in Good condition are valued at about 50% of the Very Good values shown here. Cards in Fair condition are valued at 25% or less of VG.

COMPLIMENTS OF
Mr. F. F. Proctor
TO
BABE RUTH'S
MANY MT. VERNON
FRIENDS

APPEARING AT
PROCTOR'S
MOUNT VERNON
Nov. 3rd-4th-5th

	NM	EX	VG
Babe Ruth	9,000	4,500	2,700

1946-47 Propagandas Montiel Los Reyes del Deporte

The 180 athletes in this issue of "Sporting Kings" cards are featured in a couple of different styles. Most cards from #1-101 have only the athlete's photo on front, surrounded by a yellow or orange border. Most cards #100-180 also have the card number and player ID on front, with a chest-to-cap photo set a colored frame. All are roughly 2-1/8" x 3-1/8". Backs have biographical data, the issuer's name and, sometimes, an ad for a Cuban novelty store or radio program. Most examples in the hobby today were once pasted in the colorful album accompanying the issue and it is rare to find cards in better than VG condition. The set opens with a run of boxers, then a group of Cuban baseball stars of the past and present, former big league greats and contemporary major leaguers, plus a few wrestlers. Cards #100-180 (except 101) feature players from the Florida International League, a Class B circuit within Organized Baseball with teams in Havana, Miami, Miami Beach, Lakeland and Tampa included. Curiously, the West Palm Beach team is not represented.

		NM	EX	VG
Complete Set (180):		20,000	8,800	4,000
Common Baseball Player:		45.00	20.00	9.00
Album:		300.00	135.00	60.00
1	John L. Sullivan (Boxer)	135.00	60.00	27.50
2	James J. Corbett (Boxer)	85.00	37.50	17.50
3	Bob Fitzsimmons (Boxer)	70.00	30.00	15.00
4	James J. Jeffries (Boxer)	85.00	37.50	17.50
5	Tommy Burns (Boxer)	70.00	30.00	15.00
6	Jack Johnson (Boxer)	90.00	40.00	18.00
7	Jess Willard (Boxer)	75.00	35.00	15.00
8	Jack Dempsey (Boxer)	135.00	60.00	27.50
9	Gene Tunney (Boxer)	75.00	35.00	15.00
10	Max Schmeling (Boxer)	75.00	35.00	15.00
11	Jack Sharkey (Boxer)	70.00	30.00	15.00
12	Primo Carnera (Boxer)	70.00	30.00	15.00
13	Max Baer (Boxer)	70.00	30.00	15.00
14	James J. Braddock (Boxer)	70.00	30.00	15.00
15	Joe Louis (Boxer)	135.00	60.00	27.50
16	Georges Carpentier (Boxer)	70.00	30.00	15.00
17	Tommy Loughran (Boxer)	70.00	30.00	15.00
18	Tony Zale (Boxer)	70.00	30.00	15.00
19	Johnny Dundee (Boxer)	55.00	25.00	10.00
20	Billy Conn (Boxer)	70.00	30.00	15.00
21	Holman Williams (Boxer)	55.00	25.00	10.00
22	Kid Tuncro (Tunero) (Boxer)	55.00	25.00	10.00
23	Lazaro Salazar	300.00	135.00	60.00
24	Napoleon Reyes	120.00	55.00	25.00
25	Roberto Estalella	110.00	50.00	22.50
26	Juan Oliva (Boxer)	55.00	25.00	10.00
27	Gilberto Torres	75.00	35.00	15.00
28	Heberto Blanco	75.00	35.00	15.00
29	Adolfo Luque	375.00	175.00	75.00
30	Luis Galvani (Boxer)	55.00	25.00	10.00
31	Miguel Angel Gonzalez	195.00	90.00	40.00
32	Chuck Klein	110.00	50.00	22.50
33	Joe Legon (Boxer)	55.00	25.00	10.00
34	Carlos Blanco	75.00	35.00	15.00

35	Santos Amaro	225.00	100.00	45.00
36	Kid Chocolate (Boxer)	85.00	37.50	17.50
37	Henry Armstrong (Boxer)	55.00	25.00	10.00
38	Silvio Garcia	300.00	135.00	60.00
39	Martin Dihigo	3,000	1,350	600.00
40	Fermin Guerra	120.00	55.00	25.00
41	Babe Ruth	1,250	560.00	250.00
42	Ty Cobb	450.00	200.00	90.00
43	Alejandro Crespo	75.00	35.00	15.00
44	Ted Williams	900.00	400.00	180.00
45	Jose Maria Fernandez	85.00	37.50	17.50
46	Dom DiMaggio	110.00	50.00	22.50
47	Julio Rojo	75.00	35.00	15.00
48	Armando Marsans	110.00	50.00	22.50
49	Dick Sisler	75.00	35.00	15.00
50	Antonio Rodriguez	75.00	35.00	15.00
51	Joscito Rodriguez	75.00	35.00	15.00
52	Antonio Ordenana	80.00	35.00	15.00
53	Armandito Pi (Boxer)	55.00	25.00	10.00
54	Paul Derringer	75.00	35.00	15.00
55	Bob Feller	185.00	85.00	37.50
56a	Bill Dickey (Photo is Gabby Hartnett.)(Light cap.)	150.00	65.00	30.00
56b	Bill Dickey (Corrected photo.) (Dark cap.)	225.00	100.00	45.00
57	Lou Gehrig	750.00	335.00	150.00
58	Joe DiMaggio	1,575	710.00	315.00
59	Hank Greenberg	165.00	75.00	35.00
60	Red Ruffing	110.00	50.00	22.50
61	Tex Hughson	75.00	35.00	15.00
62	Bucky Walters	75.00	35.00	15.00
63	Stanley Hack	75.00	35.00	15.00
64	Stanley Musial	600.00	275.00	125.00
65	Melvin Ott	135.00	60.00	27.50
66	Dutch Leonard	75.00	35.00	15.00
67	Frank Overmire	75.00	35.00	15.00
68	Mort Cooper	75.00	35.00	15.00
69	Edward Miller	75.00	35.00	15.00
70	Jimmie Foxx	165.00	75.00	35.00
71	Joseph Cronin	110.00	50.00	22.50
72	James Vernon	75.00	35.00	15.00
73	Carl Hubbell	165.00	75.00	35.00
74	Andrew Pafko	75.00	35.00	15.00
75	David Ferris	75.00	35.00	15.00
76	John Mize	110.00	50.00	22.50
77	Spud Chandler	75.00	35.00	15.00
78	Joseph Medwick	110.00	50.00	22.50
79	Christy Mathewson	450.00	200.00	90.00
80	Nelson Potter	75.00	35.00	15.00
81	James Tabor	75.00	35.00	15.00
82	Martin Marion	75.00	35.00	15.00
83	Rip Sewell	75.00	35.00	15.00
84	Philip Cavaretta (Cavarretta)	75.00	35.00	15.00
85	Al Lopez	110.00	50.00	22.50
86	Rudy York	75.00	35.00	15.00
87	Walter Masterson	75.00	35.00	15.00
88	Roger Wolff	75.00	35.00	15.00
89	Jacob Early	75.00	35.00	15.00
90	Oswald Bluege	75.00	35.00	15.00
91	Zoco Godoy/Wrestler	45.00	20.00	9.00
92	John Kelly Lewis	75.00	35.00	15.00
93	Well Stewart/Wrestler	45.00	20.00	9.00
94	Bruce Campbell	75.00	35.00	15.00
95	Sherrod Robertson	75.00	35.00	15.00
96	Rose Evans/Wrestler	45.00	20.00	9.00
97	Maurice "El Angel" Tillet/ Wrestler	45.00	20.00	9.00
98	Nicholas Altrock	75.00	35.00	15.00
99	Helen Willis/Tennis	70.00	30.00	15.00
100	Borrest Smith	45.00	20.00	9.00
101	Merito Acosta	80.00	35.00	15.00
102	Oscar Rodriguez	45.00	20.00	9.00
103	Octavio Rubert	45.00	20.00	9.00
104	Antonio Lorenzo	45.00	20.00	9.00
105	Agustin del Toro	45.00	20.00	9.00
106	Hector Arago	45.00	20.00	9.00
107	Agustin de la Ville	45.00	20.00	9.00
108	Valeriano (Lilo) Fano	45.00	20.00	9.00
109	Orlando Moreno	45.00	20.00	9.00
110	"Bicho" Dunabeitia	45.00	20.00	9.00
111	Rafael Rivas	45.00	20.00	9.00
112	Jose Traspuestro	45.00	20.00	9.00
113	Mario Diaz	45.00	20.00	9.00
114	Armando Valdes	45.00	20.00	9.00
115	Alberto Matos	45.00	20.00	9.00
116	Humberto Baez	45.00	20.00	9.00
117	Orlando (Tango) Suarez	45.00	20.00	9.00
118	Manuel (Chino) Hidalgo	45.00	20.00	9.00
119	Fernando Rodriguez	45.00	20.00	9.00
120	Jose Cendan	45.00	20.00	9.00
121	Francisco Gallardo	45.00	20.00	9.00
122	Orlando Mejido	45.00	20.00	9.00
123	Julio (Jiqui) Moreno	45.00	20.00	9.00
124	Efrain Vinajcras	45.00	20.00	9.00
125	Luis Suarez	45.00	20.00	9.00
126	Oscar del Calvo	45.00	20.00	9.00
127	Julio Gomez	45.00	20.00	9.00
128	Ernesto Morillas	45.00	20.00	9.00
129	Leonardo Goicochea	45.00	20.00	9.00
130	Max Rosenfeld	300.00	135.00	60.00
131	Oscar Garmendia	45.00	20.00	9.00
132	Fernando Solis	45.00	20.00	9.00
133	Oliverio Ortiz	55.00	25.00	10.00
134	Osmaro Blanco	45.00	20.00	9.00
135	Oral Ratliff	45.00	20.00	9.00
136	Deo Grose	45.00	20.00	9.00
137	Homer Daugherty	45.00	20.00	9.00
138	Frank Matthews	45.00	20.00	9.00
139	Roger LaFrance	45.00	20.00	9.00
140	Harold Cowan	45.00	20.00	9.00
141	Richard Henton	45.00	20.00	9.00
142	Banks McDowell	45.00	20.00	9.00
143	Harold Graham	45.00	20.00	9.00
144	Jack Sweeting	45.00	20.00	9.00
145	Bill Wixted	45.00	20.00	9.00
146	Larry Graham	45.00	20.00	9.00
147	Ralph Brown	45.00	20.00	9.00
148	Felipe Jimenez	45.00	20.00	9.00
149	John Ippolito	45.00	20.00	9.00
150	Joe Benito	45.00	20.00	9.00
151	Bernardo Fernandez	45.00	20.00	9.00
152	Buckey Winkler	45.00	20.00	9.00
153	Carl Armstrong	45.00	20.00	9.00
154	Jack Bearden	45.00	20.00	9.00
155	George Bucci	45.00	20.00	9.00
156	John Pere (Pare)	45.00	20.00	9.00
157	Mickey O'Brien	45.00	20.00	9.00
158	Lamar Murphy	45.00	20.00	9.00
159	Devon Chaptman (Choptman)	45.00	20.00	9.00
160	Hal Johnson	45.00	20.00	9.00
161	"Bitsy" Mott	45.00	20.00	9.00
162	Charles Cuellar	45.00	20.00	9.00
163	Chester Covington	45.00	20.00	9.00
164	Howard Ermisch	45.00	20.00	9.00
165	Bill Lewis	45.00	20.00	9.00
166	Roy Knepper	45.00	20.00	9.00
167	Bull Enos	45.00	20.00	9.00
168	Joe Wilder	45.00	20.00	9.00
169	Jake Baker	45.00	20.00	9.00
170	Joe Bodner	45.00	20.00	9.00
171	Jackie Myer	45.00	20.00	9.00
172	Mel Fisher	45.00	20.00	9.00
173	Larry Baldwin	45.00	20.00	9.00
174	Richard Farkas	45.00	20.00	9.00
175	Alston McGahgin	45.00	20.00	9.00
176	Ray Weiss	45.00	20.00	9.00
177	Paul Waner	400.00	180.00	80.00
178	Frank Miller	45.00	20.00	9.00
179	John Sabatie	45.00	20.00	9.00
180	John Maire	45.00	20.00	9.00

1966 Pro's Pizza Chicago Cubs

These black-and-white player cards were printed on boxes in which individual-serving pizzas were sold, reportedly only at Wrigley Field. The panel measures 6" x 6" and has a black-and-white player photo at left, with his name in a white strip at bottom. At right are drawn sports action scenes and toward the top is a black box with "the pro's PIZZA" in white. The backs are blank. The unnumbered pieces are listed here alphabetically. The example pictured was autographed by the player, no facsimile signature was printed originally.

		NM	EX	VG
Complete Set (15):		3,250	1,600	975.00
Common Player:		160.00	80.00	50.00
(1)	Ted Abernathy	160.00	80.00	50.00
(2)	Joe Amalfitano	160.00	80.00	50.00
(3)	George Altman	160.00	80.00	50.00
(4)	Ernie Banks	650.00	325.00	200.00
(5)	Ernie Broglio	160.00	80.00	50.00
(6)	Billy Connors	160.00	80.00	50.00
(7)	Dick Ellsworth	160.00	80.00	50.00
(8)	Bill Hoeft	160.00	80.00	50.00
(9)	Ken Holtzman	160.00	80.00	50.00
(10)	Randy Hundley	160.00	80.00	50.00
(11)	Ferguson Jenkins	325.00	160.00	100.00
(12)	Chris Krug	160.00	80.00	50.00
(13)	Ron Santo	245.00	120.00	75.00
(14)	Carl Warwick	160.00	80.00	50.00
(15)	Billy Williams	400.00	200.00	120.00

1967 Pro's Pizza - B & W

For a second year, Chicago players - Cubs and White Sox - were featured on boxes of individual-serving pizza reportedly sold only at the ballparks. The panel on which the player photos (black-and-white) are printed measures 4-3/4" x 5-3/4" and is similar in design to the 1966 issue, except there is a vertical perforation allowing most of the player photo to be torn away in a 3-1/16" x 5-3/4" size. Cards are unnumbered and listed here alphabetically. Values are for unseparated panels. Those separated at the perforation line are worth 60-75 percent.

		NM	EX	VG
Complete Set (10):		1,500	750.00	450.00
Common Player:		125.00	65.00	35.00
(1)	Ernie Banks	325.00	160.00	100.00
(2)	Glenn Beckert	125.00	65.00	35.00
(3)	Byron Browne	125.00	65.00	35.00
(4)	Don Buford	125.00	65.00	35.00
(5)	Joel Horlen	125.00	65.00	35.00
(6)	Randy Hundley	125.00	65.00	35.00
(7)	Don Kessinger	125.00	65.00	35.00
(8)	Gary Peters	125.00	65.00	35.00
(9)	Ron Santo	175.00	85.00	50.00
(10)	Billy Williams	200.00	100.00	60.00

1967 Pro's Pizza - Color

Only Chicago Cubs are included in this set of cards printed on the top of individual serving pizza boxes, reportedly sold only at Wrigley Field. The color player poses are printed in a 4-3/4" diameter circle on top of the box, with the player's name in a white panel at bottom. The player's name was also printed in large black letters on one side of the box. Values shown here for the unnumbered cards are for the complete box top. A similar issue of Chicago Bears players was also produced.

		NM	EX	VG
Complete Set (12):		5,000	2,500	1,500
Common Player:		400.00	200.00	120.00
(1)	Joe Amalfitano	400.00	200.00	120.00
(2)	Ernie Banks	1,100	550.00	330.00
(3)	Glenn Beckert	400.00	200.00	120.00
(4)	John Boccabella	400.00	200.00	120.00
(5)	Bill Hands	400.00	200.00	120.00
(6)	Ken Holtzman	400.00	200.00	120.00
(7)	Randy Hundley	400.00	200.00	120.00
(8)	Ferguson Jenkins	675.00	335.00	200.00
(9)	Don Kessinger	400.00	200.00	120.00
(10)	Adolfo Phillips	400.00	200.00	120.00
(11)	Ron Santo	600.00	300.00	180.00
(12)	Billy Williams	850.00	425.00	255.00

1972 Pro Star Promotions

This set of postcard-sized (3-1/2" x 5-1/2") color photocards features players from 14 major league teams, with a heavy emphasis on Montreal Expos. Uniforms in the photos have had team logos removed. Cards have a facsimile autograph on front. In the white border at bottom is the player name, league, copyright notice and "Printed in Canada." The unnumbered cards are checklisted here in alphabetical order.

		NM	EX	VG
Complete Set (40):		275.00	135.00	85.00
Common Player:		3.00	1.50	.90
(1)	Hank Aaron	17.50	8.75	5.25
(2)	Bob Bailey	3.00	1.50	.90
(3)	Johnny Bench	12.50	6.25	3.75
(4)	Vida Blue	3.00	1.50	.90
(5)	John Boccabella	3.00	1.50	.90
(6)	Roberto Clemente	20.00	10.00	6.00
(7)	Boots Day	3.00	1.50	.90
(8)	Jim Fairey	3.00	1.50	.90
(9)	Tim Foli	3.00	1.50	.90

		NM	EX	VG
(10)	Ron Hunt	3.00	1.50	.90
(11)	Catfish Hunter	7.50	3.75	2.25
(12)	Reggie Jackson	15.00	7.50	4.50
(13)	Fergy Jenkins	10.00	5.00	3.00
(14)	Mike Jorgensen	3.00	1.50	.90
(15)	Al Kaline	12.50	6.25	3.75
(16)	Harmon Killebrew	12.50	6.25	3.75
(17)	Mickey Lolich	3.00	1.50	.90
(18)	Juan Marichal	7.50	3.75	2.25
(19)	Willie Mays	17.50	8.75	5.25
(20)	Willie McCovey	10.00	5.00	3.00
(21)	Ernie McAnally	3.00	1.50	.90
(22)	Dave McNally	3.00	1.50	.90
(23)	Bill Melton	3.00	1.50	.90
(24)	Carl Morton	3.00	1.50	.90
(25)	Bobby Murcer	3.00	1.50	.90
(26)	Fritz Peterson	3.00	1.50	.90
(27)	Boog Powell	6.00	3.00	1.75
(28)	Steve Renko	3.00	1.50	.90
(29)	Merv Rettenmund	3.00	1.50	.90
(30)	Brooks Robinson	12.50	6.25	3.75
(31)	Frank Robinson	12.50	6.25	3.75
(32)	Pete Rose	17.50	8.75	5.25
(33)	Tom Seaver	12.50	6.25	3.75
(34)	Ken Singleton	3.00	1.50	.90
(35)	Willie Stargell	10.00	5.00	3.00
(36)	Bill Stoneman	3.00	1.50	.90
(37)	Joe Torre	6.00	3.00	1.75
(38)	Checklist - American League	1.50	.70	.45
(39)	Checklist - National League	1.50	.70	.45
(40)	Checklist - Montreal Expos	1.50	.70	.45

1971 Pro Stars Publications Montreal Expos

Posed action photos of the Expos are featured on this postcard-size (3-1/2" x 5-1/2") issue. The color photos are surrounded by a white border and have a facsimile autograph. Printed in the bottom border is, "Copyright Pro Stars Publications 1971 Printed in Canada." Backs are blank. The unnumbered cards are checklisted here in alphabetical order.

		NM	EX	VG
Complete Set (28):		175.00	85.00	50.00
Common Player:		6.00	3.00	1.80
(1)	Bob Bailey	6.00	3.00	1.80
(2)	John Bateman	6.00	3.00	1.80
(3)	John Boccabella	6.00	3.00	1.80
(4)	Ron Brand	6.00	3.00	1.80
(5)	Boots Day	6.00	3.00	1.80
(6)	Jim Fairey	6.00	3.00	1.80
(7)	Ron Fairly	7.50	3.75	2.25
(8)	Jim Gosger	6.00	3.00	1.80
(9)	Don Hahn	6.00	3.00	1.80
(10)	Ron Hunt	6.00	3.00	1.80
(11)	Mack Jones	6.00	3.00	1.80
(12)	Coco Laboy	6.00	3.00	1.80
(13)	Mike Marshall	7.50	3.75	2.25
(14)	Clyde Mashore	6.00	3.00	1.80
(15)	Gene Mauch	7.50	3.75	2.25
(16)	Dan McGinn	6.00	3.00	1.80
(17)	Carl Morton	6.00	3.00	1.80
(18)	John O'Donoghue	6.00	3.00	1.80
(19)	Adolfo Phillips	6.00	3.00	1.80
(20)	Claude Raymond	6.00	3.00	1.80
(21)	Howie Reed	6.00	3.00	1.80
(22)	Steve Renko	6.00	3.00	1.80
(23)	Rusty Staub	10.00	5.00	3.00
(24)	Bill Stoneman	6.00	3.00	1.80
(25)	John Strohmayer	6.00	3.00	1.80
(26)	Gary Sutherland	6.00	3.00	1.80
(27)	Mike Wegener	6.00	3.00	1.80
(28)	Bobby Wine	6.00	3.00	1.80

1950s Publix Markets

It is not known whether this is a one-card set or whether similar cards exist for other subjects. Without information on other subjects it is impossible to date the issue more precisely. The black-and-white card is printed on thin, semi-gloss cardboard in 4" x 4-3/4" format. The front has a facsimile autograph. The back has a message to Little Leaguers from the Red Sox pitcher and a list of sponsors, along with the Publix logo.

	NM	EX	VG
Tom Brewer	150.00	75.00	45.00

1972 Puerto Rican League Stickers

Often mistakenly called "minor league" cards, this issue consists of 231 ungummed stickers pertinent to the Puerto Rican winter baseball league. A colorful album was available in which to paste the stickers, though obviously stickers that have evidence of glue or torn paper have little collector value. Besides individual player photos, there are stickers of "old-timers" and groups of stickers which make up composite photos of all-star teams and of the island's god of baseball, Roberto Clemente. Team emblem stickers are also included. Many big league stars who were either beginning or ending their pro careers can be found in the set, including some current and future Hall of Famers. Stickers have color photos on the front, with backs printed in Spanish. They measure 2-1/4" x 3".

		NM	EX	VG
Complete Set (231):		1,000	500.00	300.00
Complete Set in Album:		1,200	600.00	350.00
Common Player:		5.00	2.50	1.50
Album:		200.00	100.00	60.00
Unopened Pack:		50.00		
1	Santurce All-Star Team Composite Photo	10.00	5.00	3.00
2	Santurce All-Star Team Composite Photo	10.00	5.00	3.00
3	Santurce All-Star Team Composite Photo	10.00	5.00	3.00
4	Santurce All-Star Team Composite Photo	10.00	5.00	3.00
5	Santurce All-Star Team Composite Photo	10.00	5.00	3.00
6	Santurce All-Star Team Composite Photo	10.00	5.00	3.00
7	Santurce All-Star Team Composite Photo	10.00	5.00	3.00
8	Santurce All-Star Team Composite Photo	10.00	5.00	3.00
9	Santurce All-Star Team Composite Photo	10.00	5.00	3.00
10	Ponce All-Star Team Composite Photo	10.00	5.00	3.00
11	Ponce All-Star Team Composite Photo	10.00	5.00	3.00
12	Ponce All-Star Team Composite Photo	10.00	5.00	3.00
13	Ponce All-Star Team Composite Photo	10.00	5.00	3.00
14	Ponce All-Star Team Composite Photo	10.00	5.00	3.00
15	Ponce All-Star Team Composite Photo	10.00	5.00	3.00
16	Ponce All-Star Team Composite Photo	10.00	5.00	3.00
17	Ponce All-Star Team Composite Photo	10.00	5.00	3.00
18	Ponce All-Star Team Composite Photo	10.00	5.00	3.00
19	Arecibo Team Emblem	5.00	2.50	1.50
20	Caguas-Guayana Team Emblem	5.00	2.50	1.50
21	Mayaguez Team Emblem	5.00	2.50	1.50
22	Ponce Team Emblem	5.00	2.50	1.50
23	San Juan Team Emblem	5.00	2.50	1.50
24	Santurce Team Emblem	5.00	2.50	1.50
25	Steve Boros	5.00	2.50	1.50
26	Luis Isaac	5.00	2.50	1.50
27	Emmanuel Toledo	5.00	2.50	1.50
28	Gregorio Perez	5.00	2.50	1.50
29	Rosario Llanos	5.00	2.50	1.50
30	Jose Geigel	5.00	2.50	1.50
31	Eduardo Figueroa	5.00	2.50	1.50
32	Julian Muniz	5.00	2.50	1.50

		NM	EX	VG
33	Fernando Gonzalez	5.00	2.50	1.50
34	Bennie Ayala	5.00	2.50	1.50
35	Miguel Villaran	5.00	2.50	1.50
36	Efrain Vazquez	5.00	2.50	1.50
37	Ramon Ariles	5.00	2.50	1.50
38	Angel Alcaraz	5.00	2.50	1.50
39	Henry Cruz	5.00	2.50	1.50
40	Jose Silva	5.00	2.50	1.50
41	Jose Alcaide	5.00	2.50	1.50
42	Pepe Mangual	5.00	2.50	1.50
43	Mike Jackson	5.00	2.50	1.50
44	Lynn McGlothen	5.00	2.50	1.50
45	Frank Ortenzio	5.00	2.50	1.50
46	Norm Angelini	5.00	2.50	1.50
47	Richard Coggins	5.00	2.50	1.50
48	Lance Clemons	5.00	2.50	1.50
49	Mike Kelleher	5.00	2.50	1.50
50	Ken Wright	5.00	2.50	1.50
51	Buck Martinez	5.00	2.50	1.50
52	Billy De Mars	5.00	2.50	1.50
53	Elwood Huyke	5.00	2.50	1.50
54	Pedro Garcia	5.00	2.50	1.50
55	Bob Boone	15.00	7.50	4.50
56	Jose Laboy	5.00	2.50	1.50
57	Eduardo Rodriguez	5.00	2.50	1.50
58	Jesus Hernaiz	5.00	2.50	1.50
59	Joaquin Quintana	5.00	2.50	1.50
60	Domingo Figueroa	5.00	2.50	1.50
61	Juan Lopez	5.00	2.50	1.50
62	Luis Alvarado	5.00	2.50	1.50
63	Otoniel Velez	5.00	2.50	1.50
64	Mike Schmidt	300.00	150.00	90.00
65	Felix Millan	5.00	2.50	1.50
66	Guillermo Montanez	5.00	2.50	1.50
67	Ivan de Jesus	7.50	3.75	2.25
68	Sixto Lezcano	5.00	2.50	1.50
69	Jerry Morales	5.00	2.50	1.50
70	Bombo Rivera	5.00	2.50	1.50
71	Mike Ondina	5.00	2.50	1.50
72	Grant Jackson	5.00	2.50	1.50
73	Roger Freed	5.00	2.50	1.50
74	Steve Rogers	5.00	2.50	1.50
75	Mac Scarce	5.00	2.50	1.50
76	Mike Jorgensen	5.00	2.50	1.50
77	Jerry Crider	5.00	2.50	1.50
78	Fred Beene	5.00	2.50	1.50
79	Carl Ermer	5.00	2.50	1.50
80	Luis Marquez	5.00	2.50	1.50
81	Hector Valle	5.00	2.50	1.50
82	Ramon Vega	5.00	2.50	1.50
83	Cirito Cruz	5.00	2.50	1.50
84	Fernando Vega	5.00	2.50	1.50
85	Porfiro Sanchez	5.00	2.50	1.50
86	Jose Sevillano	5.00	2.50	1.50
87	Felix Roque	5.00	2.50	1.50
88	Enrique Rivera	5.00	2.50	1.50
89	Wildredo Rios	5.00	2.50	1.50
90	Javier Andino	5.00	2.50	1.50
91	Milton Ramirez	5.00	2.50	1.50
92	Max Oliveras	5.00	2.50	1.50
93	Jose Calero	5.00	2.50	1.50
94	Esteban Vazquez	5.00	2.50	1.50
95	Hector Cruz	5.00	2.50	1.50
96	Felix Arce	5.00	2.50	1.50
97	Gilberto Rivera	5.00	2.50	1.50
98	Rafael Rodriguez	5.00	2.50	1.50
99	Julio Gonzalez	5.00	2.50	1.50
100	Rosendo Cedeno	5.00	2.50	1.50
101	Pedro Cintron	5.00	2.50	1.50
102	Osvaldo Ortiz	5.00	2.50	1.50
103	Frank Verdi	5.00	2.50	1.50
104	Carlos Santiago	5.00	2.50	1.50
105	Ramon Conde	5.00	2.50	1.50
106	Pat Corrales	5.00	2.50	1.50
107	Jose Morales	5.00	2.50	1.50
108	Jack Whillock	5.00	2.50	1.50
109	Raul Mercado	5.00	2.50	1.50
110	Bonifacio Aponte	5.00	2.50	1.50
111	Angel Alicea	5.00	2.50	1.50
112	Santos Alomar	10.00	5.00	3.00
113	Francisco Libran	5.00	2.50	1.50
114	Edwin Pacheco	5.00	2.50	1.50
115	Luis Gonzalez	5.00	2.50	1.50
116	Juan Rios	5.00	2.50	1.50
117	Jorge Roque	5.00	2.50	1.50
118	Carlos Velez	5.00	2.50	1.50
119	David Gonzalez	5.00	2.50	1.50
120	Jose Cruz	7.50	3.75	2.25
121	Luis Melendez	5.00	2.50	1.50
122	Jose Ortiz	5.00	2.50	1.50
123	David Rosello	5.00	2.50	1.50
124	Juan Veintidos	5.00	2.50	1.50
125	Arnaldo Nazario	5.00	2.50	1.50
126	Dave Lemonds	5.00	2.50	1.50
127	Jim Magnuson	5.00	2.50	1.50
128	Tom Kelley	7.50	3.75	2.25
129	Chris Zachary	5.00	2.50	1.50
130	Hal Breeden	5.00	2.50	1.50
131	Jackie Hernandez	5.00	2.50	1.50
132	Rick Gossage	30.00	15.00	9.00
133	Frank Luchessi	5.00	2.50	1.50
134	Nino Escalera	5.00	2.50	1.50
135	Julio Navarro	5.00	2.50	1.50
136	Manny Sanguillen	15.00	7.50	4.50
137	Bob Johnson	5.00	2.50	1.50
138	Chuck Coggins	5.00	2.50	1.50
139	Orlando Gomez	5.00	2.50	1.50
140	William Melendez	5.00	2.50	1.50
141	Jose Del Moral	5.00	2.50	1.50
142	Jacinto Camacho	5.00	2.50	1.50
143	Emiliano Rivera	5.00	2.50	1.50
144	Luis Peraza	5.00	2.50	1.50
145	Carlos Velazquez	5.00	2.50	1.50
146	Luis Raul Garcia	5.00	2.50	1.50
147	Eliseo Rodriguez	5.00	2.50	1.50
148	Santiago Rosario	5.00	2.50	1.50
149	Ruben Castillo	5.00	2.50	1.50
150	Sergio Ferrer	5.00	2.50	1.50

(Within image 2) "HI, LITTLE LEAGUERS"

"It was a real pleasure meeting you in person at Publix Food Markets. My visit here was made possible by the fine products listed below. Tell Mom to look for them next time she shops at Publix."

TOM BREWER

- COTT QUALITY BEVERAGES
- PRINCE PREPARED FOODS
- COLONIAL MEAT PRODUCTS
- QUALITY BRAND GRATED CHEESE
- DRAGONE RICOTTA CHEESE
- GEM All-Beef FRANKFURTS

publix markets

(Within image 3)

BASEBALL DE PUERTO RICO

64

MIKE SCHMIDT

Jardinero corto y tercera base. Tira y batea a la derecha. Bateó para .267 con 9 cuadrangulares y 24 carreras empujadas en la pasada temporada. Pertenece a los Phillies de Philadelphia.

Ediciones EVA   Printed in Spain

151	Jose Pagan	5.00	2.50	1.50
152	Raul Colon	5.00	2.50	1.50
153	Robert Rauch	5.00	2.50	1.50
154	Luis Rosado	5.00	2.50	1.50
155	Francisco Lopez	5.00	2.50	1.50
156	Richard Zisk	5.00	2.50	1.50
157	Orlando Alvarez	5.00	2.50	1.50
158	Jaime Rosario	5.00	2.50	1.50
159	Rosendo Torres	5.00	2.50	1.50
160	Jim McKee	5.00	2.50	1.50
161	Mike Nagy	5.00	2.50	1.50
162	Brent Strom	5.00	2.50	1.50
163	Tom Walker	5.00	2.50	1.50
164	Angel Davila	5.00	2.50	1.50
165	Jose Cruz	5.00	2.50	1.50
166	Frank Robinson	25.00	12.50	7.50
167	German Rivera	5.00	2.50	1.50
168	Reinaldo Oliver	5.00	2.50	1.50
169	Geraldo Rodriguez	5.00	2.50	1.50
170	Elrod Hendricks	5.00	2.50	1.50
171	Gilberto Flores	5.00	2.50	1.50
172	Ruben Gomez	5.00	2.50	1.50
173	Juan Pizarro	5.00	2.50	1.50
174	William De Jesus	5.00	2.50	1.50
175	Rogelio Morel	5.00	2.50	1.50
176	Victor Agosto	5.00	2.50	1.50
177	Esteban Texidor	5.00	2.50	1.50
178	Ramon Hernandez	5.00	2.50	1.50
179	Gilberto Rondon Olivo	5.00	2.50	1.50
180	Juan Beniquez	5.00	2.50	1.50
181	Arturo Miranda	5.00	2.50	1.50
182	Manuel Ruiz	5.00	2.50	1.50
183	Julio Gotay	5.00	2.50	1.50
184	Arsenio Rodriguez	5.00	2.50	1.50
185	Luis Delgado	5.00	2.50	1.50
186	Jorge Rivera	5.00	2.50	1.50
187	Willie Crawford	5.00	2.50	1.50
188	Angel Mangual	5.00	2.50	1.50
189	Mike Strahler	5.00	2.50	1.50
190	Doyle Alexander	5.00	2.50	1.50
191	Bob Reynolds	5.00	2.50	1.50
192	Ron Cey	7.50	3.75	2.25
193	Jerr Da Vanon	5.00	2.50	1.50
194	Don Baylor	12.50	6.25	3.75
195	Tony Perez	25.00	12.50	7.50
196	Lloyd Allen	5.00	2.50	1.50
197	Orlando Cepeda	20.00	10.00	6.00
198	Roberto Clemente Composite Photo	15.00	7.50	4.50
199	Roberto Clemente Composite Photo	15.00	7.50	4.50
200	Roberto Clemente Composite Photo	15.00	7.50	4.50
201	Roberto Clemente Composite Photo	15.00	7.50	4.50
202	Roberto Clemente Composite Photo	15.00	7.50	4.50
203	Roberto Clemente Composite Photo	15.00	7.50	4.50
204	Roberto Clemente Composite Photo	15.00	7.50	4.50
205	Roberto Clemente Composite Photo	15.00	7.50	4.50
206	Roberto Clemente Composite Photo	15.00	7.50	4.50
207	Jaime Almendro	5.00	2.50	1.50
208	Jose R. Santiago	5.00	2.50	1.50
209	Luis Cabrera	5.00	2.50	1.50
210	Jorge Tirado	5.00	2.50	1.50
211	Radames Lopez	5.00	2.50	1.50
212	Juan Vargas	5.00	2.50	1.50
213	Francisco Coimbre	5.00	2.50	1.50
214	Freddie Thon	5.00	2.50	1.50
215	Manuel Alvarez	5.00	2.50	1.50
216	Luis Olmo	5.00	2.50	1.50
217	Jose Santiago	7.50	3.75	2.25
218	Hiram Bithorn	12.50	6.25	3.75
219	Willard Brown	30.00	15.00	9.00
220	Robert Thurman	10.00	5.00	3.00
221	Buster Clarkson	7.50	3.75	2.25
222	Satchel Paige	40.00	20.00	12.00
223	Raymond Brown	30.00	15.00	9.00
224	Alonso Perry	7.50	3.75	2.25
225	Quincy Trouppe	12.50	6.25	3.75
226	Santiago Muratti	5.00	2.50	1.50
227	Johnny Davis	5.00	2.50	1.50
228	Lino Suarez	5.00	2.50	1.50
229	Demetrio Pesante	5.00	2.50	1.50
230	Luis Arroyo	5.00	2.50	1.50
231	Jose Garcia	5.00	2.50	1.50

1905 Harry Pulliam Cigar Label

The attributed dated is speculative. Pulliam was the first president of the modern National League. These colorful gold-leaf highlighted lithographed cigar box labels measure 4-1/4" square with clipped corners. Since all examples seen appear to be unused it is believed that the cigar brand never materialized, possibly having been aborted when Pulliam committed suicide in 1909.

	NM	EX	VG
Harry Pulliam	100.00	50.00	30.00

1910 Punch Cigars

By virtue of its age, scarcity and checklist, this is among the most popular of the Cuban card sets. Issued contemporary with a visit by the Detroit Tigers and Philadelphia A's for an exhibition series in Cuba, these cards feature an approximately 1-1/4" x 1-7/8" black-and-white portrait photo attached to a decorative cardboard backing of about 1-3/4" x 2-1/4". Known cards include a dozen each of the Major League teams and, it is speculated, an equal number from Cuba's professional Almendares and Havana clubs; though the complete checklist remains unknown. The scarcity of surviving specimens may be traced to the copy on the original cardboard backing that offers an album for anybody turning in a complete set. Only a tiny percentage of Punch cards are known with their cardboard backing attached. Because most cards seen to date have been in wretched condition, no values are quoted above VG condition. Cards with backing should command a 3X premium.

	NM	EX	VG
Common Cuban Player:			750.00
Common Major Leaguer:			1,125

ALMENDARES

(1)	Armando Cabanas	1,125
(2)	Alfredo Cabrera	750.00
(3)	Gervasio Gonzalez	1,500
(4)	Eleadoro Hidalgo	1,500
(5)	Armando Marzans (Marsans)	2,000
(6)	Jose Mendez	30,000
(7)	Evaristo Pia (trainer)	750.00
(8)	Carlos Roggers (Royer)	1,125
(9)	Rogelio Valdes	750.00
		500.00

HAVANA

(1)	P. (Pete) Hill	5,250
(2)	Carlos Moran	2,250
(3)	Agustin Molina	4,500
(4)	Luis Padron	2,250
(5)	Agustin Parpetti	1,500
		500.00

DETROIT TIGERS

(1)	Joe Casey	1,125
(2)	Ty Cobb	11,250
(3)	Sam Crawford	5,250
(4)	Tom Jones	1,125
(5)	Matty McIntyre	1,125
(6)	George Moriarty	1,125
(7)	George Mullin	1,125
(8)	Charley O'Leary	1,125
(9)	Germany Schaefer	1,125
(10)	Oscar Stanage	1,125
(11)	Ed Summers	1,125
(12)	Ed Willetts (Willett)	1,125
		500.00

PHILADELPHIA A'S

(1)	Jack Barry	1,125
(2)	Chief Bender	5,250
(3)	Jack Coombs	1,125
(4)	Harry Davis	1,125
(5)	Claude Derrick	1,125
(6)	Topsy Hartsel	1,125
(7)	Jack Lapp	1,125
(8)	Bris Lord	1,125
(9)	Stuffy McInnis	1,125
(10)	Danny Murphy	1,125
(11)	Eddie Plank	6,000
(12)	Ira Thomas	1,125

1966 Pure Oil Atlanta Braves

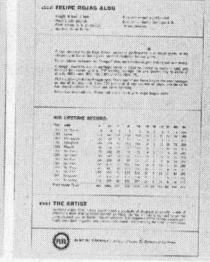

In their first year in Atlanta a set of Braves premium pictures done by noted portrait artist Nicholas Volpe was sponsored by Pure Oil. The 8-1/2" x 11" pictures were given away with gas purchases. Fronts featured a large pastel portrait and smaller full-figure action picture of the player set against a black background. A facsimile player autograph was pencilled at the bottom, along with the artist's signature. The player's name was printed in black in the white bottom border. Backs are printed in black-and-white and include biographical and career notes, full major and minor league stats, a short biography of the artist and the sponsoring company's logo. The unnumbered cards are checklisted here alphabetically.

		NM	EX	VG
Complete Set (12):		75.00	37.50	22.00
Common Player:		5.00	2.50	1.50
(1)	Hank Aaron	25.00	12.50	7.50
(2)	Felipe Alou	6.00	3.00	1.75
(3)	Frank Bolling	5.00	2.50	1.50
(4)	Bobby Bragan	5.00	2.50	1.50
(5)	Rico Carty	5.00	2.50	1.50
(6)	Tony Cloninger	5.00	2.50	1.50
(7)	Mack Jones	5.00	2.50	1.50
(8)	Denny LeMaster	5.00	2.50	1.50
(9)	Eddie Mathews	15.00	7.50	4.50
(10)	Denis Menke	5.00	2.50	1.50
(11)	Lee Thomas	5.00	2.50	1.50
(12)	Joe Torre	7.50	3.75	2.25

1933 PX3 Double Header Coins

Issued by Gum Inc. circa 1933, this unnumbered set consists of 43 metal discs approximately 1-1/4" in diameter. The front lists the player's name and team beneath his picture. The numbers "1" or "2" also appear inside a small circle at the bottom of the disc, and the wrapper advised collectors to "put 1 and 2 together and make a double header." Some players are found in more than one color. The set is designated as PX3 in the American Card Catalog.

		NM	EX	VG
Complete Set (43):		1,750	875.00	525.00
Common Player:		40.00	20.00	12.00
(1)	Sparky Adams	40.00	20.00	12.00
(2)	Dale Alexander	40.00	20.00	12.00
(3)	Earl Averill	75.00	37.00	22.00
(4)	Dick Bartell	40.00	20.00	12.00
(5)	Walter Berger	40.00	20.00	12.00
(6)	Jim Bottomley	75.00	37.00	22.00
(7)	Lefty Brandt	40.00	20.00	12.00
(8)	Owen Carroll	40.00	20.00	12.00
(9)	Lefty Clark	40.00	20.00	12.00
(10)	Mickey Cochrane	75.00	37.00	22.00
(11)	Joe Cronin	75.00	37.00	22.00
(12)	Jimmy Dykes	40.00	20.00	12.00
(13)	George Earnshaw	40.00	20.00	12.00
(14)	Wes Ferrell	40.00	20.00	12.00
(15)	Neal Finn	40.00	20.00	12.00
(16)	Lew Fonseca	40.00	20.00	12.00
(17)	Jimmy Foxx	100.00	50.00	30.00
(18)	Frankie Frisch	75.00	37.00	22.00
(19)	Chick Fullis	40.00	20.00	12.00
(20)	Charley Gehringer	75.00	37.00	22.00
(21)	Goose Goslin	75.00	37.00	22.00
(22)	Johnny Hodapp	40.00	20.00	12.00
(23)	Frank Hogan	40.00	20.00	12.00
(24)	Si Johnson	40.00	20.00	12.00
(25)	Joe Judge	40.00	20.00	12.00
(26)	Chuck Klein	75.00	37.00	22.00
(27)	Al Lopez	75.00	37.00	22.00
(28)	Ray Lucas	40.00	20.00	12.00
(29)	Red Lucas	40.00	20.00	12.00
(30)	Ted Lyons	75.00	37.00	22.00
(31)	Firpo Marberry	40.00	20.00	12.00
(32)	Oscar Melillo	40.00	20.00	12.00
(33)	Lefty O'Doul	50.00	25.00	15.00
(34)	George Pipgras	40.00	20.00	12.00
(35)	Flint Rhem	40.00	20.00	12.00
(36)	Sam Rice	75.00	37.00	22.00
(37)	Muddy Ruel	40.00	20.00	12.00
(38)	Harry Seibold	40.00	20.00	12.00
(39)	Al Simmons	75.00	37.00	22.00
(40)	Joe Vosmik	40.00	20.00	12.00
(41)	Gerald Walker	40.00	20.00	12.00
(42)	Pinky Whitney	40.00	20.00	12.00
(43)	Hack Wilson	75.00	37.00	22.00

The Mint-Mint examples of vintage cards carry a significant premium over the Near Mint values shown here. This premium reflects limited availability of the highest-grade cards as well as demand for particular cards or sets in the best possible condition.

Q

1934 Quaker Oats Babe Ruth Premium Photo (8x10)

Members of the cereal company's Babe Ruth Baseball Club could obtain this souvenir photo among many other promotional items endorsed by the slugger. This 8" x 10" black-and-white photo has a facsimile autograph and is inscribed, "To My Pal." Advertising for Quaker Oats appears in the white border at bottom.

	NM	EX	VG
Babe Ruth	600.00	350.00	150.00

1954 Quaker Sports Oddities

Available both as cereal-box premiums and a mail-away set, this issue of horizontal-format 3-1/2" x 2-1/2", round-corner cards depicts "Odd but True" moments in sports. Fronts of the multi-sports set feature portrait and action color art. Backs describe the sports oddity.

	NM	EX	VG
Complete Set (27):	200.00	100.00	60.00
Common Card:	3.00	1.50	.90
1 Johnny Miller/Football	4.00	2.00	1.25
2 Fred Snite Jr./Golf	3.00	1.50	.90
3 George Quam/Handball	3.00	1.50	.90
4 John B. Maypole/ Speed Boating	3.00	1.50	.90
5 Harold (Bunny) Leavitt/ Basketball	5.00	2.50	1.50
6 Wake Forest College/ Football	5.00	1.50	1.50
7 Amos Alonzo Stagg/Football	20.00	10.00	6.00
8 Catherine Fellmuth/Bowling	3.00	1.50	.90
9 Bill Wilson/Golf	3.00	1.50	.90
10 Chicago Blackhawks/Hockey	20.00	10.00	6.00
11 Betty Robinson/Track	3.00	1.50	.90
12 Dartmouth College/ University of Utah/Basketball	5.00	2.50	1.50
13 Ab Jenkins/Auto Racing	3.00	1.50	.90
14 Capt. Eddie Rickenbacker/ Auto Racing	5.00	2.50	1.50
15 Jackie LaVine/Swimming	3.00	1.50	.90
16 Jack Riley/Wrestling	3.00	1.50	.90
17 Carl Stockton/Biking	3.00	1.50	.90
18 Jimmy Smilgoff/Baseball	3.00	1.50	.90
19 George Halas/Football	20.00	10.00	6.00
20 Joyce Rosenbom/Basketball	5.00	2.50	1.50
21 Squatters Rights/Baseball	3.00	1.50	.90
22 Richard Dwyer/Skating	3.00	1.50	.90
23 Harlem Globetrotters/ Basketball	25.00	12.50	7.50
24 Everett Dean/Basketball	3.00	1.50	.90
25 Texas U./Northwestern U./ Football	5.00	2.50	1.50
26 Bronko Nagurski/Football	25.00	12.50	7.50
27 Yankee Stadium/Baseball	20.00	10.00	6.00

R

1909 Ramly Cigarettes (T204)

While issued with both Ramly and T.T.T. brand Turkish tobacco cigarettes, the cards in this set take their name from the more common of the two brands. By whatever name, the set is one of the more interesting and attractive of the early 20th Century. The 2" x 2-1/2" cards carry black-and-white photographic portraits with impressive gold embossed frames and borders on the front. Toward the bottom appears the player's last name, position, team and league. The backs carry only the most basic information on the cigarette company. The complete set price does not include the scarce variations of some players' cards on which the photos are square and surrounded by a heavy gold frame with white borders.

	NM	EX	VG
Complete Set (121):	175,000	75,000	35,000
Common Player:	1,000	250.00	125.00
T.T.T.: 4-5X			
(1) Whitey Alperman	1,000	250.00	125.00
(2a) John Anderson (Photo inside oval frame.)	1,000	250.00	125.00
(2b) John Anderson (Photo inside square frame.)	22,500	9,000	4,500
(3) Jimmy Archer	1,000	250.00	125.00
(4) Frank Arrelanes (Arellanes)	1,000	250.00	125.00
(5) Jim Ball	1,000	250.00	125.00
(6) Neal Ball	1,000	250.00	125.00
(7a) Frank C. Bancroft (Photo inside oval frame.)	1,000	250.00	125.00
(7b) Frank C. Bancroft (Photo inside square frame.)	30,000	12,000	6,000
(8) Johnny Bates	1,000	250.00	125.00
(9) Fred Beebe	1,000	250.00	125.00
(10) George Bell	1,000	250.00	125.00
(11) Chief Bender	3,400	1,400	700.00
(12) Walter Blair	1,000	250.00	125.00
(13) Cliff Blankenship	1,000	250.00	125.00
(14) Frank Bowerman	1,000	250.00	125.00
(15a) Wm. Bransfield (Photo inside oval frame.)	1,000	250.00	125.00
(15b) Wm. Bransfield (Photo inside square frame.)	22,500	9,000	4,500
(16) Roger Bresnahan	3,400	1,400	700.00
(17) Al Bridwell	1,000	250.00	125.00
(18) Mordecai Brown	3,400	1,400	700.00
(19) Fred Burchell	1,000	250.00	125.00
(20a) Jesse C. Burkett (Photo inside oval frame.)	15,600	6,250	3,100
(20b) Jesse C. Burkett (Photo inside square frame.)	22,500	9,000	4,500
(21) Bobby Byrnes (Byrne)	1,000	250.00	125.00
(22) Bill Carrigan	1,000	250.00	125.00
(23) Frank Chance	3,400	1,400	700.00
(24) Charlie Chech	1,000	250.00	125.00
(25) Ed Cicolte (Cicotte)	3,000	1,200	600.00
(26) Otis Clymer	1,000	250.00	125.00
(27) Andy Coakley	1,000	250.00	125.00
(28) Jimmy Collins	3,400	1,400	700.00
(29) Ed. Collins	3,400	1,400	700.00
(30) Wid Conroy	1,000	250.00	125.00
(31) Jack Coombs	1,000	250.00	125.00
(32) Doc Crandall	1,000	250.00	125.00
(33) Lou Criger	1,000	250.00	125.00
(84) Harry Davis	1,000	250.00	125.00
(35) Art Devlin	1,000	250.00	125.00
(36a) Wm. H. Dineen (Dinneen)	1,000	250.00	125.00
(36b) Wm. H. Dineen (Dinneen) (Photo inside square frame.)	22,500	9,000	4,500
(37) Jiggs Donahue	1,000	250.00	125.00
(38) Mike Donlin	1,000	250.00	125.00
(39) Wild Bill Donovan	1,000	250.00	125.00
(40) Gus Dorner	1,000	250.00	125.00
(41) Joe Dunn	1,000	250.00	125.00
(42) Kid Elberfield (Elberfeld)	1,000	250.00	125.00
(43) Johnny Evers	3,400	1,400	700.00
(44) Bob Ewing	1,000	250.00	125.00
(45) Cecil Ferguson	1,000	250.00	125.00
(46) Hobe Ferris	1,000	250.00	125.00
(47) Jerry Freeman	1,000	250.00	125.00
(48) Art Fromme	1,000	250.00	125.00
(49) Bob Ganley	1,000	250.00	125.00
(50) Doc Gessler	1,000	250.00	125.00
(51) Peaches Graham	1,000	250.00	125.00
(52) Clark Griffith	3,400	1,400	700.00
(53) Roy Hartzell	1,000	250.00	125.00
(54) Charlie Hemphill	1,000	250.00	125.00
(55) Dick Hoblitzel (Hoblitzell)	1,000	250.00	125.00
(56a) Geo. Howard (Photo inside oval frame.)	1,000	250.00	125.00
(56b) Geo. Howard (Photo inside square frame.)	22,500	9,000	4,500
(57) Harry Howell	1,000	250.00	125.00
(58) Miller Huggins	3,400	1,400	700.00
(59) John Hummell (Hummel)	1,000	250.00	125.00
(60) Walter Johnson	50,000	20,000	10,000
(61) Thos. Jones	1,000	250.00	125.00
(62) Mike Kahoe	1,000	250.00	125.00
(63) Ed Kargar	1,000	250.00	125.00
(64) Wee Willie Keeler	3,400	1,400	700.00
(65) Red Kleinon (Kleinow)	1,000	250.00	125.00
(66) Jack Knight	1,000	250.00	125.00
(67) Ed Konetchey	1,000	250.00	125.00
(68) Vive Lindaman	1,000	250.00	125.00
(69) Hans Loebert (Lobert)	1,000	250.00	125.00
(70) Harry Lord	1,000	250.00	125.00
(71) Harry Lumley	1,000	250.00	125.00
(72) Johnny Lush	1,000	250.00	125.00
(73) Rube Manning	1,000	250.00	125.00
(74) Jimmy McAleer	1,000	250.00	125.00
(75) Amby McConnell	1,000	250.00	125.00
(76) Moose McCormick	1,000	250.00	125.00
(77) Harry McIntyre	1,000	250.00	125.00
(78) Larry McLean	1,000	250.00	125.00
(79) Fred Merkle	1,000	250.00	125.00
(80) Clyde Milan	1,000	250.00	125.00
(81) Mike Mitchell	1,005	250.00	125.00
(82a) Pat Moran (Photo inside oval frame.)	1,000	250.00	125.00
(82b) Pat Moran (Photo inside square frame.)	22,500	9,000	4,500
(83) Cy Morgan	1,000	250.00	125.00
(84) Tim Murname (Murnane)	1,005	250.00	125.00
(85) Danny Murphy	1,000	250.00	125.00
(86) Red Murray	1,000	250.00	125.00
(87) Doc Newton	1,000	250.00	125.00
(88) Simon Nichols (Nicholls)	1,000	250.00	125.00
(89) Harry Niles	1,000	250.00	125.00
(90) Bill O'Hare (O'Hara)	1,000	250.00	125.00
(91) Charley O'Leary	1,000	250.00	125.00
(92) Dode Paskert	1,000	250.00	125.00
(93) Barney Pelty	1,000	250.00	125.00
(94) Jake Pfeister	1,000	250.00	125.00
(95) Ed Plank	9,400	3,800	1,900
(96) Jack Powell	1,000	250.00	125.00
(97) Bugs Raymond	1,000	250.00	125.00
(98) Tom Reilly	1,000	250.00	125.00
(99) Claude Ritchey	1,000	250.00	125.00
(100) Nap Rucker	1,000	250.00	125.00
(101) Ed Ruelbach (Reulbach)	1,000	250.00	125.00
(102) Slim Sallee	1,000	250.00	125.00
(103) Germany Schaefer	1,005	250.00	125.00
(104) Jimmy Schekard (Sheckard)	1,000	250.00	125.00
(105) Admiral Schlei	1,000	250.00	125.00
(106) Wildfire Schulte	1,000	400.00	200.00
(107) Jimmy Sebring	1,000	250.00	125.00
(108) Bill Shipke	1,000	250.00	125.00
(109) Charlie Smith	1,000	250.00	125.00
(110) Tubby Spencer	1,000	250.00	125.00
(111) Jake Stahl	1,000	250.00	125.00
(112) Jim Stephens	1,000	250.00	125.00
(113) Harry Stienfeldt (Steinfeldt)	1,000	250.00	125.00
(114) Gabby Street	1,000	250.00	125.00
(115) Bill Sweeney	1,000	250.00	125.00
(116) Fred Tenney	1,000	250.00	125.00
(117) Ira Thomas	1,000	250.00	125.00
(118) Joe Tinker	3,400	1,400	700.00
(119) Bob Unglane (Unglaub)	1,000	250.00	125.00
(120) Heinie Wagner	1,000	250.00	125.00
(121) Bobby Wallace	3,400	1,400	700.00

1910 Ramly Team Composite Premiums

Pittsburg National 1910.

At least two versions of coupons found in boxes of Ramly (and possibly T.T.T.) cigarettes offered a large-format (about 23" x 18-1/2") black-and-white photogravure premium featuring a composite of player portraits for five, or six, popular teams of the era. Players are identified in the bottom border, which also has a credit line for the tobacco company. To date, only the 1909 pennant winners' premiums have been confirmed as surviving.

(1) Boston Red Sox (Unconfirmed)
(2) Boston Rustlers
(3) Detroit Tigers
(4) New York Giants (Unconfirmed)
(5) Philadelphia A's (Unconfirmed)
(6) Pittsburgh Pirates (5/04 auction, trimmed, $3,163)

1881 Randall Studio Cabinets

What the players of the 1881 Boston Beaneaters were doing posing in their Sunday best suits at the Detroit studio of Randall the photographer is open to speculation, as is the question of whether other teams' players were also photographed there. These cabinets are about 4-1/4" x 6-1/2" and blank-backed. On most of them the player name and city and in small type on the portrait.

Common Player:	NM	EX	VG
(1) Tommy Bond	2,000	1,000	600.00
(2) Tom Deasley	2,000	1,000	600.00
(3) John Morrill	2,000	1,000	600.00
(4) John Richmond	2,000	1,000	600.00
(5) Ezra Sutton	2,000	1,000	600.00
(6) Jim Whitney	2,000	1,000	600.00

1950s-70s Rawlings Advisory Staff Photos

Advisory staff photos were a promtional item which debuted in the early 1950s, flourished in the Sixties and died in the early 1970s. Generally 8" x 10" (sometimes a little larger), these black-and-white (a few later were color) glossy photos picture players who had contracted with a major baseball equipment company to endorse and use their product. Usually the product - most often a glove - was prominently displayed in the photo. The pictures were often displayed in the windows of sporting goods stores or the walls of sports departments and were sometimes made available to customers. Because the companies tended to stick with players over the years, some photos were reissued, sometimes with and sometimes without a change of team, pose or style. All advisory staff photos of the era are checklisted here in alphabetical order. A pose description is given for each known picture. The photos are checklisted here in alphabetical order. It is unlikely this list is complete. In general, Rawlings advisory staff photos feature a white box within the photo which contains the glove-company logo and a facsimile autograph of the player. Gaps have been left in the checklist numbering to accommodate possible additions.

Common Player:	NM	EX	VG
(1) Joe Adcock/Kneeling (Braves)	35.00	17.50	10.50
(2) Joe Adcock (Braves, locker room.)	25.00	12.50	7.50
(3) Joe Adcock (Braves, upper body.)	25.00	12.50	7.50
(4) Hank Aguirre (Tigers, glove on knee.)	25.00	12.50	7.50
(5) Bobby Avila (Indians, upper body.)	25.00	12.50	7.50
(6) Bob Bailey/Kneeling (Pirates)	25.00	12.50	7.50
(7) Ed Bailey (Reds, gearing up in dugout.)	25.00	12.50	7.50
(8) Ed Bailey (Giants, catching crouch.)	25.00	12.50	7.50
(9) Earl Battey (Twins, catching crouch.)	25.00	12.50	7.50
(10) Earl Battey (Twins, kneeling w/bat.)	25.00	12.50	7.50
(11) Johnny Bench/Crouching (No catcher's gear.)	45.00	22.00	13.50
(12) Dick Bertell (Cubs, catching crouch.)	25.00	12.50	7.50
(13) John Blanchard (Yankees, catching crouch.)	25.00	12.50	7.50
(14) John Blanchard (Yankees, dugout step.)	25.00	12.50	7.50
(15) "Clete" Boyer/Fielding (Yankees)	25.00	12.50	7.50
(16) Ken Boyer (Cardinals, in front of locker.)	25.00	12.50	7.50
(17) Ken Boyer (Cardinals, b/w, kneeling.)	25.00	12.50	7.50
(18) Ken Boyer (Mets, b/w, full-length.)	25.00	12.50	7.50
(19) Ken Boyer (Mets, color, leaning on bat.)	25.00	12.50	7.50
(20) Ken Boyer (White Sox, upper body.)	30.00	15.00	9.00
(21) Lew Burdette (Braves, beginning windup.)	25.00	12.50	7.50
(22) Lew Burdette (Braves, upper body w/ball.)	35.00	17.50	10.50
(23) Bob Cerv (A's, at bat rack.)	25.00	12.50	7.50
(24) Gordon Coleman (Reds, kneeling w/bat.)	25.00	12.50	7.50
(25) Tony Conigliaro (Red Sox, glove at chest.)	45.00	22.00	13.50
(26) Wes Covington (Braves, upper body.)	25.00	12.50	7.50
(27) Joe Cunningham (White Sox, glove at knee.)	25.00	12.50	7.50
(28) Joe Cunningham (Cardinals, chest-up.)	25.00	12.50	7.50
(29) Tommy Davis (Dodgers, dugout step.)	25.00	12.50	7.50
(30) Don Demeter (Dodgers, upper body.)	25.00	12.50	7.50
(31) Don Demeter (Phillies, hands on knees.)	25.00	12.50	7.50
(32) Dick Dietz (Giants, catching pose.)	25.00	12.50	7.50
(33) Tito Francona (Indians, sitting w/glove.)	25.00	12.50	7.50
(34) Steve Garvey (Dodgers, horizontal, pose and action.)	25.00	12.50	7.50
(35) Mudcat Grant (Indians, horizontal, upper body.)	25.00	12.50	7.50
(36) Dick Groat (Pirates, b/w, full-length.)	25.00	12.50	7.50
(37) Dick Groat (Pirates, b/w, upper body.)	25.00	12.50	7.50
(38) Dick Groat (Cardinals, b/w, kneeling w/bat.)	25.00	12.50	7.50
(39) Dick Groat/Kneeling (Cardinals, b/w)	25.00	12.50	7.50
(40) Harvey Haddix/Kneeling (Pirates)	25.00	12.50	7.50
(41) Harvey Haddix (Pirates, locker room.)	25.00	12.50	7.50
(42) Ken Holtzman (Cubs, hands on knees.)	25.00	12.50	7.50
(43) Ken Holtzman (A's, horizontal, two poses.)	25.00	12.50	7.50
(44) Elston Howard (Yankees, catching crouch.)	30.00	15.00	9.00
(45) Al Hrabosky (Cardinals, upper body.)	25.00	12.50	7.50
(46) Larry Jackson/Kneeling (Cubs)	25.00	12.50	7.50
(47) Larry Jackson/Fielding (Cardinals)	25.00	12.50	7.50
(48) Larry Jackson (Cardinals, full-length on mound.)	25.00	12.00	7.50
(49) Reggie Jackson (A's, full-length.)	40.00	20.00	12.00
(50) Joey Jay (Reds, dugout step, glove on rail.)	25.00	12.50	7.50
(51) Fergie Jenkins (Cubs, hands on knees.)	25.00	12.50	7.50
(52) Ed Kranepool/Btg (Mets, color)	25.00	12.50	7.50
(53) Tony Kubek/Fielding (Full-length.)	25.00	12.50	7.50
(54) Tony Kubek/Kneeling (No bat.)	25.00	12.50	7.50
(55) Tony Kubek (Kneeling w/bat.)	25.00	12.50	7.50
(56) Tony Kubek (Horizontal, upper body.)	25.00	12.50	7.50
(57) Vern Law (Locker room.)	25.00	12.50	7.50
(58) Jim Lefebvre (Dodgers, kneeling, bat on shoulder.)	25.00	12.50	7.50
(59) Sherman Lollar (White Sox, throwing from crouch.)	25.00	12.50	7.50
(60) Art Mahaffey (Phillies, upper body.)	25.00	12.50	7.50
(61) Mickey Mantle (Upper body, road uniform.)	150.00	75.00	45.00
(62) Mickey Mantle/Leaning (Hands on knees.)	100.00	50.00	30.00
(63) Mickey Mantle (Seated w/bat, glove on knee.)	130.00	65.00	40.00
(64) Mickey Mantle/Kneeling	150.00	75.00	45.00
(65) Mickey Mantle (Seated at locker, pointing to glove.)	150.00	75.00	45.00
(66) Eddie Mathews (Braves, full-length.)	45.00	22.00	13.50
(67) Eddie Mathews (Braves, sepia, upper body.)	45.00	22.00	13.50
(68) Eddie Mathews (Braves, upper body, glove in front)	45.00	22.00	13.50
(69) Eddie Mathews (Braves, upper body, looking at glove.)	45.00	22.00	13.50
(70) Dal Maxvill (Cardinals, bat on shoulder.)	25.00	12.50	7.50
(71) Dal Maxvill/Fielding (Cardinals)	25.00	12.50	7.50
(72) Charlie Maxwell (Tigers, horizontal, upper body.)	25.00	12.50	7.50
(73) Tim McCarver (Cardinals, catching crouch.)	25.00	12.50	7.50
(74) Lindy McDaniel (Cardinals, b/w, on dugout steps.)	25.00	12.50	7.50
(75) Dave McNally (Orioes, upper body.)	25.00	12.50	7.50
(76) Wilmer Mizell (Cardinals, upper body.)	25.00	12.50	7.50
(77) Wally Moon/Kneeling (Dodgers)	25.00	12.50	7.50
(78) Wally Moon/Standing (Dodgers)	25.00	12.50	7.50
(79) Stan Musial (Upper body.)	50.00	25.00	15.00
(80) Stan Musial/Btg (horizontal)	50.00	25.00	15.00
(81) Stan Musial (Upper body, holding glove and bat.)	50.00	25.00	15.00
(82) Stan Musial (Kneeling on bat.)	50.00	25.00	15.00
(83) Stan Musial (Kneeling on bat, glove on ground.)	50.00	25.00	15.00
(84) Stan Musial/Kneeling (Glove in front, Busch Stadium.)	50.00	25.00	15.00
(85) Stan Musial (Full-length, hands on knees.)	80.00	40.00	24.00
(86) Stan Musial (Socks to cap, white background, in proposed '56 road uniform.)	125.00	62.00	37.00
(87) Charlie Neal/Kneeling (Dodgers)	25.00	12.50	7.50
(88) Charlie Neal (Dodgers, looking into glove.)	25.00	12.50	7.50
(89) Rocky Nelson/Kneeling (Pirates)	25.00	12.50	7.50
(90) Rocky Nelson/Fielding (Pirates)	25.00	12.50	7.50
(91) Amos Otis (Royals, upper body.)	25.00	12.50	7.50
(92) Jim Perry/Pitching (Indians)	25.00	12.50	7.50
(93) Boog Powell (Orioles, full-length.)	25.00	12.50	7.50
(94) Rick Reichardt (Angels, full-length.)	25.00	12.50	7.50
(95) Brooks Robinson (Dugout step.)	45.00	22.00	13.50
(96) Brooks Robinson/Throwing	45.00	22.00	13.50
(97) Brooks Robinson (Standing w/glove.)	45.00	22.00	13.50
(98) Brooks Robinson (Tying shoe.)	45.00	22.00	13.50
(99) John Romano (Indians, adjusting shinguard.)	25.00	12.50	7.50
(101) Manny Sanguillen (Pirates, catching crouch.)	25.00	12.50	7.50
(102) Chuck Schilling (Full-length.)	25.00	12.50	7.50
(103) Herb Score/Pitching (Indians	25.00	12.50	7.50
(104) Norm Siebern/Vest (A's)	25.00	12.50	7.50
(105) Norm Siebern/Jsy (A's)	25.00	12.50	7.50
(106) Roy Sievers (Senators, full-length.)	25.00	12.50	7.50
(107) Roy Sievers (White Sox, drinking fountain.)	25.00	12.50	7.50
(108) Roy Sievers/Kneeling (Phillies)	25.00	12.50	7.50
(109) Bob Skinner (Pirates, upper body.)	25.00	12.50	7.50
(110) Duke Snider (Brooklyn Dodgers, full-length.)	45.00	22.00	13.50
(111) Duke Snider (L.A. Dodgers, upper body.)	45.00	22.00	13.50
(112) Warren Spahn (Braves, b/w, wind-up.)	45.00	22.00	13.50
(114) Willie Stargell (Upper body.)	35.00	17.50	10.50
(115) Willie Stargell (Full-length.)	35.00	17.50	10.50
(116) Tom Tresh/Fielding (Yankees)	25.00	12.50	7.50
(117) Tom Tresh (Yankees, full-length.)	25.00	12.50	7.50
(119) Bob Turley (Yankees, upper body.)	25.00	12.50	7.50
(120) Bob Turley (At water fountain.)	25.00	12.50	7.50
(121) Bill White (Cardinals, glove over rail.)	25.00	12.50	7.50
(122) Bill White (Phillies, b/w, full-length.)	25.00	12.50	7.50
(123) Bill White (Phillies, color, full-length.)	25.00	12.50	7.50
(124) Billy Williams (Cubs, full-length.)	35.00	17.50	10.50
(126) Steve Yeager (Dodgers, upper body.)	25.00	12.50	7.50

1952 Rawlings Stan Musial Premium Photo

In this black-and-white, blank-backed premium photo, Musial is shown in a batting stance superimposed over a game-action photo at Sportsman's Park. A white facsimile autograph is at lower-right. The wide bottom border of the 5" x 7" picture has the Rawlings logoscript and address.

	NM	EX	VG
Stan Musial	40.00	20.00	12.00

1954 Rawlings Stan Musial

The date of issue is speculation although the picture is certainly from 1955 or earlier. This 5-1/2" x 7-1/2" colorized photo is actually part of a cardboard Rawlings glove box. The panel at lower-right of the card identifies it as "A GENUINE RAWLINGS FACSIMILE AUTOGRAPH PICTURE." Back is blank.

	NM	EX	VG
Stan Musial	300.00	150.00	90.00

1955 Rawlings Stan Musial

Though missing from Topps and Bowman card sets from 1954-57, Cardinals superstar Stan Musial wasn't entirely unavailable on baseball cards. About 1955 he appeared on a series of six cards found on boxes of Rawlings baseball gloves carrying Musial's endorsement. The cards feature black-and-white photos of Musial set against a blue background. Because the cards were part of a display box, they are blank-backed. Depending on the position on the box, the cards measure approximately 2" x 3" (#1A and 2A) or 2-1/2" x 3-3/4" (#1-4). Cards are numbered in a yellow star at upper left.

		NM	EX	VG
Complete Set (6):		2,500	1,250	750.00
Complete Box:		3,000	1,500	900.00
Common Card:		450.00	225.00	125.00
1	Stan Musial/Portrait	450.00	225.00	125.00
1A	Stan Musial (Portrait with bat.)	450.00	225.00	125.00
2	Stan Musial/Kneeling	450.00	225.00	125.00
2A	Stan Musial/Portrait	450.00	225.00	125.00
3	Stan Musial/Swinging (Horizontal)	450.00	225.00	125.00
4	Stan Musial (Batting pose.)	450.00	225.00	125.00

1963 Rawlings Stan Musial Premium

This premium was available by mail and commemorates the career of long-time Rawlings spokesman Stan Musial upon his retirement. The package contains an approximately 9" x 10" color portrait photo of Musial with a facsimile autograph, a sheet illustrated with four portraits of Musial during his career and listing his many records, and a note from the company indicating future availability of Musial gloves.

	NM	EX	VG
Complete Package:			
Stan Musial	60.00	30.00	18.00

1964 Rawlings Glove Box

Measuring about 2-3/8" x 4" when properly cut off the glove boxes on which they were printed, these full-color cards show stars of the day posing with their Raw-

lings glove prominently displayed. The blank-backed unnumbered cards are checklisted here alphabetically. The quality of cutting should be considered in grading these cards. In actuality, the cards were not meant to be cut from the boxes, but rather to show which premium photo was packed inside the glove box. Two cards of each player appear on the box.

		NM	EX	VG
Complete Set (8):		450.00	225.00	135.00
Common Player:		25.00	12.50	7.50
Complete Box:		750.00	375.00	225.00
(1)	Ken Boyer	35.00	17.50	10.50
(2)	Tommy Davis	25.00	12.50	7.50
(3)	Dick Groat	25.00	12.50	7.50
(4)	Mickey Mantle	200.00	100.00	60.00
(5)	Brooks Robinson	60.00	30.00	18.00
(6)	Warren Spahn	50.00	25.00	15.00
(7)	Tom Tresh	25.00	12.50	7.50
(8)	Billy Williams	45.00	22.00	13.50

1964-66 Rawlings Premium Photos

One premium photo was inserted into each baseball glove box sold by Rawlings beginning in 1964 and continuing at least into 1966, when some changes in players and pictures were added. The 8" x 9-1/2" full-color photos were advertised on the outside of the boxes in miniature form. Each of the photos pictures a player posed with his Rawlings leather prominently displayed. A black facsimile autograph is printed on the front.

		NM	EX	VG
Complete Set (12):		600.00	300.00	180.00
Common Player:		20.00	10.00	6.00
(1a)	Ken Boyer (Cardinals, 1964)	25.00	12.50	7.50
(1b)	Ken Boyer (Mets, 1966)	25.00	12.50	7.50
(2)	Tommy Davis	20.00	10.00	6.00
(3)	Dick Groat	20.00	10.00	6.00
(4a)	Mickey Mantle (No undershirt, 1964.)	150.00	75.00	45.00
(4b)	Mickey Mantle (Black undershirt, 1966.)	150.00	75.00	45.00
(5a)	Brooks Robinson (Full-bird cap, 1964.)	70.00	35.00	21.00
(5b)	Brooks Robinson (Bird's-head cap, 1966.)	85.00	42.00	25.00
(6)	Warren Spahn	75.00	37.00	22.00
(7)	Tom Tresh	20.00	10.00	6.00
(8)	Bill White (1966)	20.00	10.00	6.00
(9)	Billy Williams	50.00	25.00	15.00

1965 Rawlings MVP Premiums

The American and National League MVPs are featured in this pair of 8-1/8" x 10-1/4" premium pictures sponsored by the sporting goods manufacturer. The manner of their distribution is unknown. Printed on thin card stock, the premiums feature the artwork of Amadee Wohlschlaeger.

Checklists showing card numbers in parentheses ( ) indicates the numbers do not appear on the cards.

		NM	EX	VG
Complete Set (2):		125.00	65.00	40.00
(1)	Ken Boyer	65.00	35.00	20.00
(2)	Brooks Robinson	75.00	40.00	25.00

1969 Rawlings

How these cards were distributed is not certain today, nor is the extent of the series known. The approximately 3" x 5" black-and-white cards feature a portrait photo on front, with a wide white border at bottom that holds a facsimile autograph. The back has complete major and minor league stats, career highlights and a Rawlings ad.

	NM	EX	VG
Reggie Jackson	900.00	450.00	275.00
Mickey Mantle	2,500	1,250	750.00

1930 Ray-O-Print Photo Kits

This was one of several contemporary kits for do-it-yourself production of photo prints. The outfits were produced by M.P. & Co., of New York. The novelty kit consists of a 4-1/8" x 2-1/2" kraft paper envelope with production instructions printed on the outside and the name of the subject rubber-stamped on one end. Inside was a film negative, a piece of light-sensitive photo paper (each 1-7/8" x 2-15/16") and a tin stand for exposing and displaying the photo. Values shown are for complete kits. Individual components would be pro-rated, with the negative being the most valuable of the pieces. Anyone with a negative could make unlimited prints today, and even make them look old; collectors should use caution in purchasing prints alone.

		NM	EX	VG
Complete Set (8):		1,000	500.00	300.00
Common Kit:		125.00	67.00	38.00
Card: 20%				
(1)	Lou Gehrig	250.00	125.00	75.00
(2)	Babe Ruth	400.00	200.00	120.00
(3)	Jack Dempsey (Boxer)	100.00	50.00	30.00
(4)	Herbert Hoover/President	75.00	37.00	22.00
(5)	"Lindy" (Charles Lindbergh)/ Aviator	150.00	75.00	45.00
(6)	Mary Pickford/Actress	50.00	25.00	15.00
(7)	Will Rogers/Humorist	50.00	25.00	15.00
(8)	We (Charles Lindberg) (w/ plane, Spirit of St. Louis.)	150.00	75.00	45.00

1899 Henry Reccius Cigars Honus Wagner

The date of this card's issue is probable, though it could have been issued anytime between 1897-99 during Wagner's stay in Louisville. The 3-3/8" x 4-11/16" card is printed in black-on-orange with an oval photograph of Wagner at center. Advertising for the company that marketed cigars under his name is around the border. The back has a lengthy pro-trade union poem. Only one example of the card is known. It was graded by PSA sometime after 1998 and given a Poor-Fair designation. The card was auctioned in November 2001, for $21,850, and again in April 2006, for $52,040.

HENRY RECCIUS

Honus Wagner

1912 Recruit Little Cigars

This is the most common of the back advertisements found in T207. Factory 606 (Maryland) backs are much scarcer than those with Factory 240 (Pennsylvania), but currently carry little premium on that basis. Back printing is usually found in black, but several examples have been authenticated with brown ink printing on back. Their value is undetermined.

(See 1912 T207.)

1976 Red Barn Discs

The scarcest among the several regional sponsors of player disc sets issued in 1976 are those of the Red Barn family restaurant chain in Southeastern Wisconsin. The discs are 3-3/8" diameter with a black-and-white player portrait photo in the center of the baseball design. A line of red stars is above, while the left and right panels feature one of several bright colors. Produced by Michael Schecter Associates under license from the Major League Baseball Players Association, the player photos have had uniform and cap logos removed. Backs are printed in red and purple. The unnumbered checklist here is presented in alphabetical order.

		NM	EX	VG
Complete Set (70):		500.00	250.00	150.00
Common Player:		8.00	4.00	2.50
(1)	Henry Aaron	65.00	32.00	19.50
(2)	Johnny Bench	25.00	12.50	7.50
(3)	Vida Blue	8.00	4.00	2.50
(4)	Larry Bowa	8.00	4.00	2.50
(5)	Lou Brock	20.00	10.00	6.00
(6)	Jeff Burroughs	8.00	4.00	2.50
(7)	John Candelaria	8.00	4.00	2.50
(8)	Jose Cardenal	8.00	4.00	2.50
(9)	Rod Carew	20.00	10.00	6.00
(10)	Steve Carlton	25.00	12.50	7.50
(11)	Dave Cash	8.00	4.00	2.50
(12)	Cesar Cedeno	8.00	4.00	2.50
(13)	Ron Cey	8.00	4.00	2.50
(14)	Carlton Fisk	20.00	10.00	6.00
(15)	Tito Fuentes	8.00	4.00	2.50
(16)	Steve Garvey	12.00	6.00	3.50
(17)	Ken Griffey	8.00	4.00	2.50
(18)	Don Gullett	8.00	4.00	2.50
(19)	Willie Horton	8.00	4.00	2.50
(20)	Al Hrabosky	8.00	4.00	2.50
(21)	Catfish Hunter	20.00	10.00	6.00
(22)	Reggie Jackson	40.00	20.00	12.00

(23)	Randy Jones	8.00	4.00	2.50
(24)	Jim Kaat	8.00	4.00	2.50
(25)	Don Kessinger	8.00	4.00	2.50
(26)	Dave Kingman	8.00	4.00	2.50
(27)	Jerry Koosman	8.00	4.00	2.50
(28)	Mickey Lolich	8.00	4.00	2.50
(29)	Greg Luzinski	8.00	4.00	2.50
(30)	Fred Lynn	10.00	5.00	3.00
(31)	Bill Madlock	8.00	4.00	2.50
(32)	Carlos May	8.00	4.00	2.50
(33)	John Mayberry	8.00	4.00	2.50
(34)	Bake McBride	8.00	4.00	2.50
(35)	Doc Medich	8.00	4.00	2.50
(36)	Andy Messersmith	8.00	4.00	2.50
(37)	Rick Monday	8.00	4.00	2.50
(38)	John Montefusco	8.00	4.00	2.50
(39)	Jerry Morales	8.00	4.00	2.50
(40)	Joe Morgan	20.00	10.00	6.00
(41)	Thurman Munson	15.00	7.50	4.50
(42)	Bobby Murcer	8.00	4.00	2.50
(43)	Al Oliver	8.00	4.00	2.50
(44)	Jim Palmer	20.00	10.00	6.00
(45)	Dave Parker	8.00	4.00	2.50
(46)	Tony Perez	20.00	10.00	6.00
(47)	Jerry Reuss	8.00	4.00	2.50
(48)	Brooks Robinson	25.00	12.50	7.50
(49)	Frank Robinson	25.00	12.50	7.50
(50)	Steve Rogers	8.00	4.00	2.50
(51)	Pete Rose	65.00	32.00	19.50
(52)	Nolan Ryan	100.00	50.00	30.00
(53)	Manny Sanguillen	8.00	4.00	2.50
(54)	Mike Schmidt	45.00	22.00	13.50
(55)	Tom Seaver	25.00	12.50	7.50
(56)	Ted Simmons	8.00	4.00	2.50
(57)	Reggie Smith	8.00	4.00	2.50
(58)	Willie Stargell	20.00	10.00	6.00
(59)	Rusty Staub	12.00	6.00	3.50
(60)	Rennie Stennett	8.00	4.00	2.50
(61)	Don Sutton	20.00	10.00	6.00
(62)	Andy Thornton	8.00	4.00	2.50
(63)	Luis Tiant	8.00	4.00	2.50
(64)	Joe Torre	12.00	6.00	3.50
(65)	Mike Tyson	8.00	4.00	2.50
(66)	Bob Watson	8.00	4.00	2.50
(67)	Wilbur Wood	8.00	4.00	2.50
(68)	Jimmy Wynn	8.00	4.00	2.50
(69)	Carl Yastrzemski	25.00	12.50	7.50
(70)	Richie Zisk	8.00	4.00	2.50

1912 Red Cross Tobacco (T207)

Russell Blackburne

Among the rarest back variations known in the tobacco card series is the Red Cross back on T207. Only a handful of examples have ever been seen. Determination of values is an inexact science.

	NM	EX	VG

(See T207 for checklist. A Fair-condition "common" was bid to $3,500 in a 12/00 auction but was not sold.)

Russell Blackburne	9,183		
(4/02 auction G-VG)			
George Weaver	10,187		
(9/02 auction - Fair)			

1910-12 Red Cross Tobacco Type 1 (T215)

The T215 set issued by Red Cross Tobacco is another of the Louisiana regional sets closely related to the T206 "White Border" tobacco cards. Very similar to the T213 Coupon cards, the Red Cross Tobacco cards are found in two distinct types, both featuring color player lithographs and measuring approximately 1-1/2" x 2-5/8", the standard tobacco card size. Type 1 Red Cross cards, issued from 1910 to 1912, have brown captions; while Type 2 cards, most of which appear to be from 1912-13, have blue printing. The backs of both types are identical, displaying the Red Cross name and emblem, which can be used to positively identify the set and differentiate it from the other Louisiana sets of the same period. Several variations have been found, most of them

involving caption changes. Gaps have been left in the assigned numbering to accommodate future additions to these checklists.

		NM	EX	VG
Common Player:		825.00	330.00	165.00
(1)	Red Ames	825.00	330.00	165.00
(2)	Home Run Baker	2,500	1,000	500.00
(3)	Neal Ball	825.00	330.00	165.00
(4)	Chief Bender (No trees in background.)	2,500	1,000	500.00
(5)	Chief Bender (Trees in background.)	2,500	1,000	500.00
(6)	Al Bridwell	825.00	330.00	165.00
(7)	Bobby Byrne	825.00	330.00	165.00
(8)	Howie Camnitz	825.00	330.00	165.00
(9)	Frank Chance	2,500	1,000	500.00
(10)	Hal Chase	1,875	750.00	375.00
(11)	Ty Cobb	9,375	3,750	1,875
(12)	Eddie Collins	2,500	1,000	500.00
(13)	Wid Conroy	825.00	330.00	165.00
(14)	Doc Crandall	825.00	330.00	165.00
(15)	Sam Crawford	2,500	1,000	500.00
(16)	Birdie Cree	825.00	330.00	165.00
(17)	Harry Davis	825.00	330.00	165.00
(18)	Josh Devore	825.00	330.00	165.00
(19)	Mike Donlin	825.00	330.00	165.00
(20)	Mickey Doolan	825.00	330.00	165.00
(21)	Patsy Dougherty	825.00	330.00	165.00
(22)	Larry Doyle/Btg	825.00	330.00	165.00
(23)	Larry Doyle/Portrait	825.00	330.00	165.00
(24)	Kid Elberfeld	825.00	330.00	165.00
(25)	Russ Ford	825.00	330.00	165.00
(26)	Art Fromme	825.00	330.00	165.00
(27)	Clark Griffith	2,500	1,000	500.00
(28)	Topsy Hartsel	825.00	330.00	165.00
(29)	Dick Hoblitzell	825.00	330.00	165.00
(30)	Solly Hofman	825.00	330.00	165.00
(31)	Del Howard	825.00	330.00	165.00
(32)	Miller Huggins (Hands at mouth.)	2,500	1,000	500.00
(33)	Miller Huggins/Portrait	2,500	1,000	500.00
(34)	John Hummel	825.00	330.00	165.00
(35)	Hughie Jennings (Both hands showing.)	2,500	1,000	500.00
(36)	Hughie Jennings (One hand showing.)	2,500	1,000	500.00
(37)	Walter Johnson	4,375	1,750	875.00
(38)	Ed Konetchy	825.00	330.00	165.00
(39)	Harry Krause	825.00	330.00	165.00
(41)	Nap Lajoie	2,500	1,000	500.00
(42)	Joe Lake	825.00	330.00	165.00
(43)	Arlie Latham	825.00	330.00	165.00
(44)	Tommy Leach	825.00	330.00	165.00
(45)	Lefty Leifield	825.00	330.00	165.00
(46)	Harry Lord	825.00	330.00	165.00
(47)	Sherry Magee	825.00	330.00	165.00
(48)	Rube Marquard/Pitching	2,500	1,000	500.00
(49)	Rube Marquard/Portrait	2,500	1,000	500.00
(51)	Christy Mathewson (Dark cap.)	6,250	2,500	1,250
(52)	Christy Mathewson (White cap.)	6,250	2,500	1,250
(53)	Joe McGinnity	2,500	1,000	500.00
(54)	John McGraw (Glove at hip.)	2,500	1,000	500.00
(55)	John McGraw/Portrait	2,500	1,000	500.00
(56)	Harry McIntyre	825.00	330.00	165.00
(57)	Fred Merkle	825.00	330.00	165.00
(58)	Chief Meyers	825.00	330.00	165.00
(59)	Dots Miller	825.00	330.00	165.00
(61)	Mike Mowrey	825.00	330.00	165.00
(62)	Danny Murphy	825.00	330.00	165.00
(63)	Red Murray	825.00	330.00	165.00
(64)	Rebel Oakes	825.00	330.00	165.00
(65)	Charley O'Leary	825.00	330.00	165.00
(66)	Dode Paskert	825.00	330.00	165.00
(67)	Barney Pelty	825.00	330.00	165.00
(68)	Jack Quinn	825.00	330.00	165.00
(69)	Ed Reulbach	825.00	330.00	165.00
(71)	Nap Rucker	825.00	330.00	165.00
(72)	Germany Schaefer	825.00	330.00	165.00
(73)	Wildfire Schulte	825.00	330.00	165.00
(74)	Jimmy Sheckard	825.00	330.00	165.00
(75)	Frank Smith	825.00	330.00	165.00
(76)	Frank Smither (Smith)	825.00	330.00	165.00
(77)	Tris Speaker	3,125	1,250	625.00
(78)	Jake Stahl	825.00	330.00	165.00
(79)	Harry Steinfeldt	825.00	330.00	165.00
(81)	Gabby Street/Catching	825.00	330.00	165.00
(82)	Gabby Street/Portrait	825.00	330.00	165.00
(83)	Jeff Sweeney	825.00	330.00	165.00
(84)	Lee Tannehill	825.00	330.00	165.00
(85)	Joe Tinker (Bat off shoulder.)	2,500	1,000	500.00
(86)	Joe Tinker (Bat on shoulder.)	2,500	1,000	500.00
(87)	Heinie Wagner	825.00	330.00	165.00
(88)	Jack Warhop	825.00	330.00	165.00
(89)	Zach Wheat	2,500	1,000	500.00
(91)	Doc White	825.00	330.00	165.00
(92)	Ed Willetts (Willett)	825.00	330.00	165.00
(93)	Owen Wilson	825.00	330.00	165.00
(94)	Hooks Wiltse/Pitching	825.00	330.00	165.00
(95)	Hooks Wiltse/Portrait	825.00	330.00	165.00
(96)	Cy Young	6,250	2,500	1,250

1912-13 Red Cross Tobacco Type 2 (T215)

		NM	EX	VG
Common Player:		825.00	330.00	165.00
(1)	Red Ames	825.00	330.00	165.00
(2)	Neal Ball	825.00	330.00	165.00
(3)	Home Run Baker	2,375	950.00	475.00
(4)	Chief Bender (No trees in background.)	2,375	950.00	475.00
(5)	Chief Bender (Trees in background.)	2,375	950.00	475.00

(6)	Roger Bresnahan	2,375	950.00	475.00
(7)	Al Bridwell	825.00	330.00	165.00
(8)	Mordecai Brown	2,375	950.00	475.00
(9)	Bobby Byrne	825.00	330.00	165.00
(10)	Howie Camnitz	825.00	330.00	165.00
(11)	Frank Chance	2,375	950.00	475.00
(12)	Hal Chase	1,500	600.00	300.00
(13)	Ty Cobb	9,375	3,750	1,875
(14)	Eddie Collins	2,375	950.00	475.00
(15)	Doc Crandall	825.00	330.00	165.00
(16)	Sam Crawford	2,375	950.00	475.00
(17)	Birdie Cree	825.00	330.00	165.00
(18)	Harry Davis	825.00	330.00	165.00
(19)	Josh Devore	825.00	330.00	165.00
(21)	Mike Donlin	825.00	330.00	165.00
(22)	Mickey Doolan/Btg	825.00	330.00	165.00
(23)	Mickey Doolan/Fielding	825.00	330.00	165.00
(24)	Patsy Dougherty	825.00	330.00	165.00
(25)	Larry Doyle/Btg	825.00	330.00	165.00
(26)	Larry Doyle/Portrait	825.00	330.00	165.00
(27)	Jean Dubuc	825.00	330.00	165.00
(28)	Kid Elberfeld	825.00	330.00	165.00
(29)	Johnny Evers	2,375	950.00	475.00
(30)	Russ Ford	825.00	330.00	165.00
(31)	Art Fromme	825.00	330.00	165.00
(32)	Clark Griffith	2,375	950.00	475.00
(33)	Bob Groom	825.00	330.00	165.00
(34)	Topsy Hartsel	825.00	330.00	165.00
(35)	Buck Herzog	825.00	330.00	165.00
(36)	Dick Hoblitzell	825.00	330.00	165.00
(37)	Solly Hofman	825.00	330.00	165.00
(38)	Miller Huggins (Hands at mouth.)	2,375	950.00	475.00
(39)	Miller Huggins/Portrait	2,375	950.00	475.00
(41)	John Hummel	825.00	330.00	165.00
(42)	Hughie Jennings	2,375	950.00	475.00
(43)	Walter Johnson	3,125	1,250	625.00
(44)	Joe Kelley	2,375	950.00	475.00
(45)	Ed Konetchy	825.00	330.00	165.00
(46)	Harry Krause	825.00	330.00	165.00
(47)	Nap Lajoie	2,375	950.00	475.00
(48)	Joe Lake	825.00	330.00	165.00
(49)	Tommy Leach	825.00	330.00	165.00
(50)	Lefty Leifield	825.00	330.00	165.00
(51)	Harry Lord	825.00	330.00	165.00
(52)	Sherry Magee	825.00	330.00	165.00
(53)	Rube Marquard/Pitching	2,375	950.00	475.00
(54)	Rube Marquard/Portrait	2,375	950.00	475.00
(55)	Christy Mathewson	3,440	1,375	690.00
(56)	John McGraw (Glove at side.)	2,300	950.00	475.00
(57)	John McGraw/Portrait	2,375	950.00	475.00
(58)	Harry McIntire	825.00	330.00	165.00
(59)	Larry McLean	825.00	330.00	165.00
(61)	Fred Merkle	825.00	330.00	165.00
(62)	Dots Miller	825.00	330.00	165.00
(63)	Mike Mitchell	825.00	330.00	165.00
(64)	Mike Mowrey	825.00	330.00	165.00
(65)	George Mullin	825.00	330.00	165.00
(66)	Danny Murphy	825.00	330.00	165.00
(67)	Red Murray	825.00	330.00	165.00
(68)	Rebel Oakes	825.00	330.00	165.00
(69)	Rube Oldring	825.00	330.00	165.00
(70)	Charley O'Leary	825.00	330.00	165.00
(71)	Dode Paskert	825.00	330.00	165.00
(72)	Barney Pelty	825.00	330.00	165.00
(73)	Billy Purtell	825.00	330.00	165.00
(74)	Ed Reulbach	825.00	330.00	165.00
(75)	Nap Rucker	825.00	330.00	165.00
(76)	Germany Schaefer (Chicago)	825.00	330.00	165.00
(77)	Germany Schaefer (Washington)	825.00	330.00	165.00
(78)	Wildfire Schulte	825.00	330.00	165.00
(79)	Frank Smith	825.00	330.00	165.00
(80)	Frank Smither (Smith)	825.00	330.00	165.00
(82)	Tris Speaker	2,375	950.00	475.00
(83)	Jake Stahl	825.00	330.00	165.00
(84)	Harry Steinfeldt	825.00	330.00	165.00
(85)	Ed Summers	825.00	330.00	165.00
(86)	Jeff Sweeney	825.00	330.00	165.00
(87)	Ira Thomas	825.00	330.00	165.00
(88)	Joe Tinker (Bat off shoulder.)	2,375	950.00	475.00
(89)	Joe Tinker (Bat on shoulder.)	2,375	950.00	475.00
(90)	Heinie Wagner	825.00	330.00	165.00
(91)	Jack Warhop	825.00	330.00	165.00
(92)	Doc White	825.00	330.00	165.00
(93)	Hooks Wiltse/Pitching	825.00	330.00	165.00
(94)	Hooks Wiltse/Portrait	825.00	330.00	165.00

1954 Red Heart Dog Food

 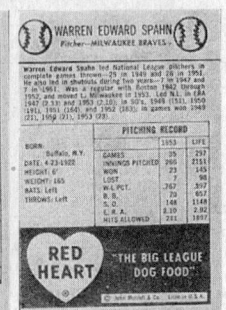

This set of 33 cards was issued in three color-coded series by the Red Heart Dog Food Co. Card fronts feature hand-colored photos on either a blue, green or red background. The 11 red-background cards are scarcer than the 11-card blue or green series. Backs of the 2-5/8" x 3-3/4" cards contain biographical and statistical information along with a Red Heart ad. Each 11-card series was available via a mail-in offer. As late as the early 1970s, the company was still sending cards to collectors who requested them.

		NM	EX	VG
Complete Set (33):		2,150	900.00	450.00
Common Player:		30.00	15.00	9.00
(1)	Richie Ashburn	100.00	40.00	20.00
(2)	Frankie Baumholtz	40.00	16.00	8.00
(3)	Gus Bell	30.00	15.00	9.00
(4)	Billy Cox	40.00	16.00	8.00
(5)	Alvin Dark	30.00	15.00	9.00
(6)	Carl Erskine	75.00	30.00	15.00
(7)	Ferris Fain	40.00	16.00	8.00
(8)	Dee Fondy	30.00	15.00	9.00
(9)	Nelson Fox	85.00	35.00	17.50
(10)	Jim Gilliam	50.00	20.00	10.00
(11)	Jim Hegan	40.00	16.00	8.00
(12)	George Kell	45.00	18.00	9.00
(13)	Ted Kluszewski	65.00	25.00	13.00
(14)	Ralph Kiner	60.00	24.00	12.00
(15)	Harvey Kuenn	30.00	12.00	6.00
(16)	Bob Lemon	55.00	22.50	11.00
(17)	Sherman Lollar	30.00	15.00	9.00
(18)	Mickey Mantle	430.00	175.00	90.00
(19)	Billy Martin	65.00	25.00	13.00
(20)	Gil McDougald	55.00	22.50	11.00
(21)	Roy McMillan	30.00	15.00	9.00
(22)	Minnie Minoso	50.00	20.00	10.00
(23)	Stan Musial	260.00	100.00	50.00
(24)	Billy Pierce	40.00	16.00	8.00
(25)	Al Rosen	45.00	18.00	9.00
(26)	Hank Sauer	30.00	15.00	9.00
(27)	Red Schoendienst	75.00	30.00	15.00
(28)	Enos Slaughter	65.00	25.00	13.00
(29)	Duke Snider	120.00	50.00	25.00
(30)	Warren Spahn	65.00	25.00	13.00
(31)	Sammy White	30.00	15.00	9.00
(32)	Eddie Yost	30.00	12.00	6.00
(33)	Gus Zernial	30.00	12.00	6.00

1952 Red Man Tobacco

This was the first national set of tobacco cards produced since the golden days of tobacco sets in the early part of the century. There are 52 cards in the set, with 25 top players and one manager from each league. Player selection was made by editor J.G. Taylor Spink of The Sporting News. Cards measure 3-1/2" x 4", including a 1/2" tab at the bottom of each card. These tabs were redeemable for a free baseball cap from Red Man. Cards are harder to find with tabs intact, and thus more valuable in that form. Values quoted here are for cards with tabs. Cards with the tabs removed would be valued about 25-35 percent of the quoted figures. Card fronts are full color paintings of each player with biographical information inset in the portrait area. Card backs contain company advertising. Cards are numbered and dated only on the tabs. The 1952 Red Man cards can be found with either of two expiration dates on back, March 31 or June 1, 1953; neither commands a premium.

		NM	EX	VG
Complete Set, W/Tab (52):		10,000	4,000	2,000
Common Player, W/Tab:		100.00	40.00	20.00
Complete Set, No Tab (52):		2,250	550.00	275.00
Common Player, No Tab:		20.00	8.00	4.00
WITH TAB				
1A	Casey Stengel	250.00	100.00	50.00
1N	Leo Durocher	200.00	80.00	40.00
2A	Roberto Avila	100.00	40.00	20.00
2N	Richie Ashburn	240.00	95.00	45.00
3A	Larry "Yogi" Berra	375.00	150.00	75.00
3N	Ewell Blackwell	120.00	50.00	25.00
4A	Gil Coan	100.00	40.00	20.00
4N	Cliff Chambers	100.00	40.00	20.00
5A	Dom DiMaggio	140.00	55.00	27.50
5N	Murry Dickson	100.00	40.00	20.00
6A	Larry Doby	215.00	85.00	45.00
6N	Sid Gordon	100.00	40.00	20.00
7A	Ferris Fain	100.00	40.00	20.00
7N	Granny Hamner	100.00	40.00	20.00
8A	Bob Feller	325.00	130.00	65.00
8N	Jim Hearn	100.00	40.00	20.00
9A	Nelson Fox	215.00	85.00	45.00
9N	Monte Irvin	215.00	85.00	45.00
10A	Johnny Groth	100.00	40.00	20.00
10N	Larry Jansen	100.00	40.00	20.00
11A	Jim Hegan	100.00	40.00	20.00
11N	Willie Jones	100.00	40.00	20.00
12A	Eddie Joost	100.00	40.00	20.00
12N	Ralph Kiner	215.00	85.00	45.00
13A	George Kell	215.00	85.00	45.00
13N	Whitey Lockman	100.00	40.00	20.00
14A	Gil McDougald	100.00	40.00	20.00
14N	Sal Maglie	100.00	40.00	20.00

15A	Orestes Minoso	100.00	40.00	20.00
15N	Willie Mays	600.00	240.00	120.00
16A	Bill Pierce	100.00	40.00	20.00
16N	Stan Musial	575.00	230.00	115.00
17A	Bob Porterfield	100.00	40.00	20.00
17N	Pee Wee Reese	340.00	135.00	65.00
18A	Eddie Robinson	100.00	40.00	20.00
18N	Robin Roberts	215.00	85.00	45.00
19A	Saul Rogovin	100.00	40.00	20.00
19N	Al Schoendienst	215.00	85.00	45.00
20A	Bobby Shantz	100.00	40.00	20.00
20N	Enos Slaughter	215.00	85.00	45.00
21A	Vern Stephens	100.00	40.00	20.00
21N	Duke Snider	275.00	110.00	55.00
22A	Vic Wertz	100.00	40.00	20.00
22N	Warren Spahn	215.00	85.00	45.00
23A	Ted Williams	1,800	725.00	360.00
23N	Eddie Stanky	100.00	40.00	20.00
24A	Early Wynn	215.00	85.00	45.00
24N	Bobby Thomson	100.00	40.00	20.00
25A	Eddie Yost	100.00	40.00	20.00
25N	Earl Torgeson	100.00	40.00	20.00
26A	Gus Zernial	100.00	40.00	20.00
26N	Wes Westrum	100.00	40.00	20.00
NO TAB				
1A	Casey Stengel	45.00	18.00	9.00
1N	Leo Durocher	35.00	14.00	7.00
2A	Roberto Avila	20.00	8.00	4.00
2N	Richie Ashburn	55.00	22.00	11.00
3A	Larry "Yogi" Berra	85.00	35.00	17.50
3N	Ewell Blackwell	25.00	10.00	5.00
4A	Gil Coan	20.00	8.00	4.00
4N	Cliff Chambers	20.00	8.00	4.00
5A	Dom DiMaggio	30.00	12.00	6.00
5N	Murry Dickson	20.00	8.00	4.00
6A	Larry Doby	45.00	18.00	9.00
6N	Sid Gordon	20.00	8.00	4.00
7A	Ferris Fain	20.00	8.00	4.00
7N	Granny Hamner	20.00	8.00	4.00
8A	Bob Feller	80.00	32.00	16.00
8N	Jim Hearn	20.00	8.00	4.00
9A	Nelson Fox	50.00	20.00	10.00
9N	Monte Irvin	45.00	18.00	9.00
10A	Johnny Groth	20.00	8.00	4.00
10N	Larry Jansen	20.00	8.00	4.00
11A	Jim Hegan	20.00	8.00	4.00
11N	Willie Jones	20.00	8.00	4.00
12A	Eddie Joost	20.00	8.00	4.00
12N	Ralph Kiner	45.00	18.00	9.00
13A	George Kell	45.00	18.00	9.00
13N	Whitey Lockman	20.00	8.00	4.00
14A	Gil McDougald	25.00	10.00	5.00
14N	Sal Maglie	20.00	8.00	4.00
15A	Orestes Minoso	30.00	12.00	6.00
15N	Willie Mays	200.00	80.00	40.00
16A	Bill Pierce	20.00	8.00	4.00
16N	Stan Musial	175.00	70.00	35.00
17A	Bob Porterfield	20.00	8.00	4.00
17N	Pee Wee Reese	70.00	28.00	14.00
18A	Eddie Robinson	20.00	8.00	4.00
18N	Robin Roberts	45.00	18.00	9.00
19A	Saul Rogovin	20.00	8.00	4.00
19N	Al Schoendienst	45.00	18.00	9.00
20A	Bobby Shantz	20.00	8.00	4.00
20N	Enos Slaughter	45.00	18.00	9.00
21A	Vern Stephens	20.00	8.00	4.00
21N	Duke Snider	85.00	35.00	17.50
22A	Vic Wertz	20.00	8.00	4.00
22N	Warren Spahn	45.00	18.00	9.00
23A	Ted Williams	375.00	150.00	75.00
23N	Eddie Stanky	20.00	8.00	4.00
24A	Early Wynn	45.00	18.00	9.00
24N	Bobby Thomson	20.00	8.00	4.00
25A	Eddie Yost	20.00	8.00	4.00
25N	Earl Torgeson	20.00	8.00	4.00
26A	Gus Zernial	20.00	8.00	4.00
26N	Wes Westrum	20.00	8.00	4.00

1953 Red Man Tobacco

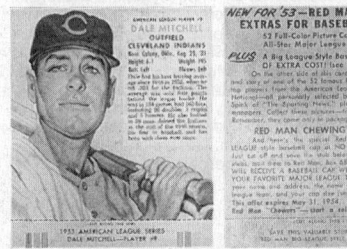

This was the chewing tobacco company's second annual set of 3-1/2" x 4" cards, including the tabs at the bottom of the cards. Formats for front and back are similar to the '52 edition. The 1953 Red Man cards, however, include card numbers within the player biographical section, and the card backs are headlined "New for '53." Once again, cards with intact tabs (which were redeemable for a free cap.) are more valuable. Prices below are for cards with tabs. Cards with tabs removed are worth about 25-35 percent of the stated values. Each league is represented by 25 players and a manager on the full-color cards, a total of 52. Values quoted here are for cards with tabs. Cards with the tabs removed would be valued about 35-40 percent of the quoted figures. The 1953 Red Man cards can be found with either of two expiration dates on back, March 31 or May 31, 1954; neither commands a premium.

Left column table

	NM	EX	VG
Complete Set, W/Tab (52):	5,500	2,200	1,100
Common Player:	60.00	24.00	12.00
Complete Set, No Tab (52):	1,400	550.00	275.00
Common Player, No Tab:	12.50	5.00	2.50
WITH TAB			
1A Casey Stengel	150.00	60.00	30.00
1N Charlie Dressen	75.00	30.00	15.00
2A Hank Bauer	75.00	30.00	15.00
2N Bobby Adams	60.00	24.00	12.00
3A Larry "Yogi" Berra	300.00	120.00	60.00
3N Richie Ashburn	125.00	50.00	25.00
4A Walt Dropo	60.00	24.00	12.00
4N Joe Black	100.00	40.00	20.00
5A Nelson Fox	125.00	50.00	25.00
5N Roy Campanella	300.00	120.00	60.00
6A Jackie Jensen	75.00	30.00	15.00
6N Ted Kluszewski	95.00	40.00	20.00
7A Eddie Joost	60.00	24.00	12.00
7N Whitey Lockman	60.00	24.00	12.00
8A George Kell	125.00	50.00	25.00
8N Sal Maglie	60.00	24.00	12.00
9A Dale Mitchell	60.00	24.00	12.00
9N Andy Pafko	60.00	24.00	12.00
10A Phil Rizzuto	225.00	90.00	45.00
10N Pee Wee Reese	250.00	100.00	50.00
11A Eddie Robinson	60.00	24.00	12.00
11N Robin Roberts	125.00	50.00	25.00
12A Gene Woodling	70.00	28.00	14.00
12N Red Schoendienst	125.00	50.00	25.00
13A Gus Zernial	60.00	24.00	12.00
13N Enos Slaughter	125.00	50.00	25.00
14A Early Wynn	125.00	50.00	25.00
14N Edwin "Duke" Snider	300.00	120.00	60.00
15A Joe Dobson	60.00	24.00	12.00
15N Ralph Kiner	125.00	50.00	25.00
16A Billy Pierce	60.00	24.00	12.00
16N Hank Sauer	60.00	24.00	12.00
17A Bob Lemon	125.00	50.00	25.00
17N Del Ennis	60.00	24.00	12.00
18A Johnny Mize	145.00	60.00	30.00
18N Granny Hamner	60.00	24.00	12.00
19A Bob Porterfield	60.00	24.00	12.00
19N Warren Spahn	145.00	60.00	30.00
20A Bobby Shantz	60.00	24.00	12.00
20N Wes Westrum	60.00	24.00	12.00
21A "Mickey" Vernon	60.00	24.00	12.00
21N Hoyt Wilhelm	125.00	50.00	25.00
22A Dom DiMaggio	75.00	30.00	15.00
22N Murry Dickson	60.00	24.00	12.00
23A Gil McDougald	70.00	28.00	14.00
23N Warren Hacker	60.00	24.00	12.00
24A Al Rosen	70.00	28.00	14.00
24N Gerry Staley	60.00	24.00	12.00
25A Mel Parnell	60.00	24.00	12.00
25N Bobby Thomson	60.00	24.00	12.00
26A Roberto Avila	60.00	24.00	12.00
26N Stan Musial	700.00	280.00	140.00
NO TAB			
1A Casey Stengel	35.00	14.00	7.00
1N Charlie Dressen	17.50	7.00	3.50
2A Hank Bauer	17.50	7.00	3.50
2N Bobby Adams	12.50	5.00	2.50
3A Larry "Yogi" Berra	65.00	26.00	13.00
3N Richie Ashburn	40.00	16.00	8.00
4A Walt Dropo	12.50	5.00	2.50
4N Joe Black	20.00	8.00	4.00
5A Nelson Fox	40.00	16.00	8.00
5N Roy Campanella	65.00	26.00	13.00
6A Jackie Jensen	20.00	8.00	4.00
6N Ted Kluszewski	25.00	10.00	5.00
7A Eddie Joost	12.50	5.00	2.50
7N Whitey Lockman	12.50	5.00	2.50
8A George Kell	40.00	16.00	8.00
8N Sal Maglie	15.00	6.00	3.00
9A Dale Mitchell	12.50	5.00	2.50
9N Andy Pafko	12.50	5.00	2.50
10A Phil Rizzuto	50.00	20.00	10.00
10N Pee Wee Reese	60.00	24.00	12.00
11A Eddie Robinson	12.50	5.00	2.50
11N Robin Roberts	40.00	16.00	8.00
12A Gene Woodling	15.00	6.00	3.00
12N Red Schoendienst	40.00	16.00	8.00
13A Gus Zernial	12.50	5.00	2.50
13N Enos Slaughter	40.00	16.00	8.00
14A Early Wynn	40.00	16.00	8.00
14N Edwin "Duke" Snider	75.00	30.00	15.00
15A Joe Dobson	12.50	5.00	2.50
15N Ralph Kiner	40.00	16.00	8.00
16A Billy Pierce	15.00	6.00	3.00
16N Hank Sauer	12.50	5.00	2.50
17A Bob Lemon	40.00	16.00	8.00
17N Del Ennis	12.50	5.00	2.50
18A Johnny Mize	40.00	16.00	8.00
18N Granny Hamner	12.50	5.00	2.50
19A Bob Porterfield	12.50	5.00	2.50
19N Warren Spahn	45.00	18.00	9.00
20A Bobby Shantz	12.50	5.00	2.50
20N Wes Westrum	12.50	5.00	2.50
21A "Mickey" Vernon	12.50	5.00	2.50
21N Hoyt Wilhelm	35.00	14.00	7.00
22A Dom DiMaggio	25.00	10.00	5.00
22N Murry Dickson	12.50	5.00	2.50
23A Gil McDougald	15.00	6.00	3.00
23N Warren Hacker	12.50	5.00	2.50
24A Al Rosen	17.50	7.00	3.50
24N Gerry Staley	12.50	5.00	2.50
25A Mel Parnell	12.50	5.00	2.50
25N Bobby Thomson	12.50	5.00	2.50
26A Roberto Avila	12.50	5.00	2.50
26N Stan Musial	125.00	50.00	25.00

1954 Red Man Tobacco

In 1954, the Red Man set eliminated managers from the set, and issued only 25 player cards for each

league. There are, however, four variations which bring the total set size to 54 full-color cards. Two cards exist for Gus Bell and Enos Slaughter, while American Leaguers George Kell, Sam Mele and Dave Philley are each shown with two different teams. Complete set prices quoted below do not include the scarcer of the variation pairs. Cards measure 3-1/2" x 4" with tabs intact. Cards without tabs are worth about 25-35 percent of the values quoted below. Formats for the cards remain virtually unchanged, with card numbers included within the player information boxes as well as on the tabs. Cards can be found with either of two expiration dates on back, March 31 or May 31, 1955; neither commands a premium.

	NM	EX	VG
Complete Set, W/Tab (50):	4,000	1,600	800.00
Common Player, W/Tab:	45.00	18.00	9.00
Complete Set, No Tab (50):	1,400	550.00	275.00
Common Player, No Tab:	15.00	6.00	3.00
WITH TAB			
1A Bobby Avila	45.00	18.00	9.00
1N Richie Ashburn	90.00	36.00	18.00
2A Jim Busby	45.00	18.00	9.00
2N Billy Cox	55.00	22.00	11.00
3A Nelson Fox	90.00	36.00	18.00
3N Del Crandall	45.00	18.00	9.00
4Aa George Kell (Boston)	125.00	50.00	25.00
4Ab George Kell (Chicago)	180.00	70.00	35.00
4N Carl Erskine	60.00	24.00	12.00
5A Sherman Lollar	45.00	18.00	9.00
5N Monte Irvin	90.00	36.00	18.00
6Aa Sam Mele (Baltimore)	90.00	36.00	18.00
6Ab Sam Mele (Chicago)	110.00	44.00	22.00
6N Ted Kluszewski	100.00	40.00	20.00
7A Orestes Minoso	65.00	26.00	13.00
7N Don Mueller	45.00	18.00	9.00
8A Mel Parnell	45.00	18.00	9.00
8N Andy Pafko	45.00	18.00	9.00
9Aa Dave Philley (Cleveland)	75.00	30.00	15.00
9Ab Dave Philley (Philadelphia)	145.00	60.00	30.00
9N Del Rice	45.00	18.00	9.00
10A Billy Pierce	45.00	18.00	9.00
10N Al Schoendienst	90.00	36.00	18.00
11A Jim Piersall	60.00	24.00	12.00
11N Warren Spahn	100.00	40.00	20.00
12A Al Rosen	50.00	20.00	10.00
12N Curt Simmons	45.00	18.00	9.00
13A "Mickey" Vernon	45.00	18.00	9.00
13N Roy Campanella	215.00	85.00	45.00
14A Sammy White	45.00	18.00	9.00
14N Jim Gilliam	60.00	24.00	12.00
15A Gene Woodling	60.00	24.00	12.00
15N "Pee Wee" Reese	160.00	64.00	32.00
16A Ed "Whitey" Ford	140.00	56.00	28.00
16N Edwin "Duke" Snider	215.00	85.00	45.00
17A Phil Rizzuto	140.00	56.00	28.00
17N Rip Repulski	45.00	18.00	9.00
18A Bob Porterfield	45.00	18.00	9.00
18N Robin Roberts	90.00	36.00	18.00
19A Al "Chico" Carrasquel	45.00	18.00	9.00
19Na Enos Slaughter	215.00	85.00	45.00
19Nb Gus Bell	190.00	75.00	35.00
20A Larry "Yogi" Berra	200.00	80.00	40.00
20N Johnny Logan	45.00	18.00	9.00
21A Bob Lemon	90.00	36.00	18.00
21N Johnny Antonelli	45.00	18.00	9.00
22A Ferris Fain	45.00	18.00	9.00
22N Gil Hodges	90.00	36.00	18.00
23A Hank Bauer	50.00	20.00	10.00
23N Eddie Mathews	100.00	40.00	20.00
24A Jim Delsing	45.00	18.00	9.00
24N Lew Burdette	45.00	18.00	9.00
25A Gil McDougald	55.00	22.00	11.00
25N Willie Mays	425.00	170.00	85.00
NO TAB			
1A Bobby Avila	15.00	6.00	3.00
1N Richie Ashburn	35.00	14.00	7.00
2A Jim Busby	15.00	6.00	3.00
2N Billy Cox	20.00	8.00	4.00
3A Nelson Fox	35.00	14.00	7.00
3N Del Crandall	15.00	6.00	3.00
4Aa George Kell (Boston)	50.00	20.00	10.00
4Ab George Kell (Chicago)	65.00	26.00	13.00
4N Carl Erskine	22.50	9.00	4.50
5A Sherman Lollar	15.00	6.00	3.00
5N Monte Irvin	35.00	14.00	7.00
6Aa Sam Mele (Baltimore)	30.00	12.00	6.00
6Ab Sam Mele (Chicago)	55.00	22.00	11.00
6N Ted Kluszewski	30.00	12.00	6.00
7A Orestes Minoso	25.00	10.00	5.00
7N Don Mueller	15.00	6.00	3.00
8A Mel Parnell	15.00	6.00	3.00
8N Andy Pafko	15.00	6.00	3.00
9Aa Dave Philley (Cleveland)	30.00	12.00	6.00
9Ab Dave Philley (Philadelphia)	65.00	26.00	13.00
9N Del Rice	15.00	6.00	3.00
10A Billy Pierce	15.00	6.00	3.00
10N Al Schoendienst	35.00	14.00	7.00
11A Jim Piersall	20.00	8.00	4.00
11N Warren Spahn	35.00	14.00	7.00
12A Al Rosen	20.00	8.00	4.00
12N Curt Simmons	15.00	6.00	3.00
13A "Mickey" Vernon	15.00	6.00	3.00
13N Roy Campanella	65.00	26.00	13.00
14A Sammy White	15.00	6.00	3.00
14N Jim Gilliam	22.50	9.00	4.50
15A Gene Woodling	22.50	9.00	4.50
15N "Pee Wee" Reese	55.00	22.00	11.00
16A Ed "Whitey" Ford	45.00	18.00	9.00
16N Edwin "Duke" Snider	65.00	26.00	13.00
17A Phil Rizzuto	50.00	20.00	10.00
17N Rip Repulski	15.00	6.00	3.00
18A Bob Porterfield	15.00	6.00	3.00
18N Robin Roberts	35.00	14.00	7.00
19A Al "Chico" Carrasquel	20.00	8.00	4.00
19Na Enos Slaughter	70.00	28.00	14.00
19Nb Gus Bell	70.00	28.00	14.00
20A Larry "Yogi" Berra	65.00	26.00	13.00
20N Johnny Logan	15.00	6.00	3.00
21A Bob Lemon	35.00	14.00	7.00
21N Johnny Antonelli	15.00	6.00	3.00
22A Ferris Fain	15.00	6.00	3.00
22N Gil Hodges	35.00	14.00	7.00
23A Hank Bauer	20.00	8.00	4.00
23N Eddie Mathews	35.00	14.00	7.00
24A Jim Delsing	15.00	6.00	3.00
24N Lew Burdette	15.00	6.00	3.00
25A Gil McDougald	20.00	8.00	4.00
25N Willie Mays	130.00	55.00	25.00

1955 Red Man Tobacco

These 50 cards are quite similar to the 1954 edition, with card fronts virtually unchanged except for the data in the biographical box on the color picture area. This set of the 3-1/2" x 4" cards includes 25 players from each league, with no known variations. As with all Red Man sets, those cards complete with the redeemable tabs are more valuable. Values quoted below are for cards with tabs. Cards with the tabs removed are worth about 25-35 percent of those figures. Each card can be found with two different expiration dates on back, April 15 or June 15, 1956; neither version commands a premium.

	NM	EX	VG
Complete Set, W/Tab (50):	3,750	1,500	750.00
Common Player, W/Tab:	60.00	24.00	12.00
Complete Set, No Tab (50):	900.00	360.00	180.00
Common Player, No Tab:	10.00	4.00	2.00
WITH TAB			
1A Ray Boone	60.00	24.00	12.00
1N Richie Ashburn	95.00	38.00	19.00
2A Jim Busby	60.00	24.00	12.00
2N Del Crandall	60.00	24.00	12.00
3A Ed "Whitey" Ford	125.00	50.00	25.00
3N Gil Hodges	90.00	36.00	18.00
4A Nelson Fox	90.00	36.00	18.00
4N Brooks Lawrence	60.00	24.00	12.00
5A Bob Grim	60.00	24.00	12.00
5N Johnny Logan	60.00	24.00	12.00
6A Jack Harshman	60.00	24.00	12.00
6N Sal Maglie	60.00	24.00	12.00
7A Jim Hegan	60.00	24.00	12.00
7N Willie Mays	250.00	100.00	50.00
8A Bob Lemon	90.00	36.00	18.00
8N Don Mueller	60.00	24.00	12.00
9A Irv Noren	60.00	24.00	12.00
9N Bill Sarni	60.00	24.00	12.00
10A Bob Porterfield	60.00	24.00	12.00
10N Warren Spahn	90.00	36.00	18.00
11A Al Rosen	75.00	30.00	15.00
11N Henry Thompson	60.00	24.00	12.00
12A "Mickey" Vernon	60.00	24.00	12.00
12N Hoyt Wilhelm	90.00	36.00	18.00
13A Vic Wertz	60.00	24.00	12.00
13N Johnny Antonelli	60.00	24.00	12.00
14A Early Wynn	90.00	36.00	18.00
14N Carl Erskine	75.00	30.00	15.00
15A Bobby Avila	60.00	24.00	12.00
15N Granny Hamner	60.00	24.00	12.00
16A Larry "Yogi" Berra	165.00	65.00	35.00
16N Ted Kluszewski	75.00	30.00	15.00
17A Joe Coleman	60.00	24.00	12.00
17N Pee Wee Reese	125.00	50.00	25.00
18A Larry Doby	90.00	36.00	18.00
18N Al Schoendienst	90.00	36.00	18.00
19A Jackie Jensen	65.00	26.00	13.00
19N Duke Snider	165.00	65.00	35.00
20A Pete Runnels	60.00	24.00	12.00
20N Frank Thomas	60.00	24.00	12.00
21A Jim Piersall	60.00	24.00	12.00
21N Ray Jablonski	60.00	24.00	12.00
22A Hank Bauer	65.00	26.00	13.00
22N James "Dusty" Rhodes	60.00	24.00	12.00
23A "Chico" Carrasquel	60.00	24.00	12.00

23N	Gus Bell	60.00	24.00	12.00
24A	Orestes Minoso	75.00	30.00	15.00
24N	Curt Simmons	60.00	24.00	12.00
25A	Sandy Consuegra	60.00	24.00	12.00
25N	Marvin Grissom	60.00	24.00	12.00
	NO TAB			
1A	Ray Boone	10.00	4.00	2.00
1N	Richie Ashburn	30.00	12.00	6.00
2A	Jim Busby	10.00	4.00	2.00
2N	Del Crandall	10.00	4.00	2.00
3A	Ed "Whitey" Ford	35.00	14.00	7.00
3N	Gil Hodges	30.00	12.00	6.00
4A	Nelson Fox	30.00	12.00	6.00
4N	Brooks Lawrence	10.00	4.00	2.00
5A	Bob Grim	10.00	4.00	2.00
5N	Johnny Logan	10.00	4.00	2.00
6A	Jack Harshman	10.00	4.00	2.00
6N	Sal Maglie	10.00	4.00	2.00
7A	Jim Hegan	10.00	4.00	2.00
7N	Willie Mays	100.00	40.00	20.00
8A	Bob Lemon	30.00	12.00	6.00
8N	Don Mueller	10.00	4.00	2.00
9A	Irv Noren	10.00	4.00	2.00
9N	Bill Sarni	10.00	4.00	2.00
10A	Bob Porterfield	10.00	4.00	2.00
10N	Warren Spahn	30.00	12.00	6.00
11A	Al Rosen	13.50	5.50	2.75
11N	Henry Thompson	10.00	4.00	2.00
12A	"Mickey" Vernon	10.00	4.00	2.00
12N	Hoyt Wilhelm	30.00	12.00	6.00
13A	Vic Wertz	10.00	4.00	2.00
13N	Johnny Antonelli	10.00	4.00	2.00
14A	Early Wynn	30.00	12.00	6.00
14N	Carl Erskine	15.00	6.00	3.00
15A	Bobby Avila	10.00	4.00	2.00
15N	Granny Hamner	10.00	4.00	2.00
16A	Larry "Yogi" Berra	50.00	20.00	10.00
16N	Ted Kluszewski	20.00	8.00	4.00
17A	Joe Coleman	10.00	4.00	2.00
17N	Pee Wee Reese	50.00	20.00	10.00
18A	Larry Doby	30.00	12.00	6.00
18N	Al Schoendienst	30.00	12.00	6.00
19A	Jackie Jensen	13.50	5.50	2.75
19N	Duke Snider	55.00	22.00	11.00
20A	Pete Runnels	10.00	4.00	2.00
20N	Frank Thomas	10.00	4.00	2.00
21A	Jim Piersall	13.50	5.50	2.75
21N	Ray Jablonski	10.00	4.00	2.00
22A	Hank Bauer	13.50	5.50	2.75
22N	James "Dusty" Rhodes	10.00	4.00	2.00
23A	"Chico" Carrasquel	10.00	4.00	2.00
23N	Gus Bell	10.00	4.00	2.00
24A	Orestes Minoso	15.00	6.00	3.00
24N	Curt Simmons	10.00	4.00	2.00
25A	Sandy Consuegra	10.00	4.00	2.00
25N	Marvin Grissom	10.00	4.00	2.00

1952-1954 Red Man Posters

These colorful lithographed paper posters, 11" x 15-1/2", were intended as point-of-purchase displays to encourage sales of the chewing tobacco and offer a baseball cap in exchange for the tabs found on the bottom of each card. The posters were reproduced in 11" x 16" format on cardboard in the 1980s.

		NM	EX	VG
1952	Ralph Kiner (11" x 15")	200.00	100.00	60.00
1953	Enos Slaughter (11" x 15")	300.00	150.00	90.00
1954	Johnny Mize (12" x 15-1/2")	325.00	160.00	95.00

"1952-54" Red Man Posters

Some 30 years after the original 11" x 15-1/2" paper posters were used to advertise Red Man chewing tobacco and the baseball cards and caps available as premiums, three of the pieces were reproduced. Posters which are printed on cardboard in a 11" x 16" size are modern reproductions with only decorative, rather than collectible, value.

No Collector Value
1952 Ralph Kiner
1953 Enos Slaughter
1954 Johnny Mize

1976 Redpath Sugar Expos

Among the more unusual baseball collectibles of the late 1970s are the Montreal Expos sugar packs produced by Redpath Sugar for distribution in Quebec. About 1-1/2" x 2-3/4" in size, the sugar packs feature color portraits of the players on front, along with bi-lingual personal information and a uniform number. Backs have a color team logo and career highlights. Uncut sheets or the packaging are known which indicate several players were double- or triple-printed. The checklist here is arranged by uniform number.

		NM	EX	VG
	Complete Set (36):	75.00	37.00	22.00
	Common Player:	2.00	1.00	.60
1	Osvaldo Jose Virgil	2.00	1.00	.60
5	Peter Mackanin, Jr.	2.00	1.00	.60
6	Karl Otto Kuehl	2.00	1.00	.60
8	Gary Edmund Carter	15.00	7.50	4.50
9	Barry Clifton Foote	2.00	1.00	.60
11	Jose Manuel Mangual	2.00	1.00	.60
14	Lawrence Eugene Doby	6.00	3.00	1.75
15	Larry Alton Parrish	2.00	1.00	.60
16	Michael Jorgensen	2.00	1.00	.60
17	Andre Thornton	4.00	2.00	1.25
18	Joseph Thomas Kerrigan	2.00	1.00	.60
19	Timothy John Foli/DP	2.00	1.00	.60
20	James Lawrence Lyttle, Jr.	2.00	1.00	.60
21	Frederick John Scherman, Jr.	2.00	1.00	.60
22	Ellis Clarence Valentine	2.00	1.00	.60
26	Donald Joseph Stanhouse	2.00	1.00	.60
27	Dale Albert Murray	2.00	1.00	.60
31	Clayton Laws Kirby, Jr.	2.00	1.00	.60
33	Robert David Lang	2.00	1.00	.60
34	Jose Manuel Morales	2.00	1.00	.60
35	Woodrow Thompson Fryman	3.00	1.50	.90
36	Steven John Dunning	2.00	1.00	.60
37	Jerome Cardell White	2.00	1.00	.60
38	Jesus Maria Frias (Andujar)	2.00	1.00	.60
39	Daniel Dean Warthen	2.00	1.00	.60
40	Donald George Carrithers (3P)	2.00	1.00	.60
41	Ronald Jacques Piche	2.00	1.00	.60
43	James Edward Dwyer	2.00	1.00	.60
44	Jesus Rivera (Torres), Jr.	2.00	1.00	.60
45	Stephen Douglas Rogers/DP	2.00	1.00	.60
46	Marion Danne Adair	2.00	1.00	.60
47	Wayne Allen Granger	2.00	1.00	.60
48	Lawrence Donald Bearnarth	2.00	1.00	.60
---	Roland Wayne Garrett	2.00	1.00	.60
---	Charles Gilbert Taylor	2.00	1.00	.60
---	Delbert Bernard Unser	2.00	1.00	.60

1977 Redpath Sugar Expos

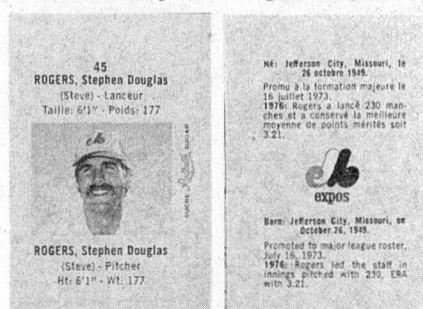

One of the more obscure regional Canadian issues, this 30-player set features members of the Expos and was printed on sugar packets distributed in the Montreal area in 1977. The front of the packet fea-

tures a color photo of the player with his name, uniform number, position, height and weight listed in both English and French. A line identifying Redpath Sugar appears alongside the photo. The backs display the Expos logo and brief player highlights (again printed in both French and English). The set has been seen in uncut sheets, revealing that the packets of Steve Rogers and David Cash, Jr. were double printed.

		NM	EX	VG
	Complete Set (30):	75.00	37.00	22.00
	Common Player:	1.50	.70	.45
1	Osvaldo Jose Virgil	1.50	.70	.45
2	James Thomas Brewer	1.50	.70	.45
3	James Barton Vernon	1.50	.70	.45
4	Chris Edward Speier	1.50	.70	.45
5	Peter Mackanin Jr.	1.50	.70	.45
7	William Frederick Gardner	1.50	.70	.45
8	Gary Edmund Carter	15.00	7.50	4.50
9	Barry Clifton Foote	1.50	.70	.45
10	Andre Dawson	6.00	3.00	1.75
11	Ronald Wayne Garrett	1.50	.70	.45
14	Samuel Elias Mejias	1.50	.70	.45
15	Larry Alton Parrish	2.00	1.00	.60
16	Michael Jorgensen	1.50	.70	.45
17	Ellis Clarence Valentine	1.50	.70	.45
18	Joseph Thomas Kerrigan	1.50	.70	.45
23	William Henry McEnaney	1.50	.70	.45
23	Richard Hirshfield Williams	2.00	1.00	.60
24	Atanasio Rigal Perez	3.00	1.50	.90
25	Delbert Bernard Unser	1.50	.70	.45
26	Donald Joseph Stanhouse	1.50	.70	.45
30	David Cash, Jr.	1.50	.70	.45
31	Jackie Gene Brown	1.50	.70	.45
34	Jose Manual Morales	1.50	.70	.45
35	Gerald Ellis Hannahs	1.50	.70	.45
38	Jesus Maria Frias (Andujar)	1.50	.70	.45
39	Daniel Dean Warthen	1.50	.70	.45
42	William Cecil Glenn Atkinson	1.50	.70	.45
45	Stephen Douglas Rogers	2.25	1.25	.70
48	Jeffrey Michael Terpko	1.50	.70	.45
49	Warren Livingston Cromartie	1.50	.70	.45

1886 Red Stocking Cigars

This set of Boston Red Stockings schedule cards was issued in 1886, and the three known cards measure 6-1/2" x 3-3/4". The cards were printed in black and red. One side carries the 1886 Boston schedule, while the other side features a full-length player drawing. Both sides include advertising for "Red Stocking" cigars. Only three different players are known.

		NM	EX	VG
	Complete Set (3):	160,000	64,000	28,000
	Common Player:	30,000	8,000	4,000
(1)	C.G. Buffington	30,000	8,000	4,000
(2)	Capt. John F. Morrill	30,000	8,000	4,000
(3)	Charles Radbourn	100,000	50,000	20,000

1972 Regent Glove Hang Tag

This 2-1/4" x 3" card was distributed as an attachment to baseball gloves sold at retail outlets. A hole punched at top allowed the card to be strung to the glove. Front has a blue background and black-and-white portrait photo of 1971 MVP Vida Blue. His facsimile autograph is on back.

	NM	EX	VG
Vida Blue	15.00	7.50	4.50

1964-68 Requena N.Y. Yankees Postcards

Over a period of several years in the 1960s a series of Yankee color player postcards was issued with the identifier "Photo by Requena." Similar in format, the 3-1/2" x 5-1/2" cards have borderless color photos on front. Except for facsimile autographs on some players' cards, there are no other front graphics. Backs are printed in dark green with player ID at upper-left, a "K"-within-diamond Kodachrome logo at bottom-left, a card number centered at bottom, the Requena line vertically at center and standard postcard markings at right.

		NM	EX	VG
Complete Set (17):		300.00	150.00	90.00
Common Player:		15.00	7.50	4.50
66443	Phil Linz	15.00	7.50	4.50
66880	Clete Boyer	15.00	7.50	4.50
66881	Jim Bouton	20.00	10.00	6.00
66882	Tom Tresh	20.00	10.00	6.00
66883	Joe Pepitone	20.00	10.00	6.00
66884	Tony Kubek	20.00	10.00	6.00
66885	Elston Howard	20.00	10.00	6.00
66886	Ralph Terry	15.00	7.50	4.50
66887	Bill Stafford	15.00	7.50	4.50
66888	Whitey Ford	30.00	15.00	9.00
66889	Bob Richardson	20.00	10.00	6.00
69891	Yogi Berra (Signature at top.)	30.00	15.00	9.00
69891	Yogi Berra (Signature at bottom.)	30.00	15.00	9.00
74284	John Blanchard	15.00	7.50	4.50
78909	Pedro Ramos	15.00	7.50	4.50
78910	Mel Stottlemyre	15.00	7.50	4.50
98553	Fritz Peterson	15.00	7.50	4.50
101461	Steve Barber	15.00	7.50	4.50

1964-66 Requena N.Y. Yankees 8x10s

Many of the same Yankees players and poses which appear in the standard (3-1/2" x 5-1/2") Requena postcard series can also be found, along with additional subjects, in an 8" x 10" blank-back format. The large format cards are listed here in alphabetical order.

		NM	EX	VG
Complete Set (18):		300.00	150.00	90.00
Common Player:		9.00	4.50	2.75
(1)	Yogi Berra	20.00	10.00	6.00
(2)	John Blanchard	9.00	4.50	2.75
(3)	Jim Bouton	12.50	6.25	3.75
(4)	Clete Boyer	9.00	4.50	2.75
(5)	Al Downing	9.00	4.50	2.75
(6)	Whitey Ford	20.00	10.00	6.00
(7)	Ralph Houk	9.00	4.50	2.75
(8)	Elston Howard	12.50	6.25	3.75
(9)	Tony Kubek	12.50	6.25	3.75
(10)	Phil Linz	9.00	4.50	2.75
(11)	Mickey Mantle	35.00	17.50	10.00
(12)	Mickey Mantle, Roger Maris	30.00	15.00	9.00
(13a)	Roger Maris (Facsimile autograph.)	25.00	12.50	7.50
(13b)	Roger Maris (No facsimile autograph.)	25.00	12.50	7.50
(14)	Joe Pepitone	12.50	6.25	3.75
(15)	Pedro Ramos	9.00	4.50	2.75
(16)	Bobby Richardson	12.50	6.25	3.75
(17)	Bill Stafford	9.00	4.50	2.75
(18)	Mel Stottlemyre	9.00	4.50	2.75
(19)	Ralph Terry	9.00	4.50	2.75
(20)	Tom Tresh	12.50	6.25	3.75

1953 R.G. Dun Cigars Milwaukee Braves

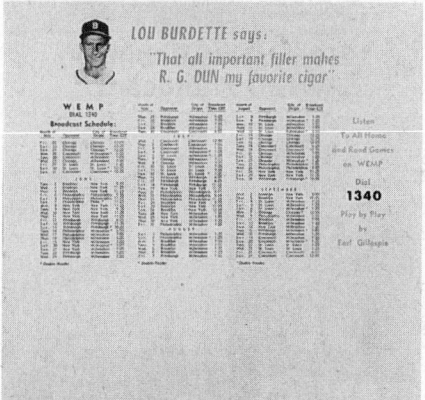

This series of counter cards was issued by a cigar company and features the radio schedule for the 1953 Braves. The cards are printed in red and black on cream cardboard and measure 10" x 9-1/2". They are unnumbered and blank-backed. The cards have vertical slits from bottom to about 1/3 the height of the cards, probably so they could be inserted into some type of counter display for Dun cigars. It's unknown how many players were represented in the series.

		NM	EX	VG
Common Player:		35.00	17.50	10.00
(1)	Lew Burdette	35.00	17.50	10.00
(2)	Jim Wilson	35.00	17.50	10.00

1935 Rice-Stix (UM7)

This two-card set was distributed in packages of shirts from a St. Louis firm. Measuring about 2-1/4" x 3", the cards feature color painting of the pitchers on front, along with a facsimile autograph and photo credits. Backs have a short career summary and an ad for the issuer.

		NM	EX	VG
Complete Set (2):		1,800	725.00	450.00
(1)	Dizzy Dean	1,200	475.00	300.00
(2)	Paul Dean	625.00	250.00	150.00

1927 Rinkeydink Stamps

These 1-1/4" x 1-1/2" pieces are not actually stamps, but rather are printed on newsprint with unrelated matter on back. The printing is in red, green and black and each stamp has a "denomination" of 2 in a baseball design at top. The "stamps" were featured in the heading of the "Winnie Winkle" comic strip in the Sunday funnies section of newspapers.

		NM	EX	VG
Complete Set (10):		450.00	225.00	135.00
Common Player:		30.00	15.00	9.00
(1)	Grover C. Alexander	40.00	20.00	12.00
(2)	Ty Cobb	75.00	37.50	22.00
(3)	Eddie Collins	30.00	15.00	9.00
(4)	Bucky Harris	30.00	15.00	9.00
(5)	Rogers Hornsby	40.00	20.00	12.00
(6)	Walter Johnson	50.00	25.00	15.00
(7)	George Kelly	30.00	15.00	9.00
(8)	Herb Pennock	30.00	15.00	9.00
(9)	Babe Ruth	100.00	50.00	30.00
(10)	Tris Speaker	40.00	20.00	12.00

1933 Rittenhouse Candy (E285)

Designed to resemble a set of playing cards, this set, issued circa 1933 by the Rittenhouse Candy Co. of Philadelphia, carries the ACC designation E285 and is generally considered to be the last of the E-card issues. Each card measures 1-7/16" x 2-1/4" and features a small player photo in the center of the playing card design. Cards are known printed in red, orange, blue and green. The backs of the cards usually consist of just one large letter and were part of a promotion in which collectors were instructed to find enough different letters to spell "Rittenhouse Candy Co." Other backs explaining the contest and the prizes available were also issued, as were backs with numbers. Because it was designed as a deck of playing cards, the set is complete at 52 cards, featuring 46 different players (six are pictured on two cards each).

		NM	EX	VG
Complete Set (52):		9,000	3,600	1,800
Common Player:		100.00	40.00	20.00
(1)	Dick Bartell	100.00	40.00	20.00
(2)	Walter Berger	100.00	40.00	20.00
(3)	Max Bishop	100.00	40.00	20.00
(4)	James Bottomley	200.00	80.00	40.00
(5)	Fred Brickell	100.00	40.00	20.00
(6)	Sugar Cain	100.00	40.00	20.00
(7)	Ed. Cihocki	100.00	40.00	20.00
(8)	Phil Collins	100.00	40.00	20.00
(9)	Roger Cramer	100.00	40.00	20.00
(10)	Hughie Critz	100.00	40.00	20.00
(11)	Joe Cronin	200.00	80.00	40.00
(12)	Hazen (Kiki) Cuyler	200.00	80.00	40.00
(13)	Geo. Davis	100.00	40.00	20.00
(14)	Spud Davis	100.00	40.00	20.00
(15)	Jimmy Dykes	100.00	40.00	20.00
(16)	George Earnshaw	100.00	40.00	20.00
(17)	Jumbo Elliot	100.00	40.00	20.00
(18)	Lou Finney	100.00	40.00	20.00
(19)	Jimmy Foxx	275.00	110.00	55.00
(20)	Frankie Frisch (3 of Spades.)	200.00	80.00	40.00
(21)	Frankie Frisch (7 of Spades.)	200.00	80.00	40.00
(22)	Robert (Lefty) Grove	225.00	90.00	45.00
(23)	Mule Haas	100.00	40.00	20.00
(24)	Chick Hafey	200.00	80.00	40.00
(25)	Chas. Leo Hartnett	200.00	80.00	40.00
(26)	Babe Herman	110.00	45.00	25.00
(27)	Wm. Herman	200.00	80.00	40.00
(28)	Kid Higgins	100.00	40.00	20.00
(29)	Rogers Hornsby	235.00	95.00	45.00
(30)	Don Hurst (Jack of Diamonds.)	100.00	40.00	20.00
(31)	Don Hurst (6 of Spades.)	100.00	40.00	20.00
(32)	Chuck Klein	200.00	80.00	40.00
(33)	Leroy Mahaffey	100.00	40.00	20.00
(34)	Gus Mancuso	100.00	40.00	20.00
(35)	Rabbit McNair	100.00	40.00	20.00
(36)	Bing Miller	100.00	40.00	20.00
(37)	Frank (Lefty) O'Doul	115.00	45.00	25.00
(38)	Mel Ott	200.00	80.00	40.00
(39)	Babe Ruth (Ace of Spades.)	1,000	400.00	200.00
(40)	Babe Ruth (King of Clubs.)	1,000	400.00	200.00
(41)	Al Simmons	200.00	80.00	40.00
(42)	Bill Terry	200.00	80.00	40.00
(43)	Pie Traynor	200.00	80.00	40.00
(44)	Rube Wallberg (Walberg)	100.00	40.00	20.00
(45)	Lloyd Waner	200.00	80.00	40.00
(46)	Paul Waner	200.00	80.00	40.00
(47)	Lloyd Warner (Waner)	200.00	80.00	40.00
(48)	Paul Warner (Waner)	200.00	80.00	40.00
(49)	Pinkey Whitney	100.00	40.00	20.00
(50)	Dib Williams	100.00	40.00	20.00
(51)	Hack Wilson (9 of Spades.)	200.00	80.00	40.00
(52)	Hack Wilson (9 of Clubs.)	200.00	80.00	40.00

1948 R.K.O. Theaters Babe Ruth Premium

The attributed date is speculative, based on the similarity of the back copy to the 1948 American Association Babe Ruth memorial card. Apparently issued as a premium at moviehouses, this 8" x 9-1/2" picture is printed on thin cardboard. On front is a sepia action photo of Ruth in the 1932 World Series.

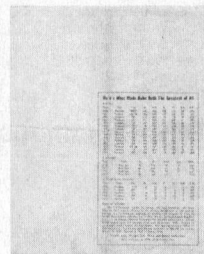

In the bottom border is the R.K.O. attribution. Back has biographical details, career highlights and complete major league stats.

	NM	EX	VG
Babe Ruth	400.00	200.00	125.00

1951 Roadmaster Photos

Black-and-white glossy photos of at least two major league stars were available as a premium from Roadmaster bicycles. Contemporary ads said that for a dime, an 8" x 10" photo could be obtained. The photos show the uniformed players seated on Roadmaster bikes inside a ballpark. There is a facsimile autograph on each. Backs are blank. It's possible other player photos may yet be seen.

		NM	EX	VG
(1)	Bob Feller	200.00	100.00	60.00
(2)	Pee Wee Reese	250.00	125.00	75.00

1947 Jackie Robinson Pins

In his historic debut season with the Brooklyn Dodgers, a number of celluloid pinback buttons featuring Jackie Robinson were issued. Ranging in size from about 1-1/4" to 1-3/4", the pins usually feature a black-and-white portrait photo at center and were originally sold with a silk pennant and plastic or pot-metal baseball charms attached.

		NM	EX	VG
(1)	Brooklyn 1947 Dodgers Congratulations "Jackie" (1-1/4" white background.)	600.00	300.00	180.00
(2)	HI TEAMMATES (1-3/8", batting, blue background.)	250.00	125.00	75.00
(3)	I'M FOR JACKIE (Blue type on white ball, no photo.)	200.00	100.00	60.00
(4)	I'm Rooting for Jackie Robinson (1-3/4", red border.)	275.00	135.00	80.00
(5)	I'm Rooting for Jackie Robinson (1-1/4", white background.)	350.00	175.00	100.00
(6)	I'm Rooting for Jackie Robinson (1-3/4", gray background.)	300.00	150.00	90.00
(7)	JACKIE ROBINSON / DODGERS (1-3/4", b/w photo batting in pinstripes and plain cap.)	400.00	200.00	125.00
(8)	JACKIE ROBINSON / DODGERS (1-1/4", white background.)	200.00	100.00	60.00

		NM	EX	VG
(9)	Jackie Robinson Outstanding Rookie (3-3/8" white border.)	200.00	100.00	60.00
(10)	19 Rookie of the Year 47 (1-3/4" red border.)(Modern reproductions exist.)	325.00	160.00	100.00

1950s Jackie Robinson WNBC Photocard

This black-and-white 5-3/4" x 7-1/2" photocard pictures Robinson in his post-playing days career as a broadcaster for the NBC radio network's flagship station in New York.

	NM	EX	VG
Jackie Robinson	35.00	17.50	10.50

1911 Rochester Baking Philadelphia A's (D359)

The 1911 Rochester Baking set, an 18-card Philadelphia Athletics set, is among the scarcest of early 20th Century bakery issues. The set commemorates the Athletics' 1910 Championship season, and, except for pitcher Jack Coombs, the checklist includes nearly all key members of the club, including manager Connie Mack. The cards are the standard size for the era, 1-1/2" x 2-5/8". The front of each card features a player portrait set against a colored background. The player's name and the word "Athletics" appear at the bottom, while "World's Champions 1910" is printed along the top. The backs of the cards advertise the set as the "Athletics Series." Collectors should be aware that the same checklist was used for a similar Athletics set issued by Williams Baking and Cullivan's Firesdie tobacco (T208), and also that blank-backed versions are also known to exist, but these are classified as E104 cards in the American Card Catalog.

		NM	EX	VG
Complete Set (18):		85,000	35,000	17,000
Common Player:		4,000	2,000	1,000
(1)	Home Run Baker	7,000	3,500	1,750
(2)	Jack Barry	4,000	2,000	1,000
(3)	Chief Bender	7,000	3,500	1,750
(4)	Eddie Collins	7,000	3,500	1,750
(5)	Harry Davis	4,000	2,000	1,000
(6)	Jimmy Dygert	4,000	2,000	1,000
(7)	Topsy Hartsel	4,000	2,000	1,000
(8)	Harry Krause	4,000	2,000	1,000
(9)	Jack Lapp	4,000	2,000	1,000
(10)	Paddy Livingston	4,000	2,000	1,000
(11)	Bris Lord	4,000	2,000	1,000
(12)	Connie Mack	14,000	7,900	4,575
(13)	Cy Morgan	4,000	2,000	1,000
(14)	Danny Murphy	4,000	2,000	1,000
(15)	Rube Oldring	4,000	2,000	1,000
(16)	Eddie Plank	14,000	7,900	4,575
(17)	Amos Strunk	4,000	2,000	1,000
(18)	Ira Thomas	4,000	2,000	1,000

1955 Rodeo Meats Athletics

This set of 2-1/2" x 3-1/2" color cards was issued by a local meat company to commemorate the first year of the Athletics in Kansas City. There are 38 different players included in the set, with nine players known to ap-

Don Bollweg

pear in two different variations for a total of 47 cards in the set. Most variations are in background colors, although Bobby Shantz is also listed incorrectly as "Schantz" on one variation. The cards are unnumbered, with the Rodeo logo and player name on the fronts, and an ad for a scrapbook album listed on the backs.

		NM	EX	VG
Complete Set (47):		12,500	6,250	3,750
Common Player:		225.00	110.00	45.00
Album:		550.00	275.00	125.00
(1)	Joe Astroth	225.00	110.00	45.00
(2)	Harold Bevan	275.00	135.00	55.00
(3)	Charles Bishop	275.00	135.00	55.00
(4)	Don Bollweg	275.00	135.00	55.00
(5)	Lou Boudreau	600.00	300.00	120.00
(6)	Cloyd Boyer (Blue background.)	275.00	135.00	55.00
(7)	Cloyd Boyer (Pink background.)	225.00	110.00	45.00
(8)	Ed Burtschy	275.00	135.00	55.00
(9)	Art Ceccarelli	225.00	110.00	45.00
(10)	Joe DeMaestri (Pea green background.)	275.00	135.00	55.00
(11)	Joe DeMaestri (Light green background.)	225.00	110.00	45.00
(12)	Art Ditmar	225.00	110.00	45.00
(13)	John Dixon	275.00	135.00	55.00
(14)	Jim Finigan	225.00	110.00	45.00
(15)	Marion Fricano	275.00	135.00	55.00
(16)	Tom Gorman	275.00	135.00	55.00
(17)	John Gray	225.00	110.00	45.00
(18)	Ray Herbert	225.00	110.00	45.00
(19)	Forest "Spook" Jacobs (Forrest)	275.00	135.00	55.00
(20)	Alex Kellner	275.00	135.00	55.00
(21)	Harry Kraft (Craft)	225.00	110.00	45.00
(22)	Jack Littrell	225.00	110.00	45.00
(23)	Hector Lopez	275.00	135.00	55.00
(24)	Oscar Melillo	225.00	110.00	45.00
(25)	Arnold Portocarrero (Purple background.)	275.00	135.00	55.00
(26)	Arnold Portocarrero (Grey background.)	225.00	110.00	45.00
(27)	Vic Power (pink background.)	275.00	135.00	55.00
(28)	Vic Power (Yellow background.)	250.00	125.00	50.00
(29)	Vic Raschi	275.00	135.00	55.00
(30)	Bill Renna (Dark pink background.)	275.00	135.00	55.00
(31)	Bill Renna (Light pink background.)	225.00	110.00	45.00
(32)	Al Robertson	275.00	135.00	55.00
(33)	Johnny Sain	275.00	135.00	55.00
(34a)	Bobby Schantz (Incorrect spelling.)	900.00	450.00	180.00
(34b)	Bobby Shantz (Correct spelling.)	300.00	150.00	60.00
(35)	Wilmer Shantz (Orange background.)	275.00	135.00	55.00
(36)	Wilmer Shantz (Purple background.)	225.00	110.00	45.00
(37)	Harry Simpson	225.00	110.00	45.00
(38)	Enos Slaughter	650.00	325.00	130.00
(39)	Lou Sleater	225.00	110.00	45.00
(40)	George Susce	225.00	110.00	45.00
(41)	Bob Trice	275.00	135.00	55.00
(42)	Elmer Valo (Yellow background.)	275.00	135.00	55.00
(43)	Elmer Valo (Green background.)	225.00	110.00	45.00
(44)	Bill Wilson (Yellow background.)	275.00	135.00	55.00
(45)	Bill Wilson (Purple background.)	225.00	110.00	45.00
(46)	Gus Zernial	250.00	125.00	50.00

1956 Rodeo Meats Athletics

Gus Zernial

Rodeo Meats issued another Kansas City Athletics set in 1956, but this one was a much smaller 13-card set. The 2-1/2" x 3-1/2" cards are again unnumbered, with the player name and Rodeo logo on the fronts. Card backs feature some of the same graphics and copy as the 1955 cards, but the album offer is omitted. The full-color cards were only available in packages of Rodeo hot dogs.

		NM	EX	VG
Complete Set (12):		2,750	1,100	550.00
Common Player:		200.00	80.00	40.00
(1)	Joe Astroth	200.00	80.00	40.00
(2)	Lou Boudreau	350.00	140.00	70.00
(3)	Joe DeMaestri	200.00	80.00	40.00
(4)	Art Ditmar	200.00	80.00	40.00
(5)	Jim Finigan	200.00	80.00	40.00
(6)	Hector Lopez	200.00	80.00	40.00
(7)	Vic Power	200.00	80.00	40.00
(8)	Bobby Shantz	225.00	90.00	45.00
(9)	Harry Simpson	200.00	80.00	40.00
(10)	Enos Slaughter	475.00	190.00	95.00
(11)	Elmer Valo	200.00	80.00	40.00
(12)	Gus Zernial	200.00	80.00	40.00

1976 Rodeo Meats Athletics Commemorative

Bobby Shantz

This collectors' issue essentially reprints many of the 1955-56 Rodeo Meats cards in a 2-1/2" x 3-1/2" black-and-white format. Fronts have player photos, the Rodeo logo and the player name in the white border at bottom. Backs, instead of the original Rodeo ads, have player identification, biographical information and career summary, along with a reprint notice.

		NM	EX	VG
Complete Set (30):		20.00	10.00	6.00
Common Player:		2.00	1.00	.60
1	Header Card	.50	.25	.15
2	Checklist Vard	.50	.25	.15
3	Joe Astroth	2.00	1.00	.60
4	Lou Boudreau	3.00	1.50	.90
5	Cloyd Boyer	2.00	1.00	.60
6	Art Ceccarelli	2.00	1.00	.60
7	Harry Craft	2.00	1.00	.60
8	Joe DeMaestri	2.00	1.00	.60
9	Art Ditmar	2.00	1.00	.60
10	Jim Finigan	2.00	1.00	.60
11	Ray Herbert	2.00	1.00	.60
12	Tom Gorman	2.00	1.00	.60
13	Alex Kellner	2.00	1.00	.60
14	Jack Littrell	2.00	1.00	.60
15	Hector Lopez	2.00	1.00	.60
16	Oscar Melillo	2.00	1.00	.60
17	Arnie Portocarrero	2.00	1.00	.60
18	Vic Power	2.50	1.25	.70
19	Vic Raschi	2.50	1.25	.70
20	Bill Renna	2.00	1.00	.60
21	Johnny Sain	2.50	1.25	.70
22	Bobby Shantz	2.50	1.25	.70
23	Wilmer Shantz	2.00	1.00	.60
24	Harry Simpson	2.50	1.25	.70
25	Enos Slaughter	4.00	2.00	1.25
26	Lou Sleator	2.00	1.00	.60
27	George Susce	2.00	1.00	.60
28	Elmer Valo	2.00	1.00	.60
29	Bill Wilson	2.00	1.00	.60
30	Gus Zernial	2.50	1.25	.70

1930s Rogers Peet Sport Album

18.— HERB PENNOCK

This is one of the scarcest multi-sport issues of the 1930s. It was the promotion of a New York-Boston chain of stores (boys' clothing?) in the form of a frequent customer program. Boys visiting the store with a parent could receive a set of four cards to be placed in a 14-page 4-1/2" x 7-1/4" album. Individual cards are about 1-7/8" x 2-1/2" and feature black-and-white with a white border. The athlete's name and card number are printed in the bottom border. Numbers correspond to spaces in the album. Only the "Baseball Stars" from the issue are checklisted here. Others include hockey, football, track, swimming, golf, tennis, aviation, etc.

		NM	EX	VG
Complete Set (44):		7,500	3,750	2,250
Complete Set in Album:		5,000	2,500	1,500
Common Sticker:		30.00	15.00	9.00
Album:		500.00	250.00	150.00
5	Dazzy Vance	225.00	110.00	65.00
13	Walter Johnson	650.00	325.00	195.00
16	Rogers Hornsby	450.00	225.00	135.00
18	Herb Pennock	225.00	110.00	65.00
28	Lou Gehrig	2,400	1,200	725.00
34	Ty Cobb	1,100	550.00	330.00
38	Tris Speaker	450.00	225.00	135.00
48	Babe Ruth	2,600	1,300	780.00

1960s Rogers Printing Co. Postcards

The extent to which this Columbus, Ohio, firm may have provided baseball players with postcards to answer fan mail requests is unknown. At present, only a single card is known, that of Bob Wills, who played his entire major league career (1957-63) with the Cubs. The card is printed in black-and-white on glossy stock in a 3-1/2" x 5-1/2" format. A facsimile autograph message is printed on front. Postcard-style backs have the imprint of the printer.

	NM	EX	VG
Bob Will	3.00	1.50	.90

1970 Rold Gold Pretzels

The 1970 Rold Gold Pretzels set of 15 cards honors the "Greatest Players Ever" in the first 100 years of baseball as chosen by the Baseball Writers of America. The cards, which measure 2-1/4" x 3-1/2" in size, feature a simulated 3-D effect. The set was re-released in 1972 by Kellogg's in packages of Danish-Go-Rounds. Rold Gold cards can be differentiated from the Kellogg's cards of 1972 by the 1970 copyright date found on the card reverse.

		NM	EX	VG
Complete Set (15):		50.00	25.00	15.00
Common Player:		2.00	1.00	.60
1	Walter Johnson	6.00	3.00	1.75
2	Rogers Hornsby	3.00	1.50	.90
3	John McGraw	2.00	1.00	.60
4	Mickey Cochrane	2.00	1.00	.60
5	George Sisler	2.00	1.00	.60
6	Babe Ruth ("Greatest Ever")	15.00	7.50	4.50
7	Robert "Lefty" Grove	2.00	1.00	.60
8	Harold "Pie" Traynor	2.00	1.00	.60
9	Honus Wagner	7.50	3.75	2.25

		NM	EX	VG
10	Eddie Collins	2.00	1.00	.60
11	Tris Speaker	3.00	1.50	.90
12	Cy Young	5.00	2.50	1.50
13	Lou Gehrig	10.00	5.00	3.00
14	Babe Ruth ("Greatest Right Fielder")	15.00	7.50	4.50
15	Ty Cobb	9.00	4.50	2.75

1908-1909 Rose Company Postcards

Among the most ornate and attractive baseball cards of the pre-1910 period is the set of postcards produced by The Rose Co., between 1908-09. The 3-1/2" x 5-1/2" cards feature a black-and-white player portrait photo at center, surrounded by an embossed round gold frame. The player's surname and (usually) team are in a white panel under the photo. The background of the card's front is in green and includes crossed bats and a baseball, a diamond diagram and pictures of a fielder and batter. The postcard-format back is printed in black-and-white with a TRC logo at bottom-center. The unnumbered postcards are checklisted here alphabetically; including 11 minor league players from Scranton in the New York State League. It is possible future discoveries will be added to this checklist; gaps have been left in the numbering to accommodate them.

		NM	EX	VG
Common Player:		2,000	800.00	400.00
(1)	Ed Abbaticchio	2,000	800.00	400.00
(2)	Bill Abstein	2,000	800.00	400.00
(3)	Whitey Alperman	2,000	800.00	400.00
(4)	Nick Altrock	2,000	800.00	400.00
(5)	John Anderson	2,000	800.00	400.00
(6)	Shad Barry	2,000	800.00	400.00
(7)	Ginger Beaumont	2,000	800.00	400.00
(8)	Heinie Beckendorf	2,000	800.00	400.00
(9)	Fred Beebe	2,000	800.00	400.00
(10)	Harry Bemis	2,000	800.00	400.00
(11)	Chief Bender	3,000	1,200	600.00
(12)	Bills	2,000	800.00	400.00
(13)	Joe Birmingham	2,000	800.00	400.00
(14)	Frank Bowerman	2,000	800.00	400.00
(15)	Bill Bradley	2,000	800.00	400.00
(16)	Kitty Bransfield	2,000	800.00	400.00
(17)	Roger Bresnahan	3,000	1,200	600.00
(18)	Al Bridwell	2,000	800.00	400.00
(19)	Buster Brown (Philadelphia) (Photo actually Mordeai Brown.)	2,000	800.00	400.00
(20)	Samuel Brown (Boston)	2,000	800.00	400.00
(21)	Mordecai Brown (Chicago)	3,000	1,200	600.00
(22)	Bobby Byrne	2,000	800.00	400.00
(23)	Howie Camnitz	2,000	800.00	400.00
(24)	Billy Campbell	2,000	800.00	400.00
(26)	Frank Chance	3,000	1,200	600.00
(27)	Hal Chase	1,750	700.00	350.00
(28)	Charlie Chech	2,000	800.00	400.00
(29)	Jack Chesbro	3,000	1,200	600.00
(30)	Fred Clarke (Pittsburg)	3,000	1,200	600.00
(31)	Nig Clarke (Cleveland)	2,000	800.00	400.00
(32)	Otis Clymer	2,000	800.00	400.00
(33a)	Andy Coakley (Cincinnati)	2,000	800.00	400.00
(33b)	Andy Coakley (No team name.)	2,000	800.00	400.00
(34)	Ty Cobb	16,000	6,400	3,200
(35)	Jimmy Collins	3,000	1,200	600.00
(36)	Wid Conroy	2,000	800.00	400.00
(37)	Jack Coombs	2,000	800.00	400.00
(38)	Frank Corridon	2,000	800.00	400.00
(39)	Bill Coughlin	2,000	800.00	400.00
(40)	Sam Crawford	3,000	1,200	600.00
(41a)	Lou Criger (Boston)	2,000	800.00	400.00
(41b)	Lou Criger (No team.)	2,000	800.00	400.00
(42)	Bill Dahlen	2,000	800.00	400.00
(43)	Harry Davis	2,000	800.00	400.00
(44)	Joe Delahanty (St. Louis)	1,500	600.00	300.00
(45)	Frank Delehanty (Delahanty) (Washington; team actually N.Y., A.L.)	1,500	600.00	300.00
(46)	Art Devlin	2,000	800.00	400.00
(47)	Mike Donlin	2,000	800.00	400.00
(48)	Jiggs Donohue (Donahue)	2,000	800.00	400.00
(49)	Wild Bill Donovan	2,000	800.00	400.00
(51)	Red Dooin	2,000	800.00	400.00
(52)	Mickey Doolan	2,000	800.00	400.00
(53)	Jimmy Doyle	2,000	800.00	400.00
(54)	Jimmy Dygert	2,000	800.00	400.00
(55)	Kid Elberfeld	2,000	800.00	400.00
(56)	Eley	2,000	800.00	400.00
(57)	Johnny Evers	3,000	1,200	600.00

(58)	Bob Ewing	2,000	800.00	400.00
(59)	George Ferguson	2,000	800.00	400.00
(60)	Hobe Ferris	2,000	800.00	400.00
(61)	Jerry Freeman	2,000	800.00	400.00
(62)	Bob Ganley	2,000	800.00	400.00
(63)	John Ganzel	2,000	800.00	400.00
(64)	Doc Gessler	2,000	800.00	400.00
(65)	George Gibson	2,000	800.00	400.00
(66)	Billy Gilbert	2,000	800.00	400.00
(67)	Fred Glade	2,000	800.00	400.00
(68)	Ralph Glaze	2,000	800.00	400.00
(69)	Graham	2,000	800.00	400.00
(70)	Eddie Grant	1,500	600.00	300.00
(71)	Groh	2,000	800.00	400.00
(72)	Charley Hale (Hall)	2,000	800.00	400.00
(73)	Halligan	2,000	800.00	400.00
(74)	Topsy Hartsel	2,000	800.00	400.00
(75)	Charlie Hemphill	2,000	800.00	400.00
(76)	Bill Hinchman	2,000	800.00	400.00
(77)	Art Hoelskoetter	2,000	800.00	400.00
(78)	Danny Hoffman	2,000	800.00	400.00
(79)	Solly Hofmann	2,000	800.00	400.00
(80)	Houser	2,000	800.00	400.00
(81)	Harry Howell	2,000	800.00	400.00
(82)	Miller Huggins	3,000	1,200	600.00
(83)	Rudy Hulswitt	2,000	800.00	400.00
(84)	John Hummel	2,000	800.00	400.00
(85a)	Frank Isbel (Isbell)(Chicago)	2,000	800.00	400.00
(85b)	Frank Isbel (Isbell)(No team.)	2,000	800.00	400.00
(86)	Walter Johnson	7,500	3,000	1,500
(87)	Fielder Jones (Chicago)	2,000	800.00	400.00
(88)	Tom Jones (St. Louis)	2,000	800.00	400.00
(89)	Tim Jordan	2,000	800.00	400.00
(90)	Addie Joss	3,500	1,400	700.00
(91)	Johnny Kane	2,000	800.00	400.00
(92)	Ed Karger	2,000	800.00	400.00
(93)	Wee Willie Keeler	3,000	1,200	600.00
(94)	Kellogg	2,000	800.00	400.00
(95)	Ed Killian	2,000	800.00	400.00
(96)	Malachi Kittredge (Kittridge)	2,000	800.00	400.00
(97)	Red Kleinow	2,000	800.00	400.00
(98)	Johnny Kling	2,000	800.00	400.00
(99)	Otto Knabe	2,000	800.00	400.00
(101)	John Knight	2,000	800.00	400.00
(102)	Ed Konetchy	2,000	800.00	400.00
(103)	Nap Lajoie	3,250	1,300	650.00
(104)	Frank LaPorte	2,000	800.00	400.00
(105)	Tommy Leach	2,000	800.00	400.00
(106)	Glenn Leibhardt (Liebhardt)	2,000	800.00	400.00
(107)	Phil Lewis	2,000	800.00	400.00
(108)	Vive Lindamann (Lindaman)	2,000	800.00	400.00
(109)	Hans Lobert	2,000	800.00	400.00
(110)	Harry Lord	2,000	800.00	400.00
(111)	Harry Lumley	2,000	800.00	400.00
(112)	Johnny Lush	2,000	800.00	400.00
(113)	Nick Maddox	2,000	800.00	400.00
(114)	Sherry Magee	2,000	800.00	400.00
(115)	Billy Maloney	2,000	800.00	400.00
(116)	Christy Mathewson	9,000	3,600	1,800
(117)	George McBride	2,000	800.00	400.00
(118)	Joe McGinnity	3,000	1,200	600.00
(119)	Stoney McGlynn	2,000	800.00	400.00
(120)	Harry McIntyre (McIntire) (Brooklyn)	2,000	800.00	400.00
(121)	Matty McIntyre (Detroit)	2,000	800.00	400.00
(122)	Larry McLean	2,000	800.00	400.00
(123)	George McQuillen (McQuillan)	2,000	800.00	400.00
(124)	Clyde Milan	2,000	800.00	400.00
(126)	Mike Mitchell	2,000	800.00	400.00
(127)	Moran	2,000	800.00	400.00
(128)	Mike Mowrey	2,000	800.00	400.00
(129)	George Mullin	2,000	800.00	400.00
(130)	Danny Murphy	2,000	800.00	400.00
(131)	J.J. Murray	2,000	800.00	400.00
(132)	Doc Newton	2,000	800.00	400.00
(133)	Simon Nicholls	2,000	800.00	400.00
(134)	Harry Niles	2,000	800.00	400.00
(135)	Rebel Oakes	2,000	800.00	400.00
(136)	Rube Oldring	2,000	800.00	400.00
(137)	Charley O'Leary	2,000	800.00	400.00
(138)	Patsy O'Rourke	2,000	800.00	400.00
(139)	Al Orth	2,000	800.00	400.00
(140)	Fred Osborne (Osborn)	2,000	800.00	400.00
(141)	Orval Overall	2,000	800.00	400.00
(142)	Freddy Parent	2,000	800.00	400.00
(143)	George Paskert	2,000	800.00	400.00
(144)	Case Patten	2,000	800.00	400.00
(145)	Deacon Phillippi (Phillippe)	2,000	800.00	400.00
(146)	Eddie Plank	3,500	1,400	700.00
(147)	Jack Powell	2,000	800.00	400.00
(148)	Tex Pruiett	2,000	800.00	400.00
(149)	Ed Reulbach	2,000	800.00	400.00
(151)	Bob Rhoades (Rhoads)	2,000	800.00	400.00
(152)	Claude Ritchey	2,000	800.00	400.00
(153)	Claude Rossman	2,000	800.00	400.00
(154)	Nap Rucker	2,000	800.00	400.00
(155)	Germany Schaefer	2,000	800.00	400.00
(156)	George Schlei	2,000	800.00	400.00
(157)	Boss Schmidt	2,000	800.00	400.00
(158)	Ossie Schreck	2,000	800.00	400.00
(159)	Wildfire Schulte	2,000	800.00	400.00
(160)	Schultz	2,000	800.00	400.00
(161)	Socks Seybold	2,000	800.00	400.00
(162)	Cy Seymour	2,000	800.00	400.00
(163)	Spike Shannon	2,000	800.00	400.00
(164)	Jimmy Sheckard	2,000	800.00	400.00
(165)	Tommy Sheehan	2,000	800.00	400.00
(166)	Bill Shipke	2,000	800.00	400.00
(167)	Jimmy Slagle	2,000	800.00	400.00
(168)	Charlie Smith (Chicago)	2,000	800.00	400.00
(169)	Frank Smith (Washington)	2,000	800.00	400.00
(170)	Bob Spade	2,000	800.00	400.00
(171)	Tully Sparks	2,000	800.00	400.00
(172)	Tris Speaker	3,000	1,200	600.00
(173)	Tubby Spencer	2,000	800.00	400.00
(174)	Jake Stahl	2,000	800.00	400.00
(176)	Steele	2,000	800.00	400.00

(177)	Harry Steinfeldt	2,000	800.00	400.00
(178)	George Stone	2,000	800.00	400.00
(179)	George Stovall	2,000	800.00	400.00
(180)	Billy Sullivan	2,000	800.00	400.00
(181)	Ed Summers	2,000	800.00	400.00
(182)	Bill Sweeney	2,000	800.00	400.00
(183)	Lee Tannehill	2,000	800.00	400.00
(184)	Dummy Taylor	1,750	700.00	350.00
(185)	Fred Tenney	2,000	800.00	400.00
(186)	Ira Thomas (No team.)	2,000	800.00	400.00
(187)	Roy Thomas (Pittsburg)	2,000	800.00	400.00
(188)	Jack Thoney	2,000	800.00	400.00
(189)	Joe Tinker	3,000	1,200	600.00
(190)	John Titus	2,000	800.00	400.00
(191)	Terry Turner	2,000	800.00	400.00
(192)	Bob Unglaub	2,000	800.00	400.00
(193)	Rube Waddell	3,000	1,200	600.00
(194)	Heinie Wagner (Boston)	2,000	800.00	400.00
(195)	Honus Wagner (Pittsburg)	12,500	5,000	2,500
(196)	Ed Walsh	3,000	1,200	600.00
(197)	Jack Warner	2,000	800.00	400.00
(198a)	Jake Weimer (Cincinnati)	2,000	800.00	400.00
(198b)	Jake Weimer (No team.)	2,000	800.00	400.00
(199)	Doc White	2,000	800.00	400.00
(201)	Jimmy Williams	2,000	800.00	400.00
(202)	Chief Wilson	2,000	800.00	400.00
(203)	Hooks Wiltse	2,000	800.00	400.00
(204)	George Winter	2,000	800.00	400.00
(205)	Cy Young (Boston)	7,500	3,000	1,500
(206)	Harley Young (Pittsburg)	2,000	800.00	400.00

1905 Rotograph Postcards

LUTHER TAYLOR

Only New York players have been seen on this series of 3-1/4" x 5-3/8" black-and-white or blue-and-white duotone postcards. Cards have player portrait photos with a white strip at bottom identifying the player; a "Rotograph / Series" notation is at left. Backs have typical postcard markings. This checklist may not be complete. The set was listed in the American Card Catalog under the number PC782.

		NM	EX	VG
Common Player:		800.00	400.00	250.00
(1)	Geo. Brown (Browne)	800.00	400.00	250.00
(2)	J.D. Chesbro	1,000	500.00	300.00
(3)	Wm. F. Dahlen	800.00	400.00	250.00
(4)	Clark Griffill (Griffith)	1,350	675.00	405.00
(5)	Joseph McGinnity	1,000	500.00	300.00
(6)	John McGraw	1,500	750.00	450.00
(7)	A. Puttmann	800.00	400.00	250.00
(8)	Luther Taylor	1,250	625.00	375.00

1977 Jim Rowe 4-on-1 Exhibits

This collectors' edition set harkens back to the four-player cards issued in the 1930s by Exhibit Supply Co. The 1977 version is printed in black on yellow in a 3-1/4" x 5-1/2" format. Backs are blank. Each of the four player photos on front is identified by name. The cards are checklisted here in order of team name.

	NM	EX	VG
Complete Set (16):	90.00	45.00	27.00

Common Card:		5.00	2.50	1.50
(1)	Boston Braves (Al Lopez, Rabbit Maranville, Warren Spahn, Casey Stengel)	5.00	2.50	1.50
(2)	Boston Red Sox (Joe Cronin, Herb Pennock, Babe Ruth, Ted Williams)	15.00	7.50	4.50
(3)	Brooklyn Dodgers (Max Carey, Burleigh Grimes, Joe Medwick, Dazzy Vance)	5.00	2.50	1.50
(4)	Chicago Cubs (Kiki Cuyler, Gabby Hartnett, Billy Herman, Freddy Lindstrom)	5.00	2.50	1.50
(5)	Chicago White Sox (Luke Appling, Red Faber, Ted Lyons, Red Ruffing)	5.00	2.50	1.50
(6)	Cincinnati Reds (Chick Hafey, George Kelly, Bill McKechnie, Edd Roush)	5.00	2.50	1.50
(7)	Cleveland Indians (Earl Averill, Lou Boudreau, Bob Feller, Bob Lemon)	5.00	2.50	1.50
(8)	Detroit Tigers (Ty Cobb, Charlie Gehringer, Goose Goslin, Hank Greenberg)	11.00	5.50	3.25
(9)	New York Giants (Dave Bancroft, Carl Hubbell, Mel Ott, Bill Terry)	5.00	2.50	1.50
(10)	New York Yankees (Bill Dickey, Joe DiMaggio, Lou Gehrig, Lefty Gomez)	12.00	6.00	3.50
(11)	Philadelphia Athletics (Mickey Cochrane, Eddie Collins, Lefty Grove, Al Simmons)	5.00	2.50	1.50
(12)	Philadelphia Phillies (Grover Alexander, Jimmie Foxx, Eppa Rixey, Robin Roberts)	5.00	2.50	1.50
(13)	Pittsburgh Pirates (Pie Traynor, Honus Wagner, Lloyd Waner, Paul Waner)	6.00	3.00	1.75
(14)	St. Louis Browns (Jim Bottomley, Earle Combs, Rogers Hornsby, George Sisler)	5.00	2.50	1.50
(15)	St. Louis Cardinals (Dizzy Dean, Frankie Frisch, Jesse Haines, Stan Musial)	5.00	2.50	1.50
(16)	Washington Senators (Bucky Harris, Walter Johnson, Heinie Manush, Sam Rice)	6.00	3.00	1.75

1977 Jim Rowe 1929 Cubs Postcards

Originally retailed for $3 per set, these collector-issue postcards feature on front borderless black-and-white photos in 3-1/2" x 5-7/16" format. Backs are standard Kodak postcard style, with no mention of the issuer. The player name is usually found penned at top.

		NM	EX	VG
Complete Set (13):		30.00	20.00	12.00
Common Player:		3.00	1.50	.90
(1)	Guy Bush	3.00	1.50	.90
(2)	Kiki Cuyler	3.00	1.50	.90
(3)	Woody English	3.00	1.50	.90
(4)	Charlie Grimm	3.00	1.50	.90
(5)	Gabby Hartnett	3.00	1.50	.90
(6)	Rogers Hornsby	3.00	1.50	.90
(7)	Pat Malone	3.00	1.50	.90
(8)	Norman McMillan	3.00	1.50	.90
(9)	Charlie Root	3.00	1.50	.90
(10)	Riggs Stephenson	3.00	1.50	.90
(11)	Zach Taylor	3.00	1.50	.90
(12)	Hack Wilson	3.00	1.50	.90
(13)	Team photo	3.00	1.50	.90

1977 Jim Rowe 1956 Braves Postcards

Originally retailed for $4 per set, these collector-issue postcards feature on front borderless black-and-white photos in 3-1/2" x 5-7/16" format. Backs are standard Kodak postcard style, with no mention of the issuer. The player name is usually found penned at top.

	NM	EX	VG
Complete Set (16):	35.00	17.50	10.50

Common Player:	3.00	1.50	.90
(1) Hank Aaron	4.00	2.00	1.25
(2) Joe Adcock	3.00	1.50	.90
(3) Bill Bruton	3.00	1.50	.90
(4) Bob Buhl	3.00	1.50	.90
(5) Lew Burdette	3.00	1.50	.90
(6) Gene Conley	3.00	1.50	.90
(7) Del Crandall	3.00	1.50	.90
(8) Charlie Grimm	3.00	1.50	.90
(9) Fred Haney	3.00	1.50	.90
(10) Joey Jay	3.00	1.50	.90
(11) Johnny Logan	3.00	1.50	.90
(12) Chet Nichols	3.00	1.50	.90
(13) Danny O'Connell	3.00	1.50	.90
(14) Andy Pafko	3.00	1.50	.90
(15) Warren Spahn	3.00	1.50	.90
(16) Bobby Thomson	3.00	1.50	.90

1978 Royal Crown Cola Iron-Ons

These iron-on color transfers were available in team strips of five players for 50 cents and six bottle cap liners. Because they were licensed only by the Players Association, and not MLB, the approximately 4-1/4" x 6-1/4" transfers do not show team logos or nicknames.

	NM	EX	VG
Complete Set (130):	750.00	375.00	225.00
Common Player:	6.00	3.00	1.75
Atlanta Strip	25.00	12.50	7.50
(1) Jeff Burroughs	6.00	3.00	1.75
(2) Gary Matthews	6.00	3.00	1.75
(3) Phil Niekro	7.50	3.75	2.25
(4) Biff Pocoroba	6.00	3.00	1.75
(5) Dick Ruthven	6.00	3.00	1.75
Baltimore Strip	50.00	25.00	15.00
(6) Al Bumbry	6.00	3.00	1.75
(7) Lee May	6.00	3.00	1.75
(8) Eddie Murray	30.00	15.00	9.00
(9) Jim Palmer	15.00	7.50	4.50
(10) Ken Singleton	6.00	3.00	1.75
Boston Strip	40.00	20.00	12.00
(11) Bill Campbell	6.00	3.00	1.75
(12) Fred Lynn	6.00	3.00	1.75
(13) Jim Rice	7.50	3.75	2.25
(14) George Scott	6.00	3.00	1.75
(15) Carl Yastrzemski	25.00	12.50	7.50
California Strip	75.00	37.50	22.50
(16) Dave Chalk	6.00	3.00	1.75
(17) Bobby Grich	6.00	3.00	1.75
(18) Joe Rudi	6.00	3.00	1.75
(19) Nolan Ryan	60.00	30.00	18.00
(20) Frank Tanana	6.00	3.00	1.75
Chicago (Cubs) Strip	30.00	15.00	9.00
(21) Bill Buckner	6.00	3.00	1.75
(22) Dave Kingman	6.00	3.00	1.75
(23) Steve Ontiveros	6.00	3.00	1.75
(24) Bruce Sutter	7.50	3.75	2.25
(25) Manny Trillo	6.00	3.00	1.75
Chicago (White Sox) Strip	25.00	12.50	7.50
(26) Ron Blomberg	6.00	3.00	1.75
(27) Bobby Bonds	6.00	3.00	1.75
(28) Ralph Garr	6.00	3.00	1.75
(29) Jorge Orta	6.00	3.00	1.75
(30) Eric Soderholm	6.00	3.00	1.75
Cincinnati Strip			
(31) Johnny Bench	15.00	7.50	4.50
(32) Unknown			
(33) Joe Morgan	15.00	7.50	4.50
(34) Unknown			
(35) Pete Rose	40.00	20.00	12.00
Cleveland Strip	25.00	12.50	7.50
(36) Buddy Bell	6.00	3.00	1.75
(37) Wayne Garland	6.00	3.00	1.75
(38) Johnny Grubb	6.00	3.00	1.75
(39) Rick Manning	6.00	3.00	1.75
(40) Andre Thornton	6.00	3.00	1.75
Detroit Strip	25.00	12.50	7.50
(41) Mark Fidrych	6.00	3.00	1.75
(42) John Hiller	6.00	3.00	1.75
(43) Ron LeFlore	6.00	3.00	1.75
(44) Milt May	6.00	3.00	1.75
(45) Jason Thompson	6.00	3.00	1.75
Houston Strip	25.00	12.50	7.50
(46) Enos Cabell	6.00	3.00	1.75
(47) Cesar Cedeno	6.00	3.00	1.75

(48) Joe Ferguson	6.00	3.00	1.75
(49) J.R. Richard	6.00	3.00	1.75
(50) Bobby Watson	6.00	3.00	1.75
Kansas City Strip	45.00	22.50	13.50
(51) George Brett	30.00	15.00	9.00
(52) Al Cowens	6.00	3.00	1.75
(53) Hal McRae	6.00	3.00	1.75
(54) Amos Otis	6.00	3.00	1.75
(55) Fred Patek	6.00	3.00	1.75
Los Angeles Strip	30.00	15.00	9.00
(56) Ron Cey	6.00	3.00	1.75
(57) Steve Garvey	7.50	3.75	2.25
(58) Tommy John	6.00	3.00	1.75
(59) Bill Russell	6.00	3.00	1.75
(60) Don Sutton	7.50	3.75	2.25
Milwaukee Strip	30.00	15.00	9.00
(61) Sal Bando	6.00	3.00	1.75
(62) Ray Fosse	6.00	3.00	1.75
(63) Larry Hisle	6.00	3.00	1.75
(64) Sixto Lezcano	6.00	3.00	1.75
(65) Robin Yount	15.00	7.50	4.50
Minnesota Strip	30.00	15.00	9.00
(66) Rod Carew	15.00	7.50	4.50
(67) Dan Ford	6.00	3.00	1.75
(68) Dave Goltz	6.00	3.00	1.75
(69) Roy Smalley	6.00	3.00	1.75
(70) Butch Wynegar	6.00	3.00	1.75
Montreal Strip	30.00	15.00	9.00
(71) Dave Cash	6.00	3.00	1.75
(72) Andre Dawson	7.50	3.75	2.25
(73) Tony Perez	7.50	3.75	2.25
(74) Steve Rogers	6.00	3.00	1.75
(75) Ellis Valentine	6.00	3.00	1.75
New York (Mets) Strip	25.00	12.50	7.50
(76) Steve Henderson	6.00	3.00	1.75
(77) Jerry Koosman	6.00	3.00	1.75
(78) Elliott Maddox	6.00	3.00	1.75
(79) Willie Montanez	6.00	3.00	1.75
(80) Lenny Randle	6.00	3.00	1.75
New York (Yankees) Strip	30.00	15.00	9.00
(81) Sparky Lyle	6.00	3.00	1.75
(82) Thurman Munson	7.50	3.75	2.25
(83) Lou Piniella	6.00	3.00	1.75
(84) Willie Randolph	6.00	3.00	1.75
(85) Mickey Rivers	6.00	3.00	1.75
Oakland Strip	25.00	12.50	7.50
(86) Wayne Gross	6.00	3.00	1.75
(87) Rick Langford	6.00	3.00	1.75
(88) Bill North	6.00	3.00	1.75
(89) Mitchell Page	6.00	3.00	1.75
(90) Gary Thomasson	6.00	3.00	1.75
Philadelphia Strip	60.00	30.00	18.00
(91) Larry Bowa	6.00	3.00	1.75
(92) Steve Carlton	15.00	7.50	4.50
(93) Greg Luzinski	6.00	3.00	1.75
(94) Garry Maddox	6.00	3.00	1.75
(95) Mike Schmidt	35.00	17.50	10.50
Pittsburgh Strip	30.00	15.00	9.00
(96) John Candelaria	6.00	3.00	1.75
(97) Dave Parker	6.00	3.00	1.75
(98) Bill Robinson	6.00	3.00	1.75
(99) Willie Stargell	15.00	7.50	4.50
(100) Rennie Stennett	6.00	3.00	1.75
San Diego Strip	35.00	17.50	10.00
(101) Rollie Fingers	7.50	3.75	2.25
(102) Oscar Gamble	6.00	3.00	1.75
(103) Randy Jones	6.00	3.00	1.75
(104) Gene Tenace	6.00	3.00	1.75
(105) Dave Winfield	15.00	7.50	4.50
San Francisco Strip	30.00	15.00	9.00
(106) Vida Blue	6.00	3.00	1.75
(107) Gary Lavelle	6.00	3.00	1.75
(108) Bill Madlock	6.00	3.00	1.75
(109) Willie McCovey	15.00	7.50	4.50
(110) John Montefusco	6.00	3.00	1.75
Seattle Strip	25.00	12.50	7.50
(111) Bruce Bochte	6.00	3.00	1.75
(112) Ruppert Jones	6.00	3.00	1.75
(113) Dan Meyer	6.00	3.00	1.75
(114) Lee Stanton	6.00	3.00	1.75
(115) Bill Stein	6.00	3.00	1.75
St. Louis Strip	30.00	15.00	9.00
(116) Lou Brock	15.00	7.50	4.50
(117) Bob Forsch	6.00	3.00	1.75
(118) Ken Reitz	6.00	3.00	1.75
(119) Ted Simmons	6.00	3.00	1.75
(120) Garry Templeton	6.00	3.00	1.75
Texas Strip	25.00	12.50	7.50
(121) Mike Hargrove	6.00	3.00	1.75
(122) Toby Harrah	6.00	3.00	1.75
(123) Jon Matlack	6.00	3.00	1.75
(124) Jim Sundberg	6.00	3.00	1.75
(125) Richie Zisk	6.00	3.00	1.75
Toronto Strip	25.00	12.50	7.50
(126) Doug Ault	6.00	3.00	1.75
(127) Bob Bailor	6.00	3.00	1.75
(128) Jerry Garvin	6.00	3.00	1.75
(129) Roy Howell	6.00	3.00	1.75
(130) Al Woods	6.00	3.00	1.75

1950 Royal Desserts

This set was issued one per box on the backs of various Royal Dessert products over a period of three years. The basic set contains 24 players, however a number of variations create the much higher total for the set. In 1950, Royal issued cards with two different tints - black and white with red, or blue and white with red. Over the next two years, various sentences of the cards' biographies were updated; up to three times in some cases. Some players from the set left the majors after 1950 and others were apparently never updated, but the 23 biography updates that do exist, added to the original 24 cards issued in 1950, give the set a total of 47 cards. The 2-5/8" x 3-1/4"

ROYAL STARS OF BASEBALL No. 21

VIRGIL TRUCKS

Detroit Tigers' great master of the speedball, Virgil is known around the American League as "Fire" Trucks.

Born in Birmingham, Ala., April 26, 1919, the 198 lb., 5'11" pitcher has been a Tiger since 1941, except for a hitch in military service.

Trucks' string of 19 wins in 1949 was his top big league mark to date. He was also official winner of the All Star game that year.

Send for a Plastic Album to Hold Your Royal Stars Collection!

Eight clear envelopes, bound with colorful cover; displays 16 photographs. Mail 15¢ and 3 Royal Desserts package fronts to Royal, Box 89, New York 46, N.Y.

Virgil Trucks

cards are blank-backed with personal and playing biographies alongside the card front photos. Some sample cards can be found with advertising for the desserts on back; they are valued at about double regular card prices. A comb-bound album with seven pages to hold 14 cards was also issued in a 3-1/4" x 3-3/8" format with "Royal Stars" and a crown logo printed in red on white.

		NM	EX	VG
Common Player:		125.00	55.00	25.00
Album:		200.00	90.00	40.00
1a	Stan Musial (2nd paragraph begins "Musial's 207...")	525.00	235.00	100.00
1b	Stan Musial (2nd paragraph begins "Musial batted...")	525.00	235.00	100.00
2a	Pee Wee Reese (2nd paragraph begins "Pee Wee's...)	330.00	150.00	65.00
2b	Pee Wee Reese (2nd paragraph begins "Captain...")	330.00	150.00	65.00
3a	George Kell (2nd paragraph ends "...in 1945, '46.")	200.00	90.00	40.00
3b	George Kell (2nd paragraph ends "...two base hits, 56.")	200.00	90.00	40.00
4a	Dom DiMaggio (2nd paragraph ends "...during 1947.")	165.00	75.00	35.00
4b	Dom DiMaggio (2nd paragraph ends "...with 11.")	165.00	75.00	35.00
5a	Warren Spahn (2nd paragraph ends "...shutouts 7.")	265.00	120.00	55.00
5b	Warren Spahn (2nd paragraph ends "...with 191.")	265.00	120.00	55.00
6a	Andy Pafko (2nd paragraph ends "...7 games.")	125.00	56.00	25.00
6b	Andy Pafko (2nd paragraph ends "...National League.")	125.00	55.00	25.00
6c	Andy Pafko (2nd paragraph ends "...weighs 190.")	125.00	55.00	25.00
7a	Andy Seminick (2nd paragraph ends "...as outfield.")	125.00	55.00	25.00
7b	Andy Seminick (2nd paragraph ends "...since 1916.")	125.00	55.00	25.00
7c	Andy Seminick (2nd paragraph ends "...in the outfield.")	125.00	55.00	25.00
7d	Andy Seminick (2nd paragraph ends "...right handed.")	125.00	55.00	25.00
8a	Lou Brissie (2nd paragraph ends "...when pitching.")	125.00	55.00	25.00
8b	Lou Brissie (2nd paragraph ends "...weighs 215.")	125.00	55.00	25.00
9a	Ewell Blackwell (2nd paragraph begins "Despite recent illness...")	145.00	65.00	30.00
9b	Ewell Blackwell (2nd paragraph begins "Blackwell's...")	145.00	65.00	30.00
10a	Bobby Thomson (2nd paragraph begins "In 1949...")	165.00	75.00	35.00
10b	Bobby Thomson (2nd paragraph begins "Thomson is...")	165.00	75.00	35.00
11a	Phil Rizzuto (2nd paragraph ends "...one 1942 game.")	330.00	150.00	65.00
11b	Phil Rizzuto (2nd paragraph ends "...Most Valuable Player.")	330.00	150.00	65.00
12	Tommy Henrich	155.00	70.00	30.00
13	Joe Gordon	125.00	55.00	25.00
14a	Ray Scarborough (Senators)	125.00	55.00	25.00
14b	Ray Scarborough (White Sox, 2nd paragraph ends "...military service.")	125.00	55.00	25.00
14c	Ray Scarborough (White Sox, 2nd paragraph ends "...the season.")	125.00	55.00	25.00
14d	Ray Scarborough (Red Sox)	125.00	55.00	25.00
15a	Stan Rojek (Pirates)	125.00	55.00	25.00
15b	Stan Rojek (Browns)	125.00	55.00	25.00
16	Luke Appling	180.00	80.00	35.00
17	Willard Marshall	125.00	55.00	25.00
18	Alvin Dark	125.00	55.00	25.00
19a	Dick Sisler (2nd paragraph ends "...service record.")	125.00	55.00	25.00

		NM	EX	VG
19b	Dick Sisler (2nd paragraph ends "...National League flag.")	125.00	55.00	25.00
19c	Dick Sisler (2nd paragraph ends "...Nov. 2, 1920.")	125.00	55.00	25.00
19d	Dick Sisler (2nd paragraph ends "...from '46 to '48. ")	125.00	55.00	25.00
20a	Johnny Ostrowski (White Sox)	125.00	55.00	25.00
20b	Johnny Ostrowski (Senators)	125.00	55.00	25.00
21a	Virgil Trucks (2nd paragraph ends "...in military service.")	125.00	55.00	25.00
21b	Virgil Trucks (2nd paragraph ends "...that year.")	125.00	55.00	25.00
21c	Virgil Trucks (2nd paragraph ends "...for military service.")	125.00	55.00	25.00
22	Eddie Robinson	125.00	55.00	25.00
23	Nanny Fernandez	125.00	55.00	25.00
24	Ferris Fain	125.00	55.00	25.00

1952 Royal Desserts

This set, issued as a premium by Royal Desserts in 1952, consists of 16 unnumbered black and white cards, each measuring 5" x 7". The cards include the inscription "To A Royal Fan" along with the player's facsimile autograph. Backs are blank.

		NM	EX	VG
	Complete Set (16):	1,400	625.00	275.00
	Common Player:	55.00	25.00	10.00
(1)	Ewell Blackwell	55.00	25.00	10.00
(2)	Leland V. Brissie Jr.	55.00	25.00	10.00
(3)	Alvin Dark	55.00	25.00	10.00
(4)	Dom DiMaggio	100.00	45.00	20.00
(5)	Ferris Fain	55.00	25.00	10.00
(6)	George Kell	100.00	45.00	20.00
(7)	Stan Musial	280.00	125.00	55.00
(8)	Andy Pafko	55.00	25.00	10.00
(9)	Pee Wee Reese	175.00	80.00	35.00
(10)	Phil Rizzuto	160.00	70.00	30.00
(11)	Eddie Robinson	55.00	25.00	10.00
(12)	Ray Scarborough	55.00	25.00	10.00
(13)	Andy Seminick	55.00	25.00	10.00
(14)	Dick Sisler	55.00	25.00	10.00
(15)	Warren Spahn	140.00	65.00	25.00
(16)	Bobby Thomson	80.00	35.00	15.00

1920 Babe Ruth "Headin' Home"

This was one of several series of promotional cards issued to advertise the Bambino's starring role in the 1920 silent film, "Headin' Home." The black-and-white cards measure about 1-1/2" x 2-7/16". They feature borderless photos with the three-line caption: BABE RUTH / IN / "HEADIN' HOME." The cards are frequently found miscut with a portion of another card showing at one or more of the edges. Backs may be blank or carry the advertising of a local theater.

		NM	EX	VG
	Complete Set (6):	16,000	8,000	4,750
	Common Card:	3,000	1,500	900.00
(1)	Babe Ruth (Bat at shoulder, crotch-to-cap.)	3,000	1,500	900.00
(2)	Babe Ruth (Bat extended to his right.)	3,000	1,500	900.00
(3)	Babe Ruth (Bat on shoulder, full-length.)	3,000	1,500	900.00
(4)	Babe Ruth (Follow-through, bat head-high.)	3,000	1,500	900.00
(5)	Babe Ruth (Follow-through, bat below waist.)	3,000	1,500	900.00
(6)	Babe Ruth (Horizontal card, holding bat.)	3,000	1,500	900.00

1920 Babe Ruth "Headin' Home" Theater Cards

To promote the showing of "Headin' Home," a silent movie starring Babe Ruth, theaters had these cards printed up with details of show dates. Fronts of the 1-3/4" x 3-1/4" cards have a sepia photo of Ruth swinging the bat. On back is an advertisement from a local theater. This is one of the first cards ever to picture Ruth as a N.Y. Yankee.

	NM	EX	VG
Babe Ruth (Both hands on bat.)	2,750	1,375	825.00
Babe Ruth (One hand on bat.)	2,750	1,375	825.00

1920 Babe Ruth "Headin' Home" (Tex Rickard)

Taking advantage of the Babe's enormous popularity in the Taking advantage of the Babe's enormous popularity in the pinstripes of his new team, he was given a starring role in a 1920 silent movie titled "Headin Home." To promote the flick, a small set of cards was issued. The 1-7/8" x 3-1/4" black-and-white cards have posed photos of Ruth on front. Dropped out in white in the lower portion of the photo is his name and movie title. Backs have an ad for the movie (some cards are known with blank backs, as well). Tex Rickard was the Ebbets Field announcer for the Brooklyn Dodgers for over 30 years.

		NM	EX	VG
	Common Card:	5,000	2,500	1,500
(1)	Babe Ruth (Bat on shoulder, crotch to cap.)	5,000	2,500	1,500
(2)	Babe Ruth (Bat on shoulder, full-length.)	5,000	2,500	1,500
(3)	Babe Ruth (Batting follow-through.)	5,000	2,500	1,500

1920s Babe Ruth Postcard

There is no indication of publisher or specific date of issue on this standard-size, typically marked black-and-white photo postcard which pictures the Babe in street clothes informally posed with a cane chair. The number "210" near the bottom of the photo indicates it was part of a series. The horizontal divided back has typical postcard markings.

		NM	EX	VG
210	Babe Ruth	750.00	375.00	225.00

1920s Babe Ruth Underwear Premium Photo

While the product itself and the boxes and display pieces are collectibles in their own right, among the scarcest pieces associated with the Babe Ruth brand underwear is this approximately 8" x 10" premium photo which was apparently only included in some forms of packaging. The blank-back photo shows a buff Babe in the product and has a facsimile autograph on his right bicep.

	NM	EX	VG
Babe Ruth	500.00	250.00	150.00

1927 "Babe Comes Home" Strip Cards (R94)

This strip card set of unknown scope (at least 75 known) was cataloged as "Movie Stars and Scenes (R94)" in the American Card Catalog. At least two of the cards depict Babe Ruth as "Babe Dugan" in scenes from his silent film. Cards are nominally about 2-7/8" x 2-5/16" and can be found printed in black-and-white or as red, blue or green duotones. The name of the movie is printed in white at bottom. Backs and blank.

	NM	EX	VG
Babe Ruth (In suit w/ police.)	1,350	675.00	400.00
Babe Ruth (In uniform, locker room.)	1,350	675.00	400.00

1928 Babe Ruth Home Run Candy Club Membership Card

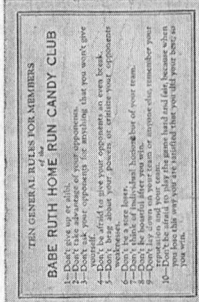

In conjunction with his candy bar, Ruth created the "Babe Ruth Home Run Candy Club," and issued this membership card. Front has a black-and-white portrait photo. Back of the 2-3/4" x 4" card has 10 rules of sportsmanship for members. The card folds open to reveal a membership certificate with a facsimile autograph.

	NM	EX	VG
Babe Ruth	2,500	1,250	750.00

1928 George Ruth Candy Co.

② "BABE" RUTH
Knocked out 60 Home
Runs in 1927.
His Candy Helped Him.

This circa 1928 issue features sepia-toned photos of Babe Ruth. According to the back of the cards, it was issued by the Geo. H. Ruth Candy Co. Cards measure 1-7/8" x 4" and picture Ruth during a 1924 promotional West Coast tour and in scenes from the movie "Babe Comes Home." The cards are numbered and include photo captions at the bottom. The backs of most cards contain an offer to exchange the six cards for an autographed baseball, which may explain their scarcity today. Cards have been seen with the address to mail for exchange as Cleveland and as San Francisco. Cards can also be found with blank backs. This issue was deceptively counterfeited in the early 21st Century.

	NM	EX	VG
Complete Set (6):	7,000	3,150	1,400
Common Card:	1,250	650.00	300.00
Wrapper:	3,500	2,000	1,250
1 "Babe" Ruth ("King of them all...")	1,250	650.00	300.00
2 "Babe" Ruth ("Knocked out 60 Home Runs...")	1,250	650.00	300.00
3 "Babe" Ruth ("The only player...")	1,250	650.00	300.00
4 "Babe" Ruth ("The Popular Bambino...")	1,250	650.00	300.00
5 "Babe" Ruth ("A favorite with the Kiddies...")	1,250	650.00	300.00
6 "Babe" Ruth ("The King of Swat...")	1,250	650.00	300.00

1936 R311 Glossy Finish

The cards in this 28-card set, which was available as a premium in 1936, measure 6" x 8" and were printed on a glossy cardboard. The photos are either black and white or sepia-toned and include a facsimile autograph. The unnumbered set includes individual players and team photos. The Boston Red Sox team card can be found in two varieties; one shows the sky above the building on the card's right side, while the other does not. Some of the cards are scarcer than others in the set and command a premium. Babe Ruth is featured on the Boston Braves team card.

	NM	EX	VG
Complete Set (27):	3,750	1,850	1,100
Common Player:	60.00	30.00	18.00
(1) Earl Averill	100.00	50.00	30.00
(2) James L. "Jim" Bottomley	100.00	50.00	30.00
(3) Gordon S. "Mickey" Cochrane	100.00	50.00	30.00
(4) Joe Cronin	100.00	50.00	30.00
(5) Jerome "Dizzy" Dean	150.00	75.00	45.00
(6) Jimmy Dykes	60.00	30.00	18.00
(7) Jimmy Foxx	125.00	65.00	35.00
(8) Frankie Frisch	100.00	50.00	30.00
(9) Henry "Hank" Greenberg	120.00	60.00	35.00

(10) Mel Harder/SP	120.00	60.00	35.00
(11) Pepper Martin/SP	225.00	110.00	65.00
(12) Lynwood "Schoolboy" Rowe/SP	120.00	60.00	35.00
(13) William "Bill" Terry	100.00	50.00	30.00
(14) Harold "Pie" Traynor	100.00	50.00	30.00
(15) American League All-Stars - 1935	275.00	135.00	80.00
(16) American League Pennant Winners - 1934 (Detroit Tigers)	125.00	65.00	35.00
(17) Boston Braves - 1935	300.00	150.00	90.00
(18a) Boston Red Sox (sky visible above building at right)	100.00	50.00	30.00
(18b) Boston Red Sox (No sky visible.)	180.00	90.00	55.00
(19) Brooklyn Dodgers - 1935/SP	225.00	110.00	65.00
(20) Chicago White Sox - 1935	100.00	50.00	30.00
(21) Columbus Red Birds (1934 Pennant Winners of American Association)/SP	150.00	75.00	45.00
(22) National League All-Stars - 1935	180.00	90.00	55.00
(23) National League Champions - 1935 (Chicago Cubs)	100.00	50.00	30.00
(24) New York Yankees - 1935	180.00	90.00	55.00
(25) Pittsburgh Pirates - 1935/SP	200.00	100.00	60.00
(26) St. Louis Browns - 1935	100.00	50.00	30.00
(27) The World Champions, 1934 (St. Louis Cardinals)	100.00	50.00	30.00

1936 R311 Leather Finish

This set of 15 unnumbered cards, issued as a premium in 1936, is distinctive because of its uneven, leather-like surface. The cards measure 6" x 8" and display a facsimile autograph on the black and white photo surrounded by a plain border. The cards are unnumbered and include individual player photos, multi-player photos and team photos of the 1935 pennant winners.

	NM	EX	VG
Complete Set (15):	2,750	1,325	825.00
Common Player:	90.00	45.00	25.00
(1) Frank Crosetti, Joe DiMaggio, Tony Lazzeri	825.00	410.00	245.00
(2) Paul Derringer	90.00	45.00	25.00
(3) Wes Ferrell	90.00	45.00	25.00
(4) Jimmy (Jimmie) Foxx	180.00	90.00	55.00
(5) Charlie Gehringer	165.00	80.00	50.00
(6) Mel Harder	90.00	45.00	25.00
(7) Gabby Hartnett	165.00	80.00	50.00
(8) Rogers Hornsby	190.00	95.00	55.00
(9) Connie Mack	165.00	80.00	50.00
(10) Van Mungo	90.00	45.00	25.00
(11) Steve O'Neill	90.00	45.00	25.00
(12) Charles Ruffing	165.00	80.00	50.00
(13) Arky Vaughan, Honus Wagner	245.00	120.00	75.00
(14) American League Pennant Winners - 1935 (Detroit Tigers)	165.00	80.00	50.00
(15) National League Pennant Winners - 1935 (Chicago Cubs)	165.00	80.00	50.00

1936 R312

Gordon Cochrane

The 50 cards in this set of 4" x 5-3/8" point-of-purchase premiums are black-and-white photos that have been tinted in soft pastel colors. The set includes 25 individual player portraits, 14 multi-player cards and 11

action photos. Six of the action photos include facsimilie autographs, while the other five have printed legends. The Allen card is scarcer than the others in the set.

	NM	EX	VG
Complete Set (50):	8,500	4,250	2,500
Common Player:	90.00	35.00	20.00
(1) John Thomas Allen	90.00	35.00	20.00
(2) Nick Altrock, Al Schact	140.00	55.00	35.00
(3) Ollie Bejma, Rolly Hemsley	90.00	35.00	20.00
(4) Les Bell, Zeke Bonura	90.00	35.00	20.00
(5) Cy Blanton	90.00	35.00	20.00
(6) Cliff Bolton, Earl Whitehill	90.00	35.00	20.00
(7) Frenchy Bordagaray, George Earnshaw	90.00	35.00	20.00
(8) Mace Brown	90.00	35.00	20.00
(9) Dolph Camilli	90.00	35.00	20.00
(10) Phil Cavaretta (Cavarretta), Frank Demaree, Augie Galan, Stan Hack, Gabby Hartnett, Billy Herman, Billy Jurges, Chuck Klein, Fred Lindstrom	185.00	75.00	45.00
(11) Phil Cavaretta (Cavarretta), Stan Hack, Billy Herman, Billy Jurges	185.00	75.00	45.00
(12) Gordon Cochrane	185.00	75.00	45.00
(13) Jim Collins, Stan Hack	90.00	35.00	20.00
(14) Rip Collins	90.00	35.00	20.00
(15) Joe Cronin, Buckey Harris (Bucky)	125.00	50.00	30.00
(16) Alvin Crowder	90.00	35.00	20.00
(17) Kiki Cuyler	185.00	75.00	45.00
(18) Kiki Cuyler, Tris Speaker, Danny Taylor	225.00	90.00	55.00
(19) "Bill" Dickey	185.00	75.00	45.00
(20) Joe DiMagio (DiMaggio)	2,200	850.00	550.00
(21) "Chas." Dressen	90.00	35.00	20.00
(22) Rick Ferrell, Russ Van Atta	125.00	50.00	30.00
(23) Pete Fox, Goose Goslin, "Jo Jo" White	165.00	65.00	40.00
(24) Jimmey Foxx, Luke Sewell	215.00	85.00	55.00
(25) Benny Frey	90.00	35.00	20.00
(26) Augie Galan, "Pie" Traynor	165.00	65.00	40.00
(27) Lefty Gomez, Myril Hoag	165.00	65.00	40.00
(28) "Hank" Greenberg	185.00	75.00	45.00
(29) Lefty Grove, Connie Mack	250.00	100.00	65.00
(30) Muel Haas (Mule), Mike Kreevich, Dixie Walker	90.00	35.00	20.00
(31) Mel Harder	90.00	35.00	20.00
(32) Gabby Hartnett (Mickey Cochrane, Frank Demaree, Ernie Quigley (ump) in photo)	165.00	65.00	40.00
(33) Gabby Hartnett, Lonnie Warnecke (Warneke)	135.00	55.00	35.00
(34) Roger Hornsby (Rogers)	250.00	100.00	65.00
(35) Rogers Hornsby, Allen Sothoron (Sothoron)	185.00	75.00	45.00
(36) Ernie Lombardi	185.00	75.00	45.00
(37) Al Lopez	185.00	75.00	45.00
(38) Pepper Martin	110.00	45.00	25.00
(39) "Johnny" Mize	185.00	75.00	45.00
(40) Van L. Mungo	100.00	40.00	25.00
(41) Bud Parmelee	90.00	35.00	20.00
(42) Schoolboy Rowe	90.00	35.00	20.00
(43) Chas. Ruffing	185.00	75.00	45.00
(44) Eugene Schott	90.00	35.00	20.00
(45) Casey Stengel	185.00	75.00	45.00
(46) Bill Sullivan	90.00	35.00	20.00
(47) Bill Swift	90.00	35.00	20.00
(48) Floyd Vaughan, Hans Wagner	225.00	90.00	55.00
(49) L. Waner, P. Waner, Big Jim Weaver	215.00	85.00	55.00
(50) Ralph Winegarner	90.00	35.00	20.00

1936 R313

(See 1936 National Chicle "Fine Pens.")

1936 R314

(See 1936 Goudey "Wide Pen" Premiums.)

1929-1930 R315

Bob Shawkey "YANKEES"

Apparently issued over a period of at least two years, based on observed player/team combinations, the 58 cards in this set can be found in either black-and-white or yellow-and-black. The unnumbered, blank-backed cards measure a nominal 3-1/4" x 5-1/4" though original cutting variances abound. The cards feature either portraits or posed action photos. The set includes several different types of cards, depending on the caption. Cards can be found with the player's name and team inside a white box in a lower corner; other cards add the position and team in small type in the bottom border; a third type has the player's name in hand lettering near the bottom; and the final type includes the position and team printed in small type along the bottom border.

	NM	EX	VG
Complete Set (46):	6,000	2,400	1,200
Common Player:	45.00	20.00	10.00
(1) Earl Averill	90.00	35.00	25.00
(2) "Benny" Bengough	45.00	20.00	10.00
(3) Laurence Benton (Lawrence)	45.00	20.00	10.00
(4) "Max" Bishop	45.00	20.00	10.00
(5) "Sunny Jim" Bottomley	90.00	35.00	20.00
(6) Bill Cissell	45.00	20.00	10.00
(7) Bud Clancey (Clancy)	45.00	20.00	10.00
(8) "Freddy" Fitzsimmons	45.00	20.00	10.00
(9) "Jimmy" Foxx	260.00	100.00	65.00
(10) "Johnny" Fredericks (Frederick)	45.00	20.00	10.00
(11) Frank Frisch	110.00	45.00	25.00
(12) "Lou" Gehrig	1,500	600.00	375.00
(13) "Goose" Goslin	90.00	35.00	20.00
(14) Burleigh Grimes	90.00	35.00	20.00
(15) "Lefty" Grove	110.00	45.00	25.00
(16) "Mule" Haas	45.00	20.00	10.00
(17) Harvey Hendricks (Hendrick)	45.00	20.00	10.00
(18) "Babe" Herman	60.00	25.00	15.00
(19) "Roger" Hornsby (Rogers)	135.00	55.00	35.00
(20) Karl Hubbell (Carl)	90.00	35.00	20.00
(21) "Stonewall" Jackson	90.00	35.00	20.00
(22) Smead Jolley	45.00	20.00	10.00
(23) "Chuck" Klein	90.00	35.00	20.00
(24) Mark Koenig	45.00	20.00	10.00
(25) "Tony" Lazerri (Lazzeri)	90.00	35.00	20.00
(26) Fred Leach	45.00	20.00	10.00
(27) "Freddy" Lindstrom	90.00	35.00	20.00
(28) Fred Marberry	45.00	20.00	10.00
(29) "Bing" Miller	45.00	20.00	10.00
(30) "Bob" O'Farrell	45.00	20.00	10.00
(31) Frank O'Doul	75.00	30.00	18.50
(32) "Herbie" Pennock	90.00	35.00	20.00
(33) George Pipgras	45.00	20.00	10.00
(34) Andrew Reese	45.00	20.00	10.00
(35) Carl Reynolds	45.00	20.00	10.00
(36) "Babe" Ruth	1,600	640.00	400.00
(37) "Bob" Shawkey	45.00	20.00	10.00
(38) Art Shires	45.00	20.00	10.00
(39) "Al" Simmons	90.00	35.00	20.00
(40) "Riggs" Stephenson	45.00	20.00	10.00
(41) "Bill" Terry	90.00	35.00	20.00
(42) "Pie" Traynor	90.00	35.00	20.00
(43) "Dazzy" Vance	90.00	35.00	20.00
(44) Paul Waner	90.00	35.00	20.00
(45) Hack Wilson	90.00	35.00	20.00
(46) "Tom" Zachary	45.00	20.00	10.00

1929 R316

(See Kashin Publications.)

1929 R316 5x7 Photos

There is nothing concrete to connect this set of player photos with the Kashin Publications card set which carried the R316 designation in the American Card Catalog except that these 4-7/8" x 6-3/4" heavy-paper pictures use the same photos and graphics as the smaller cards. It is thought that the photos are the work of Charles M. Conlon and that the 5x7s may have some connection to the Spalding sporting goods company for whom he worked. Pictures feature white borders and facsimile autographs on front, along with the player's city and league on two lines of type at bottom. While the photos are all the same as seen on R316, the city/league designation on some of the photos is sometimes in black instead of white as on the card, or vice versa. Because almost every card from R316 is known in the 5x7 series, it is reasonable to expect that pictures of Frank Hogan and Jimmy Welsh may also exist. A number of players in the 5x7 set do not appear in the Kashin Publications set, and are noted here with an asterisk.

	NM	EX	VG
Complete Set (111):	7,000	3,500	2,100
Common Player:	50.00	25.00	15.00
(1) Dale Alexander	50.00	25.00	15.00
(2) Ethan N. Allen	50.00	25.00	15.00
(3) Ray Benge (*)	50.00	25.00	15.00
(4) Larry Benton	50.00	25.00	15.00
(5) Moe Berg	65.00	32.50	20.00
(6) Max Bishop	50.00	25.00	15.00

	NM	EX	VG
(7) Del Bissonette	50.00	25.00	15.00
(8) Lucerne A. Blue	50.00	25.00	15.00
(9) James Bottomley	75.00	37.50	22.50
(10) Raymond B. Bressler (*)	50.00	25.00	15.00
(11) Fred Brickell (*)	50.00	25.00	15.00
(12) Guy T. Bush	50.00	25.00	15.00
(13) Harold G. Carlson	50.00	25.00	15.00
(14) Owen Carroll	50.00	25.00	15.00
(15) Chalmers W. Cissell (Chalmer)	50.00	25.00	15.00
(16) Mickey Cochrane (*)	85.00	45.00	25.00
(17) Earl (Earle) Combs	75.00	37.50	22.50
(18) Hugh M. Critz	50.00	25.00	15.00
(19) H.J. DeBerry	50.00	25.00	15.00
(20) Pete Donohue	50.00	25.00	15.00
(21) Taylor Douthit	50.00	25.00	15.00
(22) Chas. W. Dressen	50.00	25.00	15.00
(23) Clise Dudley (*)	50.00	25.00	15.00
(24) Jimmy Dykes	50.00	25.00	15.00
(25) Howard Ehmke	50.00	25.00	15.00
(26) Elwood English	50.00	25.00	15.00
(27) Urban Faber	75.00	37.50	22.50
(28) Fred Fitzsimmons	50.00	25.00	15.00
(29) Lewis A. Fonseca	50.00	25.00	15.00
(30) Horace H. Ford	50.00	25.00	15.00
(31) Jimmy Foxx	85.00	45.00	25.00
(32) Frank Frisch	75.00	37.50	22.50
(33) Lou Gehrig	335.00	165.00	100.00
(34) Charles Gehringer	75.00	37.50	22.50
(35) Walter Gilbert (*)	50.00	25.00	15.00
(36) Leon Goslin	75.00	37.50	22.50
(37) George Grantham	50.00	25.00	15.00
(38) Burleigh Grimes	75.00	37.50	22.50
(39) Robert Grove	85.00	45.00	25.00
(40) Bump Hadley	50.00	25.00	15.00
(41) Charlie Hafey	75.00	37.50	22.50
(42) Jesse J. Haines	75.00	37.50	22.50
(43) Harvey Hendrick	50.00	25.00	15.00
(44) Floyd C. Herman	50.00	25.00	15.00
(45) Andy High	50.00	25.00	15.00
(46) Urban J. Hodapp	50.00	25.00	15.00
(47) Frank Hogan (Existence not confirmed.)			
(48) Rogers Hornsby	90.00	45.00	25.00
(49) Waite Hoyt	75.00	37.50	22.50
(50) Willis Hudlin	50.00	25.00	15.00
(51) Frank O. Hurst	50.00	25.00	15.00
(52) Charlie Jamieson	50.00	25.00	15.00
(53) Roy C. Johnson	50.00	25.00	15.00
(54) Percy Jones	50.00	25.00	15.00
(55) Sam Jones	50.00	25.00	15.00
(56) Joseph Judge	50.00	25.00	15.00
(57) Willie Kamm	50.00	25.00	15.00
(58) Charles Klein	75.00	37.50	22.50
(59) Mark Koenig	50.00	25.00	15.00
(60) Ralph Kress	50.00	25.00	15.00
(61) Fred M. Leach	50.00	25.00	15.00
(62) Carl Lind (*)	50.00	25.00	15.00
(63) Fred Lindstrom	75.00	37.50	22.50
(64) Ad Liska	50.00	25.00	15.00
(65) Fred Lucas (Red)	50.00	25.00	15.00
(66) Fred Maguire	50.00	25.00	15.00
(67) Perce L. Malone	50.00	25.00	15.00
(68) Harry Manush (Henry)	75.00	37.50	22.50
(69) Walter Maranville	75.00	37.50	22.50
(70) Earl McNeely (*)	50.00	25.00	15.00
(71) Douglas McWeeney (McWeeny)	50.00	25.00	15.00
(72) Oscar Melillo	50.00	25.00	15.00
(73) Alex Metzler (*)	50.00	25.00	15.00
(74) Ed "Bing" Miller	50.00	25.00	15.00
(75) Clarence Mitchell (*)	50.00	25.00	15.00
(76) Ed Morgan (*)	50.00	25.00	15.00
(77) Chas. S. Myer (*)	50.00	25.00	15.00
(78) Frank O'Doul	65.00	32.50	20.00
(79) Melvin Ott	85.00	45.00	25.00
(80) Herbert Pennock	75.00	37.50	22.50
(81) William W. Regan	50.00	25.00	15.00
(82) Harry F. Rice	50.00	25.00	15.00
(83) Sam Rice	75.00	37.50	22.50
(84) Lance Richbourgh (Richbourg)	50.00	25.00	15.00
(85) Eddie Rommel	50.00	25.00	15.00
(86) Chas. H. Root	50.00	25.00	15.00
(87) Ed Roush	75.00	37.50	22.50
(88) Harold Ruel (Herold)	50.00	25.00	15.00
(89) Charles Ruffing	75.00	37.50	22.50
(90) Jack Russell	50.00	25.00	15.00
(91) Babe Ruth	425.00	210.00	125.00
(92) Fred Schulte	50.00	25.00	15.00
(93) Harry Seibold	50.00	25.00	15.00
(94) Joe Sewell	75.00	37.50	22.50
(95) Luke Sewell	50.00	25.00	15.00
(96) Art Shires	50.00	25.00	15.00
(97) Al Simmons	75.00	37.50	22.50
(98) Bob Smith	50.00	25.00	15.00
(99) Riggs Stephenson	50.00	25.00	15.00
(100) Wm. H. Terry	75.00	37.50	22.50
(101) Alphonse Thomas	50.00	25.00	15.00
(102) Lafayette F. Thompson	50.00	25.00	15.00
(103) Phil Todt	50.00	25.00	15.00
(104) Harold J. Traynor	75.00	37.50	22.50
(105) Dazzy Vance	75.00	37.50	22.50
(106) Lloyd Waner	75.00	37.50	22.50
(107) Paul Waner	75.00	37.50	22.50
(108) Jimmy Welsh (Existence unconfirmed.)			
(109) Earl Whitehill	50.00	25.00	15.00
(110) A.C. Whitney	50.00	25.00	15.00
(111) Claude Willoughby	50.00	25.00	15.00
(112) Hack Wilson	75.00	37.50	22.50
(113) Tom Zachary	50.00	25.00	15.00

1933 R337

(See 1933 Eclipse Import.)

1948 R346 Blue Tint

JACKIE ROBINSON
BROOKLYN
36

Issued circa 1948-49, the cards in this set derive their name from the distinctive blue coloring used to tint the black-and-white photos. The cards have blank backs and measure 2" x 2-5/8". The set has a high percentage of New York players and was originally issued in strips of six or eight cards each and therefore would have been more appropriately cataloged as a "W" strip card set. The set includes several variations of team designations. It appears that all cards #25-48, along with possibly some of the team variations can also be found in black-and-white, rather than blue printing. The complete set price does not include the variations. Proof cards have been found with printing on the back indicating they were photographed by Al Weinstein of Brooklyn.

	NM	EX	VG
Complete Set (48):	1,300	650.00	375.00
Common Player:	15.00	7.50	4.50
Black-and-White: 1.5-3X			
1 Bill Johnson	15.00	7.50	4.50
2a Leo Durocher (Brooklyn)	30.00	15.00	9.00
2b Leo Durocher (New York)	30.00	15.00	9.00
3 Marty Marion	20.00	10.00	6.00
4 Ewell Blackwell	15.00	7.50	4.50
5 John Lindell	15.00	7.50	4.50
6 Larry Jansen	15.00	7.50	4.50
7 Ralph Kiner	30.00	15.00	9.00
8 Chuck Dressen	15.00	7.50	4.50
9 Bobby Brown	15.00	7.50	4.50
10 Luke Appling	30.00	15.00	9.00
11 Bill Nicholson	15.00	7.50	4.50
12 Phil Masi	15.00	7.50	4.50
13 Frank Shea	15.00	7.50	4.50
14 Bob Dillinger	15.00	7.50	4.50
15 Pete Suder	15.00	7.50	4.50
16 Joe DiMaggio	225.00	110.00	65.00
17 John Corriden	15.00	7.50	4.50
18a Mel Ott (New York)	40.00	20.00	12.00
18b Mel Ott (no team)	40.00	20.00	12.00
19 Warren Rosar	15.00	7.50	4.50
20 Warren Spahn	35.00	17.50	10.00
21 Allie Reynolds	20.00	10.00	6.00
22 Lou Boudreau	30.00	15.00	9.00
23 Harry Majeski (Hank)(Photo actually Randy Gumpert.)	15.00	7.50	4.50
24 Frank Crosetti	15.00	7.50	4.50
25 Gus Niarhos	15.00	7.50	4.50
26 Bruce Edwards	15.00	7.50	4.50
27 Rudy York	15.00	7.50	4.50
28 Don Black	15.00	7.50	4.50
29 Lou Gehrig	225.00	110.00	65.00
30 Johnny Mize	30.00	15.00	9.00
31 Ed Stanky	15.00	7.50	4.50
32 Vic Raschi	20.00	10.00	6.00
33 Cliff Mapes	15.00	7.50	4.50
34 Enos Slaughter	30.00	15.00	9.00
35 Hank Greenberg	35.00	17.50	10.00
36 Jackie Robinson	125.00	65.00	40.00
37 Frank Hiller	15.00	7.50	4.50
38 Bob Elliot (Elliott)	15.00	7.50	4.50
39 Harry Walker	15.00	7.50	4.50
40 Ed Lopat	15.00	7.50	4.50
41 Bobby Thomson	20.00	10.00	6.00
42 Tommy Henrich	20.00	10.00	6.00
43 Bobby Feller	35.00	17.50	10.00
44 Ted Williams	100.00	50.00	30.00
45 Dixie Walker	15.00	7.50	4.50
46 Johnnie Vander Meer	20.00	10.00	6.00
47 Clint Hartung	15.00	7.50	4.50
(48) Charlie Keller	20.00	10.00	6.00

1950 R423

102. AL SIMMONS
Ball

These tiny (5/8" x 7/8") cards are numbered roughly in alphabetical order from 1 through 120. They were issued in 13-card perforated strips from vending machines. The black-and-white cards are printed on thin stock and include the player's name beneath his photo. The backs - most commonly printed in orange, but sometimes purple or green - display a rough drawing of a baseball infield with tiny figures at the various positions. It appears the cards were intended to be used to play a game of baseball. Many of the cards were printed on more than one strip, creating varying levels of scarcity not necessarily reflected in pricing.

		NM	EX	VG
Complete Set (119):		850.00	425.00	250.00
Common Player:		6.00	3.00	1.75
1	Richie Ashburn	12.50	6.25	3.75
2	Grover Alexander	10.00	5.00	3.00
3	Frank Baumholtz	6.00	3.00	1.75
4	Ralph Branca	6.00	3.00	1.75
5	Yogi Berra	15.00	7.50	4.50
6	Ewell Blackwell	7.50	3.75	2.25
7	Lou Boudreau	7.50	3.75	2.25
8	Harry Brecheen	6.00	3.00	1.75
9	Chico Carrasquel	6.00	3.00	1.75
10	Jerry Coleman	6.00	3.00	1.75
11	Walker Cooper	6.00	3.00	1.75
12	Roy Campanella	17.50	8.75	5.25
13	Phil Cavaretta (Cavarretta)	6.00	3.00	1.75
14a	Ty Cobb (W/facsimile autograph.)	30.00	15.00	9.00
14b	Ty Cobb (No facsimile autograph.)	40.00	20.00	12.00
15	Mickey Cochrane	7.50	3.75	2.25
16	Ed Collins	7.50	3.75	2.25
17	Frank Crosetti	7.50	3.75	2.25
18	Larry Doby	7.50	3.75	2.25
19	Walter Dropo	6.00	3.00	1.75
20	Alvin Dark	6.00	3.00	1.75
21	Dizzy Dean	17.50	8.75	5.25
22	Bill Dickey	15.00	7.50	4.50
23	Murray Dickson (Murry)	6.00	3.00	1.75
24	Dom DiMaggio	7.50	3.75	2.25
25	Joe DiMaggio	50.00	25.00	15.00
26	Leo Durocher	7.50	3.75	2.25
27	Luke Easter	6.00	3.00	1.75
28	Bob Elliott	6.00	3.00	1.75
29	Del Ennis	6.00	3.00	1.75
30	Ferris Fain	6.00	3.00	1.75
31	Bob Feller	15.00	7.50	4.50
32	Frank Frisch	7.50	3.75	2.25
33	Billy Goodman	6.00	3.00	1.75
34	Lefty Gomez	7.50	3.75	2.25
35	Lou Gehrig	40.00	20.00	12.00
36	Joe Gordon	6.00	3.00	1.75
37	Sid Gordon	6.00	3.00	1.75
38	Hank Greenberg	15.00	7.50	4.50
39	Lefty Grove	10.00	5.00	3.00
40	Art Houtteman	6.00	3.00	1.75
41	Sid Hudson	6.00	3.00	1.75
42	Ken Heintzelman	6.00	3.00	1.75
43	Gene Hermanski	6.00	3.00	1.75
44	Jim Hearn	6.00	3.00	1.75
45	Gil Hodges	12.50	6.25	3.75
46	Harry Heilman (Heilmann)	7.50	3.75	2.25
47	Tommy Henrich	7.50	3.75	2.25
48	Roger Hornsby (Rogers)	10.00	5.00	3.00
49	Carl Hubbell	10.00	5.00	3.00
50	Edwin Joost	6.00	3.00	1.75
51	John Jorgensen	6.00	3.00	1.75
52	Larry Jansen	6.00	3.00	1.75
53	Nippy Jones	6.00	3.00	1.75
54	Walter Johnson	12.50	6.25	3.75
55	Ellis Kinder	6.00	3.00	1.75
56	Jim Konstanty	6.00	3.00	1.75
57	George Kell	7.50	3.75	2.25
58	Ralph Kiner	7.50	3.75	2.25
59	Bob Lemon	7.50	3.75	2.25
60	Whitey Lockman	6.00	3.00	1.75
61	Ed Lopat	7.50	3.75	2.25
62	Tony Lazzeri	7.50	3.75	2.25
63	Cass Michaels	6.00	3.00	1.75
64	Cliff Mapes	6.00	3.00	1.75
65	Willard Marshall	6.00	3.00	1.75
66	Clyde McCullough	6.00	3.00	1.75
67	Connie Mack	7.50	3.75	2.25
68	Christy Mathewson	17.50	8.75	5.25
69	Joe Medwick	7.50	3.75	2.25
70	Johnny Mize	7.50	3.75	2.25
71	Terry Moore	6.00	3.00	1.75
72	Stan Musial	20.00	10.00	6.00
73	Hal Newhouser	7.50	3.75	2.25
74	Don Newcombe	7.50	3.75	2.25
75	Lefty O'Doul	7.50	3.75	2.25
76	Mel Ott	10.00	5.00	3.00
77	Mel Parnell	6.00	3.00	1.75
78	Johnny Pesky	6.00	3.00	1.75
79	Gerald Priddy	6.00	3.00	1.75
80	Dave Philley	6.00	3.00	1.75
81	Bob Porterfield	6.00	3.00	1.75
82	Andy Pafko	6.00	3.00	1.75
83	Howie Pollet	6.00	3.00	1.75
84	Herb Pennock	7.50	3.75	2.25
85	Al Rosen	7.50	3.75	2.25
86	Pee Wee Reese	15.00	7.50	4.50
87	Del Rice	6.00	3.00	1.75
88	Vic Raschi	7.50	3.75	2.25
89	Allie Reynolds	7.50	3.75	2.25
90	Phil Rizzuto	15.00	7.50	4.50
91	Jackie Robinson	35.00	17.50	10.50
92	Babe Ruth	40.00	20.00	12.00
93	Casey Stengel	15.00	7.50	4.50
94	Vern Stephens	6.00	3.00	1.75
95	Duke Snider	15.00	7.50	4.50
96	Enos Slaughter	7.50	3.75	2.25
97	Al Schoendienst	7.50	3.75	2.25
98	Gerald Staley	6.00	3.00	1.75
99	Clyde Shoun	6.00	3.00	1.75
100	Unknown			
101	Hank Sauer	6.00	3.00	1.75
102	Al Simmons	7.50	3.75	2.25
103	George Sisler	7.50	3.75	2.25
104	Tris Speaker	12.50	6.25	3.75
105	Ed Stanky	6.00	3.00	1.75
106	Virgil Trucks	6.00	3.00	1.75
107	Henry Thompson	6.00	3.00	1.75
108	Bobby Thomson	7.50	3.75	2.25
109	Dazzy Vance	7.50	3.75	2.25
110	Lloyd Waner	7.50	3.75	2.25
111	Paul Waner	7.50	3.75	2.25
112	Gene Woodling	7.50	3.75	2.25
113	Ted Williams	35.00	17.50	10.50
114	Vic Wertz	6.00	3.00	1.75
115	Wes Westrom (Westrum)	6.00	3.00	1.75
116	Johnny Wyrostek	6.00	3.00	1.75
117	Eddie Yost	6.00	3.00	1.75
118	Allen Zarilla	6.00	3.00	1.75
119	Gus Zernial	6.00	3.00	1.75
120	Sam Zoldack (Zoldak)	6.00	3.00	1.75
(47)	Arky Vaughan (Vaughn)	30.00	15.00	9.00
(48)	Joe Vosmik	12.50	6.25	3.75
(49)	Lloyd Waner	30.00	15.00	9.00
(50)	Paul Waner	30.00	15.00	9.00
(51)	Lon Warneke	12.50	6.25	3.75
(52)	Floyd Young	12.50	6.25	3.75

S

1936 S and S Game

Small black-and-white player photos are featured on the fronts of this 52-card game set. Measuring about 2-1/4" x 3-1/2", with rounded corners, the cards feature plain green or cream-colored backs. Besides the player photo on front, there are a few biographical details and stats, and a pair of game scenarios. The cards are unnumbered and are checklisted here alphabetically. The complete game included a special scoreboard, at least two "directions" cards and a contest card.

		NM	EX	VG
Complete Set (52):		1,000	500.00	300.00
Complete Boxed Set:		1,250	625.00	375.00
Common Player:		12.50	6.25	3.75
(1)	Luke Appling	30.00	15.00	9.00
(2)	Earl Averill	30.00	15.00	9.00
(3)	Zeke Bonura	12.50	6.25	3.75
(4)	Dolph Camilli	12.50	6.25	3.75
(5)	Ben Cantwell	12.50	6.25	3.75
(6)	Phil Cavaretta (Cavarretta)	12.50	6.25	3.75
(7)	Rip Collins	12.50	6.25	3.75
(8)	Joe Cronin	30.00	15.00	9.00
(9)	Frank Crosetti	20.00	10.00	6.00
(10)	Kiki Cuyler	30.00	15.00	9.00
(11)	Virgil Davis	12.50	6.25	3.75
(12)	Frank Demaree	12.50	6.25	3.75
(13)	Paul Derringer	12.50	6.25	3.75
(14)	Bill Dickey	50.00	25.00	15.00
(15)	Woody English	12.50	6.25	3.75
(16)	Fred Fitzsimmons	12.50	6.25	3.75
(17)	Richard Ferrell	30.00	15.00	9.00
(18)	Pete Fox	12.50	6.25	3.75
(19)	Jimmy (Jimmie) Foxx	60.00	30.00	18.00
(20)	Larry French	12.50	6.25	3.75
(21)	Frank Frisch	30.00	15.00	9.00
(22)	August Galan	12.50	6.25	3.75
(23)	Chas. Gehringer	30.00	15.00	9.00
(24)	John Gill	12.50	6.25	3.75
(25)	Charles Grimm	12.50	6.25	3.75
(26)	Mule Haas	12.50	6.25	3.75
(27)	Stanley Hack	12.50	6.25	3.75
(28)	Bill Hallahan	12.50	6.25	3.75
(29)	Melvin Harder	12.50	6.25	3.75
(30)	Gabby Hartnett	30.00	15.00	9.00
(31)	Ray Hayworth	12.50	6.25	3.75
(32)	Ralston Hemsley	12.50	6.25	3.75
(33)	Bill Herman	30.00	15.00	9.00
(34)	Frank Higgins	12.50	6.25	3.75
(35)	Carl Hubbell	40.00	20.00	12.00
(36)	Bill Jurges	12.50	6.25	3.75
(37)	Vernon Kennedy	12.50	6.25	3.75
(38)	Chuck Klein	30.00	15.00	9.00
(39)	Mike Kreevich	12.50	6.25	3.75
(40)	Bill Lee	12.50	6.25	3.75
(41)	Jos. Medwick	30.00	15.00	9.00
(42)	Van Mungo	12.50	6.25	3.75
(43)	James O'Dea	12.50	6.25	3.75
(44)	Mel Ott	50.00	25.00	15.00
(45)	Rip Radcliff	12.50	6.25	3.75
(46)	Pie Traynor	30.00	15.00	9.00

1948-50 Safe-T-Card

The earliest known safety issue is this series sponsored by a children's television show which was in turn sponsored by a Washington, D.C. auto dealer. Player selection and team indications on the cards point to a three-year (1948-50) range of issue dates for the cards. Minor differences in typography and information printed on the front probably differentiate the years of issue. All cards are about 2-1/2" x 3-1/2" with rounded corners. Fronts feature rather crude black-and-white drawings of the players with a facsimile autograph superimposed. A safety message is at top and, on most cards, the player's position and team are printed at bottom. Backs are printed in one of several colors and have a picture of the TV host and an ad for the program and its sponsors. The set is checklisted here alphabetically, though it's possible other cards may be added in the future. Only the baseball players from the set are listed here. Cards featuring football, basketball and other sports figures were also produced, along with cards for team executives, sports reporters and broadcasters.

		NM	EX	VG
Complete (Baseball) Set (21):		2,925	1,450	875.00
Common Player:		125.00	65.00	35.00
(1)	Ossie Bluege	125.00	65.00	35.00
(2)	Gil Coan	125.00	65.00	35.00
(3)	Sam Dente	125.00	65.00	35.00
(4)	Jake Early	125.00	65.00	35.00
(5)	Al Evans	125.00	65.00	35.00
(6)	Calvin Griffith	250.00	125.00	75.00
(7)	Clark Griffith	150.00	75.00	45.00
(8)	Bucky Harris	150.00	75.00	45.00
(9)	Sid Hudson	125.00	65.00	35.00
(10)	Joe Kuhel	125.00	65.00	35.00
(11)	Bob Lemon	150.00	75.00	45.00
(12)	Bill McGowan	400.00	200.00	120.00
(13)	George McQuinn	125.00	65.00	35.00
(14)	Don Newcombe	250.00	125.00	75.00
(15)	Joe Ostrowski	125.00	65.00	35.00
(16)	Sam Rice	150.00	75.00	45.00
(17)	Bert Shepard	150.00	75.00	45.00
(18)	Ray Scarborough	125.00	65.00	35.00
(19)	Mickey Vernon	125.00	65.00	35.00
(20)	Early Wynn	150.00	75.00	45.00
(21)	Eddie Yost	125.00	65.00	35.00

1976 Safelon Discs

One of several regional sponsors of player disc sets in 1976, Safelon, of New York, advertised its "Super Star Lunch Bags" in red and purple on the backs of its discs. The discs are 3-3/8" diameter with a black-and-white player portrait photo in the center of the baseball design. A line of red stars is above, while the left and right panels feature one of several bright colors. Produced by Michael Schechter Associates under license from the Major League Baseball Players Association, the player photos have had uniform and cap logos removed. The unnumbered checklist here is presented in alphabetical order.

		NM	EX	VG
Complete Set (70):		100.00	50.00	30.00
Common Player:		3.00	1.50	.90
(1)	Henry Aaron	17.50	8.75	5.25
(2)	Johnny Bench	9.00	4.50	2.75
(3)	Vida Blue	3.00	1.50	.90
(4)	Larry Bowa	3.00	1.50	.90

(5)	Lou Brock	6.00	3.00	1.75
(6)	Jeff Burroughs	3.00	1.50	.90
(7)	John Candelaria	3.00	1.50	.90
(8)	Jose Cardenal	3.00	1.50	.90
(9)	Rod Carew	6.00	3.00	1.75
(10)	Steve Carlton	6.00	3.00	1.75
(11)	Dave Cash	3.00	1.50	.90
(12)	Cesar Cedeno	3.00	1.50	.90
(13)	Ron Cey	3.00	1.50	.90
(14)	Carlton Fisk	6.00	3.00	1.75
(15)	Tito Fuentes	3.00	1.50	.90
(16)	Steve Garvey	4.50	2.25	1.25
(17)	Ken Griffey	3.00	1.50	.90
(18)	Don Gullett	3.00	1.50	.90
(19)	Willie Horton	3.00	1.50	.90
(20)	Al Hrabosky	3.00	1.50	.90
(21)	Catfish Hunter	6.00	3.00	1.75
(22)	Reggie Jackson (A's)	12.00	6.00	3.50
(23)	Randy Jones	3.00	1.50	.90
(24)	Jim Kaat	3.00	1.50	.90
(25)	Don Kessinger	3.00	1.50	.90
(26)	Dave Kingman	3.00	1.50	.90
(27)	Jerry Koosman	3.00	1.50	.90
(28)	Mickey Lolich	3.00	1.50	.90
(29)	Greg Luzinski	3.00	1.50	.90
(30)	Fred Lynn	3.00	1.50	.90
(31)	Bill Madlock	3.00	1.50	.90
(32)	Carlos May (White Sox)	3.00	1.50	.90
(33)	John Mayberry	3.00	1.50	.90
(34)	Bake McBride	3.00	1.50	.90
(35)	Doc Medich	3.00	1.50	.90
(36)	Andy Messersmith	3.00	1.50	.90
(37)	Rick Monday	3.00	1.50	.90
(38)	John Montefusco	3.00	1.50	.90
(39)	Jerry Morales	3.00	1.50	.90
(40)	Joe Morgan	6.00	3.00	1.75
(41)	Thurman Munson	5.00	2.50	1.50
(42)	Bobby Murcer	3.00	1.50	.90
(43)	Al Oliver	3.00	1.50	.90
(44)	Jim Palmer	6.00	3.00	1.75
(45)	Dave Parker	3.00	1.50	.90
(46)	Tony Perez	6.00	3.00	1.75
(47)	Jerry Reuss	3.00	1.50	.90
(48)	Brooks Robinson	9.00	4.50	2.75
(49)	Frank Robinson	9.00	4.50	2.75
(50)	Steve Rogers	3.00	1.50	.90
(51)	Pete Rose	15.00	7.50	4.50
(52)	Nolan Ryan	40.00	20.00	12.00
(53)	Manny Sanguillen	3.00	1.50	.90
(54)	Mike Schmidt	12.00	6.00	3.50
(55)	Tom Seaver	9.00	4.50	2.75
(56)	Ted Simmons	3.00	1.50	.90
(57)	Reggie Smith	3.00	1.50	.90
(58)	Willie Stargell	6.00	3.00	1.75
(59)	Rusty Staub	3.00	1.50	.90
(60)	Rennie Stennett	3.00	1.50	.90
(61)	Don Sutton	6.00	3.00	1.75
(62)	Andy Thornton (Cubs)	3.00	1.50	.90
(63)	Luis Tiant	3.00	1.50	.90
(64)	Joe Torre	3.00	1.50	.90
(65)	Mike Tyson	3.00	1.50	.90
(66)	Bob Watson	3.00	1.50	.90
(67)	Wilbur Wood	3.00	1.50	.90
(68)	Jimmy Wynn	3.00	1.50	.90
(69)	Carl Yastrzemski	9.00	4.50	2.75
(70)	Richie Zisk	3.00	1.50	.90

(16)	Ron Cey	12.50	6.25	3.75
(17)	Dave Concepcion	12.50	6.25	3.75
(18)	Dennis Eckersley	35.00	17.50	10.50
(19)	Mark Fidrych	17.50	8.75	5.25
(20)	Rollie Fingers	35.00	17.50	10.50
(21)	Carlton Fisk	35.00	17.50	10.50
(22)	George Foster	12.50	6.25	3.75
(23)	Wayne Garland	12.50	6.25	3.75
(24)	Ralph Garr	12.50	6.25	3.75
(25)	Steve Garvey	25.00	12.50	7.50
(26)	Cesar Geronimo	12.50	6.25	3.75
(27)	Bobby Grich	12.50	6.25	3.75
(28)	Ken Griffey Sr.	12.50	6.25	3.75
(29)	Don Gullett	12.50	6.25	3.75
(30)	Mike Hargrove	12.50	6.25	3.75
(31)	Al Hrabosky	12.50	6.25	3.75
(32)	Jim Hunter	35.00	17.50	10.50
(33)	Reggie Jackson	50.00	25.00	15.00
(34)	Randy Jones	12.50	6.25	3.75
(35)	Dave Kingman	15.00	7.50	4.50
(36)	Jerry Koosman	12.50	6.25	3.75
(37)	Dave LaRoche	12.50	6.25	3.75
(38)	Greg Luzinski	12.50	6.25	3.75
(39)	Fred Lynn	12.50	6.25	3.75
(40)	Bill Madlock	12.50	6.25	3.75
(41)	Rick Manning	12.50	6.25	3.75
(42)	Jon Matlock	12.50	6.25	3.75
(43)	John Mayberry	12.50	6.25	3.75
(44)	Hal McRae	12.50	6.25	3.75
(45)	Andy Messersmith	12.50	6.25	3.75
(46)	Rick Monday	12.50	6.25	3.75
(47)	John Montefusco	12.50	6.25	3.75
(48)	Joe Morgan	35.00	17.50	10.50
(49)	Thurman Munson	30.00	15.00	9.00
(50)	Bobby Murcer	12.50	6.25	3.75
(51)	Bill North	12.50	6.25	3.75
(52)	Jim Palmer	35.00	17.50	10.50
(53)	Tony Perez	35.00	17.50	10.50
(54)	Jerry Reuss	12.50	6.25	3.75
(55)	Brooks Robinson	40.00	20.00	12.00
(56)	Pete Rose	110.00	55.00	33.00
(57)	Joe Rudi	12.50	6.25	3.75
(58)	Nolan Ryan	135.00	67.00	40.00
(59)	Manny Sanguillen	12.50	6.25	3.75
(60)	Mike Schmidt	75.00	37.00	22.00
(61)	Tom Seaver	40.00	20.00	12.00
(62)	Bill Singer	12.50	6.25	3.75
(63)	Willie Stargell	35.00	17.50	10.50
(64)	Rusty Staub	15.00	7.50	4.50
(65)	Luis Tiant	12.50	6.25	3.75
(66)	Bob Watson	12.50	6.25	3.75
(67)	Butch Wynegar	12.50	6.25	3.75
(68)	Carl Yastrzemski	40.00	20.00	12.00
(69)	Robin Yount	35.00	17.50	10.50
(70)	Richie Zisk	12.50	6.25	3.75

1978 Saga Discs

One player from each major league team was selected for inclusion in this disc set distributed by Saga, a provider of school lunches; discs were given one per lunch purchase at selected schools. The 3-3/8" diameter discs have a sepia-toned player portrait photo at center within a white diamond and surrounded by a brightly colored border with four colored stars at top. Licensed by the players' association through Michael Schechter Associates, the photos have had uniform logos removed. Backs are nearly identical to the previous year, but printed in red. The unnumbered Saga discs are checklisted here according to the numbers found on the Big T/Tastee Freeze versions.

		NM	EX	VG
Complete Set (26):		130.00	65.00	40.00
Common Player:		6.00	3.00	1.75
(1)	Buddy Bell	6.00	3.00	1.75
(2)	Jim Palmer	12.50	6.25	3.75
(3)	Steve Garvey	7.50	3.75	2.25
(4)	Jeff Burroughs	6.00	3.00	1.75
(5)	Greg Luzinski	6.00	3.00	1.75
(6)	Lou Brock	12.50	6.25	3.75
(7)	Thurman Munson	10.00	5.00	3.00
(8)	Rod Carew	12.50	6.25	3.75
(9)	George Brett	50.00	25.00	15.00
(10)	Tom Seaver	15.00	7.50	4.50
(11)	Willie Stargell	12.50	6.25	3.75
(12)	Jerry Koosman	6.00	3.00	1.75
(13)	Bill North	6.00	3.00	1.75
(14)	Richie Zisk	6.00	3.00	1.75
(15)	Bill Madlock	6.00	3.00	1.75
(16)	Carl Yastrzemski	15.00	7.50	4.50
(17)	Dave Cash	6.00	3.00	1.75
(18)	Bob Watson	6.00	3.00	1.75
(19)	Dave Kingman	6.50	3.25	2.00
(20)	Gene Tenance (Tenace)	6.00	3.00	1.75
(21)	Ralph Garr	6.00	3.00	1.75
(22)	Mark Fidrych	6.50	3.25	2.00
(23)	Frank Tanana	6.00	3.00	1.75
(24)	Larry Hisle	6.00	3.00	1.75
(25)	Bruce Bochte	6.00	3.00	1.75
(26)	Bob Bailor	6.00	3.00	1.75

1977 Saga Discs

Virtually identical in format to the several locally sponsored disc sets of the previous year, these 3-3/8" diameter player discs were given away with the purchase of school lunches in the Philadelphia area. They are the scarcest of the 1977 disc sets. Discs once again feature black-and-white player portrait photos in the center of a baseball design. The left and right panels are in one of several bright colors. Licensed by the players' association through Mike Schechter Associates, the player photos carry no uniform logos. Backs are printed in orange with background art of a sunrise over the mountains. The unnumbered discs are checklisted here alphabetically.

		NM	EX	VG
Complete Set (70):		850.00	425.00	250.00
Common Player:		12.50	6.25	3.75
(1)	Sal Bando	12.50	6.25	3.75
(2)	Buddy Bell	12.50	6.25	3.75
(3)	Johnny Bench	40.00	20.00	12.00
(4)	Larry Bowa	12.50	6.25	3.75
(5)	Steve Braun	12.50	6.25	3.75
(6)	George Brett	125.00	62.00	37.00
(7)	Lou Brock	35.00	17.50	10.50
(8)	Jeff Burroughs	12.50	6.25	3.75
(9)	Bert Campaneris	12.50	6.25	3.75
(10)	John Candelaria	12.50	6.25	3.75
(11)	Jose Cardenal	12.50	6.25	3.75
(12)	Rod Carew	35.00	17.50	10.50
(13)	Steve Carlton	35.00	17.50	10.50
(14)	Dave Cash	12.50	6.25	3.75
(15)	Cesar Cedeno	12.50	6.25	3.75

1962 John Sain Spinner Promotional Postcard

The attributed date of issue is approximate. This 3-7/16" x 5-7/16" color postcard was issued to promote the John Sain Spinner, a device to teach pitching mechanics. The front pictures the Yankees pitching coach in four views demonstrating the device, which is itself pictured at top. Black-and-white back is in traditional postcard divided-back format with information on the spinner and ordering information.

	NM	EX	VG
John Sain	15.00	7.50	4.50

1962 Salada-Junket Coins

These 1-3/8" diameter plastic coins were issued in packages of Salada Tea and Junket Pudding mix. There are 221 different players available, with variations bringing the total of different coins to 265. Each coin has a paper color photo inserted in the front which contains the player's name and position plus the coin number. The plastic rims come in six different colors, coded by team. Production began with 180 coins, but the addition of the New York Mets and Houston Colt .45's to the National League allowed the company to expand the set's size. Twenty expansion players were added along with 21 other players. Several players' coins were dropped after the initial 180 run, causing some scarcities. Embossed green plastic shields into which 10 coins could be placed were available via a mail-in offer. About 9" x 10-1/2", the shields have a banner near the top with the team name. Many of the players in the 180 series can be found with variations in the placement of the front typography relative to the colored portrait. Though these variations seem to affect a tiny percentage of some players' 180 coins, they are in most cases too difficult to distinguish except by direct comparison between specimens and are of interest only to the most dedicated Salada collectors.

		NM	EX	VG
Complete Set, no variations (221):		3,000	1,500	900.00
Complete Set, w/ variations (265):		6,500	3,250	2,000
Complete Boxed Presentation Set (180):		1,900	950.00	575.00
Complete Boxed Presentation Set (200):		2,600	1,300	800.00
Uncut Sheet (180):		1,800	900.00	550.00
Common Player (1-180):		4.00	2.00	1.25
Common Player (181-221):		10.00	5.00	3.00
Team Shield (Empty):		60.00	30.00	18.00
1	Jim Gentile	5.00	2.50	1.50
2	Bill Pierce	65.00	32.50	20.00
3a	Chico Fernandez (Light blue jersey piping.)	4.00	2.00	1.25
3b	Chico Fernandez (Dark blue jersey piping.)	12.00	6.00	3.50
4	Tom Brewer	15.00	7.50	4.50
5	Woody Held	4.00	2.00	1.25
6	Ray Herbert	22.50	11.00	7.00
7a	Ken Aspromonte (Angels)	10.00	5.00	3.00
7b	Ken Aspromonte (Indians)	10.00	5.00	3.00
8	Whitey Ford	20.00	10.00	6.00
9	Jim Lemon	4.00	2.00	1.25
10	Billy Klaus	4.00	2.00	1.25
11	Steve Barber	27.50	13.50	8.25
12	Nellie Fox	17.50	8.75	5.25
13	Jim Bunning	15.00	7.50	4.50
14	Frank Malzone	5.00	2.50	1.50
15	Tito Francona	4.00	2.00	1.25
16	Bobby Del Greco	4.00	2.00	1.25

17a	Steve Bilko (Red shirt buttons.)	9.00	4.50	2.75
17b	Steve Bilko (White shirt buttons.)	9.00	4.50	2.75
18	Tony Kubek	35.00	17.50	10.00
19	Earl Battey	4.00	2.00	1.25
20	Chuck Cottier	4.00	2.00	1.25
21	Willie Tasby	4.00	2.00	1.25
22	Bob Allison	6.00	3.00	1.75
23	Roger Maris	25.00	12.50	7.50
24a	Earl Averill (Red shirt buttons.)	9.00	4.50	2.75
24b	Earl Averill (White shirt buttons.)	5.00	2.50	1.50
25	Jerry Lumpe	4.00	2.00	1.25
26	Jim Grant	17.50	8.75	5.25
27	Carl Yastrzemski	30.00	15.00	9.00
28a	Rocky Colavito (Light blue jersey piping.)	20.00	10.00	6.00
28b	Rocky Colavito (Dark blue jersey piping.)	12.50	6.25	3.75
29	Al Smith	4.00	2.00	1.25
30	Jim Busby	30.00	15.00	9.00
31	Dick Howser	4.00	2.00	1.25
32	Jim Perry	4.00	2.00	1.25
33	Yogi Berra	25.00	12.50	7.50
34a	Ken Hamlin (Red shirt buttons.)	7.00	3.50	2.00
34b	Ken Hamlin (White shirt buttons.)	4.00	2.00	1.25
35	Dale Long	4.00	2.00	1.25
36	Harmon Killebrew	20.00	10.00	6.00
37a	Dick Brown (Light blue jersey piping.)	12.00	6.00	3.50
37b	Dick Brown (Dark blue jersey piping.)	4.00	2.00	1.25
38	Gary Geiger	4.00	2.00	1.25
39a	Minnie Minoso (White Sox)	20.00	10.00	6.00
39b	Minnie Minoso (Cardinals)	9.00	4.50	2.75
40	Brooks Robinson	20.00	10.00	6.00
41	Mickey Mantle	70.00	35.00	20.00
42	Bennie Daniels	4.00	2.00	1.25
43	Billy Martin	12.00	6.00	3.50
44	Vic Power	5.00	2.50	1.50
45	Joe Pignatano	4.00	2.00	1.25
46a	Ryne Duren (Red shirt buttons.)	9.00	4.50	2.75
46b	Ryne Duren (White shirt buttons.)	8.00	4.00	2.50
47a	Pete Runnels (2B)	12.00	6.00	3.50
47b	Pete Runnels (1B)	7.50	3.75	2.25
48a	Dick Williams (Name on right.)	1,800	900.00	550.00
48b	Dick Williams (Name on left.)	4.00	2.00	1.25
49	Jim Landis	4.00	2.00	1.25
50	Steve Boros	4.00	2.00	1.25
51a	Zoilo Versalles (Red shirt buttons.)	7.00	3.50	2.00
51b	Zoilo Versalles (White shirt buttons.)	7.00	3.50	2.00
52a	Johnny Temple (Indians)	12.50	6.25	3.75
52b	Johnny Temple (Orioles)	5.00	2.50	1.50
53a	Jackie Brandt (Oriole)	15.00	7.50	4.50
53b	Jackie Brandt (Orioles)	1,600	800.00	475.00
54	Joe McClain	4.00	2.00	1.25
55	Sherman Lollar	5.00	2.50	1.50
56	Gene Stephens	4.00	2.00	1.25
57a	Leon Wagner (Red shirt buttons.)	7.00	3.50	2.00
57b	Leon Wagner (White shirt buttons.)	5.00	2.50	1.50
58	Frank Lary	6.00	3.00	1.75
59	Bill Skowron	10.00	5.00	3.00
60	Vic Wertz	20.00	10.00	6.00
61	Willie Kirkland	4.00	2.00	1.25
62	Leo Posada	4.00	2.00	1.25
63a	Albie Pearson (Red shirt buttons.)	9.00	4.50	2.75
63b	Albie Pearson (White shirt buttons.)	8.00	4.00	2.50
64	Bobby Richardson	15.00	7.50	4.50
65a	Marv Breeding (SS)	9.00	4.50	2.75
65b	Marv Breeding (2B)	12.00	6.00	3.50
66	Roy Sievers	70.00	35.00	20.00
67	Al Kaline	25.00	12.50	7.50
68a	Don Buddin (Red Sox)	15.00	7.50	4.50
68b	Don Buddin (Colts)	5.00	2.50	1.50
69a	Lenny Green (Red shirt buttons.)	8.00	4.00	2.50
69b	Lenny Green (White shirt buttons.)	6.00	3.00	1.75
70	Gene Green	40.00	20.00	12.00
71	Luis Aparicio	12.00	6.00	3.50
72	Norm Cash	16.00	8.00	4.75
73	Jackie Jensen	20.00	10.00	6.00
74	Bubba Phillips	6.00	3.00	1.75
75	Jim Archer	4.00	2.00	1.25
76a	Ken Hunt (Red shirt buttons.)	9.00	4.50	2.75
76b	Ken Hunt (White shirt buttons)	4.00	2.00	1.25
77	Ralph Terry	4.00	2.00	1.25
78	Camilo Pascual	4.00	2.00	1.25
79	Marty Keough	27.50	13.50	8.25
80	Cletis Boyer	10.00	5.00	3.00
81	Jim Pagliaroni	4.00	2.00	1.25
82a	Gene Leek (Red shirt buttons.)	9.00	4.50	2.75
82b	Gene Leek (White shirt buttons.)	4.00	2.00	1.25
83	Jake Wood	5.00	2.50	1.50
84	Coot Veal	25.00	12.50	7.50
85	Norm Siebern	5.00	2.50	1.50
86a	Andy Carey (White Sox)	25.00	12.50	7.50
86b	Andy Carey (Phillies)	9.00	4.50	2.75
87a	Bill Tuttle (Red shirt buttons.)	9.00	4.50	2.75
87b	Bill Tuttle (White shirt buttons.)	25.00	12.50	7.50
88a	Jimmy Piersall (Indians)	20.00	10.00	6.00
88b	Jimmy Piersall (Senators)	20.00	10.00	6.00
89	Ron Hansen	25.00	12.50	7.50
90a	Chuck Stobbs (Red shirt buttons.)	8.00	4.00	2.50
90b	Chuck Stobbs (White shirt buttons.)	4.00	2.00	1.25
91a	Ken McBride (Red shirt buttons.)	9.00	4.50	2.75
91b	Ken McBride (White shirt buttons.)	7.50	3.75	2.25
92	Bill Bruton	4.00	2.00	1.25
93	Gus Triandos	4.00	2.00	1.25
94	John Romano	4.00	2.00	1.25
95	Elston Howard	10.00	5.00	3.00
96	Gene Woodling	6.00	3.00	1.75
97a	Early Wynn (Pitching pose.)	45.00	22.00	13.50
97b	Early Wynn/Portrait	15.00	7.50	4.50
98	Milt Pappas	4.00	2.00	1.25
99	Bill Monbouquette	4.00	2.00	1.25
100	Wayne Causey	4.00	2.00	1.25
101	Don Elston	4.00	2.00	1.25
102a	Charlie Neal (Dodgers)	12.00	6.00	3.50
102b	Charlie Neal (Mets)	4.00	2.00	1.25
103	Don Blasingame	4.00	2.00	1.25
104	Frank Thomas	30.00	15.00	9.00
105	Wes Covington	4.00	2.00	1.25
106	Chuck Hiller	5.00	2.50	1.50
107	Don Hoak	4.00	2.00	1.25
108a	Bob Lillis (Cardinals)	27.50	13.50	8.25
108b	Bob Lillis (Colts)	4.00	2.00	1.25
109	Sandy Koufax	30.00	15.00	9.00
110	Gordy Coleman	4.00	2.00	1.25
111	Ed Matthews (Mathews)	20.00	10.00	6.00
112	Art Mahaffey	4.00	2.00	1.25
113a	Ed Bailey (Partial left shoulder; "C" level w/ear.)	1,400	700.00	425.00
113b	Ed Bailey (Full left shoulder; second button red.)	10.00	5.00	3.00
113c	Ed Bailey (Full left shoulder; second button white.)	4.00	2.00	1.25
114	Smoky Burgess	7.00	3.50	2.00
115	Bill White	6.00	3.00	1.75
116	Ed Bouchee	25.00	12.50	7.50
117	Bob Buhl	8.00	4.00	2.50
118	Vada Pinson	4.00	2.00	1.25
119	Carl Sawatski	4.00	2.00	1.25
120	Dick Stuart	6.00	3.00	1.75
121	Harvey Kuenn	40.00	20.00	12.00
122	Pancho Herrera	4.00	2.00	1.25
123a	Don Zimmer (Cubs)	12.50	6.25	3.75
123b	Don Zimmer (Mets)	5.00	2.50	1.50
124	Wally Moon	6.00	3.00	1.75
125	Joe Adcock	9.00	4.50	2.75
126	Joey Jay	4.00	2.00	1.25
127a	Maury Wills (Blue "3" on shirt.)	10.00	5.00	3.00
127b	Maury Wills (Red "3" on shirt.)	10.00	5.00	3.00
128	George Altman	4.00	2.00	1.25
129a	John Buzhardt (Phillies)	30.00	15.00	9.00
129b	John Buzhardt (White Sox)	10.00	5.00	3.00
130	Felipe Alou	4.00	2.00	1.25
131	Bill Mazeroski	15.00	7.50	4.50
132	Ernie Broglio	4.00	2.00	1.25
133	John Roseboro	4.00	2.00	1.25
134	Mike McCormick	4.00	2.00	1.25
135a	Chuck Smith (Phillies)	15.00	7.50	4.50
135b	Chuck Smith (White Sox)	10.00	5.00	3.00
136	Ron Santo	12.00	6.00	3.50
137	Gene Freese	4.00	2.00	1.25
138	Dick Groat	5.00	2.50	1.50
139	Curt Flood	4.00	2.00	1.25
140	Frank Bolling	4.00	2.00	1.25
141	Clay Dalrymple	4.00	2.00	1.25
142	Willie McCovey	16.00	8.00	4.75
143	Bob Skinner	4.00	2.00	1.25
144	Lindy McDaniel	4.00	2.00	1.25
145	Glen Hobbie	4.00	2.00	1.25
146a	Gil Hodges (Dodgers)	30.00	15.00	9.00
146b	Gil Hodges (Mets)	22.50	11.00	6.75
147	Eddie Kasko	4.00	2.00	1.25
148	Gino Cimoli	25.00	12.50	7.50
149	Willie Mays	30.00	15.00	9.00
150	Roberto Clemente	55.00	27.50	16.50
151	Red Schoendienst	15.00	7.50	4.50
152	Joe Torre	5.00	2.50	1.50
153	Bob Purkey	4.00	2.00	1.25
154a	Tommy Davis (3B)	7.50	3.75	2.25
154b	Tommy Davis (OF)	12.00	6.00	3.50
155a	Andre Rogers (Incorrect spelling, 1B.)	7.50	3.75	2.25
155b	Andre Rodgers (Correct spelling, SS.)	12.00	6.00	3.50
156	Tony Taylor	4.00	2.00	1.25
157	Bob Friend	4.00	2.00	1.25
158a	Gus Bell (Redlegs)	20.00	10.00	6.00
158b	Gus Bell (Mets)	4.00	2.00	1.25
159	Roy McMillan	4.00	2.00	1.25
160	Carl Warwick	4.00	2.00	1.25
161	Willie Davis	4.00	2.00	1.25
162	Sam Jones	60.00	30.00	18.00
163	Ruben Amaro	6.00	3.00	1.75
164	Sam Taylor	4.00	2.00	1.25
165	Frank Robinson	15.00	7.50	4.50
166	Lou Burdette	5.00	2.50	1.50
167	Ken Boyer	13.50	6.75	4.00
168	Bill Virdon	4.00	2.00	1.25
169	Jim Davenport	4.00	2.00	1.25
170	Don Demeter	4.00	2.00	1.25
171	Richie Ashburn	40.00	20.00	12.00
172	John Podres	8.00	4.00	2.50
173a	Joe Cunningham (Cardinals)	30.00	15.00	9.00
173b	Joe Cunningham (White Sox)	12.50	6.25	3.75
174	ElRoy Face	5.00	2.50	1.50
175	Orlando Cepeda	12.00	6.00	3.50
176a	Bobby Gene Smith (Phillies)	15.00	7.50	4.50
176b	Bobby Gene Smith (Mets)	6.00	3.00	1.75
177a	Ernie Banks (OF)	25.00	12.50	7.50
177b	Ernie Banks (SS)	20.00	10.00	6.00
178a	Daryl Spencer (3B)	20.00	10.00	6.00
178b	Daryl Spencer (1B)	12.00	6.00	3.50
179	Bob Schmidt	25.00	12.50	7.50
180	Hank Aaron	35.00	17.50	10.50
181	Hobie Landrith	10.00	5.00	3.00
182a	Ed Broussard (Bressoud)	400.00	200.00	120.00
182b	Ed Bressoud	25.00	12.50	7.50
183	Felix Mantilla	10.00	5.00	3.00
184	Dick Farrell	10.00	5.00	3.00
185	Bob Miller	10.00	5.00	3.00
186	Don Taussig	15.00	7.50	4.50
187	Pumpsie Green	10.00	5.00	3.00
188	Bobby Shantz	10.00	5.00	3.00
189	Roger Craig	10.00	5.00	3.00
190	Hal Smith	10.00	5.00	3.00
191	John Edwards	10.00	5.00	3.00
192	John DeMerit	10.00	5.00	3.00
193	Joe Amalfitano	10.00	5.00	3.00
194	Norm Larker	10.00	5.00	3.00
195	Al Heist	10.00	5.00	3.00
196	Al Spangler	10.00	5.00	3.00
197	Alex Grammas	10.00	5.00	3.00
198	Gerry Lynch	10.00	5.00	3.00
199	Jim McKnight	15.00	7.50	4.50
200	Jose Pagen (Pagan)	10.00	5.00	3.00
201	Junior Gilliam	20.00	10.00	6.00
202	Art Ditmar	10.00	5.00	3.00
203	Pete Daley	10.00	5.00	3.00
204	Johnny Callison	20.00	10.00	6.00
205	Stu Miller	10.00	5.00	3.00
206	Russ Snyder	10.00	5.00	3.00
207	Billy Williams	25.00	12.50	7.50
208	Walter Bond	10.00	5.00	3.00
209	Joe Koppe	10.00	5.00	3.00
210	Don Schwall	16.00	8.00	4.75
211	Billy Gardner	15.00	7.50	4.50
212	Chuck Estrada	10.00	5.00	3.00
213	Gary Bell	15.00	7.50	4.50
214	Floyd Robinson	10.00	5.00	3.00
215	Duke Snider	25.00	12.50	7.50
216	Lee Maye	10.00	5.00	3.00
217	Howie Bedell	10.00	5.00	3.00
218	Bob Will	10.00	5.00	3.00
219	Dallas Green	15.00	7.50	4.50
220	Carroll Hardy	15.00	7.50	4.50
221	Danny O'Connell	10.00	5.00	3.00

1962 Salada-Junket Coins - Clip Back

A very rare version of the Salada Tea/Junket Dessert plastic coins exists in a clip-back format. An extruded tab at back center would allow the coin to be slid onto a cap bill or shirt flap as a decoration. With the exception of Averill (Angels), all clip-back Saladas confirmed thus far depict Boston Red Sox players. It has been reported that the clip-back coins were created for use in Opening Day stadium promotions by the Red Sox, Yankees and Mets.

Common Player:		NM	EX	VG
14	Frank Malzone	450.00	225.00	135.00
24	Earl Averill	450.00	225.00	135.00
27	Carl Yastrzemski	600.00	300.00	180.00
38	Gary Geiger	450.00	225.00	135.00
47	Pete Runnels	450.00	225.00	135.00
73	Jackie Jensen	450.00	225.00	135.00
81	Jim Pagliaroni	450.00	225.00	135.00
99	Bill Monbouquette	450.00	225.00	135.00
182	Ed Broussard (Bressoud)	450.00	225.00	135.00
187	Pumpsie Green	450.00	225.00	135.00
210	Don Schwall	450.00	225.00	135.00
220	Carroll Hardy	450.00	225.00	135.00

1963 Salada-Junket Coins

A much smaller set of baseball coins was issued by Salada/Junket in 1963. The 63 coins issued were called "All-Star Baseball Coins" and included most of the top players of the day. Unlike 1962, the coins were made of metal and measured a slightly larger 1-1/2" diameter. American League players have blue rims on their coins, while National Leaguers are rimmed in red.

Coin fronts contain no printing on the full-color player photos, while backs list coin number, player name, team and position, along with brief statistics and the sponsors' logos.

		NM	EX	VG
Complete Set (63):		650.00	325.00	200.00
Common Player:		6.00	3.00	1.75
1	Don Drysdale	12.50	6.25	3.75
2	Dick Farrell	6.00	3.00	1.75
3	Bob Gibson	12.50	6.25	3.75
4	Sandy Koufax	35.00	17.50	10.00
5a	Juan Marichal (No buttons.)	12.50	6.25	3.75
5b	Juan Marichal	10.00	5.00	3.00
	(Jersey buttons.)			
6	Bob Purkey	6.00	3.00	1.75
7	Bob Shaw	6.00	3.00	1.75
8	Warren Spahn	12.50	6.25	3.75
9	Johnny Podres	7.50	3.75	2.25
10	Art Mahaffey	6.00	3.00	1.75
11	Del Crandall	6.00	3.00	1.75
12	John Roseboro	6.00	3.00	1.75
13	Orlando Cepeda	10.00	5.00	3.00
14	Bill Mazeroski	10.00	5.00	3.00
15	Ken Boyer	7.50	3.75	2.25
16	Dick Groat	6.00	3.00	1.75
17	Ernie Banks	15.00	7.50	4.50
18	Frank Bolling	6.00	3.00	1.75
19	Jim Davenport	6.00	3.00	1.75
20	Maury Wills	7.50	3.75	2.25
21	Tommy Davis	6.00	3.00	1.75
22	Willie Mays	35.00	17.50	10.00
23	Roberto Clemente	45.00	22.50	13.50
24	Henry Aaron	30.00	15.00	9.00
25	Felipe Alou	7.50	3.75	2.25
26	Johnny Callison	6.00	3.00	1.75
27	Richie Ashburn	12.50	6.25	3.75
28	Eddie Mathews	12.50	6.25	3.75
29	Frank Robinson	10.00	5.00	3.00
30	Billy Williams	10.00	5.00	3.00
31	George Altman	6.00	3.00	1.75
32	Hank Aguirre	6.00	3.00	1.75
33	Jim Bunning	10.00	5.00	3.00
34	Dick Donovan	6.00	3.00	1.75
35	Bill Monbouquette	6.00	3.00	1.75
36	Camilo Pascual	6.00	3.00	1.75
37	David Stenhouse	6.00	3.00	1.75
38	Ralph Terry	6.00	3.00	1.75
39	Hoyt Wilhelm	10.00	5.00	3.00
40	Jim Kaat	7.50	3.75	2.25
41	Ken McBride	6.00	3.00	1.75
42	Ray Herbert	6.00	3.00	1.75
43	Milt Pappas	6.00	3.00	1.75
44	Earl Battey	6.00	3.00	1.75
45	Elston Howard	7.50	3.75	2.25
46	John Romano	6.00	3.00	1.75
47	Jim Gentile	6.00	3.00	1.75
48	Billy Moran	6.00	3.00	1.75
49	Rich Rollins	6.00	3.00	1.75
50	Luis Aparicio	10.00	5.00	3.00
51	Norm Siebern	6.00	3.00	1.75
52	Bobby Richardson	7.50	3.75	2.25
53	Brooks Robinson	15.00	7.50	4.50
54	Tom Tresh	7.50	3.75	2.25
55	Leon Wagner	6.00	3.00	1.75
56	Mickey Mantle	85.00	45.00	25.00
57	Roger Maris	25.00	12.50	7.50
58	Rocky Colavito	20.00	10.00	6.00
59	Lee Thomas	6.00	3.00	1.75
60	Jim Landis	6.00	3.00	1.75
61	Pete Runnels	6.00	3.00	1.75
62	Yogi Berra	22.50	11.00	6.75
63	Al Kaline	15.00	7.50	4.50

1961 Sam's Family Restaurants Roger Maris

This postcard was issued to commemorate the presentation of Roger Maris' historic 61st home run ball back to the slugger. Pictured with Maris on this color 3-1/2" x 5-1/2" postcard is Sam Gordon, owner of a chain of family restaurants in northern California. Gordon purchased the ball from the fan who caught it, Sal Durante, and flew Durante and his wife, and Maris to Sacramento where he paid $5,000 for the ball and presented it to Maris, who later donated it to the Hall of Fame. On front is a borderless color photo of the presentation. Back has the historical details and the traditional postcard indicia.

		NM	EX	VG
61	Roger Maris, Sam Gordon	50.00	25.00	15.00

1886 W.H. Sanders New York Baseball Club (H812)

This rare 19th Century baseball issue can be classified under the general category of "trade" cards, a popular advertising vehicle of the period. The cards measure 3" x 4-3/4" and feature blue line-drawing portraits of members of the "New York Base Ball Club," which is printed along the top. As was common with this type of trade card, the bottom was left blank to accomodate various messages. The known examples of this set carry ads for local tobacco merchants and other businesses. The portraits are all based on the photographs used in the 1886 Old Judge set. The cards, which were assigned an ACC designation of H812, are printed on thin paper rather than cardboard.

(See 1889 New York Baseball Club for checklist and values.)

1969 San Diego Padres Premium Pictures

Unlike most of the contemporary large-format (8-1/2" x 11") premium pictures, this issue carries no advertising and appears to have been a team-issue in the Padres inaugural year. Fronts feature large portraits and smaller action pictures of the player against a dark background with a facsimile auto-graph at the bottom and the player's name printed in the white bottom border. The signature of the artist appears in the lower-left corner. The artwork was done by Nicholas Volpe, who produced many similar items for teams in all sports in the '60s, '70s and '80s. Backs have a large team logo at center and a sketch of the artist at bottom. There is evidence to suggest that the picture of Cito Gaston is scarcer than the other seven.

		NM	EX	VG
Complete Set (8):		60.00	30.00	18.00
Common Player:		7.50	3.75	2.25
(1)	Ollie Brown	7.50	3.75	2.25
(2)	Tommy Dean	7.50	3.75	2.25
(3)	Al Ferrara	7.50	3.75	2.25
(4)	Clarence Gaston	10.00	5.00	3.00
(5)	Preston Gomez	7.50	3.75	2.25
(6)	Johnny Podres	9.00	4.50	2.75
(7)	Al Santorini	7.50	3.75	2.25
(8)	Ed Spiezio	7.50	3.75	2.25

1977 San Diego Padres Schedule Cards

Members of the 1977 San Diego Padres, players and management, are featured in this set. The 2-1/4" x 3-3/8" cards are printed in brown on thin white stock. Fronts have a player photo with a pinstripe around and the team and player name at bottom. Backs have the team logo at top, a list of promotional dates in the center and ticket information at bottom. While some card

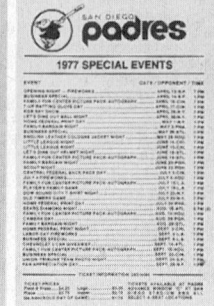

backs state "One in a Series of 40 Player Photos," more than 80 variations are known, including some poses with blank backs. The unnumbered cards are checklisted here in alphabetical order, within three types differentiated by back printing.

		NM	EX	VG
Complete Set (89):		60.00	30.00	18.00
Common Player:		1.00	.50	.30
Type 1 - "Series of 40"				
(1)	Bill Almon	1.00	.50	.30
(2)	Joe Amalfitano	1.00	.50	.30
(3)	Buzzy Bavasi/GM	1.00	.50	.30
(4)	Vic Bernal	1.00	.50	.30
(5)	Mike Champion	1.00	.50	.30
(6)	Billy Champion, Bill Almon	1.00	.50	.30
(7)	Roger Craig	1.00	.50	.30
(8)	John D'Acquisto	1.00	.50	.30
(9)	Bob Davis	1.00	.50	.30
(10)	Rollie Fingers	3.00	1.50	.90
(11)	Dave Freisleben	1.00	.50	.30
(12)	Tom Griffin	1.00	.50	.30
(13)	George Hendrick	1.00	.50	.30
(14)	Enzo Hernandez	1.00	.50	.30
(15)	Mike Ivie	1.00	.50	.30
(16)	Randy Jones	1.00	.50	.30
	(Follow-through.)			
(17)	Randy Jones	1.00	.50	.30
	(Cy Young Award)			
(18)	John McNamara	1.00	.50	.30
(19)	Luis Melendez	1.00	.50	.30
(20)	Butch Metzger	1.00	.50	.30
(21)	Bob Owchinko	1.00	.50	.30
(22)	Doug Rader	1.00	.50	.30
(23)	Merv Rettenmund	1.00	.50	.30
(24)	Gene Richards	1.00	.50	.30
(25)	Dave Roberts	1.00	.50	.30
(26)	Rick Sawyer	1.00	.50	.30
(27)	Bob Shirley	1.00	.50	.30
(28)	Bob Skinner	1.00	.50	.30
(29)	Dan Spillner	1.00	.50	.30
(30)	Brent Strom	1.00	.50	.30
(31)	Gary Sutherland	1.00	.50	.30
(32)	Gene Tenace	1.00	.50	.30
(33)	Dave Tomlin	1.00	.50	.30
(34)	Jerry Turner	1.00	.50	.30
(35)	Bobby Valentine	1.00	.50	.30
(36)	Dan Wehrmeister	1.00	.50	.30
(37)	Whitey Wietelmann	1.00	.50	.30
(38)	Don Williams	1.00	.50	.30
(39)	Dave Winfield (One bat.)	10.00	5.00	3.00
(40)	Dave Winfield (Two bats.)	5.00	2.50	1.50
Type 2 - No "Series of 40"				
(1)	Bill Almon	1.00	.50	.30
(2)	Matty Alou	1.00	.50	.30
(3)	Steve Arlin (Glove to ches.)	1.00	.50	.30
(4)	Steve Arlin (Follow-through.)	1.00	.50	.30
(5)	Bob Barton	1.00	.50	.30
(6)	Glenn Beckert	1.50	.75	.45
(7)	Ollie Brown	1.00	.50	.30
(8)	Dave Campbell	1.00	.50	.30
	(Bat on shoulder.)			
(9)	Dave Campbell/Kneeling	1.00	.50	.30
(10)	Enzo Hernandez,	1.00	.50	.30
	Nate Colbert			
(11)	Nate Colbert	1.00	.50	.30
(12)	Colbert and Friend	1.00	.50	.30
	(With child.)			
(13)	Jerry Coleman/Announcer	1.00	.50	.30
(14)	Willie Davis	1.00	.50	.30
(15)	Jim Eakle ("TUBA MAN")	1.00	.50	.30
(16)	Rollie Fingers	3.00	1.50	.90
(17)	Cito Gaston (Bare hands.)	1.00	.50	.30
(18)	Cito Gaston (Batting gloves.)	1.00	.50	.30
(19)	Johnny Grubb	1.00	.50	.30
(20)	George Hendrick	1.00	.50	.30
(21)	Mike Ivie	1.00	.50	.30
(22)	Fred Kendall/Btg	1.00	.50	.30
(23)	Fred Kendall (Holding ball.)	1.00	.50	.30
(24)	Clay Kirby (Follow-through.)	1.00	.50	.30
(25)	Clay Kirby (Glove to chest.)	1.00	.50	.30
(26)	Dave Marshall	1.00	.50	.30
(27)	Willie McCovey (Moustache)	5.00	2.50	1.50
(28)	John McNamara	1.00	.50	.30
(29)	Bob Miller	1.00	.50	.30
(30)	Fred Norman	1.00	.50	.30
	(Arms above head.)			
(31)	Fred Norman/Kneeling	1.00	.50	.30
(32)	Gene Richards	1.00	.50	.30
(33)	Ballard Smith/GM	1.00	.50	.30
(34)	Ed Spiezio	1.00	.50	.30
(35)	Derrell (Darrel) Thomas	1.00	.50	.30
	(Glasses)			
(36)	Derrel Thomas (No glasses.)	1.00	.50	.30
(37)	Bobby Tolan/Btg	1.00	.50	.30
(38)	Bobby Tolan/Kneeling	1.00	.50	.30

		NM	EX	VG
(39)	Jerry Turner	1.00	.50	.30
(40)	Dave Winfield	5.00	2.50	1.50

Type 3 - Blank back

(1)	Nate Colbert	1.00	.50	.30
(2)	Dave Freisleben	1.00	.50	.30
(3)	Mike Ivie	1.00	.50	.30
(4)	Randy Jones and Bowie Kuhn	1.00	.50	.30
(5)	Mike Kilkenny	1.00	.50	.30
(6)	Ray Kroc/Owner	1.00	.50	.30
(7)	Willie McCovey	5.00	2.50	1.50
(8)	John McNamara (Facing his right.)	1.00	.50	.30
(9)	Dave Winfield	7.50	3.75	2.25

1932 Sanella Margarine

One of several "foreign" Babe Ruth cards issued during his prime was included in a 112-card set produced as premiums for Sanella margarine in Germany. Ruth is the only major league ballplayer in the issue. Cards are in full color, measuring 2-3/4" x 4-1/8". Backs of the unnumbered cards are printed in German. Four types of backs can be found on the Ruth card. Type 1 has the Sanella name nearly centered. The Type 2 back has the brand name printed closer to the bottom of the card, with only four lines of type under it. Type 3 is a variation of Type 2 on which the appropriate page number (83) of the accompanying album is mentioned on the line immediately above "Handbuch des Sports" near the top. Type 4 cards also mention the page number and have the brand name near the center. One card was given with the purchase of each 1/2 pound of margarine and the album could be ordered by mail. See also Astra Margarine.

	NM	EX	VG
Type 1 Babe Ruth (Centered)	200.00	100.00	60.00
Type 2 Babe Ruth (At bottom.)	140.00	70.00	42.00
Type 3 Babe Ruth (At bottom w/83.)	200.00	100.00	60.00
Type 4 Babe Ruth (Centered w/83.)	250.00	125.00	75.00

1958 San Francisco Call-Bulletin Giants

These unnumbered cards, picturing members of the San Francisco Giants, were inserted in copies of the San Francisco Call-Bulletin newspaper as part of a promotional contest. The 25 cards in the set measure 2" x 4" and were printed on orange paper. The top of the card contains a black and white player photo, while the bottom contains a perforated stub with a serial number used to win prizes. (Cards without the stub intact are approximately 50 percent of the prices listed.) The contest name, "Giant Payoff," appears prominently on both sides of the stub. The back of the card contains a 1958 Giants schedule.

	NM	EX	VG
Complete Set (25):	1,800	900.00	550.00
Common Player:	25.00	12.50	7.50
(1) Johnny Antonelli	25.00	12.50	7.50
(2) Curt Barclay	25.00	12.50	7.50
(3) Tom Bowers/SP	400.00	200.00	120.00
(4) Ed Bressoud/SP	150.00	75.00	45.00
(5) Orlando Cepeda	250.00	125.00	75.00
(6) Ray Crone	25.00	12.50	7.50
(7) Jim Davenport	25.00	12.50	7.50
(8) Paul Giel	25.00	12.50	7.50
(9) Ruben Gomez	25.00	12.50	7.50
(10) Marv Grissom	25.00	12.50	7.50
(11) Ray Jablonski/SP	150.00	75.00	45.00
(12) Willie Kirkland/SP	150.00	75.00	45.00
(13) Whitey Lockman	25.00	12.50	7.50
(14) Willie Mays	250.00	125.00	75.00
(15) Mike McCormick	25.00	12.50	7.50
(16) Stu Miller	25.00	12.50	7.50
(17) Ramon Monzant	25.00	12.50	7.50
(18) Danny O'Connell	25.00	12.50	7.50
(19) Bill Rigney	25.00	12.50	7.50
(20) Hank Sauer	25.00	12.50	7.50
(21) Bob Schmidt	25.00	12.50	7.50
(22) Daryl Spencer	25.00	12.50	7.50
(23) Valmy Thomas	25.00	12.50	7.50
(24) Bobby Thomson	45.00	22.50	13.50
(25) Allan Worthington	25.00	12.50	7.50

1971-1982 San Francisco Giants Autograph Cards

RANDY MOFFITT   Chris Arnold - infielder

Randy Moffitt   Chris Arnold

Giants autograph card courtesy of Redwood City Tribune

For more than 10 years the Giants issued a number of different types of cards bearing facsimile autographs that the players could use to respond to fan mail. The cards vary in size from 3" x 5" to 3" x 6" and have a black-and-white photo (usually a portrait). The cards are blank-backed. Besides the cards with pre-printed autographs, a number of special cards in similar format were issued without facsimile signature. The listings are presented here in two major styles, those with player name in all-capital letters and those with names in upper and lower case.

		NM	EX	VG
Common Player:		6.00	3.00	1.75

NAME IN ALL-CAPITAL LETTERS
TYPE 1 - Name only, letters 1/8" wide

		NM	EX	VG
(1)	Doyle Alexander	6.00	3.00	1.75
(2)	Gary Alexander	6.00	3.00	1.75
(3)	Joe Altobelli	6.00	3.00	1.75
(4)	Rob Andrews/Portrait	6.00	3.00	1.75
(5)	Rob Andrews/Fielding	6.00	3.00	1.75
(6)	Jim Barr/Pitching	6.00	3.00	1.75
(7)	Dave Bergman	6.00	3.00	1.75
(8)	Vida Blue/Portrait	8.00	4.00	2.50
(9)	Vida Blue/Pitching	8.00	4.00	2.50
(10)	Bill Bordley	6.00	3.00	1.75
(11)	Fred Breining	6.00	3.00	1.75
(12)	Dave Bristol	6.00	3.00	1.75
(13)	Enos Cabell	6.00	3.00	1.75
(14)	Jack Clark (Ready to bat.)	8.00	4.00	2.50
(15)	Jack Clark (Swinging bat.)	8.00	4.00	2.50
(16)	Terry Cornutt	6.00	3.00	1.75
(17)	Heity Cruz	6.00	3.00	1.75
(18)	John Curtis	6.00	3.00	1.75
(19)	Jim Dwyer	6.00	3.00	1.75
(20)	Randy Elliott	6.00	3.00	1.75
(21)	Darrell Evans/Portrait	8.00	4.00	2.50
(22)	Darrell Evans/Btg	8.00	4.00	2.50
(23)	Tim Foli/Fielding	6.00	3.00	1.75
(24)	Tom Griffin	6.00	3.00	1.75
(25)	Ed Halicki/Portrait	6.00	3.00	1.75
(26)	Ed Halicki/Pitching	6.00	3.00	1.75
(27)	Vic Harris	6.00	3.00	1.75
(28)	Dave Heaverlo/Action	6.00	3.00	1.75
(29)	Tom Heintzelman	6.00	3.00	1.75
(30)	Larry Herndon	6.00	3.00	1.75
(31)	Marc Hill	6.00	3.00	1.75
(32)	Al Holland	6.00	3.00	1.75
(33)	Mike Ivie (Looks to side.)	6.00	3.00	1.75
(34)	Mike Ivie (Looks to front.)	6.00	3.00	1.75
(35)	Skip James	6.00	3.00	1.75
(36)	Bob Knepper	6.00	3.00	1.75
(37)	Gary Lavelle/Portrait	6.00	3.00	1.75
(38)	Gary Lavelle/Pitching	6.00	3.00	1.75
(39)	Johnnie Lemaster/Fielding	6.00	3.00	1.75
(40)	Dennis Littlejohn	6.00	3.00	1.75
(41)	Bill Madlock (Picture reversed.)	8.00	4.00	2.50
(42)	Bill Madlock (Corrected)	8.00	4.00	2.50
(43)	Jerry Martin	6.00	3.00	1.75
(44)	Milt May	6.00	3.00	1.75
(45)	Willie McCovey/Portrait	15.00	7.50	4.50
(46)	Willie McCovey/Btg	15.00	7.50	4.50
(47)	Lynn McGlothen/Pitching	6.00	3.00	1.75
(48)	Roger Metzger	6.00	3.00	1.75
(49)	Greg Minton	6.00	3.00	1.75
(50)	Randy Moffitt/Portrait	6.00	3.00	1.75
(51)	Randy Moffitt/Pitching	6.00	3.00	1.75
(52)	John Montefusco (To neck.)	6.00	3.00	1.75
(53)	John Montefusco (To letters.)	6.00	3.00	1.75
(54)	Joe Morgan	15.00	7.50	4.50
(55)	Rich Murray	6.00	3.00	1.75
(56)	Phil Nastu	6.00	3.00	1.75
(57)	Bill North	6.00	3.00	1.75
(58)	Joe Pettini	6.00	3.00	1.75
(59)	Allen Ripley	6.00	3.00	1.75
(60)	Dave Roberts	6.00	3.00	1.75
(61)	Frank Robinson	20.00	10.00	6.00
(62)	Mike Sadek (To neck.)	6.00	3.00	1.75
(63)	Mike Sadek (To letters.)	6.00	3.00	1.75
(64)	Billy Smith	6.00	3.00	1.75
(65)	Rennie Stennett	6.00	3.00	1.75
(66)	Joe Strain	6.00	3.00	1.75
(67)	John Tamargo	6.00	3.00	1.75
(68)	Derrel Thomas/Throwing	6.00	3.00	1.75
(69)	Gary Thomasson	6.00	3.00	1.75
(70)	Max Venable	6.00	3.00	1.75
(71)	Terry Whitfield	6.00	3.00	1.75
(72)	Ed Whitson	6.00	3.00	1.75
(73)	Charlie Williams	6.00	3.00	1.75
(74)	Jim Wohlford	6.00	3.00	1.75

TYPE 2 - Name only, letters 1/16" wide

		NM	EX	VG
(1)	Jim Barr (Mouth closed.)	6.00	3.00	1.75
(2)	Jim Barr (Mouth open, fence.)	6.00	3.00	1.75
(3)	Jim Barr (Mouth open, no fence.)	6.00	3.00	1.75
(4)	Bobby Bonds	9.00	4.50	2.75
(5)	Tom Bradley	6.00	3.00	1.75
(6)	Ron Bryant	6.00	3.00	1.75
(7)	Don Carrithers (To neck.)	6.00	3.00	1.75
(8)	Don Carrithers (To letters.)	6.00	3.00	1.75
(9)	Pete Falcone	6.00	3.00	1.75
(10)	Charlie Fox	6.00	3.00	1.75
(11)	Tito Fuentes (To neck.)	6.00	3.00	1.75
(12)	Tito Fuentes (To letters.)	6.00	3.00	1.75
(13)	Alan Gallagher	6.00	3.00	1.75
(14)	Russ Gibson	6.00	3.00	1.75
(15)	Ed Goodson	6.00	3.00	1.75
(16)	Ed Halicki/Pitching	6.00	3.00	1.75
(17)	Marc Hill	6.00	3.00	1.75
(18)	Jim Howarth	6.00	3.00	1.75
(19)	Jerry Johnson	6.00	3.00	1.75
(20)	Von Joshua	6.00	3.00	1.75
(21)	Gary Lavelle/Pitching	6.00	3.00	1.75
(22)	Garry Maddox	6.00	3.00	1.75
(23)	Juan Marichal	15.00	7.50	4.50
(24)	Gary Matthews	8.00	4.00	2.50
(25)	Randy Moffitt	6.00	3.00	1.75
(26)	Willie McCovey	15.00	7.50	4.50
(27)	Willie Montanez	6.00	3.00	1.75
(28)	John Montefusco/Pitching	6.00	3.00	1.75
(29)	Bobby Murcer/Btg	8.00	4.00	2.50
(30)	Dave Rader	6.00	3.00	1.75
(31)	Ken Reitz/Btg	6.00	3.00	1.75
(32)	Bill Rigney	6.00	3.00	1.75
(33)	Mike Sadek	6.00	3.00	1.75
(34)	Elias Sosa	6.00	3.00	1.75
(35)	Chris Speier (To neck.)	6.00	3.00	1.75
(36)	Chris Speier (To shoulders.)	6.00	3.00	1.75
(37)	Steve Stone	8.00	4.00	2.50
(38)	Derrel Thomas	6.00	3.00	1.75
(39)	Gary Thomasson	6.00	3.00	1.75
(40)	Jim Willoughby	6.00	3.00	1.75

TYPE 3 - 25th Anniversary logo

		NM	EX	VG
(1)	Jim Barr	6.00	3.00	1.75
(2)	Bob Brenly	6.00	3.00	1.75
(3)	Don Buford (1-1/2" autograph.)	6.00	3.00	1.75
(4)	Don Buford (2-1/2" autograph.)	6.00	3.00	1.75
(5)	Jim Davenport	6.00	3.00	1.75
(6)	Chili Davis	8.00	4.00	2.50
(7)	Alan Fowlkes	6.00	3.00	1.75
(8)	Rich Gale	6.00	3.00	1.75
(9)	Atlee Hammaker	6.00	3.00	1.75
(10)	Al Holland	6.00	3.00	1.75
(11)	Duane Kuiper	6.00	3.00	1.75
(12)	Bill Laskey	6.00	3.00	1.75
(13)	Jim Lefebvre	6.00	3.00	1.75
(14)	Johnnie Lemaster	6.00	3.00	1.75
(15)	Jeff Leonard (Chain in background.)	8.00	4.00	2.50
(16)	Jeff Leonard (No chain.)	8.00	4.00	2.50
(17)	Renie Martin	6.00	3.00	1.75
(18)	Willie McCovey	15.00	7.50	4.50
(19)	Don McMahon (2-3/8" autograph.)	6.00	3.00	1.75
(20)	Don McMahon (2-5/8" autograph.)	6.00	3.00	1.75
(21)	Greg Minton	6.00	3.00	1.75
(22)	Joe Morgan	15.00	7.50	4.50
(23)	Tom O'Malley	6.00	3.00	1.75
(24)	Frank Robinson	20.00	10.00	6.00
(25)	Mike Sadek	6.00	3.00	1.75
(26)	Reggie Smith	6.00	3.00	1.75
(27)	Guy Sularz	6.00	3.00	1.75
(28)	Champ Summers	6.00	3.00	1.75
(29)	John Van Ornum (2" autograph.)	6.00	3.00	1.75
(30)	John Van Ornum (2-1/4" autograph.)	6.00	3.00	1.75
(31)	Jim Wohlford	6.00	3.00	1.75

TYPE 4 - Position after name, no autograph

		NM	EX	VG
(1)	Chris Speier	6.00	3.00	1.75

TYPE 5 - Courtesy Chevrolet, no autograph

(1)	Bobby Bonds	9.00	4.50	2.75
(2)	Dick Dietz	6.00	3.00	1.75
(3)	Tito Fuentes	6.00	3.00	1.75
(4)	Ken Henderson	6.00	3.00	1.75
	TYPE 6 - West Valley Bicycles, no autograph			
(1)	Alan Gallagher	6.00	3.00	1.75
	TYPE 7 - Best Chevrolet, no autograph			
(1)	Tito Fuentes	6.00	3.00	1.75
(2)	Chris Speier	6.00	3.00	1.75
	TYPE 8 - Redwood City Tribune, no autograph			
(1)	Jim Barr	6.00	3.00	1.75
	NAME IN UPPER- AND LOWER CASE LETTERS			
	TYPE A - Name only			
(1)	John D'Acquisto	6.00	3.00	1.75
(2)	Mike Caldwell	6.00	3.00	1.75
(3)	Ed Goodson	6.00	3.00	1.75
(4)	Dave Kingman	8.00	4.00	2.50
(5)	Steve Ontiveros	6.00	3.00	1.75
(6)	Mike Phillips	6.00	3.00	1.75
(7)	"Wes" Westrum	6.00	3.00	1.75
(8)	Charlie Williams	6.00	3.00	1.75
	TYPE B - Team after name, no autograph			
(1)	Rich Robertson	6.00	3.00	1.75
	TYPE C - Courtesy Chevrolet, no autograph			
(1)	Rich Robertson	6.00	3.00	1.75
	TYPE D - Position after name			
(1)	Garry Maddox	6.00	3.00	1.75
	TYPE E - Redwood City Tribune, no logo, no autograph			
(1)	Chris Arnold	6.00	3.00	1.75
(2)	Jim Barr	6.00	3.00	1.75
(3)	Jim Howarth	6.00	3.00	1.75
(4)	Garry Maddox	6.00	3.00	1.75
(5)	Dave Rader	6.00	3.00	1.75
(6)	Chris Speier	6.00	3.00	1.75
	TYPE F - Redwood City Tribune, with newspaper logo, no autograph			
(1)	Chris Arnold	6.00	3.00	1.75
(2)	Jim Barr	6.00	3.00	1.75
(3)	Ed Goodson	6.00	3.00	1.75
	TYPE G - Name only, old Giants logo			
(1)	Dave Kingman	8.00	4.00	2.50
(2)	Juan Marichal	15.00	7.50	4.50

1977 San Francisco Giants Team Issue

Skip James
Infielder

These 3-1/2" x 5" blank-back cards feature black-and-white player photos surrounded by an orange frame with black borders. The manager, coaches and instructors are featured along with players in the issue. The unnumbered cards are checklisted here in alphabetical order.

		NM	EX	VG
	Complete Set (25):	15.00	7.50	4.50
	Common Player:	1.50	.75	.45
(1)	Joe Altobelli	1.50	.75	.45
(2)	Jim Barr	1.50	.75	.45
(3)	Jack Clark	2.50	1.25	.70
(4)	Terry Cornutt	1.50	.75	.45
(5)	Rob Dressler	1.50	.75	.45
(6)	Darrell Evans	2.50	1.25	.70
(7)	Frank Funk	1.50	.75	.45
(8)	Ed Halicki	1.50	.75	.45
(9)	Tom Haller	1.50	.75	.45
(10)	Marc Hill	1.50	.75	.45
(11)	Skip James	1.50	.75	.45
(12)	Bob Knepper	1.50	.75	.45
(13)	Gary Lavelle	1.50	.75	.45
(14)	Bill Madlock	1.75	.90	.50
(15)	Willie McCovey	6.00	3.00	1.75
(16)	Randy Moffitt	1.50	.75	.45
(17)	John Montefusco	1.50	.75	.45
(18)	Marty Perez	1.50	.75	.45
(19)	Frank Riccelli	1.50	.75	.45
(20)	Mike Sadek	1.50	.75	.45
(21)	Hank Sauer	1.50	.75	.45
(22)	Chris Speier	1.50	.75	.45
(23)	Gary Thomasson	1.50	.75	.45
(24)	Tommy Toms	1.50	.75	.45
(25)	Bobby Winkles	1.50	.75	.45

1979 San Francisco Giants Police

3 Mike Sadek
Catcher

Tips from the Giants

Balk

A pitcher bluffing a throw to a base while standing on the pitcher's rubber is charged with a balk. Runners on base are allowed to advance one base.

Don't balk if someone needs help. Take time to call the Police and offer assistance if needed.

Each of the full-color cards measures 2-5/8" x 4-1/8" and is numbered by player uniform number. The set includes players and coaches. The player's name, position and facsimile autograph are on front, along with the Giants logo. Backs have a "Tip from the Giants" and sponsor logos for the Giants and radio station KNBR, all printed in orange and black. Half of the set was distributed as a ballpark promotion, while the other cards were available from police agencies in several San Francisco Bay area counties.

		NM	EX	VG
	Complete Set (29):	10.00	5.00	3.00
	Common Player:	.50	.25	.15
1	Dave Bristol	.50	.25	.15
2	Marc Hill	.50	.25	.15
3	Mike Sadek	.50	.25	.15
5	Tom Haller	.50	.25	.15
6	Joe Altobelli	.50	.25	.15
8	Larry Shepard	.50	.25	.15
9	Heity Cruz	.50	.25	.15
10	Johnnie LeMaster	.50	.25	.15
12	Jim Davenport	.50	.25	.15
14	Vida Blue	.75	.40	.25
15	Mike Ivie	.50	.25	.15
16	Roger Metzger	.50	.25	.15
17	Randy Moffitt	.50	.25	.15
18	Bill Madlock	.60	.30	.20
21	Rob Andrews	.50	.25	.15
22	Jack Clark	.75	.40	.25
25	Dave Roberts	.50	.25	.15
26	John Montefusco	.50	.25	.15
28	Ed Halicki	.50	.25	.15
30	John Tamargo	.50	.25	.15
31	Larry Herndon	.50	.25	.15
36	Bill North	.50	.25	.15
39	Bob Knepper	.50	.25	.15
40	John Curtis	.50	.25	.15
41	Darrell Evans	.75	.40	.25
43	Tom Griffin	.50	.25	.15
44	Willie McCovey	5.00	2.50	1.50
46	Gary Lavelle	.50	.25	.15
49	Max Venable	.50	.25	.15

1980 San Francisco Giants Police

44 Willie McCovey
Infielder

Tips from the Giants

Triple Play

Putting three men out on the same play, a triple play, can't happen with fewer than two runners on base.

There are three things you should always know. The phone numbers of the Police Department, Fire Department and Emergency Ambulance service.

The 1980 Giants police set is virtually identical in format to its 1979 forerunner, with radio station KNBR and the San Francisco Police Department once again co-sponsors. The 2-5/8" x 4-1/8" cards feature full-color photos and facsimile autographs. Backs are in the team's orange and black colors. The set includes players and coaches, with each card numbered by uniform number. As in 1979, half the cards were distributed as a stadium promotion, with the remainder available only from police officers.

		NM	EX	VG
	Complete Set (31):	9.00	4.50	2.75
	Common Player:	.50	.25	.15
1	Dave Bristol	.50	.25	.15
2	Marc Hill	.50	.25	.15
3	Mike Sadek	.50	.25	.15
5	Jim Lefebvre	.50	.25	.15
6	Rennie Stennett	.50	.25	.15

7	Milt May	.50	.25	.15
8	Vern Benson	.50	.25	.15
9	Jim Wohlford	.50	.25	.15
10	Johnnie LeMaster	.50	.25	.15
12	Jim Davenport	.50	.25	.15
14	Vida Blue	.75	.40	.25
15	Mike Ivie	.50	.25	.15
16	Roger Metzger	.50	.25	.15
17	Randy Moffitt	.50	.25	.15
19	Al Holland	.50	.25	.15
20	Joe Strain	.50	.25	.15
22	Jack Clark	.50	.25	.15
26	John Montefusco	.50	.25	.15
28	Ed Halicki	.50	.25	.15
31	Larry Herndon	.50	.25	.15
32	Ed Whitson	.50	.25	.15
36	Bill North	.50	.25	.15
38	Greg Minton	.50	.25	.15
39	Bob Knepper	.50	.25	.15
41	Darrell Evans	.60	.30	.20
42	John Van Ornum	.50	.25	.15
43	Tom Griffin	.50	.25	.15
44	Willie McCovey	4.00	2.00	1.25
45	Terry Whitfield	.50	.25	.15
46	Gary Lavelle	.50	.25	.15
47	Don McMahon	.50	.25	.15

1940s Sarra Trade Cards

STAN MUSIAL   CARDENALES

AGUA DE COLONIA
SUPREMA
EXTRA - FUERTE
SARRA
MUY REFINADA
MUY CONCENTRADA
INSUPERABLE

While the cards are undated, one of the uniforms shown places its issue between 1940-1950. These ad cards are about 3-1/2" x 5-3/8" and printed in sepia on thick cream-colored paper stock. The backs picture examples of the company's personal care products, including cologne, available in sizes up to one quart!

	NM	EX	VG
Stan Musial	350.00	175.00	100.00
Babe Ruth	550.00	275.00	165.00

1938 Sawyer Biscuit Cubs/White Sox

In the late 1930s, a local baker ran a promotion by which fans could redeem a coupon found in its product along with a dime for a matted black-and-white portrait photo of a favorite Chicago ballplayer. The photo was delivered in a thick textured maroon frame about 4-3/4" x 5-3/4" in size that had a punch-out stand on back. The Sawyer company name is not found on the actual photo, but is seen on the envelope and cover letter which are sometimes found with the pictures. It is unknown whether the list presented here is complete.

		NM	EX	VG
	Common Player:	600.00	300.00	180.00
	CHICAGO CUBS			
(1)	Jim Asbell	600.00	300.00	180.00
(2)	Clay Bryant	600.00	300.00	180.00
(3)	Tex Carleton	600.00	300.00	180.00
(4)	Phil Cavarretta	600.00	300.00	180.00
(5)	Rip Collins	600.00	300.00	180.00
(6)	Jerome "Dizzy" Dean	1,200	600.00	360.00
(7)	Frank Demaree	600.00	300.00	180.00
(8)	Al Epperly	600.00	300.00	180.00
(9)	Larry French	600.00	300.00	180.00
(10)	Augie Galan	600.00	300.00	180.00
(11)	Bob Garbark	600.00	300.00	180.00
(12)	Charlie Grimm	600.00	300.00	180.00
(13)	Stan Hack	650.00	325.00	195.00
(14)	Gabby Hartnett	750.00	375.00	225.00

		NM	EX	VG
(15)	Billy Herman	750.00	375.00	225.00
(16)	Bill Jurges	600.00	300.00	180.00
(17)	Tony Lazzeri	750.00	375.00	225.00
(18)	Bill Lee	600.00	300.00	180.00
(19)	Bob Logan	600.00	300.00	180.00
(20)	Joe Marty	600.00	300.00	180.00
(21)	Ken O'Dea	600.00	300.00	180.00
(22)	Carl Reynolds	600.00	300.00	180.00
(23)	Charlie Root	600.00	300.00	180.00
(24)	Jack Russell	600.00	300.00	180.00

CHICAGO WHITE SOX

(1)	Luke Appling	750.00	375.00	225.00
(2)	Boze Berger	600.00	300.00	180.00
(3)	Clint Brown	600.00	300.00	180.00
(4)	Frog Dietrich	600.00	300.00	180.00
(5)	Jimmie Dykes	600.00	300.00	180.00
(6)	Frank Gabler	600.00	300.00	180.00
(7)	Jackie Hayes	600.00	300.00	180.00
(8)	Jack Knott	600.00	300.00	180.00
(9)	Mike Kreevich	600.00	300.00	180.00
(10)	Joe Kuhel	600.00	300.00	180.00
(11)	Thornton Lee	600.00	300.00	180.00
(12)	Ted Lyons	750.00	375.00	225.00
(13)	Marv Owen	600.00	300.00	180.00
(14)	Tony Rensa	600.00	300.00	180.00
(15)	Dunc Rigney	600.00	300.00	180.00
(16)	Larry Rosenthal	600.00	300.00	180.00
(17)	Norm Schlueter	600.00	300.00	180.00
(18)	Luke Sewell	600.00	300.00	180.00
(19)	Henk Steinbacher	600.00	300.00	180.00
(20)	Monty Stratton	625.00	310.00	185.00
(21)	Gee Gee Walker	600.00	300.00	180.00
(22)	Porkshops Whitehead	600.00	300.00	180.00

BROADCASTER

	Bob Elson	600.00	300.00	180.00

1921-22 Schapira Bros. Big Show Candy

The players known, with the teams on which they are pictured, can pinpoint the issue date no closer than 1921-22. Nominally about 1-3/4" or 1-7/8" x 2-3/8" (size varies because the cards were printed without borders in sheet form, and are often found crudely cut), the cards were one of several types of insert cards and toys found in boxes of Schapira's "Big Show" candy. The cards have black-and-white borderless photos on which the player name is (usually) printed diagonally in script at lower right. Most cards have an Underwood & Underwood credit line on front, as well. Backs are blank. The unnumbered cards are listed here alphabetically, though the checklist may not be complete. Most cards are found with a horizontal crease at center, possibly to get them into the tight-fitting candy box.

		NM	EX	VG
	Common Player:	200.00	100.00	60.00
(1)	George J. Burns	200.00	80.00	40.00
(2)	Ty Cobb	1,800	725.00	350.00
(3)	Stan Coveleski	250.00	100.00	50.00
(4)	(Jake) Daubert	200.00	80.00	40.00
(5)	Joe Dugan	200.00	80.00	40.00
(6)	Jimmy Dykes	200.00	80.00	40.00
(7)	Walter Holke	200.00	80.00	40.00
(8)	Walter Johnson	600.00	240.00	120.00
(9)	Joe Judge	200.00	80.00	40.00
(10)	Dick Kerr	200.00	80.00	40.00
(11)	Rabbit Maranville	250.00	100.00	50.00
(12)	Bob Meusel	200.00	80.00	40.00
(13)	Hy Meyers (Myers)	200.00	80.00	40.00
(14)	O'Neil (Mickey?)	200.00	80.00	40.00
(15)	Roger Peckinpaugh	200.00	80.00	40.00
(16)	Edd Rousch (Roush)	250.00	100.00	50.00
(17)	Ray Schalk	200.00	80.00	40.00
(18)	Everett Scott	200.00	80.00	40.00
(19)	Aaron Ward	200.00	80.00	40.00

1921 Schapira Bros. Candy Babe Ruth

The date assigned to this rare candy issue is a best guess based on the uniform in which the Babe is shown on the various cards. The blank-back cards measure between 1-5/8" and 1-3/4" in width, and are 2-1/2" tall. Printed in red, white and blue the cards were printed on a candy box and come in two types. Apparently each box contained a portrait card of Ruth which offered "a base ball autographed by Babe

Ruth" for 250 of the pictures, plus one of five action photos. The portrait card would thus be much more common than any particular action pose, unless great numbers of them were redeemed. The cards illustrated here are not front and back, but show a typical action card and the portrait card. The unnumbered cards are checklisted here in alphabetical order based on the card's caption.

		NM	EX	VG
	Complete Set (6):	5,500	2,200	1,100
(1)	Cleared the Bags (Babe Ruth)	1,000	400.00	200.00
(2)	Home Run (Babe Ruth)	1,000	400.00	200.00
(3)	Over the Fence (Babe Ruth)	1,000	400.00	200.00
(4)	They Passed Him (Babe Ruth)	1,000	400.00	200.00
(5)	Waiting for a High One (Babe Ruth)	1,000	400.00	200.00
(6)	Babe Ruth/Portrait	900.00	360.00	180.00

1975 Michael Schechter Associates Test Discs

Prior to rolling out is 70-disc set in 1976, Michael Schecter Associates issued this sample set of discs the previous year. Slightly larger, at 3-9/16" diameter, than the '76 issues, the '75 sample discs share a similar format. Fronts have a black-and-white player photo from which uniform logo details have been removed due to lack of licensing by Major League Baseball. Backs are blank. The Seaver and Bench discs are considerably scarcer than the other four players in the set.

		NM	EX	VG
	Complete Set (6):	175.00	90.00	55.00
	Common Player:	6.00	3.00	1.75
(1)	Hank Aaron	15.00	7.50	4.50
(2)	Johnny Bench	60.00	30.00	18.00
(3)	Catfish Hunter	6.00	3.00	1.75
(4)	Fred Lynn	6.00	3.00	1.75
(5)	Pete Rose	10.00	5.00	3.00
(6)	Tom Seaver	100.00	50.00	30.00

1976 Michael Schechter Associates Discs

Following its test issue of 1975, Michael Schechter Associates ran out its baseball player disc issues on a large scale in 1976. While most were sold with specific sponsor advertising on back, they were also made available with blank backs. The discs are 3-3/8" diameter with a black-and-white player portrait photo in the center of the baseball design. A line of red stars is above, while the left and right panels feature one of several bright colors. Produced by MSA under license from the Major League Players Association, the player photos have had uniform and cap logos removed. The unnumbered discs are presented in alphabetical order.

		NM	EX	VG
	Complete Set (70):	60.00	30.00	18.00
	Common Player:	.50	.25	.15
(1)	Henry Aaron	12.50	6.25	3.75
(2)	Johnny Bench	6.00	3.00	1.75
(3)	Vida Blue	.50	.25	.15
(4)	Larry Bowa	.50	.25	.15
(5)	Lou Brock	4.50	2.25	1.25
(6)	Jeff Burroughs	.50	.25	.15
(7)	John Candelaria	.50	.25	.15
(8)	Jose Cardenal	.50	.25	.15
(9)	Rod Carew	6.00	3.00	1.75
(10)	Steve Carlton	4.50	2.25	1.25
(11)	Dave Cash	.50	.25	.15
(12)	Cesar Cedeno	.50	.25	.15
(13)	Ron Cey	.50	.25	.15
(14)	Carlton Fisk	4.50	2.25	1.25
(15)	Tito Fuentes	.50	.25	.15
(16)	Steve Garvey	3.00	1.50	.90
(17)	Ken Griffey	.50	.25	.15
(18)	Don Gullett	.50	.25	.15
(19)	Willie Horton	.50	.25	.15
(20)	Al Hrabosky	.50	.25	.15
(21)	Catfish Hunter	4.50	2.25	1.25
(22)	Reggie Jackson (A's)	9.00	4.50	2.75
(23)	Randy Jones	.50	.25	.15
(24)	Jim Kaat	.50	.25	.15
(25)	Don Kessinger	.50	.25	.15
(26)	Dave Kingman	.50	.25	.15
(27)	Jerry Koosman	.50	.25	.15
(28)	Mickey Lolich	.60	.30	.20
(29)	Greg Luzinski	.50	.25	.15
(30)	Fred Lynn	.50	.25	.15
(31)	Bill Madlock	.50	.25	.15
(32)	Carlos May (White Sox)	.50	.25	.15
(33)	John Mayberry	.50	.25	.15
(34)	Bake McBride	.50	.25	.15
(35)	Doc Medich	.50	.25	.15
(36)	Andy Messersmith	.50	.25	.15
(37)	Rick Monday	.50	.25	.15
(38)	John Montefusco	.50	.25	.15
(39)	Jerry Morales	.50	.25	.15
(40)	Joe Morgan	4.50	2.25	1.25
(41)	Thurman Munson	4.50	2.25	1.25
(42)	Bobby Murcer	.50	.25	.15
(43)	Al Oliver	.50	.25	.15
(44)	Jim Palmer	4.50	2.25	1.25
(45)	Dave Parker	.50	.25	.15
(46)	Tony Perez	4.50	2.25	1.25
(47)	Jerry Reuss	.50	.25	.15
(48)	Brooks Robinson	6.00	3.00	1.75
(49)	Frank Robinson	6.00	3.00	1.75
(50)	Steve Rogers	.50	.25	.15
(51)	Pete Rose	10.00	5.00	3.00
(52)	Nolan Ryan	15.00	7.50	4.50
(53)	Manny Sanguillen	.50	.25	.15
(54)	Mike Schmidt	10.00	5.00	3.00
(55)	Tom Seaver	6.00	3.00	1.75
(56)	Ted Simmons	.50	.25	.15
(57)	Reggie Smith	.50	.25	.15
(58)	Willie Stargell	4.50	2.25	1.25
(59)	Rusty Staub	.75	.40	.25
(60)	Rennie Stennett	.50	.25	.15
(61)	Don Sutton	4.50	2.25	1.25
(62)	Andy Thornton	.50	.25	.15
(63)	Luis Tiant	.50	.25	.15
(64)	Joe Torre	.50	.25	.15
(65)	Mike Tyson	.50	.25	.15
(66)	Bob Watson	.50	.25	.15
(67)	Wilbur Wood	.50	.25	.15
(68)	Jimmy Wynn	.50	.25	.15
(69)	Carl Yastrzemski	6.00	3.00	1.75
(70)	Richie Zisk	.50	.25	.15

1977 Michael Schechter Associates Cup Lids

One of MSA's early baseball novelty issues was a set of drink-cup lids. The 3-1/2" diameter pieces are made of pressed and waxed cardboard. They are 3/16" thick and have a 3/8" die-cut hole for inserting a straw. Design is similar to other MSA issues of the era, with a black-and-white player portrait photo at center of a simulated baseball design. Personal data is printed in colored panels at left and right, and there is a row of colored stars above the photo. Player caps do not show team insignia because the issue was licensed only by the players' union, and not the owners. The unnumbered lids are checklisted here in alphabetical order.

		NM	EX	VG
	Complete Set (49):	700.00	350.00	225.00
	Common Player:	10.00	5.00	3.00

(1)	Sal Bando	10.00	5.00	3.00
(2)	Johnny Bench	30.00	15.00	9.00
(3)	Larry Bowa	10.00	5.00	3.00
(4)	Steve Braun	10.00	5.00	3.00
(5)	George Brett	100.00	50.00	30.00
(6)	Lou Brock	30.00	15.00	9.00
(7)	Bert Campaneris	10.00	5.00	3.00
(8)	Bill Campbell	10.00	5.00	3.00
(9)	Jose Cardenal	10.00	5.00	3.00
(10)	Rod Carew	30.00	15.00	9.00
(11)	Dave Cash	10.00	5.00	3.00
(12)	Cesar Cedeno	10.00	5.00	3.00
(13)	Chris Chambliss	10.00	5.00	3.00
(14)	Dave Concepcion	10.00	5.00	3.00
(15)	Mark Fidrych	10.00	5.00	3.00
(16)	Rollie Fingers	20.00	10.00	6.00
(17)	George Foster	10.00	5.00	3.00
(18)	Wayne Garland	10.00	5.00	3.00
(19)	Steve Garvey	20.00	10.00	6.00
(20)	Cesar Geronimo	10.00	5.00	3.00
(21)	Bobby Grich	10.00	5.00	3.00
(22)	Don Gullett	10.00	5.00	3.00
(23)	Mike Hargrove	10.00	5.00	3.00
(24)	Catfish Hunter	20.00	10.00	6.00
(25)	Randy Jones	10.00	5.00	3.00
(26)	Dave Kingman	15.00	7.50	4.50
(27)	Dave LaRoche	10.00	5.00	3.00
(28)	Greg Luzinski	10.00	5.00	3.00
(29)	Fred Lynn	10.00	5.00	3.00
(30)	Jon Matlack	10.00	5.00	3.00
(31)	Bake McBride	10.00	5.00	3.00
(32)	Joe Morgan	25.00	12.50	7.50
(33)	Phil Niekro	20.00	10.00	6.00
(34)	Jim Palmer	25.00	12.50	7.50
(35)	Dave Parker	10.00	5.00	3.00
(36)	Fred Patek	10.00	5.00	3.00
(37)	Mickey Rivers	10.00	5.00	3.00
(38)	Brooks Robinson	30.00	15.00	9.00
(39)	Pete Rose	75.00	37.00	22.00
(40)	Nolan Ryan	100.00	50.00	30.00
(41)	Tom Seaver/1976	60.00	30.00	18.00
(42)	Mike Schmidt	50.00	25.00	15.00
(43)	Bill Singer	10.00	5.00	3.00
(44)	Chris Speier	10.00	5.00	3.00
(45)	Willie Stargell	25.00	12.50	7.50
(46)	Luis Tiant	12.50	6.25	3.75
(47)	Butch Wynegar	10.00	5.00	3.00
(48)	Robin Yount	20.00	10.00	6.00
(49)	Richie Zisk	10.00	5.00	3.00

1977 Mike Schechter Associates Customized Sports Discs

Virtually identical in format to the several locally sponsored disc sets of the previous year, these 3-3/8" diameter player discs once again feature black-and-white player portrait photos in the center of a baseball design. The left and right panels are in one of several bright colors. Licensed by the Players' Association, the photos carry no uniform logos. Backs of the discs are printed in dark blue and carry an ad from MSA for "Customized Sports Discs" and novelties for which Schechter held the licenses. The unnumbered discs are checklisted here alphabetically.

		NM	EX	VG
Complete Set (70):		350.00	175.00	100.00
Common Player:		3.00	1.50	.90
(1)	Sal Bando	3.00	1.50	.90
(2)	Buddy Bell	3.00	1.50	.90
(3)	Johnny Bench	20.00	10.00	6.00
(4)	Larry Bowa	3.00	1.50	.90
(5)	Steve Braun	3.00	1.50	.90
(6)	George Brett	125.00	62.00	37.00
(7)	Lou Brock	15.00	7.50	4.50
(8)	Jeff Burroughs	3.00	1.50	.90
(9)	Bert Campaneris	3.00	1.50	.90
(10)	John Candelaria	3.00	1.50	.90
(11)	Jose Cardenal	3.00	1.50	.90
(12)	Rod Carew	20.00	10.00	6.00
(13)	Steve Carlton	20.00	10.00	6.00
(14)	Dave Cash	3.00	1.50	.90
(15)	Cesar Cedeno	3.00	1.50	.90
(16)	Ron Cey	3.00	1.50	.90
(17)	Dave Concepcion	3.00	1.50	.90
(18)	Dennis Eckersley	15.00	7.50	4.50
(19)	Mark Fidrych	6.00	3.00	1.75
(20)	Rollie Fingers	15.00	7.50	4.50
(21)	Carlton Fisk	15.00	7.50	4.50
(22)	George Foster	3.00	1.50	.90
(23)	Wayne Garland	3.00	1.50	.90
(24)	Ralph Garr	3.00	1.50	.90
(25)	Steve Garvey	12.50	6.25	3.75
(26)	Cesar Geronimo	3.00	1.50	.90
(27)	Bobby Grich	3.00	1.50	.90
(28)	Ken Griffey Sr.	3.00	1.50	.90
(29)	Don Gullett	3.00	1.50	.90
(30)	Mike Hargrove	3.00	1.50	.90
(31)	Al Hrabosky	3.00	1.50	.90
(32)	Jim Hunter	15.00	7.50	4.50

(33)	Reggie Jackson	30.00	15.00	9.00
(34)	Randy Jones	3.00	1.50	.90
(35)	Dave Kingman	5.00	2.50	1.50
(36)	Jerry Koosman	3.00	1.50	.90
(37)	Dave LaRoche	3.00	1.50	.90
(38)	Greg Luzinski	3.00	1.50	.90
(39)	Fred Lynn	3.00	1.50	.90
(40)	Bill Madlock	3.00	1.50	.90
(41)	Rick Manning	3.00	1.50	.90
(42)	Jon Matlock	3.00	1.50	.90
(43)	John Mayberry	3.00	1.50	.90
(44)	Hal McRae	3.00	1.50	.90
(45)	Andy Messersmith	3.00	1.50	.90
(46)	Rick Monday	3.00	1.50	.90
(47)	John Montefusco	3.00	1.50	.90
(48)	Joe Morgan	15.00	7.50	4.50
(49)	Thurman Munson	12.50	6.25	3.75
(50)	Bobby Murcer	3.00	1.50	.90
(51)	Bill North	3.00	1.50	.90
(52)	Jim Palmer	15.00	7.50	4.50
(53)	Tony Perez	15.00	7.50	4.50
(54)	Jerry Reuss	3.00	1.50	.90
(55)	Brooks Robinson	20.00	10.00	6.00
(56)	Pete Rose	75.00	37.00	22.00
(57)	Joe Rudi	3.00	1.50	.90
(58)	Nolan Ryan	125.00	62.00	37.00
(59)	Manny Sanguillen	3.00	1.50	.90
(60)	Mike Schmidt	100.00	50.00	30.00
(61)	Tom Seaver	20.00	10.00	6.00
(62)	Bill Singer	3.00	1.50	.90
(63)	Willie Stargell	15.00	7.50	4.50
(64)	Rusty Staub	5.00	2.50	1.50
(65)	Luis Tiant	3.00	1.50	.90
(66)	Bob Watson	3.00	1.50	.90
(67)	Butch Wynegar	3.00	1.50	.90
(68)	Carl Yastrzemski	20.00	10.00	6.00
(69)	Robin Yount	15.00	7.50	4.50
(70)	Richie Zisk	3.00	1.50	.90

1915 Schmelzer's Sporting Goods Pins

The date of issue attributed is speculative, based on the limited checklist currently available. These pin-back celluloid buttons measure about 1-1/4" in diameter. A color lithographed figure of a generic ballplayer shares the front with a smaller inset black-and-white photo of an actual player and a fancy script position designation. The player's last name appears at the bottom of the photo. Issuer identification is on back. It is presumed at least one pinback was issued for each of the nine positions.

		NM	EX	VG
Common Player:		350.00	175.00	105.00
RF	"Ty" Cobb	26,250	13,125	7,500
3B	Charlie Deal	5,625	2,813	1,688
C	Hank Gowdy	5,625	2,813	1,688
LF	Hoffman	5,625	2,813	1,688
CF	Joe Jackson	12,000	6,000	3,600
P	Christy Mathewson	6,750	3,375	2,025
1B	Butch Schmidt	5,625	2,813	1,688

1921 C. Shulz Baseball Card Game

While this catalog generally does not attempt to list game cards which do not depict actual ballplayers, this set is considered exceptional due to its format similarity to the popularly collected 1922 American Caramel issue known as E120. Backs of the game cards are printed in blue on white and reproduce the border design of the National League

cards of E120. The unnamed photo of Heinie Groh on back is identical to that on E120, except uniform lettering has been airbrushed away on the game card. Backs are printed in red with a ballgame situation. The credit line on back reads, "Instructions Copyrighted 1921 by C. Schulz." The game cards measure about 2-1/2" x 3-1/2".

	NM	EX	VG
Common Card:	35.00	17.50	10.00

1949 Schumacher Service Station

Because some of these cards have been found with the advertising of Schumacher Service Station (location unknown) printed in red on the back, the issue is so designated for cataloging purposes. Given that the (living) players from this set were with their respective teams in 1949-1950, the issue date could be either year. Measuring 2-5/8" x 3-9/16", the cards are black-and-white on the front. It is unknown whether other players were issued in these series.

		NM	EX	VG
Complete Set (9):		2,200	1,100	650.00
Common Player:		200.00	100.00	60.00
(1)	Joe Garagiola	250.00	125.00	75.00
(2)	Marty Marion	225.00	110.00	65.00
(3)	Les Moss	200.00	100.00	60.00
(4)	George (Red) Munger	200.00	100.00	60.00
(5)	Don Newcomb (Newcombe)	250.00	125.00	75.00
(6)	Howard Pollet	200.00	100.00	60.00
(7)	George Herman (Babe) Ruth	600.00	300.00	180.00
(8)	Red Schoendienst	250.00	125.00	75.00
(9)	Vernon Stephens	200.00	100.00	60.00

1935 Schutter-Johnson (R332)

This 50-card set was issued by the Schutter-Johnson Candy Corp. of Chicago and Brooklyn circa 1930 and features drawings of major league players offering baseball playing tips. The cards measure 2-1/4" x 2-7/8". The drawings on the front are set against a red background while the backs are titled "Major League Secrets" and give the player's advice on some aspect of the game. The Scutter-Johnson name appears at the bottom.

		NM	EX	VG
Complete Set (50):		17,500	7,000	3,500
Common Player:		200.00	100.00	50.00
1	Al Simmons	350.00	140.00	70.00
2	Lloyd Waner	275.00	110.00	55.00
3	Kiki Cuyler	275.00	110.00	55.00
4	Frank Frisch	275.00	110.00	55.00
5	Chick Hafey	275.00	110.00	55.00
6	Bill Klem (Umpire)	450.00	180.00	90.00
7	Rogers Hornsby	300.00	120.00	60.00
8	Carl Mays	200.00	100.00	50.00
9	Chas. Wrigley (Umpire)	275.00	110.00	55.00
10	Christy Mathewson	900.00	360.00	180.00
11	Bill Dickey	275.00	110.00	55.00
12	Walter Berger	200.00	100.00	50.00
13	George Earnshaw	200.00	100.00	50.00
14	Hack Wilson	275.00	110.00	55.00
15	Charley Grimm	200.00	100.00	50.00
16	Lloyd Waner, Paul Waner	275.00	110.00	55.00
17	Chuck Klein	275.00	110.00	55.00
18	Woody English	200.00	100.00	50.00
19	Grover Alexander	300.00	120.00	60.00
20	Lou Gehrig	2,000	800.00	400.00
21	Wes Ferrell	200.00	100.00	50.00
22	Carl Hubbell	300.00	120.00	60.00

		NM	EX	VG
23	Pie Traynor	275.00	110.00	55.00
24	Gus Mancuso	200.00	100.00	50.00
25	Ben Cantwell	200.00	100.00	50.00
26	Babe Ruth	2,350	940.00	470.00
27	"Goose" Goslin	275.00	110.00	55.00
28	Earle Combs	275.00	110.00	55.00
29	"Kiki" Cuyler	275.00	110.00	55.00
30	Jimmy Wilson	200.00	100.00	50.00
31	Dizzy Dean	450.00	180.00	90.00
32	Mickey Cochrane	275.00	110.00	55.00
33	Ted Lyons	275.00	110.00	55.00
34	Si Johnson	200.00	100.00	50.00
35	Dizzy Dean	450.00	180.00	90.00
36	Pepper Martin	225.00	90.00	45.00
37	Joe Cronin	275.00	110.00	55.00
38	Gabby Hartnett	275.00	110.00	55.00
39	Oscar Melillo	200.00	100.00	50.00
40	Ben Chapman	200.00	100.00	50.00
41	John McGraw	275.00	110.00	55.00
42	Babe Ruth	2,350	940.00	470.00
43	"Red" Lucas	200.00	100.00	50.00
44	Charley Root	200.00	100.00	50.00
45	Dazzy Vance	275.00	110.00	55.00
46	Hugh Critz	200.00	100.00	50.00
47	"Firpo" Marberry	200.00	100.00	50.00
48	Grover Alexander	300.00	120.00	60.00
49	Lefty Grove	325.00	130.00	65.00
50	Heinie Meine	200.00	100.00	50.00

1888 "Scrapps Tobacco" Die-Cuts

The origin of these die-cut, embossed player busts is not known, but they were apparently part of a book of "punch-outs" issued in the late 1880s. When out of their original album, they apparently resembled scraps of paper, presumably leading to their unusual name. An earlier theory that they were issued by "Scrapps Tobacco" has since been disocunted after research indicated there never was such a company. The die-cuts include 18 different players - nine members of the American Association St. Louis Browns and nine from the National League Detroit Wolverines. Although they vary slightly in size, the player busts are generally about 2" wide and 3" high. The drawings for the St. Louis player busts were taken from the Old Judge "Brown's Champions" set. The player's name appears along the bottom.

		NM	EX	VG
	Complete Set (18):	35,000	14,000	7,000
	Common Player:	1,800	725.00	360.00
(1)	C.W. Bennett	1,800	725.00	360.00
(2)	D. Brouthers	2,400	960.00	480.00
(3)	A.J. Bushong	1,800	725.00	360.00
(4)	Robert L. Caruthers	1,800	725.00	360.00
(5)	Charles Comiskey	2,400	960.00	480.00
(6)	F. Dunlap	1,800	725.00	360.00
(7)	David L. Foutz	1,800	725.00	360.00
(8)	C.H. Getzen (Getzien)	1,800	725.00	360.00
(9)	Wm. Gleason	1,800	725.00	360.00
(10)	E. Hanlon	2,400	960.00	480.00
(11)	Walter A. Latham	1,800	725.00	360.00
(12)	James O'Neill	1,800	725.00	360.00
(13)	H. Richardson	1,800	725.00	360.00
(14)	Wm. Robinson	2,400	960.00	480.00
(15)	J.C. Rowe	1,800	725.00	360.00
(16)	S. Thompson	2,400	960.00	480.00
(17)	Curtis Welch	1,800	725.00	360.00
(18)	J.L. White	1,800	725.00	360.00

1949 Sealtest Phillies Stickers

This regional Phillies set was issued in the Philadelphia area in 1949 by Sealtest Dairy. It consisted of 12 large (3-1/2" by 4-1/4") sticker cards with peel-off backs. The front of the unnumbered cards featured an action photo with facsimilie autograph, while the back has an advertisement for Sealtest products. The same format, photos and checklist were also used for the Lummis Peanut Butter card set issued in Philadelphia the same year.

		NM	EX	VG
	Complete Set (12):	2,800	1,400	850.00
	Common Player:	250.00	125.00	75.00
(1)	Rich Ashburn	700.00	350.00	210.00
(2)	Hank Borowy	250.00	125.00	75.00
(3)	Del Ennis	260.00	130.00	78.00
(4)	Granny Hamner	250.00	125.00	75.00
(5)	Puddinhead Jones	250.00	125.00	75.00
(6)	Russ Meyer	250.00	125.00	75.00
(7)	Bill Nicholson	250.00	125.00	75.00
(8)	Robin Roberts	700.00	350.00	210.00
(9)	"Schoolboy" Rowe	250.00	125.00	75.00
(10)	Andy Seminick	250.00	125.00	75.00
(11)	Curt Simmons	300.00	150.00	90.00
(12)	Eddie Waitkus	250.00	125.00	75.00

1946 Sears St. Louis Browns/ Cardinals Postcards

One of the more popular issues of the immediate post-war period are the black-and-white postcards of St. Louis Browns and Cardinals players issued by Sears in East St. Louis. The 3-1/2" x 5-3/8" postcards have posed player portraits on front with the player's name and Sears "Compliments of" line in the white border beneath. Backs are stamped "POST CARD / ACTUAL PHOTOGRAPH." The cards were reported to have been issued in groups of five on a bi-weekly basis, sold both at the Sears store and through the mail. The unnumbered cards are checklisted here alphabetically within team.

		NM	EX	VG
	Complete Set (69):	8,000	4,000	2,400
	Common Player:	100.00	50.00	30.00
	St. Louis Browns Set (33):	3,000	1,500	900.00
(1)	John Berardino	200.00	100.00	60.00
(2)	Frank Biscan	100.00	50.00	30.00
(3)	Mark Christman	100.00	50.00	30.00
(4)	Babe Dahlgren	100.00	50.00	30.00
(5)	Bob Dillinger	100.00	50.00	30.00
(6)	Stanley Ferens	100.00	50.00	30.00
(7)	Denny Galehouse	100.00	50.00	30.00
(8)	Joe Grace	100.00	50.00	30.00
(9)	Jeff Heath	100.00	50.00	30.00
(10)	Henry Helf	100.00	50.00	30.00
(11)	Fred Hoffman	100.00	50.00	30.00
(12)	Walt Judnich	100.00	50.00	30.00
(13)	Ellis Kinder	100.00	50.00	30.00
(14)	Jack Kramer	100.00	50.00	30.00
(15)	Chet Laabs	100.00	50.00	30.00
(16)	Al LaMacchia	125.00	65.00	35.00
(17)	John Lucadello	100.00	50.00	30.00
(18)	Frank Mancuso	100.00	50.00	30.00
(19)	Glenn McQuillen	100.00	50.00	30.00
(20)	John Miller	100.00	50.00	30.00
(21)	Al Milnar	150.00	75.00	45.00
(22)	Bob Muncrief	100.00	50.00	30.00
(23)	Nelson Potter	100.00	50.00	30.00
(24)	Ken Sears	100.00	50.00	30.00
(25)	Len Schulte	100.00	50.00	30.00
(26)	Luke Sewell	100.00	50.00	30.00
(27)	Joe Schultz	100.00	50.00	30.00
(28)	Tex Shirley	100.00	50.00	30.00
(29)	Vern Stephens	100.00	50.00	30.00
(30)	Chuck Stevens	100.00	50.00	30.00
(31)	Zack Taylor	100.00	50.00	30.00
(32)	Al Zarilla	100.00	50.00	30.00
(33)	Sam Zoldak	100.00	50.00	30.00
	St. Louis Cardinals Set (36):	5,000	2,500	1,500
(1)	Buster Adams	100.00	50.00	30.00
(2)	Red Barrett	100.00	50.00	30.00
(3)	Johnny Beazley	100.00	50.00	30.00
(4)	Al Brazle	100.00	50.00	30.00
(5)	Harry Brecheen	100.00	50.00	30.00
(6)	Ken Burkhart	100.00	50.00	30.00
(7)	Joffre Cross	100.00	50.00	30.00
(8)	Murray Dickson	100.00	50.00	30.00
(9)	George Dockins	100.00	50.00	30.00
(10)	Blix Donnelly	150.00	75.00	45.00
(11)	Erv Dusak	100.00	50.00	30.00
(12)	Eddie Dyer	100.00	50.00	30.00
(13)	Bill Endicott	100.00	50.00	30.00
(14)	Joe Garagiola	400.00	200.00	120.00
(15)	Mike Gonzales (Gonzalez)	125.00	65.00	35.00
(16)	Lou Klein	100.00	50.00	30.00
(17)	Clyde Kluttz	100.00	50.00	30.00
(18)	Howard Krist	100.00	50.00	30.00
(19)	George Kurowski	100.00	50.00	30.00
(20)	Danny Litwhiler	100.00	50.00	30.00
(21)	Marty Marion	150.00	75.00	45.00
(22)	Fred Martin	100.00	50.00	30.00
(23)	Terry Moore	125.00	65.00	35.00
(24)	Stan Musial	1,000	500.00	300.00
(25)	Ken O'Dea	100.00	50.00	30.00
(26)	Howard Pollet	100.00	50.00	30.00
(27)	Del Rice	100.00	50.00	30.00
(28)	Red Schoendienst	300.00	150.00	90.00
(29)	Walt Sessi	100.00	50.00	30.00
(30)	Dick Sisler	100.00	50.00	30.00
(31)	Enos Slaughter	300.00	150.00	90.00
(32)	Max Surkont	100.00	50.00	30.00
(33)	Harry Walker	100.00	50.00	30.00
(34)	Buzzy Wares	100.00	50.00	30.00
(35)	Ernie White	100.00	50.00	30.00
(36)	Ted Wilks	100.00	50.00	30.00

1969 Seattle Pilots Premium Pictures

This set of 8-1/2" x 11" premium pictures is based on the artwork of John Wheeldon, who did contemporary issues for the Mets, Twins and Red Sox, as well. The pastels feature large portraits and smaller action pictures with a large facsimile autograph at bottom. Backs are in black-and-white and feature biographical data, comprehensive career summary and complete minor and major league stats. There is a self-portrait and biographical sketch of the artist on back, as well. The premiums were given away at selected Pilots home games during their lone season in Seattle. They were later sold for 25 cents each in the concession stand. The unnumbered pictures are checklisted here in alphabetical order.

		NM	EX	VG
	Complete Set (8):	75.00	37.00	22.00
	Common Player:	8.00	4.00	2.50
(1)	Wayne Comer	8.00	4.00	2.50
(2)	Tommy Harper	10.00	5.00	3.00
(3)	Mike Hegan	8.00	4.00	2.50
(4)	Jerry McNertney	8.00	4.00	2.50
(5)	Don Mincher	8.00	4.00	2.50
(6)	Ray Oyler	8.00	4.00	2.50
(7)	Marty Pattin	8.00	4.00	2.50
(8)	Diego Segui	8.00	4.00	2.50

1963 Mickey Sego S.F. Giants

These self-framing picutres feature the artwork of Mickey Sego, but the method of their distribution is unknown. Measuring 7" x 8-1/2", the pieces have a dark frame around a large black-and-white portrait and smaller cartoon drawing of the player. There are also a few words about the player's career. A simulated plaque at the bottom of the frame bears a facsimile autograph. Each picture has a hole at top for hanging.

		NM	EX	VG
	Common Player:	15.00	7.50	4.50
(1)	Chuck Hiller	15.00	7.50	4.50
(2)	Harvey Kuenn	20.00	10.00	6.00
(3)	Willie Mays	85.00	42.00	25.00
(4)	Billy Pierce	17.50	8.75	5.25

1914 Lawrence Semon Postcards

RICHARD (RUBE) W. MARQUARD

Seven players are currently known in this series, but it's possible others remain to be reported. The approximately 3-1/2" x 5-1/2" postcards feature on their fronts either portrait or action drawings of star players by Lawrence Semon. A few biographical and career details are printed at bottom, which have allowed the assignment of 1914 as the year of issue. Backs are standard postcard style. The unnumbered cards are checklisted here alphabetically.

	NM	EX	VG
Common Player:	250.00	125.00	75.00
(1) George Burns	250.00	125.00	75.00
(2) Frank Chance	500.00	250.00	150.00
(3) Ty Cobb	2,500	1,250	750.00
(4) Walter Johnson	2,250	1,125	675.00
(5) Cornelius McGillicuddy (Connie Mack)	400.00	200.00	120.00
(6) Richard (Rube) Marquard	400.00	200.00	120.00
(7) John J. McGraw	400.00	200.00	120.00

1946-1947 Sensacion Premiums

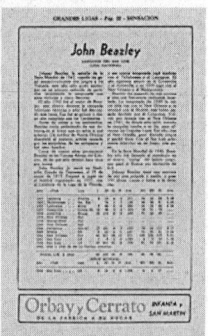

Two types of baseball premium pictures were issued by the magazine "Sensacion" during the winter league season of 1946-47. One series of 27 features Cuban stars (some of whom played in the Major Leagues), while a series of 11 Major League stars was also issued. Printed in color on newspaper stock, the pictures measure about 7-3/4" x 11". Fronts have large portraits or posed action photos with the player name in a fancy bottom border. Backs have lengthy career summaries and full stats, along with a small ad. The premiums were issued in magazines as well as in a complete album of each type. They are numbered according to the apparent order of their appearance.

	NM	EX	VG
Complete Set, Cubans (27):	1,500	750.00	450.00
Complete Set, Major Leaguers (11):	600.00	300.00	175.00
Common Cuban Player:	30.00	15.00	9.00
Common Major Leaguer:	45.00	22.50	13.50
Estrellas del Base Ball Cubano			
(1) Napoleon Reyes	45.00	22.50	13.50
(2) Fermin Guerra	30.00	15.00	9.00
(3) Gilberto Torres	30.00	15.00	9.00
(4) Martin Dihigo	750.00	375.00	225.00
(5) Lazaro Salazar	100.00	50.00	30.00
(6) Silvio Garcia	100.00	50.00	30.00
(7) Pollo Rodriguez	30.00	15.00	9.00
(8) Herberto Blanco	30.00	15.00	9.00
(9) Andres Fleitas	30.00	15.00	9.00
(10) Jorge J. Torres	30.00	15.00	9.00
(11) Salvador Hernandez	30.00	15.00	9.00
(12) Agapito Mayor	30.00	15.00	9.00
(13) Tomas de la Cruz	30.00	15.00	9.00
(14) Gilberto Valdivia	30.00	15.00	9.00
(15) Julio Moreno	30.00	15.00	9.00
(16) Regino Otero	30.00	15.00	9.00
(17) Claro Duany	50.00	25.00	15.00
(18) Pedro Jimenez	30.00	15.00	9.00
(19) Tony Castanos	30.00	15.00	9.00

(20) Alberto Hernandez	30.00	15.00	9.00
(21) Hector Rodriguez	40.00	20.00	12.00
(22) Carlos Blanco	30.00	15.00	9.00
(23) Roberto Ortiz	50.00	25.00	15.00
(24) Rene Monteagudo	30.00	15.00	9.00
(25) Pedro Pages	30.00	15.00	9.00
(26) Conrado Marrero	40.00	20.00	12.00
(27) Chino Hidalgo	30.00	15.00	9.00
Estrellas de las Grandes Ligas			
(1) Stan Musial	150.00	75.00	45.00
(2) Jim (Mickey) Vernon	50.00	25.00	15.00
(3) Dave Ferris	45.00	22.50	13.50
(4) Johnny Pesky	45.00	22.50	13.50
(5) Howie Pollett	45.00	22.50	13.50
(6) Ted Williams	200.00	100.00	60.00
(7) Johnny Hopp	45.00	22.50	13.50
(8) Dom DiMaggio	75.00	37.00	22.00
(9) Tex Hughson	45.00	22.50	13.50
(10) Johnny Beazley	45.00	22.50	13.50
(11) Tommy Holmes	45.00	22.50	13.50

1977 Sertoma Stars

This collectors' issue was produced by an Indianapolis service club. The 3" x 4" cards are printed in black on a textured yellow stock. Fronts have borderless player poses, many of which were lifted from earlier-issued cards. Backs have the Sertoma logo, set name and player name at top. Beneath a squiggly line is a business-card size ad for different members of the organization.

	NM	EX	VG
Complete Set (24):	45.00	22.50	13.50
Common Player:	2.00	1.00	.60
(1) Hank Aaron	10.00	5.00	3.00
(2) Bob Allison	2.00	.75	.60
(3) Clete Boyer	2.00	.75	.60
(4) Don Buford	2.00	.75	.60
(5) Rod Carew	3.00	1.50	.90
(6) Rico Carty	2.00	.75	.60
(7) Roberto Clemente	15.00	7.50	4.50
(8) Jim Ray Hart	2.00	.75	.60
(9) Dave Johnson	2.00	.75	.60
(10) Harmon Killebrew	3.00	1.50	.90
(11) Mickey Mantle	20.00	10.00	6.00
(12) Juan Marichal	3.00	1.50	.90
(13) Bill Mazeroski	3.00	1.50	.90
(14) Joe Morgan	3.00	1.50	.90
(15) Phil Niekro	2.50	1.25	.70
(16) Tony Oliva	2.00	1.00	.60
(17) Gaylord Perry	2.50	1.25	.70
(18) Boog Powell	2.00	1.00	.60
(19) Brooks Robinson	3.50	1.75	1.00
(20) Frank Robinson	3.50	1.75	1.00
(21) John Roseboro	2.00	.75	.60
(22) Rusty Staub	2.00	.75	.60
(23) Joe Torre	2.00	1.00	.60
(24) Jim Wynn	2.00	.75	.60

1977 Sertoma Stars - Puzzle Backs

This collectors set was issued in conjunction with the Indianapolis Sports Collectors Convention in 1977. The set was sold for $3 with proceeds benefiting the local Sertoma (Service to Mankind) Club's charity works. Cards measure 2-3/4" x 4-1/8". A 2-1/2" black circle at center contains a black-and-white player photo. The background on front is yellow, with red and black printing. Backs are borderless and form an old Pittsburgh Pirates team photo puzzle. Sets were originally sold for $3.50.

	NM	EX	VG
Complete Set (25):	75.00	37.50	22.50
Common Player:	2.00	1.00	.60
(1) Bernie Allen	2.00	1.00	.60
(2) Home Run Baker	2.00	1.00	.60
(3) Ted Beard	2.00	1.00	.60
(4) Don Buford	2.00	1.00	.60
(5) Eddie Cicotte	4.00	2.00	1.25
(6) Roberto Clemente	20.00	10.00	6.00
(7) Dom Dallessandro	2.00	1.00	.60
(8) Carl Erskine	2.00	1.00	.60
(9) Nellie Fox	6.00	3.00	1.75
(10) Lou Gehrig	20.00	10.00	6.00
(11) Joe Jackson	20.00	10.00	6.00
(12) Len Johnston	2.00	1.00	.60
(13) Benny Kauff	2.00	1.00	.60
(14) Dick Kenworthy	2.00	1.00	.60
(15) Harmon Killebrew	6.00	3.00	1.75
(16) "Lefty Bob" Logan	2.00	1.00	.60
(17) Willie Mays	15.00	7.50	4.50
(18) Satchel Paige	9.00	4.50	2.75
(19) Edd Roush	2.00	1.00	.60
(20) Chico Ruiz	2.00	1.00	.60
(21) Babe Ruth	20.00	10.00	6.00
(22) Herb Score	2.00	1.00	.60
(23) George Sisler	2.00	1.00	.60
(24) Buck Weaver	5.00	2.50	1.50
(25) Early Wynn	2.00	1.00	.60

1961 7-11

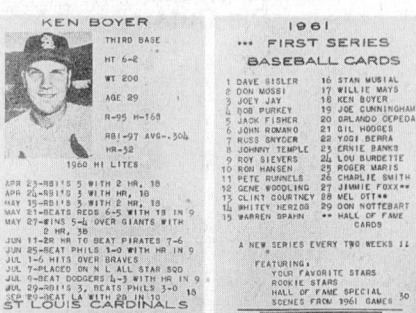

The first of 7-11's baseball card issues was a crude attempt which was abruptly halted. The checklist for the 30-card set indicated that it was the first of planned series to be issued two weeks apart. No follow-up to the first series was ever distributed. The 2-7/16" x 3-3/8" cards are printed on pink cardboard stock, with blank backs. Small black-and-white player portraits appear in the upper-left, with the player name at top, team name at bottom and card number in the lower-right corner. There are a few biographical bits and stats to the right of the photo, and several lines of 1960 season highlights below. The cards were sold seven for a nickel in vending machines.

	NM	EX	VG
Complete Set (30):	2,400	1,200	725.00
Common Player:	50.00	25.00	15.00
1 Dave Sisler	50.00	25.00	15.00
2 Don Mossi	50.00	25.00	15.00
3 Joey Jay	50.00	25.00	15.00
4 Bob Purkey	50.00	25.00	15.00
5 Jack Fisher	50.00	25.00	15.00
6 John Romano	50.00	25.00	15.00
7 Russ Snyder	50.00	25.00	15.00
8 Johnny Temple	50.00	25.00	15.00
9 Roy Sievers	50.00	25.00	15.00
10 Ron Hansen	50.00	25.00	15.00
11 Pete Runnels	50.00	25.00	15.00
12 Gene Woodling	50.00	25.00	15.00
13 Clint Courtney	50.00	25.00	15.00
14 Whitey Herzog	50.00	25.00	15.00
15 Warren Spahn	120.00	60.00	35.00
16 Stan Musial	250.00	125.00	75.00
17 Willie Mays	400.00	200.00	120.00
18 Ken Boyer	60.00	30.00	18.00
19 Joe Cunningham	50.00	25.00	15.00
20 Orlando Cepeda	90.00	45.00	27.00
21 Gil Hodges	125.00	65.00	35.00
22 Yogi Berra	150.00	75.00	45.00
23 Ernie Banks	200.00	100.00	60.00
24 Lou Burdette	50.00	25.00	15.00
25 Roger Maris	250.00	125.00	75.00
26 Charlie Smith	50.00	25.00	15.00
27 Jimmie Foxx	50.00	25.00	15.00
28 Mel Ott	50.00	25.00	15.00
29 Don Nottebart	50.00	25.00	15.00
---- Checklist	50.00	25.00	15.00

1975 Shakey's Pizza West Coast Greats

This collectors' issue was sponsored by Seattle area Shakey's Pizza restaurants in conjunction with the 1975 convention of the Washington State Sports Collectors Assn. Two thousand sets were produced featuring players who were born and/or played on the West Coast. The first 1,000 attendees at the convention were given a free sample of card #1, DiMaggio. Cards are 2-3/4" x about 3-5/8". Fronts have a black-and-white photo at center with black and red graphics. A large Shakey's logo is at lower-left. The card number, player name, position and connection to the

West Coast are printed at lower-right. Backs are in red and white with the pizza chain's logo and a list of four Seattle-area locations.

		NM	EX	VG
Complete Set (18):		30.00	15.00	9.00
Common Player:		4.00	2.00	1.25
1	Joe DiMaggio	15.00	7.50	4.50
2	Paul Waner	4.00	2.00	1.25
3	Lefty Gomez	4.00	2.00	1.25
4	Earl Averill	4.00	2.00	1.25
5	Ernie Lombardi	4.00	2.00	1.25
6	Joe Cronin	4.00	2.00	1.25
7	George Burns	4.00	2.00	1.25
8	Casey Stengel	5.00	2.50	1.50
9	Wahoo Sam Crawford	4.00	2.00	1.25
10	Ted Williams	12.50	6.25	3.75
11	Fred Hutchinson	4.00	2.00	1.25
12	Duke Snider	7.50	3.75	2.25
13	Hal Chase	4.00	2.00	1.25
14	Bobby Doerr	4.00	2.00	1.25
15	Arky Vaughan	4.00	2.00	1.25
16	Tony Lazzeri	4.00	2.00	1.25
17	Lefty O'Doul	4.00	2.00	1.25
18	Stan Hack	4.00	2.00	1.25

1976 Shakey's Pizza Hall of Fame

Between 1975-77 the Washington State Sports Collectors Assn. worked with the Shakey's pizza chain in the Seattle area to produce and distribute several sets of "old timers" cards. Generally one card from the set was given away to hobbyists attending the club's annual convention, with other cards available at the pizza places. Complete sets were also widely sold within the hobby. Interpretation of whether these are "legitimate" cards or a collector issue is up to each collector. The 1976 cards were issued in four series: Hall of Fame, Greatest Players, Immortals and All-Time Greats. The format was identical, with the (approximately) 2-1/2" x 3-1/2" cards featuring black-and-white player photos on front, surrounded by a red frame and bright blue border. Backs are in red, black and white with large Shakey ads at top and bottom. Also on back are player biographies and career stats. The cards were issued in order of the players' induction into the Hall of Fame. All four series are skip-numbered. Cards of Sam Thompson and Robin Roberts were re-issued in Series 2 to correct errors.

		NM	EX	VG
Complete Set (160):		100.00	50.00	30.00
Complete Set, no coupons (158):		75.00	37.50	22.00
Common Player:		2.00	1.00	.60
	Series 1 - Baseball's Hall of Fame	35.00	17.50	10.50
A	Earl Averill ($1 off pizza coupon on back; card show giveaway.)	4.00	2.00	1.25
1	Ty Cobb	7.50	3.75	2.25
3	Walter Johnson	3.00	1.50	.90
12	Connie Mack	2.00	1.00	.60
18	Lou Gehrig	9.00	4.50	2.75
20	George Sisler	2.00	1.00	.60
21	Cap Anson	2.00	1.00	.60
36	Mike "King" Kelly	2.00	1.00	.60
41	Jack Chesbro	2.00	1.00	.60
50	Mickey Cochrane	2.00	1.00	.60
52	Lefty Grove	2.00	1.00	.60
54	Herb Pennock	2.00	1.00	.60
55	Pie Traynor	2.00	1.00	.60
56	Charlie Gehringer	2.00	1.00	.60
57	Three-Finger Brown	2.00	1.00	.60
58	Kid Nichols	2.00	1.00	.60
59	Jimmie Foxx	2.00	1.00	.60

64	Al Simmons	2.00	1.00	.60
72	Rabbit Maranville	2.00	1.00	.60
73	Bill Terry	2.00	1.00	.60
80	Joe Cronin	2.00	1.00	.60
83	Joe McCarthy	2.00	1.00	.60
86	Bill Hamilton	2.00	1.00	.60
88	Jackie Robinson	7.50	3.75	2.25
89	Bill McKechnie	2.00	1.00	.60
93	Sam Rice	2.00	1.00	.60
95	Luke Appling	2.00	1.00	.60
103	Ted Williams	7.50	3.75	2.25
104	Casey Stengel	2.00	1.00	.60
107	Lloyd Waner	2.00	1.00	.60
108	Joe Medwick	2.00	1.00	.60
115	Lou Boudreau	2.00	1.00	.60
122	Harry Hooper	2.00	1.00	.60
127	Yogi Berra	3.00	1.50	.90
129	Lefty Gomez	2.00	1.00	.60
131	Sandy Koufax	7.50	3.75	2.25
143	Jocko Conlan	2.00	1.00	.60
144	Whitey Ford	2.00	1.00	.60
146	Sam Thompson	2.00	1.00	.60
147	Earl Averill	2.00	1.00	.60
149	Billy Herman	2.00	1.00	.60
154	Cal Hubbard	2.00	1.00	.60
156	Fred Lindstrom	2.00	1.00	.60
157	Robin Roberts	2.00	1.00	.60
	Series 2 - Baseball's Greatest Players	35.00	17.50	10.50
A	Earl Averill (Card show giveaway, coupon on back.)	2.00	1.00	.60
4	Christy Mathewson	3.00	1.50	.90
6	Nap Lajoie	2.00	1.00	.60
7	Tris Speaker	2.00	1.00	.60
9	Morgan Bulkeley	2.00	1.00	.60
10	Ban Johnson	2.00	1.00	.60
11	John McGraw	2.00	1.00	.60
14	Grover Alexander	2.00	1.00	.60
17	Eddie Collins	2.00	1.00	.60
19	Willie Keeler	2.00	1.00	.60
22	Charles Comiskey	2.00	1.00	.60
24	Buck Ewing	2.00	1.00	.60
31	Fred Clarke	2.00	1.00	.60
32	Jimmy Collins	2.00	1.00	.60
34	Hugh Duffy	2.00	1.00	.60
35	Hugh Jennings	2.00	1.00	.60
38	Wilbert Robinson	2.00	1.00	.60
40	Frank Chance	2.00	1.00	.60
42	John Evers	2.00	1.00	.60
43	Clark Griffith	2.00	1.00	.60
47	Joe Tinker	2.00	1.00	.60
51	Frank Frisch	2.00	1.00	.60
53	Carl Hubbell	2.00	1.00	.60
65	Ed Barrow	2.00	1.00	.60
66	Chief Bender	2.00	1.00	.60
67	Tommy Connolly	2.00	1.00	.60
74	Joe DiMaggio	12.50	6.25	3.75
75	Gabby Hartnett	2.00	1.00	.60
78	Home Run Baker	2.00	1.00	.60
81	Hank Greenberg	3.00	1.50	.90
87	Bob Feller	2.00	1.00	.60
90	Edd Roush	2.00	1.00	.60
109	Kiki Cuyler	2.00	1.00	.60
111	Roy Campanella	4.00	2.00	1.25
113	Stan Coveleski	2.00	1.00	.60
116	Earle Combs	2.00	1.00	.60
120	Jake Beckley	2.00	1.00	.60
125	Satchel Paige	4.00	2.00	1.25
130	Josh Gibson	3.00	1.50	.90
135	Roberto Clemente	10.00	5.00	3.00
141	Cool Papa Bell	2.00	1.00	.60
142	Jim Bottomley	2.00	1.00	.60
146	Sam Thompson	2.00	1.00	.60
150	Judy Johnson	2.00	1.00	.60
152	Oscar Charleston	2.00	1.00	.60
158	Robin Roberts	2.00	1.00	.60
	Series 3 - Baseball's Immortals	25.00	12.50	7.50
5	Honus Wagner	3.50	1.75	1.00
8	George Wright	2.00	1.00	.60
15	Alexander Cartwright	2.00	1.00	.60
16	Henry Chadwick	2.00	1.00	.60
23	Candy Cummings	2.00	1.00	.60
25	Old Hoss Radbourne	2.00	1.00	.60
26	Al Spalding	2.00	1.00	.60
28	Judge Landis	2.00	1.00	.60
29	Roger Bresnahan	2.00	1.00	.60
30	Dan Brouthers	2.00	1.00	.60
33	Ed Delahanty	2.00	1.00	.60
37	Jim O'Rourke	2.00	1.00	.60
39	Jesse Burkett	2.00	1.00	.60
44	Tommy McCarthy	2.00	1.00	.60
45	Joe McGinnity	2.00	1.00	.60
46	Eddie Plank	2.00	1.00	.60
49	Ed Walsh	2.00	1.00	.60
61	Harry Heilmann	2.00	1.00	.60
68	Bill Klem	2.00	1.00	.60
70	Harry Wright	2.00	1.00	.60
85	Max Carey	2.00	1.00	.60
91	John Clarkson	2.00	1.00	.60
92	Elmer Flick	2.00	1.00	.60
96	Red Faber	2.00	1.00	.60
97	Burleigh Grimes	2.00	1.00	.60
98	Miller Huggins	2.00	1.00	.60
99	Tim Keefe	2.00	1.00	.60
101	Monte Ward	2.00	1.00	.60
102	Pud Galvin	2.00	1.00	.60
110	Goose Goslin	2.00	1.00	.60
114	Waite Hoyt	2.00	1.00	.60
117	Ford Frick	2.00	1.00	.60
118	Jesse Haines	2.00	1.00	.60
126	George Weiss	2.00	1.00	.60
130	William Harridge	2.00	1.00	.60
132	Buck Leonard	2.00	1.00	.60
133	Early Wynn	2.00	1.00	.60
136	Billy Evans	2.00	1.00	.60
137	Monte Irvin	2.00	1.00	.60
138	George Kelly	2.00	1.00	.60

140	Mickey Welch	2.00	1.00	.60
148	Bucky Harris	2.00	1.00	.60
151	Ralph Kiner	2.00	1.00	.60
153	Roger Connor	2.00	1.00	.60
	Series 4 - Ball's All-Time Greats	20.00	10.00	6.00
2	Babe Ruth	12.50	6.25	3.75
8	Cy Young	2.50	1.25	.70
27	Rogers Hornsby	2.00	1.00	.60
48	Rube Waddell	2.00	1.00	.60
62	Paul Waner	2.00	1.00	.60
63	Dizzy Dean	2.50	1.25	.70
69	Bobby Wallace	2.00	1.00	.60
71	Bill Dickey	2.00	1.00	.60
77	Dazzy Vance	2.00	1.00	.60
79	Ray Schalk	2.00	1.00	.60
82	Sam Crawford	2.00	1.00	.60
84	Zack Wheat	2.00	1.00	.60
94	Eppa Rixey	2.00	1.00	.60
100	Heinie Manush	2.00	1.00	.60
105	Red Ruffing	2.00	1.00	.60
106	Branch Rickey	2.00	1.00	.60
112	Stan Musial	5.00	2.50	1.50
119	Dave Bancroft	2.00	1.00	.60
121	Chick Hafey	2.00	1.00	.60
123	Joe Kelley	2.00	1.00	.60
124	Rube Marquard	2.00	1.00	.60
134	Ross Youngs	2.00	1.00	.60
139	Warren Spahn	2.00	1.00	.60
145	Mickey Mantle	16.00	8.00	4.75
155	Bob Lemon	2.00	1.00	.60

1977 Shakey's All-Time Superstars

This set of baseball's all-time greatest (at least through the 1950s) was the final production of the Washington State Sports Collectors Assn. and local Shakey's restaurants. About 2-3/8" x 3", the cards feature black-and-white player photos at center with a red border around. A facsimile autograph appears in blue on the photo. Backs are similar to earlier Shakey's issues, with large logos for the pizza chain, player information and "Seasonal Bests" stats, all printed in red and black on white. Several special cards were produced for distribution at the 1977 annual convention and other venues.

		NM	EX	VG
Complete Set (28):		35.00	17.50	10.00
Complete Set (25):		25.00	12.50	7.50
Common Player:		2.00	1.00	.60
	Welcome to WSSCA Show card (Collectibles collage.)	3.00	1.50	.90
A	Earl Averill	3.00	1.50	.90
B	John Mize ($1 coupon on back.)	3.00	1.50	.90
C	Robert Lee Johnson	3.00	1.50	.90
1	Connie Mack	2.00	1.00	.60
2	John J. McGraw	2.00	1.00	.60
3	Denton T. (Cy) Young	4.00	2.00	1.25
4	Walter Johnson	4.00	2.00	1.25
5	G.C. Alexander	2.00	1.00	.60
6	Christy Mathewson	4.00	2.00	1.25
7	Lefty Grove	2.00	1.00	.60
8	Mickey Cochrane	2.00	1.00	.60
9	Bill Dickey	2.00	1.00	.60
10	Lou Gehrig	7.50	3.75	2.25
11	George Sisler	2.00	1.00	.60
12	Cap Anson	2.00	1.00	.60
13	Jimmie Foxx	2.00	1.00	.60
14	Rogers Hornsby	2.00	1.00	.60
15	Nap Lajoie	2.00	1.00	.60
16	Eddie Collins	2.00	1.00	.60
17	Pie Traynor	2.00	1.00	.60
18	Honus Wagner	4.00	2.00	1.25
19	Ty Cobb	7.50	3.75	2.25
20	Babe Ruth	10.00	5.00	3.00
21	Joe Jackson	10.00	5.00	3.00
22	Tris Speaker	2.00	1.00	.60
23	Ted Williams	6.00	3.00	1.75
24	Joe DiMaggio	7.50	3.75	2.25
25	Stan Musial	5.00	2.50	1.50
---	WSSCA Club Information Card	2.00	1.00	1.25

1952 Shelby Bicycles

The year of issue stated is conjectural, based on the familiar picture of Berra used for this promotional photo. The photo shows Yogi kneeling in full catcher's gear, except mask, ready to throw the ball; it is seen on his '50 Bowman card, among others. The blank-back, black-and-white photos is 5" x 7" with a white border all around. Scripted at bottom is, "Ride Shelby / The Winner's Bike / Sincerely / Yogi Berra."

	NM	EX	VG
Yogi Berra	150.00	75.00	45.00

1958-1959 Shillito's Boys' Shop Cincinnati Reds

This rare regional set was issued by a Cincinnati-area chain department store. The 2-1/2" x 3-1/2" black-and-white glossy cards are essentially a version of contemporary team-issued photos except for the presence (usually) on the otherwise blank back of a purple "SHILLITO'S / BOYS' SHOPS" rubber-stamp. Some cards have been seen without the ad on back. The unnumbered pictures are listed here in alphabetical order.

		NM	EX	VG
Complete Set (23):		3,500	1,750	1,050
Common Player:		200.00	100.00	60.00
(1)	Tom Acker	200.00	100.00	60.00
(2)	Ed Bailey	200.00	100.00	60.00
(3)	Gus Bell	200.00	100.00	60.00
(4)	John "Dutch" Dotterer	200.00	100.00	60.00
(5)	Walt Dropo	200.00	100.00	60.00
(6)	Del Ennis	200.00	100.00	60.00
(7)	Jay Hook	200.00	100.00	60.00
(8)	Hal Jeffcoat	200.00	100.00	60.00
(9)	Eddie Kasko	200.00	100.00	60.00
(10)	Brooks Lawrence	200.00	100.00	60.00
(11)	Jerry Lynch	200.00	100.00	60.00
(12)	Roy McMillan	200.00	100.00	60.00
(13)	Eddie Miksis	200.00	100.00	60.00
(14)	Don Newcombe	230.00	115.00	69.00
(15)	Joe Nuxhall	250.00	125.00	75.00
(16)	Jim O'Toole	200.00	100.00	60.00
(17)	Vada Pinson	250.00	125.00	75.00
(18)	Bob Purkey	200.00	100.00	60.00
(19)	Frank Robinson	500.00	250.00	150.00
(20)	Frank Thomas	200.00	100.00	60.00
(21)	Johnny Temple	200.00	100.00	60.00
(22)	Bob Thurman	200.00	100.00	60.00
(23)	Pete Whisenant	200.00	100.00	60.00

1974 Shillito's Pete Rose

PETE ROSE, 3rd Base CINCINNATI REDS
SHILLITO'S

Probably issued in conjunction with an autograph-signing appearance at the Cincinnati department store, this picture could have been issued in either 1974 or 1975. The glossy black-and-white, blank-back photo measures 5-1/2" x 8". The autograph on the example shown is genuine, the photo does not have a facsimile signature.

	NM	EX	VG
Pete Rose	150.00	75.00	45.00

1976 Shillito's Kahn's Reds Clubhouse

shillito's

Though the format for each photo differs, this series of Reds player photos was issued under the sponsorship of the Shillito's department store and Kahn's meats. In about 5" x 7-3/16" format, the blank-back photos are black-and-white with at least one (Bench) having red highlights. The pictures were given out at player autograph appearances at various Shillito's locations between June 21 and August 13. Youngsters enrolled in the club received a membership card, probably entitling them to an autograph at each event. With five dates specifically mentioned, it is likely at least one more photo exists in this series.

		NM	EX	VG
Common Player:				
(1)	Johnny Bench (Kenwood Plaza)	100.00	50.00	30.00
(2)	Dave Concepcion (Kahn's - WLW Radio)	30.00	15.00	9.00
(3)	Doug Flynn (No sponsor.)	12.00	6.00	3.50
(4)	George Foster (Four sponsors listed.)	15.00	7.50	4.50
(5)	Pete Rose (Shillito's)	100.00	50.00	30.00
---	Membership Card	10.00	5.00	3.00

1962 Shirriff Coins

This is a Canadian version of the better-known Salada-Junket plastic player coins issued in the U.S. Backs specify an issue of 200; 21 of the players from the Salada set were not issued by Shirriff. Because the Canadian coins were produced after the U.S. version they are not found with all the variations known in Salada, nor the differing levels of scarcity. Shirriff coins were packed in bags of potato chips, with each coin sealed in a clear cellophane wrapper. Although the Canadian coins are much scarcer than the U.S., significantly less demand keeps prices lower, as well.

		NM	EX	VG
Complete Set (200):		1,600	800.00	525.00
Common Player:		6.00	3.00	1.75
1	Jim Gentile	7.00	3.50	2.00
2	NOT ISSUED (Bill Pierce)			
3	Chico Fernandez (Light blue piping.)	6.00	3.00	1.75
4	NOT ISSUED (Tom Brewer)			
5	Woody Held	6.00	3.00	1.75
6	NOT ISSUED (Ray Herbert)			
7	Ken Aspromonte (Indians)	6.00	3.00	1.75
8	Whitey Ford	40.00	20.00	12.00
9	Jim Lemon	6.00	3.00	1.75
10	Billy Klaus	6.00	3.00	1.75
11	NOT ISSUED (Steve Barber)			
12	Nellie Fox	25.00	12.50	7.50
13	Jim Bunning	25.00	12.50	7.50
14	Frank Malzone	6.00	3.00	1.75
15	Tito Francona	6.00	3.00	1.75
16	Bobby Del Greco	6.00	3.00	1.75
17	Steve Bilko	6.00	3.00	1.75
18	NOT ISSUED (Tony Kubek)			
19	Earl Battey	6.00	3.00	1.75
20	Chuck Cottier	6.00	3.00	1.75
21	Willie Tasby	6.00	3.00	1.75

		NM	EX	VG
22	Bob Allison	7.00	3.50	2.00
23	Roger Maris	40.00	20.00	12.00
24	Earl Averill	6.00	3.00	1.75
25	Jerry Lumpe			
26	NOT ISSUED (Jim Grant)			
27	Carl Yastrzemski	50.00	25.00	15.00
28	Rocky Colavito (Blue piping.)	20.00	10.00	6.00
29	Al Smith	6.00	3.00	1.75
30	NOT ISSUED (Jim Busby)			
31	Dick Howser	6.00	3.00	1.75
32	Jim Perry	6.00	3.00	1.75
33	Yogi Berra	50.00	25.00	15.00
34	Ken Hamlin	6.00	3.00	1.75
35	Dale Long	6.00	3.00	1.75
36	Harmon Killebrew	35.00	17.50	10.50
37	Dick Brown	6.00	3.00	1.75
38	Gary Geiger	6.00	3.00	1.75
39	Minnie Minoso (Cardinals)	9.00	4.50	2.75
40	Brooks Robinson	35.00	17.50	10.50
41	Mickey Mantle	180.00	90.00	54.00
42	Bennie Daniels	6.00	3.00	1.75
43	Billy Martin	15.00	7.50	4.50
44	Vic Power	7.00	3.50	2.00
45	Joe Pignatano	6.00	3.00	1.75
46	Ryne Duren	7.00	3.50	2.00
47	Pete Runnels (1B)	6.00	3.00	1.75
48	Dick Williams	6.00	3.00	1.75
49	Jim Landis	6.00	3.00	1.75
50	Steve Boros	6.00	3.00	1.75
51	Zoilo Versalles	7.00	3.50	2.00
52	Johnny Temple (Orioles)	6.00	3.00	1.75
53	Jackie Brandt	6.00	3.00	1.75
54	Joe McClain	6.00	3.00	1.75
55	Sherman Lollar	6.00	3.00	1.75
56	Gene Stephens	6.00	3.00	1.75
57	Leon Wagner	6.00	3.00	1.75
58	Frank Lary	6.00	3.00	1.75
59	Bill Skowron	12.00	6.00	3.50
60	NOT ISSUED (Vic Wertz)			
61	Willie Kirkland	6.00	3.00	1.75
62	Leo Posada	6.00	3.00	1.75
63	Albie Pearson	7.00	3.50	2.00
64	Bobby Richardson	15.00	7.50	4.50
65	Marv Breeding (SS)	6.00	3.00	1.75
66	NOT ISSUED (Roy Sievers)			
67	Al Kaline	35.00	17.50	10.50
68	Don Buddin (Colts)	6.00	3.00	1.75
69	Lenny Green (White top button)	6.00	3.00	1.75
70	NOT ISSUED (Gene Green)			
71	Luis Aparicio	25.00	12.50	7.50
72	Norm Cash	12.00	6.00	3.50
73	NOT ISSUED (Jackie Jensen)			
74	Bubba Phillips	6.00	3.00	1.75
75	Jim Archer	6.00	3.00	1.75
76	Ken Hunt	6.00	3.00	1.75
77	Ralph Terry	6.00	3.00	1.75
78	Camilo Pascual	6.00	3.00	1.75
79	NOT ISSUED (Marty Keough)			
80	Cletis Boyer	9.00	4.50	2.75
81	Jim Pagliaroni	6.00	3.00	1.75
82	Gene Leek	6.00	3.00	1.75
83	Jake Wood	6.00	3.00	1.75
84	NOT ISSUED (Coot Veal)			
85	Norm Siebern	6.00	3.00	1.75
86	Andy Carey (Phillies)	6.00	3.00	1.75
87	Bill Tuttle (White top button.)	6.00	3.00	1.75
88	Jimmy Piersall	6.00	3.00	1.75
89	NOT ISSUED (Ron Hansen)			
90	Chuck Stobbs	6.00	3.00	1.75
91	Ken McBride	6.00	3.00	1.75
92	Bill Bruton	6.00	3.00	1.75
93	Gus Triandos	6.00	3.00	1.75
94	John Romano	6.00	3.00	1.75
95	Elston Howard	12.00	6.00	3.50
96	Gene Woodling	6.00	3.00	1.75
97	Early Wynn/Portrait	20.00	10.00	6.00
98	Milt Pappas	6.00	3.00	1.75
99	Bill Monbouquette	6.00	3.00	1.75
100	Wayne Causey	6.00	3.00	1.75
101	Don Elston	6.00	3.00	1.75
102	Charlie Neal	6.00	3.00	1.75
103	Don Blasingame	6.00	3.00	1.75
104	NOT ISSUED (Frank Thomas)			
105	Wes Covington	6.00	3.00	1.75
106	Chuck Hiller	6.00	3.00	1.75
107	Don Hoak	6.00	3.00	1.75
108	Bob Lillis (Colts)	6.00	3.00	1.75
109	Sandy Koufax	65.00	32.00	19.50
110	Gordy Coleman	6.00	3.00	1.75
111	Ed Matthews (Mathews)	30.00	15.00	9.00
112	Art Mahaffey	6.00	3.00	1.75
113	Ed Bailey (Name above ear.)	6.00	3.00	1.75
114	Smoky Burgess	7.00	3.50	2.00
115	Bill White	7.00	3.50	2.00
116	NOT ISSUED (Ed Bouchee)			
117	Bob Buhl	6.00	3.00	1.75
118	Vada Pinson	7.00	3.50	2.00
119	Carl Sawatski	6.00	3.00	1.75
120	Dick Stuart	7.00	3.50	2.00
121	NOT ISSUED (Harvey Kuenn)			
122	Pancho Herrera	6.00	3.00	1.75
123	Don Zimmer	7.00	3.50	2.00
124	Wally Moon	7.00	3.50	2.00
125	Joe Adcock	6.00	3.00	1.75
126	Joey Jay	6.00	3.00	1.75
127	Maury Wills (Red 3 on uniform.)	12.00	6.00	3.50
128	George Altman	6.00	3.00	1.75
129	John Buzhardt	6.00	3.00	1.75
130	Felipe Alou	7.00	3.50	2.00
131	Bill Mazeroski	25.00	12.50	7.50
132	Ernie Broglio	6.00	3.00	1.75
133	John Roseboro	7.00	3.50	2.00
134	Mike McCormick	6.00	3.00	1.75
135	Chuck Smith (White Sox)	6.00	3.00	1.75
136	Ron Santo	12.00	6.00	3.50
137	Gene Freese	6.00	3.00	1.75

138	Dick Groat	7.00	3.50	2.00
139	Curt Flood	7.00	3.50	2.00
140	Frank Bolling	6.00	3.00	1.75
141	Clay Dalrymple	6.00	3.00	1.75
142	Willie McCovey	30.00	15.00	9.00
143	Bob Skinner	6.00	3.00	1.75
144	Lindy McDaniel	6.00	3.00	1.75
145	Glen Hobbie	6.00	3.00	1.75
146	Gil Hodges	20.00	10.00	6.00
147	Eddie Kasko	6.00	3.00	1.75
148	NOT ISSUED (Gino Cimoli)			
149	Willie Mays	75.00	37.00	22.00
150	Roberto Clemente	90.00	45.00	27.00
151	Red Schoendienst	25.00	12.50	7.50
152	Joe Torre	9.00	4.50	2.75
153	Bob Purkey	6.00	3.00	1.75
154	Tommy Davis (3B)	7.50	3.75	2.25
155	Andre Rogers (Rodgers)	6.00	3.00	1.75
156	Tony Taylor	6.00	3.00	1.75
157	Bob Friend	6.00	3.00	1.75
158	Gus Bell	6.00	3.00	1.75
159	Roy McMillan	6.00	3.00	1.75
160	Carl Warwick	6.00	3.00	1.75
161	Willie Davis	6.00	3.00	1.75
162	NOT ISSUED (Sam Jones)			
163	Ruben Amaro	6.00	3.00	1.75
164	Sam Taylor	6.00	3.00	1.75
165	Frank Robinson	35.00	17.50	10.50
166	Lou Burdette	6.00	3.00	1.75
167	Ken Boyer	10.00	5.00	3.00
168	Bill Virdon	6.00	3.00	1.75
169	Jim Davenport	6.00	3.00	1.75
170	Don Demeter	6.00	3.00	1.75
171	NOT ISSUED (Richie Ashburn)			
172	John Podres	7.50	3.75	2.25
173	Joe Cunningham (White Sox)	6.00	3.00	1.75
174	ElRoy Face	6.00	3.00	1.75
175	Orlando Cepeda	25.00	12.50	7.50
176	Bobby Gene Smith	6.00	3.00	1.75
177	Ernie Banks (SS)	50.00	25.00	15.00
178	Daryl Spencer (1B)	6.00	3.00	1.75
179	NOT ISSUED (Bob Schmidt)			
180	Hank Aaron	75.00	37.00	22.00
181	Hobie Landrith	6.00	3.00	1.75
182	Ed Bressoud	6.00	3.00	1.75
183	Felix Mantilla	6.00	3.00	1.75
184	Dick Farrell	6.00	3.00	1.75
185	Bob Miller	6.00	3.00	1.75
186	Don Taussig	6.00	3.00	1.75
187	Pumpsie Green	6.00	3.00	1.75
188	Bobby Shantz	7.50	3.75	2.25
189	Roger Craig	6.00	3.00	1.75
190	Hal Smith	6.00	3.00	1.75
191	John Edwards	6.00	3.00	1.75
192	John DeMerit	6.00	3.00	1.75
193	Joe Amalfitano	6.00	3.00	1.75
194	Norm Larker	6.00	3.00	1.75
195	Al Heist	6.00	3.00	1.75
196	Al Spangler	6.00	3.00	1.75
197	Alex Grammas	6.00	3.00	1.75
198	Gerry Lynch	6.00	3.00	1.75
199	Jim McKnight	6.00	3.00	1.75
200	Jose Pagen (Pagan)	6.00	3.00	1.75
201	Junior Gilliam	7.50	3.75	2.25
202	Art Ditmar	6.00	3.00	1.75
203	Pete Daley	6.00	3.00	1.75
204	Johnny Callison	6.00	3.00	1.75
205	Stu Miller	6.00	3.00	1.75
206	Russ Snyder	6.00	3.00	1.75
207	Billy Williams	25.00	12.50	7.50
208	Walter Bond	6.00	3.00	1.75
209	Joe Koppe	6.00	3.00	1.75
210	Don Schwall	6.00	3.00	1.75
211	Billy Gardner	6.00	3.00	1.75
212	Chuck Estrada	6.00	3.00	1.75
213	Gary Bell	6.00	3.00	1.75
214	Floyd Robinson	6.00	3.00	1.75
215	Duke Snider	35.00	17.50	10.50
216	Lee Maye	6.00	3.00	1.75
217	Howie Bedell	6.00	3.00	1.75
218	Bob Will	6.00	3.00	1.75
219	Dallas Green	7.50	3.75	2.25
220	Carroll Hardy	6.00	3.00	1.75
221	Danny O'Connell	6.00	3.00	1.75

1928 Shonen Kulubu Babe Ruth Postcard

This card, which the Japanese inscription describes as picturing Babe Ruth hitting his first home run of 1926, was part of a multi-sport premium issue by the Japanese magazine Shonen Kubulu ("Youth Club"). The front has a colorized black-and-white photo, with blue inscriptions at right. Back is in blue with standard international postcard indicia.

	NM	EX	VG
Babe Ruth	500.00	250.00	150.00

1889 G. Waldon Smith Boston Beaneaters Cabinets

Whether the scope of his issue encompassed a greater portion of the 1889 Boston National Leaguers or just the four currently known players is currently unknown. Boston photographer G. Waldon Smith immortalized the players in a series of 4-1/4" x 6-1/2" cabinet cards. Each card features a capless, chest-up portrait of a mustachioed ballplayer. The studio's name and location are printed in red at bottom. The players are not identified on the pieces. The 1889 pictures can be differentiated from the 1890 issue by the ornateness of the studio address; the earlier is in plain type, the later is more ornate and includes the state abbreviation.

		NM	EX	VG
Common Player:		3,600	1,800	1,080
(1)	Tom Brown	3,600	1,800	1,080
(2)	Harry Ganzel	3,600	1,800	1,080
(3)	Billy Nash	3,600	1,800	1,080
(4)	Pop Smith	3,600	1,800	1,080
(6)	The Boston Base Ball Club (Team photo, 21" x 18")	18,000	9,000	5,400

1890 G. Waldon Smith Cabinets

As little as is known about the 1889 Smith baseball cabinets, the 1890 issue is even less well documented. Only a single player is currently recorded, Tom Brown, who also appears in the 1889 issue. In 1890, Brown was a member of the Boston Players League team; whether or not his teammates or those of the Boston National League club can be found in this issue remains unknown. Like the 1889 cabinets, size is about 4-1/4" x 6-1/2" and no player identification is presented. The 1890 cabinets can be differentiated from the 1889s by the more elaborate presentation of the studio address at bottom-right, including the state abbreviation.

	NM	EX	VG
Tom Brown	3,000	1,500	900.00
Boston Base Ball Club / Players' League (Team photo, 22" x 18")	20,000	10,000	6,000

1904 G. Waldon Smith Cabinets

Following a move down Tremont St. to No. 164A, this Boston photographer was still producing baseball player cabinet photos. Like his earlier photos, the circa 1904 pieces have black-and-white photographs mounted on stiff 4-1/4" x 6-1/2" cardboard backings. The only currently known picture in this series is a full-length portrait of Kip Selbach. Others almost certainly exist.

	NM	EX	VG
Kip Selbach	2,500	1,250	750.00

1909 W.W. Smith Postcards

Only two subjects are known in this series of postcards issued contemporary with the 1909 World Series between the Tigers and Pirates, though it is possible a card of Ty Cobb might have also been issued. The 3-1/2" x 5-1/2" black-and-white cards have pencil portraits by W.W. Smith. Backs have standard postcard markings.

THE MIGHTY HONUS

		NM	EX	VG
Complete Set (2):		3,750	1,800	1,100
(1)	The Mighty Honus (Honus Wagner)	750.00	375.00	225.00
(2)	Two of a Kind (Ty Cobb, Honus Wagner)	3,000	1,500	900.00

1957 Sohio Gas Indians/Reds

In 1957 Sohio (Standard Oil of Ohio) gas stations in Ohio issued sets of Cleveland Indians and Cincinnati Reds photocards and team albums. The blank-backed cards are 5" x 7" and printed in black-and-white with one perforated edge. The cards have a facsimile autograph as the only identification. The unnumbered cards are checklisted here alphabetically within team.

		NM	EX	VG
Complete Set (36):		650.00	325.00	195.00
Common Player:		10.00	5.00	3.00
CLEVELAND INDIANS				
	Complete Set (18):	300.00	150.00	90.00
(1)	Bob Avila	10.00	5.00	3.00
(2)	Jim Busby	10.00	5.00	3.00
(3)	Chico Carrasquel	10.00	5.00	3.00
(4)	Rocky Colavito	75.00	37.00	22.00
(5)	Mike Garcia	10.00	5.00	3.00
(6)	Jim Hegan	10.00	5.00	3.00
(7)	Bob Lemon	20.00	10.00	6.00
(8)	Roger Maris	150.00	75.00	45.00
(9)	Don Mossi	10.00	5.00	3.00
(10)	Ray Narleski	10.00	5.00	3.00
(11)	Russ Nixon	10.00	5.00	3.00
(12)	Herb Score	15.00	7.50	4.50
(13)	Al Smith	10.00	5.00	3.00
(14)	George Strickland	10.00	5.00	3.00
(15)	Bob Usher	10.00	5.00	3.00
(16)	Vic Wertz	10.00	5.00	3.00
(17)	Gene Woodling	10.00	5.00	3.00
(18)	Early Wynn	20.00	10.00	6.00
----	Cleveland Indians Album	60.00	30.00	18.00
CINCINNATI REDS				
	Complete Set (18):	325.00	160.00	97.00
(1)	Ed Bailey	10.00	5.00	3.00
(2)	Gus Bell	10.00	5.00	3.00
(3)	Rocky Bridges	10.00	5.00	3.00
(4)	Smoky Burgess	10.00	5.00	3.00
(5)	Hersh Freeman	10.00	5.00	3.00
(6)	Alex Grammas	10.00	5.00	3.00
(7)	Don Gross	10.00	5.00	3.00
(8)	Warren Hacker	10.00	5.00	3.00
(9)	Don Hoak	10.00	5.00	3.00
(10)	Hal Jeffcoat	10.00	5.00	3.00
(11)	Johnny Klippstein	10.00	5.00	3.00
(12)	Ted Kluszewski	60.00	30.00	18.00
(13)	Brooks Lawrence	10.00	5.00	3.00
(14)	Roy McMillan	10.00	5.00	3.00
(15)	Joe Nuxhall	12.50	6.25	3.75
(16)	Wally Post	10.00	5.00	3.00
(17)	Frank Robinson	150.00	75.00	45.00
(18)	Johnny Temple	10.00	5.00	3.00
----	Cincinnati Redlegs Album	60.00	30.00	18.00

1969 Solon Kansas City Royals

This collectors' issue is believed to have originated with Illinois hobbyist Bob Solon. The black-and-white, blank-back cards feature members of the expansion Royals. The border beneath the posed photos features a team logo and player identification at bottom. Cards measure 2-1/8" x 3-5/8". The checklist here is arranged alphabetically, as the cards are unnumbered.

		NM	EX	VG
Complete Set (15):		16.00	8.00	4.75
Common Player:		2.00	1.00	.60
(1)	Jerry Adair	2.00	1.00	.60
(2)	Wally Bunker	2.00	1.00	.60
(3)	Moe Drabowsky	3.00	1.50	.90
(4)	Dick Drago	2.00	1.00	.60
(5)	Joe Foy	2.00	1.00	.60
(6)	Joe Gordon	2.00	1.00	.60
(7)	Chuck Harrison	2.00	1.00	.60
(8)	Mike Hedlund	2.00	1.00	.60
(9)	Jack Hernandez	2.00	1.00	.60
(10)	Pat Kelly	2.00	1.00	.60
(11)	Roger Nelson	2.00	1.00	.60
(12)	Bob Oliver	2.00	1.00	.60
(13)	Lou Piniella	6.00	3.00	1.75
(14)	Ellie Rodriguez	2.00	1.00	.60
(15)	Dave Wickersham	2.00	1.00	.60

1905 Souvenir Post Card Shop of Cleveland

Formal portraits of the 1905 Cleveland Naps are featured in this set of black-and-white postcards. The 3-1/4" x 5-1/2" cards have a wide white border at bottom which carries the legend, "SOUVENIR POST CARD SHOP OF CLEVELAND." The player name is in white at the bottom of the photo. Backs have postage rate information and a notice, "NOTHING BUT ADDRESS ON THIS SIDE."

		NM	EX	VG
Complete Set (18):		16,500	8,250	5,000
Common Player:		950.00	475.00	285.00
(1)	Harry Bay	950.00	475.00	285.00
(2)	Harry Bemis	950.00	475.00	285.00
(3)	Bill Bernhard	950.00	475.00	285.00
(4)	Bill Bradley	950.00	475.00	285.00
(5)	Fred Buelow	950.00	475.00	285.00
(6)	Charles C. Carr	950.00	475.00	285.00
(7)	Frank Donahue	950.00	475.00	285.00
(8)	Elmer Flick	1,425	710.00	425.00
(9)	Otto Hess	950.00	475.00	285.00
(10)	Jay Jackson	950.00	475.00	285.00
(11)	Addie Joss	2,750	1,375	825.00
(12)	Nick Kahl	950.00	475.00	285.00
(13)	Napoleon Lajoie	2,000	1,000	600.00
(14)	Earl Moore	950.00	475.00	285.00
(15)	Robert Rhoads	950.00	475.00	285.00
(16)	George Stovall	950.00	475.00	285.00
(17)	Terry Turner	950.00	475.00	285.00

(18)	Ernest Vinson	950.00	475.00	285.00
(19)	Team Portraits Composite	1,500	750.00	450.00

1909-11 Sovereign Cigarettes

Premiums shown are for common-player cards. Hall of Famers or other high-demand cards generally realize little or no premium with Sovereign back. On T205s, the backs are printed in green.

PREMIUMS
T205: 1.25X
T206 150 Subjects: 1X
T206 350 Subjects: 1.5X
T206 460 Subjects: 1.5X
(See T205, T206 for checklists and base card values.)

1949 Spalding Joe DiMaggio Glove Premium Photos

The attributed date is only approximate. Lucky youngsters who received a Spalding Joe DiMaggio fielder's glove also got a pair of 8" x 10" black-and-white posed action photos of the Yankee Clipper. Each blank-back, borderless photo has a facsimile autograph.

		NM	EX	VG
(1)	Joe DiMaggio (No ball in photo.)	125.00	65.00	40.00
(2)	Joe DiMaggio (Ball in photo.)	125.00	65.00	40.00

1950s-70s Spalding Advisory Staff Photos

Advisory staff photos were a promtional item which debuted in the early 1950s, flourished in the Sixties and died in the early 1970s. Generally 8" x 10" (sometimes a little larger), these black-and-white (a few later were color) glossy photos picture players who had contracted with a major baseball equipment company to endorse and use their product. Usually the product - most often a glove - was prominently displayed in the photo. The pictures were often displayed in the windows of sporting goods stores or the walls of sports departments and were sometimes made available to customers. Because the compa- nies tended to stick with players over the years, some photos were reissued, sometimes with and sometimes without a change of team, pose or typography. Spalding staff photos of the era are checklisted here in alphabetical order. Team designation and pose description is given for each known picture. The photos are checklisted here in alphabetical order. It is unlikely this list is complete. Several arrangements of typography in the bottom border are seen for Spalding advisory staff pictures.

		NM	EX	VG
Common Player:		12.00	6.00	3.50
(1)	Richie Allen (Phillies, batting helmet.)	20.00	10.00	6.00
(2)	Gene Alley (Pirates, upper body.)	12.00	6.00	3.50
(3)	Mike Andrews (Red Sox, upper body.)	12.00	6.00	3.50
(4)	Bob Aspromonte (Dodgers, upper body.)	12.00	6.00	3.50
(5)	Sal Bando (A's, upper body.)	12.00	6.00	3.50
(7)	Steve Barber (Orioles, chest-to-cap.)	12.00	6.00	3.50
(8)	John Bateman (Colt .45s, upper body.)	12.00	6.00	3.50
(9)	Yogi Berra/Btg (Yankees)	30.00	15.00	9.00
(10)	Yogi Berra (Mets, upper body.)	30.00	15.00	9.00
(11)	Don Bessent (Brooklyn, follow-through.)	20.00	10.00	6.00
(12)	Frank Bolling/Fielding (Tigers)	15.00	7.50	4.50
(13)	Jim Bouton (Yankees, upper body.)	15.00	7.50	4.50
(14)	Jim Bunning (Phillies, upper body.)	20.00	10.00	6.00
(16)	John Callison (Phillies, batson shoulder.)	12.00	6.00	3.50
(17)	Rocky Colavito/Btg (Tigers)	25.00	12.50	7.50
(18)	Roger Craig (Brooklyn, follow-through.)	15.00	7.50	4.50
(19)	Clay Dalrymple (Phillies, upper body.)	12.00	6.00	3.50
(20)	Alvin Dark (Cardinals, batting follow-through.)	20.00	10.00	6.00
(21)	Don Drysdale (Dodgers, pitching follow-through.)	25.00	12.50	7.50
(22)	Sam Esposito (White Sox, hands on knees.)	12.00	6.00	3.50
(23)	Ron Fairly (Dodgers, upper body.)	12.00	6.00	3.50
(24)	Dick Farrell (Phillies, follow-through.)	25.00	12.50	7.50
(25)	Whitey Ford (Yankees, hands over head.)	30.00	15.00	9.00
(26)	Jim Fregosi (L.A. Angels, upper body.)	15.00	7.50	4.50
(27)	Jim Fregosi (California Angels, upper body, looking front.)	15.00	7.50	4.50
(28)	Jim Fregosi (California Angels, upper body, looking right.)	15.00	7.50	4.50
(29)	Jim Fregosi (Angels, green borders, b/w portrait.)	15.00	7.50	4.50
(30)	Bob Gibson (color, stretch position.)	25.00	12.50	7.50
(33)	Tom Haller (Giants, catching crouch.)	12.00	6.00	3.50
(34)	Richie Hebner (Pirates, full-length.)	12.00	6.00	3.50
(35)	Mike Hegan (Brewers, upper body.)	12.00	6.00	3.50
(36)	Jim Hickman (Mets, upper body.)	12.00	6.00	3.50
(37)	Ken Hunt (Reds, follow-through.)	20.00	10.00	6.00
(38)	Jerry Koosman (Mets, ready to pitch.)	15.00	7.50	4.50
(39)	Jerry Koosman (Mets, upper body.)	15.00	7.50	4.50
(40)	Don Larsen (Yankees, follow-through.)	25.00	12.50	7.50
(41)	Charlie Lau (Braves, upper body.)	15.00	7.50	4.50
(42)	Mickey Lolich (Tigers, upper body, ready to pitch.)	15.00	7.50	4.50
(43)	Jerry Lumpe (Tigers, belt-up.)	12.00	6.00	3.50
(45)	Roger Maris/Btg (Yankees)	30.00	15.00	9.00
(46)	Roger Maris (Yankees, full-length.)	30.00	15.00	9.00
(47)	Roger Maris (Cardinals, "picture-frame," b/w photo.)	30.00	15.00	9.00
(49)	Dick McAuliffe/Portrait (Tigers)	12.00	6.00	3.50
(50)	Bill Monbouquette (Red Sox, wind-up.)	12.00	6.00	3.50
(51)	Bobby Murcer (Yankees, upper body.)	12.00	6.00	3.50
(53)	Jim Northrup/Btg (Tigers)	12.00	6.00	3.50
(56)	Jim Pagliaroni/Btg (Pirates)	12.00	6.00	3.50
(58)	Jim Palmer (Upper body.)	25.00	12.50	7.50
(60)	Joe Pepitone/Btg (Yankees)	15.00	7.50	4.50
(61)	Gary Peters (White Sox, green borders, b/w portrait.)	12.00	6.00	3.50
(62)	Rico Petrocelli (Red Sox, upper body.)	12.00	6.00	3.50
(64)	Joe Pignatano (A's, hands on hips.)	12.00	6.00	3.50
(66)	Bob Rodgers/Portrait (Angels)	12.00	6.00	3.50
(67)	Rich Rollins (Twins, arms crossed.)	12.00	6.00	3.50
(69)	Nolan Ryan/Pitching (Angels, color.)	75.00	37.00	22.00
(72)	Tom Seaver (Mets, waist-to-cap.)	30.00	15.00	9.00

		NM	EX	VG
(73)	Tom Seaver/Pitching (Mets, color.)	30.00	15.00	9.00
(75)	Mel Stottlemyre (Yankees, rust borders, b/w pitching pose.)	12.00	6.00	3.50
(76)	Dick Stuart/Btg (Pirates)	15.00	7.50	4.50
(78)	Joe Torre (Braves, upper body/)	15.00	7.50	4.50
(79)	Joe Torre (Cardinals, red borders, b/w portrait/)	15.00	7.50	4.50
(85)	Pete Ward/Portrait (White Sox)	12.00	6.00	3.50
(86)	Fred Whitfield/Portrait (Indians)	12.00	6.00	3.50
(87)	Maury Wills (Dodgers, chest-to-cap.)	15.00	7.50	4.50
(88)	Maury Wills (No team, full-length batting.)	12.00	6.00	3.50
(90)	Carl Yastrzemski (Kneeling w/ bats.)	30.00	15.00	9.00
(91)	Carl Yastrzemski (Picture-frame border, b/w portrait.)	30.00	15.00	9.00

1969 Spare-Time Products Minnesota Twins Discs

The intended use and manner of distribution of these 8" uniface color discs is unknown. The hard composition discs have a baseball design on which is centered a player portrait. A facsimile autograph is at bottom and there is a hole at top for hanging. Copyright information appears at lower-right.

		NM	EX	VG
Complete Set (8):		400.00	200.00	125.00
Common Player:		30.00	15.00	9.00
(1)	Dave Boswell	30.00	22.00	9.00
(2)	Leo Cardenas	30.00	15.00	9.00
(3)	Dean Chance	30.00	15.00	9.00
(4)	Jim Kaat	45.00	22.00	13.50
(5)	Tony Oliva/SP	150.00	75.00	45.00
(6)	Ron Perranoski	30.00	22.00	9.00
(7)	Jim Perry	30.00	15.00	9.00
(8)	John Roseboro	30.00	15.00	9.00

1948 Speedway 79 Tiger of the Week Photos

This set of blank-back, black-and-white 8" x 10" photos was issued by one of the Tigers radio sponsors. One photo, bearing a facsimile autograph on front, was given away each week to honor the outstanding Tigers performer. The photos have no markings identifying the issuer and they are unnumbered. They are checklisted here alphabetically.

		NM	EX	VG
Complete Set (14):		350.00	175.00	100.00
Common Player:		30.00	15.00	9.00
(1)	Neil Berry	30.00	15.00	9.00
(2)	"Hoot" Evers	30.00	15.00	9.00
(3)	Ted Gray	30.00	15.00	9.00
(4)	Art Houtteman	30.00	15.00	9.00
(5)	Fred Hutchinson	30.00	15.00	9.00
(6)	George Kell	50.00	25.00	15.00
(7)	Eddie Lake	30.00	15.00	9.00
(8)	Johnny Lipon	30.00	15.00	9.00
(9)	Hal Newhouser	50.00	25.00	15.00
(10)	Dizzy Trout	30.00	15.00	9.00
(11)	Virgil Trucks	30.00	15.00	9.00
(12)	George Vico	30.00	15.00	9.00
(13)	Dick Wakefield	30.00	15.00	9.00
(14)	Bill Wertz	30.00	15.00	9.00

1936 Spencer Shoes Jimmie Foxx Premium Photo

The attributed date is speculative, based on the uniform in which the player is pictured on this 7" x 9", blank-back, black-and-white premium photo. The picture has a facsimile autograph at left. At bottom-right in script is, "Courtesy of Spencer Shoes."

	NM	EX	VG
Jimmie Foxx	350.00	175.00	105.00

1953-55 Spic and Span Braves

 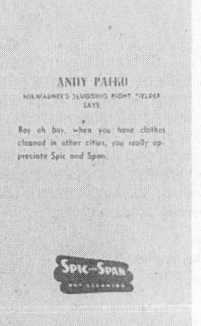

The first of several regional issues from a Milwaukee dry cleaner, the 1953-55 Spic and Span Braves set consists of black-and-white cards, 3-1/4" x 5-1/2". The fronts of the card have a facsimile autograph beneath the player photo. Cards are found with blank backs or with a ,Spic and Span advertising message on the back. Blank-backed cards are believed to have been issued by Wisco gas stations.

		NM	EX	VG
Complete Set (29):		1,800	900.00	540.00
Common Player:		50.00	25.00	15.00
(1)	Hank Aaron	600.00	300.00	180.00
(2)	Joe Adcock	50.00	25.00	15.00
(3)	John Antonelli	50.00	25.00	15.00
(4)	Vern Bickford	50.00	25.00	15.00
(5)	Bill Bruton	50.00	25.00	15.00
(6)	Bob Buhl	50.00	25.00	15.00
(7)	Lew Burdette	50.00	25.00	15.00
(8)	Dick Cole	50.00	25.00	15.00
(9)	Walker Cooper	50.00	25.00	15.00
(10)	Del Crandall	50.00	25.00	15.00
(11)	George Crowe	50.00	25.00	15.00
(12)	Jack Dittmer	50.00	25.00	15.00
(13)	Sid Gordon	50.00	25.00	15.00
(14)	Ernie Johnson	50.00	25.00	15.00
(15)	Dave Jolly	50.00	25.00	15.00
(16)	Don Liddle	50.00	25.00	15.00
(17)	John Logan	50.00	25.00	15.00
(18)	Ed Mathews	200.00	100.00	60.00
(19)	Chet Nichols	50.00	25.00	15.00
(20)	Dan O'Connell	50.00	25.00	15.00
(21)	Andy Pafko	50.00	25.00	15.00
(22)	Jim Pendleton	50.00	25.00	15.00
(23)	Ebba St. Claire	50.00	25.00	15.00
(24)	Warren Spahn	200.00	100.00	60.00
(25)	Max Surkont	50.00	25.00	15.00
(26)	Bob Thomson	75.00	37.50	22.00
(27)	Bob Thorpe	50.00	25.00	15.00
(28)	Roberto Vargas	50.00	25.00	15.00
(29)	Jim Wilson	50.00	25.00	15.00

1953-57 Spic and Span Braves 7x10 Photos

This regional set was issued by Spic and Span Dry Cleaners of Milwaukee over a four-year period and consists of large (7" x 10") photos of Braves players. Of all the various Spic and Span sets, this one seems to be the easiest to find. The fronts feature a player photo with a facsimile autograph below. The Spic and Span logo also appears on the fronts, while the backs are blank. A header card picturing Milwaukee County Stadium also exists.

		NM	EX	VG
Complete Set (14):		335.00	165.00	100.00
Common Player:		25.00	12.50	7.50
(1)	Joe Adcock	25.00	12.50	7.50
(2)	William H. Bruton	25.00	12.50	7.50
(3)	Robert Buhl	25.00	12.50	7.50
(4)	Lou Burdette	25.00	12.50	7.50
(5)	Del Crandall	25.00	12.50	7.50
(6)	Jack Dittmer	25.00	12.50	7.50
(7)	Johnny Logan	25.00	12.50	7.50
(8)	Edwin L. Mathews, Jr.	75.00	37.50	22.00
(9)	Chet Nichols	25.00	12.50	7.50
(10)	Danny O'Connell	25.00	12.50	7.50
(11)	Andy Pafko	25.00	12.50	7.50
(12)	Warren E. Spahn	75.00	37.50	22.00
(13)	Bob Thomson	35.00	17.50	10.00
(14)	Milwaukee County Stadium	35.00	17.50	10.00

1954 Spic and Span Braves

Player selection points to 1954 as the date of this issue, making it contemporary with several other card sets produced by the chain of Wisconsin dry cleaners. These cards are printed in blue on 5-1/2" x 8-1/2" yellow cardstock. Fronts have player portraits by an artist signed as "Warmuth," facsimile autographs, a promotional quote from the player and the sponsor's logo. Backs are blank. It is not known whether the set is complete at 13.

		NM	EX	VG
Complete Set (13):		1,200	600.00	350.00
Common Player:		75.00	37.50	22.50
(1)	Joe Adcock	90.00	45.00	27.50
(2)	William H. Bruton	75.00	37.50	22.50
(3)	Robert Buhl	75.00	37.50	22.50
(4)	Lou Burdette	75.00	37.50	22.50
(5)	Del Crandall	75.00	37.50	22.50
(6)	Jack Dittmer	75.00	37.50	22.50
(7)	Johnny Logan	75.00	37.50	22.50
(8)	Edwin L. Mathews Jr.	225.00	110.00	70.00
(9)	Chet Nichols	75.00	37.50	22.50
(10)	Danny O'Connell	75.00	37.50	22.50
(11)	Andy Pafko	75.00	37.50	22.50
(12)	Warren E. Spahn	225.00	110.00	70.00
(13)	Bob Thomson	90.00	45.00	27.50

1954-56 Spic and Span Braves

Issued during the three-year period from 1954-1956, this Spic and Span set consists of 18 postcard-size (4" x 6") cards. The front of the cards include a facsimile autograph printed in white and the Spic and Span logo.

		NM	EX	VG
Complete Set (18):		1,350	675.00	400.00
Common Player:		35.00	17.50	10.00
(1)	Hank Aaron	400.00	200.00	120.00
(2)	Joe Adcock	35.00	17.50	10.00
(3)	William H. Bruton	35.00	17.50	10.00
(4)	Robert Buhl	35.00	17.50	10.00
(5)	Lou Burdette	35.00	17.50	10.00
(6)	Gene Conley	35.00	17.50	10.00
(7)	Del Crandall	35.00	17.50	10.00
(8)	Ray Crone	35.00	17.50	10.00
(9)	Jack Dittmer	35.00	17.50	10.00
(10)	Ernie Johnson	35.00	17.50	10.00
(11)	Dave Jolly	35.00	17.50	10.00
(12)	Johnny Logan	35.00	17.50	10.00
(13)	Edwin L. Mathews, Jr.	225.00	110.00	70.00
(14)	Chet Nichols	35.00	17.50	10.00
(15)	Danny O'Connell	35.00	17.50	10.00
(16)	Andy Pafko	35.00	17.50	10.00
(17)	Warren E. Spahn	220.00	110.00	70.00
(18)	Bob Thomson	60.00	30.00	18.00

1955 Spic and Span Braves Die-cuts

This 17-card, die-cut set is the rarest of all the Spic and Span issues. The stand-ups, which measure approximately 7-1/2" x 7", picture the players in action poses and were designed to be punched out, allowing them to stand up. Most cards were used in this fashion, making better-condition cards very rare today. The front of the card includes a facsimile autograph and the Spic and Span logo.

		NM	EX	VG
Complete Set (18):		4,400	2,200	1,250
Common Player:		175.00	90.00	55.00
(1)	Hank Aaron	900.00	450.00	275.00
(2)	Joe Adcock	175.00	90.00	55.00
(3)	Bill Bruton	175.00	90.00	55.00
(4)	Bob Buhl	175.00	90.00	55.00
(5)	Lew Burdette	175.00	90.00	55.00
(6)	Gene Conley	175.00	90.00	55.00
(7)	Del Crandall	175.00	90.00	55.00
(8)	Jack Dittmer	175.00	90.00	55.00
(9)	Ernie Johnson	175.00	90.00	55.00
(10)	Dave Jolly	175.00	90.00	55.00
(11)	John Logan	175.00	90.00	55.00
(12)	Ed Mathews	450.00	225.00	135.00
(13)	Chet Nichols	175.00	90.00	55.00
(14)	Dan O'Connell	175.00	90.00	55.00
(15)	Andy Pafko	175.00	90.00	55.00
(16)	Warren Spahn	450.00	225.00	135.00
(17)	Bob Thomson	225.00	110.00	65.00
(18)	Jim Wilson	175.00	90.00	55.00

1957 Spic and Span Braves

This 20-card set was issued in 1957, the year the Braves were World Champions and is a highly desirable set. The cards measure 4" x 5" and have a wide white border surrounding the player photo. A blue Spic and Span logo appears in the lower-right corner and the card includes a salutation and facsimile autograph, also in blue.

	NM	EX	VG
Complete Set (20):	1,250	625.00	375.00
Common Player:	25.00	12.50	7.50

		NM	EX	VG
(1)	Hank Aaron	400.00	200.00	120.00
(2)	Joe Adcock	25.00	12.50	7.50
(3)	Bill Bruton	25.00	12.50	7.50
(4)	Bob Buhl	25.00	12.50	7.50
(5)	Lew Burdette	25.00	12.50	7.50
(6)	Gene Conley	25.00	12.50	7.50
(7)	Wes Covington/SP	50.00	25.00	15.00
(8)	Del Crandall	25.00	12.50	7.50
(9)	Ray Crone	25.00	12.50	7.50
(10)	Fred Haney	25.00	12.50	7.50
(11)	Ernie Johnson	25.00	12.50	7.50
(12)	John Logan	25.00	12.50	7.50
(13)	Felix Mantilla/SP	50.00	25.00	15.00
(14)	Ed Mathews	85.00	45.00	25.00
(15)	Dan O'Connell	25.00	12.50	7.50
(16)	Andy Pafko	25.00	12.50	7.50
(17)	Red Schoendienst/SP	110.00	55.00	35.00
(18)	Warren Spahn	85.00	45.00	25.00
(19)	Bob Thomson	45.00	22.50	13.50
(20)	Bob Trowbridge/SP	50.00	25.00	15.00

1960 Spic and Span Braves

Spic and Span's final Milwaukee Braves issue consists of 26 cards, each measuring 2-3/4" x 3-1/8". The fronts contain a white-bordered photo with no printing, while the backs include a facsimile autograph and the words "Photographed and Autographed Exclusively for Spic and Span." The 1960 set includes the only known variation in the Spic and Span sets; a "flopped" negative error showing catcher Del Crandall batting left-handed was later corrected.

		NM	EX	VG
Complete Set (26):		1,650	825.00	500.00
Common Player:		35.00	17.50	10.00
(1)	Hank Aaron	650.00	325.00	200.00
(2)	Joe Adcock	35.00	17.50	10.00
(3)	Bill Bruton	35.00	17.50	10.00
(4)	Bob Buhl	35.00	17.50	10.00
(5)	Lew Burdette	35.00	17.50	10.00
(6)	Chuck Cottier	35.00	17.50	10.00
(7a)	Del Crandall (Photo reversed.)	60.00	30.00	18.00
(7b)	Del Crandall (Correct photo.)	35.00	17.50	10.00
(8)	Chuck Dressen	35.00	17.50	10.00
(9)	Joey Jay	35.00	17.50	10.00
(10)	John Logan	35.00	17.50	10.00
(11)	Felix Mantilla	35.00	17.50	10.00
(12)	Ed Mathews	125.00	65.00	35.00
(13)	Lee Maye	35.00	17.50	10.00
(14)	Don McMahon	35.00	17.50	10.00
(15)	George Myatt	35.00	17.50	10.00
(16)	Andy Pafko	35.00	17.50	10.00
(17)	Juan Pizarro	35.00	17.50	10.00
(18)	Mel Roach	35.00	17.50	10.00
(19)	Bob Rush	35.00	17.50	10.00
(20)	Bob Scheffing	35.00	17.50	10.00
(21)	Red Schoendienst	90.00	45.00	27.50
(22)	Warren Spahn	125.00	65.00	35.00
(23)	Al Spangler	35.00	17.50	10.00
(24)	Frank Torre	35.00	17.50	10.00
(25)	Carl Willey	35.00	17.50	10.00
(26)	Whit Wyatt	35.00	17.50	10.00

1964-67 Sport Hobbyist Famous Card Series

These very early collectors issues were produced over a period of several years in the mid-1960s during Frank Nagy's ownership of the "Sport Hobbyist" magazine. The 2-1/4" x 3-3/4" black-and-white cards picture on their fronts reproductions of rare and famous baseball cards from Nagy's

unequaled collection, including eight of the very rare Tarzan Bread issue of the mid-1930s which few collectors even today have seen. Backs have identification of the pictured card, utilizing the then-standard "American Card Catalog" set designations.

		NM	EX	VG
Complete Set (30):		90.00	45.00	27.50
Common Player:		5.00	2.50	1.50
1	T206 Honus Wagner	12.50	6.25	3.75
2	T212 Henley	5.00	2.50	1.50
3	C46 Simmons	5.00	2.50	1.50
4	M116 Christy Mathewson	5.00	2.50	1.50
5	M101-5 Jack Barry	5.00	2.50	1.50
6	T204 Mordecai Brown	5.00	2.50	1.50
7	D322 Tip Top Bread Webb	5.00	2.50	1.50
8	S74 Lou Criger	5.00	2.50	1.50
9	R333 DeLong Kiki Cuyler	5.00	2.50	1.50
10	R319 Nap Lajoie	7.50	3.75	2.25
11	T205 John McGraw	5.00	2.50	1.50
12	E107 Addie Joss	5.00	2.50	1.50
13	W502 George Sisler	5.00	2.50	1.50
14	Allen & Ginter N29 Buck Ewing	5.00	2.50	1.50
15	E90 Chief Bender	5.00	2.50	1.50
16	E104 George Mullin	5.00	2.50	1.50
17	E95 Fred Merkle	5.00	2.50	1.50
18	E121 Walter Schang	5.00	2.50	1.50
19	Allen & Ginter N28 Tim Keefe	5.00	2.50	1.50
20	E120 Harold (Muddy) Ruel	5.00	2.50	1.50
21	D382 Irving (Jack) Burns	5.00	2.50	1.50
22	D382 George Connally	5.00	2.50	1.50
23	D382 Myril Hoag	5.00	2.50	1.50
24	D382 Willie Kamm	5.00	2.50	1.50
25	D382 Dutch Leonard	5.00	2.50	1.50
26	D382 Clyde Manion	5.00	2.50	1.50
27	D382 Johnny Vergez	5.00	2.50	1.50
28	D382 Tom Zachary	5.00	2.50	1.50
29	E145 Ty Cobb	7.50	3.75	2.25
30	Playing Card, Richardson	5.00	2.50	1.50

1971 Sport Hobbyist Famous Card Series

A new series of collector cards, designed as the first-ever attempt to reproduce the T206 tobacco set, was begun under the hobby paper's new ownership but quickly abandoned. The 2" x 3" cards have a black-and-white picture of a card at center, surrounded by a red frame (except Bescher, which has a black frame). Backs identify the card and include a card number.

		NM	EX	VG
Complete Set (21):		90.00	45.00	27.50
Common Card:		5.00	2.50	1.50
31	T206 Abbaticchio	5.00	2.50	1.50
32	T206 Barbeau	5.00	2.50	1.50
33	T206 Burch	5.00	2.50	1.50
34	T206 M. Brown	5.00	2.50	1.50
35	T206 Chase	5.00	2.50	1.50
36	T206 Ball	5.00	2.50	1.50
37	T206 Abstein	5.00	2.50	1.50
38	T206 Bowerman	5.00	2.50	1.50
39	T206 Chase	5.00	2.50	1.50
40	T206 Criss	5.00	2.50	1.50
41	T206 Beck	5.00	2.50	1.50
42	T206 Bresnahan	5.00	2.50	1.50
43	T206 Bradley	5.00	2.50	1.50
44	T206 Berger	5.00	2.50	1.50
45	T206 Bransfield	5.00	2.50	1.50
46	T206 Bescher	5.00	2.50	1.50
47	T206 Bell	5.00	2.50	1.50
48	T206 Bergen	5.00	2.50	1.50
49	T206 Bender	5.00	2.50	1.50
50	T206 Bush	5.00	2.50	1.50
51	T206 Chesbro	5.00	2.50	1.50

1975 Sport Hobbyist

This was one of several series of collectors issues produced in the 1960s and 1970s by the Sport Hobbyist, one of the card hobby's earliest periodicals. This series features the past greats of the game in postcard size (3-1/2" x 5-1/2"). Cards are found either blank-backed or with an ad offering various new-card products. Fronts of cards numbered through 115 have watercolor portraits in an oval frame. A box below offers a career summary. Higher number cards feature photos and/or artwork, some-

JOE DiMAGGIO
Joe DiMaggio hit safely in 56 consecutive games for a major league record. Was MVP in 1939-41 and 47. Batted over .300 11 times in 13 seasons, seven times consecutively. Elected to Hall of Famer in 1955.

times with a caption, and sometimes with no identification. Cards are numbered with an SH prefix. Each series of 18 were originally sold for $1.50.

	NM	EX	VG
Complete Set (48):	150.00	75.00	45.00
Common Player:	5.00	2.50	1.50
98 Lou Gehrig	15.00	7.50	4.50
99 Ty Cobb	12.50	6.25	3.75
100 Joe DiMaggio	15.00	7.50	4.50
101 Mel Ott	5.00	2.50	1.50
102 Carl Hubbell	5.00	2.50	1.50
103 Babe Ruth	20.00	10.00	6.00
104 Rogers Hornsby	7.50	3.75	2.25
105 Tris Speaker	7.50	3.75	2.25
106 Hank Greenberg	7.50	3.75	2.25
107 Jimmy (Jimmie) Foxx	7.50	3.75	2.25
108 Ted Williams	15.00	7.50	4.50
109 Mickey Cochrane	5.00	2.50	1.50
110 Bob Feller	7.50	3.75	2.25
111 Cy Young	9.00	4.50	2.75
112 George Sissler (Sisler)	5.00	2.50	1.50
113 Honus Wagner	9.00	4.50	2.75
114 Lefty Grove	5.00	2.50	1.50
115 Dizzy Dean	7.50	3.75	2.25
116 Babe Ruth (Farewell address.)	9.00	4.50	2.75
117 Jackie Robinson	7.50	3.75	2.25
118 Mike Kelly (Woodcut)	5.00	2.50	1.50
119 Honus Wagner (Portrait and action.)	5.00	2.50	1.50
120 Babe Ruth (W/mascot Ray Kelly.)	9.00	4.50	2.75
121 Babe Ruth (Photos/artwork.)	5.00	2.50	1.50
122 John M. Ward (Newsboy cabinet.)	5.00	2.50	1.50
123 Babe Ruth (Photos/artwork)	5.00	2.50	1.50
124 Babe Ruth (Artwork)	5.00	2.50	1.50
125 Hall of Fame Dedication, 1939	5.00	2.50	1.50
126 Babe Ruth (At microphone.)	5.00	2.50	1.50
127 Babe Ruth, Jacob Ruppert	7.50	3.75	2.25
128 Stan Musial	7.50	3.75	2.25
129 Babe Ruth (W/others.)	5.00	2.50	1.50
130 George Kell	5.00	2.50	1.50
131 Luke Appling	5.00	2.50	1.50
132 Cecil Travis	5.00	2.50	1.50
133 Larry "Yogi" Berra	7.50	3.75	2.25
134 Harry Heilman (Heilmann)	5.00	2.50	1.50
135 Johnny Mize	5.00	2.50	1.50
136 Christy Mathewson	7.50	3.75	2.25
137 Ralph Kiner	5.00	2.50	1.50
138 Bill Dickey	5.00	2.50	1.50
139 Hank Sauer	5.00	2.50	1.50
140 Hank Greenberg	7.50	3.75	2.25
141 Charlie Gehringer	5.00	2.50	1.50
142 Walter Evers	5.00	2.50	1.50
143 John Pepper Martin	5.00	2.50	1.50
144 Vern Stephens	5.00	2.50	1.50
145 Bobbie (Bobby) Doerr	5.00	2.50	1.50

1975 Sport Hobbyist Team Composites

This was one of several series of collectors issues produced in the 1960s and 1970s by the Sport Hobbyist, one of the card hobby's earliest periodicals. This series features black-and-white postcard

size (about 3-1/2" x 5-1/4") reproductions of team composite photos from the 1931 Spalding Guide. Cards are blank-backed. Most of the cards are numbered, with an SH prefix, though some are not.

		NM	EX	VG
Common Card:		6.00	3.00	1.80
70	Chicago Cubs	6.00	3.00	1.80
71				
72	N.Y. Giants	6.00	3.00	1.80
73				
74	Pittsburgh Pirates	6.00	3.00	1.80
75	Chicago Cubs	6.00	3.00	1.80
76				
77	Boston Braves	6.00	3.00	1.80
78	Cincinnati Reds	6.00	3.00	1.80
79	Brooklyn Dodgers	6.00	3.00	1.80
80				
81	Philadelphia A's	6.00	3.00	1.80
82	Cleveland Indians	6.00	3.00	1.80
83	Detroit Tigers	6.00	3.00	1.80
84	Chicago White Sox	6.00	3.00	1.80
85	Chicago White Sox	6.00	3.00	1.80
86	Boston Red Sox	6.00	3.00	1.80
87	Boston Red Sox	6.00	3.00	1.80
88	N.Y. Yankees	10.00	5.00	3.00
89	Cleveland Indians	6.00	3.00	1.80
90	St. Louis Browns	6.00	3.00	1.80
91	Washington Senators	6.00	3.00	1.80
92	Boston Braves	6.00	3.00	1.80
93	St. Louis Browns	6.00	3.00	1.80
94	Washington Senators	6.00	3.00	1.80
95	Philadelphia Phillies	6.00	3.00	1.80
96	Cincinnati Reds	6.00	3.00	1.80
97	Philadelphia Phillies	6.00	3.00	1.80
UNNUMBERED				
---	Brooklyn Dodgers	6.00	3.00	1.80
---	Detroit Tigers	6.00	3.00	1.80
---	N.Y. Yankees	10.00	5.00	3.00
---	Pittsburgh Pirates	6.00	3.00	1.80

1888-1889 Sporting Extra World Tour Imperial Cabinets

These large-format (about 9-3/4" x 6-1/2") imperial cabinet cards were issued in conjunction with "Spalding's World Base Ball Tour" of 1888-1889, though their method of distribution is unknown. The cards feature team portraits on a heavy cardboard, gilt-edge mount. At top is the name of the sponsoring cigarette brand, at bottom is the team name, printed in red. Backs are blank. Each of the cards that appeared in a 12/05 auction is believed unique.

(1) THE ALL AMERICA B.B. TOURISTS
(2) THE CHICAGO B.B. TOURISTS
Pair sold in 12/05 auction for $27,709.

1902-11 Sporting Life Cabinets (W600)

From 1902 through 1911, Sporting Life, a weekly newspaper published in Philadelphia, produced and sold a lengthy run of 5" x 7-1/2" "Cabinet Phototypes of Well-known Baseball Players." They were collectively given the catalog number of W600 in "The American Card Catalog." Because many players were issued with different team designations as they moved about over the years, and because there are new discoveries from this issue being made even today, it is likely this checklist will remain in flux for some time to come. For that reason, gaps in the assigned card numbers in this checklist have been left to accommodate additions. Several different styles and colors of mattes were used over the years, with many players issued in more than one of them. Many of the earliest cabinets picture the players in suit-and-tie, while later issues show them in uniform. Where verified, cabinets showing players in street clothes are noted. The black-and-white player portraits are mounted on heavy cardboard mattes. The player's name, position, team and league are printed beneath the photo. Backs are blank. Each cabinet was issued in a transparent envelope. They were originally given away for three two-cents stamps and a coupon found in the paper; later they were offered for sale for 10 cents apiece; 12 for a dollar. The checklist here is presented in alphabetical order. Most of the names are as presented in contemporary ads from the newspaper; rife with misspellings and misidentifications, and may or may not represent

the actual spelling shown on the cards. The year shown in parentheses indicates the first year the player was issued with that team. Because these cards were sold individually upon fan request, this is an issue in which the superstars of the day are more common than the benchwarmers. It is also likely that some of the cards on this list were never issued or do not survive.

		NM	EX	VG
Common Player:		2,000	1,000	600.00
(1)	Edward Abbatichio (Abbaticchio) (Boston NL, 1903)	3,000	1,500	900.00
(2)	Edward Abbatichio (Pittsburg, 1907)	2,000	1,000	600.00
(3)	William Abstein (St. Louis AL, 1910)	2,000	1,000	600.00
(4)	Charles B. Adams (Pittsburg, 1909)	2,000	1,000	600.00
(5)	C.A. Alperman (Brooklyn, 1906)	2,000	1,000	600.00
(6)	David Altizer (Washington, 1907)	2,000	1,000	600.00
(7)	Nick Altrock (Chicago AL, 1903)	3,600	1,800	1,080
(8)	Leon Ames (New York, NL, 1904)	2,000	1,000	600.00
(9)	John Anderson (St. Louis AL, 1902, street)	3,000	1,500	900.00
(10)	John Anderson (New York AL, 1904)	2,000	1,000	600.00
(11)	John Anderson (Washington, 1905)	2,000	1,000	600.00
(12)	Frank Arelanes (Arellanes) (Boston AL, 1910)	2,000	1,000	600.00
(13)	Charles Armbruster (Boston AL, 1906)	2,000	1,000	600.00
(14)	William R. Armour (Detroit, 1906)	2,000	1,000	600.00
(15)	Harry Arndt (St. Louis NL, 1906)	2,000	1,000	600.00
(16)	Harry J. Aubrey (Boston NL, 1903)	3,000	1,500	900.00
(17)	James Austin (New York AL, 1910)	2,000	1,000	600.00
(18)	Charles Babb (New York NL, 1903)	3,000	1,500	900.00
(19)	Charles Babb (Brooklyn, 1904)	2,000	1,000	600.00
(20)	William Bailey (St. Louis NL, 1910)	2,000	1,000	600.00
(21)	Frank Baker (Philadelphia AL, 1910)	5,400	2,700	1,620
(22)	J. Barbeau (Cleveland, 1906)	2,000	1,000	600.00
(23)	G.O. Barclay (Boston NL, 1904)	2,000	1,000	600.00
(24)	Edward Barger (First name Eros)(Brooklyn, 1910.)	2,000	1,000	600.00
(25)	James Barrett (Detroit, 1902, street)	3,000	1,500	900.00
(26)	James Barrett (Boston AL, 1906)	2,000	1,000	600.00
(27)	John C. Barry (Philadelphia NL, 1902)	3,000	1,500	900.00
(28)	John C. Barry (Chicago NL, 1904)	2,000	1,000	600.00
(29)	John C. Barry (Cincinnati, 1905)	2,000	1,000	600.00
(30)	John C. Barry (St. Louis NL, 1906)	2,000	1,000	600.00
(31)	John J. Barry (Philadelphia AL, 1910)	2,000	1,000	600.00
(32)	Harry L. Barton (Philadelphia AL, 1905)	2,000	1,000	600.00
(33)	Henry Batch (Brooklyn, 1906)	2,000	1,000	600.00
(34)	Joseph Bates (Johnny)(Boston NL, 1907)	2,000	1,000	600.00
(35)	Harry Bay (Cleveland, 1903)	3,000	1,500	900.00
(36)	Clarence H. Beaumont (Pittsburg, 1902, street)	3,000	1,500	900.00
(37)	Clarence H. Beaumont (Pittsburg, 1902, uniform)	3,000	1,500	900.00
(38)	Clarence H. Beaumont (Boston NL, 1907)	2,000	1,000	600.00
(39)	Fred Beck (Boston NL, 1910)	2,000	1,000	600.00
(40)	Harry Beckendorf (Detroit, 1910)	2,000	1,000	600.00
(41)	Jacob Beckley (Cincinnati, 1902)	6,600	3,300	1,980
(42)	Jacob Beckley (St. Louis NL, 1904)	5,400	2,700	1,620
(43)	Fred L. Beebe (St. Louis NL, 1906)	2,000	1,000	600.00
(44)	George C. Bell (Brooklyn, 1910)	2,000	1,000	600.00
(45)	Harry Bemis (Cleveland, 1903)	3,000	1,500	900.00
(46)	Charles Bender (Philadelphia AL, 1903, street)	6,600	3,300	1,980
(47)	Charles Bender (Philadelphia AL, 1903, uniform)	6,600	3,300	1,980
(48)	Justin J. Bennett (St. Louis NL, 1907)	2,000	1,000	600.00
(49)	William Bergen (Brooklyn, 1904)	2,000	1,000	600.00
(50)	Charles Berger (Cleveland, 1907)	2,000	1,000	600.00
(51)	William Bernhardt (Bernhard) (Cleveland, 1902, street)	3,000	1,500	900.00
(52)	Robert Bescher (Cincinnati, 1910)	2,000	1,000	600.00
(53)	Walter Beville (Henry "Monte") (New York, AL 1903)	3,000	1,500	900.00

#	Name (Team, Year)			
(54)	Walter Beville (Henry "Monte") (Detroit, 1904)	2,000	1,000	600.00
(55)	Russell Blackburne (Chicago AL, 1910)	2,000	1,000	600.00
(56)	Elmer Bliss (St. Louis NL, 1910)	2,000	1,000	600.00
(57)	Frank Bowerman (New York NL, 1903)	3,000	1,500	900.00
(58)	Frank (William J.) Bradley (Cleveland, 1903)	3,000	1,500	900.00
(59)	William J. Bradley (Cleveland, 1903)	3,000	1,500	900.00
(60)	David L. Brain (St. Louis NL, 1903)	3,000	1,500	900.00
(61)	David L. Brain (Pittsburg, 1905)	2,000	1,000	600.00
(62)	David L. Brain (Boston NL, 1906)	2,000	1,000	600.00
(63)	William Bransfield (Pittsburg, 1902, street)	3,000	1,500	900.00
(64)	William Bransfield (Pittsburg, 1902, uniform)	3,000	1,500	900.00
(65)	William Bransfield (Philadelphia NL, 1905)	2,000	1,000	600.00
(66)	Roger Bresnahan (New York NL, 1903)	6,600	3,300	1,980
(67)	Roger Bresnahan (St. Louis NL, 1909)	5,400	2,700	1,620
(68)	Albert Bridwell (Boston NL, 1906)	2,000	1,000	600.00
(69)	Herbert Briggs (Chicago NL, 1905)	2,000	1,000	600.00
(70)	Herbert Briggs (Brooklyn, 1906)	2,000	1,000	600.00
(71)	Charles E. Brown (St. Louis NL, 1906)	2,000	1,000	600.00
(72)	Charles E. Brown (Philadelphia NL, 1907)	2,000	1,000	600.00
(73)	Mordecai Brown (Chicago NL, 1904)	5,400	2,700	1,620
(74)	Samuel Brown (Boston NL, 1907)	2,000	1,000	600.00
(75)	George Browne (New York NL, 1903)	3,000	1,500	900.00
(76)	Fred Buelow (Detroit, 1903)	3,000	1,500	900.00
(77)	Fred Buelow (Cleveland, 1904)	2,000	1,000	600.00
(78)	James T. Burke (St. Louis NL, 1903)	3,000	1,500	900.00
(79)	James T. Burke (Philadelphia AL, 1906)	2,000	1,000	600.00
(80)	Jesse Burkett (St. Louis AL, 1903)	36,000	18,000	10,800
(81)	Jesse Burkett (Boston AL, 1905)	5,400	2,700	1,620
(82)	James J. Callahan (Chicago AL, 1903)	3,000	1,500	900.00
(83)	Howard Camnitz (Pittsburg, 1910)	2,000	1,000	600.00
(84)	Wirt V. Cannell (Virgin Wirt)(Boston NL, 1903)	3,000	1,500	900.00
(85)	Joseph Cantillion (Washington, 1907)	2,000	1,000	600.00
(86)	George Carey (Washington, 1903)	3,000	1,500	900.00
(87)	P.J. Carney (Boston NL, 1903)	3,000	1,500	900.00
(88)	Charles C. Carr (Cleveland, 1904)	2,000	1,000	600.00
(89)	Charles C. Carr (Cincinnati, 1906)	2,000	1,000	600.00
(90)	William Carrigan (Boston AL, 1910)	2,000	1,000	600.00
(91)	James P. Casey (Chicago NL, 1902, street)	3,000	1,500	900.00
(92)	James P. Casey (Brooklyn, 1906)	2,000	1,000	600.00
(93)	Joseph Cassidy (Washington, 1904)	2,000	1,000	600.00
(94)	Luis Castro (Philadelphia AL, 1902, street)	2,000	1,000	600.00
(95)	Frank Chance (Chicago NL, 1902, street)	6,600	3,300	1,980
(96)	Frank Chance (Chicago NL, 1902, uniform)	6,600	3,300	1,980
(97)	Harold Chase (New York AL, 1906)	4,200	2,150	1,200
(98)	John Chesbro (Pittsburg, 1902, street)	6,600	3,300	1,980
(99)	John Chesbro (New York AL, 1903, uniform)	6,600	3,300	1,980
(100)	Edw. V. Cicotte (Boston AL, 1910)	5,400	2,700	1,620
(101)	William Clark (Clarke)(Washington, 1903)	3,000	1,500	900.00
(102)	William Clark (Clarke)(New York NL, 1905)	2,000	1,000	600.00
(103)	Fred Clarke (Pittsburg, 1902, street)	6,600	3,300	1,980
(104)	Fred Clarke (Pittsburg, 1902, uniform)	6,600	3,300	1,980
(104)	Justin J. Clarke (Cleveland, 1906)	2,000	1,000	600.00
(105)	Thomas Clarke (Cincinnati, 1910)	2,000	1,000	600.00
(106)	Walter Clarkson (New York AL, 1906)	2,000	1,000	600.00
(107)	Walter Clarkson (Cleveland, 1907)	2,000	1,000	600.00
(108)	Otis Clymer (Pittsburg, 1905)	2,000	1,000	600.00
(109)	Otis Clymer (Washington, 1907)	2,000	1,000	600.00
(110)	Andrew Coakley (Philadelphia AL, 1905)	2,000	1,000	600.00
(111)	Andrew Coakley (Cincinnati, 1907)	2,000	1,000	600.00
(112)	Tyrus R. Cobb (Detroit, 1907)	18,000	9,000	5,400
(115)	Edward Collins (Philadelphia AL, 1907)	5,400	2,700	1,620
(116)	James Collins (Boston AL, 1902, uniform)	6,000	3,000	1,800
(117)	W.M. Congalton (Cleveland, 1906)	2,000	1,000	600.00
(118)	W.A. Congalton (Boston AL, 1907)	2,000	1,000	600.00
(119)	William Conroy (New York AL, 1903)	3,000	1,500	900.00
(120)	Richard Cooley (Boston NL, 1902, street)	3,000	1,500	900.00
(121)	Richard Cooley (Detroit, 1905)	2,000	1,000	600.00
(122)	John W. Coombs (Philadelphia AL, 1910)	2,000	1,000	600.00
(123)	T.W. Corcoran (Cincinnati, 1904)	2,000	1,000	600.00
(124)	T.W. Corcoran (New York NL, 1907)	2,000	1,000	600.00
(125)	Frank J. Corridon (Philadelphia NL, 1907)	2,000	1,000	600.00
(126)	William Coughlin (Washington, 1903)	3,000	1,500	900.00
(127)	William Coughlin (Detroit, 1904)	2,000	1,000	600.00
(128)	Ernest Courtney (Philadelphia NL, 1905)	2,000	1,000	600.00
(129)	Otis Crandall (New York NL, 1910)	2,000	1,000	600.00
(130)	Samuel Crawford (Cincinnati, 1902, street)	6,600	3,300	1,980
(131)	Samuel Crawford (Detroit, 1903)	6,600	3,300	1,980
(132)	Burde Cree (Birdie) (New York AL, 1911)	2,000	1,000	600.00
(134)	Louis Criger (Boston AL, 1903)	3,000	1,500	900.00
(135)	Dode Criss (St. Louis AL, 1910)	2,000	1,000	600.00
(136)	John Cronin (New York NL, 1903)	3,000	1,500	900.00
(137)	John Cronin (Brooklyn, 1904)	2,000	1,000	600.00
(138)	Lafayette Cross (Philadelphia AL, 1902, street)	3,000	1,500	900.00
(139)	Lafayette Cross (Washington, 1906)	2,000	1,000	600.00
(140)	Monte Cross (Philadelphia AL, 1902)	3,000	1,500	900.00
(142)	Clarence Currie (St. Louis NL, 1903)	3,000	1,500	900.00
(143)	Clarence Currie (Chicago NL, 1903)	3,000	1,500	900.00
(145)	William Dahlen (Brooklyn, 1902, street)	3,600	1,800	1,080
(146)	William Dahlen (New York NL, 1904)	2,000	1,000	600.00
(147)	Thomas Daly (Chicago AL, 1903, street)	3,000	1,500	900.00
(148)	Thomas Daly (Cincinnati, 1903)	3,000	1,500	900.00
(148)	George Davis (Chicago AL, 1902)	6,600	3,300	1,980
(150)	Harry Davis (Philadelphia AL, 1902, street)	3,000	1,500	900.00
(152)	Edward J. Delahanty (Washington, 1902, street)	16,200	8,100	4,860
(153)	James Delahanty (Boston NL, 1904)	2,000	1,000	600.00
(154)	James Delahanty (Cincinnati, 1906)	2,000	1,000	600.00
(155)	James Delahanty (St. Louis AL, 1907)	2,000	1,000	600.00
(156)	James Delahanty (Washington, 1907)	2,000	1,000	600.00
(158)	Arthur Devlin (New York NL, 1905)	2,000	1,000	600.00
(159)	Joshua Devore (New York NL, 1911)	2,000	1,000	600.00
(160)	Charles Dexter (Boston NL, 1903)	3,000	1,500	900.00
(161)	Frank Dillon (Brooklyn, 1903)	3,000	1,500	900.00
(162)	William Dinneen (Boston AL, 1903)	3,000	1,500	900.00
(163)	William Dineen (St. Louis AL, 1907)	2,000	1,000	600.00
(164)	John Dobbs (Brooklyn, 1903)	3,000	1,500	900.00
(164)	Edward Doheny (Pittsburg, 1903)	3,000	1,500	900.00
(165)	Harry Dolan (Patrick Henry "Cozy")(Cincinnati, 1904)	2,000	1,000	600.00
(166)	Harry Dolan (Patrick Henry "Cozy")(Boston NL, 1905)	2,000	1,000	600.00
(167)	Frank Donahue (St. Louis NL, 1903)	3,000	1,500	900.00
(168)	Frank Donahue (Cleveland, 1903)	3,000	1,500	900.00
(169)	Frank Donahue (Detroit, 1906)	2,000	1,000	600.00
(170)	J. "Jiggs" Donahue (Chicago AL, 1906)	3,000	1,500	900.00
(171)	Michael Donlin (Cincinnati, 1902, street)	3,000	1,500	900.00
(172)	Michael Donlin (New York NL, 1904)	2,000	1,000	600.00
(173)	P.J. (Patrick) Donovan (St. Louis NL, 1902, street)	3,000	1,500	900.00
(174)	Patrick J. Donovan (Washington, 1904)	2,000	1,000	600.00
(175)	Patrick J. Donovan (Brooklyn, 1906, street)	2,000	1,000	600.00
(176)	William Donovan (Detroit, 1903)	3,000	1,500	900.00
(177)	Charles Dooin (Philadelphia NL, 1903)	3,000	1,500	900.00
(178)	Michael Doolin (Doolan) (Philadelphia NL, 1906)	2,000	1,000	600.00
(180)	Thomas Doran (Boston AL, 1904)	2,000	1,000	600.00
(181)	Thomas Doran (Detroit, 1905)	2,000	1,000	600.00
(182)	August Dorner (Boston NL, 1907)	2,000	1,000	600.00
(183)	Patrick Dougherty (Boston AL, 1903)	3,000	1,500	900.00
(184)	Patrick Dougherty (New York AL, 1904)	2,000	1,000	600.00
(185)	Patrick Dougherty (Chicago AL, 1906)	2,000	1,000	600.00
(186)	William Douglas (Douglass) (Philadelphia NL, 1902)	3,000	1,500	900.00
(187)	Thomas Downey (Cincinnati, 1910)	2,000	1,000	600.00
(188)	J.W. Downs (Detroit, 1907)	2,000	1,000	600.00
(189)	Joe Doyle (New York AL, 1907)	2,000	1,000	600.00
(190)	John Doyle (Brooklyn, 1903)	3,000	1,500	900.00
(191)	John Doyle (Philadelphia NL, 1904)	2,000	1,000	600.00
(192)	Larry J. Doyle (New York NL, 1908)	2,000	1,000	600.00
(194)	Louis Drill (Washington, 1903)	3,000	1,500	900.00
(195)	Louis Drill (Detroit, 1904)	2,000	1,000	600.00
(196)	Hugh Duffy (Philadelphia NL, 1905)	5,400	2,700	1,620
(197)	William Duggleby (Philadelphia NL, 1903)	3,000	1,500	900.00
(198)	William Duggleby (Pittsburg, 1907)	2,000	1,000	600.00
(199)	August Dundon (Chicago AL, 1904)	2,000	1,000	600.00
(200)	Edward Dunkle (Washington, 1903)	3,000	1,500	900.00
(201)	James Dunleavy (John) (St. Louis NL, 1904)	2,000	1,000	600.00
(202)	John Dunn (New York NL, 1903)	3,000	1,500	900.00
(203)	James H. Dygert (Philadelphia AL, 1905)	2,000	1,000	600.00
(204)	Malcolm Eason (Brooklyn, 1906)	2,000	1,000	600.00
(205)	Harry Eells (Cleveland, 1906)	2,000	1,000	600.00
(206)	Richard J. Egan (Cincinnati, 1910)	2,000	1,000	600.00
(207)	Norman Elberfeld (Detroit, 1903)	3,000	1,500	900.00
(208)	Norman Elberfeld (New York AL, 1903)	3,000	1,500	900.00
(209)	Claude Elliott (New York NL, 1904)	2,000	1,000	600.00
(210)	George W. Ellis (St. Louis NL, 1910)	2,000	1,000	600.00
(212)	John Eubank (Detroit, 1906)	2,000	1,000	600.00
(213)	John Evers (Chicago NL, 1903)	6,600	3,300	1,980
(214)	Robert Ewing (George L.)(Cincinnati, 1904)	2,000	1,000	600.00
(216)	Fred Falkenberg (Washington, 1906)	2,000	1,000	600.00
(217)	Charles Farrell (Brooklyn, 1902, street)	3,000	1,500	900.00
(218)	Charles Farrell (Boston AL, 1903)	3,000	1,500	900.00
(219)	John S. Farrell (St. Louis NL, 1903)	3,000	1,500	900.00
(220)	Cecil Ferguson (George) (New York NL, 1906)	2,000	1,000	600.00
(221)	Hobe Ferris (Boston AL, 1903)	3,000	1,500	900.00
(222)	Thomas S. Fisher (Middle initial C.)(Boston NL, 1904)	2,000	1,000	600.00
(223)	Patrick Flaherty (Chicago AL, 1903)	3,000	1,500	900.00
(224)	Patrick Flaherty (Pittsburg, 1904)	2,000	1,000	600.00
(225)	Patrick Flaherty (Boston NL, 1907)	2,000	1,000	600.00
(226)	Elmer Flick (Cleveland, 1903)	6,600	3,300	1,980
(227)	John Flynn (Pittsburg, 1910)	2,000	1,000	600.00
(229)	William Foxen (Chicago NL, 1910)	2,000	1,000	600.00
(231)	Charles Fraser (Philadelphia NL, 1903, street)	3,000	1,500	900.00
(232)	Charles Fraser (Boston NL, 1905)	2,000	1,000	600.00
(233)	Charles Fraser (Chicago NL, 1907)	2,000	1,000	600.00
(234)	John ("Buck") Freeman (Boston AL, 1902)	3,600	1,800	1,080
(235)	William Friel (St. Louis AL, 1903)	3,000	1,500	900.00
(236)	Arthur Fromme (Cincinnati, 1910)	2,000	1,000	600.00
(237)	David L. Fultz (Philadelphia AL, 1902, street)	3,000	1,500	900.00
(238)	David L. Fultz (New York AL, 1903)	3,000	1,500	900.00
(240)	Robert S. Ganley (Pittsburg, 1906)	2,000	1,000	600.00
(241)	Robert S. Ganley (Washington, 1907)	2,000	1,000	600.00
(242)	John Ganzell (Ganzel) (New York AL, 1903)	3,000	1,500	900.00
(243)	John Ganzell (Ganzell) (Cincinnati, 1907)	2,000	1,000	600.00
(244)	Virgil Garvin (Brooklyn, 1903)	3,000	1,500	900.00
(245)	Harry L. Gaspar (Cincinnati, 1910)	2,000	1,000	600.00
(246)	Philip Geier (Boston NL, 1904)	2,000	1,000	600.00
(247)	Harry Gessler (Brooklyn, 1903)	3,000	1,500	900.00
(248)	Harry Gessler (Chicago NL, 1906)	2,000	1,000	600.00

No.	Name			
(250)	George Gibson (Pittsburg, 1905)	2,000	1,000	600.00
(251)	Norwood Gibson (Boston AL, 1903)	3,000	1,500	900.00
(252)	William Gilbert (New York NL, 1903)	3,000	1,500	900.00
(253)	Frederick Glade (St. Louis AL, 1904)	2,000	1,000	600.00
(254)	Harry Gleason (Boston AL, 1903)	3,000	1,500	900.00
(255)	Harry Gleason (St. Louis AL, 1904)	2,000	1,000	600.00
(256)	William Gleason (Philadelphia NL, 1903)	3,000	1,500	900.00
(258)	William Gochnauer (John Gochnaur)(Cleveland, 1903)	3,000	1,500	900.00
(259)	Michael Grady (St. Louis NL, 1904)	2,000	1,000	600.00
(260)	Edward L. Grant (Philadelphia NL, 1910)	2,880	1,440	870.00
(262)	Daniel Green (Chicago AL, 1903)	3,000	1,500	900.00
(263)	E.W. Greminger (Boston NL, 1903)	3,000	1,500	900.00
(264)	E.W. Greminger (Detroit, 1904)	2,000	1,000	600.00
(265)	Clarke Griffith (Clark) (Chicago AL, 1902)	6,600	3,300	1,980
(266)	Clarke Griffith (Clark) (New York AL, 1903)	6,600	3,300	1,980
(267)	Myron Grimshaw (Boston AL, 1906)	2,000	1,000	600.00
(269)	James Hackett (St. Louis NL, 1903)	3,000	1,500	900.00
(270)	Edgar Hahn (Chicago AL, 1906)	2,000	1,000	600.00
(271)	Frank Hahn (Cincinnati, 1902, street)	2,000	1,000	600.00
(272)	Frank Hahn (New York AL, 1905)	2,000	1,000	600.00
(273)	Charles Hall (Cincinnati, 1907)	2,000	1,000	600.00
(274)	William H. Hallman (Philadelphia NL, 1903)	3,000	1,500	900.00
(275)	William H. Hallman (Pittsburg, 1906)	2,000	1,000	600.00
(276)	Edward Hanlon (Brooklyn, 1905, street)	5,400	2,700	1,620
(277)	Edward Hanlon (Cincinnati, 1906)	5,400	2,700	1,620
(278)	Richard Harley (Chicago NL, 1903)	3,000	1,500	900.00
(279)	Robert Harmon (St. Louis NL, 1910)	2,000	1,000	600.00
(280)	Charles Harper (Cincinnati, 1903)	3,000	1,500	900.00
(281)	Charles Harper (Chicago NL, 1906)	2,000	1,000	600.00
(282)	Joseph Harris (Boston AL, 1906)	2,000	1,000	600.00
(283)	Harry Hart (Chicago AL, 1906)	2,000	1,000	600.00
(284)	Frederick L. Hartzell (Hartsel) (Philadelphia AL, 1902)	3,000	1,500	900.00
(285)	Roy A. Hartzell (St. Louis AL, 1906)	2,000	1,000	600.00
(287)	J.E. Heidrick (St. Louis NL, 1903)	3,000	1,500	900.00
(288)	Charles Hemphill (St. Louis AL, 1903)	3,000	1,500	900.00
(289)	Weldon Henley (Philadelphia AL, 1903, street)	3,000	1,500	900.00
(290)	Otto Hess (Cleveland, 1904)	2,000	1,000	600.00
(291)	Edward Heydon (Mike)(Washington, 1906)	2,000	1,000	600.00
(292)	Charles Hickman (Cleveland, 1903)	3,000	1,500	900.00
(293)	Charles Hickman (Detroit, 1904)	2,000	1,000	600.00
(294)	Charles Hickman (Washington, 1905)	2,000	1,000	600.00
(295)	Charles Hickman (Chicago AL, 1907)	2,000	1,000	600.00
(296)	Hunter Hill (St. Louis AL, 1903)	3,000	1,500	900.00
(297)	Hunter Hill (Washington, 1904)	2,000	1,000	600.00
(298)	Homer Hillebrand (Pittsburg, 1905)	2,000	1,000	600.00
(299)	Harry Hinchman (Cleveland, 1907)	2,000	1,000	600.00
(300)	William Hinchman (Cleveland, 1907)	2,000	1,000	600.00
(303)	R. C. Hoblitzel (Cincinnati, 1910)	2,000	1,000	600.00
(304)	Daniel Hoffman (Philadelphia AL, 1903)	3,000	1,500	900.00
(305)	Daniel Hoffman (New York AL, 1906)	2,000	1,000	600.00
(306)	Arthur Hofman (Chicago NL, 1906)	2,000	1,000	600.00
(307)	William Hogg (New York AL, 1906)	2,000	1,000	600.00
(308)	A. Holesketter (St. Louis NL, 1907)	2,000	1,000	600.00
(309)	William Holmes (James Wm. "Ducky")(Chicago AL, 1903)	3,000	1,500	900.00
(310)	George Howard (Pittsburg, 1905)	2,000	1,000	600.00
(311)	George Howard (Boston NL, 1906)	2,000	1,000	600.00
(312)	Harry Howell (Baltimore, 1902, street)	3,000	1,500	900.00
(313)	Harry Howell (New York AL, 1903, street)	3,000	1,500	900.00
(314)	Harry Howell (St. Louis AL, 1904)	2,000	1,000	600.00
(315)	Miller Huggins (Cincinnati, 1906)	5,400	2,700	1,620
(316)	James Hughes (Brooklyn, 1902, street)	3,000	1,500	900.00
(317)	Thomas Hughes (Boston AL, 1902)	3,000	1,500	900.00
(318)	Thomas Hughes (New York AL, 1904)	2,000	1,000	600.00
(319)	Thomas Hughes (Washington, 1904)	2,000	1,000	600.00
(320)	John Hulseman (Frank Huelsman) (Washington, 1904)	2,000	1,000	600.00
(321)	Rudolph Hulswitt (Philadelphia NL, 1903)	3,000	1,500	900.00
(322)	John Hummell (Hummel) (Brooklyn, 1906)	2,000	1,000	600.00
(323)	Berthold J. Husting (Philadelphia AL, 1902, street)	3,000	1,500	900.00
(324)	Hamilton Hyatt (Pittsburg, 1909)	2,000	1,000	600.00
(325)	Frank Isbell (Chicago AL, 1903)	3,000	1,500	900.00
(326)	Fred Jacklitsch (Brooklyn, 1903, street)	3,000	1,500	900.00
(327)	Fred Jacklitsch (Philadelphia NL, 1907)	2,000	1,000	600.00
(328)	James Jackson (Cleveland, 1906)	2,000	1,000	600.00
(329)	Harry Jacobson (Albert "Beany")(Washington, 1904)	2,000	1,000	600.00
(330)	Harry Jacobson (Albert "Beany)(St. Louis AL, 1906)	2,000	1,000	600.00
(331)	Harry Jacobson (Albert "Beany")(Boston AL, 1907)	2,000	1,000	600.00
(333)	Hugh Jennings (Philadelphia NL, 1902)	6,600	3,300	1,980
(334)	Hugh Jennings (Detroit, 1907)	5,400	2,700	1,620
(335)	Charles Jones (Washington, 1905)	2,000	1,000	600.00
(336)	David Jones (Chicago NL, 1904)	2,000	1,000	600.00
(337)	David Jones (Detroit, 1906)	2,000	1,000	600.00
(338)	Fielder Jones (Chicago AL, 1902)	3,000	1,500	900.00
(339)	Oscar Jones (Brooklyn, 1903)	3,000	1,500	900.00
(340)	Thomas Jones (St. Louis AL, 1904)	2,000	1,000	600.00
(341)	Otto Jordan ("Dutch")(Brooklyn, 1903)	3,000	1,500	900.00
(342)	Otto Jordan ("Dutch")(Cleveland, 1905)	2,000	1,000	600.00
(343)	Tim Jordan (Brooklyn, 1906)	2,000	1,000	600.00
(344)	Adrian Joss (Cleveland, 1903)	7,200	3,600	2,160
(345)	Michael Kahoe (St. Louis AL, 1903)	3,000	1,500	900.00
(346)	Michael Kahoe (Philadelphia NL, 1905)	2,000	1,000	600.00
(347)	Michael Kahoe (Chicago NL, 1907)	2,000	1,000	600.00
(348)	Michael Kahoe (Washington, 1907)	2,000	1,000	600.00
(349)	Edward Karger (Edwin)(Boston AL, 1910)	2,000	1,000	600.00
(350)	Robert Keefe (New York AL, 1906)	2,000	1,000	600.00
(351)	William Keeler (Brooklyn, 1902, street)	6,600	3,300	1,980
(352)	William Keeler (New York, AL 1903, street)	6,600	3,300	1,980
(353)	William Keister (Philadelphia NL, 1903)	3,000	1,500	900.00
(355)	Joseph J. Kelley (Cincinnati, 1902, street)	10,800	5,400	3,240
(356)	William Kennedy (Pittsburg, 1903, street)	3,000	1,500	900.00
(357)	Edward Killian (Detroit, 1904)	2,000	1,000	600.00
(358)	James Kissinger (Chas. "Rube" Kisinger) (Detroit, 1903)	3,000	1,500	900.00
(359)	Frank Kitson (Brooklyn, 1902, street)	3,000	1,500	900.00
(360)	Frank Kitson (Detroit, 1903)	3,000	1,500	900.00
(361)	Frank Kitson (Washington, 1906)	2,000	1,000	600.00
(362)	Frank Kitson (New York AL, 1907)	2,000	1,000	600.00
(363)	Malachi Kittridge (Washington, 1903)	3,000	1,500	900.00
(365)	John Kleinow (New York AL, 1905, street)	2,000	1,000	600.00
(366)	John Kleinow (New York AL, 1905, uniform)	2,000	1,000	600.00
(367)	John Kling (Chicago NL, 1903)	3,000	1,500	900.00
(368)	F. Otto Knabe (Philadelphia NL, 1910)	2,000	1,000	600.00
(369)	John Knight (Philadelphia AL, 1905)	2,000	1,000	600.00
(370)	John Knight (Boston AL, 1907)	2,000	1,000	600.00
(371)	Bernard Koehler (St. Louis AL, 1906)	2,000	1,000	600.00
(372)	Edward Konetchy (St. Louis NL, 1907)	2,000	1,000	600.00
(373)	Harry Krause (Philadelphia AL, 1910)	2,000	1,000	600.00
(374)	Otto Krueger (Pittsburg, 1903)	3,000	1,500	900.00
(375)	Otto Krueger (Philadelphia NL, 1905)	2,000	1,000	600.00
(376)	George LaChance (Boston AL, 1903)	3,000	1,500	900.00
(377)	Napoleon Lajoie (Cleveland, 1902, street)	6,600	3,300	1,980
(378)	Napoleon Lajoie (Cleveland, 1902, uniform)	6,600	3,300	1,980
(379)	Joseph Lake (St. Louis AL, 1910)	2,000	1,000	600.00
(380)	Frank Laporte (LaPorte) (New York AL, 1906)	2,000	1,000	600.00
(381)	Louis Laroy (LeRoy)	2,000	1,000	600.00
(382)	William Lauder (New York NL, 1903)	3,000	1,500	900.00
(383)	Thomas Leach (Pittsburg, 1902)	3,000	1,500	900.00
(384)	Wyatt Lee (Washington, 1903)	3,000	1,500	900.00
(385)	Wyatt Lee (Pittsburg, 1904)	2,000	1,000	600.00
(386)	Samuel Leever (Pittsburg, 1902, street)	3,000	1,500	900.00
(387)	Samuel Leever (Pittsburg, 1902, uniform)	2,000	1,000	600.00
(388)	Philip Lewis (Brooklyn, 1908)	2,000	1,000	600.00
(389)	Vive A. Lindaman (Boston NL, 1906)	2,000	1,000	600.00
(390)	Paddy Livingstone (Livingston) (Philadelphia AL, 1910)	2,000	1,000	600.00
(391)	John Lobert (Cincinnati, 1907)	2,000	1,000	600.00
(392)	Herman Long (Boston NL, 1902)	2,000	1,000	600.00
(393)	Herman Long (Detroit, 1903)	3,000	1,500	900.00
(394)	Herman Long (New York AL, 1903)	3,000	1,500	900.00
(395)	Briscoe Lord (Philadelphia AL, 1905)	2,000	1,000	600.00
(396)	Harry D. Lord (Chicago AL, 1910)	2,000	1,000	600.00
(397)	Robert H. Lowe (Detroit, 1907)	2,000	1,000	600.00
(398)	Harry Lumley (Brooklyn, 1904)	2,000	1,000	600.00
(399)	Carl Lundgren (Chicago NL, 1903)	3,000	1,500	900.00
(400)	John Lush (St. Louis NL, 1903)	2,000	1,000	600.00
(401)	William L. Lush (Detroit, 1903)	3,000	1,500	900.00
(402)	William L. Lush (Cleveland, 1904)	2,000	1,000	600.00
(403)	Michael M. Lynch (Pittsburg, 1906)	2,000	1,000	600.00
(404)	Michael M. Lynch (New York NL, 1907)	2,000	1,000	600.00
(405)	Connie Mack (Philadelphia AL, 1902, street)	6,600	3,300	1,980
(406)	Nick Maddox (Pittsburg, 1909)	2,000	1,000	600.00
(407)	Sherwood Magee (Philadelphia NL, 1905)	2,000	1,000	600.00
(408)	George H. Magoon (Chicago AL, 1903)	3,000	1,500	900.00
(409)	John Malarkey (Boston NL, 1903)	3,000	1,500	900.00
(410)	William Maloney (Chicago NL, 1905)	2,000	1,000	600.00
(411)	William Maloney (Brooklyn, 1906)	2,000	1,000	600.00
(412)	William R. Marshall (New York NL, 1905)	2,000	1,000	600.00
(413)	William R. Marshall (St. Louis NL, 1906)	2,000	1,000	600.00
(414)	William R. Marshall (Brooklyn, 1909)	2,000	1,000	600.00
(415)	Christopher Matthewson (Mathewson) (New York NL, 1902, street)	18,000	9,000	5,400
(416a)	Christopher Matthewson (Mathewson) (New York NL, 1902, uniform)	16,200	8,100	4,860
(416b)	Christopher Mathewson (New York, NL, uniform, corrected)	14,400	7,200	4,320
(417)	James A. McAleer (St. Louis AL, 1906)	2,000	1,000	600.00
(418)	Louis McAllister (Lewis)(Detroit, 1903)	3,000	1,500	900.00
(419)	John McCarthy (Cleveland, 1903)	3,000	1,500	900.00
(420)	John McCarthy (Chicago NL, 1903)	3,000	1,500	900.00
(421)	John McCarthy (Brooklyn, 1906)	2,000	1,000	600.00
(422)	John J. McCloskey (St. Louis NL, 1906)	2,000	1,000	600.00
(423)	Ambrose McConnell (Boston AL, 1910)	2,000	1,000	600.00
(424)	George W. McQuillan (Philadelphia NL, 1907)	2,000	1,000	600.00
(425)	Barry McCormick (St. Louis AL, 1903)	3,000	1,500	900.00
(426)	Barry McCormick (Washington, 1903)	3,000	1,500	900.00
(427)	Michael McCormick (Brooklyn, 1904)	2,000	1,000	600.00
(428)	Charles McFarland (St. Louis NL, 1903)	3,000	1,500	900.00
(429)	Charles McFarland (Pittsburg, 1906)	2,000	1,000	600.00
(430)	Edward McFarland (Chicago AL, 1902, street)	3,000	1,500	900.00
(431)	Herm McFarland (Hermas) (New York AL, 1903)	3,000	1,500	900.00
(432)	John McFetridge (Philadelphia NL, 1903)	3,000	1,500	900.00
(433)	Dan McGann (New York NL, 1903)	3,000	1,500	900.00
(434)	Joseph McGinnity (New York NL, 1902, street)	6,600	3,300	1,980
(435)	Joseph McGinnity (New York NL, 1902, uniform)	6,600	3,300	1,980
(436)	John J. McGraw (infielder, New York NL, 1902, street)	6,600	3,300	1,980
(437)	John J. McGraw (manager, New York NL, 1902, street)	6,600	3,300	1,980
(438)	James McGuire (Detroit, 1903)	2,000	1,000	600.00
(439)	James McGuire (New York AL, 1904)	2,000	1,000	600.00
(440)	James McGuire (Boston AL, 1907)	2,000	1,000	600.00

(441) Harry McIntyre (McIntire) (Brooklyn, 1905)	2,000	1,000	600.00
(442) Matty McIntyre (Detroit, 1904, street)	2,000	1,000	600.00
(443) John B. McLean (Cincinnati, 1910)	2,000	1,000	600.00
(444) John Menefee (Chicago NL, 1903)	3,000	1,500	900.00
(445) Fred Merkle (New York NL, 1908)	2,000	1,000	600.00
(446) Samuel Mertes (New York NL, 1903)	3,000	1,500	900.00
(447) Samuel Mertes (St. Louis NL, 1906)	2,000	1,000	600.00
(448) Samuel Mertes (Boston NL, 1907)	2,000	1,000	600.00
(451) Clyde Milan (Washington, 1910)	2,000	1,000	600.00
(452) John B. Miller (Pittsburg, 1909)	2,000	1,000	600.00
(453) Roscoe Miller (New York NL, 1903)	3,000	1,500	900.00
(454) Roscoe Miller (Pittsburg, 1903)	3,000	1,500	900.00
(455) William Milligan (New York NL, 1904)	2,000	1,000	600.00
(456) Frederick Mitchell (Philadelphia NL, 1903, street)	3,000	1,500	900.00
(457) Frederick Mitchell (Brooklyn, 1904)	2,000	1,000	600.00
(458) M.F. Mitchell (Cincinnati, 1910)	2,000	1,000	600.00
(461) Earl Moore (Cleveland, 1903)	3,000	1,500	900.00
(462) Earl Moore (New York AL, 1907)	2,000	1,000	600.00
(463) Charles P. Moran (Middle initial V)(Washington, 1904)	2,000	1,000	600.00
(464) Charles P. Moran (Middle initial V)(St. Louis AL, 1904)	2,000	1,000	600.00
(465) Patrick J. Moran (Boston NL, 1902, street)	3,000	1,500	900.00
(466) Patrick J. Moran (Chicago NL, 1906)	2,000	1,000	600.00
(467) Lewis Moren (Philadelphia NL, 1910)	2,000	1,000	600.00
(468) Harry R. Morgan (Philadelphia AL, 1910)	2,000	1,000	600.00
(469) Eugene Moriarty (George) (New York AL, 1906)	2,000	1,900	600.00
(470) John Morrissey (Cincinnati, 1903)	3,000	1,500	900.00
(471) Michael Mowery (Cincinnati, 1907)	2,000	1,000	600.00
(472) George Mullin (Detroit, 1903)	3,000	1,500	900.00
(473) Daniel Murphy (Philadelphia AL, 1902, street)	3,000	1,500	900.00
(474) John J. Murray (St. Louis NL, 1907)	2,000	1,000	600.00
(475) William Murray (Boston NL, 1907)	2,000	1,000	600.00
(477) Joseph Nealon (Jim)(Pittsburg, 1906)	2,000	1,000	600.00
(478) Daniel Needham (Thomas) (Boston NL, 1904)	2,000	1,000	600.00
(479) Eustace J. Newto (New York AL, 1906)	2,000	1,000	600.00
(481) Simon Nicholls (Philadelphia AL, 1907)	2,000	1,000	600.00
(482) Harry Niles (St. Louis AL, 1906)	2,000	1,000	600.00
(483) George Nill (Washington, 1906)	2,000	1,000	600.00
(484) George Nill (Cleveland, 1907)	2,000	1,000	600.00
(485) Pete Noonan (St. Louis NL, 1906)	2,000	1,000	600.00
(486) John O'Brien (Boston AL, 1903)	2,000	1,500	900.00
(487) Peter O'Brien (St. Louis AL, 1906)	2,000	1,000	600.00
(488) Peter O'Brien (Cleveland, 1907)	2,000	1,000	600.00
(489) Peter O'Brien (Washington, 1907)	2,000	1,000	600.00
(490) John O'Connor (Pittsburg, 1902)	3,000	1,500	900.00
(491) John O'Connor (New York AL, 1903)	3,000	1,500	900.00
(492) John O'Connor (St. Louis AL, 1904)	2,000	1,000	600.00
(493) Reuben Oldring (Philadelphia AL, 1906)	2,000	1,000	600.00
(494) Charles O'Leary (Detroit, 1904)	2,000	1,000	600.00
(495) John J. O'Neil (O'Neill) (St. Louis NL, 1903)	2,500	1,250	750.00
(496) John J. O'Neil (O'Neill)(Chicago NL, 1904)	2,000	1,000	600.00
(497) John O'Neil (O'Neill) (Boston NL, 1906)	2,000	1,000	600.00
(498) Michael J. O'Neil (O'Neill)(St. Louis NL, 1903)	3,000	1,500	900.00
(499) Michael J. O'Neil (O'Neill)(Brooklyn, 1906)	2,000	1,000	600.00
(500) Albert Orth (Washington, 1903)	3,000	1,500	900.00
(501) Albert Orth (New York AL, 1904)	2,000	1,000	600.00
(502) Orville Overall (Orval) (Chicago NL, 1906)	2,000	1,000	600.00
(503) Frank Owen (Chicago AL, 1903)	3,000	1,500	900.00
(504) Richard Padden (St. Louis AL, 1903)	3,000	1,500	900.00
(505) Frederick Parent (Boston AL, 1902)	3,000	1,500	900.00
(506) Frederick Parent (Chicago AL, 1908)	2,000	1,000	600.00
(508) George Paskert (Cincinnati, 1910)	2,000	1,000	600.00

(509) James Pastorious (Brooklyn, 1906)	2,000	1,000	600.00
(510) Case Patten (Washington, 1903)	3,000	1,500	900.00
(511) Roy Patterson (Chicago AL, 1903)	3,000	1,500	900.00
(512) Frederick Payne (Detroit, 1906)	2,000	1,000	600.00
(513) Henry Peitz (Cincinnati, 1904)	2,000	1,000	600.00
(514) Henry Peitz (Pittsburg, 1905)	2,000	1,000	600.00
(515) Barney Pelty (St. Louis AL, 1904)	2,000	1,000	600.00
(516) Frank Pfeiffer ("Big Jeff" Pfeffer)(Chicago NL, 1905)	2,000	1,000	600.00
(517) Frank Pfeiffer ("Big Jeff" Pfeffer)(Boston NL, 1906)	2,000	1,000	600.00
(518) John Pfiester (Chicago NL, 1907)	2,000	1,000	600.00
(519) Edward Phelps (Pittsburg, 1903)	3,000	1,500	900.00
(520) Edward Phelps (Cincinnati, 1905)	2,000	1,000	600.00
(521) Charles Phillippe (Pittsburg, 1903)	3,000	1,150	900.00
(522) William Phillips (Cincinnati, 1902, street)	3,000	1,500	900.00
(523) Wiley Piatt (Boston NL, 1903)	3,000	1,500	900.00
(524) Oliver Pickering (Philadelphia AL, 1903)	3,000	1,500	900.00
(525) Oliver Pickering (St. Louis AL, 1906)	2,000	1,000	600.00
(526) Charles Pittinger (Boston NL, 1903)	3,000	1,500	900.00
(527) Charles Pittinger (Philadelphia NL, 1905)	2,000	1,000	600.00
(528) Edward S. Plank (Philadelphia AL, 1902 street)	6,600	3,300	1,980
(529) Edward S. Plank (Philadelphia AL, 1902, uniform)	6,600	3,300	1,980
(530) Edward Poole (Cincinnati, 1903)	3,000	1,500	900.00
(531) Edward Poole (Brooklyn, 1904)	2,000	1,000	600.00
(532) John Powell (St. Louis AL, 1903)	3,000	1,500	900.00
(533) John Powell (New York AL, 1904)	2,000	1,000	600.00
(534) Maurice R. Powers (Michael) (Philadelphia AL, 1902, street)	3,000	1,500	900.00
(535) William Purtell (Boston AL, 1910)	2,000	1,000	600.00
(536) Ambrose Puttmann (New York AL, 1905)	2,000	1,000	600.00
(539) Thomas Raub (Chicago NL, 1903)	3,000	1,500	900.00
(540) Frederick Raymer (Boston NL, 1904)	2,000	1,000	600.00
(541) William Reidy (Brooklyn, 1903)	3,000	1,500	900.00
(542) Ed Reulbach (Chicago NL, 1907)	2,000	1,000	600.00
(543) R.B. Rhoades (Rhoads) (Cleveland, 1903)	3,000	1,500	900.00
(544) Lewis Richie (Chicago NL, 1910)	2,000	1,000	600.00
(545) Branch Rickey (New York AL, 1907)	5,400	2,700	1,620
(546) Claude Ritchey (Pittsburg, 1902, street)	3,000	1,500	900.00
(547) Claude Ritchey (Boston NL, 1907)	2,000	1,000	600.00
(548) Louis Ritter (Lewis) (Brooklyn, 1903)	3,000	1,500	900.00
(549) Clyde Robinson (Detroit, 1904)	2,000	1,000	600.00
(550) George Rohe (Chicago AL, 1906)	2,000	1,000	600.00
(553) Claude Rossman (Cleveland, 1906)	2,000	1,000	600.00
(554) Claude Rossman (Detroit, 1907)	2,000	1,000	600.00
(555) Frank Roth (Philadelphia NL, 1903)	3,000	1,500	900.00
(556) Frank Roth (St. Louis AL, 1905)	2,000	1,000	600.00
(557) Frank Roth (Chicago AL, 1906)	2,000	1,000	600.00
(558) John A. Rowan (Cincinnati, 1910)	2,000	1,000	600.00
(559) James Ryan (Washington, 1902, street)	3,000	1,500	900.00
(562) Harry Sallee (St. Louis NL, 1910)	2,000	1,000	600.00
(563) Herman Schaefer (Detroit, 1907)	2,000	1,000	600.00
(564) George Schlei (Cincinnati, 1906)	2,000	1,000	600.00
(565) Charles Schmidt (Detroit, 1906)	2,000	1,000	600.00
(566) Harry Schmidt (Henry) (Brooklyn, 1903)	3,000	1,500	900.00
(567) Osee F. Schreckengost (Ossee) (Philadelphia AL, 1902, street)	3,000	1,500	900.00
(568) Osee F. Schreckengost (Ossee)(Philadelphia AL, 1902, uniform)	3,000	1,500	900.00
(569) Frank Schulte (Chicago NL, 1905)	2,000	1,000	600.00
(570) Al Schweitzer (St. Louis AL, 1910)	2,000	1,000	600.00
(571) James Sebring (Pittsburg, 1903)	3,000	1,500	900.00
(572) James Sebring (Cincinnati, 1904)	2,000	1,000	600.00
(573) James Sebring (Chicago NL, 1905)	2,000	1,000	600.00

(575) Albert Selbach (Washington, 1903)	3,000	1,500	900.00
(576) Albert Selbach (Boston AL, 1904)	2,000	1,000	600.00
(577) Ralph O. "Socks" Seybold (Philadelphia AL, 1902, street)	3,000	1,500	900.00
(578) J. Bentley Seymour (Cincinnati, 1903)	3,000	1,500	900.00
(579) J. Bentley Seymour (New York NL, 1906)	2,000	1,000	600.00
(580) Arthur Shafer (New York NL, 1910)	2,000	1,000	600.00
(581) W.P. Shannon (St. Louis NL, 1904)	2,000	1,000	600.00
(582) W.P. Shannon (New York NL, 1906)	2,000	1,000	600.00
(583) Daniel Shay (St. Louis NL, 1904)	2,000	1,000	600.00
(586) David Shean (Boston NL, 1910)	2,000	1,000	600.00
(587) James Sheckard (Brooklyn, 1902, street)	3,000	1,500	900.00
(588) James Sheckard (Chicago NL, 1906)	2,000	1,000	600.00
(589) Edward Siever (Detroit, 1903)	3,000	1,500	900.00
(590) Edward Siever (St. Louis AL, 1903)	3,000	1,500	900.00
(591) James Slagle (Chicago NL, 1903)	3,000	1,500	900.00
(592) John Slattery (Chicago AL, 1903)	3,000	1,500	900.00
(593) Alexander Smith ("Broadway Aleck")(Boston AL, 1903)	3,000	1,500	900.00
(594) Alexander Smith ("Broadway Aleck")(Chicago NL, 1904)	2,000	1,000	600.00
(595) Alexander Smith ("Broadway Aleck")(New York NL, 1906)	2,000	1,000	600.00
(596) Charles Smith (Boston AL, 1910)	2,000	1,000	600.00
(597) Edward Smith (St. Louis AL, 1906)	2,000	1,000	600.00
(598) Frank Smith (Chicago AL, 1904)	2,000	1,000	600.00
(599) Harry Smith (Pittsburg, 1902, street)	3,000	1,500	900.00
(600) Heinie Smith (Detroit, 1903, street)	3,000	1,500	900.00
(602) Homer Smoot (St. Louis NL, 1903)	3,000	1,500	900.00
(603) Homer Smoot (Cincinnati, 1906)	2,000	1,000	600.00
(604) Frank Sparks (T. Frank "Tully") (Philadelphia, NL, 1903)	3,000	1,500	900.00
(605) Charles ("Chic") Stahl (Boston AL, 1902)	3,300	1,650	990.00
(606) Jacob G. Stahl (Washington, 1904)	2,000	1,000	600.00
(607) Jacob G. Stahl (Washington)	2,000	1,000	600.00
(609) J.B. Stanley (Boston NL, 1903)	3,000	1,500	900.00
(610) J.B. Stanley (Washington, 1905)	2,000	1,000	600.00
(611) Harry Steinfeldt (Cincinnati, 1902, street)	3,000	1,500	900.00
(612) Harry Steinfeldt (Chicago NL, 1905)	2,000	1,000	600.00
(615) James Stephens (St. Louis AL, 1910)	2,000	1,000	600.00
(616) George Stone (St. Louis AL, 1905)	2,000	1,000	600.00
(617) George Stovall (Cleveland, 1904)	2,000	1,000	600.00
(618) Jesse Stovall (Detroit, 1904)	2,000	1,000	600.00
(619) Samuel Strang (Brooklyn, 1903)	3,000	1,500	900.00
(620) Samuel Strang (New York NL, 1905)	2,000	1,000	600.00
(621) Elmer Stricklett (Brooklyn, 1906)	2,000	1,000	600.00
(622) Willie Sudhoff (St. Louis AL, 1903)	3,000	1,500	900.00
(623) Willie Sudhoff (Washington, 1906)	2,000	1,000	600.00
(624) Joseph Sugden (St. Louis AL, 1903)	3,000	1,500	900.00
(625) George Suggs (Cincinnati, 1910)	2,000	1,000	600.00
(628) William D. Sullivan (Middle initial J.)(Chicago AL, 1902)	3,000	1,500	900.00
(629) Edgar Summers (Detroit, 1909)	2,000	1,000	600.00
(630) William J. Sweeney (Boston NL, 1910)	2,000	1,000	600.00
(632) Jesse Tannehill (New York AL, 1903)	3,000	1,500	900.00
(633) Jesse Tannehill (Boston NL, 1904)	2,000	1,000	600.00
(634) Lee Tannehill (Chicago AL, 1903)	3,000	1,500	900.00
(636) John Taylor (Chicago NL, 1902)	3,000	1,500	900.00
(637) John Taylor (St. Louis NL, 1904)	2,000	1,000	600.00
(638) Luther H. Taylor (New York NL, 1903)	6,600	3,300	1,980
(639) Fred Tenney (Boston NL, 1903)	3,000	1,500	900.00
(640) Ira Thomas (New York AL, 1906)	2,000	1,000	600.00
(641) Roy Thomas (Philadelphia NL, 1903)	3,000	1,500	900.00
(642) John Thoney (Cleveland, 1903)	3,000	1,500	900.00
(643) John Thoney (Washington, 1904)	2,000	1,000	600.00

		NM	EX	VG
(644)	John Thoney (New York AL, 1904)	2,000	1,000	600.00
(645)	Joseph B. Tinker (Chicago NL, 1903)	6,600	3,300	1,980
(646)	John Townsend (Washington, 1903)	3,000	1,500	900.00
(647)	John Townsend (Cleveland, 1906)	2,000	1,000	600.00
(648)	Terrence Turner (Cleveland, 1906)	2,000	1,000	600.00
(650)	Robert Unglaub (Boston AL, 1905)	2,000	1,000	600.00
(652)	George Van Haltren (New York NL, 1902, street)	3,600	1,800	1,080
(653)	George Van Haltren (New York NL, 1902, uniform)	3,600	1,800	1,080
(654)	Fred Veil (Pittsburg, 1903)	3,000	1,500	900.00
(655)	Ernest Vinson (Cleveland, 1905)	2,000	1,000	600.00
(656)	Ernest Vinson (Chicago AL, 1905)	2,000	1,000	600.00
(660)	George Edward "Rube" Waddell (Philadelphia AL, 1902, street)	6,600	3,300	1,980
(661)	George Edward Waddell (St. Louis AL, 1908)	5,400	2,700	1,620
(663)	Charles Wagner (Boston AL, 1910)	2,000	1,000	600.00
(664)	John ("Hans") Wagner (Pittsburg, 1902, street)	16,200	8,150	4,860
(665)	John ("Hans") Wagner (Pittsburg, 1905, uniform)	9,600	4,800	2,880
(666)	Robert Wallace (St. Louis AL, 1902)	6,600	3,300	1,980
(668)	Edward A. Walsh (Chicago AL, 1904)	5,400	2,700	1,620
(670)	John Warner (New York NL, 1903)	3,000	1,500	900.00
(671)	John Warner (St. Louis NL, 1905)	2,000	1,000	600.00
(672)	John Warner (Detroit, 1905)	2,000	1,000	600.00
(673)	John Warner (Washington, 1906)	2,000	1,000	600.00
(674)	Arthur Weaver (Pittsburg, 1903)	3,000	1,500	900.00
(675)	Arthur Weaver (St. Louis AL, 1905)	2,000	1,000	600.00
(676)	Jacob Weimer (Chicago NL, 1903)	3,000	1,500	900.00
(677)	Jacob Weimer (Cincinnati, 1906)	2,000	1,000	600.00
(678)	G. Harry White (G. Harris "Doc")(Chicago AL, 1903)	3,000	1,500	900.00
(679)	Robert Wicker (Chicago NL, 1903)	3,000	1,500	900.00
(680)	Robert Wicker (Cincinnati, 1906)	2,000	1,000	600.00
(681)	Fredrick Wilhelm (Irvin "Kaiser")(Pittsburg, 1903)	3,000	1,500	900.00
(682)	Fredrick Wilhelm (Irvin "Kaiser")(Boston NL, 1904)	2,000	1,000	600.00
(683)	Edgar Willett (Detroit, 1907)	2,000	1,000	600.00
(684)	James Williams (Baltimore, 1902, street)	3,000	1,500	900.00
(685)	James Williams (New York AL, 1903, street)	3,000	1,500	900.00
(686)	James Williams (New York AL, 1903, uniform)	3,000	1,500	900.00
(687)	Otto G. Williams (Chicago NL, 1904)	2,000	1,000	600.00
(688)	Otto G. Williams (Philadelphia AL, 1905)	2,000	1,000	600.00
(689)	Otto G. Williams (Washington, 1906)	2,000	1,000	600.00
(692)	Victor J. Willis (Boston NL, 1903)	6,600	3,300	1,980
(693)	Victor J. Willis (Pittsburg, 1906)	5,400	2,700	1,620
(694)	Howard P. Wilson (Philadelphia AL, 1902, street)	3,000	1,500	900.00
(695)	Howard P. Wilson (Washington, 1903)	3,000	1,500	900.00
(696)	Howard P. Wilson (Cleveland, 1906)	2,000	1,000	600.00
(698)	J. Owen Wilson (Pittsburg, 1910)	2,000	1,000	600.00
(699)	George Wiltse (New York NL, 1904)	2,000	1,000	600.00
(700)	Louis Wiltse (Lewis)(Baltimore, 1902)	3,000	1,500	900.00
(701)	Louis Wiltse (Lewis)(New York AL, 1903)	3,000	1,500	900.00
(702)	George Winters (Winter) (Boston AL, 1902, street)	3,000	1,500	900.00
(705)	William Wolfe (Wilbert)(Washington, 1904)	2,000	1,000	600.00
(706)	Harry Wolverton (Philadelphia NL, 1902, street)	3,000	1,500	900.00
(707)	Harry Wolverton (Boston NL, 1905)	2,000	1,000	600.00
(708)	Robert Wood (Detroit, 1904)	2,000	1,000	600.00
(710)	Eugene Wright (Clarence Eugene)(Cleveland, 1903)	3,000	1,500	900.00
(711)	Eugene Wright (Clarence Eugene)(St. Louis AL, 1903)	3,000	1,500	900.00
(712)	Joseph Yeager (Detroit, 1902, street)	3,000	1,500	900.00
(713)	Joseph Yeager (New York AL, 1905)	2,000	1,000	600.00
(714)	Joseph Yeager (St. Louis AL, 1907)	2,000	1,000	600.00
(715)	Denton ("Cy") Young (Boston AL, 1902)	16,200	8,100	4,860
(716)	Irving Young (Boston NL, 1905)	2,000	1,000	600.00

		NM	EX	VG
(717)	David Zearfoss (St. Louis NL, 1904)	2,000	1,000	600.00
(718)	Charles Zimmer (Pittsburg, 1902)	3,000	1,500	900.00
(719)	Charles Zimmer (Philadelphia NL, 1903)	3,000	1,500	900.00
(720)	H. Zimmerman (Chicago NL, 1910)	2,000	1,000	600.00

TRAP SHOOTERS

(T1)	Neas Apgar	800.00	400.00	240.00
(T2)	Chas. W. Budd	800.00	400.00	240.00
(T3)	W.R. Crosby	800.00	400.00	240.00
(T4)	J.A.R. Elliott	800.00	400.00	240.00
(T5)	J.S. Fanning	800.00	400.00	240.00
(T6)	Fred Gilbert	800.00	400.00	240.00
(T7)	Rolla O. Heikes	800.00	400.00	240.00
(T8)	H.C. Hirschy	800.00	400.00	240.00
(T9)	Tom A. Marshall	800.00	400.00	240.00
(T10)	Harvey McMurchy	800.00	400.00	240.00
(T11)	Ralph Trimble	800.00	400.00	240.00

1902 Sporting Life Team Composites (W601)

Printed on heavy 13" x 14" paper and featuring a composite of player photos arranged around that of the manager and a notice of league championship status, these prints were offered to readers of the weekly sports paper for six cents in postage stamps or 50 cents per dozen. The art was often found on the covers of "Sporting Life." While the prints were issued in 1902, they specify the teams as champions "for 1903." The Buck Weaver shown on the Butte composite is not the future Black Sox shortstop.

		NM	EX	VG
Complete Set:		4,500	2,200	1,350
Common Team:		300.00	150.00	90.00
(1)	Philadelphia, American League	500.00	250.00	150.00
(2)	Pittsburg, National League	500.00	250.00	150.00
(3)	Albany, New York State League	300.00	150.00	90.00
(4)	Butte, Pacific Northwest League	400.00	200.00	120.00
(5)	Indianapolis, American Assoc.	400.00	200.00	120.00
(6)	Kansas City, Western League	400.00	200.00	120.00
(7)	Manchester, New England League	300.00	150.00	90.00
(8)	Nashville, Southern League	350.00	175.00	105.00
(9)	New Haven, Connecticut League	300.00	150.00	90.00
(10)	Rockford, Illinois-Indiana-Iowa League	300.00	150.00	90.00
(11)	Toronto, Eastern League	400.00	200.00	120.00

1903 Sporting Life Team Composites (W601)

Portraits of the individual players, usually identified by name and position, surround the manager's portrait in this series of team composites sold by Sporting Life newspaper. The 1903 series is the first in which all major league team composites were available. The 13" x 14" pictures are printed on heavy enamel paper and were sold for six cents in postage stamps, 50 cents per dozen. In some years bound portfolio complete sets were also offered, as were some of the more popular minor league teams. Notations of league and World Championships were incorporated into the design where appropriate. While issued in 1903, the pictures of league championship teams carry the notation "For 1904."

		NM	EX	VG
Complete Set (25):		5,550	2,700	1,650
Common (Major League) Team:		400.00	200.00	120.00
(1)	Boston, National League	400.00	200.00	120.00
(2)	Brooklyn, National League	400.00	200.00	120.00
(3)	Chicago, National League	600.00	300.00	180.00
(4)	Cincinnati, National League	400.00	200.00	120.00
(5)	New York, National League	500.00	250.00	150.00
(6)	Philadelphia, National League	400.00	200.00	120.00
(7)	Pittsburgh, National League	500.00	250.00	150.00
(8)	St. Louis, National League	400.00	200.00	120.00
(9)	Boston, American League	450.00	225.00	135.00
(10)	Chicago, American League	400.00	200.00	120.00
(11)	Cleveland, American League	400.00	200.00	120.00
(12)	Detroit, American League	400.00	200.00	120.00
(13)	New York, American League	450.00	225.00	135.00
(14)	Philadelphia, American League	450.00	225.00	135.00
(15)	St. Louis, American League	400.00	200.00	120.00
(16)	Washington, American League	400.00	200.00	120.00
(17)	Ft. Wayne, Central League	250.00	125.00	75.00
(18)	Holyoke, Connecticut League	250.00	125.00	75.00
(19)	Jersey City, Eastern League	300.00	150.00	90.00
(20)	Los Angeles, Pacific Coast League	300.00	150.00	90.00
(21)	Lowell, New England League	250.00	125.00	75.00
(22)	Memphis, Southern League	250.00	125.00	75.00
(23)	Schenectady, New York State League	250.00	125.00	75.00
(24)	Sedalia, Missouri Valley League	250.00	125.00	75.00
(25)	St. Paul, American Association	300.00	150.00	90.00

1904 Sporting Life Team Composites (W601)

Portraits of the individual players, usually identified by name and position, surround the manager's portrait in this series of team composites sold by Sporting Life newspaper. The 13" x 14" pictures are printed on heavy enamel paper and were sold for a dime apiece postpaid. In some years bound portfolio complete sets were also offered, as were some of the more popular minor league teams. Notations of league and World Championships were incorporated into the design where appropriate.

		NM	EX	VG
Complete Set (24):		5,550	2,700	1,650
Common (Major League) Team:		400.00	200.00	120.00
(1)	Boston, National League	400.00	200.00	120.00
(2)	Brooklyn, National League	400.00	200.00	120.00
(3)	Chicago, National League	600.00	300.00	180.00
(4)	Cincinnati, National League	400.00	200.00	120.00
(5)	New York, National League	500.00	250.00	150.00
(6)	Philadelphia, National League	400.00	200.00	120.00
(7)	Pittsburgh, National League	550.00	275.00	165.00
(8)	St. Louis, National League	400.00	200.00	120.00
(9)	Boston, American League	450.00	225.00	135.00
(10)	Chicago, American League	400.00	200.00	120.00
(11)	Cleveland, American League	400.00	200.00	120.00
(12)	Detroit, American League	400.00	200.00	120.00
(13)	New York, American League	450.00	225.00	135.00
(14)	Philadelphia, American League	450.00	225.00	135.00
(15)	St. Louis, American League	400.00	200.00	120.00
(16)	Washington, American League	400.00	200.00	120.00
(17)	Buffalo, Eastern League	300.00	150.00	90.00
(18)	Ft. Wayne, Central League	200.00	100.00	60.00
(19)	Haverhill, New England League	200.00	100.00	60.00
(20)	Macon, South Atlantic League	200.00	100.00	60.00
(21)	Memphis, Southern League	200.00	100.00	60.00
(22)	Springfield, Indiana-Illinois-Iowa League	200.00	100.00	60.00
(23)	St. Paul, American Assoc.	250.00	125.00	75.00
(24)	Syracuse, New York League (1903 Indiana-Illinois-Iowa League Champs)	200.00	100.00	60.00

1905 Sporting Life Team Composites (W601)

Portraits of the individual players, usually identified by name and position, surround the manager's portrait in this series of team composites sold by Sporting Life newspaper. The 13" x 14" pictures are printed on heavy enamel paper and were sold for a dime apiece postpaid. In some years bound portfolio complete sets were also offered, as were some of the more popular minor league teams. Notations of league and World Championships were incorporated into the design where appropriate.

		NM	EX	VG
Complete Set (23):		5,500	2,700	1,650
Common (Major League) Team:		400.00	200.00	120.00
(1)	Boston, National League	400.00	200.00	120.00
(2)	Brooklyn, National League	400.00	200.00	120.00
(3)	Chicago, National League	600.00	300.00	180.00
(4)	Cincinnati, National League	400.00	200.00	120.00
(5)	New York, National League	450.00	225.00	135.00
(6)	Philadelphia, National League	400.00	200.00	120.00
(7)	Pittsburgh, National League	750.00	375.00	225.00
(8)	St. Louis, National League	400.00	200.00	120.00
(9)	Boston, American League	400.00	200.00	120.00
(10)	Chicago, American League	400.00	200.00	120.00
(11)	Cleveland, American League	400.00	200.00	120.00
(12)	Detroit, American League	400.00	200.00	120.00
(13)	New York, American League	600.00	300.00	180.00
(14)	Philadelphia, American League	600.00	300.00	180.00
(15)	St. Louis, American League	400.00	200.00	120.00
(16)	Washington, American League	400.00	200.00	120.00
(17)	A., J. & G., New York League	200.00	100.00	60.00
(18)	Columbus, American Assoc.	250.00	125.00	75.00
(19)	Concord, New England League	200.00	100.00	60.00
(20)	Des Moines, Western League	200.00	100.00	60.00
(21)	Macon, South Atlantic League	200.00	100.00	60.00
(22)	New Orleans, Southern League	250.00	125.00	75.00
(23)	Providence, Eastern League	250.00	125.00	75.00

1906-07 Sporting Life Team Composite Postcards

A miniature version of the Sporting Life's team composite lithographs was utilized to create a postcard set. In 3-5/8" x 5-7/16" format, the postcards have a composite of player portraits surrounding that of the manager, with a wide white right margin. Backs have standard postcard indicia. Some cards have been found with backs containing an ad offering either league's set for 10 cents in stamps.

		NM	EX	VG
Complete Set (16):		13,500	6,750	4,150
Common Team:		675.00	335.00	200.00
(1)	Boston, National League	675.00	335.00	200.00
(2)	Brooklyn, National League	900.00	450.00	270.00
(3)	Chicago, National League	900.00	450.00	270.00
(4)	Cincinnati, National League	850.00	425.00	255.00
(5)	New York, National League	850.00	425.00	255.00
(6)	Philadelphia, National League	675.00	335.00	200.00
(7)	Pittsburg, National League	1,000	500.00	300.00
(8)	St. Louis, National League	675.00	335.00	200.00

(9)	Boston, American League	700.00	350.00	210.00
(10)	Chicago, American League	750.00	375.00	225.00
(11)	Cleveland, American League	1,100	550.00	330.00
(12)	Detroit, American League	1,200	600.00	360.00
(13)	New York, American League	1,100	550.00	330.00
(14)	Philadelphia, American League	900.00	450.00	270.00
(15)	St. Louis, American League	900.00	450.00	270.00
(16)	Washington, American League	800.00	400.00	240.00

1906 Sporting Life Team Composites (W601)

Originally sold as a string-bound "Premier Art Portfolio" containing 24 major and minor league team composite pictures, single pieces from this premium issue are not uncommonly found as they were later offered individually for 10 cents apiece. The individual pieces measure 13" x 14" and are printed in black-and-white on heavy enameled paper. Individual player pictures are arranged around a baseball containing the manager's picture. Each player is identified beneath his photo by name and position. By 1906 the year printed on the pictures corresponds to the year of issue.

		NM	EX	VG
Complete Set (24):		12,000	6,000	3,500
Common Major League Team:		550.00	275.00	165.00
Common Minor League Team:		300.00	150.00	90.00
(1)	Boston, National League	750.00	375.00	225.00
(2)	Brooklyn, National League	550.00	275.00	165.00
(3)	Chicago, National League	800.00	400.00	240.00
(4)	Cincinnati, National League	550.00	275.00	165.00
(5)	New York, National League	650.00	325.00	195.00
(6)	Philadelphia, National League	675.00	335.00	200.00
(7)	Pittsburg, National League	650.00	325.00	195.00
(8)	St. Louis, National League	550.00	275.00	165.00
(9)	Boston, American League	800.00	400.00	240.00
(10)	Chicago, American League	650.00	325.00	195.00
(11)	Cleveland, American League	1,200	600.00	360.00
(12)	Detroit, American League	1,200	600.00	360.00
(13)	New York, American League	800.00	400.00	240.00
(14)	Philadelphia, American League	800.00	400.00	240.00
(15)	St. Louis, American League	550.00	275.00	165.00
(16)	Washington, American League	550.00	275.00	165.00
(17)	National League president, managers	600.00	300.00	180.00
(18)	American League president, managers	600.00	300.00	180.00
(19)	Birmingham, Southern League	300.00	150.00	90.00
(20)	Buffalo, Eastern League	300.00	150.00	90.00
(21)	Columbus, American Assoc.	300.00	150.00	90.00
(22)	Grand Rapids, Central League	300.00	150.00	90.00
(23)	Norwich, Connecticut League	300.00	150.00	90.00
(24)	Scranton, New York League	300.00	150.00	90.00

1907 Sporting Life Team Composites (W601)

Portraits of the individual players, usually identified by name and position, surround the manager's portrait in this series of team composites sold by Sporting Life newspaper. The 13" x 14" pictures are printed on heavy enamel paper and were sold for a dime apiece postpaid. In some years bound portfolio

complete sets were also offered, as were some of the more popular minor league teams. Notations of league and World Championships were incorporated into the design where appropriate.

		NM	EX	VG
Complete Set (20):		5,500	2,700	1,600
Common (Major League) Team:		400.00	200.00	120.00
(1)	Boston, National League	400.00	200.00	120.00
(2)	Brooklyn, National League	400.00	200.00	120.00
(3)	Chicago, National League	500.00	250.00	150.00
(4)	Cincinnati, National League	400.00	200.00	120.00
(5)	New York, National League	500.00	250.00	150.00
(6)	Philadelphia, National League	400.00	200.00	120.00
(7)	Pittsburgh, National League	450.00	225.00	135.00
(8)	St. Louis, National League	400.00	200.00	120.00
(9)	Boston, American League	400.00	200.00	120.00
(10)	Chicago, American League	400.00	200.00	120.00
(11)	Cleveland, American League	400.00	200.00	120.00
(12)	Detroit, American League	600.00	300.00	180.00
(13)	New York, American League	450.00	225.00	135.00
(14)	Philadelphia, American League	400.00	200.00	120.00
(15)	St. Louis, American League	400.00	200.00	120.00
(16)	Washington, American League	500.00	250.00	150.00
(17)	Toronto, Eastern League	300.00	150.00	90.00
(18)	Columbus, American Assoc.	300.00	150.00	90.00
(19)	Williamsport, Tri-State League	200.00	100.00	60.00
(20)	Albany, New York League	200.00	100.00	60.00
(21)	Atlanta, Southern League	200.00	100.00	60.00
(22)	Holyoke, Connecticut League	200.00	100.00	60.00
(23)	Norfolk, Virginia League	200.00	100.00	60.00

1908 Sporting Life Team Composites (W601)

Portraits of the individual players, usually identified by name and position, surround the manager's portrait in this series of team composites sold by Sporting Life newspaper. The 13" x 14" pictures are printed on heavy enamel paper and were sold for a dime apiece postpaid. In some years bound portfolio complete sets were also offered, as were some of the more popular minor league teams. Notations of league and World Championships were incorporated into the design where appropriate.

		NM	EX	VG
Complete Set (16):		4,500	2,250	1,350
Common Team:		400.00	200.00	120.00
(1)	Boston, National League	400.00	200.00	120.00
(2)	Brooklyn, National League	400.00	200.00	120.00
(3)	Chicago, National League	500.00	250.00	150.00
(4)	Cincinnati, National League	400.00	200.00	120.00
(5)	New York, National League	425.00	210.00	125.00
(6)	Philadelphia, National League	400.00	200.00	120.00
(7)	Pittsburgh, National League	450.00	225.00	135.00
(8)	St. Louis, National League	400.00	200.00	120.00
(9)	Boston, American League	400.00	200.00	120.00
(10)	Chicago, American League	400.00	200.00	120.00
(11)	Cleveland, American League	400.00	200.00	120.00
(12)	Detroit, American League	600.00	300.00	180.00
(13)	New York, American League	450.00	225.00	135.00
(14)	Philadelphia, American League	400.00	200.00	120.00
(15)	St. Louis, American League	400.00	200.00	120.00
(16)	Washington, American League	450.00	225.00	135.00

1909 Sporting Life Team Composites (W601)

Portraits of the individual players, usually identified by name and position, surround the manager's portrait in this series of team composites sold by Sporting Life newspaper. The 13" x 14" pictures are printed on heavy enamel paper and were sold for a dime apiece postpaid. In some years bound portfolio complete sets were also offered, as were some of the more popular minor league teams. Notations of league and World Championships were incorporated into the design where appropriate.

		NM	EX	VG
Complete Set (16):		6,500	3,250	1,850
Common Team:		600.00	300.00	180.00
(1)	Boston, National League	600.00	300.00	180.00

		NM	EX	VG
(2)	Brooklyn, National League	600.00	300.00	180.00
(3)	Chicago, National League	750.00	375.00	225.00
(4)	Cincinnati, National League	600.00	300.00	180.00
(5)	New York, National League	675.00	335.00	200.00
(6)	Philadelphia, National League	600.00	300.00	180.00
(7)	Pittsburgh, National League	1,125	560.00	335.00
(8)	St. Louis, National League	1,000	500.00	300.00
(9)	Boston, American League	600.00	300.00	180.00
(10)	Chicago, American League	600.00	300.00	180.00
(11)	Cleveland, American League	600.00	300.00	180.00
(12)	Detroit, American League	900.00	450.00	270.00
(13)	New York, American League	675.00	335.00	200.00
(14)	Philadelphia, American League	600.00	300.00	180.00
(15)	St. Louis, American League	600.00	300.00	180.00
(16)	Washington, American League	675.00	335.00	200.00

1910 Sporting Life Team Composites (W601)

After several years of issuing composite team photos for all major league teams (and some minor league teams), Sporting Life in 1910 began issuing them only for the league and World's Champions. Like the others, they are 13" x 14", printed on heavy enamel paper with individual player portrait photos surrounding the manager at center.

		NM	EX	VG
Complete Set (2):		1,200	600.00	350.00
Common Team:		300.00	150.00	90.00
(1)	Chicago Cubs (N.L. champs.)	450.00	225.00	135.00
(2)	Philadelphia Athletics (World's Champions)	750.00	375.00	225.00

1910-11 Sporting Life (M116)

Hans Wagner, Pitts. Nationals

This set of nominally 1-1/2" x 2-5/8" (individual card sizes vary even moreso than typically found on early 20th Century cards, notably with the "high numbers" often found somewhat larger) cards was offered to subscribers to "Sporting Life," a major competitor of "The Sporting News" in the early part of the century. The cards were issued in 24 series of 12 cards each, sold by mail for four cents per series. Card fronts feature color-tinted black-and-white portrait photos with the name and team printed below. Backs have various ads for the weekly paper. The last three 24-card series are scarcer than the earlier cards. These 72 cards have "Over 300 subjects" printed on back. Values in this checklist are adjusted according to that scarcity. The scarce blue-background cards appear to have been a second printing of the first two 12-card series which no doubt sold out quickly in the original pastel-background version due to the popularity of the players included. The 12 players in the Third Series can be found in an original printing with the ad on back printed in black, and a later version with a blue back. Each of the Third Series cards also exhibits on front subtle differences in the size and coloring of the player portrait. The complete set price does not include variations.

		NM	EX	VG
Common Player:		360.00	180.00	110.00
(1)	Ed Abbaticchio	360.00	180.00	110.00
(2a)	Babe Adams (Black back.)	520.00	260.00	155.00
(2b)	Babe Adams (Blue back.)	360.00	180.00	110.00
(3)	Red Ames	1,000	500.00	300.00
(4)	Jimmy Archer	1,000	500.00	300.00
(5)	Frank Arrelanes (Arellanes)	360.00	180.00	110.00
(6)	Tommy Atkins	1,000	500.00	300.00
(7)	Jimmy Austin	1,000	500.00	300.00
(8)	Les Bachman (Backman)	360.00	180.00	110.00
(9)	Bill Bailey	360.00	180.00	110.00
(10a)	Home Run Baker (Black back.)	2,400	1,200	720.00
(10b)	Home Run Baker (Blue back.)	1,600	800.00	480.00
(11)	Cy Barger	360.00	180.00	110.00
(12)	Jack Barry	360.00	180.00	110.00
(13a)	Johnny Bates (Philadelphia)	360.00	180.00	110.00
(13b)	Johnny Bates (Cincinnati)(A G-VG example sold at auction 4/06 for $22,987.)			
(14)	Ginger Beaumont	360.00	180.00	110.00
(15)	Fred Beck	360.00	180.00	110.00
(16)	Heinie Beckendorf	360.00	180.00	110.00
(17)	Fred Beebe	360.00	180.00	110.00
(18)	George Bell	360.00	180.00	110.00
(19)	Harry Bemis	360.00	180.00	110.00
(20a)	Chief Bender (Blue background.)	2,400	1,200	720.00
(20b)	Chief Bender (Pastel background.)	1,600	800.00	480.00
(21)	Bill Bergen	360.00	180.00	110.00
(22)	Heinie Berger	360.00	180.00	110.00
(23)	Bob Bescher	360.00	180.00	110.00
(24)	Joe Birmingham	360.00	180.00	110.00
(25)	Lena Blackburn (Blackburne)	360.00	180.00	110.00
(26)	John Bliss	1,000	500.00	300.00
(27)	Bruno Block	1,000	500.00	300.00
(28)	Bill Bradley	360.00	180.00	110.00
(29)	Kitty Bransfield	360.00	180.00	110.00
(30a)	Roger Bresnahan (Blue)	2,400	1,200	720.00
(30b)	Roger Bresnahan (Pastel)	1,600	800.00	480.00
(31)	Al Bridwell	360.00	180.00	110.00
(32)	Buster Brown (Boston)	360.00	180.00	110.00
(33a)	Mordecai Brown (Blue, Chicago)	2,400	1,200	720.00
(33b)	Mordecai Brown (Pastel, Chicago)	1,600	800.00	480.00
(34)	Al Burch	360.00	180.00	110.00
(35)	Donie Bush	360.00	180.00	110.00
(36)	Bobby Byrne	360.00	180.00	110.00
(37)	Howie Camnitz	360.00	180.00	110.00
(38)	Vin Campbell	1,000	500.00	300.00
(39)	Bill Carrigan	360.00	180.00	110.00
(40a)	Frank Chance (Blue)	2,400	1,200	720.00
(40b)	Frank Chance (Pastel)	1,600	800.00	480.00
(41)	Chappy Charles	360.00	180.00	110.00
(42a)	Hal Chase (Blue)	1,600	800.00	480.00
(42b)	Hal Chase (Pastel)	1,100	550.00	330.00
(43)	Ed Cicotte	1,800	900.00	540.00
(44a)	Fred Clarke (Pittsburgh, black back.)	2,400	1,200	720.00
(44b)	Fred Clarke (Pittsburgh, blue back.)	1,600	800.00	480.00
(45)	Nig Clarke (Cleveland)	360.00	180.00	110.00
(46)	Tommy Clarke (Cincinnati)	1,000	500.00	300.00
(47a)	Ty Cobb (Blue)	6,000	3,000	1,800
(47b)	Ty Cobb (pastel)	18,000	9,000	5,400
(48a)	Eddie Collins (Blue)	2,400	1,200	720.00
(48b)	Eddie Collins (Pastel)	1,600	800.00	480.00
(49)	Ray Collins	1,000	500.00	300.00
(50)	Wid Conroy	360.00	180.00	110.00
(51)	Jack Coombs	360.00	180.00	110.00
(52)	Frank Corridon	360.00	180.00	110.00
(53)	Harry Coveleskie (Coveleski)	2,000	1,000	600.00
(54)	Doc Crandall	360.00	180.00	110.00
(55a)	Sam Crawford (Blue)	2,400	1,200	720.00
(55b)	Sam Crawford (Pastel)	1,600	800.00	480.00
(56)	Birdie Cree	360.00	180.00	110.00
(57)	Lou Criger	360.00	180.00	110.00
(58)	Dode Criss	1,000	500.00	300.00
(59)	Cliff Curtis	1,000	500.00	300.00
(60)	Bill Dahlen	360.00	180.00	110.00
(61)	Bill Davidson	1,000	500.00	300.00
(62a)	Harry Davis (Blue)	1,000	500.00	300.00
(62b)	Harry Davis (pastel)	360.00	180.00	110.00
(63)	Jim Delehanty (Delahanty)	360.00	180.00	110.00
(64)	Ray Demmitt	1,000	500.00	300.00
(65)	Rube Dessau	1,000	500.00	300.00
(66a)	Art Devlin (Black back)	520.00	260.00	155.00
(66b)	Art Devlin (Blue back)	360.00	180.00	110.00
(67)	Josh Devore	1,000	500.00	300.00
(68)	Pat Donahue	360.00	180.00	110.00
(69)	Patsy Donovan	1,000	500.00	300.00
(70a)	Wild Bill Donovan (Blue)	1,000	500.00	300.00
(70b)	Wild Bill Donovan (Pastel)	360.00	180.00	110.00
(71a)	Red Dooin (Blue)	1,000	500.00	300.00
(71b)	Red Dooin (Pastel)	360.00	180.00	110.00
(72)	Mickey Doolan	360.00	180.00	110.00
(73)	Patsy Dougherty	360.00	180.00	110.00
(74)	Tom Downey	360.00	180.00	110.00
(75)	Jim Doyle	360.00	180.00	110.00
(76a)	Larry Doyle (Blue)	1,000	500.00	300.00
(76b)	Larry Doyle (Pastel)	360.00	180.00	110.00
(77)	Hugh Duffy	1,600	800.00	480.00
(78)	Jimmy Dygert	360.00	180.00	110.00
(79)	Dick Eagan (Egan)	360.00	180.00	110.00
(80)	Kid Elberfeld	360.00	180.00	110.00
(81)	Rube Ellis	360.00	180.00	110.00
(82)	Clyde Engle	360.00	180.00	110.00
(83)	Tex Erwin	1,000	500.00	300.00
(84)	Steve Evans	1,000	500.00	300.00
(85a)	Johnny Evers (Black back)	2,400	1,200	720.00
(85b)	Johnny Evers (Blue back)	1,600	800.00	480.00
(86)	Bob Ewing	360.00	180.00	110.00
(87)	Cy Falkenberg	360.00	180.00	110.00
(88)	George Ferguson	360.00	180.00	110.00
(89)	Art Fletcher	1,000	500.00	300.00
(90)	Elmer Flick	1,600	800.00	480.00
(91)	John Flynn	1,000	500.00	300.00
(92)	Russ Ford	1,000	500.00	300.00
(93)	Eddie Foster	1,000	500.00	300.00
(94)	Bill Foxen	360.00	180.00	110.00
(95)	John Frill	1,000	500.00	300.00
(96)	Sam Frock	1,000	500.00	300.00
(97)	Art Fromme	360.00	180.00	110.00
(98)	Earl Gardner (New York)	1,000	500.00	300.00
(99)	Larry Gardner (Boston)	1,000	500.00	300.00
(100)	Harry Gaspar	1,000	500.00	300.00
(101)	Doc Gessler	360.00	180.00	110.00
(102a)	George Gibson (Blue)	1,000	500.00	300.00
(102b)	George Gibson (Pastel)	360.00	180.00	110.00
(103)	Bill Graham (St. Louis)	360.00	180.00	110.00
(104)	Peaches Graham (Boston)	360.00	180.00	110.00
(105)	Eddie Grant	360.00	180.00	110.00
(106)	Clark Griffith	1,600	800.00	480.00
(107)	Ed Hahn	360.00	180.00	110.00
(108)	Charley Hall	360.00	180.00	110.00
(109)	Bob Harmon	1,000	500.00	300.00
(110)	Topsy Hartsel	360.00	180.00	110.00
(111)	Roy Hartzell	360.00	180.00	110.00
(112)	Heinie Heitmuller	360.00	180.00	110.00
(113)	Buck Herzog	360.00	180.00	110.00
(114)	Dick Hoblitzel (Hoblitzell)	360.00	180.00	110.00
(115)	Danny Hoffman	360.00	180.00	110.00
(116)	Solly Hofman	360.00	180.00	110.00
(117)	Harry Hooper	1,600	800.00	480.00
(118)	Harry Howell	360.00	180.00	110.00
(119)	Miller Huggins	1,600	800.00	480.00
(120)	Long Tom Hughes	1,000	500.00	300.00
(121)	Rudy Hulswitt	360.00	180.00	110.00
(122)	John Hummel	360.00	180.00	110.00
(123)	George Hunter	360.00	180.00	110.00
(124)	Ham Hyatt	360.00	180.00	110.00
(125)	Fred Jacklitsch	360.00	180.00	110.00
(126a)	Hughie Jennings (Blue)	2,400	1,200	720.00
(126b)	Hughie Jennings (Pastel)	1,600	800.00	480.00
(127)	Walter Johnson	7,000	3,500	2,100
(128a)	Davy Jones (Blue)	1,000	500.00	300.00
(128b)	Davy Jones (Pastel)	360.00	180.00	110.00
(129)	Tom Jones	360.00	180.00	110.00
(130a)	Tim Jordan (Blue)	1,000	500.00	300.00
(130b)	Tim Jordan (Pastel)	360.00	180.00	110.00
(131)	Addie Joss	1,800	900.00	540.00
(132)	Johnny Kane	360.00	180.00	110.00
(133)	Ed Karger	360.00	180.00	110.00
(134)	Red Killifer (Killefer)	1,000	500.00	300.00
(135)	Johnny Kling	360.00	180.00	110.00
(136)	Otto Knabe	360.00	180.00	110.00
(137)	John Knight	1,000	500.00	300.00
(138)	Ed Konetchy	360.00	180.00	110.00
(139)	Harry Krause	360.00	180.00	110.00
(140)	Rube Kroh	360.00	180.00	110.00
(141)	Art Krueger	1,600	800.00	480.00
(142a)	Nap Lajoie (Blue)	2,400	1,200	720.00
(142b)	Nap Lajoie (Pastel)	1,600	800.00	480.00
(143)	Fred Lake (Boston)	360.00	180.00	110.00
(144)	Joe Lake (St. Louis)	1,000	500.00	300.00
(145)	Frank LaPorte	360.00	180.00	110.00
(146)	Jack Lapp	1,000	500.00	300.00
(147)	Chick Lathers	1,000	500.00	300.00
(148a)	Tommy Leach (Blue)	1,000	500.00	300.00
(148b)	Tommy Leach (Pastel)	360.00	180.00	110.00
(149)	Sam Leever	360.00	180.00	110.00
(150)	Lefty Leifeld	360.00	180.00	110.00
(151)	Ed Lennox	360.00	180.00	110.00
(152)	Fred Linke (Link)	1,000	500.00	300.00
(153)	Paddy Livingstone (Livingston)	360.00	180.00	110.00
(154)	Hans Lobert	360.00	180.00	110.00
(155)	Bris Lord	360.00	180.00	110.00
(156a)	Harry Lord (Blue)	1,000	500.00	300.00
(156b)	Harry Lord (pastel)	360.00	180.00	110.00
(157)	Johnny Lush	360.00	180.00	110.00
(158)	Connie Mack	1,600	800.00	480.00
(159)	Tom Madden	1,000	500.00	300.00
(160)	Nick Maddox	360.00	180.00	110.00
(161)	Sherry Magee	360.00	180.00	110.00
(162a)	Christy Mathewson (Blue)	10,000	5,000	3,000
(162b)	Christy Mathewson (Pastel)	5,400	2,700	1,625
(163)	Al Mattern	360.00	180.00	110.00
(164)	Jimmy McAleer	360.00	180.00	110.00
(165)	George McBride	1,000	500.00	300.00
(166a)	Amby McConnell (Boston)	360.00	180.00	110.00
(166b)	Amby McConnell (Chicago)	10,000	5,000	3,000
(167)	Pryor McElveen	360.00	180.00	110.00
(168)	John McGraw	1,600	800.00	480.00
(169)	Deacon McGuire	360.00	180.00	110.00
(170)	Stuffy McInnes (McInnis)	1,000	500.00	300.00
(171)	Harry McIntire (McIntyre)	360.00	180.00	110.00
(172)	Matty McIntyre	360.00	180.00	110.00
(173)	Larry McLean	360.00	180.00	110.00
(174)	Tommy McMillan	360.00	180.00	110.00
(175a)	George McQuillan (Blue, Philadelphia)	1,000	500.00	300.00
(175b)	George McQuillan (Pastel, Philadelphia)	360.00	180.00	110.00
(175c)	George McQuillan (Cincinnati)	5,000	2,500	1,500
(176)	Paul Meloan	1,000	500.00	300.00
(177)	Fred Merkle	360.00	180.00	110.00
(178)	Clyde Milan	360.00	180.00	110.00
(179)	Dots Miller (Pittsburgh)	360.00	180.00	110.00
(180)	Warren Miller (Washington)	1,000	500.00	300.00
(181)	Fred Mitchell	1,000	500.00	300.00
(182)	Mike Mitchell	360.00	180.00	110.00
(183)	Earl Moore	360.00	180.00	110.00
(184)	Pat Moran	360.00	180.00	110.00
(185a)	Lew Moren (Black back)	520.00	260.00	155.00
(185b)	Lew Moren (Blue back)	360.00	180.00	110.00
(186)	Cy Morgan	360.00	180.00	110.00
(187)	George Moriarty	360.00	180.00	110.00
(188)	Mike Mowery (Mowrey)	1,000	500.00	300.00
(189a)	George Mullin (Black back)	520.00	260.00	155.00
(189b)	George Mullin (Blue back.)	360.00	180.00	110.00

		NM	EX	VG
(190)	Danny Murphy	360.00	180.00	110.00
(191)	Red Murray	360.00	180.00	110.00
(192)	Chief Myers (Meyers)	1,000	500.00	300.00
(193)	Tom Needham	360.00	180.00	110.00
(194)	Harry Niles	360.00	180.00	110.00
(195)	Rebel Oakes	1,000	500.00	300.00
(196)	Jack O'Connor	360.00	180.00	110.00
(197)	Paddy O'Connor	360.00	180.00	110.00
(198)	Bill O'Hara	1,000	500.00	300.00
(199)	Rube Oldring	360.00	180.00	110.00
(200)	Charley O'Leary	360.00	180.00	110.00
(201)	Orval Overall	360.00	180.00	110.00
(202)	Freddy Parent	360.00	180.00	110.00
(203)	Dode Paskert	1,000	500.00	300.00
(204)	Fred Payne	360.00	180.00	110.00
(205)	Barney Pelty	360.00	180.00	110.00
(206)	Hub Pernoll	1,000	500.00	300.00
(207)	George Perring	1,000	500.00	300.00
(208)	Big Jeff Pfeffer	1,000	500.00	300.00
(209)	Jack Pfiester	360.00	180.00	110.00
(210)	Art Phelan	1,000	500.00	300.00
(211)	Ed Phelps	360.00	180.00	110.00
(212)	Deacon Phillippe	360.00	180.00	110.00
(213)	Eddie Plank	4,800	2,400	1,450
(214)	Jack Powell	360.00	180.00	110.00
(215)	Billy Purtell	360.00	180.00	110.00
(216)	Farmer Ray	1,000	500.00	300.00
(217)	Bugs Raymond	360.00	180.00	110.00
(218)	Doc Reisling	360.00	180.00	110.00
(219)	Ed Reulbach	360.00	180.00	110.00
(220)	Lew Richie	360.00	180.00	110.00
(221)	Jack Rowan	360.00	180.00	110.00
(222a)	Nap Rucker (Black back.)	520.00	260.00	155.00
(222b)	Nap Rucker (Blue back.)	360.00	180.00	110.00
(223)	Slim Sallee	360.00	180.00	110.00
(224)	Doc Scanlon	360.00	180.00	110.00
(225)	Germany Schaefer	360.00	180.00	110.00
(226)	Lou Schettler	1,000	500.00	300.00
(227)	Admiral Schlei	360.00	180.00	110.00
(228)	Boss Schmidt	360.00	180.00	110.00
(229)	Wildfire Schulte	360.00	180.00	110.00
(230)	Al Schweitzer	360.00	180.00	110.00
(231)	Jim Scott	1,000	500.00	300.00
(232a)	Cy Seymour (N.Y.)	360.00	180.00	110.00
(232b)	Cy Seymour (Baltimore) (Two known; 4/04 auction $18,000+ Fair-Good.)			
(233)	Tillie Shafer	360.00	180.00	110.00
(234)	Bud Sharpe	1,000	500.00	300.00
(235)	Dave Shean	1,000	500.00	300.00
(236)	Jimmy Sheckard	360.00	180.00	110.00
(237)	Mike Simon	1,000	500.00	300.00
(238)	Charlie Smith (Boston)	1,000	500.00	300.00
(239)	Frank Smith (Chicago)	360.00	180.00	110.00
(240)	Harry Smith (Boston)	360.00	180.00	110.00
(241)	Fred Snodgrass	360.00	180.00	110.00
(242)	Bob Spade	360.00	180.00	110.00
(243)	Tully Sparks	360.00	180.00	110.00
(244)	Tris Speaker	3,000	1,500	900.00
(245)	Jake Stahl	360.00	180.00	110.00
(246)	George Stallings	360.00	180.00	110.00
(247)	Oscar Stanage	360.00	180.00	110.00
(248)	Harry Steinfeldt	360.00	180.00	110.00
(249)	Jim Stephens	360.00	180.00	110.00
(250)	George Stone	360.00	180.00	110.00
(251)	George Stovall	360.00	180.00	110.00
(252)	Gabby Street	360.00	180.00	110.00
(253)	Sailor Stroud	1,000	500.00	300.00
(254)	Amos Strunk	1,000	500.00	300.00
(255)	George Suggs	360.00	180.00	110.00
(256)	Billy Sullivan	360.00	180.00	110.00
(257a)	Ed Summers (Black back.)	520.00	260.00	155.00
(257b)	Ed Summers (Blue back.)	360.00	180.00	110.00
(258)	Bill Sweeney (Boston)	360.00	180.00	110.00
(259)	Jeff Sweeney (New York)	1,000	500.00	300.00
(260)	Lee Tannehill	360.00	180.00	110.00
(261a)	Fred Tenney (Blue)	1,000	500.00	300.00
(261b)	Fred Tenney (pastel)	360.00	180.00	110.00
(262a)	Ira Thomas (Blue)	1,000	500.00	300.00
(262b)	Ira Thomas (pastel)	360.00	180.00	110.00
(263)	Jack Thoney	360.00	180.00	110.00
(264a)	Joe Tinker (Black back.)	2,400	1,200	720.00
(264b)	Joe Tinker (Blue back.)	1,600	800.00	480.00
(265)	John Titus	1,000	500.00	300.00
(266)	Terry Turner	360.00	180.00	110.00
(267)	Bob Unglaub	360.00	180.00	110.00
(268a)	Rube Waddell (Black back.)	2,400	1,200	720.00
(268b)	Rube Waddell (Blue back.)	1,600	800.00	480.00
(269a)	Hans Wagner (Pittsburgh, blue)	22,000	11,000	6,600
(269b)	Hans Wagner (Pittsburgh, pastel)	4,000	2,000	1,200
(270)	Heinie Wagner (Boston)	360.00	180.00	110.00
(271)	Bobby Wallace	1,600	800.00	480.00
(272)	Ed Walsh (Chicago)	1,600	800.00	480.00
(273a)	Jimmy Walsh (gray background, Philadelphia)	1,400	700.00	420.00
(273b)	Jimmy Walsh (White background, Philadelphia)	1,400	700.00	420.00
(274)	Doc White	360.00	180.00	110.00
(275)	Kaiser Wilhelm	360.00	180.00	110.00
(276)	Ed Willett	360.00	180.00	110.00
(277)	Vic Willis	1,600	800.00	480.00
(278)	Art Wilson (New York)	1,000	500.00	300.00
(279)	Owen Wilson (Pittsburgh)	360.00	180.00	110.00
(280)	Hooks Wiltse	360.00	180.00	110.00
(281)	Harry Wolter	360.00	180.00	110.00
(282)	Smokey Joe Wood	2,700	1,350	810.00
(283)	Ralph Works	360.00	180.00	110.00
(284a)	Cy Young (Black back.)	4,800	2,400	1,450
(284b)	Cy Young (Blue back.)	3,600	1,800	1,075
(285)	Irv Young	360.00	180.00	110.00
(286)	Heinie Zimmerman	1,000	500.00	300.00
(287)	Dutch Zwilling	360.00	180.00	110.00

1911 Sporting Life Cabinets (M110)

This set of 5-5/8" x 7-1/2" premium photos is similar to, but much scarcer than, the contemporary T3 Turkey Red cabinets. Like those, the Sporting Life cabinets feature a pastel player picture surrounded by a gray frame with a "gold" nameplate at bottom. Backs have advertising for the weekly sports paper printed in blue.

		NM	EX	VG
Complete Set (6):		90,000	35,000	17,500
Common Player:		5,500	2,200	1,325
(1)	Frank Chance	10,000	4,000	2,000
(2)	Hal Chase	8,000	3,200	1,600
(3)	Ty Cobb	25,000	10,000	5,000
(4)	Napoleon Lajoie	10,000	4,000	2,000
(5)	Christy Mathewson	20,000	8,000	4,000
(6)	Honus Wagner	22,500	9,000	4,500

1911 Sporting Life Team Composites (W601)

After several years of issuing composite team photos for all major league teams (and some minor league teams), Sporting Life in 1910 began issuing them only for the league and World's Champions. Like the others, they are 13" x 14", printed on heavy enamel paper with individual player portrait photos surrounding the manager at center.

		NM	EX	VG
Complete Set (2):		1,200	600.00	350.00
Common Team:		300.00	150.00	90.00
(1)	New York Giants (N.L. champs.)	600.00	300.00	180.00
(2)	Philadelphia Athletics (World's Champions)	750.00	375.00	225.00

1899-1900 Sporting News Supplements (M101-1)

For much of 1899 and 1900, the weekly issues of The Sporting News included a baseball player portrait supplement. About 10" x 13", the pictures offered vignetted photos of the era's stars on a glossy paper stock. Virtually all pictures were formal head-and-shoulders portraits; some in uniform, some in civilian clothes. A handful of players are depicted in full-length poses. The pictures were produced for the

sports paper by National Copper Plate Co., (which issued its own set of prints listed elsewhere in this catalog). The TSN supplements have a logotype above the photo and the date in which it was included in the paper. Full player name and team/year are printed at bottom. Backs have a small box offering career information. Besides offering the pictures with weekly issues, portfolios of 50 could be had by starting or renewing a subscription for $2 a year.

		NM	EX	VG
Complete Set (62):		60,000	24,000	12,000
Common Player:		750.00	300.00	150.00
	1899			
(1)	William Lange (Apr. 22)	750.00	300.00	150.00
(2)	Hugh Duffy (Apr. 29)	1,250	500.00	250.00
(3)	Charles A. Nichols (May 6)	1,250	500.00	250.00
(4)	Martin Bergen (May 13)	750.00	300.00	150.00
(5)	Michael Griffin (May 20)	750.00	300.00	150.00
(6)	Wilbert Robinson (May 27)	1,250	500.00	250.00
(7)	Clark C. Griffith (June 3)	1,250	500.00	250.00
(8)	John J. Doyle (June 10)	750.00	300.00	150.00
(9)	R.J. Wallace (June 17)	1,250	500.00	250.00
(10)	John O'Connor (June 24)	750.00	300.00	150.00
(11)	Louis Criger (July 1)	750.00	300.00	150.00
(12)	Jerry H. Nops (July 8)	750.00	300.00	150.00
(13)	William Kennedy (July 15)	750.00	300.00	150.00
(14)	P.J. Donovan (July 22)	750.00	300.00	150.00
(15)	William H. Keeler (July 29)	1,250	500.00	250.00
(16)	John J. McGraw (Aug. 5)	1,250	500.00	250.00
(17)	James Hughes (Aug. 12)	750.00	300.00	150.00
(18)	John Wagner (Aug. 19)	7,500	3,000	1,500
(19)	Victor G. Willis (Aug. 26)	1,250	500.00	250.00
(20)	James J. Collins (Sept. 2)	1,250	500.00	250.00
(21)	Eugene DeMontreville (Sept. 9)	750.00	300.00	150.00
(22)	Joseph J. Kelley (Sept. 16)	1,250	500.00	250.00
(23)	Frank L. Donahue (Francis R. "Red")(Sept. 23)	750.00	300.00	150.00
(24)	Edward J. Delehanty (Delahanty)(Sept. 30)	750.00	300.00	50.00
(25)	Fred C. Clark (Clarke) (Oct. 7)	1,250	500.00	250.00
(26)	Napoleon Lajoie (Oct. 14)	1,250	500.00	250.00
(27)	Edward Hanlon (Oct. 21)	1,250	500.00	250.00
(28)	Charles Stahl (Oct. 28)	750.00	300.00	150.00
(29)	Lave N. Cross (Nov. 4)	750.00	300.00	150.00
(30)	Elmer H. Flick (Nov. 11)	1,250	500.00	250.00
(31)	Frank LeRoy Chance (Nov. 18)	1,250	500.00	250.00
(32)	George S. Davis (Nov. 25)	1,250	500.00	250.00
(33)	Hugh J. Jennings (Dec. 2)	1,250	500.00	250.00
(34)	Denton T. Young (Dec. 9)	2,500	1,000	500.00
	1900			
(35)	George E. Waddell (Apr. 14)	1,250	500.00	250.00
(36)	John Dunn (Apr. 21)	750.00	300.00	150.00
(37)	Clarence Beaumont (Apr. 28)	750.00	300.00	150.00
(38)	James T. McGuire (May 5)	750.00	300.00	150.00
(39)	William H. Dineen (May 12)	750.00	300.00	150.00
(40)	James T. Williams (May 19)	750.00	300.00	150.00
(41)	Thomas W. Corcoran (May 26)	750.00	300.00	150.00
(42)	John Freeman (June 2)	750.00	300.00	150.00
(43)	Henry Peitz (June 9)	750.00	300.00	150.00
(44)	Charles Phillippe (June 16)	750.00	300.00	150.00
(45)	Frank Hahn (June 23)	750.00	300.00	150.00
(46)	J. Emmet Heidrick (June 30)	750.00	300.00	150.00
(47)	Joseph McGinnity (July 7)	1,250	500.00	250.00
(48)	John D. Chesbro (July 14)	1,250	500.00	250.00
(49)	William R. Hamilton (July 21)	750.00	300.00	150.00
(50)	Samuel Leever (July 28)	750.00	300.00	150.00
(51)	Mike Donlin (Aug. 4)	750.00	300.00	150.00
(52)	William F. Dahlen (Aug. 11)	750.00	300.00	150.00
(53)	Frederick Tenney (Aug. 18)	750.00	300.00	150.00
(54)	Edward P. Scott (Aug. 25)	750.00	300.00	150.00
(55)	Edward M. Lewis (Sept. 1)	750.00	300.00	150.00
(56)	Theodore Breitenstein (Sept. 8)	750.00	300.00	150.00
(57)	Herman C. Long (Sept. 15)	750.00	300.00	150.00
(58)	Jesse Tannehill (Sept. 22)	750.00	300.00	150.00
(59)	Burt E. Jones (Sept. 29)	750.00	300.00	150.00
(60)	J. Callahan (Nixey)(Oct. 6)	750.00	300.00	150.00
(61)	Claude Ritchey (Oct. 13)	750.00	300.00	150.00
(62)	Roy Thomas (Oct. 20)	750.00	300.00	150.00

1909-1913 Sporting News Supplements (M101-2)

Among the finest large-format baseball collectibles published in the early part of the 20th Century was the 100-piece series of sepia-toned supplements issued by The Sporting News. Initially issued in a size of about 7-1/2" x 10", by late 1909 the size evolved to about 8-1/2" x 10" with the team photos issued in a 16" x 10" format. The series was begun with the insertion of a supplement in the July 22, 1909, issue of TSN. One supplement was issued with each week's paper through April 7, 1910. There were several gaps over the course of the next several years, until the final piece was issued with the TSN dated Dec. 11, 1913. Most of the supplements feature full-length poses of the players. Each is labeled "Supplement to The Sporting News" with the issue date at top. At bottom is a box with the player's name and team. Backs are usually blank, but some supplements are found with colored advertising on back for various other collectibles from the newspaper. The TSN supplements were printed on heavy paper and are usually found with corner creases or other signs of wear.

		NM	EX	VG
Complete Set (100):		25,000	12,500	7,500
Common Player:		80.00	40.00	25.00
Ad backs: 3X				
1909				
(1)	Roger Bresnahan (7/22)	600.00	300.00	180.00
(2)	Denton Young, Louis Criger (7/29)	450.00	225.00	135.00
(3)	Christopher Mathewson (8/5)	1,000	500.00	300.00
(4)	Tyrus R. Cobb (8/12)	1,200	600.00	360.00
(5)	Napoleon Lajoie (8/19)	550.00	275.00	165.00
(6)	Sherwood N. Magee (8/26)	80.00	40.00	25.00
(7)	Frank L. Chance (9/2)	500.00	250.00	150.00
(8)	Edward Walsh (9/9)	500.00	250.00	150.00
(9)	Nap Rucker (9/16)	80.00	40.00	25.00
(10)	Honus Wagner (9/23)	1,000	500.00	300.00
(11)	Hugh Jennings (9/30)	550.00	275.00	165.00
(12)	Fred C. Clarke (10/7)	550.00	275.00	165.00
(13)	Byron Bancroft Johnson (10/14)	550.00	275.00	165.00
(14)	Charles A. Comiskey (10/21)	550.00	275.00	165.00
(15)	Edward Collins (10/28)	550.00	275.00	165.00
(16)	James A. McAleer (11/4)	160.00	80.00	50.00
(17)	Pittsburgh Team (11/11)	350.00	175.00	100.00
(18)	Detroit Team (11/18)	350.00	175.00	100.00
(19)	George Bell (11/25)	160.00	80.00	50.00
(20)	Tris Speaker (12/2)	650.00	325.00	195.00
(21)	Mordecai Brown (12/9)	550.00	275.00	165.00
(22)	Hal Chase (12/16)	550.00	275.00	165.00
(23)	Thomas W. Leach (12/23)	160.00	80.00	50.00
(24)	Owen Bush (12/30)	160.00	80.00	50.00
1910				
(25)	John J. Evers (1/6)	400.00	200.00	120.00
(26)	Harry Krause (1/13)	80.00	40.00	25.00
(27)	Chas. B. Adams (1/20)	80.00	40.00	25.00
(28)	Addie Joss (1/27)	400.00	200.00	120.00
(29)	Orval Overall (2/3)	80.00	40.00	25.00
(30)	Samuel E. Crawford (2/10)	400.00	200.00	120.00
(31)	Fred Merkle (2/17)	90.00	45.00	25.00
(32)	George Mullin (2/24)	80.00	40.00	25.00
(33)	Edward Konetchy (3/3)	80.00	40.00	25.00
(34)	George Gibson, Arthur Raymond (3/10)	80.00	40.00	25.00
(35)	Ty Cobb, Hans Wagner (3/17)	2,000	1,000	600.00
(36)	Connie Mack (3/24)	400.00	200.00	120.00
(37)	Wm. Evans, "Silk" O'Loughlin, William Klem, Wm. Johnston (3/31)	550.00	275.00	165.00
(38)	Edward Plank (4/7)	325.00	160.00	95.00
(39)	Walter Johnson, Charles E. Street (9/1)	500.00	250.00	150.00
(40)	John C. Kling (9/8)	80.00	40.00	25.00
(41)	Frank Baker (9/15)	400.00	200.00	120.00
(42)	Charles S. Dooin (9/22)	80.00	40.00	25.00
(43)	Wm. F. Carrigan (9/29)	80.00	40.00	25.00
(44)	John B. McLean (10/6)	80.00	40.00	25.00
(45)	John W. Coombs (10/13)	80.00	40.00	25.00
(46)	Jos. B. Tinker (10/20)	350.00	175.00	100.00
(47)	John I. Taylor (10/27)	80.00	40.00	25.00
(48)	Russell Ford (11/3)	80.00	40.00	25.00
(49)	Leonard L. Cole (11/10)	80.00	40.00	25.00
(50)	Harry Lord (11/17)	80.00	40.00	25.00
(51)	Philadelphia-A Team (11/24)	130.00	65.00	40.00
(52)	Chicago-N Team (12/1)	130.00	65.00	40.00
(53)	Charles A. Bender (12/8)	400.00	200.00	120.00
(54)	Arthur Hofman (12/15)	80.00	40.00	25.00
(55)	Bobby Wallace (12/21)	325.00	160.00	95.00
(56)	Jno. J. McGraw (12/28)	325.00	160.00	95.00
1911				
(57)	Harry H. Davis (1/5)	80.00	40.00	25.00
(58)	James P. Archer (1/12)	80.00	40.00	25.00
(59)	Ira Thomas (1/19)	80.00	40.00	25.00
(60)	Robert Byrnes (1/26)	80.00	40.00	25.00
(61)	Clyde Milan (2/2)	80.00	40.00	25.00
(62)	John T. Meyer (2/9)(Meyers)	80.00	40.00	25.00
(63)	Robert Bescher (2/16)	80.00	40.00	25.00
(64)	John J. Barry (2/23)	80.00	40.00	25.00
(65)	Frank Schulte (3/2)	80.00	40.00	25.00
(66)	C. Harris White (3/9)	80.00	40.00	25.00
(67)	Lawrence Doyle (3/16)	80.00	40.00	25.00
(68)	Joe Jackson (3/23)	2,500	1,250	750.00
(69)	Martin O'Toole, William Kelly (10/26)	80.00	40.00	25.00
(70)	Vean Gregg (11/2)	80.00	40.00	25.00
(71)	Richard W. Marquard (11/9)	325.00	160.00	95.00
(72)	John E. McInnis (11/16)	80.00	40.00	25.00
(73)	Grover C. Alexander (11/23)	350.00	175.00	100.00
(74)	Del Gainor (11/30)	80.00	40.00	25.00
(75)	Fred Snodgrass (12/7)	80.00	40.00	25.00
(76)	James J. Callahan (12/14)	80.00	40.00	25.00
(77)	Robert Harmon (12/21)	80.00	40.00	25.00
(78)	George Stovall (12/28)	80.00	40.00	25.00
1912				
(79)	Zack D. Wheat (1/4)	325.00	160.00	95.00

(80)	Frank "Ping" Bodie (1/11)	80.00	40.00	25.00
(81)	Boston-A Team (10/10)	130.00	65.00	40.00
(82)	New York-N Team (10/17)	130.00	65.00	40.00
(83)	Jake Stahl (10/24)	80.00	40.00	25.00
(84)	Joe Wood (10/31)	275.00	135.00	80.00
(85)	Charles Wagner (11/7)	80.00	40.00	25.00
(86)	Lew Ritchie (11/14)	80.00	40.00	25.00
(87)	Clark Griffith (11/21)	325.00	160.00	95.00
(88)	Arnold Hauser (11/28)	80.00	40.00	25.00
(89)	Charles Herzog (12/5)	80.00	40.00	25.00
(90)	James Lavender (12/12)	80.00	40.00	25.00
(91)	Jeff Tesreau (12/19)	80.00	40.00	25.00
(92)	August Herrmann (12/26)	110.00	55.00	30.00
1913				
(93)	Jake Daubert (10/23)	80.00	40.00	25.00
(94)	Heinie Zimmerman (10/30)	80.00	40.00	25.00
(95)	Ray Schalk (11/6)	325.00	160.00	95.00
(96)	Hans Lobert (11/13)	80.00	40.00	25.00
(97)	Albert W. Demaree (11/20)	80.00	40.00	25.00
(98)	Arthur Fletcher (11/27)	80.00	40.00	25.00
(99)	Charles A. Somers (12/4)	80.00	40.00	25.00
(100)	Joe Birmingham (12/11)	80.00	40.00	25.00

1913 Sporting News Postcards (M101-3)

This six-card set was issued as a premium by the weekly sports newspaper. The 3-1/2" x 5-1/2" cards have borderless front photos printed in duotone color. Along with the player and team names at bottom is a "Published by The Sporting News" tag line. Postcard-format backs are in black-and-white. The unnumbered cards are checklisted here alphabetically.

		NM	EX	VG
Complete Set (6):		4,250	2,125	1,275
Common Player:		275.00	135.00	80.00
(1)	Roger Bresnahan	450.00	225.00	135.00
(2)	Ty Cobb	2,000	1,000	600.00
(3)	Eddie Collins	450.00	225.00	135.00
(4)	Vean Gregg	275.00	135.00	80.00
(5)	Walter Johnson, Gabby Street	750.00	375.00	225.00
(6)	Rube Marquard	450.00	225.00	135.00

1916 The Sporting News (M101-5)

(Though listed in catalogs for more than 25 years, it is now believed M101-5 cards with Sporting News backs do not exist.)

1916 The Sporting News (M101-4)

The "update" version of the promotional premium issued by The Sporting News is nearly identical to the earlier cards. The 200 black-and-white cards once again are printed with player photo, name, position, team and card number on front and advertising on the backs. The set checklist, and, generally, values are the same for sets issued by several other businesses around the country. Most of the players included on the 1-5/8" x 3" cards also appear in the prior edition. Despite being labeled in the American Card Catalog as M101-4, this version was issued after the M101-5 version, with the first advertising

appearing in August, 1916. Cards could be ordered in series of 20 for a dime, or the complete set was free with a $2 subscription. The complete set price does not include variations.

		NM	EX	VG
Complete Set (200):		60,000	30,000	18,000
Common Player:		95.00	50.00	30.00
1	Babe Adams	110.00	50.00	30.00
2	Sam Agnew	95.00	50.00	30.00
3	Eddie Ainsmith	95.00	50.00	30.00
4	Grover Alexander	600.00	300.00	180.00
5	Leon Ames	95.00	50.00	30.00
6	Jimmy Archer	95.00	50.00	30.00
7	Jimmy Austin	95.00	50.00	30.00
8	H.D. Baird	95.00	50.00	30.00
9	J. Franklin Baker	390.00	190.00	115.00
10	Dave Bancroft	390.00	190.00	115.00
11	Jack Barry	95.00	50.00	30.00
12	Zinn Beck	95.00	50.00	30.00
13	"Chief" Bender	390.00	190.00	115.00
14	Joe Benz	95.00	50.00	30.00
15	Bob Bescher	95.00	50.00	30.00
16	Al Betzel	95.00	50.00	30.00
17	Mordecai Brown	390.00	190.00	115.00
18	Eddie Burns	95.00	50.00	30.00
19	George Burns	95.00	50.00	30.00
20	Geo. J. Burns	95.00	50.00	30.00
21	Joe Bush	95.00	50.00	30.00
22	"Donie" Bush	95.00	50.00	30.00
23	Art Butler	95.00	50.00	30.00
24	Bobbie Byrne	95.00	50.00	30.00
25	Forrest Cady	95.00	50.00	30.00
26	Jimmy Callahan	95.00	50.00	30.00
27	Ray Caldwell	95.00	50.00	30.00
28	Max Carey	390.00	190.00	115.00
29	George Chalmers	95.00	50.00	30.00
30	Ray Chapman	95.00	50.00	30.00
31	Larry Cheney	95.00	50.00	30.00
32	Eddie Cicotte	390.00	190.00	115.00
33	Tom Clarke	95.00	50.00	30.00
34	Eddie Collins	390.00	190.00	155.00
35	"Shauno" Collins	95.00	50.00	30.00
36	Charles Comiskey	390.00	190.00	115.00
37	Joe Connolly	95.00	50.00	30.00
38	Ty Cobb	4,800	2,400	1,440
39	Harry Coveleskie (Coveleski)	95.00	50.00	30.00
40	Gavvy Cravath	95.00	50.00	30.00
41	Sam Crawford	390.00	190.00	115.00
42	Jean Dale	95.00	50.00	30.00
43	Jake Daubert	95.00	50.00	30.00
44	Charles Deal	95.00	50.00	30.00
45	Al Demaree	95.00	50.00	30.00
46	Josh Devore	95.00	50.00	30.00
47	William Doak	95.00	50.00	30.00
48	Bill Donovan	95.00	50.00	30.00
49	Charles Dooin	95.00	50.00	30.00
50	Mike Doolan	95.00	50.00	30.00
51	Larry Doyle	95.00	50.00	30.00
52	Jean Dubuc	95.00	50.00	30.00
53	Oscar Dugey	95.00	50.00	30.00
54	Johnny Evers	390.00	190.00	115.00
55	Urban Faber	390.00	190.00	115.00
56	"Hap" Felsch	1,000	285.00	170.00
57	Bill Fischer	95.00	50.00	30.00
58	Ray Fisher	95.00	50.00	30.00
59	Max Flack	95.00	50.00	30.00
60	Art Fletcher	95.00	50.00	30.00
61	Eddie Foster	95.00	50.00	30.00
62	Jacques Fournier	95.00	50.00	30.00
63	Del Gainer (Gainor)	95.00	50.00	30.00
64	"Chic" Gandil	1,000	190.00	115.00
65	Larry Gardner	95.00	50.00	30.00
66	Joe Gedeon	95.00	50.00	30.00
67	Gus Getz	95.00	50.00	30.00
68	Geo. Gibson	95.00	50.00	30.00
69	Wilbur Good	95.00	50.00	30.00
70	Hank Gowdy	95.00	50.00	30.00
71	John Graney	95.00	50.00	30.00
72	Clark Griffith	390.00	190.00	115.00
73	Tom Griffith	95.00	50.00	30.00
74	Heinie Groh	95.00	50.00	30.00
75	Earl Hamilton	95.00	50.00	30.00
76	Bob Harmon	95.00	50.00	30.00
77	Roy Hartzell	95.00	50.00	30.00
78	Claude Hendrix	95.00	50.00	30.00
79	Olaf Henriksen	95.00	50.00	30.00
80	John Henry	95.00	50.00	30.00
81	"Buck" Herzog	95.00	50.00	30.00
82	Hugh High	95.00	50.00	30.00
83	Dick Hoblitzell	95.00	50.00	30.00
84	Harry Hooper	390.00	190.00	115.00
85	Ivan Howard	95.00	50.00	30.00
86	Miller Huggins	390.00	190.00	115.00
87	Joe Jackson	15,000	5,400	3,240
88	William James	95.00	50.00	30.00
89	Harold Janvrin	95.00	50.00	30.00
90	Hugh Jennings	390.00	190.00	115.00
91	Walter Johnson	1,140	570.00	345.00
92	Fielder Jones	95.00	50.00	30.00
93	Joe Judge	95.00	50.00	30.00
94	Bennie Kauff	95.00	50.00	30.00
95	Wm. Killefer Jr.	95.00	50.00	30.00
96	Ed. Konetchy	95.00	50.00	30.00
97	Napoleon Lajoie	390.00	190.00	115.00
98	Jack Lapp	95.00	50.00	30.00
99	John Lavan	95.00	50.00	30.00
100	Jimmy Lavender	95.00	50.00	30.00
101	"Nemo" Leibold	95.00	50.00	30.00
102	H.B. Leonard	95.00	50.00	30.00
103	Duffy Lewis	95.00	50.00	30.00
104	Hans Lobert	95.00	50.00	30.00
105	Tom Long	95.00	50.00	30.00
106	Fred Luderus	95.00	50.00	30.00
107	Connie Mack	390.00	190.00	115.00
108	Lee Magee	95.00	50.00	30.00
109	Sherwood Magee	95.00	50.00	30.00

		NM	EX	VG
110	Al. Mamaux	95.00	50.00	30.00
111	Leslie Mann	95.00	50.00	30.00
112	"Rabbit" Maranville	390.00	190.00	115.00
113	Rube Marquard	390.00	190.00	115.00
114	J. Erskine Mayer	150.00	80.00	45.00
115	George McBride	95.00	50.00	30.00
116	John J. McGraw	390.00	190.00	115.00
117	Jack McInnis	95.00	50.00	30.00
118	Fred Merkle	95.00	50.00	30.00
119	Chief Meyers	95.00	50.00	30.00
120	Clyde Milan	95.00	50.00	30.00
121	John Miller	95.00	50.00	30.00
122	Otto Miller	95.00	50.00	30.00
123	Willie Mitchell	95.00	50.00	30.00
124	Fred Mollwitz	95.00	50.00	30.00
125	Pat Moran	95.00	50.00	30.00
126	Ray Morgan	95.00	50.00	30.00
127	Geo. Moriarty	95.00	50.00	30.00
128	Guy Morton	95.00	50.00	30.00
129	Mike Mowrey	95.00	50.00	30.00
130	Ed. Murphy	95.00	50.00	30.00
131	"Hy" Myers	95.00	50.00	30.00
132	J.A. Niehoff	95.00	50.00	30.00
133	Rube Oldring	95.00	50.00	30.00
134	Oliver O'Mara	95.00	50.00	30.00
135	Steve O'Neill	95.00	50.00	30.00
136	"Dode" Paskert	95.00	50.00	30.00
137	Roger Peckinpaugh	95.00	50.00	30.00
138	Walter Pipp	95.00	50.00	30.00
139	Derril Pratt (Derrill)	95.00	50.00	30.00
140	Pat Ragan	95.00	50.00	30.00
141	Bill Rariden	95.00	50.00	30.00
142	Eppa Rixey	390.00	190.00	115.00
143	Davey Robertson	95.00	50.00	30.00
144	Wilbert Robinson	390.00	190.00	115.00
145	Bob Roth	95.00	50.00	30.00
146	Ed. Roush	390.00	190.00	115.00
147	Clarence Rowland	95.00	50.00	30.00
148	"Nap" Rucker	95.00	50.00	30.00
149	Dick Rudolph	95.00	50.00	30.00
150	Reb Russell	95.00	50.00	30.00
151	Babe Ruth	30,000	15,000	9,000
152	Vic Saier	95.00	50.00	30.00
153	"Slim" Sallee	95.00	50.00	30.00
154	Ray Schalk	390.00	190.00	115.00
155	Walter Schang	95.00	50.00	30.00
156	Frank Schulte	95.00	50.00	30.00
157	Everett Scott	95.00	50.00	30.00
158	Jim Scott	95.00	50.00	30.00
159	Tom Seaton	95.00	50.00	30.00
160	Howard Shanks	95.00	50.00	30.00
161	Bob Shawkey	95.00	50.00	30.00
162	Ernie Shore	95.00	50.00	30.00
163	Burt Shotton	95.00	50.00	30.00
164	Geo. Sisler	390.00	190.00	115.00
165	J. Carlisle Smith	95.00	50.00	30.00
166	Fred Snodgrass	95.00	50.00	30.00
167	Geo. Stallings	95.00	50.00	30.00
168a	Oscar Stanage/Catching	95.00	50.00	30.00
168b	Oscar Stanage (Portrait to thighs.)	900.00	450.00	270.00
169	Charles Stengel	390.00	190.00	115.00
170	Milton Stock	95.00	50.00	30.00
171	Amos Strunk	95.00	50.00	30.00
172	Billy Sullivan	95.00	50.00	30.00
173	"Jeff" Tesreau	95.00	50.00	30.00
174	Joe Tinker	390.00	190.00	115.00
175	Fred Toney	95.00	50.00	30.00
176	Terry Turner	95.00	50.00	30.00
177	George Tyler	95.00	50.00	30.00
178	Jim Vaughn	95.00	50.00	30.00
179	Bob Veach	95.00	50.00	30.00
180	James Viox	95.00	50.00	30.00
181	Oscar Vitt	95.00	50.00	30.00
182	Hans Wagner	2,500	660.00	395.00
183	Clarence Walker	95.00	50.00	30.00
184	Ed. Walsh	390.00	190.00	115.00
185	W. Wambsganss (photo actually Fritz Coumbe)	95.00	50.00	30.00
186	Buck Weaver	1,000	285.00	170.00
187	Carl Weilman	95.00	50.00	30.00
188	Zach Wheat	390.00	190.00	115.00
189	Geo. Whitted	95.00	50.00	30.00
190	Fred Williams	95.00	50.00	30.00
191	Art Wilson	95.00	50.00	30.00
192	J. Owen Wilson	95.00	50.00	30.00
193	Ivy Wingo	95.00	50.00	30.00
194	"Mel" Wolfgang	95.00	50.00	30.00
195	Joe Wood	500.00	120.00	75.00
196	Steve Yerkes	95.00	50.00	30.00
197	"Pep" Young	95.00	50.00	30.00
198	Rollie Zeider	95.00	50.00	30.00
199	Heiny Zimmerman	95.00	50.00	30.00
200	Ed. Zwilling	95.00	50.00	30.00

1919 Sporting News (M101-6)

(The issue listed in previous editions as 1919 Sporting News Supplements (M101-6) is now listed as 1917-1920 Felix Mendelsohn.)

1926 Sporting News Supplements (M101-7)

This set of 11 player photos was issued as a post-World Series weekly supplement by The Sporting News in 1926. Sepia-toned portrait or posed photos are featured on the 7" x 10" supplements. The player's name and team are printed at the bottom, while a line identifying The Sporting News and the date appear in the upper left corner. The unnumbered set includes a half-dozen Hall of Famers. Large-format (10" x 14-1/4") team photos of the 1926

Yankees (October 28) and Cardinals were also issued in the weeks preceding the start of issue for the weekly player supplements.

		NM	EX	VG
Complete Set (13):		2,000	800.00	400.00
Common Player:		40.00	16.00	8.00
(1)	Hazen "Kiki" Cuyler	100.00	40.00	20.00
(2)	Rogers Hornsby	125.00	50.00	25.00
(3)	Tony Lazzeri	100.00	40.00	20.00
(4)	Harry E. Manush (Henry)	100.00	40.00	20.00
(5)	John Mostil	40.00	16.00	8.00
(6)	Harry Rice	40.00	16.00	8.00
(7)	George Herman "Babe" Ruth	1,200	480.00	240.00
(8)	Al Simmons	100.00	40.00	20.00
(9)	Harold "Pie" Traynor	100.00	40.00	20.00
(10)	George Uhle	40.00	16.00	8.00
(11)	Glenn Wright	40.00	16.00	8.00
(12)	1926 Cardinals Team Photo	100.00	40.00	20.00
(13)	1926 Yankees Team Photo	200.00	80.00	40.00

1927-1928 Sporting News Ad-Back Supplements (M101-7)

Evidently faced with a surplus of player supplements from its 1926 issue, The Sporting News recycled at least some of them in subsequent years as subscription sales advertising. Fronts of the supplements differ in that the sports paper's logo and the original issue date from 1926 have been removed from the upper-left border. Instead of blank backs, however, the re-issues have color (blue or red seen to date) advertising on back. Respond-by dates in 1927 have been seen rubber-stamped on the back of some pieces, while that of Kiki Cuyler mentions his team as being the Cubs, who he joined in 1928.

	NM	EX	VG
Kiki Cuyler	300.00	125.00	65.00
Babe Ruth	1,500	600.00	300.00

1932 Sporting News Supplements (M101-8)

This issue of player-picture supplements from TSN is unusual not only in its brevity - only four were issued - but also in that the pictures have printed matter on back, consisting of player personal data and complete major/minor league stats. Only the Grimm piece has an issue date: Sept. 1, 1932. The pictures

are on thin card stock in an 8-1/4" x 10-1/2" format. Fronts have a black-and-white photo with the player named in the wide bottom border.

		NM	EX	VG
Complete Set (4):		2,000	1,000	600.00
Common Player:		240.00	120.00	72.00
(1)	Jerome H. (Dizzy) Dean	900.00	450.00	270.00
(2)	Vernon Gomez	600.00	300.00	180.00
(3)	Charles John Grimm	250.00	125.00	75.00
(4)	Lonnie Warneke	250.00	125.00	75.00

1939 Sporting News Supplements (M101-9)

These dated supplements feature a trio of team photos and two star players as individuals. The team pictures are about 15" x 10-1/2" and comprise double-page spreads; the single players are 7-1/2" x 10".

		NM	EX	VG
Complete Set (5):		800.00	400.00	240.00
Common:		150.00	75.00	45.00
(1)	Joseph DiMaggio (Oct. 26)	200.00	100.00	60.00
(2)	Robert Feller (Nov. 9)	150.00	75.00	45.00
(3)	Cincinnati Reds Team (Nov. 2)	150.00	75.00	45.00
(4)	N.Y. Yankees Team (Oct. 19)	200.00	100.00	60.00
(5)	St. Louis Cardinals Team (Nov. 16)	150.00	75.00	45.00

1888 Sporting Times (M117)

Examples of these cards, issued in 1888 and 1889 by the Sporting Times weekly newspaper, are very rare. The complete set price includes all variations. The cabinet-size cards (7-1/4" x 4-1/2") feature line drawings of players in action poses on soft cardboard stock. The cards came in a variety of pastel colors surrounded by a 1/4" white border. The player's last name is printed on each drawing, as are the words "Courtesy Sporting Times New York." A pair of crossed bats and a baseball appear along the bottom of the card. Twenty-seven different players are known to exist. The drawing of Cap Anson is the same one used in the N28 Allen & Ginter series, and some of the other drawings are based on photos used in the popular Old Judge series.

		NM	EX	VG
Common Player:		15,000	10,000	6,000
(1)	Cap Anson	35,000	17,500	10,000
(2)	Jersey Bakely	15,000	10,000	6,000
(3)	Dan Brouthers	25,000	12,500	7,500
(4)	Doc Bushong	15,000	10,000	6,000
(5)	Jack Clements	15,000	10,000	6,000
(6)	Charlie Comiskey	25,000	12,500	7,500
(7)	Jerry Denny	15,000	10,000	6,000
(8)	Buck Ewing	25,000	12,500	7,500
(9)	Dude Esterbrook	15,000	10,000	6,000
(10)	Jay Faatz	15,000	10,000	6,000
(11)	Pud Galvin	25,000	12,500	7,500
(12)	Jack Glasscock	15,000	10,000	6,000
(13)	Tim Keefe	25,000	12,500	7,500
(14)	King Kelly	30,000	15,000	9,000

		NM	EX	VG
(15)	Matt Kilroy	15,000	10,000	6,000
(16)	Arlie Latham	15,000	10,000	6,000
(17)	Doggie Miller	15,000	10,000	6,000
(18)	Hank O'Day	15,000	10,000	6,000
(19)	Fred Pfeffer	15,000	10,000	6,000
(20)	Henry Porter	15,000	10,000	6,000
(21)	Toad Ramsey	15,000	10,000	6,000
(22)	Long John Reilly	15,000	10,000	6,000
(23)	Mike Smith	15,000	10,000	6,000
(24)	Harry Stovey	15,000	10,000	6,000
(25)	Sam Thompson	25,000	12,500	7,500
(26)	John Ward	25,000	12,500	7,500
(27)	Mickey Welch	25,000	12,500	7,500

1933 Sport Kings (R338)

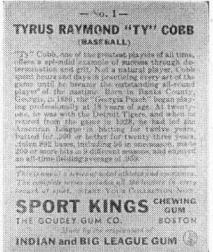

This 48-card set was issued by the Goudey Gum Co. Participants in 18 different sports are included in the set, which honors the top sports figures of the era. Three baseball players are pictured on the 2-3/8" x 2-7/8" cards and are listed here. The card fronts are color portraits and include the player's name and silhouette representations of the respective sport. The card backs are numbered and list biographical information and a company ad.

		NM	EX	VG
Complete (Baseball) Set (3):		10,000	5,000	3,000
Advertising Poster:		7,500	4,000	2,400
1	Ty Cobb	2,800	1,400	840.00
2	Babe Ruth	6,500	3,250	1,950
3	Nat Holman	200.00	100.00	60.00
4	Harold "Red" Grange	200.00	100.00	60.00
5	Ed Wachter	200.00	100.00	60.00
6	Jim Thorpe	200.00	100.00	60.00
7	Bobby Walthour, Jr.	200.00	100.00	60.00
8	Walter Hagen	200.00	100.00	60.00
9	Ed Blood	200.00	100.00	60.00
10	Anton Lekang	200.00	100.00	60.00
11	Charles Jewtraw	200.00	100.00	60.00
12	Bobby McLean	200.00	100.00	60.00
13	LaVerne Fatour	200.00	100.00	60.00
14	Jim Londos	200.00	100.00	60.00
15	Reggie McNamara	200.00	100.00	60.00
16	William Tilden	200.00	100.00	60.00
17	Jack Dempsey	200.00	100.00	60.00
18	Gene Tunney	200.00	100.00	60.00
19	Eddie Shore	200.00	100.00	60.00
20	Duke Kahanamoku	200.00	100.00	60.00
21	Johnny Weissmuller	200.00	100.00	60.00
22	Gene Sarazen	200.00	100.00	60.00
23	Vincent Richards	200.00	100.00	60.00
24	Howie Morenz	200.00	100.00	60.00
25	Ralph Snoddy	200.00	100.00	60.00
26	James R. Wedell	200.00	100.00	60.00
27	Roscoe Turner	200.00	100.00	60.00
28	Jimmy Doolittle	200.00	100.00	60.00
29	Ace Bailey	200.00	100.00	60.00
30	Ching Johnson	200.00	100.00	60.00
31	Bobby Walthour, Jr.	200.00	100.00	60.00
32	Joe Lopchick	200.00	100.00	60.00
33	Eddie Burke	200.00	100.00	60.00
34	Irving Jaffee	200.00	100.00	60.00
35	Knute Rockne	200.00	100.00	60.00
36	Willie Hoppe	200.00	100.00	60.00
37	Helene Madison	200.00	100.00	60.00
38	Bobby Jones	200.00	100.00	60.00
39	Jack Westrope	200.00	100.00	60.00
40	Don George	200.00	100.00	60.00
41	Jim Browning	200.00	100.00	60.00
42	Carl Hubbell	1,000	500.00	300.00
43	Primo Carnera	200.00	100.00	60.00
44	Max Baer	200.00	100.00	60.00
45	Babe Didrickson	200.00	100.00	60.00
46	Ellsworth Vines	200.00	100.00	60.00
47	J. Hubert Stevens	200.00	100.00	60.00
48	Leonhard Seppala	200.00	100.00	60.00

1947 Sport Magazine Premium

This 8-1/2" x 11", blank-back, paper-stock picture appears to have been a premium issued in conjunction with Sport magazine's premiere issue in March, 1947, perhaps as a send-away offer. The picture has a black-and-white portrait photo on a bright orange background, surrounded with a white border. In the lower-left corner is "March '47." "15 Sport" appears at lower-right.

		NM	EX	VG
15	Joe DiMaggio	35.00	17.50	10.50

1953 Sport Magazine All-Star Portfolio

STANLEY FRANK MUSIAL

This set of 5-3/8" x 7" glossy color pictures was used by Sport Magazine as a subscription premium. Featuring the outstanding photography of Ozzie Sweet, all but the Bob Mathias pictures are portraits, surrounded with a white border and the player name at bottom. Backs are blank. The heavy cardboard mailing envelope contains short athlete biographies.

		NM	EX	VG
Complete Set (10):		175.00	85.00	50.00
Common Player:		20.00	10.00	6.00
(1)	Joe Black	25.00	12.50	7.50
(2)	Robert Cousy/Basketball	20.00	10.00	6.00
(3)	Elroy Hirsch/Football	20.00	10.00	6.00
(4)	Rocky Marciano/Boxing	30.00	15.00	9.00
(5)	Robert Bruce Mathias/ Track and field	20.00	10.00	6.00
(6)	Stanley Frank Musial	45.00	22.50	13.50
(7)	John Olszewski/Football	20.00	10.00	6.00
(8)	Allie Pierce Reynolds	20.00	10.00	6.00
(9)	Robin Evan Roberts	30.00	15.00	9.00
(10)	Robert Clayton Shantz	20.00	10.00	6.00

1968-69 Sports Cards for Collectors

These Myron Aronstein-drawn 3-1/2" x 4-1/4" postcards feature 78 pre-1950 players. Cards 1-36 feature blank backs, and 37-78 have brief biographical and statistical data. The last four are checklists.

		NM	EX	VG
Complete Set (82):		100.00	50.00	30.00
Common Player:		2.00	1.00	.60
1	Babe Ruth	15.00	7.50	5.00
2	Rube Marquard	2.00	1.00	.60
3	Zack Wheat	2.00	1.00	.60
4	John Clarkson	2.00	1.00	.60
5	Honus Wagner	2.00	1.00	.60
6	Johnny Evers	2.00	1.00	.60
7	Bill Dickey	2.00	1.00	.60
8	Elmer Smith	2.00	1.00	.60
9	Ty Cobb	10.00	5.00	3.00
10	Jack Chesbro	2.00	1.00	.60
11	George Gibson	2.00	1.00	.60
12	Bullet Joe Bush	2.00	1.00	.60
13	George Mullin	2.00	1.00	.60
14	Buddy Meyer	2.00	1.00	.60
15	Jimmy Collins	2.00	1.00	.60
16	Bill Wambsganss	2.00	1.00	.60
17	Jack Barry	2.00	1.00	.60
18	Dickie Kerr	2.00	1.00	.60
19	Connie Mack	2.00	1.00	.60
20	Rabbit Maranville	2.00	1.00	.60
21	Roger Peckinpaugh	2.00	1.00	.60
22	Mickey Cochrane	2.00	1.00	.60
23	George Kelly	2.00	1.00	.60
24	Frank "Home Rune" Baker	2.00	1.00	.60
25	Wally Schang	2.00	1.00	.60
26	Eddie Plank	2.00	1.00	.60
27	Bill Donovan	2.00	1.00	.60
28	Red Faber	2.00	1.00	.60
29	Hack Wilson	2.00	1.00	.60
30	Mordecai "3 Finger" Brown	2.00	1.00	.60
31	Fred Merkle	2.00	1.00	.60
32	Heinie Groh	2.00	1.00	.60
33	Stuffy McInnis	2.00	1.00	.60
34	Hal Chase	2.00	1.00	.60
35	Judge Kenesaw Mountain Landis	2.00	1.00	.60
36	Chief Bender	2.00	1.00	.60
37	Fred Snodgrass	2.00	1.00	.60
38	Tony Lazzeri	2.00	1.00	.60
39	John McGraw	2.00	1.00	.60
40	Mel Ott	10.00	5.00	3.00
41	Grover Alexander	2.00	1.00	.60
42	Rube Waddell	2.00	1.00	.60
43	Wilbert Robinson	2.00	1.00	.60
44	Cap Anson	2.00	1.00	.60
45	Eddie Cicotte	2.00	1.00	.60
46	Hank Gowdy	2.00	1.00	.60
47	Frankie Frisch	2.00	1.00	.60
48	Charles Comiskey	2.00	1.00	.60
49	Clyde Milan	2.00	1.00	.60
50	Jimmy Wilson	2.00	1.00	.60
51	Christy Mathewson	10.00	5.00	3.00
52	Tim Keefe	2.00	1.00	.60
53	Abner Doubleday	2.00	1.00	.60
54	Ed Walsh	2.00	1.00	.60
55	Jim Thorpe	10.00	5.00	3.00
56	Roger Bresnahan	2.00	1.00	.60
57	Frank Chance	2.00	1.00	.60
58	Heinie Manush	2.00	1.00	.60
59	Max Carey	2.00	1.00	.60
60	Joe Tinker	2.00	1.00	.60
61	Benny Kauff	2.00	1.00	.60
62	Fred Clarke	2.00	1.00	.60
63	Smokey Joe Wood	2.00	1.00	.60
64	George Burns	2.00	1.00	.60
65	Walter Johnson	10.00	5.00	3.00
66	Ferdie Schupp	2.00	1.00	.60
67	Jimmy McAleer	2.00	1.00	.60
68	Larry Gardner	2.00	1.00	.60
69	Buck Ewing	2.00	1.00	.60
70	George Sisler	2.00	1.00	.60
71	Charley Robertson	2.00	1.00	.60
72	Bill Dineen	2.00	1.00	.60
73	Kid Gleason	2.00	1.00	.60
74	Jim Bottomley	2.00	1.00	.60
75	Sam Crawford	2.00	1.00	.60
76	Kid Nichols	2.00	1.00	.60
77	Dick Rudolph	2.00	1.00	.60
78	Bill Klem	2.00	1.00	.60
79	Checklist	2.00	1.00	.60
80	Checklist	2.00	1.00	.60
81	Checklist	2.00	1.00	.60
82	Checklist	2.00	1.00	.60

1970 Sports Cards for Collectors Old Timer Postcards

LAWRENCE EUGENE DOBY "LARRY" | MESSAGE

The date of issue given here is approximate. This collectors issue "Old Timer Postcard Series" features black-and-white photos bordered in white in a 3-1/2" x 5-1/2" format. Player identification in the bottom border usually offers his complete name on one line and his nickname below. Backs are divided by a card number and the name and address of the issuer. At left is a space for "MESSAGE:."

		NM	EX	VG
Complete Set (32):		75.00	37.50	22.00
Common Player:		4.00	2.00	1.25
1	Babe Ruth, Lou Gehrig	12.00	6.00	3.50
2	Larry Doby	6.00	3.00	1.75
3	Mike Garcia	4.00	2.00	1.25
4	Bob Feller	10.00	5.00	3.00
5	Early Wynn	4.00	2.00	1.25
6	Burleigh Grimes	4.00	2.00	1.25
7	Rabbit Maranville	4.00	2.00	1.25
8	Babe Ruth	15.00	7.50	4.50
9	Lou Gehrig	12.00	6.00	3.50
10	Joe DiMaggio	12.00	6.00	3.50
11	Ty Cobb	10.00	5.00	3.00
12	Lou Boudreau	4.00	2.00	1.25
13	Jimmie Foxx	4.00	2.00	1.25
14	Casey Stengel	6.00	3.00	1.75
15	Kenesaw M. Landis	4.00	2.00	1.25
16	Max Carey	4.00	2.00	1.25
17	Wilbert Robinson	4.00	2.00	1.25
18	Paul Richards	4.00	2.00	1.25
19	Zack Wheat	4.00	2.00	1.25
20	Rube Marquard	4.00	2.00	1.25
21	Dave Bancroft	4.00	2.00	1.25
22	Bobby Thomson	4.00	2.00	1.25
23	Mel Ott	4.00	2.00	1.25

		NM	EX	VG
24	Bobo Newsom	4.00	2.00	1.25
25	Johnny Mize	4.00	2.00	1.25
26	Walker Cooper	4.00	2.00	1.25
27	Fred "Dixie" Walker	4.00	2.00	1.25
28	Augie Galan	4.00	2.00	1.25
29	"Snuffy" Sturnweiss (Stirnweiss)	4.00	2.00	1.25
30	Floyd Caves "Babe" Herman	4.00	2.00	1.25
31	Babe Ruth	15.00	7.50	4.50
32	Babe Ruth	15.00	7.50	4.50

1970 Sports Cards for Collectors Sports Stuff

This set includes 10 Myron Aronsten-drawn 3-1/2" x 4-1/4" postcards depicting pre-1920 baseball luminaries, trivia, and legends.

		NM	EX	VG
Complete Set (10):		20.00	10.00	6.00
Common Player:		2.00	1.00	.60
1	Manager Trivia	2.00	1.00	.60
2	1914 Miracle Braves	2.00	1.00	.60
3	1919 Black Sox	2.00	1.00	.60
4	Eddie Plank, Fred Clarke, Roger Bresnahan, Babe Ruth	5.00	2.50	1.50
5	Bobby Lowe	2.00	1.00	.60
6	$100,000 Athletics Infield	2.00	1.00	.60
7	Joe Bush, Eddie Plank, Chief Bender	2.00	1.00	.60
8	Joe Tinker, Johnny Evers, Frank Chance	2.00	1.00	.60
9	Wilbert Robinson, John McGraw, Roger Peckinpaugh	2.00	1.00	.60
10	Ty Cobb	5.00	2.50	1.50

1977-79 Sportscaster

This massive set of full-color cards includes players from dozens of different sports - some of them very obscure - among more than 2,000 different subjects, making it one of the biggest sets of trading cards ever issued. Available by mail subscription from 1977 through 1979, the Sportscaster cards are large, measuring 4-3/4" x 6-1/4". Subscribers were mailed one series of 24 cards for $1.89 plus postage every month or so. The set has an international flavor to it, including such sports as rugby, soccer, lawn bowling, fencing, karate, bicycling, curling, skiing, bullfighting, auto racing, mountain climbing, hang gliding, yachting, sailing, badminton, bobsledding, etc. Each card has a series of icons in the upper-right corner to assist collectors in the various methods of sorting. Most popular among American collectors are the baseball, football and basketball stars in the set, which includes the 140 baseball subjects listed here. The checklist includes many Hall of Famers. Backs contain detailed write-ups of the player featured. Because the set was issued in series, and many collectors dropped out of the program before the end, cards in the higher series are especially scarce. This accounts for prices on some of the superstar cards, issued in early series, being lower than for some of the lesser-known players. The cards of Aaron and Bench are quite common because they were mailed to large numbers of persons as samples to introduce the program. The cards were also sold in several European countries and can be found with backs printed in French, Swedish and other languages.

		NM	EX	VG
Complete (Baseball) Set (140):		350.00	175.00	100.00
Common Player:		1.00	.50	.30
(1)	Henry Aaron	4.00	2.00	1.25
(2)	Danny Ainge	30.00	15.00	9.00
(3)	Emmett Ashford (Umpire)	2.50	1.25	.70
(4)	Ernie Banks	2.75	1.50	.80
(5)	Johnny Bench	7.50	3.75	2.25
(6)	Vida Blue	1.75	.90	.50
(7)	Bert Blyleven	1.25	.60	.40
(8)	Bobby Bonds	3.25	1.75	1.00
(9)	Lyman Bostock	1.25	.60	.40
(10)	George Brett	5.00	2.50	1.50
(11)	Lou Brock	3.25	1.75	1.00
(12)	Jeff Burroughs	1.25	.60	.40
(13)	Roy Campanella	8.00	4.00	2.50
(14)	John Candelaria	1.25	.60	.40
(15)	Rod Carew	3.25	1.75	1.00
(16)	Steve Carlton	4.00	2.00	1.25
(17)	Ron Cey	1.00	.50	.30
(18)	Roberto Clemente	10.00	5.00	3.00
(19)	Steve Dembowski	2.25	1.25	.70
(20)	Joe DiMaggio	5.00	2.50	1.50

		NM	EX	VG
(21)	Dennis Eckersley	4.00	2.00	1.25
(22)	Mark Fidrych	1.75	.90	.50
(23)	Carlton Fisk	6.00	3.00	1.75
(24)	Mike Flanagan	3.00	1.50	.90
(25)	Steve Garvey	5.00	2.50	1.50
(26)	Ron Guidry	3.00	1.50	.90
(27)	Gil Hodges	4.00	2.00	1.25
(28)	Catfish Hunter	4.00	2.00	1.25
(29)	Tommy John	1.25	.60	.40
(30)	Randy Jones	1.00	.50	.30
(31)	Dave Kingman	1.75	.90	.50
(32)	Sandy Koufax	6.00	3.00	1.75
(33)	Tommy Lasorda	6.50	3.25	2.00
(34)	Ron LeFlore	1.25	.60	.40
(35)	Greg Luzinski	1.00	.50	.30
(36)	Billy Martin	3.25	1.75	1.00
(37)	Willie Mays	4.00	2.00	1.25
(38)	Lee Mazzilli	5.00	2.50	1.50
(39)	Willie McCovey	3.75	2.00	1.25
(40)	Joe Morgan	2.75	1.50	.80
(41)	Thurman Munson	4.00	2.00	1.25
(42)	Stan Musial	5.00	2.50	1.50
(43)	Phil Niekro	4.00	2.00	1.25
(44)	Jim Palmer	3.00	1.50	.90
(45)	Dave Parker	1.75	.90	.50
(46)	Freddie Patek	1.25	.60	.40
(47)	Gaylord Perry	2.25	1.25	.70
(48)	Jim Piersall	2.75	1.50	.80
(49)	Vada Pinson	1.25	.60	.40
(50)	Rick Reuschel	1.25	.60	.40
(51)	Jim Rice	6.00	3.00	1.75
(52)	J.R. Richard	2.25	1.25	.70
(53)	Brooks Robinson	3.75	2.00	1.25
(54)	Frank Robinson	5.00	2.50	1.50
(55)	Jackie Robinson	5.00	2.50	1.50
(56)	Pete Rose	6.00	3.00	1.75
(57)	Joe Rudi	1.00	.50	.30
(58)	Babe Ruth	6.00	3.00	1.75
(59)	Nolan Ryan	7.00	3.50	2.00
(60)	Tom Seaver	3.75	2.00	1.25
(61)	Warren Spahn	3.75	2.00	1.25
(62)	Monty Stratton	2.25	1.25	.70
(63)	Craig Swan	1.75	.90	.50
(64)	Frank Tanana	1.00	.50	.30
(65)	Ron Taylor	2.25	1.25	.70
(66)	Garry Templeton	1.00	.50	.30
(67)	Gene Tenace	1.00	.50	.30
(68)	Bobby Thomson	1.75	.90	.50
(69)	Andre Thornton	1.25	.60	.40
(70)	Johnny VanderMeer	1.75	.90	.50
(71)	Ted Williams	7.00	3.50	2.00
(72)	Maury Wills	1.00	.50	.30
(73)	Hack Wilson	3.25	1.75	1.00
(74)	Dave Winfield/Hitting	8.00	4.00	2.50
(75)	Dave Winfield/Portrait	4.00	2.00	1.25
(76)	Cy Young	2.75	1.50	.80
(77)	The 1927 Yankees	2.75	1.50	.80
(78)	1969 Mets	6.50	3.25	2.00
(79)	All-Star Game (Steve Garvey, Joe Morgan)	2.75	1.50	.80
(80)	Amateur Draft (Rick Monday)	1.25	.60	.40
(81)	At-A-Glance Reference (Tom Seaver)	5.00	2.50	1.50
(82)	Babe Ruth Baseball (Ed Figueroa)	6.50	3.25	2.00
(83)	Baltimore Memorial Stadium	3.00	1.50	.90
(84)	Boston's Fenway Park	5.00	2.50	1.50
(85)	Brother vs. Brother (Joe Niekro)	2.75	1.50	.80
(86)	Busch Memorial Stadium	2.50	1.25	.70
(87)	Candlestick Park	2.00	1.00	.60
(88)	Cape Cod League (Jim Beattie)	6.00	3.00	1.75
(89)	A Century and a Half of Baseball (Johnny Bench)	1.75	.90	.50
(90)	Cy Young Award (Tom Seaver)	2.75	1.50	.80
(91)	The Dean Brothers (Dizzy Dean, Paul Dean)	5.00	2.50	1.50
(92)	Designated Hitter (Rusty Staub)	2.25	1.25	.70
(93)	Dodger Stadium	2.75	1.50	.80
(94)	Perfect Game (Don Larsen)	3.25	1.75	1.00
(95)	The Double Steal (Davey Lopes)	5.00	2.50	1.50
(96)	Fenway Park	4.00	2.00	1.25
(97)	The Firemen (Goose Gossage)	4.00	2.00	1.25
(98)	Forever Blowing Bubbles (Davey Lopes)	2.00	1.00	.60
(99)	The Forsch Brothers (Bob Forsch, Ken Forsch)	5.00	2.50	1.50
(100)	Four Home Runs In A Game (Mike Schmidt)	6.50	3.25	2.00
(101)	400-Homer Club (Duke Snider)	5.00	2.50	1.50
(102)	Great Moments (Bob Gibson)	3.25	1.75	1.00
(103)	Great Moments (Ferguson Jenkins)	2.25	1.25	.70
(104)	Great Moments (Mickey Lolich)	1.75	.90	.50
(105)	Great Moments (Carl Yastrzemski)	3.25	1.75	1.00
(106)	Hidden Ball Trick (Carl Yastrzemski)	2.75	1.50	.80
(107)	Hit And Run (George Foster)	1.25	.60	.40
(108)	Hitting The Cutoff Man	1.00	.50	.30
(109)	Hitting Pitchers (Don Drysdale)	3.25	1.75	1.00
(110)	Infield Fly Rule (Bobby Grich)	1.25	.60	.40
(111)	Instruction (Rod Carew)	2.75	1.50	.80
(112)	Interference (Johnny Bench)	2.75	1.50	.80
(113)	Iron Mike (Pitching Machine)	2.75	1.50	.80
(114)	Keeping Score	1.75	.90	.50
(115)	Like Father, Like Son (Roy Smalley)	3.75	2.00	1.25
(116)	Lingo I (Gary Carter)	1.75	.90	.50

		NM	EX	VG
(117)	Lingo II (Earl Weaver)	2.75	1.50	.80
(118)	Little Leagues To Big Leagues (Hector Torres)	1.75	.90	.50
(119)	Maris and Mantle (Mickey Mantle, Roger Maris)	4.00	2.00	1.25
(120)	Measurements (Memorial Stadium)	1.00	.50	.30
(121)	The Money Game (Dennis Eckersley)	6.00	3.00	1.75
(122)	NCAA Tournament (Aggies-Longhorns)	1.75	.90	.50
(123)	The Oakland A's, 1971-75	3.00	1.50	.90
(124)	The Perfect Game (Sandy Koufax)	3.50	1.75	1.00
(125)	Pickoff (Luis Tiant)	1.25	.60	.40
(126)	The Presidential Ball (William Howard Taft)	1.75	.90	.50
(127)	Relief Pitching (Mike Marshall)	1.25	.60	.40
(128)	The Rules (Hank Aaron)	2.75	1.50	.80
(129)	Rundown (Mets vs. Astros)	1.75	.90	.50
(130)	7th Game of the World Series (Bert Campaneris)	2.25	1.25	.70
(131)	Shea Stadium	2.50	1.25	.70
(132)	The 3000 Hit Club (Roberto Clemente)	8.00	4.00	2.50
(133)	Training Camps (Orioles)	2.75	1.50	.80
(134)	Triple Crown (Carl Yastrzemski)	16.00	8.00	4.75
(135)	Triple Play (Rick Burleson)	2.75	1.50	.80
(136)	Triple Play (Bill Wambsganss)	1.75	.90	.50
(137)	Umpires Strike	1.75	.90	.50
(138)	Veterans Stadium	2.50	1.25	.70
(139)	Wrigley Marathon (Mike Schmidt)	8.00	4.00	2.50
(140)	Yankee Stadium	1.00	.50	.30

Beyond Sports (Baseball) Set: (6):

		NM	EX	VG
(1)	Clemente Award (Andre Thornton)	5.00	2.50	1.50
(2)	Clowns (Al Schact, Nick Altrock)	4.00	2.00	1.25
(3)	Fellowship of Christian Athletes (Don Kessinger)	4.00	2.00	1.25
(4)	High School Record Book (David Clyde)	2.50	1.25	.70
(5)	Hutchinson Award (Al Kaline)	40.00	20.00	12.00
(6)	Walkie-Talkie (Yogi Berra)	5.00	2.50	1.50

1977 Sports Challenge Records

Taped highlights and an interview with the player are featured on this series of 33-1/3 RPM records. The 6" diameter records have a centerhole to be punched out to play the record. Fronts have a stylized picture of the player, his name and a title. Backs describe the highlight and give other career details.

		NM	EX	VG
Complete Set (12):		250.00	125.00	75.00
Common Player:		20.00	10.00	6.00
(1)	Henry Aaron (Hits 715th Homer)	45.00	22.50	13.50
(2)	Johnny Bench (Beats Pirates in '72 Playoff)	30.00	15.00	9.00
(3)	Jerry Koosman, Donn Clendenon (1969 Miracle Mets)	20.00	10.00	6.00
(4)	Don Larsen ('56 World Series Perfect Game)	20.00	10.00	6.00
(5)	Fred Lynn (Has Incredible Day in Detroit)	20.00	10.00	6.00
(6)	Willie Mays (Hits 1st Met Homer)	35.00	17.50	10.50
(7)	Bill Mazeroski (Wins 1960 World Series)	25.00	12.50	7.50
(8)	Frank Robinson (Homers 1st Time as Indian)	20.00	10.00	6.00
(9)	Nolan Ryan (4th No Hitter)	45.00	22.50	13.50
(10)	Tom Seaver (Cubs Ruin Perfect Game)	25.00	12.50	7.50
(11)	Bobby Thomson (Shot Heard 'Round the World)	20.00	10.00	6.00
(12)	Ted Williams (Last Time at Bat in Boston)	35.00	17.50	10.50

1926 Sports Co. of America Champions

Little was known of these small (1-1/2" x 2-1/4") black-and-white cards until an original store display was discovered in the late 1980s. Carrying a copyright date of Nov., 1926, from Sports Co. of America, a San Francisco publishing firm, these cards were produced for A. G. Spalding & Bros., the sporting goods firm. Each card was issued in a wax paper baggie with a

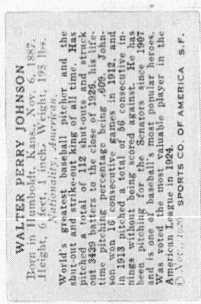

like-sized red, white and blue "Sport-Scrip" which was serial numbered for use in a candy prize drawing at the store or could be redeemed for 10 cents on Spalding equipment. The cards themselves feature ornately framed photos at center, with "CHAMPIONS" in a cartouche at top and the player's name and sport in a second ornate frame at bottom. Most backs have biographical data and career notes, but some are seen with advertising offering an album for the pieces. Nearly 50 baseball players are known from a list of over 175 male and female athletes from sports as diverse as fishing, chess and balloon racing. The unnumbered baseball players from the set are checklisted here in alphabetical order.

		NM	EX	VG
Common Baseball Player:		45.00	20.00	10.00
Ad Back: 2X				
(1)	"Babe" Adams	45.00	20.00	10.00
(2)	Grover Alexander	275.00	110.00	55.00
(3)	Nick Altrock	45.00	20.00	10.00
(4)	Dave Bancroft	220.00	90.00	45.00
(5)	Jesse Barnes	45.00	20.00	10.00
(6)	Oswald Bluege	45.00	20.00	10.00
(7)	Jim Bottomley	220.00	90.00	45.00
(8)	Max Carey	220.00	90.00	45.00
(9)	Ty Cobb	825.00	330.00	165.00
(10)	Mickey Cochrane	220.00	90.00	45.00
(11)	Eddie Collins	220.00	90.00	45.00
(12)	Stan Coveleskie (Coveleski)	220.00	90.00	45.00
(13)	Kiki Cuyler	220.00	90.00	45.00
(14)	Hank DeBerry	45.00	20.00	10.00
(15)	Jack Fournier	45.00	20.00	10.00
(16)	Goose Goslin	220.00	90.00	45.00
(17)	Charlie Grimm	45.00	20.00	10.00
(18)	Bucky Harris	220.00	90.00	45.00
(19)	Gabby Hartnett	220.00	90.00	45.00
(20)	Fred Hofmann	45.00	20.00	10.00
(21)	Rogers Hornsby	275.00	110.00	55.00
(22)	Waite Hoyt	220.00	90.00	45.00
(23)	Walter Johnson	715.00	290.00	145.00
(24)	Joe Judge	45.00	20.00	10.00
(25)	Willie Kamm	45.00	20.00	10.00
(26)	Tony Lazzeri	220.00	90.00	45.00
(27)	Rabbit Maranville	220.00	90.00	45.00
(28)	Fred Marberry	45.00	20.00	10.00
(29)	Rube Marquard	220.00	90.00	45.00
(30)	"Stuffy" McInnis	45.00	20.00	10.00
(31)	"Babe" Pinelli	45.00	20.00	10.00
(32)	Wally Pipp	45.00	20.00	10.00
(33)	Sam Rice	220.00	90.00	45.00
(34)	Emory Rigney	45.00	20.00	10.00
(35)	Dutch Ruether	45.00	20.00	10.00
(36a)	Babe Ruth (1926 copyright.)	2,000	705.00	350.00
(36b)	Babe Ruth (1927 copyright.)	4,000	1,320	660.00
(37)	Ray Schalk	220.00	90.00	45.00
(38)	Joey Sewell	220.00	90.00	45.00
(39)	Urban Shocker	45.00	20.00	10.00
(40)	Al Simmons	220.00	90.00	45.00
(41)	George Sisler	220.00	90.00	45.00
(42)	Tris Speaker	275.00	110.00	55.00
(43)	Pie Traynor	220.00	90.00	45.00
(44)	George Uhle	45.00	20.00	10.00
(45)	Paul Waner	220.00	90.00	45.00
(46)	Aaron L. Ward	45.00	20.00	10.00
(47)	Ken Williams	45.00	20.00	10.00
(48)	Glenn Wright	45.00	20.00	10.00
(49)	Emil Yde	45.00	20.00	10.00

1946-49 Sports Exchange All-Star Picture File

Produced and sold (originally at 50 cents per series) by "The Trading Post," one of the first card collectors' publications, over a period which spanned several years in the late 1940s, this 113-card set was issued in 12 series. Most of the series were nine cards each, printed in black-and-white, unnumbered and blank-backed in a 7" x 10" format. The first 27 cards carry no series designation but were advertised as Series 1A and 1B and Series 2. Series 3 features 11 cards and is printed in sepia tones rather than black-and-white. The fourth series is also unmarked. The final two series consist of 12 cards each, printed two per sheet in smaller format. The photos are labeled as originating with the International News Service. Most of the same players and photos appearing in this set are also found in the Sports Exchange Baseball Miniatures set. Because this was one of the first baseball card sets issued after World War II, it contains cards of several players not found in other issues. The set carries a W603 designation in the "American Card Catalog." Cards are listed alphabetically within series in the checklist which follows.

		NM	EX	VG
Complete Set (113):		2,750	1,350	825.00
Common Card:		15.00	7.50	4.50
SERIES 1A				
(1)	Phil Cavaretta	15.00	7.50	4.50
(2)	Walker Cooper	15.00	7.50	4.50
(3)	Dave Ferriss	15.00	7.50	4.50
(4)	Les Fleming	15.00	7.50	4.50
(5)	Whitey Kurowski	15.00	7.50	4.50
(6)	Marty Marion	20.00	10.00	6.00
(7)	Rip Sewell	15.00	7.50	4.50
(8)	Eddie Stanky	20.00	10.00	6.00
(9)	Dixie Walker	15.00	7.50	4.50
SERIES 1B				
(10)	Bill Dickey	40.00	20.00	12.00
(11)	Bobby Doerr	30.00	15.00	9.00
(12)	Bob Feller	40.00	20.00	12.00
(13)	Hank Greenberg	75.00	37.00	22.00
(14)	George McQuinn	15.00	7.50	4.50
(15)	Ray Mueller	15.00	7.50	4.50
(16)	Hal Newhouser	30.00	15.00	9.00
(17)	Dick Wakefield	15.00	7.50	4.50
(18)	Ted Williams	150.00	75.00	45.00
SERIES 2				
(19)	Al Benton	15.00	7.50	4.50
(20)	Lou Boudreau	30.00	15.00	9.00
(21)	Spud Chandler	15.00	7.50	4.50
(22)	Jeff Heath	15.00	7.50	4.50
(23)	Kirby Higbe	15.00	7.50	4.50
(24)	Tex Hughson	15.00	7.50	4.50
(25)	Stan Musial	175.00	90.00	55.00
(26)	Howie Pollet	15.00	7.50	4.50
(27)	Enos Slaughter	40.00	20.00	12.00
SERIES 3				
(28)	Harry Brecheen	15.00	7.50	4.50
(29)	Dom DiMaggio	30.00	15.00	9.00
(30)	Del Ennis	15.00	7.50	4.50
(31)	Al Evans	15.00	7.50	4.50
(32)	Johnny Lindell	15.00	7.50	4.50
(33)	Johnny Mize	35.00	17.50	10.50
(34)	Johnny Pesky	15.00	7.50	4.50
(35)	Pete Reiser	15.00	7.50	4.50
(36a)	Aaron Robinson/Throwing	15.00	7.50	4.50
(36b)	Aaron Robinson/Fielding	15.00	7.50	4.50
(37)	1946 Boston Red Sox Team	30.00	15.00	9.00
(38)	1946 St. Louis Cardinals Team	30.00	15.00	9.00
SERIES 4				
(39)	Jimmie Foxx	45.00	22.00	13.50
(40)	Frank Frisch	30.00	15.00	9.00
(41)	Lou Gehrig	150.00	75.00	45.00
(42)	Lefty Grove	35.00	17.50	10.50
(43)	Bill Hallahan	15.00	7.50	4.50
(44)	Rogers "Rajah" Hornsby	45.00	22.00	13.50
(45)	Carl Hubbell	30.00	15.00	9.00
(46)	Babe Ruth	250.00	125.00	75.00
(47)	Hack Wilson	30.00	15.00	9.00
SERIES 5				
(48)	Eddie Dyer	15.00	7.50	4.50
(49)	Charlie Grimm	15.00	7.50	4.50
(50)	Billy Herman	30.00	15.00	9.00
(51)	Ted Lyons	30.00	15.00	9.00
(52)	Lefty O'Doul	25.00	12.50	7.50
(53)	Steve O'Neill	15.00	7.50	4.50
(54)	Herb Pennock	30.00	15.00	9.00
(55)	Luke Sewell	15.00	7.50	4.50
(56)	Billy Southworth	15.00	7.50	4.50
SERIES 6				
(57)	Ewell Blackwell	25.00	12.50	7.50
(58)	Jimmy Outlaw	15.00	7.50	4.50
(59)	Andy Pafko	15.00	7.50	4.50
(60)	Pee Wee Reese	75.00	37.00	22.00
(61)	Phil Rizzuto	60.00	30.00	18.00
(62)	Buddy Rosar	15.00	7.50	4.50
(63)	Johnny Sain	25.00	12.50	7.50
(64)	Dizzy Trout	15.00	7.50	4.50
(65)	Harry Walker	15.00	7.50	4.50
SERIES 7				
(66)	Floyd Bevens	15.00	7.50	4.50
(67)	Hugh Casey	15.00	7.50	4.50
(68)	Sam Chapman	15.00	7.50	4.50
(69)	Joe DiMaggio	150.00	75.00	45.00
(70)	Tommy Henrich	25.00	12.50	7.50
(71)	Ralph Kiner	30.00	15.00	9.00
(72)	Cookie Lavagetto	15.00	7.50	4.50
(73)	Vic Lombardi	15.00	7.50	4.50
(74)	Cecil Travis	15.00	7.50	4.50
SERIES 8				
(75)	Nick Altrock	20.00	10.00	6.00
(76)	Mark Christman	15.00	7.50	4.50
(77)	Earle Combs	30.00	15.00	9.00
(78)	Travis Jackson	30.00	15.00	9.00
(79)	Bob Muncrief	15.00	7.50	4.50
(80)	Earl Neale	25.00	12.50	7.50
(81)	Joe Page	15.00	7.50	4.50
(82)	Honus Wagner	75.00	37.00	22.00
(83)	Mickey Witek	15.00	7.50	4.50
SERIES 9				
(84)	George Case	15.00	7.50	4.50
(85)	Jake Early	15.00	7.50	4.50
(86)	Carl Furillo	30.00	15.00	9.00
(87)	Augie Galan	15.00	7.50	4.50
(88)	Bert Haas	15.00	7.50	4.50
(89)	Johnny Hopp	15.00	7.50	4.50
(90)	Ray Lamanno	15.00	7.50	4.50
(91)	Buddy Lewis	15.00	7.50	4.50
(92)	Warren Spahn	40.00	20.00	12.00
SERIES 10				
(93)	Lu Blue	15.00	7.50	4.50
q94)	Bruce Edwards	15.00	7.50	4.50
(95)	Elbie Fletcher	15.00	7.50	4.50
(96)	Joe Gordon	15.00	7.50	4.50
(97)	Tommy Holmes	15.00	7.50	4.50
(98)	Billy Johnson	15.00	7.50	4.50
(99)	Phil Masi	15.00	7.50	4.50
(100)	Red Munger	15.00	7.50	4.50
(101)	Vern Stephens	15.00	7.50	4.50
SERIES 11				
(102)	Ralph Branca, Ken Keltner	20.00	10.00	6.00
(103)	Mickey Cochrane, Bob Dillinger	40.00	20.00	12.00
(104)	Dizzy Dean, Eddie Joost	80.00	40.00	24.00
(105)	Joe Jackson, Wally Westlake	400.00	200.00	120.00
(106)	Larry Jansen, Yogi Berra	80.00	40.00	24.00
(107)	Peanuts Lowrey, Heinie Manush	40.00	20.00	12.00
SERIES 12				
(108)	Gene Bearden, Dale Mitchell	45.00	22.00	13.50
(109)	Steve Gromek, Earl Torgeson	45.00	22.00	13.50
(110)	Jim Hegan, Mickey Vernon	45.00	22.00	13.50
(111)	Bob Lemon, Red Rolfe	100.00	50.00	30.00
(112)	Billy Meyer, Ben Chapman	45.00	22.00	13.50
(113)	Sibbi Sisti, Zach Taylor	45.00	22.00	13.50

1947 Sports Exchange Baseball Miniatures

Heinie Manush

Produced and sold (originally at $1 per series) by one of the hobby's first periodicals, "The Trading Post," this 108-card set was released in three series, designated by red, green and gold borders. The blank-back, unnumbered cards are printed in black-and-white and were sold in sheets of six. When cut from the sheets, individual cards in the red- and green-bordered series measure 2-1/2" x 3", while the gold-bordered cards measure 2-1/2" x 3-1/8". The set is checklisted here alphabetically within series. The set carries an American Card Catalog designation of W602.

		NM	EX	VG
Complete Set (108):		4,750	2,400	1,400
Common Player:		15.00	7.50	4.50
GREEN BORDER SERIES				
(1)	Nick Altrock	20.00	10.00	6.00
(2)	Floyd Bevens	15.00	7.50	4.50
(3)	Ewell Blackwell	20.00	10.00	6.00
(4)	Lou Boudreau	35.00	17.50	10.50
(5)	Harry Brecheen	15.00	7.50	4.50
(6)	Hugh Casey	15.00	7.50	4.50
(7)	Phil Cavaretta	15.00	7.50	4.50
(8)	Sam Chapman	15.00	7.50	4.50
(9)	Mark Christman	15.00	7.50	4.50
(10)	Bill Dickey	40.00	20.00	12.00
(11)	Dom DiMaggio	25.00	12.50	7.50
(12)	Joe DiMaggio	400.00	200.00	120.00
(13)	Eddie Dyer	15.00	7.50	4.50
(14)	Frank Frisch	40.00	20.00	12.00
(15)	Lou Gehrig	275.00	135.00	82.00
(16)	Charlie Grimm	15.00	7.50	4.50
(17)	Lefty Grove	40.00	20.00	12.00
(18)	Tommy Henrich	20.00	10.00	6.00
(19)	Ralph Kiner	35.00	17.50	10.50
(20)	Cookie Lavagetto	15.00	7.50	4.50
(21)	Vic Lombardi	15.00	7.50	4.50
(22)	Ted Lyons	35.00	17.50	10.50
(23)	Bob Muncrief	15.00	7.50	4.50
(24)	Stan Musial	160.00	80.00	48.00
(25)	Steve O'Neill	15.00	7.50	4.50
(26)	Jimmy Outlaw	15.00	7.50	4.50
(27)	Joe Page	15.00	7.50	4.50
(28)	Pee Wee Reese	65.00	32.00	19.50
(29)	Phil Rizzuto	65.00	32.00	19.50
(30)	Buddy Rosar	15.00	7.50	4.50
(31)	Johnny Sain	20.00	10.00	6.00

		NM	EX	VG
(32)	Billy Southworth	15.00	7.50	4.50
(33)	Cecil Travis	15.00	7.50	4.50
(34)	Honus Wagner	90.00	45.00	27.00
(35)	Harry Walker	15.00	7.50	4.50
(36)	Mickey Witek	15.00	7.50	4.50

RED BORDER SERIES

		NM	EX	VG
(37)	Yogi Berra	80.00	40.00	24.00
(38)	Lu Blue	15.00	7.50	4.50
(39)	Ben Chapman	15.00	7.50	4.50
(40)	Mickey Cochrane	35.00	17.50	10.50
(41)	Earle Combs	35.00	17.50	10.50
(42)	Dizzy Dean	95.00	47.00	28.00
(43)	Bob Dillinger	15.00	7.50	4.50
(44)	Bobby Doerr	35.00	17.50	10.50
(45)	Al Evans	15.00	7.50	4.50
(46)	Jimmy (Jimmie) Foxx	50.00	25.00	15.00
(47)	Joe Gordon	15.00	7.50	4.50
(48)	Bill Hallahan	15.00	7.50	4.50
(49)	Tommy Holmes	15.00	7.50	4.50
(50)	Rogers Hornsby	50.00	25.00	15.00
(51)	Carl Hubbell	45.00	22.00	13.50
(52)	Travis Jackson	35.00	17.50	10.50
(53)	Bill Johnson	15.00	7.50	4.50
(54)	Ken Keltner	15.00	7.50	4.50
(55)	Whitey Kurowski	15.00	7.50	4.50
(56)	Ray Lamanno	15.00	7.50	4.50
(57)	Johnny Lindell	15.00	7.50	4.50
(58)	Peanuts Lowrey	15.00	7.50	4.50
(59)	Phil Masi	15.00	7.50	4.50
(60)	Earl Neale	20.00	10.00	6.00
(61)	Hal Newhouser	35.00	17.50	10.50
(62)	Lefty O'Doul	25.00	12.50	7.50
(63)	Herb Pennock	35.00	17.50	10.50
(64)	Red Rolfe	35.00	17.50	10.50
(65)	Babe Ruth	450.00	225.00	135.00
(66)	Luke Sewell	15.00	7.50	4.50
(67)	Rip Sewell	15.00	7.50	4.50
(68)	Warren Spahn	60.00	30.00	18.00
(69)	Vern Stephens	15.00	7.50	4.50
(70)	Dizzy Trout	15.00	7.50	4.50
(71)	Wally Westlake	15.00	7.50	4.50
(72)	Hack Wilson	50.00	25.00	15.00

GOLD BORDER SERIES

		NM	EX	VG
(73)	Al Benton	30.00	15.00	9.00
(74)	Ralph Branca	25.00	12.50	7.50
(75)	George Case	30.00	15.00	9.00
(76)	Spud Chandler	30.00	15.00	9.00
(77)	Jake Early	30.00	15.00	9.00
(78)	Bruce Edwards	30.00	15.00	9.00
(79)	Del Ennis	30.00	15.00	9.00
(80)	Bob Feller	80.00	40.00	24.00
(81)	Dave Ferriss	30.00	15.00	9.00
(82)	Les Fleming	30.00	15.00	9.00
(83)	Carl Furillo	150.00	75.00	45.00
(84)	Augie Galan	30.00	15.00	9.00
(85)	Hank Greenberg	100.00	50.00	30.00
(86)	Bert Haas	30.00	15.00	9.00
(87)	Jeff Heath	30.00	15.00	9.00
(88)	Billy Herman	60.00	30.00	18.00
(89)	Kirby Higbe	30.00	15.00	9.00
(90)	Tex Hughson	30.00	15.00	9.00
(91)	Johnny Hopp	30.00	15.00	9.00
(92)	Joe Jackson	650.00	325.00	195.00
(93)	Larry Jansen	30.00	15.00	9.00
(94)	Eddie Joost	30.00	15.00	9.00
(95)	Buddy Lewis	30.00	15.00	9.00
(96)	Heinie Manush	60.00	30.00	18.00
(97)	Marty Marion	30.00	15.00	9.00
(98)	George McQuinn	30.00	15.00	9.00
(99)	Johnny Mize	60.00	30.00	18.00
(100)	Red Munger	30.00	15.00	9.00
(101)	Andy Pafko	30.00	15.00	9.00
(102)	Johnny Pesky	30.00	15.00	9.00
(103)	Howie Pollet	30.00	15.00	9.00
(104)	Pete Reiser	30.00	15.00	9.00
(105)	Aaron Robinson	30.00	15.00	9.00
(106)	Enos Slaughter	60.00	30.00	18.00
(107)	Dixie Walker	30.00	15.00	9.00
(108)	Ted Williams (Photo actually Bobby Doerr.)	200.00	100.00	60.00

1963 Sports "Hall of Fame" Busts

Licensed by the National Baseball Hall of Fame, this set of 20 plastic player busts was produced by Sports "Hall of Fame," Inc., of New York. Each six-inch statue has a white player figure atop a wood-look pedestal with a plaque providing career details.

The busts were sold in a red, white and gold display box with photos of the players on the back. Though the box back promised "Many More," only the 20 players pictured were ever issued. Retail price at issue was $1-1.25. The first 12 busts are more common than the final eight, with Foxx and Greenberg especially scarce. Values quoted are for busts alone, add $25 for accompanying box and $50 or more for unopened box with cellophane.

		NM	EX	VG
Complete Set (20):		3,000	1,500	900.00
Common Player:		75.00	35.00	20.00
(1)	Babe Ruth	110.00	55.00	30.00
(2)	Ty Cobb	90.00	45.00	25.00
(3)	Joe DiMaggio	110.00	55.00	30.00
(4)	Rogers Hornsby	80.00	40.00	24.00
(5)	Lou Gehrig	100.00	50.00	30.00
(6)	Pie Traynor	75.00	35.00	20.00
(7)	Honus Wagner	150.00	75.00	45.00
(8)	Bill Dickey	110.00	55.00	30.00
(9)	Walter Johnson	135.00	65.00	40.00
(10)	Christy Mathewson	110.00	55.00	30.00
(11)	Jimmie Foxx	335.00	165.00	100.00
(12)	Tris Speaker	75.00	35.00	20.00
(13)	Joe Cronin	180.00	90.00	50.00
(14)	Paul Waner	165.00	80.00	45.00
(15)	Bobby Feller	225.00	110.00	65.00
(16)	Hank Greenberg	275.00	135.00	80.00
(17)	Jackie Robinson	260.00	130.00	75.00
(18)	George Sisler	200.00	100.00	60.00
(19)	John McGraw	200.00	100.00	60.00
(20)	Mickey Cochrane	200.00	100.00	60.00

1954 Sports Illustrated Topps Foldouts

To illustrate a feature about baseball card collecting in its very first issue, Sports Illustrated included a three-page foldout featuring 27 contemporary Topps cards. Printed on glossy paper stock in full color, the paper cards are exact front and back reproductions of the real thing. The foldout panel is found in the August 16, 1954, issue of SI which features on its cover a photo of Eddie Mathews at bat during a night game. The magazine's second issue also contains a 27-card foldout of New York Yankees. The insert reproduces all of Topps' 1954 Yankees cards in full color, and supplements them with black-and-white "cards" in the general style of '54 Topps for those Yankees who appeared only on Bowman cards or on no cards in 1954. The Aug. 23 issue of SI features a stand of golf clubs on its cover. Surviving examples of SI issue #2 are actually scarcer than the debut issue. Singles of the paper cards are rarely encountered. In 2001, SI reprinted 50,000 copies of issue #1 as a subscription premium. These copies are unmarked as reprints and difficult to distinguish from the originals. Many surviving original copies have a mail-in subscription offer card which the reprint does not.

		NM	EX	VG
	Aug. 16, 1954 Issue (Original)	250.00	125.00	75.00
	Aug. 16, 1954 Issue (2001 Reprint)	30.00	15.00	9.00
1	Ted Williams			
2	Gus Zernial			
4	Hank Sauer			
6	Pete Runnels			
7	Ted Kluszewski			
9	Harvey Haddix			
10	Jackie Robinson			
15	Al Rosen			
24	Granny Hamner			
25	Harvey Kuenn			
26	Ray Jablonski			
27	Ferris Fain			
29	Jim Hegan			
30	Ed Mathews			
32	Duke Snider			
34	Jim Rivera			
40	Mel Parnell			
45	Richie Ashburn			
70	Larry Doby			
77	Ray Boone			
85	Bob Turley			
90	Willie Mays			
100	Bob Keegan			
102	Gil Hodges			
119	Johnny Antonelli			
137	Wally Moon			

		NM	EX	VG
235	Vern Law			
	Aug. 23, 1954 issue	350.00	175.00	100.00
5	Ed Lopat			
17	Phil Rizzuto			
37	Whitey Ford			
50	Yogi Berra			
56	Willie Miranda			
62	Eddie Robinson			
83	Joe Collins			
96	Charlie Silvera			
101	Gene Woodling			
105	Andy Carey			
130	Hank Bauer			
175	Frank Leja			
205	Johnny Sain			
230	Bob Kuzava			
239	Bill Skowron			
	Harry Byrd			
	Bob Cerv			
	Jerry Coleman			
	Tom Gorman			
	Bob Grim			
	Mickey Mantle			
	Jim McDonald			
	Gil McDougald			
	Tom Morgan			
	Irv Noren			
	Allie Reynolds			
	Enos Slaughter			

1955 Sports Illustrated Topps Foldouts

SI kicked off the 1955 baseball season by including a page of 1955 Topps card reproductions in its April 11 and April 18 issues. Unlike the tri-fold panels of 1954, the 1955 issues contain only eight reproductions per magazine. Printed in full size in full color on glossy magazine paper, the pages are exact front and back replicas of regular-issue 1955 Topps cards. The April 11 issue features on its cover Willie Mays, Leo Durocher and Lorraine Day (Mrs. D.); the April 18 issue has Al Rosen at bat. Surviving examples of these 1955 SI issues are scarce and the paper cards are seldom seen as singles.

		NM	EX	VG
	April 11, 1955 issue	200.00	100.00	60.00
1	Dusty Rhodes			
26	Dick Groat			
28	Ernie Banks			
31	Warren Spahn			
56	Ray Jablonski			
67	Wally Moon			
79	Danny Schell			
90	Karl Spooner			
8	**April 18, 1955 issue** Hal Smith	60.00	30.00	18.00
10	Bob Keegan			
11	Ferris Fain			
16	Roy Sievers			
38	Bob Turley			
70	Al Rosen			
77	Arnie Portocarrero			
106	Frank Sullivan			

1968-70 Sports Illustrated Posters

Between 1968-70, Sports Illustrated issued a series of baseball player posters. The 2' x 3' blank-back posters have borderless color action or posed photos. In an upper corner are the player identification, copyright, poster number, etc., in small type. Values for the posters issued in 1969 and 1970 are higher than those produced in 1968. Current market values reflect the fact that many superstars' posters were sold in larger quantities than those of journeyman players and survive in greater numbers. The posters are listed here alphabetically within year of issue. Original selling price of the posters was $1.50 each, plus postage.

		NM	EX	VG
Complete Set (86):		2,500	1,250	750.00
Common Player:		10.00	5.00	3.00
	1968			
(1)	Hank Aaron	45.00	22.50	13.50
(2)	Rich Allen	30.00	15.00	9.00
(3)	Gene Alley	15.00	7.50	4.50

(4)	Felipe Alou	15.00	7.50	4.50
(5)	Max Alvis	10.00	5.00	3.00
(6)	Bob Aspromonte	10.00	5.00	3.00
(7)	Ernie Banks (Photo actually Billy Williams.)	35.00	17.50	10.50
(8)	Clete Boyer	12.50	6.25	3.75
(9)	Lou Brock	15.00	7.50	4.50
(10)	John Callison	15.00	7.50	4.50
(11)	Campy Campaneris	12.50	6.25	3.75
(12)	Leo Cardenas	12.50	6.25	3.75
(13)	Paul Casanova	17.50	8.75	5.25
(14)	Orlando Cepeda	17.50	8.75	5.25
(15)	Roberto Clemente	185.00	95.00	55.00
(16)	Tony Conigliaro	20.00	10.00	6.00
(17)	Willie Davis	15.00	7.50	4.50
(18)	Don Drysdale	17.50	8.75	5.25
(19)	Al Ferrara	12.50	6.25	3.75
(20)	Curt Flood	15.00	7.50	4.50
(21)	Bill Freehan	30.00	15.00	9.00
(22)	Jim Fregosi	10.00	5.00	3.00
(23)	Bob Gibson	15.00	7.50	4.50
(24)	Bud Harrelson (Photo actually Ken Harrelson.)	20.00	10.00	6.00
(25)	Joe Horlen	10.00	5.00	3.00
(26)	Tony Horton	15.00	7.50	4.50
(27)	Tommy John	12.50	6.25	3.75
(28)	Al Kaline	40.00	20.00	12.00
(29)	Harmon Killebrew	17.50	8.75	5.25
(30)	Jim Lonborg	17.50	8.75	5.25
(31)	Jim Maloney	12.50	6.25	3.75
(32)	Mickey Mantle	185.00	92.00	55.00
(33)	Juan Marichal	17.50	8.75	5.25
(34)	Willie Mays	110.00	55.00	35.00
(35)	Bill Mazeroski	25.00	12.50	7.50
(36)	Tim McCarver	17.50	8.75	5.25
(37)	Mike McCormick	15.00	7.50	4.50
(38)	Willie McCovey	45.00	22.50	13.50
(39a)	Don Mincher (Angels)	15.00	7.50	4.50
(39b)	Don Mincher (Pilots)	20.00	10.00	6.00
(40)	Rick Monday	12.50	6.25	3.75
(41)	Tony Oliva	15.00	7.50	4.50
(42)	Rick Reichardt	10.00	5.00	3.00
(43)	Brooks Robinson	175.00	90.00	50.00
(44)	Frank Robinson	75.00	37.50	22.00
(45)	Pete Rose	100.00	50.00	30.00
(46)	Ron Santo	17.50	8.75	5.25
(47)	Tom Seaver	130.00	65.00	39.00
(48)	Chris Short	15.00	7.50	4.50
(49)	Reggie Smith	12.50	6.25	3.75
(50)	Rusty Staub	17.50	8.75	5.25
(51)	Mel Stottlemyre	20.00	10.00	6.00
(52)	Ron Swoboda	25.00	12.50	7.50
(53)	Cesar Tovar	15.00	7.50	4.50
(54)	Earl Wilson	17.50	8.75	5.25
(55)	Jim Wynn	10.00	5.00	3.00
(56)	Carl Yastrzemski	25.00	12.50	7.50

1969

(1)	Tommie Agee	17.50	8.75	5.25
(2)	Mike Andrews	12.50	6.25	3.75
(3)	Ernie Banks/Btg	15.00	7.50	4.50
(4a)	Gary Bell (Indians)	20.00	10.00	6.00
(4b)	Gary Bell (Pilots)	20.00	10.00	6.00
(5a)	Tommy Davis (White Sox)	17.50	8.75	5.25
(5b)	Tommy Davis (Pilots)	20.00	10.00	6.00
(6)	Frank Howard	20.00	10.00	6.00
(7)	Reggie Jackson	95.00	47.00	28.00
(8)	Fergie Jenkins	45.00	22.00	13.50
(9)	Let's Go Mets (Tommie Agee, Jerry Grote, Cleon Jones, Jerry Koosman, Ed Kranepool, Tom Seaver, Ron Swoboda)	20.00	10.00	6.00
(10)	Denny McLain	15.00	7.50	4.50
(11)	Bobby Murcer	45.00	22.00	13.50
(12)	John Odom	17.50	8.75	5.25
(13)	Rico Petrocelli	17.50	8.75	5.25
(14)	Boog Powell	20.00	10.00	6.00
(15)	Roy White	25.00	12.50	7.50

1970

(1)	Glenn Beckert	17.50	8.75	5.25
(2)	Bobby Bonds	20.00	10.00	6.00
(3)	Rod Carew	17.50	8.75	5.25
(4)	Mike Cuellar	17.50	8.75	5.25
(5)	Mike Epstein	15.00	7.50	4.50
(6)	Ken Holtzman	15.00	7.50	4.50
(7)	Cleon Jones	15.00	7.50	4.50
(8)	Mickey Lolich	15.00	7.50	4.50
(9)	Sam McDowell	20.00	10.00	6.00
(10)	Phil Niekro	35.00	17.50	10.50
(11)	Wes Parker	17.50	8.75	5.25
(12)	Tony Perez	25.00	12.50	7.50
(13)	Bill Singer	10.00	5.00	3.00
(14)	Walt Williams	20.00	10.00	6.00

1968 Sports Memorabilia All Time Baseball Team

"BABE" RUTH

This is one of the earliest collectors' issue baseball card sets created for distribution solely within the hobby. The 2-1/2" x 3-1/2" cards feature the artwork of Art Oulette done in sepia tones on a white background and surrounded by a yellow border. Backs have career information, copyright and player identification. Issue price was $2.50.

		NM	EX	VG
	Complete Set (15):	35.00	17.50	10.00
	Common Player:	2.00	1.00	.60
1	Checklist	.50	.25	.15
2	"Connie" Mack	2.00	1.00	.60
3	Walter Johnson	4.00	2.00	1.25
4	Warren Spahn	2.00	1.00	.60
5	Christy Mathewson	4.00	2.00	1.25
6	Lefty Grove	2.00	1.00	.60
7	Mickey Cochrane	2.00	1.00	.60
8	Bill Dickey	2.00	1.00	.60
9	"Tris" Speaker	2.50	1.25	.75
10	"Ty" Cobb	6.00	3.00	2.00
11	"Babe" Ruth	10.00	5.00	3.00
12	"Lou" Gehrig	7.50	3.75	2.25
13	Rogers Hornsby	2.50	1.25	.75
14	"Honus" Wagner	5.00	2.50	1.50
15	"Pie" Traynor	2.00	1.00	.60

1960 Sports Novelties Inc. Genuine Baseball Photos

GEORGE ANDERSON
SECOND BASE—PHILADELPHIA PHILLIES

(See 1960 Leaf for checklist and price guide.)

1960s Sports Pix Premiums

These black-and-white blank-back pictures were distributed as a premium for Sports Pix magazine in the early 1960s. Two sizes are known: A smaller (about 8" x 10") style was issued in the early 1960s, while a larger (about 8-1/2" x 10-1/2") format was produced after 1963. Both styles have the photo bordered in white, with the player name centered at bottom. In the bottom-right corner is a three-line credit to the magazine and its Washington, D.C. address. Gaps have been left in the assigned numbering to accommodate future additions.

		NM	EX	VG
	Common Player:	10.00	5.00	3.00
(1)	Ty Cobb (Large)	7.50	3.75	2.25
(2)	Mickey Cochrane (Large)	3.00	1.50	.90
(3)	Rocky Colavito (Large)	5.00	2.50	1.50
(3)	Joe Cronin (Large)	3.00	1.50	.90
(4)	Bill Dickey (Large)	3.00	2.00	1.00
(5)	Joe DiMaggio (Large, glossy, w/caption)	7.50	3.75	2.25
(7)	Bob Feller (Large)	3.00	2.00	1.00
(8)	Lou Gehrig (Large)	7.50	3.75	2.25
(9)	Charlie Gehringer (Large)	3.00	2.00	1.00
(11)	"Lefty" Grove (Large)		2.00	1.00
(12)	Rogers Hornsby (Large)	3.00	2.00	1.00
(13)	Walter Johnson (Large)	5.00	2.50	1.50
(14)	Sandy Koufax (Small)	5.00	2.50	1.50
(15)	Sandy Koufax (Large)	5.00	2.50	1.50
(16)	Mickey Mantle (Large)	15.00	7.50	4.50
(17)	Mickey Mantle (Small)	15.00	7.50	4.50
(18)	Roger Maris (Large)	4.50	2.25	1.25
(19)	Willie Mays (Large)	7.50	3.75	2.25
(20)	Willie Mays (small)	7.50	3.75	2.25
(21)	John McGraw (Large)	3.00	2.00	1.00
(22)	Stan Musial (Large)	5.00	2.50	1.50
(23)	Babe Ruth (Large)	7.50	3.75	2.25
(24)	George Sisler (Large)	3.00	2.00	1.00
(26)	Warren Spahn (Large)	2.00	1.00	1.00
(27)	"Casey" Stengel (Large)	3.00	2.00	1.00
(28)	"Pie" Traynor (Large)	3.00	2.00	1.00
(30)	"Honus" Wagner (Large)	4.50	2.25	1.25
(32)	Ted Williams (Large)	7.50	3.75	2.25

1979 Sports Reading Series

This set of large-format (abouyt 8-1/2" x 14") was designed to encourage youthful readers. The black-and-white cards have one or more photos and lengthy text describing the player and/or action depicted.

		NM	EX	VG
	Complete Set (50):	250.00	125.00	75.00
	Common Player:	5.00	2.50	1.50
1	Carlos May	5.00	2.50	1.50
2	Babe Ruth	10.00	5.00	3.00
3	Eddie Gaedel	6.00	3.00	1.75
4	Cesar Gutierrez	5.00	2.50	1.50
5	Ted Williams	7.50	3.75	2.25
6	Pete Gray	6.00	3.00	1.75
7	Hank Aaron	7.50	3.75	2.25
8	Lou Brock	5.00	2.50	1.50
9	Virgil Trucks	5.00	2.50	1.50
10	Cesar Tovar	5.00	2.50	1.50
11	Wrigley Field	5.00	2.50	1.50
12	Ron Guidry	5.00	2.50	1.50
13	Bill Davis	5.00	2.50	1.50
14	Jimmy Piersall	5.00	2.50	1.50
15	Eddie Gaedel	6.00	3.00	1.75
16	Reggie Jackson	7.50	3.75	2.25
17	Mark Fidrych	5.00	2.50	1.50
18	Sandy Koufax	7.50	3.75	2.25
19	Dale Long	5.00	2.50	1.50
20	Herb Score	5.00	2.50	1.50
21	Dizzy Dean, Daffy Dean	5.00	2.50	1.50
22	Stan Musial	7.50	3.75	2.25
23	1903 N.Y. Giants	5.00	2.50	1.50
24	Pete Rose	7.50	3.75	2.25
25	Cy Young	5.00	2.50	1.50
26	Ferguson Jenkins	5.00	2.50	1.50
27	Minnie Minoso	5.00	2.50	1.50
28	Mort Cooper, Walker Cooper	5.00	2.50	1.50
29	Jim Thorpe	7.50	3.75	2.25
30	Lefty Grove	5.00	2.50	1.50
31	Roberto Clemente	9.00	4.50	2.75
32	Pres. Coolidge Throws Out First Ball	5.00	2.50	1.50
33	Lou Gehrig	7.50	3.75	2.25
34	Nolan Ryan	10.00	5.00	3.00
35	1969 N.Y. Mets	5.00	2.50	1.50
36	Yankee Stadium	5.00	2.50	1.50
37	Jackie Robinson	7.50	3.75	2.25
38	Carl Hubbell	5.00	2.50	1.50
39	Willie Mays	7.50	3.75	2.25
40	Mike Schmidt	6.00	3.00	1.75
41	Harvey Haddix	5.00	2.50	1.50
42	Pete Reiser	5.00	2.50	1.50
43	Gary Cooper (Pride of the Yankees)	5.00	2.50	1.50
44	Jackie Robinson	7.50	3.75	2.25
45	Walter Johnson	5.00	2.50	1.50
46	Hall of Fame	5.00	2.50	1.50
47	Jose Morales	5.00	2.50	1.50
48	Rod Carew	5.00	2.50	1.50
49	Lou Boudreau	5.00	2.50	1.50
50	Hank Greenberg	5.00	2.50	1.50

1950 Sport Stars Luckee Key Charms

This series of 1-3/8" square, diamond-format aluminum tags depicts on front an action picture of a player along with his facsimile autograph. A good luck and sportsmanship message appears on back. The charms are holed at the top to accomodate a beaded chain. While the charms themselves are not so marked, they were produced by Ralpat Co., of Cleveland, and sold on an approximately 3" x 5" cardboard backing card which has a line-art portrait of the player, his name, "Sport Stars" and "Luckee Key Charm." Values shown are for complete card/charm combinations. The metal charms themselves would be valued at about 35-50 percent.

		NM	EX	VG
	Complete Set (5):	150.00	75.00	45.00
	Common Player:	15.00	7.50	4.50
(1)	Ewell Blackwell	15.00	7.50	4.50

		NM	EX	VG
(2)	Bob Feller	30.00	15.00	9.00
(3)	Ralph Kiner	20.00	10.00	6.00
(4)	Hal Newhouser	17.50	8.75	5.25
(5)	Ted Williams	100.00	50.00	30.00

1976 Sportstix

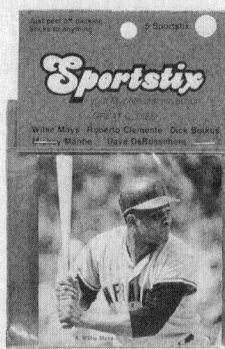

These peel-off player stickers were sold in five-piece plastic packs, with specific contents noted on the header. Stickers are found in three formats: 3-1/2" square, 3-1/2" square with clipped corners and 3" diameter round. The set includes 10 numbered current players and three retired baseball superstars identified as A, B and D. Stickers have full-color player pictures on front with no border. The player's name and sticker number are printed in black. Backs are blank. Besides the baseball players, there were stickers for football and basketball players, in a total issue of 30.

		NM	EX	VG
Complete Baseball Set (13):		40.00	20.00	12.00
Common Player:		1.00	.50	.30
A	Willie Mays	10.00	5.00	3.00
C	Roberto Clemente	12.50	6.25	3.75
D	Mickey Mantle	15.00	7.50	4.50
1	Dave Kingman	1.00	.50	.30
2	Steve Busby	1.00	.50	.30
3	Bill Madlock	1.00	.50	.30
4	Jeff Burroughs	1.00	.50	.30
5	Ted Simmons	1.00	.50	.30
6	Randy Jones	1.00	.50	.30
7	Buddy Bell	1.00	.50	.30
8	Dave Cash	1.00	.50	.30
9	Jerry Grote	1.00	.50	.30
10	Davey Lopes	1.00	.50	.30

1975 SSPC Promo Cards

1976
BASEBALL CARDS

Complete Set of 630 Cards

$12.99 + $1.00 Postage

You get the complete set of 630 cards in full color.
In depth biography and uniform number on the back of every card.

NOT AVAILABLE IN STORES

All the players on your favorite team - $1.00 + 50¢ postage.

SPORTS STARS PUBLISHING CO.
P. O. BOX #132 DEPT JG
Valley Cottage, N. Y. 10989

The six players in this sample set can each be found with three different backs. Some backs are similar to the cards issued in 1976, with player data and career summary. Some cards will have an ad message on back offering the complete 1976 SSPC set and team sets. Still others have blank backs. All cards are in 2-1/2" x 3-1/2" format with color photos on front surrounded by a white border and no extraneous graphics. Blank-back versions are worth 2-4X the values quoted here.

		NM	EX	VG
Complete Set (6):		15.00	7.50	4.50
Common Player:		1.50	.75	.45
(1)	Hank Aaron	4.00	2.00	1.25
(2)	Catfish Hunter	2.00	1.00	.60
(3)	Dave Kingman	1.50	.75	.45
(4)	Mickey Mantle	7.50	3.75	2.25
(5)	Willie Mays	4.00	2.00	1.25
(6)	Tom Seaver	3.00	1.50	.90

Near Mint-Mint and Mint examples of vintage cards carry a significant premium over the Near Mint values shown here. This premium reflects limited availability of the highest-grade cards as well as demand for particular cards or sets in the best possible condition.

1975 SSPC Sample Cards

The Winter 1975 issue of "Collector's Quarterly" magazine (an advertising vehicle for Mike Aronstein, SSPC's principal) contained a two-page cardboard insert previewing the 1976 SSPC set. The cards could be cut apart into singles and represented something of a traded set, as each player or manager changed teams between the end of the 1975 season and the start of 1976. The cards have the players pictured on front in their old uniforms, with their new teams identified on back. Backs of the 2-1/2" x 3-1/2" cards are printed in red and black with a player biography and uniform number. "SAMPLE CARD 1975" is printed around the uniform number. A card number is in the lower-left corner, with 1975 copyright at bottom-right.

		NM	EX	VG
Complete Set, Uncut Sheet:		25.00	12.50	7.50
Complete Set, Singles (18):		20.00	10.00	6.00
Common Card:		1.50	.75	.45
1	Harry Parker	1.50	.75	.45
2	Jim Bibby	1.50	.75	.45
3	Mike Wallace	1.50	.75	.45
4	Tony Muser	1.50	.75	.45
5	Yogi Berra	7.50	3.75	2.25
6	Preston Gomez	1.50	.75	.45
7	Jack McKeon	1.50	.75	.45
8	Sam McDowell	1.50	.70	.45
9	Gaylord Perry	4.00	2.00	1.25
10	Fred Stanley	1.50	.75	.45
11	Willie Davis	1.50	.70	.45
12	Don Hopkins	1.50	.75	.45
13	Whitey Herzog	1.50	.70	.45
14	Ray Sadecki	1.50	.75	.45
15	Stan Bahnsen	1.50	.75	.45
16	Bob Oliver	1.50	.75	.45
17	Denny Doyle	1.50	.75	.45
18	Deron Johnson	1.50	.70	.45

1975 SSPC

This set, produced by the Sport Star Publishing Co. in 1975 as a collectors' issue (though not actually issued until 1976), was withdrawn from the market because of legal entanglements. Because SSPC agreed never to reprint the issue, some collectors feel it has an air of legitimacy. The complete set contains 630 full-color cards, each 2-1/2" x 3-1/2" in size. The cards look similar to 1953 Bowmans, with only the player picture (no identification) on the fronts. Card backs are in a vertical format, with personal stats, brief biographies, uniform and card numbers printed in a variety of colors. Sets originally sold for $9.99.

		NM	EX	VG
Complete Set (630):		60.00	30.00	18.00
Common Player:		.10	.05	.03
1	Lee William (Buzz) Capra	.10	.05	.03
2	Thomas Ross House	.10	.05	.03
3	Maximino Leon	.10	.05	.03
4	Carl Wendle Morton	.10	.05	.03
5	Philip Henry Niekro	1.50	.70	.45
6	Michael Wayne Thompson	.10	.05	.03
7	Elias Sosa (Martinez)	.10	.05	.03
8	Larvell Blanks	.10	.05	.03
9	Darrell Wayne Evans	.10	.05	.03
10	Rodney Joe Gilbreath	.10	.05	.03
11	Michael Ken-Wai Lum	.10	.05	.03
12	Craig George Robinson	.10	.05	.03
13	Earl Craig Williams, Jr.	.10	.05	.03
14	Victor Crosby Correll	.10	.05	.03
15	Biff Pocoroba	.10	.05	.03
16	Johnny B. (Dusty) Baker, Jr.	.35	.20	.11
17	Ralph Allen Garr	.10	.05	.03
18	Clarence Edward (Cito) Gaston	.10	.05	.03
19	David LaFrance May	.10	.05	.03
20	Rowland Johnnie Office	.10	.05	.03
21	Robert Brooks Beall	.10	.05	.03
22	George Lee (Sparky) Anderson	1.00	.50	.30
23	John Eugene Billingham	.10	.05	.03
24	Pedro Rodriguez Borbon	.10	.05	.03
25	Clay Palmer Carroll	.10	.05	.03
26	Patrick Leonard Darcy	.10	.05	.03
27	Donald Edward Gullett	.10	.05	.03
28	Clayton Laws Kirby	.10	.05	.03
29	Gary Lynn Nolan	.10	.05	.03
30	Fredie Hubert Norman	.10	.05	.03
31	Johnny Lee Bench	2.50	1.25	.70
32	William Francis Plummer	.10	.05	.03
33	Darrel Lee Chaney	.10	.05	.03
34	David Ismael Concepcion	.10	.05	.03
35	Terrence Michael Crowley	.10	.05	.03
36	Daniel Driessen	.10	.05	.03
37	Robert Douglas Flynn, Jr.	.10	.05	.03
38	Joe Leonard Morgan	2.00	1.00	.60
39	Atanasio Rigal (Tony) Perez	1.50	.70	.45
40	George Kenneth (Ken) Griffey	.35	.20	.11
41	Peter Edward Rose	5.00	2.50	1.50
42	Edison Rosanda Armbrister	.10	.05	.03
43	John Christopher Vukovich	.10	.05	.03
44	George Arthur Foster	.10	.05	.03
45	Cesar Francisco Geronimo	.10	.05	.03
46	Mervin Weldon Rettenmund	.10	.05	.03
47	James Frederick Crawford	.10	.05	.03
48	Kenneth Roth Forsch	.10	.05	.03
49	Douglas James Konieczny	.10	.05	.03
50	Joseph Franklin Niekro	.10	.05	.03
51	Clifford Johnson	.10	.05	.03
52	Alfred Henry (Skip) Jutze	.10	.05	.03
53	Milton Scott May	.10	.05	.03
54	Robert Patrick Andrews	.10	.05	.03
55	Kenneth George Boswell	.10	.05	.03
56	Tommy Vann Helms	.10	.05	.03
57	Roger Henry Metzger	.10	.05	.03
58	Lawrence William Milbourne	.10	.05	.03
59	Douglas Lee Rader	.10	.05	.03
60	Robert Jose Watson	.10	.05	.03
61	Enos Milton Cabell, Jr.	.10	.05	.03
62	Jose Delan Cruz	.10	.05	.03
63	Cesar Cedeno	.10	.05	.03
64	Gregory Eugene Gross	.10	.05	.03
65	Wilbur Leon Howard	.10	.05	.03
66	Alphonso Erwin Downing	.10	.05	.03
67	Burt Carlton Hooton	.10	.05	.03
68	Charles Oliver Hough	.10	.05	.03
69	Thomas Edward John	.25	.13	.08
70	John Alexander Messersmith	.10	.05	.03
71	Douglas James Rau	.10	.05	.03
72	Richard Alan Rhoden	.10	.05	.03
73	Donald Howard Sutton	1.50	.70	.45
74	Frederick Steven Auerbach	.10	.05	.03
75	Ronald Charles Cey	.10	.05	.03
76	Ivan De Jesus	.10	.05	.03
77	Steven Patrick Garvey	1.00	.50	.30
78	Leonadus Lacy	.10	.05	.03
79	David Earl Lopes	.10	.05	.03
80	Kenneth Lee McMullen	.10	.05	.03
81	Joseph Vance Ferguson	.10	.05	.03
82	Paul Ray Powell	.10	.05	.03
83	Stephen Wayne Yeager	.10	.05	.03
84	Willie Murphy Crawford	.10	.05	.03
85	Henry Cruz	.10	.05	.03
86	Charles Fuqua Manuel	.10	.05	.03
87	Manuel Mota	.10	.05	.03
88	Thomas Marian Paciorek	.10	.05	.03
89	James Sherman Wynn	.10	.05	.03
90	Walter Emmons Alston	1.00	.50	.30
91	William Joseph Buckner	.10	.05	.03
92	James Leland Barr	.10	.05	.03
93	Ralph Michael (Mike) Caldwell	.10	.05	.03
94	John Francis D'Acquisto	.10	.05	.03
95	David Wallace Heaverlo	.10	.05	.03
96	Gary Robert Lavelle	.10	.05	.03
97	John Joseph Montefusco, Jr.	.10	.05	.03
98	Charles Prosek Williams	.10	.05	.03
99	Christopher Paul Arnold	.10	.05	.03
100	Mark Kevin Hill (Marc)	.10	.05	.03
101	David Martin Rader	.10	.05	.03
102	Charles Bruce Miller	.10	.05	.03
103	Guillermo Naranjo (Willie) Montano	.10	.05	.03
104	Steven Robert Ontiveros	.10	.05	.03
105	Chris Edward Speier	.10	.05	.03
106	Derrel Osbon Thomas	.10	.05	.03
107	Gary Leah Thomasson	.10	.05	.03
108	Glenn Charles Adams	.10	.05	.03
109	Von Everett Joshua	.10	.05	.03
110	Gary Nathaniel Matthews	.10	.05	.03
111	Bobby Ray Murcer	.10	.05	.03
112	Horace Arthur Speed III	.10	.05	.03
113	Wesley Noreen Westrum	.10	.05	.03
114	Richard Nevin Folkers	.10	.05	.03
115	Alan Benton Foster	.10	.05	.03
116	David James Freisleben	.10	.05	.03
117	Daniel Vincent Frisella	.10	.05	.03
118	Randall Leo Jones	.10	.05	.03
119	Daniel Ray Spillner	.10	.05	.03
120	Howard Lawrence (Larry) Hardy	.10	.05	.03
121	Cecil Randolph (Randy) Hundley	.10	.05	.03
122	Fred Lyn Kendall	.10	.05	.03
123	John Francis McNamara	.10	.05	.03
124	Rigoberto (Tito) Fuentes	.10	.05	.03
125	Enzo Octavio Hernandez	.10	.05	.03
126	Stephen Michael Huntz	.10	.05	.03
127	Michael Wilson Ivie	.10	.05	.03
128	Hector Epitacio Torres	.10	.05	.03
129	Theodore Rodger Kubiak	.10	.05	.03
130	John Maywood Grubb, Jr.	.10	.05	.03
131	John Henry Scott	.10	.05	.03
132	Robert Tolan	.10	.05	.03
133	David Mark Winfield	2.50	1.25	.70
134	William Joseph Gogolewski	.10	.05	.03
135	Danny L. Osborn	.10	.05	.03
136	James Lee Kaat	.25	.13	.08
137	Claude Wilson Osteen	.10	.05	.03
138	Cecil Lee Upshaw, Jr.	.10	.05	.03

139	Wilbur Forrester Wood, Jr.	.10	.05	.03
140	Lloyd Cecil Allen	.10	.05	.03
141	Brian Jay Downing	.10	.05	.03
142	James Sarkis Essian, Jr.	.10	.05	.03
143	Russell Earl (Bucky) Dent	.50	.25	.15
144	Jorge Orta	.10	.05	.03
145	Lee Edward Richard	.10	.05	.03
146	William Allen Stein	.10	.05	.03
147	Kenneth Joseph Henderson	.10	.05	.03
148	Carlos May	.10	.05	.03
149	Nyls Wallace Rex Nyman	.10	.05	.03
150	Robert Pasquali Coluccio, Jr.	.10	.05	.03
151	Charles William Tanner, Jr.	.10	.05	.03
152	Harold Patrick (Pat) Kelly	.10	.05	.03
153	Jerry Wayne Hairston Sr.	.10	.05	.03
154	Richard Fred (Pete) Varney, Jr.	.10	.05	.03
155	William Edwin Melton	.10	.05	.03
156	Richard Michael Gossage	.50	.25	.15
157	Terry Jay Forster	.10	.05	.03
158	Richard Michael Hinton	.10	.05	.03
159	Nelson Kelley Briles	.10	.05	.03
160	Alan James Fitzmorris	.10	.05	.03
161	Stephen Bernard Mingori	.10	.05	.03
162	Martin William Pattin	.10	.05	.03
163	Paul William Splittorff, Jr.	.10	.05	.03
164	Dennis Patrick Leonard	.10	.05	.03
165	John Albert (Buck) Martinez	.10	.05	.03
166	Gorrell Robert (Bob) Stinson III	.10	.05	.03
167	George Howard Brett	7.50	3.75	2.25
168	Harmon Clayton Killebrew, Jr.	2.50	1.25	.70
169	John Claiborn Mayberry	.10	.05	.03
170	Freddie Joe Patek	.10	.05	.03
171	Octavio (Cookie) Rojas	.10	.05	.03
172	Rodney Darrell Scott	.10	.05	.03
173	Tolia (Tony) Solaita	.10	.05	.03
174	Frank White, Jr.	.10	.05	.03
175	Alfred Edward Cowens, Jr.	.10	.05	.03
176	Harold Abraham McRae	.10	.05	.03
177	Amos Joseph Otis	.10	.05	.03
178	Vada Edward Pinson, Jr.	.50	.25	.15
179	James Eugene Wohlford	.10	.05	.03
180	James Douglas Bird	.10	.05	.03
181	Mark Alan Littell	.10	.05	.03
182	Robert McClure	.10	.05	.03
183	Steven Lee Busby	.10	.05	.03
184	Francis Xavier Healy	.10	.05	.03
185	Dorrel Norman Elvert (Whitey) Herzog	.10	.05	.03
186	Andrew Earl Hassler	.10	.05	.03
187	Lynn Nolan Ryan, Jr.	7.50	3.75	2.25
188	William Robert Singer	.10	.05	.03
189	Frank Daryl Tanana	.10	.05	.03
190	Eduardo Figueroa	.10	.05	.03
191	David S. Collins	.10	.05	.03
192	Richard Hirshfeld Williams	.10	.05	.03
193	Eliseo Rodriguez	.10	.05	.03
194	David Lee Chalk	.10	.05	.03
195	Winston Enriquillo Llenas	.10	.05	.03
196	Rudolph Bart Meoli	.10	.05	.03
197	Orlando Ramirez	.10	.05	.03
198	Gerald Peter Remy	.10	.05	.03
199	Billy Edward Smith	.10	.05	.03
200	Bruce Anton Bochte	.10	.05	.03
201	Joseph Michael Lahoud, Jr.	.10	.05	.03
202	Morris Nettles, Jr.	.10	.05	.03
203	John Milton (Mickey) Rivers	.10	.05	.03
204	Leroy Bobby Stanton	.10	.05	.03
205	Victor Albury	.10	.05	.03
206	Thomas Henry Burgmeier	.10	.05	.03
207	William Franklin Butler	.10	.05	.03
208	William Richard Campbell	.10	.05	.03
209	Alton Ray Corbin	.10	.05	.03
210	George Henry (Joe) Decker, Jr.	.10	.05	.03
211	James Michael Hughes	.10	.05	.03
212	Edward Norman Bane (photo actually Mike Pazik)	.10	.05	.03
213	Glenn Dennis Borgmann	.10	.05	.03
214	Rodney Cline Carew	2.50	1.25	.70
215	Stephen Robert Brye	.10	.05	.03
216	Darnell Glenn (Dan) Ford	.10	.05	.03
217	Antonio Oliva	.35	.20	.11
218	David Allan Goltz	.10	.05	.03
219	Rikalbert Blyleven	.25	.13	.08
220	Larry Eugene Hisle	.10	.05	.03
221	Stephen Russell Braun, III	.10	.05	.03
222	Jerry Wayne Terrell	.10	.05	.03
223	Eric Thane Soderholm	.10	.05	.03
224	Philip Anthony Roof	.10	.05	.03
225	Danny Leon Thompson	.10	.05	.03
226	James William Colborn	.10	.05	.03
227	Thomas Andrew Murphy	.10	.05	.03
228	Eduardo Rodriguez	.10	.05	.03
229	James Michael Slaton	.10	.05	.03
230	Edward Nelson Sprague	.10	.05	.03
231	Charles William Moore, Jr.	.10	.05	.03
232	Darrell Ray Porter	.10	.05	.03
233	Kurt Anthony Bevacqua	.10	.05	.03
234	Pedro Garcia	.10	.05	.03
235	James Michael (Mike) Hegan	.10	.05	.03
236	Donald Wayne Money	.10	.05	.03
237	George C. Scott, Jr.	.10	.05	.03
238	Robin Roy Yount	5.00	2.50	1.50
239	Henry Louis Aaron	5.00	2.50	1.50
240	Robert Walker Ellis	.10	.05	.03
241	Sixto Lezcano	.10	.05	.03
242	Robert Vance Mitchell	.10	.05	.03
243	James Gorman Thomas, III	.10	.05	.03
244	William Edward Travers	.10	.05	.03
245	Peter Sven Broberg	.10	.05	.03
246	William Howard Sharp	.10	.05	.03
247	Arthur Bobby Lee Darwin	.10	.05	.03
248	Rick Gerald Austin (photo actually Larry Anderson)	.10	.05	.03
249	Lawrence Dennis Anderson (photo actually Rick Austin)	.10	.05	.03
250	Thomas Antony Bianco	.10	.05	.03
251	DeLancy LaFayette Currence	.10	.05	.03
252	Steven Raymond Foucault	.10	.05	.03
253	William Alfred Hands, Jr.	.10	.05	.03
254	Steven Lowell Hargan	.10	.05	.03
255	Ferguson Arthur Jenkins	1.50	.70	.45
256	Bob Mitchell Sheldon	.10	.05	.03
257	James Umbarger	.10	.05	.03
258	Clyde Wright	.10	.05	.03
259	William Roger Fahey	.10	.05	.03
260	James Howard Sundberg	.10	.05	.03
261	Leonardo Alfonso Cardenas	.10	.05	.03
262	James Louis Fregosi	.10	.05	.03
263	Dudley Michael (Mike) Hargrove	.10	.05	.03
264	Colbert Dale (Toby) Harrah	.10	.05	.03
265	Roy Lee Howell	.10	.05	.03
266	Leonard Shenoff Randle	.10	.05	.03
267	Roy Frederick Smalley III	.10	.05	.03
268	James Lloyd Spencer	.10	.05	.03
269	Jeffrey Alan Burroughs	.10	.05	.03
270	Thomas Alan Grieve	.10	.05	.03
271	Joseph Lovitto, Jr.	.10	.05	.03
272	Frank Joseph Lucchesi	.10	.05	.03
273	David Earl Nelson	.10	.05	.03
274	Ted Lyle Simmons	.10	.05	.03
275	Louis Clark Brock	2.00	1.00	.60
276	Ronald Ray Fairly	.10	.05	.03
277	Arnold Ray (Bake) McBride	.10	.05	.03
278	Carl Reginald (Reggie) Smith	.10	.05	.03
279	William Henry Davis	.10	.05	.03
280	Kenneth John Reitz	.10	.05	.03
281	Charles William (Buddy) Bradford	.10	.05	.03
282	Luis Antonio Melendez	.10	.05	.03
283	Michael Ray Tyson	.10	.05	.03
284	Ted Crawford Sizemore	.10	.05	.03
285	Mario Miguel Guerrero	.10	.05	.03
286	Larry Lintz	.10	.05	.03
287	Kenneth Victor Rudolph	.10	.05	.03
288	Richard Arlin Billings	.10	.05	.03
289	Jerry Wayne Mumphrey	.10	.05	.03
290	Michael Sherman Wallace	.10	.05	.03
291	Alan Thomas Hrabosky	.10	.05	.03
292	Kenneth Lee Reynolds	.10	.05	.03
293	Michael Douglas Garman	.10	.05	.03
294	Robert Herbert Forsch	.10	.05	.03
295	John Allen Denny	.10	.05	.03
296	Harold R. Rasmussen	.10	.05	.03
297	Lynn Everratt McGlothen (Everett)	.10	.05	.03
298	Michael Roswell Barlow	.10	.05	.03
299	Gregory John Terlecky	.10	.05	.03
300	Albert Fred (Red) Schoendienst	1.00	.50	.30
301	Ricky Eugene Reuschel	.10	.05	.03
302	Steven Michael Stone	.10	.05	.03
303	William Gordon Bonham	.10	.05	.03
304	Oscar Joseph Zamora	.10	.05	.03
305	Kenneth Douglas Frailing	.10	.05	.03
306	Milton Edward Wilcox	.10	.05	.03
307	Darold Duane Knowles	.10	.05	.03
308	Rufus James (Jim) Marshall	.10	.05	.03
309	Bill Madlock, Jr.	.10	.05	.03
310	Jose Domec Cardenal	.10	.05	.03
311	Robert James (Rick) Monday, Jr.	.10	.05	.03
312	Julio Ruben (Jerry) Morales	.10	.05	.03
313	Timothy Kenneth Hosley	.10	.05	.03
314	Gene Taylor Hiser	.10	.05	.03
315	Donald Eulon Kessinger	.10	.05	.03
316	Jesus Manuel (Manny) Trillo	.10	.05	.03
317	Ralph Pierre (Pete) LaCock, Jr.	.10	.05	.03
318	George Eugene Mitterwald	.10	.05	.03
319	Steven Eugene Swisher	.10	.05	.03
320	Robert Walter Sperring	.10	.05	.03
321	Victor Lanier Harris	.10	.05	.03
322	Ronald Ray Dunn	.10	.05	.03
323	Jose Manuel Morales	.10	.05	.03
324	Peter MacKanin, Jr.	.10	.05	.03
325	James Charles Cox	.10	.05	.03
326	Larry Alton Parrish	.10	.05	.03
327	Michael Jorgensen	.10	.05	.03
328	Timothy John Foli	.10	.05	.03
329	Harold Noel Breeden	.10	.05	.03
330	Nathan Colbert, Jr.	.10	.05	.03
331	Jesus Maria (Pepe) Frias	.10	.05	.03
332	James Patrick (Pat) Scanlon	.10	.05	.03
333	Robert Sherwood Bailey	.10	.05	.03
334	Gary Edmund Carter	2.00	1.00	.60
335	Jose Mauel (Pepe) Mangual	.10	.05	.03
336	Lawrence David Biittner	.10	.05	.03
337	James Lawrence Lyttle, Jr.	.10	.05	.03
338	Gary Roenicke	.10	.05	.03
339	Anthony Scott	.10	.05	.03
340	Jerome Cardell White	.10	.05	.03
341	James Edward Dwyer	.10	.05	.03
342	Ellis Clarence Valentine	.10	.05	.03
343	Frederick John Scherman, Jr.	.10	.05	.03
344	Dennis Herman Blair	.10	.05	.03
345	Woodrow Thompson Fryman	.10	.05	.03
346	Charles Gilbert Taylor	.10	.05	.03
347	Daniel Dean Warthen	.10	.05	.03
348	Donald George Carrithers	.10	.05	.03
349	Stephen Douglas Rogers	.10	.05	.03
350	Dale Albert Murray	.10	.05	.03
351	Edwin Donald (Duke) Snider	3.00	1.50	.90
352	Ralph George Houk	.10	.05	.03
353	John Frederick Hiller	.10	.05	.03
354	Michael Stephen Lolich	.10	.05	.03
355	David Lawrence Lemancyzk	.10	.05	.03
356	Lerrin Harris LaGrow	.10	.05	.03
357	Fred Arroyo	.10	.05	.03
358	Joseph Howard Coleman	.10	.05	.03
359	Benjamin A. Oglivie	.10	.05	.03
360	Willie Wattison Horton	.10	.05	.03
361	John Clinton Knox	.10	.05	.03
362	Leon Kauffman Roberts	.10	.05	.03
363	Ronald LeFlore	.10	.05	.03
364	Gary Lynn Sutherland	.10	.05	.03
365	Daniel Thomas Meyer	.10	.05	.03
366	Aurelio Rodriguez	.10	.05	.03
367	Thomas Martin Veryzer	.10	.05	.03
368	Lavern Jack Pierce	.10	.05	.03
369	Eugene Richard Michael	.10	.05	.03
370	Robert (Billy) Baldwin	.10	.05	.03
371	William James Gates Brown	.10	.05	.03
372	Mitchell Jack (Mickey) Stanley	.10	.05	.03
373	Terryal Gene Humphrey	.10	.05	.03
374	Doyle Lafayette Alexander	.10	.05	.03
375	Miguel Angel (Mike) Cuellar	.10	.05	.03
376	Marcus Wayne Garland	.10	.05	.03
377	Ross Albert Grimsley III	.10	.05	.03
378	Grant Dwight Jackson	.10	.05	.03
379	Dyar K. Miller	.10	.05	.03
380	James Alvin Palmer	2.00	1.00	.60
381	Michael Augustine Torrez	.10	.05	.03
382	Michael Henry Willis	.10	.05	.03
383	David Edwin Duncan	.10	.05	.03
384	Elrod Jerome Hendricks	.10	.05	.03
385	James Neamon Hutto Jr.	.10	.05	.03
386	Robert Michael Bailor	.10	.05	.03
387	Douglas Vernon DeCinces	.10	.05	.03
388	Robert Anthony Grich	.10	.05	.03
389	Lee Andrew May	.10	.05	.03
390	Anthony Joseph Muser	.10	.05	.03
391	Timothy C. Nordbrook	.10	.05	.03
392	Brooks Calbert Robinson, Jr.	2.50	1.25	.70
393	Royle Stillman	.10	.05	.03
394	Don Edward Baylor	.10	.05	.03
395	Paul L.D. Blair	.10	.05	.03
396	Alonza Benjamin Bumbry	.10	.05	.03
397	Larry Duane Harlow	.10	.05	.03
398	Herman Thomas (Tommy) Davis, Jr.	.10	.05	.03
399	James Thomas Northrup	.10	.05	.03
400	Kenneth Wayne Singleton	.10	.05	.03
401	Thomas Michael Shopay	.10	.05	.03
402	Fredrick Michael Lynn	.75	.40	.25
403	Carlton Ernest Fisk	2.00	1.00	.60
404	Cecil Celester Cooper	.10	.05	.03
405	James Edward Rice	1.00	.50	.30
406	Juan Jose Beniquez	.10	.05	.03
407	Robert Dennis Doyle	.10	.05	.03
408	Dwight Michael Evans	.10	.05	.03
409	Carl Michael Yastrzemski	3.00	1.50	.90
410	Richard Paul Burleson	.10	.05	.03
411	Bernardo Carbo	.10	.05	.03
412	Douglas Lee Griffin, Jr.	.10	.05	.03
413	Americo P. Petrocelli	.10	.05	.03
414	Robert Edward Montgomery	.10	.05	.03
415	Timothy P. Blackwell	.10	.05	.03
416	Richard Alan Miller	.10	.05	.03
417	Darrell Dean Johnson	.10	.05	.03
418	Jim Scott Burton	.10	.05	.03
419	James Arthur Willoughby	.10	.05	.03
420	Rogelio (Roger) Moret	.10	.05	.03
421	William Francis Lee, III	.10	.05	.03
422	Richard Anthony Drago	.10	.05	.03
423	Diego Pablo Segui	.10	.05	.03
424	Luis Clemente Tiant	.10	.05	.03
425	James Augustus (Catfish) Hunter	1.50	.70	.45
426	Richard Clyde Sawyer	.10	.05	.03
427	Rudolph May Jr.	.10	.05	.03
428	Richard William Tidrow	.10	.05	.03
429	Albert Walter (Sparky) Lyle	.10	.05	.03
430	George Francis (Doc) Medich	.10	.05	.03
431	Patrick Edward Dobson, Jr.	.10	.05	.03
432	David Percy Pagan	.10	.05	.03
433	Thurman Lee Munson	2.00	1.00	.60
434	Carroll Christopher Chambliss	.10	.05	.03
435	Roy Hilton White	.10	.05	.03
436	Walter Allen Williams	.10	.05	.03
437	Graig Nettles	.10	.05	.03
438	John Rikard (Rick) Dempsey	.10	.05	.03
439	Bobby Lee Bonds	.25	.13	.08
440	Edward Martin Hermann (Herrmann)	.10	.05	.03
441	Santos Alomar	.10	.05	.03
442	Frederick Blair Stanley	.10	.05	.03
443	Terry Bertland Whitfield	.10	.05	.03
444	Richard Alan Bladt	.10	.05	.03
445	Louis Victor Piniella	.50	.25	.15
446	Richard Allen Coggins	.10	.05	.03
447	Edwin Albert Brinkman	.10	.05	.03
448	James Percy Mason	.10	.05	.03
449	Larry Murray	.10	.05	.03
450	Ronald Mark Blomberg	.10	.05	.03
451	Elliott Maddox	.10	.05	.03
452	Kerry Dineen	.10	.05	.03
453	Alfred Manuel (Billy) Martin	.50	.25	.15
454	Dave Bergman	.10	.05	.03
455	Otoniel Velez	.10	.05	.03
456	Joseph Walter Hoerner	.10	.05	.03
457	Frank Edwin (Tug) McGraw, Jr.	.10	.05	.03
458	Henry Eugene (Gene) Garber	.10	.05	.03
459	Steven Norman Carlton	2.00	1.00	.60
460	Larry Richard Christenson	.10	.05	.03
461	Thomas Gerald Underwood	.10	.05	.03
462	James Reynold Lonborg	.10	.05	.03
463	John William (Jay) Johnstone	.10	.05	.03
464	Lawrence Robert Bowa	.10	.05	.03
465	David Cash, Jr.	.10	.05	.03
466	Ollie Lee Brown	.10	.05	.03
467	Gregory Michael Luzinski	.10	.05	.03
468	Johnny Lane Oates	.10	.05	.03
469	Michael Allen Anderson	.10	.05	.03
470	Michael Jack Schmidt	4.00	2.00	1.25
471	Robert Raymond Boone	.10	.05	.03
472	Thomas George Hutton	.10	.05	.03

473	Richard Anthony Allen	.50	.25	.15
474	Antonio Taylor	.10	.05	.03
475	Jerry Lindsey Martin	.10	.05	.03
476	Daniel Leonard Ozark	.10	.05	.03
477	Richard David Ruthven	.10	.05	.03
478	James Richard Todd, Jr.	.10	.05	.03
479	Paul Aaron Lindblad	.10	.05	.03
480	Roland Glen Fingers	1.50	.70	.45
481	Vida Blue, Jr.	.10	.05	.03
482	Kenneth Dale Holtzman	.10	.05	.03
483	Richard Allen Bosman	.10	.05	.03
484	Wilfred Charles (Sonny) Siebert	.10	.05	.03
485	William Glenn Abbott	.10	.05	.03
486	Stanley Raymond Bahnsen	.10	.05	.03
487	Michael Norris	.10	.05	.03
488	Alvin Ralph Dark	.10	.05	.03
489	Claudell Washington	.10	.05	.03
490	Joseph Oden Rudi	.10	.05	.03
491	William Alex North	.10	.05	.03
492	Dagoberto Blanco (Bert) Campaneris	.10	.05	.03
493	Fury Gene Tenace	.10	.05	.03
494	Reginald Martinez Jackson	4.00	2.00	1.25
495	Philip Mason Garner	.10	.05	.03
496	Billy Leo Williams	2.00	1.00	.60
497	Salvatore Leonard Bando	.10	.05	.03
498	James William Holt	.10	.05	.03
499	Teodoro Noel Martinez	.10	.05	.03
500	Raymond Earl Fosse	.10	.05	.03
501	Matthew Alexander	.10	.05	.03
502	Wallace Larry Haney	.10	.05	.03
503	Angel Luis Mangual	.10	.05	.03
504	Fred Ray Beene	.10	.05	.03
505	Thomas William Buskey	.10	.05	.03
506	Dennis Lee Eckersley	2.00	1.00	.60
507	Roric Edward Harrison	.10	.05	.03
508	Donald Harris Hood	.10	.05	.03
509	James Lester Kern	.10	.05	.03
510	David Eugene LaRoche	.10	.05	.03
511	Fred Ingels (Fritz) Peterson	.10	.05	.03
512	James Michael Strickland	.10	.05	.03
513	Michael Richard (Rick) Waits	.10	.05	.03
514	Alan Dean Ashby	.10	.05	.03
515	John Charles Ellis	.10	.05	.03
516	Rick Cerone	.10	.05	.03
517	David Gus (Buddy) Bell	.10	.05	.03
518	John Anthony Brohamer, Jr.	.10	.05	.03
519	Ricardo Adolfo Jacobo Carty	.10	.05	.03
520	Edward Carlton Crosby	.10	.05	.03
521	Frank Thomas Duffy	.10	.05	.03
522	Duane Eugene Kuiper (Photo actually Rick Manning.)	.10	.05	.03
523	Joseph Anthony Lis	.10	.05	.03
524	John Wesley (Boog) Powell	.50	.25	.15
525	Frank Robinson	2.50	1.25	.70
526	Oscar Charles Gamble	.10	.05	.03
527	George Andrew Hendrick	.10	.05	.03
528	John Lee Lowenstein	.10	.05	.03
529	Richard Eugene Manning (photo actually Duane Kuiper)	.10	.05	.03
530	Tommy Alexander Smith	.10	.05	.03
531	Leslie Charles (Charlie) Spikes	.10	.05	.03
532	Steve Jack Kline	.10	.05	.03
533	Edward Emil Kranepool	.10	.05	.03
534	Michael Vail	.10	.05	.03
535	Delbert Bernard Unser	.10	.05	.03
536	Felix Bernardo Martinez Millan	.10	.05	.03
537	Daniel Joseph (Rusty) Staub	.25	.13	.08
538	Jesus Maria Rojas Alou	.10	.05	.03
539	Ronald Wayne Garrett	.10	.05	.03
540	Michael Dwaine Phillips	.10	.05	.03
541	Joseph Paul Torre	.10	.05	.03
542	David Arthur Kingman	.10	.05	.03
543	Eugene Anthony Clines	.10	.05	.03
544	Jack Seale Heidemann	.10	.05	.03
545	Derrel McKinley (Bud) Harrelson	.10	.05	.03
546	John Hardin Stearns	.10	.05	.03
547	John David Milner	.10	.05	.03
548	Robert John Apodaca	.10	.05	.03
549	Claude Edward (Skip) Lockwood Jr.	.10	.05	.03
550	Kenneth George Sanders	.10	.05	.03
551	George Thomas (Tom) Seaver	3.00	1.50	.90
552	Ricky Alan Baldwin	.10	.05	.03
553	Jonathan Trumpbour Matlack	.10	.05	.03
554	Henry Gaylon Webb	.10	.05	.03
555	Randall Lee Tate	.10	.05	.03
556	Tom Edward Hall	.10	.05	.03
557	George Heard Stone Jr.	.10	.05	.03
558	Craig Steven Swan	.10	.05	.03
559	Gerald Allen Cram	.10	.05	.03
560	Roy J. Staiger	.10	.05	.03
561	Kenton C. Tekulve	.10	.05	.03
562	Jerry Reuss	.10	.05	.03
563	John R. Candelaria	.10	.05	.03
564	Lawrence C. Demery	.10	.05	.03
565	David John Giusti Jr.	.10	.05	.03
566	James Phillip Rooker	.10	.05	.03
567	Ramon Gonzalez Hernandez	.10	.05	.03
568	Bruce Anthony Kison	.10	.05	.03
569	Kenneth Alven Brett (Alvin)	.10	.05	.03
570	Robert Ralph Moose Jr.	.10	.05	.03
571	Manuel Jesus Sanguillen	.10	.05	.03
572	David Gene Parker	.10	.05	.03
573	Wilver Dornel Stargell	2.00	1.00	.60
574	Richard Walter Zisk	.10	.05	.03
575	Renaldo Antonio Stennett	.10	.05	.03
576	Albert Oliver Jr.	.25	.13	.08
577	William Henry Robinson Jr.	.10	.05	.03
578	Robert Eugene Robertson	.10	.05	.03
579	Richard Joseph Hebner	.10	.05	.03
580	Edgar Leon Kirkpatrick	.10	.05	.03

581	Don Robert (Duffy) Dyer	.10	.05	.03
582	Craig Reynolds	.10	.05	.03
583	Franklin Fabian Taveras	.10	.05	.03
584	William Larry Randolph	.10	.05	.03
585	Arthur H. Howe	.10	.05	.03
586	Daniel Edward Murtaugh	.10	.05	.03
587	Charles Richard (Rich) McKinney	.10	.05	.03
588	James Edward Goodson	.10	.05	.03
589	George Brett, Al Cowans/Checklist	1.50	.70	.45
590	Keith Hernandez, Lou Brock/Checklist	.15	.08	.05
591	Jerry Koosman, Duke Snider/Checklist	.25	.13	.08
592	John Knox, Maury Wills/Checklist	.10	.05	.03
593a	Catfish Hunter, Noland Ryan/Checklist	4.00	2.00	1.25
593b	Catfish Hunter, Nolan Ryan/Checklist	3.00	1.50	.90
594	Pee Wee Reese, Ralph Branca, Carl Erskine	1.00	.50	.30
595	Willie Mays, Herb Score/Checklist	1.00	.50	.30
596	Larry Eugene Cox	.10	.05	.03
597	Eugene William Mauch	.10	.05	.03
598	William Frederick (Whitey) Wietelmann	.10	.05	.03
599	Wayne Kirby Simpson	.10	.05	.03
600	Melvin Erskine Thomason	.10	.05	.03
601	Issac Bernard (Ike) Hampton	.10	.05	.03
602	Kenneth S. Crosby	.10	.05	.03
603	Ralph Emanuel Rowe	.10	.05	.03
604	James Vernon Tyrone	.10	.05	.03
605	Michael Dennis Kelleher	.10	.05	.03
606	Mario Mendoza	.10	.05	.03
607	Michael George Rogodzinski	.10	.05	.03
608	Robert Collins Gallagher	.10	.05	.03
609	Jerry Martin Koosman	.10	.05	.03
610	Joseph Filmore Frazier	.10	.05	.03
611	Karl Kuehl	.10	.05	.03
612	Frank J. LaCorte	.10	.05	.03
613	Raymond Douglas Bare	.10	.05	.03
614	Billy Arnold Muffett	.10	.05	.03
615	William Harry Laxton	.10	.05	.03
616	Willie Howard Mays	5.00	2.50	1.50
617	Philip Joseph Cavaretta (Cavarretta)	.10	.05	.03
618	Theodore Bernard Kluszewski	.50	.25	.15
619	Elston Gene Howard	.10	.05	.03
620	Alexander Peter Grammas	.10	.05	.03
621	James Barton (Mickey) Vernon	.10	.05	.03
622	Richard Allan Sisler	.10	.05	.03
623	Harvey Haddix, Jr.	.10	.05	.03
624	Bobby Brooks Winkles	.10	.05	.03
625	John Michael Pesky	.10	.05	.03
626	James Houston Davenport	.10	.05	.03
627	David Allen Tomlin	.10	.05	.03
628	Roger Lee Craig	.10	.05	.03
629	John Joseph Amalfitano	.10	.05	.03
630	James Harrison Reese	.25	.13	.08

1975 SSPC Mets/Yankees

Team sets of the New York clubs were issued by SSPC bearing a 1975 copyright date and in the same "pure card" format as most of the company's other issues. The 2-1/2" x 3-1/2" cards have a posed color photo on front with a thin white border and no extraneous graphics - not even the player's name. Backs are printed in red and blue with personal data and a career summary, along with the player's full formal name. The checklist lists the player as he is best known. Issue price was $1.25 per team set.

		NM	EX	VG
Complete Set (45):		15.00	7.50	4.50
Common Player:		.25	.13	.08
	New York Mets Team Set:	9.00	4.50	2.75
1	John Milner	.25	.13	.08
2	Henry Webb	.25	.13	.08
3	Tom Hall	.25	.13	.08
4	Del Unser	.25	.13	.08
5	Wayne Garrett	.25	.13	.08
6	Jesus Alou	.25	.13	.08
7	Rusty Staub	.40	.20	.12
8	John Stearns	.25	.13	.08
9	Dave Kingman	.75	.40	.25
10	Ed Kranepool	.35	.20	.11
11	Cleon Jones	.40	.20	.12
12	Tom Seaver	4.00	2.00	1.25
13	George Stone	.25	.13	.08
14	Jerry Koosman	.35	.20	.11
15	Bob Apodaca	.25	.13	.08
16	Felix Millan	.25	.13	.08
17	Gene Clines	.25	.13	.08
18	Mike Phillips	.25	.13	.08

19	Yogi Berra	3.00	1.50	.90
20	Joe Torre	1.50	.70	.45
21	Jon Matlack	.25	.13	.08
22	Ricky Baldwin	.25	.13	.08
	New York Yankees Team Set:	9.00	4.50	2.75
1	Catfish Hunter	1.00	.50	.30
2	Bobby Bonds	.35	.20	.11
3	Ed Brinkman	.25	.13	.08
4	Ron Blomberg	.25	.13	.08
5	Thurman Munson	3.50	1.75	1.00
6	Roy White	.35	.20	.11
7	Larry Gura	.25	.13	.08
8	Ed Herrman	.25	.13	.08
9	Bill Virdon	.25	.13	.08
10	Elliott Maddox	.25	.13	.08
11	Lou Piniella	.50	.25	.15
12	Rick Dempsey	.25	.13	.08
13	Fred Stanley	.25	.13	.08
14	Chris Chambliss	.25	.13	.08
15	Doc Medich	.25	.13	.08
16	Pat Dobson	.25	.13	.08
17	Alex Johnson	.25	.13	.08
18	Jim Mason	.25	.13	.08
19	Sandy Alomar	.25	.13	.08
20	Graig Nettles	.50	.25	.15
21	Walt Williams	.25	.13	.08
22	Sparky Lyle	.35	.20	.11
23	Dick Tidrow	.25	.13	.08

1975 SSPC Puzzle Backs

A large black-and-white puzzle picture of Nolan Ryan and Catfish Hunter can be assembled with the backs of these cards. Fronts of the 3-9/16" x 4-1/4" cards have a color player pose with a white border. The player's name, position and team are printed at bottom. Fronts have a glossy surface. The SSPC identification only appears around the border of the puzzle. The unnumbered cards are checklisted here alphabetically. Issue price was $2.

		NM	EX	VG
Complete Set, Uncut Sheet:		40.00	20.00	12.00
Complete Set (24):		20.00	10.00	6.00
Common Player:		.30	.15	.09
(1)	Hank Aaron	4.00	2.00	1.25
(2)	Johnny Bench	1.75	.90	.50
(3)	Bobby Bonds	.35	.20	.11
(4)	Jeff Burroughs	.30	.15	.09
(5)	Rod Carew	1.75	.90	.50
(6)	Dave Cash	.30	.15	.09
(7)	Cesar Cedeno	.30	.15	.09
(8)	Bucky Dent	.30	.15	.09
(9)	Rollie Fingers	1.25	.60	.40
(10)	Steve Garvey	1.00	.50	.30
(11)	John Grubb	.30	.15	.09
(12)	Reggie Jackson	2.00	1.00	.60
(13)	Jim Kaat	.30	.15	.09
(14)	Greg Luzinski	.30	.15	.09
(15)	Fred Lynn	.50	.25	.15
(16)	Bill Madlock	.30	.15	.09
(17)	Andy Messersmith	.30	.15	.09
(18)	Thurman Munson	1.50	.70	.45
(19)	Jim Palmer	1.25	.60	.40
(20)	Dave Parker	.30	.15	.09
(21)	Jim Rice	.50	.25	.15
(22)	Pete Rose	4.00	2.00	1.25
(23)	Tom Seaver	1.75	.90	.50
(24)	Chris Speier	.30	.15	.09

1975 SSPC Superstars

 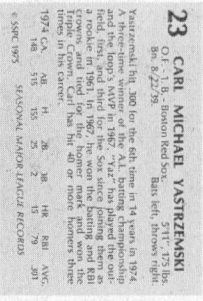

Nearly four dozen of the game's contemporary and former stars are featured in this set. Like other SSPC issues of 1975, fronts of the 2-1/2" x 3-1/2" cards have posed color photos with a white border. There are no other graphics, not even the player's name. The horizontal backs feature the player's full formal name (checklist here uses popular name) along with personal data, career summary and stats. Issue price was $4.

	NM	EX	VG
Complete Set (42):	25.00	12.50	7.50
Common Player:	.25	.13	.08
1 Wilbur Wood	.25	.13	.08
2 Johnny Sain	.25	.13	.08
3 Bill Melton	.25	.13	.08
4 Dick Allen	.50	.25	.15
5 Jim Palmer	1.00	.50	.30
6 Brooks Robinson	1.50	.70	.45
7 Tommy Davis	.25	.13	.08
8 Frank Robinson	1.50	.70	.45
9 Vada Pinson (Nolan Ryan in background of photo.)	1.00	.50	.30
10 Nolan Ryan	4.00	2.00	1.25
11 Reggie Jackson	3.00	1.50	.90
12 Vida Blue	.25	.13	.08
13 Sal Bando	.25	.13	.08
14 Bert Campaneris	.25	.13	.08
15 Tom Seaver	2.00	1.00	.60
16 Bud Harrelson	.25	.13	.08
17 Jerry Koosman	.25	.13	.08
18 Dave Nelson	.25	.13	.08
19 Ted Williams	3.50	1.75	1.00
20 Tony Oliva	.35	.20	.11
21 Mickey Lolich	.25	.13	.08
22 Amos Otis	.25	.13	.08
23 Carl Yastrzemski	2.00	1.00	.60
24 Mike Cuellar	.25	.13	.08
25 Doc Medich	.25	.13	.08
26 Cesar Cedeno	.25	.13	.08
27 Jeff Burroughs	.25	.13	.08
28 Ted Williams, Sparky Lyle	.75	.40	.25
29 Johnny Bench	2.00	1.00	.60
30 Gaylord Perry	1.00	.50	.30
31 John Mayberry	.25	.13	.08
32 Rod Carew	1.00	.50	.30
33 Whitey Ford	2.00	1.00	.60
34 Al Kaline	2.00	1.00	.60
35 Willie Mays	3.50	1.75	1.00
36 Warren Spahn	1.00	.50	.30
37 Mickey Mantle	5.00	2.50	1.50
38 Norm Cash	.35	.20	.11
39 Steve Busby	.25	.13	.08
40 Yogi Berra	2.00	1.00	.60
41 Harvey Kuenn	.25	.13	.08
42 Felipe Alou, Jesus Alou, Matty Alou	.60	.30	.20

1976 SSPC Yankees Old Timers Day

JOE DIMAGGIO

The Spring 1976 edition of "Collectors Quarterly" magazine contained a nine-card sheet of players who had appeared at an old timers' games in Yankees Stadium. The sheet could be cut into individual 2-1/2" x 3-1/2" cards with a color player photo and name on front. Backs form a black-and-white puzzle picture of Joe DiMaggio, Mickey Mantle, Whitey Ford, and Billy Martin. Cards are checklisted here alphabetically.

	NM	EX	VG
Complete Magazine:	25.00	12.50	7.50
Complete Set, Singles:	15.00	7.50	4.50
Common Player:	.35	.20	.11
(1) Earl Averill	.35	.20	.11
(2) Joe DiMaggio	6.00	3.00	1.75
(3) Tommy Henrich	.35	.20	.11
(4) Billy Herman	.35	.20	.11
(5) Monte Irvin	.35	.20	.11
(6) Jim Konstanty	.35	.20	.11
(7) Mickey Mantle	7.50	3.75	2.25
(8) Pee Wee Reese	3.00	1.50	.90
(9) Bobby Thompson (Thomson)	.50	.25	.15

1976 SSPC 1887 World Series

WORLD'S SERIES 1887
DETROIT vs. ST. LOUIS

BUSHONG, the veteran backstop, was given the task of educating young Boyle in the tricks of their trade, and did not see much action for St. Louis in the '87 series. His infrequent performances were, however, typical of his considerable excellence.

ALBERT JOHN BUSHONG has a degree in dentistry, hence his moniker "Doc." He first made the big time in 1875, joining the old Brooklyn Atlantics. He was then bought for Philadelphia, Worcester, Cleveland, and the Browns, hitting that club in '80. '87 saw him bat .288 in 14 contests, while enjoying a huge. Bushong has gone to Brooklyn for 1888, where he will likely split the backstopping with the incumbent, Peoples. Never a strong hitter, he has made himself very valuable with the canny pitch calling and agile fielding in back of the bat, and his willingness to have a go at other positions.

A.J. Bushong   C   NO. 13 of 18   SSPC 1976

The history of the 1887 "World Series" between the Detroit Wolverines of the National League and the St. Louis Browns of the American Association is told on the backs of this collector's issue. The 2-1/2" x 3-1/2" cards were printed on a pair of uncut sheets inserted in the Fall 1976 issue of "Collectors Quarterly" magazine. Fronts of the cards reproduce in full color the Scrapps tobacco die-cut cards originally issued in 1888. Backs recount the individual players' performances in the series as well as giving a career summary; they are printed in red and black. Detroit won the Series, a best-of-15 contest.

		NM	EX	VG
Complete Magazine:		15.00	7.50	4.50
Complete Set, Singles:		12.00	6.00	3.50
Common Player:		.75	.40	.25
1	Bob Caruthers	.75	.40	.25
2	David Foutz	.75	.40	.25
3	W.A. Latham	.75	.40	.25
4	Charles H. Getzin (Getzien)	.75	.40	.25
5	J.C. Rowe	.75	.40	.25
6	Fred Dunlap	.75	.40	.25
7	James O'Neill	.75	.40	.25
8	Curtis Welch	.75	.40	.25
9	William Gleason	.75	.40	.25
10	Sam Thompson	.75	.40	.25
11	Ned Hanlon	.75	.40	.25
12	Dan Brothers (Brouthers)	.75	.40	.25
13	Albert Bushong	.75	.40	.25
14	Charles Comiskey	.75	.40	.25
15	Wm. Robinson	.75	.40	.25
16	Charles Bennett	.75	.40	.25
17	Hardy Richardson	.75	.40	.25
18	Deacon White	.75	.40	.25

1976 SSPC 1963 New York Mets

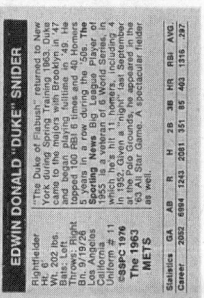

EDWIN DONALD "DUKE" SNIDER

The Duke of Flatbush" returned to New York including Sporting News' rating back when came to the majors with Brooklyn in '47 and began enjoying fulltime in '49 his 5 years in a row during the '50s. The Sporting News Big League Player of which he's hit 11 homers, including 4 in 1952. Given a "night" last September in 1952. His 40 HR in '53 with 4 '63 All Star Game. A spectacular fielder as well.

Rightfielder
Wt. 202 lbs.
Bats: Left
Throws: Left
Bn. 9/19/26
Los Angeles
Uniform #11
#SSPC 1976
The 1963
METS

Statistics GA	AB	R	H	2B	3B	HR	RBI	AVG
Career 2052	6994	1243	2061	351	85	463	1316	.297

Issued in the Summer 1976 issue of "Collectors Quarterly" magazine as a two-page uncut sheet, this 18-card issue features the 1963 Mets. Like contemporary collectors' issues from SSPC, the cards feature white-bordered color photos on front with no other graphics or player identification. Backs are printed in black-and-white, contain player biographical data, a career summary and uniform number, by which the checklist is arranged. Size is standard 2-1/2" x 3-1/2".

		NM	EX	VG
Complete Magazine:		25.00	12.50	7.50
Complete Set, Singles (18):		15.00	7.50	4.50
Common Player:		1.00	.50	.30
1	Duke Carmel	1.00	.50	.30
5	Norman Burt Sherry	1.00	.50	.30
7	Casey Stengel	5.00	2.50	1.50
9	Jim Hickman	1.00	.50	.30
10	Rod Kanehl	1.00	.50	.30
11	Duke Snider	7.50	3.75	2.25
12	Jesse Gonder	1.00	.50	.30
16	Dick Smith	1.00	.50	.30
17	Clarence Coleman	1.00	.50	.30
18	Pumpsie Green	1.00	.50	.30
23	Joe Christopher	1.00	.50	.30
36	Tracy Stallard	1.00	.50	.30
39	Steve Dillon	1.00	.50	.30
40	Rich Moran	1.00	.50	.30
41	Grover Powell	1.00	.50	.30
43	Ted Schreiber	1.00	.50	.30
53	Ernest White	1.00	.50	.30
56	Ed Bauta	1.00	.50	.30

1978 SSPC All-Star Gallery

AMERICAN LEAGUE   BOSTON RED SOX   Uniform No. 34

DONALD WILLIAM (ZIM) ZIMMER
Manager–Throws (R)–Bats (R)
Ht. 5'9 Wt. 185 Bn. 1/17/31

The Red Sox had one of their most successful seasons in years in '77. Don's 1st as Boston manager. The 97 wins was the most since the .46 pennant winner and they went down to the last game of the season before being eliminated. Zim's record of 139–98 (.586) is 5th best among all-time Sox skippers. Beginning a 12-year M.L. career in '54, Don played with the Dodgers, Cubs, Mets, Reds and Senators. He was out for a year in his '56–'57 after being hit with a pitch in the cheek. Since his return, he has been noted as one of baseball's most courageous players.

© 1978 SSPC   0179

A series of team "Photo Fact Cards" was produced by Sports Stars Publishing Co., for insertion into its 48-page "All Star Gallery" magazine, sold for $2. Fully licensed by MLB and the players' union, the 27 cards in each team set are printed on a triple-fold 24" x 10-7/8" cardboard sheet stapled into the center of the magazine. Fronts are full color poses with no extraneous graphics. Backs are in black-and-white with a few vital data, a career summary, uniform number and a card number from within the overall issue of 270. Only eight teams are represented in the All-Star Gallery magazine series. The Yankees (#001-027) and Phillies cards (#028-054) issued with other magazines that year may be considered part of the All-Star Gallery issue.

	NM	EX	VG
Complete Set, Magazines (8):	135.00	65.00	40.00
Complete Set, Singles (216):	125.00	60.00	35.00
Common Player:	.50	.25	.15
Los Angeles Dodgers magazine:	15.00	7.50	4.50
0055 Burt Hooton	.50	.25	.15
0056 Bill Russell	.50	.25	.15
0057 Dusty Baker	.60	.30	.20
0058 Reggie Smith	.50	.25	.15
0059 Dick Rhoden	.50	.25	.15
0060 Jerry Grote	.50	.25	.15
0061 Bill Butler	.50	.25	.15
0062 Ron Cey	.50	.25	.15
0063 Ron Cey	.50	.25	.15
0064 Ted Martinez	.50	.25	.15
0065 Ed Goodson	.50	.25	.15
0066 Vic Davalillo	.50	.25	.15
0067 Davey Lopes	.50	.25	.15
0068 Terry Forster	.50	.25	.15
0069 Lee Lacy	.50	.25	.15
0070 Mike Garman	.50	.25	.15
0071 Steve Garvey	1.50	.70	.45
0072 Johnny Oates	.50	.25	.15
0073 Steve Yeager	.50	.25	.15
0074 Rafael Landestoy	.50	.25	.15
0075 Tommy John	.60	.30	.20
0076 Glenn Burke	.50	.25	.15
0077 Rick Monday	.50	.25	.15
0078 Doug Rau	.50	.25	.15
0079 Manny Mota	.50	.25	.15
0080 Don Sutton	2.00	1.00	.60
0081 Charlie Hough	.50	.25	.15
Texas Rangers Magazine:	12.50	6.25	3.75
0082 Mike Hargrove	.50	.25	.15
0083 Jim Sundberg	.50	.25	.15
0084 Fergie Jenkins	2.00	1.00	.60
0085 Paul Lindblad	.50	.25	.15
0086 Sandy Alomar	.50	.25	.15
0087 John Lowenstein	.50	.25	.15
0088 Claudell Washington	.50	.25	.15
0089 Toby Harrah	.50	.25	.15
0090 Jim Umbarger	.50	.25	.15
0091 Len Barker	.50	.25	.15
0092 Dave May	.50	.25	.15
0093 Kurt Bevacqua	.50	.25	.15
0094 Jim Mason	.50	.25	.15
0095 Bump Wills	.50	.25	.15
0096 Dock Ellis	.50	.25	.15
0097 Bill Fahey	.50	.25	.15
0098 Richie Zisk	.50	.25	.15
0099 Jon Matlack	.50	.25	.15
0100 John Ellis	.50	.25	.15
0101 Bert Campaneris	.50	.25	.15
0102 Doc Medich	.50	.25	.15
0103 Juan Beniquez	.50	.25	.15
0104 Bill Hunter	.50	.25	.15
0105 Doyle Alexander	.50	.25	.15
0106 Roger Moret	.50	.25	.15
0107 Mike Jorgensen	.50	.25	.15
0108 Al Oliver	.60	.30	.20
Cincinnati Reds Magazine:	15.00	7.50	4.50
0109 Fred Norman	.50	.25	.15
0110 Ray Knight	.50	.25	.15
0111 Pedro Borbon	.50	.25	.15
0112 Bill Bonham	.50	.25	.15
0113 George Foster	.60	.30	.20
0114 Doug Bair	.50	.25	.15
0115 Cesar Geronimo	.50	.25	.15
0116 Tom Seaver	3.50	1.75	1.00
0117 Mario Soto	.50	.25	.15
0118 Ken Griffey	.50	.25	.15
0119 Mike Lum	.50	.25	.15
0120 Tom Hume	.50	.25	.15
0121 Joe Morgan	2.50	1.25	.70
0122 Manny Sarmiento	.50	.25	.15
0123 Dan Driessen	.50	.25	.15
0124 Ed Armbrister	.50	.25	.15
0125 John Summers	.50	.25	.15
0126 Fred Auerbach	.50	.25	.15
0127 Doug Capilla	.50	.25	.15
0128 Johnny Bench	3.50	1.75	1.00
0129 Sparky Anderson	1.50	.70	.45
0130 Raul Ferreyra	.50	.25	.15
0131 Dale Murray	.50	.25	.15
0132 Pete Rose	7.50	3.75	2.25
0133 Dave Concepcion	.50	.25	.15
0134 Junior Kennedy	.50	.25	.15
0135 Dave Collins	.50	.25	.15
Chicago White Sox Magazine:	12.50	6.25	3.75
0136 Mike Eden	.50	.25	.15
0137 Lamar Johnson	.50	.25	.15
0138 Ron Schueler	.50	.25	.15
0139 Bob Lemon	.75	.40	.25
0140 Thad Bosley	.50	.25	.15
0141 Bobby Bonds	.60	.30	.20
0142 Wilbur Wood	.50	.25	.15

		NM	EX	VG
0143	Jorge Orta	.50	.25	.15
0144	Francisco Barrios	.50	.25	.15
0145	Greg Pryor	.50	.25	.15
0146	Chet Lemon	.50	.25	.15
0147	Mike Squires	.50	.25	.15
0148	Eric Soderholm	.50	.25	.15
0149	Reggie Sanders	.50	.25	.15
0150	Kevin Bell	.50	.25	.15
0151	Alan Bannister	.50	.25	.15
0152	Henry Cruz	.50	.25	.15
0153	Larry Doby	2.00	1.00	.60
0154	Don Kessinger	.50	.25	.15
0155	Ralph Garr	.50	.25	.15
0156	Bill Nahorodny	.50	.25	.15
0157	Ron Blomberg	.50	.25	.15
0158	Bob Molinaro	.50	.25	.15
0159	Junior Moore	.50	.25	.15
0160	Minnie Minoso	1.50	.70	.45
0161	Lerrin LaGrow	.50	.25	.15
0162	Wayne Nordhagen	.50	.25	.15
	Boston Red Sox Magazine:	20.00	10.00	6.00
0163	Ramon Aviles	.50	.25	.15
0164	Bob Stanley	.50	.25	.15
0165	Reggie Cleveland	.50	.25	.15
0166	John Brohamer	.50	.25	.15
0167	Bill Lee	.50	.25	.15
0168	Jim Burton	.50	.25	.15
0169	Bill Campbell	.50	.25	.15
0170	Mike Torrez	.50	.25	.15
0171	Dick Drago	.50	.25	.15
0172	Butch Hobson	.50	.25	.15
0173	Bob Bailey	.50	.25	.15
0174	Fred Lynn	.50	.25	.15
0175	Rick Burleson	.50	.25	.15
0176	Luis Tiant	.50	.25	.15
0177	Ted Williams	6.00	3.00	1.75
0178	Dennis Eckersley	2.00	1.00	.60
0179	Don Zimmer	.50	.25	.15
0180	Carlton Fisk	2.50	1.25	.70
0181	Dwight Evans	.50	.25	.15
0182	Fred Kendall	.50	.25	.15
0183	George Scott	.50	.25	.15
0184	Frank Duffy	.50	.25	.15
0185	Bernie Carbo	.50	.25	.15
0186	Jerry Remy	.50	.25	.15
0187	Carl Yastrzemski	4.00	2.00	1.25
0188	Allen Ripley	.50	.25	.15
0189	Jim Rice	.90	.45	.25
	California Angels Magazine:	20.00	10.00	6.00
0190	Ken Landreaux	.50	.25	.15
0191	Paul Hartzell	.50	.25	.15
0192	Ken Brett	.50	.25	.15
0193	Dave Garcia	.50	.25	.15
0194	Bobby Grich	.50	.25	.15
0195	Lyman Bostock	.50	.25	.15
0196	Isaac Hampton	.50	.25	.15
0197	Dave LaRoche	.50	.25	.15
0198	Dave Chalk	.50	.25	.15
0199	Rick Miller	.50	.25	.15
0200	Floyd Rayford	.50	.25	.15
0201	Willie Aikens	.50	.25	.15
0202	Balor Moore	.50	.25	.15
0203	Nolan Ryan	10.00	5.00	3.00
0204	Dan Goodwin	.50	.25	.15
0205	Ron Fairly	.50	.25	.15
0206	Dyar Miller	.50	.25	.15
0207	Carney Lansford	.50	.25	.15
0208	Don Baylor	.60	.30	.20
0209	Gil Flores	.50	.25	.15
0210	Terry Humphrey	.50	.25	.15
0211	Frank Tanana	.50	.25	.15
0212	Chris Knapp	.50	.25	.15
0213	Ron Jackson	.50	.25	.15
0214	Joe Rudi	.50	.25	.15
0215	Tony Solaita	.50	.25	.15
0216	Steve Mulliniks	.50	.25	.15
	Kansas City Royals Magazine:	20.00	10.00	6.00
0217	George Brett	6.00	3.00	1.75
0218	Doug Bird	.50	.25	.15
0219	Hal McRae	.50	.25	.15
0220	Dennis Leonard	.50	.25	.15
0221	Darrell Porter	.50	.25	.15
0222	Randy McGilberry	.50	.25	.15
0223	Pete LaCock	.50	.25	.15
0224	Whitey Herzog	.50	.25	.15
0225	Andy Hassler	.50	.25	.15
0226	Joe Lahoud	.50	.25	.15
0227	Amos Otis	.50	.25	.15
0228	Al Hrabosky	.50	.25	.15
0229	Clint Hurdle	.50	.25	.15
0230	Paul Splittorff	.50	.25	.15
0231	Marty Pattin	.50	.25	.15
0232	Frank White	.50	.25	.15
0233	John Wathan	.50	.25	.15
0234	Freddie Patek	.50	.25	.15
0235	Rich Gale	.50	.25	.15
0236	U.L. Washington	.50	.25	.15
0237	Larry Gura	.50	.25	.15
0238	Jim Colborn	.50	.25	.15
0239	Tom Poquette	.50	.25	.15
0240	Al Cowens	.50	.25	.15
0241	Willie Wilson	.50	.25	.15
0242	Steve Mingori	.50	.25	.15
0243	Jerry Terrell	.50	.25	.15
	Chicago Cubs magazine:	12.50	6.25	3.75
0244	Larry Biittner	.50	.25	.15
0245	Rick Reuschel	.50	.25	.15
0246	Dave Rader	.50	.25	.15
0247	Paul Reuschel	.50	.25	.15
0248	Hector Cruz	.50	.25	.15
0249	Woody Fryman	.50	.25	.15
0250	Steve Ontiveros	.50	.25	.15
0251	Mike Gordon	.50	.25	.15
0252	Dave Kingman	.50	.25	.15
0253	Gene Clines	.50	.25	.15
0254	Bruce Sutter	2.00	1.00	.60
0255	Guillermo Hernandez	.50	.25	.15
0256	Ivan DeJesus	.50	.25	.15

		NM	EX	VG
0257	Greg Gross	.50	.25	.15
0258	Larry Cox	.50	.25	.15
0259	Joe Wallis	.50	.25	.15
0260	Dennis Lamp	.50	.25	.15
0261	Ray Burris	.50	.25	.15
0262	Bill Caudill	.50	.25	.15
0263	Donnie Moore	.50	.25	.15
0264	Bill Buckner	.60	.30	.20
0265	Bobby Murcer	.60	.30	.20
0266	Dave Roberts	.50	.25	.15
0267	Mike Krukow	.50	.25	.15
0268	Herman Franks	.50	.25	.15
0269	Mike Kelleher	.50	.25	.15
0270	Rudy Meoli	.50	.25	.15

1978 SSPC Baseball the Phillies Way

This team set was produced on a tri-fold insert in an SSPC magazine titled, "Baseball the Phillies Way." The magazine offered playing tips. Cards are in the contemporary SSPC format of a posed front photo with a white border and no other graphics. Backs are printed in red, white and black with player ID, career data and card numbers between 0028-0054, continuing the sequence begun with the Yankees yearbook team set which continues with the All-Star Gallery set. Cards could be cut from the sheets into 2-1/2" x 3-1/2" singles.

		NM	EX	VG
	Complete Magazine:	15.00	7.50	4.50
	Complete Set, Singles (27):	12.00	6.00	3.50
	Common Player:	.50	.25	.15
0028	Garry Maddox	.50	.25	.15
0029	Steve Carlton	2.50	1.25	.70
0030	Ron Reed	.50	.25	.15
0031	Greg Luzinski	.50	.25	.15
0032	Bobby Wine	.50	.25	.15
0033	Bob Boone	1.50	.70	.45
0034	Carroll Beringer	.50	.25	.15
0035	Dick Hebner	.50	.25	.15
0036	Ray Rippelmeyer	.50	.25	.15
0037	Terry Harmon	.50	.25	.15
0038	Gene Garber	.50	.25	.15
0039	Ted Sizemore	.50	.25	.15
0040	Barry Foote	.50	.25	.15
0041	Tony Taylor	.50	.25	.15
0042	Tug McGraw	.75	.40	.25
0043	Jay Johnstone	.65	.35	.20
0044	Randy Lerch	.50	.25	.15
0045	Billy DeMars	.50	.25	.15
0046	Mike Schmidt	5.00	2.50	1.50
0047	Larry Christenson	.50	.25	.15
0048	Tim McCarver	1.00	.50	.30
0049	Larry Bowa	.65	.35	.20
0050	Danny Ozark	.50	.25	.15
0051	Jerry Martin	.50	.25	.15
0052	Jim Lonborg	.50	.25	.15
0053	Bake McBride	.50	.25	.15
0054	Warren Brusstar	.50	.25	.15

1978 SSPC Yankees Yearbook

This team set was printed on a tri-fold insert found both in the 1978 Yankees yearbook and a magazine titled "Diary of a Champion Yankee," produced by SSPC. The nine cards on each sheet could be cut apart into 2-1/2" x 3-1/2" singles. Cards follow the basic SSPC format of a posed color photo on front with a white border and no graphic elements. Backs have player identification, career summary and "CHAMPIONSHIP SEASON" highlights, printed

in black and blue on white. Cards are numbered from 0001-0027, and may be considered part of the larger All-Star Gallery issue.

		NM	EX	VG
	Complete Magazine:	12.50	6.25	3.75
	Complete Set, Singles (27):	10.00	5.00	3.00
	Common Player:	.50	.25	.15
0001	Thurman Munson	3.00	1.50	.90
0002	Cliff Johnson	.50	.25	.15
0003	Lou Piniella	.75	.40	.25
0004	Dell Alston	.50	.25	.15
0005	Yankee Stadium	1.00	.50	.30
0006	Ken Holtzman	.50	.25	.15
0007	Chris Chambliss	.50	.25	.15
0008	Roy White	.60	.30	.20
0009	Ed Figueroa	.50	.25	.15
0010	Dick Tidrow	.50	.25	.15
0011	Sparky Lyle	.60	.30	.20
0012	Fred Stanley	.50	.25	.15
0013	Mickey Rivers	.50	.25	.15
0014	Billy Martin	.75	.40	.25
0015	George Zeber	.50	.25	.15
0016	Ken Clay	.50	.25	.15
0017	Ron Guidry	.75	.40	.25
0018	Don Gullett	.50	.25	.15
0019	Fran Healy	.50	.25	.15
0020	Paul Blair	.50	.25	.15
0021	Mickey Klutts	.50	.25	.15
0022	Yankee Team	.50	.25	.15
0023	Catfish Hunter	1.50	.70	.45
0024	Bucky Dent	.75	.40	.25
0025	Graig Nettles	.75	.40	.25
0026	Reggie Jackson	3.00	1.50	.90
0027	Willie Randolph	.60	.30	.20

1889 "The Stage" Stars of the Diamond

Titled "Stars of the Diamond" and issued weekly between May 25-Aug. 31, 1889, these numbered supplements were printed in "The Stage" newspaper, a Philadelphia-based publication. Two types of supplements are found, those picturing New York players in uniforms (from Joseph Hall photos), and those picturing members of the Philadelphia National League and American Association teams in street clothes. The black-and-white portraits are printed in a 9" x 12" format on newsprint, making surviving examples very rare today.

		NM	EX	VG
	Common Player:	250.00	125.00	75.00
1	Charles Buffington	250.00	125.00	75.00
2	John Clements	250.00	125.00	75.00
3	Harry D. Stovey	250.00	125.00	75.00
4	"Gus" Weyhing	250.00	125.00	75.00
5	L.M. Cross	250.00	125.00	75.00
6	Edward Seward	250.00	125.00	75.00
7	Wm. Robinson (Wilbert)	375.00	185.00	110.00
8	Denny Lyons	375.00	185.00	110.00
9	A.B. Sanders	250.00	125.00	75.00
10	William Schriver	250.00	125.00	75.00
11	Daniel M. Casey	250.00	125.00	75.00
12	"Tim" Keefe	375.00	185.00	110.00
13	"Buck" Ewing	375.00	185.00	110.00
14	John Ward	375.00	185.00	110.00

1953 Stahl-Meyer Franks

These nine cards, issued in packages of hot dogs by a New York area meat company, feature three players from each of the New York teams of the day - Dodgers Giants and Yankees. Cards in the set measure 3-1/4" x 4-1/2". The card fronts in this unnumbered set feature color photos with player name and facsimile autograph. The backs list both biographical and statistical information on half the card and a ticket offer promotion on the other half. The card corners are cut diagonally, although some cards (apparantly cut from sheets) with square corners have been seen. Cards are white-bordered.

		NM	EX	VG
	Complete Set (9):	20,000	9,000	4,000
	Common Player:	500.00	225.00	100.00
(1)	Hank Bauer	550.00	245.00	110.00
(2)	Roy Campanella	2,000	900.00	400.00
(3)	Gil Hodges	1,250	560.00	250.00
(4)	Monte Irvin	750.00	335.00	150.00
(5)	Whitey Lockman	500.00	225.00	100.00
(6)	Mickey Mantle	13,500	6,100	2,750
(7)	Phil Rizzuto	1,250	560.00	250.00
(8)	Duke Snider	2,000	900.00	400.00
(9)	Bobby Thomson	650.00	290.00	130.00

1954 Stahl-Meyer Franks

 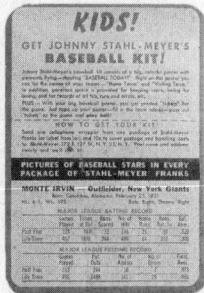

The 1954 set of Stahl-Meyer Franks was increased to 12 cards which retained the 3-1/4" x 4-1/2" size. The most prominent addition to the '54 set was New York Giants slugger Willie Mays. The card fronts are identical in format to the previous year's set. However, the backs are different as they are designed on a vertical format. The backs also contain an advertisement for a "Johnny Stahl-Meyer Baseball Kit." The cards in the set are unnumbered.

		NM	EX	VG
Complete Set (12):		30,000	13,500	6,000
Common Player:		650.00	290.00	130.00
(1)	Hank Bauer	750.00	335.00	150.00
(2)	Carl Erskine	750.00	335.00	150.00
(3)	Gil Hodges	2,000	900.00	400.00
(4)	Monte Irvin	1,000	450.00	200.00
(5)	Whitey Lockman	650.00	290.00	130.00
(6)	Gil McDougald	750.00	335.00	150.00
(7)	Mickey Mantle	12,000	5,400	2,400
(8)	Willie Mays	8,500	3,825	1,700
(9)	Don Mueller	650.00	290.00	130.00
(10)	Don Newcombe	750.00	335.00	150.00
(11)	Phil Rizzuto	2,000	900.00	400.00
(12)	Duke Snider	2,000	900.00	400.00

1955 Stahl-Meyer Franks

 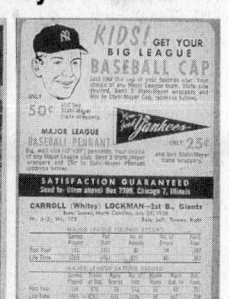

Eleven of the 12 players in the 1955 set are the same as those featured in 1954. The exception is the New York Giants Dusty Rhodes, who replaced Willie Mays on the 3-1/4" x 4-1/2" cards. The card fronts are again full-color photos bordered in yellow with diagonal corners, and four players from each of the three New York teams are featured. The backs offer a new promotion, with a drawing of Mickey Mantle and advertisements selling pennants and caps. Player statistics are still included on the vertical card backs. The cards in the set are unnumbered.

		NM	EX	VG
Complete Set (12):		20,000	9,000	4,000
Common Player:		500.00	225.00	100.00
(1)	Hank Bauer	600.00	275.00	125.00
(2)	Carl Erskine	600.00	275.00	125.00
(3)	Gil Hodges	1,500	675.00	300.00
(4)	Monte Irvin	800.00	360.00	160.00
(5)	Whitey Lockman	500.00	225.00	100.00
(6)	Mickey Mantle	12,000	5,400	2,400
(7)	Gil McDougald	600.00	275.00	125.00
(8)	Don Mueller	500.00	225.00	100.00
(9)	Don Newcombe	600.00	275.00	125.00
(10)	Jim Rhodes	500.00	225.00	100.00
(11)	Phil Rizzuto	1,500	675.00	300.00
(12)	Duke Snider	1,500	675.00	300.00

1916 Standard Biscuit (D350-1)

The range of cards in this issue is uncertain as examples can be found corresponding to the checklists of both of the 1916 sets known as M101-5 and M101-4 Blank Backs. Standard Biscuit cards in this format are also known that correspond to neither M101-5 nor M101-4. The approximately 1-5/8" x 3" black-and-white cards usually command a modest premium from collectors seeking to enhance a type collection or superstar collection. A trial checklist is begun herewith.

HAROLD JANVRIN
S.S.—Boston Red Sox

		NM	EX	VG
Common Player:		90.00	45.00	30.00
1	Babe Adams	90.00	45.00	30.00
3	Ed Ainsmith	90.00	45.00	30.00
6	Jimmy Archer	90.00	45.00	30.00
12	Beals Becker	90.00	45.00	30.00
13	Joe Benz	90.00	45.00	30.00
14	Bob Bescher	90.00	45.00	30.00
15	Al Betzel	90.00	45.00	30.00
18	Eddie Burns	90.00	45.00	30.00
27	George Chalmers	90.00	45.00	30.00
37	Joe Connolly	90.00	45.00	30.00
39	Harry Coveleskie (Coveleski)	90.00	45.00	30.00
42	Sam Crawford	400.00	200.00	130.00
48	William Doak	90.00	45.00	30.00
50	Charles Dooin	90.00	45.00	30.00
60	Max Flack	90.00	45.00	30.00
61	Art Fletcher	90.00	45.00	30.00
63	Jacques Fournier	90.00	45.00	30.00
64	"Chic" Gandil	900.00	450.00	300.00
66	Joe Gedeon	90.00	45.00	30.00
68	George Gibson	90.00	45.00	30.00
69	Wilbur Good	90.00	45.00	30.00
71	John Graney	90.00	45.00	30.00
72	Tom Griffith	90.00	45.00	30.00
73	Heinie Groh	90.00	45.00	30.00
75	Bob Harmon	90.00	45.00	30.00
77	Claude Hendrix	90.00	45.00	30.00
79	John Henry	90.00	45.00	30.00
80	Buck Herzog	90.00	45.00	30.00
82	Dick Hoblitzell	90.00	45.00	30.00
84	Ivan Howard	90.00	45.00	30.00
87	Joe Jackson	10,000	5,000	3,300
89	Hugh Jennings	400.00	200.00	130.00
131	Les Nunamaker	90.00	45.00	30.00
137	E.J. Pfeffer	90.00	45.00	30.00
164	Ernie Shore	90.00	45.00	30.00
172a	Milton Stock	90.00	45.00	30.00
172b	Billy Sullivan	90.00	45.00	30.00
176	Jim Thorpe	17,500	8,750	5,775
186	Bobby Wallace	600.00	300.00	200.00
191	Fred Williams	90.00	45.00	30.00
195	Joe Wood	350.00	175.00	115.00
196	Joe Wood	350.00	175.00	115.00
199	Heiny Zimmerman	90.00	45.00	30.00

1917 Standard Biscuit (D350-2)

BOBBIE BYRNE
3rd B.—Philadelphia Nationals
23

The 200 cards in this set are more commonly found with the advertising of Collins-McCarthy Candy Co. on the back. The cards measure about 2" x 3-1/4" and are printed in black-and-white. Though the Standard Biscuit cards are scarcer than the Collins-McCarthy version, collectors do not attach much premium to them.

		NM	EX	VG
Complete Set (200):		70,000	35,000	21,000
Common Player:		150.00	75.00	45.00
1	Sam Agnew	150.00	75.00	45.00
2	Grover Alexander	600.00	300.00	180.00
3	W.S. Alexander (W.E.)	150.00	75.00	45.00
4	Leon Ames	150.00	75.00	45.00
5	Fred Anderson	150.00	75.00	45.00
6	Ed Appleton	150.00	75.00	45.00
7	Jimmy Archer	150.00	75.00	45.00
8	Jimmy Austin	150.00	75.00	45.00
9	Jim Bagby	150.00	75.00	45.00
10	H.D. Baird	150.00	75.00	45.00
11	J. Franklin Baker	350.00	175.00	100.00
12	Dave Bancroft	350.00	175.00	100.00
13	Jack Barry	150.00	75.00	45.00
14	Joe Benz	150.00	75.00	45.00
15	Al Betzel	150.00	75.00	45.00
16	Ping Bodie	150.00	75.00	45.00
17	Joe Boehling	150.00	75.00	45.00
18	Eddie Burns	150.00	75.00	45.00
19	George Burns	150.00	75.00	45.00
20	Geo. J. Burns	150.00	75.00	45.00
21	Joe Bush	150.00	75.00	45.00
22	Owen Bush	150.00	75.00	45.00
23	Bobby Byrne	150.00	75.00	45.00
24	Forrest Cady	150.00	75.00	45.00
25	Max Carey	350.00	175.00	100.00
26	Ray Chapman	200.00	100.00	60.00
27	Larry Cheney	150.00	75.00	45.00
28	Eddie Cicotte	450.00	225.00	135.00
29	Tom Clarke	150.00	75.00	45.00
30	Ty Cobb	4,500	2,250	1,350
31	Eddie Collins	350.00	175.00	100.00
32	"Shauno" Collins (Shano)	150.00	75.00	45.00
33	Fred Coumbe	150.00	75.00	45.00
34	Harry Coveleskie (Coveleski)	150.00	75.00	45.00
35	Gavvy Cravath	150.00	75.00	45.00
36	Sam Crawford	350.00	175.00	100.00
37	Geo. Cutshaw	150.00	75.00	45.00
38	Jake Daubert	150.00	75.00	45.00
39	Geo. Dauss	150.00	75.00	45.00
40	Charles Deal	150.00	75.00	45.00
41	"Wheezer" Dell	150.00	75.00	45.00
42	William Doak	150.00	75.00	45.00
43	Bill Donovan	150.00	75.00	45.00
44	Larry Doyle	150.00	75.00	45.00
45	Johnny Evers	350.00	175.00	100.00
46	Urban Faber	350.00	175.00	100.00
47	"Hap" Felsch	750.00	375.00	225.00
48	Bill Fischer	150.00	75.00	45.00
49	Ray Fisher	150.00	75.00	45.00
50	Art Fletcher	150.00	75.00	45.00
51	Eddie Foster	150.00	75.00	45.00
52	Jacques Fournier	150.00	75.00	45.00
53	Del Gainer (Gainor)	150.00	75.00	45.00
54	Bert Gallia	150.00	75.00	45.00
55	"Chic" Gandil (Chick)	450.00	225.00	135.00
56	Larry Gardner	150.00	75.00	45.00
57	Joe Gedeon	150.00	75.00	45.00
58	Gus Getz	150.00	75.00	45.00
59	Frank Gilhooley	150.00	75.00	45.00
60	Wm. Gleason	150.00	75.00	45.00
61	M.A. Gonzales (Gonzalez)	165.00	80.00	50.00
62	Hank Gowdy	150.00	75.00	45.00
63	John Graney	150.00	75.00	45.00
64	Tom Griffith	150.00	75.00	45.00
65	Heinie Groh	150.00	75.00	45.00
66	Bob Groom	150.00	75.00	45.00
67	Louis Guisto	150.00	75.00	45.00
68	Earl Hamilton	150.00	75.00	45.00
69	Harry Harper	150.00	75.00	45.00
70	Grover Hartley	150.00	75.00	45.00
71	Harry Heilmann	350.00	175.00	100.00
72	Claude Hendrix	150.00	75.00	45.00
73	Olaf Henriksen	150.00	75.00	45.00
74	John Henry	150.00	75.00	45.00
75	"Buck" Herzog	150.00	75.00	45.00
76	Hugh High	150.00	75.00	45.00
77	Dick Hoblitzell	150.00	75.00	45.00
78	Walter Holke	150.00	75.00	45.00
79	Harry Hooper	350.00	175.00	100.00
80	Rogers Hornsby	650.00	325.00	195.00
81	Ivan Howard	150.00	75.00	45.00
82	Joe Jackson	15,000	7,500	4,500
83	Harold Janvrin	150.00	75.00	45.00
84	William James	150.00	75.00	45.00
85	C. Jamieson	150.00	75.00	45.00
86	Hugh Jennings	350.00	175.00	100.00
87	Walter Johnson	750.00	375.00	225.00
88	James Johnston	150.00	75.00	45.00
89	Fielder Jones	150.00	75.00	45.00
90	Joe Judge	150.00	75.00	45.00
91	Hans Lobert	150.00	75.00	45.00
92	Benny Kauff	150.00	75.00	45.00
93	Wm. Killefer Jr.	150.00	75.00	45.00
94	Ed. Konetchy	150.00	75.00	45.00
95	John Lavan	150.00	75.00	45.00
96	Jimmy Lavender	150.00	75.00	45.00
97	"Nemo" Leibold	150.00	75.00	45.00
98	H.B. Leonard	150.00	75.00	45.00
99	Duffy Lewis	150.00	75.00	45.00
100	Tom Long	150.00	75.00	45.00
101	Wm. Louden	150.00	75.00	45.00
102	Fred Luderus	150.00	75.00	45.00
103	Lee Magee	150.00	75.00	45.00
104	Sherwood Magee	150.00	75.00	45.00
105	Al Mamaux	150.00	75.00	45.00
106	Leslie Mann	150.00	75.00	45.00
107	"Rabbit" Maranville	350.00	175.00	100.00
108	Rube Marquard	350.00	175.00	100.00
109	Armando Marsans	165.00	85.00	50.00
110	J. Erskine Mayer	175.00	85.00	50.00
111	George McBride	150.00	75.00	45.00
112	Lew McCarty	150.00	75.00	45.00
113	John J. McGraw	350.00	175.00	100.00
114	Jack McInnis	150.00	75.00	45.00
115	Lee Meadows	150.00	75.00	45.00
116	Fred Merkle	150.00	75.00	45.00
117	"Chief" Meyers	150.00	75.00	45.00
118	Clyde Milan	150.00	75.00	45.00
119	Otto Miller	150.00	75.00	45.00
120	Clarence Mitchell	150.00	75.00	45.00
121	Ray Morgan	150.00	75.00	45.00
122	Guy Morton	150.00	75.00	45.00
123	"Mike" Mowrey	150.00	75.00	45.00
124	Elmer Myers	150.00	75.00	45.00
125	"Hy" Myers	150.00	75.00	45.00
126	A.E. Neale	175.00	85.00	50.00
127	Arthur Nehf	150.00	75.00	45.00
128	J.A. Niehoff	150.00	75.00	45.00

		NM	EX	VG
129	Steve O'Neill	150.00	75.00	45.00
130	"Dode" Paskert	150.00	75.00	45.00
131	Roger Peckinpaugh	150.00	75.00	45.00
132	"Pol" Perritt	150.00	75.00	45.00
133	"Jeff" Pfeffer	150.00	75.00	45.00
134	Walter Pipp	150.00	75.00	45.00
135	Derril Pratt (Derrill)	150.00	75.00	45.00
136	Bill Rariden	150.00	75.00	45.00
137	E.C. Rice	350.00	175.00	100.00
138	Wm. A. Ritter (Wm. H.)	150.00	75.00	45.00
139	Eppa Rixey	350.00	175.00	100.00
140	Davey Robertson	150.00	75.00	45.00
141	"Bob" Roth	150.00	75.00	45.00
142	Ed. Roush	350.00	175.00	100.00
143	Clarence Rowland	150.00	75.00	45.00
144	Dick Rudolph	150.00	75.00	45.00
145	William Rumler	150.00	75.00	45.00
146	Reb Russell	150.00	75.00	45.00
147	"Babe" Ruth	12,500	6,250	3,750
148	Vic Saier	150.00	75.00	45.00
149	"Slim" Sallee	150.00	75.00	45.00
150	Ray Schalk	350.00	175.00	100.00
151	Walter Schang	150.00	75.00	45.00
152	Frank Schulte	150.00	75.00	45.00
153	Ferd Schupp	150.00	75.00	45.00
154	Everett Scott	150.00	75.00	45.00
155	Hank Severeid	150.00	75.00	45.00
156	Howard Shanks	150.00	75.00	45.00
157	Bob Shawkey	150.00	75.00	45.00
158	Jas. Sheckard	150.00	75.00	45.00
159	Ernie Shore	150.00	75.00	45.00
160	C.H. Shorten	150.00	75.00	45.00
161	Burt Shotton	150.00	75.00	45.00
162	Geo. Sisler	350.00	175.00	100.00
163	Elmer Smith	150.00	75.00	45.00
164	J. Carlisle Smith	150.00	75.00	45.00
165	Fred Snodgrass	150.00	75.00	45.00
166	Tris Speaker	650.00	325.00	195.00
167	Oscar Stanage	150.00	75.00	45.00
168	Charles Stengel	350.00	175.00	100.00
169	Milton Stock	150.00	75.00	45.00
170	Amos Strunk	150.00	75.00	45.00
171	"Zeb" Terry	150.00	75.00	45.00
172	"Jeff" Tesreau	150.00	75.00	45.00
173	Chester Thomas	150.00	75.00	45.00
174	Fred Toney	150.00	75.00	45.00
175	Terry Turner	150.00	75.00	45.00
176	George Tyler	150.00	75.00	45.00
177	Jim Vaughn	150.00	75.00	45.00
178	Bob Veach	150.00	75.00	45.00
179	Oscar Vitt	150.00	75.00	45.00
180	Hans Wagner	3,500	1,750	1,050
181	Clarence Walker	150.00	75.00	45.00
182	Jim Walsh	150.00	75.00	45.00
183	Al Walters	150.00	75.00	45.00
184	W. Wambsganss	150.00	75.00	45.00
185	Buck Weaver	1,000	500.00	300.00
186	Carl Weilman	150.00	75.00	45.00
187	Zack Wheat	350.00	175.00	100.00
188	Geo. Whitted	150.00	75.00	45.00
189	Joe Wilhoit	150.00	75.00	45.00
190	Claude Williams	750.00	375.00	225.00
191	Fred Williams	150.00	75.00	45.00
192	Art Wilson	150.00	75.00	45.00
193	Lawton Witt	150.00	75.00	45.00
194	Joe Wood	150.00	75.00	45.00
195	William Wortman	150.00	75.00	45.00
196	Steve Yerkes	150.00	75.00	45.00
197	Earl Yingling	150.00	75.00	45.00
198	"Pep" (Ralph) Young	150.00	75.00	45.00
199	Rollie Zeider	150.00	75.00	45.00
200	Henry Zimmerman	150.00	75.00	45.00

1921 Standard Biscuit (D350-3)

CHESTER THOMAS
C.—Cleveland Americans

A photograph of a member of either the American or National League will be found in every 5 and 10 cent package of our products. There are 80 to the set.

STANDARD BISCUIT COMPANY

San Francisco, Cal.

Sole Makers of Paradise Sodas.

It is unknown to what extent this scarcest of the three Standard Biscuit advertising issues actually parallels the E121 Series of 80, on which American Caramel Co. backs are more commonly found. This uncertainty contributes to the relatively low premium value (about 2X) attached to the Standard Biscuit versions. Backs have been seen in two styles; one mentions "80 to the set", the other mentions "contains 80 photographs". Cards are printed in black-and-white in a size of about 2" x 3-1/4". A checklist has been started here in an effort to better understand the issue.

PREMIUM: 2X
(12)	Max Carey (Hands at hips.)
(14)	Ty Cobb/Throwing (Looking front.)
(19)	Dave Davenport
(37)	Tom Griffith

(40)	John Henry
(52)	James Johnston
(62)	"Rabbit" Maranville
(83)	Eppa Rixey, Jr.
(86)	Babe Ruth
(90)	Ray Schalk
(103)	Chester Thomas
(109)	Jim Vaughn (Dark cap.)
(113)	Oscar Vitt
(116)	Zach Wheat
(120)	Joe Wood

1910 Standard Caramel Co. (E93)

WILTSE, N.Y. Nat'l

This 30-card set issued in 1910 by Standard Caramel Co. of Lancaster, Pa., is closely related to several other candy sets from this period which share the same format and, in many cases, the same player poses. The cards measure 1-1/2" x 2-3/4" and utilize tinted black-and-white player photos. The back of each card contains an alphabetical checklist of the set plus a line indicating it was manufactured by Standard Caramel Co., Lancaster, Pa. The set carries the ACC designation of E93.

		NM	EX	VG
Complete Set (30):		100,000	40,000	20,000
Common Player:		1,500	600.00	300.00
(1)	Red Ames	1,500	600.00	300.00
(2)	Chief Bender	3,000	1,200	600.00
(3)	Mordecai Brown	3,000	1,200	600.00
(4)	Frank Chance	3,000	1,200	600.00
(5)	Hal Chase	2,200	880.00	440.00
(6)	Fred Clarke	3,000	1,200	600.00
(7)	Ty Cobb	15,000	6,000	3,000
(8)	Eddie Collins	3,000	1,200	600.00
(9)	Harry Coveleskie (Coveleski)	1,500	600.00	300.00
(10)	Jim Delehanty	1,500	600.00	300.00
(11)	Wild Bill Donovan	1,500	600.00	300.00
(12)	Red Dooin	1,500	600.00	300.00
(13)	Johnny Evers	3,000	1,200	600.00
(14)	George Gibson	1,500	600.00	300.00
(15)	Clark Griffith	3,000	1,200	600.00
(16)	Hugh Jennings	3,000	1,200	600.00
(17)	Davy Jones	1,500	600.00	300.00
(18)	Addie Joss	3,300	1,320	660.00
(19)	Nap Lajoie	3,000	120.00	600.00
(20)	Tommy Leach	1,500	600.00	300.00
(21)	Christy Mathewson	8,000	3,200	1,600
(22)	John McGraw	3,000	1,200	600.00
(23)	Jim Pastorious	1,500	600.00	300.00
(24)	Deacon Phillippi (Phillippe)	1,500	600.00	300.00
(25)	Eddie Plank	5,000	2,000	1,000
(26)	Joe Tinker	3,000	1,200	600.00
(27)	Rube Waddell	3,000	1,200	600.00
(28)	Honus Wagner	12,000	4,800	2,400
(29)	Hooks Wiltse	1,500	600.00	300.00
(30)	Cy Young	7,000	2,800	1,400

1960-70s Stan Musial & Biggie's Restaurant

Compliments of
STAN MUSIAL & BIGGIE'S RESTAURANT
5130 Oakland Ave., St. Louis, Mo. 63110

These black-and-white photocards were prepared for Musial's use while glad-handing patrons at his St. Louis eatery. The pictures have a facsimile autograph. A "Compliments of . . ." message is printed in the bottom border. Backs are blank.

		NM	EX	VG
(1)	Stan Musial (Batting pose, 5" x 7".)	10.00	5.00	3.00
(2)	Stan Musial (Batting pose, 3-1/2" x 5-1/2".)	10.00	5.00	3.00
(3)	Stan Musial (Standing w/glove, 5" x 7".)	10.00	5.00	3.00

1952 Star-Cal Decals Type 1

The Meyercord Co., of Chicago issued two sets of baseball player decals in 1952. The Type I Star-Cal Decal set consists of 68 different major leaguers, each pictured on a large (4-1/8" x 6-1/8") decal. The player's name and facsimile autograph appear on the decal, along with the decal number listed on the checklist here. Values shown are for decals complete with outer directions envelope.

		NM	EX	VG
Complete Set (68):		7,500	3,750	2,250
Common Player:		45.00	22.50	13.50
70A	Allie Reynolds	50.00	25.00	15.00
70B	Ed Lopat	50.00	25.00	15.00
70C	Yogi Berra	200.00	100.00	60.00
70D	Vic Raschi	50.00	25.00	15.00
70E	Jerry Coleman	45.00	22.50	13.50
70F	Phil Rizzuto	110.00	55.00	35.00
70G	Mickey Mantle	1,750	875.00	525.00
71A	Mel Parnell	45.00	22.50	13.50
71B	Ted Williams	400.00	200.00	120.00
71C	Ted Williams	400.00	200.00	120.00
71D	Vern Stephens	45.00	22.50	13.50
71E	Billy Goodman	45.00	22.50	13.50
71F	Dom DiMaggio	50.00	25.00	15.00
71G	Dick Gernert	45.00	22.50	13.50
71H	Hoot Evers	45.00	22.50	13.50
72A	George Kell	50.00	25.00	15.00
72B	Hal Newhouser	50.00	25.00	15.00
72C	Hoot Evers	45.00	22.50	13.50
72D	Vic Wertz	45.00	22.50	13.50
72E	Fred Hutchinson	45.00	22.50	13.50
72F	Johnny Groth	45.00	22.50	13.50
73A	Al Zarilla	45.00	22.50	13.50
73B	Billy Pierce	45.00	22.50	13.50
73C	Eddie Robinson	45.00	22.50	13.50
73D	Chico Carrasquel	50.00	25.00	15.00
73E	Minnie Minoso	50.00	25.00	15.00
73F	Jim Busby	45.00	22.50	13.50
73G	Nellie Fox	55.00	27.50	16.50
73H	Sam Mele	45.00	22.50	13.50
74A	Larry Doby	55.00	27.50	16.50
74B	Al Rosen	50.00	25.00	15.00
74C	Bob Lemon	55.00	27.00	16.50
74D	Jim Hegan	45.00	22.50	13.50
74E	Bob Feller	90.00	45.00	27.00
74F	Dale Mitchell	45.00	22.50	13.50
75A	Ned Garver	45.00	22.50	13.50
76A	Gus Zernial	45.00	22.50	13.50
76B	Ferris Fain	45.00	22.50	13.50
76C	Bobby Shantz	45.00	22.50	13.50
77A	Richie Ashburn	60.00	30.00	18.00
77B	Ralph Kiner	55.00	27.50	16.50
77C	Curt Simmons	45.00	22.50	13.50
78A	Bobby Thomson	55.00	27.50	16.50
78B	Alvin Dark	45.00	22.50	13.50
78C	Sal Maglie	45.00	22.50	13.50
78D	Larry Jansen	45.00	22.50	13.50
78E	Willie Mays	425.00	210.00	125.00
78F	Monte Irvin	55.00	27.50	16.50
78G	Whitey Lockman	45.00	22.50	13.50
79A	Gil Hodges	90.00	45.00	27.00
79B	Pee Wee Reese	110.00	55.00	35.00
79C	Roy Campanella	110.00	55.00	35.00
79D	Don Newcombe	55.00	27.50	16.50
79E	Duke Snider	110.00	55.00	35.00
79F	Preacher Roe	50.00	25.00	15.00
79G	Jackie Robinson	350.00	175.00	105.00
80A	Eddie Miksis	45.00	22.50	13.50
80B	Dutch Leonard	45.00	22.50	13.50
80C	Randy Jackson	45.00	22.50	13.50
80D	Bob Rush	45.00	22.50	13.50
80E	Hank Sauer	45.00	22.50	13.50
80F	Phil Cavarretta	45.00	22.50	13.50
80G	Warren Hacker	45.00	22.50	13.50
81A	Red Schoendienst	55.00	27.50	16.50
81B	Wally Westlake	45.00	22.50	13.50
81C	Cliff Chambers	45.00	22.50	13.50
81D	Enos Slaughter	55.00	27.50	16.50
81E	Stan Musial	275.00	135.00	85.00
81F	Stan Musial	275.00	135.00	85.00
81G	Jerry Staley	45.00	22.50	13.50

1952 Star-Cal Decals Type 2

Also produced by Chicago's Meyercord Co. in 1952, these Star-cal decals are similar to the Type I

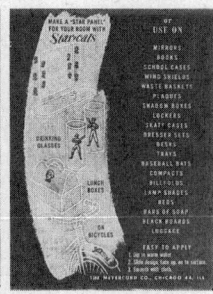

variety, except the decal sheets are smaller, measuring 4-1/8" x 3-1/16" , and each sheet features two players instead of one.

	NM	EX	VG
Complete Set (32):	3,000	1,500	900.00
Common Player:	45.00	22.50	13.50
84A Vic Raschi, Allie Reynolds	80.00	40.00	25.00
84B Yogi Berra, Ed Lopat	165.00	80.00	50.00
84C Jerry Coleman, Phil Rizzuto	135.00	65.00	40.00
85A Ted Williams, Ted Williams	450.00	225.00	135.00
85B Dom DiMaggio, Mel Parnell	60.00	30.00	18.00
85C Billy Goodman, Vern Stephens	45.00	22.50	13.50
86A George Kell, Hal Newhouser	80.00	40.00	25.00
86B Hoot Evers, Vic Wertz	45.00	22.50	13.50
86C Johnny Groth, Fred Hutchinson	45.00	22.50	13.50
87A Eddie Robinson, Eddie Robinson	45.00	22.50	13.50
87B Chico Carrasquel, Minnie Minoso	60.00	30.00	18.00
87C Nellie Fox, Billy Pierce	65.00	32.50	20.00
87D Jim Busby, Al Zarilla	45.00	22.50	13.50
88A Jim Hegan, Bob Lemon	65.00	32.50	20.00
88B Larry Doby, Bob Feller	165.00	80.00	50.00
88C Dale Mitchell, Al Rosen	45.00	22.50	13.50
89A Ned Garver, Ned Garver	45.00	22.50	13.50
89B Ferris Fain, Gus Zernial	45.00	22.50	13.50
89C Richie Ashburn, Richie Ashburn	75.00	37.50	22.00
89D Ralph Kiner, Ralph Kiner	75.00	37.50	22.00
90A Monty Irvin, Willie Mays (Monte)	300.00	150.00	90.00
90B Larry Jansen, Sal Maglie	45.00	22.50	13.50
90C Al Dark, Bobby Thomson	55.00	27.50	16.50
91A Gil Hodges, Pee Wee Reese	225.00	110.00	65.00
91B Roy Campanella, Jackie Robinson	300.00	150.00	90.00
91C Preacher Roe, Duke Snider	200.00	100.00	60.00
92A Phil Cavarretta, Dutch Leonard	45.00	22.50	13.50
92B Randy Jackson, Eddie Miksis	45.00	22.50	13.50
92C Bob Rush, Hank Sauer	45.00	22.50	13.50
93A Stan Musial, Stan Musial	350.00	175.00	105.00
93B Red Schoendienst, Enos Slaughter	90.00	45.00	27.00
93C Cliff Chambers, Wally Westlake	45.00	22.50	13.50

1976 Star Market Red Sox

Only Red Sox are featured in this set issued by the Star Market chain in the Boston area. Players are photographed hatless in jerseys which feature the Massachusetts Bicentennial logo. Pictures measure 5-7/8" x 9" and have a 3-16" white border all around. A facsimile autograph is printed on the front in black. Backs are blank. The unnumbered pictures are checklisted here alphabetically.

	NM	EX	VG
Complete Set (16):	35.00	17.50	10.00
Common Player:	1.50	.75	.45
(1) Rick Burleson	1.50	.75	.45
(2) Reggie Cleveland	1.50	.75	.45
(3) Cecil Cooper	2.50	1.25	.70
(4) Denny Doyle	1.50	.75	.45
(5) Dwight Evans	2.50	1.25	.70
(6) Carlton Fisk	5.00	2.50	1.50
(7) Tom House	1.50	.75	.45
(8) Fergie Jenkins	4.00	2.00	1.25
(9) Bill Lee	1.50	.75	.45
(10) Fred Lynn	2.50	1.25	.70

(11) Rick Miller	1.50	.75	.45
(12) Rico Petrocelli	2.50	1.25	.70
(13) Jim Rice	3.50	1.75	1.00
(14) Luis Tiant	2.50	1.25	.70
(15) Rick Wise	1.50	.75	.45
(16) Carl Yastrzemski	10.00	5.00	3.00

1928 Star Player Candy

WALLY SCHANG

Little is known about the origin of this set. The producer is not identified, but experienced collectors generally refer to it as the Star Player Candy set, possibly because it was distributed with a product of that name. The cards measure 1-7/8" x 2-7/8", are sepia-toned, blank-backed and printed on thin paper. The player's name (but no team designation) appears in the border below the photo in brown capital letters. To date the checklist of baseball players numbers 73, but more may exist, and cards of football players have also been found.

	NM	EX	VG
Common Player:	900.00	360.00	180.00
(1) Dave Bancroft	2,000	800.00	400.00
(2) Emile Barnes	900.00	360.00	180.00
(3) L.A. Blue	900.00	360.00	180.00
(4) Garland Buckeye	900.00	360.00	180.00
(5) George Burns	900.00	360.00	180.00
(6) Guy T. Bush	900.00	360.00	180.00
(7) Owen T. Carroll	900.00	360.00	180.00
(8) Chalmer Cissell	900.00	360.00	180.00
(9) Ty Cobb	20,000	8,000	4,000
(10) Gordon Cochrane	2,000	800.00	400.00
(11) Richard Coffman	900.00	360.00	180.00
(12) Eddie Collins	2,000	800.00	400.00
(13) Stanley Coveleskie (Coveleski)	2,000	800.00	400.00
(14) Hugh Critz	900.00	360.00	180.00
(15) Hazen Cuyler	2,000	800.00	400.00
(16) Charles Dressen	900.00	360.00	180.00
(17) Joe Dugan	900.00	360.00	180.00
(18) Elwood English	900.00	360.00	180.00
(19) Bib Falk (Bibb)	900.00	360.00	180.00
(20) Ira Flagstead	900.00	360.00	180.00
(21) Bob Fothergill	900.00	360.00	180.00
(22) Frank T. Frisch	2,000	800.00	400.00
(23) Foster Ganzel	900.00	360.00	180.00
(24) Lou Gehrig	22,500	9,000	4,500
(25) Chas. Gihringer (Gehringer)	2,000	800.00	400.00
(26) George Gerken	900.00	360.00	180.00
(27) Grant Gillis	900.00	360.00	180.00
(28) Miguel Gonzales (Gonzalez)	900.00	360.00	180.00
(29) Sam Gray	900.00	360.00	180.00
(30) Chas. J. Grimm	900.00	360.00	180.00
(31) Robert M. Grove	2,250	900.00	450.00
(32) Chas. J. Hafey	2,000	800.00	400.00
(33) Jesse Haines	2,000	800.00	400.00
(34) Chas. L. Hartnett	2,000	800.00	400.00
(35) Clifton Heathcote	900.00	360.00	180.00
(36) Harry Heilmann	2,000	800.00	400.00
(37) John Heving	900.00	360.00	180.00
(38) Waite Hoyt	2,000	800.00	400.00
(39) Chas. Jamieson	900.00	360.00	180.00
(40) Joe Judge	900.00	360.00	180.00
(41) Willie Kamm	900.00	360.00	180.00
(42) George Kelly	2,000	800.00	400.00
(43) Tony Lazzeri	2,000	800.00	400.00
(44) Adolfo Luque	900.00	360.00	180.00
(45) Ted Lyons	2,000	800.00	400.00
(46) Hugh McMullen	900.00	360.00	180.00
(47) Bob Meusel	2,000	800.00	400.00
(48) Wilcey Moore (Wilcy)	900.00	360.00	180.00
(49) Ed C. Morgan	900.00	360.00	180.00
(50) Buddy Myer	900.00	360.00	180.00
(51) Herb Pennock	2,000	800.00	400.00
(52) Everett Purdy	900.00	360.00	180.00
(53) William Regan	900.00	360.00	180.00
(54) Eppa Rixey	2,000	800.00	400.00
(55) Charles Root	900.00	360.00	180.00
(56) Jack Rothrock	900.00	360.00	180.00
(57) Harold Ruel (Herold)	900.00	360.00	180.00
(58) Babe Ruth	32,500	13,000	6,500
(59) Wally Schang	900.00	360.00	180.00
(60) Joe Sewell	2,000	800.00	400.00
(61) Luke Sewell	900.00	360.00	180.00
(62) Joe Shaute	900.00	360.00	180.00
(63) George Sisler	2,000	800.00	400.00
(64) Tris Speaker	2,500	1,000	500.00
(65) Riggs Stephenson	900.00	360.00	180.00
(66) Jack Tavener	900.00	360.00	180.00
(67) Al Thomas	900.00	360.00	180.00
(68) Harold J. Traynor	2,000	800.00	400.00
(69) George Uhle	900.00	360.00	180.00
(70) Dazzy Vance	2,000	800.00	400.00
(71) Cy Williams	900.00	360.00	180.00
(72) Ken Williams	900.00	360.00	180.00
(73) Lewis R. Wilson	2,000	800.00	400.00

1929 Star Player Candy

BABE RUTH

BABE RUTH, "Sultan of Swat," has reigned supreme as home run king for eight consecutive years. His record of 60 home runs in one season will probably remain unbroken for some years to come.

The actual year of issue can only be approximated from the write-ups on the cards' backs. Only two players can be checklisted thus far, though the numbers on the backs would seem to indicate an issue of at least 32. The 1-7/8" x 2-7/8" cards are printed in sepia with wide borders on front and player name below the photo. Unlike the 1928 Star Candy issue, this series has printed and numbered backs.

	NM	EX	VG
21 Babe Ruth	20,000	10,000	6,000
32 Lou Gehrig	22,500	11,250	6,750

1892 J.U. Stead Studio Cabinets

J.U. STEAD. 383 6th Ave. N.Y.

Only members of the N.Y. Giants are thus far known in this series of cabinet cards from New York City photographer J.U. Stead. About standard cabinet size (4-1/2" x 6-1/2") the cards have black-and-white portraits. On the thick cardboard mount's bottom border is the name and address of the studio. Backs repeat that information and have three lines of type at bottom extolling "Instantaneous Photographs." Unless the player name was penciled on the card by a previous owner, the players are not otherwise identified. Fortunately, the plethora of contemporary issues from other sources makes matching names and photos fairly easy. The issue date attributed is speculative.

	NM	EX	VG
Common Player:	3,000	1,500	900.00
Roger Connor	4,000	2,000	1,200
Willie Keeler	7,500	3,750	2,250
Mike Tiernan	3,000	1,500	900.00

1909-16 Max Stein Postcards (PC758)

Issued over a period of several years these sepia-toned photo postcards depict most of the stars of the day. In standard 3-1/2" x 5-1/2" format they have typical postcard indicia on the back. Some cards have been seen with a "United States Pub." legend on the back. Most of the subjects played in Stein's Chicago location. Besides the baseball players listed here, the series also included "Statesmen, etc., Aeroplanes and Flyers, Fighters, etc.," and, "Dancing Girls," according to advertising found on the back of some cards. Wholesale prices when issued were 35 cents per hundred, $2.75 per thousand.

		NM	EX	VG
Common Player:		200.00	80.00	40.00
Advertising Back: 1.5X				
(1)	Ping Bodie	200.00	80.00	40.00
(2)	Frank Chance	400.00	160.00	80.00
(3)	Ty Cobb	2,250	900.00	450.00
(4)	Johnny Evers	400.00	160.00	80.00
(5)	Rube Marquard	400.00	160.00	80.00
(6)	Christy Mathewson	1,200	480.00	240.00
(7)	John McGraw	400.00	160.00	80.00
(8)	Chief Meyers	200.00	80.00	40.00
(9)	Marty O'Toole	200.00	80.00	40.00
(10)	Wildfire Schulte	200.00	80.00	40.00
(11)	Tris Speaker	450.00	180.00	90.00
(12)	Jake Stahl	200.00	80.00	40.00
(13)	Jim Thorpe	2,500	1,000	500.00
(14)	Joe Tinker	400.00	160.00	80.00
(15)	Honus Wagner	1,500	600.00	300.00
(16)	Ed Walsh	400.00	160.00	80.00
(17)	Buck Weaver	1,750	700.00	350.00
(18)	Joe Wood	200.00	80.00	40.00
(19)	Heinie Zimmerman	200.00	80.00	40.00
(20)	Chicago Cubs (Jimmy Archer, Roger Bresnahan, Johnny Evers, Mike Hechinger, Tom Needham)	200.00	80.00	40.00
(21)	Chicago Cubs (Bill Clymer, Wilbur Good, Ward Miller, Mike Mitchell, Wildfire Schulte)	200.00	80.00	40.00
(22)	Boston Americans Team Photo	200.00	80.00	40.00
(23)	1916 Chicago Cubs Team Photo	300.00	120.00	60.00
(24)	1916 Cincinnati Reds Team Photo	200.00	80.00	40.00
(25)	New York Nationals Team Photo	200.00	80.00	40.00
(26)	Johnny Coulon, Jess Willard (Boxers)	200.00	80.00	40.00

1904 Stenzel's Rooter Buttons

The extent of the checklist for this rare Cincinnati 1-1/4" pinback celluloid button issue is unknown. According to a paper label found in the back of well-preserved examples, the buttons are the issue of "Jake Stenzel B.B. Exchange located opposite Ball Park." Fronts have "STENZEL'S ROOTER BUTTON" at top and a player portrait photo at center with last name and position below.

		NM	EX	VG
(1)	Mike Donlin	750.00	375.00	225.00
(2)	Bob Ewing	600.00	300.00	180.00
(3)	Jack Harper	600.00	300.00	180.00
(4)	Joe Kelley	1,750	875.00	525.00
(5)	Win Kellum	600.00	300.00	180.00
(6)	Peaches O'Neil (O'Neill)	900.00	450.00	275.00
(7)	Heinie Pietz (Peitz)	600.00	300.00	180.00
(8)	Admiral Schlei	600.00	300.00	180.00
(9)	Jack Sutthoff	600.00	300.00	180.00
(10)	Sam Woodruff	600.00	300.00	180.00

1911 Stevens Firearms Philadelphia Athletics

Riding on the coattails of the A's American League pennant (and eventual World Series) win, Stevens Firearms created this set of cards to promote its rifles and shotguns. About 6-3/16" x 3-7/16", the blank-back, medium-weight cards have a black-and-white posed action photo at left with the player identified by name, position and team. At top right is advertising, at bottom-right is a box where local retailers' addresses could be stamped or printed. Cards have been seen printed on several different colors of stock. In actuality, these are really ink blotters from the old fountain pen days as opposed to "cards." Other players are likely to have been issued.

		NM	EX	VG
Common Player:		1,000	500.00	300.00
(1)	Frank Baker	1,500	750.00	450.00
(2)	Chief Bender	1,500	750.00	450.00
(3)	Bris Lord	1,000	500.00	300.00
(4)	Connie Mack	1,500	750.00	450.00
(5)	Danny Murphy	1,000	500.00	300.00
(6)	Rube Oldring	1,000	500.00	300.00
(7)	Harry Davis	1,000	500.00	300.00
(8)	Ira Thomas	1,000	500.00	300.00

1888-1889 Stevens Studio Australian Tour Cabinets

After the 1888 season, Albert Spalding toured to Australia with a group of major league players to increase interest in baseball Down Under (as well as to increase demand for the baseball equipment his firm sold). Prior to departure, many of the players gathered at Stevens Studio in Chicago for portrait photos to be made into cabinet cards, presumably for sale as souvenirs on the junket. Vignetted portraits present the players in their Sunday best. Below a decorative dividing line is "Spalding's Australian Base Ball Tour / Stevens 1888-89 Chicago." Back has a large ornate ad for the photographer. The full extent of the checklist is unknown.

		NM	EX	VG
Common Player:		3,500	1,750	1,000
	Cap Anson	10,000	5,000	3,000
	Jim Donnelly	3,500	1,750	1,000
	Jim Fogarty	3,500	1,750	1,000
	Ned Williamson	3,500	1,750	1,000

1890 Stevens Studio Chicago Pirates Cabinets

The single-season players' revolution that spawned the Players League is marked with this issue of cabinet cards from the Stevens studio of Chicago. Only members of the Chicago Pirates P.L. team have been seen in this issue, all in street clothes and identified by a name penned on the front. A composite-photo card is also known, providing reasonable expectations that more individual player cabinets will be discovered. The studio advertising on back is ornately printed in maroon.

		NM	EX	VG
Common Player:		1,650	825.00	500.00
(1)	Charles Comiskey	3,500	1,750	1,000

(2)	Hugh Duffy	3,500	1,750	1,000
(3)	Silver Flint	1,650	825.00	500.00
(4)	Jimmy Ryan	1,650	825.00	500.00
(5)	Team Composite	9,000	4,500	2,700

1890 Stevens Studio Chicago White Stockings Cabinets

Cabinet cards in the standard 4-1/4" x 6-1/2" format of at least three of the 1890 Chicago National Leaguers, as well as a team composite picture are known to have been produced by the Stevens Art Studio. Fronts have vignetted portraits of the players in dress clothes. Backs have an ornate ad for the photographer, which includes the note, "DUPLICATES OF THIS PICTURE CAN BE HAD AT ANY TIME, AT REDUCED RATES." Player names are often found penned on the cards, as the photos are otherwise unidentified. At least two styles of cardboard mounts are seen with the White Stockings cabinets. The extent of the checklist is also unknown.

		NM	EX	VG
Common Player:		1,650	825.00	500.00
(1)	Cap Anson	7,500	3,750	2,250
(2)	Mike Sullivan	1,650	825.00	500.00
(3)	Pat Wright	1,650	825.00	500.00
(4)	1890 Chicago White Stockings	4,000	2,000	1,200

1941 St. Louis Browns Team Issue (W753)

Measuring 2-1/8" x 2-5/8", this unnumbered boxed set of cards features the St. Louis Browns in black-and-white portrait photos on front. Backs have player name, position and personal and statistical information. There are also cards for coaches and one of the the club's two managers that season (Luke Sewell). As the Browns weren't much of a team in 1941 (or in most seasons for that matter) there are no major stars in the set. The issue was cataloged as W753 in the ACC.

		NM	EX	VG
Complete Set (30):		850.00	425.00	250.00
Common Player:		35.00	17.50	10.00
Box:		75.00	35.00	25.00
(1)	Johnny Allen	35.00	17.50	10.00
(2)	Elden Auker (Eldon)	35.00	17.50	10.00
(3)	Donald L Barnes	35.00	17.50	10.00
(4)	Johnny Berardino	50.00	25.00	15.00
(5)	George Caster	35.00	17.50	10.00
(6)	Harlond Benton (Darky) Clift	35.00	17.50	10.00
(7)	Roy J. Cullenbine	35.00	17.50	10.00
(8)	William O. DeWitt, Vice-president)	35.00	17.50	10.00
(9)	Roberto Estalella	35.00	17.50	10.00
(10)	Richard Benjamin (Rick) Ferrell	60.00	30.00	18.00
(11)	Dennis W. Galehouse	35.00	17.50	10.00
(12)	Joseph L. Grace	35.00	17.50	10.00
(13)	Frank Grube	35.00	17.50	10.00
(14)	Robert A. Harris	35.00	17.50	10.00
(15)	Donald Henry Heffner	35.00	17.50	10.00
(16)	Fred Hofmann	35.00	17.50	10.00
(17)	Walter Franklin Judnich	35.00	17.50	10.00
(18)	John Henry (Jack) Kramer	35.00	17.50	10.00
(19)	Chester (Chet) Laabs	35.00	17.50	10.00
(20)	John Lucadello	35.00	17.50	10.00
(21)	George Hartley McQuinn	35.00	17.50	10.00
(22)	Robert Cleveland Muncrief, Jr.	35.00	17.50	10.00
(23)	John Niggeling	35.00	17.50	10.00
(24)	Fred Raymond (Fritz) Ostermueller	35.00	17.50	10.00
(25)	James Luther (Luke) Sewell	35.00	17.50	10.00
(26)	Alan Cochran Strange (Cochrane)	35.00	17.50	10.00
(27)	Robert Virgil (Bob) Swift	35.00	17.50	10.00
(28)	James W. (Zack) Taylor	35.00	17.50	10.00
(29)	William Felix (Bill) Trotter	35.00	17.50	10.00
(30)	Presentation card/order form	10.00	5.00	3.00

1952 St. Louis Browns Postcards

This series of player postcards features black-and-white glossy photos on front with a white border. The cards bear no player identification and were evidently intended for use in honoring fan requests for autographs. The 1952 issue can be differentiated from that of 1953 by the absence of a stamp box on back. The unnumbered cards are checklisted here alphabetically, though the list may be incomplete. Multiple player names indicate known different poses.

		NM	EX	VG
Common Player:		50.00	25.00	15.00
(1)	Tommy Byrne	50.00	25.00	15.00
(2)	Bob Cain	50.00	25.00	15.00
(3)	Bob Cain	50.00	25.00	15.00
(4)	Clint Courtney	50.00	25.00	15.00
(5)	Jim Delsing	50.00	25.00	15.00
(6)	Jim Dyck	50.00	25.00	15.00
(7)	Jim Dyck	50.00	25.00	15.00
(8)	Ned Garver	50.00	25.00	15.00
(9)	Marty Marion	60.00	30.00	18.00
(10)	Cass Michaels	50.00	25.00	15.00
(11)	Bob Nieman	50.00	25.00	15.00
(12)	Satchel Paige	200.00	100.00	60.00
(13)	Duane Pillette	50.00	25.00	15.00
(14)	Jim Rivera	50.00	25.00	15.00
(15)	Bill Veeck	75.00	37.00	22.00
(16)	Bobby Young	50.00	25.00	15.00

1953 St. Louis Browns Postcards

This series of player postcards from the team's final year in St. Louis features black-and-white glossy photos on front with a white border. The cards bear no player identification and were evidently intended for use in honoring fan requests for autographs. The 1953 issue can be differentiated from that of 1952 by the presence of a stamp box on back identifying the issuer as Deorite Peerless. The unnumbered cards are checklisted here alphabetically though the list is likely incomplete.

		NM	EX	VG
Common Player:		50.00	25.00	15.00
(1)	Connie Berry	50.00	25.00	15.00
(2)	Mike Blyzka	50.00	25.00	15.00
(3)	Harry Brecheen	50.00	25.00	15.00
(4)	Bob Cain	50.00	25.00	15.00
(5)	Clint Courtney	50.00	25.00	15.00
(6)	Jim Dyck	50.00	25.00	15.00
(7)	Hank Edwards	50.00	25.00	15.00
(8)	Ned Garver	50.00	25.00	15.00
(9)	Johnny Groth	50.00	25.00	15.00
(11)	Bobo Holloman	50.00	25.00	15.00
(12)	Billy Hunter	50.00	25.00	15.00
(13)	Dick Kokos	50.00	25.00	15.00
(14)	Dick Kryhoski	50.00	25.00	15.00
(15)	Max Lanier	50.00	25.00	15.00
(16)	Don Larsen	75.00	37.50	22.00
(17)	Don Lenhardt	50.00	25.00	15.00
(18)	Dick Littlefield	50.00	25.00	15.00
(19)	Marty Marion	60.00	30.00	18.00
(21)	Babe Martin	50.00	25.00	15.00
(22)	Willy Miranda	50.00	25.00	15.00
(23)	Les Moss	50.00	25.00	15.00
(24)	Bill Norman	50.00	25.00	15.00
(25)	Satchel Paige/Kneeling	200.00	100.00	60.00
(26)	Satchel Paige/Pitching	200.00	100.00	60.00
(27)	Duane Pillette	50.00	25.00	15.00
(28)	Bob Scheffing	50.00	25.00	15.00
(29)	Roy Sievers	60.00	30.00	18.00
(31)	Marlin Stuart	50.00	25.00	15.00
(32)	Virgil Trucks	65.00	32.00	19.50
(33)	Bill Veeck	75.00	37.00	22.00
(34)	Vic Wertz	50.00	25.00	15.00
(35)	Bobby Young	50.00	25.00	12.00

1941 St. Louis Cardinals Team Issue (W754)

 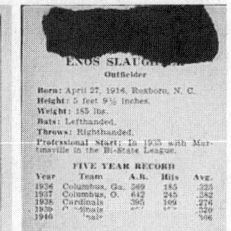

A companion set to W753, this time featuring the National League team in St. Louis. Cards measure 2-1/8" x 2-5/8" and are unnumbered. Like the Browns set, this issue features black-and-white portrait photos on front and the individual's name, position and personal and statistical information on back. One interesting addition to the set is a card of Branch Rickey which, coupled with cards of Enos Slaughter and Johnny Mize, gives the set a bit more appeal than the Browns set. ACC designation is W754.

		NM	EX	VG
Complete Set (30):		1,000	500.00	300.00
Common Player:		35.00	17.50	10.00
Box:		75.00	35.00	25.00
(1)	Sam Breadon	35.00	17.50	10.00
(2)	James Brown	35.00	17.50	10.00
(3)	Morton Cooper	35.00	17.50	10.00
(4)	William Walker Cooper	35.00	17.50	10.00
(5)	Estel Crabtree	35.00	17.50	10.00
(6)	Frank Crespi	35.00	17.50	10.00
(7)	William Crouch	35.00	17.50	10.00
(8)	Miguel Mike Gonzalez	50.00	25.00	15.00
(9)	Harry Gumbert	35.00	17.50	10.00
(10)	John Hopp	35.00	17.50	10.00
(11)	Ira Hutchinson	35.00	17.50	10.00
(12)	Howard Krist	35.00	17.50	10.00
(13)	Edward E. Lake	35.00	17.50	10.00
(14)	Hubert Max Lanier	35.00	17.50	10.00
(15)	Gus Mancuso	35.00	17.50	10.00
(16)	Martin Marion	55.00	27.50	16.50
(17)	Steve Mesner	35.00	17.50	10.00
(18)	John Mize	100.00	50.00	30.00
(19)	Capt. Terry Moore	50.00	25.00	15.00
(20)	Sam Nahem	35.00	17.50	10.00
(21)	Don Padgett	35.00	17.50	10.00
(22)	Branch Rickey/Vice President	60.00	30.00	18.00
(23)	Clyde Shoun	35.00	17.50	10.00
(24)	Enos Slaughter	100.00	50.00	30.00
(25)	William H. (Billy) Southworth	35.00	17.50	10.00
(26)	Herman Coaker Triplett	35.00	17.50	10.00
(27)	Clyde Buzzy Wares	35.00	17.50	10.00
(28)	Lon Warneke	35.00	17.50	10.00
(29)	Ernest White	35.00	17.50	10.00
(30)	Presentation card/order form	10.00	5.00	3.00

1966 St. Louis Cardinals Busch Stadium Immortals Coins

A dozen all-time great Cardinals are included in this set of commemorative medallions. Each 1-1/2" bright bronze "coin" has a portrait and career summary. The coins were issued in a 9" x 10-1/2" cardinal-red cardboard holder with gold logo and graphics.

		NM	EX	VG
Complete Board/Coin Set:		75.00	37.50	22.50
Common Player:		7.50	3.75	2.25
(1)	Dizzy Dean	10.00	5.00	3.00
(2)	Frank Frisch	7.50	3.75	2.25
(3)	Chick Hafey	7.50	3.75	2.25
(4)	Jesse Haines	7.50	3.75	2.25
(5)	Marty Marion	7.50	3.75	2.25
(6)	Joe Medwick	7.50	3.75	2.25
(7)	Johnny Mize	7.50	3.75	2.25
(8)	Terry Moore	7.50	3.75	2.25
(9)	Stan Musial	15.00	7.50	4.50
(10)	Red Schoendienst	7.50	3.75	2.25
(11)	George Sisler	7.50	3.75	2.25
(12)	Enos Slaughter	7.50	3.75	2.25

1953 Stop & Shop Boston Red Sox

Four of the early 1950s Red Sox appear in this series issued by a Boston grocery chain. The cards may have been distributed in conjunction with players' in-store appearances. The cards measure 3-3/4" x 5" and are printed in black-and-white. A facsimile autograph appears on the front. Backs have the sponsor's advertising. The unnumbered cards are checklisted here alphabetically. See also 1953 First National Super Market Boston Red Sox.

		NM	EX	VG
Complete Set (4):		3,000	1,500	900.00
Common Player:		750.00	375.00	225.00
(1)	Billy Goodman	750.00	375.00	225.00
(2)	Ellis Kinder	750.00	375.00	225.00
(3)	Mel Parnell	750.00	375.00	225.00
(4)	Sammy White	750.00	375.00	225.00

1888 Sub Rosa Cigarettes Girl Baseball Players (N508)

(See 1888 Allen & Ginter Girl Baseball Players.)

1916 Successful Farming

Best known for its use as a promotional medium for The Sporting News (M101-5), this 200-card set can be found with ads on the back for several local and regional businesses. Among them is Successful Farming magazine of Des Moines, Iowa. Type card collectors and superstar collectors can expect to pay a modest premium for individual cards with the magazine's advertising. Cards measure about 1-5/8" x 3" and are printed in black-and-white.

PREMIUM: 2-3X
(See 1916 Sporting News M101-5 for checklist and base card values.)

1976 Sugar Daddy Sports World

Two baseball related cards were issued as part of this multi-sport candy insert set. Each card is titled "BASEBALL" and they detail the 1974 and 1975 World Series and depict a player - though not naming him - in action. The cards are 1" x 2-3/4" and have a white-bordered color photo on front. Backs include various advertising details.

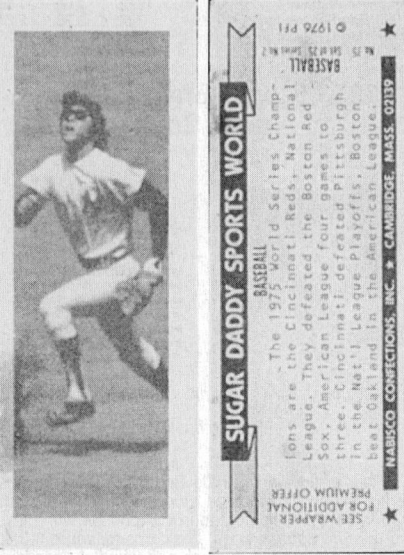

	NM	EX	VG
Complete Set (25):	60.00	30.00	18.00
12 Pete Rose (Series 1, 1974 World Series)	25.00	12.50	7.50
25 Bobby Murcer (Series 2, 1975 World Series)	17.50	9.00	5.00

1962 Sugardale Weiners

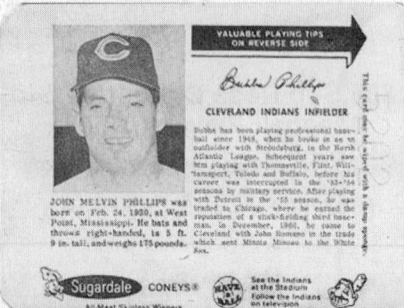

The Sugardale Meats set of black and white cards measure 5-1/8" x 3-3/4". The 22-card set includes 18 Cleveland Indians and four Pittsburgh Pirates players. The Indians cards are numbered from 1-19 with card number 6 not issued. The Pirates cards are lettered from A to D. The card fronts contain a relatively small player photo, with biographical information and Sugardale logo. The backs are printed in red and offer playing tips and another company logo. Card number 10 (Bob Nieman) is considerably more scarce than other cards in the set.

	NM	EX	VG
Complete Set (22):	10,000	4,000	2,000
Common Player:	325.00	130.00	65.00
A Dick Groat	325.00	130.00	65.00
B Roberto Clemente	3,250	1,300	650.00
C Don Hoak	325.00	130.00	65.00
D Dick Stuart	325.00	130.00	65.00
1 Barry Latman	325.00	130.00	65.00
2 Gary Bell	325.00	130.00	65.00
3 Dick Donovan	325.00	130.00	65.00
4 Frank Funk	325.00	130.00	65.00
5 Jim Perry	325.00	130.00	65.00
6 Not Issued			
7 Johnny Romano	325.00	130.00	65.00
8 Ty Cline	325.00	130.00	65.00
9 Tito Francona	325.00	130.00	65.00
10 Bob Nieman/SP	1,200	480.00	240.00
11 Willie Kirkland	325.00	130.00	65.00
12 Woodie Held	325.00	130.00	65.00
13 Jerry Kindall	325.00	130.00	65.00
14 Bubba Phillips	325.00	130.00	65.00
15 Mel Harder	325.00	130.00	65.00
16 Salty Parker	325.00	130.00	65.00
17 Ray Katt	325.00	130.00	65.00
18 Mel McGaha	325.00	130.00	65.00
19 Pedro Ramos	325.00	130.00	65.00

1963 Sugardale Weiners

Sugardale Meats again featured Cleveland and Pittsburgh players in its 1963 set, which grew to 31 cards. The black and white cards again measure 5-1/8" x 3-3/4", and consist of 28 Indians and five Pirates players. Card formats are virtually identical to the 1962 cards, with the only real difference being the information included in the player biographies. The cards are numbered 1-38, with numbers 6, 21, 22 and 29-32 not

issued. Cards for Bob Skinner (#35) and Jim Perry (#5) are scarce as these two players were traded during the season and their cards withdrawn from distribution. The red card backs again offer playing tips.

		NM	EX	VG
Complete Set (31):		10,000	4,000	2,000
Common Player:		325.00	130.00	65.00
A	Don Cardwell	325.00	130.00	65.00
B	Robert R. Skinner/SP	600.00	240.00	120.00
C	Donald B. Schwall	325.00	130.00	65.00
D	Jim Pagliaroni	325.00	130.00	65.00
E	Dick Schofield	325.00	130.00	65.00
1	Barry Latman	325.00	130.00	65.00
2	Gary Bell	325.00	130.00	65.00
3	Dick Donovan	325.00	130.00	65.00
4	Joe Adcock	400.00	160.00	80.00
5	Jim Perry/SP	600.00	240.00	120.00
6	Not Issued			
7	Johnny Romano	325.00	130.00	65.00
8	Mike de la Hoz	325.00	130.00	65.00
9	Tito Francona	325.00	130.00	65.00
10	Gene Green	325.00	130.00	65.00
11	Willie Kirkland	325.00	130.00	65.00
12	Woodie Held	325.00	130.00	65.00
13	Jerry Kindall	325.00	130.00	65.00
14	Max Alvis	325.00	130.00	65.00
15	Mel Harder	325.00	130.00	65.00
16	George Strickland	325.00	130.00	65.00
17	Elmer Valo	325.00	130.00	65.00
18	Birdie Tebbetts	325.00	130.00	65.00
19	Pedro Ramos	325.00	130.00	65.00
20	Al Luplow	325.00	130.00	65.00
21	Not Issued			
22	Not Issued			
23	Jim Grant	325.00	130.00	65.00
24	Victor Davalillo	325.00	130.00	65.00
25	Jerry Walker	325.00	130.00	65.00
26	Sam McDowell	400.00	160.00	80.00
27	Fred Whitfield	325.00	130.00	65.00
28	Jack Kralick	325.00	130.00	65.00
29	Not Issued			
30	Not Issued			
31	Not Issued			
32	Not Issued			
33	Bob Allen	325.00	130.00	65.00

1933 Sulima Cigarettes

This is one of several early 1930s German cigarette cards to picture Babe Ruth. In this case he is pictured on the 1-5/8" x 2-3/8" black-and-white card with American comedic actor Harold Lloyd. The card is part of a numbered set of 272 movie star cards. Backs are printed in German. The card is identical in format to the Josetti cigarette cards.

		NM	EX	VG
151	Babe Ruth, Harold Lloyd	1,100	550.00	330.00

1936 Sunday Advertiser Sport Stamps

(See 1936 Boston American Sport Stamps.)

1974 Sun-Glo Pop Al Kaline

This 2-1/4" x 4-1/2" card was issued as an attachment to bottles of soda pop. The blank-back card features a modishly dressed portrait of the former Tigers great and his endorsement for the soda. Cards are printed in black on various brightly colored backgrounds.

	NM	EX	VG
Al Kaline	6.00	3.00	1.75

1969 Sunoco Cubs/ Brewers Pins

Fans in Southern Wisconsin and Northern Illinois could acquire 1-1/8" lithographed steel baseball player pins of the Cubs and Brewers at participating Sunoco gas stations. The blue-and-white (Cubs) or red-and-white (Brewers) pins have black-and-white player portrait photos at center on which cap logos have been removed. The Brewers pins are somewhat scarcer than those of the Cubs.

		NM	EX	VG
Complete Set (18):		100.00	50.00	30.00
Common Player:		4.00	2.00	1.25
	Chicago Cubs Team Set:	65.00	32.50	20.00
(1)	Ernie Banks	25.00	12.50	7.50
(2)	Glenn Beckert	4.00	2.00	1.25
(3)	Jim Hickman	4.00	2.00	1.25
(4)	Randy Hundley	4.00	2.00	1.25
(5)	Ferguson Jenkins	7.50	3.75	2.25
(6)	Don Kessinger	6.00	3.00	1.75
(7)	Joe Pepitone	6.00	3.00	1.75
(8)	Ron Santo	10.00	5.00	3.00
(9)	Billy Williams	12.50	6.25	3.75
	Milwaukee Brewers Team Set:	50.00	25.00	15.00
(1)	Tommy Harper	6.00	3.00	1.75
(2)	Mike Hegan	6.00	3.00	1.75
(3)	Lew Krausse	6.00	3.00	1.75
(4)	Ted Kubiak	6.00	3.00	1.75
(5)	Marty Pattin	6.00	3.00	1.75
(6)	Phil Roof	6.00	3.00	1.75
(7)	Ken Sanders	6.00	3.00	1.75
(8)	Ted Savage	6.00	3.00	1.75
(9)	Danny Walton	6.00	3.00	1.75

1931 Sun Pictures Photo Kits

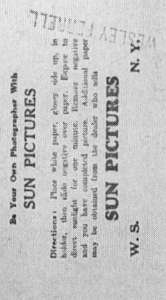

One of several contemporary kits for do-it-yourself production of photos, this issue was produced in New York City by a firm identified only as "W.S." A complete outfit consists of a 4-1/4" x 2-1/2" pink or kraft paper envelope with the name of the subject inside rubber-stamped on one end, a film negative, a piece of photo paper and a stand for producing/displaying the photo. The negative and resulting print measure 2-5/16" x 3-1/4". The set is listed in the American Card Catalog as W626. Prices shown are for complete kits; individual pieces would be pro-rated, with the negative the most valuable component. Because individual prints can be easily made even today, they have little collectible value. Only the baseball players are listed here.

		NM	EX	VG
	Common Player Kit:	125.00	62.00	37.50
(1)	George Earnshaw	125.00	62.00	38.00
(2)	Wesley Ferrell	125.00	62.00	37.00
(3)	Lefty Grove	250.00	125.00	75.00
(4)	Leo Hartnett	225.00	112.00	67.00
(5)	Tony Lazzeri	250.00	125.00	75.00
(6)	Herb Pennock	225.00	112.00	67.00
(7)	Babe Ruth	2,400	1,200	725.00
(8)	Al Simmons	225.00	112.00	67.00
(9)	Dazzy Vance	225.00	112.00	67.00
(10)	Hack Wilson	250.00	125.00	75.00

1960s Sunny Ayr Farms Johnny Callison

In the absence of other player cardsm, it is impossible to date this issue any more precisely than Callison's tenure with the Phillies which encompassed the 1960s. The 3-1/2" x 5-1/2" black-and-white card had a facsimile autograph on front. The divided back is printed in red.

	NM	EX	VG
Johnny Callison	100.00	50.00	30.00

1970 Superballs

Manufactured by Chemtoy (though not credited on the balls), these high-bouncing hard rubber balls are composed of see-through material in which is imbedded a disc with a baseball player's portrait and identification. About 1-1/8" in diameter, the balls identify the player by name, team and position and include a four-digit number. In this checklist, the balls are listed alphabetically for lack of access to a complete list of the actual numbers. It is also possible the checklist in incomplete.

		NM	EX	VG
	Complete Set (286):	1,650	825.00	500.00
	Common Player:	5.00	2.50	1.50
(1)	Hank Aaron	40.00	20.00	12.00
(2)	Jerry Adair	5.00	2.50	1.50
(3)	Tommie Agee	5.00	2.50	1.50
(4)	Bernie Allen	5.00	2.50	1.50
(5)	Lloyd Allen	5.00	2.50	1.50
(6)	Gene Alley	5.00	2.50	1.50
(7)	Bob Allison	5.00	2.50	1.50
(8)	Sandy Alomar	5.00	2.50	1.50
(9)	Jesus Alou	5.00	2.50	1.50
(10)	Matty Alou	5.00	2.50	1.50
(11)	Max Alvis	5.00	2.50	1.50
(12)	Mike Andrews	5.00	2.50	1.50
(13)	Luis Aparicio	17.50	8.75	5.25
(14)	Jose Arcia	5.00	2.50	1.50
(15)	Bob Aspromonte	5.00	2.50	1.50
(16)	Jose Azcue	5.00	2.50	1.50
(17)	Bob Bailey	5.00	2.50	1.50
(18)	Jack Baldschun	5.00	2.50	1.50
(19)	Sal Bando	5.00	2.50	1.50
(20)	Ernie Banks	25.00	12.50	7.50
(21)	John Bateman	5.00	2.50	1.50
(22)	Glenn Beckert	5.00	2.50	1.50
(23)	Mark Belanger	5.00	2.50	1.50
(24)	Ken Berry	5.00	2.50	1.50
(25)	Paul Blair	5.00	2.50	1.50
(26)	Curt Blefary	5.00	2.50	1.50
(27)	John Boccabella	5.00	2.50	1.50
(28)	Bobby Bonds	5.00	2.50	1.50
(29)	John Boozer	5.00	2.50	1.50
(30)	Ken Boswell	5.00	2.50	1.50
(31)	Clete Boyer	5.00	2.50	1.50
(32)	Gene Brabender	5.00	2.50	1.50
(33)	Ron Brand	5.00	2.50	1.50
(34)	Jim Brewer	5.00	2.50	1.50
(35)	Johnny Briggs	5.00	2.50	1.50
(36)	Nelson Briles	5.00	2.50	1.50
(37)	Ed Brinkman	5.00	2.50	1.50
(38)	Lou Brock	17.50	8.75	5.25
(39)	Don Buford	5.00	2.50	1.50
(40)	Tom Burgmeier	5.00	2.50	1.50
(41)	Bill Butler	5.00	2.50	1.50
(42)	Johnny Callison	5.00	2.50	1.50
(43)	Bert Campaneris	5.00	2.50	1.50
(44)	Jim Campanis	5.00	2.50	1.50
(45)	Chris Cannizzaro	5.00	2.50	1.50
(46)	Jose Cardenal	5.00	2.50	1.50
(47)	Leo Cardenas	5.00	2.50	1.50
(48)	Rod Carew	20.00	10.00	6.00
(49)	Clay Carroll	5.00	2.50	1.50
(50)	Rico Carty	5.00	2.50	1.50
(51)	Paul Casanova	5.00	2.50	1.50
(52)	Norm Cash	10.00	5.00	3.00
(53)	Orlando Cepeda	17.50	8.75	5.25
(54)	Billy Champion	5.00	2.50	1.50
(55)	Dean Chance	5.00	2.50	1.50
(56a)	Roberto Clemente (Red insert.)	60.00	30.00	18.00
(56b)	Roberto Clemente (Blue insert.)	50.00	25.00	15.00
(57)	Tony Cloninger	5.00	2.50	1.50
(58)	Nate Colbert	5.00	2.50	1.50
(59)	Joe Coleman	5.00	2.50	1.50
(60)	Kevin Collins	5.00	2.50	1.50
(61)	Wayne Comer	5.00	2.50	1.50
(62)	Tony Conigliaro	10.00	5.00	3.00
(63)	Billy Cowan	5.00	2.50	1.50
(64)	Casey Cox	5.00	2.50	1.50
(65)	Willie Crawford	5.00	2.50	1.50
(66)	Mike Cuellar	5.00	2.50	1.50
(67)	Al Dark	5.00	2.50	1.50
(68)	Vic Davalillo	5.00	2.50	1.50
(69)	Jim Davenport	5.00	2.50	1.50
(70)	Willie Davis	5.00	2.50	1.50
(71)	Tommy Dean	5.00	2.50	1.50
(72)	Larry Dierker	5.00	2.50	1.50
(73)	Dick Dietz	5.00	2.50	1.50
(74)	Moe Drabowsky	5.00	2.50	1.50
(75)	Leo Durocher	13.50	6.75	4.00
(76)	Johnny Edwards	5.00	2.50	1.50
(77)	Dock Ellis	5.00	2.50	1.50
(78)	Dick Ellsworth	5.00	2.50	1.50
(79)	Mike Epstein	5.00	2.50	1.50
(80)	Andy Etchebarren	5.00	2.50	1.50
(81)	Ron Fairly	5.00	2.50	1.50
(82)	Al Ferrera	5.00	2.50	1.50
(83)	Rollie Fingers	13.50	6.75	4.00
(84)	Mike Fiore	5.00	2.50	1.50
(85)	Eddie Fisher	5.00	2.50	1.50
(86)	Jack Fisher	5.00	2.50	1.50
(87)	Ray Fosse	5.00	2.50	1.50
(88)	Bill Freehan	5.00	2.50	1.50
(89)	Jim Fregosi	5.00	2.50	1.50
(90)	Tito Fuentes	5.00	2.50	1.50
(91)	Vern Fuller	5.00	2.50	1.50
(92)	Woody Fryman	5.00	2.50	1.50
(93)	Len Gabrielson	5.00	2.50	1.50
(94)	Gary Gentry	5.00	2.50	1.50
(95)	Jake Gibbs	5.00	2.50	1.50
(96)	Russ Gibson	5.00	2.50	1.50
(97)	Billy Grabarkewitz	5.00	2.50	1.50
(98)	Dick Green	5.00	2.50	1.50
(99)	Tom Griffin	5.00	2.50	1.50
(100)	Jerry Grote	5.00	2.50	1.50
(101)	Tom Haller	5.00	2.50	1.50
(102)	Steve Hamilton	5.00	2.50	1.50
(103)	Ron Hansen	5.00	2.50	1.50
(104)	Tommy Harmon	5.00	2.50	1.50
(105)	Tommy Harper	5.00	2.50	1.50
(106)	Bud Harrelson	5.00	2.50	1.50
(107)	Jim Ray Hart	5.00	2.50	1.50
(108)	Richie Hebner	5.00	2.50	1.50
(109)	Mike Hedlund	5.00	2.50	1.50
(110)	Mike Hegan	5.00	2.50	1.50
(111)	Tommy Helms	5.00	2.50	1.50
(112)	Angel Hermoso	5.00	2.50	1.50
(113)	Ed Herrmann	5.00	2.50	1.50
(114)	Mike Hershberger	5.00	2.50	1.50
(115)	Jim Hickman	5.00	2.50	1.50
(116)	Jim Hicks	5.00	2.50	1.50
(117)	Chuck Hinton	5.00	2.50	1.50
(118)	Larry Hisle	5.00	2.50	1.50
(119)	Gil Hodges	13.50	6.75	4.00
(120)	Ken Holtzman	5.00	2.50	1.50
(121)	Joel Horlen	5.00	2.50	1.50
(122)	Willie Horton	5.00	2.50	1.50
(123)	Ralph Houk	5.00	2.50	1.50
(124)	Frank Howard	7.50	3.75	2.25
(125)	Randy Hundley	5.00	2.50	1.50
(126)	Ron Hunt	5.00	2.50	1.50
(127)	Jim Hunter	13.50	6.75	4.00
(128)	Steve Huntz	5.00	2.50	1.50
(129)	Al Jackson	5.00	2.50	1.50
(130)	Reggie Jackson	35.00	17.50	10.50
(131)	Pat Jarvis	5.00	2.50	1.50
(132)	Julian Javier	5.00	2.50	1.50
(133)	Tommy John	10.00	5.00	3.00
(134)	Dave Johnson	5.00	2.50	1.50
(135)	Jerry Johnson	5.00	2.50	1.50
(136)	Jay Johnstone	5.00	2.50	1.50
(137)	Cleon Jones	5.00	2.50	1.50
(138)	Dalton Jones	5.00	2.50	1.50
(139)	Jim Kaat	7.50	3.75	2.25
(140)	Al Kaline	20.00	10.00	6.00
(141)	Dick Kelley	5.00	2.50	1.50
(142)	Pat Kelly	5.00	2.50	1.50
(143)	John Kennedy	5.00	2.50	1.50
(144)	Joe Keough	5.00	2.50	1.50
(145)	Don Kessinger	5.00	2.50	1.50
(146)	Harmon Killebrew	20.00	10.00	6.00
(147)	Clay Kirby	5.00	2.50	1.50
(148)	Darold Knowles	5.00	2.50	1.50
(149)	Jerry Koosman	5.00	2.50	1.50
(150)	Andy Kosco	5.00	2.50	1.50
(151)	Ed Kranepool	5.00	2.50	1.50
(152)	Lew Krausse	5.00	2.50	1.50
(153)	Coco Laboy	5.00	2.50	1.50
(154)	Hal Lanier	5.00	2.50	1.50
(155)	George Lauzerique	5.00	2.50	1.50
(156)	Denny Lemaster	5.00	2.50	1.50
(157)	Bob Locker	5.00	2.50	1.50
(158)	Mickey Lolich	5.00	2.50	1.50
(159)	Jim Lonborg	5.00	2.50	1.50
(160)	Mike Lum	5.00	2.50	1.50
(161)	Jim Maloney	5.00	2.50	1.50
(162)	Juan Marichal	13.50	6.75	4.00
(163)	Dal Maxvill	5.00	2.50	1.50
(164)	Carlos May	5.00	2.50	1.50
(165)	Lee May	5.00	2.50	1.50
(166)	Willie Mays	40.00	20.00	12.00
(167)	Bill Mazeroski	17.50	8.75	5.25
(168)	Dick McAuliffe	5.00	2.50	1.50
(169)	Mike McCormick	5.00	2.50	1.50
(170)	Willie McCovey	20.00	10.00	6.00
(171)	Denny McLain	5.00	2.50	1.50
(172)	Jerry McNertney	5.00	2.50	1.50
(173)	Bill Melton	5.00	2.50	1.50
(174)	Denis Menke	5.00	2.50	1.50
(175)	Jim Merritt	5.00	2.50	1.50
(176)	Gene Michael	5.00	2.50	1.50
(177)	Pete Mikkelsen	5.00	2.50	1.50
(178)	Felix Millan	5.00	2.50	1.50
(179)	Norm Miller	5.00	2.50	1.50
(180)	Don Mincher	5.00	2.50	1.50
(181)	George Mitterwald	5.00	2.50	1.50
(182)	Rick Monday	5.00	2.50	1.50
(183)	Don Money	5.00	2.50	1.50
(184)	Bob Moose	5.00	2.50	1.50
(185)	Dave Morehead	5.00	2.50	1.50
(186)	Joe Morgan	20.00	10.00	6.00
(187)	Bobby Mercer (Murcer)	7.50	3.75	2.25
(188)	Ivan Murrell	5.00	2.50	1.50
(189)	Phil Niekro	13.50	6.75	4.00
(190)	Jim Northrup	5.00	2.50	1.50
(191)	Tony Oliva	10.00	5.00	3.00
(192)	Al Oliver	5.00	2.50	1.50
(193)	Claude Osteen	5.00	2.50	1.50
(194)	Jose Pagan	5.00	2.50	1.50
(195)	Jim Pagliaroni	5.00	2.50	1.50
(196)	Jim Palmer	20.00	10.00	6.00
(197)	Lowell Palmer	5.00	2.50	1.50
(198)	Milt Pappas	5.00	2.50	1.50
(199)	Marty Pattin	5.00	2.50	1.50
(200)	Roberto Pena	5.00	2.50	1.50
(201)	Joe Pepitone	7.50	3.75	2.25
(202)	Tony Perez	17.50	8.75	5.25
(203)	Gaylord Perry	13.50	6.75	4.00
(204)	Jim Perry	5.00	2.50	1.50
(205)	Fritz Peterson	5.00	2.50	1.50
(206)	Rico Petroceli (Petrocelli)	5.00	2.50	1.50
(207)	Lefty Phillips	5.00	2.50	1.50
(208)	Tom Phoebus	5.00	2.50	1.50
(209)	Lou Piniella	7.50	3.75	2.25
(210)	Vada Pinson	7.50	3.75	2.25
(211)	Boog Powell	10.00	5.00	3.00
(212)	Frank Quilici	5.00	2.50	1.50
(213)	Doug Rader	5.00	2.50	1.50
(214)	Ron Reed	5.00	2.50	1.50
(215)	Rich Reese	5.00	2.50	1.50
(216)	Rick Reichardt	5.00	2.50	1.50
(217)	Phil Regan	5.00	2.50	1.50
(218)	Roger Repoz	5.00	2.50	1.50
(219)	Juan Rios	5.00	2.50	1.50
(220)	Brooks Robinson	20.00	10.00	6.00
(221)	Frank Robinson	20.00	10.00	6.00
(222)	Cookie Rojas	5.00	2.50	1.50
(223)	Rich Rollins	5.00	2.50	1.50
(224)	Pete Rose	40.00	20.00	12.00
(225)	Gary Ross	5.00	2.50	1.50
(226)	Joe Rudi	5.00	2.50	1.50
(227)	Manny Sanguillen	5.00	2.50	1.50
(228)	Jose Santiago	5.00	2.50	1.50
(229)	Ron Santo	10.00	5.00	3.00
(230)	Tom Satriano	5.00	2.50	1.50
(231)	Richie Scheinblum	5.00	2.50	1.50
(232)	Red Schoendienst	13.50	6.75	4.00
(233)	George Scott	5.00	2.50	1.50
(234)	Tom Seaver	20.00	10.00	6.00
(235)	Norm Siebern	5.00	2.50	1.50
(236)	Sonny Siebert	5.00	2.50	1.50
(237)	Duke Sims	5.00	2.50	1.50
(238)	Tommie Sisk	5.00	2.50	1.50
(239)	Ted Sizemore	5.00	2.50	1.50
(240)	Mayo Smith	5.00	2.50	1.50
(241)	Reggie Smith	5.00	2.50	1.50
(242)	Willie Smith	5.00	2.50	1.50
(243)	Russ Snyder	5.00	2.50	1.50
(244)	Joe Sparma	5.00	2.50	1.50
(245)	Lee Stange	5.00	2.50	1.50
(246)	Mickey Stanley	5.00	2.50	1.50
(247)	Willie Stargell	17.50	8.75	5.25
(248)	Rusty Staub	7.50	3.75	2.25
(249)	Ron Stone	5.00	2.50	1.50
(250)	Bill Stoneman	5.00	2.50	1.50

		NM	EX	VG
(251)	Mel Stottlemyre	5.00	2.50	1.50
(252)	Ed Stroud	5.00	2.50	1.50
(253)	Bill Sudakis	5.00	2.50	1.50
(254)	Gary Sutherland	5.00	2.50	1.50
(255)	Ron Swoboda	5.00	2.50	1.50
(256)	Carl Taylor	5.00	2.50	1.50
(257)	Tony Taylor	5.00	2.50	1.50
(258)	Bob Tillman	5.00	2.50	1.50
(259)	Bobby Tolan	5.00	2.50	1.50
(260)	Cesar Tovar	5.00	2.50	1.50
(261)	Jeff Torborg	5.00	2.50	1.50
(262)	Joe Torre	10.00	5.00	3.00
(263)	Hector Torres	5.00	2.50	1.50
(264)	Tom Tresh	7.50	3.75	2.25
(265)	Ted Uhlaender	5.00	2.50	1.50
(266)	Del Unser	5.00	2.50	1.50
(267)	Bob Veale	5.00	2.50	1.50
(268)	Zoilo Versalles	5.00	2.50	1.50
(269)	Bill Voss	5.00	2.50	1.50
(270)	Pete Ward	5.00	2.50	1.50
(271)	Greg Washburn	5.00	2.50	1.50
(272)	Eddie Watt	5.00	2.50	1.50
(273)	Ramon Webster	5.00	2.50	1.50
(274)	Al Weis	5.00	2.50	1.50
(275)	Roy White	5.00	2.50	1.50
(276)	Billy Williams	17.50	8.75	5.25
(277)	Ted Williams	30.00	15.00	9.00
(278)	Walt Williams	5.00	2.50	1.50
(279)	Billy Wilson	5.00	2.50	1.50
(280)	Don Wilson	5.00	2.50	1.50
(281)	Earl Wilson	5.00	2.50	1.50
(282)	Rick Wise	5.00	2.50	1.50
(283)	Bobby Wine	5.00	2.50	1.50
(284)	Wilbur Wood	5.00	2.50	1.50
(285)	Woody Woodward	5.00	2.50	1.50
(286)	Billy Wynne	5.00	2.50	1.50

1980 Superstar

This collectors' issue, probably produced by Card Collectors Closet in Springfield, Mass., included up to five cards each of the most famous former players. The 2-1/2" x 3-1/2" cards have black-and-white photos on front, with yellow, white and blue graphics. Backs are in black-and-white with career narrative. The set sold originally for $3.50.

		NM	EX	VG
Complete Set (45):		20.00	10.00	6.00
Common Player:		.75	.35	.20
1	Babe Ruth	1.25	.60	.40
2	Roberto Clemente	1.00	.50	.30
3	Roberto Clemente	1.00	.50	.30
4	Roberto Clemente	1.00	.50	.30
5	Lou Gehrig, Joe DiMaggio	.75	.35	.20
6	Mickey Mantle, Roger Maris	1.75	.90	.50
7	Roger Maris, Yogi Berra, Mickey Mantle	1.25	.60	.40
8	Whitey Ford, Sandy Koufax	.75	.35	.20
9	Babe Ruth	1.25	.60	.40
10	Roger Maris, Mickey Mantle	1.75	.90	.50
11	Ted Williams, Stan Musial, Willie Mays	.75	.35	.20
12	Mickey Mantle, Hank Aaron	1.25	.60	.40
13	Sandy Koufax	.75	.35	.20
14	Sandy Koufax	.75	.35	.20
15	Thurman Munson	.75	.35	.20
16	Sandy Koufax	.75	.35	.20
17	Sandy Koufax	.75	.35	.20
18	Willie Mays	.75	.35	.20
19	Willie Mays	.75	.35	.20
20	Willie Mays	.75	.35	.20
21	Willie Mays	.75	.35	.20
22	Ted Williams	.75	.35	.20
23	Ted Williams	.75	.35	.20
24	Ted Williams	.75	.35	.20
25	Ted Williams	.75	.35	.20
26	Lou Gehrig	.75	.35	.20
27	Lou Gehrig	.75	.35	.20
28	Lou Gehrig	.75	.35	.20
29	Lou Gehrig	.75	.35	.20
30	Mickey Mantle	2.00	1.00	.60
31	Mickey Mantle	2.00	1.00	.60
32	Mickey Mantle	2.00	1.00	.60
33	Mickey Mantle	2.00	1.00	.60
34	Hank Aaron	.75	.35	.20
35	Joe DiMaggio	.75	.35	.20
36	Joe DiMaggio	.75	.35	.20
37	Joe DiMaggio	.75	.35	.20
38	Joe DiMaggio	.75	.35	.20
39	Roberto Clemente	1.00	.50	.30
40	Babe Ruth	1.25	.60	.40
41	Babe Ruth	1.25	.60	.40
42	Babe Ruth	1.25	.60	.40
43	Hank Aaron	.75	.35	.20
44	Hank Aaron	.75	.35	.20
45	Hank Aaron	.75	.35	.20

1970 Super Valu Minnesota Twins

One of many Minnesota Twins regional issues from the team's first decade, this set of player portraits was painted by noted celebrity artist John Wheeldon. Individual player pictures were given away at Super Valu grocery stores. The premiums feature large portraits and smaller action pictures, painted in pastels, against a pastel background. A facsimile autograph is printed below the pictures and the player's name is printed in the bottom border. At 7-3/4" x 9-3/8", the Twins portraits are somewhat smaller than similar contemporary issues. Backs are printed in black-and-white and include a self-portrait and biography of the artist. Player information includes biographical bits, a lengthy career summary and complete major and minor league stats. Team and sponsor logo are also included on the unnumbered card backs. The set is checklisted here alphabetically.

		NM	EX	VG
Complete Set (12):		90.00	45.00	27.50
Common Player:		6.00	3.00	1.75
(1)	Brant Alyea	6.00	3.00	1.75
(2)	Leo Cardenas	6.00	3.00	1.75
(3)	Rod Carew	20.00	10.00	6.00
(4)	Jim Kaat	9.00	4.50	2.75
(5)	Harmon Killebrew	20.00	10.00	6.00
(6)	George Mitterwald	6.00	3.00	1.75
(7)	Tony Oliva	9.00	4.50	2.75
(8)	Ron Perranoski	6.00	3.00	1.75
(9)	Jim Perry	6.00	3.00	1.75
(10)	Rich Reese	6.00	3.00	1.75
(11)	Luis Tiant	7.50	3.75	2.25
(12)	Cesar Tovar	6.00	3.00	1.75

1874 Suppards & Fennemore Cabinets

Only members of the hometown 1874 Athletics (National Association) have been reported in this issue of cabinet cards from the Philadelphia studio. The 4-1/4" x 6-1/2" cards have full-length poses on front. Backs carry an ornate ad for the photographer. The players are not identified on the cards, unless an earlier owner has written the name. Thus far the team's most famous player, Cap Anson, has not been reported.

		NM	EX	VG
Common Player:		3,000	1,500	900.00
(1)	Joe Battin (Bat on shoulder.)	3,000	1,500	900.00
(2)	John Clapp (Cap on floor to his right.)	3,000	1,500	900.00
(3)	Wes Fisler (Bat at right side, no cap on floor.)	3,000	1,500	900.00
(4)	Dick McBride (Ball in hands at waist.)	3,000	1,500	900.00
(5)	Mike McGeary (Bat in crook of arm.)	3,000	1,500	900.00
(6)	John McMullin (Bat at his left, cap on floor at left.)	3,000	1,500	900.00
(7)	Tim Murnane (Bat at his right, cap on floor at left.)	3,250	1,625	975.00

1966 Swap-N-Save Album

While this 4" x 9" album pictures 1965 and 1966 Topps cards in full color on front and back, it is not connected with Topps. The album's interior pages feature die-cuts which allow the central panel to be removed so both front and back of each card can be viewed. Informational pages include team rosters.

	NM	EX	VG
Album:	80.00	40.00	20.00

1909-11 Sweet Caporal

 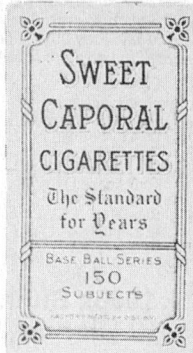

Among the most common of the American Tobacco Co. brands advertising on the backs of 1909-11 T206 and 1911 T205 is Sweet Caporal. T206s can be found with factory designations of No. 25, No. 30, No. 42 (overprinted), No. 649 and No. 649 (overprinted). In T205, Sweet Cap backs can be found printed in red (no factory number, or No. 42) or black, No. 25, No. 42.

(See T205, T206)

1909-12 Sweet Caporal Domino Discs (PX7)

Domino Discs, distributed by Sweet Caporal Cigarettes from 1909 to 1912, are among the more obscure 20th Century tobacco issues. Although the disc set contains many of the same players - some even pictured in the same poses - as the later Sweet Caporal pin set, the discs have always lagged behind the pins in collector appeal. The Domino Discs, so called because each disc has a large, white domino printed on the back, measure approximately 1-1/8" in diameter and are made of thin cardboard surrounded by a metal rim. The fronts of the discs contain a player portrait set against a background of either red, green or blue. The words "Sweet Caporal Cigarettes" appear on the front along with the player's last name and team. There are 129 different major leaguers featured in the set. Each player can be found with two picture variations involving uniform or cap details, or just the size of the portrait. Also known to exist as part of the set is a disc which pictures a generic player and contains the words "Home Team" against a red background on one side and "Visiting Team" with a green background on the reverse. Because each of the players can theoretically be found in two pictures, with three different background colors and with varying numbers of dots on the dominoes, there is almost an impossible number of variations available. Collectors, however, generally collect the discs without regard to background color or domino arrangement. The Domino Disc set was assigned the designation PX7 in the American Card Catalog.

		NM	EX	VG
Complete Set (129):		10,000	5,000	3,000
Common Player:		60.00	30.00	18.00
(1)	Red Ames	60.00	30.00	18.00
(2)	Jimmy Archer	60.00	30.00	18.00
(3)	Jimmy Austin	60.00	30.00	18.00
(4)	Home Run Baker	130.00	65.00	40.00
(5)	Neal Ball	60.00	30.00	18.00
(6)	Cy Barger	60.00	30.00	18.00
(7)	Jack Barry	60.00	30.00	18.00
(8)	Johnny Bates	60.00	30.00	18.00
(9)	Beals Becker	60.00	30.00	18.00
(10)	George Bell	60.00	30.00	18.00
(11)	Chief Bender	130.00	65.00	40.00
(12)	Bill Bergen	60.00	30.00	18.00

		NM	EX	VG
(13)	Bob Bescher	60.00	30.00	18.00
(14)	Joe Birmingham	60.00	30.00	18.00
(15)	Roger Bresnahan	130.00	65.00	40.00
(16)	Al Bridwell	60.00	30.00	18.00
(17)	Mordecai Brown	130.00	65.00	40.00
(18)	Bobby Byrne	60.00	30.00	18.00
(19)	Nixey Callahan	60.00	30.00	18.00
(20)	Howie Camnitz	60.00	30.00	18.00
(21)	Bill Carrigan	60.00	30.00	18.00
(22)	Frank Chance	130.00	65.00	40.00
(23)	Hal Chase	60.00	30.00	18.00
(24)	Ed Cicotte	60.00	30.00	18.00
(25)	Fred Clarke	130.00	65.00	40.00
(26a)	Ty Cobb ("D" on cap.)	600.00	300.00	180.00
(26b)	Ty Cobb (no "D" on cap.)	600.00	300.00	180.00
(27)	Eddie Collins	130.00	65.00	40.00
(28)	Doc Crandall	60.00	30.00	18.00
(29)	Birdie Cree	60.00	30.00	18.00
(30)	Bill Dahlen	60.00	30.00	18.00
(31)	Jim Delahanty	60.00	30.00	18.00
(32)	Art Devlin	60.00	30.00	18.00
(33)	Josh Devore	60.00	30.00	18.00
(34)	Red Dooin	60.00	30.00	18.00
(35)	Mickey Doolan	60.00	30.00	18.00
(36)	Patsy Dougherty	60.00	30.00	18.00
(37)	Tom Downey	60.00	30.00	18.00
(38)	Larry Doyle	60.00	30.00	18.00
(39)	Louis Drucke	60.00	30.00	18.00
(40)	Clyde Engle	60.00	30.00	18.00
(41)	Tex Erwin	60.00	30.00	18.00
(42)	Steve Evans	60.00	30.00	18.00
(43)	Johnny Evers	130.00	65.00	40.00
(44)	Cecil Ferguson	60.00	30.00	18.00
(45)	Russ Ford	60.00	30.00	18.00
(46)	Art Fromme	60.00	30.00	18.00
(47)	Harry Gaspar	60.00	30.00	18.00
(48)	George Gibson	60.00	30.00	18.00
(49)	Eddie Grant	65.00	32.50	20.00
(50)	Clark Griffith	130.00	65.00	40.00
(51)	Bob Groom	60.00	30.00	18.00
(52)	Bob Harmon	60.00	30.00	18.00
(53)	Topsy Hartsel	60.00	30.00	18.00
(54)	Arnold Hauser	60.00	30.00	18.00
(55)	Dick Hoblitzell	60.00	30.00	18.00
(56)	Danny Hoffman	60.00	30.00	18.00
(57)	Miller Huggins	130.00	65.00	40.00
(58)	John Hummel	60.00	30.00	18.00
(59)	Hugh Jennings	130.00	65.00	40.00
(60)	Walter Johnson	350.00	175.00	100.00
(61)	Ed Karger	60.00	30.00	18.00
(62a)	Jack Knight (Yankees)	60.00	30.00	18.00
(62b)	Jack Knight (Senators)	60.00	30.00	18.00
(63)	Ed Konetchy	60.00	30.00	18.00
(64)	Harry Krause	60.00	30.00	18.00
(65)	Frank LaPorte	60.00	30.00	18.00
(66)	Nap Lajoie	130.00	65.00	40.00
(67)	Tommy Leach	60.00	30.00	18.00
(68)	Sam Leever	60.00	30.00	18.00
(69)	Lefty Leifield	60.00	30.00	18.00
(70)	Paddy Livingston	60.00	30.00	18.00
(71)	Hans Lobert	60.00	30.00	18.00
(72)	Harry Lord	60.00	30.00	18.00
(73)	Nick Maddox	60.00	30.00	18.00
(74)	Sherry Magee	60.00	30.00	18.00
(75)	Rube Marquard	130.00	65.00	40.00
(76)	Christy Mathewson	400.00	200.00	120.00
(77)	Al Mattern	60.00	30.00	18.00
(78)	George McBride	60.00	30.00	18.00
(79)	John McGraw	130.00	65.00	40.00
(80)	Harry McIntire	60.00	30.00	18.00
(81)	Matty McIntyre	60.00	30.00	18.00
(82)	Larry McLean	60.00	30.00	18.00
(83)	Fred Merkle	60.00	30.00	18.00
(84)	Chief Meyers	60.00	30.00	18.00
(85)	Clyde Milan	60.00	30.00	18.00
(86)	Dots Miller	60.00	30.00	18.00
(87)	Mike Mitchell	60.00	30.00	18.00
(88a)	Pat Moran (Cubs)	60.00	30.00	18.00
(88b)	Pat Moran (Phillies)	60.00	30.00	18.00
(89)	George Mullen (Mullin)	60.00	30.00	18.00
(90)	Danny Murphy	60.00	30.00	18.00
(91)	Red Murray	60.00	30.00	18.00
(92)	Tom Needham	60.00	30.00	18.00
(93)	Rebel Oakes	60.00	30.00	18.00
(94)	Rube Oldring	60.00	30.00	18.00
(95)	Fred Parent	60.00	30.00	18.00
(96)	Dode Paskert	60.00	30.00	18.00
(97)	Barney Pelty	60.00	30.00	18.00
(98)	Eddie Phelps	60.00	30.00	18.00
(99)	Deacon Phillippe	60.00	30.00	18.00
(100)	Jack Quinn	60.00	30.00	18.00
(101)	Ed Reulbach	60.00	30.00	18.00
(102)	Lew Richie	60.00	30.00	18.00
(103)	Jack Rowan	60.00	30.00	18.00
(104)	Nap Rucker	60.00	30.00	18.00
(105a)	Doc Scanlon (Scanlan) (Superbas)	60.00	30.00	18.00
(105b)	Doc Scanlon (Scanlan) (Phillies)	60.00	30.00	18.00
(106)	Germany Schaefer	60.00	30.00	18.00
(107)	Boss Schmidt	60.00	30.00	18.00
(108)	Wildfire Schulte	60.00	30.00	18.00
(109)	Jimmy Sheckard	60.00	30.00	18.00
(110)	Hap Smith	60.00	30.00	18.00
(111)	Tris Speaker	150.00	75.00	45.00
(112)	Harry Stovall	60.00	30.00	18.00
(113a)	Gabby Street (Senators)	60.00	30.00	18.00
(113b)	Gabby Street (Yankees)	60.00	30.00	18.00
(114)	George Suggs	60.00	30.00	18.00
(115)	Ira Thomas	60.00	30.00	18.00
(116)	Joe Tinker	130.00	65.00	40.00
(117)	John Titus	60.00	30.00	18.00
(118)	Terry Turner	60.00	30.00	18.00
(119)	Heinie Wagner	60.00	30.00	18.00
(120)	Bobby Wallace	130.00	65.00	40.00
(121)	Ed Walsh	130.00	65.00	40.00
(122)	Jack Warhop	60.00	30.00	18.00
(123)	Zach Wheat	130.00	65.00	40.00
(124)	Doc White	60.00	30.00	18.00
(125a)	Art Wilson (Dark cap, Pirates.)	60.00	30.00	18.00
(125b)	Art Wilson (Dark cap, Giants.)	60.00	30.00	18.00
(126a)	Owen Wilson (White cap, Giants.)	60.00	30.00	18.00
(126b)	Owen Wilson (White cap, Pirates.)	60.00	30.00	18.00
(127)	Hooks Wiltse	60.00	30.00	18.00
(128)	Harry Wolter	60.00	30.00	18.00
(129)	Cy Young	400.00	200.00	120.00

1910-12 Sweet Caporal Pins (P2)

Expanding its premiums to include more than just trading cards, the American Tobacco Co. issued a series of baseball pins circa 1910-12. The sepia-colored pins measure 7/8" in diameter. The set includes 152 different players, but because of numerous "large letter" and "small letter" variations, collectors generally consider the set complete at 205 different pins. Fifty of the players are pictured on a second pin that usually displays the same photo but has the player's name and team designation printed in larger letters. Three players (Bresnahan, Mullin and Wallace) have three pins each. It is now generally accepted that there are 153 pins with "small letters" and another 52 "large letter" variations in a complete set. Research among advanced collectors has shown that 19 of the pins, including six of the "large letter" variations, are considered more difficult to find. The back of each pin has a variously colored paper insert advertising Sweet Caporal Cigarettes. The red backings are generally less common. The Sweet Caporal pins are closely related to the popular T205 Gold Border tobacco cards, also issued by the American Tobacco Co. about the same time. All but nine of the players featured in the pin set were also pictured on T205 cards, and in nearly all cases the photos are identical. The Sweet Caporal pins are designated as P2 in the American Card Catalog. The complete set price includes all variations.

		NM	EX	VG
	Complete Set (204):	10,000	5,000	3,000
	Common Player:	30.00	15.00	9.00
(1)	Ed Abbaticchio	30.00	15.00	9.00
(2)	Red Ames	30.00	15.00	9.00
(3a)	Jimmy Archer (Small letters.)	30.00	15.00	9.00
(3b)	Jimmy Archer (Large letters.)	35.00	17.50	10.00
(4a)	Jimmy Austin (Small letters.)	30.00	15.00	9.00
(4b)	Jimmy Austin (Large letters.)	35.00	17.50	10.00
(5)	Home Run Baker	90.00	45.00	27.00
(6)	Neal Ball	30.00	15.00	9.00
(7)	Cy Barger	30.00	15.00	9.00
(8)	Jack Barry	30.00	15.00	9.00
(9)	Johnny Bates	30.00	15.00	9.00
(10)	Beals Becker	30.00	15.00	9.00
(11)	Fred Beebe	30.00	15.00	9.00
(12a)	George Bell (Small letters.)	30.00	15.00	9.00
(12b)	George Bell (large letters)	35.00	17.50	10.00
(13a)	"Chief" Bender (Small letters.)	90.00	45.00	27.00
(13b)	"Chief" Bender (Large letters.)	100.00	50.00	30.00
(14)	Bill Bergen	30.00	15.00	9.00
(15)	Bob Bescher	30.00	15.00	9.00
(16)	Joe Birmingham	30.00	15.00	9.00
(17)	Kitty Bransfield	65.00	32.50	20.00
(18a)	Roger Bresnahan (Mouth closed, small letters.)	90.00	45.00	27.00
(18b)	Roger Bresnahan (Mouth closed, large letters.)	100.00	50.00	30.00
(19)	Roger Bresnahan (Mouth open.)	90.00	45.00	27.00
(20)	Al Bridwell	30.00	15.00	9.00
(21a)	Mordecai Brown (Small letters.)	90.00	45.00	27.00
(21b)	Mordecai Brown (Large letters.)	100.00	50.00	30.00
(22)	Bobby Byrne	30.00	15.00	9.00
(23)	Nixey Callahan	30.00	15.00	9.00
(24a)	Howie Camnitz (Small letters.)	30.00	15.00	9.00
(24b)	Howie Camnitz (Large letters.)	35.00	17.50	10.00
(25a)	Bill Carrigan (Small letters.)	30.00	15.00	9.00
(25b)	Bill Carrigan (Large letters.)	35.00	17.50	10.00
(26a)	Frank Chance (Small letters.)	90.00	45.00	27.00
(26b)	Frank Chance (Large letters.)	100.00	50.00	30.00
(27)	Hal Chase (Small letters.)	50.00	25.00	15.00
(28)	Hal Chase (Large letters.)	90.00	45.00	27.00
(29)	Ed Cicotte	90.00	45.00	27.00
(30a)	Fred Clarke (Small letters.)	90.00	45.00	27.00
(30b)	Fred Clarke (Large letters.)	100.00	50.00	30.00
(31a)	Ty Cobb (Small letters, "D" on cap.)	600.00	300.00	180.00
(31b)	Ty Cobb (Large letters, no "D" on cap.)	675.00	335.00	200.00
(32a)	Eddie Collins (Small letters.)	90.00	45.00	27.00
(32b)	Eddie Collins (Large letters.)	100.00	50.00	30.00
(33)	Doc Crandall	30.00	15.00	9.00
(34)	Birdie Cree	65.00	32.50	20.00
(35)	Bill Dahlen	30.00	15.00	9.00
(36)	Jim Delahanty	30.00	15.00	9.00
(37)	Art Devlin	30.00	15.00	9.00
(38)	Josh Devore	30.00	15.00	9.00
(39)	Wild Bill Donovan	65.00	32.50	20.00
(40a)	Red Dooin (Small letters.)	30.00	15.00	9.00
(40b)	Red Dooin (Large letters.)	35.00	17.50	10.00
(41a)	Mickey Doolan (Small letters.)	30.00	15.00	9.00
(41b)	Mickey Doolan (Large letters.)	35.00	17.50	10.00
(42)	Patsy Dougherty	30.00	15.00	9.00
(43a)	Tom Downey (Small letters.)	30.00	15.00	9.00
(43b)	Tom Downey (Large letters.)	35.00	17.50	10.00
(44a)	Larry Doyle (Small letters.)	30.00	15.00	9.00
(44b)	Larry Doyle (Large letters.)	35.00	17.50	10.00
(45)	Louis Drucke	30.00	15.00	9.00
(46a)	Hugh Duffy (Small letters.)	90.00	45.00	27.00
(46b)	Hugh Duffy (Large letters.)	100.00	50.00	30.00
(47)	Jimmy Dygert	30.00	15.00	9.00
(48a)	Kid Elberfeld (Small letters.)	30.00	15.00	9.00
(48b)	Kid Elberfeld (Large letters.)	35.00	17.50	10.00
(49a)	Clyde Engle (Small letters.)	30.00	15.00	9.00
(49b)	Clyde Engle (Large letters.)	35.00	17.50	10.00
(50)	Tex Erwin	30.00	15.00	9.00
(51)	Steve Evans	30.00	15.00	9.00
(52)	Johnny Evers	90.00	45.00	27.00
(53)	Cecil Ferguson	30.00	15.00	9.00
(54)	John Flynn	30.00	15.00	9.00
(55a)	Russ Ford (Small letters.)	30.00	15.00	9.00
(55b)	Russ Ford (Large letters.)	35.00	17.50	10.00
(56)	Art Fromme	30.00	15.00	9.00
(57)	Harry Gaspar	30.00	15.00	9.00
(58a)	George Gibson (Small letters.)	30.00	15.00	9.00
(58b)	George Gibson (Large letters.)	35.00	17.50	10.00
(59)	Eddie Grant	65.00	32.50	20.00
(60)	Dolly Gray	30.00	15.00	9.00
(61a)	Clark Griffith (Small letters.)	90.00	45.00	27.00
(61b)	Clark Griffith (Large letters.)	100.00	50.00	30.00
(62)	Bob Groom	30.00	15.00	9.00
(63)	Bob Harmon	30.00	15.00	9.00
(64)	Topsy Hartsel	30.00	15.00	9.00
(65)	Arnold Hauser	65.00	32.50	20.00
(66)	Ira Hemphill	30.00	15.00	9.00
(67a)	Buck Herzog (Small letters.)	30.00	15.00	9.00
(67b)	Buck Herzog (Large letters.)	35.00	17.50	10.00
(68)	Dick Hoblitzell	30.00	15.00	9.00
(69)	Danny Hoffman	30.00	15.00	9.00
(70)	Harry Hooper	90.00	45.00	27.00
(71a)	Miller Huggins (Small letters.)	90.00	45.00	27.00
(71b)	Miller Huggins (Large letters.)	100.00	50.00	30.00
(72)	John Hummel	30.00	15.00	9.00
(73)	Hugh Jennings (Small letters.)	90.00	45.00	27.00
(74)	Hugh Jennings (Large letters.)	100.00	50.00	30.00
(75a)	Walter Johnson (Small letters.)	225.00	110.00	65.00
(75b)	Walter Johnson (Large letters.)	275.00	135.00	85.00
(76)	Tom Jones	65.00	32.50	20.00
(77)	Ed Karger	30.00	15.00	9.00
(78)	Ed Killian	65.00	32.50	20.00
(79a)	Jack Knight (Small letters.)	30.00	15.00	9.00
(79b)	Jack Knight (Large letters.)	35.00	17.50	10.00
(80)	Ed Konetchy	30.00	15.00	9.00
(81)	Harry Krause	30.00	15.00	9.00
(82)	Rube Kroh	30.00	15.00	9.00
(83)	Nap Lajoie	90.00	45.00	27.00
(84a)	Frank LaPorte (Small letters.)	30.00	15.00	9.00
(84b)	Frank LaPorte (Large letters.)	35.00	17.50	10.00
(85)	Arlie Latham	30.00	15.00	9.00
(86a)	Tommy Leach (Small letters.)	30.00	15.00	9.00
(86b)	Tommy Leach (Large letters.)	35.00	17.50	10.00
(87)	Sam Leever	30.00	15.00	9.00
(88)	Lefty Leifield	30.00	15.00	9.00
(89)	Hans Lobert	30.00	15.00	9.00
(90a)	Harry Lord (Small letters.)	30.00	15.00	9.00
(90b)	Harry Lord (Large letters.)	35.00	17.50	10.00
(91)	Paddy Livingston	30.00	15.00	9.00
(92)	Nick Maddox	30.00	15.00	9.00
(93)	Sherry Magee	30.00	15.00	9.00
(94)	Rube Marquard	90.00	45.00	27.00
(95a)	Christy Mathewson (Small letters.)	225.00	110.00	65.00
(95b)	Christy Mathewson (Large letters.)	275.00	135.00	80.00
(96a)	Al Mattern (Small letters.)	30.00	15.00	9.00
(96b)	Al Mattern (Large letters.)	35.00	17.50	10.00
(97)	George McBride	30.00	15.00	9.00
(98a)	John McGraw (Small letters.)	90.00	45.00	27.00
(98b)	John McGraw (Large letters.)	100.00	50.00	30.00
(99)	Harry McIntire (Cubs)	30.00	15.00	9.00
(100a)	Matty McIntyre (White Sox, small letters.)	30.00	15.00	9.00
(100b)	Matty McIntyre (White Sox, large letters.)	35.00	17.50	10.00
(101a)	John McLean (Small letters.)	30.00	15.00	9.00
(101b)	John McLean (Large letters.)	35.00	17.50	10.00
(102)	Fred Merkle	30.00	15.00	9.00
(103)	Chief Meyers	30.00	15.00	9.00
(104)	Clyde Milan	30.00	15.00	9.00
(105)	Dots Miller	30.00	15.00	9.00
(106)	Mike Mitchell	30.00	15.00	9.00
(107)	Pat Moran	30.00	15.00	9.00
(108a)	George Mullen (Mullin) (Small letters.)	30.00	15.00	9.00
(108b)	George Mullin (Large letters, white cap.)	90.00	45.00	27.00
(109)	Danny Murphy	30.00	15.00	9.00
(110a)	Red Murray (Small letters.)	35.00	17.50	10.00
(110b)	Red Murray (Large letters.)	30.00	15.00	9.00
(111)	Tom Needham	65.00	32.50	20.00
(112a)	Rebel Oakes (Small letters.)	30.00	15.00	9.00
(112b)	Rebel Oakes (Large letters.)	35.00	17.50	10.00

		NM	EX	VG
(113)	Rube Oldring	30.00	15.00	9.00
(114)	Charley O'Leary	30.00	15.00	9.00
(115)	Orval Overall	65.00	32.50	20.00
(116)	Fred Parent	30.00	15.00	9.00
(117a)	Dode Paskert (Small letters.)	30.00	15.00	9.00
(117b)	Dode Paskert (Large letters.)	35.00	17.50	10.00
(118)	Barney Pelty	30.00	15.00	9.00
(119)	Jake Pfeister	30.00	15.00	9.00
(120)	Eddie Phelps	30.00	15.00	9.00
(121)	Deacon Phillippe	30.00	15.00	9.00
(122)	Jack Quinn	30.00	15.00	9.00
(123)	Ed Reulbach	30.00	15.00	9.00
(124)	Lew Richie	30.00	15.00	9.00
(125)	Jack Rowan	30.00	15.00	9.00
(126a)	Nap Rucker (Small letters.)	30.00	15.00	9.00
(126b)	Nap Rucker (Large letters.)	35.00	17.50	10.00
(127)	Doc Scanlon (Scanlan)	65.00	32.50	20.00
(128)	Germany Schaefer	30.00	15.00	9.00
(129)	Jimmy Scheckard (Sheckard)	30.00	15.00	9.00
(130a)	Boss Schmidt (Small letters.)	30.00	15.00	9.00
(130b)	Boss Schmidt (Large letters.)	35.00	17.50	10.00
(131)	Wildfire Schulte	30.00	15.00	9.00
(132)	Hap Smith	30.00	15.00	9.00
(133a)	Tris Speaker (Small letters.)	150.00	75.00	45.00
(133b)	Tris Speaker (Large letters.)	175.00	85.00	50.00
(134)	Oscar Stanage	30.00	15.00	9.00
(135)	Harry Steinfeldt	30.00	15.00	9.00
(136)	George Stone	30.00	15.00	9.00
(137a)	George Stoval (Stovall) (Small letters.)	30.00	15.00	9.00
(137b)	George Stoval (Stovall) (Large letters.)	35.00	17.50	10.00
(138a)	Gabby Street (Small letters.)	30.00	15.00	9.00
(138b)	Gabby Street (Large letters.)	35.00	17.50	10.00
(139)	George Suggs	30.00	15.00	9.00
(140a)	Ira Thomas (Small letters.)	30.00	15.00	9.00
(140b)	Ira Thomas (Large letters.)	35.00	17.50	10.00
(141a)	Joe Tinker (Small letters.)	90.00	45.00	27.00
(141b)	Joe Tinker (Large letters.)	100.00	50.00	30.00
(142a)	John Titus (Small letters.)	30.00	15.00	9.00
(142b)	John Titus (Large letters.)	35.00	17.50	10.00
(143)	Terry Turner	30.00	15.00	9.00
(144)	Heinie Wagner	30.00	15.00	9.00
(145a)	Bobby Wallace (With cap, small letters.)	90.00	45.00	27.00
(145b)	Bobby Wallace (With cap, large letters.)	100.00	50.00	30.00
(146)	Bobby Wallace (Without cap.)	90.00	45.00	27.00
(147)	Ed Walsh	90.00	45.00	27.00
(148)	Jack Warhop	30.00	15.00	9.00
(149a)	Zach Wheat (Small letters.)	90.00	45.00	27.00
(149b)	Zach Wheat (Large letters.)	100.00	50.00	30.00
(150)	Doc White	30.00	15.00	9.00
(151)	Art Wilson (Giants)	30.00	15.00	9.00
(152)	Owen Wilson (Pirates)	30.00	15.00	9.00
(153)	Hooks Wiltse	30.00	15.00	9.00
(154)	Harry Wolter	30.00	15.00	9.00
(155a)	"Cy" Young ("C" on cap.)	200.00	100.00	60.00
(155b)	Old Cy Young (Plain cap.)	225.00	110.00	65.00

1928 Sweetman

(27) TY COBB

This set consists of 60 of the most prominent Baseball players in the big Leagues. We have made up an album which will hold the complete set. On receipt of 15 cents in stamps we will send a blank album to any address in the United States.

Manufactured only by the SWEETMAN CO. INC. 1611 Cass Ave. St. Louis, Mo.

The cards of this St. Louis firm share the format - about 1-3/8" x 2-1/2", black-and-white with card number in parentheses to the left of player name on front - and checklist with the 1928 York Caramels Type 2 issue, but are less frequently encountered. Backs of the Sweetman cards offer an album for 15 cents in stamps. The type of business is which Sweetman Co., Inc., was engaged is unknown.

		NM	EX	VG
	Complete Set (60):	25,000	12,500	7,500
	Common Player:	250.00	125.00	75.00
1	Burleigh Grimes	400.00	200.00	120.00
2	Walter Reuther (Ruether)	250.00	125.00	75.00
3	Joe Dugan	250.00	125.00	75.00
4	Red Faber	400.00	200.00	120.00
5	Gabby Hartnett	400.00	200.00	120.00
6	Babe Ruth	6,000	3,000	1,800
7	Bob Meusel	250.00	125.00	75.00
8	Herb Pennock	400.00	200.00	120.00
9	George Burns	250.00	125.00	75.00
10	Joe Sewell	400.00	200.00	120.00
11	George Uhle	250.00	125.00	75.00
12	Bob O'Farrell	250.00	125.00	75.00
13	Rogers Hornsby	500.00	250.00	150.00
14	"Pie" Traynor	400.00	200.00	120.00

		NM	EX	VG
15	Clarence Mitchell	250.00	125.00	75.00
16	Eppa Jepha Rixey	400.00	200.00	120.00
17	Carl Mays	300.00	150.00	90.00
18	Adolfo Luque	250.00	125.00	75.00
19	Dave Bancroft	400.00	200.00	120.00
20	George Kelly	400.00	200.00	120.00
21	Earl (Earle) Combs	400.00	200.00	120.00
22	Harry Heilmann	400.00	200.00	120.00
23	Ray W. Schalk	400.00	200.00	120.00
24	Johnny Mostil	250.00	125.00	75.00
25	Hack Wilson	400.00	200.00	120.00
26	Lou Gehrig	4,000	2,000	1,200
27	Ty Cobb	4,000	2,000	1,200
28	Tris Speaker	500.00	250.00	150.00
29	Tony Lazzeri	400.00	200.00	120.00
30	Waite Hoyt	400.00	200.00	120.00
31	Sherwood Smith	250.00	125.00	75.00
32	Max Carey	400.00	200.00	120.00
33	Eugene Hargrave	250.00	125.00	75.00
34	Miguel L. Gonzales (Miguel A. Gonzalez)	250.00	125.00	75.00
35	Joe Judge	250.00	125.00	75.00
36	E.C. (Sam) Rice	400.00	200.00	120.00
37	Earl Sheely	250.00	125.00	75.00
38	Sam Jones	250.00	125.00	75.00
39	Bib (Bibb) A. Falk	250.00	125.00	75.00
40	Willie Kamm	250.00	125.00	75.00
41	Stanley Harris	400.00	200.00	120.00
42	John J. McGraw	400.00	200.00	120.00
43	Artie Nehf	250.00	125.00	75.00
44	Grover Alexander	500.00	250.00	150.00
45	Paul Waner	400.00	200.00	120.00
46	William H. Terry	400.00	200.00	120.00
47	Glenn Wright	250.00	125.00	75.00
48	Earl Smith	250.00	125.00	75.00
49	Leon (Goose) Goslin	400.00	200.00	120.00
50	Frank Frisch	400.00	200.00	120.00
51	Joe Harris	250.00	125.00	75.00
52	Fred (Cy) Williams	250.00	125.00	75.00
53	Eddie Roush	400.00	200.00	120.00
54	George Sisler	400.00	200.00	120.00
55	Ed. Rommel	250.00	125.00	75.00
56	Rogers Peckinpaugh (Roger)	250.00	125.00	75.00
57	Stanley Coveleskie (Coveleski)	400.00	200.00	120.00
58	Lester Bell	250.00	125.00	75.00
59	Clyde Barnhart	250.00	125.00	75.00
60	John P. McInnis	250.00	125.00	75.00

1948 Swell Babe Ruth Story

The Philadelphia Gum Co., in 1948, created a card set about the movie "The Babe Ruth Story," which starred William Bendix and Claire Trevor. The set, whose American Card Catalog designation is R421, contains 28 black and white, numbered cards which measure 2" x 2-1/2". The Babe Ruth Story set was originally intended to consist of sixteen cards. Twelve additional cards (#'s 17-28) were added when Ruth died before the release of the film. The card backs include an offer for an autographed photo of William Bendix, starring as the Babe, for five Swell Bubble Gum wrappers and five cents.

		NM	EX	VG
	Complete Set (28):	2,750	1,100	550.00
	Common Card (1-16):	45.00	20.00	10.00
	Common Card (17-28):	125.00	55.00	30.00
1	"The Babe Ruth Story" in the Making	150.00	65.00	35.00
2	Batboy Becomes the Babe (William Bendix)	45.00	20.00	10.00
3	Claire Hodgson (Claire Trevor)	45.00	20.00	10.00
4	Babe Ruth and Claire Hodgson	45.00	20.00	10.00
5	Brother Mathias (Charles Bickford)	45.00	20.00	10.00
6	Phil Conrad (Sam Levene)	45.00	20.00	10.00
7	Nightclub Singer (Gertrude Niesen)	45.00	20.00	10.00
8	Baseball's Famous Deal, Jack Dunn (William Frawley)	45.00	20.00	10.00
9	Mr. and Mrs. Babe Ruth	45.00	20.00	10.00
10	Babe Ruth, Claire Ruth and Brother Mathias	45.00	20.00	10.00
11	Babe Ruth and Miller Huggins (Fred Lightner)	45.00	20.00	10.00
12	Babe at Bed of Ill Boy Johnny Sylvester (Gregory Marshall)	45.00	20.00	10.00
13	Sylvester Family Listening to Game	45.00	20.00	10.00
14	"When a Feller Needs a Friend" (With dog at police station.)	45.00	20.00	10.00
15	Dramatic Home Run	45.00	20.00	10.00
16	The Homer That Set the Record - #60 (#60)	75.00	34.00	18.50
17	"The Slap That Started Baseball's Famous Career"	125.00	55.00	30.00
18	The Babe Plays Santa Claus	125.00	55.00	30.00
19	Meeting of Owner and Manager	125.00	55.00	30.00
20	"Broken Window Paid Off"	125.00	55.00	30.00
21	Babe in a Crowd of Autograph Collectors	200.00	90.00	50.00
22	Charley Grimm, William Bendix	125.00	55.00	30.00
23	Ted Lyons, William Bendix	125.00	55.00	30.00
24	Lefty Gomez, William Bendix, Bucky Harris	150.00	65.00	35.00
25	Babe Ruth, William Bendix	400.00	180.00	100.00
26	Babe Ruth, William Bendix	400.00	180.00	100.00
27	Babe Ruth, Claire Trevor	400.00	180.00	100.00
28	William Bendix, Babe Ruth, Claire Trevor	400.00	180.00	100.00

1948 Swell Sport Thrills

This is a set of black-and-white cards which depicts memorable events in baseball history. The cards measure 2-1/2" x 3" and have a picture frame border and event title on the card fronts. The card backs describe the event in detail. Twenty cards were produced in this set by the Swell Gum Company of Philadelphia. Each card is numbered, and card numbers 9, 11, 16 and 20 are considered more difficult to obtain.

		NM	EX	VG
	Complete Set (20):	1,500	675.00	375.00
	Common Player:	30.00	13.50	7.00
1	Greatest Single Inning (Mickey Cochrane, Jimmy (Jimmie) Foxx, George Haas, Bing Miller, Al Simmons)	85.00	37.50	20.00
2	Amazing Record (Pete Reiser)	30.00	13.50	7.00
3	Dramatic Debut (Jackie Robinson)	175.00	80.00	45.00
4	Greatest Pitcher (Walter Johnson)	75.00	35.00	17.50
5	Three Strikes Not Out! (Tommy Henrich, Mickey Owen)	30.00	13.50	7.00
6	Home Run Wins Series (Bill Dickey)	35.00	16.00	9.00
7	Never Say Die Pitcher (Hal Schumacher)	30.00	13.50	7.00
8	Five Strikeouts! (Carl Hubbell)	40.00	18.00	10.00
9	Greatest Catch! (Al Gionfriddo)	55.00	25.00	13.50
10	No Hits! No Runs! (Johnny VanderMeer)	30.00	13.50	7.00
11	Bases Loaded! (Tony Lazzeri, Bob O'Farrell)	35.00	16.00	9.00
12	Most Dramatic Home Run (Lou Gehrig, Babe Ruth)	200.00	90.00	50.00
13	Winning Run (Tommy Bridges, Mickey Cochrane, Goose Goslin)	30.00	13.50	7.00
14	Great Slugging (Lou Gehrig)	225.00	100.00	55.00
15	Four Men to Stop Him! (Jim Bagby, Al Smith)	50.00	22.50	12.50
16	Three Run Homer in Ninth! (Joe DiMaggio, Joe Gordon, Ted Williams)	200.00	90.00	50.00
17	Football Block! (Whitey Kurowski, Johnny Lindell)	30.00	13.50	7.00
18	Home Run to Fame (Pee Wee Reese)	85.00	37.50	20.00
19	Strikeout Record! (Bob Feller)	50.00	22.50	12.50
20	Rifle Arm! (Carl Furillo)	50.00	22.50	12.50

1957 Swift Meats

One of the really different baseball card issues of the Fifties was the set of 18 3-D baseball player figures which could be punched out and assembled from cards included in packages of hot dogs. The unpunched cards measure approximately 3-1/2" x 4".

Prices below are for unpunched cards. Values for assembled figures are problematical.

		NM	EX	VG
Complete Set, Singles (18):		1,500	750.00	450.00
Complete Set w/ Mailer, Playing Board:		2,650	1,300	775.00
Common Player:		60.00	30.00	18.00
1	John Podres	75.00	37.50	22.50
2	Gus Triandos	60.00	30.00	18.00
3	Dale Long	60.00	30.00	18.00
4	Billy Pierce	60.00	30.00	18.00
5	Ed Bailey	60.00	30.00	18.00
6	Vic Wertz	60.00	30.00	18.00
7	Nelson Fox	130.00	65.00	40.00
8	Ken Boyer	75.00	37.50	22.50
9	Gil McDougald	75.00	37.50	22.50
10	Junior Gilliam	75.00	37.50	22.50
11	Eddie Yost	60.00	30.00	18.00
12	Johnny Logan	60.00	30.00	18.00
13	Hank Aaron	200.00	100.00	60.00
14	Bill Tuttle	60.00	30.00	18.00
15	Jackie Jensen	60.00	30.00	18.00
16	Frank Robinson	200.00	100.00	60.00
17	Richie Ashburn	130.00	65.00	40.00
18	Rocky Colavito	200.00	100.00	60.00

1951 Sylvania Leo Durocher Postcard

The N.Y. Giants manager endorses Sylvania radio/television service on this large-format (8-1/2" x 5-1/2") postcard. Color artwork features Durocher with a quotation endorsing Sylvania parts and service.

	NM	EX	VG
Leo Durocher	50.00	25.00	15.00

1910-11 S74 Silks - White

Designated as S74 in the "American Card Catalog," these delicate fabric collectibles are popular with advanced collectors. The silks were issued as premiums with several different brands of cigarettes: Turkey Red, Old Mill, Red Sun, and, rarely, Helmar. The satin-like silks can be found in two different styles, either "white" or "colored." The white silks measure 1-7/8" x 3" and were originally issued with a brown paper backing that carried an advertisement for one of the cigarette brands. The backing also advised that the silks were "useful in making pillow covers and other fancy articles for home decoration." Many undoubtedly were used for such purposes, making silks with the paper backing still intact more difficult to find. White silks must have the backing intact to command top values shown here. Ninety-two subjects are known in the "white" silks. The silks feature the player pictures found in the popular T205 Gold Border tobacco card set.

		NM	EX	VG
Complete Set (92):		16,000	6,400	4,150
Common Player:		135.00	55.00	35.00
No Paper Backing: 50%				
(1)	Home Run Baker	300.00	120.00	75.00
(2)	Cy Barger	135.00	55.00	35.00
(3)	Jack Barry	135.00	55.00	35.00
(4)	Johnny Bates	135.00	55.00	35.00
(5)	Fred Beck	135.00	55.00	35.00
(6)	Beals Becker	135.00	55.00	35.00
(7)	George Bell	135.00	55.00	35.00
(8)	Chief Bender	300.00	120.00	75.00
(9)	Roger Bresnahan	300.00	120.00	75.00
(10)	Al Bridwell	135.00	55.00	35.00
(11)	Mordecai Brown	300.00	120.00	75.00
(12)	Bobby Byrne	135.00	55.00	35.00
(13)	Howie Camnitz	135.00	55.00	35.00
(14)	Bill Carrigan	135.00	55.00	35.00
(15)	Frank Chance	300.00	120.00	75.00
(16)	Hal Chase	250.00	100.00	60.00
(17)	Fred Clarke	300.00	120.00	75.00
(18)	Ty Cobb	1,350	550.00	350.00
(19)	Eddie Collins	300.00	120.00	75.00
(20)	Doc Crandall	135.00	55.00	35.00
(21)	Lou Criger	135.00	55.00	35.00
(22)	Jim Delahanty	135.00	55.00	35.00
(23)	Art Devlin	135.00	55.00	35.00
(24)	Red Dooin	135.00	55.00	35.00
(25)	Mickey Doolan	135.00	55.00	35.00
(26)	Larry Doyle	135.00	55.00	35.00
(27)	Jimmy Dygert	135.00	55.00	35.00
(28)	Kid Elberfield (Elberfeld)	135.00	55.00	35.00
(29)	Steve Evans	135.00	55.00	35.00
(30)	Johnny Evers	300.00	120.00	75.00
(31)	Bob Ewing	135.00	55.00	35.00
(32)	Art Fletcher	135.00	55.00	35.00
(33)	John Flynn	135.00	55.00	35.00
(34)	Bill Foxen	135.00	55.00	35.00
(35)	George Gibson	135.00	55.00	35.00
(36)	Peaches Graham (Cubs)	135.00	55.00	35.00
(37)	Peaches Graham (Rustlers)	135.00	55.00	35.00
(38)	Clark Griffith	300.00	120.00	75.00
(39)	Topsy Hartsel	135.00	55.00	35.00
(40)	Arnold Hauser	135.00	55.00	35.00
(41)	Charlie Hemphill	135.00	55.00	35.00
(42)	Davy Jones	135.00	55.00	35.00
(43)	Jack Knight	135.00	55.00	35.00
(44)	Ed Konetchy	135.00	55.00	35.00
(45)	Harry Krause	135.00	55.00	35.00
(46)	Tommy Leach	135.00	55.00	35.00
(47)	Rube Marquard	300.00	120.00	75.00
(48)	Christy Mathewson	650.00	260.00	160.00
(49)	Al Mattern	135.00	55.00	35.00
(50)	Amby McConnell	135.00	55.00	35.00
(51)	John McGraw	300.00	120.00	75.00
(52)	Harry McIntire (McIntyre)	135.00	55.00	35.00
(53)	Fred Merkle	135.00	55.00	35.00
(54)	Chief Meyers	135.00	55.00	35.00
(55)	Dots Miller	135.00	55.00	35.00
(56)	Danny Murphy	135.00	55.00	35.00
(57)	Red Murray	135.00	55.00	35.00
(58)	Tom Needham	135.00	55.00	35.00
(59)	Rebel Oakes	135.00	55.00	35.00
(60)	Rube Oldring	135.00	55.00	35.00
(61)	Orval Overall	135.00	55.00	35.00
(62)	Fred Parent	135.00	55.00	35.00
(63)	Fred Payne	135.00	55.00	35.00
(64)	Barney Pelty	135.00	55.00	35.00
(65)	Deacon Phillippe	135.00	55.00	35.00
(66)	Jack Quinn	135.00	55.00	35.00
(67)	Bugs Raymond	135.00	55.00	35.00
(68)	Ed Reulbach	135.00	55.00	35.00
(69)	Doc Scanlon (Scanlan)	135.00	55.00	35.00
(70)	Germany Schaefer	135.00	55.00	35.00
(71)	Geo. Schlei	135.00	55.00	35.00
(72)	Wildfire Schulte	135.00	55.00	35.00
(73)	Dave Shean	135.00	55.00	35.00
(74)	Jimmy Sheckard	135.00	55.00	35.00
(75)	Tony Smith (Superbas)	135.00	55.00	35.00
(76)	Harry Smith (Rustlers)	500.00	200.00	125.00
(77)	Fred Snodgrass	135.00	55.00	35.00
(78)	Tris Speaker	350.00	140.00	87.00
(79)	Harry Steinfeldt (Cubs)	135.00	55.00	35.00
(80)	Harry Steinfeldt (Rustlers)	135.00	55.00	35.00
(81)	George Stone	135.00	55.00	35.00
(82)	Gabby Street	135.00	55.00	35.00
(83)	Ed Summers	135.00	55.00	35.00
(84)	Lee Tannehill	135.00	55.00	35.00
(85)	Joe Tinker	300.00	120.00	75.00
(86)	John Titus	135.00	55.00	35.00
(87)	Terry Turner	135.00	55.00	35.00
(88)	Bobby Wallace	300.00	120.00	75.00
(89)	Doc White	135.00	55.00	35.00
(90)	Ed Willett	135.00	55.00	35.00
(91)	Art Wilson	135.00	55.00	35.00
(92)	Harry Wolter	135.00	55.00	35.00

1911 S74 Silks - Colored

Designated as S74 in the "American Card Catalog," these delicate fabric collectibles are popular with advanced collectors. The silks were issued as premiums with several different brands of cigarettes: Turkey Red, Old Mill, Helmar, and, rarely, Red Sun. The satin-like silks can be found in two different styles, either "white" or "colored." The S74 "colored" silks, as their name indicates, were issued in a variety of colors. They are slightly larger than the white version, measuring 1-7/8" x 3-1/2", and were issued without a paper backing, carrying the cigarette brand name on the lower front of the fabric. (No color silks advertising the Helmar brand are known to exist.) In the colored silks, 120 subjects are known. The silks feature the same player pictures found in the popular T205 Gold Border tobacco card set.

		NM	EX	VG
Complete Set (120):		20,000	8,000	5,000
Common Player:		150.00	60.00	35.00
(1)	Red Ames	150.00	60.00	35.00
(2)	Jimmy Archer	150.00	60.00	35.00
(3)	Home Run Baker	300.00	120.00	70.00
(4)	Cy Barger	150.00	60.00	35.00
(5)	Jack Barry	150.00	60.00	35.00
(6)	Johnny Bates	150.00	60.00	35.00
(7)	Beals Becker	150.00	60.00	35.00
(8)	George Bell	150.00	60.00	35.00
(9)	Chief Bender	300.00	120.00	70.00
(10)	Bill Bergen	150.00	60.00	35.00
(11)	Bob Bescher	150.00	60.00	35.00
(12)	Roger Bresnahan (Mouth closed.)	300.00	120.00	70.00
(13)	Roger Bresnahan (Mouth openm)	300.00	120.00	70.00
(14)	Al Bridwell	150.00	60.00	35.00
(15)	Mordecai Brown	300.00	120.00	70.00
(16)	Bobby Byrne	150.00	60.00	35.00
(17)	Howie Camnitz	150.00	60.00	35.00
(18)	Bill Carrigan	150.00	60.00	35.00
(19)	Frank Chance	300.00	120.00	70.00
(20)	Hal Chase	225.00	90.00	55.00
(21)	Ed Cicotte	300.00	120.00	70.00
(22)	Fred Clarke	300.00	120.00	70.00
(23)	Ty Cobb	1,200	480.00	290.00
(24)	Eddie Collins	300.00	120.00	70.00
(25)	Doc Crandall	150.00	60.00	35.00
(26)	Bill Dahlen	150.00	60.00	35.00
(27)	Jake Daubert	150.00	60.00	35.00
(28)	Jim Delahanty	150.00	60.00	35.00
(29)	Art Devlin	150.00	60.00	35.00
(30)	Josh Devore	150.00	60.00	35.00
(31)	Red Dooin	150.00	60.00	35.00
(32)	Mickey Doolan	150.00	60.00	35.00
(33)	Tom Downey	150.00	60.00	35.00
(34)	Larry Doyle	150.00	60.00	35.00
(35)	Hugh Duffy	300.00	120.00	70.00
(36)	Jimmy Dygert	150.00	60.00	35.00
(37)	Kid Elberfield (Elberfeld)	150.00	60.00	35.00
(38)	Steve Evans	150.00	60.00	35.00
(39)	Johnny Evers	300.00	120.00	70.00
(40)	Bob Ewing	150.00	60.00	35.00
(41)	Art Fletcher	150.00	60.00	35.00
(42)	John Flynn	150.00	60.00	35.00
(43)	Russ Ford	150.00	60.00	35.00
(44)	Bill Foxen	150.00	60.00	35.00
(45)	Art Fromme	150.00	60.00	35.00
(46)	George Gibson	150.00	60.00	35.00
(47)	Peaches Graham	150.00	60.00	35.00
(48)	Eddie Grant	150.00	60.00	35.00
(49)	Clark Griffith	300.00	120.00	70.00
(50)	Topsy Hartsel	150.00	60.00	35.00
(51)	Arnold Hauser	150.00	60.00	35.00
(52)	Charlie Hemphill	150.00	60.00	35.00
(53)	Dick Hoblitzell	150.00	60.00	35.00
(54)	Miller Huggins	300.00	120.00	70.00
(55)	John Hummel	150.00	60.00	35.00
(56)	Walter Johnson	600.00	240.00	145.00
(57)	Davy Jones	150.00	60.00	35.00
(58)	Johnny Kling	150.00	60.00	35.00
(59)	Jack Knight	150.00	60.00	35.00
(60)	Ed Konetchy	150.00	60.00	35.00
(61)	Harry Krause	150.00	60.00	35.00
(62)	Tommy Leach	150.00	60.00	35.00
(63)	Lefty Leifield	150.00	60.00	35.00
(64)	Hans Lobert	150.00	60.00	35.00
(65)	Rube Marquard	300.00	120.00	70.00
(66)	Christy Mathewson	750.00	300.00	180.00
(67)	Al Mattern	150.00	60.00	35.00
(68)	Amby McConnell	150.00	60.00	35.00
(69)	John McGraw	300.00	120.00	70.00
(70)	Harry McIntire (McIntyre)	150.00	60.00	35.00
(71)	Fred Merkle	150.00	60.00	35.00
(72)	Chief Meyers	150.00	60.00	35.00
(73)	Dots Miller	150.00	60.00	35.00
(74)	Mike Mitchell	150.00	60.00	35.00
(75)	Pat Moran	150.00	60.00	35.00
(76)	George Moriarty	150.00	60.00	35.00
(77)	George Mullin	150.00	60.00	35.00
(78)	Danny Murphy	150.00	60.00	35.00
(79)	Red Murray	150.00	60.00	35.00
(80)	Tom Needham	150.00	60.00	35.00
(81)	Rebel Oakes	150.00	60.00	35.00
(82)	Rube Oldring	150.00	60.00	35.00
(83)	Orval Overall	150.00	60.00	35.00
(84)	Fred Parent	150.00	60.00	35.00
(85)	Dode Paskert	150.00	60.00	35.00
(86)	Fred Payne	150.00	60.00	35.00
(87)	Barney Pelty	150.00	60.00	35.00
(88)	Deacon Phillippe	150.00	60.00	35.00
(89)	Jack Quinn	150.00	60.00	35.00
(90)	Bugs Raymond	150.00	60.00	35.00
(91)	Ed Reulbach	150.00	60.00	35.00
(92)	Jack Rowan	150.00	60.00	35.00
(93)	Nap Rucker	150.00	60.00	35.00

(94)	Doc Scanlon (Scanlan)	150.00	60.00	35.00
(95)	Germany Schaefer	150.00	60.00	35.00
(96)	Geo. Schlei	150.00	60.00	35.00
(97)	Wildfire Schulte	150.00	60.00	35.00
(98)	Dave Shean	150.00	60.00	35.00
(99)	Jimmy Sheckard	150.00	60.00	35.00
(100)	Happy Smith	150.00	60.00	35.00
(101)	Fred Snodgrass	150.00	60.00	35.00
(102)	Tris Speaker	400.00	160.00	95.00
(103)	Jake Stahl	150.00	60.00	35.00
(104)	Harry Steinfeldt	150.00	60.00	35.00
(105)	George Stone	150.00	60.00	35.00
(106)	Gabby Street	150.00	60.00	35.00
(107)	Ed Summers	150.00	60.00	35.00
(108)	Lee Tannehill	150.00	60.00	35.00
(109)	Joe Tinker	300.00	120.00	70.00
(110)	John Titus	150.00	60.00	35.00
(111)	Terry Turner	150.00	60.00	35.00
(112)	Bobby Wallace	300.00	120.00	70.00
(113)	Zack Wheat	300.00	120.00	70.00
(114)	Doc White (White Sox)	150.00	60.00	35.00
(115)	Kirby White (Pirates)	150.00	60.00	35.00
(116)	Ed Willett	150.00	60.00	35.00
(117)	Owen Wilson	150.00	60.00	35.00
(118)	Hooks Wiltse	150.00	60.00	35.00
(119)	Harry Wolter	150.00	60.00	35.00
(120)	Cy Young	750.00	300.00	180.00

1912 S81 Silks

The 1912 S81 "Silks," so-called because they featured pictures of baseball players on a satin-like fabric rather than paper or cardboard, are closely related to the better-known T3 Turkey Red cabinet cards of the same era. The silks, which featured 25 of the day's top baseball players among its other various subjects, were available as a premium with Helmar "Turkish Trophies" cigarettes. According to an advertising sheet, one silk could be obtained for 25 Helmar coupons. The silks measure about 6-3/4" x 8-3/4" and, with a few exceptions, used the same pictures featured on the popular Turkey Red cards. Five players (Rube Marquard, Rube Benton, Marty O'Toole, Grover Alexander and Russ Ford) appear in the "Silks" set that were not included in the T3 set. In addition, an error involving the Frank Baker card was corrected for the "Silks" set. (In the T3 set, Baker's card actually pictured Jack Barry.) Several years ago a pair of New England collectors found a small stack of Christy Mathewson "Silks," making his, by far, the most common. Otherwise, the "Silks" are generally so rare that it is difficult to determine the relative scarcity of the others. Baseball enthusiasts are usually only attrached to the 25 baseball players in the "Silks" premium set, but it is interesting to note that the promotion also offered dozens of other subjects, including "beautiful women in bathing and athletic costumes, charming dancers in gorgeous attire, natiional flags and generals on horseback."

		NM	EX	VG
Complete Set (25):		145,000	50,000	27,500
Common Player:		3,000	1,000	575.00
86	Rube Marquard	6,500	2,275	1,225
87	Marty O'Toole	3,000	1,000	575.00
88	Rube Benton	3,000	1,000	575.00
89	Grover Alexander	9,000	3,150	1,700
90	Russ Ford	3,000	1,000	575.00
91	John McGraw	6,500	2,275	1,225
92	Nap Rucker	3,000	1,000	575.00
93	Mike Mitchell	3,000	1,000	575.00
94	Chief Bender	6,500	2,275	1,225
95	Home Run Baker	6,500	2,275	1,225
96	Nap Lajoie	6,500	2,275	1,225
97	Joe Tinker	6,500	2,275	1,225
98	Sherry Magee	3,000	1,000	575.00
99	Howie Camnitz	3,000	1,000	575.00
100	Eddie Collins	6,500	2,275	1,225
101	Red Dooin	3,000	1,000	575.00
102	Ty Cobb	15,000	5,250	2,850
103	Hugh Jennings	6,500	2,275	1,225
104	Roger Bresnahan	6,500	2,275	1,225
105	Jake Stahl	3,000	1,000	575.00
106	Tris Speaker	8,000	2,800	1,525
107	Ed Walsh	6,500	2,275	1,225
108	Christy Mathewson	6,000	2,100	1,150
109	Johnny Evers	6,500	2,275	1,225
110	Walter Johnson	12,000	4,200	2,275

1912 S110 Baseball Player Silks Pillow Case

Closely related to the S81 silks, and issued as a premuim for 100 coupons, this approximately 23" x 23" pillow case shares the same designs as the individual silks of the players thereon. Cross-stich borders for the player images on the cloth pillow case would indicate the silks were meant to be sewn on as they were acquired. Besides the baseball players pillow cases, similar premiums are known for the other Turkey Red/Helmar silks -- Indians, generals, etc.

		NM	EX	VG
(1)	Home Run Baker, Ty Cobb, Walter Johnson, Christy Mathewson, Tris Speaker	8,500	4,250	2,550
(2)	Home Run Baker, Ty Cobb, Christy Mathewson, Marty O'Toole, Tris Speaker	8,000	4,000	2,400

T

1928 Tabacalera la Morena

Believed to have been issued in El Salvador in the late 1920s, the extent of this card issue is not yet known. It is possible other American baseball players are included in the issue. Approximately 1-7/8" x 2-5/8", the cards are printed in black-and-white with some color tints added. The borderless front that includes the card number at bottom. Backs are printed in Spanish and repeat the card number along with player identification and a few words about the pictured players. An ad at bottom attributes the card (roughly): "Courtesy of Rich Brown Tobacco, the Champion among Consumers."

		NM	EX	VG
96	St. Louis Cardinals Team	100.00	50.00	30.00
97	Everett Scott	50.00	25.00	15.00
98	Babe Ruth	900.00	450.00	270.00
100	Lou Gehrig, Babe Ruth	500.00	250.00	150.00
101	George Kelly	100.00	50.00	30.00
103	Earl Webb	50.00	25.00	15.00
105	Ty Cobb, Babe Ruth	300.00	150.00	90.00
106	Jim Bottomley	100.00	50.00	30.00
107	Christy Mathewson, John McGraw	150.00	75.00	45.00
109	John J. Mc. Graw	100.00	50.00	30.00
110	Ullmann	50.00	25.00	15.00
111	Lee Todd, P Todd	50.00	25.00	15.00
114	St. Louis Cardinals/ Brooklyn Robins	50.00	25.00	15.00
120	St. Louis Cardinals/ Brooklyn Robins	50.00	25.00	15.00

1916 Tango Eggs

Unknown until the discovery of a hoard of "fewer than 500" cards in 1991, this 20-card set was produced for L. Frank & Co. of New Orleans to be distributed in an as-yet unknown manner in connection with its Tango brand eggs. Similar in size (1-7/16" x 2-3/4") and format to contemporary caramel cards, the Tango set features familiar player pictures from those issues. In fact, several of the Tango cards have player designations which differ from the same pictures used in the E106 American Caramel issue of 1915. The Tango cards feature a glossy front surface, and are brightly colored. The hoard varied greatly in the number of each player's card. Some were found in quantities as low as one, while some were represented by more than 50 specimens. Because several of the cards exist in only a single specimen, no price for a complete set is quoted.

		NM	EX	VG
Common Player:		240.00	95.00	50.00
(1)	Bob Bescher	240.00	95.00	50.00
(2)	Roger Bresnahan (Four known.)	2,400	960.00	480.00
(3)	Al Bridwell (Fewer than 10 known.)	870.00	350.00	175.00
(4)	Hal Chase	1,080	430.00	215.00
(5)	Ty Cobb (One known, VG, value undetermined.)			
(6)	Eddie Collins	1,920	770.00	385.00
(7)	Sam Crawford (Fewer than five known.)	2,400	960.00	480.00
(8)	Red Dooin	430.00	175.00	85.00
(9)	Johnny Evers (One known, G/VG, value undetermined.)			
(10)	Happy Felsch (Picture actually Ray Demmitt.) (2-3 known.)	2,880	1,150	575.00
(11)	Hughie Jennings (20 known.)	660.00	265.00	135.00
(12)	George McQuillen	510.00	205.00	100.00
(13)	Billy Meyer (Picture actually Fred Jacklitsch.)	450.00	180.00	90.00
(14)	Ray Morgan (Picture actually Mike Doolan.)(2-3 known.)	1,920	770.00	385.00
(15)	Danny Murphy	270.00	110.00	55.00
(16)	Germany Schaefer (1-2 known.)	2,400	960.00	480.00
(17)	Joe Tinker (Unconfirmed)	2,880	1,150	575.00
(18)	Honus Wagner (None confirmed.)			
(19)	Buck Weaver (Picture actually Joe Tinker.)	1,500	600.00	300.00
(20)	Heinie Zimmerman (Fewer than 10 known.)	870.00	350.00	175.00

1934 Tarzan Bread (D382)

Among the rarest issues of the 1930s is this set sponsored by an unusually named brand of bread from a bakery whose location is unknown. The cards are printed in black-and-white in 2-1/4" x 3-1/4" format. Borderless front photos have the player name in capital letters. Backs have the sponsor's name and a short career summary. The checklist here, almost certainly incomplete, is arranged alphabetically; the cards are unnumbered.

		NM	EX	VG
Common Player:		2,200	1,100	650.00
(1)	Sparky Adams	2,200	1,100	650.00
(2)	Walter Betts	2,200	1,100	650.00
(3)	Ed Brandt	2,200	1,100	650.00
(4)	Tommy Bridges	2,200	1,100	650.00
(5)	Irving "Jack" Burns	2,200	1,100	650.00
(6)	Bruce Campbell	2,200	1,100	650.00
(7)	Tex Carleton	2,200	1,100	650.00
(8)	Dick Coffman	2,200	1,100	650.00
(9)	George Connally	2,200	1,100	650.00
(10)	Tony Cuccinello	2,200	1,100	650.00
(11)	Debs Garms	2,200	1,100	650.00
(12)	Milt Gaston	2,200	1,100	650.00
(13)	Bill Hallahan	2,200	1,100	650.00
(14)	Myril Hoag	2,200	1,100	650.00
(15)	Chief Hogsett	2,200	1,100	650.00
(16)	Arndt Jorgens	2,200	1,100	650.00
(17)	Willie Kamm	2,200	1,100	650.00
(18)	Dutch Leonard	2,200	1,100	650.00
(19)	Clyde Manion	2,200	1,100	650.00
(20)	Eric McNair	2,200	1,100	650.00
(21)	Oscar Melillo	2,200	1,100	650.00
(22)	Bob O'Farrell	2,200	1,100	650.00
(23)	Gus Suhr	2,200	1,100	650.00
(24)	Evar Swanson	2,200	1,100	650.00
(25)	Billy Urbanski	2,200	1,100	650.00
(26)	Johnny Vergez	2,200	1,100	650.00
(27)	Robert Worthington	2,200	1,100	650.00
(28)	Tom Zachary	2,200	1,100	650.00

1969 Tasco All-Star Collection Caricatures

This set of large - 11-1/2" x 16" - player posters features colorful caricatures with an emphasis on Tigers players, befitting the Detroit address of the publisher. Licensed by MLBPA, the pictures are listed here alphabetically. They were originally sold for less than $1 apiece.

		NM	EX	VG
Complete Set (46):		450.00	225.00	135.00
Common Player:		7.50	3.75	2.25
(1)	Hank Aaron	35.00	17.50	10.50
(2)	Richie Allen	12.50	6.25	3.75
(3)	Luis Aparicio	17.50	8.75	5.25
(4)	Ernie Banks	25.00	12.50	7.50
(5)	Glenn Beckert	7.50	3.75	2.25
(6)	Johnny Bench	20.00	10.00	6.00
(7)	Norm Cash	10.00	5.00	3.00
(8)	Danny Cater	7.50	3.75	2.25
(9)	Pat Dobson	7.50	3.75	2.25
(10)	Don Drysdale	17.50	8.75	5.25
(11)	Bill Freehan	7.50	3.75	2.25
(12)	Jim Fregosi	7.50	3.75	2.25
(13)	Bob Gibson	17.50	8.75	5.25
(14)	Bill Hands	7.50	3.75	2.25
(15)	Ken Holtzman	7.50	3.75	2.25
(16)	Willie Horton	7.50	3.75	2.25
(17)	Frank Howard	9.00	4.50	2.75
(18)	Randy Hundley	7.50	3.75	2.25
(19)	Ferguson Jenkins	17.50	8.75	5.25
(20)	Al Kaline	25.00	12.50	7.50
(21)	Don Kessinger	7.50	3.75	2.25
(22)	Jerry Koosman	7.50	3.75	2.25
(23)	Mickey Lolich	7.50	3.75	2.25
(24)	Juan Marichal	17.50	8.75	5.25
(25)	Willie Mays	35.00	17.50	10.50
(26)	Bill Mazeroski	17.50	8.75	5.25
(27)	Dick McAuliffe	7.50	3.75	2.25
(28)	Denny McLain	7.50	3.75	2.25
(29)	Dave McNally	7.50	3.75	2.25
(30)	Jim Northrup	7.50	3.75	2.25
(31)	Tony Oliva	9.00	4.50	2.75
(32)	Adolfo Phillips	7.50	3.75	2.25
(33)	Jim Price	7.50	3.75	2.25
(34)	Brooks Robinson	20.00	10.00	6.00
(35)	Pete Rose	35.00	17.50	10.50
(36)	Ron Santo	15.00	7.50	4.50
(37)	Joe Sparma	7.50	3.75	2.25
(38)	Mickey Stanley	7.50	3.75	2.25
(39)	Mel Stottlemyre	7.50	3.75	2.25
(40)	Luis Tiant	7.50	3.75	2.25
(41)	Joe Torre	9.00	4.50	2.75
(42)	Dick Tracewski	7.50	3.75	2.25
(43)	Don Wert	7.50	3.75	2.25
(44)	Billy Williams	17.50	8.75	5.25
(45)	Earl Wilson	7.50	3.75	2.25
(46)	Carl Yastrzemski	25.00	12.50	7.50

1970 Tasco Caricatures

This group of colorful player caricatures was sold in a four-pack featuring two each baseball and foot-

ball players. The 8-1/2" x 10-7/8" blank-back pictures have central images surrounded by colorful borders.

		NM	EX	VG
Complete Set (4):		150.00	75.00	45.00
Common Player:		40.00	20.00	12.00
(1)	Jim "Catfish" Hunter	40.00	20.00	12.00
(2)	Al Kaline	50.00	25.00	15.00
(3)	Joe Namath	75.00	37.00	22.00
(4)	O.J. Simpson	50.00	25.00	15.00

1933 Tattoo Orbit (R305)

Found in 1¢ packages of Tattoo gum, these 2" x 2-1/4" cards were produced by the Orbit Gum Co., of Chicago, a subsidiary of Wrigley's. Fronts feature a black-and-white photo which is tinted to give the skin some color. Stylized ballpark backgrounds are separated from the photograph by a black line. The rest of the background is printed in vivid red, yellow and green. Backs have player identification and vitals. Cards of Bump Hadley and George Blaeholder are the most elusive, followed by those of Ivy Andrews and Rogers Hornsby:

		NM	EX	VG
Complete Set (60):		20,000	8,000	4,000
Common Player:		250.00	100.00	60.00
(1)	Dale Alexander	250.00	100.00	60.00
(2)	Ivy Paul Andrews	900.00	360.00	225.00
(3)	Earl Averill	400.00	160.00	100.00
(4)	Richard Bartell	250.00	100.00	60.00
(5)	Walter Berger	250.00	100.00	60.00
(6)	George F. Blaeholder	1,000	400.00	250.00
(7)	Irving J. Burns	250.00	100.00	60.00
(8)	Guy T. Bush	250.00	100.00	60.00
(9)	Bruce D. Campbell	250.00	100.00	60.00
(10)	William Cissell	250.00	100.00	60.00
(11)	Lefty Clark	250.00	100.00	60.00
(12)	Mickey Cochrane	400.00	160.00	100.00
(13)	Phil Collins	250.00	100.00	60.00
(14)	Hazen Kiki Cuyler	400.00	160.00	100.00
(15)	Dizzy Dean	575.00	230.00	145.00
(16)	Jimmy Dykes	250.00	100.00	60.00
(17)	George L. Earnshaw	250.00	100.00	60.00
(18)	Woody English	250.00	100.00	60.00
(19)	Lewis A. Fonseca	250.00	100.00	60.00
(20)	Jimmy Foxx	750.00	300.00	185.00
(21)	Burleigh A. Grimes	400.00	160.00	100.00
(22)	Charles John Grimm	250.00	100.00	60.00
(23)	Robert M. Grove	500.00	200.00	125.00
(24)	Frank Grube	250.00	100.00	60.00
(25)	George W. Haas	250.00	100.00	60.00
(26)	Irving D. Hadley	1,000	400.00	250.00
(27)	Chick Hafey	400.00	160.00	100.00
(28)	Jesse Joseph Haines	400.00	160.00	100.00
(29)	William Hallahan	250.00	100.00	60.00
(30)	Melvin Harder	250.00	100.00	60.00
(31)	Gabby Hartnett	400.00	160.00	100.00
(32)	Babe Herman	250.00	100.00	60.00
(33)	William Herman	400.00	160.00	100.00
(34)	Rogers Hornsby	1,200	480.00	300.00
(35)	Roy C. Johnson	250.00	100.00	60.00
(36)	J. Smead Jolley	250.00	100.00	60.00
(37)	William Jurges	250.00	100.00	60.00
(38)	William Kamm	250.00	100.00	60.00
(39)	Mark A. Koenig	250.00	100.00	60.00
(40)	James J. Levey	450.00	180.00	110.00
(41)	Ernie Lombardi	400.00	160.00	100.00
(42)	Red Lucas	250.00	100.00	60.00
(43)	Ted Lyons	400.00	160.00	100.00
(44)	Connie Mack	400.00	160.00	100.00
(45)	Pat Malone	250.00	100.00	60.00
(46)	Pepper Martin	300.00	125.00	75.00
(47)	Marty McManus	250.00	100.00	60.00
(48)	Frank J. O'Doul	350.00	140.00	87.00
(49)	Richard Porter	250.00	100.00	60.00
(50)	Carl N. Reynolds	250.00	100.00	60.00
(51)	Charles Henry Root	250.00	100.00	60.00
(52)	Robert Seeds	250.00	100.00	60.00
(53)	Al H. Simmons	400.00	160.00	100.00
(54)	Jackson Riggs Stephenson	250.00	100.00	60.00
(55)	Bud Tinning	250.00	100.00	60.00
(56)	Joe Vosmik	250.00	100.00	60.00
(57)	Rube Walberg	250.00	100.00	60.00
(58)	Paul Waner	400.00	160.00	100.00
(59)	Lonnie Warneke	250.00	100.00	60.00
(60)	Arthur C. Whitney	250.00	100.00	60.00

1933 Tattoo Orbit (R308)

This obscure set of cards, issued with Tattoo Orbit gum, is numbered from 151 through 207, with a few of the numbers still unknown. Most surviving examples measure 1-7/8" x 1-1/4", but larger pieces (2-1/2" x 3-7/8") are also known with the same players and numbers. The player pictures on the cards "developed" when moistened and rubbed with a piece of blotting paper. Besides the baseball players, there were also pictures of movie stars and other celebrities.

		NM	EX	VG
Common Player:		200.00	90.00	50.00
Large-Format: 4X				
151	Vernon Gomez	500.00	225.00	125.00
152	Kiki Cuyler	500.00	225.00	125.00
153	Jimmy Foxx	850.00	380.00	210.00
154	Al Simmons	500.00	225.00	125.00
155	Chas. J. Grimm	200.00	90.00	50.00
156	William Jurges	200.00	90.00	50.00
157	Chuck Klein	500.00	225.00	125.00
158	Richard Bartell	200.00	90.00	50.00
159	Pepper Martin	275.00	125.00	69.00
160	Earl Averill	500.00	225.00	125.00
161	William Dickey	500.00	225.00	125.00
162	Wesley Ferrell	200.00	90.00	50.00
163	Oral Hildebrand	200.00	90.00	50.00
164	Wm. Kamm	200.00	90.00	50.00
165	Earl Whitehill	200.00	90.00	50.00
166	Charles Fullis	200.00	90.00	50.00
167	Jimmy Dykes	200.00	90.00	50.00
168	Ben Cantwell	200.00	90.00	50.00
169	George Earnshaw	200.00	90.00	50.00
170	Jackson Stephenson	200.00	90.00	50.00
171	Randolph Moore	200.00	90.00	50.00
172	Ted Lyons	500.00	225.00	125.00
173	Goose Goslin	500.00	225.00	125.00
174	E. Swanson	200.00	90.00	50.00
175	Lee Roy Mahaffey	200.00	90.00	50.00
176	Joe Cronin	500.00	225.00	125.00
177	Tom Bridges	200.00	90.00	50.00
178	Henry Manush	500.00	225.00	125.00
179	Walter Stewart	200.00	90.00	50.00
180	Frank Pytlak	200.00	90.00	50.00
181	Dale Alexander	200.00	90.00	50.00
182	Robert Grove	600.00	270.00	150.00
183	Charles Gehringer	500.00	225.00	125.00
184	Lewis Fonseca	200.00	90.00	50.00
185	Alvin Crowder	200.00	90.00	50.00
186	Mickey Cochrane	500.00	225.00	125.00
187	Max Bishop	200.00	90.00	50.00
188	Connie Mack	500.00	225.00	125.00
189	Guy Bush	200.00	90.00	50.00
190	Charlie Root	200.00	90.00	50.00
191a	Burleigh Grimes	500.00	225.00	125.00
191b	Gabby Hartnett	500.00	225.00	125.00
192	Pat Malone	200.00	90.00	50.00
193	Woody English	200.00	90.00	50.00
194	Lonnie Warneke	200.00	90.00	50.00
195	Babe Herman	275.00	125.00	69.00
196	Unknown			
197	Unknown			
198	Unknown			
199	Unknown			
200	Gabby Hartnett	500.00	225.00	125.00
201	Paul Waner	500.00	225.00	125.00
202	Dizzy Dean	750.00	335.00	185.00
203	Unknown			
204	Unknown			
205	Jim Bottomley	500.00	225.00	125.00
206	Unknown			
207	Charles Hafey	500.00	225.00	125.00
208	Unknown			
209	Unknown			
210	Unknown			

1907-09 H.M. Taylor Detroit Tigers Postcards

Various players and groups of players are featured in this issue of hometown heroes from H. M. Taylor in Detroit. The 5-1/2" x 3-1/2" black-and-white cards have white borders on front. Undivided backs have a gothic "Post Card" at top, a one-cent stamp box and, at bottom-left, "Rights reserved by H. M. Taylor, Detroit."

	NM	EX	VG
Complete Set (7):	5,000	2,500	1,500
Common Card:	525.00	260.00	150.00
(1) Tyrus Cobb (at Bat.)	1,800	900.00	550.00
(2) Bill Coughlin/Btg	525.00	260.00	150.00
(3) Sam Crawford (Ready for the Ball.)	750.00	375.00	225.00
(4) Detroit Club (Team photo.)	850.00	425.00	250.00
(5) Wild Bill Donovan (Floral horseshoe presented at Philadelphia.)	525.00	260.00	150.00
(6) Hughie Jennings ("WEE'AH")	525.00	260.00	150.00
(7) Hughie Jennings, Wild Bill Donovan, Frank Chance (In dugout.)	525.00	260.00	150.00

1972 TCMA The 1930's

Extending to over 500 cards, this was one of TCMA's first ventures into the business of creating collectors' edition card sets of former players. Over the length of the series there were a number of style differences. The set was issued in 21 series of 24 cards each. All cards were printed in black-and-white (except for Series 18-19 printed in blue) and feature player photos on usually borderless fronts. Dimensions were about 2" x 2-3/4" for most series, with Series 15-16 in a 2-1/2" x 3-1/2" format. Except for a TCMA copyright line on some of the earlier cards, there is no other printing on front. Backs have player identification, team affiliations, TCMA copyright and, after #72, a card number. Production is reported as 1,000 sets. Blank-bank versions and uncut panels of 12 exist.

	NM	EX	VG
Complete Set (504):	400.00	200.00	120.00
Common Player:	3.00	1.50	.90
(1) Roy Bell	3.00	1.50	.90
(2) Max Bishop	3.00	1.50	.90
(3) Bob Boken	3.00	1.50	.90
(4) Cliff Bolton	3.00	1.50	.90
(5) John Broaca	3.00	1.50	.90
(6) Bill Brubaker	3.00	1.50	.90
(7) Slick Castleman	3.00	1.50	.90
(8) Dick Coffman	3.00	1.50	.90
(9) Phil Collins	3.00	1.50	.90
(10) Earle Combs	3.00	1.50	.90
(11) Doc Cramer	3.00	1.50	.90
(12) Joe Cronin	3.00	1.50	.90
(13) Jack Crouch	3.00	1.50	.90
(14) Tony Cuccinello	3.00	1.50	.90
(15) Babe Dahlgren	3.00	1.50	.90
(16) Spud Davis	3.00	1.50	.90
(17) Dizzy Dean	6.00	3.00	1.75
(18) Paul Dean	3.00	1.50	.90
(19) Bill Dickey	3.00	1.50	.90
(20) Joe DiMaggio	10.00	5.00	3.00
(21) George Earnshaw	3.00	1.50	.90
(22) Woody English	3.00	1.50	.90
(23) Woody English	3.00	1.50	.90
(24) Hal Finney	3.00	1.50	.90
(25) Freddie Fitzsimmons, Bump Hadley	3.00	1.50	.90
(26) Tony Freitas	3.00	1.50	.90
(27) Frank Frisch	3.00	1.50	.90
(28) Milt Gaston	3.00	1.50	.90
(29) Sid Gautreaux	3.00	1.50	.90
(30) Charlie Gehringer	3.00	1.50	.90
(31) Charley Gelbert	3.00	1.50	.90
(32) Lefty Gomez	3.00	1.50	.90
(33) Lefty Grove	5.00	2.50	1.50
(34) Chick Hafey	3.00	1.50	.90
(35) Jesse Haines	3.00	1.50	.90
(36) Bill Hallahan	3.00	1.50	.90
(37) Bucky Harris	3.00	1.50	.90
(38) Ed Heusser	3.00	1.50	.90
(39) Carl Hubbell	3.00	1.50	.90
(40) Carl Hubbell	3.00	1.50	.90
(41) Jimmy Jordan	3.00	1.50	.90
(42) Joe Judge	3.00	1.50	.90
(43) Len Koenecke	3.00	1.50	.90
(44) Mark Koenig	3.00	1.50	.90
(45) Cookie Lavagetto	3.00	1.50	.90
(46) Roxie Lawson	3.00	1.50	.90
(47) Tony Lazzeri	3.00	1.50	.90
(48) Gus Mancuso	3.00	1.50	.90
(49) John McCarthy	3.00	1.50	.90
(50) Joe Medwick	3.00	1.50	.90
(51) Cliff Melton	3.00	1.50	.90
(52) Terry Moore	3.00	1.50	.90
(53) John Murphy	3.00	1.50	.90
(54) Ken O'Dea	3.00	1.50	.90
(55) Bob O'Farrell	3.00	1.50	.90
(56) Manuel Onis	3.00	1.50	.90
(57) Monte Pearson	3.00	1.50	.90
(58) Paul Richards	3.00	1.50	.90
(59) Max Rosenfeld	6.00	3.00	1.75
(60) Red Ruffing	3.00	1.50	.90
(61) Red Ruffing	3.00	1.50	.90
(62) Hal Schumacher	3.00	1.50	.90
(63) George Selkirk	3.00	1.50	.90
(64) Joe Shaute	3.00	1.50	.90
(65) Gordon Slade	3.00	1.50	.90
(66) Lindo Storti	3.00	1.50	.90
(67) Smokey Sundra	3.00	1.50	.90
(68) Bill Terry	3.00	1.50	.90
(69) Jack Tising	3.00	1.50	.90
(70) Sandy Vance	3.00	1.50	.90
(71) Rube Walberg	3.00	1.50	.90
(72) Sammy West	3.00	1.50	.90
73 Vito Tamulis	3.00	1.50	.90
74 Kemp Wicker	3.00	1.50	.90
75 Bob Seeds	3.00	1.50	.90
76 Jack Saltzgaver	3.00	1.50	.90
77 Walter Brown	3.00	1.50	.90
78 Spud Chandler	3.00	1.50	.90
79 Myril Hoag	3.00	1.50	.90
80 Joe Glenn	3.00	1.50	.90
81 Lefty Gomez	3.00	1.50	.90
82 Arndt Jorgens	3.00	1.50	.90
83 Jesse Hill	3.00	1.50	.90
84 Red Rolfe	3.00	1.50	.90
85 Wes Ferrell	3.00	1.50	.90
86 Joe Morrissey	3.00	1.50	.90
87 Tony Piet	3.00	1.50	.90
88 Fred Walker	3.00	1.50	.90
89 Bill Dietrich	3.00	1.50	.90
90 Lyn Lary	3.00	1.50	.90
91 Lyn Lary	3.00	1.50	.90
92 Lyn Lary	3.00	1.50	.90
93 Lyn Lary	3.00	1.50	.90
94 Buzz Boyle	3.00	1.50	.90
95 Tony Malinosky	3.00	1.50	.90
96 Al Lopez	3.00	1.50	.90
97 Linus Frey	3.00	1.50	.90
98 Tony Malinosky	3.00	1.50	.90
99 Owen Carroll	3.00	1.50	.90
100 Buddy Hassett	3.00	1.50	.90
101 Gib Brack	3.00	1.50	.90
102 Sam Leslie	3.00	1.50	.90
103 Fred Heimach	3.00	1.50	.90
104 Burleigh Grimes	3.00	1.50	.90
105 Ray Benge	3.00	1.50	.90
106 Joe Stripp	3.00	1.50	.90
107 Joe Becker	3.00	1.50	.90
108 Oscar Melillo	3.00	1.50	.90
109 Charley O'Leary, Rogers Hornsby	3.00	1.50	.90
110 Luke Appling	3.00	1.50	.90
111 Stan Hack	3.00	1.50	.90
112 Ray Hayworth	3.00	1.50	.90
113 Charles Wilson	3.00	1.50	.90
114 Hal Trosky	3.00	1.50	.90
115 Wes Ferrell	3.00	1.50	.90
116 Lyn Lary	3.00	1.50	.90
117 Milt Gaston	3.00	1.50	.90
118 Eldon Auker	3.00	1.50	.90
119 Heinie Manush	3.00	1.50	.90
120 Jimmie Foxx	6.00	3.00	1.75
121 Don Heffner	3.00	1.50	.90
122 George Pipgras	3.00	1.50	.90
123 Bump Hadley	3.00	1.50	.90
124 Tommy Henrich	3.00	1.50	.90
125 Joe McCarthy	3.00	1.50	.90
126 Joe Sewell	3.00	1.50	.90
127 Frank Crosetti	3.00	1.50	.90
128 Fred Walker	3.00	1.50	.90
129 Ted Kleinhans	3.00	1.50	.90
130 Jake Powell	3.00	1.50	.90
131 Ben Chapman	3.00	1.50	.90
132 John Murphy	3.00	1.50	.90
133 Lon Warneke	3.00	1.50	.90
134 Augie Galan	3.00	1.50	.90
135 Gene Lillard	3.00	1.50	.90
136 Stan Hack	3.00	1.50	.90
137 Frank Demaree	3.00	1.50	.90
138 Tony Piet	3.00	1.50	.90
139 Tony Piet	3.00	1.50	.90
140 Don Brennan	3.00	1.50	.90
141 Hal Schumacher, Lefty Gomez	3.00	1.50	.90
142 Bump Hadley	3.00	1.50	.90
143 Ollie Bejma	3.00	1.50	.90
144 Jim Bottomley	3.00	1.50	.90
145 Clay Bryant	3.00	1.50	.90
146 Charlie Grimm	3.00	1.50	.90
147 Flea Clifton	3.00	1.50	.90
148 Rollie Stiles	3.00	1.50	.90
149 Al Simmons	3.00	1.50	.90
150 Al Simmons	3.00	1.50	.90
151 Lyn Lary	3.00	1.50	.90
152 Roy Weatherly	3.00	1.50	.90
153 Whit Wyatt	3.00	1.50	.90
154 Oscar Vitt	3.00	1.50	.90
155 Jack Kroner	3.00	1.50	.90
156 Ted Lyons	3.00	1.50	.90
157 Joe Malay	3.00	1.50	.90
158 John McCarthy	3.00	1.50	.90
159 Hy Vandenberg	3.00	1.50	.90
160 Hank Leiber	3.00	1.50	.90
161 Joe Moore	3.00	1.50	.90
162 Cliff Melton	3.00	1.50	.90
163 Harry Danning	3.00	1.50	.90
164 Ray Harrell	3.00	1.50	.90
165 Bruce Ogrodowski	3.00	1.50	.90
166 Leo Durocher	3.00	1.50	.90
167 Leo Durocher	3.00	1.50	.90
168 William Walker	3.00	1.50	.90
169 Alvin Crowder	3.00	1.50	.90
170 Gus Suhr	3.00	1.50	.90
171 Monty Stratton	4.50	2.25	1.25
172 Boze Berger	3.00	1.50	.90
173 John Whitehead	3.00	1.50	.90
174 Joe Heving	3.00	1.50	.90
175 Merv Shea	3.00	1.50	.90
176 Ed Durham	3.00	1.50	.90
177 Buddy Myer	3.00	1.50	.90
178 Earl Whitehill	3.00	1.50	.90
179 Joe Cronin	3.00	1.50	.90
180 Zeke Bonura	3.00	1.50	.90
181 John Knott	3.00	1.50	.90
182 John Allen	3.00	1.50	.90
183 William Knickerbocker	3.00	1.50	.90
184 Earl Averill	3.00	1.50	.90
185 Bob Feller	4.50	2.25	1.25
186 Steve O'Neill	3.00	1.50	.90
187 Bruce Campbell	3.00	1.50	.90
188 Ivy Andrews	3.00	1.50	.90
189 Ivy Andrews	3.00	1.50	.90
190 Muddy Ruel	3.00	1.50	.90
191 Art Scharein	3.00	1.50	.90
192 Merv Shea	3.00	1.50	.90
193 George Myatt	3.00	1.50	.90
194 Bill Werber	3.00	1.50	.90
195 Red Lucas	3.00	1.50	.90
196 Hugh Luby	3.00	1.50	.90
197 Vic Sorrell	3.00	1.50	.90
198 Mickey Cochrane	3.00	1.50	.90
199 Rudy York	3.00	1.50	.90
200 Ray Mack	3.00	1.50	.90
201 Vince DiMaggio	4.50	2.25	1.25
202 Mel Ott	4.50	2.25	1.25
203 John Lucadello	3.00	1.50	.90
204 Debs Garms	3.00	1.50	.90
205 John Murphy, Pat Malone, Bump Hadley, Kemp Wicker, John Broaca	3.00	1.50	.90
206 Stan Sperry	3.00	1.50	.90
207 Hal Schumacher	3.00	1.50	.90
208 Blondy Ryan	3.00	1.50	.90
209 Bob Seeds	3.00	1.50	.90
210 Danny MacFayden	3.00	1.50	.90
211 Fran Healy	3.00	1.50	.90
212 Al Spohrer	3.00	1.50	.90
213 Ed Linke	3.00	1.50	.90
214 Joe Schultz	3.00	1.50	.90
215 Casey Stengel	3.00	1.50	.90
216 Casey Stengel	3.00	1.50	.90
217 Phil Hensick	3.00	1.50	.90
218 Rollie Hemsley	3.00	1.50	.90
219 Ace Parker	4.50	2.25	1.25
220 Henry Helf	3.00	1.50	.90
221 Bill Schuster	3.00	1.50	.90
222 Heinie Schuble	3.00	1.50	.90
223 John Salveson	3.00	1.50	.90
224 Robert Grace	3.00	1.50	.90
225 Sig Gryska	3.00	1.50	.90
226 Mickey Haslin	3.00	1.50	.90
227 Randy Gumpert	3.00	1.50	.90
228 Frank Gustine	3.00	1.50	.90
229 Marv Gudat	3.00	1.50	.90
230 Bob Logan	3.00	1.50	.90
231 Marvin Owen	3.00	1.50	.90
232 Bucky Walters	3.00	1.50	.90
233 Marty Hopkins	3.00	1.50	.90
234 Jimmy Dykes	3.00	1.50	.90
235 Lefty O'Doul	3.00	1.50	.90
236 Larry Rosenthal	3.00	1.50	.90
237 Mickey Haslin	3.00	1.50	.90
238 Eugene Schott	3.00	1.50	.90
239 Sad Sam Jones	3.00	1.50	.90
240 Edwin Rommel	3.00	1.50	.90
241 Rip Collins	3.00	1.50	.90
242 Rosy Ryan	3.00	1.50	.90
243 James Bucher	3.00	1.50	.90
244 Ethan Allen	3.00	1.50	.90
245 Dick Bartell	3.00	1.50	.90
246 Henry Leiber	3.00	1.50	.90
247 Lou Chiozza	3.00	1.50	.90
248 Babe Herman	3.00	1.50	.90
249 Tommy Henrich	3.00	1.50	.90
250 Thornton Lee	3.00	1.50	.90
251 Joe Kuhel	3.00	1.50	.90
252 George Pipgras	3.00	1.50	.90
253 Luke Sewell	3.00	1.50	.90
254 Tony Lazzeri	3.00	1.50	.90
255 Ival Goodman	3.00	1.50	.90

256	George Rensa	3.00	1.50	.90
257	Hal Newhouser	3.00	1.50	.90
258	Rogers Hornsby	5.00	2.50	1.50
259	Tuck Stainback	3.00	1.50	.90
260	Vance Page	3.00	1.50	.90
261	Art Scharein	3.00	1.50	.90
262	Mike Ryba	3.00	1.50	.90
263	James Lindsey	3.00	1.50	.90
264	Ed Parsons	3.00	1.50	.90
265	Elon Hogsett	3.00	1.50	.90
266	Bud Hafey	3.00	1.50	.90
267	John Gill	3.00	1.50	.90
268	Owen Bush	3.00	1.50	.90
269	Ethan Allen	3.00	1.50	.90
270	Jim Bagby	3.00	1.50	.90
271	Bill Atwood	3.00	1.50	.90
272	Phil Cavarretta	3.00	1.50	.90
273	Travis Jackson	3.00	1.50	.90
274	Ted Olson	3.00	1.50	.90
275	Boze Berger	3.00	1.50	.90
276	Norb Kleinke	3.00	1.50	.90
277	Rip Radcliff	3.00	1.50	.90
278	Mule Haas	3.00	1.50	.90
279	Julius Solters	3.00	1.50	.90
280	Ivey Shiver	3.00	1.50	.90
281	Wes Schulmerich	3.00	1.50	.90
282	Ray Kolp	3.00	1.50	.90
283	Si Johnson	3.00	1.50	.90
284	Al Hollingsworth	3.00	1.50	.90
285	D'Arcy Flowers	3.00	1.50	.90
286	Adam Comorosky	3.00	1.50	.90
287	Allen Cooke	3.00	1.50	.90
288	Clyde Kimsey	3.00	1.50	.90
289	Fred Ostermueller	3.00	1.50	.90
290	Angelo Giuliani	3.00	1.50	.90
291	John Wilson	3.00	1.50	.90
292	George Dickman	3.00	1.50	.90
293	Jim DeShong	3.00	1.50	.90
294	Red Evans	3.00	1.50	.90
295	Curtis Davis	3.00	1.50	.90
296	Charlie Berry	3.00	1.50	.90
297	George Gibson	3.00	1.50	.90
298	Fern Bell	3.00	1.50	.90
299	Irv Bartling	3.00	1.50	.90
300	Babe Barna	3.00	1.50	.90
301	Henry Johnson	3.00	1.50	.90
302	Harlond Clift	3.00	1.50	.90
303	Lu Blue	3.00	1.50	.90
304	George Hockette	3.00	1.50	.90
305	Walt Bashore	3.00	1.50	.90
306	Walter Beck	3.00	1.50	.90
307	Jewel Ens	3.00	1.50	.90
308	Doc Prothro	3.00	1.50	.90
309	Morrie Arnovich	3.00	1.50	.90
310	Bill Killefer	3.00	1.50	.90
311	Pete Appleton	3.00	1.50	.90
312	Fred Archer	3.00	1.50	.90
313	Bill Lohrman	3.00	1.50	.90
314	Fred Haney	3.00	1.50	.90
315	Jimmy Ripple	3.00	1.50	.90
316	Johnny Kerr	3.00	1.50	.90
317	Harry Gumbert	3.00	1.50	.90
318	Samuel Derringer	3.00	1.50	.90
319	Firpo Marberry	3.00	1.50	.90
320	Waite Hoyt	3.00	1.50	.90
321	Rick Ferrell	3.00	1.50	.90
322	Hank Greenberg	6.00	3.00	1.75
323	Carl Reynolds	3.00	1.50	.90
324	Roy Johnson	3.00	1.50	.90
325	Gil English	3.00	1.50	.90
326	Al Smith	3.00	1.50	.90
327	Dolph Camilli	3.00	1.50	.90
328	Oscar Grimes	3.00	1.50	.90
329	Ray Berres	3.00	1.50	.90
330	Norm Schlueter	3.00	1.50	.90
331	Joe Vosmik	3.00	1.50	.90
332	Jimmy Dykes	3.00	1.50	.90
333	Vern Washington	3.00	1.50	.90
334	"Bad News" Hale	3.00	1.50	.90
335	Lew Fonseca	3.00	1.50	.90
336	Mike Kreevich	3.00	1.50	.90
337	Bob Johnson	3.00	1.50	.90
338	"Jeep" Handley	3.00	1.50	.90
339	Gabby Hartnett	3.00	1.50	.90
340	Freddie Lindstrom	3.00	1.50	.90
341	Bert Haas	3.00	1.50	.90
342	Elbie Fletcher	3.00	1.50	.90
343	Tom Hafey	3.00	1.50	.90
344	Rip Collins	3.00	1.50	.90
345	John Babich	3.00	1.50	.90
346	Joe Beggs	3.00	1.50	.90
347	Bobo Newsom	3.00	1.50	.90
348	Wally Berger	3.00	1.50	.90
349	Bud Thomas	3.00	1.50	.90
350	Tom Heath	3.00	1.50	.90
351	Cecil Travis	3.00	1.50	.90
352	Jack Redmond	3.00	1.50	.90
353	Fred Schulte	3.00	1.50	.90
354	Pat Malone	3.00	1.50	.90
355	Hugh Critz	3.00	1.50	.90
356	Frank Pytlak	3.00	1.50	.90
357	Glenn Liebhardt	3.00	1.50	.90
358	Al Milnar	3.00	1.50	.90
359	Al Benton	3.00	1.50	.90
360	Moe Berg	6.00	3.00	1.75
361	Al Brancato	3.00	1.50	.90
362	Mark Christman	3.00	1.50	.90
363	Fabian Gaffke	3.00	1.50	.90
364	George Gill	3.00	1.50	.90
365	Oral Hildebrand	3.00	1.50	.90
366	Lou Fette	3.00	1.50	.90
367	Tex Carleton	3.00	1.50	.90
368	Don Gutteridge	3.00	1.50	.90
369	Pete Fox	3.00	1.50	.90
370	George Blaeholder	3.00	1.50	.90
371	George Caster	3.00	1.50	.90
372	Joe Cascarella	3.00	1.50	.90
373	Jimmy Hitchcock	3.00	1.50	.90

374	Frank Croucher	3.00	1.50	.90
375	LeRoy Parmelee	3.00	1.50	.90
376	Joe Mulligan	3.00	1.50	.90
377	John Welch	3.00	1.50	.90
378	Donald McNair	3.00	1.50	.90
379	Frenchy Bordagaray	3.00	1.50	.90
380	Denny Galehouse	3.00	1.50	.90
381	Robert Harris	3.00	1.50	.90
382	Max Butcher	3.00	1.50	.90
383	Sam Byrd	3.00	1.50	.90
384	Pete Coscarart	3.00	1.50	.90
385	George Case	3.00	1.50	.90
386	John Hudson	3.00	1.50	.90
387	Frank Crespi	3.00	1.50	.90
388	Gene Desautels	3.00	1.50	.90
389	Bill Cissell	3.00	1.50	.90
390	John Burns	3.00	1.50	.90
391	Larry Benton	3.00	1.50	.90
392	James Holbrook	3.00	1.50	.90
393	Ernie Koy	3.00	1.50	.90
394	Bobby Doerr	3.00	1.50	.90
395	Harry Boyles	3.00	1.50	.90
396	Pinky Higgins	3.00	1.50	.90
397	Mel Almada	3.00	1.50	.90
398	Carl Fischer	3.00	1.50	.90
399	Rabbit Maranville, Johnny Evers, Hank Gowdy	3.00	1.50	.90
400	Lou Gehrig	10.00	5.00	3.00
401	Lincoln Blakely	3.00	1.50	.90
402	James Henry	3.00	1.50	.90
403	Ed Holley	3.00	1.50	.90
404	Elmer Hodgin	3.00	1.50	.90
405	Bob Garbark	3.00	1.50	.90
406	John Burnett	3.00	1.50	.90
407	David Harris	3.00	1.50	.90
408	Johnny Dickshot	3.00	1.50	.90
409	Ray Mueller	3.00	1.50	.90
410	John Welaj	3.00	1.50	.90
411	Les McCrabb	3.00	1.50	.90
412	George Uhle	3.00	1.50	.90
413	Leo Mangum	3.00	1.50	.90
414	Howard Maple	3.00	1.50	.90
415	Syl Johnson	3.00	1.50	.90
416	Hershel Martin	3.00	1.50	.90
417	Joe Martin	3.00	1.50	.90
418	Phil Masi	3.00	1.50	.90
419	Bobby Mattick	3.00	1.50	.90
420	Marshall Mauldin	3.00	1.50	.90
421	Frank May	3.00	1.50	.90
422	Merrill May	3.00	1.50	.90
423	Bill McAfee	3.00	1.50	.90
424	Benny McCoy	3.00	1.50	.90
425	Charlie George	3.00	1.50	.90
426	Roy Hughes	3.00	1.50	.90
427	Bill Kerksieck	3.00	1.50	.90
428	Wes Kingdon	3.00	1.50	.90
429	Lynn King	3.00	1.50	.90
430	Harry Kinzy	3.00	1.50	.90
431	Harry Kimberlin	3.00	1.50	.90
432	Bob Klinger	3.00	1.50	.90
433	Wilfred Knothe	3.00	1.50	.90
434	Lou Finney	3.00	1.50	.90
435	Roy Johnson	3.00	1.50	.90
436	Woody Jensen	3.00	1.50	.90
437	George Jeffcoat	3.00	1.50	.90
438	Roy Joiner	3.00	1.50	.90
439	Baxter Jordan	3.00	1.50	.90
440	Edwin Joost	3.00	1.50	.90
441	Bubber Jonnard	3.00	1.50	.90
442	Bucky Jacobs	3.00	1.50	.90
443	Art Jacobs	3.00	1.50	.90
444	Orville Jorgens	3.00	1.50	.90
445	Hal Kelleher	3.00	1.50	.90
446	Harry Kelley	3.00	1.50	.90
447	Ken Keltner	3.00	1.50	.90
448	Paul Kardon	3.00	1.50	.90
449	Alex Kampouris	3.00	1.50	.90
450	Willie Kamm	3.00	1.50	.90
451	Bob Kahle	3.00	1.50	.90
452	Billy Jurges	3.00	1.50	.90
453	Ken Jungles	3.00	1.50	.90
454	John Juelich	3.00	1.50	.90
455	John Marcum	3.00	1.50	.90
456	Walt Masterson	3.00	1.50	.90
457	Clint Brown	3.00	1.50	.90
458	Buddy Lewis	3.00	1.50	.90
459	Watty Clark	3.00	1.50	.90
460	Johnny Cooney	3.00	1.50	.90
461	Mel Harder	3.00	1.50	.90
462	Justin McLaughlin	3.00	1.50	.90
463	Frank Grube	3.00	1.50	.90
464	Jeff Heath	3.00	1.50	.90
465	Cliff Heathcote	3.00	1.50	.90
466	Harvey Hendrick	3.00	1.50	.90
467	Johnny Hodapp	3.00	1.50	.90
468	Bob Holland	3.00	1.50	.90
469	Otto Huber	3.00	1.50	.90
470	Rudy Hulswitt	3.00	1.50	.90
471	Roy Johnson	3.00	1.50	.90
472	Smead Jolley	3.00	1.50	.90
473	Rollie Hemsley; Bob Smith, John Moore	3.00	1.50	.90
474	John Jones	3.00	1.50	.90
475	Harry Kelley	3.00	1.50	.90
476	George Kelly	3.00	1.50	.90
477	Chuck Klein	3.00	1.50	.90
478	Joe Krakauskas	3.00	1.50	.90
479	Mike Kreevich	3.00	1.50	.90
480	Dick Lanahan	3.00	1.50	.90
481	Emil "Dutch" Leonard	3.00	1.50	.90
482	Harl Maggert	3.00	1.50	.90
483	Cyrus Malis	3.00	1.50	.90
484	Dario Lodigiani	3.00	1.50	.90
485	Walt Masterson	3.00	1.50	.90
486	Rabbit Maranville	3.00	1.50	.90
487	Ed Marshall	3.00	1.50	.90
488	Tim McKeithan	3.00	1.50	.90
489	Patrick McLaughlin	3.00	1.50	.90

490	Bob McNamara	3.00	1.50	.90
491	Steve Mesner	3.00	1.50	.90
492	Clarence Mitchell	3.00	1.50	.90
493	Mal Moss	3.00	1.50	.90
494	Joe Murray	3.00	1.50	.90
495	Pete Naktenis	3.00	1.50	.90
496	Bill Nicholson	3.00	1.50	.90
497	John Rigney	3.00	1.50	.90
498	Clyde Sukeforth	3.00	1.50	.90
499	Evar Swanson	3.00	1.50	.90
500	Dan Taylor	3.00	1.50	.90
501	Sloppy Thurston	3.00	1.50	.90
502	Forrest Wright	3.00	1.50	.90
503	Ray Lucas	3.00	1.50	.90
504	Nig Lipscomb	3.00	1.50	.90

1973-80 TCMA All-Time Greats Postcards

One of the longest collectors' series issued by TCMA in the 1970s was this set of player postcards. Measuring 3-1/2" x 5-1/2" the black-and-white cards have large photos on front, bordered in black and highlighted with banners and baseball equipment. Backs have postcard markings. Six series of cards were issued between 1973-80 and the unnumbered cards are checklisted here in alphabetical order within series.

		NM	EX	VG
Complete Set (156):		150.00	75.00	45.00
Common Player:		3.00	1.50	.90
	SERIES 1			
(1)	Luke Appling	3.00	1.50	.90
(2)	Mickey Cochrane	3.00	1.50	.90
(3)	Eddie Collins	3.00	1.50	.90
(4)	Kiki Cuyler	3.00	1.50	.90
(5)	Bill Dickey	3.00	1.50	.90
(6)	Joe DiMaggio	7.50	3.75	2.25
(7)	Bob Feller	3.00	1.50	.90
(8)	Frank Frisch	3.00	1.50	.90
(9)	Lou Gehrig	7.50	3.75	2.25
(10)	Goose Goslin	3.00	1.50	.90
(11)	Chick Hafey	3.00	1.50	.90
(12)	Gabby Hartnett	3.00	1.50	.90
(13)	Rogers Hornsby	4.00	2.00	1.25
(14)	Ted Lyons	3.00	1.50	.90
(15)	Connie Mack	3.00	1.50	.90
(16)	Heinie Manush	3.00	1.50	.90
(17)	Rabbit Maranville	3.00	1.50	.90
(18)	Ducky Medwick	3.00	1.50	.90
(19)	Al Simmons	3.00	1.50	.90
(20)	Bill Terry	3.00	1.50	.90
(21)	Pie Traynor	3.00	1.50	.90
(22)	Dazzy Vance	3.00	1.50	.90
(23)	Cy Young	5.00	2.50	1.50
(24)	Gabby Hartnett, Babe Ruth	6.00	3.00	1.75
	SERIES 2			
(1)	Roger Bresnahan	3.00	1.50	.90
(2)	Dizzy Dean	4.00	2.00	1.25
(3)	Buck Ewing & mascot	3.00	1.50	.90
(4)	Jimmie Foxx	4.50	2.25	1.25
(5)	Hank Greenberg	4.50	2.25	1.25
(6)	Burleigh Grimes	3.00	1.50	.90
(7)	Harry Heilmann	3.00	1.50	.90
(8)	Waite Hoyt	3.00	1.50	.90
(9)	Walter Johnson	5.00	2.50	1.50
(10)	George Kelly	3.00	1.50	.90
(11)	Christy Mathewson	5.00	2.50	1.50
(12)	John McGraw	3.00	1.50	.90
(13)	Stan Musial	4.00	2.00	1.25
(14)	Mel Ott	3.00	1.50	.90
(15)	Satchel Paige	6.00	3.00	1.75
(16)	Sam Rice	3.00	1.50	.90
(17)	Edd Roush	3.00	1.50	.90
(18)	Red Ruffing	3.00	1.50	.90
(19)	Casey Stengel	3.00	1.50	.90
(20)	Honus Wagner	6.00	3.00	1.75
(21)	Lloyd Waner	3.00	1.50	.90
(22)	Paul Waner	3.00	1.50	.90
(23)	Harry Wright	3.00	1.50	.90
(24)	Ross Youngs	3.00	1.50	.90
	SERIES 3			
(1)	Home Run Baker	3.00	1.50	.90
(2)	Chief Bender	3.00	1.50	.90
(3)	Jim Bottomley	3.00	1.50	.90
(4)	Lou Boudreau	3.00	1.50	.90
(5)	Mordecai Brown	3.00	1.50	.90
(6)	Roy Campanella	3.50	1.75	1.00
(7)	Max Carey	3.00	1.50	.90
(8)	Ty Cobb	7.50	3.75	2.25
(9)	Earle Combs	3.00	1.50	.90
(10)	Jocko Conlan	3.00	1.50	.90

		NM	EX	VG
(11)	Hugh Duffy	3.00	1.50	.90
(12)	Red Faber	3.00	1.50	.90
(13)	Lefty Grove	3.00	1.50	.90
(14)	Judge K.M. Landis	3.00	1.50	.90
(15)	Eddie Plank	3.00	1.50	.90
(16)	Hoss Radbourne	3.00	1.50	.90
(17)	Eppa Rixey	3.00	1.50	.90
(18)	Jackie Robinson	6.00	3.00	1.75
(19)	Babe Ruth	7.50	3.75	2.25
(20)	George Sisler	3.00	1.50	.90
(21)	Zack Wheat	3.00	1.50	.90
(22)	Ted Williams	6.00	3.00	1.75
(23)	Mel Ott, Babe Ruth	6.00	3.00	1.75
(24)	Tris Speaker, Wilbert Robinson	3.00	1.50	.90

SERIES 4

		NM	EX	VG
(1)	Grover C. Alexander	3.50	1.75	1.00
(2)	Cap Anson	3.00	1.50	.90
(3)	Earl Averill	3.00	1.50	.90
(4)	Ed Barrow	3.00	1.50	.90
(5)	Yogi Berra	3.50	1.75	1.00
(6)	Roberto Clemente	6.00	3.00	1.75
(7)	Jimmy Collins	3.00	1.50	.90
(8)	Whitey Ford	3.50	1.75	1.00
(9)	Ford Frick	3.00	1.50	.90
(10)	Vernon Gomez	3.00	1.50	.90
(11)	Bucky Harris	3.00	1.50	.90
(12)	Billy Herman	3.00	1.50	.90
(13)	Carl Hubbell	3.00	1.50	.90
(14)	Miller Huggins	3.00	1.50	.90
(15)	Monte Irvin	3.00	1.50	.90
(16)	Ralph Kiner	3.00	1.50	.90
(17)	Bill Klem	3.00	1.50	.90
(18)	Sandy Koufax	6.00	3.00	1.75
(19)	Napoleon Lajoie	3.00	1.50	.90
(20)	Bob Lemon	3.00	1.50	.90
(21)	Mickey Mantle	7.50	3.75	2.25
(22)	Rube Marquard	3.00	1.50	.90
(23)	Joe McCarthy	3.00	1.50	.90
(24)	Bill McKechnie	3.00	1.50	.90
(25)	Herb Pennock	3.00	1.50	.90
(26)	Warren Spahn	3.00	1.50	.90
(27)	Joe Tinker	3.00	1.50	.90
(28)	Early Wynn	3.00	1.50	.90
(29)	Joe Cronin, Honus Wagner, Bill Terry	3.00	1.50	.90
(30)	Jimmie Foxx, Lou Gehrig	6.00	3.00	1.75
(31)	Hank Greenberg, Ralph Kiner	3.00	1.50	.90
(32)	Walter Johnson, Connie Mack	3.00	1.50	.90
(33)	Connie Mack, Bob Feller	3.00	1.50	.90
(34)	Mel Ott, Lou Gehrig	6.00	3.00	1.75
(35)	Al Simmons, Tris Speaker, Ty Cobb	3.00	1.50	.90
(36)	Ted Williams, Lou Boudreau	3.00	1.50	.90

SERIES 5

		NM	EX	VG
(1)	Dave Bancroft	3.00	1.50	.90
(2)	Ernie Banks	3.50	1.75	1.00
(3)	Frank Chance	3.00	1.50	.90
(4)	Stan Coveleski	3.00	1.50	.90
(5)	Billy Evans	3.00	1.50	.90
(6)	Clark Griffith	3.00	1.50	.90
(7)	Jesse Haines	3.00	1.50	.90
(8)	Will Harridge	3.00	1.50	.90
(9)	Harry Hooper	3.00	1.50	.90
(10)	Cal Hubbard	3.00	1.50	.90
(11)	Hugh Jennings	3.00	1.50	.90
(12)	Wee Willie Keeler	3.00	1.50	.90
(13)	Fred Lindstrom	3.00	1.50	.90
(14)	Pop Lloyd	3.00	1.50	.90
(15)	Al Lopez	3.00	1.50	.90
(16)	Robin Roberts	3.00	1.50	.90
(17)	Amos Rusie	3.00	1.50	.90
(18)	Ray Schalk	3.00	1.50	.90
(19)	Joe Sewell	3.00	1.50	.90
(20)	Rube Waddell	3.00	1.50	.90
(21)	George Weiss	3.00	1.50	.90
(22)	Dizzy Dean, Gabby Hartnett	3.00	1.50	.90
(23)	Joe DiMaggio, Mickey Mantle	7.50	3.75	2.25
(24)	Ted Williams, Joe DiMaggio	6.00	3.00	1.75

SERIES 6

		NM	EX	VG
(1)	Jack Chesbro	3.00	1.50	.90
(2)	Tom Connolly	3.00	1.50	.90
(3)	Sam Crawford	3.00	1.50	.90
(4)	Elmer Flick	3.00	1.50	.90
(5)	Charlie Gehringer	3.00	1.50	.90
(6)	Warren Giles	3.00	1.50	.90
(7)	Ban Johnson	3.00	1.50	.90
(8)	Addie Joss	3.00	1.50	.90
(9)	Al Kaline	3.00	1.50	.90
(10)	Willie Mays	6.00	3.00	1.75
(11)	Joe McGinnity	3.00	1.50	.90
(12)	Larry McPhail (MacPhail)	3.00	1.50	.90
(13)	Branch Rickey	3.00	1.50	.90
(14)	Wilbert Robinson	3.00	1.50	.90
(15)	Duke Snider	3.00	1.50	.90
(16)	Tris Speaker	4.00	2.00	1.25
(17)	Bobby Wallace	3.00	1.50	.90
(18)	Hack Wilson	.45	.25	.14
(19)	Yogi Berra, Casey Stengel	4.00	2.00	1.25
(20)	Warren Giles, Roberto Clemente	4.50	2.25	1.25
(21)	Mickey Mantle, Willie Mays	6.00	3.00	1.75
(22)	John McGraw, Babe Ruth	6.00	3.00	1.75
(23)	Satchel Paige, Bob Feller	5.00	2.50	1.50
(24)	Paul Waner, Lloyd Waner	4.00	2.00	1.25

1973 TCMA All Time New York Yankees Team

Printed in black-and-white in 3-1/2" x 5-1/2" format, these cards have borderless photos on front with a white strip at bottom in which the player's position and name appear. Backs list the all-time roster but are not numbered or dated. Production was 1,000 sets.

Outfield-Mickey Mantle

		NM	EX	VG
Complete Set (12):		25.00	12.50	7.50
Common Player:		3.50	1.75	1.00
(1)	Bill Dickey	3.50	1.75	1.00
(2)	Joe DiMaggio	10.00	5.00	3.00
(3)	Whitey Ford	5.00	2.50	1.50
(4)	Lou Gehrig	10.00	5.00	3.00
(5)	Tony Lazzeri	3.50	1.75	1.00
(6)	Mickey Mantle	15.00	7.50	4.50
(7)	Johnny Murphy	3.50	1.75	1.00
(8)	Phil Rizzuto	5.00	2.50	1.50
(9)	Red Rolfe	3.50	1.75	1.00
(10)	Red Ruffing	3.50	1.75	1.00
(11)	Babe Ruth	10.00	5.00	3.00
(12)	Casey Stengel	3.50	1.75	1.00

1973 TCMA Autographs & Drawings Postcards

These black-and-white postcards feature drawings of the players, along with facsimile autographs.

		NM	EX	VG
Complete Set (12):		50.00	25.00	15.00
Common Player:		5.00	2.50	1.50
1	Mickey Cockran (Cochrane)	5.00	2.50	1.50
2	Christy Mathewson	5.00	2.50	1.50
3	Roberto Clemente	10.00	5.00	3.00
4	Rogers Hornsby	5.00	2.50	1.50
5	Pie Traynor	5.00	2.50	1.50
6	Frankie Frisch	5.00	2.50	1.50
7	Ty Cobb	7.50	3.75	2.25
8	Connie Mack	5.00	2.50	1.50
9	Babe Ruth	10.00	5.00	3.00
10	Lou Gehrig	8.00	4.00	2.50
11	Gil Hodges	5.00	2.50	1.50
12	Jackie Robinson	8.00	4.00	2.50

1973-1974 TCMA Autograph Series

These postcard-size black-and-white cards have borderless front photos with a wide white strip at bottom to accomodate an autograph. They are blank-backed.

		NM	EX	VG
Complete Set (36):		125.00	65.00	35.00
Common Player:		4.00	2.00	1.20
1	Satchel Paige	7.50	3.75	2.25
2	Phil Rizzuto	6.00	3.00	1.75
3	Sid Gordon	4.00	2.00	1.20
4	Ernie Lombardi	4.00	2.00	1.20
5	Jesse Haines	4.00	2.00	1.20
6	Joe Gordon	4.00	2.00	1.20
7	Bill Terry	4.00	2.00	1.20
8	Bill Dickey	6.00	3.00	1.75
9	Joe DiMaggio	12.00	6.00	3.50
10	Carl Hubbell	5.00	2.50	1.50
11	Fred Lindstrom	4.00	2.00	1.20
12	Ted Lyons	4.00	2.00	1.20
13	Red Ruffing	4.00	2.00	1.20
14	Joe Gordon	4.00	2.00	1.20
15	Bob Feller	6.00	3.00	1.75
16	Yogi Berra	7.50	3.75	2.25
17	Ford Frick, Whitey Ford	5.00	2.50	1.50
18	Sandy Koufax	12.00	6.00	3.50
19	Ted Williams	10.00	5.00	3.00
20	Warren Spahn	5.00	2.50	1.50
21	Al Rosen	4.00	2.00	1.20
22	Luke Appling	4.00	2.00	1.20
23	Joe Bush	4.00	2.00	1.20
24	Joe Medwick	4.00	2.00	1.20
25	Lou Boudreau	4.00	2.00	1.20
26	Ralph Kiner	4.00	2.00	1.20
27	Lloyd Waner	4.00	2.00	1.20
28	Pee Wee Reese	7.50	3.75	2.25
29	Duke Snider	7.50	3.75	2.25
30	Sal Maglie	4.00	2.00	1.20
31	Monte Irvin	4.00	2.00	1.20
32	Lefty Gomez	4.00	2.00	1.20
33	George Kelly	4.00	2.00	1.20
34	Joe Adcock	4.00	2.00	1.20
35	Max Carey	4.00	2.00	1.20
36	Rube Marquard	4.00	2.00	1.20

1973 TCMA "Bobo"

The major league travels of Bobo Newsom are chronicled in this set of 3-1/2" x 5-1/2" black-and-white cards depicting the pitcher in the uniforms of the nine teams for whom he played between 1929-53.

		NM	EX	VG
Complete Set (10):		25.00	12.50	7.50
Common Card:		4.00	2.00	1.25
(1)	Bobo Newsom (A's)	4.00	2.00	1.25
(2)	Bobo Newsom (A's, with Bobby Shantz)	4.00	2.00	1.25
(3)	Bobo Newsom (Browns)	4.00	2.00	1.25
(4)	Bobo Newsom (Cubs)	4.00	2.00	1.25
(5)	Bobo Newsom (Dodgers, with Leo Durocher)	4.00	2.00	1.25
(6)	Bobo Newsom (Giants)	4.00	2.00	1.25
(7)	Bobo Newsom (Red Sox)	4.00	2.00	1.25
(8)	Bobo Newsom (Senators, with Ossie Bluege)	4.00	2.00	1.25
(9)	Bobo Newsom (Tigers, with Paul Derringer)	4.00	2.00	1.25
(10)	Bobo Newsom (Yankees, with Vic Rashi, Bucky Harris)	4.00	2.00	1.25

1973 TCMA Pudge Gautreaux

This custom-published postcard of the Brooklyn Dodgers catcher (1936-37) was printed in black-and-white in a 3-1/2" x 6" format. The issue date is approximate.

	NM	EX	VG
Sid "Pudge" Gautreaux	4.00	2.00	1.25

1973-78 TCMA League Leaders

One of TCMA's earliest major series of collectors cards was this run of postcard-size (3-1/2" x 5-1/2") black-and-whites honoring various statistical leaders in each league from the 1920s through the 1950s. Backs have a list of the leaders by year within decade, with one of them pictured on the front. The unnumbered cards are checklisted here in alphabetical order within decade, as they were issued.

		NM	EX	VG
	Complete Set (96):	190.00	95.00	55.00
	Common Player:	5.00	2.50	1.50
	Complete set, The 1920s	50.00	25.00	15.00
(1)	Grover C. Alexander	5.00	2.50	1.50
(2)	Jim Bagby, Sr.	5.00	2.50	1.50
(3)	Jim Bottomley	5.00	2.50	1.50
(4)	Eddie Collins	5.00	2.50	1.50
(5)	Earle Combs	5.00	2.50	1.50
(6)	Kiki Cuyler	5.00	2.50	1.50
(7)	Urban "Red" Faber	5.00	2.50	1.50
(8)	Johnny Frederick	5.00	2.50	1.50
(9)	Charlie Gehringer	5.00	2.50	1.50
(10)	Goose Goslin	5.00	2.50	1.50
(11)	Rogers Hornsby	5.00	2.50	1.50
(12)	Walter Johnson	6.00	3.00	1.75
(13)	Freddie Lindstrom	5.00	2.50	1.50
(14)	Bob Meusel	5.00	2.50	1.50
(15)	Charlie Root	5.00	2.50	1.50
(16)	Babe Ruth, Rogers Hornsby	7.50	3.75	2.25
(17)	Al Simmons, Babe Ruth	7.50	3.75	2.25
(18)	Tris Speaker	5.00	2.50	1.50
(19)	Dazzy Vance	5.00	2.50	1.50
(20)	Lloyd Waner	5.00	2.50	1.50
(21)	Cy Williams	5.00	2.50	1.50
(22)	Ken Williams	5.00	2.50	1.50
(23)	Hack Wilson	5.00	2.50	1.50
(24)	Ross Youngs	5.00	2.50	1.50
	Complete set, The 1930s	50.00	25.00	15.00
(1)	Johnny Allen	5.00	2.50	1.50
(2)	Beau Bell	5.00	2.50	1.50
(3)	Cy Blanton	5.00	2.50	1.50
(4)	Ben Chapman	5.00	2.50	1.50
(5)	Joe Cronin	5.00	2.50	1.50
(6)	Dizzy Dean	6.50	3.25	2.00
(7)	Joe DiMaggio	20.00	10.00	6.00
(8)	Jimmie Foxx	5.00	2.50	1.50
(9)	Lou Gehrig	15.00	7.50	4.50
(10)	Charlie Gehringer	5.00	2.50	1.50
(11)	Lefty Gomez	5.00	2.50	1.50
(12)	Ival Goodman	5.00	2.50	1.50
(13)	Lefty Grove	5.00	2.50	1.50
(14)	Billy Herman	5.00	2.50	1.50
(15)	Ernie Lombardi	5.00	2.50	1.50
(16)	Chuck Klein	5.00	2.50	1.50
(17)	Heinie Manush	5.00	2.50	1.50
(18)	Pepper Martin	5.00	2.50	1.50
(19)	Joe Medwick	5.00	2.50	1.50
(20)	Van Mungo	5.00	2.50	1.50
(21)	Mel Ott	5.00	2.50	1.50
(22)	Bill Terry	5.00	2.50	1.50
(23)	Hal Trosky	5.00	2.50	1.50
(24)	Arky Vaughan	5.00	2.50	1.50
	Complete set, The 1940s	50.00	25.00	15.00
(1)	Gene Bearden	5.00	2.50	1.50
(2)	Lou Boudreau	5.00	2.50	1.50
(3)	George Case	5.00	2.50	1.50
(4)	Phil Cavarretta	5.00	2.50	1.50
(5)	Bob Feller	6.00	3.00	1.75
(6)	Boo Ferriss	5.00	2.50	1.50
(7)	Hank Greenberg	9.00	4.50	2.75
(8)	Jeff Heath	5.00	2.50	1.50
(9)	Tommy Holmes	5.00	2.50	1.50
(10)	Larry Jansen	5.00	2.50	1.50
(11)	George Kell	5.00	2.50	1.50
(12)	Ralph Kiner	5.00	2.50	1.50
(13)	Marty Marion	5.00	2.50	1.50
(14)	Johnny Mize	5.00	2.50	1.50
(15)	Stan Musial	10.00	5.00	3.00
(16)	Bill Nicholson	5.00	2.50	1.50
(17)	Johnny Pesky	5.00	2.50	1.50
(18)	Jackie Robinson	10.00	5.00	3.00
(19)	Enos Slaughter	5.00	2.50	1.50
(20)	Snuffy Stirnweiss	5.00	2.50	1.50
(21)	Bill Voiselle	5.00	2.50	1.50
(22)	Bucky Walters	5.00	2.50	1.50
(23)	Ted Williams	10.00	5.00	3.00
(24)	Ted Williams, Joe DiMaggio	10.00	5.00	3.00
	Complete set, The 1950s	50.00	25.00	15.00
(1)	Luis Aparicio	5.00	2.50	1.50
(2)	Ernie Banks	5.00	2.50	1.50
(3)	Bill Bruton	5.00	2.50	1.50
(4)	Lew Burdette	5.00	2.50	1.50
(5)	Rocky Colavito	5.00	2.50	1.50
(6)	Dom DiMaggio	5.00	2.50	1.50
(7)	Ferris Fain	5.00	2.50	1.50
(8)	Whitey Ford	5.00	2.50	1.50
(9)	Don Hoak	5.00	2.50	1.50
(10)	Sam Jethroe	5.00	2.50	1.50
(11)	Ted Kluszewski	5.00	2.50	1.50
(12)	Harvey Kuenn	5.00	2.50	1.50
(13)	Bob Lemon	5.00	2.50	1.50
(14)	Mickey Mantle	30.00	15.00	9.00
(15)	Willie Mays	15.00	7.50	4.50
(16)	Willie Mays, Bobby Avila	5.00	2.50	1.50
(17)	Minnie Minoso	5.00	2.50	1.50
(18)	Don Newcombe	5.00	2.50	1.50
(19)	Robin Roberts	5.00	2.50	1.50
(20)	Hank Sauer	5.00	2.50	1.50
(21)	Bobby Shantz	5.00	2.50	1.50
(22)	Roy Sievers	5.00	2.50	1.50
(23)	Duke Snider	6.00	3.00	1.75
(24)	Mickey Vernon	5.00	2.50	1.50

1973 TCMA Sports Scoop Hall of Fame

This set of large-format (3-1/2" x 5-1/2") black-and-white cards was produced by TCMA for the collectors' magazine Sports Scoop, which was promoting the players to be inducted into the Hall of Fame. Backs have information about the player's career and HoF credentials.

		NM	EX	VG
	Complete Set (12):	20.00	10.00	6.00
	Common Player:	2.00	1.00	.60
(1)	Earl Averill	2.50	1.25	.70
(2)	Ben Chapman	2.00	1.00	.60
(3)	Doc Cramer	2.00	1.00	.60
(4)	Spud Davis	2.00	1.00	.60
(5)	Babe Herman	2.00	1.00	.60
(6)	Billy Herman	2.50	1.25	.70
(7)	Chuck Klein	2.50	1.25	.70
(8)	Bob Meusel	2.00	1.00	.60
(9)	Johnny Mize	3.00	1.50	.90
(10)	Joe Sewell	2.50	1.25	.70
(11)	Enos Slaughter	3.00	1.50	.90
(12)	Hal Trosky	2.00	1.00	.60

1973 TCMA 1874 Philadelphia Athletics

This early collectors' issue reproduces woodcuts of the A's as they appeared in the July 25, 1874, edition of Harper's Weekly. The 3-1/16" x 4-1/2" cards are printed in black-and-white with the player name and position in the white border at bottom. Identical backs credit the pictures' original source and state "TCMA Reprint 1973." The unnumbered cards are checklisted here alphabetically.

		NM	EX	VG
	Complete Set (9):	25.00	12.50	7.50
	Common Player:	3.00	1.50	.90
(1)	Cap Anson	10.00	5.00	3.00
(2)	Joseph Battin	3.00	1.50	.90
(3)	John Clapp	3.00	1.50	.90
(4)	Wes Fisler	3.00	1.50	.90
(5)	Count Gedney	3.00	1.50	.90
(6)	Dick McBride	3.00	1.50	.90
(7)	Mike McGeary	3.00	1.50	.90
(8)	J.F. McMullen	3.00	1.50	.90
(9)	Ezra Sutton	3.00	1.50	.90

1973 TCMA 1890 Base-ball Season

This set commemorates the baseball "war" of 1890 when many National League players - stars and journeymen alike - defected to a new player-owned league called, appropriately enough, the Players League. Fronts of these 3-1/8" x 4-1/2" black-and-white cards feature reproductions of woodcuts originally printed in Harper's Weekly. Backs have information about the

teams in each league. The unnumbered cards are checklisted here in alphabetical order. Original issue price of the set was $3.

		NM	EX	VG
	Complete Set (30):	48.00	24.00	14.50
	Common Player:	2.00	1.00	.60
(1)	Cap Anson	2.00	1.00	.60
(2)	Dan Brouthers	2.00	1.00	.60
(3)	Thomas E. Burns	2.00	1.00	.60
(4)	John Clarkson	2.00	1.00	.60
(5)	C.A. Comiskey	2.00	1.00	.60
(6)	Roger Connor	2.00	1.00	.60
(7)	E.N. Crane	2.00	1.00	.60
(8)	Jeremiah Denny	2.00	1.00	.60
(9)	William B. Ewing	2.00	1.00	.60
(10)	D.L. Foutz	2.00	1.00	.60
(11)	John W. Glasscock	2.00	1.00	.60
(12)	W. Hallman	2.00	1.00	.60
(13)	Edward Hanlon	2.00	1.00	.60
(14)	Timothy J. Keefe	2.00	1.00	.60
(15)	M.J. Kelly	2.00	1.00	.60
(16)	M. Kilroy	2.00	1.00	.60
(17)	W.A. Latham	2.00	1.00	.60
(18)	J.A. McPhee	2.00	1.00	.60
(19)	Joseph Mulvey	2.00	1.00	.60
(20)	W.D. O'Brien	2.00	1.00	.60
(21)	David Orr	2.00	1.00	.60
(22)	John G. Reilly	2.00	1.00	.60
(23)	S.L. Thompson	2.00	1.00	.60
(24)	M. Tiernan	2.00	1.00	.60
(25)	John M. Ward	2.00	1.00	.60
(26)	M. Welsh (Welch)	2.00	1.00	.60
(27)	A. Weyhing	2.00	1.00	.60
(28)	Charles Zimmer	2.00	1.00	.60
(29)	A dive for second base	1.00	.50	.30
(30)	Brotherhood Players Header Card	1.00	.50	.30

1973 TCMA 1930's No Hit Pitchers and 6 for 6 Hitters

These large-format (3-1/2" x 5-1/2") cards feature the no-hit pitchers and 6-for-6 hitters of the 1930s. Borderless front photos are in black-and-white. On back of the pitchers' cards is a list of the decade's no-hitters, the date, score and opposing team. A similar list of the 6-for-6 hitters is on the back of their cards. The cards are unnumbered.

		NM	EX	VG
	Complete Set (12):	40.00	20.00	12.00
	Common Player:	4.00	2.00	1.25
	PITCHERS			
(1)	Paul Dean	6.00	3.00	1.75
(2)	Bill Dietrich	4.00	2.00	1.25
(3)	Vern Kennedy	4.00	2.00	1.25
(4)	Monte Pearson	4.00	2.00	1.25
(5)	Johnny Vander Meer	5.00	2.50	1.50
	HITTERS			
(6)	Jim Bottomley	6.00	3.00	1.75
(7)	Bruce Campbell	4.00	2.00	1.25
(8)	Doc Cramer	4.00	2.00	1.25
(9)	Myril Hoag	4.00	2.00	1.25
(10)	Cookie Lavagetto	4.00	2.00	1.25
(11)	Terry Moore	5.00	2.50	1.50
(12)	Henry Steinbacher	4.00	2.00	1.25

1973 TCMA 1941 Brooklyn Dodgers

These 3-3/8" x 2-1/2" cards are printed in blue-and-white. The unnumbered cards do not have player names on front.

		NM	EX	VG
	Complete Set (32):	50.00	25.00	15.00
	Common Player	2.00	1.00	.60
(1)	Title card	1.00	.50	.60
(2)	John Allen	2.00	1.00	.60
(3)	Mace Brown	2.00	1.00	.60
(4)	Dolph Camilli	2.00	1.00	.60
(5)	Hugh Casey	2.00	1.00	.60
(6)	Curt Davis	2.00	1.00	.60
(7)	Tom Drake	2.00	1.00	.60
(8)	Leo Durocher	4.00	2.00	1.25
(9)	Fred Fitzsimmons	2.00	1.00	.60
(10)	Herman Franks	2.00	1.00	.60
(11)	Augie Galan	2.00	1.00	.60
(12)	Tony Giuliani	2.00	1.00	.60
(13)	Luke Hamlin	2.00	1.00	.60
(14)	Billy Herman	4.00	2.00	1.25
(15)	Kirby Higbe	2.00	1.00	.60
(16)	Alex Kampouris	2.00	1.00	.60

		NM	EX	VG
(17)	Newt Kimball	2.00	1.00	.60
(18)	Cookie Lavagetto	2.00	1.00	.60
(19)	Ducky Medwick	4.00	2.00	1.25
(20)	Van Mungo	2.00	1.00	.60
(21)	Mickey Owen	2.00	1.00	.60
(22)	Babe Phelps	2.00	1.00	.60
(23)	Pee Wee Reese	8.00	4.00	2.50
(24)	Pete Reiser	2.00	1.00	.60
(25)	Lew Riggs	2.00	1.00	.60
(26)	Bill Swift	2.00	1.00	.60
(27)	Vito Tamulis	2.00	1.00	.60
(28)	Joe Vosmik	2.00	1.00	.60
(29)	Dixie Walker	2.00	1.00	.60
(30)	Paul Waner	4.00	2.00	1.25
(31)	Jimmy Wasdell	2.00	1.00	.60
(32)	Whit Wyatt	2.00	1.00	.60

1973 TCMA Stan Martucci Postcards

This set of postcards was custom-produced by TCMA for card dealer Stan Martucci who apparently used them as "ride alongs" when filling orders. Approximately 3-1/2" x 5-1/2", the fronts have borderless, unidentified black-and-white photos of popular former stars. The back is in standard postcard format and had the player identified at top-left and a note from Martucci in the message area.

		NM	EX	VG
Complete Set (16):		15.00	7.50	4.50
Common Player:		1.00	.50	.30
(1)	Joe Cronin	1.00	.50	.30
(2)	Dizzy Dean	2.00	1.00	.60
(3)	Joe DiMaggio	5.00	2.50	1.50
(4)	Jimmie Foxx	2.00	1.00	.60
(5)	Lou Gehrig	5.00	2.50	1.50
(6)	Charlie Gehringer	1.00	.50	.30
(7)	Lefty Gomez	1.00	.50	.30
(8)	Lefty Grove	1.00	.50	.30
(9)	Carl Hubbell	1.00	.50	.30
(10)	Ted Lyons	1.00	.50	.30
(11)	Heinie Manush	1.00	.50	.30
(12)	Joe Medwick	1.00	.50	.30
(13)	Mel Ott	1.00	.50	.30
(14)	Red Ruffing	1.00	.50	.30
(15)	Bill Terry	1.00	.50	.30
(16)	Paul Waner	1.00	.50	.30

1974 TCMA Nicknames

Nicknames of notable ballplayers of the 1930s-40s are featured in this early collectors' set. Fronts of the 2-5/16" x 3-1/2" cards have a black-and-white photo with the player's nickname in the bottom border and "Nicknames" in the top border, both printed in red. Backs have a card number, the player's full name, position and the teams and years he played in the major leagues. The set originally sold for $3.

		NM	EX	VG
Complete Set (28):		40.00	20.00	12.00
Common Player:		3.00	1.50	.90
1	Rapid Robert Feller	4.50	2.25	1.25
2	Babe Dahlgren	3.00	1.50	.90
3	Spud Chandler	3.00	1.50	.90
4	Ducky Medwick	3.00	1.50	.90
5	Silent Cal Benge	3.00	1.50	.90
6	Goose Goslin	3.00	1.50	.90
7	Mule Haas	3.00	1.50	.90
8	Dizzy Dean	6.00	3.00	1.75
9	Cowboy Harrell	3.00	1.50	.90
10	Buzz Boyle	3.00	1.50	.90
11	Coonskin Davis	3.00	1.50	.90
12	Moose Solters	3.00	1.50	.90
13	Sad Sam Jones	3.00	1.50	.90
14	Bad News Hale	3.00	1.50	.90
15	Bucky Harris	3.00	1.50	.90
16	Lord Jim Jordan	3.00	1.50	.90
17	Zeke Bonura	3.00	1.50	.90
18	Heave-o Hafey	3.00	1.50	.90
19	Spud Davis	3.00	1.50	.90
20	Bing Miller	3.00	1.50	.90
21	Preacher Roe	3.00	1.50	.90
22	Wild Bill Hallahan	3.00	1.50	.90
23	Indian Bob Johnson	3.00	1.50	.90
24	Flash Gordon	3.00	1.50	.90
25	Tot Pressnell	3.00	1.50	.90
26	Hot Potato Hamlin	3.00	1.50	.90
27	Old Reliable Henrich	3.00	1.50	.90
28	Tom Hafey	3.00	1.50	.90

1974 TCMA Sports Nostalgia Store Postcards

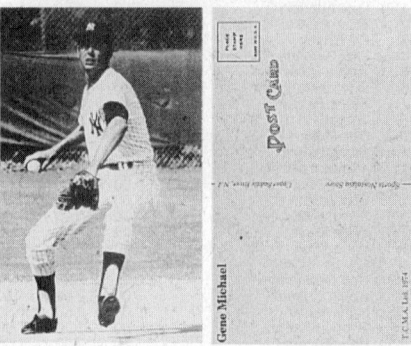

Gene Michael

To celebrate the opening of one of the first, if not the first, sports collectors' retail stores, TCMA issued a set of four 3-1/2" x 51/2" black-and-white postcards. The set includes one current N.Y. Yankees player and three former boxers. The set was issued in an edition of 1,000.

		NM	EX	VG
Complete Set (4):		20.00	10.00	6.00
Common Card:		5.00	2.50	1.50
(1)	Gene Michael	7.50	3.75	2.25
(2)	Emile Griffith	5.00	2.50	1.50
(3)	Floyd Patterson	5.00	2.50	1.50
(4)	Willie Pep	5.00	2.50	1.50

1974 TCMA Stadium Postcards

These 5" x 3-1/2" black-and-white postcards are not numbered and are listed here alphabetically.

		NM	EX	VG
Complete Set (12):		35.00	17.50	10.50
Common Card:		4.00	2.00	1.20
(1)	Baltimore Stadium	4.00	2.00	1.20
(2)	Boston Braves Field	4.00	2.00	1.20
(3)	Crosley Field	4.00	2.00	1.20
(4)	Ebbet's (Ebbets) Field	6.00	3.00	1.75
(5)	Forbes Field	4.00	2.00	1.20
(6)	Griffith Field	4.00	2.00	1.20
(7)	Milwaukee County Stadium	4.00	2.00	1.20
(8)	Narvin (Navin) Field	4.00	2.00	1.20
(9)	Polo Grounds	4.00	2.00	1.20
(10)	Shea Stadium	4.00	2.00	1.20
(11)	Wrigley Field	5.00	2.50	1.50
(12)	Yankee Stadium	7.50	3.75	2.25

1974-75 TCMA St. Louis Browns

St. Louis Browns 1902 - 1953

OSTERMUELLER, Frederick Raymond "Fritz"

	G.	W-L
1941	16	0-3
1942	10	3-1
1943	11	0-2

FRITZ OSTER MUELLER

THE BROWNS

2nd Series

1974 TCMA, Ltd.

Some of baseball's most loveable losers from about the 1930s through the team's flight to Baltimore in 1953 are presented in this multi-series collectors' issue. Cards are printed in a 2-1/4" x 3-7/8" format, with brown ink used on front and on back of Series 1 and 2; Series 3 cards have black ink on back. Some cards have player identification on front, some only on back. All cards have a TCMA copyright date line and a few player stats for his years with the Brownies. The unnumbered cards are checklisted here alphabetically by series.

		NM	EX	VG
Complete Set (108):		80.00	40.00	20.00
Common Player:		1.50	.75	.45
	Series 1 - 1974	25.00	12.50	7.50
(1)	Ethan Allen	1.50	.75	.45
(2)	Mel Almada	2.00	1.00	.60
(3)	Ed Baecht	1.50	.75	.45
(4)	John Berardino	4.00	2.00	1.25
(5)	Emil Bildilli	1.50	.75	.45
(6)	John Blake	1.50	.75	.45
(7)	Julio Bonetti	1.50	.75	.45
(8)	Earl Caldwell	1.50	.75	.45
(9)	Scoops Carey	1.50	.75	.45
(10)	Stinky Davis	1.50	.75	.45
(11)	Fred Haney	1.50	.75	.45
(12)	Jeff Heath	1.50	.75	.45
(13)	Don Heffner	1.50	.75	.45

		NM	EX	VG
(14)	Rollie Hemsley	1.50	.75	.45
(15)	Oral Hildebrand	1.50	.75	.45
(16)	Elon Hogsett	1.50	.75	.45
(17)	Ben Huffman	1.50	.75	.45
(18)	Sig Jakucki	1.50	.75	.45
(19)	Billy Knickerbocker	1.50	.75	.45
(20)	John Knott	1.50	.75	.45
(21)	Jack Kramer	1.50	.75	.45
(22)	Red Kress	1.50	.75	.45
(23)	Chet Laabs	1.50	.75	.45
(24)	Gerard "Nig" Lipscomb	1.50	.75	.45
(25)	John Lucadello	1.50	.75	.45
(26)	Mel Mazzera	1.50	.75	.45
(27)	Red McQuillen	1.50	.75	.45
(28)	George McQuinn	1.50	.75	.45
(29)	Oscar Melillo	1.50	.75	.45
(30)	Howard Mills	1.50	.75	.45
(31)	Bob Muncrief	1.50	.75	.45
(32)	Hank Thompson	1.50	.75	.45
(33)	Russell "Sheriff" Van Atta	1.50	.75	.45
(34)	Joe Vosmik	1.50	.75	.45
(35)	Jim Walkup	1.50	.75	.45
(36)	Sam West	1.50	.75	.45
	Series 2 - 1974	30.00	15.00	9.00
(37)	Floyd Baker	1.50	.75	.45
(38)	John Bassler	1.50	.75	.45
(39)	Ollie Bejma	1.50	.75	.45
(40)	Jim Bottomley	2.00	1.00	.60
(41)	Willard Brown	4.50	2.25	1.25
(42)	Bob Dillinger	1.50	.75	.45
(43)	Owen Red" Friend	1.50	.75	.45
(44)	Eddie Gaedel	5.00	2.50	1.50
(45)	Dennis Galehouse	1.50	.75	.45
(46)	Joseph Gallagher	1.50	.75	.45
(47)	Ned Garver	1.50	.75	.45
(48)	Robert Harris	1.50	.75	.45
(49)	Al Hollingsworth	1.50	.75	.45
(50)	Walter Judnich	1.50	.75	.45
(51)	William "Lefty" Kennedy	1.50	.75	.45
(52)	Lou Kretlow	1.50	.75	.45
(53)	Martin Marion	1.50	.70	.45
(54)	Les Moss	1.50	.75	.45
(55)	Louis "Bobo" Newsom	1.50	.75	.45
(56)	Fritz Ostermueller	1.50	.75	.45
(57)	Joe Ostrowski	1.50	.75	.45
(58)	Edward Pellagrini	1.50	.75	.45
(59)	Duane Pillette	1.50	.75	.45
(60)	Nelson Potter	1.50	.75	.45
(61)	Raymond "Rip" Radcliff	1.50	.75	.45
(62)	Harry Rice	1.50	.75	.45
(63)	Jim Rivera	1.50	.75	.45
(64)	John "Fred" Sanford	1.50	.75	.45
(65)	Luke Sewell	1.50	.75	.45
(66)	Al Shirley	1.50	.75	.45
(67)	Junior Stephens	1.50	.75	.45
(68)	Thomas Turner	1.50	.75	.45
(69)	Ken Wood	1.50	.75	.45
(70)	Allen "Zeke" Zarilla	1.50	.75	.45
(71)	Samuel "Sad Sam" Zoldak	1.50	.75	.45
(72)	1944 Infield	1.50	.75	.45
	Series 3 - 1975	30.00	15.00	9.00
(73)	Bow-Wow Arft	1.50	.75	.45
(74)	Matthew Batts	1.50	.75	.45
(75)	Tommy Byrne	1.50	.75	.45
(76)	Skippy Byrnes	1.50	.75	.45
(77)	Raymond Coleman	1.50	.75	.45
(78)	Scrap Iron Courtney	1.50	.75	.45
(79)	James Delsing	1.50	.75	.45
(80)	William "Kid" DeMars	1.50	.75	.45
(81)	Clifford "Mule" Fannin	1.50	.75	.45
(82)	Tom Fine	1.50	.75	.45
(83)	Pete Gray	5.00	2.50	1.50
(84)	Red Hayworth	1.50	.75	.45
(85)	Procopio Herrera	1.50	.70	.45
(86)	Fred Hoffman	1.50	.75	.45
(87)	Walter "Union Man" Holke	1.50	.75	.45
(88)	Hal Hudson	1.50	.70	.45
(89)	Richard Kokos	1.50	.75	.45
(90)	Michael Kreevich	1.50	.75	.45
(91)	Richard Kryhoski	1.50	.75	.45
(92)	Paul "Peanuts" Lehner	1.50	.75	.45
(93)	Footsie Lenhardt	1.50	.75	.45
(94)	Joe Lutz	1.50	.75	.45
(95)	Robert Mahoney	1.50	.75	.45
(96)	Frank Mancuso	1.50	.75	.45
(97)	Clifford Mapes	1.50	.75	.45
(98)	Cass Michaels	1.50	.75	.45
(99)	Frank "Stubby" Overmire	1.50	.75	.45
(100)	Satchel Paige	5.00	2.50	1.50
(101)	Roy Sievers	1.50	.75	.45
(102)	Louis Sleator	1.50	.75	.45
(103)	Richard Starr	1.50	.75	.45
(104)	Thomas "Muscles" Upton	1.50	.75	.45
(105)	Jerome Witte	1.50	.75	.45
(106)	Robert Young	1.50	.75	.45
(107)	1951 Browns	1.50	.75	.45
(108)	1952 Browns	1.50	.75	.45

1974 TCMA The Babe Postcards

This set of black-and-white postcards features photos of Ruth with contemporary players and managers. Cards measure 5-1/2" x 3-1/2" and have standard postcard indicia on the backs.

	NM	EX	VG
Complete Set (6):	20.00	10.00	6.00
Common Card:	5.00	2.50	1.50
1 Babe Ruth, Bill Terry	5.00	2.50	1.50
2 Babe Ruth, Walter Johnson	5.00	2.50	1.50
3 Babe Ruth, Lou Gehrig, Joe McCarthy	5.00	2.50	1.50
4 Babe Ruth, Miller Huggins	5.00	2.50	1.50
5 Babe Ruth, Tony Lazzeri	5.00	2.50	1.50
6 Babe Ruth and 1934 All-Stars	5.00	2.50	1.50

1974 TCMA 1890 Brooklyn Club

The National League champion Brooklyn Bridegrooms are featured in this collectors issue. Fronts of the 3-1/2" x 3-3/4" black-and-white cards picture the players in dress suits with ornate designs around the border. The design was copied from an 1890 Brooklyn scorecard/yearbook. Backs have biographical information and career highlights, also copied from the earlier publication. The back also includes a 1974 TCMA reprint notice. The unnumbered cards are checklisted here in alphabetical order.

	NM	EX	VG
Complete Set (16):	30.00	15.00	9.00
Common Player:	3.00	1.50	.90
(1) Thomas P. Burns	3.00	1.50	.90
(2) Albert J. Bushong	3.00	1.50	.90
(3) Robert Lee Caruthers	3.00	1.50	.90
(4) Robert H. Clark	3.00	1.50	.90
(5) Hubbert Collins	3.00	1.50	.90
(6) John S. Corkhill	3.00	1.50	.90
(7) Thomas P. Daly	3.00	1.50	.90
(8) D.L. Foutz	3.00	1.50	.90
(9) Michael F. Hughes	3.00	1.50	.90
(10) Thomas J. Lovett	3.00	1.50	.90
(11) W.H. McGunnigle	3.00	1.50	.90
(12) Wm. D. O'Brien	3.00	1.50	.90
(13) George Burton Pinkney	3.00	1.50	.90
(14) George J. Smith	3.00	1.50	.90
(15) George T. Stallings	3.00	1.50	.90
(16) Wm. H. Terry	3.00	1.50	.90

1974 TCMA 1910-14 Philadelphia Athletics Postcards

This series of collectors' issue postcards (about 3-1/2" x 5-3/4") was issued in two forms; printed front and back in black-and-white or in blue-and-white. While numbered between 501 and 518, only 12 cards were issued. The cards are reproductions of the images from the 1911 Pinkerton cabinets (T5). The postcard-format backs have a "1974 TCMA Reprint" notice along with the list of the dynasty's league and world championships.

	NM	EX	VG
Complete Set (12):	10.00	5.00	3.00
Common Player:	1.00	.50	.30
501 Chas. Bender	1.50	.70	.45
502 John Coombs	1.00	.50	.30
503 Eddie Plank	1.50	.70	.45
504 Amos Strunk	1.00	.50	.30
506 Ira Thomas	1.00	.50	.30
508 Stuffy McInnis	1.00	.50	.30

510 Rube Oldring	1.00	.50	.30
511 Eddie Collins	1.50	.70	.45
512 Frank Baker	1.50	.70	.45
515 Jack Barry	1.00	.50	.30
516 Jack Lapp	1.00	.50	.30
518 Danny Murphy	1.00	.50	.30

1974 TCMA 1929-31 Athletics

Stars of the Philadelphia A's dynasty which won two World Series and an A.L. pennant from 1929-31 are featured in this collectors issue. The 2-5/8" x 4" cards have black-and-white player photos at center. Printed in green in the white border at top is "1929-31 Athletics." At bottom, printed in black, is the player's name and position. Backs are in black-and-white with stats for 1929, 1930 and 1931, as appropriate. The unnumbered cards are checklisted here in alphabetical order.

	NM	EX	VG
Complete Set (29):	30.00	15.00	9.00
Common Player:	2.00	1.00	.60
(1) Max Bishop	2.00	1.00	.60
(2) Joe Boley	2.00	1.00	.60
(3) George Burns	2.00	1.00	.60
(4) Mickey Cochrane	3.00	1.50	.90
(5) Eddie Collins, Lew Krausse	2.00	1.00	.60
(6) "Doc" Cramer	2.00	1.00	.60
(7) Jimmy Dykes	2.00	1.00	.60
(8) George Earnshaw	2.00	1.00	.60
(9) Howard Ehmke	2.00	1.00	.60
(10) Lou Finney, John Heving	2.00	1.00	.60
(11) Jimmie Foxx	4.00	2.00	1.25
(12) Walt French, Waite Hoyt	2.00	1.00	.60
(13) "Lefty" Grove	3.00	1.50	.90
(14) "Mule" Haas	2.00	1.00	.60
(15) Sammy Hale	2.00	1.00	.60
(16) "Pinky" Higgins, Phil Todt	2.00	1.00	.60
(17) Earle Mack, Connie Mack	2.00	1.00	.60
(18) Roy Mahaffey	2.00	1.00	.60
(19) Eric McNair	2.00	1.00	.60
(20) Bing Miller	2.00	1.00	.60
(21) Jim Moore, Jim Peterson	2.00	1.00	.60
(22) Jack Quinn	2.00	1.00	.60
(23) Eddie Rommel	2.00	1.00	.60
(24) Wally Schang	2.50	1.25	.70
(25) Al Simmons	2.50	1.25	.70
(26) Homer Summa	2.00	1.00	.60
(27) Rube Walberg	2.00	1.00	.60
(28) "Dib" Williams	2.00	1.00	.60
(29) Team photo card (10" x 5")	10.00	5.00	3.00

1974 TCMA 1934 St. Louis Cardinals

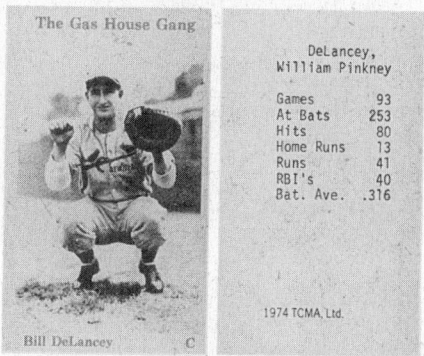

The "Gas House Gang" (as some of these cards are designated) is featured in this collectors' issue. Cards are 2-1/4" x 3-5/8" (#27-31 are 4-1/2" x 3-3/4") and feature black-and-white photos on front with red typography. Backs have a few stats in black-and-white. Some cards have a title at top front reading "1934 Cardinals". The unnumbered cards are checklisted here in alphabetical order.

	NM	EX	VG
Complete Set (31):	50.00	25.00	15.00
Common Player:	2.00	1.00	.60
(1) "Tex" Carleton	2.00	1.00	.60
(2) "Ripper" Collins	2.00	1.00	.60

(3) "Pat" Crawford	2.00	1.00	.60
(4) "Spud" Davis	2.00	1.00	.60
(5) "Daffy" Dean	2.50	1.25	.70
(6) "Dizzy" Dean	4.00	2.00	1.25
(7) Bill DeLancey	2.00	1.00	.60
(8) Leo Durocher	2.50	1.25	.70
(9) Frank Frisch	2.50	1.25	.70
(10) "Chick" Fullis	2.00	1.00	.60
(11) "Mike" Gonzalez	2.50	1.25	.70
(12) "Pop" Haines	2.50	1.25	.70
(13) Bill Hallahan	2.00	1.00	.60
(14) Francis Healey (Healy)	2.00	1.00	.60
(15) Jim Lindsey	2.00	1.00	.60
(16) "Pepper" Martin	2.00	1.00	.60
(17) "Ducky" Medwick	2.50	1.25	.70
(18) Jim Mooney	2.00	1.00	.60
(19) Ernie Orsatti	2.00	1.00	.60
(20) Flint Rhem	2.00	1.00	.60
(21) John Rothrock	2.00	1.00	.60
(22) "Dazzy" Vance	2.50	1.25	.70
(23) Bill Walker	2.00	1.00	.60
(24) "Buzzy" Wares	2.00	1.00	.60
(25) "Whitey" Whitehead	2.00	1.00	.60
(26) Jim Winford	2.00	1.00	.60
(27) "Daffy" & "Dizzy" (Daffy Dean, Dizzy Dean)	6.00	3.00	1.75
(28) Dizzy & Leo Celebrate (Dizzy Dean, Leo Durocher)	4.00	2.00	1.25
(29) Durocher Scores (Leo Durocher) (1934 World Series)	4.00	2.00	1.25
(30) Medwick Out Cochrane Catcher (Mickey Cochrane, Ducky Medwick) (1934 World Series)	4.00	2.00	1.25
(31) 1934 St. Louis Cardinals World Champions	4.00	2.00	1.25

1974 TCMA 1934-5 Detroit Tigers

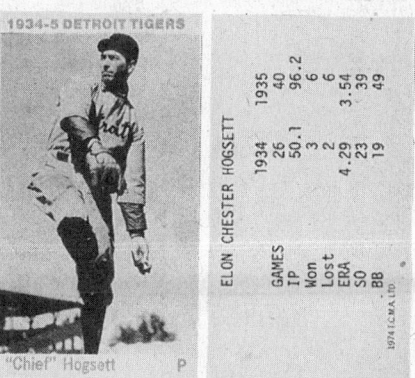

Members of the 1934 A.L. Champion and 1935 World's Champion teams are featured in this collectors issue team set. Except for a pair of large-format (4-1/4" x 3-3/4") cards, the cards measure about 2-1/8" x 3-5/8". Fronts have black-and-white photos. Above and below the photo are white stripes with the set title, player name and position. Backs are in black-and-white with 1934 and/or 1935 stats. The unnumbered cards are checklisted here alphabetically.

	NM	EX	VG
Complete Set (36):	35.00	17.50	10.00
Common Player:	2.00	1.00	.60
(1) Eldon Auker	2.00	1.00	.60
(2) Del Baker	2.00	1.00	.60
(3) Tommy Bridges	2.00	1.00	.60
(4) "Flea" Clifton	2.00	1.00	.60
(5) Mickey Cochrane	4.00	2.00	1.25
(6) "General" Crowder	2.00	1.00	.60
(7) Frank Doljack	2.00	1.00	.60
(8) Carl Fischer	2.00	1.00	.60
(9) Pete Fox	2.00	1.00	.60
(10) Vic Frasier	2.00	1.00	.60
(11) Charlie Gehringer	4.00	2.00	1.25
(12) Goose Goslin	2.00	1.00	.60
(13) Hank Greenberg	5.00	2.50	1.50
(14) Luke Hamlin	2.00	1.00	.60
(15) Clyde Hatter	2.00	1.00	.60
(16) Ray Hayworth	2.00	1.00	.60
(17) "Chief" Hogsett	2.00	1.00	.60
(18) Roxie Lawson	2.00	1.00	.60
(19) "Firpo" Marberry	2.00	1.00	.60
(20) Chet Morgan	2.00	1.00	.60
(21) Marv Owen	2.00	1.00	.60
(22) "Cy" Perkins	2.00	1.00	.60
(23) "Red" Phillips	2.00	1.00	.60
(24) Frank Reiber	2.00	1.00	.60
(25) Billy Rogell	2.00	1.00	.60
(26) "Schoolboy" Rowe	2.00	1.00	.60
(27) "Heinie" Schuble	2.00	1.00	.60
(28) Hugh Shelley	2.00	1.00	.60
(29) Vic Sorrell	2.00	1.00	.60
(30) Joe Sullivan	2.00	1.00	.60
(31) "Gee" Walker	2.00	1.00	.60
(32) "Hub" Walker	2.00	1.00	.60
(33) "Jo-Jo" White	2.00	1.00	.60
(34) Rudy York	2.00	1.00	.60
(35) 1934 Pitchers (Eldon Auker, Firpo Marberry, Tommy Bridges, Schoolboy Rowe) (4-1/4" x 3-3/4")	5.00	2.50	1.50

		NM	EX	VG
(36)	1935 Outfield (Goose Goslin, Jo-Jo White, Pete Fox) (4-1/4" x 3-3/4")	5.00	2.50	1.50

1974 TCMA 1936-37 New York Giants

This is the rarest of the TCMA Great Teams sets. Fewer than half of the 1,000 sets got into the hands of customers before legal action by Dick Bartell forced the company to halt sales and destroy more than 500 sets. The 2-5/8" x 3-3/8" cards are printed in black-and-orange. They are unnumbered and checklisted here in alphabetical order.

		NM	EX	VG
Complete Set (36):		90.00	45.00	27.50
Common Player:		2.50	1.25	.75
(1)	Title card	1.00	.50	.30
(2)	Tom Baker	2.50	1.25	.75
(3)	Dick Bartell	2.50	1.25	.75
(4)	Wally Berger	2.50	1.25	.75
(5)	Don Brennan	2.50	1.25	.75
(6)	Walter Brown	2.50	1.25	.75
(7)	Clyde Castleman	2.50	1.25	.75
(8)	Lou Chiozza	2.50	1.25	.70
(9)	Dick Coffman	2.50	1.25	.75
(10)	Harry Danning	2.50	1.25	.75
(11)	George Davis	2.50	1.25	.75
(12)	Charlie English	2.50	1.25	.75
(13)	Freddie Fitzsimmons	2.50	1.25	.75
(14)	Frank Gabler	2.50	1.25	.75
(15)	Harry Gumbert	2.50	1.25	.75
(16)	Mickey Haslin	2.50	1.25	.75
(17)	Carl Hubbell	6.00	3.00	1.75
(18)	Travis Jackson	4.00	2.00	1.25
(19)	Mark Koenig	2.50	1.25	.75
(20)	Hank Leiber	2.50	1.25	.75
(21)	Sam Leslie	2.50	1.25	.75
(22)	Bill Lohrman	2.50	1.25	.75
(23)	Eddie Mayo	2.50	1.25	.75
(24)	John McCarthy	2.50	1.25	.75
(25)	Cliff Melton	2.50	1.25	.75
(26)	Jo Jo Moore	2.50	1.25	.75
(27)	Mel Ott	6.00	3.00	1.75
(28)	Jimmy Ripple	2.50	1.25	.75
(29)	Hal Schumacher	2.50	1.25	.75
(30)	Al Smith	2.50	1.25	.75
(31)	Roy Spencer	2.50	1.25	.75
(32)	Bill Terry	5.00	2.50	1.50
(33)	Hy Vandenberg	2.50	1.25	.75
(34)	Phil Weintraub	2.50	1.25	.75
(35)	Burgess Whitehead	2.50	1.25	.75
(36)	Babe Young	2.50	1.25	.75

1974 TCMA 1936-1939 Yankee Dynasty

Johnny Murphy   P

JOHN JOSEPH MURPHY

Many of the players who participated in one or more of the Yankees' four consecutive World Champion seasons in the late 1930s are included in this collectors' edition. Cards are 2-3/4" x 4" and feature black-and-white photos on front. In the white borders at top and bottom, the set name and player identification are printed in blue. Backs have stats for each season and are printed in black-and-white on a white background. A virtual reprint of the set was made circa 1983 with two player cards added and a brown background on back. The unnumbered cards are checklisted here alphabetically.

		NM	EX	VG
Complete Set (56):		75.00	37.50	22.50
Complete Set (51):		45.00	22.50	13.50
Common Player:		2.00	1.00	.60
(1)	"Poison Ivy" Andrews	2.00	1.00	.60
(2)	Joe Beggs	2.00	1.00	.60
(3)	Marv Breuer	2.00	1.00	.60
(4)	Johnny Broaca	2.00	1.00	.60
(5)	"Jumbo" Brown	2.00	1.00	.60
(6)	"Spud" Chandler	2.00	1.00	.60
(7)	Ben Chapman	2.00	1.00	.60
(8)	Earle Combs	2.00	1.00	.60
(9)	Frankie Crosetti	2.00	1.00	.60
(10)	"Babe" Dahlgren	2.00	1.00	.60
(11)	Bill Dickey	2.50	1.25	.70
(12)	Joe DiMaggio	10.00	5.00	3.00
(13)	Atley Donald	2.00	1.00	.60
(14)	Wes Ferrell	2.00	1.00	.60
(15)	Artie Fletcher	2.00	1.00	.60
(16)	Joe Gallagher	2.00	1.00	.60
(17)	Lou Gehrig	10.00	5.00	3.00

		NM	EX	VG
(18)	Joe Glenn	2.00	1.00	.60
(19)	"Lefty" Gomez	2.00	1.00	.60
(20)	Joe Gordon	2.00	1.00	.60
(21)	"Bump" Hadley	2.00	1.00	.60
(22)	Don Heffner	2.00	1.00	.60
(23)	Tommy Henrich	2.00	1.00	.60
(24)	Oral Hildebrand	2.00	1.00	.60
(25)	Myril Hoag	2.00	1.00	.60
(26)	Roy Johnson	2.00	1.00	.60
(27)	Arndt Jorgens	2.00	1.00	.60
(28)	Charlie Keller	2.00	1.00	.60
(29)	Ted Kleinhans	2.00	1.00	.60
(30)	Billy Knickerbocker	2.00	1.00	.60
(31)	Tony Lazzeri	2.50	1.25	.70
(32)	Frank Makosky	2.00	1.00	.60
(33)	"Pat" Malone	2.00	1.00	.60
(34)	Johnny Murphy	2.00	1.00	.60
(35)	"Monty" Pearson	2.00	1.00	.60
(36)	"Jake" Powell	2.00	1.00	.60
(37)	"Red" Rolfe	2.00	1.00	.60
(38)	"Buddy" Rosar	2.00	1.00	.60
(39)	"Red" Ruffing	2.50	1.25	.70
(40)	Marius Russo	2.00	1.00	.60
(41)	"Jack" Saltzgaver	2.00	1.00	.60
(42)	Paul Schreiber	2.00	1.00	.60
(43)	Johnny Schulte	2.00	1.00	.60
(44)	Bob Seeds	2.00	1.00	.60
(45)	"Twinkletoes" Selkirk	2.00	1.00	.60
(46)	Lee Stine	2.00	1.00	.60
(47)	Steve Sundra	2.00	1.00	.60
(48)	"Sandy" Vance	2.00	1.00	.60
(49)	Dixie Walker	2.00	1.00	.60
(50)	Kemp Wicker	2.00	1.00	.60
(51)	Joe McCarthy, Jacob Ruppert	2.00	1.00	.60
5-1/2" x 4" FEATURE CARDS				
(52)	Joe DiMaggio, Frank Crosetti, Tony Lazzeri, Bill Dickey, Lou Gehrig, Jake Powell, George Selkirk	5.00	2.50	1.50
(53)	Lou Gehrig, Joe DiMaggio	7.50	3.75	2.25
(54)	Gehrig Hits Another	6.00	3.00	1.75
(55)	Red Rolfe, Tony Lazzeri, Lou Gehrig, Frank Crosetti	5.00	2.50	1.50
(56)	World Champions - 1936	6.00	3.00	1.75

1974 TCMA 1952 Brooklyn Dodgers

1952 BROOKLYN DODGERS
ALBERT BLUFORD WALKER
Catcher   #10

Games	46
AB	139
Hits	36
Runs	9
HR	1
RBI	19
BA	.259

Rube

T.C.M.A. 1974

The National League champion '52 Dodgers are featured in this collectors issue. Nominally 2-3/4" x 3-3/8", the cards are often found with minor variations in size. Fronts are printed in red and blue with a white border. The only identification on front is the player's first name or nickname. Backs are black-and-white with the player's full name, position, uniform number, 1952 stats and TCMA copyright. Cards are checklisted here in alphabetical order.

		NM	EX	VG
Complete Set (40):		25.00	15.00	7.50
Common Player:		2.00	1.00	.60
(1)	Header/Team History Card (Jackie Robinson, Gil Hodges, Roy Campanella, Billy Cox, Pee Wee Reese)	2.00	1.00	.60
(2)	Cal Abrams	2.00	1.00	.60
(3)	Sandy Amoros	2.00	1.00	.60
(4)	Joe Black	2.00	1.00	.60
(5)	Ralph Branca	2.00	1.00	.60
(6)	Rocky Bridges	2.00	1.00	.60
(7)	Roy Campanella	4.00	2.00	1.25
(8)	Billy Cox	2.00	1.00	.60
(9)	Chuck Dressen	2.00	1.00	.60
(10)	Carl Erskine	2.00	1.00	.60
(11)	Carl Furillo	3.00	1.50	.90
(12)	Billy Herman	2.00	1.00	.60
(13)	Gil Hodges	4.00	2.00	1.25
(14)	Tommy Holmes	2.00	1.00	.60
(15)	Jim Hughes	2.00	1.00	.60
(16)	Clyde King	2.00	1.00	.60
(17)	Clem Labine	2.00	1.00	.60
(18)	Joe Landrum	2.00	1.00	.60
(19)	Cookie Lavagetto	2.00	1.00	.60
(20)	Ken Lehman	2.00	1.00	.60
(21)	Steve Lembo	2.00	1.00	.60
(22)	Billy Loes	2.00	1.00	.60
(23)	Ray Moore	2.00	1.00	.60
(24)	Bobby Morgan	2.00	1.00	.60
(25)	Ron Negray	2.00	1.00	.60
(26)	Rocky Nelson	2.00	1.00	.60
(27)	Andy Pafko	2.00	1.00	.60
(28)	Jake Pitler	2.00	1.00	.60
(29)	Bud Podbielan	2.00	1.00	.60
(30)	Pee Wee Reese	4.00	2.00	1.25
(31)	Jackie Robinson	7.50	3.75	2.25
(32)	Preacher Roe	2.00	1.00	.60

		NM	EX	VG
(33)	Johnny Rutherford	2.00	1.00	.60
(34)	Johnny Schmitz	2.00	1.00	.60
(35)	George Shuba	2.00	1.00	.60
(36)	Duke Snider	4.00	2.00	1.25
(37)	Chris Van Cuyk	2.00	1.00	.60
(38)	Ben Wade	2.00	1.00	.60
(39)	Rube Walker	2.00	1.00	.60
(40)	Dick Williams	2.00	1.00	.60

1975 TCMA All Time Brooklyn/ Los Angeles Dodgers

LHP   Sandy Koufax

ALL TIME BROOKLYN/LOS ANGELES DODGERS	
1b	Gil Hodges
2b	Jackie Robinson
ss	Pee Wee Reese
3b	Junior Gilliam
OF	Duke Snider
OF	Dixie Walker
OF	Zack Wheat
C	Roy Campanella
RHP	Don Drysdale
LHP	Sandy Koufax
RP	Hugh Casey
Mgr	Walter Alston

A picked team of former Dodgers stars is featured in this collectors issue team set. Cards are in black-and-white in the standard 2-1/2" x 3-1/2" format. Fronts have player identification in the border beneath the photo. Backs have a checklist by position and a TCMA copyright line. The unnumbered cards are checklisted here in the order presented on back.

		NM	EX	VG
Complete Set (12):		36.00	18.00	11.00
Common Player:		2.25	1.25	.70
(1)	Gil Hodges	3.00	1.50	.90
(2)	Jackie Robinson	10.00	5.00	3.00
(3)	Pee Wee Reese	3.00	1.50	.90
(4)	Junior Gilliam	2.25	1.25	.70
(5)	Duke Snider	3.00	1.50	.90
(6)	Dixie Walker	2.25	1.25	.70
(7)	Zack Wheat	2.25	1.25	.70
(8)	Roy Campanella	4.00	2.00	1.25
(9)	Don Drysdale	3.00	1.50	.90
(10)	Sandy Koufax	8.00	4.00	2.50
(11)	Hugh Casey	2.25	1.25	.70
(12)	Walter Alston	2.25	1.25	.70

1975 TCMA All-Time Greats

LOUIS BOUDREAU	
Shortstop	
Indians Red Sox	
1938 - 1952	
Games	1646
At Bats	6030
Hits	1779
Home Runs	68
Batting Ave.	.295
Hall of Fame	1970

This is a smaller - both in size and number - version of TCMA's Hall of Famer postcard set issued between 1973-80. These collectors' edition cards measure 2-3/8" x 3-3/4" and were issued in strips of six. Two printings were done, the first with blue-and-white fronts and red backs, the second in black-and-white, blank-backed. Surrounding the photo on front is a blue or black border with baseball equipment ornamentation. The unnumbered cards are checklisted here in alphabetical order.

		NM	EX	VG
Complete Set (39):		40.00	20.00	12.00
Common Player:		2.00	1.00	.60
(1)	"Luke" Appling	2.00	1.00	.60
(2)	Roger Bresnahan	2.00	1.00	.60
(3)	Ty Cobb	8.00	4.00	2.50
(4)	Mickey Cochrane	2.00	1.00	.60
(5)	Eddie Collins	2.00	1.00	.60
(6)	Kiki Cuyler	2.00	1.00	.60
(7)	Dizzy Dean	4.00	2.00	1.25
(8)	Bill Dickey	2.00	1.00	.60
(9)	Joe DiMaggio	8.00	4.00	2.50
(10)	Bob Feller	2.00	1.00	.60
(11)	Elmer Flick	2.00	1.00	.60
(12)	Frank Frisch	2.00	1.00	.60
(13)	Lou Gehrig	8.00	4.00	2.50
(14)	Hank Greenberg	4.00	2.00	1.25
(15)	Goose Goslin	2.00	1.00	.60
(16)	Chick Hafey	2.00	1.00	.60
(17)	Gabby Hartnett	2.00	1.00	.60
(18)	Harry Heilmann	2.00	1.00	.60
(19)	Rogers Hornsby	2.00	1.00	.60
(20)	Waite Hoyt	2.00	1.00	.60
(21)	Walter Johnson	4.00	2.00	1.25

		NM	EX	VG
(22)	George Kelly	2.00	1.00	.60
(23)	Ted Lyons	2.00	1.00	.60
(24)	Connie Mack	2.00	1.00	.60
(25)	Mickey Mantle	10.00	5.00	3.00
(26)	Rabbit Maranville	2.00	1.00	.60
(27)	Mel Ott	2.00	1.00	.60
(28)	Edd Roush	2.00	1.00	.60
(29)	Red Ruffing	2.00	1.00	.60
(30)	Babe Ruth	10.00	5.00	3.00
(31)	Al Simmons	2.00	1.00	.60
(32)	Casey Stengel	2.00	1.00	.60
(33)	Pie Traynor	2.00	1.00	.60
(34)	Dazzy Vance	2.00	1.00	.60
(35)	Honus Wagner	4.00	2.00	1.25
(36)	Lloyd Waner	2.00	1.00	.60
(37)	Paul Waner	2.00	1.00	.60
(38)	Ted Williams	6.00	3.00	1.75
(39)	Harry Wright	2.00	1.00	.60

1975 TCMA All Time New York Giants

ss Alvin Dark

ALL TIME NEW YORK GIANTS

1b	Bill Terry
2b	Frankie Frisch
ss	Alvin Dark
3b	Fred Lindstrom
LF	Bobby Thomson
CF	Willie Mays
RF	Mel Ott
C	Wes Westrum
LHP	Carl Hubbell
RHP	Christy Mathewson
RP	Hoyt Wilhelm
Mgr	John McGraw

TCMA Ltd. 1975

An all-time line-up of Giants is presented in this collector issue. Fronts of the 2-1/2" x 3-1/2" cards have black-and-white player photos with the player's name and position printed in red in the white bottom border. Backs are in black-and-white and present the all-time roster. The unnumbered cards are checklisted here alphabetically.

		NM	EX	VG
Complete Set (12):		30.00	15.00	9.00
Common Player:		2.00	1.00	.60
(1)	Alvin Dark	2.00	1.00	.60
(2)	Frankie Frisch	2.00	1.00	.60
(3)	Carl Hubbell	2.00	1.00	.60
(4)	Freddie Lindstrom	2.00	1.00	.60
(5)	Christy Mathewson	4.00	2.00	1.25
(6)	Willie Mays	15.00	7.50	4.50
(7)	John McGraw	2.00	1.00	.60
(8)	Mel Ott	2.00	1.00	.60
(9)	Bill Terry	2.00	1.00	.60
(10)	Bobby Thomson	2.00	1.00	.60
(11)	Wes Westrum	2.00	1.00	.60
(12)	Hoyt Wilhelm	2.00	1.00	.60

1975 TCMA All Time New York Yankees

SS Phil Rizzuto

ALL TIME NEW YORK YANKEE TEAM

1B	Lou Gehrig
2B	Tony Lazzeri
3B	Red Rolfe
SS	Phil Rizzuto
OF	Babe Ruth
OF	Mickey Mantle
OF	Joe DiMaggio
C	Bill Dickey
P	Red Ruffing
P	Whitey Ford
RP	Johnny Murphy
Mgr	Casey Stengel

T.C.M.A. LTD 1975

The best players on the best team in baseball history are featured in this collectors' edition. Cards measure 2-1/2" x 3-3/4" and feature black-and-white photos on front, with white borders. Player name and position are printed in a white strip toward the bottom of the picture. Backs have a list of the all-time team. The unnumbered cards are listed here in that order.

		NM	EX	VG
Complete Set (12):		15.00	7.50	4.50
Common Player:		2.00	1.00	.60
(1)	Lou Gehrig	4.00	2.00	1.25
(2)	Tony Lazzeri	2.00	1.00	.60
(3)	Red Rolfe	2.00	1.00	.60
(4)	Phil Rizzuto	2.50	1.25	.70
(5)	Babe Ruth	5.00	2.50	1.50
(6)	Mickey Mantle	6.00	3.00	1.75
(7)	Joe DiMaggio	4.00	2.00	1.25
(8)	Bill Dickey	2.00	1.00	.60
(9)	Red Ruffing	2.00	1.00	.60
(10)	Whitey Ford	2.50	1.25	.70
(11)	Johnny Murphy	2.00	1.00	.60
(12)	Casey Stengel	2.00	1.00	.60

1975 TCMA Larry French Postcards

The career of National League pitcher Larry French is recounted in this set of 3-1/2" x 5-1/2" black-and-white postcard-size cards. Fronts have photos of him with the Pirates, Cubs and Dodgers. Backs have a continuing biography.

		NM	EX	VG
Complete Set (6):		15.00	7.50	4.50
Common Card:		3.00	1.50	.90
1	Larry French (Pittsburgh Pirates)	3.00	1.50	.90
2	Larry French (Chicago Cubs)	3.00	1.50	.90
3	Larry French (w/Bill Lee, Charlie Root, Tuck Stainback)	3.00	1.50	.90
4	Larry French (w/Charlie Grimm, Fred Lindstrom)	3.00	1.50	.90
5	Larry French (Brooklyn Dodgers)	3.00	1.50	.90
6	Larry French (w/Mickey Owen)	3.00	1.50	.90

1975 TCMA Guam WW2

1. PHIL RIZZUTO • TERRY MOORE

This set of 3-1/2" x 5-1/2" black-and-white cards details the connection between Major League Baseball and the Pacific island of Guam during WWII. Some cards picture players in their military uniforms, others shown them in baseball uniforms. Backs contain a narrative of the series.

		NM	EX	VG
Complete Set (18):		25.00	12.50	7.50
Common Card:		1.00	.50	.30
1	Phil Rizzuto, Terry Moore	5.00	2.50	1.50
2	Gab Gab Guam 1945	1.00	.50	.30
3	Team Photo	1.00	.50	.30
4	Merrill May, Pee Wee Reese, Johnny Vander Meer	2.50	1.25	.70
5	Team Photo	1.00	.50	.30
6	Team Photo	1.00	.50	.30
7	Del Ennis	2.00	1.00	.60
8	Mace Brown	2.00	1.00	.60
9	Pee Wee Reese, Joe Gordon, Bill Dickey	3.50	1.75	1.00
10	Glenn McQuillen	2.00	1.00	.60
11	Mike Budnick	2.00	1.00	.60
12	Team Photo	1.00	.50	.30
13	"Skeets" Dickey	2.00	1.00	.60
14	Connie Ryan	2.00	1.00	.60
15	Hal White	2.00	1.00	.60
16	Mickey Cochrane	7.50	3.75	2.25
17	Barney McCosky	2.00	1.00	.60
18	Ben Huffman	2.00	1.00	.60

1975 TCMA 1913 Philadelphia Athletics

1913 Philadelphia Athletics World Champions

CHARLES ALBERT BENDER "Chief"

Pitcher

Games	48
IP	237
Won	21
Lost	10
Pct.	.677
SO	135
BB	59
ERA	2.21

BENDER   TCMA 1975

Members of the World Champion A's of 1913 are featured in this collectors' edition card set. In an unusual 3-1/8" x 5-11/16" format, the cards have black-and-white photos on front, with white borders and player identification at bottom. Backs feature season statistics. The unnumbered cards are checklisted here alphabetically.

		NM	EX	VG
Complete Set (16):		20.00	10.00	6.00
Common Player:		3.00	1.50	.90
(1)	Home Run Baker	3.00	1.50	.90
(2)	Jack Barry	3.00	1.50	.90
(3)	Chief Bender	3.00	1.50	.90
(4)	Joe Bush	3.00	1.50	.90
(5)	Eddie Collins	3.00	1.50	.90
(6)	Jack Coombs	3.00	1.50	.90
(7)	Jack Lapp	3.00	1.50	.90
(8)	Connie Mack	3.00	1.50	.90
(9)	Stuffy McInnis	3.00	1.50	.90
(10)	Dan Murphy	3.00	1.50	.90
(11)	Eddie Murphy	3.00	1.50	.90
(12)	Rube Oldring	3.00	1.50	.90
(13)	William Orr	3.00	1.50	.90
(14)	Ed Plank	3.00	1.50	.90
(15)	Walter Schang	3.00	1.50	.90
(16)	Amos Strunk	3.00	1.50	.90

1975 TCMA 1919 Chicago White Sox

Joe Jackson   OF
1919 CHICAGO WHITE SOX

JOSEPH JEFFERSON JACKSON

Games	139
At Bats	516
Hits	181
Runs	79
Home Runs	7
RBI's	96
Bat. Ave.	.351

T.C.M.A. 1975

The infamous Black Sox who threw the 1919 World Series, and their teammates, are featured in this collectors' edition. The 2-1/2" x 3-1/2" cards are printed in black-and-white. Fronts have player photos with identification in the white border at bottom. Backs have 1919 season stats. The unnumbered cards are checklisted here alphabetically.

		NM	EX	VG
Complete Set (28):		35.00	17.50	10.00
Common Player:		1.00	.50	.30
(1)	Joe Benz	1.00	.50	.30
(2)	Eddie Cicotte	3.50	1.75	1.00
(3)	Eddie Collins	2.50	1.25	.70
(4)	Shano Collins	1.00	.50	.30
(5)	Dave Danforth	1.00	.50	.30
(6)	Red Faber	1.00	.40	.25
(7)	Happy Felsch	3.50	1.75	1.00
(8)	Chick Gandil	5.00	2.50	1.50
(9)	Kid Gleason	1.00	.50	.30
(10)	Joe Jackson	10.00	5.00	3.00
(11)	Bill James	1.00	.50	.30
(12)	Dickie Kerr	1.00	.50	.30
(13)	Nemo Leibold	1.00	.50	.30
(14)	Byrd Lynn	1.00	.50	.30
(15)	Erskine Mayer	2.00	1.00	.60
(16)	Harvey McClellan	1.00	.50	.30
(17)	Fred McMullin	4.00	2.00	1.25
(18)	Eddie Murphy	1.00	.50	.30
(19)	Pat Ragan	1.00	.50	.30
(20)	Swede Risberg	4.00	2.00	1.25
(21)	Charlie Robertson	1.00	.50	.30
(22)	Reb Russell	1.00	.50	.30
(23)	Ray Schalk	1.00	.40	.25
(24)	Buck Weaver	6.00	3.00	1.75
(25)	Roy Wilkinson	1.00	.50	.30
(26)	Lefty Williams	4.00	2.00	1.25
(27)	Frank Shellenback, Grover Lowdermilk, Joe Jenkins, Dickie Kerr, Ray Schalk	1.00	.50	.30
(28)	Team photo (4-3/4" x 3-1/2")	7.50	3.75	2.25

1975 TCMA 1924-1925 Washington Senators

1924 - 1925 Washington Senators

Bennie Tate   C

HENRY BENNETT TATE

	1924	1925
Games	21	16
At Bats	43	27
Hits	13	13
Runs	2	0
HR	0	0
RBI's	7	7
AVE.	.302	.481

T.C.M.A. Ltd. 1975

The back-to-back American League champion Senators of 1924-25 are featured in this collectors' edition card set. Cards measure 2-3/8" x 3-7/16". Fronts have black-and-white photos with blue captions and white borders. Backs have player stats for the two seasons. The unnmubered cards are checklisted here in alphabetical order.

		NM	EX	VG
Complete Set (42):		30.00	15.00	9.00
Common Player:		1.50	.75	.45
(1)	Spencer Adams	1.50	.75	.45
(2)	Nick Altrock	1.50	.75	.45
(3)	Ossie Bluege	1.50	.75	.45
(4)	Stan Coveleski	1.50	.75	.45
(5)	Alex Ferguson	1.50	.75	.45
(6)	Showboat Fisher	1.50	.75	.45
(7)	Goose Goslin	1.50	.75	.45
(8)	Bart Griffith	1.50	.75	.45
(9)	Pinky Hargrave	1.50	.75	.45
(10)	Bucky Harris	1.50	.75	.45
(11)	Joe Harris	1.50	.75	.45
(12)	Tex Jeanes	1.50	.75	.45
(13)	Walter Johnson	4.00	2.00	1.25
(14)	Joe Judge	1.50	.75	.45
(15)	Wade Lefler	1.50	.75	.45
(16)	Nemo Leibold	1.50	.75	.45
(17)	Firpo Marberry	1.50	.75	.45
(18)	Joe Martina	1.50	.75	.45
(19)	Wid Matthews	1.50	.75	.45
(20)	Mike McNally	1.50	.75	.45
(21)	Earl McNeely	1.50	.75	.45
(22)	Ralph Miller	1.50	.75	.45
(23)	George Mogridge	1.50	.75	.45
(24)	Buddy Myer	1.50	.75	.45
(25)	Curly Ogden	1.50	.75	.45
(26)	Roger Peckinpaugh	1.50	.75	.45
(27)	Spencer Pumpelly	1.50	.75	.45
(28)	Sam Rice	1.50	.75	.45
(29)	Muddy Ruel	1.50	.75	.45
(30)	Dutch Ruether	1.50	.75	.45
(31)	Allen Russell	1.50	.75	.45
(32)	Everett Scott	1.50	.75	.45
(33)	Hank Severeid	1.50	.75	.45
(34)	Mule Shirley	1.50	.75	.45
(35)	Byron Speece	1.50	.75	.45
(36)	Benny Tate	1.50	.75	.45
(37)	Bobby Veach	1.50	.75	.45
(38)	Tom Zachary	1.50	.75	.45
(39)	Paul Zahniser	1.50	.75	.45
	5" x 3-1/2" FEATURE CARDS			
(40)	Bucky Harris, Bill McKechnie	2.00	1.00	.60
(41)	Ossie Bluege, Roger Peckinpaugh, Bucky Harris, Joe Judge	2.00	1.00	.60
(42)	Tom Zachary, Firpo Marberry, Alex Ferguson, Walter Johnson	2.50	1.25	.70

1975 TCMA 1927 New York Yankees

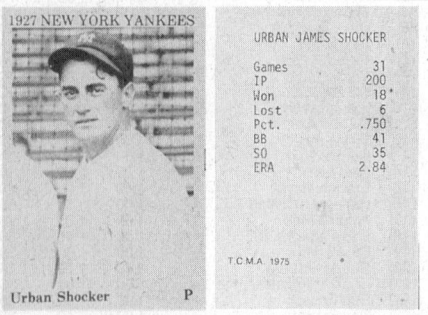

1927 NEW YORK YANKEES

URBAN JAMES SHOCKER

Games	31
IP	200
Won	18
Lost	6
Pct.	.750
BB	41
SO	35
ERA	2.84

T.C.M.A. 1975

Urban Shocker   P

One of the greatest teams in baseball history is featured in this set of collectors' cards. The 2-1/2" x 3-1/2" cards have black-and-white photos with a white border. At top is the team identification, at bottom is player name and position. The back has the player's 1927 season stats. The unnumbered cards are checklisted here alphabetically.

		NM	EX	VG
Complete Set (30):		40.00	20.00	12.00
Common Player:		2.00	1.00	.60
(1)	Walter Beall	2.00	1.00	.60
(2)	Benny Bengough	2.00	1.00	.60
(3)	Pat Collins	2.00	1.00	.60
(4)	Earle Combs	2.00	1.00	.60
(5)	Joe Dugan	2.00	1.00	.60
(6)	Cedric Durst	2.00	1.00	.60
(7)	Mike Gazella	2.00	1.00	.60
(8)	Lou Gehrig	7.50	3.75	2.25
(9)	Joe Giard	2.00	1.00	.60
(10)	Johnny Grabowski	2.00	1.00	.60
(11)	Waite Hoyt	2.00	1.00	.60
(12)	Miller Huggins	2.00	1.00	.60
(13)	Mark Koenig	2.00	1.00	.60
(14)	Tony Lazzeri	2.00	1.00	.60
(15)	Bob Meusel	2.00	1.00	.60
(16)	Wilcy Moore	2.00	1.00	.60
(17)	Ray Morehart	2.00	1.00	.60
(18)	Ben Paschal	2.00	1.00	.60
(19)	Herb Pennock	2.00	1.00	.60
(20)	George Pipgras	2.00	1.00	.60
(21)	Dutch Ruether	2.00	1.00	.60
(22)	Jacob Ruppert	2.00	1.00	.60
(23)	Babe Ruth	12.00	6.00	3.50
(24)	Bob Shawkey	2.00	1.00	.60
(25)	Urban Shocker	2.00	1.00	.60
(26)	Myles Thomas	2.00	1.00	.60

(27)	Julie Wera	2.00	1.00	.60
(28)	Yankee Coaches and Manager (Charlie O'Leary, Miller Huggins, Artie Fletcher)	2.00	1.00	.60
(29)	Yankee Stadium	3.00	1.50	.90
(30)	Yankees infield (Lou Gehrig, Tony Lazzeri, Mark Koenig, Joe Dugan) (5" x 3-5/8")	9.00	4.50	2.75

1975 TCMA 1942-46 St. Louis Cardinals

1942 St. Louis Cardinals

This collectors' issue set features players and staff from the Cards' war-years dynasty. In 2-1/2" x 3-5/8" format, the cards have black-and-white photos with red printing on front. The unnumbered cards have statistics on back.

		NM	EX	VG
Complete Set (66):		40.00	20.00	12.00
Common Player:		1.00	.50	.30
(1)	Buster Adams	1.00	.50	.30
(2)	Red Barrett	1.00	.50	.30
(3)	John Beazley	1.00	.50	.30
(4)	Al Brazle	1.00	.50	.30
(5)	Harry Brecheen	1.00	.50	.30
(6)	Jimmy Brown	1.00	.50	.30
(7)	Ken Burkhart	1.00	.50	.30
(8)	Bud Byerly	1.00	.50	.30
(9)	Mort Cooper	1.00	.50	.30
(10)	Walker Cooper	1.00	.50	.30
(11)	Estel Crabtree	1.00	.50	.30
(12)	Creepy Crespi	1.00	.50	.30
(13)	Jeff Cross	1.00	.50	.30
(14)	Frank Demaree	1.00	.50	.30
(15)	Murrey Dickson (Murry)	1.00	.50	.30
(16)	Blix Donnelly	1.00	.50	.30
(17)	Erv Dusak	1.00	.50	.30
(18)	Eddie Dyer	1.00	.50	.30
(19)	Bill Endicott	1.00	.50	.30
(20)	George Fallon	1.00	.50	.30
(21)	Joe Garagiola	3.00	1.50	.90
(22)	Debs Garms	1.00	.50	.30
(23)	Mike Gonzalez	1.25	.60	.40
(24)	Johnny Grodzicki	1.00	.50	.30
(25)	Harry Gumbert	1.00	.50	.30
(26)	Johnny Hopp	1.00	.50	.30
(27)	Nippy Jones	1.00	.50	.30
(28)	Lou Klein	1.00	.50	.30
(29)	Clyde Kluttz	1.00	.50	.30
(30)	Howie Krist	1.00	.50	.30
(31)	Whitey Kurowski	1.00	.50	.30
(32)	Max Lanier	1.00	.50	.30
(33)	Danny Litwhiler	1.00	.50	.30
(34)	Bill Lohrman	1.00	.50	.30
(35)	Marty Marion	1.50	.70	.45
(36)	Freddie Martin	1.00	.50	.30
(37)	Pepper Martin	2.00	1.00	.60
(38)	Terry Moore	1.00	.50	.30
(39)	Red Munger	1.00	.50	.30
(40)	Stan Musial	5.00	2.50	1.50
(41)	Sam Narron	1.00	.50	.30
(42)	Ken O'Dea	1.00	.50	.30
(43)	Howie Pollet	1.00	.50	.30
(44)	Del Rice	1.00	.50	.30
(45)	Ray Sanders	1.00	.50	.30
(46)	Fred Schmidt	1.00	.50	.30
(47)	Red Schoendienst	3.00	1.50	.90
(48)	Walt Sessi	1.00	.50	.30
(49)	Clyde Shoun	1.00	.50	.30
(50)	Dick Sisler	1.00	.50	.30
(51)	Enos Slaughter	3.00	1.50	.90
(52)	Billy Southworth	1.00	.50	.30
(53)	Coaker Triplett	1.00	.50	.30
(54)	Emil Verban	1.00	.50	.30
(55)	Harry Walker	1.00	.50	.30
(56)	Buzzy Wares	1.00	.50	.30
(57)	Lon Warneke	1.00	.50	.30
(58)	Ernie White	1.00	.50	.30
(59)	Del Wilber	1.00	.50	.30
(60)	Ted Wilks	1.00	.50	.30
(61)	Leo Durocher, Eddie Dyer	1.00	.50	.30
(62)	Stan Musial, Billy Southworth, Johnny Hopp	1.00	.50	.30
(63)	Stan Musial, Billy Southworth, Ray Sanders	1.00	.50	.30
(64)	Red Ruffing, Johnny Beazley	1.00	.50	.30
(65)	1942 St. Louis Cardinals (5" x 3-1/2")	3.00	1.50	.90
(66)	Sportsman's Park (5" x 3-1/2")	2.50	1.25	.70

1975 TCMA 1946 Boston Red Sox

The Red Sox American League champions of 1946 are featured in this collectors' issue. Blue-and-

BENJAMIN SAUNDERS STEINER

Games	3
At Bats	4
Hits	1
Runs	1
Home Runs	0
Runs Batted In	0
Batting Average	.250

Ben Steiner   3b
1946 BOSTON RED SOX   TCMA, Ltd. 1975

white player photos appear on front, with the player's name and position in black below. At bottom-front is the team name in red. Backs of the 2-1/2" x 3-1/2" cards have the player's 1946 stats. The unnumbered cards are checklisted here in alphabetical order.

		NM	EX	VG
Complete Set (43):		45.00	22.50	13.50
Common Player:		1.50	.75	.45
(1)	Jim Bagby	1.50	.75	.45
(2)	Del Baker	1.50	.75	.45
(3)	Mace Brown	1.50	.75	.45
(4)	Bill Butland	1.50	.75	.45
(5)	Paul Campbell	1.50	.75	.45
(6)	Tom Carey	1.50	.75	.45
(7)	Joe Cronin	2.00	1.00	.60
(8)	Leon Culberson	1.50	.75	.45
(9)	Tom Daly	1.50	.75	.45
(10)	Dom DiMaggio	2.50	1.25	.70
(11)	Joe Dobson	1.50	.75	.45
(12)	Bobby Doerr	1.50	.75	.45
(13)	Clem Dreisewerd	1.50	.75	.45
(14)	"Boo" Ferriss	1.50	.75	.45
(15)	Andy Gilbert	1.50	.75	.45
(16)	Don Gutteridge	1.50	.75	.45
(17)	Mickey Harris	1.50	.75	.45
(18)	Randy Heflin	1.50	.75	.45
(19)	"Pinky" Higgins	1.50	.75	.45
(20)	"Tex" Hughson	1.50	.75	.45
(21)	Earl Johnson	1.50	.75	.45
(22)	Bob Klinger	1.50	.75	.45
(23)	Johnny Lazor	1.50	.75	.45
(24)	Tom McBride	1.50	.75	.45
(25)	Ed McGah	1.50	.75	.45
(26)	"Catfish" Metkovich	1.50	.75	.45
(27)	Wally Moses	1.50	.75	.45
(28)	Roy Partee	1.50	.75	.45
(29)	Eddie Pellagrini	1.50	.75	.45
(30)	Johnny Pesky	1.50	.75	.45
(31)	Frank Pytlak	1.50	.75	.45
(32)	"Rip" Russell	1.50	.75	.45
(33)	Mike Ryba	1.50	.75	.45
(34)	Ben Steiner	1.50	.70	.45
(35)	Charlie Wagner	1.50	.75	.45
(36)	Hal Wagner	1.50	.75	.45
(37)	Ted Williams	7.50	3.75	2.25
(38)	Larry Woodall	1.50	.75	.45
(39)	Rudy York	1.50	.75	.45
(40)	Bill Zuber	1.50	.75	.45
(41)	Team photo	2.00	1.00	.60
(42)	Larry Woodall, Hal Wagner, Del Baker	1.50	.75	.45
(43)	Rudy York, Wally Moses, Dom DiMaggio, Bobby Doerr, Charlie Wagner (5" x 3-1/2")	4.00	2.00	1.25

1975 TCMA 1950 Philadelphia Phillies/Whiz Kids

Whiz Kids

EDWARD STEPHEN WAITKUS

Games	154
At Bats	641
Hits	182
Runs	102
HR	2
RBI	44
Bat. Ave.	.284

Eddie Waitkus   1b   T.C.M.A. Ltd. 1975

The National League Champion "Whiz Kids" are featured in this collectors issue. The 2-1/2" x 3-1/2" cards have black-and-white photos on front with the player's name and position in red at bottom and either "Whiz Kids" or "1950 Philadelphia Phillies" in red at top. Black-and-white backs have 1950 season stats. The unnumbered cards are checklisted here alphabetically. The large-format multiple-player card was issued coincidentally with the set.

		NM	EX	VG
Complete Set (32):		45.00	22.50	13.50
Common Player:		2.00	1.00	.60
(1)	Richie Ashburn	11.00	5.50	3.25

		NM	EX	VG
(2)	Benny Bengough	2.00	1.00	.60
(3)	Jimmy Bloodworth	2.00	1.00	.60
(4)	Hank Borowy	2.00	1.00	.60
(5)	"Putsy" Caballero	2.00	1.00	.60
(6)	"Bubba" Church	2.00	1.00	.60
(7)	Dusty Cooke	2.00	1.00	.60
(8)	Blix Donnelly	2.00	1.00	.60
(9)	Del Ennis	2.00	1.00	.60
(10)	Mike Goliat	2.00	1.00	.60
(11)	Granny Hamner	2.00	1.00	.60
(12)	Ken Heintzelman	2.00	1.00	.60
(13)	Stan Hollmig	2.00	1.00	.60
(14)	Ken Johnson	2.00	1.00	.60
(15)	"Puddin-Head" Jones	2.00	1.00	.60
(16)	Jim Konstanty	2.00	1.00	.60
(17)	Stan Lopata	2.00	1.00	.60
(18)	Jackie Mayo	2.00	1.00	.60
(19)	Russ Meyer	2.00	1.00	.60
(20)	Bob Miller	2.00	1.00	.60
(21)	Bill Nicholson	2.00	1.00	.60
(22)	Cy Perkins	2.00	1.00	.60
(23)	Robin Roberts	11.00	5.50	3.25
(24)	Eddie Sawyer	2.00	1.00	.60
(25)	Andy Seminick	2.00	1.00	.60
(26)	Ken Silvestri	2.00	1.00	.60
(27)	Curt Simmons	2.00	1.00	.60
(28)	Dick Sisler	2.00	1.00	.60
(29)	"Jocko" Thompson	2.00	1.00	.60
(30)	Eddie Waitkus	2.00	1.00	.60
(31)	Dick Whitman	2.00	1.00	.60
(32)	Russ Meyer, Hank Borowy, Bill Nicholson, Willie Jones (4-7/8" x 3-1/2")	15.00	7.50	4.50

1975 TCMA 1951 New York Giants

Artie Wilson   OF
1951 NEW YORK GIANTS

The National League Champion Giants of 1951 are honored in this collectors' issue card set. The 2-1/2" x 3-1/2" cards have black-and-white photos on front, with player name, team and position in the bottom border in red-orange ink. Backs are black-and-white with 1951 stats. The unnumbered cards are listed here in alphabetical order.

		NM	EX	VG
	Complete Set (34):	35.00	17.50	10.00
	Common Player:	1.50	.75	.45
(1)	George Bamberger	1.50	.75	.45
(2)	Roger Bowman	1.50	.75	.45
(3)	Al Corwin	1.50	.75	.45
(4)	Alvin Dark	2.00	1.00	.60
(5)	Allen Gettel	1.50	.75	.45
(6)	Clint Hartung	1.50	.75	.45
(7)	Jim Hearn	1.50	.75	.45
(8)	Monte Irvin	2.00	1.00	.60
(9)	Larry Jansen	1.50	.75	.45
(10)	Sheldon Jones	1.50	.75	.45
(11)	"Spider" Jorgensen	1.50	.75	.45
(12)	Monte Kennedy	1.50	.75	.45
(13)	Alex Konikowski	1.50	.70	.45
(14)	Dave Koslo	1.50	.75	.45
(15)	Jack Kramer	1.50	.75	.45
(16)	Whitey Lockman	1.50	.75	.45
(17)	"Lucky" Lohrke	1.50	.75	.45
(18)	Sal Maglie	1.50	.70	.45
(19)	Jack Maguire	1.50	.70	.45
(20)	Willie Mays	10.00	5.00	3.00
(21)	Don Mueller	1.50	.75	.45
(22)	Ray Noble	1.50	.75	.45
(23)	Earl Rapp	1.50	.75	.45
(24)	Bill Rigney	1.50	.75	.45
(25)	George Spencer	1.50	.75	.45
(26)	Eddie Stanky	1.50	.70	.45
(27)	Hank Thompson	1.50	.75	.45
(28)	Bobby Thomson	2.50	1.20	.70
(29)	Wes Westrum	1.50	.75	.45
(30)	Davey Williams	1.50	.75	.45
(31)	Artie Wilson	1.50	.75	.45
(32)	Sal Yvars	1.50	.75	.45
(33)	Leo Durocher, Willie Mays (3-5/8" x 5")	7.00	3.50	2.00
(34)	Durocher and coaches (3-5/8" x 5")	3.00	1.50	.90

1975 TCMA 1954 Cleveland Indians

The American League Champions of 1954 are featured in this collectors issue. Individual player cards are 2-1/2" x 3-1/2" printed in black-and-white. Backs have 1954 season stats. Three large-format (3-3/4" x 5-1/8") multi-player cards were issued with the complete set. The unnumbered cards are check-listed here alphabetically.

1954 CLEVELAND INDIANS

ARTHUR JOSEPH HOUTTEMAN

Games	32
IP	188
Won	15
Lost	7
Pct.	6.82
BB	59
SO	68
ERA	3.35

T.C.M.A. 1975

Art Houtteman   P

		NM	EX	VG
	Complete Set (39):	35.00	17.50	10.00
	Common Player:	1.50	.75	.45
(1)	Bobby Avila	2.00	1.00	.60
(2)	Bob Chakales	1.50	.75	.45
(3)	Tony Cuccinello	1.50	.75	.45
(4)	Sam Dente	1.50	.75	.45
(5)	Larry Doby	3.50	1.75	1.00
(6)	Luke Easter	2.00	1.00	.60
(7)	Bob Feller	5.00	2.50	1.50
(8)	Mike Garcia	2.00	1.00	.60
(9)	Joe Ginsberg	1.50	.75	.45
(10)	Bill Glynn	1.50	.75	.45
(11)	Mickey Grasso	1.50	.75	.45
(12)	Mel Harder	1.50	.75	.45
(13)	Jim Hegan	1.50	.75	.45
(14)	Bob Hooper	1.50	.75	.45
(15)	Dave Hoskins	1.50	.75	.45
(16)	Art Houtteman	1.50	.75	.45
(17)	Bob Kennedy	1.50	.75	.45
(18)	Bob Lemon	2.50	1.25	.70
(19)	Al Lopez	2.50	1.25	.70
(20)	Hank Majeski	1.50	.75	.45
(21)	Dale Mitchell	1.50	.75	.45
(22)	Don Mossi	1.50	.75	.45
(23)	Hal Naragon	1.50	.75	.45
(24)	Ray Narleski	1.50	.75	.45
(25)	Rocky Nelson	1.50	.75	.45
(26)	Hal Newhouser	2.50	1.25	.70
(27)	Dave Philley	1.50	.75	.45
(28)	Dave Pope	1.50	.75	.45
(29)	Rudy Regalado	1.50	.75	.45
(30)	Al Rosen	2.00	1.00	.60
(31)	Jose Santiago	1.50	.75	.45
(32)	Al Smith	1.50	.75	.45
(33)	George Strickland	1.50	.75	.45
(34)	Vic Wertz	1.50	.75	.45
(35)	Wally Westlake	1.50	.75	.45
(36)	Early Wynn	2.50	1.25	.70
	Large format cards	1.50	.75	.45
(37)	Al Lopez and coaches	5.00	2.50	1.50
(38)	Al Lopez and pitchers	5.00	2.50	1.50
(39)	Indians outfielders	5.00	2.50	1.50

1975 TCMA/ASCCA Ad Card

To promote the American Sports Card Collectors Association Show in New York City, this 3-1/2" x 5-1/2" black-and-white card done in the format of the All-Time Greats postcards was issued. The front pictures two of the game's greatest pitchers and offers a discount on show admission. The back provides a detailed description of the show.

	NM	EX	VG
Dizzy Dean, Lefty Grove	6.00	3.00	1.80

1976 TCMA DiMaggio Brothers Postcard

This black-and-white postcard was issued singly circa the mid-1970s. It measures approximately 3-1/2" x 5-1/2".

	NM	EX	VG
Dom DiMaggio, Joe DiMaggio, Vince DiMaggio	12.00	6.00	3.50

1976 TCMA Larry Rosenthal

This custom-published card of the long-time American League outfielder (1936-1945) was printed in red, black and white in a 2-5/8" x 4-5/8" format. The issue date is approximate.

	NM	EX	VG
Larry Rosenthal	6.00	3.00	2.00

1976 TCMA Umpires

American League

Don Denkinger   Umpire

Eight of the better-known umpires of the era apparently commissioned TCMA to produce cards for them. The cards are black-and-white in the standard 2-1/2" x 3-1/2" format.

		NM	EX	VG
	Complete Set (8):	25.00	12.50	7.50
	Common Card:	4.00	2.00	1.25
(1)	Larry Barnett	4.00	2.00	1.25
(2)	Al Clark	4.00	2.00	1.25
(3)	Nick Colosi	4.00	2.00	1.25
(4)	Don Denkinger	4.00	2.00	1.25
(5)	Art Frantz	4.00	2.00	1.25
(6)	Marty Springstead	4.00	2.00	1.25
(7)	Ed Sudol	4.00	2.00	1.25
(8)	Bill Williams	4.00	2.00	1.25

1976 TCMA 1911 N.Y. Highlanders Postcard

This black-and-white postcard was issued singly circa the mid-1970s. It measures approximately 6" x 3-1/2".

	NM	EX	VG
1911 N.Y. Highlanders Team Photo	12.00	6.00	3.50

1976 TCMA 1938 Chicago Cubs

AUGUST JOHN GALAN

Games	110
At Bats	395
Hits	113
Runs	52
Home Runs	6
RBI	69
Bat. Ave.	.286

Augie Galan   OF

1938 CHICAGO CUBS
NATIONAL LEAGUE CHAMPIONS
1976 TCMA LTD.

The National League Champion Chicago Cubs of 1938 are featured in this collectors issue. The 2-1/2" x 3-1/2" cards have black-and-white player photos on front with the player's name and position in blue at bottom. Backs are in black-and-white with season stats. The unnumbered cards are checklisted here alphabetically.

		NM	EX	VG
	Complete Set (33):	40.00	20.00	12.00
	Common Player:	2.00	1.00	.60
(1)	Jim Asbell	2.00	1.00	.60
(2)	Clay Bryant	2.00	1.00	.60
(3)	Tex Carleton	2.00	1.00	.60
(4)	Phil Cavarretta	2.00	1.00	.60
(5)	Ripper Collins	2.00	1.00	.60
(6)	"Red" Corriden	2.00	1.00	.60
(7)	Dizzy Dean	7.50	3.75	2.25
(8)	Frank Demaree	2.00	1.00	.60
(9)	Al Epperly	2.00	1.00	.60
(10)	Larry French	2.00	1.00	.60
(11)	Augie Galan	2.00	1.00	.60
(12)	Bob Garbark	2.00	1.00	.60
(13)	Charlie Grimm	2.00	1.00	.60
(14)	Stan Hack	2.00	1.00	.60
(15)	Gabby Hartnett	3.00	1.50	.90
(16)	Billy Herman	3.00	1.50	.90
(17)	Kirby Higbe	2.00	1.00	.60
(18)	Hardrock Johnson	2.00	1.00	.60
(19)	Billy Jurges	2.00	1.00	.60
(20)	Newt Kimball	2.00	1.00	.60
(21)	Tony Lazzeri	3.00	1.50	.90
(22)	Bill Lee	2.00	1.00	.60
(23)	Bob Logan	2.00	1.00	.60
(24)	Joe Marty	2.00	1.00	.60
(25)	Bobby Mattick	2.00	1.00	.60
(26)	Steve Mesner	2.00	1.00	.60
(27)	Ken O'Dea	2.00	1.00	.60
(28)	Vance Page	2.00	1.00	.60
(29)	Carl Reynolds	2.00	1.00	.60
(30)	Charlie Root	2.00	1.00	.60
(31)	Jack Russell	2.00	1.00	.60
(32)	Coaker Triplett	2.00	1.00	.60
(33)	Team history card	.70	.35	.20

1977 TCMA All-Time White Sox

All-Time Chicago White Sox	
Eddie Robinson	1B
Eddie Collins	2B
Willie Kamm	3B
Luke Appling	SS
Ray Schalk	C
Al Simmons	LF
Johnny Mostil	CF
Harry Hooper	RF
Ted Lyons	RHP
Billy Pierce	LHP
Gerry Staley	RP
Al Lopez	Mgr

Ray Schalk   C

Because this is one of the few early TCMA issues not to have a date printed on the back, the quoted year of issue is approximate. Fronts of the 2-1/2" x 3-1/2" cards have black-and-white player photos with name and position printed in red in the bottom border. Black-and-white backs have an all-time team roster of position players, pitchers and manager. The unnumbered cards are checklisted here in alphabetical order.

	NM	EX	VG
Complete Set (12):	24.00	12.00	7.25
Common Player:	2.00	1.00	.60
(1) Luke Appling	2.50	1.25	.70
(2) Eddie Collins	2.50	1.25	.70
(3) Harry Hooper	2.00	1.00	.60
(4) Willie Kamm	2.00	1.00	.60
(5) Al Lopez	2.00	1.00	.60
(6) Ted Lyons	2.00	1.00	.60
(7) Johnny Mostil	2.00	1.00	.60
(8) Billy Pierce	2.00	1.00	.60
(9) Eddie Robinson	2.00	1.00	.60
(10) Ray Schalk	2.00	1.00	.60
(11) Al Simmons	2.00	1.00	.60
(12) Gerry Staley	2.00	1.00	.60

1977 TCMA Chicago Cubs All Time Team

Chicago Cubs
All Time Team

1B - Charlie Grimm
2B - Rogers Hornsby
SS - Ernie Banks
3B - Ron Santo
C - Gabby Hartnett
LF - Billy Williams
RF - Kiki Cuyler
CF - Hack Wilson
RHP - Charlie Root
LHR - Larry French
RP - Emil Kush
MGR - Charlie Grimm
INF - Billy Herman

ALL TIME TEAM

RF - Kiki Cuyler

The best of the Cubs are presented in this collectors issue. An all-time great at each position is featured on the 2-1/2" x 3-1/2" card. Fronts have black-and-white photos with orange graphics. Backs are in black-and-white and list the team by position. The unnumbered cards are checklisted here in that order.

	NM	EX	VG
Complete Set (12):	30.00	15.00	9.00
Common Player:	3.00	1.50	.90
(1) Charlie Grimm	3.00	1.50	.90
(2) Rogers Hornsby	4.00	2.00	1.25
(3) Ernie Banks	4.00	2.00	1.25
(4) Ron Santo	3.00	1.50	.90
(5) Gabby Hartnett	3.00	1.50	.90
(6) Billy Williams	3.00	1.50	.90
(7) Kiki Cuyler	3.00	1.50	.90
(8) Hack Wilson	4.00	2.00	1.25
(9) Charlie Root	3.00	1.50	.90
(10) Larry French	3.00	1.50	.90
(11) Emil Kush	3.00	1.50	.90
(12) Billy Herman	3.00	1.50	.90

1977 TCMA Stars of the Twenties

CHICAGO

Six players are featured on this 22" x 11" triple-folder which was glued into issues of the Summer, 1977, "Baseball Quarterly" magazine from TCMA. The pictures feature artwork by John Anderson in sepia tones on heavy cream-colored textured paper stock. The pictures are back-to-back in pairs as listed here, with individual pictures varying in width from 7-1/4" to 7-1/2".

	NM	EX	VG
Complete Foldout:	10.00	5.00	3.00
Common Pair:	3.00	1.50	.90
(1/2) Joe Bush, Gabby Hartnett	3.00	1.50	.90
(3/4) Jim Bottomley, "Mule" Haas	3.00	1.50	.90
(5/6) Sam Rice, Buddy Myer	3.00	1.50	.90

1977-80 TCMA The War Years

 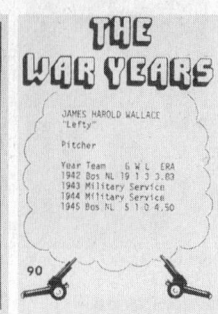

THE WAR YEARS

JAMES HAROLD WALLACE
"Lefty"

Pitcher

Year	Team	G	W	L	ERA
1942	Bos NL	19	1	3	3.83
1943	Military Service				
1944	Military Service				
1945	Bos NL	5	1	0	4.50

90

The decimated major league rosters circa 1942-46 are reflected in this collectors' card set. The 2-1/2" x 3-1/2" cards have black-and-white player photos on front, with a white border around. There is no typography on front. Backs have player identification, stats and the set title. Series 1, cards #1-45 was issued in 1977 and is much scarcer than Series 2, #46-90, which was issued in 1980.

	NM	EX	VG
Complete Set (90):	140.00	70.00	42.50
Common Player:	2.00	1.00	.60
1 Samuel Narron	3.00	1.50	.90
2 Raymond Mack	3.00	1.50	.90
3 Arnold (Mickey) Owen	3.00	1.50	.90
4 John Peacock	3.00	1.50	.90
5 Paul (Dizzy) Trout	3.00	1.50	.90
6 George (Birdie) Tebbetts	3.00	1.50	.90
7 Alfred Todd	3.00	1.50	.90
8 Harlond Clift	3.00	1.50	.90
9 Don G.N. (Gil) Torres	3.00	1.50	.90
10 Alfonso Lopez	4.00	2.00	1.25
11 Ulysses (Tony) Lupien	3.00	1.50	.90
12 Lucius Appling	4.00	2.00	1.25
13 James (Pat) Seery	3.00	1.50	.90
14 Phil Masi	3.00	1.50	.90
15 Thomas Turner	3.00	1.50	.90
16 Nicholas Piccuito	3.00	1.50	.90
17 Mel Ott	7.50	3.75	2.25
18 Thadford Treadway	3.00	1.50	.90
19 Sam Naham (Neham)	3.00	1.50	.90
20 Truett (Rip) Sewell	3.00	1.50	.90
21 Roy Partee	3.00	1.50	.90
22 Richard Siebert	3.00	1.50	.90
23 Francis (Red) Barrett	3.00	1.50	.90
24 Paul O'Dea	3.00	1.50	.90
25 Lou Parisse	3.00	1.50	.90
26 Martin Marion	4.00	2.00	1.25
27 Eugene Moore	3.00	1.50	.90
28 Walter Beck	3.00	1.50	.90
29 Donald Manno	3.00	1.50	.90
30 Harold Newhouser	4.00	2.00	1.25
31 August Mancuso	3.00	1.50	.90
32 Merrill May	3.00	1.50	.90
33 Gerald Priddy	3.00	1.50	.90
34 Herman Besse	3.00	1.50	.90
35 Luis Olmo	3.00	1.50	.90
36 Robert O'Neill	3.00	1.50	.90
37 John Barrett	3.00	1.50	.90
38 Gordon Maltzberger	3.00	1.50	.90
39 William Nicholson	3.00	1.50	.90
40 Ron Northey	3.00	1.50	.90
41 Howard Pollet	3.00	1.50	.90
42 Aloysius Piechota	3.00	1.50	.90
43 Albert Shepard	7.50	3.75	2.25
44 Alfred Anderson	3.00	1.50	.90
45 Damon Phillips	3.00	1.50	.90
46 Herman Franks	2.00	1.00	.60
47 Aldon Wilke	2.00	1.00	.60
48 Max Macon	2.00	1.00	.60
49 Lester Webber	2.00	1.00	.60
50 Robert Swift	2.00	1.00	.60
51 Philip Weintraub	2.00	1.00	.60
52 Nicholas Strincevich	2.00	1.00	.60
53 Michael Tresh	2.00	1.00	.60
54 William Trotter	2.00	1.00	.60
55 1943 Yankees (Spud Chandler, Frank Crosetti, Bill Dickey, Nick Etten, Joe Gordon, Billy Johnson, Charlie Keller, John Lindell, Bud Metheny)	4.00	2.00	1.25
56 John Sturm	2.00	1.00	.60
57 Silas Johnson	2.00	1.00	.60
58 Donald Kolloway	2.00	1.00	.60
59 Cecil Vaughn (Vaughan)	2.00	1.00	.60
60 St. Louis Browns Bombers (Harlond Clift, Walt Judnich, Chet Laabs)	3.00	1.50	.90
61 Harold Wagner	2.00	1.00	.60
62 Alva Javery	2.00	1.00	.60
63 1941 Boston Bees Pitchers (George Barnicle, Ed Carnett, Art Johnson, Frank LaManna, Casey Stengel, Bob Williams)	3.00	1.50	.90
64 Adolph Camilli	2.00	1.00	.60
65 Myron McCormick	2.00	1.00	.60
66 Richard Wakefield	2.00	1.00	.60
67 James (Mickey) Vernon	3.00	1.50	.90
68 John Vander Meer	3.00	1.50	.90
69 James McDonnell	4.00	2.00	1.25
70 Thomas Jordan	2.00	1.00	.60
71 Maurice Van Robays	2.00	1.00	.60
72 Charles Stanceau	2.00	1.00	.60
73 Samuel Zoldak	2.00	1.00	.60
74 Raymond Starr	2.00	1.00	.60
75 Roger Wolff	2.00	1.00	.60
76 Cecil Travis	2.00	1.00	.60
77 Arthur Johnson	2.00	1.00	.60
78 Louis (Lewis) Riggs	2.00	1.00	.60
79 Peter Suder	2.00	1.00	.60
80 Thomas Warren	2.00	1.00	.60
81 John Welaj	2.00	1.00	.60
82 Gerald Walker	2.00	1.00	.60
83 Dewey Williams	2.00	1.00	.60
84 Leonard Merullo	2.00	1.00	.60
85 John Johnson	2.00	1.00	.60
86 Eugene Thompson	2.00	1.00	.60
87 William Zuber	2.00	1.00	.60
88 Earl Johnson	2.00	1.00	.60
89 Norman Young	2.00	1.00	.60
90 James Wallace	2.00	1.00	.60

1977 TCMA 1920 Cleveland Indians

The World Champion Indians are pictured on this collectors' issue team set. In standard 2-1/2" x 3-1/2" size with black-and-white photos, the cards are unnumbered. Some of the players are pictured in their 1921 uniforms with the "World Champions" lettering.

	NM	EX	VG
Complete Set (22):	25.00	12.50	7.50
Common Player:	2.00	1.00	.60
(1) Jim Bagby	2.00	1.00	.60
(2) George Burns	2.00	1.00	.60
(3) Ray Caldwell	2.00	1.00	.60
(4) Ray Chapman	3.00	1.50	.90
(5) Stan Coveleski	2.50	1.25	.70
(6) Joe Evans	2.00	1.00	.60
(7) Larry Gardner	2.00	1.00	.60
(8) Jack Graney	2.00	1.00	.60
(9) Charlie Jamieson	2.00	1.00	.60
(10) Doc Johnston	2.00	1.00	.60
(11) Harry Lunte	2.00	1.00	.60
(12) Duster Mails	2.00	1.00	.60
(13) Guy Morton	2.00	1.00	.60
(14) Les Nunamaker	2.00	1.00	.60
(15) Steve O'Neill	2.00	1.00	.60
(16) Joe Sewell	2.50	1.25	.70
(17) Elmer Smith	2.00	1.00	.60
(18) Tris Speaker	4.00	2.00	1.25
(19) George Uhle	2.00	1.00	.60
(20) Bill Wambsganss	2.50	1.25	.70
(21) Joe Wood	2.50	1.25	.70
(22) World Series Foes (Wilbert Robinson, Tris Speaker) (5-1/2" x 3")	4.00	2.00	1.25

1977 TCMA 1927 Yankees 50th Anniversary

Henry Louis Gehrig

First Baseman
Ht. 6-0 Wt. 200
Ba. Left Th. Left
Brn. 6/19/03
Dd. 6/2/41

As an insert in its inaugural issue of "Baseball Quarterly" magazine dated Winter, 1977, TCMA included a 16-3/4" x 11" cardboard panel with 18 black-and-white cards featuring members of the 1927 N.Y. Yankees. Measuring about 2-1/2" x 3-3/8" if cut apart, the individual cards have unadorned photos on front framed in black with a white border. Backs have player identification, a 50th anniversary logo, career summary and 1927 and career stats. The unnumbered cards are listed here in alphabetical order.

	NM	EX	VG
Complete Panel:	35.00	17.50	10.50
Complete Set (18):	25.00	12.50	7.50
Common Player:	2.00	1.00	.60
(1) Bernard Oliver Bengough	2.00	1.00	.60
(2) Tharon Patrick Collins	2.00	1.00	.60
(3) Earle Bryan Combs	2.00	1.00	.60
(4) Joseph Anthony Dugan	2.00	1.00	.60
(5) Henry Louis Gehrig	6.00	3.00	1.75
(6) John Patrick Grabowski	2.00	1.00	.60
(7) Waite Charles Hoyt	2.00	1.00	.60
(8) Miller James Huggins	2.00	1.00	.60
(9) Mark Anthony Koenig	2.00	1.00	.60
(10) Anthony Michael Lazzeri	2.00	1.00	.60
(11) Robert Williams Meusel	2.00	1.00	.60
(12) William Wilcy Moore	2.00	1.00	.60
(13) Herbert Jeffries Pennock	2.00	1.00	.60
(14) George William Pipgras	2.00	1.00	.60
(15) Walter Henry Ruether	2.00	1.00	.60
(16) George Herman Ruth	8.00	4.00	2.50
(17) James Robert Shawkey	2.00	1.00	.60
(18) Urban James Shocker	2.00	1.00	.60

1977 TCMA 1939-40 Cincinnati Reds

The National League Champion Reds of 1939 and the World's Champion team of 1940 are featured in this collectors issue. The 2-1/2" x 3-1/2" cards have black-and-white photos on front surrounded by red borders. Backs, also in black-and-white, have 1939 and/or 1940 season stats.

	NM	EX	VG
Complete Set (45):	35.00	17.50	10.00
Common Player:	1.50	.75	.45
1 Vince DiMaggio	2.50	1.25	.70
2 Wally Berger	1.50	.75	.45
3 Nolan Richardson (Nolen)	1.50	.75	.45
4 Ernie Lombardi	2.50	1.25	.70
5 Ival Goodman	1.50	.75	.45
6 Jim Turner	1.50	.75	.45
7 Bucky Walters	1.50	.75	.45
8 Jimmy Ripple	1.50	.75	.45
9 Hank Johnson	1.50	.75	.45
10 Bill Baker	1.50	.75	.45
11 Al Simmons	2.00	1.00	.60
12 Johnny Hutchings	1.50	.75	.45
13 Peaches Davis	1.50	.75	.45
14 Willard Hershberger	2.50	1.25	.70
15 Bill Werber	1.50	.75	.45
16 Harry Craft	1.50	.75	.45
17 Milt Galatzer	1.50	.75	.45
18 Dick West	1.50	.75	.45
19 Art Jacobs	1.50	.75	.45
20 Joe Beggs	1.50	.75	.45
21 Frenchy Bordagaray	1.50	.75	.45
22 Lee Gamble	1.50	.75	.45
23 Lee Grissom	1.50	.75	.45
24 Eddie Joost	1.50	.75	.45
25 Milt Shofner	1.50	.75	.45
26 Morrie Arnovich	1.50	.75	.45
27 Pete Naktenis	1.50	.75	.45
28 Jim Weaver	1.50	.75	.45
29 Mike McCormick	1.50	.75	.45
30 John Niggeling	1.50	.75	.45
31 Les Scarsella	1.50	.75	.45
32 Lonny Frey	1.50	.75	.45
33 Bill Myers	1.50	.75	.45
34 Frank McCormick	1.50	.75	.45
35 Lew Riggs	1.50	.75	.45
36 Nino Bongiovanni	1.50	.75	.45
37 Johnny Rizzo	1.50	.75	.45
38 Wes Livengood	1.50	.75	.45
39 Junior Thompson	1.50	.75	.45
40 Mike Dejan	1.50	.75	.45
41 Jimmy Wilson	1.50	.75	.45
42 Paul Derringer	1.50	.75	.45
43 Johnny Vander Meer	2.00	1.00	.60
44 Whitey Moore	1.50	.75	.45
45 Bill McKechnie	2.00	1.00	.60

1977 TCMA 1960 Pittsburgh Pirates

The World's Champions Pirates are featured on this collector issue. The 2-1/2" x 3-1/2" cards have black-and-white photos on front surrounded by orange borders. Backs, also in black-and-white, have a card number, player name and position at top and season stats.

	NM	EX	VG
Complete Set (42):	100.00	50.00	30.00
Common Player:	3.00	1.50	.90
1 Danny Murtaugh	3.00	1.50	.90
2 Dick Stuart	4.00	2.00	1.25
3 Bill Mazeroski	10.00	5.00	3.00
4 Dick Groat	4.00	2.00	1.25
5 Don Hoak	3.00	1.50	.90
6 Roberto Clemente	20.00	10.00	6.00
7 Bill Virdon	3.00	1.50	.90
8 Bob Skinner	3.00	1.50	.90
9 Smoky Burgess	3.00	1.50	.90
10 Gino Cimoli	3.00	1.50	.90
11 Rocky Nelson	3.00	1.50	.90
12 Hal Smith	3.00	1.50	.90
13 Dick Schofield	3.00	1.50	.90
14 Joe Christopher	3.00	1.50	.90
15 Gene Baker	3.00	1.50	.90
16 Bob Oldis	3.00	1.50	.90
17 Vern Law	3.00	1.50	.90
18 Bob Friend	3.00	1.50	.90
19 Wilmer Mizell	3.00	1.50	.90
20 Harvey Haddix	3.00	1.50	.90
21 Roy Face	3.00	1.50	.90
22 Fred Green	3.00	1.50	.90
23 Joe Gibbon	3.00	1.50	.90
24 Clem Labine	3.00	1.50	.90
25 Paul Giel	3.00	1.50	.90
26 Tom Cheney	3.00	1.50	.90
27 Earl Francis	3.00	1.50	.90
28 Jim Umbricht	3.00	1.50	.90
29 George Witt	3.00	1.50	.90
30 Bennie Daniels	3.00	1.50	.90
31 Don Gross	3.00	1.50	.90
32 Diomedes Olivo	4.00	2.00	1.25
33 Roman Mejias	3.00	1.50	.90
34 R.C. Stevens	3.00	1.50	.90
35 Mickey Vernon	3.00	1.50	.90
36 Danny Kravitz	3.00	1.50	.90
37 Harry Bright	3.00	1.50	.90
38 Dick Barone	3.00	1.50	.90
39 Bill Burwell	3.00	1.50	.90
40 Lenny Levy	4.00	2.00	1.25
41 Sam Narron	3.00	1.50	.90
42 Team card (Bob Friend)	3.00	1.50	.90

1977 TCMA/ASCCA Ad Card

To promote the American Sports Card Collectors Association Show in New York City, this 2-1/2" x 3-1/2" black-and-white, gold highlighted card was issued. The front pictures Babe Ruth and offers a 25-cent discount on show admission. The back provides a detailed description of the show.

	NM	EX	VG
Babe Ruth	6.00	3.00	1.80

1977-84 TCMA/Renata Galasso

This issue of six 45-card series is in similar format but with different players, checklists and copyright dates produced by TCMA and marketed by Renata Galasso. In 2-1/2" x 3-1/2" format the cards have black-and-white photos on front. Backs are printed in red and blue and include a career summary, large Galasso ad and TCMA dateline.

	NM	EX	VG
Complete Set (270):	50.00	25.00	15.00
Common Player:	.25	.13	.08
SERIES 1 - 1977	12.50	6.25	3.75
1 Joe DiMaggio	4.00	2.00	1.25
2 Ralph Kiner	.25	.13	.08
3 Don Larsen	.25	.13	.08
4 Robin Roberts	.25	.13	.08
5 Roy Campanella	.50	.25	.15
6 Smoky Burgess	.25	.13	.08
7 Mickey Mantle	6.00	3.00	1.75
8 Willie Mays	3.00	1.50	.90
9 George Kell	.25	.13	.08
10 Ted Williams	3.00	1.50	.90
11 Carl Furillo	.25	.13	.08
12 Bob Feller	.25	.13	.08
13 Casey Stengel	.25	.13	.08
14 Richie Ashburn	.25	.13	.08
15 Gil Hodges	.25	.13	.08
16 Stan Musial	.75	.40	.25
17 Don Newcombe	.25	.13	.08
18 Jackie Jensen	.25	.13	.08
19 Lou Boudreau	.25	.13	.08
20 Jackie Robinson	2.00	1.00	.60
21 Billy Goodman	.25	.13	.08
22 Satchel Paige	1.00	.50	.30
23 Hoyt Wilhelm	.25	.13	.08
24 Duke Snider	.25	.13	.08
25 Whitey Ford	.25	.13	.08
26 Monte Irvin	.25	.13	.08
27 Hank Sauer	.25	.13	.08
28 Sal Maglie	.25	.13	.08
29 Ernie Banks	.25	.13	.08
30 Billy Pierce	.25	.13	.08
31 Pee Wee Reese	.25	.13	.08
32 Al Lopez	.25	.13	.08
33 Allie Reynolds	.25	.13	.08
34 Eddie Mathews	.25	.13	.08
35 Al Rosen	.25	.13	.08
36 Early Wynn	.25	.13	.08
37 Phil Rizzuto	.25	.13	.08
38 Warren Spahn	.25	.13	.08
39 Bobby Thomson	.25	.13	.08
40 Enos Slaughter	.25	.13	.08
41 Roberto Clemente	4.00	2.00	1.25
42 Luis Aparicio	.25	.13	.08
43 Roy Sievers	.25	.13	.08
44 Hank Aaron	4.00	2.00	1.25
45 Mickey Vernon	.25	.13	.08
SERIES 2 - 1979	10.00	5.00	3.00
46 Lou Gehrig	3.00	1.50	.90
47 Lefty O'Doul	.25	.13	.08
48 Chuck Klein	.25	.13	.08
49 Paul Waner	.25	.13	.08
50 Mel Ott	.25	.13	.08
51 Riggs Stephenson	.25	.13	.08
52 Dizzy Dean	.50	.25	.15
53 Frankie Frisch	.25	.13	.08
54 Red Ruffing	.25	.13	.08
55 Lefty Grove	.25	.13	.08
56 Heinie Manush	.25	.13	.08
57 Jimmie Foxx	.25	.13	.08
58 Al Simmons	.25	.13	.08
59 Charlie Root	.25	.13	.08
60 Goose Goslin	.25	.13	.08
61 Mickey Cochrane	.25	.13	.08
62 Gabby Hartnett	.25	.13	.08
63 Ducky Medwick	.25	.13	.08
64 Ernie Lombardi	.25	.13	.08
65 Joe Cronin	.25	.13	.08
66 Pepper Martin	.25	.13	.08
67 Jim Bottomley	.25	.13	.08
68 Bill Dickey	.25	.13	.08
69 Babe Ruth	5.00	2.50	1.50
70 Joe McCarthy	.25	.13	.08
71 Doc Cramer	.25	.13	.08
72 Kiki Cuyler	.25	.13	.08
73 Johnny Vander Meer	.25	.13	.08
74 Paul Derringer	.25	.13	.08
75 Freddie Fitzsimmons	.25	.13	.08
76 Lefty Gomez	.25	.13	.08
77 Arky Vaughan	.25	.13	.08
78 Stan Hack	.25	.13	.08
79 Earl Averill	.25	.13	.08
80 Luke Appling	.25	.13	.08
81 Mel Harder	.25	.13	.08
82 Hank Greenberg	.25	.13	.08
83 Schoolboy Rowe	.25	.13	.08
84 Billy Herman	.25	.13	.08
85 Gabby Street	.25	.13	.08
86 Lloyd Waner	.25	.13	.08
87 Jocko Conlan	.25	.13	.08
88 Carl Hubbell	.25	.13	.08
89 Series 1 checklist	.25	.13	.08
90 Series 2 checklist	.25	.13	.08
SERIES 3 - 1980	7.50	3.75	2.25
91 Babe Ruth	3.00	1.50	.90
92 Rogers Hornsby	.25	.13	.08
93 Edd Roush	.25	.13	.08
94 George Sisler	.25	.13	.08
95 Harry Heilmann	.25	.13	.08
96 Tris Speaker	.25	.13	.08
97 Burleigh Grimes	.25	.13	.08
98 John McGraw	.25	.13	.08
99 Eppa Rixey	.25	.13	.08
100 Ty Cobb	1.00	.50	.30
101 Zack Wheat	.25	.13	.08
102 Pie Traynor	.25	.13	.08
103 Max Carey	.25	.13	.08
104 Dazzy Vance	.25	.13	.08
105 Walter Johnson	.50	.25	.15
106 Herb Pennock	.25	.13	.08
107 Joe Sewell	.25	.13	.08
108 Sam Rice	.25	.13	.08
109 Earle Combs	.25	.13	.08
110 Ted Lyons	.25	.13	.08
111 Eddie Collins	.25	.13	.08
112 Bill Terry	.25	.13	.08
113 Hack Wilson	.25	.13	.08
114 Rabbit Maranville	.25	.13	.08
115 Charlie Grimm	.25	.13	.08
116 Tony Lazzeri	.25	.13	.08
117 Waite Hoyt	.25	.13	.08
118 Stan Coveleski	.25	.13	.08
119 George Kelly	.25	.13	.08
120 Jimmy Dykes	.25	.13	.08
121 Red Faber	.25	.13	.08
122 Dave Bancroft	.25	.13	.08
123 Judge Landis	.25	.13	.08
124 Branch Rickey	.25	.13	.08
125 Jesse Haines	.25	.13	.08
126 Carl Mays	.25	.13	.08
127 Fred Lindstrom	.25	.13	.08
128 Miller Huggins	.25	.13	.08
129 Sad Sam Jones	.25	.13	.08
130 Joe Judge	.25	.13	.08
131 Ross Young (Youngs)	.25	.13	.08
132 Bucky Harris	.25	.13	.08
133 Bob Meusel	.25	.13	.08
134 Billy Evans	.25	.13	.08
135 1927 N.Y. Yankees Team Photo/Checklist	.50	.25	.15
SERIES 4 - 1981	7.50	3.75	2.25
136 Ty Cobb	1.00	.50	.30
137 Nap Lajoie	.25	.13	.08
138 Tris Speaker	.25	.13	.08
139 Heinie Groh	.25	.13	.08
140 Sam Crawford	.25	.13	.08
141 Clyde Milan	.25	.13	.08
142 Chief Bender	.25	.13	.08
143 Big Ed Walsh	.25	.13	.08
144 Walter Johnson	.50	.25	.15

#	Player	NM	EX	VG
145	Connie Mack	.25	.13	.08
146	Hal Chase	.25	.13	.08
147	Hugh Duffy	.25	.13	.08
148	Honus Wagner	.50	.25	.15
149	Tom Connolly	.25	.13	.08
150	Clark Griffith	.25	.13	.08
151	Zack Wheat	.25	.13	.08
152	Christy Mathewson	.50	.25	.15
153	Grover C. Alexander	.25	.13	.08
154	Joe Jackson	3.00	1.50	.90
155	Home Run Baker	.25	.13	.08
156	Ed Plank	.25	.13	.08
157	Larry Doyle	.25	.13	.08
158	Rube Marquard	.25	.13	.08
159	Johnny Evers	.25	.13	.08
160	Joe Tinker	.25	.13	.08
161	Frank Chance	.25	.13	.08
162	Wilbert Robinson	.25	.13	.08
163	Roger Peckinpaugh	.25	.13	.08
164	Fred Clarke	.25	.13	.08
165	Babe Ruth	3.00	1.50	.90
166	Wilbur Cooper	.25	.13	.08
167	Germany Schaefer	.25	.13	.08
168	Addie Joss	.25	.13	.08
169	Cy Young	.50	.25	.15
170	Ban Johnson	.25	.13	.08
171	Joe Judge	.25	.13	.08
172	Harry Hooper	.25	.13	.08
173	Bill Klem	.25	.13	.08
174	Ed Barrow	.25	.13	.08
175	Ed Cicotte	.25	.13	.08
176	Hughie Jennings	.25	.13	.08
177	Ray Schalk	.25	.13	.08
178	Nick Altrock	.25	.13	.08
179	Roger Bresnahan	.25	.13	.08
180	$100,000 Infield	.25	.13	.08
SERIES 5 - 1983		**7.50**	**3.75**	**2.25**
181	Lou Gehrig	3.00	1.50	.90
182	Eddie Collins	.25	.13	.08
183	Art Fletcher	.25	.13	.08
184	Jimmie Foxx	.25	.13	.08
185	Lefty Gomez	.25	.13	.08
186	Oral Hildebrand	.25	.13	.08
187	General Crowder	.25	.13	.08
188	Bill Dickey	.25	.13	.08
189	Wes Ferrell	.25	.13	.08
190	Al Simmons	.25	.13	.08
191	Tony Lazzeri	.25	.13	.08
192	Sam West	.25	.13	.08
193	Babe Ruth	3.00	1.50	.90
194	Connie Mack	.25	.13	.08
195	Lefty Grove	.25	.13	.08
196	Eddie Rommel	.25	.13	.08
197	Ben Chapman	.25	.13	.08
198	Joe Cronin	.25	.13	.08
199	Rich Ferrell (Rick)	.25	.13	.08
200	Charlie Gehringer	.25	.13	.08
201	Jimmy Dykes	.25	.13	.08
202	Earl Averill	.25	.13	.08
203	Pepper Martin	.25	.13	.08
204	Bill Terry	.25	.13	.08
205	Pie Traynor	.25	.13	.08
206	Gabby Hartnett	.25	.13	.08
207	Frank Frisch	.25	.13	.08
208	Carl Hubbell	.25	.13	.08
209	Paul Waner	.25	.13	.08
210	Woody English	.25	.13	.08
211	Bill Hallahan	.25	.13	.08
212	Dick Bartell	.25	.13	.08
213	Bill McKechnie	.25	.13	.08
214	Max Carey	.25	.13	.08
215	John McGraw	.25	.13	.08
216	Jimmie Wilson	.25	.13	.08
217	Chick Hafey	.25	.13	.08
218	Chuck Klein	.25	.13	.08
219	Lefty O'Doul	.25	.13	.08
220	Wally Berger	.25	.13	.08
221	Hal Schumacher	.25	.13	.08
222	Lon Warneke	.25	.13	.08
223	Tony Cuccinello	.25	.13	.08
(224)	1933 A.L. All-Stars	.50	.25	.15
(225)	1933 N.L. All-Stars	.50	.25	.15
SERIES 6 - 1984		**15.00**	**7.50**	**4.50**
226	Roger Maris	.75	.40	.25
227	Babe Ruth	3.00	1.50	.90
228	Jackie Robinson	2.00	1.00	.60
229	Pete Gray	.75	.40	.25
230	Ted Williams	3.00	1.50	.90
231	Hank Aaron	3.00	1.50	.90
232	Mickey Mantle	5.00	2.50	1.50
233	Gil Hodges	.25	.13	.08
234	Walter Johnson	.50	.25	.15
235	Joe DiMaggio	3.00	1.50	.90
236	Lou Gehrig	3.00	1.50	.90
237	Stan Musial	.75	.40	.25
238	Mickey Cochrane	.25	.13	.08
239	Denny McLain	.25	.13	.08
240	Carl Hubbell	.25	.13	.08
241	Harvey Haddix	.25	.13	.08
242	Christy Mathewson	.50	.25	.15
243	Johnny VanderMeer	.25	.13	.08
244	Sandy Koufax	3.00	1.50	.90
245	Willie Mays	3.00	1.50	.90
246	Don Drysdale	.25	.13	.08
247	Bobby Richardson	.25	.13	.08
248	Hoyt Wilhelm	.25	.13	.08
249	Yankee Stadium	.25	.13	.08
250	Bill Terry	.25	.13	.08
251	Roy Campanella	.50	.25	.15
252	Roberto Clemente	3.00	1.50	.90
253	Casey Stengel	.25	.13	.08
254	Ernie Banks	.50	.25	.15
255	Bobby Thomson	.25	.13	.08
256	Mel Ott	.25	.13	.08
257	Tony Oliva	.25	.13	.08
258	Satchel Paige	1.00	.50	.30
259	Joe Jackson	3.00	1.50	.90
260	Larry Lajoie	.25	.13	.08
261	Bill Mazeroski	.25	.13	.08
262	Bill Wambsganss	.25	.13	.08
263	Willie McCovey	.25	.13	.08
264	Warren Spahn	.25	.13	.08
265	Lefty Gomez	.25	.13	.08
266	Dazzy Vance	.25	.13	.08
267	Sam Crawford	.25	.13	.08
268	Tris Speaker	.25	.13	.08
269	Lou Brock	.25	.13	.08
270	Cy Young	.25	.13	.08

1978 TCMA Baseball Nostalgia Postcard

Vernon "Whitey" Wilshere

Baseball Nostalgia Inc.
Doubleday Plaza
Cooperstown, N.Y. 13326

TCMA produced this card for Baseball Nostalgia, Inc., a Cooperstown, N.Y., hobby shop, in an edition of 500. The card pictures a Cooperstown resident who taught at the local high school following a short (1934-36) major league pitching career. The 3-1/2" x 5-1/2" black-and-white card has standard postcard markings on back.

	NM	EX	VG
Vernon "Whitey" Wilshere	6.00	3.00	1.80

1978 TCMA The 1960's

Nearly 300 players of the 1960s are featured in this collectors issue. Fronts of the 2-1/2" x 3-1/2" cards have a color photo with a black frameline and white border. There are no other graphics. Backs are printed in green and include a lengthy career summary. On some cards the set's title, "The 1960's" is printed at top. Several mistakes in card numbering are noted in the accompanying checklist.

#	Player	NM	EX	VG
	Complete Set (293):	40.00	20.00	12.00
	Common Player:	.25	.13	.08
1	Smoky Burgess	.25	.13	.08
2	Juan Marichal	1.00	.50	.30
3	Don Drysdale	1.00	.50	.30
4	Jim Gentile	.25	.13	.08
5	Roy Face	.25	.13	.08
6	Joe Pepitone	.25	.13	.08
7	Joe Christopher	.25	.13	.08
8	Wayne Causey	.25	.13	.08
9	Frank Bolling	.25	.13	.08
10	Jim Maloney	.25	.13	.08
11	Roger Maris	2.50	1.25	.70
12	Bill White	.25	.13	.08
13	Roberto Clemente	7.50	3.75	2.25
14	Bob Saverine	.25	.13	.08
15	Barney Schultz	.25	.13	.08
16	Albie Pearson	.25	.13	.08
17	Denny Lemaster	.25	.13	.08
18	Ernie Broglio	.25	.13	.08
19	Bobby Klaus	.25	.13	.08
20	Tony Cloninger	.25	.13	.08
21	Whitey Ford	1.50	.70	.45
22	Ron Santo	.60	.30	.20
23	Jim Duckworth	.25	.13	.08
24	Willie Davis	.25	.13	.08
25	Ed Charles	.25	.13	.08
26	Bob Allison	.25	.13	.08
27	Fritz Ackley	.25	.13	.08
28	Ruben Amaro	.25	.13	.08
29	Johnny Callison	.25	.13	.08
30	Greg Bollo	.25	.13	.08
31	Felix Millan	.25	.13	.08
32	Camilo Pascual	.25	.13	.08
33	Jackie Brandt	.25	.13	.08
34	Don Lock	.25	.13	.08
35	Chico Ruiz	.25	.13	.08
36	Joe Azcue	.25	.13	.08
37	Ed Bailey	.25	.13	.08
38	Pete Ramos	.25	.13	.08
39	Eddie Bressoud	.25	.13	.08
40	Al Kaline	1.50	.70	.45
41	Ron Brand	.25	.13	.08
42	Bob Lillis	.25	.13	.08
43	Not issued (See #125.)	.25	.13	.08
44	Buster Narum	.25	.13	.08
45	Jim Gilliam	.25	.13	.08
46	Claude Raymond	.25	.13	.08
47	Billy Bryan	.25	.13	.08
48	Marshall Bridges	.25	.13	.08
49	Norm Cash	.45	.25	.14
50	Orlando Cepeda	1.00	.50	.30
51	Lee Maye	.25	.13	.08
52	Andre Rodgers	.25	.13	.08
53	Ken Berry	.25	.13	.08
54	Don Mincher	.25	.13	.08
55	Jerry Lumpe	.25	.13	.08
56	Milt Pappas	.25	.13	.08
57	Steve Barber	.25	.18	.08
58	Denis Menke	.25	.13	.08
59	Larry Maxie	.25	.13	.08
60	Bob Gibson	1.00	.50	.30
61	Larry Bearnarth	.25	.13	.08
62	Bill Mazeroski	1.00	.50	.30
63	Bob Rodgers	.25	.13	.08
64	Jerry Arrigo	.25	.13	.08
65	Joe Nuxhall	.25	.13	.08
66	Dean Chance	.25	.13	.08
67	Ken Boyer	.60	.30	.20
68	John Odom	.25	.13	.08
69	Chico Cardenas	.25	.13	.08
70	Maury Wills	.35	.20	.11
71	Tony Oliva	.45	.25	.14
72	Don Nottebart	.25	.13	.08
73	Joe Adcock	.25	.13	.08
74	Felipe Alou	.25	.13	.08
75	Matty Alou	.25	.13	.08
76	Dick Radatz	.25	.13	.08
77	Jim Bouton	.25	.13	.08
78	John Blanchard	.25	.13	.08
79	Juan Pizarro	.25	.13	.08
80	Boog Powell	.45	.25	.14
81	Earl Robinson	.25	.13	.08
82	Bob Chance	.25	.13	.08
83	Max Alvis	.25	.13	.08
84	Don Blasingame	.25	.13	.08
85	Tom Cheney	.25	.13	.08
86	Jerry Arrigo	.25	.13	.08
87	Tommy Davis	.25	.13	.08
88	Steve Boros	.25	.13	.08
89	Don Cardwell	.25	.13	.08
90	Harmon Killebrew	1.50	.70	.45
91	Jim Pagliaroni	.25	.13	.08
92	Jim O'Toole	.25	.13	.08
93	Dennis Bennett	.25	.13	.08
94	Dick McAuliffe	.25	.13	.08
95	Dick Brown	.25	.13	.08
96	Joe Amalfitano	.25	.13	.08
97	Phil Linz	.25	.13	.08
98	Not issued (see #165)	.25	.13	.08
99	Dave Nicholson	.25	.13	.08
100	Hoyt Wilhelm	1.00	.50	.30
101	Don Leppert	.25	.13	.08
102	Jose Pagan	.25	.13	.08
103	Sam McDowell	.25	.13	.08
104	Jack Baldschun	.25	.13	.08
105	Jim Perry	.25	.13	.08
106	Hal Reniff	.25	.13	.08
107	Lee Maye	.25	.13	.08
108	Joe Adcock	.25	.13	.08
109	Bob Bolin	.25	.13	.08
110	Don Leppert	.25	.13	.08
111	Bill Monbouquette	.25	.13	.08
112	Bobby Richardson	.45	.25	.14
113	Earl Battey	.25	.13	.08
114	Bob Veale	.25	.13	.08
115	Lou Jackson	.25	.13	.08
116	Frank Kreutzer	.25	.13	.08
117	Jerry Zimmerman	.25	.13	.08
118	Don Schwall	.25	.13	.08
119	Rich Rollins	.25	.13	.08
120	Pete Ward	.25	.13	.08
121	Moe Drabowsky	.25	.13	.08
122	Jesse Gonder	.25	.13	.08
123	Hal Woodeshick	.25	.13	.08
124	John Herrnstein	.25	.13	.08
125a	Gary Peters (Should be #43.)	.25	.13	.08
125b	Leon Wagner	.25	.13	.08
126	Dwight Siebler	.25	.13	.08
027	Gary Kroll	.25	.13	.08
128	Tony Horton	.25	.13	.08
129	John DeMerit	.25	.13	.08
130	Sandy Koufax	6.00	3.00	1.75
131	Jim Davenport	.25	.13	.08
132	Wes Covington	.25	.13	.08
133	Tony Taylor	.25	.13	.08
134	Jack Kralick	.25	.13	.08
135	Bill Pleis	.25	.13	.08
136	Russ Snyder	.25	.13	.08
137	Joe Torre	.75	.40	.25
138	Ted Wills	.25	.13	.08
139	Wes Stock	.25	.13	.08
140	Frank Robinson	1.50	.70	.45
141	Dave Stenhouse	.25	.13	.08
142	Ron Hansen	.25	.13	.08
143	Don Elston	.25	.13	.08
144	Del Crandall	.25	.13	.08
145	Bennie Daniels	.25	.13	.08
146	Vada Pinson	.45	.25	.14
147	Bill Spanswick	.25	.13	.08
148	Earl Wilson	.25	.13	.08
149	Ty Cline	.25	.13	.08
150	Dick Groat	.25	.13	.08

		NM	EX	VG
151	Jim Duckworth	.25	.13	.08
152	Jimmie Schaffer	.25	.13	.08
153	George Thomas	.25	.13	.08
154	Wes Stock	.25	.13	.08
155	Mike White	.25	.13	.08
156	John Podres	.25	.13	.08
157	Willie Crawford	.25	.13	.08
158	Fred Gladding	.25	.13	.08
159	John Wyatt	.25	.13	.08
160	Bob Friend	.25	.13	.08
161	Ted Uhlaender	.25	.13	.08
162	Dick Stigman	.25	.13	.08
163	Don Wert	.25	.13	.08
164	Eddie Bressoud	.25	.13	.08
165a	Ed Roebuck (Should be #98)	.25	.13	.08
165b	Leon Wagner	.25	.13	.08
166	Al Spangler	.25	.13	.08
167	Bob Sadowski	.25	.13	.08
168	Ralph Terry	.25	.13	.08
169	Jimmie Schaffer	.25	.13	.08
170a	Jim Fregosi (should be #180)	.25	.13	.08
170b	Dick Hall	.25	.13	.08
171	Al Spangler	.25	.13	.08
172	Bob Tillman	.25	.13	.08
173	Ed Bailey	.25	.13	.08
174	Cesar Tovar	.25	.13	.08
175	Morrie Stevens	.25	.13	.08
176	Floyd Weaver	.25	.13	.08
177	Frank Malzone	.25	.13	.08
178	Norm Siebern	.25	.13	.08
179	Dick Phillips	.25	.13	.08
180	Not issued (see #170)	.25	.13	.08
181	Bobby Wine	.25	.13	.08
182	Masanori Murakami	.75	.40	.25
183	Chuck Schilling	.25	.13	.08
184	Jimmie Schaffer	.25	.13	.08
185	John Roseboro	.25	.13	.08
186	Jake Wood	.25	.13	.08
187	Dallas Green	.25	.13	.08
188	Tom Haller	.25	.13	.08
189	Chuck Cottier	.25	.13	.08
190	Brooks Robinson	1.50	.70	.45
191	Ty Cline	.25	.13	.08
192	Bubba Phillips	.25	.13	.08
193	Al Jackson	.25	.13	.08
194	Herm Starrette	.25	.13	.08
195	Dave Wickersham	.25	.13	.08
196	Vic Power	.25	.13	.08
197	Ray Culp	.25	.13	.08
198	Don Demeter	.25	.13	.08
199	Dick Schofield	.25	.13	.08
200	Stephen Grant	.25	.13	.08
201	Roger Craig	.25	.13	.08
202	Dick Farrell	.25	.13	.08
203	Clay Dalrymple	.25	.13	.08
204	Jim Duffalo	.25	.13	.08
205	Tito Francona	.25	.13	.08
206	Tony Conigliaro	.45	.25	.14
207	Jim King	.25	.13	.08
208	Joe Gibbon	.25	.13	.08
209	Arnold Earley	.25	.13	.08
210	Denny McLain	.25	.13	.08
211	Don Larsen	.25	.13	.08
212	Ron Hunt	.25	.13	.08
213	Deron Johnson	.25	.13	.08
214	Harry Bright	.25	.13	.08
215	Ernie Fazio	.25	.13	.08
216	Joey Jay	.25	.13	.08
217	Jim Coates	.25	.13	.08
218	Jerry Kindall	.25	.13	.08
219	Joe Gibbon	.25	.13	.08
220	Frank Howard	.35	.20	.11
221	Howie Koplitz	.25	.13	.08
222	Larry Jackson	.25	.13	.08
223	Dale Long	.25	.13	.08
224	Jimmy Dykes	.25	.13	.08
225	Hank Aguirre	.25	.13	.08
226	Earl Francis	.25	.13	.08
227	Vic Wertz	.25	.13	.08
228	Larry Haney	.25	.13	.08
229	Tony LaRussa	.45	.25	.14
230	Moose Skowron	.35	.20	.11
231a	Tito Francona (Should be #235.)	.25	.13	.08
231b	Lee Thomas	.25	.13	.08
232	Ken Johnson	.25	.13	.08
233	Dick Howser	.25	.13	.08
234	Bobby Knoop	.25	.13	.08
235	Not issued (See #231.)	.25	.13	.08
236	Elston Howard	.35	.20	.11
237	Donn Clendenon	.25	.13	.08
238	Jesse Gonder	.25	.13	.08
239	Vern Law	.25	.13	.08
240	Curt Flood	.25	.13	.08
241	Dal Maxvill	.25	.13	.08
242	Roy Sievers	.25	.13	.08
243	Jim Brewer	.25	.13	.08
244	Harry Craft	.25	.13	.08
245	Dave Eilers	.25	.13	.08
246	Dave DeBusschere	.25	.13	.08
247	Ken Harrelson	.25	.13	.08
248	Not issued (See #249.)	.25	.13	.08
249a	Jim Duffalo	.25	.13	.08
249b	Eddie Kasko (Should be #248.)	.25	.13	.08
250	Luis Aparicio	1.00	.50	.30
251	Ron Kline	.25	.13	.08
252	Chuck Hinton	.25	.13	.08
253	Frank Lary	.25	.13	.08
254	Stu Miller	.25	.13	.08
255	Ernie Banks	2.00	1.00	.60
256	Dick Farrell	.25	.13	.08
257	Bud Daley	.25	.13	.08
258	Luis Arroyo	.25	.13	.08
259	Bob Del Greco	.25	.13	.08
260	Ted Williams	6.00	3.00	1.75
261	Mike Epstein	.25	.13	.08
262	Mickey Mantle	10.00	5.00	3.00

		NM	EX	VG
263	Jim LeFebvre	.25	.13	.08
264	Pat Jarvis	.25	.13	.08
265	Chuck Hinton	.25	.13	.08
266	Don Larsen	.25	.13	.08
267	Jim Coates	.25	.13	.08
268	Gary Kolb	.25	.13	.08
269	Jim Ray Hart	.25	.13	.08
270	Dave McNally	.25	.13	.08
271	Jerry Kindall	.25	.13	.08
272	Hector Lopez	.25	.13	.08
273	Claude Osteen	.25	.13	.08
274	Jack Aker	.25	.13	.08
275	Mike Shannon	.25	.13	.08
276	Lew Burdette	.25	.13	.08
277	Mack Jones	.25	.13	.08
278	Art Shamsky	.25	.13	.08
279	Bob Johnson	.25	.13	.08
280	Willie Mays	6.00	3.00	1.75
281	Rich Nye	.25	.13	.08
282	Bill Cowan	.25	.13	.08
283	Gary Kolb	.25	.13	.08
284	Woody Held	.25	.13	.08
285	Bill Freehan	.25	.13	.08
286	Larry Jackson	.25	.13	.08
287	Mike Hershberger	.25	.13	.08
288	Julian Javier	.25	.13	.08
289	Charley Smith	.25	.13	.08
290	Hank Aaron	6.00	3.00	1.75
291	John Boccabella	.25	.13	.08
292	Charley James	.25	.13	.08
293	Sammy Ellis	.25	.13	.08

1978 TCMA 1941 Brooklyn Dodgers

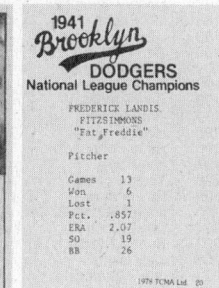

The National League Champion Brooklyn Dodgers are featured in the collectors' edition card set. Measuring 2-1/2" x 3-1/2", the cards have blue duotone player photos on front with the name and position overprinted in black at bottom. A white border surrounds the photo. Backs are in black-and-white with a large championship logo and a few stats from the 1941 season.

		NM	EX	VG
Complete Set (43):		25.00	12.50	7.50
Common Player:		1.50	.75	.45
1	Mickey Owen	2.50	1.25	.70
2	Pee Wee Reese	7.50	3.75	2.25
3	Hugh Casey	1.50	.75	.45
4	Larry French	1.50	.75	.45
5	Tom Drake	1.50	.75	.45
6	Ed Albosta	1.50	.75	.45
7	Tommy Tatum	1.50	.75	.45
8	Paul Waner	3.50	1.75	1.00
9	Van Lingle Mungo	2.50	1.25	.70
10	Bill Swift	1.50	.75	.45
11	Dolph Camilli	2.50	1.25	.70
12	Pete Coscarart	1.50	.75	.45
13	Vito Tamulis	1.50	.75	.45
14	John Allen	1.50	.75	.45
15	Lee Grissom	1.50	.75	.45
16	Billy Herman	2.50	1.25	.70
17	Joe Vosmik	1.50	.75	.45
18	Babe Phelps	1.50	.75	.45
19	Mace Brown	1.50	.75	.45
20	Freddie Fitzsimmons	1.50	.75	.45
21	Angelo Giuliani	1.50	.75	.45
22	Lewis Riggs	1.50	.75	.45
23	Jimmy Wasdell	1.50	.75	.45
24	Herman Franks	1.50	.75	.45
25	Alex Kampouris	1.50	.75	.45
26	Kirby Higbe	1.50	.75	.45
27	Joe Medwick	2.50	1.25	.70
28	Newt Kimball	1.50	.75	.45
29	Curt Davis	1.50	.75	.45
30	Augie Galan	1.50	.75	.45
31	Luke Hamlin	1.50	.75	.45
32	Cookie Lavagetto	1.50	.75	.45
33	Joe Gallagher	1.50	.75	.45
34	Whitlow Wyatt	1.50	.75	.45
35	Dixie Walker	1.50	.75	.45
36	Pete Reiser	1.50	.75	.45
37	Leo Durocher	2.50	1.25	.70
38	Pee Wee Reese, Joe Medwick (3" x 5")	4.50	2.25	1.25
39	Dixie Walker, Joe Medwick, Dolph Camilli, Pete Reiser (3" x 5")	4.50	2.25	1.25
40	Team photo	3.00	1.50	.90
41	Kemp Wicker	1.50	.75	.45
42	George Pfister	2.00	1.00	.60
43	Chuck Dressen	1.50	.75	.45

1979 TCMA All Time Tigers

ALL TIME DETROIT TIGER TEAM	
Hank Greenberg	1B
Charlie Gehringer	2B
George Kell	3B
Billy Rogell	SS
Ty Cobb	OF
Harry Heilmann	OF
Al Kaline	OF
Mickey Cochrane	C
Denny McLain	RHP
Hal Newhouser	LHP
Terry Fox	RP
Steve O'Neil	Mgr

Utilizing a format similar to its several minor league team sets of the same year, this collectors' issue from TCMA features an "All Time" Tigers team selection of position players, pitchers and manager. The 2-1/2" x 3-1/2" cards have black-and-white photos on front with the player's name and position in an orange "wave" at bottom; the whole is surrounded by a white border. Backs are in black-and-white and detail the all-time line-up. The unnumbered cards are checklisted here alphabetically.

		NM	EX	VG
Complete Set (12):		20.00	10.00	6.00
Common Player:		1.50	.70	.45
(1)	Ty Cobb	6.00	3.00	1.75
(2)	Mickey Cochrane	1.50	.70	.45
(3)	Terry Fox	1.50	.70	.45
(4)	Charlie Gehringer	2.50	1.25	.70
(5)	Hank Greenberg	5.00	2.50	1.50
(6)	Harry Heilmann	1.50	.70	.45
(7)	Al Kaline	5.00	2.50	1.50
(8)	George Kell	1.50	.70	.45
(9)	Denny McLain	1.50	.70	.45
(10)	Hal Newhouser	1.50	.70	.45
(11)	Steve O'Neil (O'Neill)	1.50	.70	.45
(12)	Billy Rogell	1.50	.70	.45

1979 TCMA Baseball History Series: The Fifties

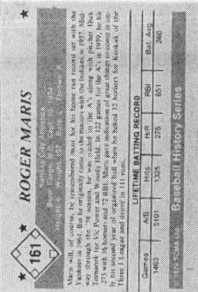

The "pure" format of the 1953 Bowman set was borrowed in this collectors issue featuring the stars and journeymen of baseball in the 1950s. The 2-1/2" x 3-1/2" cards have color photos on front with white borders. Backs are in red and black with personal data and career summary and stats. Each set originally sold by TCMA came with two large-format (5" x 3-1/2") team-photo cards.

		NM	EX	VG
Complete Set (291):		35.00	17.50	10.00
Common Player:		.25	.13	.08
1	Joe DiMaggio	7.50	3.75	2.25
2	Yogi Berra	1.50	.70	.45
3	Warren Spahn	.75	.40	.25
4	Robin Roberts	.60	.30	.20
5	Ernie Banks	1.50	.70	.45
6	Willie Mays	5.00	2.50	1.50
7	Mickey Mantle	10.00	5.00	3.00
8	Roy Campanella	1.50	.70	.45
9	Stan Musial	4.00	2.00	1.25
10	Ted Williams	5.00	2.50	1.50
11	Ed Bailey	.25	.13	.08
12	Ted Kluszewski	.60	.30	.20
13	Ralph Kiner	.60	.30	.20
14	Dick Littlefield	.25	.13	.08
15	Nellie Fox	.60	.30	.20
16	Billy Pierce	.25	.13	.08
17	Richie Ashburn	.60	.30	.20
18	Del Ennis	.25	.13	.08
19	Bob Lemon	.50	.25	.15
20	Early Wynn	.50	.25	.15
21	Joe Collins	.25	.13	.08
22	Hank Bauer	.25	.13	.08
23	Roberto Clemente	6.00	3.00	1.75
24	Frank Thomas	.25	.13	.08
25	Alvin Dark	.25	.13	.08
26	Whitey Lockman	.25	.13	.08
27	Larry Doby	.60	.30	.20
28	Bob Feller	.75	.40	.25
29	Willie Jones	.25	.13	.08
30	Granny Hamner	.25	.13	.08
31	Clem Labine	.25	.13	.08

32	Ralph Branca	.25	.13	.08
33	Jack Harshman	.25	.13	.08
34	Dick Donovan	.25	.13	.08
35	Tommy Henrich	.25	.13	.08
36	Jerry Coleman	.25	.13	.08
37	Billy Hoeft	.25	.13	.08
38	Johnny Groth	.25	.13	.08
39	Harvey Haddix	.25	.13	.08
40	Gerry Staley	.25	.13	.08
41	Dale Long	.25	.13	.08
42	Vern Law	.25	.13	.08
43	Dodger Power	1.50	.70	.45
44	Sam Jethroe	.25	.13	.08
45	Vic Wertz	.25	.13	.08
46	Wes Westrum	.25	.13	.08
47	Dee Fondy	.25	.13	.08
48	Gene Baker	.25	.13	.08
49	Sandy Koufax	5.00	2.50	1.50
50	Billy Loes	.25	.13	.08
51	Chuck Diering	.25	.13	.08
52	Joe Ginsberg	.25	.13	.08
53	Jim Konstanty	.25	.13	.08
54	Curt Simmons	.25	.13	.08
55	Alex Kellner	.25	.13	.08
56	Charlie Dressen	.25	.13	.08
57	Frank Sullivan	.25	.13	.08
58	Mel Parnell	.25	.13	.08
59	Bobby Hofman	.25	.13	.08
60	Bill Connelly	.25	.13	.08
61	Corky Valentine	.25	.13	.08
62	Johnny Klippstein	.25	.13	.08
63	Chuck Tanner	.25	.13	.08
64	Dick Drott	.25	.13	.08
65	Dean Stone	.25	.13	.08
66	Jim Busby	.25	.13	.08
67	Sid Gordon	.25	.13	.08
68	Del Crandall	.25	.13	.08
69	Walker Cooper	.25	.13	.08
70	Hank Sauer	.25	.13	.08
71	Gil Hodges	.75	.40	.25
72	Duke Snider	1.00	.50	.30
73	Sherman Lollar	.25	.13	.08
74	Chico Carrasquel	.25	.13	.08
75	Gus Triandos	.25	.13	.08
76	Bob Harrison	.25	.13	.08
77	Eddie Waitkus	.25	.13	.08
78	Ken Heintzelman	.25	.13	.08
79	Harry Simpson	.25	.13	.08
80	Luke Easter	.25	.13	.08
81	Ed Dick	.25	.13	.08
82	Jim DePaola	.25	.13	.08
83	Billy Cox	.25	.13	.08
84	Pee Wee Reese	1.00	.50	.30
85	Virgil Trucks	.25	.13	.08
86	George Kell	.50	.25	.15
87	Mickey Vernon	.25	.13	.08
88	Eddie Yost	.25	.13	.08
89	Gus Bell	.25	.13	.08
90	Wally Post	.25	.13	.08
91	Ed Lopat	.25	.13	.08
92	Dick Wakefield	.25	.13	.08
93	Solly Hemus	.25	.13	.08
94	Al "Red" Schoendienst	.60	.30	.20
95	Sammy White	.25	.13	.08
96	Billy Goodman	.25	.13	.08
97	Jim Hearn	.25	.13	.08
98	Ruben Gomez	.25	.13	.08
99	Marty Marion	.25	.13	.08
100	Bill Virdon	.25	.13	.08
101	Chuck Stobbs	.25	.13	.08
102	Ron Samford	.25	.13	.08
103	Bill Tuttle	.25	.13	.08
104	Harvey Kuenn	.25	.13	.08
105	Joe Cunningham	.25	.13	.08
106	Bill Sarni	.25	.13	.08
107	Jack Kramer	.25	.13	.08
108	Eddie Stanky	.25	.13	.08
109	Carmen Mauro	.25	.13	.08
110	Wayne Belardi	.25	.13	.08
111	Preston Ward	.25	.13	.08
112	Jack Shepard	.25	.13	.08
113	Buddy Kerr	.25	.13	.08
114	Vern Bickford	.25	.13	.08
115	Ellis Kinder	.25	.13	.08
116	Walt Dropo	.25	.13	.08
117	Duke Maas	.25	.13	.08
118	Billy Hunter	.25	.13	.08
119	Ewell Blackwell	.25	.13	.08
120	Hershell Freeman	.25	.13	.08
121	Freddie Martin	.25	.13	.08
122	Erv Dusak	.25	.13	.08
123	Roy Hartsfield	.25	.13	.08
124	Willard Marshall	.25	.13	.08
125	Jack Sanford	.25	.13	.08
126	Herm Wehmeier	.25	.13	.08
127	Hal Smith	.25	.13	.08
128	Jim Finigan	.25	.13	.08
129	Bob Hale	.25	.13	.08
130	Jim Wilson	.25	.13	.08
131	Bill Wight	.25	.13	.08
132	Mike Fornieles	.25	.13	.08
133	Steve Gromek	.25	.13	.08
134	Herb Score	.35	.20	.11
135	Ryne Duren	.25	.13	.08
136	Bob Turley	.25	.13	.08
137	Wally Moon	.25	.13	.08
138	Fred Hutchinson	.25	.13	.08
139	Jim Hegan	.25	.13	.08
140	Dale Mitchell	.25	.13	.08
141	Walt Moryn	.25	.13	.08
142	Cal Neeman	.25	.13	.08
143	Billy Martin	.50	.25	.15
144	Phil Rizzuto	1.00	.50	.30
145	Preacher Roe	.25	.13	.08
146	Carl Erskine	.25	.13	.08
147	Vic Power	.25	.13	.08
148	Elmer Valo	.25	.13	.08
149	Don Mueller	.25	.13	.08
150	Hank Thompson	.25	.13	.08
151	Stan Lopata	.25	.13	.08
152	Dick Sisler	.25	.13	.08
153	Willard Schmidt	.25	.13	.08
154	Roy McMillan	.25	.13	.08
155	Gil McDougald	.25	.13	.08
156	Gene Woodling	.25	.13	.08
157	Eddie Mathews	.75	.40	.25
158	Johnny Logan	.25	.13	.08
159	Dan Bankhead	.25	.13	.08
160	Joe Black	.25	.13	.08
161	Roger Maris	1.50	.70	.45
162	Bob Cerv	.25	.13	.08
163	Paul Minner	.25	.13	.08
164	Bob Rush	.25	.13	.08
165	Gene Hermanski	.25	.13	.08
166	Harry Brecheen	.25	.13	.08
167	Davey Williams	.25	.13	.08
168	Monte Irvin	.60	.30	.20
169	Clint Courtney	.25	.13	.08
170	Sandy Consuegra	.25	.13	.08
171	Bobby Shantz	.25	.13	.08
172	Harry Byrd	.25	.13	.08
173	Marv Throneberry	.25	.13	.08
174	Woody Held	.25	.13	.08
175	Al Rosen	.25	.13	.08
176	Rance Pless	.25	.13	.08
177	Steve Bilko	.25	.13	.08
178	Joe Presko	.25	.13	.08
179	Ray Boone	.25	.13	.08
180	Jim Lemon	.25	.13	.08
181	Andy Pafko	.25	.13	.08
182	Don Newcombe	.35	.20	.11
183	Frank Lary	.25	.13	.08
184	Al Kaline	.75	.40	.25
185	Allie Reynolds	.25	.13	.08
186	Vic Raschi	.25	.13	.08
187	Dodger Braintrust	.50	.25	.15
188	Jim Piersall	.25	.13	.08
189	George Wilson	.25	.13	.08
190	Jim "Dusty" Rhodes	.25	.13	.08
191	Duane Pillette	.25	.13	.08
192	Dave Philley	.25	.13	.08
193	Bobby Morgan	.25	.13	.08
194	Russ Meyer	.25	.13	.08
195	Hector Lopez	.25	.13	.08
196	Arnie Portocarrero	.25	.13	.08
197	Joe Page	.25	.13	.08
198	Tommy Byrne	.25	.13	.08
199	Ray Monzant	.25	.13	.08
200	John "Windy" McCall	.25	.13	.08
201	Leo Durocher	.50	.25	.15
202	Bobby Thomson	.35	.20	.11
203	Jack Banta	.25	.13	.08
204	Joe Pignatano	.25	.13	.08
205	Carlos Paula	.25	.13	.08
206	Roy Sievers	.25	.13	.08
207	Mickey McDermott	.25	.13	.08
208	Ray Scarborough	.25	.13	.08
209	Bill Miller	.25	.13	.08
210	Bill Skowron	.25	.13	.08
211	Bob Nieman	.25	.13	.08
212	Al Pilarcik	.25	.13	.08
213	Jerry Priddy	.25	.13	.08
214	Frank House	.25	.13	.08
215	Don Mossi	.25	.13	.08
216	Rocky Colavito	.60	.30	.20
217	Brooks Lawrence	.25	.13	.08
218	Ted Wilks	.25	.13	.08
219	Zack Monroe	.25	.13	.08
220	Art Ditmar	.25	.13	.08
221	Cal McLish	.25	.13	.08
222	Gene Bearden	.25	.13	.08
223	Norm Siebern	.25	.13	.08
224	Bob Wiesler	.25	.13	.08
225	Foster Castleman	.25	.13	.08
226	Daryl Spencer	.25	.13	.08
227	Dick Williams	.25	.13	.08
228	Don Zimmer	.25	.13	.08
229	Jackie Jensen	.25	.13	.08
230	Billy Johnson	.25	.13	.08
231	Dave Koslo	.25	.13	.08
232	Al Corwin	.25	.13	.08
233	Erv Palica	.25	.13	.08
234	Bob Milliken	.25	.13	.08
235	Ray Katt	.25	.13	.08
236	Sammy Calderone	.25	.13	.08
237	Don Demeter	.25	.13	.08
238	Karl Spooner	.25	.13	.08
239	The Veteran and The Rookie	.50	.25	.15
240	Enos Slaughter	.50	.25	.15
241	Dick Kryhoski	.25	.13	.08
242	Art Houtteman	.25	.13	.08
243	Andy Carey	.25	.13	.08
244	Tony Kubek	.35	.20	.11
245	Mike McCormick	.25	.13	.08
246	Bob Schmidt	.25	.13	.08
247	Nelson King	.25	.13	.08
248	Bob Skinner	.25	.13	.08
249	Dick Bokelmann	.25	.13	.08
250	Eddie Kazak	.25	.13	.08
251	Billy Klaus	.25	.13	.08
252	Norm Zauchin	.25	.13	.08
253	Art Schult	.25	.13	.08
254	Bob Martyn	.25	.13	.08
255	Larry Jansen	.25	.13	.08
256	Sal Maglie	.25	.13	.08
257	Bob Darnell	.25	.13	.08
258	Ken Lehman	.25	.13	.08
259	Jim Blackburn	.25	.13	.08
260	Bob Purkey	.25	.13	.08
261	Harry Walker	.25	.13	.08
262	Joe Garagiola	.35	.20	.11
263	Gus Zernial	.25	.13	.08
264	Walter "Hoot" Evers	.25	.13	.08
265	Mark Freeman	.25	.13	.08
266	Charlie Silvera	.25	.13	.08
267	Johnny Podres	.25	.13	.08
268	Jim Hughes	.25	.13	.08
269	Al Worthington	.25	.13	.08
270	Hoyt Wilhelm	.50	.25	.15
271	Elston Howard	.25	.13	.08
272	Don Larsen	.40	.20	.12
273	Don Hoak	.25	.13	.08
274	Chico Fernandez	.25	.13	.08
275	Gail Harris	.25	.13	.08
276	Valmy Thomas	.25	.13	.08
277	George Shuba	.25	.13	.08
278	Al "Rube" Walker	.25	.13	.08
279	Willard Ramsdell	.25	.13	.08
280	Lindy McDaniel	.25	.13	.08
281	Bob Wilson	.25	.13	.08
282	Chuck Templeton	.25	.13	.08
283	Eddie Robinson	.25	.13	.08
284	Bob Porterfield	.25	.13	.08
285	Larry Miggins	.25	.13	.08
286	Minnie Minoso	.25	.13	.08
287	Lou Boudreau	.50	.25	.15
288	Jim Davenport	.25	.13	.08
289	Bob Miller	.25	.13	.08
290	Jim Gilliam	.25	.13	.08
291	Jackie Robinson	4.00	2.00	1.25
Bonus 1	1955 Brooklyn Dodgers Team Card	10.00	5.00	3.00
Bonus 2	1957 Milwaukee Braves Team	10.00	5.00	3.00

1979 TCMA Japan Pro Baseball

 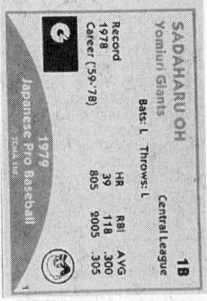

Stars of Japan's Pacific and Central "major" leagues are featured in this collectors issue. More than a dozen Americans playing or managing in Japan at the time are included in the set, as well as several Japanese Hall of Famers including home-run king Sadaharu Oh. Cards feature a color posed portrait with a light blue semi-circle at bottom containing the team and player name in royal blue. Backs are printed in red and black on white and have a few personal data, 1978 and career stats, plus league and team logos and TCMA copyright. Cards are nominally standard 2-1/2" x 3-1/2" in size, but actual size varies a bit due to cutting discrepancies.

		NM	EX	VG
	Complete Set (90):	50.00	25.00	15.00
	Common Player:	.50	.25	.15
1	Sadaharu Oh	15.00	7.50	4.50
2	Jinten Haku	.50	.25	.15
3	Toshizo Sakamoto	.50	.25	.15
4	Tony Muser	1.00	.50	.30
5	Makoto Matsubara	.50	.25	.15
6	Masayuki Nakaysuka	.50	.25	.15
7	Daisuke Yamashita	.50	.25	.15
8	Koji Yamamoto	.50	.25	.15
9	Sachio Kinugasa	4.00	2.00	1.25
10	Bernie Williams	.60	.30	.20
11	Bobby Marcano	.60	.30	.20
12	Koichi Tabuchi	.50	.25	.15
13	Katsuya Nomura	3.00	1.50	.90
14	Jack Maloof	.60	.30	.20
15	Masahiro Doi	.50	.25	.15
16	Hiroyuki Yamazaki	.50	.25	.15
17	Vernon Law	2.00	1.00	.60
18	Dave Hilton	.60	.30	.20
19	Katsuo Osugi	.50	.25	.15
20	Tsutomu Wakamatsu	.50	.25	.15
21	John Scott	.60	.30	.20
22	Toru Sugiura	.50	.25	.15
23	Akihiko Kondo	.50	.25	.15
24	Shintaro Mizutani	.50	.25	.15
25	Tatsuro Hirooka	.50	.25	.15
26	Kojiro Ikegaya	.50	.25	.15
27	Yutaka Enatsu	1.50	.70	.45
28	Tomehiro Kaneda	.50	.25	.15
29	Yoshihiko Takahashi	.50	.25	.15
30	Jitsuo Mizutani	.50	.25	.15
31	Adrian Garrett	.60	.30	.20
32	Jim Lyttle	.60	.30	.20
33	Takeshi Koba	.50	.25	.15
34	Sam Ewing	.60	.30	.20
35	Kazumi Takahashi	.50	.25	.15
36	Kazushi Saeki	.50	.25	.15
37	Masanori Murakami	7.50	3.75	2.25
38	Toshiro Kato	.50	.25	.15
39	Junichi Kashiwabara	.50	.25	.15
40	Masaru Tomita	.50	.25	.15
41	Bobby Mitchell	.60	.30	.20
42	Mikio Sendoh	.50	.25	.15
43	Chris Arnold	.60	.30	.20
44	Charlie Manuel	.60	.30	.20
45	Keiji Suzuki	.50	.25	.15
46	Toru Ogawa	.50	.25	.15
47	Shigeru Ishiwata	.50	.25	.15

		NM	EX	VG
48	Kyosuke Sasaki	.50	.25	.15
49	Iwao Ikebe	.50	.25	.15
50	Kaoru Betto	.50	.25	.15
51	Gene Martin	.60	.30	.20
52	Felix Millan	1.00	.50	.30
53	Mitsuo Motoi	.50	.25	.15
54	Tomio Tashiro	.50	.25	.15
55	Shigeo Nagashima	7.50	3.75	2.25
56	Yoshikazu Takagi	.50	.25	.15
57	Keiichi Nagasaki	.50	.25	.15
58	Rick Krueger	.60	.30	.20
59	John Sipin	.60	.30	.20
60	Osao Shibata	.50	.25	.15
61	Isao Harimoto	.50	.25	.15
62	Shigeru Takada	.50	.25	.15
63	Michiyo Arito	.50	.25	.15
64	Hisao Niura	.50	.25	.15
65	Teruhide Sakurai	.50	.25	.15
66	Yoshito Oda	.50	.25	.15
67	Leron Lee	.60	.30	.20
68	Carlos May	.60	.30	.20
69	Frank Ortenzio	.60	.30	.20
70	Leon Lee	.60	.30	.20
71	Mitsuru Fujiwara	.50	.25	.15
72	Senichi Hoshino	.50	.25	.15
73	Tatsuhiko Kimata	.50	.25	.15
74	Morimichi Takagi	.50	.25	.15
75	Yasunori Oshima	.50	.25	.15
76	Yasushi Tao	.50	.25	.15
77	Wayne Garrett	.60	.30	.20
78	Bob Jones	.60	.30	.20
79	Toshiro Naka	.50	.25	.15
80	Don Blasingame	3.00	1.50	.90
81	Mike Reinbach	.60	.30	.20
82	Masashi Takenouchi	.50	.25	.15
83	Masayuki Kakefu	.50	.25	.15
84	Katsuhiro Nakamura	.50	.25	.15
85	Shigeru Kobayashi	.50	.25	.15
86	Lee Stanton	.60	.30	.20
87	Takenori Emoto	.50	.25	.15
88	Sohachi Aniya	.50	.25	.15
89	Wally Yonamine	4.00	2.00	1.25
90	Kazuhiro Yamauchi	.50	.25	.15

1979 TCMA 1927 New York Yankees

Perhaps the finest baseball team of all time is featured in this collectors' set. The sepia oval photos at center are surrounded by black-and-white graphics of baseball equipment and other ornamentation. Player name and position are in a strip beneath the photo. Backs have personal data and a career summary. The cards are in standard 2-1/2" x 3-1/2".

		NM	EX	VG
Complete Set (32):		20.00	10.00	6.00
Common Player:		1.00	.50	.30
1	Babe Ruth	6.00	3.00	1.75
2	Lou Gehrig	4.00	2.00	1.25
3	Tony Lazzeri	1.00	.50	.30
4	Mark Koenig	1.00	.50	.30
5	Julie Wera	1.00	.50	.30
6	Ray Morehart	1.00	.50	.30
7	Art Fletcher	1.00	.50	.30
8	Joe Dugan	1.00	.50	.30
9	Charley O'Leary	1.00	.50	.30
10	Bob Meusel	1.00	.50	.30
11	Earle Combs	1.00	.50	.30
12	Cedric Durst	1.00	.50	.30
13	Johnny Grabowski	1.00	.50	.30
14	Mike Gazella	1.00	.50	.30
15	Pat Collins	1.00	.50	.30
16	Waite Hoyt	1.00	.50	.30
17	Myles Thomas	1.00	.50	.30
18	Benny Bengough	1.00	.50	.30
19	Herb Pennock	1.00	.50	.30
20	Wilcy Moore	1.00	.50	.30
21	Urban Shocker	1.00	.50	.30
22	Dutch Ruether	1.00	.50	.30
23	George Pipgras	1.00	.50	.30
24	Jacob Ruppert	1.00	.50	.30
25	Eddie Bennett	1.00	.50	.30
26	Ed Barrow	1.00	.50	.30
27	Ben Paschal	1.00	.50	.30
28	Miller Huggins	1.00	.50	.30
29	Joe Giard	1.00	.50	.30
30	Bob Shawkey	1.00	.50	.30
31	Walter Beall	1.00	.50	.30
32	Don Miller	1.00	.50	.30

1980 TCMA All-Time Teams

In 1980, TCMA began a new series of sets featuring 11 all-time great players and a manager from several of the 26 teams. In standard 2-1/2" x 3-1/2"

format, most of the cards utilize black-and-white player photos, though some more recent stars are pictured in color. Several decorative borders, varying by team, surround the front photos. On most team sets there is an "All Time" designation at top, with the player name and (usually) position at bottom. Backs are fairly uniform, printed in blue or black, and offering a few biographical details and career highlights or a checklist. Besides hobby sales, these old-timers' sets were also sold in several major retail chains.

(Team sets listed individually.)

1980 TCMA All-Time Brooklyn Dodgers

		NM	EX	VG
Complete Set (12):		6.00	3.00	1.80
Common Player:		.50	.25	.15
1	Gil Hodges	1.00	.50	.30
2	Jim Gilliam	.50	.25	.15
3	Pee Wee Reese	1.00	.50	.30
4	Jackie Robinson	3.00	1.50	.90
5	Sandy Koufax	3.00	1.50	.90
6	Zach Wheat	.50	.25	.15
7	Dixie Walker	.50	.25	.15
8	Hugh Casey	.50	.25	.15
9	Dazzy Vance	.50	.25	.15
10	Duke Snider	1.00	.50	.30
11	Roy Campanella	1.50	.70	.45
12	Walter Alston	.50	.25	.15

1980 TCMA All-Time Cubs

		NM	EX	VG
Complete Set (12):		6.00	3.00	1.80
Common Player:		.50	.25	.15
1	Billy Williams	1.50	.70	.45
2	Charlie Root	.50	.25	.15
3	Ron Santo	1.50	.70	.45
4	Larry French	.50	.25	.15
5	Gabby Hartnett	.50	.25	.15
6	Emil Kush	.50	.25	.15
7	Charlie Grimm	.50	.25	.15
8	Kiki Cuyler	.50	.25	.15
9	Billy Herman	.50	.25	.15
10	Hack Wilson	1.00	.50	.30
11	Rogers Hornsby	1.00	.50	.30
12	Ernie Banks	4.00	2.00	1.25

1980 TCMA All-Time N.Y. Giants

		NM	EX	VG
Complete Set (12):		6.00	3.00	1.80
Common Player:		.50	.25	.15
1	Willie Mays	4.00	2.00	1.25
2	Wes Westrum	.50	.25	.15
3	Carl Hubbell	.50	.25	.15
4	Hoyt Wilhelm	.50	.25	.15
5	Bobby Thomson	1.00	.50	.30
6	Frankie Frisch	.50	.25	.15
7	Bill Terry	.50	.25	.15
8	Alvin Dark	.50	.25	.15
9	Mel Ott	1.00	.50	.30
10	Christy Mathewson	2.50	1.25	.70
11	Freddie Lindstrom	.50	.25	.15
12	John McGraw	.50	.25	.15

1980 TCMA All-Time Tigers

Sets printed with blue or red borders.

		NM	EX	VG
Complete Set (12):		6.00	3.00	1.80
Common Player:		.50	.25	.15
1	George Kell	.50	.25	.15
2	Billy Rogell	.50	.25	.15
3	Ty Cobb	4.00	2.00	1.25
4	Hank Greenberg	2.50	1.25	.70
5	Al Kaline	1.50	.70	.45
6	Charlie Gehringer	.75	.40	.25
7	Harry Heilmann	.50	.25	.15
8	Hal Newhouser	.50	.25	.15
9	Steve O'Neill	.50	.25	.15
10	Denny McLain	.50	.25	.15
11	Mickey Cochrane	.50	.25	.15
12	John Hiller	.50	.25	.15

1980 TCMA All-Time White Sox

		NM	EX	VG
Complete Set (12):		6.00	3.00	1.80
Common Player:		.50	.25	.15
1	Ted Lyons	.50	.25	.15
2	Eddie Collins	2.00	1.00	.60
3	Al Lopez	.75	.40	.25
4	Luke Appling	2.00	1.00	.60
5	Billy Pierce	.75	.40	.25
6	Willie Kamm	.50	.25	.15
7	Johnny Mostil	.50	.25	.15
8	Al Simmons	.75	.40	.25
9	Ray Schalk	.50	.25	.15
10	Gerry Staley	.50	.25	.15
11	Harry Hooper	.50	.25	.15
12	Eddie Robinson	.50	.25	.15

1980 TCMA All-Time Yankees

Casey Stengel

		NM	EX	VG
Complete Set (12):		16.00	8.00	4.75
Common Player:		.50	.25	.15
1	Lou Gehrig	4.00	2.00	1.25
2	Tony Lazzeri	.50	.25	.15
3	Red Rolfe	.50	.25	.15
4	Phil Rizzuto	1.00	.50	.30
5	Babe Ruth	4.00	2.00	1.25
6	Mickey Mantle	5.00	2.50	1.50
7	Joe DiMaggio	4.00	2.00	1.25
8	Bill Dickey	.75	.40	.25
9	Red Ruffing	.50	.25	.15
10	Whitey Ford	1.00	.50	.30
11	Johnny Murphy	.50	.25	.15
12	Casey Stengel	.75	.40	.25

1980 TCMA 1914 Miracle (Boston) Braves

The 1914 Boston Braves team which went from dead last in the National League in mid-July to winning the pennant by 10-1/2 games and sweeping the Philadelphia A's in the World Series is featured on this collectors' issue. In standard 2-1/2" x 3-1/2" format, the cards feature sepia photos in fancy borders. Backs have details of the person's contribution to the "Miracle," along with stats and biographical data.

		NM	EX	VG
Complete Set (32):		30.00	15.00	9.00
Common Player:		1.00	.50	.30
1	Joe Connolly	1.00	.50	.30
2	Lefty Tyler	1.00	.50	.30
3	Tom Hughes	1.00	.50	.30
4	Hank Gowdy	1.00	.50	.30
5	Gene Cochreham (Cocreham)	1.25	.60	.40
6	Larry Gilbert	1.00	.50	.30
7	George Davis	1.00	.50	.30
8	Hub Perdue	1.00	.50	.30
9	Otto Hess	1.00	.50	.30
10	Clarence Kraft	1.25	.60	.40
11	Tommy Griffith	1.00	.50	.30
12	1914 World Series	1.00	.50	.30
13	Oscar Dugey	1.00	.50	.30
14	Josh Devore	1.00	.50	.30
15	George Stallings	1.00	.50	.30
16	Rabbit Maranville	1.50	.70	.45
17	Paul Strand	1.00	.50	.30
18	Charlie Deal	1.00	.50	.30
19	Dick Rudolph	1.00	.50	.30
20	Butch Schmidt	1.00	.50	.30
21	Johnny Evers	2.00	1.00	.60
22	Dick Crutcher	1.25	.60	.40
23	Possum Whitted	1.00	.50	.30
24	Fred Mitchell	1.00	.50	.30
25	Herbie Moran	1.00	.50	.30
26	Bill James	1.00	.50	.30
27	Ted Cather	1.00	.50	.30
28	Red Smith	1.00	.50	.30
29	Les Mann	1.00	.50	.30
30	Herbie Moran, Wally Schrang (Schang)	1.00	.50	.30
31	NOT ISSUED			
32	Johnny Evers (1914 MVP)	1.00	.50	.30
33	Jim Gaffney	1.25	.60	.40

1980 TCMA 1950 Philadelphia Phillies/Whiz Kids

JACKIE MAYO

The National League Champions of 1950 are featured in this collectors issue team-set. The 2-1/2" x 3-1/2" cards have black-and-white player photo sur-

rounded by red borders. Backs are in black-and-white with player personal data, career summary and 1950 and lifetime stats.

		NM	EX	VG
Complete Set (31):		20.00	10.00	6.00
Common Player:		.60	.30	.20
1	Ken Silvestri	.50	.25	.15
2	Hank Borowy	.50	.25	.15
3	Bob Miller	.50	.25	.15
4	Jocko Thompson	.50	.25	.15
5	Curt Simmons	.50	.25	.15
6	Dick Sisler	.50	.25	.15
7	Eddie Waitkus	.50	.25	.15
8	Dick Whitman	.50	.25	.15
9	Andy Seminick	.50	.25	.15
10	Richie Ashburn	5.00	2.50	1.50
11	Bubba Church	.50	.25	.15
12	Jackie Mayo	.50	.25	.15
13	Eddie Sawyer	.50	.25	.15
14	Benny Bengough	.50	.25	.15
15	Jim Konstanty	.50	.25	.15
16	Robin Roberts	5.00	2.50	1.50
17	Del Ennis	.50	.25	.15
18	Dusty Cooke	.50	.25	.15
19	Mike Goliat	.50	.25	.15
20	Russ Meyer	.50	.25	.15
21	Granny Hamner	.50	.25	.15
22	Stan Lopata	.50	.25	.15
23	Willie Jones	.50	.25	.15
24	Stan Hollmig	.50	.25	.15
25	Jimmy Bloodworth	.50	.25	.15
26	Ken Johnson	.50	.25	.15
27	Bill Nicholson	.50	.25	.15
28	Ken Heintzelman	.50	.25	.15
29	Blix Donnelly	.50	.25	.15
30	Putsy Caballero	.50	.25	.15
31	Cy Perkins	.50	.25	.15

1980 TCMA 1957 Milwaukee Braves

CHARLIE ROOT

The World Champion Milwaukee Braves are featured in this collectors' issue. The 2-1/2" x 3-1/2" cards have blue-and-white player photos with white borders, blue typography and red graphics. Backs are in blue-and-white with a few bits of player data, career information and stats, along with a TCMA copyright line.

		NM	EX	VG
Complete Set (42):		30.00	15.00	9.00
Common Player:		.50	.25	.15
1	Don McMahon	.50	.25	.15
2	Joey Jay	.75	.40	.25
3	Phil Paine	.50	.25	.15
4	Bob Trowbridge	.50	.25	.15
5	Bob Buhl	.50	.25	.15
6	Lew Burdette	.75	.40	.25
7	Ernie Johnson	.50	.25	.15
8	Ray Crone	.50	.25	.15
9	Taylor Phillips	.50	.25	.15
10	Johnny Logan	.50	.25	.15
11	Frank Torre	.50	.25	.15
12	John DeMerit	.50	.25	.15
13	Red Murff	.50	.25	.15
14	Nippy Jones	.50	.25	.15
15	Bobby Thomson	.75	.40	.25
16	Chuck Tanner	.50	.25	.15
17	Charlie Root	.50	.25	.15
18	Juan Pizarro	.50	.25	.15
19	Hawk Taylor	.50	.25	.15
20	Mel Roach	.50	.25	.15
21	Bob Hazle	.75	.40	.25
22	Del Rice	.50	.25	.15
23	Felix Mantilla	.50	.25	.15
24	Andy Pafko	.50	.25	.15
25	Del Crandall	.75	.40	.25
26	Wes Covington	.50	.25	.15
27	Eddie Mathews	5.00	2.50	1.50
28	Joe Adcock	.75	.40	.25
29	Dick Cole	.50	.25	.15
30	Carl Sawatski	.50	.25	.15
31	Warren Spahn	5.00	2.50	1.50
32	Hank Aaron	10.00	5.00	3.00
33	Bob Keely	.50	.25	.15
34	Johnny Riddle	.50	.25	.15
35	Connie Ryan	.50	.25	.15
36	Harry Hanebrink	.50	.25	.15
37	Danny O'Connell	.50	.25	.15
38	Fred Haney	.50	.25	.15
39	Dave Jolly	.50	.25	.15
40	Red Schoendienst	3.50	1.75	1.00
41	Gene Conley	.50	.25	.15
42	Bill Bruton	.50	.25	.15

1980 TCMA 1959 L.A. Dodgers

CHUCK CHURN P

This collectors' issue features the members of the 1959 World Champion L.A. Dodgers. The 2-1/2" x 3-1/2" cards can be found printed in either black-and-white or blue-and-white on front and back. Fronts have player photos with white borders. Backs have personal data, 1959 and career stats and a few sentences about the player's performance in the championship season.

		NM	EX	VG
Complete Set (40):		40.00	20.00	12.00
Common Player:		1.00	.50	.30
1	Joe Pignatano	1.00	.50	.30
2	Carl Furillo	1.50	.70	.45
3	Bob Lillis	1.00	.50	.30
4	Chuck Essegian	1.00	.50	.30
5	Dick Gray	1.00	.50	.30
6	Rip Repulski	1.00	.50	.30
7	Jim Baxes	1.00	.50	.30
8	Frank Howard	2.50	1.25	.70
9	Solly Drake	1.00	.50	.30
10	Sandy Amoros	1.50	.70	.45
11	Norm Sherry	1.50	.70	.45
12	Tommy Davis	1.50	.70	.45
13	Jim Gilliam	1.50	.70	.45
14	Duke Snider	5.00	2.50	1.50
15	Maury Wills	2.50	1.25	.70
16	Don Demeter	1.00	.50	.30
17	Wally Moon	1.50	.70	.45
18	John Roseboro	1.50	.70	.45
19	Ron Fairly	1.50	.70	.45
20	Norm Larker	1.50	.70	.45
21	Charlie Neal	1.50	.70	.45
22	Don Zimmer	1.50	.70	.45
23	Chuck Dressen	1.00	.50	.30
24	Gil Hodges	4.00	2.00	1.25
25	Joe Becker	1.00	.50	.30
26	Walter Alston	1.50	.70	.45
27	Greg Mulleavy	1.00	.50	.30
28	Don Drysdale	4.00	2.00	1.25
29	Johnny Podres	1.50	.70	.45
30	Sandy Koufax	7.50	3.75	2.25
31	Roger Craig	1.50	.70	.45
32	Danny McDevitt	1.00	.50	.30
33	Bill Harris	1.00	.50	.30
34	Larry Sherry	1.00	.50	.30
35	Stan Williams	1.50	.70	.45
36	Clem Labine	1.50	.70	.45
37	Chuck Churn	1.00	.50	.30
38	Johnny Klippstein	1.00	.50	.30
39	Carl Erskine	1.50	.70	.45
40	Fred Kipp	1.00	.50	.30

1980 TCMA 1960 Pittsburgh Pirates

GINO CIMOLI

The World Champion 1960 Pirates are featured in this collectors issue team-set. Black-and-white player photos are bordered in gold on the fronts of the 2-1/2" x 3-1/2" cards. Backs are in black-and-white with personal data, career summary and stats for the 1960 season and career. The Cimoli error card #39 was pulled from distribution and replaced with the unnumbered corrected version.

		NM	EX	VG
Complete Set (41):		30.00	15.00	9.00
(No #39 Cimoli error.)				
Common Player:		.50	.25	.15
1	Clem Labine	.50	.25	.15
2	Bob Friend	.75	.40	.25
3	Roy Face	.75	.40	.25
4	Vern Law	.75	.40	.25

		NM	EX	VG
5	Harvey Haddix	.75	.40	.25
6	Vinegar Bend Mizell	.50	.25	.15
7	Bill Burwell	.50	.25	.15
8	Diomedes Olivo	.50	.25	.15
9	Don Gross	.50	.25	.15
10	Fred Green	.50	.25	.15
11	Jim Umbricht	.50	.25	.15
12	George Witt	.50	.25	.15
13	Tom Cheney	.50	.25	.15
14	Bennie Daniels	.50	.25	.15
15	Earl Francis	.50	.25	.15
16	Joe Gibbon	.50	.25	.15
17	Paul Giel	.50	.25	.15
18	Danny Kravitz	.50	.25	.15
19	R.C. Stevens	.50	.25	.15
20	Roman Mejias	.50	.25	.15
21	Dick Barone	.50	.25	.15
22	Sam Narron	.50	.25	.15
23	Harry Bright	.50	.25	.15
24	Mickey Vernon	.50	.25	.15
25	Bob Skinner	.60	.30	.20
26	Smoky Burgess	.60	.30	.20
27	Bill Virdon	.60	.30	.20
28	NOT ISSUED			
29	Don Hoak	.60	.30	.20
30	Bill Mazeroski	6.00	3.00	1.75
31	Dick Stuart	1.50	.70	.45
32	Dick Groat	1.50	.70	.45
33	Bob Oldis	.50	.25	.15
34	Gene Baker	.50	.25	.15
35	Joe Christopher	.50	.25	.15
36	Dick Schofield	.60	.30	.20
37	Hal Smith	.50	.25	.15
38	Rocky Nelson	.50	.25	.15
39	Gino Cimoli (Photo actually Dick Schofield.)	6.00	3.00	1.75
40	Danny Murtaugh	.50	.25	.15
41	Lenny Levy	.50	.25	.15
---	Gino Cimoli	.50	.25	.15
---	Roberto Clemente	12.00	6.00	3.50

1980 TCMA 1961 Cincinnati Reds

Virtually every member of the World Champion Cincinnati Reds team of 1961 is included in this collectors issue. Fronts of the 2-1/2" x 3-1/2" cards feature black-and-white player poses with red graphics. Backs are in black-and-white with personal data, 1961 and career stats and a short career summary.

		NM	EX	VG
Complete Set (41):		30.00	15.00	9.00
Common Player:		1.00	.50	.30
1	Eddie Kasko	1.00	.50	.30
2	Wally Post	1.00	.50	.30
3	Vada Pinson	2.50	1.25	.70
4	Frank Robinson	7.50	3.75	2.25
5	Pete Whisenant	1.00	.50	.30
6	Reggie Otero	1.00	.50	.30
7	Dick Sisler	1.00	.50	.30
8	Jim Turner	1.00	.50	.30
9	Fred Hutchinson	1.00	.50	.30
10	Gene Freese	1.00	.50	.30
11	Gordy Coleman	1.00	.50	.30
12	Don Blasingame	1.00	.50	.30
13	Gus Bell	1.00	.50	.30
14	Leo Cardenas	1.00	.50	.30
15	Elio Chacon	1.00	.50	.30
16	Dick Gernert	1.00	.50	.30
17	Jim Baumer	1.00	.50	.30
18	Willie Jones	1.00	.50	.30
19	Joe Gaines	1.00	.50	.30
20	Cliff Cook	1.00	.50	.30
21	Harry Anderson	1.00	.50	.30
22	Jerry Zimmerman	1.00	.50	.30
23	Johnny Edwards	1.00	.50	.30
24	Bob Schmidt	1.00	.50	.30
25	Darrell Johnson	1.00	.50	.30
26	Ed Bailey	1.00	.50	.30
27	Joey Jay	1.00	.50	.30
28	Jim O'Toole	1.00	.50	.30
29	Bob Purkey	1.00	.50	.30
30	Jim Brosnan	1.00	.50	.30
31	Ken Hunt	1.00	.50	.30
32	Ken Johnson	1.00	.50	.30
33	Jim Mahoney	1.00	.50	.30
34	Bill Henry	1.00	.50	.30
35	Jerry Lynch	1.00	.50	.30
36	Hal Bevan	1.00	.50	.30
37	Howie Nunn	1.00	.50	.30
38	Sherman Jones	1.00	.50	.30
39	Jay Hook	1.00	.50	.30
40	Claude Osteen	1.00	.50	.30
41	Marshall Bridges	1.00	.50	.30

1980 TCMA/Sports Nostalgia Store Babe Ruth

The same photo on the Babe Ruth card which appeared in TCMA's 1927 N.Y. Yankees set from 1979 was utilized by Sports Nostalgia as an advertising medium. On the back of the ad card is store information and an offer to redeem the card there for a free picture of Ruth. Production was 500 cards.

	NM	EX	VG
Babe Ruth	7.50	3.75	2.25

1978 Allen P. Terach Immortals of Baseball

These souvenir cards were issued as the first of what was intended to be a series honoring baseball's greatest players. No succeeding issues were forthcoming. The images on the 9" x 6-1/2" blank-back cards are printed in black-and-white and sepia. Fine print at the bottom states the card is part of an edition of 3,500. Issue price was just under $5 apiece.

		NM	EX	VG
Souvenir Card:				
1	Babe Ruth, Joe DiMaggio	9.00	4.50	2.75
2	Ty Cobb, Stan Musial	6.00	3.00	1.75

1914 Texas Tommy Type 1 (E224)

Designated as E224 in the American Card Catalog these cards measure about 2-3/8" x 3-1/2". Fronts feature sepia-toned action photos with the player's name in capital letters and his team below in parenthesis. The back carries a lengthy player biography and most cards, although not all, include year-by-year statistics at the bottom. The words "Texas Tommy" appear at the top. Texas Tommy was a candy bar brand from the Cardinet Candy Co., Oakland, Calif. The candy bar took its name from a popular dance of the era. Most examples of this set have been found in northern California. There is also a second variety of the set, smaller in size (1-7/8" x 3"), which have borderless pictures and a glossy finish. Gaps have been left in the assigned numbers on this checklist to accomodate future additions.

		NM	EX	VG
Common Player:		5,850	2,925	1,755
(1)	Jimmy Archer	5,850	2,925	1,755
(2)	Jimmy Austin	5,850	2,925	1,755
(3)	Home Run Baker	9,750	4,875	2,925
(4)	Chief Bender	9,750	4,875	2,925
(5)	Bob Bescher	5,850	2,925	1,755
(6)	Ping Bodie	5,850	2,925	1,755
(7)	Donie Bush	5,850	2,925	1,755
(8)	Bobby Byrne	5,850	2,925	1,755
(9)	Nixey Callanan (Callahan)	5,850	2,925	1,755
(10)	Howie Camnitz	5,850	2,925	1,755
(11)	Frank Chance	9,750	4,875	2,925
(12)	Hal Chase	8,450	4,225	2,535
(13)	Ty Cobb	45,500	22,750	13,000
(14)	Jack Coombs	5,850	2,925	1,755
(15)	Sam Crawford	9,750	4,875	2,925
(16)	Birdie Cree	5,850	2,925	1,755
(17)	Al Demaree	5,850	2,925	1,755
(18)	Red Dooin	5,850	2,925	1,755
(19)	Larry Doyle	5,850	2,925	1,755
(20)	Johnny Evers	9,750	4,875	2,925
(21)	Vean Gregg	5,850	2,925	1,755
(22)	Bob Harmon	5,850	2,925	1,755
(23)	Joe Jackson	58,500	29,250	17,550
(24)	Walter Johnson	19,500	9,750	5,850
(25)	Otto Knabe	5,850	2,925	1,755
(26)	Nap Lajoie	9,750	4,875	2,925
(27)	Harry Lord	5,850	2,925	1,755
(28)	Connie Mack	9,750	4,875	2,925
(29)	Armando Marsans	5,850	2,925	1,755
(30)	Christy Mathewson	9,750	4,875	2,925
(31)	George McBride	5,850	2,925	1,755
(32)	John McGraw	9,750	4,875	2,925
(33)	Stuffy McInnis	5,850	2,925	1,755
(34)	Chief Meyers	5,850	2,925	1,755
(35)	Earl Moore	5,850	2,925	1,755
(36)	Mike Mowrey	5,850	2,925	1,755
(37)	Rebel Oakes	5,850	2,925	1,755
(38)	Marty O'Toole	5,850	2,925	1,755
(39)	Eddie Plank	13,000	6,500	3,900
(41)	Bud Ryan	5,850	2,925	1,755
(42)	Tris Speaker	16,250	8,125	4,875
(43)	Jake Stahl	5,850	2,925	1,755
(44)	Oscar Strange (Stanage)	5,850	2,925	1,755
(45)	Bill Sweeney	5,850	2,925	1,755
(46)	Honus Wagner	39,000	19,500	11,700
(47)	Ed Walsh	9,750	4,875	2,925
(48)	Zach Wheat	9,750	4,875	2,925
(49)	Harry Wolter	5,850	2,925	1,755
(50)	Joe Wood	7,150	3,575	2,145
(51)	Steve Yerkes	5,850	2,925	1,755
(52)	Heinie Zimmerman	5,850	2,925	1,755

1914 Texas Tommy Type 2 (E224)

Type 2 Texas Tommy cards are smaller in size, at about 1-7/8" x 3" to 3-1/16", have a glossy front surface and are blank-backed. Their only real link to the Type 1 Texas Tommy cards is the shared front on those players who appear in both checklists.

		NM	EX	VG
Common Player:		6,000	3,000	1,800
(1)	Ping Bodie	6,000	3,000	1,800
(2)	Larry Doyle	6,000	3,000	1,800
(3)	Vean Gregg	6,000	3,000	1,800
(4)	Harry Hooper	7,800	3,900	2,340
(5)	Walter Johnson	12,000	6,000	3,600
(6)	Connie Mack	7,800	3,900	2,340
(7)	Rube Marquard	7,800	3,900	2,340
(8)	Christy Mathewson	14,400	7,200	4,320
(9)	John McGraw	7,800	3,900	2,340
(10)	Chief Meyers	6,000	3,000	1,800
(11)	Fred Snodgrass	6,000	3,000	1,800
(12)	Jake Stahl	6,000	3,000	1,800
(13)	Honus Wagner	16,200	8,100	4,860
(14)	Joe Wood	6,600	3,300	1,980
(15)	Steve Yerkes	6,000	3,000	1,800

1928 Tharp's Ice Cream

(6) BABE RUTH

SAVE THESE PICTURES

One ice cream bar will be given free for each picture of Babe Ruth.

ALSO

One gallon of Tharp's ice cream will be delivered free to the holder of a complete set of sixty different Baseball Stars, upon surrender of same to any Tharp dealer.

Sharing the same format and checklist with several other contemporary ice cream sets this 60-card set includes all of the top stars of the day. Cards are printed in black-and-white on a 1-3/8" x 2-1/2" format. There appears to have been two different types issued, but the extent of each version is unknown. The variations are found in the player's name and card number which can appear either in a strip within the frame of the photo, or printed in the border beneath the photo. Card backs have a redemption offer that includes an ice cream bar in exchange for a Babe Ruth card, or a gallon of ice cream for a complete set of 60.

		NM	EX	VG
Complete Set (60):		20,000	8,000	4,000
Common Player:		115.00	45.00	20.00
1	Burleigh Grimes	225.00	90.00	45.00
2	Walter Reuther (Ruether)	115.00	45.00	20.00
3	Joe Dugan	115.00	45.00	20.00
4	Red Faber	225.00	90.00	45.00
5	Gabby Hartnett	225.00	90.00	45.00
6a	Babe Ruth/Portrait	7,500	3,000	1,500
6b	Babe Ruth/Throwing	7,500	3,000	1,500
7	Bob Meusel	115.00	45.00	20.00
8	Herb Pennock	225.00	90.00	45.00
9	George Burns	115.00	45.00	20.00
10	Joe Sewell	225.00	90.00	45.00
11	George Uhle	115.00	45.00	20.00
12	Bob O'Farrell	115.00	45.00	20.00
13	Rogers Hornsby	350.00	140.00	70.00
14	"Pie" Traynor	225.00	90.00	45.00
15	Clarence Mitchell	115.00	45.00	20.00
16a	Eppa Jepha Rixey	225.00	90.00	45.00
16b	Eppa Rixey	225.00	90.00	45.00
17	Carl Mays	115.00	45.00	20.00
18	Adolfo Luque	125.00	50.00	25.00
19	Dave Bancroft	225.00	90.00	45.00
20	George Kelly	225.00	90.00	45.00
21	Earl (Earle) Combs	225.00	90.00	45.00
22	Harry Heilmann	225.00	90.00	45.00
23a	Ray W. Schalk	225.00	90.00	45.00
23b	Ray Schalk	225.00	90.00	45.00
24	Johnny Mostil	115.00	45.00	20.00
25	Hack Wilson	225.00	90.00	45.00
26	Lou Gehrig	2,500	1,000	500.00
27	Ty Cobb	1,500	600.00	300.00
28	Tris Speaker	350.00	140.00	70.00
29	Tony Lazzeri	225.00	90.00	45.00
30	Waite Hoyt	115.00	45.00	20.00
31	Sherwood Smith	115.00	45.00	20.00
32	Max Carey	225.00	90.00	45.00
33	Eugene Hargrave	115.00	45.00	20.00
34	Miguel L. Gonzalez (Middle initial A.)	125.00	50.00	25.00
35	Joe Judge	115.00	45.00	20.00
36	E.C. (Sam) Rice	225.00	90.00	45.00
37	Earl Sheely	115.00	45.00	20.00
38	Sam Jones	115.00	45.00	20.00
39	Bib (Bibb) A. Falk	115.00	45.00	20.00
40	Willie Kamm	115.00	45.00	20.00
41	Stanley Harris	225.00	90.00	45.00
42	John J. McGraw	225.00	90.00	45.00
43	Artie Nehf	115.00	45.00	20.00
44	Grover Alexander	700.00	280.00	140.00
45	Paul Waner	225.00	90.00	45.00
46	William H. Terry (photo actually Zeb Terry)	225.00	90.00	45.00
47	Glenn Wright	115.00	45.00	20.00
48	Earl Smith	115.00	45.00	20.00
49	Leon (Goose) Goslin	225.00	90.00	45.00
50	Frank Frisch	225.00	90.00	45.00
51	Joe Harris	115.00	45.00	20.00
52	Fred (Cy) Williams	225.00	90.00	45.00
53	Eddie Roush	225.00	90.00	45.00
54	George Sisler	225.00	90.00	45.00
55	Ed. Rommel	115.00	45.00	20.00
56	Rogers Peckinpaugh (Roger)	115.00	45.00	20.00
57	Stanley Coveleskie (Coveleski)	225.00	90.00	45.00
58	Lester Bell	115.00	45.00	20.00
59	L. Waner	225.00	90.00	45.00
60	John P. McInnis	115.00	45.00	20.00

1978 The Card Coach Milwaukee Braves Greats

JOE ADCOCK

Stars of the Milwaukee Braves from the early 1950s through the early 1960s are featured in this collectors' issue. The 2-1/2" x 3-1/2" cards have black-and-white player photos on front with the player name in the white border at bottom. Backs are also in black-and-white with personal data, career summary and stats. Cards are numbered by uniform number.

		NM	EX	VG
Complete Set (15):		10.00	5.00	3.00
Common Player:		2.00	1.00	.60
1	Del Crandall	2.00	1.00	.60
4	Red Schoendienst	2.00	1.00	.60
8	Bob Uecker	2.50	1.25	.70
9	Joe Adcock	2.00	1.00	.60
10	Bob Buhl	2.00	1.00	.60
15	Joe Torre	2.50	1.25	.70
16	Carlton Willey	2.00	1.00	.60
21	Warren Spahn	3.00	1.50	.90
22	Johnny Logan	2.00	1.00	.60
33	Lew Burdette	2.00	1.00	.60
34	Billy Bruton	2.00	1.00	.60
41	Eddie Mathews	3.00	1.50	.90
43	Wes Covington	2.00	1.00	.60
44	Hank Aaron	7.50	3.75	2.25
48	Andy Pafko (Checklist)	2.00	1.00	.60

1971 Ticketron L.A. Dodgers/S.F. Giants

Essentially large team schedule cards with promotional dates noted and an ad for the ticket service, the Ticketron Dodgers/Giants cards of 1971 are similar in format. Each has a color photo on front with facsimile autograph. The Dodgers cards are 4" x 6" with no borders on fronts; the 3-3/4" x 5-3/4" Giants cards have a white border. Backs are white with red and blue printing. The unnumbered cards are checklisted here alphabetically within team.

		NM	EX	VG
Complete Dodgers Set (20):		75.00	37.00	22.00
Complete Giants Set (10):		150.00	75.00	45.00
Common Dodger Player:		3.00	1.50	.90
Common Giant Player:		6.00	3.00	1.75
LOS ANGELES DODGERS				
(1)	Richie Allen	15.00	7.50	4.50
(2)	Walter Alston	6.00	3.00	1.75
(3)	Jim Brewer	3.00	1.50	.90
(4)	Willie Crawford	3.00	1.50	.90
(5)	Willie Davis	4.50	2.25	1.25
(6)	Steve Garvey	20.00	10.00	6.00
(7)	Bill Grabarkewitz	3.00	1.50	.90
(8)	Jim Lefebvre	3.00	1.50	.90
(9)	Pete Mikkelsen	3.00	1.50	.90
(10)	Joe Moeller	3.00	1.50	.90
(11)	Manny Mota	4.50	2.25	1.25
(12)	Claude Osteen	3.00	1.50	.90
(13)	Wes Parker	3.00	1.50	.90
(14)	Bill Russell	4.50	2.25	1.25
(15)	Duke Sims	3.00	1.50	.90
(16)	Bill Singer	3.00	1.50	.90
(17)	Bill Sudakis	3.00	1.50	.90
(18)	Don Sutton	20.00	10.00	6.00
(19)	Maury Wills	7.50	3.75	2.25
(20)	Jerry Doggett, Vin Scully	3.00	1.50	.90
SAN FRANSICO GIANTS				
(1)	Bobby Bonds	9.00	4.50	2.75
(2)	Dick Dietz	6.00	3.00	1.75
(3)	Charles Fox	6.00	3.00	1.75
(4)	Tito Fuentes	6.00	3.00	1.75
(5)	Ken Henderson	6.00	3.00	1.75
(6)	Juan Marichal	20.00	10.00	6.00
(7)	Willie Mays	60.00	30.00	18.00
(8)	Willie McCovey	25.00	12.50	7.50
(9)	Don McMahon	3.00	1.50	.90
(10)	Gaylord Perry	15.00	7.50	4.50

1972 Ticketron Phillies

The Phillies' main off-site ticket outlet produced this set of schedule cards. Fronts are in horizontal 6" x 3-7/8" format with a color player photo at center. Backs are in black-and-white and include a Phillies home schedule and sponsor advertising. Because he was traded to the Expos in mid-season, the card of Tim McCarver is scarcer than the others.

		NM	EX	VG
Complete Set (10):		95.00	47.00	28.00
Common Player:		8.00	4.00	2.50
(1)	Mike Anderson	8.00	4.00	2.50
(2)	Larry Bowa	8.00	4.00	2.50
(3)	Steve Carlton	15.00	7.50	4.50
(4)	Deron Johnson	8.00	4.00	2.50
(5)	Frank Lucchesi	8.00	4.00	2.50
(6)	Greg Luzinski	10.00	5.00	3.00
(7)	Tim McCarver	35.00	17.50	10.50
(8)	Don Money	8.00	4.00	2.50
(9)	Willie Montanez	8.00	4.00	2.50
(10)	Dick Selma	8.00	4.00	2.50

1959 Ticoa Tires Frank Malzone

This black-and-white J.D. McCarthy postcard of the former Red Sox infielder was issued in conjunction with Malzone's endorsement of the Boston area tire store chain. The card measures 3-1/4" x 5-1/2" and has a blue facsimile autograph on front. A similar promotional postcard is listed under Molinari's Restaurant.

	NM	EX	VG
Frank Malzone	25.00	12.50	7.50

1910 Tip-Top Bread Pittsburgh Pirates (D322)

The previous season's World Champion Pittsburgh Pirates are featured in this issue. The cards have an unusual - for the era - nearly square (1-13/16" x 2-3/8") format. Fronts have pastel paintings of the subjects with identification in the white border below as "World's Champions". Backs have a checklist, ad for the bakery and offer to send the complete set of cards for 50 bread labels.

		NM	EX	VG
Complete Set (25):		90,000	45,000	27,000
Common Player:		2,300	1,150	700.00
1	Barney Dreyfuss/President	3,000	1,500	900.00
2	William H. Locke/Secretary	2,300	1,150	700.00
3	Fred Clarke	7,000	3,800	2,600
4	Honus Wagner	40,000	22,000	12,000
5	Tom Leach	2,300	1,150	700.00
6	George Gibson	2,300	1,150	700.00
7	Dots Miller	2,300	1,150	700.00
8	Howie Camnitz	2,300	1,125	700.00
9	Babe Adams	2,300	1,150	700.00
10	Lefty Leifield	2,300	1,150	700.00
11	Nick Maddox	2,300	1,150	700.00
12	Deacon Philippe	2,300	1,150	700.00
13	Bobby Byrne	2,300	1,150	700.00
14	Ed Abbaticchio	2,300	1,150	700.00
15	Lefty Webb	2,300	1,150	700.00
16	Vin Campbell	2,300	1,150	700.00
17	Owen Wilson	2,300	1,150	700.00
18	Sam Leever	2,300	1,150	700.00
19	Mike Simon	2,300	1,150	700.00
20	Ham Hyatt	2,300	1,150	700.00
21	Paddy O'Connor	2,300	1,150	700.00
22	John Flynn	2,350	1,150	700.00

		NM	EX	VG
23	Kirby White	2,300	1,150	700.00
24	Tip Top Boy Mascot	3,500	1,850	1,100
25	Forbes Field	5,000	2,500	1,500

1939 Tip-Top Bread Joe DiMaggio Pin

This 1-1/4" black-and-white photo portrait pin has a white background and printed endorsement for the Ward's brand. Similar pins were issued of boxer Billy Conn and hockey star Eddie Shore.

	NM	EX	VG
Joe DiMaggio	600.00	300.00	180.00

1947 Tip Top Bread

Tip-Top is a "pennant winner" every day at every meal

Look for the stars on the TIP-TOP wrapper and the stars on the diamond.

Enriched TIP-TOP is Better Bread.

There are 163 photos of your favorite baseball players in this club group. Should you get duplicate photos (two or more of same player) trade cards until you have the complete set. Root for your home team and for TIP-TOP BREAD.

Compliments of TIP-TOP Bakers

ENOS SLAUGHTER
Outfield, St. Louis, N.L.

This 163-card set actually consists of a group of regional issues, some of which are scarcer than others. The 2-1/4" x 3" cards are borderless at top and sides, with a black-and-white player photo below which is a white strip containing the player identification. Backs carry an illustrated advertisement. The set is known for a quantity of obscure players, many of whom played during the talent-lean World War II seasons.

		NM	EX	VG
	Complete Set (163):	16,000	6,400	3,200
	Common Player:	60.00	25.00	12.50
(1)	Bill Ayers	60.00	25.00	12.50
(2)	Floyd Baker	100.00	40.00	20.00
(3)	Charles Barrett	100.00	40.00	20.00
(4)	Eddie Basinski	60.00	25.00	12.50
(5)	John Berardino	100.00	40.00	20.00
(6)	Larry Berra	500.00	200.00	100.00
(7)	Bill Bevens	100.00	40.00	20.00
(8)	Robert Blattner	60.00	25.00	12.50
(9)	Ernie Bonham	60.00	25.00	12.50
(10)	Bob Bragan	80.00	32.00	16.00
(11)	Ralph Branca	125.00	50.00	25.00
(12)	Alpha Brazle	60.00	25.00	12.50
(13)	Bobbie Brown (Bobby)	100.00	40.00	20.00
(14)	Mike Budnick	60.00	25.00	12.50
(15)	Ken Burkhart	60.00	25.00	12.50
(16)	Thomas Byrne	100.00	40.00	20.00
(17)	Earl Caldwell	100.00	40.00	20.00
(18)	"Hank" Camelli	100.00	40.00	20.00
(19)	Hugh Casey	80.00	32.00	16.00
(20)	Phil Cavarretta	100.00	40.00	20.00
(21)	Bob Chipman	100.00	40.00	20.00
(22)	Lloyd Christopher	100.00	40.00	20.00
(23)	Bill Cox	60.00	25.00	12.50
(24)	Bernard Creger	60.00	25.00	12.50
(25)	Frank Crosetti	100.00	40.00	20.00
(26)	Joffre Cross	60.00	25.00	12.50
(27)	Leon Culberson	100.00	40.00	20.00
(28)	Dick Culler	100.00	40.00	20.00
(29)	Dom DiMaggio	200.00	80.00	40.00
(30)	George Dickey	100.00	40.00	20.00
(31)	Chas. E. Diering	60.00	25.00	12.50
(32)	Joseph Dobson	100.00	40.00	20.00
(33)	Bob Doerr	260.00	105.00	52.00
(34)	Ervin Dusak	60.00	25.00	12.50
(35)	Bruce Edwards	60.00	24.00	12.00
(36)	Walter "Hoot" Evers	130.00	52.00	26.00
(37)	Clifford Fannin	60.00	25.00	12.50
(38)	"Nanny" Fernandez	100.00	40.00	20.00
(39)	Dave "Boo" Ferriss	100.00	40.00	20.00
(40)	Elbie Fletcher	60.00	25.00	12.50
(41)	Dennis Galehouse	60.00	25.00	12.50
(42)	Joe Garagiola	225.00	90.00	45.00
(43)	Sid Gordon	60.00	25.00	12.50
(44)	John Gorsica	100.00	40.00	20.00
(45)	Hal Gregg	60.00	24.00	12.00
(46)	Frank Gustine	60.00	25.00	12.50
(47)	Stanley Hack	100.00	40.00	20.00

		NM	EX	VG
(48)	Mickey Harris	100.00	40.00	20.00
(49)	Clinton Hartung	60.00	25.00	12.50
(50)	Joe Hatten	60.00	24.00	12.00
(51)	Frank Hayes	100.00	40.00	20.00
(52)	"Jeff" Heath	60.00	25.00	12.50
(53)	Tom Henrich	130.00	52.00	26.00
(54)	Gene Hermanski	60.00	24.00	12.00
(55)	Kirby Higbe	60.00	25.00	12.50
(56)	Ralph Hodgin	100.00	40.00	20.00
(57)	Tex Hughson	100.00	40.00	20.00
(58)	Fred Hutchinson	150.00	60.00	30.00
(59)	LeRoy Jarvis	60.00	25.00	12.50
(60)	"Si" Johnson	100.00	40.00	20.00
(61)	Don Johnson	100.00	40.00	20.00
(62)	Earl Johnson	80.00	32.00	16.00
(63)	John Jorgensen	60.00	24.00	12.00
(64)	Walter Judnick (Judnich)	60.00	25.00	12.50
(65)	Tony Kaufmann	60.00	25.00	12.50
(66)	George Kell	260.00	105.00	52.00
(67)	Charlie Keller	100.00	40.00	20.00
(68)	Bob Kennedy	100.00	40.00	20.00
(69)	Montia Kennedy	60.00	25.00	12.50
(70)	Ralph Kiner	140.00	56.00	28.00
(71)	Dave Koslo	60.00	25.00	12.50
(72)	Jack Kramer	60.00	25.00	12.50
(73)	Joe Kuhel	100.00	40.00	20.00
(74)	George Kurowski	60.00	25.00	12.50
(75)	Emil Kush	100.00	40.00	20.00
(76)	"Eddie" Lake	100.00	40.00	20.00
(77)	Harry Lavagetto	80.00	32.00	16.00
(78)	Bill Lee	100.00	40.00	20.00
(79)	Thornton Lee	100.00	40.00	20.00
(80)	Paul Lehner	60.00	25.00	12.50
(81)	John Lindell	100.00	40.00	20.00
(82)	Danny Litwhiler	100.00	40.00	20.00
(83)	"Mickey" Livingston	100.00	40.00	20.00
(84)	Carroll Lockman	60.00	25.00	12.50
(85)	Jack Lohrke	60.00	25.00	12.50
(86)	Ernie Lombardi	140.00	56.00	28.00
(87)	Vic Lombardi	60.00	24.00	12.00
(88)	Edmund Lopat	130.00	52.00	26.00
(89)	Harry Lowrey	100.00	40.00	20.00
(90)	Marty Marion	80.00	32.00	16.00
(91)	Willard Marshall	60.00	25.00	12.50
(92)	Phil Masi	100.00	40.00	20.00
(93)	Edward J. Mayo	100.00	40.00	20.00
(94)	Clyde McCullough	100.00	40.00	20.00
(95)	Frank Melton	100.00	40.00	20.00
(96)	Cass Michaels	100.00	40.00	20.00
(97)	Ed Miksis	100.00	40.00	20.00
(98)	Arthur Mills	100.00	40.00	20.00
(99)	Johnny Mize	140.00	56.00	28.00
(100)	Lester Moss	60.00	25.00	12.50
(101)	"Pat" Mullin	100.00	40.00	20.00
(102)	"Bob" Muncrief	60.00	25.00	12.50
(103)	George Munger	60.00	25.00	12.50
(104)	Fritz Ostermueller	60.00	25.00	12.50
(105)	James P. Outlaw	100.00	40.00	20.00
(106)	Frank "Stub" Overmire	60.00	25.00	12.50
(107)	Andy Pafko	100.00	40.00	20.00
(108)	Joe Page	100.00	40.00	20.00
(109)	Roy Partee	100.00	40.00	20.00
(110)	Johnny Pesky	100.00	40.00	20.00
(111)	Nelson Potter	60.00	25.00	12.50
(112)	Mel Queen	100.00	40.00	20.00
(113)	Marion Rackley	60.00	24.00	12.00
(114)	Al Reynolds	125.00	50.00	25.00
(115)	Del Rice	60.00	25.00	12.50
(116)	Marv Rickert	100.00	40.00	20.00
(117)	John Rigney	100.00	40.00	20.00
(118)	Phil Rizzuto	375.00	150.00	75.00
(119)	Aaron Robinson	100.00	40.00	20.00
(120)	"Preacher" Roe	80.00	32.00	16.00
(121)	Carvel Rowell	100.00	40.00	20.00
(122)	Jim Russell	60.00	25.00	12.50
(123)	Rip Russell	100.00	40.00	20.00
(124)	Connie Ryan	100.00	40.00	20.00
(125)	John Sain	100.00	40.00	20.00
(126)	Ray Sanders	100.00	40.00	20.00
(127)	Fred Sanford	60.00	25.00	12.50
(128)	Johnny Schmitz	100.00	40.00	20.00
(129)	Joe Schultz	60.00	25.00	12.50
(130)	"Rip" Sewell	60.00	25.00	12.50
(131)	Dick Sisler	60.00	25.00	12.50
(132)	"Sibby" Sisti	100.00	40.00	20.00
(133)	Enos Slaughter	130.00	52.00	26.00
(134)	"Billy" Southworth	100.00	40.00	20.00
(135)	Warren Spahn	475.00	190.00	95.00
(136)	Verne Stephens (Vern)	60.00	25.00	12.50
(137)	George Sternweiss (Stirnweiss)	100.00	40.00	20.00
(138)	Ed Stevens	60.00	24.00	12.00
(139)	Nick Strincevich	60.00	25.00	12.50
(140)	"Bobby" Sturgeon	100.00	40.00	20.00
(141)	Robt. "Bob" Swift	100.00	40.00	20.00
(142)	Geo. "Birdie" Tibbetts (Tebbetts)	100.00	40.00	20.00
(143)	"Mike" Tresh	100.00	40.00	20.00
(144)	Ken Trinkle	60.00	25.00	12.50
(145)	Paul "Diz" Trout	100.00	40.00	20.00
(146)	Virgil "Fire" Trucks	100.00	40.00	20.00
(147)	Thurman Tucker	100.00	40.00	20.00
(148)	Bill Voiselle	60.00	25.00	12.50
(149)	Hal Wagner	100.00	40.00	20.00
(150)	Honus Wagner	475.00	190.00	95.00
(151)	Eddy Waitkus	100.00	40.00	20.00
(152)	Richard "Dick" Wakefield	100.00	40.00	20.00
(153)	Jack Wallaesa	100.00	40.00	20.00
(154)	Charles Wensloff	100.00	40.00	20.00
(155)	Ted Wilks	60.00	25.00	12.50
(156)	Mickey Witek	60.00	25.00	12.50
(157)	"Jerry" Witte	60.00	25.00	12.50
(158)	Ed Wright	100.00	40.00	20.00
(159)	Taft Wright	100.00	40.00	20.00
(160)	Henry Wyse	100.00	40.00	20.00
(161)	"Rudy" York	100.00	40.00	20.00
(162)	Al Zarilla	60.00	25.00	12.50
(163)	Bill Zuber	125.00	50.00	25.00

1952 Tip Top Bread Labels

DUKE SNIDER — Brooklyn Dodgers

This unnumbered set of bread end-labels consists of 48 different labels, including two of Phil Rizzuto. The player's photo, name and team appear inside a star, with the words "Tip Top" printed above. The labels measure approximately 2-1/2" x 2-3/4". An advertising message appears in red on back. A large fold-out sheet to collect and display the labels was also issued. Each space is labeled with a player name and basic information, and is die-cut to allow the label to be slid in.

		NM	EX	VG
	Complete Set (48):	20,000	9,000	4,500
	Common Player:	400.00	180.00	100.00
	Display Sheet:	250.00	125.00	75.00
(1)	Hank Bauer	450.00	200.00	110.00
(2)	Yogi Berra	700.00	315.00	175.00
(3)	Ralph Branca	450.00	200.00	110.00
(4)	Lou Brissie	400.00	180.00	100.00
(5)	Roy Campanella	700.00	315.00	175.00
(6)	Phil Cavarreta (Cavarretta)	400.00	180.00	100.00
(7)	Murray Dickson (Murry)	400.00	180.00	100.00
(8)	Ferris Fain	400.00	180.00	100.00
(9)	Carl Furillo	450.00	200.00	110.00
(10)	Ned Garver	400.00	180.00	100.00
(11)	Sid Gordon	400.00	180.00	100.00
(12)	John Groth	400.00	180.00	100.00
(13)	Gran Hamner	400.00	180.00	100.00
(14)	Jim Hearn	400.00	180.00	100.00
(15)	Gene Hermanski	400.00	180.00	100.00
(16)	Gil Hodges	550.00	245.00	135.00
(17)	Larry Jansen	400.00	180.00	100.00
(18)	Eddie Joost	400.00	180.00	100.00
(19)	George Kell	500.00	225.00	125.00
(20)	Dutch Leonard	400.00	180.00	100.00
(21)	Whitey Lockman	400.00	180.00	100.00
(22)	Ed Lopat	450.00	200.00	110.00
(23)	Sal Maglie	400.00	180.00	100.00
(24)	Mickey Mantle	4,500	2,000	1,125
(25)	Gil McDougald	450.00	200.00	110.00
(26)	Dale Mitchell	400.00	180.00	100.00
(27)	Don Mueller	400.00	180.00	100.00
(28)	Andy Pafko	400.00	180.00	100.00
(29)	Bob Porterfield	400.00	180.00	100.00
(30)	Ken Raffensberger	400.00	180.00	100.00
(31)	Allie Reynolds	450.00	200.00	110.00
(32a)	Phil Rizutto (Rizzuto) ("NY" shows on shirt.)	600.00	275.00	150.00
(32b)	Phil Rizutto (Rizzuto) (No "NY" visible on shirt.)	600.00	275.00	150.00
(33)	Robin Roberts	550.00	245.00	135.00
(34)	Saul Rogovin	400.00	180.00	100.00
(35)	Ray Scarborough	400.00	180.00	100.00
(36)	Red Schoendienst	500.00	225.00	125.00
(37)	Dick Sisler	400.00	180.00	100.00
(38)	Enos Slaughter	500.00	225.00	125.00
(39)	Duke Snider	600.00	275.00	150.00
(40)	Warren Spahn	600.00	275.00	150.00
(41)	Vern Stephens	400.00	180.00	100.00
(42)	Earl Torgeson	400.00	180.00	100.00
(43)	Mickey Vernon	400.00	180.00	100.00
(44)	Ed Waitkus	400.00	180.00	100.00
(45)	Wes Westrum	400.00	180.00	100.00
(46)	Eddie Yost	400.00	180.00	100.00
(47)	Al Zarilla	400.00	180.00	100.00

1887 Tobin Lithographs - Color

New York

WHERE'S YOU HAVE IT! (TIM KEEFE)

The Tobin lithographs, measuring about 3" x 4-1/2", are typical of the "trade" cards that were popular advertising vehicles in the late 19th Century. Found in both black-and-white and color, the lithos include 10 cards depicting caricature action drawings of popular baseball players of the era. Each cartoon-like drawing is accompanied by a colorful caption along with the player's name in parenthesis below. The team affiliation is printed in the upper-left corner, while a large space in the upper-right corner was left blank to accomodate advertising messages. As a result, Tobin cards can be found with ads for various products and services or left blank. Similarly the backs of the cards are also found either blank or with advertising. The set takes its name from the manufacturer, whose name ("Tobin N.Y.") appears in the lower-right corner of each card.

	NM	EX	VG
Complete Set (10):	6,650	2,650	1,325
Common Player:	675.00	275.00	135.00
(1) "Go It Old Boy" (Ed Andrews)	675.00	275.00	135.00
(2) "Oh, Come Off!" (Cap Anson)	1,325	525.00	275.00
(3) "Watch Me Soak it" (Dan Brouthers)	800.00	325.00	160.00
(4) "Not Onto It" (Charlie Ferguson)	675.00	275.00	135.00
(5) "Struck By A Cyclone" (Pebbly Jack Glasscock)	675.00	275.00	135.00
(6) "An Anxious Moment" (Paul Hines)	675.00	275.00	135.00
(7) "Where'l You Have It?" (Tim Keefe)	800.00	325.00	160.00
(8) "The Flower Of The Flock" (Our Own Kelly)	1,000	400.00	200.00
(9) "A Slide For Home" (Jim M'Cormick) (McCormick)	675.00	275.00	135.00
(10) "Ain't It A Daisy?" (Smiling Mickey Welch)	800.00	325.00	160.00

1887 Tobin Lithographs - B/W

The black-and-white Tobin Lithographs were likely created to offer 19th Century advertisers a lower-cost venue than the lavishly colored version of the same cards. It appears, however, that most advertisers opted for the color type and/or that the color cards were saved more often because the black-and-white cards are today many times scarcer than their color counterparts. Despite the disparity in rarity, the black-and-whites carry only a modest premium value over the color, again probably attributable to the grander overall appearance of the colored cards.

	NM	EX	VG
Complete Set (10):	12,500	5,000	2,500
Common Player:	1,250	500.00	250.00
(1) "Go It Old Boy" (Ed Andrews)	1,250	500.00	250.00
(2) "Oh, Come Off!" (Cap Anson)	2,500	1,000	500.00
(3) "Watch Me Soak it" (Dan Brouthers)	1,500	600.00	300.00
(4) "Not Onto It" (Charlie Ferguson)	1,250	500.00	250.00
(5) "Struck By A Cyclone" (Pebbly Jack Glasscock)	1,250	500.00	250.00
(6) "An Anxious Moment" (Paul Hines)	1,250	500.00	250.00
(7) "Where'l You Have It? (Tim Keefe)	1,500	600.00	300.00
(8) "The Flower Of The Flock" (Our Own Kelly)	1,900	760.00	380.00
(9) "A Slide For Home" (Jim M'Cormick) (McCormick)	1,250	500.00	250.00
(10) "Ain't It A Daisy?" (Smiling Mickey Welch)	1,500	600.00	300.00

1948-1949 Toleteros

This was the first of three annual issues during the Puerto Rican League winter seasons. Cards are about 1-1/2" x 2-1/4", printed in sepia on thin cardboard. Backs are printed in black-and-white and have a "play" designation for use in a card game. They are numbered, but the numbers are not unique to specific players. Several of the cards were issued in photographic format, rather than printed. It is believed these are scarcer than the regular cards and may account for most of the seven cards which are not currently check-listed. They are designated here with a (P) notation. This checklist is presented alphabetically. An album

was issued with the set, and like most contemporary Caribbean issues, card are usually found in well-used condition with evidence of past mounting. Toleteros is roughly translated as "sluggers."

	NM	EX	VG
Complete Set (168):			
Value Undetermined			
Common Player:	150.00	75.00	45.00
Album:			
(1) Yuyo Acosta	150.00	75.00	45.00
(2) Hector Agosto	150.00	75.00	45.00
(3) Alberto Alberdeston	150.00	75.00	45.00
(4) Alberto Alicea	150.00	75.00	45.00
(5) Jaime Almendro	150.00	75.00	45.00
(6) Guinea Alomar	150.00	75.00	45.00
(7) Pedro Alomar	150.00	75.00	45.00
(8) Alfredo Alonso	150.00	75.00	45.00
(9) Yiyo Alonso	150.00	75.00	45.00
(10) Pablo Andino	150.00	75.00	45.00
(11) Jueyito Andrade	150.00	75.00	45.00
(12) Paday Anglero	150.00	75.00	45.00
(13) Luis Arroyo	200.00	100.00	60.00
(14) Pedro J. Arroyo	150.00	75.00	45.00
(15) Joe Atkins (P)	300.00	150.00	90.00
(16) Eugene Baker	300.00	150.00	90.00
(17) Dan Bankhead	300.00	150.00	90.00
(18) Bennett	150.00	75.00	45.00
(19) Carlos Bernier	200.00	100.00	60.00
(20) Hiram Bithorn	250.00	125.00	75.00
(21) Efrain Blasini	150.00	75.00	45.00
(22) Oswaldo Brau	150.00	75.00	45.00
(23) Johnny Britton	150.00	75.00	45.00
(24) George Brown	150.00	75.00	45.00
(25) Willard Brown	4,500	2,250	1,350
(26) Jose Burgos	150.00	75.00	45.00
(27) Tommy Butts	1,200	600.00	360.00
(28) Joe Buzas	150.00	75.00	45.00
(29) Luis R. Cabrera	150.00	75.00	45.00
(30) Marzo Cabrera	150.00	75.00	45.00
(31) Eugenio Camara	150.00	75.00	45.00
(32) Juan Carrero	150.00	75.00	45.00
(33) Medina Chapman	150.00	75.00	45.00
(34) Fernando Clara	150.00	75.00	45.00
(35) Buster Clarkson (P)	800.00	400.00	240.00
(36) Francisco Coimbre	1,000	500.00	300.00
(37) Eugene Collins	400.00	200.00	120.00
(38) Cefo Conde	150.00	75.00	45.00
(39) Johnny Cox	150.00	75.00	45.00
(40) Vitin Cruz	150.00	75.00	45.00
(41) Johnny Davis	500.00	250.00	150.00
(42) Piper Davis	500.00	250.00	150.00
(43) Felle Delgado	150.00	75.00	45.00
(44) Luke Easter	500.00	250.00	150.00
(45) Howard Easterling	600.00	300.00	180.00
(46) Saturnino Escalera	150.00	75.00	45.00
(47) Teggy Espinosa	150.00	75.00	45.00
(48) Coco Ferrer	150.00	75.00	45.00
(49) Wilmer Fields	400.00	200.00	120.00
(50) Tite Figueroa	150.00	75.00	45.00
(51) Oscar Mir Flores	150.00	75.00	45.00
(52) Jesus M. Freyre	150.00	75.00	45.00
(53) Cinque Garcia	150.00	75.00	45.00
(54) Alfonso Gerard	150.00	75.00	45.00
(55) Jim Gilliam (P)	800.00	400.00	240.00
(56) Charlie Glock	150.00	75.00	45.00
(57) Ruben Gomez	250.00	125.00	75.00
(58) David Gonzalez	150.00	75.00	45.00
(59) Gely Goyco	150.00	75.00	45.00
(60) Jack Graham	150.00	75.00	45.00
(61) Roberto Griffith	600.00	300.00	180.00
(62) Jesus Guilbe	150.00	75.00	45.00
(63) Juan Guilbe	150.00	75.00	45.00
(64) Hector Haddock	150.00	75.00	45.00
(65) Sam Hairston	200.00	100.00	60.00
(66) Van Harrington	150.00	75.00	45.00
(67) Luman Harris	150.00	75.00	45.00
(68) Manuel Hernandez	150.00	75.00	45.00
(69) Efrain Hidalgo	150.00	75.00	45.00
(70) Dixie Howell	150.00	75.00	45.00
(71) Jim Lamarque (P)	800.00	400.00	240.00
(72) Carlos Lanauze	150.00	75.00	45.00
(73) Ramon Lasa	150.00	75.00	45.00
(74) Lee Layton	150.00	75.00	45.00
(75) Liebould	150.00	75.00	45.00
(76) Royce Lint	150.00	75.00	45.00
(77) Radames Lopez	150.00	75.00	45.00
(78) Louis Louden	250.00	125.00	75.00
(79) Robert Lynn	150.00	75.00	45.00
(80) Caro Maldonado	150.00	75.00	45.00
(81) Canena Marquez	500.00	250.00	150.00
(82) Antonio Marrero	150.00	75.00	45.00
(83) Gilberto Marrero	150.00	75.00	45.00
(84) Humberto Marti	150.00	75.00	45.00
(85) Millito Martinez	150.00	75.00	45.00
(86) Jose E. Montalvo	150.00	75.00	45.00

(90) Luis Morales	150.00	75.00	45.00
(91) Willie Morales	150.00	75.00	45.00
(92) Howard Moss	150.00	75.00	45.00
(93) Chaguin Muratti	150.00	75.00	45.00
(94) Domingo Navarro	150.00	75.00	45.00
(95) Millito Navarro	200.00	100.00	60.00
(97) Alfredo Olivencia	150.00	75.00	45.00
(98) Guayubin Olivo	200.00	100.00	60.00
(99) Noel Oquendo	150.00	75.00	45.00
(100) Otoniel Ortiz	150.00	75.00	45.00
(101) Rafaelito Ortiz	150.00	75.00	45.00
(102) Alberto Padilla	150.00	75.00	45.00
(103) Fernando Diaz Pedroso	200.00	100.00	60.00
(104) Victor Pellot (Power)	250.00	125.00	75.00
(105) Pedro Pena	150.00	75.00	45.00
(106) Pepin Pereira	150.00	75.00	45.00
(107) Ismael Perez	150.00	75.00	45.00
(108) Juan Perez	150.00	75.00	45.00
(109) Palomo Perez	150.00	75.00	45.00
(110) Villodas Perez	150.00	75.00	45.00
(111) Alonso Perry	500.00	250.00	150.00
(112) Jose Polanco	150.00	75.00	45.00
(113) Bill Powell	200.00	100.00	60.00
(114) Tomas Quinones	200.00	100.00	60.00
(115) R. Cuebas Quintana	150.00	75.00	45.00
(116) Milton Ralat	150.00	75.00	45.00
(117) Otto Ralat	150.00	75.00	45.00
(118) Fernando Ramos	150.00	75.00	45.00
(119) Xavier Rescigno	150.00	75.00	45.00
(121) Miguel L. Rivera	150.00	75.00	45.00
(122) Charlie Rivero	150.00	75.00	45.00
(123) Bienvenido Rodriguez	150.00	75.00	45.00
(124) Pedro Rodriguez	150.00	75.00	45.00
(125) Anastasio Rosario	150.00	75.00	45.00
(126) Jorge Rosas	150.00	75.00	45.00
(127) Cafe Salaberrios	150.00	75.00	45.00
(128) Wilfredo Salas	150.00	75.00	45.00
(129) Juan Sanchez	150.00	75.00	45.00
(130) Carlos M. Santiago	150.00	75.00	45.00
(131) Jose G. Santiago (P)	400.00	200.00	120.00
(132) Ed Sauer	150.00	75.00	45.00
(133) George Scales	1,200	600.00	360.00
(134) Kermit Schmidt	150.00	75.00	45.00
(135) Ken Sears (P)	400.00	200.00	120.00
(136) Herbert Sewell (Souell)	250.00	125.00	75.00
(137) Dwain Sloat	150.00	75.00	45.00
(138) Eugene Smith	200.00	100.00	60.00
(139) Hilton Smith	20,000	10,000	6,000
(140) John Ford Smith	400.00	200.00	120.00
(141) Fernando Sola	150.00	75.00	45.00
(142) Ismael Solla	150.00	75.00	45.00
(143) Francisco Sostre	150.00	75.00	45.00
(144) Earl Taborn	200.00	100.00	60.00
(145) Freddie Thon	150.00	75.00	45.00
(146) Bob Thurman	400.00	200.00	120.00
(147) Griffin Tirado	150.00	75.00	45.00
(148) Leon Tirado	150.00	75.00	45.00
(149) Pedro J. Toro	150.00	75.00	45.00
(150) Bin Torres	150.00	75.00	45.00
(151) Carmelo Torres	150.00	75.00	45.00
(152) Onofre Torres	150.00	75.00	45.00
(153) Penpen Torres	150.00	75.00	45.00
(154) Quincy Trouppe	1,000	500.00	300.00
(155) Foca Valentin	150.00	75.00	45.00
(156) Roberto Vargas	150.00	75.00	45.00
(157) Tetelo Vargas	1,000	500.00	300.00
(158) Rafael Vasquez	150.00	75.00	45.00
(159) Guillermo Vega	150.00	75.00	45.00
(160) Jose L. Velazquez	150.00	75.00	45.00
(161) Laru Velazquez	150.00	75.00	45.00
(162) Vicente Villafane	150.00	75.00	45.00
(165) Luis Villodas	200.00	100.00	60.00
(166) Jesse Williams	200.00	100.00	60.00
(167) Artie Wilson	500.00	250.00	150.00
(168) Rogelio Wiscovich	150.00	75.00	45.00

1949-1950 Toleteros

The second of three annual issues during the Puerto Rican League winter seasons, these cards are similar in format to the previous year's set. Front photos are printed in black-and-white, and the backs are printed in red. Cards are about 1-1/2" x 2-1/4", printed on thin cardboard with a light gloss. Backs have a "play" designation for use in a card game and are numbered, though the numbers are not unique to specific players. This checklist is presented alphabetically. Some players can be found in two different poses. Where the variations are known, they are described parenthetically; where the poses are not known, an asterisk is shown. Players with a (P) designation were produced on photographic, rather than printed stock and are scarcer than the regular cards. An album was issued with the set, and like most contemporary Caribbean issues, cards are usually found in well-used condition with evidence of past mounting. Toleteros is roughly translated as "sluggers."

		NM	EX	VG
Complete Set (216):				
Value Undetermined				
Common Player:		100.00	50.00	30.00
Album:		600.00	300.00	180.00
(1)	Hector Agosto	100.00	50.00	30.00
(2)	Alberto Alberdeston	100.00	50.00	30.00
(3)	Alberto Alicea	100.00	50.00	30.00
(4)	Jaime Almendro (*)	100.00	50.00	30.00
(5)	Guinea Alomar	100.00	50.00	30.00
(6)	Pedro Alomar	100.00	50.00	30.00
(7)	Alfredo Alonso	100.00	50.00	30.00
(8)	Yiyo Alonso	100.00	50.00	30.00
(9)	Ismael Alvarado	100.00	50.00	30.00
(10)	Manuel Alvarez (*)	100.00	50.00	30.00
(11)	Pablo Andino	100.00	50.00	30.00
(12)	Jueyito Andrade	100.00	50.00	30.00
(13)	Paday Anglero	100.00	50.00	30.00
(14)	Luis Arroyo (*)	125.00	65.00	40.00
(15)	Pedro J. Arroyo	100.00	50.00	30.00
(16)	Eugene Baker	150.00	75.00	45.00
(17)	Dan Bankhead	150.00	75.00	45.00
(18)	Sammy Bankhead	300.00	150.00	90.00
(19)	Ramon Bayron	100.00	50.00	30.00
(20)	Carlos Bernier	125.00	65.00	40.00
(21)	Hiram Bithorn	200.00	100.00	60.00
(22)	Efrain Blasini	100.00	50.00	30.00
(23)	Anil Bonilla (*)	100.00	50.00	30.00
(24)	Stan Bread (Breard)	100.00	50.00	30.00
(25)	Chester Brewer	1,000	500.00	300.00
(26)	Johnny Britton	100.00	50.00	30.00
(27)	George Brown	100.00	50.00	30.00
(28)	Willard Brown (*)	3,600	1,800	1,075
(29)	J.A. Burgos (*)	100.00	50.00	30.00
(30)	Tommy Butts	300.00	150.00	90.00
(31)	Joe Buzas	100.00	50.00	30.00
(32)	Rafael Cabezudo	100.00	50.00	30.00
(33)	Luis R. Cabrera	100.00	50.00	30.00
(34)	Marzo Cabrera	100.00	50.00	30.00
(35)	Manolete Caceres (*)	100.00	50.00	30.00
(36)	Eugenio Camara	100.00	50.00	30.00
(37)	Maximo Casals	100.00	50.00	30.00
(38)	Rafael Casanovas	100.00	50.00	30.00
(39)	Nino Zurdo Castro	100.00	50.00	30.00
(40)	Perucho Cepeda (*)	500.00	250.00	150.00
(41)	Medina Chapman	100.00	50.00	30.00
(42)	T. Gomez Checo	100.00	50.00	30.00
(43)	Buster Clarkson	300.00	150.00	90.00
(44)	Francisco Coimbre	400.00	200.00	120.00
(45a)	Eugene Collins (Chest-up.)	200.00	100.00	60.00
(45b)	Eugene Collins (Waist-up.)	200.00	100.00	60.00
(46)	Luis Colmenero	100.00	50.00	30.00
(47)	Luis Colon	100.00	50.00	30.00
(48)	Monchile Concepcion (*)	125.00	65.00	40.00
(49)	Cefo Conde	100.00	50.00	30.00
(50)	Omar Cordero	100.00	50.00	30.00
(51)	Johnny Cox	100.00	50.00	30.00
(52)	Vitin Cruz	100.00	50.00	30.00
(53)	Johnny Davis	400.00	200.00	120.00
(54)	Lomax Davis	125.00	65.00	40.00
(55)	Piper Davis	200.00	100.00	60.00
(56)	Leon Day	12,000	6,000	3,600
(57)	Felle Delgado	100.00	50.00	30.00
(58)	Carmelo Delpin	100.00	50.00	30.00
(59)	Ruben Diaz	100.00	50.00	30.00
(60)	Lucius Easter	300.00	150.00	90.00
(61)	Howard Easterling	200.00	100.00	60.00
(62)	Saturnino Escalera	100.00	50.00	30.00
(63)	Teggy Espinosa	100.00	50.00	30.00
(64)	George Fallon	100.00	50.00	30.00
(65)	Coco Ferrer (*)	100.00	50.00	30.00
(66)	Walter Fialla (Fiala)	100.00	50.00	30.00
(67)	Wilmer Fields (*)	300.00	150.00	90.00
(68)	Tite Figueroa	100.00	50.00	30.00
(69)	Oscar Mir Flores	100.00	50.00	30.00
(70)	Jesus M. Freyre	100.00	50.00	30.00
(71)	Les Fusselmann (Fusselman)	100.00	50.00	30.00
(72)	Cinque Garcia	100.00	50.00	30.00
(73)	Alfonso Gerard	100.00	50.00	30.00
(74)	Alban Glossopp (Glossop)	100.00	50.00	30.00
(75)	Ruben Gomez (*)	150.00	75.00	45.00
(76)	Faelo Gonzalez (P)	200.00	100.00	60.00
(77)	Rafael Gonzalez	100.00	50.00	30.00
(78)	Gely Goyco	100.00	50.00	30.00
(79)	Jack Graham	100.00	50.00	30.00
(80)	Bill Greason	125.00	65.00	40.00
(81)	Felo Guilbe	100.00	50.00	30.00
(82)	Jesus Guilbe	100.00	50.00	30.00
(83)	Juan Guilbe	100.00	50.00	30.00
(84)	Hector Haddock	100.00	50.00	30.00
(85)	Sam Hairston	150.00	75.00	45.00
(86)	Luman Harris	100.00	50.00	30.00
(87a)	Vic Harris (Black background.)	1,000	500.00	300.00
(87b)	Vic Harris (Outdoors background.)	1,000	500.00	300.00
(88)	Angel Hernaiz (P)	200.00	100.00	60.00
(89)	Manuel Hernandez	100.00	50.00	30.00
(90)	Efrain Hidalgo	100.00	50.00	30.00
(91)	Dixie Howell	100.00	50.00	30.00
(92)	Roy Hughes (*)	100.00	50.00	30.00
(93)	Natalio Irizarry	100.00	50.00	30.00
(94)	Walter James	100.00	50.00	30.00
(95)	Cecyl Kayser (P)	300.00	150.00	90.00
(96)	Jack Krauss	100.00	50.00	30.00
(97)	Jim Lamarque	200.00	100.00	60.00
(98)	Carlos Lanauze	100.00	50.00	30.00
(99)	Ramon Lasa	100.00	50.00	30.00
(100)	Rafael Lastra	100.00	50.00	30.00
(101)	Lee Layton	100.00	50.00	30.00
(102)	Lettish	100.00	50.00	30.00
(103)	Johnny Logan	100.00	50.00	30.00
(104)	Radames Lopez	100.00	50.00	30.00
(105)	Louis Louden	150.00	75.00	45.00
(106)	Robert Lynn	100.00	50.00	30.00
(107)	Al Lyons	100.00	50.00	30.00
(108)	Cirico Machuca	100.00	50.00	30.00
(109)	Caro Maldonado	100.00	50.00	30.00
(110)	Clifford Mapes	100.00	50.00	30.00
(111)	Jim Markland (P)	200.00	100.00	60.00
(112)	Canena Marquez	200.00	100.00	60.00
(113)	Leo Marquez	100.00	50.00	30.00
(114)	Antonio Marrero (*)	100.00	50.00	30.00
(115)	Gilberto Marrero	100.00	50.00	30.00
(116)	Humberto Marti	100.00	50.00	30.00
(117)	Achin Matos	100.00	50.00	30.00
(118)	Booker McDaniels	150.00	75.00	45.00
(119)	George McQuillen	100.00	50.00	30.00
(120)	Agustin Medina	100.00	50.00	30.00
(121)	John Medina	100.00	50.00	30.00
(122)	Vicente Medina	100.00	50.00	30.00
(123)	Henry Miller (P)	300.00	150.00	90.00
(124)	Jose E. Montalvo	100.00	50.00	30.00
(125)	Luis A. Morales (*)	100.00	50.00	30.00
(126)	Pedroso Morales	100.00	50.00	30.00
(127)	Willie Morales	100.00	50.00	30.00
(128)	Howard Moss	100.00	50.00	30.00
(129)	Gallego Munoz	100.00	50.00	30.00
(130)	Digno Navarro	100.00	50.00	30.00
(131)	Domingo Navarro	100.00	50.00	30.00
(132)	Millito Navarro	125.00	65.00	40.00
(133)	Earl Naylor (P)	200.00	100.00	60.00
(134)	Alfredo Olivencia	100.00	50.00	30.00
(135)	Guayubin Olivo	125.00	65.00	40.00
(136)	Noel Oquendo	100.00	50.00	30.00
(137)	Otoniel Ortiz	100.00	50.00	30.00
(138)	Rafaelito Ortiz	100.00	50.00	30.00
(139)	Alberto Padilla	100.00	50.00	30.00
(140)	Miguel Payano (P)	200.00	100.00	60.00
(141)	Fernando Diaz Pedroso (*)	125.00	65.00	40.00
(142)	Victor Pellot (Power)	150.00	75.00	45.00
(143)	Pedro Pena	100.00	50.00	30.00
(144)	Pepin Pereira (*)	100.00	50.00	30.00
(145)	Ismael Perez	100.00	50.00	30.00
(146)	Juan Perez	100.00	50.00	30.00
(147)	Palomo Perez	100.00	50.00	30.00
(148)	Rogelio Perez	100.00	50.00	30.00
(149)	Villodas Perez	100.00	50.00	30.00
(150)	Alonso Perry	200.00	100.00	60.00
(151)	Russ Peters	100.00	50.00	30.00
(152)	Jose Polanco	100.00	50.00	30.00
(153)	Bill Powell	100.00	50.00	30.00
(154)	Thomas Quinones (*)	125.00	65.00	40.00
(155)	Milton Ralat	100.00	50.00	30.00
(156)	Otto Ralat	100.00	50.00	30.00
(157)	Fernando Ramos	100.00	50.00	30.00
(158)	Lionel Richards	100.00	50.00	30.00
(159)	Enrique Reinoso	100.00	50.00	30.00
(160)	Xavier Rescigno	100.00	50.00	30.00
(161)	Miguel L. Rivera	100.00	50.00	30.00
(162)	Bienvenido Rodriguez	100.00	50.00	30.00
(163)	Pedro Rodriguez	100.00	50.00	30.00
(164)	Jose M. Roque	100.00	50.00	30.00
(165)	Fachy Rosado	100.00	50.00	30.00
(166)	Jorge Rosas	100.00	50.00	30.00
(167)	Ramon Salgado (*)	100.00	50.00	30.00
(168)	Juan Sanchez	100.00	50.00	30.00
(169)	Carlos M. Santiago	100.00	50.00	30.00
(170)	Jose G. Santiago	100.00	50.00	30.00
(171)	Ed Sauer (*)	100.00	50.00	30.00
(172)	George Scales	800.00	400.00	240.00
(173)	Kermit Schmidt (*)	100.00	50.00	30.00
(174)	Ken Sears	100.00	50.00	30.00
(175)	Dick Seay	700.00	350.00	210.00
(176)	Jose Seda	100.00	50.00	30.00
(177)	Barney Serrell	200.00	100.00	60.00
(178)	McDuffie Sevilla (*)	100.00	50.00	30.00
(179)	Dwain Sloat	100.00	50.00	30.00
(180)	Eugene Smith	125.00	65.00	40.00
(181)	Hilton Smith	12,000	6,000	3,600
(182)	John Ford Smith	150.00	75.00	45.00
(183)	Jerome Snider	100.00	50.00	30.00
(184)	Ismael Solla	100.00	50.00	30.00
(185)	Francisco Sostre	100.00	50.00	30.00
(186)	Herb Souell	100.00	50.00	30.00
(187)	Luis St. Clair	100.00	50.00	30.00
(188)	Tetelo Sterling	100.00	50.00	30.00
(189)	Lonnie Summers	125.00	65.00	40.00
(190)	Jim Tabor (*)	100.00	50.00	30.00
(191)	Earl Taborn	100.00	50.00	30.00
(192)	Israel Ten (*)	100.00	50.00	30.00
(193)	Leo Thomas	100.00	50.00	30.00
(194)	Freddie Thon	100.00	50.00	30.00
(195)	Bob Thurman (*)	200.00	100.00	60.00
(196)	Griffin Tirado (*)	100.00	50.00	30.00
(197)	Leon Tirado	100.00	50.00	30.00
(198)	Bin Torres	100.00	50.00	30.00
(199)	Carmelo Torres	100.00	50.00	30.00
(200)	Indian Torres	100.00	50.00	30.00
(201)	Quincy Trouppe	700.00	350.00	210.00
(202)	Hector Trussa	100.00	50.00	30.00
(203)	Foca Valentin	100.00	50.00	30.00
(204)	Roberto Vargas	100.00	50.00	30.00
(205)	Tetelo Vargas	300.00	150.00	90.00
(206)	Rafael Vazquez	100.00	50.00	30.00
(207)	Guillermo Vega	100.00	50.00	30.00
(208)	Jose L. Velazquez	100.00	50.00	30.00
(209)	Vicente Villafane (*)	100.00	50.00	30.00
(210)	Luis Villodas	100.00	50.00	30.00
(211)	Curley Williams (P)	300.00	150.00	90.00
(212)	Marvin Williams (P)	300.00	150.00	90.00
(213)	Artie Wilson	300.00	150.00	90.00
(214)	Robert Wilson (*)	100.00	50.00	30.00
(215)	Rogelio Wiscovich	100.00	50.00	30.00
(216)	Rafael Zavala	100.00	50.00	30.00

1950-1951 Toleteros

The last of three annual issues during the Puerto Rican League winter seasons, these cards are similar in

JOSHUA GIBSON

format to the previous years' sets, with the principal difference being that the approximately 1-3/4" x 2-1/2" cards are printed in color rather than black-and-white. Most are printed on thin cardboard, but some are produced on photographic stock and believed to be scarcer than the others. Those are designated with a (P) in the checklist. Unlike the previous years' issues, backs are blank. This checklist is presented alphabetically. An album was issued with the set, and like most contemporary Caribbean issues, card are usually found in well-used condition with evidence of past mounting. Toleteros is roughly translated as "sluggers."

		NM	EX	VG
Complete Set (192): VALUE				
UNDETERMINED				
Common Player:		60.00	30.00	18.00
Album:		300.00	150.00	90.00
(1)	Hector Agosto	60.00	30.00	18.00
(2)	Robert Alexander	60.00	30.00	18.00
(3)	Alberto Alicea	60.00	30.00	18.00
(4)	Jaime Almendro (Blue Senadores.)	60.00	30.00	18.00
(5)	Jaime Almendro (Red Senadores.)	60.00	30.00	18.00
(6)	Pedro Alomar	60.00	30.00	18.00
(7)	Ismael Alvarado (Ponce)	60.00	30.00	18.00
(8)	Ismael Alvarado (Aguadilla)	60.00	30.00	18.00
(9)	Jueyito Andrade	60.00	30.00	18.00
(10)	Nick Andromidas	60.00	30.00	18.00
(11)	Pacay Anglero	60.00	30.00	18.00
(12)	Luis (Tite) Arroyo	75.00	37.50	22.50
(13)	Pedro J. Arroyo	60.00	30.00	18.00
(14)	Dan Bankhead	100.00	50.00	30.00
(15)	Babe Barna	60.00	30.00	18.00
(16)	Carlos Bernier	75.00	37.50	22.50
(17)	John Bero	60.00	30.00	18.00
(18)	Wayne Blackburn	60.00	30.00	18.00
(19)	Efrain Blasini	60.00	30.00	18.00
(20)	Bill Boyd	75.00	37.50	22.50
(21)	Stan Breard	60.00	30.00	18.00
(22)	Willard Brown	4,000	2,000	1,200
(23)	Lou Burdette (P)	125.00	65.00	35.00
(24)	Jose A. Burgos	60.00	30.00	18.00
(25)	Rafael Cabezudo	60.00	30.00	18.00
(26)	Luis R. Cabrera	60.00	30.00	18.00
(27)	Marzo Cabrera	60.00	30.00	18.00
(28)	Manolete Caceres	60.00	30.00	18.00
(29)	Rafael Casanova	60.00	30.00	18.00
(30)	Medina Chapman	60.00	30.00	18.00
(31)	Al Cihosky (P)	125.00	65.00	35.00
(32)	Mike Clark	60.00	30.00	18.00
(33)	Buster Clarkson (Santurce)	250.00	125.00	75.00
(34)	Buster Clarkson (Ponce)	250.00	125.00	75.00
(35)	Francisco Coimbre	300.00	150.00	90.00
(36)	Rafael Colmenero	60.00	30.00	18.00
(37)	Luis Colon	60.00	30.00	18.00
(38)	Monchile Concepcion	75.00	37.50	22.50
(39)	Cefo Conde	60.00	30.00	18.00
(40)	Omar Cordero	60.00	30.00	18.00
(41)	William Costa	60.00	30.00	18.00
(42)	Clinton Courtney	75.00	37.50	22.50
(43)	George Crowe	75.00	37.50	22.50
(44)	Johnny Davis (Mayaguez)	150.00	75.00	45.00
(45)	Johnny Davis (San Juan)	150.00	75.00	45.00
(46)	Piper Davis	200.00	100.00	60.00
(47)	Ellis Deal	75.00	37.50	22.50
(48)	Felle Delgado	60.00	30.00	18.00
(49)	Luke Easter	175.00	85.00	50.00
(50)	Jaime A. Escalera	60.00	30.00	18.00
(51)	Saturnino Escalera	60.00	30.00	18.00
(52)	Luis Ferbe	60.00	30.00	18.00
(53)	L.E. Fernandez	60.00	30.00	18.00
(54)	Coco Ferrer	60.00	30.00	18.00
(55)	Walter Fialla (Fiala)	60.00	30.00	18.00
(56)	Wilmer Fields	150.00	75.00	45.00
(57)	Jose A. Figueroa	75.00	37.50	22.50
(58)	Oscar Mir Flores	60.00	30.00	18.00
(59)	Jesus M. Freyre	60.00	30.00	18.00
(60)	Dominic Galata	60.00	30.00	18.00
(61)	Felipe Garcia	60.00	30.00	18.00
(62)	Alfonso Gerard	60.00	30.00	18.00
(63)	Al Gerheauser (P)	125.00	65.00	35.00
(64)	Joshua Gibson	75,000	37,500	20,000
(65)	Jim Gilliam	150.00	75.00	45.00
(66)	Ruben Gomez	75.00	37.50	22.50
(67)	Rafael Gonzalez	60.00	30.00	18.00
(68)	Felo Guilbe (Ponce)	60.00	30.00	18.00
(69)	Felo Guilbe (San Juan)	60.00	30.00	18.00
(70)	Juan Guilbe	60.00	30.00	18.00
(71)	Hector Haddock	60.00	30.00	18.00
(72)	Red Hardy (P)	125.00	60.00	35.00
(73)	Van Harrington (P)	125.00	60.00	35.00

(74)	Ray Hathaway	60.00	30.00	18.00
(75)	Ralston Hemsley	75.00	37.50	22.50
(76)	Angel Hernaiz	60.00	30.00	18.00
(77)	Rudy Hernandez	60.00	30.00	18.00
(78)	Don Hoak	100.00	50.00	30.00
(79)	Rogers Hornsby	500.00	250.00	150.00
(80)	Dixie Howell	60.00	30.00	18.00
(81)	Natalio Irizarry (P)	125.00	60.00	35.00
(82)	Walter James	60.00	30.00	18.00
(83)	Stan Karpinsky (P)	125.00	60.00	35.00
(84)	Cecyl Kayser	100.00	50.00	30.00
(85)	Carlos Lanauze	60.00	30.00	18.00
(86)	Rafael Lastra	60.00	30.00	18.00
(87)	Quique Leon	60.00	30.00	18.00
(88)	George Lerchen (P)	125.00	60.00	35.00
(89)	Lou Limmer	60.00	30.00	18.00
(90)	Royce Lint	60.00	30.00	18.00
(91)	Al Lyons	60.00	30.00	18.00
(92)	Glenn MacQuillen	60.00	30.00	18.00
(93)	Jim Markland	60.00	30.00	18.00
(94)	Luis A. Marquez	225.00	110.00	65.00
(95)	Bob Marquis	60.00	30.00	18.00
(96)	Antonio Marrero	60.00	30.00	18.00
(97)	Humberto Marti	60.00	30.00	18.00
(98)	Vicente Medina	60.00	30.00	18.00
(99)	M. Monserrate Jr.	60.00	30.00	18.00
(100)	Jose E. Montalvo (Blue Senadores.)	60.00	30.00	18.00
(101)	Jose E. Montalvo (Red Senadores.)	60.00	30.00	18.00
(102)	Luis Morales	60.00	30.00	18.00
(103)	Pedroso Morales	60.00	30.00	18.00
(104)	Willie Morales	60.00	30.00	18.00
(105)	Luis M. Munoz (Blue Senadores.)	60.00	30.00	18.00
(106)	Luis M. Munoz (Red Senadores.)	60.00	30.00	18.00
(107)	Napier	60.00	30.00	18.00
(108)	Digno Navarro	60.00	30.00	18.00
(109)	Ernest Nevel	60.00	30.00	18.00
(110)	Alfredo Olivencia	60.00	30.00	18.00
(111)	L. Rodriguez Olmo	75.00	37.50	22.50
(112)	Noel Oquendo	60.00	30.00	18.00
(113)	Otoniel Ortiz	60.00	30.00	18.00
(114)	Rafaelito Ortiz	60.00	30.00	18.00
(115)	Roy Partlow	175.00	85.00	50.00
(116)	Miguel Payano (Red Senadores.)	60.00	30.00	18.00
(117)	Miguel Payano (Mayaguez)	60.00	30.00	18.00
(118)	Fernando Pedroso	75.00	37.50	22.50
(119)	Victor Pellot (Power)	100.00	50.00	30.00
(120)	Pedro Pena	60.00	30.00	18.00
(121)	Jose Pereira	60.00	30.00	18.00
(122)	Ismael Perez	60.00	30.00	18.00
(123)	Juan Perez	60.00	30.00	18.00
(124)	Villodas Perez	60.00	30.00	18.00
(125)	Alonso Perry	225.00	110.00	65.00
(126)	Alonso Perry	225.00	110.00	65.00
(127)	Jose D. Polanco	60.00	30.00	18.00
(128)	A. Portocarrero	60.00	30.00	18.00
(129)	Bill Powell	75.00	37.50	22.50
(130)	Tomas Quinones	75.00	37.50	22.50
(131)	Milton Ralat	60.00	30.00	18.00
(132)	Fernando Ramos	60.00	30.00	18.00
(133)	Henry Rementeria	60.00	30.00	18.00
(134)	Luis Renta	60.00	30.00	18.00
(135)	Herminio Reyes	60.00	30.00	18.00
(136)	Lionel Richards	60.00	30.00	18.00
(137)	Gene Richardson	75.00	37.50	22.50
(138)	Jim Rivera	60.00	30.00	18.00
(139)	Miguel A. Rivera	60.00	30.00	18.00
(140)	Roberto Rivera	60.00	30.00	18.00
(141)	Jack Robinson	60.00	30.00	18.00
(142)	Ministro Rodriguez	60.00	30.00	18.00
(143)	Pedro Rodriguez	60.00	30.00	18.00
(144)	Jorge Rosas	60.00	30.00	18.00
(145)	Miguel Ruiz	60.00	30.00	18.00
(146)	Ramon Salgado	60.00	30.00	18.00
(147)	Juan Sanchez	60.00	30.00	18.00
(148)	Carlos M. Santiago	60.00	30.00	18.00
(149)	Jose G. Santiago	60.00	30.00	18.00
(150)	George Scales	600.00	300.00	180.00
(151)	Scarpatte	60.00	30.00	18.00
(152)	Kermit Schmidt (Ponce)	60.00	30.00	18.00
(153)	Kermit Schmidt (Red Senadores.)	60.00	30.00	18.00
(154)	Ken Sears	60.00	30.00	18.00
(155)	Dick Seay	300.00	150.00	90.00
(156)	Pedro Seda	60.00	30.00	18.00
(157)	McDuffie Sevilla	60.00	30.00	18.00
(158)	Vincent Shuppe	60.00	30.00	18.00
(159)	William Skowron	150.00	75.00	45.00
(160)	Dwain Sloat	60.00	30.00	18.00
(161)	John Ford Smith	175.00	85.00	50.00
(162)	Francisco Sostre	60.00	30.00	18.00
(163)	Jose St. Clair (Looking forward.)	60.00	30.00	18.00
(164)	Jose St. Clair (Looking left.)	60.00	30.00	18.00
(165)	Luis St. Clair	60.00	30.00	18.00
(166)	Jimmy Starks	75.00	37.50	22.50
(167)	Israel Ten	60.00	30.00	18.00
(168)	Leo Thomas	60.00	30.00	18.00
(169)	Valmy Thomas (P)	150.00	75.00	45.00
(170)	Freddie Thon	60.00	30.00	18.00
(171)	Bob Thurman	175.00	85.00	50.00
(172)	Miguel A. Tineo	60.00	30.00	18.00
(173)	Griffin Tirado (Blue background.)	60.00	30.00	18.00
(174)	Griffin Tirado (Trees in background.)	60.00	30.00	18.00
(175)	Bin Torres	60.00	30.00	18.00
(176)	Clarkson Torres	60.00	30.00	18.00
(177)	Manuel Traboux	60.00	30.00	18.00
(178)	Gilberto Valentin	60.00	30.00	18.00
(179)	Roberto Vargas	60.00	30.00	18.00
(180)	Tetelo Vargas	350.00	175.00	100.00
(181)	Rafael Vazquez	60.00	30.00	18.00
(182)	Guillermo Vega	60.00	30.00	18.00
(183)	Jose L. Velazquez	60.00	30.00	18.00
(184)	Vicente Villafane	60.00	30.00	18.00
(185)	Luis Villodas	75.00	37.50	22.50
(186)	Curley Williams (P)	150.00	75.00	45.00
(187)	Artie Wilson	225.00	110.00	65.00
(188)	Robert Wilson (P)	150.00	75.00	45.00
(189)	Jerry Witte (P)	125.00	60.00	35.00
(190)	Pete Wojey	60.00	30.00	18.00
(191)	Andres Zabala	60.00	30.00	18.00
(192)	Rafael Zavala	60.00	30.00	18.00

1950-1951 Toleteros In Action

90. Piper intenta sacar a Tetelo- SAFE

		NM	EX	VG
Complete Set (178):		6,500	3,250	2,000
Common Card:		50.00	25.00	15.00
1	Pellot fildea con elegencia. (Victor Pellot (Power))	60.00	30.00	18.00
2	Burgos conecta hit de piernas. (Jose Burgos)	50.00	25.00	15.00
3	OUT por medio paso.	50.00	25.00	15.00
4	Te gusta el mamabo, Canena? (Canena Marquez)	65.00	32.50	20.00
5	OUT!!	50.00	25.00	15.00
6	Lanauze se eleva tras la bola. (Carlos Lanauze)	50.00	25.00	15.00
7	Simpson se escurre en tercera. . .	50.00	25.00	15.00
8	Si no se la cae la bola. . .	50.00	25.00	15.00
9	Escalera realiza brillante cogida. (Saturnino Escalera)	50.00	25.00	15.00
10	Lucha Grecoromana?	50.00	25.00	15.00
11	Gallego a punto deslizarse. . . (Gallego Munoz)	50.00	25.00	15.00
12	Parece. . .pero no lo empuja. . .	50.00	25.00	15.00
13	Ramos da out a Felo en primera. (Fernando Ramos)	50.00	25.00	15.00
14	El Chiquitin y El Magnifico.	50.00	25.00	15.00
15	Limmer llege de pie tras triple. (Lou Limmer)	50.00	25.00	15.00
16	Arroyo toca a Costa. . .OUT. (Luis Arroyo)	50.00	25.00	15.00
17	Thon a salvo en tercera. (Freddie Thon)	50.00	25.00	15.00
18	Thurman hacia home Scales lo felicita. (Bob Thurman, George Scales)	65.00	32.50	20.00
19	NOT ISSUED			
20	NOT ISSUED			
21	Coca trata de escurrirse - OUT. (Coco Ferrer)	50.00	25.00	15.00
22	Thurman out a manos de Lanauze (Bob Thurman, Carlos Lanauzue)	65.00	32.50	20.00
23	Santiago felicita a Atkins (Carlos M. Santiago, Joe Atkins)	50.00	25.00	15.00
24	Griffin captura a Miller en home. (Griffin Tirado, Henry Miller)	50.00	25.00	15.00
25	"Detente Villodas": Escalera. (Luis Villodas, Saturnino Escalera)	50.00	25.00	15.00
26	Felo se desliza. . .SAFE. (Felo Guilbe)	50.00	25.00	15.00
27	Gallego llega safe a Home. (Gallego Munoz)	50.00	25.00	15.00
28	Que pena! Se cayo la bola. . .	50.00	25.00	15.00
29	Easterling esperando la bola - OUT. (Howard Easterling)	50.00	25.00	15.00
30	Pitcher McDuffie anotando. (McDuffie Sevilla)	50.00	25.00	15.00
31	El raudo Roberto se desliza - SAFE. (Roberto Vargas)	50.00	25.00	15.00
32	Harris felicita Brown tras homerun (Willard Brown)	200.00	100.00	60.00
33	Burgos intenta sacar Easter - SAFE. (Jose Burgos, Luke Easter)	65.00	32.50	20.00
34	Los Leones felicitan a Clarkson. (Buster Clarkson)	65.00	32.50	20.00
35	Otoniel realiza dificil cogida. . . (Otoniel Ortiz)	50.00	25.00	15.00
36	Thurman safe en tercera. . . (Bob Thurman)	65.00	32.50	20.00
37	Bernier safe en home. (Carlos Bernier)	50.00	25.00	15.00
38	Chifflan Clark se va de homerun. (Chiflan Clark)	50.00	25.00	15.00
39	El gran Easter llega tras homerun. (Luke Easter)	65.00	32.50	20.00
40	Se cae bola a Fields; Graham safe. (Wilmer Fields, Jack Graham)	60.00	30.00	18.00
41	Otoniel trata sacar Taborn - SAFE. (Otoniel Ortiz, Earl Taborn)	50.00	25.00	15.00
42	McQuillen se desliza tercera - SAFE. (George McQuillen)	50.00	25.00	15.00
43	Uno, dos y tres. . .Y anota Coimbre (Francisco Coimbre)	90.00	45.00	27.50
44	Carlos Manuel llega trade. . .OUT. (Carlos M. Santiago)	50.00	25.00	15.00
45	Aprieta el paso, Griffin. . . (Griffin Tirado)	50.00	25.00	15.00
46	Pepe Lucas saca out a Resbaloso. (Pepe Lucas)	50.00	25.00	15.00
47	"No hay quien pase", dice Howell (Dixie Howell)	50.00	25.00	15.00
48	Y que dice el Umpiere?	50.00	25.00	15.00
49	Pedroso intenta robo home - OUT. (Fernando Pedroso)	50.00	25.00	15.00
50	Se formo el nudo. . .	50.00	25.00	15.00
51	Cogelo con calma, Leo. . . (Leo Thomas)	50.00	25.00	15.00
52	Tetelo galopando hacia primera. . . (Tetelo Vargas)	90.00	45.00	27.50
53	Haciendose burla?	50.00	25.00	15.00
54	Los tiburones felicitan. . .	50.00	25.00	15.00
55	La No. 29 de Bernier. (Carlos Bernier)	50.00	25.00	15.00
56	Jockey entra facilmente a primera.	50.00	25.00	15.00
57	Buzas felicita a Collins. (Joe Buzas, Eugene Collins)	50.00	25.00	15.00
58	Ya es tarde, Jose Enrique. . .	50.00	25.00	15.00
59	Lomax Davis entra tras homerun (Lomax Davis)	50.00	25.00	15.00
60	Haddock no puede sacar Villafane. (Hector Haddock)	50.00	25.00	15.00
61	Otoniel Ortiz se va de hom,erun. . . (Otoniel Ortiz)	50.00	25.00	15.00
62	Otra mas para Bernier (Carlos Bernier)	50.00	25.00	15.00
63	Montalvo se desliza en tercera (?) (Jose E. Montalvo)	50.00	25.00	15.00
64	Willie es todo ojos. . . (Willie Morales)	50.00	25.00	15.00
65	La Mucura esta llegando. . . (Johnny Davis)	60.00	30.00	18.00
66	Chapman da out espectacular. (Medina Chapman)	50.00	25.00	15.00
67	McQuilen pisa plato tras homerun (George McQuillen)	50.00	25.00	15.00
68	"Coimbre, Safe". . .dice el Umpire. (Francisco Coimbre)	90.00	45.00	27.50
69	Llega Perry despues de Homerun. . . (Alonso Perry)	65.00	32.50	20.00
70	Griffin, ya es tuyo. . . (Griffin Tirado)	50.00	25.00	15.00
71	Fields pisa plato tras Homerun. . . (Wilmer Fields)	50.00	25.00	15.00
72	EL HOMBRE ESE. . . (Willard Brown)	200.00	100.00	60.00
73	Jockey se desliza violentamente.	50.00	25.00	15.00
74	Montalvo esperando a Tite - OUT. (Jose E. Montalvo)	50.00	25.00	15.00
75	Perry anota transqueando. . . (Alonso Perry)	65.00	32.50	20.00
76	Fields pivotea para double-play. (Wilmer Fields)	60.00	30.00	18.00
77	Andando en la cuerda, Piper? (Piper Davis)	65.00	32.50	20.00
78	Montalvo en pie de combate. . . (Jose E. Montalvo)	50.00	25.00	15.00
79	EN GRAN EXPECTATIVA. . .	50.00	25.00	15.00
80	Indios reciben Gachito tras homer	50.00	25.00	15.00
81	Butts esquiva la bola - SAFE. (Pee Wee Butts)	50.00	25.00	15.00
82	Otro para el Gaucho Davis. . . (Johnny Davis)	60.00	30.00	18.00
83	Los leones se alborotan. . . (Piper Davis)	60.00	30.00	18.00
84	Lanauze safe en home. . . (Carlos Lanauze)	50.00	25.00	15.00
85	Lanauze se alarga - OUT. (Carlos Lanauze)	50.00	25.00	15.00
86	Thurman llega tras homerun. (Bob Thurman)	65.00	32.50	20.00
87	Sauer anota home espectacularmente (Ed Sauer)	50.00	25.00	15.00
88	PERRY SE ESTIRA. . .OUT. (Alonso Perry)	65.00	32.50	20.00
89	Clarkson conecta otro homerun. (Buster Clarkson)	65.00	32.50	20.00
90	Piper intenta sacar a Tetelo - SAFE (Tetelo Vargas, Piper Davis)	90.00	45.00	27.50
91	QUE QUE USTED DICE. . .?	50.00	25.00	15.00
92	Bernier se roba el home. . . (Carlos Bernier)	50.00	25.00	15.00
93	UNA ESCENA DE RUTINA. . . (Willard Brown)	200.00	100.00	60.00
94	Taborn trata de esquvarse - OUT. (Earl Taborn)	50.00	25.00	15.00
95	Pita Marti safe en tercera. (Humberto Marti)	50.00	25.00	15.00
96	PIE CONTRA PIE. . .(?)	50.00	25.00	15.00
97	NO QUIERE NI VERLO. . .	50.00	25.00	15.00
98	SUDOR Y ARENA. . .	50.00	25.00	15.00
99	Jueyito safe en primera. (Jueyito Andrade)	50.00	25.00	15.00
100	QUIÉN LLEGO PRIMERO?	50.00	25.00	15.00
101	LLEGO TARDE EL TIRO..SAFE.	50.00	25.00	15.00
102	Escalera se estira. . .pero es SAFE. (Saturnino Escalera)	50.00	25.00	15.00

103	Howell aspera. . .Almendro observa. (Dixie Howell)	50.00	25.00	15.00
104	A todo vapor hacia tercera. .	50.00	25.00	15.00
105	Buena cogida, pero es SAFE.	50.00	25.00	15.00
106	El arbitro observa. . .SAFE.	50.00	25.00	15.00
107	SAFE EN HOME.	50.00	25.00	15.00
108	Regreso a tiempo. . .SAFE.	50.00	25.00	15.00
109	Canena es felicitados tras Homer. (Canena Marquez)	65.00	32.50	20.00
110	"COC SAFE", canta el umpiere. (Coco Ferrer)	50.00	25.00	15.00
111	Taft Wright jonronen. . . (Taft Wright)	50.00	25.00	15.00
112	Esta solo. . .pero siempre gana.	50.00	25.00	15.00
113	????????, CANTE!	50.00	25.00	15.00
114	Casanovas quieto en tercera. . . (Rafael Casanovas)	50.00	25.00	15.00
115	Wilson espera pero no llega. . .SAFE. (Artie Wilson)	65.00	32.50	20.00
116	FELLE FELICITA MONTALVO (Felle Delgado, Jose E. Montalvo)	50.00	25.00	15.00
117	El tigre tambien se desliza. . .Safe.	50.00	25.00	15.00
118	Limmer se adelanta. . .Montalvo out. (Lou Limmer, Jose E. Montalvo)	50.00	25.00	15.00
119	TIRO MALO. . .BUTTS SAFE. (Pee Wee Butts)	50.00	25.00	15.00
120	SAFE EN TERCERA.	50.00	25.00	15.00
121	EL JIBARO CONECTA HIT. . .	50.00	25.00	15.00
122	Chapman no puede alcanzarla. . . (Medina Chapman)	50.00	25.00	15.00
123	Guinea Alomar da OUT en Home. (Guinea Alomar)	50.00	25.00	15.00
124	INDIO ANOTA EN SLIDE. . .	50.00	25.00	15.00
125	Miller saca a Serrel en primera. (Henry Miller, Barney Serrell)	50.00	25.00	15.00
126	El gran COIMBRE llega SAFE. (Francisco Coimbre)	90.00	45.00	27.50
127	El arbitro tome impulsa. . .OUT!	50.00	25.00	15.00
128	TROUPPE DA OUT EN HOME. (Quincy Trouppe)	90.00	45.00	27.50
129	BANKHEAD OUT EN PRIMERA. (Bankhead)	60.00	30.00	18.00
130	Tiene que pensarlo bien. . .	50.00	25.00	15.00
131	Escalera a salvo en tercera. . . (Saturnino Escalera)	50.00	25.00	15.00
132	DOS MANOS QUE BUSCAN.	50.00	25.00	15.00
133	FIGUEROA SE DESLIZA - SAFE (Tite Figueroa)	50.00	25.00	15.00
134	VIENE LA BOLA. . .OUT.	50.00	25.00	15.00
135	Esperando el tiro. . .OUT.	50.00	25.00	15.00
136	KAYSER SAFE EN PRIMERA. (Cecyl Kayser)	50.00	25.00	15.00
137	COCO FERRER DA OUT. . . (Coco Ferrer)	50.00	25.00	15.00
138	Lo atajaron a tiempo. . .OUT.	50.00	25.00	15.00
139	Limmer da su primer homer. (Lou Limmer)	50.00	25.00	15.00
140	Starks y Blasini alegan. . . (Jimmy Starks, Efrain Blasini)	50.00	25.00	15.00
141	BARNA SE VA DE HOMERUN. (Babe Barna)	50.00	25.00	15.00
142	"La antesala del gran choque. . . (George Scales)	60.00	30.00	18.00
143	"QUIETO". DICE EL UMPIRE.	50.00	25.00	15.00
144	LO SACARON POR UN PELO.	50.00	25.00	15.00
145	Un recibimiento poco agradable.	50.00	25.00	15.00
146	Montalvo se desliza. . .OUT. (Jose E. Montalvo)	50.00	25.00	15.00
147	ALOMAR OUT EN HOME. . . (Alomar)	50.00	25.00	15.00
148	EASTER SAFE EN HOME. . . (Luke Easter)	65.00	32.50	20.00
149	Grillo se anota hit de piernas. . .	50.00	25.00	15.00
150	BARNA SAFE EN TERCERA. (Babe Barna)	50.00	25.00	15.00
151	Esta en la base pero es OUT.	50.00	25.00	15.00
152	TYBOR DA OUT A TABORN. (Jim Tabor, Earl Taborn)	50.00	25.00	15.00
153	BUTTS OUT EN PRIMERA. (Pee Wee Butts)	50.00	25.00	15.00
154	Viene la bola. . .Hernaiz SAFE. (Angel Hernaiz)	50.00	25.00	15.00
155	VILLODAS LO ESPERA. . .OUT. (Luis Villodas)	50.00	25.00	15.00
156	TYBOR SACA A COCA FERRER. (Jim Tabor, Coco Ferrer)	50.00	25.00	15.00
157	LO FUSILAN EN TERCERA.	50.00	25.00	15.00
158	BLOQUEADO. . .	50.00	25.00	15.00
159	"Estoy firme en base", dice Coco. (Coco Ferrer)	50.00	25.00	15.00
160	Ruben Gomez se tira slide. . .SAFE. (Ruben Gomez)	50.00	25.00	15.00
161	HOWELL OUT EN PRIMERA. (Dixie Howell)	50.00	25.00	15.00
162	SAFE EN HOME.	50.00	25.00	15.00
163	PERRY ES ESCURRE. . .SAFE. (Alonso Perry)	65.00	32.50	20.00
164	PEDROSO SE LESIONA. (Fernando Pedroso)	50.00	25.00	15.00
165	LA APOTEOSIS DEL TRIUNFO.	50.00	25.00	15.00
166	Ruben jonroneo ganar su juego. (Ruben Gomez)	50.00	25.00	15.00
167	Primer homerun CANENA 1950-51. (Canena Marquez)	65.00	32.50	20.00
168	GOLPE DE IZQUIRDA? SAFE.	50.00	25.00	15.00

169	PELLOT OUT EN HOME. (Victor Pellot) (Power)	65.00	32.50	20.00
170	Muchos ojos tras Scales y Mullens. (George Scales)	60.00	30.00	18.00
171	Nube de polvo en el Castillo.	50.00	25.00	15.00
172	Bero participa carnaval jonrones. (John Bero)	50.00	25.00	15.00
173	Lanauze completa out a Butts. (Carlos Lanauze, Pee Wee Butts)	50.00	25.00	15.00
174	SE LE ESCAPO LA PILDORA.	50.00	25.00	15.00
175	EL UMPIRE DECIDIRA. . .	50.00	25.00	15.00
176	Llego tarde el HOMBRE ESE. (Willard Brown)	200.00	100.00	60.00
177	THON SE DESLIZA. . .SAFE. (Freddie Thon)	50.00	25.00	15.00
178	AL REVES, PERO SAFE. . .	50.00	25.00	15.00
179	Hughes no puede sacar al corredor. (Roy Hughes)	50.00	25.00	15.00
180	"Chiflan Safe". . .dice el Umpiere. (Chiflan Clark)	50.00	25.00	15.00

1909-11 Tolstoi Cigarettes

 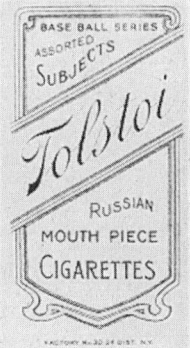

PREMIUMS:
Commons: 1.5-2X
Hall of Famers: 1-2X
(See T206 for checklist and base values.)

1887 Tomlinson Studios Cabinets

The extent to which this Detroit photographer promulgated individual player cabinet cards of the 1887 Wolverines is unknown. However, since the portrait on the known Bennett card is the same as that found on a team-composite cabinet card, it is not unreasonable to expect that each of the other 13 players pictured on the team card may have been issued individually. The cabinet is in the typical 4-1/4" x 6-1/2" format, with blank back.

	NM	EX	VG
C.W. Bennett	5,000	2,500	1,500
Jimmy Manning	5,000	2,500	1,500

1909 Topping & Co. Detroit Tigers Postcards

This set of postcards features the members of the 1909 American League Champion Detroit Tigers. About 3-1/2" x 5-1/2" in size, vertically formatted fronts have black-and-white player portraits at center within a yellow six-pointed star. "Tiger Stars" appears in script in a yellow stripe at top, while the player name and position are in a similar strip at bottom. Black trim surrounds the design elements. Backs are black-and-white with standard postcard markings and a credit line for Topping and Publishers Co., Detroit. The unnumbered cards are listed here alphabetically.

		NM	EX	VG
Complete Set (21):		12,000	6,000	3,500
Common Player:		400.00	200.00	120.00
(1)	Henry Beckendorf	400.00	200.00	120.00
(2)	Donie Bush	400.00	200.00	120.00
(3)	Ty Cobb	3,500	1,750	1,000
(4)	Sam Crawford	1,000	500.00	300.00
(5)	Jim Delehanty	400.00	200.00	120.00
(6)	Bill Donovan	400.00	200.00	120.00
(7)	Hughie Jennings	400.00	200.00	120.00
(8)	Davy Jones	400.00	200.00	120.00
(9)	Tom Jones	400.00	200.00	120.00
(10)	Ed Killian	400.00	200.00	120.00
(11)	Matty McIntyre	400.00	200.00	120.00
(12)	George Moriarty	400.00	200.00	120.00
(13)	George Mullin	400.00	200.00	120.00
(14)	Charley O'Leary	400.00	200.00	120.00
(15)	Germany Schaefer	400.00	200.00	120.00
(16)	Charlie Schmidt	400.00	200.00	120.00
(17)	George Speer	400.00	200.00	120.00
(18)	Oscar Stanage	400.00	200.00	120.00
(19)	Eddie Summers	400.00	200.00	120.00
(20)	Ed Willett	400.00	200.00	120.00
(21)	Ralph Works	400.00	200.00	120.00

1948 Topps Magic Photos

 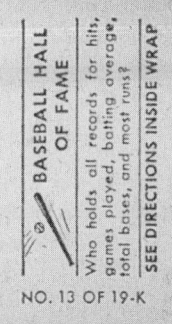

The first Topps baseball cards appeared as a subset of 19 cards from an issue of 252 "Magic Photos." The set takes its name from the self-developing nature of the cards. The cards were blank on the front when first taken from the wrapper. By spitting on the wrapper and holding it to the card while exposing it to light the black-and-white photo appeared. Measuring 7/8" x 1-1/2", the cards are very similar to Topps 1955 and 1956 "Hocus Focus" issues.

		NM	EX	VG
Complete Set (19):		2,400	1,200	725.00
Common Card:		60.00	30.00	18.00
1	Lou Boudreau	75.00	37.50	22.50
2	Cleveland Indians	60.00	30.00	18.00
3	Bob Eliott	75.00	37.50	22.50
4	Cleveland Indians 4-3	60.00	30.00	18.00
5	Cleveland Indians 4-1	60.00	30.00	18.00
6	Babe Ruth	450.00	225.00	135.00
7	Tris Speaker	90.00	45.00	27.50
8	Rogers Hornsby	90.00	45.00	27.50
9	Connie Mack	75.00	37.50	22.50
10	Christy Mathewson	150.00	75.00	45.00
11	Hans Wagner	100.00	50.00	30.00
12	Grover Alexander	90.00	45.00	27.50
13	Ty Cobb	275.00	135.00	80.00
14	Lou Gehrig	275.00	135.00	80.00
15	Walter Johnson	125.00	65.00	35.00
16	Cy Young	125.00	65.00	35.00
17	George Sisler	75.00	37.50	22.50
18	Tinker and Evers	125.00	65.00	35.00
19	Third Base Cleveland Indians	75.00	37.50	22.50

1951 Topps Red Backs

Like the Blue Backs, the Topps Red Backs which were sold at the same time came two to a package for 1¢. Their black-and-white photographs appear on a red, white, blue and yellow background. The back printing is red on white. Their 2" x 2-5/8" size is the same as Blue Backs. Also identical is the set size (52 cards) and the game situations to be found on the fronts of the cards, for use in playing a card game of baseball. Red Backs are more common than the Blue Backs by virtue of a 1980s discovery of a large hoard of unopened boxes. Red Backs are also known to have been sold in a plastic-bagged set along with a foldout paper game board for 29 cents.

		NM	EX	VG
Complete Set (52):		900.00	450.00	275.00
Common Player:		12.00	6.00	3.50
Wax Pack (2):		75.00		
1	Larry (Yogi) Berra	75.00	37.50	22.00
2	Sid Gordon	12.00	6.00	3.50
3	Ferris Fain	12.00	6.00	3.50
4	Verne Stephens	12.00	6.00	3.50
5	Phil Rizzuto	40.00	20.00	12.00
6	Allie Reynolds	20.00	10.00	6.00
7	Howie Pollet	12.00	6.00	3.50
8	Early Wynn	25.00	12.50	7.50
9	Roy Sievers	12.00	6.00	3.50
10	Mel Parnell	12.00	6.00	3.50
11	Gene Hermanski	12.00	6.00	3.50
12	Jim Hegan	12.00	6.00	3.50
13	Dale Mitchell	12.00	6.00	3.50
14	Wayne Terwilliger	12.00	6.00	3.50
15	Ralph Kiner	25.00	12.50	7.50
16	Preacher Roe	20.00	10.00	6.00
17	Dave Bell	12.00	6.00	3.50
18	Gerry Coleman	15.00	7.50	4.50
19	Dick Kokos	12.00	6.00	3.50
20	Dominick DiMaggio	20.00	10.00	6.00
21	Larry Jansen	12.00	6.00	3.50
22	Bob Feller	45.00	22.50	13.50
23	Ray Boone	12.00	6.00	3.50
24	Hank Bauer	15.00	7.50	4.50
25	Cliff Chambers	12.00	6.00	3.50
26	Luke Easter	15.00	7.50	4.50
27	Wally Westlake	12.00	6.00	3.50
28	Elmer Valo	12.00	6.00	3.50
29	Bob Kennedy	12.00	6.00	3.50
30	Warren Spahn	45.00	22.00	13.50
31	Gil Hodges	35.00	17.50	10.50
32	Henry Thompson	12.00	6.00	3.50
33	William Werle	12.00	6.00	3.50
34	Grady Hatton	12.00	6.00	3.50
35	Al Rosen	15.00	7.50	4.50
36a	Gus Zernial (Chicago in bio.)	50.00	25.00	15.00
36b	Gus Zernial (Philadelphia in bio.)	22.50	11.00	6.75
37	Wes Westrum	12.00	6.00	3.50
38	Ed (Duke) Snider	50.00	25.00	15.00
39	Ted Kluszewski	20.00	10.00	6.00
40	Mike Garcia	12.00	6.00	3.50
41	Whitey Lockman	12.00	6.00	3.50
42	Ray Scarborough	12.00	6.00	3.50
43	Maurice McDermott	12.00	6.00	3.50
44	Sid Hudson	12.00	6.00	3.50
45	Andy Seminick	12.00	6.00	3.50
46	Billy Goodman	12.00	6.00	3.50
47	Tommy Glaviano	12.00	6.00	3.50
48	Eddie Stanky	12.00	6.00	3.50
49	Al Zarilla	12.00	6.00	3.50
50	Monte Irvin	25.00	12.50	7.50
51	Eddie Robinson	12.00	6.00	3.50
52a	Tommy Holmes (Boston in bio.)	50.00	25.00	15.00
52b	Tommy Holmes (Hartford in bio.)	22.50	11.00	6.75

1951 Topps Blue Backs

Sold two cards in a package with a piece of candy for 1¢, the Topps Blue Backs are considerably scarcer than their Red Back counterparts. The 2" x 2-5/8" cards carry a black-and-white player photograph on a red, white, yellow and green background along with the player's name and other information including their 1950 record on the front. The back is printed

in blue on a white background. The 52-card set has varied baseball situations on them, making the playing of a rather elementary game of baseball possible. Although scarce, Blue Backs were printed on thick cardboard and have survived quite well over the years. There are, however, few stars in the set.

		NM	EX	VG
Complete Set (52):		1,900	950.00	575.00
Common Player:		25.00	12.50	7.50
Wax Pack (2):		175.00		
1	Eddie Yost	35.00	12.50	7.50
2	Henry (Hank) Majeski	25.00	12.50	7.50
3	Richie Ashburn	225.00	110.00	65.00
4	Del Ennis	25.00	12.50	7.50
5	Johnny Pesky	25.00	12.50	7.50
6	Albert (Red) Schoendienst	125.00	65.00	35.00
7	Gerald Staley	25.00	12.50	7.50
8	Dick Sisler	25.00	12.50	7.50
9	Johnny Sain	35.00	17.50	10.00
10	Joe Page	25.00	12.50	7.50
11	Johnny Groth	25.00	12.50	7.50
12	Sam Jethroe	25.00	12.50	7.50
13	James (Mickey) Vernon	25.00	12.50	7.50
14	George Munger	25.00	12.50	7.50
15	Eddie Joost	25.00	12.50	7.50
16	Murry Dickson	25.00	12.50	7.50
17	Roy Smalley	25.00	12.50	7.50
18	Ned Garver	25.00	12.50	7.50
19	Phil Masi	25.00	12.50	7.50
20	Ralph Branca	35.00	17.50	10.00
21	Billy Johnson	25.00	12.50	7.50
22	Bob Kuzava	25.00	12.50	7.50
23	Paul (Dizzy) Trout	25.00	12.50	7.50
24	Sherman Lollar	25.00	12.50	7.50
25	Sam Mele	25.00	12.50	7.50
26	Chico Carrasquel	25.00	12.50	7.50
27	Andy Pafko	25.00	12.50	7.50
28	Harry (The Cat) Brecheen	25.00	12.50	7.50
29	Granville Hamner	25.00	12.50	7.50
30	Enos (Country) Slaughter	125.00	65.00	35.00
31	Lou Brissie	25.00	12.50	7.50
32	Bob Elliott	25.00	12.50	7.50
33	Don Lenhardt	25.00	12.50	7.50
34	Earl Torgeson	25.00	12.50	7.50
35	Tommy Byrne	25.00	12.50	7.50
36	Cliff Fannin	25.00	12.50	7.50
37	Bobby Doerr	125.00	65.00	35.00
38	Irv Noren	25.00	12.50	7.50
39	Ed Lopat	35.00	17.50	10.00
40	Vic Wertz	25.00	12.50	7.50
41	Johnny Schmitz	25.00	12.50	7.50
42	Bruce Edwards	25.00	12.50	7.50
43	Willie (Puddin' Head) Jones	25.00	12.50	7.50
44	Johnny Wyrostek	25.00	12.50	7.50
45	Bill Pierce	25.00	12.50	7.50
46	Gerry Priddy	25.00	12.50	7.50
47	Herman Wehmeier	25.00	12.50	7.50
48	Billy Cox	25.00	12.50	7.50
49	Henry (Hank) Sauer	25.00	12.50	7.50
50	Johnny Mize	125.00	62.00	37.00
51	Eddie Waitkus	25.00	12.50	7.50
52	Sam Chapman	25.00	12.50	7.50

1951 Topps Connie Mack's All-Stars

A set of die-cut, 2-1/16" x 5-1/4" cards, all 11 players are Hall of Famers. The cards feature a black-and-white action player photograph printed on a red background with a colored name plaque underneath. Like the "Current All-Stars," with which they were issued, the background could be folded, making it possible for the card to stand up. This practice, however, resulted in the card's mutilation and lowers its condition in the eyes of today's collectors. Connie Mack All-Stars are scarce today and, despite being relatively expensive, retain a certain popularity as one of Topps first issues.

		NM	EX	VG
Complete Set (11):		16,000	8,000	4,750
Common Player:		525.00	260.00	155.00
(1)	Grover Cleveland Alexander	900.00	450.00	275.00
(2)	Gordon Stanley Cochrane	600.00	300.00	180.00
(3)	Edward Trowbridge Collins	600.00	300.00	180.00
(4)	James J. Collins	600.00	300.00	180.00
(5)	Lou Gehrig	4,500	2,250	1,350
(6)	Walter Johnson	1,000	500.00	300.00
(7)	Connie Mack	600.00	300.00	180.00
(8)	Christopher Mathewson	1,125	560.00	335.00
(9)	George Herman Ruth	5,500	2,750	1,650
(10)	Tris Speaker	600.00	300.00	180.00
(11)	Honus Wagner	1,250	625.00	375.00

1951 Topps Major League All-Stars

The Topps Major League All-Stars are very similar to the Connie Mack All-Stars of the same year. The 2-1/16" x 5-1/4" cards have a black-and-white photograph on a red die-cut background. Most of the background could be folded over so that the card would stand up. A plaque at the base carries brief biographical information. The set was to contain 11 cards, but only eight were actually issued in gum packs. Those of Konstanty, Roberts and Stanky were not issued and are very rare, with only a handful of each known. A big problem with the set is that if the card was used as it was intended it was folded and, thus, damaged from a collector's viewpoint. That makes top quality examples of any players difficult to find and quite expensive.

		NM	EX	VG
Complete Set (8):		14,000	7,000	4,200
Common Player:		1,025	510.00	305.00
(1)	Yogi Berra	3,000	1,500	900.00
(2)	Larry Doby	1,900	950.00	575.00
(3)	Walt Dropo	900.00	450.00	270.00
(4)	"Hoot" Evers	900.00	450.00	270.00
(5)	George Clyde Kell	1,600	800.00	480.00
(6)	Ralph Kiner	1,600	800.00	480.00
(7)	Jim Konstanty	30,000	15,000	9,000
(8)	Bob Lemon	1,600	800.00	480.00
(9)	Phil Rizzuto	2,750	1,375	825.00
(10)	Robin Roberts	35,000	17,500	10,500
(11)	Ed Stanky	30,000	15,000	9,000

1951 Topps Teams

An innovative issue for 1951, the Topps team cards were a nine-card set, 5-1/4" x 2-1/16", which carry a black-and-white picture of a major league team surrounded by a yellow border on the front. The back identifies team members with red printing on white cardboard. There are two versions of each card, with and without the date "1950" in the banner that carries the team name. Undated versions are valued slightly higher than the cards with dates. Strangely only nine teams were issued. Scarcity varies, with the Cardinals and Red Sox being the most difficult to obtain.

		NM	EX	VG
(1a)	Boston Red Sox/1950	475.00	235.00	140.00
(1b)	Boston Red Sox (Undated)	500.00	250.00	150.00
(2a)	Brooklyn Dodgers/1950	375.00	185.00	110.00
(2b)	Brooklyn Dodgers (Undated)	400.00	200.00	120.00
(3a)	Chicago White Sox/1950	275.00	135.00	80.00
(3b)	Chicago White Sox (Undated)	250.00	125.00	75.00
(4a)	Cincinnati Reds/1950	300.00	150.00	90.00
(4b)	Cincinnati Reds (Undated)	325.00	160.00	95.00
(5a)	New York Giants/1950	300.00	150.00	90.00
(5b)	New York Giants (Undated)	325.00	160.00	95.00
(6a)	Philadelphia Athletics/1950	225.00	110.00	65.00
(6b)	Philadelphia Athletics (Undated)	250.00	125.00	75.00
(7a)	Philadelphia Phillies /1950	225.00	110.00	65.00
(7b)	Philadelphia Phillies (Undated)	400.00	200.00	120.00
(8a)	St. Louis Cardinals /1950	400.00	200.00	120.00
(8b)	St. Louis Cardinals (Undated)	425.00	210.00	125.00
(9a)	Washington Senators/1950	250.00	125.00	75.00
(9b)	Washington Senators (Undated)	300.00	150.00	90.00

1952 Topps

At 407 cards, the 1952 Topps set was the largest set of its day, both in number of cards and physical dimensions of the cards. Cards are 2-5/8" x 3-3/4" with a colorized black-and-white photo on front. Major baseball card innovations presented in the set include the first-ever use of color team logos as part of the design, and the inclusion of stats for the previous season and career on the backs. The first 80 cards in the set can be found with backs printed entirely in black or black and red. While "Black Backs" used to command a significant premium over the "Red Back" version, that differential has diminished in recent years to the point of insignificance. Several cards in the #1-80 range can be found with noticeable color differences on front depending on whether they are Red Back or Black Back. Cards #311-407, known as the "high numbers," were distributed in limited areas and are extremely rare.

		NM	EX	VG
	Complete Set (407):	90,000	42,500	24,000
	Common Player (1-250):	45.00	22.50	13.50
	Common Player (251-310):	60.00	30.00	18.00
	Common Player (311-407):	275.00	135.00	80.00
1	Andy Pafko	3,500	375.00	190.00
2	*James E. Runnels*	400.00	40.00	20.00
3	Hank Thompson	45.00	22.50	13.50
4	Don Lenhardt	45.00	22.50	13.50
5	Larry Jansen	45.00	22.50	13.50
6	Grady Hatton	45.00	22.50	13.50
7	Wayne Terwilliger	55.00	27.50	16.50
8	Fred Marsh	45.00	22.50	13.50
9	Bobby Hogue	55.00	27.50	16.50
10	Al Rosen	160.00	80.00	45.00
11	Phil Rizzuto	375.00	185.00	110.00
12	Monty Basgall	45.00	22.50	13.50
13	Johnny Wyrostek	45.00	22.50	13.50
14	Bob Elliott	45.00	22.50	13.50
15	Johnny Pesky	45.00	22.50	13.50
16	Gene Hermanski	45.00	22.50	13.50
17	Jim Hegan	45.00	22.50	13.50
18	Merrill Combs	45.00	22.50	13.50
19	Johnny Bucha	45.00	22.50	13.50
20	*Billy Loes*	225.00	110.00	65.00
21	Ferris Fain	60.00	30.00	18.00
22	Dom DiMaggio	145.00	75.00	45.00
23	Billy Goodman	45.00	22.50	13.50
24	Luke Easter	60.00	30.00	18.00
25	Johnny Groth	45.00	22.50	13.50
26	Monty Irvin	125.00	65.00	35.00
27	Sam Jethroe	45.00	22.50	13.50
28	Jerry Priddy	45.00	22.50	13.50
29	Ted Kluszewski	225.00	110.00	65.00
30	Mel Parnell	45.00	22.50	13.50
31	Gus Zernial	125.00	65.00	35.00
32	Eddie Robinson	45.00	22.50	13.50
33	Warren Spahn	225.00	110.00	65.00
34	Elmer Valo	45.00	22.50	13.50
35	Hank Sauer	45.00	22.50	13.50
36	Gil Hodges	225.00	110.00	65.00
37	Duke Snider	350.00	175.00	100.00
38	Wally Westlake	45.00	22.50	13.50
39	"Dizzy" Trout	45.00	22.50	13.50

40	Irv Noren	45.00	22.50	13.50
41	Bob Wellman	45.00	22.50	13.50
42	Lou Kretlow	45.00	22.50	13.50
43	Ray Scarborough	45.00	22.50	13.50
44	Con Dempsey	45.00	22.50	13.50
45	Eddie Joost	45.00	22.50	13.50
46	Gordon Goldsberry	45.00	22.50	13.50
47	Willie Jones	45.00	22.50	13.50
48a	Joe Page (Wrong (Sain) back.)	850.00	425.00	255.00
48b	Joe Page (Correct bac.)	165.00	80.00	50.00
49a	Johnny Sain (Wrong (Page) back.)	900.00	450.00	275.00
49b	Johnny Sain (Correct back.)	175.00	85.00	50.00
50	Marv Rickert	45.00	22.50	13.50
51	Jim Russell	55.00	27.50	16.50
52	Don Mueller	45.00	22.50	13.50
53	Chris Van Cuyk	55.00	27.50	16.50
54	Leo Kiely	45.00	22.50	13.50
55	Ray Boone	45.00	22.50	13.50
56	Tommy Glaviano	45.00	22.50	13.50
57	Ed Lopat	90.00	45.00	25.00
58	Bob Mahoney	45.00	22.50	13.50
59	Robin Roberts	200.00	100.00	60.00
60	Sid Hudson	45.00	22.50	13.50
61	"Tookie" Gilbert	45.00	22.50	13.50
62	Chuck Stobbs	45.00	22.50	13.50
63	Howie Pollet	45.00	22.50	13.50
64	Roy Sievers	45.00	22.50	13.50
65	Enos Slaughter	130.00	65.00	40.00
66	"Preacher" Roe	115.00	55.00	35.00
67	Allie Reynolds	120.00	60.00	35.00
68	Cliff Chambers	45.00	22.50	13.50
69	Virgil Stallcup	45.00	22.50	13.50
70	Al Zarilla	45.00	22.50	13.50
71	Tom Upton	45.00	22.50	13.50
72	Karl Olson	45.00	22.50	13.50
73	William Werle	45.00	22.50	13.50
74	Andy Hansen	45.00	22.50	13.50
75	Wes Westrum	45.00	22.50	13.50
76	Eddie Stanky	45.00	22.50	13.50
77	Bob Kennedy	45.00	22.50	13.50
78	Ellis Kinder	45.00	22.50	13.50
79	Gerald Staley	45.00	22.50	13.50
80	Herman Wehmeier	45.00	22.50	13.50
81	Vernon Law	45.00	22.50	13.50
82	Duane Pillette	45.00	22.50	13.50
83	Billy Johnson	45.00	22.50	13.50
84	Vern Stephens	45.00	22.50	13.50
85	Bob Kuzava	55.00	27.50	16.50
86	Ted Gray	45.00	22.50	13.50
87	Dale Coogan	45.00	22.50	13.50
88	Bob Feller	190.00	95.00	60.00
89	Johnny Lipon	45.00	22.50	13.50
90	Mickey Grasso	45.00	22.50	13.50
91	Al Schoendienst	135.00	65.00	40.00
92	Dale Mitchell	45.00	22.50	13.50
93	Al Sima	45.00	22.50	13.50
94	Sam Mele	45.00	22.50	13.50
95	Ken Holcombe	45.00	22.50	13.50
96	Willard Marshall	45.00	22.50	13.50
97	Earl Torgeson	45.00	22.50	13.50
98	Bill Pierce	55.00	27.50	16.50
99	Gene Woodling	80.00	40.00	24.00
100	Del Rice	45.00	22.50	13.50
101	Max Lanier	45.00	22.50	13.50
102	Bill Kennedy	45.00	22.50	13.50
103	Cliff Mapes	45.00	22.50	13.50
104	Don Kolloway	45.00	22.50	13.50
105	John Pramesa	45.00	22.50	13.50
106	Mickey Vernon	45.00	22.50	13.50
107	Connie Ryan	45.00	22.50	13.50
108	Jim Konstanty	45.00	22.50	13.50
109	Ted Wilks	45.00	22.50	13.50
110	Dutch Leonard	45.00	22.50	13.50
111	Harry Lowrey	45.00	22.50	13.50
112	Henry Majeski	45.00	22.50	13.50
113	Dick Sisler	45.00	22.50	13.50
114	Willard Ramsdell	45.00	22.50	13.50
115	George Munger	45.00	22.50	13.50
116	Carl Scheib	45.00	22.50	13.50
117	Sherman Lollar	45.00	22.50	13.50
118	Ken Raffensberger	45.00	22.50	13.50
119	Maurice McDermott	45.00	22.50	13.50
120	Bob Chakales	45.00	22.50	13.50
121	Gus Niarhos	45.00	22.50	13.50
122	Jack Jensen	100.00	50.00	30.00
123	Eddie Yost	45.00	22.50	13.50
124	Monte Kennedy	45.00	22.50	13.50
125	Bill Rigney	45.00	22.50	13.50
126	Fred Hutchinson	45.00	22.50	13.50
127	Paul Minner	45.00	22.50	13.50
128	Don Bollweg	55.00	27.50	16.50
129	Johnny Mize	200.00	100.00	60.00
130	Sheldon Jones	45.00	22.50	13.50
131	Morrie Martin	45.00	22.50	13.50
132	Clyde Kluttz	45.00	22.50	13.50
133	Al Widmar	45.00	22.50	13.50
134	Joe Tipton	45.00	22.50	13.50
135	Dixie Howell	45.00	22.50	13.50
136	Johnny Schmitz	45.00	22.50	13.50
137	*Roy McMillan*	50.00	25.00	15.00
138	Bill MacDonald	45.00	22.50	13.50
139	Ken Wood	45.00	22.50	13.50
140	John Antonelli	45.00	22.50	13.50
141	Clint Hartung	45.00	22.50	13.50
142	Harry Perkowski	45.00	22.50	13.50
143	Les Moss	45.00	22.50	13.50
144	Ed Blake	45.00	22.50	13.50
145	Joe Haynes	45.00	22.50	13.50
146	Frank House	45.00	22.50	13.50
147	Bob Young	45.00	22.50	13.50
148	Johnny Klippstein	45.00	22.50	13.50
149	Dick Kryhoski	45.00	22.50	13.50
150	Ted Beard	45.00	22.50	13.50
151	*Wally Post*	55.00	27.50	16.50
152	Al Evans	45.00	22.50	13.50
153	Bob Rush	45.00	22.50	13.50

154	Joe Muir	45.00	22.50	13.50
155	Frank Overmire	55.00	27.50	16.50
156	Frank Hiller	45.00	22.50	13.50
157	Bob Usher	45.00	22.50	13.50
158	Eddie Waitkus	45.00	22.50	13.50
159	Saul Rogovin	45.00	22.50	13.50
160	Owen Friend	45.00	22.50	13.50
161	Bud Byerly	45.00	22.50	13.50
162	Del Crandall	45.00	22.50	13.50
163	Stan Rojek	45.00	22.50	13.50
164	Walt Dubiel	45.00	22.50	13.50
165	Eddie Kazak	45.00	22.50	13.50
166	Paul LaPalme	45.00	22.50	13.50
167	Bill Howerton	45.00	22.50	13.50
168	*Charlie Silvera*	75.00	37.50	22.50
169	Howie Judson	45.00	22.50	13.50
170	Gus Bell	65.00	32.50	20.00
171	Ed Erautt	45.00	22.50	13.50
172	Eddie Miksis	45.00	22.50	13.50
173	Roy Smalley	45.00	22.50	13.50
174	Clarence Marshall	45.00	22.50	13.50
175	*Billy Martin*	375.00	185.00	110.00
176	Hank Edwards	45.00	22.50	13.50
177	Bill Wight	45.00	22.50	13.50
178	Cass Michaels	45.00	22.50	13.50
179	Frank Smith	45.00	22.50	13.50
180	*Charley Maxwell*	60.00	30.00	18.00
181	Bob Swift	45.00	22.50	13.50
182	Billy Hitchcock	45.00	22.50	13.50
183	Erv Dusak	45.00	22.50	13.50
184	Bob Ramazzotti	45.00	22.50	13.50
185	Bill Nicholson	45.00	22.50	13.50
186	Walt Masterson	45.00	22.50	13.50
187	Bob Miller	45.00	22.50	13.50
188	Clarence Podbielan	45.00	22.50	13.50
189	Pete Reiser	45.00	22.50	13.50
190	Don Johnson	45.00	22.50	13.50
191	Yogi Berra	750.00	375.00	225.00
192	Myron Ginsberg	45.00	22.50	13.50
193	Harry Simpson	45.00	22.50	13.50
194	Joe Hatten	45.00	22.50	13.50
195	*Orestes Minoso*	135.00	65.00	40.00
196	Solly Hemus	45.00	22.50	13.50
197	George Strickland	45.00	22.50	13.50
198	Phil Haugstad	50.00	25.00	15.00
199	George Zuverink	45.00	22.50	13.50
200	Ralph Houk	100.00	50.00	30.00
201	Alex Kellner	45.00	22.50	13.50
202	Joe Collins	60.00	30.00	18.00
203	Curt Simmons	45.00	22.50	13.50
204	Ron Northey	45.00	22.50	13.50
205	Clyde King	45.00	22.50	13.50
206	Joe Ostrowski	55.00	27.50	16.50
207	Mickey Harris	45.00	22.50	13.50
208	Marlin Stuart	45.00	22.50	13.50
209	Howie Fox	45.00	22.50	13.50
210	Dick Fowler	45.00	22.50	13.50
211	Ray Coleman	45.00	22.50	13.50
212	Ned Garver	45.00	22.50	13.50
213	Nippy Jones	45.00	22.50	13.50
214	Johnny Hopp	55.00	27.50	16.50
215	Hank Bauer	95.00	45.00	25.00
216	Richie Ashburn	185.00	90.00	55.00
217	George Stirnweiss	45.00	22.50	13.50
218	Clyde McCullough	45.00	22.50	13.50
219	Bobby Shantz	55.00	27.50	16.50
220	Joe Presko	45.00	22.50	13.50
221	Granny Hamner	45.00	22.50	13.50
222	"Hoot" Evers	45.00	22.50	13.50
223	Del Ennis	45.00	22.50	13.50
224	Bruce Edwards	45.00	22.50	13.50
225	Frank Baumholtz	45.00	22.50	13.50
226	Dave Philley	45.00	22.50	13.50
227	Joe Garagiola	110.00	55.00	35.00
228	Al Brazle	45.00	22.50	13.50
229	Gene Bearden	45.00	22.50	13.50
230	Matt Batts	45.00	22.50	13.50
231	Sam Zoldak	45.00	22.50	13.50
232	Billy Cox	90.00	45.00	25.00
233	*Bob Friend*	75.00	37.50	22.50
234	Steve Souchock	45.00	22.50	13.50
235	Walt Dropo	45.00	22.50	13.50
236	Ed Fitz Gerald	45.00	22.50	13.50
237	Jerry Coleman	60.00	30.00	18.00
238	Art Houtteman	45.00	22.50	13.50
239	*Rocky Bridges*	45.00	22.50	13.50
240	Jack Phillips	45.00	22.50	13.50
241	Tommy Byrne	45.00	22.50	13.50
242	Tom Poholsky	45.00	22.50	13.50
243	Larry Doby	150.00	75.00	45.00
244	Vic Wertz	45.00	22.50	13.50
245	Sherry Robertson	45.00	22.50	13.50
246	George Kell	110.00	55.00	35.00
247	Randy Gumpert	45.00	22.50	13.50
248	Frank Shea	45.00	22.50	13.50
249	Bobby Adams	45.00	22.50	13.50
250	Carl Erskine	120.00	60.00	35.00
251	Chico Carrasquel	95.00	47.50	27.50
252	Vern Bickford	60.00	30.00	18.00
253	Johnny Berardino	75.00	37.50	22.50
254	Joe Dobson	60.00	30.00	18.00
255	Clyde Vollmer	60.00	30.00	18.00
256	Pete Suder	60.00	30.00	18.00
257	Bobby Avila	60.00	30.00	18.00
258	Steve Gromek	60.00	30.00	18.00
259	Bob Addis	60.00	30.00	18.00
260	Pete Castiglione	60.00	30.00	18.00
261	Willie Mays	1,750	750.00	375.00
262	Virgil Trucks	60.00	30.00	18.00
263	Harry Brecheen	60.00	30.00	18.00
264	Roy Hartsfield	60.00	30.00	18.00
265	Chuck Diering	60.00	30.00	18.00
266	Murry Dickson	60.00	30.00	18.00
267	Sid Gordon	60.00	30.00	18.00
268	Bob Lemon	135.00	65.00	40.00
269	Willard Nixon	60.00	30.00	18.00
270	Lou Brissie	60.00	30.00	18.00
271	Jim Delsing	60.00	30.00	18.00

272	Mike Garcia	60.00	30.00	18.00
273	Erv Palica	70.00	35.00	20.00
274	Ralph Branca	160.00	80.00	45.00
275	Pat Mullin	60.00	30.00	18.00
276	Jim Wilson	60.00	30.00	18.00
277	Early Wynn	175.00	85.00	50.00
278	Al Clark	60.00	30.00	18.00
279	Ed Stewart	60.00	30.00	18.00
280	Cloyd Boyer	60.00	30.00	18.00
281	Tommy Brown	60.00	30.00	18.00
282	Birdie Tebbetts	60.00	30.00	18.00
283	Phil Masi	60.00	30.00	18.00
284	Hank Arft	60.00	30.00	18.00
285	Cliff Fannin	60.00	30.00	18.00
286	Joe De Maestri	60.00	30.00	18.00
287	Steve Bilko	60.00	30.00	18.00
288	Chet Nichols	60.00	30.00	18.00
289	Tommy Holmes	60.00	30.00	18.00
290	Joe Astroth	60.00	30.00	18.00
291	Gil Coan	60.00	30.00	18.00
292	Floyd Baker	60.00	30.00	18.00
293	Sibby Sisti	60.00	30.00	18.00
294	Walker Cooper	60.00	30.00	18.00
295	Phil Cavarretta	60.00	30.00	18.00
296	"Red" Rolfe	60.00	30.00	18.00
297	Andy Seminick	60.00	30.00	18.00
298	Bob Ross	60.00	30.00	18.00
299	Ray Murray	60.00	30.00	18.00
300	Barney McCosky	60.00	30.00	18.00
301	Bob Porterfield	60.00	30.00	18.00
302	Max Surkont	60.00	30.00	18.00
303	Harry Dorish	60.00	30.00	18.00
304	Sam Dente	60.00	30.00	18.00
305	Paul Richards	60.00	30.00	18.00
306	Lou Sleator	60.00	30.00	18.00
307a	Frank Campos (Black star on back to right of "TOPPS BASEBALL")(Graded "Good" example auctioned 4/06 for $4,640.)			
307b	Frank Campos (Red star on back to right of "TOPPS BASEBALL")	60.00	30.00	18.00
308	Luis Aloma	60.00	30.00	18.00
309	Jim Busby	60.00	30.00	18.00
310	George Metkovich	125.00	30.00	18.00
311	Mickey Mantle (DP)	27,500	13,750	8,000
312	Jackie Robinson (DP)	1,700	895.00	350.00
313	Bobby Thomson (DP)	275.00	135.00	80.00
314	Roy Campanella	1,350	675.00	400.00
315	Leo Durocher	475.00	235.00	140.00
316	Davey Williams	275.00	135.00	80.00
317	Connie Marrero	275.00	135.00	80.00
318	Hal Gregg	275.00	135.00	80.00
319	Al Walker	300.00	150.00	90.00
320	John Rutherford	300.00	150.00	90.00
321	*Joe Black*	600.00	300.00	180.00
322	Randy Jackson	275.00	135.00	80.00
323	Bubba Church	275.00	135.00	80.00
324	Warren Hacker	275.00	135.00	80.00
325	Bill Serena	275.00	135.00	80.00
326	George Shuba	325.00	160.00	95.00
327	Archie Wilson	275.00	135.00	80.00
328	Bob Borkowski	275.00	135.00	80.00
329	Ivan Delock	275.00	135.00	80.00
330	Turk Lown	275.00	135.00	80.00
331	Tom Morgan	275.00	135.00	80.00
332	Tony Bartirome	275.00	135.00	80.00
333	Pee Wee Reese	1,200	600.00	360.00
334	Wilmer Mizell	275.00	135.00	80.00
335	Ted Lepcio	275.00	135.00	80.00
336	Dave Koslo	275.00	135.00	80.00
337	Jim Hearn	275.00	135.00	80.00
338	Sal Yvars	275.00	135.00	80.00
339	Russ Meyer	275.00	135.00	80.00
340	Bob Hooper	275.00	135.00	80.00
341	Hal Jeffcoat	275.00	135.00	80.00
342	*Clem Labine*	750.00	375.00	225.00
343	Dick Gernert	275.00	135.00	80.00
344	Ewell Blackwell	275.00	135.00	80.00
345	Sam White	275.00	135.00	80.00
346	George Spencer	275.00	135.00	80.00
347	Joe Adcock	350.00	175.00	100.00
348	Bob Kelly	275.00	135.00	80.00
349	Bob Cain	275.00	135.00	80.00
350	Cal Abrams	275.00	135.00	80.00
351	Al Dark	300.00	150.00	90.00
352	Karl Drews	275.00	135.00	80.00
353	Bob Del Greco	275.00	135.00	80.00
354	Fred Hatfield	275.00	135.00	80.00
355	Bobby Morgan	300.00	150.00	90.00
356	Toby Atwell	275.00	135.00	80.00
357	Smoky Burgess	350.00	175.00	100.00
358	John Kucab	275.00	135.00	80.00
359	Dee Fondy	275.00	135.00	80.00
360	George Crowe	275.00	135.00	80.00
361	Bill Posedel	275.00	135.00	80.00
362	Ken Heintzelman	275.00	135.00	80.00
363	Dick Rozek	275.00	135.00	80.00
364	Clyde Sukeforth	275.00	135.00	80.00
365	"Cookie" Lavagetto	275.00	135.00	80.00
366	Dave Madison	275.00	135.00	80.00
367	Bob Thorpe	275.00	135.00	80.00
368	Ed Wright	275.00	135.00	80.00
369	*Dick Groat*	400.00	200.00	120.00
370	Billy Hoeft	275.00	135.00	80.00
371	Bob Hofman	275.00	135.00	80.00
372	*Gil McDougald*	500.00	250.00	150.00
373	Jim Turner	300.00	150.00	90.00
374	Al Benton	275.00	135.00	80.00
375	Jack Merson	275.00	135.00	80.00
376	Faye Throneberry	275.00	135.00	80.00
377	Chuck Dressen	275.00	135.00	80.00
378	Les Fusselman	275.00	135.00	80.00
379	Joe Rossi	275.00	135.00	80.00
380	Clem Koshorek	275.00	135.00	80.00
381	Milton Stock	275.00	135.00	80.00
382	Sam Jones	275.00	135.00	80.00

383	Del Wilber	275.00	135.00	80.00
384	Frank Crosetti	400.00	200.00	120.00
385	Herman Franks	275.00	135.00	80.00
386	Eddie Yuhas	275.00	135.00	80.00
387	Billy Meyer	275.00	135.00	80.00
388	Bob Chipman	275.00	135.00	80.00
389	Ben Wade	300.00	150.00	90.00
390	Glenn Nelson	300.00	150.00	90.00
391	Ben Chapman (Photo actually Sam Chapman.)	275.00	135.00	80.00
392	*Hoyt Wilhelm*	750.00	375.00	225.00
393	Ebba St. Claire	275.00	135.00	80.00
394	Billy Herman	400.00	200.00	120.00
395	Jake Pitler	300.00	150.00	90.00
396	*Dick Williams*	400.00	200.00	120.00
397	Forrest Main	275.00	135.00	80.00
398	Hal Rice	275.00	135.00	80.00
399	Jim Fridley	275.00	135.00	80.00
400	Bill Dickey	800.00	400.00	240.00
401	Bob Schultz	275.00	135.00	80.00
402	Earl Harrist	275.00	135.00	80.00
403	Bill Miller	300.00	150.00	90.00
404	Dick Brodowski	275.00	135.00	80.00
405	Eddie Pellagrini	275.00	135.00	80.00
406	*Joe Nuxhall*	600.00	300.00	180.00
407	*Eddie Mathews*	10,000	3,600	1,525

1952 Topps "Canadian"

Perhaps because the "gray back" 1954 Topps cards have long been known as the "Canadian" issue, there is growing hobby support for the belief that a similar abbreviated set was printed in Canada for distribution there. The cards differ from the regular 1952 Topps of the same numerical range in that they are printed on a gray-backed cardboard stock, distinctly different from the cream-colored stock found on most '52 Topps #131-190. Additionally, the fronts of most, but not all, of the "Canadian" cards have colors which are subjectively darker or more muted than the the "U.S.A." versions. The market is just beginning to differentiate values between the two types, though the gray-backs are considered scarcer.

		NM	EX	VG
Complete Set (60):		5,000	2,500	1,500
Common Player:		80.00	40.00	24.00
131	Morrie Martin	80.00	40.00	24.00
132	Clyde Kluttz	80.00	40.00	24.00
133	Al Widmar	80.00	40.00	24.00
134	Joe Tipton	80.00	40.00	24.00
135	Dixie Howell	80.00	40.00	24.00
136	Johnny Schmitz	85.00	42.50	25.00
137	Roy McMillan	80.00	40.00	24.00
138	Bill MacDonald	80.00	40.00	24.00
139	Ken Wood	80.00	40.00	24.00
140	John Antonelli	80.00	40.00	24.00
141	Clint Hartung	80.00	40.00	24.00
142	Harry Perkowski	80.00	40.00	24.00
143	Les Moss	80.00	40.00	24.00
144	Ed Blake	80.00	40.00	24.00
145	Joe Haynes	80.00	40.00	24.00
146	Frank House	80.00	40.00	24.00
147	Bob Young	80.00	40.00	24.00
148	Johnny Klippstein	80.00	40.00	24.00
149	Dick Kryhoski	80.00	40.00	24.00
150	Ted Beard	80.00	40.00	24.00
151	Wally Post	80.00	40.00	24.00
152	Al Evans	80.00	40.00	24.00
153	Bob Rush	80.00	40.00	24.00
154	Joe Muir	80.00	40.00	24.00
155	Frank Overmire	85.00	42.50	25.00
156	Frank Hiller	80.00	40.00	24.00
157	Bob Usher	80.00	40.00	24.00
158	Eddie Waitkus	80.00	40.00	24.00
159	Saul Rogovin	80.00	40.00	24.00
160	Owen Friend	80.00	40.00	24.00
161	Bud Byerly	80.00	40.00	24.00
162	Del Crandall	80.00	40.00	24.00
163	Stan Rojek	80.00	40.00	24.00
164	Walt Dubiel	80.00	40.00	24.00
165	Eddie Kazak	80.00	40.00	24.00
166	Paul LaPalme	80.00	40.00	24.00
167	Bill Howerton	80.00	40.00	24.00
168	Charlie Silvera	100.00	50.00	30.00
169	Howie Judson	80.00	40.00	24.00
170	Gus Bell	100.00	50.00	30.00
171	Ed Erautt	80.00	40.00	24.00
172	Eddie Miksis	80.00	40.00	24.00
173	Roy Smalley	80.00	40.00	24.00
174	Clarence Marshall	80.00	40.00	24.00
175	Billy Martin	500.00	250.00	150.00
176	Hank Edwards	80.00	40.00	24.00
177	Bill Wight	80.00	40.00	24.00
178	Cass Michaels	80.00	40.00	24.00
179	Frank Smith	80.00	40.00	24.00

180	Charley Maxwell	80.00	40.00	24.00
181	Bob Swift	80.00	40.00	24.00
182	Billy Hitchcock	80.00	40.00	24.00
183	Erv Dusak	80.00	40.00	24.00
184	Bob Ramazzotti	80.00	40.00	24.00
185	Bill Nicholson	80.00	40.00	24.00
186	Walt Masterson	80.00	40.00	24.00
187	Bob Miller	80.00	40.00	24.00
188	Clarence Podbielan	80.00	40.00	24.00
189	Pete Reiser	80.00	40.00	24.00
190	Don Johnson	80.00	40.00	24.00

1953 Topps

 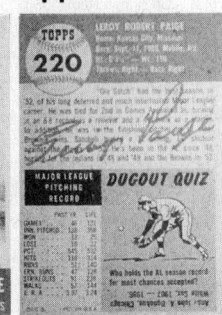

The 1953 Topps set reflects the company's continuing legal battles with Bowman. The set, originally intended to consist of 280 cards, is lacking six numbers (253, 261, 267, 268, 271 and 275) that represent players whose contracts were lost to the competition. The 2-5/8" x 3-3/4" cards feature painted player pictures. A color team logo appears at a bottom panel (red for American League and black for National). Card backs contain the first baseball-card trivia questions along with brief statistics and player biographies. In the red panel at the top, which lists the player's personal data, cards from the 2nd Series (#86-165 plus 10, 44, 61, 72 and 81) can be found with that data printed in either black or white, black being the marginally scarcer variety. Eighty-five cards between #1-165 were printed in noticeably larger quantities than the others, and are indicated in these listings with a double-print (DP) notation. Cards #221-280, the high numbers, were printed late in the season, in smaller quantities than the earlier series. Among the high numbers, even scarcer short-printed/SP cards are interspersed in the series.

		NM	EX	VG
Complete Set (274):		20,000	9,250	5,250
Common Player (1-165):		30.00	15.00	9.00
Common Player (166-220):		35.00	17.50	10.00
Common Player (221-280):		60.00	30.00	18.00
Short-print Player (221-280):		90.00	45.00	27.50
1	Jackie Robinson/DP	900.00	200.00	100.00
2	Luke Easter/DP	40.00	20.00	12.00
3	George Crowe	40.00	20.00	12.00
4	Ben Wade	45.00	22.50	13.50
5	Joe Dobson	40.00	20.00	12.00
6	Sam Jones	40.00	20.00	12.00
7	Bob Borkowski/DP	30.00	15.00	9.00
8	Clem Koshorek/DP	30.00	15.00	9.00
9	Joe Collins	45.00	22.50	13.50
10	Smoky Burgess/SP	70.00	35.00	20.00
11	Sal Yvars	40.00	20.00	12.00
12	Howie Judson/DP	30.00	15.00	9.00
13	Connie Marrero/D	30.00	15.00	9.00
14	Clem Labine/DP	60.00	30.00	18.00
15	Bobo Newsom/DP	30.00	15.00	9.00
16	Harry Lowrey/DP	30.00	15.00	9.00
17	Billy Hitchcock	40.00	20.00	12.00
18	Ted Lepcio/DP	30.00	15.00	9.00
19	Mel Parnell/DP	30.00	15.00	9.00
20	Hank Thompson	40.00	20.00	12.00
21	Billy Johnson	40.00	20.00	12.00
22	Howie Fox	40.00	20.00	12.00
23	Toby Atwell/DP	30.00	15.00	9.00
24	Ferris Fain	40.00	20.00	12.00
25	Ray Boone	40.00	20.00	12.00
26	Dale Mitchell/DP	30.00	15.00	9.00
27	Roy Campanella/DP	180.00	90.00	55.00
28	Eddie Pellagrini	40.00	20.00	12.00
29	Hal Jeffcoat	40.00	20.00	12.00
30	Willard Nixon	40.00	20.00	12.00
31	Ewell Blackwell	55.00	27.50	16.50
32	Clyde Vollmer	40.00	20.00	12.00
33	Bob Kennedy/DP	30.00	15.00	9.00
34	George Shuba	60.00	30.00	18.00
35	Irv Noren/DP	35.00	17.50	10.00
36	Johnny Groth/DP	30.00	15.00	9.00
37	Ed Mathews/DP	135.00	65.00	40.00
38	Jim Hearn/DP	30.00	15.00	9.00
39	Eddie Miksis	40.00	20.00	12.00
40	John Lipon	40.00	20.00	12.00
41	Enos Slaughter	80.00	40.00	24.00
42	Gus Zernial/DP	30.00	15.00	9.00
43	Gil McDougald	75.00	37.50	22.50
44	Ellis Kinder/SP	75.00	37.50	22.50
45	Grady Hatton/DP	30.00	15.00	9.00
46	Johnny Klippstein/DP	30.00	15.00	9.00
47	Bubba Church/DP	30.00	15.00	9.00
48	Bob Del Greco/DP	30.00	15.00	9.00
49	Faye Throneberry/DP	30.00	15.00	9.00
50	Chuck Dressen/DP	40.00	20.00	12.00
51	Frank Campos/DP	30.00	15.00	9.00

		NM	EX	VG
52	Ted Gray/DP	30.00	15.00	9.00
53	Sherman Lollar/DP	30.00	15.00	9.00
54	Bob Feller/DP	160.00	80.00	50.00
55	Maurice McDermott/DP	30.00	15.00	9.00
56	Gerald Staley/DP	30.00	15.00	9.00
57	Carl Scheib	40.00	20.00	12.00
58	George Metkovich	40.00	20.00	12.00
59	Karl Drews/DP	30.00	15.00	9.00
60	Cloyd Boyer/DP	30.00	15.00	9.00
61	Early Wynn/SP	90.00	45.00	27.50
62	Monte Irvin/SP	100.00	50.00	30.00
63	Gus Niarhos/DP	30.00	15.00	9.00
64	Dave Philley	40.00	20.00	12.00
65	Earl Harrist	40.00	20.00	12.00
66	Orestes Minoso	70.00	35.00	20.00
67	Roy Sievers/DP	30.00	15.00	9.00
68	Del Rice	40.00	20.00	12.00
69	Dick Brodowski	40.00	20.00	12.00
70	Ed Yuhas	40.00	20.00	12.00
71	Tony Bartirome	40.00	20.00	12.00
72	Fred Hutchinson/SP	75.00	37.50	22.50
73	Eddie Robinson	40.00	20.00	12.00
74	Joe Rossi	40.00	20.00	12.00
75	Mike Garcia	40.00	20.00	12.00
76	Pee Wee Reese	180.00	90.00	55.00
77	Johnny Mize/DP	75.00	37.50	22.50
78	Al Schoendienst	100.00	50.00	30.00
79	Johnny Wyrostek	40.00	20.00	12.00
80	Jim Hegan	40.00	20.00	12.00
81	Joe Black/SP	120.00	60.00	35.00
82	Mickey Mantle	2,600	1,000	475.00
83	Howie Pollet	40.00	20.00	12.00
84	Bob Hooper/DP	30.00	15.00	9.00
85	Bobby Morgan/DP	35.00	17.50	10.00
86	Billy Martin	140.00	70.00	40.00
87	Ed Lopat	60.00	30.00	18.00
88	Willie Jones/DP	30.00	15.00	9.00
89	Chuck Stobbs/DP	30.00	15.00	9.00
90	Hank Edwards/DP	30.00	15.00	9.00
91	Ebba St. Claire/DP	30.00	15.00	9.00
92	Paul Minner/DP	30.00	15.00	9.00
93	Hal Rice/DP	30.00	15.00	9.00
94	William Kennedy/DP	30.00	15.00	9.00
95	Willard Marshall/DP	30.00	15.00	9.00
96	Virgil Trucks	40.00	20.00	12.00
97	Don Kolloway/DP	30.00	15.00	9.00
98	Cal Abrams/DP	30.00	15.00	9.00
99	Dave Madison	40.00	20.00	12.00
100	Bill Miller	40.00	20.00	12.00
101	Ted Wilks	40.00	20.00	12.00
102	Connie Ryan/DP	30.00	15.00	9.00
103	Joe Astroth/DP	30.00	15.00	9.00
104	Yogi Berra	260.00	130.00	75.00
105	Joe Nuxhall/DP	35.00	17.50	10.00
106	John Antonelli	40.00	20.00	12.00
107	Danny O'Connell/DP	30.00	15.00	9.00
108	Bob Porterfield/DP	30.00	15.00	9.00
109	Alvin Dark	40.00	20.00	12.00
110	Herman Wehmeier/DP	30.00	15.00	9.00
111	Hank Sauer/DP	30.00	15.00	9.00
112	Ned Garver/DP	30.00	15.00	9.00
113	Jerry Priddy	40.00	20.00	12.00
114	Phil Rizzuto	160.00	80.00	45.00
115	George Spencer	40.00	20.00	12.00
116	Frank Smith/DP	30.00	15.00	9.00
117	Sid Gordon/DP	30.00	15.00	9.00
118	Gus Bell/DP	30.00	15.00	9.00
119	John Sain	75.00	37.50	22.50
120	Davey Williams	40.00	20.00	12.00
121	Walt Dropo	40.00	20.00	12.00
122	Elmer Valo	40.00	20.00	12.00
123	Tommy Byrne/DP	30.00	15.00	9.00
124	Sibby Sisti/DP	30.00	15.00	9.00
125	Dick Williams/DP	35.00	17.50	10.00
126	Bill Connelly/DP	30.00	15.00	9.00
127	Clint Courtney/DP	30.00	15.00	9.00
128	Wilmer Mizell/DP	30.00	15.00	9.00
129	Keith Thomas	40.00	20.00	12.00
130	Turk Lown/DP	30.00	15.00	9.00
131	Harry Byrd/DP	30.00	15.00	9.00
132	Tom Morgan	45.00	22.50	13.50
133	Gil Coan	40.00	20.00	12.00
134	Rube Walker	45.00	22.50	13.50
135	Al Rosen/DP	45.00	22.50	13.50
136	Ken Heintzelman/DP	30.00	15.00	9.00
137	John Rutherford/DP	35.00	17.50	10.00
138	George Kell	55.00	27.50	16.50
139	Sammy White	40.00	20.00	12.00
140	Tommy Glaviano	40.00	20.00	12.00
141	Allie Reynolds/DP	75.00	37.50	22.50
142	Vic Wertz	40.00	20.00	12.00
143	Billy Pierce	40.00	20.00	12.00
144	Bob Schultz/DP	30.00	15.00	9.00
145	Harry Dorish/DP	30.00	15.00	9.00
146	Granville Hamner	40.00	20.00	12.00
147	Warren Spahn	165.00	85.00	50.00
148	Mickey Grasso	40.00	20.00	12.00
149	Dom DiMaggio/DP	65.00	32.50	20.00
150	Harry Simpson/DP	30.00	15.00	9.00
151	Hoyt Wilhelm	80.00	40.00	24.00
152	Bob Adams/DP	30.00	15.00	9.00
153	Andy Seminick/DP	30.00	15.00	9.00
154	Dick Groat	40.00	20.00	12.00
155	Dutch Leonard	40.00	20.00	12.00
156	Jim Rivera/DP	30.00	15.00	9.00
157	Bob Addis/DP	30.00	15.00	9.00
158	John Logan	40.00	20.00	12.00
159	Wayne Terwilliger/DP	30.00	15.00	9.00
160	Bob Young	40.00	20.00	12.00
161	Vern Bickford/DP	30.00	15.00	9.00
162	Ted Kluszewski	80.00	40.00	24.00
163	Fred Hatfield/DP	30.00	15.00	9.00
164	Frank Shea/DP	30.00	15.00	9.00
165	Billy Hoeft	40.00	20.00	12.00
166	Bill Hunter	35.00	17.50	10.00
167	Art Schult	35.00	17.50	10.00
168	Willard Schmidt	35.00	17.50	10.00
169	Dizzy Trout	35.00	17.50	10.00
170	Bill Werle	35.00	17.50	10.00
171	Bill Glynn	35.00	17.50	10.00
172	Rip Repulski	35.00	17.50	10.00
173	Preston Ward	35.00	17.50	10.00
174	Billy Loes	45.00	22.50	13.50
175	Ron Kline	35.00	17.50	10.00
176	Don Hoak	40.00	20.00	12.00
177	Jim Dyck	35.00	17.50	10.00
178	Jim Waugh	35.00	17.50	10.00
179	Gene Hermanski	35.00	17.50	10.00
180	Virgil Stallcup	35.00	17.50	10.00
181	Al Zarilla	35.00	17.50	10.00
182	Bob Hofman	35.00	17.50	10.00
183	Stu Miller	35.00	17.50	10.00
184	Hal Brown	35.00	17.50	10.00
185	Jim Pendleton	35.00	17.50	10.00
186	Charlie Bishop	35.00	17.50	10.00
187	Jim Fridley	35.00	17.50	10.00
188	Andy Carey	60.00	30.00	18.00
189	Ray Jablonski	35.00	17.50	10.00
190	Dixie Walker	35.00	17.50	10.00
191	Ralph Kiner	90.00	45.00	27.50
192	Wally Westlake	35.00	17.50	10.00
193	Mike Clark	35.00	17.50	10.00
194	Eddie Kazak	35.00	17.50	10.00
195	Ed McGhee	35.00	17.50	10.00
196	Bob Keegan	35.00	17.50	10.00
197	Del Crandall	35.00	17.50	10.00
198	Forrest Main	35.00	17.50	10.00
199	Marion Fricano	35.00	17.50	10.00
200	Gordon Goldsberry	35.00	17.50	10.00
201	Paul La Palme	35.00	17.50	10.00
202	Carl Sawatski	35.00	17.50	10.00
203	Cliff Fannin	35.00	17.50	10.00
204	Dick Bokelmann	35.00	17.50	10.00
205	Vern Benson	35.00	17.50	10.00
206	Ed Bailey	35.00	17.50	10.00
207	Whitey Ford	210.00	100.00	65.00
208	Jim Wilson	35.00	17.50	10.00
209	Jim Greengrass	35.00	17.50	10.00
210	Bob Cerv	45.00	22.20	13.50
211	J.W. Porter	35.00	17.50	10.00
212	Jack Dittmer	35.00	17.50	10.00
213	Ray Scarborough	35.00	17.50	10.00
214	Bill Bruton	35.00	17.50	10.00
215	Gene Conley	35.00	17.50	10.00
216	Jim Hughes	40.00	20.00	12.00
217	Murray Wall	35.00	17.50	10.00
218	Les Fusselman	35.00	17.50	10.00
219	Pete Runnels (Picture actually Don Johnson.)	35.00	17.50	10.00
220	Satchell Paige	500.00	200.00	110.00
221	Bob Milliken/SP	100.00	50.00	30.00
222	Vic Janowicz	100.00	50.00	30.00
223	John O'Brien	60.00	30.00	18.00
224	Lou Sleater	60.00	30.00	18.00
225	Bobby Shantz/SP	90.00	45.00	27.50
226	Ed Erautt/SP	90.00	45.00	27.50
227	Morris Martin/SP	90.00	45.00	27.50
228	Hal Newhouser/SP	140.00	70.00	45.00
229	Rocky Krsnich/SP	90.00	45.00	27.50
230	Johnny Lindell	60.00	30.00	18.00
231	Solly Hemus	60.00	30.00	18.00
232	Dick Kokos/SP	90.00	45.00	27.50
233	Al Aber/SP	90.00	45.00	27.50
234	Ray Murray	60.00	30.00	18.00
235	John Hetki	60.00	30.00	18.00
236	Harry Perkowski	60.00	30.00	18.00
237	Clarence Podbielan	60.00	30.00	18.00
238	Cal Hogue	60.00	30.00	18.00
239	Jim Delsing/SP	90.00	45.00	27.50
240	Freddie Marsh/SP	90.00	45.00	27.50
241	Al Sima	60.00	30.00	18.00
242	Charlie Silvera/SP	100.00	50.00	30.00
243	Carlos Bernier	60.00	30.00	18.00
244	Willie Mays/SP	2,600	650.00	300.00
245	Bill Norman	90.00	45.00	27.50
246	Roy Face	75.00	37.50	22.50
247	Mike Sandlock	60.00	30.00	18.00
248	Gene Stephens	60.00	30.00	18.00
249	Ed O'Brien/SP	90.00	45.00	27.50
250	Bob Wilson/SP	90.00	45.00	27.50
251	Sid Hudson/SP	90.00	45.00	27.50
252	Henry Foiles/SP	90.00	45.00	27.50
253	Not Issued			
254	Preacher Roe	125.00	65.00	35.00
255	Dixie Howell/SP	100.00	50.00	30.00
256	Les Peden/SP	90.00	45.00	27.50
257	Bob Boyd/SP	90.00	45.00	27.50
258	Jim Gilliam/SP	265.00	130.00	80.00
259	Roy McMillan	60.00	30.00	18.00
260	Sam Calderone/SP	90.00	45.00	27.50
261	Not Issued			
262	Bob Oldis/SP	90.00	45.00	27.50
263	Johnny Podres/SP	275.00	135.00	85.00
264	Gene Woodling	95.00	47.50	27.50
265	Jackie Jensen/SP	100.00	50.00	30.00
266	Bob Cain/SP	90.00	45.00	27.50
267	Not Issued			
268	Not Issued			
269	Duane Pillette/SP	90.00	45.00	27.50
270	Vern Stephens/SP	90.00	45.00	27.50
271	Not Issued			
272	Bill Antonello/SP	100.00	50.00	30.00
273	Harvey Haddix/SP	160.00	80.00	47.50
274	John Riddle/SP	90.00	45.00	27.50
275	Not Issued			
276	Ken Raffensberger/SP	90.00	45.00	27.50
277	Don Lund/SP	90.00	45.00	27.50
278	Willie Miranda/SP	90.00	45.00	27.50
279	Joe Coleman	60.00	30.00	18.00
280	Milt Bolling/SP	400.00	115.00	45.00

1954 Topps

The first issue to use two player pictures on the front, the 1954 Topps set remains popular today.

Solid color backgrounds frame both color portraits and black-and-white action pictures of the player. The player's name, position, team and team logo appear at the top. Backs include an "Inside Baseball" cartoon regarding the player as well as statistics and biography. The 250-card, 2-5/8" x 3-3/4", set includes manager and coaches cards. A gray-back version of cards #1-50 is known, distinguished by the use of dark gray cardboard on back. These are often attributed to Canadian issue and carry a modest premium.

		NM	EX	VG
Complete Set (250):		9,250	4,000	2,400
Common Player (1-50):		20.00	10.00	6.00
Common Player (51-75):		35.00	17.50	10.00
Common Player (76-250):		20.00	10.00	6.00
1	Ted Williams	675.00	175.00	80.00
2	Gus Zernial	35.00	10.00	6.00
3	Monte Irvin	60.00	30.00	18.00
4	Hank Sauer	20.00	10.00	6.00
5	Ed Lopat	25.00	12.50	7.50
6	Pete Runnels	20.00	10.00	6.00
7	Ted Kluszewski	35.00	17.50	10.00
8	Bobby Young	20.00	10.00	6.00
9	Harvey Haddix	20.00	10.00	6.00
10	Jackie Robinson	235.00	115.00	70.00
11	Paul Smith	20.00	10.00	6.00
12	Del Crandall	20.00	10.00	6.00
13	Billy Martin	75.00	37.50	22.00
14	Preacher Roe	35.00	17.50	10.00
15	Al Rosen	30.00	15.00	9.00
16	Vic Janowicz	25.00	12.50	7.50
17	Phil Rizzuto	85.00	42.50	25.00
18	Walt Dropo	20.00	10.00	6.00
19	Johnny Lipon	20.00	10.00	6.00
20	Warren Spahn	85.00	42.50	25.00
21	Bobby Shantz	20.00	10.00	6.00
22	Jim Greengrass	20.00	10.00	6.00
23	Luke Easter	25.00	12.50	7.50
24	Granny Hamner	20.00	10.00	6.00
25	Harvey Kuenn	35.00	17.50	10.00
26	Ray Jablonski	20.00	10.00	6.00
27	Ferris Fain	20.00	10.00	6.00
28	Paul Minner	20.00	10.00	6.00
29	Jim Hegan	20.00	10.00	6.00
30	Ed Mathews	70.00	35.00	20.00
31	Johnny Klippstein	20.00	10.00	6.00
32	Duke Snider	130.00	65.00	40.00
33	Johnny Schmitz	20.00	10.00	6.00
34	Jim Rivera	20.00	10.00	6.00
35	Junior Gilliam	35.00	17.50	10.00
36	Hoyt Wilhelm	40.00	20.00	12.00
37	Whitey Ford	100.00	50.00	30.00
38	Eddie Stanky	20.00	10.00	6.00
39	Sherm Lollar	20.00	10.00	6.00
40	Mel Parnell	20.00	10.00	6.00
41	Willie Jones	20.00	10.00	6.00
42	Don Mueller	20.00	10.00	6.00
43	Dick Groat	20.00	10.00	6.00
44	Ned Garver	20.00	10.00	6.00
45	Richie Ashburn	60.00	30.00	18.00
46	Ken Raffensberger	20.00	10.00	6.00
47	Ellis Kinder	20.00	10.00	6.00
48	Billy Hunter	20.00	10.00	6.00
49	Ray Murray	20.00	10.00	6.00
50	Yogi Berra	165.00	80.00	50.00
51	Johnny Lindell	35.00	17.50	10.00
52	Vic Power	40.00	20.00	12.00
53	Jack Dittmer	35.00	17.50	10.00
54	Vern Stephens	35.00	17.50	10.00
55	Phil Cavarretta	35.00	17.50	10.00
56	Willie Miranda	35.00	17.50	10.00
57	Luis Aloma	35.00	17.50	10.00
58	Bob Wilson	35.00	17.50	10.00
59	Gene Conley	35.00	17.50	10.00
60	Frank Baumholtz	35.00	17.50	10.00
61	Bob Cain	35.00	17.50	10.00
62	Eddie Robinson	40.00	20.00	12.00
63	Johnny Pesky	35.00	17.50	10.00
64	Hank Thompson	35.00	17.50	10.00
65	Bob Swift	35.00	17.50	10.00
66	Ted Lepcio	35.00	17.50	10.00
67	Jim Willis	35.00	17.50	10.00
68	Sammy Calderone	35.00	17.50	10.00
69	Bud Podbielan	35.00	17.50	10.00
70	Larry Doby	85.00	42.50	25.00
71	Frank Smith	35.00	17.50	10.00
72	Preston Ward	35.00	17.50	10.00
73	Wayne Terwilliger	35.00	17.50	10.00
74	Bill Taylor	35.00	17.50	10.00
75	Fred Haney	35.00	17.50	10.00
76	Bob Scheffing	20.00	10.00	6.00
77	Ray Boone	20.00	10.00	6.00
78	Ted Kazanski	20.00	10.00	6.00
79	Andy Pafko	20.00	10.00	6.00
80	Jackie Jensen	30.00	15.00	9.00

		NM	EX	VG
81	Dave Hoskins	20.00	10.00	6.00
82	Milt Bolling	20.00	10.00	6.00
83	Joe Collins	25.00	12.50	7.50
84	Dick Cole	20.00	10.00	6.00
85	*Bob Turley*	35.00	17.50	10.00
86	Billy Herman	45.00	22.50	13.50
87	Roy Face	20.00	10.00	6.00
88	Matt Batts	20.00	10.00	6.00
89	Howie Pollet	20.00	10.00	6.00
90	Willie Mays	375.00	185.00	110.00
91	Bob Oldis	20.00	10.00	6.00
92	Wally Westlake	20.00	10.00	6.00
93	Sid Hudson	20.00	10.00	6.00
94	*Ernie Banks*	850.00	300.00	180.00
95	Hal Rice	20.00	10.00	6.00
96	Charlie Silvera	25.00	12.50	7.50
97	Jerry Lane	20.00	10.00	6.00
98	Joe Black	55.00	27.50	16.50
99	Bob Hofman	20.00	10.00	6.00
100	Bob Keegan	20.00	10.00	6.00
101	Gene Woodling	50.00	25.00	15.00
102	Gil Hodges	95.00	47.50	27.00
103	*Jim Lemon*	25.00	12.50	7.50
104	Mike Sandlock	20.00	10.00	6.00
105	Andy Carey	25.00	12.50	7.50
106	Dick Kokos	20.00	10.00	6.00
107	Duane Pillette	20.00	10.00	6.00
108	Thornton Kipper	20.00	10.00	6.00
109	Bill Bruton	20.00	10.00	6.00
110	Harry Dorish	20.00	10.00	6.00
111	Jim Delsing	20.00	10.00	6.00
112	Bill Renna	20.00	10.00	6.00
113	Bob Boyd	20.00	10.00	6.00
114	Dean Stone	20.00	10.00	6.00
115	"Rip" Repulski	20.00	10.00	6.00
116	Steve Bilko	20.00	10.00	6.00
117	Solly Hemus	20.00	10.00	6.00
118	Carl Scheib	20.00	10.00	6.00
119	Johnny Antonelli	20.00	10.00	6.00
120	Roy McMillan	20.00	10.00	6.00
121	Clem Labine	45.00	22.50	13.50
122	Johnny Logan	20.00	10.00	6.00
123	Bobby Adams	20.00	10.00	6.00
124	Marion Fricano	20.00	10.00	6.00
125	Harry Perkowski	20.00	10.00	6.00
126	Ben Wade	25.00	12.50	7.50
127	Steve O'Neill	20.00	10.00	6.00
128	*Hank Aaron*	1,400	500.00	275.00
129	Forrest Jacobs	20.00	10.00	6.00
130	Hank Bauer	45.00	22.50	13.50
131	Reno Bertoia	20.00	10.00	6.00
132	*Tom Lasorda*	135.00	65.00	40.00
133	Del Baker	20.00	10.00	6.00
134	Cal Hogue	20.00	10.00	6.00
135	Joe Presko	20.00	10.00	6.00
136	Connie Ryan	20.00	10.00	6.00
137	*Wally Moon*	35.00	17.50	10.00
138	Bob Borkowski	20.00	10.00	6.00
139	Ed O'Brien, Johnny O'Brien	75.00	37.50	22.50
140	Tom Wright	20.00	10.00	6.00
141	*Joe Jay*	40.00	20.00	12.00
142	Tom Poholsky	20.00	10.00	6.00
143	Rollie Hemsley	20.00	10.00	6.00
144	Bill Werle	20.00	10.00	6.00
145	Elmer Valo	20.00	10.00	6.00
146	Don Johnson	20.00	10.00	6.00
147	John Riddle	20.00	10.00	6.00
148	Bob Trice	20.00	10.00	6.00
149	Jim Robertson	20.00	10.00	6.00
150	Dick Kryhoski	20.00	10.00	6.00
151	Alex Grammas	20.00	10.00	6.00
152	Mike Blyzka	20.00	10.00	6.00
153	Rube Walker	25.00	12.50	7.50
154	Mike Fornieles	20.00	10.00	6.00
155	Bob Kennedy	20.00	10.00	6.00
156	Joe Coleman	20.00	10.00	6.00
157	Don Lenhardt	20.00	10.00	6.00
158	"Peanuts" Lowrey	20.00	10.00	6.00
159	Dave Philley	20.00	10.00	6.00
160	"Red" Kress	20.00	10.00	6.00
161	John Hetki	20.00	10.00	6.00
162	Herman Wehmeier	20.00	10.00	6.00
163	Frank House	20.00	10.00	6.00
164	Stu Miller	20.00	10.00	6.00
165	Jim Pendleton	20.00	10.00	6.00
166	Johnny Podres	45.00	22.50	13.50
167	Don Lund	20.00	10.00	6.00
168	Morrie Martin	20.00	10.00	6.00
169	Jim Hughes	25.00	12.50	7.50
170	*Jim Rhodes*	40.00	20.00	12.00
171	Leo Kiely	20.00	10.00	6.00
172	Hal Brown	20.00	10.00	6.00
173	Jack Harshman	20.00	10.00	6.00
174	Tom Qualters	20.00	10.00	6.00
175	*Frank Leja*	25.00	12.50	7.50
176	Bob Keely	20.00	10.00	6.00
177	Bob Milliken	25.00	12.50	7.50
178	Bill Gynn (Glynn)	20.00	10.00	6.00
179	Gair Allie	20.00	10.00	6.00
180	Wes Westrum	20.00	10.00	6.00
181	Mel Roach	20.00	10.00	6.00
182	Chuck Harmon	20.00	10.00	6.00
183	Earle Combs	25.00	12.50	7.50
184	Ed Bailey	20.00	10.00	6.00
185	Chuck Stobbs	20.00	10.00	6.00
186	Karl Olson	20.00	10.00	6.00
187	"Heinie" Manush	25.00	12.50	7.50
188	Dave Jolly	20.00	10.00	6.00
189	Bob Ross	20.00	10.00	6.00
190	Ray Herbert	20.00	10.00	6.00
191	*Dick Schofield*	25.00	12.50	7.50
192	"Cot" Deal	20.00	10.00	6.00
193	Johnny Hopp	20.00	10.00	6.00
194	Bill Sarni	20.00	10.00	6.00
195	Bill Consolo	20.00	10.00	6.00
196	Stan Jok	20.00	10.00	6.00
197	"Schoolboy" Rowe	25.00	12.50	7.50
198	Carl Sawatski	20.00	10.00	6.00
199	"Rocky" Nelson	20.00	10.00	6.00
200	Larry Jansen	20.00	10.00	6.00
201	*Al Kaline*	425.00	200.00	100.00
202	*Bob Purkey*	20.00	10.00	6.00
203	Harry Brecheen	20.00	10.00	6.00
204	Angel Scull	20.00	10.00	6.00
205	Johnny Sain	30.00	15.00	9.00
206	Ray Crone	20.00	10.00	6.00
207	Tom Oliver	20.00	10.00	6.00
208	Grady Hatton	20.00	10.00	6.00
209	Charlie Thompson	25.00	12.50	7.50
210	*Bob Buhl*	25.00	12.50	7.50
211	Don Hoak	25.00	12.50	7.50
212	Mickey Micelotta	20.00	10.00	6.00
213	John Fitzpatrick	20.00	10.00	6.00
214	Arnold Portocarrero	20.00	10.00	6.00
215	Ed McGhee	20.00	10.00	6.00
216	Al Sima	20.00	10.00	6.00
217	Paul Schreiber	20.00	10.00	6.00
218	Fred Marsh	20.00	10.00	6.00
219	Charlie Kress	20.00	10.00	6.00
220	Ruben Gomez	20.00	10.00	6.00
221	Dick Brodowski	20.00	10.00	6.00
222	Bill Wilson	20.00	10.00	6.00
223	Joe Haynes	20.00	10.00	6.00
224	Dick Weik	20.00	10.00	6.00
225	Don Liddle	20.00	10.00	6.00
226	Jehosie Heard	20.00	10.00	6.00
227	Buster Mills	20.00	10.00	6.00
228	Gene Hermanski	20.00	10.00	6.00
229	Bob Talbot	20.00	10.00	6.00
230	Bob Kuzava	25.00	12.50	7.50
231	Roy Smalley	20.00	10.00	6.00
232	Lou Limmer	20.00	10.00	6.00
233	Augie Galan	20.00	10.00	6.00
234	*Jerry Lynch*	20.00	10.00	6.00
235	Vern Law	20.00	10.00	6.00
236	Paul Penson	20.00	10.00	6.00
237	Mike Ryba	20.00	10.00	6.00
238	Al Aber	20.00	10.00	6.00
239	*Bill Skowron*	85.00	42.50	25.00
240	Sam Mele	20.00	10.00	6.00
241	Bob Miller	20.00	10.00	6.00
242	Curt Roberts	20.00	10.00	6.00
243	Ray Blades	20.00	10.00	6.00
244	Leroy Wheat	20.00	10.00	6.00
245	Roy Sievers	20.00	10.00	6.00
246	Howie Fox	20.00	10.00	6.00
247	Eddie Mayo	20.00	10.00	6.00
248	*Al Smith*	20.00	10.00	6.00
249	Wilmer Mizell	20.00	10.00	6.00
250	Ted Williams	600.00	190.00	100.00

1954 Topps "Canadian"

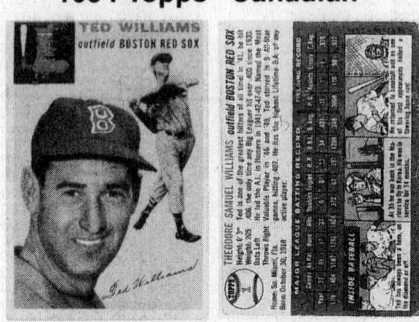

This version of the first 50 cards from 1954 Topps has long been known as the "Canadian" issue. It is widely believed that the abbreviated set was intended solely for Canadian distribution. The cards differ from the regular 1954 Topps in that they are printed on a gray-backed cardboard stock, distinctly different from the white stock found on most '54 Topps. Later series white-back Topps cards were sold in Canada in O-Pee-Chee marked wrappers at four for a nickel as opposed to six for five cents in the U.S.

		NM	EX	VG
Complete Set (50):		5,500	2,750	1,750
Common Player:		40.00	20.00	12.00
1	Ted Williams	1,500	700.00	450.00
2	Gus Zernial	60.00	30.00	12.00
3	Monte Irvin	115.00	55.00	35.00
4	Hank Sauer	40.00	20.00	12.00
5	Ed Lopat	50.00	25.00	15.00
6	Pete Runnels	40.00	20.00	12.00
7	Ted Kluszewski	75.00	35.00	22.50
8	Bobby Young	40.00	20.00	12.00
9	Harvey Haddix	40.00	20.00	12.00
10	Jackie Robinson	525.00	250.00	150.00
11	Paul Smith	40.00	20.00	12.00
12	Del Crandall	40.00	20.00	12.00
13	Billy Martin	225.00	100.00	65.00
14	Preacher Roe	75.00	35.00	22.50
15	Al Rosen	85.00	40.00	25.00
16	Vic Janowicz	45.00	22.00	13.50
17	Phil Rizzuto	225.00	110.00	65.00
18	Walt Dropo	40.00	20.00	12.00
19	Johnny Lipon	40.00	20.00	12.00
20	Warren Spahn	215.00	100.00	60.00
21	Bobby Shantz	45.00	22.50	13.50
22	Jim Greengrass	40.00	20.00	12.00
23	Luke Easter	40.00	20.00	12.00
24	Granny Hamner	40.00	20.00	12.00
25	Harvey Kuenn	75.00	35.00	22.50
26	Ray Jablonski	40.00	20.00	12.00
27	Ferris Fain	40.00	20.00	12.00
28	Paul Minner	40.00	20.00	12.00
29	Jim Hegan	40.00	20.00	12.00
30	Ed Mathews	165.00	80.00	47.50
31	Johnny Klippstein	40.00	20.00	12.00
32	Duke Snider	315.00	150.00	90.00
33	Johnny Schmitz	40.00	20.00	12.00
34	Jim Rivera	40.00	20.00	12.00
35	Junior Gilliam	85.00	40.00	25.00
36	Hoyt Wilhelm	115.00	55.00	32.50
37	Whitey Ford	215.00	100.00	60.00
38	Eddie Stanky	45.00	22.50	13.50
39	Sherm Lollar	40.00	20.00	12.00
40	Mel Parnell	40.00	20.00	12.00
41	Willie Jones	40.00	20.00	12.00
42	Don Mueller	40.00	20.00	12.00
43	Dick Groat	40.00	20.00	12.00
44	Ned Garver	40.00	20.00	12.00
45	Richie Ashburn	140.00	70.00	40.00
46	Ken Raffensberger	40.00	20.00	12.00
47	Ellis Kinder	40.00	20.00	12.00
48	Billy Hunter	40.00	20.00	12.00
49	Ray Murray	40.00	20.00	12.00
50	Yogi Berra	365.00	175.00	100.00

1954 Topps Look 'N See

Among the 135 historical figures in this set is only one baseball player - Babe Ruth. These 2-1/16" x 2-15/16" cards feature colorful portrait paintings on the front and biographies on the back. The answer to a trivia question on back can be discovered by laying a piece of red cellophane over the question box.

		NM	EX	VG
Complete Set (135):		3,000	1,500	900.00
Common Card:		4.00	2.00	1.25
15	Babe Ruth	150.00	75.00	45.00

1954 Topps Scoops

World - and sports - history from the mid-18th Century through October 1953, is chronicled in this 156-card set. Four baseball subjects are presented in the set. Cards are 2-1/16" x 2-15/16" and feature on the front a color painting with a dated caption box at bottom. Originally a black scratch-off ink covered the caption box (cards with the black ink removed can still be considered Mint as those with the ink currently command little premium value). Backs feature a simulated newspaper front page with banner headline and picture, along with a description of the event.

		NM	EX	VG
Complete Set (156):		1,750	875.00	525.00
Common Card:		6.00	3.00	1.75
27	Bob Feller Strikeout King, Oct. 2, 1938 (Bob Feller)	60.00	30.00	18.00
41	Babe Ruth Sets Record, Sept. 30, 1927 (Babe Ruth)	250.00	125.00	75.00
130	Braves Go to Milwaukee	40.00	20.00	12.00
154	26-Inning Tie Game May 1, 1920	60.00	30.00	18.00

1955 Topps

The 1955 Topps set is numerically the smallest of the regular annual issues. The 3-3/4" x 2-5/8" cards mark the first time that Topps used a horizontal format for the entire set. While that format was new, the design was not; they are very similar to the 1954 cards to the point many pictures appeared in both years. Although it was slated for a 210-card set, the 1955 Topps set turned out to be only 206 cards with numbers 175, 186, 203 and 209 never being released. The scarce high numbers in this set begin with #161.

	NM	EX	VG
Complete Set (206):	8,000	3,750	2,250
Common Player (1-150):	20.00	10.00	6.00
Common Player (151-160):	25.00	12.50	7.50
Common Player (161-210):	45.00	22.50	13.50
1 "Dusty" Rhodes	85.00	20.00	6.00
2 Ted Williams	400.00	175.00	90.00
3 Art Fowler	20.00	10.00	6.00
4 Al Kaline	150.00	75.00	45.00
5 Jim Gilliam	40.00	20.00	12.00
6 Stan Hack	25.00	12.50	7.50
7 Jim Hegan	20.00	10.00	6.00
8 Hal Smith	20.00	10.00	6.00
9 Bob Miller	20.00	10.00	6.00
10 Bob Keegan	20.00	10.00	6.00
11 Ferris Fain	20.00	10.00	6.00
12 "Jake" Thies	20.00	10.00	6.00
13 Fred Marsh	20.00	10.00	6.00
14 Jim Finigan	20.00	10.00	6.00
15 Jim Pendleton	20.00	10.00	6.00
16 Roy Sievers	20.00	10.00	6.00
17 Bobby Hofman	20.00	10.00	6.00
18 Russ Kemmerer	20.00	10.00	6.00
19 Billy Herman	45.00	22.50	13.50
20 Andy Carey	25.00	12.50	7.50
21 Alex Grammas	20.00	10.00	6.00
22 Bill Skowron	35.00	17.50	10.00
23 Jack Parks	20.00	10.00	6.00
24 Hal Newhouser	50.00	25.00	15.00
25 Johnny Podres	40.00	20.00	12.00
26 Dick Groat	20.00	10.00	6.00
27 *Billy Gardner*	20.00	10.00	6.00
28 Ernie Banks	135.00	65.00	40.00
29 Herman Wehmeier	20.00	10.00	6.00
30 Vic Power	20.00	10.00	6.00
31 Warren Spahn	90.00	45.00	27.50
32 Ed McGhee	20.00	10.00	6.00
33 Tom Qualters	20.00	10.00	6.00
34 Wayne Terwilliger	20.00	10.00	6.00
35 Dave Jolly	20.00	10.00	6.00
36 Leo Kiely	20.00	10.00	6.00
37 *Joe Cunningham*	20.00	10.00	6.00
38 Bob Turley	27.50	13.50	8.25
39 Bill Glynn	20.00	10.00	6.00
40 Don Hoak	25.00	12.50	7.50
41 Chuck Stobbs	20.00	10.00	6.00
42 "Windy" McCall	20.00	10.00	6.00
43 Harvey Haddix	20.00	10.00	6.00
44 "Corky" Valentine	20.00	10.00	6.00
45 Hank Sauer	20.00	10.00	6.00
46 Ted Kazanski	20.00	10.00	6.00
47 Hank Aaron	265.00	130.00	80.00
48 Bob Kennedy	20.00	10.00	6.00
49 J.W. Porter	20.00	10.00	6.00
50 Jackie Robinson	260.00	130.00	80.00
51 Jim Hughes	25.00	12.50	7.50
52 Bill Tremel	20.00	10.00	6.00
53 Bill Taylor	20.00	10.00	6.00
54 Lou Limmer	20.00	10.00	6.00
55 "Rip" Repulski	20.00	10.00	6.00
56 Ray Jablonski	20.00	10.00	6.00
57 *Billy O'Dell*	20.00	10.00	6.00
58 Jim Rivera	20.00	10.00	6.00
59 Gair Allie	20.00	10.00	6.00
60 Dean Stone	20.00	10.00	6.00
61 "Spook" Jacobs	20.00	10.00	6.00
62 Thornton Kipper	20.00	10.00	6.00
63 Joe Collins	25.00	12.50	7.50
64 *Gus Triandos*	25.00	12.50	7.50
65 Ray Boone	20.00	10.00	6.00
66 Ron Jackson	20.00	10.00	6.00
67 Wally Moon	20.00	10.00	6.00
68 Jim Davis	20.00	10.00	6.00
69 Ed Bailey	20.00	10.00	6.00
70 Al Rosen	40.00	20.00	12.00
71 Ruben Gomez	20.00	10.00	6.00
72 Karl Olson	20.00	10.00	6.00
73 Jack Shepard	20.00	10.00	6.00
74 Bob Borkowski	20.00	10.00	6.00
75 *Sandy Amoros*	45.00	22.50	13.50
76 Howie Pollet	20.00	10.00	6.00
77 Arnold Portocarrero	20.00	10.00	6.00
78 Gordon Jones	20.00	10.00	6.00
79 Danny Schell	20.00	10.00	6.00
80 Bob Grim	25.00	12.50	7.50
81 Gene Conley	20.00	10.00	6.00
82 Chuck Harmon	20.00	10.00	6.00
83 Tom Brewer	20.00	10.00	6.00
84 *Camilo Pascual*	35.00	17.50	10.00
85 *Don Mossi*	35.00	17.50	10.00
86 Bill Wilson	20.00	10.00	6.00
87 Frank House	20.00	10.00	6.00
88 *Bob Skinner*	20.00	10.00	6.00
89 *Joe Frazier*	20.00	10.00	6.00
90 Karl Spooner	25.00	12.50	7.50
91 Milt Bolling	20.00	10.00	6.00
92 *Don Zimmer*	90.00	45.00	27.50
93 Steve Bilko	20.00	10.00	6.00
94 Reno Bertoia	20.00	10.00	6.00
95 Preston Ward	20.00	10.00	6.00
96 Charlie Bishop	20.00	10.00	6.00
97 Carlos Paula	20.00	10.00	6.00
98 Johnny Riddle	20.00	10.00	6.00
99 Frank Leja	25.00	12.50	7.50
100 Monte Irvin	40.00	20.00	12.00
101 Johnny Gray	20.00	10.00	6.00
102 Wally Westlake	20.00	10.00	6.00
103 Charlie White	20.00	10.00	6.00
104 Jack Harshman	20.00	10.00	6.00
105 Chuck Diering	20.00	10.00	6.00
106 *Frank Sullivan* (Several variations exist in the size, shape and density of the dot over the "i" in the facsimile autograph.)			
107 Curt Roberts	20.00	10.00	6.00
108 "Rube" Walker	25.00	12.50	7.50
109 Ed Lopat	30.00	15.00	9.00
110 Gus Zernial	20.00	10.00	6.00
111 Bob Milliken	25.00	12.50	7.50
112 Nelson King	20.00	10.00	6.00
113 Harry Brecheen	20.00	10.00	6.00
114 Lou Ortiz	20.00	10.00	6.00
115 Ellis Kinder	20.00	10.00	6.00
116 Tom Hurd	20.00	10.00	6.00
117 Mel Roach	20.00	10.00	6.00
118 Bob Purkey	20.00	10.00	6.00
119 Bob Lennon	20.00	10.00	6.00
120 Ted Kluszewski	45.00	22.50	13.50
121 Bill Renna	20.00	10.00	6.00
122 Carl Sawatski	20.00	10.00	6.00
123 "Sandy" Koufax	575.00	250.00	160.00
124 *Harmon Killebrew*	200.00	80.00	35.00
125 Ken Boyer	80.00	40.00	24.00
126 *Dick Hall*	20.00	10.00	6.00
127 *Dale Long*	20.00	10.00	6.00
128 Ted Lepcio	20.00	10.00	6.00
129 Elvin Tappe	20.00	10.00	6.00
130 Mayo Smith	20.00	10.00	6.00
131 Grady Hatton	20.00	10.00	6.00
132 Bob Trice	20.00	10.00	6.00
133 Dave Hoskins	20.00	10.00	6.00
134 Joe Jay	20.00	10.00	6.00
135 Johnny O'Brien	20.00	10.00	6.00
136 "Bunky" Stewart	20.00	10.00	6.00
137a Harry Elliott (Last line in bio is, "the Cards in '53.")			
137b Harry Elliott (Last line in bio ends, "the Cards in (crescent mark)")	20.00	10.00	6.00
137c Harry Elliott (Last line in bio ends, "the Cards in.")	20.00	10.00	6.00
138 Ray Herbert	20.00	10.00	6.00
139 Steve Kraly	25.00	12.50	7.50
140 Mel Parnell	20.00	10.00	6.00
141 Tom Wright	20.00	10.00	6.00
142 Jerry Lynch	20.00	10.00	6.00
143 Dick Schofield	20.00	10.00	6.00
144 *Joe Amalfitano*	20.00	10.00	6.00
145 Elmer Valo	20.00	10.00	6.00
146 *Dick Donovan*	20.00	10.00	6.00
147 Laurin Pepper	20.00	10.00	6.00
148 Hal Brown	20.00	10.00	6.00
149 Ray Crone	20.00	10.00	6.00
150 Mike Higgins	20.00	10.00	6.00
151 "Red" Kress	25.00	12.50	7.50
152 *Harry Agganis*	135.00	65.00	40.00
153 "Bud" Podbielan	25.00	12.50	7.50
154 Willie Miranda	25.00	12.50	7.50
155 Ed Mathews	110.00	55.00	35.00
156 Joe Black	60.00	30.00	18.00
157 Bob Miller	25.00	12.50	7.50
158 Tom Carroll	35.00	17.50	10.50
159 Johnny Schmitz	25.00	12.50	7.50
160 Ray Narleski	25.00	12.50	7.50
161 *Chuck Tanner*	50.00	25.00	15.00
162 Joe Coleman	45.00	22.50	13.50
163 Faye Throneberry	45.00	22.50	13.50
164 *Roberto Clemente*	1,400	575.00	350.00
165 Don Johnson	45.00	22.50	13.50
166 Hank Bauer	60.00	30.00	18.00
167 Tom Casagrande	45.00	22.50	13.50
168 Duane Pillette	45.00	22.50	13.50
169 Bob Oldis	45.00	22.50	13.50
170 Jim Pearce	45.00	22.50	13.50
171 Dick Brodowski	45.00	22.50	13.50
172 Frank Baumholtz	45.00	22.50	13.50
173 Bob Kline	45.00	22.50	13.50
174 Rudy Minarcin	45.00	22.50	13.50
175 Not Issued			
176 Norm Zauchin	45.00	22.50	13.50
177 Jim Robertson	45.00	22.50	13.50
178 Bobby Adams	45.00	22.50	13.50
179 Jim Bolger	45.00	22.50	13.50
180 Clem Labine	60.00	30.00	18.00
181 Roy McMillan	45.00	22.50	13.50
182 Humberto Robinson	45.00	22.50	13.50
183 Tony Jacobs	45.00	22.50	13.50
184 Harry Perkowski	45.00	22.50	13.50
185 Don Ferrarese	45.00	22.50	13.50
186 Not Issued			
187 Gil Hodges	140.00	70.00	40.00
188 Charlie Silvera	50.00	25.00	15.00
189 Phil Rizzuto	160.00	80.00	50.00
190 Gene Woodling	50.00	25.00	15.00
191 Ed Stanky	45.00	22.50	13.50
192 Jim Delsing	45.00	22.50	13.50
193 Johnny Sain	55.00	27.50	16.50
194 Willie Mays	475.00	175.00	100.00
195 Ed Roebuck	50.00	25.00	15.00
196 Gale Wade	45.00	22.50	13.50
197 Al Smith	45.00	22.50	13.50
198 Yogi Berra	250.00	125.00	75.00
199 Bert Hamric	50.00	25.00	15.00
200 Jack Jensen	60.00	30.00	18.00
201 Sherm Lollar	45.00	22.50	13.50
202 Jim Owens	45.00	22.50	13.50
203 Not Issued			
204 Frank Smith	45.00	22.50	13.50
205 Gene Freese	45.00	22.50	13.50
206 Pete Daley	45.00	22.50	13.50
207 Bill Consolo	45.00	22.50	13.50
208 Ray Moore	45.00	22.50	13.50
209 Not Issued			
210 Duke Snider	600.00	130.00	80.00

1955 Topps Doubleheaders

This set is a throwback to the 1911 T201 Mecca Double Folders. The cards are perforated through the middle, allowing them to be folded. Open, there is a color painting of a player set against a stadium background. When folded, a different player and stadium appears; both players share the same lower legs and feet. Backs have abbreviated career histories and stats. Placed side by side in reverse numerical order, the backgrounds form a continuous stadium scene. When open the cards measure 2-1/16" x 4-7/8". The 66 cards in the set mean 132 total players, all of whom also appeared in the lower numbers of the regular 1955 Topps set.

	NM	EX	VG
Complete Set (66):	4,000	2,000	1,200
Common Card:	45.00	22.50	13.50
Wax Pack:	240.00		
1-2 Al Rosen, Chuck Diering	60.00	25.00	15.00
3-4 Monte Irvin, Russ Kemmerer	60.00	30.00	18.00
5-6 Ted Kazanski, Gordon Jones	45.00	22.50	13.50
7-8 Bill Taylor, Billy O'Dell	45.00	22.50	13.50
9-10 J.W. Porter, Thornton Kipper	45.00	22.50	13.50
11-12 Curt Roberts, Arnie Portocarrero	45.00	22.50	13.50
13-14 Wally Westlake, Frank House	45.00	22.50	13.50
15-16 Rube Walker, Lou Limmer	45.00	22.50	13.50
17-18 Dean Stone, Charlie White	45.00	22.50	13.50
19-20 Karl Spooner, Jim Hughes	50.00	25.00	15.00
21-22 Bill Skowron, Frank Sullivan	60.00	30.00	18.00
23-24 Jack Shepard, Stan Hack	45.00	22.50	13.50
25-26 Jackie Robinson, Don Hoak	325.00	160.00	100.00
27-28 Dusty Rhodes, Jim Davis	45.00	22.50	13.50
29-30 Vic Power, Ed Bailey	45.00	22.50	13.50
31-32 Howie Pollet, Ernie Banks	200.00	100.00	60.00
33-34 Jim Pendleton, Gene Conley	45.00	22.50	13.50
35-36 Karl Olson, Andy Carey	45.00	22.50	13.50
37-38 Wally Moon, Joe Cunningham	45.00	22.50	13.50
39-40 Fred Marsh, "Jake" Thies	45.00	22.50	13.50
41-42 Ed Lopat, Harvey Haddix	45.00	22.50	13.50
43-44 Leo Kiely, Chuck Stobbs	45.00	22.50	13.50
45-46 Al Kaline, "Corky" Valentine	225.00	110.00	65.00
47-48 "Spook" Jacobs, Johnny Gray	45.00	22.50	13.50
49-50 Ron Jackson, Jim Finigan	45.00	22.50	13.50
51-52 Ray Jablonski, Bob Keegan	45.00	22.50	13.50
53-54 Billy Herman, Sandy Amoros	60.00	30.00	18.00
55-56 Chuck Harmon, Bob Skinner	45.00	22.50	13.50
57-58 Dick Hall, Bob Grim	45.00	22.50	13.50
59-60 Bill Glynn, Bob Miller	45.00	22.50	13.50
61-62 Billy Gardner, John Hetki	45.00	22.50	13.50
63-64 Bob Borkowski, Bob Turley	45.00	22.50	13.50
65-66 Joe Collins, Jack Harshman	45.00	22.50	13.50
67-68 Jim Hegan, Jack Parks	45.00	22.50	13.50
69-70 Ted Williams, Hal Smith	425.00	210.00	125.00
71-72 Gair Allie, Grady Hatton	45.00	22.50	13.50
73-74 Jerry Lynch, Harry Brecheen	45.00	22.50	13.50
75-76 Tom Wright, "Bunky" Stewart	45.00	22.50	13.50
77-78 Dave Hoskins, Ed McGhee	45.00	22.50	13.50
79-80 Roy Sievers, Art Fowler	45.00	22.50	13.50
81-82 Danny Schell, Gus Triandos	45.00	22.50	13.50
83-84 Joe Frazier, Don Mossi	45.00	22.50	13.50
85-86 Elmer Valo, Hal Brown	45.00	22.50	13.50
87-88 Bob Kennedy, "Windy" McCall	45.00	22.50	13.50
89-90 Ruben Gomez, Jim Rivera	45.00	22.50	13.50
91-92 Lou Ortiz, Milt Bolling	45.00	22.50	13.50
93-94 Carl Sawatski, Elvin Tappe	45.00	22.50	13.50
95-96 Dave Jolly, Bobby Hofman	45.00	22.50	13.50
97-98 Preston Ward, Don Zimmer	45.00	22.50	13.50
99-100 Bill Renna, Dick Groat	45.00	22.50	13.50

101-102	Bill Wilson, Bill Tremel	45.00	22.50	13.50
103-104	Hank Sauer, Camilo Pascual	45.00	22.50	13.50
105-106	Hank Aaron, Ray Herbert	400.00	200.00	120.00
107-108	Alex Grammas, Tom Qualters	45.00	22.50	13.50
109-110	Hal Newhouser, Charlie Bishop	60.00	30.00	18.00
111-112	Harmon Killebrew, John Podres	225.00	110.00	65.00
113-114	Ray Boone, Bob Purkey	45.00	22.50	13.50
115-116	Dale Long, Ferris Fain	45.00	22.50	13.50
117-118	Steve Bilko, Bob Milliken	45.00	22.50	13.50
119-120	Mel Parnell, Tom Hurd	45.00	22.50	13.50
121-122	Ted Kluszewski, Jim Owens	60.00	30.00	18.00
123-124	Gus Zernial, Bob Trice	45.00	22.50	13.50
125-126	"Rip" Repulski, Ted Lepcio	45.00	22.50	13.50
127-128	Warren Spahn, Tom Brewer	150.00	75.00	45.00
129-130	Jim Gilliam, Ellis Kinder	60.00	30.00	18.00
131-132	Herm Wehmeier, Wayne Terwilliger	45.00	22.50	13.50

1955 Topps Hocus Focus

This set is a direct descendant of the 1948 "Topps Magic Photo" issue. Again, the baseball players were part of a larger overall series covering several topical areas. The cards, 7/8" x 1-3/8", state on the back that they are a series of 23, though only 14 are known. The photos on these cards were developed by wetting the card's surface and exposing to light. Prices below are for cards with well-developed pictures. Cards with poorly developed photos are worth significantly less.

		NM	EX	VG
	Common Player:	255.00	125.00	76.00
1	Babe Ruth	3,500	1,750	1,000
2	Lou Gehrig	3,500	1,750	1,000
3	Dick Groat	275.00	135.00	80.00
4	Ed Lopat	400.00	200.00	120.00
5	Hank Sauer	250.00	125.00	75.00
6	"Dusty" Rhodes	250.00	125.00	75.00
7	Ted Williams	1,950	975.00	585.00
8	Harvey Haddix	250.00	125.00	75.00
9	Ray Boone	250.00	125.00	75.00
10	Al Rosen	450.00	225.00	135.00
11	Unknown			
12	Warren Spahn	600.00	300.00	180.00
13	Jim Rivera	250.00	125.00	75.00
14	Ted Kluszewski	600.00	300.00	180.00
15	Gus Zernial	250.00	125.00	75.00
16	Jackie Robinson	1,750	875.00	525.00
17	Unknown			
18	Johnny Schmitz	250.00	125.00	75.00
19	Unknown			
20	Karl Spooner	275.00	135.00	80.00
21	Ed Mathews	600.00	300.00	180.00
22	Unknown			
23	Unknown			

1955 Topps Stamps

An extremely rare and enigmatic test issue, these stamps are the same size as Topps' 1955 card issue and have a blank, gummed back. Most of the specimens currently known are imperforate along one of the sides. All of the known examples have counterparts in the regular set which range from card #6 through 108. The unnumbered stamps are checklisted here alphabetically, with gaps left in the numbering to accommodate future discoveries.

	NM	EX	VG
Common Player:	750.00	375.00	225.00

(1)	Ray Boone	750.00	375.00	225.00
(2)	Joe Cunningham	750.00	375.00	225.00
(3)	Jim Davis	750.00	375.00	225.00
(4)	Chuck Diering	750.00	375.00	225.00
(5)	Ruben Gomez	750.00	375.00	225.00
(6)	Alex Grammas	750.00	375.00	225.00
(7)	Stan Hack	750.00	375.00	225.00
(8)	Harvey Haddix	750.00	375.00	225.00
(9)	Bobby Hofman	750.00	375.00	225.00
(11)	Ray Jablonski	750.00	375.00	225.00
(12)	Dave Jolly	750.00	375.00	225.00
(13)	Ted Kazanski	750.00	375.00	225.00
(14)	Don Mossi	775.00	385.00	230.00
(15)	Jim Pendleton	750.00	375.00	225.00
(16)	Howie Pollet	750.00	375.00	225.00
(17)	Jack Shepard	750.00	375.00	225.00
(18)	Bob Skinner	750.00	375.00	225.00
(19)	Bill Skowron	975.00	485.00	290.00
(20)	Karl Spooner	775.00	385.00	230.00
(21)	Bill Tremel	750.00	375.00	225.00
(22)	Corky Valentine	750.00	375.00	225.00
(23)	Rube Walker	775.00	385.00	230.00
(24)	Charlie White	750.00	375.00	225.00

1956 Topps

This set is similar in format to the 1955 Topps set, again using both a portrait and an "action" picture. Some portraits are the same as those used in 1955 (and even 1954). Innovations found in the 1956 Topps set of 2-5/8" x 3-3/4" cards include team cards introduced as part of a regular set. Additionally, there are two unnumbered checklist cards (the complete set price quoted below does not include the checklist cards). Finally, there are cards of the two league presidents, William Harridge and Warren Giles. On the backs, a three-panel cartoon depicts big moments from the player's career while biographical information appears above the cartoon and the statistics below. Card backs for numbers 1-180 can be found with either white or gray cardboard. Some hobbyists feel a premium is warranted for gray backs between #1-100 and white backs from #101-180.

		NM	EX	VG
	Complete Set (340):	9,000	4,250	2,550
	Common Player (1-180):	15.00	7.50	4.50
	Common Player (181-340):	20.00	10.00	6.00
1	William Harridge	125.00	25.00	15.00
2	Warren Giles	65.00	12.00	6.00
3	Elmer Valo	15.00	7.50	4.50
4	Carlos Paula	15.00	7.50	4.50
5	Ted Williams	375.00	130.00	70.00
6	Ray Boone	15.00	7.50	4.50
7	Ron Negray	15.00	7.50	4.50
8	Walter Alston	45.00	22.50	13.50
9	Ruben Gomez	15.00	7.50	4.50
10	Warren Spahn	75.00	37.50	22.50
11a	Chicago Cubs - 1955	125.00	65.00	35.00
11b	Chicago Cubs (No date, name centered.)	60.00	30.00	18.00
11c	Chicago Cubs (No date, name at left.)	70.00	35.00	20.00
12	Andy Carey	20.00	10.00	6.00
13	Roy Face	15.00	7.50	4.50
14	Ken Boyer	25.00	12.50	7.50
15	Ernie Banks	100.00	50.00	30.00
16	Hector Lopez	20.00	10.00	6.00
17	Gene Conley	15.00	7.50	4.50
18	Dick Donovan	15.00	7.50	4.50
19	Chuck Diering	15.00	7.50	4.50
20	Al Kaline	75.00	37.50	22.50
21	Joe Collins	20.00	10.00	6.00
22	Jim Finigan	15.00	7.50	4.50
23	Freddie Marsh	20.00	10.00	6.00
24	Dick Groat	20.00	10.00	6.00
25	Ted Kluszewski	35.00	17.50	10.00
26	Grady Hatton	15.00	7.50	4.50
27	Nelson Burbrink	15.00	7.50	4.50
28	Bobby Hofman	15.00	7.50	4.50
29	Jack Harshman	15.00	7.50	4.50
30	Jackie Robinson	165.00	85.00	50.00
31	Hank Aaron	225.00	110.00	65.00
32	Frank House	15.00	7.50	4.50
33	Roberto Clemente	250.00	125.00	75.00
34	Tom Brewer	15.00	7.50	4.50
35	Al Rosen	20.00	10.00	6.00
36	Rudy Minarcin	15.00	7.50	4.50
37	Alex Grammas	15.00	7.50	4.50
38	Bob Kennedy	15.00	7.50	4.50
39	Don Mossi	15.00	7.50	4.50
40	Bob Turley	25.00	12.50	7.50
41	Hank Sauer	15.00	7.50	4.50
42	Sandy Amoros	25.00	12.50	7.50
43	Ray Moore	15.00	7.50	4.50
44	"Windy" McCall	15.00	7.50	4.50
45	Gus Zernial	15.00	7.50	4.50
46	Gene Freese	15.00	7.50	4.50
47	Art Fowler	15.00	7.50	4.50
48	Jim Hegan	15.00	7.50	4.50
49	Pedro Ramos	20.00	10.00	6.00
50	"Dusty" Rhodes	15.00	7.50	4.50
51	Ernie Oravetz	15.00	7.50	4.50
52	Bob Grim	20.00	10.00	6.00
53	Arnold Portocarrero	15.00	7.50	4.50
54	Bob Keegan	15.00	7.50	4.50
55	Wally Moon	15.00	7.50	4.50
56	Dale Long	15.00	7.50	4.50
57	"Duke" Maas	15.00	7.50	4.50
58	Ed Roebuck	20.00	10.00	6.00
59	Jose Santiago	15.00	7.50	4.50
60	Mayo Smith	15.00	7.50	4.50
61	Bill Skowron	35.00	17.50	10.00
62	Hal Smith	15.00	7.50	4.50
63	Roger Craig	27.50	13.50	8.00
64	Luis Arroyo	15.00	7.50	4.50
65	Johnny O'Brien	15.00	7.50	4.50
66	Bob Speake	15.00	7.50	4.50
67	Vic Power	15.00	7.50	4.50
68	Chuck Stobbs	15.00	7.50	4.50
69	Chuck Tanner	15.00	7.50	4.50
70	Jim Rivera	15.00	7.50	4.50
71	Frank Sullivan	15.00	7.50	4.50
72a	Philadelphia Phillies - 1955	80.00	40.00	24.00
72b	Philadelphia Phillies	40.00	20.00	12.00
72c	Philadelphia Phillies (No date, name at left.)	60.00	30.00	18.00
73	Wayne Terwilliger	15.00	7.50	4.50
74	Jim King	15.00	7.50	4.50
75	Roy Sievers	15.00	7.50	4.50
76	Ray Crone	15.00	7.50	4.50
77	Harvey Haddix	15.00	7.50	4.50
78	Herman Wehmeier	15.00	7.50	4.50
79	Sandy Koufax	185.00	90.00	50.00
80	Gus Triandos	15.00	7.50	4.50
81	Wally Westlake	15.00	7.50	4.50
82	Bill Renna	15.00	7.50	4.50
83	Karl Spooner	20.00	10.00	6.00
84	"Babe" Birrer	15.00	7.50	4.50
85a	Cleveland Indians - 1955	85.00	42.50	25.00
85b	Cleveland Indians (no date, name centered)	50.00	25.00	15.00
85c	Cleveland Indians (no date, name at left)	60.00	30.00	18.00
86	Ray Jablonski	15.00	7.50	4.50
87	Dean Stone	15.00	7.50	4.50
88	Johnny Kucks	20.00	10.00	6.00
89	Norm Zauchin	15.00	7.50	4.50
90a	Cincinnati Redlegs - 1955	100.00	50.00	30.00
90b	Cincinnati Redlegs (No date, name centered.)	45.00	22.50	13.50
90c	Cincinnati Redlegs (No date, name at left.)	90.00	45.00	27.50
91	Gail Harris	15.00	7.50	4.50
92	"Red" Wilson	15.00	7.50	4.50
93	George Susce, Jr.	15.00	7.50	4.50
94	Ronnie Kline	15.00	7.50	4.50
95a	Milwaukee Braves - 1955	160.00	80.00	50.00
95b	Milwaukee Braves (No date, name centered.)	60.00	30.00	18.00
95c	Milwaukee Braves (No date, name at left.)	55.00	27.50	16.50
96	Bill Tremel	15.00	7.50	4.50
97	Jerry Lynch	15.00	7.50	4.50
98	Camilo Pascual	15.00	7.50	4.50
99	Don Zimmer	30.00	15.00	9.00
100a	Baltimore Orioles - 1955	160.00	80.00	45.00
100b	Baltimore Orioles (No date, name centered.)	110.00	55.00	35.00
100c	Baltimore Orioles (No date, name at left.)	110.00	55.00	35.00
101	Roy Campanella	100.00	50.00	30.00
102	Jim Davis	15.00	7.50	4.50
103	Willie Miranda	15.00	7.50	4.50
104	Bob Lennon	15.00	7.50	4.50
105	Al Smith	15.00	7.50	4.50
106	Joe Astroth	15.00	7.50	4.50
107	Ed Mathews	70.00	35.00	20.00
108	Laurin Pepper	15.00	7.50	4.50
109	Enos Slaughter	32.50	16.00	10.00
110	Yogi Berra	115.00	55.00	35.00
111	Boston Red Sox	35.00	17.50	10.00
112	Dee Fondy	15.00	7.50	4.50
113	Phil Rizzuto	95.00	47.50	27.50
114	Jim Owens	15.00	7.50	4.50
115	Jackie Jensen	20.00	10.00	6.00
116	Eddie O'Brien	15.00	7.50	4.50
117	Virgil Trucks	15.00	7.50	4.50
118	"Nellie" Fox	50.00	25.00	15.00
119	Larry Jackson	15.00	7.50	4.50
120	Richie Ashburn	50.00	25.00	15.00
121	Pittsburgh Pirates	65.00	32.50	20.00
122	Willard Nixon	15.00	7.50	4.50
123	Roy McMillan	15.00	7.50	4.50
124	Don Kaiser	15.00	7.50	4.50
125	"Minnie" Minoso	30.00	15.00	9.00
126	Jim Brady	15.00	7.50	4.50
127	Willie Jones	15.00	7.50	4.50
128	Eddie Yost	15.00	7.50	4.50
129	"Jake" Martin	15.00	7.50	4.50
130	Willie Mays	225.00	110.00	65.00
131	Bob Roselli	15.00	7.50	4.50
132	Bobby Avila	15.00	7.50	4.50
133	Ray Narleski	15.00	7.50	4.50
134	St. Louis Cardinals	25.00	12.50	7.50
135	Mickey Mantle	875.00	400.00	215.00
136	Johnny Logan	15.00	7.50	4.50
137	Al Silvera	15.00	7.50	4.50
138	Johnny Antonelli	15.00	7.50	4.50
139	Tommy Carroll	20.00	10.00	6.00
140	Herb Score	35.00	17.50	10.00

#	Player	NM	EX	VG
141	Joe Frazier	15.00	7.50	4.50
142	Gene Baker	15.00	7.50	4.50
143	Jim Piersall	20.00	10.00	6.00
144	Leroy Powell	15.00	7.50	4.50
145	Gil Hodges	55.00	27.50	16.50
146	Washington Nationals	40.00	20.00	12.00
147	Earl Torgeson	15.00	7.50	4.50
148	Alvin Dark	15.00	7.50	4.50
149	"Dixie" Howell	15.00	7.50	4.50
150	"Duke" Snider	95.00	47.50	27.50
151	"Spook" Jacobs	15.00	7.50	4.50
152	Billy Hoeft	15.00	7.50	4.50
153	Frank Thomas	15.00	7.50	4.50
154	Dave Pope	15.00	7.50	4.50
155	Harvey Kuenn	15.00	7.50	4.50
156	Wes Westrum	15.00	7.50	4.50
157	Dick Brodowski	15.00	7.50	4.50
158	Wally Post	15.00	7.50	4.50
159	Clint Courtney	15.00	7.50	4.50
160	Billy Pierce	15.00	7.50	4.50
161	Joe De Maestri	15.00	7.50	4.50
162	"Gus" Bell	15.00	7.50	4.50
163	Gene Woodling	15.00	7.50	4.50
164	Harmon Killebrew	100.00	50.00	30.00
165	"Red" Schoendienst	35.00	17.50	10.00
166	Brooklyn Dodgers	135.00	65.00	40.00
167	Harry Dorish	15.00	7.50	4.50
168	Sammy White	15.00	7.50	4.50
169	Bob Nelson	15.00	7.50	4.50
170	Bill Virdon	15.00	7.50	4.50
171	Jim Wilson	15.00	7.50	4.50
172	*Frank Torre*	20.00	10.00	6.00
173	Johnny Podres	30.00	15.00	9.00
174	Glen Gorbous	15.00	7.50	4.50
175	Del Crandall	15.00	7.50	4.50
176	Alex Kellner	15.00	7.50	4.50
177	Hank Bauer	30.00	15.00	9.00
178	Joe Black	20.00	10.00	6.00
179	Harry Chiti	15.00	7.50	4.50
180	Robin Roberts	40.00	20.00	12.00
181	Billy Martin	50.00	25.00	15.00
182	Paul Minner	20.00	10.00	6.00
183	Stan Lopata	20.00	10.00	6.00
184	Don Bessent	25.00	12.50	7.50
185	Bill Bruton	20.00	10.00	6.00
186	Ron Jackson	20.00	10.00	6.00
187	Early Wynn	55.00	27.50	16.50
188	Chicago White Sox	75.00	37.50	22.50
189	Ned Garver	20.00	10.00	6.00
190	Carl Furillo	45.00	22.50	13.50
191	Frank Lary	20.00	10.00	6.00
192	"Smoky" Burgess	20.00	10.00	6.00
193	Wilmer Mizell	20.00	10.00	6.00
194	Monte Irvin	55.00	27.50	16.50
195	George Kell	45.00	22.50	13.50
196	Tom Poholsky	20.00	10.00	6.00
197	Granny Hamner	20.00	10.00	6.00
198	Ed Fitzgerald	20.00	10.00	6.00
199	Hank Thompson	20.00	10.00	6.00
200	Bob Feller	100.00	50.00	30.00
201	"Rip" Repulski	20.00	10.00	6.00
202	Jim Hearn	20.00	10.00	6.00
203	Bill Tuttle	20.00	10.00	6.00
204	Art Swanson	20.00	10.00	6.00
205	"Whitey" Lockman	20.00	10.00	6.00
206	Erv Palica	20.00	10.00	6.00
207	Jim Small	20.00	10.00	6.00
208	Elston Howard	45.00	22.50	13.50
209	Max Surkont	20.00	10.00	6.00
210	Mike Garcia	20.00	10.00	6.00
211	Murry Dickson	20.00	10.00	6.00
212	Johnny Temple	20.00	10.00	6.00
213	Detroit Tigers	60.00	30.00	18.00
214	Bob Rush	20.00	10.00	6.00
215	Tommy Byrne	25.00	12.50	7.50
216	Jerry Schoonmaker	20.00	10.00	6.00
217	Billy Klaus	20.00	10.00	6.00
218	Joe Nuxall (Nuxhall)	25.00	12.50	7.50
219	Lew Burdette	20.00	10.00	6.00
220	Del Ennis	20.00	10.00	6.00
221	Bob Friend	20.00	10.00	6.00
222	Dave Philley	20.00	10.00	6.00
223	Randy Jackson	25.00	12.50	7.50
224	"Bud" Podbielan	20.00	10.00	6.00
225	Gil McDougald	35.00	17.50	10.00
226	New York Giants	50.00	25.00	15.00
227	Russ Meyer	20.00	10.00	6.00
228	"Mickey" Vernon	20.00	10.00	6.00
229	Harry Brecheen	20.00	10.00	6.00
230	"Chico" Carrasquel	20.00	10.00	6.00
231	Bob Hale	20.00	10.00	6.00
232	"Toby" Atwell	20.00	10.00	6.00
233	Carl Erskine	30.00	15.00	9.00
234	"Pete" Runnels	20.00	10.00	6.00
235	Don Newcombe	55.00	27.50	16.50
236	Kansas City Athletics	35.00	17.50	10.00
237	Jose Valdivielso	20.00	10.00	6.00
238	Walt Dropo	20.00	10.00	6.00
239	Harry Simpson	20.00	10.00	6.00
240	"Whitey" Ford	90.00	45.00	27.50
241	Don Mueller	20.00	10.00	6.00
242	Hershell Freeman	20.00	10.00	6.00
243	Sherm Lollar	20.00	10.00	6.00
244	Bob Buhl	20.00	10.00	6.00
245	Billy Goodman	20.00	10.00	6.00
246	Tom Gorman	20.00	10.00	6.00
247	Bill Sarni	20.00	10.00	6.00
248	Bob Porterfield	20.00	10.00	6.00
249	Johnny Klippstein	20.00	10.00	6.00
250	Larry Doby	45.00	22.50	13.50
251	New York Yankees	250.00	125.00	75.00
252	Vernon Law	20.00	10.00	6.00
253	Irv Noren	25.00	12.50	7.50
254	George Crowe	20.00	10.00	6.00
255	Bob Lemon	35.00	17.50	10.00
256	Tom Hurd	20.00	10.00	6.00
257	Bobby Thomson	25.00	12.50	7.50
258	Art Ditmar	20.00	10.00	6.00
259	Sam Jones	20.00	10.00	6.00
260	"Pee Wee" Reese	120.00	60.00	35.00
261	Bobby Shantz	20.00	10.00	6.00
262	Howie Pollet	20.00	10.00	6.00
263	Bob Miller	20.00	10.00	6.00
264	Ray Monzant	20.00	10.00	6.00
265	Sandy Consuegra	20.00	10.00	6.00
266	Don Ferrarese	20.00	10.00	6.00
267	Bob Nieman	20.00	10.00	6.00
268	Dale Mitchell	20.00	10.00	6.00
269	Jack Meyer	20.00	10.00	6.00
270	Billy Loes	25.00	12.50	7.50
271	Foster Castleman	20.00	10.00	6.00
272	Danny O'Connell	20.00	10.00	6.00
273	Walker Cooper	20.00	10.00	6.00
274	Frank Baumholtz	20.00	10.00	6.00
275	Jim Greengrass	20.00	10.00	6.00
276	George Zuverink	20.00	10.00	6.00
277	Daryl Spencer	20.00	10.00	6.00
278	Chet Nichols	20.00	10.00	6.00
279	Johnny Groth	20.00	10.00	6.00
280	Jim Gilliam	45.00	22.50	13.50
281	Art Houtteman	20.00	10.00	6.00
282	Warren Hacker	20.00	10.00	6.00
283	Hal Smith	20.00	10.00	6.00
284	Ike Delock	20.00	10.00	6.00
285	Eddie Miksis	20.00	10.00	6.00
286	Bill Wight	20.00	10.00	6.00
287	Bobby Adams	20.00	10.00	6.00
288	Bob Cerv/SP	45.00	22.50	13.50
289	Hal Jeffcoat	20.00	10.00	6.00
290	Curt Simmons	20.00	10.00	6.00
291	Frank Kellert	20.00	10.00	6.00
292	*Luis Aparicio*	100.00	50.00	30.00
293	Stu Miller	20.00	10.00	6.00
294	Ernie Johnson	20.00	10.00	6.00
295	Clem Labine	30.00	15.00	9.00
296	Andy Seminick	20.00	10.00	6.00
297	Bob Skinner	20.00	10.00	6.00
298	Johnny Schmitz	20.00	10.00	6.00
299	Charley Neal/SP	35.00	17.50	10.00
300	Vic Wertz	20.00	10.00	6.00
301	Marv Grissom	20.00	10.00	6.00
302	Eddie Robinson	25.00	12.50	7.50
303	Jim Dyck	20.00	10.00	6.00
304	Frank Malzone	20.00	10.00	6.00
305	Brooks Lawrence	20.00	10.00	6.00
306	Curt Roberts	20.00	10.00	6.00
307	Hoyt Wilhelm	40.00	20.00	12.00
308	"Chuck" Harmon	20.00	10.00	6.00
309	*Don Blasingame*	25.00	12.50	7.50
310	Steve Gromek	20.00	10.00	6.00
311	Hal Naragon	20.00	10.00	6.00
312	Andy Pafko	20.00	10.00	6.00
313	Gene Stephens	20.00	10.00	6.00
314	Hobie Landrith	20.00	10.00	6.00
315	Milt Bolling	20.00	10.00	6.00
316	Jerry Coleman	25.00	12.50	7.50
317	Al Aber	20.00	10.00	6.00
318	Fred Hatfield	20.00	10.00	6.00
319	Jack Crimian	20.00	10.00	6.00
320	Joe Adcock	20.00	10.00	6.00
321	Jim Konstanty	25.00	12.50	7.50
322	Karl Olson	20.00	10.00	6.00
323	Willard Schmidt	20.00	10.00	6.00
324	"Rocky" Bridges	20.00	10.00	6.00
325	Don Liddle	20.00	10.00	6.00
326	Connie Johnson	20.00	10.00	6.00
327	Bob Wiesler	20.00	10.00	6.00
328	Preston Ward	20.00	10.00	6.00
329	Lou Berberet	20.00	10.00	6.00
330	Jim Busby	20.00	10.00	6.00
331	Dick Hall	20.00	10.00	6.00
332	Don Larsen	55.00	27.50	16.50
333	"Rube" Walker	25.00	12.50	7.50
334	Bob Miller	20.00	10.00	6.00
335	Don Hoak	20.00	10.00	6.00
336	Ellis Kinder	20.00	10.00	6.00
337	Bobby Morgan	20.00	10.00	6.00
338	Jim Delsing	20.00	10.00	6.00
339	Rance Pless	20.00	10.00	6.00
340	Mickey McDermott	45.00	15.00	8.00
----	Checklist 1/3	150.00	45.00	30.00
----	Checklist 2/4	190.00	60.00	35.00

1956 Topps Hocus Focus

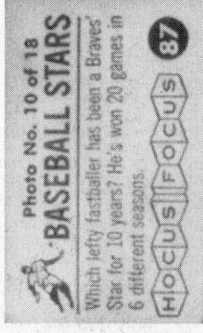

Following its 1955 issue with a somewhat larger format (1" x 1-5/8") the following year, the baseball players in this set are part of a larger overall series covering several topical areas. Cards backs specify an issue of 18 baseball stars. The black-and-white photos on these cards were developed by wetting the card's surface and exposing to light. Prices below are for cards with well-developed pictures. Cards with poorly developed photos are worth significantly less.

		NM	EX	VG
Complete Set (18):		7,000	3,500	2,100
Common Player:		220.00	110.00	66.00
1	Dick Groat	225.00	110.00	65.00
2	Ed Lopat	425.00	210.00	125.00
3	Hank Sauer	225.00	110.00	65.00
4	"Dusty" Rhodes	225.00	110.00	65.00
5	Ted Williams	1,600	800.00	480.00
6	Harvey Haddix	225.00	110.00	65.00
7	Ray Boone	225.00	110.00	65.00
8	Al Rosen	250.00	125.00	75.00
9	Mayo Smith	225.00	110.00	65.00
10	Warren Spahn	550.00	275.00	165.00
11	Jim Rivera	225.00	110.00	65.00
12	Ted Kluszewski	450.00	225.00	135.00
13	Gus Zernial	225.00	110.00	65.00
14	Jackie Robinson	1,350	675.00	400.00
15	Hal Smith	225.00	110.00	65.00
16	Johnny Schmitz	225.00	110.00	65.00
17	"Spook" Jacobs	225.00	110.00	65.00
18	Mel Parnell	225.00	110.00	65.00

1956 Topps Pins

One of Topps first specialty issues, the 60-pin set of ballplayers issued in 1956 contains a high percentage of big-name stars which, combined with the scarcity of the pins, makes collecting a complete set extremely challenging. Compounding the situation is the fact that some pins are seen far less often than others, though the reason is unknown. Chuck Stobbs, Hector Lopez and Chuck Diering are unaccountably scarce. Measuring 1-1/8" in diameter, the pins utilize the same portraits found on 1956 Topps baseball cards. The photos are set against a solid color background. The pins were sold in a box picturing the Ted Williams pin, with a piece of bubblegum for five cents.

		NM	EX	VG
Complete Set (60):		3,600	1,800	1,100
Common Player:		40.00	20.00	12.00
Box:		500.00	250.00	150.00
(1)	Hank Aaron	200.00	100.00	60.00
(2)	Sandy Amoros	50.00	25.00	15.00
(3)	Luis Arroyo	40.00	20.00	12.00
(4)	Ernie Banks	150.00	75.00	45.00
(5)	Yogi Berra	150.00	75.00	45.00
(6)	Joe Black	60.00	30.00	18.00
(7)	Ray Boone	40.00	20.00	12.00
(8)	Ken Boyer	45.00	22.50	13.50
(9)	Joe Collins	45.00	22.50	13.50
(10)	Gene Conley	40.00	20.00	12.00
(11)	Chuck Diering	275.00	135.00	85.00
(12)	Dick Donovan	40.00	20.00	12.00
(13)	Jim Finigan	40.00	20.00	12.00
(14)	Art Fowler	40.00	20.00	12.00
(15)	Ruben Gomez	40.00	20.00	12.00
(16)	Dick Groat	40.00	20.00	12.00
(17)	Harvey Haddix	40.00	20.00	12.00
(18)	Jack Harshman	40.00	20.00	12.00
(19)	Grady Hatton	40.00	20.00	12.00
(20)	Jim Hegan	40.00	20.00	12.00
(21)	Gil Hodges	100.00	50.00	30.00
(22)	Bobby Hofman	40.00	20.00	12.00
(23)	Frank House	40.00	20.00	12.00
(24)	Jackie Jensen	45.00	22.50	13.50
(25)	Al Kaline	100.00	50.00	30.00
(26)	Bob Kennedy	40.00	20.00	12.00
(27)	Ted Kluszewski	85.00	42.50	25.00
(28)	Dale Long	40.00	20.00	12.00
(29)	Hector Lopez	400.00	200.00	120.00
(30)	Ed Mathews	100.00	50.00	30.00
(31)	Willie Mays	200.00	100.00	60.00
(32)	Roy McMillan	40.00	20.00	12.00
(33)	Willie Miranda	40.00	20.00	12.00
(34)	Wally Moon	40.00	20.00	12.00
(35)	Don Mossi	40.00	20.00	12.00
(36)	Ron Negray	40.00	20.00	12.00
(37)	Johnny O'Brien	40.00	20.00	12.00
(38)	Carlos Paula	40.00	20.00	12.00
(39)	Vic Power	40.00	20.00	12.00
(40)	Jim Rivera	40.00	20.00	12.00
(41)	Phil Rizzuto	150.00	75.00	45.00
(42)	Jackie Robinson	180.00	90.00	55.00
(43)	Al Rosen	45.00	22.50	13.50
(44)	Hank Sauer	40.00	20.00	12.00
(45)	Roy Sievers	40.00	20.00	12.00
(46)	Bill Skowron	45.00	22.50	13.50
(47)	Al Smith	40.00	20.00	12.00
(48)	Hal Smith	40.00	20.00	12.00
(49)	Mayo Smith	40.00	20.00	12.00
(50)	Duke Snider	125.00	65.00	35.00
(51)	Warren Spahn	100.00	50.00	30.00
(52)	Karl Spooner	45.00	22.50	13.50
(53)	Chuck Stobbs	225.00	110.00	65.00

	NM	EX	VG
(54) Frank Sullivan	40.00	20.00	12.00
(55) Bill Tremel	40.00	20.00	12.00
(56) Gus Triandos	40.00	20.00	12.00
(57) Bob Turley	50.00	25.00	15.00
(58) Herman Wehmeier	40.00	20.00	12.00
(59) Ted Williams	225.00	110.00	65.00
(60) Gus Zernial	40.00	20.00	12.00

1957 Topps

For 1957, Topps reduced the size of its cards to the now-standard 2-1/2" x 3-1/2". Set size was increased to 407 cards. Another change came in the form of the use of real color photographs as opposed to the hand-colored black and whites of previous years. For the first time since 1954, there were also cards with more than one player. The two, "Dodger Sluggers" and "Yankees' Power Hitters" began a trend toward the increased use of multiple-player cards. Another first-time innovation, found on the backs, is complete players statistics. The scarce cards in the set are not the highest numbers, but rather numbers 265-352. Four unnumbered checklist cards were issued along with the set. They are quite expensive and are not included in the complete set prices quoted below.

	NM	EX	VG
Complete Set (407):	10,000	5,000	3,000
Common Player (1-264):	12.00	6.00	3.50
Common Player (265-352):	25.00	12.50	7.50
Common Player (353-407):	12.00	6.00	3.50
1 Ted Williams	375.00	135.00	65.00
2 Yogi Berra	120.00	60.00	35.00
3 Dale Long	12.00	6.00	3.50
4 Johnny Logan	12.00	6.00	3.50
5 Sal Maglie	20.00	10.00	6.00
6 Hector Lopez	12.00	6.00	3.50
7 Luis Aparicio	40.00	20.00	12.00
8 Don Mossi	12.00	6.00	3.50
9 Johnny Temple	12.00	6.00	3.50
10 Willie Mays	215.00	100.00	65.00
11 George Zuverink	12.00	6.00	3.50
12 Dick Groat	12.00	6.00	3.50
13 Wally Burnette	12.00	6.00	3.50
14 Bob Nieman	12.00	6.00	3.50
15 Robin Roberts	50.00	25.00	15.00
16 Walt Moryn	12.00	6.00	3.50
17 Billy Gardner	12.00	6.00	3.50
18 *Don Drysdale*	165.00	80.00	50.00
19 Bob Wilson	12.00	6.00	3.50
20 Hank Aaron	200.00	100.00	60.00
(Photo reversed.)			
21 Frank Sullivan	12.00	6.00	3.50
22 Jerry Snyder (Photo actually	12.00	6.00	3.50
Ed Fitz Gerald.)			
23 Sherman Lollar	12.00	6.00	3.50
24 *Bill Mazeroski*	75.00	37.50	22.50
25 Whitey Ford	90.00	45.00	27.50
26 Bob Boyd	12.00	6.00	3.50
27 Ted Kazanski	12.00	6.00	3.50
28 Gene Conley	12.00	6.00	3.50
29 *Whitey Herzog*	15.00	7.50	4.50
30 Pee Wee Reese	75.00	37.50	22.50
31 Ron Northey	12.00	6.00	3.50
32 Hersh Freeman	12.00	6.00	3.50
33 Jim Small	12.00	6.00	3.50
34 Tom Sturdivant	15.00	7.50	4.50
35 *Frank Robinson*	180.00	75.00	35.00
36 Bob Grim	15.00	7.50	4.50
37 Frank Torre	12.00	6.00	3.50
38 Nellie Fox	40.00	20.00	12.00
39 Al Worthington	12.00	6.00	3.50
40 Early Wynn	30.00	15.00	9.00
41 Hal Smith	12.00	6.00	3.50
42 Dee Fondy	12.00	6.00	3.50
43 Connie Johnson	12.00	6.00	3.50
44 Joe DeMaestri	12.00	6.00	3.50
45 Carl Furillo	40.00	20.00	12.00
46 Bob Miller	12.00	6.00	3.50
47 Don Blasingame	12.00	6.00	3.50
48 Bill Bruton	12.00	6.00	3.50
49 Daryl Spencer	12.00	6.00	3.50
50 Herb Score	25.00	12.50	7.50
51 Clint Courtney	12.00	6.00	3.50
52 Lee Walls	12.00	6.00	3.50
53 Clem Labine	20.00	10.00	6.00
54 Elmer Valo	12.00	6.00	3.50
55 Ernie Banks	85.00	42.50	25.00
56 Dave Sisler	12.00	6.00	3.50
57 Jim Lemon	12.00	6.00	3.50
58 Ruben Gomez	12.00	6.00	3.50
59 Dick Williams	12.00	6.00	3.50
60 Billy Hoeft	12.00	6.00	3.50
61 Dusty Rhodes	12.00	6.00	3.50
62 Billy Martin	40.00	20.00	12.00
63 Ike Delock	12.00	6.00	3.50
64 Pete Runnels	12.00	6.00	3.50
65 Wally Moon	12.00	6.00	3.50
66 Brooks Lawrence	12.00	6.00	3.50
67 Chico Carrasquel	12.00	6.00	3.50
68 Ray Crone	12.00	6.00	3.50
69 Roy McMillan	12.00	6.00	3.50
70 Richie Ashburn	45.00	22.50	13.50
71 Murry Dickson	12.00	6.00	3.50
72 Bill Tuttle	12.00	6.00	3.50
73 George Crowe	12.00	6.00	3.50
74 Vito Valentinetti	12.00	6.00	3.50
75 Jim Piersall	15.00	7.50	4.50
76 Bob Clemente	175.00	90.00	45.00
77 Paul Foytack	12.00	6.00	3.50
78 Vic Wertz	12.00	6.00	3.50
79 *Lindy McDaniel*	15.00	7.50	4.50
80 Gil Hodges	45.00	22.50	13.50
81 Herm Wehmeier	12.00	6.00	3.50
82 Elston Howard	30.00	15.00	9.00
83 Lou Skizas	12.00	6.00	3.50
84 Moe Drabowsky	12.00	6.00	3.50
85 Larry Doby	40.00	20.00	12.00
86 Bill Sarni	12.00	6.00	3.50
87 Tom Gorman	12.00	6.00	3.50
88 Harvey Kuenn	12.00	6.00	3.50
89 Roy Sievers	12.00	6.00	3.50
90 Warren Spahn	60.00	30.00	18.00
91 Mack Burk	12.00	6.00	3.50
92 Mickey Vernon	12.00	6.00	3.50
93 Hal Jeffcoat	12.00	6.00	3.50
94 Bobby Del Greco	12.00	6.00	3.50
95 Mickey Mantle	650.00	275.00	180.00
96 *Hank Aguirre*	12.00	6.00	3.50
97 New York Yankees Team	65.00	32.50	20.00
98 Al Dark	12.00	6.00	3.50
99 Bob Keegan	12.00	6.00	3.50
100 League Presidents (Warren	60.00	30.00	18.00
Giles, William Harridge)			
101 Chuck Stobbs	12.00	6.00	3.50
102 Ray Boone	12.00	6.00	3.50
103 Joe Nuxhall	12.00	6.00	3.50
104 Hank Foiles	12.00	6.00	3.50
105 Johnny Antonelli	12.00	6.00	3.50
106 Ray Moore	12.00	6.00	3.50
107 Jim Rivera	12.00	6.00	3.50
108 Tommy Byrne	15.00	7.50	4.50
109 Hank Thompson	12.00	6.00	3.50
110 Bill Virdon	12.00	6.00	3.50
111 Hal Smith	12.00	6.00	3.50
112 Tom Brewer	12.00	6.00	3.50
113 Wilmer Mizell	12.00	6.00	3.50
114 Milwaukee Braves Team	30.00	15.00	9.00
115 Jim Gilliam	27.50	13.50	8.25
116 Mike Fornieles	12.00	6.00	3.50
117 Joe Adcock	12.00	6.00	3.50
118 Bob Porterfield	12.00	6.00	3.50
119 Stan Lopata	12.00	6.00	3.50
120 Bob Lemon	35.00	17.50	10.00
121 *Cletis Boyer*	30.00	15.00	9.00
122 Ken Boyer	20.00	10.00	6.00
123 Steve Ridzik	12.00	6.00	3.50
124 Dave Philley	12.00	6.00	3.50
125 Al Kaline	75.00	37.50	22.50
126 Bob Wiesler	12.00	6.00	3.50
127 Bob Buhl	12.00	6.00	3.50
128 Ed Bailey	12.00	6.00	3.50
129 Saul Rogovin	12.00	6.00	3.50
130 Don Newcombe	25.00	12.50	7.50
131 Milt Bolling	12.00	6.00	3.50
132 Art Ditmar	12.00	6.00	3.50
133 Del Crandall	12.00	6.00	3.50
134 Don Kaiser	12.00	6.00	3.50
135 Bill Skowron	30.00	15.00	9.00
136 Jim Hegan	12.00	6.00	3.50
137 Bob Rush	12.00	6.00	3.50
138 Minnie Minoso	25.00	12.50	7.50
139 Lou Kretlow	12.00	6.00	3.50
140 Frank Thomas	12.00	6.00	3.50
141 Al Aber	12.00	6.00	3.50
142 Charley Thompson	12.00	6.00	3.50
143 Andy Pafko	12.00	6.00	3.50
144 Ray Narleski	12.00	6.00	3.50
145 Al Smith	12.00	6.00	3.50
146 Don Ferrarese	12.00	6.00	3.50
147 Al Walker	15.00	7.50	4.50
148 Don Mueller	12.00	6.00	3.50
149 Bob Kennedy	12.00	6.00	3.50
150 Bob Friend	12.00	6.00	3.50
151 Willie Miranda	12.00	6.00	3.50
152 Jack Harshman	12.00	6.00	3.50
153 Karl Olson	12.00	6.00	3.50
154 Red Schoendienst	30.00	15.00	9.00
155 Jim Brosnan	12.00	6.00	3.50
156 Gus Triandos	12.00	6.00	3.50
157 Wally Post	12.00	6.00	3.50
158 Curt Simmons	12.00	6.00	3.50
159 Solly Drake	12.00	6.00	3.50
160 Billy Pierce	12.00	6.00	3.50
161 Pittsburgh Pirates Team	20.00	10.00	6.00
162 Jack Meyer	12.00	6.00	3.50
163 Sammy White	12.00	6.00	3.50
164 Tommy Carroll	15.00	7.50	4.50
165 Ted Kluszewski	65.00	32.50	20.00
166 Roy Face	12.00	6.00	3.50
167 Vic Power	12.00	6.00	3.50
168 Frank Lary	12.00	6.00	3.50
169 Herb Plews	12.00	6.00	3.50
170 Duke Snider	95.00	47.50	27.50
171 Boston Red Sox Team	32.50	16.00	10.00
172 Gene Woodling	12.00	6.00	3.50
173 Roger Craig	15.00	7.50	4.50
174 Willie Jones	12.00	6.00	3.50
175 Don Larsen	35.00	17.50	10.00
176a Gene Baker	12.00	6.00	3.50
176b Gene Baker (Error on back,	650.00	360.00	215.00
"EUGENF W. BAKEP.")			
177 Eddie Yost	12.00	6.00	3.50
178 Don Bessent	15.00	7.50	4.50
179 Ernie Oravetz	12.00	6.00	3.50
180 Gus Bell	12.00	6.00	3.50
181 Dick Donovan	12.00	6.00	3.50
182 Hobie Landrith	12.00	6.00	3.50
183 Chicago Cubs Team	25.00	12.50	7.50
184 *Tito Francona*	12.00	6.00	3.50
185 Johnny Kucks	15.00	7.50	4.50
186 Jim King	12.00	6.00	3.50
187 Virgil Trucks	12.00	6.00	3.50
188 Felix Mantilla	12.00	6.00	3.50
189 Willard Nixon	12.00	6.00	3.50
190 Randy Jackson	15.00	7.50	4.50
191 Joe Margoneri	12.00	6.00	3.50
192 Jerry Coleman	15.00	7.50	4.50
193 Del Rice	12.00	6.00	3.50
194 Hal Brown	12.00	6.00	3.50
195 Bobby Avila	12.00	6.00	3.50
196 Larry Jackson	12.00	6.00	3.50
197 Hank Sauer	12.00	6.00	3.50
198 Detroit Tigers Team	20.00	10.00	6.00
199 Vernon Law	12.00	6.00	3.50
200 Gil McDougald	25.00	12.50	7.50
201 Sandy Amoros	25.00	12.50	7.50
202 Dick Gernert	12.00	6.00	3.50
203 Hoyt Wilhelm	25.00	12.50	7.50
204 Kansas City A's Team	20.00	10.00	6.00
205 Charley Maxwell	12.00	6.00	3.50
206 Willard Schmidt	12.00	6.00	3.50
207 Billy Hunter	12.00	6.00	3.50
208 Lew Burdette	12.00	6.00	3.50
209 Bob Skinner	12.00	6.00	3.50
210 Roy Campanella	95.00	47.50	27.50
211 Camilo Pascual	12.00	6.00	3.50
212 *Rocky Colavito*	70.00	35.00	20.00
213 Les Moss	12.00	6.00	3.50
214 Philadelphia Phillies Team	25.00	12.50	7.50
215 Enos Slaughter	35.00	17.50	10.00
216 Marv Grissom	12.00	6.00	3.50
217 Gene Stephens	12.00	6.00	3.50
218 Ray Jablonski	12.00	6.00	3.50
219 Tom Acker	12.00	6.00	3.50
220 Jackie Jensen	17.50	8.75	5.25
221 Dixie Howell	12.00	6.00	3.50
222 Alex Grammas	12.00	6.00	3.50
223 Frank House	12.00	6.00	3.50
224 Marv Blaylock	12.00	6.00	3.50
225 Harry Simpson	12.00	6.00	3.50
226 Preston Ward	12.00	6.00	3.50
227 Jerry Staley	12.00	6.00	3.50
228 Smoky Burgess	12.00	6.00	3.50
229 George Susce	12.00	6.00	3.50
230 George Kell	25.00	12.50	7.50
231 Solly Hemus	12.00	6.00	3.50
232 Whitey Lockman	12.00	6.00	3.50
233 Art Fowler	12.00	6.00	3.50
234 Dick Cole	12.00	6.00	3.50
235 Tom Poholsky	12.00	6.00	3.50
236 Joe Ginsberg	12.00	6.00	3.50
237 Foster Castleman	12.00	6.00	3.50
238 Eddie Robinson	12.00	6.00	3.50
239 Tom Morgan	12.00	6.00	3.50
240 Hank Bauer	30.00	15.00	9.00
241 Joe Lonnett	12.00	6.00	3.50
242 Charley Neal	15.00	7.50	4.50
243 St. Louis Cardinals Team	20.00	10.00	6.00
244 Billy Loes	12.00	6.00	3.50
245 Rip Repulski	12.00	6.00	3.50
246 Jose Valdivielso	12.00	6.00	3.50
247 Turk Lown	12.00	6.00	3.50
248 Jim Finigan	12.00	6.00	3.50
249 Dave Pope	12.00	6.00	3.50
250 Ed Mathews	55.00	27.50	16.50
251 Baltimore Orioles Team	20.00	10.00	6.00
252 Carl Erskine	20.00	10.00	6.00
253 Gus Zernial	12.00	6.00	3.50
254 Ron Negray	12.00	6.00	3.50
255 Charlie Silvera	12.00	6.00	3.50
256 Ronnie Kline	12.00	6.00	3.50
257 Walt Dropo	12.00	6.00	3.50
258 Steve Gromek	12.00	6.00	3.50
259 Eddie O'Brien	12.00	6.00	3.50
260 Del Ennis	12.00	6.00	3.50
261 Bob Chakales	12.00	6.00	3.50
262 Bobby Thomson	15.00	7.50	4.50
263 George Strickland	12.00	6.00	3.50
264 Bob Turley	25.00	12.50	7.50
265 Harvey Haddix	25.00	12.50	7.50
266 Ken Kuhn	25.00	12.50	7.50
267 Danny Kravitz	25.00	12.50	7.50
268 Jackie Collum	25.00	12.50	7.50
269 Bob Cerv	25.00	12.50	7.50
270 Washington Senators Team	45.00	22.50	13.50
271 Danny O'Connell	25.00	12.50	7.50
272 Bobby Shantz	40.00	20.00	12.00
273 Jim Davis	25.00	12.50	7.50
274 Don Hoak	25.00	12.50	7.50
275 Cleveland Indians Team	40.00	20.00	12.00
276 Jim Pyburn	25.00	12.50	7.50
277 Johnny Podres	40.00	20.00	12.00
278 Fred Hatfield	25.00	12.50	7.50
279 Bob Thurman	25.00	12.50	7.50
280 Alex Kellner	25.00	12.50	7.50
281 Gail Harris	25.00	12.50	7.50
282 Jack Dittmer	25.00	12.50	7.50
283 *Wes Covington*	25.00	12.50	7.50
284 Don Zimmer	40.00	20.00	12.00
285 Ned Garver	25.00	12.50	7.50
286 *Bobby Richardson*	100.00	50.00	30.00
287 Sam Jones	25.00	12.50	7.50
288 Ted Lepcio	25.00	12.50	7.50
289 Jim Bolger	25.00	12.50	7.50
290 Andy Carey	35.00	17.50	10.00
291 Windy McCall	25.00	10.00	6.00
292 Billy Klaus	25.00	12.50	7.50
293 Ted Abernathy	25.00	12.50	7.50
294 Rocky Bridges	25.00	12.50	7.50
295 Joe Collins	35.00	17.50	10.50

#	Player	NM	EX	VG
296	Johnny Klippstein	25.00	12.50	7.50
297	Jack Crimian	25.00	12.50	7.50
298	Irv Noren	25.00	12.50	7.50
299	Chuck Harmon	25.00	12.50	7.50
300	Mike Garcia	25.00	12.50	7.50
301	Sam Esposito	25.00	12.50	7.50
302	Sandy Koufax	225.00	110.00	65.00
303	Billy Goodman	25.00	12.50	7.50
304	Joe Cunningham	25.00	12.50	7.50
305	Chico Fernandez	25.00	12.50	7.50
306	*Darrell Johnson*	35.00	17.50	10.00
307	Jack Phillips	25.00	12.50	7.50
308	Dick Hall	25.00	12.50	7.50
309	Jim Busby	25.00	12.50	7.50
310	Max Surkont	25.00	12.50	7.50
311	Al Pilarcik	25.00	12.50	7.50
312	*Tony Kubek*	70.00	35.00	20.00
313	Mel Parnell	25.00	12.50	7.50
314	Ed Bouchee	25.00	12.50	7.50
315	Lou Berberet	25.00	12.50	7.50
316	Billy O'Dell	25.00	12.50	7.50
317	New York Giants Team	40.00	20.00	12.00
318	Mickey McDermott	25.00	12.50	7.50
319	*Gino Cimoli*	30.00	15.00	9.00
320	Neil Chrisley	25.00	12.50	7.50
321	Red Murff	25.00	12.50	7.50
322	Cincinnati Redlegs Team	45.00	22.50	13.50
323	Wes Westrum	25.00	12.50	7.50
324	Brooklyn Dodgers Team	100.00	50.00	30.00
325	Frank Bolling	25.00	12.50	7.50
326	Pedro Ramos	25.00	12.50	7.50
327	Jim Pendleton	25.00	12.50	7.50
328	*Brooks Robinson*	245.00	130.00	65.00
329	Chicago White Sox Team	45.00	22.50	13.50
330	Jim Wilson	25.00	12.50	7.50
331	Ray Katt	25.00	12.50	7.50
332	Bob Bowman	25.00	12.50	7.50
333	Ernie Johnson	25.00	12.50	7.50
334	Jerry Schoonmaker	25.00	12.50	7.50
335	Granny Hamner	25.00	12.50	7.50
336	*Haywood Sullivan*	25.00	12.50	7.50
337	Rene Valdes (Valdez)	30.00	15.00	9.00
338	*Jim Bunning*	85.00	42.50	25.00
339	Bob Speake	25.00	12.50	7.50
340	Bill Wight	25.00	12.50	7.50
341	Don Gross	25.00	12.50	7.50
342	Gene Mauch	25.00	12.50	7.50
343	Taylor Phillips	25.00	12.50	7.50
344	Paul LaPalme	25.00	12.50	7.50
345	Paul Smith	25.00	12.50	7.50
346	Dick Littlefield	25.00	12.50	7.50
347	Hal Naragon	25.00	12.50	7.50
348	Jim Hearn	25.00	12.50	7.50
349	Nelson King	25.00	12.50	7.50
350	Eddie Miksis	25.00	12.50	7.50
351	Dave Hillman	25.00	12.50	7.50
352	Ellis Kinder	25.00	12.50	7.50
353	Cal Neeman	12.00	6.00	3.50
354	Rip Coleman	12.00	6.00	3.50
355	Frank Malzone	12.00	6.00	3.50
356	Faye Throneberry	12.00	6.00	3.50
357	Earl Torgeson	12.00	6.00	3.50
358	Jerry Lynch	12.00	6.00	3.50
359	Tom Cheney	12.00	6.00	3.50
360	Johnny Groth	12.00	6.00	3.50
361	Curt Barclay	12.00	6.00	3.50
362	Roman Mejias	12.00	6.00	3.50
363	Eddie Kasko	12.00	6.00	3.50
364	*Cal McLish*	12.00	6.00	3.50
365	Ossie Virgil	12.00	6.00	3.50
366	Ken Lehman	15.00	7.50	4.50
367	Ed FitzGerald	12.00	6.00	3.50
368	Bob Purkey	12.00	6.00	3.50
369	Milt Graff	12.00	6.00	3.50
370	Warren Hacker	12.00	6.00	3.50
371	Bob Lennon	12.00	6.00	3.50
372	Norm Zauchin	12.00	6.00	3.50
373	Pete Whisenant	12.00	6.00	3.50
374	Don Cardwell	12.00	6.00	3.50
375	*Jim Landis*	12.00	6.00	3.50
376	Don Elston	15.00	7.50	4.50
377	Andre Rodgers	12.00	6.00	3.50
378	Elmer Singleton	12.00	6.00	3.50
379	Don Lee	12.00	6.00	3.50
380	Walker Cooper	12.00	6.00	3.50
381	Dean Stone	12.00	6.00	3.50
382	Jim Brideweser	12.00	6.00	3.50
383	*Juan Pizarro*	12.00	6.00	3.50
384	Bobby Gene Smith	12.00	6.00	3.50
385	Art Houtteman	12.00	6.00	3.50
386	Lyle Luttrell	12.00	6.00	3.50
387	*Jack Sanford*	12.00	6.00	3.50
388	Pete Daley	12.00	6.00	3.50
389	Dave Jolly	12.00	6.00	3.50
390	Reno Bertoia	12.00	6.00	3.50
391	*Ralph Terry*	15.00	7.50	4.50
392	Chuck Tanner	12.00	6.00	3.50
393	Raul Sanchez	12.00	6.00	3.50
394	Luis Arroyo	12.00	6.00	3.50
395	Bubba Phillips	12.00	6.00	3.50
396	Casey Wise	12.00	6.00	3.50
397	Roy Smalley	12.00	6.00	3.50
398	Al Cicotte	15.00	7.50	4.50
399	Billy Consolo	12.00	6.00	3.50
400	Dodgers' Sluggers (Roy Campanella, Carl Furillo, Gil Hodges, Duke Snider)	150.00	75.00	45.00
401	*Earl Battey*	15.00	7.50	4.50
402	Jim Pisoni	12.00	6.00	3.50
403	Dick Hyde	12.00	6.00	3.50
404	Harry Anderson	12.00	6.00	3.50
405	Duke Maas	12.00	6.00	3.50
406	Bob Hale	12.00	6.00	3.50
407	Yankees' Power Hitters (Mickey Mantle, Yogi Berra)	325.00	140.00	65.00
----	Checklist Series 1-2 (Big Blony ad on back.)	300.00	140.00	90.00

#	Player	NM	EX	VG
----	Checklist Series 1-2 (Bazooka ad on back)	300.00	140.00	90.00
----	Checklist Series 2-3 (Big Blony)	350.00	200.00	130.00
----	Checklist Series 2-3 (Bazooka)	350.00	200.00	130.00
----	Checklist Series 3-4 (Twin Blony)	800.00	300.00	195.00
----	Checklist Series 3-4 (Bazooka)	800.00	300.00	195.00
----	Checklist Series 4-5 (Twin Blony)	1,150	575.00	345.00
----	Checklist Series 4-5 (Bazooka)	1,150	575.00	345.00
----	Contest May 4	120.00	60.00	35.00
----	Contest May 25	135.00	65.00	40.00
----	Contest June 22	145.00	75.00	45.00
----	Contest July 19	200.00	100.00	60.00
----	Lucky Penny Insert Card	300.00	150.00	90.00

1958 Topps

Topps continued to expand its set size in 1958 with the release of a 494-card set. One card (#145) was not issued after Ed Bouchee was suspended from baseball. Cards retained the 2-1/2" x 3-1/2" size. There are a number of variations, including player or team names found in either yellow or white lettering on 33 cards between numbers 2-108 (higher priced yellow-letter variations checklisted below are not included in the complete set prices). The number of multiple-player cards was increased. A major innovation is the addition of 20 "All-Star" cards. For the first time, checklists were incorporated into the numbered series, on the backs of team cards.

#	Player	NM	EX	VG
	Complete Set (494):	8,500	4,250	2,500
	Common Player (1-495):	9.00	4.50	2.57
1	Ted Williams	360.00	115.00	55.00
2a	Bob Lemon (Yellow team.)	80.00	40.00	24.00
2b	Bob Lemon (White team.)	30.00	15.00	9.00
3	Alex Kellner	9.00	4.50	2.57
4	Hank Foiles	9.00	4.50	2.57
5	Willie Mays	190.00	95.00	55.00
6	George Zuverink	9.00	4.50	2.57
7	Dale Long	9.00	4.50	2.57
8a	Eddie Kasko (Yellow name.)	60.00	30.00	18.00
8b	Eddie Kasko (White name.)	9.00	4.50	2.57
9	Hank Bauer	20.00	10.00	6.00
10	Lou Burdette	9.00	4.50	2.57
11a	Jim Rivera (Yellow team.)	60.00	30.00	18.00
11b	Jim Rivera (White team.)	9.00	4.50	2.57
12	George Crowe	9.00	4.50	2.57
13a	Billy Hoeft (Yellow name.)	60.00	30.00	18.00
13b	Billy Hoeft (White name, orange triangle by foot.)	9.00	4.50	2.57
13c	Billy Hoeft (White name, red triangle by foot.)	9.00	4.50	2.57
14	Rip Repulski	9.00	4.50	2.57
15	Jim Lemon	9.00	4.50	2.57
16	Charley Neal	9.00	4.50	2.57
17	Felix Mantilla	9.00	4.50	2.57
18	Frank Sullivan	9.00	4.50	2.57
19	1957 Giants Team	40.00	20.00	12.00
20a	Gil McDougald (Yellow name.)	75.00	37.50	22.00
20b	Gil McDougald (White name.)	20.00	10.00	6.00
21	Curt Barclay	9.00	4.50	2.57
22	Hal Naragon	9.00	4.50	2.57
23a	Bill Tuttle (Yellow name.)	60.00	30.00	18.00
23b	Bill Tuttle (White name.)	9.00	4.50	2.57
24a	Hobie Landrith (Yellow name.)	60.00	30.00	18.00
24b	Hobie Landrith (White name.)	9.00	4.50	2.57
25	Don Drysdale	45.00	22.50	13.50
26	Ron Jackson	9.00	4.50	2.57
27	Bud Freeman	9.00	4.50	2.57
28	Jim Busby	9.00	4.50	2.57
29	Ted Lepcio	9.00	4.50	2.57
30a	Hank Aaron (Yellow name.)	380.00	165.00	95.00
30b	Hank Aaron (White name.)	165.00	80.00	45.00
31	Tex Clevenger	9.00	4.50	2.57
32a	J.W. Porter (Yellow name.)	60.00	30.00	18.00
32b	J.W. Porter (White name.)	9.00	4.50	2.57
33a	Cal Neeman (Yellow team.)	60.00	30.00	18.00
33b	Cal Neeman (White team.)	9.00	4.50	2.57
34	Bob Thurman	9.00	4.50	2.57
35a	Don Mossi (Yellow team.)	60.00	30.00	18.00
35b	Don Mossi (White team.)	9.00	4.50	2.57
36	Ted Kazanski	9.00	4.50	2.57
37	*Mike McCormick* (Photo actually Ray Monzant.)	9.00	4.50	2.57
38	Dick Gernert	9.00	4.50	2.57
39	Bob Martyn	9.00	4.50	2.57

#	Player	NM	EX	VG
40	George Kell	20.00	10.00	6.00
41	Dave Hillman	9.00	4.50	2.57
42	*John Roseboro*	25.00	12.50	7.50
43	Sal Maglie	12.50	6.25	3.75
44	Wash. Senators Team	20.00	10.00	6.00
45	Dick Groat	9.00	4.50	2.57
46a	Lou Sleater (Yellow name.)	60.00	30.00	18.00
46b	Lou Sleater (White name.)	9.00	4.50	2.57
47	*Roger Maris*	285.00	140.00	85.00
48	Chuck Harmon	9.00	4.50	2.57
49	Smoky Burgess	9.00	4.50	2.57
50a	Billy Pierce (Yellow team.)	60.00	30.00	18.00
50b	Billy Pierce (White team.)	9.00	4.50	2.57
51	Del Rice	9.00	4.50	2.57
52a	Bob Clemente (Yellow team.)	425.00	210.00	125.00
52b	Bob Clemente (White team.)	200.00	100.00	60.00
53a	Morrie Martin (Yellow name.)	60.00	30.00	18.00
53b	Morrie Martin (White name.)	9.00	4.50	2.57
54	*Norm Siebern*	12.50	6.25	3.75
55	Chico Carrasquel	9.00	4.50	2.57
56	Bill Fischer	9.00	4.50	2.57
57a	Tim Thompson (Yellow name.)	60.00	30.00	18.00
57b	Tim Thompson (White name.)	9.00	4.50	2.57
58a	Art Schult (Yellow team.)	60.00	30.00	18.00
58b	Art Schult (White team.)	9.00	4.50	2.57
59	Dave Sisler	9.00	4.50	2.57
60a	Del Ennis (Yellow name.)	60.00	30.00	18.00
60b	Del Ennis (White name.)	9.00	4.50	2.57
61a	Darrell Johnson (Yellow name.)	100.00	50.00	30.00
61b	Darrell Johnson (White name.)	15.00	7.50	4.50
62	Joe DeMaestri	9.00	4.50	2.57
63	Joe Nuxhall	9.00	4.50	2.57
64	Joe Lonnett	9.00	4.50	2.57
65a	Von McDaniel (Yellow name.)	60.00	30.00	18.00
65b	Von McDaniel (White name.)	9.00	4.50	2.57
66	Lee Walls	9.00	4.50	2.57
67	Joe Ginsberg	9.00	4.50	2.57
68	Daryl Spencer	9.00	4.50	2.57
69	Wally Burnette	9.00	4.50	2.57
70a	Al Kaline (Yellow name.)	225.00	110.00	65.00
70b	Al Kaline (White name.)	65.00	32.50	20.00
71	1957 Dodgers Team	60.00	30.00	18.00
72	Bud Byerly (Photo actually Hal Griggs.)	9.00	4.50	2.57
73	Pete Daley	9.00	4.50	2.57
74	Roy Face	9.00	4.50	2.57
75	Gus Bell	9.00	4.50	2.57
76a	Dick Farrell (Yellow name.)	60.00	30.00	18.00
76b	Dick Farrell (White name.)	9.00	4.50	2.57
77a	Don Zimmer (Yellow name.)	80.00	40.00	24.00
77b	Don Zimmer (White name.)	15.00	7.50	4.50
78a	Ernie Johnson (Yellow name.)	60.00	30.00	18.00
78b	Ernie Johnson (White name.)	9.00	4.50	2.57
79a	Dick Williams (Yellow name.)	60.00	30.00	18.00
79b	Dick Williams (White name.)	9.00	4.50	2.57
80	Dick Drott	9.00	4.50	2.57
81a	*Steve Boros* (Yellow name.)	60.00	30.00	18.00
81b	*Steve Boros* (White name.)	9.00	4.50	2.57
82	Ronnie Kline	9.00	4.50	2.57
83	*Bob Hazle*	9.00	4.50	2.57
84	Billy O'Dell	9.00	4.50	2.57
85a	Luis Aparicio (Yellow name.)	140.00	70.00	40.00
85b	Luis Aparicio (White name.)	30.00	15.00	9.00
86	Valmy Thomas	9.00	4.50	2.57
87	Johnny Kucks	10.00	5.00	3.00
88	Duke Snider	45.00	22.50	13.50
89	Billy Klaus	9.00	4.50	2.57
90	Robin Roberts	30.00	15.00	9.00
91	Chuck Tanner	9.00	4.50	2.57
92a	Clint Courtney (Yellow name.)	60.00	30.00	18.00
92b	Clint Courtney (White name.)	9.00	4.50	2.57
93	Sandy Amoros	12.00	6.00	3.50
94	Bob Skinner	9.00	4.50	2.57
95	Frank Bolling	9.00	4.50	2.57
96	Joe Durham	9.00	4.50	2.57
97a	Larry Jackson (Yellow name.)	60.00	30.00	18.00
97b	Larry Jackson (White name.)	9.00	4.50	2.57
98a	Billy Hunter (Yellow name.)	60.00	30.00	18.00
98b	Billy Hunter (White name.)	9.00	4.50	2.57
99	Bobby Adams	9.00	4.50	2.57
100a	Early Wynn (Yellow name.)	90.00	45.00	27.50
100b	Early Wynn (White name.)	20.00	10.00	6.00
101a	Bobby Richardson (Yellow name.)	100.00	50.00	30.00
101b	Bobby Richardson (White name.)	30.00	15.00	9.00
102	George Strickland	9.00	4.50	2.57
103	Jerry Lynch	9.00	4.50	2.57
104	Jim Pendleton	9.00	4.50	2.57
105	Billy Gardner	9.00	4.50	2.57
106	Dick Schofield	9.00	4.50	2.57
107	Ossie Virgil	9.00	4.50	2.57
108a	Jim Landis (Yellow name.)	60.00	30.00	18.00
108b	Jim Landis (White name.)	9.00	4.50	2.57
109	Herb Plews	9.00	4.50	2.57
110	Johnny Logan	9.00	4.50	2.57
111	Stu Miller	9.00	4.50	2.57
112	Gus Zernial	9.00	4.50	2.57
113	Jerry Walker	9.00	4.50	2.57
114	Irv Noren	9.00	4.50	2.57
115	Jim Bunning	20.00	10.00	6.00
116	Dave Philley	9.00	4.50	2.57
117	Frank Torre	9.00	4.50	2.57
118	Harvey Haddix	9.00	4.50	2.57
119	Harry Chiti	9.00	4.50	2.57
120	Johnny Podres	12.00	6.00	3.50
121	Eddie Miksis	9.00	4.50	2.57
122	Walt Moryn	9.00	4.50	2.57
123	Dick Tomanek	9.00	4.50	2.57
124	Bobby Usher	9.00	4.50	2.57
125	Al Dark	9.00	4.50	2.57
126	Stan Palys	9.00	4.50	2.57
127	Tom Sturdivant	10.00	5.00	3.00
128	*Willie Kirkland*	9.00	4.50	2.57

129	Jim Derrington	9.00	4.50	2.57
130	Jackie Jensen	10.00	5.00	3.00
131	Bob Henrich	9.00	4.50	2.57
132	Vernon Law	9.00	4.50	2.57
133	Russ Nixon	9.00	4.50	2.57
134	Phila. Phillies Team	16.00	8.00	4.75
135	Mike Drabowsky	9.00	4.50	2.57
136	Jim Finingan	9.00	4.50	2.57
137	Russ Kemmerer	9.00	4.50	2.57
138	Earl Torgeson	9.00	4.50	2.57
139	George Brunet	9.00	4.50	2.57
140	Wes Covington	9.00	4.50	2.57
141	Ken Lehman	9.00	4.50	2.57
142	Enos Slaughter	25.00	12.50	7.50
143	Billy Muffett	9.00	4.50	2.57
144	Bobby Morgan	9.00	4.50	2.57
145	Not Issued			
146	Dick Gray	9.00	4.50	2.57
147	*Don McMahon*	9.00	4.50	2.57
148	Billy Consolo	9.00	4.50	2.57
149	Tom Acker	9.00	4.50	2.57
150	Mickey Mantle	615.00	250.00	135.00
151	Buddy Pritchard	9.00	4.50	2.57
152	Johnny Antonelli	9.00	4.50	2.57
153	Les Moss	9.00	4.50	2.57
154	Harry Byrd	9.00	4.50	2.57
155	Hector Lopez	9.00	4.50	2.57
156	Dick Hyde	9.00	4.50	2.57
157	Dee Fondy	9.00	4.50	2.57
158	Cleve. Indians Team	25.00	12.50	7.50
159	Taylor Phillips	9.00	4.50	2.57
160	Don Hoak	9.00	4.50	2.57
161	Don Larsen	25.00	12.50	7.50
162	Gil Hodges	30.00	15.00	9.00
163	Jim Wilson	9.00	4.50	2.57
164	Bob Taylor	9.00	4.50	2.57
165	Bob Nieman	9.00	4.50	2.57
166	Danny O'Connell	9.00	4.50	2.57
167	Frank Baumann	9.00	4.50	2.57
168	Joe Cunningham	9.00	4.50	2.57
169	Ralph Terry	9.00	4.50	2.57
170	Vic Wertz	9.00	4.50	2.57
171	Harry Anderson	9.00	4.50	2.57
172	Don Gross	9.00	4.50	2.57
173	Eddie Yost	9.00	4.50	2.57
174	K.C. Athletics Team	20.00	10.00	6.00
175	*Marv Throneberry*	25.00	12.50	7.50
176	Bob Buhl	9.00	4.50	2.57
177	Al Smith	9.00	4.50	2.57
178	Ted Kluszewski	20.00	10.00	6.00
179	Willy Miranda	9.00	4.50	2.57
180	Lindy McDaniel	9.00	4.50	2.57
181	Willie Jones	9.00	4.50	2.57
182	Joe Caffie	9.00	4.50	2.57
183	Dave Jolly	9.00	4.50	2.57
184	Elvin Tappe	9.00	4.50	2.57
185	Ray Boone	9.00	4.50	2.57
186	Jack Meyer	9.00	4.50	2.57
187	Sandy Koufax	160.00	80.00	45.00
188	Milt Bolling (Photo actually Lou Berberet.)	9.00	4.50	2.57
189	George Susce	9.00	4.50	2.57
190	Red Schoendienst	20.00	10.00	6.00
191	Art Ceccarelli	9.00	4.50	2.57
192	Milt Graff	9.00	4.50	2.57
193	*Jerry Lumpe*	12.50	6.25	3.75
194	Roger Craig	9.00	4.50	2.57
195	Whitey Lockman	9.00	4.50	2.57
196	Mike Garcia	9.00	4.50	2.57
197	Haywood Sullivan	9.00	4.50	2.57
198	Bill Virdon	9.00	4.50	2.57
199	Don Blasingame	9.00	4.50	2.57
200	Bob Keegan	9.00	4.50	2.57
201	Jim Bolger	9.00	4.50	2.57
202	*Woody Held*	9.00	4.50	2.57
203	Al Walker	9.00	4.50	2.57
204	Leo Kiely	9.00	4.50	2.57
205	Johnny Temple	9.00	4.50	2.57
206	Bob Shaw	9.00	4.50	2.57
207	Solly Hemus	9.00	4.50	2.57
208	Cal McLish	9.00	4.50	2.57
209	Bob Anderson	9.00	4.50	2.57
210	Wally Moon	9.00	4.50	2.57
211	Pete Burnside	9.00	4.50	2.57
212	Bubba Phillips	9.00	4.50	2.57
213	Red Wilson	9.00	4.50	2.57
214	Willard Schmidt	9.00	4.50	2.57
215	Jim Gilliam	12.50	6.25	3.75
216	St. Louis Cards Team	25.00	12.50	7.50
217	Jack Harshman	9.00	4.50	2.57
218	Dick Rand	9.00	4.50	2.57
219	Camilo Pascual	9.00	4.50	2.57
220	Tom Brewer	9.00	4.50	2.57
221	Jerry Kindall	9.00	4.50	2.57
222	Bud Daley	9.00	4.50	2.57
223	Andy Pafko	9.00	4.50	2.57
224	Bob Grim	10.00	5.00	3.00
225	Billy Goodman	9.00	4.50	2.57
226	Bob Smith (Photo actually Bobby Gene Smith.)	9.00	4.50	2.57
227	Gene Stephens	9.00	4.50	2.57
228	Duke Maas	9.00	4.50	2.57
229	Frank Zupo	9.00	4.50	2.57
230	Richie Ashburn	30.00	15.00	9.00
231	Lloyd Merritt	9.00	4.50	2.57
232	Reno Bertoia	9.00	4.50	2.57
233	Mickey Vernon	9.00	4.50	2.57
234	Carl Sawatski	9.00	4.50	2.57
235	Tom Gorman	9.00	4.50	2.57
236	Ed FitzGerald	9.00	4.50	2.57
237	Bill Wight	9.00	4.50	2.57
238	Bill Mazeroski	30.00	15.00	9.00
239	Chuck Stobbs	9.00	4.50	2.57
240	Moose Skowron	20.00	10.00	6.00
241	Dick Littlefield	9.00	4.50	2.57
242	Johnny Klippstein	9.00	4.50	2.57
243	Larry Raines	9.00	4.50	2.57
244	*Don Demeter*	9.00	4.50	2.57
245	*Frank Lary*	9.00	4.50	2.57
246	New York Yankees Team	75.00	37.50	22.50
247	Casey Wise	9.00	4.50	2.57
248	Herm Wehmeier	9.00	4.50	2.57
249	Ray Moore	9.00	4.50	2.57
250	Roy Sievers	9.00	4.50	2.57
251	Warren Hacker	9.00	4.50	2.57
252	Bob Trowbridge	9.00	4.50	2.57
253	Don Mueller	9.00	4.50	2.57
254	Alex Grammas	9.00	4.50	2.57
255	Bob Turley	25.00	12.50	7.50
256	Chicago White Sox Team	20.00	10.00	6.00
257	Hal Smith	9.00	4.50	2.57
258	Carl Erskine	17.50	8.75	5.25
259	Al Pilarcik	9.00	4.50	2.57
260	Frank Malzone	9.00	4.50	2.57
261	Turk Lown	9.00	4.50	2.57
262	Johnny Groth	9.00	4.50	2.57
263	Eddie Bressoud	9.00	4.50	2.57
264	Jack Sanford	9.00	4.50	2.57
265	Pete Runnels	9.00	4.50	2.57
266	Connie Johnson	9.00	4.50	2.57
267	Sherm Lollar	9.00	4.50	2.57
268	Granny Hamner	9.00	4.50	2.57
269	Paul Smith	9.00	4.50	2.57
270	Warren Spahn	50.00	25.00	15.00
271	Billy Martin	20.00	10.00	6.00
272	Ray Crone	9.00	4.50	2.57
273	Hal Smith	9.00	4.50	2.57
274	Rocky Bridges	9.00	4.50	2.57
275	Elston Howard	20.00	10.00	6.00
276	Bobby Avila	9.00	4.50	2.57
277	Virgil Trucks	9.00	4.50	2.57
278	Mack Burk	9.00	4.50	2.57
279	Bob Boyd	9.00	4.50	2.57
280	Jim Piersall	9.00	4.50	2.57
281	Sam Taylor	9.00	4.50	2.57
282	Paul Foytack	9.00	4.50	2.57
283	Ray Shearer	9.00	4.50	2.57
284	Ray Katt	9.00	4.50	2.57
285	Frank Robinson	60.00	30.00	18.00
286	Gino Cimoli	9.00	4.50	2.57
287	Sam Jones	9.00	4.50	2.57
288	Harmon Killebrew	60.00	30.00	18.00
289	Series Hurling Rivals (Lou Burdette, Bobby Shantz)	25.00	12.50	7.50
290	Dick Donovan	9.00	4.50	2.57
291	Don Landrum	9.00	4.50	2.57
292	Ned Garver	9.00	4.50	2.57
293	Gene Freese	9.00	4.50	2.57
294	Hal Jeffcoat	9.00	4.50	2.57
295	Minnie Minoso	20.00	10.00	6.00
296	*Ryne Duren*	50.00	25.00	15.00
297	Don Buddin	9.00	4.50	2.57
298	Jim Hearn	9.00	4.50	2.57
299	Harry Simpson	9.00	4.50	2.57
300	League Presidents (Warren Giles, William Harridge)	35.00	17.50	10.00
301	Randy Jackson	9.00	4.50	2.57
302	Mike Baxes	9.00	4.50	2.57
303	Neil Chrisley	9.00	4.50	2.57
304	Tigers' Big Bats (Al Kaline, Harvey Kuenn)	35.00	17.50	10.00
305	Clem Labine	12.50	6.25	3.75
306	Whammy Douglas	9.00	4.50	2.57
307	Brooks Robinson	75.00	37.50	22.00
308	Paul Giel	9.00	4.50	2.57
309	Gail Harris	9.00	4.50	2.57
310	Ernie Banks	75.00	37.50	22.50
311	Bob Purkey	9.00	4.50	2.57
312	Boston Red Sox Team	25.00	12.50	7.50
313	Bob Rush	9.00	4.50	2.57
314	Dodgers' Boss & Power (Duke Snider, Walter Alston)	35.00	17.50	10.00
315	Bob Friend	9.00	4.50	2.57
316	Tito Francona	9.00	4.50	2.57
317	*Albie Pearson*	10.00	5.00	3.00
318	Frank House	9.00	4.50	2.57
319	Lou Skizas	9.00	4.50	2.57
320	Whitey Ford	60.00	30.00	18.00
321	Sluggers Supreme (Ted Kluszewski, Ted Williams)	65.00	32.50	20.00
322	Harding Peterson	9.00	4.50	2.57
323	Elmer Valo	9.00	4.50	2.57
324	Hoyt Wilhelm	20.00	10.00	6.00
325	Joe Adcock	9.00	4.50	2.57
326	Bob Miller	9.00	4.50	2.57
327	Chicago Cubs Team	20.00	10.00	6.00
328	Ike Delock	9.00	4.50	2.57
329	Bob Cerv	9.00	4.50	2.57
330	Ed Bailey	9.00	4.50	2.57
331	Pedro Ramos	9.00	4.50	2.57
332	Jim King	9.00	4.50	2.57
333	Andy Carey	10.00	5.00	3.00
334	Mound Aces (Bob Friend, Billy Pierce)	12.00	6.00	3.50
335	Ruben Gomez	9.00	4.50	2.57
336	Bert Hamric	9.00	4.50	2.57
337	Hank Aguirre	9.00	4.50	2.57
338	Walt Dropo	9.00	4.50	2.57
339	Fred Hatfield	9.00	4.50	2.57
340	Don Newcombe	25.00	12.50	7.50
341	Pittsburgh Pirates Team	30.00	15.00	9.00
342	Jim Brosnan	9.00	4.50	2.57
343	*Orlando Cepeda*	70.00	35.00	20.00
344	Bob Porterfield	9.00	4.50	2.57
345	Jim Hegan	9.00	4.50	2.57
346	Steve Bilko	9.00	4.50	2.57
347	Don Rudolph	9.00	4.50	2.57
348	Chico Fernandez	9.00	4.50	2.57
349	Murry Dickson	9.00	4.50	2.57
350	Ken Boyer	12.50	6.25	3.75
351	Braves' Fence Busters (Hank Aaron, Joe Adcock, Del Crandall, Eddie Mathews)	60.00	30.00	18.00
352	Herb Score	12.50	6.25	3.75
353	Stan Lopata	9.00	4.50	2.57
354	Art Ditmar	10.00	5.00	3.00
355	Bill Bruton	9.00	4.50	2.57
356	Bob Malkmus	9.00	4.50	2.57
357	Danny McDevitt	9.00	4.50	2.57
358	Gene Baker	9.00	4.50	2.57
359	Billy Loes	9.00	4.50	2.57
360	Roy McMillan	9.00	4.50	2.57
361	Mike Fornieles	9.00	4.50	2.57
362	Ray Jablonski	9.00	4.50	2.57
363	Don Elston	9.00	4.50	2.57
364	Earl Battey	9.00	4.50	2.57
365	Tom Morgan	9.00	4.50	2.57
366	Gene Green	9.00	4.50	2.57
367	Jack Urban	9.00	4.50	2.57
368	Rocky Colavito	50.00	25.00	15.00
369	Ralph Lumenti	9.00	4.50	2.57
370	Yogi Berra	80.00	40.00	25.00
371	Marty Keough	9.00	4.50	2.57
372	Don Cardwell	9.00	4.50	2.57
373	Joe Pignatano	9.00	4.50	2.57
374	Brooks Lawrence	9.00	4.50	2.57
375	Pee Wee Reese	45.00	22.50	13.50
376	Charley Rabe	9.00	4.50	2.57
377a	Milwaukee Braves Team (Alphabetical checklist.)	20.00	10.00	6.00
377b	Milwaukee Braves Team (Numerical checklist.)	140.00	70.00	40.00
378	Hank Sauer	9.00	4.50	2.57
379	Ray Herbert	9.00	4.50	2.57
380	Charley Maxwell	9.00	4.50	2.57
381	Hal Brown	9.00	4.50	2.57
382	Al Cicotte	10.00	5.00	3.00
383	Lou Berberet	9.00	4.50	2.57
384	John Goryl	9.00	4.50	2.57
385	Wilmer Mizell	9.00	4.50	2.57
386	Birdie's Young Sluggers (Ed Bailey, Frank Robinson, Birdie Tebbetts)	20.00	10.00	6.00
387	Wally Post	9.00	4.50	2.57
388	Billy Moran	9.00	4.50	2.57
389	Bill Taylor	9.00	4.50	2.57
390	Del Crandall	9.00	4.50	2.57
391	Dave Melton	9.00	4.50	2.57
392	Bennie Daniels	9.00	4.50	2.57
393	Tony Kubek	20.00	10.00	6.00
394	*Jim Grant*	10.00	5.00	3.00
395	Willard Nixon	9.00	4.50	2.57
396	Dutch Dotterer	9.00	4.50	2.57
397a	Detroit Tigers Team (Alphabetical checklist.)	15.00	7.50	4.50
397b	Detroit Tigers Team (Numerical checklist.)	125.00	65.00	35.00
398	Gene Woodling	9.00	4.50	2.57
399	Marv Grissom	9.00	4.50	2.57
400	Nellie Fox	25.00	12.50	7.50
401	Don Bessent	9.00	4.50	2.57
402	Bobby Gene Smith	9.00	4.50	2.57
403	Steve Korcheck	9.00	4.50	2.57
404	Curt Simmons	9.00	4.50	2.57
405	Ken Aspromonte	9.00	4.50	2.57
406	Vic Power	9.00	4.50	2.57
407	Carlton Willey	9.00	4.50	2.57
408a	Baltimore Orioles Team (Alphabetical checklist.)	15.00	7.50	4.50
408b	Baltimore Orioles Team (Numerical checklist.)	125.00	65.00	35.00
409	Frank Thomas	9.00	4.50	2.57
410	Murray Wall	9.00	4.50	2.57
411	*Tony Taylor*	9.00	4.50	2.57
412	Jerry Staley	9.00	4.50	2.57
413	*Jim Davenport*	9.00	4.50	2.57
414	Sammy White	9.00	4.50	2.57
415	Bob Bowman	9.00	4.50	2.57
416	Foster Castleman	9.00	4.50	2.57
417	Carl Furillo	15.00	7.50	4.50
418	World Series Foes (Hank Aaron, Mickey Mantle)	215.00	105.00	65.00
419	Bobby Shantz	15.00	7.50	4.50
420	*Vada Pinson*	20.00	10.00	6.00
421	Dixie Howell	9.00	4.50	2.57
422	Norm Zauchin	9.00	4.50	2.57
423	Phil Clark	9.00	4.50	2.57
424	Larry Doby	20.00	10.00	6.00
425	Sam Esposito	9.00	4.50	2.57
426	Johnny O'Brien	9.00	4.50	2.57
427	Al Worthington	9.00	4.50	2.57
428a	Cincinnati Redlegs Team (Alphabetical checklist.)	15.00	7.50	4.50
428b	Cincinnati Redlegs Team (Numerical checklist.)	125.00	65.00	35.00
429	Gus Triandos	9.00	4.50	2.57
430	Bobby Thomson	12.00	6.00	3.50
431	Gene Conley	9.00	4.50	2.57
432	John Powers	9.00	4.50	2.57
433	Pancho Herrera	9.00	4.50	2.57
433a	Pancho Herrera (Printing error, no "a" in Herrera.)	4,000	2,000	1,200
434	Harvey Kuenn	9.00	4.50	2.57
435	Ed Roebuck	9.00	4.50	2.57
436	Rival Fence Busters (Willie Mays, Duke Snider)	75.00	37.50	22.50
437	Bob Speake	9.00	4.50	2.57
438	Whitey Herzog	9.00	4.50	2.57
439	Ray Narleski	9.00	4.50	2.57
440	Ed Mathews	65.00	32.50	20.00
441	Jim Marshall	9.00	4.50	2.57
442	Phil Paine	9.00	4.50	2.57
443	Billy Harrell/SP	15.00	7.50	4.50
444	Danny Kravitz	9.00	4.50	2.57
445	Bob Smith	9.00	4.50	2.57
446	Carroll Hardy/SP	15.00	7.50	4.50
447	Ray Monzant	9.00	4.50	2.57
448	*Charlie Lau*	13.50	7.00	4.00
449	Gene Fodge	9.00	4.50	2.57
450	Preston Ward/SP	15.00	7.50	4.50
451	Joe Taylor	9.00	4.50	2.57
452	Roman Mejias	9.00	4.50	2.57
453	Tom Qualters	9.00	4.50	2.57
454	Harry Hanebrink	9.00	4.50	2.57

		NM	EX	VG
455	Hal Griggs (Photo actually Bud Byerly.)	9.00	4.50	2.57
456	Dick Brown	9.00	4.50	2.57
457	*Milt Pappas*	10.00	5.00	3.00
458	Julio Becquer	9.00	4.50	2.57
459	Ron Blackburn	9.00	4.50	2.57
460	Chuck Essegian	9.00	4.50	2.57
461	Ed Mayer	9.00	4.50	2.57
462	Gary Geiger/SP	15.00	7.50	4.50
463	Vito Valentinetti	9.00	4.50	2.57
464	*Curt Flood*	30.00	15.00	9.00
465	Arnie Portocarrero	9.00	4.50	2.57
466	Pete Whisenant	9.00	4.50	2.57
467	Glen Hobbie	9.00	4.50	2.57
468	Bob Schmidt	9.00	4.50	2.57
469	Don Ferrarese	9.00	4.50	2.57
470	R.C. Stevens	9.00	4.50	2.57
471	Lenny Green	9.00	4.50	2.57
472	Joe Jay	9.00	4.50	2.57
473	Bill Renna	9.00	4.50	2.57
474	Roman Semproch	9.00	4.50	2.57
475	All-Star Managers (Fred Haney, Casey Stengel)	30.00	15.00	9.00
476	Stan Musial (All-Star)	35.00	17.50	10.00
477	Bill Skowron (All-Star)	15.00	7.50	4.50
478	Johnny Temple (All-Star)	10.00	5.00	3.00
479	Nellie Fox (All-Star)	15.00	7.50	4.50
480	Eddie Mathews (All-Star)	25.00	12.50	7.50
481	Frank Malzone (All-Star)	10.00	5.00	3.00
482	Ernie Banks (All-Star)	30.00	15.00	9.00
483	Luis Aparicio (All-Star)	20.00	10.00	6.00
484	Frank Robinson (All-Star)	30.00	15.00	9.00
485	Ted Williams (All-Star)	75.00	37.50	22.00
486	Willie Mays (All-Star)	55.00	27.50	16.50
487	Mickey Mantle (All-Star)(Triple Print)	110.00	55.00	35.00
488	Hank Aaron (All-Star)	55.00	27.50	16.50
489	Jackie Jensen (All-Star)	12.00	6.00	3.50
490	Ed Bailey (All-Star)	10.00	5.00	3.00
491	Sherman Lollar (All-Star)	10.00	5.00	3.00
492	Bob Friend (All-Star)	10.00	5.00	3.00
493	Bob Turley (All-Star)	15.00	7.50	4.50
494	Warren Spahn (All-Star)	25.00	12.50	7.50
495	Herb Score (All-Star)	15.00	7.50	4.50
----	Contest Card (All-Star Game, July 8)	70.00	35.00	20.00
----	Felt Emblems Insert Card	45.00	22.50	13.50

1959 Topps

These 2-1/2" x 3-1/2" cards have a round photograph on front with a solid-color background above and below and a white border. A facsimile autograph is found across the photo. The 572-card set marks the largest set issued to that time. Card numbers below 507 have red and green printing on back with the card number in white in a green box. On high number cards beginning with #507, the printing is black and red and the card number is in a black box. Specialty cards include multiple-player cards, team cards with checklists on back, "All-Star" cards, "Baseball Thrills", and 31 "Rookie Stars." There is also a card of the commissioner, Ford Frick, and one of Roy Campanella in a wheelchair. A handful of cards can be found with and without lines added to the biographies on back indicating trades or demotions; those without the added lines are scarcer and more valuable and are not included in the complete set price. Card numbers 199-286 can be found with either white or grey backs, with the grey stock being the less common.

		NM	EX	VG
	Complete Set (572):	6,500	3,250	1,900
	Common Player (1-506):	7.00	3.50	2.00
	Common Player (507-572):	15.00	7.50	4.50
1	Ford Frick	100.00	25.00	4.00
2	Eddie Yost	12.00	3.50	2.00
3	Don McMahon	7.00	3.50	2.00
4	Albie Pearson	7.00	3.50	2.00
5	Dick Donovan	7.00	3.50	2.00
6	Alex Grammas	7.00	3.50	2.00
7	Al Pilarcik	7.00	3.50	2.00
8	Philadelphia Phillies Team /SP	90.00	45.00	27.50
9	Paul Giel	7.00	3.50	2.00
10	Mickey Mantle	515.00	225.00	125.00
11	Billy Hunter	7.00	3.50	2.00
12	Vern Law	7.00	3.50	2.00
13	Dick Gernert	7.00	3.50	2.00
14	Pete Whisenant	7.00	3.50	2.00
15	Dick Drott	7.00	3.50	2.00
16	Joe Pignatano	7.00	3.50	2.00
17	Danny's All-Stars (Ted Kluszewski, Danny Murtaugh, Frank J. Thomas)	13.50	7.00	4.00
18	Jack Urban	7.00	3.50	2.00
19	Ed Bressoud	7.00	3.50	2.00
20	Duke Snider	40.00	20.00	12.00
21	Connie Johnson	7.00	3.50	2.00
22	Al Smith	7.00	3.50	2.00
23	Murry Dickson	7.00	3.50	2.00
24	Red Wilson	7.00	3.50	2.00
25	Don Hoak	7.00	3.50	2.00
26	Chuck Stobbs	7.00	3.50	2.00
27	Andy Pafko	7.00	3.50	2.00
28	Red Worthington	7.00	3.50	2.00
29	Jim Bolger	7.00	3.50	2.00
30	Nellie Fox	30.00	15.00	9.00
31	Ken Lehman	7.00	3.50	2.00
32	Don Buddin	7.00	3.50	2.00
33	Ed Fitz Gerald	7.00	3.50	2.00
34	Pitchers Beware (Al Kaline, Charlie Maxwell)	25.00	12.50	7.50
35	Ted Kluszewski	17.50	8.75	5.25
36	Hank Aguirre	7.00	3.50	2.00
37	Gene Green	7.00	3.50	2.00
38	Morrie Martin	7.00	3.50	2.00
39	Ed Bouchee	7.00	3.50	2.00
40a	Warren Spahn (Born 1931)	85.00	42.50	25.00
40b	Warren Spahn (Born 1931, "3" partially obscured.)	75.00	37.50	22.50
40c	Warren Spahn (Born 1921.)	65.00	32.50	20.00
41	Bob Martyn	7.00	3.50	2.00
42	Murray Wall	7.00	3.50	2.00
43	Steve Bilko	7.00	3.50	2.00
44	Vito Valentinetti	7.00	3.50	2.00
45	Andy Carey	9.00	4.50	2.75
46	Bill Henry	7.00	3.50	2.00
47	Jim Finigan	7.00	3.50	2.00
48	Baltimore Orioles Team	17.50	8.75	5.25
49	Bill Hall	7.00	3.50	2.00
50	Willie Mays	115.00	55.00	35.00
51	Rip Coleman	7.00	3.50	2.00
52	Coot Veal	7.00	3.50	2.00
53	*Stan Williams*	20.00	10.00	6.00
54	Mel Roach	7.00	3.50	2.00
55	Tom Brewer	7.00	3.50	2.00
56	Carl Sawatski	7.00	3.50	2.00
57	Al Cicotte	7.00	3.50	2.00
58	Eddie Miksis	7.00	3.50	2.00
59	Irv Noren	7.00	3.50	2.00
60	Bob Turley	15.00	7.50	4.50
61	Dick Brown	7.00	3.50	2.00
62	Tony Taylor	7.00	3.50	2.00
63	Jim Hearn	7.00	3.50	2.00
64	Joe DeMaestri	7.00	3.50	2.00
65	Frank Torre	7.00	3.50	2.00
66	Joe Ginsberg	7.00	3.50	2.00
67	Brooks Lawrence	7.00	3.50	2.00
68	Dick Schofield	7.00	3.50	2.00
69	San Francisco Giants Team	17.50	8.75	5.25
70	Harvey Kuenn	7.00	3.50	2.00
71	Don Bessent	7.00	3.50	2.00
72	Bill Renna	7.00	3.50	2.00
73	Ron Jackson	7.00	3.50	2.00
74	Directing the Power (Cookie Lavagetto, Jim Lemon, Roy Sievers)	9.00	4.50	2.75
75	Sam Jones	7.00	3.50	2.00
76	Bobby Richardson	25.00	12.50	7.50
77	John Goryl	7.00	3.50	2.00
78	Pedro Ramos	7.00	3.50	2.00
79	Harry Chiti	7.00	3.50	2.00
80	Minnie Minoso	15.00	7.50	4.50
81	Hal Jeffcoat	7.00	3.50	2.00
82	Bob Boyd	7.00	3.50	2.00
83	Bob Smith	7.00	3.50	2.00
84	Reno Bertoia	7.00	3.50	2.00
85	Harry Anderson	7.00	3.50	2.00
86	Bob Keegan	7.00	3.50	2.00
87	Danny O'Connell	7.00	3.50	2.00
88	Herb Score	15.00	7.50	4.50
89	Billy Gardner	7.00	3.50	2.00
90	Bill Skowron/SP	60.00	30.00	18.00
91	Herb Moford	7.00	3.50	2.00
92	Dave Philley	7.00	3.50	2.00
93	Julio Becquer	7.00	3.50	2.00
94	Chicago White Sox Team	17.50	8.75	5.25
95	Carl Willey	7.00	3.50	2.00
96	Lou Berberet	7.00	3.50	2.00
97	Jerry Lynch	7.00	3.50	2.00
98	Arnie Portocarrero	7.00	3.50	2.00
99	Ted Kazanski	7.00	3.50	2.00
100	Bob Cerv	7.00	3.50	2.00
101	Alex Kellner	7.00	3.50	2.00
102	*Felipe Alou*	25.00	12.50	7.50
103	Billy Goodman	7.00	3.50	2.00
104	Del Rice	7.00	3.50	2.00
105	Lee Walls	7.00	3.50	2.00
106	Hal Woodeshick	7.00	3.50	2.00
107	*Norm Larker*	10.00	5.00	3.00
108	Zack Monroe	9.00	4.50	2.75
109	Bob Schmidt	7.00	3.50	2.00
110	George Witt	7.00	3.50	2.00
111	Cincinnati Red Legs Team	16.00	8.00	4.75
112	Billy Consolo	7.00	3.50	2.00
113	Taylor Phillips	7.00	3.50	2.00
114	Earl Battey	7.00	3.50	2.00
115	Mickey Vernon	7.00	3.50	2.00
116	*Bob Allison*	13.50	7.00	4.00
117	*John Blanchard*	15.00	7.50	4.50
118	John Buzhardt	7.00	3.50	2.00
119	*John Callison*	12.50	6.25	3.75
120	Chuck Coles	7.00	3.50	2.00
121	Bob Conley	7.00	3.50	2.00
122	Bennie Daniels	7.00	3.50	2.00
123	Don Dillard	7.00	3.50	2.00
124	Dan Dobbek	7.00	3.50	2.00
125	*Ron Fairly*	13.50	6.75	4.00
126	Eddie Haas	7.00	3.50	2.00
127	Kent Hadley	7.00	3.50	2.00
128	Bob Hartman	7.00	3.50	2.00
129	Frank Herrera	7.00	3.50	2.00
130	Lou Jackson	7.00	3.50	2.00
131	*Deron Johnson*	10.00	5.00	3.00
132	Don Lee	7.00	3.50	2.00
133	*Bob Lillis*	7.00	3.50	2.00
134	Jim McDaniel	7.00	3.50	2.00
135	Gene Oliver	7.00	3.50	2.00
136	*Jim O'Toole*	7.50	3.75	2.25
137	Dick Ricketts	7.00	3.50	2.00
138	John Romano	7.00	3.50	2.00
139	Ed Sadowski	7.00	3.50	2.00
140	Charlie Secrest	7.00	3.50	2.00
141	Joe Shipley	7.00	3.50	2.00
142	Dick Stigman	7.00	3.50	2.00
143	Willie Tasby	7.00	3.50	2.00
144	Jerry Walker	7.00	3.50	2.00
145	Dom Zanni	7.00	3.50	2.00
146	Jerry Zimmerman	7.00	3.50	2.00
147	Cubs' Clubbers (Ernie Banks, Dale Long, Walt Moryn)	20.00	10.00	6.00
148	Mike McCormick	7.00	3.50	2.00
149	Jim Bunning	20.00	10.00	6.00
150	Stan Musial	80.00	40.00	24.00
151	Bob Malkmus	7.00	3.50	2.00
152	Johnny Klippstein	7.00	3.50	2.00
153	Jim Marshall	7.00	3.50	2.00
154	Ray Herbert	7.00	3.50	2.00
155	Enos Slaughter	20.00	10.00	6.00
156	Ace Hurlers (Billy Pierce, Robin Roberts)	12.50	6.25	3.75
157	Felix Mantilla	7.00	3.50	2.00
158	Walt Dropo	7.00	3.50	2.00
159	Bob Shaw	7.00	3.50	2.00
160	Dick Groat	7.00	3.50	2.00
161	Frank Baumann	7.00	3.50	2.00
162	Bobby G. Smith	7.00	3.50	2.00
163	Sandy Koufax	130.00	65.00	40.00
164	Johnny Groth	7.00	3.50	2.00
165	Bill Bruton	7.00	3.50	2.00
166	Destruction Crew (Rocky Colavito, Larry Doby, Minnie Minoso)	20.00	10.00	6.00
167	Duke Maas	7.00	3.50	2.00
168	Carroll Hardy	7.00	3.50	2.00
169	Ted Abernathy	7.00	3.50	2.00
170	Gene Woodling	7.00	3.50	2.00
171	Willard Schmidt	7.00	3.50	2.00
172	Kansas City Athletics Team	16.00	8.00	4.75
173	*Bill Monbouquette*	7.00	3.50	2.00
174	Jim Pendleton	7.00	3.50	2.00
175	Dick Farrell	7.00	3.50	2.00
176	Preston Ward	7.00	3.50	2.00
177	Johnny Briggs	7.00	3.50	2.00
178	Ruben Amaro	7.00	3.50	2.00
179	Don Rudolph	7.00	3.50	2.00
180	Yogi Berra	65.00	32.50	20.00
181	Bob Porterfield	7.00	3.50	2.00
182	Milt Graff	7.00	3.50	2.00
183	Stu Miller	7.00	3.50	2.00
184	Harvey Haddix	7.00	3.50	2.00
185	Jim Busby	7.00	3.50	2.00
186	Mudcat Grant	7.00	3.50	2.00
187	Bubba Phillips	7.00	3.50	2.00
188	Juan Pizarro	7.00	3.50	2.00
189	Neil Chrisley	7.00	3.50	2.00
190	Bill Virdon	7.00	3.50	2.00
191	Russ Kemmerer	7.00	3.50	2.00
192	Charley Beamon	7.00	3.50	2.00
193	Sammy Taylor	7.00	3.50	2.00
194	Jim Brosnan	7.00	3.50	2.00
195	Rip Repulski	7.00	3.50	2.00
196	Billy Moran	7.00	3.50	2.00
197	Ray Semproch	7.00	3.50	2.00
198	Jim Davenport	7.00	3.50	2.00
199	Leo Kiely	7.00	3.50	2.00
200	Warren Giles	20.00	10.00	6.00
201	Tom Acker	7.00	3.50	2.00
202	Roger Maris	85.00	42.50	25.00
203	Ozzie Virgil	7.00	3.50	2.00
204	Casey Wise	7.00	3.50	2.00
205	Don Larsen	17.50	8.75	5.25
206	Carl Furillo	17.50	8.75	5.25
207	George Strickland	7.00	3.50	2.00
208	Willie Jones	7.00	3.50	2.00
209	Lenny Green	7.00	3.50	2.00
210	Ed Bailey	7.00	3.50	2.00
211	Bob Blaylock	7.00	3.50	2.00
212	Fence Busters (Hank Aaron, Eddie Mathews)	50.00	25.00	15.00
213	Jim Rivera	7.00	3.50	2.00
214	Marcelino Solis	7.00	3.50	2.00
215	Jim Lemon	7.00	3.50	2.00
216	Andre Rodgers	7.00	3.50	2.00
217	Carl Erskine	12.50	6.25	3.75
218	Roman Mejias	7.00	3.50	2.00
219	George Zuverink	7.00	3.50	2.00
220	Frank Malzone	7.00	3.50	2.00
221	Bob Bowman	7.00	3.50	2.00
222	Bobby Shantz	15.00	7.50	4.50
223	St. Louis Cardinals Team	20.00	10.00	6.00
224	*Claude Osteen*	7.50	3.75	2.25
225	Johnny Logan	7.00	3.50	2.00
226	Art Ceccarelli	7.00	3.50	2.00
227	Hal Smith	7.00	3.50	2.00
228	Don Gross	7.00	3.50	2.00
229	Vic Power	7.00	3.50	2.00
230	Bill Fischer	7.00	3.50	2.00
231	Ellis Burton	7.00	3.50	2.00
232	Eddie Kasko	7.00	3.50	2.00
233	Paul Foytack	7.00	3.50	2.00
234	Chuck Tanner	7.00	3.50	2.00
235	Valmy Thomas	7.00	3.50	2.00
236	Ted Bowsfield	7.00	3.50	2.00
237	Run Preventers (Gil McDougald, Bobby Richardson, Bob Turley)	20.00	10.00	6.00

238	Gene Baker	7.00	3.50	2.00
239	Bob Trowbridge	7.00	3.50	2.00
240	Hank Bauer	13.50	7.00	4.00
241	Billy Muffett	7.00	3.50	2.00
242	Ron Samford	7.00	3.50	2.00
243	Marv Grissom	7.00	3.50	2.00
244	Dick Gray	7.00	3.50	2.00
245	Ned Garver	7.00	3.50	2.00
246	J.W. Porter	7.00	3.50	2.00
247	Don Ferrarese	7.00	3.50	2.00
248	Boston Red Sox Team	16.00	8.00	4.75
249	Bobby Adams	7.00	3.50	2.00
250	Billy O'Dell	7.00	3.50	2.00
251	Cletis Boyer	15.00	7.50	4.50
252	Ray Boone	7.00	3.50	2.00
253	Seth Morehead	7.00	3.50	2.00
254	Zeke Bella	7.00	3.50	2.00
255	Del Ennis	7.00	3.50	2.00
256	Jerry Davie	7.00	3.50	2.00
257	*Leon Wagner*	9.00	4.50	2.75
258	Fred Kipp	7.00	3.50	2.00
259	Jim Pisoni	7.00	3.50	2.00
260	Early Wynn	20.00	10.00	6.00
261	Gene Stephens	7.00	3.50	2.00
262	Hitters' Foes (Don Drysdale, Clem Labine, Johnny Podres)	20.00	10.00	6.00
263	Buddy Daley	7.00	3.50	2.00
264	Chico Carrasquel	7.00	3.50	2.00
265	Ron Kline	7.00	3.50	2.00
266	Woody Held	7.00	3.50	2.00
267	John Romonosky	7.00	3.50	2.00
268	Tito Francona	7.00	3.50	2.00
269	Jack Meyer	7.00	3.50	2.00
270	Gil Hodges	20.00	10.00	6.00
271	*Orlando Pena*	7.00	3.50	2.00
272	Jerry Lumpe	9.00	4.50	2.75
273	Joe Jay	7.00	3.50	2.00
274	Jerry Kindall	7.00	3.50	2.00
275	Jack Sanford	7.00	3.50	2.00
276	Pete Daley	7.00	3.50	2.00
277	Turk Lown	7.00	3.50	2.00
278	Chuck Essegian	7.00	3.50	2.00
279	Ernie Johnson	7.00	3.50	2.00
280	Frank Bolling	7.00	3.50	2.00
281	Walt Craddock	7.00	3.50	2.00
282	R.C. Stevens	7.00	3.50	2.00
283	Russ Heman	7.00	3.50	2.00
284	Steve Korcheck	7.00	3.50	2.00
285	Joe Cunningham	7.00	3.50	2.00
286	Dean Stone	7.00	3.50	2.00
287	Don Zimmer	12.50	6.25	3.75
288	Dutch Dotterer	7.00	3.50	2.00
289	Johnny Kucks	9.00	4.50	2.75
290	Wes Covington	7.00	3.50	2.00
291	Pitching Partners (Camilo Pascual, Pedro Ramos)	9.00	4.50	2.75
292	Dick Williams	7.00	3.50	2.00
293	Ray Moore	7.00	3.50	2.00
294	Hank Foiles	7.00	3.50	2.00
295	Billy Martin	17.50	8.75	5.25
296	*Ernie Broglio*	7.00	3.50	2.00
297	*Jackie Brandt*	7.00	3.50	2.00
298	Tex Clevenger	7.00	3.50	2.00
299	Billy Klaus	7.00	3.50	2.00
300	Richie Ashburn	25.00	12.50	7.50
301	Earl Averill	7.00	3.50	2.00
302	Don Mossi	7.00	3.50	2.00
303	Marty Keough	7.00	3.50	2.00
304	Chicago Cubs Team	16.00	8.00	4.75
305	Curt Raydon	7.00	3.50	2.00
306	Jim Gilliam	12.00	6.00	3.50
307	Curt Barclay	7.00	3.50	2.00
308	Norm Siebern	9.00	4.50	2.75
309	Sal Maglie	7.00	3.50	2.00
310	Luis Aparicio	25.00	12.50	7.50
311	Norm Zauchin	7.00	3.50	2.00
312	Don Newcombe	9.00	4.50	2.75
313	Frank House	7.00	3.50	2.00
314	Don Cardwell	7.00	3.50	2.00
315	Joe Adcock	7.00	3.50	2.00
316a	Ralph Lumenti (No optioned statement.)	75.00	37.50	22.50
316b	Ralph Lumenti (Optioned statement.)	7.00	3.50	2.00
317	N.L. Hitting Kings (Richie Ashburn, Willie Mays)	45.00	22.50	13.50
318	Rocky Bridges	7.00	3.50	2.00
319	Dave Hillman	7.00	3.50	2.00
320	Bob Skinner	7.00	3.50	2.00
321a	Bob Giallombardo (No optioned statement.)	75.00	37.50	22.50
321b	Bob Giallombardo (Optioned statement.)	7.00	3.50	2.00
322a	Harry Hanebrink (No trade statement.)	90.00	45.00	27.50
322b	Harry Hanebrink (Trade statement.)	7.00	3.50	2.00
323	Frank Sullivan	7.00	3.50	2.00
324	Don Demeter	7.00	3.50	2.00
325	Ken Boyer	13.50	7.00	4.00
326	Marv Throneberry	10.00	5.00	3.00
327	*Gary Bell*	7.00	3.50	2.00
328	Lou Skizas	7.00	3.50	2.00
329	Detroit Tigers Team	17.50	8.75	5.25
330	Gus Triandos	7.00	3.50	2.00
331	Steve Boros	7.00	3.50	2.00
332	Ray Monzant	7.00	3.50	2.00
333	Harry Simpson	7.00	3.50	2.00
334	Glen Hobbie	7.00	3.50	2.00
335	Johnny Temple	7.00	3.50	2.00
336a	Billy Loes (No trade statement.)	75.00	37.50	22.50
336b	Billy Loes (Trade statement.)	7.00	3.50	2.00
337	George Crowe	7.00	3.50	2.00
338	*George Anderson* (Sparky)	30.00	15.00	9.00
339	Roy Face	7.00	3.50	2.00
340	Roy Sievers	7.00	3.50	2.00
341	Tom Qualters	7.00	3.50	2.00

342	Ray Jablonski	7.00	3.50	2.00
343	Billy Hoeft	7.00	3.50	2.00
344	Russ Nixon	7.00	3.50	2.00
345	Gil McDougald	12.50	6.25	3.75
346	Batter Bafflers (Tom Brewer, Dave Sisler)	9.00	4.50	2.75
347	Bob Buhl	7.00	3.50	2.00
348	Ted Lepcio	7.00	3.50	2.00
349	Hoyt Wilhelm	15.00	7.50	4.50
350	Ernie Banks	50.00	25.00	15.00
351	Earl Torgeson	7.00	3.50	2.00
352	Robin Roberts	20.00	10.00	6.00
353	Curt Flood	12.00	6.00	3.50
354	Pete Burnside	7.00	3.50	2.00
355	Jim Piersall	9.00	4.50	2.75
356	Bob Mabe	7.00	3.50	2.00
357	*Dick Stuart*	10.00	5.00	3.00
358	Ralph Terry	7.00	3.50	2.00
359	*Bill White*	12.50	6.25	3.75
360	Al Kaline	35.00	17.50	10.00
361	Willard Nixon	7.00	3.50	2.00
362a	Dolan Nichols (No optioned statement.)	80.00	40.00	24.00
362b	Dolan Nichols (Optioned statement.)	7.00	3.50	2.00
363	Bobby Avila	7.00	3.50	2.00
364	Danny McDevitt	7.00	3.50	2.00
365	Gus Bell	7.00	3.50	2.00
366	Humberto Robinson	7.00	3.50	2.00
367	Cal Neeman	7.00	3.50	2.00
368	Don Mueller	7.00	3.50	2.00
369	Dick Tomanek	7.00	3.50	2.00
370	Pete Runnels	7.00	3.50	2.00
371	Dick Brodowski	7.00	3.50	2.00
372	Jim Hegan	7.00	3.50	2.00
373	Herb Plews	7.00	3.50	2.00
374	Art Ditmar	9.00	4.50	2.75
375	Bob Nieman	7.00	3.50	2.00
376	Hal Naragon	7.00	3.50	2.00
377	Johnny Antonelli	7.00	3.50	2.00
378	Gail Harris	7.00	3.50	2.00
379	Bob Miller	7.00	3.50	2.00
380	Hank Aaron	110.00	55.00	35.00
381	Mike Baxes	7.00	3.50	2.00
382	Curt Simmons	7.00	3.50	2.00
383	Words of Wisdom (Don Larsen, Casey Stengel)	16.00	8.00	4.75
384	Dave Sisler	7.00	3.50	2.00
385	Sherm Lollar	7.00	3.50	2.00
386	Jim Delsing	7.00	3.50	2.00
387	Don Drysdale	25.00	12.50	7.50
388	Bob Will	7.00	3.50	2.00
389	Joe Nuxhall	7.00	3.50	2.00
390	Orlando Cepeda	25.00	12.50	7.50
391	Milt Pappas	7.00	3.50	2.00
392	Whitey Herzog	7.00	3.50	2.00
393	Frank Lary	7.00	3.50	2.00
394	Randy Jackson	7.00	3.50	2.00
395	Elston Howard	15.00	7.50	4.50
396	Bob Rush	7.00	3.50	2.00
397	Washington Senators Team	16.00	8.00	4.75
398	Wally Post	7.00	3.50	2.00
399	Larry Jackson	7.00	3.50	2.00
400	Jackie Jensen	10.00	5.00	3.00
401	Ron Blackburn	7.00	3.50	2.00
402	Hector Lopez	7.00	3.50	2.00
403	Clem Labine	12.50	6.25	3.75
404	Hank Sauer	7.00	3.50	2.00
405	Roy McMillan	7.00	3.50	2.00
406	Solly Drake	7.00	3.50	2.00
407	Moe Drabowsky	7.00	3.50	2.00
408	Keystone Combo (Luis Aparicio, Nellie Fox)	20.00	10.00	6.00
409	Gus Zernial	7.00	3.50	2.00
410	Billy Pierce	7.00	3.50	2.00
411	Whitey Lockman	7.00	3.50	2.00
412	Stan Lopata	7.00	3.50	2.00
413	Camilo (Camilo) Pascual	7.00	3.50	2.00
414	Dale Long	7.00	3.50	2.00
415	Bill Mazeroski	20.00	10.00	6.00
416a	Haywood Sullivan (No circle around copyright symbol, no period after "A" in "U.S.A.")	15.00	7.50	4.50
416b	Haywood Sullivan (No circle around copyright symbol, period added after "A" in "U.S.A.")	7.00	3.50	2.00
416c	Haywood Sullivan (Circle around copyright symbol, period after "A" in "U.S.A.")	7.00	3.50	2.00
417	Virgil Trucks	7.00	3.50	2.00
418	Gino Cimoli	7.00	3.50	2.00
419	Milwaukee Braves Team	16.00	8.00	4.75
420	Rocky Colavito	20.00	10.00	6.00
421	Herm Wehmeier	7.00	3.50	2.00
422	Hobie Landrith	7.00	3.50	2.00
423	Bob Grim	7.00	3.50	2.00
424	Ken Aspromonte	7.00	3.50	2.00
425	Del Crandall	7.00	3.50	2.00
426	Jerry Staley	7.00	3.50	2.00
427	Charlie Neal	7.00	3.50	2.00
428	Buc Hill Aces (Roy Face, Bob Friend, Ron Kline, Vern Law)	9.00	4.50	2.75
429	Bobby Thomson	9.00	4.50	2.75
430	Whitey Ford	40.00	20.00	12.00
431	Whammy Douglas	7.00	3.50	2.00
432	Smoky Burgess	7.00	3.50	2.00
433	Billy Harrell	7.00	3.50	2.00
434	Hal Griggs	7.00	3.50	2.00
435	Frank Robinson	30.00	15.00	9.00
436	Granny Hamner	7.00	3.50	2.00
437	Ike Delock	7.00	3.50	2.00
438	Sam Esposito	7.00	3.50	2.00
439	Brooks Robinson	30.00	15.00	9.00
440	Lou Burdette	7.00	3.50	2.00
441	John Roseboro	7.00	3.50	2.00
442	Ray Narleski	7.00	3.50	2.00

443	Daryl Spencer	7.00	3.50	2.00
444	*Ronnie Hansen*	7.00	3.50	2.00
445	Cal McLish	7.00	3.50	2.00
446	Rocky Nelson	7.00	3.50	2.00
447	Bob Anderson	7.00	3.50	2.00
448	Vada Pinson	7.00	3.50	2.00
449	Tom Gorman	7.00	3.50	2.00
450	Ed Mathews	45.00	22.50	13.50
451	Jimmy Constable	7.00	3.50	2.00
452	Chico Fernandez	7.00	3.50	2.00
453	Les Moss	7.00	3.50	2.00
454	Phil Clark	7.00	3.50	2.00
455	Larry Doby	15.00	7.50	4.50
456	Jerry Casale	7.00	3.50	2.00
457	Los Angeles Dodgers Team	20.00	10.00	6.00
458	Gordon Jones	7.00	3.50	2.00
459	Bill Tuttle	7.00	3.50	2.00
460	Bob Friend	7.00	3.50	2.00
461	Mantle Hits 42nd Homer For Crown (Mickey Mantle)	70.00	35.00	20.00
462	Colavito's Great Catch Saves Game (Rocky Colavito)	12.50	6.25	3.75
463	Kaline Becomes Youngest Batting Champ (Al Kaline)	15.00	7.50	4.50
464	Mays' Catch Makes Series History (Willie Mays)	35.00	17.50	10.00
465	Sievers Sets Homer Mark (Roy Sievers)	7.00	3.50	2.00
466	Pierce All-Star Starter (Billy Pierce)	7.00	3.50	2.00
467	Aaron Clubs World Series Homer (Hank Aaron)	25.00	12.50	7.50
468	Snider's Play Brings L.A. Victory (Duke Snider)	15.00	7.50	4.50
469	Hustler Banks Wins M.V.P. Award (Ernie Banks)	16.00	8.00	5.00
470	Musial Raps Out 3,000th Hit (Stan Musial)	25.00	12.50	7.50
471	Tom Sturdivant	9.00	4.50	2.75
472	Gene Freese	7.00	3.50	2.00
473	Mike Fornieles	7.00	3.50	2.00
474	Moe Thacker	7.00	3.50	2.00
475	Jack Harshman	7.00	3.50	2.00
476	Cleveland Indians Team	16.00	8.00	4.75
477	Barry Latman	7.00	3.50	2.00
478	Bob Clemente	110.00	55.00	35.00
479	Lindy McDaniel	7.00	3.50	2.00
480	Red Schoendienst	20.00	10.00	6.00
481	Charley Maxwell	7.00	3.50	2.00
482	Russ Meyer	7.00	3.50	2.00
483	Clint Courtney	7.00	3.50	2.00
484	Willie Kirkland	7.00	3.50	2.00
485	Ryne Duren	10.00	5.00	3.00
486	Sammy White	7.00	3.50	2.00
487	Hal Brown	7.00	3.50	2.00
488	Walt Moryn	7.00	3.50	2.00
489	John C. Powers	7.00	3.50	2.00
490	Frank Thomas	7.00	3.50	2.00
491	Don Blasingame	7.00	3.50	2.00
492	Gene Conley	7.00	3.50	2.00
493	Jim Landis	7.00	3.50	2.00
494	Don Pavletich	7.00	3.50	2.00
495	Johnny Podres	11.00	5.50	3.25
496	Wayne Terwilliger	7.00	3.50	2.00
497	Hal R. Smith	7.00	3.50	2.00
498	Dick Hyde	7.00	3.50	2.00
499	Johnny O'Brien	7.00	3.50	2.00
500	Vic Wertz	7.00	3.50	2.00
501	Bobby Tiefenauer	7.00	3.50	2.00
502	Al Dark	7.00	3.50	2.00
503	Jim Owens	7.00	3.50	2.00
504	Ossie Alvarez	7.00	3.50	2.00
505	Tony Kubek	20.00	10.00	6.00
506	Bob Purkey	7.00	3.50	2.00
507	Bob Hale	15.00	7.50	4.50
508	Art Fowler	15.00	7.50	4.50
509	*Norm Cash*	60.00	30.00	18.00
510	New York Yankees Team	80.00	40.00	24.00
511	George Susce	15.00	7.50	4.50
512	George Altman	15.00	7.50	4.50
513	Tom Carroll	15.00	7.50	4.50
514	*Bob Gibson*	200.00	90.00	55.00
515	Harmon Killebrew	95.00	47.50	27.50
516	Mike Garcia	15.00	7.50	4.50
517	Joe Koppe	15.00	7.50	4.50
518	*Mike Cuellar*	20.00	10.00	6.00
519	Infield Power (Dick Gernert, Frank Malzone, Pete Runnels)	17.50	8.75	5.25
520	Don Elston	15.00	7.50	4.50
521	Gary Geiger	15.00	7.50	4.50
522	Gene Snyder	15.00	7.50	4.50
523	Harry Bright	15.00	7.50	4.50
524	Larry Osborne	15.00	7.50	4.50
525	Jim Coates	17.50	8.75	5.25
526	Bob Speake	15.00	7.50	4.50
527	Solly Hemus	15.00	7.50	4.50
528	Pittsburgh Pirates Team	40.00	20.00	12.00
529	*George Bamberger*	15.00	7.50	4.50
530	Wally Moon	15.00	7.50	4.50
531	Ray Webster	15.00	7.50	4.50
532	Mark Freeman	15.00	7.50	4.50
533	Darrell Johnson	17.50	8.75	5.25
534	Faye Throneberry	15.00	7.50	4.50
535	Ruben Gomez	15.00	7.50	4.50
536	Dan Kravitz	15.00	7.50	4.50
537	Rodolfo Arias	15.00	7.50	4.50
538	Chick King	15.00	7.50	4.50
539	Gary Blaylock	15.00	7.50	4.50
540	Willy Miranda	15.00	7.50	4.50
541	Bob Thurman	15.00	7.50	4.50
542	*Jim Perry*	30.00	15.00	9.00
543	Corsair Outfield Trio (Roberto Clemente, Bob Skinner, Bill Virdon)	60.00	30.00	18.00
544	Lee Tate	15.00	7.50	4.50
545	Tom Morgan	15.00	7.50	4.50
546	Al Schroll	15.00	7.50	4.50
547	Jim Baxes	15.00	7.50	4.50

	NM	EX	VG
548 Elmer Singleton	15.00	7.50	4.50
549 Howie Nunn	15.00	7.50	4.50
550 Roy Campanella (Symbol of Courage)	90.00	45.00	27.50
551 Fred Haney (All-Star)	15.00	7.50	4.50
552 Casey Stengel (All-Star)	25.00	12.50	7.50
553 Orlando Cepeda (All-Star)	25.00	12.50	7.50
554 Bill Skowron (All-Star)	22.50	11.00	6.75
555 Bill Mazeroski (All-Star)	25.00	12.50	7.50
556 Nellie Fox (All-Star)	27.50	13.50	8.25
557 Ken Boyer (All-Star)	20.00	10.00	6.00
558 Frank Malzone (All-Star)	15.00	7.50	4.50
559 Ernie Banks (All-Star)	45.00	22.50	13.50
560 Luis Aparicio (All-Star)	20.00	10.00	6.00
561 Hank Aaron (All-Star)	75.00	37.50	22.50
562 Al Kaline (All-Star)	30.00	15.00	9.00
563 Willie Mays (All-Star)	70.00	35.00	20.00
564 Mickey Mantle (All-Star)	250.00	125.00	60.00
565 Wes Covington (All-Star)	15.00	7.50	4.50
566 Roy Sievers (All-Star)	15.00	7.50	4.50
567 Del Crandall (All-Star)	15.00	7.50	4.50
568 Gus Triandos (All-Star)	15.00	7.50	4.50
569 Bob Friend (All-Star)	15.00	7.50	4.50
570 Bob Turley (All-Star)	17.50	8.75	5.25
571 Warren Spahn (All-Star)	27.50	13.50	8.25
572 Billy Pierce (All-Star)	150.00	10.00	6.00
---- Elect Your Favorite Rookie Insert (Paper stock, September 29 date on back.)	30.00	15.00	9.00
---- Felt Pennants Insert (Paper stock.)	30.00	15.00	9.00

1960 Topps

In 1960, Topps opted for a horizontal format in standard 3-1/2" x 2-1/2" size. Basic fronts have a large color portrait or pose at right and black-and-white action photograph at left. After a one-year hiatus, backs returned to the use of lifetime statistics along with a cartoon and short career summary or previous season highlights. Specialty cards in the 572-card set are multi-player cards, managers and coaches cards, and highlights of the 1959 World Series. Two groups of rookie cards are included. The first are numbers 117-148, which are the Sport Magazine rookies. The second group is called "Topps All-Star Rookies." Finally, there is a run of All-Star cards to close out the set in the scarcer high numbers. Cards #375-440 can be found with backs printed on either white or grey cardboard, with the white stock being the less common. Team cards have checklists on the back.

	NM	EX	VG
Complete Set (572):	6,500	3,250	2,000
Common Player (1-440):	6.00	3.00	1.75
Common Player (441-506):	9.00	4.50	2.75
Common Player (507-572):	15.00	7.50	4.50
1 Early Wynn	40.00	10.00	6.00
2 Roman Mejias	20.00	4.00	1.75
3 Joe Adcock	6.00	3.00	1.75
4 Bob Purkey	6.00	3.00	1.75
5 Wally Moon	6.00	3.00	1.75
6 Lou Berberet	6.00	3.00	1.75
7 Master and Mentor (Willie Mays, Bill Rigney)	20.00	10.00	6.00
8 Bud Daley	6.00	3.00	1.75
9 Faye Throneberry	6.00	3.00	1.75
10 Ernie Banks	50.00	25.00	15.00
11 Norm Siebern	6.00	3.00	1.75
12 Milt Pappas	6.00	3.00	1.75
13 Wally Post	6.00	3.00	1.75
14 Jim Grant	6.00	3.00	1.75
15 Pete Runnels	6.00	3.00	1.75
16 Ernie Broglio	6.00	3.00	1.75
17 Johnny Callison	6.00	3.00	1.75
18 Los Angeles Dodgers Team	35.00	17.50	10.00
19 Felix Mantilla	6.00	3.00	1.75
20 Roy Face	6.00	3.00	1.75
21 Dutch Dotterer	6.00	3.00	1.75
22 Rocky Bridges	6.00	3.00	1.75
23 Eddie Fisher	6.00	3.00	1.75
24 Dick Gray	6.00	3.00	1.75
25 Roy Sievers	6.00	3.00	1.75
26 Wayne Terwilliger	6.00	3.00	1.75
27 Dick Drott	6.00	3.00	1.75
28 Brooks Robinson	40.00	20.00	12.00
29 Clem Labine	8.00	4.00	2.50
30 Tito Francona	6.00	3.00	1.75
31 Sammy Esposito	6.00	3.00	1.75
32 Sophomore Stalwarts (Jim O'Toole, Vada Pinson)	9.00	4.50	2.75
33 Tom Morgan	6.00	3.00	1.75
34 George Anderson (Sparky)	20.00	10.00	6.00
35 Whitey Ford	35.00	17.50	10.00
36 Russ Nixon	6.00	3.00	1.75
37 Bill Bruton	6.00	3.00	1.75
38 Jerry Casale	6.00	3.00	1.75
39 Earl Averill	6.00	3.00	1.75
40 Joe Cunningham	6.00	3.00	1.75
41 Barry Latman	6.00	3.00	1.75
42 Hobie Landrith	6.00	3.00	1.75
43 Washington Senators Team	15.00	7.50	4.50
44 Bobby Locke	6.00	3.00	1.75
45 Roy McMillan	6.00	3.00	1.75
46 Jack Fisher	6.00	3.00	1.75
47 Don Zimmer	12.00	6.00	3.50
48 Hal Smith	6.00	3.00	1.75
49 Curt Raydon	6.00	3.00	1.75
50 Al Kaline	35.00	17.50	10.00
51 Jim Coates	6.00	3.00	1.75
52 Dave Philley	6.00	3.00	1.75
53 Jackie Brandt	6.00	3.00	1.75
54 Mike Fornieles	6.00	3.00	1.75
55 Bill Mazeroski	20.00	10.00	6.00
56 Steve Korcheck	6.00	3.00	1.75
57 Win-Savers (Turk Lown, Gerry Staley)	6.00	3.00	1.75
58 Gino Cimoli	6.00	3.00	1.75
59 Juan Pizarro	6.00	3.00	1.75
60 Gus Triandos	6.00	3.00	1.75
61 Eddie Kasko	6.00	3.00	1.75
62 Roger Craig	6.00	3.00	1.75
63 George Strickland	6.00	3.00	1.75
64 Jack Meyer	6.00	3.00	1.75
65 Elston Howard	15.00	7.50	4.50
66 Bob Trowbridge	6.00	3.00	1.75
67 *Jose Pagan*	6.00	3.00	1.75
68 Dave Hillman	6.00	3.00	1.75
69 Billy Goodman	6.00	3.00	1.75
70 Lou Burdette	6.00	3.00	1.75
71 Marty Keough	6.00	3.00	1.75
72 Detroit Tigers Team	15.00	7.50	4.50
73 Bob Gibson	50.00	25.00	15.00
74 Walt Moryn	6.00	3.00	1.75
75 Vic Power	6.00	3.00	1.75
76 Bill Fischer	6.00	3.00	1.75
77 Hank Foiles	6.00	3.00	1.75
78 Bob Grim	6.00	3.00	1.75
79 Walt Dropo	6.00	3.00	1.75
80 Johnny Antonelli	6.00	3.00	1.75
81 Russ Snyder	6.00	3.00	1.75
82 Ruben Gomez	6.00	3.00	1.75
83 Tony Kubek	25.00	12.50	7.50
84 Hal Smith	6.00	3.00	1.75
85 Frank Lary	6.00	3.00	1.75
86 Dick Gernert	6.00	3.00	1.75
87 John Romonosky	6.00	3.00	1.75
88 John Roseboro	6.00	3.00	1.75
89 Hal Brown	6.00	3.00	1.75
90 Bobby Avila	6.00	3.00	1.75
91 Bennie Daniels	6.00	3.00	1.75
92 Whitey Herzog	6.00	3.00	1.75
93 Art Schult	6.00	3.00	1.75
94 Leo Kiely	6.00	3.00	1.75
95 Frank Thomas	6.00	3.00	1.75
96 Ralph Terry	7.50	3.75	2.25
97 Ted Lepcio	6.00	3.00	1.75
98 Gordon Jones	6.00	3.00	1.75
99 Lenny Green	6.00	3.00	1.75
100 Nellie Fox	20.00	10.00	6.00
101 Bob Miller	6.00	3.00	1.75
102 Kent Hadley	6.00	3.00	1.75
103 Dick Farrell	6.00	3.00	1.75
104 Dick Schofield	6.00	3.00	1.75
105 *Larry Sherry*	12.00	6.00	3.50
106 Billy Gardner	6.00	3.00	1.75
107 Carl Willey	6.00	3.00	1.75
108 Pete Daley	6.00	3.00	1.75
109 Cletis Boyer	13.50	6.75	4.00
110 Cal McLish	6.00	3.00	1.75
111 Vic Wertz	6.00	3.00	1.75
112 Jack Harshman	6.00	3.00	1.75
113 Bob Skinner	6.00	3.00	1.75
114 Ken Aspromonte	6.00	3.00	1.75
115 Fork and Knuckler (Roy Face, Hoyt Wilhelm)	9.00	4.50	2.75
116 Jim Rivera	6.00	3.00	1.75
117 Tom Borland	6.00	3.00	1.75
118 Bob Bruce	6.00	3.00	1.75
119 *Chico Cardenas*	6.00	3.00	1.75
120 Duke Carmel	6.00	3.00	1.75
121 Camilo Carreon	6.00	3.00	1.75
122 Don Dillard	6.00	3.00	1.75
123 Dan Dobbek	6.00	3.00	1.75
124 Jim Donohue	6.00	3.00	1.75
125 *Dick Ellsworth*	6.00	3.00	1.75
126 *Chuck Estrada*	6.00	3.00	1.75
127 Ronnie Hansen	6.00	3.00	1.75
128 Bill Harris	6.00	3.00	1.75
129 Bob Hartman	6.00	3.00	1.75
130 Frank Herrera	6.00	3.00	1.75
131 Ed Hobaugh	6.00	3.00	1.75
132 *Frank Howard*	20.00	10.00	6.00
133 *Manuel Javier*	6.00	3.00	1.75
134 Deron Johnson	7.50	3.75	2.25
135 Ken Johnson	6.00	3.00	1.75
136 *Jim Kaat*	20.00	10.00	6.00
137 Lou Klimchock	6.00	3.00	1.75
138 *Art Mahaffey*	6.00	3.00	1.75
139 Carl Mathias	6.00	3.00	1.75
140 Julio Navarro	6.00	3.00	1.75
141 Jim Proctor	6.00	3.00	1.75
142 Bill Short	6.00	3.00	1.75
143 Al Spangler	6.00	3.00	1.75
144 Al Stieglitz	6.00	3.00	1.75
145 Jim Umbricht	6.00	3.00	1.75
146 Ted Wieand	6.00	3.00	1.75
147 Bob Will	6.00	3.00	1.75
148 *Carl Yastrzemski*	130.00	65.00	35.00
149 Bob Nieman	6.00	3.00	1.75
150 Billy Pierce	6.00	3.00	1.75
151 San Francisco Giants Team	15.00	7.50	4.50
152 Gail Harris	6.00	3.00	1.75
153 Bobby Thomson	7.50	3.75	2.25
154 Jim Davenport	6.00	3.00	1.75
155 Charlie Neal	6.00	3.00	1.75
156 Art Ceccarelli	6.00	3.00	1.75
157 Rocky Nelson	6.00	3.00	1.75
158 Wes Covington	6.00	3.00	1.75
159 Jim Piersall	8.00	4.00	2.50
160 Rival All-Stars (Ken Boyer, Mickey Mantle)	60.00	30.00	18.00
161 Ray Narleski	6.00	3.00	1.75
162 Sammy Taylor	6.00	3.00	1.75
163 Hector Lopez	6.00	3.00	1.75
164 Cincinnati Reds Team	15.00	7.50	4.50
165 Jack Sanford	6.00	3.00	1.75
166 Chuck Essegian	6.00	3.00	1.75
167 Valmy Thomas	6.00	3.00	1.75
168 Alex Grammas	6.00	3.00	1.75
169 Jake Striker	6.00	3.00	1.75
170 Del Crandall	6.00	3.00	1.75
171 Johnny Groth	6.00	3.00	1.75
172 Willie Kirkland	6.00	3.00	1.75
173 Billy Martin	10.00	5.00	3.00
174 Cleveland Indians Team	15.00	7.50	4.50
175 Pedro Ramos	6.00	3.00	1.75
176 Vada Pinson	10.00	5.00	3.00
177 Johnny Kucks	6.00	3.00	1.75
178 Woody Held	6.00	3.00	1.75
179 Rip Coleman	6.00	3.00	1.75
180 Harry Simpson	6.00	3.00	1.75
181 Billy Loes	6.00	3.00	1.75
182 Glen Hobbie	6.00	3.00	1.75
183 Eli Grba	6.00	3.00	1.75
184 Gary Geiger	6.00	3.00	1.75
185 Jim Owens	6.00	3.00	1.75
186 Dave Sisler	6.00	3.00	1.75
187 Jay Hook	6.00	3.00	1.75
188 Dick Williams	6.00	3.00	1.75
189 Don McMahon	6.00	3.00	1.75
190 Gene Woodling	6.00	3.00	1.75
191 Johnny Klippstein	6.00	3.00	1.75
192 Danny O'Connell	6.00	3.00	1.75
193 Dick Hyde	6.00	3.00	1.75
194 Bobby Gene Smith	6.00	3.00	1.75
195 Lindy McDaniel	6.00	3.00	1.75
196 Andy Carey	6.00	3.00	1.75
197 Ron Kline	6.00	3.00	1.75
198 Jerry Lynch	6.00	3.00	1.75
199 Dick Donovan	6.00	3.00	1.75
200 Willie Mays	90.00	45.00	27.50
201 Larry Osborne	6.00	3.00	1.75
202 Fred Kipp	6.00	3.00	1.75
203 Sammy White	6.00	3.00	1.75
204 Ryne Duren	7.50	3.75	2.25
205 Johnny Logan	6.00	3.00	1.75
206 Claude Osteen	6.00	3.00	1.75
207 Bob Boyd	6.00	3.00	1.75
208 Chicago White Sox Team	15.00	7.50	4.50
209 Ron Blackburn	6.00	3.00	1.75
210 Harmon Killebrew	30.00	15.00	9.00
211 Taylor Phillips	6.00	3.00	1.75
212 Walt Alston	12.00	6.00	3.50
213 Chuck Dressen	6.00	3.00	1.75
214 Jimmie Dykes	6.00	3.00	1.75
215 Bob Elliott	6.00	3.00	1.75
216 Joe Gordon	6.00	3.00	1.75
217 Charley Grimm	6.00	3.00	1.75
218 Solly Hemus	6.00	3.00	1.75
219 Fred Hutchinson	6.00	3.00	1.75
220 Billy Jurges	6.00	3.00	1.75
221 Cookie Lavagetto	6.00	3.00	1.75
222 Al Lopez	10.00	5.00	3.00
223 Danny Murtaugh	6.00	3.00	1.75
224 Paul Richards	6.00	3.00	1.75
225 Bill Rigney	6.00	3.00	1.75
226 Eddie Sawyer	6.00	3.00	1.75
227 Casey Stengel	17.50	8.75	5.25
228 Ernie Johnson	6.00	3.00	1.75
229 Joe Morgan	6.00	3.00	1.75
230 Mound Magicians (Bob Buhl, Lou Burdette, Warren Spahn)	17.50	8.75	5.25
231 Hal Naragon	6.00	3.00	1.75
232 Jim Busby	6.00	3.00	1.75
233 Don Elston	6.00	3.00	1.75
234 Don Demeter	6.00	3.00	1.75
235 Gus Bell	6.00	3.00	1.75
236 Dick Ricketts	6.00	3.00	1.75
237 Elmer Valo	6.00	3.00	1.75
238 Danny Kravitz	6.00	3.00	1.75
239 Joe Shipley	6.00	3.00	1.75
240 Luis Aparicio	17.50	8.75	5.25
241 Albie Pearson	6.00	3.00	1.75
242 St. Louis Cardinals Team	15.00	7.50	4.50
243 Bubba Phillips	6.00	3.00	1.75
244 Hal Griggs	6.00	3.00	1.75
245 Eddie Yost	6.00	3.00	1.75
246 Lee Maye	6.00	3.00	1.75
247 Gil McDougald	12.00	6.00	3.50
248 Del Rice	6.00	3.00	1.75
249 *Earl Wilson*	6.00	3.00	1.75
250 Stan Musial	65.00	32.50	20.00
251 Bobby Malkmus	6.00	3.00	1.75
252 Ray Herbert	6.00	3.00	1.75
253 Eddie Bressoud	6.00	3.00	1.75
254 Arnie Portocarrero	6.00	3.00	1.75
255 Jim Gilliam	10.00	5.00	3.00
256 Dick Brown	6.00	3.00	1.75
257 Gordy Coleman	6.00	3.00	1.75
258 Dick Groat	6.00	3.00	1.75
259 George Altman	6.00	3.00	1.75
260 Power Plus (Rocky Colavito, Tito Francona)	11.00	5.50	3.25
261 Pete Burnside	6.00	3.00	1.75
262 Hank Bauer	7.50	3.75	2.25
263 Darrell Johnson	6.00	3.00	1.75
264 Robin Roberts	12.50	6.25	3.75
265 Rip Repulski	6.00	3.00	1.75
266 Joe Jay	6.00	3.00	1.75
267 Jim Marshall	6.00	3.00	1.75

268	Al Worthington	6.00	3.00	1.75
269	Gene Green	6.00	3.00	1.75
270	Bob Turley	10.00	5.00	3.00
271	Julio Becquer	6.00	3.00	1.75
272	Fred Green	6.00	3.00	1.75
273	Neil Chrisley	6.00	3.00	1.75
274	Tom Acker	6.00	3.00	1.75
275	Curt Flood	9.00	4.50	2.75
276	Ken McBride	6.00	3.00	1.75
277	Harry Bright	6.00	3.00	1.75
278	Stan Williams	6.00	3.00	1.75
279	Chuck Tanner	6.00	3.00	1.75
280	Frank Sullivan	6.00	3.00	1.75
281	Ray Boone	6.00	3.00	1.75
282	Joe Nuxhall	6.00	3.00	1.75
283	John Blanchard	7.50	3.75	2.25
284	Don Gross	6.00	3.00	1.75
285	Harry Anderson	6.00	3.00	1.75
286	Ray Semproch	6.00	3.00	1.75
287	Felipe Alou	7.50	3.75	2.25
288	Bob Mabe	6.00	3.00	1.75
289	Willie Jones	6.00	3.00	1.75
290	Jerry Lumpe	6.00	3.00	1.75
291	Bob Keegan	6.00	3.00	1.75
292	Dodger Backstops (Joe Pignatano, John Roseboro)	7.50	3.75	2.25
293	Gene Conley	6.00	3.00	1.75
294	Tony Taylor	6.00	3.00	1.75
295	Gil Hodges	15.00	7.50	4.50
296	Nelson Chittum	6.00	3.00	1.75
297	Reno Bertoia	6.00	3.00	1.75
298	George Witt	6.00	3.00	1.75
299	Earl Torgeson	6.00	3.00	1.75
300	Hank Aaron	115.00	55.00	35.00
301	Jerry Davie	6.00	3.00	1.75
302	Philadelphia Phillies Team	15.00	7.50	4.50
303	Billy O'Dell	6.00	3.00	1.75
304	Joe Ginsberg	6.00	3.00	1.75
305	Richie Ashburn	15.00	7.50	4.50
306	Frank Baumann	6.00	3.00	1.75
307	Gene Oliver	6.00	3.00	1.75
308	Dick Hall	6.00	3.00	1.75
309	Bob Hale	6.00	3.00	1.75
310	Frank Malzone	6.00	3.00	1.75
311	Raul Sanchez	6.00	3.00	1.75
312	Charlie Lau	6.00	3.00	1.75
313	Turk Lown	6.00	3.00	1.75
314	Chico Fernandez	6.00	3.00	1.75
315	Bobby Shantz	11.00	5.50	3.25
316	*Willie McCovey*	90.00	45.00	27.50
317	Pumpsie Green	7.50	3.75	2.25
318	Jim Baxes	6.00	3.00	1.75
319	Joe Koppe	6.00	3.00	1.75
320	Bob Allison	6.00	3.00	1.75
321	Ron Fairly	6.00	3.00	1.75
322	Willie Tasby	6.00	3.00	1.75
323	Johnny Romano	6.00	3.00	1.75
324	Jim Perry	7.50	3.75	2.25
325	Jim O'Toole	6.00	3.00	1.75
326	Bob Clemente	95.00	47.50	27.50
327	*Ray Sadecki*	6.00	3.00	1.75
328	Earl Battey	6.00	3.00	1.75
329	Zack Monroe	6.00	3.00	1.75
330	Harvey Kuenn	6.00	3.00	1.75
331	Henry Mason	6.00	3.00	1.75
332	New York Yankees Team	37.50	18.50	11.00
333	Danny McDevitt	6.00	3.00	1.75
334	Ted Abernathy	6.00	3.00	1.75
335	Red Schoendienst	12.50	6.25	3.75
336	Ike Delock	6.00	3.00	1.75
337	Cal Neeman	6.00	3.00	1.75
338	Ray Monzant	6.00	3.00	1.75
339	Harry Chiti	6.00	3.00	1.75
340	Harvey Haddix	6.00	3.00	1.75
341	Carroll Hardy	6.00	3.00	1.75
342	Casey Wise	6.00	3.00	1.75
343	Sandy Koufax	85.00	42.50	25.00
344	Clint Courtney	6.00	3.00	1.75
345	Don Newcombe	7.50	3.75	2.25
346	J.C. Martin (Photo actually Gary Peters.)	6.00	3.00	1.75
347	Ed Bouchee	6.00	3.00	1.75
348	Barry Shetrone	6.00	3.00	1.75
349	Moe Drabowsky	6.00	3.00	1.75
350	Mickey Mantle	350.00	160.00	95.00
351	Don Nottebart	6.00	3.00	1.75
352	Cincy Clouters (Gus Bell, Jerry Lynch, Frank Robinson)	12.00	6.00	3.50
353	Don Larsen	8.00	4.00	2.50
354	Bob Lillis	6.00	3.00	1.75
355	Bill White	6.00	3.00	1.75
356	Joe Amalfitano	6.00	3.00	1.75
357	Al Schroll	6.00	3.00	1.75
358	Joe De Maestri	6.00	3.00	1.75
359	Buddy Gilbert	6.00	3.00	1.75
360	Herb Score	7.50	3.75	2.25
361	Bob Oldis	6.00	3.00	1.75
362	Russ Kemmerer	6.00	3.00	1.75
363	Gene Stephens	6.00	3.00	1.75
364	Paul Foytack	6.00	3.00	1.75
365	Minnie Minoso	12.50	6.25	3.75
366	*Dallas Green*	9.00	4.50	2.75
367	Bill Tuttle	6.00	3.00	1.75
368	Daryl Spencer	6.00	3.00	1.75
369	Billy Hoeft	6.00	3.00	1.75
370	Bill Skowron	17.50	8.75	5.25
371	Bud Byerly	6.00	3.00	1.75
372	Frank House	6.00	3.00	1.75
373	Don Hoak	6.00	3.00	1.75
374	Bob Buhl	6.00	3.00	1.75
375	Dale Long	6.00	3.00	1.75
376	Johnny Briggs	6.00	3.00	1.75
377	Roger Maris	80.00	40.00	24.00
378	Stu Miller	6.00	3.00	1.75
379	Red Wilson	6.00	3.00	1.75
380	Bob Shaw	6.00	3.00	1.75
381	Milwaukee Braves Team	16.00	8.00	4.75
382	Ted Bowsfield	6.00	3.00	1.75
383	Leon Wagner	6.00	3.00	1.75
384	Don Cardwell	6.00	3.00	1.75
385	World Series Game 1 (Neal Steals Second)	10.00	5.00	3.00
386	World Series Game 2 (Neal Belts 2nd Homer)	10.00	5.00	3.00
387	World Series Game 3 (Furillo Breaks Up Game)	10.00	5.00	3.00
388	World Series Game 4 (Hodges' Winning Homer)	10.00	5.00	3.00
389	World Series Game 5 (Luis Swipes Base)	12.00	6.00	3.50
390	World Series Game 6 (Scrambling After Ball)	10.00	5.00	3.00
391	World Series Summary (The Champs Celebrate)	10.00	5.00	3.00
392	Tex Clevenger	6.00	3.00	1.75
393	Smoky Burgess	6.00	3.00	1.75
394	Norm Larker	6.00	3.00	1.75
395	Hoyt Wilhelm	13.50	6.75	4.00
396	Steve Bilko	6.00	3.00	1.75
397	Don Blasingame	6.00	3.00	1.75
398	Mike Cuellar	6.00	3.00	1.75
399	Young Hill Stars (Jack Fisher, Milt Pappas, Jerry Walker)	6.00	3.00	1.75
400	Rocky Colavito	20.00	10.00	6.00
401	Bob Duliba	6.00	3.00	1.75
402	Dick Stuart	6.00	3.00	1.75
403	Ed Sadowski	6.00	3.00	1.75
404	Bob Rush	6.00	3.00	1.75
405	Bobby Richardson	25.00	12.50	7.50
406	Billy Klaus	6.00	3.00	1.75
407	Gary Peters (Photo actually J.C. Martin.)	6.00	3.00	1.75
408	Carl Furillo	11.00	5.50	3.25
409	Ron Samford	6.00	3.00	1.75
410	Sam Jones	6.00	3.00	1.75
411	Ed Bailey	6.00	3.00	1.75
412	Bob Anderson	6.00	3.00	1.75
413	Kansas City Athletics Team	15.00	7.50	4.50
414	Don Williams	6.00	3.00	1.75
415	Bob Cerv	6.00	3.00	1.75
416	Humberto Robinson	6.00	3.00	1.75
417	Chuck Cottier	6.00	3.00	1.75
418	Don Mossi	6.00	3.00	1.75
419	George Crowe	6.00	3.00	1.75
420	Ed Mathews	25.00	12.50	7.50
421	Duke Maas	6.00	3.00	1.75
422	Johnny Powers	6.00	3.00	1.75
423	Ed Fitz Gerald	6.00	3.00	1.75
424	Pete Whisenant	6.00	3.00	1.75
425	Johnny Podres	10.00	5.00	3.00
426	Ron Jackson	6.00	3.00	1.75
427	Al Grunwald	6.00	3.00	1.75
428	Al Smith	6.00	3.00	1.75
429	American League Kings (Nellie Fox, Harvey Kuenn)	12.50	6.25	3.75
430	Art Ditmar	6.00	3.00	1.75
431	Andre Rodgers	6.00	3.00	1.75
432	Chuck Stobbs	6.00	3.00	1.75
433	Irv Noren	6.00	3.00	1.75
434	Brooks Lawrence	6.00	3.00	1.75
435	Gene Freese	6.00	3.00	1.75
436	Marv Throneberry	6.00	3.00	1.75
437	Bob Friend	6.00	3.00	1.75
438	Jim Coker	6.00	3.00	1.75
439	Tom Brewer	6.00	3.00	1.75
440	Jim Lemon	6.00	3.00	1.75
441	Gary Bell	9.00	4.50	2.75
442	Joe Pignatano	9.00	4.50	2.75
443	Charlie Maxwell	9.00	4.50	2.75
444	Jerry Kindall	9.00	4.50	2.75
445	Warren Spahn	35.00	17.50	10.00
446	Ellis Burton	9.00	4.50	2.75
447	Ray Moore	9.00	4.50	2.75
448	*Jim Gentile*	15.00	7.50	4.50
449	Jim Brosnan	9.00	4.50	2.75
450	Orlando Cepeda	30.00	15.00	9.00
451	Curt Simmons	9.00	4.50	2.75
452	Ray Webster	9.00	4.50	2.75
453	Vern Law	9.00	4.50	2.75
454	Hal Woodeshick	9.00	4.50	2.75
455	Baltimorre Orioles Coaches (Harry Brecheen, Lum Harris, Eddie Robinson)	9.00	4.50	2.75
456	Boston Red Sox Coaches (Del Baker, Billy Herman, Sal Maglie, Rudy York)	15.00	7.50	4.50
457	Chicago Cubs Coaches (Lou Klein, Charlie Root, Elvin Tappe)	9.00	4.50	2.75
458	Chicago White Sox Coaches (Ray Berres, Johnny Cooney, Tony Cuccinello, Don Gutteridge)	9.00	4.50	2.75
459	Cincinnati Reds Coaches (Cot Deal, Wally Moses, Reggie Otero)	9.00	4.50	2.75
460	Cleveland Indians Coaches (Mel Harder, Red Kress, Bob Lemon, Jo-Jo White)	10.00	5.00	3.00
461	Detroit Tigers Coaches (Luke Appling, Tom Ferrick, Billy Hitchcock)	10.00	5.00	3.00
462	Kansas City A's Coaches (Walker Cooper, Fred Fitzsimmons, Don Heffner)	9.00	4.50	2.75
463	L.A. Dodgers Coaches (Joe Becker, Bobby Bragan, Greg Mulleavy, Pete Reiser)	9.00	4.50	2.75
464	Milwaukee Braves Coaches (George Myatt, Andy Pafko, Bob Scheffing, Whitlow Wyatt)	9.00	4.50	2.75
465	N.Y. Yankees Coaches (Frank Crosetti, Bill Dickey, Ralph Houk, Ed Lopat)	20.00	10.00	6.00
466	Phila. Phillies Coaches (Dick Carter, Andy Cohen, Ken Silvestri)	9.00	4.50	2.75
467	Pitts. Pirates Coaches (Bill Burwell, Sam Narron, Frank Oceak, Mickey Vernon)	9.00	4.50	2.75
468	St. Louis Cards Coaches (Ray Katt, Johnny Keane, Howie Pollet, Harry Walker)	9.00	4.50	2.75
469	San Fran. Giants Coaches (Salty Parker, Bill Posedel, Wes Westrum)	9.00	4.50	2.75
470	Wash. Senators Coaches (Ellis Clary, Sam Mele, Bob Swift)	9.00	4.50	2.75
471	Ned Garver	9.00	4.50	2.75
472	Al Dark	9.00	4.50	2.75
473	Al Cicotte	9.00	4.50	2.75
474	Haywood Sullivan	9.00	4.50	2.75
475	Don Drysdale	35.00	17.50	10.00
476	Lou Johnson	9.00	4.50	2.75
477	Don Ferrarese	9.00	4.50	2.75
478	Frank Torre	9.00	4.50	2.75
479	Georges Maranda	9.00	4.50	2.75
480	Yogi Berra	65.00	32.50	20.00
481	Wes Stock	9.00	4.50	2.75
482	Frank Bolling	9.00	4.50	2.75
483	Camilo Pascual	9.00	4.50	2.75
484	Pittsburgh Pirates Team	25.00	12.50	7.50
485	Ken Boyer	15.00	7.50	4.50
486	Bobby Del Greco	9.00	4.50	2.75
487	Tom Sturdivant	9.00	4.50	2.75
488	Norm Cash	15.00	7.50	4.50
489	Steve Ridzik	9.00	4.50	2.75
490	Frank Robinson	40.00	20.00	12.00
491	Mel Roach	9.00	4.50	2.75
492	Larry Jackson	9.00	4.50	2.75
493	Duke Snider	40.00	20.00	12.00
494	Baltimore Orioles Team	20.00	10.00	6.00
495	Sherm Lollar	9.00	4.50	2.75
496	Bill Virdon	9.00	4.50	2.75
497	John Tsitouris	9.00	4.50	2.75
498	Al Pilarcik	9.00	4.50	2.75
499	Johnny James	9.00	4.50	2.75
500	Johnny Temple	9.00	4.50	2.75
501	Bob Schmidt	9.00	4.50	2.75
502	Jim Bunning	20.00	10.00	6.00
503	Don Lee	9.00	4.50	2.75
504	Seth Morehead	9.00	4.50	2.75
505	Ted Kluszewski	15.00	7.50	4.50
506	Lee Walls	9.00	4.50	2.75
507	Dick Stigman	15.00	7.50	4.50
508	Billy Consolo	15.00	7.50	4.50
509	*Tommy Davis*	20.00	10.00	6.00
510	Jerry Staley	15.00	7.50	4.50
511	Ken Walters	15.00	7.50	4.50
512	Joe Gibbon	15.00	7.50	4.50
513	Chicago Cubs Team	20.00	10.00	6.00
514	*Steve Barber*	17.50	8.75	5.25
515	Stan Lopata	15.00	7.50	4.50
516	Marty Kutyna	15.00	7.50	4.50
517	Charley James	15.00	7.50	4.50
518	*Tony Gonzalez*	15.00	7.50	4.50
519	Ed Roebuck	15.00	7.50	4.50
520	Don Buddin	15.00	7.50	4.50
521	Mike Lee	15.00	7.50	4.50
522	Ken Hunt	15.00	7.50	4.50
523	*Clay Dalrymple*	15.00	7.50	4.50
524	Bill Henry	15.00	7.50	4.50
525	Marv Breeding	15.00	7.50	4.50
526	Paul Giel	15.00	7.50	4.50
527	Jose Valdivielso	15.00	7.50	4.50
528	Ben Johnson	15.00	7.50	4.50
529	Norm Sherry	17.50	8.75	5.25
530	Mike McCormick	15.00	7.50	4.50
531	Sandy Amoros	15.00	7.50	4.50
532	Mike Garcia	15.00	7.50	4.50
533	Lu Clinton	15.00	7.50	4.50
534	Ken MacKenzie	15.00	7.50	4.50
535	Whitey Lockman	15.00	7.50	4.50
536	Wynn Hawkins	15.00	7.50	4.50
537	Boston Red Sox Team	25.00	12.50	7.50
538	Frank Barnes	15.00	7.50	4.50
539	Gene Baker	15.00	7.50	4.50
540	Jerry Walker	15.00	7.50	4.50
541	Tony Curry	15.00	7.50	4.50
542	Ken Hamlin	15.00	7.50	4.50
543	Elio Chacon	15.00	7.50	4.50
544	Bill Monbouquette	15.00	7.50	4.50
545	Carl Sawatski	15.00	7.50	4.50
546	Hank Aguirre	15.00	7.50	4.50
547	*Bob Aspromonte*	17.50	8.75	5.25
548	*Don Mincher*	15.00	7.50	4.50
549	John Buzhardt	15.00	7.50	4.50
550	Jim Landis	15.00	7.50	4.50
551	Ed Rakow	15.00	7.50	4.50
552	Walt Bond	15.00	7.50	4.50
553	Bill Skowron (All-Star)	20.00	10.00	6.00
554	Willie McCovey (All-Star)	35.00	17.50	10.00
555	Nellie Fox (All-Star)	20.00	10.00	6.00
556	Charlie Neal (All-Star)	17.50	8.75	5.25
557	Frank Malzone (All-Star)	17.50	8.75	5.25
558	Eddie Mathews (All-Star)	25.00	12.50	7.50
559	Luis Aparicio (All-Star)	20.00	10.00	6.00
560	Ernie Banks (All-Star)	35.00	17.50	10.00
561	Al Kaline (All-Star)	30.00	15.00	9.00
562	Joe Cunningham (All-Star)	17.50	8.75	5.25
563	Mickey Mantle (All-Star)	150.00	75.00	45.00
564	Willie Mays (All-Star)	60.00	30.00	18.00
565	Roger Maris (All-Star)	70.00	35.00	20.00
566	Hank Aaron (All-Star)	65.00	32.50	20.00
567	Sherm Lollar (All-Star)	17.50	8.75	5.25
568	Del Crandall (All-Star)	17.50	8.75	5.25
569	Camilo Pascual (All-Star)	17.50	8.75	5.25
570	Don Drysdale (All-Star)	25.00	12.50	7.50
571	Billy Pierce (All-Star)	17.50	8.75	5.25
572	Johnny Antonelli (All-Star)	25.00	9.00	5.25

----	Elect Your Favorite Rookie Insert (Paper stock, no date on back.)	30.00	15.00	9.00
----	Hot Iron Transfer Insert (Paper stock.)	30.00	15.00	9.00

1960 Topps Proofs

KENTHDE
NEW YORK YANKEES — FIRST BASE

Subsequent to a pair of December, 1959, trades, the 1960 Topps cards of three players were significantly changed. Whether the change occurred prior to regular production printing and packaging or while the cards were still in the proofing stage is unknown. The changes affect the cards of Gino Cimoli, Kent Hadley and, reportedly, Marv Throneberry. In the very rare versions each player's card has at bottom left the logo of his team prior to the trade. The common regular-issue version has the new team logo. The front of Hadley's rare card names his team as the Yankees, while Cimoli's rare version says Cardinals.

		NM	EX	VG
58	Gino Cimoli (Cardinals logo)(No recent sales)			
102	Kent Hadley (A's logo) (Nov., 1999 auction record)	13,500		
436	Marv Throneberry (Yankees logo)(Existence not confirmed)			

1960 Topps Tattoos

BASEBALL TATTOO BUBBLE GUM

STAN MUSIAL

CERTIFIED FOOD COLOR

Probably the least popular of all Topps products among parents and teachers, the Tattoos were printed on the reverse of the wrappers of Topps "Tattoo Bubble Gum." The entire wrapper was 1-9/16" x 3-1/2". The owner moistened his skin and applied the back of the wrapper to the wet spot, producing a colorful "tattoo" (although often blurred by running colors). The set offered 96 tattoo possibilities of which 55 were players, 16 teams, 15 action pictures and 10 autographed balls. Because the packaged gum slides easily in and out of the "sealed" wrapper, allowing the tattoo to be easily seen, unopened packs command little premium.

		NM	EX	VG
	Complete Set (96):	2,750	1,350	825.00
	Common Player:	20.00	10.00	6.00
	Common Non-player:	12.00	6.00	3.50
(1)	Hank Aaron	150.00	75.00	45.00
(2)	Bob Allison	20.00	10.00	6.00
(3)	John Antonelli	20.00	10.00	6.00
(4)	Richie Ashburn	40.00	20.00	12.00
(5)	Ernie Banks	65.00	32.00	19.50
(6)	Yogi Berra	60.00	30.00	18.00
(7)	Lew Burdette	20.00	10.00	6.00
(8)	Orlando Cepeda	35.00	17.50	10.50
(9)	Rocky Colavito	35.00	17.50	10.50
(10)	Joe Cunningham	20.00	10.00	6.00
(11)	Buddy Daley	20.00	10.00	6.00
(12)	Don Drysdale	40.00	20.00	12.00

(13)	Ryne Duren	20.00	10.00	6.00
(14)	Roy Face	20.00	10.00	6.00
(15)	Whitey Ford	60.00	30.00	18.00
(16)	Nellie Fox	35.00	17.50	10.50
(17)	Tito Francona	20.00	10.00	6.00
(18)	Gene Freese	20.00	10.00	6.00
(19)	Jim Gilliam	20.00	10.00	6.00
(20)	Dick Groat	20.00	10.00	6.00
(21)	Ray Herbert	20.00	10.00	6.00
(22)	Glen Hobbie	20.00	10.00	6.00
(23)	Jackie Jensen	20.00	10.00	6.00
(24)	Sam Jones	20.00	10.00	6.00
(25)	Al Kaline	60.00	30.00	18.00
(26)	Harmon Killebrew	40.00	20.00	12.00
(27)	Harvey Kuenn	20.00	10.00	6.00
(28)	Frank Lary	20.00	10.00	6.00
(29)	Vernon Law	20.00	10.00	6.00
(30)	Frank Malzone	20.00	10.00	6.00
(31)	Mickey Mantle	300.00	150.00	90.00
(32)	Roger Maris	75.00	37.00	22.00
(33)	Ed Mathews	40.00	20.00	12.00
(34)	Willie Mays	150.00	75.00	45.00
(35)	Cal Mclish	20.00	10.00	6.00
(36)	Wally Moon	20.00	10.00	6.00
(37)	Walt Moryn	20.00	10.00	6.00
(38)	Don Mossi	20.00	10.00	6.00
(39)	Stan Musial	100.00	50.00	30.00
(40)	Charlie Neal	20.00	10.00	6.00
(41)	Don Newcombe	20.00	10.00	6.00
(42)	Milt Pappas	20.00	10.00	6.00
(43)	Camilo Pascual	20.00	10.00	6.00
(44)	Billie (Billy) Pierce	20.00	10.00	6.00
(45)	Robin Roberts	35.00	17.50	10.50
(46)	Frank Robinson	40.00	20.00	12.00
(47)	Pete Runnels	20.00	10.00	6.00
(48)	Herb Score	20.00	10.00	6.00
(49)	Warren Spahn	35.00	17.50	10.50
(50)	Johnny Temple	20.00	10.00	6.00
(51)	Gus Triandos	20.00	10.00	6.00
(52)	Jerry Walker	20.00	10.00	6.00
(53)	Bill White	20.00	10.00	6.00
(54)	Gene Woodling	20.00	10.00	6.00
(55)	Early Wynn	35.00	17.50	10.50
(56)	Chicago Cubs Logo	15.00	7.50	4.50
(57)	Cincinnati Reds Logo	15.00	7.50	4.50
(58)	Los Angeles Dodgers Logo	15.00	7.50	4.50
(59)	Milwaukee Braves Logo	15.00	7.50	4.50
(60)	Philadelphia Phillies Logo	15.00	7.50	4.50
(61)	Pittsburgh Pirates Logo	20.00	10.00	6.00
(62)	San Francisco Giants Logo	15.00	7.50	4.50
(63)	St. Louis Cardinals Logo	15.00	7.50	4.50
(64)	Baltimore Orioles Logo	15.00	7.50	4.50
(65)	Boston Red Sox Logo	15.00	7.50	4.50
(66)	Chicago White Sox Logo	15.00	7.50	4.50
(67)	Cleveland Indians Logo	15.00	7.50	4.50
(68)	Detroit Tigers Logo	15.00	7.50	4.50
(69)	Kansas City Athletics Logo	15.00	7.50	4.50
(70)	New York Yankees Logo	20.00	10.00	6.00
(71)	Washington Senators Logo	15.00	7.50	4.50
(72)	Autograph (Richie Ashburn)	20.00	10.00	6.00
(73)	Autograph (Rocky Colavito)	25.00	12.50	7.50
(74)	Autograph (Roy Face)	15.00	7.50	4.50
(75)	Autograph (Jackie Jensen)	15.00	7.50	4.50
(76)	Autograph (Harmon Killebrew)	25.00	12.50	7.50
(77)	Autograph (Mickey Mantle)	100.00	50.00	30.00
(78)	Autograph (Willie Mays)	50.00	25.00	15.00
(79)	Autograph (Stan Musial)	50.00	25.00	15.00
(80)	Autograph (Billy Pierce)	15.00	7.50	4.50
(81)	Autograph (Jerry Walker)	15.00	7.50	4.50
(82)	Run-Down	12.00	6.00	3.50
(83)	Out At First	12.00	6.00	3.50
(84)	The Final Word	12.00	6.00	3.50
(85)	Twisting Foul	12.00	6.00	3.50
(86)	Out At Home	12.00	6.00	3.50
(87)	Circus Catch	12.00	6.00	3.50
(88)	Great Catch	12.00	6.00	3.50
(89)	Stolen Base	12.00	6.00	3.50
(90)	Grand Slam Homer	12.00	6.00	3.50
(91)	Double Play	12.00	6.00	3.50
(92)	Right-Handed Follow Thru	12.00	6.00	3.50
(93)	Right-Handed High Leg Kick	12.00	6.00	3.50
(94)	Left-handed pitcher	12.00	6.00	3.50
(95)	Right-handed batter	12.00	6.00	3.50
(96)	Left-handed batter	12.00	6.00	3.50

1950s-60s Topps "PROMOTIONAL SAMPLES"

PROMOTIONAL SAMPLE THE TOPPS CO BROOKLYN, N.Y.

These mini sample cards are fantasy items created in the late 1990s to defraud collectors. Often sold grouped in an older frame or otherwise made to look old, they are pictures which have been cut out of the "Topps Baseball Cards" books or the team-issued Surf books which reproduced Topps cards in about 1-1/4" x

1-3/4" format. The color glossy pictures were then glued to a cardboard back which has been rubber-stamped "PROMOTIONAL / SAMPLE / THE TOPPS CO / BROOKLYN, N.Y." There were no legitimate miniature Topps promotional or sample cards produced.

(No Collectible Value.)

1961 Topps

STAN MUSIAL — Outfield — St. Louis Cardinals
TOPPS 290

Except for some of the specialty cards, Topps returned to a vertical format with their 1961 cards. The set is numbered through 598, however only 587 cards were printed. No numbers 426, 587 and 588 were issued. Two cards numbered 463 exist (one a Braves team card and one a player card of Jack Fisher). Actually, the Braves team card is checklisted as #426. Designs for 1961 are basically large color portraits; the backs return to extensive statistics. A three-panel cartoon highlighting the player's career appears on the card backs. Innovations include numbered checklists, cards for statistical leaders, and 10 "Baseball Thrills" cards. The scarce high numbers are card numbers 523-589.

		NM	EX	VG
	Complete Set (587):	7,500	3,750	2,250
	Common Player (1-522):	6.00	3.00	1.75
	Common Player (523-589):	20.00	10.00	6.00
1	Dick Groat	25.00	6.00	2.00
2	Roger Maris	145.00	50.00	30.00
3	John Buzhardt	6.00	3.00	1.75
4	Lenny Green	6.00	3.00	1.75
5	Johnny Romano	6.00	3.00	1.75
6	Ed Roebuck	6.00	3.00	1.75
7	Chicago White Sox Team	10.00	5.00	3.00
8	Dick Williams	6.00	3.00	1.75
9	Bob Purkey	6.00	3.00	1.75
10	Brooks Robinson	30.00	15.00	9.00
11	Curt Simmons	6.00	3.00	1.75
12	Moe Thacker	6.00	3.00	1.75
13	Chuck Cottier	6.00	3.00	1.75
14	Don Mossi	6.00	3.00	1.75
15	Willie Kirkland	6.00	3.00	1.75
16	Billy Muffett	6.00	3.00	1.75
17	1st Series Checklist (1-88)	12.00	6.00	3.50
18	Jim Grant	6.00	3.00	1.75
19	Cletis Boyer	10.00	5.00	3.00
20	Robin Roberts	15.00	7.50	4.50
21	*Zoilo Versalles*	12.50	6.25	3.75
22	Clem Labine	6.00	3.00	1.75
23	Don Demeter	6.00	3.00	1.75
24	Ken Johnson	6.00	3.00	1.75
25	Reds' Heavy Artillery (Gus Bell, Vada Pinson, Frank Robinson)	15.00	7.50	4.50
26	Wes Stock	6.00	3.00	1.75
27	Jerry Kindall	6.00	3.00	1.75
28	Hector Lopez	6.00	3.00	1.75
29	Don Nottebart	6.00	3.00	1.75
30	Nellie Fox	20.00	10.00	6.00
31	Bob Schmidt	6.00	3.00	1.75
32	Ray Sadecki	6.00	3.00	1.75
33	Gary Geiger	6.00	3.00	1.75
34	Wynn Hawkins	6.00	3.00	1.75
35	*Ron Santo*	35.00	17.50	10.00
36	Jack Kralick	6.00	3.00	1.75
37	Charlie Maxwell	6.00	3.00	1.75
38	Bob Lillis	6.00	3.00	1.75
39	Leo Posada	6.00	3.00	1.75
40	Bob Turley	10.00	5.00	3.00
41	N.L. Batting Leaders (Roberto Clemente, Dick Groat, Norm Larker, Willie Mays)	20.00	10.00	6.00
42	A.L. Batting Leaders (Minnie Minoso, Pete Runnels, Bill Skowron, Al Smith)	9.00	4.50	2.75
43	N.L. Home Run Leaders (Hank Aaron, Ernie Banks, Ken Boyer, Eddie Mathews)	17.50	8.75	5.25
44	A.L. Home Run Leaders (Rocky Colavito, Jim Lemon, Mickey Mantle, Roger Maris)	45.00	22.00	13.50
45	N.L. E.R.A. Leaders (Ernie Broglio, Don Drysdale, Bob Friend, Mike McCormick, Stan Williams)	7.00	3.50	2.00
46	A.L. E.R.A. Leaders (Frank Baumann, Hal Brown, Jim Bunning, Art Ditmar)	9.00	4.50	2.75

47a	N.L. Pitching Leaders (Ernie Broglio, Lou Burdette, Vern Law, Warren Spahn) (vertical black bar in Burdette's box to right of 19)	12.00	6.00	3.50
47b	N.L. Pitching Leaders (Ernie Broglio, Lew Burdette, Vern Law, Warren Spahn) (No black bar.)	12.00	6.00	3.50
48	A.L. Pitching Leaders (Bud Daley, Art Ditmar, Chuck Estrada, Frank Lary, Milt Pappas, Jim Perry)	7.00	3.50	2.00
49	N.L. Strikeout Leaders (Ernie Broglio, Don Drysdale, Sam Jones, Sandy Koufax)	16.00	8.00	4.75
50	A.L. Strikeout Leaders (Jim Bunning, Frank Lary, Pedro Ramos, Early Wynn)	12.00	6.00	3.50
51	Detroit Tigers Team	10.00	5.00	3.00
52	George Crowe	6.00	3.00	1.75
53	Russ Nixon	6.00	3.00	1.75
54	Earl Francis	6.00	3.00	1.75
55	Jim Davenport	6.00	3.00	1.75
56	Russ Kemmerer	6.00	3.00	1.75
57	Marv Throneberry	6.00	3.00	1.75
58	Joe Schaffernoth	6.00	3.00	1.75
59	Jim Woods	6.00	3.00	1.75
60	Woodie Held	6.00	3.00	1.75
61	Ron Piche	6.00	3.00	1.75
62	Al Pilarcik	6.00	3.00	1.75
63	Jim Kaat	9.00	4.50	2.75
64	Alex Grammas	6.00	3.00	1.75
65	Ted Kluszewski	10.00	5.00	3.00
66	Bill Henry	6.00	3.00	1.75
67	Ossie Virgil	6.00	3.00	1.75
68	Deron Johnson	6.00	3.00	1.75
69	Earl Wilson	6.00	3.00	1.75
70	Bill Virdon	6.00	3.00	1.75
71	Jerry Adair	6.00	3.00	1.75
72	Stu Miller	6.00	3.00	1.75
73	Al Spangler	6.00	3.00	1.75
74	Joe Pignatano	6.00	3.00	1.75
75	Lindy Shows Larry (Larry Jackson, Lindy McDaniel)	6.00	3.00	1.75
76	Harry Anderson	6.00	3.00	1.75
77	Dick Stigman	6.00	3.00	1.75
78	Lee Walls	6.00	3.00	1.75
79	Joe Ginsberg	6.00	3.00	1.75
80	Harmon Killebrew	25.00	12.50	7.50
81	Tracy Stallard	6.00	3.00	1.75
82	Joe Christopher	6.00	3.00	1.75
83	Bob Bruce	6.00	3.00	1.75
84	Lee Maye	6.00	3.00	1.75
85	Jerry Walker	6.00	3.00	1.75
86	Los Angeles Dodgers Team	11.00	5.50	3.25
87	Joe Amalfitano	6.00	3.00	1.75
88	Richie Ashburn	15.00	7.50	4.50
89	Billy Martin	9.00	4.50	2.75
90	Jerry Staley	6.00	3.00	1.75
91	Walt Moryn	6.00	3.00	1.75
92	Hal Naragon	6.00	3.00	1.75
93	Tony Gonzalez	6.00	3.00	1.75
94	Johnny Kucks	6.00	3.00	1.75
95	Norm Cash	12.50	6.25	3.75
96	Billy O'Dell	6.00	3.00	1.75
97	Jerry Lynch	6.00	3.00	1.75
98a	2nd Series Checklist (9-176) ("Checklist" in red on front)	12.00	6.00	3.50
98b	2nd Series Checklist (89-176) ("Checklist" in yellow, 98 on back in black.)	12.00	6.00	3.50
98c	2nd Series Checklist (89-176) ("Checklist" in yellow, 98 on back in white.)	12.00	6.00	3.50
99	Don Buddin	6.00	3.00	1.75
100	Harvey Haddix	6.00	3.00	1.75
101	Bubba Phillips	6.00	3.00	1.75
102	Gene Stephens	6.00	3.00	1.75
103	Ruben Amaro	6.00	3.00	1.75
104	John Blanchard	7.50	3.75	2.25
105	Carl Willey	6.00	3.00	1.75
106	Whitey Herzog	6.00	3.00	1.75
107	Seth Morehead	6.00	3.00	1.75
108	Dan Dobbek	6.00	3.00	1.75
109	Johnny Podres	7.50	3.75	2.25
110	Vada Pinson	9.00	4.50	2.75
111	Jack Meyer	6.00	3.00	1.75
112	Chico Fernandez	6.00	3.00	1.75
113	Mike Fornieles	6.00	3.00	1.75
114	Hobie Landrith	6.00	3.00	1.75
115	Johnny Antonelli	6.00	3.00	1.75
116	Joe DeMaestri	6.00	3.00	1.75
117	Dale Long	6.00	3.00	1.75
118	Chris Cannizzaro	6.00	3.00	1.75
119	A's Big Armor (Hank Bauer, Jerry Lumpe, Norm Siebern)	9.00	4.50	2.75
120	Ed Mathews	20.00	10.00	6.00
121	Eli Grba	6.00	3.00	1.75
122	Chicago Cubs Team	10.00	5.00	3.00
123	Billy Gardner	6.00	3.00	1.75
124	J.C. Martin	6.00	3.00	1.75
125	Steve Barber	6.00	3.00	1.75
126	Dick Stuart	6.00	3.00	1.75
127	Ron Kline	6.00	3.00	1.75
128	Rip Repulski	6.00	3.00	1.75
129	Ed Hobaugh	6.00	3.00	1.75
130	Norm Larker	6.00	3.00	1.75
131	Paul Richards	6.00	3.00	1.75
132	Al Lopez	12.50	6.25	3.75
133	Ralph Houk	25.00	12.50	7.50
134	Mickey Vernon	6.00	3.00	1.75
135	Fred Hutchinson	6.00	3.00	1.75
136	Walt Alston	12.50	6.25	3.75
137	Chuck Dressen	6.00	3.00	1.75
138	Danny Murtaugh	6.00	3.00	1.75
139	Solly Hemus	6.00	3.00	1.75
140	Gus Triandos	6.00	3.00	1.75
141	*Billy Williams*	35.00	17.50	10.00
142	Luis Arroyo	6.00	3.00	1.75
143	Russ Snyder	6.00	3.00	1.75
144	Jim Coker	6.00	3.00	1.75
145	Bob Buhl	6.00	3.00	1.75
146	Marty Keough	6.00	3.00	1.75
147	Ed Rakow	6.00	3.00	1.75
148	Julian Javier	6.00	3.00	1.75
149	Bob Oldis	6.00	3.00	1.75
150	Willie Mays	60.00	30.00	18.00
151	Jim Donohue	6.00	3.00	1.75
152	Earl Torgeson	6.00	3.00	1.75
153	Don Lee	6.00	3.00	1.75
154	Bobby Del Greco	6.00	3.00	1.75
155	Johnny Temple	6.00	3.00	1.75
156	Ken Hunt	6.00	3.00	1.75
157	Cal McLish	6.00	3.00	1.75
158	Pete Daley	6.00	3.00	1.75
159	Baltimore Orioles Team	10.00	5.00	3.00
160	Whitey Ford	30.00	15.00	9.00
161	Sherman Jones	6.00	3.00	1.75
162	Jay Hook	6.00	3.00	1.75
163	Ed Sadowski	6.00	3.00	1.75
164	Felix Mantilla	6.00	3.00	1.75
165	Gino Cimoli	6.00	3.00	1.75
166	Danny Kravitz	6.00	3.00	1.75
167	San Francisco Giants Team	10.00	5.00	3.00
168	Tommy Davis	6.00	3.00	1.75
169	Don Elston	6.00	3.00	1.75
170	Al Smith	6.00	3.00	1.75
171	Paul Foytack	6.00	3.00	1.75
172	Don Dillard	6.00	3.00	1.75
173	Beantown Bombers (Jackie Jensen, Frank Malzone, Vic Wertz)	9.00	4.50	2.75
174	Ray Semproch	6.00	3.00	1.75
175	Gene Freese	6.00	3.00	1.75
176	Ken Aspromonte	6.00	3.00	1.75
177	Don Larsen	7.50	3.75	2.25
178	Bob Nieman	6.00	3.00	1.75
179	Joe Koppe	6.00	3.00	1.75
180	Bobby Richardson	15.00	7.50	4.50
181	Fred Green	6.00	3.00	1.75
182	*Dave Nicholson*	6.00	3.00	1.75
183	Andre Rodgers	6.00	3.00	1.75
184	Steve Bilko	6.00	3.00	1.75
185	Herb Score	6.00	3.00	1.75
186	Elmer Valo	6.00	3.00	1.75
187	Billy Klaus	6.00	3.00	1.75
188	Jim Marshall	6.00	3.00	1.75
189a	3rd Series Checklist (177-264) (no "4" on player at left)	10.00	5.00	3.00
189b	3rd Series Checklist (177-264) ("4" shows on player at left.)	10.00	5.00	3.00
190	Stan Williams	6.00	3.00	1.75
191	Mike de la Hoz	6.00	3.00	1.75
192	Dick Brown	6.00	3.00	1.75
193	Gene Conley	6.00	3.00	1.75
194	Gordy Coleman	6.00	3.00	1.75
195	Jerry Casale	6.00	3.00	1.75
196	Ed Bouchee	6.00	3.00	1.75
197	Dick Hall	6.00	3.00	1.75
198	Carl Sawatski	6.00	3.00	1.75
199	Bob Boyd	6.00	3.00	1.75
200	Warren Spahn	25.00	12.50	7.50
201	Pete Whisenant	6.00	3.00	1.75
202	Al Neiger	6.00	3.00	1.75
203	Eddie Bressoud	6.00	3.00	1.75
204	Bob Skinner	6.00	3.00	1.75
205	Bill Pierce	6.00	3.00	1.75
206	Gene Green	6.00	3.00	1.75
207	Dodger Southpaws (Sandy Koufax, Johnny Podres)	20.00	10.00	6.00
208	Larry Osborne	6.00	3.00	1.75
209	Ken McBride	6.00	3.00	1.75
210	Pete Runnels	6.00	3.00	1.75
211	Bob Gibson	25.00	12.50	7.50
212	Haywood Sullivan	6.00	3.00	1.75
213	*Bill Stafford*	6.00	3.00	1.75
214	Danny Murphy	6.00	3.00	1.75
215	Gus Bell	6.00	3.00	1.75
216	Ted Bowsfield	6.00	3.00	1.75
217	Mel Roach	6.00	3.00	1.75
218	Hal Brown	6.00	3.00	1.75
219	Gene Mauch	6.00	3.00	1.75
220	Al Dark	6.00	3.00	1.75
221	Mike Higgins	6.00	3.00	1.75
222	Jimmie Dykes	6.00	3.00	1.75
223	Bob Scheffing	6.00	3.00	1.75
224	Joe Gordon	6.00	3.00	1.75
225	Bill Rigney	6.00	3.00	1.75
226	Harry Lavagetto	6.00	3.00	1.75
227	Juan Pizarro	6.00	3.00	1.75
228	New York Yankees Team	40.00	20.00	12.00
229	Rudy Hernandez	6.00	3.00	1.75
230	Don Hoak	6.00	3.00	1.75
231	Dick Drott	6.00	3.00	1.75
232	Bill White	6.00	3.00	1.75
233	Joe Jay	6.00	3.00	1.75
234	Ted Lepcio	6.00	3.00	1.75
235	Camilo Pascual	6.00	3.00	1.75
236	Don Gile	6.00	3.00	1.75
237	Billy Loes	6.00	3.00	1.75
238	Jim Gilliam	7.50	3.75	2.25
239	Dave Sisler	6.00	3.00	1.75
240	Ron Hansen	6.00	3.00	1.75
241	Al Cicotte	6.00	3.00	1.75
242	Hal W. Smith	6.00	3.00	1.75
243	Frank Lary	6.00	3.00	1.75
244	Chico Cardenas	6.00	3.00	1.75
245	Joe Adcock	6.00	3.00	1.75
246	Bob Davis	6.00	3.00	1.75
247	Billy Goodman	6.00	3.00	1.75
248	Ed Keegan	6.00	3.00	1.75
249	Cincinnati Reds Team	10.00	5.00	3.00
250	Buc Hill Aces (Roy Face, Vern Law)	9.00	4.50	2.75
251	Bill Bruton	6.00	3.00	1.75
252	Bill Short	6.00	3.00	1.75
253	Sammy Taylor	6.00	3.00	1.75
254	Ted Sadowski	6.00	3.00	1.75
255	Vic Power	6.00	3.00	1.75
256	Billy Hoeft	6.00	3.00	1.75
257	Carroll Hardy	6.00	3.00	1.75
258	Jack Sanford	6.00	3.00	1.75
259	John Schaive	6.00	3.00	1.75
260	Don Drysdale	25.00	12.50	7.50
261	Charlie Lau	6.00	3.00	1.75
262	Tony Curry	6.00	3.00	1.75
263	Ken Hamlin	6.00	3.00	1.75
264	Glen Hobbie	6.00	3.00	1.75
265	Tony Kubek	15.00	7.50	4.50
266	Lindy McDaniel	6.00	3.00	1.75
267	Norm Siebern	6.00	3.00	1.75
268	Ike DeLock (Delock)	6.00	3.00	1.75
269	Harry Chiti	6.00	3.00	1.75
270	Bob Friend	6.00	3.00	1.75
271	Jim Landis	6.00	3.00	1.75
272	Tom Morgan	6.00	3.00	1.75
273a	4th Series Checklist (265-352) (Copyright ends opposite fifth name.)	12.00	6.00	3.50
273b	4th Series Checklist (265-352) (Copyright ends opposite top name.)	12.00	6.00	3.50
274	Gary Bell	6.00	3.00	1.75
275	Gene Woodling	6.00	3.00	1.75
276	Ray Rippelmeyer	6.00	3.00	1.75
277	Hank Foiles	6.00	3.00	1.75
278	Don McMahon	6.00	3.00	1.75
279	Jose Pagan	6.00	3.00	1.75
280	Frank Howard	9.00	4.50	2.75
281	Frank Sullivan	6.00	3.00	1.75
282	Faye Throneberry	6.00	3.00	1.75
283	Bob Anderson	6.00	3.00	1.75
284	Dick Gernert	6.00	3.00	1.75
285	Sherm Lollar	6.00	3.00	1.75
286	George Witt	6.00	3.00	1.75
287	Carl Yastrzemski	45.00	22.50	13.50
288	Albie Pearson	6.00	3.00	1.75
289	Ray Moore	6.00	3.00	1.75
290	Stan Musial	50.00	25.00	15.00
291	Tex Clevenger	6.00	3.00	1.75
292	Jim Baumer	6.00	3.00	1.75
293	Tom Sturdivant	6.00	3.00	1.75
294	Don Blasingame	6.00	3.00	1.75
295	Milt Pappas	6.00	3.00	1.75
296	Wes Covington	6.00	3.00	1.75
297	Kansas City Athletics Team	10.00	5.00	3.00
298	Jim Golden	6.00	3.00	1.75
299	Clay Dalrymple	6.00	3.00	1.75
300	Mickey Mantle	325.00	135.00	85.00
301	Chet Nichols	6.00	3.00	1.75
302	Al Heist	6.00	3.00	1.75
303	Gary Peters	6.00	3.00	1.75
304	Rocky Nelson	6.00	3.00	1.75
305	Mike McCormick	6.00	3.00	1.75
306	World Series Game 1 (Virdon Saves Game)	9.00	4.50	2.75
307	World Series Game 2 (Mantle Slams 2 Homers)	45.00	22.50	13.50
308	World Series Game 3 (Richardson Is Hero)	20.00	10.00	6.00
309	World Series Game 4 (Cimoli Safe In Crucial Play)	9.00	4.50	2.75
310	World Series Game 5 (Face Saves The Day)	10.00	5.00	3.00
311	World Series Game 6 (Ford Pitches Second Shutout)	15.00	7.50	4.50
312	World Series Game 7 (Mazeroski's Homer Wins It!)	25.00	12.50	7.50
313	World Series (The Winners Celebrate)	12.50	6.25	3.75
314	Bob Miller	6.00	3.00	1.75
315	Earl Battey	6.00	3.00	1.75
316	Bobby Gene Smith	6.00	3.00	1.75
317	*Jim Brewer*	6.00	3.00	1.75
318	Danny O'Connell	6.00	3.00	1.75
319	Valmy Thomas	6.00	3.00	1.75
320	Lou Burdette	6.00	3.00	1.75
321	Marv Breeding	6.00	3.00	1.75
322	Bill Kunkel	6.00	3.00	1.75
323	Sammy Esposito	6.00	3.00	1.75
324	Hank Aguirre	6.00	3.00	1.75
325	Wally Moon	6.00	3.00	1.75
326	Dave Hillman	6.00	3.00	1.75
327	*Matty Alou*	12.50	6.25	3.75
328	Jim O'Toole	6.00	3.00	1.75
329	Julio Becquer	6.00	3.00	1.75
330	Rocky Colavito	15.00	7.50	4.50
331	Ned Garver	6.00	3.00	1.75
332	Dutch Dotterer (Photo actually Tommy Dotterer.)	6.00	3.00	1.75
333	Fritz Brickell	6.00	3.00	1.75
334	Walt Bond	6.00	3.00	1.75
335	Frank Bolling	6.00	3.00	1.75
336	Don Mincher	6.00	3.00	1.75
337	Al's Aces (Al Lopez, Herb Score, Early Wynn)	9.00	4.50	2.75
338	Don Landrum	6.00	3.00	1.75
339	Gene Baker	6.00	3.00	1.75
340	Vic Wertz	6.00	3.00	1.75
341	Jim Owens	6.00	3.00	1.75
342	Clint Courtney	6.00	3.00	1.75
343	Earl Robinson	6.00	3.00	1.75
344	Sandy Koufax	60.00	30.00	18.00
345	Jim Piersall	7.50	3.75	2.25
346	Howie Nunn	6.00	3.00	1.75
347	St. Louis Cardinals Team	10.00	5.00	3.00
348	Steve Boros	6.00	3.00	1.75
349	Danny McDevitt	6.00	3.00	1.75
350	Ernie Banks	30.00	15.00	9.00
351	Jim King	6.00	3.00	1.75
352	Bob Shaw	6.00	3.00	1.75
353	Howie Bedell	6.00	3.00	1.75

#	Player	NM	EX	VG
354	Billy Harrell	6.00	3.00	1.75
355	Bob Allison	6.00	3.00	1.75
356	Ryne Duren	7.50	3.75	2.25
357	Daryl Spencer	6.00	3.00	1.75
358	Earl Averill	6.00	3.00	1.75
359	Dallas Green	7.50	3.75	2.25
360	Frank Robinson	25.00	12.50	7.50
361a	5th Series Checklist (353-429) ("Topps Baseball" in black on front.)	10.00	5.00	3.00
361b	5th Series Checklist (353-429) ("Topps Baseball" in yellow.)	12.00	6.00	3.50
362	Frank Funk	6.00	3.00	1.75
363	John Roseboro	6.00	3.00	1.75
364	Moe Drabowsky	6.00	3.00	1.75
365	Jerry Lumpe	6.00	3.00	1.75
366	Eddie Fisher	6.00	3.00	1.75
367	Jim Rivera	6.00	3.00	1.75
368	Bennie Daniels	6.00	3.00	1.75
369	Dave Philley	6.00	3.00	1.75
370	Roy Face	6.00	3.00	1.75
371	Bill Skowron/SP	40.00	20.00	12.00
372	Bob Hendley	6.00	3.00	1.75
373	Boston Red Sox Team	10.00	5.00	3.00
374	Paul Giel	6.00	3.00	1.75
375	Ken Boyer	13.50	6.75	4.00
376	Mike Roarke	6.00	3.00	1.75
377	Ruben Gomez	6.00	3.00	1.75
378	Wally Post	6.00	3.00	1.75
379	Bobby Shantz	6.00	3.00	1.75
380	Minnie Minoso	9.00	4.50	2.75
381	Dave Wickersham	6.00	3.00	1.75
382	Frank Thomas	6.00	3.00	1.75
383	Frisco First Liners (Mike McCormick, Billy O'Dell, Jack Sanford)	7.50	3.75	2.25
384	Chuck Essegian	6.00	3.00	1.75
385	Jim Perry	6.00	3.00	1.75
386	Joe Hicks	6.00	3.00	1.75
387	Duke Maas	6.00	3.00	1.75
388	Bob Clemente	70.00	35.00	20.00
389	Ralph Terry	6.00	3.00	1.75
390	Del Crandall	6.00	3.00	1.75
391	Winston Brown	6.00	3.00	1.75
392	Reno Bertoia	6.00	3.00	1.75
393	Batter Bafflers (Don Cardwell, Glen Hobbie)	7.50	3.75	2.25
394	Ken Walters	6.00	3.00	1.75
395	Chuck Estrada	6.00	3.00	1.75
396	Bob Aspromonte	6.00	3.00	1.75
397	Hal Woodeshick	6.00	3.00	1.75
398	Hank Bauer	7.50	3.75	2.25
399	Cliff Cook	6.00	3.00	1.75
400	Vern Law	6.00	3.00	1.75
401	Babe Ruth Hits 60th Homer	50.00	25.00	15.00
402	Larsen Pitches Perfect Game /SP	25.00	12.50	7.50
403	Brooklyn-Boston Play 26-Inning Tie	6.00	3.00	1.75
404	Hornsby Tops N.L. with .424 Average	9.00	4.50	2.75
405	Gehrig Benched After 2,130 Games	35.00	17.50	10.00
406	Mantle Blasts 565 ft. Home Run	45.00	22.50	13.50
407	Jack Chesbro Wins 41st Game	6.00	3.00	1.75
408	Mathewson Strikes Out 267 Batters /SP	17.50	8.75	5.25
409	Johnson Hurls 3rd Shutout In 4 Days	9.00	4.50	2.75
410	Haddix Pitches 12 Perfect Innings	7.50	3.75	2.25
411	Tony Taylor	6.00	3.00	1.75
412	Larry Sherry	6.00	3.00	1.75
413	Eddie Yost	6.00	3.00	1.75
414	Dick Donovan	6.00	3.00	1.75
415	Hank Aaron	85.00	42.50	25.00
416	*Dick Howser*/SP	12.50	6.25	3.75
417	*Juan Marichal*	60.00	30.00	18.00
418	Ed Bailey	6.00	3.00	1.75
419	Tom Borland	6.00	3.00	1.75
420	Ernie Broglio	6.00	3.00	1.75
421	Ty Cline/SP	12.50	6.25	3.75
422	Bud Daley	6.00	3.00	1.75
423	Charlie Neal/SP	12.50	6.25	3.75
424	Turk Lown	6.00	3.00	1.75
425	Yogi Berra	50.00	25.00	15.00
426	Not issued (see #463)			
427	Dick Ellsworth	6.00	3.00	1.75
428	Ray Barker/SP	12.50	6.25	3.75
429	Al Kaline	30.00	15.00	9.00
430	Bill Mazeroski/SP	35.00	17.50	10.00
431	Chuck Stobbs	6.00	3.00	1.75
432	Coot Veal	6.00	3.00	1.75
433	Art Mahaffey	6.00	3.00	1.75
434	Tom Brewer	6.00	3.00	1.75
435	Orlando Cepeda	15.00	7.50	4.50
436	*Jim Maloney*/SP	20.00	10.00	6.00
437a	6th Series Checklist (430-506) (#440 is Louis Aparicio)	12.00	6.00	3.50
437b	6th Series Checklist (430-506) (#440 is Luis Aparicio)	10.00	5.00	3.00
438	Curt Flood	7.50	3.75	2.25
439	*Phil Regan*	6.00	3.00	1.75
440	Luis Aparicio	15.00	7.50	4.50
441	Dick Bertell	6.00	3.00	1.75
442	Gordon Jones	6.00	3.00	1.75
443	Duke Snider	30.00	15.00	9.00
444	Joe Nuxhall	6.00	3.00	1.75
445	Frank Malzone	6.00	3.00	1.75
446	Bob "Hawk" Taylor	6.00	3.00	1.75
447	Harry Bright	6.00	3.00	1.75
448	Del Rice	6.00	3.00	1.75
449	*Bobby Bolin*	6.00	3.00	1.75
450	Jim Lemon	6.00	3.00	1.75

#	Player	NM	EX	VG
451	Power For Ernie (Ernie Broglio, Daryl Spencer, Bill White)	7.50	3.75	2.25
452	Bob Allen	6.00	3.00	1.75
453	Dick Schofield	6.00	3.00	1.75
454	Pumpsie Green	6.00	3.00	1.75
455	Early Wynn	12.50	6.25	3.75
456	Hal Bevan	6.00	3.00	1.75
457	Johnny James	6.00	3.00	1.75
458	Willie Tasby	6.00	3.00	1.75
459	Terry Fox	6.00	3.00	1.75
460	Gil Hodges	12.50	6.25	3.75
461	Smoky Burgess	6.00	3.00	1.75
462	Lou Klimchock	6.00	3.00	1.75
463a	Milwaukee Braves Team (Should be card #426.)	10.00	5.00	3.00
463b	Jack Fisher	6.00	3.00	1.75
464	*Leroy Thomas*	6.00	3.00	1.75
465	Roy McMillan	6.00	3.00	1.75
466	Ron Moeller	6.00	3.00	1.75
467	Cleveland Indians Team	10.00	5.00	3.00
468	Johnny Callison	6.00	3.00	1.75
469	Ralph Lumenti	6.00	3.00	1.75
470	Roy Sievers	6.00	3.00	1.75
471	Phil Rizzuto/MVP	25.00	12.50	7.50
472	Yogi Berra/MVP	45.00	22.50	13.50
473	Bobby Shantz/MVP	7.50	3.75	2.25
474	Al Rosen/MVP	7.50	3.75	2.25
475	Mickey Mantle/MVP	120.00	60.00	36.00
476	Jackie Jensen/MVP	7.50	3.75	2.25
477	Nellie Fox/MVP	17.50	8.75	5.25
478	Roger Maris/MVP	40.00	20.00	12.00
479	Jim Konstanty/MVP	6.00	3.00	1.75
480	Roy Campanella/MVP	25.00	12.50	7.50
481	Hank Sauer/MVP	6.00	3.00	1.75
482	Willie Mays/MVP	40.00	20.00	12.00
483	Don Newcombe/MVP	7.50	3.75	2.25
484	Hank Aaron/MVP	35.00	17.50	10.00
485	Ernie Banks/MVP	20.00	10.00	6.00
486	Dick Groat/MVP	7.50	3.75	2.25
487	Gene Oliver	6.00	3.00	1.75
488	Joe McClain	6.00	3.00	1.75
489	Walt Dropo	6.00	3.00	1.75
490	Jim Bunning	12.50	6.25	3.75
491	Philadelphia Phillies Team	10.00	5.00	3.00
492	Ron Fairly	6.00	3.00	1.75
493	Don Zimmer	7.50	3.75	2.25
494	Tom Cheney	6.00	3.00	1.75
495	Elston Howard	15.00	7.50	4.50
496	Ken MacKenzie	6.00	3.00	1.75
497	Willie Jones	6.00	3.00	1.75
498	Ray Herbert	6.00	3.00	1.75
499	*Chuck Schilling*	6.00	3.00	1.75
500	Harvey Kuenn	6.00	3.00	1.75
501	John DeMerit	6.00	3.00	1.75
502	Clarence Coleman	6.00	3.00	1.75
503	Tito Francona	6.00	3.00	1.75
504	Billy Consolo	6.00	3.00	1.75
505	Red Schoendienst	12.50	6.25	3.75
506	*Willie Davis*	13.50	6.75	4.00
507	Pete Burnside	6.00	3.00	1.75
508	Rocky Bridges	6.00	3.00	1.75
509	Camilo Carreon	6.00	3.00	1.75
510	Art Ditmar	6.00	3.00	1.75
511	Joe Morgan	6.00	3.00	1.75
512	Bob Will	6.00	3.00	1.75
513	Jim Brosnan	6.00	3.00	1.75
514	Jake Wood	6.00	3.00	1.75
515	Jackie Brandt	6.00	3.00	1.75
516a	7th Series Checklist (507-587) (second "C" of "CHECK" above #13's cap.)	12.00	6.00	3.50
516b	7th Series Checklist (506-587) (Second "C" of "CHECK" covers top of #13's cap.)	12.00	6.00	3.50
517	Willie McCovey	25.00	12.50	7.50
518	Andy Carey	6.00	3.00	1.75
519	Jim Pagliaroni	6.00	3.00	1.75
520	Joe Cunningham	6.00	3.00	1.75
521	Brother Battery (Larry Sherry, Norm Sherry)	10.00	5.00	3.00
522	Dick Farrell	6.00	3.00	1.75
523	Joe Gibbon	20.00	10.00	6.00
524	Johnny Logan	20.00	10.00	6.00
525	*Ron Perranoski*	25.00	12.50	7.50
526	R.C. Stevens	20.00	10.00	6.00
527	Gene Leek	20.00	10.00	6.00
528	Pedro Ramos	20.00	10.00	6.00
529	Bob Roselli	20.00	10.00	6.00
530	Bobby Malkmus	20.00	10.00	6.00
531	Jim Coates	20.00	10.00	6.00
532	Bob Hale	20.00	10.00	6.00
533	Jack Curtis	20.00	10.00	6.00
534	Eddie Kasko	20.00	10.00	6.00
535	Larry Jackson	20.00	10.00	6.00
536	Bill Tuttle	20.00	10.00	6.00
537	Bobby Locke	20.00	10.00	6.00
538	Chuck Hiller	20.00	10.00	6.00
539	Johnny Klippstein	20.00	10.00	6.00
540	Jackie Jensen	22.50	11.00	7.00
541	Roland Sheldon	20.00	10.00	6.00
542	Minnesota Twins Team	35.00	17.50	10.00
543	Roger Craig	20.00	10.00	6.00
544	George Thomas	20.00	10.00	6.00
545	Hoyt Wilhelm	32.50	16.00	10.00
546	Marty Kutyna	20.00	10.00	6.00
547	Leon Wagner	20.00	10.00	6.00
548	Ted Wills	20.00	10.00	6.00
549	Hal R. Smith	20.00	10.00	6.00
550	Frank Baumann	20.00	10.00	6.00
551	George Altman	20.00	10.00	6.00
552	Jim Archer	20.00	10.00	6.00
553	Bill Fischer	20.00	10.00	6.00
554	Pittsburgh Pirates Team	45.00	22.50	13.50
555	Sam Jones	20.00	10.00	6.00
556	Ken R. Hunt	20.00	10.00	6.00
557	Jose Valdivielso	20.00	10.00	6.00
558	Don Ferrarese	20.00	10.00	6.00

#	Player	NM	EX	VG
559	Jim Gentile	75.00	37.50	22.50
560	Barry Latman	20.00	10.00	6.00
561	Charley James	20.00	10.00	6.00
562	Bill Monbouquette	20.00	10.00	6.00
563	Bob Cerv	20.00	10.00	6.00
564	Don Cardwell	20.00	10.00	6.00
565	Felipe Alou	30.00	15.00	9.00
566	Paul Richards (All-Star)	20.00	10.00	6.00
567	Danny Murtaugh (All-Star)	20.00	10.00	6.00
568	Bill Skowron (All-Star)	25.00	12.50	7.50
569	Frank Herrera (All-Star)	20.00	10.00	6.00
570	Nellie Fox (All-Star)	30.00	15.00	9.00
571	Bill Mazeroski (All-Star)	32.50	16.00	10.00
572	Brooks Robinson (All-Star)	50.00	25.00	15.00
573	Ken Boyer (All-Star)	22.50	11.00	6.75
574	Luis Aparicio (All-Star)	30.00	15.00	9.00
575	Ernie Banks (All-Star)	60.00	30.00	18.00
576	Roger Maris (All-Star)	100.00	50.00	30.00
577	Hank Aaron (All-Star)	100.00	50.00	30.00
578	Mickey Mantle (All-Star)	285.00	140.00	85.00
579	Willie Mays (All-Star)	90.00	45.00	27.00
580	Al Kaline (All-Star)	50.00	25.00	15.00
581	Frank Robinson (All-Star)	50.00	25.00	15.00
582	Earl Battey (All-Star)	20.00	10.00	6.00
583	Del Crandall (All-Star)	20.00	10.00	6.00
584	Jim Perry (All-Star)	20.00	10.00	6.00
585	Bob Friend (All-Star)	20.00	10.00	6.00
586	Whitey Ford (All-Star)	60.00	30.00	18.00
587	Not Issued			
588	Not Issued			
589	Warren Spahn (All-Star)	60.00	30.00	18.00

1961 Topps Dice Game

One of the more obscure Topps test issues that may have never actually been issued is the 1961 Topps Dice Game. Eighteen black and white cards, each measuring 2-1/2" x 3-1/2" in size, comprise the set. Interestingly, there are no identifying marks, such as copyrights or trademarks, to indicate the set was produced by Topps. The card backs contain various baseball plays that occur when a certain pitch is called and a specific number of the dice is rolled.

	Common Player:	NM	EX	VG
(1)	Earl Battey	1,850	925.00	550.00
(2)	Del Crandall	1,850	925.00	550.00
(3)	Jim Davenport	1,850	925.00	550.00
(4)	Don Drysdale	4,500	2,250	1,350
(5)	Dick Groat	1,850	925.00	550.00
(6)	Al Kaline	7,500	3,750	2,250
(7)	Tony Kubek	3,250	1,625	975.00
(8)	Mickey Mantle	45,000	22,500	13,500
(9)	Willie Mays	20,000	8,500	5,100
(10)	Bill Mazeroski	4,500	2,250	1,350
(11)	Stan Musial	20,000	10,000	6,000
(12)	Camilo Pascual	1,850	925.00	550.00
(13)	Bobby Richardson	3,500	1,750	1,050
(14)	Brooks Robinson	7,500	3,750	2,250
(15)	Frank Robinson	7,500	3,750	2,250
(16)	Norm Siebern	1,850	925.00	550.00
(17)	Leon Wagner	1,850	925.00	550.00
(18)	Bill White	1,850	925.00	550.00

1961 Topps Magic Rub-Offs

Not too different in concept from the tattoos of the previous year, the Topps Magic Rub-Off was designed to leave impressions of team themes or individual players when properly applied. Measuring 2-1/16" x 3-1/16", the Magic Rub-Off was not designed specifically for application to the owner's skin. The set features team themes that are a far cry from official logos, and the players (one per team) seem to have been included for their nicknames.

		NM	EX	VG
	Complete Set (36):	200.00	100.00	60.00
	Common Player:	6.00	3.00	1.75
(1)	Baltimore Orioles Pennant	6.00	3.00	1.75
(2)	Ernie "Bingo" Banks	15.00	7.50	4.50
(3)	Yogi Berra	15.00	7.50	4.50
(4)	Boston Red Sox Pennant	6.00	3.00	1.75
(5)	Jackie "Ozark" Brandt	6.00	3.00	1.75
(6)	Jim "Professor" Brosnan	6.00	3.00	1.75
(7)	Chicago Cubs Pennant	6.00	3.00	1.75
(8)	Chicago White Sox Pennant	6.00	3.00	1.75
(9)	Cincinnati Red Legs Pennant	6.00	3.00	1.75
(10)	Cleveland Indians Pennant	6.00	3.00	1.75
(11)	Detroit Tigers Pennant	6.00	3.00	1.75
(12)	Henry "Dutch" Dotterer	6.00	3.00	1.75
(13)	Joe "Flash" Gordon	6.00	3.00	1.75
(14)	Harvey "The Kitten" Haddix	6.00	3.00	1.75
(15)	Frank "Pancho" Hererra	6.00	3.00	1.75
(16)	Frank "Tower" Howard	7.50	3.75	2.25
(17)	"Sad" Sam Jones	6.00	3.00	1.75
(18)	Kansas City Athletics Pennant	6.00	3.00	1.75
(19)	Los Angeles Angels Pennant	7.50	3.75	2.25
(20)	Los Angeles Dodgers Pennant	7.50	3.75	2.25
(21)	Omar "Turk" Lown	6.00	3.00	1.75
(22)	Billy "The Kid" Martin	7.50	3.75	2.25
(23)	Duane "Duke" Mass (Maas)	6.00	3.00	1.75
(24)	Charlie "Paw Paw" Maxwell	6.00	3.00	1.75
(25)	Milwaukee Braves Pennant	6.00	3.00	1.75
(26)	Minnesota Twins Pennant	7.50	3.75	2.25
(27)	"Farmer" Ray Moore	6.00	3.00	1.75
(28)	Walt "Moose" Moryn	6.00	3.00	1.75
(29)	New York Yankees Pennant	9.00	4.50	2.75
(30)	Philadelphia Phillies Pennant	6.00	3.00	1.75
(31)	Pittsburgh Pirates Pennant	6.00	3.00	1.75
(32)	John "Honey" Romano	6.00	3.00	1.75
(33)	"Pistol Pete" Runnels	6.00	3.00	1.75
(34)	St. Louis Cardinals Pennant	6.00	3.00	1.75
(35)	San Francisco Giants Pennant	6.00	3.00	1.75
(36)	Washington Senators Pennant	9.00	4.50	2.75

1961 Topps Stamps

JOHNNY CALLISON
PHILA. PHILLIES   OUTFIELD

Issued as an added insert to 1961 Topps wax packs these 1-3/8" x 1-3/16" stamps were desigend to be collected and placed in an album which could be bought for an additional 10¢. Packs of cards contained two stamps. There are 208 stamps in a complete set which depict 207 different players (Al Kaline appears twice). There are 104 players on brown stamps and 104 on green. While there are many Hall of Famers on the stamps, prices remain low because there is relatively little interest in what is a non-card set.

		NM	EX	VG
	Complete Set (208):	750.00	375.00	225.00
	Common Player:	2.00	1.00	.60
	Stamp Album (Green):	65.00	30.00	20.00
(1)	Hank Aaron	20.00	10.00	6.00
(2)	Joe Adcock	2.00	1.00	.60
(3)	Hank Aguirre	2.00	1.00	.60
(4)	Bob Allison	2.00	1.00	.60
(5)	George Altman	2.00	1.00	.60
(6)	Bob Anderson	2.00	1.00	.60
(7)	Johnny Antonelli	2.00	1.00	.60
(8)	Luis Aparicio	12.00	6.00	3.50
(9)	Luis Arroyo	2.00	1.00	.60
(10)	Richie Ashburn	13.50	6.75	4.00
(11)	Ken Aspromonte	2.00	1.00	.60
(12)	Ed Bailey	2.00	1.00	.60
(13)	Ernie Banks	13.50	6.75	4.00
(14)	Steve Barber	2.00	1.00	.60
(15)	Earl Battey	2.00	1.00	.60
(16)	Hank Bauer	2.00	1.00	.60
(17)	Gus Bell	2.00	1.00	.60
(18)	Yogi Berra	13.50	6.75	4.00
(19)	Reno Bertoia	2.00	1.00	.60
(20)	John Blanchard	2.00	1.00	.60
(21)	Don Blasingame	2.00	1.00	.60
(22)	Frank Bolling	2.00	1.00	.60
(23)	Steve Boros	2.00	1.00	.60
(24)	Ed Bouchee	2.00	1.00	.60
(25)	Bob Boyd	2.00	1.00	.60
(26)	Cletis Boyer	2.00	1.00	.60
(27)	Ken Boyer	3.00	1.50	.90

(28)	Jackie Brandt	2.00	1.00	.60
(29)	Marv Breeding	2.00	1.00	.60
(30)	Eddie Bressoud	2.00	1.00	.60
(31)	Jim Brewer	2.00	1.00	.60
(32)	Tom Brewer	2.00	1.00	.60
(33)	Jim Brosnan	2.00	1.00	.60
(34)	Bill Bruton	2.00	1.00	.60
(35)	Bob Buhl	2.00	1.00	.60
(36)	Jim Bunning	10.00	5.00	3.00
(37)	Smoky Burgess	2.00	1.00	.60
(38)	John Buzhardt	2.00	1.00	.60
(39)	Johnny Callison	2.00	1.00	.60
(40)	Chico Cardenas	2.00	1.00	.60
(41)	Andy Carey	2.00	1.00	.60
(42)	Jerry Casale	2.00	1.00	.60
(43)	Norm Cash	4.00	2.00	1.25
(44)	Orlando Cepeda	10.00	5.00	3.00
(45)	Bob Cerv	2.00	1.00	.60
(46)	Harry Chiti	2.00	1.00	.60
(47)	Gene Conley	2.00	1.00	.60
(48)	Wes Covington	2.00	1.00	.60
(49)	Del Crandall	2.00	1.00	.60
(50)	Tony Curry	2.00	1.00	.60
(51)	Bud Daley	2.00	1.00	.60
(52)	Pete Daley	2.00	1.00	.60
(53)	Clay Dalrymple	2.00	1.00	.60
(54)	Jim Davenport	2.00	1.00	.60
(55)	Tommy Davis	2.00	1.00	.60
(56)	Bobby Del Greco	2.00	1.00	.60
(57)	Ike Delock	2.00	1.00	.60
(58)	Art Ditmar	2.00	1.00	.60
(59)	Dick Donovan	2.00	1.00	.60
(60)	Don Drysdale	13.50	6.75	4.00
(61)	Dick Ellsworth	2.00	1.00	.60
(62)	Don Elston	2.00	1.00	.60
(63)	Chuck Estrada	2.00	1.00	.60
(64)	Roy Face	2.00	1.00	.60
(65)	Dick Farrell	2.00	1.00	.60
(66)	Chico Fernandez	2.00	1.00	.60
(67)	Curt Flood	2.00	1.00	.60
(68)	Whitey Ford	13.50	6.75	4.00
(69)	Tito Francona	2.00	1.00	.60
(70)	Gene Freese	2.00	1.00	.60
(71)	Bob Friend	2.00	1.00	.60
(72)	Billy Gardner	2.00	1.00	.60
(73)	Ned Garver	2.00	1.00	.60
(74)	Gary Geiger	2.00	1.00	.60
(75)	Jim Gentile	2.00	1.00	.60
(76)	Dick Gernert	2.00	1.00	.60
(77)	Tony Gonzalez	2.00	1.00	.60
(78)	Alex Grammas	2.00	1.00	.60
(79)	Jim Grant	2.00	1.00	.60
(80)	Dick Groat	2.00	1.00	.60
(81)	Dick Hall	2.00	1.00	.60
(82)	Ron Hansen	2.00	1.00	.60
(83)	Bob Hartman	2.00	1.00	.60
(84)	Woodie Held	2.00	1.00	.60
(85)	Ray Herbert	2.00	1.00	.60
(86)	Frank Herrera	2.00	1.00	.60
(87)	Whitey Herzog	2.00	1.00	.60
(88)	Don Hoak	2.00	1.00	.60
(89)	Elston Howard	5.00	2.50	1.50
(90)	Frank Howard	4.00	2.00	1.25
(91)	Ken Hunt	2.00	1.00	.60
(92)	Larry Jackson	2.00	1.00	.60
(93)	Julian Javier	2.00	1.00	.60
(94)	Joe Jay	2.00	1.00	.60
(95)	Jackie Jensen	2.00	1.00	.60
(96)	Jim Kaat	2.50	1.25	.70
(97a)	Al Kaline (Green)	25.00	12.50	7.50
(97b)	Al Kaline (brown)	15.00	7.50	4.50
(98)	Eddie Kasko	2.00	1.00	.60
(99)	Russ Kemmerer	2.00	1.00	.60
(100)	Harmon Killebrew	13.50	6.75	4.00
(101)	Billy Klaus	2.00	1.00	.60
(102)	Ron Kline	2.00	1.00	.60
(103)	Johnny Klippstein	2.00	1.00	.60
(104)	Ted Kluszewski	10.00	5.00	3.00
(105)	Tony Kubek	5.00	2.50	1.50
(106)	Harvey Kuenn	2.00	1.00	.60
(107)	Jim Landis	2.00	1.00	.60
(108)	Hobie Landrith	2.00	1.00	.60
(109)	Norm Larker	2.00	1.00	.60
(110)	Frank Lary	2.00	1.00	.60
(111)	Barry Latman	2.00	1.00	.60
(112)	Vern Law	2.00	1.00	.60
(113)	Jim Lemon	2.00	1.00	.60
(114)	Sherman Lollar	2.00	1.00	.60
(115)	Dale Long	2.00	1.00	.60
(116)	Jerry Lumpe	2.00	1.00	.60
(117)	Jerry Lynch	2.00	1.00	.60
(118)	Art Mahaffey	2.00	1.00	.60
(119)	Frank Malzone	2.00	1.00	.60
(120)	Felix Mantilla	2.00	1.00	.60
(121)	Mickey Mantle	60.00	30.00	18.00
(122)	Juan Marichal	13.50	6.75	4.00
(123)	Roger Maris	25.00	12.50	7.50
(124)	Billy Martin	5.00	2.50	1.50
(125)	J.C. Martin	2.00	1.00	.60
(126)	Ed Mathews	13.50	6.75	4.00
(127)	Charlie Maxwell	2.00	1.00	.60
(128)	Willie Mays	20.00	10.00	6.00
(129)	Bill Mazeroski	12.00	6.00	3.50
(130)	Mike McCormick	2.00	1.00	.60
(131)	Willie McCovey	13.50	6.75	4.00
(132)	Lindy McDaniel	2.00	1.00	.60
(133)	Roy McMillan	2.00	1.00	.60
(134)	Minnie Minoso	3.00	1.50	.90
(135)	Bill Monbouquette	2.00	1.00	.60
(136)	Wally Moon	2.00	1.00	.60
(137)	Stan Musial	20.00	10.00	6.00
(138)	Charlie Neal	2.00	1.00	.60
(139)	Rocky Nelson	2.00	1.00	.60
(140)	Russ Nixon	2.00	1.00	.60
(141)	Billy O'Dell	2.00	1.00	.60
(142)	Jim O'Toole	2.00	1.00	.60
(143)	Milt Pappas	2.00	1.00	.60
(144)	Camilo Pascual	2.00	1.00	.60

(145)	Jim Perry	2.00	1.00	.60
(146)	Bubba Phillips	2.00	1.00	.60
(147)	Bill Pierce	2.00	1.00	.60
(148)	Jim Piersall	2.00	1.00	.60
(149)	Vada Pinson	3.00	1.50	.90
(150)	Johnny Podres	2.50	1.25	.70
(151)	Wally Post	2.00	1.00	.60
(152)	Vic Powers (Power)	2.00	1.00	.60
(153)	Pedro Ramos	2.00	1.00	.60
(154)	Robin Roberts	10.00	5.00	3.00
(155)	Brooks Robinson	13.50	6.75	4.00
(156)	Frank Robinson	13.50	6.75	4.00
(157)	Ed Roebuck	2.00	1.00	.60
(158)	John Romano	2.00	1.00	.60
(159)	John Roseboro	2.00	1.00	.60
(160)	Pete Runnels	2.00	1.00	.60
(161)	Ed Sadowski	2.00	1.00	.60
(162)	Jack Sanford	2.00	1.00	.60
(163)	Ron Santo	3.00	1.50	.90
(164)	Ray Semproch	2.00	1.00	.60
(165)	Bobby Shantz	2.00	1.00	.60
(166)	Bob Shaw	2.00	1.00	.60
(167)	Larry Sherry	2.00	1.00	.60
(168)	Norm Siebern	2.00	1.00	.60
(169)	Roy Sievers	2.00	1.00	.60
(170)	Curt Simmons	2.00	1.00	.60
(171)	Dave Sisler	2.00	1.00	.60
(172)	Bob Skinner	2.00	1.00	.60
(173)	Al Smith	2.00	1.00	.60
(174)	Hal Smith	2.00	1.00	.60
(175)	Hal Smith	2.00	1.00	.60
(176)	Duke Snider	13.50	6.75	4.00
(177)	Warren Spahn	13.50	6.75	4.00
(178)	Daryl Spencer	2.00	1.00	.60
(179)	Bill Stafford	2.00	1.00	.60
(180)	Jerry Staley	2.00	1.00	.60
(181)	Gene Stephens	2.00	1.00	.60
(182)	Chuck Stobbs	2.00	1.00	.60
(183)	Dick Stuart	2.00	1.00	.60
(184)	Willie Tasby	2.00	1.00	.60
(185)	Sammy Taylor	2.00	1.00	.60
(186)	Tony Taylor	2.00	1.00	.60
(187)	Johnny Temple	2.00	1.00	.60
(188)	Marv Throneberry	2.00	1.00	.60
(189)	Gus Triandos	2.00	1.00	.60
(190)	Bob Turley	2.00	1.00	.60
(191)	Bill Tuttle	2.00	1.00	.60
(192)	Zoilo Versalles	2.00	1.00	.60
(193)	Bill Virdon	2.00	1.00	.60
(194)	Lee Walls	2.00	1.00	.60
(195)	Vic Wertz	2.00	1.00	.60
(196)	Pete Whisenant	2.00	1.00	.60
(197)	Bill White	2.00	1.00	.60
(198)	Hoyt Wilhelm	10.00	5.00	3.00
(199)	Bob Will	2.00	1.00	.60
(200)	Carl Willey	2.00	1.00	.60
(201)	Billy Williams	12.00	6.00	3.50
(202)	Dick Williams	2.00	1.00	.60
(203)	Stan Williams	2.00	1.00	.60
(204)	Gene Woodling	2.00	1.00	.60
(205)	Early Wynn	10.00	5.00	3.00
(206)	Carl Yastrzemski	13.50	6.75	4.00
(207)	Eddie Yost	2.00	1.00	.60

1961 Topps Stamps Panels

BILLY MARTIN
CINCINNATI REDS   2nd BASE

WHITEY HERZOG
KANSAS CITY A's   OUTFIELD

Some advanced collectors pursue the 1961 Topps stamps in the form of the two-stamp panels in which they were issued. The 208 different stamps which make up the issue can be found on 182 different two-stamp panels. The unnumbered stamps are listed here alphabetically according to the name of the player which appears on the left end of the panel. Values shown are for complete panels of two players stamps plus the attached tab at left.

		NM	EX	VG
	Complete Panel Set (182):	3,000	1,500	900.00
	Common Panel:	9.00	4.50	2.75
(1)	Hank Aguirre/Bob Boyd	9.00	4.50	2.75
(2)	Bob Allison/Orlando Cepeda	20.00	10.00	6.00
(3)	Bob Allison/Early Wynn	20.00	10.00	6.00
(4)	George Altman/Andy Carey	9.00	4.50	2.75
(5)	George Altman/ Lindy McDaniel	9.00	4.50	2.75
(6)	Johnny Antonelli/Ken Hunt	9.00	4.50	2.75
(7)	Richie Ashburn/ Don Drysdale	30.00	15.00	9.00
(8)	Richie Ashburn/Joe Jay	25.00	12.50	7.50
(9)	Ken Aspromonte/ Chuck Estrada	9.00	4.50	2.75
(10)	Ken Aspromonte/ Jerry Lynch	9.00	4.50	2.75
(11)	Ed Bailey/Marv Breeding	9.00	4.50	2.75
(12)	Ed Bailey/Smoky Burgess	9.00	4.50	2.75
(13)	Ernie Banks/Chico Fernandez	30.00	15.00	9.00
(14)	Ernie Banks/Pedro Ramos	30.00	15.00	9.00
(15)	Steve Barber/Eddie Kasko	9.00	4.50	2.75
(16)	Steve Barber/Roy Sievers	9.00	4.50	2.75

(17)	Earl Battey/Art Ditmar	9.00	4.50	2.75
(18)	Earl Battey/Bill White	9.00	4.50	2.75
(19)	Gus Bell/Gary Geiger	9.00	4.50	2.75
(20)	Gus Bell/Early Wynn	20.00	10.00	6.00
(21)	John Blanchard/Dick Donovan	9.00	4.50	2.75
(22)	John Blanchard/Ray Semproch	9.00	4.50	2.75
(23)	Don Blasingame/Elston Howard	12.00	6.00	3.50
(24)	Don Blasingame/Charlie Maxwell	9.00	4.50	2.75
(25)	Frank Bolling/Luis Aparicio	20.00	10.00	6.00
(26)	Frank Bolling/Whitey Herzog	9.00	4.50	2.75
(27)	Steve Boros/Ike Delock	9.00	4.50	2.75
(28)	Steve Boros/Russ Nixon	9.00	4.50	2.75
(29)	Ed Bouchee/Larry Sherry	9.00	4.50	2.75
(30)	Ed Bouchee/Willie Tasby	9.00	4.50	2.75
(31)	Cletis Boyer/Johnny Klippstein	9.00	4.50	2.75
(32)	Jim Brewer/Vern Law	9.00	4.50	2.75
(33)	Jim Brewer/Camilo Pascual	9.00	4.50	2.75
(34)	Tom Brewer/Tommy Davis	9.00	4.50	2.75
(35)	Tom Brewer/Larry Sherry	9.00	4.50	2.75
(36)	Jim Brosnan/Roy McMillan	9.00	4.50	2.75
(37)	Jim Brosnan/Calr Willey	9.00	4.50	2.75
(38)	Bill Bruton/Ken Boyer	12.00	6.00	3.50
(39)	Bill Bruton/Mickey Mantle	200.00	100.00	60.00
(40)	Bob Buhl/Willie Mays	60.00	30.00	18.00
(41)	Bob Buhl/Roy Sievers	9.00	4.50	2.75
(42)	Jim Bunning/Bob Boyd	20.00	10.00	6.00
(43)	Jim Bunning/Ron Hansen	20.00	10.00	6.00
(44)	John Buzhardt/Brooks Robinson	30.00	15.00	9.00
(45)	John Buzhardt/Dick Williams	9.00	4.50	2.75
(46)	Johnny Callison/Jim Landis	9.00	4.50	2.75
(47)	Johnny Callison/Ed Roebuck	9.00	4.50	2.75
(48)	Harry Chiti/Jackie Brandt	9.00	4.50	2.75
(49)	Harry Chiti/Gene Conley	9.00	4.50	2.75
(50)	Del Crandall/Billy Gardner	9.00	4.50	2.75
(51)	Bud Daley/Al Kaline	30.00	15.00	9.00
(52)	Bud Daley/Dave Sisler	9.00	4.50	2.75
(53)	Pete Daley/Dick Ellsworth	9.00	4.50	2.75
(54)	Pete Daley/Hal (R.) Smith	9.00	4.50	2.75
(55)	Clay Dalrymple/Norm Larker	9.00	4.50	2.75
(56)	CLay Dalrymple/Stan Williams	9.00	4.50	2.75
(57)	Jim Davenport/Reno Bertoia	9.00	4.50	2.75
(58)	Jim Davenport/Jerry Lynch	9.00	4.50	2.75
(59)	Bobby Del Greco/Roy Face	9.00	4.50	2.75
(60)	Bobby Del Greco/Frank Howard	12.00	6.00	3.50
(61)	Gene Freese/Wes Covington	9.00	4.50	2.75
(62)	Gene Freese/Vada Pinson	9.00	4.50	2.75
(63)	Bob Friend/Hank Aaron	60.00	30.00	18.00
(64)	Bob Friend/Lee Walls	9.00	4.50	2.75
(65)	Jim Gentile/Chuck Estrada	9.00	4.50	2.75
(66)	Jim Gentile/Bill O'Dell	9.00	4.50	2.75
(67)	Dick Gernert/Russ Nixon	9.00	4.50	2.75
(68)	Alex Grammas/Eddie Bressoud	9.00	4.50	2.75
(69)	Frank Herrera/Joe Jay	9.00	4.50	2.75
(70)	Frank Herrera/Jim Landis	9.00	4.50	2.75
(71)	Julian Javier/Eddie Kasko	9.00	4.50	2.75
(72)	Jackie Jensen/Hank Bauer	15.00	7.50	4.50
(73)	Jackie Jensen/Mickey Mantle	200.00	100.00	60.00
(74)	Al Kaline/Dick Hall	30.00	15.00	9.00
(75)	Al Kaline/Ray Herbert	30.00	15.00	9.00
(76)	Russ Kemmerer/Ed Sadowski	9.00	4.50	2.75
(77)	Harmon Killebrew/Bill Stafford	30.00	15.00	9.00
(78)	Harmon Killebrew/Bill White	30.00	15.00	9.00
(79)	Billy Klaus/Bob Anderson	9.00	4.50	2.75
(80)	Ron Kline/Juan Marichal	20.00	10.00	6.00
(81)	Ron Kline/Curt Simmons	9.00	4.50	2.75
(82)	Tony Kubek/Reno Bertoia	12.00	6.00	3.50
(83)	Frank Lary/Andy Carey	9.00	4.50	2.75
(84)	Barry Latman/Hank Bauer	9.00	4.50	2.75
(85)	Jim Lemon/Tony Curry	9.00	4.50	2.75
(86)	Jim Lemon/Dick Williams	9.00	4.50	2.75
(87)	Sherm Lollar/Willie Mays	60.00	30.00	18.00
(88)	Sherm Lollar/Duke Snider	30.00	15.00	9.00
(89)	Dale Long/Bob Anderson	9.00	4.50	2.75
(90)	Dale Long/Don Elston	9.00	4.50	2.75
(91)	Art Mahaffey/Vada Pinson	9.00	4.50	2.75
(92)	Art Mahaffey/Robin Roberts	20.00	10.00	6.00
(93)	Frank Malzone/Dick Hall	9.00	4.50	2.75
(94)	Frank Malzone/Bob Hartman	9.00	4.50	2.75
(95)	Felix Mantilla/Billy Gardner	9.00	4.50	2.75
(96)	Felix Mantilla/Gary Geiger	9.00	4.50	2.75
(97)	Roger Maris/Johnny Klippstein	45.00	22.00	13.50
(98)	Roger Maris/Ray Semproch	45.00	22.00	13.50
(99)	Billy Martin/Hank Aaron	60.00	30.00	18.00
(100)	Billy Martin/Whitey Herzog	15.00	7.50	4.50
(101)	J.C. Martin/Bob Cerv	9.00	4.50	2.75
(102)	J.C. Martin/Eddie Yost	9.00	4.50	2.75
(103)	Ed Mathews/Chico Cardenas	30.00	15.00	9.00
(104)	Bill Mazeroski/Joe Adcock	20.00	10.00	6.00
(105)	Bill Mazeroski/Elston Howard	20.00	10.00	6.00
(106)	Mike McCormick/Rocky Nelson	9.00	4.50	2.75
(107)	Mike McCormick/Curt Simmons	9.00	4.50	2.75
(108)	Wille McCovey/Smoky Burgess	30.00	15.00	9.00
(109)	Minnie Minoso/Ted Kluszewski	15.00	7.50	4.50
(110)	Minnie Minoso/Eddie Yost	12.00	6.00	3.50
(111)	Bikll Monbouquette/Tony Curry	9.00	4.50	2.75
(112)	Bill Monbouquette/Sammy Taylor	9.00	4.50	2.75
(113)	Wally Moon/Roy Face	9.00	4.50	2.75
(114)	Stan Musial/Rocky Nelson	60.00	30.00	18.00
(115)	Charlie Neal/Marv Breeding	9.00	4.50	2.75

(116)	Charlie Neal/Jim Grant	9.00	4.50	2.75
(117)	Jim O'Toole/Chico Cardenas	9.00	4.50	2.75
(118)	Jim O'Toole/Roy McMillan	9.00	4.50	2.75
(119)	Milt Pappas/Tito Francona	9.00	4.50	2.75
(120)	Milt Pappas/Jim Piersall	9.00	4.50	2.75
(121)	Jim Perry/Bob Cerv	9.00	4.50	2.75
(122)	Jim Perry/Ken Hunt	9.00	4.50	2.75
(123)	Bubba Phillips/Art Ditmar	9.00	4.50	2.75
(124)	Bubba Phillips/Jim Kaat	15.00	7.50	4.50
(125)	Johnny Podres/Dick Farrell	9.00	4.50	2.75
(126)	Wally Post/Dick Farrell	9.00	4.50	2.75
(127)	Wally Post/Robin Roberts	10.00	5.00	6.00
(128)	Frank Robinson/Jim Grant	30.00	15.00	9.00
(129)	Frank Robinson/Don Hoak	30.00	15.00	9.00
(130)	John Romano/Al Kaline	30.00	15.00	9.00
(131)	John Roseboro/Dick Groat	9.00	4.50	2.75
(132)	Pete Runnels/Larry Jackson	9.00	4.50	2.75
(133)	Jack Sanford/Whitey Ford	30.00	15.00	9.00
(134)	Jack Sanford/Pedro Ramos	9.00	4.50	2.75
(135)	Ron Santo/Harvey Kuenn	15.00	7.50	4.50
(136)	Ron Santo/Vern Law	15.00	7.50	4.50
(137)	Bobby Shantz/Joe Adcock	9.00	4.50	2.75
(138)	Bobby Shantz/Dick Groat	9.00	4.50	2.75
(139)	Bob Shaw/Jerry Casale	9.00	4.50	2.75
(140)	Bob Shaw/Ned Garver	9.00	4.50	2.75
(141)	Norm Siebern/Tony Gonzalez	9.00	4.50	2.75
(142)	Norm Siebern/Woodie Held	9.00	4.50	2.75
(143)	Bob Skinner/Hobie Landrith	9.00	4.50	2.75
(144)	Bob Skinner/Juan Marichal	20.00	10.00	6.00
(145)	Al Smith/Don Drysdale	25.00	12.50	7.50
(146)	Hal (W.) Smith/Eddie Bressoud	9.00	4.50	2.75
(147)	Hal (W.) Smith/Harvey Kuenn	9.00	4.50	2.75
(148)	Daryl Spencer/Norm Cash	9.00	4.50	2.75
(149)	Daryl Spencer/Vic Powers (Power)	9.00	4.50	2.75
(150)	Jerry Staley/Ned Garver	9.00	4.50	2.75
(151)	Jerry Staley/Ed Sadowski	9.00	4.50	2.75
(152)	Gene Stephens/Gene Conley	9.00	4.50	2.75
(153)	Gene Stephens/Ike Delock	9.00	4.50	2.75
(154)	Chuck Stobbs/Ken Boyer	12.00	6.00	3.50
(155)	Chuck Stobbs/Curt Flood	9.00	4.50	2.75
(156)	Dick Stuart/Whitey Ford	30.00	15.00	9.00
(157)	Dick Stuart/Larry Jackson	9.00	4.50	2.75
(158)	Tony Taylor/Frank Howard	12.00	6.00	3.50
(159)	Tony Taylor/Norm Larker	9.00	4.50	2.75
(160)	Johnny Temple/Norm Cash	9.00	4.50	2.75
(161)	Johnny Temple/Dave Sisler	9.00	4.50	2.75
(162)	Marv Throneberry/Yogi Berra	45.00	22.00	13.50
(163)	Marv Throneberry/Tommy Davis	9.00	4.50	2.75
(164)	Gus Triandos/Sammy Taylor	9.00	4.50	2.75
(165)	Bob Turley/Luis Aparicio	20.00	10.00	6.00
(166)	Bill Tuttle/Jerry Casale	9.00	4.50	2.75
(167)	Bill Tuttle/Billy Pierce	9.00	4.50	2.75
(168)	Zoilo Versalles/Bill Stafford	9.00	4.50	2.75
(169)	Bill Virdon/Yogi Berra	30.00	15.00	9.00
(170)	Vic Wertz/Bob Hartman	9.00	4.50	2.75
(171)	Vic Wertz/Jerry Lumpe	9.00	4.50	2.75
(172)	Pete Whisenant/Luis Arroyo	9.00	4.50	2.75
(173)	Pete Whisenant/Dick Donovan	9.00	4.50	2.75
(174)	Hoyt Wilhelm/Ron Hansen	20.00	10.00	6.00
(175)	Hoyt Wilhelm/Jim Piersall	20.00	10.00	6.00
(176)	Bob Will/Tony Gonzalez	9.00	4.50	2.75
(177)	Bob Will/Lindy McDaniel	9.00	4.50	2.75
(178)	Billy Williams/Warren Spahn	30.00	15.00	9.00
(179)	Billy Williams/Carl Willey	25.00	12.50	7.50
(180)	Gene Woodling/Don Elston	9.00	4.50	2.75
(181)	Gene Woodling/Hal (R.) Smith	9.00	4.50	2.75
(182)	Carl Yastrzemski/Jerry Lumpe	60.00	30.00	18.00

1962 Topps

The 1962 Topps set established another plateau for set size with 598 cards. The 2-1/2" x 3-1/2" cards feature a photograph set against a woodgrain background. The lower-right corner has been made to look like it is curling away. Many established specialty cards dot the set including statistical leaders, multi-player cards, team cards, checklists, World Series cards and All-Stars. Of note is that 1962 was the first year of the multi-player rookie card. There is a 9-card "In Action" subset and a 10-card run of special Babe Ruth cards. Photo variations of several cards in the 2nd Series (#110-196) exist. All cards in the 2nd Series can be found with two distinct printing variations, an early printing with the cards containing a very noticeable greenish tint, having been corrected to clear photos in subsequent print runs. The complete set price in the checklist that follows does not

include the higher-priced variations. Among the high numbers (#523-598) certain cards were "short-printed," produced in lesser quantities. These cards carry a higher value and are indicated in the checklist by the notation/SP after the player name.

		NM	EX	VG
	Complete Set (598):	5,500	2,750	1,650
	Common Player (1-446):	4.00	2.00	1.25
	Common Player (447-522):	7.00	3.50	2.00
	Common Player (523-598):	10.00	5.00	3.00
1	Roger Maris	270.00	70.00	40.00
2	Jim Brosnan	4.00	2.00	1.25
3	Pete Runnels	4.00	2.00	1.25
4	John DeMerit	4.00	2.00	1.25
5	Sandy Koufax	100.00	50.00	30.00
6	Marv Breeding	4.00	2.00	1.25
7	Frank Thomas	4.00	2.00	1.25
8	Ray Herbert	4.00	2.00	1.25
9	Jim Davenport	4.00	2.00	1.25
10	Bob Clemente	95.00	47.50	27.50
11	Tom Morgan	4.00	2.00	1.25
12	Harry Craft	4.00	2.00	1.25
13	Dick Howser	4.00	2.00	1.25
14	Bill White	4.00	2.00	1.25
15	Dick Donovan	4.00	2.00	1.25
16	Darrell Johnson	4.00	2.00	1.25
17	Johnny Callison	4.00	2.00	1.25
18	Managers' Dream (Mickey Mantle, Willie Mays)	120.00	60.00	35.00
19	*Ray Washburn*	4.00	2.00	1.25
20	Rocky Colavito	15.00	7.50	4.50
21	Jim Kaat	6.00	3.00	1.75
22a	1st Series Checklist (1-88) (numbers 121-176 on back)	6.00	3.00	1.75
22b	1st Series Checklist (1-88) (numbers 33-88 on back)	9.00	4.50	2.75
23	Norm Larker	4.00	2.00	1.25
24	Detroit Tigers Team	7.00	3.50	2.00
25	Ernie Banks	40.00	20.00	12.00
26	Chris Cannizzaro	4.00	2.00	1.25
27	Chuck Cottier	4.00	2.00	1.25
28	Minnie Minoso	9.00	4.50	2.75
29	Casey Stengel	13.50	6.75	4.00
30	Ed Mathews	25.00	12.50	7.50
31	*Tom Tresh*	13.50	6.75	4.00
32	John Roseboro	4.00	2.00	1.25
33	Don Larsen	4.00	2.00	1.25
34	Johnny Temple	4.00	2.00	1.25
35	*Don Schwall*	4.00	2.00	1.25
36	Don Leppert	4.00	2.00	1.25
37	Tribe Hill Trio (Barry Latman, Jim Perry, Dick Stigman)	6.00	3.00	1.75
38	Gene Stephens	4.00	2.00	1.25
39	Joe Koppe	4.00	2.00	1.25
40	Orlando Cepeda	16.00	8.00	4.75
41	Cliff Cook	4.00	2.00	1.25
42	Jim King	4.00	2.00	1.25
43	Los Angeles Dodgers Team	10.00	5.00	3.00
44	Don Taussig	4.00	2.00	1.25
45	Brooks Robinson	25.00	12.50	7.50
46	*Jack Baldschun*	4.00	2.00	1.25
47	Bob Will	4.00	2.00	1.25
48	Ralph Terry	4.00	2.00	1.25
49	Hal Jones	4.00	2.00	1.25
50	Stan Musial	50.00	25.00	15.00
51	A.L. Batting Leaders (Norm Cash, Elston Howard, Al Kaline, Jim Piersall)	12.50	6.25	3.75
52	N.L. Batting Leaders (Ken Boyer, Roberto Clemente, Wally Moon, Vada Pinson)	15.00	7.50	4.50
53	A.L. Home Run Leaders (Jim Gentile, Harmon Killebrew, Mickey Mantle, Roger Maris)	55.00	27.50	16.50
54	N.L. Home Run Leaders (Orlando Cepeda, Willie Mays, Frank Robinson)	12.50	6.25	3.75
55	A.L. E.R.A. Leaders (Dick Donovan, Don Mossi, Milt Pappas, Bill Stafford)	6.00	3.00	1.75
56	N.L. E.R.A. Leaders (Mike McCormick, Jim O'Toole, Curt Simmons, Warren Spahn)	7.00	3.50	2.00
57	A.L. Win Leaders (Steve Barber, Jim Bunning, Whitey Ford, Frank Lary)	10.00	5.00	3.00
58	N.L. Win Leaders (Joe Jay, Jim O'Toole, Warren Spahn)	7.00	3.50	2.00
59	A.L. Strikeout Leaders (Jim Bunning, Whitey Ford, Camilo Pascual, Juan Pizzaro)	7.50	3.75	2.25
60	N.L. Strikeout Leaders (Don Drysdale, Sandy Koufax, Jim O'Toole, Stan Williams)	16.00	8.00	4.75
61	St. Louis Cardinals Team	7.00	3.50	2.00
62	Steve Boros	4.00	2.00	1.25
63	*Tony Cloninger*	7.00	3.50	2.00
64	Russ Snyder	4.00	2.00	1.25
65	Bobby Richardson	15.00	7.50	4.50
66	Cuno Barragon (Barragan)	4.00	2.00	1.25
67	Harvey Haddix	4.00	2.00	1.25
68	Ken L. Hunt	4.00	2.00	1.25
69	Phil Ortega	4.00	2.00	1.25
70	Harmon Killebrew	25.00	12.50	7.50
71	Dick LeMay	4.00	2.00	1.25
72	Bob's Pupils (Steve Boros, Bob Scheffing, Jake Wood)	4.50	2.25	1.25
73	Nellie Fox	16.00	8.00	4.75
74	Bob Lillis	4.00	2.00	1.25
75	Milt Pappas	4.00	2.00	1.25
76	Howie Bedell	4.00	2.00	1.25
77	Tony Taylor	4.00	2.00	1.25
78	Gene Green	4.00	2.00	1.25
79	Ed Hobaugh	4.00	2.00	1.25

80	Vada Pinson	7.00	3.50	2.00
81	Jim Pagliaroni	4.00	2.00	1.25
82	Deron Johnson	4.00	2.00	1.25
83	Larry Jackson	4.00	2.00	1.25
84	Lenny Green	4.00	2.00	1.25
85	Gil Hodges	15.00	7.50	4.50
86	Donn Clendenon	6.00	3.00	1.75
87	Mike Roarke	4.00	2.00	1.25
88	Ralph Houk	10.00	5.00	3.00
89	Barney Schultz	4.00	2.00	1.25
90	Jim Piersall	6.00	3.00	1.75
91	J.C. Martin	4.00	2.00	1.25
92	Sam Jones	4.00	2.00	1.25
93	John Blanchard	5.00	2.50	1.50
94	Jay Hook	4.00	2.00	1.25
95	Don Hoak	4.00	2.00	1.25
96	Eli Grba	4.00	2.00	1.25
97	Tito Francona	4.00	2.00	1.25
98	2nd Series Checklist (89-176)	6.00	3.00	1.75
99	John Powell (Boog)	20.00	10.00	6.00
100	Warren Spahn	30.00	15.00	9.00
101	Carroll Hardy	4.00	2.00	1.25
102	Al Schroll	4.00	2.00	1.25
103	Don Blasingame	4.00	2.00	1.25
104	Ted Savage	4.00	2.00	1.25
105	Don Mossi	4.00	2.00	1.25
106	Carl Sawatski	4.00	2.00	1.25
107	Mike McCormick	4.00	2.00	1.25
108	Willie Davis	5.00	2.50	1.50
109	Bob Shaw	4.00	2.00	1.25
110	Bill Skowron	22.50	11.00	7.00
111	Dallas Green	4.00	2.00	1.25
112	Hank Foiles	4.00	2.00	1.25
113	Chicago White Sox Team	7.00	3.50	2.00
114	Howie Koplitz	4.00	2.00	1.25
115	Bob Skinner	4.00	2.00	1.25
116	Herb Score	4.00	2.00	1.25
117	Gary Geiger	4.00	2.00	1.25
118	Julian Javier	4.00	2.00	1.25
119	Danny Murphy	4.00	2.00	1.25
120	Bob Purkey	4.00	2.00	1.25
121	Billy Hitchcock	4.00	2.00	1.25
122	Norm Bass	4.00	2.00	1.25
123	Mike de la Hoz	4.00	2.00	1.25
124	Bill Pleis	4.00	2.00	1.25
125	Gene Woodling	4.00	2.00	1.25
126	Al Cicotte	4.00	2.00	1.25
127	Pride of the A's (Hank Bauer, Jerry Lumpe, Norm Siebern)	4.50	2.25	1.25
128	Art Fowler	4.00	2.00	1.25
129a	Lee Walls (Pinstriped jersey.)	20.00	10.00	6.00
129b	Lee Walls (Plain jersey.)	6.00	3.00	1.75
130	Frank Bolling	4.00	2.00	1.25
131	Pete Richert	4.00	2.00	1.25
132a	Los Angeles Angels Team (with inset photos)	13.50	6.75	4.00
132b	Los Angeles Angels Team (No inset photos.)	7.00	3.50	2.00
133	Felipe Alou	9.00	4.50	2.75
134a	Billy Hoeft (Green sky)	15.00	7.50	4.50
134b	Billy Hoeft (Blue sky)	12.00	6.00	3.50
135	Babe as a Boy (Babe Ruth)	20.00	10.00	6.00
136	Babe Joins Yanks (Babe Ruth)	20.00	10.00	6.00
137	Babe and Mgr. Huggins (Babe Ruth)	20.00	10.00	6.00
138	The Famous Slugger (Babe Ruth)	20.00	10.00	6.00
139a	Hal Reniff/Pitching	40.00	20.00	12.00
139b	Hal Reniff/Portrait	15.00	7.50	4.50
139c	Babe Hits 60 (Babe Ruth) (pole in background at left)	35.00	17.50	10.00
139d	Babe Hits 60 (Babe Ruth) (No pole.)	35.00	17.50	10.00
140	Gehrig and Ruth (Babe Ruth)	35.00	17.50	10.00
141	Twilight Years (Babe Ruth)	20.00	10.00	6.00
142	Coaching for the Dodgers (Babe Ruth)	20.00	10.00	6.00
143	Greatest Sports Hero (Babe Ruth)	20.00	10.00	6.00
144	Farewell Speech (Babe Ruth)	20.00	10.00	6.00
145	Barry Latman	4.00	2.00	1.25
146	Don Demeter	4.00	2.00	1.25
147a	Bill Kunkel (Ball in hand.)	17.50	8.75	5.25
147b	Bill Kunkel/Portrait	12.00	6.00	3.50
148	Wally Post	4.00	2.00	1.25
149	Bob Duliba	4.00	2.00	1.25
150	Al Kaline	30.00	15.00	9.00
151	Johnny Klippstein	4.00	2.00	1.25
152	Mickey Vernon	4.00	2.00	1.25
153	Pumpsie Green	4.00	2.00	1.25
154	Lee Thomas	4.00	2.00	1.25
155	Stu Miller	4.00	2.00	1.25
156	Merritt Ranew	4.00	2.00	1.25
157	Wes Covington	4.00	2.00	1.25
158	Milwaukee Braves Team	7.00	3.50	2.00
159	Hal Reniff	4.00	2.00	1.25
160	Dick Stuart	4.00	2.00	1.25
161	Frank Baumann	4.00	2.00	1.25
162	Sammy Drake	4.00	2.00	1.25
163	Hot Corner Guardians (Cletis Boyer, Billy Gardner)	10.00	5.00	3.00
164	Hal Naragon	4.00	2.00	1.25
165	Jackie Brandt	4.00	2.00	1.25
166	Don Lee	4.00	2.00	1.25
167	Tim McCarver	17.50	8.75	5.25
168	Leo Posada	4.00	2.00	1.25
169	Bob Cerv	4.00	2.00	1.25
170	Ron Santo	12.50	6.25	3.75
171	Dave Sisler	4.00	2.00	1.25
172	Fred Hutchinson	4.00	2.00	1.25
173	Chico Fernandez	4.00	2.00	1.25
174a	Carl Willey (With cap.)	15.00	7.50	4.50
174b	Carl Willey (No cap.)	8.00	4.00	2.50
175	Frank Howard	5.00	2.50	1.50
176a	Eddie Yost/Btg	15.00	7.50	4.50
176b	Eddie Yost/Portrait	4.00	2.00	1.25
177	Bobby Shantz	4.00	2.00	1.25
178	Camilo Carreon	4.00	2.00	1.25
179	Tom Sturdivant	4.00	2.00	1.25
180	Bob Allison	4.00	2.00	1.25
181	Paul Brown	4.00	2.00	1.25
182	Bob Nieman	4.00	2.00	1.25
183	Roger Craig	4.00	2.00	1.25
184	Haywood Sullivan	4.00	2.00	1.25
185	Roland Sheldon	4.00	2.00	1.25
186	Mack Jones	4.00	2.00	1.25
187	Gene Conley	4.00	2.00	1.25
188	Chuck Hiller	4.00	2.00	1.25
189	Dick Hall	4.00	2.00	1.25
190a	Wally Moon (with cap.)	20.00	10.00	6.00
190b	Wally Moon (no cap.)	6.00	3.00	1.75
191	Jim Brewer	4.00	2.00	1.25
192a	3rd Series Checklist (177-264) (192 is Check List, 3)	7.00	3.50	2.00
192b	3rd Series Checklist (177-264) (192 is Check List 3)	8.00	4.00	2.50
193	Eddie Kasko	4.00	2.00	1.25
194	Dean Chance	12.50	6.25	3.75
195	Joe Cunningham	4.00	2.00	1.25
196	Terry Fox	4.00	2.00	1.25
197	Daryl Spencer	4.00	2.00	1.25
198	Johnny Keane	4.00	2.00	1.25
199	Gaylord Perry	55.00	27.50	16.50
200	Mickey Mantle	410.00	145.00	65.00
201	Ike Delock	4.00	2.00	1.25
202	Carl Warwick	4.00	2.00	1.25
203	Jack Fisher	4.00	2.00	1.25
204	Johnny Weekly	4.00	2.00	1.25
205	Gene Freese	4.00	2.00	1.25
206	Washington Senators Team	7.00	3.50	2.00
207	Pete Burnside	4.00	2.00	1.25
208	Billy Martin	12.00	6.00	3.50
209	Jim Fregosi	15.00	7.50	4.50
210	Roy Face	4.00	2.00	1.25
211	Midway Masters (Frank Bolling, Roy McMillan)	4.50	2.25	1.25
212	Jim Owens	4.00	2.00	1.25
213	Richie Ashburn	20.00	10.00	6.00
214	Dom Zanni	4.00	2.00	1.25
215	Woody Held	4.00	2.00	1.25
216	Ron Kline	4.00	2.00	1.25
217	Walt Alston	10.00	5.00	3.00
218	Joe Torre	55.00	27.50	16.50
219	Al Downing	12.00	6.00	3.50
220	Roy Sievers	4.00	2.00	1.25
221	Bill Short	4.00	2.00	1.25
222	Jerry Zimmerman	4.00	2.00	1.25
223	Alex Grammas	4.00	2.00	1.25
224	Don Rudolph	4.00	2.00	1.25
225	Frank Malzone	4.00	2.00	1.25
226	San Francisco Giants Team	7.00	3.50	2.00
227	Bobby Tiefenauer	4.00	2.00	1.25
228	Dale Long	4.00	2.00	1.25
229	Jesus McFarlane	4.00	2.00	1.25
230	Camilo Pascual	4.00	2.00	1.25
231	Ernie Bowman	4.00	2.00	1.25
232	World Series Game 1 (Yanks Win Opener)	8.00	4.00	2.50
233	World Series Game 2 (Jay Ties It Up)	10.00	5.00	3.00
234	World Series Game 3 (Maris Wins It In the 9th)	22.50	11.00	7.00
235	World Series Game 4 (Ford Sets New Mark)	17.50	8.75	5.25
236	World Series Game 5 (Yanks Crush Reds in Finale)	7.00	3.50	2.00
237	World Series (The Winners Celebrate)	10.00	5.00	3.00
238	Norm Sherry	4.00	2.00	1.25
239	Cecil Butler	4.00	2.00	1.25
240	George Altman	4.00	2.00	1.25
241	Johnny Kucks	4.00	2.00	1.25
242	Mel McGaha	4.00	2.00	1.25
243	Robin Roberts	15.00	7.50	4.50
244	Don Gile	4.00	2.00	1.25
245	Ron Hansen	4.00	2.00	1.25
246	Art Ditmar	4.00	2.00	1.25
247	Joe Pignatano	4.00	2.00	1.25
248	Bob Aspromonte	4.00	2.00	1.25
249	Ed Keegan	4.00	2.00	1.25
250	Norm Cash	12.00	6.00	3.50
251	New York Yankees Team	32.50	16.00	10.00
252	Earl Francis	4.00	2.00	1.25
253	Harry Chiti	4.00	2.00	1.25
254	Gordon Windhorn	4.00	2.00	1.25
255	Juan Pizarro	4.00	2.00	1.25
256	Elio Chacon	4.00	2.00	1.25
257	Jack Spring	4.00	2.00	1.25
258	Marty Keough	4.00	2.00	1.25
259	Lou Klimchock	4.00	2.00	1.25
260	Bill Pierce	4.00	2.00	1.25
261	George Alusik	4.00	2.00	1.25
262	Bob Schmidt	4.00	2.00	1.25
263	The Right Pitch (Joe Jay, Bob Purkey, Jim Turner)	4.50	2.25	1.25
264	Dick Ellsworth	4.00	2.00	1.25
265	Joe Adcock	4.00	2.00	1.25
266	John Anderson	4.00	2.00	1.25
267	Dan Dobbek	4.00	2.00	1.25
268	Ken McBride	4.00	2.00	1.25
269	Bob Oldis	4.00	2.00	1.25
270	Dick Groat	4.00	2.00	1.25
271	Ray Rippelmeyer	4.00	2.00	1.25
272	Earl Robinson	4.00	2.00	1.25
273	Gary Bell	4.00	2.00	1.25
274	Sammy Taylor	4.00	2.00	1.25
275	Norm Siebern	4.00	2.00	1.25
276	Hal Kostad	4.00	2.00	1.25
277	4th Series Checklist (265-352)	7.00	3.50	2.00
278	Ken Johnson	4.00	2.00	1.25
279	Hobie Landrith	4.00	2.00	1.25
280	Johnny Podres	7.50	3.75	2.25
281	Jake Gibbs	7.50	3.75	2.25
282	Dave Hillman	4.00	2.00	1.25
283	Charlie Smith	4.00	2.00	1.25
284	Ruben Amaro	4.00	2.00	1.25
285	Curt Simmons	4.00	2.00	1.25
286	Al Lopez	9.00	4.50	2.75
287	George Witt	4.00	2.00	1.25
288	Billy Williams	25.00	12.50	7.50
289	Mike Krsnich	4.00	2.00	1.25
290	Jim Gentile	6.00	3.00	1.75
291	Hal Stowe	4.00	2.00	1.25
292	Jerry Kindall	4.00	2.00	1.25
293	Bob Miller	4.00	2.00	1.25
294	Philadelphia Phillies Team	7.50	3.75	2.25
295	Vern Law	4.00	2.00	1.25
296	Ken Hamlin	4.00	2.00	1.25
297	Ron Perranoski	4.00	2.00	1.25
298	Bill Tuttle	4.00	2.00	1.25
299	Don Wert	4.00	2.00	1.25
300	Willie Mays	150.00	75.00	45.00
301	Galen Cisco	4.00	2.00	1.25
302	John Edwards	4.00	2.00	1.25
303	Frank Torre	4.00	2.00	1.25
304	Dick Farrell	4.00	2.00	1.25
305	Jerry Lumpe	4.00	2.00	1.25
306	Redbird Rippers (Larry Jackson, Lindy McDaniel)	5.00	2.50	1.50
307	Jim Grant	4.00	2.00	1.25
308	Neil Chrisley	4.00	2.00	1.25
309	Moe Morhardt	4.00	2.00	1.25
310	Whitey Ford	32.50	16.00	10.00
311	Kubek Makes The Double Play (Tony Kubek)	12.00	6.00	3.50
312	Spahn Shows No-Hit Form (Warren Spahn)	15.00	7.50	4.50
313	Maris Blasts 61st (Roger Maris)	40.00	20.00	12.00
314	Colavito's Power (Rocky Colavito)	11.00	5.50	3.25
315	Ford Tosses a Curve (Whitey Ford)	20.00	10.00	6.00
316	Killebrew Sends One into Orbit (Harmon Killebrew)	20.00	10.00	6.00
317	Musial Plays 21st Season (Stan Musial)	17.50	8.75	5.25
318	The Switch Hitter Connects (Mickey Mantle)	90.00	45.00	25.00
319	McCormick Shows His Stuff (Mike McCormick)	6.00	3.00	1.75
320	Hank Aaron	100.00	50.00	30.00
321	Lee Stange	4.00	2.00	1.25
322	Al Dark	4.00	2.00	1.25
323	Don Landrum	4.00	2.00	1.25
324	Joe McClain	4.00	2.00	1.25
325	Luis Aparicio	15.00	7.50	4.50
326	Tom Parsons	4.00	2.00	1.25
327	Ozzie Virgil	4.00	2.00	1.25
328	Ken Walters	4.00	2.00	1.25
329	Bob Bolin	4.00	2.00	1.25
330	Johnny Romano	4.00	2.00	1.25
331	Moe Drabowsky	4.00	2.00	1.25
332	Don Buddin	4.00	2.00	1.25
333	Frank Cipriani	4.00	2.00	1.25
334	Boston Red Sox Team	9.00	4.50	2.75
335	Bill Bruton	4.00	2.00	1.25
336	Billy Muffett	4.00	2.00	1.25
337	Jim Marshall	4.00	2.00	1.25
338	Billy Gardner	4.00	2.00	1.25
339	Jose Valdivielso	4.00	2.00	1.25
340	Don Drysdale	30.00	15.00	9.00
341	Mike Hershberger	4.00	2.00	1.25
342	Ed Rakow	4.00	2.00	1.25
343	Albie Pearson	4.00	2.00	1.25
344	Ed Bauta	4.00	2.00	1.25
345	Chuck Schilling	4.00	2.00	1.25
346	Jack Kralick	4.00	2.00	1.25
347	Chuck Hinton	4.00	2.00	1.25
348	Larry Burright	4.00	2.00	1.25
349	Paul Foytack	4.00	2.00	1.25
350	Frank Robinson	40.00	20.00	12.00
351	Braves' Backstops (Del Crandall, Joe Torre)	12.00	6.00	3.50
352	Frank Sullivan	4.00	2.00	1.25
353	Bill Mazeroski	20.00	10.00	6.00
354	Roman Mejias	4.00	2.00	1.25
355	Steve Barber	4.00	2.00	1.25
356	Tom Haller	4.00	2.00	1.25
357	Jerry Walker	4.00	2.00	1.25
358	Tommy Davis	4.00	2.00	1.25
359	Bobby Locke	4.00	2.00	1.25
360	Yogi Berra	50.00	25.00	15.00
361	Bob Hendley	4.00	2.00	1.25
362	Ty Cline	4.00	2.00	1.25
363	Bob Roselli	4.00	2.00	1.25
364	Ken Hunt	4.00	2.00	1.25
365	Charley Neal	4.00	2.00	1.25
366	Phil Regan	4.00	2.00	1.25
367	5th Checklist (353-429)	8.00	4.00	2.50
368	Bob Tillman	4.00	2.00	1.25
369	Ted Bowsfield	4.00	2.00	1.25
370	Ken Boyer	7.50	3.75	2.25
371	Earl Battey	4.00	2.00	1.25
372	Jack Curtis	4.00	2.00	1.25
373	Al Heist	4.00	2.00	1.25
374	Gene Mauch	4.00	2.00	1.25
375	Ron Fairly	4.00	2.00	1.25
376	Bud Daley	4.00	2.00	1.25
377	Johnny Orsino	4.00	2.00	1.25
378	Bennie Daniels	4.00	2.00	1.25
379	Chuck Essegian	4.00	2.00	1.25
380	Lou Burdette	4.00	2.00	1.25
381	Chico Cardenas	4.00	2.00	1.25
382	Dick Williams	4.00	2.00	1.25
383	Ray Sadecki	4.00	2.00	1.25
384	Kansas City Athletics Team	8.00	4.00	2.50
385	Early Wynn	12.00	6.00	3.50

		NM	EX	VG
386	Don Mincher	4.00	2.00	1.25
387	*Lou Brock*	95.00	45.00	25.00
388	Ryne Duren	4.00	2.00	1.25
389	Smoky Burgess	4.00	2.00	-1.25
390	Orlando Cepeda (All-Star)	10.00	5.00	3.00
391	Bill Mazeroski (All-Star)	12.00	6.00	3.50
392	Ken Boyer (All-Star)	7.00	3.50	2.00
393	Roy McMillan (All-Star)	4.00	2.00	1.25
394	Hank Aaron (All-Star)	32.50	16.00	10.00
395	Willie Mays (All-Star)	32.50	16.00	10.00
396	Frank Robinson (All-Star)	13.50	6.75	4.00
397	John Roseboro (All-Star)	4.00	2.00	1.25
398	Don Drysdale (All-Star)	13.50	6.75	4.00
399	Warren Spahn (All-Star)	13.50	6.75	4.00
400	Elston Howard	11.00	7.50	4.50
401	AL & NL Homer Kings (Roger Maris, Orlando Cepeda)	45.00	22.50	13.50
402	Gino Cimoli	4.00	2.00	1.25
403	Chet Nichols	4.00	2.00	1.25
404	Tim Harkness	4.00	2.00	1.25
405	Jim Perry	4.00	2.00	1.25
406	Bob Taylor	4.00	2.00	1.25
407	Hank Aguirre	4.00	2.00	1.25
408	Gus Bell	4.00	2.00	1.25
409	Pittsburgh Pirates Team	11.00	5.50	3.25
410	Al Smith	4.00	2.00	1.25
411	Danny O'Connell	4.00	2.00	1.25
412	Charlie James	4.00	2.00	1.25
413	Matty Alou	4.00	2.00	1.25
414	Joe Gaines	4.00	2.00	1.25
415	Bill Virdon	4.00	2.00	1.25
416	Bob Scheffing	4.00	2.00	1.25
417	Joe Azcue	4.00	2.00	1.25
418	Andy Carey	4.00	2.00	1.25
419	Bob Bruce	4.00	2.00	1.25
420	Gus Triandos	4.00	2.00	1.25
421	Ken MacKenzie	4.00	2.00	1.25
422	Steve Bilko	4.00	2.00	1.25
423	Rival League Relief Aces (Roy Face, Hoyt Wilhelm)	9.00	4.50	2.75
424	Al McBean	4.00	2.00	1.25
425	Carl Yastrzemski	75.00	37.50	22.00
426	Bob Farley	4.00	2.00	1.25
427	Jake Wood	4.00	2.00	1.25
428	Joe Hicks	4.00	2.00	1.25
429	Bill O'Dell	4.00	2.00	1.25
430	Tony Kubek	15.00	7.50	4.50
431	*Bob Rodgers*	4.00	2.00	1.25
432	Jim Pendleton	4.00	2.00	1.25
433	Jim Archer	4.00	2.00	1.25
434	Clay Dalrymple	4.00	2.00	1.25
435	Larry Sherry	4.00	2.00	1.25
436	Felix Mantilla	4.00	2.00	1.25
437	Ray Moore	4.00	2.00	1.25
438	Dick Brown	4.00	2.00	1.25
439	Jerry Buchek	4.00	2.00	1.25
440	Joe Jay	4.00	2.00	1.25
441a	6th Series Checklist (430-506) (Large "CHECKLIST.")	9.00	4.50	2.75
441b	6th Series Checklist (430-506) (Small "CHECKLIST.")	9.00	4.50	2.75
442	Wes Stock	4.00	2.00	1.25
443	Del Crandall	4.00	2.00	1.25
444	Ted Wills	4.00	2.00	1.25
445	Vic Power	4.00	2.00	1.25
446	Don Elston	4.00	2.00	1.25
447	Willie Kirkland	7.00	3.50	2.00
448	Joe Gibbon	7.00	3.50	2.00
449	Jerry Adair	7.00	3.50	2.00
450	Jim O'Toole	7.00	3.50	2.00
451	*Jose Tartabull*	7.00	3.50	2.00
452	Earl Averill	7.00	3.50	2.00
453	Cal McLish	7.00	3.50	2.00
454	Floyd Robinson	7.00	3.50	2.00
455	Luis Arroyo	7.00	3.50	2.00
456	Joe Amalfitano	7.00	3.50	2.00
457	Lou Clinton	7.00	3.50	2.00
458a	Bob Buhl ("M" on cap.)	17.50	8.75	5.25
458b	Bob Buhl (plain cap.)	15.00	7.50	4.50
459	Ed Bailey	7.00	3.50	2.00
460	Jim Bunning	20.00	10.00	6.00
461	*Ken Hubbs*	15.00	7.50	4.50
462a	Willie Tasby ("W" on cap.)	17.50	8.75	5.25
462b	Willie Tasby (plain cap.)	16.00	8.00	4.75
463	Hank Bauer	9.00	4.50	2.75
464	*Al Jackson*	7.00	3.50	2.00
465	Cincinnati Reds Team	11.00	5.50	3.25
466	Norm Cash (All-Star)	13.50	6.75	4.00
467	Chuck Schilling (All-Star)	7.00	3.50	2.00
468	Brooks Robinson (All-Star)	15.00	7.50	4.50
469	Luis Aparicio (All-Star)	11.00	5.50	3.25
470	Al Kaline (All-Star)	20.00	10.00	6.00
471	Mickey Mantle (All-Star)	125.00	60.00	35.00
472	Rocky Colavito (All-Star)	12.00	6.00	3.50
473	Elston Howard (All-Star)	10.00	5.00	3.00
474	Frank Lary (All-Star)	7.00	3.50	2.00
475	Whitey Ford (All-Star)	15.00	7.50	4.50
476	Baltimore Orioles Team	12.50	6.25	3.75
477	Andre Rodgers	7.00	3.50	2.00
478	Don Zimmer	12.50	6.25	3.75
479	*Joel Horlen*	7.00	3.50	2.00
480	Harvey Kuenn	7.00	3.50	2.00
481	Vic Wertz	7.00	3.50	2.00
482	Sam Mele	7.00	3.50	2.00
483	Don McMahon	7.00	3.50	2.00
484	Dick Schofield	7.00	3.50	2.00
485	Pedro Ramos	7.00	3.50	2.00
486	Jim Gilliam	12.00	6.00	3.50
487	Jerry Lynch	7.00	3.50	2.00
488	Hal Brown	7.00	3.50	2.00
489	Julio Gotay	7.00	3.50	2.00
490	Clete Boyer	13.50	6.75	4.00
491	Leon Wagner	7.00	3.50	2.00
492	Hal Smith	7.00	3.50	2.00
493	Danny McDevitt	7.00	3.50	2.00
494	Sammy White	7.00	3.50	2.00
495	Don Cardwell	7.00	3.50	2.00
496	Wayne Causey	7.00	3.50	2.00
497	Ed Bouchee	7.00	3.50	2.00
498	Jim Donohue	7.00	3.50	2.00
499	Zoilo Versalles	7.00	3.50	2.00
500	Duke Snider	40.00	20.00	12.00
501	Claude Osteen	7.00	3.50	2.00
502	Hector Lopez	7.00	3.50	2.00
503	Danny Murtaugh	7.00	3.50	2.00
504	Eddie Bressoud	7.00	3.50	2.00
505	Juan Marichal	30.00	15.00	9.00
506	Charley Maxwell	7.00	3.50	2.00
507	Ernie Broglio	7.00	3.50	2.00
508	Gordy Coleman	7.00	3.50	2.00
509	*Dave Giusti*	7.00	3.50	2.00
510	Jim Lemon	7.00	3.50	2.00
511	Bubba Phillips	7.00	3.50	2.00
512	Mike Fornieles	7.00	3.50	2.00
513	Whitey Herzog	7.00	3.50	2.00
514	Sherm Lollar	7.00	3.50	2.00
515	Stan Williams	7.00	3.50	2.00
516a	7th Series Checklist (507-598) (Boxes are yellow.)	9.00	4.50	2.75
516b	7th Series Checklist (507-598) (Boxes are white.)	9.00	4.50	2.75
517	Dave Wickersham	7.00	3.50	2.00
518	Lee Maye	7.00	3.50	2.00
519	Bob Johnson	7.00	3.50	2.00
520	Bob Friend	7.00	3.50	2.00
521	Jacke Davis	7.00	3.50	2.00
522	Lindy McDaniel	7.00	3.50	2.00
523	Russ Nixon/SP	15.00	7.50	4.50
524	Howie Nunn/SP	15.00	7.50	4.50
525	George Thomas	10.00	5.00	3.00
526	Hal Woodeshick/SP	15.00	7.50	4.50
527	*Dick McAuliffe*	10.00	5.00	3.00
528	Turk Lown	10.00	5.00	3.00
529	John Schaive/SP	15.00	7.50	4.50
530	Bob Gibson	85.00	42.50	25.00
531	Bobby G. Smith	10.00	5.00	3.00
532	Dick Stigman	10.00	5.00	3.00
533	Charley Lau/SP	15.00	7.50	4.50
534	Tony Gonzalez/SP	15.00	7.50	4.50
535	Ed Roebuck	10.00	5.00	3.00
536	Dick Gernert	10.00	5.00	3.00
537	Cleveland Indians Team	20.00	10.00	6.00
538	Jack Sanford	10.00	5.00	3.00
539	Billy Moran	10.00	5.00	3.00
540	Jim Landis/SP	15.00	7.50	4.50
541	Don Nottebart/SP	15.00	7.50	4.50
542	Dave Philley	10.00	5.00	3.00
543	Bob Allen/SP	15.00	7.50	4.50
544	Willie McCovey/SP	70.00	35.00	20.00
545	Hoyt Wilhelm/SP	40.00	20.00	12.00
546	Moe Thacker/SP	15.00	7.50	4.50
547	Don Ferrarese	10.00	5.00	3.00
548	Bobby Del Greco	10.00	5.00	3.00
549	Bill Rigney/SP	15.00	7.50	4.50
550	Art Mahaffey/SP	15.00	7.50	4.50
551	Harry Bright	10.00	5.00	3.00
552	Chicago Cubs Team /SP	35.00	17.50	10.00
553	Jim Coates	10.00	5.00	3.00
554	Bubba Morton/SP	15.00	7.50	4.50
555	John Buzhardt/SP	15.00	7.50	4.50
556	Al Spangler	10.00	5.00	3.00
557	Bob Anderson/SP	15.00	7.50	4.50
558	John Goryl	10.00	5.00	3.00
559	Mike Higgins	10.00	5.00	3.00
560	Chuck Estrada/SP	15.00	7.50	4.50
561	Gene Oliver/SP	15.00	7.50	4.50
562	Bill Henry	10.00	5.00	3.00
563	Ken Aspromonte	10.00	5.00	3.00
564	Bob Grim	10.00	5.00	3.00
565	Jose Pagan	10.00	5.00	3.00
566	Marty Kutyna/SP	15.00	7.50	4.50
567	Tracy Stallard/SP	15.00	7.50	4.50
568	Jim Golden	10.00	5.00	3.00
569	Ed Sadowski/SP	15.00	7.50	4.50
570	Bill Stafford	10.00	5.00	3.00
571	Billy Klaus/SP	15.00	7.50	4.50
572	Bob Miller/SP	15.00	7.50	4.50
573	Johnny Logan	10.00	5.00	3.00
574	Dean Stone	10.00	5.00	3.00
575	Red Schoendienst	25.00	12.50	7.50
576	Russ Kemmerer/SP	15.00	7.50	4.50
577	Dave Nicholson/SP	15.00	7.50	4.50
578	Jim Duffalo	10.00	5.00	3.00
579	Jim Schaffer/SP	15.00	7.50	4.50
580	Bill Monbouquette	10.00	5.00	3.00
581	Mel Roach	10.00	5.00	3.00
582	Ron Piche	10.00	5.00	3.00
583	Larry Osborne	10.00	5.00	3.00
584	Minnesota Twins Team /SP	40.00	20.00	12.00
585	Glen Hobbie/SP	15.00	7.50	4.50
586	Sammy Esposito/SP	15.00	7.50	4.50
587	Frank Funk/SP	15.00	7.50	4.50
588	Birdie Tebbetts	10.00	5.00	3.00
589	Bob Turley	17.50	8.75	5.25
590	Curt Flood	17.50	8.75	5.25
591	Rookie Parade Pitchers (*Sam McDowell, Ron Nischwitz, Art Quirk, Dick Radatz, Ron Taylor*)	40.00	20.00	12.00
592	Rookie Parade Pitchers (Bo Belinsky, Joe Bonikowski, Jim Bouton, Dan Pfister, Dave Stenhouse)	45.00	22.50	13.50
593	Rookie Parade Pitchers (*Craig Anderson, Jack Hamilton, Jack Lamabe, Bob Moorhead, Bob Veale*)	40.00	20.00	12.00
594	Rookie Parade Catchers (*Doug Camilli, Doc Edwards, Don Pavletich, Ken Retzer, Bob Uecker*)	65.00	32.50	20.00
595	Rookie Parade Infielders (Ed Charles, Marlin Coughtry, Bob Sadowski, Felix Torres)	25.00	12.50	7.50
596	Rookie Parade Infielders (*Bernie Allen, Phil Linz, Joe Pepitone, Rich Rollins*)	55.00	27.50	16.50
597	Rookie Parade Infielders (Rod Kanehl, Jim McKnight, Denis Menke, Amado Samuel)	40.00	20.00	12.00
598	Rookie Parade Outfielders (*Howie Goss, Jim Hickman, Manny Jimenez, Al Luplow, Ed Olivares*)	70.00	20.00	12.00

1962 Topps Baseball Bucks

Issued in their own 1-cent package, "Baseball Bucks" measure 4-1/8" x 1-3/4", were printed in black on green paper and designed to resemble dollar bills. The center player portrait has a banner underneath with the player's name. His home park is shown on the right and there is some biographical information at left. The back features a large denomination, with the player's league and team logo on either side. Poorly centered examples of this issue are the rule, rather than the exception. Sixty-two of the players appear on facsimile $1 notes. There are 24 $5 stars and 10 $10 superstars. Baseball Bucks are graded without regard to the vertical fold with which they were issued.

		NM	EX	VG
	Complete Set (96):	2,000	1,000	600.00
	Common Player:	7.50	3.75	2.25
	Wax Pack:	175.00		
(1)	Hank Aaron ($5)	50.00	25.00	15.00
(2)	Joe Adcock	7.50	3.75	2.25
(3)	George Altman	7.50	3.75	2.25
(4)	Jim Archer	7.50	3.75	2.25
(5)	Richie Ashburn ($5)	40.00	20.00	12.00
(6)	Ernie Banks ($10)	45.00	22.00	13.50
(7)	Earl Battey	7.50	3.75	2.25
(8)	Gus Bell	7.50	3.75	2.25
(9)	Yogi Berra ($5)	40.00	20.00	12.00
(10)	Ken Boyer ($10)	15.00	7.50	4.50
(11)	Jackie Brandt	7.50	3.75	2.25
(12)	Jim Bunning	15.00	7.50	4.50
(13)	Lou Burdette ($5)	7.50	3.75	2.25
(14)	Don Cardwell	7.50	3.75	2.25
(15)	Norm Cash ($5)	15.00	7.50	4.50
(16)	Orlando Cepeda ($5)	30.00	15.00	9.00
(17)	Roberto Clemente ($5)	200.00	100.00	60.00
(18)	Rocky Colavito ($5)	25.00	12.50	7.50
(19)	Chuck Cottier	7.50	3.75	2.25
(20)	Roger Craig	7.50	3.75	2.25
(21)	Bennie Daniels	7.50	3.75	2.25
(22)	Don Demeter	7.50	3.75	2.25
(23)	Don Drysdale	30.00	15.00	9.00
(24)	Chuck Estrada	7.50	3.75	2.25
(25)	Dick Farrell	7.50	3.75	2.25
(26)	Whitey Ford ($10)	40.00	20.00	12.00
(27)	Nellie Fox ($5)	30.00	15.00	9.00
(28)	Tito Francona	7.50	3.75	2.25
(29)	Bob Friend	7.50	3.75	2.25
(30)	Jim Gentile ($5)	15.00	7.50	4.50
(31)	Dick Gernert	7.50	3.75	2.25
(32)	Lenny Green	7.50	3.75	2.25
(33)	Dick Groat	7.50	3.75	2.25
(34)	Woody Held	7.50	3.75	2.25
(35)	Don Hoak	7.50	3.75	2.25
(36)	Gil Hodges ($5)	25.00	12.50	7.50
(37)	Frank Howard	10.00	5.00	3.00
(38)	Elston Howard	10.00	5.00	3.00
(39)	Dick Howser	7.50	3.75	2.25
(40)	Ken Hunt	7.50	3.75	2.25
(41)	Larry Jackson	7.50	3.75	2.25
(42)	Joe Jay	7.50	3.75	2.25
(43)	Al Kaline	30.00	15.00	9.00
(44)	Harmon Killebrew ($5)	40.00	20.00	12.00
(45)	Sandy Koufax ($5)	75.00	37.00	22.00
(46)	Harvey Kuenn	7.50	3.75	2.25
(47)	Jim Landis	7.50	3.75	2.25
(48)	Norm Larker	7.50	3.75	2.25
(49)	Frank Lary ($5)	7.50	3.75	2.25
(50)	Jerry Lumpe	7.50	3.75	2.25
(51)	Art Mahaffey	7.50	3.75	2.25
(52)	Frank Malzone	7.50	3.75	2.25
(53)	Felix Mantilla	7.50	3.75	2.25
(54)	Mickey Mantle ($10)	350.00	175.00	105.00
(55)	Roger Maris ($10)	45.00	22.00	13.50
(56)	Ed Mathews ($10)	35.00	17.50	10.50
(57)	Willie Mays ($10)	65.00	32.00	19.50
(58)	Ken McBride	7.50	3.75	2.25
(59)	Mike McCormick	7.50	3.75	2.25

		NM	EX	VG
(60)	Stu Miller	7.50	3.75	2.25
(61)	Minnie Minoso	10.00	5.00	3.00
(62)	Wally Moon ($5)	7.50	3.75	2.25
(63)	Stan Musial ($10)	60.00	30.00	18.00
(64)	Danny O'Connell	7.50	3.75	2.25
(65)	Jim O'Toole	7.50	3.75	2.25
(66)	Camilo Pascual ($5)	7.50	3.75	2.25
(67)	Jim Perry	7.50	3.75	2.25
(68)	Jimmy Piersall ($5)	12.00	6.00	3.50
(69)	Vada Pinson ($5)	12.00	6.00	3.50
(70)	Juan Pizarro	7.50	3.75	2.25
(71)	Johnny Podres	10.00	5.00	3.00
(72)	Vic Power ($5)	7.50	3.75	2.25
(73)	Bob Purkey	7.50	3.75	2.25
(74)	Pedro Ramos	7.50	3.75	2.25
(75)	Brooks Robinson ($5)	30.00	15.00	9.00
(76)	Floyd Robinson	7.50	3.75	2.25
(77)	Frank Robinson ($10)	35.00	17.50	10.50
(78)	Johnny Romano	7.50	3.75	2.25
(79)	Pete Runnels ($5)	7.50	3.75	2.25
(80)	Don Schwall	7.50	3.75	2.25
(81)	Bobby Shantz ($5)	7.50	3.75	2.25
(82)	Norm Siebern	7.50	3.75	2.25
(83)	Roy Sievers ($5)	7.50	3.75	2.25
(84)	Hal (W.) Smith	7.50	3.75	2.25
(85)	Warren Spahn ($10)	40.00	20.00	12.00
(86)	Dick Stuart	7.50	3.75	2.25
(87)	Tony Taylor	7.50	3.75	2.25
(88)	Lee Thomas	7.50	3.75	2.25
(89)	Gus Triandos	7.50	3.75	2.25
(90)	Leon Wagner	7.50	3.75	2.25
(91)	Jerry Walker	7.50	3.75	2.25
(92)	Bill White	7.50	3.75	2.25
(93)	Billy Williams	15.00	7.50	4.50
(94)	Gene Woodling	7.50	3.75	2.25
(95)	Early Wynn ($5)	15.00	7.50	4.50
(96)	Carl Yastrzemski	40.00	20.00	12.00

1962 Topps Stamps

CARL YASTRZEMSKI
BOST. RED SOX   OUTFIELD

An artistic improvement over the somewhat drab Topps stamps of the previous year, the 1962 stamps, 1-3/8" x 1-7/8", had color player photographs set on red or yellow backgrounds. As in 1961, they were issued in two-stamp panels as insert with Topps baseball cards. A change from 1961 was the inclusion of team emblems in the set. A complete set consists of 201 stamps; Roy Sievers was originally portrayed on the wrong team - Athletics - and was later corrected to the Phillies.

		NM	EX	VG
Complete Set (200):		800.00	400.00	240.00
Common Player:		3.00	1.50	.90
Stamp Album (Red):		60.00	30.00	18.00
(1)	Hank Aaron	15.00	7.50	4.50
(2)	Jerry Adair	3.00	1.50	.90
(3)	Joe Adcock	3.00	1.50	.90
(4)	Bob Allison	3.00	1.50	.90
(5)	Felipe Alou	4.00	2.00	1.25
(6)	George Altman	3.00	1.50	.90
(7)	Joe Amalfitano	3.00	1.50	.90
(8)	Ruben Amaro	3.00	1.50	.90
(9)	Luis Aparicio	6.00	3.00	1.75
(10)	Jim Archer	3.00	1.50	.90
(11)	Bob Aspromonte	3.00	1.50	.90
(12)	Ed Bailey	3.00	1.50	.90
(13)	Jack Baldschun	3.00	1.50	.90
(14)	Ernie Banks	9.00	4.50	2.75
(15)	Earl Battey	3.00	1.50	.90
(16)	Gus Bell	3.00	1.50	.90
(17)	Yogi Berra	12.00	6.00	3.50
(18)	Dick Bertell	3.00	1.50	.90
(19)	Steve Bilko	3.00	1.50	.90
(20)	Frank Bolling	3.00	1.50	.90
(21)	Steve Boros	3.00	1.50	.90
(22)	Ted Bowsfield	3.00	1.50	.90
(23)	Clete Boyer	3.00	1.50	.90
(24)	Ken Boyer	4.00	2.00	1.25
(25)	Jackie Brandt	3.00	1.50	.90
(26)	Bill Bruton	3.00	1.50	.90
(27)	Jim Bunning	6.00	3.00	1.75
(28)	Lou Burdette	3.00	1.50	.90
(29)	Smoky Burgess	3.00	1.50	.90
(30)	Johnny Callizon (Callison)	3.00	1.50	.90
(31)	Don Cardwell	3.00	1.50	.90
(32)	Camilo Carreon	3.00	1.50	.90
(33)	Norm Cash	4.00	2.00	1.25
(34)	Orlando Cepeda	6.00	3.00	1.75
(35)	Roberto Clemente	20.00	10.00	6.00
(36)	Ty Cline	3.00	1.50	.90
(37)	Rocky Colavito	6.00	3.00	1.75
(38)	Gordon Coleman	3.00	1.50	.90
(39)	Chuck Cottier	3.00	1.50	.90
(40)	Roger Craig	3.00	1.50	.90

		NM	EX	VG
(41)	Del Crandall	3.00	1.50	.90
(42)	Pete Daley	3.00	1.50	.90
(43)	Clay Dalrymple	3.00	1.50	.90
(44)	Bennie Daniels	3.00	1.50	.90
(45)	Jim Davenport	3.00	1.50	.90
(46)	Don Demeter	3.00	1.50	.90
(47)	Dick Donovan	3.00	1.50	.90
(48)	Don Drysdale	10.00	5.00	3.00
(49)	John Edwards	3.00	1.50	.90
(50)	Dick Ellsworth	3.00	1.50	.90
(51)	Chuck Estrada	3.00	1.50	.90
(52)	Roy Face	3.00	1.50	.90
(53)	Ron Fairly	3.00	1.50	.90
(54)	Dick Farrell	3.00	1.50	.90
(55)	Whitey Ford	12.00	6.00	3.50
(56)	Mike Fornieles	3.00	1.50	.90
(57)	Nellie Fox	7.00	3.50	2.00
(58)	Tito Francona	3.00	1.50	.90
(59)	Gene Freese	3.00	1.50	.90
(60)	Bob Friend	3.00	1.50	.90
(61)	Gary Geiger	3.00	1.50	.90
(62)	Jim Gentile	3.00	1.50	.90
(63)	Tony Gonzalez	3.00	1.50	.90
(64)	Lenny Green	3.00	1.50	.90
(65)	Dick Groat	3.00	1.50	.90
(66)	Ron Hansen	3.00	1.50	.90
(67)	Al Heist	3.00	1.50	.90
(68)	Woody Held	3.00	1.50	.90
(69)	Ray Herbert	3.00	1.50	.90
(70)	Chuck Hinton	3.00	1.50	.90
(71)	Don Hoak	3.00	1.50	.90
(72)	Glen Hobbie	3.00	1.50	.90
(73)	Gil Hodges	6.00	3.00	1.75
(74)	Jay Hook	3.00	1.50	.90
(75)	Elston Howard	4.00	2.00	1.25
(76)	Frank Howard	3.00	1.50	.90
(77)	Dick Howser	3.00	1.50	.90
(78)	Ken Hunt	3.00	1.50	.90
(79)	Larry Jackson	3.00	1.50	.90
(80)	Julian Javier	3.00	1.50	.90
(81)	Joe Jay	3.00	1.50	.90
(82)	Bob Johnson	3.00	1.50	.90
(83)	Sam Jones	3.00	1.50	.90
(84)	Al Kaline	9.00	4.50	2.75
(85)	Eddie Kasko	3.00	1.50	.90
(86)	Harmon Killebrew	10.00	5.00	3.00
(87)	Sandy Koufax	15.00	7.50	4.50
(88)	Jack Kralick	3.00	1.50	.90
(89)	Tony Kubek	4.00	2.00	1.25
(90)	Harvey Kuenn	3.00	1.50	.90
(91)	Jim Landis	3.00	1.50	.90
(92)	Hobie Landrith	3.00	1.50	.90
(93)	Frank Lary	3.00	1.50	.90
(94)	Barry Latman	3.00	1.50	.90
(95)	Jerry Lumpe	3.00	1.50	.90
(96)	Art Mahaffey	3.00	1.50	.90
(97)	Frank Malzone	3.00	1.50	.90
(98)	Felix Mantilla	3.00	1.50	.90
(99)	Mickey Mantle	50.00	25.00	15.00
(100)	Juan Marichal	6.00	3.00	1.75
(101)	Roger Maris	13.50	6.75	4.00
(102)	J.C. Martin	3.00	1.50	.90
(103)	Ed Mathews	9.00	4.50	2.75
(104)	Willie Mays	15.00	7.50	4.50
(105)	Bill Mazeroski	6.00	3.00	1.75
(106)	Ken McBride	3.00	1.50	.90
(107)	Tim McCarver	3.00	1.50	.90
(108)	Joe McClain	3.00	1.50	.90
(109)	Mike McCormick	3.00	1.50	.90
(110)	Lindy McDaniel	3.00	1.50	.90
(111)	Roy McMillan	3.00	1.50	.90
(112)	Bob L. Miller	3.00	1.50	.90
(113)	Stu Miller	3.00	1.50	.90
(114)	Minnie Minoso	6.00	3.00	1.75
(115)	Bill Monbouquette	3.00	1.50	.90
(116)	Wally Moon	3.00	1.50	.90
(117)	Don Mossi	3.00	1.50	.90
(118)	Stan Musial	15.00	7.50	4.50
(119)	Russ Nixon	3.00	1.50	.90
(120)	Danny O'Connell	3.00	1.50	.90
(121)	Jim O'Toole	3.00	1.50	.90
(122)	Milt Pappas	3.00	1.50	.90
(123)	Camilo Pascual	3.00	1.50	.90
(124)	Albie Pearson	3.00	1.50	.90
(125)	Jim Perry	3.00	1.50	.90
(126)	Bubba Phillips	3.00	1.50	.90
(127)	Jimmy Piersall	3.00	1.50	.90
(128)	Vada Pinson	3.00	1.50	.90
(129)	Juan Pizarro	3.00	1.50	.90
(130)	Johnny Podres	3.00	1.50	.90
(131)	Leo Posada	3.00	1.50	.90
(132)	Vic Power	3.00	1.50	.90
(133)	Bob Purkey	3.00	1.50	.90
(134)	Pedro Ramos	3.00	1.50	.90
(135)	Bobby Richardson	4.00	2.00	1.25
(136)	Brooks Robinson	10.00	5.00	3.00
(137)	Floyd Robinson	3.00	1.50	.90
(138)	Frank Robinson	10.00	5.00	3.00
(139)	Bob Rodgers	3.00	1.50	.90
(140)	Johnny Romano	3.00	1.50	.90
(141)	John Roseboro	3.00	1.50	.90
(142)	Pete Runnels	3.00	1.50	.90
(143)	Ray Sadecki	3.00	1.50	.90
(144)	Ron Santo	3.00	1.50	.90
(145)	Chuck Schilling	3.00	1.50	.90
(146)	Barney Schultz	3.00	1.50	.90
(147)	Don Schwall	3.00	1.50	.90
(148)	Bobby Shantz	3.00	1.50	.90
(149)	Bob Shaw	3.00	1.50	.90
(150)	Norm Siebern	3.00	1.50	.90
(151a)	Roy Sievers (Kansas City)	4.00	2.00	1.25
(151b)	Roy Sievers (Philadelphia)	3.00	1.50	.90
(152)	Bill Skowron	4.00	2.00	1.25
(153)	Hal (W.) Smith	3.00	1.50	.90
(154)	Duke Snider	12.00	6.00	3.50
(155)	Warren Spahn	9.00	4.50	2.75
(156)	Al Spangler	3.00	1.50	.90
(157)	Daryl Spencer	3.00	1.50	.90

		NM	EX	VG
(158)	Gene Stephens	3.00	1.50	.90
(159)	Dick Stuart	3.00	1.50	.90
(160)	Haywood Sullivan	3.00	1.50	.90
(161)	Tony Taylor	3.00	1.50	.90
(162)	George Thomas	3.00	1.50	.90
(163)	Lee Thomas	3.00	1.50	.90
(164)	Bob Tiefenauer	3.00	1.50	.90
(165)	Joe Torre	6.00	3.00	1.75
(166)	Gus Triandos	3.00	1.50	.90
(167)	Bill Tuttle	3.00	1.50	.90
(168)	Zoilo Versalles	3.00	1.50	.90
(169)	Bill Virdon	3.00	1.50	.90
(170)	Leon Wagner	3.00	1.50	.90
(171)	Jerry Walker	3.00	1.50	.90
(172)	Lee Walls	3.00	1.50	.90
(173)	Bill White	3.00	1.50	.90
(174)	Hoyt Wilhelm	4.00	2.00	1.25
(175)	Billy Williams	6.00	3.00	1.75
(176)	Jake Wood	3.00	1.50	.90
(177)	Gene Woodling	3.00	1.50	.90
(178)	Early Wynn	4.00	2.00	1.25
(179)	Carl Yastrzemski	12.00	6.00	3.50
(180)	Don Zimmer	3.00	1.50	.90
(181)	Baltimore Orioles Logo	3.00	1.50	.90
(182)	Boston Red Sox Logo	3.00	1.50	.90
(183)	Chicago Cubs Logo	3.00	1.50	.90
(184)	Chicago White Sox Logo	3.00	1.50	.90
(185)	Cincinnati Reds Logo	3.00	1.50	.90
(186)	Cleveland Indians Logo	3.00	1.50	.90
(187)	Detroit Tigers Logo	3.00	1.50	.90
(188)	Houston Colts Logo	3.00	1.50	.90
(189)	Kansas City Athletics Logo	3.00	1.50	.90
(190)	Los Angeles Angels Logo	3.00	1.50	.90
(191)	Los Angeles Dodgers Logo	3.00	1.50	.90
(192)	Milwaukee Braves Logo	3.00	1.50	.90
(193)	Minnesota Twins Logo	3.00	1.50	.90
(194)	New York Mets Logo	3.00	1.50	.90
(195)	New York Yankees Logo	6.00	3.00	1.75
(196)	Philadelphia Phillies Logo	3.00	1.50	.90
(197)	Pittsburgh Pirates Logo	3.00	1.50	.90
(198)	St. Louis Cardinals Logo	3.00	1.50	.90
(199)	San Francisco Giants Logo	3.00	1.50	.90
(200)	Washington Senators Logo	3.00	1.50	.90

1962 Topps Stamps Panels

ELSTON HOWARD
N.Y. YANKEES   CATCHER

BOB CLEMENTE
PITT. PIRATES   OUTFIELD

Some advanced collectors pursue the 1962 Topps stamps in the form of the two-stamp panels in which they were issued. The 200 different stamps which make up the issue can be found on 245 different two-stamp panels, flanked at left by a smaller tab advertising the accompanying album. The unnumbered stamps are listed here alphabetically according to the name of the player or team which appears on the left end of the panel. Values shown are for full three-piece panels.

		NM	EX	VG
Complete Panel Set (245):		2,750	1,375	825.00
Common Panel:		4.00	2.00	1.25
(1)	Hank Aaron/Ted Bowsfield	35.00	17.50	10.50
(2)	Jerry Adair/Tony Gonzalez	8.00	4.00	2.50
(3)	Joe Adcock/George Thomas	8.00	4.00	2.50
(4)	Bob Allison/Jim Davenport	8.00	4.00	2.50
(5)	Felipe Alou/Mickey Mantle	100.00	50.00	30.00
(6)	Felipe Alou/Chuck Schilling	9.00	4.50	2.75
(7)	George Altman/Rocky Colavito	10.00	5.00	3.00
(8)	George Altman/Don Schwall	8.00	4.00	2.50
(9)	Joe Amalfitano/Jim Gentile	8.00	4.00	2.50
(10)	Joe Amalfitano/Vic Power	8.00	4.00	2.50
(11)	Ruben Amaro/Carl Yastrzemski	30.00	15.00	9.00
(12)	Luis Aparicio/Dick Farrell	10.00	5.00	3.00
(13)	Luis Aparicio/Al Heist	10.00	5.00	3.00
(14)	Bob Aspromonte/Al Kaline	15.00	7.50	4.50
(15)	Ed Bailey/Jim Piersall	8.00	4.00	2.50
(16)	Ernie Banks/Milt Pappas	20.00	10.00	6.00
(17)	Earl Battey/Bob Clemente	35.00	17.50	10.50
(18)	Earl Battey/Ed Mathews	12.00	6.00	3.50
(19)	Gus Bell/Steve Boros	8.00	4.00	2.50
(20)	Gus Bell/Ty Cline	8.00	4.00	2.50
(21)	Yogi Berra/Roy Face	20.00	10.00	6.00
(22)	Yogi Berra/Jack Kralick	15.00	7.50	4.50
(23)	Dick Bertell/Hoyt Wilhelm	10.00	5.00	3.00
(24)	Dick Bertell/Don Zimmer	9.00	4.50	2.75
(25)	Steve Bilko/Ruben Amaro	8.00	4.00	2.50
(26)	Steve Bilko/Roy Sievers	8.00	4.00	2.50
(27)	Frank Bolling/Nellie Fox	10.00	5.00	3.00
(28)	Steve Boros/Art Mahaffey	8.00	4.00	2.50
(29)	Clete Boyer/Chuck Cottier	9.00	4.50	2.75
(30)	Ken Boyer/Bob Friend	9.00	4.50	2.75
(31)	Jackie Brandt/Frank Robinson	15.00	7.50	4.50
(32)	Bill Bruton/Ernie Banks	20.00	10.00	6.00
(33)	Bill Bruton/Jay Hook	8.00	4.00	2.50
(34)	Jim Bunning/Bob Miller	10.00	5.00	3.00
(35)	Jim Bunning/Jim O'Toole	10.00	5.00	3.00
(36)	Jim Bunning/Daryl Spencer	10.00	5.00	3.00

(37)	Lou Burdette/Ed Mathews	12.00	6.00	3.50
(38)	Lou Burdette/Willie Mays	35.00	17.50	10.50
(39)	Smoky Burgess/Bobby Richardson	9.00	4.50	2.75
(40)	Johnny Callizon (Callison)/Barry Latman	9.00	4.50	2.75
(41)	Johnny Callizon (Callison)/Frank Malzone	9.00	4.50	2.75
(42)	Johnny Callizon (Callison)/Willie Mays	35.00	17.50	10.50
(43)	Don Cardwell/Hoyt Wilhelm	10.00	5.00	3.00
(44)	Norm Cash/Dick Bertell	9.00	4.50	2.75
(45)	Norm Cash/Don Cardwell	9.00	4.50	2.75
(46)	Norm Cash/Dick Howser	9.00	4.50	2.75
(47)	Ty Cline/Art Mahaffey	8.00	4.00	2.50
(48)	Rocky Colavito/Sam Jones	10.00	5.00	3.00
(49)	Gordon Coleman/Pete Daley	8.00	4.00	2.50
(50)	Gordon Coleman/Danny O'Connell	8.00	4.00	2.50
(51)	Roger Craig/Ted Bowsfield	8.00	4.00	2.50
(52)	Roger Craig/Minnie Minoso	9.00	4.50	2.75
(53)	Del Crandall/Clete Boyer	9.00	4.50	2.75
(54)	Del Crandall/Ray Sadecki	8.00	4.00	2.50
(55)	Pete Daley/Bob Friend	8.00	4.00	2.50
(56)	Pete Daley/Mike McCormick	8.00	4.00	2.50
(57)	Clay Dalrymple/Woody Held	8.00	4.00	2.50
(58)	Clay Dalrymple/Pedro Ramos	8.00	4.00	2.50
(59)	Bennie Daniels/Jerry Walker	8.00	4.00	2.50
(60)	Jim Davenport/Harmon Killebrew	15.00	7.50	4.50
(61)	Don Demeter/Haywood Sullivan	8.00	4.00	2.50
(62)	Don Demeter/Gus Triandos	8.00	4.00	2.50
(63)	Don Demeter/Lee Walls	8.00	4.00	2.50
(64)	Dick Donovan/Jerry Adair	8.00	4.00	2.50
(65)	Dick Donovan/Jim Perry	8.00	4.00	2.50
(66)	Dick Donovan/Vada Pinson	9.00	4.50	2.75
(67)	John Edwards/Jerry Walker	8.00	4.00	2.50
(68)	Dick Ellsworth/Glen Hobbie	8.00	4.00	2.50
(69)	Dick Ellsworth/Pete Runnels	8.00	4.00	2.50
(70)	Chuck Estrada/Don Drysdale	12.00	6.00	3.50
(71)	Chuck Estrada/Al Kaline	15.00	7.50	4.50
(72)	Roy Face/Minnie Minoso	9.00	4.50	2.75
(73)	Ron Fairly/Jim Landis	8.00	4.00	2.50
(74)	Dick Farrell/Frank Lary	8.00	4.00	2.50
(75)	Whitey Ford/Joe Torre	15.00	7.50	4.50
(76)	Nellie Fox/Willie Mays	35.00	17.50	10.50
(77)	Tito Francona/Ken Boyer	9.00	4.50	2.75
(78)	Tito Francona/Bob Johnson	8.00	4.00	2.50
(79)	Gene Freese/Bob Allison	8.00	4.00	2.50
(80)	Gene Freese/Ernie Banks	15.00	7.50	4.50
(81)	Gary Geiger/Bobby Richardson	9.00	4.50	2.75
(82)	Jim Gentile/Hal W. Smith	8.00	4.00	2.50
(83)	Dick Groat/Joe McClain	8.00	4.00	2.50
(84)	Al Heist/Frank Lary	8.00	4.00	2.50
(85)	Woody Held/Orlando Cepeda	10.00	5.00	3.00
(86)	Ray Herbert/Frank Bolling	8.00	4.00	2.50
(87)	Ray Herbert/Eddie Kasko	8.00	4.00	2.50
(88)	Chuck Hinton/Dick Groat	8.00	4.00	2.50
(89)	Chuck Hinton/Stu Miller	8.00	4.00	2.50
(90)	Don Hoak/Bob Allison	8.00	4.00	2.50
(91)	Gil Hodges/Bennie Daniels	10.00	5.00	3.00
(92)	Gil Hodges/John Edwards	10.00	5.00	3.00
(93)	Elston Howard/Bob Clemente	35.00	17.50	10.50
(94)	Dick Howser/Don Zimmer	9.00	4.50	2.75
(95)	Ken Hunt/Lenny Green	8.00	4.00	2.50
(96)	Larry Jackson/Smoky Burgess	8.00	4.00	2.50
(97)	Larry Jackson/Gary Geiger	8.00	4.00	2.50
(98)	Joe Jay/Johnny Romano	8.00	4.00	2.50
(99)	Bob Johnson/Bob Friend	8.00	4.00	2.50
(100)	Al Kaline/Don Hoak	15.00	7.50	4.50
(101)	Eddie Kasko/Nellie Fox	10.00	5.00	3.00
(102)	Sandy Koufax/Joe Adcock	30.00	15.00	9.00
(103)	Sandy Koufax/Hobie Landrith	30.00	15.00	9.00
(104)	Sandy Koufax/Bob Shaw	30.00	15.00	9.00
(105)	Jack Kralick/Minnie Minoso	9.00	4.50	2.75
(106)	Harvey Kuenn/Ken Hunt	8.00	4.00	2.50
(107)	Havey Kuenn/Gene Woodling	8.00	4.00	2.50
(108)	Hobie Landrith/Mike Fornieles	8.00	4.00	2.50
(109)	Barry Latman/Tony Kubek	9.00	4.50	2.75
(110)	Barry Latman/Johnny Podres	8.00	4.00	2.50
(111)	Frank Malzone/Johnny Podres	8.00	4.00	2.50
(112)	Frank Malzone/Duke Snider	15.00	7.50	4.50
(113)	Felix Mantilla/Camilo Carreon	8.00	4.00	2.50
(114)	Mickey Mantle/Hank Aaron	125.00	62.00	37.00
(115)	Mickey Mantle/Dick Stuart	110.00	55.00	33.00
(116)	Juan Marichal/Bill Bruton	12.00	6.00	3.50
(117)	Juan Marichal/Gene Freese	12.00	6.00	3.50
(118)	Juan Marichal/Don Hoak	12.00	6.00	3.50
(119)	Roger Maris/Lou Burdette	20.00	10.00	6.00
(120)	Roger Maris/Nellie Fox	20.00	10.00	6.00
(121)	Roger Maris/Lee Thomas	20.00	10.00	6.00
(122)	J.C. Martin/Felix Mantilla	8.00	4.00	2.50
(123)	J.C. Martin/Barney Schultz	8.00	4.00	2.50
(124)	Willie Mays/Tony Kubek	35.00	17.50	10.50
(125)	Bill Mazeroski/Earl Battey	10.00	5.00	3.00
(126)	Bill Mazeroski/Elston Howard	10.00	5.00	3.00
(127)	Bill Mazeroski/Early Wynn	12.00	6.00	3.50
(128)	Ken McBride/Joe Torre	9.00	4.50	2.75
(129)	Tim McCarver/Bill Tuttle	9.00	4.50	2.75
(130)	Lindy McDaniel/Jim Piersall	8.00	4.00	2.50
(131)	Roy McMillan/Bob Allison	8.00	4.00	2.50
(132)	Roy McMillan/Albie Pearson	8.00	4.00	2.50
(133)	Roy McMillan/Leon Wagner	8.00	4.00	2.50
(134)	Bob Miller/Ron Hansen	8.00	4.00	2.50
(135)	Stu Miller/Joe McCain	8.00	4.00	2.50
(136)	Bill Monbouquette/Don Hoak	8.00	4.00	2.50
(137)	Bill Monbouquette/Joe Torre	9.00	4.50	2.75
(138)	Wally Moon/Frank Malzone	8.00	4.00	2.50
(139)	Wally Moon/Juan Pizarro	8.00	4.00	2.50
(140)	Wally Moon/Brooks Robinson	20.00	10.00	6.00
(141)	Don Mossi/Bill Bruton	8.00	4.00	2.50
(142)	Don Mossi/Johnny Podres	8.00	4.00	2.50
(143)	Don Mossi/Al Spangler	8.00	4.00	2.50
(144)	Stan Musial/Whitey Ford	30.00	15.00	9.00
(145)	Stan Musial/Joe Torre	30.00	15.00	9.00
(146)	Russ Nixon/Ed Bailey	8.00	4.00	2.50
(147)	Russ Nixon/Lindy McDaniel	8.00	4.00	2.50
(148)	Danny O'Connell/Mike McCormick	8.00	4.00	2.50
(149)	Jim O'Toole/Ron Hansen	8.00	4.00	2.50
(150)	Jim O'Toole/Gene Stephens	8.00	4.00	2.50
(151)	Camilo Pascual/Pete Daley	8.00	4.00	2.50
(152)	Camilo Pascual/Tim McCarver	9.00	4.00	2.75
(153)	Camilo Pascual/Bill Virdon	8.00	4.00	2.50
(154)	Albie Pearson/Julian Javier	8.00	4.00	2.50
(155)	Jim Perry/Frank Howard	8.00	4.00	2.50
(156)	Bubba Phillips/Don Drysdale	12.00	6.00	3.50
(157)	Vada Pinson/Tony Gonzalez	9.00	4.50	2.75
(158)	Vada Pinson/Frank Howard	9.00	4.50	2.75
(159)	Juan Pizarro/Jack Baldschun	8.00	4.00	2.50
(160)	Johnny Podres/Jim Archer	8.00	4.00	2.50
(161)	Leo Posada/Milt Pappas	8.00	4.00	2.50
(162)	Leo Posada/Johnny Romano	8.00	4.00	2.50
(163)	Vic Power/Hal W. Smith	8.00	4.00	2.50
(164)	Bob Purkey/Harmon Killebrew	15.00	7.50	4.50
(165)	Pedro Ramos/Orlando Cepeda	10.00	5.00	3.00
(166)	Brooks Robinson/Jack Baldschun	15.00	7.50	4.50
(167)	Brooks Robinson/Duke Snider	20.00	10.00	6.00
(168)	Floyd Robinson/Ron Fairly	8.00	4.00	2.50
(169)	Floyd Robinson/Tony Taylor	8.00	4.00	2.50
(170)	Bob Rodgers/Hank Aaron	35.00	17.50	10.50
(171)	Bob Rodgers/Roger Craig	8.00	4.00	2.50
(172)	Bob Rodgers/Johnny Romano	8.00	4.00	2.50
(173)	Johnny Romano/Minnie Minoso	9.00	4.50	2.75
(174)	John Roseboro/Bob Aspromonte	8.00	4.00	2.50
(175)	John Roseboro/Chuck Estrada	8.00	4.00	2.50
(176)	John Roseboro/Bubba Phillips	8.00	4.00	2.50
(177)	Ray Sadecki/Chuck Cottier	8.00	4.00	2.50
(178)	Ron Santo/Ernie Banks	20.00	10.00	6.00
(179)	Ron Santo/Joe Jay	9.00	4.50	2.75
(180)	Ron Santo/Leo Posada	9.00	4.50	2.75
(181)	Chuck Schilling/Hank Aaron	35.00	17.50	10.50
(182)	Chuck Schilling/Dick Stuart	8.00	4.00	2.50
(183)	Barney Schultz/Camilo Carreon	8.00	4.00	2.50
(184)	Don Schwall/Sam Jones	8.00	4.00	2.50
(185)	Bobby Shantz/Pete Runnels	8.00	4.00	2.50
(186)	Bob Shaw/Mike Fornieles	8.00	4.00	2.50
(187)	Bob Shaw/George Thomas	8.00	4.00	2.50
(188)	Norm Siebern/Dick Ellsworth	8.00	4.00	2.50
(189)	Norm Siebern/Bobby Shantz	8.00	4.00	2.50
(190)	Norm Siebern/Early Wynn	10.00	5.00	3.00
(191)	Roy Sievers/Carl Yastrzemski	30.00	15.00	9.00
(192)	Bill Skowron/Jim Davenport	9.00	4.50	2.75
(193)	Bill Skowron/Bob Purkey	9.00	4.50	2.75
(194)	Warren Spahn/Whitey Ford	20.00	10.00	6.00
(195)	Al Spangler/Jim Archer	8.00	4.00	2.50
(196)	Al Spangler/Jay Hook	8.00	4.00	2.50
(197)	Daryl Spencer/Gene Stephens	8.00	4.00	2.50
(198)	Haywood Sullivan/Jerry Lumpe	8.00	4.00	2.50
(199)	Haywood Sullivan/Billy Williams	10.00	5.00	3.00
(200)	Tony Taylor/Jim Landis	8.00	4.00	2.50
(201)	Lee Thomas/Ed Mathews	12.00	6.00	3.50
(202)	Bob Tiefenauer/Jackie Brandt	8.00	4.00	2.50
(203)	Bob Tiefenauer/Jake Wood	8.00	4.00	2.50
(204)	Gus Triandos/Billy Williams	10.00	5.00	3.00
(205)	Zoilo Versalles/Whitey Ford	12.50	6.25	3.75
(206)	Zoilo Versalles/Stan Musial	30.00	15.00	9.00
(207)	Zoilo Veraalles/Warren Spahn	12.00	6.00	3.50
(208)	Bill Virdon/Bob Friend	8.00	4.00	2.50
(209)	Bill Virdon/Bill Tuttle	8.00	4.00	2.50
(210)	Leon Wagner/Jim Davenport	8.00	4.00	2.50
(211)	Leon Wagner/Julian Javier	8.00	4.00	2.50
(212)	Lee Walls/Jerry Lumpe	8.00	4.00	2.50
(213)	Bill White/Al Kaline	15.00	7.50	4.50
(214)	Bill White/Ken McBride	8.00	4.00	2.50
(215)	Bill White/Bill Monbouquette	8.00	4.00	2.50
(216)	Jake Wood/Frank Robinson	12.00	6.00	3.50
(217)	Gene Woodling/Lenny Green	8.00	4.00	2.50
(218)	Early Wynn/Glen Hobbie	10.00	5.00	3.00
(219)	Early Wynn/Ed Mathews	15.00	7.50	4.50
(220)	Angels/Athletics	8.00	4.00	2.50
(221)	Angels/Colts	9.00	4.50	2.75
(222)	Angels/Orioles	8.00	4.00	2.50
(223)	Athletics/Mets	10.00	5.00	3.00
(224)	Athletics/Pirates	9.00	4.50	2.75
(225)	Cardinals/Indians	9.00	4.50	2.75
(226)	Colts/Mets	12.00	6.00	3.50
(227)	Colts/Twins	9.00	4.50	2.75
(228)	Cubs/Senators	9.00	4.50	2.75
(229)	Giants/Red Sox	9.00	4.50	2.75
(230)	Giants/Tigers	9.00	4.50	2.75
(231)	Giants/White Sox	12.00	6.00	3.50
(232)	Indians/Reds	9.00	4.50	2.75
(233)	Mets/Dodgers	10.00	5.00	3.00
(234)	Orioles/Pirates	9.00	4.50	2.75
(235)	Phillies/Senators	9.00	4.50	2.75
(236)	Red Sox/Braves	9.00	4.50	2.75
(237)	Red Sox/Phillies	9.00	4.50	2.75
(238)	Reds/Indians	9.00	4.50	2.75
(239)	Reds/Yankees	12.50	6.25	3.75
(240)	Tigers/Braves	9.00	4.50	2.75
(241)	Twins/Dodgers	12.50	6.25	3.75
(242)	White Sox/Cubs	10.00	5.00	3.00
(243)	White Sox/Phillies	10.00	5.00	3.00
(244)	Yankees/Cardinals	12.50	6.25	3.75
(245)	Yankees/Reds	12.50	6.25	3.75

1963 Topps

Although the number of cards dropped to 576, the 1963 Topps set is among the most popular of the 1960s. A color photo dominates the 2-1/2" x 3-1/2" card, but a colored circle at the bottom carries a black and white portrait as well. A colored band gives the player's name, team and position. The backs again feature career statistics and a cartoon, career summary and brief biographical details. The set is somewhat unlike those immediately preceding it in that there are fewer specialty cards. The major groupings are statistical leaders, World Series highlights and rookies. It is one rookie which makes the set special - Pete Rose. As one of most avidly sought cards in history and a high-numbered card at that, the Rose rookie card accounts for much of the value of a complete set.

		NM	EX	VG
	Complete Set (576):	5,250	2,600	1,550
	Common Player (1-446):	4.00	2.00	1.25
	Common Player (447-576):	9.00	4.50	2.75
1	N.L. Batting Leaders (Hank Aaron, Bill White, Frank Robinson, Tommy Davis, Stan Musial)	60.00	15.00	9.00
2	A.L. Batting Leaders (Chuck Hinton, Mickey Mantle, Floyd Robinson, Pete Runnels, Norm Siebern)	30.00	15.00	9.00
3	N.L. Home Run Leaders (Hank Aaron, Ernie Banks, Orlando Cepeda, Willie Mays, Frank Robinson)	40.00	20.00	12.00
4	A.L. Home Run Leaders (Norm Cash, Rocky Colavito, Jim Gentile, Harmon Killebrew, Roger Maris, Leon Wagner)	20.00	10.00	6.00
5	N.L. E.R.A. Leaders (Don Drysdale, Bob Gibson, Sandy Koufax, Bob Shaw, Bob Purkey)	17.50	8.75	5.25
6	A.L. E.R.A. Leaders (Hank Aguirre, Dean Chance, Eddie Fisher, Whitey Ford, Robin Roberts)	10.00	5.00	3.00
7	N.L. Pitching Leaders (Don Drysdale, Joe Jay, Art Mahaffey, Billy O'Dell, Bob Purkey, Jack Sanford)	12.00	6.00	3.50
8	A.L. Pitching Leaders (Jim Bunning, Dick Donovan, Ray Herbert, Camilo Pascual, Ralph Terry)	10.00	5.00	3.00
9	N.L. Strikeout Leaders (Don Drysdale, Dick Farrell, Bob Gibson, Sandy Koufax, Billy O'Dell)	20.00	10.00	6.00
10	A.L. Strikeout Leaders (Jim Bunning, Jim Kaat, Camilo Pascual, Juan Pizarro, Ralph Terry)	9.00	4.50	2.75
11	Lee Walls	4.00	2.00	1.25
12	Steve Barber	4.00	2.00	1.25
13	Philadelphia Phillies Team	7.00	3.50	2.00
14	Pedro Ramos	4.00	2.00	1.25
15	Ken Hubbs	10.00	5.00	3.00
16	Al Smith	4.00	2.00	1.25
17	Ryne Duren	4.00	2.00	1.25
18	Buc Blasters (Smoky Burgess, Roberto Clemente, Bob Skinner, Dick Stuart)	40.00	20.00	12.00
19	Pete Burnside	4.00	2.00	1.25
20	Tony Kubek	12.50	6.25	3.75
21	Marty Keough	4.00	2.00	1.25
22	Curt Simmons	4.00	2.00	1.25
23	Ed Lopat	4.00	2.00	1.25
24	Bob Bruce	4.00	2.00	1.25
25	Al Kaline	35.00	17.50	10.00
26	Ray Moore	4.00	2.00	1.25
27	Choo Choo Coleman	4.00	2.00	1.25
28	Mike Fornieles	4.00	2.00	1.25
29a	1962 Rookie Stars (Sammy Ellis, Ray Culp, John Boozer, Jesse Gonder)	6.00	3.00	1.75
29b	1963 Rookie Stars (Sammy Ellis, Ray Culp, John Boozer, Jesse Gonder)	4.00	2.00	1.25
30	Harvey Kuenn	4.00	2.00	1.25

31	Cal Koonce	4.00	2.00	1.25
32	Tony Gonzalez	4.00	2.00	1.25
33	Bo Belinsky	4.00	2.00	1.25
34	Dick Schofield	4.00	2.00	1.25
35	John Buzhardt	4.00	2.00	1.25
36	Jerry Kindall	4.00	2.00	1.25
37	Jerry Lynch	4.00	2.00	1.25
38	Bud Daley	4.00	2.00	1.25
39	Los Angeles Angels Team	7.00	3.50	2.00
40	Vic Power	4.00	2.00	1.25
41	Charlie Lau	4.00	2.00	1.25
42	Stan Williams	4.00	2.00	1.25
43	Veteran Masters (Casey Stengel, Gene Woodling)	7.50	3.75	2.25
44	Terry Fox	4.00	2.00	1.25
45	Bob Aspromonte	4.00	2.00	1.25
46	*Tommie Aaron*	5.00	2.50	1.50
47	Don Lock	4.00	2.00	1.25
48	Birdie Tebbetts	4.00	2.00	1.25
49	*Dal Maxvill*	4.00	2.00	1.25
50	Bill Pierce	4.00	2.00	1.25
51	George Alusik	4.00	2.00	1.25
52	Chuck Schilling	4.00	2.00	1.25
53	Joe Moeller	4.00	2.00	1.25
54a	1962 Rookie Stars (*Nelson Mathews, Harry Fanok, Jack Cullen, Dave DeBusschere*)	10.00	5.00	3.00
54b	1963 Rookie Stars (*Jack Cullen, Dave DeBusschere, Harry Fanok, Nelson Mathews*)	8.00	4.00	2.50
55	Bill Virdon	4.00	2.00	1.25
56	Dennis Bennett	4.00	2.00	1.25
57	Billy Moran	4.00	2.00	1.25
58	Bob Will	4.00	2.00	1.25
59	Craig Anderson	4.00	2.00	1.25
60	Elston Howard	9.00	4.50	2.75
61	Ernie Bowman	4.00	2.00	1.25
62	Bob Hendley	4.00	2.00	1.25
63	Cincinnati Reds Team	7.00	3.50	2.00
64	Dick McAuliffe	4.00	2.00	1.25
65	Jackie Brandt	4.00	2.00	1.25
66	Mike Joyce	4.00	2.00	1.25
67	Ed Charles	4.00	2.00	1.25
68	Friendly Foes (Gil Hodges, Duke Snider)	15.00	7.50	4.50
69	Bud Zipfel	4.00	2.00	1.25
70	Jim O'Toole	4.00	2.00	1.25
71	*Bobby Wine*	4.00	2.00	1.25
72	Johnny Romano	4.00	2.00	1.25
73	Bobby Bragan	4.00	2.00	1.25
74	*Denver Lemaster*	4.00	2.00	1.25
75	Bob Allison	4.00	2.00	1.25
76	Earl Wilson	4.00	2.00	1.25
77	Al Spangler	4.00	2.00	1.25
78	Marv Throneberry	4.00	2.00	1.25
79	1st Series Checklist (1-88)	6.00	3.00	1.75
80	Jim Gilliam	6.00	3.00	1.75
81	Jimmie Schaffer	4.00	2.00	1.25
82	Ed Rakow	4.00	2.00	1.25
83	Charley James	4.00	2.00	1.25
84	Ron Kline	4.00	2.00	1.25
85	Tom Haller	4.00	2.00	1.25
86	Charley Maxwell	4.00	2.00	1.25
87	Bob Veale	4.00	2.00	1.25
88	Ron Hansen	4.00	2.00	1.25
89	Dick Stigman	4.00	2.00	1.25
90	Gordy Coleman	4.00	2.00	1.25
91	Dallas Green	4.00	2.00	1.25
92	Hector Lopez	4.00	2.00	1.25
93	Galen Cisco	4.00	2.00	1.25
94	Bob Schmidt	4.00	2.00	1.25
95	Larry Jackson	4.00	2.00	1.25
96	Lou Clinton	4.00	2.00	1.25
97	Bob Duliba	4.00	2.00	1.25
98	George Thomas	4.00	2.00	1.25
99	Jim Umbricht	4.00	2.00	1.25
100	Joe Cunningham	4.00	2.00	1.25
101	Joe Gibbon	4.00	2.00	1.25
102a	2nd Series Checklist (89-176) ("Checklist" in red on yellow)	6.00	3.00	1.75
102b	2nd Series Checklist (89-176) ("Checklist" in white on red)	10.00	5.00	3.00
103	Chuck Essegian	4.00	2.00	1.25
104	Lew Krausse	4.00	2.00	1.25
105	Ron Fairly	4.00	2.00	1.25
106	Bob Bolin	4.00	2.00	1.25
107	Jim Hickman	4.00	2.00	1.25
108	Hoyt Wilhelm	15.00	7.50	4.50
109	Lee Maye	4.00	2.00	1.25
110	Rich Rollins	4.00	2.00	1.25
111	Al Jackson	4.00	2.00	1.25
112	Dick Brown	4.00	2.00	1.25
113	Don Landrum (Photo actally Ron Santo.)	4.00	2.00	1.25
114	Dan Osinski	4.00	2.00	1.25
115	Carl Yastrzemski	40.00	20.00	12.00
116	Jim Brosnan	4.00	2.00	1.25
117	Jacke Davis	4.00	2.00	1.25
118	Sherm Lollar	4.00	2.00	1.25
119	Bob Lillis	4.00	2.00	1.25
120	Roger Maris	60.00	30.00	18.00
121	Jim Hannan	4.00	2.00	1.25
122	Julio Gotay	4.00	2.00	1.25
123	Frank Howard	4.00	2.00	1.25
124	Dick Howser	4.00	2.00	1.25
125	Robin Roberts	15.00	7.50	4.50
126	Bob Uecker	17.50	8.75	5.25
127	Bill Tuttle	4.00	2.00	1.25
128	Matty Alou	4.00	2.00	1.25
129	Gary Bell	4.00	2.00	1.25
130	Dick Groat	4.00	2.00	1.25
131	Washington Senators Team	7.00	3.50	2.00
132	Jack Hamilton	4.00	2.00	1.25
133	Gene Freese	4.00	2.00	1.25
134	Bob Scheffing	4.00	2.00	1.25
135	Richie Ashburn	15.00	7.50	4.50
136	Ike Delock	4.00	2.00	1.25
137	Mack Jones	4.00	2.00	1.25
138	Pride of N.L. (Willie Mays, Stan Musial)	40.00	20.00	12.00
139	Earl Averill	4.00	2.00	1.25
140	Frank Lary	4.00	2.00	1.25
141	Manny Mota	6.00	3.00	1.75
142	World Series Game 1 (Yanks' Ford Wins Series Opener)	11.00	5.50	3.25
143	World Series Game 2 (Sanford Flashes Shutout Magic)	5.00	2.50	1.50
144	World Series Game 3 (Maris Sparks Yankee Rally)	12.00	6.00	3.50
145	World Series Game 4 (Hiller Blasts Grand Slammer)	5.00	2.50	1.50
146	World Series Game 5 (Tresh's Homer Defeats Giants)	6.00	3.00	1.75
147	World Series Game 6 (Pierce Stars in 3-Hit Victory)	6.00	3.00	1.75
148	World Series Game 7 (Yanks Celebrate as Terry Wins)	7.00	3.50	2.00
149	Marv Breeding	4.00	2.00	1.25
150	Johnny Podres	6.00	3.00	1.75
151	Pittsburgh Pirates Team	10.00	5.00	3.00
152	Ron Nischwitz	4.00	2.00	1.25
153	Hal Smith	4.00	2.00	1.25
154	Walt Alston	7.50	3.75	2.25
155	Bill Stafford	4.00	2.00	1.25
156	Roy McMillan	4.00	2.00	1.25
157	*Diego Segui*	4.00	2.00	1.25
158	1963 Rookie Stars (Rogelio Alvarez, Tommy Harper, Dave Roberts, Bob Saverine)	6.00	3.00	1.75
159	Jim Pagliaroni	4.00	2.00	1.25
160	Juan Pizarro	4.00	2.00	1.25
161	Frank Torre	4.00	2.00	1.25
162	Minnesota Twins Team	7.00	3.50	2.00
163	Don Larsen	4.00	2.00	1.25
164	Bubba Morton	4.00	2.00	1.25
165	Jim Kaat	5.00	2.50	1.50
166	Johnny Keane	4.00	2.00	1.25
167	Jim Fregosi	4.00	2.00	1.25
168	Russ Nixon	4.00	2.00	1.25
169	1963 Rookie Stars (*Dick Egan, Julio Navarro, Gaylord Perry, Tommie Sisk*)	17.50	8.75	5.25
170	Joe Adcock	4.00	2.00	1.25
171	Steve Hamilton	4.00	2.00	1.25
172	Gene Oliver	4.00	2.00	1.25
173	Bombers' Best (Tom Tresh, Mickey Mantle, Bobby Richardson)	75.00	37.50	22.00
174	Larry Burright	4.00	2.00	1.25
175	Bob Buhl	4.00	2.00	1.25
176	Jim King	4.00	2.00	1.25
177	Bubba Phillips	4.00	2.00	1.25
178	Johnny Edwards	4.00	2.00	1.25
179	Ron Piche	4.00	2.00	1.25
180	Bill Skowron	10.00	5.00	3.00
181	Sammy Esposito	4.00	2.00	1.25
182	Albie Pearson	4.00	2.00	1.25
183	Joe Pepitone	10.00	5.00	3.00
184	Vern Law	4.00	2.00	1.25
185	Chuck Hiller	4.00	2.00	1.25
186	Jerry Zimmerman	4.00	2.00	1.25
187	Willie Kirkland	4.00	2.00	1.25
188	Eddie Bressoud	4.00	2.00	1.25
189	Dave Giusti	4.00	2.00	1.25
190	Minnie Minoso	6.00	3.00	1.75
191	3rd Series Checklist (177-264)	8.00	4.00	2.50
192	Clay Dalrymple	4.00	2.00	1.25
193	Andre Rodgers	4.00	2.00	1.25
194	Joe Nuxhall	4.00	2.00	1.25
195	Manny Jimenez	4.00	2.00	1.25
196	Doug Camilli	4.00	2.00	1.25
197	Roger Craig	4.00	2.00	1.25
198	Lenny Green	4.00	2.00	1.25
199	Joe Amalfitano	4.00	2.00	1.25
200	Mickey Mantle	300.00	150.00	90.00
201	Cecil Butler	4.00	2.00	1.25
202	Boston Red Sox Team	7.00	3.50	2.00
203	Chico Cardenas	4.00	2.00	1.25
204	Don Nottebart	4.00	2.00	1.25
205	Luis Aparicio	15.00	7.50	4.50
206	Ray Washburn	4.00	2.00	1.25
207	Ken Hunt	4.00	2.00	1.25
208	1963 Rookie Stars (Ron Herbel, John Miller, Ron Taylor, Wally Wolf)	4.00	2.00	1.25
209	Hobie Landrith	4.00	2.00	1.25
210	Sandy Koufax	125.00	60.00	35.00
211	Fred Whitfield	4.00	2.00	1.25
212	Glen Hobbie	4.00	2.00	1.25
213	Billy Hitchcock	4.00	2.00	1.25
214	Orlando Pena	4.00	2.00	1.25
215	Bob Skinner	4.00	2.00	1.25
216	Gene Conley	4.00	2.00	1.25
217	Joe Christopher	4.00	2.00	1.25
218	Tiger Twirlers (Jim Bunning, Frank Lary, Don Mossi)	7.50	3.75	2.25
219	Chuck Cottier	4.00	2.00	1.25
220	Camilo Pascual	4.00	2.00	1.25
221	*Cookie Rojas*	4.00	2.00	1.25
222	Chicago Cubs Team	7.00	3.50	2.00
223	Eddie Fisher	4.00	2.00	1.25
224	Mike Roarke	4.00	2.00	1.25
225	Joe Jay	4.00	2.00	1.25
226	Julian Javier	4.00	2.00	1.25
227	Jim Grant	4.00	2.00	1.25
228	1963 Rookie Stars (*Max Alvis, Bob Bailey, Ed Kranepool, Tony Oliva*)	40.00	20.00	12.00
229	Willie Davis	4.00	2.00	1.25
230	Pete Runnels	4.00	2.00	1.25
231	Eli Grba (Photo actually Ryne Duren.)	4.00	2.00	1.25
232	Frank Malzone	4.00	2.00	1.25
233	Casey Stengel	15.00	7.50	4.50
234	Dave Nicholson	4.00	2.00	1.25
235	Billy O'Dell	4.00	2.00	1.25
236	Bill Bryan	4.00	2.00	1.25
237	Jim Coates	4.00	2.00	1.25
238	Lou Johnson	4.00	2.00	1.25
239	Harvey Haddix	4.00	2.00	1.25
240	Rocky Colavito	17.50	8.75	5.25
241	Billy Smith	4.00	2.00	1.25
242	Power Plus (Hank Aaron, Ernie Banks)	50.00	25.00	15.00
243	Don Leppert	4.00	2.00	1.25
244	John Tsitouris	4.00	2.00	1.25
245	Gil Hodges	12.50	6.25	3.75
246	Lee Stange	4.00	2.00	1.25
247	New York Yankees Team	30.00	15.00	9.00
248	Tito Francona	4.00	2.00	1.25
249	Leo Burke	4.00	2.00	1.25
250	Stan Musial	65.00	32.50	20.00
251	Jack Lamabe	4.00	2.00	1.25
252	Ron Santo	13.50	6.75	4.00
253	1963 Rookie Stars (Len Gabrielson, Pete Jernigan, Deacon Jones, John Wojcik)	4.00	2.00	1.25
254	Mike Hershberger	4.00	2.00	1.25
255	Bob Shaw	4.00	2.00	1.25
256	Jerry Lumpe	4.00	2.00	1.25
257	Hank Aguirre	4.00	2.00	1.25
258	Alvin Dark	4.00	2.00	1.25
259	Johnny Logan	4.00	2.00	1.25
260	Jim Gentile	4.00	2.00	1.25
261	Bob Miller	4.00	2.00	1.25
262	Ellis Burton	4.00	2.00	1.25
263	Dave Stenhouse	4.00	2.00	1.25
264	Phil Linz	4.00	2.00	1.25
265	Vada Pinson	7.00	3.50	2.00
266	Bob Allen	4.00	2.00	1.25
267	Carl Sawatski	4.00	2.00	1.25
268	Don Demeter	4.00	2.00	1.25
269	Don Mincher	4.00	2.00	1.25
270	Felipe Alou	5.00	2.50	1.50
271	Dean Stone	4.00	2.00	1.25
272	Danny Murphy	4.00	2.00	1.25
273	Sammy Taylor	4.00	2.00	1.25
274	6th Series Checklist (265-352)	8.00	4.00	2.50
275	Ed Mathews	25.00	12.50	7.50
276	Barry Shetrone	4.00	2.00	1.25
277	Dick Farrell	4.00	2.00	1.25
278	Chico Fernandez	4.00	2.00	1.25
279	Wally Moon	4.00	2.00	1.25
280	Bob Rodgers	4.00	2.00	1.25
281	Tom Sturdivant	4.00	2.00	1.25
282	Bob Del Greco	4.00	2.00	1.25
283	Roy Sievers	4.00	2.00	1.25
284	Dave Sisler	4.00	2.00	1.25
285	Dick Stuart	4.00	2.00	1.25
286	Stu Miller	4.00	2.00	1.25
287	Dick Bertell	4.00	2.00	1.25
288	Chicago White Sox Team	8.00	4.00	2.50
289	Hal Brown	4.00	2.00	1.25
290	Bill White	4.00	2.00	1.25
291	Don Rudolph	4.00	2.00	1.25
292	Pumpsie Green	4.00	2.00	1.25
293	Bill Pleis	4.00	2.00	1.25
294	Bill Rigney	4.00	2.00	1.25
295	Ed Roebuck	4.00	2.00	1.25
296	Doc Edwards	4.00	2.00	1.25
297	Jim Golden	4.00	2.00	1.25
298	Don Dillard	4.00	2.00	1.25
299	1963 Rookie Stars (Tom Butters, Bob Dustal, Dave Morehead, Dan Schneider)	4.00	2.00	1.25
300	Willie Mays	110.00	55.00	35.00
301	Bill Fischer	4.00	2.00	1.25
302	Whitey Herzog	4.00	2.00	1.25
303	Earl Francis	4.00	2.00	1.25
304	Harry Bright	4.00	2.00	1.25
305	Don Hoak	4.00	2.00	1.25
306	Star Receivers (Earl Battey, Elston Howard)	5.00	2.50	1.50
307	Chet Nichols	4.00	2.00	1.25
308	Camilo Carreon	4.00	2.00	1.25
309	Jim Brewer	4.00	2.00	1.25
310	Tommy Davis	6.00	3.00	1.75
311	Joe McClain	4.00	2.00	1.25
312	Houston Colt .45s Team	13.50	6.75	4.00
313	Ernie Broglio	4.00	2.00	1.25
314	John Goryl	4.00	2.00	1.25
315	Ralph Terry	4.00	2.00	1.25
316	Norm Sherry	4.00	2.00	1.25
317	Sam McDowell	5.00	2.50	1.50
318	Gene Mauch	4.00	2.00	1.25
319	Joe Gaines	4.00	2.00	1.25
320	Warren Spahn	40.00	20.00	12.00
321	Gino Cimoli	4.00	2.00	1.25
322	Bob Turley	4.00	2.00	1.25
323	Bill Mazeroski	20.00	10.00	6.00
324	1963 Rookie Stars (Vic Davalillo, Phil Roof, Pete Ward, George Williams)	6.00	3.00	1.75
325	Jack Sanford	4.00	2.00	1.25
326	Hank Foiles	4.00	2.00	1.25
327	Paul Foytack	4.00	2.00	1.25
328	Dick Williams	4.00	2.00	1.25
329	Lindy McDaniel	4.00	2.00	1.25
330	Chuck Hinton	4.00	2.00	1.25
331	Series Foes (Bill Pierce, Bill Stafford)	7.00	3.50	2.00
332	Joel Horlen	4.00	2.00	1.25

333	Carl Warwick	4.00	2.00	1.25
334	Wynn Hawkins	4.00	2.00	1.25
335	Leon Wagner	4.00	2.00	1.25
336	Ed Bauta	4.00	2.00	1.25
337	Los Angeles Dodgers Team	15.00	7.50	4.50
338	Russ Kemmerer	4.00	2.00	1.25
339	Ted Bowsfield	4.00	2.00	1.25
340	Yogi Berra	70.00	35.00	20.00
341a	Jack Baldschun (White slash across body in inset photo.)	8.00	4.00	2.50
341b	Jack Baldschun (Slash repaired with red/mottling.)	4.00	2.00	1.25
342	Gene Woodling	4.00	2.00	1.25
343	Johnny Pesky	4.00	2.00	1.25
344	Don Schwall	4.00	2.00	1.25
345	Brooks Robinson	40.00	20.00	12.00
346	Billy Hoeft	4.00	2.00	1.25
347	Joe Torre	17.50	8.75	5.25
348	Vic Wertz	4.00	2.00	1.25
349	Zoilo Versalles	4.00	2.00	1.25
350	Bob Purkey	4.00	2.00	1.25
351	Al Luplow	4.00	2.00	1.25
352	Ken Johnson	4.00	2.00	1.25
353	Billy Williams	20.00	10.00	6.00
354	Dom Zanni	4.00	2.00	1.25
355	Dean Chance	4.00	2.00	1.25
356	John Schaive	4.00	2.00	1.25
357	George Altman	4.00	2.00	1.25
358	Milt Pappas	4.00	2.00	1.25
359	Haywood Sullivan	4.00	2.00	1.25
360	Don Drysdale	40.00	20.00	12.00
361	Clete Boyer	9.00	4.50	2.75
362	5th Series Checklist (353-429)	9.00	4.50	2.75
363	Dick Radatz	4.00	2.00	1.25
364	Howie Goss	4.00	2.00	1.25
365	Jim Bunning	13.50	6.75	4.00
366	Tony Taylor	4.00	2.00	1.25
367	Tony Cloninger	4.00	2.00	1.25
368	Ed Bailey	4.00	2.00	1.25
369	Jim Lemon	4.00	2.00	1.25
370	Dick Donovan	4.00	2.00	1.25
371	Rod Kanehl	4.00	2.00	1.25
372	Don Lee	4.00	2.00	1.25
373	Jim Campbell	4.00	2.00	1.25
374	Claude Osteen	4.00	2.00	1.25
375	Ken Boyer	10.00	5.00	3.00
376	Johnnie Wyatt	4.00	2.00	1.25
377	Baltimore Orioles Team	9.00	4.50	2.75
378	Bill Henry	4.00	2.00	1.25
379	Bob Anderson	4.00	2.00	1.25
380	Ernie Banks	65.00	32.50	20.00
381	Frank Baumann	4.00	2.00	1.25
382	Ralph Houk	6.00	3.00	1.75
383	Pete Richert	4.00	2.00	1.25
384	Bob Tillman	4.00	2.00	1.25
385	Art Mahaffey	4.00	2.00	1.25
386	1963 Rookie Stars (John Bateman, Larry Bearnarth, Ed Kirkpatrick, Garry Roggenburk)	5.00	2.50	1.50
387	Al McBean	4.00	2.00	1.25
388	Jim Davenport	4.00	2.00	1.25
389	Frank Sullivan	4.00	2.00	1.25
390	Hank Aaron	110.00	55.00	35.00
391	Bill Dailey	4.00	2.00	1.25
392	Tribe Thumpers (Tito Francona, Johnny Romano)	4.50	2.25	1.25
393	Ken MacKenzie	4.00	2.00	1.25
394	Tim McCarver	9.00	4.50	2.75
395	Don McMahon	4.00	2.00	1.25
396	Joe Koppe	4.00	2.00	1.25
397	Kansas City Athletics Team	9.00	4.50	2.75
398	Boog Powell	12.50	6.25	3.75
399	Dick Ellsworth	4.00	2.00	1.25
400	Frank Robinson	45.00	22.50	13.50
401	Jim Bouton	12.00	6.00	3.50
402	Mickey Vernon	4.00	2.00	1.25
403	Ron Perranoski	4.00	2.00	1.25
404	Bob Oldis	4.00	2.00	1.25
405	Floyd Robinson	4.00	2.00	1.25
406	Howie Koplitz	4.00	2.00	1.25
407	1963 Rookie Stars (Larry Elliot, Frank Kostro, Chico Ruiz, Dick Simpson)	4.00	2.00	1.25
408	Billy Gardner	4.00	2.00	1.25
409	Roy Face	4.00	2.00	1.25
410	Earl Battey	4.00	2.00	1.25
411	Jim Constable	4.00	2.00	1.25
412	Dodgers' Big Three (Johnny Podres, Don Drysdale, Sandy Koufax)	75.00	37.50	22.50
413	Jerry Walker	4.00	2.00	1.25
414	Ty Cline	4.00	2.00	1.25
415	Bob Gibson	45.00	22.50	13.50
416	Alex Grammas	4.00	2.00	1.25
417	San Francisco Giants Team	9.00	4.50	2.75
418	Johnny Orsino	4.00	2.00	1.25
419	Tracy Stallard	4.00	2.00	1.25
420	Bobby Richardson	12.50	6.25	3.75
421	Tom Morgan	4.00	2.00	1.25
422	Fred Hutchinson	4.00	2.00	1.25
423	Ed Hobaugh	4.00	2.00	1.25
424	Charley Smith	4.00	2.00	1.25
425	Smoky Burgess	4.00	2.00	1.25
426	Barry Latman	4.00	2.00	1.25
427	Bernie Allen	4.00	2.00	1.25
428	Carl Boles	4.00	2.00	1.25
429	Lou Burdette	4.00	2.00	1.25
430	Norm Siebern	4.00	2.00	1.25
431a	6th Series Checklist (430-506) ("Checklist" in black on front.)	8.00	4.00	2.50
431b	6th Series Checklist (430-506) ("Checklist" in white.)	20.00	10.00	6.00
432	Roman Mejias	4.00	2.00	1.25
433	Denis Menke	4.00	2.00	1.25
434	Johnny Callison	4.00	2.00	1.25
435	Woody Held	4.00	2.00	1.25
436	Tim Harkness	4.00	2.00	1.25
437	Bill Bruton	4.00	2.00	1.25
438	Wes Stock	4.00	2.00	1.25
439	Don Zimmer	6.00	3.00	1.75
440	Juan Marichal	25.00	12.50	7.50
441	Lee Thomas	4.00	2.00	1.25
442	J.C. Hartman	4.00	2.00	1.25
443	Jim Piersall	7.00	3.50	2.00
444	Jim Maloney	4.00	2.00	1.25
445	Norm Cash	9.00	4.50	2.75
446	Whitey Ford	40.00	20.00	12.00
447	Felix Mantilla	9.00	4.50	2.75
448	Jack Kralick	9.00	4.50	2.75
449	Jose Tartabull	9.00	4.50	2.75
450	Bob Friend	9.00	4.50	2.75
451	Cleveland Indians Team	20.00	10.00	6.00
452	Barney Schultz	9.00	4.50	2.75
453	Jake Wood	9.00	4.50	2.75
454a	Art Fowler (Card # on orange background.)	9.00	4.50	2.75
454b	Art Fowler (Card # on white background.)	30.00	15.00	9.00
455	Ruben Amaro	9.00	4.50	2.75
456	Jim Coker	9.00	4.50	2.75
457	Tex Clevenger	9.00	4.50	2.75
458	Al Lopez	20.00	10.00	6.00
459	Dick LeMay	9.00	4.50	2.75
460	Del Crandall	9.00	4.50	2.75
461	Norm Bass	9.00	4.50	2.75
462	Wally Post	9.00	4.50	2.75
463	Joe Schaffernoth	9.00	4.50	2.75
464	Ken Aspromonte	9.00	4.50	2.75
465	Chuck Estrada	9.00	4.50	2.75
466	1963 Rookie Stars (Bill Freehan, Tony Martinez, Nate Oliver, Jerry Robinson)	32.50	16.00	10.00
467	Phil Ortega	9.00	4.50	2.75
468	Carroll Hardy	9.00	4.50	2.75
469	Jay Hook	9.00	4.50	2.75
470	Tom Tresh/SP	35.00	17.50	10.00
471	Ken Retzer	9.00	4.50	2.75
472	Lou Brock	65.00	32.50	20.00
473	New York Mets Team	40.00	20.00	12.00
474	Jack Fisher	9.00	4.50	2.75
475	Gus Triandos	9.00	4.50	2.75
476	Frank Funk	9.00	4.50	2.75
477	Donn Clendenon	9.00	4.50	2.75
478	Paul Brown	9.00	4.50	2.75
479	*Ed Brinkman*	9.00	4.50	2.75
480	Bill Monbouquette	9.00	4.50	2.75
481	Bob Taylor	9.00	4.50	2.75
482	Felix Torres	9.00	4.50	2.75
483	Jim Owens	9.00	4.50	2.75
484	Dale Long/SP	15.00	7.50	4.50
485	Jim Landis	9.00	4.50	2.75
486	Ray Sadecki	9.00	4.50	2.75
487	John Roseboro	9.00	4.50	2.75
488	Jerry Adair	9.00	4.50	2.75
489	Paul Toth	9.00	4.50	2.75
490	Willie McCovey	60.00	30.00	18.00
491	Harry Craft	9.00	4.50	2.75
492	Dave Wickersham	9.00	4.50	2.75
493	Walt Bond	9.00	4.50	2.75
494	Phil Regan	9.00	4.50	2.75
495	Frank Thomas/SP	15.00	7.50	4.50
496	1963 Rookie Stars (Carl Bouldin, Steve Dalkowski, Fred Newman, Jack Smith)	20.00	10.00	6.00
497	Bennie Daniels	9.00	4.50	2.75
498	Eddie Kasko	9.00	4.50	2.75
499	J.C. Martin	9.00	4.50	2.75
500	Harmon Killebrew/SP	80.00	40.00	24.00
501	Joe Azcue	9.00	4.50	2.75
502	Daryl Spencer	9.00	4.50	2.75
503	Milwaukee Braves Team	15.00	7.50	4.50
504	Bob Johnson	9.00	4.50	2.75
505	Curt Flood	15.00	7.50	4.50
506	Gene Green	9.00	4.50	2.75
507	Roland Sheldon	9.00	4.50	2.75
508	Ted Savage	9.00	4.50	2.75
509a	7th Series Checklist (507-576) (Copyright centered.)	17.50	8.75	5.25
509b	7th Series Checklist (509-576) (Copyright to right.)	17.50	8.75	5.25
510	Ken McBride	9.00	4.50	2.75
511	Charlie Neal	9.00	4.50	2.75
512	Cal McLish	9.00	4.50	2.75
513	Gary Geiger	9.00	4.50	2.75
514	Larry Osborne	9.00	4.50	2.75
515	Don Elston	9.00	4.50	2.75
516	Purnal Goldy	9.00	4.50	2.75
517	Hal Woodeshick	9.00	4.50	2.75
518	Don Blasingame	9.00	4.50	2.75
519	Claude Raymond	9.00	4.50	2.75
520	Orlando Cepeda	30.00	15.00	9.00
521	Dan Pfister	9.00	4.50	2.75
522	1963 Rookie Stars (Mel Nelson, Gary Peters, Art Quirk, Jim Roland)	9.00	4.50	2.75
523	Bill Kunkel	9.00	4.50	2.75
524	St. Louis Cardinals Team	20.00	10.00	6.00
525	Nellie Fox	30.00	15.00	9.00
526	Dick Hall	9.00	4.50	2.75
527	Ed Sadowski	9.00	4.50	2.75
528	Carl Willey	9.00	4.50	2.75
529	Wes Covington	9.00	4.50	2.75
530	Don Mossi	9.00	4.50	2.75
531	Sam Mele	9.00	4.50	2.75
532	Steve Boros	9.00	4.50	2.75
533	Bobby Shantz	9.00	4.50	2.75
534	Ken Walters	9.00	4.50	2.75
535	Jim Perry	9.00	4.50	2.75
536	Norm Larker	9.00	4.50	2.75
537	1963 Rookie Stars (*Pedro Gonzalez, Ken McMullen, Pete Rose, Al Weis*)	550.00	270.00	180.00
538	George Brunet	9.00	4.50	2.75
539	Wayne Causey	9.00	4.50	2.75
540	Bob Clemente	150.00	75.00	45.00
541	Ron Moeller	9.00	4.50	2.75
542	Lou Klimchock	9.00	4.50	2.75
543	Russ Snyder	9.00	4.50	2.75
544	1963 Rookie Stars (*Duke Carmel, Bill Haas, Dick Phillips, Rusty Staub*)	30.00	15.00	9.00
545	Jose Pagan	9.00	4.50	2.75
546	Hal Reniff	9.00	4.50	2.75
547	Gus Bell	9.00	4.50	2.75
548	Tom Satriano	9.00	4.50	2.75
549	1963 Rookie Stars (Marcelino Lopez, Pete Lovrich, Elmo Plaskett, Paul Ratliff)	11.00	5.50	3.25
550	Duke Snider	45.00	22.50	13.50
551	Billy Klaus	9.00	4.50	2.75
552	Detroit Tigers Team	25.00	12.50	7.50
553	1963 Rookie Stars (*Brock Davis, Jim Gosger, John Herrnstein, Willie Stargell*)	80.00	40.00	24.00
554	Hank Fischer	9.00	4.50	2.75
555	John Blanchard	12.00	6.00	3.50
556	Al Worthington	9.00	4.50	2.75
557	Cuno Barragan	9.00	4.50	2.75
558	1963 Rookie Stars (*Bill Faul, Ron Hunt, Bob Lipski, Al Moran*)	11.00	5.50	3.25
559	Danny Murtaugh	9.00	4.50	2.75
560	Ray Herbert	9.00	4.50	2.75
561	Mike de la Hoz	9.00	4.50	2.75
562	1963 Rookie Stars (*Randy Cardinal, Dave McNally, Don Rowe, Ken Rowe*)	25.00	12.50	7.50
563	Mike McCormick	9.00	4.50	2.75
564	George Banks	9.00	4.50	2.75
565	Larry Sherry	9.00	4.50	2.75
566	Cliff Cook	9.00	4.50	2.75
567	Jim Duffalo	9.00	4.50	2.75
568	Bob Sadowski	9.00	4.50	2.75
569	Luis Arroyo	9.00	4.50	2.75
570	Frank Bolling	9.00	4.50	2.75
571	Johnny Klippstein	9.00	4.50	2.75
572	Jack Spring	9.00	4.50	2.75
573	Coot Veal	9.00	4.50	2.75
574	Hal Kolstad	9.00	4.50	2.75
575	Don Cardwell	9.00	4.50	2.75
576	Johnny Temple	13.50	5.00	3.00

1963 Topps Famous Americans Stamps

Actually marketed as "Stamp Gum," this obscure test issue features 80 perforated stamps depicting great Americans from all walks of life, including two baseball players. The 2-9/16" x 1-3/8" stamps are printed in black, blue and yellow and combine a photographic portrait with a cartoon drawing. Centering is often a problem with these pieces. Only the baseball players are listed here.

		NM	EX	VG
50	Babe Ruth	300.00	150.00	90.00
60	Lou Gehrig	250.00	125.00	75.00

1963 Topps Mickey Mantle Plaque

Advertised as a "mask" on high-number 1963 Topps wax wrappers, this is actually a plastic plaque. About 6" x 8", the plaque features a color picture of Mantle in embossed plastic with a faux wood frame, also embossed plastic, around it. A holed tab at top allows hanging.

	NM	EX	VG
Mickey Mantle	900.00	450.00	270.00

1963 Topps Peel-Offs

JIM BUNNING
DET. TIGERS   PITCHER

Measuring 1-1/4" x 2-3/4", Topps Peel-Offs were an insert with 1963 Topps baseball cards. There are 46 players in the unnumbered set, each pictured in a color photo inside an oval with the player's name, team and position in a band below. The back of the Peel-Off is removable, leaving a sticky surface that made the Peel-Off a popular decorative item among youngsters of the day. Naturally, that makes them quite scarce today. The stickers can be found both blank-backed and with instructions printed on the peel-off backing.

		NM	EX	VG
Complete Set (46):		525.00	275.00	160.00
Common Player:		4.00	2.00	1.25
(1)	Hank Aaron	35.00	17.50	10.00
(2)	Luis Aparicio	12.50	6.25	3.75
(3)	Richie Ashburn	17.50	8.75	5.25
(4)	Bob Aspromonte	4.00	2.00	1.25
(5)	Ernie Banks	22.50	11.00	6.75
(6)	Ken Boyer	7.50	3.75	2.25
(7)	Jim Bunning	10.00	5.00	3.00
(8)	Johnny Callison	4.00	2.00	1.25
(9)	Orlando Cepeda	10.00	5.00	3.00
(10)	Roberto Clemente	40.00	20.00	12.00
(11)	Rocky Colavito	9.00	4.50	2.75
(12)	Tommy Davis	4.00	2.00	1.25
(13)	Dick Donovan	4.00	2.00	1.25
(14)	Don Drysdale	15.00	7.50	4.50
(15)	Dick Farrell	4.00	2.00	1.25
(16)	Jim Gentile	4.00	2.00	1.25
(17)	Ray Herbert	4.00	2.00	1.25
(18)	Chuck Hinton	4.00	2.00	1.25
(19)	Ken Hubbs	7.50	3.75	2.25
(20)	Al Jackson	4.00	2.00	1.25
(21)	Al Kaline	17.50	8.75	5.25
(22)	Harmon Killebrew	17.50	8.75	5.25
(23)	Sandy Koufax	40.00	20.00	12.00
(24)	Jerry Lumpe	4.00	2.00	1.25
(25)	Art Mahaffey	4.00	2.00	1.25
(26)	Mickey Mantle	100.00	50.00	30.00
(27)	Willie Mays	35.00	17.50	10.00
(28)	Bill Mazeroski	12.50	6.25	3.75
(29)	Bill Monbouquette	4.00	2.00	1.25
(30)	Stan Musial	35.00	17.50	10.00
(31)	Camilo Pascual	4.00	2.00	1.25
(32)	Bob Purkey	4.00	2.00	1.25
(33)	Bobby Richardson	9.00	4.50	2.75
(34)	Brooks Robinson	17.50	8.75	5.25
(35)	Floyd Robinson	4.00	2.00	1.25
(36)	Frank Robinson	17.50	8.75	5.25
(37)	Bob Rodgers	4.00	2.00	1.25
(38)	Johnny Romano	4.00	2.00	1.25
(39)	Jack Sanford	4.00	2.00	1.25
(40)	Norm Siebern	4.00	2.00	1.25
(41)	Warren Spahn	17.50	8.75	5.25
(42)	Dave Stenhouse	4.00	2.00	1.25
(43)	Ralph Terry	4.00	2.00	1.25
(44)	Lee Thomas	4.00	2.00	1.25
(45)	Bill White	4.00	2.00	1.25
(46)	Carl Yastrzemski	20.00	10.00	6.00

1963 Topps Valentine Foldees

Featuring the artwork of 1960s cartoonist Jack Davis, this set of specialty cards had the left and right panels of the 4-1/2" x 2-3/8" pieces slit to allow either the top or the bottom half of the portrait to be folded over the central panel to create funny combinations. There were 55 cards in the series; Babe Ruth is the only baseball player included.

		NM	EX	VG
Complete Set (55):		150.00	75.00	45.00
6	Babe Ruth	25.00	12.50	7.50

1964 Topps

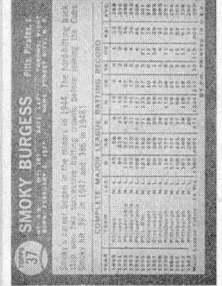

SMOKY BURGESS   catcher

The 1964 Topps set is a 587-card issue of 2-1/2" x 3-1/2" cards which is considered by many as being among the company's best efforts. Card fronts feature a large color photo which blends into a top panel which contains the team name, while a panel below the picture carries the player's name and position. An interesting innovation on the back is a baseball quiz question which required the rubbing of a white panel to reveal the answer. As in 1963, specialty cards remained modest in number with a 12-card set of statistical leaders, a few multi-player cards, rookies and World Series highlights. An interesting card is an "In Memoriam" card for Ken Hubbs who was killed in an airplane crash.

		NM	EX	VG
Complete Set (587):		4,250	2,125	1,250
Common Player (1-370):		3.50	1.75	1.00
Common Player (371-522):		6.00	3.00	1.75
Common Player (523-587):		9.00	4.50	2.75
1	N.L. E.R.A. Leaders (Dick Ellsworth, Bob Friend, Sandy Koufax)	20.00	10.00	6.00
2	A.L. E.R.A. Leaders (Camilo Pascual, Gary Peters, Juan Pizarro)	12.00	3.00	2.00
3	N.L. Pitching Leaders (Sandy Koufax, Jim Maloney, Juan Marichal, Warren Spahn)	20.00	10.00	6.00
4a	A.L. Pitching Leaders (Jim Bouton, Whitey Ford, Camilo Pascual) (apostrophe after "Pitching" on back)	17.50	8.75	5.25
4b	A.L. Pitching Leaders (Jim Bouton, Whitey Ford, Camilo Pascual) (no apostrophe)	17.50	8.75	5.25
5	N.L. Strikeout Leaders (Don Drysdale, Sandy Koufax, Jim Maloney)	20.00	10.00	6.00
6	A.L. Strikeout Leaders (Jim Bunning, Camilo Pascual, Dick Stigman)	12.50	6.25	3.75
7	N.L. Batting Leaders (Hank Aaron, Roberto Clemente, Tommy Davis, Dick Groat)	16.00	8.00	4.75
8	A.L. Batting Leaders (Al Kaline, Rich Rollins, Carl Yastrzemski)	12.50	6.25	3.75
9	N.L. Home Run Leaders (Hank Aaron, Orlando Cepeda, Willie Mays, Willie McCovey)	20.00	10.00	6.00
10	A.L. Home Run Leaders (Bob Allison, Harmon Killebrew, Dick Stuart)	12.00	6.00	3.50
11	N.L. R.B.I. Leaders (Hank Aaron, Ken Boyer, Bill White)	12.50	6.25	3.75
12	A.L. R.B.I. Leaders (Al Kaline, Harmon Killebrew, Dick Stuart)	13.50	6.75	4.00
13	Hoyt Wilhelm	15.00	7.50	4.50
14	Dodgers Rookies (Dick Nen, Nick Willhite)	3.50	1.75	1.00
15	Zoilo Versalles	3.50	1.75	1.00
16	John Boozer	3.50	1.75	1.00
17	Willie Kirkland	3.50	1.75	1.00
18	Billy O'Dell	3.50	1.75	1.00
19	Don Wart	3.50	1.75	1.00
20	Bob Friend	3.50	1.75	1.00
21	Yogi Berra	35.00	17.50	10.00
22	Jerry Adair	3.50	1.75	1.00
23	Chris Zachary	3.50	1.75	1.00
24	Carl Sawatski	3.50	1.75	1.00
25	Bill Monbouquette	3.50	1.75	1.00
26	Gino Cimoli	3.50	1.75	1.00
27	New York Mets Team	7.50	3.75	2.25
28	Claude Osteen	3.50	1.75	1.00
29	Lou Brock	24.00	12.00	7.25
30	Ron Perranoski	3.50	1.75	1.00
31	Dave Nicholson	3.50	1.75	1.00
32	Dean Chance	3.50	1.75	1.00
33	Reds Rookies (Sammy Ellis, Mel Queen)	3.50	1.75	1.00
34	Jim Perry	3.50	1.75	1.00
35	Ed Mathews	20.00	10.00	6.00
36	Hal Reniff	3.50	1.75	1.00
37	Smoky Burgess	3.50	1.75	1.00
38	*Jim Wynn*	5.00	2.50	1.50
39	Hank Aguirre	3.50	1.75	1.00
40	Dick Groat	3.50	1.75	1.00
41	Friendly Foes (Willie McCovey, Leon Wagner)	10.00	5.00	3.00
42	Moe Drabowsky	3.50	1.75	1.00
43	Roy Sievers	3.50	1.75	1.00
44	Duke Carmel	3.50	1.75	1.00
45	Milt Pappas	3.50	1.75	1.00
46	Ed Brinkman	3.50	1.75	1.00
47	Giants Rookies (Jesus Alou, Ron Herbel)	5.00	2.50	1.75
48	Bob Perry	3.50	1.75	1.00
49	Bill Henry	3.50	1.75	1.00
50	Mickey Mantle	225.00	100.00	65.00
51	Pete Richert	3.50	1.75	1.00
52	Chuck Hinton	3.50	1.75	1.00
53	Denis Menke	3.50	1.75	1.00
54	Sam Mele	3.50	1.75	1.00
55	Ernie Banks	35.00	17.50	10.00
56	Hal Brown	3.50	1.75	1.00
57	Tim Harkness	3.50	1.75	1.00
58	Don Demeter	3.50	1.75	1.00
59	Ernie Broglio	3.50	1.75	1.00
60	Frank Malzone	3.50	1.75	1.00
61	Angel Backstops (Bob Rodgers, Ed Sadowski)	3.50	1.75	1.00
62	Ted Savage	3.50	1.75	1.00
63	Johnny Orsino	3.50	1.75	1.00
64	Ted Abernathy	3.50	1.75	1.00
65	Felipe Alou	4.50	2.25	1.25
66	Eddie Fisher	3.50	1.75	1.00
67	Detroit Tigers Team	6.00	3.00	1.75
68	Willie Davis	3.50	1.75	1.00
69	Clete Boyer	10.00	5.00	3.00
70	Joe Torre	12.00	6.00	3.50
71	Jack Spring	3.50	1.75	1.00
72	Chico Cardenas	3.50	1.75	1.00
73	*Jimmie Hall*	3.50	1.75	1.00
74	Pirates Rookies (Tom Butters, Bob Priddy)	3.50	1.75	1.00
75	Wayne Causey	3.50	1.75	1.00
76	1st Series Checklist (1-88)	5.00	2.50	1.50
77	Jerry Walker	3.50	1.75	1.00
78	Merritt Ranew	3.50	1.75	1.00
79	Bob Heffner	3.50	1.75	1.00
80	Vada Pinson	9.00	4.50	2.75
81	All-Star Vets (Nellie Fox, Harmon Killebrew)	12.50	6.25	3.75
82	Jim Davenport	3.50	1.75	1.00
83	Gus Triandos	3.50	1.75	1.00
84	Carl Willey	3.50	1.75	1.00
85	Pete Ward	3.50	1.75	1.00
86	Al Downing	3.50	1.75	1.00
87	St. Louis Cardinals Team	6.00	3.00	1.75
88	John Roseboro	3.50	1.75	1.00
89	Boog Powell	7.50	3.75	2.25
90	Earl Battey	3.50	1.75	1.00
91	Bob Bailey	3.50	1.75	1.00
92	Steve Ridzik	3.50	1.75	1.00
93	Gary Geiger	3.50	1.75	1.00
94	Braves Rookies (Jim Britton, Larry Maxie)	3.50	1.75	1.00
95	George Altman	3.50	1.75	1.00
96	Bob Buhl	3.50	1.75	1.00
97	Jim Fregosi	3.50	1.75	1.00
98	Bill Bruton	3.50	1.75	1.00
99	Al Stanek	3.50	1.75	1.00
100	Elston Howard	12.50	6.25	3.75
101	Walt Alston	6.00	3.00	1.75
102	2nd Series Checklist (89-176)	6.00	3.00	1.75
103	Curt Flood	5.00	2.50	1.50
104	Art Mahaffey	3.50	1.75	1.00
105	Woody Held	3.50	1.75	1.00
106	Joe Nuxhall	3.50	1.75	1.00
107	White Sox Rookies (Bruce Howard, Frank Kreutzer)	3.50	1.75	1.00
108	John Wyatt	3.50	1.75	1.00
109	Rusty Staub	10.00	5.00	3.00
110	Albie Pearson	3.50	1.75	1.00
111	Don Elston	3.50	1.75	1.00
112	Bob Tillman	3.50	1.75	1.00
113	Grover Powell	3.50	1.75	1.00
114	Don Lock	3.50	1.75	1.00
115	Frank Bolling	3.50	1.75	1.00
116	Twins Rookies (Tony Oliva, Jay Ward)	9.00	4.50	2.75
117	Earl Francis	3.50	1.75	1.00
118	John Blanchard	5.00	2.50	1.50
119	Gary Kolb	3.50	1.75	1.00
120	Don Drysdale	17.50	8.75	5.25
121	Pete Runnels	3.50	1.75	1.00
122	Don McMahon	3.50	1.75	1.00
123	Jose Pagan	3.50	1.75	1.00
124	Orlando Pena	3.50	1.75	1.00
125	Pete Rose	140.00	70.00	40.00
126	Russ Snyder	3.50	1.75	1.00
127	Angels Rookies (Aubrey Gatewood, Dick Simpson)	3.50	1.75	1.00
128	*Mickey Lolich*	12.50	6.25	3.75
129	Amado Samuel	3.50	1.75	1.00
130	Gary Peters	3.50	1.75	1.00
131	Steve Boros	3.50	1.75	1.00
132	Milwaukee Braves Team	6.00	3.00	1.75
133	Jim Grant	3.50	1.75	1.00
134	Don Zimmer	5.00	2.50	1.50
135	Johnny Callison	3.50	1.75	1.00

No.	Player	NM	EX	VG
136	World Series Game 1 (Koufax Strikes Out 15)	30.00	15.00	9.00
137	World Series Game 2 (Davis Sparks Rally)	9.00	4.50	2.75
138	World Series Game 3 (L.A. Takes 3rd Straight)	9.00	4.50	2.75
139	World Series Game 4 (Sealing Yanks' Doom)	7.00	3.50	2.00
140	World Series (The Dodgers Celebrate)	7.00	3.50	2.00
141	Danny Murtaugh	3.50	1.75	1.00
142	John Bateman	3.50	1.75	1.00
143	Bubba Phillips	3.50	1.75	1.00
144	Al Worthington	3.50	1.75	1.00
145	Norm Siebern	3.50	1.75	1.00
146	Indians Rookies (**Bob Chance, Tommy John**)	17.50	8.75	5.25
147	Ray Sadecki	3.50	1.75	1.00
148	J.C. Martin	3.50	1.75	1.00
149	Paul Foytack	3.50	1.75	1.00
150	Willie Mays	90.00	45.00	27.50
151	K.C. Athletics Team	6.00	3.00	1.75
152	Denver Lemaster	3.50	1.75	1.00
153	Dick Williams	3.50	1.75	1.00
154	Dick Tracewski	3.50	1.75	1.00
155	Duke Snider	15.00	7.50	4.50
156	Bill Dailey	3.50	1.75	1.00
157	Gene Mauch	3.50	1.75	1.00
158	Ken Johnson	3.50	1.75	1.00
159	Charlie Dees	3.50	1.75	1.00
160	Ken Boyer	8.00	4.00	2.50
161	Dave McNally	3.50	1.75	1.00
162	Hitting Area (Vada Pinson, Dick Sisler)	5.00	2.50	1.50
163	Donn Clendenon	3.50	1.75	1.00
164	Bud Daley	3.50	1.75	1.00
165	Jerry Lumpe	3.50	1.75	1.00
166	Marty Keough	3.50	1.75	1.00
167	Senators Rookies (**Mike Brumley, Lou Piniella**)	27.50	13.50	8.25
168	Al Weis	3.50	1.75	1.00
169	Del Crandall	3.50	1.75	1.00
170	Dick Radatz	3.50	1.75	1.00
171	Ty Cline	3.50	1.75	1.00
172	Cleveland Indians Team	6.00	3.00	1.75
173	Ryne Duren	3.50	1.75	1.00
174	Doc Edwards	3.50	1.75	1.00
175	Billy Williams	17.50	8.75	5.25
176	Tracy Stallard	3.50	1.75	1.00
177	Harmon Killebrew	22.50	11.00	7.00
178	Hank Bauer	4.50	2.25	1.25
179	Carl Warwick	3.50	1.75	1.00
180	Tommy Davis	3.50	1.75	1.00
181	Dave Wickersham	3.50	1.75	1.00
182	Sox Sockers (Chuck Schilling, Carl Yastrzemski)	17.50	8.75	5.25
183	Ron Taylor	3.50	1.75	1.00
184	Al Luplow	3.50	1.75	1.00
185	Jim O'Toole	3.50	1.75	1.00
186	Roman Mejias	3.50	1.75	1.00
187	Ed Roebuck	3.50	1.75	1.00
188	3rd Series Checklist (177-264)	5.00	2.50	1.50
189	Bob Hendley	3.50	1.75	1.00
190	Bobby Richardson	12.50	6.25	3.75
191	Clay Dalrymple	3.50	1.75	1.00
192	Cubs Rookies (John Boccabella, Billy Cowan)	3.50	1.75	1.00
193	Jerry Lynch	3.50	1.75	1.00
194	John Goryl	3.50	1.75	1.00
195	Floyd Robinson	3.50	1.75	1.00
196	Jim Gentile	3.50	1.75	1.00
197	Frank Lary	3.50	1.75	1.00
198	Len Gabrielson	3.50	1.75	1.00
199	Joe Azcue	3.50	1.75	1.00
200	Sandy Koufax	70.00	35.00	20.00
201	Orioles Rookies (**Sam Bowens, Wally Bunker**)	3.50	1.75	1.00
202	Galen Cisco	3.50	1.75	1.00
203	John Kennedy	3.50	1.75	1.00
204	Matty Alou	3.50	1.75	1.00
205	Nellie Fox	12.50	6.25	3.75
206	Steve Hamilton	3.50	1.75	1.00
207	Fred Hutchinson	3.50	1.75	1.00
208	Wes Covington	3.50	1.75	1.00
209	Bob Allen	3.50	1.75	1.00
210	Carl Yastrzemski	35.00	17.50	10.00
211	Jim Coker	3.50	1.75	1.00
212	Pete Lovrich	3.50	1.75	1.00
213	Los Angeles Angels Team	6.00	3.00	1.75
214	Ken McMullen	3.50	1.75	1.00
215	Ray Herbert	3.50	1.75	1.00
216	Mike de la Hoz	3.50	1.75	1.00
217	Jim King	3.50	1.75	1.00
218	Hank Fischer	3.50	1.75	1.00
219	Young Aces (Jim Bouton, Al Downing)	8.00	4.00	2.50
220	Dick Ellsworth	3.50	1.75	1.00
221	Bob Saverine	3.50	1.75	1.00
222	Bill Pierce	3.50	1.75	1.00
223	George Banks	3.50	1.75	1.00
224	Tommie Sisk	3.50	1.75	1.00
225	Roger Maris	55.00	27.50	16.50
226	Colts Rookies (Gerald Grote, Larry Yellen)	5.00	2.50	1.50
227	Barry Latman	3.50	1.75	1.00
228	Felix Mantilla	3.50	1.75	1.00
229	Charley Lau	3.50	1.75	1.00
230	Brooks Robinson	22.50	11.00	6.75
231	Dick Calmus	3.50	1.75	1.00
232	Al Lopez	6.00	3.00	1.75
233	Hal Smith	3.50	1.75	1.00
234	Gary Bell	3.50	1.75	1.00
235	Ron Hunt	3.50	1.75	1.00
236	Bill Faul	3.50	1.75	1.00
237	Chicago Cubs Team	6.50	3.25	2.00
238	Roy McMillan	3.50	1.75	1.00
239	Herm Starrette	3.50	1.75	1.00
240	Bill White	3.50	1.75	1.00
241	Jim Owens	3.50	1.75	1.00
242	Harvey Kuenn	3.50	1.75	1.00
243	Phillies Rookies (Richie Allen, John Herrnstein)	17.50	8.75	5.25
244	**Tony LaRussa**	17.50	8.75	5.25
245	Dick Stigman	3.50	1.75	1.00
246	Manny Mota	3.50	1.75	1.00
247	Dave DeBusschere	5.00	2.50	1.50
248	Johnny Pesky	3.50	1.75	1.00
249	Doug Camilli	3.50	1.75	1.00
250	Al Kaline	22.50	11.00	7.00
251	Choo Choo Coleman	3.50	1.75	1.00
252	Ken Aspromonte	3.50	1.75	1.00
253	Wally Post	3.50	1.75	1.00
254	Don Hoak	3.50	1.75	1.00
255	Lee Thomas	3.50	1.75	1.00
256	Johnny Weekly	3.50	1.75	1.00
257	San Francisco Giants Team	6.00	3.00	1.75
258	Garry Roggenburk	3.50	1.75	1.00
259	Harry Bright	3.50	1.75	1.00
260	Frank Robinson	22.50	11.00	7.00
261	Jim Hannan	3.50	1.75	1.00
262	Cardinals Rookies (**Harry Fanok, Mike Shannon**)	9.00	4.50	2.75
263	Chuck Estrada	3.50	1.75	1.00
264	Jim Landis	3.50	1.75	1.00
265	Jim Bunning	12.50	6.25	3.75
266	Gene Freese	3.50	1.75	1.00
267	**Wilbur Wood**	5.00	2.50	1.50
268	Bill's Got It (Danny Murtaugh, Bill Virdon)	3.50	1.75	1.00
269	Ellis Burton	3.50	1.75	1.00
270	Rich Rollins	3.50	1.75	1.00
271	Bob Sadowski	3.50	1.75	1.00
272	Jake Wood	3.50	1.75	1.00
273	Mel Nelson	3.50	1.75	1.00
274	4th Series Checklist (265-352)	6.00	3.00	1.75
275	John Tsitouris	3.50	1.75	1.00
276	Jose Tartabull	3.50	1.75	1.00
277	Ken Retzer	3.50	1.75	1.00
278	Bobby Shantz	3.50	1.75	1.00
279	Joe Koppe	3.50	1.75	1.00
280	Juan Marichal	12.50	6.25	3.75
281	Yankees Rookies (Jake Gibbs, Tom Metcalf)	5.00	2.50	1.50
282	Bob Bruce	3.50	1.75	1.00
283	**Tommy McCraw**	3.50	1.75	1.00
284	Dick Schofield	3.50	1.75	1.00
285	Robin Roberts	12.50	6.25	3.75
286	Don Landrum	3.50	1.75	1.00
287	Red Sox Rookies (Tony Conigliaro, Bill Spanswick)	35.00	17.50	10.00
288	Al Moran	3.50	1.75	1.00
289	Frank Funk	3.50	1.75	1.00
290	Bob Allison	3.50	1.75	1.00
291	Phil Ortega	3.50	1.75	1.00
292	Mike Roarke	3.50	1.75	1.00
293	Phillies Team	6.00	3.00	1.75
294	Ken Hunt	3.50	1.75	1.00
295	Roger Craig	3.50	1.75	1.00
296	Ed Kirkpatrick	3.50	1.75	1.00
297	Ken MacKenzie	3.50	1.75	1.00
298	Harry Craft	3.50	1.75	1.00
299	Bill Stafford	3.50	1.75	1.00
300	Hank Aaron	70.00	35.00	20.00
301	Larry Brown	3.50	1.75	1.00
302	Dan Pfister	3.50	1.75	1.00
303	Jim Campbell	3.50	1.75	1.00
304	Bob Johnson	3.50	1.75	1.00
305	Jack Lamabe	3.50	1.75	1.00
306	Giant Gunners (Orlando Cepeda, Willie Mays)	25.00	12.50	7.50
307	Joe Gibbon	3.50	1.75	1.00
308	Gene Stephens	3.50	1.75	1.00
309	Paul Toth	3.50	1.75	1.00
310	Jim Gilliam	5.00	2.50	1.50
311	Tom Brown	3.50	1.75	1.00
312	Tigers Rookies (Fritz Fisher, Fred Gladding)	3.50	1.75	1.00
313	Chuck Hiller	3.50	1.75	1.00
314	Jerry Buchek	3.50	1.75	1.00
315	Bo Belinsky	3.50	1.75	1.00
316	Gene Oliver	3.50	1.75	1.00
317	Al Smith	3.50	1.75	1.00
318	Twins Team	6.00	3.00	1.75
319	Paul Brown	3.50	1.75	1.00
320	Rocky Colavito	12.50	6.25	3.75
321	Bob Lillis	3.50	1.75	1.00
322	George Brunet	3.50	1.75	1.00
323	John Buzhardt	3.50	1.75	1.00
324	Casey Stengel	12.50	6.25	3.75
325	Hector Lopez	3.50	1.75	1.00
326	Ron Brand	3.50	1.75	1.00
327	Don Blasingame	3.50	1.75	1.00
328	Bob Shaw	3.50	1.75	1.00
329	Russ Nixon	3.50	1.75	1.00
330	Tommy Harper	3.50	1.75	1.00
331	A.L. Bombers (Norm Cash, Al Kaline, Mickey Mantle, Roger Maris)	100.00	50.00	30.00
332	Ray Washburn	3.50	1.75	1.00
333	Billy Moran	3.50	1.75	1.00
334	Lew Krausse	3.50	1.75	1.00
335	Don Mossi	3.50	1.75	1.00
336	Andre Rodgers	3.50	1.75	1.00
337	Dodgers Rookies (**Al Ferrara, Jeff Torborg**)	6.00	3.00	1.75
338	Jack Kralick	3.50	1.75	1.00
339	Walt Bond	3.50	1.75	1.00
340	Joe Cunningham	3.50	1.75	1.00
341	Jim Roland	3.50	1.75	1.00
342	Willie Stargell	25.00	12.50	7.50
343	Senators Team	6.00	3.00	1.75
344	Phil Linz	3.50	1.75	1.00
345	Frank Thomas	3.50	1.75	1.00
346	Joe Jay	3.50	1.75	1.00
347	Bobby Wine	3.50	1.75	1.00
348	Ed Lopat	3.50	1.75	1.00
349	Art Fowler	3.50	1.75	1.00
350	Willie McCovey	20.00	10.00	6.00
351	Dan Schneider	3.50	1.75	1.00
352	Eddie Bressoud	3.50	1.75	1.00
353	Wally Moon	3.50	1.75	1.00
354	Dave Giusti	3.50	1.75	1.00
355	Vic Power	3.50	1.75	1.00
356	Reds Rookies (Bill McCool, Chico Ruiz)	3.50	1.75	1.00
357	Charley James	3.50	1.75	1.00
358	Ron Kline	3.50	1.75	1.00
359	Jim Schaffer	3.50	1.75	1.00
360	Joe Pepitone	4.50	2.25	1.25
361	Jay Hook	3.50	1.75	1.00
362	5th Series Checklist (353-429)	6.00	3.00	1.75
363	Dick McAuliffe	3.50	1.75	1.00
364	Joe Gaines	3.50	1.75	1.00
365	Cal McLish	3.50	1.75	1.00
366	Nelson Mathews	3.50	1.75	1.00
367	Fred Whitfield	3.50	1.75	1.00
368	White Sox Rookies (**Fritz Ackley, Don Buford**)	5.50	2.75	1.75
369	Jerry Zimmerman	3.50	1.75	1.00
370	Hal Woodeshick	3.50	1.75	1.00
371	Frank Howard	7.50	3.75	2.25
372	Howie Koplitz	6.00	3.00	1.75
373	Pittsburgh Pirates Team	11.00	5.50	3.25
374	Bobby Bolin	6.00	3.00	1.75
375	Ron Santo	20.00	10.00	6.00
376	Dave Morehead	6.00	3.00	1.75
377	Bob Skinner	6.00	3.00	1.75
378	Braves Rookies (**Jack Smith, Woody Woodward**)	6.00	3.00	1.75
379	Tony Gonzalez	6.00	3.00	1.75
380	Whitey Ford	30.00	15.00	9.00
381	Bob Taylor	6.00	3.00	1.75
382	Wes Stock	6.00	3.00	1.75
383	Bill Rigney	6.00	3.00	1.75
384	Ron Hansen	6.00	3.00	1.75
385	Curt Simmons	6.00	3.00	1.75
386	Lenny Green	6.00	3.00	1.75
387	Terry Fox	6.00	3.00	1.75
388	Athletics Rookies (John O'Donoghue, George Williams)	6.00	3.00	1.75
389	Jim Umbricht	6.00	3.00	1.75
390	Orlando Cepeda	17.50	8.75	5.25
391	Sam McDowell	6.00	3.00	1.75
392	Jim Pagliaroni	6.00	3.00	1.75
393	Casey Teaches (Ed Kranepool, Casey Stengel)	12.50	6.25	3.75
394	Bob Miller	6.00	3.00	1.75
395	Tom Tresh	13.50	6.75	4.00
396	Dennis Bennett	6.00	3.00	1.75
397	Chuck Cottier	6.00	3.00	1.75
398	Mets Rookies (Bill Haas, Dick Smith)	6.00	3.00	1.75
399	Jackie Brandt	6.00	3.00	1.75
400	Warren Spahn	30.00	15.00	9.00
401	Charlie Maxwell	6.00	3.00	1.75
402	Tom Sturdivant	6.00	3.00	1.75
403	Cincinnati Reds Team	10.00	5.00	3.00
404	Tony Martinez	6.00	3.00	1.75
405	Ken McBride	6.00	3.00	1.75
406	Al Spangler	6.00	3.00	1.75
407	Bill Freehan	6.00	3.00	1.75
408	Cubs Rookies (Fred Burdette, Jim Stewart)	6.00	3.00	1.75
409	Bill Fischer	6.00	3.00	1.75
410	Dick Stuart	6.00	3.00	1.75
411	Lee Walls	6.00	3.00	1.75
412	Ray Culp	6.00	3.00	1.75
413	Johnny Keane	6.00	3.00	1.75
414	Jack Sanford	6.00	3.00	1.75
415	Tony Kubek	12.50	6.25	3.75
416	Lee Maye	6.00	3.00	1.75
417	Don Cardwell	6.00	3.00	1.75
418	Orioles Rookies (Darold Knowles, Les Narum)	6.00	3.00	1.75
419	**Ken Harrelson**	9.00	4.50	2.75
420	Jim Maloney	6.00	3.00	1.75
421	Camilo Carreon	6.00	3.00	1.75
422	Jack Fisher	6.00	3.00	1.75
423	Tops in N.L. (Hank Aaron, Willie Mays)	85.00	42.50	25.00
424	Dick Bertell	6.00	3.00	1.75
425	Norm Cash	12.00	6.00	3.50
426	Bob Rodgers	6.00	3.00	1.75
427	Don Rudolph	6.00	3.00	1.75
428	Red Sox Rookies (Archie Skeen, Pete Smith)	6.00	3.00	1.75
429	Tim McCarver	12.50	6.25	3.75
430	Juan Pizarro	6.00	3.00	1.75
431	George Alusik	6.00	3.00	1.75
432	Ruben Amaro	6.00	3.00	1.75
433	New York Yankees Team	20.00	10.00	6.00
434	Don Nottebart	6.00	3.00	1.75
435	Vic Davalillo	6.00	3.00	1.75
436	Charlie Neal	6.00	3.00	1.75
437	Ed Bailey	6.00	3.00	1.75
438	6th Series Checklist (430-506)	11.00	5.50	3.25
439	Harvey Haddix	6.00	3.00	1.75
440	Bob Clemente	145.00	75.00	45.00
441	Bob Duliba	6.00	3.00	1.75
442	Pumpsie Green	6.00	3.00	1.75
443	Chuck Dressen	6.00	3.00	1.75
444	Larry Jackson	6.00	3.00	1.75
445	Bill Skowron	9.00	4.50	2.75
446	Julian Javier	6.00	3.00	1.75
447	Ted Bowsfield	6.00	3.00	1.75
448	Cookie Rojas	6.00	3.00	1.75
449	Deron Johnson	6.00	3.00	1.75
450	Steve Barber	6.00	3.00	1.75
451	Joe Amalfitano	6.00	3.00	1.75

		NM	EX	VG
452	Giants Rookies (**Gil Garrido, Jim Hart**)	7.50	3.75	2.25
453	Frank Baumann	6.00	3.00	1.75
454	Tommie Aaron	6.00	3.00	1.75
455	Bernie Allen	6.00	3.00	1.75
456	Dodgers Rookies (Wes Parker, John Werhas)	6.00	3.00	1.75
457	Jesse Gonder	6.00	3.00	1.75
458	Ralph Terry	6.00	3.00	1.75
459	Red Sox Rookies (Pete Charton, Dalton Jones)	6.00	3.00	1.75
460	Bob Gibson	25.00	12.50	7.50
461	George Thomas	6.00	3.00	1.75
462	Birdie Tebbetts	6.00	3.00	1.75
463	Don Leppert	6.00	3.00	1.75
464	Dallas Green	6.00	3.00	1.75
465	Mike Hershberger	6.00	3.00	1.75
466	Athletics Rookies (Dick Green, Aurelio Monteagudo)	6.00	3.00	1.75
467	Bob Aspromonte		6.00	3.00	1.75
468	Gaylord Perry	20.00	10.00	6.00
469	Cubs Rookies (Fred Norman, Sterling Slaughter)	6.00	3.00	1.75
470	Jim Bouton	10.00	5.00	3.00
471	**Gates Brown**	6.50	3.25	2.00
472	Vern Law	6.00	3.00	1.75
473	Baltimore Orioles Team	9.00	4.50	3.75
474	Larry Sherry	6.00	3.00	1.75
475	Ed Charles	6.00	3.00	1.75
476	Braves Rookies (Rico Carty, Dick Kelley)	9.00	4.50	2.75
477	Mike Joyce	6.00	3.00	1.75
478	Dick Howser	6.00	3.00	1.75
479	Cardinals Rookies (Dave Bakenhaster, Johnny Lewis)	6.00	3.00	1.75
480	Bob Purkey	6.00	3.00	1.75
481	Chuck Schilling	6.00	3.00	1.75
482	Phillies Rookies (**John Briggs, Danny Cater**)	6.00	3.00	1.75
483	Fred Valentine	6.00	3.00	1.75
484	Bill Pleis	6.00	3.00	1.75
485	Tom Haller	6.00	3.00	1.75
486	Bob Kennedy	6.00	3.00	1.75
487	Mike McCormick	6.00	3.00	1.75
488	Yankees Rookies (Bob Meyer, Pete Mikkelsen)	6.00	3.00	1.75
489	Julio Navarro	6.00	3.00	1.75
490	Ron Fairly	6.00	3.00	1.75
491	Ed Rakow	6.00	3.00	1.75
492	Colts Rookies (Jim Beauchamp, Mike White)	6.00	3.00	1.75
493	Don Lee	6.00	3.00	1.75
494	Al Jackson	6.00	3.00	1.75
495	Bill Virdon	6.00	3.00	1.75
496	Chicago White Sox Team	9.00	4.50	2.75
497	Jeoff Long	6.00	3.00	1.75
498	Dave Stenhouse	6.00	3.00	1.75
499	Indians Rookies (Chico Salmon, Gordon Seyfried)	6.00	3.00	1.75
500	Camilo Pascual	6.00	3.00	1.75
501	Bob Veale	6.00	3.00	1.75
502	Angels Rookies (Bobby Knoop, Bob Lee)	6.00	3.00	1.75
503	Earl Wilson	6.00	3.00	1.75
504	Claude Raymond	6.00	3.00	1.75
505	Stan Williams	6.00	3.00	1.75
506	Bobby Bragan	6.00	3.00	1.75
507	John Edwards	6.00	3.00	1.75
508	Diego Segui	6.00	3.00	1.75
509	Pirates Rookies (Gene Alley, Orlando McFarlane)	6.00	3.00	1.75
510	Lindy McDaniel	6.00	3.00	1.75
511	Lou Jackson	6.00	3.00	1.75
512	Tigers Rookies (**Willie Horton, Joe Sparma**)	22.50	11.00	6.75
513	Don Larsen	6.00	3.00	1.75
514	Jim Hickman	6.00	3.00	1.75
515	Johnny Romano	6.00	3.00	1.75
516	Twins Rookies (Jerry Arrigo, Dwight Siebler)	6.00	3.00	1.75
517a	7th Series Checklist (507-587) (Wrong numbering on back.)	15.00	7.50	4.50
517b	7th Series Checklist (507-587) (Correct numbering on back.)	11.00	5.50	3.25
518	Carl Bouldin	6.00	3.00	1.75
519	Charlie Smith	6.00	3.00	1.75
520	Jack Baldschun	6.00	3.00	1.75
521	Tom Satriano	6.00	3.00	1.75
522	Bobby Tiefenauer	6.00	3.00	1.75
523	Lou Burdette	9.00	4.50	2.75
524	Reds Rookies (Jim Dickson, Bobby Klaus)	9.00	4.50	2.75
525	Al McBean	9.00	4.50	2.75
526	Lou Clinton	9.00	4.50	2.75
527	Larry Bearnarth	9.00	4.50	2.75
528	Athletics Rookies (Dave Duncan, Tom Reynolds)	9.00	4.50	2.75
529	Al Dark	9.00	4.50	2.75
530	Leon Wagner	9.00	4.50	2.75
531	L.A. Dodgers Team	17.50	8.75	5.25
532	Twins Rookies (Bud Bloomfield, Joe Nossek)	9.00	4.50	2.75
533	Johnny Klippstein	9.00	4.50	2.75
534	Gus Bell	9.00	4.50	2.75
535	Phil Regan	9.00	4.50	2.75
536	Mets Rookies (Larry Elliot, John Stephenson)	9.00	4.50	2.75
537	Dan Osinski	9.00	4.50	2.75
538	Minnie Minoso	13.50	6.75	4.00
539	Roy Face	9.00	4.50	2.75
540	Luis Aparicio	35.00	17.50	10.00
541	Braves Rookies (Phil Niekro, Phil Roof)	50.00	25.00	15.00
542	Don Mincher	9.00	4.50	2.75
543	Bob Uecker	30.00	15.00	9.00
544	Colts Rookies (Steve Hertz, Joe Hoerner)	9.00	4.50	2.75
545	Max Alvis	9.00	4.50	2.75
546	Joe Christopher	9.00	4.50	2.75
547	Gil Hodges	15.00	7.50	4.50
548	N.L. Rookies (Wayne Schurr, Paul Speckenbach)	9.00	4.50	2.75
549	Joe Moeller	9.00	4.50	2.75
550	Ken Hubbs - In Memoriam	20.00	10.00	6.00
551	Billy Hoeft	9.00	4.50	2.75
552	Indians Rookies (**Tom Kelley, Sonny Siebert**)	11.00	5.50	3.25
553	Jim Brewer	9.00	4.50	2.75
554	Hank Foiles	9.00	4.50	2.75
555	Lee Stange	9.00	4.50	2.75
556	Mets Rookies (Steve Dillon, Ron Locke)	9.00	4.50	2.75
557	Leo Burke	9.00	4.50	2.75
558	Don Schwall	9.00	4.50	2.75
559	Dick Phillips	9.00	4.50	2.75
560	Dick Farrell	9.00	4.50	2.75
561	Phillies Rookies (**Dave Bennett, Rick Wise**)	11.00	5.50	3.25
562	Pedro Ramos	9.00	4.50	2.75
563	Dal Maxvill	9.00	4.50	2.75
564	A.L. Rookies (Joe McCabe, Jerry McNertney)	9.00	4.50	2.75
565	Stu Miller	9.00	4.50	2.75
566	Ed Kranepool	9.00	4.50	2.75
567	Jim Kaat	12.50	6.25	3.75
568	N.L. Rookies (Phil Gagliano, Cap Peterson)	9.00	4.50	2.75
569	Fred Newman	9.00	4.50	2.75
570	Bill Mazeroski	25.00	12.50	7.50
571	Gene Conley	9.00	4.50	2.75
572	A.L. Rookies (Dick Egan, Dave Gray)	9.00	4.50	2.75
573	Jim Duffalo	9.00	4.50	2.75
574	Manny Jimenez	9.00	4.50	2.75
575	Tony Cloninger	9.00	4.50	2.75
576	Mets Rookies (Jerry Hinsley, Bill Wakefield)	9.00	4.50	2.75
577	Gordy Coleman	9.00	4.50	2.75
578	Glen Hobbie	9.00	4.50	2.75
579	Boston Red Sox Team	17.50	8.75	5.25
580	Johnny Podres	11.00	5.50	3.25
581	Yankees Rookies (Pedro Gonzalez, Archie Moore)	9.00	4.50	2.75
582	Rod Kanehl	9.00	4.50	2.75
583	Tito Francona	9.00	4.50	2.75
584	Joel Horlen	9.00	4.50	2.75
585	Tony Taylor	9.00	4.50	2.75
586	Jim Piersall	10.00	5.00	3.00
587	Bennie Daniels	12.00	6.00	3.50

1964 Topps Coins

The 164 metal coins in this set were issued by Topps as inserts in the company's baseball card wax packs. The series is divided into two principal types, 120 "regular" coins and 44 All-Star coins. The 1 1/2" diameter coins feature a full-color background for the player photos in the "regular" series, while the players in the All-Star series are featured against plain red or blue backgrounds. There are two variations each of the Mantle, Causey and Hinton coins among the All-Star subset.

		NM	EX	VG
Complete Set (164):		1,125	550.00	325.00
Common Player:		6.00	3.00	1.75
1	Don Zimmer	6.00	3.00	1.75
2	Jim Wynn	6.00	3.00	1.75
3	Johnny Orsino	6.00	3.00	1.75
4	Jim Bouton	7.50	3.75	2.25
5	Dick Groat	6.00	3.00	1.75
6	Leon Wagner	6.00	3.00	1.75
7	Frank Malzone	6.00	3.00	1.75
8	Steve Barber	6.00	3.00	1.75
9	Johnny Romano	6.00	3.00	1.75
10	Tom Tresh	7.50	3.75	2.25
11	Felipe Alou	6.00	3.00	1.75
12	Dick Stuart	6.00	3.00	1.75
13	Claude Osteen	6.00	3.00	1.75
14	Juan Pizarro	6.00	3.00	1.75
15	Donn Clendenon	6.00	3.00	1.75
16	Jimmie Hall	6.00	3.00	1.75
17	Larry Jackson	6.00	3.00	1.75
18	Brooks Robinson	15.00	7.50	4.50
19	Bob Allison	6.00	3.00	1.75
20	Ed Roebuck	6.00	3.00	1.75
21	Pete Ward	6.00	3.00	1.75
22	Willie McCovey	12.50	6.25	3.75
23	Elston Howard	7.00	3.50	2.00
24	Diego Segui	6.00	3.00	1.75
25	Ken Boyer	7.00	3.50	2.00
26	Carl Yastrzemski	20.00	10.00	6.00
27	Bill Mazeroski	12.50	6.25	3.75
28	Jerry Lumpe	6.00	3.00	1.75
29	Woody Held	6.00	3.00	1.75
30	Dick Radatz	6.00	3.00	1.75

		NM	EX	VG
31	Luis Aparicio	10.00	5.00	3.00
32	Dave Nicholson	6.00	3.00	1.75
33	Ed Mathews	15.00	7.50	4.50
34	Don Drysdale	15.00	7.50	4.50
35	Ray Culp	6.00	3.00	1.75
36	Juan Marichal	10.00	5.00	3.00
37	Frank Robinson	15.00	7.50	4.50
38	Chuck Hinton	6.00	3.00	1.75
39	Floyd Robinson	6.00	3.00	1.75
40	Tommy Harper	6.00	3.00	1.75
41	Ron Hansen	6.00	3.00	1.75
42	Ernie Banks	20.00	10.00	6.00
43	Jesse Gonder	6.00	3.00	1.75
44	Billy Williams	10.00	5.00	3.00
45	Vada Pinson	7.00	3.50	2.00
46	Rocky Colavito	9.00	4.50	2.75
47	Bill Monbouquette	6.00	3.00	1.75
48	Max Alvis	6.00	3.00	1.75
49	Norm Siebern	6.00	3.00	1.75
50	John Callison	6.00	3.00	1.75
51	Rich Rollins	6.00	3.00	1.75
52	Ken McBride	6.00	3.00	1.75
53	Don Lock	6.00	3.00	1.75
54	Ron Fairly	6.00	3.00	1.75
55	Roberto Clemente	30.00	15.00	9.00
56	Dick Ellsworth	6.00	3.00	1.75
57	Tommy Davis	6.00	3.00	1.75
58	Tony Gonzalez	6.00	3.00	1.75
59	Bob Gibson	15.00	7.50	4.50
60	Jim Maloney	6.00	3.00	1.75
61	Frank Howard	7.00	3.50	2.00
62	Jim Pagliaroni	6.00	3.00	1.75
63	Orlando Cepeda	10.00	5.00	3.00
64	Ron Perranoski	6.00	3.00	1.75
65	Curt Flood	6.00	3.00	1.75
66	Al McBean	6.00	3.00	1.75
67	Dean Chance	6.00	3.00	1.75
68	Ron Santo	7.50	3.75	2.25
69	Jack Baldschun	6.00	3.00	1.75
70	Milt Pappas	6.00	3.00	1.75
71	Gary Peters	6.00	3.00	1.75
72	Bobby Richardson	7.50	3.75	2.25
73	Lee Thomas	6.00	3.00	1.75
74	Hank Aguirre	6.00	3.00	1.75
75	Carl Willey	6.00	3.00	1.75
76	Camilo Pascual	6.00	3.00	1.75
77	Bob Friend	6.00	3.00	1.75
78	Bill White	6.00	3.00	1.75
79	Norm Cash	7.50	3.75	2.25
80	Willie Mays	30.00	15.00	9.00
81	Duke Carmel	6.00	3.00	1.75
82	Pete Rose	35.00	17.50	10.50
83	Hank Aaron	30.00	15.00	9.00
84	Bob Aspromonte	6.00	3.00	1.75
85	Jim O'Toole	6.00	3.00	1.75
86	Vic Davalillo	6.00	3.00	1.75
87	Bill Freehan	6.00	3.00	1.75
88	Warren Spahn	15.00	7.50	4.50
89	Ron Hunt	6.00	3.00	1.75
90	Denis Menke	6.00	3.00	1.75
91	Turk Farrell	6.00	3.00	1.75
92	Jim Hickman	6.00	3.00	1.75
93	Jim Bunning	9.00	4.50	2.75
94	Bob Hendley	6.00	3.00	1.75
95	Ernie Broglio	6.00	3.00	1.75
96	Rusty Staub	7.00	3.50	2.00
97	Lou Brock	10.00	5.00	3.00
98	Jim Fregosi	6.00	3.00	1.75
99	Jim Grant	6.00	3.00	1.75
100	Al Kaline	15.00	7.50	4.50
101	Earl Battey	6.00	3.00	1.75
102	Wayne Causey	6.00	3.00	1.75
103	Chuck Schilling	6.00	3.00	1.75
104	Boog Powell	7.50	3.75	2.25
105	Dave Wickersham	6.00	3.00	1.75
106	Sandy Koufax	30.00	15.00	9.00
107	John Bateman	6.00	3.00	1.75
108	Ed Brinkman	6.00	3.00	1.75
109	Al Downing	6.00	3.00	1.75
110	Joe Azcue	6.00	3.00	1.75
111	Albie Pearson	6.00	3.00	1.75
112	Harmon Killebrew	15.00	7.50	4.50
113	Tony Taylor	6.00	3.00	1.75
114	Alvin Jackson	6.00	3.00	1.75
115	Billy O'Dell	6.00	3.00	1.75
116	Don Demeter	6.00	3.00	1.75
117	Ed Charles	6.00	3.00	1.75
118	Joe Torre	7.50	3.75	2.25
119	Don Nottebart	6.00	3.00	1.75
120	Mickey Mantle	65.00	32.00	19.50
121	Joe Pepitone (All-Star)	7.50	3.75	2.25
122	Dick Stuart (All-Star)	6.00	3.00	1.75
123	Bobby Richardson (All-Star)	7.50	3.75	2.25
124	Jerry Lumpe (All-Star)	6.00	3.00	1.75
125	Brooks Robinson (All-Star)	12.50	6.25	3.75
126	Frank Malzone (All-Star)	6.00	3.00	1.75
127	Luis Aparicio (All-Star)	9.00	4.50	2.75
128	Jim Fregosi (All-Star)	6.00	3.00	1.75
129	Al Kaline (All-Star)	12.50	6.25	3.75
130	Leon Wagner (All-Star)	6.00	3.00	1.75
131a	Mickey Mantle (All-Star, lefthanded.)	45.00	22.00	13.50
131b	Mickey Mantle (All-Star, righthanded.)	50.00	25.00	15.00
132	Albie Pearson (All-Star)	6.00	3.00	1.75
133	Harmon Killebrew (All-Star)	12.50	6.25	3.75
134	Carl Yastrzemski (All-Star)	17.50	8.75	5.25
135	Elston Howard (All-Star)	7.00	3.50	2.00
136	Earl Battey (All-Star)	6.00	3.00	1.75
137	Camilo Pascual (All-Star)	6.00	3.00	1.75
138	Jim Bouton (All-Star)	7.00	3.50	2.00
139	Whitey Ford (All-Star)	15.00	7.50	4.50
140	Gary Peters (All-Star)	6.00	3.00	1.75
141	Bill White (All-Star)	6.00	3.00	1.75
142	Orlando Cepeda (All-Star)	9.00	4.50	2.75
143	Bill Mazeroski (All-Star)	10.00	5.00	3.00
144	Tony Taylor (All-Star)	6.00	3.00	1.75
145	Ken Boyer (All-Star)	7.00	3.50	2.00

		NM	EX	VG
146	Ron Santo (All-Star)	7.50	3.75	2.25
147	Dick Groat (All-Star)	6.00	3.00	1.75
148	Roy McMillan (All-Star)	6.00	3.00	1.75
149	Hank Aaron (All-Star)	27.50	13.50	8.25
150	Roberto Clemente (All-Star)	27.50	13.50	8.25
151	Willie Mays (All-Star)	27.50	13.50	8.25
152	Vada Pinson (All-Star)	7.00	3.50	2.00
153	Tommy Davis (All-Star)	6.00	3.00	1.75
154	Frank Robinson (All-Star)	12.50	6.25	3.75
155	Joe Torre (All-Star)	7.50	3.75	2.25
156	Tim McCarver (All-Star)	6.00	3.00	1.75
157	Juan Marichal (All-Star)	10.00	5.00	3.00
158	Jim Maloney (All-Star)	6.00	3.00	1.75
159	Sandy Koufax (All-Star)	27.50	13.50	8.25
160	Warren Spahn (All-Star)	12.50	6.25	3.75
161a	Wayne Causey (All-Star, N.L. on back.)	20.00	10.00	6.00
161b	Wayne Causey (All-Star, A.L. on back.)	6.00	3.00	1.75
162a	Chuck Hinton (All-Star, N.L. on back.)	20.00	10.00	6.00
162b	Chuck Hinton (All-Star, A.L. on back.)	6.00	3.00	1.75
163	Bob Aspromonte (All-Star)	6.00	3.00	1.75
164	Ron Hunt (All-Star)	6.00	3.00	1.75

1964 Topps Giants

Measuring 3-1/8" x 5-1/4" the Topps Giants were the company's first postcard-size issue. The cards feature large color photographs surrounded by white borders with a white baseball containing the player's name, position and team. Card backs carry another photo of the player surrounded by a newspaper-style explanation of the depicted career highlight. The 60-card set contains primarily stars which means it's an excellent place to find inexpensive cards of Hall of Famers. The '64 Giants were not printed in equal quantity and seven of the cards, including Sandy Koufax and Willie Mays, are significantly scarcer than the remainder of the set.

		NM	EX	VG
	Complete Set (60):	265.00	135.00	80.00
	Common Player:	3.00	1.50	.90
1	Gary Peters	3.00	1.50	.90
2	Ken Johnson	3.00	1.50	.90
3	Sandy Koufax/SP	35.00	17.50	10.00
4	Bob Bailey	3.00	1.50	.90
5	Milt Pappas	3.00	1.50	.90
6	Ron Hunt	3.00	1.50	.90
7	Whitey Ford	10.00	5.00	3.00
8	Roy McMillan	3.00	1.50	.90
9	Rocky Colavito	6.00	3.00	1.75
10	Jim Bunning	6.00	3.00	1.75
11	Roberto Clemente	17.50	8.75	5.25
12	Al Kaline	9.00	4.50	2.75
13	Nellie Fox	7.00	3.50	2.00
14	Tony Gonzalez	3.00	1.50	.90
15	Jim Gentile	3.00	1.50	.90
16	Dean Chance	3.00	1.50	.90
17	Dick Ellsworth	3.00	1.50	.90
18	Jim Fregosi	3.00	1.50	.90
19	Dick Groat	3.00	1.50	.90
20	Chuck Hinton	3.00	1.50	.90
21	Elston Howard	4.50	2.25	1.25
22	Dick Farrell	3.00	1.50	.90
23	Albie Pearson	3.00	1.50	.90
24	Frank Howard	4.00	2.00	1.25
25	Mickey Mantle	35.00	17.50	10.00
26	Joe Torre	5.00	2.50	1.50
27	Ed Brinkman	3.00	1.50	.90
28	Bob Friend/SP	12.50	6.25	3.75
29	Frank Robinson	8.00	4.00	2.50
30	Bill Freehan	3.00	1.50	.90
31	Warren Spahn	8.00	4.00	2.50
32	Camilo Pascual	3.00	1.50	.90
33	Pete Ward	3.00	1.50	.90
34	Jim Maloney	3.00	1.50	.90
35	Dave Wickersham	3.00	1.50	.90
36	Johnny Callison	3.00	1.50	.90
37	Juan Marichal	7.00	3.50	2.00
38	Harmon Killebrew	9.00	4.50	2.75
39	Luis Aparicio	7.00	3.50	2.00
40	Dick Radatz	3.00	1.50	.90
41	Bob Gibson	7.00	3.50	2.00
42	Dick Stuart/SP	15.00	7.50	4.50
43	Tommy Davis	3.00	1.50	.90
44	Tony Oliva	3.50	1.75	1.00
45	Wayne Causey/SP	15.00	7.50	4.50
46	Max Alvis	3.00	1.50	.90
47	Galen Cisco/SP	13.50	6.75	4.00

		NM	EX	VG
48	Carl Yastrzemski	9.00	4.50	2.75
49	Hank Aaron	17.50	8.75	5.25
50	Brooks Robinson	9.00	4.50	2.75
51	Willie Mays/SP	35.00	17.50	10.00
52	Billy Williams	8.00	4.00	2.50
53	Juan Pizarro	3.00	1.50	.90
54	Leon Wagner	3.00	1.50	.90
55	Orlando Cepeda	7.00	3.50	2.00
56	Vada Pinson	3.50	1.75	1.00
57	Ken Boyer	3.50	1.75	1.00
58	Ron Santo	5.00	2.50	1.50
59	John Romano	3.00	1.50	.90
60	Bill Skowron/SP	16.00	8.00	4.75

1964 Topps Photo Tatoos

Apparently not content to leave the skin of American children without adornment, Topps jumped back into the tattoo field in 1964 with the release of a new series, measuring 1-9/16" x 3-1/2". The picture side for the 20 team tattoos gives the team logo and name.

		NM	EX	VG
	Complete Set (79):	3,000	1,500	900.00
	Common Player:	15.00	7.50	4.50
	Unopened Pack:	160.00		
(1)	Hank Aaron	135.00	65.00	40.00
(2)	Hank Aguirre	15.00	7.50	4.50
(3)	Max Alvis	15.00	7.50	4.50
(4)	Ernie Banks	80.00	40.00	24.00
(5)	Steve Barber	15.00	7.50	4.50
(6)	Ken Boyer	20.00	10.00	6.00
(7)	Johnny Callison	15.00	7.50	4.50
(8)	Norm Cash	20.00	10.00	6.00
(9)	Wayne Causey	15.00	7.50	4.50
(10)	Orlando Cepeda	50.00	25.00	15.00
(11)	Rocky Colavito	50.00	25.00	15.00
(12)	Ray Culp	15.00	7.50	4.50
(13)	Vic Davalillo	15.00	7.50	4.50
(14)	Moe Drabowsky	15.00	7.50	4.50
(15)	Dick Ellsworth	15.00	7.50	4.50
(16)	Curt Flood	15.00	7.50	4.50
(17)	Bill Freehan	15.00	7.50	4.50
(18)	Jim Fregosi	15.00	7.50	4.50
(19)	Bob Friend	15.00	7.50	4.50
(20)	Dick Groat	15.00	7.50	4.50
(21)	Woody Held	15.00	7.50	4.50
(22)	Frank Howard	20.00	10.00	6.00
(23)	Al Jackson	15.00	7.50	4.50
(24)	Larry Jackson	15.00	7.50	4.50
(25)	Ken Johnson	15.00	7.50	4.50
(26)	Al Kaline	60.00	30.00	18.00
(27)	Harmon Killebrew (Green background.)	60.00	30.00	18.00
(28)	Harmon Killebrew (Red background.)	60.00	30.00	18.00
(29)	Sandy Koufax (Horizontal band.)	135.00	65.00	40.00
(30)	Sandy Koufax (Diagonal band.)	145.00	75.00	45.00
(31)	Don Lock	15.00	7.50	4.50
(32)	Frank Malzone	15.00	7.50	4.50
(33)	Mickey Mantle (Diagonal yellow band.)	325.00	160.00	100.00
(34)	Mickey Mantle (Red triangle.)	325.00	160.00	100.00
(35)	Eddie Mathews	60.00	30.00	18.00
(36)	Willie Mays (Yellow background encompasses head.)	135.00	65.00	40.00
(37)	Willie Mays (Yellow background ears-to-chin.)	135.00	65.00	40.00
(38)	Bill Mazeroski	60.00	30.00	18.00
(39)	Ken McBride	15.00	7.50	4.50
(40)	Bill Monbouquette	15.00	7.50	4.50
(41)	Dave Nicholson	15.00	7.50	4.50
(42)	Claude Osteen	15.00	7.50	4.50
(43)	Milt Pappas	15.00	7.50	4.50
(44)	Camilo Pascual	15.00	7.50	4.50
(45)	Albie Pearson	15.00	7.50	4.50
(46)	Ron Perranoski	15.00	7.50	4.50
(47)	Gary Peters	15.00	7.50	4.50
(48)	Boog Powell	20.00	10.00	6.00
(49)	Frank Robinson	60.00	30.00	18.00
(50)	John Romano	15.00	7.50	4.50
(51)	Norm Siebern	15.00	7.50	4.50
(52)	Warren Spahn	60.00	30.00	18.00
(53)	Dick Stuart	15.00	7.50	4.50
(54)	Lee Thomas	15.00	7.50	4.50
(55)	Joe Torre	25.00	12.50	7.50
(56)	Pete Ward	15.00	7.50	4.50
(57)	Carlton Willey	15.00	7.50	4.50

		NM	EX	VG
(58)	Billy Williams	60.00	30.00	18.00
(59)	Carl Yastrzemski	75.00	37.50	22.50
(60)	Baltimore Orioles Logo	20.00	10.00	6.00
(61)	Boston Red Sox Logo	20.00	10.00	6.00
(62)	Chicago Cubs Logo	20.00	10.00	6.00
(63)	Chicago White Sox Logo	20.00	10.00	6.00
(64)	Cincinnati Reds Logo	20.00	10.00	6.00
(65)	Cleveland Indians Logo	20.00	10.00	6.00
(66)	Detroit Tigers Logo	20.00	10.00	6.00
(67)	Houston Colts Logo	25.00	12.50	7.50
(68)	Kansas City Athletics Logo	20.00	10.00	6.00
(69)	Los Angeles Angels Logo	20.00	10.00	6.00
(70)	Los Angeles Dodgers Logo	20.00	10.00	6.00
(71)	Milwaukee Braves Logo	20.00	10.00	6.00
(72)	Minnesota Twins Logo	20.00	10.00	6.00
(73)	New York Mets Logo	25.00	12.50	7.50
(74)	New York Yankees Logo	25.00	12.50	7.50
(75)	Philadelphia Phillies Logo	20.00	10.00	6.00
(76)	Pittsburgh Pirates Logo	20.00	10.00	6.00
(77)	St. Louis Cardinals Logo	20.00	10.00	6.00
(78)	San Francisco Giants Logo	20.00	10.00	6.00
(79)	Washington Senators Logo	20.00	10.00	6.00

1964 Topps Rookie All-Star Banquet

Since 1959 Topps has sponsored a formal post-season banquet to honor its annual Rookie All-Star team. In 1964, the gum company deviated from the tradition dinner program by issuing a 36-card boxed set. Each of the cards is printed in black-and-white, with red or light blue graphic highlights. The first seven cards in the set feature Topps staff and baseball dignitaries involved in the selection of the rookie team. Cards #8-12 are composite photos of the 1959-63 Rookie All-Star team. Cards #13-34A showcase the '64 honorees. Each player's card is matched with a card from the team's public relations officer extolling the rookie's virtues. Each card in this unique dinner program measures 3" x 5-1/4" and is numbered as a "PAGE" in the lower-right corner.

		NM	EX	VG
	Complete Boxed Set (36):	2,800	1,400	850.00
	Common Player:	17.50	8.75	5.25
1	"6th Annual Topps Rookie All-Star Team Awards" header card	17.50	8.75	5.25
2	The Baseball World Votes (Tommy Davis, Jeff Torborg, Ron Santo, Billy Williams)	17.50	8.75	5.25
3	The Baseball World Votes (Six more clubhouse scenes)	17.50	8.75	5.25
4	Topps Rookie All-Star Team Honorary Election Committee (photos of media and Hall of Famers Hank Greenberg and Fran Frisch)	55.00	27.00	16.50
5	Topps Rookie All-Star Team Honorary Election Committee (photos of five media, Topps' VP Joel Shorin and Jackie Robinson)	120.00	60.00	35.00
6	Executive Director of the Committee and His Associates (Topps' Cy Berger, three others)	17.50	8.75	5.25
7	Topps Salutes Joe Garagiola (Joe Garagiola)	95.00	45.00	25.00
8	The 1959 Topps Rookie All-Star Team (Willie McCovey, Pumpsie Green, Joe Koppe, Jim Baxes, Bobby Allison, Ron Fairly, Willie Tasby, John Romano, Jim Perry, Jim O'Toole)	225.00	110.00	65.00
9	The 1960 Topps Rookie All-Star Team (Jim Gentile, Julian Javier, Ron Hansen, Ron Santo, Tommy Davis, Frank Howard, Tony Curry, Jimmie Coker, Chuck Estrada, Dick Stigman)	225.00	110.00	65.00
10	The 1961 Topps Rookie All-Star Team (J.C. Martin, Jake Wood, Dick Howser, Charlie Smith, Billy Williams, Lee Thomas, Floyd Robinson, Joe Torre, Don Schwall, Jack Curtis)	185.00	90.00	55.00

11	The 1962 Topps Rookie All-Star Team (Fred Whitfield, Bernie Allen, Tom Tresh, Ed Charles, Manny Jiminez, Al Luplow, Boog Powell, Buck Rodgers, Dean Chance, Al Jackson)	185.00	90.00	55.00
12	The 1963 Topps Rookie All-Star Team (Pete Rose, Rusty Staub, Al Weis, Pete Ward, Jimmie Hall, Vic Davalillo, Tommy Harper, Jesse Gonder, Ray Culp, Gary Peters)	1,400	700.00	425.00
13	1964 Topps Rookie All-Star Team header card	17.50	8.75	5.25
14	Ed Uhas, Cleveland Indians PR	17.50	8.75	5.25
15	Bob Chance	135.00	65.00	40.00
16	Garry Schumacher, S.F. Giants PR	17.50	8.75	5.25
17	Hal Lanier	135.00	65.00	40.00
18	Larry Shenk, Phillies PR	17.50	8.75	5.25
19	Richie Allen	300.00	150.00	90.00
20	Jim Schaaf, Athletics PR	17.50	8.75	5.25
21	Bert Campaneris	160.00	80.00	45.00
22	Ernie Johnson, Braves PR	17.50	8.75	5.25
23	Rico Carty	160.00	80.00	45.00
24	Bill Crowley, Red Sox PR	17.50	8.75	5.25
25	Tony Conigliaro	345.00	175.00	100.00
26	Tom Mee, Twins PR	17.50	8.75	5.25
27	Tony Oliva	210.00	100.00	60.00
28	Burt Hawkins, Senators PR	17.50	8.75	5.25
29	Mike Brumley	135.00	65.00	40.00
30	Hank Zureick, Reds PR	17.50	8.75	5.25
31	Bill McCool	135.00	65.00	40.00
32	Rob Brown, Orioles PR	17.50	8.75	5.25
33	Wally Bunker	135.00	65.00	40.00
34	"5th Annual Topps Minor League Player of the Year" header card	17.50	8.75	5.25
34A	Luis Tiant (Minor League Player of the Year)	160.00	80.00	45.00
35	Rookie All-Star trophy	17.50	8.75	5.25

1964 Topps Stand-Ups

These 2-1/2" x 3-1/2" cards were the first since the All-Star sets of 1951 to be die-cut. This made it possible for a folded card to stand on display. The 77-cards in the set feature color photographs of the player with yellow and green backgrounds. Directions for folding are on the yellow top background, and when folded only the green background remains. Of the 77 cards, 55 were double-printed while 22 were single-printed, making them twice as scarce.

	NM	EX	VG
Complete Set (77):	2,250	1,125	650.00
Common Player:	12.00	6.00	3.50
Wax Pack (1):	600.00		
(1) Hank Aaron	90.00	45.00	27.50
(2) Hank Aguirre	12.00	6.00	3.50
(3) George Altman	12.00	6.00	3.50
(4) Max Alvis	12.00	6.00	3.50
(5) Bob Aspromonte	12.00	6.00	3.50
(6) Jack Baldschun/SP	20.00	10.00	6.00
(7) Ernie Banks	55.00	27.50	16.50
(8) Steve Barber	12.00	6.00	3.50
(9) Earl Battey	12.00	6.00	3.50
(10) Ken Boyer	20.00	10.00	6.00
(11) Ernie Broglio	12.00	6.00	3.50
(12) Johnny Callison	12.00	6.00	3.50
(13) Norm Cash/SP	50.00	25.00	15.00
(14) Wayne Causey	12.00	6.00	3.50
(15) Orlando Cepeda	27.50	13.50	8.25
(16) Ed Charles	12.00	6.00	3.50
(17) Roberto Clemente	150.00	75.00	45.00
(18) Donn Clendenon/SP	20.00	10.00	6.00
(19) Rocky Colavito	25.00	12.50	7.50
(20) Ray Culp/SP	20.00	10.00	6.00
(21) Tommy Davis	12.00	6.00	3.50
(22) Don Drysdale/SP	55.00	27.50	16.50
(23) Dick Ellsworth	12.00	6.00	3.50
(24) Dick Farrell	12.00	6.00	3.50
(25) Jim Fregosi	12.00	6.00	3.50
(26) Bob Friend	12.00	6.00	3.50
(27) Jim Gentile	12.00	6.00	3.50
(28) Jesse Gonder/SP	20.00	10.00	6.00
(29) Tony Gonzalez/SP	20.00	10.00	6.00
(30) Dick Groat	12.50	6.25	3.75
(31) Woody Held	12.00	6.00	3.50
(32) Chuck Hinton	12.00	6.00	3.50
(33) Elston Howard	20.00	10.00	6.00

(34)	Frank Howard/SP	27.50	13.50	8.25
(35)	Ron Hunt	12.00	6.00	3.50
(36)	Al Jackson	12.00	6.00	3.50
(37)	Ken Johnson	12.00	6.00	3.50
(38)	Al Kaline	40.00	20.00	12.00
(39)	Harmon Killebrew	50.00	25.00	15.00
(40)	Sandy Koufax	100.00	50.00	30.00
(41)	Don Lock/SP	20.00	10.00	6.00
(42)	Jerry Lumpe/SP	20.00	10.00	6.00
(43)	Jim Maloney	12.00	6.00	3.50
(44)	Frank Malzone	12.00	6.00	3.50
(45)	Mickey Mantle	465.00	230.00	140.00
(46)	Juan Marichal/SP	50.00	25.00	15.00
(47)	Ed Mathews/SP	60.00	30.00	18.00
(48)	Willie Mays	135.00	65.00	40.00
(49)	Bill Mazeroski	22.50	11.00	7.00
(50)	Ken McBride	12.00	6.00	3.50
(51)	Willie McCovey/SP	50.00	25.00	15.00
(52)	Claude Osteen	12.00	6.00	3.50
(53)	Jim O'Toole	12.00	6.00	3.50
(54)	Camilo Pascual	12.00	6.00	3.50
(55)	Albie Pearson/SP	20.00	10.00	6.00
(56)	Gary Peters	12.00	6.00	3.50
(57)	Vada Pinson	15.00	7.50	4.50
(58)	Juan Pizarro	12.00	6.00	3.50
(59)	Boog Powell	20.00	10.00	6.00
(60)	Bobby Richardson	20.00	10.00	6.00
(61)	Brooks Robinson	60.00	30.00	18.00
(62)	Floyd Robinson	12.00	6.00	3.50
(63)	Frank Robinson	50.00	25.00	15.00
(64)	Ed Roebuck/SP	20.00	10.00	6.00
(65)	Rich Rollins	12.00	6.00	3.50
(66)	Johnny Romano	12.00	6.00	3.50
(67)	Ron Santo/SP	35.00	17.50	10.00
(68)	Norm Siebern	12.00	6.00	3.50
(69)	Warren Spahn/SP	60.00	30.00	18.00
(70)	Dick Stuart/SP	20.00	10.00	6.00
(71)	Lee Thomas	12.00	6.00	3.50
(72)	Joe Torre	30.00	15.00	9.00
(73)	Pete Ward	12.00	6.00	3.50
(74)	Bill White/SP	25.00	12.50	7.50
(75)	Billy Williams/SP	45.00	22.50	13.50
(76)	Hal Woodeshick/SP	20.00	10.00	6.00
(77)	Carl Yastrzemski/SP	225.00	110.00	65.00

1965 Topps

The 1965 Topps set features a large color photograph of the player surrounded by a colored, round-cornered frame and a white border. The bottom of the 2-1/2" x 3-1/2" cards includes a pennant with a color team logo and name over the left side of a rectangle which features the player's name and position. Backs feature statistics and, if space allowed, a cartoon and headline about the player. There are no multi-player cards in the 1965 set other than the usual team cards and World Series highlights. Rookie cards include team, as well as league groupings from two to four players per card. Also present in the 598-card set are statistical leaders. Certain cards in the high-number series (#523-598) were produced in lesser quantities than the rest of the series. Known as "short-prints," and valued somewhat higher than the other high numbers, they are indicated in the checklist by an (SP) after the player name.

		NM	EX	VG
	Complete Set (598):	4,000	2,000	1,200
	Common Player (1-370):	3.00	1.50	.90
	Common Player (371-598):	6.00	3.00	1.75
1	A.L. Batting Leaders (Elston Howard, Tony Oliva, Brooks Robinson)	17.50	8.75	5.25
2	N.L. Batting Leaders (Hank Aaron, Rico Carty, Roberto Clemente)	25.00	12.50	7.50
3	A.L. Home Run Leaders (Harmon Killebrew, Mickey Mantle, Boog Powell)	35.00	17.50	10.00
4	N.L. Home Run Leaders (Johnny Callison, Orlando Cepeda, Jim Hart, Willie Mays, Billy Williams)	20.00	10.00	6.00
5	A.L. RBI Leaders (Harmon Killebrew, Mickey Mantle, Brooks Robinson, Dick Stuart)	35.00	17.50	10.00
6	N.L. RBI Leaders (Ken Boyer, Willie Mays, Ron Santo)	13.50	6.75	4.00
7	A.L. ERA Leaders (Dean Chance, Joel Horlen)	3.50	1.75	1.00
8	N.L. ERA Leaders (Don Drysdale, Sandy Koufax)	25.00	12.50	7.50

9	A.L. Pitching Leaders (Wally Bunker, Dean Chance, Gary Peters, Juan Pizarro, Dave Wickersham)	3.50	1.75	1.00
10	N.L. Pitching Leaders (Larry Jackson, Juan Marichal, Ray Sadecki)	4.50	2.25	1.25
11	A.L. Strikeout Leaders (Dean Chance, Al Downing, Camilo Pascual)	3.50	1.75	1.00
12	N.L. Strikeout Leaders (Don Drysdale, Bob Gibson, Bob Veale)	12.00	6.00	3.50
13	Pedro Ramos	3.00	1.50	.90
14	Len Gabrielson	3.00	1.50	.90
15	Robin Roberts	12.50	6.25	3.75
16	Astros Rookies (Sonny Jackson, Joe Morgan)	50.00	25.00	15.00
17	Johnny Romano	3.00	1.50	.90
18	Bill McCool	3.00	1.50	.90
19	Gates Brown	3.00	1.50	.90
20	Jim Bunning	10.00	5.00	3.00
21	Don Blasingame	3.00	1.50	.90
22	Charlie Smith	3.00	1.50	.90
23	Bob Tiefenauer	3.00	1.50	.90
24	Twins Team	7.50	3.75	2.25
25	Al McBean	3.00	1.50	.90
26	Bobby Knoop	3.00	1.50	.90
27	Dick Bertell	3.00	1.50	.90
28	Barney Schultz	3.00	1.50	.90
29	Felix Mantilla	3.00	1.50	.90
30	Jim Bouton	4.50	2.25	1.25
31	Mike White	3.00	1.50	.90
32	Herman Franks	3.00	1.50	.90
33	Jackie Brandt	3.00	1.50	.90
34	Cal Koonce	3.00	1.50	.90
35	Ed Charles	3.00	1.50	.90
36	Bobby Wine	3.00	1.50	.90
37	Fred Gladding	3.00	1.50	.90
38	Jim King	3.00	1.50	.90
39	Gerry Arrigo	3.00	1.50	.90
40	Frank Howard	4.50	2.25	1.25
41	White Sox Rookies (Bruce Howard, Marv, Staehle)	3.00	1.50	.90
42	Earl Wilson	3.00	1.50	.90
43	Mike Shannon	3.00	1.50	.90
44	Wade Blasingame	3.00	1.50	.90
45	Roy McMillan	3.00	1.50	.90
46	Bob Lee	3.00	1.50	.90
47	Tommy Harper	3.00	1.50	.90
48	Claude Raymond	3.00	1.50	.90
49	Orioles Rookies (Curt Blefary, John Miller)	3.00	1.50	.90
50	Juan Marichal	13.50	6.75	4.00
51	Billy Bryan	3.00	1.50	.90
52	Ed Roebuck	3.00	1.50	.90
53	Dick McAuliffe	3.00	1.50	.90
54	Joe Gibbon	3.00	1.50	.90
55	Tony Conigliaro	12.00	6.00	3.50
56	Ron Kline	3.00	1.50	.90
57	Cards Team	7.50	3.75	2.25
58	Fred Talbot	3.00	1.50	.90
59	Nate Oliver	3.00	1.50	.90
60	Jim O'Toole	3.00	1.50	.90
61	Chris Cannizzaro	3.00	1.50	.90
62	Jim Katt (Kaat)	3.50	1.75	1.00
63	Ty Cline	3.00	1.50	.90
64	Lou Burdette	3.00	1.50	.90
65	Tony Kubek	11.00	5.50	3.25
66	Bill Rigney	3.00	1.50	.90
67	Harvey Haddix	3.00	1.50	.90
68	Del Crandall	3.00	1.50	.90
69	Bill Virdon	3.00	1.50	.90
70	Bill Skowron	3.50	1.75	1.00
71	John O'Donoghue	3.00	1.50	.90
72	Tony Gonzalez	3.00	1.50	.90
73	Dennis Ribant	3.00	1.50	.90
74	Red Sox Rookies (Rico Petrocelli, Jerry Stephenson)	13.50	6.75	4.00
75	Deron Johnson	3.00	1.50	.90
76	Sam McDowell	3.00	1.50	.90
77	Doug Camilli	3.00	1.50	.90
78	Dal Maxvill	3.00	1.50	.90
79a	1st Series Checklist (1-88) (61 is C. Cannizzaro)	3.50	1.75	1.00
79b	1st Series Checklist (1-88) (61 is Cannizzaro)	7.00	3.50	2.00
80	Turk Farrell	3.00	1.50	.90
81	Don Buford	3.00	1.50	.90
82	Braves Rookies (Santos Alomar, John Braun)	4.50	2.25	1.25
83	George Thomas	3.00	1.50	.90
84	Ron Herbel	3.00	1.50	.90
85	Willie Smith	3.00	1.50	.90
86	Les Narum	3.00	1.50	.90
87	Nelson Mathews	3.00	1.50	.90
88	Jack Lamabe	3.00	1.50	.90
89	Mike Hershberger	3.00	1.50	.90
90	Rich Rollins	3.00	1.50	.90
91	Cubs Team	7.50	3.75	2.25
92	Dick Howser	3.00	1.50	.90
93	Jack Fisher	3.00	1.50	.90
94	Charlie Lau	3.00	1.50	.90
95	Bill Mazeroski	12.50	6.25	3.75
96	Sonny Siebert	3.00	1.50	.90
97	Pedro Gonzalez	3.00	1.50	.90
98	Bob Miller	3.00	1.50	.90
99	Gil Hodges	9.00	4.50	2.75
100	Ken Boyer	4.50	2.25	1.25
101	Fred Newman	3.00	1.50	.90
102	Steve Boros	3.00	1.50	.90
103	Harvey Kuenn	3.00	1.50	.90
104	2nd Series Checklist (89-176)	4.00	2.00	1.25
105	Chico Salmon	3.00	1.50	.90
106	Gene Oliver	3.00	1.50	.90
107	Phillies Rookies (Pat Corrales, Costen Shockley)	4.00	2.00	1.25

108	Don Mincher	3.00	1.50	.90
109	Walt Bond	3.00	1.50	.90
110	Ron Santo	12.00	6.00	3.50
111	Lee Thomas	3.00	1.50	.90
112	Derrell Griffith	3.00	1.50	.90
113	Steve Barber	3.00	1.50	.90
114	Jim Hickman	3.00	1.50	.90
115	Bobby Richardson	12.00	6.00	3.50
116	Cardinals Rookies	3.00	1.50	.90
	(*Dave Dowling, Bob Tolan*)			
117	Wes Stock	3.00	1.50	.90
118	*Hal Lanier*	3.00	1.50	.90
119	John Kennedy	3.00	1.50	.90
120	Frank Robinson	20.00	10.00	6.00
121	Gene Alley	3.00	1.50	.90
122	Bill Pleis	3.00	1.50	.90
123	Frank Thomas	3.00	1.50	.90
124	Tom Satriano	3.00	1.50	.90
125	Juan Pizarro	3.00	1.50	.90
126	Dodgers Team	7.50	3.75	2.25
127	Frank Lary	3.00	1.50	.90
128	Vic Davalillo	3.00	1.50	.90
129	Bennie Daniels	3.00	1.50	.90
130	Al Kaline	20.00	10.00	6.00
131	Johnny Keane	4.00	2.00	1.25
132	World Series Game 1	10.00	5.00	3.00
	(Cards Take Opener)			
133	World Series Game 2	12.50	6.25	3.75
	(Stottlemyre Wins)			
134	World Series Game 3	40.00	20.00	12.00
	(Mantle's Clutch HR)			
135	World Series Game 4	10.00	5.00	3.00
	(Boyer's Grand-Slam)			
136	World Series Game 5	7.00	3.50	2.00
	(10th Inning Triumph)			
137	World Series Game 6	10.00	5.00	3.00
	(Bouton Wins Again)			
138	World Series Game 7	15.00	7.50	4.50
	(Gibson Wins Finale)			
139	World Series	9.00	4.50	2.75
	(The Cards Celebrate)			
140	Dean Chance	3.00	1.50	.90
141	Charlie James	3.00	1.50	.90
142	Bill Monbouquette	3.00	1.50	.90
143	Pirates Rookies	3.00	1.50	.90
	(*John Gelnar, Jerry May*)			
144	Ed Kranepool	3.00	1.50	.90
145	*Luis Tiant*	12.00	6.00	3.50
146	Ron Hansen	3.00	1.50	.90
147	Dennis Bennett	3.00	1.50	.90
148	Willie Kirkland	3.00	1.50	.90
149	Wayne Schurr	3.00	1.50	.90
150	Brooks Robinson	20.00	10.00	6.00
151	Athletics Team	7.50	3.75	2.25
152	Phil Ortega	3.00	1.50	.90
153	Norm Cash	9.00	4.50	2.75
154	Bob Humphreys	3.00	1.50	.90
155	Roger Maris	50.00	25.00	15.00
156	Bob Sadowski	3.00	1.50	.90
157	Zoilo Versalles	3.00	1.50	.90
158	Dick Sisler	3.00	1.50	.90
159	Jim Duffalo	3.00	1.50	.90
160	Bob Clemente	95.00	47.50	27.50
161	Frank Baumann	3.00	1.50	.90
162	Russ Nixon	3.00	1.50	.90
163	John Briggs	3.00	1.50	.90
164	Al Spangler	3.00	1.50	.90
165	Dick Ellsworth	3.00	1.50	.90
166	Indians Rookies (*Tommie*	9.00	4.50	2.75
	Agee, George Culver)			
167	Bill Wakefield	3.00	1.50	.90
168	Dick Green	3.00	1.50	.90
169	Dave Vineyard	3.00	1.50	.90
170	Hank Aaron	80.00	40.00	24.00
171	Jim Roland	3.00	1.50	.90
172	Jim Piersall	6.00	3.00	1.75
173	Tigers Team	8.00	4.00	2.50
174	Joe Jay	3.00	1.50	.90
175	Bob Aspromonte	3.00	1.50	.90
176	Willie McCovey	17.50	8.75	5.25
177	Pete Mikkelsen	3.00	1.50	.90
178	Dalton Jones	3.00	1.50	.90
179	Hal Woodeshick	3.00	1.50	.90
180	Bob Allison	3.00	1.50	.90
181	Senators Rookies	3.00	1.50	.90
	(*Don Loun, Joe McCabe*)			
182	Mike de la Hoz	3.00	1.50	.90
183	Dave Nicholson	3.00	1.50	.90
184	John Boozer	3.00	1.50	.90
185	Max Alvis	3.00	1.50	.90
186	Billy Cowan	3.00	1.50	.90
187	Casey Stengel	12.50	6.25	3.75
188	Sam Bowens	3.00	1.50	.90
189	3rd Series Checklist	6.50	3.25	2.00
	(177-264)			
190	Bill White	3.00	1.50	.90
191	Phil Regan	3.00	1.50	.90
192	Jim Coker	3.00	1.50	.90
193	Gaylord Perry	12.00	6.00	3.50
194	Angels Rookies	3.00	1.50	.90
	(*Bill Kelso, Rick Reichardt*)			
195	Bob Veale	3.00	1.50	.90
196	Ron Fairly	3.00	1.50	.90
197	Diego Segui	3.00	1.50	.90
198	Smoky Burgess	3.00	1.50	.90
199	Bob Heffner	3.00	1.50	.90
200	Joe Torre	12.00	6.00	3.50
201	Twins Rookies (*Cesar*	3.00	1.50	.90
	Tovar, Sandy Valdespino)			
202	Leo Burke	3.00	1.50	.90
203	Dallas Green	3.00	1.50	.90
204	Russ Snyder	3.00	1.50	.90
205	Warren Spahn	20.00	10.00	6.00
206	Willie Horton	3.00	1.50	.90
207	Pete Rose	100.00	50.00	30.00
208	Tommy John	6.00	3.00	1.75
209	Pirates Team	7.50	3.75	2.25
210	Jim Fregosi	3.00	1.50	.90
211	Steve Ridzik	3.00	1.50	.90
212	Ron Brand	3.00	1.50	.90
213	Jim Davenport	3.00	1.50	.90
214	Bob Purkey	3.00	1.50	.90
215	Pete Ward	3.00	1.50	.90
216	Al Worthington	3.00	1.50	.90
217	Walt Alston	9.00	4.50	2.75
218	Dick Schofield	3.00	1.50	.90
219	Bob Meyer	3.00	1.50	.90
220	Billy Williams	25.00	12.50	7.50
221	John Tsitouris	3.00	1.50	.90
222	Bob Tillman	3.00	1.50	.90
223	Dan Osinski	3.00	1.50	.90
224	Bob Chance	3.00	1.50	.90
225	Bo Belinsky	3.00	1.50	.90
226	Yankees Rookies	9.00	4.50	2.75
	(*Jake Gibbs, Elvio Jimenez*)			
227	Bobby Klaus	3.00	1.50	.90
228	Jack Sanford	3.00	1.50	.90
229	Lou Clinton	3.00	1.50	.90
230	Ray Sadecki	3.00	1.50	.90
231	Jerry Adair	3.00	1.50	.90
232	*Steve Blass*	3.00	1.50	.90
233	Don Zimmer	6.00	3.00	1.75
234	White Sox Team	7.50	3.75	2.25
235	Chuck Hinton	3.00	1.50	.90
236	*Dennis McLain*	15.00	7.50	4.50
237	Bernie Allen	3.00	1.50	.90
238	Joe Moeller	3.00	1.50	.90
239	Doc Edwards	3.00	1.50	.90
240	Bob Bruce	3.00	1.50	.90
241	Mack Jones	3.00	1.50	.90
242	George Brunet	3.00	1.50	.90
243	Reds Rookies (*Ted*	3.00	1.50	.90
	Davidson, Tommy Helms)			
244	Lindy McDaniel	3.00	1.50	.90
245	Joe Pepitone	10.00	5.00	3.00
246	Tom Butters	3.00	1.50	.90
247	Wally Moon	3.00	1.50	.90
248	Gus Triandos	3.00	1.50	.90
249	Dave McNally	3.00	1.50	.90
250	Willie Mays	85.00	42.50	25.00
251	Billy Herman	7.50	3.75	2.25
252	Pete Richert	3.00	1.50	.90
253	Danny Cater	3.00	1.50	.90
254	Roland Sheldon	3.00	1.50	.90
255	Camilo Pascual	3.00	1.50	.90
256	Tito Francona	3.00	1.50	.90
257	Jim Wynn	3.00	1.50	.90
258	Larry Bearnarth	3.00	1.50	.90
259	Tigers Rookies (*Jim*	4.00	2.00	1.25
	Northrup, Ray Oyler)			
260	Don Drysdale	20.00	10.00	6.00
261	Duke Carmel	3.00	1.50	.90
262	Bud Daley	3.00	1.50	.90
263	Marty Keough	3.00	1.50	.90
264	Bob Buhl	3.00	1.50	.90
265	Jim Pagliaroni	3.00	1.50	.90
266	*Bert Campaneris*	15.00	7.50	4.50
267	Senators Team	7.50	3.75	2.25
268	Ken McBride	3.00	1.50	.90
269	Frank Bolling	3.00	1.50	.90
270	Milt Pappas	3.00	1.50	.90
271	Don Wert	3.00	1.50	.90
272	Chuck Schilling	3.00	1.50	.90
273	4th Series Checklist	7.50	3.75	2.25
	(265-352)			
274	Lum Harris	3.00	1.50	.90
275	Dick Groat	3.00	1.50	.90
276	Hoyt Wilhelm	12.50	6.25	3.75
277	Johnny Lewis	3.00	1.50	.90
278	Ken Retzer	3.00	1.50	.90
279	Dick Tracewski	3.00	1.50	.90
280	Dick Stuart	3.00	1.50	.90
281	Bill Stafford	3.00	1.50	.90
282	Giants Rookies	20.00	10.00	6.00
	(*Dick Estelle, Masanori*			
	Murakami)			
283	Fred Whitfield	3.00	1.50	.90
284	Nick Willhite	3.00	1.50	.90
285	Ron Hunt	3.00	1.50	.90
286	Athletics Rookies (*Jim*	3.00	1.50	.90
	Dickson, Aurelio Monteagudo)			
287	Gary Kolb	3.00	1.50	.90
288	Jack Hamilton	3.00	1.50	.90
289	Gordy Coleman	3.00	1.50	.90
290	Wally Bunker	3.00	1.50	.90
291	Jerry Lynch	3.00	1.50	.90
292	Larry Yellen	3.00	1.50	.90
293	Angels Team	7.50	3.75	2.25
294	Tim McCarver	8.00	4.00	2.50
295	Dick Radatz	3.00	1.50	.90
296	Tony Taylor	3.00	1.50	.90
297	Dave DeBusschere	4.00	2.00	1.25
298	Jim Stewart	3.00	1.50	.90
299	Jerry Zimmerman	3.00	1.50	.90
300	Sandy Koufax	95.00	47.50	27.50
301	Birdie Tebbetts	3.00	1.50	.90
302	Al Stanek	3.00	1.50	.90
303	Johnny Orsino	3.00	1.50	.90
304	Dave Stenhouse	3.00	1.50	.90
305	Rico Carty	3.00	1.50	.90
306	Bubba Phillips	3.00	1.50	.90
307	Barry Latman	3.00	1.50	.90
308	Mets Rookies (*Cleon Jones,*	8.00	4.00	2.50
	Tom Parsons)			
309	Steve Hamilton	3.00	1.50	.90
310	Johnny Callison	3.00	1.50	.90
311	Orlando Pena	3.00	1.50	.90
312	Joe Nuxhall	3.00	1.50	.90
313	Jimmie Schaffer	3.00	1.50	.90
314	Sterling Slaughter	3.00	1.50	.90
315	Frank Malzone	3.00	1.50	.90
316	Reds Team	7.00	3.50	2.00
317	Don McMahon	3.00	1.50	.90
318	Matty Alou	3.00	1.50	.90
319	Ken McMullen	3.00	1.50	.90
320	Bob Gibson	25.00	12.50	7.50
321	Rusty Staub	7.50	3.75	2.25
322	Rick Wise	3.00	1.50	.90
323	Hank Bauer	3.00	1.50	.90
324	Bobby Locke	3.00	1.50	.90
325	Donn Clendenon	3.00	1.50	.90
326	Dwight Siebler	3.00	1.50	.90
327	Denis Menke	3.00	1.50	.90
328	Eddie Fisher	3.00	1.50	.90
329	Hawk Taylor	3.00	1.50	.90
330	Whitey Ford	25.00	12.50	7.50
331	Dodgers Rookies	3.00	1.50	.90
	(*Al Ferrara, John Purdin*)			
332	Ted Abernathy	3.00	1.50	.90
333	Tommie Reynolds	3.00	1.50	.90
334	Vic Roznovsky	3.00	1.50	.90
335	Mickey Lolich	6.00	3.00	1.75
336	Woody Held	3.00	1.50	.90
337	Mike Cuellar	3.00	1.50	.90
338	Phillies Team	7.50	3.75	2.25
339	Ryne Duren	3.00	1.50	.90
340	Tony Oliva	15.00	7.50	4.50
341	Bobby Bolin	3.00	1.50	.90
342	Bob Rodgers	3.00	1.50	.90
343	Mike McCormick	3.00	1.50	.90
344	Wes Parker	3.00	1.50	.90
345	Floyd Robinson	3.00	1.50	.90
346	Bobby Bragan	3.00	1.50	.90
347	Roy Face	3.00	1.50	.90
348	George Banks	3.00	1.50	.90
349	Larry Miller	3.00	1.50	.90
350	Mickey Mantle	325.00	155.00	95.00
351	Jim Perry	3.00	1.50	.90
352	*Alex Johnson*	3.50	1.75	1.00
353	Jerry Lumpe	3.00	1.50	.90
354	Cubs Rookies	3.00	1.50	.90
	(*Billy Ott, Jack Warner*)			
355	Vada Pinson	8.00	4.00	2.50
356	Bill Spanswick	3.00	1.50	.90
357	Carl Warwick	3.00	1.50	.90
358	Albie Pearson	3.00	1.50	.90
359	Ken Johnson	3.00	1.50	.90
360	Orlando Cepeda	20.00	10.00	6.00
361	5th Series Checklist	9.00	4.50	2.75
	(353-429)			
362	Don Schwall	3.00	1.50	.90
363	Bob Johnson	3.00	1.50	.90
364	Galen Cisco	3.00	1.50	.90
365	Jim Gentile	3.00	1.50	.90
366	Dan Schneider	3.00	1.50	.90
367	Leon Wagner	3.00	1.50	.90
368	White Sox Rookies (*Ken*	3.00	1.50	.90
	Berry, Joel Gibson)			
369	Phil Linz	3.00	1.50	.90
370	Tommy Davis	3.00	1.50	.90
371	Frank Kreutzer	7.50	3.75	2.25
372	Clay Dalrymple	7.50	3.75	2.25
373	Curt Simmons	7.50	3.75	2.25
374	Angels Rookies (*Jose*	9.00	4.50	2.75
	Cardenal, Dick Simpson)			
375	Dave Wickersham	7.50	3.75	2.25
376	Jim Landis	7.50	3.75	2.25
377	Willie Stargell	20.00	10.00	6.00
378	Chuck Estrada	7.50	3.75	2.25
379	Giants Team	10.00	5.00	3.00
380	Rocky Colavito	12.00	6.00	3.50
381	Al Jackson	7.50	3.75	2.25
382	J.C. Martin	7.50	3.75	2.25
383	Felipe Alou	9.00	4.50	2.75
384	Johnny Klippstein	7.50	3.75	2.25
385	Carl Yastrzemski	35.00	17.50	10.00
386	Cubs Rookies (*Paul*	7.50	3.75	2.25
	Jaeckel, Fred Norman)			
387	Johnny Podres	9.00	4.50	2.75
388	John Blanchard	7.50	3.75	2.25
389	Don Larsen	7.50	3.75	2.25
390	Bill Freehan	7.50	3.75	2.25
391	Mel McGaha	7.50	3.75	2.25
392	Bob Friend	7.50	3.75	2.25
393	Ed Kirkpatrick	7.50	3.75	2.25
394	Jim Hannan	7.50	3.75	2.25
395	Jim Hart	7.50	3.75	2.25
396	Frank Bertaina	7.50	3.75	2.25
397	Jerry Buchek	7.50	3.75	2.25
398	Reds Rookies (*Dan Neville,*	7.50	3.75	2.25
	Art Shamsky)			
399	Ray Herbert	7.50	3.75	2.25
400	Harmon Killebrew	35.00	17.50	10.00
401	Carl Willey	7.50	3.75	2.25
402	Joe Amalfitano	7.50	3.75	2.25
403	Red Sox Team	10.00	5.00	3.00
404	Stan Williams	7.50	3.75	2.25
405	John Roseboro	7.50	3.75	2.25
406	Ralph Terry	7.50	3.75	2.25
407	Lee Maye	7.50	3.75	2.25
408	Larry Sherry	7.50	3.75	2.25
409	Astros Rookies (*Jim*	9.00	4.50	2.75
	Beauchamp, Larry Dierker)			
410	Luis Aparicio	17.50	8.75	5.25
411	Roger Craig	7.50	3.75	2.25
412	Bob Bailey	7.50	3.75	2.25
413	Hal Reniff	7.50	3.75	2.25
414	Al Lopez	12.50	6.25	3.75
415	Curt Flood	12.50	6.25	3.75
416	Jim Brewer	7.50	3.75	2.25
417	Ed Brinkman	7.50	3.75	2.25
418	Johnny Edwards	7.50	3.75	2.25
419	Ruben Amaro	7.50	3.75	2.25
420	Larry Jackson	7.50	3.75	2.25
421	Twins Rookies	7.50	3.75	2.25
	(*Gary Dotter, Jay Ward*)			
422	Aubrey Gatewood	7.50	3.75	2.25
423	Jesse Gonder	7.50	3.75	2.25
424	Gary Bell	7.50	3.75	2.25
425	Wayne Causey	7.50	3.75	2.25
426	Braves Team	10.00	5.00	3.00
427	Bob Saverine	7.50	3.75	2.25
428	Bob Shaw	7.50	3.75	2.25
429	Don Demeter	7.50	3.75	2.25

		NM	EX	VG
430	Gary Peters	7.50	3.75	2.25
431	Cardinals Rookies (Nelson Briles, Wayne Spiezio)	9.00	4.50	2.75
432	Jim Grant	7.50	3.75	2.25
433	John Bateman	7.50	3.75	2.25
434	Dave Morehead	7.50	3.75	2.25
435	Willie Davis	7.50	3.75	2.25
436	Don Elston	7.50	3.75	2.25
437	Chico Cardenas	7.50	3.75	2.25
438	Harry Walker	7.50	3.75	2.25
439	Moe Drabowsky	7.50	3.75	2.25
440	Tom Tresh	12.50	6.25	3.75
441	Denver Lemaster	7.50	3.75	2.25
442	Vic Power	7.50	3.75	2.25
443	6th Series Checklist (430-506)	9.00	4.50	2.75
444	Bob Hendley	7.50	3.75	2.25
445	Don Lock	7.50	3.75	2.25
446	Art Mahaffey	7.50	3.75	2.25
447	Julian Javier	7.50	3.75	2.25
448	Lee Stange	7.50	3.75	2.25
449	Mets Rookies (Jerry Hinsley, Gary Kroll)	7.50	3.75	2.25
450	Elston Howard	12.00	6.00	3.50
451	Jim Owens	7.50	3.75	2.25
452	Gary Geiger	7.50	3.75	2.25
453	Dodgers Rookies (Willie Crawford, John Werhas)	7.50	3.75	2.25
454	Ed Rakow	7.50	3.75	2.25
455	Norm Siebern	7.50	3.75	2.25

		NM	EX	VG
49	Tommy Davis	4.00	1.50	.60
50	Walt Bond	4.00	1.50	.60
51	John Orsino	4.00	1.50	.60
52	Joe Christopher	4.00	1.50	.60
53	Al Spangler	4.00	1.50	.60
54	Jim King	4.00	1.50	.60
55	Mickey Lolich	4.00	1.50	.60
56	Harmon Killebrew	10.00	3.50	1.50
57	Bob Shaw	4.00	1.50	.60
58	Ernie Banks	15.00	5.25	2.25
59	Hank Aaron	25.00	9.00	4.00
60	Chuck Hinton	4.00	1.50	.60
61	Bob Aspromonte	4.00	1.50	.60
62	Lee Maye	4.00	1.50	.60
63	Joe Cunningham	4.00	1.50	.60
64	Pete Ward	4.00	1.50	.60
65	Bobby Richardson	6.00	2.00	.90
66	Dean Chance	4.00	1.50	.60
67	Dick Ellsworth	4.00	1.50	.60
68	Jim Maloney	4.00	1.50	.60
69	Bob Gibson	9.00	3.25	1.25
70	Earl Battey	4.00	1.50	.60
71	Tony Kubek	5.00	1.75	.70
72	Jack Kralick	4.00	1.50	.60

1965 Topps Push-Pull

Part of a 36-card set combining sports and non-sport subjects, the Push-Pull novelties have a louvered shutter attached to a tab at the bottom. When the tab is moved, from position to position, each of the underlying photos is revealed in turn. The cards measure 2-1/2" x 4-11/16". Backs are printed in black-and-white and contain biographical data. Three of the cards in the set feature baseball players.

		NM	EX	VG
Complete Set (36):		3,650	1,800	1,050
(1)	Lou Gehrig, Babe Ruth	500.00	250.00	150.00
(2)	Casey Stengel Wins/Loses	75.00	37.00	22.00
(3)	Yogi Berra, Mickey Mantle	950.00	475.00	285.00

1965 Topps Transfers

Issued as strips of three players each as inserts in 1965, the Topps Transfers were 2" x 3" portraits of players. The transfers have blue or red bands at the top and bottom with the team name and position in the top band and the player's name in the bottom. As is so often the case, the superstars in the transfer set can be quite expensive, but like many of Topps non-card products, the common transfers are neither terribly expensive or popular today.

		NM	EX	VG
Complete Set (72):		750.00	375.00	225.00
Common Player:		6.00	3.00	1.75
(1)	Hank Aaron	50.00	25.00	15.00
(2)	Richie Allen	12.00	6.00	3.50
(3)	Bob Allison	6.00	3.00	1.75
(4)	Max Alvis	6.00	3.00	1.75
(5)	Luis Aparicio	17.50	8.75	5.25
(6)	Bob Aspromonte	6.00	3.00	1.75
(7)	Walt Bond	6.00	3.00	1.75
(8)	Jim Bouton	9.00	4.50	2.75
(9)	Ken Boyer	10.00	5.00	3.00

		NM	EX	VG
(10)	Jim Bunning	17.50	8.75	5.25
(11)	John Callison	6.00	3.00	1.75
(12)	Rico Carty	6.00	3.00	1.75
(13)	Wayne Causey	6.00	3.00	1.75
(14)	Orlando Cepeda	17.50	8.75	5.25
(15)	Bob Chance	6.00	3.00	1.75
(16)	Dean Chance	6.00	3.00	1.75
(17)	Joe Christopher	6.00	3.00	1.75
(18)	Roberto Clemente	60.00	30.00	18.00
(19)	Rocky Colavito	15.00	7.50	4.50
(20)	Tony Conigliaro	10.00	5.00	3.00
(21)	Tommy Davis	6.00	3.00	1.75
(22)	Don Drysdale	17.50	8.75	5.25
(23)	Bill Freehan	6.00	3.00	1.75
(24)	Jim Fregosi	6.00	3.00	1.75
(25)	Bob Gibson	17.50	8.75	5.25
(26)	Dick Groat	6.00	3.00	1.75
(27)	Tom Haller	6.00	3.00	1.75
(28)	Chuck Hinton	6.00	3.00	1.75
(29)	Elston Howard	9.00	4.50	2.75
(30)	Ron Hunt	6.00	3.00	1.75
(31)	Al Jackson	6.00	3.00	1.75
(32)	Al Kaline	25.00	12.50	7.50
(33)	Harmon Killebrew	20.00	10.00	6.00
(34)	Jim King	6.00	3.00	1.75
(35)	Ron Kline	6.00	3.00	1.75
(36)	Bobby Knoop	6.00	3.00	1.75
(37)	Sandy Koufax	45.00	22.00	13.50
(38)	Ed Kranepool	6.00	3.00	1.75
(39)	Jim Maloney	6.00	3.00	1.75
(40)	Mickey Mantle	90.00	45.00	27.00
(41)	Juan Marichal	17.50	8.75	5.25
(42)	Lee Maye	6.00	3.00	1.75
(43)	Willie Mays	50.00	25.00	15.00
(44)	Bill Mazeroski	17.50	8.75	5.25
(45)	Tony Oliva	7.50	3.75	2.25
(46)	Jim O'Toole	6.00	3.00	1.75
(47)	Milt Pappas	6.00	3.00	1.75
(48)	Camilo Pascual	6.00	3.00	1.75
(49)	Gary Peters	6.00	3.00	1.75
(50)	Vada Pinson	6.00	3.00	1.75
(51)	Juan Pizarro	6.00	3.00	1.75
(52)	Boog Powell	10.00	5.00	3.00
(53)	Dick Radatz	6.00	3.00	1.75
(54)	Bobby Richardson	10.00	5.00	3.00
(55)	Brooks Robinson	20.00	10.00	6.00
(56)	Frank Robinson	20.00	10.00	6.00
(57)	Bob Rodgers	6.00	3.00	1.75
(58)	John Roseboro	6.00	3.00	1.75
(59)	Ron Santo	12.00	6.00	3.50
(60)	Diego Segui	6.00	3.00	1.75
(61)	Bill Skowron	9.00	4.50	2.75
(62)	Al Spangler	6.00	3.00	1.75
(63)	Dick Stuart	6.00	3.00	1.75
(64)	Luis Tiant	6.00	3.00	1.75
(65)	Joe Torre	12.00	6.00	3.50
(66)	Bob Veale	6.00	3.00	1.75
(67)	Leon Wagner	6.00	3.00	1.75
(68)	Pete Ward	6.00	3.00	1.75
(69)	Bill White	6.00	3.00	1.75
(70)	Dave Wickersham	6.00	3.00	1.75
(71)	Billy Williams	17.50	8.75	5.25
(72)	Carl Yastrzemski	25.00	12.50	7.50

1965 Topps Embossed

Inserted in regular packs, the 2-1/8" x 3-1/2" Topps Embossed cards feature a 3-D profile portrait on gold foil-like cardboard (some collectors report finding the cards with silver cardboard). The player's name, team and position are below the portrait - which is good, because most of the embossed portraits are otherwise unrecognizeable. There is a gold border with American League players framed in blue and National Leaguers in red.

		NM	EX	VG
Complete Set (72):		400.00	140.00	60.00
Common Player:		4.00	1.50	.60
1	Carl Yastrzemski	15.00	5.25	2.25
2	Ron Fairly	4.00	1.50	.60
3	Max Alvis	4.00	1.50	.60
4	Jim Ray Hart	4.00	1.50	.60
5	Bill Skowron	5.00	1.75	.70
6	Ed Kranepool	4.00	1.50	.60
7	Tim McCarver	5.00	1.75	.70
8	Sandy Koufax	25.00	9.00	4.00
9	Donn Clendenon	4.00	1.50	.60
10	John Romano	4.00	1.50	.60
11	Mickey Mantle	60.00	20.00	9.00
12	Joe Torre	6.00	2.00	.90
13	Al Kaline	15.00	5.25	2.25
14	Al McBean	4.00	1.50	.60
15	Don Drysdale	10.00	3.50	1.50
16	Brooks Robinson	12.50	4.50	2.00
17	Jim Bunning	9.00	3.25	1.25
18	Gary Peters	4.00	1.50	.60
19	Roberto Clemente	40.00	14.00	6.00
20	Milt Pappas	4.00	1.50	.60
21	Wayne Causey	4.00	1.50	.60
22	Frank Robinson	12.50	4.50	2.00
23	Bill Mazeroski	9.00	3.25	1.25
24	Diego Segui	4.00	1.50	.60
25	Jim Bouton	4.00	1.50	.60
26	Ed Mathews	10.00	3.50	1.50
27	Willie Mays	25.00	9.00	4.00
28	Ron Santo	6.00	2.00	.90
29	Boog Powell	6.00	2.00	.90
30	Ken McBride	4.00	1.50	.60
31	Leon Wagner	4.00	1.50	.60
32	John Callison	4.00	1.50	.60
33	Zoilo Versalles	4.00	1.50	.60
34	Jack Baldschun	4.00	1.50	.60
35	Ron Hunt	4.00	1.50	.60
36	Richie Allen	6.00	2.00	.90
37	Frank Malzone	4.00	1.50	.60
38	Bob Allison	4.00	1.50	.60
39	Jim Fregosi	4.00	1.50	.60
40	Billy Williams	9.00	3.25	1.25
41	Bill Freehan	4.00	1.50	.60
42	Vada Pinson	5.00	1.75	.70
43	Bill White	4.00	1.50	.60
44	Roy McMillan	4.00	1.50	.60
45	Orlando Cepeda	9.00	3.25	1.25
46	Rocky Colavito	7.50	2.75	1.25
47	Ken Boyer	5.00	1.75	.70
48	Dick Radatz	4.00	1.50	.60

Abbreviation Key

IS: Interleague Showdown

OPS: Overprinted "Promotional Sample"

ED: Expansion Draft

AS: All-Star

HL: Hit List

RC: Rookie Class

RC or (RC): Rookie Card

UPT: Unlimited Potential/Talent

SF: Star Factor

SP: Short Print

DT: Double Team

GLS: Gold Leaf Stars

CC: Curtain Calls

GLR: Gold Leaf Rookies

TP: Top Performers

FF: Future Foundation

DK: Diamond King

RR: Rated Rookie

DP: Double Print

IA: In Action

PC: Promo Card

SR: Star Rookie

1966 Topps

PETE ROSE 2nd base

In 1966, Topps produced another 598-card set. The 2-1/2" x 3-1/2" cards feature the traditional color photograph with a diagonal strip in the upper left-hand corner carrying the team name. A band at the bottom carries the player's name and position. Multi-player cards returned in 1966 after a year's hiatus. The statistical leader cards feature the categorical leader and two runners-up. Most team managers have cards as well. The 1966 set features a handful of cards found with or without a notice of the player's sale or trade to another team. Cards without the notice bring higher prices and are not included in the complete set prices. Some cards in the high series (#523-598) were short-printed - produced in lesser quantities than the rest of the series. They are valued somewhat higher than the others and are indicated in the checklist by an SP notation following the player name.

		NM	EX	VG
	Complete Set (598):	4,600	2,300	1,375
	Common Player (1-370):	4.00	2.00	1.25
	Common Player (371-446):	7.50	3.75	2.25
	Common Player (447-522):	9.00	4.50	2.75
	Common Player (523-598):	12.50	6.25	3.75
1	Willie Mays	200.00	50.00	30.00
2	Ted Abernathy	4.00	2.00	1.25
3	Sam Mele	4.00	2.00	1.25
4	Ray Culp	4.00	2.00	1.25
5	Jim Fregosi	4.00	2.00	1.25
6	Chuck Schilling	4.00	2.00	1.25
7	Tracy Stallard	4.00	2.00	1.25
8	Floyd Robinson	4.00	2.00	1.25
9	Clete Boyer	8.00	4.00	2.50
10	Tony Cloninger	4.00	2.00	1.25
11	Senators Rookies (*Brant Alyea, Pete Craig*)	4.00	2.00	1.25
12	John Tsitouris	4.00	2.00	1.25
13	Lou Johnson	4.00	2.00	1.25
14	Norm Siebern	4.00	2.00	1.25
15	Vern Law	4.00	2.00	1.25
16	Larry Brown	4.00	2.00	1.25
17	Johnny Stephenson	4.00	2.00	1.25
18	Roland Sheldon	4.00	2.00	1.25
19	Giants Team	7.50	3.75	2.25
20	Willie Horton	4.00	2.00	1.25
21	Don Nottebart	4.00	2.00	1.25
22	Joe Nossek	4.00	2.00	1.25
23	Jack Sanford	4.00	2.00	1.25
24	*Don Kessinger*	7.50	3.75	2.25
25	Pete Ward	4.00	2.00	1.25
26	Ray Sadecki	4.00	2.00	1.25
27	Orioles Rookies (*Andy Etchebarren, Darold Knowles*)	6.00	3.00	1.75
28	Phil Niekro	15.00	7.50	4.50
29	Mike Brumley	4.00	2.00	1.25
30	Pete Rose	60.00	30.00	18.00
31	Jack Cullen	4.00	2.00	1.25
32	Adolfo Phillips	4.00	2.00	1.25
33	Jim Pagliaroni	4.00	2.00	1.25
34	1st Series Checklist (1-88)	7.50	3.75	2.25
35	Ron Swoboda	4.00	2.00	1.25
36	Jim Hunter	15.00	7.50	4.50
37	Billy Herman	6.00	3.00	1.75
38	Ron Nischwitz	4.00	2.00	1.25
39	Ken Henderson	4.00	2.00	1.25
40	Jim Grant	4.00	2.00	1.25
41	Don LeJohn	4.00	2.00	1.25
42	Aubrey Gatewood	4.00	2.00	1.25
43a	Don Landrum (No button on pants.)	4.00	2.00	1.25
43b	Don Landrum (Partial button on pants.)	6.00	3.00	1.75
43c	Don Landrum (Full button on pants.)	6.00	3.00	1.75
44	Indians Rookies (*Bill Davis, Tom Kelley*)	4.00	2.00	1.25
45	Jim Gentile	4.00	2.00	1.25
46	Howie Koplitz	4.00	2.00	1.25
47	J.C. Martin	4.00	2.00	1.25
48	Paul Blair	4.00	2.00	1.25
49	Woody Woodward	4.00	2.00	1.25
50	Mickey Mantle	180.00	90.00	55.00
51	Gordon Richardson	4.00	2.00	1.25
52	Power Plus (Johnny Callison, Wes Covington)	4.00	2.00	1.25
53	Bob Duliba	4.00	2.00	1.25
54	Jose Pagan	4.00	2.00	1.25
55	Ken Harrelson	4.00	2.00	1.25
56	Sandy Valdespino	4.00	2.00	1.25
57	Jim Lefebvre	4.00	2.00	1.25
58	Dave Wickersham	4.00	2.00	1.25
59	Reds Team	7.00	3.50	2.00

60	Curt Flood	4.00	2.00	1.25
61	Bob Bolin	4.00	2.00	1.25
62a	Merritt Ranew (No sold statement.)	20.00	10.00	6.00
62b	Merritt Ranew (With sold statement.)	4.00	2.00	1.25
63	Jim Stewart	4.00	2.00	1.25
64	Bob Bruce	4.00	2.00	1.25
65	Leon Wagner	4.00	2.00	1.25
66	Al Weis	4.00	2.00	1.25
67	Mets Rookies (*Cleon Jones, Dick Selma*)	4.00	2.00	1.25
68	Hal Reniff	4.00	2.00	1.25
69	Ken Hamlin	4.00	2.00	1.25
70	Carl Yastrzemski	30.00	15.00	9.00
71	Frank Carpin	4.00	2.00	1.25
72	Tony Perez	22.50	11.00	7.00
73	Jerry Zimmerman	4.00	2.00	1.25
74	Don Mossi	4.00	2.00	1.25
75	Tommy Davis	4.00	2.00	1.25
76	Red Schoendienst	7.50	3.75	2.25
77	Johnny Orsino	4.00	2.00	1.25
78	Frank Linzy	4.00	2.00	1.25
79	Joe Pepitone	8.00	4.00	2.50
80	Richie Allen	6.00	3.00	1.75
81	Ray Oyler	4.00	2.00	1.25
82	Bob Hendley	4.00	2.00	1.25
83	Albie Pearson	4.00	2.00	1.25
84	Braves Rookies (*Jim Beauchamp, Dick Kelley*)	4.00	2.00	1.25
85	Eddie Fisher	4.00	2.00	1.25
86	John Bateman	4.00	2.00	1.25
87	Dan Napoleon	4.00	2.00	1.25
88	Fred Whitfield	4.00	2.00	1.25
89	Ted Davidson	4.00	2.00	1.25
90	Luis Aparicio	15.00	7.50	4.50
91a	Bob Uecker (No trade statement.)	60.00	30.00	18.00
91b	Bob Uecker (With trade statement.)	20.00	10.00	6.00
92	Yankees Team	15.00	7.50	4.50
93	Jim Lonborg	4.00	2.00	1.25
94	Matty Alou	4.00	2.00	1.25
95	Pete Richert	4.00	2.00	1.25
96	Felipe Alou	6.00	3.00	1.75
97	Jim Merritt	4.00	2.00	1.25
98	Don Demeter	4.00	2.00	1.25
99	Buc Belters (Donn Clendenon, Willie Stargell)	8.00	4.00	2.50
100	Sandy Koufax	65.00	32.50	20.00
101a	2nd Series Checklist (89-176) (115 is Spahn)	12.50	6.25	3.75
101b	2nd Series Checklist (89-176) (115 is Henry)	7.50	3.75	2.25
102	Ed Kirkpatrick	4.00	2.00	1.25
103a	Dick Groat (No trade statement.)	20.00	10.00	6.00
103b	Dick Groat (With trade statement.)	4.00	2.00	1.25
104a	Alex Johnson (No trade statement.)	20.00	10.00	6.00
104b	Alex Johnson (With trade statement.)	4.00	2.00	1.25
105	Milt Pappas	4.00	2.00	1.25
106	Rusty Staub	6.00	3.00	1.75
107	Athletics Rookies (*Larry Stahl, Ron Tompkins*)	4.00	2.00	1.25
108	Bobby Klaus	4.00	2.00	1.25
109	Ralph Terry	4.00	2.00	1.25
110	Ernie Banks	30.00	15.00	9.00
111	Gary Peters	4.00	2.00	1.25
112	Manny Mota	4.00	2.00	1.25
113	Hank Aguirre	4.00	2.00	1.25
114	Jim Gosger	4.00	2.00	1.25
115	Bill Henry	4.00	2.00	1.25
116	Walt Alston	6.00	3.00	1.75
117	Jake Gibbs	4.00	2.00	1.25
118	Mike McCormick	4.00	2.00	1.25
119	Art Shamsky	4.00	2.00	1.25
120	Harmon Killebrew	20.00	10.00	6.00
121	Ray Herbert	4.00	2.00	1.25
122	Joe Gaines	4.00	2.00	1.25
123	Pirates Rookies (*Frank Bork, Jerry May*)	4.00	2.00	1.25
124	Tug McGraw	4.00	2.00	1.25
125	Lou Brock	20.00	10.00	6.00
126	*Jim Palmer*	55.00	27.50	16.50
127	Ken Berry	4.00	2.00	1.25
128	Jim Landis	4.00	2.00	1.25
129	Jack Kralick	4.00	2.00	1.25
130	Joe Torre	6.00	3.00	1.75
131	Angels Team	7.50	3.75	2.25
132	Orlando Cepeda	15.00	7.50	4.50
133	Don McMahon	4.00	2.00	1.25
134	Wes Parker	4.00	2.00	1.25
135	Dave Morehead	4.00	2.00	1.25
136	Woody Held	4.00	2.00	1.25
137	Pat Corrales	4.00	2.00	1.25
138	Roger Repoz	4.00	2.00	1.25
139	Cubs Rookies (*Byron Browne, Don Young*)	4.00	2.00	1.25
140	Jim Maloney	4.00	2.00	1.25
141	Tom McCraw	4.00	2.00	1.25
142	Don Dennis	4.00	2.00	1.25
143	Jose Tartabull	4.00	2.00	1.25
144	Don Schwall	4.00	2.00	1.25
145	Bill Freehan	4.00	2.00	1.25
146	George Altman	4.00	2.00	1.25
147	Lum Harris	4.00	2.00	1.25
148	Bob Johnson	4.00	2.00	1.25
149	Dick Nen	4.00	2.00	1.25
150	Rocky Colavito	12.00	6.00	3.50
151	Gary Wagner	4.00	2.00	1.25
152	Frank Malzone	4.00	2.00	1.25
153	Rico Carty	4.00	2.00	1.25
154	Chuck Hiller	4.00	2.00	1.25
155	Marcelino Lopez	4.00	2.00	1.25

156	D P Combo (Hal Lanier, Dick Schofield)	4.00	2.00	1.25
157	Rene Lachemann	4.00	2.00	1.25
158	Jim Brewer	4.00	2.00	1.25
159	Chico Ruiz	4.00	2.00	1.25
160	Whitey Ford	25.00	12.50	7.50
161	Jerry Lumpe	4.00	2.00	1.25
162	Lee Maye	4.00	2.00	1.25
163	Tito Francona	4.00	2.00	1.25
164	White Sox Rookies (*Tommie Agee, Marv Staehle*)	4.00	2.00	1.25
165	Don Lock	4.00	2.00	1.25
166	Chris Krug	4.00	2.00	1.25
167	Boog Powell	6.00	3.00	1.75
168	Dan Osinski	4.00	2.00	1.25
169	Duke Sims	4.00	2.00	1.25
170	Cookie Rojas	4.00	2.00	1.25
171	Nick Willhite	4.00	2.00	1.25
172	Mets Team	6.00	3.00	1.75
173	Al Spangler	4.00	2.00	1.25
174	Ron Taylor	4.00	2.00	1.25
175	Bert Campaneris	4.00	2.00	1.25
176	Jim Davenport	4.00	2.00	1.25
177	Hector Lopez	4.00	2.00	1.25
178	Bob Tillman	4.00	2.00	1.25
179	Cardinals Rookies (*Dennis Aust, Bob Tolan*)	4.00	2.00	1.25
180	Vada Pinson	7.50	3.75	2.25
181	Al Worthington	4.00	2.00	1.25
182	Jerry Lynch	4.00	2.00	1.25
183a	3rd Series Checklist (177-264) (Large print on front.)	7.50	3.75	2.25
183b	3rd Series Checklist (177-264) (Small print on front.)	9.00	4.50	2.75
184	Denis Menke	4.00	2.00	1.25
185	Bob Buhl	4.00	2.00	1.25
186	Ruben Amaro	4.00	2.00	1.25
187	Chuck Dressen	4.00	2.00	1.25
188	Al Luplow	4.00	2.00	1.25
189	John Roseboro	4.00	2.00	1.25
190	Jimmie Hall	4.00	2.00	1.25
191	Darrell Sutherland	4.00	2.00	1.25
192	Vic Power	4.00	2.00	1.25
193	Dave McNally	4.00	2.00	1.25
194	Senators Team	6.00	3.00	1.75
195	Joe Morgan	25.00	12.50	7.50
196	Don Pavletich	4.00	2.00	1.25
197	Sonny Siebert	4.00	2.00	1.25
198	*Mickey Stanley*	6.00	3.00	1.75
199	Chisox Clubbers (Floyd Robinson, Johnny Romano, Bill Skowron)	6.00	3.00	1.75
200	Ed Mathews	20.00	10.00	6.00
201	Jim Dickson	4.00	2.00	1.25
202	Clay Dalrymple	4.00	2.00	1.25
203	Jose Santiago	4.00	2.00	1.25
204	Cubs Team	7.50	3.75	2.25
205	Tom Tresh	9.00	4.50	2.75
206	Alvin Jackson	4.00	2.00	1.25
207	Frank Quilici	4.00	2.00	1.25
208	Bob Miller	4.00	2.00	1.25
209	Tigers Rookies (*Fritz Fisher, John Hiller*)	4.00	2.00	1.25
210	Bill Mazeroski	17.50	8.75	5.25
211	Frank Kreutzer	4.00	2.00	1.25
212	Ed Kranepool	4.00	2.00	1.25
213	Fred Newman	4.00	2.00	1.25
214	Tommy Harper	4.00	2.00	1.25
215	N.L. Batting Leaders (Hank Aaron, Roberto Clemente, Willie Mays)	40.00	20.00	12.00
216	A.L. Batting Leaders (Vic Davalillo, Tony Oliva, Carl Yastrzemski)	16.00	8.00	4.75
217	N.L. Home Run Leaders (Willie Mays, Willie McCovey, Billy Williams)	25.00	12.50	7.50
218	A.L. Home Run Leaders (Norm Cash, Tony Conigliaro, Willie Horton)	12.50	6.25	3.75
219	N.L. RBI Leaders (Deron Johnson, Willie Mays, Frank Robinson)	20.00	10.00	6.00
220	A.L. RBI Leaders (Rocky Colavito, Willie Horton, Tony Oliva)	12.00	6.00	3.50
221	N.L. ERA Leaders (Sandy Koufax, Vern Law, Juan Marichal)	15.00	7.50	4.50
222	A.L. ERA Leaders (Eddie Fisher, Sam McDowell, Sonny Siebert)	6.00		1.75
223	N.L. Pitching Leaders (Tony Cloninger, Don Drysdale, Sandy Koufax)	16.00	8.00	4.75
224	A.L. Pitching Leaders (Jim Grant, Jim Kaat, Mel Stottlemyre)	9.00	4.50	2.75
225	N.L. Strikeout Leaders (Bob Gibson, Sandy Koufax, Bob Veale)	15.00	7.50	4.50
226	A.L. Strikeout Leaders (Mickey Lolich, Sam McDowell, Denny McLain, Sonny Siebert)	10.00	5.00	3.00
227	Russ Nixon	4.00	2.00	1.25
228	Larry Dierker	4.00	2.00	1.25
229	Hank Bauer	4.50	2.25	1.25
230	Johnny Callison	4.00	2.00	1.25
231	Floyd Weaver	4.00	2.00	1.25
232	Glenn Beckert	4.00	2.00	1.25
233	Dom Zanni	4.00	2.00	1.25
234	Yankees Rookies (*Rich Beck, Roy White*)	15.00	7.50	4.50
235	Don Cardwell	4.00	2.00	1.25
236	Mike Hershberger	4.00	2.00	1.25
237	Billy O'Dell	4.00	2.00	1.25
238	Dodgers Team	9.00	4.50	2.75

239	Orlando Pena	4.00	2.00	1.25
240	Earl Battey	4.00	2.00	1.25
241	Dennis Ribant	4.00	2.00	1.25
242	Jesus Alou	4.00	2.00	1.25
243	Nelson Briles	4.00	2.00	1.25
244	Astros Rookies (*Chuck Harrison, Sonny Jackson*)	4.00	2.00	1.25
245	John Buzhardt	4.00	2.00	1.25
246	Ed Bailey	4.00	2.00	1.25
247	Carl Warwick	4.00	2.00	1.25
248	Pete Mikkelsen	4.00	2.00	1.25
249	Bill Rigney	4.00	2.00	1.25
250	Sam Ellis	4.00	2.00	1.25
251	Ed Brinkman	4.00	2.00	1.25
252	Denver Lemaster	4.00	2.00	1.25
253	Don Wert	4.00	2.00	1.25
254	Phillies Rookies (*Fergie Jenkins, Bill Sorrell*)	45.00	22.50	13.50
255	Willie Stargell	20.00	10.00	6.00
256	Lew Krausse	4.00	2.00	1.25
257	Jeff Torborg	4.00	2.00	1.25
258	Dave Giusti	4.00	2.00	1.25
259	Red Sox Team	7.50	3.75	2.25
260	Bob Shaw	4.00	2.00	1.25
261	Ron Hansen	4.00	2.00	1.25
262	Jack Hamilton	4.00	2.00	1.25
263	Tom Egan	4.00	2.00	1.25
264	Twins Rookies (*Andy Kosco, Ted Uhlaender*)	4.00	2.00	1.25
265	Stu Miller	4.00	2.00	1.25
266	Pedro Gonzalez	4.00	2.00	1.25
267	Joe Sparma	4.00	2.00	1.25
268	John Blanchard	4.00	2.00	1.25
269	Don Heffner	4.00	2.00	1.25
270	Claude Osteen	4.00	2.00	1.25
271	Hal Lanier	4.00	2.00	1.25
272	Jack Baldschun	4.00	2.00	1.25
273	Astro Aces (Bob Aspromonte, Rusty Staub)	6.00	3.00	1.75
274	Buster Narum	4.00	2.00	1.25
275	Tim McCarver	7.50	3.75	2.25
276	Jim Bouton	6.00	3.00	1.75
277	George Thomas	4.00	2.00	1.25
278	Calvin Koonce	4.00	2.00	1.25
279a	4th Series Checklist (265-352) (Player's cap black.)	7.00	3.50	2.00
279b	4th Series Checklist (265-352) (Player's cap red.)	7.50	3.75	2.25
280	Bobby Knoop	4.00	2.00	1.25
281	Bruce Howard	4.00	2.00	1.25
282	Johnny Lewis	4.00	2.00	1.25
283	Jim Perry	4.00	2.00	1.25
284	Bobby Wine	4.00	2.00	1.25
285	Luis Tiant	4.00	2.00	1.25
286	Gary Geiger	4.00	2.00	1.25
287	Jack Aker	4.00	2.00	1.25
288	Dodgers Rookies (*Bill Singer, Don Sutton*)	40.00	20.00	12.00
289	Larry Sherry	4.00	2.00	1.25
290	Ron Santo	12.50	6.25	3.75
291	Moe Drabowsky	4.00	2.00	1.25
292	Jim Coker	4.00	2.00	1.25
293	Mike Shannon	4.00	2.00	1.25
294	Steve Ridzik	4.00	2.00	1.25
295	Jim Hart	4.00	2.00	1.25
296	Johnny Keane	4.00	2.00	1.25
297	Jim Owens	4.00	2.00	1.25
298	Rico Petrocelli	6.00	3.00	1.75
299	Lou Burdette	4.00	2.00	1.25
300	Bob Clemente	100.00	50.00	30.00
301	Greg Bollo	4.00	2.00	1.25
302	Ernie Bowman	4.00	2.00	1.25
303a	Indians Team (Dot between "PLACE" and "AMERICAN.")	6.00	3.00	1.75
303b	Indians Team (No dot.)	6.00	3.00	1.75
304	John Herrnstein	4.00	2.00	1.25
305	Camilo Pascual	4.00	2.00	1.25
306	Ty Cline	4.00	2.00	1.25
307	Clay Carroll	4.00	2.00	1.25
308	Tom Haller	4.00	2.00	1.25
309	Diego Segui	4.00	2.00	1.25
310	Frank Robinson	35.00	17.50	10.00
311	Reds Rookies (*Tommy Helms, Dick Simpson*)	4.00	2.00	1.25
312	Bob Saverine	4.00	2.00	1.25
313	Chris Zachary	4.00	2.00	1.25
314	Hector Valle	4.00	2.00	1.25
315	Norm Cash	11.00	5.50	3.25
316	Jack Fisher	4.00	2.00	1.25
317	Dalton Jones	4.00	2.00	1.25
318	Harry Walker	4.00	2.00	1.25
319	Gene Freese	4.00	2.00	1.25
320	Bob Gibson	30.00	15.00	9.00
321	Rick Reichardt	4.00	2.00	1.25
322	Bill Faul	4.00	2.00	1.25
323	Ray Barker	4.00	2.00	1.25
324	John Boozer	4.00	2.00	1.25
325	Vic Davalillo	4.00	2.00	1.25
326a	Braves Team (Dot between "PLACE" and "NATIONAL.")	7.50	3.75	2.25
326b	Braves Team (No dot.)	7.50	3.75	2.25
327	Bernie Allen	4.00	2.00	1.25
328	Jerry Grote	4.00	2.00	1.25
329	Pete Charton	4.00	2.00	1.25
330	Ron Fairly	4.00	2.00	1.25
331	Ron Herbel	4.00	2.00	1.25
332	Billy Bryan	4.00	2.00	1.25
333	Senators Rookies (*Joe Coleman, Jim French*)	4.00	2.00	1.25
334	Marty Keough	4.00	2.00	1.25
335	Juan Pizarro	4.00	2.00	1.25
336	Gene Alley	4.00	2.00	1.25
337	Fred Gladding	4.00	2.00	1.25
338	Dal Maxvill	4.00	2.00	1.25
339	Del Crandall	4.00	2.00	1.25
340	Dean Chance	4.00	2.00	1.25
341	Wes Westrum	4.00	2.00	1.25
342	Bob Humphreys	4.00	2.00	1.25
343	Joe Christopher	4.00	2.00	1.25
344	Steve Blass	4.00	2.00	1.25
345	Bob Allison	4.00	2.00	1.25
346	Mike de la Hoz	4.00	2.00	1.25
347	Phil Regan	4.00	2.00	1.25
348	Orioles Team	8.00	4.00	2.50
349	Cap Peterson	4.00	2.00	1.25
350	Mel Stottlemyre	6.00	3.00	1.75
351	Fred Valentine	4.00	2.00	1.25
352	Bob Aspromonte	4.00	2.00	1.25
353	Al McBean	4.00	2.00	1.25
354	Smoky Burgess	4.00	2.00	1.25
355	Wade Blasingame	4.00	2.00	1.25
356	Red Sox Rookies (*Owen Johnson, Ken Sanders*)	4.00	2.00	1.25
357	Gerry Arrigo	4.00	2.00	1.25
358	Charlie Smith	4.00	2.00	1.25
359	Johnny Briggs	4.00	2.00	1.25
360	Ron Hunt	4.00	2.00	1.25
361	Tom Satriano	4.00	2.00	1.25
362	Gates Brown	4.00	2.00	1.25
363	5th Series Checklist (353-429)	9.00	4.50	2.75
364	Nate Oliver	4.00	2.00	1.25
365	Roger Maris	45.00	22.50	13.50
366	Wayne Causey	4.00	2.00	1.25
367	Mel Nelson	4.00	2.00	1.25
368	Charlie Lau	4.00	2.00	1.25
369	Jim King	4.00	2.00	1.25
370	Chico Cardenas	4.00	2.00	1.25
371	Lee Stange	7.50	3.75	2.25
372	Harvey Kuenn	7.50	3.75	2.25
373	Giants Rookies (*Dick Estelle, Jack Hiatt*)	7.50	3.75	2.25
374	Bob Locker	7.50	3.75	2.25
375	Donn Clendenon	7.50	3.75	2.25
376	Paul Schaal	7.50	3.75	2.25
377	Turk Farrell	7.50	3.75	2.25
378	Dick Tracewski	7.50	3.75	2.25
379	Cards Team	10.00	5.00	3.00
380	Tony Conigliaro	12.50	6.25	3.75
381	Hank Fischer	7.50	3.75	2.25
382	Phil Roof	7.50	3.75	2.25
383	Jackie Brandt	7.50	3.75	2.25
384	Al Downing	7.50	3.75	2.25
385	Ken Boyer	10.00	5.00	3.00
386	Gil Hodges	11.00	5.50	3.25
387	Howie Reed	7.50	3.75	2.25
388	Don Mincher	7.50	3.75	2.25
389	Jim O'Toole	7.50	3.75	2.25
390	Brooks Robinson	35.00	17.50	10.00
391	Chuck Hinton	7.50	3.75	2.25
392	Cubs Rookies (*Bill Hands, Randy Hundley*)	12.00	6.00	3.50
393	George Brunet	7.50	3.75	2.25
394	Ron Brand	7.50	3.75	2.25
395	Len Gabrielson	7.50	3.75	2.25
396	Jerry Stephenson	7.50	3.75	2.25
397	Bill White	7.50	3.75	2.25
398	Danny Cater	7.50	3.75	2.25
399	Ray Washburn	7.50	3.75	2.25
400	Zoilo Versalles	7.50	3.75	2.25
401	Ken McMullen	7.50	3.75	2.25
402	Jim Hickman	7.50	3.75	2.25
403	Fred Talbot	7.50	3.75	2.25
404a	Pirates Team (Dot between "PLACE" and "NATIONAL.")	12.50	6.25	3.75
404b	Pirates Team (No dot.)	12.50	6.25	3.75
405	Elston Howard	9.00	4.50	2.75
406	Joe Jay	7.50	3.75	2.25
407	John Kennedy	7.50	3.75	2.25
408	Lee Thomas	7.50	3.75	2.25
409	Billy Hoeft	7.50	3.75	2.25
410	Al Kaline	35.00	17.50	10.00
411	Gene Mauch	7.50	3.75	2.25
412	Sam Bowens	7.50	3.75	2.25
413	John Romano	7.50	3.75	2.25
414	Dan Coombs	7.50	3.75	2.25
415	Max Alvis	7.50	3.75	2.25
416	Phil Ortega	7.50	3.75	2.25
417	Angels Rookies (*Jim McGlothlin, Ed Sukla*)	7.50	3.75	2.25
418	Phil Gagliano	7.50	3.75	2.25
419	Mike Ryan	7.50	3.75	2.25
420	Juan Marichal	20.00	10.00	6.00
421	Roy McMillan	7.50	3.75	2.25
422	Ed Charles	7.50	3.75	2.25
423	Ernie Broglio	7.50	3.75	2.25
424	Reds Rookies (*Lee May, Darrell Osteen*)	10.00	5.00	3.00
425	Bob Veale	7.50	3.75	2.25
426	White Sox Team	10.00	5.00	3.00
427	John Miller	7.50	3.75	2.25
428	Sandy Alomar	7.50	3.75	2.25
429	Bill Monbouquette	7.50	3.75	2.25
430	Don Drysdale	20.00	10.00	6.00
431	Walt Bond	7.50	3.75	2.25
432	Bob Heffner	7.50	3.75	2.25
433	Alvin Dark	7.50	3.75	2.25
434	Willie Kirkland	7.50	3.75	2.25
435	Jim Bunning	15.00	7.50	4.50
436	Julian Javier	7.50	3.75	2.25
437	Al Stanek	7.50	3.75	2.25
438	Willie Smith	7.50	3.75	2.25
439	Pedro Ramos	7.50	3.75	2.25
440	Deron Johnson	7.50	3.75	2.25
441	Tommie Sisk	7.50	3.75	2.25
442	Orioles Rookies (*Ed Barnowski, Eddie Watt*)	7.50	3.75	2.25
443	Bill Wakefield	7.50	3.75	2.25
444a	6th Series Checklist (430-506) (456 is R. Sox Rookies)	7.50	3.75	2.25
444b	6th Series Checklist (430-506) (456 is Red Sox Rookies)	9.00	4.50	2.75
445	Jim Kaat	9.00	4.50	2.75
446	Mack Jones	7.50	3.75	2.25
447	Dick Ellsworth (Photo actually Ken Hubbs.)	12.50	6.25	3.75
448	Eddie Stanky	9.00	4.50	2.75
449	Joe Moeller	9.00	4.50	2.75
450	Tony Oliva	15.00	7.50	4.50
451	Barry Latman	9.00	4.50	2.75
452	Joe Azcue	9.00	4.50	2.75
453	Ron Kline	9.00	4.50	2.75
454	Jerry Buchek	9.00	4.50	2.75
455	Mickey Lolich	9.00	4.50	2.75
456	Red Sox Rookies (*Darrell Brandon, Joe Foy*)	9.00	4.50	2.75
457	Joe Gibbon	9.00	4.50	2.75
458	Manny Jiminez (Jimenez)	9.00	4.50	2.75
459	Bill McCool	9.00	4.50	2.75
460	Curt Blefary	9.00	4.50	2.75
461	Roy Face	9.00	4.50	2.75
462	Bob Rodgers	9.00	4.50	2.75
463	Phillies Team	12.00	6.00	3.50
464	Larry Bearnarth	9.00	4.50	2.75
465	Don Buford	9.00	4.50	2.75
466	Ken Johnson	9.00	4.50	2.75
467	Vic Roznovsky	9.00	4.50	2.75
468	Johnny Podres	9.00	4.50	2.75
469	Yankees Rookies (*Bobby Murcer, Dooley Womack*)	22.50	11.00	6.75
470	Sam McDowell	9.00	4.50	2.75
471	Bob Skinner	9.00	4.50	2.75
472	Terry Fox	9.00	4.50	2.75
473	Rich Rollins	9.00	4.50	2.75
474	Dick Schofield	9.00	4.50	2.75
475	Dick Radatz	9.00	4.50	2.75
476	Bobby Bragan	9.00	4.50	2.75
477	Steve Barber	9.00	4.50	2.75
478	Tony Gonzalez	9.00	4.50	2.75
479	Jim Hannan	9.00	4.50	2.75
480	Dick Stuart	9.00	4.50	2.75
481	Bob Lee	9.00	4.50	2.75
482	Cubs Rookies (*John Boccabella, Dave Dowling*)	9.00	4.50	2.75
483	Joe Nuxhall	9.00	4.50	2.75
484	Wes Covington	9.00	4.50	2.75
485	Bob Bailey	9.00	4.50	2.75
486	Tommy John	9.00	4.50	2.75
487	Al Ferrara	9.00	4.50	2.75
488	George Banks	9.00	4.50	2.75
489	Curt Simmons	9.00	4.50	2.75
490	Bobby Richardson	15.00	7.50	4.50
491	Dennis Bennett	9.00	4.50	2.75
492	Athletics Team	12.00	6.00	3.50
493	Johnny Klippstein	9.00	4.50	2.75
494	Gordon Coleman	9.00	4.50	2.75
495	Dick McAuliffe	9.00	4.50	2.75
496	Lindy McDaniel	9.00	4.50	2.75
497	Chris Cannizzaro	9.00	4.50	2.75
498	Pirates Rookies (*Woody Fryman, Luke Walker*)	9.00	4.50	2.75
499	Wally Bunker	9.00	4.50	2.75
500	Hank Aaron	100.00	50.00	30.00
501	John O'Donoghue	9.00	4.50	2.75
502	Lenny Green	9.00	4.50	2.75
503	Steve Hamilton	9.00	4.50	2.75
504	Grady Hatton	9.00	4.50	2.75
505	Jose Cardenal	9.00	4.50	2.75
506	Bo Belinsky	9.00	4.50	2.75
507	John Edwards	9.00	4.50	2.75
508	*Steve Hargan*	9.00	4.50	2.75
509	Jake Wood	9.00	4.50	2.75
510	Hoyt Wilhelm	16.00	8.00	4.75
511	Giants Rookies (*Bob Barton, Tito Fuentes*)	9.00	4.50	2.75
512	Dick Stigman	9.00	4.50	2.75
513	Camilo Carreon	9.00	4.50	2.75
514	Hal Woodeshick	9.00	4.50	2.75
515	Frank Howard	9.00	4.50	2.75
516	Eddie Bressoud	9.00	4.50	2.75
517a	7th Series Checklist (507-598) (529 is W. Sox Rookies)	11.00	5.50	3.25
517b	7th Series Checklist (507-598) (529 is White Sox Rookies)	13.50	6.75	4.00
518	Braves Rookies (*Herb Hippauf, Arnie Umbach*)	9.00	4.50	2.75
519	Bob Friend	9.00	4.50	2.75
520	Jim Wynn	9.00	4.50	2.75
521	John Wyatt	9.00	4.50	2.75
522	Phil Linz	9.00	4.50	2.75
523	Bob Sadowski	12.50	6.25	3.75
524	Giants Rookies (*Ollie Brown, Don Mason*)/SP	16.00	8.00	4.75
525	Gary Bell/SP	16.00	8.00	4.75
526	Twins Team/SP	60.00	30.00	18.00
527	Julio Navarro	12.50	6.25	3.75
528	Jesse Gonder/SP	16.00	8.00	4.75
529	White Sox Rookies (*Lee Elia, Dennis Higgins, Bill Voss*)	12.50	6.25	3.75
530	Robin Roberts	25.00	12.50	7.50
531	Joe Cunningham	12.50	6.25	3.75
532	Aurelio Monteagudo/SP	16.00	8.00	4.75
533	Jerry Adair/SP	16.00	8.00	4.75
534	Mets Rookies (*Dave Eilers, Rob Gardner*)	12.50	6.25	3.75
535	Willie Davis/SP	16.00	8.00	4.75
536	Dick Egan	12.50	6.25	3.75
537	Herman Franks	12.50	6.25	3.75
538	Bob Allen/SP	16.00	8.00	4.75
539	Astros Rookies (*Bill Heath, Carroll Sembera*)	12.50	6.25	3.75
540	Denny McLain/SP	50.00	25.00	15.00
541	Gene Oliver/SP	16.00	8.00	4.75
542	George Smith	12.50	6.25	3.75
543	Roger Craig/SP	16.00	8.00	4.75
544	Cardinals Rookies (*Joe Hoerner, George Kernek, Jimmy Williams*)/SP	16.00	8.00	4.75
545	Dick Green/SP	16.00	8.00	4.75

#	Player	NM	EX	VG
546	Dwight Siebler	12.50	6.25	3.75
547	*Horace Clarke*/SP	60.00	30.00	18.00
548	Gary Kroll/SP	16.00	8.00	4.75
549	Senators Rookies (*Al Closter, Casey Cox*)	12.50	6.25	3.75
550	Willie McCovey/SP	60.00	30.00	18.00
551	Bob Purkey/SP	16.00	8.00	4.75
552	Birdie Tebbetts/SP	16.00	8.00	4.75
553	Major League Rookies (*Pat Garrett, Jackie Warner*)	12.50	6.25	3.75
554	Jim Northrup/SP	16.00	8.00	4.75
555	Ron Perranoski/SP	16.00	8.00	4.75
556	Mel Queen/SP	16.00	8.00	4.75
557	Felix Mantilla/SP	16.00	8.00	4.75
558	Red Sox Rookies (*Guido Grilli, Pete Magrini, George Scott*)	20.00	10.00	6.00
559	Roberto Pena/SP	16.00	8.00	4.75
560	Joel Horlen/SP	12.50	6.25	3.75
561	Choo Choo Coleman/SP	30.00	15.00	9.00
562	Russ Snyder	12.50	6.25	3.75
563	Twins Rookies (*Pete Cimino, Cesar Tovar*)	12.50	6.25	3.75
564	Bob Chance/SP	16.00	8.00	4.75
565	Jimmy Piersall/SP	17.50	8.75	5.25
566	Mike Cuellar/SP	16.00	8.00	4.75
567	Dick Howser/SP	16.00	8.00	4.75
568	Athletics Rookies (*Paul Lindblad, Ron Stone*)	12.50	6.25	3.75
569	Orlando McFarlane/SP	16.00	8.00	4.75
570	Art Mahaffey/SP	16.00	8.00	4.75
571	Dave Roberts/SP	16.00	8.00	4.75
572	Bob Priddy	12.50	6.25	3.75
573	Derrell Griffith	12.50	6.25	3.75
574	Mets Rookies (*Bill Hepler, Bill Murphy*)	12.50	6.25	3.75
575	Earl Wilson	12.50	6.25	3.75
576	Dave Nicholson/SP	16.00	8.00	4.75
577	Jack Lamabe/SP	16.00	8.00	4.75
578	Chi Chi Olivo/SP	16.00	8.00	4.75
579	Orioles Rookies (*Frank Bertaina, Gene Brabender, Dave Johnson*)	17.50	8.75	5.25
580	Billy Williams/SP	45.00	22.50	13.50
581	Tony Martinez	12.50	6.25	3.75
582	Garry Roggenburk	12.50	6.25	3.75
583	Tigers Team/SP	75.00	37.50	22.50
584	Yankees Rookies (*Frank Fernandez, Fritz Peterson*)	15.00	7.50	4.50
585	Tony Taylor	12.50	6.25	3.75
586	Claude Raymond/SP	16.00	8.00	4.75
587	Dick Bertell	12.50	6.25	3.75
588	Athletics Rookies (*Chuck Dobson, Ken Suarez*)	12.50	6.25	3.75
589	Lou Klimchock/SP	16.00	8.00	4.75
590	Bill Skowron/SP	25.00	12.50	7.50
591	N.L. Rookies (*Grant Jackson, Bart Shirley*)/SP	16.00	8.00	4.75
592	Andre Rodgers	12.50	6.25	3.75
593	Doug Camilli/SP	16.00	8.00	4.75
594	Chico Salmon	12.50	6.25	3.75
595	Larry Jackson	12.50	6.25	3.75
596	Astros Rookies (*Nate Colbert, Greg Sims*)/SP	20.00	10.00	6.00
597	John Sullivan	12.50	6.25	3.75
598	Gaylord Perry/SP	100.00	30.00	15.00

1966 Topps Comic Book Foldees

Comic book heroes and other fictional characters were the focus of this set of 44 "foldees." The pictures on the left and right ends of the 4-1/2" x 2-3/8" cards were cut through the middle to allow them to be folded over the central picture and each other to create funny combinations. Babe Ruth, in a rather generic drawing, is the only baseball player represented in the issue. A version of the set exists which carries a "T.G.C. PRINTED IN CANADA" copyright line; it is valued similarly.

	NM	EX	VG
Complete Set (44):	100.00	50.00	30.00
12 Babe Ruth	20.00	10.00	7.25

1966 Topps Punch-Outs

Only a handful of surviving examples of this issue are known. It is believed they represent a prototype for the 1967 Topps Punch-Outs which were themselves issued only on a test basis. The cards are blank-backed, measuring about 2-1/2" x 4-5/8" and perforated at center to allow the American League and National League to be separated for game play. A team captain is pictured in black-and-white on each half of the card. The A.L. side has a red background with 35 yellow baseballs to be punched out to determine game action. Background on the N.L. side is blue. Because of their rarity and lack of recent sales records, valuations for most pieces are not provided. This checklist is likely incomplete.

		NM	EX	VG
(1)	Ernie Banks, Mel Stottlemyre			
(2)	Johnny Callison/Jim Grant			
(3)	Donn Clendenon, Al Kaline			
(4)	Curt Flood, Bill Skowron			
(5)	Jim Ray Hart, Mickey Mantle			
(6)	Sandy Koufax, Carl Yastrzemski (12/04 auction)	6,700		
(7)	John Roseboro, Bobby Richardson			

1966 Topps Rub-Offs

Returning to a concept last tried in 1961, Topps tried an expanded version of Rub-Offs in 1966. Measuring 2-1/16" x 3", the Rub-Offs are in vertical format for the 100 players and horizontal for the 20 team pennants. The player Rub-Offs feature a color photo. Cutting procedures left well-centered examples in the distinct minority.

		NM	EX	VG
	Complete Set (120):	800.00	265.00	120.00
	Common Player:	5.00	1.50	.75
(1)	Hank Aaron	30.00	11.00	5.00
(2)	Jerry Adair	5.00	1.50	.75
(3)	Richie Allen	6.00	2.00	.90
(4)	Jesus Alou	5.00	1.50	.75
(5)	Max Alvis	5.00	1.50	.75
(6)	Bob Aspromonte	5.00	1.50	.75
(7)	Ernie Banks	15.00	5.00	2.50
(8)	Earl Battey	5.00	1.50	.75
(9)	Curt Blefary	5.00	1.50	.75
(10)	Ken Boyer	6.00	2.00	.90
(11)	Bob Bruce	5.00	1.50	.75
(12)	Jim Bunning	10.00	3.50	1.50
(13)	Johnny Callison	5.00	1.50	.75
(14)	Bert Campaneris	5.00	1.50	.75
(15)	Jose Cardenal	5.00	1.50	.75
(16)	Dean Chance	5.00	1.50	.75
(17)	Ed Charles	5.00	1.50	.75
(18)	Bob Clemente	35.00	12.00	5.00
(19)	Tony Cloninger	5.00	1.50	.75
(20)	Rocky Colavito	6.00	2.00	.90
(21)	Tony Conigliaro	6.50	2.25	1.00
(22)	Vic Davalillo	5.00	1.50	.75
(23)	Willie Davis	5.00	1.50	.75
(24)	Don Drysdale	10.00	3.50	1.50
(25)	Sammy Ellis	5.00	1.50	.75
(26)	Dick Ellsworth	5.00	1.50	.75
(27)	Ron Fairly	5.00	1.50	.75
(28)	Dick Farrell	5.00	1.50	.75
(29)	Eddie Fisher	5.00	1.50	.75
(30)	Jack Fisher	5.00	1.50	.75
(31)	Curt Flood	5.00	1.50	.75
(32)	Whitey Ford	15.00	5.25	2.25
(33)	Bill Freehan	5.00	1.50	.75
(34)	Jim Fregosi	5.00	1.50	.75
(35)	Bob Gibson	10.00	3.50	1.50
(36)	Jim Grant	5.00	1.50	.75
(37)	Jimmie Hall	5.00	1.50	.75
(38)	Ken Harrelson	5.00	1.50	.75
(39)	Jim Hart	5.00	1.50	.75
(40)	Joel Horlen	5.00	1.50	.75
(41)	Willie Horton	5.00	1.50	.75
(42)	Frank Howard	6.00	2.00	.90
(43)	Deron Johnson	5.00	1.50	.75
(44)	Al Kaline	12.50	4.50	2.00
(45)	Harmon Killebrew	10.00	3.50	1.50
(46)	Bobby Knoop	5.00	1.50	.75
(47)	Sandy Koufax	30.00	10.00	5.00
(48)	Ed Kranepool	5.00	1.50	.75
(49)	Gary Kroll	5.00	1.50	.75
(50)	Don Landrum	5.00	1.50	.75
(51)	Vernon Law	5.00	1.50	.75
(52)	Johnny Lewis	5.00	1.50	.75
(53)	Don Lock	5.00	1.50	.75
(54)	Mickey Lolich	5.00	1.50	.75
(55)	Jim Maloney	5.00	1.50	.75
(56)	Felix Mantilla	5.00	1.50	.75
(57)	Mickey Mantle	55.00	20.00	8.00
(58)	Juan Marichal	10.00	3.50	1.50
(59)	Ed Mathews	10.00	3.50	1.50
(60)	Willie Mays	30.00	10.00	5.00
(61)	Bill Mazeroski	10.00	3.50	1.50
(62)	Dick McAuliffe	5.00	1.50	.75
(63)	Tim McCarver	6.00	2.00	.90
(64)	Willie McCovey	10.00	3.50	1.50
(65)	Sammy McDowell	5.00	1.50	.75
(66)	Ken McMullen	5.00	1.50	.75
(67)	Denis Menke	5.00	1.50	.75
(68)	Bill Monbouquette	5.00	1.50	.75
(69)	Joe Morgan	10.00	3.50	1.50
(70)	Fred Newman	5.00	1.50	.75
(71)	John O'Donoghue	5.00	1.50	.75
(72)	Tony Oliva	6.00	2.00	.90
(73)	Johnny Orsino	5.00	1.50	.75
(74)	Phil Ortega	5.00	1.50	.75
(75)	Milt Pappas	5.00	1.50	.75
(76)	Dick Radatz	5.00	1.50	.75
(77)	Bobby Richardson	6.50	2.25	1.00
(78)	Pete Richert	5.00	1.50	.75
(79)	Brooks Robinson	12.50	4.50	2.00
(80)	Floyd Robinson	5.00	1.50	.75
(81)	Frank Robinson	12.50	4.50	2.00
(82)	Cookie Rojas	5.00	1.50	.75
(83)	Pete Rose	25.00	9.00	4.00
(84)	John Roseboro	5.00	1.50	.75
(85)	Ron Santo	6.50	2.25	1.00
(86)	Bill Skowron	5.00	1.75	.70
(87)	Willie Stargell	10.00	3.50	1.50
(88)	Mel Stottlemyre	5.00	1.50	.75
(89)	Dick Stuart	5.00	1.50	.75
(90)	Ron Swoboda	5.00	1.50	.75
(91)	Fred Talbot	5.00	1.50	.75
(92)	Ralph Terry	5.00	1.50	.75
(93)	Joe Torre	6.50	2.25	1.00
(94)	Tom Tresh	5.00	1.50	.75
(95)	Bob Veale	5.00	1.50	.75
(96)	Pete Ward	5.00	1.50	.75
(97)	Bill White	5.00	1.50	.75
(98)	Billy Williams	10.00	3.50	1.50
(99)	Jim Wynn	5.00	1.50	.75
(100)	Carl Yastrzemski	15.00	5.25	2.25
(101)	Angels Pennant	7.00	2.50	1.00
(102)	Astros Pennant	7.00	2.50	1.00
(103)	Athletics Pennant	7.00	2.50	1.00
(104)	Braves Pennant	7.00	2.50	1.00
(105)	Cards Pennant	7.00	2.50	1.00
(106)	Cubs Pennant	7.00	2.50	1.00
(107)	Dodgers Pennant	7.00	2.50	1.00
(108)	Giants Pennant	7.00	2.50	1.00
(109)	Indians Pennant	7.00	2.50	1.00
(110)	Mets Pennant	7.00	2.50	1.00
(111)	Orioles Pennant	7.00	2.50	1.00
(112)	Phillies Pennant	7.00	2.50	1.00
(113)	Pirates Pennant	7.00	2.50	1.00
(114)	Red Sox Pennant	7.00	2.50	1.00
(115)	Reds Pennant	7.00	2.50	1.00
(116)	Senators Pennant	7.00	2.50	1.00
(117)	Tigers Pennant	7.00	2.50	1.00
(118)	Twins Pennant	7.00	2.50	1.00
(119)	White Sox Pennant	7.00	2.50	1.00
(120)	Yankees Pennant	9.00	3.25	1.25

1967 Topps

This 609-card set of 2-1/2" x 3-1/2" cards marked the largest set up to that time for Topps. Card fronts feature large color photographs bordered by white. The player's name and position are printed at the top with the team at the bottom. Across the front of the card with the exception of #254 (Milt Pappas) there is a facsimile autograph. The backs were the first to be done vertically, although they continued to carry familiar statistical and biographical information. The only subsets are statistical leaders and World Series highlights. Rookie cards are done by team or league with two players per card. The high numbers (#534-609) in '67 are quite scarce, and while it is known that some are even scarcer, by virtue of having been short-printed in relation to the rest of the series, there is no general agreement on which cards are involved. Cards in the high series which are generally believed to have been double-printed - and thus worth somewhat less than the other cards in the series - are indicated in the checklist by a (DP) notation following the player name.

		NM	EX	VG
	Complete Set (609):	4,500	2,250	1,350
	Common Player (1-370):	2.00	1.00	.60
	Common Player (371-457):	4.00	2.00	1.25
	Common Player (458-533):	7.00	3.50	2.00
	Common Player (534-609):	12.00	6.00	3.50
1	The Champs (Hank Bauer, Brooks Robinson, Frank Robinson)	20.00	9.00	5.00
2	Jack Hamilton	2.00	1.00	.60
3	Duke Sims	2.00	1.00	.60
4	Hal Lanier	2.00	1.00	.60
5	Whitey Ford	25.00	12.50	7.50
6	Dick Simpson	2.00	1.00	.60
7	Don McMahon	2.00	1.00	.60
8	Chuck Harrison	2.00	1.00	.60
9	Ron Hansen	2.00	1.00	.60
10	Matty Alou	2.00	1.00	.60
11	Barry Moore	2.00	1.00	.60
12	Dodgers Rookies (*Jimmy Campanis, Bill Singer*)			
13	Joe Sparma	2.00	1.00	.60
14	Phil Linz	2.00	1.00	.60
15	Earl Battey	2.00	1.00	.60
16	Bill Hands	2.00	1.00	.60
17	Jim Gosger	2.00	1.00	.60
18	Gene Oliver	2.00	1.00	.60
19	Jim McGlothlin	2.00	1.00	.60
20	Orlando Cepeda	15.00	7.50	4.50
21	Dave Bristol	2.00	1.00	.60
22	Gene Brabender	2.00	1.00	.60
23	Larry Elliot	2.00	1.00	.60
24	Bob Allen	2.00	1.00	.60
25	Elston Howard	7.00	3.50	2.00
26a	Bob Priddy (No trade statement.)	30.00	15.00	9.00
26b	Bob Priddy (With trade statement.)	2.00	1.00	.60
27	Bob Saverine	2.00	1.00	.60
28	Barry Latman	2.00	1.00	.60
29	Tommy McCraw	2.00	1.00	.60
30	Al Kaline	20.00	10.00	6.00
31	Jim Brewer	2.00	1.00	.60
32	Bob Bailey	2.00	1.00	.60
33	Athletics Rookies (*Sal Bando, Randy Schwartz*)	4.00	2.00	1.25
34	Pete Cimino	2.00	1.00	.60
35	Rico Carty	2.00	1.00	.60
36	Bob Tillman	2.00	1.00	.60
37	Rick Wise	2.00	1.00	.60
38	Bob Johnson	2.00	1.00	.60
39	Curt Simmons	2.00	1.00	.60
40	Rick Reichardt	2.00	1.00	.60
41	Joe Hoerner	2.00	1.00	.60
42	Mets Team	8.00	4.00	2.50
43	Chico Salmon	2.00	1.00	.60
44	Joe Nuxhall	2.00	1.00	.60
45a	Roger Maris (Cards on front.)	35.00	17.50	10.00
45b	Roger Maris (Yankees on front, blank-back proof.)	2,250	1,125	635.00
46	Lindy McDaniel	2.00	1.00	.60
47	Ken McMullen	2.00	1.00	.60
48	Bill Freehan	2.00	1.00	.60
49	Roy Face	2.00	1.00	.60
50	Tony Oliva	6.00	3.00	1.75
51	Astros Rookies (*Dave Adlesh, Wes Bales*)	2.00	1.00	.60
52	Dennis Higgins	2.00	1.00	.60
53	Clay Dalrymple	2.00	1.00	.60
54	Dick Green	2.00	1.00	.60
55	Don Drysdale	20.00	10.00	6.00
56	Jose Tartabull	2.00	1.00	.60
57	*Pat Jarvis*			
58a	Paul Schaal (Bat green above name.)	15.00	7.50	4.50
58b	Paul Schaal (Bat natural above name.)	2.00	1.00	.60
59	Ralph Terry	2.00	1.00	.60
60	Luis Aparicio	15.00	7.50	4.50
61	Gordy Coleman	2.00	1.00	.60
62a	1st Series Check List (1-109) (Frank Robinson) (Copyright symbol beneath T of Tribe.)	7.00	3.50	2.00
62b	1st Series Check List (1-109) (Frank Robinson) (Copyright symbol beneath r of Tribe.)	7.00	3.50	2.00
63	Cards Clubbers (Lou Brock, Curt Flood)	12.00	6.00	3.50
64	Fred Valentine	2.00	1.00	.60
65	Tom Haller	2.00	1.00	.60
66	Manny Mota	2.00	1.00	.60
67	Ken Berry	2.00	1.00	.60
68	Bob Buhl	2.00	1.00	.60
69	Vic Davalillo	2.00	1.00	.60
70	Ron Santo	6.00	3.00	1.75
71	Camilo Pascual	2.00	1.00	.60
72	Tigers Rookies (George Korince, John Matchick) (Korince photo actually James M. Brown.)	2.00	1.00	.60
73	Rusty Staub	3.00	1.50	.90
74	Wes Stock	2.00	1.00	.60
75	George Scott	2.00	1.00	.60
76	Jim Barbieri	2.00	1.00	.60
77	Dooley Womack	2.00	1.00	.60
78	Pat Corrales	2.00	1.00	.60
79	Bubba Morton	2.00	1.00	.60
80	Jim Maloney	2.00	1.00	.60
81	Eddie Stanky	2.00	1.00	.60
82	Steve Barber	2.00	1.00	.60
83	Ollie Brown	2.00	1.00	.60
84	Tommie Sisk	2.00	1.00	.60
85	Johnny Callison	2.00	1.00	.60
86a	Mike McCormick (No trade statement.)	30.00	15.00	9.00
86b	Mike McCormick (With trade statement.)	2.00	1.00	.60
87	George Altman	2.00	1.00	.60
88	Mickey Lolich	2.00	1.00	.60
89	*Felix Millan*	2.00	1.00	.60
90	Jim Nash	2.00	1.00	.60
91	Johnny Lewis	2.00	1.00	.60
92	Ray Washburn	2.00	1.00	.60
93	Yankees Rookies (*Stan Bahnsen, Bobby Murcer*)	12.00	6.00	3.50
94	Ron Fairly	2.00	1.00	.60
95	Sonny Siebert	2.00	1.00	.60
96	Art Shamsky	2.00	1.00	.60
97	Mike Cuellar	2.00	1.00	.60
98	Rich Rollins	2.00	1.00	.60
99	Lee Stange	2.00	1.00	.60
100	Frank Robinson	20.00	10.00	6.00
101	Ken Johnson	2.00	1.00	.60
102	Phillies Team	3.50	1.75	1.00
103a	2nd Series Check List (110-196) (Mickey Mantle) (170 is D McAuliffe)	25.00	12.50	7.50
103b	2nd Series Check List (110-196) (Mickey Mantle) (170 is D. McAuliffe)	25.00	12.50	7.50
104	Minnie Rojas	2.00	1.00	.60
105	Ken Boyer	5.00	2.50	1.50
106	Randy Hundley	2.00	1.00	.60
107	Joel Horlen	2.00	1.00	.60
108	Alex Johnson	2.00	1.00	.60
109	Tribe Thumpers (Rocky Colavito, Leon Wagner)	9.00	4.50	2.75
110	Jack Aker	2.00	1.00	.60
111	John Kennedy	2.00	1.00	.60
112	Dave Wickersham	2.00	1.00	.60
113	Dave Nicholson	2.00	1.00	.60
114	Jack Baldschun	2.00	1.00	.60
115	Paul Casanova	2.00	1.00	.60
116	Herman Franks	2.00	1.00	.60
117	Darrell Brandon	2.00	1.00	.60
118	Bernie Allen	2.00	1.00	.60
119	Wade Blasingame	2.00	1.00	.60
120	Floyd Robinson	2.00	1.00	.60
121	Ed Bressoud	2.00	1.00	.60
122	George Brunet	2.00	1.00	.60
123	Pirates Rookies (*Jim Price, Luke Walker*)	2.00	1.00	.60
124	Jim Stewart	2.00	1.00	.60
125	Moe Drabowsky	2.00	1.00	.60
126	Tony Taylor	2.00	1.00	.60
127	John O'Donoghue	2.00	1.00	.60
128a	Ed Spiezio (Most of "SPIE" missing at top.)	75.00	37.50	22.50
128b	Ed Spiezio (Lettering all there.)	2.00	1.00	.60
129	Phil Roof	2.00	1.00	.60
130	Phil Regan	2.00	1.00	.60
131	Yankees Team	9.00	4.50	2.75
132	Ozzie Virgil	2.00	1.00	.60
133	Ron Kline	2.00	1.00	.60
134	Gates Brown	2.00	1.00	.60
135	Deron Johnson	2.00	1.00	.60
136	Carroll Sembera	2.00	1.00	.60
137	Twins Rookies (*Ron Clark, Jim Ollom*)	2.00	1.00	.60
138	Dick Kelley	2.00	1.00	.60
139	Dalton Jones	2.00	1.00	.60
140	Willie Stargell	20.00	10.00	6.00
141	John Miller	2.00	1.00	.60
142	Jackie Brandt	2.00	1.00	.60
143	Sox Sockers (Don Buford, Pete Ward)	2.00	1.00	.60
144	Bill Hepler	2.00	1.00	.60
145	Larry Brown	2.00	1.00	.60
146	Steve Carlton	27.50	13.50	8.25
147	Tom Egan	2.00	1.00	.60
148	Adolfo Phillips	2.00	1.00	.60
149a	Joe Moeller (White streak between "M" and cap.)	30.00	15.00	9.00
149b	Joe Moeller (No white streak.)	2.00	1.00	.60
150	Mickey Mantle	180.00	90.00	55.00
151	World Series Game 1 (Moe Mows Down 11)	6.00	3.00	1.75
152	World Series Game 2 (Palmer Blanks Dodgers)	11.00	5.50	3.25
153	World Series Game 3 (Blair's Homer Defeats L.A.)	6.00	3.00	1.75
154	World Series Game 4 (Orioles Win 4th Straight)	6.00	3.00	1.75
155	World Series (The Winners Celebrate)	7.50	3.75	2.25
156	Ron Herbel	2.00	1.00	.60
157	Danny Cater	2.00	1.00	.60
158	Jimmy Coker	2.00	1.00	.60
159	Bruce Howard	2.00	1.00	.60
160	Willie Davis	2.00	1.00	.60
161	Dick Williams	2.00	1.00	.60
162	Billy O'Dell	2.00	1.00	.60
163	Vic Roznovsky	2.00	1.00	.60
164	Dwight Siebler	2.00	1.00	.60
165	Cleon Jones	2.00	1.00	.60
166	Ed Mathews	20.00	10.00	6.00
167	Senators Rookies (*Joe Coleman, Tim Cullen*)	2.00	1.00	.60
168	Ray Culp	2.00	1.00	.60
169	Horace Clarke	2.00	1.00	.60
170	Dick McAuliffe	2.00	1.00	.60
171	Calvin Koonce	2.00	1.00	.60
172	Bill Heath	2.00	1.00	.60
173	Cards Team	5.00	2.50	1.50
174	Dick Radatz	2.00	1.00	.60
175	Bobby Knoop	2.00	1.00	.60
176	Sammy Ellis	2.00	1.00	.60
177	Tito Fuentes	2.00	1.00	.60
178	John Buzhardt	2.00	1.00	.60
179	Braves Rookies (*Cecil Upshaw, Chas. Vaughan*)	2.00	1.00	.60
180	Curt Blefary	2.00	1.00	.60
181	Terry Fox	2.00	1.00	.60
182	Ed Charles	2.00	1.00	.60
183	Jim Pagliaroni	2.00	1.00	.60
184	George Thomas	2.00	1.00	.60
185	*Ken Holtzman*	4.00	2.00	1.25
186	Mets Maulers (Ed Kranepool, Ron Swoboda)	3.50	1.75	1.00
187	Pedro Ramos	2.00	1.00	.60
188	Ken Harrelson	2.00	1.00	.60
189	Chuck Hinton	2.00	1.00	.60
190	Turk Farrell	2.00	1.00	.60
191a	3rd Series Check List (197-283) (Willie Mays) (214 is Dick Kelley)	9.00	4.50	2.75
191b	3rd Series Check List (197-283) (Willie Mays) (214 is Tom Kelley)	12.00	6.00	3.50
192	Fred Gladding	2.00	1.00	.60
193	Jose Cardenal	2.00	1.00	.60
194	Bob Allison	2.00	1.00	.60
195	Al Jackson	2.00	1.00	.60
196	Johnny Romano	2.00	1.00	.60
197	Ron Perranoski	2.00	1.00	.60
198	Chuck Hiller	2.00	1.00	.60
199	Billy Hitchcock	2.00	1.00	.60
200	Willie Mays	65.00	32.50	20.00
201	Hal Reniff	2.00	1.00	.60
202	Johnny Edwards	2.00	1.00	.60
203	Al McBean	2.00	1.00	.60
204	Orioles Rookies (*Mike Epstein, Tom Phoebus*)	2.00	1.00	.60
205	Dick Groat	2.00	1.00	.60
206	Dennis Bennett	2.00	1.00	.60
207	John Orsino	2.00	1.00	.60
208	Jack Lamabe	2.00	1.00	.60
209	Joe Nossek	2.00	1.00	.60
210	Bob Gibson	20.00	10.00	6.00
211	Twins Team	6.00	3.00	1.75
212	Chris Zachary	2.00	1.00	.60
213	*Jay Johnstone*	4.00	2.00	1.25
214	Tom Kelley	2.00	1.00	.60
215	Ernie Banks	25.00	12.50	7.50
216	Bengal Belters (Norm Cash, Al Kaline)	15.00	7.50	4.50
217	Rob Gardner	2.00	1.00	.60
218	Wes Parker	2.00	1.00	.60
219	Clay Carroll	2.00	1.00	.60
220	Jim Hart	2.00	1.00	.60
221	Woody Fryman	2.00	1.00	.60
222	Reds Rookies (*Lee May, Darrell Osteen*)	2.00	1.00	.60
223	Mike Ryan	2.00	1.00	.60
224	Walt Bond	2.00	1.00	.60
225	Mel Stottlemyre	4.00	2.00	1.25
226	Julian Javier	2.00	1.00	.60
227	Paul Lindblad	2.00	1.00	.60
228	Gil Hodges	9.00	4.50	2.75
229	Larry Jackson	2.00	1.00	.60
230	Boog Powell	6.00	3.00	1.75
231	John Bateman	2.00	1.00	.60
232	Don Buford	2.00	1.00	.60
233	A.L. ERA Leaders (Steve Hargan, Joel Horlen, Gary Peters)	3.00	1.50	.90
234	N.L. ERA Leaders (Mike Cuellar, Sandy Koufax, Juan Marichal)	12.00	6.00	3.50
235	A.L. Pitching Leaders (Jim Kaat, Denny McLain, Earl Wilson)	3.50	1.75	1.00
236	N.L. Pitching Leaders (Bob Gibson, Sandy Koufax, Juan Marichal, Gaylord Perry)	16.00	8.00	4.75
237	A.L. Strikeout Leaders (Jim Kaat, Sam McDowell, Earl Wilson)	3.50	1.75	1.00
238	N.L. Strikeout Leaders (Jim Bunning, Sandy Koufax, Bob Veale)	12.00	6.00	3.50
239	A.L. Batting Leaders (Al Kaline, Tony Oliva, Frank Robinson)	16.00	8.00	4.75
240	N.L. Batting Leaders (Felipe Alou, Matty Alou, Rico Carty)	11.00	5.50	3.25
241	A.L. RBI Leaders (Harmon Killebrew, Boog Powell, Frank Robinson)	11.00	5.50	3.25
242	N.L. RBI Leaders (Hank Aaron, Richie Allen, Bob Clemente)	17.50	8.75	5.25
243	A.L. Home Run Leaders (Harmon Killebrew, Boog Powell, Frank Robinson)	11.00	5.50	3.25
244	N.L. Home Run Leaders (Hank Aaron, Richie Allen, Willie Mays)	15.00	7.50	4.50
245	Curt Flood	5.00	2.50	1.50
246	Jim Perry	2.00	1.00	.60

#	Player			
247	Jerry Lumpe	2.00	1.00	.60
248	Gene Mauch	2.00	1.00	.60
249	Nick Willhite	2.00	1.00	.60
250	Hank Aaron	65.00	32.50	20.00
251	Woody Held	2.00	1.00	.60
252a	Bob Bolin (White streak between Bob and Bolin.)	60.00	30.00	18.00
252b	Bob Bolin (No white streak.)	2.00	1.00	.60
253	Indians Rookies (*Bill Davis, Gus Gil*)	2.00	1.00	.60
254	Milt Pappas	2.00	1.00	.60
255	Frank Howard	2.50	1.25	.70
256	Bob Hendley	2.00	1.00	.60
257	Charley Smith	2.00	1.00	.60
258	Lee Maye	2.00	1.00	.60
259	Don Dennis	2.00	1.00	.60
260	Jim Lefebvre	2.00	1.00	.60
261	John Wyatt	2.00	1.00	.60
262	Athletics Team	6.00	3.00	1.75
263	Hank Aguirre	2.00	1.00	.60
264	Ron Swoboda	2.00	1.00	.60
265	Lou Burdette	2.00	1.00	.60
266	Pitt Power (Donn Clendenon, Willie Stargell)	12.00	6.00	3.50
267	Don Schwall	2.00	1.00	.60
268	John Briggs	2.00	1.00	.60
269	Don Nottebart	2.00	1.00	.60
270	Zoilo Versalles	2.00	1.00	.60
271	Eddie Watt	2.00	1.00	.60
272	Cubs Rookies (*Bill Connors, Dave Dowling*)	2.00	1.00	.60
273	Dick Lines	2.00	1.00	.60
274	Bob Aspromonte	2.00	1.00	.60
275	Fred Whitfield	2.00	1.00	.60
276	Bruce Brubaker	2.00	1.00	.60
277	Steve Whitaker	2.00	1.00	.60
278	4th Series Check List (284-370) (Jim Kaat)	7.00	3.50	2.00
279	Frank Linzy	2.00	1.00	.60
280	Tony Conigliaro	9.00	4.50	2.75
281	Bob Rodgers	2.00	1.00	.60
282	Johnny Odom	2.00	1.00	.60
283	Gene Alley	2.00	1.00	.60
284	Johnny Podres	3.00	1.50	.90
285	Lou Brock	17.50	8.75	5.25
286	Wayne Causey	2.00	1.00	.60
287	Mets Rookies (*Greg Goossen, Bart Shirley*)	2.00	1.00	.60
288	Denver Lemaster	2.00	1.00	.60
289	Tom Tresh	6.00	3.00	1.75
290	Bill White	2.00	1.00	.60
291	Jim Hannan	2.00	1.00	.60
292	Don Pavletich	2.00	1.00	.60
293	Ed Kirkpatrick	2.00	1.00	.60
294	Walt Alston	7.00	3.50	2.00
295	Sam McDowell	2.00	.70	.60
296	Glenn Beckert	2.00	1.00	.60
297	Dave Morehead	2.00	1.00	.60
298	Ron Davis	2.00	1.00	.60
299	Norm Siebern	2.00	1.00	.60
300	Jim Kaat	4.00	2.00	1.25
301	Jesse Gonder	2.00	1.00	.60
302	Orioles Team	6.00	3.00	1.75
303	Gil Blanco	2.00	1.00	.60
304	Phil Gagliano	2.00	1.00	.60
305	Earl Wilson	2.00	1.00	.60
306	Bud Harrelson	7.00	3.50	2.00
307	Jim Beauchamp	2.00	1.00	.60
308	Al Downing	2.00	1.00	.60
309	Hurlers Beware (Richie Allen, Johnny Callison)	6.00	3.00	1.75
310	Gary Peters	2.00	1.00	.60
311	Ed Brinkman	2.00	1.00	.60
312	Don Mincher	2.00	1.00	.60
313	Bob Lee	2.00	1.00	.60
314	Red Sox Rookies (*Mike Andrews, Reggie Smith*)	12.00	6.00	3.50
315	Billy Williams	17.50	8.75	5.25
316	Jack Kralick	2.00	1.00	.60
317	Cesar Tovar	2.00	1.00	.60
318	Dave Giusti	2.00	1.00	.60
319	Paul Blair	2.00	1.00	.60
320	Gaylord Perry	15.00	7.50	4.50
321	Mayo Smith	2.00	1.00	.60
322	Jose Pagan	2.00	1.00	.60
323	Mike Hershberger	2.00	1.00	.60
324	Hal Woodeshick	2.00	1.00	.60
325	Chico Cardenas	2.00	1.00	.60
326	Bob Uecker	12.00	6.00	3.50
327	Angels Team	6.00	3.00	1.75
328	Clete Boyer	4.00	2.00	1.25
329	Charlie Lau	2.00	1.00	.60
330	Claude Osteen	2.00	1.00	.60
331	Joe Foy	2.00	1.00	.60
332	Jesus Alou	2.00	1.00	.60
333	Fergie Jenkins	16.00	8.00	4.75
334	Twin Terrors (Bob Allison, Harmon Killebrew)	15.00	7.50	4.50
335	Bob Veale	2.00	1.00	.60
336	Joe Azcue	2.00	1.00	.60
337	Joe Morgan	17.50	8.75	5.25
338	Bob Locker	2.00	1.00	.60
339	Chico Ruiz	2.00	1.00	.60
340	Joe Pepitone	4.00	2.00	1.25
341	Giants Rookies (*Dick Dietz, Bill Sorrell*)	2.00	1.00	.60
342	Hank Fischer	2.00	1.00	.60
343	Tom Satriano	2.00	1.00	.60
344	Ossie Chavarria	2.00	1.00	.60
345	Stu Miller	2.00	1.00	.60
346	Jim Hickman	2.00	1.00	.60
347	Grady Hatton	2.00	1.00	.60
348	Tug McGraw	3.00	1.50	.90
349	Bob Chance	2.00	1.00	.60
350	Joe Torre	7.00	3.50	2.00
351	Vern Law	2.00	1.00	.60
352	Ray Oyler	2.00	1.00	.60
353	Bill McCool	2.00	1.00	.60
354	Cubs Team	6.00	3.00	1.75
355	Carl Yastrzemski	45.00	22.50	13.50
356	Larry Jaster	2.00	1.00	.60
357	Bill Skowron	5.00	2.50	1.50
358	Ruben Amaro	2.00	1.00	.60
359	Dick Ellsworth	2.00	1.00	.60
360	Leon Wagner	2.00	1.00	.60
361	5th Series Check List (371-457) (Roberto Clemente)	9.00	4.50	2.75
362	Darold Knowles	2.00	1.00	.60
363	Dave Johnson	2.00	1.00	.60
364	Claude Raymond	2.00	1.00	.60
365	John Roseboro	2.00	1.00	.60
366	Andy Kosco	2.00	1.00	.60
367	Angels Rookies (*Bill Kelso, Don Wallace*)	2.00	1.00	.60
368	Jack Hiatt	2.00	1.00	.60
369	Jim Hunter	15.00	7.50	4.50
370	Tommy Davis	2.00	1.00	.60
371	Jim Lonborg	4.00	2.00	1.25
372	Mike de la Hoz	4.00	2.00	1.25
373	White Sox Rookies (Duane Josephson, Fred Klages)	4.00	2.00	1.25
374a	Mel Queen (Rule under stats totals nearly gone.)	4.00	2.00	1.25
374b	Mel Queen (Full rule.)	4.00	2.00	1.25
375	Jake Gibbs	4.00	2.00	1.25
376	Don Lock	4.00	2.00	1.25
377	Luis Tiant	4.00	2.00	1.25
378	Tigers Team	7.00	3.50	2.00
379	Jerry May	4.00	2.00	1.25
380	Dean Chance	4.00	2.00	1.25
381	Dick Schofield	4.00	2.00	1.25
382	Dave McNally	4.00	2.00	1.25
383	Ken Henderson	4.00	2.00	1.25
384	Cards Rookies (*Jim Cosman, Dick Hughes*)	4.00	2.00	1.25
385	Jim Fregosi	4.00	2.00	1.25
386	Dick Selma	4.00	2.00	1.25
387	Cap Peterson	4.00	2.00	1.25
388	Arnold Earley	4.00	2.00	1.25
389	Al Dark	4.00	2.00	1.25
390	Jim Wynn	4.00	2.00	1.25
391	Wilbur Wood	4.00	2.00	1.25
392	Tommy Harper	4.00	2.00	1.25
393	Jim Bouton	7.00	3.50	2.00
394	Jake Wood	4.00	2.00	1.25
395	Chris Short	4.00	2.00	1.25
396	Atlanta Aces (Tony Cloninger, Denis Menke)	7.00	3.50	2.00
397	Willie Smith	4.00	2.00	1.25
398	Jeff Torborg	4.00	2.00	1.25
399	Al Worthington	4.00	2.00	1.25
400	Roberto Clemente	80.00	40.00	24.00
401	Jim Coates	4.00	2.00	1.25
402a	Phillies Rookies (*Grant Jackson, Billy Wilson*) (Incomplete line under Wilson's stats.)	6.50	3.25	2.00
402b	Grant Jackson, Billy Wilson (Complete line.)	4.00	2.00	1.25
403	Dick Nen	4.00	2.00	1.25
404	Nelson Briles	4.00	2.00	1.25
405	Russ Snyder	4.00	2.00	1.25
406	Lee Elia	4.00	2.00	1.25
407	Reds Team	7.00	3.50	2.00
408	Jim Northrup	4.00	2.00	1.25
409	Ray Sadecki	4.00	2.00	1.25
410	Lou Johnson	4.00	2.00	1.25
411	Dick Howser	4.00	2.00	1.25
412	Astros Rookies (*Norm Miller, Doug Rader*)	5.00	2.50	1.50
413	Jerry Grote	4.00	2.00	1.25
414	Casey Cox	4.00	2.00	1.25
415	Sonny Jackson	4.00	2.00	1.25
416	Roger Repoz	4.00	2.00	1.25
417a	Bob Bruce (RBAVES on back)	30.00	15.00	9.00
417b	Bob Bruce (Corrected)	4.00	2.00	1.25
418	Sam Mele	4.00	2.00	1.25
419	Don Kessinger	4.00	2.00	1.25
420	Denny McLain	7.00	3.50	2.00
421	Dal Maxvill	4.00	2.00	1.25
422	Hoyt Wilhelm	15.00	7.50	4.50
423	Fence Busters (Willie Mays, Willie McCovey)	25.00	12.50	7.50
424	Pedro Gonzalez	4.00	2.00	1.25
425	Pete Mikkelsen	4.00	2.00	1.25
426	Lou Clinton	4.00	2.00	1.25
427a	Ruben Gomez (Stats totals line nearly gone.)	12.00	6.00	3.50
427b	Ruben Gomez (Full stats totals line.)	4.00	2.00	1.25
428	Dodgers Rookies (*Tom Hutton, Gene Michael*)	6.00	3.00	1.75
429	Garry Roggenburk	4.00	2.00	1.25
430	Pete Rose	65.00	32.50	20.00
431	Ted Uhlaender	4.00	2.00	1.25
432	Jimmie Hall	4.00	2.00	1.25
433	Al Luplow	4.00	2.00	1.25
434	Eddie Fisher	4.00	2.00	1.25
435	Mack Jones	4.00	2.00	1.25
436	Pete Ward	4.00	2.00	1.25
437	Senators Team	7.00	3.50	2.00
438	Chuck Dobson	4.00	2.00	1.25
439	Byron Browne	4.00	2.00	1.25
440	Steve Hargan	4.00	2.00	1.25
441	Jim Davenport	4.00	2.00	1.25
442	Yankees Rookies (Bill Robinson, Joe Verbanic)	6.00	3.00	1.75
443	Tito Francona	4.00	2.00	1.25
444	George Smith	4.00	2.00	1.25
445	Don Sutton	15.00	7.50	4.50
446	Russ Nixon	4.00	2.00	1.25
447a	Bo Belinsky (1966 S.D. stats nearly gone)	6.00	3.00	1.75
447b	Bo Belinsky (Full 1966 S.D. stats line.)	4.00	2.00	1.25
448	Harry Walker	4.00	2.00	1.25
449	Orlando Pena	4.00	2.00	1.25
450	Richie Allen	12.00	6.00	3.50
451	Fred Newman	4.00	2.00	1.25
452	Ed Kranepool	4.00	2.00	1.25
453	Aurelio Monteagudo	4.00	2.00	1.25
454a	6th Series Check List (458-533) (Juan Marichal) (Left ear shows.)	9.00	4.50	2.75
454b	6th Series Check List (458-533) (Juan Marichal) (No left ear.)	12.00	6.00	3.50
455	Tommie Agee	4.00	2.00	1.25
456	Phil Niekro	15.00	7.50	4.50
457	Andy Etchebarren	4.00	2.00	1.25
458	Lee Thomas	7.00	3.50	2.00
459	Senators Rookies (*Dick Bosman, Pete Craig*)	7.00	3.50	2.00
460	Harmon Killebrew	35.00	17.50	10.00
461	Bob Miller	7.00	3.50	2.00
462	Bob Barton	7.00	3.50	2.00
463	Hill Aces (Sam McDowell, Sonny Siebert)	11.00	5.50	3.25
464	Dan Coombs	7.00	3.50	2.00
465	Willie Horton	7.00	3.50	2.00
466	Bobby Wine	7.00	3.50	2.00
467	Jim O'Toole	7.00	3.50	2.00
468	Ralph Houk	7.00	3.50	2.00
469	Len Gabrielson	7.00	3.50	2.00
470	Bob Shaw	7.00	3.50	2.00
471	Rene Lachemann	7.00	3.50	2.00
472	Pirates Rookies (*John Gelnar, George Spriggs*)	7.00	3.50	2.00
473	Jose Santiago	7.00	3.50	2.00
474	Bob Tolan	7.00	3.50	2.00
475	Jim Palmer	35.00	17.50	10.00
476	Tony Perez/SP	40.00	20.00	12.00
477	Braves Team	11.00	5.50	3.25
478	Bob Humphreys	7.00	3.50	2.00
479	Gary Bell	7.00	3.50	2.00
480	Willie McCovey	35.00	17.50	10.00
481	Leo Durocher	12.00	6.00	3.50
482	Bill Monbouquette	7.00	3.50	2.00
483	Jim Landis	7.00	3.50	2.00
484	Jerry Adair	7.00	3.50	2.00
485	Tim McCarver	17.50	8.75	5.25
486	Twins Rookies (*Rich Reese, Bill Whitby*)	7.00	3.50	2.00
487	Tom Reynolds	7.00	3.50	2.00
488	Gerry Arrigo	7.00	3.50	2.00
489	Doug Clemens	7.00	3.50	2.00
490	Tony Cloninger	7.00	3.50	2.00
491	Sam Bowens	7.00	3.50	2.00
492	Pirates Team	16.00	8.00	4.75
493	Phil Ortega	7.00	3.50	2.00
494	Bill Rigney	7.00	3.50	2.00
495	Fritz Peterson	7.00	3.50	2.00
496	Orlando McFarlane	7.00	3.50	2.00
497	Ron Campbell	7.00	3.50	2.00
498	Larry Dierker	7.00	3.50	2.00
499	Indians Rookies (*George Culver, Jose Vidal*)	7.00	3.50	2.00
500	Juan Marichal	25.00	12.50	7.50
501	Jerry Zimmerman	7.00	3.50	2.00
502	Derrell Griffith	7.00	3.50	2.00
503	Dodgers Team	16.00	8.00	4.75
504	Orlando Martinez	7.00	3.50	2.00
505	Tommy Helms	7.00	3.50	2.00
506	Smoky Burgess	7.00	3.50	2.00
507	Orioles Rookies (*Ed Barnowski, Larry Haney*)	7.00	3.50	2.00
508	Dick Hall	7.00	3.50	2.00
509	Jim King	7.00	3.50	2.00
510	Bill Mazeroski	20.00	10.00	6.00
511	Don Wert	7.00	3.50	2.00
512	Red Schoendienst	15.00	7.50	4.50
513	Marcelino Lopez	7.00	3.50	2.00
514	John Werhas	7.00	3.50	2.00
515	Bert Campaneris	7.00	3.50	2.00
516	Giants Team	17.50	8.75	5.25
517	Fred Talbot	7.00	3.50	2.00
518	Denis Menke	7.00	3.50	2.00
519	Ted Davidson	7.00	3.50	2.00
520	Max Alvis	7.00	3.50	2.00
521	Bird Bombers (Curt Blefary, Boog Powell)	7.50	3.75	2.25
522	John Stephenson	7.00	3.50	2.00
523	Jim Merritt	7.00	3.50	2.00
524	Felix Mantilla	7.00	3.50	2.00
525	Ron Hunt	7.00	3.50	2.00
526	Tigers Rookies (*Pat Dobson, George Korince*)	11.00	5.50	3.25
527	Dennis Ribant	7.00	3.50	2.00
528	Rico Petrocelli	12.50	6.25	3.75
529	Gary Wagner	7.00	3.50	2.00
530	Felipe Alou	12.00	6.00	3.50
531	7th Series Check List (534-609) (Brooks Robinson)	12.00	6.00	3.50
532	Jim Hicks	7.00	3.50	2.00
533	Jack Fisher	7.00	3.50	2.00
534	Hank Bauer/DP	8.00	4.00	2.50
535	Donn Clendenon	12.00	6.00	3.50
536	Cubs Rookies (Joe Niekro, Paul Popovich)	32.50	16.00	10.00
537	Chuck Estrada/DP	8.00	4.00	2.50
538	J.C. Martin	12.00	6.00	3.50
539	Dick Egan/DP	8.00	4.00	2.50
540	Norm Cash	45.00	22.50	13.50
541	Joe Gibbon	12.00	6.00	3.50
542	Athletics Rookies (*Rick Monday, Tony Pierce*)/DP	12.50	6.25	3.75
543	Dan Schneider	12.00	6.00	3.50
544	Indians Team	40.00	20.00	12.00
545	Jim Grant	12.00	6.00	3.50
546	Woody Woodward	12.00	6.00	3.50
547	Red Sox Rookies (*Russ Gibson, Bill Rohr*)/DP	8.00	4.00	2.50
548	Tony Gonzalez/DP	8.00	4.00	2.50

		NM	EX	VG
549	Jack Sanford	12.00	6.00	3.50
550	Vada Pinson/DP	12.00	6.00	3.50
551	Doug Camilli/DP	8.00	4.00	2.50
552	Ted Savage	12.00	6.00	3.50
553	Yankees Rookies (*Mike Hegan, Thad Tillotson*)	25.00	12.50	7.50
554	Andre Rodgers/DP	8.00	4.00	2.50
555	Don Cardwell	12.00	6.00	3.50
556	Al Weis/DP	8.00	4.00	2.50
557	Al Ferrara	12.00	6.00	3.50
558	Orioles Rookies (*Mark Belanger, Bill Dillman*)	45.00	22.50	13.50
559	Dick Tracewski/DP	8.00	4.00	2.50
560	Jim Bunning	50.00	25.00	15.00
561	Sandy Alomar	12.00	6.00	3.50
562	Steve Blass/DP	8.00	4.00	2.50
563	Joe Adcock	15.00	7.50	4.50
564	Astros Rookies (*Alonzo Harris, Aaron Pointer*)/DP	8.00	4.00	2.50
565	Lew Krausse	12.00	6.00	3.50
566	Gary Geiger (DP)	8.00	4.00	2.50
567	Steve Hamilton	12.00	6.00	3.50
568	John Sullivan	12.00	6.00	3.50
569	A.L. Rookies (*Hank Allen, Rod Carew*)/DP	165.00	80.00	50.00
570	Maury Wills	70.00	35.00	20.00
571	Larry Sherry	12.00	6.00	3.50
572	Don Demeter	12.00	6.00	3.50
573	White Sox Team (Indians team stats on back.)	25.00	12.50	7.50
574	Jerry Buchek	12.00	6.00	3.50
575	*Dave Boswell*	12.00	6.00	3.50
576	N.L. Rookies (*Norm Gigon, Ramon Hernandez*)	12.00	6.00	3.50
577	Bill Short	12.00	6.00	3.50
578	John Boccabella	12.00	6.00	3.50
579	Bill Henry	12.00	6.00	3.50
580	Rocky Colavito	70.00	35.00	20.00
581	Mets Rookies (*Bill Denehy, Tom Seaver*)	340.00	170.00	100.00
582	Jim Owens/DP	8.00	4.00	2.50
583	Ray Barker	12.00	6.00	3.50
584	Jim Piersall	20.00	10.00	6.00
585	Wally Bunker	12.00	6.00	3.50
586	Manny Jimenez	12.00	6.00	3.50
587	N.L. Rookies (*Don Shaw, Gary Sutherland*)	12.00	6.00	3.50
588	Johnny Klippstein/DP	8.00	4.00	2.50
589	Dave Ricketts/DP	8.00	4.00	2.50
590	Pete Richert	12.00	6.00	3.50
591	Ty Cline	12.00	6.00	3.50
592	N.L. Rookies (*Jim Shellenback, Ron Willis*)	12.00	6.00	3.50
593	Wes Westrum	12.00	6.00	3.50
594	Dan Osinski	12.00	6.00	3.50
595	Cookie Rojas	12.00	6.00	3.50
596	Galen Cisco (DP)	8.00	4.00	2.50
597	Ted Abernathy	12.00	6.00	3.50
598	White Sox Rookies (*Ed Stroud, Walt Williams*)	12.00	6.00	3.50
599	Bob Duliba (DP)	8.00	4.00	2.50
600	Brooks Robinson/SP	155.00	75.00	45.00
601	Bill Bryan (DP)	8.00	4.00	2.50
602	Juan Pizarro	12.00	6.00	3.50
603	Athletics Rookies (*Tim Talton, Ramon Webster*)	12.00	6.00	3.50
604	Red Sox Team	85.00	42.50	25.00
605	Mike Shannon	45.00	22.50	13.50
606	Ron Taylor	12.00	6.00	3.50
607	Mickey Stanley	25.00	12.50	7.50
608	Cubs Rookies (*Rich Nye, John Upham*)/DP	8.00	4.00	2.50
609	Tommy John	60.00	20.00	12.00

1967 Topps Discs

Similar to the more common 28-piece set of 1968, this set of all-stars is known only in proof form, evidently intended to be pressed onto a pin-back button issue which never materialized. Printed on blank-backed silver foil about 2-3/8" square, the pieces have a 2-1/4" diameter center with color player portrait with name and position printed in black across the chest. Some pieces have a team name to the left and right of the player's picture. "JAPAN" is printed in tiny black letters at top-left, apparently intended to be folded under the rim of the button. The unnumbered discs are checklisted here alphabetically.

		NM	EX	VG
Complete Set (24):		12,500	6,250	3,750
Common Player:		185.00	90.00	55.00
(1)	Hank Aaron	1,400	700.00	420.00
(2)	Johnny Callison	185.00	90.00	55.00
(3)	Bert Campaneris	185.00	90.00	55.00
(4)	Leo Cardenas	185.00	90.00	55.00
(5)	Orlando Cepeda	600.00	300.00	180.00
(6)	Roberto Clemente	1,850	925.00	555.00
(7)	Frank Howard	210.00	105.00	63.00
(8)	Cleon Jones	185.00	90.00	55.00
(9)	Bobby Knoop	185.00	90.00	55.00
(10)	Sandy Koufax	1,150	575.00	345.00
(11)	Mickey Mantle	2,800	1,400	840.00
(12)	Juan Marichal	600.00	300.00	180.00
(13)	Willie Mays	1,400	700.00	420.00
(14)	Sam McDowell	185.00	90.00	55.00
(15)	Denny McLain	210.00	105.00	63.00
(16)	Joe Morgan	600.00	300.00	180.00
(17)	Tony Oliva	185.00	90.00	55.00
(18)	Boog Powell	225.00	110.00	67.00
(19)	Brooks Robinson	750.00	375.00	225.00
(20)	Frank Robinson	750.00	375.00	225.00
(21)	Johnny Romano	185.00	90.00	55.00
(22)	Ron Santo	210.00	105.00	63.00
(23)	Joe Torre	450.00	225.00	135.00
(24)	Carl Yastrzemski	750.00	375.00	225.00

1967 Topps S.F. Giants Discs

One of several prototypes for pinback button sets which were never issued. Generally found in the form of a silver-foil cardboard square, about 2-3/8" a side, the 2-1/4" round center features color player photos or team booster slogans. The player's name and position are printed across his chest, the team name at top. At top-left is a tiny black "JAPAN." The unnumbered discs are checklisted here alphabetically.

		NM	EX	VG
Complete Set (24):		8,000	4,000	2,400
Common Player:		185.00	92.00	55.00
(1)	Jesus Alou	185.00	92.00	55.00
(2)	Bob Bolin	185.00	92.00	55.00
(3)	Ollie Brown	185.00	92.00	55.00
(4)	Jim Davenport	185.00	92.00	55.00
(5)	Herman Franks	185.00	92.00	55.00
(6)	Len Gabrielson	185.00	92.00	55.00
(7)	Joe Gibbon	185.00	92.00	55.00
(8)	Tom Haller	185.00	92.00	55.00
(9)	Jim Ray Hart	185.00	92.00	55.00
(10)	Ron Herbel	185.00	92.00	55.00
(11)	Hal Lanier	185.00	92.00	55.00
(12)	Frank Linzy	185.00	92.00	55.00
(13)	Juan Marichal	925.00	460.00	275.00
(14)	Willie Mays	1,625	810.00	485.00
(15)	Willie McCovey	925.00	460.00	275.00
(16)	Lindy McDaniel	185.00	92.00	55.00
(17)	Gaylord Perry	825.00	410.00	245.00
(18)	Cap Peterson	185.00	92.00	55.00
(19)	Bob Priddy	185.00	92.00	55.00
(20)	Happiness is a Giant Win	115.00	57.00	34.00
(21)	I Love the Giants	115.00	57.00	34.00
(22)	Let's Go Giants	115.00	57.00	34.00
(23)	Willie Mays for Mayor (Willie Mays)	700.00	350.00	210.00
(24)	S.F. Giants Logo	115.00	57.00	34.00

1967 Topps Pin-Ups

The 5" x 7" "All Star Pin-ups" were wax pack inserts. They feature a full color picture with the player's name, position and team in a circle in one of the lower corners on the front. The numbered set consists of 32 players (generally big names). Because the large paper pin-ups had to be folded several times to fit into the wax packs, the factory-created folds are not considered when grading unless paper separations have developed along the seams. At least one of the pin-ups (Clemente) has been seen in an unnumbered version printed on better-quality sticker stock and not having fold lines.

	NM	EX	VG
Complete Set (32):	150.00	65.00	35.00
Common Player:	2.00	.70	.30
1 Boog Powell	2.50	.90	.40
2 Bert Campaneris	2.00	.70	.30
3 Brooks Robinson	9.00	3.25	1.25
4 Tommie Agee	2.00	.70	.30
5 Carl Yastrzemski	9.00	3.25	1.25
6 Mickey Mantle	40.00	14.00	6.00
7 Frank Howard	2.50	.90	.40
8 Sam McDowell	2.00	.70	.30
9 Orlando Cepeda	6.00	2.00	.90
10 Chico Cardenas	2.00	.70	.30
11 Roberto Clemente	20.00	7.00	3.00
12 Willie Mays	15.00	5.25	2.25
13 Cleon Jones	2.00	.70	.30
14 John Callison	2.00	.70	.30
15 Hank Aaron	15.00	5.25	2.25
16 Don Drysdale	7.50	2.75	1.25
17 Bobby Knoop	2.00	.70	.30
18 Tony Oliva	2.50	.90	.40
19 Frank Robinson	9.00	3.25	1.25
20 Denny McLain	2.50	.90	.40
21 Al Kaline	9.00	3.25	1.25
22 Joe Pepitone	3.00	1.00	.45
23 Harmon Killebrew	7.50	2.75	1.25
24 Leon Wagner	2.00	.70	.30
25 Joe Morgan	7.50	2.75	1.25
26 Ron Santo	3.00	1.00	.45
27 Joe Torre	4.50	1.50	.70
28 Juan Marichal	6.00	2.00	.90
29 Matty Alou	2.00	.70	.30
30 Felipe Alou	2.00	.70	.30
31 Ron Hunt	2.00	.70	.30
32 Willie McCovey	7.50	2.75	1.25

1967 Topps Punch-Outs

This test issue was reportedly released around Maryland in cello packs containing two perforated strips of three game cards each. Cards are printed in black, white and red and measure 2-1/2" x 4-2/3". Backs have instructions on how to play a baseball game by punching out the small squares. Only the "Team Captain" is pictured on the card; each captain can be found with at least two different line-ups on his team, creating a large number of collectible variations. Variations in some player photos have also been noted. The unnumbered issue is checklisted here in alphabetical order.

		NM	EX	VG
Complete Set (91):		19,000	9,500	5,750
Common Player:		80.00	40.00	24.00
(1)	Hank Aaron	1,500	750.00	450.00
(2)	Richie Allen	150.00	75.00	45.00
(3)	Gene Alley	80.00	40.00	24.00
(4)	Felipe Alou	90.00	45.00	27.00
(5)	Matty Alou	80.00	40.00	24.00
(6)	Max Alvis	80.00	40.00	24.00
(7)	Luis Aparicio	200.00	100.00	60.00
(8)	Steve Barber	80.00	40.00	24.00
(9)	Earl Battey	80.00	40.00	24.00
(10)	Clete Boyer	80.00	40.00	24.00
(11)	Ken Boyer	100.00	50.00	30.00
(12)	Lou Brock	200.00	100.00	60.00
(13)	Jim Bunning	175.00	87.00	52.00
(14)	Johnny Callison	80.00	40.00	24.00
(15)	Bert Campaneris	80.00	40.00	24.00
(16)	Leo Cardenas	80.00	40.00	24.00
(17)	Rico Carty	80.00	40.00	24.00
(18)	Norm Cash	90.00	45.00	27.00
(19)	Orlando Cepeda	175.00	87.00	52.00
(20)	Ed Charles	80.00	40.00	24.00
(21a)	Roberto Clemente (Plain background photo.)	1,500	750.00	450.00
(21b)	Roberto Clemente (Stadium background photo.)	2,000	1,000	600.00
(22)	Donn Clendenon	80.00	40.00	24.00
(23)	Rocky Colavito	150.00	75.00	45.00
(24)	Tony Conigliaro	90.00	45.00	27.00
(25)	Willie Davis	80.00	40.00	24.00
(26)	Johnny Edwards	80.00	40.00	24.00
(27)	Andy Etchebarren	80.00	40.00	24.00
(28)	Curt Flood	80.00	40.00	24.00
(29)	Bill Freehan	80.00	40.00	24.00
(30)	Jim Fregosi	80.00	40.00	24.00
(31)	Bob Gibson	300.00	150.00	90.00
(32)	Dick Green	80.00	40.00	24.00
(33)	Dick Groat	80.00	40.00	24.00

		NM	EX	VG
(34)	Jerry Grote	80.00	40.00	24.00
(35)	Tom Haller	80.00	40.00	24.00
(36)	Jim Ray Hart	80.00	40.00	24.00
(37)	Mike Hershberger	80.00	40.00	24.00
(38)	Elston Howard	100.00	50.00	30.00
(39)	Frank Howard	90.00	45.00	27.00
(40)	Ron Hunt	80.00	40.00	24.00
(41)	Sonny Jackson	80.00	40.00	24.00
(42)	Cleon Jones	80.00	40.00	24.00
(43)	Jim Kaat	100.00	50.00	30.00
(44)	Al Kaline	400.00	200.00	120.00
(45)	Harmon Killebrew	300.00	150.00	90.00
(46)	Bobby Knoop	80.00	40.00	24.00
(47)	Sandy Koufax	1,500	750.00	450.00
(48)	Ed Kranepool	80.00	40.00	24.00
(49)	Jim Lefebvre	80.00	40.00	24.00
(50)	Don Lock	80.00	40.00	24.00
(51)	Jerry Lumpe	80.00	40.00	24.00
(52)	Mickey Mantle	2,400	1,200	720.00
(53)	Juan Marichal	175.00	87.00	52.00
(54)	Willie Mays	1,500	750.00	450.00
(55)	Bill Mazeroski	175.00	87.00	52.00
(56)	Dick McAuliffe	80.00	40.00	24.00
(57)	Tim McCarver	90.00	45.00	27.00
(58)	Willie McCovey	200.00	100.00	60.00
(59)	Denny McLain	90.00	45.00	27.00
(60)	Roy McMillan	80.00	40.00	24.00
(61)	Denis Menke	80.00	40.00	24.00
(62)	Joe Morgan	200.00	100.00	60.00
(63)	Tony Oliva	90.00	45.00	27.00
(64)	Joe Pepitone	100.00	50.00	30.00
(65)	Gaylord Perry	175.00	87.00	52.00
(66)	Vada Pinson	90.00	45.00	27.00
(67)	Boog Powell	100.00	50.00	30.00
(68)	Rick Reichardt	80.00	40.00	24.00
(69)	Brooks Robinson	400.00	200.00	120.00
(70)	Floyd Robinson	80.00	40.00	24.00
(71)	Frank Robinson	400.00	200.00	120.00
(72)	Johnny Romano	80.00	40.00	24.00
(73)	Pete Rose	1,250	625.00	375.00
(74)	John Roseboro	80.00	40.00	24.00
(75)	Ron Santo	100.00	50.00	30.00
(76)	Chico Salmon	80.00	40.00	24.00
(77)	George Scott	80.00	40.00	24.00
(78)	Sonny Siebert	80.00	40.00	24.00
(79)	Russ Snyder	80.00	40.00	24.00
(80)	Willie Stargell	200.00	100.00	60.00
(81)	Mel Stottlemyre	80.00	40.00	24.00
(82)	Joe Torre	120.00	60.00	36.00
(83)	Cesar Tovar	80.00	40.00	24.00
(84)	Tom Tresh	90.00	45.00	27.00
(85)	Zoilo Versalles	80.00	40.00	24.00
(86)	Leon Wagner	80.00	40.00	24.00
(87)	Bill White	80.00	40.00	24.00
(88)	Fred Whitfield	80.00	40.00	24.00
(89)	Billy Williams	175.00	87.00	52.00
(90)	Jimmy Wynn	80.00	40.00	24.00
(91)	Carl Yastrzemski	450.00	225.00	135.00

1967 Topps Stand-Ups

Never actually issued, no more than a handful of each of these rare test issues have made their way into the hobby market. Designed so that the color photo of the player's head could be popped out of the black background and placed into a punch-out base to create a stand-up display, examples of these 3-1/8" x 5-1/4" cards can be found either on thick stock, die-cut around the portrait and with a die-cut stand, or as thin-stock proofs without the die-cutting. Blank-backed, there are 24 cards in the set, numbered on the front at bottom left.

		NM	EX	VG
Complete Set, Thick (24):		75,000	37,500	22,500
Complete Set, Thin (24):		60,000	30,000	18,000
Common Player, Thick:		1,250	625.00	375.00
Common Player, Thin:		1,000	500.00	300.00
THICK STOCK, DIE-CUT				
1	Pete Rose	4,750	2,375	1,425
2	Gary Peters	1,250	625.00	375.00
3	Frank Robinson	2,400	1,200	720.00
4	Jim Lonborg	1,250	625.00	375.00
5	Ron Swoboda	1,250	625.00	375.00
6	Harmon Killebrew	2,100	1,050	630.00
7	Roberto Clemente	8,500	4,250	2,550
8	Mickey Mantle	12,500	6,250	3,750
9	Jim Fregosi	1,250	625.00	375.00
10	Al Kaline	3,000	1,500	900.00
11	Don Drysdale	2,500	1,250	750.00

12	Dean Chance	1,250	625.00	375.00
13	Orlando Cepeda	1,750	875.00	525.00
14	Tim McCarver	1,400	700.00	420.00
15	Frank Howard	1,250	625.00	375.00
16	Max Alvis	1,250	625.00	375.00
17	Rusty Staub	1,400	700.00	420.00
18	Richie Allen	1,400	700.00	420.00
19	Willie Mays	8,500	4,250	2,550
20	Hank Aaron	8,500	4,250	2,550
21	Carl Yastrzemski	7,000	3,500	2,100
22	Ron Santo	1,400	700.00	420.00
23	Catfish Hunter	1,750	875.00	525.00
24	Jim Wynn	1,250	625.00	375.00
THIN STOCK, PROOFS				
1	Pete Rose	3,750	1,875	1,125
2	Gary Peters	1,000	500.00	300.00
3	Frank Robinson	1,900	950.00	570.00
4	Jim Lonborg	1,000	500.00	300.00
5	Ron Swoboda	1,000	500.00	300.00
6	Harmon Killebrew	1,650	825.00	495.00
7	Roberto Clemente	6,500	3,250	1,950
8	Mickey Mantle	10,000	5,000	3,000
9	Jim Fregosi	1,000	500.00	300.00
10	Al Kaline	2,500	1,250	750.00
11	Don Drysdale	2,000	1,000	600.00
12	Dean Chance	1,000	500.00	300.00
13	Orlando Cepeda	1,400	700.00	420.00
14	Tim McCarver	1,100	550.00	330.00
15	Frank Howard	1,100	550.00	330.00
16	Max Alvis	1,000	500.00	300.00
17	Rusty Staub	1,100	550.00	330.00
18	Richie Allen	1,100	550.00	330.00
19	Willie Mays	7,000	3,500	2,100
20	Hank Aaron	7,000	3,500	2,100
21	Carl Yastrzemski	5,500	2,750	1,650
22	Ron Santo	1,100	550.00	330.00
23	Catfish Hunter	1,400	700.00	420.00
24	Jim Wynn	1,000	500.00	300.00

1967 Topps Pirates Stickers

Considered a "test" issue, this 33-sticker set of 2-1/2" x 3-1/2" stickers is very similar to the Red Sox stickers which were produced the same year. Player stickers have a color picture (often just the player's head) and the player's name in large "comic book" letters. Besides the players, there are other topics such as "I Love the Pirates," "Bob Clemente for Mayor," and a number of similar sentiments. The stickers have blank backs and are rather scarce.

		NM	EX	VG
Complete Set (33):		750.00	375.00	225.00
Common Player:		15.00	7.50	4.50
1	Gene Alley	15.00	7.50	4.50
2	Matty Alou	15.00	7.50	4.50
3	Dennis Ribant	15.00	7.50	4.50
4	Steve Blass	15.00	7.50	4.50
5	Juan Pizarro	15.00	7.50	4.50
6	Bob Clemente	175.00	85.00	50.00
7	Donn Clendenon	15.00	7.50	4.50
8	Roy Face	15.00	7.50	4.50
9	Woody Fryman	15.00	7.50	4.50
10	Jesse Gonder	15.00	7.50	4.50
11	Vern Law	15.00	7.50	4.50
12	Al McBean	15.00	7.50	4.50
13	Jerry May	15.00	7.50	4.50
14	Bill Mazeroski	35.00	17.50	10.00
15	Pete Mikkelsen	15.00	7.50	4.50
16	Manny Mota	15.00	7.50	4.50
17	Billy O'Dell	15.00	7.50	4.50
18	Jose Pagan	15.00	7.50	4.50
19	Jim Pagliaroni	15.00	7.50	4.50
20	Johnny Pesky	15.00	7.50	4.50
21	Tommie Sisk	15.00	7.50	4.50
22	Willie Stargell	60.00	30.00	18.00
23	Bob Veale	15.00	7.50	4.50
24	Harry Walker	15.00	7.50	4.50
25	I Love The Pirates	20.00	10.00	6.00
26	Let's Go Pirates	20.00	10.00	6.00
27	Bob Clemente For Mayor	100.00	50.00	30.00
28	National League Batting Champion (Matty Alou)	15.00	7.50	4.50
29	Happiness Is A Pirate Win	20.00	10.00	6.00
30	Donn Clendenon Is My Hero	15.00	7.50	4.50
31	Pirates' Home Run Champion (Willie Stargell)	30.00	15.00	9.00
32	Pirates Logo	20.00	10.00	6.00
33	Pirates Pennant	25.00	12.50	7.50

1967 Topps Red Sox Stickers

Like the 1967 Pirates Stickers, the Red Sox Stickers were part of the same test procedure. The Red Sox Stickers have the same 2-1/2" x 3-1/2" dimensions, color picture and large player's name on the front. A set is complete at 33 stickers. The majority are players, but themes such as "Let's Go Red Sox" are also included.

		NM	EX	VG
Complete Set (33):		500.00	250.00	150.00
Common Player:		10.00	5.00	3.00
1	Dennis Bennett	10.00	5.00	3.00
2	Darrell Brandon	10.00	5.00	3.00
3	Tony Conigliaro	35.00	17.50	10.00
4	Don Demeter	10.00	5.00	3.00
5	Hank Fischer	10.00	5.00	3.00
6	Joe Foy	10.00	5.00	3.00
7	Mike Andrews	10.00	5.00	3.00
8	Dalton Jones	10.00	5.00	3.00
9	Jim Lonborg	10.00	5.00	3.00
10	Don McMahon	10.00	5.00	3.00
11	Dave Morehead	10.00	5.00	3.00
12	George Smith	10.00	5.00	3.00
13	Rico Petrocelli	15.00	7.50	4.50
14	Mike Ryan	10.00	5.00	3.00
15	Jose Santiago	10.00	5.00	3.00
16	George Scott	10.00	5.00	3.00
17	Sal Maglie	10.00	5.00	3.00
18	Reggie Smith	10.00	5.00	3.00
19	Lee Stange	10.00	5.00	3.00
20	Jerry Stephenson	10.00	5.00	3.00
21	Jose Tartabull	10.00	5.00	3.00
22	George Thomas	10.00	5.00	3.00
23	Bob Tillman	10.00	5.00	3.00
24	Johnnie Wyatt	10.00	5.00	3.00
25	Carl Yastrzemski	90.00	45.00	27.50
26	Dick Williams	10.00	5.00	3.00
27	I Love The Red Sox	12.50	6.25	3.75
28	Let's Go Red Sox	12.50	6.25	3.75
29	Carl Yastrzemski For Mayor	50.00	25.00	15.00
30	Tony Conigliaro Is My Hero	27.50	13.50	8.25
31	Happiness Is A Boston Win	12.50	6.25	3.75
32	Red Sox Logo	15.00	7.50	4.50
33	Red Sox Pennant	20.00	10.00	6.00

1967 Topps Who Am I?

A cartoon caption and goofy facial features were printed on the front of these 2-1/2" x 3-1/2" cards and were designed to be scratched off to reveal the portrait, name and claim to fame of the person beneath. This 44-card set includes all manner of U.S. and international historical figures, including four baseball players. Backs are printed in red and have a large question mark with several hints printed thereon. Unscratched cards are much rarer than scratched cards, though they carry only about a 50 percent premium.

		NM	EX	VG
Complete Set (44):		850.00	425.00	250.00
Wax Pack:		350.00		
12	Babe Ruth	100.00	50.00	30.00
22	Mickey Mantle	225.00	110.00	65.00
33	Willie Mays	100.00	50.00	30.00
41	Sandy Koufax	100.00	50.00	30.00

1968 Topps

In 1968, Topps returned to a 598-card set of 2-1/2" x 3-1/2" cards. It is not, however, more of the same by way of appearance as the cards feature a

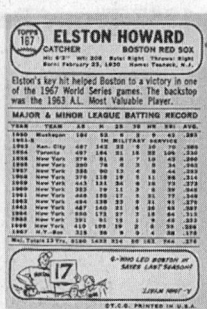

color photograph on a background of what appears to be a burlap fabric. The player's name is below the photo but on the unusual background. A colored circle on the lower right carries the team and position. Backs were also changed, while retaining the vertical format introduced the previous year, with stats in the middle and cartoon at the bottom. The set features many of the old favorite subsets, including statistical leaders, World Series highlights, multi-player cards, checklists, rookie cards and the return of All-Star cards. Most checklist cards are double-printed, once in the series preceding the series it lists and once within the series it lists; subtle variations between the pairs are listed where known.

		NM	EX	VG
	Complete Set (598):	3,000	1,500	900.00
	Common Player (1-457):	2.00	1.00	.60
	Common Player (458-598):	5.00	2.50	1.50
1	N.L. Batting Leaders (Matty Alou, Roberto Clemente, Tony Gonzalez)	12.50	6.25	3.75
2	A.L. Batting Leaders (Al Kaline, Frank Robinson, Carl Yastrzemski)	20.00	10.00	6.00
3	N.L. RBI Leaders (Hank Aaron, Orlando Cepeda, Roberto Clemente)	22.50	11.00	6.75
4	A.L. RBI Leaders (Harmon Killebrew, Frank Robinson, Carl Yastrzemski)	12.00	6.00	3.50
5	N.L. Home Run Leaders (Hank Aaron, Willie McCovey, Ron Santo, Jim Wynn)	20.00	10.00	6.00
6	A.L. Home Run Leaders (Frank Howard, Harmon Killebrew, Carl Yastrzemski)	12.00	6.00	3.50
7	N.L. ERA Leaders (Jim Bunning, Phil Niekro, Chris Short)	7.00	3.50	2.00
8	A.L. ERA Leaders (Joe Horlen, Gary Peters, Sonny Siebert)	2.00	1.00	.60
9	N.L. Pitching Leaders (Jim Bunning, Fergie Jenkins, Mike McCormick, Claude Osteen)	7.00	3.50	2.00
10a	A.L. Pitching Leaders (Dean Chance, Jim Lonborg, Earl Wilson) ("Lonberg" on back)	9.00	4.50	2.75
10b	A.L. Pitching Leaders (Dean Chance, Jim Lonborg, Earl Wilson) ("Lonberg" on back)	7.00	3.50	2.00
11	N.L. Strikeout Leaders (Jim Bunning, Fergie Jenkins, Gaylord Perry)	7.00	3.50	2.00
12	A.L. Strikeout Leaders (Dean Chance, Jim Lonborg, Sam McDowell)	7.00	3.50	2.00
13	Chuck Hartenstein	2.00	1.00	.60
14	Jerry McNertney	2.00	1.00	.60
15	Ron Hunt	2.00	1.00	.60
16	Indians Rookies (*Lou Piniella, Richie Scheinblum*)	5.00	2.50	1.50
17	Dick Hall	2.00	1.00	.60
18	Mike Hershberger	2.00	1.00	.60
19	Juan Pizarro	2.00	1.00	.60
20	Brooks Robinson	15.00	7.50	4.50
21	Ron Davis	2.00	1.00	.60
22	Pat Dobson	2.00	1.00	.60
23	Chico Cardenas	2.00	1.00	.60
24	Bobby Locke	2.00	1.00	.60
25	Julian Javier	2.00	1.00	.60
26	Darrell Brandon	2.00	1.00	.60
27	Gil Hodges	7.50	3.75	2.25
28	Ted Uhlaender	2.00	1.00	.60
29	Joe Verbanic	2.00	1.00	.60
30	Joe Torre	8.00	4.00	2.50
31	Ed Stroud	2.00	1.00	.60
32	Joe Gibbon	2.00	1.00	.60
33	Pete Ward	2.00	1.00	.60
34	Al Ferrara	2.00	1.00	.60
35	Steve Hargan	2.00	1.00	.60
36	Pirates Rookies (*Bob Moose, Bob Robertson*)	2.00	1.00	.60
37	Billy Williams	13.50	6.75	4.00
38	Tony Pierce	2.00	1.00	.60
39	Cookie Rojas	2.00	1.00	.60
40	Denny McLain	6.00	3.00	1.75
41	Julio Gotay	2.00	1.00	.60
42	Larry Haney	2.00	1.00	.60
43	Gary Bell	2.00	1.00	.60
44	Frank Kostro	2.00	1.00	.60
45	Tom Seaver	30.00	15.00	9.00

46	Dave Ricketts	2.00	1.00	.60
47	Ralph Houk	2.50	1.25	.70
48	Ted Davidson	2.00	1.00	.60
49a	Ed Brinkman (Yellow team.)	120.00	60.00	36.00
49b	Ed Brinkman (White team.)	2.00	1.00	.60
50	Willie Mays	50.00	25.00	15.00
51	Bob Locker	2.00	1.00	.60
52	Hawk Taylor	2.00	1.00	.60
53	Gene Alley	2.00	1.00	.60
54	Stan Williams	2.00	1.00	.60
55	Felipe Alou	5.00	2.50	1.50
56	Orioles Rookies (*Dave Leonhard, Dave May*)	2.00	1.00	.60
57	Dan Schneider	2.00	1.00	.60
58	Ed Mathews	13.50	6.75	4.00
59	Don Lock	2.00	1.00	.60
60	Ken Holtzman	2.00	1.00	.60
61	Reggie Smith	2.00	1.00	.60
62	Chuck Dobson	2.00	1.00	.60
63	Dick Kenworthy	2.00	1.00	.60
64	Jim Merritt	2.00	1.00	.60
65	John Roseboro	2.00	1.00	.60
66a	Casey Cox (Yellow team.)	120.00	60.00	36.00
66b	Casey Cox (White team.)	2.00	1.00	.60
67	1st Series Check List (1-109) (Jim Kaat)	5.00	2.50	1.50
68	Ron Willis	2.00	1.00	.60
69	Tom Tresh	6.00	3.00	1.75
70	Bob Veale	2.00	1.00	.60
71	Vern Fuller	2.00	1.00	.60
72	Tommy John	5.00	2.50	1.50
73	Jim Hart	2.00	1.00	.60
74	Milt Pappas	2.00	1.00	.60
75	Don Mincher	2.00	1.00	.60
76	Braves Rookies (*Jim Britton, Ron Reed*)	2.00	1.00	.60
77	*Don Wilson*	2.00	1.00	.60
78	Jim Northrup	2.00	1.00	.60
79	Ted Kubiak	2.00	1.00	.60
80	Rod Carew	17.50	8.75	5.25
81	Larry Jackson	2.00	1.00	.60
82	Sam Bowens	2.00	1.00	.60
83	John Stephenson	2.00	1.00	.60
84	Bob Tolan	2.00	1.00	.60
85	Gaylord Perry	9.00	4.50	2.75
86	Willie Stargell	12.00	6.00	3.50
87	Dick Williams	2.00	1.00	.60
88	Phil Regan	2.00	1.00	.60
89	Jake Gibbs	2.00	1.00	.60
90	Vada Pinson	5.00	2.50	1.50
91	Jim Ollom	2.00	1.00	.60
92	Ed Kranepool	2.00	1.00	.60
93	Tony Cloninger	2.00	1.00	.60
94	Lee Maye	2.00	1.00	.60
95	Bob Aspromonte	2.00	1.00	.60
96	Senators Rookies (*Frank Coggins, Dick Nold*)	2.00	1.00	.60
97	Tom Phoebus	2.00	1.00	.60
98	Gary Sutherland	2.00	1.00	.60
99	Rocky Colavito	7.00	3.50	2.00
100	Bob Gibson	17.50	8.75	5.25
101	Glenn Beckert	2.00	1.00	.60
102	Jose Cardenal	2.00	1.00	.60
103	Don Sutton	9.00	4.50	2.75
104	Dick Dietz	2.00	1.00	.60
105	Al Downing	2.00	1.00	.60
106	Dalton Jones	2.00	1.00	.60
107	2nd Series Check List (110-196) (Juan Marichal)	5.00	2.50	1.50
108	Don Pavletich	2.00	1.00	.60
109	Bert Campaneris	2.00	1.00	.60
110	Hank Aaron	45.00	22.50	13.50
111	Rich Reese	2.00	1.00	.60
112	Woody Fryman	2.00	1.00	.60
113	Tigers Rookies (*Tom Matchick, Daryl Patterson*)	2.00	1.00	.60
114	Ron Swoboda	2.00	1.00	.60
115	Sam McDowell	2.00	1.00	.60
116	Ken McMullen	2.00	1.00	.60
117	Larry Jaster	2.00	1.00	.60
118	Mark Belanger	2.00	1.00	.60
119	Ted Savage	2.00	1.00	.60
120	Mel Stottlemyre	5.00	2.50	1.50
121	Jimmie Hall	2.00	1.00	.60
122	Gene Mauch	2.00	1.00	.60
123	Jose Santiago	2.00	1.00	.60
124	Nate Oliver	2.00	1.00	.60
125	Joe Horlen	2.00	1.00	.60
126	Bobby Etheridge	2.00	1.00	.60
127	Paul Lindblad	2.00	1.00	.60
128	Astros Rookies (*Tom Dukes, Alonzo Harris*)	2.00	1.00	.60
129	Mickey Stanley	2.00	1.00	.60
130	Tony Perez	10.00	5.00	3.00
131	Frank Bertaina	2.00	1.00	.60
132	Bud Harrelson	2.00	1.00	.60
133	Fred Whitfield	2.00	1.00	.60
134	Pat Jarvis	2.00	1.00	.60
135	Paul Blair	2.00	1.00	.60
136	Randy Hundley	2.00	1.00	.60
137	Twins Team	5.00	2.50	1.50
138	Ruben Amaro	2.00	1.00	.60
139	Chris Short	2.00	1.00	.60
140	Tony Conigliaro	5.00	2.50	1.50
141	Dal Maxvill	2.00	1.00	.60
142	White Sox Rookies (*Buddy Bradford, Bill Voss*)	2.00	1.00	.60
143	Pete Cimino	2.00	1.00	.60
144	Joe Morgan	12.00	6.00	3.50
145	Don Drysdale	15.00	7.50	4.50
146	Sal Bando	2.00	1.00	.60
147	Frank Linzy	2.00	1.00	.60
148	Dave Bristol	2.00	1.00	.60
149	Bob Saverine	2.00	1.00	.60
150	Roberto Clemente	50.00	25.00	15.00
151	World Series Game 1 (Brock Socks 4 Hits in Opener)	6.00	3.00	1.75

152	World Series Game 2 (Yaz Smashes Two Homers)	10.00	5.00	3.00
153	World Series Game 3 (Briles Cools Off Boston)	3.00	1.50	.90
154	World Series Game 4 (Gibson Hurls Shutout)	9.00	4.50	2.75
155	World Series Game 5 (Lonborg Wins Again)	6.00	3.00	1.75
156	World Series Game 6 (Petrocelli Socks Two Homers)	6.00	3.00	1.75
157	World Series Game 7 (St. Louis Wins It)	6.00	3.00	1.75
158	1967 World Series (The Cardinals Celebrate)	5.00	2.50	1.50
159	Don Kessinger	2.00	1.00	.60
160	Earl Wilson	2.00	1.00	.60
161	Norm Miller	2.00	1.00	.60
162	Cards Rookies (*Hal Gilson, Mike Torrez*)	2.00	1.00	.60
163	Gene Brabender	2.00	1.00	.60
164	Ramon Webster	2.00	1.00	.60
165	Tony Oliva	5.00	2.50	1.50
166	Claude Raymond	2.00	1.00	.60
167	Elston Howard	5.00	2.50	1.50
168	Dodgers Team	5.00	2.50	1.50
169	Bob Bolin	2.00	1.00	.60
170	Jim Fregosi	2.00	1.00	.60
171	Don Nottebart	2.00	1.00	.60
172	Walt Williams	2.00	1.00	.60
173	John Boozer	2.00	1.00	.60
174	Bob Tillman	2.00	1.00	.60
175	Maury Wills	2.00	1.00	.60
176	Bob Allen	2.00	1.00	.60
177	Mets Rookies (*Jerry Koosman, Nolan Ryan*)	375.00	175.00	85.00
178	Don Wert	2.00	1.00	.60
179	Bill Stoneman	2.00	1.00	.60
180	Curt Flood	3.00	1.50	.90
181	Jerry Zimmerman	2.00	1.00	.60
182	Dave Giusti	2.00	1.00	.60
183	Bob Kennedy	2.00	1.00	.60
184	Lou Johnson	2.00	1.00	.60
185	Tom Haller	2.00	1.00	.60
186	Eddie Watt	2.00	1.00	.60
187	Sonny Jackson	2.00	1.00	.60
188	Cap Peterson	2.00	1.00	.60
189	Bill Landis	2.00	1.00	.60
190	Bill White	2.00	1.00	.60
191	Dan Frisella	2.00	1.00	.60
192a	3rd Series Check List (197-283) (Carl Yastrzemski) ("To increase the..." on back.)	6.00	3.00	1.75
192b	3rd Series Check List (197-283) (Carl Yastrzemski) ("To increase your..." on back.)	6.00	3.00	1.75
193	Jack Hamilton	2.00	1.00	.60
194	Don Buford	2.00	1.00	.60
195	Joe Pepitone	5.00	2.50	1.50
196	Gary Nolan	2.00	1.00	.60
197	Larry Brown	2.00	1.00	.60
198	Roy Face	2.00	1.00	.60
199	A's Rookies (*Darrell Osteen, Roberto Rodriguez*)	2.00	1.00	.60
200	Orlando Cepeda	11.00	5.50	3.25
201	*Mike Marshall*	3.00	1.50	.90
202	Adolfo Phillips	2.00	1.00	.60
203	Dick Kelley	2.00	1.00	.60
204	Andy Etchebarren	2.00	1.00	.60
205	Juan Marichal	9.00	4.50	2.75
206	Cal Ermer	2.00	1.00	.60
207	Carroll Sembera	2.00	1.00	.60
208	Willie Davis	2.00	1.00	.60
209	Tim Cullen	2.00	1.00	.60
210	Gary Peters	2.00	1.00	.60
211	J.C. Martin	2.00	1.00	.60
212	Dave Morehead	2.00	1.00	.60
213	Chico Ruiz	2.00	1.00	.60
214	Yankees Rookies (*Stan Bahnsen, Frank Fernandez*)	2.00	1.00	.60
215	Jim Bunning	9.00	4.50	2.75
216	Bubba Morton	2.00	1.00	.60
217	Turk Farrell	2.00	1.00	.60
218	Ken Suarez	2.00	1.00	.60
219	Rob Gardner	2.00	1.00	.60
220	Harmon Killebrew	17.50	8.75	5.25
221	Braves Team	5.00	2.50	1.50
222	Jim Hardin	2.00	1.00	.60
223	Ollie Brown	2.00	1.00	.60
224	Jack Aker	2.00	1.00	.60
225	Richie Allen	6.00	3.00	1.75
226	Jimmie Price	2.00	1.00	.60
227	Joe Hoerner	2.00	1.00	.60
228	Dodgers Rookies (*Jack Billingham, Jim Fairey*)	2.00	1.00	.60
229	Fred Klages	2.00	1.00	.60
230	Pete Rose	45.00	22.50	13.50
231	Dave Baldwin	2.00	1.00	.60
232	Denis Menke	2.00	1.00	.60
233	George Scott	2.00	1.00	.60
234	Bill Monbouquette	2.00	1.00	.60
235	Ron Santo	6.00	3.00	1.75
236	Tug McGraw	2.00	1.00	.60
237	Alvin Dark	2.00	1.00	.60
238	Tom Satriano	2.00	1.00	.60
239	Bill Henry	2.00	1.00	.60
240	Al Kaline	20.00	10.00	6.00
241	Felix Millan	2.00	1.00	.60
242	Moe Drabowsky	2.00	1.00	.60
243	Rich Rollins	2.00	1.00	.60
244	John Donaldson	2.00	1.00	.60
245	Tony Gonzalez	2.00	1.00	.60
246	Fritz Peterson	2.00	1.00	.60
247	Reds Rookies (*Johnny Bench, Ron Tompkins*)	85.00	40.00	25.00
248	Fred Valentine	2.00	1.00	.60
249	Bill Singer	2.00	1.00	.60
250	Carl Yastrzemski	20.00	10.00	6.00

No.	Name			
251	*Manny Sanguillen*	4.50	2.25	1.25
252	Angels Team	5.00	2.50	1.50
253	Dick Hughes	2.00	1.00	.60
254	Cleon Jones	2.00	1.00	.60
255	Dean Chance	2.00	1.00	.60
256	Norm Cash	7.00	3.50	2.00
257	Phil Niekro	9.00	4.50	2.75
258	Cubs Rookies (*Jose Arcia, Bill Schlesinger*)	2.00	1.00	.60
259	Ken Boyer	5.00	2.50	1.50
260	Jim Wynn	2.00	1.00	.60
261	Dave Duncan	2.00	1.00	.60
262	Rick Wise	2.00	1.00	.60
263	Horace Clarke	2.00	1.00	.60
264	Ted Abernathy	2.00	1.00	.60
265	Tommy Davis	2.00	1.00	.60
266	Paul Popovich	2.00	1.00	.60
267	Herman Franks	2.00	1.00	.60
268	Bob Humphreys	2.00	1.00	.60
269	Bob Tiefenauer	2.00	1.00	.60
270	Matty Alou	2.00	1.00	.60
271	Bobby Knoop	2.00	1.00	.60
272	Ray Culp	2.00	1.00	.60
273	Dave Johnson	2.00	1.00	.60
274	Mike Cuellar	2.00	1.00	.60
275	Tim McCarver	5.00	2.50	1.50
276	Jim Roland	2.00	1.00	.60
277	Jerry Buchek	2.00	1.00	.60
278a	4th Series Check List (284-370) (Orlando Cepeda) (Copyright at right.)	5.00	2.50	1.50
278b	4th Series Check List (284-370) (Orlando Cepeda) (Copyright at left.)	5.50	2.75	1.75
279	Bill Hands	2.00	1.00	.60
280	Mickey Mantle	155.00	75.00	45.00
281	Jim Campanis	2.00	1.00	.60
282	Rick Monday	2.00	1.00	.60
283	Mel Queen	2.00	1.00	.60
284	John Briggs	2.00	1.00	.60
285	Dick McAuliffe	2.00	1.00	.60
286	Cecil Upshaw	2.00	1.00	.60
287	White Sox Rookies (*Mickey Abarbanel, Cisco Carlos*)	2.00	1.00	.60
288	Dave Wickersham	2.00	1.00	.60
289	Woody Held	2.00	1.00	.60
290	Willie McCovey	17.50	8.75	5.25
291	Dick Lines	2.00	1.00	.60
292	Art Shamsky	2.00	1.00	.60
293	Bruce Howard	2.00	1.00	.60
294	Red Schoendienst	7.00	3.50	2.00
295	Sonny Siebert	2.00	1.00	.60
296	Byron Browne	2.00	1.00	.60
297	Russ Gibson	2.00	1.00	.60
298	Jim Brewer	2.00	1.00	.60
299	Gene Michael	2.00	1.00	.60
300	Rusty Staub	2.50	1.25	.70
301	Twins Rookies (*George Mitterwald, Rick Renick*)	2.00	1.00	.60
302	Gerry Arrigo	2.00	1.00	.60
303	Dick Green	2.00	1.00	.60
304	Sandy Valdespino	2.00	1.00	.60
305	Minnie Rojas	2.00	1.00	.60
306	Mike Ryan	2.00	1.00	.60
307	John Hiller	2.00	1.00	.60
308	Pirates Team	6.00	3.00	1.75
309	Ken Henderson	2.00	1.00	.60
310	Luis Aparicio	11.00	5.50	3.25
311	Jack Lamabe	2.00	1.00	.60
312	Curt Blefary	2.00	1.00	.60
313	Al Weis	2.00	1.00	.60
314	Red Sox Rookies (*Bill Rohr, George Spriggs*)	2.00	1.00	.60
315	Zoilo Versalles	2.00	1.00	.60
316	Steve Barber	2.00	1.00	.60
317	Ron Brand	2.00	1.00	.60
318	Chico Salmon	2.00	1.00	.60
319	George Culver	2.00	1.00	.60
320	Frank Howard	2.50	1.25	.70
321	Leo Durocher	6.00	3.00	1.75
322	Dave Boswell	2.00	1.00	.60
323	Deron Johnson	2.00	1.00	.60
324	Jim Nash	2.00	1.00	.60
325	Manny Mota	2.00	1.00	.60
326	Dennis Ribant	2.00	1.00	.60
327	Tony Taylor	2.00	1.00	.60
328	Angels Rookies (*Chuck Vinson, Jim Weaver*)	2.00	1.00	.60
329	Duane Josephson	2.00	1.00	.60
330	Roger Maris	30.00	15.00	9.00
331	Dan Osinski	2.00	1.00	.60
332	Doug Rader	2.00	1.00	.60
333	Ron Herbel	2.00	1.00	.60
334	Orioles Team	5.00	2.50	1.50
335	Bob Allison	2.00	1.00	.60
336	John Purdin	2.00	1.00	.60
337	Bill Robinson	2.00	1.00	.60
338	Bob Johnson	2.00	1.00	.60
339	Rich Nye	2.00	1.00	.60
340	Max Alvis	2.00	1.00	.60
341	Jim Lemon	2.00	1.00	.60
342	Ken Johnson	2.00	1.00	.60
343	Jim Gosger	2.00	1.00	.60
344	Donn Clendenon	2.00	1.00	.60
345	Bob Hendley	2.00	1.00	.60
346	Jerry Adair	2.00	1.00	.60
347	George Brunet	2.00	1.00	.60
348	Phillies Rookies (*Larry Colton, Dick Thoenen*)	2.00	1.00	.60
349	Ed Spiezio	2.00	1.00	.60
350	Hoyt Wilhelm	9.00	4.50	2.75
351	Bob Barton	2.00	1.00	.60
352	Jackie Hernandez	2.00	1.00	.60
353	Mack Jones	2.00	1.00	.60
354	Pete Richert	2.00	1.00	.60
355	Ernie Banks	20.00	10.00	6.00
356a	5th Series Check List (371-457) (Ken Holtzman) (Top of cap away from black circle.)	5.00	2.50	1.50
356b	5th Series Check List (371-457) (Ken Holtzman) (Top of cap near black circle.)	5.00	2.50	1.50
357	Len Gabrielson	2.00	1.00	.60
358	Mike Epstein	2.00	1.00	.60
359	Joe Moeller	2.00	1.00	.60
360	Willie Horton	2.00	1.00	.60
361	Harmon Killebrew (All-Star)	7.50	3.75	2.25
362	Orlando Cepeda (All-Star)	5.00	2.50	1.50
363	Rod Carew (All-Star)	6.50	3.25	2.00
364	Joe Morgan (All-Star)	6.00	3.00	1.75
365	Brooks Robinson (All-Star)	7.50	3.75	2.25
366	Ron Santo (All-Star)	5.00	2.50	1.50
367	Jim Fregosi (All-Star)	2.00	1.00	.60
368	Gene Alley (All-Star)	2.00	1.00	.60
369	Carl Yastrzemski (All-Star)	7.50	3.75	2.25
370	Hank Aaron (All-Star)	16.00	8.00	4.75
371	Tony Oliva (All-Star)	2.50	1.25	.70
372	Lou Brock (All-Star)	6.00	3.00	1.75
373	Frank Robinson (All-Star)	7.50	3.75	2.25
374	Roberto Clemente (All-Star)	20.00	10.00	6.00
375	Bill Freehan (All-Star)	2.00	1.00	.60
376	Tim McCarver (All-Star)	3.00	1.50	.90
377	Joe Horlen (All-Star)	2.00	1.00	.60
378	Bob Gibson (All-Star)	7.00	3.50	2.00
379	Gary Peters (All-Star)	2.00	1.00	.60
380	Ken Holtzman (All-Star)	2.00	1.00	.60
381	Boog Powell	3.00	1.50	.90
382	Ramon Hernandez	2.00	1.00	.60
383	Steve Whitaker	2.00	1.00	.60
384	Reds Rookies (*Bill Henry, Hal McRae*)	6.00	3.00	1.75
385	Jim Hunter	10.00	5.00	3.00
386	Greg Goossen	2.00	1.00	.60
387	Joe Foy	2.00	1.00	.60
388	Ray Washburn	2.00	1.00	.60
389	Jay Johnstone	2.00	1.00	.60
390	Bill Mazeroski	10.00	5.00	3.00
391	Bob Priddy	2.00	1.00	.60
392	Grady Hatton	2.00	1.00	.60
393	Jim Perry	2.00	1.00	.60
394	Tommie Aaron	2.00	1.00	.60
395	Camilo Pascual	2.00	1.00	.60
396	Bobby Wine	2.00	1.00	.60
397	Vic Davalillo	2.00	1.00	.60
398	Jim Grant	2.00	1.00	.60
399	Ray Oyler	2.00	1.00	.60
400a	Mike McCormick (White team.)	450.00	225.00	135.00
400b	Mike McCormick (Yellow team.)	2.00	1.00	.60
401	Mets Team	5.00	2.50	1.50
402	Mike Hegan	2.00	1.00	.60
403	John Buzhardt	2.00	1.00	.60
404	Floyd Robinson	2.00	1.00	.60
405	Tommy Helms	2.00	1.00	.60
406	Dick Ellsworth	2.00	1.00	.60
407	Gary Kolb	2.00	1.00	.60
408	Steve Carlton	15.00	7.50	4.50
409	Orioles Rookies (*Frank Peters, Ron Stone*)	2.00	1.00	.60
410	Fergie Jenkins	10.00	5.00	3.00
411	Ron Hansen	2.00	1.00	.60
412	Clay Carroll	2.00	1.00	.60
413	Tommy McCraw	2.00	1.00	.60
414	Mickey Lolich	2.00	1.00	.60
415	Johnny Callison	2.00	1.00	.60
416	Bill Rigney	2.00	1.00	.60
417	Willie Crawford	2.00	1.00	.60
418	Eddie Fisher	2.00	1.00	.60
419	Jack Hiatt	2.00	1.00	.60
420	Cesar Tovar	2.00	1.00	.60
421	Ron Taylor	2.00	1.00	.60
422	Rene Lachemann	2.00	1.00	.60
423	Fred Gladding	2.00	1.00	.60
424	White Sox Team	5.00	2.50	1.50
425	Jim Maloney	2.00	1.00	.60
426	Hank Allen	2.00	1.00	.60
427	Dick Calmus	2.00	1.00	.60
428	Vic Roznovsky	2.00	1.00	.60
429	Tommie Sisk	2.00	1.00	.60
430	Rico Petrocelli	2.00	1.00	.60
431	Dooley Womack	2.00	1.00	.60
432	Indians Rookies (Bill Davis, Jose Vidal)	2.00	1.00	.60
433	Bob Rodgers	2.00	1.00	.60
434	Ricardo Joseph	2.00	1.00	.60
435	Ron Perranoski	2.00	1.00	.60
436	Hal Lanier	2.00	1.00	.60
437	Don Cardwell	2.00	1.00	.60
438	Lee Thomas	2.00	1.00	.60
439	Luman Harris	2.00	1.00	.60
440	Claude Osteen	2.00	1.00	.60
441	Alex Johnson	2.00	1.00	.60
442	Dick Bosman	2.00	1.00	.60
443	Joe Azcue	2.00	1.00	.60
444	Jack Fisher	2.00	1.00	.60
445	Mike Shannon	2.00	1.00	.60
446	Ron Kline	2.00	1.00	.60
447	Tigers Rookies (George Korince, Fred Lasher)	2.00	1.00	.60
448	Gary Wagner	2.00	1.00	.60
449	Gene Oliver	2.00	1.00	.60
450	Jim Kaat	2.50	1.25	.70
451	Al Spangler	2.00	1.00	.60
452	Jesus Alou	2.00	1.00	.60
453	Sammy Ellis	2.00	1.00	.60
454a	6th Series Check List (458-533) (Frank Robinson) (Neck chain shows.)	6.00	3.00	1.75
454b	6th Series Check List (458-533) (Frank Robinson) (No neck chain.)	6.00	3.00	1.75
455	Rico Carty	2.00	1.00	.60
456	John O'Donoghue	2.00	1.00	.60
457	Jim Lefebvre	2.00	1.00	.60
458	Lew Krausse	5.00	2.50	1.50
459	Dick Simpson	5.00	2.50	1.50
460	Jim Lonborg	5.00	2.50	1.50
461	Chuck Hiller	5.00	2.50	1.50
462	Barry Moore	5.00	2.50	1.50
463	Jimmie Schaffer	5.00	2.50	1.50
464	Don McMahon	5.00	2.50	1.50
465	Tommie Agee	5.00	2.50	1.50
466	Bill Dillman	5.00	2.50	1.50
467	Dick Howser	5.00	2.50	1.50
468	Larry Sherry	5.00	2.50	1.50
469	Ty Cline	5.00	2.50	1.50
470	Bill Freehan	5.00	2.50	1.50
471	Orlando Pena	5.00	2.50	1.50
472	Walt Alston	8.00	4.00	2.50
473	Al Worthington	5.00	2.50	1.50
474	Paul Schaal	5.00	2.50	1.50
475	Joe Niekro	5.00	2.50	1.50
476	Woody Woodward	5.00	2.50	1.50
477	Phillies Team	6.00	3.00	1.75
478	Dave McNally	5.00	2.50	1.50
479	Phil Gagliano	5.00	2.50	1.50
480	Manager's Dream (Chico Cardenas, Roberto Clemente, Tony Oliva)	40.00	20.00	12.00
481	John Wyatt	5.00	2.50	1.50
482	Jose Pagan	5.00	2.50	1.50
483	Darold Knowles	5.00	2.50	1.50
484	Phil Roof	5.00	2.50	1.50
485	Ken Berry	5.00	2.50	1.50
486	Cal Koonce	5.00	2.50	1.50
487	Lee May	5.00	2.50	1.50
488	Dick Tracewski	5.00	2.50	1.50
489	Wally Bunker	5.00	2.50	1.50
490	Super Stars (Harmon Killebrew, Mickey Mantle, Willie Mays)	110.00	55.00	35.00
491	Denny Lemaster	5.00	2.50	1.50
492	Jeff Torborg	5.00	2.50	1.50
493	Jim McGlothlin	5.00	2.50	1.50
494	Ray Sadecki	5.00	2.50	1.50
495	Leon Wagner	5.00	2.50	1.50
496	Steve Hamilton	5.00	2.50	1.50
497	Cards Team	6.00	3.00	1.75
498	Bill Bryan	5.00	2.50	1.50
499	Steve Blass	5.00	2.50	1.50
500	Frank Robinson	25.00	12.50	7.50
501	John Odom	5.00	2.50	1.50
502	Mike Andrews	5.00	2.50	1.50
503	Al Jackson	5.00	2.50	1.50
504	Russ Snyder	5.00	2.50	1.50
505	Joe Sparma	5.00	2.50	1.50
506	Clarence Jones	5.00	2.50	1.50
507	Wade Blasingame	5.00	2.50	1.50
508	Duke Sims	5.00	2.50	1.50
509	Dennis Higgins	5.00	2.50	1.50
510	Ron Fairly	5.00	2.50	1.50
511	Bill Kelso	5.00	2.50	1.50
512	Grant Jackson	5.00	2.50	1.50
513	Hank Bauer	5.00	2.50	1.50
514	Al McBean	5.00	2.50	1.50
515	Russ Nixon	5.00	2.50	1.50
516	Pete Mikkelsen	5.00	2.50	1.50
517	Diego Segui	5.00	2.50	1.50
518a	7th Series Check List (534-598) (Clete Boyer) (539 is Maj. L. Rookies)	6.00	3.00	1.75
518b	7th Series Check List (534-598) (Clete Boyer) (539 is Amer. L. Rookies)	10.00	5.00	3.00
519	Jerry Stephenson	5.00	2.50	1.50
520	Lou Brock	20.00	10.00	6.00
521	Don Shaw	5.00	2.50	1.50
522	Wayne Causey	5.00	2.50	1.50
523	John Tsitouris	5.00	2.50	1.50
524	Andy Kosco	5.00	2.50	1.50
525	Jim Davenport	5.00	2.50	1.50
526	Bill Denehy	5.00	2.50	1.50
527	Tito Francona	5.00	2.50	1.50
528	Tigers Team	30.00	15.00	9.00
529	Bruce Von Hoff	5.00	2.50	1.50
530	Bird Belters (Brooks Robinson, Frank Robinson)	27.50	13.50	8.25
531	Chuck Hinton	5.00	2.50	1.50
532	Luis Tiant	5.00	2.50	1.50
533	Wes Parker	5.00	2.50	1.50
534	Bob Miller	5.00	2.50	1.50
535	Danny Cater	5.00	2.50	1.50
536	Bill Short	5.00	2.50	1.50
537	Norm Siebern	5.00	2.50	1.50
538	Manny Jimenez	5.00	2.50	1.50
539	Major League Rookies (*Mike Ferraro, Jim Ray*)	5.00	2.50	1.50
540	Nelson Briles	5.00	2.50	1.50
541	Sandy Alomar	5.00	2.50	1.50
542	John Boccabella	5.00	2.50	1.50
543	Bob Lee	5.00	2.50	1.50
544	Mayo Smith	5.00	2.50	1.50
545	Lindy McDaniel	5.00	2.50	1.50
546	Roy White	4.50	2.25	1.25
547	Dan Coombs	5.00	2.50	1.50
548	Bernie Allen	5.00	2.50	1.50
549	Orioles Rookies (*Curt Motton, Roger Nelson*)	5.00	2.50	1.50
550	Clete Boyer	5.00	2.50	1.50
551	Darrell Sutherland	5.00	2.50	1.50
552	Ed Kirkpatrick	5.00	2.50	1.50
553	Hank Aguirre	5.00	2.50	1.50
554	A's Team	6.00	3.00	1.75
555	Jose Tartabull	5.00	2.50	1.50
556	Dick Selma	5.00	2.50	1.50
557	Frank Quilici	5.00	2.50	1.50
558	John Edwards	5.00	2.50	1.50
559	Pirates Rookies (*Carl Taylor, Luke Walker*)	5.00	2.50	1.50
560	Paul Casanova	5.00	2.50	1.50
561	Lee Elia	5.00	2.50	1.50

		NM	EX	VG
562	Jim Bouton	6.00	3.00	1.75
563	Ed Charles	5.00	2.50	1.50
564	Eddie Stanky	5.00	2.50	1.50
565	Larry Dierker	5.00	2.50	1.50
566	Ken Harrelson	5.00	2.50	1.50
567	Clay Dalrymple	5.00	2.50	1.50
568	Willie Smith	5.00	2.50	1.50
569	N.L. Rookies	5.00	2.50	1.50
	(Ivan Murrell, Les Rohr)			
570	Rick Reichardt	5.00	2.50	1.50
571	Tony LaRussa	6.00	3.00	1.75
572	Don Bosch	5.00	2.50	1.50
573	Joe Coleman	5.00	2.50	1.50
574	Reds Team	7.50	3.75	2.25
575	Jim Palmer	20.00	10.00	6.00
576	Dave Adlesh	5.00	2.50	1.50
577	Fred Talbot	5.00	2.50	1.50
578	Orlando Martinez	5.00	2.50	1.50
579	N.L. Rookies	5.00	2.50	1.50
	(Larry Hisle, Mike Lum)			
580	Bob Bailey	5.00	2.50	1.50
581	Garry Roggenburk	5.00	2.50	1.50
582	Jerry Grote	5.00	2.50	1.50
583	Gates Brown	6.00	3.00	1.75
584	Larry Shepard	5.00	2.50	1.50
585	Wilbur Wood	5.00	2.50	1.50
586	Jim Pagliaroni	5.00	2.50	1.50
587	Roger Repoz	5.00	2.50	1.50
588	Dick Schofield	5.00	2.50	1.50
589	Twins Rookies	5.00	2.50	1.50
	(Ron Clark, Moe Ogier)			
590	Tommy Harper	5.00	2.50	1.50
591	Dick Nen	5.00	2.50	1.50
592	John Bateman	5.00	2.50	1.50
593	Lee Stange	5.00	2.50	1.50
594	Phil Linz	5.00	2.50	1.50
595	Phil Ortega	5.00	2.50	1.50
596	Charlie Smith	5.00	2.50	1.50
597	Bill McCool	5.00	2.50	1.50
598	Jerry May	11.00	2.00	1.25

1968 Topps Action All-Star Stickers

Another of the many Topps test issues of the late 1960s, Action All-Star stickers were sold in a strip of three, with bubblegum, for 10 cents. The strip is comprised of three 3-1/4" x 5-1/4" panels, perforated at the joints for separation. The numbered central panel contains a large photo of a star player. The top and bottom panels each contain smaller pictures of three players. While there are 16 numbered center panels, only 12 of them are different; panels 13-16 are double-prints. Similarly, the triple-player panels at top and bottom of stickers 13-16 repeat panels from #1-4. Prices below are for stickers which have all three panels still joined. Individual panels are priced signicantly lower.

		NM	EX	VG
Complete Set (16):		3,850	1,900	1,150
Common Panel:		100.00	50.00	30.00
1	Orlando Cepeda, Joe Horlen, Al Kaline, Bill Mazeroski, Claude Osteen, Mel Stottlemyre, Carl Yastrzemski	300.00	150.00	90.00
2	Don Drysdale, Harmon Killebrew, Mike McCormick, Tom Phoebus, George Scott, Ron Swoboda, Pete Ward	125.00	65.00	35.00
3	Hank Aaron, Paul Casanova, Jim Maloney, Joe Pepitone, Rick Reichardt, Frank Robinson, Tom Seaver	115.00	55.00	35.00

		NM	EX	VG
4	Bob Aspromonte, Johnny Callison, Dean Chance, Jim Lefebvre, Jim Lonborg, Frank Robinson, Ron Santo	150.00	75.00	45.00
5	Bert Campaneris, Al Downing, Willie Horton, Ed Kranepool, Willie Mays, Pete Rose, Ron Santo	375.00	185.00	110.00
6	Max Alvis, Ernie Banks, Al Kaline, Tim McCarver, Rusty Staub, Walt Williams, Carl Yastrzemski	300.00	150.00	90.00
7	Rod Carew, Tony Gonzalez, Steve Hargan, Mickey Mantle, Willie McCovey, Rick Monday, Billy Williams	500.00	250.00	150.00
8	Clete Boyer, Jim Bunning, Tony Conigliaro, Mike Cuellar, Joe Horlen, Ken McMullen, Don Mincher	100.00	50.00	30.00
9	Orlando Cepeda, Bob Clemente, Jim Fregosi, Harmon Killebrew, Willie Mays, Chris Short, Earl Wilson	300.00	150.00	90.00
10	Hank Aaron, Bob Gibson, Bud Harrelson, Jim Hunter, Mickey Mantle, Gary Peters, Vada Pinson	375.00	185.00	110.00
11	Don Drysdale, Bill Freehan, Frank Howard, Ferguson Jenkins, Tony Oliva, Bob Veale, Jim Wynn	235.00	115.00	70.00
12	Richie Allen, Bob Clemente, Sam McDowell, Jim McGlothlin, Tony Perez, Brooks Robinson, Joe Torre	850.00	425.00	255.00
13	Dean Chance, Don Drysdale, Jim Lefebvre, Tom Phoebus, Frank Robinson, George Scott, Carl Yastrzemski	300.00	150.00	90.00
14	Paul Casanova, Orlando Cepeda, Joe Horlen, Harmon Killebrew, Bill Mazeroski, Rick Reichardt, Tom Seaver	175.00	85.00	50.00
15	Bob Aspromonte, Johnny Callison, Jim Lonborg, Mike McCormick, Frank Robinson, Ron Swoboda, Pete Ward	125.00	62.00	37.00
16	Hank Aaron, Al Kaline, Jim Maloney, Claude Osteen, Joe Pepitone, Ron Santo, Mel Stottlemyre	225.00	110.00	65.00

1968 Topps "Batter Up" Game

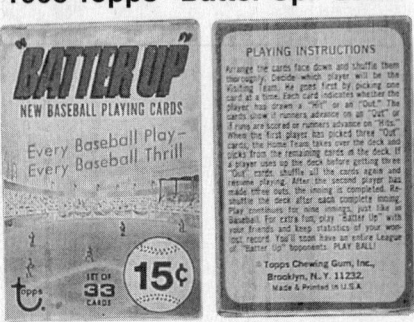

The same cards which were issued as pack inserts in 1968 Topps were sold in a much scarcer boxed-set form. Packaged in a colorful cardboard box with game rules on back, the set is labeled "Batter Up" and can be found in versions with 10 or 15 original retail price.

	NM	EX	VG
Complete Boxed Set:	275.00	85.00	45.00

(See 1968 Topps Game for individual card checklist and values.)

1968 Topps Deckle Edge Proofs

While most Topps proofs are so rare as to preclude their listing in this catalog, the 1968 Deckle Edge test set is an exception. Usually found in the form of a 7-3/4" x 11" uncut sheet of nine black-and-white cards, single cards are sometimes encountered. The blank-backed sheet and cards can be found with the players' facsimile autographs printed in red, black or blue. Unnumbered cards are checklisted here alphabetically.

		NM	EX	VG
Complete Set, Singles (9):		700.00	350.00	225.00
Uncut Sheet:		700.00	350.00	225.00
Common Player:		50.00	25.00	15.00
(1)	Dave Adlesh	50.00	25.00	15.00
(2)	Hank Aguire	50.00	25.00	15.00
(3)	Sandy Alomar	50.00	25.00	15.00
(4)	Sonny Jackson	50.00	25.00	15.00
(5)	Bob Johnson	50.00	25.00	15.00
(6)	Claude Osteen	50.00	25.00	15.00
(7)	Juan Pizarro	50.00	25.00	15.00
(8)	Hal Woodeshick	50.00	25.00	15.00
(9)	Carl Yastrzemski	400.00	200.00	120.00

1968 Topps Discs

One of the scarcer Topps baseball collectibles, this set was apparently a never-completed test issue. These full-color, cardboard discs, which measure approximately 2-1/4" in diameter, were probably intended to be made into a pin set but production was never completed and no actual pins are known to exist. Uncut sheets of the player discs have been found. The discs include a player portrait photo with the name beneath and (usually) the city and team nickname along the sides.

		NM	EX	VG
Complete Set (29):		8,000	4,000	2,400
Common Player:		125.00	65.00	35.00
(1)	Hank Aaron	625.00	310.00	185.00
(2)	Richie Allen	140.00	75.00	40.00
(3)	Gene Alley	125.00	65.00	35.00
(4)	Rod Carew	350.00	175.00	100.00
(5)	Orlando Cepeda	300.00	150.00	90.00
(6)	Dean Chance	125.00	65.00	35.00
(7)	Roberto Clemente	850.00	425.00	255.00
(8)	Tommy Davis	125.00	65.00	35.00
(9)	Bill Freehan	125.00	65.00	35.00
(10)	Jim Fregosi	125.00	65.00	35.00
(11)	Steve Hargan	125.00	65.00	35.00
(12)	Frank Howard	125.00	65.00	35.00
(13)	Al Kaline	350.00	175.00	100.00
(14)	Harmon Killebrew	350.00	175.00	100.00
(15)	Mickey Mantle	1,750	875.00	525.00
(16)	Willie Mays	625.00	310.00	185.00
(17)	Mike McCormick	125.00	65.00	35.00
(18)	Rick Monday	125.00	65.00	35.00
(19)	Claude Osteen	125.00	65.00	35.00
(20)	Gary Peters	125.00	65.00	35.00
(21)	Brooks Robinson	350.00	175.00	100.00
(22)	Frank Robinson	350.00	175.00	100.00
(23)	Pete Rose	550.00	275.00	165.00
(24)	Ron Santo	150.00	75.00	45.00
(25)	Rusty Staub	135.00	70.00	40.00
(26)	Joe Torre	125.00	65.00	35.00
(27)	Bob Veale	125.00	65.00	35.00
(28)	Carl Yastrzemski	350.00	175.00	100.00

1968 Topps Game

A throwback to the Red and Blue Back sets of 1951, the 33-cards in the 1968 Topps Game set, inserted into packs of regular '68 Topps cards or purchases as a complete boxed set, enable the owner to play a game of baseball based on the game situations on each card. Also on the 2-1/4" x 3-1/4" cards were a color photograph of a player and his facsimile autograph. One redeeming social value of the set (assuming you're not mesmerized by the game) is that it affords an inexpensive way to get big-name cards as the set is loaded with stars, but not at all popular with collectors.

		NM	EX	VG
	Complete Set (33):	115.00	55.00	35.00
	Common Player:	2.00	1.00	.60
1	Mateo Alou	2.00	1.00	.60
2	Mickey Mantle	30.00	15.00	9.00
3	Carl Yastrzemski	10.00	5.00	3.00
4	Henry Aaron	12.00	6.00	3.50
5	Harmon Killebrew	9.00	4.50	2.75
6	Roberto Clemente	15.00	7.50	4.50
7	Frank Robinson	9.00	4.50	2.75
8	Willie Mays	12.00	6.00	3.50
9	Brooks Robinson	9.00	4.50	2.75
10	Tommy Davis	2.00	1.00	.60
11	Bill Freehan	2.00	1.00	.60
12	Claude Osteen	2.00	1.00	.60
13	Gary Peters	2.00	1.00	.60
14	Jim Lonborg	2.00	1.00	.60
15	Steve Hargan	2.00	1.00	.60
16	Dean Chance	2.00	1.00	.60
17	Mike McCormick	2.00	1.00	.60
18	Tim McCarver	3.00	1.50	.90
19	Ron Santo	6.00	3.00	1.75
20	Tony Gonzalez	2.00	1.00	.60
21	Frank Howard	3.00	1.50	.90
22	George Scott	2.00	1.00	.60
23	Rich Allen	6.00	3.00	1.75
24	Jim Wynn	2.00	1.00	.60
25	Gene Alley	2.00	1.00	.60
26	Rick Monday	2.00	1.00	.60
27	Al Kaline	9.00	4.50	2.75
28	Rusty Staub	3.00	1.50	.90
29	Rod Carew	9.00	4.50	2.75
30	Pete Rose	12.00	6.00	3.50
31	Joe Torre	6.00	3.00	1.75
32	Orlando Cepeda	6.00	3.00	1.75
33	Jim Fregosi	2.00	1.00	.60

1968 Topps Plaks

Among the scarcest Topps test issues of the late 1960s, the "All Star Baseball Plaks" were plastic busts of two dozen stars of the era which came packaged like model airplane parts. The busts had to be snapped off a sprue and could be inserted into a base which carried the player's name. Packed with the plastic plaks was one of two checklist cards which featured six color photos per side. The 2-1/8" x 4" checklist cards are popular with superstar collectors and are considerably easier to find today than the actual plaks. Wax packs of three plaks and two sticks of bubblegum were sold for a dime.

		NM	EX	VG
	Complete Set (24):	9,000	4,500	2,750
	Common Player:	100.00	50.00	30.00
1	Max Alvis	100.00	50.00	30.00
2	Dean Chance	100.00	50.00	30.00
3	Jim Fregosi	100.00	50.00	30.00
4	Frank Howard	125.00	62.00	37.00
5	Jim Hunter	250.00	125.00	75.00
6	Al Kaline	400.00	200.00	120.00
7	Harmon Killebrew	400.00	200.00	120.00
8	Jim Lonborg	100.00	50.00	30.00
9	Mickey Mantle	1,850	925.00	555.00
10	Gary Peters	100.00	50.00	30.00
11	Frank Robinson	400.00	200.00	120.00
12	Carl Yastrzemski	450.00	225.00	135.00
13	Hank Aaron	750.00	375.00	225.00
14	Richie Allen	125.00	62.00	37.00
15	Orlando Cepeda	300.00	150.00	90.00
16	Roberto Clemente	1,350	675.00	400.00
17	Tommy Davis	100.00	50.00	30.00
18	Don Drysdale	400.00	200.00	120.00
19	Willie Mays	750.00	375.00	225.00
20	Tim McCarver	125.00	62.00	37.00
21	Ron Santo	125.00	62.00	37.00
22	Rusty Staub	125.00	62.00	37.00
23	Pete Rose	650.00	325.00	195.00
24	Jim Wynn	100.00	50.00	30.00
---	Checklist Card 1-12	1,000	500.00	300.00
---	Checklist Card 13-24	1,500	750.00	450.00

1968 Topps Posters

Yet another innovation from the creative minds at Topps appeared in 1968; a set of color player posters. Measuring 9-3/4" x 18-1/8", each poster was sold separately with its own piece of gum, rather than as an insert. The posters feature a large color photograph with a star at the bottom containing the player's name, position and team. There are 24 different posters which were folded numerous times to fit into the package they were sold in. Unless the paper has split at the folds, they are not considered in grading.

		NM	EX	VG
	Complete Set (24):	650.00	325.00	200.00
	Common Player:	15.00	7.50	4.50
	Unopened Pack:	175.00		
1	Dean Chance	15.00	7.50	4.50
2	Max Alvis	15.00	7.50	4.50
3	Frank Howard	17.50	8.75	5.25
4	Jim Fregosi	15.00	7.50	4.50
5	Catfish Hunter	20.00	10.00	6.00
6	Roberto Clemente	60.00	30.00	18.00
7	Don Drysdale	25.00	12.50	7.50
8	Jim Wynn	15.00	7.50	4.50
9	Al Kaline	25.00	12.50	7.50
10	Harmon Killebrew	25.00	12.50	7.50
11	Jim Lonborg	15.00	7.50	4.50
12	Orlando Cepeda	20.00	10.00	6.00
13	Gary Peters	15.00	7.50	4.50
14	Hank Aaron	50.00	25.00	15.00
15	Richie Allen	17.50	8.75	5.25
16	Carl Yastrzemski	30.00	15.00	9.00
17	Ron Swoboda	15.00	7.50	4.50
18	Mickey Mantle	80.00	40.00	24.00
19	Tim McCarver	15.00	7.50	4.50
20	Willie Mays	50.00	25.00	15.00
21	Ron Santo	17.50	8.75	5.25
22	Rusty Staub	17.50	8.75	5.25
23	Pete Rose	50.00	25.00	15.00
24	Frank Robinson	25.00	12.50	7.50

1968 Tipps From Topps Book

While the Bazooka brand is not referenced in this booklet, it presents the baseball playing tips that appeared on box backs of Bazooka gum. The player photo and cartoon tips are printed in blue in the interior pages of the 5-7/8" x 3" book. The front and back covers are black, white and green. The manner of distribution for this premium is not known.

	NM	EX	VG
Tipps From Topps Book	150.00	75.00	45.00

1968 Topps 3-D Prototype

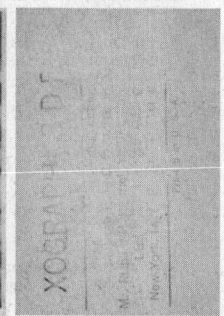

Apparently produced as a prototype for the 3-D cards which Topps issued as a test in 1968, this prototype card is 2-1/4" x 3-1/4" with square corners. The team name is in red block letters at top. The back carries a rubber-stamped notice which identifies the card as a "Xograph 3-D" product from New York City.

	NM	EX	VG
Brooks Robinson	20,000	10,000	6,000

1968 Topps 3-D

These very rare test-issue cards measure 2-1/4" x 3-1/2" with rounded corners and blank backs. They simulate a three- dimensional effect with backgrounds purposely blurred, in front of which is a sharp color player photograph. The outer layer is a thin coating of ribbed plastic. The special process gives the picture the illusion of depth when the card is moved or tilted. As this was done two years before Kellogg's began its 3-D cards, this test issue really was breaking new ground. Production and distribution were limited, making the cards very tough to find. Some cards, said to have been the first produced, are stamped on back with a notice from Visual Panographics of New York. "This is an experimental XOGRAPH card produced as a limited edition. Not for public circulation or distribution. Not for resale. To be returned to:."

		NM	EX	VG
	Complete Set (12):	17,500	8,750	5,250
	Common Player:	500.00	250.00	150.00
	Wrapper:	900.00	450.00	275.00
(1)	Bob Clemente	12,000	6,000	3,600
(2)	Willie Davis	500.00	250.00	150.00
(3)	Ron Fairly	500.00	250.00	150.00
(4)	Curt Flood	650.00	325.00	200.00
(5)	Jim Lonborg	500.00	250.00	150.00
(6)	Jim Maloney	500.00	250.00	150.00
(7)	Tony Perez	1,000	500.00	300.00
(8)	Boog Powell	750.00	375.00	225.00
(9)	Bill Robinson	500.00	250.00	150.00
(10)	Rusty Staub	750.00	375.00	225.00
(11)	Mel Stottlemyre	500.00	250.00	150.00
(12)	Ron Swoboda	500.00	250.00	150.00

1968 Topps/Milton Bradley

As part of a Win-A-Card trading card board game, Milton Bradley contracted with Topps to print 132 special versions of its 1968 baseball cards, 1967 football cards and hot rod cards. The baseball cards can be differentiated from regular-issue 1968 Topps in that the yellow ink on back is much lighter and brighter than the dark yellow/gold ink usually found on back. Also, some of the card fronts show evidence of the white-bordered football and hot rod cards at one or more edges. Collectors currently will pay only a small premium for the MB version, but that gap is likely to widen in the future.

		NM	EX	VG
	Complete (Baseball) Set (76):			
	Common Player:			
7	N.L. ERA Leaders	7.00	3.50	2.00
	(Jim Bunning, Phil Niekro,			
	Chris Short)			

8	A.L. ERA Leaders (Joe Horlen, Gary Peters, Sonny Siebert)	2.00	1.00	.60
10	A.L. Pitching Leaders (Dean Chance, Jim Lonborg, Earl Wilson)	9.00	4.50	2.75
13	Chuck Hartenstein	2.00	1.00	.60
16	Indians Rookies (**Lou Piniella, Richie Scheinblum**)	4.00	2.00	1.25
17	Dick Hall	2.00	1.00	.60
18	Mike Hershberger	2.00	1.00	.60
19	Juan Pizarro	2.00	1.00	.60
20	Brooks Robinson	15.00	7.50	4.50
24	Bobby Locke	2.00	1.00	.60
26	Darrell Brandon	2.00	1.00	.60
34	Al Ferrara	2.00	1.00	.60
36	Pirates Rookies (**Bob Moose, Bob Robertson**)	2.00	1.00	.60
38	Tony Pierce	2.00	1.00	.60
43	Gary Bell	2.00	1.00	.60
44	Frank Kostro	2.00	1.00	.60
45	Tom Seaver	30.00	15.00	9.00
48	Ted Davidson	2.00	1.00	.60
49	Ed Brinkman (Yellow team.)	50.00	25.00	15.00
53	Gene Alley	2.00	1.00	.60
57	Dan Schneider	2.00	1.00	.60
58	Ed Mathews	13.50	6.75	4.00
60	Ken Holtzman	2.00	1.00	.60
61	Reggie Smith	2.00	1.00	.60
62	Chuck Dobson	2.00	1.00	.60
64	Jim Merritt	2.00	1.00	.60
66	Casey Cox (Yellow team.)	50.00	25.00	15.00
68	Ron Willis	2.00	1.00	.60
72	Tommy John	4.00	2.00	1.25
74	Milt Pappas	2.00	1.00	.60
77	**Don Wilson**	2.00	1.00	.60
78	Jim Northrup	2.00	1.00	.60
80	Rod Carew	17.50	8.75	5.25
81	Larry Jackson	2.00	1.00	.60
85	Gaylord Perry	9.00	4.50	2.75
89	Jake Gibbs	2.00	1.00	.60
94	Lee Maye	2.00	1.00	.60
98	Gary Sutherland	2.00	1.00	.60
99	Rocky Colavito	7.00	3.50	2.00
100	Bob Gibson	17.50	8.75	5.25
105	Al Downing	2.00	1.00	.60
106	Dalton Jones	2.00	1.00	.60
107	2nd Series Check List (110-196) (Juan Marichal)	4.00	2.00	1.25
108	Don Pavletich	2.00	1.00	.60
110	Hank Aaron	40.00	20.00	12.00
112	Woody Fryman	2.00	1.00	.60
113	Tigers Rookies (**Tom Matchick, Daryl Patterson**)	2.00	1.00	.60
117	Larry Jaster	2.00	1.00	.60
118	Mark Belanger	2.00	1.00	.60
119	Ted Savage	2.00	1.00	.60
120	Mel Stottlemyre	4.00	2.00	1.25
121	Jimmie Hall	2.00	1.00	.60
124	Nate Oliver	2.00	1.00	.60
127	Paul Lindblad	2.00	1.00	.60
128	Astros Rookies (**Tom Dukes, Alonzo Harris**)	2.00	1.00	.60
129	Mickey Stanley	2.00	1.00	.60
136	Randy Hundley	2.00	1.00	.60
139	Chris Short	2.00	1.00	.60
143	Pete Cimino	2.00	1.00	.60
146	Sal Bando	2.00	1.00	.60
149	Bob Saverine	2.00	1.00	.60
155	World Series Game 5 (Lonborg Wins Again)	6.00	3.00	1.75
156	World Series Game 6 (Petrocelli Socks Two Homers)	6.00	3.00	1.75
165	Tony Oliva	4.00	2.00	1.25
168	Dodgers Team	5.00	2.50	1.50
172	Walt Williams	2.00	1.00	.60
175	Maury Wills	2.00	1.00	.60
176	Bob Allen	2.00	1.00	.60
177	Mets Rookies (**Jerry Koosman, Nolan Ryan**)	335.00	190.00	95.00
179	Bill Stoneman	2.00	1.00	.60
180	Curt Flood	3.00	1.50	.90
185	Tom Haller	2.00	1.00	.60
189	Bill Landis	2.00	1.00	.60
191	Dan Frisella	2.00	1.00	.60
193	Jack Hamilton	2.00	1.00	.60
195	Joe Pepitone	4.00	2.00	1.25

1969 Topps

The 1969 Topps set broke yet another record for quantity as the issue is officially a whopping 664 cards. With substantial numbers of variations, the number of possible cards runs closer to 700. The design of the 2-1/2" x 3-1/2" cards in the set feature a color photo with the team name printed in block letters underneath. A circle contains the player's name and position. Card backs returned to a horizontal format. Despite the size of the set, it contains no team cards. It does, however, have multi-player cards, All-Stars, statistical leaders, and World Series highlights. Most significant among the varieties are white and yellow letter cards from the run of #'s 440-511. The complete set prices below do not include the scarcer and more expensive "white letter" variations.

		NM	EX	VG
	Complete Set (664):	3,150	1,550	925.00
	Common Player (1-588):	2.00	1.00	.60
	Common Player (589-664):	3.00	1.50	.90
1	A.L. Batting Leaders (Danny Cater, Tony Oliva, Carl Yastrzemski)	11.00	5.50	3.25
2	N.L. Batting Leaders (Felipe Alou, Matty Alou, Pete Rose)	15.00	7.50	4.50
3	A.L. RBI Leaders (Ken Harrelson, Frank Howard, Jim Northrup)	2.50	1.25	.75
4	N.L. RBI Leaders (Willie McCovey, Ron Santo, Billy Williams)	9.00	4.50	2.75
5	A.L. Home Run Leaders (Ken Harrelson, Willie Horton, Frank Howard)	6.00	3.00	1.75
6	N.L. Home Run Leaders (Richie Allen, Ernie Banks, Willie McCovey)	8.00	4.00	2.50
7	A.L. ERA Leaders (Sam McDowell, Dave McNally, Luis Tiant)	3.00	1.50	.90
8	N.L. ERA Leaders (Bobby Bolin, Bob Gibson, Bob Veale)	4.00	2.00	1.25
9	A.L. Pitching Leaders (Denny McLain, Dave McNally, Mel Stottlemyre, Luis Tiant)	4.00	2.00	1.25
10	N.L. Pitching Leaders (Bob Gibson, Fergie Jenkins, Juan Marichal)	5.00	2.50	1.50
11	A.L. Strikeout Leaders (Sam McDowell, Denny McLain, Luis Tiant)	3.00	1.50	.90
12	N.L. Strikeout Leaders (Bob Gibson, Fergie Jenkins, Bill Singer)	5.00	2.50	1.50
13	Mickey Stanley	2.00	1.00	.60
14	Al McBean	2.00	1.00	.60
15	Boog Powell	3.00	1.50	.90
16	Giants Rookies (Cesar Gutierrez, Rich Robertson)	2.00	1.00	.60
17	Mike Marshall	2.00	1.00	.60
18	Dick Schofield	2.00	1.00	.60
19	Ken Suarez	2.00	1.00	.60
20	Ernie Banks	25.00	12.50	7.50
21	Jose Santiago	2.00	1.00	.60
22	Jesus Alou	2.00	1.00	.60
23	Lew Krausse	2.00	1.00	.60
24	Walt Alston	4.00	2.00	1.25
25	Roy White	2.00	1.00	.60
26	Clay Carroll	2.00	1.00	.60
27	Bernie Allen	2.00	1.00	.60
28	Mike Ryan	2.00	1.00	.60
29	Dave Morehead	2.00	1.00	.60
30	Bob Allison	2.00	1.00	.60
31	Mets Rookies (**Gary Gentry, Amos Otis**)	3.00	1.50	.90
32	Sammy Ellis	2.00	1.00	.60
33	Wayne Causey	2.00	1.00	.60
34	Gary Peters	2.00	1.00	.60
35	Joe Morgan	10.00	5.00	3.00
36	Luke Walker	2.00	1.00	.60
37	Curt Motton	2.00	1.00	.60
38	Zoilo Versalles	2.00	1.00	.60
39	Dick Hughes	2.00	1.00	.60
40	Mayo Smith	2.00	1.00	.60
41	Bob Barton	2.00	1.00	.60
42	Tommy Harper	2.00	1.00	.60
43	Joe Niekro	2.00	1.00	.60
44	Danny Cater	2.00	1.00	.60
45	Maury Wills	2.00	1.00	.60
46	Fritz Peterson	2.00	1.00	.60
47a	Paul Popovich (Emblem visible thru airbrush.)	15.00	7.50	4.50
47b	Paul Popovich (Helmet emblem completely airbrushed.)	2.00	1.00	.60
48	Brant Alyea	2.00	1.00	.60
49a	Royals Rookies (**Steve Jones, Eliseo Rodriguez**) (Rodriquez on front.)	15.00	7.50	4.50
49b	Royals Rookies (**Steve Jones, Eliseo Rodriguez**) (Rodriguez on front.)	2.00	1.00	.60
50	Roberto Clemente	40.00	20.00	12.00
51	Woody Fryman	2.00	1.00	.60
52	Mike Andrews	2.00	1.00	.60
53	Sonny Jackson	2.00	1.00	.60
54	Cisco Carlos	2.00	1.00	.60
55	Jerry Grote	2.00	1.00	.60
56	Rich Reese	2.00	1.00	.60
57	1st Series Check List (1-109) (Denny McLain)	4.00	2.00	1.25
58	Fred Gladding	2.00	1.00	.60
59	Jay Johnstone	2.00	1.00	.60
60	Nelson Briles	2.00	1.00	.60
61	Jimmie Hall	2.00	1.00	.60
62	Chico Salmon	2.00	1.00	.60
63	Jim Hickman	2.00	1.00	.60
64	Bill Monbouquette	2.00	1.00	.60
65	Willie Davis	2.00	1.00	.60
66	Orioles Rookies (**Mike Adamson, Merv Rettenmund**)	2.00	1.00	.60
67	Bill Stoneman	2.00	1.00	.60
68	Dave Duncan	2.00	1.00	.60
69	Steve Hamilton	2.00	1.00	.60
70	Tommy Helms	2.00	1.00	.60
71	Steve Whitaker	2.00	1.00	.60
72	Ron Taylor	2.00	1.00	.60
73	Johnny Briggs	2.00	1.00	.60
74	Preston Gomez	2.00	1.00	.60
75	Luis Aparicio	9.00	4.50	2.75
76	Norm Miller	2.00	1.00	.60
77a	Ron Perranoski (LA visible thru airbrush.)	25.00	12.50	7.50
77b	Ron Perranoski (Cap emblem completely airbrushed.)	2.00	1.00	.60
78	Tom Satriano	2.00	1.00	.60
79	Milt Pappas	2.00	1.00	.60
80	Norm Cash	6.00	3.00	1.75
81	Mel Queen	2.00	1.00	.60
82	Pirates Rookies (**Rich Hebner, Al Oliver**)	10.00	5.00	3.00
83	Mike Ferraro	2.00	1.00	.60
84	Bob Humphreys	2.00	1.00	.60
85	Lou Brock	20.00	10.00	6.00
86	Pete Richert	2.00	1.00	.60
87	Horace Clarke	2.00	1.00	.60
88	Rich Nye	2.00	1.00	.60
89	Russ Gibson	2.00	1.00	.60
90	Jerry Koosman	2.00	1.00	.60
91	Al Dark	2.00	1.00	.60
92	Jack Billingham	2.00	1.00	.60
93	Joe Foy	2.00	1.00	.60
94	Hank Aguirre	2.00	1.00	.60
95	Johnny Bench	50.00	25.00	15.00
96	Denver Lemaster	2.00	1.00	.60
97	Buddy Bradford	2.00	1.00	.60
98	Dave Giusti	2.00	1.00	.60
99a	Twins Rookies (**Danny Morris, Graig Nettles**) (Black loop above "Twins.")	13.50	6.75	4.00
99b	Twins Rookies (**Danny Morris, Graig Nettles**) (No black loop.)	12.50	6.25	3.75
100	Hank Aaron	50.00	25.00	15.00
101	Daryl Patterson	2.00	1.00	.60
102	Jim Davenport	2.00	1.00	.60
103	Roger Repoz	2.00	1.00	.60
104	Steve Blass	2.00	1.00	.60
105	Rick Monday	2.00	1.00	.60
106	Jim Hannan	2.00	1.00	.60
107a	2nd Series Check List (110-218) (Bob Gibson) (161 is Jim Purdin)	4.00	2.00	1.25
107b	2nd Series Check List (110-218) (Bob Gibson) (161 is John Purdin)	6.00	3.00	1.75
108	Tony Taylor	2.00	1.00	.60
109	Jim Lonborg	2.00	1.00	.60
110	Mike Shannon	2.00	1.00	.60
111	Johnny Morris	2.00	1.00	.60
112	J.C. Martin	2.00	1.00	.60
113	Dave May	2.00	1.00	.60
114	Yankees Rookies (**Alan Closter, John Cumberland**)	2.00	1.00	.60
115	Bill Hands	2.00	1.00	.60
116	Chuck Harrison	2.00	1.00	.60
117	Jim Fairey	2.00	1.00	.60
118	Stan Williams	2.00	1.00	.60
119	Doug Rader	2.00	1.00	.60
120	Pete Rose	35.00	17.50	10.00
121	Joe Grzenda	2.00	1.00	.60
122	Ron Fairly	2.00	1.00	.60
123	Wilbur Wood	2.00	1.00	.60
124	Hank Bauer	2.00	1.00	.60
125	Ray Sadecki	2.00	1.00	.60
126	Dick Tracewski	2.00	1.00	.60
127	Kevin Collins	2.00	1.00	.60
128	Tommie Aaron	2.00	1.00	.60
129	Bill McCool	2.00	1.00	.60
130	Carl Yastrzemski	25.00	12.50	7.50
131	Chris Cannizzaro	2.00	1.00	.60
132	Dave Baldwin	2.00	1.00	.60
133	Johnny Callison	2.00	1.00	.60
134	Jim Weaver	2.00	1.00	.60
135	Tommy Davis	2.00	1.00	.60
136	Cards Rookies (**Steve Huntz, Mike Torrez**)	2.00	1.00	.60
137	Wally Bunker	2.00	1.00	.60
138	John Bateman	2.00	1.00	.60
139	Andy Kosco	2.00	1.00	.60
140	Jim Lefebvre	2.00	1.00	.60
141	Bill Dillman	2.00	1.00	.60
142	Woody Woodward	2.00	1.00	.60
143	Joe Nossek	2.00	1.00	.60
144	Bob Hendley	2.00	1.00	.60
145	Max Alvis	2.00	1.00	.60
146	Jim Perry	2.00	1.00	.60
147	Leo Durocher	5.00	2.50	1.50
148	Lee Stange	2.00	1.00	.60
149	Ollie Brown	2.00	1.00	.60
150	Denny McLain	5.00	2.50	1.50
151a	Clay Dalrymple (Phillies)	22.50	11.00	6.75
151b	Clay Dalrymple (Orioles)	2.00	1.00	.60
152	Tommie Sisk	2.00	1.00	.60
153	Ed Brinkman	2.00	1.00	.60
154	Jim Britton	2.00	1.00	.60
155	Pete Ward	2.00	1.00	.60
156	Astros Rookies (**Hal Gilson, Leon McFadden**)	2.00	1.00	.60
157	Bob Rodgers	2.00	1.00	.60
158	Joe Gibbon	2.00	1.00	.60
159	Jerry Adair	2.00	1.00	.60
160	Vada Pinson	3.00	1.50	.90
161	John Purdin	2.00	1.00	.60

#	Player			
162	World Series Game 1 (Gibson Fans 17; Sets New Record)	15.00	7.50	4.50
163	World Series Game 2 (Tiger Homers Deck The Cards)	6.00	3.00	1.75
164	World Series Game 3 (McCarver's Homer Puts St. Louis Ahead)	7.00	3.50	2.00
165	World Series Game 4 (Brock's Lead-Off HR Starts Cards' Romp)	7.00	3.50	2.00
166	World Series Game 5 (Kaline's Key Hit Sparks Tiger Rally)	7.00	3.50	2.00
167	World Series Game 6 (Tiger 10-Run Inning Ties Mark)	6.00	3.00	1.75
168	World Series Game 7 (Lolich Series Hero Outduels Gibson)	9.00	4.50	2.75
169	World Series (Tigers Celebrate Their Victory)	12.00	6.00	3.50
170	Frank Howard	3.00	1.50	.90
171	Glenn Beckert	2.00	1.00	.60
172	Jerry Stephenson	2.00	1.00	.60
173	White Sox Rookies (*Bob Christian, Gerry Nyman*)	2.00	1.00	.60
174	Grant Jackson	2.00	1.00	.60
175	Jim Bunning	8.00	4.00	2.50
176	Joe Azcue	2.00	1.00	.60
177	Ron Reed	2.00	1.00	.60
178	Ray Oyler	2.00	1.00	.60
179	Don Pavletich	2.00	1.00	.60
180	Willie Horton	2.00	1.00	.60
181	Mel Nelson	2.00	1.00	.60
182	Bill Rigney	2.00	1.00	.60
183	Don Shaw	2.00	1.00	.60
184	Roberto Pena	2.00	1.00	.60
185	Tom Phoebus	2.00	1.00	.60
186	John Edwards	2.00	1.00	.60
187	Leon Wagner	2.00	1.00	.60
188	Rick Wise	2.00	1.00	.60
189	Red Sox Rookies (*Joe Lahoud, John Thibdeau*)	2.00	1.00	.60
190	Willie Mays	55.00	27.50	16.50
191	Lindy McDaniel	2.00	1.00	.60
192	Jose Pagan	2.00	1.00	.60
193	Don Cardwell	2.00	1.00	.60
194	Ted Uhlaender	2.00	1.00	.60
195	John Odom	2.00	1.00	.60
196	Lum Harris	2.00	1.00	.60
197	Dick Selma	2.00	1.00	.60
198	Willie Smith	2.00	1.00	.60
199	Jim French	2.00	1.00	.60
200	Bob Gibson	15.00	7.50	4.50
201	Russ Snyder	2.00	1.00	.60
202	Don Wilson	2.00	1.00	.60
203	Dave Johnson	2.00	1.00	.60
204	Jack Hiatt	2.00	1.00	.60
205	Rick Reichardt	2.00	1.00	.60
206	Phillies Rookies (Larry Hisle, Barry Lersch)	2.00	1.00	.60
207	Roy Face	2.00	1.00	.60
208a	Donn Clendenon (Expos)	25.00	12.50	7.50
208b	Donn Clendenon (Houston)	2.00	1.00	.60
209	Larry Haney (Photo reversed.)	2.00	1.00	.60
210	Felix Millan	2.00	1.00	.60
211	Galen Cisco	2.00	1.00	.60
212	Tom Tresh	6.00	3.00	1.75
213	Gerry Arrigo	2.00	1.00	.60
214	3rd Series Check List (219-327)	4.00	2.00	1.25
215	Rico Petrocelli	2.00	1.00	.60
216	Don Sutton	8.00	4.00	2.50
217	John Donaldson	2.00	1.00	.60
218	John Roseboro	2.00	1.00	.60
219	*Freddie Patek*	2.00	1.00	.60
220	Sam McDowell	2.00	1.00	.60
221	Art Shamsky	2.00	1.00	.60
222	Duane Josephson	2.00	1.00	.60
223	Tom Dukes	2.00	1.00	.60
224	Angels Rookies (*Bill Harrelson, Steve Kealey*)	2.00	1.00	.60
225	Don Kessinger	2.00	1.00	.60
226	Bruce Howard	2.00	1.00	.60
227	Frank Johnson	2.00	1.00	.60
228	Dave Leonhard	2.00	1.00	.60
229	Don Lock	2.00	1.00	.60
230	Rusty Staub	3.00	1.50	.90
231	Pat Dobson	2.00	1.00	.60
232	Dave Ricketts	2.00	1.00	.60
233	Steve Barber	2.00	1.00	.60
234	Dave Bristol	2.00	1.00	.60
235	Jim Hunter	9.00	4.50	2.75
236	Manny Mota	2.00	1.00	.60
237	*Bobby Cox*	12.00	6.00	3.50
238	Ken Johnson	2.00	1.00	.60
239	Bob Taylor	2.00	1.00	.60
240	Ken Harrelson	2.00	1.00	.60
241	Jim Brewer	2.00	1.00	.60
242	Frank Kostro	2.00	1.00	.60
243	Ron Kline	2.00	1.00	.60
244	Indians Rookies (*Ray Fosse, George Woodson*)	3.50	1.75	1.00
245	Ed Charles	2.00	1.00	.60
246	Joe Coleman	2.00	1.00	.60
247	Gene Oliver	2.00	1.00	.60
248	Bob Priddy	2.00	1.00	.60
249	Ed Spiezio	2.00	1.00	.60
250	Frank Robinson	25.00	12.50	7.50
251	Ron Herbel	2.00	1.00	.60
252	Chuck Cottier	2.00	1.00	.60
253	Jerry Johnson	2.00	1.00	.60
254	Joe Schultz	2.00	1.00	.60
255	Steve Carlton	15.00	7.50	4.50
256	Gates Brown	2.00	1.00	.60
257	Jim Ray	2.00	1.00	.60
258	Jackie Hernandez	2.00	1.00	.60
259	Bill Short	2.00	1.00	.60
260	*Reggie Jackson*	170.00	60.00	40.00
261	Bob Johnson	2.00	1.00	.60
262	Mike Kekich	2.00	1.00	.60
263	Jerry May	2.00	1.00	.60
264	Bill Landis	2.00	1.00	.60
265	Chico Cardenas	2.00	1.00	.60
266	Dodgers Rookies (*Alan Foster, Tom Hutton*)	2.00	1.00	.60
267	Vicente Romo	2.00	1.00	.60
268	Al Spangler	2.00	1.00	.60
269	Al Weis	2.00	1.00	.60
270	Mickey Lolich	2.00	1.00	.60
271	Larry Stahl	2.00	1.00	.60
272	Ed Stroud	2.00	1.00	.60
273	Ron Willis	2.00	1.00	.60
274	Clyde King	2.00	1.00	.60
275	Vic Davalillo	2.00	1.00	.60
276	Gary Wagner	2.00	1.00	.60
277	*Rod Hendricks*	2.00	1.00	.60
278	Gary Geiger	2.00	1.00	.60
279	Roger Nelson	2.00	1.00	.60
280	Alex Johnson	2.00	1.00	.60
281	Ted Kubiak	2.00	1.00	.60
282	Pat Jarvis	2.00	1.00	.60
283	Sandy Alomar	2.00	1.00	.60
284	Expos Rookies (*Jerry Robertson, Mike Wegener*)	2.00	1.00	.60
285	Don Mincher	2.00	1.00	.60
286	*Dock Ellis*	3.00	1.50	.90
287	Jose Tartabull	2.00	1.00	.60
288	Ken Holtzman	2.00	1.00	.60
289	Bart Shirley	2.00	1.00	.60
290	Jim Kaat	3.00	1.50	.90
291	Vern Fuller	2.00	1.00	.60
292	Al Downing	2.00	1.00	.60
293	Dick Dietz	2.00	1.00	.60
294	Jim Lemon	2.00	1.00	.60
295	Tony Perez	10.00	5.00	3.00
296	*Andy Messersmith*	3.00	1.50	.90
297	Deron Johnson	2.00	1.00	.60
298	Dave Nicholson	2.00	1.00	.60
299	Mark Belanger	2.00	1.00	.60
300	Felipe Alou	4.00	2.00	1.25
301	Darrell Brandon	2.00	1.00	.60
302	Jim Pagliaroni	2.00	1.00	.60
303	Cal Koonce	2.00	1.00	.60
304	Padres Rookies (*Bill Davis, Clarence Gaston*)	4.00	2.00	1.25
305	Dick McAuliffe	2.00	1.00	.60
306	Jim Grant	2.00	1.00	.60
307	Gary Kolb	2.00	1.00	.60
308	Wade Blasingame	2.00	1.00	.60
309	Walt Williams	2.00	1.00	.60
310	Tom Haller	2.00	1.00	.60
311	*Sparky Lyle*	6.00	3.00	1.75
312	Lee Elia	2.00	1.00	.60
313	Bill Robinson	2.00	1.00	.60
314	4th Series Check List (328-425)	5.00	2.50	1.50
315	Eddie Fisher	2.00	1.00	.60
316	Hal Lanier	2.00	1.00	.60
317	Bruce Look	2.00	1.00	.60
318	Jack Fisher	2.00	1.00	.60
319	Ken McMullen	2.00	1.00	.60
320	Dal Maxvill	2.00	1.00	.60
321	Jim McAndrew	2.00	1.00	.60
322	Jose Vidal	2.00	1.00	.60
323	Larry Miller	2.00	1.00	.60
324	Tigers Rookies (*Les Cain, Dave Campbell*)	2.00	1.00	.60
325	Jose Cardenal	2.00	1.00	.60
326	Gary Sutherland	2.00	1.00	.60
327	Willie Crawford	2.00	1.00	.60
328	Joe Horlen	2.00	1.00	.60
329	Rick Joseph	2.00	1.00	.60
330	Tony Conigliaro	6.00	3.00	1.75
331	Braves Rookies (*Gil Garrido, Tom House*)	2.00	1.00	.60
332	Fred Talbot	2.00	1.00	.60
333	Ivan Murrell	2.00	1.00	.60
334	Phil Roof	2.00	1.00	.60
335	Bill Mazeroski	10.00	5.00	3.00
336	Jim Roland	2.00	1.00	.60
337	Marty Martinez	2.00	1.00	.60
338	*Del Unser*	2.00	1.00	.60
339	Reds Rookies (Steve Mingori, Jose Pena)	2.00	1.00	.60
340	Dave McNally	2.00	1.00	.60
341	Dave Adlesh	2.00	1.00	.60
342	Bubba Morton	2.00	1.00	.60
343	Dan Frisella	2.00	1.00	.60
344	Tom Matchick	2.00	1.00	.60
345	Frank Linzy	2.00	1.00	.60
346	Wayne Comer	2.00	1.00	.60
347	Randy Hundley	2.00	1.00	.60
348	Steve Hargan	2.00	1.00	.60
349	Dick Williams	2.00	1.00	.60
350	Richie Allen	4.00	2.00	1.25
351	Carroll Sembera	2.00	1.00	.60
352	Paul Schaal	2.00	1.00	.60
353	Jeff Torborg	2.00	1.00	.60
354	Nate Oliver	2.00	1.00	.60
355	Phil Niekro	8.00	4.00	2.50
356	Frank Quilici	2.00	1.00	.60
357	Carl Taylor	2.00	1.00	.60
358	Athletics Rookies (George Lauzerique, Roberto Rodriguez)	2.00	1.00	.60
359	Dick Kelley	2.00	1.00	.60
360	Jim Wynn	2.00	1.00	.60
361	Gary Holman	2.00	1.00	.60
362	Jim Maloney	2.00	1.00	.60
363	Russ Nixon	2.00	1.00	.60
364	Tommie Agee	2.00	1.00	.60
365	Jim Fregosi	2.00	1.00	.60
366	Bo Belinsky	2.00	1.00	.60
367	Lou Johnson	2.00	1.00	.60
368	Vic Roznovsky	2.00	1.00	.60
369	Bob Skinner	2.00	1.00	.60
370	Juan Marichal	8.00	4.00	2.50
371	Sal Bando	2.00	1.00	.60
372	Adolfo Phillips	2.00	1.00	.60
373	Fred Lasher	2.00	1.00	.60
374	Bob Tillman	2.00	1.00	.60
375	Harmon Killebrew	20.00	10.00	6.00
376	Royals Rookies (*Mike Fiore, Jim Rooker*)	2.00	1.00	.60
377	Gary Bell	2.00	1.00	.60
378	Jose Herrera	2.00	1.00	.60
379	Ken Boyer	2.00	1.00	.60
380	Stan Bahnsen	2.00	1.00	.60
381	Ed Kranepool	2.00	1.00	.60
382	Pat Corrales	2.00	1.00	.60
383	Casey Cox	2.00	1.00	.60
384	Larry Shepard	2.00	1.00	.60
385	Orlando Cepeda	10.00	5.00	3.00
386	Jim McGlothlin	2.00	1.00	.60
387	Bobby Klaus	2.00	1.00	.60
388	Tom McCraw	2.00	1.00	.60
389	Dan Coombs	2.00	1.00	.60
390	Bill Freehan	2.00	1.00	.60
391	Ray Culp	2.00	1.00	.60
392	Bob Burda	2.00	1.00	.60
393	Gene Brabender	2.00	1.00	.60
394	Pilots Rookies (*Lou Piniella, Marv Staehle*)	4.00	2.00	1.25
395	Chris Short	2.00	1.00	.60
396	Jim Campanis	2.00	1.00	.60
397	Chuck Dobson	2.00	1.00	.60
398	Tito Francona	2.00	1.00	.60
399	Bob Bailey	2.00	1.00	.60
400	Don Drysdale	15.00	7.50	4.50
401	Jake Gibbs	2.00	1.00	.60
402	Ken Boswell	2.00	1.00	.60
403	Bob Miller	2.00	1.00	.60
404	Cubs Rookies (*Vic LaRose, Gary Ross*)	2.00	1.00	.60
405	Lee May	2.00	1.00	.60
406	Phil Ortega	2.00	1.00	.60
407	Tom Egan	2.00	1.00	.60
408	Nate Colbert	2.00	1.00	.60
409	Bob Moose	2.00	1.00	.60
410	Al Kaline	20.00	10.00	6.00
411	Larry Dierker	2.00	1.00	.60
412	5th Series Check List (426-512) (Mickey Mantle)	17.50	8.75	5.25
413	Roland Sheldon	2.00	1.00	.60
414	Duke Sims	2.00	1.00	.60
415	Ray Washburn	2.00	1.00	.60
416	Willie McCovey (All-Star)	7.00	3.50	2.00
417	Ken Harrelson (All-Star)	2.00	1.00	.60
418	Tommy Helms (All-Star)	2.00	1.00	.60
419	Rod Carew (All-Star)	8.00	4.00	2.50
420	Ron Santo (All-Star)	4.00	2.00	1.25
421	Brooks Robinson (All-Star)	9.00	4.50	2.75
422	Don Kessinger (All-Star)	2.00	1.00	.60
423	Bert Campaneris (All-Star)	2.00	1.00	.60
424	Pete Rose (All-Star)	20.00	10.00	6.00
425	Carl Yastrzemski (All-Star)	13.50	6.75	4.00
426	Curt Flood (All-Star)	3.00	1.50	.90
427	Tony Oliva (All-Star)	3.00	1.50	.90
428	Lou Brock (All-Star)	7.00	3.50	2.00
429	Willie Horton (All-Star)	2.00	1.00	.60
430	Johnny Bench (All-Star)	12.50	6.25	3.75
431	Bill Freehan (All-Star)	2.00	1.00	.60
432	Bob Gibson (All-Star)	8.00	4.00	2.50
433	Denny McLain (All-Star)	3.00	1.50	.90
434	Jerry Koosman (All-Star)	2.00	1.00	.60
435	Sam McDowell (All-Star)	2.00	1.00	.60
436	Gene Alley	2.00	1.00	.60
437	Luis Alcaraz	2.00	1.00	.60
438	Gary Waslewski	2.00	1.00	.60
439	White Sox Rookies (Ed Herrmann, Dan Lazar)	2.00	1.00	.60
440a	Willie McCovey (Last name in white.)	150.00	75.00	45.00
440b	Willie McCovey (Last name in yellow.)	13.50	6.75	4.00
441a	Dennis Higgins (Last name in white.)	60.00	30.00	18.00
441b	Dennis Higgins (Last name in yellow.)	2.00	1.00	.60
442	Ty Cline	2.00	1.00	.60
443	Don Wert	2.00	1.00	.60
444a	Joe Moeller (Last name in white.)	60.00	30.00	18.00
444b	Joe Moeller (Last name in yellow.)	2.00	1.00	.60
445	Bobby Knoop	2.00	1.00	.60
446	Claude Raymond	2.00	1.00	.60
447a	Ralph Houk (Last name in white.)	80.00	40.00	24.00
447b	Ralph Houk (Last name in yellow.)	5.00	2.50	1.50
448	Bob Tolan	2.00	1.00	.60
449	Paul Lindblad	2.00	1.00	.60
450	Billy Williams	13.50	6.75	4.00
451a	Rich Rollins (First name in white.)	60.00	30.00	18.00
451b	Rich Rollins (First name in yellow.)	2.00	1.00	.60
452a	Al Ferrara (First name in white.)	60.00	30.00	18.00
452b	Al Ferrara (First name in yellow.)	2.00	1.00	.60
453	Mike Cuellar	2.00	1.00	.60
454a	Phillies Rookies (*Larry Colton, Don Money*) (Names in white.)	60.00	30.00	18.00
454b	Phillies Rookies (*Larry Colton, Don Money*) (Names in yellow.)	2.00	1.00	.60
455	Sonny Siebert	2.00	1.00	.60
456	Bud Harrelson	2.00	1.00	.60
457	Dalton Jones	2.00	1.00	.60

No.	Player	NM	EX	VG
458	Curt Blefary	2.00	1.00	.60
459	Dave Boswell	2.00	1.00	.60
460	Joe Torre	5.00	2.50	1.50
461a	Mike Epstein (Last name in white.)	60.00	30.00	18.00
461b	Mike Epstein (Last name in yellow.)	2.00	1.00	.60
462	Red Schoendienst	7.00	3.50	2.00
463	Dennis Ribant	2.00	1.00	.60
464a	Dave Marshall (Last name in white.)	60.00	30.00	18.00
464b	Dave Marshall (Last name in yellow.)	2.00	1.00	.60
465	Tommy John	4.00	2.00	1.25
466	John Boccabella	2.00	1.00	.60
467	Tom Reynolds	2.00	1.00	.60
468a	Pirates Rookies (*Bruce Dal Canton, Bob Robertson*) (Names in white.)	60.00	30.00	18.00
468b	Pirates Rookies (*Bruce Dal Canton, Bob Robertson*) (Names in yellow.)			
469	Chico Ruiz	2.00	1.00	.60
470a	Mel Stottlemyre (Last name in white.)	60.00	30.00	18.00
470b	Mel Stottlemyre (Last name in yellow.)	3.00	1.50	.90
471a	Ted Savage (Last name in white.)	60.00	30.00	18.00
471b	Ted Savage (Last name in yellow.)	2.00	1.00	.60
472	Jim Price	2.00	1.00	.60
473a	Jose Arcia (First name in white.)	60.00	30.00	18.00
473b	Jose Arcia (First name in yellow.)	2.00	1.00	.60
474	Tom Murphy	2.00	1.00	.60
475	Tim McCarver	3.00	1.50	.90
476a	Red Sox Rookies (Ken Brett, Gerry Moses) (Names in white.)	60.00	30.00	18.00
476b	Red Sox Rookies (Ken Brett, Gerry Moses) (Names in yellow.)	3.00	1.50	.90
477	Jeff James	2.00	1.00	.60
478	Don Buford	2.00	1.00	.60
479	Richie Scheinblum	2.00	1.00	.60
480	Tom Seaver	30.00	15.00	9.00
481	*Bill Melton*	2.00	1.00	.60
482a	Jim Gosger (First name in white.)	60.00	30.00	18.00
482b	Jim Gosger (First name in yellow.)	2.00	1.00	.60
483	Ted Abernathy	2.00	1.00	.60
484	Joe Gordon	2.00	1.00	.60
485a	Gaylord Perry (Last name in white.)	90.00	45.00	27.50
485b	Gaylord Perry (Last name in yellow.)	8.00	4.00	2.50
486a	Paul Casanova (Last name in white.)	60.00	30.00	18.00
486b	Paul Casanova (Last name in yellow.)	2.00	1.00	.60
487	Denis Menke	2.00	1.00	.60
488	Joe Sparma	2.00	1.00	.60
489	Clete Boyer	3.00	1.50	.90
490	Matty Alou	2.00	1.00	.60
491a	Twins Rookies (*Jerry Crider, George Mitterwald*) (Names in white.)	60.00	30.00	18.00
491b	Twins Rookies (*Jerry Crider, George Mitterwald*) (Names in yellow.)			
492	Tony Cloninger	2.00	1.00	.60
493a	Wes Parker (Last name in white.)	60.00	30.00	18.00
493b	Wes Parker (Last name in yellow.)	2.00	1.00	.60
494	Ken Berry	2.00	1.00	.60
495	Bert Campaneris	2.00	1.00	.60
496	Larry Jaster	2.00	1.00	.60
497	Julian Javier	2.00	1.00	.60
498	Juan Pizarro	2.00	1.00	.60
499	Astros Rookies (Don Bryant, Steve Shea)	2.00	1.00	.60
500a	Mickey Mantle (Last name in white.)	1,750	600.00	375.00
500b	Mickey Mantle (Last name in yellow.)	200.00	90.00	55.00
501a	Tony Gonzalez (First name in white.)	60.00	30.00	18.00
501b	Tony Gonzalez (First name in yellow.)	2.00	1.00	.60
502	Minnie Rojas	2.00	1.00	.60
503	Larry Brown	2.00	1.00	.60
504	6th Series Check List (513-588) (Brooks Robinson)	7.00	3.50	2.00
505a	Bobby Bolin (Last name in white.)	60.00	30.00	18.00
505b	Bobby Bolin (Last name in yellow.)	2.00	1.00	.60
506	Paul Blair	2.00	1.00	.60
507	Cookie Rojas	2.00	1.00	.60
508	Moe Drabowsky	2.00	1.00	.60
509	Manny Sanguillen	2.00	1.00	.60
510	Rod Carew	20.00	10.00	6.00
511a	Diego Segui (First name in white.)	60.00	30.00	18.00
511b	Diego Segui (First name in yellow.)	2.00	1.00	.60
512	Cleon Jones	2.00	1.00	.60
513	Camilo Pascual	2.00	1.00	.60
514	Mike Lum	2.00	1.00	.60
515	Dick Green	2.00	1.00	.60
516	Earl Weaver	9.00	4.50	2.75
517	Mike McCormick	2.00	1.00	.60
518	Fred Whitfield	2.00	1.00	.60
519	Yankees Rookies (*Len Boehmer, Gerry Kenney*)	2.00	1.00	.60
520	Bob Veale	2.00	1.00	.60
521	George Thomas	2.00	1.00	.60
522	Joe Hoerner	2.00	1.00	.60
523	Bob Chance	2.00	1.00	.60
524	Expos Rookies (*Jose Laboy, Floyd Wicker*)	2.00	1.00	.60
525	Earl Wilson	2.00	1.00	.60
526	Hector Torres	2.00	1.00	.60
527	Al Lopez	6.00	3.00	1.75
528	Claude Osteen	2.00	1.00	.60
529	Ed Kirkpatrick	2.00	1.00	.60
530	Cesar Tovar	2.00	1.00	.60
531	Dick Farrell	2.00	1.00	.60
532	Bird Hill Aces (Mike Cuellar, Jim Hardin, Dave McNally, Tom Phoebus)	3.50	1.75	1.00
533	Nolan Ryan	135.00	50.00	30.00
534	Jerry McNertney	2.00	1.00	.60
535	Phil Regan	2.00	1.00	.60
536	Padres Rookies (*Danny Breeden, Dave Roberts*)	2.00	1.00	.60
537	Mike Paul	2.00	1.00	.60
538	Charlie Smith	2.00	1.00	.60
539	Ted Shows How (Mike Epstein, Ted Williams)	13.50	6.75	4.00
540	Curt Flood	3.00	1.50	.90
541	Joe Verbanic	2.00	1.00	.60
542	Bob Aspromonte	2.00	1.00	.60
543	Fred Newman	2.00	1.00	.60
544	Tigers Rookies (*Mike Kilkenny, Ron Woods*)	2.00	1.00	.60
545	Willie Stargell	15.00	7.50	4.50
546	Jim Nash	2.00	1.00	.60
547	Billy Martin	6.00	3.00	1.75
548	Bob Locker	2.00	1.00	.60
549	Ron Brand	2.00	1.00	.60
550	Brooks Robinson	25.00	12.50	7.50
551	Wayne Granger	2.00	1.00	.60
552	Dodgers Rookies (*Ted Sizemore, Bill Sudakis*)	3.00	1.50	.90
553	Ron Davis	2.00	1.00	.60
554	Frank Bertaina	2.00	1.00	.60
555	Jim Hart	2.00	1.00	.60
556	A's Stars (Sal Bando, Bert Campaneris, Danny Cater)	3.00	1.50	.90
557	Frank Fernandez	2.00	1.00	.60
558	*Tom Burgmeier*	2.00	1.00	.60
559	Cards Rookies (*Joe Hague, Jim Hicks*)	2.00	1.00	.60
560	Luis Tiant	2.00	1.00	.60
561	Ron Clark	2.00	1.00	.60
562	*Bob Watson*	4.00	2.00	1.25
563	Marty Pattin	2.00	1.00	.60
564	Gil Hodges	7.00	3.50	2.00
565	Hoyt Wilhelm	8.00	4.00	2.50
566	Ron Hansen	2.00	1.00	.60
567a	Pirates Rookies (*Elvio Jimenez, Jim Shellenback*) (No black outline around title letters.)	45.00	22.50	13.50
567b	Pirates Rookies (*Elvio Jiminez, Jim Shellenback*) (Title letters outlined in black.)	2.00	1.00	.60
568	Cecil Upshaw	2.00	1.00	.60
569	Billy Harris	2.00	1.00	.60
570	Ron Santo	10.00	5.00	3.00
571	Cap Peterson	2.00	1.00	.60
572	Giants Heroes (Juan Marichal, Willie McCovey)	9.00	4.50	2.75
573	Jim Palmer	13.50	6.75	4.00
574	George Scott	2.00	1.00	.60
575	Bill Singer	2.00	1.00	.60
576	Phillies Rookies (*Ron Stone, Bill Wilson*)	2.00	1.00	.60
577	Mike Hegan	2.00	1.00	.60
578	Don Bosch	2.00	1.00	.60
579	*Dave Nelson*	2.00	1.00	.60
580	Jim Northrup	2.00	1.00	.60
581	Gary Nolan	2.00	1.00	.60
582a	7th Series Check List (589-664) (Tony Oliva) (Red circle on back.)	4.50	2.25	1.25
582b	7th Series Check List (589-664) (Tony Oliva) (White circle on back.)	3.00	1.50	.90
583	*Clyde Wright*	2.00	1.00	.60
584	Don Mason	2.00	1.00	.60
585	Ron Swoboda	2.00	1.00	.60
586	Tim Cullen	2.00	1.00	.60
587	*Joe Rudi*	5.00	2.50	1.50
588	Bill White	3.00	1.50	.90
589	Joe Pepitone	6.00	3.00	1.75
590	Rico Carty	3.00	1.50	.90
591	Mike Hedlund	3.00	1.50	.90
592	Padres Rookies (*Rafael Robles, Al Santorini*)	3.00	1.50	.90
593	Don Nottebart	3.00	1.50	.90
594	Dooley Womack	3.00	1.50	.90
595	Lee Maye	3.00	1.50	.90
596	Chuck Hartenstein	3.00	1.50	.90
597	A.L. Rookies (*Larry Burchart, Rollie Fingers, Bob Floyd*)	25.00	12.50	7.50
598	Ruben Amaro	3.00	1.50	.90
599	John Boozer	3.00	1.50	.90
600	Tony Oliva	6.00	3.00	1.75
601	Tug McGraw	4.00	2.00	1.25
602	Cubs Rookies (*Alec Distaso, Jim Qualls, Don Young*)	3.00	1.50	.90
603	Joe Keough	3.00	1.50	.90
604	Bobby Etheridge	3.00	1.50	.90
605	Dick Ellsworth	3.00	1.50	.90
606	Gene Mauch	3.00	1.50	.90
607	Dick Bosman	3.00	1.50	.90
608	Dick Simpson	3.00	1.50	.90
609	Phil Gagliano	3.00	1.50	.90
610	Jim Hardin	3.00	1.50	.90
611	Braves Rookies (*Bob Didier, Walt Hriniak, Gary Neibauer*)	3.00	1.50	.90
612	Jack Aker	3.00	1.50	.90
613	Jim Beauchamp	3.00	1.50	.90
614	Astros Rookies (*Tom Griffin, Skip Guinn*)	3.00	1.50	.90
615	Len Gabrielson	3.00	1.50	.90
616	Don McMahon	3.00	1.50	.90
617	Jesse Gonder	3.00	1.50	.90
618	Ramon Webster	3.00	1.50	.90
619	Royals Rookies (*Bill Butler, Pat Kelly, Juan Rios*)	3.00	1.50	.90
620	Dean Chance	3.00	1.50	.90
621	Bill Voss	3.00	1.50	.90
622	Dan Osinski	3.00	1.50	.90
623	Hank Allen	3.00	1.50	.90
624	N.L. Rookies (*Darrel Chaney, Duffy Dyer, Terry Harmon*)	3.00	1.50	.90
625	Mack Jones	3.00	1.50	.90
626	Gene Michael	3.00	1.50	.90
627	George Stone	3.00	1.50	.90
628	Red Sox Rookies (*Bill Conigliaro, Syd O'Brien, Fred Wenz*)	4.00	2.00	1.25
629	Jack Hamilton	3.00	1.50	.90
630	*Bobby Bonds*	25.00	12.50	7.50
631	John Kennedy	3.00	1.50	.90
632	Jon Warden	3.00	1.50	.90
633	Harry Walker	3.00	1.50	.90
634	Andy Etchebarren	3.00	1.50	.90
635	George Culver	3.00	1.50	.90
636	Woodie Held	3.00	1.50	.90
637	Padres Rookies (*Jerry DaVanon, Clay Kirby, Frank Reberger*)	3.00	1.50	.90
638	Ed Sprague	3.00	1.50	.90
639	Barry Moore	3.00	1.50	.90
640	Fergie Jenkins	12.50	6.25	3.75
641	N.L. Rookies (*Bobby Darwin, Tommy Dean, John Miller*)	3.00	1.50	.90
642	John Hiller	3.00	1.50	.90
643	Billy Cowan	3.00	1.50	.90
644	Chuck Hinton	3.00	1.50	.90
645	George Brunet	3.00	1.50	.90
646	Expos Rookies (*Dan McGinn, Carl Morton*)	3.00	1.50	.90
647	Dave Wickersham	3.00	1.50	.90
648	Bobby Wine	3.00	1.50	.90
649	Al Jackson	3.00	1.50	.90
650	Ted Williams	20.00	10.00	6.00
651	Gus Gil	3.00	1.50	.90
652	Eddie Watt	3.00	1.50	.90
653	*Aurelio Rodriguez* (Photo actually batboy Leonard Garcia.)	6.00	3.00	1.75
654	White Sox Rookies (*Carlos May, Rich Morales, Don Secrist*)	3.50	1.75	1.00
655	Mike Hershberger	3.00	1.50	.90
656	Dan Schneider	3.00	1.50	.90
657	Bobby Murcer	6.00	3.00	1.75
658	A.L. Rookies (*Bill Burbach, Tom Hall, Jim Miles*)	3.00	1.50	.90
659	Johnny Podres	3.00	1.50	.90
660	Reggie Smith	3.00	1.50	.90
661	Jim Merritt	3.00	1.50	.90
662	Royals Rookies (*Dick Drago, Bob Oliver, George Spriggs*)	3.00	1.50	.90
663	Dick Radatz	4.50	2.25	1.25
664	Ron Hunt	13.50	3.00	1.00

1969 Topps Decals

Designed as an insert for 1969 regular issue card packs, these decals are virtually identical in format to the '69 cards. The 48 decals in the set measure 1" x 2-1/2", although they are mounted on white paper backing which measures 1-3/4" x 2-1/8". In March 2001, a hoard consisting of two original 10,000-piece rolls - 833 each of half the players in the set - was sold at auction. The players represented in that find are indicated in these listings with an asterisk.

		NM	EX	VG
Complete Set (48):		350.00	175.00	100.00
Common Player:		4.00	2.00	1.25
(1)	Hank Aaron	25.00	12.50	7.50
(2)	Richie Allen	7.00	3.50	2.00
(3)	Felipe Alou	5.00	2.50	1.50

(4)	Matty Alou	4.00	2.00	1.25
(5)	Luis Aparicio	9.00	4.50	2.75
(6)	Bob Clemente	30.00	15.00	9.00
(7)	Donn Clendenon	4.00	2.00	1.25
(8)	Tommy Davis (*)	4.00	2.00	1.25
(9)	Don Drysdale (*)	10.00	5.00	3.00
(10)	Joe Foy (*)	4.00	2.00	1.25
(11)	Jim Fregosi	4.00	2.00	1.25
(12)	Bob Gibson (*)	10.00	5.00	3.00
(13)	Tony Gonzalez	4.00	2.00	1.25
(14)	Tom Haller	4.00	2.00	1.25
(15)	Ken Harrelson	4.00	2.00	1.25
(16)	Tommy Helms	4.00	2.00	1.25
(17)	Willie Horton (*)	4.00	2.00	1.25
(18)	Frank Howard	4.50	2.25	1.25
(19)	Reggie Jackson (*)	20.00	10.00	6.00
(20)	Fergie Jenkins	9.00	4.50	2.75
(21)	Harmon Killebrew (*)	10.00	5.00	3.00
(22)	Jerry Koosman (*)	4.00	2.00	1.25
(23)	Mickey Mantle	40.00	20.00	12.00
(24)	Willie Mays (*)	20.00	10.00	6.00
(25)	Tim McCarver	4.50	2.25	1.25
(26)	Willie McCovey	10.00	5.00	3.00
(27)	Sam McDowell (*)	4.00	2.00	1.25
(28)	Denny McLain (*)	4.00	2.00	1.25
(29)	Dave McNally (*)	4.00	2.00	1.25
(30)	Don Mincher	4.00	2.00	1.25
(31)	Rick Monday	4.00	2.00	1.25
(32)	Tony Oliva (*)	4.50	2.25	1.25
(33)	Camilo Pascual	4.00	2.00	1.25
(34)	Rick Reichardt (*)	4.00	2.00	1.25
(35)	Frank Robinson (*)	10.00	5.00	3.00
(36)	Pete Rose (*)	20.00	10.00	6.00
(37)	Ron Santo (*)	5.00	2.50	1.50
(38)	Tom Seaver (*)	12.00	6.00	3.50
(39)	Dick Selma (*)	4.00	2.00	1.25
(40)	Chris Short (*)	4.00	2.00	1.25
(41)	Rusty Staub	4.00	2.00	1.25
(42)	Mel Stottlemyre	4.00	2.00	1.25
(43)	Luis Tiant (*)	4.00	2.00	1.25
(44)	Pete Ward	4.00	2.00	1.25
(45)	Hoyt Wilhelm (*)	7.50	3.75	2.25
(46)	Maury Wills (*)	4.00	2.00	1.25
(47)	Jim Wynn	4.00	2.00	1.25
(48)	Carl Yastrzemski (*)	12.00	6.00	3.50

1969 Topps Deckle Edge

PETE ROSE
No. 21 of 33 photos

These 2-1/4" x 3-1/4" inch cards take their name from their borders which have a scalloped effect. Fronts have a black-and-white player photo along with a blue facsimile autograph. Backs have the player's name and the card number in light blue ink in a small box at the bottom of the card. While there are only 33 numbered cards, there are actually 35 possible players; both Jim Wynn and Hoyt Wilhelm cards are found as #11 while cards of Joe Foy and Rusty Staub as #22. Straight-edged proof cards are sometimes found but these were never formally issued; they carry a premium.

		NM	EX	VG
	Complete Set (33):	80.00	40.00	25.00
	Common Player:	1.00	.50	.30
	Proofs: 6-8X			
1	Brooks Robinson	9.00	4.50	2.75
2	Boog Powell	1.50	.70	.45
3	Ken Harrelson	1.00	.50	.30
4	Carl Yastrzemski	9.00	4.50	2.75
5	Jim Fregosi	1.00	.50	.30
6	Luis Aparicio	7.50	3.75	2.25
7	Luis Tiant	1.00	.50	.30
8	Denny McLain	1.00	.50	.30
9	Willie Horton	1.00	.50	.30
10	Bill Freehan	1.00	.50	.30
11a	Hoyt Wilhelm	6.00	3.00	1.75
11b	Jim Wynn	12.00	6.00	3.50
12	Rod Carew	7.50	3.75	2.25
13	Mel Stottlemyre	1.00	.50	.30
14	Rick Monday	1.00	.50	.30
15	Tommy Davis	1.00	.50	.30
16	Frank Howard	1.50	.70	.45
17	Felipe Alou	1.00	.50	.30
18	Don Kessinger	1.00	.50	.30
19	Ron Santo	2.00	1.00	.60
20	Tommy Helms	1.00	.50	.30
21	Pete Rose	15.00	7.50	4.50
22a	Rusty Staub	2.00	1.00	.60
22b	Joe Foy	9.00	4.50	2.75
23	Tom Haller	1.00	.50	.30
24	Maury Wills	1.00	.50	.30
25	Jerry Koosman	1.00	.50	.30
26	Richie Allen	3.00	1.50	.90
27	Roberto Clemente	20.00	10.00	6.00
28	Curt Flood	1.00	.50	.30
29	Bob Gibson	7.50	3.75	2.25
30	Al Ferrara	1.00	.50	.30
31	Willie McCovey	7.50	3.75	2.25
32	Juan Marichal	6.00	3.00	1.75
33	Willie Mays	15.00	7.50	4.50

1969 Topps Stamps

Topps continued to refine its efforts at baseball stamps in 1969 with the release of 240 player stamps, each measuring 1" x 1-7/16". Each stamp has a color photo along with the player's name, position and team. Unlike prior stamp issues, the 1969 stamps have 24 separate albums (one per team). The stamps were issued in strips of 12, many players appearing on two different strips.

		NM	EX	VG
	Complete Sheet Set (24):	200.00	100.00	60.00
	Common Sheet:	5.00	2.50	1.50
	Complete Stamp Album Set (24):	80.00	40.00	20.00
	Single Stamp Album:	3.00	1.50	.90
	Unopened Pack:	50.00		
(1)	Tommie Agee, Sandy Alomar, Jose Cardenal, Dean Chance, Joe Foy, Jim Grant, Don Kessinger, Mickey Mantle, Jerry May, Bob Rodgers, Cookie Rojas, Gary Sutherland	55.00	27.50	16.50
(2)	Jesus Alou, Mike Andrews, Larry Brown, Moe Drabowsky, Alex Johnson, Lew Krausse, Jim Lefebvre, Dal Maxvill, John Odom, Claude Osteen, Rick Reichardt, Luis Tiant	5.00	2.50	1.50
(3)	Hank Aaron, Matty Alou, Max Alvis, Nelson Briles, Eddie Fisher, Bud Harrelson, Willie Horton, Randy Hundley, Larry Jaster, Jim Kaat, Gary Peters, Pete Ward	20.00	10.00	6.00
(4)	Don Buford, John Callison, Tommy Davis, Jackie Hernandez, Fergie Jenkins, Lee May, Denny McLain, Bob Oliver, Roberto Pena, Tony Perez, Joe Torre, Tom Tresh	7.50	3.75	2.25
(5)	Jim Bunning, Dean Chance, Joe Foy, Sonny Jackson, Don Kessinger, Rick Monday, Gaylord Perry, Roger Repoz, Cookie Rojas, Mel Stottlemyre, Leon Wagner, Jim Wynn	7.50	3.75	2.25
(6)	Felipe Alou, Gerry Arrigo, Bob Aspromonte, Gary Bell, Clay Dalrymple, Jim Fregosi, Tony Gonzalez, Duane Josephson, Dick McAuliffe, Tony Oliva, Brooks Robinson, Willie Stargell	20.00	10.00	6.00
(7)	Steve Barber, Donn Clendenon, Joe Coleman, Vic Davalillo, Russ Gibson, Jerry Grote, Tom Haller, Andy Kosco, Willie McCovey, Don Mincher, Joe Morgan, Don Wilson	7.50	3.75	2.25
(8)	George Brunet, Don Buford, John Callison, Danny Cater, Tommy Davis, Willie Davis, John Edwards, Jim Hart, Mickey Lolich, Willie Mays, Roberto Pena, Mickey Stanley	25.00	12.50	7.50
(9)	Ernie Banks, Glenn Beckert, Ken Berry, Horace Clarke, Roberto Clemente, Larry Dierker, Len Gabrielson, Jake Gibbs, Jerry Koosman, Sam McDowell, Tom Satriano, Bill Singer	25.00	12.50	7.50
(10)	Gene Alley, Lou Brock, Larry Brown, Moe Drabowsky, Frank Howard, Tommie John, Roger Nelson, Claude Osteen, Phil Regan, Rick Reichardt, Tony Taylor, Roy White	7.50	3.75	2.25
(11)	Bob Allison, John Bateman, Don Drysdale, Dave Johnson, Harmon Killebrew, Jim Maloney, Bill Mazeroski, Gerry McNertney, Ron Perranoski, Rico Petrocelli, Pete Rose, Billy Williams	35.00	17.50	10.50
(12)	Bernie Allen (Senators), Jose Arcia, Stan Bahnsen, Sal Bando, Jim Davenport, Tito Francona, Dick Green, Ron Hunt, Mack Jones, Vada Pinson, George Scott, Don Wert	5.00	2.50	1.50
(13)	Gerry Arrigo, Bob Aspromonte, Joe Azcue, Curt Blefary, Orlando Cepeda, Bill Freehan, Jim Fregosi, Dave Giusti, Duane Josephson, Tim McCarver, Jose Santiago, Bob Tolan	7.50	3.75	2.25
(14)	Jerry Adair, Johnny Bench, Clete Boyer, John Briggs, Bert Campaneris, Woody Fryman, Ron Kline, Bobby Knoop, Ken McMullen, Adolfo Phillips, John Roseboro, Tom Seaver	20.00	10.00	6.00
(15)	Norm Cash, Ron Fairly, Bob Gibson, Bill Hands, Cleon Jones, Al Kaline, Paul Schaal, Mike Shannon, Duke Sims, Reggie Smith, Steve Whitaker, Carl Yastrzemski	15.00	7.50	4.50
(16)	Steve Barber, Paul Casanova, Dick Dietz, Russ Gibson, Jerry Grote, Tom Haller, Ed Kranepool, Juan Marichal, Denis Menke, Jim Nash, Bill Robinson, Frank Robinson	15.00	7.50	4.50
(17)	Bobby Bolin, Ollie Brown, Rod Carew, Mike Epstein, Bud Harrelson, Larry Jaster, Dave McNally, Willie Norton, Milt Pappas, Gary Peters, Paul Popovich, Stan Williams	7.50	3.75	2.25
(18)	Ted Abernathy, Bob Allison, Ed Brinkman, Don Drysdale, Jim Hardin, Julian Javier, Hal Lanier, Jim McGlothlin, Ron Perranoski, Rich Rollins, Ron Santo, Billy Williams	15.00	7.50	4.50
(19)	Richie Allen, Luis Aparicio, Wally Bunker, Curt Flood, Ken Harrelson, Jim Hunter, Denver Lemaster, Felix Millan, Jim Northrop (Northrup), Art Shamsky, Larry Stahl, Ted Uhlaender	7.50	3.75	2.25
(20)	Bob Bailey, Johnny Bench, Woody Fryman, Jim Hannan, Ron Kline, Al McBean, Camilo Pascual, Joe Pepitone, Doug Rader, Ron Reed, John Roseboro, Sonny Siebert	7.50	3.75	2.25
(21)	Jack Aker, Tommy Harper, Tommy Helms, Dennis Higgins, Jim Hunter, Don Lock, Felix Millan, Jim Northrop (Northrup), Larry Stahl, Don Sutton, Zoilo Versalles	7.50	3.75	2.25
(22)	Norm Cash, Ed Charles, Joe Horlen, Pat Jarvis, Jim Lonborg, Manny Mota, Boog Powell, Dick Selma, Mike Shannon, Duke Sims, Steve Whitaker, Hoyt Wilhelm	7.50	3.75	2.25
(23)	Bernie Allen (Senator), Ray Culp, Al Ferrara, Tito Francona, Dick Green, Ron Hunt, Ray Oyler, Tom Phoebus, Rusty Staub, Bob Veale, Maury Wills, Wilbur Wood	5.00	2.50	1.50
(24)	Ernie Banks, Mark Belanger, Steve Blass, Horace Clarke, Bob Clemente, Larry Dierker, Dave Duncan, Chico Salmon, Chris Short, Ron Swoboda, Cesar Tovar, Rick Wise	20.00	10.00	6.00

1969 Topps Super

JOSE CARDENAL
Cleveland Indians   Outfield
No. 13 of 66 Super Baseball Cards

These 2-1/4" x 3-1/4" cards are not the bigger "Super" cards which would be seen in following years.

Rather, what enabled Topps to dub them "Super Baseball Cards" is their high-gloss finish which enhances the bright color photograph used on their fronts. The only other design element on the front is a facsimile autograph. The backs contain a box at the the bottom which carries the player's name, team, position, a copyright line and the card number. Another unusual feature is that the cards have rounded corners, although square-cornered proof cards are also known, completely printed on front and back.

	NM	EX	VG
Complete Set (66):	6,000	3,000	1,800
Common Player:	20.00	10.00	6.00
Proofs: 2-3X			
1 Dave McNally	20.00	10.00	6.00
2 Frank Robinson	175.00	85.00	50.00
3 Brooks Robinson	175.00	85.00	50.00
4 Ken Harrelson	20.00	10.00	6.00
5 Carl Yastrzemski	250.00	125.00	75.00
6 Ray Culp	20.00	10.00	6.00
7 James Fregosi	20.00	10.00	6.00
8 Rick Reichardt	20.00	10.00	6.00
9 Vic Davalillo	20.00	10.00	6.00
10 Luis Aparicio	100.00	50.00	30.00
11 Pete Ward	20.00	10.00	6.00
12 Joe Horlen	20.00	10.00	6.00
13 Luis Tiant	20.00	10.00	6.00
14 Sam McDowell	20.00	10.00	6.00
15 Jose Cardenal	20.00	10.00	6.00
16 Willie Horton	20.00	10.00	6.00
17 Denny McLain	20.00	10.00	6.00
18 Bill Freehan	20.00	10.00	6.00
19 Harmon Killebrew	175.00	85.00	50.00
20 Tony Oliva	20.00	10.00	6.00
21 Dean Chance	20.00	10.00	6.00
22 Joe Foy	20.00	10.00	6.00
23 Roger Nelson	20.00	10.00	6.00
24 Mickey Mantle	1,100	550.00	350.00
25 Mel Stottlemyre	20.00	10.00	6.00
26 Roy White	20.00	10.00	6.00
27 Rick Monday	20.00	10.00	6.00
28 Reggie Jackson	400.00	200.00	120.00
29 Bert Campaneris	20.00	10.00	6.00
30 Frank Howard	20.00	10.00	6.00
31 Camilo Pascual	20.00	10.00	6.00
32 Tommy Davis	20.00	10.00	6.00
33 Don Mincher	20.00	10.00	6.00
34 Henry Aaron	400.00	200.00	120.00
35 Felipe Alou	20.00	10.00	6.00
36 Joe Torre	50.00	25.00	15.00
37 Fergie Jenkins	100.00	50.00	30.00
38 Ronald Santo	35.00	17.50	10.00
39 Billy Williams	100.00	50.00	30.00
40 Tommy Helms	20.00	10.00	6.00
41 Pete Rose	400.00	200.00	120.00
42 Joe Morgan	100.00	50.00	30.00
43 Jim Wynn	20.00	10.00	6.00
44 Curt Blefary	20.00	10.00	6.00
45 Willie Davis	20.00	10.00	6.00
46 Don Drysdale	135.00	65.00	40.00
47 Tom Haller	20.00	10.00	6.00
48 Rusty Staub	35.00	17.50	10.00
49 Maurice Wills	20.00	10.00	6.00
50 Cleon Jones	20.00	10.00	6.00
51 Jerry Koosman	20.00	10.00	6.00
52 Tom Seaver	175.00	87.00	52.00
53 Rich Allen	45.00	22.50	13.50
54 Chris Short	20.00	10.00	6.00
55 Cookie Rojas	20.00	10.00	6.00
56 Mateo Alou	20.00	10.00	6.00
57 Steve Blass	20.00	10.00	6.00
58 Roberto Clemente	500.00	250.00	150.00
59 Curt Flood	20.00	10.00	6.00
60 Bob Gibson	125.00	65.00	35.00
61 Tim McCarver	35.00	17.50	10.00
62 Dick Selma	20.00	10.00	6.00
63 Ollie Brown	20.00	10.00	6.00
64 Juan Marichal	100.00	50.00	30.00
65 Willie Mays	400.00	200.00	120.00
66 Willie McCovey	120.00	60.00	36.00

1969 Topps Team Posters

Picking up where the 1968 posters left off, the 1969 poster is larger at about 12" x 20". The posters each have a team focus with a large pennant carrying the team name, along with nine or ten photos of players. Each of the photos has a facsimile autograph. The size of posters meant they had to be folded to fit

in their packages. These original folds are not considered when grading, unless the paper has split on those seams.

	NM	EX	VG
Complete Set (24):	2,250	1,125	675.00
Common Poster:	55.00	27.50	16.00
Unopened Pack:	190.00		
1 Detroit Tigers (Norm Cash, Bill Freehan, Willie Horton, Al Kaline, Mickey Lolich, Dick McAuliffe, Denny McLain, Jim Northrup, Mickey Stanley, Don Wert, Earl Wilson)	125.00	65.00	35.00
2 Atlanta Braves (Hank Aaron, Felipe Alou, Clete Boyer, Rico Carty, Tito Francona, Sonny Jackson, Pat Jarvis, Felix Millan, Phil Niekro, Milt Pappas, Joe Torre)	90.00	45.00	27.00
3 Boston Red Sox (Mike Andrews, Tony Conigliaro, Ray Culp, Russ Gibson, Ken Harrelson, Jim Lonborg, Rico Petrocelli, Jose Santiago, George Scott, Reggie Smith, Carl Yastrzemski)	100.00	50.00	30.00
4 Chicago Cubs (Ernie Banks, Glenn Beckert, Bill Hands, Jim Hickman, Ken Holtzman, Randy Hundley, Fergie Jenkins, Don Kessinger, Adolfo Phillips, Ron Santo, Billy Williams)	90.00	45.00	27.00
5 Baltimore Orioles (Mark Belanger, Paul Blair, Don Buford, Andy Etchebarren, Jim Hardin, Dave Johnson, Dave McNally, Tom Phoebus, Boog Powell, Brooks Robinson, Frank Robinson)	80.00	40.00	24.00
6 Houston Astros (Curt Blefary, Donn Clendenon, Larry Dierker, John Edwards, Denny Lemaster, Denis Menke, Norm Miller, Joe Morgan, Doug Rader, Don Wilson, Jim Wynn)	55.00	27.50	16.00
7 Kansas City Royals (Jerry Adair, Wally Bunker, Mike Fiore, Joe Foy, Jackie Hernandez, Pat Kelly, Dave Morehead, Roger Nelson, Dave Nicholson, Eliseo Rodriguez, Steve Whitaker)	55.00	27.50	16.00
8 Philadelphia Phillies (Richie Allen, Johnny Callison, Woody Fryman, Larry Hisle, Don Money, Cookie Rojas, Mike Ryan, Chris Short, Tony Taylor, Bill White, Rick Wise)	60.00	30.00	18.00
9 Seattle Pilots (Jack Aker, Steve Barber, Gary Bell, Tommy Davis, Jim Gosger, Tommy Harper, Gerry McNertney, Don Mincher, Ray Oyler, Rich Rollins, Chico Salmon)	150.00	75.00	45.00
10 Montreal Expos (Bob Bailey, John Bateman, Jack Billingham, Jim Grant, Larry Jaster, Mack Jones, Manny Mota, Rusty Staub, Gary Sutherland, Jim Williams, Maury Wills)	50.00	25.00	15.00
11 Chicago White Sox (Sandy Alomar, Luis Aparicio, Ken Berry, Buddy Bradford, Joe Horlen, Tommy John, Duane Josephson, Tom McCraw, Bill Melton, Pete Ward, Wilbur Wood)	55.00	27.50	16.00
12 San Diego Padres (Jose Arcia, Danny Breeden, Ollie Brown, Bill Davis, Ron Davis, Tony Gonzalez, Dick Kelley, Al McBean, Roberto Pena, Dick Selma, Ed Spiezio)	55.00	27.50	16.00
13 Cleveland Indians (Max Alvis, Joe Azcue, Jose Cardenal, Vern Fuller, Lou Johnson, Sam McDowell, Sonny Siebert, Duke Sims, Russ Snyder, Luis Tiant, Zoilo Versalles)	75.00	37.00	22.00
14 San Francisco Giants (Bobby Bolin, Jim Davenport, Dick Dietz, Jim Hart, Ron Hunt, Hal Lanier, Juan Marichal, Willie Mays, Willie McCovey, Gaylord Perry, Charlie Smith)	125.00	65.00	35.00
15 Minnesota Twins (Bob Allison, Chico Cardenas, Rod Carew, Dean Chance, Jim Kaat, Harmon Killebrew, Tony Oliva, Jim Perry, John Roseboro, Cesar Tovar, Ted Uhlaender)	100.00	50.00	30.00
16 Pittsburgh Pirates (Gene Alley, Matty Alou, Steve Blass, Jim Bunning, Bob Clemente, Rich Hebner, Jerry May, Bill Mazeroski, Bob Robertson, Willie Stargell, Bob Veale)	135.00	65.00	40.00
17 California Angels (Ruben Amaro, George Brunet, Bob Chance, Vic Davalillo, Jim Fregosi, Bobby Knoop, Jim McGlothlin, Rick Reichardt, Roger Repoz, Bob Rodgers, Hoyt Wilhelm)	60.00	30.00	18.00
18 St. Louis Cardinals (Nelson Briles, Lou Brock, Orlando Cepeda, Curt Flood, Bob Gibson, Julian Javier, Dal Maxvill, Tim McCarver, Vada Pinson, Mike Shannon, Ray Washburn)	75.00	37.50	22.00
19 New York Yankees (Stan Bahnsen, Horace Clarke, Bobby Cox, Jake Gibbs, Mickey Mantle, Joe Pepitone, Fritz Peterson, Bill Robinson, Mel Stottlemyre, Tom Tresh, Roy White)	165.00	82.00	49.00
20 Cincinnati Reds (Gerry Arrigo, Johnny Bench, Tommy Helms, Alex Johnson, Jim Maloney, Lee May, Gary Nolan, Tony Perez, Pete Rose, Bob Tolan, Woody Woodward)	110.00	55.00	33.00
21 Oakland Athletics (Sal Bando, Bert Campaneris, Danny Cater, Dick Green, Mike Hershberger, Jim Hunter, Reggie Jackson, Rick Monday, Jim Nash, John Odom, Jim Pagliaroni)	100.00	50.00	30.00
22 Los Angeles Dodgers (Willie Crawford, Willie Davis, Don Drysdale, Ron Fairly, Tom Haller, Andy Kosco, Jim Lefebvre, Claude Osteen, Paul Popovich, Bill Singer, Bill Sudakis)	80.00	40.00	24.00
23 Washington Senators (Bernie Allen, Brant Alyea, Ed Brinkman, Paul Casanova, Joe Coleman, Mike Epstein, Jim Hannan, Frank Howard, Ken McMullen, Camilo Pascual, Del Unser)	80.00	40.00	24.00
24 New York Mets (Tommie Agee, Ken Boswell, Ed Charles, Jerry Grote, Bud Harrelson, Cleon Jones, Jerry Koosman, Jim McAndrew, Tom Seaver, Ron Swoboda)	150.00	75.00	45.00

1969 Topps 4-On-1 Mini Stickers

Another in the long line of Topps test issues, the 4-on-1s are 2-1/2" x 3-1/2" cards with blank backs featuring a quartet of miniature stickers in the design of the same cards from the 1969 Topps regular set. There are 25 different cards, for a total of 100 different stickers. As they are not common, Mint cards bring fairly strong prices on today's market. As the set was drawn from the 3rd Series of the regular cards, it includes some rookie stickers and World Series highlight stickers.

	NM	EX	VG
Complete Set (25):	2,250	1,125	675.00
Common 4-in-1:	50.00	25.00	15.00
Unopened Pack:	375.00		
(1) Jerry Adair, Willie Mays, Johnny Morris, Don Wilson	400.00	200.00	120.00
(2) Tommie Aaron, Jim Britton, Donn Clendenon, Woody Woodward	50.00	25.00	15.00
(3) Tommy Davis, Don Pavletich, Vada Pinson, World Series Game 4 (Lou Brock)	75.00	37.50	22.00
(4) Max Alvis, Glenn Beckert, Ron Fairly, Rick Wise	50.00	25.00	15.00
(5) Johnny Callison, Jim French, Lum Harris, Dick Selma	50.00	25.00	15.00
(6) Bob Gibson, Larry Haney, Rick Reichardt, World Series Game 3 (Tim McCarver)	125.00	65.00	35.00

		NM	EX	VG
(7)	Wally Bunker, Don Cardwell, Joe Gibbon, Astros Rookies (Gilsen, McFadden)	50.00	25.00	15.00
(8)	Ollie Brown, Jim Bunning, Andy Kosco, Ron Reed	50.00	25.00	15.00
(9)	Bill Dillman, Jim Lefebvre, John Purdin, John Roseboro	50.00	25.00	15.00
(10)	Bill Hands, Chuck Harrison, Lindy McDaniel, Felix Millan	50.00	25.00	15.00
(11)	Jack Hiatt, Dave Johnson, Mel Nelson, Tommie Sisk	50.00	25.00	15.00
(12)	Clay Dalrymple, Leo Durocher, John Odom, Wilbur Wood	50.00	25.00	15.00
(13)	Hank Bauer, Kevin Collins, Ray Oyler, Russ Snyder	50.00	25.00	15.00
(14)	Gerry Arrigo, Jim Perry, Red Sox Rookies (Lahoud, Thibodeau), World Series Game 7 (Mickey Lolich)	50.00	25.00	15.00
(15)	Bill McCool, Roberto Pena, Doug Rader, World Series Game 2 (Willie Horton)	75.00	37.50	22.00
(16)	Ed Brinkman, Roy Face, Willie Horton, Bob Rodgers	50.00	25.00	15.00
(17)	Dave Baldwin, J.C. Martin, Dave May, Ray Sadecki	50.00	25.00	15.00
(18)	Jose Pagan, Tom Phoebus, Mike Shannon, World Series Game 1 (Bob Gibson)	50.00	25.00	15.00
(19)	Pete Rose, Lee Stange, Don Sutton, Ted Uhlaender	500.00	250.00	150.00
(20)	Joe Grzenda, Frank Howard, Dick Tracewski, Jim Weaver	50.00	25.00	15.00
(21)	Joe Azcue, Grant Jackson, Denny McLain, White Sox Rookies (Christman, Nyman)	50.00	25.00	15.00
(22)	John Edwards, Jim Fairey, Phillies Rookies, Stan Williams	50.00	25.00	15.00
(23)	John Bateman, Willie Smith, Leon Wagner, World Series Summary	50.00	25.00	15.00
(24)	Chris Cannizzaro, Bob Hendley, World Series Game 5 (Al Kaline), Yankees Rookies (Closter, Cumberland)	50.00	25.00	15.00
(25)	Joe Nossek, Rico Petrocelli, Carl Yastrzemski, Cardinals Rookies (Huntz, Torrez)	350.00	175.00	105.00

1969 Topps Bowie Kuhn

 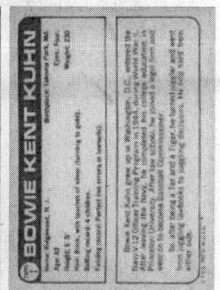

Following Kuhn's election as Commissioner in February 1969, Topps produced this special card, presumably for his personal use. In standard 2-1/2" x 3-1/2" format, but printed on thinner than usual card stock, the front has a photo of Kuhn's face composited with the drawing of a crowned baseball player sitting on top of the world. The horizontal back has a few personal data and a career summary.

		NM	EX	VG
1	Bowie Kuhn	90.00	45.00	27.50

1970 Topps

 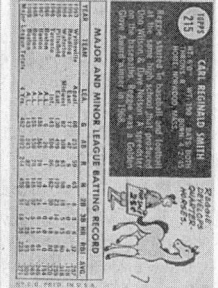

Topps established another set size record by coming out with 720 cards in 1970. The 2-1/2" x 3-1/2" cards have a color photo with a thin white frame. The photos have the player's team overprinted at the top, while the player's name in script and his position are at the bottom. A gray border surrounds the front. Card backs follow the normal design pattern, although they are more readable than some issues of the past. Team cards returned and were joined with many of the usual specialty cards. The World Series highlights were joined by cards with playoff highlights. Statistical leaders and All-Stars are also included in the set. High-numbered cards provide the most expensive cards in the set.

		NM	EX	VG
	Complete Set (720):	2,400	1,200	725.00
	Common Player (1-546):	1.50	.75	.45
	Common Player (547-633):	4.00	2.00	1.00
	Common Player (634-720):	8.00	4.00	2.25
1	World Champions (Mets team.)	25.00	12.50	7.50
2	Diego Segui	1.50	.75	.45
3	Darrel Chaney	1.50	.75	.45
4	Tom Egan	1.50	.75	.45
5	Wes Parker	1.50	.75	.45
6	Grant Jackson	1.50	.75	.45
7	Indians Rookies (*Gary Boyd, Russ Nagelson*)	1.50	.75	.45
8	Jose Martinez	1.50	.75	.45
9	1st Series Check List (1-132)	8.00	4.00	2.50
10	Carl Yastrzemski	25.00	12.50	7.50
11	Nate Colbert	1.50	.75	.45
12	John Hiller	1.50	.75	.45
13	Jack Hiatt	1.50	.75	.45
14	Hank Allen	1.50	.75	.45
15	Larry Dierker	1.50	.75	.45
16	Charlie Metro	1.50	.75	.45
17	Hoyt Wilhelm	6.00	3.00	1.75
18	Carlos May	1.50	.75	.45
19	John Boccabella	1.50	.75	.45
20	Dave McNally	1.50	.75	.45
21	Athletics Rookies (*Vida Blue, Gene Tenace*)	8.00	4.00	2.50
22	Ray Washburn	1.50	.75	.45
23	Bill Robinson	1.50	.75	.45
24	Dick Selma	1.50	.75	.45
25	Cesar Tovar	1.50	.75	.45
26	Tug McGraw	1.50	.75	.45
27	Chuck Hinton	1.50	.75	.45
28	Billy Wilson	1.50	.75	.45
29	Sandy Alomar	1.50	.75	.45
30	Matty Alou	1.50	.75	.45
31	Marty Pattin	1.50	.75	.45
32	Harry Walker	1.50	.75	.45
33	Don Wert	1.50	.75	.45
34	Willie Crawford	1.50	.75	.45
35	Joe Horlen	1.50	.75	.45
36	Reds Rookies (*Danny Breeden, Bernie Carbo*)	1.50	.75	.45
37	Dick Drago	1.50	.75	.45
38	Mack Jones	1.50	.75	.45
39	Mike Nagy	1.50	.75	.45
40	Rich Allen	3.00	1.50	.90
41	George Lauzerique	1.50	.75	.45
42	Tito Fuentes	1.50	.75	.45
43	Jack Aker	1.50	.75	.45
44	Roberto Pena	1.50	.75	.45
45	Dave Johnson	1.50	.75	.45
46	Ken Rudolph	1.50	.75	.45
47	Bob Miller	1.50	.75	.45
48	Gill Garrido (Gil)	1.50	.75	.45
49	Tim Cullen	1.50	.75	.45
50	Tommie Agee	1.50	.75	.45
51	Bob Christian	1.50	.75	.45
52	Bruce Dal Canton	1.50	.75	.45
53	John Kennedy	1.50	.75	.45
54	Jeff Torborg	1.50	.75	.45
55	John Odom	1.50	.75	.45
56	Phillies Rookies (*Joe Lis, Scott Reid*)	1.50	.75	.45
57	Pat Kelly	1.50	.75	.45
58	Dave Marshall	1.50	.75	.45
59	Dick Ellsworth	1.50	.75	.45
60	Jim Wynn	1.50	.75	.45
61	N.L. Batting Leaders (Roberto Clemente, Cleon Jones, Pete Rose)	20.00	10.00	6.00
62	A.L. Batting Leaders (Rod Carew, Tony Oliva, Reggie Smith)	6.00	3.00	1.75
63	N.L. RBI Leaders (Willie McCovey, Tony Perez, Ron Santo)	5.00	2.50	1.50
64	A.L. RBI Leaders (Reggie Jackson, Harmon Killebrew, Boog Powell)	10.00	5.00	3.00
65	N.L. Home Run Leaders (Hank Aaron, Lee May, Willie McCovey)	10.00	5.00	3.00
66	A.L. Home Run Leaders (Frank Howard, Reggie Jackson, Harmon Killebrew)	8.00	4.00	2.50
67	N.L. ERA Leaders (Steve Carlton, Bob Gibson, Juan Marichal)	8.00	4.00	2.50
68	A.L. ERA Leaders (Dick Bosman, Mike Cuellar, Jim Palmer)	4.00	2.00	1.25
69	N.L. Pitching Leaders (Fergie Jenkins, Juan Marichal, Phil Niekro, Tom Seaver)	10.00	5.00	3.00
70	A.L. Pitching Leaders (Dave Boswell, Mike Cuellar, Dennis McLain, Dave McNally, Jim Perry, Mel Stottlemyre)	4.00	2.00	1.25
71	N.L. Strikeout Leaders (Bob Gibson, Fergie Jenkins, Bill Singer)	6.00	3.00	1.75
72	A.L. Strikeout Leaders (Mickey Lolich, Sam McDowell, Andy Messersmith)	4.00	2.00	1.25
73	Wayne Granger	1.50	.75	.45

		NM	EX	VG
74	Angels Rookies (*Greg Washburn, Wally Wolf*)	1.50	.75	.45
75	Jim Kaat	1.50	.75	.45
76	Carl Taylor	1.50	.75	.45
77	Frank Linzy	1.50	.75	.45
78	Joe Lahoud	1.50	.75	.45
79	Clay Kirby	1.50	.75	.45
80	Don Kessinger	1.50	.75	.45
81	Dave May	1.50	.75	.45
82	Frank Fernandez	1.50	.75	.45
83	Don Cardwell	1.50	.75	.45
84	Paul Casanova	1.50	.75	.45
85	Max Alvis	1.50	.75	.45
86	Lum Harris	1.50	.75	.45
87	Steve Renko	1.50	.75	.45
88	Pilots Rookies (*Dick Baney, Miguel Fuentes*)	1.50	.75	.45
89	Juan Rios	1.50	.75	.45
90	Tim McCarver	3.00	1.50	.90
91	Rich Morales	1.50	.75	.45
92	George Culver	1.50	.75	.45
93	Rick Renick	1.50	.75	.45
94	Fred Patek	1.50	.75	.45
95	Earl Wilson	1.50	.75	.45
96	Cards Rookies (*Leron Lee, Jerry Reuss*)	3.00	1.50	.90
97	Joe Moeller	1.50	.75	.45
98	Gates Brown	1.50	.75	.45
99	Bobby Pfeil	1.50	.75	.45
100	Mel Stottlemyre	1.50	.75	.45
101	Bobby Floyd	1.50	.75	.45
102	Joe Rudi	1.50	.75	.45
103	Frank Reberger	1.50	.75	.45
104	Gerry Moses	1.50	.75	.45
105	Tony Gonzalez	1.50	.75	.45
106	Darold Knowles	1.50	.75	.45
107	Bobby Etheridge	1.50	.75	.45
108	Tom Burgmeier	1.50	.75	.45
109	Expos Rookies (*Garry Jestadt, Carl Morton*)	1.50	.75	.45
110	Bob Moose	1.50	.75	.45
111	Mike Hegan	1.50	.75	.45
112	Dave Nelson	1.50	.75	.45
113	Jim Ray	1.50	.75	.45
114	Gene Michael	1.50	.75	.45
115	Alex Johnson	1.50	.75	.45
116	Sparky Lyle	1.50	.75	.45
117	Don Young	1.50	.75	.45
118	George Mitterwald	1.50	.75	.45
119	Chuck Taylor	1.50	.75	.45
120	Sal Bando	1.50	.75	.45
121	Orioles Rookies (*Fred Beene, Terry Crowley*)	1.50	.75	.45
122	George Stone	1.50	.75	.45
123	Don Gutteridge	1.50	.75	.45
124	Larry Jaster	1.50	.75	.45
125	Deron Johnson	1.50	.75	.45
126	Marty Martinez	1.50	.75	.45
127	Joe Coleman	1.50	.75	.45
128a	2nd Series Check List (133-263) (226 is R Perranoski)	5.00	2.50	1.50
128b	2nd Series Check List (133-263) (226 is R. Perranoski)	5.00	2.50	1.50
129	Jimmie Price	1.50	.75	.45
130	Ollie Brown	1.50	.75	.45
131	Dodgers Rookies (*Ray Lamb, Bob Stinson*)	1.50	.75	.45
132	Jim McGlothlin	1.50	.75	.45
133	Clay Carroll	1.50	.75	.45
134	Danny Walton	1.50	.75	.45
135	Dick Dietz	1.50	.75	.45
136	Steve Hargan	1.50	.75	.45
137	Art Shamsky	1.50	.75	.45
138	Joe Foy	1.50	.75	.45
139	Rich Nye	1.50	.75	.45
140	Reggie Jackson	40.00	20.00	12.00
141	Pirates Rookies (*Dave Cash, Johnny Jeter*)	1.50	.75	.45
142	Fritz Peterson	1.50	.75	.45
143	Phil Gagliano	1.50	.75	.45
144	Ray Culp	1.50	.75	.45
145	Rico Carty	1.50	.75	.45
146	Danny Murphy	1.50	.75	.45
147	Angel Hermoso	1.50	.75	.45
148	Earl Weaver	4.00	2.00	1.25
149	Billy Champion	1.50	.75	.45
150	Harmon Killebrew	10.00	5.00	3.00
151	Dave Roberts	1.50	.75	.45
152	Ike Brown	1.50	.75	.45
153	Gary Gentry	1.50	.75	.45
154	Senators Rookies (*Jan Dukes, Jim Miles*)	1.50	.75	.45
155	Denis Menke	1.50	.75	.45
156	Eddie Fisher	1.50	.75	.45
157	Manny Mota	1.50	.75	.45
158	Jerry McNertney	1.50	.75	.45
159	Tommy Helms	1.50	.75	.45
160	Phil Niekro	6.00	3.00	1.75
161	Richie Scheinblum	1.50	.75	.45
162	Jerry Johnson	1.50	.75	.45
163	Syd O'Brien	1.50	.75	.45
164	Ty Cline	1.50	.75	.45
165	Ed Kirkpatrick	1.50	.75	.45
166	Al Oliver	2.00	1.00	.60
167	Bill Burbach	1.50	.75	.45
168	Dave Watkins	1.50	.75	.45
169	Tom Hall	1.50	.75	.45
170	Billy Williams	8.00	4.00	2.50
171	Jim Nash	1.50	.75	.45
172	Braves Rookies (*Ralph Garr, Garry Hill*)	2.00	1.00	.60
173	Jim Hicks	1.50	.75	.45
174	Ted Sizemore	1.50	.75	.45
175	Dick Bosman	1.50	.75	.45
176	Jim Hart	1.50	.75	.45
177	Jim Northrup	1.50	.75	.45
178	Denny Lemaster	1.50	.75	.45
179	Ivan Murrell	1.50	.75	.45

180	Tommy John	2.00	1.00	.60
181	Sparky Anderson	6.00	3.00	1.75
182	Dick Hall	1.50	.75	.45
183	Jerry Grote	1.50	.75	.45
184	Ray Fosse	1.50	.75	.45
185	Don Mincher	1.50	.75	.45
186	Rick Joseph	1.50	.75	.45
187	Mike Hedlund	1.50	.75	.45
188	Manny Sanguillen	1.50	.75	.45
189	Yankees Rookies (*Dave McDonald, Thurman Munson*)	75.00	37.00	22.00
190	Joe Torre	6.00	3.00	1.75
191	Vicente Romo	1.50	.75	.45
192	Jim Qualls	1.50	.75	.45
193	Mike Wegener	1.50	.75	.45
194	Chuck Manuel	1.50	.75	.45
195	N.L.C.S. Game 1 (Seaver Wins Opener!)	10.00	5.00	3.00
196	N.L.C.S. Game 2 (Mets Show Muscle!)	6.00	3.00	1.75
197	N.L.C.S. Game 3 (Ryan Saves the Day!)	20.00	10.00	6.00
198	Mets Celebrate (We're Number One!)(Nolan Ryan)	15.00	7.50	4.50
199	A.L.C.S. Game 1 (Orioles Win A Squeaker!)	4.00	2.00	1.25
200	A.L.C.S. Game 2 (Powell Scores Winning Run!)	4.00	2.00	1.25
201	A.L.C.S. Game 3 (Birds Wrap It Up!)	3.00	1.50	.90
202	Oriole Celebrate (Sweep Twins In Three!)	3.00	1.50	.90
203	Rudy May	1.50	.75	.45
204	Len Gabrielson	1.50	.75	.45
205	Bert Campaneris	1.50	.75	.45
206	Clete Boyer	1.50	.75	.45
207	Tigers Rookies (*Norman McRae, Bob Reed*)	1.50	.75	.45
208	Fred Gladding	1.50	.75	.45
209	Ken Suarez	1.50	.75	.45
210	Juan Marichal	6.00	3.00	1.75
211	Ted Williams	15.00	7.50	4.50
212	Al Santorini	1.50	.75	.45
213	Andy Etchebarren	1.50	.75	.45
214	Ken Boswell	1.50	.75	.45
215	Reggie Smith	1.50	.75	.45
216	Chuck Hartenstein	1.50	.75	.45
217	Ron Hansen	1.50	.75	.45
218	Ron Stone	1.50	.75	.45
219	Jerry Kenney	1.50	.75	.45
220	Steve Carlton	10.00	5.00	3.00
221	Ron Brand	1.50	.75	.45
222	Jim Rooker	1.50	.75	.45
223	Nate Oliver	1.50	.75	.45
224	Steve Barber	1.50	.75	.45
225	Lee May	1.50	.75	.45
226	Ron Perranoski	1.50	.75	.45
227	Astros Rookies (*John Mayberry, Bob Watkins*)	1.50	.75	.45
228	Aurelio Rodriguez	1.50	.75	.45
229	Rich Robertson	1.50	.75	.45
230	Brooks Robinson	20.00	10.00	6.00
231	Luis Tiant	1.50	.75	.45
232	Bob Didier	1.50	.75	.45
233	Lew Krausse	1.50	.75	.45
234	Tommy Dean	1.50	.75	.45
235	Mike Epstein	1.50	.75	.45
236	Bob Veale	1.50	.75	.45
237	Russ Gibson	1.50	.75	.45
238	Jose Laboy	1.50	.75	.45
239	Ken Berry	1.50	.75	.45
240	Fergie Jenkins	6.00	3.00	1.75
241	Royals Rookies (*Al Fitzmorris, Scott Northey*)	1.50	.75	.45
242	Walter Alston	4.00	2.00	1.25
243	Joe Sparma	1.50	.75	.45
244a	3rd Series Check List (264-372) (Red bat on front.)	6.00	3.00	1.75
244b	3rd Series Check List (264-372) (Brown bat on front.)	6.00	3.00	1.75
245	Leo Cardenas	1.50	.75	.45
246	Jim McAndrew	1.50	.75	.45
247	Lou Klimchock	1.50	.75	.45
248	Jesus Alou	1.50	.75	.45
249	Bob Locker	1.50	.75	.45
250	Willie McCovey	10.00	5.00	3.00
251	Dick Schofield	1.50	.75	.45
252	Lowell Palmer	1.50	.75	.45
253	Ron Woods	1.50	.75	.45
254	Camilo Pascual	1.50	.75	.45
255	*Jim Spencer*	1.50	.75	.45
256	Vic Davalillo	1.50	.75	.45
257	Dennis Higgins	1.50	.75	.45
258	Paul Popovich	1.50	.75	.45
259	Tommie Reynolds	1.50	.75	.45
260	Claude Osteen	1.50	.75	.45
261	Curt Motton	1.50	.75	.45
262	Padres Rookies (*Jerry Morales, Jim Williams*)	1.50	.75	.45
263	Duane Josephson	1.50	.75	.45
264	Rich Hebner	1.50	.75	.45
265	Randy Hundley	1.50	.75	.45
266	Wally Bunker	1.50	.75	.45
267	Twins Rookies (*Herman Hill, Paul Ratliff*)	1.50	.75	.45
268	Claude Raymond	1.50	.75	.45
269	Cesar Gutierrez	1.50	.75	.45
270	Chris Short	1.50	.75	.45
271	Greg Goossen	1.50	.75	.45
272	Hector Torres	1.50	.75	.45
273	Ralph Houk	4.00	2.00	1.25
274	Gerry Arrigo	1.50	.75	.45
275	Duke Sims	1.50	.75	.45
276	Ron Hunt	1.50	.75	.45
277	Paul Doyle	1.50	.75	.45
278	Tommie Aaron	1.50	.75	.45
279	*Bill Lee*	1.50	.75	.45
280	Donn Clendenon	1.50	.75	.45
281	Casey Cox	1.50	.75	.45
282	Steve Huntz	1.50	.75	.45
283	Angel Bravo	1.50	.75	.45
284	Jack Baldschun	1.50	.75	.45
285	Paul Blair	1.50	.75	.45
286	Dodgers Rookies (*Bill Buckner, Jack Jenkins*)	6.00	3.00	1.75
287	Fred Talbot	1.50	.75	.45
288	Larry Hisle	1.50	.75	.45
289	Gene Brabender	1.50	.75	.45
290	Rod Carew	10.00	5.00	3.00
291	Leo Durocher	4.00	2.00	1.25
292	Eddie Leon	1.50	.75	.45
293	Bob Bailey	1.50	.75	.45
294	Jose Azcue	1.50	.75	.45
295	Cecil Upshaw	1.50	.75	.45
296	Woody Woodward	1.50	.75	.45
297	Curt Blefary	1.50	.75	.45
298	Ken Henderson	1.50	.75	.45
299	Buddy Bradford	1.50	.75	.45
300	Tom Seaver	25.00	12.50	7.50
301	Chico Salmon	1.50	.75	.45
302	Jeff James	1.50	.75	.45
303	Brant Alyea	1.50	.75	.45
304	*Bill Russell*	4.00	2.00	1.25
305	World Series Game 1 (Buford Belts Leadoff Homer!)	4.00	2.00	1.25
306	World Series Game 2 (Clendenon's HR Breaks Ice!)	4.00	2.00	1.25
307	World Series Game 3 (Agee's Catch Saves The Day!)	4.00	2.00	1.25
308	World Series Game 4 (Martin's Bunt Ends Deadlock!)	4.00	2.00	1.25
309	World Series Game 5 (Koosman Shuts The Door!)	4.00	2.00	1.25
310	World Series Celebration (Mets Whoop It Up!)	8.00	4.00	2.50
311	Dick Green	1.50	.75	.45
312	Mike Torrez	1.50	.75	.45
313	Mayo Smith	1.50	.75	.45
314	Bill McCool	1.50	.75	.45
315	Luis Aparicio	8.00	4.00	2.50
316	Skip Guinn	1.50	.75	.45
317	Red Sox Rookies (*Luis Alvarado, Billy Conigliaro*)	1.50	.75	.45
318	Willie Smith	1.50	.75	.45
319	Clayton Dalrymple	1.50	.75	.45
320	Jim Maloney	1.50	.75	.45
321	Lou Piniella	3.00	1.50	.90
322	Luke Walker	1.50	.75	.45
323	Wayne Comer	1.50	.75	.45
324	Tony Taylor	1.50	.75	.45
325	Dave Boswell	1.50	.75	.45
326	Bill Voss	1.50	.75	.45
327	Hal King	1.50	.75	.45
328	George Brunet	1.50	.75	.45
329	Chris Cannizzaro	1.50	.75	.45
330	Lou Brock	10.00	5.00	3.00
331	Chuck Dobson	1.50	.75	.45
332	Bobby Wine	1.50	.75	.45
333	Bobby Murcer	3.00	1.50	.90
334	Phil Regan	1.50	.75	.45
335	Bill Freehan	1.50	.75	.45
336	Del Unser	1.50	.75	.45
337	Mike McCormick	1.50	.75	.45
338	Paul Schaal	1.50	.75	.45
339	Johnny Edwards	1.50	.75	.45
340	Tony Conigliaro	4.00	2.00	1.25
341	Bill Sudakis	1.50	.75	.45
342	Wilbur Wood	1.50	.75	.45
343a	4th Series Check List (373-459) (Red bat on front.)	5.00	2.50	1.50
343b	4th Series Check List (373-459) (Brown bat on front.)	5.00	2.50	1.50
344	Marcelino Lopez	1.50	.75	.45
345	Al Ferrara	1.50	.75	.45
346	Red Schoendienst	4.00	2.00	1.25
347	Russ Snyder	1.50	.75	.45
348	Mets Rookies (*Jesse Hudson, Mike Jorgensen*)	1.50	.75	.45
349	Steve Hamilton	1.50	.75	.45
350	Roberto Clemente	50.00	25.00	15.00
351	Tom Murphy	1.50	.75	.45
352	Bob Barton	1.50	.75	.45
353	Stan Williams	1.50	.75	.45
354	Amos Otis	1.50	.75	.45
355	Doug Rader	1.50	.75	.45
356	Fred Lasher	1.50	.75	.45
357	Bob Burda	1.50	.75	.45
358	*Pedro Borbon*	1.50	.75	.45
359	Phil Roof	1.50	.75	.45
360	Curt Flood	2.00	1.00	.60
361	Ray Jarvis	1.50	.75	.45
362	Joe Hague	1.50	.75	.45
363	Tom Shopay	1.50	.75	.45
364	Dan McGinn	1.50	.75	.45
365	Zoilo Versalles	1.50	.75	.45
366	Barry Moore	1.50	.75	.45
367	Mike Lum	1.50	.75	.45
368	Ed Herrmann	1.50	.75	.45
369	Alan Foster	1.50	.75	.45
370	Tommy Harper	1.50	.75	.45
371	Rod Gaspar	1.50	.75	.45
372	Dave Giusti	1.50	.75	.45
373	Roy White	2.50	1.25	.75
374	Tommie Sisk	1.50	.75	.45
375	Johnny Callison	1.50	.75	.45
376	Lefty Phillips	1.50	.75	.45
377	Bill Butler	1.50	.75	.45
378	Jim Davenport	1.50	.75	.45
379	Tom Tischinski	1.50	.75	.45
380	Tony Perez	8.00	4.00	2.50
381	Athletics Rookies (*Bobby Brooks, Mike Olivo*)	1.50	.75	.45
382	Jack DiLauro	1.50	.75	.45
383	Mickey Stanley	1.50	.75	.45
384	Gary Neibauer	1.50	.75	.45
385	George Scott	1.50	.75	.45
386	Bill Dillman	1.50	.75	.45
387	Baltimore Orioles Team	3.00	1.50	.90
388	Byron Browne	1.50	.75	.45
389	Jim Shellenback	1.50	.75	.45
390	Willie Davis	1.50	.75	.45
391	Larry Brown	1.50	.75	.45
392	Walt Hriniak	1.50	.75	.45
393	John Gelnar	1.50	.75	.45
394	Gil Hodges	6.00	3.00	1.75
395	Walt Williams	1.50	.75	.45
396	Steve Blass	1.50	.75	.45
397	Roger Repoz	1.50	.75	.45
398	Bill Stoneman	1.50	.75	.45
399	New York Yankees Team	8.00	4.00	2.50
400	Denny McLain	1.50	.70	.45
401	Giants Rookies (*John Harrell, Bernie Williams*)	1.50	.75	.45
402	Ellie Rodriguez	1.50	.75	.45
403	Jim Bunning	6.00	3.00	1.75
404	Rich Reese	1.50	.75	.45
405	Bill Hands	1.50	.75	.45
406	Mike Andrews	1.50	.75	.45
407	Bob Watson	1.50	.75	.45
408	Paul Lindblad	1.50	.75	.45
409	Bob Tolan	1.50	.75	.45
410	Boog Powell	5.00	2.50	1.50
411	Los Angeles Dodgers Team	6.00	3.00	1.75
412	Larry Burchart	1.50	.75	.45
413	Sonny Jackson	1.50	.75	.45
414	Paul Edmondson	1.50	.75	.45
415	Julian Javier	1.50	.75	.45
416	Joe Verbanic	1.50	.75	.45
417	John Bateman	1.50	.75	.45
418	John Donaldson	1.50	.75	.45
419	Ron Taylor	1.50	.75	.45
420	Ken McMullen	1.50	.75	.45
421	Pat Dobson	1.50	.75	.45
422	Kansas City Royals Team	3.00	1.50	.90
423	Jerry May	1.50	.75	.45
424	Mike Kilkenny	1.50	.75	.45
425	Bobby Bonds	3.00	1.50	.90
426	Bill Rigney	1.50	.75	.45
427	Fred Norman	1.50	.75	.45
428	Don Buford	1.50	.75	.45
429	Cubs Rookies (*Randy Bobb, Jim Cosman*)	1.50	.75	.45
430	A. Messersmith	1.50	.75	.45
431	Ron Swoboda	1.50	.75	.45
432a	5th Series Check List (460-546) ("Baseball" on front in yellow.)	4.00	2.00	1.25
432b	5th Series Check List (460-546) ("Baseball" on front in white.)	4.00	2.00	1.25
433	Ron Bryant	1.50	.75	.45
434	Felipe Alou	2.50	1.25	.75
435	Nelson Briles	1.50	.75	.45
436	Philadelphia Phillies Team	3.00	1.50	.90
437	Danny Cater	1.50	.75	.45
438	Pat Jarvis	1.50	.75	.45
439	Lee Maye	1.50	.75	.45
440	Bill Mazeroski	8.00	4.00	2.50
441	John O'Donoghue	1.50	.75	.45
442	Gene Mauch	1.50	.75	.45
443	Al Jackson	1.50	.75	.45
444	White Sox Rookies (*Bill Farmer, John Matias*)	1.50	.75	.45
445	Vada Pinson	2.00	1.00	.60
446	*Billy Grabarkewitz*	1.50	.75	.45
447	Lee Stange	1.50	.75	.45
448	Houston Astros Team	3.00	1.50	.90
449	Jim Palmer	8.00	4.00	2.50
450	Willie McCovey (All-Star)	6.00	3.00	1.75
451	Boog Powell (All-Star)	2.00	1.00	.60
452	Felix Millan (All-Star)	1.50	.75	.45
453	Rod Carew (All-Star)	6.00	3.00	1.75
454	Ron Santo (All-Star)	3.00	1.50	.90
455	Brooks Robinson (All-Star)	6.00	3.00	1.75
456	Don Kessinger (All-Star)	1.50	.75	.45
457	Rico Petrocelli (All-Star)	1.50	.75	.45
458	Pete Rose (All-Star)	20.00	10.00	6.00
459	Reggie Jackson (All-Star)	10.00	5.00	3.00
460	Matty Alou (All-Star)	1.50	.75	.45
461	Carl Yastrzemski (All-Star)	10.00	5.00	3.00
462	Hank Aaron (All-Star)	25.00	12.50	7.50
463	Frank Robinson (All-Star)	8.00	4.00	2.50
464	Johnny Bench (All-Star)	10.00	5.00	3.00
465	Bill Freehan (All-Star)	1.50	.75	.45
466	Juan Marichal (All-Star)	6.00	3.00	1.75
467	Denny McLain (All-Star)	1.50	.70	.45
468	Jerry Koosman (All-Star)	1.50	.75	.45
469	Sam McDowell (All-Star)	1.50	.75	.45
470	Willie Stargell	10.00	5.00	3.00
471	Chris Zachary	1.50	.75	.45
472	Atlanta Braves Team	3.00	1.50	.90
473	Don Bryant	1.50	.75	.45
474	Dick Kelley	1.50	.75	.45
475	Dick McAuliffe	1.50	.75	.45
476	Don Shaw	1.50	.75	.45
477	Orioles Rookies (*Roger Freed, Al Severinsen*)	1.50	.75	.45
478	Bob Heise	1.50	.75	.45
479	Dick Woodson	1.50	.75	.45
480	Glenn Beckert	1.50	.75	.45
481	Jose Tartabull	1.50	.75	.45
482	Tom Hilgendorf	1.50	.75	.45
483	Gail Hopkins	1.50	.75	.45
484	Gary Nolan	1.50	.75	.45
485	Jay Johnstone	1.50	.75	.45
486	Terry Harmon	1.50	.75	.45
487	Cisco Carlos	1.50	.75	.45
488	J.C. Martin	1.50	.75	.45
489	Eddie Kasko	1.50	.75	.45
490	Bill Singer	1.50	.75	.45
491	Graig Nettles	3.00	2.00	.90

#	Player	NM	EX	VG
492	Astros Rookies (*Keith Lampard, Scipio Spinks*)	1.50	.75	.45
493	Lindy McDaniel	1.50	.75	.45
494	Larry Stahl	1.50	.75	.45
495	Dave Morehead	1.50	.75	.45
496	Steve Whitaker	1.50	.75	.45
497	Eddie Watt	1.50	.75	.45
498	Al Weis	1.50	.75	.45
499	Skip Lockwood	1.50	.75	.45
500	Hank Aaron	40.00	20.00	12.00
501	Chicago White Sox Team	3.00	1.50	.90
502	Rollie Fingers	8.00	4.00	2.50
503	Dal Maxvill	1.50	.75	.45
504	Don Pavletich	1.50	.75	.45
505	Ken Holtzman	1.50	.75	.45
506	Ed Stroud	1.50	.75	.45
507	Pat Corrales	1.50	.75	.45
508	Joe Niekro	1.50	.75	.45
509	Montreal Expos Team	3.00	1.50	.90
510	Tony Oliva	3.50	1.75	1.00
511	Joe Hoerner	1.50	.75	.45
512	Billy Harris	1.50	.75	.45
513	Preston Gomez	1.50	.75	.45
514	Steve Hovley	1.50	.75	.45
515	Don Wilson	1.50	.75	.45
516	Yankees Rookies (*John Ellis, Jim Lyttle*)	1.50	.75	.45
517	Joe Gibbon	1.50	.75	.45
518	Bill Melton	1.50	.75	.45
519	Don McMahon	1.50	.75	.45
520	Willie Horton	1.50	.75	.45
521	Cal Koonce	1.50	.75	.45
522	California Angels Team	3.00	1.50	.90
523	Jose Pena	1.50	.75	.45
524	Alvin Dark	1.50	.75	.45
525	Jerry Adair	1.50	.75	.45
526	Ron Herbel	1.50	.75	.45
527	Don Bosch	1.50	.75	.45
528	Elrod Hendricks	1.50	.75	.45
529	Bob Aspromonte	1.50	.75	.45
530	Bob Gibson	12.00	6.00	3.50
531	Ron Clark	1.50	.75	.45
532	Danny Murtaugh	1.50	.75	.45
533	Buzz Stephen	1.50	.75	.45
534	Minnesota Twins Team	3.00	1.50	.90
535	Andy Kosco	1.50	.75	.45
536	Mike Kekich	1.50	.75	.45
537	Joe Morgan	10.00	5.00	3.00
538	Bob Humphreys	1.50	.75	.45
539	Phillies Rookies (*Larry Bowa, Dennis Doyle*)	6.00	3.00	1.75
540	Gary Peters	1.50	.75	.45
541	Bill Heath	1.50	.75	.45
542a	6th Series Check List (547-633) (Gray bat on front.)	5.00	2.50	1.50
542b	6th Series Check List (547-633) (Brown bat on front.)	5.00	2.50	1.50
543	Clyde Wright	1.50	.75	.45
544	Cincinnati Reds Team	5.00	2.50	1.50
545	Ken Harrelson	1.50	.75	.45
546	Ron Reed	1.50	.75	.45
547	Rick Monday	4.00	2.00	1.25
548	Howie Reed	3.00	1.50	.90
549	St. Louis Cardinals Team	6.00	3.00	1.75
550	Frank Howard	5.00	2.50	1.50
551	Dock Ellis	4.00	2.00	1.25
552	Royals Rookies (*Don O'Riley, Dennis Paepke, Fred Rico*)	4.00	2.00	1.25
553	Jim Lefebvre	4.00	2.00	1.25
554	Tom Timmermann	4.00	2.00	1.25
555	Orlando Cepeda	12.00	6.00	3.50
556	Dave Bristol	4.00	2.00	1.25
557	Ed Kranepool	4.00	2.00	1.25
558	Vern Fuller	4.00	2.00	1.25
559	Tommy Davis	4.00	2.00	1.25
560	Gaylord Perry	8.00	4.00	2.50
561	Tom McCraw	4.00	2.00	1.25
562	Ted Abernathy	4.00	2.00	1.25
563	Boston Red Sox Team	8.00	4.00	2.50
564	Johnny Briggs	4.00	2.00	1.25
565	Jim Hunter	8.00	4.00	2.50
566	Gene Alley	4.00	2.00	1.25
567	Bob Oliver	4.00	2.00	1.25
568	Stan Bahnsen	4.00	2.00	1.25
569	Cookie Rojas	4.00	2.00	1.25
570	Jim Fregosi	5.00	2.50	1.50
571	Jim Brewer	4.00	2.00	1.25
572	Frank Quilici	4.00	2.00	1.25
573	Padres Rookies (*Mike Corkins, Rafael Robles, Ron Slocum*)	4.00	2.00	1.25
574	Bobby Bolin	4.00	2.00	1.25
575	Cleon Jones	4.00	2.00	1.25
576	Milt Pappas	4.00	2.00	1.25
577	Bernie Allen	4.00	2.00	1.25
578	Tom Griffin	4.00	2.00	1.25
579	Detroit Tigers Team	8.00	4.00	2.50
580	Pete Rose	50.00	25.00	15.00
581	Tom Satriano	4.00	2.00	1.25
582	Mike Paul	4.00	2.00	1.25
583	Hal Lanier	4.00	2.00	1.25
584	Al Downing	5.00	2.50	1.50
585	Rusty Staub	6.00	3.00	1.75
586	Rickey Clark	4.00	2.00	1.25
587	Jose Arcia	4.00	2.00	1.25
588a	7th Series Check List (634-720) (666 is Adolpho Phillips)	6.00	3.00	1.75
588b	7th Series Check List (634-720) (666 is Adolfo Phillips)	6.00	3.00	1.75
589	Joe Keough	4.00	2.00	1.25
590	Mike Cuellar	4.00	2.00	1.25
591	Mike Ryan	4.00	2.00	1.25
592	Daryl Patterson	4.00	2.00	1.25
593	Chicago Cubs Team	8.00	4.00	2.50
594	Jake Gibbs	4.00	2.00	1.25
595	Maury Wills	4.00	2.00	1.25
596	Mike Hershberger	4.00	2.00	1.25
597	Sonny Siebert	4.00	2.00	1.25
598	Joe Pepitone	5.00	2.50	1.50
599	Senators Rookies (*Gene Martin, Dick Stelmaszek, Dick Such*)	4.00	2.00	1.25
600	Willie Mays	60.00	30.00	18.00
601	Pete Richert	4.00	2.00	1.25
602	Ted Savage	4.00	2.00	1.25
603	Ray Oyler	4.00	2.00	1.25
604	Clarence Gaston	6.00	3.00	1.75
605	Rick Wise	4.00	2.00	1.25
606	Chico Ruiz	4.00	2.00	1.25
607	Gary Waslewski	4.00	2.00	1.25
608	Pittsburgh Pirates Team	8.00	4.00	2.50
609	*Buck Martinez*	6.00	3.00	1.75
610	Jerry Koosman	6.00	3.00	1.75
611	Norm Cash	6.00	3.00	1.75
612	Jim Hickman	4.00	2.00	1.25
613	Dave Baldwin	4.00	2.00	1.25
614	Mike Shannon	4.00	2.00	1.25
615	Mark Belanger	4.00	2.00	1.25
616	Jim Merritt	4.00	2.00	1.25
617	Jim French	4.00	2.00	1.25
618	Billy Wynne	4.00	2.00	1.25
619	Norm Miller	4.00	2.00	1.25
620	Jim Perry	4.00	2.00	1.25
621	Braves Rookies (*Darrell Evans, Rick Kester, Mike McQueen*)	10.00	5.00	3.00
622	Don Sutton	8.00	4.00	2.50
623	Horace Clarke	4.00	2.00	1.25
624	Clyde King	4.00	2.00	1.25
625	Dean Chance	4.00	2.00	1.25
626	Dave Ricketts	4.00	2.00	1.25
627	Gary Wagner	4.00	2.00	1.25
628	Wayne Garrett	4.00	2.00	1.25
629	Merv Rettenmund	4.00	2.00	1.25
630	Ernie Banks	40.00	20.00	12.00
631	Oakland Athletics Team	8.00	4.00	2.50
632	Gary Sutherland	4.00	2.00	1.25
633	Roger Nelson	4.00	2.00	1.25
634	Bud Harrelson	8.00	4.00	2.50
635	Bob Allison	8.00	4.00	2.50
636	Jim Stewart	8.00	4.00	2.50
637	Cleveland Indians Team	12.00	6.00	3.50
638	Frank Bertaina	8.00	4.00	2.50
639	Dave Campbell	8.00	4.00	2.50
640	Al Kaline	40.00	20.00	12.00
641	Al McBean	8.00	4.00	2.50
642	Angels Rookies (*Greg Garrett, Gordon Lund, Jarvis Tatum*)	8.00	4.00	2.50
643	Jose Pagan	8.00	4.00	2.50
644	Gerry Nyman	8.00	4.00	2.50
645	Don Money	8.00	4.00	2.50
646	Jim Britton	8.00	4.00	2.50
647	Tom Matchick	8.00	4.00	2.50
648	Larry Haney	8.00	4.00	2.50
649	Jimmie Hall	8.00	4.00	2.50
650	Sam McDowell	10.00	5.00	3.00
651	Jim Gosger	8.00	4.00	2.50
652	Rich Rollins	10.00	5.00	3.00
653	Moe Drabowsky	8.00	4.00	2.50
654	N.L. Rookies (*Boots Day, Oscar Gamble, Angel Mangual*)	10.00	5.00	3.00
655	John Roseboro	8.00	4.00	2.50
656	Jim Hardin	8.00	4.00	2.50
657	San Diego Padres Team	15.00	7.50	4.50
658	Ken Tatum	8.00	4.00	2.50
659	Pete Ward	8.00	4.00	2.50
660	Johnny Bench	60.00	30.00	18.00
661	Jerry Robertson	8.00	4.00	2.50
662	Frank Lucchesi	8.00	4.00	2.50
663	Tito Francona	8.00	4.00	2.50
664	Bob Robertson	8.00	4.00	2.50
665	Jim Lonborg	8.00	4.00	2.50
666	Adolfo Phillips	8.00	4.00	2.50
667	Bob Meyer	8.00	4.00	2.50
668	Bob Tillman	8.00	4.00	2.50
669	White Sox Rookies (*Bart Johnson, Dan Lazar, Mickey Scott*)	8.00	4.00	2.50
670	Ron Santo	15.00	7.50	4.50
671	Jim Campanis	10.00	5.00	3.00
672	Leon McFadden	8.00	4.00	2.50
673	Ted Uhlaender	8.00	4.00	2.50
674	Dave Leonhard	8.00	4.00	2.50
675	Jose Cardenal	10.00	5.00	3.00
676	Washington Senators Team	15.00	7.50	4.50
677	Woodie Fryman	8.00	4.00	2.50
678	Dave Duncan	15.00	7.50	4.50
679	Ray Sadecki	8.00	4.00	2.50
680	Rico Petrocelli	10.00	5.00	3.00
681	Bob Garibaldi	8.00	4.00	2.50
682	Dalton Jones	8.00	4.00	2.50
683	Reds Rookies (*Vern Geishert, Hal McRae, Wayne Simpson*)	10.00	5.00	3.00
684	Jack Fisher	8.00	4.00	2.50
685	Tom Haller	8.00	4.00	2.50
686	Jackie Hernandez	8.00	4.00	2.50
687	Bob Priddy	8.00	4.00	2.50
688	Ted Kubiak	8.00	4.00	2.50
689	Frank Tepedino	8.00	4.00	2.50
690	Ron Fairly	8.00	4.00	2.50
691	Joe Grzenda	8.00	4.00	2.50
692	Duffy Dyer	8.00	4.00	2.50
693	Bob Johnson	8.00	4.00	2.50
694	Gary Ross	8.00	4.00	2.50
695	Bobby Knoop	8.00	4.00	2.50
696	San Francisco Giants Team	15.00	7.50	4.50
697	Jim Hannan	8.00	4.00	2.50
698	Tom Tresh	10.00	5.00	3.00
699	Hank Aguirre	8.00	4.00	2.50
700	Frank Robinson	40.00	20.00	12.00
701	Jack Billingham	8.00	4.00	2.50
702	A.L. Rookies (*Bob Johnson, Ron Klimkowski, Bill Zepp*)	8.00	4.00	2.50
703	Lou Marone	8.00	4.00	2.50
704	Frank Baker	8.00	4.00	2.50
705	Tony Cloninger	8.00	4.00	2.50
706	John McNamara	8.00	4.00	2.50
707	Kevin Collins	8.00	4.00	2.50
708	Jose Santiago	8.00	4.00	2.50
709	Mike Fiore	8.00	4.00	2.50
710	Felix Millan	8.00	4.00	2.50
711	Ed Brinkman	8.00	4.00	2.50
712	Nolan Ryan	180.00	90.00	54.00
713	Seattle Pilots Team	20.00	10.00	6.00
714	Al Spangler	8.00	4.00	2.50
715	Mickey Lolich	8.00	4.00	2.50
716	Cards Rookies (*Sal Campisi, Reggie Cleveland, Santiago Guzman*)	10.00	5.00	3.00
717	Tom Phoebus	8.00	4.00	2.50
718	Ed Spiezio	8.00	4.00	2.50
719	Jim Roland	8.00	4.00	2.50
720	Rick Reichardt	12.00	5.00	2.50

1970 Topps Candy Lids

The 1970 Topps Candy Lids are a test issue that was utilized again in 1973. The set is made up of 24 lids that measure 1-7/8" in diameter and were the tops of small 1.1 oz. tubs of "Baseball Stars Candy." Unlike the 1973 versions, the 1970 lids have no border surrounding the full-color photos. Frank Howard, Tom Seaver and Carl Yastrzemski photos are found on the top (outside) of the candy lid.

		NM	EX	VG
	Complete Set (24):	2,800	1,400	840.00
	Common Player:	40.00	20.00	12.00
(1)	Hank Aaron	350.00	175.00	105.00
(2)	Rich Allen	75.00	37.00	22.00
(3)	Luis Aparicio	140.00	70.00	42.00
(4)	Johnny Bench	225.00	110.00	67.00
(5)	Ollie Brown	40.00	20.00	12.00
(6)	Willie Davis	40.00	20.00	12.00
(7)	Jim Fregosi	40.00	20.00	12.00
(8)	Mike Hegan	40.00	20.00	12.00
(9)	Frank Howard	60.00	30.00	18.00
(10)	Reggie Jackson	275.00	135.00	82.00
(11)	Fergie Jenkins	130.00	65.00	39.00
(12)	Harmon Killebrew	175.00	87.00	52.00
(13)	Juan Marichal	140.00	70.00	42.00
(14)	Bill Mazeroski	140.00	70.00	42.00
(15)	Tim McCarver	60.00	30.00	18.00
(16)	Sam McDowell	40.00	20.00	12.00
(17)	Denny McLain	60.00	30.00	18.00
(18)	Lou Piniella	45.00	22.00	13.50
(19)	Frank Robinson	175.00	87.00	52.00
(20)	Tom Seaver	200.00	100.00	60.00
(21)	Rusty Staub	60.00	30.00	18.00
(22)	Mel Stottlemyre	40.00	20.00	12.00
(23)	Jim Wynn	40.00	20.00	12.00
(24)	Carl Yastrzemski	225.00	110.00	67.00

1970 Topps Cloth Stickers

The earliest and rarest of the Topps cloth sticker test issues, only 15 subjects are known, and only a single specimen apiece is known for many of them. In the same 2-1/2" x 3-1/2" size, and with the same design as the 1970 Topps baseball cards, the stickers are blank-backed. The stickers of Denny Lemaster, Dennis Higgins and Rich Nye use photos that are different from their '70 Topps cards. It is quite likely that the checklist presented here is incomplete. The stickers are unnumbered and are checklisted alphabetically.

Common Player:	NM	EX	VG
(1) A.L. Playoff Game 2	1,750	875.00	525.00
(Boog Powell)	1,900	950.00	570.00
(2) Bill Burbach	1,750	875.00	525.00
(3) Gary Gentry	1,750	875.00	525.00
(4) Tom Hall	1,750	875.00	525.00
(5) Chuck Hartenstein	1,750	875.00	525.00
(6) Dennis Higgins	1,750	875.00	525.00
(7) Jose Laboy	1,750	875.00	525.00
(8) Denny Lemaster	1,750	875.00	525.00
(9) Juan Marichal	2,200	1,100	660.00
(10) Jerry McNertney	1,750	875.00	525.00
(11) Curt Motton	1,750	875.00	525.00
(12) Ivan Murrell	1,750	875.00	525.00
(13) N.L. Playoff Game 1	1,750	875.00	525.00
(Tom Seaver)			
(14) N.L. Playoff Game 3	3,000	1,500	900.00
(Nolan Ryan)			
(15) Phil Niekro	2,100	1,050	630.00
(16) Jim Northrup	1,750	875.00	525.00
(17) Rich Nye	1,750	875.00	525.00
(18) Ron Perranoski	1,750	875.00	525.00
(19) Al Santorini	1,750	875.00	525.00

1970 Topps Posters

Helping to ease a price increase, Topps included extremely fragile 8-11/16" x 9-5/8" posters in packs of regular cards. The posters feature color portraits and a smaller black and white "action" pose as well as the player's name, team and position at the top. Although there are Hall of Famers in the 24-poster set, all the top names are not represented. Folds from original packaging are not considered in grading unless they split the paper.

		NM	EX	VG
	Complete Set (24):	60.00	30.00	18.00
	Common Player:	3.00	1.50	.90
1	Joe Horlen	3.00	1.50	.90
2	Phil Niekro	6.00	3.00	1.75
3	Willie Davis	3.00	1.50	.90
4	Lou Brock	7.00	3.50	2.00
5	Ron Santo	4.00	2.00	1.25
6	Ken Harrelson	3.00	1.50	.90
7	Willie McCovey	7.00	3.50	2.00
8	Rick Wise	3.00	1.50	.90
9	Andy Messersmith	3.00	1.50	.90
10	Ron Fairly	3.00	1.50	.90
11	Johnny Bench	10.00	5.00	3.00
12	Frank Robinson	10.00	5.00	3.00
13	Tommie Agee	3.00	1.50	.90
14	Roy White	3.00	1.50	.90
15	Larry Dierker	3.00	1.50	.90
16	Rod Carew	9.00	4.50	2.75
17	Don Mincher	3.00	1.50	.90
18	Ollie Brown	3.00	1.50	.90
19	Ed Kirkpatrick	3.00	1.50	.90
20	Reggie Smith	3.00	1.50	.90
21	Roberto Clemente	25.00	12.50	7.50
22	Frank Howard	3.00	1.50	.90
23	Bert Campaneris	3.00	1.50	.90
24	Denny McLain	3.00	1.50	.90

1970 Topps Scratch-Offs

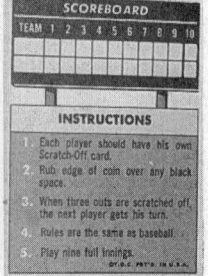

Not having given up on the idea of a game which could be played with baseball cards, Topps provided a new game - the baseball scratch-off - in 1970. Unfolded, cards measure 3-3/8" x 5", and reveal a baseball game played by rubbing the black ink off playing squares to determine the "action." Fronts have a player picture as "captain," while backs have instructions and a scoreboard. Inserts with white centers are from 1970 while those with red centers are from 1971.

		NM	EX	VG
	Complete Set (24):	60.00	30.00	18.00
	Common Player:	1.50	.75	.45
(1)	Hank Aaron	12.00	6.00	3.50
(2)	Rich Allen	2.50	1.25	.70
(3)	Luis Aparicio	3.50	1.75	1.00
(4)	Sal Bando	1.50	.75	.45
(5)	Glenn Beckert	1.50	.75	.45
(6)	Dick Bosman	1.50	.75	.45
(7)	Nate Colbert	1.50	.75	.45
(8)	Mike Hegan	1.50	.75	.45
(9)	Mack Jones	1.50	.75	.45
(10)	Al Kaline	4.50	2.25	1.25
(11)	Harmon Killebrew	4.50	2.25	1.25
(12)	Juan Marichal	3.50	1.75	1.00
(13)	Tim McCarver	2.50	1.25	.70
(14)	Sam McDowell	1.50	.75	.45
(15)	Claude Osteen	1.50	.75	.45
(16)	Tony Perez	3.50	1.75	1.00
(17)	Lou Piniella	1.50	.75	.45
(18)	Boog Powell	2.50	1.25	.70
(19)	Tom Seaver	4.50	2.25	1.25
(20)	Jim Spencer	1.50	.75	.45
(21)	Willie Stargell	3.50	1.75	1.00
(22)	Mel Stottlemyre	1.50	.75	.45
(23)	Jim Wynn	1.50	.75	.45
(24)	Carl Yastrzemski	6.00	3.00	1.75

1970 Topps Story Booklets

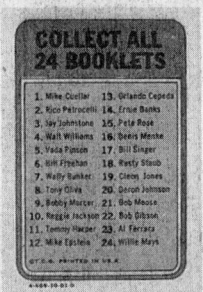

Measuring 2-1/2" x 3-7/16", the Topps Story Booklet was a 1970 regular pack insert. The booklet feature a photo, title and booklet number on the "cover." Inside are six pages of comic book story. The backs give a checklist of other available booklets. Not every star had a booklet as the set is only 24 in number.

		NM	EX	VG
	Complete Set (24):	65.00	32.50	20.00
	Common Player:	1.50	.75	.45
1	Mike Cuellar	1.50	.75	.45
2	Rico Petrocelli	1.50	.75	.45
3	Jay Johnstone	1.50	.75	.45
4	Walt Williams	1.50	.75	.45
5	Vada Pinson	2.25	1.25	.70
6	Bill Freehan	1.50	.75	.45
7	Wally Bunker	1.50	.75	.45
8	Tony Oliva	2.25	1.25	.70
9	Bobby Murcer	2.00	1.00	.60
10	Reggie Jackson	9.00	4.50	2.75
11	Tommy Harper	1.50	.75	.45
12	Mike Epstein	1.50	.75	.45
13	Orlando Cepeda	4.00	2.00	1.25
14	Ernie Banks	7.00	3.50	2.00
15	Pete Rose	10.00	5.00	3.00
16	Denis Menke	1.50	.75	.45
17	Bill Singer	1.50	.75	.45
18	Rusty Staub	2.00	1.00	.60
19	Cleon Jones	1.50	.75	.45
20	Deron Johnson	1.50	.75	.45
21	Bob Moose	1.50	.75	.45
22	Bob Gibson	5.00	2.50	1.50
23	Al Ferrara	1.50	.75	.45
24	Willie Mays	10.00	5.00	3.00

1970 Topps Super

Representing a refinement of the concept begun in 1969, the 1970 Topps Supers had a new 3-1/8" x 5-1/4" size. Printed on thick stock with rounded corners, card fronts feature a borderless color photograph and facsimile autograph. Backs are an enlarged version of the player's regular 1970 Topps card. Probably due to the press sheet configuration,

eight of the 42 cards were short-printed. The most elusive is card #38 (Boog Powell). The set was more widely produced than was the case in 1969. Square-cornered proofs, either with blank or printed backs, are known, valued from 1X-2X the regular-card price.

		NM	EX	VG
	Complete Set (42):	250.00	125.00	75.00
	Common Player:	4.00	2.00	1.25
	Unopened Pack:	95.00		
	Proofs: 1-2X			
1	Claude Osteen/SP	10.00	5.00	3.00
2	Sal Bando/SP	10.00	5.00	3.00
3	Luis Aparicio	9.00	4.50	2.75
4	Harmon Killebrew	15.00	7.50	4.50
5	Tom Seaver/SP	25.00	12.50	7.50
6	Larry Dierker	4.00	2.00	1.25
7	Bill Freehan	4.00	2.00	1.25
8	Johnny Bench	20.00	10.00	6.00
9	Tommy Harper	4.00	2.00	1.25
10	Sam McDowell	4.00	2.00	1.25
11	Lou Brock	12.00	6.00	3.50
12	Roberto Clemente	40.00	20.00	12.00
13	Willie McCovey	12.00	6.00	3.50
14	Rico Petrocelli	4.00	2.00	1.25
15	Phil Niekro	9.00	4.50	2.75
16	Frank Howard	4.00	2.00	1.25
17	Denny McLain	4.00	2.00	1.25
18	Willie Mays	35.00	17.50	10.00
19	Willie Stargell	12.00	6.00	3.50
20	Joe Horlen	4.00	2.00	1.25
21	Ron Santo	6.00	3.00	1.75
22	Dick Bosman	4.00	2.00	1.25
23	Tim McCarver	5.00	2.50	1.50
24	Henry Aaron	35.00	17.50	10.00
25	Andy Messersmith	4.00	2.00	1.25
26	Tony Oliva	5.00	2.50	1.50
27	Mel Stottlemyre	4.00	2.00	1.25
28	Reggie Jackson	30.00	15.00	9.00
29	Carl Yastrzemski	20.00	10.00	6.00
30	James Fregosi	4.00	2.00	1.25
31	Vada Pinson	5.00	2.50	1.50
32	Lou Piniella	4.00	2.00	1.25
33	Robert Gibson	10.00	5.00	3.00
34	Pete Rose	35.00	17.50	10.00
35	Jim Wynn	4.00	2.00	1.25
36	Ollie Brown/SP	10.00	5.00	3.00
37	Frank Robinson/SP	35.00	17.50	10.00
38	Boog Powell/SP	60.00	30.00	18.00
39	Willie Davis/SP	10.00	5.00	3.00
40	Billy Williams/SP	20.00	10.00	6.00
41	Rusty Staub	5.00	2.50	1.50
42	Tommie Agee	4.00	2.00	1.25

1971 Topps

In 1971, Topps again increased the size of its set to 752 cards. These 2-1/2" x 3-1/2" cards feature a large color photo with a thin white frame. Above the picture, in the card's overall black border, is the player's name, team and position. A facsimile autograph completes the front. Backs feature a major change as a black-and-white "snapshot" of the player appears. Abbreviated statistics, a line giving the player's first pro and major league games and a short biography complete the back. Specialty cards in this issue are limited. There are statistical leaders as well as World Series and playoff highlights. High-number cards #644-752 are scarce, with about half of the cards being short-printed.

		NM	EX	VG
	Complete Set (752):	3,000	1,500	900.00
	Common Player (1-523):	2.00	1.00	.60
	Common Player (524-643):	4.00	2.00	1.00
	Common Player (644-752):	6.00	3.00	1.75
1	World Champions	20.00	10.00	6.00
	(Orioles team.)			
2	Dock Ellis	2.00	1.00	.60
3	Dick McAuliffe	2.00	1.00	.60
4	Vic Davalillo	2.00	1.00	.60
5	Thurman Munson	120.00	60.00	36.00
6	Ed Spiezio	2.00	1.00	.60
7	Jim Holt	2.00	1.00	.60
8	Mike McQueen	2.00	1.00	.60
9	George Scott	2.00	1.00	.60
10	Claude Osteen	2.00	1.00	.60
11	*Elliott Maddox*	2.00	1.00	.60
12	Johnny Callison	2.00	1.00	.60
13	White Sox Rookies (*Charlie Brinkman, Dick Moloney*)	2.00	1.00	.60
14	*Dave Concepcion*	15.00	7.50	4.50
15	Andy Messersmith	2.00	1.00	.60
16	*Ken Singleton*	4.00	2.00	1.25
17	Billy Sorrell	2.00	1.00	.60

No.	Player			
18	Norm Miller	2.00	1.00	.60
19	Skip Pitlock	2.00	1.00	.60
20	Reggie Jackson	50.00	25.00	15.00
21	Dan McGinn	2.00	1.00	.60
22	Phil Roof	2.00	1.00	.60
23	Oscar Gamble	2.00	1.00	.60
24	Rich Hand	2.00	1.00	.60
25	Clarence Gaston	2.00	1.00	.60
26	*Bert Blyleven*	20.00	10.00	6.00
27	Pirates Rookies (*Fred Cambria, Gene Clines*)	2.00	1.00	.60
28	Ron Klimkowski	2.00	1.00	.60
29	Don Buford	2.00	1.00	.60
30	Phil Niekro	8.00	4.00	2.50
31	Eddie Kasko	2.00	1.00	.60
32	Jerry DaVanon	2.00	1.00	.60
33	Del Unser	2.00	1.00	.60
34	Sandy Vance	2.00	1.00	.60
35	Lou Piniella	4.00	2.00	1.25
36	Dean Chance	2.00	1.00	.60
37	Rich McKinney	2.00	1.00	.60
38	*Jim Colborn*	2.00	1.00	.60
39	Tigers Rookies (*Gene Lamont, Lerrin LaGrow*)	2.00	1.00	.60
40	Lee May	2.00	1.00	.60
41	Rick Austin	2.00	1.00	.60
42a	Boots Day (Stadium lights behind ear.)	8.00	4.00	2.50
42b	Boots Day (No stadium lights.)	8.00	4.00	2.50
43	Steve Kealey	2.00	1.00	.60
44	Johnny Edwards	2.00	1.00	.60
45	Jim Hunter	8.00	4.00	2.50
46	Dave Campbell	2.00	1.00	.60
47	Johnny Jeter	2.00	1.00	.60
48	Dave Baldwin	2.00	1.00	.60
49	Don Money	2.00	1.00	.60
50	Willie McCovey	10.00	5.00	3.00
51	Steve Kline	2.00	1.00	.60
52	Braves Rookies (*Oscar Brown, Earl Williams*)	2.00	1.00	.60
53	Paul Blair	2.00	1.00	.60
54	1st Series Checklist (1-132)	5.00	2.50	1.50
55	Steve Carlton	20.00	10.00	6.00
56	Duane Josephson	2.00	1.00	.60
57	Von Joshua	2.00	1.00	.60
58	Bill Lee	2.00	1.00	.60
59	Gene Mauch	2.00	1.00	.60
60	Dick Bosman	2.00	1.00	.60
61	A.L. Batting Leaders (Alex Johnson, Tony Oliva, Carl Yastrzemski)	8.00	4.00	2.50
62	N.L. Batting Leaders (Rico Carty, Manny Sanguillen, Joe Torre)	6.00	3.00	1.75
63	A.L. RBI Leaders (Tony Conigliaro, Frank Howard, Boog Powell)	6.00	3.00	1.75
64	N.L. RBI Leaders (Johnny Bench, Tony Perez, Billy Williams)	8.00	4.00	2.50
65	A.L. Home Run Leaders (Frank Howard, Harmon Killebrew, Carl Yastrzemski)	8.00	4.00	2.50
66	N.L. Home Run Leaders (Johnny Bench, Tony Perez, Billy Williams)	10.00	5.00	3.00
67	A.L. ERA Leaders (Jim Palmer, Diego Segui, Clyde Wright)	6.00	3.00	1.75
68	N.L. ERA Leaders (Tom Seaver, Wayne Simpson, Luke Walker)	6.00	3.00	1.75
69	A.L. Pitching Leaders (Mike Cuellar, Dave McNally, Jim Perry)	3.00	1.50	.90
70	N.L. Pitching Leaders (Bob Gibson, Fergie Jenkins, Gaylord Perry)	8.00	4.00	2.50
71	A.L. Strikeout Leaders (Bob Johnson, Mickey Lolich, Sam McDowell)	3.00	1.50	.90
72	N.L. Strikeout Leaders (Bob Gibson, Fergie Jenkins, Tom Seaver)	8.00	4.00	2.50
73	George Brunet	2.00	1.00	.60
74	Twins Rookies (*Pete Hamm, Jim Nettles*)	2.00	1.00	.60
75	Gary Nolan	2.00	1.00	.60
76	Ted Savage	2.00	1.00	.60
77	Mike Compton	2.00	1.00	.60
78	Jim Spencer	2.00	1.00	.60
79	Wade Blasingame	2.00	1.00	.60
80	Bill Melton	2.00	1.00	.60
81	Felix Millan	2.00	1.00	.60
82	Casey Cox	2.00	1.00	.60
83	Mets Rookies (*Randy Bobb, Tim Foli*)	2.00	1.00	.60
84	Marcel Lachemann	2.00	1.00	.60
85	Billy Grabarkewitz	2.00	1.00	.60
86	Mike Kilkenny	2.00	1.00	.60
87	Jack Heidemann	2.00	1.00	.60
88	Hal King	2.00	1.00	.60
89	Ken Brett	2.00	1.00	.60
90	Joe Pepitone	2.00	1.00	.60
91	Bob Lemon	4.00	2.00	1.25
92	Fred Wenz	2.00	1.00	.60
93	Senators Rookies (*Norm McRae, Denny Riddleberger*)	2.00	1.00	.60
94	Don Hahn	2.00	1.00	.60
95	Luis Tiant	2.00	1.00	.60
96	Joe Hague	2.00	1.00	.60
97	Floyd Wicker	2.00	1.00	.60
98	Joe Decker	2.00	1.00	.60
99	Mark Belanger	2.00	1.00	.60
100	Pete Rose	85.00	42.00	25.00
101	Les Cain	2.00	1.00	.60
102	Astros Rookies (*Ken Forsch, Larry Howard*)	2.00	1.00	.60
103	Rich Severson	2.00	1.00	.60
104	Dan Frisella	2.00	1.00	.60
105	Tony Conigliaro	6.00	3.00	1.75
106	Tom Dukes	2.00	1.00	.60
107	Roy Foster	2.00	1.00	.60
108	John Cumberland	2.00	1.00	.60
109	Steve Hovley	2.00	1.00	.60
110	Bill Mazeroski	10.00	5.00	3.00
111	Yankees Rookies (*Loyd Colson, Bobby Mitchell*)	2.00	1.00	.60
112	Manny Mota	2.00	1.00	.60
113	Jerry Crider	2.00	1.00	.60
114	Billy Conigliaro	2.00	1.00	.60
115	Donn Clendenon	2.00	1.00	.60
116	Ken Sanders	2.00	1.00	.60
117	*Ted Simmons*	8.00	4.00	2.50
118	Cookie Rojas	2.00	1.00	.60
119	Frank Lucchesi	2.00	1.00	.60
120	Willie Horton	2.00	1.00	.60
121	Cubs Rookies (*Jim Dunegan, Roe Skidmore*)	2.00	1.00	.60
122	Eddie Watt	2.00	1.00	.60
123a	2nd Series Checklist (133-263) (Card # on right, orange helmet.)	5.00	2.50	1.50
123b	2nd Series Checklist (133-263) (Card # on right, red helmet.)	5.00	2.50	1.50
123c	2nd Series Checklist (133-263) (Card # centered.)	5.00	2.50	1.50
124	*Don Gullett*	2.00	1.00	.60
125	Ray Fosse	2.00	1.00	.60
126	Danny Coombs	2.00	1.00	.60
127	*Danny Thompson*	2.00	1.00	.60
128	Frank Johnson	2.00	1.00	.60
129	Aurelio Monteagudo	2.00	1.00	.60
130	Denis Menke	2.00	1.00	.60
131	Curt Blefary	2.00	1.00	.60
132	Jose Laboy	2.00	1.00	.60
133	Mickey Lolich	2.00	1.00	.60
134	Jose Arcia	2.00	1.00	.60
135	Rick Monday	2.00	1.00	.60
136	Duffy Dyer	2.00	1.00	.60
137	Marcelino Lopez	2.00	1.00	.60
138	Phillies Rookies (*Joe Lis, Willie Montanez*)	2.00	1.00	.60
139	Paul Casanova	2.00	1.00	.60
140	Gaylord Perry	8.00	4.00	2.50
141	Frank Quilici	2.00	1.00	.60
142	Mack Jones	2.00	1.00	.60
143	Steve Blass	2.00	1.00	.60
144	Jackie Hernandez	2.00	1.00	.60
145	Bill Singer	2.00	1.00	.60
146	Ralph Houk	2.00	1.00	.60
147	Bob Priddy	2.00	1.00	.60
148	John Mayberry	2.00	1.00	.60
149	Mike Hershberger	2.00	1.00	.60
150	Sam McDowell	2.00	1.00	.60
151	Tommy Davis	2.00	1.00	.60
152	Angels Rookies (*Lloyd Allen, Winston Llenas*)	2.00	1.00	.60
153	Gary Ross	2.00	1.00	.60
154	Cesar Gutierrez	2.00	1.00	.60
155	Ken Henderson	2.00	1.00	.60
156	Bart Johnson	2.00	1.00	.60
157	Bob Bailey	2.00	1.00	.60
158	Jerry Reuss	2.00	1.00	.60
159	Jarvis Tatum	2.00	1.00	.60
160	Tom Seaver	25.00	12.50	7.50
161	Coins Checklist	4.00	2.00	1.25
162	Jack Billingham	2.00	1.00	.60
163	Buck Martinez	2.00	1.00	.60
164	Reds Rookies (*Frank Duffy, Milt Wilcox*)	2.00	1.00	.60
165	Cesar Tovar	2.00	1.00	.60
166	Joe Hoerner	2.00	1.00	.60
167	Tom Grieve	2.00	1.00	.60
168	Bruce Dal Canton	2.00	1.00	.60
169	Ed Herrmann	2.00	1.00	.60
170	Mike Cuellar	2.00	1.00	.60
171	Bobby Wine	2.00	1.00	.60
172	Duke Sims	2.00	1.00	.60
173	Gil Garrido	2.00	1.00	.60
174	*Dave LaRoche*	2.00	1.00	.60
175	Jim Hickman	2.00	1.00	.60
176	Red Sox Rookies (*Doug Griffin, Bob Montgomery*)	2.00	1.00	.60
177	Hal McRae	2.00	1.00	.60
178	Dave Duncan	2.00	1.00	.60
179	Mike Corkins	2.00	1.00	.60
180	Al Kaline	20.00	10.00	6.00
181	Hal Lanier	2.00	1.00	.60
182	Al Downing	2.00	1.00	.60
183	Gil Hodges	10.00	5.00	3.00
184	Stan Bahnsen	2.00	1.00	.60
185	Julian Javier	2.00	1.00	.60
186	Bob Spence	2.00	1.00	.60
187	Ted Abernathy	2.00	1.00	.60
188	Dodgers Rookies (*Mike Strahler, Bob Valentine*)	4.00	2.00	1.25
189	George Mitterwald	2.00	1.00	.60
190	Bob Tolan	2.00	1.00	.60
191	Mike Andrews	2.00	1.00	.60
192	Billy Wilson	2.00	1.00	.60
193	*Bob Grich*	5.00	2.50	1.50
194	Mike Lum	2.00	1.00	.60
195	A.L. Playoff Game 1 (Powell Muscles Twins!)	5.00	2.50	1.50
196	A.L. Playoff Game 2 (McNally Makes It Two Straight!)	3.00	1.50	.90
197	A.L. Playoff Game 3 (Palmer Mows 'Em Down!)	6.00	3.00	1.75
198	Orioles Celebrate! (A Team Effort!)	3.00	1.50	.90
199	N.L. Playoff Game 1 (Cline Pinch-Triple Decides It!)	3.00	1.50	.90
200	N.L. Playoff Game 2 (Tolan Scores For Third Time!)	3.00	1.50	.90
201	N.L. Playoff Game 3 (Cline Scores Winning Run!)	3.00	1.50	.90
202	Reds Celebrate! (World Series Bound!)	3.00	1.50	.90
203	*Larry Gura*	2.00	1.00	.60
204	Brewers Rookies (*George Kopacz, Bernie Smith*)	2.00	1.00	.60
205	Gerry Moses	2.00	1.00	.60
206a	3rd Series Checklist (264-393) (Orange helmet.)	6.00	3.00	1.75
206b	3rd Series Checklist (264-393) (Red helmet.)	6.00	3.00	1.75
207	Alan Foster	2.00	1.00	.60
208	Billy Martin	8.00	4.00	2.50
209	Steve Renko	2.00	1.00	.60
210	Rod Carew	15.00	7.50	4.50
211	Phil Hennigan	2.00	1.00	.60
212	Rich Hebner	2.00	1.00	.60
213	Frank Baker	2.00	1.00	.60
214	Al Ferrara	2.00	1.00	.60
215	Diego Segui	2.00	1.00	.60
216	Cards Rookies (*Reggie Cleveland, Luis Melendez*)	2.00	1.00	.60
217	Ed Stroud	2.00	1.00	.60
218	Tony Cloninger	2.00	1.00	.60
219	Elrod Hendricks	2.00	1.00	.60
220	Ron Santo	8.00	4.00	2.50
221	Dave Morehead	2.00	1.00	.60
222	Bob Watson	2.00	1.00	.60
223	Cecil Upshaw	2.00	1.00	.60
224	Alan Gallagher	2.00	1.00	.60
225	Gary Peters	2.00	1.00	.60
226	Bill Russell	2.00	1.00	.60
227	Floyd Weaver	2.00	1.00	.60
228	Wayne Garrett	2.00	1.00	.60
229	Jim Hannan	2.00	1.00	.60
230	Willie Stargell	15.00	7.50	4.50
231	Indians Rookies (*Vince Colbert, John Lowenstein*)	2.00	1.00	.60
232	John Strohmayer	2.00	1.00	.60
233	Larry Bowa	2.00	1.00	.60
234	Jim Lyttle	2.00	1.00	.60
235	Nate Colbert	2.00	1.00	.60
236	Bob Humphreys	2.00	1.00	.60
237	*Cesar Cedeno*	6.00	3.00	1.75
238	Chuck Dobson	2.00	1.00	.60
239	Red Schoendienst	6.00	3.00	1.75
240	Clyde Wright	2.00	1.00	.60
241	Dave Nelson	2.00	1.00	.60
242	Jim Ray	2.00	1.00	.60
243	Carlos May	2.00	1.00	.60
244	Bob Tillman	2.00	1.00	.60
245	Jim Kaat	3.00	1.50	.90
246	Tony Taylor	2.00	1.00	.60
247	Royals Rookies (*Jerry Cram, Paul Splittorff*)	2.00	1.00	.60
248	Hoyt Wilhelm	8.00	4.00	2.50
249	Chico Salmon	2.00	1.00	.60
250	Johnny Bench	60.00	30.00	18.00
251	Frank Reberger	2.00	1.00	.60
252	Eddie Leon	2.00	1.00	.60
253	Bill Sudakis	2.00	1.00	.60
254	Cal Koonce	2.00	1.00	.60
255	Bob Robertson	2.00	1.00	.60
256	Tony Gonzalez	2.00	1.00	.60
257	Nelson Briles	2.00	1.00	.60
258	Dick Green	2.00	1.00	.60
259	Dave Marshall	2.00	1.00	.60
260	Tommy Harper	2.00	1.00	.60
261	Darold Knowles	2.00	1.00	.60
262	Padres Rookies (*Dave Robinson, Jim Williams*)	2.00	1.00	.60
263	John Ellis	2.00	1.00	.60
264	Joe Morgan	12.00	6.00	3.50
265a	Jim Northrup (Black "dot" at right of photo.)	2.00	1.00	.60
265b	Jim Northrup (Black "blob" at right of photo.)	2.00	1.00	.60
266	Bill Stoneman	2.00	1.00	.60
267	Rich Morales	2.00	1.00	.60
268	Phillies Team	4.00	2.00	1.25
269	Gail Hopkins	2.00	1.00	.60
270	Rico Carty	2.00	1.00	.60
271	Bill Zepp	2.00	1.00	.60
272	Tommy Helms	2.00	1.00	.60
273	Pete Richert	2.00	1.00	.60
274	Ron Slocum	2.00	1.00	.60
275	Vada Pinson	5.00	2.50	1.50
276	Giants Rookies (*Mike Davison, George Foster*)	15.00	7.50	4.50
277	Gary Waslewski	2.00	1.00	.60
278	Jerry Grote	2.00	1.00	.60
279	Lefty Phillips	2.00	1.00	.60
280	Fergie Jenkins	10.00	5.00	3.00
281	Danny Walton	2.00	1.00	.60
282	Jose Pagan	2.00	1.00	.60
283	Dick Such	2.00	1.00	.60
284	Jim Gosger	2.00	1.00	.60
285	Sal Bando	2.00	1.00	.60
286	Jerry McNertney	2.00	1.00	.60
287	Mike Fiore	2.00	1.00	.60
288	Joe Moeller	2.00	1.00	.60
289	White Sox Team	4.00	2.00	1.25
290	Tony Oliva	4.00	2.00	1.25
291	George Culver	2.00	1.00	.60
292	Jay Johnstone	2.00	1.00	.60
293	Pat Corrales	2.00	1.00	.60
294	Steve Dunning	2.00	1.00	.60
295	Bobby Bonds	4.00	2.00	1.25
296	Tom Timmermann	2.00	1.00	.60
297	Johnny Briggs	2.00	1.00	.60
298	Jim Nelson	2.00	1.00	.60
299	Ed Kirkpatrick	2.00	1.00	.60
300	Brooks Robinson	20.00	10.00	6.00

301	Earl Wilson	2.00	1.00	.60
302	Phil Gagliano	2.00	1.00	.60
303	Lindy McDaniel	2.00	1.00	.60
304	Ron Brand	2.00	1.00	.60
305	Reggie Smith	2.00	1.00	.60
306a	Jim Nash (Black blob, left center.)	4.00	2.00	1.25
306b	Jim Nash (Blob airbrushed away.)	2.00	1.00	.60
307	Don Wert	2.00	1.00	.60
308	Cards Team	3.00	1.50	.90
309	Dick Ellsworth	2.00	1.00	.60
310	Tommie Agee	2.00	1.00	.60
311	Lee Stange	2.00	1.00	.60
312	Harry Walker	2.00	1.00	.60
313	Tom Hall	2.00	1.00	.60
314	Jeff Torborg	2.00	1.00	.60
315	Ron Fairly	2.00	1.00	.60
316	Fred Scherman	2.00	1.00	.60
317	Athletics Rookies (*Jim Driscoll, Angel Mangual*)	2.00	1.00	.60
318	Rudy May	2.00	1.00	.60
319	Ty Cline	2.00	1.00	.60
320	Dave McNally	2.00	1.00	.60
321	Tom Matchick	2.00	1.00	.60
322	Jim Beauchamp	2.00	1.00	.60
323	Billy Champion	2.00	1.00	.60
324	Graig Nettles	4.00	2.00	1.25
325	Juan Marichal	8.00	4.00	2.50
326	Richie Scheinblum	2.00	1.00	.60
327	World Series Game 1 (Powell Homers To Opposite Field!)	3.00	1.50	.90
328	World Series Game 2 (Buford Goes 2-For-4!)	2.00	1.00	.60
329	World Series Game 3 (F. Robinson Shows Muscle!)	6.00	3.00	1.75
330	World Series Game 4 (Reds Stay Alive!)	2.00	1.00	.60
331	World Series Game 5 (B. Robinson Commits Robbery!)	8.00	4.00	2.50
332	World Series Celebration! (Convincing Performance!)	5.00	2.50	1.50
333	Clay Kirby	2.00	1.00	.60
334	Roberto Pena	2.00	1.00	.60
335	Jerry Koosman	2.00	1.00	.60
336	Tigers Team	4.00	2.00	1.25
337	Jesus Alou	2.00	1.00	.60
338	Gene Tenace	2.00	1.00	.60
339	Wayne Simpson	2.00	1.00	.60
340	Rico Petrocelli	2.00	1.00	.60
341	*Steve Garvey*	30.00	15.00	9.00
342	Frank Tepedino	2.00	1.00	.60
343	Pirates Rookies (*Ed Acosta, Milt May*)	2.00	1.00	.60
344	Ellie Rodriguez	2.00	1.00	.60
345	Joe Horlen	2.00	1.00	.60
346	Lum Harris	2.00	1.00	.60
347	Ted Uhlaender	2.00	1.00	.60
348	Fred Norman	2.00	1.00	.60
349	Rich Reese	2.00	1.00	.60
350	Billy Williams	12.00	6.00	3.50
351	Jim Shellenback	2.00	1.00	.60
352	Denny Doyle	2.00	1.00	.60
353	Carl Taylor	2.00	1.00	.60
354	Don McMahon	2.00	1.00	.60
355	Bud Harrelson	2.00	1.00	.60
356	Bob Locker	2.00	1.00	.60
357	Reds Team	4.00	2.00	1.25
358	Danny Cater	2.00	1.00	.60
359	Ron Reed	2.00	1.00	.60
360	Jim Fregosi	2.00	1.00	.60
361	Don Sutton	8.00	4.00	2.50
362	Orioles Rookies (*Mike Adamson, Roger Freed*)	2.00	1.00	.60
363	Mike Nagy	2.00	1.00	.60
364	Tommy Dean	2.00	1.00	.60
365	Bob Johnson	2.00	1.00	.60
366	Ron Stone	2.00	1.00	.60
367	Dalton Jones	2.00	1.00	.60
368	Bob Veale	2.00	1.00	.60
369a	4th Series Checklist (394-523) (Orange helmet.)	5.00	2.50	1.50
369b	4th Series Checklist (394-523) (Red helmet, black line above ear.)	6.00	3.00	1.75
369c	4th Series Checklist (394-523) (Red helmet, no line.)	6.00	3.00	1.75
370	Joe Torre	6.00	3.00	1.75
371	Jack Hiatt	2.00	1.00	.60
372	Lew Krausse	2.00	1.00	.60
373	Tom McCraw	2.00	1.00	.60
374	Clete Boyer	2.00	1.00	.60
375	Steve Hargan	2.00	1.00	.60
376	Expos Rookies (*Clyde Mashore, Ernie McAnally*)	2.00	1.00	.60
377	Greg Garrett	2.00	1.00	.60
378	Tito Fuentes	2.00	1.00	.60
379	Wayne Granger	2.00	1.00	.60
380	Ted Williams	12.00	6.00	3.50
381	Fred Gladding	2.00	1.00	.60
382	Jake Gibbs	2.00	1.00	.60
383	Rod Gaspar	2.00	1.00	.60
384	Rollie Fingers	8.00	4.00	2.50
385	Maury Wills	4.00	2.00	1.25
386	Red Sox Team	4.00	2.00	1.25
387	Ron Herbel	2.00	1.00	.60
388	Al Oliver	2.00	1.00	.60
389	Ed Brinkman	2.00	1.00	.60
390	Glenn Beckert	2.00	1.00	.60
391	Twins Rookies (*Steve Brye, Cotton Nash*)	2.00	1.00	.60
392	Grant Jackson	2.00	1.00	.60
393	Merv Rettenmund	2.00	1.00	.60
394	Clay Carroll	2.00	1.00	.60
395	Roy White	2.00	1.00	.60
396	Dick Schofield	2.00	1.00	.60
397	Alvin Dark	2.00	1.00	.60
398	Howie Reed	2.00	1.00	.60
399	Jim French	2.00	1.00	.60
400	Hank Aaron	70.00	35.00	21.00
401	Tom Murphy	2.00	1.00	.60
402	Dodgers Team	4.00	2.00	1.25
403	Joe Coleman	2.00	1.00	.60
404	Astros Rookies (*Buddy Harris, Roger Metzger*)	2.00	1.00	.60
405	Leo Cardenas	2.00	1.00	.60
406	Ray Sadecki	2.00	1.00	.60
407	Joe Rudi	2.00	1.00	.60
408	Rafael Robles	2.00	1.00	.60
409	Don Pavletich	2.00	1.00	.60
410	Ken Holtzman	2.00	1.00	.60
411	George Spriggs	2.00	1.00	.60
412	Jerry Johnson	2.00	1.00	.60
413	Pat Kelly	2.00	1.00	.60
414	Woodie Fryman	2.00	1.00	.60
415	Mike Hegan	2.00	1.00	.60
416	Gene Alley	2.00	1.00	.60
417	Dick Hall	2.00	1.00	.60
418	Adolfo Phillips	2.00	1.00	.60
419	Ron Hansen	2.00	1.00	.60
420	Jim Merritt	2.00	1.00	.60
421	John Stephenson	2.00	1.00	.60
422	Frank Bertaina	2.00	1.00	.60
423	Tigers Rookies (*Tim Marting, Dennis Saunders*)	2.00	1.00	.60
424	Roberto Rodriquez (Rodriguez)	2.00	1.00	.60
425	Doug Rader	2.00	1.00	.60
426	Chris Cannizzaro	2.00	1.00	.60
427	Bernie Allen	2.00	1.00	.60
428	Jim McAndrew	2.00	1.00	.60
429	Chuck Hinton	2.00	1.00	.60
430	Wes Parker	2.00	1.00	.60
431	Tom Burgmeier	2.00	1.00	.60
432	Bob Didier	2.00	1.00	.60
433	Skip Lockwood	2.00	1.00	.60
434	Gary Sutherland	2.00	1.00	.60
435	Jose Cardenal	2.00	1.00	.60
436	Wilbur Wood	2.00	1.00	.60
437	Danny Murtaugh	2.00	1.00	.60
438	Mike McCormick	2.00	1.00	.60
439	Phillies Rookies (*Greg Luzinski, Scott Reid*)	5.00	2.50	1.50
440	Bert Campaneris	2.00	1.00	.60
441	Milt Pappas	2.00	1.00	.60
442	Angels Team	4.00	2.00	1.25
443	Rich Robertson	2.00	1.00	.60
444	Jimmie Price	2.00	1.00	.60
445	Art Shamsky	2.00	1.00	.60
446	Bobby Bolin	2.00	1.00	.60
447	*Cesar Geronimo*	3.00	1.50	.90
448	Dave Roberts	2.00	1.00	.60
449	Brant Alyea	2.00	1.00	.60
450	Bob Gibson	15.00	7.50	4.50
451	Joe Keough	2.00	1.00	.60
452	John Boccabella	2.00	1.00	.60
453	Terry Crowley	2.00	1.00	.60
454	Mike Paul	2.00	1.00	.60
455	Don Kessinger	2.00	1.00	.60
456	Bob Meyer	2.00	1.00	.60
457	Willie Smith	2.00	1.00	.60
458	White Sox Rookies (*Dave Lemonds, Ron Lolich*)	2.00	1.00	.60
459	Jim Lefebvre	2.00	1.00	.60
460	Fritz Peterson	2.00	1.00	.60
461	Jim Hart	2.00	1.00	.60
462	Senators Team	5.00	2.50	1.50
463	Tom Kelley	2.00	1.00	.60
464	Aurelio Rodriguez	2.00	1.00	.60
465	Tim McCarver	6.00	3.00	1.75
466	Ken Berry	2.00	1.00	.60
467	Al Santorini	2.00	1.00	.60
468	Frank Fernandez	2.00	1.00	.60
469	Bob Aspromonte	2.00	1.00	.60
470	Bob Oliver	2.00	1.00	.60
471	Tom Griffin	2.00	1.00	.60
472	Ken Rudolph	2.00	1.00	.60
473	Gary Wagner	2.00	1.00	.60
474	Jim Fairey	2.00	1.00	.60
475	Ron Perranoski	2.00	1.00	.60
476	Dal Maxvill	2.00	1.00	.60
477	Earl Weaver	5.00	2.50	1.50
478	Bernie Carbo	2.00	1.00	.60
479	Dennis Higgins	2.00	1.00	.60
480	Manny Sanguillen	2.00	1.00	.60
481	Daryl Patterson	2.00	1.00	.60
482	Padres Team	5.00	2.50	1.50
483	Gene Michael	2.00	1.00	.60
484	Don Wilson	2.00	1.00	.60
485	Ken McMullen	2.00	1.00	.60
486	Steve Huntz	2.00	1.00	.60
487	Paul Schaal	2.00	1.00	.60
488	Jerry Stephenson	2.00	1.00	.60
489	Luis Alvarado	2.00	1.00	.60
490	Deron Johnson	2.00	1.00	.60
491	Jim Hardin	2.00	1.00	.60
492	Ken Boswell	2.00	1.00	.60
493	Dave May	2.00	1.00	.60
494	Braves Rookies (*Ralph Garr, Rick Kester*)	2.00	1.00	.60
495	Felipe Alou	3.00	1.50	.90
496	Woody Woodward	2.00	1.00	.60
497	Horacio Pina	2.00	1.00	.60
498	John Kennedy	2.00	1.00	.60
499	5th Series Checklist (524-643)	6.00	3.00	1.75
500	Jim Perry	2.00	1.00	.60
501	Andy Etchebarren	2.00	1.00	.60
502	Cubs Team	5.00	2.50	1.50
503	Gates Brown	2.00	1.00	.60
504	Ken Wright	2.00	1.00	.60
505	Ollie Brown	2.00	1.00	.60
506	Bobby Knoop	2.00	1.00	.60
507	George Stone	2.00	1.00	.60
508	Roger Repoz	2.00	1.00	.60
509	Jim Grant	2.00	1.00	.60
510	Ken Harrelson	2.00	1.00	.60
511	Chris Short	2.00	1.00	.60
512	Red Sox Rookies (*Mike Garman, Dick Mills*)	2.00	1.00	.60
513	Nolan Ryan	140.00	70.00	42.00
514	Ron Woods	2.00	1.00	.60
515	Carl Morton	2.00	1.00	.60
516	Ted Kubiak	2.00	1.00	.60
517	Charlie Fox	2.00	1.00	.60
518	Joe Grzenda	2.00	1.00	.60
519	Willie Crawford	2.00	1.00	.60
520	Tommy John	5.00	2.50	1.50
521	Leron Lee	2.00	1.00	.60
522	Twins Team	4.00	2.00	1.25
523	John Odom	2.00	1.00	.60
524	Mickey Stanley	4.00	2.00	1.25
525	Ernie Banks	40.00	20.00	12.00
526	Ray Jarvis	4.00	2.00	1.25
527	Cleon Jones	4.00	2.00	1.25
528	Wally Bunker	4.00	2.00	1.25
529	N.L. Rookies (*Bill Buckner, Enzo Hernandez, Marty Perez*)	6.00	3.00	1.75
530	Carl Yastrzemski	25.00	12.50	7.50
531	Mike Torrez	4.00	2.00	1.25
532	Bill Rigney	4.00	2.00	1.25
533	Mike Ryan	4.00	2.00	1.25
534	Luke Walker	4.00	2.00	1.25
535	Curt Flood	5.00	2.50	1.50
536	Claude Raymond	4.00	2.00	1.25
537	Tom Egan	4.00	2.00	1.25
538	Angel Bravo	4.00	2.00	1.25
539	Larry Brown	4.00	2.00	1.25
540	Larry Dierker	4.00	2.00	1.25
541	Bob Burda	4.00	2.00	1.25
542	Bob Miller	4.00	2.00	1.25
543	Yankees Team	8.00	4.00	2.50
544	Vida Blue	5.00	2.50	1.50
545	Dick Dietz	4.00	2.00	1.25
546	John Matias	4.00	2.00	1.25
547	Pat Dobson	4.00	2.00	1.25
548	Don Mason	4.00	2.00	1.25
549	Jim Brewer	4.00	2.00	1.25
550	Harmon Killebrew	25.00	12.50	7.50
551	Frank Linzy	4.00	2.00	1.25
552	Buddy Bradford	4.00	2.00	1.25
553	Kevin Collins	4.00	2.00	1.25
554	Lowell Palmer	4.00	2.00	1.25
555	Walt Williams	4.00	2.00	1.25
556	Jim McGlothlin	4.00	2.00	1.25
557	Tom Satriano	4.00	2.00	1.25
558	Hector Torres	4.00	2.00	1.25
559	A.L. Rookies (*Terry Cox, Bill Gogolewski, Gary Jones*)	4.00	2.00	1.25
560	Rusty Staub	5.00	2.50	1.50
561	Syd O'Brien	4.00	2.00	1.25
562	Dave Giusti	4.00	2.00	1.25
563	Giants Team	10.00	5.00	3.00
564	Al Fitzmorris	4.00	2.00	1.25
565	Jim Wynn	4.00	2.00	1.25
566	Tim Cullen	4.00	2.00	1.25
567	Walt Alston	6.00	3.00	1.75
568	Sal Campisi	4.00	2.00	1.25
569	Ivan Murrell	4.00	2.00	1.25
570	Jim Palmer	25.00	12.50	7.50
571	Ted Sizemore	4.00	2.00	1.25
572	Jerry Kenney	4.00	2.00	1.25
573	Ed Kranepool	4.00	2.00	1.25
574	Jim Bunning	8.00	4.00	2.50
575	Bill Freehan	4.00	2.00	1.25
576	Cubs Rookies (*Brock Davis, Adrian Garrett, Garry Jestadt*)	4.00	2.00	1.25
577	Jim Lonborg	4.00	2.00	1.25
578	Ron Hunt	4.00	2.00	1.25
579	Marty Pattin	4.00	2.00	1.25
580	Tony Perez	20.00	10.00	6.00
581	Roger Nelson	4.00	2.00	1.25
582	Dave Cash	4.00	2.00	1.25
583	Ron Cook	4.00	2.00	1.25
584	Indians Team	10.00	5.00	3.00
585	Willie Davis	4.00	2.00	1.25
586	Dick Woodson	4.00	2.00	1.25
587	Sonny Jackson	4.00	2.00	1.25
588	Tom Bradley	4.00	2.00	1.25
589	Bob Barton	4.00	2.00	1.25
590	Alex Johnson	4.00	2.00	1.25
591	Jackie Brown	4.00	2.00	1.25
592	Randy Hundley	4.00	2.00	1.25
593	Jack Aker	4.00	2.00	1.25
594	Cards Rookies (*Bob Chlupsa, Al Hrabosky, Bob Stinson*)	6.00	3.00	1.75
595	Dave Johnson	4.00	2.00	1.25
596	Mike Jorgensen	4.00	2.00	1.25
597	Ken Suarez	4.00	2.00	1.25
598	Rick Wise	4.00	2.00	1.25
599	Norm Cash	6.00	3.00	1.75
600	Willie Mays	100.00	50.00	30.00
601	Ken Tatum	4.00	2.00	1.25
602	Marty Martinez	4.00	2.00	1.25
603	Pirates Team	8.00	4.00	2.50
604	John Gelnar	4.00	2.00	1.25
605	Orlando Cepeda	15.00	7.50	4.50
606	Chuck Taylor	4.00	2.00	1.25
607	Paul Ratliff	4.00	2.00	1.25
608	Mike Wegener	4.00	2.00	1.25
609	Leo Durocher	8.00	4.00	2.50
610	Amos Otis	4.00	2.00	1.25
611	Tom Phoebus	4.00	2.00	1.25
612	Indians Rookies (*Lou Camilli, Ted Ford, Steve Mingori*)	4.00	2.00	1.25
613	Pedro Borbon	4.00	2.00	1.25
614	Billy Cowan	4.00	2.00	1.25

615	Mel Stottlemyre	6.00	3.00	1.75
616	Larry Hisle	4.00	2.00	1.25
617	Clay Dalrymple	4.00	2.00	1.25
618	Tug McGraw	4.00	2.00	1.25
619a	6th Series Checklist (644-752) (No copyright on back.)	5.00	2.50	1.50
619b	6th Series Checklist (644-752) (With copyright, no wavy line on helmet brim.)	4.00	2.00	1.25
619c	6th Series Checklist (644-752) (With copyright, wavy line on helmet brim.)	4.00	2.00	1.25
620	Frank Howard	5.00	2.50	1.50
621	Ron Bryant	4.00	2.00	1.25
622	Joe Lahoud	4.00	2.00	1.25
623	Pat Jarvis	4.00	2.00	1.25
624	Athletics Team	10.00	5.00	3.00
625	Lou Brock	25.00	12.50	7.50
626	Freddie Patek	4.00	2.00	1.25
627	Steve Hamilton	4.00	2.00	1.25
628	John Bateman	4.00	2.00	1.25
629	John Hiller	4.00	2.00	1.25
630	Roberto Clemente	140.00	70.00	42.00
631	Eddie Fisher	4.00	2.00	1.25
632	Darrel Chaney	4.00	2.00	1.25
633	A.L. Rookies (*Bobby Brooks, Pete Koegel, Scott Northey*)	4.00	2.00	1.25
634	Phil Regan	4.00	2.00	1.25
635	Bobby Murcer	15.00	7.50	4.50
636	Denny Lemaster	4.00	2.00	1.25
637	Dave Bristol	4.00	2.00	1.25
638	Stan Williams	4.00	2.00	1.25
639	Tom Haller	4.00	2.00	1.25
640	Frank Robinson	40.00	20.00	12.00
641	Mets Team	10.00	5.00	3.00
642	Jim Roland	4.00	2.00	1.25
643	Rick Reichardt	4.00	2.00	1.25
644	Jim Stewart/SP	8.00	4.00	2.50
645	Jim Maloney/SP	8.00	4.00	2.50
646	Bobby Floyd/SP	8.00	4.00	2.50
647	Juan Pizarro	6.00	3.00	1.75
648	Mets Rookies (*Rich Folkers, Ted Martinez, Jon Matlack*)/SP	20.00	10.00	6.00
649	Sparky Lyle/SP	10.00	5.00	3.00
650	Rich Allen/SP	30.00	15.00	9.00
651	Jerry Robertson/SP	8.00	4.00	2.50
652	Braves Team	10.00	5.00	3.00
653	Russ Snyder/SP	8.00	4.00	2.50
654	Don Shaw/SP	8.00	4.00	2.50
655	Mike Epstein/SP	8.00	4.00	2.50
656	Gerry Nyman/SP	8.00	4.00	2.50
657	Jose Azcue	6.00	3.00	1.75
658	Paul Lindblad/SP	8.00	4.00	2.50
659	Byron Browne/SP	8.00	4.00	2.50
660	Ray Culp	6.00	3.00	1.75
661	Chuck Tanner/SP	8.00	4.00	2.50
662	Mike Hedlund/SP	8.00	4.00	2.50
663	Marv Staehle	6.00	3.00	1.75
664	Major League Rookies (*Archie Reynolds, Bob Reynolds, Ken Reynolds*)/SP	8.00	4.00	2.50
665	Ron Swoboda/SP	8.00	4.00	2.50
666	Gene Brabender/SP	8.00	4.00	2.50
667	Pete Ward	6.00	3.00	1.75
668	Gary Neibauer	6.00	3.00	1.75
669	Ike Brown/SP	8.00	4.00	2.50
670	Bill Hands	6.00	3.00	1.75
671	Bill Voss/SP	8.00	4.00	2.50
672	Ed Crosby/SP	8.00	4.00	2.50
673	Gerry Janeski/SP	8.00	4.00	2.50
674	Expos Team	12.00	6.00	3.50
675	Dave Boswell	6.00	3.00	1.75
676	Tommie Reynolds	6.00	3.00	1.75
677	Jack DiLauro/SP	8.00	4.00	2.50
678	George Thomas	6.00	3.00	1.75
679	Don O'Riley	6.00	3.00	1.75
680	Don Mincher/SP	8.00	4.00	2.50
681	Bill Butler	6.00	3.00	1.75
682	Terry Harmon	6.00	3.00	1.75
683	Bill Burbach/SP	8.00	4.00	2.50
684	Curt Motton	6.00	3.00	1.75
685	Moe Drabowsky	6.00	3.00	1.75
686	Chico Ruiz/SP	8.00	4.00	2.50
687	Ron Taylor/SP	8.00	4.00	2.50
688	Sparky Anderson/SP	25.00	12.50	7.50
689	Frank Baker	6.00	3.00	1.75
690	Bob Moose	6.00	3.00	1.75
691	Bob Heise	6.00	3.00	1.75
692	A.L. Rookies (*Hal Haydel, Rogelio Moret, Wayne Twitchell*)/SP	8.00	4.00	2.50
693	Jose Pena/SP	8.00	4.00	2.50
694	Rick Renick/SP	8.00	4.00	2.50
695	Joe Niekro	6.00	3.00	1.75
696	Jerry Morales	6.00	3.00	1.75
697	Rickey Clark/SP	8.00	4.00	2.50
698	Brewers Team /SP	20.00	10.00	6.00
699	Jim Britton	6.00	3.00	1.75
700	Boog Powell/SP	20.00	10.00	6.00
701	Bob Garibaldi	6.00	3.00	1.75
702	Milt Ramirez	6.00	3.00	1.75
703	Mike Kekich	6.00	3.00	1.75
704	J.C. Martin/SP	8.00	4.00	2.50
705	Dick Selma/SP	8.00	4.00	2.50
706	Joe Foy/SP	8.00	4.00	2.50
707	Fred Lasher	6.00	3.00	1.75
708	Russ Nagelson/SP	8.00	4.00	2.50
709	Major League Rookies (*Dusty Baker, Don Baylor, Tom Paciorek*)/SP	60.00	30.00	18.00
710	Sonny Siebert	6.00	3.00	1.75
711	Larry Stahl/SP	8.00	4.00	2.50
712	Jose Martinez	6.00	3.00	1.75
713	Mike Marshall/SP	8.00	4.00	2.50
714	Dick Williams/SP	8.00	4.00	2.50
715	Horace Clarke/SP	8.00	4.00	2.50
716	Dave Leonhard	6.00	3.00	1.75
717	Tommie Aaron/SP	8.00	4.00	2.50
718	Billy Wynne	6.00	3.00	1.75
719	Jerry May/SP	8.00	4.00	2.50
720	Matty Alou	6.00	3.00	1.75
721	John Morris	6.00	3.00	1.75
722	Astros Team/SP	15.00	7.50	4.50
723	Vicente Romo/SP	8.00	4.00	2.50
724	Tom Tischinski/SP	8.00	4.00	2.50
725	Gary Gentry/SP	8.00	4.00	2.50
726	Paul Popovich	6.00	3.00	1.75
727	Ray Lamb/SP	8.00	4.00	2.50
728	N.L. Rookies (*Keith Lampard, Wayne Redmond, Bernie Williams*)	6.00	3.00	1.75
729	Dick Billings	6.00	3.00	1.75
730	Jim Rooker	6.00	3.00	1.75
731	Jim Qualls/SP	8.00	4.00	2.50
732	Bob Reed	6.00	3.00	1.75
733	Lee Maye/SP	8.00	4.00	2.50
734	Rob Gardner/SP	8.00	4.00	2.50
735	Mike Shannon/SP	8.00	4.00	2.50
736	Mel Queen/SP	8.00	4.00	2.50
737	Preston Gomez/SP	8.00	4.00	2.50
738	Russ Gibson/SP	8.00	4.00	2.50
739	Barry Lersch/SP	8.00	4.00	2.50
740	Luis Aparicio/SP	25.00	12.50	7.50
741	Skip Guinn	6.00	3.00	1.75
742	Royals Team	10.00	5.00	3.00
743	John O'Donoghue/SP	8.00	4.00	2.50
744	Chuck Manuel/SP	8.00	4.00	2.50
745	Sandy Alomar/SP	8.00	4.00	2.50
746	Andy Kosco	6.00	3.00	1.75
747	N.L. Rookies (*Balor Moore, Al Severinsen, Scipio Spinks*)	6.00	3.00	1.75
748	John Purdin/SP	8.00	4.00	2.50
749	Ken Szotkiewicz	6.00	3.00	1.75
750	Denny McLain/SP	20.00	10.00	6.00
751	Al Weis/SP	6.00	3.00	1.75
752	Dick Drago	10.00	5.00	3.00

1971 Topps All-Star Rookies Artist's Proofs

There exists only one set of these artist's proofs for a proposed set of All-Star Rookie cards. The standard-size card fronts are pasted onto 9-1/2" x 6-1/2" cardboard backing. It may have been intended that these be issued in card form for Topps' annual banquet. There is a player for each position on the 1970 All-Rookie Team, plus right- and left-handed pitchers. Players are listed here in alphabetical order.

		NM	EX	VG
Complete Set (10):		1,500	750.00	450.00
Common Player:		200.00	100.00	60.00
(1)	Larry Bowa	350.00	175.00	105.00
(2)	Les Cain	200.00	100.00	60.00
(3)	Bernie Carbo	200.00	100.00	60.00
(4)	Dave Cash	200.00	100.00	60.00
(5)	Billy Conigliaro	200.00	100.00	60.00
(6)	John Ellis	200.00	100.00	60.00
(7)	Roy Foster	200.00	100.00	60.00
(8)	Alan Gallagher	200.00	100.00	60.00
(9)	Carl Morton	200.00	100.00	60.00
(10)	Thurman Munson	750.00	375.00	225.00

1971 Topps Coins

Measuring 1-1/2" in diameter, the latest edition of the Topps coins was a 153-piece set. The coins feature a color photograph surrounded by a colored band on the front. The band carries the player's name, team, position and several stars. Backs have a short biography, the coin number and encourage-

ment to collect the entire set. Back colors differ, with #s 1-51 having a brass back, #s 52-102 chrome backs, and the rest have blue backs. Most of the stars of the period are included in the set.

		NM	EX	VG
Complete Set (153):		500.00	250.00	150.00
Common Player:		2.00	1.00	.60
1	Cito Gaston	2.00	1.00	.60
2	Dave Johnson	2.00	1.00	.60
3	Jim Bunning	8.00	4.00	2.50
4	Jim Spencer	2.00	1.00	.60
5	Felix Millan	2.00	1.00	.60
6	Gerry Moses	2.00	1.00	.60
7	Fergie Jenkins	8.00	4.00	2.50
8	Felipe Alou	2.50	1.25	.70
9	Jim McGlothlin	2.00	1.00	.60
10	Dick McAuliffe	2.00	1.00	.60
11	Joe Torre	5.00	2.50	1.50
12	Jim Perry	2.00	1.00	.60
13	Bobby Bonds	2.00	1.00	.60
14	Danny Cater	2.00	1.00	.60
15	Bill Mazeroski	8.00	4.00	2.50
16	Luis Aparicio	8.00	4.00	2.50
17	Doug Rader	2.00	1.00	.60
18	Vada Pinson	3.00	1.50	.90
19	John Bateman	2.00	1.00	.60
20	Lew Krausse	2.00	1.00	.60
21	Billy Grabarkewitz	2.00	1.00	.60
22	Frank Howard	2.00	1.00	.60
23	Jerry Koosman	2.00	1.00	.60
24	Rod Carew	10.00	5.00	3.00
25	Al Ferrara	2.00	1.00	.60
26	Dave McNally	2.00	1.00	.60
27	Jim Hickman	2.00	1.00	.60
28	Sandy Alomar	2.00	1.00	.60
29	Lee May	2.00	1.00	.60
30	Rico Petrocelli	2.00	1.00	.60
31	Don Money	2.00	1.00	.60
32	Jim Rooker	2.00	1.00	.60
33	Dick Dietz	2.00	1.00	.60
34	Roy White	2.00	1.00	.60
35	Carl Morton	2.00	1.00	.60
36	Walt Williams	2.00	1.00	.60
37	Phil Niekro	8.00	4.00	2.50
38	Bill Freehan	2.00	1.00	.60
39	Julian Javier	2.00	1.00	.60
40	Rick Monday	2.00	1.00	.60
41	Don Wilson	2.00	1.00	.60
42	Ray Fosse	2.00	1.00	.60
43	Art Shamsky	2.00	1.00	.60
44	Ted Savage	2.00	1.00	.60
45	Claude Osteen	2.00	1.00	.60
46	Ed Brinkman	2.00	1.00	.60
47	Matty Alou	2.00	1.00	.60
48	Bob Oliver	2.00	1.00	.60
49	Danny Coombs	2.00	1.00	.60
50	Frank Robinson	10.00	5.00	3.00
51	Randy Hundley	2.00	1.00	.60
52	Cesar Tovar	2.00	1.00	.60
53	Wayne Simpson	2.00	1.00	.60
54	Bobby Murcer	2.00	1.00	.60
55	Tony Taylor	2.00	1.00	.60
56	Tommy John	3.00	1.50	.90
57	Willie McCovey	9.00	4.50	2.75
58	Carl Yastrzemski	13.50	6.75	4.00
59	Bob Bailey	2.00	1.00	.60
60	Clyde Wright	2.00	1.00	.60
61	Orlando Cepeda	8.00	4.00	2.50
62	Al Kaline	10.00	5.00	3.00
63	Bob Gibson	9.00	4.50	2.75
64	Bert Campaneris	2.00	1.00	.60
65	Ted Sizemore	2.00	1.00	.60
66	Duke Sims	2.00	1.00	.60
67	Bud Harrelson	2.00	1.00	.60
68	Jerry McNertney	2.00	1.00	.60
69	Jim Wynn	2.00	1.00	.60
70	Dick Bosman	2.00	1.00	.60
71	Roberto Clemente	30.00	15.00	9.00
72	Rich Reese	2.00	1.00	.60
73	Gaylord Perry	8.00	4.00	2.50
74	Boog Powell	3.00	1.50	.90
75	Billy Williams	9.00	4.50	2.75
76	Bill Melton	2.00	1.00	.60
77	Nate Colbert	2.00	1.00	.60
78	Reggie Smith	2.00	1.00	.60
79	Deron Johnson	2.00	1.00	.60
80	Catfish Hunter	8.00	4.00	2.50
81	Bob Tolan	2.00	1.00	.60
82	Jim Northrup	2.00	1.00	.60
83	Ron Fairly	2.00	1.00	.60
84	Alex Johnson	2.00	1.00	.60
85	Pat Jarvis	2.00	1.00	.60
86	Sam McDowell	2.00	1.00	.60
87	Lou Brock	9.00	4.50	2.75
88	Danny Walton	2.00	1.00	.60
89	Denis Menke	2.00	1.00	.60
90	Jim Palmer	9.00	4.50	2.75
91	Tommie Agee	2.00	1.00	.60
92	Duane Josephson	2.00	1.00	.60
93	Willie Davis	2.00	1.00	.60
94	Mel Stottlemyre	2.00	1.00	.60
95	Ron Santo	5.00	2.50	1.50
96	Amos Otis	2.00	1.00	.60
97	Ken Henderson	2.00	1.00	.60
98	George Scott	2.00	1.00	.60
99	Dock Ellis	2.00	1.00	.60
100	Harmon Killebrew	10.00	5.00	3.00
101	Pete Rose	20.00	10.00	6.00
102	Rick Reichardt	2.00	1.00	.60
103	Cleon Jones	2.00	1.00	.60
104	Ron Perranoski	2.00	1.00	.60
105	Tony Perez	9.00	4.50	2.75
106	Mickey Lolich	2.00	1.00	.60
107	Tim McCarver	3.00	1.50	.90
108	Reggie Jackson	15.00	7.50	4.50
109	Chris Cannizzaro	2.00	1.00	.60

		NM	EX	VG
110	Steve Hargan	2.00	1.00	.60
111	Rusty Staub	3.00	1.50	.90
112	Andy Messersmith	2.00	1.00	.60
113	Rico Carty	2.00	1.00	.60
114	Brooks Robinson	10.00	5.00	3.00
115	Steve Carlton	9.00	4.50	2.75
116	Mike Hegan	2.00	1.00	.60
117	Joe Morgan	9.00	4.50	2.75
118	Thurman Munson	8.00	4.00	2.50
119	Don Kessinger	2.00	1.00	.60
120	Joe Horlen	2.00	1.00	.60
121	Wes Parker	2.00	1.00	.60
122	Sonny Siebert	2.00	1.00	.60
123	Willie Stargell	9.00	4.50	2.75
124	Ellie Rodriguez	2.00	1.00	.60
125	Juan Marichal	8.00	4.00	2.50
126	Mike Epstein	2.00	1.00	.60
127	Tom Seaver	10.00	5.00	3.00
128	Tony Oliva	3.00	1.50	.90
129	Jim Merritt	2.00	1.00	.60
130	Willie Horton	2.00	1.00	.60
131	Rick Wise	2.00	1.00	.60
132	Sal Bando	2.00	1.00	.60
133	Ollie Brown	2.00	1.00	.60
134	Ken Harrelson	2.00	1.00	.60
135	Mack Jones	2.00	1.00	.60
136	Jim Fregosi	2.00	1.00	.60
137	Hank Aaron	25.00	12.50	7.50
138	Fritz Peterson	2.00	1.00	.60
139	Joe Hague	2.00	1.00	.60
140	Tommy Harper	2.00	1.00	.60
141	Larry Dierker	2.00	1.00	.60
142	Tony Conigliaro	4.00	2.00	1.25
143	Glenn Beckert	2.00	1.00	.60
144	Carlos May	2.00	1.00	.60
145	Don Sutton	8.00	4.00	2.50
146	Paul Casanova	2.00	1.00	.60
147	Bob Moose	2.00	1.00	.60
148	Leo Cardenas	2.00	1.00	.60
149	Johnny Bench	10.00	5.00	3.00
150	Mike Cuellar	2.00	1.00	.60
151	Donn Clendenon	2.00	1.00	.60
152	Lou Piniella	3.00	1.50	.90
153	Willie Mays	25.00	12.50	7.50

1971 Topps Greatest Moments

This 55-card set features highlights from the careers of top players of the day. The front of the 2-1/2" x 4-3/4" cards features a portrait photo of the player at left and deckle-edge action photo at right. There is a small headline on the white border of the action photo. The player's name and "One of Baseball's Greatest Moments" along with a black border complete the front. The back features a detail from the front photo and the story of the event. The newspaper style presentation includes the name of real newspapers. Relatively scarce, virtually every card in this set is a star or at least an above-average player. Because of their unusual size, 22 of the cards were double-printed, as indicated in the checklist here. Because of endemic centering problems there is a greater than usual value difference between NM and lower-grade cards.

		NM	EX	VG
Complete Set (55):		4,500	2,250	1,350
Common Player:		20.00	10.00	6.00
1	Thurman Munson/DP	300.00	150.00	90.00
2	Hoyt Wilhelm	75.00	37.50	22.50
3	Rico Carty	65.00	32.50	20.00
4	Carl Morton/DP	20.00	10.00	6.00
5	Sal Bando/DP	20.00	10.00	6.00
6	Bert Campaneris/DP	20.00	10.00	6.00
7	Jim Kaat	70.00	35.00	20.00
8	Harmon Killebrew	225.00	110.00	65.00
9	Brooks Robinson	250.00	125.00	75.00
10	Jim Perry	45.00	22.50	13.50
11	Tony Oliva	125.00	62.50	37.50
12	Vada Pinson	125.00	62.50	37.50
13	Johnny Bench	300.00	150.00	90.00
14	Tony Perez	100.00	50.00	30.00
15	Pete Rose/DP	145.00	75.00	45.00

		NM	EX	VG
16	Jim Fregosi/DP	20.00	10.00	6.00
17	Alex Johnson/DP	20.00	10.00	6.00
18	Clyde Wright/DP	20.00	10.00	6.00
19	Al Kaline/DP	100.00	50.00	30.00
20	Denny McLain	50.00	25.00	15.00
21	Jim Northrup	45.00	22.50	13.50
22	Bill Freehan	50.00	25.00	15.00
23	Mickey Lolich	60.00	30.00	18.00
24	Bob Gibson/DP	75.00	37.50	22.50
25	Tim McCarver/DP	35.00	17.50	10.00
26	Orlando Cepeda/DP	45.00	22.50	13.50
27	Lou Brock/DP	60.00	30.00	18.00
28	Nate Colbert/DP	20.00	10.00	6.00
29	Maury Wills	50.00	25.00	15.00
30	Wes Parker	65.00	32.50	20.00
31	Jim Wynn	55.00	27.50	16.50
32	Larry Dierker	60.00	30.00	18.00
33	Bill Melton	60.00	30.00	18.00
34	Joe Morgan	75.00	37.50	22.50
35	Rusty Staub	65.00	32.50	20.00
36	Ernie Banks/DP	95.00	47.50	27.50
37	Billy Williams	75.00	37.50	22.50
38	Lou Piniella	80.00	40.00	24.00
39	Rico Petrocelli/DP	35.00	17.50	10.00
40	Carl Yastrzemski/DP	95.00	47.50	27.50
41	Willie Mays/DP	175.00	85.00	55.00
42	Tommy Harper	45.00	22.50	13.50
43	Jim Bunning/DP	25.00	12.50	7.50
44	Fritz Peterson	60.00	30.00	18.00
45	Roy White	75.00	37.50	22.50
46	Bobby Murcer	165.00	80.00	50.00
47	Reggie Jackson	600.00	300.00	180.00
48	Frank Howard	60.00	30.00	18.00
49	Dick Bosman	50.00	25.00	15.00
50	Sam McDowell /DP	25.00	12.50	7.50
51	Luis Aparicio /DP	45.00	22.50	13.50
52	Willie McCovey/DP	65.00	32.50	20.00
53	Joe Pepitone	65.00	32.50	20.00
54	Jerry Grote	45.00	22.50	13.50
55	Bud Harrelson	90.00	45.00	27.50

1971 Topps Scratch-Offs

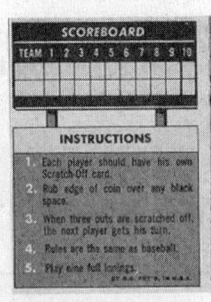

For a second year in 1971, Topps continued its scratch-off baseball card game with the same checklist of 24 players from the previous year. Unfolded, cards measure 3-3/8" x 5", and reveal a baseball game played by rubbing the black ink off squares to determine the "action." Fronts of the cards have a player picture as "captain," while backs have instructions and a scoreboard. Inserts with white centers are from 1970 while those with red centers are from 1971.

		NM	EX	VG
Complete Set (24):		65.00	32.50	20.00
Common Player:		1.50	.75	.45
(1)	Hank Aaron	7.50	3.75	2.25
(2)	Rich Allen	2.00	1.00	.60
(3)	Luis Aparicio	3.50	1.75	1.00
(4)	Sal Bando	1.50	.75	.45
(5)	Glenn Beckert	1.50	.75	.45
(6)	Dick Bosman	1.50	.75	.45
(7)	Nate Colbert	1.50	.75	.45
(8)	Mike Hegan	1.50	.75	.45
(9)	Mack Jones	1.50	.75	.45
(10)	Al Kaline	5.00	2.50	1.50
(11)	Harmon Killebrew	5.00	2.50	1.50
(12)	Juan Marichal	3.50	1.75	1.00
(13)	Tim McCarver	2.00	1.00	.60
(14)	Sam McDowell	1.50	.75	.45
(15)	Claude Osteen	1.50	.75	.45
(16)	Tony Perez	3.50	1.75	1.00
(17)	Lou Piniella	1.50	.75	.45
(18)	Boog Powell	2.00	1.00	.60
(19)	Tom Seaver	5.00	2.50	1.50
(20)	Jim Spencer	1.50	.75	.45
(21)	Willie Stargell	3.50	1.75	1.00
(22)	Mel Stottlemyre	1.50	.75	.45
(23)	Jim Wynn	1.50	.75	.45
(24)	Carl Yastrzemski	5.00	2.50	1.50

1971 Topps Super

Topps continued to produce its special oversized cards in 1971. Measuring 3-1/8" x 5-1/4" with rounded corners, they feature a borderless color photograph with a facsimile autograph on front. Backs are basically enlargements of the player's regular Topps card. The set size was enlarged to 63 cards in 1971, so there are no short-printed cards as in 1970. Proof cards with square corners and blank backs, measuring about 3-3/8" x 5-1/2", are known.

		NM	EX	VG
Complete Set (63):		300.00	150.00	90.00
Common Player:		3.00	1.50	.90
Wax Pack (3):		50.00		
Proofs: 1-2X				
1	Reggie Smith	3.00	1.50	.90
2	Gaylord Perry	7.50	3.75	2.25
3	Ted Savage	3.00	1.50	.90
4	Donn Clendenon	3.00	1.50	.90
5	Boog Powell	4.50	2.25	1.25
6	Tony Perez	7.50	3.75	2.25
7	Dick Bosman	3.00	1.50	.90
8	Alex Johnson	3.00	1.50	.90
9	Rusty Staub	3.50	1.75	1.00
10	Mel Stottlemyre	3.00	1.50	.90
11	Tony Oliva	4.00	2.00	1.25
12	Bill Freehan	3.00	1.50	.90
13	Fritz Peterson	3.00	1.50	.90
14	Wes Parker	3.00	1.50	.90
15	Cesar Cedeno	3.00	1.50	.90
16	Sam McDowell	3.00	1.50	.90
17	Frank Howard	3.00	1.50	.90
18	Dave McNally	3.00	1.50	.90
19	Rico Petrocelli	3.00	1.50	.90
20	Pete Rose	25.00	12.50	7.50
21	Luke Walker	3.00	1.50	.90
22	Nate Colbert	3.00	1.50	.90
23	Luis Aparicio	7.50	3.75	2.25
24	Jim Perry	3.00	1.50	.90
25	Louis Brock	9.00	4.50	2.75
26	Roy White	3.00	1.50	.90
27	Claude Osteen	3.00	1.50	.90
28	Carl W. Morton	3.00	1.50	.90
29	Rico Carty	3.00	1.50	.90
30	Larry Dierker	3.00	1.50	.90
31	Bert Campaneris	3.00	1.50	.90
32	Johnny Bench	10.00	5.00	3.00
33	Felix Millan	3.00	1.50	.90
34	Tim McCarver	3.50	1.75	1.00
35	Ronald Santo	6.00	3.00	1.75
36	Tommie Agee	3.00	1.50	.90
37	Roberto Clemente	40.00	20.00	12.00
38	Reggie Jackson	20.00	10.00	6.00
39	Clyde Wright	3.00	1.50	.90
40	Rich Allen	4.50	2.25	1.25
41	Curt Flood	3.50	1.75	1.00
42	Fergie Jenkins	7.50	3.75	2.25
43	Willie Stargell	9.00	4.50	2.75
44	Henry Aaron	25.00	12.50	7.50
45	Amos Otis	3.00	1.50	.90
46	Willie McCovey	9.00	4.50	2.75
47	William Melton	3.00	1.50	.90
48	Bob Gibson	9.00	4.50	2.75
49	Carl Yastrzemski	12.00	6.00	3.50
50	Glenn Beckert	3.00	1.50	.90
51	Ray Fosse	3.00	1.50	.90
52	Clarence Gaston	3.00	1.50	.90
53	Tom Seaver	10.00	5.00	3.00
54	Al Kaline	10.00	5.00	3.00
55	Jim Northrup	3.00	1.50	.90
56	Willie Mays	25.00	12.50	7.50
57	Sal Bando	3.00	1.50	.90
58	Deron Johnson	3.00	1.50	.90
59	Brooks Robinson	10.00	5.00	3.00
60	Harmon Killebrew	9.00	4.50	2.75
61	Joseph Torre	4.50	2.25	1.25
62	Lou Piniella	4.50	2.25	1.25
63	Tommy Harper	3.00	1.50	.90

1971 Topps Tattoos

Topps once again produced baseball tattoos in 1971. This time, the tattoos came in a variety of sizes, shapes and themes. The sheets of tattoos measure 3-1/2" x 14-1/4". Each sheet contains an assortment of tattoos in two sizes, 1-3/4" x 2-3/8" or 1-3/16" x 1-3/4". There are players, facsimile autographed baseballs, team pennants and assorted baseball cartoon figures carried on the 16 different sheets. Listings below are for complete sheets; with the exception of the biggest-name stars, individual tattoos have little or no collector value.

	NM	EX	VG
Complete Sheet Set (16):	350.00	175.00	100.00
Common Sheet:	10.00	5.00	3.00
Unopened Pack:	25.00		

1 Brooks Robinson Autograph Montreal Expos Pennant San Francisco Giants Pennant (Sal Bando, Dick Bosman, Nate Colbert, Cleon Jones, Juan Marichal) 25.00 12.50 7.50
2 Red Sox Pennant Carl Yastrzemski Autograph New York Mets Pennant (Glenn Beckert, Tommy Harper, Ken Henderson, Fritz Peterson, Bob Robertson, Carl Yastrzemski) 35.00 17.50 10.00
3 Jim Fregosi Autograph New York Yankees Pennant Philadelphia Phillies Pennant (Orlando Cepeda, Jim Fregosi, Randy Hundley, Reggie Jackson, Jerry Koosman, Jim Palmer) 35.00 17.50 10.00
4 Kansas City Royals Pennant Oakland Athletics Pennant Sam McDowell Autograph (Dick Dietz, Cito Gaston, Dave Johnson, Sam McDowell, Gary Nolan, Amos Otis) 10.00 5.00 3.00
5 Al Kaline Autograph Braves Pennant L.A. Dodgers Pennant (Bill Grabarkewitz, Al Kaline, Lee May, Tom Murphy, Vada Pinson, Manny Sanguillen) 20.00 10.00 6.00
6 Chicago Cubs Pennant Cincinnati Reds Pennant Harmon Kilebrew Autograph (Luis Aparicio, Paul Blair, Chris Cannizzaro, Donn Clendenon, Larry Dieker, Harmon Killebrew) 25.00 12.50 7.50
7 Boog Powell Autograph Cleveland Indians Pennant Milwaukee Brewers Pennant (Rich Allen, Bert Campaneris, Don Money, Boog Powell, Ted Savage, Rusty Staub) 15.00 7.50 4.50
8 Chicago White Sox Pennant Frank Howard Autograph San Diego Padres Pennant (Leo Cardenas, Bill Hands, Frank Howard, Wes Parker, Reggie Smith, Willie Stargell) 10.00 5.00 3.00
9 Detroit Tigers Pennant Henry Aaron Autograph (Hank Aaron, Tommy Agee, Jim Hunter, Dick McAuliffe, Tony Perez, Lou Piniella) 35.00 17.50 10.00
10 Baltimore Orioles Pennant Fergie Jenkins Autograph (Roberto Clemente, Tony Conigliaro, Fergie Jenkins, Thurman Munson, Gary Peters, Joe Torre) 50.00 25.00 15.00
11 Johnny Bench Autograph Washington Senators Pennant (Johnny Bench, Rico Carty, Bill Mazeroski, Bob Oliver, Rico Petrocelli, Frank Robinson) 35.00 17.50 10.00
12 Billy Williams Autograph Houston Astros Pennant (Bill Freehan, Dave McNally, Felix Millan, Mel Stottlemyre, Bob Tolan, Billy Williams) 15.00 7.50 4.50
13 Pittsburgh Pirates Pennant Willie McCovey Aut zograph (Ray Culp, Bud Harrelson, Mickey Lolich, Willie McCovey, Ron Santo, Roy White) 20.00 10.00 6.00
14 Minnesota Twins Pennant Tom Seaver Autograph (Bill Melton, Jim Perry, Pete Rose, Tom Seaver, Maury Wills, Clyde Wright) 45.00 22.00 13.50
15 Robert Gibson Autograph St. Louis Cardinals Pennant (Rod Carew, Bob Gibson, Alex Johnson, Don Kessinger, Jim Merritt, Rick Monday) 20.00 10.00 6.00
16 Angels Pennant Willie Mays Autograph (Larry Bowa, Mike Cuellar, Ray Fosse, Willie Mays, Carl Morton, Tony Oliva) 25.00 12.50 7.50

1972 Topps

The largest Topps issue of its time appeared in 1972, with the set size reaching the 787 mark. The 2-1/2" x 3-1/2" cards are something special as well. Their fronts have a color photo which is shaped into an arch and surrounded by two different color borders, all of which is inside the overall white border. The player's name is in a white panel below the picture while the team name is above the picture in what might best be described as "superhero" type in a variety of colors. No mention of the player's position appears on the front. Cards backs are tame by comparison, featuring statistics and a trivia question. The set features a record number of specialty cards including more than six dozen "In Action" (shown as "IA" in checklists below) cards featuring action shots of popular players. There are the usual statistical leaders, playoff and World Series highlights. Other innovations are 16 "Boyhood Photo" cards which depict scrapbook black and white photos of 1972's top players, and a group of cards depicting the trophies which comprise baseball's major awards. Finally, a group of seven "Traded" cards was included which feature a large "Traded" across the front of the card.

		NM	EX	VG
	Complete Set (787):	1,600	800.00	475.00
	Common Player (1-525):	1.50	.70	.45
	Common Player (526-656):	3.00	1.50	.90
	Common Player (657-787):	10.00	5.00	3.00
1	Pirates Team (World Champions)	8.00	4.00	2.50
2	Ray Culp	1.50	.70	.45
3	Bob Tolan	1.50	.70	.45
4	1st Series Checklist (1-132)	4.00	2.00	1.25
5	John Bateman	1.50	.70	.45
6	Fred Scherman	1.50	.70	.45
7	Enzo Hernandez	1.50	.70	.45
8	Ron Swoboda	1.50	.70	.45
9	Stan Williams	1.50	.70	.45
10	Amos Otis	1.50	.70	.45
11	Bobby Valentine	1.50	.70	.45
12	Jose Cardenal	1.50	.70	.45
13	Joe Grzenda	1.50	.70	.45
14	Phillies Rookies (**Mike Anderson, Pete Koegel, Wayne Twitchell**)	1.50	.70	.45
15	Walt Williams	1.50	.70	.45
16	Mike Jorgensen	1.50	.70	.45
17	Dave Duncan	1.50	.70	.45
18a	Juan Pizarro (Green under "C" and "S.")	7.50	3.75	2.25
18b	Juan Pizarro (Yellow under "C" and "S.")	1.50	.70	.45
19	Billy Cowan	1.50	.70	.45
20	Don Wilson	1.50	.70	.45
21	Braves Team	3.00	1.50	.90
22	Rob Gardner	1.50	.70	.45
23	Ted Kubiak	1.50	.70	.45
24	Ted Ford	1.50	.70	.45
25	Bill Singer	1.50	.70	.45
26	Andy Etchebarren	1.50	.70	.45
27	Bob Johnson	1.50	.70	.45
28	Twins Rookies (**Steve Brye, Bob Gebhard, Hal Haydel**)	1.50	.70	.45
29a	Bill Bonham (Green under "C" and "S.")	7.50	3.75	2.25
29b	Bill Bonham (Yellow under "C" and "S.")	1.50	.70	.45
30	Rico Petrocelli	1.50	.70	.45
31	Cleon Jones	1.50	.70	.45
32	Cleon Jones (In Action)	1.50	.70	.45
33	Billy Martin	6.00	3.00	1.75
34	Billy Martin (In Action)	2.00	1.00	.60
35	Jerry Johnson	1.50	.70	.45
36	Jerry Johnson (In Action)	1.50	.70	.45
37	Carl Yastrzemski	8.00	4.00	2.50
38	Carl Yastrzemski (In Action)	5.00	2.50	1.50
39	Bob Barton	1.50	.70	.45
40	Bob Barton (In Action)	1.50	.70	.45
41	Tommy Davis	1.50	.70	.45
42	Tommy Davis (In Action)	1.50	.70	.45
43	Rick Wise	1.50	.70	.45
44	Rick Wise (In Action)	1.50	.70	.45
45a	Glenn Beckert (Green under "C" and "S.")	7.50	3.75	2.25
45b	Glenn Beckert (Yellow under "C" and "S.")	1.50	.70	.45
46	Glenn Beckert (In Action)	1.50	.70	.45
47	John Ellis	1.50	.70	.45
48	John Ellis (In Action)	1.50	.70	.45
49	Willie Mays	40.00	20.00	12.00
50	Willie Mays (In Action)	20.00	10.00	6.00
51	Harmon Killebrew	8.00	4.00	2.50
52	Harmon Killebrew (In Action)	5.00	2.50	1.50
53	Bud Harrelson	1.50	.70	.45
54	Bud Harrelson (In Action)	1.50	.70	.45
55	Clyde Wright	1.50	.70	.45
56	Rich Chiles	1.50	.70	.45
57	Bob Oliver	1.50	.70	.45
58	Ernie McAnally	1.50	.70	.45
59	*Fred Stanley*	1.50	.70	.45
60	Manny Sanguillen	1.50	.70	.45
61	Cubs Rookies (**Gene Hiser, Burt Hooton, Earl Stephenson**)	1.50	.70	.45
62	Angel Mangual	1.50	.70	.45
63	Duke Sims	1.50	.70	.45
64	Pete Broberg	1.50	.70	.45
65	Cesar Cedeno	1.50	.70	.45
66	Ray Corbin	1.50	.70	.45
67	Red Schoendienst	4.00	2.00	1.25
68	Jim York	1.50	.70	.45
69	Roger Freed	1.50	.70	.45
70	Mike Cuellar	1.50	.70	.45
71	Angels Team	3.00	1.50	.90
72	*Bruce Kison*	1.50	.70	.45
73	Steve Huntz	1.50	.70	.45
74	Cecil Upshaw	1.50	.70	.45
75	Bert Campaneris	1.50	.70	.45
76	Don Carrithers	1.50	.70	.45
77	Ron Theobald	1.50	.70	.45
78	Steve Arlin	1.50	.70	.45
79	Red Sox Rookies (**Cecil Cooper, Carlton Fisk, Mike Garman**)	40.00	20.00	12.00
80	Tony Perez	6.00	3.00	1.75
81	Mike Hedlund	1.50	.70	.45
82	Ron Woods	1.50	.70	.45
83	Dalton Jones	1.50	.70	.45
84	Vince Colbert	1.50	.70	.45
85	N.L. Batting Leaders (Glenn Beckert, Ralph Garr, Joe Torre)	4.00	2.00	1.25
86	A.L. Batting Leaders (Bobby Murcer, Tony Oliva, Merv Rettenmund)	3.00	1.50	.90
87	N.L. R.B.I. Leaders (Hank Aaron, Willie Stargell, Joe Torre)	6.00	3.00	1.75
88	A.L. R.B.I. Leaders (Harmon Killebrew, Frank Robinson, Reggie Smith)	3.00	1.50	.90
89	N.L. Home Run Leaders (Hank Aaron, Lee May, Willie Stargell)	6.00	3.00	1.75
90	A.L. Home Run Leaders (Norm Cash, Reggie Jackson, Bill Melton)	4.00	2.00	1.25
91	N.L. E.R.A. Leaders (Dave Roberts (Picture is Denny Coombs), Tom Seaver, Don Wilson.)	2.50	1.25	.70
92	A.L. E.R.A. Leaders (Vida Blue, Jim Palmer, Wilbur Wood)	2.00	1.00	.60
93	N.L. Pitching Leaders (Steve Carlton, Al Downing, Fergie Jenkins, Tom Seaver)	4.00	2.00	1.25
94	A.L. Pitching Leaders (Vida Blue, Mickey Lolich, Wilbur Wood)	1.50	.70	.45
95	N.L. Strikeout Leaders (Fergie Jenkins, Tom Seaver, Bill Stoneman)	4.00	2.00	1.25
96	A.L. Strikeout Leaders (Vida Blue, Joe Coleman, Mickey Lolich)	1.50	.70	.45
97	Tom Kelley	1.50	.70	.45
98	Chuck Tanner	1.50	.70	.45
99	*Ross Grimsley*	1.50	.70	.45
100	Frank Robinson	8.00	4.00	2.50
101	Astros Rookies (**Ray Busse, Bill Grief, J.R. Richard**)	4.00	2.00	1.25
102	Lloyd Allen	1.50	.70	.45
103	2nd Series Checklist (133-263)	2.00	1.00	.60
104	*Toby Harrah*	1.50	.70	.45
105	Gary Gentry	1.50	.70	.45
106	Brewers Team	3.00	1.50	.90
107	*Jose Cruz*	3.00	1.50	.90
108	Gary Waslewski	1.50	.70	.45
109	Jerry May	1.50	.70	.45
110	Ron Hunt	1.50	.70	.45
111	Jim Grant	1.50	.70	.45
112	Greg Luzinski	1.50	.70	.45
113	Rogelio Moret	1.50	.70	.45
114	Bill Buckner	1.50	.70	.45
115	Jim Fregosi	1.50	.70	.45
116	*Ed Farmer*	1.50	.70	.45
117a	Cleo James (Green under "C" and "S.")	7.50	3.75	2.25
117b	Cleo James (Yellow under "C" and "S.")	1.50	.70	.45
118	Skip Lockwood	1.50	.70	.45
119	Marty Perez	1.50	.70	.45
120	Bill Freehan	1.50	.70	.45
121	Ed Sprague	1.50	.70	.45
122	Larry Biittner	1.50	.70	.45
123	Ed Acosta	1.50	.70	.45
124	Yankees Rookies (**Alan Closter, Roger Hambright, Rusty Torres**)	1.50	.70	.45
125	Dave Cash	1.50	.70	.45
126	Bart Johnson	1.50	.70	.45
127	Duffy Dyer	1.50	.70	.45
128	Eddie Watt	1.50	.70	.45
129	Charlie Fox	1.50	.70	.45
130	Bob Gibson	8.00	4.00	2.50
131	Jim Nettles	1.50	.70	.45
132	Joe Morgan	8.00	4.00	2.50

133	Joe Keough	1.50	.70	.45
134	Carl Morton	1.50	.70	.45
135	Vada Pinson	2.50	1.25	.70
136	Darrel Chaney	1.50	.70	.45
137	Dick Williams	1.50	.70	.45
138	Mike Kekich	1.50	.70	.45
139	Tim McCarver	3.00	1.50	.90
140	Pat Dobson	1.50	.70	.45
141	Mets Rookies	1.50	.70	.45
	(*Buzz Capra, Jon Matlack, Leroy Stanton*)			
142	*Chris Chambliss*	3.00	1.50	.90
143	Garry Jestadt	1.50	.70	.45
144	Marty Pattin	1.50	.70	.45
145	Don Kessinger	1.50	.70	.45
146	Steve Kealey	1.50	.70	.45
147	*Dave Kingman*	6.00	3.00	1.75
148	Dick Billings	1.50	.70	.45
149	Gary Neibauer	1.50	.70	.45
150	Norm Cash	2.50	1.25	.70
151	Jim Brewer	1.50	.70	.45
152	Gene Clines	1.50	.70	.45
153	Rick Auerbach	1.50	.70	.45
154	Ted Simmons	4.00	2.00	1.25
155	Larry Dierker	1.50	.70	.45
156	Twins Team	3.00	1.50	.90
157	Don Gullett	1.50	.70	.45
158	Jerry Kenney	1.50	.70	.45
159	John Boccabella	1.50	.70	.45
160	Andy Messersmith	1.50	.70	.45
161	Brock Davis	1.50	.70	.45
162	Brewers Rookies	1.50	.70	.45
	(*Jerry Bell, Darrell Porter, Bob Reynolds*) (Bell and Porter photos transposed.)			
163	Tug McGraw	1.50	.70	.45
164	Tug McGraw (In Action)	1.50	.70	.45
165	*Chris Speier*	1.50	.70	.45
166	Chris Speier (In Action)	1.50	.70	.45
167	Deron Johnson	1.50	.70	.45
168	Deron Johnson (In Action)	1.50	.70	.45
169	Vida Blue	4.00	2.00	1.25
170	Vida Blue (In Action)	2.00	1.00	.60
171	Darrell Evans	3.00	1.50	.90
172	Darrell Evans (In Action)	2.00	1.00	.60
173	Clay Kirby	1.50	.70	.45
174	Clay Kirby (In Action)	1.50	.70	.45
175	Tom Haller	1.50	.70	.45
176	Tom Haller (In Action)	1.50	.70	.45
177	Paul Schaal	1.50	.70	.45
178	Paul Schaal (In Action)	1.50	.70	.45
179	Dock Ellis	1.50	.70	.45
180	Dock Ellis (In Action)	1.50	.70	.45
181	Ed Kranepool	1.50	.70	.45
182	Ed Kranepool (In Action)	1.50	.70	.45
183	Bill Melton	1.50	.70	.45
184	Bill Melton (In Action)	1.50	.70	.45
185	Ron Bryant	1.50	.70	.45
186	Ron Bryant (In Action)	1.50	.70	.45
187	Gates Brown	1.50	.70	.45
188	Frank Lucchesi	1.50	.70	.45
189	Gene Tenace	1.50	.70	.45
190	Dave Giusti	1.50	.70	.45
191	*Jeff Burroughs*	3.00	1.50	.90
192	Cubs Team	4.00	2.00	1.25
193	*Kurt Bevacqua*	1.50	.70	.45
194	Fred Norman	1.50	.70	.45
195	Orlando Cepeda	6.00	3.00	1.75
196	Mel Queen	1.50	.70	.45
197	Johnny Briggs	1.50	.70	.45
198	Dodgers Rookies	5.00	2.50	1.50
	(*Charlie Hough, Bob O'Brien, Mike Strahler*)			
199	Mike Fiore	1.50	.70	.45
200	Lou Brock	8.00	4.00	2.50
201	Phil Roof	1.50	.70	.45
202	Scipio Spinks	1.50	.70	.45
203	*Ron Blomberg*	2.50	1.25	.70
204	Tommy Helms	1.50	.70	.45
205	Dick Drago	1.50	.70	.45
206	Dal Maxvill	1.50	.70	.45
207	Tom Egan	1.50	.70	.45
208	Milt Pappas	1.50	.70	.45
209	Joe Rudi	1.50	.70	.45
210	Denny McLain	3.00	1.50	.90
211	Gary Sutherland	1.50	.70	.45
212	Grant Jackson	1.50	.70	.45
213	Angels Rookies	1.50	.70	.45
	(*Art Kusnyer, Billy Parker, Tom Silverio*)			
214	Mike McQueen	1.50	.70	.45
215	Alex Johnson	1.50	.70	.45
216	Joe Niekro	1.50	.70	.45
217	Roger Metzger	1.50	.70	.45
218	Eddie Kasko	1.50	.70	.45
219	*Rennie Stennett*	1.50	.70	.45
220	Jim Perry	1.50	.70	.45
221	N.L. Playoffs (Bucs Champs)	4.00	2.00	1.25
222	A.L. Playoffs (Orioles Champs)	5.00	2.50	1.50
223	World Series Game 1	4.00	2.00	1.25
224	World Series Game 2	4.00	2.00	1.25
225	World Series Game 3	4.00	2.00	1.25
226	World Series Game 4 (Roberto Clemente)	10.00	5.00	3.00
227	World Series Game 5	4.00	2.00	1.25
228	World Series Game 6	4.00	2.00	1.25
229	World Series Game 7	4.00	2.00	1.25
230	Series Celebration (On Top of the World)	4.00	2.00	1.25
231	Casey Cox	1.50	.70	.45
232	Giants Rookies	1.50	.70	.45
	(*Chris Arnold, Jim Barr, Dave Rader*)			
233	Jay Johnstone	1.50	.70	.45
234	Ron Taylor	1.50	.70	.45
235	Merv Rettenmund	1.50	.70	.45
236	Jim McGlothlin	1.50	.70	.45

237	Yankees Team	4.00	2.00	1.25
238	Leron Lee	1.50	.70	.45
239	Tom Timmermann	1.50	.70	.45
240	Rich Allen	3.00	1.50	.90
241	Rollie Fingers	6.00	3.00	1.75
242	Don Mincher	1.50	.70	.45
243	Frank Linzy	1.50	.70	.45
244	Steve Braun	1.50	.70	.45
245	Tommie Agee	1.50	.70	.45
246	Tom Burgmeier	1.50	.70	.45
247	Milt May	1.50	.70	.45
248	Tom Bradley	1.50	.70	.45
249	Harry Walker	1.50	.70	.45
250	Boog Powell	2.00	1.00	.60
251a	3rd Series Checklist (264-394) (Small print on front.)	3.00	1.50	.90
251b	3rd Series Checklist (264-394) (Large print on front.)	3.00	1.50	.90
252	Ken Reynolds	1.50	.70	.45
253	Sandy Alomar	1.50	.70	.45
254	Boots Day	1.50	.70	.45
255	Jim Lonborg	1.50	.70	.45
256	George Foster	2.50	1.25	.70
257	Tigers Rookies (*Jim Foor, Tim Hosley, Paul Jata*)	1.50	.70	.45
258	Randy Hundley	1.50	.70	.45
259	Sparky Lyle	1.50	.70	.45
260	Ralph Garr	1.50	.70	.45
261	Steve Mingori	1.50	.70	.45
262	Padres Team	3.00	1.50	.90
263	Felipe Alou	2.00	1.00	.60
264	Tommy John	2.00	1.00	.60
265	Wes Parker	1.50	.70	.45
266	Bobby Bolin	1.50	.70	.45
267	Dave Concepcion	2.00	1.00	.60
268	A's Rookies (*Dwain Anderson, Chris Floethe*)	1.50	.70	.45
269	Don Hahn	1.50	.70	.45
270	Jim Palmer	8.00	4.00	2.50
271	Ken Rudolph	1.50	.70	.45
272	*Mickey Rivers*	2.00	1.00	.60
273	Bobby Floyd	1.50	.70	.45
274	Al Severinsen	1.50	.70	.45
275	Cesar Tovar	1.50	.70	.45
276	Gene Mauch	1.50	.70	.45
277	Elliott Maddox	1.50	.70	.45
278	Dennis Higgins	1.50	.70	.45
279	Larry Brown	1.50	.70	.45
280	Willie McCovey	8.00	4.00	2.50
281	Bill Parsons	1.50	.70	.45
282	Astros Team	4.00	2.00	1.25
283	Darrell Brandon	1.50	.70	.45
284	Ike Brown	1.50	.70	.45
285	Gaylord Perry	6.00	3.00	1.75
286	Gene Alley	1.50	.70	.45
287	Jim Hardin	1.50	.70	.45
288	Johnny Jeter	1.50	.70	.45
289	Syd O'Brien	1.50	.70	.45
290	Sonny Siebert	1.50	.70	.45
291	Hal McRae	2.50	1.25	.70
292	Hal McRae (In Action)	1.50	.70	.45
293	Danny Frisella	1.50	.70	.45
294	Danny Frisella (In Action)	1.50	.70	.45
295	Dick Dietz	1.50	.70	.45
296	Dick Dietz (In Action)	1.50	.70	.45
297	Claude Osteen	1.50	.70	.45
298	Claude Osteen (In Action)	1.50	.70	.45
299	Hank Aaron	40.00	20.00	12.00
300	Hank Aaron (In Action)	25.00	12.50	7.50
301	George Mitterwald	1.50	.70	.45
302	George Mitterwald (In Action)	1.50	.70	.45
303	Joe Pepitone	2.00	1.00	.60
304	Joe Pepitone (In Action)	1.50	.70	.45
305	Ken Boswell	1.50	.70	.45
306	Ken Boswell (In Action)	1.50	.70	.45
307	Steve Renko	1.50	.70	.45
308	Steve Renko (In Action)	1.50	.70	.45
309	Roberto Clemente	50.00	25.00	15.00
310	Roberto Clemente (In Action)	30.00	15.00	9.00
311	Clay Carroll	1.50	.70	.45
312	Clay Carroll (In Action)	1.50	.70	.45
313	Luis Aparicio	6.00	3.00	1.75
314	Luis Aparicio (In Action)	4.00	2.00	1.25
315	Paul Splittorff	1.50	.70	.45
316	Cardinals Rookies (*Jim Bibby, Santiago Guzman, Jorge Roque*)	1.50	.70	.45
317	Rich Hand	1.50	.70	.45
318	Sonny Jackson	1.50	.70	.45
319	Aurelio Rodriguez	1.50	.70	.45
320	Steve Blass	1.50	.70	.45
321	Joe Lahoud	1.50	.70	.45
322	Jose Pena	1.50	.70	.45
323	Earl Weaver	5.00	2.50	1.50
324	Mike Ryan	1.50	.70	.45
325	Mel Stottlemyre	1.50	.70	.45
326	Pat Kelly	1.50	.70	.45
327	*Steve Stone*	3.00	1.50	.90
328	Red Sox Team	5.00	2.50	1.50
329	Roy Foster	1.50	.70	.45
330	Jim Hunter	6.00	3.00	1.75
331	Stan Swanson	1.50	.70	.45
332	Buck Martinez	1.50	.70	.45
333	Steve Barber	1.50	.70	.45
334	Rangers Rookies (*Bill Fahey, Jim Mason, Tom Ragland*)	1.50	.70	.45
335	Bill Hands	1.50	.70	.45
336	Marty Martinez	1.50	.70	.45
337	Mike Kilkenny	1.50	.70	.45
338	Bob Grich	1.50	.70	.45
339	Ron Cook	1.50	.70	.45
340	Roy White	1.50	.70	.45
341	Joe Torre (Boyhood Photo)	2.50	1.25	.70
342	Wilbur Wood (Boyhood Photo)	1.50	.70	.45

343	Willie Stargell (Boyhood Photo)	2.00	1.00	.60
344	Dave McNally (Boyhood Photo)	1.50	.70	.45
345	Rick Wise (Boyhood Photo)	1.50	.70	.45
346	Jim Fregosi (Boyhood Photo)	1.50	.70	.45
347	Tom Seaver (Boyhood Photo)	3.00	1.50	.90
348	Sal Bando (Boyhood Photo)	1.50	.70	.45
349	Al Fitzmorris	1.50	.70	.45
350	Frank Howard	2.00	1.00	.60
351	Braves Rookies	1.50	.70	.45
	(*Jimmy Britton, Tom House, Rick Kester*)			
352	Dave LaRoche	1.50	.70	.45
353	Art Shamsky	1.50	.70	.45
354	Tom Murphy	1.50	.70	.45
355	Bob Watson	1.50	.70	.45
356	Gerry Moses	1.50	.70	.45
357	Woodie Fryman	1.50	.70	.45
358	Sparky Anderson	4.00	2.00	1.25
359	Don Pavletich	1.50	.70	.45
360	Dave Roberts	1.50	.70	.45
361	Mike Andrews	1.50	.70	.45
362	Mets Team	4.00	2.00	1.25
363	Ron Klimkowski	1.50	.70	.45
364	Johnny Callison	1.50	.70	.45
365	Dick Bosman	1.50	.70	.45
366	Jimmy Rosario	1.50	.70	.45
367	Ron Perranoski	1.50	.70	.45
368	Danny Thompson	1.50	.70	.45
369	Jim Lefebvre	1.50	.70	.45
370	Don Buford	1.50	.70	.45
371	Denny Lemaster	1.50	.70	.45
372	Royals Rookies	1.50	.70	.45
	(*Lance Clemons, Monty Montgomery*)			
373	John Mayberry	1.50	.70	.45
374	Jack Heidemann	1.50	.70	.45
375	Reggie Cleveland	1.50	.70	.45
376	Andy Kosco	1.50	.70	.45
377	Terry Harmon	1.50	.70	.45
378	4th Series Checklist (395-525)	3.00	1.50	.90
379	Ken Berry	1.50	.70	.45
380	Earl Williams	1.50	.70	.45
381	White Sox Team	3.00	1.50	.90
382	Joe Gibbon	1.50	.70	.45
383	Brant Alyea	1.50	.70	.45
384	Dave Campbell	1.50	.70	.45
385	Mickey Stanley	1.50	.70	.45
386	Jim Colborn	1.50	.70	.45
387	Horace Clarke	1.50	.70	.45
388	Charlie Williams	1.50	.70	.45
389	Bill Rigney	1.50	.70	.45
390	Willie Davis	1.50	.70	.45
391	Ken Sanders	1.50	.70	.45
392	Pirates Rookies	2.00	1.00	.60
	(*Fred Cambria, Richie Zisk*)			
393	Curt Motton	1.50	.70	.45
394	Ken Forsch	1.50	.70	.45
395	Matty Alou	1.50	.70	.45
396	Paul Lindblad	1.50	.70	.45
397	Phillies Team	4.00	2.00	1.25
398	Larry Hisle	2.00	1.00	.60
399	Milt Wilcox	1.50	.70	.45
400	Tony Oliva	3.00	1.50	.90
401	Jim Nash	1.50	.70	.45
402	Bobby Heise	1.50	.70	.45
403	John Cumberland	1.50	.70	.45
404	Jeff Torborg	1.50	.70	.45
405	Ron Fairly	1.50	.70	.45
406	*George Hendrick*	2.00	1.00	.60
407	Chuck Taylor	1.50	.70	.45
408	Jim Northrup	1.50	.70	.45
409	Frank Baker	1.50	.70	.45
410	Fergie Jenkins	6.00	3.00	1.75
411	Bob Montgomery	1.50	.70	.45
412	Dick Kelley	1.50	.70	.45
413	White Sox Rookies	1.50	.70	.45
	(*Don Eddy, Dave Lemonds*)			
414	Bob Miller	1.50	.70	.45
415	Cookie Rojas	1.50	.70	.45
416	Johnny Edwards	1.50	.70	.45
417	Tom Hall	1.50	.70	.45
418	Tom Shopay	1.50	.70	.45
419	Jim Spencer	1.50	.70	.45
420	Steve Carlton	15.00	7.50	4.50
421	Ellie Rodriguez	1.50	.70	.45
422	Ray Lamb	1.50	.70	.45
423	Oscar Gamble	1.50	.70	.45
424	Bill Gogolewski	1.50	.70	.45
425	Ken Singleton	1.50	.70	.45
426	Ken Singleton (In Action)	1.50	.70	.45
427	Tito Fuentes	1.50	.70	.45
428	Tito Fuentes (In Action)	1.50	.70	.45
429	Bob Robertson	1.50	.70	.45
430	Bob Robertson (In Action)	1.50	.70	.45
431	Clarence Gaston	1.50	.70	.45
432	Clarence Gaston (In Action)	1.50	.70	.45
433	Johnny Bench	20.00	10.00	6.00
434	Johnny Bench (In Action)	10.00	5.00	3.00
435	Reggie Jackson	25.00	12.50	7.50
436	Reggie Jackson (In Action)	12.00	6.00	3.50
437	Maury Wills	1.50	.70	.45
438	Maury Wills (In Action)	1.50	.70	.45
439	Billy Williams	8.00	4.00	2.50
440	Billy Williams (In Action)	5.00	2.50	1.50
441	Thurman Munson	15.00	7.50	4.50
442	Thurman Munson (In Action)	10.00	5.00	3.00
443	Ken Henderson	1.50	.70	.45
444	Ken Henderson (In Action)	1.50	.70	.45
445	Tom Seaver	25.00	12.50	7.50
446	Tom Seaver (In Action)	15.00	7.50	4.50
447	Willie Stargell	8.00	4.00	2.50
448	Willie Stargell (In Action)	5.00	2.50	1.50
449	Bob Lemon	4.00	2.00	1.25

450	Mickey Lolich	1.50	.70	.45
451	Tony LaRussa	2.50	1.25	.70
452	Ed Herrmann	1.50	.70	.45
453	Barry Lersch	1.50	.70	.45
454	A's Team	4.00	2.00	1.25
455	Tommy Harper	1.50	.70	.45
456	Mark Belanger	1.50	.70	.45
457	Padres Rookies (*Darcy Fast, Mike Ivie, Derrel Thomas*)	1.50	.70	.45
458	Aurelio Monteagudo	1.50	.70	.45
459	Rick Renick	1.50	.70	.45
460	Al Downing	1.50	.70	.45
461	Tim Cullen	1.50	.70	.45
462	Rickey Clark	1.50	.70	.45
463	Bernie Carbo	1.50	.70	.45
464	Jim Roland	1.50	.70	.45
465	Gil Hodges	4.00	2.00	1.25
466	Norm Miller	1.50	.70	.45
467	Steve Kline	1.50	.70	.45
468	Richie Scheinblum	1.50	.70	.45
469	Ron Herbel	1.50	.70	.45
470	Ray Fosse	1.50	.70	.45
471	Luke Walker	1.50	.70	.45
472	Phil Gagliano	1.50	.70	.45
473	Dan McGinn	1.50	.70	.45
474	Orioles Rookies (*Don Baylor, Roric Harrison, Johnny Oates*)	10.00	5.00	3.00
475	Gary Nolan	1.50	.70	.45
476	Lee Richard	1.50	.70	.45
477	Tom Phoebus	1.50	.70	.45
478a	5th Series Checklist (526-656) (Small print on front.)	2.50	1.25	.70
478b	5th Series Checklist (526-656) (Large printing on front.)	2.50	1.25	.70
479	Don Shaw	1.50	.70	.45
480	Lee May	1.50	.70	.45
481	Billy Conigliaro	1.50	.70	.45
482	Joe Hoerner	1.50	.70	.45
483	Ken Suarez	1.50	.70	.45
484	Lum Harris	1.50	.70	.45
485	Phil Regan	1.50	.70	.45
486	John Lowenstein	1.50	.70	.45
487	Tigers Team	5.00	2.50	1.50
488	Mike Nagy	1.50	.70	.45
489	Expos Rookies (*Terry Humphrey, Keith Lampard*)	1.50	.70	.45
490	Dave McNally	1.50	.70	.45
491	Lou Piniella (Boyhood Photo)	1.50	.70	.45
492	Mel Stottlemyre (Boyhood Photo)	1.50	.70	.45
493	Bob Bailey (Boyhood Photo)	1.50	.70	.45
494	Willie Horton (Boyhood Photo)	1.50	.70	.45
495	Bill Melton (Boyhood Photo)	1.50	.70	.45
496	Bud Harrelson (Boyhood Photo)	1.50	.70	.45
497	Jim Perry (Boyhood Photo)	1.50	.70	.45
498	Brooks Robinson (Boyhood Photo)	4.00	2.00	1.25
499	Vicente Romo	1.50	.70	.45
500	Joe Torre	5.00	2.50	1.50
501	Pete Hamm	1.50	.70	.45
502	Jackie Hernandez	1.50	.70	.45
503	Gary Peters	1.50	.70	.45
504	Ed Spiezio	1.50	.70	.45
505	Mike Marshall	1.50	.70	.45
506	Indians Rookies (*Terry Ley, Jim Moyer, Dick Tidrow*)	1.50	.70	.45
507	Fred Gladding	1.50	.70	.45
508	Ellie Hendricks	1.50	.70	.45
509	Don McMahon	1.50	.70	.45
510	Ted Williams	10.00	5.00	3.00
511	Tony Taylor	1.50	.70	.45
512	Paul Popovich	1.50	.70	.45
513	Lindy McDaniel	1.50	.70	.45
514	Ted Sizemore	1.50	.70	.45
515	Bert Blyleven	3.00	1.50	.90
516	Oscar Brown	1.50	.70	.45
517	Ken Brett	1.50	.70	.45
518	Wayne Garrett	1.50	.70	.45
519	Ted Abernathy	1.50	.70	.45
520	Larry Bowa	1.50	.70	.45
521	Alan Foster	1.50	.70	.45
522	Dodgers Team	4.00	2.00	1.25
523	Chuck Dobson	1.50	.70	.45
524	Reds Rookies (*Ed Armbrister, Mel Behney*)	1.50	.70	.45
525	Carlos May	1.50	.70	.45
526	Bob Bailey	3.00	1.50	.90
527	Dave Leonhard	3.00	1.50	.90
528	Ron Stone	3.00	1.50	.90
529	Dave Nelson	3.00	1.50	.90
530	Don Sutton	10.00	5.00	3.00
531	Freddie Patek	4.00	2.00	1.25
532	Fred Kendall	3.00	1.50	.90
533	Ralph Houk	6.00	3.00	1.75
534	Jim Hickman	3.00	1.50	.90
535	Ed Brinkman	3.00	1.50	.90
536	Doug Rader	3.00	1.50	.90
537	Bob Locker	3.00	1.50	.90
538	Charlie Sands	3.00	1.50	.90
539	*Terry Forster*	4.00	2.00	1.25
540	Felix Millan	3.00	1.50	.90
541	Roger Repoz	3.00	1.50	.90
542	Jack Billingham	3.00	1.50	.90
543	Duane Josephson	3.00	1.50	.90
544	Ted Martinez	3.00	1.50	.90
545	Wayne Granger	3.00	1.50	.90
546	Joe Hague	3.00	1.50	.90
547	Indians Team	6.00	3.00	1.75
548	Frank Reberger	3.00	1.50	.90
549	Dave May	3.00	1.50	.90
550	Brooks Robinson	25.00	12.50	7.50
551	Ollie Brown	3.00	1.50	.90
552	Ollie Brown (In Action)	3.00	1.50	.90

553	Wilbur Wood	3.00	1.50	.90
554	Wilbur Wood (In Action)	3.00	1.50	.90
555	Ron Santo	8.00	4.00	2.50
556	Ron Santo (In Action)	4.00	2.00	1.25
557	John Odom	3.00	1.50	.90
558	John Odom (In Action)	3.00	1.50	.90
559	Pete Rose	50.00	25.00	15.00
560	Pete Rose (In Action)	30.00	15.00	9.00
561	Leo Cardenas	3.00	1.50	.90
562	Leo Cardenas (In Action)	3.00	1.50	.90
563	Ray Sadecki	3.00	1.50	.90
564	Ray Sadecki (In Action)	3.00	1.50	.90
565	Reggie Smith	3.00	1.50	.90
566	Reggie Smith (In Action)	3.00	1.50	.90
567	Juan Marichal	10.00	5.00	3.00
568	Juan Marichal (In Action)	5.00	2.50	1.50
569	Ed Kirkpatrick	3.00	1.50	.90
570	Ed Kirkpatrick (In Action)	3.00	1.50	.90
571	Nate Colbert	3.00	1.50	.90
572	Nate Colbert (In Action)	3.00	1.50	.90
573	Fritz Peterson	3.00	1.50	.90
574	Fritz Peterson (In Action)	3.00	1.50	.90
575	Al Oliver	4.00	2.00	1.25
576	Leo Durocher	5.00	2.50	1.50
577	Mike Paul	3.00	1.50	.90
578	Billy Grabarkewitz	3.00	1.50	.90
579	*Doyle Alexander*	4.00	2.00	1.25
580	Lou Piniella	5.00	2.50	1.50
581	Wade Blasingame	3.00	1.50	.90
582	Expos Team	6.00	3.00	1.75
583	Darold Knowles	3.00	1.50	.90
584	Jerry McNertney	3.00	1.50	.90
585	George Scott	3.00	1.50	.90
586	Denis Menke	3.00	1.50	.90
587	Billy Wilson	3.00	1.50	.90
588	Jim Holt	3.00	1.50	.90
589	Hal Lanier	3.00	1.50	.90
590	Graig Nettles	3.00	1.50	.90
591	Paul Casanova	3.00	1.50	.90
592	Lew Krausse	3.00	1.50	.90
593	Rich Morales	3.00	1.50	.90
594	Jim Beauchamp	3.00	1.50	.90
595	Nolan Ryan	100.00	50.00	30.00
596	Manny Mota	3.00	1.50	.90
597	Jim Magnuson	3.00	1.50	.90
598	Hal King	3.00	1.50	.90
599	Billy Champion	3.00	1.50	.90
600	Al Kaline	25.00	12.50	7.50
601	George Stone	3.00	1.50	.90
602	Dave Bristol	3.00	1.50	.90
603	Jim Ray	3.00	1.50	.90
604a	6th Series Checklist (657-787) (Copyright on right.)	6.00	3.00	1.75
604b	6th Series Checklist (657-787) (Copyright on left.)	6.00	3.00	1.75
605	Nelson Briles	3.00	1.50	.90
606	Luis Melendez	3.00	1.50	.90
607	Frank Duffy	3.00	1.50	.90
608	Mike Corkins	3.00	1.50	.90
609	Tom Grieve	3.00	1.50	.90
610	Bill Stoneman	3.00	1.50	.90
611	Rich Reese	3.00	1.50	.90
612	Joe Decker	3.00	1.50	.90
613	Mike Ferraro	3.00	1.50	.90
614	Ted Uhlaender	3.00	1.50	.90
615	Steve Hargan	3.00	1.50	.90
616	*Joe Ferguson*	3.00	1.50	.90
617	Royals Team	6.00	3.00	1.75
618	Rich Robertson	3.00	1.50	.90
619	Rich McKinney	3.00	1.50	.90
620	Phil Niekro	10.00	5.00	3.00
621	Commissioners Award	3.00	1.50	.90
622	Most Valuable Player Award	3.00	1.50	.90
623	Cy Young Award	3.00	1.50	.90
624	Minor League Player Of The Year Award	3.00	1.50	.90
625	Rookie of the Year Award	3.00	1.50	.90
626	Babe Ruth Award	3.00	1.50	.90
627	Moe Drabowsky	3.00	1.50	.90
628	Terry Crowley	3.00	1.50	.90
629	Paul Doyle	3.00	1.50	.90
630	Rich Hebner	3.00	1.50	.90
631	John Strohmayer	3.00	1.50	.90
632	Mike Hegan	3.00	1.50	.90
633	Jack Hiatt	3.00	1.50	.90
634	Dick Woodson	3.00	1.50	.90
635	Don Money	3.00	1.50	.90
636	Bill Lee	3.00	1.50	.90
637	Preston Gomez	3.00	1.50	.90
638	Ken Wright	3.00	1.50	.90
639	J.C. Martin	3.00	1.50	.90
640	Joe Coleman	3.00	1.50	.90
641	Mike Lum	3.00	1.50	.90
642	Denny Riddleberger	3.00	1.50	.90
643	Russ Gibson	3.00	1.50	.90
644	Bernie Allen	3.00	1.50	.90
645	Jim Maloney	3.00	1.50	.90
646	Chico Salmon	3.00	1.50	.90
647	Bob Moose	3.00	1.50	.90
648	Jim Lyttle	3.00	1.50	.90
649	Pete Richert	3.00	1.50	.90
650	Sal Bando	3.00	1.50	.90
651	Reds Team	8.00	4.00	2.50
652	Marcelino Lopez	3.00	1.50	.90
653	Jim Fairey	3.00	1.50	.90
654	Horacio Pina	3.00	1.50	.90
655	Jerry Grote	3.00	1.50	.90
656	Rudy May	3.00	1.50	.90
657	Bobby Wine	10.00	5.00	3.00
658	Steve Dunning	10.00	5.00	3.00
659	Bob Aspromonte	10.00	5.00	3.00
660	Paul Blair	10.00	5.00	3.00
661	Bill Virdon	10.00	5.00	3.00
662	Stan Bahnsen	10.00	5.00	3.00
663	Fran Healy	10.00	5.00	3.00
664	Bobby Knoop	10.00	5.00	3.00
665	Chris Short	10.00	5.00	3.00
666	Hector Torres	10.00	5.00	3.00

667	Ray Newman	10.00	5.00	3.00
668	Rangers Team	20.00	10.00	6.00
669	Willie Crawford	10.00	5.00	3.00
670	Ken Holtzman	10.00	5.00	3.00
671	Donn Clendenon	10.00	5.00	3.00
672	Archie Reynolds	10.00	5.00	3.00
673	Dave Marshall	10.00	5.00	3.00
674	John Kennedy	10.00	5.00	3.00
675	Pat Jarvis	10.00	5.00	3.00
676	Danny Cater	10.00	5.00	3.00
677	Ivan Murrell	10.00	5.00	3.00
678	Steve Luebber	10.00	5.00	3.00
679	Astros Rookies (*Bob Fenwick, Bob Stinson*)	10.00	5.00	3.00
680	Dave Johnson	10.00	5.00	3.00
681	Bobby Pfeil	10.00	5.00	3.00
682	Mike McCormick	10.00	5.00	3.00
683	Steve Hovley	10.00	5.00	3.00
684	Hal Breeden	10.00	5.00	3.00
685	Joe Horlen	10.00	5.00	3.00
686	Steve Garvey	25.00	12.50	7.50
687	Del Unser	10.00	5.00	3.00
688	Cardinals Team	20.00	10.00	6.00
689	Eddie Fisher	10.00	5.00	3.00
690	Willie Montanez	10.00	5.00	3.00
691	Curt Blefary	10.00	5.00	3.00
692	Curt Blefary (In Action)	10.00	5.00	3.00
693	Alan Gallagher	10.00	5.00	3.00
694	Alan Gallagher (In Action)	10.00	5.00	3.00
695	Rod Carew	50.00	25.00	15.00
696	Rod Carew (In Action)	25.00	12.50	7.50
697	Jerry Koosman	15.00	7.50	4.50
698	Jerry Koosman (In Action)	10.00	5.00	3.00
699	Bobby Murcer	12.00	6.00	3.50
700	Bobby Murcer (In Action)	10.00	5.00	3.00
701	Jose Pagan	10.00	5.00	3.00
702	Jose Pagan (In Action)	10.00	5.00	3.00
703	Doug Griffin	10.00	5.00	3.00
704	Doug Griffin (In Action)	10.00	5.00	3.00
705	Pat Corrales	10.00	5.00	3.00
706	Pat Corrales (In Action)	10.00	5.00	3.00
707	Tim Foli	10.00	5.00	3.00
708	Tim Foli (In Action)	10.00	5.00	3.00
709	Jim Kaat	15.00	7.50	4.50
710	Jim Kaat (In Action)	10.00	5.00	3.00
711	Bobby Bonds	15.00	7.50	4.50
712	Bobby Bonds (In Action)	10.00	5.00	3.00
713	Gene Michael	10.00	5.00	3.00
714	Gene Michael (In Action)	10.00	5.00	3.00
715	Mike Epstein	10.00	5.00	3.00
716	Jesus Alou	10.00	5.00	3.00
717	Bruce Dal Canton	10.00	5.00	3.00
718	Del Rice	10.00	5.00	3.00
719	Cesar Geronimo	10.00	5.00	3.00
720	Sam McDowell	10.00	5.00	3.00
721	Eddie Leon	10.00	5.00	3.00
722	Bill Sudakis	10.00	5.00	3.00
723	Al Santorini	10.00	5.00	3.00
724	A.L. Rookies (*John Curtis, Rich Hinton, Mickey Scott*)	10.00	5.00	3.00
725	Dick McAuliffe	10.00	5.00	3.00
726	Dick Selma	10.00	5.00	3.00
727	Jose Laboy	10.00	5.00	3.00
728	Gail Hopkins	10.00	5.00	3.00
729	Bob Veale	10.00	5.00	3.00
730	Rick Monday	10.00	5.00	3.00
731	Orioles Team	15.00	7.50	4.50
732	George Culver	10.00	5.00	3.00
733	Jim Hart	10.00	5.00	3.00
734	Bob Burda	10.00	5.00	3.00
735	Diego Segui	10.00	5.00	3.00
736	Bill Russell	10.00	5.00	3.00
737	*Lenny Randle*	10.00	5.00	3.00
738	Jim Merritt	10.00	5.00	3.00
739	Don Mason	10.00	5.00	3.00
740	Rico Carty	10.00	5.00	3.00
741	Major League Rookies (*Tom Hutton, Rick Miller, John Milner*)	10.00	5.00	3.00
742	Jim Rooker	10.00	5.00	3.00
743	Cesar Gutierrez	10.00	5.00	3.00
744	*Jim Slaton*	10.00	5.00	3.00
745	Julian Javier	10.00	5.00	3.00
746	Lowell Palmer	10.00	5.00	3.00
747	Jim Stewart	10.00	5.00	3.00
748	Phil Hennigan	10.00	5.00	3.00
749	Walter Alston	15.00	7.50	4.50
750	Willie Horton	10.00	5.00	3.00
751	Steve Carlton (Traded)	30.00	15.00	9.00
752	Joe Morgan (Traded)	30.00	15.00	9.00
753	Denny McLain (Traded)	15.00	7.50	4.50
754	Frank Robinson (Traded)	40.00	20.00	12.00
755	Jim Fregosi (Traded)	15.00	7.50	4.50
756	Rick Wise (Traded)	10.00	5.00	3.00
757	Jose Cardenal (Traded)	10.00	5.00	3.00
758	Gil Garrido	10.00	5.00	3.00
759	Chris Cannizzaro	10.00	5.00	3.00
760	Bill Mazeroski	20.00	10.00	6.00
761	A.L.-N.L. Rookies (*Ron Cey, Ben Oglivie, Bernie Williams*)	20.00	10.00	6.00
762	Wayne Simpson	10.00	5.00	3.00
763	Ron Hansen	10.00	5.00	3.00
764	Dusty Baker	15.00	7.50	4.50
765	Ken McMullen	10.00	5.00	3.00
766	Steve Hamilton	10.00	5.00	3.00
767	Tom McCraw	10.00	5.00	3.00
768	Denny Doyle	10.00	5.00	3.00
769	Jack Aker	10.00	5.00	3.00
770	Jim Wynn	10.00	5.00	3.00
771	Giants Team	20.00	10.00	6.00
772	Ken Tatum	10.00	5.00	3.00
773	Ron Brand	10.00	5.00	3.00
774	Luis Alvarado	10.00	5.00	3.00
775	Jerry Reuss	10.00	5.00	3.00
776	Bill Voss	10.00	5.00	3.00
777	Hoyt Wilhelm	25.00	12.50	7.50

		NM	EX	VG
778	Twins Rookies (*Vic Albury, Rick Dempsey, Jim Strickland*)	20.00	10.00	6.00
779	Tony Cloninger	10.00	5.00	3.00
780	Dick Green	10.00	5.00	3.00
781	Jim McAndrew	10.00	5.00	3.00
782	Larry Stahl	10.00	5.00	3.00
783	Les Cain	10.00	5.00	3.00
784	Ken Aspromonte	10.00	5.00	3.00
785	Vic Davalillo	10.00	5.00	3.00
786	Chuck Brinkman	10.00	5.00	3.00
787	Ron Reed	12.00	5.00	3.00

1972 Topps Candy Lid Test Issue

Between the production of its regular-issue candy lid sets of 1970 and 1973, Topps was working on another issue that survives today in proof form, either as uncropped squares or cut to the 1-7/8" diameter tabbed lid form meant to cover a plastic bucket of bubblegum nuggets. The 1972 proofs are very close to the 1973 issue in format; the principal difference is the player portrait does not have a solid-color border as on the 1973s, and that the pictures of Seaver and Yaz on the front are set against green, rather than orange, stars. The extent of the checklist is unknown.

		NM	EX	VG
	Common Player:	100.00	50.00	30.00
(1)	Hank Aaron	900.00	450.00	275.00
(2)	Dick Allen	150.00	75.00	45.00
(3)	Dusty Baker	100.00	50.00	35.00
(4)	Sal Bando	100.00	50.00	30.00
(5)	Johnny Bench	450.00	225.00	135.00
(6)	Bobby Bonds	100.00	50.00	30.00
(7)	Dick Bosman	100.00	50.00	30.00
(8)	Lou Brock	250.00	125.00	75.00
(9)	Rod Carew	300.00	150.00	90.00
(10)	Steve Carlton	300.00	150.00	90.00
(11)	Nate Colbert	100.00	50.00	30.00
(12)	Willie Davis	100.00	50.00	30.00
(13)	Larry Dierker	100.00	50.00	30.00
(14)	Mike Epstein	100.00	50.00	30.00
(15)	Carlton Fisk	300.00	150.00	90.00
(16)	Tim Foli	100.00	50.00	30.00
(17)	Ray Fosse	100.00	50.00	30.00
(18)	Bill Freehan	100.00	50.00	30.00
(19)	Bob Gibson	300.00	150.00	90.00
(20)	Bud Harrelson	100.00	50.00	30.00
(21)	Catfish Hunter	250.00	125.00	75.00
(22)	Reggie Jackson	650.00	325.00	195.00
(23)	Fergie Jenkins	250.00	125.00	75.00
(24)	Al Kaline	350.00	175.00	100.00
(25)	Harmon Killebrew	350.00	175.00	100.00
(26)	Clay Kirby	100.00	50.00	30.00
(27)	Mickey Lolich	100.00	50.00	30.00
(28)	Greg Luzinski	100.00	50.00	30.00
(29)	Mike Marshall	100.00	50.00	30.00
(30)	Lee May	100.00	50.00	30.00
(31)	John Mayberry	100.00	50.00	30.00
(32)	Willie Mays	900.00	450.00	275.00
(33)	Willie McCovey	250.00	125.00	75.00
(34)	Thurman Munson	300.00	150.00	90.00
(35)	Bobby Murcer	150.00	75.00	45.00
(36)	Gary Nolan	100.00	50.00	30.00
(37)	Amos Otis	100.00	50.00	30.00
(38)	Jim Palmer	250.00	125.00	75.00
(39)	Gaylord Perry	250.00	125.00	75.00
(40)	Lou Piniella	150.00	75.00	45.00
(41)	Brooks Robinson	350.00	175.00	100.00
(42)	Frank Robinson	350.00	175.00	100.00
(43)	Ellie Rodriguez	100.00	50.00	30.00
(44)	Pete Rose	900.00	450.00	275.00
(45)	Nolan Ryan	2,500.00	1,250.00	750.00
(46)	Manny Sanguillen	100.00	50.00	30.00
(47)	George Scott	100.00	50.00	30.00
(48)	Tom Seaver	350.00	175.00	100.00
(49)	Chris Speier	100.00	50.00	30.00
(50)	Willie Stargell	250.00	125.00	75.00
(51)	Don Sutton	250.00	125.00	75.00
(52)	Joe Torre	150.00	75.00	45.00
(53)	Billy Williams	250.00	125.00	75.00
(54)	Wilbur Wood	100.00	50.00	30.00
(55)	Carl Yastrzemski	450.00	225.00	135.00

1972 Topps Cloth Stickers

Despite the fact they were never actually issued, examples of this test issue can readily be found within the hobby. The set of 33 contains stickers with designs identical to cards found in three contiguous rows of a regular Topps card sheet that year; thus the inclusion of a meaningless checklist card. Sometimes found in complete 33-sticker strips, or 132-piece sheets, individual stickers nominally measure 2-1/2" x 3-1/2", though

dimensions vary according to the care with which they were cut. Stickers are unnumbered and blank-backed; most are found without the original paper backing as the glue used did not hold up well over the years. Eleven of the stickers are prone to miscutting and are identified with an/SP in the checklist.

		NM	EX	VG
	Complete Set (33):	1,300	650.00	390.00
	Common Player:	20.00	10.00	6.00
(1)	Hank Aaron	200.00	100.00	60.00
(2)	Luis Aparicio (In Action)/SP	60.00	30.00	18.00
(3)	Ike Brown	20.00	10.00	6.00
(4)	Johnny Callison	20.00	10.00	6.00
(5)	Checklist 264-319	10.00	5.00	3.00
(6)	Roberto Clemente (In Action)	300.00	150.00	90.00
(7)	Dave Concepcion/SP	40.00	20.00	12.00
(8)	Ron Cook	20.00	10.00	6.00
(9)	Willie Davis	20.00	10.00	6.00
(10)	Al Fitzmorris	20.00	10.00	6.00
(11)	Bobby Floyd	20.00	10.00	6.00
(12)	Roy Foster	20.00	10.00	6.00
(13)	Jim Fregosi (Boyhood Photo)	20.00	10.00	6.00
(14)	Danny Frisella (In Action)	20.00	10.00	6.00
(15)	Woody Fryman/SP	25.00	12.50	7.50
(16)	Terry Harmon	20.00	10.00	6.00
(17)	Frank Howard/SP	40.00	20.00	12.00
(18)	Ron Klimkowski	20.00	10.00	6.00
(19)	Joe Lahoud	20.00	10.00	6.00
(20)	Jim Lefebvre	20.00	10.00	6.00
(21)	Elliott Maddox	20.00	10.00	6.00
(22)	Marty Martinez	20.00	10.00	6.00
(23)	Willie McCovey/SP	100.00	50.00	30.00
(24)	Hal McRae/SP	30.00	15.00	9.00
(25)	Syd O'Brien/SP	25.00	12.50	7.50
(26)	Red Sox Team	25.00	12.50	7.50
(27)	Aurelio Rodriguez	20.00	10.00	6.00
(28)	Al Severinsen	20.00	10.00	6.00
(29)	Art Shamsky/SP	25.00	12.50	7.50
(30)	Steve Stone/SP	30.00	15.00	9.00
(31)	Stan Swanson/SP	25.00	12.50	7.50
(32)	Bob Watson	20.00	10.00	6.00
(33)	Roy White/SP	30.00	15.00	9.00

1972 Topps Posters

Issued as a separate set, rather than as a wax pack insert, these 9-7/16" x 18" posters feature a borderless full-color picture on the front with the player's name, team and position. Printed on very thin paper, the posters were folded for packaging, causing large creases that cannot be removed. Grading of these posters is done without regard to those packaging folds.

		NM	EX	VG
	Complete Set (24):	700.00	350.00	200.00
	Common Player:	12.00	6.00	3.50
	Wax Pack:	50.00		
1	Dave McNally	12.00	6.00	3.50
2	Carl Yastrzemski	45.00	22.50	13.50
3	Bill Melton	12.00	6.00	3.50
4	Ray Fosse	12.00	6.00	3.50
5	Mickey Lolich	12.00	6.00	3.50
6	Amos Otis	12.00	6.00	3.50
7	Tony Oliva	15.00	7.50	4.50
8	Vida Blue	12.00	6.00	3.50
9	Hank Aaron	75.00	37.50	22.00
10	Fergie Jenkins	30.00	15.00	9.00
11	Pete Rose	75.00	37.50	22.00
12	Willie Davis	12.00	6.00	3.50
13	Tom Seaver	40.00	20.00	12.00
14	Rick Wise	12.00	6.00	3.50
15	Willie Stargell	30.00	15.00	9.00
16	Joe Torre	17.50	8.75	5.25
17	Willie Mays	75.00	37.50	22.00
18	Andy Messersmith	12.00	6.00	3.50
19	Wilbur Wood	12.00	6.00	3.50
20	Harmon Killebrew	35.00	17.50	10.00
21	Billy Williams	30.00	15.00	9.00
22	Bud Harrelson	12.00	6.00	3.50
23	Roberto Clemente	125.00	65.00	35.00
24	Willie McCovey	30.00	15.00	9.00

1973 Topps

 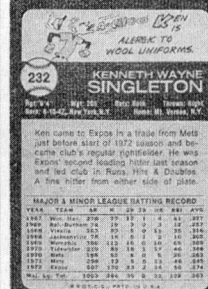

Topps cut back to 660 cards in 1973. The set is interesting for it marks the last time cards were issued by series, a procedure which had produced many a scarce high number card over the years. These 2-1/2" x 3-1/2" cards have a color photo, accented by a silhouette of a player over the front, indicative of his position. Card backs are vertical for the first time since 1968, with the usual statistical and biographical information. Specialty cards begin with card number 1, which depicted Ruth, Mays and Aaron as the all-time home run leaders. It was followed by statistical leaders, although there also were additional all-time leader cards. Also present are playoff and World Series highlights. From the age-and-youth department, the 1973 Topps set has coaches and managers as well as more "Boyhood Photos."

		NM	EX	VG
	Complete Set (660):	650.00	325.00	195.00
	Common Player (1-396):	.75	.40	.25
	Common Player (397-528):	1.00	.50	.30
	Common Player (529-660):	2.00	1.00	.60
	Series 1/2/3 Wax Pack (10):	80.00		
	Series 4 Wax Pack (10):	165.00		
	Series 5 Wax Pack (10+1):	215.00		
1	All Time Home Run Leaders (Hank Aaron, Willie Mays, Babe Ruth)	40.00	20.00	12.00
2	Rich Hebner	.75	.40	.25
3	Jim Lonborg	.75	.40	.25
4	John Milner	.75	.40	.25
5	Ed Brinkman	.75	.40	.25
6	Mac Scarce	.75	.40	.25
7	Texas Rangers Team	1.00	.50	.30
8	Tom Hall	.75	.40	.25
9	Johnny Oates	.75	.40	.25
10	Don Sutton	3.00	1.50	.90
11	Chris Chambliss	.75	.40	.25
12a	Padres Mgr./Coaches (Dave Garcia, Johnny Podres, Bob Skinner, Whitey Wietelmann, Don Zimmer) (Coaches background brown.)	1.00	.50	.30
12b	Padres Mgr./Coaches (Dave Garcia, Johnny Podres, Bob Skinner, Whitey Wietelmann, Don Zimmer) (Coaches background orange.)	1.00	.50	.30
13	George Hendrick	.75	.40	.25
14	Sonny Siebert	.75	.40	.25
15	Ralph Garr	.75	.40	.25
16	Steve Braun	.75	.40	.25
17	Fred Gladding	.75	.40	.25
18	Leroy Stanton	.75	.40	.25
19	Tim Foli	.75	.40	.25
20a	Stan Bahnsen (Small gap in left border.)	1.00	.50	.30
20b	Stan Bahnsen (No gap.)	.75	.40	.25
21	Randy Hundley	.75	.40	.25
22	Ted Abernathy	.75	.40	.25
23	Dave Kingman	1.00	.50	.30
24	Al Santorini	.75	.40	.25
25	Roy White	.75	.40	.25
26	Pittsburgh Pirates Team	2.00	1.00	.60
27	Bill Gogolewski	.75	.40	.25
28	Hal McRae	.75	.40	.25
29	Tony Taylor	.75	.40	.25
30	Tug McGraw	.75	.40	.25
31a	*Buddy Bell* (Small gap in right border.)	6.00	3.00	1.75
31b	*Buddy Bell* (No gap.)	6.00	3.00	1.75
32	Fred Norman	.75	.40	.25

No.	Card			
33	Jim Breazeale	.75	.40	.25
34	Pat Dobson	.75	.40	.25
35	Willie Davis	.75	.40	.25
36	Steve Barber	.75	.40	.25
37	Bill Robinson	.75	.40	.25
38	Mike Epstein	.75	.40	.25
39	Dave Roberts	.75	.40	.25
40	Reggie Smith	.75	.40	.25
41	Tom Walker	.75	.40	.25
42	Mike Andrews	.75	.40	.25
43	*Randy Moffitt*	.75	.40	.25
44	Rick Monday	.75	.40	.25
45	Ellie Rodriguez (Photo actually Paul Ratliff.)	.75	.40	.25
46	Lindy McDaniel	.75	.40	.25
47	Luis Melendez	.75	.40	.25
48	Paul Splittorff	.75	.40	.25
49a	Twins Mgr./Coaches (Vern Morgan, Frank Quilici, Bob Rodgers, Ralph Rowe, Al Worthington) (Coaches background brown.)	.75	.40	.25
49b	Twins Mgr./Coaches (Vern Morgan, Frank Quilici, Bob Rodgers, Al Worthington) (Coaches background orange.)	.75	.40	.25
50	Roberto Clemente	40.00	20.00	12.00
51	Chuck Seelbach	.75	.40	.25
52	Denis Menke	.75	.40	.25
53	Steve Dunning	.75	.40	.25
54	Checklist 1-132	1.00	.50	.30
55	Jon Matlack	.75	.40	.25
56	Merv Rettenmund	.75	.40	.25
57	Derrel Thomas	.75	.40	.25
58	Mike Paul	.75	.40	.25
59	*Steve Yeager*	.75	.40	.25
60	Ken Holtzman	.75	.40	.25
61	Batting Leaders (Rod Carew, Billy Williams)	1.00	.50	.30
62	Home Run Leaders (Dick Allen, Johnny Bench)	1.00	.50	.30
63	Runs Batted In Leaders (Dick Allen, Johnny Bench)	1.00	.50	.30
64	Stolen Base Leaders (Lou Brock, Bert Campaneris)	1.00	.50	.30
65	Earned Run Average Leaders (Steve Carlton, Luis Tiant)	1.00	.50	.30
66	Victory Leaders (Steve Carlton, Gaylord Perry, Wilbur Wood)	1.00	.50	.30
67	Strikeout Leaders (Steve Carlton, Nolan Ryan)	20.00	10.00	6.00
68	Leading Firemen (Clay Carroll, Sparky Lyle)	.75	.40	.25
69	Phil Gagliano	.75	.40	.25
70	Milt Pappas	.75	.40	.25
71	Johnny Briggs	.75	.40	.25
72	Ron Reed	.75	.40	.25
73	Ed Herrmann	.75	.40	.25
74	Billy Champion	.75	.40	.25
75	Vada Pinson	1.00	.50	.30
76	Doug Rader	.75	.40	.25
77	Mike Torrez	.75	.40	.25
78	Richie Scheinblum	.75	.40	.25
79	Jim Willoughby	.75	.40	.25
80	Tony Oliva ("MINNSEOTA" on front is uncorrected error.)	1.00	.50	.30
81a	Cubs Mgr./Coaches (Hank Aguirre, Ernie Banks, Larry Jansen, Whitey Lockman, Pete Reiser) (Trees in coaches background.)	1.25	.60	.40
81b	Cubs Mgr./Coaches (Hank Aguirre, Ernie Banks, Larry Jansen, Whitey Lockman, Pete Reiser) (Solid orange background.)	1.25	.60	.40
82	Fritz Peterson	.75	.40	.25
83	Leron Lee	.75	.40	.25
84	Rollie Fingers	3.00	1.50	.90
85	Ted Simmons	.75	.40	.25
86	Tom McCraw	.75	.40	.25
87	Ken Boswell	.75	.40	.25
88	Mickey Stanley	.75	.40	.25
89	Jack Billingham	.75	.40	.25
90	Brooks Robinson	8.00	4.00	2.50
91	Los Angeles Dodgers Team	2.00	1.00	.60
92	Jerry Bell	.75	.40	.25
93	Jesus Alou	.75	.40	.25
94	Dick Billings	.75	.40	.25
95	Steve Blass	.75	.40	.25
96	Doug Griffin	.75	.40	.25
97	Willie Montanez	.75	.40	.25
98	Dick Woodson	.75	.40	.25
99	Carl Taylor	.75	.40	.25
100	Hank Aaron	40.00	20.00	12.00
101	Ken Henderson	.75	.40	.25
102	Rudy May	.75	.40	.25
103	Celerino Sanchez	.75	.40	.25
104	Reggie Cleveland	.75	.40	.25
105	Carlos May	.75	.40	.25
106	Terry Humphrey	.75	.40	.25
107	Phil Hennigan	.75	.40	.25
108	Bill Russell	1.00	.50	.30
109	Doyle Alexander	.75	.40	.25
110	Bob Watson	.75	.40	.25
111	Dave Nelson	.75	.40	.25
112	Gary Ross	.75	.40	.25
113	Jerry Grote	.75	.40	.25
114	Lynn McGlothen	.75	.40	.25
115	Ron Santo	2.00	1.00	.60
116a	Yankees Mgr./Coaches (Jim Hegan, Ralph Houk, Elston Howard, Dick Howser, Jim Turner) (Coaches background brown.)	2.00	1.00	.60
116b	Yankees Mgr./Coaches (Jim Hegan, Ralph Houk, Elston Howard, Dick Howser, Jim Turner) (Coaches background orange.)	2.00	1.00	.60
117	Ramon Hernandez	.75	.40	.25
118	John Mayberry	.75	.40	.25
119	Larry Bowa	1.50	.70	.45
120	Joe Coleman	.75	.40	.25
121	Dave Rader	.75	.40	.25
122	Jim Strickland	.75	.40	.25
123	Sandy Alomar	.75	.40	.25
124	Jim Hardin	.75	.40	.25
125	Ron Fairly	.75	.40	.25
126	Jim Brewer	.75	.40	.25
127	Milwaukee Brewers Team	2.00	1.00	.60
128	Ted Sizemore	.75	.40	.25
129	Terry Forster	.75	.40	.25
130	Pete Rose	30.00	15.00	9.00
131a	Red Sox Mgr./Coaches (Doug Camilli, Eddie Kasko, Don Lenhardt, Eddie Popowski, Lee Stange) (Coaches background brown.)	.75	.40	.25
131b	Red Sox Mgr./Coaches (Doug Camilli, Eddie Kasko, Don Lenhardt, Eddie Popowski, Lee Stange) (Coaches background orange.)	.75	.40	.25
132	Matty Alou	.75	.40	.25
133	Dave Roberts	.75	.40	.25
134	Milt Wilcox	.75	.40	.25
135	Lee May	.75	.40	.25
136a	Orioles Mgr./Coaches (George Bamberger, Jim Frey, Billy Hunter, George Staller, Earl Weaver) (Coaches background brown.)	2.00	1.00	.60
136b	Orioles Mgr./Coaches (George Bamberger, Jim Frey, Billy Hunter, George Staller, Earl Weaver) (Coaches background orange.)	2.00	1.00	.60
137	Jim Beauchamp	.75	.40	.25
138	Horacio Pina	.75	.40	.25
139	Carmen Fanzone	.75	.40	.25
140	Lou Piniella	2.00	1.00	.60
141	Bruce Kison	.75	.40	.25
142	Thurman Munson	10.00	5.00	3.00
143	John Curtis	.75	.40	.25
144	Marty Perez	.75	.40	.25
145	Bobby Bonds	2.00	1.00	.60
146	Woodie Fryman	.75	.40	.25
147	Mike Anderson	.75	.40	.25
148	*Dave Goltz*	.75	.40	.25
149	Ron Hunt	.75	.40	.25
150	Wilbur Wood	1.50	.70	.45
151	Wes Parker	.75	.40	.25
152	Dave May	.75	.40	.25
153	Al Hrabosky	1.50	.70	.45
154	Jeff Torborg	.75	.40	.25
155	Sal Bando	.75	.40	.25
156	Cesar Geronimo	.75	.40	.25
157	Denny Riddleberger	.75	.40	.25
158	Houston Astros Team	2.00	1.00	.60
159	Clarence Gaston	.75	.40	.25
160	Jim Palmer	6.00	3.00	1.75
161	Ted Martinez	.75	.40	.25
162	Pete Broberg	.75	.40	.25
163	Vic Davalillo	.75	.40	.25
164	Monty Montgomery	.75	.40	.25
165	Luis Aparicio	4.00	2.00	1.25
166	Terry Harmon	.75	.40	.25
167	Steve Stone	1.00	.50	.30
168	Jim Northrup	.75	.40	.25
169	Ron Schueler	.75	.40	.25
170	Harmon Killebrew	6.00	3.00	1.75
171	Bernie Carbo	.75	.40	.25
172	Steve Kline	.75	.40	.25
173	Hal Breeden	.75	.40	.25
174	*Rich Gossage*	12.00	6.00	3.50
175	Frank Robinson	8.00	4.00	2.50
176	Chuck Taylor	.75	.40	.25
177	Bill Plummer	.75	.40	.25
178	Don Rose	.75	.40	.25
179a	A's Mgr./Coaches (Jerry Adair, Vern Hoscheit, Irv Noren, Wes Stock, Dick Williams) (Coaches background brown.)	1.00	.50	.30
179b	A's Mgr./Coaches (Jerry Adair, Vern Hoscheit, Irv Noren, Wes Stock, Dick Williams) (Coaches background orange.)	1.00	.50	.30
180	Fergie Jenkins	4.00	2.00	1.25
181	Jack Brohamer	.75	.40	.25
182	*Mike Caldwell*	.75	.40	.25
183	Don Buford	.75	.40	.25
184	Jerry Koosman	1.00	.50	.30
185	Jim Wynn	.75	.40	.25
186	Bill Fahey	.75	.40	.25
187	Luke Walker	.75	.40	.25
188	Cookie Rojas	.75	.40	.25
189	Greg Luzinski	1.50	.70	.45
190	Bob Gibson	6.00	3.00	1.75
191	Detroit Tigers Team	2.00	1.00	.60
192	Pat Jarvis	.75	.40	.25
193	Carlton Fisk	8.00	4.00	2.50
194	*Jorge Orta*	.75	.40	.25
195	Clay Carroll	.75	.40	.25
196	Ken McMullen	.75	.40	.25
197	Ed Goodson	.75	.40	.25
198	Horace Clarke	.75	.40	.25
199	Bert Blyleven	1.50	.70	.45
200	Billy Williams	5.00	2.50	1.50
201	A.L. Playoffs (Hendrick Scores Winning Run.)	1.00	.50	.30
202	N.L. Playoffs (Foster's Run Decides It.)	1.00	.50	.30
203	World Series Game 1 (Tenace The Menace.)	1.00	.50	.30
204	World Series Game 2 (A's Make It Two Straight.)	1.00	.50	.30
205	World Series Game 3 (Reds Win Squeeker.)	1.00	.50	.30
206	World Series Game 4 (Tenace Singles In Ninth.)	1.00	.50	.30
207	World Series Game 5 (Odom Out At Plate.)	1.00	.50	.30
208	World Series Game 6 (Reds' Slugging Ties Series.)	4.00	2.00	1.25
209	World Series Game 7 (Campy Starts Winning Rally.)	1.00	.50	.30
210	A's Win! (World Champions.)	1.50	.70	.45
211	Balor Moore	.75	.40	.25
212	Joe Lahoud	.75	.40	.25
213	Steve Garvey	3.00	1.50	.90
214	Dave Hamilton	.75	.40	.25
215	Dusty Baker	1.00	.50	.30
216	Toby Harrah	.75	.40	.25
217	Don Wilson	.75	.40	.25
218	Aurelio Rodriguez	.75	.40	.25
219	St. Louis Cardinals Team	2.00	1.00	.60
220	Nolan Ryan	50.00	25.00	15.00
221	Fred Kendall	.75	.40	.25
222	Rob Gardner	.75	.40	.25
223	Bud Harrelson	.75	.40	.25
224	Bill Lee	.75	.40	.25
225	Al Oliver	1.00	.50	.30
226	Ray Fosse	.75	.40	.25
227	Wayne Twitchell	.75	.40	.25
228	Bobby Darwin	.75	.40	.25
229	Roric Harrison	.75	.40	.25
230	Joe Morgan	6.00	3.00	1.75
231	Bill Parsons	.75	.40	.25
232	Ken Singleton	.75	.40	.25
233	Ed Kirkpatrick	.75	.40	.25
234	*Bill North*	.75	.40	.25
235	Jim Hunter	3.00	1.50	.90
236	Tito Fuentes	.75	.40	.25
237a	Braves Mgr./Coaches (Lew Burdette, Jim Busby, Roy Hartsfield, Eddie Mathews, Ken Silvestri) (Coaches background brown.)	1.00	.50	.30
237b	Braves Mgr./Coaches (Lew Burdette, Jim Busby, Roy Hartsfield, Eddie Mathews, Ken Silvestri) (Coaches background orange.)	1.00	.50	.30
238	Tony Muser	.75	.40	.25
239	Pete Richert	.75	.40	.25
240	Bobby Murcer	1.00	.50	.30
241	Dwain Anderson	.75	.40	.25
242	George Culver	.75	.40	.25
243	California Angels Team	2.00	1.00	.60
244	Ed Acosta	.75	.40	.25
245	Carl Yastrzemski	10.00	5.00	3.00
246	Ken Sanders	.75	.40	.25
247	Del Unser	.75	.40	.25
248	Jerry Johnson	.75	.40	.25
249	Larry Biittner	.75	.40	.25
250	Manny Sanguillen	.75	.40	.25
251	Roger Nelson	.75	.40	.25
252a	Giants Mgr./Coaches (Joe Amalfitano, Charlie Fox, Andy Gilbert, Don McMahon, John McNamara) (Coaches background brown.)			
252b	Giants Mgr./Coaches (Joe Amalfitano, Charlie Fox, Andy Gilbert, Don McMahon, John McNamara) (Coaches background orange.)	.75	.40	.25
253	Mark Belanger	.75	.40	.25
254	Bill Stoneman	.75	.40	.25
255	Reggie Jackson	12.00	6.00	3.50
256	Chris Zachary	.75	.40	.25
257a	Mets Mgr./Coaches (Yogi Berra, Roy McMillan, Joe Pignatano, Rube Walker, Eddie Yost) (Coaches background brown.)	2.00	1.00	.60
257b	Mets Mgr./Coaches (Yogi Berra, Roy McMillan, Joe Pignatano, Rube Walker, Eddie Yost) (Coaches background orange.)	2.00	1.00	.60
258	Tommy John	1.00	.50	.30
259	Jim Holt	.75	.40	.25
260	Gary Nolan	.75	.40	.25
261	Pat Kelly	.75	.40	.25
262	Jack Aker	.75	.40	.25
263	George Scott	.75	.40	.25
264	Checklist 133-264	1.00	.50	.30
265	Gene Michael	.75	.40	.25
266	Mike Lum	.75	.40	.25
267	Lloyd Allen	.75	.40	.25
268	Jerry Morales	.75	.40	.25
269	Tim McCarver	1.50	.70	.45
270	Luis Tiant	.75	.40	.25
271	Tom Hutton	.75	.40	.25
272	Ed Farmer	.75	.40	.25
273	Chris Speier	.75	.40	.25
274	Darold Knowles	.75	.40	.25
275	Tony Perez	5.00	2.50	1.50
276	Joe Lovitto	.75	.40	.25
277	Bob Miller	.75	.40	.25
278	Baltimore Orioles Team	3.00	1.50	.90
279	Mike Strahler	.75	.40	.25
280	Al Kaline	8.00	4.00	2.50
281	Mike Jorgensen	.75	.40	.25
282	Steve Hovley	.75	.40	.25
283	Ray Sadecki	.75	.40	.25

284	Glenn Borgmann	.75	.40	.25
285	Don Kessinger	.75	.40	.25
286	Frank Linzy	.75	.40	.25
287	Eddie Leon	.75	.40	.25
288	Gary Gentry	.75	.40	.25
289	Bob Oliver	.75	.40	.25
290	Cesar Cedeno	.75	.40	.25
291	Rogelio Moret	.75	.40	.25
292	Jose Cruz	.75	.40	.25
293	Bernie Allen	.75	.40	.25
294	Steve Arlin	.75	.40	.25
295	Bert Campaneris	.75	.40	.25
296	Reds Mgr./Coaches (Sparky Anderson, Alex Grammas, Ted Kluszewski, George Scherger, Larry Shepard)	2.50	1.25	.70
297	Walt Williams	.75	.40	.25
298	Ron Bryant	.75	.40	.25
299	Ted Ford	.75	.40	.25
300	Steve Carlton	8.00	4.00	2.50
301	Billy Grabarkewitz	.75	.40	.25
302	Terry Crowley	.75	.40	.25
303	Nelson Briles	.75	.40	.25
304	Duke Sims	.75	.40	.25
305	Willie Mays	40.00	20.00	12.00
306	Tom Burgmeier	.75	.40	.25
307	Boots Day	.75	.40	.25
308	Skip Lockwood	.75	.40	.25
309	Paul Popovich	.75	.40	.25
310	Dick Allen	1.50	.70	.45
311	Joe Decker	.75	.40	.25
312	Oscar Brown	.75	.40	.25
313	Jim Ray	.75	.40	.25
314	Ron Swoboda	.75	.40	.25
315	John Odom	.75	.40	.25
316	San Diego Padres Team	2.00	1.00	.60
317	Danny Cater	.75	.40	.25
318	Jim McGlothlin	.75	.40	.25
319	Jim Spencer	.75	.40	.25
320	Lou Brock	6.00	3.00	1.75
321	Rich Hinton	.75	.40	.25
322	*Garry Maddox*	1.00	.50	.30
323	Tigers Mgr./Coaches (Art Fowler, Billy Martin, Joe Schultz, Charlie Silvera, Dick Tracewski)	1.00	.50	.30
324	Al Downing	.75	.40	.25
325	Boog Powell	1.00	.50	.30
326	Darrell Brandon	.75	.40	.25
327	John Lowenstein	.75	.40	.25
328	Bill Bonham	.75	.40	.25
329	Ed Kranepool	.75	.40	.25
330	Rod Carew	6.00	3.00	1.75
331	Carl Morton	.75	.40	.25
332	*John Felske*	.75	.40	.25
333	Gene Clines	.75	.40	.25
334	Freddie Patek	.75	.40	.25
335	Bob Tolan	.75	.40	.25
336	Tom Bradley	.75	.40	.25
337	Dave Duncan	1.00	.50	.30
338	Checklist 265-396	1.00	.50	.30
339	Dick Tidrow	.75	.40	.25
340	Nate Colbert	.75	.40	.25
341	Jim Palmer (Boyhood Photo.)	1.50	.70	.45
342	Sam McDowell (Boyhood Photo.)	.75	.40	.25
343	Bobby Murcer (Boyhood Photo.)	.75	.40	.25
344	Jim Hunter (Boyhood Photo.)	1.50	.70	.45
345	Chris Speier (Boyhood Photo)	.75	.40	.25
346	Gaylord Perry (Boyhood Photo.)	1.50	.70	.45
347	Kansas City Royals Team	2.00	1.00	.60
348	Rennie Stennett	.75	.40	.25
349	Dick McAuliffe	.75	.40	.25
350	Tom Seaver	10.00	5.00	3.00
351	Jimmy Stewart	.75	.40	.25
352	*Don Stanhouse*	.75	.40	.25
353	Steve Brye	.75	.40	.25
354	Billy Parker	.75	.40	.25
355	Mike Marshall	.75	.40	.25
356	White Sox Mgr./Coaches (Joe Lonnett, Jim Mahoney, Al Monchak, Johnny Sain, Chuck Tanner)	.75	.40	.25
357	Ross Grimsley	.75	.40	.25
358	Jim Nettles	.75	.40	.25
359	Cecil Upshaw	.75	.40	.25
360	Joe Rudi (Photo actually Gene Tenace.)	.75	.40	.25
361	Fran Healy	.75	.40	.25
362	Eddie Watt	.75	.40	.25
363	Jackie Hernandez	.75	.40	.25
364	Rick Wise	.75	.40	.25
365	Rico Petrocelli	.75	.40	.25
366	Brock Davis	.75	.40	.25
367	Burt Hooton	.75	.40	.25
368	Bill Buckner	1.00	.50	.30
369	Lerrin LaGrow	.75	.40	.25
370	Willie Stargell	6.00	3.00	1.75
371	Mike Kekich	.75	.40	.25
372	Oscar Gamble	.75	.40	.25
373	Clyde Wright	.75	.40	.25
374	Darrell Evans	1.00	.50	.30
375	Larry Dierker	.75	.40	.25
376	Frank Duffy	.75	.40	.25
377	Expos Mgr./Coaches (Dave Bristol, Larry Doby, Gene Mauch, Cal McLish, Jerry Zimmerman)	1.00	.50	.30
378	Lenny Randle	.75	.40	.25
379	Cy Acosta	.75	.40	.25
380	Johnny Bench	10.00	5.00	3.00
381	Vicente Romo	.75	.40	.25
382	Mike Hegan	.75	.40	.25
383	Diego Segui	.75	.40	.25
384	Don Baylor	3.00	1.50	.90
385	Jim Perry	.75	.40	.25
386	Don Money	.75	.40	.25
387	Jim Barr	.75	.40	.25
388	Ben Oglivie	.75	.40	.25
389	New York Mets Team	4.00	2.00	1.25
390	Mickey Lolich	.75	.40	.25
391	*Lee Lacy*	.75	.40	.25
392	Dick Drago	.75	.40	.25
393	Jose Cardenal	.75	.40	.25
394	Sparky Lyle	.75	.40	.25
395	Roger Metzger	.75	.40	.25
396	Grant Jackson	.75	.40	.25
397	Dave Cash	1.00	.50	.30
398	Rich Hand	1.00	.50	.30
399	George Foster	1.00	.50	.30
400	Gaylord Perry	5.00	2.50	1.50
401	Clyde Mashore	1.00	.50	.30
402	Jack Hiatt	1.00	.50	.30
403	Sonny Jackson	1.00	.50	.30
404	Chuck Brinkman	1.00	.50	.30
405	Cesar Tovar	1.00	.50	.30
406	Paul Lindblad	1.00	.50	.30
407	Felix Millan	1.00	.50	.30
408	Jim Colborn	1.00	.50	.30
409	Ivan Murrell	1.00	.50	.30
410	Willie McCovey	8.00	4.00	2.50
411	Ray Corbin	1.00	.50	.30
412	Manny Mota	1.00	.50	.30
413	Tom Timmermann	1.00	.50	.30
414	Ken Rudolph	1.00	.50	.30
415	Marty Pattin	1.00	.50	.30
416	Paul Schaal	1.00	.50	.30
417	Scipio Spinks	1.00	.50	.30
418	Bobby Grich	1.00	.50	.30
419	Casey Cox	1.00	.50	.30
420	Tommie Agee	1.00	.50	.30
421	Angels Mgr./Coaches (Tom Morgan, Salty Parker, Jimmie Reese, John Roseboro, Bobby Winkles)	1.50	.70	.45
422	Bob Robertson	1.00	.50	.30
423	Johnny Jeter	1.00	.50	.30
424	Denny Doyle	1.00	.50	.30
425	Alex Johnson	1.00	.50	.30
426	Dave LaRoche	1.00	.50	.30
427	Rick Auerbach	1.00	.50	.30
428	Wayne Simpson	1.00	.50	.30
429	Jim Fairey	1.00	.50	.30
430	Vida Blue	1.50	.70	.45
431	Gerry Moses	1.00	.50	.30
432	Dan Frisella	1.00	.50	.30
433	Willie Horton	1.00	.50	.30
434	San Francisco Giants Team	3.00	1.50	.90
435	Rico Carty	1.00	.50	.30
436	Jim McAndrew	1.00	.50	.30
437	John Kennedy	1.00	.50	.30
438	Enzo Hernandez	1.00	.50	.30
439	Eddie Fisher	1.00	.50	.30
440	Glenn Beckert	1.00	.50	.30
441	Gail Hopkins	1.00	.50	.30
442	Dick Dietz	1.00	.50	.30
443	Danny Thompson	1.00	.50	.30
444	Ken Brett	1.00	.50	.30
445	Ken Berry	1.00	.50	.30
446	Jerry Reuss	1.00	.50	.30
447	Joe Hague	1.00	.50	.30
448	John Hiller	1.00	.50	.30
449a	Indians Mgr./Coaches (Ken Aspromonte, Rocky Colavito, Joe Lutz, Warren Spahn) (Spahn's ear pointed.)	1.50	.70	.45
449b	Indians Mgr./Coaches (Ken Aspromonte, Rocky Colavito, Joe Lutz, Warren Spahn) (Spahn's ear round.)	2.00	1.00	.60
450	Joe Torre	3.00	1.50	.90
451	John Vukovich	1.00	.50	.30
452	Paul Casanova	1.00	.50	.30
453	Checklist 397-528	1.25	.60	.40
454	Tom Haller	1.00	.50	.30
455	Bill Melton	1.00	.50	.30
456	Dick Green	1.00	.50	.30
457	John Strohmayer	1.00	.50	.30
458	Jim Mason	1.00	.50	.30
459	Jimmy Howarth	1.00	.50	.30
460	Bill Freehan	1.00	.50	.30
461	Mike Corkins	1.00	.50	.30
462	Ron Blomberg	1.00	.50	.30
463	Ken Tatum	1.00	.50	.30
464	Chicago Cubs Team	4.00	2.00	1.25
465	Dave Giusti	1.00	.50	.30
466	Jose Arcia	1.00	.50	.30
467	Mike Ryan	1.00	.50	.30
468	Tom Griffin	1.00	.50	.30
469	Dan Monzon	1.00	.50	.30
470	Mike Cuellar	1.00	.50	.30
471	All-Time Hit Leader (Ty Cobb)	10.00	5.00	3.00
472	All-Time Grand Slam Leader (Lou Gehrig)	12.00	6.00	3.50
473	All-Time Total Base Leader (Hank Aaron)	10.00	5.00	3.00
474	All-Time RBI Leader (Babe Ruth)	20.00	10.00	6.00
475	All-Time Batting Leader (Ty Cobb)	8.00	4.00	2.50
476	All-Time Shutout Leader (Walter Johnson)	3.00	1.50	.90
477	All-Time Victory Leader (Cy Young)	3.00	1.50	.90
478	All-Time Strikeout Leader (Walter Johnson)	3.00	1.50	.90
479	Hal Lanier	1.00	.50	.30
480	Juan Marichal	6.00	3.00	1.75
481	Chicago White Sox Team	3.00	1.50	.90
482	*Rick Reuschel*	2.00	1.00	.60
483	Dal Maxvill	1.00	.50	.30
484	Ernie McAnally	1.00	.50	.30
485	Norm Cash	1.50	.70	.45
486a	Phillies Mgr./Coaches (Carroll Berringer, Billy DeMars, Danny Ozark, Ray Rippelmeyer, Bobby Wine) (Coaches background brown-red.)	1.00	.50	.30
486b	Phillies Mgr./Coaches (Carroll Beringer, Billy DeMars, Danny Ozark, Ray Rippelmeyer, Bobby Wine) (Coaches background orange.)	1.00	.50	.30
487	Bruce Dal Canton	1.00	.50	.30
488	Dave Campbell	1.00	.50	.30
489	Jeff Burroughs	1.00	.50	.30
490	Claude Osteen	1.00	.50	.30
491	Bob Montgomery	1.00	.50	.30
492	Pedro Borbon	1.00	.50	.30
493	Duffy Dyer	1.00	.50	.30
494	Rich Morales	1.00	.50	.30
495	Tommy Helms	1.00	.50	.30
496	Ray Lamb	1.00	.50	.30
497	Cardinals Mgr./Coaches (Vern Benson, George Kissell, Red Schoendienst, Barney Schultz)	1.50	.70	.45
498	Graig Nettles	1.50	.70	.45
499	Bob Moose	1.00	.50	.30
500	Oakland A's Team	4.00	2.00	1.25
501	Larry Gura	1.00	.50	.30
502	Bobby Valentine	1.00	.50	.30
503	Phil Niekro	5.00	2.50	1.50
504a	Earl Williams (Small gap in each side border.)	1.25	.60	.40
504b	Earl Williams (No gaps in border.)	1.00	.50	.30
505	Bob Bailey	1.00	.50	.30
506	Bart Johnson	1.00	.50	.30
507	Darrel Chaney	1.00	.50	.30
508	Gates Brown	1.00	.50	.30
509	Jim Nash	1.00	.50	.30
510	Amos Otis	1.00	.50	.30
511	Sam McDowell	1.00	.50	.30
512	Dalton Jones	1.00	.50	.30
513	Dave Marshall	1.00	.50	.30
514	Jerry Kenney	1.00	.50	.30
515	Andy Messersmith	1.00	.50	.30
516	Danny Walton	1.00	.50	.30
517a	Pirates Mgr./Coaches (Don Leppert, Bill Mazeroski, Dave Ricketts, Bill Virdon, Mel Wright) (Coaches background brown.)	1.50	.70	.45
517b	Pirates Mgr./Coaches (Don Leppert, Bill Mazeroski, Dave Ricketts, Bill Virdon, Mel Wright) (Coaches background orange.)	1.50	.70	.45
518	Bob Veale	1.00	.50	.30
519	John Edwards	1.00	.50	.30
520	Mel Stottlemyre	1.25	.60	.40
521	Atlanta Braves Team	4.00	2.00	1.25
522	Leo Cardenas	1.00	.50	.30
523	Wayne Granger	1.00	.50	.30
524	Gene Tenace	1.00	.50	.30
525	Jim Fregosi	1.00	.50	.30
526	Ollie Brown	1.00	.50	.30
527	Dan McGinn	1.00	.50	.30
528	Paul Blair	1.00	.50	.30
529	Milt May	2.00	1.00	.60
530	Jim Kaat	4.00	2.00	1.25
531	Ron Woods	2.00	1.00	.60
532	Steve Mingori	2.00	1.00	.60
533	Larry Stahl	2.00	1.00	.60
534	Dave Lemonds	2.00	1.00	.60
535	John Callison	2.00	1.00	.60
536	Philadelphia Phillies Team	6.00	3.00	1.75
537	Bill Slayback	2.00	1.00	.60
538	Jim Hart	2.00	1.00	.60
539	Tom Murphy	2.00	1.00	.60
540	Cleon Jones	2.00	1.00	.60
541	Bob Bolin	2.00	1.00	.60
542	Pat Corrales	2.00	1.00	.60
543	Alan Foster	2.00	1.00	.60
544	Von Joshua	2.00	1.00	.60
545	Orlando Cepeda	10.00	5.00	3.00
546	Jim York	2.00	1.00	.60
547	Bobby Heise	2.00	1.00	.60
548	Don Durham	2.00	1.00	.60
549	Rangers Mgr./Coaches (Chuck Estrada, Whitey Herzog, Chuck Hiller, Jackie Moore)	2.00	1.00	.60
550	Dave Johnson	2.00	1.00	.60
551	Mike Kilkenny	2.00	1.00	.60
552	J.C. Martin	2.00	1.00	.60
553	Mickey Scott	2.00	1.00	.60
554	Dave Concepcion	2.00	1.00	.60
555	Bill Hands	2.00	1.00	.60
556	New York Yankees Team	10.00	5.00	3.00
557	Bernie Williams	2.00	1.00	.60
558	Jerry May	2.00	1.00	.60
559	Barry Lersch	2.00	1.00	.60
560	Frank Howard	3.00	1.50	.90
561	Jim Geddes	2.00	1.00	.60
562	Wayne Garrett	2.00	1.00	.60
563	Larry Haney	2.00	1.00	.60
564	Mike Thompson	2.00	1.00	.60
565	Jim Hickman	2.00	1.00	.60
566	Lew Krausse	2.00	1.00	.60
567	Bob Fenwick	2.00	1.00	.60
568	Ray Newman	2.00	1.00	.60
569	Dodgers Mgr./Coaches (Red Adams, Walt Alston, Monty Basgall, Jim Gilliam, Tom Lasorda)	5.00	2.50	1.50

570	Bill Singer	2.00	1.00	.60
571	Rusty Torres	2.00	1.00	.60
572	Gary Sutherland	2.00	1.00	.60
573	Fred Beene	2.00	1.00	.60
574	Bob Didier	2.00	1.00	.60
575	Dock Ellis	2.00	1.00	.60
576	Montreal Expos Team	5.00	2.50	1.50
577	*Eric Soderholm*	2.00	1.00	.60
578	Ken Wright	2.00	1.00	.60
579	Tom Grieve	2.00	1.00	.60
580	Joe Pepitone	2.00	1.00	.60
581	Steve Kealey	2.00	1.00	.60
582	Darrell Porter	2.00	1.00	.60
583	Bill Greif	2.00	1.00	.60
584	Chris Arnold	2.00	1.00	.60
585	Joe Niekro	2.00	1.00	.60
586	Bill Sudakis	2.00	1.00	.60
587	Rich McKinney	2.00	1.00	.60
588	Checklist 529-660	15.00	7.50	4.50
589	Ken Forsch	2.00	1.00	.60
590	Deron Johnson	2.00	1.00	.60
591	Mike Hedlund	2.00	1.00	.60
592	John Boccabella	2.00	1.00	.60
593	Royals Mgr./Coaches (Galen Cisco, Harry Dunlop, Charlie Lau, Jack McKeon)	2.00	1.00	.60
594	Vic Harris	2.00	1.00	.60
595	Don Gullett	2.00	1.00	.60
596	Boston Red Sox Team	5.00	2.50	1.50
597	Mickey Rivers	2.00	1.00	.60
598	Phil Roof	2.00	1.00	.60
599	Ed Crosby	2.00	1.00	.60
600	Dave McNally	2.00	1.00	.60
601	Rookie Catchers (George Pena, Sergio Robles, Rick Stelmaszek)	3.00	1.50	.90
602	Rookie Pitchers (*Mel Behney, Ralph Garcia, Doug Rau*)	3.00	1.50	.90
603	Rookie Third Basemen (*Terry Hughes, Bill McNulty, Ken Reitz*)	3.00	1.50	.90
604	Rookie Pitchers (Jesse Jefferson, Dennis O'Toole, Bob Strampe)	3.00	1.50	.90
605	Rookie First Basemen (Pat Bourque, Enos Cabell, Gonzalo Marquez)	3.00	1.50	.90
606	Rookie Outfielders (Gary Matthews, Tom Paciorek, Jorge Roque)	4.00	2.00	1.25
607	Rookie Shortstops (Ray Busse, Pepe Frias, Mario Guerrero)	3.00	1.50	.90
608	Rookie Pitchers (*Steve Busby, Dick Colpaert, George Medich*)	3.00	1.50	.90
609	Rookie Second Basemen (*Larvell Blanks, Pedro Garcia, Dave Lopes*)	5.00	2.50	1.50
610	Rookie Pitchers (Jimmy Freeman, Charlie Hough, Hank Webb)	4.00	2.00	1.25
611	Rookie Outfielders (Rich Coggins, Jim Wohlford, Richie Zisk)	3.00	1.50	.90
612	Rookie Pitchers (Steve Lawson, Bob Reynolds, Brent Strom)	3.00	1.50	.90
613	Rookie Catchers (Bob Boone, Mike Ivie, Skip Jutze)	15.00	7.50	4.50
614	Rookie Outfielders (Al Bumbry, Dwight Evans, Charlie Spikes)	20.00	10.00	6.00
615	Rookie Third Basemen (*Ron Cey, John Hilton, Mike Schmidt*)	150.00	75.00	45.00
616	Rookie Pitchers (Norm Angelini, Steve Blateric, Mike Garman)	3.00	1.50	.90
617	Rich Chiles	2.00	1.00	.60
618	Andy Etchebarren	2.00	1.00	.60
619	Billy Wilson	2.00	1.00	.60
620	Tommy Harper	2.00	1.00	.60
621	Joe Ferguson	2.00	1.00	.60
622	Larry Hisle	2.00	1.00	.60
623	Steve Renko	2.00	1.00	.60
624	Astros Mgr./Coaches (Leo Durocher, Preston Gomez, Grady Hatton, Hub Kittle, Jim Owens)	3.00	1.50	.90
625	Angel Mangual	2.00	1.00	.60
626	Bob Barton	2.00	1.00	.60
627	Luis Alvarado	2.00	1.00	.60
628	Jim Slaton	2.00	1.00	.60
629	Cleveland Indians Team	5.00	2.50	1.50
630	Denny McLain	6.00	3.00	1.75
631	Tom Matchick	2.00	1.00	.60
632	Dick Selma	2.00	1.00	.60
633	Ike Brown	2.00	1.00	.60
634	Alan Closter	2.00	1.00	.60
635	Gene Alley	2.00	1.00	.60
636	Rick Clark	2.00	1.00	.60
637	Norm Miller	2.00	1.00	.60
638	Ken Reynolds	2.00	1.00	.60
639	Willie Crawford	2.00	1.00	.60
640	Dick Bosman	2.00	1.00	.60
641	Cincinnati Reds Team	6.00	3.00	1.75
642	Jose Laboy	2.00	1.00	.60
643	Al Fitzmorris	2.00	1.00	.60
644	Jack Heidemann	2.00	1.00	.60
645	Bob Locker	2.00	1.00	.60
646	Brewers Mgr./Coaches (Del Crandall, Harvey Kuenn, Joe Nossek, Bob Shaw, Jim Walton)	2.00	1.00	.60
647	George Stone	2.00	1.00	.60
648	Tom Egan	2.00	1.00	.60

649	Rich Folkers	2.00	1.00	.60
650	Felipe Alou	4.00	2.00	1.25
651	Don Carrithers	2.00	1.00	.60
652	Ted Kubiak	2.00	1.00	.60
653	Joe Hoerner	2.00	1.00	.60
654	Minnesota Twins Team	4.00	2.00	1.25
655	Clay Kirby	2.00	1.00	.60
656	John Ellis	2.00	1.00	.60
657	Bob Johnson	2.00	1.00	.60
658	Elliott Maddox	2.00	1.00	.60
659	Jose Pagan	2.00	1.00	.60
660	Fred Scherman	2.00	1.00	.60

1973 Topps Candy Lids

A bit out of the ordinary, the Topps Candy Lids were the top of a product called "Baseball Stars Bubble Gum." The bottom (inside) of the lids carry a color photo of a player with a ribbon containing the name, position and team. The lids are 1-7/8" in diameter. A total of 55 different lids were made, featuring most of the stars of the day.

		NM	EX	VG
Complete Set (55):		750.00	375.00	225.00
Common Player:		6.00	3.00	1.75
Unopened Tub:		135.00		
(1)	Hank Aaron	60.00	30.00	18.00
(2)	Dick Allen	7.50	3.75	2.25
(3)	Dusty Baker	6.00	3.00	1.75
(4)	Sal Bando	6.00	3.00	1.75
(5)	Johnny Bench	30.00	15.00	9.00
(6)	Bobby Bonds	6.00	3.00	1.75
(7)	Dick Bosman	6.00	3.00	1.75
(8)	Lou Brock	15.00	7.50	4.50
(9)	Rod Carew	25.00	12.50	7.50
(10)	Steve Carlton	25.00	12.50	7.50
(11)	Nate Colbert	6.00	3.00	1.75
(12)	Willie Davis	6.00	3.00	1.75
(13)	Larry Dierker	6.00	3.00	1.75
(14)	Mike Epstein	6.00	3.00	1.75
(15)	Carlton Fisk	15.00	7.50	4.50
(16)	Tim Foli	6.00	3.00	1.75
(17)	Ray Fosse	6.00	3.00	1.75
(18)	Bill Freehan	6.00	3.00	1.75
(19)	Bob Gibson	25.00	12.50	7.50
(20)	Bud Harrelson	6.00	3.00	1.75
(21)	Catfish Hunter	15.00	7.50	4.50
(22)	Reggie Jackson	40.00	20.00	12.00
(23)	Fergie Jenkins	15.00	7.50	4.50
(24)	Al Kaline	30.00	15.00	9.00
(25)	Harmon Killebrew	30.00	15.00	9.00
(26)	Clay Kirby	6.00	3.00	1.75
(27)	Mickey Lolich	6.00	3.00	1.75
(28)	Greg Luzinski	6.00	3.00	1.75
(29)	Mike Marshall	6.00	3.00	1.75
(30)	Lee May	6.00	3.00	1.75
(31)	John Mayberry	6.00	3.00	1.75
(32)	Willie Mays	60.00	30.00	18.00
(33)	Willie McCovey	15.00	7.50	4.50
(34)	Thurman Munson	25.00	12.50	7.50
(35)	Bobby Murcer	12.50	6.25	3.75
(36)	Gary Nolan	6.00	3.00	1.75
(37)	Amos Otis	6.00	3.00	1.75
(38)	Jim Palmer	15.00	7.50	4.50
(39)	Gaylord Perry	15.00	7.50	4.50
(40)	Lou Piniella	7.50	3.75	2.25
(41)	Brooks Robinson	30.00	15.00	9.00
(42)	Frank Robinson	30.00	15.00	9.00
(43)	Ellie Rodriguez	6.00	3.00	1.75
(44)	Pete Rose	50.00	25.00	15.00
(45)	Nolan Ryan	200.00	100.00	60.00
(46)	Manny Sanguillen	6.00	3.00	1.75
(47)	George Scott	6.00	3.00	1.75
(48)	Tom Seaver	25.00	12.50	7.50
(49)	Chris Speier	6.00	3.00	1.75
(50)	Willie Stargell	15.00	7.50	4.50
(51)	Don Sutton	15.00	7.50	4.50
(52)	Joe Torre	7.50	3.75	2.25
(53)	Billy Williams	15.00	7.50	4.50
(54)	Wilbur Wood	6.00	3.00	1.75
(55)	Carl Yastrzemski	35.00	17.50	10.50

1973 Topps Comics

Strictly a test issue, if ever publicly distributed at all (most are found without any folding which would have occurred had they actually been used to wrap a piece of bubblegum), the 24 players in the 1973 Topps Comics issue appear on 4-5/8" x 3-7/16" waxed paper wrappers. The inside of the wrapper combines a color photo and facsimile autograph with a comic-style presentation of the player's career highlights. The Comics share a checklist with the 1973 Topps Pin-Ups, virtually all star players.

		NM	EX	VG
Complete Set (24):		15,000	7,500	4,500
Common Player:		200.00	100.00	60.00
(1)	Hank Aaron	1,100	550.00	330.00
(2)	Dick Allen	375.00	185.00	110.00
(3)	Johnny Bench	675.00	335.00	200.00
(4)	Steve Carlton	550.00	275.00	165.00
(5)	Nate Colbert	200.00	100.00	60.00
(6)	Willie Davis	200.00	100.00	60.00
(7)	Mike Epstein	200.00	100.00	60.00
(8)	Reggie Jackson	1,100	550.00	330.00
(9)	Harmon Killebrew	550.00	275.00	165.00
(10)	Mickey Lolich	200.00	100.00	60.00
(11)	Mike Marshall	200.00	100.00	60.00
(12)	Lee May	200.00	100.00	60.00
(13)	Willie McCovey	550.00	275.00	165.00
(14)	Bobby Murcer	300.00	150.00	90.00
(15)	Gaylord Perry	525.00	260.00	155.00
(16)	Lou Piniella	300.00	150.00	90.00
(17)	Brooks Robinson	900.00	450.00	270.00
(18)	Nolan Ryan	3,500	1,750	1,000
(19)	George Scott	200.00	100.00	60.00
(20)	Tom Seaver	750.00	375.00	225.00
(21)	Willie Stargell	550.00	275.00	165.00
(22)	Joe Torre	300.00	150.00	90.00
(23)	Billy Williams	525.00	260.00	155.00
(24)	Carl Yastrzemski	1,100	550.00	330.00

1973 Topps Pin-Ups

Another test issue of 1973, the 24 Topps Pin-Ups include the same basic format and the same checklist of star-caliber players as the Comics test issue of the same year. The 3-7/16" x 4-5/8" Pin-Ups are actually the inside of a wrapper for a piece of bubblegum. The color player photo features a decorative lozenge inserted at bottom with the player's name, team and position. There is also a facsimile autograph. Curiously, neither the Pin-Ups nor the Comics of 1973 bear team logos on the players' caps.

		NM	EX	VG
Complete Set (24):		9,000	4,500	2,750
Common Player:		250.00	125.00	75.00
(1)	Hank Aaron	800.00	400.00	240.00
(2)	Dick Allen	300.00	150.00	90.00
(3)	Johnny Bench	600.00	300.00	180.00
(4)	Steve Carlton	500.00	250.00	150.00
(5)	Nate Colbert	250.00	125.00	75.00
(6)	Willie Davis	250.00	125.00	75.00
(7)	Mike Epstein	265.00	130.00	80.00
(8)	Reggie Jackson	800.00	400.00	240.00
(9)	Harmon Killebrew	550.00	275.00	165.00
(10)	Mickey Lolich	265.00	130.00	80.00
(11)	Mike Marshall	250.00	125.00	75.00
(12)	Lee May	250.00	125.00	75.00
(13)	Willie McCovey	550.00	275.00	165.00
(14)	Bobby Murcer	300.00	150.00	90.00
(15)	Gaylord Perry	500.00	250.00	150.00
(16)	Lou Piniella	300.00	150.00	90.00
(17)	Brooks Robinson	600.00	300.00	180.00
(18)	Nolan Ryan	900.00	450.00	270.00
(19)	George Scott	250.00	125.00	75.00
(20)	Tom Seaver	600.00	300.00	180.00
(21)	Willie Stargell	550.00	275.00	165.00
(22)	Joe Torre	275.00	135.00	82.00
(23)	Billy Williams	550.00	275.00	165.00
(24)	Carl Yastrzemski	650.00	325.00	195.00

1973 Topps Team Checklists

This is a 24-card unnumbered set of 2-1/2" x 3-1/2" cards that is generally believed to have been included with the high-numbered series in 1973, while also being made available in a mail-in offer. The front of the cards have the team name at the top and a white

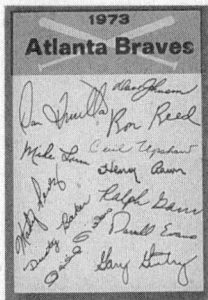

panel with various facsimile autographs takes up the rest of the space except for a blue border. Backs feature the team name and checklist. Relatively scarce, these somewhat mysterious cards are not included by many in their collections despite their obvious relationship to the regular set.

		NM	EX	VG
Complete Set (24):		100.00	50.00	30.00
Common Checklist:		3.50	1.75	1.00
(1)	Atlanta Braves	3.50	1.75	1.00
(2)	Baltimore Orioles	3.50	1.75	1.00
(3)	Boston Red Sox	5.00	2.50	1.50
(4)	California Angels	3.50	1.75	1.00
(5)	Chicago Cubs	3.50	1.75	1.00
(6)	Chicago White Sox	3.50	1.75	1.00
(7)	Cincinnati Reds	5.00	2.50	1.50
(8)	Cleveland Indians	3.50	1.75	1.00
(9)	Detroit Tigers	6.00	3.00	1.75
(10)	Houston Astros	3.50	1.75	1.00
(11)	Kansas City Royals	3.50	1.75	1.00
(12)	Los Angeles Dodgers	3.50	1.75	1.00
(13)	Milwaukee Brewers	3.50	1.75	1.00
(14)	Minnesota Twins	3.50	1.75	1.00
(15)	Montreal Expos	3.50	1.75	1.00
(16)	New York Mets	6.00	3.00	1.75
(17)	New York Yankees	6.00	3.00	1.75
(18)	Oakland A's	6.00	3.00	1.75
(19)	Philadelphia Phillies	3.50	1.75	1.00
(20)	Pittsburgh Pirates	3.50	1.75	1.00
(21)	St. Louis Cardinals	3.50	1.75	1.00
(22)	San Diego Padres	3.50	1.75	1.00
(23)	San Francisco Giants	3.50	1.75	1.00
(24)	Texas Rangers	3.50	1.75	1.00

1973 Topps 1953 Reprints

Long before Topps reprinted virtually the entire 1953 set in its "Archives" program in 1991, selected cards from the '53 set had been reprinted in a rare eight-card issue. Some sources say the cards were produced as table favors at a Topps banquet, while at least one contemporary hobby periodical said they were sold on a test-issue basis in Brooklyn. It was said only 300 of the sets were made. Unlike the original cards in 2-5/8" x 3-3/4" format, the test issue cards are modern standard 2-1/2" x 3-1/2". Three of the players in the issue were misidentified. Card backs feature a career summary written as though in 1953; the backs are formatted differently than original 1953 Topps cards and are printed in black-and-white.

		NM	EX	VG
Complete Set (8):		750.00	375.00	225.00
Common Player:		35.00	17.50	10.00
1	Satchell Paige	225.00	110.00	65.00
2	Jackie Robinson	300.00	150.00	90.00
3	Carl Furillo (Picture actually Bill Antonello.)	50.00	25.00	15.00
4	Al Rosen (Picture actually Jim Fridley.)	35.00	17.50	10.00
5	Hal Newhouser	40.00	20.00	12.00
6	Clyde McCullough (Picture actually Vic Janowicz.)	35.00	17.50	10.00
7	"Peanuts Lowrey	35.00	17.50	10.00
8	Johnny Mize	85.00	42.50	25.00

1974 Topps

Issued all at once at the beginning of the year, rather than by series throughout the baseball season as had been done since 1952, this 660-card '74 Topps set features a famous group of error cards. At the time the cards were printed, it was uncertain whether the San Diego Padres would move to Washington, D.C., and by

the time a decision was made some Padres cards had appeared with a "Washington, Nat'l League" designation on the front. A total of 15 cards were affected, and those with the Washington designation bring prices well in excess of regular cards of the same players (the Washington variations are not included in the complete set prices quoted below). The 2-1/2" x 3-1/2" cards feature color photos (frequently game-action shots) along with the player's name, team and position. Specialty cards abound, starting with a Hank Aaron tribute and running through the usual managers, statistical leaders, playoff and World Series highlights, multi-player rookie cards and All-Stars.

		NM	EX	VG
Unopened Factory Set (704):		600.00		
Complete Set (660):		350.00	175.00	100.00
Common Player:		.40	.20	.10
Wax Pack (2):		9.00		
Wax Pack (8+1 - B.T.C.):		40.00		
Wax Box (36):		1,600		
Wax Pack (12+1 - B.T.C.):		45.00		
Wax Box (24):		1,700		
Cello Pack (22):		125.00		
Rack Pack (42):		325.00		
Vending Box (500):		925.00		
1	Hank Aaron (All-Time Home Run King.)	50.00	25.00	15.00
2	Hank Aaron (Aaron Special 1954-57.)	10.00	5.00	3.00
3	Hank Aaron (Aaron Special 1958-61.)	10.00	5.00	3.00
4	Hank Aaron (Aaron Special 1962-65.)	10.00	5.00	3.00
5	Hank Aaron (Aaron Special 1966-69.)	10.00	5.00	3.00
6	Hank Aaron (Aaron Special 1970-73.)	10.00	5.00	3.00
7	Jim Hunter	4.00	2.00	1.25
8	George Theodore	.40	.20	.10
9	Mickey Lolich	.40	.20	.09
10	Johnny Bench	15.00	7.50	4.50
11	Jim Bibby	.40	.20	.10
12	Dave May	.40	.20	.10
13	Tom Hilgendorf	.40	.20	.10
14	Paul Popovich	.40	.20	.10
15	Joe Torre	2.00	1.00	.60
16	Baltimore Orioles Team	2.00	1.00	.60
17	Doug Bird	.40	.20	.10
18	Gary Thomasson	.40	.20	.10
19	Gerry Moses	.40	.20	.10
20	Nolan Ryan	40.00	20.00	12.00
21	Bob Gallagher	.40	.20	.10
22	Cy Acosta	.40	.20	.10
23	Craig Robinson	.40	.20	.10
24	John Hiller	.40	.20	.10
25	Ken Singleton	.40	.20	.10
26	*Bill Campbell*	.40	.20	.10
27	George Scott	.40	.20	.10
28	Manny Sanguillen	.40	.20	.10
29	Phil Niekro	4.00	2.00	1.25
30	Bobby Bonds	.40	.20	.09
31	Astros Mgr./Coaches (Roger Craig, Preston Gomez, Grady Hatton, Hub Kittle, Bob Lillis)	.40	.20	.09
32a	John Grubb (Washington)	3.00	1.50	.90
32b	John Grubb (San Diego)	.40	.20	.10
33	Don Newhauser	.40	.20	.10
34	Andy Kosco	.40	.20	.10
35	Gaylord Perry	4.00	2.00	1.25
36	St. Louis Cardinals Team	2.00	1.00	.60
37	Dave Sells	.40	.20	.10
38	Don Kessinger	.40	.20	.10
39	Ken Suarez	.40	.20	.10
40	Jim Palmer	6.00	3.00	1.75
41	Bobby Floyd	.40	.20	.10
42	Claude Osteen	.40	.20	.10
43	Jim Wynn	.40	.20	.10
44	Mel Stottlemyre	.75	.40	.25
45	Dave Johnson	.40	.20	.10
46	Pat Kelly	.40	.20	.10
47	*Dick Ruthven*	.40	.20	.10
48	Dick Sharon	.40	.20	.10
49	Steve Renko	.40	.20	.10
50	Rod Carew	6.00	3.00	1.75
51	Bobby Heise	.40	.20	.10
52	Al Oliver	.50	.25	.15
53a	Fred Kendall (Washington)	3.00	1.50	.90
53b	Fred Kendall (San Diego)	.40	.20	.10
54	*Elias Sosa*	.40	.20	.10
55	Frank Robinson	6.00	3.00	1.75
56	New York Mets Team	1.50	.70	.45
57	Darold Knowles	.40	.20	.10
58	Charlie Spikes	.40	.20	.10
59	Ross Grimsley	.40	.20	.10

60	Lou Brock	5.00	2.50	1.50
61	Luis Aparicio	4.00	2.00	1.25
62	Bob Locker	.40	.20	.10
63	Bill Sudakis	.40	.20	.10
64	Doug Rau	.40	.20	.10
65	Amos Otis	.40	.20	.10
66	Sparky Lyle	.40	.20	.10
67	Tommy Helms	.40	.20	.10
68	Grant Jackson	.40	.20	.10
69	Del Unser	.40	.20	.10
70	Dick Allen	.75	.40	.25
71	Danny Frisella	.40	.20	.10
72	Aurelio Rodriguez	.40	.20	.10
73	Mike Marshall	.40	.20	.10
74	Minnesota Twins Team	1.00	.50	.30
75	Jim Colborn	.40	.20	.10
76	Mickey Rivers	.40	.20	.10
77a	Rich Troedson (Washington)	3.00	1.50	.90
77b	Rich Troedson (San Diego)	.40	.20	.10
78	Giants Mgr./Coaches (Joe Amalfitano, Charlie Fox, Andy Gilbert, Don McMahon, John McNamara)	.40	.20	.10
79	Gene Tenace	.40	.20	.10
80	Tom Seaver	10.00	5.00	3.00
81	Frank Duffy	.40	.20	.10
82	Dave Giusti	.40	.20	.10
83	Orlando Cepeda	4.00	2.00	1.25
84	Rick Wise	.40	.20	.10
85	Joe Morgan	6.00	3.00	1.75
86	Joe Ferguson	.40	.20	.10
87	Fergie Jenkins	4.00	2.00	1.25
88	Freddie Patek	.40	.20	.10
89	Jackie Brown	.40	.20	.10
90	Bobby Murcer	.50	.25	.15
91	Ken Forsch	.40	.20	.10
92	Paul Blair	.40	.20	.10
93	Rod Gilbreath	.40	.20	.10
94	Detroit Tigers Team	1.00	.50	.30
95	Steve Carlton	6.00	3.00	1.75
96	*Jerry Hairston Sr.*	.40	.20	.10
97	Bob Bailey	.40	.20	.10
98	Bert Blyleven	.75	.40	.25
99	Brewers Mgr./Coaches (Del Crandall, Harvey Kuenn, Joe Nossek, Jim Walton, Al Widmar)	.40	.20	.10
100	Willie Stargell	5.00	2.50	1.50
101	Bobby Valentine	.40	.20	.10
102a	Bill Greif (Washington)	3.00	1.50	.90
102b	Bill Greif (San Diego)	.40	.20	.10
103	Sal Bando	.40	.20	.10
104	Ron Bryant	.40	.20	.10
105	Carlton Fisk	10.00	5.00	3.00
106	Harry Parker	.40	.20	.10
107	Alex Johnson	.40	.20	.10
108	Al Hrabosky	.40	.20	.10
109	Bob Grich	.40	.20	.10
110	Billy Williams	5.00	2.50	1.50
111	Clay Carroll	.40	.20	.10
112	Dave Lopes	.40	.20	.10
113	Dick Drago	.40	.20	.10
114	California Angels Team	1.00	.50	.30
115	Willie Horton	.40	.20	.10
116	Jerry Reuss	.40	.20	.10
117	Ron Blomberg	.40	.20	.10
118	Bill Lee	.40	.20	.10
119	Phillies Mgr./Coaches (Carroll Beringer, Bill DeMars, Danny Ozark, Ray Ripplemeyer, Bobby Wine)	.40	.20	.10
120	Wilbur Wood	.40	.20	.10
121	Larry Lintz	.40	.20	.10
122	Jim Holt	.40	.20	.10
123	Nelson Briles	.40	.20	.10
124	Bob Coluccio	.40	.20	.10
125a	Nate Colbert (Washington)	3.00	1.50	.90
125b	Nate Colbert (San Diego)	.40	.20	.10
126	Checklist 1-132	.75	.40	.25
127	Tom Paciorek	.40	.20	.10
128	John Ellis	.40	.20	.10
129	Chris Speier	.40	.20	.10
130	Reggie Jackson	15.00	7.50	4.50
131	Bob Boone	1.50	.70	.45
132	Felix Millan	.40	.20	.10
133	*David Clyde*	.40	.20	.10
134	Denis Menke	.40	.20	.10
135	Roy White	.40	.20	.10
136	Rick Reuschel	.40	.20	.10
137	Al Bumbry	.40	.20	.10
138	Ed Brinkman	.40	.20	.10
139	Aurelio Monteagudo	.40	.20	.10
140	Darrell Evans	.75	.40	.25
141	Pat Bourque	.40	.20	.10
142	Pedro Garcia	.40	.20	.10
143	Dick Woodson	.40	.20	.10
144	Dodgers Mgr./Coaches (Red Adams, Walter Alston, Monty Basgall, Jim Gilliam, Tom Lasorda)	1.00	.50	.30
145	Dock Ellis	.40	.20	.10
146	Ron Fairly	.40	.20	.10
147	Bart Johnson	.40	.20	.10
148a	Dave Hilton (Washington)	3.00	1.50	.90
148b	Dave Hilton (San Diego)	.40	.20	.10
149	Mac Scarce	.40	.20	.10
150	John Mayberry	.40	.20	.10
151	Diego Segui	.40	.20	.10
152	Oscar Gamble	.40	.20	.10
153	Jon Matlack	.40	.20	.10
154	Houston Astros Team	1.50	.70	.45
155	Bert Campaneris	.40	.20	.10
156	Randy Moffitt	.40	.20	.10
157	Vic Harris	.40	.20	.10
158	Jack Billingham	.40	.20	.10
159	Jim Ray Hart	.40	.20	.10
160	Brooks Robinson	6.00	3.00	1.75
161	*Ray Burris*	.40	.20	.10

162	Bill Freehan	.40	.20	.10
163	Ken Berry	.40	.20	.10
164	Tom House	.40	.20	.10
165	Willie Davis	.40	.20	.10
166	Royals Mgr./Coaches (Galen Cisco, Harry Dunlop, Charlie Lau, Jack McKeon)	.40	.20	.10
167	Luis Tiant	1.00	.50	.30
168	Danny Thompson	.40	.20	.10
169	*Steve Rogers*	.40	.20	.10
170	Bill Melton	.40	.20	.10
171	Eduardo Rodriguez	.40	.20	.10
172	Gene Clines	.40	.20	.10
173a	*Randy Jones* (Washington)	3.00	1.50	.90
173b	*Randy Jones* (San Diego)	.40	.20	.10
174	Bill Robinson	.40	.20	.10
175	Reggie Cleveland	.40	.20	.10
176	John Lowenstein	.40	.20	.10
177	Dave Roberts	.40	.20	.10
178	Garry Maddox	.40	.20	.10
179	Mets Mgr./Coaches (Yogi Berra, Roy McMillan, Joe Pignatano, Rube Walker, Eddie Yost)	1.50	.70	.45
180	Ken Holtzman	.40	.20	.10
181	Cesar Geronimo	.40	.20	.10
182	Lindy McDaniel	.40	.20	.10
183	Johnny Oates	.40	.20	.10
184	Texas Rangers Team	1.00	.50	.30
185	Jose Cardenal	.40	.20	.10
186	Fred Scherman	.40	.20	.10
187	Don Baylor	1.00	.50	.30
188	Rudy Meoli	.40	.20	.10
189	Jim Brewer	.40	.20	.10
190	Tony Oliva	1.50	.70	.45
191	Al Fitzmorris	.40	.20	.10
192	Mario Guerrero	.40	.20	.10
193	Tom Walker	.40	.20	.10
194	Darrell Porter	.40	.20	.10
195	Carlos May	.40	.20	.10
196	Jim Fregosi	.75	.40	.25
197a	Vicente Romo (Washington)	3.00	1.50	.90
197b	Vicente Romo (San Diego)	.40	.20	.10
198	Dave Cash	.40	.20	.10
199	Mike Kekich	.40	.20	.10
200	Cesar Cedeno	.40	.20	.10
201	Batting Leaders (Rod Carew, Pete Rose)	6.00	3.00	1.75
202	Home Run Leaders (Reggie Jackson, Willie Stargell)	4.00	2.00	1.25
203	RBI Leaders (Reggie Jackson, Willie Stargell)	4.00	2.00	1.25
204	Stolen Base Leaders (Lou Brock, Tommy Harper)	1.50	.70	.45
205	Victory Leaders (Ron Bryant, Wilbur Wood)	1.00	.50	.30
206	Earned Run Average Leaders (Jim Palmer, Tom Seaver)	2.00	1.00	.60
207	Strikeout Leaders (Nolan Ryan, Tom Seaver)	10.00	5.00	3.00
208	Leading Firemen (John Hiller, Mike Marshall)	1.00	.50	.30
209	Ted Sizemore	.40	.20	.10
210	Bill Singer	.40	.20	.10
211	Chicago Cubs Team	1.00	.50	.30
212	Rollie Fingers	4.00	2.00	1.25
213	Dave Rader	.40	.20	.10
214	Billy Grabarkewitz	.40	.20	.10
215	Al Kaline	10.00	5.00	3.00
216	Ray Sadecki	.40	.20	.10
217	Tim Foli	.40	.20	.10
218	Johnny Briggs	.40	.20	.10
219	Doug Griffin	.40	.20	.10
220	Don Sutton	4.00	2.00	1.25
221	White Sox Mgr./Coaches (Joe Lonnett, Jim Mahoney, Alex Monchak, Johnny Sain, Chuck Tanner)	.40	.20	.10
222	Ramon Hernandez	.40	.20	.10
223	Jeff Burroughs	.40	.20	.10
224	Roger Metzger	.40	.20	.10
225	Paul Splittorff	.40	.20	.10
226a	Washington Nat'l. Team	8.00	4.00	2.50
226b	San Diego Padres Team	2.00	1.00	.60
227	Mike Lum	.40	.20	.10
228	Ted Kubiak	.40	.20	.10
229	Fritz Peterson	.40	.20	.10
230	Tony Perez	4.00	2.00	1.25
231	Dick Tidrow	.40	.20	.10
232	Steve Brye	.40	.20	.10
233	Jim Barr	.40	.20	.10
234	John Milner	.40	.20	.10
235	Dave McNally	.40	.20	.10
236	Cardinals Mgr./Coaches (Vern Benson, George Kissell, Johnny Lewis, Red Schoendienst, Barney Schultz)	.75	.40	.25
237	Ken Brett	.40	.20	.10
238	Fran Healy	.40	.20	.10
239	Bill Russell	.40	.20	.10
240	Joe Coleman	.40	.20	.10
241a	Glenn Beckert (Washington)	3.00	1.50	.90
241b	Glenn Beckert (San Diego)	.40	.20	.10
242	Bill Gogolewski	.40	.20	.10
243	Bob Oliver	.40	.20	.10
244	Carl Morton	.40	.20	.10
245	Cleon Jones	.40	.20	.10
246	Oakland A's Team	2.00	1.00	.60
247	Rick Miller	.40	.20	.10
248	Tom Hall	.40	.20	.10
249	George Mitterwald	.40	.20	.10
250a	Willie McCovey (Washington)	20.00	10.00	6.00
250b	Willie McCovey (San Diego)	6.00	3.00	1.75
251	Graig Nettles	1.50	.70	.45
252	*Dave Parker*	8.00	4.00	2.50

253	John Boccabella	.40	.20	.10
254	Stan Bahnsen	.40	.20	.10
255	Larry Bowa	1.00	.50	.30
256	Tom Griffin	.40	.20	.10
257	Buddy Bell	.40	.20	.10
258	Jerry Morales	.40	.20	.10
259	Bob Reynolds	.40	.20	.10
260	Ted Simmons	.75	.40	.25
261	Jerry Bell	.40	.20	.10
262	Ed Kirkpatrick	.40	.20	.10
263	Checklist 133-264	1.00	.50	.30
264	Joe Rudi	.40	.20	.10
265	Tug McGraw	.40	.20	.10
266	Jim Northrup	.40	.20	.10
267	Andy Messersmith	.40	.20	.10
268	Tom Grieve	.40	.20	.10
269	Bob Johnson	.40	.20	.10
270	Ron Santo	3.00	1.50	.90
271	Bill Hands	.40	.20	.10
272	Paul Casanova	.40	.20	.10
273	Checklist 265-396	.75	.40	.25
274	Fred Beene	.40	.20	.10
275	Ron Hunt	.40	.20	.10
276	Angels Mgr./Coaches (Tom Morgan, Salty Parker, Jimmie Reese, John Roseboro, Bobby Winkles)	.40	.20	.10
277	Gary Nolan	.40	.20	.10
278	Cookie Rojas	.40	.20	.10
279	Jim Crawford	.40	.20	.10
280	Carl Yastrzemski	10.00	5.00	3.00
281	San Francisco Giants Team	1.00	.50	.30
282	Doyle Alexander	.40	.20	.10
283	Mike Schmidt	20.00	10.00	6.00
284	Dave Duncan	.40	.20	.10
285	Reggie Smith	.40	.20	.10
286	Tony Muser	.40	.20	.10
287	Clay Kirby	.40	.20	.10
288	*Gorman Thomas*	2.00	1.00	.60
289	Rick Auerbach	.40	.20	.10
290	Vida Blue	1.00	.50	.30
291	Don Hahn	.40	.20	.10
292	Chuck Seelbach	.40	.20	.10
293	Milt May	.40	.20	.10
294	Steve Foucault	.40	.20	.10
295	Rick Monday	.40	.20	.10
296	Ray Corbin	.40	.20	.10
297	Hal Breeden	.40	.20	.10
298	Roric Harrison	.40	.20	.10
299	Gene Michael	.40	.20	.10
300	Pete Rose	25.00	12.50	7.50
301	Bob Montgomery	.40	.20	.10
302	Rudy May	.40	.20	.10
303	George Hendrick	.40	.20	.10
304	Don Wilson	.40	.20	.10
305	Tito Fuentes	.40	.20	.10
306	Orioles Mgr./Coaches (George Bamberger, Jim Frey, Billy Hunter, George Staller, Earl Weaver)	2.00	1.00	.60
307	Luis Melendez	.40	.20	.10
308	Bruce Dal Canton	.40	.20	.10
309a	Dave Roberts (Washington)	3.00	1.50	.90
309b	Dave Roberts (San Diego)	.40	.20	.10
310	Terry Forster	.40	.20	.10
311	Jerry Grote	.40	.20	.10
312	Deron Johnson	.40	.20	.10
313	Berry Lersch	.40	.20	.10
314	Milwaukee Brewers Team	1.00	.50	.30
315	Ron Cey	.50	.25	.15
316	Jim Perry	.40	.20	.10
317	Richie Zisk	.40	.20	.10
318	Jim Merritt	.40	.20	.10
319	Randy Hundley	.40	.20	.10
320	Dusty Baker	1.00	.50	.30
321	Steve Braun	.40	.20	.10
322	Ernie McAnally	.40	.20	.10
323	Richie Scheinblum	.40	.20	.10
324	Steve Kline	.40	.20	.10
325	Tommy Harper	.40	.20	.10
326	Reds Mgr./Coaches (Sparky Anderson, Alex Grammas, Ted Kluszewski, George Scherger, Larry Shepard)	2.00	1.00	.60
327	Tom Timmermann	.40	.20	.10
328	Skip Jutze	.40	.20	.10
329	Mark Belanger	.40	.20	.10
330	Juan Marichal	4.00	2.00	1.25
331	All-Star Catchers (Johnny Bench, Carlton Fisk)	4.00	2.00	1.25
332	All-Star First Basemen (Hank Aaron, Dick Allen)	6.00	3.00	1.75
333	All-Star Second Basemen (Rod Carew, Joe Morgan)	3.00	1.50	.90
334	All-Star Third Basemen (Brooks Robinson, Ron Santo)	2.00	1.00	.60
335	All-Star Shortstops (Bert Campaneris, Chris Speier)	1.00	.50	.30
336	All-Star Left Fielders (Bobby Murcer, Pete Rose)	5.00	2.50	1.50
337	All-Star Center Fielders (Cesar Cedeno, Amos Otis)	.75	.40	.25
338	All-Star Right Fielders (Reggie Jackson, Billy Williams)	4.00	2.00	1.25
339	All-Star Pitchers (Jim Hunter, Rick Wise)	2.00	1.00	.60
340	Thurman Munson	8.00	4.00	2.50
341	*Dan Driessen*	.40	.20	.10
342	Jim Lonborg	.40	.20	.10
343	Kansas City Royals Team	1.00	.50	.30
344	Mike Caldwell	.40	.20	.10
345	Bill North	.40	.20	.10
346	Ron Reed	.40	.20	.10
347	Sandy Alomar	.40	.20	.10
348	Pete Richert	.40	.20	.10
349	John Vukovich	.40	.20	.10
350	Bob Gibson	6.00	3.00	1.75

351	Dwight Evans	1.00	.50	.30
352	Bill Stoneman	.40	.20	.10
353	Rich Coggins	.40	.20	.10
354	Cubs Mgr./Coaches fz (Hank Aguirre, Whitey Lockman, Jim Marshall, J.C. Martin, Al Spangler)	.40	.20	.10
355	Dave Nelson	.40	.20	.10
356	Jerry Koosman	.40	.20	.10
357	Buddy Bradford	.40	.20	.10
358	Dal Maxvill	.40	.20	.10
359	Brent Strom	.40	.20	.10
360	Greg Luzinski	1.00	.50	.30
361	Don Carrithers	.40	.20	.10
362	Hal King	.40	.20	.10
363	New York Yankees Team	2.00	1.00	.60
364a	Clarence Gaston (Washington)	3.00	1.50	.90
364b	Clarence Gaston (San Diego)	.40	.20	.10
365	Steve Busby	.40	.20	.10
366	Larry Hisle	.40	.20	.10
367	Norm Cash	1.00	.50	.30
368	Manny Mota	.40	.20	.10
369	Paul Lindblad	.40	.20	.10
370	Bob Watson	.40	.20	.10
371	Jim Slaton	.40	.20	.10
372	Ken Reitz	.40	.20	.10
373	John Curtis	.40	.20	.10
374	Marty Perez	.40	.20	.10
375	Earl Williams	.40	.20	.10
376	Jorge Orta	.40	.20	.10
377	Ron Woods	.40	.20	.10
378	Burt Hooton	.40	.20	.10
379	Rangers Mgr./Coaches (Art Fowler, Frank Lucchesi, Billy Martin, Jackie Moore, Charlie Silvera)	.45	.25	.15
380	Bud Harrelson	.40	.20	.10
381	Charlie Sands	.40	.20	.10
382	Bob Moose	.40	.20	.10
383	Philadelphia Phillies Team	1.00	.50	.30
384	Chris Chambliss	.75	.40	.25
385	Don Gullett	.40	.20	.10
386	Gary Matthews	.40	.20	.10
387a	Rich Morales (Washington)	3.00	1.50	.90
387b	Rich Morales (San Diego)	.40	.20	.10
388	Phil Roof	.40	.20	.10
389	Gates Brown	.40	.20	.10
390	Lou Piniella	2.00	1.00	.60
391	Billy Champion	.40	.20	.10
392	Dick Green	.40	.20	.10
393	Orlando Pena	.40	.20	.10
394	Ken Henderson	.40	.20	.10
395	Doug Rader	.40	.20	.10
396	Tommy Davis	.40	.20	.10
397	George Stone	.40	.20	.10
398	Duke Sims	.40	.20	.10
399	Mike Paul	.40	.20	.10
400	Harmon Killebrew	5.00	2.50	1.50
401	Elliott Maddox	.40	.20	.10
402	Jim Rooker	.40	.20	.10
403	Red Sox Mgr./Coaches (Don Bryant, Darrell Johnson, Eddie Popowski, Lee Stange, Don Zimmer)	.40	.20	.10
404	Jim Howarth	.40	.20	.10
405	Ellie Rodriguez	.40	.20	.10
406	Steve Arlin	.40	.20	.10
407	Jim Wohlford	.40	.20	.10
408	Charlie Hough	1.00	.50	.30
409	Ike Brown	.40	.20	.10
410	Pedro Borbon	.40	.20	.10
411	Frank Baker	.40	.20	.10
412	Chuck Taylor	.40	.20	.10
413	Don Money	.40	.20	.10
414	Checklist 397-528	2.00	1.00	.60
415	Gary Gentry	.40	.20	.10
416	Chicago White Sox Team	1.00	.50	.30
417	Rich Folkers	.40	.20	.10
418	Walt Williams	.40	.20	.10
419	Wayne Twitchell	.40	.20	.10
420	Ray Fosse	.40	.20	.10
421	Dan Fife	.40	.20	.10
422	Gonzalo Marquez	.40	.20	.10
423	Fred Stanley	.40	.20	.10
424	Jim Beauchamp	.40	.20	.10
425	Pete Broberg	.40	.20	.10
426	Rennie Stennett	.40	.20	.10
427	Bobby Bolin	.40	.20	.10
428	Gary Sutherland	.40	.20	.10
429	Dick Lange	.40	.20	.10
430	Matty Alou	.40	.20	.10
431	*Gene Garber*	.40	.20	.10
432	Chris Arnold	.40	.20	.10
433	Lerrin LaGrow	.40	.20	.10
434	Ken McMullen	.40	.20	.10
435	Dave Concepcion	1.00	.50	.30
436	Don Hood	.40	.20	.10
437	Jim Lyttle	.40	.20	.10
438	Ed Herrmann	.40	.20	.10
439	Norm Miller	.40	.20	.10
440	Jim Kaat	1.50	.70	.45
441	Tom Ragland	.40	.20	.10
442	Alan Foster	.40	.20	.10
443	Tom Hutton	.40	.20	.10
444	Vic Davalillo	.40	.20	.10
445	George Medich	.40	.20	.10
446	Len Randle	.40	.20	.10
447	Twins Mgr./Coaches (Vern Morgan, Frank Quilici, Bob Rodgers, Ralph Rowe)	.40	.20	.10
448	Ron Hodges	.40	.20	.10
449	Tom McCraw	.40	.20	.10
450	Rich Hebner	.40	.20	.10
451	Tommy John	1.00	.50	.30
452	Gene Hiser	.40	.20	.10
453	Balor Moore	.40	.20	.10

454	Kurt Bevacqua	.40	.20	.10
455	Tom Bradley	.40	.20	.10
456	*Dave Winfield*	50.00	25.00	15.00
457	Chuck Goggin	.40	.20	.10
458	Jim Ray	.40	.20	.10
459	Cincinnati Reds Team	1.50	.70	.45
460	Boog Powell	1.00	.50	.30
461	John Odom	.40	.20	.10
462	Luis Alvarado	.40	.20	.10
463	Pat Dobson	.40	.20	.10
464	Jose Cruz	.40	.20	.10
465	Dick Bosman	.40	.20	.10
466	Dick Billings	.40	.20	.10
467	Winston Llenas	.40	.20	.10
468	Pepe Frias	.40	.20	.10
469	Joe Decker	.40	.20	.10
470	A.L. Playoffs (Reggie Jackson)	4.00	2.00	1.25
471	N.L. Playoffs (Jon Matlack)	.50	.25	.15
472	World Series Game 1 (Darold Knowles)	.50	.25	.15
473	World Series Game 2 (Willie Mays)	6.00	3.00	1.75
474	World Series Game 3	1.00	.50	.30
475	World Series Game 4	1.00	.50	.30
476	World Series Game 5	1.00	.50	.30
477	World Series Game 6 (Reggie Jackson)	4.00	2.00	1.25
478	World Series Game 7	1.50	.75	.45
479	A's Celebrate (Win 2nd Consecutive Championship!)	1.00	.50	.30
480	Willie Crawford	.40	.20	.10
481	Jerry Terrell	.40	.20	.10
482	Bob Didier	.40	.20	.10
483	Atlanta Braves Team	1.00	.50	.30
484	Carmen Fanzone	.40	.20	.10
485	Felipe Alou	.50	.25	.15
486	Steve Stone	.40	.20	.10
487	Ted Martinez	.40	.20	.10
488	Andy Etchebarren	.40	.20	.10
489	Pirates Mgr./Coaches (Don Leppert, Bill Mazeroski, Danny Murtaugh, Don Osborn, Bob Skinner)	.75	.40	.25
490	Vada Pinson	1.00	.50	.30
491	Roger Nelson	.40	.20	.10
492	Mike Rogodzinski	.40	.20	.10
493	Joe Hoerner	.40	.20	.10
494	Ed Goodson	.40	.20	.10
495	Dick McAuliffe	.40	.20	.10
496	Tom Murphy	.40	.20	.10
497	Bobby Mitchell	.40	.20	.10
498	Pat Corrales	.40	.20	.10
499	Rusty Torres	.40	.20	.10
500	Lee May	.75	.40	.25
501	Eddie Leon	.40	.20	.10
502	Dave LaRoche	.40	.20	.10
503	Eric Soderholm	.40	.20	.10
504	Joe Niekro	.75	.40	.25
505	Bill Buckner	.75	.40	.25
506	Ed Farmer	.40	.20	.10
507	Larry Stahl	.40	.20	.10
508	Montreal Expos Team	1.00	.50	.30
509	Jesse Jefferson	.40	.20	.10
510	Wayne Garrett	.40	.20	.10
511	Toby Harrah	.40	.20	.10
512	Joe Lahoud	.40	.20	.10
513	Jim Campanis	.40	.20	.10
514	Paul Schaal	.40	.20	.10
515	Willie Montanez	.40	.20	.10
516	Horacio Pina	.40	.20	.10
517	Mike Hegan	.40	.20	.10
518	Derrel Thomas	.40	.20	.10
519	Bill Sharp	.40	.20	.10
520	Tim McCarver	1.50	.70	.45
521	Indians Mgr./Coaches (Ken Aspromonte, Clay Bryant, Tony Pacheco)	.40	.20	.10
522	J.R. Richard	1.00	.50	.30
523	Cecil Cooper	1.00	.50	.30
524	Bill Plummer	.40	.20	.10
525	Clyde Wright	.40	.20	.10
526	Frank Tepedino	.40	.20	.10
527	Bobby Darwin	.40	.20	.10
528	Bill Bonham	.40	.20	.10
529	Horace Clarke	.40	.20	.10
530	Mickey Stanley	.40	.20	.10
531	Expos Mgr./Coaches (Dave Bristol, Larry Doby, Gene Mauch, Cal McLish, Jerry Zimmerman)	.40	.20	.10
532	Skip Lockwood	.40	.20	.10
533	Mike Phillips	.40	.20	.10
534	Eddie Watt	.40	.20	.10
535	Bob Tolan	.40	.20	.10
536	Duffy Dyer	.40	.20	.10
537	Steve Mingori	.40	.20	.10
538	Cesar Tovar	.40	.20	.10
539	Lloyd Allen	.40	.20	.10
540	Bob Robertson	.40	.20	.10
541	Cleveland Indians Team	1.00	.50	.30
542	Rich Gossage	4.00	2.00	1.25
543	Danny Cater	.40	.20	.10
544	Ron Schueler	.40	.20	.10
545	Billy Conigliaro	.40	.20	.10
546	Mike Corkins	.40	.20	.10
547	Glenn Borgmann	.40	.20	.10
548	Sonny Siebert	.40	.20	.10
549	Mike Jorgensen	.40	.20	.10
550	Sam McDowell	.40	.20	.10
551	Von Joshua	.40	.20	.10
552	Denny Doyle	.40	.20	.10
553	Jim Willoughby	.40	.20	.10
554	Tim Johnson	.40	.20	.10
555	Woodie Fryman	.40	.20	.10
556	Dave Campbell	.40	.20	.10
557	Jim McGlothlin	.40	.20	.10
558	Bill Fahey	.40	.20	.10
559	Darrel Chaney	.40	.20	.10

560	Mike Cuellar	.40	.20	.10
561	Ed Kranepool	.40	.20	.10
562	Jack Aker	.40	.20	.10
563	Hal McRae	.75	.40	.25
564	Mike Ryan	.40	.20	.10
565	Milt Wilcox	.40	.20	.10
566	Jackie Hernandez	.40	.20	.10
567	Boston Red Sox Team	1.50	.75	.45
568	Mike Torrez	.40	.20	.10
569	Rick Dempsey	.40	.20	.10
570	Ralph Garr	.40	.20	.10
571	Rich Hand	.40	.20	.10
572	Enzo Hernandez	.40	.20	.10
573	Mike Adams	.40	.20	.10
574	Bill Parsons	.40	.20	.10
575	Steve Garvey	2.00	1.00	.60
576	Scipio Spinks	.40	.20	.10
577	Mike Sadek	.40	.20	.10
578	Ralph Houk	.75	.40	.25
579	Cecil Upshaw	.40	.20	.10
580	Jim Spencer	.40	.20	.10
581	Fred Norman	.40	.20	.10
582	*Bucky Dent*	2.00	1.00	.60
583	Marty Pattin	.40	.20	.10
584	Ken Rudolph	.40	.20	.10
585	Merv Rettenmund	.40	.20	.10
586	Jack Brohamer	.40	.20	.10
587	*Larry Christenson*	.40	.20	.10
588	Hal Lanier	.40	.20	.10
589	Boots Day	.40	.20	.10
590	Rogelio Moret	.40	.20	.10
591	Sonny Jackson	.40	.20	.10
592	Ed Bane	.40	.20	.10
593	Steve Yeager	.40	.20	.10
594	Leroy Stanton	.40	.20	.10
595	Steve Blass	.40	.20	.10
596	Rookie Pitchers (Wayne Garland, Fred Holdsworth, Mark Littell, Dick Pole)	.40	.20	.10
597	Rookie Shortstops (*Dave Chalk, John Gamble, Pete Mackanin, Manny Trillo*)	1.00	.50	.30
598	Rookie Outfielders (*Dave Augustine, Ken Griffey, Steve Ontiveros, Jim Tyrone*)	10.00	5.00	3.00
599a	Rookie Pitchers (Ron Diorio, Dave Freisleben, Frank Riccelli, Greg Shanahan) (Freisleben- Washington)	1.00	.50	.30
599b	Rookie Pitchers (Ron Diorio, Dave Freisleben, Frank Riccelli, Greg Shanahan) (Freisleben- San Diego large print.)	3.00	1.50	.90
599c	Rookie Pitchers (Ron Diorio, Dave Freisleben, Frank Riccelli, Greg Shanahan) (Freisleben- San Diego small print.)	5.00	2.50	1.50
600	Rookie Infielders (*Ron Cash, Jim Cox, Bill Madlock, Reggie Sanders*)	5.00	2.50	1.50
601	Rookie Outfielders (*Ed Armbrister, Rich Bladt, Brian Downing, Bake McBride*)	2.00	1.00	.60
602	Rookie Pitchers (Glenn Abbott, Rick Henninger, Craig Swan, Dan Vossler)	.75	.40	.25
603	Rookie Catchers (Barry Foote, Tom Lundstedt, Charlie Moore, Sergio Robles)	.75	.40	.25
604	Rookie Infielders (*Terry Hughes, John Knox, Andy Thornton, Frank White*)	4.00	2.00	1.25
605	Rookie Pitchers (*Vic Albury, Ken Frailing, Kevin Kobel, Frank Tanana*)	3.00	1.50	.90
606	Rookie Outfielders (Jim Fuller, Wilbur Howard, Tommy Smith, Otto Velez)	.75	.40	.25
607	Rookie Shortstops (*Leo Foster, Tom Heintzelman, Dave Rosello, Frank Taveras*)	.75	.40	.25
608a	Rookie Pitchers (Bob Apodaca, Dick Baney, John D'Acquisto, Mike Wallace) (Apodaca incorrect)	1.50	.75	.45
608b	Rookie Pitchers (Bob Apodaca, Dick Baney, John D'Acquisto, Mike Wallace) (corrected)	.75	.40	.25
609	Rico Petrocelli	1.00	.50	.30
610	Dave Kingman	.75	.40	.25
611	Rick Stelmaszek	.40	.20	.10
612	Luke Walker	.40	.20	.10
613	Dan Monzon	.40	.20	.10
614	Adrian Devine	.40	.20	.10
615	Johnny Jeter	.40	.20	.10
616	Larry Gura	.40	.20	.10
617	Ted Ford	.40	.20	.10
618	Jim Mason	.40	.20	.10
619	Mike Anderson	.40	.20	.10
620	Al Downing	.40	.20	.10
621	Bernie Carbo	.40	.20	.10
622	Phil Gagliano	.40	.20	.10
623	Celerino Sanchez	.40	.20	.10
624	Bob Miller	.40	.20	.10
625	Ollie Brown	.40	.20	.10
626	Pittsburgh Pirates Team	1.00	.50	.30
627	Carl Taylor	.40	.20	.10
628	Ivan Murrell	.40	.20	.10
629	Rusty Staub	.75	.40	.25
630	Tommie Agee	.40	.20	.10
631	Steve Barber	.40	.20	.10
632	George Culver	.40	.20	.10

633	Dave Hamilton	.40	.20	.10
634	Braves Mgr./Coaches (Jim Busby, Eddie Mathews, Connie Ryan, Ken Silvestri, Herm Starrette)	2.00	1.00	.60
635	John Edwards	.40	.20	.10
636	Dave Goltz	.40	.20	.10
637	Checklist 529-660	1.00	.50	.30
638	Ken Sanders	.40	.20	.10
639	Joe Lovitto	.40	.20	.10
640	Milt Pappas	.40	.20	.10
641	Chuck Brinkman	.40	.20	.10
642	Terry Harmon	.40	.20	.10
643	Los Angeles Dodgers Team	2.50	1.25	.75
644	Wayne Granger	.40	.20	.10
645	Ken Boswell	.40	.20	.10
646	George Foster	.75	.40	.25
647	*Juan Beniquez*	.40	.20	.10
648	Terry Crowley	.40	.20	.10
649	Fernando Gonzalez	.40	.20	.10
650	Mike Epstein	.40	.20	.10
651	Leron Lee	.40	.20	.10
652	Gail Hopkins	.40	.20	.10
653	Bob Stinson	.40	.20	.10
654a	Jesus Alou (No position.)	4.00	2.00	1.25
654b	Jesus Alou ("Outfield")	.40	.20	.10
655	Mike Tyson	.40	.20	.10
656	Adrian Garrett	.40	.20	.10
657	Jim Shellenback	.40	.20	.10
658	Lee Lacy	.40	.20	.10
659	Joe Lis	.40	.20	.10
660	Larry Dierker	1.50	.70	.45

1974 Topps Traded

Appearing late in the season, these 2-1/2" x 3-1/2" cards share the format of the regular-issue Topps cards. The major change is a large yellow panel with the word "Traded" in red, added below the player photo. Backs feature a "Baseball News" design that contains the details of the trade. Card numbers correspond to the player's regular card number in 1974 except that the suffix "T" is added. The set consists of 43 player cards and a checklist. In most cases, Topps did not obtain pictures of the players in their new uniforms. Instead, the Topps artists simply provided the needed changes to existing photos.

		NM	EX	VG
	Complete Set (44):	25.00	12.50	7.50
	Common Player:	.50	.25	.15
23T	Craig Robinson	.50	.25	.15
42T	Claude Osteen	.50	.25	.15
43T	Jim Wynn	.50	.25	.15
51T	Bobby Heise	.50	.25	.15
59T	Ross Grimsley	.50	.25	.15
62T	Bob Locker	.50	.25	.15
63T	Bill Sudakis	.50	.25	.15
73T	Mike Marshall	.50	.25	.15
123T	Nelson Briles	.50	.25	.15
139T	Aurelio Monteagudo	.50	.25	.15
151T	Diego Segui	.50	.25	.15
165T	Willie Davis	.50	.25	.15
175T	Reggie Cleveland	.50	.25	.15
182T	Lindy McDaniel	.50	.25	.15
186T	Fred Scherman	.50	.25	.15
249T	George Mitterwald	.50	.25	.15
262T	Ed Kirkpatrick	.50	.25	.15
269T	Bob Johnson	.50	.25	.15
270T	Ron Santo	3.00	1.50	.90
313T	Barry Lersch	.50	.25	.15
319T	Randy Hundley	.50	.25	.15
330T	Juan Marichal	4.00	2.00	1.25
348T	Pete Richert	.50	.25	.15
373T	John Curtis	.50	.25	.15
390T	Lou Piniella	2.00	1.00	.60
428T	Gary Sutherland	.50	.25	.15
454T	Kurt Bevacqua	.50	.25	.15
458T	Jim Ray	.50	.25	.15
485T	Felipe Alou	.75	.40	.25
486T	Steve Stone	.75	.40	.25
496T	Tom Murphy	.50	.25	.15
516T	Horacio Pina	.50	.25	.15
534T	Eddie Watt	.50	.25	.15
538T	Cesar Tovar	.50	.25	.15
544T	Ron Schueler	.50	.25	.15
579T	Cecil Upshaw	.50	.25	.15
585T	Merv Rettenmund	.50	.25	.15
612T	Luke Walker	.50	.25	.15
616T	Larry Gura	.50	.25	.15
618T	Jim Mason	.50	.25	.15
630T	Tommie Agee	.50	.25	.15
648T	Terry Crowley	.50	.25	.15
649T	Fernando Gonzalez	.50	.25	.15
----	Traded Checklist	.50	.25	.15

1974 Topps Action Emblem Cloth Stickers

This enigmatic Topps test issue has never found favor with collectors because no actual ballplayers are pictured. In fact, official team logos are not used either, negating the necessity of licensing from either Major League Baseball or the players' association. The 2-1/2" x 3-1/2" cloth stickers were sold with a rub-off baseball game card in a Topps white test wrapper with a sticker describing them as "Topps Baseball Action Emblems Cloth Stickers." Each sticker features a generic ballplayer on front with a city (not team) name. At bottom is a pennant with another major league city named and a generic baseball symbol at its left. Backs are blank. This issue can be found in either a cloth sticker version or cardboard version. The cardboard pieces are worth about 4X the cloth type.

	NM	EX	VG
Complete Set (24):	900.00	450.00	275.00
Common Sticker:	40.00	20.00	12.00
Wax Pack:	75.00		
Cardboard: 4X			
(1) Atlanta/Baltimore	40.00	20.00	12.00
(2) Baltimore/Montreal	40.00	20.00	12.00
(3) Boston/Oakland	40.00	20.00	12.00
(4) California/St. Louis	40.00	20.00	12.00
(5) Chicago/Houston	40.00	20.00	12.00
(6) Chicago/Pittsburgh	40.00	20.00	12.00
(7) Cincinnati/Minnesota	40.00	20.00	12.00
(8) Cleveland/San Diego	40.00	20.00	12.00
(9) Detroit/New York	40.00	20.00	12.00
(10) Houston/Chicago	40.00	20.00	12.00
(11) Kansas City/Philadelphia	40.00	20.00	12.00
(12) Los Angeles/Milwaukee	40.00	20.00	12.00
(13) Milwaukee/New York	40.00	20.00	12.00
(14) Minnesota/California	40.00	20.00	12.00
(15) Montreal/San Francisco	40.00	20.00	12.00
(16) New York/Cincinnati	40.00	20.00	12.00
(17) New York/Texas	40.00	20.00	12.00
(18) Oakland/Boston	40.00	20.00	12.00
(19) Philadelphia/Los Angeles	40.00	20.00	12.00
(20) Pittsburgh/Cleveland	40.00	20.00	12.00
(21) St. Louis/Kansas City	40.00	20.00	12.00
(22) San Diego/Detroit	40.00	20.00	12.00
(23) San Francisco/Chicago	40.00	20.00	12.00
(24) Texas/Atlanta	40.00	20.00	12.00

1974 Topps Deckle Edge

 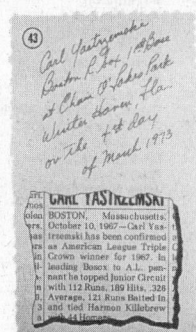

These borderless 2-7/8" x 5" cards feature a black-and-white photograph with a blue facsimile autograph on the front. The backs have in handwritten script the player's name, team, position and the date and location of the picture. Below is a mock newspaper clipping providing a detail from the player's career. Backs can be found in either gray or white (somewhat scarcer). The cards take their names from their specially cut edges which give them a scalloped appearance. The 72-card set was a test issue and received rather limited distribution around Massachusetts. The cards were sold three per pack for five cents with a piece of gum, or in two-card pack with no gum. Proof versions with straight edges and white or gray backs are known; they are slightly larger, at about 3-1/8" x 5-1/4".

	NM	EX	VG
Complete Set (72):	5,000	2,500	1,500
Common Player:	20.00	10.00	6.00
White Backs: 1.5X			
Proofs: .75-1X			
Wax Pack (5):	375.00		
1 Amos Otis	20.00	10.00	6.00
2 Darrell Evans	20.00	10.00	6.00
3 Bob Gibson	135.00	65.00	40.00
4 David Nelson	20.00	10.00	6.00
5 Steve Carlton	135.00	65.00	40.00
6 Catfish Hunter	90.00	45.00	27.50
7 Thurman Munson	135.00	65.00	40.00
8 Bob Grich	20.00	10.00	6.00
9 Tom Seaver	150.00	75.00	45.00
10 Ted Simmons	20.00	10.00	6.00
11 Bobby Valentine	20.00	10.00	6.00
12 Don Sutton	90.00	45.00	27.50
13 Wilbur Wood	20.00	10.00	6.00
14 Doug Rader	20.00	10.00	6.00
15 Chris Chambliss	20.00	10.00	6.00
16 Pete Rose	275.00	135.00	80.00
17 John Hiller	20.00	10.00	6.00
18 Burt Hooton	20.00	10.00	6.00
19 Tim Foli	20.00	10.00	6.00
20 Lou Brock	100.00	50.00	30.00
21 Ron Bryant	20.00	10.00	6.00
22 Manuel Sanguillen	20.00	10.00	6.00
23 Bobby Tolan	20.00	10.00	6.00
24 Greg Luzinski	20.00	10.00	6.00
25 Brooks Robinson	150.00	75.00	45.00
26 Felix Millan	20.00	10.00	6.00
27 Luis Tiant	20.00	10.00	6.00
28 Willie McCovey	100.00	50.00	30.00
29 Chris Speier	20.00	10.00	6.00
30 George Scott	20.00	10.00	6.00
31 Willie Stargell	100.00	50.00	30.00
32 Rod Carew	135.00	65.00	40.00
33 Charlie Spikes	20.00	10.00	6.00
34 Nate Colbert	20.00	10.00	6.00
35 Richie Hebner	20.00	10.00	6.00
36 Bobby Bonds	20.00	10.00	6.00
37 Buddy Bell	20.00	10.00	6.00
38 Claude Osteen	20.00	10.00	6.00
39 Rich Allen	55.00	27.50	16.50
40 Bill Russell	20.00	10.00	6.00
41 Nolan Ryan	900.00	450.00	275.00
42 Willie Davis	20.00	10.00	6.00
43 Carl Yastrzemski	160.00	80.00	45.00
44 Jon Matlack	20.00	10.00	6.00
45 Jim Palmer	135.00	65.00	40.00
46 Bert Campaneris	20.00	10.00	6.00
47 Bert Blyleven	20.00	10.00	6.00
48 Jeff Burroughs	20.00	10.00	6.00
49 Jim Colborn	20.00	10.00	6.00
50 Dave Johnson	20.00	10.00	6.00
51 John Mayberry	20.00	10.00	6.00
52 Don Kessinger	20.00	10.00	6.00
53 Joe Coleman	20.00	10.00	6.00
54 Tony Perez	90.00	45.00	27.50
55 Jose Cardenal	20.00	10.00	6.00
56 Paul Splittorff	20.00	10.00	6.00
57 Henry Aaron	275.00	135.00	80.00
58 David May	20.00	10.00	6.00
59 Fergie Jenkins	90.00	45.00	27.50
60 Ron Blomberg	20.00	10.00	6.00
61 Reggie Jackson	175.00	85.00	50.00
62 Tony Oliva	40.00	20.00	12.00
63 Bobby Murcer	45.00	22.50	13.50
64 Carlton Fisk	100.00	50.00	30.00
65 Steve Rogers	20.00	10.00	6.00
66 Frank Robinson	150.00	75.00	45.00
67 Joe Ferguson	20.00	10.00	6.00
68 Bill Melton	20.00	10.00	6.00
69 Bob Watson	20.00	10.00	6.00
70 Larry Bowa	20.00	10.00	6.00
71 Johnny Bench	150.00	75.00	45.00
72 Willie Horton	20.00	10.00	6.00

1974 Topps Puzzles

One of many test issues by Topps in the mid-1970s, the 12-player jigsaw puzzle set was an innovation which never caught on with collectors. The 40-piece puzzles (4-3/4" x 7-1/2") feature color photos with a decorative lozenge at bottom naming the player, team and position. The 29-cent puzzles came in individual wrappers picturing Tom Seaver. Centering, particularly of the Ryan puzzle, is a plague with the puzzles, accounting for the greater than usual spread between NM and lower-grade values.

	NM	EX	VG
Complete Set (12):	2,000	700.00	300.00
Common Player:	65.00	32.50	20.00

	NM	EX	VG
Wax Pack:	225.00		
Wrapper:	20.00		
(1) Hank Aaron	250.00	90.00	35.00
(2) Dick Allen	75.00	30.00	15.00
(3) Johnny Bench	125.00	44.00	18.50
(4) Bobby Bonds	65.00	25.00	10.00
(5) Bob Gibson	125.00	44.00	18.50
(6) Reggie Jackson	200.00	70.00	30.00
(7) Bobby Murcer	65.00	25.00	10.00
(8) Jim Palmer	100.00	35.00	15.00
(9) Nolan Ryan	650.00	225.00	100.00
(10) Tom Seaver	125.00	44.00	18.50
(11) Willie Stargell	100.00	35.00	15.00
(12) Carl Yastrzemski	250.00	87.00	37.00

1974 Topps Stamps

Topps continued to market baseball stamps in 1974 through the release of 240 unnumbered stamps featuring color player portraits. The player's name, team and position are found in an oval at the bottom of the 1" x 1-1/2" stamps. The stamps, sold separately rather than issued as an insert, came in panels of 12. Two dozen team albums designed to hold 10 stamps were also issued.

	NM	EX	VG
Complete Sheet Set (24):	90.00	45.00	25.00
Common Sheet:	2.00	1.00	.60
Complete Stamp Album Set (24):	300.00	150.00	90.00
Single Stamp Album:	5.00	2.50	1.50
(1) Hank Aaron, Luis Aparicio, Bob Bailey, Johnny Bench, Ron Blomberg, Bob Boone, Lou Brock, Bud Harrelson, Randy Jones, Dave Rader, Nolan Ryan, Joe Torre	15.00	7.50	4.50
(2) Buddy Bell, Steve Braun, Jerry Grote, Tommy Helms, Bill Lee, Mike Lum, Dave May, Brooks Robinson, Bill Russell, Del Unser, Wilbur Wood, Carl Yastrzemski	9.00	4.50	2.75
(3) Jerry Bell, Jim Colborn, Toby Harrah, Ken Henderson, John Hiller, Randy Hundley, Don Kessinger, Jerry Koosman, Dave Lopes, Felix Millan, Thurman Munson, Ted Simmons	6.00	3.00	1.75
(4) Jerry Bell, Bill Buckner, Jim Colborn, Ken Henderson, Don Kessinger, Felix Millan, George Mitterwald, Dave Roberts, Ted Simmons, Jim Slaton, Charlie Spikes, Paul Splittorff	2.00	1.00	.60
(5) Glenn Beckert, Jim Bibby, Bill Buckner, Jim Lonborg, George Mitterwald, Dave Parker, Dave Roberts, Jim Slaton, Reggie Smith, Charlie Spikes, Paul Splittorff, Bob Watson	2.00	1.00	.60
(6) Paul Blair, Bobby Bonds, Ed Brinkman, Norm Cash, Mike Epstein, Tommy Harper, Mike Marshall, Phil Niekro, Cookie Rojas, George Scott, Mel Stottlemyre, Jim Wynn	2.00	1.00	.60
(7) Jack Billingham, Reggie Cleveland, Bobby Darwin, Dave Duncan, Tim Foli, Ed Goodson, Cleon Jones, Mickey Lolich, George Medich, John Milner, Rick Monday, Bobby Murcer	2.00	1.00	.60
(8) Steve Carlton, Orlando Cepeda, Joe Decker, Reggie Jackson, Dave Johnson, John Mayberry, Bill Melton, Roger Metzger, Dave Nelson, Jim Reuss, Jim Spencer, Bobby Valentine	10.00	5.00	3.00
(9) Dan Driessen, Pedro Garcia, Grant Jackson, Al Kaline, Clay Kirby, Carlos May, Willie Montanez, Rogelio Moret, Jim Palmer, Doug Rader, J. R. Richard, Frank Robinson	7.50	3.75	2.25

		NM	EX	VG
(10)	Pedro Garcia, Ralph Garr, Wayne Garrett, Ron Hunt, Al Kaline, Fred Kendall, Carlos May, Jim Palmer, Doug Rader, Frank Robinson, Rick Wise, Richie Zisk	7.50	3.75	2.25
(11)	Dusty Baker, Larry Bowa, Steve Busby, Chris Chambliss, Dock Ellis, Cesar Geronimo, Fran Healy, Deron Johnson, Jorge Orta, Joe Rudi, Mickey Stanley, Rennie Stennett	2.00	1.00	.60
(12)	Bob Coluccio, Ray Corbin, John Ellis, Oscar Gamble, Dave Giusti, Bill Greif, Alex Johnson, Mike Jorgensen, Andy Messersmith, Bill Robinson, Elias Sosa, Willie Stargell	2.00	1.00	.60
(13)	Ron Bryant, Nate Colbert, Jose Cruz, Dan Driessen, Billy Grabarkewitz, Don Gullett, Willie Horton, Grant Jackson, Clay Kirby, Willie Montanez, Rogelio Moret, J. R. Richard	2.00	1.00	.60
(14)	Carlton Fisk, Bill Freehan, Bobby Grich, Vic Harris, George Hendrick, Ed Herrmann, Jim Holt, Ken Holtzman, Fergie Jenkins, Lou Piniella, Steve Rogers, Ken Singleton	5.00	2.50	1.50
(15)	Stan Bahnsen, Sal Bando, Mark Belanger, David Clyde, Willie Crawford, Burt Hooton, Jon Matlack, Tim McCarver, Joe Morgan, Gene Tenace, Dick Tidrow, Dave Winfield	7.50	3.75	2.25
(16)	Hank Aaron, Stan Bahnsen, Bob Bailey, Johnny Bench, Bob Boone, Jon Matlack, Tim McCarver, Joe Morgan, Dave Rader, Gene Tenace, Dick Tidrow, Joe Torre	10.00	5.00	3.00
(17)	John Boccabella, Frank Duffy, Darrell Evans, Sparky Lyle, Lee May, Don Money, Bill North, Ted Sizemore, Chris Speier, Wayne Twitchell, Billy Williams, Earl Williams	2.00	1.00	.60
(18)	John Boccabella, Bobby Darwin, Frank Duffy, Dave Duncan, Tim Foli, Cleon Jones, Mickey Lolich, Sparky Lyle, Lee May, Rick Monday, Bill North, Billy Williams	2.00	1.00	.60
(19)	Don Baylor, Vida Blue, Tom Bradley, Jose Cardenal, Ron Cey, Greg Luzinski, Johnny Oates, Tony Oliva, Al Oliver, Tony Perez, Darrell Porter, Roy White	3.00	1.50	.90
(20)	Pedro Borbon, Rod Carew, Roric Harrison, Jim Hunter, Ed Kirkpatrick, Garry Maddox, Gene Michael, Rick Miller, Claude Osteen, Amos Otis, Rich Reuschel, Mike Tyson	5.00	2.50	1.50
(21)	Sandy Alomar, Bert Campaneris, Dave Concepcion, Tommy Davis, Joe Ferguson, Tito Fuentes, Jerry Morales, Carl Morton, Gaylord Perry, Vada Pinson, Dave Roberts, Ellie Rodriguez	2.00	1.00	.60
(22)	Dick Allen, Jeff Burroughs, Joe Coleman, Terry Forster, Bob Gibson, Harmon Killebrew, Tug McGraw, Bob Oliver, Steve Renko, Pete Rose, Luis Tiant, Otto Velez	12.00	6.00	3.50
(23)	Johnny Briggs, Willie Davis, Jim Fregosi, Rich Hebner, Pat Kelly, Dave Kingman, Willie McCovey, Graig Nettles, Freddie Patek, Marty Pattin, Manny Sanguillen, Richie Scheinblum	5.00	2.50	1.50
(24)	Bert Blyleven, Nelson Briles, Cesar Cedeno, Ron Fairly, Johnny Grubb, Dave McNally, Aurelio Rodriguez, Ron Santo, Tom Seaver, Bill Singer, Bill Sudakis, Don Sutton	6.00	3.00	1.75

1974 Topps Team Checklists

This set is a repeat of the 1973 set in the form of 24 unnumbered 2-1/2" x 3-1/2" checklist cards. Cards feature a team name on the front at the top with a white panel and a number of facsimile autographs below. Backs feature the team name and a checklist. The big difference between the 1973 and 1974 checklists is that the 1973s have blue borders while the 1974s have red borders. The 1974s were inserted into packages of the regular issue Topps cards and were also available in uncut sheet form as a wrapper redemption.

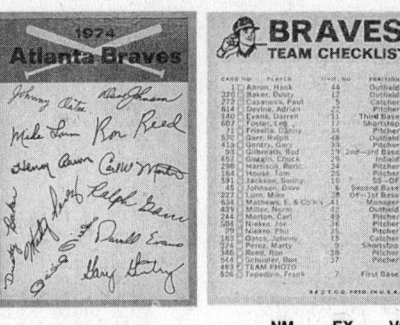

		NM	EX	VG
Complete Set (24):		25.00	12.50	7.50
Common Checklist:		1.50	.75	.45
Uncut Sheet:		25.00	12.50	7.50
(1)	Atlanta Braves	1.50	.75	.45
(2)	Baltimore Orioles	1.50	.75	.45
(3)	Boston Red Sox	1.50	.75	.45
(4)	California Angels	1.50	.75	.45
(5)	Chicago Cubs	1.50	.75	.45
(6)	Chicago White Sox	1.50	.75	.45
(7)	Cincinnati Reds	1.50	.75	.45
(8)	Cleveland Indians	1.50	.75	.45
(9)	Detroit Tigers	1.50	.75	.45
(10)	Houston Astros	1.50	.75	.45
(11)	Kansas City Royals	1.50	.75	.45
(12)	Los Angeles Dodgers	1.50	.75	.45
(13)	Milwaukee Brewers	1.50	.75	.45
(14)	Minnesota Twins	1.50	.75	.45
(15)	Montreal Expos	1.50	.75	.45
(16)	New York Mets	1.50	.75	.45
(17)	New York Yankees	1.50	.75	.45
(18)	Oakland A's	1.50	.75	.45
(19)	Philadelphia Phillies	1.50	.75	.45
(20)	Pittsburgh Pirates	1.50	.75	.45
(21)	St. Louis Cardinals	1.50	.75	.45
(22)	San Diego Padres	1.50	.75	.45
(23)	San Francisco Giants	1.50	.75	.45
(24)	Texas Rangers	1.50	.75	.45

1975 Topps

 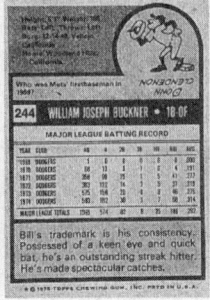

What was once seen as the strongest rookie card crop of any modern card set made this a collector favorite from the outset. Featuring the most colorful designs since 1972, cards feature large front photos with facsimile autographs. Red-and-green backs include a cartoon trivia fact and complete stats. A subset of 1951-74 MVP cards which reproduces or creates contemporary cards of past stars is one of several special features of the set, as are a group of four-on-one rookie cards. While the cards were all issued at one time, the first 132 cards have been discovered to have been printed in somewhat lesser quantities than the rest of the issue. This scarcity is not noted among the mini-version of the set which was produced as a test issue. Team/manager cards are sometimes found on thinner, white cardboard stock; these are a special version produced for a mail-in offer.

		NM	EX	VG
Complete Set (660):		450.00	225.00	135.00
Common Player:		.40	.20	.10
Mini-Stars/Rookies: 1-1.5X				
Wax Pack (10):		50.00		
Wax Box (36):		1,200		
Cello Pack (18):		80.00		
Rack Pack (42):		175.00		
Vending Box (500):				
1	Hank Aaron ('74 Highlights)	30.00	15.00	9.00
2	Lou Brock ('74 Highlights)	2.00	1.00	.60
3	Bob Gibson ('74 Highlights)	2.00	1.00	.60
4	Al Kaline ('74 Highlights)	4.00	2.00	1.25
5	Nolan Ryan ('74 Highlights)	12.00	6.00	3.50
6	Mike Marshall ('74 Highlights)	.40	.20	.10
7	Dick Bosman, Steve Busby, Nolan Ryan ('74 Highlights)	8.00	4.00	2.50
8	Rogelio Moret	.40	.20	.10
9	Frank Tepedino	.40	.20	.10
10	Willie Davis	.40	.20	.10
11	Bill Melton	.40	.20	.10
12	David Clyde	.40	.20	.10
13	Gene Locklear	.40	.20	.10
14	Milt Wilcox	.40	.20	.10
15	Jose Cardenal	.40	.20	.10
16	Frank Tanana	.40	.20	.10
17	Dave Concepcion	.40	.20	.10

		NM	EX	VG
18	Tigers Team (Ralph Houk)	1.50	.70	.45
19	Jerry Koosman	.40	.20	.10
20	Thurman Munson	8.00	4.00	2.50
21	Rollie Fingers	3.00	1.50	.90
22	Dave Cash	.40	.20	.10
23	Bill Russell	.75	.40	.25
24	Al Fitzmorris	.40	.20	.10
25	Lee May	.75	.40	.25
26	Dave McNally	.40	.20	.10
27	Ken Reitz	.40	.20	.10
28	Tom Murphy	.40	.20	.10
29	Dave Parker	1.50	.70	.45
30	Bert Blyleven	1.50	.70	.45
31	Dave Rader	.40	.20	.10
32	Reggie Cleveland	.40	.20	.10
33	Dusty Baker	1.50	.70	.45
34	Steve Renko	.40	.20	.10
35	Ron Santo	2.00	1.00	.60
36	Joe Lovitto	.40	.20	.10
37	Dave Freisleben	.40	.20	.10
38	Buddy Bell	.75	.40	.25
39	Andy Thornton	.75	.40	.25
40	Bill Singer	.40	.20	.10
41	Cesar Geronimo	.40	.20	.10
42	Joe Coleman	.40	.20	.10
43	Cleon Jones	.40	.20	.10
44	Pat Dobson	.40	.20	.10
45	Joe Rudi	.40	.20	.10
46	Phillies Team (Danny Ozark)	1.50	.70	.45
47	Tommy John	1.50	.70	.45
48	Freddie Patek	.40	.20	.10
49	Larry Dierker	.75	.40	.25
50	Brooks Robinson	8.00	4.00	2.50
51	*Bob Forsch*	.75	.40	.25
52	Darrell Porter	.75	.40	.25
53	Dave Giusti	.40	.20	.10
54	Eric Soderholm	.40	.20	.10
55	Bobby Bonds	1.50	.70	.45
56	Rick Wise	.40	.20	.10
57	Dave Johnson	.75	.40	.25
58	Chuck Taylor	.40	.20	.10
59	Ken Henderson	.40	.20	.10
60	Fergie Jenkins	3.00	1.50	.90
61	Dave Winfield	12.00	6.00	3.50
62	Fritz Peterson	.40	.20	.10
63	Steve Swisher	.40	.20	.10
64	Dave Chalk	.40	.20	.10
65	Don Gullett	.40	.20	.10
66	Willie Horton	.40	.20	.10
67	Tug McGraw	.40	.20	.10
68	Ron Blomberg	.40	.20	.10
69	John Odom	.40	.20	.10
70	Mike Schmidt	20.00	10.00	6.00
71	Charlie Hough	.75	.40	.25
72	Royals Team (Jack McKeon)	1.00	.50	.30
73	J.R. Richard	.40	.20	.10
74	Mark Belanger	.40	.20	.10
75	Ted Simmons	1.00	.50	.30
76	Ed Sprague	.40	.20	.10
77	Richie Zisk	.40	.20	.10
78	Ray Corbin	.40	.20	.10
79	Gary Matthews	.75	.40	.25
80	Carlton Fisk	6.00	3.00	1.75
81	Ron Reed	.40	.20	.10
82	Pat Kelly	.40	.20	.10
83	Jim Merritt	.40	.20	.10
84	Enzo Hernandez	.40	.20	.10
85	Bill Bonham	.40	.20	.10
86	Joe Lis	.40	.20	.10
87	George Foster	1.00	.50	.30
88	Tom Egan	.40	.20	.10
89	Jim Ray	.40	.20	.10
90	Rusty Staub	1.00	.50	.30
91	Dick Green	.40	.20	.10
92	Cecil Upshaw	.40	.20	.10
93	Dave Lopes	1.00	.50	.30
94	Jim Lonborg	.75	.40	.25
95	John Mayberry	.75	.40	.25
96	Mike Cosgrove	.40	.20	.10
97	Earl Williams	.40	.20	.10
98	Rich Folkers	.40	.20	.10
99	Mike Hegan	.40	.20	.10
100	Willie Stargell	4.00	2.00	1.25
101	Expos Team (Gene Mauch)	1.00	.50	.30
102	Joe Decker	.40	.20	.10
103	Rick Miller	.40	.20	.10
104	Bill Madlock	.75	.40	.25
105	Buzz Capra	.40	.20	.10
106	*Mike Hargrove*	2.00	1.00	.60
107	Jim Barr	.40	.20	.10
108	Tom Hall	.40	.20	.10
109	George Hendrick	.40	.20	.10
110	Wilbur Wood	.40	.20	.10
111	Wayne Garrett	.40	.20	.10
112	Larry Hardy	.40	.20	.10
113	Elliott Maddox	.40	.20	.10
114	Dick Lange	.40	.20	.10
115	Joe Ferguson	.40	.20	.10
116	Lerrin LaGrow	.40	.20	.10
117	Orioles Team (Earl Weaver)	3.00	1.50	.90
118	Mike Anderson	.40	.20	.10
119	Tommy Helms	.40	.20	.10
120	Steve Busby (Photo actually Fran Healy.)	.40	.20	.10
121	Bill North	.40	.20	.10
122	Al Hrabosky	.75	.40	.25
123	Johnny Briggs	.40	.20	.10
124	Jerry Reuss	.75	.40	.25
125	Ken Singleton	.75	.40	.25
126	Checklist 1-132	2.00	1.00	.60
127	Glen Borgmann	.40	.20	.10
128	Bill Lee	.40	.20	.10
129	Rick Monday	.40	.20	.10
130	Phil Niekro	3.00	1.50	.90
131	Toby Harrah	.40	.20	.10
132	Randy Moffitt	.40	.20	.10
133	Dan Driessen	.40	.20	.10
134	Ron Hodges	.40	.20	.10

135	Charlie Spikes	.40	.20	.10
136	Jim Mason	.40	.20	.10
137	Terry Forster	.40	.20	.10
138	Del Unser	.40	.20	.10
139	Horacio Pina	.40	.20	.10
140	Steve Garvey	2.00	1.00	.60
141	Mickey Stanley	.40	.20	.10
142	Bob Reynolds	.40	.20	.10
143	*Cliff Johnson*	.40	.20	.10
144	Jim Wohlford	.40	.20	.10
145	Ken Holtzman	.40	.20	.10
146	Padres Team (John McNamara)	1.00	.50	.30
147	Pedro Garcia	.40	.20	.10
148	Jim Rooker	.40	.20	.10
149	Tim Foli	.40	.20	.10
150	Bob Gibson	5.00	2.50	1.50
151	Steve Brye	.40	.20	.10
152	Mario Guerrero	.40	.20	.10
153	Rick Reuschel	.40	.20	.10
154	Mike Lum	.40	.20	.10
155	Jim Bibby	.40	.20	.10
156	Dave Kingman	1.00	.50	.30
157	Pedro Borbon	.40	.20	.10
158	Jerry Grote	.40	.20	.10
159	Steve Arlin	.40	.20	.10
160	Graig Nettles	1.00	.50	.30
161	Stan Bahnsen	.40	.20	.10
162	Willie Montanez	.40	.20	.10
163	Jim Brewer	.40	.20	.10
164	Mickey Rivers	.40	.20	.10
165	Doug Rader	.40	.20	.10
166	Woodie Fryman	.40	.20	.10
167	Rich Coggins	.40	.20	.10
168	Bill Greif	.40	.20	.10
169	Cookie Rojas	.40	.20	.10
170	Bert Campaneris	.40	.20	.10
171	Ed Kirkpatrick	.40	.20	.10
172	Red Sox Team (Darrell Johnson)	1.50	.70	.45
173	Steve Rogers	.40	.20	.10
174	Bake McBride	.40	.20	.10
175	Don Money	.40	.20	.10
176	Burt Hooton	.40	.20	.10
177	Vic Correll	.40	.20	.10
178	Cesar Tovar	.40	.20	.10
179	Tom Bradley	.40	.20	.10
180	Joe Morgan	5.00	2.50	1.50
181	Fred Beene	.40	.20	.10
182	Don Hahn	.40	.20	.10
183	Mel Stottlemyre	.40	.20	.10
184	Jorge Orta	.40	.20	.10
185	Steve Carlton	5.00	2.50	1.50
186	Willie Crawford	.40	.20	.10
187	Denny Doyle	.40	.20	.10
188	Tom Griffin	.40	.20	.10
189	1951-MVPs (Yogi Berra, Roy Campanella)	3.00	1.50	.90
190	1952-MVPs (Hank Sauer, Bobby Shantz)	1.00	.50	.30
191	1953-MVPs (Roy Campanella, Al Rosen)	1.50	.70	.45
192	1954-MVPs (Yogi Berra, Willie Mays)	4.00	2.00	1.25
193	1955-MVPs (Yogi Berra, Roy Campanella)	3.00	1.50	.90
194	1956-MVPs (Mickey Mantle, Don Newcombe)	10.00	5.00	3.00
195	1957-MVPs (Hank Aaron, Mickey Mantle)	12.00	6.00	3.50
196	1958-MVPs (Ernie Banks, Jackie Jensen)	2.50	1.25	.70
197	1959-MVPs (Ernie Banks, Nellie Fox)	2.00	1.00	.60
198	1960-MVPs (Dick Groat, Roger Maris)	1.50	.70	.45
199	1961-MVPs (Roger Maris, Frank Robinson)	2.00	1.00	.60
200	1962-MVPs (Mickey Mantle, Maury Wills)	10.00	5.00	3.00
201	1963-MVPs (Elston Howard, Sandy Koufax)	2.50	1.25	.70
202	1964-MVPs (Ken Boyer, Brooks Robinson)	1.00	.50	.30
203	1965-MVPs (Willie Mays, Zoilo Versalles)	2.00	1.00	.60
204	1966-MVPs (Roberto Clemente, Frank Robinson)	5.00	2.50	1.50
205	1967-MVPs (Orlando Cepeda, Carl Yastrzemski)	1.50	.70	.45
206	1968-MVPs (Bob Gibson, Denny McLain)	1.50	.70	.45
207	1969-MVPs (Harmon Killebrew, Willie McCovey)	2.00	1.00	.60
208	1970-MVPs (Johnny Bench, Boog Powell)	2.00	1.00	.60
209	1971-MVPs (Vida Blue, Joe Torre)	1.00	.50	.30
210	1972-MVPs (Rich Allen, Johnny Bench)	2.00	1.00	.60
211	1973-MVPs (Reggie Jackson, Pete Rose)	4.00	2.00	1.25
212	1974-MVPs (Jeff Burroughs, Steve Garvey)	1.00	.50	.30
213	Oscar Gamble	.40	.20	.10
214	Harry Parker	.40	.20	.10
215	Bobby Valentine	.40	.20	.10
216	Giants Team (Wes Westrum)	1.00	.50	.30
217	Lou Piniella	1.50	.70	.45
218	Jerry Johnson	.40	.20	.10
219	Ed Herrmann	.40	.20	.10
220	Don Sutton	3.00	1.50	.90
221	Aurelio Rodriquez (Rodriguez)	.40	.20	.10
222	Dan Spillner	.40	.20	.10
223	*Robin Yount*	50.00	25.00	15.00
224	Ramon Hernandez	.40	.20	.10
225	Bob Grich	.75	.40	.25
226	Bill Campbell	.40	.20	.10
227	Bob Watson	.40	.20	.10
228	*George Brett*	70.00	35.00	21.00
229	Barry Foote	.40	.20	.10
230	Jim Hunter	3.00	1.50	.90
231	Mike Tyson	.40	.20	.10
232	Diego Segui	.40	.20	.10
233	Billy Grabarkewitz	.40	.20	.10
234	Tom Grieve	.40	.20	.10
235	Jack Billingham	.40	.20	.10
236	Angels Team (Dick Williams)	1.00	.50	.30
237	Carl Morton	.40	.20	.10
238	Dave Duncan	.75	.40	.25
239	George Stone	.40	.20	.10
240	Garry Maddox	.40	.20	.10
241	Dick Tidrow	.40	.20	.10
242	Jay Johnstone	.40	.20	.10
243	Jim Kaat	1.50	.70	.45
244	Bill Buckner	.75	.40	.25
245	Mickey Lolich	1.00	.50	.30
246	Cardinals Team (Red Schoendienst)	1.00	.50	.30
247	Enos Cabell	.40	.20	.10
248	Randy Jones	.40	.20	.10
249	Danny Thompson	.40	.20	.10
250	Ken Brett	.40	.20	.10
251	Fran Healy	.40	.20	.10
252	Fred Scherman	.40	.20	.10
253	Jesus Alou	.40	.20	.10
254	Mike Torrez	.40	.20	.10
255	Dwight Evans	1.00	.50	.30
256	Billy Champion	.40	.20	.10
257	Checklist 133-264	2.00	1.00	.60
258	Dave LaRoche	.40	.20	.10
259	Len Randle	.40	.20	.10
260	Johnny Bench	15.00	7.50	4.50
261	Andy Hassler	.40	.20	.10
262	Rowland Office	.40	.20	.10
263	Jim Perry	.40	.20	.10
264	John Milner	.40	.20	.10
265	Ron Bryant	.40	.20	.10
266	Sandy Alomar	.40	.20	.10
267	Dick Ruthven	.40	.20	.10
268	Hal McRae	.75	.40	.25
269	Doug Rau	.40	.20	.10
270	Ron Fairly	.40	.20	.10
271	Jerry Moses	.40	.20	.10
272	Lynn McGlothen	.40	.20	.10
273	Steve Braun	.40	.20	.10
274	Vicente Romo	.40	.20	.10
275	Paul Blair	.40	.20	.10
276	White Sox Team (Chuck Tanner)	1.00	.50	.30
277	Frank Taveras	.40	.20	.10
278	Paul Lindblad	.40	.20	.10
279	Milt May	.40	.20	.10
280	Carl Yastrzemski	10.00	5.00	3.00
281	Jim Slaton	.40	.20	.10
282	Jerry Morales	.40	.20	.10
283	Steve Foucault	.40	.20	.10
284	Ken Griffey	2.00	1.00	.60
285	Ellie Rodriguez	.40	.20	.10
286	Mike Jorgensen	.40	.20	.10
287	Roric Harrison	.40	.20	.10
288	Bruce Ellingsen	.40	.20	.10
289	Ken Rudolph	.40	.20	.10
290	Jon Matlack	.40	.20	.10
291	Bill Sudakis	.40	.20	.10
292	Ron Schueler	.40	.20	.10
293	Dick Sharon	.40	.20	.10
294	*Geoff Zahn*	.40	.20	.10
295	Vada Pinson	1.50	.70	.45
296	Alan Foster	.40	.20	.10
297	Craig Kusick	.40	.20	.10
298	Johnny Grubb	.40	.20	.10
299	Bucky Dent	1.00	.50	.30
300	Reggie Jackson	12.00	6.00	3.50
301	Dave Roberts	.40	.20	.10
302	*Rick Burleson*	.75	.40	.25
303	Grant Jackson	.40	.20	.10
304	Pirates Team (Danny Murtaugh)	1.50	.70	.45
305	Jim Colborn	.40	.20	.10
306	Batting Leaders (Rod Carew, Ralph Garr)	1.50	.70	.45
307	Home Run Leaders (Dick Allen, Mike Schmidt)	3.00	1.50	.90
308	Runs Batted In Leaders (Johnny Bench, Jeff Burroughs)	1.50	.70	.45
309	Stolen Base Leaders (Lou Brock, Bill North)	1.50	.70	.45
310	Victory Leaders (Jim Hunter, Fergie Jenkins, Andy Messersmith, Phil Niekro)	1.50	.70	.45
311	Earned Run Average Leaders (Buzz Capra, Jim Hunter)	1.50	.70	.45
312	Strikeout Leaders (Steve Carlton, Nolan Ryan)	10.00	5.00	3.00
313	Leading Firemen (Terry Forster, Mike Marshall)	1.00	.50	.30
314	Buck Martinez	.40	.20	.10
315	Don Kessinger	.40	.20	.10
316	Jackie Brown	.40	.20	.10
317	Joe Lahoud	.40	.20	.10
318	Ernie McAnally	.40	.20	.10
319	Johnny Oates	.40	.20	.10
320	Pete Rose	25.00	12.50	7.50
321	Rudy May	.40	.20	.10
322	Ed Goodson	.40	.20	.10
323	Fred Holdsworth	.40	.20	.10
324	Ed Kranepool	.40	.20	.10
325	Tony Oliva	1.50	.70	.45
326	Wayne Twitchell	.40	.20	.10
327	Jerry Hairston Sr.	.40	.20	.10
328	Sonny Siebert	.40	.20	.10
329	Ted Kubiak	.40	.20	.10
330	Mike Marshall	.40	.20	.10
331	Indians Team (Frank Robinson)	1.50	.75	.45
332	Fred Kendall	.40	.20	.10
333	Dick Drago	.40	.20	.10
334	*Greg Gross*	.40	.20	.10
335	Jim Palmer	4.00	2.00	1.25
336	Rennie Stennett	.40	.20	.10
337	Kevin Kobel	.40	.20	.10
338	Rick Stelmaszek	.40	.20	.10
339	Jim Fregosi	1.00	.50	.30
340	Paul Splittorff	.40	.20	.10
341	Hal Breeden	.40	.20	.10
342	Leroy Stanton	.40	.20	.10
343	Danny Frisella	.40	.20	.10
344	Ben Oglivie	1.00	.50	.30
345	Clay Carroll	.40	.20	.10
346	Bobby Darwin	.40	.20	.10
347	Mike Caldwell	.40	.20	.10
348	Tony Muser	.40	.20	.10
349	Ray Sadecki	.40	.20	.10
350	Bobby Murcer	.75	.40	.25
351	Bob Boone	1.50	.70	.45
352	Darold Knowles	.40	.20	.10
353	Luis Melendez	.40	.20	.10
354	Dick Bosman	.40	.20	.10
355	Chris Cannizzaro	.40	.20	.10
356	Rico Petrocelli	.75	.40	.25
357	Ken Forsch	.40	.20	.10
358	Al Bumbry	.40	.20	.10
359	Paul Popovich	.40	.20	.10
360	George Scott	.40	.20	.10
361	Dodgers Team (Walter Alston)	1.50	.75	.45
362	Steve Hargan	.40	.20	.10
363	Carmen Fanzone	.40	.20	.10
364	Doug Bird	.40	.20	.10
365	Bob Bailey	.40	.20	.10
366	Ken Sanders	.40	.20	.10
367	Craig Robinson	.40	.20	.10
368	Vic Albury	.40	.20	.10
369	Merv Rettenmund	.40	.20	.10
370	Tom Seaver	10.00	5.00	3.00
371	Gates Brown	.40	.20	.10
372	John D'Acquisto	.40	.20	.10
373	Bill Sharp	.40	.20	.10
374	Eddie Watt	.40	.20	.10
375	Roy White	.45	.25	.15
376	Steve Yeager	.40	.20	.10
377	Tom Hilgendorf	.40	.20	.10
378	Derrel Thomas	.40	.20	.10
379	Bernie Carbo	.40	.20	.10
380	Sal Bando	.40	.20	.10
381	John Curtis	.40	.20	.10
382	Don Baylor	1.50	.70	.45
383	Jim York	.40	.20	.10
384	Brewers Team (Del Crandall)	1.50	.70	.45
385	Dock Ellis	.40	.20	.10
386	Checklist 265-396	2.00	1.00	.60
387	Jim Spencer	.40	.20	.10
388	Steve Stone	.75	.40	.25
389	Tony Solaita	.40	.20	.10
390	Ron Cey	1.00	.50	.30
391	Don DeMola	.40	.20	.10
392	Bruce Bochte	.40	.20	.10
393	Gary Gentry	.40	.20	.10
394	Larvell Blanks	.40	.20	.10
395	Bud Harrelson	.40	.20	.10
396	Fred Norman	.40	.20	.10
397	Bill Freehan	.75	.40	.25
398	Elias Sosa	.40	.20	.10
399	Terry Harmon	.40	.20	.10
400	Dick Allen	1.00	.50	.30
401	Mike Wallace	.40	.20	.10
402	Bob Tolan	.40	.20	.10
403	Tom Buskey	.40	.20	.10
404	Ted Sizemore	.40	.20	.10
405	John Montague	.40	.20	.10
406	Bob Gallagher	.40	.20	.10
407	*Herb Washington*	1.00	.50	.30
408	Clyde Wright	.40	.20	.10
409	Bob Robertson	.40	.20	.10
410	Mike Cueller (Cuellar)	.40	.20	.10
411	George Mitterwald	.40	.20	.10
412	Bill Hands	.40	.20	.10
413	Marty Pattin	.40	.20	.10
414	Manny Mota	.40	.20	.10
415	John Hiller	.40	.20	.10
416	Larry Lintz	.40	.20	.10
417	Skip Lockwood	.40	.20	.10
418	Leo Foster	.40	.20	.10
419	Dave Goltz	.40	.20	.10
420	Larry Bowa	1.50	.70	.45
421	Mets Team (Yogi Berra)	2.50	1.25	.70
422	Brian Downing	.40	.20	.10
423	Clay Kirby	.40	.20	.10
424	John Lowenstein	.40	.20	.10
425	Tito Fuentes	.40	.20	.10
426	George Medich	.40	.20	.10
427	Clarence Gaston	.40	.20	.10
428	Dave Hamilton	.40	.20	.10
429	*Jim Dwyer*	.40	.20	.10
430	Luis Tiant	1.00	.50	.30
431	Rod Gilbreath	.40	.20	.10
432	Ken Berry	.40	.20	.10
433	Larry Demery	.40	.20	.10
434	Bob Locker	.40	.20	.10
435	Dave Nelson	.40	.20	.10
436	Ken Frailing	.40	.20	.10
437	*Al Cowens*	.40	.20	.10
438	Don Carrithers	.40	.20	.10
439	Ed Brinkman	.40	.20	.10
440	Andy Messersmith	.40	.20	.10
441	Bobby Heise	.40	.20	.10
442	Maximino Leon	.40	.20	.10
443	Twins Team (Frank Quilici)	1.50	.70	.30
444	Gene Garber	.40	.20	.10
445	Felix Millan	.40	.20	.10

#	Player	NM	EX	VG
446	Bart Johnson	.40	.20	.10
447	Terry Crowley	.40	.20	.10
448	Frank Duffy	.40	.20	.10
449	Charlie Williams	.40	.20	.10
450	Willie McCovey	5.00	2.50	1.50
451	Rick Dempsey	.40	.20	.10
452	Angel Mangual	.40	.20	.10
453	Claude Osteen	.40	.20	.10
454	Doug Griffin	.40	.20	.10
455	Don Wilson	.40	.20	.10
456	Bob Coluccio	.40	.20	.10
457	Mario Mendoza	.40	.20	.10
458	Ross Grimsley	.40	.20	.10
459	A.L. Championships (Brooks Robinson)	1.00	.50	.30
460	N.L. Championships (Steve Garvey)	1.00	.50	.30
461	World Series Game 1 (Reggie Jackson)	2.00	1.00	.60
462	World Series Game 2 (Joe Ferguson)	.75	.40	.25
463	World Series Game 3 (Rollie Fingers)	1.50	.70	.45
464	World Series Game 4	.75	.40	.25
465	World Series Game 5	.75	.40	.25
466	A's Do It Again! (Win 3rd Straight World Series!)	1.50	.70	.45
467	Ed Halicki	.40	.20	.10
468	Bobby Mitchell	.40	.20	.10
469	Tom Dettore	.40	.20	.10
470	Jeff Burroughs	.40	.20	.10
471	Bob Stinson	.40	.20	.10
472	Bruce Dal Canton	.40	.20	.10
473	Ken McMullen	.40	.20	.10
474	Luke Walker	.40	.20	.10
475	Darrell Evans	1.00	.50	.30
476	*Ed Figueroa*	.40	.20	.10
477	Tom Hutton	.40	.20	.10
478	Tom Burgmeier	.40	.20	.10
479	Ken Boswell	.40	.20	.10
480	Carlos May	.40	.20	.10
481	*Will McEnaney*	.40	.20	.10
482	Tom McCraw	.40	.20	.10
483	Steve Ontiveros	.40	.20	.10
484	Glenn Beckert	.40	.20	.10
485	Sparky Lyle	.40	.20	.10
486	Ray Fosse	.40	.20	.10
487	Astros Team (Preston Gomez)	1.00	.50	.30
488	Bill Travers	.40	.20	.10
489	Cecil Cooper	1.00	.50	.30
490	Reggie Smith	.75	.40	.25
491	Doyle Alexander	.40	.20	.10
492	Rich Hebner	.40	.20	.10
493	Don Stanhouse	.40	.20	.10
494	*Pete LaCock*	.40	.20	.10
495	Nelson Briles	.40	.20	.10
496	Pepe Frias	.40	.20	.10
497	Jim Nettles	.40	.20	.10
498	Al Downing	.40	.20	.10
499	Marty Perez	.40	.20	.10
500	Nolan Ryan	50.00	25.00	15.00
501	Bill Robinson	.40	.20	.10
502	Pat Bourque	.40	.20	.10
503	Fred Stanley	.40	.20	.10
504	Buddy Bradford	.40	.20	.10
505	Chris Speier	.40	.20	.10
506	Leron Lee	.40	.20	.10
507	Tom Carroll	.40	.20	.10
508	Bob Hansen	.40	.20	.10
509	Dave Hilton	.40	.20	.10
510	Vida Blue	.75	.40	.25
511	Rangers Team (Billy Martin)	1.50	.75	.45
512	Larry Milbourne	.40	.20	.10
513	Dick Pole	.40	.20	.10
514	Jose Cruz	.40	.20	.10
515	Manny Sanguillen	.40	.20	.10
516	Don Hood	.40	.20	.10
517	Checklist 397-528	2.00	1.00	.60
518	Leo Cardenas	.40	.20	.10
519	Jim Todd	.40	.20	.10
520	Amos Otis	.40	.20	.10
521	Dennis Blair	.40	.20	.10
522	Gary Sutherland	.40	.20	.10
523	Tom Paciorek	.40	.20	.10
524	John Doherty	.40	.20	.10
525	Tom House	.40	.20	.10
526	Larry Hisle	.40	.20	.10
527	Mac Scarce	.40	.20	.10
528	Eddie Leon	.40	.20	.10
529	Gary Thomasson	.40	.20	.10
530	Gaylord Perry	3.00	1.50	.90
531	Reds Team (Sparky Anderson)	5.00	2.50	1.50
532	Gorman Thomas	.40	.20	.10
533	Rudy Meoli	.40	.20	.10
534	Alex Johnson	.40	.20	.10
535	Gene Tenace	.40	.20	.10
536	Bob Moose	.40	.20	.10
537	Tommy Harper	.40	.20	.10
538	Duffy Dyer	.40	.20	.10
539	Jesse Jefferson	.40	.20	.10
540	Lou Brock	5.00	2.50	1.50
541	Roger Metzger	.40	.20	.10
542	Pete Broberg	.40	.20	.10
543	Larry Biittner	.40	.20	.10
544	Steve Mingori	.40	.20	.10
545	Billy Williams	5.00	2.50	1.50
546	John Knox	.40	.20	.10
547	Von Joshua	.40	.20	.10
548	Charlie Sands	.40	.20	.10
549	Bill Butler	.40	.20	.10
550	Ralph Garr	.40	.20	.10
551	Larry Christenson	.40	.20	.10
552	Jack Brohamer	.40	.20	.10
553	John Boccabella	.40	.20	.10
554	Rich Gossage	1.50	.70	.45
555	Al Oliver	1.00	.50	.30
556	Tim Johnson	.40	.20	.10
557	Larry Gura	.40	.20	.10
558	Dave Roberts	.40	.20	.10
559	Bob Montgomery	.40	.20	.10
560	Tony Perez	4.00	2.00	1.25
561	A's Team (Alvin Dark)	1.00	.50	.30
562	Gary Nolan	.40	.20	.10
563	Wilbur Howard	.40	.20	.10
564	Tommy Davis	.40	.20	.10
565	Joe Torre	2.00	1.00	.60
566	Ray Burris	.40	.20	.10
567	*Jim Sundberg*	1.00	.50	.30
568	Dale Murray	.40	.20	.10
569	Frank White	.40	.20	.10
570	Jim Wynn	.40	.20	.10
571	Dave Lemanczyk	.40	.20	.10
572	Roger Nelson	.40	.20	.10
573	Orlando Pena	.40	.20	.10
574	Tony Taylor	.40	.20	.10
575	Gene Clines	.40	.20	.10
576	Phil Roof	.40	.20	.10
577	John Morris	.40	.20	.10
578	Dave Tomlin	.40	.20	.10
579	Skip Pitlock	.40	.20	.10
580	Frank Robinson	6.00	3.00	1.75
581	Darrel Chaney	.40	.20	.10
582	Eduardo Rodriguez	.40	.20	.10
583	Andy Etchebarren	.40	.20	.10
584	Mike Garman	.40	.20	.10
585	Chris Chambliss	.75	.40	.25
586	Tim McCarver	1.00	.50	.30
587	Chris Ward	.40	.20	.10
588	Rick Auerbach	.40	.20	.10
589	Braves Team (Clyde King)	1.00	.50	.30
590	Cesar Cedeno	.40	.20	.10
591	Glenn Abbott	.40	.20	.10
592	Balor Moore	.40	.20	.10
593	Gene Lamont	.40	.20	.10
594	Jim Fuller	.40	.20	.10
595	Joe Niekro	.40	.20	.10
596	Ollie Brown	.40	.20	.10
597	Winston Llenas	.40	.20	.10
598	Bruce Kison	.40	.20	.10
599	Nate Colbert	.40	.20	.10
600	Rod Carew	6.00	3.00	1.75
601	Juan Beniquez	.40	.20	.10
602	John Vukovich	.40	.20	.10
603	Lew Krausse	.40	.20	.10
604	Oscar Zamora	.40	.20	.10
605	John Ellis	.40	.20	.10
606	Bruce Miller	.40	.20	.10
607	Jim Holt	.40	.20	.10
608	Gene Michael	.40	.20	.10
609	Ellie Hendricks	.40	.20	.10
610	Ron Hunt	.40	.20	.10
611	Yankees Team (Bill Virdon)	2.00	1.00	.60
612	Terry Hughes	.40	.20	.10
613	Bill Parsons	.40	.20	.10
614	Rookie Pitchers (Jack Kucek, Dyar Miller, Vern Ruhle, Paul Siebert)	.40	.20	.10
615	Rookie Pitchers (Pat Darcy, Dennis Leonard, Tom Underwood, Hank Webb)	.40	.20	.10
616	Rookie Outfielders (*Dave Augustine, Pepe Mangual, Jim Rice, John Scott*)	20.00	10.00	6.00
617	Rookie Infielders (Mike Cubbage, Doug DeCinces, Reggie Sanders, Manny Trillo)	1.50	.70	.45
618	Rookie Pitchers (*Jamie Easterly, Tom Johnson, Scott McGregor, Rick Rhoden*)	2.00	1.00	.60
619	Rookie Outfielders (Benny Ayala, Nyls Nyman, Tommy Smith, Jerry Turner)	.40	.20	.10
620	Rookie Catchers-Outfielders (*Gary Carter, Marc Hill, Danny Meyer, Leon Roberts*)	15.00	7.50	4.50
621	Rookie Pitchers (John Denny, Rawly Eastwick, Jim Kern, Juan Veintidos)	.50	.25	.15
622	Rookie Outfielders (*Ed Armbrister, Fred Lynn, Tom Poquette, Terry Whitfield*)	8.00	4.00	2.50
623	Rookie Infielders (*Phil Garner, Keith Hernandez, Bob Sheldon, Tom Veryzer*)	8.00	4.00	2.50
624	Rookie Pitchers (Doug Konieczny, Gary Lavelle, Jim Otten, Eddie Solomon)	.40	.20	.10
625	Boog Powell	1.00	.50	.30
626	Larry Haney	.40	.20	.10
627	Tom Walker	.40	.20	.10
628	*Ron LeFlore*	.75	.40	.25
629	Joe Hoerner	.40	.20	.10
630	Greg Luzinski	1.00	.50	.30
631	Lee Lacy	.40	.20	.10
632	Morris Nettles	.40	.20	.10
633	Paul Casanova	.40	.20	.10
634	Cy Acosta	.40	.20	.10
635	Chuck Dobson	.40	.20	.10
636	Charlie Moore	.40	.20	.10
637	Ted Martinez	.40	.20	.10
638	Cubs Team (Jim Marshall)	1.50	.70	.45
639	Steve Kline	.40	.20	.10
640	Harmon Killebrew	6.00	3.00	1.75
641	Jim Northrup	.40	.20	.10
642	Mike Phillips	.40	.20	.10
643	Brent Strom	.40	.20	.10
644	Bill Fahey	.40	.20	.10
645	Danny Cater	.40	.20	.10
646	Checklist 529-660	1.00	.50	.30
647	*Claudell Washington*	.75	.40	.25
648	Dave Pagan	.40	.20	.10
649	Jack Heidemann	.40	.20	.10
650	Dave May	.40	.20	.10
651	John Morlan	.40	.20	.10
652	Lindy McDaniel	.40	.20	.10
653	Lee Richards	.40	.20	.10
654	Jerry Terrell	.40	.20	.10
655	Rico Carty	.40	.20	.10
656	Bill Plummer	.40	.20	.10
657	Bob Oliver	.40	.20	.10
658	Vic Harris	.40	.20	.10
659	Bob Apodaca	.40	.20	.10
660	Hank Aaron	30.00	15.00	9.00

1975 Topps Mini

 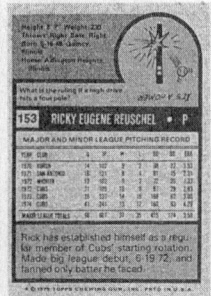

This popular set was actually a test issue to see how collectors would react to cards which were 20 percent smaller than the standard 2-1/2" x 3-1/2". Other than their 2-1/4" x 3-1/8" size, they are exactly the same, front and back as the regular-issue '75 Topps. The experimental cards were sold in Michigan and on the West Coast, where they were quickly gobbled up by collectors, dealers and speculators. While the minis for many years enjoyed a 2X premium over regular 1975 Topps values, that differential has shrunk in recent years.

	NM	EX	VG
Complete Set (660):	425.00	210.00	125.00
Common Player:	.50	.25	.15
Wax Pack (10):	40.00		
Wax Box (36):	1,600		
Cello Pack (18):	100.00		
Rack Pack (42):	200.00		

(Stars and rookies valued 1X to 1.5X regular 1975 Topps.)

1975 Topps Team Checklist Sheet

Via a mail-in wrapper redemption, collectors could receive an uncut sheet of the 24 team photo/checklist cards from the 1975 Topps baseball set. Measuring about 10-1/2" x 20-1/8", the sheet could be cut into individual team cards of standard size. They sheet-cut cards differ from issued versions in that they have white backs and are printed on thinner stock than the pack-issued versions.

	NM	EX	VG
Complete Sheet:	50.00	25.00	15.00

1976 Topps

 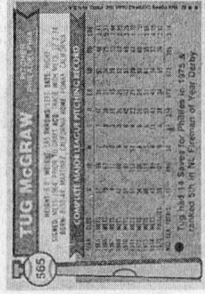

These 2-1/2" x 3-1/2" cards begin a design trend for Topps. The focus was more on the photo quality than in past years with a corresponding trend toward simplicity in the borders. The front of the cards has the player's name and team in two strips while his position is in the lower-left corner under a drawing of a player representing that position. The backs have a bat and ball with the card number on the left; statistics and personal information and career highlights on the right. The 660-card set features a number of specialty sets including record-setting performances, statistical leaders, playoff and World Series highlights, the Sporting News All-Time All-Stars and father and son combinations.

	NM	EX	VG
Complete Set (660):	250.00	125.00	75.00
Common Player:	.40	.20	.10
Wax Pack (6):	40.00		
Wax Box (36 6-Card):	1,350		
Wax Pack (10):	65.00		

	Wax Box (36 10-card):	2,400		
	Cello Pack (18):	75.00		
	Cello Box (24):	1,950		
	Rack Pack (42):	135.00		
	Vending Box (500):	550.00		
1	Hank Aaron (Record Breaker)	12.00	6.00	3.50
2	Bobby Bonds (Record Breaker)	1.50	.70	.45
3	Mickey Lolich (Record Breaker)	.40	.20	.10
4	Dave Lopes (Record Breaker)	.40	.20	.10
5	Tom Seaver (Record Breaker)	3.00	1.50	.90
6	Rennie Stennett (Record Breaker)	.40	.20	.10
7	Jim Umbarger	.40	.20	.10
8	Tito Fuentes	.40	.20	.10
9	Paul Lindblad	.40	.20	.10
10	Lou Brock	5.00	2.50	1.50
11	Jim Hughes	.40	.20	.10
12	Richie Zisk	.40	.20	.10
13	Johnny Wockenfuss	.40	.20	.10
14	Gene Garber	.40	.20	.10
15	George Scott	.40	.20	.10
16	Bob Apodaca	.40	.20	.10
17	New York Yankees Team (Billy Martin)	1.50	.70	.45
18	Dale Murray	.40	.20	.10
19	George Brett	25.00	12.50	7.50
20	Bob Watson	.40	.20	.10
21	Dave LaRoche	.40	.20	.10
22	Bill Russell	1.00	.50	.30
23	Brian Downing	.40	.20	.10
24	Cesar Geronimo	.40	.20	.10
25	Mike Torrez	.40	.20	.10
26	Andy Thornton	.75	.40	.25
27	Ed Figueroa	.40	.20	.10
28	Dusty Baker	1.50	.70	.45
29	Rick Burleson	.40	.20	.10
30	*John Montefusco*	.40	.20	.10
31	Len Randle	.40	.20	.10
32	Danny Frisella	.40	.20	.10
33	Bill North	.40	.20	.10
34	Mike Garman	.40	.20	.10
35	Tony Oliva	1.00	.50	.30
36	Frank Taveras	.40	.20	.10
37	John Hiller	.40	.20	.10
38	Garry Maddox	.40	.20	.10
39	Pete Broberg	.40	.20	.10
40	Dave Kingman	.75	.40	.25
41	*Tippy Martinez*	.75	.40	.25
42	Barry Foote	.40	.20	.10
43	Paul Splittorff	.40	.20	.10
44	Doug Rader	.40	.20	.10
45	Boog Powell	.75	.40	.25
46	Los Angeles Dodgers Team (Walter Alston)	1.00	.50	.30
47	Jesse Jefferson	.40	.20	.10
48	Dave Concepcion	.40	.20	.10
49	Dave Duncan	.40	.20	.10
50	Fred Lynn	.75	.40	.25
51	Ray Burris	.40	.20	.10
52	Dave Chalk	.40	.20	.10
53	Mike Beard	.40	.20	.10
54	Dave Rader	.40	.20	.10
55	Gaylord Perry	3.00	1.50	.90
56	Bob Tolan	.40	.20	.10
57	Phil Garner	.40	.20	.10
58	Ron Reed	.40	.20	.10
59	Larry Hisle	.40	.20	.10
60	Jerry Reuss	.40	.20	.10
61	Ron LeFlore	.40	.20	.10
62	Johnny Oates	.40	.20	.10
63	Bobby Darwin	.40	.20	.10
64	Jerry Koosman	.40	.20	.10
65	Chris Chambliss	.40	.20	.10
66	Father & Son (Buddy Bell, Gus Bell)	.40	.20	.10
67	Father & Son (Bob Boone, Ray Boone)	.40	.20	.12
68	Father & Son (Joe Coleman, Joe Coleman, Jr.)	.40	.20	.10
69	Father & Son (Jim Hegan, Mike Hegan)	.40	.20	.10
70	Father & Son (Roy Smalley, III, Roy Smalley, Jr.)	.40	.20	.10
71	Steve Rogers	.40	.20	.10
72	Hal McRae	.40	.20	.10
73	Baltimore Orioles Team (Earl Weaver)	1.00	.50	.30
74	Oscar Gamble	.40	.20	.10
75	Larry Dierker	.40	.20	.10
76	Willie Crawford	.40	.20	.10
77	Pedro Borbon	.40	.20	.10
78	Cecil Cooper	.40	.20	.10
79	Jerry Morales	.40	.20	.10
80	Jim Kaat	.75	.40	.25
81	Darrell Evans	.75	.40	.25
82	Von Joshua	.40	.20	.10
83	Jim Spencer	.40	.20	.10
84	Brent Strom	.40	.20	.10
85	Mickey Rivers	.40	.20	.10
86	Mike Tyson	.40	.20	.10
87	Tom Burgmeier	.40	.20	.10
88	Duffy Dyer	.40	.20	.10
89	Vern Ruhle	.40	.20	.10
90	Sal Bando	.40	.20	.10
91	Tom Hutton	.40	.20	.10
92	Eduardo Rodriguez	.40	.20	.10
93	Mike Phillips	.40	.20	.10
94	Jim Dwyer	.40	.20	.10
95	Brooks Robinson	6.00	3.00	1.75
96	Doug Bird	.40	.20	.10
97	Wilbur Howard	.40	.20	.10
98	*Dennis Eckersley*	25.00	12.50	7.50
99	Lee Lacy	.40	.20	.10
100	Jim Hunter	3.00	1.50	.90
101	Pete LaCock	.40	.20	.10
102	Jim Willoughby	.40	.20	.10
103	Biff Pocoroba	.40	.20	.10
104	Cincinnati Reds Team (Sparky Anderson)	1.00	.50	.30
105	Gary Lavelle	.40	.20	.10
106	Tom Grieve	.40	.20	.10
107	Dave Roberts	.40	.20	.10
108	Don Kirkwood	.40	.20	.10
109	Larry Lintz	.40	.20	.10
110	Carlos May	.40	.20	.10
111	Danny Thompson	.40	.20	.10
112	*Kent Tekulve*	.75	.40	.25
113	Gary Sutherland	.40	.20	.10
114	Jay Johnstone	.40	.20	.10
115	Ken Holtzman	.40	.20	.10
116	Charlie Moore	.40	.20	.10
117	Mike Jorgensen	.40	.20	.10
118	Boston Red Sox Team (Darrell Johnson)	1.00	.50	.30
119	Checklist 1-132	1.00	.50	.30
120	Rusty Staub	.75	.40	.25
121	Tony Solaita	.40	.20	.10
122	Mike Cosgrove	.40	.20	.10
123	Walt Williams	.40	.20	.10
124	Doug Rau	.40	.20	.10
125	Don Baylor	1.50	.70	.45
126	Tom Dettore	.40	.20	.10
127	Larvell Blanks	.40	.20	.10
128	Ken Griffey	1.00	.50	.30
129	Andy Etchebarren	.40	.20	.10
130	Luis Tiant	1.00	.50	.30
131	Bill Stein	.40	.20	.10
132	Don Hood	.40	.20	.10
133	Gary Matthews	.40	.20	.10
134	Mike Ivie	.40	.20	.10
135	Bake McBride	.40	.20	.10
136	Dave Goltz	.40	.20	.10
137	Bill Robinson	.40	.20	.10
138	Lerrin LaGrow	.40	.20	.10
139	Gorman Thomas	.75	.40	.25
140	Vida Blue	1.00	.50	.30
141	*Larry Parrish*	1.00	.50	.30
142	Dick Drago	.40	.20	.10
143	Jerry Grote	.40	.20	.10
144	Al Fitzmorris	.40	.20	.10
145	Larry Bowa	1.00	.50	.30
146	George Medich	.40	.20	.10
147	Houston Astros Team (Bill Virdon)	1.00	.50	.30
148	Stan Thomas	.40	.20	.10
149	Tommy Davis	.40	.20	.10
150	Steve Garvey	2.00	1.00	.60
151	Bill Bonham	.40	.20	.10
152	Leroy Stanton	.40	.20	.10
153	Buzz Capra	.40	.20	.10
154	Bucky Dent	.40	.20	.10
155	Jack Billingham	.40	.20	.10
156	Rico Carty	.40	.20	.10
157	Mike Caldwell	.40	.20	.10
158	Ken Reitz	.40	.20	.10
159	Jerry Terrell	.40	.20	.10
160	Dave Winfield	8.00	4.00	2.50
161	Bruce Kison	.40	.20	.10
162	Jack Pierce	.40	.20	.10
163	Jim Slaton	.40	.20	.10
164	Pepe Mangual	.40	.20	.10
165	Gene Tenace	.40	.20	.10
166	Skip Lockwood	.40	.20	.10
167	Freddie Patek	.40	.20	.10
168	Tom Hilgendorf	.40	.20	.10
169	Graig Nettles	.75	.40	.25
170	Rick Wise	.40	.20	.10
171	Greg Gross	.40	.20	.10
172	Texas Rangers Team (Frank Lucchesi)	1.00	.50	.30
173	Steve Swisher	.40	.20	.10
174	Charlie Hough	.75	.40	.25
175	Ken Singleton	.40	.20	.10
176	Dick Lange	.40	.20	.10
177	Marty Perez	.40	.20	.10
178	Tom Buskey	.40	.20	.10
179	George Foster	.75	.40	.25
180	Rich Gossage	1.00	.50	.30
181	Willie Montanez	.40	.20	.10
182	Harry Rasmussen	.40	.20	.10
183	Steve Braun	.40	.20	.10
184	Bill Greif	.40	.20	.10
185	Dave Parker	1.00	.50	.30
186	Tom Walker	.40	.20	.10
187	Pedro Garcia	.40	.20	.10
188	Fred Scherman	.40	.20	.10
189	Claudell Washington	.40	.20	.10
190	Jon Matlack	.40	.20	.10
191	N.L. Batting Leaders (Bill Madlock, Manny Sanguillen, Ted Simmons)	.75	.40	.25
192	A.L. Batting Leaders (Rod Carew, Fred Lynn, Thurman Munson)	1.00	.50	.30
193	N.L. Home Run Leaders (Dave Kingman, Greg Luzinski, Mike Schmidt)	2.00	1.00	.60
194	A.L. Home Run Leaders (Reggie Jackson, John Mayberry, George Scott)	2.00	1.00	.60
195	N.L. RBI Leaders (Johnny Bench, Greg Luzinski, Tony Perez)	1.00	.50	.30
196	A.L. RBI Leaders (Fred Lynn, John Mayberry, George Scott)	1.00	.50	.30
197	N.L. Stolen Base Leaders (Lou Brock, Dave Lopes, Joe Morgan)	1.50	.70	.45
198	A.L. Stolen Base Leaders (Amos Otis, Mickey Rivers, Claudell Washington)	.40	.20	.10
199	N.L. Victory Leaders (Randy Jones, Andy Messersmith, Tom Seaver)	2.00	1.00	.60
200	A.L. Victory Leaders (Vida Blue, Jim Hunter, Jim Palmer)	1.00	.50	.30
201	N.L. ERA Leaders (Randy Jones, Andy Messersmith, Tom Seaver)	1.00	.50	.30
202	A.L. ERA Leaders (Dennis Eckersley, Jim Hunter, Jim Palmer)	2.00	1.00	.60
203	N.L. Strikeout Leaders (Andy Messersmith, John Montefusco, Tom Seaver)	1.50	.70	.45
204	A.L. Strikeout Leaders (Bert Blyleven, Gaylord Perry, Frank Tanana)	1.00	.50	.30
205	Major League Leading Firemen (Rich Gossage, Al Hrabosky)	.75	.40	.25
206	Manny Trillo	.40	.20	.10
207	Andy Hassler	.40	.20	.10
208	Mike Lum	.40	.20	.10
209	Alan Ashby	.40	.20	.10
210	Lee May	.40	.20	.10
211	Clay Carroll	.40	.20	.10
212	Pat Kelly	.40	.20	.10
213	Dave Heaverlo	.40	.20	.10
214	Eric Soderholm	.40	.20	.10
215	Reggie Smith	.40	.20	.10
216	Montreal Expos Team (Karl Kuehl)	1.00	.50	.30
217	Dave Freisleben	.40	.20	.10
218	John Knox	.40	.20	.10
219	Tom Murphy	.40	.20	.10
220	Manny Sanguillen	.40	.20	.10
221	Jim Todd	.40	.20	.10
222	Wayne Garrett	.40	.20	.10
223	Ollie Brown	.40	.20	.10
224	Jim York	.40	.20	.10
225	Roy White	.40	.20	.10
226	Jim Sundberg	.40	.20	.10
227	Oscar Zamora	.40	.20	.10
228	John Hale	.40	.20	.10
229	*Jerry Remy*	.40	.20	.10
230	Carl Yastrzemski	10.00	5.00	3.00
231	Tom House	.40	.20	.10
232	Frank Duffy	.40	.20	.10
233	Grant Jackson	.40	.20	.10
234	Mike Sadek	.40	.20	.10
235	Bert Blyleven	1.00	.50	.30
236	Kansas City Royals Team (Whitey Herzog)	1.00	.50	.30
237	Dave Hamilton	.40	.20	.10
238	Larry Biittner	.40	.20	.10
239	John Curtis	.40	.20	.10
240	Pete Rose	25.00	12.50	7.50
241	Hector Torres	.40	.20	.10
242	Dan Meyer	.40	.20	.10
243	Jim Rooker	.40	.20	.10
244	Bill Sharp	.40	.20	.10
245	Felix Millan	.40	.20	.10
246	Cesar Tovar	.40	.20	.10
247	Terry Harmon	.40	.20	.10
248	Dick Tidrow	.40	.20	.10
249	Cliff Johnson	.40	.20	.10
250	Fergie Jenkins	3.00	1.50	.90
251	Rick Monday	.40	.20	.10
252	Tim Nordbrook	.40	.20	.10
253	Bill Buckner	.75	.40	.25
254	Rudy Meoli	.40	.20	.10
255	Fritz Peterson	.40	.20	.10
256	Rowland Office	.40	.20	.10
257	Ross Grimsley	.40	.20	.10
258	Nyls Nyman	.40	.20	.10
259	Darrel Chaney	.40	.20	.10
260	Steve Busby	.40	.20	.10
261	Gary Thomasson	.40	.20	.10
262	Checklist 133-264	1.00	.50	.30
263	*Lyman Bostock*	.75	.40	.25
264	Steve Renko	.40	.20	.10
265	Willie Davis	.40	.20	.10
266	Alan Foster	.40	.20	.10
267	Aurelio Rodriguez	.40	.20	.10
268	Del Unser	.40	.20	.10
269	Rick Austin	.40	.20	.10
270	Willie Stargell	4.00	2.00	1.25
271	Jim Lonborg	.40	.20	.10
272	Rick Dempsey	.40	.20	.10
273	Joe Niekro	.40	.20	.10
274	Tommy Harper	.40	.20	.10
275	*Rick Manning*	.75	.40	.25
276	Mickey Scott	.40	.20	.10
277	Chicago Cubs Team (Jim Marshall)	1.00	.50	.30
278	Bernie Carbo	.40	.20	.10
279	Roy Howell	.40	.20	.10
280	Burt Hooton	.40	.20	.10
281	Dave May	.40	.20	.10
282	Dan Osborn	.40	.20	.10
283	Merv Rettenmund	.40	.20	.10
284	Steve Ontiveros	.40	.20	.10
285	Mike Cuellar	.40	.20	.10
286	Jim Wohlford	.40	.20	.10
287	Pete Mackanin	.40	.20	.10
288	Bill Campbell	.40	.20	.10
289	Enzo Hernandez	.40	.20	.10
290	Ted Simmons	.40	.20	.10
291	Ken Sanders	.40	.20	.10
292	Leon Roberts	.40	.20	.10
293	Bill Castro	.40	.20	.10
294	Ed Kirkpatrick	.40	.20	.10
295	Dave Cash	.40	.20	.10
296	Pat Dobson	.40	.20	.10
297	Roger Metzger	.40	.20	.10
298	Dick Bosman	.40	.20	.10
299	Champ Summers	.40	.20	.10

300	Johnny Bench	10.00	5.00	3.00
301	Jackie Brown	.40	.20	.10
302	Rick Miller	.40	.20	.10
303	Steve Foucault	.40	.20	.10
304	California Angels Team (Dick Williams)	1.00	.50	.30
305	Andy Messersmith	.40	.20	.10
306	Rod Gilbreath	.40	.20	.10
307	Al Bumbry	.40	.20	.10
308	Jim Barr	.40	.20	.10
309	Bill Melton	.40	.20	.10
310	Randy Jones	.40	.20	.10
311	Cookie Rojas	.40	.20	.10
312	Don Carrithers	.40	.20	.10
313	*Dan Ford*	.40	.20	.10
314	Ed Kranepool	.40	.20	.10
315	Al Hrabosky	.40	.20	.10
316	Robin Yount	12.00	6.00	3.50
317	*John Candelaria*	1.00	.50	.30
318	Bob Boone	.75	.40	.25
319	Larry Gura	.40	.20	.10
320	Willie Horton	.40	.20	.10
321	Jose Cruz	.75	.40	.25
322	Glenn Abbott	.40	.20	.10
323	Rob Sperring	.40	.20	.10
324	Jim Bibby	.40	.20	.10
325	Tony Perez	4.00	2.00	1.25
326	Dick Pole	.40	.20	.10
327	Dave Moates	.40	.20	.10
328	Carl Morton	.40	.20	.10
329	Joe Ferguson	.40	.20	.10
330	Nolan Ryan	25.00	12.50	7.50
331	San Diego Padres Team (John McNamara)	1.00	.50	.30
332	Charlie Williams	.40	.20	.10
333	Bob Coluccio	.40	.20	.10
334	Dennis Leonard	.40	.20	.10
335	Bob Grich	.75	.40	.25
336	Vic Albury	.40	.20	.10
337	Bud Harrelson	.40	.20	.10
338	Bob Bailey	.40	.20	.10
339	John Denny	.40	.20	.10
340	Jim Rice	3.00	1.50	.90
341	Lou Gehrig (All Time 1B)	10.00	5.00	3.00
342	Rogers Homsby (All Time 2B)	2.50	1.25	.70
343	Pie Traynor (All Time 3B)	1.00	.50	.30
344	Honus Wagner (All Time SS)	5.00	2.50	1.50
345	Babe Ruth (All Time OF)	15.00	7.50	4.50
346	Ty Cobb (All Time OF)	10.00	5.00	3.00
347	Ted Williams (All Time OF)	10.00	5.00	3.00
348	Mickey Cochrane (All Time C)	1.00	.50	.30
349	Walter Johnson (All Time RHP)	4.00	2.00	1.25
350	Lefty Grove (All Time LHP)	1.00	.50	.30
351	Randy Hundley	.40	.20	.10
352	Dave Giusti	.40	.20	.10
353	*Sixto Lezcano*	.75	.40	.25
354	Ron Blomberg	.40	.20	.10
355	Steve Carlton	4.00	2.00	1.25
356	Ted Martinez	.40	.20	.10
357	Ken Forsch	.40	.20	.10
358	Buddy Bell	.40	.20	.10
359	Rick Reuschel	.40	.20	.10
360	Jeff Burroughs	.40	.20	.10
361	Detroit Tigers Team (Ralph Houk)	1.00	.50	.30
362	Will McEnaney	.40	.20	.10
363	*Dave Collins*	.40	.20	.12
364	Elias Sosa	.40	.20	.10
365	Carlton Fisk	5.00	2.50	1.50
366	Bobby Valentine	.40	.20	.10
367	Bruce Miller	.40	.20	.10
368	Wilbur Wood	.40	.20	.10
369	Frank White	.75	.40	.25
370	Ron Cey	.75	.40	.25
371	Ellie Hendricks	.40	.20	.10
372	Rick Baldwin	.40	.20	.10
373	Johnny Briggs	.40	.20	.10
374	Dan Warthen	.40	.20	.10
375	Ron Fairly	.40	.20	.10
376	Rich Hebner	.40	.20	.10
377	Mike Hegan	.40	.20	.10
378	Steve Stone	.40	.20	.10
379	Ken Boswell	.40	.20	.10
380	Bobby Bonds	1.00	.50	.30
381	Denny Doyle	.40	.20	.10
382	Matt Alexander	.40	.20	.10
383	John Ellis	.40	.20	.10
384	Philadelphia Phillies Team (Danny Ozark)	1.00	.50	.30
385	Mickey Lolich	.75	.40	.25
386	Ed Goodson	.40	.20	.10
387	Mike Miley	.40	.20	.10
388	Stan Perzanowski	.40	.20	.10
389	Glenn Adams	.40	.20	.10
390	Don Gullett	.40	.20	.10
391	Jerry Hairston Sr.	.40	.20	.10
392	Checklist 265-396	1.00	.50	.30
393	Paul Mitchell	.40	.20	.10
394	Fran Healy	.40	.20	.10
395	Jim Wynn	.40	.20	.10
396	Bill Lee	.40	.20	.10
397	Tim Foli	.40	.20	.10
398	Dave Tomlin	.40	.20	.10
399	Luis Melendez	.40	.20	.10
400	Rod Carew	5.00	2.50	1.50
401	Ken Brett	.40	.20	.10
402	Don Money	.40	.20	.10
403	Geoff Zahn	.40	.20	.10
404	Enos Cabell	.40	.20	.10
405	Rollie Fingers	3.00	1.50	.90
406	Ed Herrmann	.40	.20	.10
407	Tom Underwood	.40	.20	.10
408	Charlie Spikes	.40	.20	.10
409	Dave Lemanczyk	.40	.20	.10
410	Ralph Garr	.40	.20	.10
411	Bill Singer	.40	.20	.10
412	Toby Harrah	.40	.20	.10
413	Pete Varney	.40	.20	.10
414	Wayne Garland	.40	.20	.10
415	Vada Pinson	1.00	.50	.30
416	Tommy John	1.00	.50	.30
417	Gene Clines	.40	.20	.10
418	Jose Morales	.40	.20	.10
419	Reggie Cleveland	.40	.20	.10
420	Joe Morgan	4.00	2.00	1.25
421	Oakland A's Team	1.00	.50	.30
422	Johnny Grubb	.40	.20	.10
423	Ed Halicki	.40	.20	.10
424	Phil Roof	.40	.20	.10
425	Rennie Stennett	.40	.20	.10
426	Bob Forsch	.40	.20	.10
427	Kurt Bevacqua	.40	.20	.10
428	Jim Crawford	.40	.20	.10
429	Fred Stanley	.40	.20	.10
430	Jose Cardenal	.40	.20	.10
431	Dick Ruthven	.40	.20	.10
432	Tom Veryzer	.40	.20	.10
433	Rick Waits	.40	.20	.10
434	Morris Nettles	.40	.20	.10
435	Phil Niekro	3.00	1.50	.90
436	Bill Fahey	.40	.20	.10
437	Terry Forster	.40	.20	.10
438	Doug DeCinces	.40	.20	.10
439	Rick Rhoden	.40	.20	.10
440	John Mayberry	.40	.20	.10
441	Gary Carter	6.00	3.00	1.75
442	Hank Webb	.40	.20	.10
443	San Francisco Giants Team	1.00	.50	.30
444	Gary Nolan	.40	.20	.10
445	Rico Petrocelli	.40	.20	.10
446	Larry Haney	.40	.20	.10
447	Gene Locklear	.40	.20	.10
448	Tom Johnson	.40	.20	.10
449	Bob Robertson	.40	.20	.10
450	Jim Palmer	4.00	2.00	1.25
451	Buddy Bradford	.40	.20	.10
452	Tom Hausman	.40	.20	.10
453	Lou Piniella	1.50	.70	.45
454	Tom Griffin	.40	.20	.10
455	Dick Allen	.75	.40	.25
456	Joe Coleman	.40	.20	.10
457	Ed Crosby	.40	.20	.10
458	Earl Williams	.40	.20	.10
459	Jim Brewer	.40	.20	.10
460	Cesar Cedeno	.40	.20	.10
461	NL & AL Championships	.75	.40	.25
462	1975 World Series	.75	.40	.25
463	Steve Hargan	.40	.20	.10
464	Ken Henderson	.40	.20	.10
465	Mike Marshall	.40	.20	.10
466	Bob Stinson	.40	.20	.10
467	Woodie Fryman	.40	.20	.10
468	Jesus Alou	.40	.20	.10
469	Rawly Eastwick	.40	.20	.10
470	Bobby Murcer	.75	.40	.25
471	Jim Burton	.40	.20	.10
472	Bob Davis	.40	.20	.10
473	Paul Blair	.40	.20	.10
474	Ray Corbin	.40	.20	.10
475	Joe Rudi	.40	.20	.10
476	Bob Moose	.40	.20	.10
477	Cleveland Indians Team (Frank Robinson)	1.50	.70	.45
478	Lynn McGlothen	.40	.20	.10
479	Bobby Mitchell	.40	.20	.10
480	Mike Schmidt	15.00	7.50	4.50
481	Rudy May	.40	.20	.10
482	Tim Hosley	.40	.20	.10
483	Mickey Stanley	.40	.20	.10
484	Eric Raich	.40	.20	.10
485	Mike Hargrove	.40	.20	.10
486	Bruce Dal Canton	.40	.20	.10
487	Leron Lee	.40	.20	.10
488	Claude Osteen	.40	.20	.10
489	Skip Jutze	.40	.20	.10
490	Frank Tanana	.40	.20	.10
491	Terry Crowley	.40	.20	.10
492	Marty Pattin	.40	.20	.10
493	Derrel Thomas	.40	.20	.10
494	Craig Swan	.40	.20	.10
495	Nate Colbert	.40	.20	.10
496	Juan Beniquez	.40	.20	.10
497	Joe McIntosh	.40	.20	.10
498	Glenn Borgmann	.40	.20	.10
499	Mario Guerrero	.40	.20	.10
500	Reggie Jackson	10.00	5.00	3.00
501	Billy Champion	.40	.20	.10
502	Tim McCarver	1.00	.50	.30
503	Elliott Maddox	.40	.20	.10
504	Pittsburgh Pirates Team (Danny Murtaugh)	1.00	.50	.30
505	Mark Belanger	.40	.20	.10
506	George Mitterwald	.40	.20	.10
507	Ray Bare	.40	.20	.10
508	*Duane Kuiper*	.40	.20	.10
509	Bill Hands	.40	.20	.10
510	Amos Otis	.40	.20	.10
511	Jamie Easterly	.40	.20	.10
512	Ellie Rodriguez	.40	.20	.10
513	Bart Johnson	.40	.20	.10
514	Dan Driessen	.40	.20	.10
515	Steve Yeager	.40	.20	.10
516	Wayne Granger	.40	.20	.10
517	John Milner	.40	.20	.10
518	*Doug Flynn*	.40	.20	.10
519	Steve Brye	.40	.20	.10
520	Willie McCovey	4.00	2.00	1.25
521	Jim Colborn	.40	.20	.10
522	Ted Sizemore	.40	.20	.10
523	Bob Montgomery	.40	.20	.10
524	Pete Falcone	.40	.20	.10
525	Billy Williams	4.00	2.00	1.25
526	Checklist 397-528	1.00	.50	.30
527	Mike Anderson	.40	.20	.10
528	Dock Ellis	.40	.20	.10
529	Deron Johnson	.40	.20	.10
530	Don Sutton	3.00	1.50	.90
531	New York Mets Team (Joe Frazier)	1.00	.50	.30
532	Milt May	.40	.20	.10
533	Lee Richard	.40	.20	.10
534	Stan Bahnsen	.40	.20	.10
535	Dave Nelson	.40	.20	.10
536	Mike Thompson	.40	.20	.10
537	Tony Muser	.40	.20	.10
538	Pat Darcy	.40	.20	.10
539	John Balaz	.40	.20	.10
540	Bill Freehan	.40	.20	.10
541	Steve Mingori	.40	.20	.10
542	Keith Hernandez	1.00	.50	.30
543	Wayne Twitchell	.40	.20	.10
544	Pepe Frias	.40	.20	.10
545	Sparky Lyle	.40	.20	.10
546	Dave Rosello	.40	.20	.10
547	Roric Harrison	.40	.20	.10
548	Manny Mota	.40	.20	.10
549	Randy Tate	.40	.20	.10
550	Hank Aaron	25.00	12.50	7.50
551	Jerry DaVanon	.40	.20	.10
552	Terry Humphrey	.40	.20	.10
553	Randy Moffitt	.40	.20	.10
554	Ray Fosse	.40	.20	.10
555	Dyar Miller	.40	.20	.10
556	Minnesota Twins Team (Gene Mauch)	1.00	.50	.30
557	Dan Spillner	.40	.20	.10
558	Clarence Gaston	.40	.20	.10
559	Clyde Wright	.40	.20	.10
560	Jorge Orta	.40	.20	.10
561	Tom Carroll	.40	.20	.10
562	Adrian Garrett	.40	.20	.10
563	Larry Demery	.40	.20	.10
564	Kurt Bevacqua (Bubble Gum Blowing Champ)	.40	.20	.10
565	Tug McGraw	.75	.40	.25
566	Ken McMullen	.40	.20	.10
567	George Stone	.40	.20	.10
568	Rob Andrews	.40	.20	.10
569	Nelson Briles	.40	.20	.10
570	George Hendrick	.40	.20	.10
571	Don DeMola	.40	.20	.10
572	Rich Coggins	.40	.20	.10
573	Bill Travers	.40	.20	.10
574	Don Kessinger	.40	.20	.10
575	Dwight Evans	.75	.40	.25
576	Maximino Leon	.40	.20	.10
577	Marc Hill	.40	.20	.10
578	Ted Kubiak	.40	.20	.10
579	Clay Kirby	.40	.20	.10
580	Bert Campaneris	.40	.20	.10
581	St. Louis Cardinals Team (Red Schoendienst)	1.50	.70	.45
582	Mike Kekich	.40	.20	.10
583	Tommy Helms	.40	.20	.10
584	Stan Wall	.40	.20	.10
585	Joe Torre	1.50	.70	.45
586	Ron Schueler	.40	.20	.10
587	Leo Cardenas	.40	.20	.10
588	Kevin Kobel	.40	.20	.10
589	Rookie Pitchers (Santo Alcala, Mike Flanagan, Joe Pactwa, Pablo Torrealba)	1.00	.50	.30
590	Rookie Outfielders (Henry Cruz, Chet Lemon, Ellis Valentine, Terry Whitfield)	.75	.40	.25
591	Rookie Pitchers (Steve Grilli, Craig Mitchell, Jose Sosa, George Throop)	.40	.20	.10
592	Rookie Infielders (*Dave McKay, Willie Randolph, Jerry Royster, Roy Staiger*)	6.00	3.00	1.75
593	Rookie Pitchers (*Larry Anderson, Ken Crosby, Mark Littell, Butch Metzger*)	.40	.20	.10
594	Rookie Catchers & Outfielders (Andy Merchant, Ed Ott, Royle Stillman, Jerry White)	.40	.20	.10
595	Rookie Pitchers (Steve Barr, Art DeFilippis, Randy Lerch, Sid Monge)	.40	.20	.10
596	Rookie Infielders (*Lamar Johnson, Johnny LeMaster, Jerry Manuel, Craig Reynolds*)	.40	.20	.10
597	Rookie Pitchers (Don Aase, Jack Kucek, Frank LaCorte, Mike Pazik)	.40	.20	.10
598	Rookie Outfielders (Hector Cruz, Jamie Quirk, Jerry Turner, Joe Wallis)	.40	.20	.10
599	Rookie Pitchers (*Rob Dressler, Ron Guidry, Bob McClure, Pat Zachry*)	8.00	4.00	2.50
600	Tom Seaver	8.00	4.00	2.50
601	Ken Rudolph	.40	.20	.10
602	Doug Konieczny	.40	.20	.10
603	Jim Holt	.40	.20	.10
604	Joe Lovitto	.40	.20	.10
605	Al Downing	.40	.20	.10
606	Milwaukee Brewers Team (Alex Grammas)	1.00	.50	.30
607	Rich Hinton	.40	.20	.10
608	Vic Correll	.40	.20	.10
609	Fred Norman	.40	.20	.10
610	Greg Luzinski	.75	.40	.25
611	Rich Folkers	.40	.20	.10
612	Joe Lahoud	.40	.20	.10
613	Tim Johnson	.40	.20	.10
614	Fernando Arroyo	.40	.20	.10
615	Mike Cubbage	.40	.20	.10
616	Buck Martinez	.40	.20	.10

		NM	EX	VG
617	Darold Knowles	.40	.20	.10
618	Jack Brohamer	.40	.20	.10
619	Bill Butler	.40	.20	.10
620	Al Oliver	.75	.40	.25
621	Tom Hall	.40	.20	.10
622	Rick Auerbach	.40	.20	.10
623	Bob Allietta	.40	.20	.10
624	Tony Taylor	.40	.20	.10
625	J.R. Richard	.40	.20	.10
626	Bob Sheldon	.40	.20	.10
627	Bill Plummer	.40	.20	.10
628	John D'Acquisto	.40	.20	.10
629	Sandy Alomar	.40	.20	.10
630	Chris Speier	.40	.20	.10
631	Atlanta Braves Team (Dave Bristol)	1.00	.50	.30
632	Rogelio Moret	.40	.20	.10
633	*John Stearns*	.40	.20	.10
634	Larry Christenson	.40	.20	.10
635	Jim Fregosi	.40	.20	.10
636	Joe Decker	.40	.20	.10
637	Bruce Bochte	.40	.20	.10
638	Doyle Alexander	.40	.20	.10
639	Fred Kendall	.40	.20	.10
640	Bill Madlock	.75	.40	.25
641	Tom Paciorek	.40	.20	.10
642	Dennis Blair	.40	.20	.10
643	Checklist 529-660	1.00	.50	.30
644	Tom Bradley	.40	.20	.10
645	Darrell Porter	.40	.20	.10
646	John Lowenstein	.40	.20	.10
647	Ramon Hernandez	.40	.20	.10
648	Al Cowens	.40	.20	.10
649	Dave Roberts	.40	.20	.10
650	Thurman Munson	6.00	3.00	1.75
651	John Odom	.40	.20	.10
652	Ed Armbrister	.40	.20	.10
653	*Mike Norris*	.40	.20	.10
654	Doug Griffin	.40	.20	.10
655	Mike Vail	.40	.20	.10
656	Chicago White Sox Team (Chuck Tanner)	1.00	.50	.30
657	*Roy Smalley*	.40	.20	.10
658	Jerry Johnson	.40	.20	.10
659	Ben Oglivie	.40	.20	.10
660	Dave Lopes	1.00	.50	.30

1976 Topps Traded

 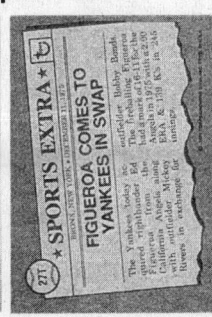

Similar to the Topps Traded set of 1974, the 2-1/2" x 3-1/2" cards feature photos of players traded after the printing deadline. The style of the cards is essentially the same as the regular issue, but with a large "Sports Extra" headline announcing the trade and its date. The backs continue in newspaper style to detail the specifics of the trade. There are 43 player cards and one checklist in the set. Numbers remain the same as the player's regular card, with the addition of a "T" suffix.

		NM	EX	VG
Complete Set (44):		20.00	10.00	6.00
Common Player:		.75	.35	.20
27T	Ed Figueroa	.75	.35	.20
28T	Dusty Baker	1.25	.60	.40
44T	Doug Rader	.75	.35	.20
58T	Ron Reed	.75	.35	.20
74T	Oscar Gamble	.75	.35	.20
80T	Jim Kaat	.75	.35	.20
83T	Jim Spencer	.75	.35	.20
85T	Mickey Rivers	.75	.35	.20
99T	Lee Lacy	.75	.35	.20
120T	Rusty Staub	.75	.35	.20
127T	Larvell Blanks	.75	.35	.20
146T	George Medich	.75	.35	.20
158T	Ken Reitz	.75	.35	.20
208T	Mike Lum	.75	.35	.20
211T	Clay Carroll	.75	.35	.20
231T	Tom House	.75	.35	.20
250T	Fergie Jenkins	3.00	1.50	.90
259T	Darrel Chaney	.75	.35	.20
292T	Leon Roberts	.75	.35	.20
296T	Pat Dobson	.75	.35	.20
309T	Bill Melton	.75	.35	.20
338T	Bob Bailey	.75	.35	.20
380T	Bobby Bonds	.75	.35	.20
383T	John Ellis	.75	.35	.20
385T	Mickey Lolich	.75	.35	.20
401T	Ken Brett	.75	.35	.20
410T	Ralph Garr	.75	.35	.20
411T	Bill Singer	.75	.35	.20
428T	Jim Crawford	.75	.35	.20
434T	Morris Nettles	.75	.35	.20
464T	Ken Henderson	.75	.35	.20
497T	Joe McIntosh	.75	.35	.20
524T	Pete Falcone	.75	.35	.20

		NM	EX	VG
527T	Mike Anderson	.75	.35	.20
528T	Dock Ellis	.75	.35	.20
532T	Milt May	.75	.35	.20
554T	Ray Fosse	.75	.35	.20
579T	Clay Kirby	.75	.35	.20
583T	Tommy Helms	.75	.35	.20
592T	Willie Randolph	.75	.35	.20
618T	Jack Brohamer	.75	.35	.20
632T	Rogelio Moret	.75	.35	.20
649T	Dave Roberts	.75	.35	.20
----	Traded Checklist	.75	.35	.20

1976 Topps Cloth Sticker Prototypes

Apparently produced to test different materials for the cloth sticker set which would be issued the following year, these prototypes were never issued. Each of the players can be found on four different types of material. The blank-backed stickers feature the card fronts as they appeared in the regular 1976 issue. It is unknown whether other players were produced for the test.

	NM	EX	VG
Common Player:	30.00	15.00	9.00
(1a) Bob Apodaca (Silk)	30.00	15.00	9.00
(1b) Bob Apodaca (Thin felt.)	30.00	15.00	9.00
(1c) Bob Apodaca (Textured felt.)	60.00	30.00	18.00
(1d) Bob Apodaca (Thick felt.)	30.00	15.00	9.00
(2a) Duffy Dyer (Silk)	30.00	15.00	9.00
(2b) Duffy Dyer (Thin felt.)	30.00	15.00	9.00
(2c) Duffy Dyer (Textured felt.)	60.00	30.00	18.00
(2d) Duffy Dyer (Thick felt.)	30.00	15.00	9.00

1976 Topps Team Checklist Sheet

Via a mail-in redemption (50¢ and a wrapper), collectors could receive an uncut sheet of the 24 team photo/checklist cards from the 1976 Topps baseball set. Measuring about 10-1/2" x 20-1/8", the sheet could be cut into individual team cards of standard size, though printed on stock that is lighter than pack-issued versions.

	NM	EX	VG
Complete Sheet:	35.00	17.50	10.00

1976 Topps Joe Garagiola

Topps produced this personal business card for long-time NBC announcer and former major leaguer Joe Garagiola. The front is in the format of a 1973 Topps card and has a color portrait. The back resembles the 1976 Topps card, is in black-and-white and provides contact information.

		NM	EX	VG
1	Joe Garagiola	20.00	10.00	6.00

1976 Topps/Dynamite Magazine Panels

In at least one issue of its "Dynamite" kids' magazine, Scholastic Book Club teamed with Topps to insert a six-card panel of its 1976 baseball issue. Values shown are for just the uncut panel; complete magazines would bear a small premium.

		NM	EX	VG
Complete Panel:		20.00	10.00	6.00
469	Rawly Eastwick			

		NM	EX	VG
471	Jim Burton			
474	Ray Corbin			
481	Rudy May			
482	Tim Hosley			
522	Ted Sizemore			

1977 Topps

 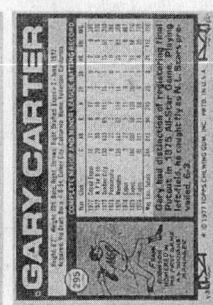

The 1977 Topps Set is a 660-card effort featuring front designs dominated by a color photograph on which there is a facsimile autograph. Above the picture are the player's name, team and position. The backs of the 2-1/2" x 3-1/2" cards include personal and career statistics along with newspaper-style highlights and a cartoon. Specialty cards include statistical leaders, record performances, a new "Turn Back The Clock" feature which highlighted great past moments and a "Big League Brothers" feature.

		NM	EX	VG
Complete Set (660):		200.00	95.00	55.00
Common Player:		.25	.10	.06
Wax Pack (10):		22.50		
Wax Box (36):		625.00		
Cello Pack (18):		50.00		
Cello Box (24):		1,200		
Rack Pack (39):		60.00		
Rack Box (24):		1,850		
Vending Box (500):		300.00		
1	Batting Leaders (George Brett, Bill Madlock)	6.00	3.00	1.75
2	Home Run Leaders (Graig Nettles, Mike Schmidt)	2.00	1.00	.60
3	RBI Leaders (George Foster, Lee May)	.75	.40	.25
4	Stolen Base Leaders (Dave Lopes, Bill North)	.50	.25	.15
5	Victory Leaders (Randy Jones, Jim Palmer)	1.00	.50	.30
6	Strikeout Leaders (Nolan Ryan, Tom Seaver)	10.00	5.00	3.00
7	ERA Leaders (John Denny, Mark Fidrych)	.50	.25	.15
8	Leading Firemen (Bill Campbell, Rawly Eastwick)	.25	.10	.06
9	Doug Rader	.25	.10	.06
10	Reggie Jackson	8.00	4.00	2.50
11	Rob Dressler	.25	.10	.06
12	Larry Haney	.25	.10	.06
13	Luis Gomez	.25	.10	.06
14	Tommy Smith	.25	.10	.06
15	Don Gullett	.25	.10	.06
16	Bob Jones	.25	.10	.06
17	Steve Stone	.25	.10	.06
18	Indians Team (Frank Robinson)	1.50	.70	.45
19	John D'Acquisto	.25	.10	.06
20	Graig Nettles	.75	.40	.25
21	Ken Forsch	.25	.10	.06
22	Bill Freehan	.25	.10	.06
23	Dan Driessen	.25	.10	.06
24	Carl Morton	.25	.10	.06
25	Dwight Evans	.75	.40	.25
26	Ray Sadecki	.25	.10	.06
27	Bill Buckner	.75	.40	.25
28	Woodie Fryman	.25	.10	.06
29	Bucky Dent	.50	.25	.15
30	Greg Luzinski	.50	.25	.15
31	Jim Todd	.25	.10	.06
32	Checklist 1-132	1.00	.50	.30
33	Wayne Garland	.25	.10	.06
34	Angels Team (Norm Sherry)	1.00	.50	.30
35	Rennie Stennett	.25	.10	.06
36	John Ellis	.25	.10	.06
37	Steve Hargan	.25	.10	.06
38	Craig Kusick	.25	.10	.06
39	Tom Griffin	.25	.10	.06
40	Bobby Murcer	.50	.25	.15
41	Jim Kern	.25	.10	.06
42	Jose Cruz	.25	.10	.06
43	Ray Bare	.25	.10	.06
44	Bud Harrelson	.25	.10	.06
45	Rawly Eastwick	.25	.10	.06
46	Buck Martinez	.25	.10	.06
47	Lynn McGlothen	.25	.10	.06
48	Tom Paciorek	.25	.10	.06
49	Grant Jackson	.25	.10	.06
50	Ron Cey	.50	.25	.15
51	Brewers Team (Alex Grammas)	1.00	.50	.30
52	Ellis Valentine	.25	.10	.06
53	Paul Mitchell	.25	.10	.06
54	Sandy Alomar	.25	.10	.06
55	Jeff Burroughs	.25	.10	.06
56	Rudy May	.25	.10	.06
57	Marc Hill	.25	.10	.06

58	Chet Lemon	.25	.10	.06
59	Larry Christenson	.25	.10	.06
60	Jim Rice	2.00	1.00	.60
61	Manny Sanguillen	.25	.10	.06
62	Eric Raich	.25	.10	.06
63	Tito Fuentes	.25	.10	.06
64	Larry Biittner	.25	.10	.06
65	Skip Lockwood	.25	.10	.06
66	Roy Smalley	.25	.10	.06
67	*Joaquin Andujar*	.50	.25	.15
68	Bruce Bochte	.25	.10	.06
69	Jim Crawford	.25	.10	.06
70	Johnny Bench	6.00	3.00	1.75
71	Dock Ellis	.25	.10	.06
72	Mike Anderson	.25	.10	.06
73	Charlie Williams	.25	.10	.06
74	A's Team (Jack McKeon)	1.00	.50	.30
75	Dennis Leonard	.25	.10	.06
76	Tim Foli	.25	.10	.06
77	Dyar Miller	.25	.10	.06
78	Bob Davis	.25	.10	.06
79	Don Money	.25	.10	.06
80	Andy Messersmith	.25	.10	.06
81	Juan Beniquez	.25	.10	.06
82	Jim Rooker	.25	.10	.06
83	Kevin Bell	.25	.10	.06
84	Ollie Brown	.25	.10	.06
85	Duane Kuiper	.25	.10	.06
86	Pat Zachry	.25	.10	.06
87	Glenn Borgmann	.25	.10	.06
88	Stan Wall	.25	.10	.06
89	*Butch Hobson*	.25	.10	.06
90	Cesar Cedeno	.25	.10	.06
91	John Verhoeven	.25	.10	.06
92	Dave Rosello	.25	.10	.06
93	Tom Poquette	.25	.10	.06
94	Craig Swan	.25	.10	.06
95	Keith Hernandez	.75	.40	.25
96	Lou Piniella	.75	.40	.25
97	Dave Heaverlo	.25	.10	.06
98	Milt May	.25	.10	.06
99	Tom Hausman	.25	.10	.06
100	Joe Morgan	3.00	1.50	.90
101	Dick Bosman	.25	.10	.06
102	Jose Morales	.25	.10	.06
103	Mike Bacsik	.25	.10	.06
104	*Omar Moreno*	.50	.25	.15
105	Steve Yeager	.50	.25	.15
106	Mike Flanagan	.50	.25	.15
107	Bill Melton	.25	.10	.06
108	Alan Foster	.25	.10	.06
109	Jorge Orta	.25	.10	.06
110	Steve Carlton	4.00	2.00	1.25
111	Rico Petrocelli	.50	.25	.15
112	Bill Greif	.25	.10	.06
113	Blue Jays Mgr./Coaches (Roy Hartsfield, Don Leppert, Bob Miller, Jackie Moore, Harry Warner)	.75	.40	.25
114	Bruce Dal Canton	.25	.10	.06
115	Rick Manning	.25	.10	.06
116	Joe Niekro	.25	.10	.06
117	Frank White	.25	.10	.06
118	Rick Jones	.25	.10	.06
119	John Stearns	.25	.10	.06
120	Rod Carew	3.00	1.50	.90
121	Gary Nolan	.25	.10	.06
122	Ben Oglivie	.25	.10	.06
123	Fred Stanley	.25	.10	.06
124	George Mitterwald	.25	.10	.06
125	Bill Travers	.25	.10	.06
126	Rod Gilbreath	.25	.10	.06
127	Ron Fairly	.25	.10	.06
128	Tommy John	.50	.25	.15
129	Mike Sadek	.25	.10	.06
130	Al Oliver	.75	.40	.25
131	Orlando Ramirez	.25	.10	.06
132	Chip Lang	.25	.10	.06
133	Ralph Garr	.25	.10	.06
134	Padres Team (John McNamara)	.75	.40	.25
135	Mark Belanger	.25	.10	.06
136	*Jerry Mumphrey*	.25	.10	.06
137	Jeff Terpko	.25	.10	.06
138	Bob Stinson	.25	.10	.06
139	Fred Norman	.25	.10	.06
140	Mike Schmidt	10.00	5.00	3.00
141	Mark Littell	.25	.10	.06
142	Steve Dillard	.25	.10	.06
143	Ed Herrmann	.25	.10	.06
144	*Bruce Sutter*	15.00	7.50	4.50
145	Tom Veryzer	.25	.10	.06
146	Dusty Baker	1.00	.50	.30
147	Jackie Brown	.25	.10	.06
148	Fran Healy	.25	.10	.06
149	Mike Cubbage	.25	.10	.06
150	Tom Seaver	6.00	3.00	1.75
151	Johnnie LeMaster	.25	.10	.06
152	Gaylord Perry	2.50	1.25	.70
153	Ron Jackson	.25	.10	.06
154	Dave Giusti	.25	.10	.06
155	Joe Rudi	.25	.10	.06
156	Pete Mackanin	.25	.10	.06
157	Ken Brett	.25	.10	.06
158	Ted Kubiak	.25	.10	.06
159	Bernie Carbo	.25	.10	.06
160	Will McEnaney	.25	.10	.06
161	*Garry Templeton*	1.00	.50	.30
162	Mike Cuellar	.25	.10	.06
163	Dave Hilton	.25	.10	.06
164	Tug McGraw	.25	.10	.06
165	Jim Wynn	.25	.10	.06
166	Bill Campbell	.25	.10	.06
167	Rich Hebner	.25	.10	.06
168	Charlie Spikes	.25	.10	.06
169	Darold Knowles	.25	.10	.06
170	Thurman Munson	6.00	3.00	1.75
171	Ken Sanders	.25	.10	.06
172	John Milner	.25	.10	.06
173	Chuck Scrivener	.25	.10	.06
174	Nelson Briles	.25	.10	.06
175	*Butch Wynegar*	.25	.10	.06
176	Bob Robertson	.25	.10	.06
177	Bart Johnson	.25	.10	.06
178	Bombo Rivera	.25	.10	.06
179	Paul Hartzell	.25	.10	.06
180	Dave Lopes	.50	.25	.15
181	Ken McMullen	.25	.10	.06
182	Dan Spillner	.25	.10	.06
183	Cardinals Team (Vern Rapp)	1.00	.50	.30
184	Bo McLaughlin	.25	.10	.06
185	Sixto Lezcano	.25	.10	.06
186	Doug Flynn	.25	.10	.06
187	Dick Pole	.25	.10	.06
188	Bob Tolan	.25	.10	.06
189	Rick Dempsey	.25	.10	.06
190	Ray Burris	.25	.10	.06
191	Doug Griffin	.25	.10	.06
192	Clarence Gaston	.25	.10	.06
193	Larry Gura	.25	.10	.06
194	Gary Matthews	.25	.10	.06
195	Ed Figueroa	.25	.10	.06
196	Len Randle	.25	.10	.06
197	Ed Ott	.25	.10	.06
198	Wilbur Wood	.25	.10	.06
199	Pepe Frias	.25	.10	.06
200	Frank Tanana	.25	.10	.06
201	Ed Kranepool	.25	.10	.06
202	Tom Johnson	.25	.10	.06
203	Ed Armbrister	.25	.10	.06
204	Jeff Newman	.25	.10	.06
205	Pete Falcone	.25	.10	.06
206	Boog Powell	.75	.40	.25
207	Glenn Abbott	.25	.10	.06
208	Checklist 133-264	.75	.40	.25
209	Rob Andrews	.25	.10	.06
210	Fred Lynn	.50	.25	.15
211	Giants Team (Joe Altobelli)	.75	.40	.25
212	Jim Mason	.25	.10	.06
213	Maximino Leon	.25	.10	.06
214	Darrell Porter	.25	.10	.06
215	Butch Metzger	.25	.10	.06
216	Doug DeCinces	.25	.10	.06
217	Tom Underwood	.25	.10	.06
218	*John Wathan*	.25	.10	.06
219	Joe Coleman	.25	.10	.06
220	Chris Chambliss	.50	.25	.15
221	Bob Bailey	.25	.10	.06
222	Francisco Barrios	.25	.10	.06
223	Earl Williams	.25	.10	.06
224	Rusty Torres	.25	.10	.06
225	Bob Apodaca	.25	.10	.06
226	Leroy Stanton	.25	.10	.06
227	*Joe Sambito*	.25	.10	.06
228	Twins Team (Gene Mauch)	1.00	.50	.30
229	Don Kessinger	.25	.10	.06
230	Vida Blue	.25	.10	.06
231	George Brett (Record Breaker)	5.00	2.50	1.50
232	Minnie Minoso (Record Breaker)	.50	.25	.15
233	Jose Morales (Record Breaker)	.50	.25	.15
234	Nolan Ryan (Record Breaker)	10.00	5.00	3.00
235	Cecil Cooper	.25	.10	.06
236	Tom Buskey	.25	.10	.06
237	Gene Clines	.25	.10	.06
238	Tippy Martinez	.25	.10	.06
239	Bill Plummer	.25	.10	.06
240	Ron LeFlore	.25	.10	.06
241	Dave Tomlin	.25	.10	.06
242	Ken Henderson	.25	.10	.06
243	Ron Reed	.25	.10	.06
244	John Mayberry	.25	.10	.06
245	Rick Rhoden	.25	.10	.06
246	Mike Vail	.25	.10	.06
247	Chris Knapp	.25	.10	.06
248	Wilbur Howard	.25	.10	.06
249	Pete Redfern	.25	.10	.06
250	Bill Madlock	.50	.25	.15
251	Tony Muser	.25	.10	.06
252	Dale Murray	.25	.10	.06
253	John Hale	.25	.10	.06
254	Doyle Alexander	.25	.10	.06
255	George Scott	.25	.10	.06
256	Joe Hoerner	.25	.10	.06
257	Mike Miley	.25	.10	.06
258	Luis Tiant	.50	.25	.15
259	Mets Team (Joe Frazier)	1.00	.50	.30
260	J.R. Richard	.50	.25	.15
261	Phil Garner	.50	.25	.15
262	Al Cowens	.25	.10	.06
263	Mike Marshall	.25	.10	.06
264	Tom Hutton	.25	.10	.06
265	*Mark Fidrych*	5.00	2.50	1.50
266	Derrel Thomas	.25	.10	.06
267	Ray Fosse	.25	.10	.06
268	Rick Sawyer	.25	.10	.06
269	Joe Lis	.25	.10	.06
270	Dave Parker	.50	.25	.15
271	Terry Forster	.25	.10	.06
272	Lee Lacy	.25	.10	.06
273	Eric Soderholm	.25	.10	.06
274	Don Stanhouse	.25	.10	.06
275	Mike Hargrove	.25	.10	.06
276	A.L. Championship (Chambliss' Dramatic Homer Decides It)	.25	.13	.08
277	N.L. Championship (Reds Sweep Phillies 3 In Row)	3.00	1.50	.90
278	Danny Frisella	.25	.10	.06
279	Joe Wallis	.25	.10	.06
280	Jim Hunter	2.50	1.25	.70
281	Roy Staiger	.25	.10	.06
282	Sid Monge	.25	.10	.06
283	Jerry DaVanon	.25	.10	.06
284	Mike Norris	.25	.10	.06
285	Brooks Robinson	4.00	2.00	1.25
286	Johnny Grubb	.25	.10	.06
287	Reds Team (Sparky Anderson)	1.00	.50	.30
288	Bob Montgomery	.25	.10	.06
289	Gene Garber	.25	.10	.06
290	Amos Otis	.25	.10	.06
291	*Jason Thompson*	.25	.10	.06
292	Rogelio Moret	.25	.10	.06
293	Jack Brohamer	.25	.10	.06
294	George Medich	.25	.10	.06
295	Gary Carter	3.00	1.50	.90
296	Don Hood	.25	.10	.06
297	Ken Reitz	.25	.10	.06
298	Charlie Hough	.25	.10	.06
299	Otto Velez	.25	.10	.06
300	Jerry Koosman	.25	.10	.06
301	Toby Harrah	.25	.10	.06
302	Mike Garman	.25	.10	.06
303	Gene Tenace	.25	.10	.06
304	Jim Hughes	.25	.10	.06
305	Mickey Rivers	.25	.10	.06
306	Rick Waits	.25	.10	.06
307	Gary Sutherland	.25	.10	.06
308	Gene Pentz	.25	.10	.06
309	Red Sox Team (Don Zimmer)	1.50	.70	.45
310	Larry Bowa	.50	.25	.15
311	Vern Ruhle	.25	.10	.06
312	Rob Belloir	.25	.10	.06
313	Paul Blair	.25	.10	.06
314	Steve Mingori	.25	.10	.06
315	Dave Chalk	.25	.10	.06
316	Steve Rogers	.25	.10	.06
317	Kurt Bevacqua	.25	.10	.06
318	Duffy Dyer	.25	.10	.06
319	Rich Gossage	.75	.40	.25
320	Ken Griffey	.75	.40	.25
321	Dave Goltz	.25	.10	.06
322	Bill Russell	.50	.25	.15
323	Larry Lintz	.25	.10	.06
324	John Curtis	.25	.10	.06
325	Mike Ivie	.25	.10	.06
326	Jesse Jefferson	.25	.10	.06
327	Astros Team (Bill Virdon)	.75	.40	.25
328	Tommy Boggs	.25	.10	.06
329	Ron Hodges	.25	.10	.06
330	George Hendrick	.25	.10	.06
331	Jim Colborn	.25	.10	.06
332	Elliott Maddox	.25	.10	.06
333	Paul Reuschel	.25	.10	.06
334	Bill Stein	.25	.10	.06
335	Bill Robinson	.25	.10	.06
336	Denny Doyle	.25	.10	.06
337	Ron Schueler	.25	.10	.06
338	Dave Duncan	.25	.10	.06
339	Adrian Devine	.25	.10	.06
340	Hal McRae	.50	.25	.15
341	Joe Kerrigan	.25	.10	.06
342	Jerry Remy	.25	.10	.06
343	Ed Halicki	.25	.10	.06
344	Brian Downing	.25	.10	.06
345	Reggie Smith	.25	.10	.06
346	Bill Singer	.25	.10	.06
347	George Foster	.25	.10	.06
348	Brent Strom	.25	.10	.06
349	Jim Holt	.25	.10	.06
350	Larry Dierker	.25	.10	.06
351	Jim Sundberg	.25	.10	.06
352	Mike Phillips	.25	.10	.06
353	Stan Thomas	.25	.10	.06
354	Pirates Team (Chuck Tanner)	.75	.40	.25
355	Lou Brock	3.00	1.50	.90
356	Checklist 265-396	.75	.40	.25
357	Tim McCarver	.75	.40	.25
358	Tom House	.25	.10	.06
359	Willie Randolph	.75	.40	.25
360	Rick Monday	.25	.10	.06
361	Eduardo Rodriguez	.25	.10	.06
362	Tommy Davis	.25	.10	.06
363	Dave Roberts	.25	.10	.06
364	Vic Correll	.25	.10	.06
365	Mike Torrez	.25	.10	.06
366	Ted Sizemore	.25	.10	.06
367	Dave Hamilton	.25	.10	.06
368	Mike Jorgensen	.25	.10	.06
369	Terry Humphrey	.25	.10	.06
370	John Montefusco	.25	.10	.06
371	Royals Team (Whitey Herzog)	1.00	.50	.30
372	Rich Folkers	.25	.10	.06
373	Bert Campaneris	.25	.10	.06
374	Kent Tekulve	.25	.10	.06
375	Larry Hisle	.25	.10	.06
376	Nino Espinosa	.25	.10	.06
377	Dave McKay	.25	.10	.06
378	Jim Umbarger	.25	.10	.06
379	Larry Cox	.25	.10	.06
380	Lee May	.25	.10	.06
381	Bob Forsch	.25	.10	.06
382	Charlie Moore	.25	.10	.06
383	Stan Bahnsen	.25	.10	.06
384	Darrel Chaney	.25	.10	.06
385	Dave LaRoche	.25	.10	.06
386	Manny Mota	.25	.10	.06
387	Yankees Team (Billy Martin)	2.00	1.00	.60
388	Terry Harmon	.25	.10	.06
389	Ken Kravec	.25	.10	.06
390	Dave Winfield	3.00	1.50	.90
391	Dan Warthen	.25	.10	.06
392	Phil Roof	.25	.10	.06
393	John Lowenstein	.25	.10	.06
394	Bill Laxton	.25	.10	.06
395	Manny Trillo	.25	.10	.06
396	Tom Murphy	.25	.10	.06
397	*Larry Herndon*	.25	.10	.06
398	Tom Burgmeier	.25	.10	.06

#	Player	NM	EX	VG
399	Bruce Boisclair	.25	.10	.06
400	Steve Garvey	2.00	1.00	.60
401	Mickey Scott	.25	.10	.06
402	Tommy Helms	.25	.10	.06
403	Tom Grieve	.25	.10	.06
404	Eric Rasmussen	.25	.10	.06
405	Claudell Washington	.25	.10	.06
406	Tim Johnson	.25	.10	.06
407	Dave Freisleben	.25	.10	.06
408	Cesar Tovar	.25	.10	.06
409	Pete Broberg	.25	.10	.06
410	Willie Montanez	.25	.10	.06
411	World Series Games 1 & 2 (Joe Morgan, Johnny Bench)	2.00	1.00	.60
412	World Series Games 3 & 4 (Johnny Bench)	2.00	1.00	.60
413	World Series Summary	.75	.40	.25
414	Tommy Harper	.25	.10	.06
415	Jay Johnstone	.25	.10	.06
416	Chuck Hartenstein	.25	.10	.06
417	Wayne Garrett	.25	.10	.06
418	White Sox Team (Bob Lemon)	1.00	.50	.30
419	Steve Swisher	.25	.10	.06
420	Rusty Staub	.50	.25	.15
421	Doug Rau	.25	.10	.06
422	Freddie Patek	.25	.10	.06
423	Gary Lavelle	.25	.10	.06
424	Steve Brye	.25	.10	.06
425	Joe Torre	1.00	.50	.30
426	Dick Drago	.25	.10	.06
427	Dave Rader	.25	.10	.06
428	Rangers Team (Frank Lucchesi)	.75	.40	.25
429	Ken Boswell	.25	.10	.06
430	Fergie Jenkins	2.50	1.25	.70
431	Dave Collins	.25	.10	.06
432	Buzz Capra	.25	.10	.06
433	Nate Colbert (Turn Back The Clock)	.25	.10	.06
434	Carl Yastrzemski (Turn Back The Clock)	1.50	.70	.45
435	Maury Wills (Turn Back The Clock)	.50	.25	.15
436	Bob Keegan (Turn Back The Clock)	.25	.10	.06
437	Ralph Kiner (Turn Back The Clock)	.75	.40	.25
438	Marty Perez	.25	.10	.06
439	Gorman Thomas	.25	.10	.06
440	Jon Matlack	.25	.10	.06
441	Larvell Blanks	.25	.10	.06
442	Braves Team (Dave Bristol)	1.00	.50	.30
443	Lamar Johnson	.25	.10	.06
444	Wayne Twitchell	.25	.10	.06
445	Ken Singleton	.25	.10	.06
446	Bill Bonham	.25	.10	.06
447	Jerry Turner	.25	.10	.06
448	Ellie Rodriguez	.25	.10	.06
449	Al Fitzmorris	.25	.10	.06
450	Pete Rose	15.00	7.50	4.50
451	Checklist 397-528	1.00	.50	.30
452	Mike Caldwell	.25	.10	.06
453	Pedro Garcia	.25	.10	.06
454	Andy Etchebarren	.25	.10	.06
455	Rick Wise	.25	.10	.06
456	Leon Roberts	.25	.10	.06
457	Steve Luebber	.25	.10	.06
458	Leo Foster	.25	.10	.06
459	Steve Foucault	.25	.10	.06
460	Willie Stargell	4.00	2.00	1.25
461	Dick Tidrow	.25	.10	.06
462	Don Baylor	.30	.15	.10
463	Jamie Quirk	.25	.10	.06
464	Randy Moffitt	.25	.10	.06
465	Rico Carty	.25	.10	.06
466	Fred Holdsworth	.25	.10	.06
467	Phillies Team (Danny Ozark)	.50	.25	.15
468	Ramon Hernandez	.25	.10	.06
469	Pat Kelly	.25	.10	.06
470	Ted Simmons	.50	.25	.15
471	Del Unser	.25	.10	.06
472	Rookie Pitchers (Don Aase, Bob McClure, Gil Patterson (Photo is Sheldon Gill), Dave Wehrmeister)	.25	.10	.06
473	Rookie Outfielders (*Andre Dawson, Gene Richards, John Scott, Denny Walling*)	15.00	7.50	4.50
474	Rookie Shortstops (Bob Bailor, Kiko Garcia, Craig Reynolds, Alex Taveras)	.25	.10	.06
475	Rookie Pitchers (Chris Batton, Rick Camp, Scott McGregor, Manny Sarmiento)	.25	.10	.06
476	Rookie Catchers (*Gary Alexander, Rick Cerone, Dale Murphy, Kevin Pasley*)	12.00	6.00	3.50
477	Rookie Infielders (Doug Ault, Rich Dauer, Orlando Gonzalez, Phil Mankowski)	.25	.10	.06
478	Rookie Pitchers (Jim Gideon, Leon Hooten, Dave Johnson, Mark Lemongello)	.25	.10	.06
479	Rookie Outfielders (Brian Asselstine, Wayne Gross, Sam Mejias, Alvis Woods)	.25	.10	.06
480	Carl Yastrzemski	6.00	3.00	1.75
481	Roger Metzger	.25	.10	.06
482	Tony Solaita	.25	.10	.06
483	Richie Zisk	.25	.10	.06
484	Burt Hooton	.25	.10	.06
485	Roy White	.25	.10	.06
486	Ed Bane	.25	.10	.06
487	Rookie Pitchers (Larry Anderson, Ed Glynn, Joe Henderson, Greg Terlecky)	.25	.10	.06

#	Player	NM	EX	VG
488	Rookie Outfielders (*Jack Clark, Ruppert Jones, Lee Mazzilli, Dan Thomas*)	3.00	1.50	.90
489	Rookie Pitchers (Len Barker, Randy Lerch, Greg Minton, Mike Overy)	.75	.40	.25
490	Rookie Shortstops (Billy Almon, Mickey Klutts, Tommy McMillan, Mark Wagner)	.25	.10	.06
491	Rookie Pitchers (*Mike Dupree, Dennis Martinez, Craig Mitchell, Bob Sykes*)	3.00	1.50	.90
492	Rookie Outfielders (*Tony Armas, Steve Kemp, Carlos Lopez, Gary Woods*)	.75	.40	.25
493	Rookie Pitchers (Mike Krukow, Jim Otten, Gary Wheelock, Mike Willis)	.25	.10	.06
494	Rookie Infielders (*Juan Bernhardt, Mike Champion, Jim Gantner, Bump Wills*)	1.00	.50	.30
495	Al Hrabosky	.50	.25	.15
496	Gary Thomasson	.25	.10	.06
497	Clay Carroll	.25	.10	.06
498	Sal Bando	.25	.10	.06
499	Pablo Torrealba	.25	.10	.06
500	Dave Kingman	.75	.40	.25
501	Jim Bibby	.25	.10	.06
502	Randy Hundley	.25	.10	.06
503	Bill Lee	.25	.10	.06
504	Dodgers Team (Tom Lasorda)	1.50	.70	.45
505	Oscar Gamble	.50	.25	.15
506	Steve Grilli	.25	.10	.06
507	Mike Hegan	.25	.10	.06
508	Dave Pagan	.25	.10	.06
509	Cookie Rojas	.25	.10	.06
510	John Candelaria	.25	.10	.06
511	Bill Fahey	.25	.10	.06
512	Jack Billingham	.25	.10	.06
513	Jerry Terrell	.25	.10	.06
514	Cliff Johnson	.25	.10	.06
515	Chris Speier	.25	.10	.06
516	Bake McBride	.25	.10	.06
517	*Pete Vuckovich*	.50	.25	.15
518	Cubs Team (Herman Franks)	1.00	.50	.30
519	Don Kirkwood	.25	.10	.06
520	Garry Maddox	.50	.25	.15
521	Bob Grich	.25	.10	.06
522	Enzo Hernandez	.25	.10	.06
523	Rollie Fingers	2.50	1.25	.70
524	Rowland Office	.25	.10	.06
525	Dennis Eckersley	4.00	2.00	1.25
526	Larry Parrish	.25	.10	.06
527	Dan Meyer	.25	.10	.06
528	Bill Castro	.25	.10	.06
529	Jim Essian	.25	.10	.06
530	Rick Reuschel	.25	.10	.06
531	Lyman Bostock	.25	.10	.06
532	Jim Willoughby	.25	.10	.06
533	Mickey Stanley	.25	.10	.06
534	Paul Splittorff	.25	.10	.06
535	Cesar Geronimo	.25	.10	.06
536	Vic Albury	.25	.10	.06
537	Dave Roberts	.25	.10	.06
538	Frank Taveras	.25	.10	.06
539	Mike Wallace	.25	.10	.06
540	Bob Watson	.25	.10	.06
541	John Denny	.25	.10	.06
542	Frank Duffy	.25	.10	.06
543	Ron Blomberg	.25	.10	.06
544	Gary Ross	.25	.10	.06
545	Bob Boone	.25	.10	.06
546	Orioles Team (Earl Weaver)	1.50	.70	.45
547	Willie McCovey	3.00	1.50	.90
548	*Joel Youngblood*	.25	.10	.06
549	Jerry Royster	.25	.10	.06
550	Randy Jones	.25	.10	.06
551	Bill North	.25	.10	.06
552	Pepe Mangual	.25	.10	.06
553	Jack Heidemann	.25	.10	.06
554	Bruce Kimm	.25	.10	.06
555	Dan Ford	.25	.10	.06
556	Doug Bird	.25	.10	.06
557	Jerry White	.25	.10	.06
558	Elias Sosa	.25	.10	.06
559	Alan Bannister	.25	.10	.06
560	Dave Concepcion	.25	.10	.06
561	Pete LaCock	.25	.10	.06
562	Checklist 529-660	.75	.40	.25
563	Bruce Kison	.25	.10	.06
564	Alan Ashby	.25	.10	.06
565	Mickey Lolich	.50	.25	.15
566	Rick Miller	.25	.10	.06
567	Enos Cabell	.25	.10	.06
568	Carlos May	.25	.10	.06
569	Jim Lonborg	.25	.10	.06
570	Bobby Bonds	.75	.40	.25
571	Darrell Evans	.25	.10	.06
572	Ross Grimsley	.25	.10	.06
573	Joe Ferguson	.25	.10	.06
574	Aurelio Rodriguez	.25	.10	.06
575	Dick Ruthven	.25	.10	.06
576	Fred Kendall	.25	.10	.06
577	Jerry Augustine	.25	.10	.06
578	Bob Randall	.25	.10	.06
579	Don Carrithers	.25	.10	.06
580	George Brett	12.00	6.00	3.50
581	Pedro Borbon	.25	.10	.06
582	Ed Kirkpatrick	.25	.10	.06
583	Paul Lindblad	.25	.10	.06
584	Ed Goodson	.25	.10	.06
585	Rick Burleson	.25	.10	.06
586	Steve Renko	.25	.10	.06
587	Rick Baldwin	.25	.10	.06
588	Dave Moates	.25	.10	.06
589	Mike Cosgrove	.25	.10	.06

#	Player	NM	EX	VG
590	Buddy Bell	.25	.10	.06
591	Chris Arnold	.25	.10	.06
592	Dan Briggs	.25	.10	.06
593	Dennis Blair	.25	.10	.06
594	Biff Pocoroba	.25	.10	.06
595	John Hiller	.25	.10	.06
596	*Jerry Martin*	.25	.10	.06
597	Mariners Mgr./Coaches (Don Bryant, Jim Busby, Darrell Johnson, Vada Pinson, Wes Stock)	1.00	.50	.30
598	Sparky Lyle	.25	.10	.06
599	Mike Tyson	.25	.10	.06
600	Jim Palmer	3.00	1.50	.90
601	Mike Lum	.25	.10	.06
602	Andy Hassler	.25	.10	.06
603	Willie Davis	.25	.10	.06
604	Jim Slaton	.25	.10	.06
605	Felix Millan	.25	.10	.06
606	Steve Braun	.25	.10	.06
607	Larry Demery	.25	.10	.06
608	Roy Howell	.25	.10	.06
609	Jim Barr	.25	.10	.06
610	Jose Cardenal	.25	.10	.06
611	Dave Lemanczyk	.25	.10	.06
612	Barry Foote	.25	.10	.06
613	Reggie Cleveland	.25	.10	.06
614	Greg Gross	.25	.10	.06
615	Phil Niekro	2.50	1.25	.70
616	Tommy Sandt	.25	.10	.06
617	Bobby Darwin	.25	.10	.06
618	Pat Dobson	.25	.10	.06
619	Johnny Oates	.25	.10	.06
620	Don Sutton	2.50	1.25	.70
621	Tigers Team (Ralph Houk)	1.00	.50	.30
622	Jim Wohlford	.25	.10	.06
623	Jack Kucek	.25	.10	.06
624	Hector Cruz	.25	.10	.06
625	Ken Holtzman	.25	.10	.06
626	Al Bumbry	.25	.10	.06
627	Bob Myrick	.25	.10	.06
628	Mario Guerrero	.25	.10	.06
629	Bobby Valentine	.25	.10	.06
630	Bert Blyleven	.75	.40	.25
631	Big League Brothers (George Brett, Ken Brett)	5.00	2.50	1.50
632	Big League Brothers (Bob Forsch, Ken Forsch)	.25	.10	.06
633	Big League Brothers (Carlos May, Lee May)	.25	.10	.06
634	Big League Brothers (Paul Reuschel, Rick Reuschel) (names switched)	.25	.10	.06
635	Robin Yount	5.00	2.50	1.50
636	Santo Alcala	.25	.10	.06
637	Alex Johnson	.25	.10	.06
638	Jim Kaat	.50	.25	.15
639	Jerry Morales	.25	.10	.06
640	Carlton Fisk	4.00	2.00	1.25
641	Dan Larson	.25	.10	.06
642	Willie Crawford	.25	.10	.06
643	Mike Pazik	.25	.10	.06
644	Matt Alexander	.25	.10	.06
645	Jerry Reuss	.25	.10	.06
646	Andres Mora	.25	.10	.06
647	Expos Team (Dick Williams)	.75	.40	.25
648	Jim Spencer	.25	.10	.06
649	Dave Cash	.25	.10	.06
650	Nolan Ryan	25.00	12.50	7.50
651	Von Joshua	.25	.10	.06
652	Tom Walker	.25	.10	.06
653	Diego Segui	.25	.10	.06
654	Ron Pruitt	.25	.10	.06
655	Tony Perez	3.00	1.50	.90
656	Ron Guidry	1.00	.50	.30
657	Mick Kelleher	.25	.10	.06
658	Marty Pattin	.25	.10	.06
659	Merv Rettenmund	.25	.10	.06
660	Willie Horton	1.00	.50	.30

1977 Topps Proofs

Perhaps the most sought-after Topps proof card is the 1977 blank-back featuring Reggie Jackson in an Orioles uniform but designating his team as the Yankees, with whom he signed as a free agent prior to the 1977 season. Less well-known are a group of other players' cards that have uniform/team variations from the regularly issued versions. All of the handful of known examples were hand-cut from sheets. Backs are blank.

	NM	EX	VG
Don Baylor	350.00	175.00	100.00

	NM	EX	VG
Rollie Fingers	900.00	450.00	275.00
Al Fitzmorris	300.00	150.00	90.00
Wayne Garland	300.00	150.00	90.00
Bill Greif	200.00	100.00	60.00
Reggie Jackson	6,000		
(5/04 auction.)			
Pat Kelly	300.00	150.00	90.00
Gary Matthews	450.00	225.00	135.00
Dan Meyer	300.00	150.00	90.00
Bill Singer	200.00	100.00	60.00
Steve Stone	350.00	175.00	100.00
Gene Tenace	425.00	210.00	125.00

1977 Topps Team Checklist Sheet

A redemption offer on packs of 1977 Topps cards offered an uncut sheet of the 26 team/checklist cards by mail. Besides the perforated team cards, the 10-1/2" x 22-1/2" sheet has a card offering collectors a card locker. The cards on the sheet are identical to the single team/checklist cards issued in packs, except they are printed on thinner card stock.

	NM	EX	VG
Uncut Sheet	35.00	17.50	10.50

1977 Topps/Dynamite Magazine Panels

In at least two issues of its "Dynamite" kids' magazine, Scholastic Book Club teamed with Topps to insert a six-card panel of its 1977 baseball issue. Values shown are for just the uncut panel; complete magazines would bear a small premium.

	NM	EX	VG
Complete Panel Set (2):	50.00	25.00	15.00
PANEL 1	25.00	12.50	7.50
215 Butch Metzger			
335 Bill Robinson			
599 Mike Tyson			
625 Ken Holtzman			
630 Bert Blyleven			
641 Dan Larson			
PANEL 2	30.00	15.00	9.00
242 Ken Henderson			
294 George Medich			
415 Jay Johnstone			
535 Cesar Geronimo			
580 George Brett			
626 Al Bumbry			

1977 Topps Cloth Stickers

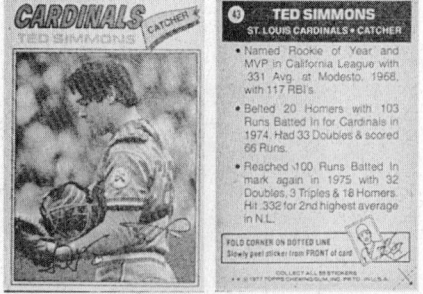

One of the few Topps specialty issues of the late 1970s, the 73-piece set of cloth stickers issued in 1977 includes 55 player stickers and 18 puzzle cards which could be joined to form a photo of the American League or National League All-Star teams. Issued as a separate issue, the 2-1/2" x 3-1/2" stickers have a paper backing which could be removed to allow the cloth to be adhered to a jacket, notebook, etc.

	NM	EX	VG
Complete Set (73):	75.00	37.70	22.50
Common Player:	1.00	.50	.30
Wax Pack:	12.50		
Wax Box (36):	325.00		
1 Alan Ashby	1.00	.50	.30
2 Buddy Bell	1.00	.50	.30

3 Johnny Bench	5.00	2.50	1.50
4 Vida Blue	1.00	.50	.30
5 Bert Blyleven	1.00	.50	.30
6 Steve Braun	1.00	.50	.30
7 George Brett	8.00	4.00	2.50
8 Lou Brock	4.00	2.00	1.25
9 Jose Cardenal	1.00	.50	.30
10 Rod Carew	5.00	2.50	1.50
11 Steve Carlton	4.00	2.00	1.25
12 Dave Cash	1.00	.50	.30
13 Cesar Cedeno	1.00	.50	.30
14 Ron Cey	1.00	.50	.30
15 Mark Fidrych	2.50	1.25	.70
16 Dan Ford	1.00	.50	.30
17 Wayne Garland	1.00	.50	.30
18 Ralph Garr	1.00	.50	.30
19 Steve Garvey	2.00	1.00	.60
20 Mike Hargrove	1.00	.50	.30
21 Catfish Hunter	3.00	1.50	.90
22 Reggie Jackson	8.00	4.00	2.50
23 Randy Jones	1.00	.50	.30
24 Dave Kingman	1.00	.50	.30
25 Bill Madlock	1.00	.50	.30
26 Lee May	1.00	.50	.30
27 John Mayberry	1.00	.50	.30
28 Andy Messersmith	1.00	.50	.30
29 Willie Montanez	1.00	.50	.30
30 John Montefusco	1.00	.50	.30
31 Joe Morgan	4.00	2.00	1.25
32 Thurman Munson	4.00	2.00	1.25
33 Bobby Murcer	1.00	.50	.30
34 Al Oliver	1.00	.50	.30
35 Dave Pagan	1.00	.50	.30
36 Jim Palmer	4.00	2.00	1.25
37 Tony Perez	3.00	1.50	.90
38 Pete Rose	10.00	5.00	3.00
39 Joe Rudi	1.00	.50	.30
40 Nolan Ryan	20.00	10.00	6.00
41 Mike Schmidt	8.00	4.00	2.50
42 Tom Seaver	5.00	2.50	1.50
43 Ted Simmons	1.00	.50	.30
44 Bill Singer	1.00	.50	.30
45 Willie Stargell	4.00	2.00	1.25
46 Rusty Staub	1.25	.60	.40
47 Don Sutton	3.00	1.50	.90
48 Luis Tiant	1.00	.50	.30
49 Bill Travers	1.00	.50	.30
50 Claudell Washington	1.00	.50	.30
51 Bob Watson	1.00	.50	.30
52 Dave Winfield	4.00	2.00	1.25
53 Carl Yastrzemski	7.00	3.50	2.00
54 Robin Yount	4.00	2.00	1.25
55 Richie Zisk	1.00	.50	.30
--- American League 9-Piece Puzzle	6.00	3.00	1.75
--- National League 9-Piece Puzzle	6.00	3.00	1.75

1978 Topps

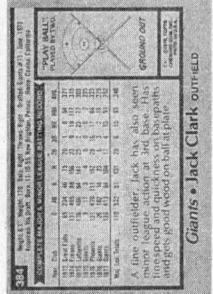

At 726 cards, this was the largest issue from Topps since 1972. In design, the color player photo is slightly larger than usual, with the player's name and team at the bottom. In the upper right-hand corner of the 2-1/2" x 3-1/2" cards, there is a small white baseball with the player's position. Most of the starting All-Stars from the previous year had a red, white and blue shield instead of the baseball. Backs feature statistics and a baseball situation which made a card game of baseball possible. Specialty cards include baseball records, statistical leaders and the World Series and playoffs. As one row of cards per sheet had to be double-printed to accommodate the 726-card set size, some cards are more common, yet that seems to have no serious impact on their prices.

	NM	EX	VG
Complete Set (726):	200.00	100.00	45.00
Common Player:	.20	.10	.06
Wax Pack (14):	15.00		
Wax Box (36):	480.00		
Cello Pack (21):	35.00		
Cello Box (24):	600.00		
Rack Pack (39):	45.00		
Rack Box (24):	925.00		
Vending Box (500):	210.00		
1 Lou Brock (Record Breaker)	1.00	.50	.30
2 Sparky Lyle (Record Breaker)	.20	.10	.06
3 Willie McCovey (Record Breaker)	.50	.25	.15
4 Brooks Robinson (Record Breaker)	2.00	1.00	.60
5 Pete Rose (Record Breaker)	4.50	2.25	1.25

6 Nolan Ryan (Record Breaker)	6.00	3.00	1.75
7 Reggie Jackson (Record Breaker)	4.00	2.00	1.25
8 Mike Sadek	.20	.10	.06
9 Doug DeCinces	.20	.10	.06
10 Phil Niekro	3.00	1.50	.90
11 Rick Manning	.20	.10	.06
12 Don Aase	.20	.10	.06
13 Art Howe	.20	.10	.06
14 Lerrin LaGrow	.20	.10	.06
15 Tony Perez	4.00	2.00	1.25
16 Roy White	.20	.10	.06
17 Mike Krukow	.20	.10	.06
18 Bob Grich	.20	.10	.06
19 Darrell Porter	.20	.10	.06
20 Pete Rose	6.00	3.00	1.75
21 Steve Kemp	.20	.10	.06
22 Charlie Hough	.20	.10	.06
23 Bump Wills	.20	.10	.06
24 Don Money	.20	.10	.06
25 Jon Matlack	.20	.10	.06
26 Rich Hebner	.20	.10	.06
27 Geoff Zahn	.20	.10	.06
28 Ed Ott	.20	.10	.06
29 Bob Lacey	.20	.10	.06
30 George Hendrick	.20	.10	.06
31 Glenn Abbott	.20	.10	.06
32 Garry Templeton	.20	.10	.06
33 Dave Lemanczyk	.20	.10	.06
34 Willie McCovey	4.00	2.00	1.25
35 Sparky Lyle	.20	.10	.06
36 *Eddie Murray*	17.50	8.75	5.25
37 Rick Waits	.20	.10	.06
38 Willie Montanez	.20	.10	.06
39 *Floyd Bannister*	.45	.25	.14
40 Carl Yastrzemski	5.00	2.50	1.50
41 Burt Hooton	.20	.10	.06
42 Jorge Orta	.20	.10	.06
43 Bill Atkinson	.20	.10	.06
44 Toby Harrah	.20	.10	.06
45 Mark Fidrych	.30	.15	.09
46 Al Cowens	.20	.10	.06
47 Jack Billingham	.20	.10	.06
48 Don Baylor	.25	.13	.08
49 Ed Kranepool	.20	.10	.06
50 Rick Reuschel	.20	.10	.06
51 Charlie Moore	.20	.10	.06
52 Jim Lonborg	.20	.10	.06
53 Phil Garner	.20	.10	.06
54 Tom Johnson	.20	.10	.06
55 Mitchell Page	.20	.10	.06
56 Randy Jones	.20	.10	.06
57 Dan Meyer	.20	.10	.06
58 Bob Forsch	.20	.10	.06
59 Otto Velez	.20	.10	.06
60 Thurman Munson	4.00	2.00	1.25
61 Larvell Blanks	.20	.10	.06
62 Jim Barr	.20	.10	.06
63 Don Zimmer	.20	.10	.06
64 Gene Pentz	.20	.10	.06
65 Ken Singleton	.20	.10	.06
66 White Sox Team	.30	.15	.09
67 Claudell Washington	.20	.10	.06
68 Steve Foucault	.20	.10	.06
69 Mike Vail	.20	.10	.06
70 Rich Gossage	.20	.10	.06
71 Terry Humphrey	.20	.10	.06
72 Andre Dawson	3.00	1.50	.90
73 Andy Hassler	.20	.10	.06
74 Checklist 1-121	.20	.10	.06
75 Dick Ruthven	.20	.10	.06
76 Steve Ontiveros	.20	.10	.06
77 Ed Kirkpatrick	.20	.10	.06
78 Pablo Torrealba	.20	.10	.06
79 Darrell Johnson/DP	.20	.10	.06
80 Ken Griffey	.20	.10	.06
81 Pete Redfern	.20	.10	.06
82 Giants Team	.30	.15	.09
83 Bob Montgomery	.20	.10	.06
84 Kent Tekulve	.20	.10	.06
85 Ron Fairly	.20	.10	.06
86 Dave Tomlin	.20	.10	.06
87 John Lowenstein	.20	.10	.06
88 Mike Phillips	.20	.10	.06
89 Ken Clay	.20	.10	.06
90 Larry Bowa	.20	.10	.06
91 Oscar Zamora	.20	.10	.06
92 Adrian Devine	.20	.10	.06
93 Bobby Cox	.40	.20	.12
94 Chuck Scrivener	.20	.10	.06
95 Jamie Quirk	.20	.10	.06
96 Orioles Team	.30	.15	.09
97 Stan Bahnsen	.20	.10	.06
98 Jim Essian	.20	.10	.06
99 *Willie Hernandez*	.30	.15	.09
100 George Brett	6.00	3.00	1.75
101 Sid Monge	.20	.10	.06
102 Matt Alexander	.20	.10	.06
103 Tom Murphy	.20	.10	.06
104 Lee Lacy	.20	.10	.06
105 Reggie Cleveland	.20	.10	.06
106 Bill Plummer	.20	.10	.06
107 Ed Halicki	.20	.10	.06
108 Von Joshua	.20	.10	.06
109 Joe Torre	.55	.30	.15
110 Richie Zisk	.20	.10	.06
111 Mike Tyson	.20	.10	.06
112 Astros Team	.30	.15	.09
113 Don Carrithers	.20	.10	.06
114 Paul Blair	.20	.10	.06
115 Gary Nolan	.20	.10	.06
116 Tucker Ashford	.20	.10	.06
117 John Montague	.20	.10	.06
118 Terry Harmon	.20	.10	.06
119 Denny Martinez	.20	.10	.06
120 Gary Carter	4.00	2.00	1.25
121 Alvis Woods	.20	.10	.06

122	Dennis Eckersley	4.00	2.00	1.25
123	Manny Trillo	.20	.10	.06
124	*Dave Rozema*	.20	.10	.06
125	George Scott	.20	.10	.06
126	Paul Moskau	.20	.10	.06
127	Chet Lemon	.20	.10	.06
128	Bill Russell	.20	.10	.06
129	Jim Colborn	.20	.10	.06
130	Jeff Burroughs	.20	.10	.06
131	Bert Blyleven	.20	.10	.06
132	Enos Cabell	.20	.10	.06
133	Jerry Augustine	.20	.10	.06
134	*Steve Henderson*	.20	.10	.06
135	Ron Guidry	.30	.15	.09
136	Ted Sizemore	.20	.10	.06
137	Craig Kusick	.20	.10	.06
138	Larry Demery	.20	.10	.06
139	Wayne Gross	.20	.10	.06
140	Rollie Fingers	3.00	1.50	.90
141	Ruppert Jones	.20	.10	.06
142	John Montefusco	.20	.10	.06
143	Keith Hernandez	.20	.10	.06
144	Jesse Jefferson	.20	.10	.06
145	Rick Monday	.20	.10	.06
146	Doyle Alexander	.20	.10	.06
147	Lee Mazzilli	.20	.10	.06
148	Andre Thornton	.20	.10	.06
149	Dale Murray	.20	.10	.06
150	Bobby Bonds	.20	.10	.06
151	Milt Wilcox	.20	.10	.06
152	*Ivan DeJesus*	.20	.10	.06
153	Steve Stone	.20	.10	.06
154	Cecil Cooper	.20	.10	.06
155	Butch Hobson	.20	.10	.06
156	Andy Messersmith	.20	.10	.06
157	Pete LaCock	.20	.10	.06
158	Joaquin Andujar	.20	.10	.06
159	Lou Piniella	.30	.15	.09
160	Jim Palmer	4.00	2.00	1.25
161	Bob Boone	.20	.10	.06
162	Paul Thormodsgard	.20	.10	.06
163	Bill North	.20	.10	.06
164	Bob Owchinko	.20	.10	.06
165	Rennie Stennett	.20	.10	.06
166	Carlos Lopez	.20	.10	.06
167	Tim Foli	.20	.10	.06
168	Reggie Smith	.20	.10	.06
169	Jerry Johnson	.20	.10	.06
170	Lou Brock	4.00	2.00	1.25
171	Pat Zachry	.20	.10	.06
172	Mike Hargrove	.20	.10	.06
173	Robin Yount	4.00	2.00	1.25
174	Wayne Garland	.20	.10	.06
175	Jerry Morales	.20	.10	.06
176	Milt May	.20	.10	.06
177	Gene Garber	.20	.10	.06
178	Dave Chalk	.20	.10	.06
179	Dick Tidrow	.20	.10	.06
180	Dave Concepcion	.20	.10	.06
181	Ken Forsch	.20	.10	.06
182	Jim Spencer	.20	.10	.06
183	Doug Bird	.20	.10	.06
184	Checklist 122-242	.20	.10	.06
185	Ellis Valentine	.20	.10	.06
186	*Bob Stanley*	.20	.10	.06
187	Jerry Royster	.20	.10	.06
188	Al Bumbry	.20	.10	.06
189	Tom Lasorda	.55	.30	.15
190	John Candelaria	.20	.10	.06
191	Rodney Scott	.20	.10	.06
192	Padres Team	.30	.15	.09
193	Rich Chiles	.20	.10	.06
194	Derrel Thomas	.20	.10	.06
195	Larry Dierker	.20	.10	.06
196	Bob Bailor	.20	.10	.06
197	Nino Espinosa	.20	.10	.06
198	Ron Pruitt	.20	.10	.06
199	Craig Reynolds	.20	.10	.06
200	Reggie Jackson	6.00	3.00	1.75
201	Batting Leaders (Rod Carew, Dave Parker)	.50	.25	.15
202	Home Run Leaders (George Foster, Jim Rice)	.25	.13	.08
203	RBI Leaders (George Foster, Larry Hisle)	.20	.10	.06
204	Stolen Base Leaders (Freddie Patek, Frank Taveras)	.20	.10	.06
205	Victory Leaders (Steve Carlton, Dave Goltz, Dennis Leonard, Jim Palmer)	.50	.25	.15
206	Strikeout Leaders (Phil Niekro, Nolan Ryan)	3.00	1.50	.90
207	ERA Leaders (John Candelaria, Frank Tanana)	.20	.10	.06
208	Leading Firemen (Bill Campbell, Rollie Fingers)	.25	.13	.08
209	Dock Ellis	.20	.10	.06
210	Jose Cardenal	.20	.10	.06
211	Earl Weaver/DP	.50	.25	.15
212	Mike Caldwell	.20	.10	.06
213	Alan Bannister	.20	.10	.06
214	Angels Team	.30	.15	.09
215	Darrell Evans	.25	.13	.08
216	Mike Paxton	.20	.10	.06
217	Rod Gilbreath	.20	.10	.06
218	Marty Pattin	.20	.10	.06
219	Mike Cubbage	.20	.10	.06
220	Pedro Borbon	.20	.10	.06
221	Chris Speier	.20	.10	.06
222	Jerry Martin	.20	.10	.06
223	Bruce Kison	.20	.10	.06
224	Jerry Tabb	.20	.10	.06
225	Don Gullett	.20	.10	.06
226	Joe Ferguson	.20	.10	.06
227	Al Fitzmorris	.20	.10	.06
228	Manny Mota	.20	.10	.06
229	Leo Foster	.20	.10	.06
230	Al Hrabosky	.20	.10	.06
231	Wayne Nordhagen	.20	.10	.06
232	Mickey Stanley	.20	.10	.06
233	Dick Pole	.20	.10	.06
234	Herman Franks	.20	.10	.06
235	Tim McCarver	.30	.15	.09
236	Terry Whitfield	.20	.10	.06
237	Rich Dauer	.20	.10	.06
238	Juan Beniquez	.20	.10	.06
239	Dyar Miller	.20	.10	.06
240	Gene Tenace	.20	.10	.06
241	Pete Vuckovich	.20	.10	.06
242	Barry Bonnell	.20	.10	.06
243	Bob McClure	.20	.10	.06
244	Expos Team	.30	.15	.09
245	Rick Burleson	.20	.10	.06
246	Dan Driessen	.20	.10	.06
247	Larry Christenson	.20	.10	.06
248	Frank White	.20	.10	.06
249	Dave Goltz	.20	.10	.06
250	Graig Nettles	.25	.13	.08
251	Don Kirkwood	.20	.10	.06
252	Steve Swisher	.20	.10	.06
253	Jim Kern	.20	.10	.06
254	Dave Collins	.20	.10	.06
255	Jerry Reuss	.20	.10	.06
256	Joe Altobelli	.20	.10	.06
257	Hector Cruz	.20	.10	.06
258	John Hiller	.20	.10	.06
259	Dodgers Team	.50	.25	.15
260	Bert Campaneris	.20	.10	.06
261	Tim Hosley	.20	.10	.06
262	Rudy May	.20	.10	.06
263	Danny Walton	.20	.10	.06
264	Jamie Easterly	.20	.10	.06
265	Sal Bando	.20	.10	.06
266	*Bob Shirley*	.20	.10	.06
267	Doug Ault	.20	.10	.06
268	Gil Flores	.20	.10	.06
269	Wayne Twitchell	.20	.10	.06
270	Carlton Fisk	4.00	2.00	1.25
271	Randy Lerch	.20	.10	.06
272	Royle Stillman	.20	.10	.06
273	Fred Norman	.20	.10	.06
274	Freddie Patek	.20	.10	.06
275	Dan Ford	.20	.10	.06
276	Bill Bonham	.20	.10	.06
277	Bruce Boisclair	.20	.10	.06
278	Enrique Romo	.20	.10	.06
279	Bill Virdon	.20	.10	.06
280	Buddy Bell	.20	.10	.06
281	Eric Rasmussen	.20	.10	.06
282	Yankees Team	1.00	.50	.30
283	Omar Moreno	.20	.10	.06
284	Randy Moffitt	.20	.10	.06
285	Steve Yeager	.20	.10	.06
286	Ben Oglivie	.20	.10	.06
287	Kiko Garcia	.20	.10	.06
288	Dave Hamilton	.20	.10	.06
289	Checklist 243-363	.20	.10	.06
290	Willie Horton	.20	.10	.06
291	Gary Ross	.20	.10	.06
292	Gene Richard	.20	.10	.06
293	Mike Willis	.20	.10	.06
294	Larry Parrish	.20	.10	.06
295	Bill Lee	.20	.10	.06
296	Biff Pocoroba	.20	.10	.06
297	Warren Brusstar	.20	.10	.06
298	Tony Armas	.20	.10	.06
299	Whitey Herzog	.20	.10	.06
300	Joe Morgan	4.00	2.00	1.25
301	Buddy Schultz	.20	.10	.06
302	Cubs Team	.30	.15	.09
303	Sam Hinds	.20	.10	.06
304	John Milner	.20	.10	.06
305	Rico Carty	.20	.10	.06
306	Joe Niekro	.20	.10	.06
307	Glenn Borgmann	.20	.10	.06
308	Jim Rooker	.20	.10	.06
309	Cliff Johnson	.20	.10	.06
310	Don Sutton	3.00	1.50	.90
311	Jose Baez	.20	.10	.06
312	Greg Minton	.20	.10	.06
313	Andy Etchebarren	.20	.10	.06
314	Paul Lindblad	.20	.10	.06
315	Mark Belanger	.20	.10	.06
316	Henry Cruz	.20	.10	.06
317	Dave Johnson	.20	.10	.06
318	Tom Griffin	.20	.10	.06
319	Alan Ashby	.20	.10	.06
320	Fred Lynn	.20	.10	.06
321	Santo Alcala	.20	.10	.06
322	Tom Paciorek	.20	.10	.06
323	Jim Fregosi (DP)	.20	.10	.06
324	Vern Rapp	.20	.10	.06
325	Bruce Sutter	3.00	1.50	.90
326	Mike Lum	.20	.10	.06
327	Rick Langford	.20	.10	.06
328	Brewers Team	.30	.15	.09
329	John Verhoeven	.20	.10	.06
330	Bob Watson	.20	.10	.06
331	Mark Littell	.20	.10	.06
332	Duane Kuiper	.20	.10	.06
333	Jim Todd	.20	.10	.06
334	John Stearns	.20	.10	.06
335	Bucky Dent	.20	.10	.06
336	Steve Busby	.20	.10	.06
337	Tom Grieve	.20	.10	.06
338	Dave Heaverlo	.20	.10	.06
339	Mario Guerrero	.20	.10	.06
340	Bake McBride	.20	.10	.06
341	Mike Flanagan	.20	.10	.06
342	Aurelio Rodriguez	.20	.10	.06
343	John Wathan (DP)	.20	.10	.06
344	Sam Ewing	.20	.10	.06
345	Luis Tiant	.20	.10	.06
346	Larry Biittner	.20	.10	.06
347	Terry Forster	.20	.10	.06
348	Del Unser	.20	.10	.06
349	Rick Camp (DP)	.20	.10	.06
350	Steve Garvey	2.00	1.00	.60
351	Jeff Torborg	.20	.10	.06
352	Tony Scott	.20	.10	.06
353	Doug Bair	.20	.10	.06
354	Cesar Geronimo	.20	.10	.06
355	Bill Travers	.20	.10	.06
356	Mets Team	.60	.30	.20
357	Tom Poquette	.20	.10	.06
358	Mark Lemongello	.20	.10	.06
359	Marc Hill	.20	.10	.06
360	Mike Schmidt	6.00	3.00	1.75
361	Chris Knapp	.20	.10	.06
362	Dave May	.20	.10	.06
363	Bob Randall	.20	.10	.06
364	Jerry Turner	.20	.10	.06
365	Ed Figueroa	.20	.10	.06
366	Larry Milbourne (DP)	.20	.10	.06
367	Rick Dempsey	.20	.10	.06
368	Balor Moore	.20	.10	.06
369	Tim Nordbrook	.20	.10	.06
370	Rusty Staub	.25	.13	.08
371	Ray Burris	.20	.10	.06
372	Brian Asselstine	.20	.10	.06
373	Jim Willoughby	.20	.10	.06
374a	Jose Morales (Red stitching on position ball.)	.20	.10	.06
374b	Jose Morales (Black overprint on red stitching.)	.20	.10	.06
375	Tommy John	.30	.15	.09
376	Jim Wohlford	.20	.10	.06
377	Manny Sarmiento	.20	.10	.06
378	Bobby Winkles	.20	.10	.06
379	Skip Lockwood	.20	.10	.06
380	Ted Simmons	.20	.10	.06
381	Phillies Team	.35	.20	.11
382	Joe Lahoud	.20	.10	.06
383	Mario Mendoza	.20	.10	.06
384	Jack Clark	.30	.15	.09
385	Tito Fuentes	.20	.10	.06
386	Bob Gorinski	.20	.10	.06
387	Ken Holtzman	.20	.10	.06
388	Bill Fahey (DP)	.20	.10	.06
389	Julio Gonzalez	.20	.10	.06
390	Oscar Gamble	.20	.10	.06
391	Larry Haney	.20	.10	.06
392	Billy Almon	.20	.10	.06
393	Tippy Martinez	.20	.10	.06
394	Roy Howell	.20	.10	.06
395	Jim Hughes	.20	.10	.06
396	Bob Stinson	.20	.10	.06
397	Greg Gross	.20	.10	.06
398	Don Hood	.20	.10	.06
399	Pete Mackanin	.20	.10	.06
400	Nolan Ryan	9.00	4.50	2.75
401	Sparky Anderson	.55	.30	.15
402	Dave Campbell	.20	.10	.06
403	Bud Harrelson	.20	.10	.06
404	Tigers Team	.30	.15	.09
405	Rawly Eastwick	.20	.10	.06
406	Mike Jorgensen	.20	.10	.06
407	Odell Jones	.20	.10	.06
408	Joe Zdeb	.20	.10	.06
409	Ron Schueler	.20	.10	.06
410	Bill Madlock	.20	.10	.06
411	A.L. Championships (Yankees Rally To Defeat Royals.)	.50	.25	.15
412	N.L. Championships (Dodgers Overpower Phillies In Four.)	.50	.25	.15
413	World Series (Reggie & Yankees Reign Supreme)	2.00	1.00	.60
414	Darold Knowles/DP	.20	.10	.06
415	Ray Fosse	.20	.10	.06
416	Jack Brohamer	.20	.10	.06
417	Mike Garman	.20	.10	.06
418	Tony Muser	.20	.10	.06
419	Jerry Garvin	.20	.10	.06
420	Greg Luzinski	.20	.10	.06
421	Junior Moore	.20	.10	.06
422	Steve Braun	.20	.10	.06
423	Dave Rosello	.20	.10	.06
424	Red Sox Team	.45	.25	.14
425	Steve Rogers	.20	.10	.06
426	Fred Kendall	.20	.10	.06
427	*Mario Soto*	.35	.20	.11
428	Joel Youngblood	.20	.10	.06
429	Mike Barlow	.20	.10	.06
430	Al Oliver	.30	.15	.09
431	Butch Metzger	.20	.10	.06
432	Terry Bulling	.20	.10	.06
433	Fernando Gonzalez	.20	.10	.06
434	Mike Norris	.20	.10	.06
435	Checklist 364-484	.20	.10	.06
436	Vic Harris (DP)	.20	.10	.06
437	Bo McLaughlin	.20	.10	.06
438	John Ellis	.20	.10	.06
439	Ken Kravec	.20	.10	.06
440	Dave Lopes	.20	.10	.06
441	Larry Gura	.20	.10	.06
442	Elliott Maddox	.20	.10	.06
443	Darrel Chaney	.20	.10	.06
444	Roy Hartsfield	.20	.10	.06
445	Mike Ivie	.20	.10	.06
446	Tug McGraw	.20	.10	.06
447	Leroy Stanton	.20	.10	.06
448	Bill Castro	.20	.10	.06
449	Tim Blackwell	.20	.10	.06
450	Tom Seaver	5.00	2.50	1.50
451	Twins Team	.30	.15	.09
452	Jerry Mumphrey	.20	.10	.06
453	Doug Flynn	.20	.10	.06
454	Dave LaRoche	.20	.10	.06
455	Bill Robinson	.20	.10	.06
456	Vern Ruhle	.20	.10	.06
457	Bob Bailey	.20	.10	.06

No.	Player	NM	EX	VG
458	Jeff Newman	.20	.10	.06
459	Charlie Spikes	.20	.10	.06
460	Jim Hunter	3.00	1.50	.90
461	Rob Andrews	.20	.10	.06
462	Rogelio Moret	.20	.10	.06
463	Kevin Bell	.20	.10	.06
464	Jerry Grote	.20	.10	.06
465	Hal McRae	.20	.10	.06
466	Dennis Blair	.20	.10	.06
467	Alvin Dark	.20	.10	.06
468	*Warren Cromartie*	.20	.10	.06
469	Rick Cerone	.20	.10	.06
470	J.R. Richard	.20	.10	.06
471	Roy Smalley	.20	.10	.06
472	Ron Reed	.20	.10	.06
473	Bill Buckner	.20	.10	.06
474	Jim Slaton	.20	.10	.06
475	Gary Matthews	.20	.10	.06
476	Bill Stein	.20	.10	.06
477	Doug Capilla	.20	.10	.06
478	Jerry Remy	.20	.10	.06
479	Cardinals Team	.30	.15	.09
480	Ron LeFlore	.20	.10	.06
481	Jackson Todd	.20	.10	.06
482	Rick Miller	.20	.10	.06
483	Ken Macha	.20	.10	.06
484	Jim Norris	.20	.10	.06
485	Chris Chambliss	.20	.10	.06
486	John Curtis	.20	.10	.06
487	Jim Tyrone	.20	.10	.06
488	Dan Spillner	.20	.10	.06
489	Rudy Meoli	.20	.10	.06
490	Amos Otis	.20	.10	.06
491	Scott McGregor	.20	.10	.06
492	Jim Sundberg	.20	.10	.06
493	Steve Renko	.20	.10	.06
494	Chuck Tanner	.20	.10	.06
495	Dave Cash	.20	.10	.06
496	*Jim Clancy*	.20	.10	.06
497	Glenn Adams	.20	.10	.06
498	Joe Sambito	.20	.10	.06
499	Mariners Team	.30	.15	.09
500	George Foster	.20	.10	.06
501	Dave Roberts	.20	.10	.06
502	Pat Rockett	.20	.10	.06
503	Ike Hampton	.20	.10	.06
504	Roger Freed	.20	.10	.06
505	Felix Millan	.20	.10	.06
506	Ron Blomberg	.20	.10	.06
507	Willie Crawford	.20	.10	.06
508	Johnny Oates	.20	.10	.06
509	Brent Strom	.20	.10	.06
510	Willie Stargell	4.00	2.00	1.25
511	Frank Duffy	.20	.10	.06
512	Larry Herndon	.20	.10	.06
513	Barry Foote	.20	.10	.06
514	Rob Sperring	.20	.10	.06
515	Tim Corcoran	.20	.10	.06
516	Gary Beare	.20	.10	.06
517	Andres Mora	.20	.10	.06
518	Tommy Boggs/DP	.20	.10	.06
519	Brian Downing	.20	.10	.06
520	Larry Hisle	.20	.10	.06
521	Steve Staggs	.20	.10	.06
522	Dick Williams	.20	.10	.06
523	*Donnie Moore*	.20	.10	.06
524	Bernie Carbo	.20	.10	.06
525	Jerry Terrell	.20	.10	.06
526	Reds Team	.45	.25	.14
527	Vic Correll	.20	.10	.06
528	Rob Picciolo	.20	.10	.06
529	Paul Hartzell	.20	.10	.06
530	Dave Winfield	4.00	2.00	1.25
531	Tom Underwood	.20	.10	.06
532	Skip Jutze	.20	.10	.06
533	Sandy Alomar	.20	.10	.06
534	Wilbur Howard	.20	.10	.06
535	Checklist 485-605	.20	.10	.06
536	Roric Harrison	.20	.10	.06
537	Bruce Bochte	.20	.10	.06
538	Johnnie LeMaster	.20	.10	.06
539	Vic Davalillo	.20	.10	.06
540	Steve Carlton	4.00	2.00	1.25
541	Larry Cox	.20	.10	.06
542	Tim Johnson	.20	.10	.06
543	Larry Harlow	.20	.10	.06
544	Len Randle	.20	.10	.06
545	Bill Campbell	.20	.10	.06
546	Ted Martinez	.20	.10	.06
547	John Scott	.20	.10	.06
548	Billy Hunter (DP)	.20	.10	.06
549	Joe Kerrigan	.20	.10	.06
550	John Mayberry	.20	.10	.06
551	Braves Team	.30	.15	.09
552	Francisco Barrios	.20	.10	.06
553	*Terry Puhl*	.25	.13	.08
554	Joe Coleman	.20	.10	.06
555	Butch Wynegar	.20	.10	.06
556	Ed Armbrister	.20	.10	.06
557	Tony Solaita	.20	.10	.06
558	Paul Mitchell	.20	.10	.06
559	Phil Mankowski	.20	.10	.06
560	Dave Parker	.20	.10	.06
561	Charlie Williams	.20	.10	.06
562	Glenn Burke	.20	.10	.06
563	Dave Rader	.20	.10	.06
564	Mick Kelleher	.20	.10	.06
565	Jerry Koosman	.20	.10	.06
566	Merv Rettenmund	.20	.10	.06
567	Dick Drago	.20	.10	.06
568	Tom Hutton	.20	.10	.06
569	*Lary Sorensen*	.20	.10	.06
570	Dave Kingman	.20	.10	.06
571	Buck Martinez	.20	.10	.06
572	Rick Wise	.20	.10	.06
573	Luis Gomez	.20	.10	.06
574	Bob Lemon	.50	.25	.15
575	Pat Dobson	.20	.10	.06
576	Sam Mejias	.20	.10	.06
577	A's Team	.30	.15	.09
578	Buzz Capra	.20	.10	.06
579	*Rance Mulliniks*	.25	.13	.08
580	Rod Carew	4.00	2.00	1.25
581	Lynn McGlothen	.20	.10	.06
582	Fran Healy	.20	.10	.06
583	George Medich	.20	.10	.06
584	John Hale	.20	.10	.06
585	Woodie Fryman	.20	.10	.06
586	Ed Goodson	.20	.10	.06
587	John Urrea	.20	.10	.06
588	Jim Mason	.20	.10	.06
589	*Bob Knepper*	.20	.10	.06
590	Bobby Murcer	.20	.10	.06
591	George Zeber	.20	.10	.06
592	Bob Apodaca	.20	.10	.06
593	Dave Skaggs	.20	.10	.06
594	Dave Freisleben	.20	.10	.06
595	Sixto Lezcano	.20	.10	.06
596	Gary Wheelock	.20	.10	.06
597	Steve Dillard	.20	.10	.06
598	Eddie Solomon	.20	.10	.06
599	Gary Woods	.20	.10	.06
600	Frank Tanana	.20	.10	.06
601	Gene Mauch	.20	.10	.06
602	Eric Soderholm	.20	.10	.06
603	Will McEnaney	.20	.10	.06
604	Earl Williams	.20	.10	.06
605	Rick Rhoden	.20	.10	.06
606	Pirates Team	.30	.15	.09
607	Fernando Arroyo	.20	.10	.06
608	Johnny Grubb	.20	.10	.06
609	John Denny	.20	.10	.06
610	Garry Maddox	.20	.10	.06
611	Pat Scanlon	.20	.10	.06
612	Ken Henderson	.20	.10	.06
613	Marty Perez	.20	.10	.06
614	Joe Wallis	.20	.10	.06
615	Clay Carroll	.20	.10	.06
616	Pat Kelly	.20	.10	.06
617	Joe Nolan	.20	.10	.06
618	Tommy Helms	.20	.10	.06
619	*Thad Bosley*	.20	.10	.06
620	Willie Randolph	.20	.10	.06
621	Craig Swan	.20	.10	.06
622	Champ Summers	.20	.10	.06
623	Eduardo Rodriguez	.20	.10	.06
624	Gary Alexander	.20	.10	.06
625	Jose Cruz	.20	.10	.06
626	Blue Jays Team	.30	.15	.09
627	Dave Johnson	.20	.10	.06
628	Ralph Garr	.20	.10	.06
629	Don Stanhouse	.20	.10	.06
630	Ron Cey	.20	.10	.06
631	Danny Ozark	.20	.10	.06
632	Rowland Office	.20	.10	.06
633	Tom Veryzer	.20	.10	.06
634	Len Barker	.20	.10	.06
635	Joe Rudi	.20	.10	.06
636	Jim Bibby	.20	.10	.06
637	Duffy Dyer	.20	.10	.06
638	Paul Splittorff	.20	.10	.06
639	Gene Clines	.20	.10	.06
640	Lee May	.20	.10	.06
641	Doug Rau	.20	.10	.06
642	Denny Doyle	.20	.10	.06
643	Tom House	.20	.10	.06
644	Jim Dwyer	.20	.10	.06
645	Mike Torrez	.20	.10	.06
646	Rick Auerbach	.20	.10	.06
647	Steve Dunning	.20	.10	.06
648	Gary Thomasson	.20	.10	.06
649	*Moose Haas*	.20	.10	.06
650	Cesar Cedeno	.20	.10	.06
651	Doug Rader	.20	.10	.06
652	Checklist 606-726	.20	.10	.06
653	Ron Hodges	.20	.10	.06
654	Pepe Frias	.20	.10	.06
655	Lyman Bostock	.20	.10	.06
656	Dave Garcia	.20	.10	.06
657	Bombo Rivera	.20	.10	.06
658	Manny Sanguillen	.20	.10	.06
659	Rangers Team	.30	.15	.09
660	Jason Thompson	.20	.10	.06
661	Grant Jackson	.20	.10	.06
662	Paul Dade	.20	.10	.06
663	Paul Reuschel	.20	.10	.06
664	Fred Stanley	.20	.10	.06
665	Dennis Leonard	.20	.10	.06
666	Billy Smith	.20	.10	.06
667	Jeff Byrd	.20	.10	.06
668	Dusty Baker	.35	.20	.11
669	Pete Falcone	.20	.10	.06
670	Jim Rice	.75	.40	.25
671	Gary Lavelle	.20	.10	.06
672	Don Kessinger	.20	.10	.06
673	Steve Brye	.20	.10	.06
674	*Ray Knight*	1.00	.50	.30
675	Jay Johnstone	.20	.10	.06
676	Bob Myrick	.20	.10	.06
677	Ed Herrmann	.20	.10	.06
678	Tom Burgmeier	.20	.10	.06
679	Wayne Garrett	.20	.10	.06
680	Vida Blue	.20	.10	.06
681	Rob Belloir	.20	.10	.06
682	Ken Brett	.20	.10	.06
683	Mike Champion	.20	.10	.06
684	Ralph Houk	.20	.10	.06
685	Frank Taveras	.20	.10	.06
686	Gaylord Perry	3.00	1.50	.90
687	*Julio Cruz*	.25	.13	.08
688	George Mitterwald	.20	.10	.06
689	Indians Team	.30	.15	.09
690	Mickey Rivers	.20	.10	.06
691	Ross Grimsley	.20	.10	.06
692	Ken Reitz	.20	.10	.06
693	Lamar Johnson	.20	.10	.06
694	Elias Sosa	.20	.10	.06
695	Dwight Evans	.20	.10	.06
696	Steve Mingori	.20	.10	.06
697	Roger Metzger	.20	.10	.06
698	Juan Bernhardt	.20	.10	.06
699	Jackie Brown	.20	.10	.06
700	Johnny Bench	5.00	2.50	1.50
701	Rookie Pitchers (Tom Hume, Larry Landreth, Steve McCatty, Bruce Taylor)	.20	.10	.06
702	Rookie Catchers (Bill Nahorodny, Kevin Pasley, Rick Sweet, Don Werner)	.20	.10	.06
703	Rookie Pitchers (*Larry Andersen, Tim Jones, Mickey Mahler, Jack Morris*)	3.50	1.75	1.00
704	Rookie 2nd Basemen (*Garth Iorg, Dave Oliver, Sam Perlozzo, Lou Whitaker*)	4.50	2.25	1.25
705	Rookie Outfielders (Dave Bergman, Miguel Dilone, Clint Hurdle, Willie Norwood)	.20	.10	.06
706	Rookie 1st Basemen (*Wayne Cage, Ted Cox, Pat Putnam, Dave Revering*)	.20	.10	.06
707	Rookie Shortstops (*Mickey Klutts, Paul Molitor, Alan Trammell, U.L. Washington*)	17.50	8.75	5.25
708	Rookie Catchers (*Bo Diaz, Dale Murphy, Lance Parrish, Ernie Whitt*)	6.00	3.00	1.75
709	Rookie Pitchers (*Steve Burke, Matt Keough, Lance Rautzhan, Dan Schatzeder*)	.20	.10	.06
710	Rookie Outfielders (Dell Alston, Rick Bosetti, Mike Easler, Keith Smith)	.20	.10	.06
711	Rookie Pitchers (Cardell Camper, Dennis Lamp, Craig Mitchell, Roy Thomas)	.20	.10	.06
712	Bobby Valentine	.20	.10	.06
713	Bob Davis	.20	.10	.06
714	Mike Anderson	.20	.10	.06
715	Jim Kaat	.20	.10	.06
716	Clarence Gaston	.20	.10	.06
717	Nelson Briles	.20	.10	.06
718	Ron Jackson	.20	.10	.06
719	Randy Elliott	.20	.10	.06
720	Fergie Jenkins	3.00	1.50	.90
721	Billy Martin	.50	.25	.15
722	Pete Broberg	.20	.10	.06
723	Johnny Wockenfuss	.20	.10	.06
724	Royals Team	.30	.15	.09
725	Kurt Bevacqua	.20	.10	.06
726	Wilbur Wood	.20	.10	.06

1978 Topps Team Checklist Sheet

A redemption offer on packs of 1978 Topps cards offered an uncut sheet of the 26 team/checklist cards by mail. Besides the team cards, the 10-1/2" x 22-1/2" sheet has a card offering collectors card boxes. The cards on the sheet are identical to the single team/checklist cards issued in packs.

	NM	EX	VG
Uncut Sheet	25.00	12.50	7.50

1978 Topps/Dynamite Magazine Panels

In issue No. 47 of its "Dynamite" kids' magazine, Scholastic Book Club teamed with Topps to insert a six-card panel of its 1978 baseball issue. Three such panels have been found thus far, one of which includes an Eddie Murray rookie card. Values shown are for just the uncut panel; complete magazines would bear a small premium.

		NM	EX	VG
Complete Panel Set (3):		60.00	30.00	18.00
PANEL 1		40.00	20.00	12.00
36	Eddie Murray			
125	George Scott			
141	Ruppert Jones			
150	Bobby Bonds			
490	Amos Otis			
550	John Mayberry			
PANEL 2		10.00	5.00	3.00
21	Steve Kemp			
168	Reggie Smith			
200	Reggie Jackson			
245	Rick Burleson			
332	Duane Kuiper			
440	Davey Lopes			
PANEL 3		15.00	7.50	4.50
44	Toby Harrah			
120	Gary Carter			
130	Jeff Burroughs			
320	Fred Lynn			
335	Bucky Dent			
670	Jim Rice			

1978 Topps/Zest Soap

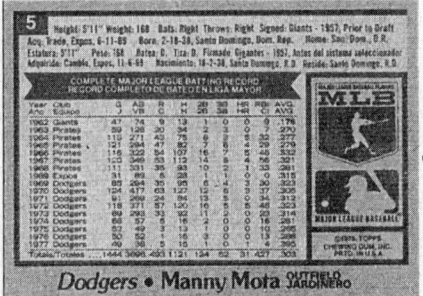

Produced by Topps for a Zest Soap promotion, the five cards in this set are almost identical to the regular issue, except the backs are printed in both Spanish and English, the game feature on back has been replaced by MLB and MLBPA logos and the card numbers are different. The cards measure 2-1/2" x 3-1/2". Because of the player selection and the bilingual back, it seems obvious that this set was aimed at the Hispanic community. Cards were issued as complete sets in a cello package.

		NM	EX	VG
Complete Set (5):				
Common Player:				
1	Joaquin Andujar	2.00	1.00	.60
2	Bert Campaneris	4.50	2.25	1.25
3	Ed Figueroa	1.50	.70	.45
4	Willie Montanez	1.50	.70	.45
5	Manny Mota	4.50	2.25	1.25

1979 Topps

 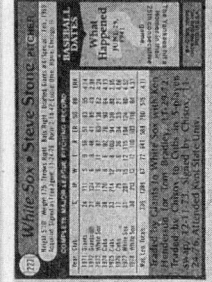

The size of this issue remained the same as in 1978 with 726 cards making their appearance. Actually, the 2-1/2" x 3-1/2" cards have a relatively minor design change from the previous year. The large color photo still dominates the front, with the player's name, team and position below it. The baseball with the player's position was moved to the lower left and the position replaced by a Topps logo. On the back, the printing color was changed and the game situation was replaced by a quiz called "Baseball Dates". Specialty cards include statistical leaders, major league records set during the season and eight cards devoted to career records. For the first time, rookies were arranged by teams under the heading of "Prospects." The key Ozzie Smith rookie card is usually seen with very poor centering.

		NM	EX	VG
Complete Set (726):		115.00	55.00	35.00
Common Player:		.15	.08	.05
Wax Pack (12):		12.00		

Wax Box (36):		295.00		
Cello Pack (18):		20.00		
Cello Box (24):		335.00		
Super Cello Pack (28):				
Super Cello Box (24):				
Rack Pack (39):		25.00		
Rack Box (24):		575.00		
Vending Box (500):		155.00		
1	Batting Leaders (Rod Carew, Dave Parker)	1.00	.50	.30
2	Home Run Leaders (George Foster, Jim Rice)	.15	.08	.05
3	RBI Leaders (George Foster, Jim Rice)	.15	.08	.05
4	Stolen Base Leaders (Ron LeFlore, Omar Moreno)	.15	.08	.05
5	Victory Leaders (Ron Guidry, Gaylord Perry)	.15	.08	.05
6	Strikeout Leaders (J.R. Richard, Nolan Ryan)	4.00	2.00	1.25
7	ERA Leaders (Ron Guidry, Craig Swan)	.15	.08	.05
8	Leading Firemen (Rollie Fingers, Rich Gossage)	.20	.10	.06
9	Dave Campbell	.15	.08	.05
10	Lee May	.15	.08	.05
11	Marc Hill	.15	.08	.05
12	Dick Drago	.15	.08	.05
13	Paul Dade	.15	.08	.05
14	Rafael Landestoy	.15	.08	.05
15	Ross Grimsley	.15	.08	.05
16	Fred Stanley	.15	.08	.05
17	Donnie Moore	.15	.08	.05
18	Tony Solaita	.15	.08	.05
19	Larry Gura	.15	.08	.05
20	Joe Morgan	3.00	1.50	.90
21	Kevin Kobel	.15	.08	.05
22	Mike Jorgensen	.15	.08	.05
23	Terry Forster	.15	.08	.05
24	Paul Molitor	6.00	3.00	1.75
25	Steve Carlton	3.00	1.50	.90
26	Jamie Quirk	.15	.08	.05
27	Dave Goltz	.15	.08	.05
28	Steve Brye	.15	.08	.05
29	Rick Langford	.15	.08	.05
30	Dave Winfield	3.00	1.50	.90
31	Tom House	.15	.08	.05
32	Jerry Mumphrey	.15	.08	.05
33	Dave Rozema	.15	.08	.05
34	Rob Andrews	.15	.08	.05
35	Ed Figueroa	.15	.08	.05
36	Alan Ashby	.15	.08	.05
37	Joe Kerrigan	.15	.08	.05
38	Bernie Carbo	.15	.08	.05
39	Dale Murphy	2.00	1.00	.60
40	Dennis Eckersley	2.50	1.25	.70
41	Twins Team (Gene Mauch)	.25	.13	.08
42	Ron Blomberg	.15	.08	.05
43	Wayne Twitchell	.15	.08	.05
44	Kurt Bevacqua	.15	.08	.05
45	Al Hrabosky	.15	.08	.05
46	Ron Hodges	.15	.08	.05
47	Fred Norman	.15	.08	.05
48	Merv Rettenmund	.15	.08	.05
49	Vern Ruhle	.15	.08	.05
50	Steve Garvey	1.50	.70	.45
51	Ray Fosse	.15	.08	.05
52	Randy Lerch	.15	.08	.05
53	Mick Kelleher	.15	.08	.05
54	Dell Alston	.15	.08	.05
55	Willie Stargell	3.00	1.50	.90
56	John Hale	.15	.08	.05
57	Eric Rasmussen	.15	.08	.05
58	Bob Randall	.15	.08	.05
59	John Denny	.15	.08	.05
60	Mickey Rivers	.15	.08	.05
61	Bo Diaz	.15	.08	.05
62	Randy Moffitt	.15	.08	.05
63	Jack Brohamer	.15	.08	.05
64	Tom Underwood	.15	.08	.05
65	Mark Belanger	.15	.08	.05
66	Tigers Team (Les Moss)	.25	.13	.08
67	Jim Mason	.15	.08	.05
68	Joe Niekro	.15	.08	.05
69	Elliott Maddox	.15	.08	.05
70	John Candelaria	.15	.08	.05
71	Brian Downing	.15	.08	.05
72	Steve Mingori	.15	.08	.05
73	Ken Henderson	.15	.08	.05
74	**Shane Rawley**	.15	.08	.05
75	Steve Yeager	.15	.08	.05
76	Warren Cromartie	.15	.08	.05
77	Dan Briggs	.15	.08	.05
78	Elias Sosa	.15	.08	.05
79	Ted Cox	.15	.08	.05
80	Jason Thompson	.15	.08	.05
81	Roger Erickson	.15	.08	.05
82	Mets Team (Joe Torre)	.75	.40	.25
83	Fred Kendall	.15	.08	.05
84	Greg Minton	.15	.08	.05
85	Gary Matthews	.15	.08	.05
86	Rodney Scott	.15	.08	.05
87	Pete Falcone	.15	.08	.05
88	Bob Molinaro	.15	.08	.05
89	Dick Tidrow	.15	.08	.05
90	Bob Boone	.15	.08	.05
91	Terry Crowley	.15	.08	.05
92	Jim Bibby	.15	.08	.05
93	Phil Mankowski	.15	.08	.05
94	Len Barker	.15	.08	.05
95	Robin Yount	3.00	1.50	.90
96	Indians Team (Jeff Torborg)	.25	.13	.08
97	Sam Mejias	.15	.08	.05
98	Ray Burris	.15	.08	.05
99	John Wathan	.15	.08	.05
100	Tom Seaver	3.50	1.75	1.00
101	Roy Howell	.15	.08	.05
102	Mike Anderson	.15	.08	.05

103	Jim Todd	.15	.08	.05
104	Johnny Oates	.15	.08	.05
105	Rick Camp	.15	.08	.05
106	Frank Duffy	.15	.08	.05
107	Jesus Alou	.15	.08	.05
108	Eduardo Rodriguez	.15	.08	.05
109	Joel Youngblood	.15	.08	.05
110	Vida Blue	.15	.08	.05
111	Roger Freed	.15	.08	.05
112	Phillies Team (Danny Ozark)	.25	.13	.08
113	Pete Redfern	.15	.08	.05
114	Cliff Johnson	.15	.08	.05
115	Nolan Ryan	6.00	3.00	1.75
116	*Ozzie Smith*	20.00	10.00	6.00
117	Grant Jackson	.15	.08	.05
118	Bud Harrelson	.15	.08	.05
119	Don Stanhouse	.15	.08	.05
120	Jim Sundberg	.15	.08	.05
121	Checklist 1-121	.15	.08	.05
122	Mike Paxton	.15	.08	.05
123	Lou Whitaker	1.00	.50	.30
124	Dan Schatzeder	.15	.08	.05
125	Rick Burleson	.15	.08	.05
126	Doug Bair	.15	.08	.05
127	Thad Bosley	.15	.08	.05
128	Ted Martinez	.15	.08	.05
129	Marty Pattin	.15	.08	.05
130	Bob Watson	.15	.08	.05
131	Jim Clancy	.15	.08	.05
132	Rowland Office	.15	.08	.05
133	Bill Castro	.15	.08	.05
134	Alan Bannister	.15	.08	.05
135	Bobby Murcer	.15	.08	.05
136	Jim Kaat	.15	.08	.05
137	Larry Wolfe	.15	.08	.05
138	Mark Lee	.15	.08	.05
139	Luis Pujols	.15	.08	.05
140	Don Gullett	.15	.08	.05
141	Tom Paciorek	.15	.08	.05
142	Charlie Williams	.15	.08	.05
143	Tony Scott	.15	.08	.05
144	Sandy Alomar	.15	.08	.05
145	Rick Rhoden	.15	.08	.05
146	Duane Kuiper	.15	.08	.05
147	Dave Hamilton	.15	.08	.05
148	Bruce Boisclair	.15	.08	.05
149	Manny Sarmiento	.15	.08	.05
150	Wayne Cage	.15	.08	.05
151	John Hiller	.15	.08	.05
152	Rick Cerone	.15	.08	.05
153	Dennis Lamp	.15	.08	.05
154	Jim Gantner	.15	.08	.05
155	Dwight Evans	.15	.08	.05
156	Buddy Solomon	.15	.08	.05
157	U.L. Washington	.15	.08	.05
158	Joe Sambito	.15	.08	.05
159	Roy White	.15	.08	.05
160	Mike Flanagan	.15	.08	.05
161	Barry Foote	.15	.08	.05
162	Tom Johnson	.15	.08	.05
163	Glenn Burke	.15	.08	.05
164	Mickey Lolich	.15	.08	.05
165	Frank Taveras	.15	.08	.05
166	Leon Roberts	.15	.08	.05
167a	Roger Metzger (Solid vertical black line between first and last names, through "A" of "GIANTS.")	.50	.25	.15
167b	Roger Metzger (Partial black line.)	.25	.13	.08
167c	Roger Metzger (No black line.)	.15	.08	.05
168	Dave Freisleben	.15	.08	.05
169	Bill Nahorodny	.15	.08	.05
170	Don Sutton	2.50	1.25	.70
171	Gene Clines	.15	.08	.05
172	Mike Bruhert	.15	.08	.05
173	John Lowenstein	.15	.08	.05
174	Rick Auerbach	.15	.08	.05
175	George Hendrick	.15	.08	.05
176	Aurelio Rodriguez	.15	.08	.05
177	Ron Reed	.15	.08	.05
178	Alvis Woods	.15	.08	.05
179	Jim Beattie	.15	.08	.05
180	Larry Hisle	.15	.08	.05
181	Mike Garman	.15	.08	.05
182	Tim Johnson	.15	.08	.05
183	Paul Splittorff	.15	.08	.05
184	Darrel Chaney	.15	.08	.05
185	Mike Torrez	.15	.08	.05
186	Eric Soderholm	.15	.08	.05
187	Mark Lemongello	.15	.08	.05
188	Pat Kelly	.15	.08	.05
189	**Eddie Whitson**	.25	.13	.08
190	Ron Cey	.15	.08	.05
191	Mike Norris	.15	.08	.05
192	Cardinals Team (Ken Boyer)	.25	.13	.08
193	Glenn Adams	.15	.08	.05
194	Randy Jones	.15	.08	.05
195	Bill Madlock	.15	.08	.05
196	Steve Kemp	.15	.08	.05
197	Bob Apodaca	.15	.08	.05
198	Johnny Grubb	.15	.08	.05
199	Larry Milbourne	.15	.08	.05
200	Johnny Bench	3.50	1.75	1.00
201	Mike Edwards (Record Breaker)	.15	.08	.05
202	Ron Guidry (Record Breaker)	.15	.08	.05
203	J.R. Richard (Record Breaker)	.15	.08	.05
204	Pete Rose (Record Breaker)	1.00	.50	.30
205	John Stearns (Record Breaker)	.15	.08	.05
206	Sammy Stewart (Record Breaker)	.15	.08	.05
207	Dave Lemanczyk	.15	.08	.05
208	Clarence Gaston	.15	.08	.05

209	Reggie Cleveland	.15	.08	.05
210	Larry Bowa	.15	.08	.05
211	Denny Martinez	.15	.08	.05
212	*Carney Lansford*	.60	.30	.20
213	Bill Travers	.15	.08	.05
214	Red Sox Team (Don Zimmer)	.25	.13	.08
215	Willie McCovey	3.00	1.50	.90
216	Wilbur Wood	.15	.08	.05
217	Steve Dillard	.15	.08	.05
218	Dennis Leonard	.15	.08	.05
219	Roy Smalley	.15	.08	.05
220	Cesar Geronimo	.15	.08	.05
221	Jesse Jefferson	.15	.08	.05
222	Bob Beall	.15	.08	.05
223	Kent Tekulve	.15	.08	.05
224	Dave Revering	.15	.08	.05
225	Rich Gossage	.25	.13	.08
226	Ron Pruitt	.15	.08	.05
227	Steve Stone	.15	.08	.05
228	Vic Davalillo	.15	.08	.05
229	Doug Flynn	.15	.08	.05
230	Bob Forsch	.15	.08	.05
231	Johnny Wockenfuss	.15	.08	.05
232	Jimmy Sexton	.15	.08	.05
233	Paul Mitchell	.15	.08	.05
234	Toby Harrah	.15	.08	.05
235	Steve Rogers	.15	.08	.05
236	Jim Dwyer	.15	.08	.05
237	Billy Smith	.15	.08	.05
238	Balor Moore	.15	.08	.05
239	Willie Horton	.15	.08	.05
240	Rick Reuschel	.15	.08	.05
241	Checklist 122-242	.15	.08	.05
242	Pablo Torrealba	.15	.08	.05
243	Buck Martinez	.15	.08	.05
244	Pirates Team (Chuck Tanner)	.25	.13	.08
245	Jeff Burroughs	.15	.08	.05
246	Darrell Jackson	.15	.08	.05
247	Tucker Ashford	.15	.08	.05
248	Pete LaCock	.15	.08	.05
249	Paul Thormodsgard	.15	.08	.05
250	Willie Randolph	.15	.08	.05
251	Jack Morris	.40	.20	.12
252	Bob Stinson	.15	.08	.05
253	Rick Wise	.15	.08	.05
254	Luis Gomez	.15	.08	.05
255	Tommy John	.30	.15	.09
256	Mike Sadek	.15	.08	.05
257	Adrian Devine	.15	.08	.05
258	Mike Phillips	.15	.08	.05
259	Reds Team (Sparky Anderson)	.75	.40	.25
260	Richie Zisk	.15	.08	.05
261	Mario Guerrero	.15	.08	.05
262	Nelson Briles	.15	.08	.05
263	Oscar Gamble	.15	.08	.05
264	*Don Robinson*	.15	.08	.05
265	Don Money	.15	.08	.05
266	Jim Willoughby	.15	.08	.05
267	Joe Rudi	.15	.08	.05
268	Julio Gonzalez	.15	.08	.05
269	Woodie Fryman	.15	.08	.05
270	Butch Hobson	.15	.08	.05
271	Rawly Eastwick	.15	.08	.05
272	Tim Corcoran	.15	.08	.05
273	Jerry Terrell	.15	.08	.05
274	Willie Norwood	.15	.08	.05
275	Junior Moore	.15	.08	.05
276	Jim Colborn	.15	.08	.05
277	Tom Grieve	.15	.08	.05
278	Andy Messersmith	.15	.08	.05
279	Jerry Grote	.15	.08	.05
280	Andre Thornton	.15	.08	.05
281	Vic Correll	.15	.08	.05
282	Blue Jays Team (Roy Hartsfield)	.25	.13	.08
283	Ken Kravec	.15	.08	.05
284	Johnnie LeMaster	.15	.08	.05
285	Bobby Bonds	.15	.08	.05
286	Duffy Dyer	.15	.08	.05
287	Andres Mora	.15	.08	.05
288	Milt Wilcox	.15	.08	.05
289	Jose Cruz	.15	.08	.05
290	Dave Lopes	.15	.08	.05
291	Tom Griffin	.15	.08	.05
292	Don Reynolds	.15	.08	.05
293	Jerry Garvin	.15	.08	.05
294	Pepe Frias	.15	.08	.05
295	Mitchell Page	.15	.08	.05
296	Preston Hanna	.15	.08	.05
297	Ted Sizemore	.15	.08	.05
298	Rich Gale	.15	.08	.05
299	Steve Ontiveros	.15	.08	.05
300	Rod Carew	3.00	1.50	.90
301	Tom Hume	.15	.08	.05
302	Braves Team (Bobby Cox)	.45	.25	.14
303	Lary Sorensen	.15	.08	.05
304	Steve Swisher	.15	.08	.05
305	Willie Montanez	.15	.08	.05
306	Floyd Bannister	.15	.08	.05
307	Larvell Blanks	.15	.08	.05
308	Bert Blyleven	.15	.08	.05
309	Ralph Garr	.15	.08	.05
310	Thurman Munson	5.00	2.50	1.50
311	Gary Lavelle	.15	.08	.05
312	Bob Robertson	.15	.08	.05
313	Dyar Miller	.15	.08	.05
314	Larry Harlow	.15	.08	.05
315	Jon Matlack	.15	.08	.05
316	Milt May	.15	.08	.05
317	Jose Cardenal	.15	.08	.05
318	*Bob Welch*	1.50	.70	.45
319	Wayne Garrett	.15	.08	.05
320	Carl Yastrzemski	3.50	1.75	1.00
321	Gaylord Perry	2.50	1.25	.70
322	Danny Goodwin	.15	.08	.05
323	Lynn McGlothen	.15	.08	.05
324	Mike Tyson	.15	.08	.05

#	Player			
325	Cecil Cooper	.15	.08	.05
326	Pedro Borbon	.15	.08	.05
327	Art Howe	.15	.08	.05
328	A's Team (Jack McKeon)	.25	.13	.08
329	Joe Coleman	.15	.08	.05
330	George Brett	6.00	3.00	1.75
331	Mickey Mahler	.15	.08	.05
332	Gary Alexander	.15	.08	.05
333	Chet Lemon	.15	.08	.05
334	Craig Swan	.15	.08	.05
335	Chris Chambliss	.15	.08	.05
336	Bobby Thompson	.15	.08	.05
337	John Montague	.15	.08	.05
338	Vic Harris	.15	.08	.05
339	Ron Jackson	.15	.08	.05
340	Jim Palmer	3.00	1.50	.90
341	*Willie Upshaw*	.20	.10	.06
342	Dave Roberts	.15	.08	.05
343	Ed Glynn	.15	.08	.05
344	Jerry Royster	.15	.08	.05
345	Tug McGraw	.15	.08	.05
346	Bill Buckner	.15	.08	.05
347	Doug Rau	.15	.08	.05
348	Andre Dawson	1.50	.70	.45
349	Jim Wright	.15	.08	.05
350	Garry Templeton	.15	.08	.05
351	Wayne Nordhagen	.15	.08	.05
352	Steve Renko	.15	.08	.05
353	Checklist 243-363	.15	.08	.05
354	Bill Bonham	.15	.08	.05
355	Lee Mazzilli	.15	.08	.05
356	Giants Team (Joe Altobelli)	.25	.13	.08
357	Jerry Augustine	.15	.08	.05
358	Alan Trammell	2.00	1.00	.60
359	Dan Spillner	.15	.08	.05
360	Amos Otis	.15	.08	.05
361	Tom Dixon	.15	.08	.05
362	Mike Cubbage	.15	.08	.05
363	Craig Skok	.15	.08	.05
364	Gene Richards	.15	.08	.05
365	Sparky Lyle	.15	.08	.05
366	Juan Bernhardt	.15	.08	.05
367	Dave Skaggs	.15	.08	.05
368	Don Aase	.15	.08	.05
369a	Bump Wills (Blue Jays)	2.00	1.00	.60
369b	Bump Wills (Rangers)	2.00	1.00	.60
370	Dave Kingman	.15	.08	.05
371	Jeff Holly	.15	.08	.05
372	Lamar Johnson	.15	.08	.05
373	Lance Rautzhan	.15	.08	.05
374	Ed Herrmann	.15	.08	.05
375	Bill Campbell	.15	.08	.05
376	Gorman Thomas	.15	.08	.05
377	Paul Moskau	.15	.08	.05
378	Rob Picciolo	.15	.08	.05
379	Dale Murray	.15	.08	.05
380	John Mayberry	.15	.08	.05
381	Astros Team (Bill Virdon)	.25	.13	.08
382	Jerry Martin	.15	.08	.05
383	Phil Garner	.15	.08	.05
384	Tommy Boggs	.15	.08	.05
385	Dan Ford	.15	.08	.05
386	Francisco Barrios	.15	.08	.05
387	Gary Thomasson	.15	.08	.05
388	Jack Billingham	.15	.08	.05
389	Joe Zdeb	.15	.08	.05
390	Rollie Fingers	2.50	1.25	.70
391	Al Oliver	.30	.15	.09
392	Doug Ault	.15	.08	.05
393	Scott McGregor	.15	.08	.05
394	Randy Stein	.15	.08	.05
395	Dave Cash	.15	.08	.05
396	Bill Plummer	.15	.08	.05
397	Sergio Ferrer	.15	.08	.05
398	Ivan DeJesus	.15	.08	.05
399	David Clyde	.15	.08	.05
400	Jim Rice	.50	.25	.15
401	Ray Knight	.15	.08	.05
402	Paul Hartzell	.15	.08	.05
403	Tim Foli	.15	.08	.05
404	White Sox Team (Don Kessinger)	.25	.13	.08
405	Butch Wynegar	.15	.08	.05
406	Joe Wallis	.15	.08	.05
407	Pete Vuckovich	.15	.08	.05
408	Charlie Moore	.15	.08	.05
409	*Willie Wilson*	2.00	1.00	.60
410	Darrell Evans	.15	.08	.05
411	All-Time Hits Leaders (Ty Cobb, George Sisler)	.50	.25	.15
412	All-Time RBI Leaders (Hank Aaron, Hack Wilson)	.50	.25	.15
413	All-Time Home Run Leaders (Hank Aaron, Roger Maris)	4.50	2.25	1.25
414	All-Time Batting Average Leaders (Ty Cobb, Roger Hornsby)	.50	.25	.15
415	All-Time Stolen Bases Leader (Lou Brock)	.30	.15	.09
416	All-Time Wins Leaders (Jack Chesbro, Cy Young)	.25	.13	.08
417	All-Time Strikeout Leaders (Walter Johnson, Nolan Ryan)	4.50	2.25	1.25
418	All-Time ERA Leaders (Walter Johnson, Dutch Leonard)	.20	.10	.06
419	Dick Ruthven	.15	.08	.05
420	Ken Griffey	.15	.08	.05
421	Doug DeCinces	.15	.08	.05
422	Ruppert Jones	.15	.08	.05
423	Bob Montgomery	.15	.08	.05
424	Angels Team (Jim Fregosi)	.25	.13	.08
425	Rick Manning	.15	.08	.05
426	Chris Speier	.15	.08	.05
427	Andy Replogle	.15	.08	.05
428	Bobby Valentine	.15	.08	.05
429	John Urrea	.15	.08	.05

#	Player			
430	Dave Parker	.15	.08	.05
431	Glenn Borgmann	.15	.08	.05
432	Dave Heaverlo	.15	.08	.05
433	Larry Biittner	.15	.08	.05
434	Ken Clay	.15	.08	.05
435	Gene Tenace	.15	.08	.05
436	Hector Cruz	.15	.08	.05
437	Rick Williams	.15	.08	.05
438	Horace Speed	.15	.08	.05
439	Frank White	.15	.08	.05
440	Rusty Staub	.15	.08	.05
441	Lee Lacy	.15	.08	.05
442	Doyle Alexander	.15	.08	.05
443	Bruce Bochte	.15	.08	.05
444	*Aurelio Lopez*			
445	Steve Henderson	.15	.08	.05
446	Jim Lonborg	.15	.08	.05
447	Manny Sanguillen	.15	.08	.05
448	Moose Haas	.15	.08	.05
449	Bombo Rivera	.15	.08	.05
450	Dave Concepcion	.15	.08	.05
451	Royals Team (Whitey Herzog)	.25	.13	.08
452	Jerry Morales	.15	.08	.05
453	Chris Knapp	.15	.08	.05
454	Len Randle	.15	.08	.05
455	Bill Lee	.15	.08	.05
456	Chuck Baker	.15	.08	.05
457	Bruce Sutter	2.50	1.25	.70
458	Jim Essian	.15	.08	.05
459	Sid Monge	.15	.08	.05
460	Graig Nettles	.15	.08	.05
461	Jim Barr	.15	.08	.05
462	Otto Velez	.15	.08	.05
463	Steve Comer	.15	.08	.05
464	Joe Nolan	.15	.08	.05
465	Reggie Smith	.15	.08	.05
466	Mark Littell	.15	.08	.05
467	Don Kessinger	.15	.08	.05
468	Stan Bahnsen	.15	.08	.05
469	Lance Parrish	.30	.15	.09
470	Garry Maddox	.15	.08	.05
471	Joaquin Andujar	.15	.08	.05
472	Craig Kusick	.15	.08	.05
473	Dave Roberts	.15	.08	.05
474	Dick Davis	.15	.08	.05
475	Dan Driessen	.15	.08	.05
476	Tom Poquette	.15	.08	.05
477	Bob Grich	.15	.08	.05
478	Juan Beniquez	.15	.08	.05
479	Padres Team (Roger Craig)	.25	.13	.08
480	Fred Lynn	.15	.08	.05
481	Skip Lockwood	.15	.08	.05
482	Craig Reynolds	.15	.08	.05
483	Checklist 364-484	.15	.08	.05
484	Rick Waits	.15	.08	.05
485	Bucky Dent	.15	.08	.05
486	Bob Knepper	.15	.08	.05
487	Miguel Dilone	.15	.08	.05
488	Bob Owchinko	.15	.08	.05
489	Larry Cox (Photo actually Dave Rader.)	.15	.08	.05
490	Al Cowens	.15	.08	.05
491	Tippy Martinez	.15	.08	.05
492	Bob Bailor	.15	.08	.05
493	Larry Christenson	.15	.08	.05
494	Jerry White	.15	.08	.05
495	Tony Perez	2.00	1.00	.60
496	Barry Bonnell	.15	.08	.05
497	Glenn Abbott	.15	.08	.05
498	Rich Chiles	.15	.08	.05
499	Rangers Team (Pat Corrales)	.25	.13	.08
500	Ron Guidry	.20	.10	.06
501	Junior Kennedy	.15	.08	.05
502	Steve Braun	.15	.08	.05
503	Terry Humphrey	.15	.08	.05
504	*Larry McWilliams*	.15	.08	.05
505	Ed Kranepool	.15	.08	.05
506	John D'Acquisto	.15	.08	.05
507	Tony Armas	.15	.08	.05
508	Charlie Hough	.15	.08	.05
509	Mario Mendoza	.15	.08	.05
510	Ted Simmons	.15	.08	.05
511	Paul Reuschel	.15	.08	.05
512	Jack Clark	.15	.08	.05
513	Dave Johnson	.15	.08	.05
514	Mike Proly	.15	.08	.05
515	Enos Cabell	.15	.08	.05
516	Champ Summers	.15	.08	.05
517	Al Bumbry	.15	.08	.05
518	Jim Umbarger	.15	.08	.05
519	Ben Oglivie	.15	.08	.05
520	Gary Carter	3.00	1.50	.90
521	Sam Ewing	.15	.08	.05
522	Ken Holtzman	.15	.08	.05
523	John Milner	.15	.08	.05
524	Tom Burgmeier	.15	.08	.05
525	Freddie Patek	.15	.08	.05
526	Dodgers Team (Tom Lasorda)	.60	.30	.20
527	Lerrin LaGrow	.15	.08	.05
528	Wayne Gross	.15	.08	.05
529	Brian Asselstine	.15	.08	.05
530	Frank Tanana	.15	.08	.05
531	Fernando Gonzalez	.15	.08	.05
532	Buddy Schultz	.15	.08	.05
533	Leroy Stanton	.15	.08	.05
534	Ken Forsch	.15	.08	.05
535	Ellis Valentine	.15	.08	.05
536	Jerry Reuss	.15	.08	.05
537	Tom Veryzer	.15	.08	.05
538	Mike Ivie	.15	.08	.05
539	John Ellis	.15	.08	.05
540	Greg Luzinski	.15	.08	.05
541	Jim Slaton	.15	.08	.05
542	Rick Bosetti	.15	.08	.05
543	Kiko Garcia	.15	.08	.05
544	Fergie Jenkins	2.00	1.00	.60
545	John Stearns	.15	.08	.05

		NM	EX	VG
546	Bill Russell	.15	.08	.05
547	Clint Hurdle	.15	.08	.05
548	Enrique Romo	.15	.08	.05
549	Bob Bailey	.15	.08	.05
550	Sal Bando	.15	.08	.05
551	Cubs Team (Herman Franks)	.25	.13	.08
552	Jose Morales	.15	.08	.05
553	Denny Walling	.15	.08	.05
554	Matt Keough	.15	.08	.05
555	Biff Pocoroba	.15	.08	.05
556	Mike Lum	.15	.08	.05
557	Ken Brett	.15	.08	.05
558	Jay Johnstone	.15	.08	.05
559	Greg Pryor	.15	.08	.05
560	John Montefusco	.15	.08	.05
561	Ed Ott	.15	.08	.05
562	Dusty Baker	.20	.10	.06
563	Roy Thomas	.15	.08	.05
564	Jerry Turner	.15	.08	.05
565	Rico Carty	.15	.08	.05
566	Nino Espinosa	.15	.08	.05
567	Rich Hebner	.15	.08	.05
568	Carlos Lopez	.15	.08	.05
569	Bob Sykes	.15	.08	.05
570	Cesar Cedeno	.15	.08	.05
571	Darrell Porter	.15	.08	.05
572	Rod Gilbreath	.15	.08	.05
573	Jim Kern	.15	.08	.05
574	Claudell Washington	.15	.08	.05
575	Luis Tiant	.15	.08	.05
576	Mike Parrott	.15	.08	.05
577	Brewers Team (George Bamberger)	.25	.13	.08
578	Pete Broberg	.15	.08	.05
579	Greg Gross	.15	.08	.05
580	Ron Fairly	.15	.08	.05
581	Darold Knowles	.15	.08	.05
582	Paul Blair	.15	.08	.05
583	Julio Cruz	.15	.08	.05
584	Jim Rooker	.15	.08	.05
585	Hal McRae	.15	.08	.05
586	**Bob Horner**	1.00	.50	.30
587	Ken Reitz	.15	.08	.05
588	Tom Murphy	.15	.08	.05
589	Terry Whitfield	.15	.08	.05
590	J.R. Richard	.15	.08	.05
591	Mike Hargrove	.15	.08	.05
592	Mike Krukow	.15	.08	.05
593	Rick Dempsey	.15	.08	.05
594	Bob Shirley	.15	.08	.05
595	Phil Niekro	2.00	1.00	.60
596	Jim Wohlford	.15	.08	.05
597	Bob Stanley	.15	.08	.05
598	Mark Wagner	.15	.08	.05
599	Jim Spencer	.15	.08	.05
600	George Foster	.15	.08	.05
601	Dave LaRoche	.15	.08	.05
602	Checklist 485-605	.15	.08	.05
603	Rudy May	.15	.08	.05
604	Jeff Newman	.15	.08	.05
605	Rick Monday	.15	.08	.05
606	Expos Team (Dick Williams)	.25	.13	.08
607	Omar Moreno	.15	.08	.05
608	Dave McKay	.15	.08	.05
609	Silvio Martinez	.15	.08	.05
610	Mike Schmidt	6.00	3.00	1.75
611	Jim Norris	.15	.08	.05
612	**Rick Honeycutt**	.25	.13	.08
613	Mike Edwards	.15	.08	.05
614	Willie Hernandez	.15	.08	.05
615	Ken Singleton	.15	.08	.05
616	Billy Almon	.15	.08	.05
617	Terry Puhl	.15	.08	.05
618	Jerry Remy	.15	.08	.05
619	**Ken Landreaux**	.15	.08	.05
620	Bert Campaneris	.15	.08	.05
621	Pat Zachry	.15	.08	.05
622	Dave Collins	.15	.08	.05
623	Bob McClure	.15	.08	.05
624	Larry Herndon	.15	.08	.05
625	Mark Fidrych	.20	.10	.06
626	Yankees Team (Bob Lemon)	.60	.30	.20
627	Gary Serum	.15	.08	.05
628	Del Unser	.15	.08	.05
629	Gene Garber	.15	.08	.05
630	Bake McBride	.15	.08	.05
631	Jorge Orta	.15	.08	.05
632	Don Kirkwood	.15	.08	.05
633	Rob Wilfong	.15	.08	.05
634	Paul Lindblad	.15	.08	.05
635	Don Baylor	.30	.15	.09
636	Wayne Garland	.15	.08	.05
637	Bill Robinson	.15	.08	.05
638	Al Fitzmorris	.15	.08	.05
639	Manny Trillo	.15	.08	.05
640	Eddie Murray	6.00	3.00	1.75
641	**Bobby Castillo**	.15	.08	.05
642	Wilbur Howard	.15	.08	.05
643	Tom Hausman	.15	.08	.05
644	Manny Mota	.15	.08	.05
645	George Scott	.15	.08	.05
646	Rick Sweet	.15	.08	.05
647	Bob Lacey	.15	.08	.05
648	Lou Piniella	.25	.13	.08
649	John Curtis	.15	.08	.05
650	Pete Rose	6.00	3.00	1.75
651	Mike Caldwell	.15	.08	.05
652	Stan Papi	.15	.08	.05
653	Warren Brusstar	.15	.08	.05
654	Rick Miller	.15	.08	.05
655	Jerry Koosman	.15	.08	.05
656	Hosken Powell	.15	.08	.05
657	George Medich	.15	.08	.05
658	Taylor Duncan	.15	.08	.05
659	Mariners Team (Darrell Johnson)	.25	.13	.08
660	Ron LeFlore	.15	.08	.05
661	Bruce Kison	.15	.08	.05

		NM	EX	VG
662	Kevin Bell	.15	.08	.05
663	Mike Vail	.15	.08	.05
664	Doug Bird	.15	.08	.05
665	Lou Brock	3.00	1.50	.90
666	Rich Dauer	.15	.08	.05
667	Don Hood	.15	.08	.05
668	Bill North	.15	.08	.05
669	Checklist 606-726	.15	.08	.05
670	Jim Hunter	3.00	1.50	.90
671	Joe Ferguson	.15	.08	.05
672	Ed Halicki	.15	.08	.05
673	Tom Hutton	.15	.08	.05
674	Dave Tomlin	.15	.08	.05
675	Tim McCarver	.25	.13	.08
676	Johnny Sutton	.15	.08	.05
677	Larry Parrish	.15	.08	.05
678	Geoff Zahn	.15	.08	.05
679	Derrel Thomas	.15	.08	.05
680	Carlton Fisk	3.00	1.50	.90
681	*John Henry Johnson*	.15	.08	.05
682	Dave Chalk	.15	.08	.05
683	Dan Meyer	.15	.08	.05
684	Jamie Easterly	.15	.08	.05
685	Sixto Lezcano	.15	.08	.05
686	Ron Schueler	.15	.08	.05
687	Rennie Stennett	.15	.08	.05
688	Mike Willis	.15	.08	.05
689	Orioles Team (Earl Weaver)	.60	.30	.20
690	Buddy Bell	.15	.08	.05
691	Dock Ellis	.15	.08	.05
692	Mickey Stanley	.15	.08	.05
693	Dave Rader	.15	.08	.05
694	Burt Hooton	.15	.08	.05
695	Keith Hernandez	.15	.08	.05
696	Andy Hassler	.15	.08	.05
697	Dave Bergman	.15	.08	.05
698	Bill Stein	.15	.08	.05
699	Hal Dues	.15	.08	.05
700	Reggie Jackson	4.00	2.00	1.25
701	Orioles Prospects (Mark Corey, John Flinn, Sammy Stewart)	.15	.08	.05
702	Red Sox Prospects (Joel Finch, Garry Hancock, Allen Ripley)	.15	.08	.05
703	Angels Prospects (Jim Anderson, Dave Frost, Bob Slater)	.15	.08	.05
704	White Sox Prospects (*Ross Baumgarten, Mike Colbern, Mike Squires*)	.15	.08	.05
705	Indians Prospects (Alfredo Griffin, Tim Norrid, Dave Oliver)	.25	.13	.08
706	Tigers Prospects (Dave Stegman, Dave Tobik, Kip Young)	.15	.08	.05
707	Royals Prospects (Randy Bass, Jim Gaudet, Randy McGilberry)	.15	.08	.05
708	Brewers Prospects (Kevin Bass, Eddie Romero, Ned Yost)	.25	.13	.08
709	Twins Prospects (Sam Perlozzo, Rick Sofield, Kevin Stanfield)	.15	.08	.05
710	Yankees Prospects (Brian Doyle, Mike Heath, Dave Rajsich)	.20	.10	.06
711	A's Prospects (Dwayne Murphy, Bruce Robinson, Alan Wirth)	.15	.08	.05
712	Mariners Prospects (Bud Anderson, Greg Biercevicz, Byron McLaughlin)	.15	.08	.05
713	Rangers Prospects (*Danny Darwin, Pat Putnam, Billy Sample*)	.25	.13	.08
714	Blue Jays Prospects (Victor Cruz, Pat Kelly, Ernie Whitt)	.15	.08	.05
715	Braves Prospects (Bruce Benedict, Glenn Hubbard, Larry Whisenton)	.25	.13	.08
716	Cubs Prospects (*Dave Geisel, Karl Pagel, Scot Thompson*)	.15	.08	.05
717	Reds Prospects (*Mike LaCoss, Ron Oester, Harry Spilman*)	.15	.08	.05
718	Astros Prospects (Bruce Bochy, Mike Fischlin, Don Pisker)	.15	.08	.05
719	Dodgers Prospects (Pedro Guerrero, Rudy Law, Joe Simpson)	1.50	.70	.45
720	Expos Prospects (*Jerry Fry, Jerry Pirtle, Scott Sanderson*)	.30	.15	.09
721	Mets Prospects (Juan Berenguer, Dwight Bernard, Dan Norman)	.15	.08	.05
722	Phillies Prospects (*Jim Morrison, Lonnie Smith, Jim Wright*)	.50	.25	.15
723	Pirates Prospects (Dale Berra, Eugenio Cotes, Ben Wiltbank)	.15	.08	.05
724	Cardinals Prospects (*Tom Bruno, George Frazier, Terry Kennedy*)	.20	.10	.06
725	Padres Prospects (Jim Beswick, Steve Mura, Broderick Perkins)	.15	.08	.05
726	Giants Prospects (Greg Johnston, Joe Strain, John Tamargo)	.15	.08	.05

1979 Topps Team Checklist Sheet

This uncut sheet of 26 team card/checklists was available via a mail-in offer. The sheet was mailed with two folds. The sheet cards are printed on lighter stock.

	NM	EX	VG
Uncut Sheet:	20.00	10.00	6.00

1979 Topps Comics

Issued as the 3" x 3-3/4" wax wrapper for a five-cent piece of bubblegum, this "test" issue was bought up in great quantities by speculators and remains rather common. It is also inexpensive, because the comic-style player representations were not popular with collectors. The set is complete at 33 pieces. Each wax box contains only 11 different players. Original packaging folds are not considered in grading.

		NM	EX	VG
Complete Set (33):		15.00	7.50	4.50
Common Player:		.25	.13	.08
Wax Box (72):		55.00		
1	Eddie Murray	1.50	.70	.45
2	Jim Rice	.60	.30	.20
3	Carl Yastrzemski	1.50	.70	.45
4	Nolan Ryan	5.00	2.50	1.50
5	Chet Lemon	.25	.13	.08
6	Andre Thornton	.25	.13	.08
7	Rusty Staub	.25	.13	.08
8	Ron LeFlore	.25	.13	.08
9	George Brett	3.00	1.50	.90
10	Larry Hisle	.25	.13	.08
11	Rod Carew	1.50	.70	.45
12	Reggie Jackson	2.50	1.25	.70
13	Ron Guidry	.25	.13	.08
14	Mitchell Page	.25	.13	.08
15	Leon Roberts	.25	.13	.08
16	Al Oliver	.25	.13	.08
17	John Mayberry	.25	.13	.08
18	Bob Horner	.25	.13	.08
19	Phil Niekro	1.00	.50	.30
20	Dave Kingman	.25	.13	.08
21	John Bench	1.50	.70	.45
22	Tom Seaver	1.50	.70	.45
23	J.R. Richard	.25	.13	.08
24	Steve Garvey	.60	.30	.20
25	Reggie Smith	.25	.13	.08
26	Ross Grimsley	.25	.13	.08
27	Craig Swan	.25	.13	.08
28	Pete Rose	3.50	1.75	1.00
29	Dave Parker	.25	.13	.08
30	Ted Simmons	.25	.13	.08
31	Dave Winfield	1.50	.70	.45
32	Jack Clark	.25	.13	.08
33	Vida Blue	.25	.13	.08

1979 Topps/Dynamite Magazine Panels

In at least two issue of its "Dynamite" kids' magazine, Scholastic Book Club teamed with Topps to insert a six-card panel of its 1979 baseball issue. Complete magazines would bear a small premium.

		NM	EX	VG
	Complete Panel:	20.00	10.00	6.00
2	Home Run Leaders (Jim Rice, George Foster)			
5	Victory Leaders (Ron Guidry, Gaylord Perry)			
6	Strikeout Leaders (Nolan Ryan, J.R. Richard)			
201	Mike Edwards (Record Breaker)			
202	Ron Guidry (Record Breaker)			
203	J.R. Richard (Record Breaker)			
	Complete Panel:	15.00	7.50	4.50
232	Jimmy Sexton			
292	Don Reynolds			
336	Bobby Thompson			
432	Dave Heaverlo			
532	Buddy Schultz			
539	John Ellis			

1980 Topps

Again numbering 726 cards measuring 2-1/2" x 3-1/2", Topps did make some design changes in 1980. Fronts have the usual color picture with a fac-simile autograph. The player's name appears above the picture, while his position is on a pennant at the upper left and his team on another pennant in the lower right. Backs no longer feature games, returning instead to statistics, personal information, a few headlines and a cartoon about the player. Specialty cards include statistical leaders, and previous season highlights. Many rookies again appear in team threesomes.

		NM	EX	VG
	Complete Set (726):	100.00	50.00	30.00
	Common Player:	.15	.08	.05
	Wax Pack (15):	10.00		
	Wax Box (36):	260.00		
	Cello Pack (25):	12.50		
	Cello Box (24):	265.00		
	Super Cello Pack (28):	16.00		
	Super Cello Box (24):	275.00		
	Rack Pack (42):	22.50		
	Rack Box (24):	450.00		
	Vending Box (500):	120.00		
1	Lou Brock, Carl Yastrzemski (Highlights)	1.00	.50	.30
2	Willie McCovey (Highlights)	.30	.15	.09
3	Manny Mota (Highlights)	.15	.08	.05
4	Pete Rose (Highlights)	2.00	1.00	.60
5	Garry Templeton (Highlights)	.15	.08	.05
6	Del Unser (Highlights)	.15	.08	.05
7	Mike Lum	.15	.08	.05
8	Craig Swan	.15	.08	.05
9a	Steve Braun (Name in yellow.)	200.00	100.00	60.00
9b	Steve Braun (Name in red.)	.15	.08	.05
10	Denny Martinez	.15	.08	.05
11	Jimmy Sexton	.15	.08	.05
12	John Curtis	.15	.08	.05
13	Ron Pruitt	.15	.08	.05
14	Dave Cash	.15	.08	.05
15	Bill Campbell	.15	.08	.05
16	Jerry Narron	.15	.08	.05
17	Bruce Sutter	2.00	1.00	.60
18	Ron Jackson	.15	.08	.05
19	Balor Moore	.15	.08	.05
20	Dan Ford	.15	.08	.05
21	Manny Sarmiento	.15	.08	.05
22	Pat Putnam	.15	.08	.05
23	Derrel Thomas	.15	.08	.05
24	Jim Slaton	.15	.08	.05
25	Lee Mazzilli	.15	.08	.05
26	Marty Pattin	.15	.08	.05
27	Del Unser	.15	.08	.05
28	Bruce Kison	.15	.08	.05
29	Mark Wagner	.15	.08	.05
30	Vida Blue	.15	.08	.05
31	Jay Johnstone	.15	.08	.05
32	Julio Cruz	.15	.08	.05
33	Tony Scott	.15	.08	.05
34	Jeff Newman	.15	.08	.05
35	Luis Tiant	.15	.08	.05
36	Rusty Torres	.15	.08	.05
37	Kiko Garcia	.15	.08	.05
38	Dan Spillner	.15	.08	.05
39	Rowland Office	.15	.08	.05
40	Carlton Fisk	2.50	1.25	.70
41	Rangers Team (Pat Corrales)	.25	.13	.08
42	*Dave Palmer*	.15	.08	.05
43	Bombo Rivera	.15	.08	.05
44	Bill Fahey	.15	.08	.05
45	Frank White	.15	.08	.05
46	Rico Carty	.15	.08	.05
47	Bill Bonham	.15	.08	.05
48	Rick Miller	.15	.08	.05
49	Mario Guerrero	.15	.08	.05
50	J.R. Richard	.15	.08	.05
51	Joe Ferguson	.15	.08	.05
52	Warren Brusstar	.15	.08	.05
53	Ben Oglivie	.15	.08	.05
54	Dennis Lamp	.15	.08	.05
55	Bill Madlock	.15	.08	.05
56	Bobby Valentine	.15	.08	.05
57	Pete Vuckovich	.15	.08	.05
58	Doug Flynn	.15	.08	.05
59	Eddy Putman	.15	.08	.05
60	Bucky Dent	.20	.10	.06
61	Gary Serum	.15	.08	.05
62	Mike Ivie	.15	.08	.05
63	Bob Stanley	.15	.08	.05
64	Joe Nolan	.15	.08	.05
65	Al Bumbry	.15	.08	.05
66	Royals Team (Jim Frey)	.25	.13	.08
67	Doyle Alexander	.15	.08	.05
68	Larry Harlow	.15	.08	.05
69	Rick Williams	.15	.08	.05
70	Gary Carter	2.50	1.25	.70
71	John Milner	.15	.08	.05
72	Fred Howard	.15	.08	.05
73	Dave Collins	.15	.08	.05
74	Sid Monge	.15	.08	.05
75	Bill Russell	.15	.08	.05
76	John Stearns	.15	.08	.05
77	*Dave Stieb*	1.00	.50	.30
78	Ruppert Jones	.15	.08	.05
79	Bob Owchinko	.15	.08	.05
80	Ron LeFlore	.15	.08	.05
81	Ted Sizemore	.15	.08	.05
82	Astros Team (Bill Virdon)	.25	.13	.08
83	*Steve Trout*	.15	.08	.05
84	Gary Lavelle	.15	.08	.05
85	Ted Simmons	.15	.08	.05
86	Dave Hamilton	.15	.08	.05
87	Pepe Frias	.15	.08	.05
88	Ken Landreaux	.15	.08	.05
89	Don Hood	.15	.08	.05
90	Manny Trillo	.15	.08	.05
91	Rick Dempsey	.15	.08	.05
92	Rick Rhoden	.15	.08	.05
93	Dave Roberts	.15	.08	.05
94	*Neil Allen*	.15	.08	.05
95	Cecil Cooper	.15	.08	.05
96	A's Team (Jim Marshall)	.25	.13	.08
97	Bill Lee	.15	.08	.05
98	Jerry Terrell	.15	.08	.05
99	Victor Cruz	.15	.08	.05
100	Johnny Bench	3.00	1.50	.90
101	Aurelio Lopez	.15	.08	.05
102	Rich Dauer	.15	.08	.05
103	*Bill Caudill*	.15	.08	.05
104	Manny Mota	.15	.08	.05
105	Frank Tanana	.15	.08	.05
106	*Jeff Leonard*	.25	.13	.08
107	Francisco Barrios	.15	.08	.05
108	Bob Horner	.15	.08	.05
109	Bill Travers	.15	.08	.05
110	Fred Lynn	.15	.08	.05
111	Bob Knepper	.15	.08	.05
112	White Sox Team (Tony LaRussa)	.45	.25	.14
113	Geoff Zahn	.15	.08	.05
114	Juan Beniquez	.15	.08	.05
115	Sparky Lyle	.15	.08	.05
116	Larry Cox	.15	.08	.05
117	Dock Ellis	.15	.08	.05
118	Phil Garner	.15	.08	.05
119	Sammy Stewart	.15	.08	.05
120	Greg Luzinski	.15	.08	.05
121	Checklist 1-121	.15	.08	.05
122	Dave Rosello	.15	.08	.05
123	Lynn Jones	.15	.08	.05
124	Dave Lemanczyk	.15	.08	.05
125	Tony Perez	2.00	1.00	.60
126	Dave Tomlin	.15	.08	.05
127	Gary Thomasson	.15	.08	.05
128	Tom Burgmeier	.15	.08	.05
129	Craig Reynolds	.15	.08	.05
130	Amos Otis	.15	.08	.05
131	Paul Mitchell	.15	.08	.05
132	Biff Pocoroba	.15	.08	.05
133	Jerry Turner	.15	.08	.05
134	Matt Keough	.15	.08	.05
135	Bill Buckner	.15	.08	.05
136	Dick Ruthven	.15	.08	.05
137	*John Castino*	.15	.08	.05
138	Ross Baumgarten	.15	.08	.05
139	*Dane Iorg*	.15	.08	.05
140	Rich Gossage	.25	.13	.08
141	Gary Alexander	.15	.08	.05
142	Phil Huffman	.15	.08	.05
143	Bruce Bochte	.15	.08	.05
144	Steve Comer	.15	.08	.05
145	Darrell Evans	.15	.08	.05
146	Bob Welch	.15	.08	.05
147	Terry Puhl	.15	.08	.05
148	Manny Sanguillen	.15	.08	.05
149	Tom Hume	.15	.08	.05
150	Jason Thompson	.15	.08	.05
151	Tom Hausman	.15	.08	.05
152	John Fulgham	.15	.08	.05
153	Tim Blackwell	.15	.08	.05
154	Lary Sorensen	.15	.08	.05
155	Jerry Remy	.15	.08	.05
156	Tony Brizzolara	.15	.08	.05
157	Willie Wilson	.15	.08	.05
158	Rob Picciolo	.15	.08	.05
159	Ken Clay	.15	.08	.05
160	Eddie Murray	3.00	1.50	.90
161	Larry Christenson	.15	.08	.05
162	Bob Randall	.15	.08	.05
163	Steve Swisher	.15	.08	.05
164a	Greg Pryor (No name.)	200.00	100.00	60.00
164b	Greg Pryor (Name in blue.)	.15	.08	.05
165	Omar Moreno	.15	.08	.05
166	Glenn Abbott	.15	.08	.05
167	Jack Clark	.15	.08	.05
168	Rick Waits	.15	.08	.05
169	Luis Gomez	.15	.08	.05
170	Burt Hooton	.15	.08	.05
171	Fernando Gonzalez	.15	.08	.05
172	Ron Hodges	.15	.08	.05
173	John Henry Johnson	.15	.08	.05
174	Ray Knight	.15	.08	.05
175	Rick Reuschel	.15	.08	.05
176	Champ Summers	.15	.08	.05
177	Dave Heaverlo	.15	.08	.05
178	Tim McCarver	.15	.08	.05
179	*Ron Davis*	.25	.13	.08
180	Warren Cromartie	.15	.08	.05
181	Moose Haas	.15	.08	.05
182	Ken Reitz	.15	.08	.05
183	Jim Anderson	.15	.08	.05
184	Steve Renko	.15	.08	.05
185	Hal McRae	.15	.08	.05
186	Junior Moore	.15	.08	.05
187	Alan Ashby	.15	.08	.05
188	Terry Crowley	.15	.08	.05
189	Kevin Kobel	.15	.08	.05
190	Buddy Bell	.15	.08	.05
191	Ted Martinez	.15	.08	.05
192	Braves Team (Bobby Cox)	.45	.25	.14
193	Dave Goltz	.15	.08	.05
194	Mike Easler	.15	.08	.05
195	John Montefusco	.15	.08	.05
196	Lance Parrish	.15	.08	.05
197	Byron McLaughlin	.15	.08	.05
198	Dell Alston	.15	.08	.05
199	Mike LaCoss	.15	.08	.05
200	Jim Rice	.30	.15	.09
201	Batting Leaders (Keith Hernandez, Fred Lynn)	.15	.08	.05
202	Home Run Leaders (Dave Kingman, Gorman Thomas)	.15	.08	.05
203	Runs Batted In Leaders (Don Baylor, Dave Winfield)	.35	.20	.11
204	Stolen Base Leaders (Omar Moreno, Willie Wilson)	.15	.08	.05
205	Victory Leaders (Mike Flanagan, Joe Niekro, Phil Niekro)	.25	.13	.08
206	Strikeout Leaders (J.R. Richard, Nolan Ryan)	3.50	1.75	1.00
207	ERA Leaders (Ron Guidry, J.R. Richard)	.25	.13	.08
208	Wayne Cage	.15	.08	.05
209	Von Joshua	.15	.08	.05
210	Steve Carlton	2.50	1.25	.70
211	Dave Skaggs	.15	.08	.05
212	Dave Roberts	.15	.08	.05
213	Mike Jorgensen	.15	.08	.05
214	Angels Team (Jim Fregosi)	.25	.13	.08
215	Sixto Lezcano	.15	.08	.05
216	Phil Mankowski	.15	.08	.05
217	Ed Halicki	.15	.08	.05
218	Jose Morales	.15	.08	.05
219	Steve Mingori	.15	.08	.05
220	Dave Concepcion	.15	.08	.05
221	Joe Cannon	.15	.08	.05
222	*Ron Hassey*	.25	.13	.08
223	Bob Sykes	.15	.08	.05
224	Willie Montanez	.15	.08	.05
225	Lou Piniella	.25	.13	.08
226	Bill Stein	.15	.08	.05
227	Len Barker	.15	.08	.05
228	Johnny Oates	.15	.08	.05
229	Jim Bibby	.15	.08	.05
230	Dave Winfield	2.50	1.25	.70
231	Steve McCatty	.15	.08	.05
232	Alan Trammell	.60	.30	.20
233	LaRue Washington	.15	.08	.05
234	Vern Ruhle	.15	.08	.05
235	Andre Dawson	1.00	.50	.30
236	Marc Hill	.15	.08	.05
237	Scott McGregor	.15	.08	.05
238	Rob Wilfong	.15	.08	.05
239	Don Aase	.15	.08	.05
240	Dave Kingman	.15	.08	.05
241	Checklist 122-242	.15	.08	.05
242	Lamar Johnson	.15	.08	.05
243	Jerry Augustine	.15	.08	.05
244	Cardinals Team (Ken Boyer)	.25	.13	.08
245	Phil Niekro	2.00	1.00	.60
246	Tim Foli	.15	.08	.05
247	Frank Riccelli	.15	.08	.05
248	Jamie Quirk	.15	.08	.05
249	Jim Clancy	.15	.08	.05
250	Jim Kaat	.15	.08	.05
251	Kip Young	.15	.08	.05
252	Ted Cox	.15	.08	.05

#	Player			
253	John Montague	.15	.08	.05
254	Paul Dade	.15	.08	.05
255	Dusty Baker	.15	.08	.05
256	Roger Erickson	.15	.08	.05
257	Larry Herndon	.15	.08	.05
258	Paul Moskau	.15	.08	.05
259	Mets Team (Joe Torre)	.60	.30	.20
260	Al Oliver	.20	.10	.06
261	Dave Chalk	.15	.08	.05
262	Benny Ayala	.15	.08	.05
263	Dave LaRoche	.15	.08	.05
264	Bill Robinson	.15	.08	.05
265	Robin Yount	2.50	1.25	.70
266	Bernie Carbo	.15	.08	.05
267	Dan Schatzeder	.15	.08	.05
268	Rafael Landestoy	.15	.08	.05
269	Dave Tobik	.15	.08	.05
270	Mike Schmidt	4.50	2.25	1.25
271	Dick Drago	.15	.08	.05
272	Ralph Garr	.15	.08	.05
273	Eduardo Rodriguez	.15	.08	.05
274	Dale Murphy	1.50	.70	.45
275	Jerry Koosman	.15	.08	.05
276	Tom Veryzer	.15	.08	.05
277	Rick Bosetti	.15	.08	.05
278	Jim Spencer	.15	.08	.05
279	Rob Andrews	.15	.08	.05
280	Gaylord Perry	2.00	1.00	.60
281	Paul Blair	.15	.08	.05
282	Mariners Team (Darrell Johnson)	.25	.13	.08
283	John Ellis	.15	.08	.05
284	Larry Murray	.15	.08	.05
285	Don Baylor	.25	.13	.08
286	Darold Knowles	.15	.08	.05
287	John Lowenstein	.15	.08	.05
288	Dave Rozema	.15	.08	.05
289	Bruce Bochy	.15	.08	.05
290	Steve Garvey	1.00	.50	.30
291	Randy Scarbery	.15	.08	.05
292	Dale Berra	.15	.08	.05
293	Elias Sosa	.15	.08	.05
294	Charlie Spikes	.15	.08	.05
295	Larry Gura	.15	.08	.05
296	Dave Rader	.15	.08	.05
297	Tim Johnson	.15	.08	.05
298	Ken Holtzman	.15	.08	.05
299	Steve Henderson	.15	.08	.05
300	Ron Guidry	.25	.13	.08
301	Mike Edwards	.15	.08	.05
302	Dodgers Team (Tom Lasorda)	.60	.30	.20
303	Bill Castro	.15	.08	.05
304	Butch Wynegar	.15	.08	.05
305	Randy Jones	.15	.08	.05
306	Denny Walling	.15	.08	.05
307	Rick Honeycutt	.15	.08	.05
308	Mike Hargrove	.15	.08	.05
309	Larry McWilliams	.15	.08	.05
310	Dave Parker	.15	.08	.05
311	Roger Metzger	.15	.08	.05
312	Mike Barlow	.15	.08	.05
313	Johnny Grubb	.15	.08	.05
314	*Tim Stoddard*	.15	.08	.05
315	Steve Kemp	.15	.08	.05
316	Bob Lacey	.15	.08	.05
317	Mike Anderson	.15	.08	.05
318	Jerry Reuss	.15	.08	.05
319	Chris Speier	.15	.08	.05
320	Dennis Eckersley	2.00	1.00	.60
321	Keith Hernandez	.15	.08	.05
322	Claudell Washington	.15	.08	.05
323	Mick Kelleher	.15	.08	.05
324	Tom Underwood	.15	.08	.05
325	Dan Driessen	.15	.08	.05
326	Bo McLaughlin	.15	.08	.05
327	Ray Fosse	.15	.08	.05
328	Twins Team (Gene Mauch)	.25	.13	.08
329	Bert Roberge	.15	.08	.05
330	Al Cowens	.15	.08	.05
331	Rich Hebner	.15	.08	.05
332	Enrique Romo	.15	.08	.05
333	Jim Norris	.15	.08	.05
334	Jim Beattie	.15	.08	.05
335	Willie McCovey	2.50	1.25	.70
336	George Medich	.15	.08	.05
337	Carney Lansford	.15	.08	.05
338	Johnny Wockenfuss	.15	.08	.05
339	John D'Acquisto	.15	.08	.05
340	Ken Singleton	.15	.08	.05
341	Jim Essian	.15	.08	.05
342	Odell Jones	.15	.08	.05
343	Mike Vail	.15	.08	.05
344	Randy Lerch	.15	.08	.05
345	Larry Parrish	.15	.08	.05
346	Buddy Solomon	.15	.08	.05
347	*Harry Chappas*	.15	.08	.05
348	Checklist 243-363	.15	.08	.05
349	Jack Brohamer	.15	.08	.05
350	George Hendrick	.15	.08	.05
351	Bob Davis	.15	.08	.05
352	Dan Briggs	.15	.08	.05
353	Andy Hassler	.15	.08	.05
354	Rick Auerbach	.15	.08	.05
355	Gary Matthews	.15	.08	.05
356	Padres Team (Jerry Coleman)	.25	.13	.08
357	Bob McClure	.15	.08	.05
358	Lou Whitaker	.25	.13	.08
359	Randy Moffitt	.15	.08	.05
360	Darrell Porter	.15	.08	.05
361	Wayne Garland	.15	.08	.05
362	Danny Goodwin	.15	.08	.05
363	Wayne Gross	.15	.08	.05
364	Ray Burris	.15	.08	.05
365	Bobby Murcer	.25	.13	.08
366	Rob Dressler	.15	.08	.05
367	Billy Smith	.15	.08	.05
368	*Willie Aikens*	.20	.10	.06
369	Jim Kern	.15	.08	.05
370	Cesar Cedeno	.15	.08	.05
371	Jack Morris	.15	.08	.05
372	Joel Youngblood	.15	.08	.05
373	*Dan Petry*	.20	.10	.06
374	Jim Gantner	.15	.08	.05
375	Ross Grimsley	.15	.08	.05
376	Gary Allenson	.15	.08	.05
377	Junior Kennedy	.15	.08	.05
378	Jerry Mumphrey	.15	.08	.05
379	Kevin Bell	.15	.08	.05
380	Garry Maddox	.15	.08	.05
381	Cubs Team (Preston Gomez)	.25	.13	.08
382	Dave Freisleben	.15	.08	.05
383	Ed Ott	.15	.08	.05
384	Joey McLaughlin	.15	.08	.05
385	Enos Cabell	.15	.08	.05
386	Darrell Jackson	.15	.08	.05
387a	Fred Stanley (Name in yellow.)	260.00	130.00	78.00
387b	Fred Stanley (Name in red.)	.15	.08	.05
388	Mike Paxton	.15	.08	.05
389	Pete LaCock	.15	.08	.05
390	Fergie Jenkins	2.00	1.00	.60
391	Tony Armas	.15	.08	.05
392	Milt Wilcox	.15	.08	.05
393	Ozzie Smith	5.00	2.50	1.50
394	Reggie Cleveland	.15	.08	.05
395	Ellis Valentine	.15	.08	.05
396	Dan Meyer	.15	.08	.05
397	Roy Thomas	.15	.08	.05
398	Barry Foote	.15	.08	.05
399	Mike Proly	.15	.08	.05
400	George Foster	.15	.08	.05
401	Pete Falcone	.15	.08	.05
402	Merv Rettenmund	.15	.08	.05
403	Pete Redfern	.15	.08	.05
404	Orioles Team (Earl Weaver)	.60	.30	.20
405	Dwight Evans	.15	.08	.05
406	Paul Molitor	2.50	1.25	.70
407	Tony Solaita	.15	.08	.05
408	Bill North	.15	.08	.05
409	Paul Splittorff	.15	.08	.05
410	Bobby Bonds	.15	.08	.05
411	Frank LaCorte	.15	.08	.05
412	Thad Bosley	.15	.08	.05
413	Allen Ripley	.15	.08	.05
414	George Scott	.15	.08	.05
415	Bill Atkinson	.15	.08	.05
416	*Tom Brookens*	.15	.08	.05
417	Craig Chamberlain	.15	.08	.05
418	Roger Freed	.15	.08	.05
419	Vic Correll	.15	.08	.05
420	Butch Hobson	.15	.08	.05
421	Doug Bird	.15	.08	.05
422	Larry Milbourne	.15	.08	.05
423	Dave Frost	.15	.08	.05
424	Yankees Team (Dick Howser)	.45	.25	.14
425	Mark Belanger	.15	.08	.05
426	Grant Jackson	.15	.08	.05
427	Tom Hutton	.15	.08	.05
428	Pat Zachry	.15	.08	.05
429	Duane Kuiper	.15	.08	.05
430	Larry Hisle	.15	.08	.05
431	Mike Krukow	.15	.08	.05
432	Willie Norwood	.15	.08	.05
433	Rich Gale	.15	.08	.05
434	Johnnie LeMaster	.15	.08	.05
435	Don Gullett	.15	.08	.05
436	Billy Almon	.15	.08	.05
437	Joe Niekro	.15	.08	.05
438	Dave Revering	.15	.08	.05
439	Mike Phillips	.15	.08	.05
440	Don Sutton	2.00	1.00	.60
441	Eric Soderholm	.15	.08	.05
442	Jorge Orta	.15	.08	.05
443	Mike Parrott	.15	.08	.05
444	Alvis Woods	.15	.08	.05
445	Mark Fidrych	.25	.13	.08
446	Duffy Dyer	.15	.08	.05
447	Nino Espinosa	.15	.08	.05
448	Jim Wohlford	.15	.08	.05
449	Doug Bair	.15	.08	.05
450	George Brett	5.00	2.50	1.50
451	Indians Team (Dave Garcia)	.25	.13	.08
452	Steve Dillard	.15	.08	.05
453	Mike Bacsik	.15	.08	.05
454	Tom Donohue	.15	.08	.05
455	Mike Torrez	.15	.08	.05
456	Frank Taveras	.15	.08	.05
457	Bert Blyleven	.15	.08	.05
458	Billy Sample	.15	.08	.05
459	Mickey Lolich	.15	.08	.05
460	Willie Randolph	.15	.08	.05
461	Dwayne Murphy	.15	.08	.05
462	Mike Sadek	.15	.08	.05
463	Jerry Royster	.15	.08	.05
464	John Denny	.15	.08	.05
465	Rick Monday	.15	.08	.05
466	Mike Squires	.15	.08	.05
467	Jesse Jefferson	.15	.08	.05
468	Aurelio Rodriguez	.15	.08	.05
469	Randy Niemann	.15	.08	.05
470	Bob Boone	.20	.10	.06
471	Hosken Powell	.15	.08	.05
472	Willie Hernandez	.15	.08	.05
473	Bump Wills	.15	.08	.05
474	Steve Busby	.15	.08	.05
475	Cesar Geronimo	.15	.08	.05
476	Bob Shirley	.15	.08	.05
477	Buck Martinez	.15	.08	.05
478	Gil Flores	.15	.08	.05
479	Expos Team (Dick Williams)	.25	.13	.08
480	Bob Watson	.15	.08	.05
481	Tom Paciorek	.15	.08	.05
482	*Rickey Henderson*	20.00	10.00	6.00
483	Bo Diaz	.15	.08	.05
484	Checklist 364-484	.15	.08	.05
485	Mickey Rivers	.15	.08	.05
486	Mike Tyson	.15	.08	.05
487	Wayne Nordhagen	.15	.08	.05
488	Roy Howell	.15	.08	.05
489	Preston Hanna	.15	.08	.05
490	Lee May	.15	.08	.05
491	Steve Mura	.15	.08	.05
492	Todd Cruz	.15	.08	.05
493	Jerry Martin	.15	.08	.05
494	Craig Minetto	.15	.08	.05
495	Bake McBride	.15	.08	.05
496	Silvio Martinez	.15	.08	.05
497	Jim Mason	.15	.08	.05
498	Danny Darwin	.15	.08	.05
499	Giants Team (Dave Bristol)	.25	.13	.08
500	Tom Seaver	3.00	1.50	.90
501	Rennie Stennett	.15	.08	.05
502	Rich Wortham	.15	.08	.05
503	Mike Cubbage	.15	.08	.05
504	Gene Garber	.15	.08	.05
505	Bert Campaneris	.15	.08	.05
506	Tom Buskey	.15	.08	.05
507	Leon Roberts	.15	.08	.05
508	U.L. Washington	.15	.08	.05
509	Ed Glynn	.15	.08	.05
510	Ron Cey	.15	.08	.05
511	Eric Wilkins	.15	.08	.05
512	Jose Cardenal	.15	.08	.05
513	Tom Dixon	.15	.08	.05
514	Steve Ontiveros	.15	.08	.05
515	Mike Caldwell	.15	.08	.05
516	Hector Cruz	.15	.08	.05
517	Don Stanhouse	.15	.08	.05
518	Nelson Norman	.15	.08	.05
519	Steve Nicosia	.15	.08	.05
520	Steve Rogers	.15	.08	.05
521	Ken Brett	.15	.08	.05
522	Jim Morrison	.15	.08	.05
523	Ken Henderson	.15	.08	.05
524	Jim Wright	.15	.08	.05
525	Clint Hurdle	.15	.08	.05
526	Phillies Team (Dallas Green)	.60	.30	.20
527	Doug Rau	.15	.08	.05
528	Adrian Devine	.15	.08	.05
529	Jim Barr	.15	.08	.05
530	Jim Sundberg	.15	.08	.05
531	Eric Rasmussen	.15	.08	.05
532	Willie Horton	.15	.08	.05
533	Checklist 485-605	.15	.08	.05
534	Andre Thornton	.15	.08	.05
535	Bob Forsch	.15	.08	.05
536	Lee Lacy	.15	.08	.05
537	*Alex Trevino*	.15	.08	.05
538	Joe Strain	.15	.08	.05
539	Rudy May	.15	.08	.05
540	Pete Rose	5.00	2.50	1.50
541	Miguel Dilone	.15	.08	.05
542	Joe Coleman	.15	.08	.05
543	Pat Kelly	.15	.08	.05
544	*Rick Sutcliffe*	2.00	1.00	.60
545	Jeff Burroughs	.15	.08	.05
546	Rick Langford	.15	.08	.05
547a	John Wathan (Name in yellow.)	200.00	100.00	60.00
547b	John .Wathan (Name in red.)	.15	.08	.05
548	Dave Rajsich	.15	.08	.05
549	Larry Wolfe	.15	.08	.05
550	Ken Griffey	.15	.08	.05
551	Pirates Team (Chuck Tanner)	.25	.13	.08
552	Bill Nahorodny	.15	.08	.05
553	Dick Davis	.15	.08	.05
554	Art Howe	.15	.08	.05
555	Ed Figueroa	.15	.08	.05
556	Joe Rudi	.15	.08	.05
557	Mark Lee	.15	.08	.05
558	Alfredo Griffin	.15	.08	.05
559	Dale Murray	.15	.08	.05
560	Dave Lopes	.15	.08	.05
561	Eddie Whitson	.15	.08	.05
562	Joe Wallis	.15	.08	.05
563	Will McEnaney	.15	.08	.05
564	Rick Manning	.15	.08	.05
565	Dennis Leonard	.15	.08	.05
566	Bud Harrelson	.15	.08	.05
567	Skip Lockwood	.15	.08	.05
568	*Gary Roenicke*	.15	.08	.05
569	Terry Kennedy	.15	.08	.05
570	Roy Smalley	.15	.08	.05
571	Joe Sambito	.15	.08	.05
572	Jerry Morales	.15	.08	.05
573	Kent Tekulve	.15	.08	.05
574	Scot Thompson	.15	.08	.05
575	Ken Kravec	.15	.08	.05
576	Jim Dwyer	.15	.08	.05
577	Blue Jays Team (Bobby Mattick)	.25	.13	.08
578	Scott Sanderson	.15	.08	.05
579	Charlie Moore	.15	.08	.05
580	Nolan Ryan	7.50	3.75	2.25
581	Bob Bailor	.15	.08	.05
582	Brian Doyle	.15	.08	.05
583	Bob Stinson	.15	.08	.05
584	Kurt Bevacqua	.15	.08	.05
585	Al Hrabosky	.15	.08	.05
586	Mitchell Page	.15	.08	.05
587	Garry Templeton	.15	.08	.05
588	Greg Minton	.15	.08	.05
589	Chet Lemon	.15	.08	.05
590	Jim Palmer	2.50	1.25	.70
591	Rick Cerone	.15	.08	.05
592	Jon Matlack	.15	.08	.05
593	Jesus Alou	.15	.08	.05
594	Dick Tidrow	.15	.08	.05
595	Don Money	.15	.08	.05
596	Rick Matula	.15	.08	.05
597a	Tom Poquette (Name in yellow.)	200.00	100.00	60.00
597b	Tom Poquette (Name in red.)	.15	.08	.05
598	Fred Kendall	.15	.08	.05

599	Mike Norris	.15	.08	.05
600	Reggie Jackson	4.00	2.00	1.25
601	Buddy Schultz	.15	.08	.05
602	Brian Downing	.15	.08	.05
603	Jack Billingham	.15	.08	.05
604	Glenn Adams	.15	.08	.05
605	Terry Forster	.15	.08	.05
606	Reds Team (John McNamara)	.25	.13	.08
607	Woodie Fryman	.15	.08	.05
608	Alan Bannister	.15	.08	.05
609	Ron Reed	.15	.08	.05
610	Willie Stargell	2.50	1.25	.70
611	Jerry Garvin	.15	.08	.05
612	Cliff Johnson	.15	.08	.05
613	Randy Stein	.15	.08	.05
614	John Hiller	.15	.08	.05
615	Doug DeCinces	.15	.08	.05
616	Gene Richards	.15	.08	.05
617	Joaquin Andujar	.15	.08	.05
618	Bob Montgomery	.15	.08	.05
619	Sergio Ferrer	.15	.08	.05
620	Richie Zisk	.15	.08	.05
621	Bob Grich	.15	.08	.05
622	Mario Soto	.15	.08	.05
623	Gorman Thomas	.15	.08	.05
624	Lerrin LaGrow	.15	.08	.05
625	Chris Chambliss	.15	.08	.05
626	Tigers Team (Sparky Anderson)	.75	.40	.25
627	Pedro Borbon	.15	.08	.05
628	Doug Capilla	.15	.08	.05
629	Jim Todd	.15	.08	.05
630	Larry Bowa	.15	.08	.05
631	Mark Littell	.15	.08	.05
632	Barry Bonnell	.15	.08	.05
633	Bob Apodaca	.15	.08	.05
634	Glenn Borgmann	.15	.08	.05
635	John Candelaria	.15	.08	.05
636	Toby Harrah	.15	.08	.05
637	Joe Simpson	.15	.08	.05
638	*Mark Clear*	.15	.08	.05
639	Larry Biittner	.15	.08	.05
640	Mike Flanagan	.15	.08	.05
641	Ed Kranepool	.15	.08	.05
642	Ken Forsch	.15	.08	.05
643	John Mayberry	.15	.08	.05
644	Charlie Hough	.15	.08	.05
645	Rick Burleson	.15	.08	.05
646	Checklist 606-726	.15	.08	.05
647	Milt May	.15	.08	.05
648	Roy White	.15	.08	.05
649	Tom Griffin	.15	.08	.05
650	Joe Morgan	2.50	1.25	.70
651	Rollie Fingers	2.00	1.00	.60
652	Mario Mendoza	.15	.08	.05
653	Stan Bahnsen	.15	.08	.05
654	Bruce Boisclair	.15	.08	.05
655	Tug McGraw	.15	.08	.05
656	Larvell Blanks	.15	.08	.05
657	Dave Edwards	.15	.08	.05
658	Chris Knapp	.15	.08	.05
659	Brewers Team (George Bamberger)	.25	.13	.08
660	Rusty Staub	.15	.08	.05
661	Orioles Future Stars (Mark Corey, Dave Ford, Wayne Krenchicki)	.15	.08	.05
662	Red Sox Future Stars (Joel Finch, Mike O'Berry, Chuck Rainey)	.15	.08	.05
663	Angels Future Stars (*Ralph Botting, Bob Clark, Dickie Thon*)	.25	.13	.08
664	White Sox Future Stars (Mike Colbern, Guy Hoffman, Dewey Robinson)	.15	.08	.05
665	Indians Future Stars (Larry Andersen, Bobby Cuellar, Sandy Wihtol)	.15	.08	.05
666	Tigers Future Stars (Mike Chris, Al Greene, Bruce Robbins)	.15	.08	.05
667	Royals Future Stars (*Renie Martin, Bill Paschall, Dan Quisenberry*)	1.00	.50	.30
668	Brewers Future Stars (Danny Boitano, Willie Mueller, Lenn Sakata)	.15	.08	.05
669	Twins Future Stars (*Dan Graham, Rick Sofield, Gary Ward*)	.25	.13	.08
670	Yankees Future Stars (Bobby Brown, Brad Gulden, Darryl Jones)	.15	.08	.05
671	A's Future Stars (*Derek Bryant, Brian Kingman, Mike Morgan*)	.50	.25	.15
672	Mariners Future Stars (Charlie Beamon, Rodney Craig, Rafael Vasquez)	.15	.08	.05
673	Rangers Future Stars (Brian Allard, Jerry Don Gleaton, Greg Mahlberg)	.15	.08	.05
674	Blue Jays Future Stars (Butch Edge, Pat Kelly, Ted Wilborn)	.15	.08	.05
675	Braves Future Stars (Bruce Benedict, Larry Bradford, Eddie Miller)	.15	.08	.05
676	Cubs Future Stars (Dave Geisel, Steve Macko, Karl Pagel)	.15	.08	.05
677	Reds Future Stars (Art DeFreites, Frank Pastore, Harry Spilman)	.15	.08	.05
678	Astros Future Stars (*Reggie Baldwin, Alan Knicely, Pete Ladd*)	.15	.08	.05

679	Dodgers Future Stars (Joe Beckwith, Mickey Hatcher, Dave Patterson)	.25	.13	.08
680	Expos Future Stars (Tony Bernazard, Randy Miller, John Tamargo)	.15	.08	.05
681	Mets Future Stars (*Dan Norman, Jesse Orosco, Mike Scott*)	1.00	.50	.30
682	Phillies Future Stars (Ramon Aviles, Dickie Noles, Kevin Saucier)	.15	.08	.05
683	Pirates Future Stars (Dorian Boyland, Alberto Lois, Harry Saferight)	.15	.08	.05
684	Cardinals Future Stars (George Frazier, Tom Herr, Dan O'Brien)	.30	.15	.09
685	Padres Future Stars (Tim Flannery, Brian Greer, Jim Wilhelm)	.15	.08	.05
686	Giants Future Stars (Greg Johnston, Dennis Littlejohn, Phil Nastu)	.15	.08	.05
687	Mike Heath	.15	.08	.05
688	Steve Stone	.15	.08	.05
689	Red Sox Team (Don Zimmer)	.25	.13	.08
690	Tommy John	.25	.13	.08
691	Ivan DeJesus	.15	.08	.05
692	Rawly Eastwick	.15	.08	.05
693	Craig Kusick	.15	.08	.05
694	Jim Rooker	.15	.08	.05
695	Reggie Smith	.15	.08	.05
696	Julio Gonzalez	.15	.08	.05
697	David Clyde	.15	.08	.05
698	Oscar Gamble	.15	.08	.05
699	Floyd Bannister	.15	.08	.05
700	Rod Carew	2.50	1.25	.70
701	*Ken Oberkfell*	.15	.08	.05
702	Ed Farmer	.15	.08	.05
703	Otto Velez	.15	.08	.05
704	Gene Tenace	.15	.08	.05
705	Freddie Patek	.15	.08	.05
706	Tippy Martinez	.15	.08	.05
707	Elliott Maddox	.15	.08	.05
708	Bob Tolan	.15	.08	.05
709	Pat Underwood	.15	.08	.05
710	Graig Nettles	.25	.13	.08
711	Bob Galasso	.15	.08	.05
712	Rodney Scott	.15	.08	.05
713	Terry Whitfield	.15	.08	.05
714	Fred Norman	.15	.08	.05
715	Sal Bando	.15	.08	.05
716	Lynn McGlothen	.15	.08	.05
717	Mickey Klutts	.15	.08	.05
718	Greg Gross	.15	.08	.05
719	Don Robinson	.15	.08	.05
720	Carl Yastrzemski	3.00	1.50	.90
721	Paul Hartzell	.15	.08	.05
722	Jose Cruz	.15	.08	.05
723	Shane Rawley	.15	.08	.05
724	Jerry White	.15	.08	.05
725	Rick Wise	.15	.08	.05
726	Steve Yeager	.15	.08	.05

1980 Topps Team Checklist Sheet

This uncut sheet of 26 1980 Topps team cards was available via a mail-in offer. The sheet was mailed with two folds and includes an offer to picture yourself on a baseball card. The sheet cards are printed on lighter card stock.

	NM	EX	VG
Uncut Sheet	15.00	7.50	4.50

1980 Topps N.Y. Yankees Proof

One of the most popular proof cards of the era is this N.Y. Yankees team photo card with an inset photo of manager Billy Martin, who was fired in October 1979 after punching a marshmellow salesman. By the time the cards were issued, Martin's name and photo had been replaced by rookie manager Dick Howser. The card is blank-backed and usually shows evidence of having been handcut from a proof sheet.

	NM	EX	VG
N.Y. Yankees	200.00	100.00	60.00

1980 Topps Stickers Prototypes

These appear to be prototypes for a Topp sticker issue that never materialized. In 3-1/2" x 2-1/2" format, the pieces have player picture pairs stuck onto a cardboard backing. Backs are blank. It is unknown if the listed examples, all of which are unique, comprise the entirety of the samples.

		NM	EX	VG
Common Card:		125.00	60.00	35.00
(1)	Johnny Bench, Maury Wills	200.00	100.00	60.00
(2)	Nino Espinosa, Ron Cey	125.00	60.00	35.00
(3)	Dwight Evans, Carlton Fisk	150.00	75.00	45.00
(4)	Don (Ron) Guidry, Dave Parker	125.00	60.00	35.00
(5)	Reggie Jackson, J.R. Richard	200.00	100.00	60.00

1980 Topps Superstar 5x7 Photos

In actuality, these cards measure 4-7/8" x 6-7/8". These were another Topps "test" issue that was bought out almost entirely by speculators. The 60 cards have a color photo on the front and a blue ink facsimile autograph. Backs have the player's name, team, position and card number. The issue was printed on different cardboard stocks, with the first on thick cardboard with a white back and the second on thinner cardboard with a gray back. Prices below are for the more common gray backs; white backs are valued 2.5X-3X the figures shown, except for triple-print cards (indicated by "3P" in checklist), which are valued at about 7.5X the gray-back price in the white-back version. The white backs were test marketed in three-card cello packs in selected geographical areas.

		NM	EX	VG
Complete Set, Gray Backs (60):		10.00	5.00	3.00
Complete Set, White Backs (60):		20.00	10.00	6.00
Common Player, Gray Back:		.25	.13	.08
Common Player, White Back:		.75	.40	.25
Wax Box (48):		10.00		
1	Willie Stargell	1.00	.50	.30
2	Mike Schmidt (3P)	1.50	.70	.45
3	Johnny Bench	1.00	.50	.30
4	Jim Palmer	.75	.40	.25
5	Jim Rice	.50	.25	.15
6	Reggie Jackson (3P)	1.50	.70	.45
7	Ron Guidry	.45	.25	.14
8	Lee Mazzilli	.25	.13	.08
9	Don Baylor	.50	.25	.15
10	Fred Lynn	.25	.13	.08
11	Ken Singleton	.25	.13	.08
12	Rod Carew (3P)	.75	.40	.25
13	Steve Garvey (3P)	.50	.25	.15
14	George Brett (3P)	1.50	.70	.45
15	Tom Seaver	1.50	.70	.45
16	Dave Kingman	.25	.13	.08
17	Dave Parker (3P)	.25	.13	.08
18	Dave Winfield	1.00	.50	.30
19	Pete Rose	2.00	1.00	.60
20	Nolan Ryan	4.00	2.00	1.25
21	Graig Nettles	.25	.13	.08
22	Carl Yastrzemski	1.50	.70	.45
23	Tommy John	.40	.20	.12
24	George Foster	.25	.13	.08
25	J.R. Richard	.25	.13	.08
26	Keith Hernandez	.25	.13	.08
27	Bob Horner	.25	.13	.08
28	Eddie Murray	1.50	.70	.45
29	Steve Kemp	.25	.13	.08

30	Gorman Thomas	.25	.13	.08
31	Sixto Lezcano	.25	.13	.08
32	Bruce Sutter	1.00	.50	.30
33	Cecil Cooper	.25	.13	.08
34	Larry Bowa	.25	.13	.08
35	Al Oliver	.35	.20	.11
36	Ted Simmons	.25	.13	.08
37	Garry Templeton	.25	.13	.08
38	Jerry Koosman	.25	.13	.08
39	Darrell Porter	.25	.13	.08
40	Roy Smalley	.25	.13	.08
41	Craig Swan	.25	.13	.08
42	Jason Thompson	.25	.13	.08
43	Andre Thornton	.25	.13	.08
44	Rick Manning	.25	.13	.08
45	Kent Tekulve	.25	.13	.08
46	Phil Niekro	.75	.40	.25
47	Buddy Bell	.25	.13	.08
48	Randy Jones	.25	.13	.08
49	Brian Downing	.25	.13	.08
50	Amos Otis	.25	.13	.08
51	Rick Bosetti	.25	.13	.08
52	Gary Carter	.75	.40	.25
53	Larry Parrish	.25	.13	.08
54	Jack Clark	.25	.13	.08
55	Bruce Bochte	.25	.13	.08
56	Cesar Cedeno	.25	.13	.08
57	Chet Lemon	.25	.13	.08
58	Dave Revering	.25	.13	.08
59	Vida Blue	.25	.13	.08
60	Davey Lopes	.25	.13	.08

1980 Topps Test Coins

These silver-dollar size (1-3/8" diameter) metal coins appear to have been a Topps test issue. The coins have a player portrait at center on obverse. On reverse center is player personal data and a Topps copyright line. Coins have been seen in compositions resembling bronze, silver and gold. Some of the coins have a hole at top.

	NM	EX	VG
Rod Carew	150.00	75.00	45.00
Steve Garvey	150.00	75.00	45.00
Reggie Jackson	300.00	150.00	90.00

1953 Top Taste Bread Milwaukee Braves

STAR PLAYER
OF THE MILWAUKEE BRAVES
GEORGE CROWE

This series of black-and-white mini-posters (8-1/2" x 11-1/4") depicts members of the 1953 Braves holding loaves of bread. They were probably intended for grocery store window or bakery aisle display. Backs are blank. It's unknown how many players are in the set. See also, Pictsweet Milwaukee Braves.

		NM	EX	VG
	Common Player:	150.00	75.00	45.00
(1)	Lew Burdette	150.00	75.00	45.00
(2)	George Crowe	150.00	75.00	45.00
(3)	Andy Pafko	150.00	75.00	45.00
(4)	Bucky Walters	150.00	75.00	45.00

1976 Towne Club Discs

One of several regional sponsors of player disc sets in 1976 was the Towne Club Pop Centers chain. The discs are 3-3/8" diameter with a black-and-white player portrait photo in the center of the baseball design. A line of red stars is above, while the left and right panels feature one of several bright colors. Produced by Michael Schecter Associates under license from the Major League Baseball Players Association,

the player photos have had uniform and cap logos removed. Backs are printed in red. The unnumbered checklist here is presented in alphabetical order.

		NM	EX	VG
	Complete Set (70):	50.00	25.00	15.00
	Common Player:	1.00	.50	.30
(1)	Henry Aaron	10.00	5.00	3.00
(2)	Johnny Bench	5.00	2.50	1.50
(3)	Vida Blue	1.00	.50	.30
(4)	Larry Bowa	1.00	.50	.30
(5)	Lou Brock	4.00	2.00	1.25
(6)	Jeff Burroughs	1.00	.50	.30
(7)	John Candelaria	1.00	.50	.30
(8)	Jose Cardenal	1.00	.50	.30
(9)	Rod Carew	4.00	2.00	1.25
(10)	Steve Carlton	4.00	2.00	1.25
(11)	Dave Cash	1.00	.50	.30
(12)	Cesar Cedeno	1.00	.50	.30
(13)	Ron Cey	1.00	.50	.30
(14)	Carlton Fisk	4.00	2.00	1.25
(15)	Tito Fuentes	1.00	.50	.30
(16)	Steve Garvey	3.00	1.50	.90
(17)	Ken Griffey	1.00	.50	.30
(18)	Don Gullett	1.00	.50	.30
(19)	Willie Horton	1.00	.50	.30
(20)	Al Hrabosky	1.00	.50	.30
(21)	Catfish Hunter	4.00	2.00	1.25
(22)	Reggie Jackson (A's)	7.50	3.75	2.25
(23)	Randy Jones	1.00	.50	.30
(24)	Jim Kaat	1.00	.50	.30
(25)	Don Kessinger	1.00	.50	.30
(26)	Dave Kingman	1.00	.50	.30
(27)	Jerry Koosman	1.00	.50	.30
(28)	Mickey Lolich	1.00	.50	.30
(29)	Greg Luzinski	1.00	.50	.30
(30)	Fred Lynn	1.00	.50	.30
(31)	Bill Madlock	1.00	.50	.30
(32)	Carlos May	1.00	.50	.30
(33)	John Mayberry	1.00	.50	.30
(34)	Bake McBride	1.00	.50	.30
(35)	Doc Medich	1.00	.50	.30
(36)	Andy Messersmith	1.00	.50	.30
(37)	Rick Monday	1.00	.50	.30
(38)	John Montefusco	1.00	.50	.30
(39)	Jerry Morales	1.00	.50	.30
(40)	Joe Morgan	4.00	2.00	1.25
(41)	Thurman Munson	5.00	2.50	1.50
(42)	Bobby Murcer	1.00	.50	.30
(43)	Al Oliver	1.00	.50	.30
(44)	Jim Palmer	4.00	2.00	1.25
(45)	Dave Parker	1.00	.50	.30
(46)	Tony Perez	4.00	2.00	1.25
(47)	Jerry Reuss	1.00	.50	.30
(48)	Brooks Robinson	5.00	2.50	1.50
(49)	Frank Robinson	5.00	2.50	1.50
(50)	Steve Rogers	1.00	.50	.30
(51)	Pete Rose	10.00	5.00	3.00
(52)	Nolan Ryan	20.00	10.00	6.00
(53)	Manny Sanguillen	1.00	.50	.30
(54)	Mike Schmidt	7.50	3.75	2.25
(55)	Tom Seaver	5.00	2.50	1.50
(56)	Ted Simmons	1.00	.50	.30
(57)	Reggie Smith	1.00	.50	.30
(58)	Willie Stargell	4.00	2.00	1.25
(59)	Rusty Staub	1.50	.70	.45
(60)	Rennie Stennett	1.00	.50	.30
(61)	Don Sutton	4.00	2.00	1.25
(62)	Andy Thornton	1.00	.50	.30
(63)	Luis Tiant	1.00	.50	.30
(64)	Joe Torre	2.50	1.25	.70
(65)	Mike Tyson	1.00	.50	.30
(66)	Bob Watson	1.00	.50	.30
(67)	Wilbur Wood	1.00	.50	.30
(68)	Jimmy Wynn	1.00	.50	.30
(69)	Carl Yastrzemski	6.00	3.00	1.75
(70)	Richie Zisk	1.00	.50	.30

1910 Toy Town Post Office

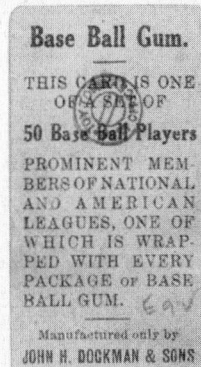

Base Ball Gum.

THIS CARD IS ONE OF A SET OF 50 Base Ball Players

PROMINENT MEMBERS OF NATIONAL AND AMERICAN LEAGUES, ONE OF WHICH IS WRAPPED WITH EVERY PACKAGE or BASE BALL GUM.

Manufactured only by JOHN H. DOCKMAN & SONS

Rather than a card issuer, this enigmatic rubber-stamp has been found on the backs of dozens of 1910-era baseball cards. Measuring 1/2" in diameter the seal is in purple ink. At center is a barred circle with "TOY TOWN" above and "POST OFFICE" below. The stamp was part of a Milton Bradley post office toy set and has been seen on different types of cards that eventually made their way into the hobby. On low-grade cards, the stamp neither greatly adds nor detracts from the value of the card on which it is placed.

(See individual card issuers for base values.)

1965 Trade Bloc Minnesota Twins

These cards were produced as part of a baseball game which was marketed at Metropolitan Stadium for $1. The blank-back cards measure 2-1/4" x 3-1/2" and are printed in either blue or sepia tones. Besides Twins players and staff, the set includes cards of various team souvenir items as well as old Met Stadium. Besides the player photo, cards include a facsimile autograph, stats and personal data. The unnumbered cards are checklisted here in alphabetical order.

		NM	EX	VG
	Complete Set (52):	600.00	300.00	175.00
	Common Player:	15.00	7.50	4.50
	Common Non-player Card:	5.00	2.50	1.50
(1)	Bernard Allen	15.00	7.50	4.50
(2)	Bob Allison	20.00	10.00	6.00
(3)	Earl Battey	15.00	7.50	4.50
(4)	Dave Boswell	15.00	7.50	4.50
(5)	Gerald Fosnow	15.00	7.50	4.50
(6)	James Grant	15.00	7.50	4.50
(7)	Calvin Griffith	20.00	10.00	6.00
(8)	Jimmie Hall	15.00	7.50	4.50
(9)	Jim Kaat	25.00	12.50	7.50
(10)	Harmon Killebrew	60.00	30.00	18.00
(11)	Jerry Kindall	15.00	7.50	4.50
(12)	Johnny Klippstein	15.00	7.50	4.50
(13)	Frank Kostro	15.00	7.50	4.50
(14)	James Lemon	15.00	7.50	4.50
(15)	George "Doc" Lentz	15.00	7.50	4.50
(16)	Alfred Martin (Billy)	30.00	15.00	9.00
(17)	Sam Mele	15.00	7.50	4.50
(18)	Donald Mincher	15.00	7.50	4.50
(19)	Harold Naragon	15.00	7.50	4.50
(20)	Melvin Nelson	15.00	7.50	4.50
(21)	Joseph Nossek	15.00	7.50	4.50
(22)	Pedro Oliva (Tony)	40.00	20.00	12.00
(23)	Camilo Pascual	20.00	10.00	6.00
(24)	James Perry	15.00	7.50	4.50
(25)	Bill Pleis	15.00	7.50	4.50
(26)	Richard Rollins	15.00	7.50	4.50
(27)	John Sain	15.00	7.50	4.50
(28)	John Sevcik	15.00	7.50	4.50
(29)	Richard Stigman	15.00	7.50	4.50
(30)	Sandy Valdespino	15.00	7.50	4.50
(31)	Zoilo Versalles	25.00	12.50	7.50
(32)	Allan Worthington	15.00	7.50	4.50
(33)	Gerald Zimmerman	15.00	7.50	4.50
(34)	Metropolitan Stadium	10.00	5.00	3.00
(35)	L.A. Angels logo	5.00	2.50	1.50
(36)	K.C. Athletics logo	5.00	2.50	1.50
(37)	Cleveland Indians logo	5.00	2.50	1.50
(38)	Baltimore Orioles logo	5.00	2.50	1.50
(39)	Boston Red Sox logo	5.00	2.50	1.50
(40)	Washington Senators logo	5.00	2.50	1.50
(41)	Detroit Tigers logo	5.00	2.50	1.50
(42)	Minnesota Twins logo	5.00	2.50	1.50
(43)	Chicago White Sox logo	5.00	2.50	1.50
(44)	N.Y. Yankees logo	5.00	2.50	1.50
(45)	Twins autographed ball	5.00	2.50	1.50
(46)	Twins autographed bat	5.00	2.50	1.50
(47)	Twins bobbin' head doll	5.00	2.50	1.50
(48)	Twins cap	5.00	2.50	1.50
(49)	Twins pennant	5.00	2.50	1.50
(50)	Twins scorebook	5.00	2.50	1.50
(51)	Twins warmup jacket	5.00	2.50	1.50
(52)	Twins yearbook	5.00	2.50	1.50

1964 Transfer-ette Chicago Cubs Iron-ons

This novelty item features artist-rendered portraits of Cubs players which were designed to be transferred to t-shirts, notebook covers or other items via an iron-on process. Each package contains three sheets of nine images; one each in blue, black and red. The sheets are about 8-3/8" x 10-3/4" with each player image about 2-1/2" x 2-3/4". According to the packaging, other teams were planned, along with larger two-color player portraits.

	NM	EX	VG
Complete Set:	50.00	25.00	15.00

BLACK SHEET
Ernie Banks
Dick Bertell
John Boccabella
Glen Hobbie
Calvin Koonce
Merritt Ranew
Andre Rodgers
Ron Santo
Jim Stewart
BLUE SHEET
Steve Boros
Lou Brock
Bob Buhl
Ellis Burton
Bill Cowan
Dick Ellsworth
Don Elston
Bob Kennedy
Jimmie Schaffer
RED SHEET
Tom Baker
Jim Brewer
Leo Burke
Larry Jackson
Don Landrum
Paul Toth
Jack Warner
Billy Williams
Chicago Cubs Logo

1964 Transfer-ette Chicago White Sox Iron-Ons

This novelty item features artist-rendered portraits of White Sox players which were designed to be transferred to t-shirts, notebook covers or other items via an iron-on process. Each package contains three sheets of nine images; one each in blue, black and red. The sheets are about 8-3/8" x 10-3/4" with each player image about 2-1/2" x 2-3/4". According to the packaging, other teams were planned, along with larger two-color player portraits.

	NM	EX	VG
Complete Set:	40.00	20.00	12.00

BLACK SHEET
Jim Brosnan
Don Buford
John Buzhardt
Joe Cunningham
Jim Golden
Joel Horlen
Charlie Maxwell
Dave Nicholson
Gene Stephens
BLUE SHEET
Fritz Ackley
Frank Bauman (Baumann)
Camilo Carreon
Dave DeBusschere
Ed Fisher
Mike Joyce
J.C. Martin
Tom McCraw
Hoyt Wilhelm
RED SHEET
Ron Hansen
Ray Herbert
Mike Hershberger
Jim Landis
Gary Peters
Floyd Robinson
Pete Ward
Al Weis
White Sox logo

1969 Transogram

These 2-1/2" x 3-1/2" cards were printed on the back of toy baseball player statue boxes. The cards feature a color photo of the player surrounded by a rounded white border. Below the photo is the player's name in red and his team and other personal details all printed in black. The overall background is yellow. The cards were designed to be cut off the box, but collectors prefer to find the box intact and, better still, with the statue inside. While the cards themselves are not numbered, there is a number on each box's end flap, which is the order in which the cards are checklisted here. Three-player boxes were also sold.

		NM	EX	VG
	CUT CARD OR STATUE			
(1)	Joe Azcue	12.50	6.25	3.75
(2)	Willie Horton	12.50	6.25	3.75
(3)	Luis Tiant	12.50	6.25	3.75
(4)	Denny McLain	12.50	6.25	3.75
(5)	Jose Cardenal	12.50	6.25	3.75
(6)	Al Kaline	30.00	15.00	9.00
(7)	Tony Oliva	15.00	7.50	4.50
(8)	Blue Moon Odom	12.50	6.25	3.75
(9)	Cesar Tovar	12.50	6.25	3.75
(10)	Rick Monday	12.50	6.25	3.75
(11)	Harmon Killebrew	25.00	12.50	7.50
(12)	Danny Cater	12.50	6.25	3.75
(13)	Brooks Robinson	35.00	17.50	10.00
(14)	Jim Fregosi	12.50	6.25	3.75
(15)	Dave McNally	12.50	6.25	3.75
(16)	Frank Robinson	35.00	17.50	10.00
(17)	Bobby Knoop	12.50	6.25	3.75
(18)	Rick Reichardt	12.50	6.25	3.75
(19)	Carl Yastrzemski	35.00	17.50	10.00
(20)	Pete Ward	12.50	6.25	3.75
(21)	Rico Petrocelli	12.50	6.25	3.75
(22)	Tommy John	15.00	7.50	4.50
(23)	Ken Harrelson	12.50	6.25	3.75
(24)	Luis Aparicio	25.00	12.50	7.50
(25)	Mike Epstein	12.50	6.25	3.75
(26)	Roy White	12.50	6.25	3.75
(27)	Camilo Pascual	12.50	6.25	3.75
(28)	Mel Stottlemyre	12.50	6.25	3.75
(29)	Frank Howard	15.00	7.50	4.50
(30)	Mickey Mantle	185.00	90.00	55.00
(31)	Lou Brock	25.00	12.50	7.50
(32)	Juan Marichal	25.00	12.50	7.50
(33)	Bob Gibson	25.00	12.50	7.50
(34)	Willie Mays	60.00	30.00	18.00
(35)	Tim McCarver	15.00	7.50	4.50
(36)	Willie McCovey	25.00	12.50	7.50
(37)	Don Wilson	12.50	6.25	3.75
(38)	Billy Williams	25.00	12.50	7.50
(39)	Dan Staub (Rusty)	15.00	7.50	4.50
(40)	Ernie Banks	45.00	22.50	13.50
(41)	Jim Wynn	12.50	6.25	3.75
(42)	Ron Santo	15.00	7.50	4.50
(43)	Tom Haller	12.50	6.25	3.75
(44)	Ron Swoboda	12.50	6.25	3.75
(45)	Willie Davis	12.50	6.25	3.75
(46)	Jerry Koosman	12.50	6.25	3.75
(47)	Jim Lefebvre	12.50	6.25	3.75
(48)	Tom Seaver	30.00	15.00	9.00
(49)	Joe Torre (Atlanta)	20.00	10.00	6.00
(50)	Tony Perez	25.00	12.50	7.50
(51)	Felipe Alou	12.50	6.25	3.75
(52)	Lee May	12.50	6.25	3.75
(53)	Hank Aaron	60.00	30.00	18.00
(54)	Pete Rose	60.00	30.00	18.00
(55)	Cookie Rojas	12.50	6.25	3.75
(56)	Roberto Clemente	60.00	30.00	18.00
(57)	Richie Allen	15.00	7.50	4.50
(58)	Matty Alou	12.50	6.25	3.75
(59)	Johnny Callison	12.50	6.25	3.75
(60)	Bill Mazeroski	25.00	12.50	7.50
	COMPLETE BOX W/STATUE			
(1)	Joe Azcue	85.00	42.50	25.00
(2)	Willie Horton	85.00	42.50	25.00
(3)	Luis Tiant	85.00	42.50	25.00
(4)	Denny McLain	85.00	42.50	25.00
(5)	Jose Cardenal	85.00	42.50	25.00
(6)	Al Kaline	175.00	85.00	50.00
(7)	Tony Oliva	100.00	50.00	30.00
(8)	Blue Moon Odom	85.00	42.50	25.00
(9)	Cesar Tovar	85.00	42.50	25.00
(10)	Rick Monday	85.00	42.50	25.00
(11)	Harmon Killebrew	200.00	100.00	60.00
(12)	Danny Cater	85.00	42.50	25.00
(13)	Brooks Robinson	250.00	125.00	75.00
(14)	Jim Fregosi	85.00	42.50	25.00
(15)	Dave McNally	85.00	42.50	25.00
(16)	Frank Robinson	250.00	125.00	75.00
(17)	Bobby Knoop	85.00	42.50	25.00
(18)	Rick Reichardt	85.00	42.50	25.00
(19)	Carl Yastrzemski	300.00	150.00	90.00
(20)	Pete Ward	85.00	42.50	25.00
(21)	Rico Petrocelli	85.00	42.50	25.00
(22)	Tommy John	120.00	60.00	36.00
(23)	Ken Harrelson	85.00	42.50	25.00
(24)	Luis Aparicio	175.00	85.00	50.00
(25)	Mike Epstein	85.00	42.50	25.00
(26)	Roy White	85.00	42.50	25.00
(27)	Camilo Pascual	85.00	42.50	25.00
(28)	Mel Stottlemyre	85.00	42.50	25.00
(29)	Frank Howard	100.00	50.00	30.00
(30)	Mickey Mantle	850.00	425.00	255.00
(31)	Lou Brock	175.00	85.00	50.00
(32)	Juan Marichal	175.00	85.00	50.00
(33)	Bob Gibson	175.00	85.00	50.00
(34)	Willie Mays	400.00	200.00	120.00
(35)	Tim McCarver	100.00	50.00	30.00
(36)	Willie McCovey	175.00	85.00	50.00
(37)	Don Wilson	85.00	42.50	25.00
(38)	Billy Williams	175.00	85.00	50.00
(39)	Dan Staub (Rusty)	120.00	60.00	36.00
(40)	Ernie Banks	350.00	175.00	100.00
(41)	Jim Wynn	85.00	42.50	25.00
(42)	Ron Santo	120.00	60.00	36.00
(43)	Tom Haller	85.00	42.50	25.00
(44)	Ron Swoboda	85.00	42.50	25.00
(45)	Willie Davis	85.00	42.50	25.00
(46)	Jerry Koosman	120.00	60.00	36.00
(47)	Jim Lefebvre	85.00	42.50	25.00
(48)	Tom Seaver	200.00	100.00	60.00
(49)	Joe Torre (Atlanta)	100.00	50.00	30.00
(50)	Tony Perez	175.00	85.00	50.00
(51)	Felipe Alou	100.00	50.00	30.00
(52)	Lee May	85.00	42.50	25.00
(53)	Hank Aaron	400.00	200.00	120.00
(54)	Pete Rose	400.00	200.00	120.00
(55)	Cookie Rojas	85.00	42.50	25.00
(56)	Roberto Clemente	450.00	225.00	135.00
(57)	Richie Allen	100.00	50.00	30.00
(58)	Matty Alou	85.00	42.50	25.00
(59)	Johnny Callison	85.00	42.50	25.00
(60)	Bill Mazeroski	175.00	85.00	50.00

1970 Transogram

The 1970 Transogram cards were found printed on boxes of three Transogram baseball player statues. The individual player cards are slightly larger than 1969's, at 2-9/16" x 3-1/2". The 30-card set has the same pictures as the 1969 set except for Joe Torre. All players in the '70 set were also in the '69 Transogram issue except for Reggie Jackson, Sam McDowell and Boog Powell. Each box contains a side panel with a series number and 1" x 1-1/4" portrait photos of the players in the series. Prices shown are for cards cut from the box.

		NM	EX	VG
Complete Set (30):		550.00	275.00	175.00
Complete Set, Boxes/Statues (10):		2,255	1,100	650.00
Common Player:		10.00	5.00	3.00
	Series 1 Boxed Set:	400.00	200.00	120.00
(1)	Pete Rose	50.00	25.00	15.00
(2)	Willie Mays	60.00	30.00	18.00
(3)	Cleon Jones	10.00	5.00	3.00
	Series 2 Boxed Set:	160.00	80.00	48.00
(4)	Ron Santo	15.00	7.50	4.50
(5)	Willie Davis	10.00	5.00	3.00
(6)	Willie McCovey	17.50	8.75	5.25
	Series 3 Boxed Set:	275.00	135.00	82.00
(7)	Juan Marichal	17.50	8.75	5.25
(8)	Joe Torre (St. Louis)	15.00	7.50	4.50
(9)	Ernie Banks	30.00	15.00	9.00
	Series 4 Boxed Set:	375.00	185.00	110.00
(10)	Hank Aaron	60.00	30.00	18.00
(11)	Jim Wynn	10.00	5.00	3.00
(12)	Tom Seaver	25.00	12.50	7.50
	Series 5 Boxed Set:	450.00	225.00	135.00
(13)	Bob Gibson	17.50	8.75	5.25
(14)	Roberto Clemente	100.00	50.00	30.00
(15)	Jerry Koosman	10.00	5.00	3.00
	Series 11 Boxed Set:	300.00	150.00	90.00
(16)	Denny McLain	12.50	6.25	3.75
(17)	Reggie Jackson	30.00	15.00	9.00
(18)	Boog Powell	15.00	7.50	4.50

		NM	EX	VG
	Series 12 Boxed Set:	175.00	87.00	52.00
(19)	Frank Robinson	25.00	12.50	7.50
(20)	Frank Howard	10.00	5.00	3.00
(21)	Rick Reichardt	10.00	5.00	3.00
	Series 13 Boxed Set:	225.00	110.00	67.00
(22)	Carl Yastrzemski	25.00	12.50	7.50
(23)	Tony Oliva	15.00	7.50	4.50
(24)	Mel Stottlemyre	10.00	5.00	3.00
	Series 14 Boxed Set:	180.00	90.00	54.00
(25)	Al Kaline	25.00	12.50	7.50
(26)	Jim Fregosi	10.00	5.00	3.00
(27)	Sam McDowell	10.00	5.00	3.00
	Series 15 Boxed Set:	180.00	90.00	54.00
(28)	Blue Moon Odom	10.00	5.00	3.00
(29)	Harmon Killebrew	25.00	12.50	7.50
(30)	Rico Petrocelli	10.00	5.00	3.00

1970 Transogram Mets

ED KRANEPOOL   AL WEIS   PITCHER TOM SEAVER

This Transogram set features members of the World Champion N.Y. Mets. Like the other 1970 Transograms, the issue was packaged in a three-statue cardboard box with cellophane front panel and cards printed on the back. Player cards are 2-9/16" x 3-1/2" and retain the basic format of Transogram cards of 1969-70: a color photo with player name in red and team, position and biographical details in black. Backs are blank. Values shown here are for cards cut from the box. Complete unopened boxes are worth 3-4X the figures shown.

		NM	EX	VG
Complete Boxed Set (5):		1,400	700.00	425.00
Complete Panel Set (5):		650.00	325.00	200.00
Complete Card Set (15):		350.00	175.00	100.00
Common Player:		12.50	6.25	3.75
	Series 21 Boxed Set	225.00	110.00	65.00
	Series 21 Uncut Box/Panel	125.00	65.00	35.00
(1)	Ed Kranepool	12.50	6.25	3.75
(2)	Al Weis	12.50	6.25	3.75
(3)	Tom Seaver	35.00	17.50	10.00
	Series 22 Boxed Set	125.00	65.00	35.00
	Series 22 Uncut Box/Panel	60.00	30.00	18.00
(4)	Ken Boswell	12.50	6.25	3.75
(5)	Jerry Koosman	12.50	6.25	3.75
(6)	Jerry Grote	12.50	6.25	3.75
	Series 23 Boxed Set	125.00	65.00	35.00
	Series 23 Uncut Box/Panel	60.00	30.00	18.00
(7)	Art Shamsky	12.50	6.25	3.75
(8)	Gary Gentry	12.50	6.25	3.75
(9)	Tommie Agee	12.50	6.25	3.75
	Series 24 Boxed Set	685.00	340.00	200.00
	Series 24 Uncut Box/Panel	350.00	175.00	100.00
(10)	Nolan Ryan	225.00	110.00	65.00
(11)	Tug McGraw	12.50	6.25	3.75
(12)	Cleon Jones	12.50	6.25	3.75
	Series 25 Boxed Set	150.00	75.00	45.00
	Series 25 Uncut Box/Panel	60.00	30.00	18.00
(13)	Ron Swoboda	12.50	6.25	3.75
(14)	Bud Harrelson	12.50	6.25	3.75
(15)	Donn Clendenon	12.50	6.25	3.75

1920s Otto Treulich & Son

OTTO TREULICH & SON
Hatters, Clothiers, Furnishers
756-760 Fullerton Avenue
N. E. COR. LINCOLN AVE. & HALSTED ST.
SUITS MADE TO MEASURE   CHICAGO
TELEPHONE LINCOLN 0486

This promotional photocard was issued, according to the blue rubber-stamped advertising on back, by Chicago clothier Otto Treulich & Son. Front of the approximately 2-3/4" x 3-1/2" card has a black-and-white studio portrait of Cubs pitcher Grover Cleveland Alexander, dressed to the nines (presumably in the haberdashery of the sponsor), and bearing a facsimile autograph.

	NM	EX	VG
Grover Alexander	400.00	200.00	120.00

1909 T.T.T. Cigarettes (T204)

 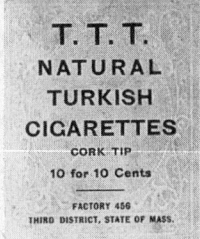

T. T. T.
NATURAL
TURKISH
CIGARETTES
CORK TIP
10 for 10 Cents
FACTORY 456
THIRD DISTRICT, STATE OF MASS.

This is one of two brands of cigarette advertising found on the backs of the ornate, gold-trimmed T204 cards. The initials stand for T.T. Tinayens, the Boston firm which also produced Ramly cigarettes, more commonly found mentioned on the cards' backs. In recent years collectors have begun paying a premium as high as 4-5X for the T.T.T. versions.

Premium: 4-5X
    (See checklist under Ramly Cigarettes listing.)

1888 Rafael Tuck & Sons Artistic Series Baseball

This series of die-cut color lithographed player figures does not represent actual players, but rather generic figures in late 19th Century uniforms labeled with the names of various major league teams of the era. The actual date of issue is unknown. The cardboard figures were issued in a sheet of 20 with duplicates. Individual figures vary in size with a typical piece about 1-1/2" wide and 2-3/4". Players are shown in batting, throwing and fielding poses. The set was lithographed in Germany and published in England by Rafael Tuck & Sons, a famous postcard publisher.

		NM	EX	VG
Complete Set (10):		3,000	1,500	900.00
Common Card:		325.00	160.00	95.00
(1)	Baltimore	325.00	160.00	95.00
(2)	Boston	325.00	160.00	95.00
(3)	Brooklyn	325.00	160.00	95.00
(4)	Chicago	325.00	160.00	95.00
(5)	Detroit	325.00	160.00	95.00
(6)	Indianapolis	325.00	160.00	95.00
(7)	New York	325.00	160.00	95.00
(8)	Philadelphia	325.00	160.00	95.00
(9)	Pittsburgh	325.00	160.00	95.00
(10)	St. Louis	325.00	160.00	95.00

1925 Turf Cigarettes

TURF
CIGARETTES
SPORTS RECORDS
Second Series, Nos. 26-50

50.—BASEBALL.
In America's great Ball-game, C. H. Sisler, of St. Louis (U.S.A.), put up the highest batting percentage known in the history of the American League. In his hit for 41,979. Mr. Sisler's name is to be inscribed on the $100,000 Base Ball Monument, which will be erected in Washington.

Alexander Boguslavsky Ltd.
55, PICCADILLY, LONDON, W.

"Sports Records" is the name of a two-series, 50-card issue by Turf Cigarettes. The last card in the set depicts George Sisler (though not named) on the front in a color action scene. Black-and-white back of the card describes Sisler's batting prowess. Like other British tobacco cards of the era, size is 2-5/8" x 1-3/8".

		NM	EX	VG
50	Baseball (George Sisler)	90.00	45.00	25.00

1909-11 Ty Cobb Tobacco (T206)

 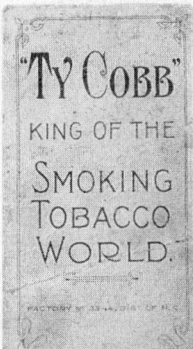

"TY COBB"
KING OF THE
SMOKING
TOBACCO
WORLD.

Much rarer than the famed Honus Wagner card from the related cigarette card series known collectively as T206, the Ty Cobb brand tobacco back was known in only about half a dozen collections until June 1997 when a find of five lower-grade specimens was auctioned. Because T206 was generally collected by front design, rather than back, through most of the hobby's history, it has only been in recent years that the value of the "Ty Cobb-back" T206 has begun to approach the other great rarities of the series. The only front known with a Cobb tobacco back is the red-background portrait. Some of the extant examples appear to have been hand-cut from a sheet. In April 2002 a PSA-graded Good example sold at an auction for $18,055. Most recently, an SGC-graded card sold at an auction for $25,000 in May 2005, and another sold at an auction for $24,655 in November 2005.

(See T206, #95b. Approximately 11 known.)

1910-1911 T3 Turkey Red Cabinets

 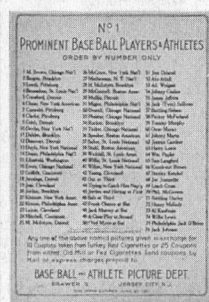

Turkey Red cabinet cards were obtained by mailing in coupons found in Turkey Red, Fez and Old Mill brand cigarettes. Turkey Reds measure 5-3/4" x 8", and feature full-color lithograph fronts with wide gray frames. Backs are known in three styles: 1) checklist with no ordering information, 2) checklist with ordering information, and, 3) with an illustrated ad for Turkey Red cigarettes. The checklist backs are found with both low- and high-number cards, the ad backs are only on cards #77-126. The series consists of 25 boxers and 100 baseball players. Coupons issued in the cigarette boxes indicate the first 50 baseball player cards were produced for spring, 1910, delivery, with the 25 boxers produced later that year and the final 50 baseball players issued in 1911.

		NM	EX	VG
Complete (Baseball) Set (100):		175,000	90,000	50,000
Common Player:		1,200	600.00	360.00
Turkey Red Ad Back: 1.5-2X				
1	Mordecai Brown	3,000	1,500	900.00
2	Bill Bergen	1,200	600.00	360.00
3	Tommy Leach	1,200	600.00	360.00
4	Roger Bresnahan	2,400	1,200	720.00
5	Sam Crawford	2,400	1,200	720.00
6	Hal Chase	1,440	720.00	435.00
7	Howie Camnitz	1,200	600.00	360.00
8	Fred Clarke	2,400	1,200	720.00
9	Ty Cobb	35,000	15,000	9,000
10	Art Devlin	1,200	600.00	360.00

#	Player			
11	Bill Dahlen	1,200	600.00	360.00
12	Wild Bill Donovan	1,200	600.00	360.00
13	Larry Doyle	1,200	600.00	360.00
14	Red Dooin	1,200	600.00	360.00
15	Kid Elberfeld	1,200	600.00	360.00
16	Johnny Evers	2,400	1,200	720.00
17	Clark Griffith	2,400	1,200	720.00
18	Hughie Jennings	2,400	1,200	720.00
19	Addie Joss	3,600	1,800	1,080
20	Tim Jordan	1,200	600.00	360.00
21	Red Kleinow	1,200	600.00	360.00
22	Harry Krause	1,200	600.00	360.00
23	Nap Lajoie	4,000	1,500	900.00
24	Mike Mitchell	1,200	600.00	360.00
25	Matty McIntyre	1,200	600.00	360.00
26	John McGraw	5,000	2,500	1,500
27	Christy Mathewson	12,000	3,600	2,160
28a	Harry McIntyre (Brooklyn)	1,200	600.00	360.00
28b	Harry McIntyre (Brooklyn and Chicago.)	1,200	600.00	360.00
29	Amby McConnell	2,000	1,000	600.00
30	George Mullin	1,200	600.00	360.00
31	Sherry Magee	1,200	600.00	360.00
32	Orval Overall	1,200	600.00	360.00
33	Jake Pfeister	1,200	600.00	360.00
34	Nap Rucker	1,200	600.00	360.00
35	Joe Tinker	2,400	1,200	720.00
36	Tris Speaker	6,000	3,000	1,800
37	Slim Sallee	1,200	600.00	360.00
38	Jake Stahl	1,200	600.00	360.00
39	Rube Waddell	2,400	1,200	720.00
40	Vic Willis	2,400	1,200	720.00
41	Hooks Wiltse	1,200	600.00	360.00
42	Cy Young	9,000	3,600	2,160
43	Out At Third	1,200	600.00	360.00
44	Trying To Catch Him Napping	1,200	600.00	360.00
45	Jordan & Herzog At First	1,200	600.00	360.00
46	Safe At Third	1,200	600.00	360.00
47	Frank Chance	2,400	1,200	720.00
48	Jack Murray	1,200	600.00	360.00
49	A Close Play At Second	1,200	600.00	360.00
50	Chief Myers	1,200	600.00	360.00
77	Red Ames	1,200	600.00	360.00
78	Home Run Baker	2,400	1,200	720.00
79	George Bell	1,200	600.00	360.00
80	Chief Bender	2,400	1,200	720.00
81	Bob Bescher	1,200	600.00	360.00
82	Kitty Bransfield	1,200	600.00	360.00
83	Al Bridwell	1,200	600.00	360.00
84	George Browne	1,200	600.00	360.00
85	Bill Burns	1,200	600.00	360.00
86	Bill Carrigan	1,200	600.00	360.00
87	Eddie Collins	2,400	1,200	720.00
88	Harry Coveleski	1,200	600.00	360.00
89	Lou Criger	1,200	600.00	360.00
90a	Mickey Doolin (Doolan)	1,320	660.00	395.00
90b	Mickey Doolan (name correct)	1,200	600.00	360.00
91	Tom Downey	1,200	600.00	360.00
92	Jimmy Dygert	1,200	600.00	360.00
93	Art Fromme	1,200	600.00	360.00
94	George Gibson	1,200	600.00	360.00
95	Peaches Graham	1,200	600.00	360.00
96	Bob Groom	1,200	600.00	360.00
97	Dick Hoblitzell	1,200	600.00	360.00
98	Solly Hofman	1,200	600.00	360.00
99	Walter Johnson	10,000	3,600	2,160
100	Davy Jones	1,200	600.00	360.00
101	Wee Willie Keeler	2,400	1,200	720.00
102	Johnny Kling	1,200	600.00	360.00
103	Ed Konetchy	1,200	600.00	360.00
104	Ed Lennox	1,200	600.00	360.00
105	Hans Lobert	1,200	600.00	360.00
106	Harry Lord	1,200	600.00	360.00
107	Rube Manning	2,000	1,000	600.00
108	Fred Merkle	1,200	600.00	360.00
109	Pat Moran	1,200	600.00	360.00
110	George McBride	1,200	600.00	360.00
111	Harry Niles	1,200	600.00	360.00
112a	Dode Paskert (Cincinnati)	1,200	600.00	360.00
112b	Dode Paskert (Cincinnati and Philadelphia)	1,200	600.00	360.00
113	Bugs Raymond	1,200	600.00	360.00
114	Bob Rhoades (Rhoads)	1,650	720.00	435.00
115	Admiral Schlei	1,200	600.00	360.00
116	Boss Schmidt	1,200	600.00	360.00
117	Wildfire Schulte	1,200	600.00	360.00
118	Frank Smith	1,200	600.00	360.00
119	George Stone	1,200	600.00	360.00
120	Gabby Street	1,200	600.00	360.00
121	Billy Sullivan	1,200	600.00	360.00
122a	Fred Tenney (New York)	1,200	600.00	360.00
122b	Fred Tenney (New York and Boston)	1,200	600.00	360.00
123	Ira Thomas	1,200	600.00	360.00
124	Bobby Wallace	2,400	1,200	720.00
125	Ed Walsh	2,400	1,200	720.00
126	Owen Wilson	1,200	600.00	360.00

1911 T5 Pinkerton Cabinets

Because they are photographs affixed to a cardboard backing, the cards in the 1911 Pinkerton set are considered "true" cabinet cards. The Pinkerton cabinets are a rather obscure issue, and because of their original method of distribution, it would be virtually impossible to assemble a complete set today. It remains uncertain how many subjects exist in the set. Pinkerton, the parent of Red Man and other tobacco products, offered the cabinets in exchange for coupons found in cigarette packages. According to an original advertising sheet, some 376 different photos were available. A consumer could exchange ten coupons for the card of his choice. The photos available included players from the 16 major league teams plus teams from the minor league

American Association, Southern Michigan Assn., and, probably, others. Pinkertons vary in both size and type of mount. The most desirable combination is a 3-3/8" x 5-1/2" photograph affixed to a thick cardboard mount measuring approximately 4-3/4" x 7-3/4". But original Pinkerton cabinets have also been found in different sizes and with less substantial backings. The most attractive mounts are embossed around the picture, but some Pinkertons have a white border surrounding the photograph. Prices listed are for cards with cardboard mounts. Cards with paper mounts are worth about 50-75 percent of listed prices. Some of the Pinkerton photos were reproduced in postcard size printed issues in later years; some with postcard style backs, some with scorecard backs and others are blank-backed (See 1911 Pinkerton).

		NM	EX	VG
Common Player:		1,000	500.00	315.00
Checklist Brochure:		625.00	315.00	190.00
Redemption Coupon:		500.00	250.00	150.00
Blank-Back Card: 5-10%				
Postcard-Back: 10-15%				
101	Jim Stephens	1,000	500.00	315.00
102	Bobby Wallace	2,190	1,095	655.00
103	Joe Lake	1,000	500.00	315.00
104	George Stone	1,000	500.00	315.00
105	Jack O'Connor	1,000	500.00	315.00
106	Bill Abstein	1,000	500.00	315.00
107	Rube Waddell	2,190	1,095	655.00
108	Roy Hartzell	1,000	500.00	315.00
109	Danny Hoffman	1,000	500.00	315.00
110	Dode Cris	1,000	500.00	315.00
111	Al Schweitzer	1,000	500.00	315.00
112	Art Griggs	1,000	500.00	315.00
113	Bill Bailey	1,000	500.00	315.00
114	Pat Newman	1,000	500.00	315.00
115	Harry Howell	1,000	500.00	315.00
117	Hobe Ferris	1,000	500.00	315.00
118	John McAleese	1,000	500.00	315.00
119	Ray Demmitt	1,000	500.00	315.00
120	Red Fisher	1,000	500.00	315.00
121	Frank Truesdale	1,000	500.00	315.00
122	Barney Pelty	1,000	500.00	315.00
123	Ed Killifer (Killefer)	1,000	500.00	315.00
151	Matty McIntyre	1,000	500.00	315.00
152	Jim Delahanty	1,000	500.00	315.00
153	Hughey Jennings	2,190	1,095	655.00
154	Ralph Works	1,000	500.00	315.00
155	George Moriarity (Moriarty)	1,000	500.00	315.00
156	Sam Crawford	2,190	1,095	655.00
157	Boss Schmidt	1,000	500.00	315.00
158	Owen Bush	1,000	500.00	315.00
159	Ty Cobb	8,750	4,375	2,625
160	Bill Donovan	1,000	500.00	315.00
161	Oscar Stanage	1,000	500.00	315.00
162	George Mullen (Mullin)	1,000	500.00	315.00
163	Davy Jones	1,000	500.00	315.00
164	Charley O'Leary	1,000	500.00	315.00
165	Tom Jones	1,000	500.00	315.00
166	Joe Casey	1,000	500.00	315.00
167	Ed Willetts (Willett)	1,000	500.00	315.00
168	Ed Lafeite (Lafitte)	1,000	500.00	315.00
169	Ty Cobb	20,000	4,530	2,720
170	Ty Cobb	20,000	4,530	2,720
201	John Evers	2,190	1,095	655.00
202	Mordecai Brown	2,190	1,095	655.00
203	King Cole	1,000	500.00	315.00
204	Johnny Cane	1,000	500.00	315.00
205	Heinie Zimmerman	1,000	500.00	315.00
206	Wildfire Schulte	1,000	500.00	315.00
207	Frank Chance	2,190	1,095	655.00
208	Joe Tinker	2,190	1,095	655.00
209	Orvall Overall	1,000	500.00	315.00
210	Jimmy Archer	1,000	500.00	315.00
211	Johnny Kling	1,000	500.00	315.00
212	Jimmy Sheckard	1,000	500.00	315.00
213	Harry McIntyre	1,000	500.00	315.00
214	Lew Richie	1,000	500.00	315.00
215	Ed Ruelbach	1,000	500.00	315.00
216	Artie Hoffman (Hofman)	1,000	500.00	315.00
217	Jake Pfeister	1,000	500.00	315.00
218	Harry Steinfeldt	1,000	500.00	315.00
219	Tom Needham	1,000	500.00	315.00
220	Ginger Beaumont	1,000	500.00	315.00
251	Christy Mathewson	10,000	2,815	1,690
252	Fred Merkle	1,000	500.00	315.00
253	Hooks Wiltsie	1,000	500.00	315.00
254	Art Devlin	1,000	500.00	315.00
255	Fred Snodgrass	1,000	500.00	315.00
256	Josh Devore	1,000	500.00	315.00

#	Player			
257	Red Murray	1,000	500.00	315.00
258	Cy Seymour	1,000	500.00	315.00
259	Rube Marquard	2,190	1,095	655.00
260	Larry Doyle	1,000	500.00	315.00
261	Bugs Raymond	1,000	500.00	315.00
262	Doc Crandall	1,000	500.00	315.00
263	Admiral Schlei	1,000	500.00	315.00
264	Chief Myers (Meyers)	1,000	500.00	315.00
265	Bill Dahlen	1,000	500.00	315.00
266	Beals Becker	1,000	500.00	315.00
267	Louis Drucke	1,000	500.00	315.00
301	Fred Luderus	1,000	500.00	315.00
302	John Titus	1,000	500.00	315.00
303	Red Dooin	1,000	500.00	315.00
304	Eddie Stack	1,000	500.00	315.00
305	Kitty Bransfield	1,000	500.00	315.00
306	Sherry Magee	1,000	500.00	315.00
307	Otto Knabe	1,000	500.00	315.00
308	Jimmy "Runt" Walsh	1,000	500.00	315.00
309	Earl Moore	1,000	500.00	315.00
310	Mickey Doolan	1,000	500.00	315.00
311	Ad Brennan	1,000	500.00	315.00
312	Bob Ewing	1,000	500.00	315.00
313	Lou Schettler	1,000	500.00	315.00
351	Joe Willis	1,000	500.00	315.00
352	Rube Ellis	1,000	500.00	315.00
353	Steve Evans	1,000	500.00	315.00
354	Miller Huggins	2,190	1,095	655.00
355	Arnold Hauser	1,000	500.00	315.00
356	Frank Corridon	1,000	500.00	315.00
357	Roger Bresnahan	2,190	1,095	655.00
358	Slim Sallee	1,000	500.00	315.00
359	Mike Mowrey	1,000	500.00	315.00
360	Ed Konetchy	1,000	500.00	315.00
361	Beckman	1,000	500.00	315.00
362	Rebel Oakes	1,000	500.00	315.00
363	Johnny Lush	1,000	500.00	315.00
364	Eddie Phelps	1,000	500.00	315.00
365	Robert Harmon	1,000	500.00	315.00
401	Lou (Pat) Moran	1,000	500.00	315.00
402	George McQuillian (McQuillan)	1,000	500.00	315.00
403	Johnny Bates	1,000	500.00	315.00
404	Eddie Grant	1,000	500.00	315.00
405	Tommy McMillan	1,000	500.00	315.00
406	Tommy Clark (Clarke)	1,000	500.00	315.00
407	Jack Rowan	1,000	500.00	315.00
408	Bob Bescher	1,000	500.00	315.00
409	Fred Beebe	1,000	500.00	315.00
410	Tom Downey	1,000	500.00	315.00
411	George Suggs	1,000	500.00	315.00
412	Hans Lobert	1,000	500.00	315.00
413	Jimmy Phelan	1,000	500.00	315.00
414	Dode Paskert	1,000	500.00	315.00
415	Ward Miller	1,000	500.00	315.00
416	Richard J. Egan	1,000	500.00	315.00
417	Art Fromme	1,000	500.00	315.00
418	Bill Burns	1,000	500.00	315.00
419	Clark Griffith	2,190	1,095	655.00
420	Dick Hoblitzell	1,000	500.00	315.00
421	Harry Gasper	1,000	500.00	315.00
422	Dave Altizer	1,000	500.00	315.00
423	Larry McLean	1,000	500.00	315.00
424	Mike Mitchell	1,000	500.00	315.00
451	John Hummel	1,000	500.00	315.00
452	Tony Smith	1,000	500.00	315.00
453	Bill Davidson	1,000	500.00	315.00
454	Ed Lennox	1,000	500.00	315.00
455	Zach Wheat	2,190	1,095	655.00
457	Elmer Knetzer	1,000	500.00	315.00
458	Rube Dessau	1,000	500.00	315.00
459	George Bell	1,000	500.00	315.00
460	Jake Daubert	1,000	500.00	315.00
461	Doc Scanlan	1,000	500.00	315.00
462	Nap Rucker	1,000	500.00	315.00
463	Cy Barger	1,000	500.00	315.00
464	Kaiser Wilhelm	1,000	500.00	315.00
465	Bill Bergen	1,000	500.00	315.00
466	Tex Erwin	1,000	500.00	315.00
501	Chas. Bender	2,190	1,095	655.00
502	John Coombs	1,000	500.00	315.00
503	Ed Plank	4,000	1,565	935.00
504	Amos Strunk	1,000	500.00	315.00
505	Connie Mack	2,190	1,095	655.00
506	Ira Thomas	1,000	500.00	315.00
507	Biscoe Lord (Briscoe)	1,000	500.00	315.00
508	Stuffy McInnis	1,000	500.00	315.00
509	Jimmy Dygert	1,000	500.00	315.00
510	Rube Oldring	1,000	500.00	315.00
511	Eddie Collins	2,190	1,095	655.00
512	Home Run Baker	2,190	1,095	655.00
513	Harry Krause	1,000	500.00	315.00
514	Harry Davis	1,000	500.00	315.00
515	Jack Barry	1,000	500.00	315.00
516	Jack Lapp	1,000	500.00	315.00
517	Cy Morgan	1,000	500.00	315.00
518	Danny Murphy	1,000	500.00	315.00
519	Topsy Hartsell	1,000	500.00	315.00
520	Paddy Livingston	1,000	500.00	315.00
521	P. Adkins	1,000	500.00	315.00
522	Eddie Collins	2,190	1,095	655.00
523	Paddy Livingston	1,000	500.00	315.00
551	Doc Gessler	1,000	500.00	315.00
552	Bill Cunningham	1,000	500.00	315.00
554	John Henry	1,000	500.00	315.00
555	Jack Lelivelt	1,000	500.00	315.00
556	Bobby Groome	1,000	500.00	315.00
557	Doc Ralston	1,000	500.00	315.00
558	Kid Elberfelt (Elberfeld)	1,000	500.00	315.00
559	Doc Reisling	1,000	500.00	315.00
560	Herman Schaefer	1,000	500.00	315.00
561	Walter Johnson	6,000	2,500	1,500
562	Dolly Gray	1,000	500.00	315.00
563	Wid Conroy	1,000	500.00	315.00
564	Charley Street	1,000	500.00	315.00
565	Bob Unglaub	1,000	500.00	315.00
566	Clyde Milan	1,000	500.00	315.00
567	George Browne	1,000	500.00	315.00

568	George McBride	1,000	500.00	315.00
569	Red Killifer (Killefer)	1,000	500.00	315.00
601	Addie Joss	2,190	1,095	655.00
602	Addie Joss	2,190	1,095	655.00
603	Napoleon Lajoie	2,190	1,095	655.00
604	Nig Clark (Clarke)	1,000	500.00	315.00
605	Cy Falkenberg	1,000	500.00	315.00
606	Harry Bemis	1,000	500.00	315.00
607	George Stovall	1,000	500.00	315.00
608	Fred Blanding	1,000	500.00	315.00
609	Elmer Koestner	1,000	500.00	315.00
610	Ted Easterly	1,000	500.00	315.00
611	Willie Mitchell	1,000	500.00	315.00
612	Hornhorst	1,000	500.00	315.00
613	Elmer Flick	2,190	1,095	655.00
614	Speck Harkness	1,000	500.00	315.00
615	Tuck Turner	1,000	500.00	315.00
616	Joe Jackson	50,000	10,000	6,000
617	Grover Land	1,000	500.00	315.00
618	Gladstone Graney	1,000	500.00	315.00
619	Dave Callahan	1,000	500.00	315.00
620	Ben DeMott	1,000	500.00	315.00
621	Neill Ball (Neal)	1,000	500.00	315.00
622	Dode Birmingham	1,000	500.00	315.00
623	George Kaler (Kahler)	1,000	500.00	315.00
624	Sid Smith	1,000	500.00	315.00
625	Bert Adams	1,000	500.00	315.00
626	Bill Bradley	1,000	500.00	315.00
627	Napoleon Lajoie	2,190	1,095	655.00
651	Bill Corrigan (Carrigan)	1,000	500.00	315.00
652	Joe Woods (Wood)	1,000	500.00	315.00
653	Heinie Wagner	1,000	500.00	315.00
654	Billy Purtell	1,000	500.00	315.00
655	Frank Smith	1,000	500.00	315.00
656	Harry Lord	1,000	500.00	315.00
657	Patsy Donovan	1,000	500.00	315.00
658	Duffy Lewis	1,000	500.00	315.00
659	Jack Kleinow	1,000	500.00	315.00
660	Ed Karger	1,000	500.00	315.00
661	Clyde Engle	1,000	500.00	315.00
662	Ben Hunt	1,000	500.00	315.00
663	Charlie Smith	1,000	500.00	315.00
664	Tris Speaker	3,000	1,155	695.00
665	Tom Madden	1,000	500.00	315.00
666	Larry Gardner	1,000	500.00	315.00
667	Harry Hooper	2,190	1,095	655.00
668	Marty McHale	1,000	500.00	315.00
669	Ray Collins	1,000	500.00	315.00
670	Jake Stahl	1,000	500.00	315.00
701	Dave Shean	1,000	500.00	315.00
702	Roy Miller	1,000	500.00	315.00
703	Fred Beck	1,000	500.00	315.00
704	Bill Collings (Collins)	1,000	500.00	315.00
705	Bill Sweeney	1,000	500.00	315.00
706	Buck Herzog	1,000	500.00	315.00
707	Bud Sharp (Sharpe)	1,000	500.00	315.00
708	Cliff Curtis	1,000	500.00	315.00
709	Al Mattern	1,000	500.00	315.00
710	Buster Brown	1,000	500.00	315.00
711	Bill Rariden	1,000	500.00	315.00
712	Grant	1,000	500.00	315.00
713	Ed Abbaticchio	1,000	500.00	315.00
714	Cecil Ferguson	1,000	500.00	315.00
715	Billy Burke	1,000	500.00	315.00
716	Sam Frock	1,000	500.00	315.00
717	Wilbur Goode (Good)	1,000	500.00	315.00
751	Charlie French	1,000	500.00	315.00
752	Patsy Dougherty	1,000	500.00	315.00
753	Shano Collins	1,000	500.00	315.00
754	Fred Parent	1,000	500.00	315.00
755	Willis Cole	1,000	500.00	315.00
756	Billy Sullivan	1,000	500.00	315.00
757	Rube Sutor (Suter)	1,000	500.00	315.00
758	Chick Gandil	2,315	1,155	695.00
759	Jim Scott	1,000	500.00	315.00
760	Ed Walsh	2,190	1,095	655.00
761	Gavvy Cravath	1,000	500.00	315.00
762	Bobby Messenger	1,000	500.00	315.00
763	Doc White	1,000	500.00	315.00
764	Rollie Zeider	1,000	500.00	315.00
765	Fred Payne	1,000	500.00	315.00
766	Lee Tannehill	1,000	500.00	315.00
767	Eddie Hahn	1,000	500.00	315.00
768	Hugh Duffy	2,190	1,095	655.00
769	Fred Olmstead	1,000	500.00	315.00
770	Lena Blackbourne (Blackburne)	1,000	500.00	315.00
771	Young "Cy" Young	1,000	500.00	315.00
801	Lew Brockett	1,000	500.00	315.00
802	Frank Laporte (LaPorte)	1,000	500.00	315.00
803	Bert Daniels	1,000	500.00	315.00
804	Walter Blair	1,000	500.00	315.00
805	Jack Knight	1,000	500.00	315.00
806	Jimmy Austin	1,000	500.00	315.00
807	Hal Chase	1,190	595.00	355.00
808	Birdie Cree	1,000	500.00	315.00
809	Jack Quinn	1,000	500.00	315.00
810	Walter Manning	1,000	500.00	315.00
811	Jack Warhop	1,000	500.00	315.00
812	Jeff Sweeney	1,000	500.00	315.00
813	Charley Hemphill	1,000	500.00	315.00
814	Harry Wolters	1,000	500.00	315.00
815	Tom Hughes	1,000	500.00	315.00
816	Earl Gardiner (Gardner)	1,000	500.00	315.00
851	John Flynn	1,000	500.00	315.00
852	Bill Powell	1,000	500.00	315.00
853	Honus Wagner	15,000	3,750	2,250
854	Bill Powell	1,000	500.00	315.00
855	Fred Clarke	2,190	1,095	655.00
856	Owen Wilson	1,000	500.00	315.00
857	George Gibson	1,000	500.00	315.00
858	Mike Simon	1,000	500.00	315.00
859	Tommy Leach	1,000	500.00	315.00
860	Lefty Leifeld (Leifield)	1,000	500.00	315.00
861	Nick Maddox	1,000	500.00	315.00
862	Dots Miller	1,000	500.00	315.00
863	Howard Camnitz	1,000	500.00	315.00
864	Deacon Phillippi (Phillippe)	1,000	500.00	315.00
865	Babe Adams	1,000	500.00	315.00
866	Ed Abbaticchio	1,000	500.00	315.00
867	Paddy O'Connor	1,000	500.00	315.00
868	Bobby Byrne	1,000	500.00	315.00
869	Vin Campbell	1,000	500.00	315.00
870	Ham Hyatt	1,000	500.00	315.00
871	Sam Leever	1,000	500.00	315.00
872	Hans Wagner	15,000	3,750	2,250
873	Hans Wagner	15,000	3,750	2,250
874	Bill McKecknie (McKechnie)	2,190	1,095	655.00
875	Kirby White	1,000	500.00	315.00
901	Jimmie Burke	1,000	500.00	315.00
902	Charlie Carr	1,000	500.00	315.00
903	Larry Cheney	1,000	500.00	315.00
904	Chet Chadbourne	1,000	500.00	315.00
905	Dan Howley	1,000	500.00	315.00
906	Jimmie Burke	1,000	500.00	315.00
907	Ray Mowe	1,000	500.00	315.00
908	Billy Milligan	1,000	500.00	315.00
909	Frank Oberlin	1,000	500.00	315.00
910	Ralph Glaze	1,000	500.00	315.00
911	O'Day	1,000	500.00	315.00
912	Kerns	1,000	500.00	315.00
913	Jim Duggan	1,000	500.00	315.00
914	Simmy Murch	1,000	500.00	315.00
915	Frank Delehanty	1,000	500.00	315.00
916	Craig	1,000	500.00	315.00
917	Jack Coffee (Coffey)	1,000	500.00	315.00
918	Lefty George	1,000	500.00	315.00
919	Otto Williams	1,000	500.00	315.00
920	M. Hayden	1,000	500.00	315.00
951	Joe Cantillon	1,000	500.00	315.00
952	Smith	1,000	500.00	315.00
953	Claud Rossman (Claude)	1,000	500.00	315.00
1001	Tony James	1,000	500.00	315.00
1002	Jack Powell	1,000	500.00	315.00
1003	Wm. J. Harbeau	1,000	500.00	315.00
1004	Homer Smoot	1,000	500.00	315.00
1051	Bill Friel	1,000	500.00	315.00
1052	Bill Friel	1,000	500.00	315.00
1053	Fred Odwell	1,000	500.00	315.00
1054	Alex Reilley	1,000	500.00	315.00
1055	Eugene Packard	1,000	500.00	315.00
1056	Irve Wrattan	1,000	500.00	315.00
1057	"Red" Nelson	1,000	500.00	315.00
1058	George Perring	1,000	500.00	315.00
1059	Glen Liebhardt	1,000	500.00	315.00
1060	Jimmie O'Rourke	1,000	500.00	315.00
1061	Fred Cook	1,000	500.00	315.00
1062	Charles Arbogast	1,000	500.00	315.00
1063	Jerry Downs	1,000	500.00	315.00
1064	"Bunk" Congalton	1,000	500.00	315.00
1065	Fred Carisch	1,000	500.00	315.00
1066	"Red" Sitton	1,000	500.00	315.00
1067	George Kaler (Kahler)	1,000	500.00	315.00
1068	Arthur Kruger	1,000	500.00	315.00
1102	Earl Yingling	1,000	500.00	315.00
1103	Jerry Freeman	1,800	500.00	315.00
1104	Harry Hinchman	1,000	500.00	315.00
1105	Jim Baskette	1,000	500.00	315.00
1106	Denny Sullivan	1,000	500.00	315.00
1107	Carl Robinson	1,000	500.00	315.00
1108	Bill Rodgers	1,000	500.00	315.00
1109	Hi West	1,000	500.00	315.00
1110	Billy Hallman	1,000	500.00	315.00
1111	Wm. Elwert	1,000	500.00	315.00
1112	Piano Legs Hickman	1,000	500.00	315.00
1113	Joe McCarthy	2,190	1,095	655.00
1114	Fred Abbott	1,000	500.00	315.00
1115	Jack Guilligan (Gilligan)	1,000	500.00	315.00
1613	C. Winger	1,000	500.00	315.00

1911 T201 Mecca Double Folders

These cards found in packages of Mecca cigarettes feature one player when the card is open, and another when the card is folded; two players sharing the same pair of legs. Mecca Double Folders measure about 2-1/8" to 2-3/16" x 4-11/16". The pictures are color lithographs, the text is printed in black. The cards contain an innovation in the form of the first use of player statistics. The 50-card set contains 100 different players including a number of Hall of Famers.

Examples authenticated and graded by major certification firms carry a much larger premium than most other cards of the era.

		NM	EX	VG
Complete Set (50):		25,000	7,000	2,650
Common Player:				
(1)	William Abstein, John Butler	385.00	85.00	30.00
(2)	Frank Baker, Edward Collins	560.00	180.00	75.00
(3)	Harry Baker, Thomas Downie (Downey)	385.00	85.00	30.00
(4)	James Barrett, Grant McGlynn	385.00	85.00	30.00
(5)	John Barry, John Lapp	385.00	85.00	30.00
(6)	Charles Bender, Reuben Oldring	435.00	135.00	55.00
(7)	William Bergen, Zack Wheat	400.00	130.00	50.00
(8)	Walter Blair, Roy Hartzell	385.00	85.00	30.00
(9)	Roger Bresnahan, Miller Huggins	650.00	200.00	80.00
(10)	Albert Bridwell, Christy Matthewson (Mathewson)	1,200	375.00	150.00
(11)	Mordecai Brown, Arthur Hofman	425.00	140.00	55.00
(12)	Robert Byrne, Fred Clarke	400.00	115.00	45.00
(13)	Frank Chance, John Evers	600.00	200.00	80.00
(14)	Harold Chase, Edward Sweeney	400.00	100.00	40.00
(15)	Edward Cicotte, John Thoney	625.00	140.00	55.00
(16)	Thomas Clarke, Harry Gaspar	385.00	85.00	30.00
(17)	Ty Cobb, Sam Crawford	3,000	1,000	400.00
(18)	Leonard Cole, John Kling	385.00	85.00	30.00
(19)	John Coombs, Ira Thomas	385.00	85.00	30.00
(20)	Jake Daubert, Nap Rucker	385.00	85.00	30.00
(21)	Bill Donovan, Ralph Stroud	385.00	85.00	30.00
(22)	Charles Dooin, John Titus	385.00	85.00	30.00
(23)	Patsy Dougherty, Harry Lord	500.00	165.00	65.00
(24)	Jerry Downs, Fred Odwell	385.00	85.00	30.00
(25)	Larry Doyle, Chief Meyers	385.00	85.00	30.00
(26)	James Dygert, Cy Seymour	385.00	85.00	30.00
(27)	Norman Elberfeld, George McBride	385.00	85.00	30.00
(28)	Fred Falkenberg, Napoleon Lajoie	575.00	190.00	75.00
(29)	Edward Fitzpatrick, Ed Killian	385.00	85.00	30.00
(30)	Russell Ford, Otis Johnson	385.00	85.00	30.00
(31)	Edward Foster, Joseph Ward	385.00	85.00	30.00
(32)	Earl Gardner, Tris Speaker	600.00	200.00	80.00
(33)	George Gibson, Thomas Leach	385.00	85.00	30.00
(34)	George Graham, Al Mattern	385.00	85.00	30.00
(35)	Edward Grant, John McLean	385.00	85.00	30.00
(36)	Arnold Hauser, Ernest Lush	385.00	85.00	30.00
(37)	Charles Herzog, Roy Miller	385.00	85.00	30.00
(38)	Charles Hickman, Harry Hinchman	385.00	85.00	30.00
(39)	Hugh Jennings, Edgar Summers	425.00	140.00	55.00
(40)	Walter Johnson, Charles Street	1,200	400.00	160.00
(41)	Frank LaPorte, James Stephens	385.00	85.00	30.00
(42)	Joseph Lake, Robert Wallace	400.00	130.00	50.00
(43)	Albert Leifield, Mike Simon	385.00	85.00	30.00
(44)	John Lobert, Earl Moore	385.00	85.00	30.00
(45)	Arthur McCabe, Charles Starr	385.00	85.00	30.00
(46)	Lewis McCarty, Joseph McGinnity	400.00	130.00	60.00
(47)	Fred Merkle, George Wiltse	385.00	85.00	30.00
(48)	Frederick Payne, Edward Walsh	400.00	130.00	60.00
(49)	George Stovall, Terrence Turner	385.00	85.00	30.00
(50)	Otto Williams, Orville Woodruff	385.00	85.00	30.00

1912 T202 Hassan Triple Folders

Measuring about 5-1/4" x 2-1/4", Hassan cigarette cards carried the concept of multiple-player cards even further than the double-fold Mecca set of the previous year. Scored so that the player pictures on each end - which are full-color and very close to exact duplicates of T205 "Gold Borders" cards - can fold over the black-and-white action-photo center panel, the Hassan Triple Folder appears like a booklet when closed. The individual player panels are not necessarily related to the action scene. The Hassan Triple Folders feature player biographies on the back of the two individual cards with a description of the action on the back of the center panel. Values depend on the player featured in the center panel, as well as the players featured on the end cards. Moreso than most contemporary cards, the value of NM or better T202s that have been graded by a major certification company well as the players featured on the end cards. Moreso than most contemporary issues, T202s that have been graded NM or better by a reputable certification company carry a larger premium over ungraded examples.

		NM	EX	VG
	Complete Set (132):	175,000	45,000	20,000
	Common Player:	1,000	250.00	100.00
(1)	A Close Play At The Home Plate (LaPorte, Wallace)	1,000	250.00	100.00
(2)	A Close Play At The Home Plate (Pelty, Wallace)	1,000	250.00	100.00
(3)	A Desperate Slide For Third (Cobb, O'Leary)	5,800	2,000	900.00
(4)	A Great Batsman (Barger, Bergen)	1,000	250.00	100.00
(5)	A Great Batsman (Bergen, Rucker)	1,000	250.00	100.00
(6)	Ambrose McConnell At Bat (Blair, Quinn)	1,000	250.00	100.00
(7)	A Wide Throw Saves Crawford (Mullin, Stanage)	1,000	250.00	100.00
(8)	Baker Gets His Man (Baker, Collins)	1,200	400.00	200.00
(9)	Birmingham Gets To Third (Johnson, Street)	1,400	500.00	200.00
(10)	Birmingham's Home Run (Birmingham, Turner)	1,000	250.00	100.00
(11)	Bush Just Misses Austin (Magee, Moran)	1,000	250.00	100.00
(12)	Carrigan Blocks His Man (Gaspar, McLean)	1,000	250.00	100.00
(13)	Carrigan Blocks His Man (Carrigan, Wagner)	1,000	250.00	100.00
(14)	Catching Him Napping (Bresnahan, Oakes)	1,000	250.00	100.00
(15)	Caught Asleep Off First (Bresnahan, Harmon)	1,000	250.00	100.00
(16)	Chance Beats Out A Hit (Chance, Foxen)	1,000	250.00	100.00
(17)	Chance Beats Out A Hit (Archer, McIntyre)	1,000	250.00	100.00
(18)	Chance Beats Out A Hit (Archer, Overall)	1,000	250.00	100.00
(19)	Chance Beats Out A Hit (Archer, Rowan)	1,000	250.00	100.00
(20)	Chance Beats Out A Hit (Chance, Shean)	1,000	250.00	100.00
(21)	Chase Dives Into Third (Chase, Wolter)	1,000	250.00	100.00
(22)	Chase Dives Into Third (Clarke, Gibson)	1,000	250.00	100.00
(23)	Chase Dives Into Third (Gibson, Phillippe)	1,000	250.00	100.00
(24)	Chase Gets Ball Too Late (Egan, Mitchell)	1,000	250.00	100.00
(25)	Chase Gets Ball Too Late (Chase, Wolter)	1,000	250.00	100.00
(26)	Chase Guarding First (Chase, Wolter)	1,000	250.00	100.00
(27)	Chase Guarding First (Clarke, Gibson)	1,000	250.00	100.00
(28)	Chase Guarding First (Gibson, Leifield)	1,000	250.00	100.00
(29)	Chase Ready For The Squeeze Play (Magee, Paskert)	1,000	250.00	100.00
(30)	Chase Safe At Third (Baker, Barry)	1,000	250.00	100.00
(31)	Chief Bender Waiting For A Good One (Bender, Thomas)	1,000	250.00	100.00
(32)	Clarke Hikes For Home (Bridwell, Kling)	1,000	250.00	100.00
(33)	Close At First (Ball, Stovall)	1,000	100.00	50.00
(34)	Close At The Plate (Payne, Walsh)	1,000	250.00	100.00
(35)	Close At The Plate (Payne, White)	1,000	250.00	100.00
(36)	Close At Third - Speaker (Speaker, Wood)	1,400	500.00	200.00
(37)	Close At Third - Wagner (Carrigan, Wagner)	1,000	250.00	100.00
(38)	Collins Easily Safe (Byrne, Clarke)	1,000	250.00	100.00
(39)	Collins Easily Safe (Baker, Collins)	1,000	250.00	100.00
(40)	Collins Easily Safe (Collins, Murphy)	1,000	250.00	100.00
(41)	Crawford About To Smash One (Stanage, Summers)	1,000	250.00	100.00
(42)	Cree Rolls Home (Daubert, Hummel)	1,000	250.00	100.00
(43)	Davy Jones' Great Slide (Delahanty, Jones)	1,000	250.00	100.00
(44)	Devlin Gets His Man (Devlin (Giants), Mathewson)	1,800	600.00	300.00
(45)	Devlin Gets His Man (Devlin (Rustlers), Mathewson)	3,500	1,200	500.00
(46)	Devlin Gets His Man (Fletcher, Mathewson)	1,900	700.00	300.00
(47)	Devlin Gets His Man (Mathewson, Meyers)	2,000	700.00	300.00
(48)	Donlin Out At First (Camnitz, Gibson)	1,000	250.00	100.00
(49)	Donlin Out At First (Doyle, Merkle)	1,000	250.00	100.00
(50)	Donlin Out At First (Leach, Wilson)	1,000	250.00	100.00
(51)	Donlin Out At First (Dooin, Magee)	1,000	250.00	100.00
(52)	Donlin Out At First (Gibson, Phillippe)	1,000	250.00	100.00
(53)	Dooin Gets His Man (Dooin, Doolan)	1,000	250.00	100.00
(54)	Dooin Gets His Man (Dooin, Lobert)	1,000	250.00	100.00
(55)	Dooin Gets His Man (Dooin, Titus)	1,000	250.00	100.00
(56)	Easy For Larry (Doyle, Merkle)	1,000	250.00	100.00
(57)	Elberfeld Beats The Throw (Elberfeld, Milan)	1,000	250.00	100.00
(58)	Elberfeld Gets His Man (Elberfeld, Milan)	1,000	250.00	100.00
(59)	Engle In A Close Play (Engle, Speaker)	1,300	400.00	200.00
(60)	Evers Makes A Safe Slide (Archer, Evers)	1,000	250.00	100.00
(61)	Evers Makes A Safe Slide (Chance, Evers)	1,700	600.00	300.00
(62)	Evers Makes A Safe Slide (Archer, Overall)	1,000	250.00	100.00
(63)	Evers Makes A Safe Slide (Archer, Reulbach)	1,000	250.00	100.00
(64)	Evers Makes A Safe Slide (Chance, Tinker)	3,000	1,000	400.00
(65)	Fast Work At Third (Cobb, O'Leary)	4,800	1,100	400.00
(66)	Ford Putting Over A Spitter (Ford, Vaughn)	1,000	250.00	100.00
(67)	Ford Putting Over A Spitter (Sweeney, Ford)	1,000	250.00	100.00
(68)	Good Play At Third (Cobb, Moriarity (Moriarty))	2,300	800.00	400.00
(69)	Grant Gets His Man (Grant, Hoblitzell)	1,000	250.00	100.00
(70)	Hal Chase Too Late (McConnell, McIntyre)	1,000	250.00	100.00
(71)	Hal Chase Too Late (McLean, Suggs)	1,000	250.00	100.00
(72)	Harry Lord At Third (Lennox, Tinker)	1,000	250.00	100.00
(73)	Hartzell Covering Third (Dahlen, Scanlan)	1,000	250.00	100.00
(74)	Hartsel Strikes Out (Gray, Groom)	1,000	250.00	100.00
(75)	Held At Third (Lord, Tannehill)	1,000	250.00	100.00
(76)	Jake Stahl Guarding First (Cicotte, Stahl)	1,300	500.00	200.00
(77)	Jim Delahanty At Bat (Delahanty, Jones)	1,000	250.00	100.00
(78)	Just Before The Battle (Ames, Meyers)	1,000	250.00	100.00
(79)	Just Before The Battle (Bresnahan, McGraw)	1,000	250.00	100.00
(80)	Just Before The Battle (Crandall, Meyers)	1,000	250.00	100.00
(81)	Just Before The Battle (Becker, Devore)	1,000	250.00	100.00
(82)	Just Before The Battle (Fletcher, Mathewson)	1,900	700.00	300.00
(83)	Just Before The Battle (Marquard, Meyers)	1,000	250.00	100.00
(84)	Just Before The Battle (Jennings, McGraw)	1,000	250.00	100.00
(85)	Just Before The Battle (Mathewson, Meyers)	1,300	500.00	200.00
(86)	Just Before The Battle (Murray, Snodgrass)	1,000	250.00	100.00
(87)	Just Before The Battle (Meyers, Wiltse)	1,000	250.00	100.00
(88)	Knight Catches A Runner (Johnson, Knight)	1,300	500.00	200.00
(89)	Lobert Almost Caught (Bridwell, Kling)	1,000	250.00	100.00
(90)	Lobert Almost Caught (Kling, Young)	1,700	400.00	200.00
(91)	Lobert Almost Caught (Kling, Mattern)	1,000	250.00	100.00
(92)	Lobert Almost Caught (Kling, Steinfeldt)	1,000	250.00	100.00
(93)	Lobert Gets Tenney (Dooin, Lobert)	1,000	250.00	100.00
(94)	Lord Catches His Man (Lord, Tannehil)	1,000	250.00	100.00
(95)	McConnell Caught (Needham, Richie)	1,000	250.00	100.00
(96)	McIntyre At Bat (McConnell, McIntyre)	1,000	250.00	100.00
(97)	Moriarty Spiked (Stanage, Willett)	1,000	250.00	100.00
(98)	Nearly Caught (Bates, Bescher)	1,000	250.00	100.00
(99)	Oldring Almost Home (Lord, Oldring)	1,000	250.00	100.00
(100)	Schaefer On First (McBride, Milan)	1,000	250.00	100.00
(101)	Schaefer Steals Second (Griffith, McBride)	1,000	250.00	100.00
(102)	Scoring From Second (Lord, Oldring)	1,000	250.00	100.00
(103)	Scrambling Back To First (Barger, Bergen)	1,000	250.00	100.00
(104)	Scrambling Back To First (Chase, Wolter)	1,000	250.00	100.00
(105)	Speaker Almost Caught (Clarke, Miller)	1,300	500.00	200.00
(106)	Speaker Rounding Third (Speaker, Wood)	2,600	900.00	400.00
(107)	Speaker Scores (Engle, Speaker)	2,000	700.00	300.00
(108)	Stahl Safe (Austin, Stovall)	1,000	250.00	100.00
(109)	Stone About To Swing (Schulte, Sheckard)	1,000	250.00	100.00
(110)	Sullivan Puts Up A High One (Evans, Huggins)	1,000	250.00	100.00
(111)	Sullivan Puts Up A High One (Gray, Groom)	1,000	250.00	100.00
(112)	Sweeney Gets Stahl (Ford, Vaughn)	1,000	250.00	100.00
(113)	Sweeney Gets Stahl (Ford, Sweeney)	1,000	250.00	100.00
(114)	Tenney Lands Safely (Latham, Raymond)	1,000	250.00	100.00
(115)	The Athletic Infield (Baker, Barry)	1,000	250.00	100.00
(116)	The Athletic Infield (Brown, Graham)	1,000	250.00	100.00
(117)	The Athletic Infield (Hauser, Konetchy)	1,000	250.00	100.00
(118)	The Athletic Infield (Krause, Thomas)	1,000	250.00	100.00
(119)	The Pinch Hitter (Egan, Hoblitzell)	1,000	250.00	100.00
(120)	The Scissors Slide (Birmingham, Turner)	1,000	250.00	100.00
(121)	Tom Jones At Bat (Fromme, McLean)	1,000	250.00	100.00
(122)	Tom Jones At Bat (Gaspar, McLean)	1,000	250.00	100.00
(123)	Too Late For Devlin (Ames, Meyers)	1,000	250.00	100.00
(124)	Too Late For Devlin (Crandall, Meyers)	1,000	250.00	100.00
(125)	Too Late For Devlin (Devlin (Giants), Mathewson)	2,000	700.00	300.00
(126)	Too Late For Devlin (Devlin (Rustlers), Mathewson)	3,900	1,400	600.00
(127)	Too Late For Devlin (Marquard, Meyers)	1,000	250.00	100.00
(128)	Too Late For Devlin (Meyers, Wiltse)	1,000	250.00	100.00
(129)	Ty Cobb Steals Third (Cobb, Jennings)	6,300	2,200	1,000
(130)	Ty Cobb Steals Third (Cobb, Moriarty)	4,400	1,500	700.00
(131)	Ty Cobb Steals Third (Austin, Stovall)	3,000	1,100	500.00
(132)	Wheat Strikes Out (Dahlen, Wheat)	1,300	500.00	200.00

1909 T204

(See 1909 Ramly Cigarettes, 1909 T.T.T. Cigarettes.)

1911 T205 Gold Border

Featuring distinctive gold-leaf borders, these cards were issued in a number of different cigarette brands. The cards nominally measure 1-7/16" x 2-5/8" although many cards, even though untrimmed or unaltered, measure somewhat less than those dimensions in length and/or width. American League cards feature a color lithograph of the player inside a stylized baseball diamond. National League cards have head-and-shoulders portraits on a plain background, plus the first-ever use of a facsimile autograph in a major card set. The 12 minor league players in the set feature three-quarter length portraits or action pictures in an elaborate frame of columns and other devices. Card backs of the major leaguers carry the player's full name (another first) and statistics. Card backs of the minor leaguers lack the statistics. The complete set price does not include the scarcer of the letter-suffixed variations. Values shown are for cards with the most common cigarette advertising on back: Piedmont and Sweet Caporal. Cards of other brands may carry a premium (see listings under brand name). The condition of the fragile gold leaf on the borders is an important grading consideration.

		NM	EX	VG
	Common Player:	700.00	100.00	50.00
(1)	Edward J. Abbaticchio	700.00	100.00	50.00
(2)	Doc Adkins	1,600	200.00	100.00
(3)	Leon K. Ames	700.00	100.00	50.00
(4)	Jas. P. Archer	700.00	100.00	50.00
(5)	Jimmy Austin	700.00	100.00	50.00
(6)	Bill Bailey	700.00	100.00	50.00
(7)	Home Run Baker	2,300	400.00	100.00
(8)	Neal Ball	700.00	100.00	50.00
(9)	E.B. Barger (Full "B" on cap.)	1,500	200.00	100.00
(10)	E.B. Barger (Partial "B" on cap.)	2,400	400.00	200.00
(11)	Jack Barry	700.00	100.00	50.00

No.	Player	NM	EX	VG
(12)	Emil Batch	1,600	200.00	100.00
(13)	John W. Bates	700.00	100.00	50.00
(14)	Fred Beck	700.00	100.00	50.00
(15)	B. Becker	700.00	100.00	50.00
(16)	George G. Bell	700.00	100.00	50.00
(17)	Chas. Bender	2,100	300.00	100.00
(18)	William Bergen	700.00	100.00	50.00
(19)	Bob Bescher	700.00	100.00	50.00
(20)	Joe Birmingham	700.00	100.00	50.00
(21)	Lena Blackburne	700.00	100.00	50.00
(22)	William E. Bransfield	700.00	100.00	50.00
(23)	Roger P. Bresnahan (Mouth closed.)	1,700	250.00	100.00
(24)	Roger P. Bresnahan (Mouth open.)	3,400	500.00	200.00
(25)	A.H. Bridwell	700.00	100.00	50.00
(26)	Mordecai Brown	2,000	300.00	100.00
(27)	Robert Byrne	700.00	100.00	50.00
(28)	Hick Cady	1,600	200.00	100.00
(29)	H. Camnitz	700.00	100.00	50.00
(30)	Bill Carrigan	700.00	100.00	50.00
(31)	Frank J. Chance	2,300	300.00	100.00
(32a)	Hal Chase (Both ears show, gold diamond frame extends below shoulders.)	1,100	200.00	100.00
(32b)	Hal Chase (Both ears show, gold diamond frame ends at shoulders.)	1,600	200.00	100.00
(33)	Hal Chase (Only left ear shows.)	3,200	500.00	200.00
(34)	Ed Cicotte	2,600	400.00	200.00
(35)	Fred C. Clarke	1,400	200.00	100.00
(36)	Ty Cobb	13,200	3,800	1,100
(37)	Eddie Collins (Mouth closed.)	2,100	300.00	100.00
(38)	Eddie Collins (Mouth open.)	4,700	700.00	300.00
(39)	Jimmy Collins	2,600	400.00	100.00
(40)	Frank J. Corridon	700.00	100.00	50.00
(41a)	Otis Crandall ("t" not crossed in name.)	1,000	200.00	100.00
(41b)	Otis Crandall ("t" crossed in name.)	1,300	200.00	100.00
(42)	Lou Criger	700.00	100.00	50.00
(43)	W.F. Dahlen	2,200	300.00	100.00
(44)	Jake Daubert	700.00	100.00	50.00
(45)	Jim Delahanty	700.00	100.00	50.00
(46)	Arthur Devlin	700.00	100.00	50.00
(47)	Josh Devore	700.00	100.00	50.00
(48)	W.R. Dickson	700.00	100.00	50.00
(49)	Jiggs Donohue (Donahue)	2,900	400.00	200.00
(50)	Chas. S. Dooin	700.00	100.00	50.00
(51)	Michael J. Doolan	700.00	100.00	50.00
(52a)	Patsy Dougherty (Red sock for team emblem.)	3,900	600.00	200.00
(52b)	Patsy Dougherty (White sock for team emblem.)	2,600	400.00	200.00
(53)	Thomas Downey	700.00	100.00	50.00
(54)	Larry Doyle	700.00	100.00	50.00
(55)	Hugh Duffy	2,800	400.00	100.00
(56)	Jack Dunn	2,600	400.00	200.00
(57)	Jimmy Dygert	700.00	100.00	50.00
(58)	R. Egan	700.00	100.00	50.00
(59)	Kid Elberfeld	700.00	100.00	50.00
(60)	Clyde Engle	700.00	100.00	50.00
(61)	Louis Evans	700.00	100.00	50.00
(62)	John J. Evers	3,300	500.00	200.00
(63)	Robert Ewing	700.00	100.00	50.00
(64)	G.C. Ferguson	700.00	100.00	50.00
(65)	Ray Fisher	2,900	400.00	200.00
(66)	Arthur Fletcher	700.00	100.00	50.00
(67)	John A. Flynn	700.00	100.00	50.00
(68)	Russ Ford (black cap)	1,100	200.00	100.00
(69)	Russ Ford (white cap)	2,200	300.00	100.00
(70)	Wm. A. Foxen	700.00	100.00	50.00
(71)	Jimmy Frick	1,600	200.00	100.00
(72)	Arthur Fromme	700.00	100.00	50.00
(73)	Earl Gardner	900.00	100.00	50.00
(74)	H.L. Gaspar	700.00	100.00	50.00
(75)	George Gibson	700.00	100.00	50.00
(76)	Wilbur Goode	700.00	100.00	50.00
(77)	George F. Graham (Rustlers)	700.00	100.00	50.00
(78)	George F. Graham (Cubs)	1,700	300.00	100.00
(79)	Edward L. Grant	2,400	400.00	100.00
(80a)	Dolly Gray (No stats on back.)	3,400	500.00	200.00
(80b)	Dolly Gray (Stats on back.)	4,800	700.00	300.00
(81)	Clark Griffith	1,800	300.00	100.00
(82)	Bob Groom	700.00	100.00	50.00
(83)	Charlie Hanford	1,600	200.00	100.00
(84)	Bob Harmon (Both ears show.)	700.00	100.00	50.00
(85)	Bob Harmon (Only left ear shows.)	2,500	400.00	200.00
(86)	Topsy Hartsel	700.00	100.00	50.00
(87)	Arnold J. Hauser	700.00	100.00	50.00
(88)	Charlie Hemphill	700.00	100.00	50.00
(89)	C.L. Herzog	700.00	100.00	50.00
(90a)	R. Hoblitzell (No stats on back.)(A PSA-graded EX-MT example was auctioned for $33,000 in 2005.)		22,000	10,000
(90b)	R. Hoblitzell ("Cin." after 2nd 1908 in stats.)	1,600	200.00	100.00
(90c)	R. Hoblitzel (Name incorrect, no "Cin." after 1908 in stats.)	3,400	500.00	200.00
(90d)	R. Hoblitzell (Name correct, no "Cin." after 1908 in stats.)	8,400	1,200	500.00
(91)	Danny Hoffman	700.00	100.00	50.00
(92)	Miller J. Huggins	1,900	300.00	100.00
(93)	John E. Hummel	700.00	100.00	50.00
(94)	Fred Jacklitsch	700.00	100.00	50.00
(95)	Hughie Jennings	1,400	200.00	100.00
(96)	Walter Johnson	8,400	1,300	500.00
(97)	D. Jones	700.00	100.00	50.00
(98)	Tom Jones	700.00	100.00	50.00
(99)	Addie Joss	9,000	1,400	500.00
(100)	Ed Karger	2,300	300.00	100.00
(101)	Ed Killian	700.00	100.00	50.00
(102)	Red Kleinow	1,600	200.00	100.00

No.	Player	NM	EX	VG
(103)	John G. Kling	700.00	100.00	50.00
(104)	Jack Knight	700.00	100.00	50.00
(105)	Ed Konetchy	700.00	100.00	50.00
(106)	Harry Krause	700.00	100.00	50.00
(107)	Floyd M. Kroh	700.00	100.00	50.00
(108)	Frank LaPorte	700.00	100.00	50.00
(109)	Frank Lang (Lange)	700.00	100.00	50.00
(110a)	A. Latham (A. Latham on back.)	1,900	300.00	100.00
(110b)	A. Latham (W.A. Latham on back.)	3,000	500.00	200.00
(111)	Thomas W. Leach	700.00	100.00	50.00
(112)	Watty Lee	1,600	200.00	100.00
(113)	Sam Leever	700.00	100.00	50.00
(114a)	A. Leifield (Initial "A." on front.)	2,400	400.00	100.00
(114b)	A.P. Leifield (Initials "A.P." on front.)	2,800	400.00	200.00
(115)	Edgar Lennox	700.00	100.00	50.00
(116)	Paddy Livingston	700.00	100.00	50.00
(117)	John B. Lobert	700.00	100.00	50.00
(118)	Bris Lord (Athletics)	700.00	100.00	50.00
(119)	Harry Lord (White Sox)	700.00	100.00	50.00
(120)	Jno. C. Lush	700.00	100.00	50.00
(121)	Nick Maddox	700.00	100.00	50.00
(122)	Sherwood R. Magee	900.00	100.00	50.00
(123)	R.W. Marquard	2,300	300.00	100.00
(124)	C. Mathewson	8,800	1,300	500.00
(125)	A.A. Mattern	700.00	100.00	50.00
(126)	Sport McAllister	1,600	200.00	100.00
(127)	George McBride	900.00	100.00	50.00
(128)	Amby McConnell	700.00	100.00	50.00
(129)	P.M. McElveen	700.00	100.00	50.00
(130)	J.J. McGraw	2,300	300.00	100.00
(131)	Harry McIntire (Cubs)	700.00	100.00	50.00
(132)	Matty McIntyre (White Sox)	700.00	100.00	50.00
(133)	M.A. McLean (initials actually J.B.)	700.00	100.00	50.00
(134)	Fred Merkle	700.00	100.00	50.00
(135)	George Merritt	1,600	200.00	100.00
(136)	J.T. Meyers	700.00	100.00	50.00
(137)	Clyde Milan	700.00	100.00	50.00
(138)	J.D. Miller	700.00	100.00	50.00
(139)	M.F. Mitchell	700.00	100.00	50.00
(140a)	P.J. Moran (Stray line of type below stats.)	12,000	1,800	700.00
(140b)	P.J. Moran (No stray line.)	700.00	100.00	50.00
(141)	George Moriarty	700.00	100.00	50.00
(142)	George Mullin	700.00	100.00	50.00
(143)	Danny Murphy	700.00	100.00	50.00
(144)	Jack Murray	700.00	100.00	50.00
(145)	John Nee	1,600	200.00	100.00
(146)	Thomas J. Needham	700.00	100.00	50.00
(147)	Rebel Oakes	700.00	100.00	50.00
(148)	Rube Oldring	700.00	100.00	50.00
(149)	Charley O'Leary	700.00	100.00	50.00
(150)	Fred Olmstead	700.00	100.00	50.00
(151)	Orval Overall	700.00	100.00	50.00
(152)	Freddy Parent	700.00	100.00	50.00
(153)	George Paskert	700.00	100.00	50.00
(154)	Fred Payne	700.00	100.00	50.00
(155)	Barney Pelty	800.00	100.00	50.00
(156)	John Pfeister	700.00	100.00	50.00
(157)	Jimmy Phelan	1,600	200.00	100.00
(158)	E.J. Phelps	700.00	100.00	50.00
(159)	C. Phillippe	700.00	100.00	50.00
(160)	Jack Quinn	700.00	100.00	50.00
(161)	A.L. Raymond	1,600	200.00	100.00
(162)	E.M. Reulbach	700.00	100.00	50.00
(163)	Lewis Richie	700.00	100.00	50.00
(164)	John A. Rowan	2,300	300.00	100.00
(165)	George N. Rucker	700.00	100.00	50.00
(166)	W.D. Scanlan	2,900	400.00	200.00
(167)	Germany Schaefer	700.00	100.00	50.00
(168)	George Schlei	700.00	100.00	50.00
(169)	Boss Schmidt	700.00	100.00	50.00
(170)	F.M. Schulte	700.00	100.00	50.00
(171)	Jim Scott	700.00	100.00	50.00
(172)	B.H. Sharpe	700.00	100.00	50.00
(173)	David Shean (Rustlers)	700.00	100.00	50.00
(174)	David Shean (Cubs)	2,500	400.00	200.00
(175)	Jas. T. Sheckard	700.00	100.00	50.00
(176)	Hack Simmons	700.00	100.00	50.00
(177)	Tony Smith	700.00	100.00	50.00
(178)	Fred C. Snodgrass	700.00	100.00	50.00
(179)	Tris Speaker	5,200	800.00	300.00
(180)	Jake Stahl	1,100	200.00	100.00
(181)	Oscar Stanage	700.00	100.00	50.00
(182)	Harry Steinfeldt	700.00	100.00	50.00
(183)	George Stone	700.00	100.00	50.00
(184)	George Stovall	700.00	100.00	50.00
(185)	Gabby Street	700.00	100.00	50.00
(186)	George F. Suggs	1,900	300.00	100.00
(187)	Ed Summers	700.00	100.00	50.00
(188)	Jeff Sweeney	2,700	400.00	200.00
(189)	Lee Tannehill	700.00	100.00	50.00
(190)	Ira Thomas	700.00	100.00	50.00
(191)	Joe Tinker	2,200	300.00	100.00
(192)	John Titus	700.00	100.00	50.00
(193)	Terry Turner	2,600	400.00	200.00
(194)	James Vaughn	2,900	400.00	200.00
(195)	Charles Wagner	3,200	500.00	200.00
(196)	Bobby Wallace (With cap.)	1,800	300.00	100.00
(197a)	Bobby Wallace (No cap, one line of 1910 stats.)	18,000	2,700	1,100
(197b)	Bobby Wallace (No cap, two lines of 1910 stats.)	7,800	1,200	500.00
(198)	Ed Walsh	5,400	800.00	300.00
(199)	Z.D. Wheat	2,300	300.00	100.00
(200)	Doc White (White Sox)	700.00	100.00	50.00
(201)	Kirb. White (Pirates)	3,100	500.00	200.00
(202a)	Irvin K. Wilhelm ("Suffered" in 18th line of bio.)	3,100	500.00	200.00
(202b)	Irvin K. Wilhelm ("Suffe ed" in 18th line of bio.)	4,500	700.00	300.00
(203)	Ed Willett	700.00	100.00	50.00
(204)	J. Owen Wilson	700.00	100.00	50.00

No.	Player	NM	EX	VG
(205)	George R. Wiltse (Both ears show.)	700.00	100.00	50.00
(206)	George R. Wiltse (Only right ear shows.)	2,600	400.00	200.00
(207)	Harry Wolter	700.00	100.00	50.00
(208)	Cy Young	11,100	1,700	700.00

1909-11 T206 White Border

SWEET CAPORAL CIGARETTES
The Standard for Years
BASE BALL SERIES
150 SUBJECTS
FACTORY No. 30, 2d DIST. N.Y.

WAGNER, PITTSBURG

The nearly 525 cards which make up the T206 set are the most popular of the early tobacco card issues. Players are depicted in color lithographs surrounded by a white border. The player's last name on the 1-7/16" x 2-5/8" cards appears at the bottom with the city and league, when a city had more than one team. Backs contain an ad for one of 16 brands of cigarettes. There are 389 major leaguer cards and 134 minor leaguer cards in the set, but with front/back varieties the number of potentially different cards runs into the thousands. The set features many expensive cards including a number of pose and/or team variations. Values shown are for cards with the most common advertising on back: Piedmont and Sweet Caporal. Other backs carry a premium depending on scarcity (see listings under brand names). Several popularly collected printing errors have been included in the listings.

No.	Player	NM	EX	VG
	Common Player:	700.00	100.00	50.00
(1)	Ed Abbaticchio (Blue sleeves.)	700.00	100.00	50.00
(2)	Ed Abbaticchio (Brown sleeves.)	700.00	100.00	50.00
(3)	Fred Abbott	700.00	100.00	50.00
(4)	Bill Abstein	700.00	100.00	50.00
(5)	Doc Adkins	700.00	100.00	50.00
(6)	Whitey Alperman	700.00	100.00	50.00
(7)	Red Ames (Hands at chest.)	700.00	100.00	50.00
(8)	Red Ames (Hands above head.)	700.00	100.00	50.00
(9)	Red Ames/Portrait	700.00	100.00	50.00
(10)	John Anderson	700.00	100.00	50.00
(11)	Frank Arellanes	700.00	100.00	50.00
(12)	Herman Armbruster	700.00	100.00	50.00
(13)	Harry Arndt	700.00	100.00	50.00
(14)	Jake Atz	700.00	100.00	50.00
(15)	Home Run Baker	1,700	400.00	200.00
(16)	Neal Ball (New York)	700.00	100.00	50.00
(17)	Neal Ball (Cleveland)	700.00	100.00	50.00
(18)	Jap Barbeau	700.00	100.00	200.00
(19)	Cy Barger	700.00	100.00	50.00
(20)	Jack Barry (Philadelphia)	700.00	100.00	50.00
(21)	Shad Barry (Milwaukee)	700.00	100.00	50.00
(22)	Jack Bastian	1,300	400.00	100.00
(23)	Emil Batch	700.00	100.00	50.00
(24)	Johnny Bates	700.00	100.00	50.00
(25)	Harry Bay	1,300	400.00	100.00
(26)	Ginger Beaumont	700.00	100.00	50.00
(27)	Fred Beck	700.00	100.00	50.00
(28)	Beals Becker	700.00	100.00	50.00
(29)	Jake Beckley	1,500	300.00	100.00
(30)	George Bell (Hands above head.)	700.00	100.00	50.00
(31)	George Bell (Pitching follow thru.)	700.00	100.00	50.00
(32)	Chief Bender/Pitching (No trees in background.)	1,800	300.00	100.00
(33)	Chief Bender/Pitching (Trees in background.)	1,900	400.00	100.00
(34)	Chief Bender/Portrait	1,350	300.00	100.00
(35)	Bill Bergen/Btg	700.00	100.00	50.00
(36)	Bill Bergen/Catching	700.00	100.00	50.00
(37)	Heinie Berger	700.00	100.00	50.00
(38)	Bill Bernhard	1,300	400.00	100.00
(39)	Bob Bescher (Hands in air.)	700.00	100.00	50.00
(40)	Bob Bescher/Portrait	700.00	100.00	50.00
(41)	Joe Birmingham	900.00	200.00	100.00
(42)	Lena Blackburne	700.00	100.00	50.00
(43)	Jack Bliss	700.00	100.00	50.00
(44)	Frank Bowerman	700.00	100.00	50.00
(45)	Bill Bradley/Portrait	700.00	100.00	50.00
(46)	Bill Bradley (With bat.)	700.00	100.00	50.00
(47)	Dave Brain	700.00	100.00	50.00
(48)	Kitty Bransfield	700.00	100.00	50.00
(49)	Roy Brashear	700.00	100.00	50.00
(50)	Ted Breitenstein	1,300	400.00	100.00
(51)	Roger Bresnahan/Portrait	1,700	300.00	100.00
(52)	Roger Bresnahan (With bat.)	1,350	300.00	100.00
(53)	Al Bridwell/Portrait (No cap.)	700.00	100.00	50.00

No.	Name			
(54)	Al Bridwell/Portrait (With cap.)	700.00	100.00	50.00
(55a)	George Brown (Browne) (Chicago)	700.00	200.00	100.00
(55b)	George Brown (Browne) (Washington)	2,100	400.00	200.00
(56)	Mordecai Brown (Chicago on shirt.)	1,600	300.00	100.00
(57)	Mordecai Brown (Cubs on shirt.)	3,600	700.00	300.00
(58)	Mordecai Brown/Portrait	1,500	300.00	100.00
(59)	Al Burch/Btg	1,100	200.00	100.00
(60)	Al Burch/Fielding	700.00	100.00	50.00
(61)	Fred Burchell	700.00	100.00	50.00
(62)	Jimmy Burke	700.00	100.00	50.00
(63)	Bill Burns	700.00	100.00	50.00
(64)	Donie Bush	700.00	100.00	50.00
(65)	John Butler	700.00	100.00	50.00
(66)	Bobby Byrne	700.00	100.00	50.00
(67)	Howie Camnitz (Arm at side.)	700.00	100.00	50.00
(68)	Howie Camnitz (Arms folded.)	700.00	100.00	50.00
(69)	Howie Camnitz (Hands above head.)	700.00	100.00	50.00
(70)	Billy Campbell	700.00	100.00	50.00
(71)	Scoops Carey	1,300	400.00	100.00
(72)	Charley Carr	700.00	100.00	50.00
(73)	Bill Carrigan	700.00	100.00	50.00
(74)	Doc Casey	700.00	100.00	50.00
(75)	Peter Cassidy	700.00	100.00	50.00
(76)	Frank Chance/Btg	1,800	300.00	100.00
(77)	Frank Chance/Portrait (Red background.)	1,900	400.00	100.00
(78)	Frank Chance/Portrait (Yellow background.)	1,400	300.00	100.00
(79)	Bill Chappelle	700.00	100.00	50.00
(80)	Chappie Charles	700.00	100.00	50.00
(81)	Hal Chase (Holding trophy.)	800.00	200.00	100.00
(82)	Hal Chase/Portrait (Blue background.)	900.00	200.00	100.00
(83)	Hal Chase/Portrait (Pink background.)	1,100	200.00	100.00
(84)	Hal Chase/Throwing (Dark cap.)	1,100	200.00	100.00
(85)	Hal Chase/Throwing (White cap.)	1,200	300.00	100.00
(86)	Jack Chesbro	1,900	300.00	100.00
(87)	Ed Cicotte	1,400	300.00	100.00
(88)	Bill Clancy (Clancey)	700.00	100.00	50.00
(89)	Josh Clark (Columbus) (Clarke)	700.00	100.00	50.00
(90)	Fred Clarke (Pittsburgh, holding bat.)	1,200	200.00	100.00
(91)	Fred Clarke/Portrait (Pittsburgh)	1,400	300.00	100.00
(92)	J.J. Clarke (Nig) (Cleveland)	700.00	100.00	50.00
(93)	Bill Clymer	700.00	100.00	50.00
(94)	Ty Cobb/Portrait (Green background.)	9,000	2,600	1,400
(95a)	Ty Cobb/Portrait (Red background.)	4,500	1,600	900.00
(95b)	Ty Cobb/Portrait (Red background, Ty Cobb brand back.)	120,000	72,000	
(96)	Ty Cobb (Bat off shoulder.)	9,600	2,300	1,000
(97)	Ty Cobb (Bat on shoulder.)	9,300	1,900	800.00
(98)	Cad Coles	1,300	400.00	100.00
(99)	Eddie Collins (Philadelphia)	1,400	300.00	100.00
(100)	Jimmy Collins (Minneapolis)	1,300	200.00	100.00
(101)	Bunk Congalton	700.00	100.00	50.00
(102)	Wid Conroy/Fielding	700.00	100.00	50.00
(103)	Wid Conroy (With bat.)	700.00	100.00	50.00
(104)	Harry Covaleski (Coveleski)	700.00	100.00	50.00
(105)	Doc Crandall/Portrait (No cap.)	700.00	100.00	50.00
(106)	Doc Crandall/Portrait (With cap.)	700.00	100.00	50.00
(107)	Bill Cranston	1,300	400.00	100.00
(108)	Gavvy Cravath	700.00	100.00	50.00
(109)	Sam Crawford/Throwing	1,700	300.00	100.00
(110)	Sam Crawford (With bat.)	1,500	300.00	100.00
(111)	Birdie Cree	700.00	100.00	50.00
(112)	Lou Criger	700.00	100.00	50.00
(113)	Dode Criss	700.00	100.00	50.00
(114)	Monte Cross	700.00	100.00	50.00
(115a)	Bill Dahlen (Boston)	1,000	200.00	100.00
(115b)	Bill Dahlen (Brooklyn)	2,100	400.00	200.00
(116)	Paul Davidson	700.00	100.00	50.00
(117)	George Davis (Chicago)	1,600	300.00	100.00
(118)	Harry Davis (Philadelphia, Davis on front.)	700.00	100.00	50.00
(119)	Harry Davis (Philadelphia, H. Davis on front.)	700.00	100.00	50.00
(120)	Frank Delehanty (Delahanty) (Louisville)	700.00	100.00	50.00
(121)	Jim Delehanty (Delahanty) (Washington)	700.00	100.00	50.00
(122a)	Ray Demmitt (New York)	700.00	100.00	50.00
(122b)	Ray Demmitt (St. Louis)	42,000	9,000	3,800
(123)	Rube Dessau	700.00	100.00	50.00
(124)	Art Devlin	700.00	100.00	50.00
(125)	Josh Devore	700.00	100.00	50.00
(126)	Bill Dineen (Dinneen)	700.00	100.00	50.00
(127)	Mike Donlin/Fielding	800.00	200.00	100.00
(128)	Mike Donlin/Seated	800.00	200.00	100.00
(129)	Mike Donlin (With bat.)	800.00	200.00	100.00
(130)	Jiggs Donohue (Donahue)	700.00	100.00	50.00
(131)	Wild Bill Donovan/Portrait	700.00	100.00	50.00
(132)	Wild Bill Donovan/Throwing	700.00	100.00	50.00
(133)	Red Dooin	700.00	100.00	50.00
(134)	Mickey Doolan/Btg	700.00	100.00	50.00
(135)	Mickey Doolan/Fielding	700.00	100.00	50.00
(136)	Mickey Doolin (Doolan)	700.00	100.00	50.00
(137)	Gus Dorner	700.00	100.00	50.00
(138)	Patsy Dougherty (Arm in air.)	700.00	100.00	50.00
(139)	Patsy Dougherty/Portrait	700.00	100.00	50.00
(140)	Tom Downey/Btg	700.00	100.00	50.00
(141)	Tom Downey/Fielding	700.00	100.00	50.00
(142)	Jerry Downs	700.00	100.00	50.00
(143a)	Joe Doyle (N.Y. Nat'l., hands above head.)			72,000
(143b)	Joe Doyle (N.Y., hands above head.)	2,200	500.00	100.00
(144)	Larry Doyle/Portrait (N.Y. Nat'l.)	700.00	100.00	50.00
(145)	Larry Doyle/Throwing (N.Y. Nat'l.)	700.00	100.00	50.00
(146)	Larry Doyle (N.Y. Nat'l., with bat.)	700.00	100.00	50.00
(147)	Jean Dubuc	700.00	100.00	50.00
(148)	Hugh Duffy	1,700	300.00	100.00
(149)	Jack Dunn (Baltimore)	700.00	100.00	50.00
(150)	Joe Dunn (Brooklyn)	700.00	100.00	50.00
(151)	Bull Durham	700.00	100.00	50.00
(152)	Jimmy Dygert	700.00	100.00	50.00
(153)	Ted Easterly	700.00	100.00	50.00
(154)	Dick Egan	700.00	100.00	50.00
(155a)	Kid Elberfeld (New York)	700.00	100.00	50.00
(155b)	Kid Elberfeld/Portrait (Washington)	6,600	1,200	500.00
(156)	Kid Elberfeld/Fielding (Washington)	700.00	100.00	50.00
(157)	Roy Ellam	1,300	400.00	100.00
(158)	Clyde Engle	700.00	100.00	50.00
(159)	Steve Evans	700.00	100.00	50.00
(160)	Johnny Evers/Portrait	3,000	600.00	200.00
(161)	Johnny Evers (With bat, Chicago on shirt.)	1,400	300.00	100.00
(162)	Johnny Evers (With bat, Cubs on shirt.)	1,900	400.00	100.00
(163)	Bob Ewing	700.00	100.00	50.00
(164)	Cecil Ferguson	700.00	100.00	50.00
(165)	Hobe Ferris	700.00	100.00	50.00
(166)	Lou Fiene/Portrait	700.00	100.00	50.00
(167)	Lou Fiene/Throwing	700.00	100.00	50.00
(168)	Steamer Flanagan	700.00	100.00	50.00
(169)	Art Fletcher	700.00	100.00	50.00
(170)	Elmer Flick	2,000	400.00	100.00
(171)	Russ Ford	700.00	100.00	50.00
(172)	Ed Foster	1,300	400.00	100.00
(173)	Jerry Freeman	700.00	100.00	50.00
(174)	John Frill	700.00	100.00	50.00
(175)	Charlie Fritz	1,300	400.00	100.00
(176)	Art Fromme	700.00	100.00	50.00
(177)	Chick Gandil	1,200	300.00	100.00
(178)	Bob Ganley	700.00	100.00	50.00
(179)	John Ganzel	700.00	100.00	50.00
(180)	Harry Gasper	700.00	100.00	50.00
(181)	Rube Geyer	700.00	100.00	50.00
(182)	George Gibson	700.00	100.00	50.00
(183)	Billy Gilbert	700.00	100.00	50.00
(184)	Wilbur Goode (Good)	700.00	100.00	50.00
(185)	Bill Graham (St. Louis)	700.00	100.00	50.00
(186)	Peaches Graham (Boston)	700.00	100.00	50.00
(187)	Dolly Gray	1,300	400.00	100.00
(188)	Ed Greminger	1,300	400.00	100.00
(189)	Clark Griffith/Btg	1,800	300.00	100.00
(190)	Clark Griffith/Portrait	1,600	300.00	100.00
(191)	Moose Grimshaw	700.00	100.00	50.00
(192)	Bob Groom	700.00	100.00	50.00
(193)	Tom Guiheen	1,300	400.00	100.00
(194)	Ed Hahn	700.00	100.00	50.00
(195)	Bob Hall	700.00	100.00	50.00
(196)	Bill Hallman	700.00	100.00	50.00
(197)	Jack Hannifan (Hannifin)	700.00	100.00	50.00
(198)	Bill Hart (Little Rock)	1,300	400.00	100.00
(199)	Jimmy Hart (Montgomery)	1,300	400.00	100.00
(200)	Topsy Hartsel	700.00	100.00	50.00
(201)	Jack Hayden	700.00	100.00	50.00
(202)	J. Ross Helm	1,300	400.00	100.00
(203)	Charlie Hemphill	700.00	100.00	50.00
(204)	Buck Herzog (Boston)	800.00	200.00	100.00
(205)	Buck Herzog (New York)	700.00	100.00	50.00
(206)	Gordon Hickman	1,300	400.00	100.00
(207)	Bill Hinchman (Cleveland)	700.00	100.00	50.00
(208)	Harry Hinchman (Toledo)	1,300	400.00	100.00
(209)	Dick Hoblitzell	700.00	100.00	50.00
(210)	Danny Hoffman (St. Louis)	700.00	100.00	50.00
(211)	Izzy Hoffman (Providence)	700.00	100.00	50.00
(212)	Solly Hofman	700.00	100.00	50.00
(213)	Bock Hooker	1,300	400.00	100.00
(214)	Del Howard (Chicago)	700.00	100.00	50.00
(215)	Ernie Howard (Savannah)	1,300	400.00	100.00
(216)	Harry Howell (Hand at waist.)	700.00	100.00	50.00
(217)	Harry Howell/Portrait	700.00	100.00	50.00
(218)	Miller Huggins (Hands at mouth.)	1,400	300.00	100.00
(219)	Miller Huggins/Portrait	1,200	200.00	100.00
(220)	Rudy Hulswitt	700.00	100.00	50.00
(221)	John Hummel	700.00	100.00	50.00
(222)	George Hunter	700.00	100.00	50.00
(223)	Frank Isbell	700.00	100.00	50.00
(224)	Fred Jacklitsch	700.00	100.00	50.00
(225)	Jimmy Jackson	700.00	100.00	50.00
(226)	Hughie Jennings (One hand showing.)	1,300	200.00	100.00
(227)	Hughie Jennings (Both hands showing.)	1,400	300.00	100.00
(228)	Hughie Jennings/Portrait	1,300	200.00	100.00
(229)	Walter Johnson (Hands at chest.)	5,400	1,000	400.00
(230)	Walter Johnson/Portrait	4,800	1,400	700.00
(231)	Fielder Jones (Chicago, hands at hips.)	700.00	100.00	50.00
(232)	Fielder Jones/Portrait (Chicago)	700.00	100.00	50.00
(233)	Davy Jones (Detroit)	700.00	100.00	50.00
(234)	Tom Jones (St. Louis)	700.00	100.00	50.00
(235)	Dutch Jordan (Atlanta)	1,300	400.00	100.00
(236)	Tim Jordan/Btg (Brooklyn)	700.00	200.00	50.00
(237)	Tim Jordan/Portrait (Brooklyn)	800.00	200.00	100.00
(238)	Addie Joss/Pitching	1,800	300.00	100.00
(239)	Addie Joss/Portrait	1,500	300.00	100.00
(240)	Ed Karger	700.00	100.00	50.00
(241)	Willie Keeler/Portrait	2,500	500.00	200.00
(242)	Willie Keeler (W/bat.)	2,500	500.00	200.00
(243)	Joe Kelley	1,300	200.00	100.00
(244)	J.F. Kiernan	1,300	400.00	100.00
(245)	Ed Killian/Pitching	700.00	100.00	50.00
(246)	Ed Killian/Portrait	700.00	100.00	50.00
(247)	Frank King	1,300	400.00	100.00
(248)	Rube Kisinger	700.00	100.00	50.00
(249a)	Red Kleinow (Boston)	2,100	400.00	200.00
(249b)	Red Kleinow/Catching (New York)	800.00	100.00	50.00
(250)	Red Kleinow (New York, with bat.)	700.00	100.00	50.00
(251)	Johnny Kling	700.00	100.00	50.00
(252)	Otto Knabe	700.00	100.00	50.00
(253)	Jack Knight/Portrait	700.00	100.00	50.00
(254)	Jack Knight (With bat.)	700.00	100.00	50.00
(255)	Ed Konetchy (Glove above head.)	700.00	100.00	50.00
(256)	Ed Konetchy (Glove near ground.)	700.00	100.00	50.00
(257)	Harry Krause/Pitching	700.00	100.00	50.00
(258)	Harry Krause/Portrait	700.00	100.00	50.00
(259)	Rube Kroh	700.00	100.00	50.00
(260)	Otto Kruger (Krueger)	700.00	100.00	50.00
(261)	James Lafitte	1,300	400.00	100.00
(262)	Nap Lajoie/Portrait	3,600	700.00	300.00
(263)	Nap Lajoie/Throwing	2,900	500.00	200.00
(264)	Nap Lajoie (With bat.)	3,600	800.00	200.00
(265)	Joe Lake (New York)	700.00	100.00	50.00
(266)	Joe Lake (St. Louis, ball in hand.)	700.00	100.00	50.00
(267)	Joe Lake (St. Louis, no ball in hand.)	700.00	100.00	50.00
(268)	Frank LaPorte	700.00	100.00	50.00
(269)	Arlie Latham	700.00	100.00	50.00
(270)	Bill Lattimore	700.00	100.00	50.00
(271)	Jimmy Lavender	700.00	100.00	50.00
(272)	Tommy Leach (Bending over.)	700.00	100.00	50.00
(273)	Tommy Leach/Portrait	700.00	100.00	50.00
(274)	Lefty Leifield/Btg	700.00	100.00	50.00
(275)	Lefty Leifield/Pitching	700.00	100.00	50.00
(276)	Ed Lennox	700.00	100.00	50.00
(277)	Harry Lentz (Sentz)	1,300	400.00	100.00
(278)	Glenn Liebhardt	700.00	100.00	50.00
(279)	Vive Lindaman	700.00	100.00	50.00
(280)	Perry Lipe	1,300	400.00	100.00
(281)	Paddy Livingstone (Livingston)	700.00	100.00	50.00
(282)	Hans Lobert	700.00	100.00	50.00
(283)	Harry Lord	700.00	100.00	50.00
(284)	Harry Lumley	700.00	100.00	50.00
(285a)	Carl Lundgren (Chicago)	3,800	800.00	300.00
(285b)	Carl Lundgren (Kansas City)	800.00	100.00	50.00
(286)	Nick Maddox	700.00	100.00	50.00
(287a)	Sherry Magie (Magee)			

Values shown represent recent auctions of examples graded by PSA, SGC or GAI. Purchase of ungraded specimens is not recommended.

VG-EX - 21,250 / 19,720
VG - 9,600
GOOD - 7,500
FAIR - 3,925
POOR - 2,875

No.	Name			
(287b)	Sherry Magee/Portrait	800.00	100.00	50.00
(288)	Sherry Magee (With bat.)	800.00	200.00	100.00
(289)	Bill Malarkey	700.00	100.00	50.00
(290)	Billy Maloney	700.00	100.00	50.00
(291)	George Manion	1,300	400.00	100.00
(292)	Rube Manning/Btg	700.00	100.00	50.00
(293)	Rube Manning/Pitching	700.00	100.00	50.00
(294)	Rube Marquard (Hands at thighs.)	1,600	300.00	100.00
(295)	Rube Marquard (Follow-through.)	1,600	300.00	100.00
(296)	Rube Marquard/Portrait	1,800	300.00	100.00
(297)	Doc Marshall	700.00	100.00	50.00
(298)	Christy Mathewson (Dark cap.)	2,700	1,000	300.00
(299)	Christy Mathewson/Portrait	5,200	1,100	400.00
(300)	Christy Mathewson (White cap.)	5,100	900.00	400.00
(301)	Al Mattern	700.00	100.00	50.00
(302)	John McAleese	700.00	100.00	50.00
(303)	George McBride	700.00	100.00	50.00
(304)	Pat McCauley	1,300	400.00	100.00
(305)	Moose McCormick	700.00	100.00	50.00
(306)	Pryor McElveen	700.00	100.00	50.00
(307)	Dan McGann	700.00	100.00	50.00
(308)	Jim McGinley	700.00	100.00	50.00
(309)	Iron Man McGinnity	1,400	200.00	100.00
(310)	Stoney McGlynn	700.00	100.00	50.00
(311)	John McGraw (Finger in air.)	2,100	400.00	200.00
(312)	John McGraw (Glove at hip.)	2,000	400.00	100.00
(313)	John McGraw/Portrait (No cap.)	1,700	300.00	100.00
(314)	John McGraw/Portrait (With cap.)	1,400	300.00	100.00
(315)	Harry McIntyre (Brooklyn)	700.00	100.00	50.00
(316)	Harry McIntyre (Brooklyn & Chicago)	700.00	100.00	50.00
(317)	Matty McIntyre (Detroit)	700.00	100.00	50.00
(318)	Larry McLean	800.00	100.00	50.00
(319)	George McQuillan (Ball in hand.)	700.00	100.00	50.00
(320)	George McQuillan (With bat.)	700.00	100.00	50.00
(321)	Fred Merkle/Portrait	700.00	300.00	50.00
(322)	Fred Merkle/Throwing	700.00	100.00	50.00
(323)	George Merritt	700.00	100.00	50.00
(324)	Chief Meyers	700.00	100.00	50.00
(325)	Clyde Milan	700.00	100.00	50.00
(326)	Dots Miller (Pittsburgh)	700.00	100.00	50.00
(327)	Molly Miller (Dallas)	1,300	400.00	100.00
(328)	Bill Milligan	700.00	100.00	50.00
(329)	Fred Mitchell (Toronto)	700.00	100.00	50.00
(330)	Mike Mitchell (Cincinnati)	700.00	100.00	50.00
(331)	Dan Moeller	700.00	100.00	50.00
(332)	Carlton Molesworth	1,300	400.00	100.00

(333) Herbie Moran (Providence) 700.00 100.00 50.00
(334) Pat Moran (Chicago) 700.00 100.00 50.00
(335) George Moriarty 700.00 100.00 50.00
(336) Mike Mowrey 700.00 100.00 50.00
(337) Dom Mullaney 1,300 400.00 100.00
(338) George Mullen (Mullin) 700.00 100.00 50.00
(339) George Mullin/Throwing 900.00 200.00 100.00
(340) George Mullin (With bat.) 700.00 100.00 50.00
(341) Danny Murphy/Btg 700.00 100.00 50.00
(342) Danny Murphy/Throwing 900.00 200.00 100.00
(343) Red Murray/Btg 700.00 100.00 50.00
(344) Red Murray/Portrait 700.00 100.00 50.00
(345) Chief Myers (Meyers)/Btg 700.00 100.00 50.00
(346) Chief Myers/Fielding (Meyers) 700.00 100.00 50.00
(347) Billy Nattress 700.00 100.00 50.00
(348) Tom Needham 700.00 100.00 50.00
(349) Simon Nicholls (Hands on knees.) 700.00 100.00 50.00
(350) Simon Nichols (Nicholls)/Btg 700.00 100.00 50.00
(351) Harry Niles 700.00 100.00 50.00
(352) Rebel Oakes 700.00 100.00 50.00
(353) Frank Oberlin 700.00 100.00 50.00
(354) Peter O'Brien 700.00 100.00 50.00
(355a) Bill O'Hara (New York) 700.00 100.00 50.00
(355b) Bill O'Hara (St. Louis) 42,000 8,700 2,900
(356) Rube Oldring/Btg 700.00 100.00 50.00
(357) Rube Oldring/Fielding 700.00 100.00 50.00
(358) Charley O'Leary (Hands on knees.) 700.00 100.00 50.00
(359) Charley O'Leary/Portrait 700.00 100.00 50.00
(360) William J. O'Neil 700.00 100.00 50.00
(361) Al Orth 1,300 400.00 100.00
(362) William Otey 1,300 400.00 100.00
(363) Orval Overall (Hand face level.) 700.00 100.00 50.00
(364) Orval Overall (Hands waist level.) 700.00 100.00 50.00
(365) Orval Overall/Portrait 700.00 100.00 50.00
(366) Frank Owen 700.00 100.00 50.00
(367) George Paige 1,300 400.00 100.00
(368) Fred Parent 700.00 100.00 50.00
(369) Dode Paskert 700.00 100.00 50.00
(370) Jim Pastorius 700.00 100.00 50.00
(371) Harry Pattee 900.00 200.00 100.00
(372) Fred Payne 700.00 100.00 50.00
(373) Barney Pelty (Horizontal photo.) 900.00 200.00 100.00
(374) Barney Pelty (Vertical photo.) 700.00 100.00 50.00
(375) Hub Perdue 1,300 400.00 100.00
(376) George Perring 700.00 100.00 50.00
(377) Arch Persons 1,300 400.00 100.00
(378) Francis (Big Jeff) Pfeffer 1,300 400.00 100.00
(379) Jake Pfeister (Pfiester)/ Seated 700.00 100.00 50.00
(380) Jake Pfeister (Pfiester)/ Throwing 700.00 100.00 50.00
(381) Jimmy Phelan 700.00 100.00 50.00
(382) Eddie Phelps 700.00 100.00 50.00
(383) Deacon Phillippe 700.00 100.00 50.00
(384) Ollie Pickering 700.00 100.00 50.00
(385) Eddie Plank
Values shown reflect recent auctions of examples graded by PSA, SGC or GAI. Purchase of ungraded specimens is not recommended.
VG-EX - 43,500
VG - 41,100
(386) Phil Poland 700.00 100.00 50.00
(387) Jack Powell 900.00 200.00 100.00
(388) Mike Powers 800.00 200.00 100.00
(389) Billy Purtell 700.00 100.00 50.00
(390) Ambrose Puttman (Puttmann) 700.00 100.00 50.00
(391) Lee Quillen (Quillin) 700.00 100.00 50.00
(392) Jack Quinn 700.00 100.00 50.00
(393) Newt Randall 700.00 100.00 50.00
(394) Bugs Raymond 700.00 100.00 50.00
(395) Ed Reagan 1,300 400.00 100.00
(396) Ed Reulbach (Glove showing.) 900.00 200.00 100.00
(397) Ed Reulbach (No glove showing.) 700.00 100.00 50.00
(398) Dutch Revelle 1,300 400.00 100.00
(399) Bob Rhoades (Rhoads) (Hands at chest.) 700.00 100.00 50.00
(400) Bob Rhoades (Rhoads) (Right arm extended.) 900.00 200.00 100.00
(401) Charlie Rhodes 700.00 100.00 50.00
(402) Claude Ritchey 700.00 100.00 50.00
(403) Lou Ritter 700.00 100.00 50.00
(404) Ike Rockenfeld 1,300 400.00 100.00
(405) Claude Rossman 700.00 100.00 50.00
(406) Nap Rucker/Portrait 700.00 100.00 50.00
(407) Nap Rucker/Throwing 700.00 100.00 50.00
(408) Dick Rudolph 700.00 100.00 50.00
(409) Ray Ryan 1,300 400.00 100.00
(410) Germany Schaefer (Detroit) 700.00 100.00 50.00
(411) Germany Schaefer (Washington) 700.00 100.00 50.00
(412) George Schirm 700.00 100.00 50.00
(413) Larry Schlafly 700.00 100.00 50.00
(414) Admiral Schlei/Btg 700.00 100.00 50.00
(415) Admiral Schlei/Catching 700.00 100.00 50.00
(416) Admiral Schlei/Portrait 700.00 100.00 50.00
(417) Boss Schmidt/Batting 700.00 100.00 50.00
(418) Boss Schmidt/Throwing 700.00 100.00 50.00
(419) Ossee Schreck (Schreckengost) 800.00 200.00 100.00
(420) Wildfire Schulte (Front view.) 700.00 100.00 50.00
(421) Wildfire Schulte (Back view.) 700.00 100.00 50.00
(422) Jim Scott 700.00 100.00 50.00
(423) Charles Seitz 1,300 400.00 100.00
(424) Cy Seymour/Btg 700.00 100.00 50.00
(425) Cy Seymour/Portrait 700.00 100.00 50.00
(426) Cy Seymour/Throwing 700.00 100.00 50.00
(427) Spike Shannon 700.00 100.00 50.00
(428) Bud Sharpe 700.00 100.00 50.00

(429) Shag Shaughnessy 1,300 400.00 100.00
(430) Al Shaw (St. Louis) 700.00 100.00 50.00
(431) Hunky Shaw (Providence) 700.00 100.00 50.00
(432) Jimmy Sheckard (Glove showing.) 700.00 100.00 50.00
(433) Jimmy Sheckard (No glove showing.) 700.00 100.00 50.00
(434) Bill Shipke 700.00 100.00 50.00
(435) Jimmy Slagle 700.00 100.00 50.00
(436) Carlos Smith (Shreveport) 1,300 400.00 100.00
(437) Frank Smith (Chicago, F. Smith on front.) 700.00 100.00 50.00
(438a) Frank Smith (Chicago, white cap.) 800.00 200.00 100.00
(438b) Frank Smith (Chicago & Boston) 1,700 300.00 100.00
(439) Happy Smith (Brooklyn) 700.00 100.00 50.00
(440) Heinie Smith (Buffalo) 700.00 100.00 50.00
(441) Sid Smith (Atlanta) 1,300 400.00 100.00
(442) Fred Snodgrass/Btg 700.00 100.00 50.00
(443) Fred Snodgrass/Catching 700.00 100.00 50.00
(444) Bob Spade 700.00 100.00 50.00
(445) Tris Speaker 4,500 800.00 300.00
(446) Tubby Spencer 700.00 100.00 50.00
(447) Jake Stahl (Glove shows.) 700.00 100.00 50.00
(448) Jake Stahl (No glove shows.) 700.00 100.00 50.00
(449) Oscar Stanage 700.00 100.00 50.00
(450) Dolly Stark 1,300 400.00 100.00
(451) Charlie Starr 700.00 100.00 50.00
(452) Harry Steinfeldt/Portrait 700.00 100.00 50.00
(453) Harry Steinfeldt (With bat.) 700.00 100.00 50.00
(454) Jim Stephens 700.00 100.00 50.00
(455) George Stone 700.00 100.00 50.00
(456) George Stovall/Btg 700.00 100.00 50.00
(457) George Stovall/Portrait 700.00 100.00 50.00
(458) Sam Strang 700.00 100.00 50.00
(459) Gabby Street/Catching 700.00 100.00 50.00
(460) Gabby Street/Portrait 700.00 100.00 50.00
(461) Billy Sullivan 700.00 100.00 50.00
(462) Ed Summers 700.00 100.00 50.00
(463) Bill Sweeney (Boston) 700.00 100.00 50.00
(464) Jeff Sweeney (New York) 700.00 100.00 50.00
(465) Jesse Tannehill (Washington) 700.00 100.00 50.00
(466) Lee Tannehill (Chicago, L. Tannehill on front.) 700.00 100.00 50.00
(467) Lee Tannehill (Chicago, Tannehill on front.) 700.00 100.00 50.00
(468) Dummy Taylor 700.00 100.00 50.00
(469) Fred Tenney 700.00 100.00 50.00
(470) Tony Thebo 1,300 400.00 100.00
(471) Jake Thielman 700.00 100.00 50.00
(472) Ira Thomas 700.00 100.00 50.00
(473) Woodie Thornton 1,300 400.00 100.00
(474) Joe Tinker (Bat off shoulder.) 1,800 400.00 100.00
(475) Joe Tinker (Bat on shoulder.) 1,700 300.00 100.00
(476) Joe Tinker (Hands on knees.) 1,700 300.00 100.00
(477) Joe Tinker/Portrait 1,800 400.00 100.00
(478) John Titus 700.00 100.00 50.00
(479) Terry Turner 700.00 100.00 50.00
(480) Bob Unglaub 700.00 100.00 50.00
(481) Juan Violat (Viola) 1,300 400.00 100.00
(482) Rube Waddell/Portrait 1,800 300.00 100.00
(483) Rube Waddell/Throwing 1,800 400.00 100.00
(484) Heinie Wagner (Bat on left shoulder.) 700.00 100.00 50.00
(485) Heinie Wagner (Bat on right shoulder.) 800.00 200.00 100.00
(486) Honus Wagner
Values shown refelct recent auctions of examples graded by PSA, SGC or GAI. Purchase of ungraded specimens is not recommended.
VG+ - 456,000
VG - 400,000.
GOOD - 235,000
FAIR - 130,000.
POOR - 90,000.
(487) Bobby Wallace 1,500 300.00 100.00
(488) Ed Walsh 2,300 400.00 200.00
(489) Jack Warhop 700.00 100.00 50.00
(490) Jake Weimer 700.00 100.00 50.00
(491) James Westlake 1,300 400.00 100.00
(492) Zack Wheat 1,500 300.00 100.00
(493) Doc White/Pitching (Chicago) 700.00 100.00 50.00
(494) Doc White/Portrait (Chicago) 700.00 100.00 50.00
(495) Foley White (Houston) 1,300 400.00 100.00
(496) Jack White (Buffalo) 700.00 100.00 50.00
(497) Kaiser Wilhelm (Hands at chest.) 700.00 100.00 50.00
(498) Kaiser Wilhelm (With bat.) 700.00 100.00 50.00
(499) Ed Willett 700.00 100.00 50.00
(500) Ed Willetts (Willett) 700.00 100.00 50.00
(501) Jimmy Williams 700.00 100.00 50.00
(502) Vic Willis/Portrait 1,700 400.00 100.00
(503) Vic Willis/Throwing 1,700 300.00 100.00
(504) Vic Willis (With bat.) 1,200 200.00 100.00
(505) Owen Wilson 700.00 100.00 50.00
(506) Hooks Wiltse/Pitching 700.00 100.00 50.00
(507) Hooks Wiltse/Portrait (No cap.) 700.00 100.00 50.00
(508) Hooks Wiltse/Portrait (With cap.) 700.00 100.00 50.00
(509) Lucky Wright 700.00 100.00 50.00
(510) Cy Young (Cleveland, glove shows.) 3,800 700.00 300.00
(511) Cy Young (Cleveland, bare hand shows.) 4,400 800.00 300.00
(512) Cy Young/Portrait (Cleveland) 8,700 1,600 700.00
(513) Irv Young (Minneapolis) 700.00 100.00 50.00
(514) Heinie Zimmerman 700.00 100.00 50.00

1909-11 T206 Errors

Because of the complexity of the lithographic process by which T206 cards were printed, a number of

SWEENEY, BOSTON NAT'L.   SWEENEY, BOSTON NAT'L.

significant printing errors - missing colors, broken or missing type, etc. - are known. Early in hobby history some of these errors were collected alongside such true design variations as the "Magie" misspelling and Joe Doyle "N.Y. Nat'l." Because of the continued popularity of T206, some of these errors remain in demand today and can command significant premium values. It should be noted, however, that not all similar errors within T206 bring such high prices; value seems dependent on the length of time the errors have been known in the hobby. Because of the ease with which various typographic elements - "S" in Snodgrass, "o" in Toronto, can be erased, many fakes of this type of error are known; collectors should be wary and consider having the cards professionally authenticated.

		NM	EX	VG
(27)	Beck, no "B"s (Missing red ink.)	1,500	750.00	450.00
(28)	Becker, no "B" (Missing red ink.)	1,500	750.00	450.00
(95a)	Cobb, orange background (Missing red ink.)	4,000	1,500	900.00
(164)	Ferguson, no "B" (Missing red ink.)	2,300	1,150	700.00
(279)	Lindaman, no "B" (Missing red ink.)	1,500	750.00	450.00
(286)	Maddox, Pittsburg (No team, name, city.)	6,000	3,000	1,800
(297)	Marshall, no "B" (Missing blue ink.)	2,000	1,000	600.00
(329)	Mitchell, "TORONT" (No last "O.")	2,000	1,000	600.00
(343)	Murray (Yellow background.)	1,500	750.00	450.00
(344)	Murr'y (Broken "A" in name, Lenox, Tolstoi, and Old Mill Back.)	7,000	3,500	2,100
(428)	Shappe, Newark (Should be Sharpe.)	4,000	2,000	1,200
(442)	nodgrass - batting (Should be Snodgrass; most of initial "S" missing.)	4,000	2,000	1,200
(443)	nodgrass - catching (All known examples, even those in grading company holders, are altered specimens with no collectible value.)			
(463)	Sweeney, no "B" (Missing magenta ink.)	9,000	4,500	2,700
(484)	Wagner, no "B" (Bat on left shoulder, missing magenta.)	2,500	1,250	750.00
	Common player (Missing one or more colors.)	500.00	250.00	150.00

1912 T207 Brown Background

Harry Lord
Harry Lord, the brilliant White Sox third baseman, came to Chicago in one of the queerest baseball deals ever recorded. Lord, first achieved success in the New England League, where, in 1908, he was lifted to the Boston Americans. Although rated as a wonderful ball player, he fell out with the club management and was traded to Comiskey, who secured a star. Lord played wonderful ball in 1911 and is rated by many as the greatest third baseman now playing—a worthy successor to Bradley and Collins. Last season he batted .321, fielded .941 and led his club with stolen bases.

RECRUIT LITTLE CIGARS

LORD-CHICAGO-AMER.

Less popular and even less understood than their T205 and T206 antecedents from American Tobacco, the T207 "Brown Background" series shares the same approximately 1-7/16" x 2-5/8" format with the earlier T-cards. A chocolate background frames the rather drab player drawings, which rely on occasional bit of color on the uniform to break up the predominant earth tones. The cards have beige borders. A white strip below the picture has the player's last name, city and league. Unlike most other cards of its time, T207 has a glossy coating on front which over the years tends to crack and/or "craze" exacerbating the appaearance of creases and other signs of wear. Card backs have the player's full name, career summary and (usually) an ad for one of several brands of cigarettes. Red Cross brand backs are virtually impossible to find, while red Cycle advertising is noticeably scarcer than more common Broadleaf or "anonymous" (no-advertising) versions. Cards with Recruit Little Cigars advertising on back are the most common. There are a number of unaccountably scarce cards in the set, including a higher than usual number of obscure players. The Davis card with blue "C" on cap carried in earlier catalogs has been removed for lack of evidence of its existence. The previously listed Carrigan-Wagner wrongbacks have also been de-listed due to their nature as wrong-back printing errors rather than true variations.

		NM	EX	VG
Common Player:		220.00	75.00	45.00
(1)	John B. Adams	1,760	615.00	355.00
(2)	Edward Ainsmith	220.00	75.00	45.00
(3)	Rafael Almeida	1,210	425.00	245.00
(4a)	James Austin (Insignia on shirt.)	440.00	155.00	90.00
(4b)	James Austin (No insignia on shirt.)	220.00	75.00	45.00
(5)	Neal Ball	200.00	75.00	45.00
(6)	Eros Barger	220.00	75.00	45.00
(7)	Jack Barry	250.00	90.00	50.00
(8)	Charles Bauman (Baumann)	1,100	385.00	220.00
(9)	Beals Becker	330.00	110.00	65.00
(10)	Chief (Albert) Bender	525.00	180.00	110.00
(11)	Joseph Benz	990.00	345.00	200.00
(12)	Robert Bescher	220.00	75.00	45.00
(13)	Joe Birmingham	880.00	310.00	175.00
(14)	Russell Blackburne	660.00	230.00	135.00
(15)	Fred Blanding	660.00	230.00	135.00
(16)	Jimmy Block	495.00	170.00	100.00
(17)	Ping Bodie	220.00	75.00	45.00
(18)	Hugh Bradley	220.00	75.00	45.00
(19)	Roger Bresnaham (Bresnahan)	495.00	170.00	100.00
(20)	J.F. Bushelman	880.00	310.00	175.00
(21)	Henry (Hank) Butcher	715.00	250.00	145.00
(22)	Robert M. Byrne	220.00	75.00	45.00
(23)	John James Callahan	220.00	75.00	45.00
(24)	Howard Camnitz	220.00	75.00	45.00
(25)	Max Carey	855.00	305.00	165.00
(26)	Bill Carrigan	220.00	75.00	45.00
(27)	George Chalmers	220.00	75.00	45.00
(28)	Frank Leroy Chance	715.00	250.00	145.00
(29)	Edward Cicotte	1,100	385.00	220.00
(30)	Tom Clarke	220.00	75.00	45.00
(31)	Leonard Cole	220.00	75.00	45.00
(32)	John Collins	305.00	105.00	60.00
(33)	Robert Coulson	220.00	75.00	45.00
(34)	Tex Covington	220.00	75.00	45.00
(35)	Otis Crandall	220.00	75.00	45.00
(36)	William Cunningham	825.00	285.00	165.00
(37)	Dave Danforth	880.00	310.00	175.00
(38)	Bert Daniels	440.00	155.00	90.00
(39)	John Daubert (Jake)	220.00	75.00	45.00
(40)	Harry Davis	250.00	90.00	50.00
(41)	Jim Delehanty	220.00	75.00	45.00
(42)	Claude Derrick	220.00	75.00	45.00
(43)	Arthur Devlin	660.00	230.00	135.00
(44)	Joshua Devore	220.00	75.00	45.00
(45)	Mike Donlin	1,500	230.00	135.00
(46)	Edward Donnelly	770.00	270.00	155.00
(47)	Charles Dooin	220.00	75.00	45.00
(48)	Tom Downey	880.00	310.00	175.00
(49)	Lawrence Doyle	440.00	155.00	90.00
(50)	Del Drake	385.00	135.00	75.00
(51)	Ted Easterly	220.00	75.00	45.00
(52)	George Ellis	660.00	230.00	135.00
(53)	Clyde Engle	360.00	125.00	70.00
(54)	R.E. Erwin	660.00	230.00	135.00
(55)	Louis Evans	220.00	75.00	45.00
(56)	John Ferry	220.00	75.00	45.00
(57a)	Ray Fisher (Blue cap.)	220.00	75.00	45.00
(57b)	Ray Fisher (White cap.)	220.00	75.00	45.00
(58)	Arthur Fletcher	220.00	75.00	45.00
(59)	Jacques Fournier	880.00	310.00	175.00
(60)	Arthur Fromme	250.00	90.00	50.00
(61)	Del Gainor	220.00	75.00	45.00
(62)	William Lawrence Gardner	330.00	110.00	65.00
(63)	Lefty George	220.00	75.00	45.00
(64)	Roy Golden	220.00	75.00	45.00
(65)	Harry Gowdy	220.00	75.00	45.00
(66)	George Graham	660.00	230.00	135.00
(67)	J.G. Graney	825.00	285.00	165.00
(68)	Vean Gregg	330.00	115.00	65.00
(69)	Casey Hageman	440.00	155.00	90.00
(70)	Charlie Hall	440.00	155.00	90.00
(71)	E.S. Hallinan	220.00	75.00	45.00
(72)	Earl Hamilton	220.00	75.00	45.00
(73)	Robert Harmon	220.00	75.00	45.00
(74)	Grover Hartley	440.00	155.00	90.00
(75)	Olaf Henriksen	230.00	110.00	60.00
(76)	John Henry	440.00	155.00	90.00
(77)	Charles Herzog	770.00	270.00	155.00
(78)	Robert Higgins	310.00	110.00	60.00
(79)	Chester Hoff	605.00	210.00	120.00
(80)	William Hogan	310.00	110.00	60.00
(81)	Harry Hooper	1,320	470.00	265.00
(82)	Ben Houser	660.00	230.00	135.00
(83)	Hamilton Hyatt	550.00	195.00	110.00
(84)	Walter Johnson	2,090	730.00	420.00
(85)	George Kaler	220.00	75.00	45.00
(86)	William Kelly	825.00	285.00	165.00
(87)	Jay Kirke	440.00	155.00	90.00
(88)	John Kling	715.00	250.00	145.00
(89)	Otto Knabe	220.00	75.00	45.00
(90)	Elmer Knetzer	220.00	75.00	45.00
(91)	Edward Konetchy	220.00	75.00	45.00
(92)	Harry Krause	220.00	75.00	45.00
(93)	"Red" Kuhn	660.00	230.00	135.00
(94)	Joseph Kutina	770.00	270.00	155.00
(95)	F.H. (Bill) Lange	440.00	155.00	90.00
(96)	Jack Lapp	220.00	75.00	45.00
(97)	W. Arlington Latham	220.00	75.00	45.00
(98)	Thomas W. Leach	220.00	75.00	45.00
(99)	Albert Leifield	220.00	75.00	45.00
(100)	Edgar Lennox	220.00	75.00	45.00
(101)	Duffy Lewis	495.00	170.00	100.00
(102a)	Irving Lewis (No emblem on sleeve.)	10,450	3,660	2,090
(102b)	Irving Lewis (Emblem on sleeve.)	10,450	3,660	2,090
(103)	Jack Lively	220.00	75.00	45.00
(104a)	Paddy Livingston ("A" on shirt.)	1,200	425.00	245.00
(104b)	Paddy Livingston (Big "C" on shirt.)	1,265	440.00	255.00
(104c)	Paddy Livingston (Small "C" on shirt.)	330.00	115.00	65.00
(105)	Briscoe Lord (Philadelphia)	440.00	155.00	90.00
(106)	Harry Lord (Chicago)	440.00	155.00	90.00
(107)	Louis Lowdermilk	10,450	3,660	2,090
(108)	Richard Marquard	605.00	210.00	120.00
(109)	Armando Marsans	770.00	270.00	155.00
(110)	George McBride	310.00	110.00	60.00
(111)	Alexander McCarthy	880.00	310.00	175.00
(112)	Edward McDonald	330.00	110.00	65.00
(113)	John J. McGraw	635.00	220.00	125.00
(114)	Harry McIntire	220.00	75.00	45.00
(115)	Matthew McIntyre	220.00	75.00	45.00
(116)	William McKechnie	880.00	310.00	175.00
(117)	Larry McLean	220.00	75.00	45.00
(118)	Clyde Milan	220.00	75.00	45.00
(119)	John B. Miller (Pittsburg)	220.00	75.00	45.00
(120)	Otto Miller (Brooklyn)	440.00	155.00	90.00
(121)	Roy Miller (Boston)	990.00	345.00	200.00
(122)	Ward Miller (Chicago)	4,400	1,540	880.00
(123)	Mike Mitchell (Cleveland, picture is Willie Mitchell.)	220.00	75.00	45.00
(124)	Mike Mitchell (Cincinnati)	330.00	110.00	65.00
(125)	Geo. Mogridge	440.00	155.00	90.00
(126)	Earl Moore	440.00	155.00	90.00
(127)	Patrick J. Moran	220.00	75.00	45.00
(128)	Cy Morgan (Philadelphia)	220.00	75.00	45.00
(129)	Ray Morgan (Washington)	220.00	75.00	45.00
(130)	George Moriarty	440.00	155.00	90.00
(131a)	George Mullin ("D" on cap.)	250.00	90.00	50.00
(131b)	George Mullin (No "D" on cap.)	745.00	260.00	150.00
(132)	Thomas Needham	330.00	110.00	65.00
(133)	Red Nelson	660.00	230.00	135.00
(134)	Herbert Northen (Hubbard)	310.00	110.00	60.00
(135)	Leslie Nunamaker	220.00	75.00	45.00
(136)	Rebel Oakes	220.00	75.00	45.00
(137)	Buck O'Brien	330.00	110.00	65.00
(138)	Rube Oldring	220.00	75.00	45.00
(139)	Ivan Olson	220.00	75.00	45.00
(140)	Martin J. O'Toole	220.00	75.00	45.00
(141)	George Paskart (Paskert)	220.00	75.00	45.00
(142)	Barney Pelty	660.00	230.00	135.00
(143)	Herbert Perdue	310.00	110.00	60.00
(144)	O.C. Peters	310.00	110.00	60.00
(145)	Arthur Phelan	660.00	230.00	135.00
(146)	Jack Quinn	440.00	155.00	90.00
(147)	Don Carlos Ragan	715.00	250.00	145.00
(148)	Arthur Rasmussen	880.00	310.00	175.00
(149)	Morris Rath	880.00	100.00	175.00
(150)	Edward Reulbach	330.00	110.00	65.00
(151)	Napoleon Rucker	440.00	155.00	90.00
(152)	J.B. Ryan	1,200	425.00	245.00
(153)	Victor Saier	2,300	810.00	470.00
(154)	William Scanlon	220.00	75.00	45.00
(155)	Germany Schaefer	220.00	75.00	45.00
(156)	Wilbur Schardt	220.00	75.00	45.00
(157)	Frank Schulte	220.00	75.00	45.00
(158)	Jim Scott	495.00	170.00	100.00
(159)	Henry Severoid (Severeid)	220.00	75.00	45.00
(160)	Mike Simon	220.00	75.00	45.00
(161)	Frank E. Smith (Cincinnati)	220.00	75.00	45.00
(162)	Wallace Smith (St. Louis)	220.00	75.00	45.00
(163)	Fred Snodgrass	220.00	75.00	45.00
(164)	Tristam Speaker	3,025	1,045	495.00
(165)	Harry Lee Spratt	220.00	75.00	45.00
(166)	Edward Stack	550.00	195.00	110.00
(167)	Oscar Stanage	220.00	75.00	45.00
(168)	William Steele	660.00	230.00	135.00
(169)	Harry Steinfeldt	440.00	155.00	90.00
(170)	George Stovall	220.00	75.00	45.00
(171)	Charles (Gabby) Street	250.00	90.00	50.00
(172)	Amos Strunk	220.00	75.00	45.00
(173)	William Sullivan	310.00	110.00	60.00
(174)	William J. Sweeney	660.00	230.00	135.00
(175)	Leeford Tannehill	220.00	75.00	45.00
(176)	C.D. Thomas	715.00	250.00	145.00
(177)	Joseph Tinker	880.00	310.00	175.00
(178)	Bert Tooley	220.00	75.00	45.00
(179)	Terence Turner (Terrence)	220.00	75.00	45.00
(180)	George Tyler	1,540	550.00	305.00
(181)	Jim Vaughn	385.00	135.00	75.00
(182)	Chas. (Heinie) Wagner	220.00	75.00	45.00
(183)	Ed (Dixie) Walker	220.00	75.00	45.00
(184)	Robert Wallace	620.00	220.00	125.00
(185)	John Warhop	220.00	75.00	45.00
(186)	George Weaver	5,225	1,815	1,045
(187)	Zach Wheat	880.00	310.00	175.00
(188)	G. Harris White	310.00	110.00	60.00
(189)	Ernest Wilie	275.00	95.00	55.00
(190)	Bob Williams	220.00	75.00	45.00
(191)	Arthur Wilson (New York)	250.00	90.00	50.00
(192)	Owen Wilson (Pittsburg)	330.00	110.00	65.00
(193)	George Wiltse	220.00	75.00	45.00
(194)	Ivey Wingo	385.00	135.00	75.00
(195)	Harry Wolverton	220.00	75.00	45.00
(196)	Joe Wood	2,640	925.00	530.00
(197)	Eugene Woodburn	880.00	310.00	175.00
(198)	Ralph Works	880.00	310.00	175.00
(199)	Stanley Yerkes	220.00	75.00	45.00
(200)	Rollie Zeider	330.00	110.00	65.00

1912 T227 Series Of Champions

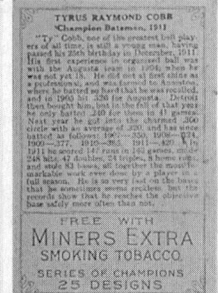

The 1912 "Series of Champions" card set issued by the "Honest Long Cut" and "Miners Extra" tobacco brands features several baseball stars among its 25 famous athletes of the day. Larger than a standard-size tobacco issue, each card in the "Champions" series measures 3-3/8" x 2-5/16". The back includes a relatively lengthy player biography, while the front features a lithograph of the player in action. Although the set includes only four baseball players, these attractive cards are popular among collectors because of the stature of the four players selected. The "Champions" series holds additional significance because it includes the only known baseball cards issued under the "Miners Extra" brand name. The set carries the American Card Catalog designation of T227.

		NM	EX	VG
Complete Set (4):		22,500	10,000	5,500
Common Player:		3,600	1,620	900.00
(1)	"Home Run" Baker	3,600	1,620	900.00
(2)	"Chief" Bender	3,600	1,620	900.00
(3)	Ty Cobb	16,200	7,200	4,200
(4)	Rube Marquard	3,600	1,620	900.00

U

1906 Ullman Postcards

The designation of Giants' players as "World's Champions" dates this issue to 1906. The 3-1/2" x 5-1/2" cards have a black-and-white photo surrounded by a greenish or reddish-brown tone wooden-look frame with a plaque printed in the bottom border. Backs are printed in brown with typical postcard markings and include mention of "Ullman's 'Art Frame' Series." This checklist is likely not complete. The card of "Harry" (name actually Henry) Mathewson is the only known baseball card appearance of Christy's kid brother.

		NM	EX	VG
Common Player:		750.00	375.00	225.00
(1)	Leon Ames	750.00	375.00	225.00
(2)	Mike Donlin	750.00	375.00	225.00
(3)	George Ferguson	750.00	375.00	225.00
(4)	Matty Fitzgerald	750.00	375.00	225.00
(5)	Billy Gilbert	750.00	375.00	225.00
(6)	Christy Matthewson (Mathewson)	3,500	1,750	1,000
(7)	Harry (Henry) Mathewson	1,200	600.00	360.00
(8)	Dan McGann (McGann on 1st Base)	750.00	375.00	225.00
(9)	"Iron Arm" McGinnity	1,000	500.00	300.00

		NM	EX	VG
(10)	Manager McGraw	1,500	750.00	450.00
(11)	Strang and Bowerman (Sammy Strang, Frank Bowerman)	900.00	450.00	250.00
(12)	Hooks Wiltse	750.00	375.00	225.00

1933 Uncle Jacks Candy

One of the lesser-known candy issues of the early 1930s was this New England regional set from Uncle Jacks, Inc., of Springfield, Mass., and Newport, R.I. The 1-7/8" x 2-7/8" blank-backed cards can be found printed in blue, red, purple or green duotone, and were sold in a see-through wax paper wrapper with a piece of candy and a coupon which could be redeemed (in quantities of 100) for a "league baseball" and a chance at a trip to the 1933 World Series. The set is among those listed in the American Card Catalog under the catchall number R317. The unnumbered cards are checklisted here alphabetically.

		NM	EX	VG
	Complete Set (30):	25,000	12,500	7,500
	Common Player:	400.00	200.00	120.00
(1)	Earl Averill	1,000	500.00	300.00
(2)	James L. Bottomley	1,000	500.00	300.00
(3)	Ed Brandt	400.00	200.00	120.00
(4)	Ben Chapman	400.00	200.00	120.00
(5)	Gordon Cochrane	1,000	500.00	300.00
(6)	Joe Cronin	1,000	500.00	300.00
(7)	Hazen Cuyler	1,000	500.00	300.00
(8)	George Earnshaw	400.00	200.00	120.00
(9)	Wesley Ferrell	400.00	200.00	120.00
(10)	Jimmie Foxx	1,500	750.00	450.00
(11)	Frank Frisch	1,000	500.00	300.00
(12)	Burleigh Grimes	1,000	500.00	300.00
(13)	"Lefty" Grove	1,250	625.00	375.00
(14)	"Wild Bill" Hallahan	400.00	200.00	120.00
(15)	Leo Hartnett	1,000	500.00	300.00
(16)	"Babe" Herman	400.00	200.00	120.00
(17)	Rogers Hornsby	1,200	600.00	360.00
(18)	Charles Klein	1,000	500.00	300.00
(19)	Tony Lazzeri	1,000	500.00	300.00
(20)	Fred Lindstrom	1,000	500.00	300.00
(21)	Ted Lyons	1,000	500.00	300.00
(22)	"Pepper" Martin	650.00	325.00	200.00
(23)	Herb Pennock	1,000	500.00	300.00
(24)	"Babe" Ruth ("King of Swat")	4,000	2,000	1,200
(25)	Al Simmons	1,000	500.00	300.00
(26)	"Bill" Terry	1,000	500.00	300.00
(27)	"Dazzy" Vance	1,000	500.00	300.00
(28)	Lloyd Waner	1,000	500.00	300.00
(29)	Paul Waner	1,000	500.00	300.00
(30)	Hack Wilson	1,000	500.00	300.00

1958 Union 76 Sports Club Booklets

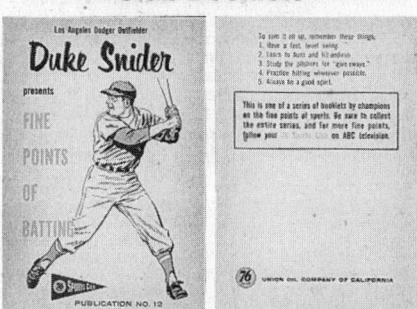

This series of sports instructional booklets was issued by Union Oil in conjunction with its Sports Club television program for youngsters. Besides seven baseball players, the series featured football, track, bowling, skiing and other stars. The booklets are 12 pages and measure about 4" x 5-1/2". Fronts have a drawing of the player and are printed in Union Oil logo colors of orange and blue. The sports tips inside are well illustrated. Books are numbered on front.

	NM	EX	VG
Complete (Baseball) Set (7):	160.00	80.00	45.00

		NM	EX	VG
	Common Player:	15.00	7.50	4.50
12	Duke Snider	35.00	17.50	10.50
14	Bob Lemon	20.00	10.00	6.00
15	Red Schoendienst	20.00	10.00	6.00
20	Bill Rigney	15.00	7.50	4.50
38	Jackie Jensen	15.00	7.50	4.50
39	Warren Spahn	25.00	12.50	7.50
41	Ernie Banks	35.00	17.50	10.50

1960 Union Oil Dodger Family Booklets

 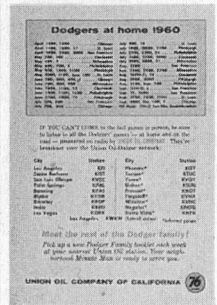

For its first major issue of Dodgers memorabilia, Union 76 gas stations in Southern California distributed a series of booklets profiling players and staff. Each 5-1/2" x 7-1/2" booklet has 16 black-and-white pages highlighted with red graphics. The covers have action poses with many other photos on the inside pages, along with a biography, personal information, career highlights, playing tips, etc. On back is a Dodgers schedule and Union 76 ad. The booklets were distributed on a one-per-week basis. They are listed here in alphabetical order.

		NM	EX	VG
	Complete Set (23):	150.00	75.00	45.00
	Common Player:	6.00	3.00	1.75
(1)	Walter Alston	7.50	3.75	2.25
(2)	Roger Craig	6.00	3.00	1.75
(3)	Tom Davis	7.50	3.75	2.25
(4)	Don Demeter	6.00	3.00	1.75
(5)	Don Drysdale	15.00	7.50	4.50
(6)	Chuck Essegian	6.00	3.00	1.75
(7)	Jim Gilliam	7.50	3.75	2.25
(8)	Gil Hodges	12.00	6.00	3.50
(9)	Frank Howard	7.50	3.75	2.25
(10)	Sandy Koufax	40.00	20.00	12.00
(11)	Norm Larker	6.00	3.00	1.75
(12)	Wally Moon	6.00	3.00	1.75
(13)	Charlie Neal	6.00	3.00	1.75
(14)	Johnny Podres	6.00	3.00	1.75
(15)	Ed Roebuck	6.00	3.00	1.75
(16)	John Roseboro	6.00	3.00	1.75
(17)	Larry Sherry	6.00	3.00	1.75
(18)	Norm Sherry	6.00	3.00	1.75
(19)	Duke Snider	15.00	7.50	4.50
(20)	Stan Williams	6.00	3.00	1.75
(21)	Maury Wills	7.50	3.75	2.25
(22)	Coaches (Joe Becker, Bobby Bragan, Greg Mulleavy, Pete Reiser)	6.00	3.00	1.75
(23)	Jerry Doggett, Vin Scully/ Announcers	6.00	3.00	1.75

1961 Union Oil Dodger Family Booklets

 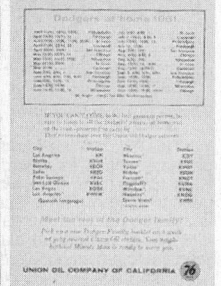

For a second consecutive year, Union 76 gas stations in Southern California distributed a series of booklets profiling team members and staff. The 5-1/2" x 7-1/2" booklets have 16 black-and-white pages highlighted with red graphics. The covers have large portraits while there are many photos on the inside pages, along with a biography, personal information, career highlights, playing tips, etc. On back is a Dodgers schedule and radio network information. The booklets were distributed on a one-per-week basis. They are listed here in alphabetical order.

		NM	EX	VG
	Complete Set (24):	175.00	85.00	50.00
	Common Player:	6.00	3.00	1.75
(1)	Walter Alston	7.50	3.75	2.25

---

(2)	Roger Craig	6.00	3.00	1.75
(3)	Tommy Davis	7.50	3.75	2.25
(4)	Willie Davis	7.50	3.75	2.25
(5)	Don Drysdale	15.00	7.50	4.50
(6)	Dick Farrell	6.00	3.00	1.75
(7)	Ron Fairly	6.00	3.00	1.75
(8)	Jim Gilliam	7.50	3.75	2.25
(9)	Gil Hodges	10.00	5.00	3.00
(10)	Frank Howard	7.50	3.75	2.25
(11)	Sandy Koufax	30.00	15.00	9.00
(12)	Norm Larker	6.00	3.00	1.75
(13)	Wally Moon	6.00	3.00	1.75
(14)	Charlie Neal	6.00	3.00	1.75
(15)	Ron Perranoski	6.00	3.00	1.75
(16)	Johnny Podres	6.00	3.00	1.75
(17)	John Roseboro	6.00	3.00	1.75
(18)	Larry Sherry	6.00	3.00	1.75
(19)	Norm Sherry	6.00	3.00	1.75
(20)	Duke Snider	15.00	7.50	4.50
(21)	Daryl Spencer	6.00	3.00	1.75
(22)	Stan Williams	6.00	3.00	1.75
(23)	Maury Wills	7.50	3.75	2.25
(24)	Jerry Doggett, Vin Scully/ Announcers	6.00	3.00	1.75

1962 Union Oil Dodgers Premium Pictures

One of many premiums issued by Union Oil during the Dodgers' early years in Los Angeles, this set of player pictures is the most popular with collectors. The 8-1/2" x 11" pictures feature a large color pastel portrait of the player on front, along with a smaller action picture. The player's name is printed in the white border below. The artist's signature and a 1962 copyright are printed below the portrait. Backs are printed in black-and-white and include a career summary and complete minor and major league stats, a profile of sports artist Nicholas Volpe and an ad at bottom for Union Oil and its Union 76 brand of gasoline. The unnumbered pictures are checklisted here alphabetically. It was reported that 200,000 of each picture were produced.

		NM	EX	VG
	Complete Set (24):	225.00	115.00	70.00
	Common Player:	8.00	4.00	2.50
(1)	Larry Burright	8.00	4.00	2.50
(2)	Doug Camilli	8.00	4.00	2.50
(3)	Andy Carey	8.00	4.00	2.50
(4)	Tom Davis	10.00	5.00	3.00
(5)	Willie Davis	10.00	5.00	3.00
(6)	Don Drysdale	20.00	10.00	6.00
(7)	Ron Fairly	8.00	4.00	2.50
(8)	Jim Gilliam	10.00	5.00	3.00
(9)	Tim Harkness	8.00	4.00	2.50
(10)	Frank Howard	10.00	5.00	3.00
(11)	Sandy Koufax	40.00	20.00	12.00
(12)	Joe Moeller	8.00	4.00	2.50
(13)	Wally Moon	8.00	4.00	2.50
(14)	Ron Perranoski	8.00	4.00	2.50
(15)	Johnny Podres	8.00	4.00	2.50
(16)	Ed Roebuck	8.00	4.00	2.50
(17)	John Roseboro	8.00	4.00	2.50
(18)	Larry Sherry	8.00	4.00	2.50
(19)	Norm Sherry	8.00	4.00	2.50
(20)	Duke Snider	25.00	12.50	7.50
(21)	Daryl Spencer	8.00	4.00	2.50
(22)	Lee Walls	8.00	4.00	2.50
(23)	Stan Williams	8.00	4.00	2.50
(24)	Maury Wills	10.00	5.00	3.00

1964 Union Oil Dodgers Premium Pictures

Paired pastel portraits, one in uniform and one in mufti, from sports artist Nicholas Volpe are featured on these large-format (8-1/2" x 11") premium pictures sponsored by Union Oil. The player's name is printed in the bottom border while the artist's signature is printed beneath the portraits. Backs are in black-and-white and feature personal data about the player and artist, complete minor and major league stats and Union Oil/Union 76 logos. The unnumbered pictures are checklisted here alphabetically.

		NM	EX	VG
Complete Set (18):		165.00	80.00	50.00
Common Player:		8.00	4.00	2.50
(1)	Tommy Davis	10.00	5.00	3.00
(2)	Willie Davis	10.00	5.00	3.00
(3)	Don Drysdale	20.00	10.00	6.00
(4)	Ron Fairly	8.00	4.00	2.50
(5)	Jim Gilliam	10.00	5.00	3.00
(6)	Frank Howard	10.00	5.00	3.00
(7)	Sandy Koufax	35.00	17.50	10.00
(8)	Bob Miller	8.00	4.00	2.50
(9)	Joe Moeller	8.00	4.00	2.50
(10)	Wally Moon	8.00	4.00	2.50
(11)	Phil Ortega	8.00	4.00	2.50
(12)	Wes Parker	8.00	4.00	2.50
(13)	Ron Perranoski	8.00	4.00	2.50
(14)	John Podres	8.00	4.00	2.50
(15)	John Roseboro	8.00	4.00	2.50
(16)	Dick Tracewski	8.00	4.00	2.50
(17)	Lee Walls	8.00	4.00	2.50
(18)	Maury Wills	10.00	5.00	3.00

1969 Union Oil Dodgers Premium Pictures

These 8-1/2" x 11" cards were given to fans attending week night "Player Portrait Night" promotional games. The premiums are similar in format to earlier and later sets sponsored by Union Oil and created by sports artist Nicholas Volpe. Fronts have pastel player portraits and action drawings against a black background. Backs are in black-and-white and have player biographies, stats and a career summary, along with a word about the artist and an ad for Union Oil/Union 76. The unnumbered pictures are checklisted here alphabetically.

		NM	EX	VG
Complete Set (13):		120.00	60.00	35.00
Common Player:		8.00	4.00	2.50
(1)	Walt Alston	10.00	5.00	3.00
(2)	Jim Brewer	8.00	4.00	2.50
(3)	Willie Davis	10.00	5.00	3.00
(4)	Don Drysdale	20.00	10.00	6.00
(5)	Ron Fairly	8.00	4.00	2.50
(6)	Tom Haller	8.00	4.00	2.50
(7)	Jim Lefebvre	8.00	4.00	2.50
(8)	Claude Osteen	8.00	4.00	2.50
(9)	Wes Parker	8.00	4.00	2.50
(10)	Paul Popovich	8.00	4.00	2.50
(11)	Bill Singer	8.00	4.00	2.50
(12)	Bill Sudakis	8.00	4.00	2.50
(13)	Don Sutton	13.50	6.75	4.00

1968 Uniroyal Keds Cincinnati Reds

These 2-1/2" x 3-1/4" cards are printed in blue duotone on thin paper. Blank backed, they were intended to be put into an accompanying album. It is unknown whether this checklist is complete.

	NM	EX	VG
Common Player:	20.00	10.00	6.00

		NM	EX	VG
(1)	Dave Bristol	20.00	10.00	6.00
(2)	Bob Johnson	20.00	10.00	6.00
(3)	Bob Lee	20.00	10.00	6.00
(4)	Jim Maloney	20.00	10.00	6.00
(5)	Lee May	20.00	10.00	6.00
(6)	Vada Pinson	25.00	12.50	7.50
(7)	Pete Rose	150.00	75.00	45.00

1979 United Press International

SPORTS NOSTALGIA

THEODORE SAMUEL WILLIAMS
(1918-)

"Ted" Williams was born in San Diego, California and during his career, he won six batting titles and hit 521 home runs. In 1946 he hit over .400, the last major league player to do so. He played for the Boston Red Sox (1939-42; 1946-60) and was elected to the Baseball Hall of Fame in 1966.

On September 28, 1960, Williams hit a 420-foot home run in the 8th inning during a game with Baltimore at Fenway Park. It was his 29th homer of the season and turned out to be Ted Williams' last 'at bat' in the majors before retiring.

UNITED PRESS INTERNATIONAL

Not widely circulated, and perhaps issued only as a prototype, these cards feature a tiny (2" x 2-1/4" clear vinyl record attached to the back. Overall, the card is 2-3/4" x 5" and has on front a black-and-white or color photo with a UPI credit line in the very wide white border at bottom. The back is headed either "Sports Nostalgia" or "Great Moments in Sports." Player identification and career highlights are printed on back. The vinyl mini-record could be played on an ancient electronic entertainment device known as a turntable. Similar card/records were produced for other sports and historical highlights.

		NM	EX	VG
Complete Set (9):		150.00	75.00	45.00
Common Player:		10.00	5.00	3.00
(1)	Hank Aaron (715th HR)	15.00	7.50	4.50
(2)	Joe DiMaggio (Hitting Streak Ends)	20.00	10.00	6.00
(3)	Lou Gehrig (Gehrig Day 7/4/39)	20.00	10.00	6.00
(4)	Mickey Mantle (Record HR)	25.00	12.50	7.50
(5)	Stan Musial (3,000th Hit)	15.00	7.50	4.50
(6)	Babe Ruth (Famous Home Run)	20.00	10.00	6.00
(7)	Gene Tenace (Record HR)	10.00	5.00	3.00
(8)	Bobby Thomson (Famous HR)	12.00	6.00	3.50
(9)	Ted Williams (Last At-Bat)	15.00	7.50	4.50

1932 Universal Pictures Babe Ruth Premium

See the Bambino Himself!
BABE RUTH
in a Humaninteresting Baseball Story
"SLIDE BABE SLIDE"
at the
KEENEY THEATRE
SUNDAY, JUNE 19th—4 Days

This 8" x 10" black-and-white photo was issued to promote what was advertised as a series of Babe Ruth shorts. The front pictures the movie star in a generic uniform with a facsimile autograph. On back is advertising for the theater bill. It is likely the pictures were distributed blank-backed, allowing local theaters to have their advertising added.

	NM	EX	VG
Babe Ruth	750.00	375.00	225.00

1925 Universal Toy & Novelty Brooklyn Dodgers (W504)

Printed on cheap paper in blue ink and intended to be cut apart into a team photo and 16 individual player cards, this set was originally issued on a 5-1/2" x 13" sheet. Single cut cards measure about 1-3/8" x 2-3/8", with the team picture about 5-1/2" x 3-1/2". Cards are blank-back. Cards are numbered in roughly alphabetical order beneath the photo, where the name, team, position and birth year are also printed.

		NM	EX	VG
Complete Sheet:		1,800	900.00	540.00
Complete Set, Singles (17):		1,200	600.00	360.00
Common Player:		50.00	25.00	15.00
101	Edward W. Brown	50.00	25.00	15.00
102	John H. De Berry	50.00	25.00	15.00
103	William L. Doak	50.00	25.00	15.00
104	Wm. C. Ehrhardt (First name Welton.)	50.00	25.00	15.00
105	J.F. Fournier	50.00	25.00	15.00
106	T.H. Griffith	50.00	25.00	15.00
107	Burleigh A. Grimes	100.00	50.00	30.00
108	C.P. Hargreaves	50.00	25.00	15.00
109	Andrew A. High	50.00	25.00	15.00
110	Andy. H. Johnston (First name Jimmy.)	50.00	25.00	15.00
111	John Mitchell	50.00	25.00	15.00
112	"Tiny" Osborne	50.00	25.00	15.00
113	Milton Stock	50.00	25.00	15.00
114	James W. Taylor	50.00	25.00	15.00
115	"Dazzy" Vance	100.00	50.00	30.00
116	Zack D. Wheat	100.00	50.00	30.00
---	Brooklyn National League Team Photo	550.00	275.00	165.00

1925 Universal Toy & Novelty New York Giants (W504)

Printed on thick cardboard and intended to be cut apart into a team photo and 16 individual player cards, this set was originally issued on a 5-1/2" x 13" sheet. Single cut cards measure about 1-3/8" x 2-3/8", with the team picture about 5" x 3-1/2". Cards are blank-back. Player cards are numbered beneath the photo, where the name, team, position and birth year are also printed.

		NM	EX	VG
Complete Sheet:		3,500	1,750	1,000
Complete Set (17):		3,000	1,500	900.00
Common Player:		125.00	60.00	35.00
133	Virgil Barnes	125.00	60.00	35.00
134	John N. Bentley	125.00	60.00	35.00
135	Frank Frisch	225.00	110.00	65.00
136	Harry Gowdy	125.00	60.00	35.00
137	Henry Groh	125.00	60.00	35.00
138	Travis Jackson	200.00	100.00	60.00
139	George Kelly	200.00	100.00	60.00
140	Emil Meusel	125.00	60.00	35.00
141	Hugh McQuillan	125.00	60.00	35.00
142	Arthur Nehf	125.00	60.00	35.00
143	Wilfred D. Ryan	125.00	60.00	35.00
144	Frank Snyder	125.00	60.00	35.00
145	Lewis R. Wilson	225.00	110.00	65.00
146	Ross Youngs	200.00	100.00	60.00
147	Hugh Jennings	200.00	100.00	60.00
148	John J. McGraw	200.00	100.00	60.00
---	New York National League Team Photo	400.00	200.00	120.00

1925 Universal Toy & Novelty N.Y. Yankees (W504)

Printed on thick cardboard and intended to be cut apart into a team photo and 16 individual player cards, this set was originally issued on a 5-1/2" x 13" sheet. Single cut cards measure about 1-3/8" x 2-3/8", with the team picture about 5" x 3-1/2". Cards are blank-back. Player cards are numbered in alphabetical order beneath the photo, where the name, team, position and birth year are also printed.

		NM	EX	VG
Complete Sheet:		4,000	2,000	1,200
Complete Set (17):		3,500	1,750	1,000
Common Player:		125.00	60.00	35.00
117	Bernard Bengough	125.00	60.00	35.00
118	Joseph Dugan	125.00	60.00	35.00
119	Waite Hoyt	200.00	100.00	60.00
120	Sam Jones	125.00	60.00	35.00
121	Robert Meusel	125.00	60.00	35.00
122	Walter C. Pipp	125.00	60.00	35.00
123	G.H. "Babe" Ruth	1,200	600.00	360.00
124	Wal. H. Schang	125.00	60.00	35.00
125	Robert J. Shawkey	125.00	60.00	35.00
126	Everett Scott	125.00	60.00	35.00
127	Urban Shocker	125.00	60.00	35.00
128	Aaron L. Ward	125.00	60.00	35.00
129	Lawton Witt	125.00	60.00	35.00
130	Carl Mays	140.00	70.00	42.00
131	Miller Huggins	200.00	100.00	60.00
132	Benj. Paschal	125.00	60.00	35.00
----	New York American League Team Photo	800.00	400.00	240.00

1925 Universal Toy & Novelty Washington Senators (W504)

Printed on thick cardboard and intended to be cut apart into a team photo and 16 individual player cards, this set was originally issued on a 5-1/2" x 13" sheet. Single cut cards measure about 1-3/8" x 2-3/8", with the team picture about 5" x 3-1/2". Cards are blank-back. Player cards are numbered beneath the photo, where the name, team, position and birth year are also printed.

		NM	EX	VG
Complete Sheet:				
Complete Set (17):				
Common Player:		50.00	25.00	15.00
149	Joe Judge	50.00	25.00	15.00
150	Wm. Hargrave	50.00	25.00	15.00
151	R. Peckinpaugh	50.00	25.00	15.00
152	O.L. Bluege	50.00	25.00	15.00
153	M.J. McNally	50.00	25.00	15.00
154	Sam Rice	200.00	100.00	60.00
155				
156				
157				
158				
159	Wm. Hargrave	50.00	25.00	15.00
160				
161				
162	Harold (Herold) Ruel	50.00	25.00	15.00
163				
164	George Mogridge	50.00	25.00	15.00

---	Washinton American League Team Photo	400.00	200.00	120.00

1933 U.S. Caramel (R328)

 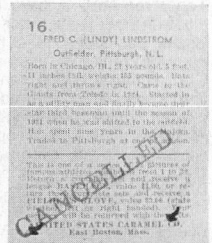

Produced by a Boston confectioner, this set is not limited to baseball, but is a set of 32 "Famous Athletes," of which 27 are baseball players. The 2-1/2" x 3" cards have a black-and-white picture on front with a red background and white border. Backs feature the player's name, position, team and league as well as a redemption ad and card number. The issue was among the last of the caramel card sets. The cards could be redeemed for a baseball and glove and were returned punch-cancelled and stamped. Card #16, short-printed to limit the number of prizes claimed, was first discovered in the late 1980s; only two examples are currently known.

		NM	EX	VG
	Common Player:	600.00	275.00	150.00
1	Edward T. (Eddie) Collins	1,000	450.00	250.00
2	Paul (Big Poison) Waner	1,000	450.00	250.00
3	Robert T. (Bobby) Jones/Golfer			
4	William (Bill) Terry	1,000	450.00	250.00
5	Earl B. Combs (Earle)	1,000	450.00	250.00
6	William (Bill) Dickey	1,000	450.00	250.00
7	Joseph (Joe) Cronin	1,000	450.00	250.00
8	Charles (Chick) Hafey	1,000	450.00	250.00
9	Gene Sarazen (golfer)			
10	Walter (Rabbit) Maranville	1,000	450.00	250.00
11	Rogers (Rajah) Hornsby	1,750	785.00	435.00
12	Gordon (Mickey) Cochrane	1,000	450.00	250.00
13	Lloyd (Little Poison) Waner	1,000	450.00	250.00
14	Tyrus (Ty) Cobb	3,000	1,350	750.00
15	Eugene (Gene) Tunney/ Boxer			
16	Charles (Lindy) Lindstrom (2 known.)			80,000
17	Al. Simmons	1,000	450.00	250.00
18	Anthony (Tony) Lazzeri	1,000	450.00	250.00
19	Walter (Wally) Berger	600.00	275.00	150.00
20	Charles (Large Charlie) Ruffing	1,000	450.00	250.00
21	Charles (Chuck) Klein	1,000	450.00	250.00
22	John (Jack) Dempsey (Boxer)			
23	James (Jimmy) Foxx	1,750	785.00	435.00
24	Frank J. (Lefty) O'Doul	750.00	335.00	185.00
25	Jack (Sailor Jack) Sharkey/ Boxer			
26	Henry (Lou) Gehrig	6,000	2,700	1,500
27	Robert (Lefty) Grove	1,200	540.00	300.00
28	Edward Brant (Brandt)	600.00	275.00	150.00
29	George Earnshaw	600.00	275.00	150.00
30	Frank (Frankie) Frisch	1,000	450.00	250.00
31	Vernon (Lefty) Gomez	1,000	450.00	250.00
32	George (Babe) Ruth	7,500	3,250	1,900

1973 U.S. Playing Card Ruth/ Gehrig

These decks of playing cards were produced for sale by the Smithsonian Institution in Washington, D.C. The 2-1/4" x 3-1/2" cards were sold as a pair. Backs have colorized pictures of the Yankees greats; Ruth on an orange background and Gehrig on red.

	NM	EX	VG
Complete Set, Ruth (54):	25.00	12.50	7.50
Single Card, Ruth:	1.50	.75	.45
Complete Set, Gehrig (54):	15.00	7.50	4.50
Single Card, Gehrig:	.75	.40	.25
(A 50% premium attaches to a complete boxed pair of decks.)			

1909-11 Uzit Cigarettes

Uzit is generally accepted as the second scarcest back advertiser (after Drum) found on T206. The typographic back is printed in light blue ink.

PREMIUMS
Commons: 35-45X
Hall of Famers: 6-8X
 (See T206 for checklist.)

1938-39 Val Decker Packing Co. Cincinnati Reds Postcards

(See 1937-39 Orcajo Cincinnati Reds postcards for checklist and values.)

1950s-70s Van Heusen Advisory Staff Photos

Not a great deal is known about the distribution of these 8" x 10" black-and-white player photos. It is likely the checklist here is not complete. The photos are bordered in white with the player name at bottom. In one of the lower corners is the logo of the clothing manufacturer. This issue is differentiated from the Phillies because of the action poses and multi-team composition of the known examples.

		NM	EX	VG
	Common Player:	20.00	10.00	6.00
(1)	Paul Blair	20.00	10.00	6.00
(2)	Curt Blefary	20.00	10.00	6.00
(3)	Jerry Coleman/Throwing (Yankees)	25.00	12.50	7.50
(4)	Tommy Davis/Btg (Dodgers)	20.00	10.00	6.00
(5)	Dick Hall/Portrait (Phillies)	20.00	10.00	6.00
(6)	Bob Hendley (Braves, follow-through.)	20.00	10.00	6.00

		NM	EX	VG
(7)	Chuck Hinton	20.00	10.00	6.00
(8)	Don Lock	20.00	10.00	6.00
	(Phillies, upper body.)			
(9)	Jim Piersall	25.00	12.50	7.50
(10)	Cookie Rojas	20.00	10.00	6.00
	(Phillies, bat on shoulder.)			
(11)	Bill Skowron	25.00	12.50	7.50
	(Dodgers, full-length.)			
(12)	Maury Wills/Btg (Dodgers)	25.00	12.50	7.50

1967 Van Heusen Phillies

Not a great deal is known about the distribution of these 8" x 10" black-and-white player portraits. It is possible the checklist here is not complete. The photos are bordered in white with the player name at bottom. At lower-right is the logo of the clothing manufacturer. This issue is differentiated from the Advisory Staff Photos because of the similitude of the portrait photos of the teammates.

		NM	EX	VG
Common Player:		20.00	10.00	6.00
(1)	Bo Belinsky	20.00	10.00	6.00
(2)	Jim Bunning	35.00	17.50	10.50
(3)	Wes Covington	20.00	10.00	6.00
(4)	Dick Ellsworth	20.00	10.00	6.00
(5)	Dick Groat	20.00	10.00	6.00
(6)	Chris Short	20.00	10.00	6.00
(7)	Bill White	20.00	10.00	6.00

1912 Vassar Sweaters

Star players of the day are pictured wearing the sponsor's product over their uniforms in this issue of 4" x 6-3/4" black-and-white cards. Player names are in the white border at bottom. It is not known whether this checklist is complete.

		NM	EX	VG
Common Player:		1,250	625.00	375.00
(1)	Ty Cobb	5,000	2,500	1,500
(2)	Sam Crawford	1,750	875.00	525.00
(3)	Walter Johnson	2,750	1,375	825.00
(4)	Napoleon Lajoie	1,750	875.00	525.00
(5)	Smokey Joe Wood	1,250	625.00	375.00

1959 Venezuelan Topps

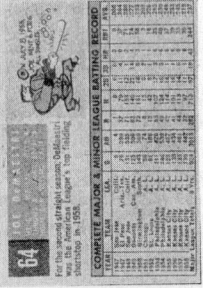

Beginning in 1959, Topps began marketing baseball cards in Venezuela, always a hotbed of baseball fandom. In most years, such as the debut set in 1959, the cards destined for the South American market represented a parallel of the first couple of series of Topps' regular U.S. issue. Print quality (usually lack of gloss on front) is the major difference between the two issues. Backs of some of the 1959 Venezuelan cards carry the credit line: "Impreso en Venezuela por Benco C.A." A reality of the Venezuelan cards is that they tend to survive in low-grade condition due to the local custom of gluing cards into albums and scrapbooks. After its 1959 issue, Topps produced Venezuelan cards only in the even-numbered years, except for 1967, until the last of the sets was issued in 1968.

		NM	EX	VG
Complete Set (196):		10,000	4,000	2,400
Common Player:		45.00	18.00	11.00
1	Ford Frick	60.00	24.00	14.50
2	Eddie Yost	45.00	18.00	11.00
3	Don McMahon	45.00	18.00	11.00
4	Albie Pearson	45.00	18.00	11.00
5	Dick Donovan	45.00	18.00	11.00
6	Alex Grammas	45.00	18.00	11.00
7	Al Pilarcik	45.00	18.00	11.00
8	Phillies Team	75.00	30.00	18.00
9	Paul Giel	45.00	18.00	11.00
10	Mickey Mantle	2,000	550.00	350.00
11	Billy Hunter	45.00	18.00	11.00
12	Vern Law	45.00	18.00	11.00
13	Dick Gernert	45.00	18.00	11.00
14	Pete Whisenant	45.00	18.00	11.00
15	Dick Drott	45.00	18.00	11.00
16	Joe Pignatano	45.00	18.00	11.00
17	Danny's All-Stars	50.00	20.00	12.00
	(Ted Kluszewski, Danny Murtaugh, Frank Thomas)			
18	Jack Urban	45.00	18.00	11.00
19	Ed Bressoud	45.00	18.00	11.00
20	Duke Snider	200.00	80.00	48.00
21	Connie Johnson	45.00	18.00	11.00
22	Al Smith	45.00	18.00	11.00
23	Murry Dickson	45.00	18.00	11.00
24	Red Wilson	45.00	18.00	11.00
25	Don Hoak	45.00	18.00	11.00
26	Chuck Stobbs	45.00	18.00	11.00
27	Andy Pafko	45.00	18.00	11.00
28	Red Worthington	45.00	18.00	11.00
29	Jim Bolger	45.00	18.00	11.00
30	Nellie Fox	100.00	40.00	24.00
31	Ken Lehman	45.00	18.00	11.00
32	Don Buddin	45.00	18.00	11.00
33	Ed Fitz Gerald	45.00	18.00	11.00
34	Pitchers Beware	90.00	36.00	22.00
	(Al Kaline, Charlie Maxwell)			
35	Ted Kluszewski	60.00	24.00	14.50
36	Hank Aguirre	45.00	18.00	11.00
37	Gene Green	45.00	18.00	11.00
38	Morrie Martin	45.00	18.00	11.00
39	Ed Bouchee	45.00	18.00	11.00
40	Warren Spahn	125.00	50.00	30.00
41	Bob Martyn	45.00	18.00	11.00
42	Murray Wall	45.00	18.00	11.00
43	Steve Bilko	45.00	18.00	11.00
44	Vito Valentinetti	45.00	18.00	11.00
45	Andy Carey	45.00	18.00	11.00
46	Bill Henry	45.00	18.00	11.00
47	Jim Finigan	45.00	18.00	11.00
48	Orioles Team/Checklist 1-88	75.00	30.00	18.00
49	Bill Hall	45.00	18.00	11.00
50	Willie Mays	450.00	180.00	108.00
51	Rip Coleman	45.00	18.00	11.00
52	Coot Veal	45.00	18.00	11.00
53	Stan Williams	45.00	18.00	11.00
54	Mel Roach	45.00	18.00	11.00
55	Tom Brewer	45.00	18.00	11.00
56	Carl Sawatski	45.00	18.00	11.00
57	Al Cicotte	45.00	18.00	11.00
58	Eddie Miksis	45.00	18.00	11.00
59	Irv Noren	45.00	18.00	11.00
60	Bob Turley	45.00	18.00	11.00
61	Dick Brown	45.00	18.00	11.00
62	Tony Taylor	45.00	18.00	11.00
63	Jim Hearn	45.00	18.00	11.00
64	Joe DeMaestri	45.00	18.00	11.00
65	Frank Torre	45.00	18.00	11.00
66	Joe Ginsberg	45.00	18.00	11.00
67	Brooks Lawrence	45.00	18.00	11.00
68	Dick Schofield	45.00	18.00	11.00
69	Giants Team/Checklist 89-176	75.00	30.00	18.00
70	Harvey Kuenn	50.00	20.00	12.00
71	Don Bessent	45.00	18.00	11.00
72	Bill Renna	45.00	18.00	11.00
73	Ron Jackson	45.00	18.00	11.00
74	Directing the Power	45.00	18.00	11.00
	(Cookie Lavagetto, Jim Lemon, Roy Sievers)			
75	Sam Jones	45.00	18.00	11.00
76	Bobby Richardson	50.00	20.00	12.00
77	John Goryl	45.00	18.00	11.00
78	Pedro Ramos	45.00	18.00	11.00
79	Harry Chiti	45.00	18.00	11.00
80	Minnie Minoso	55.00	22.00	13.00
81	Hal Jeffcoat	45.00	18.00	11.00
82	Bob Boyd	45.00	18.00	11.00
83	Bob Smith	45.00	18.00	11.00
84	Reno Bertoia	45.00	18.00	11.00
85	Harry Anderson	45.00	18.00	11.00
86	Bob Keegan	45.00	18.00	11.00
87	Danny O'Connell	45.00	18.00	11.00
88	Herb Score	45.00	18.00	11.00
89	Billy Gardner	45.00	18.00	11.00
90	Bill Skowron	55.00	22.00	13.00

		NM	EX	VG
91	Herb Moford	45.00	18.00	11.00
92	Dave Philley	45.00	18.00	11.00
93	Julio Becquer	45.00	18.00	11.00
94	White Sox Team	100.00	40.00	24.00
95	Carl Willey	45.00	18.00	11.00
96	Lou Berberet	45.00	18.00	11.00
97	Jerry Lynch	45.00	18.00	11.00
98	Arnie Portocarrero	45.00	18.00	11.00
99	Ted Kazanski	45.00	18.00	11.00
100	Bob Cerv	45.00	18.00	11.00
101	Alex Kellner	45.00	18.00	11.00
102	Felipe Alou	60.00	24.00	14.50
103	Billy Goodman	45.00	18.00	11.00
104	Del Rice	45.00	18.00	11.00
105	Lee Walls	45.00	18.00	11.00
106	Hal Woodeshick	45.00	18.00	11.00
107	Norm Larker	45.00	18.00	11.00
108	Zack Monroe	45.00	18.00	11.00
109	Bob Schmidt	45.00	18.00	11.00
110	George Witt	45.00	18.00	11.00
111	Redlegs Team/Checklist 89-176	75.00	30.00	18.00
112	Billy Consolo	45.00	18.00	11.00
113	Taylor Phillips	45.00	18.00	11.00
114	Earl Battey	45.00	18.00	11.00
115	Mickey Vernon	45.00	18.00	11.00
116	Bob Allison	45.00	18.00	11.00
117	John Blanchard	45.00	18.00	11.00
118	John Buzhardt	45.00	18.00	11.00
119	John Callison	45.00	18.00	11.00
120	Chuck Coles	45.00	18.00	11.00
121	Bob Conley	45.00	18.00	11.00
122	Bennie Daniels	45.00	18.00	11.00
123	Don Dillard	45.00	18.00	11.00
124	Dan Dobbek	45.00	18.00	11.00
125	Ron Fairly	45.00	18.00	11.00
126	Eddie Haas	45.00	18.00	11.00
127	Kent Hadley	45.00	18.00	11.00
128	Bob Hartman	45.00	18.00	11.00
129	Frank Herrera	45.00	18.00	11.00
130	Lou Jackson	45.00	18.00	11.00
131	Deron Johnson	50.00	20.00	12.00
132	Don Lee	45.00	18.00	11.00
133	Bob Lillis	45.00	18.00	11.00
134	Jim McDaniel	45.00	18.00	11.00
135	Gene Oliver	45.00	18.00	11.00
136	Jim O'Toole	45.00	18.00	11.00
137	Dick Ricketts	45.00	18.00	11.00
138	John Romano	45.00	18.00	11.00
139	Ed Sadowski	45.00	18.00	11.00
140	Charlie Secrest	45.00	18.00	11.00
141	Joe Shipley	45.00	18.00	11.00
142	Dick Stigman	45.00	18.00	11.00
143	Willie Tasby	45.00	18.00	11.00
144	Jerry Walker	45.00	18.00	11.00
145	Dom Zanni	45.00	18.00	11.00
146	Jerry Zimmerman	45.00	18.00	11.00
147	Cubs' Clubbers	90.00	36.00	22.00
	(Ernie Banks, Dale Long, Walt Moryn)			
148	Mike McCormick	45.00	18.00	11.00
149	Jim Bunning	100.00	40.00	24.00
150	Stan Musial	400.00	160.00	100.00
151	Bob Malkmus	45.00	18.00	11.00
152	Johnny Klippstein	45.00	18.00	11.00
153	Jim Marshall	45.00	18.00	11.00
154	Ray Herbert	45.00	18.00	11.00
155	Enos Slaughter	90.00	36.00	22.00
156	Ace Hurlers (Billy Pierce, Robin Roberts)	65.00	26.00	15.50
157	Felix Mantilla	45.00	18.00	11.00
158	Walt Dropo	45.00	18.00	11.00
159	Bob Shaw	45.00	18.00	11.00
160	Dick Groat	45.00	18.00	11.00
161	Frank Baumann	45.00	18.00	11.00
162	Bobby G. Smith	45.00	18.00	11.00
163	Sandy Koufax	450.00	180.00	110.00
164	Johnny Groth	45.00	18.00	11.00
165	Bill Bruton	45.00	18.00	11.00
166	Destruction Crew	125.00	50.00	30.00
	(Rocky Colavito, Larry Doby, Minnie Minoso)			
167	Duke Maas	45.00	18.00	11.00
168	Carroll Hardy	45.00	18.00	11.00
169	Ted Abernathy	45.00	18.00	11.00
170	Gene Woodling	45.00	18.00	11.00
171	Willard Schmidt	45.00	18.00	11.00
172	A's Team/Checklist 177-242	75.00	30.00	18.00
173	Bill Monbouquette	45.00	18.00	11.00
174	Jim Pendleton	45.00	18.00	11.00
175	Dick Farrell	45.00	18.00	11.00
176	Preston Ward	45.00	18.00	11.00
177	Johnny Briggs	45.00	18.00	11.00
178	Ruben Amaro	45.00	18.00	11.00
179	Don Rudolph	45.00	18.00	11.00
180	Yogi Berra	200.00	80.00	48.00
181	Bob Porterfield	45.00	18.00	11.00
182	Milt Graff	45.00	18.00	11.00
183	Stu Miller	45.00	18.00	11.00
184	Harvey Haddix	45.00	18.00	11.00
185	Jim Busby	45.00	18.00	11.00
186	Mudcat Grant	45.00	18.00	11.00
187	Bubba Phillips	45.00	18.00	11.00
188	Juan Pizarro	45.00	18.00	11.00
189	Neil Chrisley	45.00	18.00	11.00
190	Bill Virdon	45.00	18.00	11.00
191	Russ Kemmerer	45.00	18.00	11.00
192	Charley Beamon	45.00	18.00	11.00
193	Sammy Taylor	45.00	18.00	11.00
194	Jim Brosnan	45.00	18.00	11.00
195	Rip Repulski	45.00	18.00	11.00
196	Billy Moran	45.00	18.00	11.00

1960 Venezuelan Topps

Unlike its 1959 issue, which had a printed-in-Venezuela notice on the backs, Topps' 1960 issue for that South American market is virtually identical, front and back, to the company's U.S. product. The Venezuelan cards have less gloss on the frontand the black ink on their backs is lighter. The Latin American version is a parallel of the first 198 cards from Topps' set. As usual with Latin American cards, low-grade examples are the norm due to the local collecting custom of pasting cards into albums and scrapbooks.

		NM	EX	VG
	Complete Set (198):	7,900	3,150	1,900
	Common Player:	40.00	16.00	9.50
1	Early Wynn	95.00	30.00	20.00
2	Roman Mejias	40.00	16.00	9.50
3	Joe Adcock	40.00	16.00	9.50
4	Bob Purkey	40.00	16.00	9.50
5	Wally Moon	40.00	16.00	9.50
6	Lou Berberet	40.00	16.00	9.50
7	Master and Mentor	125.00	50.00	30.00
	(Willie Mays, Bill Rigney)			
8	Bud Daley	40.00	16.00	9.50
9	Faye Throneberry	40.00	16.00	9.50
10	Ernie Banks	150.00	60.00	36.00
11	Norm Siebern	40.00	16.00	9.50
12	Milt Pappas	40.00	16.00	9.50
13	Wally Post	40.00	16.00	9.50
14	Jim Grant	40.00	16.00	9.50
15	Pete Runnels	40.00	16.00	9.50
16	Ernie Broglio	40.00	16.00	9.50
17	Johnny Callison	40.00	16.00	9.50
18	Dodgers Team/	100.00	40.00	24.00
	Checklist 1-88			
19	Felix Mantilla	40.00	16.00	9.50
20	Roy Face	40.00	16.00	9.50
21	Dutch Dotterer	40.00	16.00	9.50
22	Rocky Bridges	40.00	16.00	9.50
23	Eddie Fisher	40.00	16.00	9.50
24	Dick Gray	40.00	16.00	9.50
25	Roy Sievers	40.00	16.00	9.50
26	Wayne Terwilliger	40.00	16.00	9.50
27	Dick Drott	40.00	16.00	9.50
28	Brooks Robinson	150.00	60.00	36.00
29	Clem Labine	40.00	16.00	9.50
30	Tito Francona	40.00	16.00	9.50
31	Sammy Esposito	40.00	16.00	9.50
32	Sophomore Stalwarts	40.00	16.00	9.50
	(Jim O'Toole, Vada Pinson)			
33	Tom Morgan	40.00	16.00	9.50
34	Sparky Anderson	90.00	45.00	27.00
35	Whitey Ford	150.00	60.00	36.00
36	Russ Nixon	40.00	16.00	9.50
37	Bill Bruton	40.00	16.00	9.50
38	Jerry Casale	40.00	16.00	9.50
39	Earl Averill	40.00	16.00	9.50
40	Joe Cunningham	40.00	16.00	9.50
41	Barry Latman	40.00	16.00	9.50
42	Hobie Landrith	40.00	16.00	9.50
43	Senators Team/	75.00	30.00	18.00
	Checklist 1-88			
44	Bobby Locke	40.00	16.00	9.50
45	Roy McMillan	40.00	16.00	9.50
46	Jack Fisher	40.00	16.00	9.50
47	Don Zimmer	40.00	16.00	9.50
48	Hal Smith	40.00	16.00	9.50
49	Curt Raydon	40.00	16.00	9.50
50	Al Kaline	150.00	60.00	36.00
51	Jim Coates	40.00	16.00	9.50
52	Dave Philley	40.00	16.00	9.50
53	Jackie Brandt	40.00	16.00	9.50
54	Mike Fornieles	40.00	16.00	9.50
55	Bill Mazeroski	90.00	45.00	27.00
56	Steve Korcheck	40.00	16.00	9.50
57	Win-Savers	40.00	16.00	9.50
	(Turk Lown, Gerry Staley)			
58	Gino Cimoli	40.00	16.00	9.50
59	Juan Pizarro	40.00	16.00	9.50
60	Gus Triandos	40.00	16.00	9.50
61	Eddie Kasko	40.00	16.00	9.50
62	Roger Craig	40.00	16.00	9.50
63	George Strickland	40.00	16.00	9.50
64	Jack Meyer	40.00	16.00	9.50
65	Elston Howard	45.00	18.00	11.00
66	Bob Trowbridge	40.00	16.00	9.50
67	Jose Pagan	40.00	16.00	9.50
68	Dave Hillman	40.00	16.00	9.50
69	Billy Goodman	40.00	16.00	9.50
70	Lou Burdette	40.00	16.00	9.50
71	Marty Keough	40.00	16.00	9.50
72	Tigers Team/	75.00	30.00	18.00
	Checklist 89-176			
73	Bob Gibson	100.00	40.00	24.00
74	Walt Moryn	40.00	16.00	9.50
75	Vic Power	40.00	16.00	9.50
76	Bill Fischer	40.00	16.00	9.50
77	Hank Foiles	40.00	16.00	9.50
78	Bob Grim	40.00	16.00	9.50
79	Walt Dropo	40.00	16.00	9.50
80	Johnny Antonelli	40.00	16.00	9.50
81	Russ Snyder	40.00	16.00	9.50
82	Ruben Gomez	40.00	16.00	9.50
83	Tony Kubek	40.00	16.00	9.50
84	Hal Smith	40.00	16.00	9.50
85	Frank Lary	40.00	16.00	9.50
86	Dick Gernert	40.00	16.00	9.50
87	John Romonosky	40.00	16.00	9.50
88	John Roseboro	40.00	16.00	9.50
89	Hal Brown	40.00	16.00	9.50
90	Bobby Avila	40.00	16.00	9.50
91	Bennie Daniels	40.00	16.00	9.50
92	Whitey Herzog	45.00	18.00	11.00
93	Art Schult	40.00	16.00	9.50
94	Leo Kiely	40.00	16.00	9.50
95	Frank Thomas	40.00	16.00	9.50
96	Ralph Terry	40.00	16.00	9.50
97	Ted Lepcio	40.00	16.00	9.50
98	Gordon Jones	40.00	16.00	9.50
99	Lenny Green	40.00	16.00	9.50
100	Nellie Fox	90.00	36.00	22.00
101	Bob Miller	40.00	16.00	9.50
102	Kent Hadley	40.00	16.00	9.50
103	Dick Farrell	40.00	16.00	9.50
104	Dick Schofield	40.00	16.00	9.50
105	Larry Sherry	40.00	16.00	9.50
106	Billy Gardner	40.00	16.00	9.50
107	Carl Willey	40.00	16.00	9.50
108	Pete Daley	40.00	16.00	9.50
109	Cletis Boyer	40.00	16.00	9.50
110	Cal McLish	40.00	16.00	9.50
111	Vic Wertz	40.00	16.00	9.50
112	Jack Harshman	40.00	16.00	9.50
113	Bob Skinner	40.00	16.00	9.50
114	Ken Aspromonte	40.00	16.00	9.50
115	Fork and Knuckler	45.00	18.00	11.00
	(Roy Face, Hoyt Wilhelm)			
116	Jim Rivera	40.00	16.00	9.50
117	Tom Borland	40.00	16.00	9.50
118	Bob Bruce	40.00	16.00	9.50
119	Chico Cardenas	40.00	16.00	9.50
120	Duke Carmel	40.00	16.00	9.50
121	Camilo Carreon	40.00	16.00	9.50
122	Don Dillard	40.00	16.00	9.50
123	Dan Dobbek	40.00	16.00	9.50
124	Jim Donohue	40.00	16.00	9.50
125	Dick Ellsworth	40.00	16.00	9.50
126	Chuck Estrada	40.00	16.00	9.50
127	Ronnie Hansen	40.00	16.00	9.50
128	Bill Harris	40.00	16.00	9.50
129	Bob Hartman	40.00	16.00	9.50
130	Frank Herrera	40.00	16.00	9.50
131	Ed Hobaugh	40.00	16.00	9.50
132	Frank Howard	50.00	20.00	12.00
133	Manuel Javier	40.00	16.00	9.50
134	Deron Johnson	45.00	18.00	11.00
135	Ken Johnson	40.00	16.00	9.50
136	Jim Kaat	60.00	24.00	14.50
137	Lou Klimchock	40.00	16.00	9.50
138	Art Mahaffey	40.00	16.00	9.50
139	Carl Mathias	40.00	16.00	9.50
140	Julio Navarro	40.00	16.00	9.50
141	Jim Proctor	40.00	16.00	9.50
142	Bill Short	40.00	16.00	9.50
143	Al Spangler	40.00	16.00	9.50
144	Al Stieglitz	40.00	16.00	9.50
145	Jim Umbricht	40.00	16.00	9.50
146	Ted Wieand	40.00	16.00	9.50
147	Bob Will	40.00	16.00	9.50
148	Carl Yastrzemski	550.00	275.00	165.00
149	Bob Nieman	40.00	16.00	9.50
150	Billy Pierce	40.00	16.00	9.50
151	Giants Team/	75.00	30.00	18.00
	Checklist 177-264			
152	Gail Harris	40.00	16.00	9.50
153	Bobby Thomson	40.00	16.00	9.50
154	Jim Davenport	40.00	16.00	9.50
155	Charlie Neal	40.00	16.00	9.50
156	Art Ceccarelli	40.00	16.00	9.50
157	Rocky Nelson	40.00	16.00	9.50
158	Wes Covington	40.00	16.00	9.50
159	Jim Piersall	45.00	18.00	11.00
160	Rival All-Stars	600.00	250.00	150.00
	(Ken Boyer, Mickey Mantle)			
161	Ray Narleski	40.00	16.00	9.50
162	Sammy Taylor	40.00	16.00	9.50
163	Hector Lopez	40.00	16.00	9.50
164	Reds Team/	75.00	30.00	18.00
	Checklist 89-176			
165	Jack Sanford	40.00	16.00	9.50
166	Chuck Essegian	40.00	16.00	9.50
167	Valmy Thomas	40.00	16.00	9.50
168	Alex Grammas	40.00	16.00	9.50
169	Jake Striker	40.00	16.00	9.50
170	Del Crandall	40.00	16.00	9.50
171	Johnny Groth	40.00	16.00	9.50
172	Willie Kirkland	40.00	16.00	9.50
173	Billy Martin	45.00	18.00	11.00
174	Indians Team/	75.00	30.00	18.00
	Checklist 89-176			
175	Pedro Ramos	40.00	16.00	9.50
176	Vada Pinson	45.00	18.00	11.00
177	Johnny Kucks	40.00	16.00	9.50
178	Woody Held	40.00	16.00	9.50
179	Rip Coleman	40.00	16.00	9.50
180	Harry Simpson	40.00	16.00	9.50
181	Billy Loes	40.00	16.00	9.50
182	Glen Hobbie	40.00	16.00	9.50
183	Eli Grba	40.00	16.00	9.50
184	Gary Geiger	40.00	16.00	9.50
185	Jim Owens	40.00	16.00	9.50
186	Dave Sisler	40.00	16.00	9.50
187	Jay Hook	40.00	16.00	9.50
188	Dick Williams	40.00	16.00	9.50
189	Don McMahon	40.00	16.00	9.50
190	Gene Woodling	40.00	16.00	9.50
191	Johnny Klippstein	40.00	16.00	9.50
192	Danny O'Connell	40.00	16.00	9.50
193	Dick Hyde	40.00	16.00	9.50
194	Bobby Gene Smith	40.00	16.00	9.50
195	Lindy McDaniel	40.00	16.00	9.50
196	Andy Carey	40.00	16.00	9.50
197	Ron Kline	40.00	16.00	9.50
198	Jerry Lynch	40.00	16.00	9.50

1962 Venezuelan Topps

For the first time in its short history of producing baseball cards for the Venezuelan market, Topps in 1962 reprinted virtually the entire back of each card in Spanish (except the League Leaders cards #51-60). The player personal data, career summary and even the cartoon are En Espanol; only the stats are in English. There is no Topps credit or copyright line on the backs. Otherwise identical in format to the

1962 Topps North American issue, the Venezuelan set comprises the first 198 cards of the Topps issue, though cards #197 (Daryl Spencer) and 198 (Johnny Keane) have been replaced with two local Major Leaguers. Survivors of this issue tend to be in lower grades due to the common practice of gluing cards into albums or scrapbooks.

		NM	EX	VG
	Complete Set (198):	8,000	3,200	2,000
	Common Player:	30.00	12.00	7.50
1	Roger Maris	750.00	300.00	185.00
2	Jim Brosnan	30.00	12.00	7.50
3	Pete Runnels	30.00	12.00	7.50
4	John DeMerit	30.00	12.00	7.50
5	Sandy Koufax	400.00	160.00	100.00
6	Marv Breeding	30.00	12.00	7.50
7	Frank Thomas	30.00	12.00	7.50
8	Ray Herbert	30.00	12.00	7.50
9	Jim Davenport	30.00	12.00	7.50
10	Roberto Clemente	550.00	220.00	135.00
11	Tom Morgan	30.00	12.00	7.50
12	Harry Craft	30.00	12.00	7.50
13	Dick Howser	30.00	12.00	7.50
14	Bill White	30.00	12.00	7.50
15	Dick Donovan	30.00	12.00	7.50
16	Darrell Johnson	30.00	12.00	7.50
17	Johnny Callison	30.00	12.00	7.50
18	Managers' Dream	1,500	600.00	375.00
	(Mickey Mantle, Willie Mays)			
19	Ray Washburn	30.00	12.00	7.50
20	Rocky Colavito	60.00	24.00	15.00
21	Jim Kaat	30.00	12.00	7.50
22	Checklist 1-88	30.00	12.00	7.50
23	Norm Larker	30.00	12.00	7.50
24	Tigers Team	90.00	36.00	22.00
25	Ernie Banks	175.00	70.00	45.00
26	Chris Cannizzaro	30.00	12.00	7.50
27	Chuck Cottier	30.00	12.00	7.50
28	Minnie Minoso	45.00	18.00	11.00
29	Casey Stengel	125.00	50.00	30.00
30	Eddie Mathews	125.00	50.00	30.00
31	Tom Tresh	40.00	16.00	10.00
32	John Roseboro	30.00	12.00	7.50
33	Don Larsen	30.00	12.00	7.50
34	Johnny Temple	30.00	12.00	7.50
35	Don Schwall	30.00	12.00	7.50
36	Don Leppert	30.00	12.00	7.50
37	Tribe Hill Trio (Barry Latman,	30.00	12.00	7.50
	Jim Perry, Dick Stigman)			
38	Gene Stephens	30.00	12.00	7.50
39	Joe Koppe	30.00	12.00	7.50
40	Orlando Cepeda	65.00	25.00	15.00
41	Cliff Cook	30.00	12.00	7.50
42	Jim King	30.00	12.00	7.50
43	Dodgers Team	125.00	50.00	30.00
44	Don Taussig	30.00	12.00	7.50
45	Brooks Robinson	200.00	80.00	50.00
46	Jack Baldschun	30.00	12.00	7.50
47	Bob Will	30.00	12.00	7.50
48	Ralph Terry	30.00	12.00	7.50
49	Hal Jones	30.00	12.00	7.50
50	Stan Musial	250.00	100.00	60.00
51	A.L. Batting Leaders	80.00	32.00	20.00
	(Norm Cash, Elston Howard, Al Kaline, Jim Piersall)			
52	N.L. Batting Leaders (Ken Boyer, Roberto Clemente, Wally Moon, Vada Pinson)	225.00	90.00	55.00
53	A.L. Home Run Leaders (Jim Gentile, Harmon Killebrew, Mickey Mantle, Roger Maris)	400.00	160.00	100.00
54	N.L. Home Run Leaders (Orlando Cepeda, Willie Mays, Frank Robinson)	125.00	50.00	30.00
55	A.L. E.R.A. Leaders (Dick Donovan, Don Mossi, Milt Pappas, Bill Stafford)	30.00	12.00	7.50
56	N.L. E.R.A. Leaders (Mike McCormick, Jim O'Toole, Curt Simmons, Warren Spahn)	35.00	14.00	8.75
57	A.L. Win Leaders (Steve Barber, Jim Bunning, Whitey Ford, Frank Lary)	45.00	18.00	11.00
58	N.L. Win Leaders (Joe Jay, Jim O'Toole, Warren Spahn)	35.00	14.00	8.75
59	A.L. Strikeout Leaders (Jim Bunning, Whitey Ford, Camilo Pascual, Juan Pizzaro)	45.00	18.00	11.00
60	N.L. Strikeout Leaders (Don Drysdale, Sandy Koufax, Jim O'Toole, Stan Williams)	100.00	40.00	25.00
61	Cardinals Team	90.00	36.00	22.00
62	Steve Boros	30.00	12.00	7.50
63	Tony Cloninger	30.00	12.00	7.50

64	Russ Snyder	30.00	12.00	7.50
65	Bobby Richardson	40.00	16.00	10.00
66	Cuno Barragon (Barragan)	30.00	12.00	7.50
67	Harvey Haddix	30.00	12.00	7.50
68	Ken Hunt	30.00	12.00	7.50
69	Phil Ortega	30.00	12.00	7.50
70	Harmon Killebrew	125.00	50.00	30.00
71	Dick LeMay	30.00	12.00	7.50
72	Bob's Pupils (Steve Boros, Bob Scheffing, Jake Wood)	30.00	12.00	7.50
73	Nellie Fox	125.00	50.00	30.00
74	Bob Lillis	30.00	12.00	7.50
75	Milt Pappas	30.00	12.00	7.50
76	Howie Bedell	30.00	12.00	7.50
77	Tony Taylor	30.00	12.00	7.50
78	Gene Green	30.00	12.00	7.50
79	Ed Hobaugh	30.00	12.00	7.50
80	Vada Pinson	35.00	14.00	8.75
81	Jim Pagliaroni	30.00	12.00	7.50
82	Deron Johnson	30.00	12.00	7.50
83	Larry Jackson	30.00	12.00	7.50
84	Lenny Green	30.00	12.00	7.50
85	Gil Hodges	80.00	32.00	20.00
86	Donn Clendenon	30.00	12.00	7.50
87	Mike Roarke	30.00	12.00	7.50
88	Ralph Houk	30.00	12.00	7.50
89	Barney Schultz	30.00	12.00	7.50
90	Jim Piersall	30.00	12.00	7.50
91	J.C. Martin	30.00	12.00	7.50
92	Sam Jones	30.00	12.00	7.50
93	John Blanchard	30.00	12.00	7.50
94	Jay Hook	30.00	12.00	7.50
95	Don Hoak	30.00	12.00	7.50
96	Eli Grba	30.00	12.00	7.50
97	Tito Francona	30.00	12.00	7.50
98	Checklist 89-176	30.00	12.00	7.50
99	Boog Powell	75.00	30.00	18.50
100	Warren Spahn	125.00	50.00	30.00
101	Carroll Hardy	30.00	12.00	7.50
102	Al Schroll	30.00	12.00	7.50
103	Don Blasingame	30.00	12.00	7.50
104	Ted Savage	30.00	12.00	7.50
105	Don Mossi	30.00	12.00	7.50
106	Carl Sawatski	30.00	12.00	7.50
107	Mike McCormick	30.00	12.00	7.50
108	Willie Davis	30.00	12.00	7.50
109	Bob Shaw	30.00	12.00	7.50
110	Bill Skowron	35.00	14.00	8.75
111	Dallas Green	30.00	12.00	7.50
112	Hank Foiles	30.00	12.00	7.50
113	White Sox Team	90.00	36.00	22.00
114	Howie Koplitz	30.00	12.00	7.50
115	Bob Skinner	30.00	12.00	7.50
116	Herb Score	30.00	12.00	7.50
117	Gary Geiger	30.00	12.00	7.50
118	Julian Javier	30.00	12.00	7.50
119	Danny Murphy	30.00	12.00	7.50
120	Bob Purkey	30.00	12.00	7.50
121	Billy Hitchcock	30.00	12.00	7.50
122	Norm Bass	30.00	12.00	7.50
123	Mike de la Hoz	30.00	12.00	7.50
124	Bill Pleis	30.00	12.00	7.50
125	Gene Woodling	30.00	12.00	7.50
126	Al Cicotte	30.00	12.00	7.50
127	Pride of the A's (Hank Bauer, Jerry Lumpe, Norm Siebern)	30.00	12.00	7.50
128	Art Fowler	30.00	12.00	7.50
129	Lee Walls	30.00	12.00	7.50
130	Frank Bolling	30.00	12.00	7.50
131	Pete Richert	30.00	12.00	7.50
132	Angels Team	90.00	36.00	22.00
133	Felipe Alou	45.00	18.00	11.00
134	Billy Hoeft	30.00	12.00	7.50
135	Babe as a Boy (Babe Ruth)	165.00	65.00	40.00
136	Babe Joins Yanks (Babe Ruth)	200.00	80.00	50.00
137	Babe and Mgr. Huggins (Babe Ruth)	165.00	65.00	40.00
138	The Famous Slugger (Babe Ruth)	200.00	80.00	50.00
139	Babe Hits 60 (Babe Ruth)	300.00	120.00	75.00
140	Gehrig and Ruth (Babe Ruth)	225.00	90.00	55.00
141	Twilight Years (Babe Ruth)	165.00	65.00	40.00
142	Coaching for the Dodgers (Babe Ruth)	165.00	65.00	40.00
143	Greatest Sports Hero (Babe Ruth)	165.00	65.00	40.00
144	Farewell Speech (Babe Ruth)	165.00	65.00	40.00
145	Barry Latman	30.00	12.00	7.50
146	Don Demeter	30.00	12.00	7.50
147	Bill Kunkel	30.00	12.00	7.50
148	Wally Post	30.00	12.00	7.50
149	Bob Duliba	30.00	12.00	7.50
150	Al Kaline	135.00	55.00	35.00
151	Johnny Klippstein	30.00	12.00	7.50
152	Mickey Vernon	30.00	12.00	7.50
153	Pumpsie Green	30.00	12.00	7.50
154	Lee Thomas	30.00	12.00	7.50
155	Stu Miller	30.00	12.00	7.50
156	Merritt Ranew	30.00	12.00	7.50
157	Wes Covington	30.00	12.00	7.50
158	Braves Team	90.00	36.00	22.00
159	Hal Reniff	30.00	12.00	7.50
160	Dick Stuart	30.00	12.00	7.50
161	Frank Baumann	30.00	12.00	7.50
162	Sammy Drake	30.00	12.00	7.50
163	Hot Corner Guardians (Cletis Boyer, Billy Gardner)	30.00	12.00	7.50
164	Hal Naragon	30.00	12.00	7.50
165	Jackie Brandt	30.00	12.00	7.50
166	Don Lee	30.00	12.00	7.50
167	Tim McCarver	125.00	50.00	30.00
168	Leo Posada	30.00	12.00	7.50
169	Bob Cerv	30.00	12.00	7.50
170	Ron Santo	40.00	16.00	10.00
171	Dave Sisler	30.00	12.00	7.50
172	Fred Hutchinson	30.00	12.00	7.50

173	Chico Fernandez	30.00	12.00	7.50
174	Carl Willey	30.00	12.00	7.50
175	Frank Howard	30.00	12.00	7.50
176	Eddie Yost	30.00	12.00	7.50
177	Bobby Shantz	30.00	12.00	7.50
178	Camilo Carreon	30.00	12.00	7.50
179	Tom Sturdivant	30.00	12.00	7.50
180	Bob Allison	30.00	12.00	7.50
181	Paul Brown	30.00	12.00	7.50
182	Bob Nieman	30.00	12.00	7.50
183	Roger Craig	30.00	12.00	7.50
184	Haywood Sullivan	30.00	12.00	7.50
185	Roland Sheldon	30.00	12.00	7.50
186	Mack Jones	30.00	12.00	7.50
187	Gene Conley	30.00	12.00	7.50
188	Chuck Hiller	30.00	12.00	7.50
189	Dick Hall	30.00	12.00	7.50
190	Wally Moon	30.00	12.00	7.50
191	Jim Brewer	30.00	12.00	7.50
192	Checklist 177-264	30.00	12.00	7.50
193	Eddie Kasko	30.00	12.00	7.50
194	Dean Chance	30.00	12.00	7.50
195	Joe Cunningham	30.00	12.00	7.50
196	Terry Fox	30.00	12.00	7.50
199	Elio Chacon	60.00	24.00	15.00
200	Luis Aparicio	250.00	100.00	62.00

1964 Venezuelan Topps

The first 370 cards of Topps' baseball set were issued in a parallel version for sale in Venezuela. Printed on thin cardboard with no front gloss, the cards are differentiated from the U.S. version by the use of a black border on back. Survivors of the issue are usually in low grade because of the common Latin American practice of collectors gluing the cards into the album that was available. Venezuelan Topps cards were often cut up to 1/8" smaller than their U.S. counterparts.

		NM	EX	VG
	Complete Set (370):	9,500	3,800	2,400
	Common Player:	30.00	12.00	7.50
	Album:	300.00	125.00	75.00
1	N.L. E.R.A. Leaders (Dick Ellsworth, Bob Friend, Sandy Koufax)	90.00	36.00	22.00
2	A.L. E.R.A. Leaders (Camilo Pascual, Gary Peters, Juan Pizarro)	30.00	12.00	7.50
3	N.L. Pitching Leaders (Sandy Koufax, Jim Maloney, Juan Marichal, Warren Spahn)	60.00	24.00	15.00
4	A.L. Pitching Leaders (Jim Bouton, Whitey Ford, Camilo Pascual)	45.00	18.00	11.00
5	N.L. Strikeout Leaders (Don Drysdale, Sandy Koufax, Jim Maloney)	60.00	24.00	15.00
6	A.L. Strikeout Leaders (Jim Bunning, Camilo Pascual, Dick Stigman)	35.00	14.00	8.75
7	N.L. Batting Leaders (Hank Aaron, Roberto Clemente, Tommy Davis, Dick Groat)	100.00	40.00	25.00
8	A.L. Batting Leaders (Al Kaline, Rich Rollins, Carl Yastrzemski)	50.00	20.00	12.50
9	N.L. Home Run Leaders (Hank Aaron, Orlando Cepeda, Willie Mays, Willie McCovey)	75.00	30.00	18.50
10	A.L. Home Run Leaders (Bob Allison, Harmon Killebrew, Dick Stuart)	45.00	18.00	11.00
11	N.L. R.B.I. Leaders (Hank Aaron, Ken Boyer, Bill White)	50.00	20.00	12.50
12	A.L. R.B.I. Leaders (Al Kaline, Harmon Killebrew, Dick Stuart)	45.00	18.00	11.00
13	Hoyt Wilhelm	50.00	20.00	12.50
14	Dodgers Rookies (Dick Nen, Nick Willhite)	30.00	12.00	7.50
15	Zoilo Versalles	30.00	12.00	7.50
16	John Boozer	30.00	12.00	7.50
17	Willie Kirkland	30.00	12.00	7.50
18	Billy O'Dell	30.00	12.00	7.50
19	Don Wart	30.00	12.00	7.50
20	Bob Friend	30.00	12.00	7.50
21	Yogi Berra	100.00	40.00	25.00
22	Jerry Adair	30.00	12.00	7.50
23	Chris Zachary	30.00	12.00	7.50
24	Carl Sawatski	30.00	12.00	7.50
25	Bill Monbouquette	30.00	12.00	7.50
26	Gino Cimoli	30.00	12.00	7.50
27	Mets Team	65.00	26.00	16.00
28	Claude Osteen	30.00	12.00	7.50

29	Lou Brock	75.00	30.00	18.50
30	Ron Perranoski	30.00	12.00	7.50
31	Dave Nicholson	30.00	12.00	7.50
32	Dean Chance	30.00	12.00	7.50
33	Reds Rookies (Sammy Ellis, Mel Queen)	30.00	12.00	7.50
34	Jim Perry	30.00	12.00	7.50
35	Eddie Mathews	75.00	30.00	18.50
36	Hal Reniff	30.00	12.00	7.50
37	Smoky Burgess	30.00	12.00	7.50
38	Jim Wynn	30.00	12.00	7.50
39	Hank Aguirre	30.00	12.00	7.50
40	Dick Groat	30.00	12.00	7.50
41	Friendly Foes (Willie McCovey, Leon Wagner)	35.00	14.00	8.75
42	Moe Drabowsky	30.00	12.00	7.50
43	Roy Sievers	30.00	12.00	7.50
44	Duke Carmel	30.00	12.00	7.50
45	Milt Pappas	30.00	12.00	7.50
46	Ed Brinkman	30.00	12.00	7.50
47	Giants Rookies (Jesus Alou, Ron Herbel)	30.00	12.00	7.50
48	Bob Perry	30.00	12.00	7.50
49	Bill Henry	30.00	12.00	7.50
50	Mickey Mantle	1,800	720.00	450.00
51	Pete Richert	30.00	12.00	7.50
52	Chuck Hinton	30.00	12.00	7.50
53	Denis Menke	30.00	12.00	7.50
54	Sam Mele	30.00	12.00	7.50
55	Ernie Banks	75.00	30.00	18.50
56	Hal Brown	30.00	12.00	7.50
57	Tim Harkness	30.00	12.00	7.50
58	Don Demeter	30.00	12.00	7.50
59	Ernie Broglio	30.00	12.00	7.50
60	Frank Malzone	30.00	12.00	7.50
61	Angel Backstops (Bob Rodgers, Ed Sadowski)	30.00	12.00	7.50
62	Ted Savage	30.00	12.00	7.50
63	Johnny Orsino	30.00	12.00	7.50
64	Ted Abernathy	30.00	12.00	7.50
65	Felipe Alou	35.00	14.00	8.75
66	Eddie Fisher	30.00	12.00	7.50
67	Tigers Team	50.00	20.00	12.50
68	Willie Davis	30.00	12.00	7.50
69	Clete Boyer	35.00	14.00	8.75
70	Joe Torre	45.00	18.00	11.00
71	Jack Spring	30.00	12.00	7.50
72	Chico Cardenas	30.00	12.00	7.50
73	Jimmie Hall	30.00	12.00	7.50
74	Pirates Rookies (Tom Butters, Bob Priddy)	30.00	12.00	7.50
75	Wayne Causey	30.00	12.00	7.50
76	Checklist 1-88	30.00	12.00	7.50
77	Jerry Walker	30.00	12.00	7.50
78	Merritt Ranew	30.00	12.00	7.50
79	Bob Heffner	30.00	12.00	7.50
80	Vada Pinson	45.00	18.00	11.00
81	All-Star Vets (Nellie Fox, Harmon Killebrew)	50.00	20.00	12.50
82	Jim Davenport	30.00	12.00	7.50
83	Gus Triandos	30.00	12.00	7.50
84	Carl Willey	30.00	12.00	7.50
85	Pete Ward	30.00	12.00	7.50
86	Al Downing	30.00	12.00	7.50
87	Cardinals Team	100.00	40.00	25.00
88	John Roseboro	30.00	12.00	7.50
89	Boog Powell	35.00	14.00	8.75
90	Earl Battey	30.00	12.00	7.50
91	Bob Bailey	30.00	12.00	7.50
92	Steve Ridzik	30.00	12.00	7.50
93	Gary Geiger	30.00	12.00	7.50
94	Braves Rookies (Jim Britton, Larry Maxie)	30.00	12.00	7.50
95	George Altman	30.00	12.00	7.50
96	Bob Buhl	30.00	12.00	7.50
97	Jim Fregosi	30.00	12.00	7.50
98	Bill Bruton	30.00	12.00	7.50
99	Al Stanek	30.00	12.00	7.50
100	Elston Howard	35.00	14.00	8.75
101	Walt Alston	50.00	20.00	12.50
102	Checklist 89-176	30.00	12.00	7.50
103	Curt Flood	35.00	14.00	8.75
104	Art Mahaffey	30.00	12.00	7.50
105	Woody Held	30.00	12.00	7.50
106	Joe Nuxhall	30.00	12.00	7.50
107	White Sox Rookies (Bruce Howard, Frank Kreutzer)	30.00	12.00	7.50
108	John Wyatt	30.00	12.00	7.50
109	Rusty Staub	35.00	14.00	8.75
110	Albie Pearson	30.00	12.00	7.50
111	Don Elston	30.00	12.00	7.50
112	Bob Tillman	30.00	12.00	7.50
113	Grover Powell	30.00	12.00	7.50
114	Don Lock	30.00	12.00	7.50
115	Frank Bolling	30.00	12.00	7.50
116	Twins Rookies (Tony Oliva, Jay Ward)	45.00	18.00	11.00
117	Earl Francis	30.00	12.00	7.50
118	John Blanchard	30.00	12.00	7.50
119	Gary Kolb	30.00	12.00	7.50
120	Don Drysdale	75.00	30.00	18.50
121	Pete Runnels	30.00	12.00	7.50
122	Don McMahon	30.00	12.00	7.50
123	Jose Pagan	30.00	12.00	7.50
124	Orlando Pena	30.00	12.00	7.50
125	Pete Rose	450.00	180.00	110.00
126	Russ Snyder	30.00	12.00	7.50
127	Angels Rookies (Aubrey Gatewood, Dick Simpson)	30.00	12.00	7.50
128	Mickey Lolich	35.00	14.00	8.75
129	Amado Samuel	30.00	12.00	7.50
130	Gary Peters	30.00	12.00	7.50
131	Steve Boros	30.00	12.00	7.50
132	Braves Team	50.00	20.00	12.50
133	Jim Grant	30.00	12.00	7.50
134	Don Zimmer	30.00	12.00	7.50
135	Johnny Callison	30.00	12.00	7.50

136	World Series Game 1 (Koufax Strikes Out 15)	30.00	12.00	7.50
137	World Series Game 2 (Davis Sparks Rally)	30.00	12.00	7.50
138	World Series Game 3 (L.A. Takes 3rd Straight)	30.00	12.00	7.50
139	World Series Game 4 (Sealing Yanks' Doom)	30.00	12.00	7.50
140	World Series Summary (The Dodgers Celebrate)	30.00	12.00	7.50
141	Danny Murtaugh	30.00	12.00	7.50
142	John Bateman	30.00	12.00	7.50
143	Bubba Phillips	30.00	12.00	7.50
144	Al Worthington	30.00	12.00	7.50
145	Norm Siebern	30.00	12.00	7.50
146	Indians Rookies (Bob Chance, Tommy John)	50.00	20.00	12.50
147	Ray Sadecki	30.00	12.00	7.50
148	J.C. Martin	30.00	12.00	7.50
149	Paul Foytack	30.00	12.00	7.50
150	Willie Mays	375.00	150.00	94.00
151	Athletics Team	50.00	20.00	12.50
152	Denver Lemaster	30.00	12.00	7.50
153	Dick Williams	30.00	12.00	7.50
154	Dick Tracewski	30.00	12.00	7.50
155	Duke Snider	100.00	40.00	25.00
156	Bill Dailey	30.00	12.00	7.50
157	Gene Mauch	30.00	12.00	7.50
158	Ken Johnson	30.00	12.00	7.50
159	Charlie Dees	30.00	12.00	7.50
160	Ken Boyer	35.00	14.00	8.75
161	Dave McNally	30.00	12.00	7.50
162	Hitting Area (Vada Pinson, Dick Sisler)	30.00	12.00	7.50
163	Donn Clendenon	30.00	12.00	7.50
164	Bud Daley	30.00	12.00	7.50
165	Jerry Lumpe	30.00	12.00	7.50
166	Marty Keough	30.00	12.00	7.50
167	Senators Rookies (Mike Brumley, Lou Piniella)	60.00	24.00	15.00
168	Al Weis	30.00	12.00	7.50
169	Del Crandall	30.00	12.00	7.50
170	Dick Radatz	30.00	12.00	7.50
171	Ty Cline	30.00	12.00	7.50
172	Indians Team	50.00	20.00	12.50
173	Ryne Duren	30.00	12.00	7.50
174	Doc Edwards	30.00	12.00	7.50
175	Billy Williams	50.00	20.00	12.50
176	Tracy Stallard	30.00	12.00	7.50
177	Harmon Killebrew	75.00	30.00	18.50
178	Hank Bauer	30.00	12.00	7.50
179	Carl Warwick	30.00	12.00	7.50
180	Tommy Davis	30.00	12.00	7.50
181	Dave Wickersham	30.00	12.00	7.50
182	Sox Sockers (Chuck Schilling, Carl Yastrzemski)	50.00	20.00	12.50
183	Ron Taylor	30.00	12.00	7.50
184	Al Luplow	30.00	12.00	7.50
185	Jim O'Toole	30.00	12.00	7.50
186	Roman Mejias	30.00	12.00	7.50
187	Ed Roebuck	30.00	12.00	7.50
188	Checklist 177-264	30.00	12.00	7.50
189	Bob Hendley	30.00	12.00	7.50
190	Bobby Richardson	35.00	14.00	8.75
191	Clay Dalrymple	30.00	12.00	7.50
192	Cubs Rookies (John Boccabella, Billy Cowan)	30.00	12.00	7.50
193	Jerry Lynch	30.00	12.00	7.50
194	John Goryl	30.00	12.00	7.50
195	Floyd Robinson	30.00	12.00	7.50
196	Jim Gentile	30.00	12.00	7.50
197	Frank Lary	30.00	12.00	7.50
198	Len Gabrielson	30.00	12.00	7.50
199	Joe Azcue	30.00	12.00	7.50
200	Sandy Koufax	300.00	120.00	75.00
201	Orioles Rookies (Sam Bowens, Wally Bunker)	30.00	12.00	7.50
202	Galen Cisco	30.00	12.00	7.50
203	John Kennedy	30.00	12.00	7.50
204	Matty Alou	30.00	12.00	7.50
205	Nellie Fox	65.00	26.00	16.00
206	Steve Hamilton	30.00	12.00	7.50
207	Fred Hutchinson	30.00	12.00	7.50
208	Wes Covington	30.00	12.00	7.50
209	Bob Allen	30.00	12.00	7.50
210	Carl Yastrzemski	100.00	40.00	25.00
211	Jim Coker	30.00	12.00	7.50
212	Pete Lovrich	30.00	12.00	7.50
213	Angels Team	50.00	20.00	12.50
214	Ken McMullen	30.00	12.00	7.50
215	Ray Herbert	30.00	12.00	7.50
216	Mike de la Hoz	30.00	12.00	7.50
217	Jim King	30.00	12.00	7.50
218	Hank Fischer	30.00	12.00	7.50
219	Young Aces (Jim Bouton, Al Downing)	35.00	14.00	8.75
220	Dick Ellsworth	30.00	12.00	7.50
221	Bob Saverine	30.00	12.00	7.50
222	Bill Pierce	30.00	12.00	7.50
223	George Banks	30.00	12.00	7.50
224	Tommie Sisk	30.00	12.00	7.50
225	Roger Maris	300.00	120.00	75.00
226	Colts Rookies (Gerald Grote, Larry Yellen)	30.00	12.00	7.50
227	Barry Latman	30.00	12.00	7.50
228	Felix Mantilla	30.00	12.00	7.50
229	Charley Lau	30.00	12.00	7.50
230	Brooks Robinson	110.00	45.00	25.00
231	Dick Calmus	30.00	12.00	7.50
232	Al Lopez	50.00	20.00	12.50
233	Hal Smith	30.00	12.00	7.50
234	Gary Bell	30.00	12.00	7.50
235	Ron Hunt	30.00	12.00	7.50
236	Bill Faul	30.00	12.00	7.50
237	Cubs Team	50.00	20.00	12.50
238	Roy McMillan	30.00	12.00	7.50
239	Herm Starrette	30.00	12.00	7.50
240	Bill White	30.00	12.00	7.50
241	Jim Owens	30.00	12.00	7.50
242	Harvey Kuenn	30.00	12.00	7.50
243	Phillies Rookies (Richie Allen, John Herrnstein)	50.00	20.00	12.50
244	Tony LaRussa	35.00	14.00	8.75
245	Dick Stigman	30.00	12.00	7.50
246	Manny Mota	30.00	12.00	7.50
247	Dave DeBusschere	30.00	12.00	7.50
248	Johnny Pesky	30.00	12.00	7.50
249	Doug Camilli	30.00	12.00	7.50
250	Al Kaline	110.00	45.00	25.00
251	Choo Choo Coleman	30.00	12.00	7.50
252	Ken Aspromonte	30.00	12.00	7.50
253	Wally Post	30.00	12.00	7.50
254	Don Hoak	30.00	12.00	7.50
255	Lee Thomas	30.00	12.00	7.50
256	Johnny Weekly	30.00	12.00	7.50
257	Giants Team	50.00	20.00	12.50
258	Garry Roggenburk	30.00	12.00	7.50
259	Harry Bright	30.00	12.00	7.50
260	Frank Robinson	100.00	40.00	25.00
261	Jim Hannan	30.00	12.00	7.50
262	Cardinals Rookies (Harry Fanok, Mike Shannon)	35.00	14.00	8.75
263	Chuck Estrada	30.00	12.00	7.50
264	Jim Landis	30.00	12.00	7.50
265	Jim Bunning	50.00	20.00	12.50
266	Gene Freese	30.00	12.00	7.50
267	Wilbur Wood	30.00	12.00	7.50
268	Bill's Got It (Danny Murtaugh, Bill Virdon)	30.00	12.00	7.50
269	Ellis Burton	30.00	12.00	7.50
270	Rich Rollins	30.00	12.00	7.50
271	Bob Sadowski	30.00	12.00	7.50
272	Jake Wood	30.00	12.00	7.50
273	Mel Nelson	30.00	12.00	7.50
274	Checklist 265-352	30.00	12.00	7.50
275	John Tsitouris	30.00	12.00	7.50
276	Jose Tartabull	30.00	12.00	7.50
277	Ken Retzer	30.00	12.00	7.50
278	Bobby Shantz	30.00	12.00	7.50
279	Joe Koppe	30.00	12.00	7.50
280	Juan Marichal	65.00	26.00	16.00
281	Yankees Rookies (Jake Gibbs, Tom Metcalf)	30.00	12.00	7.50
282	Bob Bruce	30.00	12.00	7.50
283	Tommy McCraw	30.00	12.00	7.50
284	Dick Schofield	30.00	12.00	7.50
285	Robin Roberts	65.00	26.00	16.00
286	Don Landrum	30.00	12.00	7.50
287	Red Sox Rookies (Tony Conigliaro, Bill Spanswick)	35.00	14.00	8.75
288	Al Moran	30.00	12.00	7.50
289	Frank Funk	30.00	12.00	7.50
290	Bob Allison	30.00	12.00	7.50
291	Phil Ortega	30.00	12.00	7.50
292	Mike Roarke	30.00	12.00	7.50
293	Phillies Team	50.00	20.00	12.50
294	Ken Hunt	30.00	12.00	7.50
295	Roger Craig	30.00	12.00	7.50
296	Ed Kirkpatrick	30.00	12.00	7.50
297	Ken MacKenzie	30.00	12.00	7.50
298	Harry Craft	30.00	12.00	7.50
299	Bill Stafford	30.00	12.00	7.50
300	Hank Aaron	375.00	150.00	94.00
301	Larry Brown	30.00	12.00	7.50
302	Dan Pfister	30.00	12.00	7.50
303	Jim Campbell	30.00	12.00	7.50
304	Bob Johnson	30.00	12.00	7.50
305	Jack Lamabe	30.00	12.00	7.50
306	Giant Gunners (Orlando Cepeda, Willie Mays)	50.00	20.00	12.50
307	Joe Gibbon	30.00	12.00	7.50
308	Gene Stephens	30.00	12.00	7.50
309	Paul Toth	30.00	12.00	7.50
310	Jim Gilliam	30.00	12.00	7.50
311	Tom Brown	30.00	12.00	7.50
312	Tigers Rookies (Fritz Fisher, Fred Gladding)	30.00	12.00	7.50
313	Chuck Hiller	30.00	12.00	7.50
314	Jerry Buchek	30.00	12.00	7.50
315	Bo Belinsky	30.00	12.00	7.50
316	Gene Oliver	30.00	12.00	7.50
317	Al Smith	30.00	12.00	7.50
318	Twins Team	50.00	20.00	12.50
319	Paul Brown	30.00	12.00	7.50
320	Rocky Colavito	50.00	20.00	12.50
321	Bob Lillis	30.00	12.00	7.50
322	George Brunet	30.00	12.00	7.50
323	John Buzhardt	30.00	12.00	7.50
324	Casey Stengel	50.00	20.00	12.50
325	Hector Lopez	30.00	12.00	7.50
326	Ron Brand	30.00	12.00	7.50
327	Don Blasingame	30.00	12.00	7.50
328	Bob Shaw	30.00	12.00	7.50
329	Russ Nixon	30.00	12.00	7.50
330	Tommy Harper	30.00	12.00	7.50
331	A.L. Bombers (Norm Cash, Al Kaline, Mickey Mantle, Roger Maris)	600.00	240.00	150.00
332	Ray Washburn	30.00	12.00	7.50
333	Billy Moran	30.00	12.00	7.50
334	Lew Krausse	30.00	12.00	7.50
335	Don Mossi	30.00	12.00	7.50
336	Andre Rodgers	30.00	12.00	7.50
337	Dodgers Rookies (Al Ferrara, Jeff Torborg)	30.00	12.00	7.50
338	Jack Kralick	30.00	12.00	7.50
339	Walt Bond	30.00	12.00	7.50
340	Joe Cunningham	30.00	12.00	7.50
341	Jim Roland	30.00	12.00	7.50
342	Willie Stargell	65.00	26.00	16.00
343	Senators Team	50.00	20.00	12.50
344	Phil Linz	30.00	12.00	7.50
345	Frank Thomas	30.00	12.00	7.50
346	Joe Jay	30.00	12.00	7.50
347	Bobby Wine	30.00	12.00	7.50
348	Ed Lopat	30.00	12.00	7.50
349	Art Fowler	30.00	12.00	7.50
350	Willie McCovey	75.00	30.00	18.50
351	Dan Schneider	30.00	12.00	7.50
352	Eddie Bressoud	30.00	12.00	7.50
353	Wally Moon	30.00	12.00	7.50
354	Dave Giusti	30.00	12.00	7.50
355	Vic Power	30.00	12.00	7.50
356	Reds Rookies (Bill McCool, Chico Ruiz)	30.00	12.00	7.50
357	Charley James	30.00	12.00	7.50
358	Ron Kline	30.00	12.00	7.50
359	Jim Schaffer	30.00	12.00	7.50
360	Joe Pepitone	30.00	12.00	7.50
361	Jay Hook	30.00	12.00	7.50
362	Checklist 353-429	30.00	12.00	7.50
363	Dick McAuliffe	30.00	12.00	7.50
364	Joe Gaines	30.00	12.00	7.50
365	Cal McLish	30.00	12.00	7.50
366	Nelson Mathews	30.00	12.00	7.50
367	Fred Whitfield	30.00	12.00	7.50
368	White Sox Rookies (Fritz Ackley, Don Buford)	30.00	12.00	7.50
369	Jerry Zimmerman	30.00	12.00	7.50
370	Hal Woodeshick	30.00	12.00	7.50

1966 Venezuelan Topps

The first 370 cards on Topps' 1966 baseball set were reprinted for sale in the Venezuelan market. Identical in design to the Topps cards, they have no Spanish on them. The South American version is printed on darker cardboard that has virtually no gloss on front and bright orange-pink highlights on back. Low-grade cards are the norm for this and other Venezuelan issues as it is common collector practice south of the border to mount cards in scrapbooks and albums. The Venezuelan cards are often found up to 1/8" smaller than their U.S. counterparts.

		NM	EX	VG
	Complete Set (370):	8,000	3,250	2,000
	Common Player:	.30.00	12.00	7.50
1	Willie Mays	400.00	160.00	100.00
2	Ted Abernathy	30.00	12.00	7.50
3	Sam Mele	30.00	12.00	7.50
4	Ray Culp	30.00	12.00	7.50
5	Jim Fregosi	30.00	12.00	7.50
6	Chuck Schilling	30.00	12.00	7.50
7	Tracy Stallard	30.00	12.00	7.50
8	Floyd Robinson	30.00	12.00	7.50
9	Clete Boyer	35.00	14.00	8.75
10	Tony Cloninger	30.00	12.00	7.50
11	Senators Rookies (Brant Alyea, Pete Craig)	30.00	12.00	7.50
12	John Tsitouris	30.00	12.00	7.50
13	Lou Johnson	30.00	12.00	7.50
14	Norm Siebern	30.00	12.00	7.50
15	Vern Law	30.00	12.00	7.50
16	Larry Brown	30.00	12.00	7.50
17	Johnny Stephenson	30.00	12.00	7.50
18	Roland Sheldon	30.00	12.00	7.50
19	Giants Team	75.00	30.00	18.50
20	Willie Horton	30.00	12.00	7.50
21	Don Nottebart	30.00	12.00	7.50
22	Joe Nossek	30.00	12.00	7.50
23	Jack Sanford	30.00	12.00	7.50
24	Don Kessinger	30.00	12.00	7.50
25	Pete Ward	30.00	12.00	7.50
26	Ray Sadecki	30.00	12.00	7.50
27	Orioles Rookies (Andy Etchebarren, Darold Knowles)	30.00	12.00	7.50
28	Phil Niekro	100.00	40.00	25.00
29	Mike Brumley	30.00	12.00	7.50
30	Pete Rose	375.00	150.00	94.00
31	Jack Cullen	30.00	12.00	7.50
32	Adolfo Phillips	30.00	12.00	7.50
33	Jim Pagliaroni	30.00	12.00	7.50
34	Checklist 1-88	30.00	12.00	7.50
35	Ron Swoboda	30.00	12.00	7.50
36	Catfish Hunter	100.00	40.00	25.00
37	Billy Herman	90.00	36.00	22.00
38	Ron Nischwitz	30.00	12.00	7.50
39	Ken Henderson	30.00	12.00	7.50
40	Jim Grant	30.00	12.00	7.50
41	Don LeJohn	30.00	12.00	7.50
42	Aubrey Gatewood	30.00	12.00	7.50
43	Don Landrum	30.00	12.00	7.50
44	Indians Rookies (Bill Davis, Tom Kelley)	30.00	12.00	7.50
45	Jim Gentile	30.00	12.00	7.50
46	Howie Koplitz	30.00	12.00	7.50
47	J.C. Martin	30.00	12.00	7.50
48	Paul Blair	30.00	12.00	7.50
49	Woody Woodward	30.00	12.00	7.50
50	Mickey Mantle	1,500	600.00	375.00

No.	Name			
51	Gordon Richardson	30.00	12.00	7.50
52	Power Plus (Johnny Callison, Wes Covington)	30.00	12.00	7.50
53	Bob Duliba	30.00	12.00	7.50
54	Jose Pagan	30.00	12.00	7.50
55	Ken Harrelson	30.00	12.00	7.50
56	Sandy Valdespino	30.00	12.00	7.50
57	Jim Lefebvre	30.00	12.00	7.50
58	Dave Wickersham	30.00	12.00	7.50
59	Reds Team	75.00	30.00	18.50
60	Curt Flood	35.00	14.00	8.75
61	Bob Bolin	30.00	12.00	7.50
62	Merritt Ranew	30.00	12.00	7.50
63	Jim Stewart	30.00	12.00	7.50
64	Bob Bruce	30.00	12.00	7.50
65	Leon Wagner	30.00	12.00	7.50
66	Al Weis	30.00	12.00	7.50
67	Mets Rookies (Cleon Jones, Dick Selma)	35.00	14.00	8.75
68	Hal Reniff	30.00	12.00	7.50
69	Ken Hamlin	30.00	12.00	7.50
70	Carl Yastrzemski	150.00	60.00	37.00
71	Frank Carpin	30.00	12.00	7.50
72	Tony Perez	150.00	60.00	37.00
73	Jerry Zimmerman	30.00	12.00	7.50
74	Don Mossi	30.00	12.00	7.50
75	Tommy Davis	30.00	12.00	7.50
76	Red Schoendienst	90.00	36.00	22.00
77	Johnny Orsino	30.00	12.00	7.50
78	Frank Linzy	30.00	12.00	7.50
79	Joe Pepitone	30.00	12.00	7.50
80	Richie Allen	45.00	18.00	11.00
81	Ray Oyler	30.00	12.00	7.50
82	Bob Hendley	30.00	12.00	7.50
83	Albie Pearson	30.00	12.00	7.50
84	Braves Rookies (Jim Beauchamp, Dick Kelley)	30.00	12.00	7.50
85	Eddie Fisher	30.00	12.00	7.50
86	John Bateman	30.00	12.00	7.50
87	Dan Napoleon	30.00	12.00	7.50
88	Fred Whitfield	30.00	12.00	7.50
89	Ted Davidson	30.00	12.00	7.50
90	Luis Aparicio	250.00	100.00	62.00
91	Bob Uecker	45.00	18.00	11.00
92	Yankees Team	125.00	50.00	30.00
93	Jim Lonborg	30.00	12.00	7.50
94	Matty Alou	30.00	12.00	7.50
95	Pete Richert	30.00	12.00	7.50
96	Felipe Alou	45.00	18.00	11.00
97	Jim Merritt	30.00	12.00	7.50
98	Don Demeter	30.00	12.00	7.50
99	Buc Belters (Donn Clendenon, Willie Stargell)	60.00	24.00	15.00
100	Sandy Koufax	300.00	120.00	75.00
101	Checklist 89-176	30.00	12.00	7.50
102	Ed Kirkpatrick	30.00	12.00	7.50
103	Dick Groat	30.00	12.00	7.50
104	Alex Johnson	30.00	12.00	7.50
105	Milt Pappas	30.00	12.00	7.50
106	Rusty Staub	35.00	14.00	8.75
107	Athletics Rookies (Larry Stahl, Ron Tompkins)	30.00	12.00	7.50
108	Bobby Klaus	30.00	12.00	7.50
109	Ralph Terry	30.00	12.00	7.50
110	Ernie Banks	200.00	80.00	50.00
111	Gary Peters	30.00	12.00	7.50
112	Manny Mota	30.00	12.00	7.50
113	Hank Aguirre	30.00	12.00	7.50
114	Jim Gosger	30.00	12.00	7.50
115	Bill Henry	30.00	12.00	7.50
116	Walt Alston	90.00	36.00	22.00
117	Jake Gibbs	30.00	12.00	7.50
118	Mike McCormick	30.00	12.00	7.50
119	Art Shamsky	30.00	12.00	7.50
120	Harmon Killebrew	150.00	60.00	37.00
121	Ray Herbert	30.00	12.00	7.50
122	Joe Gaines	30.00	12.00	7.50
123	Pirates Rookies (Frank Bork, Jerry May)	30.00	12.00	7.50
124	Tug McGraw	30.00	12.00	7.50
125	Lou Brock	125.00	50.00	30.00
126	Jim Palmer	200.00	80.00	50.00
127	Ken Berry	30.00	12.00	7.50
128	Jim Landis	30.00	12.00	7.50
129	Jack Kralick	30.00	12.00	7.50
130	Joe Torre	45.00	18.00	11.00
131	Angels Team	75.00	30.00	18.50
132	Orlando Cepeda	100.00	40.00	25.00
133	Don McMahon	30.00	12.00	7.50
134	Wes Parker	30.00	12.00	7.50
135	Dave Morehead	30.00	12.00	7.50
136	Woody Held	30.00	12.00	7.50
137	Pat Corrales	30.00	12.00	7.50
138	Roger Repoz	30.00	12.00	7.50
139	Cubs Rookies (Byron Browne, Don Young)	30.00	12.00	7.50
140	Jim Maloney	30.00	12.00	7.50
141	Tom McCraw	30.00	12.00	7.50
142	Don Dennis	30.00	12.00	7.50
143	Jose Tartabull	30.00	12.00	7.50
144	Don Schwall	30.00	12.00	7.50
145	Bill Freehan	30.00	12.00	7.50
146	George Altman	30.00	12.00	7.50
147	Lum Harris	30.00	12.00	7.50
148	Bob Johnson	30.00	12.00	7.50
149	Dick Nen	30.00	12.00	7.50
150	Rocky Colavito	75.00	30.00	18.50
151	Gary Wagner	30.00	12.00	7.50
152	Frank Malzone	30.00	12.00	7.50
153	Rico Carty	30.00	12.00	7.50
154	Chuck Hiller	30.00	12.00	7.50
155	Marcelino Lopez	30.00	12.00	7.50
156	D P Combo (Hal Lanier, Dick Schofield)			
157	Rene Lachemann	30.00	12.00	7.50
158	Jim Brewer	30.00	12.00	7.50
159	Chico Ruiz	30.00	12.00	7.50
160	Whitey Ford	150.00	60.00	37.00
161	Jerry Lumpe	30.00	12.00	7.50
162	Lee Maye	30.00	12.00	7.50
163	Tito Francona	30.00	12.00	7.50
164	White Sox Rookies (Tommie Agee, Marv Staehle)	30.00	12.00	7.50
165	Don Lock	30.00	12.00	7.50
166	Chris Krug	30.00	12.00	7.50
167	Boog Powell	45.00	18.00	11.00
168	Dan Osinski	30.00	12.00	7.50
169	Duke Sims	30.00	12.00	7.50
170	Cookie Rojas	30.00	12.00	7.50
171	Nick Willhite	30.00	12.00	7.50
172	Mets Team	150.00	60.00	37.00
173	Al Spangler	30.00	12.00	7.50
174	Ron Taylor	45.00	18.00	11.00
175	Bert Campaneris	30.00	12.00	7.50
176	Jim Davenport	30.00	12.00	7.50
177	Hector Lopez	30.00	12.00	7.50
178	Bob Tillman	30.00	12.00	7.50
179	Cardinals Rookies (Dennis Aust, Bob Tolan)	30.00	12.00	7.50
180	Vada Pinson	35.00	14.00	8.75
181	Al Worthington	30.00	12.00	7.50
182	Jerry Lynch	30.00	12.00	7.50
183	Checklist 177-264	30.00	12.00	7.50
184	Denis Menke	30.00	12.00	7.50
185	Bob Buhl	30.00	12.00	7.50
186	Ruben Amaro	30.00	12.00	7.50
187	Chuck Dressen	30.00	12.00	7.50
188	Al Luplow	30.00	12.00	7.50
189	John Roseboro	30.00	12.00	7.50
190	Jimmie Hall	30.00	12.00	7.50
191	Darrell Sutherland	30.00	12.00	7.50
192	Vic Power	30.00	12.00	7.50
193	Dave McNally	30.00	12.00	7.50
194	Senators Team	75.00	30.00	18.50
195	Joe Morgan	125.00	50.00	30.00
196	Don Pavletich	30.00	12.00	7.50
197	Sonny Siebert	30.00	12.00	7.50
198	Mickey Stanley	30.00	12.00	7.50
199	Chisox Clubbers (Floyd Robinson, Johnny Romano, Bill Skowron)	30.00	12.00	7.50
200	Eddie Mathews	125.00	50.00	30.00
201	Jim Dickson	30.00	12.00	7.50
202	Clay Dalrymple	30.00	12.00	7.50
203	Jose Santiago	30.00	12.00	7.50
204	Cubs Team	90.00	36.00	22.00
205	Tom Tresh	30.00	12.00	7.50
206	Alvin Jackson	30.00	12.00	7.50
207	Frank Quilici	30.00	12.00	7.50
208	Bob Miller	30.00	12.00	7.50
209	Tigers Rookies (Fritz Fisher, John Hiller)	30.00	12.00	7.50
210	Bill Mazeroski	75.00	30.00	18.50
211	Frank Kreutzer	30.00	12.00	7.50
212	Ed Kranepool	30.00	12.00	7.50
213	Fred Newman	30.00	12.00	7.50
214	Tommy Harper	30.00	12.00	7.50
215	N.L. Batting Leaders (Hank Aaron, Roberto Clemente, Willie Mays)	300.00	120.00	75.00
216	A.L. Batting Leaders (Vic Davalillo, Tony Oliva, Carl Yastrzemski)	150.00	60.00	37.00
217	N.L. Home Run Leaders (Willie Mays, Willie McCovey, Billy Williams)	150.00	60.00	37.00
218	A.L. Home Run Leaders (Norm Cash, Tony Conigliaro, Willie Horton)	60.00	24.00	15.00
219	N.L. RBI Leaders (Deron Johnson, Willie Mays, Frank Robinson)	90.00	36.00	22.00
220	A.L. RBI Leaders (Rocky Colavito, Willie Horton, Tony Oliva)	60.00	24.00	15.00
221	N.L. ERA Leaders (Sandy Koufax, Vern Law, Juan Marichal)	90.00	36.00	22.00
222	A.L. ERA Leaders (Eddie Fisher, Sam McDowell, Sonny Siebert)	35.00	14.00	8.75
223	N.L. Pitching Leaders (Tony Cloninger, Don Drysdale, Sandy Koufax)	90.00	36.00	22.00
224	A.L. Pitching Leaders (Jim Grant, Jim Kaat, Mel Stottlemyre)	30.00	12.00	7.50
225	N.L. Strikeout Leaders (Bob Gibson, Sandy Koufax, Bob Veale)	90.00	36.00	22.00
226	A.L. Strikeout Leaders (Mickey Lolich, Sam McDowell, Denny McLain, Sonny Siebert)	45.00	18.00	11.00
227	Russ Nixon	30.00	12.00	7.50
228	Larry Dierker	30.00	12.00	7.50
229	Hank Bauer	30.00	12.00	7.50
230	Johnny Callison	30.00	12.00	7.50
231	Floyd Weaver	30.00	12.00	7.50
232	Glenn Beckert	30.00	12.00	7.50
233	Dom Zanni	30.00	12.00	7.50
234	Yankees Rookies (Rich Beck, Roy White)	35.00	14.00	8.75
235	Don Cardwell	30.00	12.00	7.50
236	Mike Hershberger	30.00	12.00	7.50
237	Billy O'Dell	30.00	12.00	7.50
238	Dodgers Team	100.00	40.00	25.00
239	Orlando Pena	30.00	12.00	7.50
240	Earl Battey	30.00	12.00	7.50
241	Dennis Ribant	30.00	12.00	7.50
242	Jesus Alou	30.00	12.00	7.50
243	Nelson Briles	30.00	12.00	7.50
244	Astros Rookies (Chuck Harrison, Sonny Jackson)	30.00	12.00	7.50
245	John Buzhardt	30.00	12.00	7.50
246	Ed Bailey	30.00	12.00	7.50
247	Carl Warwick	30.00	12.00	7.50
248	Pete Mikkelsen	30.00	12.00	7.50
249	Bill Rigney	30.00	12.00	7.50
250	Sam Ellis	30.00	12.00	7.50
251	Ed Brinkman	30.00	12.00	7.50
252	Denver Lemaster	30.00	12.00	7.50
253	Don Wert	30.00	12.00	7.50
254	Phillies Rookies (Fergie Jenkins, Bill Sorrell)	100.00	40.00	25.00
255	Willie Stargell	125.00	50.00	30.00
256	Lew Krausse	30.00	12.00	7.50
257	Jeff Torborg	30.00	12.00	7.50
258	Dave Giusti	30.00	12.00	7.50
259	Red Sox Team	75.00	30.00	18.50
260	Bob Shaw	30.00	12.00	7.50
261	Ron Hansen	30.00	12.00	7.50
262	Jack Hamilton	30.00	12.00	7.50
263	Tom Egan	30.00	12.00	7.50
264	Twins Rookies (Andy Kosco, Ted Uhlaender)	30.00	12.00	7.50
265	Stu Miller	30.00	12.00	7.50
266	Pedro Gonzalez	30.00	12.00	7.50
267	Joe Sparma	30.00	12.00	7.50
268	John Blanchard	30.00	12.00	7.50
269	Don Heffner	30.00	12.00	7.50
270	Claude Osteen	30.00	12.00	7.50
271	Hal Lanier	30.00	12.00	7.50
272	Jack Baldschun	30.00	12.00	7.50
273	Astro Aces (Bob Aspromonte, Rusty Staub)	30.00	12.00	7.50
274	Buster Narum	30.00	12.00	7.50
275	Tim McCarver	35.00	14.00	8.75
276	Jim Bouton	35.00	14.00	8.75
277	George Thomas	30.00	12.00	7.50
278	Calvin Koonce	30.00	12.00	7.50
279	Checklist 265-352	30.00	12.00	7.50
280	Bobby Knoop	30.00	12.00	7.50
281	Bruce Howard	30.00	12.00	7.50
282	Johnny Lewis	30.00	12.00	7.50
283	Jim Perry	30.00	12.00	7.50
284	Bobby Wine	30.00	12.00	7.50
285	Luis Tiant	45.00	18.00	11.00
286	Gary Geiger	30.00	12.00	7.50
287	Jack Aker	30.00	12.00	7.50
288	Dodgers Rookies (Bill Singer, Don Sutton)	125.00	50.00	30.00
289	Larry Sherry	30.00	12.00	7.50
290	Ron Santo	45.00	18.00	11.00
291	Moe Drabowsky	30.00	12.00	7.50
292	Jim Coker	30.00	12.00	7.50
293	Mike Shannon	30.00	12.00	7.50
294	Steve Ridzik	30.00	12.00	7.50
295	Jim Hart	30.00	12.00	7.50
296	Johnny Keane	30.00	12.00	7.50
297	Jim Owens	30.00	12.00	7.50
298	Rico Petrocelli	30.00	12.00	7.50
299	Lou Burdette	30.00	12.00	7.50
300	Roberto Clemente	650.00	260.00	160.00
301	Greg Bollo	30.00	12.00	7.50
302	Ernie Bowman	30.00	12.00	7.50
303	Indians Team	75.00	30.00	18.50
304	John Herrnstein	30.00	12.00	7.50
305	Camilo Pascual	30.00	12.00	7.50
306	Ty Cline	30.00	12.00	7.50
307	Clay Carroll	30.00	12.00	7.50
308	Tom Haller	30.00	12.00	7.50
309	Diego Segui	30.00	12.00	7.50
310	Frank Robinson	125.00	50.00	30.00
311	Reds Rookies (Tommy Helms, Dick Simpson)	30.00	12.00	7.50
312	Bob Saverine	30.00	12.00	7.50
313	Chris Zachary	30.00	12.00	7.50
314	Hector Valle	30.00	12.00	7.50
315	Norm Cash	30.00	12.00	7.50
316	Jack Fisher	30.00	12.00	7.50
317	Dalton Jones	30.00	12.00	7.50
318	Harry Walker	30.00	12.00	7.50
319	Gene Freese	30.00	12.00	7.50
320	Bob Gibson	125.00	50.00	30.00
321	Rick Reichardt	30.00	12.00	7.50
322	Bill Faul	30.00	12.00	7.50
323	Ray Barker	30.00	12.00	7.50
324	John Boozer	30.00	12.00	7.50
325	Vic Davalillo	100.00	40.00	25.00
326	Braves Team	75.00	30.00	18.50
327	Bernie Allen	30.00	12.00	7.50
328	Jerry Grote	30.00	12.00	7.50
329	Pete Charton	30.00	12.00	7.50
330	Ron Fairly	30.00	12.00	7.50
331	Ron Herbel	30.00	12.00	7.50
332	Billy Bryan	30.00	12.00	7.50
333	Senators Rookies (Joe Coleman, Jim French)	30.00	12.00	7.50
334	Marty Keough	30.00	12.00	7.50
335	Juan Pizarro	30.00	12.00	7.50
336	Gene Alley	30.00	12.00	7.50
337	Fred Gladding	30.00	12.00	7.50
338	Dal Maxvill	30.00	12.00	7.50
339	Del Crandall	30.00	12.00	7.50
340	Dean Chance	30.00	12.00	7.50
341	Wes Westrum	30.00	12.00	7.50
342	Bob Humphreys	30.00	12.00	7.50
343	Joe Christopher	30.00	12.00	7.50
344	Steve Blass	30.00	12.00	7.50
345	Bob Allison	30.00	12.00	7.50
346	Mike de la Hoz	30.00	12.00	7.50
347	Phil Regan	30.00	12.00	7.50
348	Orioles Team	125.00	50.00	30.00
349	Cap Peterson	30.00	12.00	7.50
350	Mel Stottlemyre	30.00	12.00	7.50
351	Fred Valentine	30.00	12.00	7.50
352	Bob Aspromonte	30.00	12.00	7.50
353	Al McBean	30.00	12.00	7.50
354	Smoky Burgess	30.00	12.00	7.50
355	Wade Blasingame	30.00	12.00	7.50
356	Red Sox Rookies (Owen Johnson, Ken Sanders)	30.00	12.00	7.50
357	Gerry Arrigo	30.00	12.00	7.50

		NM	EX	VG
358	Charlie Smith	30.00	12.00	7.50
359	Johnny Briggs	30.00	12.00	7.50
360	Ron Hunt	30.00	12.00	7.50
361	Tom Satriano	30.00	12.00	7.50
362	Gates Brown	30.00	12.00	7.50
363	Checklist 353-429	30.00	12.00	7.50
364	Nate Oliver	30.00	12.00	7.50
365	Roger Maris	200.00	80.00	50.00
366	Wayne Causey	30.00	12.00	7.50
367	Mel Nelson	30.00	12.00	7.50
368	Charlie Lau	30.00	12.00	7.50
369	Jim King	30.00	12.00	7.50
370	Chico Cardenas	30.00	12.00	7.50

1967 Venezuelan League

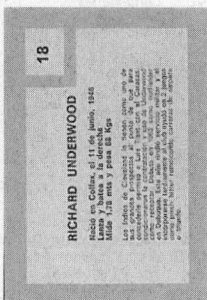

Three distinct series of baseball cards were issued in 1967 for sale in Venezuela, contiguously numbered. Cards #1-138 are players (including many future big leaguers) active in the country's Winter League. Cards are irregularly cut and somewhat smaller than the standard 2-1/2" x 3-1/2". Fronts have posed photos and a thin white border. The player name and position are at top in black, the team name is in large colored letters at bottom. Backs are printed horizontally in black on magenta with a few biographical bits and a one-paragraph career summary. Like most of the Venezuelan cards of the era, these are crudely printed on cheap cardboard. Also like most Venezuelan cards, they are virtually impossible to find in any condition above Ex. Many are found with back damage due to having been glued into an album or scrapbook.

		NM	EX	VG
Complete Set (138):		3,500	1,750	1,000
Common Player:		20.00	10.00	6.00
1	Regino Otero	40.00	20.00	12.00
2	Alejandro Carrasquel	20.00	10.00	6.00
3	Pompeyo Davilillo	25.00	12.50	7.50
4	Gonzalo Marquez	20.00	10.00	6.00
5	Octavio (Cookie) Rojas	35.00	17.50	10.50
6	Teodoro Obregon	20.00	10.00	6.00
7	Paul Schaal	25.00	12.50	7.50
8	Juan Francia	20.00	10.00	6.00
9	Luis Tiant	60.00	30.00	18.00
10	Jose Tartabull	30.00	15.00	9.00
11	Vic Davalillo	25.00	12.50	7.50
12	Cesar Tovar	25.00	12.50	7.50
13	Ron Klimkowski	20.00	10.00	6.00
14	Diego Segui	35.00	17.50	10.50
15	Luis Penalver	20.00	10.00	6.00
16	Urbano Lugo	20.00	10.00	6.00
17	Aurelio Monteagudo	20.00	10.00	6.00
18	Richard Underwood	25.00	12.50	7.50
19	Nelson Castellanos	20.00	10.00	6.00
20	Manuel Mendible	20.00	10.00	6.00
21	Fidel Garcia	40.00	20.00	12.00
22	Luis Cordoba	20.00	10.00	6.00
23	Jesus Padron	20.00	10.00	6.00
24	Lorenzo Fernandez	20.00	10.00	6.00
25	Leopoldo Tovar	20.00	10.00	6.00
26	Carlos Loreto	20.00	10.00	6.00
27	Oswaldo Blanco	20.00	10.00	6.00
28	Sid (Syd) O'Brien	20.00	10.00	6.00
29	Cesar Gutierrez	20.00	10.00	6.00
30	Luis Garcia	20.00	10.00	6.00
31	Fred Klages	20.00	10.00	6.00
32	Isaias Chavez	20.00	10.00	6.00
33	Walter Williams	25.00	12.50	7.50
34	Jim Hicks	20.00	10.00	6.00
35	Gustavo Sposito	20.00	10.00	6.00
36	Cisco Carlos	20.00	10.00	6.00
37	Jim Mooring	20.00	10.00	6.00
38	Alonso Olivares	20.00	10.00	6.00
39	Graciliano Parra	20.00	10.00	6.00
40	Merritt Ranew	20.00	10.00	6.00
41	Everest Contramaestre	20.00	10.00	6.00
42	Orlando Reyes	20.00	10.00	6.00
43	Edicto Arteaga	20.00	10.00	6.00
44	Francisco Diaz	20.00	10.00	6.00
45	Victor Colina	20.00	10.00	6.00
46a	Ramon Diaz	20.00	10.00	6.00
46b	Francisco Diaz (Blue back.)	20.00	10.00	6.00
47	Luis E. Aparicio	185.00	90.00	55.00
48	Reynaldo Cordeiro	60.00	30.00	18.00
49	Luis Aparicio, Sr.	25.00	12.50	7.50
50	Ramon Webster	20.00	10.00	6.00
51	Remigio Hermoso	20.00	10.00	6.00
52	Miguel de la Hoz	20.00	10.00	6.00
53	Enzo Hernandez	20.00	10.00	6.00
54	Ed Watt	20.00	10.00	6.00
55	Angel Bravo	20.00	10.00	6.00
56	Marv (Merv) Rettenmund	25.00	12.50	7.50
57	Jose Herrera	20.00	10.00	6.00
58	Tom Fisher	20.00	10.00	6.00

		NM	EX	VG
59	Jim Weaver	20.00	10.00	6.00
60a	Juan Quintana	20.00	10.00	6.00
60b	Frank Fernandez (Blue back.)	20.00	10.00	6.00
61	Hector Urbano	20.00	10.00	6.00
62	Hector Brito (Blue back.)	20.00	10.00	6.00
63	Jesus Romero	20.00	10.00	6.00
64	Carlos A. Moreno	20.00	10.00	6.00
65	Nestor Mendible	20.00	10.00	6.00
66	Armando Ortiz	20.00	10.00	6.00
67	Graciano Ravelo	20.00	10.00	6.00
68	Paul Knechtges	20.00	10.00	6.00
69	Marcelino Lopez	25.00	12.50	7.50
70	Wilfredo Calvino	25.00	12.50	7.50
71	Jesus Avila	20.00	10.00	6.00
72	Carlos Pascual	45.00	22.00	13.50
73	Bob Burda	20.00	10.00	6.00
74	Elio Chacon	20.00	10.00	6.00
75	Jacinto Hernandez	20.00	10.00	6.00
76	Jose M. Tovar	20.00	10.00	6.00
77	Bill Whitby	20.00	10.00	6.00
78	Enrique Izquierdo	20.00	10.00	6.00
79	Hilario Valdespino	30.00	15.00	9.00
80	John Lewis	20.00	10.00	6.00
81	Hector Martinez	40.00	20.00	12.00
82	Rene Paredes	20.00	10.00	6.00
83	Danny Morris	20.00	10.00	6.00
84	Pedro Ramos	25.00	12.50	7.50
85	Jose Ramon Lopez	20.00	10.00	6.00
86	Jesus Rizales	20.00	10.00	6.00
87	Winston Acosta	20.00	10.00	6.00
88	Pablo Bello	20.00	10.00	6.00
89	David Concepcion	200.00	100.00	60.00
90	Manuel Garcia	20.00	10.00	6.00
91	Anibal Longa	20.00	10.00	6.00
92	Francisco Moscoso	20.00	10.00	6.00
93	Mel McGaha	20.00	10.00	6.00
94	Aquiles Gomez	20.00	10.00	6.00
95	Alfonso Carrasquel (Blue back.)	40.00	20.00	12.00
96	Tom Murray	20.00	10.00	6.00
97	Gustavo Gil	20.00	10.00	6.00
98	Damaso Blanco	20.00	10.00	6.00
99	Alberto Cambero	20.00	10.00	6.00
100	Don Bryant	20.00	10.00	6.00
101	George Culver	20.00	10.00	6.00
102	Teolindo Acosta	20.00	10.00	6.00
103	Aaron Pointer	20.00	10.00	6.00
104	Ed Kirkpatrick	20.00	10.00	6.00
105	Luis Rodriguez	20.00	10.00	6.00
106	Mike Daniel	20.00	10.00	6.00
107	Cecilio Prieto (Blue back.)	20.00	10.00	6.00
108	Juan Quiroz	20.00	10.00	6.00
108				6.00
109	Juan Campos	20.00	10.00	6.00
110	Freddy Rivero	20.00	10.00	6.00
111	Dick LeMay	20.00	10.00	6.00
112	Raul Ortega	20.00	10.00	6.00
113	Bruno Estaba	20.00	10.00	6.00
114	Evangelista Nunez	20.00	10.00	6.00
115a	Robert Munoz	20.00	10.00	6.00
115b	Alfonso Carrasquel (Red back.)	40.00	20.00	12.00
116	Tony Castanos	20.00	10.00	6.00
117	Domingo Barboza	20.00	10.00	6.00
118	Lucio Celis	20.00	10.00	6.00
119	Carlos Santeliz	20.00	10.00	6.00
120	Barton Shirley	25.00	12.50	7.50
121	Neudo Morales	20.00	10.00	6.00
122	Robert Cox	100.00	50.00	30.00
123	Cruz Amaya (Blue back.)	20.00	10.00	6.00
124	Jim Campanis	75.00	37.50	22.00
125	Dave Roberts	20.00	10.00	6.00
126	Gerry Crider	20.00	10.00	6.00
127	Domingo Carrasquel	20.00	10.00	6.00
128	Leo Marentette	20.00	10.00	6.00
129	Frank Kreutzer	20.00	10.00	6.00
130	Jim Dickson	20.00	10.00	6.00
131	Bob Oliver	20.00	10.00	6.00
132	Jose Bracho	20.00	10.00	6.00
133a	Pablo Torrealba	20.00	10.00	6.00
133b	Pablo Torrealba (Different picture.)	20.00	10.00	6.00
134	Iran Paz	20.00	10.00	6.00
135	Eliecer Bueno	20.00	10.00	6.00
136	Claudio Urdaneta	20.00	10.00	6.00
137	Faustino Zabala	20.00	10.00	6.00
138	Dario Chirinos	20.00	10.00	6.00

1967 Venezuelan Retirado

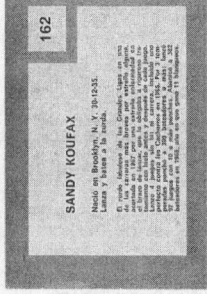

Three distinct series of baseball cards were issued in 1967 for sale in Venezuela, contiguously numbered. Cards #139-188 are former big league stars. The fronts of the roughly 2-1/2" x 3-1/2" Retirado cards have a blue background with the player's name in black at top and "RETIRADO" in red block letters at bottom. Player photos on the Retirado cards are sepia. Horizontal backs are printed in black on green with a bits of personal data and a career summary. Like most of the Venezuelan cards of the era, these are crudely printed on cheap cardboard. Also like most Venezuelan cards, they are virtually impossible to find in any condition above Ex. Many are found with back damage due to having been glued into an album or scrapbook.

		NM	EX	VG
Complete Set (50):		12,000	4,800	1,800
Common Player:		250.00	100.00	37.00
139	Walter Johnson	750.00	300.00	110.00
140	Bill Dickey	300.00	120.00	45.00
141	Lou Gehrig	1,750	700.00	260.00
142	Rogers Hornsby	300.00	120.00	45.00
143	Honus Wagner	650.00	260.00	100.00
144	Pie Traynor	250.00	100.00	35.00
145	Joe DiMaggio	1,850	740.00	275.00
146	Ty Cobb	1,350	540.00	200.00
147	Babe Ruth	2,400	960.00	360.00
148	Ted Williams	1,000	400.00	150.00
149	Mel Ott	250.00	100.00	35.00
150	Cy Young	370.00	150.00	55.00
151	Christy Mathewson	750.00	300.00	110.00
152	Warren Spahn	300.00	120.00	45.00
153	Mickey Cochrane	250.00	100.00	35.00
154	George Sisler	250.00	100.00	35.00
155	Jimmy Collins	250.00	100.00	35.00
156	Tris Speaker	300.00	120.00	45.00
157	Stan Musial	700.00	280.00	100.00
158	Luke Appling	250.00	100.00	35.00
159	Nap Lajoie	250.00	100.00	35.00
160	Bill Terry	250.00	100.00	35.00
161	Bob Feller	370.00	150.00	55.00
162	Sandy Koufax	800.00	320.00	120.00
163	Jimmie Foxx	300.00	120.00	45.00
164	Joe Cronin	250.00	100.00	35.00
165	Frankie Frisch	250.00	100.00	35.00
166	Paul Waner	250.00	100.00	35.00
167	Lloyd Waner	250.00	100.00	35.00
168	Lefty Grove	250.00	100.00	35.00
169	Bobby Doerr	250.00	100.00	35.00
170	Al Simmons	250.00	100.00	35.00
171	Grover Alexander	350.00	140.00	50.00
172	Carl Hubbell	250.00	100.00	35.00
173	Mordecai Brown	250.00	100.00	35.00
174	Ted Lyons	250.00	100.00	35.00
175	Johnny Vander Meer	250.00	100.00	35.00
176	Alex Carrasquel	300.00	120.00	45.00
177	Satchel Paige	600.00	240.00	90.00
178	Whitey Ford	500.00	200.00	75.00
179	Yogi Berra	500.00	200.00	75.00
180	Roy Campanella	450.00	180.00	65.00
181	Alfonso Carrasquel	370.00	150.00	55.00
182	Johnny Mize	250.00	100.00	35.00
183	Ted Kluszewski (Photo actually Gene Bearden.)	300.00	120.00	45.00
184	Jackie Robinson	750.00	300.00	110.00
185	Bobby Avila	250.00	100.00	35.00
186	Phil Rizzuto	300.00	120.00	45.00
187	Minnie Minoso	300.00	120.00	45.00
188	Connie Marrero	250.00	100.00	35.00

1967 Venezuelan Topps

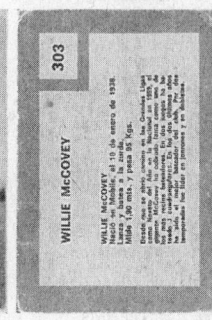

Cards numbered #189-338 in the 1967 Venezuelan issue feature then-current major leaguers. Card fronts are taken from Topps' 1967 baseball series, but are borderless, making them somewhat smaller than 2-1/2" x 3-1/2". Backs of the South American cards are horizontal and printed in black on blue and offer a few bits of personal data and a one-paragraph career summary. Like most Venezuelan cards of the era, these are crudely printed on cheap cardboard and seldom found in condition better than Ex. Many will show evidence on back of having been glued into an album or scrapbook.

		NM	EX	VG
Complete Set (150):		8,000	2,000	750.00
Common Player:		35.00	14.00	5.25
189	Luis Aparicio	150.00	60.00	22.00
190	Vic Davalillo	35.00	14.00	5.25
191	Cesar Tovar	35.00	14.00	5.25
192	Mickey Mantle	1,500	600.00	225.00
193	Carl Yastrzemski	100.00	40.00	15.00
194	Frank Robinson	100.00	40.00	15.00
195	Willie Horton	35.00	14.00	5.25
196	Gary Peters	35.00	14.00	5.25
197	Bert Campaneris	40.00	16.00	6.00
198	Norm Cash	35.00	14.00	5.25

#	Player			
199	Boog Powell	35.00	14.00	5.25
200	George Scott	35.00	14.00	5.25
201	Frank Howard	35.00	14.00	5.25
202	Rick Reichardt	35.00	14.00	5.25
203	Jose Cardenal	35.00	14.00	5.25
204	Rico Petrocelli	35.00	14.00	5.25
205	Lew Krausse	35.00	14.00	5.25
206	Harmon Killebrew	100.00	40.00	15.00
207	Leon Wagner	35.00	14.00	5.25
208	Joe Foy	35.00	14.00	5.25
209	Joe Pepitone	40.00	16.00	6.00
210	Al Kaline	100.00	40.00	15.00
211	Brooks Robinson	100.00	40.00	15.00
212	Bill Freehan	35.00	14.00	5.25
213	Jim Lonborg	35.00	14.00	5.25
214a	Ed Mathews	100.00	40.00	15.00
214b	Jim Bunning	90.00	36.00	13.50
	(Should be #174.)			
215	Dick Green	35.00	14.00	5.25
216	Tom Tresh	40.00	16.00	6.00
217	Dean Chance	35.00	14.00	5.25
218	Paul Blair	35.00	14.00	5.25
219	Larry Brown	35.00	14.00	5.25
220	Fred Valentine	35.00	14.00	5.25
221	Al Downing	35.00	14.00	5.25
222	Earl Battey	35.00	14.00	5.25
223	Don Mincher	35.00	14.00	5.25
224	Tommie Agee	35.00	14.00	5.25
225	Jim McGlothlin	35.00	14.00	5.25
226	Zoilo Versalles	35.00	14.00	5.25
227	Curt Blefary	35.00	14.00	5.25
228	Joel Horlen	35.00	14.00	5.25
229	Stu Miller	35.00	14.00	5.25
230	Tony Oliva	40.00	16.00	6.00
231	Paul Casanova	35.00	14.00	5.25
232	Orlando Pena	35.00	14.00	5.25
233	Ron Hansen	35.00	14.00	5.25
234	Earl Wilson	35.00	14.00	5.25
235	Ken Boyer	40.00	16.00	6.00
236	Jim Kaat	35.00	14.00	5.25
237	Dalton Jones	35.00	14.00	5.25
238	Pete Ward	35.00	14.00	5.25
239	Mickey Lolich	35.00	14.00	5.25
240	Jose Santiago	35.00	14.00	5.25
241	Dick McAuliffe	35.00	14.00	5.25
242	Mel Stottlemyre	35.00	14.00	5.25
243	Camilo Pascual	35.00	14.00	5.25
244	Jim Fregosi	35.00	14.00	5.25
245	Tony Conigliaro	40.00	16.00	6.00
246	Sonny Siebert	35.00	14.00	5.25
247	Jim Perry	35.00	14.00	5.25
248	Dave McNally	35.00	14.00	5.25
249	Fred Whitfield	35.00	14.00	5.25
250	Ken Berry	35.00	14.00	5.25
251	Jim Grant	35.00	14.00	5.25
252	Hank Aguirre	35.00	14.00	5.25
253	Don Wert	35.00	14.00	5.25
254	Wally Bunker	35.00	14.00	5.25
255	Elston Howard	40.00	16.00	6.00
256	Dave Johnson	35.00	14.00	5.25
257	Hoyt Wilhelm	75.00	30.00	11.00
258	Don Buford	35.00	14.00	5.25
259	Sam McDowell	35.00	14.00	5.25
260	Bobby Knoop	35.00	14.00	5.25
261	Denny McLain	35.00	14.00	5.25
262	Steve Hargan	35.00	14.00	5.25
263	Jim Nash	35.00	14.00	5.25
264	Jerry Adair	35.00	14.00	5.25
265	Tony Gonzalez	35.00	14.00	5.25
266	Mike Shannon	35.00	14.00	5.25
267	Bob Gibson	90.00	36.00	13.50
268	John Roseboro	35.00	14.00	5.25
269	Bob Aspromonte	35.00	14.00	5.25
270	Pete Rose	250.00	100.00	37.00
271	Rico Carty	40.00	16.00	6.00
272	Juan Pizarro	35.00	14.00	5.25
273	Willie Mays	250.00	100.00	37.00
274	Jim Bunning	90.00	36.00	13.50
275	Ernie Banks	100.00	40.00	15.00
276	Curt Flood	40.00	16.00	6.00
277	Mack Jones	35.00	14.00	5.25
278	Roberto Clemente	450.00	180.00	67.00
279	Sammy Ellis	35.00	14.00	5.25
280	Willie Stargell	90.00	36.00	13.50
281	Felipe Alou	40.00	16.00	6.00
282	Ed Kranepool	35.00	14.00	5.25
283	Nelson Briles	35.00	14.00	5.25
284	Hank Aaron	250.00	100.00	37.00
285	Vada Pinson	40.00	16.00	6.00
286	Jim LeFebvre	35.00	14.00	5.25
287	Hal Lanier	35.00	14.00	5.25
288	Ron Swoboda	35.00	14.00	5.25
289	Mike McCormick	35.00	14.00	5.25
290	Lou Johnson	35.00	14.00	5.25
291	Orlando Cepeda	90.00	36.00	13.50
292	Rusty Staub	40.00	16.00	6.00
293	Manny Mota	35.00	14.00	5.25
294	Tommy Harper	35.00	14.00	5.25
295	Don Drysdale	90.00	36.00	13.50
296	Mel Queen	35.00	14.00	5.25
297	Red Schoendienst	75.00	30.00	11.00
298	Matty Alou	35.00	14.00	5.25
299	Johnny Callison	35.00	14.00	5.25
300	Juan Marichal	90.00	36.00	13.50
301	Al McBean	35.00	14.00	5.25
302	Claude Osteen	35.00	14.00	5.25
303	Willie McCovey	90.00	36.00	13.50
304	Jim Owens	35.00	14.00	5.25
305	Chico Ruiz	35.00	14.00	5.25
306	Ferguson Jenkins	90.00	36.00	13.50
307	Lou Brock	90.00	36.00	13.50
308	Joe Morgan	90.00	36.00	13.50
309	Ron Santo	50.00	20.00	7.50
310	Chico Cardenas	35.00	14.00	5.25
311	Richie Allen	45.00	18.00	6.75
312	Gaylord Perry	75.00	30.00	11.00
313	Bill Mazeroski	75.00	30.00	11.00
314	Tony Taylor	35.00	14.00	5.25
315	Tommy Helms	35.00	14.00	5.25
316	Jim Wynn	35.00	14.00	5.25
317	Don Sutton	75.00	30.00	11.00
318	Mike Cuellar	45.00	18.00	6.75
319	Willie Davis	35.00	14.00	5.25
320	Julian Javier	35.00	14.00	5.25
321	Maury Wills	35.00	14.00	5.25
322	Gene Alley	35.00	14.00	5.25
323	Ray Sadecki	35.00	14.00	5.25
324	Joe Torre	45.00	18.00	6.75
325	Jim Maloney	35.00	14.00	5.25
326	Jim Davenport	35.00	14.00	5.25
327	Tony Perez	90.00	36.00	13.50
328	Roger Maris	100.00	40.00	15.00
329	Chris Short	35.00	14.00	5.25
330	Jesus Alou	35.00	14.00	5.25
331	Darron Johnson	35.00	14.00	5.25
332	Tommy Davis	35.00	14.00	5.25
333	Bob Veale	35.00	14.00	5.25
334	Bill McCool	35.00	14.00	5.25
335	Jim Hart	35.00	14.00	5.25
336	Roy Face	35.00	14.00	5.25
337	Billy Williams	75.00	30.00	11.00
338	Dick Groat	35.00	14.00	5.25

1968 Venezuelan Topps

The first 370 cards of Topps' 1968 baseball card set were reproduced in South America for sale in Venezuela. Besides being rather crudely printed on cheaper, non-gloss cardboard, the cards are virtually identical to the Topps U.S. version. The only difference is a tiny line of yellow type on back which reads: "Hecho en Venezuela - C.A. Litoven." Like most 1960s Venezuelan issues, these cards are seldom found in condition better than Excellent, and often with evidence on back of having been glued into an album or scrapbook. Venezuelan Topps cards are often found cut slightly smaller than the U.S. version, up to 1/8".

#	Player	NM	EX	VG
	Complete Set (370):	25,000	10,000	6,250
	Common Player:	30.00	12.00	7.50
1	N.L. Batting Leaders (Matty Alou, Roberto Clemente, Tony Gonzalez)	80.00	32.00	20.00
2	A.L. Batting Leaders (Al Kaline, Frank Robinson, Carl Yastrzemski)	50.00	20.00	12.50
3	N.L. RBI Leaders (Hank Aaron, Orlando Cepeda, Roberto Clemente)	80.00	32.00	20.00
4	A.L. RBI Leaders (Harmon Killebrew, Frank Robinson, Carl Yastrzemski)	50.00	20.00	12.50
5	N.L. Home Run Leaders (Hank Aaron, Willie McCovey, Ron Santo, Jim Wynn)	60.00	24.00	15.00
6	A.L. Home Run Leaders (Frank Howard, Harmon Killebrew, Carl Yastrzemski)	50.00	20.00	12.50
7	N.L. ERA Leaders (Jim Bunning, Phil Niekro, Chris Short)	30.00	12.00	7.50
8	A.L. ERA Leaders (Joe Horlen, Gary Peters, Sonny Siebert)	30.00	12.00	7.50
9	N.L. Pitching Leaders (Jim Bunning, Fergie Jenkins, Mike McCormick, Claude Osteen)	30.00	12.00	7.50
10	A.L. Pitching Leaders (Dean Chance, Jim Lonborg, Earl Wilson)	30.00	12.00	7.50
11	N.L. Strikeout Leaders (Jim Bunning, Fergie Jenkins, Gaylord Perry)	30.00	12.00	7.50
12	A.L. Strikeout Leaders (Dean Chance, Jim Lonborg, Sam McDowell)	30.00	12.00	7.50
13	Chuck Hartenstein	30.00	12.00	7.50
14	Jerry McNertney	30.00	12.00	7.50
15	Ron Hunt	30.00	12.00	7.50
16	Indians Rookies (Lou Piniella, Richie Scheinblum)	40.00	16.00	10.00
17	Dick Hall	30.00	12.00	7.50
18	Mike Hershberger	30.00	12.00	7.50
19	Juan Pizarro	30.00	12.00	7.50
20	Brooks Robinson	120.00	48.00	30.00
21	Ron Davis	30.00	12.00	7.50
22	Pat Dobson	30.00	12.00	7.50
23	Chico Cardenas	30.00	12.00	7.50
24	Bobby Locke	30.00	12.00	7.50
25	Julian Javier	30.00	12.00	7.50
26	Darrell Brandon	30.00	12.00	7.50
27	Gil Hodges	50.00	20.00	12.50
28	Ted Uhlaender	30.00	12.00	7.50
29	Joe Verbanic	30.00	12.00	7.50
30	Joe Torre	40.00	16.00	10.00
31	Ed Stroud	30.00	12.00	7.50
32	Joe Gibbon	30.00	12.00	7.50
33	Pete Ward	30.00	12.00	7.50
34	Al Ferrara	30.00	12.00	7.50
35	Steve Hargan	30.00	12.00	7.50
36	Pirates Rookies (Bob Moose, Bob Robertson)	30.00	12.00	7.50
37	Billy Williams	80.00	32.00	20.00
38	Tony Pierce	30.00	12.00	7.50
39	Cookie Rojas	30.00	12.00	7.50
40	Denny McLain	40.00	16.00	10.00
41	Julio Gotay	30.00	12.00	7.50
42	Larry Haney	30.00	12.00	7.50
43	Gary Bell	30.00	12.00	7.50
44	Frank Kostro	30.00	12.00	7.50
45	Tom Seaver	120.00	48.00	30.00
46	Dave Ricketts	30.00	12.00	7.50
47	Ralph Houk	30.00	12.00	7.50
48	Ted Davidson	30.00	12.00	7.50
49	Ed Brinkman	30.00	12.00	7.50
50	Willie Mays	350.00	140.00	90.00
51	Bob Locker	30.00	12.00	7.50
52	Hawk Taylor	30.00	12.00	7.50
53	Gene Alley	30.00	12.00	7.50
54	Stan Williams	30.00	12.00	7.50
55	Felipe Alou	40.00	16.00	10.00
56	Orioles Rookies (Dave Leonhard, Dave May)	30.00	12.00	7.50
57	Dan Schneider	30.00	12.00	7.50
58	Eddie Mathews	120.00	48.00	30.00
59	Don Lock	30.00	12.00	7.50
60	Ken Holtzman	30.00	12.00	7.50
61	Reggie Smith	30.00	12.00	7.50
62	Chuck Dobson	30.00	12.00	7.50
63	Dick Kenworthy	30.00	12.00	7.50
64	Jim Merritt	30.00	12.00	7.50
65	John Roseboro	30.00	12.00	7.50
66	Casey Cox	30.00	12.00	7.50
67	Checklist 1-109 (Jim Kaat)	30.00	12.00	7.50
68	Ron Willis	30.00	12.00	7.50
69	Tom Tresh	30.00	12.00	7.50
70	Bob Veale	30.00	12.00	7.50
71	Vern Fuller	30.00	12.00	7.50
72	Tommy John	30.00	12.00	7.50
73	Jim Hart	30.00	12.00	7.50
74	Milt Pappas	30.00	12.00	7.50
75	Don Mincher	30.00	12.00	7.50
76	Braves Rookies (Jim Britton, Ron Reed)	30.00	12.00	7.50
77	Don Wilson	30.00	12.00	7.50
78	Jim Northrup	30.00	12.00	7.50
79	Ted Kubiak	30.00	12.00	7.50
80	Rod Carew	120.00	48.00	30.00
81	Larry Jackson	30.00	12.00	7.50
82	Sam Bowens	30.00	12.00	7.50
83	John Stephenson	30.00	12.00	7.50
84	Bob Tolan	30.00	12.00	7.50
85	Gaylord Perry	80.00	32.00	20.00
86	Willie Stargell	100.00	40.00	25.00
87	Dick Williams	30.00	12.00	7.50
88	Phil Regan	30.00	12.00	7.50
89	Jake Gibbs	30.00	12.00	7.50
90	Vada Pinson	40.00	16.00	10.00
91	Jim Ollom	30.00	12.00	7.50
92	Ed Kranepool	30.00	12.00	7.50
93	Tony Cloninger	30.00	12.00	7.50
94	Lee Maye	30.00	12.00	7.50
95	Bob Aspromonte	30.00	12.00	7.50
96	Senators Rookies (Frank Coggins, Dick Nold)	30.00	12.00	7.50
97	Tom Phoebus	30.00	12.00	7.50
98	Gary Sutherland	30.00	12.00	7.50
99	Rocky Colavito	50.00	20.00	12.50
100	Bob Gibson	90.00	36.00	22.00
101	Glenn Beckert	30.00	12.00	7.50
102	Jose Cardenal	30.00	12.00	7.50
103	Don Sutton	80.00	32.00	20.00
104	Dick Dietz	30.00	12.00	7.50
105	Al Downing	30.00	12.00	7.50
106	Dalton Jones	30.00	12.00	7.50
107	Checklist 110-196 (Juan Marichal)	30.00	12.00	7.50
108	Don Pavletich	30.00	12.00	7.50
109	Bert Campaneris	40.00	16.00	10.00
110	Hank Aaron	350.00	140.00	90.00
111	Rich Reese	30.00	12.00	7.50
112	Woody Fryman	30.00	12.00	7.50
113	Tigers Rookies (Tom Matchick, Daryl Patterson)	30.00	12.00	7.50
114	Ron Swoboda	30.00	12.00	7.50
115	Sam McDowell	30.00	12.00	7.50
116	Ken McMullen	30.00	12.00	7.50
117	Larry Jaster	30.00	12.00	7.50
118	Mark Belanger	30.00	12.00	7.50
119	Ted Savage	30.00	12.00	7.50
120	Mel Stottlemyre	30.00	12.00	7.50
121	Jimmie Hall	30.00	12.00	7.50
122	Gene Mauch	30.00	12.00	7.50
123	Jose Santiago	30.00	12.00	7.50
124	Nate Oliver	30.00	12.00	7.50
125	Joe Horlen	30.00	12.00	7.50
126	Bobby Etheridge	30.00	12.00	7.50
127	Paul Lindblad	30.00	12.00	7.50
128	Astros Rookies (Tom Dukes, Alonzo Harris)	30.00	12.00	7.50
129	Mickey Stanley	30.00	12.00	7.50
130	Tony Perez	90.00	36.00	22.00
131	Frank Bertaina	30.00	12.00	7.50
132	Bud Harrelson	30.00	12.00	7.50
133	Fred Whitfield	30.00	12.00	7.50
134	Pat Jarvis	30.00	12.00	7.50
135	Paul Blair	30.00	12.00	7.50
136	Randy Hundley	30.00	12.00	7.50
137	Twins Team	40.00	16.00	10.00

#	Player	NM	EX	VG
138	Ruben Amaro	30.00	12.00	7.50
139	Chris Short	30.00	12.00	7.50
140	Tony Conigliaro	40.00	16.00	10.00
141	Dal Maxvill	30.00	12.00	7.50
142	White Sox Rookies (*Buddy Bradford, Bill Voss*)	30.00	12.00	7.50
143	Pete Cimino	30.00	12.00	7.50
144	Joe Morgan	100.00	40.00	25.00
145	Don Drysdale	100.00	40.00	25.00
146	Sal Bando	30.00	12.00	7.50
147	Frank Linzy	30.00	12.00	7.50
148	Dave Bristol	30.00	12.00	7.50
149	Bob Saverine	30.00	12.00	7.50
150	Roberto Clemente	600.00	240.00	150.00
151	World Series Game 1 (Brock Socks 4 Hits in Opener)	30.00	12.00	7.50
152	World Series Game 2 (Yaz Smashes Two Homers)	40.00	16.00	10.00
153	World Series Game 3 (Briles Cools Off Boston)	30.00	12.00	7.50
154	World Series Game 4 (Gibson Hurls Shutout)			
155	World Series Game 5 (Lonborg Wins Again)	30.00	12.00	7.50
156	World Series Game 6 (Petrocelli Socks Two Homers)	30.00	12.00	7.50
157	World Series Game 7 (St. Louis Wins It)	30.00	12.00	7.50
158	World Series Summary (The Cardinals Celebrate)	30.00	12.00	7.50
159	Don Kessinger	30.00	12.00	7.50
160	Earl Wilson	30.00	12.00	7.50
161	Norm Miller	30.00	12.00	7.50
162	Cardinals Rookies (*Hal Gilson, Mike Torrez*)	30.00	12.00	7.50
163	Gene Brabender	30.00	12.00	7.50
164	Ramon Webster	30.00	12.00	7.50
165	Tony Oliva	40.00	16.00	10.00
166	Claude Raymond	30.00	12.00	7.50
167	Elston Howard	30.00	12.00	7.50
168	Dodgers Team	50.00	20.00	12.50
169	Bob Bolin	30.00	12.00	7.50
170	Jim Fregosi	30.00	12.00	7.50
171	Don Nottebart	30.00	12.00	7.50
172	Walt Williams	30.00	12.00	7.50
173	John Boozer	30.00	12.00	7.50
174	Bob Tillman	30.00	12.00	7.50
175	Maury Wills	30.00	12.00	7.50
176	Bob Allen	30.00	12.00	7.50
177	Mets Rookies (*Jerry Koosman, Nolan Ryan*)	12,000	4,800	3,000
178	Don Wert	30.00	12.00	7.50
179	Bill Stoneman	30.00	12.00	7.50
180	Curt Flood	30.00	12.00	7.50
181	Jerry Zimmerman	30.00	12.00	7.50
182	Dave Giusti	30.00	12.00	7.50
183	Bob Kennedy	30.00	12.00	7.50
184	Lou Johnson	30.00	12.00	7.50
185	Tom Haller	30.00	12.00	7.50
186	Eddie Watt	30.00	12.00	7.50
187	Sonny Jackson	30.00	12.00	7.50
188	Cap Peterson	30.00	12.00	7.50
189	Bill Landis	30.00	12.00	7.50
190	Bill White	30.00	12.00	7.50
191	Dan Frisella	30.00	12.00	7.50
192	Checklist 197-283 (Carl Yastrzemski)	40.00	16.00	10.00
193	Jack Hamilton	30.00	12.00	7.50
194	Don Buford	30.00	12.00	7.50
195	Joe Pepitone	30.00	12.00	7.50
196	Gary Nolan	30.00	12.00	7.50
197	Larry Brown	30.00	12.00	7.50
198	Roy Face	30.00	12.00	7.50
199	A's Rookies (*Darrell Osteen, Roberto Rodriguez*)	30.00	12.00	7.50
200	Orlando Cepeda	80.00	32.00	20.00
201	Mike Marshall	30.00	12.00	7.50
202	Adolfo Phillips	30.00	12.00	7.50
203	Dick Kelley	30.00	12.00	7.50
204	Andy Etchebarren	30.00	12.00	7.50
205	Juan Marichal	90.00	36.00	22.00
206	Cal Ermer	30.00	12.00	7.50
207	Carroll Sembera	30.00	12.00	7.50
208	Willie Davis	30.00	12.00	7.50
209	Tim Cullen	30.00	12.00	7.50
210	Gary Peters	30.00	12.00	7.50
211	J.C. Martin	30.00	12.00	7.50
212	Dave Morehead	30.00	12.00	7.50
213	Chico Ruiz	30.00	12.00	7.50
214	Yankees Rookies (*Stan Bahnsen, Frank Fernandez*)	30.00	12.00	7.50
215	Jim Bunning	90.00	36.00	22.00
216	Bubba Morton	30.00	12.00	7.50
217	Turk Farrell	30.00	12.00	7.50
218	Ken Suarez	30.00	12.00	7.50
219	Rob Gardner	30.00	12.00	7.50
220	Harmon Killebrew	120.00	48.00	30.00
221	Braves Team	40.00	16.00	10.00
222	Jim Hardin	30.00	12.00	7.50
223	Ollie Brown	30.00	12.00	7.50
224	Jack Aker	30.00	12.00	7.50
225	Richie Allen	40.00	16.00	10.00
226	Jimmie Price	30.00	12.00	7.50
227	Joe Hoerner	30.00	12.00	7.50
228	Dodgers Rookies (*Jack Billingham, Jim Fairey*)	30.00	12.00	7.50
229	Fred Klages	30.00	12.00	7.50
230	Pete Rose	350.00	140.00	90.00
231	Dave Baldwin	30.00	12.00	7.50
232	Denis Menke	30.00	12.00	7.50
233	George Scott	30.00	12.00	7.50
234	Bill Monbouquette	30.00	12.00	7.50
235	Ron Santo	50.00	20.00	12.50
236	Tug McGraw	30.00	12.00	7.50
237	Alvin Dark	30.00	12.00	7.50
238	Tom Satriano	30.00	12.00	7.50
239	Bill Henry	30.00	12.00	7.50

#	Player	NM	EX	VG
240	Al Kaline	120.00	48.00	30.00
241	Felix Millan	30.00	12.00	7.50
242	Moe Drabowsky	30.00	12.00	7.50
243	Rich Rollins	30.00	12.00	7.50
244	John Donaldson	30.00	12.00	7.50
245	Tony Gonzalez	30.00	12.00	7.50
246	Fritz Peterson	30.00	12.00	7.50
247	Reds Rookies (*Johnny Bench, Ron Tompkins*)	400.00	160.00	100.00
248	Fred Valentine	30.00	12.00	7.50
249	Bill Singer	30.00	12.00	7.50
250	Carl Yastrzemski	130.00	52.00	32.00
251	Manny Sanguillen	40.00	16.00	10.00
252	Angels Team	40.00	16.00	10.00
253	Dick Hughes	30.00	12.00	7.50
254	Cleon Jones	30.00	12.00	7.50
255	Dean Chance	30.00	12.00	7.50
256	Norm Cash	40.00	16.00	10.00
257	Phil Niekro	80.00	32.00	20.00
258	Cubs Rookies (*Jose Arcia, Bill Schlesinger*)	30.00	12.00	7.50
259	Ken Boyer	30.00	12.00	7.50
260	Jim Wynn	30.00	12.00	7.50
261	Dave Duncan	30.00	12.00	7.50
262	Rick Wise	30.00	12.00	7.50
263	Horace Clarke	30.00	12.00	7.50
264	Ted Abernathy	30.00	12.00	7.50
265	Tommy Davis	30.00	12.00	7.50
266	Paul Popovich	30.00	12.00	7.50
267	Herman Franks	30.00	12.00	7.50
268	Bob Humphreys	30.00	12.00	7.50
269	Bob Tiefenauer	30.00	12.00	7.50
270	Matty Alou	30.00	12.00	7.50
271	Bobby Knoop	30.00	12.00	7.50
272	Ray Culp	30.00	12.00	7.50
273	Dave Johnson	30.00	12.00	7.50
274	Mike Cuellar	30.00	12.00	7.50
275	Tim McCarver	30.00	12.00	7.50
276	Jim Roland	30.00	12.00	7.50
277	Jerry Buchek	30.00	12.00	7.50
278	Checklist 284-370 (Orlando Cepeda)	30.00	12.00	7.50
279	Bill Hands	30.00	12.00	7.50
280	Mickey Mantle	1,900	760.00	475.00
281	Jim Campanis	30.00	12.00	7.50
282	Rick Monday	30.00	12.00	7.50
283	Mel Queen	30.00	12.00	7.50
284	John Briggs	30.00	12.00	7.50
285	Dick McAuliffe	30.00	12.00	7.50
286	Cecil Upshaw	30.00	12.00	7.50
287	White Sox Rookies (*Mickey Abarbanel, Cisco Carlos*)	30.00	12.00	7.50
288	Dave Wickersham	30.00	12.00	7.50
289	Woody Held	30.00	12.00	7.50
290	Willie McCovey	120.00	48.00	30.00
291	Dick Lines	30.00	12.00	7.50
292	Art Shamsky	30.00	12.00	7.50
293	Bruce Howard	30.00	12.00	7.50
294	Red Schoendienst	80.00	32.00	20.00
295	Sonny Siebert	30.00	12.00	7.50
296	Byron Browne	30.00	12.00	7.50
297	Russ Gibson	30.00	12.00	7.50
298	Jim Brewer	30.00	12.00	7.50
299	Gene Michael	30.00	12.00	7.50
300	Rusty Staub	40.00	16.00	10.00
301	Twins Rookies (*George Mitterwald, Rick Renick*)	30.00	12.00	7.50
302	Gerry Arrigo	30.00	12.00	7.50
303	Dick Green	30.00	12.00	7.50
304	Sandy Valdespino	30.00	12.00	7.50
305	Minnie Rojas	30.00	12.00	7.50
306	Mike Ryan	30.00	12.00	7.50
307	John Hiller	30.00	12.00	7.50
308	Pirates Team	50.00	20.00	12.50
309	Ken Henderson	30.00	12.00	7.50
310	Luis Aparicio	150.00	60.00	37.00
311	Jack Lamabe	30.00	12.00	7.50
312	Curt Blefary	30.00	12.00	7.50
313	Al Weis	30.00	12.00	7.50
314	Red Sox Rookies (*Bill Rohr, George Spriggs*)	30.00	12.00	7.50
315	Zoilo Versalles	30.00	12.00	7.50
316	Steve Barber	30.00	12.00	7.50
317	Ron Brand	30.00	12.00	7.50
318	Chico Salmon	30.00	12.00	7.50
319	George Culver	30.00	12.00	7.50
320	Frank Howard	40.00	16.00	10.00
321	Leo Durocher	50.00	20.00	12.50
322	Dave Boswell	30.00	12.00	7.50
323	Deron Johnson	30.00	12.00	7.50
324	Jim Nash	30.00	12.00	7.50
325	Manny Mota	30.00	12.00	7.50
326	Dennis Ribant	30.00	12.00	7.50
327	Tony Taylor	30.00	12.00	7.50
328	Angels Rookies (*Chuck Vinson, Jim Weaver*)	30.00	12.00	7.50
329	Duane Josephson	30.00	12.00	7.50
330	Roger Maris	120.00	48.00	30.00
331	Dan Osinski	30.00	12.00	7.50
332	Doug Rader	30.00	12.00	7.50
333	Ron Herbel	30.00	12.00	7.50
334	Orioles Team	50.00	20.00	12.50
335	Bob Allison	30.00	12.00	7.50
336	John Purdin	30.00	12.00	7.50
337	Bill Robinson	30.00	12.00	7.50
338	Bob Johnson	30.00	12.00	7.50
339	Rich Nye	30.00	12.00	7.50
340	Max Alvis	30.00	12.00	7.50
341	Jim Lemon	30.00	12.00	7.50
342	Ken Johnson	30.00	12.00	7.50
343	Jim Gosger	30.00	12.00	7.50
344	Donn Clendenon	30.00	12.00	7.50
345	Bob Hendley	30.00	12.00	7.50
346	Jerry Adair	30.00	12.00	7.50
347	George Brunet	30.00	12.00	7.50
348	Phillies Rookies (*Larry Colton, Dick Thoenen*)	30.00	12.00	7.50
349	Ed Spiezio	30.00	12.00	7.50

#	Player	NM	EX	VG
350	Hoyt Wilhelm	80.00	32.00	20.00
351	Bob Barton	30.00	12.00	7.50
352	Jackie Hernandez	30.00	12.00	7.50
353	Mack Jones	30.00	12.00	7.50
354	Pete Richert	30.00	12.00	7.50
355	Ernie Banks	130.00	55.00	35.00
356	Checklist 371-457 (Ken Holtzman)	30.00	12.00	7.50
357	Len Gabrielson	30.00	12.00	7.50
358	Mike Epstein	30.00	12.00	7.50
359	Joe Moeller	30.00	12.00	7.50
360	Willie Horton	30.00	12.00	7.50
361	Harmon Killebrew (All-Star)	50.00	20.00	12.50
362	Orlando Cepeda (All-Star)	40.00	16.00	10.00
363	Rod Carew (All-Star)	50.00	20.00	12.50
364	Joe Morgan (All-Star)	40.00	16.00	10.00
365	Brooks Robinson (All-Star)	50.00	20.00	12.50
366	Ron Santo (All-Star)	40.00	16.00	10.00
367	Jim Fregosi (All-Star)	30.00	12.00	7.50
368	Gene Alley (All-Star)	30.00	12.00	7.50
369	Carl Yastrzemski (All-Star)	50.00	20.00	12.50
370	Hank Aaron (All-Star)	250.00	100.00	62.00

1970 Ovenca Venezuelan League

After partial parallels of Topps cards were produced off and on between 1959 and 1968, Venezuelan collectors and fans were offered a completely home-brewed baseball card issue for the 1970-71 winter league season. Similar in quality (i.e., less substantial card stock) to earlier sets, these were printed by Sport Grafico for Ovenca, though neither entity is mentioned on the cards. Slightly larger than 2-1/2" x 3-1/2", cards have large color photos with color stripes above and below bearing player and team name and card number. Backs are printed in black on blue with lengthy comments about the player and his career. Gaps in this checklist will be filled as information comes to light.

	NM	EX	VG
Complete Set (300):	2,250	1,100	650.00
Common Player:	20.00	10.00	6.00
Album:	200.00	100.00	60.00

#	Player	NM	EX	VG
1	Cesar Gutierrez	20.00	10.00	6.00
2	Elio Chacon	20.00	10.00	6.00
3	Luis Rodriguez	20.00	10.00	6.00
4	David Concepcion	75.00	37.50	22.00
5	Roberto Munoz	20.00	10.00	6.00
6	Jesus Rizales	20.00	10.00	6.00
7	Virgilio Mata	20.00	10.00	6.00
8	Manuel Garcia	30.00	15.00	9.00
9	Cesar Garrido	20.00	10.00	6.00
10	Alejandro Tovar	20.00	10.00	6.00
11	William Salazar	20.00	10.00	6.00
12	Jose Lopez	20.00	10.00	6.00
13	Romulo Castillo	20.00	10.00	6.00
14	Victor Jimenez	20.00	10.00	6.00
15	Jose Saiz	20.00	10.00	6.00
16	Wilfredo Calvino	20.00	10.00	6.00
17	Jesus Avila	20.00	10.00	6.00
18	Cruz Rodriguez	20.00	10.00	6.00
19	Julio Bracho	20.00	10.00	6.00
20	David Concepcion, Cesar Gutierrez	25.00	12.50	7.50
21	Double Play (David Concepcion)	25.00	12.50	7.50
22	Tigres de Aragua Logo	10.00	5.00	3.00
23	Orlando Tavares	20.00	10.00	6.00
24	David Concepcion (In Action)	30.00	15.00	9.00
25	Aragua Action		5.00	3.00
26	Aragua Action	10.00	5.00	3.00
27	Cesar Gutierrez	20.00	10.00	6.00
28	Play at Home	10.00	5.00	3.00
29	Joe Foy	20.00	10.00	6.00
30	Dennis Paepke	20.00	10.00	6.00
31	Fred Norman	20.00	10.00	6.00
32	John Purdin	20.00	10.00	6.00
33	Steve Huntz	20.00	10.00	6.00
34	Claide (Clyde) Mashore	20.00	10.00	6.00
35	Steve Mingori	20.00	10.00	6.00
36	Jim Breazeale	20.00	10.00	6.00
37	Charles Day	20.00	10.00	6.00
38	Bob Stinson	20.00	10.00	6.00
39	Phil Hennigan	20.00	10.00	6.00
40	Aragua Checklist (Wilfredo Calvino)	25.00	12.50	7.50
41	Faustino Zabala	20.00	10.00	6.00
42	Pablo Torrealba	20.00	10.00	6.00
43	Erasmo Diaz	20.00	10.00	6.00
44	Sebastian Martinez	20.00	10.00	6.00
45	Neudo Morales	20.00	10.00	6.00
46	Iran Paz	20.00	10.00	6.00

No.	Player			
47	Franklyn Moreno	20.00	10.00	6.00
48	Claudio Urdaneta	20.00	10.00	6.00
49	Dario Chirinos	20.00	10.00	6.00
50	Domingo Carrasquel	20.00	10.00	6.00
51	Enrique Gonzalez	20.00	10.00	6.00
52	Ednio Gonzalez	20.00	10.00	6.00
53	Humberto Donquis	20.00	10.00	6.00
54	Antonio Ruiz	20.00	10.00	6.00
55	Efrain Urquiola	20.00	10.00	6.00
56	Tony Pacheco	20.00	10.00	6.00
57	Lucio Celis	20.00	10.00	6.00
58	Domingo Barboza	20.00	10.00	6.00
59	Faustino Zabala, Neudo Morales	15.00	7.50	4.50
60	Lara Action	10.00	5.00	3.00
61	Tony Pacheco, Lucio Celis, Domingo Barboza	15.00	7.50	4.50
62	Lara Team Logo	10.00	5.00	3.00
63	Alexis Corro	20.00	10.00	6.00
64	Lara Rookies in Action	10.00	5.00	3.00
65	Lara Play at First	10.00	5.00	3.00
66	Lara Play at Home	10.00	5.00	3.00
67	Lara Action	10.00	5.00	3.00
68	Jim Shellenback	20.00	10.00	6.00
69	Scipio Spinks	20.00	10.00	6.00
70	Ken Forsch	20.00	10.00	6.00
71	Oscar Zamora	20.00	10.00	6.00
72	Ronald Cook	20.00	10.00	6.00
73	Jackie Brown	20.00	10.00	6.00
74	Orlando Martinez	20.00	10.00	6.00
75	Bobby Watson	25.00	12.50	7.50
76	Jose Martinez	20.00	10.00	6.00
77	Roger Metzger	20.00	10.00	6.00
78	Tommy Reynolds	20.00	10.00	6.00
79	Cleo James	20.00	10.00	6.00
80	Lara Checkist (Tony Pacheco)	10.00	5.00	3.00
81	Gustavo Gil	20.00	10.00	6.00
82	Jesus Aristimuno	20.00	10.00	6.00
83	Armando Ortiz	20.00	10.00	6.00
84	Orlando Reyes	20.00	10.00	6.00
85	Damaso Blanco	20.00	10.00	6.00
86				
87	Victor Colina	20.00	10.00	6.00
88	Nelson Cana	20.00	10.00	6.00
89	Francisco Diaz	20.00	10.00	6.00
90	Edito Arteaga	20.00	10.00	6.00
91	Concepcion Escalona	20.00	10.00	6.00
92	Gilberto Marcano	20.00	10.00	6.00
93	Luis A. Serrano	20.00	10.00	6.00
94				
95	Raul Ortega	20.00	10.00	6.00
96	Carlos Patato Pascual	20.00	10.00	6.00
97	Leopold Tovar	20.00	10.00	6.00
98	Manuel Gonzalez	20.00	10.00	6.00
99	Magallanes Action	10.00	5.00	3.00
100	Comienza el Partido	20.00	10.00	6.00
101	Magallanes Rookies	15.00	7.50	4.50
102				
103	Marcano en la Lomita	15.00	7.50	4.50
104	Magallanes Fans	10.00	5.00	3.00
105	Magallanes Action	10.00	5.00	3.00
106				
107	Hal King, Jim Holt, Clarence Gaston, Herman Hill	15.00	7.50	4.50
108	Magallanes Caribbean Champions	10.00	5.00	3.00
109				
110	Herman Hill	20.00	10.00	6.00
111	Jim Holt	20.00	10.00	6.00
112	Orlando Pena	20.00	10.00	6.00
113	Magallanes Action	10.00	5.00	3.00
114	Hal King	20.00	10.00	6.00
115	Jorge Lauzerique	20.00	10.00	6.00
116	Rigoberto Mendoza	20.00	10.00	6.00
117	Allan (Alan) Closter	20.00	10.00	6.00
118	Clarence Gaston	25.00	12.50	7.50
119	John Morris	20.00	10.00	6.00
120	Patato Pascual, Unknown	15.00	7.50	4.50
121	Victor Davalillo	20.00	10.00	6.00
122	Cesar Tovar	20.00	10.00	6.00
123	Gonzalo Marquez	20.00	10.00	6.00
124	Luis Penalver	20.00	10.00	6.00
125	Alberto Cambero	20.00	10.00	6.00
126	Urbano Lugo	20.00	10.00	6.00
127	Juan Campos	20.00	10.00	6.00
128	William Castillo	20.00	10.00	6.00
129	Nelson Garcia	20.00	10.00	6.00
130	Ramon Guanchez	20.00	10.00	6.00
131	Jesus Marcano Trillo	40.00	20.00	12.00
132	Manuel Mendible	20.00	10.00	6.00
133	Teodoro Obregon	20.00	10.00	6.00
134	Jesus Padron	20.00	10.00	6.00
135	Ulises Urrieta	20.00	10.00	6.00
136	Antonio "Loco" Torres	20.00	10.00	6.00
137	Leopoldo Posada	20.00	10.00	6.00
138	Pompeyo Davililo	20.00	10.00	6.00
139	Alonso Olivares	20.00	10.00	6.00
140	Cesar Tovar (In Action)	15.00	7.50	4.50
141	Caracas Rookies in Action	15.00	7.50	4.50
142				
143	Andres Barrios	20.00	10.00	6.00
144	Heriberto Morillo	20.00	10.00	6.00
145	Angel Cordova	20.00	10.00	6.00
146	Freddy Rivero	20.00	10.00	6.00
147	Rafael Velasquez	20.00	10.00	6.00
148	Camilo Pascual	30.00	15.00	9.00
149	Cesar Tovar, Vic Davalillo	20.00	10.00	6.00
150	Luis Tiant	30.00	15.00	9.00
151	Roberto Musulungo Hernandez	20.00	10.00	6.00
152	Kurt Devecqua (Bevacqua)	30.00	15.00	9.00
153	Cookie Rojas	30.00	15.00	9.00
154	Larry Howard	20.00	10.00	6.00
155	Rick Scheinblum	20.00	10.00	6.00
156	Diego Segui	25.00	12.50	7.50
157	Gregory Conger	20.00	10.00	6.00
158	Richard Falker (Falkner)	20.00	10.00	6.00

No.	Player			
159	Ed Sprague	20.00	10.00	6.00
160	Zulia Checklist (Pompeyo Davililo)	15.00	7.50	4.50
161	Luis Aparicio	75.00	37.00	22.00
162	Teolindo Acosta	20.00	10.00	6.00
163	Gustavo Sposito	20.00	10.00	6.00
164	Juan Francia	20.00	10.00	6.00
165	Graciliano Parra	20.00	10.00	6.00
166	Simon Salaya	20.00	10.00	6.00
167	Nelson Castellanos	20.00	10.00	6.00
168	Edgar Urbina	20.00	10.00	6.00
169	Luis Gonzalez	20.00	10.00	6.00
170	Olinto Rojas	20.00	10.00	6.00
171	Everest Contramaestre	20.00	10.00	6.00
172	Juan Quiroz	20.00	10.00	6.00
173	Juan Quintana	20.00	10.00	6.00
174	Hugo Bello	20.00	10.00	6.00
175	Jesus Llamozas	20.00	10.00	6.00
176	Luis Aparicio (Manager)	45.00	22.00	13.50
177	Luis Aparicio, Sr.	25.00	12.50	7.50
178	Antonio Brinez	20.00	10.00	6.00
179	Carlos Dickson Bell	20.00	10.00	6.00
180	Alfonso Carrasquel	30.00	15.00	9.00
181	Zulia Action	10.00	5.00	3.00
182	Zulia Eagles Team Logo	20.00	10.00	6.00
183	Nidio Sirit	20.00	10.00	6.00
184	Zulia Action	10.00	5.00	3.00
185	Zulia Eagles Team Photo	10.00	5.00	3.00
186	Bobby Cox (In Action)	20.00	10.00	6.00
187	Zulia Play at Home	10.00	5.00	3.00
188	Alfonso Carrasquel, Luis Aparicio	25.00	12.50	7.50
189	Teolindo Acosta, Gustavo Sposito	15.00	7.50	4.50
190	Leonardo Cardenas	20.00	10.00	6.00
191	Bart Johnson	20.00	10.00	6.00
192	Jerry Crider	20.00	10.00	6.00
193	Getty Janesky (Gerry Janeski)	20.00	10.00	6.00
194	John Matias	20.00	10.00	6.00
195	Walter Williams	25.00	12.50	7.50
196	Steve Hovley	20.00	10.00	6.00
197	Frank Fernandez	20.00	10.00	6.00
198	John Donaldson	20.00	10.00	6.00
199	Donald Eddy	20.00	10.00	6.00
200	Zulia Checklist (Luis Aparicio)	30.00	15.00	9.00
201	Jose Herrera	20.00	10.00	6.00
202	Aurelio Monteagudo	20.00	10.00	6.00
203	Remigio Hermoso	20.00	10.00	6.00
204	Angel Bravo	20.00	10.00	6.00
205	Enzo Hernandez	20.00	10.00	6.00
206	Oswaldo Blanco	20.00	10.00	6.00
207	Carlos Moreno	20.00	10.00	6.00
208	Adolfo Philips (Phillips)	20.00	10.00	6.00
209	Roberto Romero	20.00	10.00	6.00
210	Euclides Camejo	20.00	10.00	6.00
211	Oswaldo Troconis	20.00	10.00	6.00
212	Roberto Marcano	20.00	10.00	6.00
213	Victor Patino	20.00	10.00	6.00
214	Hector Urbano	20.00	10.00	6.00
215	Antonio Pipo Correa	20.00	10.00	6.00
216	Dave Garcia	25.00	12.50	7.50
217	Graciano Ravelo	20.00	10.00	6.00
218	Reinaldo Cordeiro	20.00	10.00	6.00
219	La Guaira Action	10.00	5.00	3.00
220	La Tropa Completa	20.00	10.00	6.00
221	Tomas Liscano Arias	20.00	10.00	6.00
222				
223	Jesus Romero	20.00	10.00	6.00
224	Julian Yanez	20.00	10.00	6.00
225	Enrique Gutierrez	20.00	10.00	6.00
226	Dionel Durand	20.00	10.00	6.00
227	Jose Gregorio Salas	20.00	10.00	6.00
228	Luis Camaleon Garcia	20.00	10.00	6.00
229	Alfredo Ortiz	20.00	10.00	6.00
230	Luis Contreras	20.00	10.00	6.00
231	Ed Spiezio	20.00	10.00	6.00
232	Paul Casanova	25.00	12.50	7.50
233	Mike Epstein	25.00	12.50	7.50
234	Casey Cox	20.00	10.00	6.00
235	Marcelino Lopez	20.00	10.00	6.00
236	Jerry Cram	20.00	10.00	6.00
237	Danny Coombs	20.00	10.00	6.00
238	Del Unser	20.00	10.00	6.00
239	Hector Brito	20.00	10.00	6.00
240	La Guaira Checklist	10.00	5.00	3.00
241	Larry Howard, Richie Scheinblum (In Action)	15.00	7.50	4.50
242	Ed Spiezio (In Action)	15.00	7.50	4.50
243	Clarence Gaston, Cesar Tovar (In Action)	15.00	7.50	4.50
244	Paul Casanova, Unknown	15.00	7.50	4.50
245	Vitico, Cesar Tovar	15.00	7.50	4.50
246	Pasion en el Juego	10.00	5.00	3.00
247	Luis Aparicio (In Action)	35.00	17.50	10.50
248	Angel Bravo (In Action)	15.00	7.50	4.50
249	Bobby Watson (In Action)	20.00	10.00	6.00
250	Alejandro "Palon" Carrasquel (Immortal)	25.00	12.50	7.50
251	Enrique Fonseca (Veteran)	20.00	10.00	6.00
252	Manuel Pollo Malpica (Immortal)	20.00	10.00	6.00
253	Emilio Cueche	20.00	10.00	6.00
254				
255	Felix "Tirahuequito" Machado (Veteran)			
256	Herberto Leal (Veteran)	20.00	10.00	6.00
257	Chucho Ramos (Veteran)	20.00	10.00	6.00
258	Julian Ladera (Veteran)	20.00	10.00	6.00
259	Carlos Ascanio (Veteran)	20.00	10.00	6.00
260	Jose Perez Colmenare (Immortal)	20.00	10.00	6.00
261	Isaias "Latigo" Chaves (Immortal)	20.00	10.00	6.00
262	Victor Garcia (Veteran)	20.00	10.00	6.00
263	Valentin Arevalo (Immortal)	20.00	10.00	6.00

No.	Player			
264	Adolfredo Gonzalez (Veteran)	20.00	10.00	6.00
265	Hector Benitez Redondo (Veteran)	20.00	10.00	6.00
266	Ramon Fernandez (Veteran)	20.00	10.00	6.00
267	Guillermo Vento (Veteran)	20.00	10.00	6.00
268	Rafael Garcia Cedeno (Veteran)	20.00	10.00	6.00
269	Luis Oliveros (Veteran)	20.00	10.00	6.00
270	Luis Mono Zuloaga (Veteran)	20.00	10.00	6.00
271	Carlos Santeliz (Veteran)	20.00	10.00	6.00
272	Aureliano Patino	20.00	10.00	6.00
273	Rafael Olivares (Veteran)	20.00	10.00	6.00
274	Tarzan Contreras (Veteran)	20.00	10.00	6.00
275	Daniel Canonico	20.00	10.00	6.00
276	Babbino Fuenmayor (Veteran)	20.00	10.00	6.00
277	Rafael Galiz Tello (Veteran)	20.00	10.00	6.00
278	Pantaleon Espinoza	20.00	10.00	6.00
279	Miguel Sanabria (Veteran)	20.00	10.00	6.00
280				
281	Alfonso Carrasquel (Veteran)	40.00	20.00	12.00
282	Luis "Camaleon" Garcia (Veteran)	20.00	10.00	6.00
283	Balbino Inojosa (Veteran)	20.00	10.00	6.00
284	Humberto Popita Leal (Veteran)	20.00	10.00	6.00
285	Manuel Carrasquel (Veteran)	20.00	10.00	6.00
286	Ignacio Florez (Veteran)	20.00	10.00	6.00
287	Oscar Buzo Solorzino (Veteran)	20.00	10.00	6.00
288	Pelayo Chacon (Veteran)	20.00	10.00	6.00
289				
290	Micolas Berbesia (Veteran)	20.00	10.00	6.00
291	Julio Bracho (Veteran)	20.00	10.00	6.00
292	Dionisio Acosta (Veteran)	20.00	10.00	6.00
293	Gualberto Acosta (Veteran)	20.00	10.00	6.00
294	Winston Acosta (Veteran)	20.00	10.00	6.00
295	Jose Manuel Tovar (Veteran)	20.00	10.00	6.00
296	Carrao Bracho (Veteran)	20.00	10.00	6.00
297	Luis Romero Petit (Veteran)	20.00	10.00	6.00
298	Dalmiro Finol (Veteran)	20.00	10.00	6.00
299	Cerveceria Caracas Team Photo	20.00	10.00	6.00
300	Magallanes Campeones Nacionales Team	20.00	10.00	6.00

1972 Venezuelan Baseball Stamps

Utilizing most of the same photos as the 1972 Topps baseball cards, the 242 player stamps in this set feature only Major Leaguers, though with an overrepresentation of Hispanics, rather than the usual mix of U.S. and local talent. Stamps measure 2" x 2-9/16" and feature tombstone-shaped color photos at center, surrounded by a green background. The only printing is the player name, team name (in Spanish) and stamp number, all in black. A white border surrounds the whole. Backs are blank as the stamps were meant to be mounted in an album. Because stamps are seldom seen in higher grade, only a VG price is presented here. Stamps in Good should be valued at 50 percent of the price shown, and stamps grading Fair at 25 percent.

	NM	EX	VG
Complete Set (242):	4,900	1,950	980.00
Common Player:	15.00	6.00	3.00
Album:	150.00	75.00	45.00
1 Vic Davalillo	50.00	20.00	10.00
2 Doug Griffin	15.00	6.00	3.00
3 Rod Carew	150.00	60.00	30.00
4 Joel Horlen	15.00	6.00	3.00
5 Jim Fregosi	15.00	6.00	3.00
6 Rod Carew ("en acion" - In Action)	100.00	40.00	20.00
7 Billy Champion	15.00	6.00	3.00
8 Ron Hansen	15.00	6.00	3.00
9 Bobby Murcer	15.00	6.00	3.00
10 Nellie Briles	15.00	6.00	3.00
11 Fred Patek	15.00	6.00	3.00
12 Mike Epstein	15.00	6.00	3.00
13 Dave Marshall	15.00	6.00	3.00
14 Steve Hargan	15.00	6.00	3.00
15 Duane Josephson	15.00	6.00	3.00
16 Steve Garvey	22.50	9.00	4.50
17 Eddie Fisher	15.00	6.00	3.00
18 Jack Aker	15.00	6.00	3.00
19 Ron Brand	15.00	6.00	3.00

#	Player			
20	Del Rice	15.00	6.00	3.00
21	Ollie Brown	15.00	6.00	3.00
22	Jamie McAndrew	15.00	6.00	3.00
23	Willie Horton	15.00	6.00	3.00
24	Eddie Leon	15.00	6.00	3.00
25	Steve Hovley	15.00	6.00	3.00
26	Moe Drabowsky	15.00	6.00	3.00
27	Dick Selma	15.00	6.00	3.00
28	Jim Lyttle	15.00	6.00	3.00
29	Sal Bando	15.00	6.00	3.00
30	Bill Lee	15.00	6.00	3.00
31	Al Kaline	150.00	60.00	30.00
32	Mike Lum	15.00	6.00	3.00
33	Les Cain	15.00	6.00	3.00
34	Richie Hebner	15.00	6.00	3.00
35	Donn Clendenon	15.00	6.00	3.00
36	Ralph Houk	15.00	6.00	3.00
37	Luis Melendez	15.00	6.00	3.00
38	Jim Hickman	15.00	6.00	3.00
39	Manny Mota	15.00	6.00	3.00
40	Bob Locker	15.00	6.00	3.00
41	Ron Santo	20.00	8.00	4.00
42	Tony Cloninger	15.00	6.00	3.00
43	Joe Ferguson	15.00	6.00	3.00
44	Mike McCormick	15.00	6.00	3.00
45	Bobby Wine	15.00	6.00	3.00
46	Preston Gomez	15.00	6.00	3.00
47	Pat Corrales (In Action)	15.00	6.00	3.00
48	Hector Torres	15.00	6.00	3.00
49	Fritz Peterson	15.00	6.00	3.00
50	Jim Rooker	15.00	6.00	3.00
51	Chris Short	15.00	6.00	3.00
52	Juan Marichal (In Action)	22.50	9.00	4.50
53	Teddy Martinez	15.00	6.00	3.00
54	Ken Aspromonte	15.00	6.00	3.00
55	Bobby Bonds	15.00	6.00	3.00
56	Rich Robertson	15.00	6.00	3.00
57	Nate Colbert (In Action)	15.00	6.00	3.00
58	Jose Pagan (In Action)	15.00	6.00	3.00
59	Curt Blefary (In Action)	15.00	6.00	3.00
60	Bill Mazeroski	100.00	40.00	20.00
61	John Odom	15.00	6.00	3.00
62	George Stone	15.00	6.00	3.00
63	Lew Krausse	15.00	6.00	3.00
64	Bobby Knoop	15.00	6.00	3.00
65	Pete Rose (In Action)	225.00	90.00	45.00
66	Steve Luebber	15.00	6.00	3.00
67	Bill Voss	15.00	6.00	3.00
68	Chico Salmon	15.00	6.00	3.00
69	Ivan Murrell	15.00	6.00	3.00
70	Gil Garrido	15.00	6.00	3.00
71	Terry Crowley	15.00	6.00	3.00
72	Bill Russell	15.00	6.00	3.00
73	Steve Dunning	15.00	6.00	3.00
74	Ray Sadecki (In Action)	15.00	6.00	3.00
75	Al Gallagher (In Action)	15.00	6.00	3.00
76	Cesar Gutierrez	15.00	6.00	3.00
77	John Kennedy	15.00	6.00	3.00
78	Joe Hague	15.00	6.00	3.00
79	Bruce Del Canton	15.00	6.00	3.00
80	Ken Holtzman	15.00	6.00	3.00
81	Rico Carty	15.00	6.00	3.00
82	Roger Repoz	15.00	6.00	3.00
83	Fran Healy	15.00	6.00	3.00
84	Al Gallagher	15.00	6.00	3.00
85	Rich McKinney	15.00	6.00	3.00
86	Lowell Palmer	15.00	6.00	3.00
87	Jose Cardenal	15.00	6.00	3.00
88	Ed Kirkpatrick (In Action)	15.00	6.00	3.00
89	Steve Carlton	150.00	60.00	30.00
90	Gail Hopkins	15.00	6.00	3.00
91	Reggie Smith	15.00	6.00	3.00
92	Denny Riddleberger	15.00	6.00	3.00
93	Don Sutton	60.00	24.00	12.00
94	Bob Moose	15.00	6.00	3.00
95	Joe Decker	15.00	6.00	3.00
96	Bill Wilson	15.00	6.00	3.00
97	Mike Ferraro	15.00	6.00	3.00
98	Jack Hiatt	15.00	6.00	3.00
99	Bill Grabarkewitz	15.00	6.00	3.00
100	Larry Stahl	15.00	6.00	3.00
101	Jim Slaton	15.00	6.00	3.00
102	Jim Wynn	15.00	6.00	3.00
103	Phil Niekro	60.00	24.00	12.00
104	Danny Cater	15.00	6.00	3.00
105	Ray Sadecki	15.00	6.00	3.00
106	Jack Billingham	15.00	6.00	3.00
107	Dave Nelson	15.00	6.00	3.00
108	Rudy May	15.00	6.00	3.00
109	Don Money	15.00	6.00	3.00
110	Diego Segui	15.00	6.00	3.00
111	Jose Pagan	15.00	6.00	3.00
112	John Strohmayer	15.00	6.00	3.00
113	Wade Blasingame	15.00	6.00	3.00
114	Ken Wright	15.00	6.00	3.00
115	Ken Tatum	15.00	6.00	3.00
116	Mike Paul	15.00	6.00	3.00
117	Tom McCraw	15.00	6.00	3.00
118	Bob Gibson	125.00	50.00	25.00
119	Al Santorini	15.00	6.00	3.00
120	Leo Cardenas	15.00	6.00	3.00
121	Jimmy Stewart	15.00	6.00	3.00
122	Willie Crawford	15.00	6.00	3.00
123	Bob Aspromonte	15.00	6.00	3.00
124	Frank Duffy	15.00	6.00	3.00
125	Hal Lanier	15.00	6.00	3.00
126	Nate Colbert	15.00	6.00	3.00
127	Russ Gibson	15.00	6.00	3.00
128	Cesar Geronimo	15.00	6.00	3.00
129	Pat Kelly	15.00	6.00	3.00
130	Horacio Pina	15.00	6.00	3.00
131	Charlie Brinkman	15.00	6.00	3.00
132	Bill Virdon	15.00	6.00	3.00
133	Hal McRae	15.00	6.00	3.00
134	Tony Oliva (In Action)	25.00	10.00	5.00
135	Gonzalo Marquez	15.00	6.00	3.00
136	Willie Montanez	15.00	6.00	3.00
137	Dick Green	15.00	6.00	3.00
138	Jim Ray	15.00	6.00	3.00
139	Denis Menke	15.00	6.00	3.00
140	Fred Kendall	15.00	6.00	3.00
141	Vida Blue	15.00	6.00	3.00
142	Tom Grieve	15.00	6.00	3.00
143	Ed Kirkpatrick (In Action)	15.00	6.00	3.00
144	George Scott	15.00	6.00	3.00
145	Hal Breeden	15.00	6.00	3.00
146	Ken McMullen	15.00	6.00	3.00
147	Jim Perry (In Action)	15.00	6.00	3.00
148	Wayne Granger	15.00	6.00	3.00
149	Mike Hegan	15.00	6.00	3.00
150	Al Oliver	20.00	8.00	4.00
151	Frank Robinson (In Action)	100.00	40.00	20.00
152	Paul Blair	15.00	6.00	3.00
153	Phil Hennigan	15.00	6.00	3.00
154	Ron Stone	15.00	6.00	3.00
155	Gene Michael	15.00	6.00	3.00
156	Jerry McNertney	15.00	6.00	3.00
157	Marcelino Lopez	15.00	6.00	3.00
158	Dave May	15.00	6.00	3.00
159	Jim Hart	15.00	6.00	3.00
160	Joe Coleman	15.00	6.00	3.00
161	Rick Reichardt	15.00	6.00	3.00
162	Ed Brinkman	15.00	6.00	3.00
163	Dick McAuliffe	15.00	6.00	3.00
164	Paul Doyle	15.00	6.00	3.00
165	Terry Forster	15.00	6.00	3.00
166	Steve Hamilton	15.00	6.00	3.00
167	Mike Corkins	15.00	6.00	3.00
168	Dave Concepcion	75.00	30.00	15.00
169	Bill Sudakis	15.00	6.00	3.00
170	Juan Marichal	100.00	40.00	20.00
171	Harmon Killebrew	150.00	60.00	30.00
172	Luis Tiant	20.00	8.00	4.00
173	Ted Uhlaender	15.00	6.00	3.00
174	Tim Foli	15.00	6.00	3.00
175	Luis Aparicio (In Action)	200.00	80.00	40.00
176	Bert Campaneris	15.00	6.00	3.00
177	Charlie Sands	15.00	6.00	3.00
178	Darold Knowles	15.00	6.00	3.00
179	Jerry Koosman	15.00	6.00	3.00
180	Leo Cardenas (In Action)	15.00	6.00	3.00
181	Luis Alvarado	15.00	6.00	3.00
182	Graig Nettles	17.50	7.00	3.50
183	Walter Alston	20.00	8.00	4.00
184	Nolan Ryan	550.00	220.00	110.00
185	Ed Sprague	15.00	6.00	3.00
186	Rich Reese	15.00	6.00	3.00
187	Pete Rose	300.00	120.00	60.00
188	Bernie Allen	15.00	6.00	3.00
189	Lou Piniella	17.50	7.00	3.50
190	Jerry Reuss	15.00	6.00	3.00
191	Bob Pfeil	15.00	6.00	3.00
192	Bob Burda	15.00	6.00	3.00
193	Walt Williams	15.00	6.00	3.00
194	Dusty Baker	17.50	7.00	3.50
195	Rich Morales	15.00	6.00	3.00
196	Bill Stoneman	15.00	6.00	3.00
197	Hal King	15.00	6.00	3.00
198	Julian Javier	15.00	6.00	3.00
199	Dave Mason	15.00	6.00	3.00
200	Bob Veale	15.00	6.00	3.00
201	Jim Beauchamp	15.00	6.00	3.00
202	Ron Santo (In Action)	17.50	7.00	3.50
203	Tom Seaver	150.00	60.00	30.00
204	Jim Merritt	15.00	6.00	3.00
205	Jerry Koosman (In Action)	15.00	6.00	3.00
206	Dick Woodson	15.00	6.00	3.00
207	Wayne Simpson	15.00	6.00	3.00
208	Jose Laboy	15.00	6.00	3.00
209	Sam McDowell	15.00	6.00	3.00
210	Bob Bailey	15.00	6.00	3.00
211	Jim Fairey	15.00	6.00	3.00
212	Felipe Alou	25.00	10.00	5.00
213	Dave Concepcion (In Action)	50.00	20.00	10.00
214	Wilbur Wood (In Action)	15.00	6.00	3.00
215	Enzo Hernandez	15.00	6.00	3.00
216	Ron Reed	15.00	6.00	3.00
217	Stan Bahnsen	15.00	6.00	3.00
218	Ollie Brown (In Action)	15.00	6.00	3.00
219	Pat Jarvis	15.00	6.00	3.00
220	Tim Foli (In Action)	15.00	6.00	3.00
221	Denny McLain	15.00	6.00	3.00
222	Jerry Grote	15.00	6.00	3.00
223	Davey Johnson	15.00	6.00	3.00
224	John Odom (In Action)	15.00	6.00	3.00
225	Paul Casanova	15.00	6.00	3.00
226	George Culver	15.00	6.00	3.00
227	Pat Corrales	15.00	6.00	3.00
228	Jim Kaat	15.00	6.00	3.00
229	Archie Reynolds	15.00	6.00	3.00
230	Frank Reberger	15.00	6.00	3.00
231	Carl Yastrzemski	150.00	60.00	30.00
232	Jim Holt	15.00	6.00	3.00
233	Lenny Randle	15.00	6.00	3.00
234	Doug Griffin (In Action)	15.00	6.00	3.00
235	Doug Rader	15.00	6.00	3.00
236	Jesus Alou	15.00	6.00	3.00
237	Wilbur Wood (In Action)	15.00	6.00	3.00
238	Jim Kaat (In Action)	15.00	6.00	3.00
239	Fritz Peterson (In Action)	15.00	6.00	3.00
240	Dennis Leonard	15.00	6.00	3.00
241	Brooks Robinson	150.00	60.00	30.00
242	Felix Millan	15.00	6.00	3.00

LEW KRAUSSE

cartouche at bottom. The sticker number is in a circle at top-right. Because they were intended to be mounted in an accompanying album, the backs are blank. Because so many of the stickers were once pasted into albums, and due to unfavorable climactic conditions, high-grade examples of Venezuelan stickers from the era are particularly scarce.

1972 Venezuelan League Stickers

Issued in the winter league season of 1972-73, the Venezuelan League sticker set bears more than a passing similitude to the 1972 Topps baseball cards. The 2-1/2" x 3-1/2" stickers have tombstone-shaped photos framed in multi-colored borders with the team name at top and the player name in an oval

		NM	EX	VG
Complete Set (249):		1,500	750.00	450.00
Common Player:		20.00	10.00	6.00
Album:		75.00	40.00	20.00
1	Dave Concepcion	30.00	15.00	9.00
2	Luis Rodriguez	25.00	12.50	7.50
3	Roberto Munoz	25.00	12.50	7.50
4	William Castillo	25.00	12.50	7.50
5	Jose Lopez	25.00	12.50	7.50
6	Armando Chacon	25.00	12.50	7.50
7	Juan Francia	25.00	12.50	7.50
8	Roric Harrison	25.00	12.50	7.50
9	Dave Concepcion, Escalona	30.00	15.00	9.00
10	Enrique Gutierrez	25.00	12.50	7.50
11	Luis Gonzalez	25.00	12.50	7.50
12	Jose Torres	25.00	12.50	7.50
13	William Salazar	25.00	12.50	7.50
14	Everest Contramaestre	25.00	12.50	7.50
15	Jesus Rizales	25.00	12.50	7.50
16	Ramon Velasquez	25.00	12.50	7.50
17	Rafael J. Velasquez	25.00	12.50	7.50
18	Jesus Loreto	25.00	12.50	7.50
19	Orlando Galindo	25.00	12.50	7.50
20	Jose Torres	25.00	12.50	7.50
21	Victor Jimenez	25.00	12.50	7.50
22	Hernan Silva	25.00	12.50	7.50
23	Leroy Stanton	25.00	12.50	7.50
24	Jesus Yanez	25.00	12.50	7.50
25	Orlando Tavares	25.00	12.50	7.50
26	Eddie Baez	25.00	12.50	7.50
27	Jim Frey	30.00	15.00	9.00
28	Eddie Watt	25.00	12.50	7.50
29	Aragua Team Logo	10.00	5.00	3.00
30	Carlos Orea	25.00	12.50	7.50
31	Rod Carew	75.00	37.00	22.00
32	Rod Carew, Enos Cabell	35.00	17.50	10.50
33	George Mitterwald	25.00	12.50	7.50
34	Enos Cabell	25.00	12.50	7.50
35	Eddy Baez	25.00	12.50	7.50
36	Teolindo Acosta	25.00	12.50	7.50
37	Ron Theobald	25.00	12.50	7.50
38	Milt Wilcox	30.00	15.00	9.00
39	Cesar Gutierrez	25.00	12.50	7.50
40	Ed Farmer	25.00	12.50	7.50
41	Dario Chirinos	25.00	12.50	7.50
42	Alberto Cambero	25.00	12.50	7.50
43	Eddy Diaz	25.00	12.50	7.50
44	Graciliano Parra	25.00	12.50	7.50
45	Bob Lee	25.00	12.50	7.50
46	Joe Keough	25.00	12.50	7.50
47	Dario Chirinos, Pablo Torrealba	25.00	12.50	7.50
48	Rafael Alvarez	25.00	12.50	7.50
49	Lucio Celis	25.00	12.50	7.50
50	Jose Martinez	25.00	12.50	7.50
51	Faustino Zabala	25.00	12.50	7.50
52	Jose Herrera	25.00	12.50	7.50
53	Monty Montgomery	25.00	12.50	7.50
54	Al Cowens	25.00	12.50	7.50
55	Lara Team	10.00	5.00	3.00
56	Luis Aparicio	60.00	30.00	18.00
57	Virgilio Mata	25.00	12.50	7.50
58	Franklin Moreno	25.00	12.50	7.50
59	Fidel Garcia	25.00	12.50	7.50
60	Victor Montilla	25.00	12.50	7.50
61	Bobby Mitchell	25.00	12.50	7.50
62	Pablo Torrealba	25.00	12.50	7.50
63	Joe Keough	25.00	12.50	7.50
64	Al Cowens	25.00	12.50	7.50
65	Dwight Evans	35.00	17.50	10.50
66	Rick Henninger	25.00	12.50	7.50
67	Lew Krausse	25.00	12.50	7.50
68	George Manz	25.00	12.50	7.50
69	John Lowenstein	25.00	12.50	7.50
70	Juan Quiroz	25.00	12.50	7.50
71	Sebastian Martinez	25.00	12.50	7.50
72	Claudio Urdaneta	25.00	12.50	7.50
73	Barry Raziano	25.00	12.50	7.50
74	Luis Aparicio	60.00	30.00	18.00
75	Lara Team Logo	10.00	5.00	3.00
76	Bobby Mitchell	25.00	12.50	7.50
77	Harold Hunter	25.00	12.50	7.50
78	Dick Pole	25.00	12.50	7.50
79	Carlos Davila	25.00	12.50	7.50
80	Enrique Gonzalez	25.00	12.50	7.50
81	Carlos Pascual	25.00	12.50	7.50

		NM	EX	VG
82	Edito Arteaga	25.00	12.50	7.50
83	William Fahey	25.00	12.50	7.50
84	Tomas Gonzalez	25.00	12.50	7.50
85	Rigoberto Mendoza	25.00	12.50	7.50
86	Rafael Jimenez	25.00	12.50	7.50
87	Jesus Aristimuno	25.00	12.50	7.50
88	Armando Ortiz	25.00	12.50	7.50
89	Bill Butler	25.00	12.50	7.50
90	Charles Day	25.00	12.50	7.50
91	Miguel Motolongo	25.00	12.50	7.50
92	Kurt Bavacqua (Bevacqua)	25.00	12.50	7.50
93	Esteban Padron	25.00	12.50	7.50
94	Angel Baez	25.00	12.50	7.50
95	Oscar Zamora	25.00	12.50	7.50
96	Manny Sarmiento	25.00	12.50	7.50
97	Nelson Canas	25.00	12.50	7.50
98	Victor Colina	25.00	12.50	7.50
99	Jerry Pirtle	25.00	12.50	7.50
100	Charles Day	25.00	12.50	7.50
101	Miguel Motolongo	25.00	12.50	7.50
102	Magallanes Group Photo	10.00	5.00	3.00
103	Jim Holt	25.00	12.50	7.50
104	Bob Darwin	25.00	12.50	7.50
105	Magallanes Team Logo	10.00	5.00	3.00
106	Oscar Del Busto	25.00	12.50	7.50
107	Jerry Jones	25.00	12.50	7.50
108	Eddie Leon	25.00	12.50	7.50
109	Armando Ortiz	25.00	12.50	7.50
110	Magallanes Team Photo	10.00	5.00	3.00
111	Magallanes Team Photo	10.00	5.00	3.00
112	Bob Darwin (puzzle)	10.00	5.00	3.00
113	Bob Darwin	25.00	12.50	7.50
114	Rafael Cariel	25.00	12.50	7.50
115	Bob Darwin (Puzzle)	10.00	5.00	3.00
116	Bob Darwin (Puzzle)	10.00	5.00	3.00
117	Orlando Reyes	25.00	12.50	7.50
118	Edito Arteaga	25.00	12.50	7.50
119	Magallanes Roster (Carlos Pascual)	10.00	5.00	3.00
120	National Anthem	10.00	5.00	3.00
121	Barry Lersch	25.00	12.50	7.50
122	Elias Lugo	25.00	12.50	7.50
123	Simon Barreto	25.00	12.50	7.50
124	Manny Trillo	25.00	12.50	7.50
125	Joe Ferguson	25.00	12.50	7.50
126	Wilibaldo Quintana	25.00	12.50	7.50
127	Edgar Urbina	25.00	12.50	7.50
128	Nelson Garcia	25.00	12.50	7.50
129	Arguilio Freites	25.00	12.50	7.50
130	Carlos Rodriguez	25.00	12.50	7.50
131	Ozzie Virgil	25.00	12.50	7.50
132	Caracas Lions Team Logo	10.00	5.00	3.00
133	Virgilio Velasquez	25.00	12.50	7.50
134	Ed Sprague	25.00	12.50	7.50
135	Nelson Garcia	25.00	12.50	7.50
136	Jose Caldera	25.00	12.50	7.50
137	Antonio Armas	30.00	15.00	9.00
138	Dick Lange	25.00	12.50	7.50
139	Luis Sanz	25.00	12.50	7.50
140	Dave Lopez	25.00	12.50	7.50
141	Ulises Urrieta	25.00	12.50	7.50
142	Urbano Lugo	25.00	12.50	7.50
143	Bo Diaz	25.00	12.50	7.50
144	Andres Barrios	25.00	12.50	7.50
145	Victor Boll	25.00	12.50	7.50
146	Antonio Torres	25.00	12.50	7.50
147	Bert Campaneris	30.00	15.00	9.00
148	Carlos Alfonzo	25.00	12.50	7.50
149	Teodoro Obregon	25.00	12.50	7.50
150	Luis Penalver	25.00	12.50	7.50
151	Jose Ramon Jimenez	25.00	12.50	7.50
152	Cesar Tovar	25.00	12.50	7.50
153	Gonzalo Marquez	25.00	12.50	7.50
154	Dick Baney	25.00	12.50	7.50
155	Ed Armbrister	25.00	12.50	7.50
156	Ramon Webster	25.00	12.50	7.50
157	Francisco Navas	25.00	12.50	7.50
158	Hal McRae	25.00	12.50	7.50
159	Victor Davilillo	25.00	12.50	7.50
160	Geoff Zahn	25.00	12.50	7.50
161	Jesus Camacaro	25.00	12.50	7.50
162	Ruiz, Parra	25.00	12.50	7.50
163	Posada, Dick Billings	25.00	12.50	7.50
164	Tom Grieve	25.00	12.50	7.50
165	Tom Grieve	25.00	12.50	7.50
166	Dick Billings	25.00	12.50	7.50
167	Peter Broberg	25.00	12.50	7.50
168	Victor Fainette	25.00	12.50	7.50
169	Cruz Rodriguez	25.00	12.50	7.50
170	Oscar Gamble	25.00	12.50	7.50
171	Olinto Rojas	25.00	12.50	7.50
172	Nelson Paiva	25.00	12.50	7.50
173	Jackie Brown	25.00	12.50	7.50
174	Gustavo Sposito	25.00	12.50	7.50
175	Levy Ochoa	25.00	12.50	7.50
176	Larry Bittner (Biittner)	25.00	12.50	7.50
177	William Kirkpatrick	25.00	12.50	7.50
178	Nevil Romero	25.00	12.50	7.50
179	Eduardo Benitez	25.00	12.50	7.50
180	Heriberto Lemus	25.00	12.50	7.50
181	Toby Harrah	25.00	12.50	7.50
182	Alfonzo Collazo	25.00	12.50	7.50
183	Jesus Reyes	25.00	12.50	7.50
184	Hely Boscan	25.00	12.50	7.50
185	Mike (Mickey) Scott	25.00	12.50	7.50
186	Roberto Bracho	25.00	12.50	7.50
187	Walter William (Williams)	25.00	12.50	7.50
188	Nevil Romero	25.00	12.50	7.50
189	Jose Alfaro	25.00	12.50	7.50
190	Leonel Carrion	25.00	12.50	7.50
191	Jesus Padron	25.00	12.50	7.50
192	Posada, Chico Carrasquel	25.00	12.50	7.50
193	Domingo Barboza	25.00	12.50	7.50
194	Eduardo Benitez	25.00	12.50	7.50
195	Nidio Sirit	25.00	12.50	7.50
196	Jose Carrao Bracho	25.00	12.50	7.50
197	Levi Ochoa	25.00	12.50	7.50
198	Hely Boscan	25.00	12.50	7.50
199	Victor Fainette, Leonel Carrion	25.00	12.50	7.50
200	Luis Rivas	25.00	12.50	7.50
201	Luis Tiant	25.00	12.50	7.50
202	Graciano Ravelo	25.00	12.50	7.50
203	Hector Artiles	25.00	12.50	7.50
204	Enzo Hernandez	25.00	12.50	7.50
205	Remigio Hermoso	25.00	12.50	7.50
206	Hector Brito	25.00	12.50	7.50
207	Victor Patino	25.00	12.50	7.50
208	Romualdo Blanco	25.00	12.50	7.50
209	Antonio Carrera	25.00	12.50	7.50
210	Euclides Camejo	25.00	12.50	7.50
211	Carlos Moreno	25.00	12.50	7.50
212	Oswaldo Blanco	25.00	12.50	7.50
213	Jorge Padron	25.00	12.50	7.50
214	Manuel Garcia	25.00	12.50	7.50
215	La Guaira Group Photo	10.00	5.00	3.00
216	La Guaira Group Photo	10.00	5.00	3.00
217	Jose Salas	25.00	12.50	7.50
218	Luis Sanchez	25.00	12.50	7.50
219	Raul Velarde	25.00	12.50	7.50
220	Al Bumbry	25.00	12.50	7.50
221	Group Photo	10.00	5.00	3.00
222	Ivan Murrell	25.00	12.50	7.50
223	Jose Cardenal	25.00	12.50	7.50
224	Group Photo	10.00	5.00	3.00
225	Group Photo	10.00	5.00	3.00
226	Angel Bravo	25.00	12.50	7.50
227	Tom Murphy	25.00	12.50	7.50
228	Hector Urbano	25.00	12.50	7.50
229	Camilo Pascual	25.00	12.50	7.50
230	Pat Kelly	25.00	12.50	7.50
231	Robert Marcano	25.00	12.50	7.50
232	Paul Casanova	25.00	12.50	7.50
233	Preston Gomez	25.00	12.50	7.50
234	La Guaira Team Logo	10.00	5.00	3.00
235	Ken Forsch	25.00	12.50	7.50
236	Luis Tiant (puzzle)	10.00	5.00	3.00
237	Luis Tiant (puzzle)	10.00	5.00	3.00
238	Dionel Durand	25.00	12.50	7.50
239	Luis Tiant (puzzle)	10.00	5.00	3.00
240	Luis Tiant (puzzle)	10.00	5.00	3.00
241	Jim Rooker (puzzle)	10.00	5.00	3.00
242	Jim Rooker (puzzle)	10.00	5.00	3.00
243	William Parker	25.00	12.50	7.50
244	Jim Rooker (puzzle)	10.00	5.00	3.00
245	Jim Rooker (puzzle)	10.00	5.00	3.00
246	Jose Herrera	25.00	12.50	7.50
247	Aurelio Monteagudo	25.00	12.50	7.50
248	Ivan Murrell	25.00	12.50	7.50
249	Roster (Preston Gomez)	10.00	5.00	3.00

1973 Venezuelan League Stickers

These stickers were made for collection in an album and as such are typically found in low grade and/or with evidence of once having been so mounted. Several gaps in the reported checklist require further research. Many former and future Major Leaguers are included in the issue. The basic player stickers have color photos surrounded by a multi-color border with the team name at top and the player name at bottom. Stickers are about 2-1/2" x 3-1/2" and numbered on front. A colorful album to house the set was also issued.

		NM	EX	VG
Common Player:		20.00	10.00	6.00
Album:		75.00	40.00	25.00
1	Orlando Galindo	20.00	10.00	6.00
2	William Castillo	20.00	10.00	6.00
3	Everest Contramaestre	20.00	10.00	6.00
4	Luis Gonzalez	20.00	10.00	6.00
5	Jose Lopez	20.00	10.00	6.00
6	Cesar Orea	20.00	10.00	6.00
7	Luis H. Silva	20.00	10.00	6.00
8	Victor Jimenez	20.00	10.00	6.00
9	David Torres	20.00	10.00	6.00
10	Jose Torres	20.00	10.00	6.00
11	Ramon Velasquez	20.00	10.00	6.00
12	Jesus Avila	20.00	10.00	6.00
13	Carlos Loreto	20.00	10.00	6.00
14	Jesus Padron	20.00	10.00	6.00
15	Don Osborne	20.00	10.00	6.00
16	John Glass	20.00	10.00	6.00
17	Teolindo Acosta	20.00	10.00	6.00
18	Jim Todd	20.00	10.00	6.00
19	Roberto Munoz	20.00	10.00	6.00
20	Pete Lakock (LaCock)	20.00	10.00	6.00
21	Francisco Leandro	20.00	10.00	6.00
22	Jesus Rizales	20.00	10.00	6.00
23	Enos Cabell	25.00	12.50	7.50
24	Adrian Garret (Garrett)	20.00	10.00	6.00
25	Kurt Bavaqua (Bevacqua)	20.00	10.00	6.00
26	Jerry Moses	20.00	10.00	6.00
27	Jim Wiloughby (Willoughby)	20.00	10.00	6.00
28	Joel Youngblood	20.00	10.00	6.00
29	Milt Wilcox	25.00	12.50	7.50
30	Cesar Gutierrez	20.00	10.00	6.00
31	Efrain Urquiola	20.00	10.00	6.00
32	Carlos Pascual	20.00	10.00	6.00
33	Julio Bracho	20.00	10.00	6.00
34	Rafael Velasquez	20.00	10.00	6.00
35	Eddy Baez	20.00	10.00	6.00
36	Daniel Dubuc	20.00	10.00	6.00
37	Angel Leon	20.00	10.00	6.00
38	Angel Vargas	20.00	10.00	6.00
39	Motis Romero	20.00	10.00	6.00
40	Graciliano Parra	20.00	10.00	6.00
41	John Lowenstein	20.00	10.00	6.00
42	Nelson Garcia	20.00	10.00	6.00
43	Richard Burleson	25.00	12.50	7.50
44	Doug DeCinces	35.00	17.50	10.50
45	Eugene Martin	20.00	10.00	6.00
46	Jim Cox	20.00	10.00	6.00
47	Mike Adams	20.00	10.00	6.00
48	Richard Henninger	20.00	10.00	6.00
49	Sebastian Martinez	20.00	10.00	6.00
50	Lucio Celis	20.00	10.00	6.00
51	Alberto Cambero	20.00	10.00	6.00
52	Claudio Urdaneta	20.00	10.00	6.00
53	Victor Montilla	20.00	10.00	6.00
54	Pastor Perez	20.00	10.00	6.00
55	Enrique Gonzalez	20.00	10.00	6.00
56	Andres Barrios	20.00	10.00	6.00
57	Diego Herrera	20.00	10.00	6.00
58	Luis Aparicio	60.00	30.00	18.00
59	Teodoro Obregon	20.00	10.00	6.00
60	Dave Johnson	25.00	12.50	7.50
61	Roger Polanco	20.00	10.00	6.00
62	Ray Miller	20.00	10.00	6.00
63	Craig Caskey	20.00	10.00	6.00
64	David Wallace	20.00	10.00	6.00
65	Lara Team Logo	10.00	5.00	3.00
66	Herbert Hutson	20.00	10.00	6.00
67	Edgar Carusi	20.00	10.00	6.00
68	Luis Aponte	20.00	10.00	6.00
69	Joel Alcala	20.00	10.00	6.00
70	Dario Chirinos	20.00	10.00	6.00
71	Arnaldo Alvarado	20.00	10.00	6.00
72	Jose Bekis	20.00	10.00	6.00
73	Bill Moran	20.00	10.00	6.00
74	Steve McCartney	20.00	10.00	6.00
75	Lara Action	10.00	5.00	3.00
76	Rafael Alvarez	20.00	10.00	6.00
77	Juan Quiroz	20.00	10.00	6.00
78	Jim Rice	125.00	62.00	37.00
79	Ivan Murrel (Murrell)	20.00	10.00	6.00
80	James McKee	20.00	10.00	6.00
81	Rafael Cariel	20.00	10.00	6.00
82	George Theodore	20.00	10.00	6.00
83	Esteban Padron	20.00	10.00	6.00
84	Manuel Gonzalez	20.00	10.00	6.00
85	Edito Arteaga	20.00	10.00	6.00
86	Gus Gil	20.00	10.00	6.00
87	Oswaldo Olivares	20.00	10.00	6.00
88	Nelson Canas	20.00	10.00	6.00
89	Jesus Aristimuno	20.00	10.00	6.00
90	Orlando Reyes	20.00	10.00	6.00
91	Armando Ortiz	20.00	10.00	6.00
92	Gregorio Machado	20.00	10.00	6.00
93	Victor Colina	20.00	10.00	6.00
94	Alexis Ramirez	20.00	10.00	6.00
95	Jose Rios-Chiripa	20.00	10.00	6.00
96	Ed Napoleon	20.00	10.00	6.00
97	Bob Bailor	25.00	12.50	7.50
98	Dave Agustine (Augustine)	20.00	10.00	6.00
99	Bob Darwin	20.00	10.00	6.00
100	Gilberto Marcano	20.00	10.00	6.00
101	Jim Frey	25.00	12.50	7.50
102	Steve Braun	20.00	10.00	6.00
103	Don Hood	20.00	10.00	6.00
104	Mike Reinbach	20.00	10.00	6.00
105	Thomas Dettore	20.00	10.00	6.00
106	Wayne Garland	20.00	10.00	6.00
107	Mark Weens	20.00	10.00	6.00
108	Nelson Paiva	20.00	10.00	6.00
109	Manuel Sarmiento	20.00	10.00	6.00
110	Miguel Motolongo	20.00	10.00	6.00
111	Miguel Navas	20.00	10.00	6.00
112	Angel Baez	20.00	10.00	6.00
113	Raul Ortega	20.00	10.00	6.00
114	Humberto Montero	20.00	10.00	6.00
115	Tomas Gonzalez	20.00	10.00	6.00
116	Ruben Cabrera	20.00	10.00	6.00
117	Flores Bolivar	20.00	10.00	6.00
118	Felix Rodriguez	20.00	10.00	6.00
119	Ali Arape	20.00	10.00	6.00
120	Alexis Heredia	20.00	10.00	6.00
121	Arguilio Freites	20.00	10.00	6.00
122	Alfredo Ortiz	20.00	10.00	6.00
123	Simon Barreto	20.00	10.00	6.00
124	Urbano Lugo	20.00	10.00	6.00
125	Bo Diaz	20.00	10.00	6.00
126	Victor Boll	20.00	10.00	6.00
127	Jose Vinay Caldera	20.00	10.00	6.00
128	Leopoldo Tovar	20.00	10.00	6.00
129	Wilibaldo Quintana	20.00	10.00	6.00
130	Edgar Urbina	20.00	10.00	6.00
131	Ulises Urrieta	20.00	10.00	6.00
132	Antonio Torres	20.00	10.00	6.00
133	Luis Penalver	20.00	10.00	6.00
134	Heriberto Morillo	20.00	10.00	6.00
135	Tony Pacheco	20.00	10.00	6.00
136	Victor Davalillo	20.00	10.00	6.00
137	Jose Martinez	20.00	10.00	6.00
138	Jacinto Betancourt	20.00	10.00	6.00
139	Antonio Armas	40.00	20.00	12.00

Milt Wilcox

#	Player	NM	EX	VG
140	Cesar Tovar	20.00	10.00	6.00
141	Jerry Johnson	20.00	10.00	6.00
142	Mike Anderson	20.00	10.00	6.00
143	Gonzalo Marquez	20.00	10.00	6.00
144	Peter Koegel	20.00	10.00	6.00
145	Pat Dobson	20.00	10.00	6.00
146	Craig Robinson	20.00	10.00	6.00
147	Luis Saez	20.00	10.00	6.00
148	Francisco Navas	20.00	10.00	6.00
149	Elias Lugo	20.00	10.00	6.00
150	Pablo Torrealba	20.00	10.00	6.00
151	Tom Grieve	20.00	10.00	6.00
152	Manny Trillo	40.00	20.00	12.00
153	Ed Sprague	20.00	10.00	6.00
154	Virgilio Velasquez	20.00	10.00	6.00
155	Dave Hamilton	20.00	10.00	6.00
156	Rafael Jimenez	20.00	10.00	6.00
157	Ubaldo Heredia	20.00	10.00	6.00
158	Rich Dempsey	30.00	15.00	9.00
159	Bill Parson (Parsons)	20.00	10.00	6.00
160	Caracas Leones	10.00	5.00	3.00
161	Gene Garber	25.00	12.50	7.50
162	Frank White	35.00	17.50	10.50
163	John Buck Martinez	20.00	10.00	6.00
164	Manuel Garcia	20.00	10.00	6.00
165	Jesus Padron	20.00	10.00	6.00
166	Oscar Gamble	25.00	12.50	7.50
167	Nelson Castellanos	20.00	10.00	6.00
168	Leo Posada	20.00	10.00	6.00
169	Eduardo Benitez	20.00	10.00	6.00
170	Luis Rivas	20.00	10.00	6.00
171	Alfonso Collazo	20.00	10.00	6.00
172	Levy Ochoa	20.00	10.00	6.00
173	Heriberto Lemus	20.00	10.00	6.00
174	Domingo Barboza	20.00	10.00	6.00
175	Jesus Reyes Barrios	20.00	10.00	6.00
176	Inal Fainete	20.00	10.00	6.00
177	Nidio Sirit	20.00	10.00	6.00
178	Nelson Paiva	20.00	10.00	6.00
179	Alfonso Carrasquel	35.00	17.50	10.50
180	Heli Boscan	20.00	10.00	6.00
181	Leonel Carrion	20.00	10.00	6.00
182	Jose Bracho	20.00	10.00	6.00
183	Gustavo Sposito	20.00	10.00	6.00
184	Iran Paz	20.00	10.00	6.00
185	Rich Reese	20.00	10.00	6.00
186	Al Cowans (Cowens)	25.00	12.50	7.50
187	Zulio Group Photo	10.00	5.00	3.00
188	Leo Posada, Alfonso Carrasquel	15.00	7.50	4.50
189	Octavio Rojas	20.00	10.00	6.00
190	Orlando Reyes	20.00	10.00	6.00
191	Mickey Scott	20.00	10.00	6.00
192	Harold King	20.00	10.00	6.00
193	Eduardo Acosta	20.00	10.00	6.00
194	Carlos Alfonso	20.00	10.00	6.00
195	Jose Lopez	20.00	10.00	6.00
196	Jerry Martin	20.00	10.00	6.00
197	Craig Kusick	20.00	10.00	6.00
198	Charles Murray	20.00	10.00	6.00
199	Alexis Corro	20.00	10.00	6.00
200	Jose Luis Alfaro	20.00	10.00	6.00
201	Juan Fco. Monasterio	20.00	10.00	6.00
202	Oscar Zamora	20.00	10.00	6.00
203	Ramon Moreno	20.00	10.00	6.00
204	Carlos Castillo	20.00	10.00	6.00
205	Ken Forsch	20.00	10.00	6.00
206	Leroy Stanton	20.00	10.00	6.00
207	Nevil Romero	20.00	10.00	6.00
208	Romualdo Blanco	20.00	10.00	6.00
209	Remigio Hermoso	20.00	10.00	6.00
210	Paul Casanova	20.00	10.00	6.00
211	Oswaldo Blanco	20.00	10.00	6.00
212	Oswaldo Troconis	20.00	10.00	6.00
213	Antonio Pipo Correa	20.00	10.00	6.00
214	Euclides Camejo	20.00	10.00	6.00
215	Dionel Duran	20.00	10.00	6.00
216	Hector Brito	20.00	10.00	6.00
217	Reinaldo Cordeiro	20.00	10.00	6.00
218	Jose Herrera	20.00	10.00	6.00
219	Hector Urbano	20.00	10.00	6.00
220	Jose Salas	20.00	10.00	6.00
221	Robert Marcano	20.00	10.00	6.00
222	Enzo Hernandez	20.00	10.00	6.00
223	Angel Bravo	20.00	10.00	6.00
224	Tomas Liscano	20.00	10.00	6.00
225	James Granford	20.00	10.00	6.00
226	Luis Salazar	20.00	10.00	6.00
227	Carlos Moreno	20.00	10.00	6.00
228	Manuel Malave	20.00	10.00	6.00
229	Al Bumbry	25.00	12.50	7.50
230	Luis Sanchez	20.00	10.00	6.00
231	Graziano Ravelo	20.00	10.00	6.00
232	La Guaira Tiburones Logo	10.00	5.00	3.00
233	John Jetter (Jeter)	20.00	10.00	6.00
234	Unknown			
235	Orlando Martinez	20.00	10.00	6.00
236	Tom Griffin	20.00	10.00	6.00
237	Lee Pitlock	20.00	10.00	6.00
238	Ray Burry	20.00	10.00	6.00
239	Preston Gomez	20.00	10.00	6.00
240	Aurelio Monteagudo	20.00	10.00	6.00
241	Carvajal/Bat Boy	20.00	10.00	6.00
242-249	Unknown			
250	Eduardo Benitez (a-t)	20.00	10.00	6.00
251	Ted (Tom) Heintzelman (b-t)	20.00	10.00	6.00
252	Ossie Virgil (c-t)	25.00	12.50	7.50
253	Alan Closter (d-t)	20.00	10.00	6.00
254	Carlos Avila (e-t)	20.00	10.00	6.00
255	David Concepcion (g-t)	40.00	20.00	12.00
256	Enrique Colina (h-t)	20.00	10.00	6.00
257	Damaso Blanco (a-n)	20.00	10.00	6.00
258	George Manz (a-c)	20.00	10.00	6.00
259	Peter MacKanin (b-c)	20.00	10.00	6.00
260	Neldy Castillo (c-c)	20.00	10.00	6.00
261	Leovanny Baez (a-z)	20.00	10.00	6.00
262	Mike Easler (b-z)	25.00	12.50	7.50
263	Peter Broberg (c-z)	20.00	10.00	6.00
264	Reggie Cleveland (d-z)	20.00	10.00	6.00
265	Stan Perzanowky (Perzanowski) (e-z)	20.00	10.00	6.00
266	Jerry Terrel (Terrell) (f-z)	20.00	10.00	6.00
267	Toby Harrah (h-z)	30.00	15.00	9.00
268	Franklyn Moreno (y-z)	20.00	10.00	6.00
269-275	Unknown			

1974 Venezuelan League Stickers

JOEL YOUNGBLOOD — OUTFIELD TIGRES

The 1974-75 winter league set of Venezuelan League stickers is a dead ringer for the 1968 Topps baseball cards. About 2-3/8" x 3-3/16", the stickers have photos framed in orange-mottled borders. The team name and position are in a circle at bottom, along with the player name is two colors. Because they were intended to be mounted in an accompanying album, the backs are blank. Because so many of the stickers were once pasted into albums, and due to unfavorable climactic conditions, high-grade examples of Venezuelan stickers from the era are particularly scarce.

		NM	EX	VG
	Complete Set (275):	1,500	750.00	450.00
	Common Player:	20.00	10.00	6.00
	Album:	75.00	40.00	25.00
1	Arague Team Photo	10.00	5.00	3.00
2	Aragua Team Photo	10.00	5.00	3.00
3	Aragua Team Logo	10.00	5.00	3.00
4	Dave Concepcion	40.00	20.00	12.00
5	Ramon Velazquez	20.00	10.00	6.00
6	Carlos Orea	20.00	10.00	6.00
7	Francisco Leandro	20.00	10.00	6.00
8	Angel Hernandez	20.00	10.00	6.00
9	Armando Ortiz	20.00	10.00	6.00
10	Carlos Pascual	20.00	10.00	6.00
11	Argua Action	10.00	5.00	3.00
12	Milton Wilcox	25.00	12.50	7.50
13	Don Hood	20.00	10.00	6.00
14	Timothy Hosley	20.00	10.00	6.00
15	Teolindo Acosta	20.00	10.00	6.00
16	William Castillo	20.00	10.00	6.00
17	Aragua Action	10.00	5.00	3.00
18	Jesus Barron	20.00	10.00	6.00
19	Enos Cabell	25.00	12.50	7.50
20	Luis Silva	20.00	10.00	6.00
21	Aragua Action	10.00	5.00	3.00
22	Aragua Action	10.00	5.00	3.00
23	Joel Youngblood	25.00	12.50	7.50
24	Angel Vargas	20.00	10.00	6.00
25	Carlos Avila	20.00	10.00	6.00
26	Phil Gardner (Garner)	25.00	12.50	7.50
27	James Willoughby	20.00	10.00	6.00
28	Daniel Dubuc	20.00	10.00	6.00
29	Pancho	20.00	10.00	6.00
30	Angel Leon	10.00	5.00	3.00
31	Eastwick Rawlings (Rawly Eastwick)	25.00	12.50	7.50
32	David Torres	20.00	10.00	6.00
33	Robert Flynn	20.00	10.00	6.00
34	Duane Kuiper	25.00	12.50	7.50
35	Jesus Avila	20.00	10.00	6.00
36	Aragua Action	10.00	5.00	3.00
37	Aragua Action	10.00	5.00	3.00
38	Roberto Munoz	20.00	10.00	6.00
39	Eduardo Benitez	20.00	10.00	6.00
40	Aragua Action	10.00	5.00	3.00
41	Adrian Garret (Garrett)	20.00	10.00	6.00
42	Julio Bracho	20.00	10.00	6.00
43	Juan Quiroz	20.00	10.00	6.00
44	Angel Leon	20.00	10.00	6.00
45	Ossie Virgil	30.00	15.00	9.00
46	Lara Team Photo	10.00	5.00	3.00
47	Lara Team Photo	10.00	5.00	3.00
48	Lara Team Logo	10.00	5.00	3.00
49	Andres Barrios	20.00	10.00	6.00
50	Pastor Perez	20.00	10.00	6.00
51	Peter Koegel	20.00	10.00	6.00
52	Lara Action	10.00	5.00	3.00
53	Lowell Palmer	20.00	10.00	6.00
54	Alberto Cambero	20.00	10.00	6.00
55	Frank Snook	20.00	10.00	6.00
56	Steve McCartney	20.00	10.00	6.00
57	Lara Action	10.00	5.00	3.00
58	Dario Chirinos	20.00	10.00	6.00
59	Lara Action	10.00	5.00	3.00
60	Jim Cox	20.00	10.00	6.00
61	Terry Whitfield	20.00	10.00	6.00
62	Nelson Garcia	20.00	10.00	6.00
63	Lara Action	10.00	5.00	3.00
64	Sebastian Martinez	20.00	10.00	6.00
65	Lara Action	10.00	5.00	3.00
66	Rick Sawyer	20.00	10.00	6.00
67	Enrique Gonzalez	20.00	10.00	6.00
68	Tippy Martinez	30.00	15.00	9.00
69	Rafael Jimenez	20.00	10.00	6.00
70	Lara Action	10.00	5.00	3.00
71	Larvell Blanks	20.00	10.00	6.00
72	Franklin Tua	20.00	10.00	6.00
73	Craig Skok	20.00	10.00	6.00
74	Basilio Alvarado	20.00	10.00	6.00
75	Blas Arriechi	20.00	10.00	6.00
76	Dave Pagan	20.00	10.00	6.00
77	Roger Polanco	20.00	10.00	6.00
78	John Lowenstein	20.00	10.00	6.00
79	Francisco Leandro	20.00	10.00	6.00
80	Lucio Celis	20.00	10.00	6.00
81	Lara Action	10.00	5.00	3.00
82	Teodoro Obregon	20.00	10.00	6.00
83	Luis Aponte	20.00	10.00	6.00
84	Roberto Cox	40.00	20.00	12.00
85	Magallanes Team Photo	10.00	5.00	3.00
86	Magallanes Team Photo	10.00	5.00	3.00
87	Magallanes Team Logo	10.00	5.00	3.00
88	Oswaldo Olivares	20.00	10.00	6.00
89	Bob Bailor	25.00	12.50	7.50
90	Ali Arape	20.00	10.00	6.00
91	Jesus Aristimuno	20.00	10.00	6.00
92	Bob Andrews	20.00	10.00	6.00
93	Magallanes Action	10.00	5.00	3.00
94	Rick Stelmaszek	20.00	10.00	6.00
95	Damaso Blanco	20.00	10.00	6.00
96	Graciliano Parra	20.00	10.00	6.00
97	Merv Rettemund (Rettenmund)	25.00	12.50	7.50
98	Don Baylor	45.00	22.00	13.50
99	William Lister	20.00	10.00	6.00
100	Magallanes Action	10.00	5.00	3.00
101	Gregorio Machado	20.00	10.00	6.00
102	Doug Bair	20.00	10.00	6.00
103	Gilberto Marcano	20.00	10.00	6.00
104	Magallanes Action	10.00	5.00	3.00
105	Jim Sadowski	20.00	10.00	6.00
106	Miguel Nava	20.00	10.00	6.00
107	Ken (Kent) Tekulve	40.00	20.00	12.00
108	Wayne Garland	20.00	10.00	6.00
109	Magallanes Action	10.00	5.00	3.00
110	Alexis Ramirez	20.00	10.00	6.00
111	Dave Parker	60.00	30.00	18.00
112	Bob Veale	20.00	10.00	6.00
113	Manuel Sarmiento	20.00	10.00	6.00
114	Alberto Pedroza	20.00	10.00	6.00
115	Ruben Cabrera	20.00	10.00	6.00
116	Felix Rodriguez	20.00	10.00	6.00
117	Magallanes Action	10.00	5.00	3.00
118	Humberto Montero	20.00	10.00	6.00
119	Manuel Gonzalez	20.00	10.00	6.00
120	D. Flores	20.00	10.00	6.00
121	Jim Holt	20.00	10.00	6.00
122	Rafael Cariel	20.00	10.00	6.00
123	Magallanes Action	10.00	5.00	3.00
124	Deisi Bolivar	20.00	10.00	6.00
125	Edito Arteaga	20.00	10.00	6.00
126	Gustavo Gil	20.00	10.00	6.00
127	Larry Demeris (Demery)	20.00	10.00	6.00
128	Nelson Paiva	20.00	10.00	6.00
129	Steve Demeter	20.00	10.00	6.00
130	Caracas Leones Team Photo	10.00	5.00	3.00
131	Caracas Leones Team Photo	10.00	5.00	3.00
132	Caracas Leones Team Logo	10.00	5.00	3.00
133	Antonio Armas	40.00	20.00	12.00
134	Richard Dempsey	40.00	20.00	12.00
135	Toribio Garboza	20.00	10.00	6.00
136	Neldy Castillo	20.00	10.00	6.00
137	Ubaldo Heredia	20.00	10.00	6.00
138	Caracas Action	10.00	5.00	3.00
139	Jesus Marcano Trillo	40.00	20.00	12.00
140	Victor Albury	20.00	10.00	6.00
141	Uknown			
142	Peter Broberg	20.00	10.00	6.00
143	Alfredo Ortiz	20.00	10.00	6.00
144	Leopoldo Tovar	20.00	10.00	6.00
145	Caracas Action	10.00	5.00	3.00
146	Tom Buskey	20.00	10.00	6.00
147	Virgilio Velasquez	20.00	10.00	6.00
148	Cesar Tovar	20.00	10.00	6.00
149	Caracas Stadium	10.00	5.00	3.00
150	Don Stanhouse	20.00	10.00	6.00
151	Edgar Urbina	20.00	10.00	6.00
152	Pablo Torrealba	20.00	10.00	6.00
153	Jack Heidemann	20.00	10.00	6.00
154	Caracas Action	10.00	5.00	3.00
155	Luis Sanz	20.00	10.00	6.00
156	Gonzalo Marquez	20.00	10.00	6.00
157	Victor Davilillo	20.00	10.00	6.00
158	Bo Diaz	20.00	10.00	6.00
159	Caracas Action	10.00	5.00	3.00
160	Bill Butler	20.00	10.00	6.00
161	Elias Lugo	20.00	10.00	6.00
162	Tom Grieve	20.00	10.00	6.00
163	Caracas Action	10.00	5.00	3.00
164	Antonio Torres	20.00	10.00	6.00
165	Luis Penalver	20.00	10.00	6.00
166	Lenny Randle	20.00	10.00	6.00
167	Juan Gonzalez	20.00	10.00	6.00
168	Chuck Dobson	20.00	10.00	6.00
169	Urbano Lugo	20.00	10.00	6.00
170	Francisco Navas	20.00	10.00	6.00
171	Caracas Action	10.00	5.00	3.00
172	Jacinto Betancourt	20.00	10.00	6.00
173	Camilo Pascual	30.00	15.00	9.00
174	Frank White	30.00	15.00	9.00
175	Urbano Quintana	20.00	10.00	6.00
176	Jose Caldera	20.00	10.00	6.00
177	Caracas Action	10.00	5.00	3.00

#	Player	NM	EX	VG
178	Ulises Urrieta	20.00	10.00	6.00
179	Tomas Pacheco	20.00	10.00	6.00
180	La Guaira Tiburones Team Photo	10.00	5.00	3.00
181	La Guaira Tiburones Team Photo	10.00	5.00	3.00
182	La Guaira Tiburones Team Photo	10.00	5.00	3.00
183	Angel Bravo	20.00	10.00	6.00
184	Al Bumbry	25.00	12.50	7.50
185	Aurelio Monteagudo	20.00	10.00	6.00
186	Carlos Moreno	20.00	10.00	6.00
187	La Guaira Action	10.00	5.00	3.00
188	Hector Brito	20.00	10.00	6.00
189	Leroy Stanton	20.00	10.00	6.00
190	Romo Blanco	20.00	10.00	6.00
191	Marquina para Gorrias	10.00	5.00	3.00
192	Luis M. Sanchez	20.00	10.00	6.00
193	La Guaria Action	10.00	5.00	3.00
194	Jose Herrera	20.00	10.00	6.00
195	Victor Colina	20.00	10.00	6.00
196	Tiburones Team Bus	10.00	5.00	3.00
197	Jose Salas	20.00	10.00	6.00
198	La Guaira Action	10.00	5.00	3.00
199	Enzo Hernandez	20.00	10.00	6.00
200	Tomas Liscano	20.00	10.00	6.00
201	Paul Casanova	20.00	10.00	6.00
202	Machine	10.00	5.00	3.00
203	Graziano Ravelo	20.00	10.00	6.00
204	Ice Maker	10.00	5.00	3.00
205	Roland (Rowland) Office	20.00	10.00	6.00
206	Clubhouse	10.00	5.00	3.00
207	La Guaira Action	10.00	5.00	3.00
208	Dusty Baker	45.00	22.00	13.50
209	Replacements	10.00	5.00	3.00
210	Roric Harrison	20.00	10.00	6.00
211	Tom House	20.00	10.00	6.00
212	Jesus Aquino	20.00	10.00	6.00
213	Machine	10.00	5.00	3.00
214	La Guaira Action	10.00	5.00	3.00
215	Juan Monasterios	20.00	10.00	6.00
216	Angel Remigio Hermoso	20.00	10.00	6.00
217	Machine	10.00	5.00	3.00
218	Oswaldo Blanco	20.00	10.00	6.00
219	Infrared Light	10.00	5.00	3.00
220	Roberto Marcano	20.00	10.00	6.00
221	La Guaira Action	10.00	5.00	3.00
222	Jose Carvajal	20.00	10.00	6.00
223	Victor Patino	20.00	10.00	6.00
224	James Bird	20.00	10.00	6.00
225	La Guaira Action	10.00	5.00	3.00
226	Roland Sonny Jackson	25.00	12.50	7.50
227	Oscar Zamora	20.00	10.00	6.00
228	Antonio Pipo Correa	20.00	10.00	6.00
229	Manuel Malave	20.00	10.00	6.00
230	Nap Reyes	20.00	10.00	6.00
231	Zluia Aguilas Team Photo	10.00	5.00	3.00
232	Zluia Aguilas Team Photo	10.00	5.00	3.00
233	Zluia Aguilas Team Logo	10.00	5.00	3.00
234	Levy Ochoa	20.00	10.00	6.00
235	Billy Moran	20.00	10.00	6.00
236	Iran Paz	20.00	10.00	6.00
237	Alexis Corro	20.00	10.00	6.00
238	Zulia Action	10.00	5.00	3.00
239	Gus Sposito	20.00	10.00	6.00
240	Orlando Reyes	20.00	10.00	6.00
241	Carlos Alonso	20.00	10.00	6.00
242	Craig Kusick	20.00	10.00	6.00
243	Zulia Action	10.00	5.00	3.00
244	Domingo Barboza	20.00	10.00	6.00
245	Leonel Carrion	20.00	10.00	6.00
246	Jose Lopez	20.00	10.00	6.00
247	Bill Kirkpatrick	20.00	10.00	6.00
248	Alfonso Carrasquel	20.00	10.00	6.00
249	Richard Billings	20.00	10.00	6.00
250	Alfonzo Collazo	20.00	10.00	6.00
251	Orlando Ramirez	20.00	10.00	6.00
252	Ralph (Mickey) Scott	20.00	10.00	6.00
253	Luis Aparicio	60.00	30.00	18.00
254	Julio Bracho	20.00	10.00	6.00
255	Zulia Action	10.00	5.00	3.00
256	B. Jones	20.00	10.00	6.00
257	Heli Ramon Boscan	20.00	10.00	6.00
258	David Clyde	20.00	10.00	6.00
259	Cesar Gutierrez	20.00	10.00	6.00
260	Bob Randall	20.00	10.00	6.00
261	Jesus Reyes Barrios	20.00	10.00	6.00
262	Jose L. Alfaro	20.00	10.00	6.00
263	Claudio Urdaneta	20.00	10.00	6.00
264	Zulia Action	10.00	5.00	3.00
265	James Sundberg	30.00	15.00	9.00
266	Simon Barreto	20.00	10.00	6.00
267	Anthony Scott	20.00	10.00	6.00
268	Nidio Sirit	20.00	10.00	6.00
269	Zulia Action	10.00	5.00	3.00
270	Zulia Action	10.00	5.00	3.00
271	Leovanni Baez	20.00	10.00	6.00
272	Jefrey (Jeffrey) Terpko	20.00	10.00	6.00
273	Stan Perzanowski	20.00	10.00	6.00
274	Mike Easler	25.00	12.50	7.50
275	Jackie Moore	20.00	10.00	6.00

1976 Venezuelan League Stickers

The basic player stickers utilize a design very similar to Topps' 1975 baseball cards, with player photos surrounded by a colorful border with the team name in large outline letters at top and the position is a baseball at bottom. Stickers are 2-3/8" x 3-3/16" and numbered on front. Like other Latin issues of the era, they are seldom available in high grade due to their intended useage and climactic conditions. Most of the stickers after #217 are specialty pieces with action

TIGRES
34 TERRY WHITFIELD
Outfielder

photos, non-player subjects, multiple players, etc. A colorful album to house the set was also issued.

#	Player	NM	EX	VG
	Complete Set (330):	2,000	1,000	600.00
	Common Player:	20.00	10.00	6.00
	Album:	75.00	40.00	25.00
1	Ossie Virgil	30.00	15.00	9.00
2	Patato Pascual	20.00	10.00	6.00
3	Jesus Avila	20.00	10.00	6.00
4	Raul Ortega	20.00	10.00	6.00
5	Dave Concepcion	40.00	20.00	12.00
6	Jesus Araujo	20.00	10.00	6.00
7	Preston Hanna	20.00	10.00	6.00
8	Victor Davilillo	20.00	10.00	6.00
9	Jesus Padron	20.00	10.00	6.00
10	Joseph Sdeb (Zdeb)	20.00	10.00	6.00
11	Alfredo Ortiz	20.00	10.00	6.00
12	Teolindo Acosta	20.00	10.00	6.00
13	Cesar Tovar	20.00	10.00	6.00
14	Craig Kusick	20.00	10.00	6.00
15	Angel Hernandez	20.00	10.00	6.00
16	Roberto Munoz	20.00	10.00	6.00
17	Fred Andrews	20.00	10.00	6.00
18	Rafael Alvarez	20.00	10.00	6.00
19	Luis Aparicio	50.00	25.00	15.00
20	Jeffrey Newman	20.00	10.00	6.00
21	Tommy Sant (Sandt)	20.00	10.00	6.00
22	Simon Barreto	20.00	10.00	6.00
23	Willie Norwood	20.00	10.00	6.00
24	Juan Quiroz	20.00	10.00	6.00
25	Douglas Capilla	20.00	10.00	6.00
26	William Butler	20.00	10.00	6.00
27	William Castillo	20.00	10.00	6.00
28	Robert Maneely	20.00	10.00	6.00
29	Peter Bromberg (Broberg)	20.00	10.00	6.00
30	Jesse Jefferson	20.00	10.00	6.00
31	Carlos Avila	20.00	10.00	6.00
32	Aragua Action	10.00	5.00	3.00
33	Aragua Action	10.00	5.00	3.00
34	Terry Whitfield	20.00	10.00	6.00
35	Aragua Action	10.00	5.00	3.00
36	Gary Lance	20.00	10.00	6.00
37	Robert Cox	40.00	20.00	12.00
38	Leo Posada	20.00	10.00	6.00
39	Lucio Celis	20.00	10.00	6.00
40	Enrique Gonzalez	20.00	10.00	6.00
41	Jose Musiu Lopez	20.00	10.00	6.00
42	Jose Sandoval	20.00	10.00	6.00
43	Victor Correll	20.00	10.00	6.00
44	Pedro Lobaton	20.00	10.00	6.00
45	Jim Norris	20.00	10.00	6.00
46	Luis Aponte	20.00	10.00	6.00
47	Orlando Gonzalez	20.00	10.00	6.00
48	Edguardo Benitez	20.00	10.00	6.00
49	George Zeber	20.00	10.00	6.00
50	Carlos Rodriguez	20.00	10.00	6.00
51	Graig (Craig) Robinson	20.00	10.00	6.00
52	Hernan Silva	20.00	10.00	6.00
53	Bob Oliver	20.00	10.00	6.00
54	Jose Herrera	20.00	10.00	6.00
55	Pete Mackanin	20.00	10.00	6.00
56	Roger Polanco	20.00	10.00	6.00
57	Lara Stadium	10.00	5.00	3.00
58	Arnaldo Alvarado	20.00	10.00	6.00
59	Ron Selak	20.00	10.00	6.00
60	Nelson Canas	20.00	10.00	6.00
61	John Sutton	20.00	10.00	6.00
62	Nelson Garcia	20.00	10.00	6.00
63	Victor Patino	20.00	10.00	6.00
64	Francisco Navas	20.00	10.00	6.00
65	Robert Polinsky	20.00	10.00	6.00
66	Franklin Tua	20.00	10.00	6.00
67	Oscar Zamora	20.00	10.00	6.00
68	David Torres	20.00	10.00	6.00
69	Eddie Baez	20.00	10.00	6.00
70	Walter Williams	25.00	12.50	7.50
71	Cloyd Boyer	25.00	12.50	7.50
72	Carl (Garth?) Iorg	20.00	10.00	6.00
73	Pat Corrales	20.00	10.00	6.00
74	Alfonso Carrasquel	20.00	10.00	6.00
75	Antonio Torres	20.00	10.00	6.00
76	Camilo Pascual	30.00	15.00	9.00
77	Antonio Armas	40.00	20.00	12.00
78	Baudilio Diaz	20.00	10.00	6.00
79	Gary Beare	20.00	10.00	6.00
80	Steve Barr	20.00	10.00	6.00
81	Toribio Garboza	20.00	10.00	6.00
82	Mike Bassik (Bacsik)	20.00	10.00	6.00
83	Diego Segui	20.00	10.00	6.00
84	Jack Bastable	20.00	10.00	6.00
85	Ubaldo Heredia	20.00	10.00	6.00
86	Warren Cromartie	25.00	12.50	7.50
87	Elias Lugo	20.00	10.00	6.00
88	Mike (Mick) Kelleher	20.00	10.00	6.00
89	Marcano Trillo	40.00	20.00	12.00
90	Lenny Randle	20.00	10.00	6.00
91	Gonzalo Marquez	20.00	10.00	6.00
92	Jim Sadowski	20.00	10.00	6.00
93	Len Barker	25.00	12.50	7.50
94	Willi Quintana	20.00	10.00	6.00
95	Pablo Torrealba	20.00	10.00	6.00
96	Jim Hughes	20.00	10.00	6.00
97	Jose V. Caldera	20.00	10.00	6.00
98	Angel Vargas	20.00	10.00	6.00
99	Juan Gonzalez	20.00	10.00	6.00
100	Ulises Urrieta	20.00	10.00	6.00
101	Flores Bolivar	20.00	10.00	6.00
102	Robert Bowling	20.00	10.00	6.00
103	Rick Bladt	20.00	10.00	6.00
104	Luis Turner	20.00	10.00	6.00
105	Neldy Castillo	20.00	10.00	6.00
106	Adrian Garret (Garrett)	20.00	10.00	6.00
107	Bob Davis	20.00	10.00	6.00
108	La Guaira Action	10.00	5.00	3.00
109	Pompeyo Davalillo	20.00	10.00	6.00
110	Graciano Ravelo	20.00	10.00	6.00
111	Luis Lunar	20.00	10.00	6.00
112	Lester Morales	20.00	10.00	6.00
113	Enzo Hernandez	20.00	10.00	6.00
114	Aurelio Monteagudo	20.00	10.00	6.00
115	Angel Bravo	20.00	10.00	6.00
116	Carlos Moreno	20.00	10.00	6.00
117	Jose Cardenal	25.00	12.50	7.50
118	Rupert (Ruppert) Jones	20.00	10.00	6.00
119	Romo Blanco	20.00	10.00	6.00
120	Milton Ramirez	20.00	10.00	6.00
121	Antonio Correa	20.00	10.00	6.00
122	Clarence Gaston	25.00	12.50	7.50
123	Steve Lubber (Luebber)	20.00	10.00	6.00
124	Edwin Verhelst	20.00	10.00	6.00
125	Robert Johnson	20.00	10.00	6.00
126	Earl Bass	20.00	10.00	6.00
127	Jose Salas	20.00	10.00	6.00
128	Oswaldo Blanco	20.00	10.00	6.00
129	Steve Staag (Staggs)	20.00	10.00	6.00
130	Steve Patchin	20.00	10.00	6.00
131	Mike Kekish (Kekich)	20.00	10.00	6.00
132	Oswaldo Troconis	20.00	10.00	6.00
133	Dave May	20.00	10.00	6.00
134	Luis Salazar	20.00	10.00	6.00
135	Larry Gura	20.00	10.00	6.00
136	Rich Dauer	20.00	10.00	6.00
137	Pastor Perez	20.00	10.00	6.00
138	Paul Siebert	20.00	10.00	6.00
139	Luis M. Sanchez	20.00	10.00	6.00
140	Victor Colina	20.00	10.00	6.00
141	Adrian Devine	20.00	10.00	6.00
142	Robert Marcano	20.00	10.00	6.00
143	Juan Berenger (Berenguer)	25.00	12.50	7.50
144	Juan Monasterio	20.00	10.00	6.00
145	Donald Leppert	20.00	10.00	6.00
146	Gregorio Machado	20.00	10.00	6.00
147	Manuel Gonzalez	20.00	10.00	6.00
148	Wayne Granger	20.00	10.00	6.00
149	Remigio Hermoso	20.00	10.00	6.00
150	Rafael Cariel	20.00	10.00	6.00
151	Steve Dillard	20.00	10.00	6.00
152	Mitchell Page	20.00	10.00	6.00
153	Alexis Ramirez, Felix Rodriguez	15.00	7.50	4.50
154	Gary Wood	20.00	10.00	6.00
155	Ali Arape	20.00	10.00	6.00
156	Chris Batton	20.00	10.00	6.00
157	Gustavo Gil	20.00	10.00	6.00
158	Craig Reynolds	20.00	10.00	6.00
159	Jesus Aristimuno	20.00	10.00	6.00
160	Miguel Barreto	20.00	10.00	6.00
161	Alfonso Collazo	20.00	10.00	6.00
162	Steve Nicosia	20.00	10.00	6.00
163	Oswaldo Olivares	20.00	10.00	6.00
164	Robert Galasso	20.00	10.00	6.00
165	Alexis Ramirez	20.00	10.00	6.00
166	Craig Mitchell	20.00	10.00	6.00
167	Nelson Paiva	20.00	10.00	6.00
168	Ken Macha	20.00	10.00	6.00
169	Ruben Cabrera	20.00	10.00	6.00
170	Paul Reuschell (Reuschel)	20.00	10.00	6.00
171	Edito Arteaga	20.00	10.00	6.00
172	Olinto Rojas	20.00	10.00	6.00
173	Magallanes Action	10.00	5.00	3.00
174	Manny Sarmiento	20.00	10.00	6.00
175	Billy Moran	20.00	10.00	6.00
176	Eddie Watt	20.00	10.00	6.00
177	Michael Willis	20.00	10.00	6.00
178	Felix Rodriguez	20.00	10.00	6.00
179	James Easterly	20.00	10.00	6.00
180	Dave Parker	40.00	20.00	12.00
181	Luis Aparicio	50.00	25.00	15.00
182	Teodoro Obregon	20.00	10.00	6.00
183	Domingo Barboza	20.00	10.00	6.00
184	Not Issued, See #190			
185	Gilberto Marcano	20.00	10.00	6.00
186	Jose Alfaro	20.00	10.00	6.00
187	Jesus Reyes	20.00	10.00	6.00
188	Mike (Mickey) Scott	20.00	10.00	6.00
189	Carl Frost	20.00	10.00	6.00
190a	Norman Shiera	20.00	10.00	6.00
190b	Orlando Pena (See #184)	20.00	10.00	6.00
191	Orlando Reyes	20.00	10.00	6.00
192	Milt Wilcox	25.00	12.50	7.50
193	Andrew Dyes	20.00	10.00	6.00
194	J. Hernandez	20.00	10.00	6.00
195	Dario Chirinos	20.00	10.00	6.00
196	Greg Shanahan	20.00	10.00	6.00
197	Gustavo Sposito	20.00	10.00	6.00
198	Sebastian Martinez	20.00	10.00	6.00
199	Leonel Carrion	20.00	10.00	6.00
200	Dennis Lawallyn (Lewallyn)	20.00	10.00	6.00
201	Charky (Charlie) Moore	20.00	10.00	6.00
202	Steve Mallory	20.00	10.00	6.00
203	Gary Martz	20.00	10.00	6.00
204	Lamar Johnson	20.00	10.00	6.00
205	Tim Johnson	20.00	10.00	6.00
206	Levy Ochoa	20.00	10.00	6.00

		NM	EX	VG
207	Bill Dancy	20.00	10.00	6.00
208	Antonio Garcia	20.00	10.00	6.00
209	Nidio Sirit	20.00	10.00	6.00
210	Norman Shiera	20.00	10.00	6.00
211	Not Issued, See #221			
212	Jesus Alfaro	20.00	10.00	6.00
213	Bobby Darwin	20.00	10.00	6.00
214	Zulia Action	10.00	5.00	3.00
215	Mike Seoane	20.00	10.00	6.00
216	Jim Gatner (Gantner)	20.00	10.00	6.00
217	Caracas Action	10.00	5.00	3.00
218	Caracas Action	10.00	5.00	3.00
219	Caracas Action	10.00	5.00	3.00
220	Caracas Action	10.00	5.00	3.00
221a	Caracas Action	10.00	5.00	3.00
221b	Joe Chourio (See #211)	20.00	10.00	6.00
222	Lara Action	10.00	5.00	3.00
223	Ulises Urrieta, Antonio Armas, Manny Trillo	20.00	10.00	6.00
224	Magallanes Dugout	10.00	5.00	3.00
225	Remigio Hermoso, Gustavo Gil	15.00	7.50	4.50
226	Caracas Action	10.00	5.00	3.00
227	Manny Trillo, Dave Concepcion	20.00	10.00	6.00
228	Zulia Action	10.00	5.00	3.00
229	Caracas Pizarra Scoreboard	10.00	5.00	3.00
230	La Guaira Action	10.00	5.00	3.00
231	Caracas Action	10.00	5.00	3.00
232	La Guaira Action	10.00	5.00	3.00
233	Zulia Action	10.00	5.00	3.00
234	Caracas Publico	10.00	5.00	3.00
235	Magallanes Action	10.00	5.00	3.00
236	Aragua Action	10.00	5.00	3.00
237	Aragua Action	10.00	5.00	3.00
238	La Guaira Action	10.00	5.00	3.00
239	La Guaira Action	10.00	5.00	3.00
240	La Guaira Action	10.00	5.00	3.00
241	Manny Trillo, Jose Cardenal	20.00	10.00	6.00
242	Pompeyo Davilillo, Lacheman	15.00	7.50	4.50
243	La Guaira Action	10.00	5.00	3.00
244	La Guaira Action	10.00	5.00	3.00
245	Action	10.00	5.00	3.00
246	Zulia Action	10.00	5.00	3.00
247	Zulia Action	10.00	5.00	3.00
248	Tim Johnson	20.00	10.00	6.00
249	La Guaira Action	10.00	5.00	3.00
250	La Guaira Action	10.00	5.00	3.00
251	La Guaira Action	10.00	5.00	3.00
252	La Guaira Action	10.00	5.00	3.00
253	La Guaira Action	10.00	5.00	3.00
254	La Guaira Action	10.00	5.00	3.00
255	La Guaira Action	10.00	5.00	3.00
256	La Guaira Action	10.00	5.00	3.00
257	Caracas Action	10.00	5.00	3.00
258	La Guaira Action	10.00	5.00	3.00
259	Zulia Action	10.00	5.00	3.00
260	Caracas Action	10.00	5.00	3.00
261	Caracas Action	10.00	5.00	3.00
262	La Guaira Clubhouse	10.00	5.00	3.00
263	La Guaira Clubhouse	10.00	5.00	3.00
264	La Guaira Clubhouse	10.00	5.00	3.00
265	La Guaira Clubhouse	10.00	5.00	3.00
266	La Guaira Action	10.00	5.00	3.00
267	La Guaira Action	10.00	5.00	3.00
268	La Guaira Action	10.00	5.00	3.00
269	Panoramica	10.00	5.00	3.00
270	Zulia Action	10.00	5.00	3.00
271	Aragua Puzzle	10.00	5.00	3.00
272	Aragua Puzzle	10.00	5.00	3.00
273	Aragua Puzzle	10.00	5.00	3.00
274	Aragua Puzzle	10.00	5.00	3.00
275	Aragua Puzzle	10.00	5.00	3.00
276	Aragua Puzzle	10.00	5.00	3.00
277	Aragua Puzzle	10.00	5.00	3.00
278	Aragua Puzzle	10.00	5.00	3.00
279	Aragua Puzzle	10.00	5.00	3.00
280	Lara Puzzle	10.00	5.00	3.00
281	Lara Puzzle	10.00	5.00	3.00
282	Lara Puzzle	10.00	5.00	3.00
283	Lara Puzzle	10.00	5.00	3.00
284	Lara Puzzle	10.00	5.00	3.00
285	Lara Puzzle	10.00	5.00	3.00
286	Lara Puzzle	10.00	5.00	3.00
287	Lara Puzzle	10.00	5.00	3.00
288	Lara Puzzle	10.00	5.00	3.00
289	Caracas Puzzle	10.00	5.00	3.00
290	Caracas Puzzle	10.00	5.00	3.00
291	Caracas Puzzle	10.00	5.00	3.00
292	Caracas Puzzle	10.00	5.00	3.00
293	Caracas Puzzle	10.00	5.00	3.00
294	Caracas Puzzle	10.00	5.00	3.00
295	Caracas Puzzle	10.00	5.00	3.00
296	Caracas Puzzle	10.00	5.00	3.00
297	Caracas Puzzle	10.00	5.00	3.00
298	La Guaira Puzzle	10.00	5.00	3.00
299	La Guaira Puzzle	10.00	5.00	3.00
300	La Guaira Puzzle	10.00	5.00	3.00
301	La Guaira Puzzle	10.00	5.00	3.00
302	La Guaira Puzzle	10.00	5.00	3.00
303	La Guaira Puzzle	10.00	5.00	3.00
304	La Guaira Puzzle	10.00	5.00	3.00
305	La Guaira Puzzle	10.00	5.00	3.00
306	La Guaira Puzzle	10.00	5.00	3.00
307	Magallanes Puzzle	10.00	5.00	3.00
308	Magallanes Puzzle	10.00	5.00	3.00
309	Magallanes Puzzle	10.00	5.00	3.00
310	Magallanes Puzzle	10.00	5.00	3.00
311	Magallanes Puzzle	10.00	5.00	3.00
312	Magallanes Puzzle	10.00	5.00	3.00
313	Magallanes Puzzle	10.00	5.00	3.00
314	Magallanes Puzzle	10.00	5.00	3.00
315	Magallanes Puzzle	10.00	5.00	3.00
316	Zulia Puzzle	10.00	5.00	3.00
317	Zulia Puzzle	10.00	5.00	3.00
318	Zulia Puzzle	10.00	5.00	3.00
319	Zulia Puzzle	10.00	5.00	3.00
320	Zulia Puzzle	10.00	5.00	3.00
321	Zulia Puzzle	10.00	5.00	3.00
322	Zulia Puzzle	10.00	5.00	3.00
323	Zulia Puzzle	10.00	5.00	3.00
324	Zulia Puzzle	10.00	5.00	3.00
325	Magallanes Navagantes Logo	10.00	5.00	3.00
326	Aragua Tigres Logo	10.00	5.00	3.00
327	Caracas Leones Logo	10.00	5.00	3.00
328	Zulia Aguilas Logo	10.00	5.00	3.00
329	Lara Cardenales Logo	10.00	5.00	3.00
330	La Guaira Tiburones Logo	10.00	5.00	3.00

1977 Venezuelan Baseball Stickers

More than 400 pieces comprise this set of 2-3/8" x 3-1/8" blank-back stickers. The majority have color photos of winter league players with the team name, logo and position printed above, and the sticker number and name beneath the picture. There are many former and future Major League players in this group. A subset of some 50 stickers of American Major Leaguers is printed in reproduction of their 1977 Topps cards. Other stickers include group pictures, action photos, puzzle pieces, etc. The album issued to house the stickers has a player write-up in each space. Printed on very thin paper, and often removed from albums, these stickers are generally not found in condition above Very Good. For Good condition pieces, figure value at 50% of the price shown here; stickers in Fair condition should be valued at 25%. Many of the stickers have player names misspelled.

		NM	EX	VG
	Complete Set (402):	4,000	1,600	800.00
	Common Player:	15.00	6.00	3.00
	Album:	125.00	50.00	25.00
1	Aragua Tigers logo	15.00	6.00	3.00
2	Ozzie Virgil Sr.	20.00	8.00	4.00
3	Jesus Avila	15.00	6.00	3.00
4	Raul Ortega	15.00	6.00	3.00
5	Simon Barreto	15.00	6.00	3.00
6	Gustavo Quiroz	15.00	6.00	3.00
7	Jerry Cram	15.00	6.00	3.00
8	Pat Cristelli	15.00	6.00	3.00
9	Preston Hanna	15.00	6.00	3.00
10	Angel Hernandez	15.00	6.00	3.00
11	John M'Callen	15.00	6.00	3.00
12	Randy Miller	15.00	6.00	3.00
13	Dale Murray	15.00	6.00	3.00
14	Mike Nagy	15.00	6.00	3.00
15	Stan Perzanowski	15.00	6.00	3.00
16	Juan Quiroz	15.00	6.00	3.00
17	Graciano Parra	15.00	6.00	3.00
18	Larry Cox	15.00	6.00	3.00
19	Lenn Sakata	15.00	6.00	3.00
20	Lester Straker	15.00	6.00	3.00
21	Nelson Torres	15.00	6.00	3.00
22	Carlos Avila	15.00	6.00	3.00
23	Orlando Galindo	15.00	6.00	3.00
24	Dave Wagner	15.00	6.00	3.00
25	Dave Concepcion	60.00	24.00	12.00
26	Alfredo Ortiz	15.00	6.00	3.00
27	Mike Lum, Dave Concepcion, Larry Parrish	15.00	6.00	3.00
28	Jesus Padron	15.00	6.00	3.00
29	Larry Parrish	15.00	6.00	3.00
30	Rob Picciolo	15.00	6.00	3.00
31	Luis Rivas	15.00	6.00	3.00
32	Bob Slater	15.00	6.00	3.00
33	Larry Murray	15.00	6.00	3.00
34	Dave Soderholm	15.00	6.00	3.00
35	Luis Benitez	15.00	6.00	3.00
36	Cesar Tovar, Victor Davalillo	20.00	8.00	4.00
37	Luis Bravo	15.00	6.00	3.00
38	William Castillo	15.00	6.00	3.00
39	Terry Whitfield	15.00	6.00	3.00
40	Victor Davalillo	30.00	12.00	6.00
41	Mike Lum	15.00	6.00	3.00
42	Willie Norwood	15.00	6.00	3.00
43	Cesar Tovar	15.00	6.00	3.00
44	Joe Zdeb	15.00	6.00	3.00
45	Focion, Ozzie Virgil Sr.	15.00	6.00	3.00
46	Caracas Lions logo	15.00	6.00	3.00
47	Felipe Alou	20.00	8.00	4.00
48	Alfonso Carrasquel (Chico)	35.00	14.00	7.00
49	Antonio Torres	15.00	6.00	3.00
50	Len Barker	15.00	6.00	3.00
51	Gary Beare	15.00	6.00	3.00
52	Cardell Camper	15.00	6.00	3.00
53	Juan Gonzalez	15.00	6.00	3.00
54	Paul Mirabella	15.00	6.00	3.00
55	Carney Lansford	15.00	6.00	3.00
56	Ubaldo Heredia	15.00	6.00	3.00
57	Elias Lugo	15.00	6.00	3.00
58	Oswaldo Troconis	15.00	6.00	3.00
59	Diego Segui	15.00	6.00	3.00
60	Lary Sorensen	15.00	6.00	3.00
61	Pablo Torrealba	15.00	6.00	3.00
62	Gustavo Bastardo	15.00	6.00	3.00
63	Luis Sanz	15.00	6.00	3.00
64	Steve Bowling	15.00	6.00,	3.00
65	Tim Corcoran	15.00	6.00	3.00
66	Antonio Armas (Tony)	35.00	14.00	7.00
67	Toribio Garboza	15.00	6.00	3.00
68	Bob Molinaro	15.00	6.00	3.00
69	Willibaldo Quintana	15.00	6.00	3.00
70	Luis Turnes	15.00	6.00	3.00
71	Chuck Baker	15.00	6.00	3.00
72	Rob Belloir	15.00	6.00	3.00
73	Tom Brookens	15.00	6.00	3.00
74	Ron Hassey	15.00	6.00	3.00
75	Gonzalo Marquez	15.00	6.00	3.00
76	Bob Clark	15.00	6.00	3.00
77	Marceno Trillo (Manny)	30.00	12.00	6.00
78	Angel Vargas	15.00	6.00	3.00
79	Flores Bolivar	15.00	6.00	3.00
80	Baudilo Diaz (Bo)	15.00	6.00	3.00
81	Camilo Pascual	15.00	6.00	3.00
82	La Guaira Sharks logo	15.00	6.00	3.00
83	Pompeyo Davalillo	17.50	7.00	3.50
84	Jose Martinez	15.00	6.00	3.00
85	Jim Willoughby	15.00	6.00	3.00
86	Romo Blanco	15.00	6.00	3.00
87	Mark Daly	15.00	6.00	3.00
88	Tom House	15.00	6.00	3.00
89	Danny Osborne	15.00	6.00	3.00
90	David Clyde	15.00	6.00	3.00
91	Luis Lunar	15.00	6.00	3.00
92	Randy McGilberry	15.00	6.00	3.00
93	Greg Minton	15.00	6.00	3.00
94	Aurelio Monteagudo	15.00	6.00	3.00
95	Carlos Moreno	15.00	6.00	3.00
96	Luis M. Sanchez	15.00	6.00	3.00
97	George Throop	15.00	6.00	3.00
98	Victor Colina	15.00	6.00	3.00
99	Edwin Verheist	15.00	6.00	3.00
100	John Wathan	15.00	6.00	3.00
101	Ruben Alcala	15.00	6.00	3.00
102	Ossie Blanco	15.00	6.00	3.00
103	Dave Cripe	15.00	6.00	3.00
104	Bob Marcano	15.00	6.00	3.00
105	Rudy Meoli	15.00	6.00	3.00
106	Pastor Perez	15.00	6.00	3.00
107	Milton Ramirez	15.00	6.00	3.00
108	Luis Salazar	15.00	6.00	3.00
109	Angel Bravo	15.00	6.00	3.00
110	Gene Clines	15.00	6.00	3.00
111	Jose Cardenal	15.00	6.00	3.00
112	Gabriel Ferrerc	15.00	6.00	3.00
113	Clint Hurdle	15.00	6.00	3.00
114	Juan Monasterio	15.00	6.00	3.00
115	Lester Morales	15.00	6.00	3.00
116	Carlos Hernandez	15.00	6.00	3.00
117	Nelo Lira	15.00	6.00	3.00
118	Raul Perez	15.00	6.00	3.00
119	Marcos Lunar	15.00	6.00	3.00
120	Franklin Moreno	15.00	6.00	3.00
121	Jerry Manuel	15.00	6.00	3.00
122	Ossie Blanco, Raul Perez	15.00	6.00	3.00
123	Tom McMillan	15.00	6.00	3.00
124	Roric Harrison	15.00	6.00	3.00
125	Tom Griffin	15.00	6.00	3.00
126	Juan Berenguer	15.00	6.00	3.00
127	Puzzle piece (Reggie Jackson)			
128	Puzzle piece (Reggie Jackson)	15.00	6.00	3.00
129	Puzzle piece (Reggie Jackson)	15.00	6.00	3.00
130	Puzzle piece (Reggie Jackson)	15.00	6.00	3.00
131	Puzzle piece (Reggie Jackson)	15.00	6.00	3.00
132	Puzzle piece (Reggie Jackson)	15.00	6.00	3.00
133	Puzzle piece (Reggie Jackson)	15.00	6.00	3.00
134	Puzzle piece (Reggie Jackson)	15.00	6.00	3.00
135	Puzzle piece (Reggie Jackson)	15.00	6.00	3.00
136	Reggie Jackson	325.00	130.00	65.00
137	Rod Carew	175.00	70.00	35.00
138	Dave Concepcion	90.00	36.00	18.00
139	Joe Morgan	125.00	50.00	25.00
140	Dave Parker	15.00	6.00	3.00
141	Carlton Fisk	125.00	50.00	25.00
142	Garry Maddox	15.00	6.00	3.00
143	George Foster	15.00	6.00	3.00
144	Fred Lynn	15.00	6.00	3.00
145	Lou Piniella	17.50	7.00	3.50
146	Mark Fidrych	15.00	6.00	3.00
147	Lou Brock	125.00	50.00	25.00
148	Mitchell Page	15.00	6.00	3.00
149	Sparky Lyle	15.00	6.00	3.00
150	Manny Sanguillen	15.00	6.00	3.00
151	Steve Carlton	125.00	50.00	25.00
152	Al Oliver	17.50	7.00	3.50
153	Davey Lopes	15.00	6.00	3.00
154	Johnny Bench	175.00	70.00	35.00
155	Richie Hebner	15.00	6.00	3.00
156	Cesar Cedeno	15.00	6.00	3.00
157	Manny Trillo	15.00	6.00	3.00
158	Nolan Ryan	1,500	600.00	300.00
159	Tom Seaver	175.00	70.00	35.00
160	Jim Palmer	125.00	50.00	25.00
161	Randy Jones	15.00	6.00	3.00
162	George Brett	325.00	130.00	65.00
163	Bill Madlock	15.00	6.00	3.00
164	Cesar Geronimo	15.00	6.00	3.00

165	Vida Blue	15.00	6.00	3.00
166	Tony Armas	35.00	14.00	7.00
167	Bill Campbell	15.00	6.00	3.00
168	Graig Nettles	15.00	6.00	3.00
169	Mike Schmidt	325.00	130.00	65.00
170	Willie Stargell	125.00	50.00	25.00
171	Ron Cey	15.00	6.00	3.00
172	Victor Davalillo	25.00	10.00	5.00
173	Pete Rose	375.00	150.00	75.00
174	Steve Yaeger	15.00	6.00	3.00
175	Frank Tanana	15.00	6.00	3.00
176	Carl Yastrzemski	175.00	70.00	35.00
177	Willie McCovey	125.00	50.00	25.00
178	Thurman Munson	125.00	50.00	25.00
179	Chris Chambliss	15.00	6.00	3.00
180	Bill Russell	15.00	6.00	3.00
181	Lara Cardinals logo	15.00	6.00	3.00
182	Leo Posada	15.00	6.00	3.00
183	Lucio Celis	15.00	6.00	3.00
184	Enrique Gonzalez	15.00	6.00	3.00
185	Brian Abraham	15.00	6.00	3.00
186	Luis Aponte	15.00	6.00	3.00
187	Jose Lopez	15.00	6.00	3.00
188	Bobby Ramos	15.00	6.00	3.00
189	Tom Dixon	15.00	6.00	3.00
190	Gary Melson	15.00	6.00	3.00
191	Mark Budaska	15.00	6.00	3.00
192	Mark Fischlin	15.00	6.00	3.00
193	Garth Iorg	15.00	6.00	3.00
194	Mike Rowland	15.00	6.00	3.00
195	Dennis DeBarr	15.00	6.00	3.00
196	Gary Wilson	15.00	6.00	3.00
197	Dave McKay	15.00	6.00	3.00
198	Roberto Munoz	15.00	6.00	3.00
199	Roger Polanco	15.00	6.00	3.00
200	Pat Kelly	15.00	6.00	3.00
201	Hernan Silva	15.00	6.00	3.00
202	Francisco Navas	15.00	6.00	3.00
203	Pedro Lobaton	15.00	6.00	3.00
204	Pete Mackanin	15.00	6.00	3.00
205	Jose Caldera	15.00	6.00	3.00
206	Carlos Rodriguez (In Action)	15.00	6.00	3.00
207	Eddy Baez	15.00	6.00	3.00
208	Gary Metzeger	15.00	6.00	3.00
209	Rafael Sandoval	15.00	6.00	3.00
210	Arturo Sanchez	15.00	6.00	3.00
211	Franklin Tua	15.00	6.00	3.00
212	Teolindo Acosta	15.00	6.00	3.00
213	Arnaldo Alvarado	15.00	6.00	3.00
214	Orlando Gonzalez	15.00	6.00	3.00
215	Nelson Garcia	15.00	6.00	3.00
216	Terry Puhl	15.00	6.00	3.00
217	David Torres	15.00	6.00	3.00
218	Teolindo Acosta, Roberto Munoz	15.00	6.00	3.00
219	Terry Puhl, Mark Budaska	15.00	6.00	3.00
220	Gary Gray	15.00	6.00	3.00
221	Gustavo Gil	15.00	6.00	3.00
222	Epi Guerrero	15.00	6.00	3.00
223	Bobby Ramos, Enrique Gonzalez	15.00	6.00	3.00
224	Rick Sawyer	15.00	6.00	3.00
225	S. Byre	15.00	6.00	3.00
226	Magallanes Navigators logo	15.00	6.00	3.00
227	Alex Monchak	15.00	6.00	3.00
228	Manuel Gonzalez	15.00	6.00	3.00
229	Olinto Rojas	15.00	6.00	3.00
230	Gregorio Machado	15.00	6.00	3.00
231	Ali Arape	15.00	6.00	3.00
232	Miguel Barreto	15.00	6.00	3.00
233	Manny Sarmiento	15.00	6.00	3.00
234	Jesus Aristimuno, Alexis Ramirez, Felix Rodriguez	15.00	6.00	3.00
235	Ed Glynn	15.00	6.00	3.00
236	Luis Jiminez	15.00	6.00	3.00
237	Bob Adams	15.00	6.00	3.00
238	Edito Arteaga	15.00	6.00	3.00
239	Rafael Cariel	15.00	6.00	3.00
240	Eddie Solomon	15.00	6.00	3.00
241	Rick Williams	15.00	6.00	3.00
242	Miguel Nava	15.00	6.00	3.00
243	Rod Scurry	15.00	6.00	3.00
244	Mike Eduards (Edwards)	15.00	6.00	3.00
245	Earl Stephenson	15.00	6.00	3.00
246	Alfonso Collazo	15.00	6.00	3.00
247	Ruben Cabrera	15.00	6.00	3.00
248	Alfredo Torres	15.00	6.00	3.00
249	John Valle	15.00	6.00	3.00
250	Jesus Aristimuno	15.00	6.00	3.00
251	Joe Cannon	15.00	6.00	3.00
252	John Pacella	15.00	6.00	3.00
253	Oswaldo Olivares	15.00	6.00	3.00
254	Gary Hargis	15.00	6.00	3.00
255	Nelson Paiva	15.00	6.00	3.00
256	Bob Oliver	15.00	6.00	3.00
257	Alexis Ramirez	15.00	6.00	3.00
258	Larry Wolfe	15.00	6.00	3.00
259	Don Boyland (Doe)	15.00	6.00	3.00
260	Mark Wagner	15.00	6.00	3.00
261	Jim Wright	15.00	6.00	3.00
262	Mitchell Page	15.00	6.00	3.00
263	Felix Rodriguez	15.00	6.00	3.00
264	Willie Aaron	15.00	6.00	3.00
265	Justo Massaro	15.00	6.00	3.00
266	Norm Angelini	15.00	6.00	3.00
267	Fred Breining	15.00	6.00	3.00
268	Bill Sample	15.00	6.00	3.00
269	Than Smith	15.00	6.00	3.00
270	Harry Doris (Dorish)	15.00	6.00	3.00
271	Zulia Eagles logo	15.00	6.00	3.00
272	Luis Aparicio	35.00	14.00	7.00
273	Toni Taylor (Tony)	15.00	6.00	3.00
274	Teodoro Obregon	15.00	6.00	3.00
275	Gilberto Marcano	15.00	6.00	3.00
276	Jose Alfaro	15.00	6.00	3.00
277	Danny Boitano	15.00	6.00	3.00
278	Jesus Reyes	15.00	6.00	3.00
279	Johel Chourio	15.00	6.00	3.00
280	Scott Sanderson	15.00	6.00	3.00
281	Charles Kiffin	15.00	6.00	3.00
282	Bill Dancy	15.00	6.00	3.00
283	Tim Johnson	15.00	6.00	3.00
284	Norman Shiera	15.00	6.00	3.00
285	Lonnie Smith	15.00	6.00	3.00
286	Manny Seoane	15.00	6.00	3.00
287	David Wallace	15.00	6.00	3.00
288	Lareu Whashington (LaRue Washington)	15.00	6.00	3.00
289	Danny Warthen	15.00	6.00	3.00
290	Sebastian Martinez	15.00	6.00	3.00
291	Warren Brusstar	15.00	6.00	3.00
292	Steven Waterburry (Waterbury)	15.00	6.00	3.00
293	Gustavo Sposito	15.00	6.00	3.00
294	Billy Connors	15.00	6.00	3.00
295	Bod Reece (Bob)	15.00	6.00	3.00
296	Al Velasquez	15.00	6.00	3.00
297	Jesus Alfaro	15.00	6.00	3.00
298	Todd Cruz	15.00	6.00	3.00
299	Efren Chourio	15.00	6.00	3.00
300	Tim Norrid	15.00	6.00	3.00
301	Leonel Carrion	15.00	6.00	3.00
302	Dario Chirinos	15.00	6.00	3.00
303	Bobby Darwin	15.00	6.00	3.00
304	Levy Ochoa	15.00	6.00	3.00
305	Orlando Reyez (Reyes)	15.00	6.00	3.00
306	Antonio Garcia	15.00	6.00	3.00
307	Fred Andrews	15.00	6.00	3.00
308	Domingo Barboza	15.00	6.00	3.00
309	Emilio Rodriguez	15.00	6.00	3.00
310	Roger Brown (Rogers "Bobby")	15.00	6.00	3.00
311	Nelson Munoz	15.00	6.00	3.00
312	Unknown	15.00	6.00	3.00
313	Greg Pryor	15.00	6.00	3.00
314	Early Espina	15.00	6.00	3.00
315	Leonel Carrion, Dario Chirinos	15.00	6.00	3.00
316	Luis Aparicio	25.00	10.00	5.00
317	Alfonso Carrasquel (Chico)	20.00	8.00	4.00
318	Dave Concepcion	20.00	8.00	4.00
319	Antonio Armas (Tony)	20.00	8.00	4.00
320	Marcano Trillo (Manny)	20.00	8.00	4.00
321	Pablo Torrealba	15.00	6.00	3.00
322	Manny Sarmiento	15.00	6.00	3.00
323	Baudilio Diaz (Bo)	15.00	6.00	3.00
324	Victor Davalillo	15.00	6.00	3.00
325	Puzzle piece (Dave Parker)	15.00	6.00	3.00
326	Puzzle piece (Dave Parker)	15.00	6.00	3.00
327	Puzzle piece (Dave Parker)	15.00	6.00	3.00
328	Puzzle piece (Dave Parker)	15.00	6.00	3.00
329	Puzzle piece (Dave Parker)	15.00	6.00	3.00
330	Puzzle piece (Dave Parker)	15.00	6.00	3.00
331	Puzzle piece (Dave Parker)	15.00	6.00	3.00
332	Puzzle piece (Dave Parker)	15.00	6.00	3.00
333	Puzzle piece (Dave Parker)	15.00	6.00	3.00
334	Dave Parker	15.00	6.00	3.00
335	Steve Bowling	15.00	6.00	3.00
336	Jose Herrera	15.00	6.00	3.00
337	Mitchell Page	15.00	6.00	3.00
338	Enos Cabell	15.00	6.00	3.00
339	Orlando Reyes	15.00	6.00	3.00
340	Felix Rodriguez	15.00	6.00	3.00
341	Baudilio Diaz (Bo)	15.00	6.00	3.00
342	Gonzalo Marquez	15.00	6.00	3.00
343	Mike Kelleher	15.00	6.00	3.00
344	Juan Monasterio	15.00	6.00	3.00
345	Diego Segui	15.00	6.00	3.00
346	Steve Lueber (Luebber)	15.00	6.00	3.00
347	Mike Scott	15.00	6.00	3.00
348	Angel Bravo	15.00	6.00	3.00
349	Terry Whitfield	15.00	6.00	3.00
350	Bob Oliver	15.00	6.00	3.00
351	Tim Jonhson (Johnson)	15.00	6.00	3.00
352	Gustavo Sposito	15.00	6.00	3.00
353	Jim Norris	15.00	6.00	3.00
354	Marcano Trillo (Manny)	20.00	8.00	4.00
355	Gary Woods	15.00	6.00	3.00
356	Felix Rodriguez	15.00	6.00	3.00
357	Dave May	15.00	6.00	3.00
358	Don Lepper (Leppert)	15.00	6.00	3.00
359	Magallanes Team Photo	15.00	6.00	3.00
360	Magallanes Team Photo	15.00	6.00	3.00
361	Action photo	15.00	6.00	3.00
362	Action photo	15.00	6.00	3.00
363	Antonio Torres, Leo Posada	15.00	6.00	3.00
364	Action photo	15.00	6.00	3.00
365	Action photo	15.00	6.00	3.00
366	Action photo	15.00	6.00	3.00
367	Action photo	15.00	6.00	3.00
368	Action photo	15.00	6.00	3.00
369	Action photo	15.00	6.00	3.00
370	Action photo	15.00	6.00	3.00
371	Action photo	15.00	6.00	3.00
372	Action photo	15.00	6.00	3.00
373	Action photo	15.00	6.00	3.00
374	Action photo	15.00	6.00	3.00
375	Action photo	15.00	6.00	3.00
376	Action photo	15.00	6.00	3.00
377	Action photo	15.00	6.00	3.00
378	Action photo	15.00	6.00	3.00
399	Action photo (Misnumbered)	15.00	6.00	3.00
380	Action photo	15.00	6.00	3.00
381	Action photo	15.00	6.00	3.00
382	Action photo	15.00	6.00	3.00
383	Action photo	15.00	6.00	3.00
384	Action photo	15.00	6.00	3.00
385	Action photo	15.00	6.00	3.00
386	Action photo	15.00	6.00	3.00
387	Action photo	15.00	6.00	3.00
388	Action photo	15.00	6.00	3.00
389	Antonio Torres, Franklin Parra	15.00	6.00	3.00
390	Action photo	15.00	6.00	3.00
391	Angel Bravo, Luis Aparicio	20.00	8.00	4.00
392	Action photo	15.00	6.00	3.00
393	Action photo	15.00	6.00	3.00
394	Action photo	15.00	6.00	3.00
395	Action photo	15.00	6.00	3.00
396	Action photo	15.00	6.00	3.00
397	Action photo	15.00	6.00	3.00
398	Action photo	15.00	6.00	3.00
399	Action photo	15.00	6.00	3.00
400	Action photo	15.00	6.00	3.00
401	Action photo	15.00	6.00	3.00
402	Tony Armas, Manny Trillo, Gonzalo Marquez	15.00	6.00	3.00

1952 Victoria

Produced during the 1952-53 Winter League season, these paper cards were formatted in the popular Latin American manner to be pasted into a colorful accompanying album. It is possible a principal venue for the set was the ballpark at Havana, since each card urges attendance at games there. The cards are printed on paper in a 2-1/8" x 3-1/8" size. Fronts have colorized photos with white borders, but no player identification. Backs are, of course, in Spanish and include a card number player personal data, career summary and a copyright notice. Besides local players, and former, current and future major league players, the set includes league umpires and broadcasters, etc. Names as presented in this checklist may not correspond exactly with those printed on card backs and may not be correct spellings of player names.

		NM	EX	VG
Complete Set (168):		6,500	3,000	1,500
Common Player:		45.00	20.00	90.00
Album:		350.00	160.00	90.00
1	Amado Maestri/Umpire	45.00	20.00	10.00
2	John Mullen/Umpire	45.00	20.00	10.00
3	Havana Stadium	45.00	20.00	10.00
4	Bernardino Rodriguez/ Umpire	45.00	20.00	10.00
5	Raul Atan/Umpire	45.00	20.00	10.00
6	Cuco Conde/Broadcaster	45.00	20.00	10.00
7	Manolo de la Reguera/ Broadcaster	45.00	20.00	10.00
8	Rafael (Felo) Ramirez/ Broadcaster	60.00	30.00	20.00
9	Rafael Rubi/Broadcaster	45.00	20.00	10.00
10	Gabino Delgado/Broadcaster	45.00	20.00	10.00
11	Fernando Menendez/ Broadcaster	45.00	20.00	10.00
12	Buck Canel/Broadcaster	50.00	25.00	15.00
13	Orlando Sanchez Diago/ Broadcaster	45.00	20.00	10.00
14	Pedro Galiana/Broadcaster	45.00	20.00	10.00
15	Jess Losada/Broadcaster	45.00	20.00	10.00
16	Juan Ealo/Broadcaster	45.00	20.00	10.00
17	Rene Molina/Broadcaster	45.00	20.00	10.00
18	Miguel A. Ruiz/Broadcaster	45.00	20.00	10.00
19	Ruben Rodriguez/ Broadcaster	45.00	20.00	10.00
20	Havana Lions Pennant	30.00	15.00	9.00
21	Miguel Gonzalez	60.00	30.00	20.00
22	Tomas (Pipo) de la Noval	45.00	20.00	10.00
23	Salvador Hernandez	45.00	20.00	10.00
24	Manuel Garcia	45.00	20.00	10.00
25	Edilio Alfaro	45.00	20.00	10.00
26	Julio Navarro	45.00	20.00	10.00
27	Richard Rand	45.00	20.00	10.00
28	Andres Fleitas	45.00	20.00	10.00
29	Isaac Seoane	45.00	20.00	10.00
30	Jimmie Kerrigan	45.00	20.00	10.00
31	Robert Alexander	45.00	20.00	10.00
32	Charles Sipples	45.00	20.00	10.00
33	Adrian Zabala	45.00	20.00	10.00
34	Rogelio Martinez	45.00	20.00	10.00
35	Carlos Pascual	60.00	30.00	20.00
36	Mario Picone	45.00	20.00	10.00
37	Eusebio Perez (Silverio)	45.00	20.00	10.00
38	Julio Moreno	45.00	20.00	10.00
39	Gilberto Torres	45.00	20.00	10.00
40	Bert Haas	45.00	20.00	10.00
41	Johnny Jorgensen	45.00	20.00	10.00
42	Lou Klein	45.00	20.00	10.00
43	Damon Phillips	45.00	20.00	10.00
44	Orlando Varona	45.00	20.00	10.00
45	Jorge Lopez	45.00	20.00	10.00
46	Pedro Formenthal	60.00	30.00	20.00
47	Robert Usher	45.00	20.00	10.00
48	Edmundo (Sandy) Amoros	60.00	30.00	20.00
49	Alejandro Crespo	50.00	25.00	15.00
50	Oscar Sardinas	45.00	20.00	10.00
51	Almendares pennant	30.00	15.00	9.00

52	Robert Bragan	50.00	25.00	15.00
53	Clemente (Sungo) Carreras	45.00	20.00	10.00
54	Rodolfo Fernandez	45.00	20.00	10.00
55	Manuel Fernandez	45.00	20.00	10.00
56	Orlando Echevarria	45.00	20.00	10.00
57	Charles Thompson	45.00	20.00	10.00
58	Oscar Fernandez	45.00	20.00	10.00
59	Hal Erickson	45.00	20.00	10.00
60	Conrado Marrero	50.00	25.00	15.00
61	Agapito Mayor	45.00	20.00	10.00
62	Octavio Rubert	45.00	20.00	10.00
63	Edward Roebuck	45.00	20.00	10.00
64	Duke Markell	50.00	25.00	15.00
65	Rene Massip	45.00	20.00	10.00
66	Pedro Naranjo	45.00	20.00	10.00
67	Roque Contreras	45.00	20.00	10.00
68	Wayne McLeland	45.00	20.00	10.00
69	Frank Kellert	•45.00	20.00	10.00
70	Forrest Jacobs	50.00	25.00	15.00
71	Hector Rodriguez	50.00	25.00	15.00
72	Willy Miranda	50.00	25.00	15.00
73	Roberto Ortiz	50.00	25.00	15.00
74	Frank Carswell	45.00	20.00	10.00
75	Asdrubal Baro	45.00	20.00	10.00
76	Paul Smith	45.00	20.00	10.00
77	Antonio Napoles	45.00	20.00	10.00
78	Francisco Campos	45.00	20.00	10.00
79	Angel Scull	45.00	20.00	10.00
80	Raymond Coleman	45.00	20.00	10.00
81	Gino Cimolli (Cimoli)	50.00	25.00	15.00
82	Amado Ibanez	45.00	20.00	10.00
83	Avelino Canizarez	45.00	20.00	10.00
84	Conrado Perez	45.00	20.00	10.00
85	Marianao pennant	30.00	15.00	9.00
86	Fermin Guerra	50.00	25.00	15.00
87	Jose Maria Fernandez	50.00	25.00	15.00
88	Jose (Joe) Olivares	45.00	20.00	10.00
89	Ramon Carneado	45.00	20.00	10.00
90	Alejandro (Baby) Fernandez	45.00	20.00	10.00
91	Emilio Cabrera	45.00	20.00	10.00
92	Sandalio Consuegra	50.00	25.00	15.00
93	Tomas Fine	45.00	20.00	10.00
94	Miguel Fornieles	50.00	25.00	15.00
95	Camilo Pascual	60.00	30.00	18.00
96	Miguel Lopez	45.00	20.00	10.00
97	Clarence Iott	50.00	25.00	15.00
98	Dale Matthewson	45.00	20.00	10.00
99	Hampton Coleman	50.00	25.00	15.00
100	Terris McDuffie	60.00	30.00	18.00
101	Raul Sanchez	45.00	20.00	10.00
102	Lorenzo Cabrera	45.00	20.00	10.00
103	Ray Dandridge	800.00	400.00	240.00
104	Silvio Garcia	45.00	20.00	10.00
105	Carlos De Souza	45.00	20.00	10.00
106	Oreste (Minnie) Minoso	100.00	50.00	30.00
107	Sebastian Basso	45.00	20.00	10.00
108	William Wilson	45.00	20.00	10.00
109	Hank Workman	50.00	25.00	15.00
110	Fernando Pedroso	45.00	20.00	10.00
111	Juan Antonio Vistuer	45.00	20.00	10.00
112	Hiram Gonzalez	45.00	20.00	10.00
113	Julio Becquer	45.00	20.00	10.00
114	Stan Rojek	45.00	20.00	10.00
115	Ramiro (Cuco) Vasquez	45.00	20.00	10.00
116	Juan Izaguirre	45.00	20.00	10.00
117	Cienfuegos pennant	30.00	15.00	9.00
118	Billy Herman	110.00	55.00	35.00
119	Oscar Rodriguez	45.00	20.00	10.00
120	Julio Rojo	45.00	20.00	10.00
121	Pedro Pages	45.00	20.00	10.00
122	Felix Masud	45.00	20.00	10.00
123	Rafael Noble	50.00	25.00	15.00
124	Mario Diaz	45.00	20.00	10.00
125	Luis Aloma	45.00	20.00	10.00
126	Santiago Ulrich	45.00	20.00	10.00
127	Armando Roche	45.00	20.00	10.00
128	Raul Lopez	45.00	20.00	10.00
129	Armando Suarez	45.00	20.00	10.00
130	Vincente Lopez	45.00	20.00	10.00
131	Ernesto Morillas	45.00	20.00	10.00
132	Alfredo Ibanez	45.00	20.00	10.00
133	Allen J. Gettel	45.00	20.00	10.00
134	Ken Lehman	45.00	20.00	10.00
135	Pat Mc Clothin (McGlothin)	50.00	25.00	15.00
136	Rogenio Otero	45.00	20.00	10.00
137	Felipe Montemayor	45.00	20.00	10.00
138	Jack Cassini	50.00	25.00	15.00
139	Donald Zimmer	75.00	37.00	22.00
140	Robert Wilson	45.00	20.00	10.00
141	Humberto Fernandez	45.00	20.00	10.00
142	Pedro Ballester	45.00	20.00	10.00
143	Walt Morin (Moryn)	50.00	25.00	15.00
144	Roberto Fernandez	45.00	20.00	10.00
145	Claro Duany	60.00	30.00	18.00
146	Pablo Garcia	45.00	20.00	10.00
147	James Pendleton	50.00	25.00	15.00
148	Oscar Sierra	45.00	20.00	10.00
149	Adolfo Luque	80.00	40.00	25.00
150	Cando Lopez	45.00	20.00	10.00
151	Joe Black	100.00	50.00	30.00
152	Napoleon Reyes	60.00	30.00	18.00
153	Rafael (Villa) Cabrera	45.00	20.00	10.00
154	Charles (Red) Barrett	50.00	25.00	15.00
155	Fred Martin	45.00	20.00	10.00
156	Isidoro Leon	45.00	20.00	10.00
157	John Rutherford	50.00	25.00	15.00
158	Max Lanier	50.00	25.00	15.00
159	Julio Ramos	45.00	20.00	10.00
160	Manuel Hidalgo	45.00	20.00	10.00
161	Wilfredo Calvino	45.00	20.00	10.00
162	Joe Nakamura	60.00	30.00	20.00
163	Martiniano Garay	45.00	20.00	10.00
164	Fernando Rodriguez	45.00	20.00	10.00
165	Anibal Navarrette	45.00	20.00	10.00
166	Rafael Rivas	45.00	20.00	10.00
167	Wilfredo Salas	45.00	20.00	10.00
168	Jocko Thompson	45.00	20.00	10.00

1908 Victor Publishing Cy Young

Eschewing booze, broads and gambling made Cy Young famous, according to this postcard issued by an Ohio company near the end of the pitcher's career. The 3-1/2" x 5-1/2" card has a large black-and-white photographic portrait at center with maroon and black illustrations emblematic of typical ballplayers' vices in the corners. The divided-back is printed in black with typical postcard markings.

	NM	EX	VG
Cy Young	450.00	225.00	135.00

1915 Victory Tobacco (T214)

The T214 Victory set of 1915 is an obscure series of tobacco cards that is sometimes mistaken for the better-known T206 "White Border" set. The confusion is understandable because identical player poses were used for both sets. The Victory set can be easily identified, however, by the advertising for the Victory brand on the back of the cards. The set features players from the Federal League, both major leagues and at least one minor leaguer. While card backs advertise "90 Designs," fewer than 60 subjects have surfaced to date. The set had such limited distribution - apparently restricted to just the Louisiana area - and the cards are so rare that it may never be completely checklisted. Except for the advertising on the backs, the Victory cards are almost identical to the "Type 2" Coupon cards (T213), another obscure Louisiana tobacco set issued during the same period. Of the several tobacco sets issued in Louisiana in the early part of the 20th Century, the T214 Victory cards are considered the most difficult to find. Gaps have been left in the numbering sequence to accommodate future additions.

		NM	EX	VG
Common Player:		3,600	1,620	750.00
(1)	Red Ames	7,200	2,880	1,440
(2)	Chief Bender	14,400	5,760	2,880
(3)	Roger Bresnahan	14,400	5,760	2,880
(4)	Al Bridwell	7,200	2,880	1,440
(5)	Howie Camnitz	7,200	2,880	1,440
(6)	Hal Chase/Portrait	10,200	4,080	2,040
(7)	Hal Chase/Throwing	10,200	4,080	2,040
(8)	Ty Cobb/Portrait (Red background.)	30,000	12,000	6,000
(9)	Doc Crandall	7,200	2,880	1,440
(10)	Birdie Cree	7,200	2,880	1,440
(11)	Josh Devore	7,200	2,880	1,440
(12)	Ray Demmitt	7,200	2,880	1,440
(13)	Mickey Doolan	7,200	2,880	1,440
(14)	Mike Donlin	7,200	2,880	1,440
(15)	Tom Downey	7,200	2,880	1,440
(16)	Larry Doyle	7,200	2,880	1,440
(17)	Kid Elberfeld	7,200	2,880	1,440
(18)	Johnny Evers	14,400	5,760	2,880
(19)	Russ Ford	7,200	2,880	1,440
(20)	Art Fromme	7,200	2,880	1,440
(21)	Chick Gandil	14,400	5,760	2,880
(22)	Rube Geyer	7,200	2,880	1,440
(23)	Clark Griffith	14,400	5,760	2,880
(24)	Bob Groom	7,200	2,880	1,440
(25)	Buck Herzog	7,200	2,880	1,440
(26)	Hughie Jennings	14,400	5,760	2,880
(27)	Walter Johnson (Hands at chest.)	18,000	7,200	3,600
(28)	Joe Kelley	14,400	5,760	2,880
(29)	Ed Konetchy	7,200	2,880	1,440
(30)	Nap Lajoie	14,400	5,760	2,880
(31)	Ed Lennox	7,200	2,880	1,440
(32)	Sherry Magee	7,200	2,880	1,440
(33)	Rube Marquard	14,400	5,760	2,880
(34)	John McGraw	14,400	5,760	2,880
(35)	George McQuillan	7,200	2,880	1,440
(36)	Chief Meyers/Catching	7,200	2,880	1,440
(37)	Chief Meyers/Portrait	7,200	2,880	1,440
(38)	George Mullin	7,200	2,880	1,440
(41)	Red Murray	7,200	2,880	1,440
(42)	Tom Needham	7,200	2,880	1,440
(43)	Rebel Oakes	7,200	2,880	1,440
(44)	Dode Paskert	7,200	2,880	1,440
(45)	Jack Quinn	7,200	2,880	1,440
(46)	Nap Rucker	7,200	2,880	1,440
(47)	Germany Schaefer	7,200	2,880	1,440
(48)	Wildfire Schulte	7,200	2,880	1,440
(49)	Frank Smith	7,200	2,880	1,440
(51)	Tris Speaker	16,200	6,480	3,240
(52)	George Stovall	7,200	2,880	1,440
(53)	Ed Summers	7,200	2,880	1,440
(54)	Bill Sweeney	7,200	2,880	1,440
(55)	Jeff Sweeney	7,200	2,880	1,440
(56)	Ira Thomas	7,200	2,880	1,440
(57)	Joe Tinker	14,400	5,760	2,880
(58)	Heinie Wagner	7,200	2,880	1,440
(59)	Zack Wheat	14,400	5,760	2,880
(60)	Kaiser Wilhelm	7,200	2,880	1,440
(61)	Hooks Wiltse	7,200	2,880	1,440

1886 Virginia Brights Black Stocking Nine (N48)

Issued during the late 1880s, though the attributed date is speculative, this series of cabinet-size (about 5" x 7-1/2") blank-back cards was available by sending in coupons found in Allen & Ginter's Virginia Brights brand cigarettes. Fronts have a sepia photo of Rubenesque women in baseball uniforms posed before a painted ballpark backdrop. In the bottom border is "BLACK STOCKING NINE. ALLEN & GINTER'S / Virginia Brights Cigarettes. / Crop of 1884 / HAND MADE CROP OF 1884." The beveled edges of the cabinet mount were originially gilt-trimmed.

	NM	EX	VG
Common Card:	1,000	500.00	300.00

1887 Virginia Brights Polka Dot Nine

Issued during the late 1880s, though the attributed date is speculative, this series of cabinet-size (about 5" x 7-1/2") blank-back cards was available by sending in coupons found in Allen & Ginter's Virginia Brights brand cigarettes. Fronts have a sepia photo of women in baseball uniforms and polka-dot bandanas posed before a backdrop. In the top border of the yellow cardboard mount, printed in gold leaf, is "Virginia Brights / Cigarettes / CROP OF 1884." In a cartouche beneath the photo is "POLKA DOT NINE." Below that is "THE FULL SET OF THIS SERIES COMPRISES NINE DIFFERENT SUBJECTS. / REPRESENTING THE VARIOUS POSITIONS IN BASE BALL."

	NM	EX	VG
Common Card:	900.00	450.00	275.00

1888 Virginia Brights Girl Baseball Players

(See 1888 Allen & Ginter Girl Baseball Players.)

1888 Virginia Brights Black Stocking Nine

Issued during the late 1880s, this series of cabinet-size (about 5" x 7-1/2") blank-back cards was available by sending in coupons found in Allen & Ginter's Virginia Brights brand cigarettes. Fronts have a sepia photo of Rubenesque women in a baseball uniform posed before a painted ballpark backdrop. The picture is framed by a fancy design. In the border above is "Virginia Brights / Cigarettes / Crop of 1884." Below the photo is the series title "Black Stocking Nine" and "The Full Set of this Series Comprises Nine Different / Subjects Representing the Various Positions in Base-Ball."

	NM	EX	VG
Common Card:	2,400	1,200	725.00

1911-16 Virginia Extra Cigarettes (T216)

The T216 baseball card set, issued by several brands of the Peoples Tobacco Co., is the last of the Louisana cigarette sets and the most confusing. Apparently issued over a period of several years between 1911 and 1916, the set employs the same pictures as several contemporary caramel and bakery sets. Cards measure a nominal 1-1/2" x 2-5/8", thought reasonable allowance must be made in consideration of original cutting methodology. Positive identification can be made by the back of the cards. The Peoples Tobacco cards carry advertising for one of three brands of cigarettes: Kotton, Mino or Virginia Extra. The Kotton brand is the most common, while the Virginia Extra and Mino backs command a premium. T216 cards are found in two types; one has a glossy front finish, while a second scarcer type is printed on a thin paper. The thin paper cards command an additional 15 percent premium. The cards represent players from the American, National and Federal Leagues.

	NM	EX	VG
Common Player:	3,300	1,320	660.00
(1) Jack Barry/Btg	3,300	1,320	660.00

		NM	EX	VG
(2)	Jack Barry/Fielding	3,300	1,320	660.00
(3)	Harry Bemis	3,300	1,320	660.00
(4a)	Chief Bender (Philadelphia, striped cap.)	8,800	3,520	1,760
(4b)	Chief Bender (Baltimore, striped cap.)	8,800	3,520	1,760
(5a)	Chief Bender (Philadelphia, white cap.)	8,800	3,520	1,760
(5b)	Chief Bender (Baltimore, white cap.)	8,800	3,520	1,760
(6)	Bill Bergen	3,300	1,320	660.00
(7a)	Bob Bescher (Cincinnati)	3,300	1,320	660.00
(7b)	Bob Bescher (St. Louis)	3,300	1,320	660.00
(8)	Roger Bresnahan	8,800	3,520	1,760
(9)	Al Bridwell/Btg	3,300	1,320	660.00
(10a)	Al Bridwell/Sliding (New York)	3,300	1,320	660.00
(10b)	Al Bridwell/Sliding (St. Louis)	3,300	1,320	660.00
(11)	Donie Bush	3,300	1,320	660.00
(12)	Doc Casey	3,300	1,320	660.00
(13)	Frank Chance	8,800	3,520	1,760
(14a)	Hal Chase/Fielding (New York)	3,300	1,320	660.00
(14b)	Hal Chase/Fielding (Buffalo)	3,300	1,320	660.00
(15)	Hal Chase/Portrait	3,300	1,320	660.00
(16a)	Ty Cobb/Standing (Detroit Am.)	35,750	14,300	7,150
(16b)	Ty Cobb/Standing (Detroit Americans)	33,000	13,200	6,600
(17)	Ty Cobb/Btg (Detroit Americans)	33,000	13,200	6,600
(18a)	Eddie Collins (Phila. Am.)	8,800	3,520	1,760
(18b)	Eddie Collins (Phila. Amer.)	8,800	3,520	1,760
(19)	Eddie Collins (Chicago)	8,800	3,520	1,760
(20a)	Sam Crawford (Small print.)	8,800	3,520	1,760
(20b)	Sam Crawford (Large print.)	8,800	3,520	1,760
(21)	Harry Davis	3,300	1,320	660.00
(22)	Ray Demmitt	3,300	1,320	660.00
(23)	Art Devlin	3,300	1,320	660.00
(24a)	Wild Bill Donovan (Detroit)	3,300	1,320	660.00
(24b)	Wild Bill Donovan (New York)	3,300	1,320	660.00
(25a)	Red Dooin (Philadelphia)	3,300	1,320	660.00
(25b)	Red Dooin (Cincinnati)	3,300	1,320	660.00
(26a)	Mickey Doolan (Philadelphia)	3,300	1,320	660.00
(26b)	Mickey Doolan (Baltimore)	3,300	1,320	660.00
(27)	Patsy Dougherty	3,300	1,320	660.00
(28a)	Larry Doyle, Larry Doyle (N.Y. Nat'l, batting)	3,300	1,320	660.00
(28b)	Larry Doyle/Bth (New York Nat'l)	3,300	1,320	660.00
(29)	Larry Doyle/Throwing	3,300	1,320	660.00
(30)	Clyde Engle	3,300	1,320	660.00
(31a)	Johnny Evers (Chicago)	8,800	3,520	1,760
(31b)	Johnny Evers (Boston)	8,800	3,520	1,760
(32)	Art Fromme	3,300	1,320	660.00
(33a)	George Gibson (Pittsburg Nat'l, back view.)	3,300	1,320	660.00
(33b)	George Gibson (Pittsburg Nat'l., back view.)	3,300	1,320	660.00
(34a)	George Gibson (Pittsburg Nat'l, front view.)	3,300	1,320	660.00
(34b)	George Gibson (Pittsburg Nat'l., front view.)	3,300	1,320	660.00
(35a)	Topsy Hartsel (Phila. Am.)	3,300	1,320	660.00
(35b)	Topsy Hartsel (Phila. Amer.)	3,300	1,320	660.00
(36)	Roy Hartzell/Btg	3,300	1,320	660.00
(37)	Roy Hartzell/Catching	3,300	1,320	660.00
(38a)	Fred Jacklitsch (Philadelphia)	3,300	1,320	660.00
(38b)	Fred Jacklitsch (Baltimore)	3,300	1,320	660.00
(39a)	Hughie Jennings (Orange background.)	8,800	3,520	1,760
(39b)	Hughie Jennings (Red background.)	8,800	3,520	1,760
(40)	Red Kleinow	3,300	1,320	660.00
(41a)	Otto Knabe (Philadelphia)	3,300	1,320	660.00
(41b)	Otto Knabe (Baltimore)	3,300	1,320	660.00
(42)	Jack Knight	3,300	1,320	660.00
(43a)	Nap Lajoie/Fielding (Philadelphia)	13,750	5,500	2,750
(43b)	Nap Lajoie/Fielding (Cleveland)	13,750	5,500	2,750
(44)	Nap Lajoie/Portrait	13,750	5,500	2,750
(45a)	Hans Lobert (Cincinnati)	3,300	1,320	660.00
(45b)	Hans Lobert (New York)	3,300	1,320	660.00
(46)	Sherry Magee	3,300	1,320	660.00
(47)	Rube Marquard	8,800	3,520	1,760
(48a)	Christy Matthewson (Mathewson) (Large print.)	33,000	13,200	6,600
(48b)	Christy Matthewson (Mathewson) (Small print.)	33,000	13,200	6,600
(49a)	John McGraw (Large print.)	8,800	3,520	1,760
(49b)	John McGraw (Small print.)	8,800	3,520	1,760
(50)	Larry McLean	3,300	1,320	660.00
(51)	George McQuillan	3,300	1,320	660.00
(52)	Dots Miller/Btg	3,300	1,320	660.00
(53a)	Dots Miller/Fielding (Pittsburg)	3,300	1,320	660.00
(53b)	Dots Miller/Fielding (St. Louis)	3,300	1,320	660.00
(54a)	Danny Murphy (Philadelphia)	3,300	1,320	660.00
(54b)	Danny Murphy (Brooklyn)	3,300	1,320	660.00
(55)	Rebel Oakes	3,300	1,320	660.00
(56)	Bill O'Hara	3,300	1,320	660.00
(57)	Eddie Plank	8,800	3,520	1,760
(58a)	Germany Schaefer (Washington)	3,300	1,320	660.00
(58b)	Germany Schaefer (Newark)	3,300	1,320	660.00
(59)	Admiral Schlei	3,300	1,320	660.00
(60)	Boss Schmidt	3,300	1,320	660.00
(61)	Johnny Seigle	3,300	1,320	660.00
(62)	Dave Shean	3,300	1,320	660.00
(63)	Boss Smith (Schmidt)	3,300	1,320	660.00
(64)	Tris Speaker	16,500	6,600	3,300
(65)	Oscar Stanage	3,300	1,320	660.00

		NM	EX	VG
(66)	George Stovall	3,300	1,320	660.00
(67)	Jeff Sweeney	3,300	1,320	660.00
(68a)	Joe Tinker/Btg (Chicago Nat'l)	8,800	3,520	1,760
(68b)	Joe Tinker/Btg (Chicago Feds)	8,800	3,520	1,760
(69)	Joe Tinker/Portrait	8,800	3,520	1,760
(70a)	Honus Wagner/Btg (S.S.)	33,000	13,200	6,600
(70b)	Honus Wagner/Btg (2b.)	33,000	13,200	6,600
(71a)	Honus Wagner/Throwing (S.S.)	33,000	13,200	6,600
(71b)	Honus Wagner/Throwing (2b.)	33,000	13,200	6,600
(72)	Hooks Wiltse	3,300	1,320	660.00
(73)	Cy Young	22,000	8,800	4,400
(74a)	Heinie Zimmerman (2b.)	3,300	1,320	660.00
(74b)	Heinie Zimmerman (3b.)	3,300	1,320	660.00

1949 Vis-Ed Cleveland Indian Slide-Cards

These unique novelties feature the members of the World Champion 1948 Cleveland Indians. The players are pictured on a single frame of 16mm film which has been inserted into slits cut on one end of the cardboard. The cardboard holders are dark blue and yellow, with blue printing. Fronts have player personal data, career highlights, the player's name in script and identification of the issuer. Backs have a list of "Magic Slides" which could be ordered for 33 cents each. It is likely that a slide-card exists for each of the players on that list, but only those which have been confirmed to date are checklisted here, in alphabetical order. Complete slide-cards measure 3-3/4" x 2". A plastic baseball-shaped viewer was sold with the slides.

		NM	EX	VG
Common Player:		75.00	37.00	22.00
(1)	Lou Boudreau	90.00	45.00	27.00
(2)	Larry Doby	100.00	50.00	30.00
(3)	Bob Feller	125.00	62.00	37.00
(4)	Joe Gordon	75.00	37.00	22.00
(5)	Jim Hegan	75.00	37.00	22.00
(6)	Ken Keltner	75.00	37.00	22.00

1949 Vis-Ed Cleveland Indian Magic Dials

Similar in concept to a Viewmaster, these hand-held "Magic Dial Big League Viewers" feature the members of the World Champion 1948 Cleveland Indians, plus Mickey Vernon, who joined the team in 1949, and, inexplicably, Pittsburgh Pirate Ralph Kiner. Each of the players is pictured on six single frames of 8 mm movie film (once in color, but now usually faded to sepia tones) mounted on a 2" cardboard circle within a red, white and blue 2-1/4" x 2" rectangular frame; the whole is held together by a metal rivet. The pictures can be viewed by turning the round cardboard dial. The dials came with a playing tips instructional pamphlet. Original price was 29 cents apiece.

		NM	EX	VG
Complete Set (15):		1,200	600.00	350.00
Common Player:		75.00	37.00	22.00
(1)	Gene Bearden	75.00	37.00	22.00
(2)	Lou Boudreau/Btg	125.00	62.00	37.00
(3)	Lou Boudreau (Double play.)	125.00	62.00	37.00
(4)	Lou Boudreau (Shortstop.)	125.00	62.00	37.00
(5)	Larry Doby	125.00	62.00	37.00
(6)	Bob Feller	150.00	74.00	45.00
(7)	Joe Gordon (Double play.)	75.00	37.00	22.00
(8)	Joe Gordon (Second base.)	75.00	37.00	22.00
(9)	Jim Hegan	75.00	37.00	22.00

		NM	EX	VG
(10)	Ken Keltner	75.00	37.00	22.00
(11)	Ralph Kiner	125.00	62.00	37.00
(12)	Bob Lemon	125.00	62.00	37.00
(13)	Dale Mitchell	75.00	37.00	22.00
(14)	Satchel Paige	200.00	100.00	60.00
(15)	Mickey Vernon	75.00	37.00	22.00

1966 Volpe Tumblers

A number of teams co-operated in the production of baseball player 12-oz. thermal tumblers which were distributed at local gas stations for a small sum and/or a minimum fuel purchase. The plastic tumblers have artwork portraits and smaller action pictures by Nicholas Volpe and facsimile autographs on colorful backgrounds. The glasses are 5-1/4" tall and 3" in diameter at the rim.

		NM	EX	VG
Common Player:		20.00	10.00	6.00
CINCINNATI REDS				
(1)	Chico Cardenas	20.00	10.00	6.00
(2)	Gordy Coleman	20.00	10.00	6.00
(3)	John Edwards	20.00	10.00	6.00
(4)	Sammy Ellis	20.00	10.00	6.00
(5)	Tommy Harper	20.00	10.00	6.00
(6)	Deron Johnson	20.00	10.00	6.00
(7)	Jim Maloney	20.00	10.00	6.00
(8)	Billy McCool	20.00	10.00	6.00
(9)	Joe Nuxhall	20.00	10.00	6.00
(10)	Jim O'Toole	20.00	10.00	6.00
(11)	Vada Pinson	30.00	15.00	9.00
(12)	Pete Rose	75.00	37.00	22.00
CLEVELAND INDIANS				
(1)	Max Alvis	20.00	10.00	6.00
(2)	Joe Azcue	20.00	10.00	6.00
(3)	Larry Brown	20.00	10.00	6.00
(4)	Rocky Colavito	50.00	25.00	15.00
(5)	Vic Davalillo	20.00	10.00	6.00
(6)	Chuck Hinton	20.00	10.00	6.00
(7)	Dick Howser	20.00	10.00	6.00
(8)	Sam McDowell	20.00	10.00	6.00
(9)	Don McMahon	20.00	10.00	6.00
(10)	Sonny Siebert	20.00	10.00	6.00
(11)	Leon Wagner	20.00	10.00	6.00
(12)	Fred Whitfield	20.00	10.00	6.00
NEW YORK METS				
(1)	Larry Bearnarth	20.00	10.00	6.00
(2)	Yogi Berra	50.00	25.00	15.00
(3)	Jack Fisher	20.00	10.00	6.00
(4)	Rob Gardner	20.00	10.00	6.00
(5)	Jim Hickman	20.00	10.00	6.00
(6)	Ron Hunt	20.00	10.00	6.00
(7)	Ed Kranepool	20.00	10.00	6.00
(8)	Johnny Lewis	20.00	10.00	6.00
(9)	Tug McGraw	20.00	10.00	6.00
(10)	Roy McMillan	20.00	10.00	6.00
(11)	Dick Stuart	20.00	10.00	6.00
(12)	Ron Swoboda	20.00	10.00	6.00
DETROIT TIGERS				
(1)	Hank Aguirre	20.00	10.00	6.00
(2)	Norm Cash	30.00	15.00	9.00
(3)	Don Demeter	20.00	10.00	6.00
(4)	Bill Freehan	20.00	10.00	6.00
(5)	Willie Horton	20.00	10.00	6.00
(6)	Al Kaline	50.00	25.00	15.00
(7)	Mickey Lolich	20.00	10.00	6.00
(8)	Dick McAuliffe	20.00	10.00	6.00
(9)	Denny McLain	20.00	10.00	6.00
(10)	Joe Sparma	20.00	10.00	6.00
(11)	Don Wert	20.00	10.00	6.00
(12)	Dave Wickersham	20.00	10.00	6.00
LOS ANGELES DODGERS				
(1)	Tommy Davis	20.00	10.00	6.00
(2)	Willie Davis	20.00	10.00	6.00
(3)	Don Drysdale	40.00	20.00	12.00
(4)	Ron Fairly	20.00	10.00	6.00
(5)	John Kennedy	20.00	10.00	6.00
(6)	Jim Lefebvre	20.00	10.00	6.00
(7)	Sandy Koufax	60.00	30.00	18.00
(8)	Claude Osteen	20.00	10.00	6.00
(9)	Wes Parker	20.00	10.00	6.00
(10)	Ron Perranoski	20.00	10.00	6.00
(11)	Johnny Roseboro	20.00	10.00	6.00
(12)	Maury Wills	20.00	10.00	6.00

1913 Voskamp's Coffee Pittsburgh Pirates

The 1913 Pittsburgh Pirates are featured in this set of cards given away in packages of coffee and tea and redeemable for seats at Pirates games. The 2-1/4" x 3-5/8" cards have black-and-white player photos on a plain white background, along with ID and a "Photo by Johnston" credit line. The black-and-white back has a checklist of the set and details of the ticket redemption program. Pose variations of the Hofman and O'Toole cards are reported to exist. The checklist for the unnumbered cards is presented here alphabetically. Because the set was issued just after the great tobacco card era, several of the Pirates in this set are not found on any other cards.

		NM	EX	VG
Complete Set (20):		60,000	30,000	18,000
Common Player:		2,025	1,015	600.00
(1)	Babe Adams	2,025	1,015	600.00
(2)	Everitt Booe	2,025	1,015	600.00
(3)	Bobby Byrne	2,025	1,015	600.00
(4)	Howie Camnitz	2,025	1,015	600.00
(5)	Max Carey	3,000	1,500	900.00
(6)	Joe Conzelman	2,025	1,015	600.00
(7)	Jack Ferry	2,025	1,015	600.00
(8)	George Gibson	2,025	1,015	600.00
(9)	Claude Hendrix	2,025	1,015	600.00
(10)	Solly Hofman	2,025	1,015	600.00
(11)	Ham Hyatt	2,025	1,015	600.00
(12)	Bill Kelly	2,025	1,015	600.00
(13)	Ed Mensor	2,025	1,015	600.00
(14)	Dots Miller	2,025	1,015	600.00
(15)	Marty O'Toole	2,025	1,015	600.00
(16)	Hank Robinson	2,025	1,015	600.00
(17)	Mike Simon	2,025	1,015	600.00
(18)	Jim Viox	2,025	1,015	600.00
(19)	Honus Wagner	22,500	11,250	6,750
(20)	Owen Wilson	2,025	1,015	600.00

1910 Hans Wagner Cigars

Circa 1910 the Freeman Cigar Co. apparently envisioned marketing a product named for the Pirates star shortstop. While it appears the cigar was never actually produced, various packaging elements have survived in proof examples. Most pieces are embossed and have a color lithograph which features a portrait of Wagner against a ballgame background. "HANS WAGNER" is in red and gold above. Usually found in the bottom border is "Title & Design Registered by Freeman Cigar Co.". Collectors must be aware that various modern fantasy pieces purporting to be of the same genre exist in the market.

	NM	EX	VG
Hans Wagner	15,000	7,500	4,500
(7-1/4" x 6-1/2" box label)			

	NM	EX	VG
Hans Wagner	12,000	6,000	3,500
(4-1/2" octagonal label)			
Hans Wagner	15,000	7,500	4,500
(4-1/4" oval label)			
Hans Wagner (3" cigar band.)	1,600	800.00	480.00
Hans Wagner	1,500	750.00	450.00
(Typographic box-side label.)			
Hans Wagner	7,500	3,750	2,250
(Typographic box-top label.)			

1880s John M. Ward Fan

The specific date of production for this ornate hand fan is unknown. Some examples show on their back an advertisement for "C. Philpot" of Springfield, Maine. The central portion of the fan is a round piece of heavy cardboard, about 7-3/4" in diameter, that features a color lithographic portrait of Ward on a baseball background. Around the picture is a peach-colored ribbon. A wooden handle is attached on back.

	NM	EX	VG
John M. Ward	6,500	3,500	2,250

1934 Ward's Sporties Pins

The date of issue can only be approximated for this issue of 1-1/4" diameter celluloid pin-back buttons. Ward's Sporties was evidently some kind of food product; at the center of each button is a black-and-white or blue-and-white portrait photo of a player with his name above and "Eats" below the picture. Printed around the photo portion in white on a red background is: "Good Sports Enjoy / WARD'S SPORTIES." Ward's bakeries issue several type of baseball cards and collectibles over the years, such as the 1947 Tip-Top bread cards. The checklist is in alphabetical order, and may not yet be complete.

		NM	EX	VG
Complete Set (8):		4,500	2,250	1,350
Common Player:		325.00	160.00	100.00
(1)	Dizzy Dean	1,000	500.00	300.00
(2)	Jimmy Dykes	325.00	160.00	100.00
(3)	Jimmie Foxx	1,000	500.00	300.00
(4)	Frank Frisch	650.00	325.00	195.00
(5)	Charlie Gehringer	650.00	325.00	195.00
(6)	Charlie Grimm	325.00	160.00	100.00
(7)	Schoolboy Rowe	325.00	160.00	100.00
(8)	Jimmie Wilson	325.00	160.00	100.00

1916 Ware's

One of several regional advertisers to use this 200-card set as a promotional medium was this New Rochelle, N.Y., store's sporting goods department. The checklist and relative value information are listed under 1916 M101-4 Blank Backs. Collectors can expect to pay a significant premium for individual cards to enhance a type card or superstar card collection. The American Card Catalog listed these 1-5/8" x 3" black-and-white cards as H801-9.

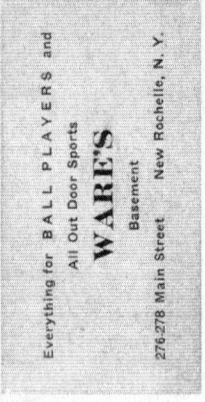

BOB VEACH
L. F.—Detroit Americans
179

PREMIUMS:
Common Players: 2-4X
Hall of Famers: 1.5-2.5X
(See 1916 Sporting News M101-4 for checklist and price guide.)

1872 Warren Studio Boston Red Stockings Cabinets

The champions from the premiere season of baseball's first professional league (some wearing their championship pins), are pictured on these cabinet cards. Members of the Boston Red Stockings were photographed in uniform at a local studio. The cards measure about 4-1/4" x 6-1/2" with sepia photos. In the bottom border is the name and address of the studio; information that is repeated on the otherwise blank back. Player identification is not found on the cards but can be deduced by studying contemporary team pictures.

	Common Player:	NM	EX	VG
	Common Player:	5,000	2,500	1,500
(1)	Ross Barnes	7,500	2,500	1,500
(2)	Dave Birdsall	6,000	2,500	1,500
(3)	Charles Gould	6,000	2,500	1,500
(4)	Andy Leonard	6,000	2,500	1,500
(5)	Cal McVey	7,500	2,500	1,500
(6)	Fraley Rogers	6,000	2,500	1,500
(7)	John Ryan	6,000	2,500	1,500
(8)	Harry Schafer	6,000	2,500	1,500
(9)	Albert Spalding	35,000	7,500	4,500
(10)	George Wright	25,000	7,500	4,500
(11)	Harry Wright	25,000	7,500	4,500

1872 Warren Studio Boston Red Stockings CDVs

WARREN   460 Washington St. Boston.

The champions from the premiere season of baseball's first professional league (some wearing their championship pins), are pictured on these cartes de visites depict. Members of the Boston Red Stockings

were photographed at a local studio, most of them being pictured in coat-and-tie with only Harry Wright in uniform. The cards measure about 2-1/2" x 4-1/4" with sepia photos bordered in white. In the bottom border is the name and address of the studio; information which is repeated on the otherwise blank back. Player identification is not found on the cards but can be deduced by studying contemporary team pictures.

	Common Player:	NM	EX	VG
	Common Player:	3,500	1,750	1,000
(1)	Ross Barnes	3,500	1,750	1,000
(2)	Dave Birdsall	3,500	1,750	1,000
(3)	Charlie Gould	3,500	1,750	1,000
(4)	Andy Leonard	3,500	1,750	1,000
(5)	Cal McVey	3,500	1,750	1,000
(6)	Fraley Rogers	3,500	1,750	1,000
(7)	John Ryan	3,500	1,750	1,000
(8)	Harry Schafer	3,500	1,750	1,000
(9)	George Wright	10,000	5,000	3,000
(10)	Harry Wright (Street clothes.)	10,000	5,000	3,000
(11)	Harry Wright (Uniform)	10,000	5,000	3,000

1874 Warren Studio Boston Red Stockings Cabinets

The champions from the National Association Boston Red Stockings were photographed in uniform at a local studio. The cards measure about 4-1/4" x 6-1/2" with sepia photos. In the bottom border is the name and address of the studio. Player identification is not found on the cards but can be deduced by studying contemporary team pictures.

	Common Player:	NM	EX	VG
	Common Player:	5,000	2,500	1,500
(1)	Ross Barnes	7,500	2,500	1,500
(2)	Tommy Beals	6,000	2,500	1,500
(3)	George Hall	6,000	2,500	1,500
(4)	Andy Leonard	5,000	2,500	1,500
(5)	Cal McVey	7,500	2,500	1,500
(6)	Harry Schafer	6,000	2,500	1,500

1931 Washington Senators Picture Pack

This set of souvenir pictures offers player photos in a black-and-white, blank-back format of about 6-1/8" x 9-1/2". Each picture has a white border and a facsimile player autograph.

		NM	EX	VG
	Complete Set (30):	800.00	400.00	240.00
	Common Player:	25.00	12.50	7.50
(1)	Nick Altrock	35.00	17.50	10.50
(2)	Oswald Bluege	25.00	12.50	7.50
(3)	Cliff Bolton	25.00	12.50	7.50
(4)	Lloyd Brown	25.00	12.50	7.50
(5)	Robert Burke	25.00	12.50	7.50
(6)	Joe Cronin	50.00	25.00	15.00
(7)	Alvin Crowder	25.00	12.50	7.50
(8)	E.B. Eynon, Jr. (Secretary-Treasurer)	25.00	12.50	7.50
(9)	Charles Fischer	25.00	12.50	7.50
(10)	Edward Gharrity	25.00	12.50	7.50
(11)	Clark Griffith	45.00	22.00	13.50
(12)	Irving Hadley	25.00	12.50	7.50
(13)	William Hargrave	25.00	12.50	7.50
(14)	David Harris	25.00	12.50	7.50
(15)	Jack Hayes	25.00	12.50	7.50
(16)	Walter Johnson	125.00	62.00	37.00
(17)	Sam Jones	25.00	12.50	7.50
(18)	Baxter Jordan	25.00	12.50	7.50
(19)	Joe Judge	25.00	12.50	7.50
(20)	Joe Kuhel	25.00	12.50	7.50
(21)	Henry Manush	50.00	25.00	15.00
(22)	Fred Marberry	25.00	12.50	7.50
(23)	Mike Martin	25.00	12.50	7.50
(24)	Walter Masters	25.00	12.50	7.50
(25)	Charles Myer	25.00	12.50	7.50
(26)	Harry Rice	25.00	12.50	7.50
(27)	Sam Rice	25.00	12.50	7.50
(28)	Al Schacht	35.00	17.50	10.50
(29)	Roy Spencer	25.00	12.50	7.50
(30)	Sam West	25.00	12.50	7.50

1970 Washington Senators Traffic Safety

EDDIE BRINKMAN
Short Stop
Washington Senators

ERRORS IN BASEBALL COST GAMES

ERRORS IN TRAFFIC COST LIVES

PLAY IT SAFE!

D.C. DEPARTMENT OF MOTOR VEHICLES
Office of Traffic Safety

Distributed in 1970 by the Washington, D.C. Department of Motor Vehicles, this issue promoting traffic safety was one of the first police sets. Featuring black-and-white player photos, the cards measure 2-1/2" x 3-7/8" and have large borders surrounding the pictures. The player's name and position are below; the team name appears in smaller type at the bottom. The set can be found on either pink card stock, used for the original print run, or on bright yellow stock, used for two subsequent printings. Aurelio Rodriguez, who joined the team after the season began, is known only in yellow; all other players can be found in both yellow and pink. The pink varieties carry a higher value. The backs of the cards offer traffic safety tips.

		NM	EX	VG
	Complete Set, Pink (10):	150.00	75.00	45.00
	Common Player, Pink:	3.50	1.75	1.00
	Complete Set, Yellow (11):	25.00	12.50	7.50
	Common Player, Yellow:	2.50	1.25	.70
(1a)	Dick Bosman (Pink)	3.50	1.75	1.00
(1b)	Dick Bosman (Yellow)	2.50	1.25	.70
(2a)	Eddie Brinkman (Pink)	3.50	1.75	1.00
(2b)	Eddie Brinkman (Yellow)	2.50	1.25	.70
(3a)	Paul Casanova (Pink)	3.50	1.75	1.00
(3b)	Paul Casanova (Yellow)	2.50	1.25	.70
(4a)	Mike Epstein (Pink)	3.50	1.75	1.00
(4b)	Mike Epstein (Yellow)	2.50	1.25	.70
(5a)	Frank Howard (Pink)	10.00	5.00	3.00
(5b)	Frank Howard (Yellow)	7.50	3.75	2.25
(6a)	Darold Knowles (Pink)	3.50	1.75	1.00
(6b)	Darold Knowles (Yellow)	2.50	1.25	.70
(7a)	Lee Maye (Pink)	3.50	1.75	1.00
(7b)	Lee Maye (Yellow)	2.50	1.25	.70
(8a)	Dave Nelson (Pink)/SP	125.00	62.00	37.00
(8b)	Dave Nelson (Yellow)	2.50	1.25	.70
(9)	Aurelio Rodriguez (Yellow)/SP	5.00	2.50	1.50
(10a)	John Roseboro (Pink)	3.50	1.75	1.00
(10b)	John Roseboro (Yellow)	2.50	1.25	.70
(11a)	Ed Stroud (Pink)	3.50	1.75	1.00
(11b)	Ed Stroud (Yellow)	2.50	1.25	.70

1971 Washington Senators Traffic Safety

DENNY McLAIN
Pitcher
Washington Senators

A FAST BALL CAN GET YOU "OUT" OF TROUBLE

A FAST CAR CAN GET YOU "INTO" TROUBLE

PLAY IT SAFE!

D.C. DEPARTMENT OF MOTOR VEHICLES
Office of Traffic Safety

The 1971 Senators safety set was again issued by the Washington, D.C., Department of Motor Vehicles and was similar in design and size (2-1/2" x 3-7/8") to the previous year, except that it was printed on a pale yellow stock. The set, which features several new players, contains no scarce cards. The backs contain traffic safety messages.

		NM	EX	VG
	Complete Set (10):	12.50	6.25	3.75
	Uncut Sheet:	12.50	6.25	3.75
	Common Player:	1.00	.50	.30
(1)	Dick Bosman	1.00	.50	.30
(2)	Paul Casanova	1.00	.50	.30
(3)	Tim Cullen	1.00	.50	.30
(4)	Joe Foy	1.00	.50	.30
(5)	Toby Harrah	1.00	.50	.30
(6)	Frank Howard	2.50	1.25	.70
(7)	Elliott Maddox	1.00	.50	.30
(8)	Tom McCraw	1.00	.50	.30
(9)	Denny McLain	3.00	1.50	.90
(10)	Don Wert	.60	.30	.20

1910 Washington Times

WALKER   WASHINGTON TIMES SERIES
WASHINGTON

Only American League players have so far been found in this issue by the Washington Times newspaper. The 2-9/16" x 3-9/16" cards have portrait or action photos of the players within a wide border. A white panel at bottom has the player name and team at left and "Washington Times Series" at right. All printing is in dark red. Backs are blank. The manner in which these cards were distributed is unknown, as is the extent of the checklist. The unnumbered cards are checklisted here in alphabetical order.

		NM	EX	VG
	Common Player:	2,500	1,250	750.00
(1)	Ty Cobb	20,000	10,000	6,000
(2)	Eddie Collins	7,500	3,750	2,250
(3)	Wid Conroy	2,500	1,250	750.00
(4)	Sam Crawford	7,500	3,750	2,250
(5)	Harry Davis	2,500	1,250	750.00
(6)	Bob Groom	2,500	1,250	750.00
(7)	Nap Lajoie	7,500	3,750	2,250
(8)	George McBride	2,500	1,250	750.00
(9)	Clyde Milan	2,500	1,250	750.00
(10)	Frank Oberlin	2,500	1,250	750.00
(11)	Rube Oldring	2,500	1,250	750.00
(12)	Freddie Parent (Freddy)	2,500	1,250	750.00
(13)	Doc Reisling	2,500	1,250	750.00
(14)	Gabby Street	2,500	1,250	750.00
(15)	Lee Tannehill	2,500	1,250	750.00
(16)	Bob Unglaub	2,500	1,250	750.00
(17)	Dixie Walker	2,500	1,250	750.00
(18)	Ed. Walsh	7,500	3,750	2,250
(19)	Joe Wood	2,000	1,000	600.00
(20)	Cy Young	12,500	6,250	3,750

1951 WBKB "Lucky Fan" Chicago Cubs

This series of black-and-white player glossies appears to have been a promotional giveaway from WBKB radio or television station in conjunction with Ben Bey's "Lucky Fan" club or contest. The 8-1/8" x 10" photos have a facsimile autograph on front. On back is a three-line rubber-stamped "COURTESY OF / BEN BEY LUCKY FAN / WBKB - CHICAGO." The checklist is arranged alphabetically.

		NM	EX	VG
	Complete Set (28):	900.00	450.00	270.00
	Common Player:	40.00	20.00	12.00
(1)	Frank Baumholtz	40.00	20.00	12.00
(2)	Bob Borkowski	40.00	20.00	12.00
(3)	Smoky Burgess	50.00	25.00	15.00
(4)	Phil Cavarretta	40.00	20.00	12.00
(5)	Chuck Connors	100.00	50.00	30.00
(6)	Jack Cusick	40.00	20.00	12.00
(7)	Bruce Edwards	40.00	20.00	12.00
(8)	Dee Fondy	40.00	20.00	12.00
(9)	Joe Hatten	40.00	20.00	12.00
(10)	Gene Hermanski	40.00	20.00	12.00
(11)	Frank Hiller	40.00	20.00	12.00
(12)	Ransom Jackson	40.00	20.00	12.00
(13)	Hal Jeffcoat	40.00	20.00	12.00
(14)	Bob Kelly	40.00	20.00	12.00
(15)	Johnny Klippstein	40.00	20.00	12.00
(16)	Dutch Leonard	40.00	20.00	12.00
(17)	Turk Lown	40.00	20.00	12.00
(18)	Cal McLish	40.00	20.00	12.00
(19)	Eddie Miksis	40.00	20.00	12.00
(20)	Paul Minner	40.00	20.00	12.00
(21)	Mickey Owen	40.00	20.00	12.00
(22)	Andy Pafko	50.00	25.00	15.00
(23)	Bob Ramazotti	40.00	20.00	12.00
(24)	Bob Rush	40.00	20.00	12.00
(25)	Hank Sauer	40.00	20.00	12.00
(26)	Bob Schultz	40.00	20.00	12.00
(27)	Bill Serena	40.00	20.00	12.00
(28)	Roy Smalley	45.00	22.00	13.50

1911-14 Weber Bakery (D304)

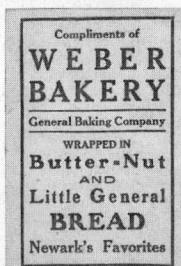

(See 1911-14 General Baking Co. for checklist and price information.)

1916 Weil Baking Co. (D329)

One of several issues by the New Orleans bakery, this 1-3/8" x 3" black-and-white set of 200 shares a checklist and relative values with the 1916 M101-4 Blank Backs set. Collectors can expect to pay a premium for a card with the Weil Baking ad on back to add to a type collection or superstar collection. The American Card Catalog lists this issue as D329.

		NM	EX	VG
	Complete Set (200):	77,000	38,500	23,100
	Common Player:	200.00	100.00	50.00
1	Babe Adams	200.00	100.00	50.00
2	Sam Agnew	200.00	100.00	50.00
3	Eddie Ainsmith	200.00	100.00	50.00
4	Grover Alexander	900.00	500.00	200.00
5	Leon Ames	200.00	100.00	50.00
6	Jimmy Archer	200.00	100.00	50.00
7	Jimmy Austin	200.00	100.00	50.00
8	H.D. Baird	200.00	100.00	50.00
9	J. Franklin Baker	700.00	400.00	200.00
10	Dave Bancroft	700.00	400.00	200.00
11	Jack Barry	200.00	100.00	50.00
12	Zinn Beck	200.00	100.00	50.00
13	"Chief" Bender	700.00	400.00	200.00
14	Joe Benz	200.00	100.00	50.00
15	Bob Bescher	200.00	100.00	50.00
16	Al Betzel	200.00	100.00	50.00
17	Mordecai Brown	700.00	400.00	200.00
18	Eddie Burns	200.00	100.00	50.00
19	George Burns	200.00	100.00	50.00
20	Geo. J. Burns	200.00	100.00	50.00
21	Joe Bush	200.00	100.00	50.00
22	"Donie" Bush	200.00	100.00	50.00
23	Art Butler	200.00	100.00	50.00
24	Bobbie Byrne	200.00	100.00	50.00
25	Forrest Cady	200.00	100.00	50.00
26	Jimmy Callahan	200.00	100.00	50.00
27	Ray Caldwell	200.00	100.00	50.00
28	Max Carey	700.00	400.00	200.00
29	George Chalmers	200.00	100.00	50.00
30	Ray Chapman	200.00	100.00	50.00
31	Larry Cheney	200.00	100.00	50.00
32	Eddie Cicotte	1,000	400.00	200.00
33	Tom Clarke	200.00	100.00	50.00
34	Eddie Collins	700.00	400.00	200.00
35	"Shauno" Collins	200.00	100.00	50.00
36	Charles Comiskey	700.00	400.00	200.00
37	Joe Connolly	200.00	100.00	50.00
38	Ty Cobb	5,500	2,900	1,400
39	Harry Coveleskie (Coveleski)	200.00	100.00	50.00
40	Gavvy Cravath	200.00	100.00	50.00
41	Sam Crawford	700.00	400.00	200.00
42	Jean Dale	200.00	100.00	50.00
43	Jake Daubert	200.00	100.00	50.00
44	Charles Deal	200.00	100.00	50.00
45	Al Demaree	200.00	100.00	50.00
46	Josh Devore	200.00	100.00	50.00
47	William Doak	200.00	100.00	50.00
48	Bill Donovan	200.00	100.00	50.00
49	Charles Dooin	200.00	100.00	50.00
50	Mike Doolan	200.00	100.00	50.00
51	Larry Doyle	200.00	100.00	50.00
52	Jean Dubuc	200.00	100.00	50.00
53	Oscar Dugey	200.00	100.00	50.00
54	Johnny Evers	700.00	400.00	200.00
55	Urban Faber	700.00	400.00	200.00
56	"Hap" Felsch	2,000	900.00	400.00
57	Bill Fischer	200.00	100.00	50.00
58	Ray Fisher	200.00	100.00	50.00
59	Max Flack	200.00	100.00	50.00
60	Art Fletcher	200.00	100.00	50.00
61	Eddie Foster	200.00	100.00	50.00
62	Jacques Fournier	200.00	100.00	50.00
63	Del Gainer (Gainor)	200.00	100.00	50.00
64	"Chic" Gandil	700.00	400.00	200.00
65	Larry Gardner	200.00	100.00	50.00
66	Joe Gedeon	200.00	100.00	50.00
67	Gus Getz	200.00	100.00	50.00
68	Geo. Gibson	200.00	100.00	50.00
69	Wilbur Good	200.00	100.00	50.00
70	Hank Gowdy	200.00	100.00	50.00
71	John Graney	200.00	100.00	50.00
72	Clark Griffith	700.00	400.00	200.00
73	Tom Griffith	200.00	100.00	50.00
74	Heinie Groh	200.00	100.00	50.00
75	Earl Hamilton	200.00	100.00	50.00
76	Bob Harmon	200.00	100.00	50.00
77	Roy Hartzell	200.00	100.00	50.00
78	Claude Hendrix	200.00	100.00	50.00
79	Olaf Henriksen	200.00	100.00	50.00
80	John Henry	200.00	100.00	50.00
81	"Buck" Herzog	200.00	100.00	50.00
82	Hugh High	200.00	100.00	50.00
83	Dick Hoblitzell	200.00	100.00	50.00
84	Harry Hooper	700.00	400.00	200.00
85	Ivan Howard	200.00	100.00	50.00
86	Miller Huggins	700.00	400.00	200.00
87	Joe Jackson	20,000	7,200	3,600
88	William James	200.00	100.00	50.00
89	Harold Janvrin	200.00	100.00	50.00
90	Hugh Jennings	700.00	400.00	200.00
91	Walter Johnson	1,800	800.00	500.00
92	Fielder Jones	200.00	100.00	50.00
93	Joe Judge	200.00	100.00	50.00
94	Bennie Kauff	200.00	100.00	50.00
95	Wm. Killefer Jr.	200.00	100.00	50.00
96	Ed. Konetchy	200.00	100.00	50.00
97	Napoleon Lajoie	700.00	400.00	200.00
98	Jack Lapp	200.00	100.00	50.00
99	John Lavan	200.00	100.00	50.00
100	Jimmy Lavender	200.00	100.00	50.00
101	"Nemo" Leibold	200.00	100.00	50.00
102	H.B. Leonard	200.00	100.00	50.00
103	Duffy Lewis	200.00	100.00	50.00
104	Hans Lobert	200.00	100.00	50.00
105	Tom Long	200.00	100.00	50.00
106	Fred Luderus	200.00	100.00	50.00
107	Connie Mack	700.00	400.00	200.00
108	Lee Magee	200.00	100.00	50.00
109	Sherwood Magee	200.00	100.00	50.00
110	Al. Mamaux	200.00	100.00	50.00
111	Leslie Mann	200.00	100.00	50.00
112	"Rabbit" Maranville	700.00	400.00	200.00
113	Rube Marquard	700.00	400.00	200.00
114	J. Erskine Mayer	200.00	100.00	50.00
115	George McBride	200.00	100.00	50.00
116	John J. McGraw	700.00	400.00	200.00
117	Jack McInnis	200.00	100.00	50.00
118	Fred Merkle	200.00	100.00	50.00
119	Chief Meyers	200.00	100.00	50.00
120	Clyde Milan	200.00	100.00	50.00
121	John Miller	200.00	100.00	50.00
122	Otto Miller	200.00	100.00	50.00
123	Willie Mitchell	200.00	100.00	50.00
124	Fred Mollwitz	200.00	100.00	50.00
125	Pat Moran	200.00	100.00	50.00
126	Ray Morgan	200.00	100.00	50.00
127	Geo. Moriarty	200.00	100.00	50.00
128	Guy Morton	200.00	100.00	50.00
129	Mike Mowrey	200.00	100.00	50.00
130	Ed. Murphy	200.00	100.00	50.00
131	"Hy" Myers	200.00	100.00	50.00
132	J.A. Niehoff	200.00	100.00	50.00
133	Rube Oldring	200.00	100.00	50.00
134	Oliver O'Mara	200.00	100.00	50.00
135	Steve O'Neill	200.00	100.00	50.00
136	"Dode" Paskert	200.00	100.00	50.00
137	Roger Peckinpaugh	200.00	100.00	50.00
138	Walter Pipp	200.00	100.00	50.00
139	Derril Pratt (Derrill)	200.00	100.00	50.00
140	Pat Ragan	200.00	100.00	50.00
141	Bill Rariden	200.00	100.00	50.00
142	Eppa Rixey	700.00	400.00	200.00
143	Davey Robertson	200.00	100.00	50.00
144	Wilbert Robinson	700.00	400.00	200.00
145	Bob Roth	200.00	100.00	50.00
146	Ed. Roush	700.00	400.00	200.00
147	Clarence Rowland	200.00	100.00	50.00
148	"Nap" Rucker	200.00	100.00	50.00
149	Dick Rudolph	200.00	100.00	50.00
150	Reb Russell	200.00	100.00	50.00
151	Babe Ruth	27,500	14,300	7,200
152	Vic Saier	200.00	100.00	50.00
153	"Slim" Sallee	200.00	100.00	50.00
154	Ray Schalk	700.00	400.00	200.00
155	Walter Schang	200.00	100.00	50.00
156	Frank Schulte	200.00	100.00	50.00
157	Everett Scott	200.00	100.00	50.00
158	Jim Scott	200.00	100.00	50.00
159	Tom Seaton	200.00	100.00	50.00
160	Howard Shanks	200.00	100.00	50.00
161	Bob Shawkey	200.00	100.00	50.00
162	Ernie Shore	200.00	100.00	50.00
163	Burt Shotton	200.00	100.00	50.00
164	Geo. Sisler	700.00	400.00	200.00
165	J. Carlisle Smith	200.00	100.00	50.00
166	Fred Snodgrass	200.00	100.00	50.00
167	Geo. Stallings	200.00	100.00	50.00
168	Oscar Stanage	200.00	100.00	50.00
169	Charles Stengel	700.00	400.00	200.00
170	Milton Stock	200.00	100.00	50.00
171	Amos Strunk	200.00	100.00	50.00
172	Billy Sullivan	200.00	100.00	50.00
173	"Jeff" Tesreau	200.00	100.00	50.00
174	Joe Tinker	700.00	400.00	200.00
175	Fred Toney	200.00	100.00	50.00
176	Terry Turner	200.00	100.00	50.00
177	George Tyler	200.00	100.00	50.00
178	Jim Vaughn	200.00	100.00	50.00
179	Bob Veach	200.00	100.00	50.00
180	James Viox	200.00	100.00	50.00
181	Oscar Vitt	200.00	100.00	50.00
182	Hans Wagner	5,000	1,400	700.00
183	Clarence Walker	200.00	100.00	50.00
184	Ed. Walsh	700.00	400.00	200.00
185	W. Wambsganss (Photo actually Fritz Coumbe)	200.00	100.00	50.00
186	Buck Weaver	1,300	700.00	300.00
187	Carl Weilman	200.00	100.00	50.00
188	Zach Wheat	700.00	400.00	200.00
189	Geo. Whitted	200.00	100.00	50.00
190	Fred Williams	200.00	100.00	50.00
191	Art Wilson	200.00	100.00	50.00
192	J. Owen Wilson	200.00	100.00	50.00

		NM	EX	VG
193	Ivy Wingo	200.00	100.00	50.00
194	"Mel" Wolfgang	200.00	100.00	50.00
195	Joe Wood	200.00	100.00	50.00
196	Steve Yerkes	200.00	100.00	50.00
197	"Pep" Young	200.00	100.00	50.00
198	Rollie Zeider	200.00	100.00	50.00
199	Heiny Zimmerman	200.00	100.00	50.00
200	Ed. Zwilling	200.00	100.00	50.00

1917 Weil Baking Co. (D328)

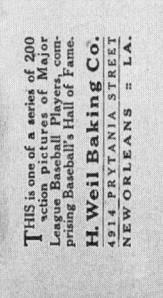

This set comprises one of several regional advertisers' use of the 200-card issue for promotional purposes. These cards are most often seen with the advertising of the Collins-McCarthy Candy Co. of San Francisco. Cards measure 2" x 3-1/4" and are printed in black-and-white. This set was listed as D328 in the American Card Catalog.

		NM	EX	VG
	Complete Set (200):	160,000	80,000	50,000
	Common Player:	300.00	200.00	100.00
1	Sam Agnew	300.00	200.00	100.00
2	Grover Alexander	1,300	700.00	400.00
3	W.S. Alexander (W.E.)	300.00	200.00	100.00
4	Leon Ames	300.00	200.00	100.00
5	Fred Anderson	300.00	200.00	100.00
6	Ed Appleton	300.00	200.00	100.00
7	Jimmy Archer	300.00	200.00	100.00
8	Jimmy Austin	300.00	200.00	100.00
9	Jim Bagby	300.00	200.00	100.00
10	H.D. Baird	300.00	200.00	100.00
11	J. Franklin Baker	800.00	400.00	200.00
12	Dave Bancroft	800.00	400.00	200.00
13	Jack Barry	300.00	200.00	100.00
14	Joe Benz	300.00	200.00	100.00
15	Al Betzel	300.00	200.00	100.00
16	Ping Bodie	300.00	200.00	100.00
17	Joe Boehling	300.00	200.00	100.00
18	Eddie Burns	300.00	200.00	100.00
19	George Burns	300.00	200.00	100.00
20	Geo. J. Burns	300.00	200.00	100.00
21	Joe Bush	300.00	200.00	100.00
22	Owen Bush	300.00	200.00	100.00
23	Bobby Byrne	300.00	200.00	100.00
24	Forrest Cady	300.00	200.00	100.00
25	Max Carey	800.00	400.00	200.00
26	Ray Chapman	400.00	200.00	100.00
27	Larry Cheney	300.00	200.00	100.00
28	Eddie Cicotte	800.00	400.00	200.00
29	Tom Clarke	300.00	200.00	100.00
30	Ty Cobb	10,000	5,000	3,000
31	Eddie Collins	800.00	400.00	200.00
32	"Shauno" Collins (Shano)	300.00	200.00	100.00
33	Fred Coumbe	300.00	200.00	100.00
34	Harry Coveleskie (Coveleski)	300.00	200.00	100.00
35	Gavvy Cravath	300.00	200.00	100.00
36	Sam Crawford	800.00	400.00	200.00
37	Geo. Cutshaw	300.00	200.00	100.00
38	Jake Daubert	300.00	200.00	100.00
39	Geo. Dauss	300.00	200.00	100.00
40	Charles Deal	300.00	200.00	100.00
41	"Wheezer" Dell	300.00	200.00	100.00
42	William Doak	300.00	200.00	100.00
43	Bill Donovan	300.00	200.00	100.00
44	Larry Doyle	300.00	200.00	100.00
45	Johnny Evers	800.00	400.00	200.00
46	Urban Faber	800.00	400.00	200.00
47	"Hap" Felsch	1,700	800.00	500.00
48	Bill Fischer	300.00	200.00	100.00
49	Ray Fisher	300.00	200.00	100.00
50	Art Fletcher	300.00	200.00	100.00
51	Eddie Foster	300.00	200.00	100.00
52	Jacques Fournier	300.00	200.00	100.00
53	Del Gainer (Gainor)	300.00	200.00	100.00
54	Bert Gallia	300.00	200.00	100.00
55	"Chic" Gandil (Chick)	1,000	500.00	300.00
56	Larry Gardner	300.00	200.00	100.00
57	Joe Gedeon	300.00	200.00	100.00
58	Gus Getz	300.00	200.00	100.00
59	Frank Gilhooley	300.00	200.00	100.00
60	Wm. Gleason	300.00	200.00	100.00
61	M.A. Gonzales (Gonzalez)	300.00	200.00	100.00
62	Hank Gowdy	300.00	200.00	100.00
63	John Graney	300.00	200.00	100.00
64	Tom Griffith	300.00	200.00	100.00
65	Heinie Groh	300.00	200.00	100.00
66	Bob Groom	300.00	200.00	100.00
67	Louis Guisto	300.00	200.00	100.00
68	Earl Hamilton	300.00	200.00	100.00
69	Harry Harper	300.00	200.00	100.00
70	Grover Hartley	300.00	200.00	100.00
71	Harry Heilmann	800.00	400.00	200.00
72	Claude Hendrix	300.00	200.00	100.00
73	Olaf Henriksen	300.00	200.00	100.00
74	John Henry	300.00	200.00	100.00
75	"Buck" Herzog	300.00	200.00	100.00
76	Hugh High	300.00	200.00	100.00
77	Dick Hoblitzell	300.00	200.00	100.00
78	Walter Holke	300.00	200.00	100.00
79	Harry Hooper	800.00	400.00	200.00
80	Rogers Hornsby	1,300	700.00	400.00
81	Ivan Howard	300.00	200.00	100.00
82	Joe Jackson	28,000	14,000	8,000
83	Harold Janvrin	300.00	200.00	100.00
84	William James	300.00	200.00	100.00
85	C. Jamieson	300.00	200.00	100.00
86	Hugh Jennings	800.00	400.00	200.00
87	Walter Johnson	1,700	800.00	500.00
88	James Johnston	300.00	200.00	100.00
89	Fielder Jones	300.00	200.00	100.00
90	Joe Judge	300.00	200.00	100.00
91	Hans Lobert	300.00	200.00	100.00
92	Benny Kauff	300.00	200.00	100.00
93	Wm. Killefer Jr.	300.00	200.00	100.00
94	Ed. Konetchy	300.00	200.00	100.00
95	John Lavan	300.00	200.00	100.00
96	Jimmy Lavender	300.00	200.00	100.00
97	"Nemo" Leibold	300.00	200.00	100.00
98	H.B. Leonard	300.00	200.00	100.00
99	Duffy Lewis	300.00	200.00	100.00
100	Tom Long	300.00	200.00	100.00
101	Wm. Louden	300.00	200.00	100.00
102	Fred Luderus	300.00	200.00	100.00
103	Lee Magee	300.00	200.00	100.00
104	Sherwood Magee	300.00	200.00	100.00
105	Al Mamaux	300.00	200.00	100.00
106	Leslie Mann	300.00	200.00	100.00
107	"Rabbit" Maranville	800.00	400.00	200.00
108	Rube Marquard	800.00	400.00	200.00
109	Armando Marsans	300.00	200.00	100.00
110	J. Erskine Mayer	300.00	200.00	100.00
111	George McBride	300.00	200.00	100.00
112	Lew McCarty	300.00	200.00	100.00
113	John J. McGraw	800.00	400.00	200.00
114	Jack McInnis	300.00	200.00	100.00
115	Lee Meadows	300.00	200.00	100.00
116	Fred Merkle	300.00	200.00	100.00
117	"Chief" Meyers	300.00	200.00	100.00
118	Clyde Milan	300.00	200.00	100.00
119	Otto Miller	300.00	200.00	100.00
120	Clarence Mitchell	300.00	200.00	100.00
121	Ray Morgan	300.00	200.00	100.00
122	Guy Morton	300.00	200.00	100.00
123	"Mike" Mowrey	300.00	200.00	100.00
124	Elmer Myers	300.00	200.00	100.00
125	"Hy" Myers	300.00	200.00	100.00
126	A.E. Neale	400.00	200.00	100.00
127	Arthur Nehf	300.00	200.00	100.00
128	J.A. Niehoff	300.00	200.00	100.00
129	Steve O'Neill	300.00	200.00	100.00
130	"Dode" Paskert	300.00	200.00	100.00
131	Roger Peckinpaugh	300.00	200.00	100.00
132	"Pol" Perritt	300.00	200.00	100.00
133	"Jeff" Pfeffer	300.00	200.00	100.00
134	Walter Pipp	300.00	200.00	100.00
135	Derril Pratt (Derrill)	300.00	200.00	100.00
136	Bill Rariden	300.00	200.00	100.00
137	E.C. Rice	800.00	400.00	200.00
138	Wm. A. Ritter (Wm. H.)	300.00	200.00	100.00
139	Eppa Rixey	800.00	400.00	200.00
140	Davey Robertson	300.00	200.00	100.00
141	"Bob" Roth	300.00	200.00	100.00
142	Ed. Roush	800.00	400.00	200.00
143	Clarence Rowland	300.00	200.00	100.00
144	Dick Rudolph	300.00	200.00	100.00
145	William Rumler	300.00	200.00	100.00
146	Reb Russell	300.00	200.00	100.00
147	"Babe" Ruth	22,000	11,000	6,600
148	Vic Saier	300.00	200.00	100.00
149	"Slim" Sallee	300.00	200.00	100.00
150	Ray Schalk	800.00	400.00	200.00
151	Walter Schang	300.00	200.00	100.00
152	Frank Schulte	300.00	200.00	100.00
153	Ferd Schupp	300.00	200.00	100.00
154	Everett Scott	300.00	200.00	100.00
155	Hank Severeid	300.00	200.00	100.00
156	Howard Shanks	300.00	200.00	100.00
157	Bob Shawkey	300.00	200.00	100.00
158	Jas. Sheckard	300.00	200.00	100.00
159	Ernie Shore	300.00	200.00	100.00
160	C.H. Shorten	300.00	200.00	100.00
161	Burt Shotton	300.00	200.00	100.00
162	Geo. Sisler	800.00	400.00	200.00
163	Elmer Smith	300.00	200.00	100.00
164	J. Carlisle Smith	300.00	200.00	100.00
165	Fred Snodgrass	300.00	200.00	100.00
166	Tris Speaker	1,300	700.00	400.00
167	Oscar Stanage	300.00	200.00	100.00
168	Charles Stengel	800.00	400.00	200.00
169	Milton Stock	300.00	200.00	100.00
170	Amos Strunk	300.00	200.00	100.00
171	"Zeb" Terry	300.00	200.00	100.00
172	"Jeff" Tesreau	300.00	200.00	100.00
173	Chester Thomas	300.00	200.00	100.00
174	Fred Toney	300.00	200.00	100.00
175	Terry Turner	300.00	200.00	100.00
176	George Tyler	300.00	200.00	100.00
177	Jim Vaughn	300.00	200.00	100.00
178	Bob Veach	300.00	200.00	100.00
179	Oscar Vitt	300.00	200.00	100.00
180	Hans Wagner	7,700	3,900	2,300
181	Clarence Walker	300.00	200.00	100.00
182	Jim Walsh	300.00	200.00	100.00
183	Al Walters	300.00	200.00	100.00
184	W. Wambsganss	300.00	200.00	100.00
185	Buck Weaver	2,200	1,100	700.00
186	Carl Weilman	300.00	200.00	100.00
187	Zack Wheat	800.00	400.00	200.00
188	Geo. Whitted	300.00	200.00	100.00
189	Joe Wilhoit	300.00	200.00	100.00
190	Claude Williams	1,700	800.00	500.00
191	Fred Williams	300.00	200.00	100.00
192	Art Wilson	300.00	200.00	100.00
193	Lawton Witt	300.00	200.00	100.00
194	Joe Wood	500.00	300.00	150.00
195	William Wortman	300.00	200.00	100.00
196	Steve Yerkes	300.00	200.00	100.00
197	Earl Yingling	300.00	200.00	100.00
198	"Pep" (Ralph) Young	300.00	200.00	100.00
199	Rollie Zeider	300.00	200.00	100.00
200	Henry Zimmerman	300.00	200.00	100.00

1886 Welton Cigars N.Y. Giants (H812)

(See "1886 New York Base Ball Club" for checklist and values.)

1977 Wendy's Discs

Virtually identical in format to the several locally sponsored disc sets of the previous year, these 3-3/8" diameter player discs were given away at participating stores in the fast-food hamburger chain. Discs once again feature black-and-white player portrait photos in the center of a baseball design. The left and right panels are in one of several bright colors. Licensed by the Players' Association through Mike Schechter Associates, the player photos carry no uniform logos. Backs are printed in green. The unnumbered discs are checklisted here alphabetically.

		NM	EX	VG
	Complete Set (70):	325.00	165.00	100.00
	Common Player:	3.00	1.50	.90
(1)	Sal Bando	3.00	1.50	.90
(2)	Buddy Bell	3.00	1.50	.90
(3)	Johnny Bench	20.00	10.00	6.00
(4)	Larry Bowa	3.00	1.50	.90
(5)	Steve Braun	3.00	1.50	.90
(6)	George Brett	50.00	25.00	15.00
(7)	Lou Brock	12.50	6.25	3.75
(8)	Jeff Burroughs	3.00	1.50	.90
(9)	Bert Campaneris	3.00	1.50	.90
(10)	John Candelaria	3.00	1.50	.90
(11)	Jose Cardenal	3.00	1.50	.90
(12)	Rod Carew	12.50	6.25	3.75
(13)	Steve Carlton	12.50	6.25	3.75
(14)	Dave Cash	3.00	1.50	.90
(15)	Cesar Cedeno	3.00	1.50	.90
(16)	Ron Cey	3.00	1.50	.90
(17)	Dave Concepcion	3.00	1.50	.90
(18)	Dennis Eckersley	12.50	6.25	3.75
(19)	Mark Fidrych	6.00	3.00	1.75
q20)	Rollie Fingers	12.50	6.25	3.75
(21)	Carlton Fisk	12.50	6.25	3.75
(22)	George Foster	3.00	1.50	.90
(23)	Wayne Garland	3.00	1.50	.90
(24)	Ralph Garr	3.00	1.50	.90
(25)	Steve Garvey	4.50	2.25	1.25
(26)	Cesar Geronimo	3.00	1.50	.90
(27)	Bobby Grich	3.00	1.50	.90
(28)	Ken Griffey Sr.	3.00	1.50	.90
(29)	Don Gullett	3.00	1.50	.90
(30)	Mike Hargrove	3.00	1.50	.90
(31)	Al Hrabosky	3.00	1.50	.90
(32)	Jim Hunter	12.50	6.25	3.75
(33)	Reggie Jackson	45.00	22.50	13.50
(34)	Randy Jones	3.00	1.50	.90
(35)	Dave Kingman	3.00	1.50	.90
(36)	Jerry Koosman	3.00	1.50	.90
(37)	Dave LaRoche	3.00	1.50	.90
(38)	Greg Luzinski	3.00	1.50	.90
(39)	Fred Lynn	3.00	1.50	.90
(40)	Bill Madlock	3.00	1.50	.90
(41)	Rick Manning	3.00	1.50	.90
(42)	Jon Matlock	3.00	1.50	.90
(43)	John Mayberry	3.00	1.50	.90

		NM	EX	VG
(44)	Hal McRae	3.00	1.50	.90
(45)	Andy Messersmith	3.00	1.50	.90
(46)	Rick Monday	3.00	1.50	.90
(47)	John Montefusco	3.00	1.50	.90
(48)	Joe Morgan	12.50	6.25	3.75
(49)	Thurman Munson	12.50	6.25	3.75
(50)	Bobby Murcer	3.00	1.50	.90
(51)	Bill North	3.00	1.50	.90
(52)	Jim Palmer	12.50	6.25	3.75
(53)	Tony Perez	12.50	6.25	3.75
(54)	Jerry Reuss	3.00	1.50	.90
(55)	Brooks Robinson	15.00	7.50	4.50
(56)	Pete Rose	55.00	27.50	16.50
(57)	Joe Rudi	3.00	1.50	.90
(58)	Nolan Ryan	65.00	32.50	20.00
(59)	Manny Sanguillen	3.00	1.50	.90
(60)	Mike Schmidt	50.00	25.00	15.00
(61)	Tom Seaver	20.00	10.00	6.00
(62)	Bill Singer	3.00	1.50	.90
(63)	Willie Stargell	12.50	6.25	3.75
(64)	Rusty Staub	4.00	2.00	1.25
(65)	Luis Tiant	3.00	1.50	.90
(66)	Bob Watson	3.00	1.50	.90
(67)	Butch Wynegar	3.00	1.50	.90
(68)	Carl Yastrzemski	20.00	10.00	6.00
(69)	Robin Yount	12.50	6.25	3.75
(70)	Richie Zisk	3.00	1.50	.90

1963 Western Oil Minnesota Twins

Issued by Mileage and DS gas stations, these 8-1/2" x 11" heavy paper portraits are the work of sports/entertainment artist Nicholas Volpe, who had done a similar series earlier for the Los Angeles Dodgers, and would do several more in the future for other baseball and NFL teams. The 1963 Twins issue features pastel portrait and action renderings against a black background on front. The player's name appears as a facsimile autograph in white on the painting and is printed in black in the white bottom border. Backs have biographical data and a career summary of the player at top. At center is a black box with complete major and minor league stats. At lower center is a biography of the artist and, on most pictures, his portrait. The DS and Mileage logos of the Western Oil and Fuel Co. appear at bottom.

		NM	EX	VG
Complete Set (24):		150.00	75.00	45.00
Common Player:		10.00	5.00	3.00
(1)	Bernie Allen	10.00	5.00	3.00
(2)	Bob Allison	15.00	7.50	4.50
(3)	George Banks	10.00	5.00	3.00
(4)	Earl Battey	12.50	6.25	3.75
(5)	Bill Dailey	10.00	5.00	3.00
(6)	John Goryl	10.00	5.00	3.00
(7)	Lenny Green	10.00	5.00	3.00
(8)	Jimmie Hall	10.00	5.00	3.00
(9)	Jim Kaat	15.00	7.50	4.50
(10)	Harmon Killebrew	30.00	15.00	9.00
(11)	Sam Mele	10.00	5.00	3.00
(12)	Don Mincher	10.00	5.00	3.00
(13)	Ray Moore	10.00	5.00	3.00
(14)	Camilo Pascual	12.50	6.25	3.75
(15)	Jim Perry	10.00	5.00	3.00
(16)	Bill Pleis	10.00	5.00	3.00
(17)	Vic Power	12.00	6.00	3.50
(18)	Garry Roggenburk	10.00	5.00	3.00
(19)	Jim Roland	10.00	5.00	3.00
(20)	Rich Rollins	10.00	5.00	3.00
(21)	Lee Stange	10.00	5.00	3.00
(22)	Dick Stigman	10.00	5.00	3.00
(23)	Zoilo Versalles	12.50	6.25	3.75
(24)	Jerry Zimmerman	10.00	5.00	3.00

1964 Western Oil Minnesota Twins

Identical in format to the previous year's issue, the 1964 set of Twins pictures features the use of a second portrait of the player in civilian dress rather than an action picture. The 1964 issue also has background of pastel colors, rather than all-black, and, on back, an oval/arrow logo for Western brand gas, along with the Mileage and DS logos.

		NM	EX	VG
Complete Set (15):		120.00	60.00	35.00
Common Player:		10.00	5.00	3.00
(1)	Bernie Allen	10.00	5.00	3.00
(2)	Bob Allison	12.50	6.25	3.75
(3)	Earl Battey	12.50	6.25	3.75
(4)	Bill Dailey	10.00	5.00	3.00
(5)	Jimmie Hall	10.00	5.00	3.00
(6)	Jim Kaat	15.00	7.50	4.50
(7)	Harmon Killebrew	30.00	15.00	9.00
(8)	Don Mincher	10.00	5.00	3.00
(9)	Tony Oliva	25.00	12.50	7.50
(10)	Camilo Pascual	12.50	6.25	3.75
(11)	Bill Pleis	10.00	5.00	3.00
(12)	Jim Roland	10.00	5.00	3.00
(13)	Rich Rollins	10.00	5.00	3.00
(14)	Dick Stigman	10.00	5.00	3.00
(15)	Zoilo Versalles	12.50	6.25	3.75

1974 Weston Expos

This 10-card set features members of the Montreal Expos. Each full-color card measures 3-1/2" x 5-1/2" and includes a facsimile autograph in black ink with the player's name printed along the bottom. The backs are distinct because they are divided in half. The top of the card lists player data and 1973 statistics in English, while the bottom carries the same information in French. The cards are numbered according to the player's uniform number.

		NM	EX	VG
Complete Set (10):		10.00	5.00	3.00
Common Player:		1.50	.75	.45
3	Bob Bailey	1.50	.75	.45
8	Boots Day	1.50	.75	.45
12	John Boccabella	1.50	.75	.45
16	Mike Jorgensen	1.50	.75	.45
18	Steve Renko	1.50	.75	.45
19	Tim Foli	1.50	.75	.45
21	Ernie McAnally	1.50	.75	.45
26	Bill Stoneman	1.50	.75	.45
29	Ken Singleton	1.50	.75	.45
33	Ron Hunt	1.50	.75	.45

1888 WG1 Base Ball Playing Cards

This little-known set of playing cards featuring drawings of real baseball players in action poses was issued in 1888 and includes members of the eight National League teams of the day. Each club is represented by nine players - one at each position - making the set complete at 72 cards. The cards measure 2-1/2" x 3-1/2" and have a blue-on-blue lathework pattern on back. The cards were sold as a boxed set. They were designed to resemble a deck of regular playing cards, and the various positions were all assigned the same denomination (for example, all of the pitchers were kings, catchers were aces, etc.). There are no cards numbered either two, three, four or five; and rather than the typical hearts, clubs, diamonds and spades, each team represents a different "suit." The American Card Catalog designation is WG1.

		NM	EX	VG
Complete Set (72):		90,000	35,000	17,500
Common Player:		900.00	360.00	180.00
Box:		5,000	2,500	1,500
(1)	Ed Andrews	900.00	360.00	180.00
(2)	Cap Anson	6,250	2,500	1,250
(3)	Charles Bassett	900.00	360.00	180.00
(4)	Charles Bastian	900.00	360.00	180.00
(5)	Charles Bennett	900.00	360.00	180.00
(6)	Henry Boyle	900.00	360.00	180.00
(7)	Dan Brouthers	3,000	1,200	600.00
(8)	Tom Brown	900.00	360.00	180.00
(9)	Tom Burns	900.00	360.00	180.00
(10)	Fred Carroll	900.00	360.00	180.00
(11)	Dan Casey	900.00	360.00	180.00
(12)	John Clarkson	3,000	1,200	600.00
(13)	Jack Clements	900.00	360.00	180.00
(14)	John Coleman	900.00	360.00	180.00
(15)	Roger Connor	3,000	1,200	600.00
(16)	Abner Dalrymple	900.00	360.00	180.00
(17)	Jerry Denny	900.00	360.00	180.00
(18)	Jim Donelly	900.00	360.00	180.00
(19)	Fred Dunlap	900.00	360.00	180.00
(20)	Dude Esterbrook	900.00	360.00	180.00
(21)	Buck Ewing	3,000	1,200	600.00
(22)	Sid Farrar	900.00	360.00	180.00
(23)	Silver Flint	900.00	360.00	180.00
(24)	Jim Fogarty	900.00	360.00	180.00
(25)	Elmer Foster	900.00	360.00	180.00
(26)	Pud Galvin	3,000	1,200	600.00
(27)	Charlie Getzein (Getzien)	900.00	360.00	180.00
(28)	Jack Glasscock	900.00	360.00	180.00
(29)	George Gore	900.00	360.00	180.00
(30)	Ned Hanlon	3,000	1,200	600.00
(31)	Paul Hines	900.00	360.00	180.00
(32)	Joe Hornung	900.00	360.00	180.00
(33)	Dummy Hoy	1,350	550.00	275.00
(34)	Arthur Irwin (Philadelphia)	900.00	360.00	180.00
(35)	John Irwin (Washington)	900.00	360.00	180.00
(36)	Dick Johnston	900.00	360.00	180.00
(37)	Tim Keefe	3,000	1,200	600.00
(38)	King Kelly	4,250	1,700	850.00
(39)	Willie Kuehne	900.00	360.00	180.00
(40)	Connie Mack	3,250	1,300	650.00
(41)	Al Maul	900.00	360.00	180.00
(42)	Al Meyers (Myers) (Washington)	900.00	360.00	180.00
(43)	George Meyers (Myers) (Indianapolis)	900.00	360.00	180.00
(44)	John Morrill	900.00	360.00	180.00
(45)	Joseph Mulvey	900.00	360.00	180.00
(46)	Billy Nash	900.00	360.00	180.00
(47)	Billy O'Brien	900.00	360.00	180.00
(48)	Orator Jim O'Rourke	3,000	1,200	600.00
(49)	Bob Pettit	900.00	360.00	180.00
(50)	Fred Pfeffer	900.00	360.00	180.00
(51)	Danny Richardson (New York)	900.00	360.00	180.00
(52)	Hardy Richardson (Detroit)	900.00	360.00	180.00
(53)	Jack Rowe	900.00	360.00	180.00
(54)	Jimmy Ryan	900.00	360.00	180.00
(55)	Emmett Seery	900.00	360.00	180.00
(56)	George Shoch	900.00	360.00	180.00
(57)	Otto Shomberg (Schomberg)	900.00	360.00	180.00
(58)	Pap Smith	900.00	360.00	180.00
(59)	Marty Sullivan	900.00	360.00	180.00
(60)	Billy Sunday	3,000	1,200	600.00
(61)	Ezra Sutton	900.00	360.00	180.00
(62)	Sam Thompson	3,000	1,200	600.00
(63)	Mike Tiernan	900.00	360.00	180.00
(64)	Larry Twitchell	900.00	360.00	180.00
(65)	Rip Van Haltren	900.00	360.00	180.00
(66)	John Ward	3,000	1,200	600.00
(67)	Deacon White	900.00	360.00	180.00
(68)	Jim Whitney	900.00	360.00	180.00
(69)	Ned Williamson	900.00	360.00	180.00
(70)	Walt Wilmot	900.00	360.00	180.00
(71)	Medoc Wise	900.00	360.00	180.00
(72)	George Wood	900.00	360.00	180.00

1932 Wheaties Babe Ruth Flip Book

This novelty item measures about 1-3/4" x 2-1/2" and is stapled at the bottom. When properly thumbed, the individual black-and-white pages inside present a simulated moving picture, "Babe Ruth Shows You How to Hit a Home Run." The covers feature orange and blue artwork.

	NM	EX	VG
Babe Ruth	750.00	375.00	225.00

1933-1934 Wheaties

Sponsored by Wheaties via mail-in offers heard on baseball games on half a dozen radio stations, these black-and-white cards are blank-backed and feature posed action photo with facsimile autographs bordered in white. In a 3-1/4" x 5-3/8" format, they are similar in design to the later 1936 National Chicle "Fine Pens" (R313) and the Gold Medal Foods World Series (R313A) issue of 1934, though each of the photos found in this set are unique. To date, this likely incomplete checklist comprises on players from the Browns, Cardinals, Cubs, White Sox, Indians and the Des Moines Demons of the Western League.

		NM	EX	VG
Common Player:				
(1)	Earl Averill	275.00	135.00	80.00
(2)	Geo. E. Blaeholder	45.00	22.50	13.50
(3)	Irving "Jack" Burns	45.00	22.50	13.50
(4)	Bruce Campbell	45.00	22.50	13.50
(5)	"Tex" Carleton	45.00	22.50	13.50
(6)	George Earnshaw	45.00	22.50	13.50
(7)	Red Faber	80.00	40.00	24.00
(8)	Fabian Gaffke	45.00	22.50	13.50
(9)	Odell Hale	180.00	90.00	55.00
(10)	Mel Harder	45.00	22.50	13.50
(11)	Roy Hudson	45.00	22.50	13.50
(12)	Chuck Klein	80.00	40.00	24.00
(13)	Jack Knott	45.00	22.50	13.50
(14)	Al Marchand	45.00	22.50	13.50
(15)	Ossie Orwoll	45.00	22.50	13.50
(16)	Al Simmons	80.00	40.00	24.00
(17)	Hal Trosky	45.00	22.50	13.50
(18)	Joe Vosmik	45.00	22.50	13.50
(19)	Bill Walker	45.00	22.50	13.50

1935 Wheaties - Series 1

This set of major leaguers (plus fictional sports hero Jack Armstrong) was issued on the back of Wheaties cereal boxes in 1935 and because of its design, is known as "Fancy Frame with Script Signature." The unnumbered cards measure 6" x 6-1/4" with frame, and 5" x 5-1/2" without the frame. The player photo is tinted blue, while the background is blue and orange. A facsimile autograph appears at the bottom of the photo. Illinois high school track star Herman "Jack" Waddlington posed for the photos of fictional Jack Armstrong "All-American Boy".

		NM	EX	VG
Complete Set (27):		3,000	1,500	900.00
Common Player:		50.00	25.00	15.50
(1)	Jack Armstrong/Btg	50.00	25.00	15.00
(2)	Jack Armstrong/Throwing	50.00	25.00	15.00
(3)	Wally Berger	50.00	25.00	15.00
(4)	Tommy Bridges	50.00	25.00	15.00
(5)	Mickey Cochrane (Black hat.)	90.00	45.00	27.00
(6)	Michey Cochrane (White hat.)	425.00	210.00	125.00
(7)	James "Rip" Collins	50.00	25.00	15.00
(8)	Dizzy Dean	325.00	160.00	97.00
(9)	Dizzy Dean, Paul Dean	250.00	125.00	75.00
(10)	Paul Dean	55.00	27.50	16.50
(11)	William Delancey	50.00	25.00	15.00
(12)	"Jimmie" Foxx	190.00	95.00	60.00
(13)	Frank Frisch	75.00	37.50	22.00
(14)	Lou Gehrig	475.00	235.00	140.00
(15)	Goose Goslin	75.00	37.50	22.00
(16)	Lefty Grove	125.00	65.00	35.00
(17)	Carl Hubbell	85.00	40.00	25.00
(18)	Travis C. Jackson	75.00	37.50	22.00
(19)	"Chuck" Klein	75.00	37.50	22.00
(20)	Gus Mancuso	50.00	25.00	15.00
(21)	Pepper Martin/Btg	55.00	27.00	16.50
(22)	Pepper Martin/Portrait	55.00	27.00	16.50
(23)	Joe Medwick	75.00	37.50	22.00
(24)	Melvin Ott	90.00	45.00	27.00
(25)	Harold Schumacher	50.00	25.00	15.00
(26)	Al Simmons	75.00	37.50	22.00
(27)	"Jo Jo" White	50.00	25.00	15.00

1936 Wheaties - Series 3

Consisting of 12 unnumbered cards, this set is similar in size (6" x 6-1/4" with frame) and design to the Wheaties of the previous year, but is known as "Fancy

Frame with Printed Name and Data" because the cards also include a few printed words describing the player.

		NM	EX	VG
Complete Set (12):		1,600	800.00	475.00
Common Player:		45.00	22.00	13.50
(1)	Earl Averill	60.00	30.00	18.00
(2)	Mickey Cochrane	60.00	30.00	18.00
(3)	Jimmy Foxx	200.00	100.00	60.00
(4)	Lou Gehrig	750.00	375.00	225.00
(5)	Hank Greenberg	175.00	90.00	50.00
(6)	"Gabby" Hartnett	60.00	30.00	18.00
(7)	Carl Hubbell	65.00	32.50	20.00
(8)	"Pepper" Martin	50.00	25.00	15.00
(9)	Van L. Mungo	45.00	22.50	13.50
(10)	"Buck" Newsom	45.00	22.50	13.50
(11)	"Arky" Vaughan	60.00	30.00	18.00
(12)	Jimmy Wilson	45.00	22.50	13.50

1936 Wheaties - Series 4

This larger size (8-1/2" x 6") card also made up the back of a Wheaties box, and because of its distinctive border which featured drawings of small athletic figures, it is referred to as "Thin Orange Border/Figures in Border." Twelve major leaguers are pictured in the unnumbered set. The photos are enclosed in a 4" x 6-1/2" box. Below the photo is an endorsement for Wheaties, the "Breakfast of Champions," and a facsimile autograph.

		NM	EX	VG
Complete Set (12):		1,200	600.00	350.00
Common Player:		45.00	22.00	13.50
(1)	Curt Davis	45.00	22.50	13.50
(2)	Lou Gehrig	500.00	250.00	150.00
(3)	Charley Gehringer	75.00	37.50	22.00
(4)	Lefty Grove	165.00	85.00	50.00
(5)	Rollie Hemsley	45.00	22.50	13.50
(6)	Billy Herman	75.00	37.50	22.00
(7)	Joe Medwick	75.00	37.50	22.00
(8)	Mel Ott	80.00	40.00	25.00
(9)	Schoolboy Rowe	45.00	22.50	13.50
(10)	Arky Vaughan	75.00	37.50	22.00
(11)	Joe Vosmik	45.00	22.50	13.50
(12)	Lon Warneke	45.00	22.50	13.50

1936 Wheaties - Series 5

Often referred to as "How to Play Winning Baseball," this 12-card set features a large player photo surrounded by blue and white drawings that illustrate various playing tips. Different major leaguers offer advice on different aspects of the game. The cards again made up the back panel of a Wheaties box and measure 8-1/2" x 6-1/2". The cards are numbered from 1 through 12, and it is now believed that each can be found or without with a small number "28" followed by a letter from "A" through "L."

		NM	EX	VG
Complete Set (12)		1,000	500.00	300.00
Common Player:		45.00	22.50	13.50
1	Lefty Gomez	85.00	45.00	25.00
2	Billy Herman	75.00	37.50	22.00
3	Luke Appling	75.00	37.50	22.00
4	Jimmie Foxx	90.00	45.00	27.00
5	Joe Medwick	75.00	37.50	22.00
6	Charles Gehringer	75.00	37.50	22.00

		NM	EX	VG
7a	Mel Ott (Tips in vertical sequence.)	95.00	45.00	25.00
7b	Mel Ott (Tips in two horizontal rows.)	95.00	45.00	25.00
8	Odell Hale	45.00	22.50	13.50
9	Bill Dickey	85.00	45.00	25.00
10	"Lefty" Grove	85.00	45.00	25.00
11	Carl Hubbell	80.00	40.00	25.00
12	Earl Averill	75.00	37.50	22.00

1937 Wheaties - Series 6

Similar to the Series 5 set, this numbered, 12-card series is known as "How to Star in Baseball" and again includes a large player photo with small instructional drawings to illustrate playing tips. The cards measure 8-1/4" x 6" and include a facsimile autograph.

		NM	EX	VG
Complete Set (12):		1,000	500.00	300.00
Common Player:		35.00	17.50	10.00
1	Bill Dickey	75.00	37.50	22.00
2	Red Ruffing	60.00	30.00	18.00
3	Zeke Bonura	35.00	17.50	10.00
4	Charlie Gehringer	60.00	30.00	18.00
5	"Arky" Vaughn (Vaughan)	60.00	30.00	18.00
6	Carl Hubbell	60.00	30.00	18.00
7	John Lewis	35.00	17.50	10.00
8	Heinie Manush	60.00	30.00	18.00
9	"Lefty" Grove	75.00	37.50	22.00
10	Billy Herman	60.00	30.00	18.00
11	Joe DiMaggio	400.00	200.00	120.00
12	Joe Medwick	60.00	30.00	18.00

1937 Wheaties - Series 7

This set of 6" x 8-1/4" panels contains several different card designs. One style (picturing Lombardi, Travis and Mungo) has a white background with an orange border and a large orange circle behind the player. Another design (showing Bonura, DiMaggio and Bridges) has the player outlined against a bright orange background with a Wheaties endorsement along the bottom. A third format (picturing Moore, Radcliff and Martin) has a distinctive red, white and blue border. And a fourth design (featuring Trosky, Demaree and Vaughan) has a tilted picture against an orange background framed in blue and white. The set also includes four Pacific Coast League Players (#29M-29P). The cards are numbered with a small "29" followed by a letter from "A" through "P."

		NM	EX	VG
Complete Set (16):		1,200	600.00	350.00
Common Player:		45.00	22.50	13.50
29A	"Zeke" Bonura	45.00	22.50	13.50
29B	Cecil Travis	45.00	22.50	13.50
29C	Frank Demaree	45.00	22.50	13.50
29D	Joe Moore	45.00	22.50	13.50
29E	Ernie Lombardi	60.00	30.00	18.00
29F	John L. "Pepper" Martin	50.00	25.00	15.00
29G	Harold Trosky	45.00	22.50	13.50
29H	Raymond Radcliff	45.00	22.50	13.50
29I	Joe DiMaggio	300.00	150.00	90.00
29J	Tom Bridges	45.00	22.50	13.50
29K	Van L. Mungo	45.00	22.50	13.50
29L	"Arky" Vaughn (Vaughan)	60.00	30.00	18.00
29M	Arnold Statz	100.00	50.00	30.00
29N	Wes Schulmerich	100.00	50.00	30.00
29O	Fred Mueller	100.00	50.00	30.00
29P	Gene Lillard	100.00	50.00	30.00

1937 Wheaties - Series 8

Another series printed on the back of Wheaties boxes in 1937, the eight cards in this set are unnumbered and measure 8-1/2" x 6". There are several different designs, but in all of them the player photo is surrounded by speckles of color, causing this series to be known as the "Speckled Orange, White and Blue" series. A facsimile autograph is included, along with brief printed 1936 season statistics.

		NM	EX	VG
Complete Set (8):		1,300	650.00	400.00
Common Player:		120.00	60.00	36.00
(1)	Luke Appling	100.00	50.00	30.00
(2)	Earl Averill	100.00	50.00	30.00
(3)	Joe DiMaggio	450.00	225.00	135.00
(4)	Robert Feller	225.00	110.00	65.00
(5)	Chas. Gehringer	100.00	50.00	30.00
(6)	Lefty Grove	125.00	65.00	35.00
(7)	Carl Hubbell	125.00	65.00	35.00
(8)	Joe Medwick	100.00	50.00	30.00

1937 Wheaties - Series 9

This unnumbered set includes one player from each of the 16 major league teams and is generally referred to as the "Color Series." The cards measure 8-1/2" x 6" and were the back panels of Wheaties boxes. The player photos are shown inside or against large stars, circles, "V" shapes, rectangles and other geometric designs. A facsimile autograph and team designation are printed near the photo, while a Wheaties endorsement and a line of player stats appear along the bottom.

		NM	EX	VG
Complete Set (16):		1,600	800.00	480.00
Common Player:		50.00	25.00	15.00
(1)	Zeke Bonura	50.00	25.00	15.00
(2)	Tom Bridges	50.00	25.00	15.00
(3)	Harland Clift (Harlond)	50.00	25.00	15.00
(4)	Kiki Cuyler	75.00	37.50	22.50
(5)	Joe DiMaggio	600.00	300.00	180.00
(6)	Robert Feller	175.00	85.00	50.00
(7)	Lefty Grove	100.00	50.00	30.00
(8)	Billy Herman	75.00	37.50	22.50
(9)	Carl Hubbell	90.00	45.00	27.50
(10)	Buck Jordan	50.00	25.00	15.00
(11)	"Pepper" Martin	60.00	30.00	18.00
(12)	John Moore	50.00	25.00	15.00
(13)	Wally Moses	50.00	25.00	15.00
(14)	Van L. Mungo	50.00	25.00	15.00
(15)	Cecil Travis	50.00	25.00	15.00
(16)	Arky Vaughan	75.00	37.50	22.50

1937 Wheaties - Series 14

Much reduced in size (2-5/8" x 3-7/8"), these unnumbered cards made up the back panels of single-serving size Wheaties boxes. The player photo (which is sometimes identical to the photos used in the larger series) is set against an orange or white background. The player's name appears in large capital letters with his position and team in smaller capitals. A facsimile autograph and Wheaties endorsement are also included. Some cards are also found with the number "29" followed by a letter.

		NM	EX	VG
Complete Set (16):		5,000	2,500	1,500
Common Player:		200.00	100.00	60.00
(1)	"Zeke" Bonura	200.00	100.00	60.00
(2)	Tom Bridges	200.00	100.00	60.00
(3)	Dolph Camilli	200.00	100.00	60.00
(4)	Frank Demaree	200.00	100.00	60.00
(5)	Joe DiMaggio	1,300	650.00	390.00
(6)	Billy Herman	300.00	150.00	90.00
(7)	Carl Hubbell	350.00	175.00	105.00
(8)	Ernie Lombardi	300.00	150.00	90.00
(9)	"Pepper" Martin	250.00	125.00	75.00
(10)	Joe Moore	200.00	100.00	60.00
(11)	Van Mungo	200.00	100.00	60.00
(12)	Mel Ott	350.00	175.00	105.00
(13)	Raymond Radcliff	200.00	100.00	60.00
(14)	Cecil Travis	200.00	100.00	60.00
(15)	Harold Trosky	200.00	100.00	60.00
(16a)	"Arky" Vaughan (29L on card.)	350.00	175.00	105.00
(16b)	"Arky" Vaughan (No 29L on card.)	350.00	175.00	105.00

1938 Wheaties - Series 10

One player from each major league team is included in this 16-card set, referred to as the "Biggest Thrills in Baseball" series. Measuring 8-1/2" x 6", each numbered card was the back panel of a Wheaties box and pictures a player along with a printed description of his biggest thrill in baseball and facsimile autograph. All 16 cards in this series have also been found on paper stock.

		NM	EX	VG
Complete Set (16):		1,700	850.00	500.00
Common Player:		45.00	22.50	13.50
1	Bob Feller	160.00	80.00	45.00
2	Cecil Travis	45.00	22.50	13.50
3	Joe Medwick	65.00	32.50	20.00
4	Gerald Walker	45.00	22.50	13.50
5	Carl Hubbell	65.00	32.50	20.00
6	Bob Johnson	45.00	22.50	13.50
7	Beau Bell	45.00	22.50	13.50
8	Ernie Lombardi	65.00	32.50	20.00
9	Lefty Grove	80.00	40.00	24.00
10	Lou Fette	45.00	22.50	13.50
11	Joe DiMaggio	600.00	300.00	180.00
12	Pinky Whitney	45.00	22.50	13.50
13	Dizzy Dean	175.00	85.00	55.00
14	Charley Gehringer	65.00	32.50	20.00
15	Paul Waner	65.00	32.50	20.00
16	Dolf Camilli	45.00	22.50	13.50

1938 Wheaties - Series 11

Cards in this unnumbered, eight-card series measure 8-1/2" x 6" and show the players in street clothes either eating or getting ready to enjoy a bowl of Wheaties. Sometimes a waitress or other person also appears in the photo. The set is sometimes called the "Dress Clothes" or "Civies" series.

		NM	EX	VG
Complete Set (8):		750.00	375.00	225.00
Common Player:		60.00	30.00	18.00
(1)	Lou Fette	60.00	30.00	18.00
(2)	Jimmie Foxx	145.00	75.00	45.00
(3)	Charlie Gehringer	115.00	55.00	35.00
(4)	Lefty Grove	115.00	55.00	35.00
(5)	Hank Greenberg, Roxie Lawson	115.00	55.00	35.00
(6)	Lee Grissom, Ernie Lombardi	85.00	40.00	25.00
(7)	Joe Medwick	85.00	40.00	25.00
(8)	Lon Warneke	60.00	30.00	18.00

1938 Wheaties - Series 15

Another set of small (2-5/8" x 3-7/8") cards, the photos in this unnumbered series made up the back panels of single-serving size Wheaties boxes. The panels have orange, blue and white backgrounds. Some of the photos are the same as those used in the larger Wheaties panels.

		NM	EX	VG
Complete Set (11):		4,500	2,250	1,350
Common Player:		160.00	80.00	45.00
(1)	"Zeke" Bonura	160.00	80.00	45.00
(2)	Joe DiMaggio	1,300	650.00	390.00
(3)	Charles Gehringer/Btg	400.00	200.00	120.00
(4)	Chas. Gehringer/Leaping	400.00	200.00	120.00
(5)	Hank Greenberg	500.00	250.00	150.00
(6)	Lefty Grove	400.00	200.00	120.00
(7)	Carl Hubbell	325.00	160.00	97.00
(8)	John (Buddy) Lewis	160.00	80.00	45.00
(9)	Heinie Manush	300.00	150.00	90.00
(10)	Joe Medwick	300.00	150.00	90.00
(11)	Arky Vaughan	300.00	150.00	90.00

1939 Wheaties - Series 12

The nine cards in this numbered series, known as the "Personal Pointers" series, measure 8-1/4" x 6" and feature an instructional format similar to earlier Wheaties issues. The cards feature a player photo along with printed tips on various aspects of hitting and pitching.

		NM	EX	VG
Complete Set (9):		1,500	750.00	450.00
Common Player:		100.00	50.00	30.00
1	Ernie Lombardi	160.00	80.00	45.00
2	Johnny Allen	100.00	50.00	30.00
3	Lefty Gomez	185.00	90.00	55.00
4	Bill Lee	100.00	50.00	30.00
5	Jimmie Foxx	250.00	125.00	75.00
6	Joe Medwick	160.00	80.00	45.00
7	Hank Greenberg	250.00	125.00	75.00
8	Mel Ott	185.00	90.00	55.00
9	Arky Vaughn (Vaughan)	160.00	80.00	45.00

1939 Wheaties - Series 13

Issued in baseball's centennial year of 1939, this set of eight 6" x 6-3/4" cards commemorates "100 Years of Baseball." Each of the numbered panels illustrates a significant event in baseball history.

		NM	EX	VG
	Complete Set (8):	650.00	325.00	200.00
	Common Panel:	75.00	37.50	22.50
1	Design of First Diamond - 1838 (Abner Doubleday)	75.00	37.50	22.50
2	Gets News of Nomination on Field - 1860 (Abraham Lincoln)	125.00	62.50	37.50
3	Crowd Boos First Baseball Glove - 1869	75.00	37.50	22.50
4	Curve Ball Just an Illusion - 1877	75.00	37.50	22.50
5	Fencer's Mask is Pattern - 1877	75.00	37.50	22.50
6	Baseball Gets "All Dressed Up" - 1895	75.00	37.50	22.50
7	Modern Bludgeon Enters Game - 1895	75.00	37.50	22.50
8	"Casey at the Bat"	100.00	50.00	30.00

1940 Wheaties Champs of the USA

This set consists of 13 numbered panels (plus seven variations). Each pictures three athletes, including one, two or three baseball players; the others include football stars, golfers, skaters, racers, etc. The entire panel measures approximately 8-1/4" x 6", while the actual card measures approximately 6" square. Each athlete is pictured in what looks like a postage stamp with a serrated edge. A brief biography appears alongside the "stamp." Some variations are known to exist among the first nine panels. The cards are numbered in the upper right corner.

		NM	EX	VG
	Complete Set (20):	1,400	700.00	425.00
	Common Player:	50.00	25.00	15.00
1A	Bob Feller, Lynn Patrick, Charles "Red" Ruffing	135.00	67.00	40.00
1B	Leo Durocher, Lynn Patrick, Charles "Red" Ruffing	90.00	45.00	27.00
2A	Joe DiMaggio, Don Budge, Hank Greenberg	300.00	150.00	90.00
2B	Joe DiMaggio, Mel Ott, Ellsworth Vines	200.00	100.00	60.00
3	Bernie Bierman, Bill Dickey, Jimmie Foxx	125.00	62.00	37.00
4	Morris Arnovich, Capt R.K. Baker, Earl "Dutch" Clark	50.00	25.00	15.00
5	Madison (Matty) Bell, Ab Jenkins, Joe Medwick	50.00	25.00	15.00
6A	Ralph Guldahl, John Mize, Davey O'Brien	50.00	25.00	15.00
6B	Bob Feller, John Mize, Rudy York	90.00	45.00	27.00
6C	Ralph Guldahl, Gabby Hartnett, Davey O'Brien	50.00	25.00	15.00
7A	Joe Cronin, Cecil Isbell, Byron Nelson	50.00	25.00	15.00
7B	Joe Cronin, Hank Greenberg, Byron Nelson	75.00	37.00	22.00
7C	Paul Derringer, Cecil Isbell, Byron Nelson	50.00	25.00	15.00

		NM	EX	VG
8A	Ernie Lombardi, Jack Manders, George I. Myers	50.00	25.00	15.00
8B	Paul Derringer, Ernie Lombardi, George I. Myers	50.00	25.00	15.00
9	Bob Bartlett, Captain R.C. Hanson, Terrell Jacobs	50.00	25.00	15.00
10	Lowell "Red" Dawson, Billy Herman, Adele Inge	50.00	25.00	15.00
11	Dolph Camilli, Antoinette Concello, Wallace Wade	50.00	25.00	15.00
12	Luke Appling, Stanley Hack, Hugh McManus	50.00	25.00	15.00
13	Felix Adler, Hal Trosky, Mabel Vinson	50.00	25.00	15.00

1941 Wheaties Champs of the USA

This eight-card series is actually a continuation of the previous year's Wheaties set, and the format is identical. The set begins with number 14, starting where the 1940 set ended.

		NM	EX	VG
	Complete Set (8):	800.00	400.00	240.00
	Common Panel:	50.00	25.00	15.00
14	Felix Adler, Jimmie Foxx, Capt. R.G. Hanson	90.00	45.00	27.00
15	Bernie Bierman, Bob Feller, Jessie McLeod	90.00	45.00	27.00
16	Lowell "Red" Dawson, Hank Greenberg, J.W. Stoker	80.00	40.00	24.00
17	Antoinette Concello, Joe DiMaggio, Byron Nelson	300.00	150.00	90.00
18	Capt. R.L. Baker, Frank "Buck" McCormick, Harold "Pee Wee" Reese	90.00	45.00	27.00
19	William W. Robbins, Gene Sarazen, Gerald "Gee" Walker	50.00	25.00	15.00
20	Harry Danning, Barney McCosky, Bucky Walters	50.00	25.00	15.00
21	Joe "Flash" Gordon, Stan Hack, George I. Myers	50.00	25.00	15.00

1951 Wheaties

Printed as the backs of single-serving size boxes of Wheaties, the six-card 1951 set includes three baseball players and one football player, basketball player and golfer. Well-trimmed cards measure 2-1/2" x 3-1/4". The cards feature blue line drawings of the athletes with a facsimile autograph and descriptive title below. There is a wide white border. A small hoard of complete sets of unused boxes made its way into the hobby in the early 1990s. Complete boxes should be priced at 1.5X the values shown here.

		NM	EX	VG
	Complete Set (6):	650.00	325.00	195.00
	Common Player:	85.00	42.00	25.00
(1)	Bob Feller/Baseball	100.00	50.00	30.00
(2)	John Lujack/Football	55.00	27.50	16.50
(3)	George Mikan/Basketball	110.00	55.00	35.00
(4)	Stan Musial/Baseball	150.00	75.00	45.00
(5)	Sam Snead/Golfer	65.00	32.50	20.00
(6)	Ted Williams/Baseball	200.00	100.00	60.00

1951 Wheaties Premium Photos

Whether or not these 5" x 7" black-and-white, blank-back photos were ever issued at all, or only on a test basis is unknown. Despite being unmarked, they are reliably attributed to General Mills, possibly

intended for use as a Wheaties premium. The photos found on several of the pictures are the same pictures used on the box-back Wheaties cards of 1952. The pictures appear in most cases to be re-uses of team-issued images from photo packs and the like. Player names are in the bottom border in capital letters. Each picture has a small alpha-numeric identifier in the lower-right corner. The scope of the issue is unknown as several letters from the sequence are missing. The letter shown in this checklist is preceded in each case by "A8491."

		NM	EX	VG
	Complete Baseball Set (8):	2,600	1,300	775.00
	Common Player:	66.00	33.00	20.00
A	Stan Musial	325.00	160.00	95.00
C	Richie Ashburn	120.00	60.00	36.00
D	Bob Feller	120.00	60.00	36.00
E	Al Rosen	65.00	32.50	20.00
F	Larry (Yogi) Berra	175.00	85.00	50.00
G	Mickey Mantle	1,600	800.00	480.00
H	Betty Schalow/Ice skater	15.00	7.50	4.50
J	Bob Lemon	65.00	32.50	20.00
K	Roy Campanella	150.00	75.00	45.00

1952 Wheaties

These 2" x 2-3/4" cards appeared on the back of the popular cereal boxes. Actually, sports figures had been appearing on the backs of the boxes for many years, but in 1952, of the 30 athletes depicted, 10 were baseball players. That means there are 20 baseball cards, as each player appears in both a portrait and an action drawing. The cards have a blue line drawing on an orange background with a white border. The player's name, team, and position appear at the bottom. The cards have rounded corners, but are often found poorly cut from the boxes. This set was extensively counterfeited circa 2002, which had a chilling effect on values of cards not professionally graded by a major certification company.

		NM	EX	VG
	Complete (Baseball) Set (20):	650.00	325.00	195.00
	Common Player:	20.00	10.00	6.00
(1)	Larry "Yogi" Berra/Portrait	50.00	25.00	15.00
(2)	Larry "Yogi" Berra/Action	50.00	25.00	15.00
(3)	Roy Campanella/Portrait	50.00	25.00	15.00
(4)	Roy Campanella/Action	50.00	25.00	15.00
(5)	Bob Feller/Portrait	30.00	15.00	9.00
(6)	Bob Feller/Action	30.00	15.00	9.00
(7)	George Kell/Portrait	25.00	12.50	7.50
(8)	George Kell/Action	25.00	12.50	7.50
(9)	Ralph Kiner/Portrait	25.00	12.50	7.50
(10)	Ralph Kiner/Action	25.00	12.50	7.50
(11)	Bob Lemon/Portrait	25.00	12.50	7.50
(12)	Bob Lemon/Action	25.00	12.50	7.50
(13)	Stan Musial/Portrait	60.00	30.00	18.00
(14)	Stan Musial/Action	60.00	30.00	18.00
(15)	Phil Rizzuto/Portrait	30.00	15.00	9.00
(16)	Phil Rizzuto/Action	30.00	15.00	9.00
(17)	Elwin "Preacher" Roe/Portrait	20.00	10.00	6.00
(18)	Elwin "Preacher" Roe/Action	20.00	10.00	6.00
(19)	Ted Williams/Portrait	100.00	50.00	30.00
(20)	Ted Williams/Action	100.00	50.00	30.00

1952 Wheaties Tin Trays

This unique cereal box premium took the shape of a 4-7/8" x 5-1/8" tin tray which was glued to the back of Wheaties boxes. A cream-colored border surrounded the 3" x 4" color photo debossed at center. A black facsimile autograph appears across the photo. At top a small hole was punched for hanging the plaque. Backs were blank, and are often found with glue and paper residue on the gold-tone metal. Most of the plates have acquired numerous scratches and dings over the years, making true Near Mint examples very scarce. The unnumbered trays are checklisted alphabetically. A George Kell tray was long believed to exist but has never been verified.

	NM	EX	VG
Complete Set (4):	1,200	600.00	350.00
Common Player:	50.00	25.00	15.00
(1) Ralph Kiner	50.00	25.00	15.00
(2) Stan Musial	125.00	65.00	35.00
(3) Phil Rizzuto	60.00	30.00	18.00
(4) Jackie Robinson	1,100	550.00	330.00

1964 Wheaties Stamps

This General Mills' promotion included 50 player stamps and a 48-page orange album called "Wheaties Major League All-Star Baseball Player Stamp Album." The 2-1/2" x 2-3/4" stamps have a color player photo at center with a facsimile autograph and surrounded by a white border. Backs are blank. The unnumbered set is checklisted here in alphabetical order.

	NM	EX	VG
Complete Set (50):	325.00	160.00	95.00
Complete Set, In Album:	125.00	65.00	35.00
Common Player:	4.00	2.00	1.25
Album:	40.00	20.00	12.00
(1) Hank Aaron	30.00	15.00	9.00
(2) Bob Allison	4.00	2.00	1.25
(3) Luis Aparicio	7.50	3.75	2.25
(4) Ed Bailey	4.00	2.00	1.25
(5) Steve Barber	4.00	2.00	1.25
(6) Earl Battey	4.00	2.00	1.25
(7) Jim Bouton	5.00	2.50	1.50
(8) Ken Boyer	5.00	2.50	1.50
(9) Jim Bunning	7.50	3.75	2.25
(10) Orlando Cepeda	10.00	5.00	3.00
(11) Roberto Clemente	45.00	22.50	13.50
(12) Ray Culp	4.00	2.00	1.25
(13) Tommy Davis	4.00	2.00	1.25
(14) John Edwards	4.00	2.00	1.25
(15) Whitey Ford	20.00	10.00	6.00
(16) Nellie Fox	10.00	5.00	3.00
(17) Bob Friend	4.00	2.00	1.25
(18) Jim Gilliam	5.00	2.50	1.50
(19) Jim Grant	4.00	2.00	1.25
(20) Dick Groat	4.00	2.00	1.25
(21) Elston Howard	5.00	2.50	1.50
(22) Larry Jackson	4.00	2.00	1.25
(23) Julian Javier	4.00	2.00	1.25
(24) Al Kaline	12.50	6.25	3.75
(25) Harmon Killebrew	12.50	6.25	3.75
(26) Don Leppert	4.00	2.00	1.25
(27) Frank Malzone	4.00	2.00	1.25
(28) Juan Marichal	7.50	3.75	2.25
(29) Willie Mays	30.00	15.00	9.00
(30) Ken McBride	4.00	2.00	1.25
(31) Willie McCovey	10.00	5.00	3.00
(32) Jim O'Toole	4.00	2.00	1.25
(33) Albie Pearson	4.00	2.00	1.25
(34) Joe Pepitone	5.00	2.50	1.50
(35) Ron Perranoski	4.00	2.00	1.25
(36) Juan Pizzaro	4.00	2.00	1.25
(37) Dick Radatz	4.00	2.00	1.25

(38) Bobby Richardson	6.00	3.00	1.75
(39) Brooks Robinson	12.50	6.25	3.75
(40) Ron Santo	6.00	3.00	1.75
(41) Norm Siebern	4.00	2.00	1.25
(42) Duke Snider	20.00	10.00	6.00
(43) Warren Spahn	12.50	6.25	3.75
(44) Joe Torre	6.00	3.00	1.75
(45) Tom Tresh	5.00	2.50	1.50
(46) Zoilo Versailles (Versalles)	4.00	2.00	1.25
(47) Leon Wagner	4.00	2.00	1.25
(48) Bill White	4.00	2.00	1.25
(49) Hal Woodeshick	4.00	2.00	1.25
(50) Carl Yastrzemski	20.00	10.00	6.00

1937 WHIO-Sy Burick Cincinnati Reds Postcards

(See 1937-39 Orcajo Cincinnati Reds postcards for checklist, values.)

1889 C.S. White & Co. Boston N.L.

(See 1889 Number 7 Cigars for checklist and value information.)

1977 Wiffle Insert Discs

Similar in concept and format to the many contemporary MSA baseball player disc sets, the pieces inserted within Wiffle brand baseball, softball and bat boxes differ in that they are smaller, at 2-3/8" diameter, and feature a larger checklist. The discs feature black-and-white player portrait photos in the center of a baseball design. The left and right panels are in one of several bright colors. Licensed by the players' association through Mike Schechter Associates, the player photos carry no uniform logos. Backs are printed in black and orange. The unnumbered discs are checklisted alphabetically.

	NM	EX	VG
Complete Set (80):	325.00	160.00	100.00
Common Player:	2.50	1.25	.70
(1) Sal Bando	2.50	1.25	.70
(2) Buddy Bell	2.50	1.25	.70
(3) Johnny Bench	7.50	3.75	2.25
(4) Vida Blue	2.50	1.25	.70
(5) Bert Blyleven	3.00	1.50	.90
(6) Bobby Bonds	2.50	1.25	.70

(7) George Brett	12.00	6.00	3.50
(8) Lou Brock	6.00	3.00	1.75
(9) Bill Buckner	2.50	1.25	.70
(10) Ray Burris	2.50	1.25	.70
(11) Jeff Burroughs	2.50	1.25	.70
(12) Bert Campaneris	2.50	1.25	.70
(13) Rod Carew	6.00	3.00	1.75
(14) Steve Carlton	6.00	3.00	1.75
(15) Dave Cash	2.50	1.25	.70
(16) Cesar Cedeno	2.50	1.25	.70
(17) Ron Cey	2.50	1.25	.70
(18) Chris Chambliss	2.50	1.25	.70
(19) Dave Concepcion	2.50	1.25	.70
(20) Dennis Eckersley	6.00	3.00	1.75
(21) Mark Fidrych	3.50	1.75	1.00
(22) Rollie Fingers	6.00	3.00	1.75
(23) Carlton Fisk	6.00	3.00	1.75
(24) George Foster	2.50	1.25	.70
(25) Wayne Garland	2.50	1.25	.70
(26) Ralph Garr	2.50	1.25	.70
(27) Steve Garvey	5.00	2.50	1.50
(28) Don Gullett	2.50	1.25	.70
(29) Larry Hisle	2.50	1.25	.70
(30) Al Hrabosky	2.50	1.25	.70
(31) Catfish Hunter	6.00	3.00	1.75
(32) Reggie Jackson	12.00	6.00	3.50
(33) Randy Jones	2.50	1.25	.70
(34) Dave Kingman	2.50	1.25	.70
(35) Jerry Koosman	2.50	1.25	.70
(36) Ed Kranepool	2.50	1.25	.70
(37) Ron LeFlore	2.50	1.25	.70
(38) Sixto Lezcano	2.50	1.25	.70
(39) Davey Lopes	2.50	1.25	.70
(40) Greg Luzinski	2.50	1.25	.70
(41) Fred Lynn	2.50	1.25	.70
(42) Garry Maddox	2.50	1.25	.70
(43) Jon Matlock	2.50	1.25	.70
(44) Gary Matthews	2.50	1.25	.70
(45) Lee May	2.50	1.25	.70
(46) John Mayberry	2.50	1.25	.70
(47) Bake McBride	2.50	1.25	.70
(48) Tug McGraw	2.50	1.25	.70
(49) Hal McRae	2.50	1.25	.70
(50) Andy Messersmith	2.50	1.25	.70
(51) Randy Moffitt	2.50	1.25	.70
(52) John Montefusco	2.50	1.25	.70
(53) Joe Morgan	6.00	3.00	1.75
(54) Thurman Munson	6.00	3.00	1.75
(55) Graig Nettles	2.50	1.25	.70
(56) Al Oliver	2.50	1.25	.70
(57) Jorge Orta	2.50	1.25	.70
(58) Jim Palmer	6.00	3.00	1.75
(59) Dave Parker	2.50	1.25	.70
(60) Tony Perez	6.00	3.00	1.75
(61) Gaylord Perry	6.00	3.00	1.75
(62) Jim Rice	3.00	1.50	.90
(63) Steve Rogers	2.50	1.25	.70
(64) Pete Rose	15.00	7.50	4.50
(65) Joe Rudi	2.50	1.25	.70
(66) Nolan Ryan	30.00	15.00	9.00
(67) Manny Sanguillen	2.50	1.25	.70
(68) Mike Schmidt	12.00	6.00	3.50
(69) Tom Seaver	7.50	3.75	2.25
(70) Ted Simmons	2.50	1.25	.70
(71) Reggie Smith	2.50	1.25	.70
(72) Willie Stargell	6.00	3.00	1.75
(73) Rusty Staub	2.50	1.25	.70
(74) Frank Tanana	2.50	1.25	.70
(75) Gene Tenace	2.50	1.25	.70
(76) Luis Tiant	2.50	1.25	.70
(77) Manny Trillo	2.50	1.25	.70
(78) Bob Watson	2.50	1.25	.70
(79) Carl Yastrzemski	7.50	3.75	2.25
(80) Richie Zisk	2.50	1.25	.70

1978 Wiffle Box-Side Discs

Similar in concept and format to the many contemporary MSA baseball player disc sets, the pieces printed on the sides of Wiffle-brand baseball boxes differ in that they are smaller, at 2-3/8" diameter, and feature a larger checklist. The discs feature black-and-white player portrait photos in the center of a baseball design. The left and right panels are in one of several bright colors. Licensed by the players' association through Mike Schechter Associates, the player photos carry no uniform logos. Backs are printed in black and orange. The unnumbered discs are checklisted here alphabetically.

	NM	EX	VG
Complete Set (88):	325.00	160.00	100.00
Common Player:	2.50	1.25	.70
(1) Sal Bando	2.50	1.25	.70
(2) Buddy Bell	2.50	1.25	.70
(3) Johnny Bench	7.50	3.75	2.25
(4) Vida Blue	2.50	1.25	.70
(5) Bert Blyleven	3.00	1.50	.90
(6) Bobby Bonds	2.50	1.25	.70
(7) George Brett	12.00	6.00	3.50
(8) Lou Brock	6.00	3.00	1.75

(9)	Bill Buckner	2.50	1.25	.70
(10)	Ray Burris	2.50	1.25	.70
(11)	Jeff Burroughs	2.50	1.25	.70
(12)	Bert Campaneris	2.50	1.25	.70
(13)	John Candelaria	2.50	1.25	.70
(14)	Jose Cardenal	2.50	1.25	.70
(15)	Rod Carew	6.00	3.00	1.75
(16)	Steve Carlton	6.00	3.00	1.75
(17)	Dave Cash	2.50	1.25	.70
(18)	Cesar Cedeno	2.50	1.25	.70
(19)	Ron Cey	2.50	1.25	.70
(20)	Chris Chambliss	2.50	1.25	.70
(21)	Dave Concepcion	2.50	1.25	.70
(22)	Dennis Eckersley	6.00	3.00	1.75
(23)	Mark Fidrych	3.50	1.75	1.00
(24)	Rollie Fingers	6.00	3.00	1.75
(25)	Carlton Fisk	6.00	3.00	1.75
(26)	George Foster	2.50	1.25	.70
(27)	Wayne Garland	2.50	1.25	.70
(28)	Ralph Garr	2.50	1.25	.70
(29)	Steve Garvey	5.00	2.50	1.50
(30)	Don Gullett	2.50	1.25	.70
(31)	Larry Hisle	2.50	1.25	.70
(32)	Al Hrabosky	2.50	1.25	.70
(33)	Catfish Hunter	6.00	3.00	1.75
(34)	Reggie Jackson	12.00	6.00	3.50
(35)	Randy Jones	2.50	1.25	.70
(36)	Von Joshua	2.50	1.25	.70
(37)	Dave Kingman	2.50	1.25	.70
(38)	Jerry Koosman	2.50	1.25	.70
(39)	Ed Kranepool	2.50	1.25	.70
(40)	Ron LeFlore	2.50	1.25	.70
(41)	Sixto Lezcano	2.50	1.25	.70
(42)	Davey Lopes	2.50	1.25	.70
(43)	Greg Luzinski	2.50	1.25	.70
(44)	Fred Lynn	2.50	1.25	.70
(45)	Garry Maddox	2.50	1.25	.70
(46)	Jon Matlock	2.50	1.25	.70
(47)	Gary Matthews	2.50	1.25	.70
(48)	Lee May	2.50	1.25	.70
(49)	John Mayberry	2.50	1.25	.70
(50)	Bake McBride	2.50	1.25	.70
(51)	Tug McGraw	2.50	1.25	.70
(52)	Hal McRae	2.50	1.25	.70
(53)	Andy Messersmith	2.50	1.25	.70
(54)	Randy Moffitt	2.50	1.25	.70
(55)	John Montefusco	2.50	1.25	.70
(56)	Joe Morgan	6.00	3.00	1.75
(57)	Thurman Munson	6.00	3.00	1.75
(58)	Graig Nettles	2.50	1.25	.70
(59)	Bill North	2.50	1.25	.70
(60)	Al Oliver	2.50	1.25	.70
(61)	Jorge Orta	2.50	1.25	.70
(62)	Jim Palmer	6.00	3.00	1.75
(63)	Dave Parker	2.50	1.25	.70
(64)	Tony Perez	6.00	3.00	1.75
(65)	Gaylord Perry	6.00	3.00	1.75
(66)	Jim Rice	3.00	1.50	.90
(67)	Ellie Rodriguez	2.50	1.25	.70
(68)	Steve Rogers	2.50	1.25	.70
(69)	Pete Rose	15.00	7.50	4.50
(70)	Joe Rudi	2.50	1.25	.70
(71)	Nolan Ryan	30.00	15.00	9.00
(72)	Manny Sanguillen	2.50	1.25	.70
(73)	Mike Schmidt	12.00	6.00	3.50
(74)	Tom Seaver	7.50	3.75	2.25
(75)	Ted Simmons	2.50	1.25	.70
(76)	Reggie Smith	2.50	1.25	.70
(77)	Jim Spencer	2.50	1.25	.70
(78)	Willie Stargell	6.00	3.00	1.75
(79)	Rusty Staub	2.50	1.25	.70
(80)	Rennie Stennett	2.50	1.25	.70
(81)	Frank Tanana	2.50	1.25	.70
(82)	Gene Tenace	2.50	1.25	.70
(83)	Luis Tiant	2.50	1.25	.70
(84)	Manny Trillo	2.50	1.25	.70
(85)	Bob Watson	2.50	1.25	.70
(86)	Butch Wynegar	2.50	1.25	.70
(87)	Carl Yastrzemski	7.50	3.75	2.25
(88)	Richie Zisk	2.50	1.25	.70

1922 Willard's Chocolates Premium

Details on distribution of this 7-1/8" x 11-1/4" premium are unclear, likely involving some sort of wrapper or coupon redemption. The blank-back piece has a central photo of Babe Ruth in action. A facsimile autograph appears in a panel at bottom.

	NM	EX	VG
Babe Ruth	4,000	2,000	1,200

1923 Willard's Chocolate (V100)

Issued circa 1923, this set was produced by the Willard Chocolate Co. of Canada and features sepia-toned photographs on cards measuring about 2" x 3-1/4". The cards are blank-backed and feature the player's name in script on the front, along with a tiny credit line: "Photo by International." The set is complete at 180 cards and nearly one-fourth of the photos used in the set are identical to the better known E120 American Caramel set. The Willard set is identified as V100 in the American Card Catalog.

		NM	EX	VG
	Complete Set (180):	30,000	15,000	9,000
	Common Player:	100.00	50.00	30.00
(1)	Chas. B. Adams	100.00	50.00	30.00
(2)	Grover C. Alexander	400.00	200.00	125.00
(3)	J.P. Austin	100.00	50.00	30.00
(4)	J.C. Bagby	100.00	50.00	30.00
(5)	J. Franklin Baker	300.00	150.00	90.00
(6)	David J. Bancroft	300.00	150.00	90.00
(7)	Turner Barber	100.00	50.00	30.00
(8)	Jesse L. Barnes	100.00	50.00	30.00
(9)	J.C. Bassler	100.00	50.00	30.00
(10)	L.A. Blue	100.00	50.00	30.00
(11)	Norman D. Boeckel	100.00	50.00	30.00
(12)	F.L. Brazil (Brazill)	100.00	50.00	30.00
(13)	G.H. Burns	100.00	50.00	30.00
(14)	Geo. J. Burns	100.00	50.00	30.00
(15)	Leon Cadore	100.00	50.00	30.00
(16)	Max G. Carey	300.00	150.00	90.00
(17)	Harold G. Carlson	100.00	50.00	30.00
(18)	Lloyd R Christenberry (Christenbury)	100.00	50.00	30.00
(19)	Vernon J. Clemons	100.00	50.00	30.00
(20)	T.R. Cobb	2,400	1,200	750.00
(21)	Bert Cole	100.00	50.00	30.00
(22)	John F. Collins	100.00	50.00	30.00
(23)	S. Coveleskie (Coveleski)	300.00	150.00	90.00
(24)	Walton E. Cruise	100.00	50.00	30.00
(25)	G.W. Cutshaw	100.00	50.00	30.00
(26)	Jacob E. Daubert	100.00	50.00	30.00
(27)	Geo. Dauss	100.00	50.00	30.00
(28)	F.T. Davis	100.00	50.00	30.00
(29)	Chas. A. Deal	100.00	50.00	30.00
(30)	William L. Doak	100.00	50.00	30.00
(31)	William E. Donovan	100.00	50.00	30.00
(32)	Hugh Duffy	300.00	150.00	90.00
(33)	J.A. Dugan	100.00	50.00	30.00
(34)	Louis B. Duncan	100.00	50.00	30.00
(35)	James Dykes	100.00	50.00	30.00
(36)	H.J. Ehmke	100.00	50.00	30.00
(37)	F.R. Ellerbe	100.00	50.00	30.00
(38)	E.G. Erickson	100.00	50.00	30.00
(39)	John J. Evers	300.00	150.00	90.00
(40)	U.C. Faber	300.00	150.00	90.00
(41)	B.A. Falk	100.00	50.00	30.00
(42)	Max Flack	100.00	50.00	30.00
(43)	Lee Fohl	100.00	50.00	30.00
(44)	Jacques F. Fournier	100.00	50.00	30.00
(45)	Frank F. Frisch	300.00	150.00	90.00
(46)	C.E. Galloway	100.00	50.00	30.00
(47)	W.C. Gardner	100.00	50.00	30.00
(48)	E.P. Gharrity	100.00	50.00	30.00
(49)	Geo. Gibson	100.00	50.00	30.00
(50)	Wm. Gleason	100.00	50.00	30.00
(51)	William Gleason	100.00	50.00	30.00
(52)	Henry M. Gowdy	100.00	50.00	30.00
(53)	I.M. Griffin	100.00	50.00	30.00
(54)	Tom Griffith	100.00	50.00	30.00
(55)	Burleigh A. Grimes	300.00	150.00	90.00
(56)	Charles J. Grimm	100.00	50.00	30.00
(57)	Jesse J. Haines	300.00	150.00	90.00
(58)	S.R. Harris	100.00	50.00	30.00
(59)	W.B. Harris	100.00	50.00	30.00
(60)	R.K. Hasty	100.00	50.00	30.00
(61)	H.E. Heilman (Heilmann)	300.00	150.00	90.00
(62)	Walter J. Henline	100.00	50.00	30.00
(63)	Walter L. Holke	100.00	50.00	30.00
(64)	Charles J. Hollocher	100.00	50.00	30.00
(65)	H.B. Hooper	300.00	150.00	90.00
(66)	Rogers Hornsby	400.00	200.00	125.00
(67)	W.C. Hoyt	300.00	150.00	90.00
(68)	Miller Huggins	300.00	150.00	90.00
(69)	W.C. Jacobsen (Jacobson)	100.00	50.00	30.00
(70)	C.D. Jamieson	100.00	50.00	30.00
(71)	Ernest Johnson	100.00	50.00	30.00
(72)	W.P. Johnson	750.00	375.00	225.00
(73)	James H. Johnston	100.00	50.00	30.00
(74)	R.W. Jones	100.00	50.00	30.00
(75)	Samuel Pond Jones	100.00	50.00	30.00
(76)	J.I. Judge	100.00	50.00	30.00
(77)	James W. Keenan	100.00	50.00	30.00
(78)	Geo. L. Kelly	300.00	150.00	90.00
(79)	Peter J. Kilduff	100.00	50.00	30.00
(80)	William Killefer	100.00	50.00	30.00
(81)	Lee King	100.00	50.00	30.00
(82)	Ray Kolp	100.00	50.00	30.00
(83)	John Lavan	100.00	50.00	30.00
(84)	H.L. Leibold	100.00	50.00	30.00
(85)	Connie Mack	300.00	150.00	90.00
(86)	J.W. Mails	100.00	50.00	30.00
(87)	Walter J. Maranville	300.00	150.00	90.00
(88)	Richard W. Marquard	300.00	150.00	90.00
(89)	C.W. Mays	100.00	50.00	30.00
(90)	Geo. F. McBride	100.00	50.00	30.00
(91)	H.M. McClellan	100.00	50.00	30.00
(92)	John J. McGraw	300.00	150.00	90.00
(93)	Austin B. McHenry	100.00	50.00	30.00
(94)	J. McInnis	100.00	50.00	30.00
(95)	Douglas McWeeney (McWeeny)	100.00	50.00	30.00
(96)	M. Menosky	100.00	50.00	30.00
(97)	Emil F. Meusel	100.00	50.00	30.00
(98)	R. Meusel	100.00	50.00	30.00
(99)	Henry W. Meyers	100.00	50.00	30.00
(100)	J.C. Milan	100.00	50.00	30.00
(101)	John K. Miljus	100.00	50.00	30.00
(102)	Edmund J. Miller	100.00	50.00	30.00
(103)	Elmer Miller	100.00	50.00	30.00
(104)	Otto L. Miller	100.00	50.00	30.00
(105)	Fred Mitchell	100.00	50.00	30.00
(106)	Geo. Mogridge	100.00	50.00	30.00
(107)	Patrick J. Moran	100.00	50.00	30.00
(108)	John D. Morrison	100.00	50.00	30.00
(109)	J.A. Mostil	100.00	50.00	30.00
(110)	Clarence F. Mueller	100.00	50.00	30.00
(111)	A. Earle Neale	100.00	50.00	30.00
(112)	Joseph Oeschger	100.00	50.00	30.00
(113)	Robert J. O'Farrell	100.00	50.00	30.00
(114)	J.C. Oldham	100.00	50.00	30.00
(115)	I.M. Olson	100.00	50.00	30.00
(116)	Geo. M. O'Neil	100.00	50.00	30.00
(117)	S.F. O'Neill	100.00	50.00	30.00
(118)	Frank J. Parkinson	100.00	50.00	30.00
(119)	Geo. H. Paskert	100.00	50.00	30.00
(120)	R.T. Peckinpaugh	100.00	50.00	30.00
(121)	H.J. Pennock	300.00	150.00	90.00
(122)	Ralph Perkins	100.00	50.00	30.00
(123)	Edw. J. Pfeffer	100.00	50.00	30.00
(124)	W.C. Pipp	100.00	50.00	30.00
(125)	Charles Elmer Ponder	100.00	50.00	30.00
(126)	Raymond R. Powell	100.00	50.00	30.00
(127)	D.B. Pratt	100.00	50.00	30.00
(128)	Joseph Rapp	100.00	50.00	30.00
(129)	John H. Rawlings	100.00	50.00	30.00
(130)	E.S. Rice (Should be E.C.)	300.00	150.00	90.00
(131)	Branch Rickey	350.00	175.00	110.00
(132)	James J. Ring	100.00	50.00	30.00
(133)	Eppa J. Rixey	300.00	150.00	90.00
(134)	Davis A. Robertson	100.00	50.00	30.00
(135)	Edwin Rommel	100.00	50.00	30.00
(136)	Edd J. Roush	300.00	150.00	90.00
(137)	Harold Ruel (Herold)	100.00	50.00	30.00
(138)	Allen Russell	100.00	50.00	30.00
(139)	G.H. Ruth	4,500	2,250	1,400
(140)	Wilfred D. Ryan	100.00	50.00	30.00
(141)	Henry F. Sallee	100.00	50.00	30.00
(142)	W.H. Schang	100.00	50.00	30.00
(143)	Raymond H. Schmandt	100.00	50.00	30.00
(144)	Everett Scott	100.00	50.00	30.00
(145)	Henry Severeid	100.00	50.00	30.00
(146)	Jos. W. Sewell	300.00	150.00	90.00
(147)	Howard S. Shanks	100.00	50.00	30.00
(148)	E.H. Sheely	100.00	50.00	30.00
(149)	Ralph Shinners	100.00	50.00	30.00
(150)	U.J. Shocker	100.00	50.00	30.00
(151)	G.H. Sisler	300.00	150.00	90.00
(152)	Earl L. Smith	100.00	50.00	30.00
(153)	Earl S. Smith	100.00	50.00	30.00
(154)	Geo. A. Smith	100.00	50.00	30.00
(155)	J.W. Smith	100.00	50.00	30.00
(156)	Tris E. Speaker	400.00	200.00	125.00
(157)	Arnold Staatz (Statz)	100.00	50.00	30.00
(158)	J.R. Stephenson	100.00	50.00	30.00
(159)	Milton J. Stock	100.00	50.00	30.00
(160)	John L. Sullivan	100.00	50.00	30.00
(161)	H.F. Tormahlen	100.00	50.00	30.00
(162)	Jas. A. Tierney	100.00	50.00	30.00
(163)	J.T. Tobin	100.00	50.00	30.00
(164)	Jas. L. Vaughn	100.00	50.00	30.00
(165)	R.H. Veach	100.00	50.00	30.00
(166)	C.W. Walker	100.00	50.00	30.00
(167)	A.L. Ward	100.00	50.00	30.00
(168)	Zack D. Wheat	300.00	150.00	90.00
(169)	George B. Whitted	100.00	50.00	30.00
(170)	Irvin K. Wilhelm	100.00	50.00	30.00
(171)	Roy H. Wilkinson	100.00	50.00	30.00
(172)	Fred C. Williams	100.00	50.00	30.00
(173)	K.R. Williams	100.00	50.00	30.00
(174)	Sam'l W. Wilson	100.00	50.00	30.00
(175)	Ivy B. Wingo	100.00	50.00	30.00
(176)	L.W. Witt	100.00	50.00	30.00
(177)	Joseph Wood	200.00	100.00	60.00
(178)	E. Yaryan	100.00	50.00	30.00
(179)	R.S. Young	100.00	50.00	30.00
(180)	Ross Young (Youngs)	300.00	150.00	90.00

1924 Willard's Chocolate Sports Champions (V122)

Three baseball players are featured among this 56-card Canadian set. The black-and-white cards are printed on thin paper measuring 1-3/8" x 3-3/8".

BABE RUTH HOME RUN CHAMPION

Backs are blank. The set features male and female athletes from many different sports, with a distinct Canadian flavor. The candy company was headquartered in Toronto.

		NM	EX	VG
2	Eddie Collins	600.00	300.00	180.00
5	Babe Ruth	3,250	1,625	975.00
39	Ty Cobb	2,250	1,125	675.00

1911 Williams Baking Philadelphia A's (D359)

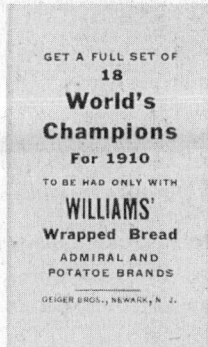

WORLD'S CHAMPIONS 1910

BARRY, ATHLETIC

GET A FULL SET OF 18 World's Champions For 1910 TO BE HAD ONLY WITH WILLIAMS' Wrapped Bread ADMIRAL AND POTATOE BRANDS

GEIGER BROS., NEWARK, N.J.

This Philadelphia Athletics team set is among the scarcest early 20th Century baking company issues. It commemorates the A's 1910 Championship season, and, except for pitcher Jack Coombs, the checklist includes nearly all key members of the club, including manager Connie Mack. The cards are the standard size for the era, 1-1/2" x 2-5/8". Fronts feature a player portrait set against a colored background. The player's name and the word "Athletics" appear at the bottom, while "World's Champions 1910" is printed along the top. Backs of the cards advertise the set as the "Athletics Series." Collectors should be aware that the same checklist was used for a similar Athletics set issued by Rochester Baking and Cullivan's Fireside tobacco (T208) and also that blank-backed versions are also known to exist, cataloged as E104 in the American Card Catalog.

		NM	EX	VG
Complete Set (18):		100,000	40,000	20,000
Common Player:		5,000	2,000	1,000
(1)	Home Run Baker	8,000	4,000	2,000
(2)	Jack Barry	5,000	2,000	1,000
(3)	Chief Bender	8,000	4,000	2,000
(4)	Eddie Collins	8,000	4,000	2,000
(5)	Harry Davis	5,000	2,000	1,000
(6)	Jimmy Dygert	5,000	2,000	1,000
(7)	Topsy Hartsel	5,000	2,000	1,000
(8)	Harry Krause	5,000	2,000	1,000
(9)	Jack Lapp	5,000	2,000	1,000
(10)	Paddy Livingston	5,000	2,000	1,000
(11)	Bris Lord	5,000	2,000	1,000
(12)	Connie Mack	13,000	6,500	3,000
(13)	Cy Morgan	5,000	2,000	1,000
(14)	Danny Murphy	5,000	2,000	1,000
(15)	Rube Oldring	5,000	2,000	1,000
(16)	Eddie Plank	13,000	6,500	3,000
(17)	Amos Strunk	5,000	2,000	1,000
(18a)	Ira Thomas (1910 at top.)	5,000	2,000	1,000
(18b)	Ira Thomas (1910 at right.)	5,000	2,000	1,000

1910 Williams Caramels (E103)

N. LAJOIE, 2d B., Cleveland
The Williams Caramel Co. Oxford, Pa.

This 30-card set issued by the Williams Caramel Co. of Oxford, Pa., in 1910 can be differentiated from other similar sets because it was printed on a thin paper stock rather than cardboard. Measuring approximately 1-3/4" x 2-5/8", each card features a player portrait set against a red background. The bottom of the card lists the player's last name, position and team; beneath that is the line, "The Williams Caramel Co. Oxford Pa." Nearly all of the photos in the set, which is designated E103 by the ACC, are identical to those in the M116 Sporting Life set.

		NM	EX	VG
Complete Set (30):		130,000	50,000	25,000
Common Player:		975.00	390.00	195.00
(1)	Chas. Bender	4,500	1,800	900.00
(2)	Roger Bresnahan	4,500	1,800	900.00
(3)	Mordecai Brown	4,500	1,800	900.00
(4)	Frank Chance	4,500	1,800	900.00
(5)	Hal Chase	3,000	1,200	600.00
(6)	Ty Cobb	37,500	15,000	7,500
(7)	Edward Collins	4,500	1,800	900.00
(8)	Sam Crawford	4,500	1,800	900.00
(9)	Harry Davis	975.00	390.00	195.00
(10)	Arthur Devlin	975.00	390.00	195.00
(11)	William Donovan	975.00	390.00	195.00
(12)	Chas. Dooin	975.00	390.00	195.00
(13)	L. Doyle	975.00	390.00	195.00
(14)	John Ewing	975.00	390.00	195.00
(15)	George Gibson	975.00	390.00	195.00
(16)	Hugh Jennings	4,500	1,800	900.00
(17)	David Jones	975.00	390.00	195.00
(18)	Tim Jordan	975.00	390.00	195.00
(19)	N. Lajoie	4,500	1,800	900.00
(20)	Thomas Leach	975.00	390.00	195.00
(21)	Harry Lord	975.00	390.00	195.00
(22)	Chris. Mathewson	15,000	6,000	3,000
(23)	John McLean	975.00	390.00	195.00
(24)	Geo. W. McQuillan	975.00	390.00	195.00
(25)	Pastorius	975.00	390.00	195.00
(26)	N. Rucker	975.00	390.00	195.00
(27)	Fred Tenny (Tenney)	975.00	390.00	195.00
(28)	Ira Thomas	975.00	390.00	195.00
(29)	Hans Wagner	30,000	12,000	6,000
(30)	Robert Wood	975.00	390.00	195.00

1889 E.R. Williams Card Game

This set of 52 playing cards came packed in its own box that advertised the set as the "Egerton R. Williams Popular Indoor Base Ball Game." Designed to look like a conventional deck of playing cards, the set included various players from the National League and the American Association. Although the set contains 52 cards (like a typical deck of playing cards) only 19 actually feature color drawings of players. Each of these cards pictures two different players (one at the top and a second at the bottom, separated by sepia-colored crossed bats in the middle), resulting in 38 different players. The remaining 33 cards in the deck are strictly game cards showing a specific baseball play (such as "Batter Out on Fly"

or "Two Base Hit," etc.). The cards have green-tinted backs and measure 2-7/16" x 3-1/2". Each one carries an 1889 copyright line by E.R. Williams.

		NM	EX	VG
Complete Boxed Set:		24,000	12,000	7,250
Common Player Card:		600.00	300.00	175.00
Common Game Action Card:		110.00	55.00	30.00
(1)	Cap Anson, Buck Ewing	2,400	1,200	720.00
(2)	Dan Brouthers, Arlie Latham	900.00	450.00	275.00
(3)	Charles Buffinton, Bob Carruthers	600.00	300.00	175.00
(4)	Hick Carpenter, Cliff Carroll	600.00	300.00	175.00
(5)	Charles Comiskey, Roger Connor	1,200	600.00	360.00
(6)	Pop Corkhill, Jim Fogarty	600.00	300.00	175.00
(7)	John Clarkson, Tim Keefe	1,200	600.00	360.00
(8)	Jerry Denny, Mike Tiernan	600.00	300.00	175.00
(9)	Dave Foutz, King Kelly	2,200	1,100	660.00
(10)	Pud Galvin, Dave Orr	900.00	450.00	275.00
(11)	Jack Glasscock, Tommy Tucker	600.00	300.00	175.00
(12)	Mike Griffin, Ed McKean	600.00	300.00	175.00
(13)	Dummy Hoy, Long John Reilley (Reilly)	900.00	450.00	275.00
(14)	Arthur Irwin, Ned Williamson	600.00	300.00	175.00
(15)	Silver King, John Tener	900.00	450.00	275.00
(16)	Al Myers, Cub Stricker	600.00	300.00	175.00
(17)	Fred Pfeffer, Chicken Wolf	600.00	300.00	175.00
(18)	Tom Ramsey, Gus Weyhing	600.00	300.00	175.00
(19)	John Ward, Curt Welch	1,000	500.00	300.00

1961 J.B. Williams Co. Roger Maris Lithograph

ROGER MARIS

The maker of Lectric Shave and Aqua Velva offered fans a lithograph of Roger Maris hitting his 59th home run at Baltimore, Sept. 20, 1961. The 16" x 11" black-and-white print on parchment paper was available by mail for 25 cents and a box top from either of the shaving products. The artwork is by Robert Riger.

	NM	EX	VG
Roger Maris	200.00	100.00	60.00

1908 R.C. Williams Cy Young Postcard

Cy, Delivering the Assets.

A mature Cy Young, about age 42, is pictured on this postcard bearing the imprint of R.C. Williams. No other contemporary cards with this imprint have been reported.

	NM	EX	VG
Cy Young	800.00	400.00	240.00

1954 Wilson Franks

The 2-5/8" x 3-3/4" cards are among the most popular and scarcest baseball card sets issued with hot dogs during the 1950s. The cards feature color-added photos on the front along with a facsimile autograph and a package of frankfurters. Backs feature personal information, a career summary and 1953 and career statistics. Cards were packaged in direct contact with the meat, resulting in many exhibiting grease stains. Survival rates of the various players differ widely, probably based on the geography of ini-

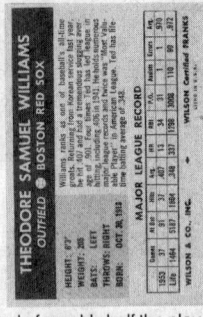

tial distribution. A small hoard of roughly half the players was discovered in unissued condition in the late 1990s, temporarily influencing the market.

	NM	EX	VG
Complete Set (20):	30,000	12,000	6,000
Common Player:	650.00	260.00	130.00
Advertising Poster:	7,500	3,500	2,000
(1) Roy Campanella	1,800	725.00	350.00
(2) Del Ennis	650.00	260.00	130.00
(3) Carl Erskine	675.00	275.00	135.00
(4) Ferris Fain	650.00	260.00	130.00
(5) Bob Feller	1,250	500.00	250.00
(6) Nelson Fox	1,250	500.00	250.00
(7) Johnny Groth	750.00	300.00	150.00
(8) Stan Hack	1,100	440.00	220.00
(9) Gil Hodges	2,750	1,100	550.00
(10) Ray Jablonski	1,250	500.00	250.00
(11) Harvey Kuenn	1,350	550.00	275.00
(12) Roy McMillan	650.00	260.00	130.00
(13) Andy Pafko	650.00	260.00	130.00
(14) Paul Richards	900.00	360.00	180.00
(15) Hank Sauer	900.00	360.00	180.00
(16) Red Schoendienst	1,000	400.00	200.00
(17) Enos Slaughter	800.00	320.00	160.00
(18) Vern Stephens	650.00	260.00	130.00
(19) Sammy White	650.00	260.00	130.00
(20) Ted Williams	13,500	6,500	3,500

1961 Wilson Meats
L.A. Dodgers/Angels

It is likely these 5-1/2" x 8-1/2" photos were prepared for promotional appearances by players on behalf of the meat company. The player name appears at the bottom of the photo and the sponsor's message appears at bottom, "Courtesy of WILSON & CO., Inc., Fine Meat Products." Backs are blank. The pictures are often found with player autographs, another indicator of their use at personal appearances.

	NM	EX	VG
(1) Ron Fairly	50.00	25.00	15.00
(2) Gil Hodges	75.00	37.00	22.00
(3) Frank Howard	50.00	25.00	15.00
(4) Ted Kluszewski	60.00	30.00	18.00

1950s-70s Wilson
Advisory Staff Photos

Advisory staff photos were a promotional item which debuted in the early 1950s, flourished in the Sixties and died in the early 1970s. Generally 8" x 10" (sometimes a little larger), these black-and-white (a few later were color) glossy photos picture players who had contracted with a major baseball equipment company to endorse and use their product. Usually the product - most often a glove - was prominently displayed in the photo. The pictures were often displayed in the windows of sporting goods stores or the walls of sports departments and were sometimes made available to customers. Because the companies tended to stick with players over the years, some photos were reissued, sometimes with and sometimes without a change of team, pose or style. The photos are checklisted here in alphabetical order. A pose description is given where known. It is unlikely this list is complete. Gaps have been left in the assigned numbering to accommodate future additions. In general, Wilson advisory staff photos feature the player name and a line of type indicating the player's status as an advisory staffer in the bottom border.

		NM	EX	VG
Common Player:		14.00	7.00	4.00
(1)	Bob Allison (Twins, full-length.)	20.00	10.00	6.00
(2)	Felipe Alou (Braves, neck-to-cap.)	25.00	12.50	7.50
(3)	Felipe Alou (Braves, upper body.)	25.00	12.50	7.50
(4)	Max Alvis (Indians, hands on knees.)	20.00	10.00	6.00
(5)	Max Alvis (Indians, upper body.)	20.00	10.00	6.00
(6)	Luis Aparicio/Fielding (White Sox, horizontal.)	50.00	25.00	15.00
(7)	Luis Aparicio (White Sox, fielding, full-length.)	40.00	20.00	12.00
(8)	Luis Aparicio (Orioles, full-length/)	50.00	25.00	15.00
(9)	Gerry Arrigo (Reds, full-length pitching.)	20.00	10.00	6.00
(10)	Ernie Banks/Btg	75.00	37.00	22.00
(11)	Ernie Banks/Fielding (horizontal)	60.00	30.00	18.00
(12)	Glenn Beckert (Cubs, fielding, ball in hand.)	25.00	12.50	7.50
(13)	Glenn Beckert (Cubs, fielding, no ball.)	25.00	12.50	7.50
(14)	Paul Blair (Orioles, full-length.)	25.00	12.50	7.50
(15)	Don Blasingame (Cardinals, belt-up.)	20.00	10.00	6.00
(16)	Bob Bolin (Giants, pitching follow-through.)	20.00	10.00	6.00
(17)	Dave Boswell (Twins, full-length.)	20.00	10.00	6.00
(18)	Dave Boswell (Twins, waist-up, stretch position.)	20.00	10.00	6.00
(19)	Jackie Brandt (Orioles, full-length.)	20.00	10.00	6.00
(20)	Smoky Burgess (Pirates, sitting on step w/3 bats.)	20.00	10.00	6.00
(21)	Rico Carty/Btg (Milwaukee Braves)	20.00	10.00	6.00
(22)	Rico Carty (Milwaukee Braves, dugout step.)	20.00	10.00	6.00
(23)	Rico Carty/Btg (Atlanta Braves)	20.00	10.00	6.00
(24)	Paul Casanova (Senators, catching crouch.)	20.00	10.00	6.00
(25)	Norm Cash/Btg (Tigers, waist-up)	25.00	12.50	7.50
(26)	Orlando Cepeda/Btg (Braves)	30.00	15.00	9.00
(27)	Orlando Cepeda (Cardinals, dugout step.)	25.00	12.50	7.50
(28)	Orlando Cepeda/Fielding (Cardinals)	25.00	12.50	7.50
(29)	Jim Davenport/Fielding (Giants)	20.00	10.00	6.00
(30)	Vic Davalillo (Indians, upper body.)	20.00	10.00	6.00
(31)	Willie Davis (Dodgers, full-length.)	20.00	10.00	6.00
(32)	Chuck Dobson (A's, full-length.)	20.00	10.00	6.00
(35)	"Moe" Drabowsky (Cubs, thighs-up.)	20.00	10.00	6.00
(36)	Don Drysdale (L.A. Dodgers, follow-through.)	25.00	12.50	7.50
(37)	Dick Ellsworth (Cubs, pitching follow-through.)	20.00	10.00	6.00
(38)	Dick Ellsworth (Phillies, full-length.)	20.00	10.00	6.00
(39)	Del Ennis/Kneeling (Cardinals.)	20.00	10.00	6.00
(40)	Bob Feller/Seated (Glove on knee.)	120.00	60.00	36.00
(41)	Nellie Fox (White Sox, chest-up.)	35.00	17.50	10.50
(42)	Nellie Fox (White Sox, fielding grounder.)	50.00	25.00	15.00
(43)	Nelson Fox/Seated (White Sox)	50.00	25.00	15.00
(44)	Nelson Fox/Btg (Colt .45s)	50.00	25.00	15.00
(45)	Bill Freehan (Catching crouch.)	20.00	10.00	6.00
(46)	Bill Freehan (Two pictures.)	20.00	10.00	6.00
(47)	Phil Gagliano/Fielding (Cardinals, photo actually Ed Spiezio.)	25.00	12.50	7.50
(48)	Jim Gentile/Btg (Orioles, chest-up.)	20.00	10.00	6.00
(49)	Vernon "Lefty" Gomez (W/ glasses)	25.00	12.50	7.50
(50)	Lefty Gomez (No glasses.)	25.00	12.50	7.50
(51)	Jim Hall/Fielding (Angels)	25.00	12.50	7.50
(52)	Don Hoak (Pirates, full-length.)	20.00	10.00	6.00
(53)	Gil Hodges (L.A. Dodgers, belt-up batting.)	50.00	25.00	15.00
(54)	Willie Horton (Tigers, full-length.)	20.00	10.00	6.00
(55)	Bruce Howard (White Sox, pitching follow-through.)	20.00	10.00	6.00
(56)	Jim Hunter (K.C. A's, beginning wind-up.)	25.00	12.50	7.50
(57)	Jim Hunter (Oakland A's, full-length, photo actually Chuck Dobson.)	25.00	12.50	7.50
(58)	Mack Jones (Reds, full-length.)	20.00	10.00	6.00
(59)	Duane Josephson (White Sox, catching crouch.)	20.00	10.00	6.00
(61)	Jim Kaat (Twins, upper body.)	25.00	12.50	7.50
(62)	Al Kaline/Bth (Full-length)	75.00	37.00	22.00
(63)	Al Kaline/Btg (Upper body.)	75.00	37.00	22.00
(64)	Al Kaline (Upper body, hands on knees.)	75.00	37.00	22.00
(65)	Al Kaline (Upper body.)	75.00	37.00	22.00
(66)	Al Kaline (Upper body, looking right.)	75.00	37.00	22.00
(67)	Harmon Killebrew/Btg (Twins, upper body.)	50.00	25.00	15.00
(68)	Harmon Killebrew (Twins, batting, looking front.)	50.00	25.00	15.00
(69)	Harmon Killebrew/Kneeling (Twins)	50.00	25.00	15.00
(70)	Cal Koonce (Cubs, pitching follow-through.)	20.00	10.00	6.00
(71)	Harvey Kuenn/Btg (Tigers)	25.00	12.50	7.50
(72)	Harvey Kuenn (Tigers, upper body.)	25.00	12.50	7.50
(73)	Hal Lanier/Throwing (Giants)	20.00	10.00	6.00
(74)	Juan Marichal (Giants, upper body.)	25.00	12.50	7.50
(75)	Willie McCovey/Btg (Giants)	25.00	12.50	7.50
(76)	Sam McDowell (Indians, seated, no cap.)	25.00	12.50	7.50
(77)	Dennis McLain (Tigers, hands at chest.)	25.00	12.50	7.50
(78)	Roy McMillan/Btg (Braves)	20.00	10.00	6.00
(79)	Roy McMillan (Reds, belt-up.)	20.00	10.00	6.00
(81)	Denis Menke/Fielding (Braves)	20.00	10.00	6.00
(82)	Denis Menke (Braves, upper body.)	20.00	10.00	6.00
(83)	Don Mincher (Angels, full-length.)	20.00	10.00	6.00
(84)	Joe Morgan/Btg (Astros)	40.00	20.00	12.00
(85)	Joe Morgan/Fielding (Astros)	40.00	20.00	12.00
(86)	Jim Nash/Pitching (A's)	20.00	10.00	6.00
(87)	Rich Nye/Pitching (Cubs)	20.00	10.00	6.00
(88)	John Odom/Pitching (Kansas City A's)	20.00	10.00	6.00
(89)	John Odom (Oakland A's, belt-up pose.)	20.00	10.00	6.00
(90)	John Orsino/Kneeling (Orioles)	20.00	10.00	6.00
(91)	Jim O'Toole (Reds, upper body, warm-up jacket.)	20.00	10.00	6.00
(92)	Jim O'Toole (White Sox, upper body.)	20.00	10.00	6.00
(93)	Ray Oyler/Fielding (Tigers)	20.00	10.00	6.00
(94)	Milt Pappas (Orioles, pitching, full-length.)	20.00	10.00	6.00
(95)	Milt Pappas (Orioles, pitching, knees-up.)	20.00	10.00	6.00
(96)	Don Pavletich (Reds, full-length.)	20.00	10.00	6.00
(97)	Don Pavletich (Reds, squatting.)	20.00	10.00	6.00
(98)	Albie Pearson (Angels, glove under left arm.)	20.00	10.00	6.00
(99)	Ron Perranoski (Dodgers, upper body.)	20.00	10.00	6.00
(100)	Ron Perranoski (Twins, belt-up from side.)	25.00	12.50	7.50
(101)	Ron Perranoski/Pitching (Twins)	20.00	10.00	6.00
(102)	Gaylord Perry/Pitching (Giants)	25.00	12.50	7.50
(103)	Billy Pierce (White Sox, knees-up.)	25.00	12.50	7.50
(104)	Bob Purkey (Reds, waist-up.)	20.00	10.00	6.00
(105)	Doug Rader/Fielding (Astros)	20.00	10.00	6.00
(106)	Dick Rodatz (Radatz) (Red Sox, upper body.)	20.00	10.00	6.00
(107)	Dick Radatz (Red Sox, upper body.)	20.00	10.00	6.00
(108)	Pete Runnels (Red Sox, kneeling on deck.)	25.00	12.50	7.50
(109)	Ron Santo/Fielding (Cubs)	25.00	12.50	7.50
(110)	George Scott (Red Sox, upper body.)	20.00	10.00	6.00
(111)	Larry Sherry (Dodgers, full-length.)	20.00	10.00	6.00
(112)	Chris Short (Phillies, upper body.)	20.00	10.00	6.00
(113)	Hal Smith/Btg (Pirates)	25.00	12.50	7.50
(114)	Mickey Stanley (Tigers, full-length.)	20.00	10.00	6.00
(115)	Tony Taylor (Phillies, bat on shoulder.)	20.00	10.00	6.00
(116)	Frank Thomas (Pirates, waist-up.)	20.00	10.00	6.00

		NM	EX	VG
(117)	Frank Thomas/Btg (Cubs)	20.00	10.00	6.00
(119)	Jeff Torborg	20.00	10.00	6.00
	(Dodgers, holding mask.)			
(121)	Al Weis	20.00	10.00	6.00
	(White Sox, ready to throw.)			
(122)	Al Weis/Fielding (Mets)	20.00	10.00	6.00
(123)	Ted Williams/Btg	125.00	62.00	37.00
(125)	Bobby Wine	20.00	10.00	6.00
	(Phillies, ready to throw.)			
(126)	Rick Wise	20.00	10.00	6.00
	(Phillies, upper body.)			
(128)	Woody Woodward	25.00	12.50	7.50
	(Reds, belt-to-cap.)			
(130)	Early Wynn	25.00	12.50	7.50
	(White Sox, full-length.)			
(131)	Jim Wynn/Btg	20.00	10.00	6.00
	(Colt .45s, upper body.)			
(132)	Jim Wynn/Btg	20.00	10.00	6.00
	(Astros, full-length.)			
(133)	Don Zimmer	20.00	10.00	6.00
	(Cubs, waist-up batting.)			

1961 Wilson Advisory Staff Cards

Similar in format to the contemporary 8" x 10" photos, these 2-3/4" x 4" cards have black-and-white player poses on front, prominently displaying a Wilson glove. In the white bottom border is: "Member-Advisory Staff, Wilson Sporting Goods Co." A blue facsimile autograph is printed across the picture. Backs are blank. The checklist, presented here alphabetically, may not be complete.

		NM	EX	VG
Common Player:		10.00	5.00	3.00
(1)	Dick Ellsworth	10.00	5.00	3.00
(2)	Don Hoak	12.00	6.00	3.50
(3)	Harvey Kuenn	12.00	6.00	3.50
(4)	Roy McMillan	10.00	5.00	3.00
(5)	Jim Piersall	12.00	6.00	3.50
(6)	Ron Santo	16.00	8.00	4.75

1977 Wilson Sporting Goods Mini-Posters

Though unmarked as such, these 6" x 9" cards are a promotion from Wilson. The blank-back cards have a color action photo with white borders and a facsimile autograph.

		NM	EX	VG
Complete Set (10):		200.00	100.00	60.00
Common Player:		10.00	5.00	3.00
(1)	Johnny Bench	35.00	17.50	10.50
(2)	George Brett	50.00	25.00	15.00
(3)	Rod Carew	30.00	15.00	9.00
(4)	Dave Concepcion	10.00	5.00	3.00
(5)	Steve Garvey	15.00	7.50	4.50
(6)	Reggie Jackson	40.00	20.00	12.00
(7)	Greg Luzinski	10.00	5.00	3.00
(8)	Pete Rose	75.00	37.00	22.00
(9)	Mike Schmidt	40.00	20.00	12.00
(10)	Tom Seaver	40.00	17.50	10.50

1955-1958 Don Wingfield Washington Nationals Postcards

This series of 3-1/2" x 5-1/2" black-and-white glossy postcards provided Nationals' players with a vehicle for accommodating fan requests. Player portraits or action poses are bordered in white with three (or in the case of Valdivielso, five) lines of type at bottom identifying the player, team and copyright holder. Most have "Photo Post Card" at top on back and "Devolite Peerless" in the stamp box. The unnumbered cards are checklisted here in alphabetical order.

		NM	EX	VG
Complete Set (12):		1,800	900.00	550.00
Common Player:		150.00	75.00	45.00
(1)	Jim Busby	150.00	75.00	45.00
(2)	Chuck Dressen	150.00	75.00	45.00
(3)	Ed Fitz Gerald	150.00	75.00	45.00
(4)	Jim Lemon	175.00	85.00	55.00
(5)	Bob Porterfield	150.00	75.00	45.00
(6)	Pete Runnels	150.00	75.00	45.00
(7)	Roy Sievers	175.00	85.00	55.00
(8)	Chuck Stobbs	150.00	75.00	45.00
(9)	Dean Stone	150.00	75.00	45.00
(10)	Jose Valdivelso (Valdivielso)	175.00	85.00	55.00
(11)	Mickey Vernon	175.00	85.00	55.00
(12)	Ed Yost	150.00	75.00	45.00

1957-1959 Don Wingfield Photocards

These black-and-white glossy photocards are usually blank-back, evidently for use as in-person handouts, rather than by mail. In 3-1/2" x 5-1/2" size, the player photos are bordered in white with an especially wide white bottom border for affixing an autograph. Other than the autograph which may appear, the player is not identified on the card. Wingfield's name may appear in white letters in the lower-right corner of the photo, may be on a credit line on back or may not appear at all.

		NM	EX	VG
Common Player:		50.00	25.00	15.00
(1)	Ted Abernathy	50.00	25.00	15.00
(2)	Bobby Allison	50.00	25.00	15.00
(3)	Tex Clevenger	50.00	25.00	15.00
(4)	Russ Kemmerer	50.00	25.00	15.00
(5)	Harmon Killebrew	100.00	50.00	30.00
(6)	Bob Usher	50.00	25.00	15.00
(7)	Hal Woodeshick	50.00	25.00	15.00

1960s Don Wingfield Postcards - b/w

A second type of player photo postcards was produced by Alexandria, Va., photographer Don Wingfield beginning around 1960. Also black-and-white, the 3-1/2" x 5-1/2" cards have (usually) borderless poses on front with no extraneous graphics. Backs have standard postcard indicia plus (on most cards) the player name and team and a copyright line with Wingfield's name and address. At top on back is "Post Card," with "Place

Stamp Here" in the postage box. Washington Senators players dominate the checklist which also includes stars of other teams. The autograph on the pictured card was added by the player after printing and is not part of the design. The currently known checklist is presented here alphabetically.

		NM	EX	VG
Common Player:		50.00	25.00	15.00
(1)	Bob Allison	55.00	27.50	16.50
(2)	Ernie Banks	100.00	50.00	30.00
(3)	Earl Battey/Btg	50.00	25.00	15.00
	(Chest to cap.)			
(4)	Earl Battey (Kneeling w/bat.)	50.00	25.00	15.00
(5)	Norm Cash	60.00	30.00	18.00
(6)	Jim Coates	50.00	25.00	15.00
(7)	Rocky Colavito	60.00	30.00	18.00
(8)	Chuck Cottier	50.00	25.00	15.00
(9)	Bennie Daniels	50.00	25.00	15.00
(10)	Dan Dobbek	50.00	25.00	15.00
(11)	Nellie Fox	60.00	30.00	18.00
(12)	Jim Gentile	50.00	25.00	15.00
(13)	Gene Green	50.00	25.00	15.00
(14)	Steve Hamilton	50.00	25.00	15.00
(15)	Ken Hamlin	50.00	25.00	15.00
(16a)	Rudy Hernandez	50.00	25.00	15.00
	(Postcard back.)			
(16b)	Rudy Hernandez	60.00	30.00	18.00
	(Restuarant ad on back.)			
(17)	Ed Hobaugh	50.00	25.00	15.00
(18)	Elston Howard	60.00	30.00	18.00
(19)	Bob Johnson	50.00	25.00	15.00
(20)	Russ Kemmerer	50.00	25.00	15.00
(21)	Harmon Killebrew	100.00	50.00	30.00
(22)	Dale Long	50.00	25.00	15.00
(23)	Mickey Mantle	325.00	160.00	100.00
(24)	Roger Maris	200.00	100.00	60.00
(25)	Willie Mays	250.00	125.00	75.00
(26)	Stan Musial	200.00	100.00	60.00
(27)	Claude Osteen	50.00	25.00	15.00
(28)	Ken Retzer	50.00	25.00	15.00
(29)	Brooks Robinson	100.00	50.00	30.00
(30)	Don Rudolph	50.00	25.00	15.00
(31)	Bill Skowron	60.00	30.00	18.00
(32)	Dave Stenhouse	50.00	25.00	15.00
(33)	Jose Valdivielso	50.00	25.00	15.00
(34)	Gene Woodling	50.00	25.00	15.00
(35)	Bud Zipfel	50.00	25.00	15.00

1960s Don Wingfield Postcards - Color

Similar in format to the contemporary series of black-and-white player photo postcards, only a single player is known to have been issued in color by Alexandria, Va., photographer Don Wingfield. The card is 3-1/2" x 5-1/2" with standard postcard indicia on back.

	NM	EX	VG
C14711 Harmon Killebrew	110.00	55.00	33.00

1951-53 Wisconsin's Athletic Hall of Fame Postcards

This set of black-and-white postcards reproduces the plaques of athletes in the state's Hall of Fame, as displayed in Milwaukee's Arena during the 1950s. Backs have typical postcard markings.

WISCONSIN'S ATHLETIC HALL OF FAME
THE ARENA
Milwaukee, Wisconsin

	NM	EX	VG
Complete Set (12):	150.00	75.00	45.00
Common Player:	10.00	5.00	3.00
(1) Addie Joss	20.00	10.00	6.00
(2) Alvin Kraenzlein/Track	10.00	5.00	3.00
(3) "Strangler" Lewis/Wrestling	12.50	6.25	3.75
(4) George McBride	10.00	5.00	3.00
(5) Ralph Metcalfe/Track	10.00	5.00	3.00
(6) Ernie Nevers	20.00	10.00	6.00
(7) "Kid" Nichols	20.00	10.00	6.00
(8) "Pa" O'Dea/Football	10.00	5.00	3.00
(9) Dave Schreiner/Football	10.00	5.00	3.00
(10) Al Simmons	20.00	10.00	6.00
(11) Billy Sullivan	12.50	6.25	3.75
(12) Bob Zuppke/Basketball	10.00	5.00	3.00

1922 Witmor Candy Co.

CHARLES DEAL
3rd B.—Chicago Nationals

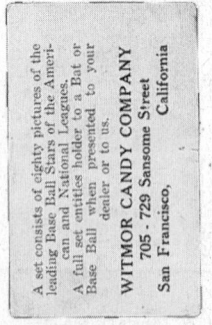

A set consists of eighty pictures of the leading Base Ball Stars of the American and National Leagues. A full set entitles holder to a Bat or Base Ball when presented to your Base Ball dealer or to us.

WITMOR CANDY COMPANY
705 - 729 Sansome Street
San Francisco, California

Two types of Witmor issues are known, both of which utilize the format of the 1921-22 W575-1 blank-back strip cards. Printed in black-and-white and measuring about 2" x 3-1/4" the two types of Witmor issues are differentiated by the ads on back for the San Francisco candy company. One type has the advertising in a horizontal format, the other has the advertising in a vertical design. Values of Witmor Candy cards carry a premium over the more common blank-back versions. The extent to which the Witmors and W575-1 share a checklist, particularly the latter's variations, is unknown.

PREMIUMS:
Common Players: 3-4X
Hall of Famers: 3-4X
(See 1921-22 W575-1 for checklist and value information.)

1907 Wolverine News Co.
Detroit Tigers

This series of postcards depicts members of the A.L. champ Tigers. The 3-5/16" x 5-5/16" black-and-white cards have poses or posed action photos on front, with a narrow white border at bottom carrying player identification. Backs are standard postcard format with a credit line to Wolverine News Co.

	NM	EX	VG
Complete Set (20):	9,000	4,500	2,700

Common Player:	100.00	50.00	30.00
(1) Ty Cobb/Btg	3,000	1,500	900.00
(2) Ty Cobb/Portrait	3,500	1,750	1,000
(3) Bill Coughlin	100.00	50.00	30.00
(4) Sam Crawford/Bunting	250.00	125.00	75.00
(5) Sam Crawford (Chest-to-cap portrait.)	250.00	125.00	75.00
(6) "Wild Bill" Donovan/Pitching	100.00	50.00	30.00
(7) "Wild Bill" Donovan ("At the Water Wagon.")	150.00	75.00	45.00
(8) Jerry Downs	100.00	50.00	30.00
(9) Hughie Jennings/Manager	250.00	125.00	75.00
(10) Hughie Jennings (On the coaching line.)	300.00	150.00	90.00
(11) Davy Jones	100.00	50.00	30.00
(12) Ed Killian	100.00	50.00	30.00
(13) George Mullin	100.00	50.00	30.00
(14) Charley O'Leary	100.00	50.00	30.00
(15) Fred Payne	100.00	50.00	30.00
(16) Claude Rossman	100.00	50.00	30.00
(17) Herman Schaefer	100.00	50.00	30.00
(18) Herman Schaefer, Charley O'Leary	100.00	50.00	30.00
(19) Charlie Schmidt	100.00	50.00	30.00
(20) Eddie Siever	100.00	50.00	30.00

1886 J. Wood Studio N.Y.
Giants Cabinets

Members of the 1886 N.Y. Giants were immortalized in this series of 4-1/4" x 6-7/8" studio cabinets. The sepia portraits are bordered in gold. The photos were likely available singly from the studio or as a complete set, with an advertising frontpiece and a 6-9/16" x 4-3/16" composite photo. It is interesting to note that on one version of the composite card, baseball caps were artificially added to the portraits. The photos became the basis for the same players' cards in several late 1880s card series.

	NM	EX	VG
Common Player:	10,000	5,000	3,000
(1) Roger Connor	25,000	7,500	4,500
(2) Larry Corcoran	10,000	5,000	3,000
(3) Pat Deasley	10,000	5,000	3,000
(4) Mike Dorgan	10,000	5,000	3,000
(5) Dude Esterbrook	10,000	5,000	3,000
(6) Buck Ewing	35,000	7,500	4,500
(7) Joe Gerhardt	10,000	5,000	3,000
(8) Pete Gillespie	10,000	5,000	3,000
(9) Tim Keefe	25,000	7,500	4,500
(10) Jim Mutrie	10,000	5,000	3,000
(11) Jim O'Rourke	30,000	7,500	4,500
(12) Danny Richardson	10,000	5,000	3,000
(13) John Ward	30,000	7,500	4,500
(14) Mickey Welch	25,000	7,500	4,500
(15) N.Y. Giants Team Composite (No caps.)	7,000	3,500	2,100
(16) N.Y. Giants Team Composite (With caps.)	25,000	10,000	6,000

1886 J. Wood Studio N.Y.
Metropolitans Cabinets

Nattily attired in dress shirts and sporty dotted ties, members of the 1886 N.Y. Metropolitans of the American Association were immortalized in this series of 4-1/2" x 6-1/2" studio cabinets. The vignetted sepia portraits are framed in gold. The photos became the basis for the same players' cards in the "dotted tie" subset of the 1887 Old Judge cigarette card issue, indicating that more of the cabinet-size photos may yet be added to this checklist.

	NM	EX	VG
Common Player:	12,500	6,250	3,750
Jos. Crotty	12,500	6,250	3,750
E.L. Cushman	12,500	6,250	3,750
E.E. Foster	12,500	6,250	3,750
Al. Mays	12,500	6,250	3,750
Jas. Roseman	12,500	6,250	3,750

1921 Wool's American-
Maid Bread

This seldom-seen variation of the W551 strip-card set appears to have been locally overprinted at an unknown location for use as a bread purchase premium. It is presumed the same checklist for W551 can

TY COBB DETROIT A. L.

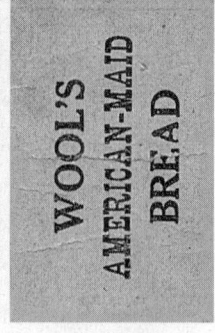

WOOL'S AMERICAN-MAID BREAD

be found with the Wool's back advertising. If ideally cut from the strip, the cards would measure 1-3/8" x 2-1/4". They feature color drawings and are unnumbered.

	NM	EX	VG
Complete Set (10):	6,000	3,000	1,800
Common Player:	160.00	80.00	48.00
(1) Frank Baker	400.00	200.00	120.00
(2) Dave Bancroft	400.00	200.00	120.00
(3) Jess Barnes	250.00	125.00	75.00
(4) Ty Cobb	2,000	1,000	600.00
(5) Walter Johnson	750.00	375.00	225.00
(6) Wally Pipp	300.00	150.00	90.00
(7) Babe Ruth	2,500	1,250	750.00
(8) George Sisler	400.00	200.00	120.00
(9) Tris Speaker	600.00	300.00	180.00
(10) Casey Stengel	450.00	225.00	135.00

1933 Worch Cigar

This set of unnumbered postcard-size (3-7/16" x 5-7/16") cards, utilizing photos from the Minneapolis Star and St. Paul Dispatch newspapers, was used as a promotion by Worch Cigar Co. of St. Paul, Minn. Although there is no advertising for Worch Cigars on the cards themselves, the cards were mailed in envelopes bearing the Worch name. The cards feature portrait or posed action photos. Player identification, which may be full name or last name, with or without team, may be found in several different styles, either printed on the background, or in a white or black box. Sometimes a photo credit is also present. Many pictures have the top of the background whited out.

	NM	EX	VG
Common Player:	90.00	40.00	25.00
(1) Sparky Adams	90.00	40.00	25.00
(2) Dale Alexander	90.00	40.00	25.00
(3) Ivy Paul Andrews	90.00	40.00	25.00
(4a) Earl Averill (Cleveland)	400.00	180.00	100.00
(4b) Earl Averill (No team designation.)	400.00	180.00	100.00
(5) Richard Bartell	90.00	40.00	25.00
(6) Herman Bell	90.00	40.00	25.00
(7) Walter Berger	90.00	40.00	25.00
(8) Huck Betts	90.00	40.00	25.00
(9) Max Bishop	90.00	40.00	25.00
(10) Jim Bottomley	400.00	180.00	100.00
(11a) Tom Bridges (Name and team in box.)	90.00	40.00	25.00
(11b) Tom Bridges (No box.)	90.00	40.00	25.00
(12) Clint Brown	90.00	40.00	25.00
(13a) Donie Bush	90.00	40.00	25.00
(13b) Donie Bush	90.00	40.00	25.00
(14a) Max Carey (Brooklyn)	400.00	180.00	100.00
(14b) Max Carey (No team designation.)	400.00	180.00	100.00
(15) Tex Carlton	90.00	40.00	25.00
(16) Ben Chapman	90.00	40.00	25.00
(17) Chalmer Cissell	90.00	40.00	25.00
(18) Mickey Cochrane	400.00	180.00	100.00
(19) Ripper Collins	90.00	40.00	25.00
(20) Earle Combs	400.00	180.00	100.00
(21) Adam Comorosky	90.00	40.00	25.00
(22) Estel Crabtree	90.00	40.00	25.00
(23) Rodger Cramer (Roger)	90.00	40.00	25.00
(24) Pat Crawford	90.00	40.00	25.00
(25) Hugh Critz	90.00	40.00	25.00

		NM	EX	VG
(26a)	Joe Cronin (Name and team in box.)	400.00	180.00	100.00
(26b)	Joe Cronin (No box.)	400.00	180.00	100.00
(27)	Frank Crosetti	150.00	67.00	37.00
(28)	Alvin Crowder	90.00	40.00	25.00
(29a)	Tony Cuccinello (Photo background.)	90.00	40.00	25.00
(29b)	Tony Cuccinello (Blank background.)	90.00	40.00	25.00
(30)	KiKi Cuyler	400.00	180.00	100.00
(31)	Geo. Davis	90.00	40.00	25.00
(32)	Dizzy Dean	750.00	335.00	185.00
(33)	Wm. Dickey	450.00	200.00	110.00
(34)	Leo Durocher	400.00	180.00	100.00
(35)	James Dykes	90.00	40.00	25.00
(36)	George Earnshaw	90.00	40.00	25.00
(37)	Woody English	90.00	40.00	25.00
(38a)	Richard Ferrell (Name and team in box.)	400.00	180.00	100.00
(38b)	Richard Ferrell (No box.)	400.00	180.00	100.00
(39a)	Wesley Ferrell (Name and team in box.)	90.00	40.00	25.00
(39b)	Wesley Ferrell (No box.)	90.00	40.00	25.00
(40)	Fred Fitzsimmons	90.00	40.00	25.00
(41)	Lew Fonseca	90.00	40.00	25.00
(42)	Bob Fothergill	90.00	40.00	25.00
(43)	James Foxx	750.00	335.00	185.00
(44)	Fred Frankhouse	90.00	40.00	25.00
(45)	Frank Frisch	400.00	180.00	100.00
(46a)	Leon Gaslin (Name incorrect.)	400.00	180.00	100.00
(46b)	Leon Goslin (Name correct.)	400.00	180.00	100.00
(47)	Lou Gehrig	1,500	675.00	375.00
(48)	Charles Gehringer	400.00	180.00	100.00
(49)	George Gibson	90.00	40.00	25.00
(50)	Vernon Gomez	400.00	180.00	100.00
(51)	George Grantham	90.00	40.00	25.00
(52)	Grimes The Lord Of Burleigh (Burleigh Grimes)	400.00	180.00	100.00
(53)	Charlie Grimm	90.00	40.00	25.00
(54)	Robt. Grove	600.00	270.00	150.00
(55)	Frank Grube	90.00	40.00	25.00
(56)	Chic Hafey (Chick)	400.00	180.00	100.00
(57)	Jess Haines	400.00	180.00	100.00
(58)	Bill Hallahan	90.00	40.00	25.00
(59)	Mel Harder	90.00	40.00	25.00
(60)	Dave Harris	90.00	40.00	25.00
(61a)	Gabby Hartnett (Small projection.)	400.00	180.00	100.00
(61b)	Gabby Hartnett (Large projection.)	400.00	180.00	100.00
(62)	George Hass (Haas)	90.00	40.00	25.00
(63)	Ray Hayworth	90.00	40.00	25.00
(64)	Harvey Hendrick	90.00	40.00	25.00
(65)	Dutch Henry	90.00	40.00	25.00
(66)	"Babe" Herman	150.00	67.00	37.00
(67)	Bill Herman	400.00	180.00	100.00
(68)	Frank Higgins	90.00	40.00	25.00
(69)	Oral Hildebrand	90.00	40.00	25.00
(70)	"Shanty" Hogan	90.00	40.00	25.00
(71)	Roger Hornsby (Rogers)	600.00	270.00	150.00
(72)	Carl Hubbell	450.00	200.00	110.00
(73)	Travis Jackson	400.00	180.00	100.00
(74)	Hank Johnson	90.00	40.00	25.00
(75)	Syl Johnson	90.00	40.00	25.00
(76)	Smead Jolley	90.00	40.00	25.00
(77)	Wm. Kamm	90.00	40.00	25.00
(78)	Wes Kingdon	90.00	40.00	25.00
(79a)	Charles Klein (Philadelphia, N.L.)	400.00	180.00	100.00
(79b)	Charles Klein (Chicago, N.L.)	400.00	180.00	100.00
(80)	Jos. Kuhel	90.00	40.00	25.00
(81a)	Tony Lazzeri (Name and team in box.)	400.00	180.00	100.00
(81b)	Tony Lazzeri (No box.)	400.00	180.00	100.00
(82)	Sam Leslie	90.00	40.00	25.00
(83)	Ernie Lombardi	400.00	180.00	100.00
(84)	Al Lopez	400.00	180.00	100.00
(85)	Red Lucas	90.00	40.00	25.00
(86)	Adolfo Luque	90.00	40.00	22.00
(87)	Ted Lyons	400.00	180.00	100.00
(88)	Connie Mack	400.00	180.00	100.00
(89)	Gus Mancuso	90.00	40.00	25.00
(90)	Henry Manush	400.00	180.00	100.00
(91)	Fred Marberry	90.00	40.00	25.00
(92)	Pepper Martin	200.00	90.00	50.00
(93)	Wm. McKechnie	400.00	180.00	100.00
(94)	Joe Medwick	400.00	180.00	100.00
(95)	Jim Mooney	90.00	40.00	25.00
(96)	Joe Moore	90.00	40.00	25.00
(97)	Joe Mowry	90.00	40.00	25.00
(98)	Van Mungo	90.00	40.00	25.00
(99)	Buddy Myer	90.00	40.00	25.00
(100)	"Lefty" O'Doul	200.00	90.00	50.00
(101)	Bob O'Farrell	90.00	40.00	25.00
(102)	Ernie Orsatti	90.00	40.00	25.00
(103)	Melvin Ott	450.00	200.00	110.00
(104)	Roy Parmelee	90.00	40.00	25.00
(105)	Homer Peel	90.00	40.00	25.00
(106)	George Pipgras	90.00	40.00	25.00
(107)	Harry Rice	90.00	40.00	25.00
(108)	Paul Richards	90.00	40.00	25.00
(109)	Eppa Rixey	400.00	180.00	100.00
(110)	Charles Ruffing	400.00	180.00	100.00
(111)	Jack Russell	90.00	40.00	25.00
(112)	Babe Ruth	2,000	900.00	500.00
(113)	"Blondy" Ryan	90.00	40.00	25.00
(114)	Wilfred Ryan	90.00	40.00	25.00
(115)	Fred Schulte	90.00	40.00	25.00
(116)	Hal Schumacher	90.00	40.00	25.00
(117a)	Luke Sewel (Sewell) (Name and team in box.)	90.00	40.00	25.00
(117b)	Luke Sewel (Sewell) (No box.)	90.00	40.00	25.00
(118)	Al Simmons	400.00	180.00	100.00
(119)	Ray Spencer	90.00	40.00	25.00
(120)	Casey Stengel	400.00	180.00	100.00

		NM	EX	VG
(121)	Riggs Stephenson	90.00	40.00	25.00
(122)	Walter Stewart	90.00	40.00	25.00
(123)	John Stone	90.00	40.00	25.00
(124)	Gabby Street	90.00	40.00	25.00
(125)	Gus Suhr	90.00	40.00	25.00
(126)	Evar Swanson	90.00	40.00	25.00
(127)	Dan Taylor	90.00	40.00	25.00
(128)	Bill Terry	400.00	180.00	100.00
(129)	Al Todd	90.00	40.00	25.00
(130)	Pie Traynor	400.00	180.00	100.00
(131)	William Urbanski	90.00	40.00	25.00
(132)	Dazzy Vance	400.00	180.00	100.00
(133)	Lloyd (Floyd) Vaughan	400.00	180.00	100.00
(134)	Johnny Vergez	90.00	40.00	25.00
(135)	George Walberg	90.00	40.00	25.00
(136)	Bill Walker	90.00	40.00	25.00
(137)	Gerald Walker	90.00	40.00	25.00
(138a)	Lloyd Waner (Photo background.)	400.00	180.00	100.00
(138b)	Lloyd Waner (Blank background.)	400.00	180.00	100.00
(139a)	Paul Waner (Photo background.)	400.00	180.00	100.00
(139b)	Paul Waner (Blank background, small projection.)	400.00	180.00	100.00
(139c)	Lloyd Waner (Blank background, large projection.)	400.00	180.00	100.00
(140)	Lon Warneke	90.00	40.00	25.00
(141)	George Watkins	90.00	40.00	25.00
(142)	Monte Weaver	90.00	40.00	25.00
(143)	Sam West	90.00	40.00	25.00
(144)	Earl Whitehill	90.00	40.00	25.00
(145)	Hack Wilson	400.00	180.00	100.00
(146)	Jimmy Wilson	90.00	40.00	25.00

1933 World Wide Gum (Canadian Goudey, V353)

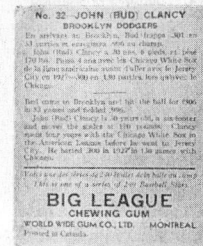

Also known as "Canadian Goudeys," this 94-card set drew heavily on its U.S. contemporary. Card fronts are identical to the '33 Goudeys and the backs are nearly so. The first 52 cards in the set carry the same card numbers as their American counterparts, while cards #53-94 have different numbers than the U.S. version. Card backs can be found printed entirely in English, or in English and French; the former being somewhat scarcer. Cards measure approximately 2-3/8" x 2-7/8".

		NM	EX	VG
Complete Set (94):		20,000	10,000	6,000
Common Player:		60.00	30.00	18.00
1	Benny Bengough	550.00	60.00	20.00
2	Arthur (Dazzy) Vance	250.00	110.00	60.00
3	Hugh Critz	60.00	30.00	18.00
4	Henry (Heinie) Schuble	60.00	30.00	18.00
5	Floyd (Babe) Herman	110.00	50.00	25.00
6	Jimmy Dykes	60.00	30.00	18.00
7	Ted Lyons	250.00	110.00	60.00
8	Roy Johnson	60.00	30.00	18.00
9	Dave Harris	60.00	30.00	18.00
10	Glenn Myatt	60.00	30.00	18.00
11	Billy Rogell	60.00	30.00	18.00
12	George Pipgras	60.00	30.00	18.00
13	Lafayette Thompson	60.00	30.00	18.00
14	Henry Johnson	60.00	30.00	18.00
15	Victor Sorrell	60.00	30.00	18.00
16	George Blaeholder	60.00	30.00	18.00
17	Watson Clark	60.00	30.00	18.00
18	Herold (Muddy) Ruel	60.00	30.00	18.00
19	Bill Dickey	275.00	125.00	70.00
20	Bill Terry	250.00	110.00	60.00
21	Phil Collins	60.00	30.00	18.00
22	Harold (Pie) Traynor	250.00	110.00	60.00
23	Hazen (Ki-Ki) Cuyler	250.00	110.00	60.00
24	Horace Ford	60.00	30.00	18.00
25	Paul Waner	250.00	110.00	60.00
26	Chalmer Cissell	60.00	30.00	18.00
27	George Connally	60.00	30.00	18.00
28	Dick Bartell	60.00	30.00	18.00
29	Jimmy Foxx	350.00	155.00	85.00
30	Frank Hogan	60.00	30.00	18.00
31	Tony Lazzeri	250.00	110.00	60.00
32	John (Bud) Clancy	60.00	30.00	18.00
33	Ralph Kress	60.00	30.00	18.00
34	Bob O'Farrell	60.00	30.00	18.00
35	Al Simmons	250.00	110.00	60.00
36	Tommy Thevenow	60.00	30.00	18.00
37	Jimmy Wilson	60.00	30.00	18.00
38	Fred Brickell	60.00	30.00	18.00
39	Mark Koenig	60.00	30.00	18.00
40	Taylor Douthit	60.00	30.00	18.00
41	Gus Mancuso	60.00	30.00	18.00
42	Eddie Collins	250.00	110.00	60.00
43	Lew Fonseca	60.00	30.00	18.00
44	Jim Bottomley	250.00	110.00	60.00

45	Larry Benton	60.00	30.00	18.00
46	Ethan Allen	60.00	30.00	18.00
47	Henry "Heinie" Manush	250.00	110.00	60.00
48	Marty McManus	60.00	30.00	18.00
49	Frank Frisch	250.00	110.00	60.00
50	Ed Brandt	60.00	30.00	18.00
51	Charlie Grimm	60.00	30.00	18.00
52	Andy Cohen	60.00	30.00	18.00
53	Jack Quinn	60.00	30.00	18.00
54	Urban (Red) Faber	250.00	110.00	60.00
55	Lou Gehrig	2,100	950.00	525.00
56	John Welch	60.00	30.00	18.00
57	Bill Walker	60.00	30.00	18.00
58	Frank (Lefty) O'Doul	90.00	40.00	22.50
59	Edmund (Bing) Miller	60.00	30.00	18.00
60	Waite Hoyt	250.00	110.00	60.00
61	Max Bishop	60.00	30.00	18.00
62	"Pepper" Martin	90.00	40.00	22.50
63	Joe Cronin	250.00	110.00	60.00
64	Burleigh Grimes	250.00	110.00	60.00
65	Milton Gaston	60.00	30.00	18.00
66	George Grantham	60.00	30.00	18.00
67	Guy Bush	60.00	30.00	18.00
68	Willie Kamm	60.00	30.00	18.00
69	Gordon (Mickey) Cochrane	250.00	110.00	60.00
70	Adam Comorosky	60.00	30.00	18.00
71	Alvin Crowder	60.00	30.00	18.00
72	Willis Hudlin	60.00	30.00	18.00
73	Eddie Farrell	60.00	30.00	18.00
74	Leo Durocher	250.00	110.00	60.00
75	Walter Stewart	60.00	30.00	18.00
76	George Walberg	60.00	30.00	18.00
77	Glenn Wright	60.00	30.00	18.00
78	Charles (Buddy) Myer	60.00	30.00	18.00
79	James (Zack) Taylor	60.00	30.00	18.00
80	George Herman (Babe) Ruth	4,000	1,800	1,000
81	D'Arcy (Jake) Flowers	60.00	30.00	18.00
82	Ray Kolp	60.00	30.00	18.00
83	Oswald Bluege	60.00	30.00	18.00
84	Morris (Moe) Berg	600.00	275.00	150.00
85	Jimmy Foxx	400.00	180.00	100.00
86	Sam Byrd	60.00	30.00	11.00
87	Danny Mcfayden (McFayden)	60.00	30.00	18.00
88	Joe Judge	60.00	30.00	18.00
89	Joe Sewell	250.00	110.00	60.00
90	Lloyd Waner	250.00	110.00	60.00
91	Luke Sewell	60.00	30.00	18.00
92	Leo Mangum	60.00	30.00	18.00
93	George Herman (Babe) Ruth	3,600	1,625	900.00
94	Al Spohrer	60.00	30.00	18.00

1934 World Wide Gum (Canadian Goudey, V354)

Again a near-clone of the American issue, the '34 "Canadian Goudeys" feature the same number (96) and size (2-3/8" x 2-7/8") of cards. Player selection is considerably different, however. Cards #1-48 feature the same front design as the '33 World Wide/Goudey sets. Cards #49-96 have the "Lou Gehrig says..." graphic on the front. Unlike the 1933 cards, backs are only found with bi-lingual text.

		NM	EX	VG
Complete Set (96):		19,000	8,500	4,500
Common Player:		75.00	35.00	20.00
1	Rogers Hornsby	900.00	400.00	250.00
2	Eddie Morgan	75.00	35.00	20.00
3	Valentine J. (Val) Picinich	75.00	35.00	20.00
4	Rabbit Maranville	250.00	120.00	75.00
5	Flint Rhem	75.00	35.00	20.00
6	Jim Elliott	75.00	35.00	20.00
7	Fred (Red) Lucas	75.00	35.00	20.00
8	Fred Marberry	75.00	35.00	20.00
9	Clifton Heathcote	75.00	35.00	20.00
10	Bernie Friberg	75.00	35.00	20.00
11	Elwood (Woody) English	75.00	35.00	20.00
12	Carl Reynolds	75.00	35.00	20.00
13	Ray Benge	75.00	35.00	20.00
14	Ben Cantwell	75.00	35.00	20.00
15	Irvin (Bump) Hadley	75.00	35.00	20.00
16	Herb Pennock	250.00	120.00	75.00
17	Fred Lindstrom	250.00	120.00	75.00
18	Edgar (Sam) Rice	250.00	120.00	75.00
19	Fred Frankhouse	75.00	35.00	20.00
20	Fred Fitzsimmons	75.00	35.00	20.00
21	Earl Coombs (Earle Combs)	250.00	120.00	75.00
22	George Uhle	75.00	35.00	20.00
23	Richard Coffman	75.00	35.00	20.00
24	Travis C. Jackson	250.00	120.00	75.00
25	Robert J. Burke	75.00	35.00	20.00
26	Randy Moore	75.00	35.00	20.00
27	John Henry (Heinie) Sand	75.00	35.00	20.00
28	George Herman (Babe) Ruth	4,200	2,000	1,600
29	Tris Speaker	300.00	145.00	90.00
30	Perce (Pat) Malone	75.00	35.00	20.00
31	Sam Jones	75.00	35.00	20.00
32	Eppa Rixey	250.00	120.00	75.00

		NM	EX	VG
33	Floyd (Pete) Scott	75.00	35.00	20.00
34	Pete Jablonowski	75.00	35.00	20.00
35	Clyde Manion	75.00	35.00	20.00
36	Dibrell Williams	75.00	35.00	20.00
37	Glenn Spencer	75.00	35.00	20.00
38	Ray Kremer	75.00	35.00	20.00
39	Phil Todt	75.00	35.00	20.00
40	Russell Rollings	75.00	35.00	20.00
41	Earl Clark	75.00	35.00	20.00
42	Jess Petty	75.00	35.00	20.00
43	Frank O'Rourke	75.00	35.00	20.00
44	Jesse Haines	250.00	120.00	75.00
45	Horace Lisenbee	75.00	35.00	20.00
46	Owen Carroll	75.00	35.00	20.00
47	Tom Zachary	75.00	35.00	20.00
48	Charlie Ruffing	250.00	120.00	75.00
49	Ray Benge	75.00	35.00	20.00
50	Elwood (Woody) English	75.00	35.00	20.00
51	Ben Chapman	75.00	35.00	20.00
52	Joe Kuhel	75.00	35.00	20.00
53	Bill Terry	250.00	120.00	75.00
54	Robert (Lefty) Grove	300.00	145.00	90.00
55	Jerome (Dizzy) Dean	450.00	220.00	140.00
56	Charles (Chuck) Klein	250.00	120.00	75.00
57	Charley Gehringer	250.00	120.00	75.00
58	Jimmy Foxx	400.00	195.00	125.00
59	Gordon (Mickey) Cochrane	250.00	120.00	75.00
60	Willie Kamm	75.00	35.00	20.00
61	Charlie Grimm	75.00	35.00	20.00
62	Ed Brandt	75.00	35.00	20.00
63	Tony Piet	75.00	35.00	20.00
64	Frank Frisch	250.00	120.00	75.00
65	Alvin Crowder	75.00	35.00	20.00
66	Frank Hogan	75.00	35.00	20.00
67	Paul Waner	250.00	120.00	75.00
68	Henry (Heinie) Manush	250.00	120.00	75.00
69	Leo Durocher	250.00	120.00	75.00
70	Floyd Vaughan	250.00	120.00	75.00
71	Carl Hubbell	275.00	135.00	85.00
72	Hugh Critz	75.00	35.00	20.00
73	John (Blondy) Ryan	75.00	35.00	20.00
74	Roger Cramer	75.00	35.00	20.00
75	Baxter Jordan	75.00	35.00	20.00
76	Ed Coleman	75.00	35.00	20.00
77	Julius Solters	75.00	35.00	20.00
78	Charles (Chick) Hafey	250.00	120.00	75.00
79	Larry French	75.00	35.00	20.00
80	Frank (Don) Hurst	75.00	35.00	20.00
81	Gerald Walker	75.00	35.00	20.00
82	Ernie Lombardi	250.00	120.00	75.00
83	Walter (Huck) Betts	75.00	35.00	20.00
84	Luke Appling	250.00	120.00	75.00
85	John Frederick	75.00	35.00	20.00
86	Fred Walker	75.00	35.00	20.00
87	Tom Bridges	75.00	35.00	20.00
88	Dick Porter	75.00	35.00	20.00
89	John Stone	75.00	35.00	20.00
90	James (Tex) Carleton	75.00	35.00	20.00
91	Joe Stripp	75.00	35.00	20.00
92	Lou Gehrig	2,500	1,225	775.00
93	George Earnshaw	75.00	35.00	20.00
94	Oscar Melillo	75.00	35.00	20.00
95	Oral Hildebrand	75.00	35.00	20.00
96	John Allen	75.00	35.00	20.00

19	Dizzy Dean	400.00	200.00	120.00
20	Roy Parmelee	125.00	55.00	30.00
21	Vic Sorrell	125.00	55.00	30.00
22	Harry Danning	125.00	55.00	30.00
23	Hal Schumacher	125.00	55.00	30.00
24	Cy Perkins	125.00	55.00	30.00
25	Speedy Durocher	250.00	125.00	75.00
26	Glenn Myatt	125.00	55.00	30.00
27	Bob Seeds	125.00	55.00	30.00
28	Jimmy Ripple	125.00	55.00	30.00
29	Al Schacht	125.00	55.00	30.00
30	Pete Fox	125.00	55.00	30.00
31	Del Baker	125.00	55.00	30.00
32	Flea Clifton	125.00	55.00	30.00
33	Tommy Bridges	125.00	55.00	30.00
34	Bill Dickey	250.00	115.00	65.00
35	Wally Berger	125.00	55.00	30.00
36	Slick Castleman	125.00	55.00	30.00
37	Dick Bartell	125.00	55.00	30.00
38	Red Rolfe	125.00	55.00	30.00
39	Waite Hoyt	250.00	125.00	75.00
40	Wes Ferrell	125.00	55.00	30.00
41	Hank Greenberg	400.00	190.00	105.00
42	Charlie Gehringer	250.00	125.00	75.00
43	Goose Goslin	250.00	125.00	75.00
44	Schoolboy Rowe	125.00	55.00	30.00
45	Mickey Cochrane	250.00	125.00	75.00
46	Joe Cronin	250.00	125.00	75.00
47	Jimmie Foxx	475.00	225.00	125.00
48	Jerry Walker	125.00	55.00	30.00
49	Charlie Gelbert	125.00	55.00	30.00
50	Roy Hayworth (Ray)	125.00	55.00	30.00
51	Joe DiMaggio	15,000	7,000	4,000
52	Billy Rogell	125.00	55.00	30.00
53	Joe McCarthy	250.00	125.00	75.00
54	Phil Cavaretta (Cavarretta)	125.00	55.00	30.00
55	Kiki Cuyler	250.00	125.00	75.00
56	Lefty Gomez	250.00	125.00	75.00
57	Gabby Hartnett	250.00	125.00	75.00
58	Johnny Marcum	125.00	55.00	30.00
59	Burgess Whitehead	125.00	55.00	30.00
60	Whitey Whitehill	125.00	55.00	30.00
61	Buckey Walters	125.00	55.00	30.00
62	Luke Sewell	125.00	55.00	30.00
63	Joey Kuhel	125.00	55.00	30.00
64	Lou Finney	125.00	55.00	30.00
65	Fred Lindstrom	250.00	125.00	75.00
66	Paul Derringer	125.00	55.00	30.00
67	Steve O'Neil (O'Neill)	125.00	55.00	30.00
68	Mule Haas	125.00	55.00	30.00
69	Freck Owen	125.00	55.00	30.00
70	Wild Bill Hallahan	125.00	55.00	30.00
71	Bill Urbanski	125.00	55.00	30.00
72	Dan Taylor	125.00	55.00	30.00
73	Heinie Manush	250.00	125.00	75.00
74	Jo-Jo White	125.00	55.00	30.00
75	Mickey Medwick (Ducky)	250.00	125.00	75.00
76	Joe Vosmik	125.00	55.00	30.00
77	Al Simmons	250.00	125.00	75.00
78	Shag Shaughnessy	125.00	55.00	30.00
79	Harry Smythe	125.00	55.00	30.00
80	Benny Tate	125.00	55.00	30.00
81	Billy Rhiel	125.00	55.00	30.00
82	Lauri Myllykangas	125.00	55.00	30.00
83	Ben Sankey	125.00	55.00	30.00
84	Crip Polli	125.00	55.00	30.00
85	Jim Bottomley	250.00	125.00	75.00
86	William Clark	125.00	55.00	30.00
87	Ossie Bluege	125.00	55.00	30.00
88	Lefty Grove	250.00	115.00	65.00
89	Charlie Grimm	125.00	55.00	30.00
90	Ben Chapman	125.00	55.00	30.00
91	Frank Crosetti	125.00	60.00	30.00
92	John Pomorski	125.00	55.00	30.00
93	Jesse Haines	250.00	125.00	75.00
94	Chick Hafey	250.00	125.00	75.00
95	Tony Piet	125.00	55.00	30.00
96	Lou Gehrig	4,000	2,000	1,400
97	Bill Jurges	125.00	55.00	30.00
98	Smead Jolley	125.00	55.00	30.00
99	Jimmy Wilson	125.00	55.00	30.00
100	Lonnie Warneke	125.00	55.00	30.00
101	Lefty Tamulis	125.00	55.00	30.00
102	Charlie Ruffing	250.00	125.00	75.00
103	Earl Grace	125.00	55.00	30.00
104	Rox Lawson	125.00	55.00	30.00
105	Stan Hack	125.00	55.00	30.00
106	August Galan	125.00	55.00	30.00
107	Frank Frisch	250.00	125.00	75.00
108	Bill McKechnie	250.00	125.00	75.00
109	Bill Lee	125.00	55.00	30.00
110	Connie Mack	250.00	125.00	75.00
111	Frank Reiber	125.00	55.00	30.00
112	Zeke Bonura	125.00	55.00	30.00
113	Luke Appling	250.00	125.00	75.00
114	Monte Pearson	125.00	55.00	30.00
115	Bob O'Farrell	125.00	55.00	30.00
116	Marvin Duke	125.00	55.00	30.00
117	Paul Florence	125.00	55.00	30.00
118	John Berley	125.00	55.00	30.00
119	Tom Oliver	125.00	55.00	30.00
120	Norman Kies	125.00	55.00	30.00
121	Hal King	125.00	55.00	30.00
122	Tom Abernathy	125.00	55.00	30.00
123	Phil Hensick	125.00	55.00	30.00
124	Roy Schalk (Ray)	250.00	125.00	75.00
125	Paul Dunlap	125.00	55.00	30.00
126	Benny Bates	125.00	55.00	30.00
127	George Puccinelli	125.00	55.00	30.00
128	Stevie Stevenson	125.00	55.00	30.00
129	Rabbit Maranville	250.00	125.00	75.00
130	Bucky Harris	250.00	125.00	75.00
131	Al Lopez	250.00	125.00	75.00
132	Buddy Myer	125.00	55.00	30.00
133	Cliff Bolton	125.00	55.00	30.00
134	Estel Crabtree	125.00	55.00	30.00
135	Phil Weintraub	3,000	1,500	900.00

1936 World Wide Gum (Canadian Goudey, V355)

This black and white Canadian set was issued by World Wide Gum in 1936. The cards measure approximately 2-1/2" x 2-7/8", and the set includes both portrait and action photos. The card number and player's name (appearing in all capital letters) are printed inside a white box below the photo.

		NM	EX	VG
Complete Set (135):		40,000	20,000	12,000
Common Player:		125.00	55.00	30.00
1	Jimmy Dykes	300.00	75.00	30.00
2	Paul Waner	250.00	125.00	75.00
3	Cy Blanton	125.00	55.00	30.00
4	Sam Leslie	125.00	55.00	30.00
5	Johnny Louis Vergez	125.00	55.00	30.00
6	Arky Vaughan	250.00	125.00	75.00
7	Bill Terry	250.00	125.00	75.00
8	Joe Moore	125.00	55.00	30.00
9	Gus Mancuso	125.00	55.00	30.00
10	Fred Marberry	125.00	55.00	30.00
11	George Selkirk	125.00	55.00	30.00
12	Spud Davis	125.00	55.00	30.00
13	Chuck Klein	250.00	125.00	75.00
14	Fred Fitzsimmons	125.00	55.00	30.00
15	Bill Delancey	125.00	55.00	30.00
16	Billy Herman	250.00	125.00	75.00
17	George Davis	125.00	55.00	30.00
18	Rip Collins	125.00	55.00	30.00

1939 World Wide Gum (Canadian Goudey, V351)

These premium pictures are analogous to the R303-A issue in the U.S. The 4" x 5-3/4" pictures were given away with the purchase of World Wide gum. The pictures are printed in sepia on cream-colored paper. Fronts have a bordered photo with facsimile autograph. Backs have a "How to . . ." baseball playing tip illustrated with drawings. Backs of the Canadian version differ from the U.S. pieces in the absence of a border line around the playing tip, and the use of a "Lithographed in Canada" notice at lower-right. The unnumbered pictures are checklisted here in alphabetical order.

		NM	EX	VG
Complete Set (25):		5,500	2,750	1,650
Common Player:		100.00	50.00	30.00
(1)	Morris Arnovich	100.00	50.00	30.00
(2)	Sam Bell	130.00	65.00	40.00
(3)	Zeke Bonura	100.00	50.00	30.00
(4)	Earl Caldwell	100.00	50.00	30.00
(5)	Flea Clifton	100.00	50.00	30.00
(6)	Frank Crosetti	140.00	70.00	40.00
(7)	Harry Danning	100.00	50.00	30.00
(8)	Dizzy Dean	250.00	125.00	75.00
(9)	Emile De Jonghe	130.00	65.00	40.00
(10)	Paul Derringer	100.00	50.00	30.00
(11)	Joe DiMaggio	1,500	750.00	450.00
(12)	Vince DiMaggio	100.00	50.00	30.00
(13)	Charlie Gehringer	225.00	110.00	67.00
(14)	Gene Hasson	130.00	65.00	40.00
(15)	Tommy Henrich	150.00	75.00	45.00
(16)	Fred Hutchinson	100.00	50.00	30.00
(17)	Phil Marchildon	100.00	50.00	30.00
(18)	Mike Meola	100.00	50.00	30.00
(19)	Arnold Moser	130.00	65.00	40.00
(20)	Frank Pytlak	100.00	50.00	30.00
(21)	Frank Reiber	100.00	50.00	30.00
(22)	Lee Rogers	100.00	50.00	30.00
(23)	Cecil Travis	100.00	50.00	30.00
(24)	Hal Trosky	100.00	50.00	30.00
(25)	Ted Williams	1,500	750.00	450.00

1975 WTMJ Milwaukee Brewers Broadcasters

To promote its schedule of radio and television broadcasts of Brewers baseball, WTMJ issued this set of broadcaster and schedule cards to potential sponsors. The standard 2-1/2" x 3-1/2" cards are printed in team colors of blue and gold. The on-air talent cards have portraits and facsimile autographs on front, with career summaries on back. The schedule cards have game-action photos on front along with the slogan, "Brewers 75: It's Gonna' Be A Whole New Ballgame!" The cards were distributed in a wax pack with gum.

		NM	EX	VG
Complete Set (7):		25.00	12.50	7.50
Common Card:		2.50	1.25	.70
1	Jim Irwin	4.00	2.00	1.25
2	Gary Bender	4.00	2.00	1.25
3	Bob Uecker	12.50	6.25	3.75
4	Merle Harmon	4.00	2.00	1.25
(5)	TV Schedule	2.50	1.25	.70
(6)	Radio Schedule, Part 1	2.50	1.25	.70
(7)	Radio Schedule, Part 2	2.50	1.25	.70

1910 W-UNC Strip Cards

MATHEWSON, N.Y.

Considerably earlier than most known strip cards, these pieces were cut from a notebook cover. The known players point to a 1910 issue date. Crudely printed on flimsy stock, the cards feature familiar colorized portraits of players on brightly colored backgrounds. The format is about 1-3/8" x 2-3/8" and some cards have evidence of a 1-16th" yellow strip around the outside of the black border. Player name and city are printed in the white border at bottom. Backs are blank. The unnumbered cards are listed here in alphabetical order, though the checklist may or may not be complete.

	Common Player:	NM	EX	VG
	Common Player:	300.00	120.00	60.00
(1)	Babe Adams	300.00	120.00	60.00
(2)	Chief Bender	600.00	240.00	120.00
(3)	Roger Bresnahan	600.00	240.00	120.00
(4)	Donie Bush	300.00	120.00	60.00
(5)	Bobby Byrne	300.00	120.00	60.00
(6)	Bill Carrigan	300.00	120.00	60.00
(7)	Frank Chance	600.00	240.00	120.00
(8)	Hal Chase	450.00	180.00	90.00
(9)	Ty Cobb	2,750	1,100	550.00
(10)	Willis Cole	300.00	120.00	60.00
(11)	Eddie Collins	600.00	240.00	120.00
(12)	Jack Coombs	300.00	120.00	60.00
(13)	Sam Crawford	600.00	240.00	120.00
(14)	Johnny Evers	600.00	240.00	120.00
(15)	Solly Hoffman	300.00	120.00	60.00
(16)	Hughie Jennings	600.00	240.00	120.00
(17)	Walter Johnston (Johnson)	1,500	600.00	300.00
(18)	Johnny Kling	300.00	120.00	60.00
(19)	Ed Konetchy	300.00	120.00	60.00
(20)	Harry Lord	300.00	120.00	60.00
(21)	Sherry Magee	300.00	120.00	60.00
(22)	Christy Mathewson	1,600	650.00	325.00
(23)	Mike Mitchell	300.00	120.00	60.00
(24)	Tris Speaker	750.00	300.00	150.00
(25)	Oscar Stanage	300.00	120.00	60.00
(26)	Honus Wagner	2,000	800.00	400.00

1912 W-UNC Strip Cards

The attributed issue date is speculative, based on the limited known roster. In much the same size and format as W555, these small (photo image area is 1-3/8" x 1-1/2") blank-back cards appear to have been cut off a box or other packaging and may actually be candy cards. Black-and-white photos are framed in dark green with the player's last name in white capital letters below.

	Common Player:	NM	EX	VG
(1)	Bill Carrigan	2,000	800.00	400.00
(2)	Tommy Leach	2,000	800.00	400.00
(3)	Oscar Stanage	2,000	800.00	400.00
(4)	Honus Wagner	7,500	3,000	1,500
(5)	Cy Young	6,500	2,600	1,300

1915 W-UNC Strip Cards

Walter Johnson, Wash. Amer.

Utilizing many photos familiar to collectors from contemporary card sets, including pictures that were several years old at the time of issue, this appears to be a strip-card issue whose scarcity has caused it to elude cataloging efforts heretofore. Cards are printed in black-and-white, blank-backed and are nominally

1-3/4" x 2-3/4". Player or photo identification appears in the bottom border, or at right on horizontally formatted cards.

	Common Player:	NM	EX	VG
	Common Player:	500.00	250.00	150.00
(1)	Ty Cobb	6,500	2,600	1,300
(2)	Larry Doyle	500.00	200.00	100.00
(3)	Johnny Evers	1,500	600.00	300.00
(4)	Joe Jackson	16,000	6,400	3,200
(5)	Walter Johnson	2,500	1,000	500.00
(6)	Sherwood Magee	500.00	200.00	100.00
(7)	Fred Maisel	500.00	200.00	100.00
(8)	Walter (Rabbit) Maranville	1,500	600.00	300.00
(9)	Rube Marquard	1,500	600.00	300.00
(10)	Christy Mathewson	2,750	1,100	550.00
(11)	Phila. Athletics, Champ.	750.00	300.00	150.00
(12)	Ready for the Wallop (Honus Wagner, Roger Bresnahan)	1,500	600.00	300.00
(13)	Nap Rucker	500.00	200.00	100.00
(14)	Hans Wagner	3,500	1,400	700.00
(15)	Joe Wood	600.00	240.00	120.00

1916-20 W-UNC "Big Head" Strip Cards

Given the known player content (perhaps not complete as listed here) and the fact that no team designations are printed on the cards, it is impossible to more accurately date this blank-back strip card issue. The 1-3/8" x 2-1/2" cards have color artwork of the players in full-body poses. The pictures are unusual in that the players' heads are out of proportion to the rest of the body. Whether the portraits were meant to be accurate portrayals is conjecture. Player names given here are as printed on the cards.

		NM	EX	VG
	Complete Set (20):	22,000	10,000	4,000
	Common Player:	500.00	350.00	150.00
(1)	Jim Bagby	500.00	350.00	150.00
(2)	Home Run Baker	800.00	475.00	300.00
(3)	Dave Bancroft	800.00	475.00	300.00
(4)	Ping Bodie	500.00	350.00	150.00
(5)	Geo. Burns	500.00	350.00	150.00
(6)	Leon Cadore	500.00	350.00	150.00
(7)	Ty Cobb	4,000	2,500	1,250
(8)	Larry Doyle	500.00	350.00	150.00
(9)	Hinie Groh	500.00	350.00	150.00
(10)	R. Hornsby	2,000	1,000	750.00
(11)	Johnston (Walter Johnson)	1,500	850.00	500.00
(12)	Joe Judge	500.00	350.00	150.00
(13)	Eddy Konetchy	500.00	350.00	150.00
(14)	Carl Mays	500.00	350.00	150.00
(15)	Zeb Milan	500.00	350.00	150.00
(16)	Sam Rice	800.00	475.00	300.00
(17)	Babe Ruth	6,500	3,000	1,800
(18)	Ray Schalk	800.00	475.00	300.00
(19)	Wally Schang	500.00	350.00	150.00
(20)	Geo. Sisler	1,500	850.00	500.00

1921 W-UNC Self-Developing Strip Cards

The technology of a self-developing photographic baseball card was popularized in the early 1930s by Ray-O-Print and again in the late late 1940s and early 1950s by Topps, but appears to have been pioneered circa 1921 by an unknown company which produced this series. Individual cards measure between 1-1/16" and 1-3/16" in width and 1-13/16" in depth. In black-and-white, they feature action poses on a dark background with the player name and team in white. A white border surrounds the picture. Backs are blank. The unnumbered cards are checklisted here alphabetically, though the list is probably incomplete.

	Common Player:	NM	EX	VG
	Common Player:	100.00	40.00	20.00
(1)	Grover Alexander	450.00	180.00	90.00
(2)	Ty Cobb	2,000	800.00	400.00
(3)	Eddie Collins	300.00	120.00	60.00
(4)	Jake Daubert	100.00	40.00	20.00
(5)	Red Faber	250.00	100.00	50.00
(6)	Max Flack	100.00	40.00	20.00
(7)	"Roger (Rogers) Hornsby"	350.00	140.00	70.00
(8)	Doc Johnston	100.00	40.00	20.00
(9)	Walter Johnston (Johnson)	900.00	360.00	180.00
(10)	Bill Killifer (Killefer)	100.00	40.00	20.00
(11)	Steve O'Neill	100.00	40.00	20.00
(12)	Derrill Pratt	100.00	40.00	20.00
(13)	"Babe" Ruth	3,500	1,400	700.00
(14)	Wallie Schang	100.00	40.00	20.00

1920s W-UNC Playing Strip Cards (1)

Because one of the baseball players (McWeeny) from this set never played for the team that is named, it is not possible to more precisely date this issue. Likely printed on a sheet similar to other playing card/strip card sets of the era, the individual cards are about 1-1/2" x 2-1/2". The front has a crude black-and-white drawing of the player inside a suit-shaped design on a red background. Back is blank.

		NM	EX	VG
6C	Shanty Hogan	150.00	75.00	45.00
7S	Doug McWeeny	150.00	75.00	45.00

1920s W-UNC Playing Strip Cards (2)

Because only three players have thus far been checklisted from this set, it is not possible to more precisely date this issue. Likely printed on a sheet similar to other playing card/strip card sets of the era, the individual cards are about 1-1/2" x 2-1/2", printed in either red (hearts, diamonds) or black (clubs, spades), with a player photo at center. Backs are blank.

Values Undetermined

6C	Bob Meusel	
9S	Tris Speaker	
AD	Babe Ruth	

1926 W-UNC Strip Cards

Ruth is the only baseball player known in this set of athletic, cinematic and historical subjects. The approximately 1-1/2" x 2-1/2" black-and-white, blue-and-white, or maroon-and-white blank-backed card identifies the player, position and team typographically within the photo and has the card number and name in the bottom border. The card has been seen with numbers 1, 52 and 71, as well as unnumbered.

		NM	EX	VG
1	Babe Ruth (Black-and-white.)	800.00	400.00	240.00
52	Babe Ruth (Blue duotone.)	800.00	400.00	240.00
71	Babe Ruth (Blue duotone.)	800.00	400.00	240.00
71	Babe Ruth (Maroon duotone.)	800.00	400.00	240.00
---	Babe Ruth (Unnumbered, maroon.)	1,100	550.00	330.00

1931 W-UNC Strip Cards

(14) ROBERT GROVE

This issue is virtually identical in format to the various 1928-1931 issues cataloged as W502, York Caramel, Yuengling Ice Cream, etc. The black-and-white, cards measure about 1-3/8" (give or take a 1/16") x 2-1/2". Player photos are bordered in white with the name printed in capital letters at bottom. At bottom-left is a card number in parentheses. This issue's checklist is identical to the 1931 W502. the only difference being these cards have blank backs.

		NM	EX	VG
	Complete Set (60):	12,500	5,000	2,500
	Common Player:	75.00	30.00	15.00
1	Muddy Ruel	75.00	30.00	15.00
2	John Grabowski	75.00	30.00	15.00
3	Mickey Cochrane	150.00	60.00	30.00
4	Bill Cissell	75.00	30.00	15.00
5	Carl Reynolds	75.00	30.00	15.00
6	Luke Sewell	75.00	30.00	15.00
7	Ted Lyons	150.00	60.00	30.00
8	Harvey Walker	75.00	30.00	15.00
9	Gerald Walker	75.00	30.00	15.00
10	Sam Byrd	75.00	30.00	15.00
11	Joe Vosmik	75.00	30.00	15.00
12	Dan MacFayden	75.00	30.00	15.00
13	William Dickey	150.00	60.00	30.00
14	Robert Grove	300.00	120.00	60.00
15	Al Simmons	150.00	60.00	30.00
16	Jimmy Foxx	300.00	120.00	60.00
17	Nick Altrock	75.00	30.00	15.00
18	Charlie Grimm	75.00	30.00	15.00
19	Bill Terry	150.00	60.00	30.00
20	Clifton Heathcote	75.00	30.00	15.00
21	Burleigh Grimes	150.00	60.00	30.00
22	Red Faber	150.00	60.00	30.00
23	Gabby Hartnett	150.00	60.00	30.00
24	Earl (Earle) Combs	150.00	60.00	30.00
25	Hack Wilson	150.00	60.00	30.00
26	Stanley Harris	150.00	60.00	30.00
27	John J. McGraw	150.00	60.00	30.00
28	Paul Waner	150.00	60.00	30.00
29	Babe Ruth	4,000	1,600	800.00
30	Herb Pennock	150.00	60.00	30.00
31	Joe Sewell	150.00	60.00	30.00
32	Lou Gehrig	2,000	800.00	400.00
33	Tony Lazzeri	150.00	60.00	30.00
34	Waite Hoyt	150.00	60.00	30.00
35	Glenn Wright	75.00	30.00	15.00
36	Leon (Goose) Goslin	150.00	60.00	30.00
37	Frank Frisch	150.00	60.00	30.00
38	George Uhle	75.00	30.00	15.00
39	Bob O'Farrell	75.00	30.00	15.00
40	Rogers Hornsby	200.00	80.00	40.00
41	"Pie" Traynor	150.00	60.00	30.00
42	Clarence Mitchell	75.00	30.00	15.00
43	Sherwood Smith	75.00	30.00	15.00
44	Miguel A. Gonzalez	75.00	30.00	15.00
45	Joe Judge	75.00	30.00	15.00
46	Eppa Rixey	150.00	60.00	30.00
47	Adolfo Luque	75.00	30.00	15.00
48	E.C. (Sam) Rice	150.00	60.00	30.00
49	Earl Sheely	75.00	30.00	15.00
50	Sam Jones	75.00	30.00	15.00
51	Bib A. Falk	75.00	30.00	15.00
52	Willie Kamm	75.00	30.00	15.00
53	Roger Peckinpaugh	75.00	30.00	15.00
54	Lester Bell	75.00	30.00	15.00
55	L. Waner	150.00	60.00	30.00
56	Eugene Hargrave	75.00	30.00	15.00
57	Harry Heilmann	150.00	60.00	30.00
58	Earl Smith	75.00	30.00	15.00
59	Dave Bancroft	150.00	60.00	30.00
60	George Kelly	150.00	60.00	30.00

1922 W501

G—4-22

TY COBB
Mgr.—Detroit Americans

This "strip card" set, known as W501 in the American Card Catalog, is closely connected to the more popular E121 American Caramel set of 1921 and 1922. Because they were handcut from strips, measurements are relative, with well-cut cards typically about 1-7/8" to 2" by about 3-3/8". The W501 cards are numbered in the upper-right corner and have the notation "G-4-22" in the upper-left corner, apparrently indicating the cards were issued in April of 1922.

		NM	EX	VG
	Complete Set (122):	30,000	12,000	6,000
	Common Player:	100.00	40.00	20.00
1	Ed Rounnel (Rommel)	100.00	40.00	20.00
2	Urban Shocker	100.00	40.00	20.00
3	Dixie Davis	100.00	40.00	20.00
4	George Sisler	350.00	140.00	70.00
5	Bob Veach	100.00	40.00	20.00
6	Harry Heilman (Heilmann)	350.00	140.00	70.00
7a	Ira Falgstead (Name incorrect.)	100.00	40.00	20.00
7b	Ira Flagstead (Name correct.)	100.00	40.00	20.00
8	Ty Cobb	3,750	1,500	750.00
9	Oscar Vitt	100.00	40.00	20.00
10	Muddy Ruel	100.00	40.00	20.00
11	Derrill Pratt	100.00	40.00	20.00
12	Ed Gharrity	100.00	40.00	20.00
13	Joe Judge	100.00	40.00	20.00
14	Sam Rice	350.00	140.00	70.00
15	Clyde Milan	100.00	40.00	20.00
16	Joe Sewell	350.00	140.00	70.00
17	Walter Johnson	900.00	360.00	180.00
18	Jack McInnis	100.00	40.00	20.00
19	Tris Speaker	450.00	180.00	90.00
20	Jim Bagby	100.00	40.00	20.00
21	Stanley Coveleskie (Coveleski)	350.00	140.00	70.00
22	Bill Wambsganss	100.00	40.00	20.00
23	Walter Mails	100.00	40.00	20.00
24	Larry Gardner	100.00	40.00	20.00
25	Aaron Ward	100.00	40.00	20.00
26	Miller Huggins	350.00	140.00	70.00
27	Wally Schang	100.00	40.00	20.00
28	Tom Rogers	100.00	40.00	20.00
29	Carl Mays	125.00	50.00	25.00
30	Everett Scott	100.00	40.00	20.00
31	Robert Shawkey	100.00	40.00	20.00
32	Waite Hoyt	350.00	140.00	70.00
33	Mike McNally	100.00	40.00	20.00
34	Joe Bush	100.00	40.00	20.00
35	Bob Meusel	100.00	40.00	20.00
36	Elmer Miller	100.00	40.00	20.00
37	Dick Kerr	100.00	40.00	20.00
38	Eddie Collins	350.00	140.00	70.00
39	Kid Gleason	100.00	40.00	20.00
40	Johnny Mostil	100.00	40.00	20.00
41	Bib Falk (Bibb)	100.00	40.00	20.00
42	Clarence Hodge	100.00	40.00	20.00
43	Ray Schalk	350.00	140.00	70.00
44	Amos Strunk	100.00	40.00	20.00
45	Eddie Mulligan	100.00	40.00	20.00
46	Earl Sheely	100.00	40.00	20.00
47	Harry Hooper	350.00	140.00	70.00
48	Urban Faber	350.00	140.00	70.00
49	Babe Ruth	6,000	2,400	1,200
50	Ivy B. Wingo	100.00	40.00	20.00
51	Earle Neale	125.00	50.00	25.00
52	Jake Daubert	100.00	40.00	20.00
53	Ed Roush	350.00	140.00	70.00
54	Eppa J. Rixey	350.00	140.00	70.00
55	Elwood Martin	100.00	40.00	20.00
56	Bill Killifer (Killefer)	100.00	40.00	20.00
57	Charles Hollocher	100.00	40.00	20.00
58	Zeb Terry	100.00	40.00	20.00
59	G.C. Alexander (Arms above head.)	600.00	240.00	120.00
60	Turner Barber	100.00	40.00	20.00
61	John Rawlings	100.00	40.00	20.00
62	Frank Frisch	350.00	140.00	70.00
63	Pat Shea	100.00	40.00	20.00
64	Dave Bancroft	350.00	140.00	70.00
65	Cecil Causey	100.00	40.00	20.00
66	Frank Snyder	100.00	40.00	20.00
67	Heinie Groh	100.00	40.00	20.00
68	Ross Young (Youngs)	350.00	140.00	70.00
69	Fred Toney	100.00	40.00	20.00
70	Arthur Nehf	100.00	40.00	20.00
71	Earl Smith	100.00	40.00	20.00
72	George Kelly	350.00	140.00	70.00
73	John J. McGraw	350.00	140.00	70.00
74	Phil Douglas	100.00	40.00	20.00
75	Bill Ryan	100.00	40.00	20.00
76	Jess Haines	350.00	140.00	70.00
77	Milt Stock	100.00	40.00	20.00
78	William Doak	100.00	40.00	20.00
79	George Toporcer	100.00	40.00	20.00
80	Wilbur Cooper	100.00	40.00	20.00
81	George Whitted	100.00	40.00	20.00
82	Chas. Grimm	100.00	40.00	20.00
83	Rabbit Maranville	350.00	140.00	70.00
84	Babe Adams	100.00	40.00	20.00
85	Carson Bigbee	100.00	40.00	20.00
86	Max Carey	350.00	140.00	70.00
87	Whitey Glazner	100.00	40.00	20.00
88	George Gibson	100.00	40.00	20.00
89	Bill Southworth	100.00	40.00	20.00
90	Hank Gowdy	100.00	40.00	20.00
91	Walter Holke	100.00	40.00	20.00
92	Joe Oeschger	100.00	40.00	20.00
93	Pete Kilduff	100.00	40.00	20.00
94	Hy Myers	100.00	40.00	20.00
95	Otto Miller	100.00	40.00	20.00
96	Wilbert Robinson	350.00	140.00	70.00
97	Zach Wheat	350.00	140.00	70.00
98	Walter Ruether	100.00	40.00	20.00
99	Curtis Walker	100.00	40.00	20.00
100	Fred Williams	100.00	40.00	20.00
101	Dave Danforth	100.00	40.00	20.00
102	Ed Rounnel (Rommel)	100.00	40.00	20.00
103	Carl Mays	125.00	50.00	25.00
104	Frank Frisch	350.00	140.00	70.00
105	Lou DeVormer	100.00	40.00	20.00
106	Tom Griffith	100.00	40.00	20.00
107	Harry Harper	100.00	40.00	20.00
108a	John Lavan	100.00	40.00	20.00
108b	John J. McGraw	350.00	140.00	70.00
109	Elmer Smith	100.00	40.00	20.00
110	George Dauss	100.00	40.00	20.00
111	Alexander Gaston	100.00	40.00	20.00
112	John Graney	100.00	40.00	20.00
113	Emil Muesel	100.00	40.00	20.00
114	Rogers Hornsby	450.00	180.00	90.00
115	Leslie Nunamaker	100.00	40.00	20.00
116	Steve O'Neill	100.00	40.00	20.00
117	Max Flack	100.00	40.00	20.00
118	Bill Southworth	100.00	40.00	20.00
119	Arthur Nehf	100.00	40.00	20.00
120	Chick Fewster	100.00	40.00	20.00

1928 W502

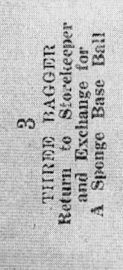

(5) BABE RUTH

3 THREE BAGGER
Return to Storekeeper
and Exchange for
A Sponge Base Ball

Issued in 1928, the manner of distribution for this set is unknown. Because some of the cards' backs indicate they were redeemable for prizes, they were most likely issued inside of a package of candy or similar product, or perhaps in an opaque envelope. The black-and-white cards measure about 1-3/8" x 2-1/2" and display the player's name at the bottom in capital letters preceded by a number in parentheses. The backs of the cards read either "One Bagger," "Three Bagger" or "Home Run." The listings here show two cards known to exist for numbers 38 and 40, which do not correspond to those numbers in 1931 W502. This raises the possibility there may have been a similar set issued in 1929 and/or 1930. The set carries the American Card Catalog designation W502.

		NM	EX	VG
	Complete Set (62):	13,500	5,400	2,700
	Common Player:	75.00	30.00	15.00
1	Burleigh Grimes	150.00	60.00	30.00
2	Walter Reuther (Ruether)	75.00	30.00	15.00
3	Joe Dugan	75.00	30.00	15.00
4	Red Faber	150.00	60.00	30.00

5	Gabby Hartnett	150.00	60.00	30.00
6	Babe Ruth	4,500	1,800	900.00
7	Bob Meusel	75.00	30.00	15.00
8	Herb Pennock	150.00	60.00	30.00
9	George Burns	75.00	30.00	15.00
	(Photo is George J., not George H. Burns.)			
10	Joe Sewell	150.00	60.00	30.00
11	George Uhle	75.00	30.00	15.00
12	Bob O'Farrell	75.00	30.00	15.00
13	Rogers Hornsby	200.00	80.00	40.00
14	"Pie" Traynor	150.00	60.00	30.00
15	Clarence Mitchell	75.00	30.00	15.00
16	Eppa Jepha Rixey	150.00	60.00	30.00
17	Carl Mays	90.00	35.00	17.50
18	Adolfo Luque	75.00	30.00	15.00
19	Dave Bancroft	150.00	60.00	30.00
20	George Kelly	150.00	60.00	30.00
21	Earl Combs (Earle)	150.00	60.00	30.00
22	Harry Heilmann	150.00	60.00	30.00
23	Ray W. Schalk	150.00	60.00	30.00
24	Johnny Mostil	75.00	30.00	15.00
25	Hack Wilson	150.00	60.00	30.00
	(Photo actually Art Wilson.)			
26	Lou Gehrig	1,750	700.00	350.00
27	Ty Cobb	1,750	700.00	350.00
28	Tris Speaker	200.00	80.00	40.00
29	Tony Lazzeri	150.00	60.00	30.00
30	Waite Hoyt	150.00	60.00	30.00
31	Sherwood Smith	75.00	30.00	15.00
32	Max Carey	150.00	60.00	30.00
33	Eugene Hargrave	75.00	30.00	15.00
34	Miguel L. Gonzales	75.00	30.00	15.00
	(Miguel A. Gonzalez)			
35	Joe Judge	75.00	30.00	15.00
36	E.C. (Sam) Rice	150.00	60.00	30.00
37	Earl Sheely	75.00	30.00	15.00
38a	Sam Jones	75.00	30.00	15.00
38b	Emory E. Rigney	75.00	30.00	15.00
39	Bib A. Falk (Bibb)	75.00	30.00	15.00
40a	Nick Altrock	75.00	30.00	15.00
40b	Willie Kamm	75.00	30.00	15.00
41	Stanley Harris	150.00	60.00	30.00
42	John J. McGraw	150.00	60.00	30.00
43	Artie Nehf	75.00	30.00	15.00
44	Grover Alexander	250.00	100.00	50.00
45	Paul Waner	150.00	60.00	30.00
46	William H. Terry	150.00	60.00	30.00
47	Glenn Wright	75.00	30.00	15.00
48	Earl Smith	75.00	30.00	15.00
49	Leon (Goose) Goslin	150.00	60.00	30.00
50	Frank Frisch	150.00	60.00	30.00
51	Joe Harris	75.00	30.00	15.00
52	Fred (Cy) Williams	75.00	30.00	15.00
53	Eddie Roush	150.00	60.00	30.00
54	George Sisler	150.00	60.00	30.00
55	Ed Rommel	75.00	30.00	15.00
56	Rogers Peckinpaugh (Roger)	75.00	30.00	15.00
57	Stanley Coveleskie (Coveleski)	150.00	60.00	30.00
58	Lester Bell	75.00	30.00	15.00
59	Dave Bancroft	150.00	60.00	30.00
60	John P. McInnis	75.00	30.00	15.00

1931 W502

(46) EPPA RIXEY

Issued in 1931, the manner of distribution for this set is unknown. Because some of the cards' backs indicate they were redeemable for prizes, they were most likely issued inside of a package of candy or similar product, or perhaps in an opaque envelope. The black-and-white cards measure about 1-3/8" x 2-1/2" and display the player's name at the bottom in capital letters preceded by a number in parentheses. The backs of the cards read either "One Bagger," "Three Bagger" or "Home Run." The set carries the American Card Catalog designation W502.

		NM	EX	VG
	Complete Set (60):	12,500	5,500	2,750
	Common Player:	90.00	35.00	17.50
1	Muddy Ruel	90.00	35.00	17.50
2	John Grabowski	90.00	35.00	17.50
3	Mickey Cochrane	150.00	60.00	30.00
4	Bill Cissell	90.00	35.00	17.50
5	Carl Reynolds	90.00	35.00	17.50
6	Luke Sewell	90.00	35.00	17.50
7	Ted Lyons	150.00	60.00	30.00
8	Harvey Walker	90.00	35.00	17.50
9	Gerald Walker	90.00	35.00	17.50
10	Sam Byrd	90.00	35.00	17.50

11	Joe Vosmik	90.00	35.00	17.50
12	Dan MacFayden	90.00	35.00	17.50
13	William Dickey	150.00	60.00	30.00
14	Robert Grove	250.00	100.00	50.00
15	Al Simmons	150.00	60.00	30.00
16	Jimmy Foxx	300.00	120.00	60.00
17	Nick Altrock	90.00	35.00	17.50
18	Charlie Grimm	90.00	35.00	17.50
19	Bill Terry	150.00	60.00	30.00
20	Clifton Heathcote	90.00	35.00	17.50
21	Burleigh Grimes	150.00	60.00	30.00
22	Red Faber	150.00	60.00	30.00
23	Gabby Hartnett	150.00	60.00	30.00
24	Earl (Earle) Combs	150.00	60.00	30.00
25	Hack Wilson	150.00	60.00	30.00
26	Stanley Harris	150.00	60.00	30.00
27	John J. McGraw	150.00	60.00	30.00
28	Paul Waner	150.00	60.00	30.00
29	Babe Ruth	4,500	1,800	900.00
30	Herb Pennock	150.00	60.00	30.00
31	Joe Sewell	150.00	60.00	30.00
32	Lou Gehrig	2,000	800.00	400.00
33	Tony Lazzeri	150.00	60.00	30.00
34	Waite Hoyt	150.00	60.00	30.00
35	Glenn Wright	90.00	35.00	17.50
36	Leon (Goose) Goslin	150.00	60.00	30.00
37	Frank Frisch	150.00	60.00	30.00
38	George Uhle	90.00	35.00	17.50
39	Bob O'Farrell	90.00	35.00	17.50
40	Rogers Hornsby	200.00	80.00	40.00
41	"Pie" Traynor	150.00	60.00	30.00
42	Clarence Mitchell	90.00	35.00	17.50
43	Sherwood Smith	90.00	35.00	17.50
44	Joe A. Gonzales	90.00	35.00	17.50
45	Joe Judge	90.00	35.00	17.50
46	Eppa Rixey	150.00	60.00	30.00
47	Adolfo Luque	90.00	35.00	17.50
48	E.C. (Sam) Rice	150.00	60.00	30.00
49	Earl Sheely	90.00	35.00	17.50
50	Sam Jones	90.00	35.00	17.50
51	Bib A. Falk	90.00	35.00	17.50
52	Willie Kamm	90.00	35.00	17.50
53	Roger Peckinpaugh	90.00	35.00	17.50
54	Lester Bell	90.00	35.00	17.50
55	L. Waner	150.00	60.00	30.00
56	Eugene Hargrave	90.00	35.00	17.50
57	Harry Heilmann	150.00	60.00	30.00
58	Earl Smith	90.00	35.00	17.50
59	Dave Bancroft	150.00	60.00	30.00
60	George Kelly	150.00	60.00	30.00

1922 W503

"IRISH" MEUSEL GIANTS N.Y. — 18

Issued circa 1923, this 64-card set of blank-backed cards, measuring 1-3/4" x 2-3/4", feature black and white player photos surrounded by a white border. The player's name and team appear on the card, along with a card number in either the left or right bottom corner. There is no indication of the set's producer, although it is believed the cards were issued with candy or gum. The set carries a W503 American Card Catalog designation.

		NM	EX	VG
	Complete Set (64):	40,000	16,000	8,000
	Common Player:	350.00	140.00	70.00
1	Joe Bush	350.00	140.00	70.00
2	Wally Schang	350.00	140.00	70.00
3	Dave Robertson	350.00	140.00	70.00
4	Wally Pipp	375.00	150.00	75.00
5	Bill Ryan	350.00	140.00	70.00
6	George Kelly	900.00	360.00	180.00
7	Frank Snyder	350.00	140.00	70.00
8	Jimmy O'Connell	350.00	140.00	70.00
9	Bill Cunningham	350.00	140.00	70.00
10	Norman McMillan	350.00	140.00	70.00
11	Waite Hoyt	900.00	360.00	180.00
12	Art Nehf	350.00	140.00	70.00
13	George Sisler	900.00	360.00	180.00
14	Al DeVormer	350.00	140.00	70.00
15	Casey Stengel	900.00	360.00	180.00
16	Ken Williams	350.00	140.00	70.00
17	Joe Dugan	350.00	140.00	70.00
18	"Irish" Meusel	350.00	140.00	70.00
19	Bob Meusel	350.00	140.00	70.00
20	Carl Mays	375.00	150.00	75.00
21	Frank Frisch	900.00	360.00	180.00
22	Jess Barnes	350.00	140.00	70.00
23	Walter Johnson	1,500	600.00	300.00
24	Claude Jonnard	350.00	140.00	70.00
25	Dave Bancroft	900.00	360.00	180.00
26	Johnny Rawlings	350.00	140.00	70.00
27	"Pep" Young	350.00	140.00	70.00
28	Earl Smith	350.00	140.00	70.00
29	Willie Kamm	350.00	140.00	70.00
30	Art Fletcher	350.00	140.00	70.00
31	"Kid" Gleason	350.00	140.00	70.00
32	"Babe" Ruth	12,000	4,800	2,400
33	Guy Morton	350.00	140.00	70.00
34	Heinie Groh	350.00	140.00	70.00
35	Leon Cadore	350.00	140.00	70.00
36	Joe Tobin	350.00	140.00	70.00
37	"Rube" Marquard	900.00	360.00	180.00
38	Grover Alexander	1,200	480.00	240.00
39	George Burns	350.00	140.00	70.00
40	Joe Oeschger	350.00	140.00	70.00
41	"Chick" Shorten	350.00	140.00	70.00
42	Roger Hornsby (Rogers)	1,100	440.00	220.00
43	Adolfo Luque	350.00	140.00	70.00
44	Zack Wheat	900.00	360.00	180.00
45	Herb Pruett (Hub)	350.00	140.00	70.00
46	Rabbit Maranville	900.00	360.00	180.00
47	Jimmy Ring	350.00	140.00	70.00
48	Sherrod Smith	350.00	140.00	70.00
49	Lea Meadows (Lee)	350.00	140.00	70.00
50	Aaron Ward	350.00	140.00	70.00
51	Herb Pennock	900.00	360.00	180.00
52	Carlson Bigbee (Carson)	350.00	140.00	70.00
53	Max Carey	900.00	360.00	180.00
54	Charles Robertson	350.00	140.00	70.00
55	Urban Shocker	350.00	140.00	70.00
56	Dutch Ruether	350.00	140.00	70.00
57	Jake Daubert	350.00	140.00	70.00
58	Louis Guisto	350.00	140.00	70.00
59	Ivy Wingo	350.00	140.00	70.00
60	Bill Pertica	350.00	140.00	70.00
61	Luke Sewell	350.00	140.00	70.00
62	Hank Gowdy	350.00	140.00	70.00
63	Jack Scott	350.00	140.00	70.00
64	Stan Coveleskie (Coveleski)	900.00	360.00	180.00

1926 W511

1. BABE RUTH

Ruth is the only baseball player known in this set of athletic, cinematic and historical subjects. The approximately 1-1/2" x 2-1/2" black-and-white, blue-and-white, or maroon-and-white blank-backed card identifies the player, position and team typographically within the photo and has the card number and name in the bottom border. The card has been seen with numbers 1, 52 and 71, as well as unnumbered.

		NM	EX	VG
1	Babe Ruth (Black-and-white.)	800.00	400.00	240.00
52	Babe Ruth (Blue duotone.)	800.00	400.00	240.00
71	Babe Ruth (Blue duotone.)	800.00	400.00	240.00
71	Babe Ruth (Maroon duotone.)	800.00	400.00	240.00
---	Babe Ruth (Unnumbered, maroon.)	1,100	550.00	330.00

1926-27 W512

3 "TY" COBB Ex-Mgr. Detroit A.L.

One of the many "strip card" sets of the period, the W512 set was initially issued in 1926 and includes 10 baseball players among its 50 cards. Also featured are boxers, golfers, tennis players, aviators, movie stars and other celebrities. The 1-3/8" x 2-1/4" cards feature crude color drawings of the subjects with their names below. A card number appears in the lower-left corner. Baseball players lead off the set and are numbered from 1 to 10. Like most strip cards, they have blank backs. At least four of the baseball player cards have been found in a second type, on which the team name is presented in a typewriter style font on the second line; these changes reflect player status as of 1927. Reprints of Ruth, Cobb, Johnson and Speaker are known.

		NM	EX	VG
Common Player:		55.00	22.50	10.00
1	Dave Bancroft	75.00	30.00	15.00
2a	Grover Alexander (Cubs)	190.00	75.00	35.00
2b	Grover Alexander (Cardinals)	95.00	40.00	20.00
3a	"Ty" Cobb	325.00	130.00	65.00
3b	"Ty" Cobb	350.00	140.00	70.00
	(Ex-Mgr. Detroit A.L.)			
4a	Tris Speaker	95.00	40.00	20.00
4b	Tris Speaker	95.00	40.00	20.00
	(Ex-Mgr. Cleveland A.L.)			
5	Glen Wright (Glenn)	55.00	22.50	10.00
6	"Babe" Ruth	360.00	145.00	70.00
7a	Everett Scott (Yankees)	75.00	30.00	15.00
7b	Everett Scott (White Sox)	55.00	22.50	10.00
8a	Frank Frisch (Giants)	75.00	30.00	15.00
8b	Frank Frisch (Cardinals)	75.00	30.00	15.00
9a	Rogers Hornsby (Cardinals)	95.00	40.00	20.00
9b	Rogers Hornsby (Giants)	95.00	40.00	20.00
10	Dazzy Vance	75.00	30.00	15.00

1928 W513

This "strip card" set, issued in 1928 was actually a continuation of the W512 set issued two years earlier and is numbered starting with number 61 where the W512 set ended. The blank-backed cards measure 1-3/8" x 2-1/4" and display color drawings of the athletes, which include 14 boxers and the 26 baseball players listed here. The cards are numbered in the lower-left corner.

		NM	EX	VG
Complete (Baseball) Set (26):		1,600	650.00	325.00
Common Player:		50.00	20.00	10.00
61	Eddie Roush	75.00	30.00	15.00
62	Waite Hoyt	75.00	30.00	15.00
63	"Gink" Hendrick	50.00	20.00	10.00
64	"Jumbo" Elliott	50.00	20.00	10.00
65	John Miljus	50.00	20.00	10.00
66	Jumping Joe Dugan	50.00	20.00	10.00
67	Smiling Bill Terry	75.00	30.00	15.00
68	Herb Pennock	75.00	30.00	15.00
69	Rube Benton	50.00	20.00	10.00
70	Paul Waner	75.00	30.00	15.00
71	Adolfo Luque	50.00	20.00	10.00
72	Burleigh Grimes	75.00	30.00	15.00
73	Lloyd Waner	75.00	30.00	15.00
74	Hack Wilson	75.00	30.00	15.00
75	Hal Carlson	50.00	20.00	10.00
76	L. Grantham	50.00	20.00	10.00
77	Wilcey Moore (Wilcy)	50.00	20.00	10.00
78	Jess Haines	75.00	30.00	15.00
79	Tony Lazzeri	75.00	30.00	15.00
80	Al DeVormer	50.00	20.00	10.00
81	Joe Harris	50.00	20.00	10.00
82	Pie Traynor	75.00	30.00	15.00
83	Mark Koenig	50.00	20.00	10.00
84	Babe Herman	60.00	24.00	12.00
85	George Harper	50.00	20.00	10.00
86	Earl Coombs (Earle Combs)	75.00	30.00	15.00

1919-21 W514

Consisting of 120 cards, the W514 set is the largest of the various "strip card" issues of its era. Issued between 1919-1921, it is also one of the earliest and most widely-collected. The 1-3/8" x 2-1/2" cards feature color drawings of the players and display the card number in the lower-left corner. The player's name, position and team appear in the bottom border of the blank-backed cards. The set holds special interest for baseball historians because it includes seven of the eight Chicago "Black Sox" who were banned from baseball

for their alleged role in throwing the 1919 World Series. The most famous of them, "Shoeless" Joe Jackson, makes his only strip card appearance in this set.

		NM	EX	VG
Complete Set (124):		30,000	12,000	6,000
Common Player:		75.00	30.00	15.00
1	Ira Flagstead	75.00	30.00	15.00
2	Babe Ruth	1,900	750.00	375.00
	(HOME RUN KING)			
3	Happy Felsch	1,200	475.00	250.00
4	Doc Lavan	75.00	30.00	15.00
5	Phil Douglas	75.00	30.00	15.00
6	Earle Neale	75.00	30.00	15.00
7	Leslie Nunamaker	75.00	30.00	15.00
8	Sam Jones	75.00	30.00	15.00
9	Claude Hendrix	75.00	30.00	15.00
10	Frank Schulte	75.00	30.00	15.00
11	Cactus Cravath	75.00	30.00	15.00
12	Pat Moran	75.00	30.00	15.00
13	Dick Rudolph	75.00	30.00	15.00
14	Arthur Fletcher	75.00	30.00	15.00
15	Joe Jackson	5,000	2,000	1,000
16	Bill Southworth	75.00	30.00	15.00
17	Ad Luque	75.00	30.00	15.00
18	Charlie Deal	75.00	30.00	15.00
19	Al Mamaux	75.00	30.00	15.00
20	Stuffy McInness (McInnis)	75.00	30.00	15.00
21a	Rabbit Maranville (Braves)	200.00	80.00	40.00
21b	Rabbit Maranville (Pirates)	200.00	80.00	40.00
22	Max Carey	200.00	80.00	40.00
23	Dick Kerr	75.00	30.00	15.00
24	George Burns	75.00	30.00	15.00
25	Eddie Collins	200.00	80.00	40.00
26	Steve O'Neil (O'Neill)	75.00	30.00	15.00
27	Bill Fisher	75.00	30.00	15.00
28	Rube Bressler	75.00	30.00	15.00
29	Bob Shawkey	75.00	30.00	15.00
30	Donie Bush	75.00	30.00	15.00
31	Chick Gandil	700.00	280.00	140.00
32	Ollie Zeider	75.00	30.00	15.00
33	Vean Gregg	75.00	30.00	15.00
34	Miller Huggins	200.00	80.00	40.00
35	Lefty Williams	800.00	325.00	160.00
36	Tub Spencer	75.00	30.00	15.00
37	Lew McCarty	75.00	30.00	15.00
38	Hod Eller	75.00	30.00	15.00
39	Joe Gedeon	75.00	30.00	15.00
40a	Dave Bancroft (Quakers)	200.00	80.00	40.00
40b	Dave Bancroft (Giants)	200.00	80.00	40.00
41	Clark Griffith	200.00	80.00	40.00
42	Wilbur Cooper	75.00	30.00	15.00
43	Ty Cobb	1,750	700.00	350.00
44	Roger Peckinpaugh	75.00	30.00	15.00
45	Nic Carter (Nick)	75.00	30.00	15.00
46	Heinie Groh	75.00	30.00	15.00
47a	Bob Roth (Indians)	75.00	30.00	15.00
47b	Bob Roth (Yankees)	75.00	30.00	15.00
48	Frank Davis	75.00	30.00	15.00
49	Leslie Mann	75.00	30.00	15.00
50	Fielder Jones	75.00	30.00	15.00
51	Bill Doak	75.00	30.00	15.00
52	John J. McGraw	200.00	80.00	40.00
53	Charles Hollocher	75.00	30.00	15.00
54	Babe Adams	75.00	30.00	15.00
55	Dode Paskert	75.00	30.00	15.00
56	Roger Hornsby (Rogers)	250.00	100.00	50.00
57	Max Rath	75.00	30.00	15.00
58	Jeff Pfeffer	75.00	30.00	15.00
59	Nick Cullop	75.00	30.00	15.00
60	Ray Schalk	200.00	80.00	40.00
61	Bill Jacobson	75.00	30.00	15.00
62	Nap Lajoie	225.00	90.00	45.00
63	George Gibson	75.00	30.00	15.00
64	Harry Hooper	200.00	80.00*	40.00
65	Grover Alexander	300.00	120.00	60.00
66	Ping Bodie	75.00	30.00	15.00
67	Hank Gowdy	75.00	30.00	15.00
68	Jake Daubert	75.00	30.00	15.00
69	Red Faber	200.00	80.00	40.00
70	Ivan Olson	75.00	30.00	15.00
71	Pickles Dilhoefer	75.00	30.00	15.00
72	Christy Mathewson	900.00	350.00	175.00
73	Ira Wingo (Ivy)	75.00	30.00	15.00
74	Fred Merkle	75.00	30.00	15.00
75	Frank Baker	200.00	80.00	40.00
76	Bert Gallia	75.00	30.00	15.00
77	Milton Watson	75.00	30.00	15.00
78	Bert Shotten (Shotton)	75.00	30.00	15.00
79	Sam Rice	200.00	80.00	40.00
80	Dan Greiner	75.00	30.00	15.00

81	Larry Doyle	75.00	30.00	15.00
82	Eddie Cicotte	750.00	300.00	150.00
83	Hugo Bezdek	75.00	30.00	15.00
84	Wally Pipp	90.00	35.00	17.50
85	Eddie Rousch (Roush)	200.00	80.00	40.00
86	Slim Sallee	75.00	30.00	15.00
87	Bill Killifer (Killefer)	75.00	30.00	15.00
88	Bob Veach	75.00	30.00	15.00
89	Jim Burke	75.00	30.00	15.00
90	Everett Scott	75.00	30.00	15.00
91	Buck Weaver	1,100	450.00	225.00
92	George Whitted	75.00	30.00	15.00
93	Ed Konetchy	75.00	30.00	15.00
94	Walter Johnson	600.00	240.00	120.00
95	Sam Crawford	200.00	80.00	40.00
96	Fred Mitchell	75.00	30.00	15.00
97	Ira Thomas	75.00	30.00	15.00
98	Jimmy Ring	75.00	30.00	15.00
99	Wally Shange (Schang)	75.00	30.00	15.00
100	Benny Kauff	75.00	30.00	15.00
101	George Sisler	200.00	80.00	40.00
102	Tris Speaker	250.00	100.00	50.00
103	Carl Mays	90.00	35.00	17.50
104	Buck Herzog	75.00	30.00	15.00
105	Swede Risberg	2,750	1,100	550.00
106a	Hugh Jennings (Tigers)	200.00	80.00	40.00
106b	Hughie Jennings (Giants)	200.00	80.00	40.00
107	Pep Young	75.00	30.00	15.00
108	Walter Reuther (Ruether)	75.00	30.00	15.00
109	Joe Gharrity (Ed)	75.00	30.00	15.00
110	Zach Wheat	200.00	80.00	40.00
111	Jim Vaughn	75.00	30.00	15.00
112	Kid Gleason	75.00	30.00	15.00
113	Casey Stengel	200.00	80.00	40.00
114	Hal Chase	150.00	60.00	30.00
115	Oscar Stange (Stanage)	75.00	30.00	15.00
116	Larry Shean	75.00	30.00	15.00
117	Steve Pendergast	75.00	30.00	15.00
118	Larry Kopf	75.00	30.00	15.00
119	Charles Whiteman	75.00	30.00	15.00
120	Jess Barnes	75.00	30.00	15.00

1923 W515-1

Cards in the 60-card "strip set" measure about 1-3/8" x 2-1/4" and feature color drawings. Backs are blank. The card number along with the player's name, position and team appear in the bottom border. Most cards also display a "U&U" copyright line, indicating that the photos on which the drawings were based were provided by Underwood & Underwood, a major news photo service of the day. The set has a heavy emphasis on New York players with 39 of the 60 cards depicting members of the Yankees, Dodgers or Giants. Babe Ruth appears on two cards and two other cards picture two players each.

		NM	EX	VG
Complete Set (60):		8,000	3,200	1,600
Common Player:		50.00	20.00	10.00
1	Bill Cunningham	50.00	20.00	10.00
2	Al Mamaux	50.00	20.00	10.00
3	"Babe" Ruth	1,600	650.00	325.00
4	Dave Bancroft	100.00	40.00	20.00
5	Ed Rommel	50.00	20.00	10.00
6	"Babe" Adams	50.00	20.00	10.00
7	Clarence Walker	50.00	20.00	10.00
8	Waite Hoyt	100.00	40.00	20.00
9	Bob Shawkey	50.00	20.00	10.00
10	"Ty" Cobb	750.00	300.00	150.00
11	George Sisler	100.00	40.00	20.00
12	Jack Bentley	50.00	20.00	10.00
13	Jim O'Connell	50.00	20.00	10.00
14	Frank Frisch	100.00	40.00	20.00
15	Frank Baker	100.00	40.00	20.00
16	Burleigh Grimes	100.00	40.00	20.00
17	Wally Schang	50.00	20.00	10.00
18	Harry Heilman (Heilmann)	100.00	40.00	20.00
19	Aaron Ward	50.00	20.00	10.00
20	Carl Mays	60.00	24.00	12.00
21	The Meusel Bros.	60.00	24.00	12.00
	(Bob Meusel, Irish Meusel)			
22	Arthur Nehf	50.00	20.00	10.00
23	Lee Meadows	50.00	20.00	10.00
24	"Casey" Stengel	100.00	40.00	20.00
25	Jack Scott	50.00	20.00	10.00
26	Kenneth Williams	50.00	20.00	10.00
27	Joe Bush	50.00	20.00	10.00

28	Tris Speaker	150.00	60.00	30.00
29	Ross Young (Youngs)	100.00	40.00	20.00
30	Joe Dugan	50.00	20.00	10.00
31	The Barnes Bros. (Jesse Barnes, Virgil Barnes)	60.00	24.00	12.00
32	George Kelly	100.00	40.00	20.00
33	Hugh McQuillen (McQuillan)	50.00	20.00	10.00
34	Hugh Jennings	100.00	40.00	20.00
35	Tom Griffith	50.00	20.00	10.00
36	Miller Huggins	100.00	40.00	20.00
37	"Whitey" Witt	50.00	20.00	10.00
38	Walter Johnson	400.00	160.00	80.00
39	"Wally" Pipp	50.00	20.00	10.00
40	"Dutch" Reuther (Ruether)	50.00	20.00	10.00
41	Jim Johnston	50.00	20.00	10.00
42	Willie Kamm	50.00	20.00	10.00
43	Sam Jones	50.00	20.00	10.00
44	Frank Snyder	50.00	20.00	10.00
45	John McGraw	100.00	40.00	20.00
46	Everett Scott	50.00	20.00	10.00
47	"Babe" Ruth	1,600	650.00	325.00
48	Urban Shocker	50.00	20.00	10.00
49	Grover Alexander	150.00	60.00	30.00
50	"Rabbit" Maranville	100.00	40.00	20.00
51	Ray Schalk	100.00	40.00	20.00
52	"Heinie" Groh	50.00	20.00	10.00
53	Wilbert Robinson	100.00	40.00	20.00
54	George Burns	50.00	20.00	10.00
55	Rogers Hornsby	150.00	60.00	30.00
56	Zack Wheat	100.00	40.00	20.00
57	Eddie Roush	100.00	40.00	20.00
58	Eddie Collins	100.00	40.00	20.00
59	Charlie Hollocher	50.00	20.00	10.00
60	Red Faber	100.00	40.00	20.00

1923 W515-2

A near duplicate of the W515-1 set in every respect except size, the W515-2 strip cards are larger in format, at about 1-1/2" x 2-1/2". Placement of the U&U copyright also differs between some players' cards in each set. Cards may be found with letters in the top border from the title, "THE LITTLE WONDER PICTURE SERIES."

		NM	EX	VG
Complete Set (60):		8,000	3,200	1,600
Common Player:		50.00	25.00	15.00
1	Bill Cunningham	50.00	25.00	15.00
2	Al Mamaux	50.00	25.00	15.00
3	"Babe" Ruth	1,600	800.00	480.00
4	Dave Bancroft	100.00	50.00	30.00
5	Ed Rommel	50.00	25.00	15.00
6	"Babe" Adams	50.00	25.00	15.00
7	Clarence Walker	50.00	25.00	15.00
8	Waite Hoyt	100.00	50.00	30.00
9	Bob Shawkey	50.00	25.00	15.00
10	"Ty" Cobb	750.00	375.00	225.00
11	George Sisler	100.00	50.00	30.00
12	Jack Bentley	50.00	25.00	15.00
13	Jim O'Connell	50.00	25.00	15.00
14	Frank Frisch	100.00	50.00	30.00
15	Frank Baker	100.00	50.00	30.00
16	Burleigh Grimes	100.00	50.00	30.00
17	Wally Schang	50.00	25.00	15.00
18	Harry Heilman (Heilmann)	100.00	50.00	30.00
19	Aaron Ward	50.00	25.00	15.00
20	Carl Mays	60.00	30.00	18.00
21	The Meusel Bros. (Bob Meusel, Irish Meusel)	60.00	30.00	18.00
22	Arthur Nehf	50.00	25.00	15.00
23	Lee Meadows	50.00	25.00	15.00
24	"Casey" Stengel	100.00	50.00	30.00
25	Jack Scott	50.00	25.00	15.00
26	Kenneth Williams	50.00	25.00	15.00
27	Joe Bush	50.00	25.00	15.00
28	Tris Speaker	150.00	75.00	45.00
29	Ross Young (Youngs)	100.00	50.00	30.00
30	Joe Dugan	50.00	25.00	15.00
31	The Barnes Bros. (Jesse Barnes, Virgil Barnes)	60.00	30.00	18.00
32	George Kelly	100.00	50.00	30.00
33	Hugh McQuillen (McQuillan)	50.00	25.00	15.00
34	Hugh Jennings	100.00	50.00	30.00
35	Tom Griffith	50.00	25.00	15.00
36	Miller Huggins	100.00	50.00	30.00
37	"Whitey" Witt	50.00	25.00	15.00
38	Walter Johnson	400.00	200.00	120.00
39	"Wally" Pipp	50.00	25.00	15.00
40	"Dutch" Reuther (Ruether)	50.00	25.00	15.00
41	Jim Johnston	50.00	25.00	15.00

42	Willie Kamm	50.00	25.00	15.00
43	Sam Jones	50.00	25.00	15.00
44	Frank Snyder	50.00	25.00	15.00
45	John McGraw	100.00	50.00	30.00
46	Everett Scott	50.00	25.00	15.00
47	"Babe" Ruth	1,600	800.00	480.00
48	Urban Shocker	50.00	25.00	15.00
49	Grover Alexander	150.00	75.00	45.00
50	"Rabbit" Maranville	100.00	50.00	30.00
51	Ray Schalk	100.00	50.00	30.00
52	"Heinie" Groh	50.00	25.00	15.00
53	Wilbert Robinson	100.00	50.00	30.00
54	George Burns	50.00	25.00	15.00
55	Rogers Hornsby	150.00	75.00	45.00
56	Zack Wheat	100.00	50.00	30.00
57	Eddie Roush	100.00	50.00	30.00
58	Eddie Collins	100.00	50.00	30.00
59	Charlie Hollocher	50.00	25.00	15.00
60	Red Faber	100.00	50.00	30.00

1920 W516-1

This "strip card" set consists of 30 cards featuring colored drawings - either portraits or full-length action poses. The blank-backed cards measure 1-1/2" x 2-1/2". The player's name, position and team appear beneath the picture in hand-printed style. To the right of the name is the card number. The set can be identified by an "IFS" copyright symbol. representing International Feature Service.

		NM	EX	VG
Complete Set (30):		5,250	2,000	1,000
Common Player:		50.00	25.00	10.00
1	Babe Ruth	2,000	800.00	400.00
2	Heinie Groh	50.00	25.00	10.00
3	Ping Bodie	50.00	25.00	10.00
4	Ray Shalk (Schalk)	100.00	40.00	20.00
5	Tris Speaker	150.00	60.00	30.00
6	Ty Cobb	750.00	300.00	150.00
7	Roger Hornsby (Rogers)	150.00	60.00	30.00
8	Walter Johnson	300.00	120.00	60.00
9	Grover Alexander	150.00	60.00	30.00
10	George Burns	50.00	25.00	10.00
11	Jimmy Ring	50.00	25.00	10.00
12	Jess Barnes	50.00	25.00	10.00
13	Larry Doyle	50.00	25.00	10.00
14	Arty Fletcher	50.00	25.00	10.00
15	Dick Rudolph	50.00	25.00	10.00
16	Benny Kauf (Kauff)	50.00	25.00	10.00
17	Art Nehf	50.00	25.00	10.00
18	Babe Adams	50.00	25.00	10.00
19	Will Cooper	50.00	25.00	10.00
20	R. Peckinpaugh	50.00	25.00	10.00
21	Eddie Cicotte	100.00	40.00	20.00
22	Hank Gowdy	50.00	25.00	10.00
23	Eddie Collins	100.00	40.00	20.00
24	Christy Mathewson	400.00	160.00	80.00
25	Clyde Milan	50.00	25.00	10.00
26	M. Kelley (Should be G. Kelly.)	100.00	40.00	20.00
27	Ed Hooper (Harry)	100.00	40.00	20.00
28	Pep. Young	50.00	25.00	10.00
29	Eddie Rousch (Roush)	100.00	40.00	20.00
30	Geo. Bancroft (Dave)	100.00	40.00	20.00

1920 W516-1-2

This set is a re-issue of the W516-1-1 set, with several changes: The pictures are reverse images of W516-1-1, and are printed only in black, red and yellow. Well cut, the blank-back cards measure a nominal 1-1/2" x 2-3/8". The cards display a backwards "IFC" copyright symbol.

		NM	EX	VG
Complete Set (30):		5,250	2,000	1,000
Common Player:		50.00	25.00	10.00
1	Babe Ruth	2,000	1,000	600.00
2	Heinie Groh	50.00	25.00	10.00
3	Ping Bodie	50.00	25.00	10.00
4	Ray Shalk (Schalk)	100.00	40.00	20.00
5	Tris Speaker	150.00	60.00	30.00
6	Ty Cobb	750.00	300.00	150.00
7	Roger Hornsby (Rogers)	150.00	75.00	45.00
8	Walter Johnson	300.00	150.00	90.00
9	Grover Alexander	150.00	60.00	30.00
10	George Burns	50.00	25.00	10.00
11	Jimmy Ring	50.00	25.00	10.00
12	Jess Barnes	50.00	25.00	10.00
13	Larry Doyle	50.00	25.00	10.00
14	Arty Fletcher	50.00	25.00	10.00
15	Dick Rudolph	50.00	25.00	10.00
16	Benny Kauf (Kauff)	50.00	25.00	10.00
17	Art Nehf	50.00	25.00	10.00
18	Babe Adams	50.00	25.00	10.00
19	Will Cooper	50.00	25.00	10.00
20	R. Peckinpaugh	50.00	25.00	10.00
21	Eddie Cicotte	100.00	50.00	30.00
22	Hank Gowdy	50.00	25.00	10.00
23	Eddie Collins	100.00	40.00	20.00
24	Christy Mathewson	400.00	200.00	120.00
25	Clyde Milan	50.00	25.00	10.00
26	M. Kelley (Should be G. Kelly.)	100.00	40.00	20.00
27	Ed Hooper (Harry)	100.00	40.00	20.00
28	Pep. Young	50.00	25.00	10.00
29	Eddie Rousch (Roush)	100.00	40.00	20.00
30	Geo. Bancroft (Dave)	100.00	40.00	20.00

1921 W516-2-1

This set is essentially a re-issue of the W516-1 set, with several changes: The pictures are reverse images of W516-1, and are printed only in red and blue. Cards have been renumbered and have player identification in typeset serifed style. The blank-backed cards measure about 1-1/2" x 2-3/8". The cards display a backwards "IFC" copyright symbol.

		NM	EX	VG
Complete Set (30):		4,500	1,800	900.00
Common Player:		50.00	25.00	10.00
1	George Burns	50.00	25.00	10.00
2	Grover Alexander	150.00	60.00	30.00
3	Walter Johnson	250.00	100.00	50.00
4	Roger Hornsby (Rogers)	125.00	50.00	25.00
5	Ty Cobb	750.00	300.00	150.00
6	Tris Speaker	125.00	50.00	25.00
7	Ray Shalk (Schalk)	75.00	30.00	15.00
8	Ping Bodie	50.00	25.00	10.00
9	Heinie Groh	50.00	25.00	10.00
10	Babe Ruth	1,500	600.00	300.00
11	R. Peckinpaugh	50.00	25.00	10.00
12	Will. Cooper	50.00	25.00	10.00
13	Babe Adams	50.00	25.00	10.00
14	Art Nehf	50.00	25.00	10.00
15	Benny Kauf (Kauff)	50.00	25.00	10.00
16	Dick Rudolph	50.00	25.00	10.00
17	Arty. Fletcher	50.00	25.00	10.00
18	Larry Doyle	50.00	25.00	10.00
19	Jess Barnes	50.00	25.00	10.00
20	Jimmy Ring	50.00	25.00	10.00
21	George Bancroft (Dave)	75.00	30.00	15.00
22	Eddie Rousch (Roush)	75.00	30.00	15.00
23	Pep Young	50.00	25.00	10.00
24	Ed Hooper (Harry)	75.00	30.00	15.00
25	M. Kelley (Should be G. Kelly.)	75.00	30.00	15.00
26	Clyde Milan	50.00	25.00	10.00
27	Christy Mathewson	350.00	140.00	70.00
28	Eddie Collins	75.00	30.00	15.00
29	Hank Gowdy	50.00	25.00	10.00
30	Eddie Cicotte	125.00	50.00	25.00

1921 W516-2-2

This set is yet another variation in the W516 "family." In numbering it parallels W516-2-1, though the typography is in the same sans-serif font as W516-1. Like W516-2-1, the player pictures have been reversed. Well cut, the blank-backed cards measure a nominal 1-1/2" x 2-1/4". The cards display a backwards "IFC" copyright symbol in the picture portion.

		NM	EX	VG
	Complete Set (30):	5,000	2,500	1,500
	Common Player:	50.00	25.00	10.00
1	George Burns	50.00	25.00	10.00
2	Grover Alexander	150.00	75.00	45.00
3	Walter Johnson	300.00	150.00	90.00
4	Roger Hornsby (Rogers)	125.00	62.00	37.00
5	Ty Cobb	750.00	375.00	225.00
6	Tris Speaker	125.00	62.00	37.00
7	Ray Shalk (Schalk)	75.00	37.50	22.50
8	Ping Bodie	50.00	25.00	10.00
9	Heinie Groh	50.00	25.00	10.00
10	Babe Ruth	2,000	1,000	600.00
11	R. Peckinpaugh	50.00	25.00	10.00
12	Will. Cooper	50.00	25.00	10.00
13	Babe Adams	50.00	25.00	10.00
14	Art Nehf	50.00	25.00	10.00
15	Benny Kauf (Kauff)	50.00	25.00	10.00
16	Dick Rudolph	50.00	25.00	10.00
17	Arty. Fletcher	50.00	25.00	10.00
18	Larry Doyle	50.00	25.00	10.00
19	Jess Barnes	50.00	25.00	10.00
20	Jimmy Ring	50.00	25.00	10.00
21	George Bancroft (Dave)	75.00	37.50	22.50
22	Eddie Rousch (Roush)	75.00	37.50	22.50
23	Pep Young	50.00	25.00	10.00
24	Ed Hooper (Harry)	75.00	37.50	22.50
25	M. Kelley	75.00	37.50	22.50
	(Should be G. Kelley.)			
26	Clyde Milan	50.00	25.00	10.00
27	Christy Mathewson	400.00	200.00	120.00
28	Eddie Collins	75.00	37.50	22.50
29	Hank Gowdy	50.00	25.00	10.00
30	Eddie Cicotte	100.00	50.00	30.00

1921 W516-2-3

This issue shares a checklist with W516-2-1, and is likewise printed only in red and blue, with typography in a serifed typeface. Unlike W516-2-1, however, the images on these cards are not reversed, as can easily be ascertained by looking at the copyright symbol and letters.

		NM	EX	VG
	Complete Set (30):	5,000	2,500	1,500
	Common Player:	50.00	25.00	10.00
1	George Burns	50.00	25.00	10.00
2	Grover Alexander	150.00	75.00	45.00
3	Walter Johnson	300.00	150.00	90.00
4	Roger Hornsby (Rogers)	125.00	62.00	37.00
5	Ty Cobb	750.00	375.00	225.00
6	Tris Speaker	125.00	62.00	37.00
7	Ray Shalk (Schalk)	75.00	30.00	15.00
8	Ping Bodie	50.00	25.00	10.00
9	Heinie Groh	50.00	25.00	10.00
10	Babe Ruth	2,000	1,000	600.00
11	R. Peckinpaugh	50.00	25.00	10.00
12	Will. Cooper	50.00	25.00	10.00
13	Babe Adams	50.00	25.00	10.00
14	Art Nehf	50.00	25.00	10.00
15	Benny Kauf (Kauff)	50.00	25.00	10.00
16	Dick Rudolph	50.00	25.00	10.00
17	Arty. Fletcher	50.00	25.00	10.00
18	Larry Doyle	50.00	25.00	10.00
19	Jess Barnes	50.00	25.00	10.00

20	Jimmy Ring	50.00	25.00	10.00
21	George Bancroft (Dave)	75.00	30.00	15.00
22	Eddie Rousch (Roush)	75.00	30.00	15.00
23	Pep Young	50.00	25.00	10.00
24	Ed Hooper (Harry)	75.00	30.00	15.00
25	M. Kelley	75.00	30.00	15.00
	(Should be G. Kelly.)			
26	Clyde Milan	50.00	25.00	10.00
27	Christy Mathewson	400.00	200.00	120.00
28	Eddie Collins	75.00	30.00	15.00
29	Hank Gowdy	50.00	25.00	10.00
30	Eddie Cicotte	100.00	50.00	30.00

1931 W517

The 54-player W517 set is an issue of 3" x 4" cards generally found in a sepia color, though other colors are known. The cards feature a player photo as well as his name and team. The card number appears in a small circle on the front, while the backs are blank. The set is heavy in stars of the period including two Babe Ruths (#4 and 20). The cards were sold in vertical strips of three cards; some cards are found with baseball plays in a line at top. Complete set prices do not include variations. The set was reprinted in three-card-strip format in 1997, with "W-517" printed in the lower-left corner of the reprints.

		NM	EX	VG
	Complete Set (59):	11,000	4,400	2,200
	Common Player:	75.00	35.00	20.00
1	Earl Combs (Earle)	160.00	70.00	40.00
2	Pie Traynor	160.00	70.00	40.00
3	Eddie Rausch (Roush)	160.00	70.00	40.00
4	Babe Ruth/Throwing	1,500	675.00	375.00
5a	Chalmer Cissell (Chicago)	75.00	35.00	20.00
5b	Chalmer Cissell (Cleveland)	75.00	35.00	20.00
6	Bill Sherdel	75.00	35.00	20.00
7	Bill Shore	75.00	35.00	20.00
8	Geo. Earnshaw	75.00	35.00	20.00
9	Bucky Harris	160.00	70.00	40.00
10	Charlie Klein	160.00	70.00	40.00
11a	Geo. Kelly (Reds)	75.00	35.00	20.00
11b	Geo. Kelly (Brooklyn)	75.00	35.00	20.00
12	Travis Jackson	160.00	70.00	40.00
13	Willie Kamm	75.00	35.00	20.00
14	Harry Heilman (Heilmann)	160.00	70.00	40.00
15	Grover Alexander	250.00	110.00	60.00
16	Frank Frisch	160.00	70.00	40.00
17	Jack Quinn	75.00	35.00	20.00
18	Cy Williams	75.00	35.00	20.00
19	Kiki Cuyler	160.00	70.00	40.00
20	Babe Ruth/Portrait	1,750	785.00	435.00
21	Jimmie Foxx	350.00	155.00	85.00
22	Jimmy Dykes	75.00	35.00	20.00
23	Bill Terry	160.00	70.00	40.00
24	Freddy Lindstrom	160.00	72.00	40.00
25	Hughey Critz	75.00	35.00	20.00
26	Pete Donahue	75.00	35.00	20.00
27	Tony Lazzeri	160.00	70.00	40.00
28	Heine Manush (Heinie)	160.00	70.00	40.00
29a	Chick Hafey (Cardinals)	160.00	70.00	40.00
29b	Chick Hafey (Cincinnati)	160.00	70.00	40.00
30	Melvin Ott	200.00	90.00	50.00
31	Bing Miller	75.00	35.00	20.00
32	Geo. Haas	75.00	35.00	20.00
33a	Lefty O'Doul (Phillies)	95.00	45.00	25.00
33b	Lefty O'Doul (Brooklyn)	95.00	45.00	25.00
(34)	Paul Waner	160.00	70.00	40.00
	(No card number.)			
34	Paul Waner	160.00	70.00	40.00
	(W/ card number.)			
35	Lou Gehrig	900.00	400.00	225.00
36	Dazzy Vance	160.00	70.00	40.00
37	Mickey Cochrane	160.00	70.00	40.00
38	Rogers Hornsby	225.00	100.00	55.00
39	Lefty Grove	200.00	90.00	50.00
40	Al Simmons	160.00	70.00	40.00
41	Rube Walberg	75.00	35.00	20.00
42	Hack Wilson	160.00	70.00	40.00
43	Art Shires	75.00	35.00	20.00
44	Sammy Hale	75.00	35.00	20.00
45	Ted Lyons	160.00	70.00	40.00
46	Joe Sewell	160.00	70.00	40.00
47	Goose Goslin	160.00	70.00	40.00
48	Lou Fonseca (Lew)	75.00	35.00	20.00
49	Bob Muesel (Meusel)	75.00	35.00	20.00
50	Lu Blue	75.00	35.00	20.00
51	Earl Averill	160.00	70.00	40.00
52	Eddy Collins (Eddie)	160.00	70.00	40.00
53	Joe Judge	75.00	35.00	20.00
54	Mickey Cochrane	160.00	70.00	40.00

1931 W517 Mini

Little is known about these smaller-format (1-3/4" x 2-3/4") versions of the W517 strip cards. They are identical in design to the more common 3" x 4" cards, although some, if not all, do not have the card number-in-circle found on regular W517s. It is presumed, though not confirmed, that all 54 of the regular versions can be found in the mini size, as well as several color variations.

PREMIUM: 2-3X
(See W517 for checklist and base card values.)

1920 W519 - Numbered 1

Cards in this 20-card "strip set" measure 1-1/2" x 2-1/2" and feature player drawings set against a brightly colored background. A card number appears in the lower-left corner followed by the player's name, printed in capital letters. The player drawings are all posed portraits, except for Joe Murphy and Ernie Kreuger, who are shown catching. Like all strip cards, the cards were sold in strips and have blank backs. The date of issue may be approximate.

		NM	EX	VG
	Complete Set (20):	5,500	2,200	1,100
	Common Player:	100.00	40.00	20.00
1	Guy Morton	100.00	40.00	20.00
2	Rube Marquard	300.00	120.00	60.00
3	Gabby Cravath (Gavvy)	100.00	40.00	20.00
4	Ernie Krueger	100.00	40.00	20.00
5	Babe Ruth	2,400	960.00	480.00
6	George Sisler	300.00	120.00	60.00
7	Rube Benton	100.00	40.00	20.00
8	Jimmie Johnston	100.00	40.00	20.00
9	Wilbur Robinson (Wilbert)	300.00	120.00	60.00
10	Johnny Griffith	100.00	40.00	20.00
11	Frank Baker	300.00	120.00	60.00
12	Bob Veach	100.00	40.00	20.00
13	Jesse Barnes	100.00	40.00	20.00
14	Leon Cadore	100.00	40.00	20.00
15	Ray Schalk	300.00	120.00	60.00
16	Kid Gleasen (Gleason)	100.00	40.00	20.00
17	Joe Murphy	100.00	40.00	20.00
18	Frank Frisch	300.00	120.00	60.00
19	Eddie Collins	300.00	120.00	60.00
20	Wallie (Wally) Schang	100.00	40.00	20.00

1920 W519 - Numbered 2

A second type of numbered version of W519 exists on which the style of the card numbers differs as does, apparently, the numbering of the players. On Type 1 cards, the card number to the left of the player name is printed in the same heavy sans-serif style as the name. Type 2 cards have the number in a lighter typewriter-style font. While only three Type 2 cards are currently confirmed to exist, it is expected the other 17 players from W519 were also issued.

20 BABE RUTH

		NM	EX	VG
12	Joe Murphy	100.00	40.00	20.00
13	Frank Frisch	300.00	120.00	60.00
14	Eddie Collins	300.00	120.00	60.00
16	Guy Morton	100.00	40.00	20.00
17	Rube Marquard	300.00	120.00	60.00
19	Ernie Kreuger	100.00	40.00	20.00
20a	Babe Ruth	2,400	960.00	480.00
20b	Wallie Schange (Wally Schang)	100.00	40.00	20.00

1920 W519 - Unnumbered

EDDIE COLLINS

Cards in this 10-card set are identical in design and size (1-1/2" x 2-1/2") to the W519 Numbered set, except the player drawings are all set against a blue background and the cards are not numbered. With the lone exception of Eddie Ciotte, all of the subjects in the unnumbered set also appear in the numbered set.

		NM	EX	VG
Complete Set (10):		3,600	1,450	725.00
Common Player:		90.00	40.00	20.00
(1)	Eddie Cicotte	350.00	140.00	70.00
(2)	Eddie Collins	275.00	110.00	55.00
(3)	Gabby Cravath (Gavvy)	90.00	40.00	20.00
(4)	Frank Frisch	275.00	110.00	55.00
(5)	Kid Gleason (Gleason)	90.00	40.00	20.00
(6)	Ernie Kreuger	90.00	40.00	20.00
(7)	Rube Marquard	275.00	110.00	55.00
(8)	Guy Morton	90.00	40.00	20.00
(9)	Joe Murphy	90.00	40.00	20.00
(10)	Babe Ruth	2,000	800.00	400.00

1920 W520

FLETCHER

Another "strip card" set issued circa 1920, cards in this set measure 1-3/8" x 2-1/4" and are numbered in the lower-right corner. The first nine cards in the set display portrait poses, while the rest are full-length action poses. Some of the poses in this set are the same as those in the W516 issue with the pictures reversed. The player's last name appears in the border beneath the picture. The cards are blank-backed.

		NM	EX	VG
Complete Set (20):		4,000	1,600	800.00
Common Player:		50.00	20.00	10.00
1	Dave Bancroft	150.00	60.00	30.00
2	Christy Mathewson	400.00	160.00	80.00
3	Larry Doyle	50.00	20.00	10.00
4	Jess Barnes	50.00	20.00	10.00
5	Art Fletcher	50.00	20.00	10.00
6	Wilbur Cooper	50.00	20.00	10.00
7	Mike Gonzales (Gonzalez)	50.00	20.00	10.00
8	Zach Wheat	150.00	60.00	30.00
9	Tris Speaker	200.00	80.00	40.00
10	Benny Kauff	50.00	20.00	10.00
11	Zach Wheat	150.00	60.00	30.00
12	Phil Douglas	50.00	20.00	10.00
13	Babe Ruth	2,000	800.00	400.00
14	Stan Koveleski (Coveleski)	150.00	60.00	30.00
15	Goldie Rapp	50.00	20.00	10.00
16	Pol Perritt	50.00	20.00	10.00
17	Otto Miller	50.00	20.00	10.00
18	George Kelly	150.00	60.00	30.00
19	Mike Gonzales (Gonzalez)	50.00	20.00	10.00
20	Les Nunamaker	50.00	20.00	10.00

1921 W521

10 JOHNNY GRIFFITH

This issue is closely related to the W519 Numbered set. In fact, it uses the same color drawings as that set with the pictures reversed, resulting in a mirror-image of the W519 cards. The player poses and the numbering system are identical, as are the various background colors. The W521 cards are blank-backed and were sold in strips.

		NM	EX	VG
Complete Set (20):		3,000	1,200	600.00
Common Player:		50.00	20.00	10.00
1	Guy Morton	50.00	20.00	10.00
2	Rube Marquard	150.00	60.00	30.00
3	Gabby Cravath (Gavvy)	50.00	20.00	10.00
4	Ernie Krueger	50.00	20.00	10.00
5	Babe Ruth	1,500	600.00	300.00
6	George Sisler	150.00	60.00	30.00
7	Rube Benton	50.00	20.00	10.00
8	Jimmie Johnston	50.00	20.00	10.00
9	Wilbur Robinson (Wilbert)	150.00	60.00	30.00
10	Johnny Griffith	50.00	20.00	10.00
11	Frank Baker	150.00	60.00	30.00
12	Bob Veach	50.00	20.00	10.00
13	Jesse Barnes	50.00	20.00	10.00
14	Leon Cadore	50.00	20.00	10.00
15	Ray Schalk	150.00	60.00	30.00
16	Kid Gleasen (Gleason)	50.00	20.00	10.00
17	Joe Murphy	50.00	20.00	10.00
18	Frank Frisch	150.00	60.00	30.00
19	Eddie Collins	150.00	60.00	30.00
20	Wallie (Wally) Schang	50.00	20.00	10.00

1920 W522

42 MIKE GONZALES

The 20 cards in this "strip card" set, issued circa 1920, are numbered from 31-50 and use the same players and drawings as the W520 set, issued about the same time. The cards measure 1-3/8" x 2-1/4" and are numbered in the lower left corner followed by the player's name. The cards have blank backs.

		NM	EX	VG
Complete Set (20):		5,000	2,000	1,000
Common Player:		75.00	30.00	15.00
31	Benny Kauf (Kauff)	75.00	30.00	15.00
32	Tris Speaker	300.00	120.00	60.00
33	Zach Wheat	225.00	90.00	45.00
34	Mike Gonzales (Gonzalez)	75.00	30.00	15.00
35	Wilbur Cooper	75.00	30.00	15.00
36	Art Fletcher	75.00	30.00	15.00
37	Jess Barnes	75.00	30.00	15.00
38	Larry Doyle	75.00	30.00	15.00
39	Christy Mathewson	900.00	360.00	180.00
40	Dave Bancroft	225.00	90.00	45.00
41	Les Nunamaker	75.00	30.00	15.00
42	Mike Gonzales (Gonzalez)	75.00	30.00	15.00
43	George Kelly	225.00	90.00	45.00
44	Otto Miller	75.00	30.00	15.00
45	Pol Perritt	75.00	30.00	15.00
46	Goldie Rapp	75.00	30.00	15.00
47	Stan Koveleski (Coveleski)	225.00	90.00	45.00
48	Babe Ruth	2,250	900.00	450.00
49	Phil Douglas	75.00	30.00	15.00
50	Zach Wheat	225.00	90.00	45.00

1921 W551

JESS BARNES "GIANTS" N. L.

Another "strip set" issued circa 1920, these ten cards measure 1-3/8" x 2-1/4" and feature color drawings. The cards are unnumbered and blank-backed.

		NM	EX	VG
Complete Set (10):		2,000	800.00	400.00
Complete Set, Uncut Strip:		2,500	1,000	500.00
Common Player:		50.00	20.00	10.00
(1)	Frank Baker	125.00	50.00	25.00
(2)	Dave Bancroft	125.00	50.00	25.00
(3)	Jess Barnes	50.00	20.00	10.00
(4)	Ty Cobb	400.00	160.00	80.00
(5)	Walter Johnson	175.00	70.00	35.00
(6)	Wally Pipp	50.00	20.00	10.00
(7)	Babe Ruth	1,100	450.00	225.00
(8)	George Sisler	125.00	50.00	25.00
(9)	Tris Speaker	150.00	60.00	30.00
(10)	Casey Stengel	125.00	50.00	25.00

1929 W553

One of the more obscure strip card sets, and one of the last of the genre, this issue also is one of the most attractive. Player photos - the same pictures used in the contemporary Kashin Publications (R316) boxed set and anonymous W554 strip cards - are printed in either black on white or as duo-tones (blue, green and magenta seen thus far), with an ornate frame. Cards measure 1-3/4" x 2-3/4". There is a facsimile autograph on front and the player's team and league are also spelled out. Backs are blank. This checklist is probably incomplete. Gaps have been left in the assigned numbering for future additions.

	NM	EX	VG
Common Player:	100.00	50.00	30.00

		NM	EX	VG
(1)	Lu Blue	100.00	50.00	30.00
(2)	Mickey Cochrane	200.00	100.00	60.00
(4)	Jimmie Foxx	300.00	150.00	90.00
(5)	Frank Frisch	200.00	100.00	60.00
(6)	Lou Gehrig	750.00	375.00	225.00
(7)	Goose Goslin	200.00	100.00	60.00
(8)	Burleigh Grimes	200.00	100.00	60.00
(9)	Lefty Grove	250.00	125.00	75.00
(11)	Rogers Hornsby	250.00	125.00	75.00
(13)	Rabbit Maranville	200.00	100.00	60.00
(14)	Bing Miller	100.00	50.00	30.00
(15)	Lefty O'Doul	150.00	75.00	45.00
(16)	Babe Ruth	1,200	600.00	360.00
(17)	Al Simmons	200.00	100.00	60.00
(18)	Pie Traynor	200.00	100.00	60.00

1930 W554

This unidentified set of black-and-white cards features most of the era's stars in action poses. A facsimile autograph appears on the front of each of the blank-back 5" x 7" pictures. Cards can be found either with and/or without player name and, sometimes, team spelled out in all-capital letters in the bottom white border, with the position in upper- and lower-case between. The unnumbered pictures are checklisted here in alphabetical order. A version of the issue has been seen with advertising for "Big Prize" on the back, printed in red. Another known back stamp is a round black ad for "A. Bonemery / ICE CREAM / CONFECTIONERY."

		NM	EX	VG
Complete Set (18):		3,500	1,400	700.00
Common Player:		60.00	25.00	12.50
(1)	Gordon S. (Mickey) Cochrane	100.00	40.00	20.00
(2)	Lewis A. Fonseca	60.00	25.00	12.50
(3)	Jimmy Foxx	200.00	80.00	40.00
(4)	Lou Gehrig	950.00	380.00	190.00
(5)	Burleigh Grimes	100.00	40.00	20.00
(6)	Robert M. Grove	125.00	50.00	25.00
(7)	Waite Hoyt	100.00	40.00	20.00
(8)	Joe Judge	60.00	25.00	12.50
(9)	Charles (Chuck) Klein	100.00	40.00	20.00
(10)	Douglas McWeeny	60.00	25.00	12.50
(11)	Frank O'Doul	75.00	25.00	15.00
(12)	Melvin Ott	125.00	50.00	25.00
(13)	Herbert Pennock	100.00	40.00	20.00
(14)	Eddie Rommel	60.00	25.00	12.50
(15)	Babe Ruth	1,200	480.00	240.00
(16)	Al Simmons	100.00	40.00	20.00
(17)	Lloyd Waner	100.00	40.00	20.00
(18)	Hack Wilson	125.00	50.00	25.00

1909-1910 W555

Designated as W555 in the American Card Catalog, very little is known about this obscure set. The nearly square cards measure only 1-1/8" x 1-3-16" and feature a sepia-colored player photo. Sixty-six different cards have been discovered to date, but others may exist. The manufacturer of the set is unknown, but the sets appear to be related to a series of contemporary candy cards (E93, E94, E97 and E98) because, with only two exceptions, the players and poses are the same. It is not known how the cards were issued. There is speculation that they may have been issued as part of a candy box.

		NM	EX	VG
Complete Set (67):		25,000	10,000	5,000
Common Player:		125.00	50.00	25.00
(1)	Red Ames	125.00	50.00	25.00

(2)	Jimmy Austin	125.00	50.00	25.00
(3)	Johnny Bates	125.00	50.00	25.00
(4)	Chief Bender	375.00	150.00	75.00
(5)	Bob Bescher	125.00	50.00	25.00
(6)	Joe Birmingham	125.00	50.00	25.00
(7)	Bill Bradley	125.00	50.00	25.00
(8)	Kitty Bransfield	125.00	50.00	25.00
(9)	Mordecai Brown	375.00	150.00	75.00
(10)	Bobby Byrne	125.00	50.00	25.00
(11)	Frank Chance	375.00	150.00	75.00
(12)	Hal Chase	375.00	150.00	75.00
(13)	Ed Cicotte	375.00	150.00	75.00
(14)	Fred Clarke	375.00	150.00	75.00
(15)	Ty Cobb	4,500	1,800	900.00
(16)	Eddie Collins (Dark uniform.)	375.00	150.00	75.00
(17)	Eddie Collins (Light uniform.)	375.00	150.00	75.00
(18)	Harry Coveleskie (Coveleski)	125.00	50.00	25.00
(19)	Sam Crawford	375.00	150.00	75.00
(20)	Harry Davis	125.00	50.00	25.00
(21)	Jim Delehanty (Delahanty)	125.00	50.00	25.00
(22)	Art Devlin	125.00	50.00	25.00
(23)	Josh Devore	125.00	50.00	25.00
(24)	Wild Bill Donovan	125.00	50.00	25.00
(25)	Red Dooin	125.00	50.00	25.00
(26)	Mickey Doolan	125.00	50.00	25.00
(27)	Bull Durham	125.00	50.00	25.00
(28)	Jimmy Dygert	125.00	50.00	25.00
(29)	Johnny Evers	375.00	150.00	75.00
(30)	Russ Ford	125.00	50.00	25.00
(31)	George Gibson	125.00	50.00·	25.00
(32)	Clark Griffith	375.00	150.00	75.00
(33)	Topsy Hartsell (Hartsel)	125.00	50.00	25.00
(34)	Bill Heinchman (Hinchman)	125.00	50.00	25.00
(35)	Ira Hemphill	125.00	50.00	25.00
(36)	Hughie Jennings	375.00	150.00	75.00
(37)	Davy Jones	125.00	50.00	25.00
(38)	Addie Joss	500.00	200.00	100.00
(39)	Wee Willie Keeler	375.00	150.00	75.00
(40)	Red Kleinow	125.00	50.00	25.00
(41)	Nap Lajoie	375.00	150.00	75.00
(42)	Joe Lake	125.00	50.00	25.00
(43)	Tommy Leach	125.00	50.00	25.00
(44)	Harry Lord	125.00	50.00	25.00
(45)	Sherry Magee	125.00	50.00	25.00
(46)	Christy Mathewson	2,000	800.00	400.00
(47)	Amby McConnell	125.00	50.00	25.00
(48)	John McGraw	375.00	150.00	75.00
(49)	Chief Meyers	125.00	50.00	25.00
(50)	Earl Moore	125.00	50.00	25.00
(51)	Mike Mowery	125.00	50.00	25.00
(52)	George Mullin	125.00	50.00	25.00
(53)	Red Murray	125.00	50.00	25.00
(54)	Nichols	125.00	50.00	25.00
(55)	Jim Pastorious (Pastorius)	125.00	50.00	25.00
(56)	Deacon Phillippi (Phillippe)	125.00	50.00	25.00
(57)	Eddie Plank	375.00	150.00	75.00
(58)	Fred Snodgrass	125.00	50.00	25.00
(59)	Harry Steinfeldt	125.00	50.00	25.00
(60)	Joe Tinker	375.00	150.00	75.00
(61)	Hippo Vaughn	125.00	50.00	25.00
(62)	Honus Wagner	2,500	1,000	500.00
(63)	Rube Waddell	375.00	150.00	75.00
(64)	Hooks Wiltse	125.00	50.00	25.00
(65)	Cy Young (Standing, full name on front.)	1,500	600.00	300.00
(66)	Cy Young (Standing, last name on front.)	1,500	600.00	300.00
(67)	Cy Young/Portrait	1,650	660.00	330.00

1927 W560

AL SIMMONS
Philadelphia Athletics

Although assigned a "W" number by the American Card Catalog, this is not a "strip card" issue in the same sense as most other "W" sets, although W560 cards are frequently found in uncut sheets of 16 cards. Cards measure a nominal 1-3/4" x 2-3/4" and are designed like a deck of playing cards, with the pictures on the various suits. The set includes aviators and other athletes in addition to baseball players. Cards can be found with designs printed in red or black, or less commonly with both and red and black on each card. Some players will also be found with different suit/value combinations.

		NM	EX	VG
Complete Set, Sheets (64):		3,250	1,625	975.00
Complete (Baseball) Set (49):		2,400	1,200	725.00
Common Player:		25.00	12.50	7.50
(1)	Vic Aldridge	25.00	12.50	7.50
(2)	Lester Bell	25.00	12.50	7.50
(3)	Larry Benton	25.00	12.50	7.50

(4)	Max Bishop	25.00	12.50	7.50
(5)	Del Bissonette	25.00	12.50	7.50
(6)	Jim Bottomley	45.00	22.50	13.50
(7)	Guy Bush	25.00	12.50	7.50
(8)	W. Clark	25.00	12.50	7.50
(9)	Andy Cohen	25.00	12.50	7.50
(10)	Mickey Cochrane	45.00	22.50	13.50
(11)	Hugh Critz	25.00	12.50	7.50
(12)	Kiki Cuyler	45.00	22.50	13.50
(13)	Taylor Douthit	25.00	12.50	7.50
(14)	Fred Fitzsimmons	25.00	12.50	7.50
(15)	Jim Foxx	110.00	55.00	35.00
(16)	Lou Gehrig	325.00	160.00	100.00
(17)	Goose Goslin	45.00	22.50	13.50
(18)	Sam Gray	25.00	12.50	7.50
(19)	Lefty Grove	60.00	30.00	18.00
(20)	Jesse Haines	45.00	22.50	13.50
(21)	Babe Herman	30.00	15.00	9.00
(22)	Roger Hornsby (Rogers)	60.00	30.00	18.00
(23)	Waite Hoyt	45.00	22.50	13.50
(24)	Henry Johnson	25.00	12.50	7.50
(25)	Walter Johnson	150.00	75.00	45.00
(26)	Willie Kamm	25.00	12.50	7.50
(27)	Remy Kremer	25.00	12.50	7.50
(28)	Fred Lindstrom	45.00	22.50	13.50
(29)	Fred Maguire	25.00	12.50	7.50
(30)	Fred Marberry	25.00	12.50	7.50
(31)	Johnny Mostil	25.00	12.50	7.50
(32)	Buddy Myer	25.00	12.50	7.50
(33)	Herb Pennock	45.00	22.50	13.50
(34)	George Pipgras	25.00	12.50	7.50
(35)	Flint Rhem	25.00	12.50	7.50
(36)	Babe Ruth	400.00	200.00	120.00
(37)	Luke Sewell	25.00	12.50	7.50
(38)	Willie Sherdel	25.00	12.50	7.50
(39)	Al Simmons	45.00	22.50	13.50
(40)	Thomas Thevenow	25.00	12.50	7.50
(41)	Fresco Thompson	25.00	12.50	7.50
(42)	George Uhle	25.00	12.50	7.50
(43)	Dazzy Vance	45.00	22.50	13.50
(44)	Rube Walberg	25.00	12.50	7.50
(45)	Lloyd Waner	45.00	22.50	13.50
(46)	Paul Waner	45.00	22.50	13.50
(47)	Fred "Cy" Williams	25.00	12.50	7.50
(48)	Jim Wilson	25.00	12.50	7.50
(49)	Glen Wright (Glenn)	25.00	12.50	7.50

1928 W565

LOU GEHRIG
N.Y. YANKEES

Similar in concept to W560, the 50 cards comprising this set were printed on two 7" x 10-1/2" sheets of cheap cardboard, one in black-and-white and one in red-and-white, each with navy blue backs. Most of the cards in the issue are of movie stars, with a few boxers, ballplayers and other notables included. While most of the cards depict the person in the center of a playing card format, it is interesting to note that a full deck of cards cannot be made up by cutting the sheets. Individual cards are 1-1/4" x 2-1/8". Only the baseball players are listed here.

		NM	EX	VG
Complete Set, Sheets (50):		450.00	225.00	135.00
Common Player:		75.00	37.50	22.50
(1)	Lou Gehrig	300.00	150.00	90.00
(2)	Harry Heilmann	75.00	37.50	22.50
(3)	Tony Lazzeri	75.00	37.50	22.50
(4)	Al Simmons	75.00	37.50	22.50

1947 W571

(See 1947 Bond Bread.)

1923 W572

These cards, designated as W572 by the American Card Catalog, measure 1-5/16" x 2-1/2" and are blank-backed. Fronts feature black-and-white or sepia player photos. The set is closely related to the popular E120 American Caramel set issued in 1922 and, with the exception of Ty Cobb, it uses the same photos. The cards were originally issued as strips of ten, with baseball players and boxers often mixed. They are found on either a white, slick stock or a dark, coarser cardboard. The player's name on the front of the cards appears in script. All cards have on front a copyright symbol and one of several alphabetical combinations indicating the source of the photo. The baseball players from the set are checklisted here in alphabetical order.

		NM	EX	VG
Complete (Baseball) Set (121):		12,500	6,250	3,750
Common Player:		50.00	25.00	15.00
(1)	Eddie Ainsmith	50.00	25.00	15.00
(2)	Vic Aldridge	50.00	25.00	15.00
(3)	Grover Alexander	250.00	125.00	75.00
(4)	Dave Bancroft	150.00	75.00	45.00
(5)	Walt Barbare	50.00	25.00	15.00
(6)	Jess Barnes	50.00	25.00	15.00
(7)	John Bassler	50.00	25.00	15.00
(8)	Lu Blue	50.00	25.00	15.00
(9)	Norman Boeckel	50.00	25.00	15.00
(10)	George Burns	50.00	25.00	15.00
(11)	Joe Bush	50.00	25.00	15.00
(12)	Leon Cadore	50.00	25.00	15.00
(13)	Virgil Cheevers (Cheeves)	50.00	25.00	15.00
(14)	Ty Cobb	1,350	675.00	400.00
(15)	Eddie Collins	150.00	75.00	45.00
(16)	John Collins	50.00	25.00	15.00
(17)	Wilbur Cooper	50.00	25.00	15.00
(18)	Stanley Coveleski	150.00	75.00	45.00
(19)	Walton Cruise	50.00	25.00	15.00
(20)	Dave Danforth	50.00	25.00	15.00
(21)	Jake Daubert	50.00	25.00	15.00
(22)	Hank DeBerry	50.00	25.00	15.00
(23)	Lou DeVormer	50.00	25.00	15.00
(24)	Bill Doak	50.00	25.00	15.00
(25)	Pete Donohue	50.00	25.00	15.00
(26)	Pat Duncan	50.00	25.00	15.00
(27)	Jimmy Dykes	50.00	25.00	15.00
(28)	Urban Faber	150.00	75.00	45.00
(29)	Bib Falk (Bibb)	50.00	25.00	15.00
(30)	Frank Frisch	150.00	75.00	45.00
(31)	C. Galloway	50.00	25.00	15.00
(32)	Ed Gharrity	50.00	25.00	15.00
(33)	Chas. Glazner	50.00	25.00	15.00
(34)	Hank Gowdy	50.00	25.00	15.00
(35)	Tom Griffith	50.00	25.00	15.00
(36)	Burleigh Grimes	150.00	75.00	45.00
(37)	Ray Grimes	50.00	25.00	15.00
(38)	Heinie Groh	50.00	25.00	15.00
(39)	Joe Harris	50.00	25.00	15.00
(40)	Stanley Harris	150.00	75.00	45.00
(41)	Joe Hauser	50.00	25.00	15.00
(42)	Harry Heilmann	150.00	75.00	45.00
(43)	Walter Henline	50.00	25.00	15.00
(44)	Chas. Hollocher	50.00	25.00	15.00
(45)	Harry Hooper	150.00	75.00	45.00
(46)	Rogers Hornsby	150.00	75.00	45.00
(47)	Waite Hoyt	150.00	75.00	45.00
(48)	Wilbur Hubbell	50.00	25.00	15.00
(49)	Wm. Jacobson	50.00	25.00	15.00
(50)	Chas. Jamieson	50.00	25.00	15.00
(51)	S. Johnson	50.00	25.00	15.00
(52)	Walter Johnson	500.00	250.00	150.00
(53)	Jimmy Johnston	50.00	25.00	15.00
(54)	Joe Judge	50.00	25.00	15.00
(55)	Geo. Kelly	150.00	75.00	45.00
(56)	Lee King	50.00	25.00	15.00
(57)	Larry Kopff (Kopf)	50.00	25.00	15.00
(58)	Geo. Leverette	50.00	25.00	15.00
(59)	Al Mamaux	50.00	25.00	15.00
(60)	"Rabbit" Maranville	150.00	75.00	45.00
(61)	"Rube" Marquard	150.00	75.00	45.00
(62)	Martin McManus	50.00	25.00	15.00
(63)	Lee Meadows	50.00	25.00	15.00
(64)	Mike Menosky	50.00	25.00	15.00
(65)	Bob Meusel	50.00	25.00	15.00
(66)	Emil Meusel	50.00	25.00	15.00
(67)	Geo. Mogridge	50.00	25.00	15.00
(68)	John Morrison	50.00	25.00	15.00
(69)	Johnny Mostil	50.00	25.00	15.00
(70)	Roliene Naylor	50.00	25.00	15.00
(71)	Art Nehf	50.00	25.00	15.00
(72)	Joe Oeschger	50.00	25.00	15.00
(73)	Bob O'Farrell	50.00	25.00	15.00
(74)	Steve O'Neill	50.00	25.00	15.00
(75)	Frank Parkinson	50.00	25.00	15.00
(76)	Ralph Perkins	50.00	25.00	15.00
(77)	H. Pillette	50.00	25.00	15.00
(78)	Ralph Pinelli	50.00	25.00	15.00
(79)	Wallie Pipp (Wally)	60.00	30.00	18.00
(80)	Ray Powell	50.00	25.00	15.00
(81)	Jack Quinn	50.00	25.00	15.00

(82)	Goldie Rapp	50.00	25.00	15.00
(83)	Walter Reuther (Ruether)	50.00	25.00	15.00
(84)	Sam Rice	150.00	75.00	45.00
(85)	Emory Rigney	50.00	25.00	15.00
(86)	Eppa Rixey	150.00	75.00	45.00
(87)	Ed Rommel	50.00	25.00	15.00
(88)	Eddie Roush	150.00	75.00	45.00
(89)	Babe Ruth	3,500	1,750	1,000
(90)	Ray Schalk	150.00	75.00	45.00
(91)	Wallie Schang (Wally)	50.00	25.00	15.00
(92)	Walter Schmidt	50.00	25.00	15.00
(93)	Joe Schultz	50.00	25.00	15.00
(94)	Hank Severeid	50.00	25.00	15.00
(95)	Joe Sewell	150.00	75.00	45.00
(96)	Bob Shawkey	50.00	25.00	15.00
(97)	Earl Sheely	50.00	25.00	15.00
(98)	Will Sherdel	50.00	25.00	15.00
(99)	Urban Shocker	50.00	25.00	15.00
(100)	George Sisler	150.00	75.00	45.00
(101)	Earl Smith	50.00	25.00	15.00
(102)	Elmer Smith	50.00	25.00	15.00
(103)	Jack Smith	50.00	25.00	15.00
(104)	Bill Southworth	50.00	25.00	15.00
(105)	Tris Speaker	150.00	75.00	45.00
(106)	Arnold Statz	50.00	25.00	15.00
(107)	Milton Stock	50.00	25.00	15.00
(108)	Jim Tierney	50.00	25.00	15.00
(109)	Harold Traynor	150.00	75.00	45.00
(110)	Geo. Uhle	50.00	25.00	15.00
(111)	Bob Veach	50.00	25.00	15.00
(112)	Clarence Walker	50.00	25.00	15.00
(113)	Curtis Walker	50.00	25.00	15.00
(114)	Bill Wambsganss	50.00	25.00	15.00
(115)	Aaron Ward	50.00	25.00	15.00
(116)	Zach Wheat	150.00	75.00	45.00
(117)	Fred Williams	50.00	25.00	15.00
(118)	Ken Williams	50.00	25.00	15.00
(119)	Ivy Wingo	50.00	25.00	15.00
(120)	Joe Wood	75.00	37.50	22.50
(121)	J.T. Zachary	50.00	25.00	15.00

1922 W573

DAVE (BEAUTY) BANCROFT
SHORT STOP, NEW YORK NATIONALS

These cards, identified as W573 in the American Card Catalog, are blank-backed, black-and-white versions of the popular E120 American Caramel set. These "strip cards," were sold in strips of 10 for a penny. The cards measure about 2-1/16" x 3-3/8", but allowances in width must be made because the cards were hand-cut from a horizontal strip. Some cards have been found with the advertising of various firms on back.

		NM	EX	VG
Complete Set (240):		22,500	11,250	6,750
Common Player:		75.00	37.50	22.50
(1)	Charles (Babe) Adams	75.00	37.50	22.50
(2)	Eddie Ainsmith	75.00	37.50	22.50
(3)	Vic Aldridge	75.00	37.50	22.50
(4)	Grover C. Alexander	300.00	150.00	90.00
(5)	Jim Bagby	75.00	37.50	22.50
(6)	Frank (Home Run) Baker	200.00	100.00	60.00
(7)	Dave (Beauty) Bancroft	200.00	100.00	60.00
(8)	Walt Barbare	75.00	37.50	22.50
(9)	Turner Barber	75.00	37.50	22.50
(10)	Jess Barnes	75.00	37.50	22.50
(11)	Clyde Barnhart	75.00	37.50	22.50
(12)	John Bassler	75.00	37.50	22.50
(13)	Will Bayne	75.00	37.50	22.50
(14)	Walter (Huck) Betts	75.00	37.50	22.50
(15)	Carson Bigbee	75.00	37.50	22.50
(16)	Lu Blue	75.00	37.50	22.50
(17)	Norman Boeckel	75.00	37.50	22.50
(18)	Sammy Bohne	75.00	37.50	22.50
(19)	George Burns	75.00	37.50	22.50
(20)	George Burns	75.00	37.50	22.50
(21)	"Bullet Joe" Bush	75.00	37.50	22.50
(22)	Leon Cadore	75.00	37.50	22.50
(23)	Marty Callaghan	75.00	37.50	22.50
(24)	Frank Calloway (Callaway)	75.00	37.50	22.50
(25)	Max Carey	200.00	100.00	60.00
(26)	Jimmy Caveney	75.00	37.50	22.50
(27)	Virgil Cheeves	75.00	37.50	22.50
(28)	Vern Clemons	75.00	37.50	22.50
(29)	Ty Cob (Cobb)	1,350	675.00	400.00
(30)	Bert Cole	75.00	37.50	22.50
(31)	Eddie Collins	200.00	100.00	60.00

(32)	John (Shano) Collins	75.00	37.50	22.50
(33)	T.P. (Pat) Collins	75.00	37.50	22.50
(34)	Wilbur Cooper	75.00	37.50	22.50
(35)	Harry Courtney	75.00	37.50	22.50
(36)	Stanley Coveleskie (Coveleski)	200.00	100.00	60.00
(37)	Elmer Cox	75.00	37.50	22.50
(38)	Sam Crane	75.00	37.50	22.50
(39)	Walton Cruise	75.00	37.50	22.50
(40)	Bill Cunningham	75.00	37.50	22.50
(41)	George Cutshaw	75.00	37.50	22.50
(42)	Dave Danforth	75.00	37.50	22.50
(43)	Jake Daubert	75.00	37.50	22.50
(44)	George Dauss	75.00	37.50	22.50
(45)	Frank (Dixie) Davis	75.00	37.50	22.50
(46)	Hank DeBerry	75.00	37.50	22.50
(47)	Albert Devormer (Lou DeVormer)	75.00	37.50	22.50
(48)	Bill Doak	75.00	37.50	22.50
(49)	Pete Donohue	75.00	37.50	22.50
(50)	"Shufflin" Phil Douglas	75.00	37.50	22.50
(51)	Joe Dugan	75.00	37.50	22.50
(52)	Louis (Pat) Duncan	75.00	37.50	22.50
(53)	Jimmy Dykes	75.00	37.50	22.50
(54)	Howard Ehmke	75.00	37.50	22.50
(55)	Frank Ellerbe	75.00	37.50	22.50
(56)	Urban (Red) Faber	200.00	100.00	60.00
(57)	Bib Falk (Bibb)	75.00	37.50	22.50
(58)	Dana Fillingim	75.00	37.50	22.50
(59)	Max Flack	75.00	37.50	22.50
(60)	Ira Flagstead	75.00	37.50	22.50
(61)	Art Fletcher	75.00	37.50	22.50
(62)	Horace Ford	75.00	37.50	22.50
(63)	Jack Fournier	75.00	37.50	22.50
(64)	Frank Frisch	200.00	100.00	60.00
(65)	Ollie Fuhrman	75.00	37.50	22.50
(66)	Clarance Galloway	75.00	37.50	22.50
(67)	Larry Gardner	75.00	37.50	22.50
(68)	Walter Gerber	75.00	37.50	22.50
(69)	Ed Gharrity	75.00	37.50	22.50
(70)	John Gillespie	75.00	37.50	22.50
(71)	Chas. (Whitey) Glazner	75.00	37.50	22.50
(72)	Johnny Gooch	75.00	37.50	22.50
(73)	Leon Goslin	200.00	100.00	60.00
(74)	Hank Gowdy	75.00	37.50	22.50
(75)	John Graney	75.00	37.50	22.50
(76)	Tom Griffith	75.00	37.50	22.50
(77)	Burleigh Grimes	200.00	100.00	60.00
(78)	Oscar Ray Grimes	75.00	37.50	22.50
(79)	Charlie Grimm	75.00	37.50	22.50
(80)	Heinie Groh	75.00	37.50	22.50
(81)	Jesse Haines	200.00	100.00	60.00
(82)	Earl Hamilton	75.00	37.50	22.50
(83)	Gene (Bubbles) Hargrave	75.00	37.50	22.50
(84)	Bryan Harris (Harriss)	75.00	37.50	22.50
(85)	Joe Harris	75.00	37.50	22.50
(86)	Stanley Harris	200.00	100.00	60.00
(87)	Chas. (Dowdy) Hartnett	200.00	100.00	60.00
(88)	Bob Hasty	75.00	37.50	22.50
(89)	Joe Hauser	100.00	50.00	30.00
(90)	Clif Heathcote	75.00	37.50	22.50
(91)	Harry Heilmann	200.00	100.00	60.00
(92)	Walter (Butch) Henline	75.00	37.50	22.50
(93)	Clarence (Shovel) Hodge	75.00	37.50	22.50
(94)	Walter Holke	75.00	37.50	22.50
(95)	Charles Hollocher	75.00	37.50	22.50
(96)	Harry Hooper	200.00	100.00	60.00
(97)	Rogers Hornsby	250.00	125.00	75.00
(98)	Waite Hoyt	200.00	100.00	60.00
(99)	Wilbur Hubbell (Wilbert)	75.00	37.50	22.50
(100)	Bernard (Bud) Hungling	75.00	37.50	22.50
(101)	Will Jacobson	75.00	37.50	22.50
(102)	Charlie Jamieson	75.00	37.50	22.50
(103)	Ernie Johnson	75.00	37.50	22.50
(104)	Sylvester Johnson	75.00	37.50	22.50
(105)	Walter Johnson	750.00	375.00	225.00
(106)	Jimmy Johnston	75.00	37.50	22.50
(107)	W.R. (Doc) Johnston	75.00	37.50	22.50
(108)	"Deacon" Sam Jones	75.00	37.50	22.50
(109)	Bob Jones	75.00	37.50	22.50
(110)	Percy Jones	75.00	37.50	22.50
(111)	Joe Judge	75.00	37.50	22.50
(112)	Ben Karr	75.00	37.50	22.50
(113)	Johnny Kelleher	75.00	37.50	22.50
(114)	George Kelly	200.00	100.00	60.00
(115)	Lee King	75.00	37.50	22.50
(116)	Wm (Larry) Kopff (Kopf)	75.00	37.50	22.50
(117)	Marty Krug	75.00	37.50	22.50
(118)	Johnny Lavan	75.00	37.50	22.50
(119)	Nemo Leibold	75.00	37.50	22.50
(120)	Roy Leslie	75.00	37.50	22.50
(121)	George Leverette (Leverett)	75.00	37.50	22.50
(122)	Adolfo Luque	75.00	37.00	22.00
(123)	Walter Mails	75.00	37.50	22.50
(124)	Al Mamaux	75.00	37.50	22.50
(125)	"Rabbit" Maranville	200.00	100.00	60.00
(126)	Cliff Markle	75.00	37.50	22.50
(127)	Richard (Rube) Marquard	200.00	100.00	60.00
(128)	Carl Mays	75.00	37.50	22.50
(129)	Hervey McClellan (Harvey)	75.00	37.50	22.50
(130)	Austin McHenry	75.00	37.50	22.50
(131)	"Stuffy" McInnis	75.00	37.50	22.50
(132)	Martin McManus	75.00	37.50	22.50
(133)	Mike McNally	75.00	37.50	22.50
(134)	Hugh McQuillan	75.00	37.50	22.50
(135)	Lee Meadows	75.00	37.50	22.50
(136)	Mike Menosky	75.00	37.50	22.50
(137)	Bob (Dutch) Meusel	75.00	37.50	22.50
(138)	Emil (Irish) Meusel	75.00	37.50	22.50
(139)	Clyde Milan	75.00	37.50	22.50
(140)	Edmund (Bing) Miller	75.00	37.50	22.50
(141)	Elmer Miller	75.00	37.50	22.50
(142)	Lawrence (Hack) Miller	75.00	37.50	22.50
(143)	Clarence Mitchell	75.00	37.50	22.50
(144)	George Mogridge	75.00	37.50	22.50
(145)	Roy Moore	75.00	37.50	22.50
(146)	John L. Mokan	75.00	37.50	22.50
(147)	John Morrison	75.00	37.50	22.50

		NM	EX	VG
(148)	Johnny Mostil	75.00	37.50	22.50
(149)	Elmer Myers	75.00	37.50	22.50
(150)	Hy Myers	75.00	37.50	22.50
(151)	Roliene Naylor (Roleine)	75.00	37.50	22.50
(152)	Earl "Greasy" Neale	75.00	37.50	22.50
(153)	Art Nehf	75.00	37.50	22.50
(154)	Les Nunamaker	75.00	37.50	22.50
(155)	Joe Oeschger	75.00	37.50	22.50
(156)	Bob O'Farrell	75.00	37.50	22.50
(157)	Ivan Olson	75.00	37.50	22.50
(158)	George O'Neil	75.00	37.50	22.50
(159)	Steve O'Neill	75.00	37.50	22.50
(160)	Frank Parkinson	75.00	37.50	22.50
(161)	Roger Peckinpaugh	75.00	37.50	22.50
(162)	Herb Pennock	200.00	100.00	60.00
(163)	Ralph (Cy) Perkins	75.00	37.50	22.50
(164)	Will Pertica	75.00	37.50	22.50
(165)	Jack Peters	75.00	37.50	22.50
(166)	Tom Phillips	75.00	37.50	22.50
(167)	Val Picinich	75.00	37.50	22.50
(168)	Herman Pillette	75.00	37.50	22.50
(169)	Ralph Pinelli	75.00	37.50	22.50
(170)	Wallie Pipp	75.00	37.50	22.50
(171)	Clark Pittenger (Clarke)	75.00	37.50	22.50
(172)	Raymond Powell	75.00	37.50	22.50
(173)	Derrill Pratt	75.00	37.50	22.50
(174)	Jack Quinn	75.00	37.50	22.50
(175)	Joe (Goldie) Rapp	75.00	37.50	22.50
(176)	John Rawlings	75.00	37.50	22.50
(177)	Walter (Dutch) Reuther (Ruether)	75.00	37.50	22.50
(178)	Sam Rice	200.00	100.00	60.00
(179)	Emory Rigney	75.00	37.50	22.50
(180)	Jimmy Ring	75.00	37.50	22.50
(181)	Eppa Rixey	200.00	100.00	60.00
(182)	Charles Robertson	75.00	37.50	22.50
(183)	Ed Rommel	75.00	37.50	22.50
(184)	Eddie Roush	200.00	100.00	60.00
(185)	Harold (Muddy) Ruel (Herold)	75.00	37.50	22.50
(186)	Babe Ruth	2,750	1,375	825.00
(187)	Ray Schalk	200.00	100.00	60.00
(188)	Wallie Schang	75.00	37.50	22.50
(189)	Ray Schmandt	75.00	37.50	22.50
(190)	Walter Schmidt	75.00	37.50	22.50
(191)	Joe Schultz	75.00	37.50	22.50
(192)	Everett Scott	75.00	37.50	22.50
(193)	Henry Severeid	75.00	37.50	22.50
(194)	Joe Sewell	200.00	100.00	60.00
(195)	Howard Shanks	75.00	37.50	22.50
(196)	Bob Shawkey	75.00	37.50	22.50
(197)	Earl Sheely	75.00	37.50	22.50
(198)	Will Sherdel	75.00	37.50	22.50
(199)	Ralph Shinners	75.00	37.50	22.50
(200)	Urban Shocker	75.00	37.50	22.50
(201)	Charles (Chick) Shorten	75.00	37.50	22.50
(202)	George Sisler	200.00	100.00	60.00
(203)	Earl Smith	75.00	37.50	22.50
(204)	Earl Smith	75.00	37.50	22.50
(205)	Elmer Smith	75.00	37.50	22.50
(206)	Jack Smith	75.00	37.50	22.50
(207)	Sherrod Smith	75.00	37.50	22.50
(208)	Colonel Snover	75.00	37.50	22.50
(209)	Frank Snyder	75.00	37.50	22.50
(210)	Al Sothoron	75.00	37.50	22.50
(211)	Bill Southworth	75.00	37.50	22.50
(212)	Tris Speaker	250.00	125.00	75.00
(213)	Arnold Statz	75.00	37.50	22.50
(214)	Milton Stock	75.00	37.50	22.50
(215)	Amos Strunk	75.00	37.50	22.50
(216)	Jim Tierney	75.00	37.50	22.50
(217)	John Tobin	75.00	37.50	22.50
(218)	Fred Toney	75.00	37.50	22.50
(219)	George Toporcer	75.00	37.50	22.50
(220)	Harold (Pie) Traynor	200.00	100.00	60.00
(221)	George Uhle	75.00	37.50	22.50
(222)	Elam Vangilder	75.00	37.50	22.50
(223)	Bob Veach	75.00	37.50	22.50
(224)	Clarence (Tillie) Walker	75.00	37.50	22.50
(225)	Curtis Walker	75.00	37.50	22.50
(226)	Al Walters	75.00	37.50	22.50
(227)	Bill Wambsganss	75.00	37.50	22.50
(228)	Aaron Ward	75.00	37.50	22.50
(229)	John Watson	75.00	37.50	22.50
(230)	Frank Welch	75.00	37.50	22.50
(231)	Zach Wheat	200.00	100.00	60.00
(232)	Fred (Cy) Williams	75.00	37.50	22.50
(233)	Kenneth Williams	75.00	37.50	22.50
(234)	Ivy Wingo	75.00	37.50	22.50
(235)	Joe Wood	75.00	37.50	22.50
(236)	Lawrence Woodall	75.00	37.50	22.50
(237)	Russell Wrightstone	75.00	37.50	22.50
(238)	Everett Yaryan	75.00	37.50	22.50
(239)	Ross Young (Youngs)	200.00	100.00	60.00
(240)	J.T. Zachary	75.00	37.50	22.50

1933 W574

WHITE SOX

Cards in this set measure an unusual 2-1/4" x 2-7/8". They are unnumbered and are listed here in alphabetical order. The black-and-white photos have a facsimile autograph and team name at bottom.

		NM	EX	VG
Complete Set (29):		3,000	1,500	900.00
Common Player:		60.00	30.00	18.00
(1)	Dale Alexander	60.00	30.00	18.00
(2)	Ivy Paul Andrews	60.00	30.00	18.00
(3)	Luke Appling	250.00	100.00	50.00
(4)	Earl Averill	250.00	100.00	50.00
(5)	George Blaeholder	60.00	30.00	18.00
(6)	Irving Burns	60.00	30.00	18.00
(7)	Pat Caraway	60.00	30.00	18.00
(8)	Chalmer Cissell	60.00	30.00	18.00
(9)	Harry Davis	60.00	30.00	18.00
(10)	Jimmy Dykes	60.00	30.00	18.00
(11)	George Earnshaw	60.00	30.00	18.00
(12)	Urban Faber	250.00	100.00	50.00
(13)	Lewis Fonseca	60.00	30.00	18.00
(14)	Jimmy Foxx	450.00	180.00	90.00
(15)	Victor Frasier	60.00	30.00	18.00
(16)	Robert Grove	350.00	140.00	70.00
(17)	Frank Grube	60.00	30.00	18.00
(18)	Irving Hadley	60.00	30.00	18.00
(19)	Willie Kamm	60.00	30.00	18.00
(20)	Bill Killefer	60.00	30.00	18.00
(21)	Ralph Kress	60.00	30.00	18.00
(22)	Fred Marberry	60.00	30.00	18.00
(23)	Roger Peckinpaugh	60.00	30.00	18.00
(24)	Frank Reiber	60.00	30.00	18.00
(25)	Carl Reynolds	60.00	30.00	18.00
(26)	Al Simmons	250.00	100.00	50.00
(27)	Joe Vosmik	60.00	30.00	18.00
(28)	Gerald Walker	60.00	30.00	18.00
(29)	Whitlow Wyatt	60.00	30.00	18.00

1921-1922 W575-1

P. J. KILDUFF
2nd B.—Brooklyn Nationals

The known variations indicate this set was issued over a period of time, likely encompassing more than one calendar year or baseball season. Designated as W575 in the American Card Catalog, these "strip cards" are essentially blank-backed versions of the contemporary American Caramel E121 set, though the checklists do not exactly correspond. Ideally cut cards in W575-1 measure 2" x 3-1/4" and are printed in black-and-white. It is almost impossible to distinguish W575-1 cards from the blank-backed Koester's Bread Yankees and Giants cards issued to commemorate the 1921 "Subway" World Series. This checklist may not be complete. Gaps have been left among the assigned numbers to accommodate future additions.

		NM	EX	VG
Common Player:		40.00	20.00	12.00
(1)	Chas. "Babe" Adams	40.00	20.00	12.00
(2)	G.C. Alexander	350.00	175.00	100.00
(3)	Grover Alexander	350.00	175.00	100.00
(4)	Jim Bagby	40.00	20.00	12.00
(5)	J. Franklin Baker	175.00	85.00	50.00
(6)	Frank Baker	175.00	85.00	50.00
(7)	Dave Bancroft/Btg	175.00	85.00	50.00
(8)	Dave Bancroft/(Fielding)	175.00	85.00	50.00
(9)	Turner Barber	40.00	20.00	12.00
(10)	Jesse Barnes	40.00	20.00	12.00
(11)	Howard Berry	40.00	20.00	12.00
(12)	L. Bigbee (Should be C.)	40.00	20.00	12.00
(13)	Ping Bodie	40.00	20.00	12.00
(14)	"Ed" Brown	40.00	20.00	12.00
(15)	George Burns	40.00	20.00	12.00
(16)	Geo. J. Burns	40.00	20.00	12.00
(17)	"Bullet Joe" Bush	40.00	20.00	12.00
(18)	Owen Bush	40.00	20.00	12.00
(19)	Max Carey/Btg	175.00	85.00	50.00
(20)	Max Carey (Hands on hips.)	175.00	85.00	50.00
(21)	Ty Cobb	2,000	1,000	600.00
(22)	Eddie Collins	175.00	85.00	50.00
(23)	"Rip" Collins	40.00	20.00	12.00
(24)	Stanley Coveleskie (Coveleski)	175.00	85.00	50.00
(25)	Bill Cunningham	40.00	20.00	12.00
(26a)	Jake Daubert (1B.)	40.00	20.00	12.00
(26b)	Jake Daubert (1st B.)	40.00	20.00	12.00
(28)	George Dauss	40.00	20.00	12.00
(29)	Dixie Davis	40.00	20.00	12.00
(30)	Charles Deal (Dark uniform.)	40.00	20.00	12.00
(31)	Charles Deal (Light uniform.)	40.00	20.00	12.00
(32)	Lou DeVormer	40.00	20.00	12.00
(33)	William Doak	40.00	20.00	12.00

		NM	EX	VG
(34)	Bill Donovan/Pitching	40.00	20.00	12.00
(35)	Bill Donovan/Portrait	40.00	20.00	12.00
(36)	Phil Douglas	40.00	20.00	12.00
(37a)	Johnny Evers/Manager	175.00	85.00	50.00
(37b)	Johnny Evers/Manager	175.00	85.00	50.00
(39)	Urban Faber (Dark uniform.)	175.00	85.00	50.00
(40)	Urban Faber (White uniform.)	175.00	85.00	50.00
(42)	Bib Falk (Bibb)	40.00	20.00	12.00
(43)	Alex Ferguson	40.00	20.00	12.00
(44)	Wm. Fewster	40.00	20.00	12.00
(45)	Ira Flagstead	40.00	20.00	12.00
(46)	Art Fletcher	40.00	20.00	12.00
(47)	Eddie Foster	40.00	20.00	12.00
(48)	Frank Frisch	175.00	85.00	50.00
(49)	W.L. Gardner	40.00	20.00	12.00
(50)	Alexander Gaston	40.00	20.00	12.00
(51)	E.P. Gharrity	40.00	20.00	12.00
(52)	Chas. "Whitey" Glazner	40.00	20.00	12.00
(53)	"Kid" Gleason	40.00	20.00	12.00
(54)	"Mike" Gonzalez	40.00	20.00	12.00
(55)	Hank Gowdy	40.00	20.00	12.00
(56a)	John Graney (Util. o.f.)	40.00	20.00	12.00
(56b)	John Graney (O.F.)	40.00	20.00	12.00
(57)	Tom Griffith	40.00	20.00	12.00
(58)	Chas. Grimm	40.00	20.00	12.00
(59a)	Heinie Groh (Cincinnati)	40.00	20.00	12.00
(59b)	Heinie Groh (New York)	40.00	20.00	12.00
(62)	Jess Haines	175.00	85.00	50.00
(63)	Harry Harper	40.00	20.00	12.00
(64)	"Chicken" Hawks	40.00	20.00	12.00
(65)	Harry Heilman (Heilmann) (holding bat)	175.00	85.00	50.00
(66)	Harry Heilman (Heilmann) (running)	175.00	85.00	50.00
(67)	John Henry	40.00	20.00	12.00
(68)	Clarence Hodge	40.00	20.00	12.00
(69)	Fred Hoffman	40.00	20.00	12.00
(70a)	Walter Holke (1st B., portrait)	40.00	20.00	12.00
(70b)	Walter Holke (1B, portrait)	40.00	20.00	12.00
(71)	Walter Holke/Throwing	40.00	20.00	12.00
(72a)	Charles Hollacher (Name incorrect.)	40.00	20.00	12.00
(72b)	Charles Hollocher (Name correct.)	40.00	20.00	12.00
(73)	Harry Hooper	175.00	85.00	50.00
(74a)	Rogers Hornsby (2nd B.)	250.00	125.00	75.00
(74b)	Rogers Hornsby (O.F.)	250.00	125.00	75.00
(75)	Waite Hoyt	175.00	85.00	50.00
(76)	Miller Huggins	175.00	85.00	50.00
(78)	Wm. C. Jacobson	40.00	20.00	12.00
(79)	Hugh Jennings	175.00	85.00	50.00
(80)	Walter Johnson (Arms at chest.)	500.00	250.00	150.00
(81)	Walter Johnson/Throwing	500.00	250.00	150.00
(82)	James Johnston	40.00	20.00	12.00
(84)	Joe Judge/Btg	40.00	20.00	12.00
(85)	Joe Judge/Fielding	40.00	20.00	12.00
(86a)	George Kelly (1st B.)	175.00	85.00	50.00
(86b)	George Kelly (1B.)	175.00	85.00	50.00
(88)	Dick Kerr	40.00	20.00	12.00
(89)	P.J. Kilduff	40.00	20.00	12.00
(90a)	Bill Killefer	40.00	20.00	12.00
(90b)	Bill Killifer (Killefer)	40.00	20.00	12.00
(92)	John Lavan	40.00	20.00	12.00
(93)	"Nemo" Leibold	40.00	20.00	12.00
(94)	Duffy Lewis	40.00	20.00	12.00
(95)	Walter Mails	40.00	20.00	12.00
(96)	Al. Mamaux	40.00	20.00	12.00
(97)	"Rabbit" Maranville	175.00	85.00	50.00
(98)	Elwood Martin	40.00	20.00	12.00
(99a)	Carl Mays (Name correct.)	40.00	20.00	12.00
(99b)	Carl May (Mays)	40.00	20.00	12.00
(100)	John McGraw/Manager	175.00	85.00	50.00
(101)	John McGraw/Manager	175.00	85.00	50.00
(102)	Jack McInnis	40.00	20.00	12.00
(103a)	M.J. McNally (3B.)	40.00	20.00	12.00
(103b)	M.J. McNally (3rd B.)	40.00	20.00	12.00
(104)	Lee Meadows	40.00	20.00	12.00
(105)	Emil Meusel	40.00	20.00	12.00
(106)	R. Meusel	40.00	20.00	12.00
(107)	Clyde Milan	40.00	20.00	12.00
(108)	Elmer Miller	40.00	20.00	12.00
(109)	Otto Miller	40.00	20.00	12.00
(110)	John Mitchell (S.S.)	40.00	20.00	12.00
(111)	John Mitchell (3rd B.)	40.00	20.00	12.00
(112)	Guy Morton	40.00	20.00	12.00
(113)	Johnny Mostil	40.00	20.00	12.00
(114)	Eddie Mulligan	40.00	20.00	12.00
(115)	Eddie Murphy	40.00	20.00	12.00
(116a)	"Hy" Myers (C.F./O.F.)	40.00	20.00	12.00
(116b)	Hy Myers (O.F.)	40.00	20.00	12.00
(117a)	A.E. Neale	75.00	37.50	22.50
(117b)	Earl Neale	75.00	37.50	22.00
(119)	Arthur Nehf	40.00	20.00	12.00
(120)	Joe Oeschger	40.00	20.00	12.00
(122)	Chas. O'Leary	40.00	20.00	12.00
(123)	Steve O'Neill	40.00	20.00	12.00
(124a)	Roger Peckinbaugh (Name incorrect.)	40.00	20.00	12.00
(124b)	Roger Peckinpaugh (Name correct.)	40.00	20.00	12.00
(125a)	Jeff Pfeffer (Brooklyn)	40.00	20.00	12.00
(125b)	Jeff Pfeffer (St. Louis)	40.00	20.00	12.00
(127)	William Piercy	40.00	20.00	12.00
(128)	Walter Pipp	40.00	20.00	12.00
(129)	D.B. Pratt	40.00	20.00	12.00
(130)	Jack Quinn	40.00	20.00	12.00
(131a)	John Rawlings (2nd B.)	40.00	20.00	12.00
(131b)	John Rawlings (2B.)	40.00	20.00	12.00
(133a)	E.S. Rice (Name incorrect.)	175.00	85.00	50.00
(133b)	E.C. Rice (Name correct.)	175.00	85.00	50.00
(134a)	Eppa Rixey	175.00	85.00	50.00
(134b)	Eppa Rixey, Jr.	175.00	85.00	50.00
(136)	Wilbert Robinson	175.00	85.00	50.00
(137)	Tom Rogers	40.00	20.00	12.00
(139)	Ed Rounnel (Rommel)	40.00	20.00	12.00
(140)	Robert Roth	40.00	20.00	12.00
(142a)	Ed Roush (O.F.)	175.00	85.00	50.00

		NM	EX	VG
(142b)	Ed Roush (C.F.)	175.00	85.00	50.00
(144)	"Muddy" Ruel	40.00	20.00	12.00
(145)	Walter Ruether	40.00	20.00	12.00
(146a)	"Babe" Ruth (R.F.)	3,500	1,750	1,000
(146b)	Babe Ruth (L.F.)	3,500	1,750	1,000
(147)	Babe Ruth (w/man, bird.)	3,500	1,750	1,000
(148a)	Bill Ryan	40.00	20.00	12.00
(148b)	"Bill" Ryan	40.00	20.00	12.00
(149a)	"Slim" Sallee (Ball in hand.)	40.00	20.00	12.00
(149b)	"Slim" Sallee (No ball in hand.)	40.00	20.00	12.00
(151)	Ray Schalk/Bunting	175.00	85.00	50.00
(152)	Ray Schalk/Catching	175.00	85.00	50.00
(153a)	Walter Schang	40.00	20.00	12.00
(153b)	Wally Schang	40.00	20.00	12.00
(154a)	Fred Schupp (Name incorrect.)	40.00	20.00	12.00
(154b)	Ferd Schupp (Name correct.)	40.00	20.00	12.00
(155a)	Everett Scott (Boston)	40.00	20.00	12.00
(155b)	Everett Scott (New York)	40.00	20.00	12.00
(157)	Hank Severeid	40.00	20.00	12.00
(159)	Robert Shawkey	40.00	20.00	12.00
(160a)	"Pat" Shea	40.00	20.00	12.00
(160b)	Pat Shea	40.00	20.00	12.00
(161)	Earl Sheely	40.00	20.00	12.00
(163)	Urban Shocker	40.00	20.00	12.00
(165)	George Sisler/Btg	175.00	85.00	50.00
(166)	George Sisler/Throwing	175.00	85.00	50.00
(168)	Earl Smith	40.00	20.00	12.00
(169)	Elmer Smith	40.00	20.00	12.00
(170)	J. Carlisle Smith	40.00	20.00	12.00
(171)	Frank Snyder	40.00	20.00	12.00
(172)	Bill Southworth	40.00	20.00	12.00
(173a)	Tris Speaker (Large projection.)	250.00	125.00	75.00
(173b)	Tris Speaker (Small projection.)	250.00	125.00	75.00
(175a)	Charles Stengel/Btg	175.00	85.00	50.00
(175b)	Charles Stengel/Portrait	175.00	85.00	50.00
(177)	Milton Stock	40.00	20.00	12.00
(178a)	Amos Strunk (C.F.)	40.00	20.00	12.00
(178b)	Amos Strunk (O.F.)	40.00	20.00	12.00
(180a)	Zeb Terry (Dark uniform, 2nd B.)	40.00	20.00	12.00
(180b)	Zeb Terry (Dark uniform, 2B.)	40.00	20.00	12.00
(181)	Zeb Terry (White uniform.)	40.00	20.00	12.00
(182)	Chester Thomas	40.00	20.00	12.00
(183)	Fred Toney (Both feet on ground.)	40.00	20.00	12.00
(184)	Fred Toney (One foot in air.)	40.00	20.00	12.00
(185)	George Toporcer	40.00	20.00	12.00
(186)	George Tyler	40.00	20.00	12.00
(187)	Jim Vaughn (Plain uniform.)	40.00	20.00	12.00
(188)	Jim Vaughn (Striped uniform.)	40.00	20.00	12.00
(189)	Bob Veach (Arm raised.)	40.00	20.00	12.00
(190)	Bob Veach (Arms folded.)	40.00	20.00	12.00
(191a)	Oscar Vitt (3rd B.)	40.00	20.00	12.00
(191b)	Oscar Vitt (3B.)	40.00	20.00	12.00
(192)	Curtis Walker	40.00	20.00	12.00
(193)	W. Wambsganss	40.00	20.00	12.00
(194)	Carl Weilman	40.00	20.00	12.00
(195)	Zach Wheat	175.00	85.00	50.00
(196)	George Whitted	40.00	20.00	12.00
(197)	Fred Williams	40.00	20.00	12.00
(198)	Ivy B. Wingo	40.00	20.00	12.00
(199)	Lawton Witt	40.00	20.00	12.00
(200)	Joe Wood	100.00	50.00	30.00
(202)	Pep Young	40.00	20.00	12.00
(203)	Ross Young (Youngs)	175.00	85.00	50.00

1922 W575-2

The blank-back, black-and-white cards in this set measure a nominal 2-1/8" x 3-3/8". Because of the design of the cards the set is sometimes called the "autograph on shoulder" series. Some cards have the player's position and team added to the name inscription. The cards were produced by Kromo Gravue Photo Co., Detroit, Mich.

		NM	EX	VG
Complete Set (40):		10,000	5,000	3,000
Common Player:		75.00	37.50	22.50
(1)	Dave Bancroft	200.00	100.00	60.00
(2)	Johnnie Bassler	75.00	37.50	22.50
(3)	Joe Bush	75.00	37.50	22.50
(4)	Ty Cobb	2,000	1,000	600.00

		NM	EX	VG
(5)	Eddie Collins	200.00	100.00	60.00
(6)	Stan Coveleskie (Coveleski)	200.00	100.00	60.00
(7)	Jake Daubert	75.00	37.50	22.50
(8)	Joe Dugan	75.00	37.50	22.50
(9)	Red Faber	200.00	100.00	60.00
(10)	Frank Frisch	200.00	100.00	60.00
(11)	Walter H. Gerber	75.00	37.50	22.50
(12)	Harry Heilmann	200.00	100.00	60.00
(13)	Harry Hooper	200.00	100.00	60.00
(14)	Rogers Hornsby	300.00	150.00	90.00
(15)	Waite Hoyt	200.00	100.00	60.00
(16)	Joe Judge	75.00	37.50	22.50
(17)	Geo. Kelly	200.00	100.00	60.00
(18)	Rabbit Maranville	200.00	100.00	60.00
(19)	Rube Marquard	200.00	100.00	60.00
(20)	Guy Morton	75.00	37.50	22.50
(21)	Art Nehf	75.00	37.50	22.50
(22)	Derrill B. Pratt	75.00	37.50	22.50
(23)	Jimmy Ring	75.00	37.50	22.50
(24)	Eppa Rixey	200.00	100.00	60.00
(25)	Gene Robertson	75.00	37.50	22.50
(26)	Ed Rommell (Rommel)	75.00	37.50	22.50
(27)	Babe Ruth	3,500	1,750	1,050
(28)	Wally Schang	75.00	37.50	22.50
(29)	Everett Scott	75.00	37.50	22.50
(30)	Henry Severeid	75.00	37.50	22.50
(31)	Joe Sewell	200.00	100.00	60.00
(32)	Geo. Sisler	200.00	100.00	60.00
(33)	Tris Speaker	300.00	150.00	90.00
(34)	(Riggs) Stephenson	75.00	37.50	22.50
(35)	Zeb Terry	75.00	37.50	22.50
(36)	Bobbie Veach	75.00	37.50	22.50
(37)	Clarence Walker	75.00	37.50	22.50
(38)	Johnnie Walker	75.00	37.50	22.50
(39)	Zach Wheat	200.00	100.00	60.00
(40)	Kenneth Williams	75.00	37.50	22.50

1925-31 W590

CHARLEY GRIMM
1st Baseman
Chicago   N.L.

Originally unlisted in the American Card Catalog, this strip-card set was given the number W590 in later editions. It is part of a larger set cataloged as W580 which includes movie stars, boxers and other athletes. These cards measure approximately 1-3/8" x 2-1/2". Fronts have black-and-white player photos with a white border. In the bottom border is the player name, position, city and league or team nickname. Some cards can be found with a "Former" designation before the position. Several variations are known in team designations, indicating the set was probably reissued at least once between 1927-31. Backs are blank. Only the baseball players are listed here, in alphabetical order.

		NM	EX	VG
Common Player:		75.00	37.00	22.00
(1a)	Grover C. Alexander (Chicago N.L.)	300.00	150.00	90.00
(1b)	Grover C. Alexander (House of David)	600.00	300.00	180.00
(2a)	Dave Bancroft (Boston N.L.)	150.00	75.00	45.00
(2b)	Dave Bancroft (New York N.L.)	150.00	75.00	45.00
(3a)	Jess Barnes ("Pitcher" Boston N.L.)	75.00	37.50	22.50
(3b)	Jess Barnes ("Former Pitcher" Boston N.L.)	75.00	37.50	22.50
(4)	Ray Blades (St. Louis Cardinals)	75.00	37.50	22.50
(5)	Pictbred Bluege (Ossie)(Third Baseman)	75.00	37.50	22.50
(6a)	George Burns (New York N.L.)	75.00	37.50	22.50
(6b)	George Burns (Philadelphia N.L.)	75.00	37.50	22.50
(7a)	George Burns (Cleveland A.L. - 1st Baseman)	75.00	37.50	22.50
(7b)	George Burns (Cleveland A.L. - Former 1st Baseman)	75.00	37.50	22.50
(8)	Max Carey (Pittsburg N.L.)	150.00	75.00	45.00
(9a)	Caveney (Jimmy)(Short Stop)	75.00	37.50	22.50
(9b)	Caveney (Jimmy) (Former Short Stop)	75.00	37.50	22.50
(10)	"Ty" Cobb	1,300	650.00	390.00
(11a)	Eddie Collins (Chicago White Sox)	175.00	85.00	50.00
(11b)	Eddie Collins (Philadelphia A.L.)	175.00	85.00	50.00

		NM	EX	VG
(12)	George Dauss (Former Pitcher - Detroit)	75.00	37.50	22.50
(13)	"Red" Faber	150.00	75.00	45.00
(14a)	Frankie Frisch (New York N.L.)	175.00	85.00	50.00
(14b)	Frank Frisch (St. Louis N.L.)	175.00	85.00	50.00
(15)	Lou Gehrig (1st Baseman)	1,125	560.00	335.00
(17a)	Hank Gowdy (Catcher)	75.00	37.50	22.50
(17b)	Hank Gowdy (Former Catcher)	75.00	37.50	22.50
(18)	Sam Gray	75.00	37.50	22.50
(19)	Charley Grimm (Chicago N.L.)	75.00	37.50	22.50
(20)	"Buckey" Harris (Manager, Washington A.L.)	150.00	75.00	45.00
(21a)	Rogers Hornsby (St. Louis N.L.)	200.00	100.00	60.00
(21b)	Rogers Hornsby (Boston N.L.)	200.00	100.00	60.00
(22)	Travis Jackson (Short Stop, New York N.L.)	150.00	75.00	45.00
(23)	Walter Johnson/Pitcher	600.00	300.00	180.00
(24a)	George Kelly (New York N.L.)	150.00	75.00	45.00
(24b)	George Kelly (Chicago N.L.)	150.00	75.00	45.00
(25)	Fred Lindstrom	150.00	75.00	45.00
(26a)	Rabbit Maranville (Chicago N.L.)	150.00	75.00	45.00
(26b)	Rabbit Maranville (Boston N.L.)	150.00	75.00	45.00
(27)	Bob Meusel/Fielder (New York A.L.)	75.00	37.50	22.50
(28)	Jack Quinn	75.00	37.50	22.50
(29)	Eppa Rixey (Cincinnati N.L.)	150.00	75.00	45.00
(31)	Eddie Rommel	75.00	37.50	22.50
(32)	"Babe" Ruth (King of the Bat)	2,250	1,125	675.00
(33)	Heinie Sand	75.00	37.50	22.50
(34)	Geo. Sissler (Sisler)	150.00	75.00	45.00
(35)	Earl Smith	75.00	37.50	22.50
(36a)	Tris Speaker (Cleveland A.L.)	200.00	100.00	60.00
(36b)	Tris Speaker/Manager (Newark)	200.00	100.00	60.00
(37)	Roy Spencer	75.00	37.50	22.50
(38)	Milton Stock	75.00	37.50	22.50
(39a)	Phil Todt (Boston A.L.)	75.00	37.50	22.50
(39b)	Phil Todt (Philadelphia A.L.)	75.00	37.50	22.50
(40)	Dazzy Vance	150.00	75.00	45.00
(41)	Zach Wheat (Brooklyn N.L.)	150.00	75.00	45.00
(42a)	Kenneth Williams (St. Louis A.L.)	75.00	37.50	22.50
(42b)	Kenneth Williams (Boston A.L.)	75.00	37.50	22.50
(43a)	Ross Young (Youngs) (Right Fielder)	150.00	75.00	45.00
(43b)	Ross Young (Youngs) (Former Right Fielder)	150.00	75.00	45.00

1921 W9316

J. BOB VEACH

As crude as many of the strip cards of the era were, this issue is the worst. In the same blank-back format and size (about 1-1/2" x 2-1/2") as many contemporary strip cards, the set features 10 of the players from W519/W521. The artwork on these cards is very crudely done, almost child-like. The most striking feature about the pictures is the ruby red lips on the players. Unlisted in the American Card Catalog, this set was given the designation W9316 in John Stirling's Sports Card Catalog.

		NM	EX	VG
Complete Set (10):		2,000	800.00	400.00
Common Player:		175.00	70.00	35.00
1	Bob Veach	175.00	70.00	35.00
2	Frank Baker	275.00	110.00	55.00
3	Wilbur (Wilbert) Robinson	275.00	110.00	55.00
4	Johnny Griffith	175.00	70.00	35.00
5	Jimmie Johnston	175.00	70.00	35.00
6	Wallie Schange (Wally Schang)	175.00	70.00	35.00
7	Leon Cadore	175.00	70.00	35.00
8	George Sisler	275.00	110.00	55.00
9	Ray Schalk	275.00	110.00	55.00
10	Jesse Barnes	175.00	70.00	35.00

1972 The Yawkey Red Sox

The Yawkey Red Sox
THE EARLY YEARS
1933 - 1938

MORRIS BERG
("Moe")

Morris Berg
BRTR   Catcher
6'1",185   B:3-2-02
      ("Moe")
      (Died 5-29-72)
Moe managed to build a
15 year career out of
being a back-up catch-
er. The last 5 seasons
of that career were in
a BoSox uniform, 1935-
1939. During that time
he was in total of 148
games, with 107 hits,
in 406 AB's, for .262.

HELP FIGHT CANCER IN
     CHILDREN
GIVE TO THE JIMMY FUND

Boston Red Sox players of the 1930s are featured in this collectors' issue. The issue date given is
only a guess. The 2-1/2" x 3-1/2" cards have black-
and-whie player photos with brown borders and black
graphics. Backs are also in black-and-white with personal data, a career summary and a promotion for
the Red Sox long-time charity, The Jimmy Fund. The
unnumbered cards are listed here alphabetically.

		NM	EX	VG
Complete Set (45):		45.00	22.50	13.50
Common Player:		3.00	1.50	.90
(1)	Mel Almada	4.50	2.25	1.25
(2)	Morris "Moe" Berg	9.00	4.50	2.75
(3)	Max Bishop	3.00	1.50	.90
(4)	Doc Bowers	3.00	1.50	.90
(5)	Joe Cascarella	3.00	1.50	.90
(6)	Ben Chapman	3.00	1.50	.90
(7)	Bill Cissell	3.00	1.50	.90
(8)	Dusty Cooke	3.00	1.50	.90
(9)	Doc Cramer	3.00	1.50	.90
(10)	Joe Cronin	4.50	2.25	1.25
(11)	George Dickey	3.00	1.50	.90
(12)	Emerson Dickman	3.00	1.50	.90
(13)	Bobby Doerr	4.50	2.25	1.25
(14)	Rick Ferrell	4.50	2.25	1.25
(15)	Wes Ferrell	3.00	1.50	.90
(16)	Jimmie Foxx	7.50	3.75	2.25
(17)	Joe Gonzales	3.00	1.50	.90
(18)	Lefty Grove	6.00	3.00	1.75
(19)	Bucky Harris	4.50	2.25	1.25
(20)	Jim Henry	3.00	1.50	.90
(21)	Pinky Higgins	3.00	1.50	.90
(22)	Lefty Hockette	3.00	1.50	.90
(23)	Roy Johnson	3.00	1.50	.90
(24)	John Kroner	3.00	1.50	.90
(25)	Heinie Manush	4.50	2.25	1.25
(26)	Archie McKain	3.00	1.50	.90
(27)	Eric McNair	3.00	1.50	.90
(28)	Oscar Melillo	3.00	1.50	.90
(29)	Bing Miller	3.00	1.50	.90
(30)	Joe Mulligan	3.00	1.50	.90
(31)	Bobo Newsom	3.00	1.50	.90
(32)	Ted Olson	3.00	1.50	.90
(33)	Fritz Ostermueller	3.00	1.50	.90
(34)	George Pipgras	3.00	1.50	.90
(35)	Dusty Rhodes	3.00	1.50	.90
(36)	Walt Ripley	3.00	1.50	.90
(37)	Buck Rogers	3.00	1.50	.90
(38)	Jack Russell	3.00	1.50	.90
(39)	Tommy Thomas	3.00	1.50	.90
(40)	Hy Vandenberg	3.00	1.50	.90
(41)	Rube Walberg	3.00	1.50	.90
(42)	Johnny Welch	3.00	1.50	.90
(43)	Bill Werber	3.00	1.50	.90
(44)	Dib Williams	3.00	1.50	.90
(45)	Black Jack Wilson	3.00	1.50	.90

1959 Yoo-Hoo

CUT OFF HERE
'Me for "YOO-HOO,"
The Drink of Champions'
says Yogi Berra

Yoo-Hoo, Fans!

Issued as a promotion for Yoo-Hoo chocolate fla-
vored soft drink (it's a New York thing), this issue features five New York Yankees players. The black-and-
white blank-backed cards measure 2-7/16" x 5-1/8",
including a tab at the bottom which could be redeemed
for various prizes. The top of the card features a posed
spring training photo and includes a facsimile autograph
and "Me for Yoo-Hoo" slogan. Prices shown here are
for complete cards; cards without tabs would be valued
at one-half of these figures. A Mickey Mantle advertising piece in larger size is often collected as an adjunct
to the set, but no card of Mantle was issued. The Berra
card is considerably scarcer than the others.

		NM	EX	VG
Complete Set, W/Tabs (5):		4,500	2,250	1,350
Complete Set, No Tabs (5):		1,350	675.00	415.00
Common Player, W/Tab:		800.00	400.00	240.00
Common Player, No Tab:				
WITH TAB				
(1)	Yogi Berra	1,200	600.00	360.00
(2)	Whitey Ford	1,200	600.00	360.00
(3)	Tony Kubek	800.00	400.00	240.00
(4)	Gil McDougald	800.00	400.00	240.00
(5)	Bill Skowron	800.00	400.00	240.00
NO TAB				
(1)	Yogi Berra	300.00	150.00	90.00
(2)	Whitey Ford	300.00	150.00	90.00
(3)	Tony Kubek	250.00	125.00	75.00
(4)	Gil McDougald	250.00	125.00	75.00
(5)	Bill Skowron	250.00	125.00	75.00

1959 Yoo-Hoo Mickey Mantle

In a different format than the other contemporary
Yoo-Hoo Yankees cards, the manner of original distribution of this card is unclear. The 2-5/8" x 3-5/8"
black-and-white card has a portrait photo and
endorsement for the product on front. Back is blank.

	NM	EX	VG
Mickey Mantle	1,600	800.00	480.00

1959 Yoo-Hoo Bottle Caps

ME FOR
MICKEY MANTLE
YOO-HOO

These lids for the chocolate soft drink feature
black-and-white player portraits with the player name
across the chest and "ME FOR" above with "YOO-
HOO" below. Caps come in two styles, the older pry-
off style and a later screw-top.

		NM	EX	VG
Complete Set (6):		2,000	1,000	450.00
Common Player:		200.00	100.00	60.00
Screw-Tops: +25%				
(1)	Yogi Berra	400.00	200.00	90.00
(2)	Whitey Ford	400.00	200.00	90.00
(3)	Tony Kubek	225.00	110.00	50.00
(4)	Mickey Mantle	800.00	400.00	175.00
(5)	Gil McDougald	200.00	100.00	45.00
(6)	Moose Skowron	225.00	110.00	50.00

1964 Yoo-Hoo Counter Sign

Seven N.Y. Yankees and Bill Skowron in a Senators' cap are pictured on this 11" x 14" easel-back
counter display for the chocolate soft drink. Printed in
brown, yellow and white, the sign has a hand holding
a bottle in front of each player's portrait.

YOGI BERRA   MICKEY MANTLE   MOOSE SKOWRON   ELSTON HOWARD

"The drink of champions!"

Yoo-Hoo
CHOCOLATE DRINK

WITH THE "MILK CHOCOLATE" FLAVOR

JOE PEPITONE   TOM TRESH   BOBBY RICHARDSON   WHITEY FORD

	NM	EX	VG
	2,000	1,000	600.00

Yogi Berra, Whitey Ford,
Elston Howard, Mickey
Mantle, Joe Pepitone, Bobby
Richardson, Moose
Skowron, Tom Tresh

1927 York Caramel Type 1 (E210)

(26) TOM ZACHARY

York Caramel Co. York, Pa.

This is one of a series of sixty of the
most prominent stars in baseball.

"He hasn't a thing." But wins just
the same

TOM ZACHARY

Issued in 1927 by the York Caramel Co. of York,
Pa., these black-and-white cards are among the last
of the caramel issues. Measuring 1-3/8" x 2-1/2", they
are similar in appearance to earlier candy and
tobacco cards. Fronts have the player's name in capital letters beneath the photo preceded by a number
in parentheses. The back also lists the player's name
in capital letters, along with a brief phrase describing
him and the line, "This is one of a series of sixty of the
most prominent stars in baseball." The bottom of the
cards reads "York Caramel Co. York, Pa." The set
includes several variations and is designated in the
ACC as E210. It is closely related to the W502 set of
the same year. Cards can be found on white or gray
card stock. Type 1 cards can be differentiated from
Type 2s by the orientation of the back printing. On
Type 1 cards, the player name on back is at right
when a normally-viewed front is turned over.

		NM	EX	VG
Complete Set (60):		40,000	16,000	8,000
Common Player:		250.00	100.00	50.00
1	Burleigh Grimes	500.00	200.00	100.00
2	Walter Reuther (Ruether)	500.00	200.00	100.00
3	Joe Duggan (Dugan)	250.00	100.00	50.00
4	Red Faber	500.00	200.00	100.00
5	Gabby Hartnett	500.00	200.00	100.00
6	Babe Ruth	15,000	4,800	2,400
7	Bob Meusel	250.00	100.00	50.00
8a	Herb Pennock (Team name on jersey.)	500.00	200.00	100.00
8b	Herb Pennock (No team name.)	500.00	200.00	100.00
9	George Burns	250.00	100.00	50.00
10	Joe Sewell	500.00	200.00	100.00
11	George Uhle	250.00	100.00	50.00
12a	Bob O'Farrel (O'Farrell) (Team name on jersey.)	250.00	100.00	50.00
12b	Bob O'Farrel (O'Farrell) (No team name.)	250.00	100.00	50.00
13	Rogers Hornsby	600.00	240.00	120.00
14	Pie Traynor	500.00	200.00	100.00
15	Clarence Mitchell	250.00	100.00	50.00
16	Eppa Jepha Rixey (Jeptha)	500.00	200.00	100.00
17	Carl Mays	250.00	100.00	50.00
18	Adolph Luque (Adolfo)	500.00	200.00	100.00
19	Dave Bancroft	500.00	200.00	100.00
20	George Kelly	500.00	200.00	100.00
21	Ira Flagstead	250.00	100.00	50.00
22	Harry Heilmann	500.00	200.00	100.00
23	Raymond W. Shalk (Schalk)	500.00	200.00	100.00
24	Johnny Mostil	250.00	100.00	50.00

No.	Player	NM	EX	VG
25	Hack Wilson (Photo actually Art Wilson.)	500.00	200.00	100.00
26	Tom Zachary	250.00	100.00	50.00
27	Ty Cobb	6,500	2,600	1,300
28	Tris Speaker	600.00	240.00	120.00
29	Ralph Perkins	250.00	100.00	50.00
30	Jess Haines	500.00	200.00	100.00
31	Sherwood Smith (Photo actually Jack Coombs.)	250.00	100.00	50.00
32	Max Carey	500.00	200.00	100.00
33	Eugene Hargraves (Hargrave)	250.00	100.00	50.00
34	Miguel L. Gonzales (Miguel A. Gonzalez)	250.00	100.00	50.00
35a	Clifton Heathcot (Heathcote) (Team name on jersey.)	250.00	100.00	50.00
35b	Clifton Heathcot (Heathcote) (No team name.)	250.00	100.00	50.00
35c	Clifton Heathcot (Correct spelling.) (Team name on jersey.)	250.00	100.00	50.00
36	E.C. (Sam) Rice	500.00	200.00	100.00
37	Earl Sheely	250.00	100.00	50.00
38a	Emory E. Rigney (Team name on jersey.)	250.00	100.00	50.00
38b	Emory E. Rigney (No team name.)	250.00	100.00	50.00
39	Bib A. Falk (Bibb)	250.00	100.00	50.00
40	Nick Altrock	250.00	100.00	50.00
41	Stanley Harris	500.00	200.00	100.00
42	John J. McGraw	500.00	200.00	100.00
43	Wilbert Robinson	500.00	200.00	100.00
44	Grover Alexander	750.00	300.00	150.00
45	Walter Johnson	1,000	400.00	200.00
46	William H. Terry (Photo actually Zeb Terry.)	500.00	200.00	100.00
47	Edward Collins	500.00	200.00	100.00
48	Marty McManus	250.00	100.00	50.00
49	Leon (Goose) Goslin	500.00	200.00	100.00
50	Frank Frisch	500.00	200.00	100.00
51	Jimmie Dykes	250.00	100.00	50.00
52	Fred (Cy) Williams	250.00	100.00	50.00
53	Eddie Roush	500.00	200.00	100.00
54	George Sisler	500.00	200.00	100.00
55	Ed Rommel	250.00	100.00	50.00
56a	Rogers Peckinpaugh (Roger) (Card number upside-down.)			
56b	Rogers Peckinpaugh (Roger) (Card number corrected.)	250.00	100.00	50.00
57	Stanley Coveleskie (Coveleski)	500.00	200.00	100.00
58	Clarence Gallaway (Galloway)	250.00	100.00	50.00
59	Bob Shawkey	250.00	100.00	50.00
60	John P. McInnis	250.00	100.00	50.00

York Caramel Type 2 (E210)

Type 2 York Caramel is in the same size and format as the Type 1 cards. They can be differentiated from Type 1 cards by the orientation of the back printing. On Type 2 cards, the player name appears at left when a normally-held card is turned over. Type 2 cards are all printed on white stock. Some players and photos were changed, and the descriptive lines about the players were changed on most cards.

No.	Player	NM	EX	VG
	Complete Set (60):	45,000	18,000	9,000
	Common Player:	250.00	100.00	50.00
1	Burleigh Grimes	500.00	200.00	100.00
2	Walter Reuther (Ruether)	250.00	100.00	50.00
3	Joe Dugan	250.00	100.00	50.00
4	Red Faber	500.00	200.00	100.00
5	Gabby Hartnett	500.00	200.00	100.00
6	Babe Ruth	12,000	4,800	2,400
7	Bob Meusel	250.00	100.00	50.00
8	Herb Pennock (Profile)	500.00	200.00	100.00
9	George Burns	500.00	200.00	100.00
10	Joe Sewell	500.00	200.00	100.00
11	George Uhle	250.00	100.00	50.00
12	Bob O'Farrell	250.00	100.00	50.00
13	Rogers Hornsby	600.00	240.00	120.00
14	Pie Traynor	500.00	200.00	100.00
15	Clarence Mitchell	250.00	100.00	50.00
16	Eppa Rixey	500.00	200.00	100.00
17	Carl Mays	250.00	100.00	50.00
18	Adolfo Luque	250.00	100.00	50.00
19	Dave Bancroft	500.00	200.00	100.00
20	George Kelly	500.00	200.00	100.00
21	Earle Combs	500.00	200.00	100.00
22	Harry Heilmann	500.00	200.00	100.00
23	Ray W. Schalk	500.00	200.00	100.00
24	Johnny Mostil	250.00	100.00	50.00
25	Hack Wilson	500.00	200.00	100.00
26	Lou Gehrig	10,000	2,600	1,300
27	Ty Cobb	6,500	2,600	1,300
28	Tris Speaker	600.00	240.00	120.00
29	Tony Lazzeri	500.00	200.00	100.00
30	Waite Hoyt	500.00	200.00	100.00
31	Sherwood Smith (Photo actually Jack Coombs.)	250.00	100.00	50.00
32	Max Carey	500.00	200.00	100.00
33	Eugene Hargrave (Hargraves)	250.00	100.00	50.00
34	Miguel L. Gonzales (Miguel A. Gonzalez)	250.00	100.00	50.00
35	Joe Judge	250.00	100.00	50.00
36	E.C. (Sam) Rice	500.00	200.00	100.00
37	Earl Sheely	250.00	100.00	50.00
38	Sam Jones	250.00	100.00	50.00
39	Bib (Bibb) A. Falk	250.00	100.00	50.00
40	Willie Kamm	250.00	100.00	50.00
41	Stanley Harris	500.00	200.00	100.00
42	John J. McGraw	500.00	200.00	100.00
43	Artie Nehf	250.00	100.00	50.00
44	Grover Alexander	750.00	300.00	150.00

No.	Player	NM	EX	VG
45	Paul Waner	500.00	200.00	100.00
46	William H. Terry (Photo actually Zeb Terry.)	500.00	200.00	100.00
47	Glenn Wright	250.00	100.00	50.00
48	Earl Smith	250.00	100.00	50.00
49	Leon (Goose) Goslin	500.00	200.00	100.00
50	Frank Frisch	500.00	200.00	100.00
51	Joe Harris	250.00	100.00	50.00
52	Fred (Cy) Williams	250.00	100.00	50.00
53	Eddie Roush	500.00	200.00	100.00
54	George Sisler	500.00	200.00	100.00
55	Ed Rommel	250.00	100.00	50.00
56	Rogers Peckinpaugh (Roger)	250.00	100.00	50.00
57	Stanley Coveleskie (Coveleski)	500.00	200.00	100.00
58	Lester Bell	250.00	100.00	50.00
59	L. Waner	500.00	200.00	100.00
60	John P. McInnis	250.00	100.00	50.00

1917 Youth's Companion Stamps

The date attributed is speculative. This set of poster-stamps was issued to promote a Boston-based weekly magazine. Although he is not named, the left-handed pitcher depicted in very Red Sox-like uniform on one of the color litho stamps evidently looks enough like Babe Ruth that collectors have been willing to pay hundreds of dollars for examples of this scarce issue. The 1-7/8" x 2-1/2" stamp is, of course, blank-backed and is part of a set which featured other sporting activities, hobbys and topics suitable for young readers.

	NM	EX	VG
(Babe Ruth?)	600.00	300.00	180.00

1928 Yuengling's Ice Cream (F50)

Issued in 1928, the Yuengling's Ice Cream issue consists of 60 black-and-white cards measuring 1-3/8" x 2-1/2". The photos are similar to those used in the E210 and W502 sets. Other ice cream companies such as Harrington's and Tharp's produced nearly identical cards. Two types of cards are seen, though whether either or both can be found for all players is unknown. Besides typographical placement differences on front, the back of one type mentions a "$5.00 skooter" as a redemption, while the other type has no mention of the toy. Collectors could redeem an entire set of Yuengling's cards for a gallon of ice cream.

No.	Player	NM	EX	VG
	Complete Set (60):	45,000	18,000	9,000
	Common Player:	250.00	100.00	50.00
1	Burleigh Grimes	500.00	200.00	100.00
2	Walter Reuther (Ruether)	250.00	100.00	50.00
3	Joe Dugan	250.00	100.00	50.00
4	Red Faber	500.00	200.00	100.00
5	Gabby Hartnett	500.00	200.00	100.00
6	Babe Ruth	12,000	4,800	2,400
7	Bob Meusel	250.00	100.00	50.00
8	Herb Pennock	500.00	200.00	100.00
9	George Burns	250.00	100.00	50.00
10	Joe Sewell	500.00	200.00	100.00
11	George Uhle	250.00	100.00	50.00
12	Bob O'Farrell	250.00	100.00	50.00
13	Rogers Hornsby	600.00	240.00	120.00
14	"Pie" Traynor	500.00	200.00	100.00
15	Clarence Mitchell	250.00	100.00	50.00
16	Eppa Jepha Rixey	500.00	200.00	100.00
17	Carl Mays	250.00	100.00	50.00
18	Adolfo Luque	250.00	100.00	50.00
19	Dave Bancroft	500.00	200.00	100.00
20	George Kelly	500.00	200.00	100.00
21	Earl (Earle) Combs	500.00	200.00	100.00
22	Harry Heilmann	500.00	200.00	100.00
23	Ray W. Schalk	500.00	200.00	100.00
24	Johnny Mostil	250.00	100.00	50.00
25	Hack Wilson	500.00	200.00	100.00
26	Lou Gehrig	6,500	2,600	1,300
27	Ty Cobb	6,500	2,600	1,300
28	Tris Speaker	600.00	240.00	120.00
29	Tony Lazzeri	500.00	200.00	100.00
30	Waite Hoyt	500.00	200.00	100.00
31	Sherwood Smith	250.00	100.00	50.00
32	Max Carey	500.00	200.00	100.00
33	Eugene Hargrave	250.00	100.00	50.00
34	Miguel L. Gonzales (Miguel A. Gonzalez)	250.00	100.00	50.00
35	Joe Judge	250.00	100.00	50.00
36	E.C. (Sam) Rice	500.00	200.00	100.00
37	Earl Sheely	250.00	100.00	50.00
38	Sam Jones	250.00	100.00	50.00
39	Bib (Bibb) A. Falk	250.00	100.00	50.00
40	Willie Kamm	250.00	100.00	50.00
41	Stanley Harris	500.00	200.00	100.00
42	John J. McGraw	500.00	200.00	100.00
43	Artie Nehf	250.00	100.00	50.00
44	Grover Alexander	750.00	300.00	150.00
45	Paul Waner	500.00	200.00	100.00
46	William H. Terry	500.00	200.00	100.00
47	Glenn Wright	250.00	100.00	50.00
48	Earl Smith	250.00	100.00	50.00
49	Leon (Goose) Goslin	500.00	200.00	100.00
50	Frank Frisch	500.00	200.00	100.00
51	Joe Harris	250.00	100.00	50.00
52	Fred (Cy) Williams	250.00	100.00	50.00
53	Eddie Roush	500.00	200.00	100.00
54	George Sisler	500.00	200.00	100.00
55	Ed. Rommel	250.00	100.00	50.00
56	Rogers Peckinpaugh (Roger)	500.00	200.00	100.00
57	Stanley Coveleskie (Coveleski)	500.00	200.00	100.00
58	Lester Bell	250.00	100.00	50.00
59	L. Waner	500.00	200.00	100.00
60	John P. McInnis	250.00	100.00	50.00

1888 Yum Yum Tobacco (N403)

An extremely rare series of tobacco cards, this set was issued in 1888 by August Beck & Co., Chicago. The cards vary slightly in size but average 1-3/8" x 2-3/4". They were distributed in packages of the company's Yum Yum smoking and chewing tobacco and are found in two distinct types: photographic portraits and full-length action drawings copied from photos used in the Old Judge sets of the same period. In both types, the player's name and position appear in capital letters below the photo, while the very bottom of the card states: "Smoke and Chew "Yum Yum" Tobacco. A. Beck & Co. Chicago, Ill." Players from all eight National League clubs, plus Brooklyn of the American Association, are included in the set. The checklist here has gaps left to accommodate future additions.

No.	Player	NM	EX	VG
	Common Player:	7,200	3,600	2,190
(3)	Cap Anson/Portrait	36,000	18,000	10,800
(4)	Cap Anson/Btg	19,000	9,000	5,400
(7)	Lady Baldwin (Left arm extended.)	7,800	3,900	2,340
(11)	Dan Brouthers/Btg	14,400	7,200	4,320
(13)	Willard "California" Brown	7,800	3,900	2,340
(15)	Charles Buffington (Buffinton)	7,800	3,900	2,340
(17)	Tom Burns/Portrait	13,200	6,600	3,960
(18)	Tom Burns (With bat.)	7,800	3,900	2,340
(21)	John Clarkson/Portrait	24,000	12,000	7,200
(22)	John Clarkson/Throwing (Arm back.)	14,400	7,200	4,320

(25)	John Coleman/Portrait	13,200	6,600	3,960
(27)	Roger Connor/Btg	14,400	7,200	4,320
(28)	Roger Connor/Portrait	24,000	12,000	7,200
(30)	Larry Corcoran/Portrait	13,200	6,600	3,960
(34)	Tom Daily (Daly)/Portrait	13,800	6,900	4,140
	(Photo actually Billy Sunday.)			
(36)	Tom Deasley/Portrait	13,200	6,600	3,960
(39)	Mike Dorgan/Portrait	13,200	6,600	3,960
(40)	Dude Esterbrook/Portrait	13,200	6,600	3,960
(41)	Buck Ewing/Portrait	24,000	12,000	7,200
(42)	Buck Ewing (With bat.)	14,400	7,200	4,320
(45)	Silver Flint/Portrait	13,200	6,600	3,960
(47)	Jim Fogarty/Throwing	7,800	3,900	2,340
(49)	Pud Galvin	14,400	7,200	4,320
	(Ball in hands at chest.)			
(51)	Joe Gerhardt	13,200	6,600	3,960
(53)	Charlie Getzein (Getzien)	7,800	3,900	2,340
	(Holding ball.)			
(55)	Pete Gillespie/Portrait	13,200	6,600	3,960
(57)	Jack Glasscock	7,800	3,900	2,340
(59)	George Gore	7,800	3,900	2,340
	(Leaning on bat.)			
(61)	Ed Greer/Portrait	13,200	6,600	3,960
(65)	Tim Keefe (pitching)	14,400	7,200	4,320
(66)	Tim Keefe/Portrait	24,000	12,000	7,200
(67)	King Kelly/Btg	15,000	7,500	4,500
(68)	King Kelly	36,000	18,000	10,800
	(Photo, standing by urn.)			
(70)	Gus Krock/Portrait	13,200	6,600	3,960
(72)	Connie Mack	14,400	7,200	4,320
(74)	Kid Madden	7,800	3,900	2,340
	(Ball in raised right hand.)			
(76)	Doggie Miller	7,800	3,900	2,340
	(Leaning on bat.)			
(78)	John Morrill (Leaning on bat.)	7,800	3,900	2,340
(80)	James Mutrie/Portrait	13,200	6,600	3,960
(82)	Billy Nash (Holding bat.)	7,800	3,900	2,340
(84)	Jim O'Rourke/Portrait	24,000	12,000	7,200
(85)	Jim O'Rourke (With bat.)	14,400	7,200	4,320
(87)	Fred Pfeffer	7,800	3,900	2,340
	(Bat on shoulder.)			
(90)	Danny Richardson/Portrait	13,200	6,600	3,960
(92)	Chief Roseman/Portrait	13,200	6,600	3,960
(94)	Jimmy Ryan/Portrait	13,200	6,600	3,960
(95)	Jimmy Ryan/Throwing	7,800	3,900	2,340
(97)	Bill Sowders	7,800	3,900	2,340
	(Ball in hands at chest.)			
(100)	Marty Sullivan/Portrait	13,200	6,600	3,960
(102)	Billy Sunday/Fielding	14,400	7,200	4,320
(103)	Billy Sunday/Portrait (Photo	14,400	7,200	4,320
	actually Mark Baldwin.)			
(105)	Ezra Sutton/Btg	7,800	3,900	2,340
(110)	Mike Tiernan/Portrait	13,200	6,600	3,960
(111)	Mike Tiernan (With bat.)	7,800	3,900	2,340
(115)	Rip Van Haltren	13,200	6,600	3,960
	(Photo not Van Haltren.)			
(119)	John Ward/Portrait	24,000	12,000	7,200
(123)	Mickey Welch	14,400	7,200	4,320
	(Ball in hands at chest.)			
(124)	Mickey Welch/Portrait	24,000	12,000	7,200
(125)	Mickey Welch	14,400	7,200	4,320
	(Right arm extended.)			
(129)	Jim Whitney/Throwing	7,800	3,900	2,340
(133)	George Wood/Throwing	7,800	3,900	2,340
	(Arm behind head.)			

Z

1977 Zip'z Discs

Virtually identical in format to the several locally sponsored disc sets of the previous year, these 3-3/8" diameter player discs were given away at the sponsor's sundae bars around the cvountry. Some are found with a black rubber-stamp on back of the specific Zip's location. Discs once again feature black-and-white player portrait photos in the center of a baseball design. The left and right panels are in one of several bright colors. Licensed by the players' association through Mike Schechter Associates, the player photos carry no uniform logos. Backs are printed in reddish-orange. The unnumbered discs are checklisted here alphabetically.

		NM	EX	VG
Complete Set (70):		120.00	60.00	35.00
Common Player:		2.00	1.00	.60
(1)	Sal Bando	2.00	1.00	.60
(2)	Buddy Bell	2.00	1.00	.60
(3)	Johnny Bench	7.50	3.75	2.25
(4)	Larry Bowa	2.00	1.00	.60
(5)	Steve Braun	2.00	1.00	.60
(6)	George Brett	20.00	10.00	6.00
(7)	Lou Brock	6.00	3.00	1.75
(8)	Jeff Burroughs	2.00	1.00	.60
(9)	Bert Campaneris	2.00	1.00	.60
(10)	John Candelaria	2.00	1.00	.60
(11)	Jose Cardenal	2.00	1.00	.60
(12)	Rod Carew	6.00	3.00	1.75
(13)	Steve Carlton	6.00	3.00	1.75
(14)	Dave Cash	2.00	1.00	.60
(15)	Cesar Cedeno	2.00	1.00	.60
(16)	Ron Cey	2.00	1.00	.60
(17)	Dave Concepcion	2.00	1.00	.60
(18)	Dennis Eckersley	6.00	3.00	1.75
(19)	Mark Fidrych	3.00	1.50	.90
(20)	Rollie Fingers	6.00	3.00	1.75
(21)	Carlton Fisk	6.00	3.00	1.75
(22)	George Foster	2.00	1.00	.60
(23)	Wayne Garland	2.00	1.00	.60
(24)	Ralph Garr	2.00	1.00	.60
(25)	Steve Garvey	5.00	2.50	1.50
(26)	Cesar Geronimo	2.00	1.00	.60
(27)	Bobby Grich	2.00	1.00	.60
(28)	Ken Griffey Sr.	2.00	1.00	.60
(29)	Don Gullett	2.00	1.00	.60
(30)	Mike Hargrove	2.00	1.00	.60
(31)	Al Hrabosky	2.00	1.00	.60
(32)	Jim Hunter	6.00	3.00	1.75
(33)	Reggie Jackson	15.00	7.50	4.50
(34)	Randy Jones	2.00	1.00	.60
(35)	Dave Kingman	2.00	1.00	.60
(36)	Jerry Koosman	2.00	1.00	.60
(37)	Dave LaRoche	2.00	1.00	.60
(38)	Greg Luzinski	2.00	1.00	.60
(39)	Fred Lynn	2.00	1.00	.60
(40)	Bill Madlock	2.00	1.00	.60
(41)	Rick Manning	2.00	1.00	.60
(42)	Jon Matlock	2.00	1.00	.60
(43)	John Mayberry	2.00	1.00	.60
(44)	Hal McRae	2.00	1.00	.60
(45)	Andy Messersmith	2.00	1.00	.60
(46)	Rick Monday	2.00	1.00	.60
(47)	John Montefusco	2.00	1.00	.60
(48)	Joe Morgan	6.00	3.00	1.75
(49)	Thurman Munson	5.00	2.50	1.50
(50)	Bobby Murcer	2.00	1.00	.60
(51)	Bill North	2.00	1.00	.60
(52)	Jim Palmer	6.00	3.00	1.75
(53)	Tony Perez	6.00	3.00	1.75
(54)	Jerry Reuss	2.00	1.00	.60
(55)	Brooks Robinson	7.50	3.75	2.25
(56)	Pete Rose	25.00	12.50	7.50
(57)	Joe Rudi	2.00	1.00	.60
(58)	Nolan Ryan	35.00	17.50	10.00
(59)	Manny Sanguillen	2.00	1.00	.60
(60)	Mike Schmidt	15.00	7.50	4.50
(61)	Tom Seaver	7.50	3.75	2.25
(62)	Bill Singer	2.00	1.00	.60
(63)	Willie Stargell	6.00	3.00	1.75
(64)	Rusty Staub	2.00	1.00	.60
(65)	Luis Tiant	2.00	1.00	.60
(66)	Bob Watson	2.00	1.00	.60
(67)	Butch Wynegar	2.00	1.00	.60
(68)	Carl Yastrzemski	10.00	5.00	3.00
(69)	Robin Yount	6.00	3.00	1.75
(70)	Richie Zisk	2.00	1.00	.60

1950s Bill Zuber's Restaurant

These 3-1/2" x 5-1/2" black-and-white cards were produced as a promotional item for an Iowa restaurant owned by the former big league pitcher (1936-47). The semi-gloss front has a portrait and facsimile autograph. One type has an advertising message at left and the inscription, "Good Hitting." On back are printed Joe McCarthy's "Ten Commandments of Baseball." A second type has the inscription, "Sincerest Wishes," with a postcard-style back featuring an advertising message in the top-left corner.

		NM	EX	VG
(1)	Bill Zuber (Ten Commandments back.)	8.00	4.00	2.50
(2)	Bill Zuber (Postcard back.)	8.00	4.00	2.50

MODERN MAJOR LEAGUE (1981-2007)

The vast majority of cards and collectibles listed in this section were issued between 1981 and May 2007 and feature only major league players.

Because modern cards are generally not collected in lower grades, cards in this section carry only a Near Mint-to-Mint (NM/M) value quote. In general, post-1980 cards that grade Near Mint will retail at about 75 percent of the NM/M price, while Excellent condition cards bring about 40 percent. Cards in lesser condition are generally not considered collectible.

Values shown are for "raw" cards, that is, cards not authenticated, graded and encapsulated by an independent certification firm. Many cards that have been graded Mint, Gem Mint or Pristine by recognized major grading companies (SCD, SGC, BGS, GAI or PSA) will sell at a premium over the values quoted here. Because the standards and reputations of these companies vary widely, prices listed here cannot be correlated to values for "slabbed" cards

A

1991 Acme Reproductions Ryan-Seaver

This collectors' issue was produced in an edition of 10,000 in an over-size (4-1/4" x 3") format and style approximating a 1967 Topps card. The future Hall of Famers are pictured in their early days with the Mets. Facsimile autographs appear at the bottom of each photo. A total of 420 of the cards was authentically autographed by both players. Backs have a cartoon and biographical data on each player, plus a career summary up to 1967. Original issue price was $29, or $109 for the autographed card. Each came in a lucite holder with numbered certificate of authenticity. A 17-1/2" x 12-1/2" lithograph was produced in an edition of 3,000, with the first 1,000 autographed by each player. The litho sold for $219 autographed and $109 unsigned.

	NM/M
Nolan Ryan, Tom Seaver	10.00
Nolan Ryan, Tom Seaver/Auto.	200.00

1988 Action Packed

Action Packed released this test set in an effort to receive a license from Major League Baseball. The cards are styled like the Action Packed football issues on the card

fronts. The flip sides are styled like Score baseball cards. The Ozzie Smith card is considered scarcer than the other five cards in the test set, while a hoard of Mattingly cards revealed in 1998 drove down the price of his card. Action Packed did not receive a license to produce baseball cards.

		NM/M
Complete Set (6):		45.00
Common Player:		4.00
(1)	Wade Boggs	12.50
(2)	Andre Dawson	7.50
(3)	Dwight Gooden	6.00
(4)	Carney Lansford	6.00
(5)	Don Mattingly	6.00
(6)	Ozzie Smith	30.00

1992 Action Packed Promos

This set was produced to preview Action Packed's All-Star Gallery card issue. The promo cards are identical in format to the regularly issued cards and use the same player photos. The only differences in the promos are found on the back, where the card number is missing from the lower-left corner and where a white "1992 Prototype" is overprinted on the gray background beneath the black career highlights. The promos were widely distributed at trade shows and to Action Packed's dealer network. The unnumbered promo cards are checklisted here alphabetically.

		NM/M
Complete Set (5):		6.00
Common Player:		1.00
(1)	Yogi Berra	1.50
(2)	Bob Gibson	1.00
(3)	Willie Mays	3.00
(4)	Warren Spahn	1.00
(5)	Willie Stargell	1.00

1992 Action Packed All-Star Gallery Series 1

Action Packed, makers of a high quality, embossed style football card for several years, entered the baseball card field in 1992 with its 84-card All-

Star Gallery Series 1. The cards feature former baseball greats, with 72 of the 84 cards in color and the remaining in sepia tone. Each foil pack of seven cards reportedly contained at least one Hall of Famer, and the company also made special 24K gold leaf stamped cards of all of the HOFers that were randomly inserted in the packs.

		NM/M
Complete Set (84):		15.00
Common Player:		.10
Wax Pack (7):		.75
Wax Box (24):		12.50
1	Yogi Berra	.50
2	Lou Brock	.25
3	Bob Gibson	.25
4	Ferguson Jenkins	.25
5	Ralph Kiner	.25
6	Al Kaline	.40
7	Lou Boudreau	.25
8	Bobby Doerr	.25
9	Billy Herman	.25
10	Monte Irvin	.25
11	George Kell	.25
12	Robin Roberts	.25
13	Johnny Mize	.25
14	Willie Mays	1.00
15	Enos Slaughter	.25
16	Warren Spahn	.25
17	Willie Stargell	.25
18	Billy Williams	.25
19	Vernon Law	.10
20	Virgil Trucks	.10
21	Mel Parnell	.10
22	Wally Moon	.10
23	Gene Woodling	.10
24	Richie Ashburn	.25
25	Mark Fidrych	.25
26	Elroy Face	.10
27	Larry Doby	.25
28	Dick Groat	.10
29	Cesar Cedeno	.10
30	Bob Horner	.10
31	Bobby Richardson	.25
32	Bobby Murcer	.10
33	Gil McDougald	.10
34	Roy White	.10
35	Bill Skowron	.25
36	Mickey Lolich	.10
37	Minnie Minoso	.10
38	Billy Pierce	.10
39	Ron Santo	.25
40	Sal Bando	.10
41	Ralph Branca	.25
42	Bert Campaneris	.10
43	Joe Garagiola	.10
44	Vida Blue	.10
45	Frank Crosetti	.10
46	Luis Tiant	.10
47	Maury Wills	.10
48	Sam McDowell	.10

49	Jimmy Piersall	.10
50	Jim Lonborg	.10
51	Don Newcombe	.15
52	Bobby Thomson	.10
53	Wilbur Wood	.10
54	Carl Erskine	.10
55	Chris Chambliss	.10
56	Dave Kingman	.10
57	Ken Holtzman	.10
58	Bud Harrelson	.10
59	Clem Labine	.10
60	Tony Oliva	.10
61	George Foster	.10
62	Bobby Bonds	.10
63	Harvey Haddix	.10
64	Steve Garvey	.15
65	Rocky Colavito	.15
66	Orlando Cepeda	.25
67	Ed Lopat	.10
68	Al Oliver	.10
69	Bill Mazeroski	.25
70	Al Rosen	.10
71	Bob Grich	.10
72	Curt Flood	.10
73	Willie Horton	.10
74	Rico Carty	.10
75	Davey Johnson	.10
76	Don Kessinger	.10
77	Frank Thomas	.10
78	Bobby Shantz	.10
79	Herb Score	.10
80	Boog Powell	.15
81	Rusty Staub	.15
82	Bill Madlock	.10
83	Manny Mota	.10
84	Bill White	.10

1993 Action Packed All-Star Gallery Series 2

The Second Series of Action Packed All-Star Gallery was released in 1993, with cards numbered from 85 to 168. In a similar fashion to the First Series, Series Two features 52 cards in color, 31 in sepia tone and one as a colorized black and white. The series also includes two tongue-in-cheek cards - "Who's on First?" duo Bud Abbot and Lou Costello, and a card highlighting the TV and radio career of Bob Uecker.

		NM/M
Complete Set (84):		10.00
Common Player:		.10
Wax Pack (7):		1.00
Wax Box (24):		17.50
85	Cy Young	.15
86	Honus Wagner	.25
87	Christy Mathewson	.15
88	Ty Cobb	1.00

89	Eddie Collins	.10
90	Walter Johnson	.15
91	Tris Speaker	.15
92	Grover Alexander	.10
93	Edd Roush	.10
94	Babe Ruth	2.00
95	Rogers Hornsby	.15
96	Pie Traynor	.10
97	Lou Gehrig	1.00
98	Mickey Cochrane	.10
99	Lefty Grove	.10
100	Jimmie Foxx	.15
101	Tony Lazzeri	.10
102	Mel Ott	.10
103	Carl Hubbell	.10
104	Al Lopez	.10
105	Lefty Gomez	.10
106	Dizzy Dean	.10
107	Hank Greenberg	.10
108	Joe Medwick	.10
109	Arky Vaughan	.10
110	Bob Feller	.15
111	Hal Newhouser	.10
112	Early Wynn	.10
113	Bob Lemon	.10
114	Red Schoendienst	.10
115	Satchel Paige	.25
116	Whitey Ford	.15
117	Eddie Mathews	.15
118	Harmon Killebrew	.15
119	Roberto Clemente	1.50
120	Brooks Robinson	.15
121	Don Drysdale	.15
122	Luis Aparicio	.15
123	Willie McCovey	.15
124	Juan Marichal	.10
125	Gaylord Perry	.10
126	Catfish Hunter	.10
127	Jim Palmer	.15
128	Rod Carew	.15
129	Tom Seaver	.15
130	Rollie Fingers	.10
131	Joe Jackson	2.00
132	Pepper Martin	.10
133	Joe Gordon	.10
134	Marty Marion	.10
135	Allie Reynolds	.10
136	Johnny Sain	.10
137	Gil Hodges	.15
138	Ted Kluszewski	.15
139	Nellie Fox	.15
140	Billy Martin	.15
141	Smoky Burgess	.10
142	Lew Burdette	.10
143	Joe Black	.10
144	Don Larsen	.10
145	Ken Boyer	.10
146	Johnny Callison	.10
147	Norm Cash	.10
148	Keith Hernandez	.10
149	Jim Kaat	.10
150	Bill Freehan	.10
151	Joe Torre	.10
152	Bob Uecker	.15
153	Dave McNally	.10
154	Denny McLain	.10
155	Dick Allen	.10
156	Jimmy Wynn	.10
157	Tommy John	.10
158	Paul Blair	.10
159	Reggie Smith	.10
160	Jerry Koosman	.10
161	Thurman Munson	.15
162	Graig Nettles	.10
163	Ron Cey	.10
164	Cecil Cooper	.10
165	Dave Parker	.10
166	Jim Rice	.10
167	Kent Tekulve	.10
168	Who's on First? (Bud Abbott, Lou Costello)	.75

1992 Action Packed Diamond Stars

The first 18 cards from Series 1 Action Packed ASG were produced in a gold-enhanced boxed-set version which included a diamond chip in 14-Karat gold setting. Each card was serially numbered from within an edition of 500.

		NM/M
Complete Set (18):		80.00
Common Player:		4.00
1G	Yogi Berra	7.50
2G	Lou Brock	4.00
3G	Bob Gibson	4.00
4G	Ferguson Jenkins	4.00
5G	Ralph Kiner	4.00
6G	Al Kaline	5.00
7G	Lou Boudreau	4.00
8G	Bobby Doerr	4.00
9G	Billy Herman	4.00
10G	Monte Irvin	4.00
11G	George Kell	4.00
12G	Robin Roberts	4.00
13G	Johnny Mize	4.00
14G	Willie Mays	12.50
15G	Enos Slaughter	4.00
16G	Warren Spahn	4.00
17G	Willie Stargell	4.00
18G	Billy Williams	4.00

1992-93 Action Packed Gold

Essentially identical to the regular-issue Action Packed All-Star Gallery cards, these premium inserts are specially numbered with a "G" prefix and highlighted with 24-Karat gold detailing.

		NM/M
Complete Set (65):		175.00
Common Player:		2.50
Series 1		
1	Yogi Berra	4.00
2	Lou Brock	2.50
3	Bob Gibson	2.50
4	Ferguson Jenkins	2.50
5	Ralph Kiner	2.50
6	Al Kaline	3.50
7	Lou Boudreau	2.50
8	Bobby Doerr	2.50
9	Billy Herman	2.50
10	Monte Irvin	2.50
11	George Kell	2.50
12	Robin Roberts	2.50
13	Johnny Mize	2.50
14	Willie Mays	7.50
15	Enos Slaughter	2.50
16	Warren Spahn	2.50
17	Willie Stargell	2.50
18	Billy Williams	2.50
Series 2		
19	Cy Young	3.50
20	Honus Wagner	5.00
21	Christy Mathewson	3.50
22	Ty Cobb	6.00
23	Eddie Collins	2.50
24	Walter Johnson	3.50
25	Tris Speaker	3.50
26	Grover Alexander	3.25

27	Edd Roush	2.50
28	Babe Ruth	12.50
29	Rogers Hornsby	3.50
30	Pie Traynor	2.50
31	Lou Gehrig	10.00
32	Mickey Cochrane	3.25
33	Lefty Grove	3.25
34	Jimmie Foxx	3.50
35	Tony Lazzeri	2.50
36	Mel Ott	2.50
37	Carl Hubbell	2.50
38	Al Lopez	2.50
39	Lefty Gomez	2.50
40	Dizzy Dean	3.50
41	Hank Greenberg	3.50
42	Joe Medwick	2.50
43	Arky Vaughan	2.50
44	Bob Feller	3.50
45	Hal Newhouser	2.50
46	Early Wynn	2.50
47	Bob Lemon	2.50
48	Red Schoendienst	2.50
49	Satchel Paige	6.00
50	Whitey Ford	3.25
51	Eddie Mathews	3.25
52	Harmon Killebrew	3.25
53	Roberto Clemente	15.00
54	Brooks Robinson	3.25
55	Don Drysdale	3.25
56	Luis Aparicio	2.50
57	Willie McCovey	3.25
58	Juan Marichal	2.50
59	Gaylord Perry	2.50
60	Catfish Hunter	2.50
61	Jim Palmer	3.25
62	Rod Carew	3.25
63	Tom Seaver	3.25
64	Rollie Fingers	2.50
65	Who's on First?	
	(Bud Abbott,	
	Lou Costello)	3.50

1992 Action Packed 24-Kt. Gold

At least the first 18 cards in 1992 AP All-Star Gallery Series 1 were also issued in a full-coverage gold-foil version (as opposed to the gold-highlighted parallels). The cards are embossed front and back in gold-foil and numbered identically to the regular-issue cards. Each has a "24-Kt. Gold" imprint on front and is ink-jet serially numbered on back within an edition of 1,000.

		NM/M
Complete Set (18):		35.00
Common Player:		2.00
1	Yogi Berra	3.50
2	Lou Brock	2.50
3	Bob Gibson	2.50
4	Ferguson Jenkins	2.50
5	Ralph Kiner	2.50
6	Al Kaline	2.50
7	Lou Boudreau	2.00
8	Bobby Doerr	2.00
9	Billy Herman	2.00
10	Monte Irvin	2.00
11	George Kell	2.00
12	Robin Roberts	2.50
13	Johnny Mize	2.50
14	Willie Mays	7.50
15	Enos Slaughter	2.50
16	Warren Spahn	2.50
17	Willie Stargell	2.50
18	Billy Williams	2.50

1993 Action Packed Amoco/Coke

A special version of 18 of its All-Star Gallery cards was created by Action Packed for use as a premium by Amoco gas stations and Coca-Cola. Card fronts feature the same embossed color or sepia player photos with a heavily lacquered finish and gold-foil and black borders. Gray backs have bio-

---

AL KALINE

graphical and career data, a few stats and sponsors' logos. Complete sets were available via a mail-in offer from Coke products. Most of these cards share card numbers and photos with AP's Series I ASG cards.

		NM/M
Complete Set (18):		4.00
Common Player:		.50
1	Yogi Berra	1.00
2	Lou Brock	.50
3	Bob Gibson	.50
4	Red Schoendienst	.50
5	Ralph Kiner	.50
6	Al Kaline	.75
7	Lou Boudreau	.50
8	Bobby Doerr	.50
9	Gaylord Perry	.50
10	Monte Irvin	.50
11	George Kell	.50
12	Robin Roberts	.60
13	Johnny Mize	.60
14	Willie Mays	2.00
15	Enos Slaughter	.50
16	Warren Spahn	.60
17	Willie Stargell	.60
18	Billy Williams	.50

1993 Action Packed 24-Kt. Gold

The first 46 cards of AP's All-Star Gallery Series II, along with the special Abbott & Costello card were produced in a limited gold edition as random pack inserts. Labeled "24-Kt. Gold" on front, the cards have the same format and design as the regular-issue, except the embossed front photo and incuse stats on back are on solid gold foil. Each gold card carries a black ink-jetted serial number on back from within an edition of either 500 or 1,000.

		NM/M
Complete Set (47):		80.00
Common Player:		2.00
85	Cy Young	3.00
86	Honus Wagner	4.00
87	Christy Mathewson	4.00
88	Ty Cobb	6.00
89	Eddie Collins	2.00
90	Walter Johnson	4.00
91	Tris Speaker	2.00
92	Grover Alexander	2.00
93	Edd Roush	2.00
94	Babe Ruth	16.00
95	Rogers Hornsby	2.00
96	Pie Traynor	2.00
97	Lou Gehrig	10.00
98	Mickey Cochrane	2.00
99	Lefty Grove	2.00
100	Jimmie Foxx	3.00
101	Tony Lazzeri	2.00
102	Mel Ott	2.00
103	Carl Hubbell	2.00
104	Al Lopez	2.00
105	Lefty Gomez	2.00
106	Dizzy Dean	3.00
107	Hank Greenberg	2.00

108	Joe Medwick	2.00
109	Arky Vaughan	2.00
110	Bob Feller	3.00
111	Hal Newhouser	2.00
112	Early Wynn	2.00
113	Bob Lemon	2.00
114	Red Schoendienst	2.00
115	Satchel Paige	4.00
116	Whitey Ford	4.00
117	Eddie Mathews	2.00
118	Harmon Killebrew	2.00
119	Roberto Clemente	12.00
120	Brooks Robinson	2.00
121	Don Drysdale	2.00
122	Luis Aparicio	2.00
123	Willie McCovey	2.00
124	Juan Marichal	2.00
125	Gaylord Perry	2.00
126	Catfish Hunter	2.00
127	Jim Palmer	2.00
128	Rod Carew	2.00
129	Tom Seaver	2.00
130	Rollie Fingers	2.00
168	Who's on First?	
	(Lou Costello,	
	Bud Abbott)	3.00

1993 Action Packed Tom Seaver Prototypes

TOM SEAVER

Tom Seaver's career was highlighted in this five-card promo set. Each card has an embossed front color photo surrounded by three gold pinstripes and a red border. Seaver's name is in red in a gold bar at bottom. Backs are printed in black and gold with a white undertype reading "1993 Prototype." Backs have biographical and career data, lifetime stats and a few sentences of career highlights. Cards have a "TS" prefix to the card number.

		NM/M
Complete Set (5):		8.00
Common Card:		2.00
1	The Franchise	2.00
2	Amazin' Mets	3.25
3	A Tearful Goodbye	2.00
4	Tom Terrific	2.00
5	Dazzling the Windy	
	City	2.00

1983 Affiliated Food Rangers

BILL STEIN

This set, featuring the Texas Rangers, was issued as a promotion by the Affiliated Food Stores chain of Arlington, Texas. Complete sets were given to youngsters 13 and under at the September 3 Rangers game. Cards measure 2-3/8" x 3-1/2" and feature a full-color photo on the front. Also on the front, located inside a blue box, is the player's name, uniform number, and "1983 Rangers." Backs

---

have a small player photo plus biographical and statistical information, along with the Affiliated logo and a brief promotional message. A total of 10,000 sets was reportedly printed. Cards are numbered by the players' uniform numbers in the checklist that follows.

		NM/M
Complete Set (28):		6.00
Common Player:		.25
1	Bill Stein	.25
2	Mike Richardt	.25
3	Wayne Tolleson	.25
5	Billy Sample	.25
6	Bobby Jones	.25
7	Bucky Dent	.35
8	Bobby Johnson	.25
9	Pete O'Brien	.25
10	Jim Sundberg	.25
11	Doug Rader	.25
12	Dave Hostetler	.25
14	Larry Biittner	.25
15	Larry Parrish	.25
17	Mickey Rivers	.30
21	Odell Jones	.25
24	Dave Schmidt	.25
25	Buddy Bell	.35
26	George Wright	.25
27	Frank Tanana	.25
29	John Butcher	.25
32	Jon Matlack	.25
40	Rick Honeycutt	.25
41	Dave Tobik	.25
44	Danny Darwin	.25
46	Jim Anderson	.25
47	Mike Smithson	.25
49	Charlie Hough	.30
---	Coaching Staff	
	(Rich Donnelly, Glenn Ezell,	
	Merv Rettenmund,	
	Dick Such,	
	Wayne Terwilliger)	.25

1990 Agfa Film

Rollie Fingers

This "old-timers" set was distributed in three-card packs with the purchase of Agfa Film. Produced by Michael Schecter Associates, whose logo appears on the back, the cards were not licensed by Major League Baseball, so team logos had to be eliminated from the photos. Cards have a white background with the film company's logos in the upper corners. Backs are in black-and-white and have full major league regular season and post-season stats.

		NM/M
Complete Set (22):		7.50
Common Player:		.50
1	Willie Mays	2.00
2	Carl Yastrzemski	1.00
3	Harmon Killebrew	1.00
4	Joe Torre	.50
5	Al Kaline	1.00
6	Hank Aaron	2.00
7	Rod Carew	.75
8	Roberto Clemente	2.50
9	Luis Aparicio	.75
10	Roger Maris	1.00
11	Joe Morgan	.75
12	Maury Wills	.75
13	Brooks Robinson	1.00
14	Tom Seaver	.75
15	Steve Carlton	.75
16	Whitey Ford	.75
17	Jim Palmer	.75
18	Rollie Fingers	.75
19	Bruce Sutter	.50
20	Willie McCovey	.75
21	Mike Schmidt	1.50
22	Yogi Berra	.75

1990 All American Baseball Team

Produced by Mike Schecter Associates, this 24-card set includes many of the top play-

---

1990 All American Baseball Team
Limited Collectors' Edition

KENT HRBEK
Minnesota Twins

ers in the game. Team logos are airbrushed from the color photo on front, which is surrounded by a red, white and blue border and the MLB Players Association logo. The backs are printed in blue on white stock, with a facsimile autograph appearing above the statistics.

		NM/M
Complete Set (24):		20.00
Common Player:		.50
1	George Brett	1.50
2	Mark McGwire	3.00
3	Wade Boggs	1.25
4	Cal Ripken, Jr.	4.00
5	Rickey Henderson	1.00
6	Dwight Gooden	.50
7	Bo Jackson	.75
8	Roger Clemens	1.50
9	Orel Hershiser	.50
10	Ozzie Smith	1.25
11	Don Mattingly	2.00
12	Kirby Puckett	1.25
13	Robin Yount	1.00
14	Tony Gwynn	1.25
15	Jose Canseco	.60
16	Nolan Ryan	4.00
17	Ken Griffey Jr.	2.50
18	Will Clark	.50
19	Ryne Sandberg	1.25
20	Kent Hrbek	.50
21	Carlton Fisk	1.00
22	Paul Molitor	1.00
23	Dave Winfield	1.00
24	Andre Dawson	.60

1987 Allstate Insurance

HANK AARON

LIFE GRAND SLAM

This six-card set was the second promotional series of baseball cards created by Allstate Insurance graphic artist Ray Lending for internal use by the company. Modeled after the famous "Diamond Stars" from the 1930s, this set features full-color player portraits of legendary sluggers. "Life Grand Slam" (the promotion theme) is printed beneath the player portrait and the player's name appears in an upper corner. Black and white backs provide personal information, player profiles and career highlights. 15,000 sets of the cards were distributed, although only a few filtered into the collecting hobby. Cards measure 2-3/4" x 3-5/8" in size. Full-color 22" x 28" reproductions of the cards in this set were produced in poster format.

		NM/M
Complete Set (6):		75.00
Common Player:		10.00
(1)	Hank Aaron	12.00
(2)	Joe DiMaggio	15.00

---

(3)	Jimmie Foxx	10.00
(4)	Lou Gehrig	15.00
(5)	Babe Ruth	20.00
(6)	Ted Williams	15.00

1994 AMC Theaters S.F. Giants

This series of large-format (about 4-1/4" x 11"), blank-back photocards was sponsored by a Bay Area movie house chain. Cards have black-and-white action photos at center with player identification below. At top is a team logo, at bottom is a sponsor's logo. The unnumbered cards are checklisted here in alphabetical order.

		NM/M
Complete Set (33):		30.00
Common Player:		1.00
(1)	Dusty Baker	1.25
(2)	Rod Beck	
	(Ready to pitch.)	1.00
(3)	Rod Beck (Piching follow	
	through.)	1.00
(4)	Mike Benjamin	1.00
(5)	Todd Benzinger	1.00
(6)	Barry Bonds	
	('93 jersey)	9.00
(7)	Barry Bonds	
	('94 jersey)	9.00
(8)	Dave Burba	1.00
(9)	John Burkett	1.00
(10)	Mark Carreon	1.00
(11)	Royce Clayton	1.00
(12)	Steve Frey	1.00
(13)	Bryan Hickerson	1.00
(14)	Mike Jackson	1.00
(15)	Darren Lewis	1.00
(16)	Kirt Manwaring	1.00
(17)	Dave Martinez	
	('93 jersey)	1.00
(18)	Dave Martinez	
	('94 jersey)	1.00
(19)	Willie McGee	1.00
(20)	Rich Monteleone	1.00
(21)	John Patterson	1.00
(22)	Mark Portugal	
	(Negative reversed,	
	pitching lefty.)	1.00
(23)	Mark Portugal (Correct,	
	pitching righty.)	1.00
(24)	Jeff Reed	1.00
(25)	Kevin Rogers/Standing	1.00
(26)	Kevin Rogers/Pitching	1.00
(27)	Steve Scarsone	1.00
(28)	Bill Swift	1.00
(29)	Robby Thompson	
	('93 jersey)	1.00
(30)	Robby Thompson	
	('94 jersey)	1.00
(31)	Salomon Torres	1.00
(32)	Matt Williams/Btg	1.50
(33)	Matt Williams/Fielding	1.50

1994 American Archives Origins of Baseball

ORIGINS of BASEBALL

BID McPHEE

This collectors' issue presents the history of baseball in America from 1744-1899. Sold in box-set form only, the cards are in standard 2-1/2" x 3-1/2" format. Fronts feature sepia-toned photos and line-art on a black background. Backs have a lengthy narrative, also printed in sepia on black. Both sides are UV coated. Individual cards feature early players, team photos, game action scenes or other historical vignettes. The set was produced by American Archives.

		NM/M
Complete Set (101):		6.00
Common Card:		.10
1	Abner Doubleday	.10

2	Doubleday Field	.10
3	Rounders 1744	.10
4	Early Baseball 700 A.D.	.10
5	The Knickerbockers	.10
6	Alex Cartwright	.10
7	Baseball in the 1850s	.10
8	Social Clubs	.10
9	Brooklyn Eckfords	.10
10	New England Baseball	.10
11	Henry Chadwick	.10
12	Brooklyn Excelsiors	.10
13	Abraham Lincoln	.10
14	Andrew Johnson	.10
15	First Enclosed Park	.10
16	Brooklyn Atlantics	.10
17	James Creighton	.10
18	Baseball in the 1860s	.10
19	1869 Red Stockings	.10
20	Cincinnati Celebration	.10
21	Harry Wright	.10
22	Boston Ball Club 1872	.10
23	Arthur Cummings	.10
24	William Hulbert	.10
25	George Wright	.10
26	Albert Spalding	.10
27	Albert Bushong	.10
28	Bid McPhee	.10
29	James O'Rourke	.10
30	Pud Galvin	.10
31	Edwin Bligh	.10
32	William Purcell	.10
33	Roger Connor	.10
34	Cincinnati Ball Club 1882	.10
35	Peter Browning	.10
36	William Gleason	.10
37	Paul Hines	.10
38	Baseball in the 1880s	.10
39	Robert Carruthers	.10
40	New York Metropolitans	.10
41	St. George's Field	.10
42	Charles Radbourne	.10
43	George Andrews	.10
44	William Hoy	.10
45	Chicago Ball Club 1886	.10
46	Cap Anson	.10
47	John Clarkson	.10
48	Mike Kelly	.10
49	Buffalo Bisons 1887	.10
50	Moses Walker	.10
51	Detroit Ball Club 1887	.10
52	Little League	.10
53	Louisville Ball Club 1888	.10
54	John Farrell	.10
55	Walter Latham	.10
56	Fred Dunlap	.10
57	Tim Keefe	.10
58	Cincinnati Ball Club 1888	.10
59	1889 World Tour	.10
60	Dan Brouthers	.10
61	John M. Ward	.10
62	Albert Spalding	.10
63	The Baseball Cap	.10
64	Tom Esterbrook	.10
65	Mark Baldwin	.10
66	Tony Mullane	.10
67	John Glasscock	.10
68	Amos Rusie	.10
69	Jake Beckley	.10
70	Jimmy Collins	.10
71	Charles Comiskey	.10
72	Tom Connolly	.10
73	Mickey Welch	.10
74	Ed Delahanty	.10
75	Hugh Duffy	.10
76	Buck Ewing	.10
77	Clark Griffith	.10
78	Kid Nichols	.10
79	Billy Hamilton	.10
80	Ban Johnson	.10
81	Willie Keeler	.10
82	Bobby Wallace	.10
83	Napoleon Lajoie	.10
84	Connie Mack	.10
85	Fred Clarke	.10
86	Tommy McCarthy	.10
87	John McGraw	.10
88	Jesse Burkett	.10
89	Frank Chance	.10
90	Mordecai Brown	.10
91	New York Nationals	.10
92	Jack Chesbro	.10
93	Sam Thompson	.10
94	Boston v. New York 1891	.10
95	Rube Waddell	.10
96	Joel Kelley	.10
97	Addie Joss	.10
98	The Boston Beaneaters	.10
99	Baltimore Baseball Club	.10
100	The Game in 1899	.10
----	Bibliography	.10

1989 Ames 20/20 Club

This 33-card set was produced by Topps for the Ames toy store chain. As its name implies, the special boxed set highlights players who have recorded 20 home runs and 20

stolen bases in the same season. The glossy cards feature action or posed photos on the front with the player's name at the top and "Ames 20/20 Club" along the bottom. The Topps logo appears in the upper-right corner. Backs have lifetime stats, biographical data and career highlights.

		NM/M
Complete Set (33):		4.00
Common Player:		.10
1	Jesse Barfield	.10
2	Kevin Bass	.10
3	Don Baylor	.10
4	George Bell	.10
5	Barry Bonds	2.00
6	Phil Bradley	.10
7	Ellis Burks	.10
8	Jose Canseco	.25
9	Joe Carter	.10
10	Kal Daniels	.10
11	Eric Davis	.10
12	Mike Davis	.10
13	Andre Dawson	.25
14	Kirk Gibson	.10
15	Pedro Guerrero	.10
16	Rickey Henderson	.45
17	Bo Jackson	.25
18	Howard Johnson	.10
19	Jeffrey Leonard	.10
20	Kevin McReynolds	.10
21	Dale Murphy	.25
22	Dwayne Murphy	.10
23	Dave Parker	.10
24	Kirby Puckett	.60
25	Juan Samuel	.10
26	Ryne Sandberg	.60
27	Mike Schmidt	.75
28	Darryl Strawberry	.10
29	Alan Trammell	.10
30	Andy Van Slyke	.10
31	Devon White	.10
32	Dave Winfield	.45
33	Robin Yount	.45

1990 Ames All-Stars

This 33-card boxed set was the second annual issue produced by Topps for the Ames toy store chain. The cards measure 2-1/2" x 3-1/2" and have a high-gloss finish on front. The set's checklist comprises the active career leaders in runs produced per game. Backs have a green-striped background and present player personal data and seasonal major league stats. Issue price for the set was $2.

		NM/M
Complete Set (33):		4.00
Common Player:		.10
1	Dave Winfield	.50
2	George Brett	.75
3	Jim Rice	.25
4	Dwight Evans	.10
5	Robin Yount	.50
6	Dave Parker	.10

7	Eddie Murray	.50
8	Keith Hernandez	.10
9	Andre Dawson	.25
10	Fred Lynn	.10
11	Dale Murphy	.35
12	Jack Clark	.10
13	Rickey Henderson	.50
14	Paul Molitor	.50
15	Cal Ripken	1.50
16	Wade Boggs	.60
17	Tim Raines	.10
18	Don Mattingly	.75
19	Kent Hrbek	.10
20	Kirk Gibson	.10
21	Julio Franco	.10
22	George Bell	.10
23	Darryl Strawberry	.10
24	Kirby Puckett	.60
25	Juan Samuel	.10
26	Alvin Davis	.10
27	Joe Carter	.10
28	Eric Davis	.10
29	Jose Canseco	.40
30	Wally Joyner	.10
31	Will Clark	.10
32	Ruben Sierra	.10
33	Danny Tartabull	.10

1999 Anaheim Angels Police

Sponsored by the Santa Ana district of the California Highway Patrol, five of the cards in this set feature players photographed with police officers. The 2-1/2" x 3-1/2" cards have borderless photos on two sides, with dark blue and gold stripes bearing player identification. The team and CHP logos are in opposite corners. Backs have a smaller version of the front photo along with player data, career information and a safety message.

		NM/M
Complete Set (10):		12.50
Common Player:		.50
1	Chuck Finley	.50
2	Shigetosi Hasegawa	.50
3	Gary DiSarcina	.50
4	Darin Erstad	2.00
5	Mo Vaughn	.50
6	Tim Salmon (w/officers)	1.00
7	Troy Percival (w/officers)	.50
8	Jim Edmonds (w/officers)	3.00
9	Troy Glaus (w/officers)	5.00
10	Santa Ana CHPs	.25

2000 Anaheim Angels Police

The California Highway Patrol sponsored this promotional set given away at an Angels game. Standard-size cards have color game-action photos which are borderless on top and right. At left and bottom are dark blue and gold stripes. A CHP badge logo appears in the lower-right. Backs have a monochrome version of the front photo, player personal data and career information and a CHP Designated Driver logo at bottom. The back photos on Jim Edmonds' and Troy Percival's cards were switched.

		NM/M
Complete Set (10):		12.50
Common Player:		1.00
1	Chuck Finley	1.00
2	Shigetoshi Hasegawa	1.00
3	Gary Disarcina	1.00
4	Darin Erstad	2.00
5	Mo Vaughn	1.00

6	Tim Salmon	2.00
7	Troy Percival	1.00
8	Jim Edmonds	2.00
9	Troy Glaus	4.00
10	CHP San Ana Area Police Officers	1.00

2000 APBA Super Stars Baseball

In the premiere edition of its board game for children, APBA included six player-image game pieces and 30 player cards, one from each team. The irregularly shaped game pieces are 1-11/16" at their widest point and 2-5/16" tall. The same player action picture appears on each side on a brightly colored background. The player cards are round-cornered, 2-1/2" x 3-1/2", with a game-action photo and green borders. The game's APBA Andy logo appears at lower-left. Backs have a few personal data and dice-throw results chart used to play the game. Player cards are unnumbered and listed here in alphabetical order. Retail price at time of issue was $19.95.

		NM/M
Complete Game:		10.00
Common Game Piece:		.50
Common Player Card:		.25
	PLAYER PIECES	
(1)	Barry Bonds	.75
(2)	Nomar Garciaparra	.45
(3)	Ken Griffey Jr.	.50
(4)	Mark McGwire	.60
(5)	Mike Piazza	.50
(6)	Alex Rodriguez	.60
	PLAYER CARDS	
(1)	Roberto Alomar	.30
(2)	Jeff Bagwell	.40
(3)	Barry Bonds	.75
(4)	Jeromy Burnitz	.25
(5)	Carlos Delgado	.35
(6)	Jermaine Dye	.25
(7)	Cliff Floyd	.25
(8)	Jason Giambi	.35
(9)	Juan Gonzalez	.30
(10)	Shawn Green	.30
(11)	Ken Griffey Jr.	.50
(12)	Vladimir Guerrero	.40
(13)	Tony Gwynn	.45
(14)	Todd Helton	.30
(15)	Derek Jeter	.75
(16)	Randy Johnson	.40
(17)	Chipper Jones	.45
(18)	Jason Kendall	.25
(19)	Matt Lawton	.25
(20)	Pedro Martinez	.40
(21)	Mark McGwire	.60
(22)	Mike Piazza	.50
(23)	Cal Ripken Jr.	.75
(24)	Alex Rodriguez	.60
(25)	Ivan Rodriguez	.50
(26)	Scott Rolen	.30
(27)	Sammy Sosa	.45
(28)	Frank Thomas	.35
(29)	Greg Vaughn	.25
(30)	Mo Vaughn	.25

1996 Arby's Cleveland Indians

These cards honor, according to the logo on front, "1995 Tribe Milestones." Fronts are bordered in black with the action photo vignetted in black. The player's milestone is printed in white on a red strip at bottom. Backs have a large baseball, bat and glove in the background with a color portrait at top. A diamond shaped

area at center has stats. Cello-wrapped cards were available one per week with a purchase.

		NM/M
Complete Set (8):		10.00
Common Player:		1.00
1	Eddie Murray (3,000th Hit)	3.00
2	Orel Hershiser (L.C.S. MVP in Both Leagues)	1.00
3	Manny Ramirez (Silver Slugger)	3.00
4	Jose Mesa (Saves Record)	1.00
5	Kenny Lofton (Gold Glove/ Most Steals)	1.00
6	Omar Vizquel (3rd Straight Gold Glove)	1.00
7	Albert Belle (50/50 Season)	1.00
8	Carlos Baerga (.310+ Ave. Four Straight Years)	1.00

2004 Archway Seattle Mariners

This stadium give-away set was sponsored by Archway Cookies and produced by Upper Deck. Fronts have green and tan borders and game-action photos. Backs repeat the color scheme and include Major League stats and licensor logos.

		NM/M
Complete Set (16):		8.00
Common Player:		.25
1	Ichiro	6.00
2	Raul Ibanez	.25
3	Randy Winn	.25
4	John Olerud	.25
5	Bret Boone	.25
6	Rich Aurilia	.25
7	Scott Spiezio	.25
8	Dan Wilson	.25
9	Edgar Martinez	.50
10	Freddy Garcia	.25
11	Jamie Moyer	.25
12	Joel Pineiro	.50
13	Gil Meche	.25
14	Ryan Franklin	.25
15	Shigetoshi Hasegawa	.25
16	Eddie Guardado	.25

2003 Arizona Diamondbacks Can Kickers Club

The attributed date is speculative, since there is no copyright date on the cards. The method of the cards' distrubtion is also unknown. These are high-tech chromium cards issued to support the team's anti-chewing tobacco program aimed at children. Fronts have color or col-

orized player photos with the player name at bottom. Backs are identical and feature a Peanuts cartoon, an anti-chew message and the club logo.

		NM/M
Complete Set (3):		10.00
Common Player:		2.00
(1)	Steve Finley	2.00
(2)	Joe Garagiola	3.00
(3)	Mark McGwire	6.00

2005 Arizona Republic Diamondbacks Deck

This stadium giveaway was sponsored by a local newspaper. Cards are 2-3/16" x 3-3/8" with rounded corners. Backs have a sponsor's logo. Each player appears four times in the deck, with an identical portrait photo on the same value card in each suit. Two Jokers complete the boxed set.

		NM/M
Complete Set (54):		10.00
Common Player:		.25
2	Koyie Hill	.25
3	Chad Tracy	.50
4	Craig Counsell	.25
5	Troy Glaus	.35
6	Royce Clayton	.25
7	Luis Gonzalez	.35
8	Jose Cruz, Jr.	.25
9	Shawn Green	.45
10	Brandon Webb	.35
J	Russ Ortiz	.25
Q	Mascot	.25
K	Bob Melvin	.25
A	Javier Vasquez	.35
Joker	Mascot	.25
Joker	Mascot	.25

1996 Arizona Lottery

BROOKS ROBINSON
ELECTED TO HALL OF FAME: 1983

To promote its Diamond Bucks scratch-off lottery game,

the Arizona Lottery issued this three-card set of Hall of Fame players' cards. Fronts have black-and-white photos which have had uniform logos airbrushed away. Borders are black. Backs are also in black-and-white, with player data and career highlights, along with the sponsors logos. Sets are given with the purchase of $5 in lottery tickets.

		NM/M
Complete Set (3):		7.50
Common Player:		2.00
(1)	Ernie Banks	4.00
(2)	Gaylord Perry	2.00
(3)	Brooks Robinson	3.00

2001 Armour Stars

FRANK THOMAS

The manner of distribution for this seven-card cello wrapped set is unknown. Produced by Playoff, the cards have game-action photos on front with red and black borders. A gold-foil Armour Stars logo is at bottom. Backs have a portrait photo, biographical data, 2000 and career stats and a trivia question about which condiments the player prefers on his hot dogs. All photos have had team logos removed.

		NM/M
Complete Set (7):		6.00
Common Player:		.50
1	Roberto Alomar	.50
2	Barry Bonds	2.00
3	Kevin Brown	.50
4	Roger Clemens	1.00
5	Greg Maddux	.75
6	Alex Rodriguez	1.50
7	Frank Thomas	.65

1997 AT&T Ambassadors of Baseball

Al Hrabosky

Taking over for the tour previously sponsored by MCI, AT&T brought a visiting team of former major league ballplayers to overseas military bases in 1997, where they played base teams in exhibition games. Card fronts feature photos (with uniform logos airbrushed away) from the players' major league days, with AT&T and Ambassadors Tour logos. Backs have typical player data.

		NM/M
Complete Set (4):		30.00
Common Player:		6.00
(1)	Jesse Barfield	6.00
(2)	Darrell Evans	12.00
(3)	Al Hrabosky	6.00
(4)	Jerry Koosman	12.00

1981 Atlanta Braves Police

Hank Aaron
Outfield
6-0—189

The first Atlanta Braves police set was a cooperative effort of the team, Hostess, Coca-Cola and the Atlanta Police Department. Card fronts feature full-color photos of 27 different Braves and manager Bobby Cox. Police and team logos are on the card backs. Card backs offer capsule biographies of the players, along with a tip for youngsters. The 2-5/8" x 4-1/8" cards are numbered by uniform number. Terry Harper (#19) appears to be somewhat scarcer than the other cards in the set. Reportedly, 33,000 sets were printed.

		NM/M
Complete Set (27):		10.00
Common Player:		.25
1	Jerry Royster	.25
3	Dale Murphy	3.00
4	Biff Pocoroba	.25
5	Bob Horner	.75
6	Bob Cox	.35
9	Luis Gomez	.25
10	Chris Chambliss	.25
15	Bill Nahorodny	.25
16	Rafael Ramirez	.25
17	Glenn Hubbard	.25
18	Claudell Washington	.25
19	Terry Harper/SP	.75
20	Bruce Benedict	.25
24	John Montefusco	.25
25	Rufino Linares	.25
26	Gene Garber	.25
28	Brian Asselstine	.25
34	Larry Bradford	.25
35	Phil Niekro	1.50
37	Rick Camp	.25
39	Al Hrabosky	.25
40	Tommy Boggs	.25
42	Rick Mahler	.25
45	Ed Miller	.25
46	Gaylord Perry	1.50
49	Preston Hanna	.25
---	Hank Aaron	5.00

1982 Atlanta Braves Police

Dale Murphy (3)
Outfield

After their successful debut in 1981, the Atlanta Braves, the Atlanta Police Department, Coca-Cola and Hostess issued another card set in '82. This 30-card set is extremely close in format to the 1981 set and again measures 2-5/8" x 4-1/8". The full-color player photos are outstanding, and each card front also bears a statement marking the 1982 Braves' record-breaking 13-

game win streak at the season's beginning. Card backs offer short biographies and "Tips from the Braves." Sponsors logos are also included. Reportedly, only 8,000 of these sets were printed.

		NM/M
Complete Set (30):		10.00
Common Player:		.25
1	Jerry Royster	.25
3	Dale Murphy	4.00
4	Biff Pocoroba	.25
6	Bob Horner	.50
8	Randy Johnson	.25
9	Bob Watson	.25
9	Joe Torre	1.00
10	Chris Chambliss	.25
15	Claudell Washington	.25
16	Rafael Ramirez	.25
17	Glenn Hubbard	.25
20	Bruce Benedict	.25
22	Brett Butler	.50
23	Tommie Aaron	.25
25	Rufino Linares	.50
26	Gene Garber	.25
27	Larry McWilliams	.25
28	Larry Whisenton	.25
35	Steve Bedrosian	.25
35	Phil Niekro	1.50
37	Rick Camp	.25
38	Joe Cowley	.25
39	Al Hrabosky	.25
42	Rick Mahler	.25
43	Bob Walk	.25
45	Bob Gibson	3.00
49	Preston Hanna	.25
52	Joe Pignatano	.25
53	Dal Maxvill	.25
54	Rube Walker	.25

1983 Atlanta Braves Police

1982 National League Western Division Champions

Brett Butler (22)
Outfielder

An almost exact replica of their 1982 set, the 1983 Atlanta Braves police set includes 30 cards numbered by uniform. Sponsors Hostess, Coca-Cola and the Atlanta Police Department returned for the third year. The cards are again 2-5/8" x 4-1/8", with full-color photos and police and team logos on the card fronts. A statement noting the team's 1982 National League Western Division title in the upper right corner is the key difference on the card fronts. As in 1982, 8,000 sets were reportedly printed.

		NM/M
Complete Set (30):		6.00
Common Player:		.15
1	Jerry Royster	.15
3	Dale Murphy	3.00
4	Biff Pocoroba	.15
5	Bob Horner	.25
8	Randy G. Johnson	.15
9	Bob Watson	.15
9	Joe Torre	.50
10	Chris Chambliss	.15
11	Ken Smith	.15
15	Claudell Washington	.15
16	Rafael Ramirez	.15
17	Glenn Hubbard	.15
19	Terry Harper	.15
20	Bruce Benedict	.15
22	Brett Butler	.25
24	Larry Owen	.15
26	Gene Garber	.15
29	Pascual Perez	.15
31	Craig McMurtry	.15
32	Steve Bedrosian	.15
33	Pete Falcone	.15
35	Phil Niekro	1.00
36	Sonny Jackson	.15
37	Rick Camp	.15
45	Bob Gibson	2.00
49	Rick Behenna	.15

51	Terry Forster	.15
52	Joe Pignatano	.15
53	Dal Maxvill	.15
54	Rube Walker	.15

1984 Atlanta Braves Police

Bob Gibson (45)
Coach

A fourth annual effort by the Braves, the Atlanta Police Department, Coca-Cola and Hostess, this 30-card set continued to be printed in a 2-5/8" x 4-1/8" format, with full-color photos plus team and police logos on the card fronts. For the first time, the cards also have a large logo and date in the upper right corner. Hostess and Coke logos again are on the card backs, with brief player information and a safety tip. Two cards in the set (Pascual Perez and Rafael Ramirez) were issued in Spanish. Cards were distributed two per week by Atlanta police officers. As in 1982 and 1983, a reported 8,000 sets were printed.

		NM/M
Complete Set (30):		8.00
Common Player:		.25
1	Jerry Royster	.25
3	Dale Murphy	3.00
5	Bob Horner	.40
6	Randy Johnson	.25
8	Bob Watson	.25
9	Joe Torre	.75
10	Chris Chambliss	.25
11	Mike Jorgensen	.25
15	Claudell Washington	.25
16	Rafael Ramirez	.25
17	Glenn Hubbard	.25
19	Terry Harper	.25
20	Bruce Benedict	.25
25	Alex Trevino	.25
26	Gene Garber	.25
28	Pascual Perez	.25
28	Gerald Perry	.25
31	Craig McMurtry	.25
32	Donnie Moore	.25
32	Steve Bedrosian	.25
33	Pete Falcone	.25
37	Rick Camp	.25
39	Len Barker	.25
42	Rick Mahler	.25
45	Bob Gibson	2.50
51	Terry Forster	.25
52	Joe Pignatano	.25
53	Dal Maxvill	.25
54	Rube Walker	.25
55	Luke Appling	2.00

1985 Atlanta Braves Police

Dale Murphy (3)
Outfielder

There are again 30 full-color cards in this fifth annual set. Hostess, Coca-Cola and the

Atlanta Police Department joined the team as sponsors again for the 2-5/8" x 4-1/8" set. Card backs are similar to previous years, with the only difference on the fronts being a swap in position for the year and team logo. The cards are checklisted by uniform number.

		NM/M
Complete Set (30):		4.00
Common Player:		.25
2	Albert Hall	.25
3	Dale Murphy	3.00
5	Rick Cerone	.25
7	Bobby Wine	.25
10	Chris Chambliss	.25
11	Bob Horner	.45
12	Paul Runge	.25
15	Claudell Washington	.25
16	Rafael Ramirez	.25
17	Glenn Hubbard	.25
18	Paul Zuvella	.25
19	Terry Harper	.25
20	Bruce Benedict	.25
22	Eddie Haas	.25
26	Ken Oberkfell	.25
26	Gene Garber	.25
27	Pascual Perez	.25
28	Gerald Perry	.25
29	Craig McMurtry	.25
32	Steve Bedrosian	.25
33	Johnny Sain	.30
34	Zane Smith	.25
36	Brad Komminsk	.25
37	Rick Camp	.25
39	Len Barker	.25
40	Bruce Sutter	1.50
42	Rick Mahler	.25
51	Terry Forster	.25
52	Leo Mazzone	.25
53	Bobby Dews	.25

1986 Atlanta Braves Police

Glenn Hubbard (17)
Second Base

The Police Athletic League of Atlanta issued a 30-card full-color set featuring Braves players and personnel. Cards measure 2-5/8" x 4-1/8". Fronts include player photos with name, uniform number and position below the photo. Backs offer the 100th Anniversary Coca-Cola logo, player information, statistics and a safety related tip. This was the sixth consecutive year that the Braves issued a safety set available from police officers in Atlanta.

		NM/M
Complete Set (30):		4.00
Common Player:		.25
2	Russ Nixon	.25
3	Dale Murphy	3.00
4	Bob Skinner	.25
5	Billy Sample	.25
7	Chuck Tanner	.25
8	Willie Stargell	1.50
9	Ozzie Virgil	.25
10	Chris Chambliss	.25
11	Bob Horner	.25
14	Andres Thomas	.25
15	Claudell Washington	.25
16	Rafael Ramirez	.25
17	Glenn Hubbard	.25
18	Omar Moreno	.25
19	Terry Harper	.25
20	Bruce Benedict	.25
23	Ted Simmons	.25
24	Ken Oberkfell	.25
26	Gene Garber	.25
29	Craig McMurtry	.25
30	Paul Assenmacher	.25
33	Johnny Sain	.25
34	Zane Smith	.25
38	Joe Johnson	.25
40	Bruce Sutter	2.00
42	Rick Mahler	.25

46	David Palmer	.25
48	Duane Ward	.25
49	Jeff Dedmon	.25
52	Al Monchak	.25

1987 Atlanta Braves Fire Safety

SIMMONS
Wildfire Prevention

These fire safety cards were given out at several different Atlanta games, with about 25,000 sets in all being distributed. The 4" x 6" cards feature Braves players in an oval frame, bordered in red, white and blue. Only the player's last name is shown on front. Backs contain the player's name, position and personal data plus a Smokey Bear cartoon fire safety message.

		NM/M
Complete Set (27):		4.00
Common Player:		.25
1	Zane Smith	.25
2	Charlie Puleo	.25
3	Randy O'Neal	.25
4	David Palmer	.25
5	Rick Mahler	.25
6	Ed Olwine	.25
7	Jeff Dedmon	.25
8	Paul Assenmacher	.25
9	Gene Garber	.25
10	Jim Acker	.25
11	Bruce Benedict	.25
12	Ozzie Virgil	.25
13	Ted Simmons	.25
14	Dale Murphy	3.00
15	Graig Nettles	.35
16	Ken Oberkfell	.25
17	Gerald Perry	.25
18	Rafael Ramirez	.25
19	Ken Griffey	.25
20	Andres Thomas	.25
21	Glenn Hubbard	.25
23	Damaso Garcia	.25
24	Gary Roenicke	.25
24	Dion James	.25
25	Albert Hall	.25
26	Chuck Tanner	.25
---	Smokey Bear Logo Card/Checklist	.10

1986 Ault Foods Blue Jays Stickers

BELL

The Ault Foods Blue Jays set is comprised of 24 full-color stickers. Designed to be placed in a special album, the stickers measure 2" x 3" in size. The attractive album measures 9" x 12" and is printed on glossy stock. While the stickers carry no information except for the player's last name and uniform number, the 20-page album contains extensive personal and statistical information about each of the 24 players.

	NM/M
Complete Set (24):	12.50
Common Player:	.50
Album:	4.00
1 Tony Fernandez	1.00
5 Rance Mulliniks	.50
7 Damaso Garcia	.50
11 George Bell	1.50
12 Ernie Whitt	.50
13 Buck Martinez	.50
15 Lloyd Moseby	.50
16 Garth Iorg	.50
17 Kelly Gruber	.50
18 Jim Clancy	.50
22 Jimmy Key	1.00
23 Cecil Fielder	5.00
25 Steve Davis	.50
26 Willie Upshaw	.50
29 Jesse Barfield	.50
31 Jim Acker	.50
33 Doyle Alexander	.50
36 Bill Caudill	.50
37 Dave Stieb	1.00
39 Don Gordon	.50
44 Cliff Johnson	.50
46 Gary Lavelle	.50
50 Tom Henke	.50
53 Dennis Lamp	.50

1982 Authentic Sports Autographs Mickey Mantle Story

1966-Hits HR No. 529

This 72-card set chronicles the life of Mickey Mantle in contemporary photos, many from Mantle's own collection and many picturing him with such stars of the era as Maris, DiMaggio, Ted Williams, Mays, etc. A total of 20,000 sets was produced; 5,000 of them feature a genuine Mantle autograph on card #1 and 15,000 sets have no autograph. Backs of cards from the autographed sets are printed in blue while the unautographed sets have backs printed in red. Issue price was $25 for the autographed set, $13 for the unsigned version.

	NM/M
Comp. Set, #1 Autographed (72):	200.00
Comp. Set, Unautographed (72):	45.00
Common Card:	1.00
1 Header card	1.00
2 Mickey & Merlyn 12/23/51	1.00
3 Spring Training 1951	1.50
4 Spring Training 1951	1.50
5 Mickey's Mom, Mickey & Merlyn	1.00
6 4/15/51 1st Homer in NY	1.00
7 1951 - DiMaggio, Mantle, Williams	1.50
8 1951- Mickey signs for 1952	1.00
9 Martin & Mickey Jr. 4/12/52	1.00
10 Brothers Roy and Ray	1.00
11 Spring Training 1952	1.00
12 1952- Bauer, Hopp, Mantle	1.50
13 1952 Season	1.00
14 Mantle & Martin 1952 Series	1.50
15 Billy & Mickey 1953	1.50
16 Knee Injury 1953	1.50
17 1953 - Before knee surgery	1.00
18 New business 1953	1.00
19 1953 World Series Power	1.00
20 1953 The long Home Run	1.50
21 1955 Hall of Fame Game	1.50
22 1955	1.00
23 1955 - Skowron, Rizzuto, Mantle	1.50
24 1954 - Jackie Robinson at 1st	1.00
25 1956 - Mickey with Ted Williams	1.50
26 1955 - Skowron, Berra, Mantle	1.50
27 1956 - Mickey safe at first	1.00
28 1956 World Series	1.00
29 1957 - Yogi, Whitey, Mickey	1.00
30 1957 - Roy Sievers with Mickey	1.00
31 1957 World Series	1.00
32 1957 Hitchcock Award	1.50
33 1957 - Mickey with Cardinal Spellman	1.00
34 1957 - Singing with Teresa Brewer	1.00
35 1957 - Brooks Robinson & Mickey	1.00
36 1958 World Series	1.00
37 1958 All Star Game with Banks	1.50
38 With Stengel 1959	1.50
39 1960 - With Roger Maris	1.50
40 1960 World Series	1.00
41 1961 All Star Game with Maris & Mays	1.00
42 Blanchard	1.50
43 1961 - with Maris & Mrs. Babe Ruth	1.50
44 1961 - Mickey Congratulates Maris	1.00
45 1961 - Maris & Mantle	1.00
46 400th Career HR 9/11/62	1.00
47 1962 World Series	1.50
48 1963 season	1.50
49 1963 World Series	1.50
50 1964 World Series	1.50
51 1964 - Pepitone, Ford, Mantle	1.00
52 1964 season	1.00
53 1965 Mickey's Day	1.50
54 1965 season	1.50
55 1966 - with Joe DiMaggio	1.50
56 Mantle family	1.50
57 1967 season	1.50
58 1968 - hits HR No. 529	1.00
59 1968 - Retirement	1.00
60 1968 - His farewell	1.50
61 Mickey's trophy room	1.00
62 1970 - Welcome back Coach	1.00
63 1973 - TV commercial	1.00
64 1974 visit	1.00
65 1974 visit	1.00
66 1974 Hall of Fame inductees	1.00
67 1979 Old Timers Game	1.00
68 1981 Old Timers Game	1.00
69 Family Day	1.00
70 The Mantle Swing	1.00
71 The Mantle Swing	1.00
72 The Mantle Swing	1.00

1983 Authentic Sports Autographs

1964 with the Giants

These collectors' issue sets of a dozen cards each present the careers of 11 Hall of Famers in pictures and words. Each 2-1/2" x 3-1/2" card has a black-and-white or color photo on front with a card title and red or green border graphics. Backs present a narrative of the player's career and some include a small portrait photo. Each set was made available in both an unautographed version and a version in which the No. 1 card was authentically autographed.

	NM/M
(1) Hank Aaron Story	15.00
(1a) Hank Aaron Story, Autographed	50.00
(2) Yogi Berra Story	6.00
(2a) Yogi Berra Story, Autographed	20.00
(3) Joe DiMaggio Story	15.00
(3a) Joe DiMaggio Story, Autographed	150.00
(4) Bob Feller Story	7.50
(4a) Bob Feller Story, Autographed	20.00
(5) Juan Marichal Story	7.50
(5a) Juan Marichal Story, Autographed	20.00
(6) Willie Mays Story	10.00
(6a) Willie Mays Story, Autographed	50.00
(7) Johnny Mize Story	6.00
(7a) Johnny Mize Story, Autogrphed	15.00
(8) Brooks Robinson Story	6.00
(8a) Brooks Robinson Story, Autographed	15.00
(9) Frank Robinson Story	6.00
(9a) Frank Robinson Story, Autographed	20.00
(10) Duke Snider Story	6.00
(10a) Duke Snider Story, Autographed	20.00
(11) Warren Spahn Story	6.00
(11a) Warren Spahn Story, Autographed	20.00

2005 Azteca Seattle Mariners Hispanic Heroes

Adrian Beltre #5 - tercera base

This set of M's Latino players was a stadium giveaway to 20,000 fans at the 3rd annual Latin American Beisbol Night, September 13 at Safeco Field.

	NM/M
Complete Set (9):	10.00
Common Player:	.50
1 Adrian Beltre	1.00
2 Yuniesky Betancourt	1.00
3 Eddie Guardado	.50
4 Felix Hernandez	1.00
5 Raul Ibanez	.50
6 Jose Lopez	1.00
7 Julio Mateo	.50
8 Joel Pineiro	.50
9 Yorvit Torrealba	.50

B

1998 Ball Park Detroit Tigers

Fans in attendance at the August 9 game at Tiger Stadium received this team set sponsored by Ball Park franks, the stadium hot dog concessionaire. Cards are standard 2-1/2" x 3-1/2" format printed on light cardboard. Fronts have color posed or action photos with white borders. Player identification is in a strip at left. Backs have a light blue background, overprinted in dark blue with the player's personal data, stats and a 1997 season highlight, along with the sponsor's logo and a picture of a moving baseball.

	NM/M
Complete Set (26):	9.00
Common Player:	.50
01 Gabe Alvarez	.50
02 Matt Anderson	.50
03 Paul Bako	.50
04 Trey Beamon	.50
05 Buddy Bell	.50
06 Geronimo Berroa	.50
07 Doug Bochtler	.50
08 Doug Brocail	.50
09 Raul Casanova	.50
10 Frank Castillo	.50
11 Frank Catalanotto	.50
12 Tony Clark	.50
13 Dean Crow	.50
14 Deivi Cruz	.50
15 Damion Easley	.50
16 Bryce Florie	.50
17 Luis Gonzalez	2.50
18 Seth Greisinger	.50
19 Bobby Higginson	.75
20 Brian Hunter	.50
21 Todd Jones	.50
22 Brian Moehler	.50
23 Brian Powell	.50
24 Joe Randa	.50
25 Sean Runyan	.50
26 Justin Thompson	.50

1994 Baltimore Orioles Program Cards

Virtually the entire O's organization, major and minor leaguers, was included in this season-long promotion. One of 12 nine-card sheets was inserted into the team's programs, which sold for $3. A reported 17,000 sets were produced. The sheets are unperforated and measure 7-1/2" x 10-1/2". Fronts have color game-action or posed photos within an orange border. A team logo is at top-right. At bottom is a black strip with the player's number (if a major leaguer), name and position in white. Backs are printed in black and orange on white with biographical details and complete major and minor league stats. The unnumbered cards are checklisted here alphabetically.

	NM/M
Complete Set, Sheets (12):	25.00
Complete Set, Singles (108):	25.00
Common Player:	.25
(1) Manny Alexander	.25
(2) Brady Anderson	.25
(3) Matt Anderson	.25
(4) Harold Baines	.25
(5) Myles Barnden	.25
(6) Kimera Bartee	.25
(7) Juan Bautista	.25
(8) Armando Benitez	.25
(9) Joe Borowski	.25
(10) Brian Brewer	.25
(11) Brandon Bridgers	.25
(12) Cory Brown	.25
(13) Damon Buford	.25
(14) Philip Byrne	.25
(15) Rocco Cafaro	.25
(16) Paul Carey	.25
(17) Carlos Chavez	.25
(18) Eric Chavez	.25
(19) Steve Chitren	.25
(20) Mike Cook	.25
(21) Shawn Curran	.25
(22) Kevin Curtis	.25
(23) Joey Dawley	.25
(24) Jim Dedrick	.25
(25) Cesar Devarez	.25
(26) Mike Devereaux	.25
(27) Brian DuBois	.25
(28) Keith Eaddy	.25
(29) Mark Eichhorn	.25
(30) Scott Emerson	.25
(31) Vaughn Eshelman	.25
(32) Craig Faulkner	.25
(33) Sid Fernandez	.25
(34) Rick Forney	.25
(35) Jim Foster	.25
(36) Jesse Garcia	.25
(37) Mike Garguilo	.25
(38) Rich Gedman	.25
(39) Leo Gomez	.25
(40) Rene Gonzalez	.25
(41) Curtis Goodwin	.25
(42) Kris Gresham	.25
(43) Shane Hale	.25
(44) Jeffrey Hammonds	.25
(45) Jimmy Haynes	.25
(46) Chris Hoiles	.25
(47) Tim Hullett	.25
(48) Matt Jarvis	.25
(49) Scott Klingenbeck	.25
(50) Rick Krivda	.25
(51) David Lamb	.25
(52) Chris Lemp	.25
(53) T.R. Lewis	.25
(54) Brian Link	.25
(55) John Lombardi	.25
(56) Rob Lukachyk	.25
(57) Calvin Maduro	.25
(58) Barry Manuel	.25
(59) Lincoln Martin	.25
(60) Scott McClain	.25
(61) Ben McDonald	.25
(62) Kevin McGehee	.25
(63) Mark McLemore	.25
(64) Miguel Mejia	.25
(65) Feliciano Mercedes	.25
(66) Jose Millares	.25
(67) Brent Miller	.25
(68) Alan Mills	.25
(69) Jamie Moyer	.25
(70) Mike Mussina	1.50
(71) Sherman Obando	.25
(72) Alex Ochoa	.25
(73) John O'Donoghue	.25
(74) Mike Oquist	.25
(75) Bo Ortiz	.25
(76) Billy Owens	.25
(77) Rafael Palmeiro	2.00
(78) Dave Paveloff	.25
(79) Brad Pennington	.25
(80) Bill Percibel	.25
(81) Jim Poole	.25
(82) Jay Powell	.25
(83) Arthur Rhodes	.25
(84) Matt Riemer	.25
(85) Cal Ripken Jr.	5.00
(86) Kevin Ryan	.25
(87) Chris Sabo	.25
(88) Brian Sackinsky	.25
(89) Francisco Saneaux	.25
(90) Jason Satre	.25
(91) David Segui	.25
(92) Jose Serra	.25
(93) Larry Shenk	.25
(94) Lee Smith	.25
(95) Lonnie Smith	.25
(96) Mark Smith	.25
(97) Garrett Stephenson	.25
(98) Jeff Tackett	.25
(99) Brad Tyler	.25
(100) Pedro Ulises	.25
(101) Jack Voight	.25
(102) Jim Walker	.25
(103) B.J. Waszgis	.25
(104) Jim Wawruck	.25
(105) Mel Wearing	.25
(106) Mark Williamson	.25
(107) Brian Wood	.25
(108) Gregg Zaun	.25

1984 Baseball Cards Magazine Repli-Cards

DALE MURPHY outfielder ATLANTA BRAVES

With its August 1984 issue, Baseball Cards Magazine pioneered the use of "repli-cards" to enhance feature articles and increase sales. The cards were printed on cardboard stock and stapled into the magazines. Most of the cards were done in the style of earlier popular card issues. though some featured original designs and others were reproductions of actual cards. Some of baseball's best artists and photographers work appears on the cards. The inclusion of repli-cards ceased after 1993 when abuses by other "publishers" caused baseball's licensors to threaten legal action. Values quoted are for single cards cut from the panel; complete panels or magazines command a premium. Cards are grouped by magazine issue and numbered with a month-designation.

		NM/M
Complete Set (3):		10.00
Aug.	Ted Williams (1953 Topps style.)	4.50
Aug.	Dale Murphy (1953 Topps style.)	3.50
Oct.	Mickey Mantle (1949 Bowman style.)	6.00

1985 Baseball Cards Magazine Repli-cards

CHUCK CONNORS

In three of its 1985 issues, Baseball Cards Magazine offered "repli-cards" to enhance feature articles and increase sales. The cards were printed on cardboard stock and stapled into the magazines. Original designs and reproductions of earlier cards were used. Values quoted are for single cards cut from the panel; complete panels or magazines command a premium. Cards are grouped by magazine issue and numbered with a month-designation.

		NM/M
Complete Set (6):		12.00
Common Player:		2.00
April	Chuck Connors (Original design.)	2.00
April	Chuck Connors (1952 Topps style.)	2.00
June	Pete Rose (Reproduction 1965 Topps.)	3.00
June	Fritz Ackley, Steve Carlton (Reproduction 1965 Topps.)	2.00
Oct.	Mickey Mantle (Reproduction 1955 Bowman #202.)	4.00
Oct.	Ernie Banks (Reproduction 1955 Bowman #242.)	2.00

1986 Baseball Cards Magazine Repli-Cards

In three of its 1986 issues, Baseball Cards Magazine offered "repli-cards" to enhance feature articles and increase sales. The cards were printed on cardboard stock and stapled into the magazines. Reproductions of existing cards and modern player cards done in the style of vintage issues were used. Values quoted are for single cards cut from the panel; complete panels or magazines command a premium. Cards are grouped by magazine issue and numbered with a month-designation.

		NM/M
Complete Set (12):		12.00
Common Player:		.50
April	Vince Coleman (Kondritz Trading Cards sample.)	.50
April	Vince Coleman (Kondritz Trading Cards sample.)	.50
June	Stan Musial (Reproduction 1953 Bowman.)	2.00
June	Roy Campanella (Reproduction 1953 Bowman.)	1.00
June	Yogi Berra (Reproduction 1953 Bowman.)	1.50
Dec.	Don Mattingly (1951 Topps Red Back style.)	3.00
Dec.	Wally Joyner (1951 Topps Red Back style.)	.50
Dec.	Wade Boggs (1951 Topps All-Stars style.)	1.50
Dec.	Dwight Gooden (1951 Topps All-Stars style.)	.50
Dec.	George Brett (Reproduction 1981 Donruss proof.)	3.00
Dec.	Reggie Jackson (Reproduction 1981 Donruss proof.)	2.50
Dec.	Lou Piniella (Reproduction 1982 Fleer proof.)	.75

1987 Baseball Cards Magazine Repli-Cards

DOUBLE TROUBLE
MCGWIRE AND DAVIS

In four of its 1987 issues, Baseball Cards Magazine offered "repli-cards" to enhance feature articles and increase sales. The cards were printed on cardboard stock and stapled into the magazines. Original designs and modern player cards done in the style of vintage issues were used. Values quoted are for single cards cut from the panel; complete panels or magazines command a premium. Cards are grouped by magazine issue and numbered with a month-designation.

		NM/M
Complete Set (10):		14.00
Common Player:		.40
April	Don Mattingly (1983 Donruss style.)	5.00
April	Don Mattingly (1983 Topps style.)	5.00
Sept.	Ozzie Canseco (Original "Future Stars" design.)	.40
Sept.	Patrick Lennon (Original "Future Stars" design.)	.40
Oct.	Eric Davis (1951 Bowman style.)	.75
Oct.	Bo Jackson (1951 Bowman style.)	.75

Oct.	Stan Musial (1951 Bowman style)	1.50
Dec.	Dale Murphy (1981 Fleer style)	1.50
Dec.	Tim Raines (1981 Fleer style)	.50
Dec.	Double Trouble Eric Davis, Mark McGwire (1981 Fleer style)	2.50

1988 Baseball Cards Magazine Repli-Cards

Mickey Mantle
OUTFIELD, NEW YORK YANKEES

In six of its 1988 issues, Baseball Cards Magazine offered "repli-cards" to enhance feature articles and increase sales. The cards were printed on cardboard stock and stapled into the magazines. Original designs, reproductions and modern player cards done in the style of vintage issues were used. Values quoted are for single cards cut from the panel; complete panels or magazines command a premium. Cards are grouped by magazine issue and numbered with a month-designation.

		NM/M
Complete Set (16):		27.50
Common Player:		.40
Feb.	Babe Ruth (1936 Diamond Stars style.)	1.50
Feb.	Wade Boggs (1936 Diamond Stars style.)	1.50
Feb.	Mark McGwire (1936 Diamond Stars style; available only via mail-in offer.)	4.00
April	Ted Williams (1952 Topps style.)	1.50
April	Ted Williams (Reproduction 1954 Bowman #66.)	2.50
June	Joey Meyer (Original design.)	.40
June	Sam Horn (Original design.)	.40
Aug.	Roger "Rocket" Clemens (1941 Play Ball style.)	2.50
Aug.	Kirk Gibson (1941 Play Ball style.)	.40
Aug.	Jack Clark (1941 Play Ball style.)	.40
Oct.	Mickey Mantle (1956 Bowman proof style.)	7.50
Oct.	Jackie Robinson (1952 Bowman style.)	1.50
Oct.	Dave Winfield (1974 Topps "Washington" style.)	1.25
Dec.	Mickey Mantle (Reproduction 1952 Bowman.)	2.50
Dec.	Mickey Mantle (reproduction 1951 Bowman)	4.50
Dec.	Mickey Mantle (Reproduction 1952 Topps.)	6.00

1989 Baseball Cards Magazine Repli-Cards

Beginning with its January 1989 issue, Baseball Cards Magazine began issuing its repli-cards in panels of six cards per month, creating an annual set of 72 insert cards. Contemporary players were presented in the designs of classic Topps sets of the 1950s-1970s. In 1989 the magazine's cards were in the style of 1959 Topps. Besides the individual player's

---

kirby puckett

MINNESOTA TWINS
OUTFIELD

cards, specialty cards included "Rookie Stars of 1989" and multi-player feature cards.

		NM/M
Complete Set (72):		20.00
Common Player:		.15
1	Keith Hernandez	.15
2	Will Clark	.15
3	Andres Galarraga	.15
4	Mark McGwire	1.50
5	Don Mattingly	1.00
6	Ricky Jordan (Rookie Stars)	.15
7	Juan Samuel	.15
8	Julio Franco	.15
9	Harold Reynolds	.15
10	Gregg Jefferies (Rookie Stars)	.15
11	Ryne Sandberg	.75
12	Lou Whitaker	.15
13	Ozzie Smith	.15
14	Gary Sheffield (Rookie Stars)	.25
15	Alan Trammell	.15
16	Cal Ripken Jr.	2.00
17	Barry Larkin	.15
18	Tony Fernandez	.15
19	Mike Schmidt	1.00
20	Wade Boggs	.75
21	Gary Gaetti	.15
22	Chris Sabo (Rookie Stars)	.15
23	Paul Molitor	.60
24	Carney Lansford	.15
25	Dave Winfield	.60
26	Darryl Strawberry	.15
27	Tony Gwynn	.75
28	Darryl Hamilton	.15
29	Jose Canseco	.45
30	Andre Dawson	.25
31	Kirby Puckett	.75
32	Cameron Drew (Rookie Stars)	.15
33	Robin Yount	.60
34	Ellis Burks	.15
35	Eric Davis	.15
36	Joe Carter	.15
37	George Bell	.15
38	Kevin McReynolds	.15
39	Tim Raines	.15
40	Luis Medina (Rookie Stars)	.15
41	Mike Greenwell	.15
42	Kal Daniels	.15
43	Dwight Gooden	.15
44	Roger Clemens	1.00
45	Nolan Ryan	2.00
46	Erik Hanson	.15
47	Orel Hershiser	.15
48	Bret Saberhagen	.15
49	Jimmy Key	.15
50	Frank Viola	.15
51	Bruce Hurst	.15
52	Norm Charlton (Rookie Stars)	.15
53	Ted Higuera	.15
54	Mark Langston	.15
55	Damon Berryhill	.15
56	Carlton Fisk	.60
57	Terry Steinbach	.15
58	Sandy Alomar (Rookie Stars)	.15
59	Benito Santiago	.15
60	Bob Boone	.15
61	Jerome Walton (Rookie Stars)	.15
62	Jaime Navarro (Rookie Stars)	.15
63	Ken Griffey Jr. (Rookie Stars)	1.50
64	Jim Abbott (Rookie Stars)	.15
65	Junior Felix (Rookie Stars)	.15
66	Tom Gordon	.15
67	Power Plus (Kirby Puckett, Don Mattingly)	.65
68	Fence Busters (Julio Franco, Eric Davis, Ruben Sierra)	.15
69	N.L. Hitting Kings (Will Clark, Tony Gwynn)	.25
70	Keystone Combo (Ozzie Smith, Ryne Sandberg)	.50

71	Dinger Duo (Howard Johnson, Kevin Mitchell)	.15
72	Texas Heat (Nolan Ryan, Mike Scott)	.75

1990 Baseball Cards Magazine Repli-Cards

PAUL MOLITOR
2B-3B

BREWERS

Beginning with its January 1989 issue, Baseball Cards Magazine began issuing its repli-cards in panels of six cards per month, creating an annual set of 72 insert cards. Contemporary players were presented in the designs of classic Topps sets of the 1950s-1970s. In 1990 the magazine's cards were in the style of 1969 Topps. Besides the individual player's cards, there were a number of multi-player "Rookie Stars" cards.

		NM/M
Complete Set (72):		25.00
Common Player:		.15
1	Craig Biggio	.15
2	Kevin Mitchell	.15
3	Orel Hershiser	.15
4	Will Clark	.15
5	Eric Davis	.15
6	Tony Gwynn	.75
7	Mike Scott	.15
8	Barry Larkin	.15
9	John Smoltz	.15
10	Glenn Davis	.15
11	Roberto Alomar	.25
12	Rick Reuschel	.15
13	N.L. West Rookie Stars (Eric Anthony, Ed Whited)	.15
14	N.L. West Rookie Stars (Andy Benes, Steve Avery)	.15
15	N.L. West Rookie Stars (John Wetteland, Joe Oliver)	.15
16	Giants Rookie Stars (Randy McCament, Greg Litton)	.15
17	Dodgers Rookie Stars (Jose Offerman, Jose Vizcaino)	.15
18	Reds Rookie Stars (Scott Scudder, Rosario Rodriguez)	.15
19	Darryl Strawberry	.15
20	Von Hayes	.15
21	Dwight Smith	.15
22	Howard Johnson	.15
23	Pedro Guerrero	.15
24	Tim Raines	.15
25	Ozzie Smith	.75
26	Barry Bonds	2.00
27	Jerome Walton	.15
28	Ryne Sandberg	.75
29	Bobby Bonilla	.15
30	Mark Grace	.15
31	Cards Rookie Stars (Todd Zeile, Alex Cole)	.15
32	N.L. East Rookie Stars (Pat Combs, Dean Wilkins)	.15
33	N.L. East Rookie Stars (Steve Carter, Jeff Huson)	.15
34	Cubs Rookie Stars (Greg Smith, Derrick May)	.15
35	Expos Rookie Stars (Marquis Grissom, Larry Walker)	.45
36	Mets Rookie Stars (Wally Whitehurst, Blaine Beatty)	.15
37	Ken Griffey Jr.	1.50
38	Kirby Puckett	.75
39	Julio Franco	.15
40	Ruben Sierra	.15
41	Bo Jackson	.25
42	Jose Canseco	.35
43	Dennis Eckersley	.50

44	Bret Saberhagen	.15
45	Wally Joyner	.15
46	Carlton Fisk	.60
47	Nolan Ryan	2.00
48	Rickey Henderson	.60
49	White Sox Rookie Stars (Robin Ventura, Sammy Sosa)	7.50
50	A.L. West Rookie Stars (John Orton, Scott Radinsky)	.15
51	A.L. West Rookie Stars (Bobby Rose, Bob Hamelin)	.15
52	Rangers Rookie Stars (Monty Fariss, Juan Gonzalez)	.50
53	Mariners Rookie Stars (Tino Martinez, Roger Salkeld)	.15
54	Twins Rookie Stars (Terry Jorgensen, Paul Sorrento)	.15
55	Don Mattingly	1.00
56	Roger Clemens	1.00
57	Cal Ripken	2.00
58	Robin Yount	.60
59	Wade Boggs	.75
60	Fred McGriff	.15
61	Cecil Fielder	.15
62	Ellis Burks	.15
63	Sandy Alomar	.15
64	Alan Trammell	.15
65	Steve Sax	.15
66	Paul Molitor	.60
67	Brewers Rookie Stars (Bert Hefferman, Matias Carillo)	.15
68	A.L. East Rookie Stars (Ben McDonald, John Olerud)	.25
69	A.L. East Rookie Stars (Mark Whiten, Phil Clark)	.15
70	Yankees Rookie Stars (Jim Leyritz, Kevin Maas)	.15
71	Indians Rookie Stars (Mark Lewis, Carlos Baerga)	.15
72	Orioles Rookie Stars (David Segui, Chris Hoiles)	.15

1991 Baseball Cards Magazine Repli-Cards

of-1st base

For the third year in 1991, Baseball Cards Magazine issued its repli-cards in panels of six cards per month, creating an annual set of 72 insert cards. Contemporary players were presented in the classic Topps design of 1966. Besides the individual players' cards, there are a number of multi-player feature cards and "Rookie Stars of 1991" multi-player cards, plus a 1952 Topps style card of Don Mattingly.

		NM/M
Complete Set (72):		18.00
Common Player:		.15
1	Eric Davis	.15
2	Cubs Rookie Stars (Lance Dickson, Hector Villanueva)	.15
3	Bobby Bonilla	.15
4	Len Dykstra	.15
5	John Franco	.15
6	Matt Williams	.15
7	Barry Bonds	2.00
8	Cards Rookie Stars (Geronimo Pena, Ray Lankford, Bernard Gilkey)	.15
9	Andre Dawson	.25
10	Dave Justice	.15
11	Triple Expos-ure (Larry Walker, Marquis Grissom, Delino DeShields)	.20

12	Howard Johnson	.15
13	Darryl Strawberry	.15
14	Astros Rookie Stars (Karl Rhodes, Andujar Cedeno, Mike Simms)	.15
15	Will Clark	.15
16	Barry Larkin	.15
17	Ramon Martinez	.15
18	Ron Gant	.15
19	Gregg Jefferies	.15
20	Giants Rookie Stars (Steve Decker, Steve Hosey, Mark Leonard)	.15
21	Todd Zeile	.15
22	Benito Santiago	.15
23	Eddie Murray	.60
24	Randy Myers	.15
25	Greg Maddux	.75
26	Phillies Rookie Stars (Mickey Morandini, Wes Chamberlain)	.15
27	Tim Wallach	.15
28	Dale Murphy	.25
29	Doug Drabek	.15
30	Kevin Mitchell	.15
31	Frank Viola	.15
32	Padres Rookie Stars (Rafael Valdez, Paul Faries)	.15
33	Hal Morris	.15
34	Pedro Guerrero	.15
35	Dwight Gooden	.15
36	Shawon Dunston	.15
37	Ken Griffey Jr.	1.00
38	Royals Rookie Stars (Sean Berry, Brian McRae)	.15
39	Roger Clemens	.85
40	Ellis Burks	.15
41	Robin Yount	.60
42	Frank Thomas	.60
43	Ruben Sierra	.15
44	Red Sox Rookie Stars (Mo Vaughn, Phil Plantier, Tim Naehring)	.15
45	Tim Raines	.15
46	Dave Parker	.15
47	Jose Canseco	.35
48	Glenn Davis	.15
49	Dave Winfield	.60
50	Chuck Knoblauch, Scott Leius, Willie Banks (Twins Rookie Stars)	.15
51	Joe Carter	.15
52	Cal Ripken	2.00
53	Carlton Fisk	.60
54	Julio Franco	.15
55	Don Mattingly	.85
56	Blue Jays Rookie Stars (Eddie Zosky, William Suero, Derek Bell)	.15
57	Sandy Alomar	.15
58	Juan Gonzalez	.30
59	Don Mattingly (1952 Topps style)	1.50
60	Mike Greenwell	.15
61	Chuck Finley	.15
62	Rangers Rookie Stars (Dean Palmer, Ivan Rodriguez, Gerald Alexander)	1.00
63	Scott Erickson	.15
64	Paul Molitor	.60
65	Triple Terrors (Cecil Fielder, Jose Canseco, Mark McGwire)	.60
66	Dennis Eckersley	.50
67	Brian Harper	.15
68	A.L. Rookie Stars (Bernie Williams, Wilson Alvarez (no designation on front banner))	.25
69	Robin Ventura	.15
70	Kirby Puckett	.75
71	Rafael Palmeiro	.50
72	Roberto Alomar	.25

1992 Baseball Cards Magazine Repli-Cards

WHITE SOX

Frank Thomas 1ST BASE

The annual repli-card series inserted in Baseball Cards

Magazine began in January with six-card panels each month. In May, panels were increased to eight cards and a UV coating was added to the front. Contemporary players were presented in the designs of classic Topps sets of the 1950s-1970s. In 1992 the magazine's cards were in the style of 1970 Topps. Besides the individual player's cards, specialty cards included "1992 Rookie Stars" multi-player and Team USA cards.

		NM/M
Complete Set (88):		20.00
Common Player:		.15
1	Eddie Murray	.50
2	Braves Rookie Stars (Ryan Klesko, Mark Wohlers)	.15
3	Barry Bonds	1.50
4	Will Clark	.15
5	Jose Canseco	.35
6	Ron Gant	.15
7	Ruben Sierra	.15
8	Reds Rookie Stars (Reggie Sanders, Mo Sanford)	.15
9	Terry Pendleton	.15
10	Hal Morris	.15
11	Kirby Puckett	.60
12	Paul Molitor	.15
13	Jack McDowell	.15
14	Dodgers Rookie Stars (Eric Karros, Tom Goodwin)	.15
15	Ramon Martinez	.15
16	Steve Avery	.15
17	Roger Clemens	.75
18	Jim Abbott	.15
19	Phil Plantier	.15
20	Giants Rookie Stars (Royce Clayton, Ted Wood)	.15
21	Frank Thomas	.50
22	Juan Gonzalez	.25
23	Felix Jose	.15
24	Chuck Knoblauch	.15
25	Tony Gwynn	.60
26	Julio Franco	.15
27	Greg Blosser, Frankie Rodriguez	.15
28	Wade Boggs	.60
29	Robin Ventura	.15
30	Shane Mack	.15
31	Roberto Alomar	.25
32	Don Mattingly	.75
33	Astros Rookie Stars (Ryan Bowen, Jeff Juden)	.15
34	Cal Ripken Jr.	1.50
35	Ozzie Smith	.60
36	Ken Griffey Jr.	1.00
37	Ivan Rodriguez	.40
38	Matt Williams	.15
39	Craig Biggio	.15
40	John Kruk	.15
41	George Brett	.75
42	Carlton Fisk	.50
43	Indians Rookie Stars (Kenny Lofton, Jim Thome)	.50
44	Andre Dawson	.25
45	Nolan Ryan	1.50
46	Robin Yount	.50
47	Ryne Sandberg	.60
48	Rickey Henderson	.50
49	Bobby Thigpen	.15
50	Dennis Eckersley	.40
51	Cards Rookie Stars (Brian Jordan, Dmitri Young)	.15
52	Jeff Reardon	.15
53	Bryan Harvey	.15
54	Tom Henke	.15
55	Lee Smith	.15
56	John Franco	.15
57	Cecil Fielder	.15
58	Darryl Strawberry	.15
59	Twins Rookie Stars (David McCarty, Scott Stahoviak)	.15
60	Mark McGwire	1.00
61	George Bell	.15
62	Fred McGriff	.15
63	Danny Tartabull	.15
64	Joe Carter	.15
65	Deion Sanders	.15
66	Roberto Alomar	.25
67	A.L. Rookie Stars (Eduardo Perez, Joe Vitiello, Bret Boone)	.15
68	Bip Roberts	.15
69	Ray Lankford	.15
70	Brady Anderson	.15
71	Tim Raines	.15
72	Marquis Grissom	.15
73	Dave Fleming	.15
74	Andy Benes	.15
75	Yankees Rookie Stars (Bob Wickman, Mark Hutton)	.15
76	Bill Swift	.15
77	Mike Mussina	.25
78	Donovan Osborne	.15
79	Juan Guzman	.15
80	Kevin Brown	.15
81	Charles Johnson (USA)	.15
82	Jeffrey Hammonds (USA)	.15
83	Rick Helling (USA)	.15
84	Chris Wimmer (USA)	.15
85	Darren Dreifort (USA)	.15
86	Calvin Murray (USA)	.15
87	Phil Nevin (USA)	.15
88	B.J. Wallace (USA)	.15

1993 Baseball Cards/Sports Cards Magazine Repli-Cards

The annual repli-card series began in Baseball Cards Magazine in 1989 continued in 1993 with eight-card panels of UV-coated repli-cards stapled into each monthly issue. (Only seven cards were included in July; there are two #32 and no #40.) Contemporary players were presented in the design of the classic 1968 Topps set. Backs are printed in black, white and yellow and include an investment advisory about the player's cards. Besides the individual player's repli-cards, there is a group of "1993 Rookie Stars" multi-player cards. Effective with its May issue, the magazine's title was changed to Sports Cards, the copyright line on back reflecting that change.

1990-92 Baseball Cards Presents Repli-Cards

Taking advantage of the boom in sports card collecting, Baseball Cards Magazine began a series of special newsstand magazine titles. Beginning with "Baseball Card Boom," dated February 1990, the series, officially known as "Baseball Cards Presents . . ." included baseball (and other sports) repli-cards in most of its issues through August 1992. Cards are listed here by issue in which they were inserted.

		NM/M
Complete Set (95):		25.00
Common Player:		.15
1	Andy Van Slyke	.15
2	Ruben Sierra	.15
3	Carlos Baerga	.15
4	Gary Sheffield	.30
5	Chuck Knoblauch	.15
6	Danny Tartabull	.15
7	Angels Rookie Stars (Chad Curtis, Tim Salmon)	.45
8	Darren Daulton	.15
9	Deion Sanders	.20
10	Pat Listach	.15
11	Albert Belle	.15
12	Frank Thomas	.60
13	Dave Hollins	.15
14	Braves Rookie Stars (Javy Lopez, Mike Kelly)	.15
15	Travis Fryman	.15
16	Edgar Martinez	.15
17	Barry Bonds	1.50
18	Dennis Eckersley	.50
19	Brady Anderson	.15
20	Fred McGriff	.15
21	Paul Molitor	.60
22	Juan Gonzalez	.30
23	Dodgers Rookie Stars (Bill Ashley, Mike Piazza)	1.50
24	Larry Walker	.15
25	Dave Winfield	.60
26	Robin Yount	.60
27	George Brett	.85
28	Jack Morris	.15
29	Eddie Murray	.60
30	Nolan Ryan	1.50
31	Carlton Fisk	.60
32a	Dale Murphy	.30
32b	Jeff Bagwell	.60
33	Eric Karros	.15
34	Roberto Alomar	.25
35	Robin Ventura	.15
36	Delino DeShields	.15
37	Ken Griffey Jr.	1.00
38	Eric Anthony	.15
39	Marquis Grissom	.15
41	Cecil Fielder	.15
42	Mark McGwire	1.25
43	Ryne Sandberg	.75
44	Kirby Puckett	.75
45	Cal Ripken Jr.	1.50
46	David McCarty	.15
47	Joe Carter	.15
48	Dean Palmer	.15
49	Jack McDowell	.15
50	Roger Clemens	.85
51	Cal Eldred	.15
52	Tom Glavine	.25
53	Steve Avery	.15
54	Mike Mussina	.35
55	Brien Taylor	.15
56	Mark Grace	.15
57	Ray Lankford	.15
58	Shane Mack	.15
59	Terry Pendleton	.15
60	Tony Gwynn	.75
61	Rafael Palmeiro	.50
62	Will Clark	.15
63	Wil Cordero	.15
64	Cliff Floyd	.15
65	Aaron Sele	.75
66	Chipper Jones	.75
67	Frank Rodriguez	.15
68	Ryan Klesko	.60
69	Manny Ramirez	.60
70	Carlos Delgado	.30
71	Paul Shuey	.15
72	Barry Bonds	1.50
73	Andre Dawson	.30
74	Paul Molitor	.60
75	Greg Maddux	.75
76	Wade Boggs	.15
77	Bryan Harvey	.15
78	Andres Galarraga	.15
79	Gregg Jefferies	.15
80	Mike Piazza	1.00
81	J.T. Snow	.15
82	Ivan Rodriguez	.50
83	Derrick May	.15
84	Tim Salmon	.15
85	Greg Vaughn	.15
86	Kenny Lofton	.15
87	John Olerud	.15
88	Sammy Sosa	.75
89	Lee Smith	.15
90	Matt Williams	.15
91	Don Mattingly	.85
92	Willie Greene	.15
93	Jim Abbott	.15
94	Mo Vaughn	.15
95	Randy Johnson	.60

		NM/M
Complete Set (61):		27.50
Common Player:		.25
1	Don Mattingly	1.25
2	Dwight Gooden	.25
3	Jose Canseco	.35
4	Bo Jackson	.35
5	Ken Griffey Jr.	1.50
1	John Olerud	.25
2	Eric Anthony	.25
3	Greg Vaughn	.25
4	Todd Zeile	.25
5	Ben McDonald	.25
6	Deion Sanders (Mail-in offer only.)	.75
1	Mark Davis	.25
2	Bret Saberhagen	.25
3	Kirby Puckett	.65
4	Rickey Henderson	.50
5	Kevin Mitchell	.25

1	Cecil Fielder	.25
2	Rickey Henderson	.50
3	Barry Bonds	2.00
4	Ryne Sandberg	.65
5	Roger Clemens	1.00
2	Nolan Ryan	2.00
2	Eric Davis	.25
3	Ryne Sandberg	.65
4	Rickey Henderson	.50
5	Kevin Maas	.25
6	Dave Justice	.25
7	Jose Canseco	.35
8	Bo Jackson	.35
9	Roger Clemens	1.00
10	Ken Griffey Jr.	1.50
1	Babe Ruth (1936 Diamond Stars style.)	1.00
1	Ted Williams (1952 Topps style.)	.75
2	Rickey Henderson (1933 Goudey style.)	.50
5	Roger Clemens (1941 Play Ball style.)	1.00
325	Stan Musial (1951 Bowman style.)	.65
11	Frank Thomas	.50
12	Dwight Gooden	.25
13	David Robinson (basketball)	.25
14	Will Clark	.25
15	Darryl Strawberry	.25
16	Kevin Mitchell	.25
17	Tony Gwynn	.65
18	Cal Ripken Jr.	2.00
19	Michael Jordan	1.50
1	Don Mattingly	1.25
1	Frank Thomas	.50
2	Scott Erickson	.25
3	Terry Pendleton	.25
4	Cal Ripken	2.00
5	Barry Bonds	2.00
1	Frank Thomas	.50
2	Jeff Bagwell	.50
3	Cecil Fielder	.50
4	Ken Griffey Jr.	1.50
5	Juan Gonzalez	.35
1	Ryne Sandberg	.65
2	Phil Plantier	.25
3	Barry Larkin	.25
4	Cecil Fielder	.25
5	Dave Justice	.25

1992 The Baseball Enquirer

This set of "Mystery Interview" cards parodies baseball players and baseball cards. The 2-1/2" x 3-1/2" cards have caricatures of well-known players on front, surrounded by a gray border and a blank white name box. A blue "Fun Stuff" trademark is at bottom-right. Backs are printed in blue and black on white with a card number, another blank name box, issuer's trademarks and a mock interview with the player. Actual player names are not seen anywhere on the cards. Issued in 10-card polypacks at 49 cents, complete sets - 184,000 of them - were also issued at $5.

		NM/M
Complete Set (64):		7.50
Common Player:		.50
Pack (7):		.50
Box (36):		7.50
1	Bo Jackson	.65
2	Jose Canseco	.50
3	Mark Langston	.50
4	Billy Ripken	.50
5	David Justice	.50
6	Rob Deer	.50
7	Jack McDowell	.50
8	Cecil Fielder	.50
9	John Smoltz	.50
10	Will Clark	.50
11	Ken Caminiti	.50
12	Kent Hrbek	.50
13	Gregg Jefferies	.50
14	Bob Uecker	.75

1980-88 Baseball Immortals

One of the most popular of the "collectors' issues," this set is produced with the permission of Major League Baseball by Renata Galasso Inc. and TCMA. The set features players in the Baseball Hall of Fame and was first issued in 1980. For several years thereafter the set was updated to include new inductees. The cards measure 2-1/2" x 3-1/2" and have colorful borders. The card fronts include the player's name, position and year of induction. The backs feature a short biography and a trivia question. The photos used are color; most players who were active before 1950 have colored black-and-white photos. The designation "first printing" appears on all cards issued in 1981 and after.

		NM/M
Complete 1980 Set (173):		15.00
Complete Set (199):		30.00
Common Player:		.10
1	Babe Ruth	2.00
2	Ty Cobb	1.00
3	Walter Johnson	.20
4	Christy Mathewson	.20
5	Honus Wagner	.20
6	Morgan Bulkeley	.10
7	Ban Johnson	.10
8	Larry Lajoie	.10
9	Connie Mack	.10
10	John McGraw	.10
11	Tris Speaker	.10
12	George Wright	.10
13	Cy Young	.10
14	Grover Alexander	.10
15	Alexander Cartwright	.10
16	Henry Chadwick	.10
17	Cap Anson	.10
18	Eddie Collins	.10
19	Charles Comiskey	.10
20	Candy Cummings	.10
21	Buck Ewing	.10
22	Lou Gehrig	1.50
23	Willie Keeler	.10
24	Hoss Radbourne	.10
25	George Sisler	.10
26	Albert Spalding	.10
27	Rogers Hornsby	.10
28	Judge Landis	.10
29	Roger Bresnahan	.10
30	Dan Brouthers	.10
31	Fred Clarke	.10
32	James Collins	.10
33	Ed Delahanty	.10
34	Hugh Duffy	.10
35	Hughie Jennings	.10
36	Mike "King" Kelly	.10
37	James O'Rourke	.10
38	Wilbert Robinson	.10
39	Jesse Burkett	.10
40	Frank Chance	.10
41	Jack Chesbro	.10
42	John Evers	.10
43	Clark Griffith	.10
44	Thomas McCarthy	.10
45	Joe McGinnity	.10
46	Eddie Plank	.10
47	Joe Tinker	.10
48	Rube Waddell	.10
49	Ed Walsh	.10
50	Mickey Cochrane	.10
51	Frankie Frisch	.10
52	Lefty Grove	.10
53	Carl Hubbell	.10
54	Herb Pennock	.10
55	Pie Traynor	.10
56	Three Finger Brown	.10
57	Charlie Gehringer	.10
58	Kid Nichols	.10
59	Jimmie Foxx	.10
60	Mel Ott	.10
61	Harry Heilmann	.10
62	Paul Waner	.10
63	Ed Barrow	.10
64	Chief Bender	.10
65	Tom Connolly	.10
66	Dizzy Dean	.10
67	Bill Klem	.10
68	Al Simmons	.10
69	Bobby Wallace	.10
70	Harry Wright	.10
71	Bill Dickey	.10
72	Rabbit Maranville	.10
73	Bill Terry	.10
74	Home Run Baker	.10
75	Joe DiMaggio	2.00
76	Gabby Hartnett	.10
77	Ted Lyons	.10
78	Ray Schalk	.10
79	Dazzy Vance	.10
80	Joe Cronin	.10
81	Hank Greenberg	.10
82	Sam Crawford	.10
83	Joe McCarthy	.10
84	Zack Wheat	.10
85	Max Carey	.10
86	Billy Hamilton	.10
87	Bob Feller	.10
88	Bill McKechnie	.10
89	Jackie Robinson	1.00
90	Edd Roush	.10
91	John Clarkson	.10
92	Elmer Flick	.10
93	Sam Rice	.10
94	Eppa Rixey	.10
95	Luke Appling	.10
96	Red Faber	.10
97	Burleigh Grimes	.10
98	Miller Huggins	.10
99	Tim Keefe	.10
100	Heinie Manush	.10
101	John Ward	.10
102	Pud Galvin	.10
103	Casey Stengel	.10
104	Ted Williams	1.00
105	Branch Rickey	.10
106	Red Ruffing	.10
107	Lloyd Waner	.10
108	Kiki Cuyler	.10
109	Goose Goslin	.10
110	Joe (Ducky) Medwick	.10
111	Roy Campanella	.20
112	Stan Coveleski	.10
113	Waite Hoyt	.10
114	Stan Musial	.50
115	Lou Boudreau	.10
116	Earle Combs	.10
117	Ford Frick	.10
118	Jesse Haines	.10
119	Dave Bancroft	.10
120	Jake Beckley	.10
121	Chick Hafey	.10
122	Harry Hooper	.10
123	Joe Kelley	.10
124	Rube Marquard	.10
125	Satchel Paige	.50
126	George Weiss	.10
127	Yogi Berra	.20
128	Josh Gibson	.10

Mike Greenwell | .50 (15)
No player | .05 (16)

129	Lefty Gomez	.10
130	Will Harridge	.10
131	Sandy Koufax	1.00
132	Buck Leonard	.10
133	Early Wynn	.10
134	Ross Youngs	.10
135	Roberto Clemente	2.00
136	Billy Evans	.10
137	Monte Irvin	.10
138	George Kelly	.10
139	Warren Spahn	.30
140	Mickey Welch	.10
141	Cool Papa Bell	.10
142	Jim Bottomley	.10
143	Jocko Conlan	.10
144	Whitey Ford	.10
145	Mickey Mantle	5.00
146	Sam Thompson	.10
147	Earl Averill	.10
148	Bucky Harris	.10
149	Billy Herman	.10
150	Judy Johnson	.10
151	Ralph Kiner	.10
152	Oscar Charleston	.10
153	Roger Connor	.10
154	Cal Hubbard	.10
155	Bob Lemon	.10
156	Fred Lindstrom	.10
157	Robin Roberts	.10
158	Ernie Banks	.25
159	Martin Dihigo	.10
160	Pop Lloyd	.10
161	Al Lopez	.10
162	Amos Rusie	.10
163	Joe Sewell	.10
164	Addie Joss	.10
165	Larry MacPhail	.10
166	Eddie Mathews	.10
167	Warren Giles	.10
168	Willie Mays	1.00
169	Hack Wilson	.10
170	Duke Snider	.20
171	Al Kaline	.10
172	Chuck Klein	.10
173	Tom Yawkey	.10
174	Bob Gibson	.10
175	Rube Foster	.10
176	Johnny Mize	.10
177	Hank Aaron	1.00
178	Frank Robinson	.10
179	Happy Chandler	.10
180	Travis Jackson	.10
181	Brooks Robinson	.10
182	Juan Marichal	.10
183	George Kell	.10
184	Walter Alston	.10
185	Harmon Killebrew	.10
186	Luis Aparicio	.10
187	Don Drysdale	.10
188	Pee Wee Reese	.10
189	Rick Ferrell	.10
190	Willie McCovey	.10
191	Ernie Lombardi	.10
192	Bobby Doerr	.10
193	Arky Vaughan	.10
194	Enos Slaughter	.10
195	Lou Brock	.10
196	Hoyt Wilhelm	.10
197	Billy Williams	.10
198	"Catfish" Hunter	.10
199	Ray Dandridge	.10

1990 Baseball Wit

15   15

This 108-card set was released in two printings. The first printing featured unnumbered cards and several errors. The second printing featured corrections and numbered cards. The set was available at several retail chains and feature trivia questions on the card backs. The set was dedicated to Little League baseball.

		NM/M
Complete Set (108):		12.50
Common Player:		.10
1	Orel Hershiser	.10
2	Tony Gwynn	.60
3	Mickey Mantle	2.50
4	Willie Stargell	.10
5	Don Baylor	.10
6	Hank Aaron	1.00
7	Don Larsen	.10
8	Lee Mazzilli	.10

9	Boog Powell	.10
10	Little League World Series	.10
11	Jose Canseco	.30
12	Mike Scott	.10
13	Bob Feller	.10
14	Ron Santo	.10
15	Mel Stottlemyre	.10
16	Shea Stadium	.10
17	Brooks Robinson	.25
18	Willie Mays	1.00
19	Ernie Banks	.30
20	Keith Hernandez	.10
21	Bret Saberhagen	.10
22	Hall of Fame	.10
23	Luis Aparicio	.10
24	Yogi Berra	.30
25	Manny Mota	.10
26	Steve Garvey	.10
27	Bill Shea	.10
28	Fred Lynn	.10
29	Todd Worrell	.10
30	Roy Campanella	.30
31	Bob Gibson	.10
32	Gary Carter	.10
33	Jim Palmer	.25
34	Carl Yastrzemski	.10
35	Dwight Gooden	.10
36	Stan Musial	.50
37	Rickey Henderson	.25
38	Dale Murphy	.25
39	Mike Schmidt	.75
40	Gaylord Perry	.10
41	Ozzie Smith	.60
42	Reggie Jackson	.25
43	Steve Carlton	.25
44	Jim Perry	.10
45	Vince Coleman	.10
46	Tom Seaver	.10
47	Marty Marion	.10
48	Frank Robinson	.10
49	Joe DiMaggio	1.50
50	Ted Williams	1.00
51	Rollie Fingers	.10
52	Jackie Robinson	1.00
53	Victor Raschi	.10
54	Johnny Bench	.25
55	Nolan Ryan	1.50
56	Ty Cobb	1.00
57	Harry Steinfeldt	.10
58	James O'Rourke	.10
59	John McGraw	.10
60	Candy Cummings	.10
61	Jimmie Foxx	.10
62	Walter Johnson	.25
63	1903 World Series	.10
64	Satchel Paige	.40
65	Bobby Wallace	.10
66	Cap Anson	.10
67	Hugh Duffy	.10
68	Buck Ewing	.10
69	Bobo Holloman	.10
70	Ed Delehanty (Delahanty)	.10
71	Dizzy Dean	.25
72	Tris Speaker	.10
73	Lou Gehrig	1.50
74	Wee Willie Keeler	.10
75	Cal Hubbell	.10
76	Eddie Collins	.10
77	Chris Von Der Ahe	.10
78	Sam Crawford	.10
79	Cy Young	.25
80	Johnny Vander Meer	.10
81	Joey Jay	.10
82	Zack Wheat	.10
83	Jim Bottomley	.10
84	Honus Wagner	.30
85	Casey Stengel	.10
86	Babe Ruth	1.50
87	John Lindemuth	.10
88	Max Carey	.10
89	Mordecai Brown	.10
90	1869 Red Stockings	.10
91	Rube Marquard	.10
92	Horse Radbourne	.10
93	Hack Wilson	.10
94	Lefty Grove	.10
95	Carl Hubbell	.10
96	A.J. Cartwright	.10
97	Rogers Hornsby	.10
98	Ernest Thayer	.10
99	Connie Mack	.10
100	1939 Centennial Celebration	.10
101	Branch Rickey	.10
102	Dan Brouthers	.10
103	First Baseball Uniform	.10
104	Christy Mathewson	.25
105	Joe Nuxhall	.10
106	1939 Centennial Celebration	.10
107	President Taft	.10
108	Abner Doubleday	.10

1987 Baseball's All-Time Greats

Though the producer is not identified anywhere on the cards, this collectors' issue was created primarily for insertion in beginner's baseball card kits. One series of 50 cards was produced about 1987, a second series some

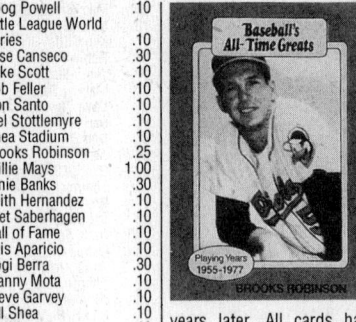

Baseball's All-Time Greats

Playing Years 1955-1977

BROOKS ROBINSON

years later. All cards have bright green or orange borders with a "window" at center in which players are pictured in either color or black-and-white photos, or artwork. The player's major league career span is in a tan oval towards bottom. Horizontal backs have a red strip at top with personal data and also include a career summary. The unnumbered cards are checklisted here in alphabetical order. Variations in photos and the presence or absence of team logos have been observed on some cards. Gaps have been left in the checklist to accommodate additions; "g" for green or "o" for orange borders is shown in parentheses where verified.

		NM/M
Common Player:		.10
(1)	Henry Aaron	1.00
(2)	Joe Adcock	.10
(3)	Richie Allen	.10
(4)	Grover C. Alexander	.10
(5)	Luis Aparicio	.10
(6)	Luke Appling	.10
(7)	Ernie Banks	.25
(8)	Hank Bauer	.10
(9)	Johnny Bench	.15
(10)	"Yogi" Berra	.15
(11)	Lou Boudreau	.10
(12)	Lou Brock	.10
(13)	"Three Finger" Brown	.10
(14)	Jim Bunning	.10
(15)	Roy Campanella	.25
(16)	Rod Carew	.10
(17)	Orlando Cepeda	.10
(18)	Roberto Clemente	1.00
(19a)	Ty Cobb (g)	1.00
(19b)	Ty Cobb (o)	1.00
(20)	Mickey Cochrane	.10
(21)	Rocky Colavito	.10
(22)	Eddie Collins	.10
(23)	Sam Crawford	.10
(24)	Joe Cronin	.10
(25)	Alvin Dark	.10
(26)	Dizzy Dean	.10
(27)	Bill Dickey	.10
(28)	Joe DiMaggio	1.00
(29)	Larry Doby	.10
(30)	Don Drysdale	.10
(31)	Leo Durocher	.10
(32)	Carl Erskine	.10
(33)	Bob Feller	.10
(34)	Curt Flood	.10
(35a)	Whitey Ford (g) (Chest, cap logos.)	.10
(36)	Jimmie Foxx	.10
(37a)	Frankie Frisch (g) (Jersey logo.)	.10
(38)	Carl Furillo	.10
(39a)	Lou Gehrig (g)	1.25
(39b)	Lou Gehrig (o)	1.25
(40)	Charlie Gehringer	.10
(41)	Bob Gibson (g)	.25
(42)	Hank Greenberg	.10
(43)	"Lefty" Grove	.10
(44)	"Gabby" Hartnett	.10
(45)	Gil Hodges	.10
(46)	Rogers Hornsby	.10
(47)	Carl Hubbell	.10
(48)	Jim Hunter	.10
(49)	Monte Irvin	.10
(50)	Ferguson Jenkins	.10
(51)	Walter Johnson	.10
(52)	Jim Kaat	.10
(53)	Al Kaline (g)	.00
(54)	George Kell	.10
(55)	Ralph Kiner	.10
(56)	Ted Kluszewski	.10
(57)	Don Larsen	.10
(58)	Bob Lemon	.10
(59)	Ernie Lombardi	.10
(61)	Eddie Lopat	.10
(62a)	Mickey Mantle (o) (Chest-up portrait.)	2.00
(63)	Juan Marichal	.10
(64)	Roger Maris	.50
(65)	Billy Martin	.10
(66)	Eddie Mathews	.10

(67)	Christy Mathewson	.25
(68)	Willie Mays	1.00
(69)	Bill Mazeroski	.10
(70)	Joe Morgan	.10
(71)	Thurman Munson	.10
(72)	Stan Musial	.50
(73)	Tony Oliva	.10
(74)	Mel Ott	.10
(75)	Jim Palmer	.10
(76)	Gaylord Perry	.10
(77)	Boog Powell	.10
(78)	Pee Wee Reese	.10
(79)	Robin Roberts	.10
(80a)	Brooks Robinson (g) (Baltimore jersey.)	.25
(81)	Frank Robinson (g)	.25
(82a)	Jackie Robinson (g)	1.00
(82b)	Jackie Robinson (o)	1.00
(83a)	Babe Ruth (g)	1.50
(83b)	Babe Ruth (o)	1.50
(84)	Tom Seaver	.10
(85)	Bobby Shantz	.10
(86)	Al Simmons	.10
(87)	George Sisler	.10
(88)	Enos Slaughter	.10
(89)	Duke Snider	.10
(90)	Warren Spahn (g)	.25
(91)	Tris Speaker	.10
(92)	Willie Stargell	.10
(93)	Bill Terry	.10
(95)	Bobby Thomson	.10
(96)	Pie Traynor	.10
(97)	Honus Wagner	.25
(98)	Ed Walsh	.10
(99)	Paul Waner	.10
(100)	Hoyt Wilhelm	.10
(101)	Billy Williams	.10
(102)	Ted Williams	1.00
(103)	Maury Wills	.10
(104)	Early Wynn	.10
(105)	Carl Yastrzemski	.25
(106)	Cy Young (o)	.25
(107)	Ross Youngs	.10

1988 Bazooka

This 22-card set from Topps marks the first Bazooka issue since 1971. Full-color player photos are bordered in white, with the player name printed on a red, white and blue bubble gum box in the lower right corner. Flip sides are also red, white and blue, printed vertically. A large, but faint, Bazooka logo backs the Topps baseball logo team name, card number, player's name and position, followed by batting records, personal information and brief career highlights. Cards were sold inside specially marked 59¢ and 79¢ Bazooka gum and candy boxes, one card per box.

		NM/M
Complete Set (22):		3.00
Common Player:		.10
1	George Bell	.10
2	Wade Boggs	.50
3	Jose Canseco	.25
4	Roger Clemens	.60
5	Vince Coleman	.10
6	Eric Davis	.10
7	Tony Fernandez	.10
8	Dwight Gooden	.10
9	Tony Gwynn	.50
10	Wally Joyner	.10
11	Don Mattingly	.60
12	Willie McGee	.10
13	Mark McGwire	.75
14	Kirby Puckett	.50
15	Tim Raines	.10
16	Dave Righetti	.10
17	Cal Ripken, Jr.	1.00
18	Juan Samuel	.10
19	Ryne Sandberg	.50
20	Benny Santiago	.10
21	Darryl Strawberry	.10
22	Todd Worrell	.10

1989 Bazooka

SHINING STAR

GREGG JEFFERIES   Bazooka STARTER SET

Topps produced this 22-card set in 1989 to be included (one card per box) in specially-marked boxes of its Bazooka brand bubblegum. The player photos have the words "Shining Star" along the top, while the player's name appears along the bottom of the card, along with the Topps Bazooka logo in the lower right corner. The cards are numbered alphabetically.

		NM/M
Complete Set (22):		3.00
Common Player:		.10
1	Tim Belcher	.10
2	Damon Berryhill	.10
3	Wade Boggs	.75
4	Jay Buhner	.10
5	Jose Canseco	.25
6	Vince Coleman	.10
7	Cecil Espy	.10
8	Dave Gallagher	.10
9	Ron Gant	.10
10	Kirk Gibson	.10
11	Paul Gibson	.10
12	Mark Grace	.10
13	Tony Gwynn	.75
14	Rickey Henderson	.50
15	Orel Hershiser	.10
16	Gregg Jefferies	.10
17	Ricky Jordan	.10
18	Chris Sabo	.10
19	Gary Sheffield	.40
20	Darryl Strawberry	.10
21	Frank Viola	.10
22	Walt Weiss	.10

1990 Bazooka

SHINING STAR

RICKEY HENDERSON   Bazooka

For the second consecutive year, Bazooka entitled its set "Shining Stars." Full-color action and posed player shots are featured on the card fronts. The flip sides feature player statistics in a style much like the cards from the previous two Bazooka issues. Unlike the past two releases, the cards are not numbered alphabetically. The cards measure 2-1/2" x 3-1/2" in size and 22 cards complete the set.

		NM/M
Complete Set (22):		3.00
Common Player:		.10
1	Kevin Mitchell	.10
2	Robin Yount	.40
3	Mark Davis	.10
4	Bret Saberhagen	.10
5	Fred McGriff	.10
6	Tony Gwynn	.50
7	Kirby Puckett	.50
8	Vince Coleman	.10
9	Rickey Henderson	.40
10	Ben McDonald	.10
11	Gregg Olson	.10
12	Todd Zeile	.10
13	Carlos Martinez	.10
14	Gregg Jefferies	.10
15	Craig Worthington	.10

16	Gary Sheffield	.25
17	Greg Briley	.10
18	Ken Griffey Jr.	1.50
19	Jerome Walton	.10
20	Bob Geren	.10
21	Tom Gordon	.10
22	Jim Abbott	.10

1991 Bazooka

SHINING STAR

GEORGE BRETT

For the third consecutive year Bazooka entitled its set "Shining Stars." The cards are styled like the 1990 issue, but include the Topps "40th Anniversary" logo. The 1991 issue is considered much scarcer than the previous releases. The cards measure 2-1/2" x 3-1/2" in size and 22 cards complete the set.

		NM/M
Complete Set (22):		5.00
Common Player:		.10
1	Barry Bonds	3.50
2	Rickey Henderson	.50
3	Bob Welch	.10
4	Doug Drabek	.10
5	Alex Fernandez	.10
6	Jose Offerman	.10
7	Frank Thomas	.50
8	Cecil Fielder	.10
9	Ryne Sandberg	.75
10	George Brett	1.00
11	Willie McGee	.10
12	Vince Coleman	.10
13	Hal Morris	.10
14	Delino DeShields	.10
15	Robin Ventura	.10
16	Jeff Huson	.10
17	Felix Jose	.10
18	Dave Justice	.10
19	Larry Walker	.10
20	Sandy Alomar, Jr.	.10
21	Kevin Appier	.10
22	Scott Radinsky	.10

1992 Bazooka

BILL BRUTON   WHITEY FORD

ED LOPAT   MICKEY VERNON

This set of 22 cards features miniature versions of the 1953 Topps Archives issue. The mini-cards are set against a blue background on front and back. Besides reproductions of issued 1953 Topps cards, these "Quadracards" include miniature versions of many of the special cards created for the Archives set. Cards feature the Bazooka logo on back, and were distributed in boxes of that bubble gum.

		NM/M
Complete Tin-Box Set (22):		16.00
Complete Set (22):		8.00
Common Player:		.25
1	Joe Adcock, Bob Lemon, Willie Mays, Vic Wertz	1.50
2	Carl Furillo, Don Newcombe, Phil Rizzuto, Hank Sauer	.25

3	Ferris Fain, John Logan, Ed Mathews, Bobby Shantz	.25
4	Yogi Berra, Del Crandall, Howie Pollett, Gene Woodling	.25
5	Richie Ashburn, Leo Durocher, Allie Reynolds, Early Wynn	.25
6	Hank Aaron, Ray Boone, Luke Easter, Dick Williams	1.50
7	Ralph Branca, Bob Feller, Rogers Hornsby, Bobby Thomson	.25
8	Jim Gilliam, Billy Martin, Orestes Minoso, Hal Newhouser	.25
9	Smoky Burgess, John Mize, Preacher Roe, Warren Spahn	.25
10	Monte Irvin, Bobo Newsom, Duke Snider, Wes Westrum	.25
11	Carl Erskine, Jackie Jensen, George Kell, Al Schoendienst	.25
12	Bill Bruton, Whitey Ford, Ed Lopat, Mickey Vernon	.25
13	Joe Black, Lew Burdette, Johnny Pesky, Enos Slaughter	.25
14	Gus Bell, Mike Garcia, Mel Parnell, Jackie Robinson	1.25
15	Alvin Dark, Dick Groat, Pee Wee Reese, John Sain	.25
16	Gil Hodges, Sal Maglie, Wilmer Mizell, Billy Pierce	.45
17	Nellie Fox, Ralph Kiner, Ted Kluszewski, Eddie Stanky	.25
18	Ewell Blackwell, Vern Law, Satchell Paige, Jim Wilson	.45
19	Lou Boudreau, Roy Face, Harvey Haddix, Bill Rigney	.25
20	Roy Campanella, Walt Dropo, Harvey Kuenn, Al Rosen	.45
21	Joe Garagiola, Robin Roberts, Casey Stengel, Hoyt Wilhelm	.25
22	John Antonelli, Bob Friend, Dixie Walker, Ted Williams	1.00

1993 Bazooka Team USA

The members of Team USA are featured on this boxed set. The 2-1/2" x 3-1/2" cards feature the same basic design as 1993 Topps baseball, except for a Bazooka gum logo in one of the upper corners. Both front and back feature posed player photos. Backs have a design simulating the U.S. flag and include amateur stats, biographical details and career highlights. The cards are virtually identical to the same players' cards in the 1993 Topps Traded set, with the addition of the Bazooka logo on front and the differences in card numbers. A special tin-boxed edition with 50 pieces of gum was produced in an edition reported as 750.

	NM/M
Complete Set (22):	100.00
Complete Tin Set (22):	150.00
Common Player:	.50

1	Terry Harvey	.50
2	Dante Powell	.50
3	Andy Barkett	.50
4	Steve Reich	.50
5	Charlie Nelson	.50
6	Todd Walker	1.00
7	Dustin Hermanson	1.00
8	Pat Clougherty	.50
9	Danny Graves	.50
10	Paul Wilson	.75
11	Todd Helton	90.00
12	Russ Johnson	.50
13	Darren Grass	.50
14	A.J. Hinch	.50
15	Mark Merila	.50
16	John Powell	.50
17	Bob Scafa	.50
18	Matt Beaumont	.50
19	Todd Dunn	.50
20	Mike Martin	.50
21	Carlton Loewer	.50
22	Bret Wagner	.50

1995 Bazooka

Topps returned to the beginner's level baseball card niche in 1995 by resurrecting its Bazooka brand name. The set was unabashedly aimed at the younger collector, offering five cards and a Bazooka Joe cartoon-wrapped chunk of bubblegum for 50 cents. Cards feature on their backs a "roulette" wheel design based on the player's 1994 stats, to be used to play a game of spinner baseball. A game instruction card and cardboard spinner was included in each pack. Limiting the set to 132 cards allowed for a concentration of established stars and hot youngsters. A 22-card Red Hot insert is found at the rate of one card per six packs, on average. Factory sets offering the 132 base cards, five Red Hot inserts and 10 pieces of bubblegum were produced.

	NM/M
Complete Set (132):	3.00
Factory Set (132+5):	5.00
Common Player:	
Pack (5):	.30
Wax Box (36):	7.00

1	Greg Maddux	
2	Cal Ripken Jr.	1.00
3	Lee Smith	
4	Sammy Sosa	.50
5	Jason Bere	.05
6	Dave Justice	
7	Kevin Mitchell	.05
8	Ozzie Guillen	.05
9	Roger Clemens	.60
10	Mike Mussina	.30
11	Sandy Alomar	.05
12	Cecil Fielder	.05
13	Dennis Martinez	.05
14	Randy Myers	.05
15	Jay Buhner	.05
16	Ivan Rodriguez	.35
17	Mo Vaughn	.05
18	Ryan Klesko	.05
19	Chuck Finley	.05
20	Barry Bonds	1.00
21	Dennis Eckersley	.35
22	Kenny Lofton	.05
23	Rafael Palmeiro	.05
24	Mike Stanley	.05
25	Gregg Jefferies	.05
26	Robin Ventura	.05
27	Mark McGwire	.75
28	Ozzie Smith	.50
29	Troy Neel	.05
30	Tony Gwynn	.50
31	Ken Griffey Jr.	.65
32	Will Clark	.05
33	Craig Biggio	.05
34	Shawon Dunston	.05
35	Wilson Alvarez	.05
36	Bobby Bonilla	.05
37	Marquis Grissom	.05
38	Ben McDonald	.05
39	Delino DeShields	.05
40	Barry Larkin	.05
41	John Olerud	.05
42	Jose Canseco	.30
43	Greg Vaughn	.05
44	Gary Sheffield	.20
45	Paul O'Neill	.05
46	Bob Hamelin	.05
47	Don Mattingly	.60
48	John Franco	.05
49	Bret Boone	.05
50	Rick Aguilera	.05
51	Tim Wallach	.05
52	Roberto Kelly	.05
53	Danny Tartabull	.05
54	Randy Johnson	.40
55	Greg McMichael	.05
56	Bip Roberts	.05
57	David Cone	.05
58	Raul Mondesi	.05
59	Travis Fryman	.05
60	Jeff Conine	.05
61	Jeff Bagwell	.40
62	Rickey Henderson	.40
63	Fred McGriff	.05
64	Matt Williams	.05
65	Rick Wilkins	.05
66	Eric Karros	.05
67	Mel Rojas	.05
68	Juan Gonzalez	.20
69	Chuck Carr	.05
70	Moises Alou	.05
71	Mark Grace	.05
72	Alex Fernandez	.05
73	Rod Beck	.05
74	Ray Lankford	.05
75	Dean Palmer	.05
76	Joe Carter	.05
77	Mike Piazza	.65
78	Eddie Murray	.40
79	Dave Nilsson	.05
80	Brett Butler	.05
81	Roberto Alomar	.10
82	Jeff Kent	.05
83	Andres Galarraga	.05
84	Brady Anderson	.05
85	Jimmy Key	.05
86	Bret Saberhagen	.05
87	Chili Davis	.05
88	Jose Rijo	.05
89	Wade Boggs	.50
90	Len Dykstra	.05
91	Steve Howe	.05
92	Hal Morris	.05
93	Larry Walker	.05
94	Jeff Montgomery	.05
95	Wil Cordero	.05
96	Jay Bell	.05
97	Tom Glavine	.15
98	Chris Hoiles	.05
99	Steve Avery	.05
100	Ruben Sierra	.05
101	Mickey Tettleton	.05
102	Paul Molitor	.40
103	Carlos Baerga	.05
104	Walt Weiss	.05
105	Darren Daulton	.05
106	Jack McDowell	.05
107	Doug Drabek	.05
108	Mark Langston	.05
109	Manny Ramirez	.40
110	Kevin Appier	.05
111	Andy Benes	.05
112	Chuck Knoblauch	.05
113	Kirby Puckett	.50
114	Dante Bichette	.05
115	Deion Sanders	.10
116	Albert Belle	.05
117	Todd Zeile	.05
118	Devon White	.05
119	Tim Salmon	.05
120	Frank Thomas	.05
121	John Wetteland	.05
122	James Mouton	.05
123	Javy Lopez	.05
124	Carlos Delgado	.25
125	Cliff Floyd	.05
126	Alex Gonzalez	.05
127	Billy Ashley	.05
128	Rondell White	.05
129	Rico Brogna	.05
130	Melvin Nieves	.05
131	Jose Oliva	.05
132	J.R. Phillips	.05

1995 Bazooka Red Hot Inserts

Twenty-two of the game's biggest stars were chosen for inclusion in 1995 Bazooka's only insert set - Red Hots. The chase cards are found at an average rate of one per six packs. Red Hots are identical to the players' cards in the regular set except that the background has been rendered in shades of red, and the player

name printed in gold foil. Card numbers have an "RH" prefix.

	NM/M
Complete Set (22):	7.00
Common Player:	.15

1	Greg Maddux	1.00
2	Cal Ripken Jr.	2.00
3	Barry Bonds	2.00
4	Kenny Lofton	.15
5	Mike Stanley	.15
6	Tony Gwynn	1.00
7	Ken Griffey Jr.	1.50
8	Barry Larkin	.15
9	Jose Canseco	.35
10	Paul O'Neill	.15
11	Randy Johnson	.75
12	David Cone	.15
13	Jeff Bagwell	.75
14	Matt Williams	.15
15	Mike Piazza	1.50
16	Roberto Alomar	.25
17	Jimmy Key	.15
18	Wade Boggs	1.00
19	Paul Molitor	.75
20	Carlos Baerga	.15
21	Albert Belle	.15
22	Frank Thomas	.75

1996 Bazooka

Topps' 1996 Bazooka set offers collectors interactive fun with its cards geared for a flipping game. Each front has an action photo of the player. The back contains one of five different Bazooka Joe characters, along with the Bazooka Ball game, the player's biographical data, and 1995 and career stats. Cards were available five per pack for 50 cents. The complete set was also offered in a factory set, packaged in an attractive gift box. As an exclusive bonus, one 1959 Bazooka Mickey Mantle reprint card is found in every factory set, along with 10 pieces of bubble gum.

	NM/M
Unopened Fact. Set (133):	9.00
Complete Set (132):	6.00
Common Player:	.05
Pack (5):	.40
Wax Box (36):	9.00

1	Ken Griffey Jr.	.75
2	J.T. Snow	.05
3	Rondell White	.05
4	Reggie Sanders	.05
5	Jeff Montgomery	.05
6	Mike Stanley	.05
7	Bernie Williams	.05
8	Mike Piazza	.75
9	Brian Hunter	.05
10	Len Dykstra	.05
11	Ray Lankford	.05
12	Kenny Lofton	.05
13	Robin Ventura	.05
14	Devon White	.05
15	Cal Ripken Jr.	1.50
16	Heathcliff Slocumb	.05
17	Ryan Klesko	.05
18	Terry Steinbach	.05
19	Travis Fryman	.05
20	Sammy Sosa	.50
21	Jim Thome	.35
22	Kenny Rogers	.05
23	Don Mattingly	.60
24	Kirby Puckett	.05
25	Matt Williams	.05
26	Larry Walker	.05
27	Tim Wakefield	.05
28	Greg Vaughn	.05
29	Denny Neagle	.05
30	Ken Caminiti	.05
31	Garret Anderson	.05
32	Brady Anderson	.05
33	Carlos Baerga	.05
34	Wade Boggs	.50
35	Roberto Alomar	.15
36	Eric Karros	.05
37	Jay Buhner	.05
38	Dante Bichette	.05
39	Darren Daulton	.05
40	Jeff Bagwell	.40
41	Jay Bell	.05
42	Dennis Eckersley	.35
43	Will Clark	.05
44	Tom Glavine	.20
45	Rick Aguilera	.05
46	Kevin Seitzer	.05
47	Bret Boone	.05
48	Mark Grace	.05
49	Ray Durham	.05
50	Rico Brogna	.05
51	Kevin Appier	.05
52	Moises Alou	.05
53	Jeff Conine	.05
54	Marty Cordova	.05
55	Jose Mesa	.05
56	Rod Beck	.05
57	Marquis Grissom	.05
58	David Cone	.05
59	Albert Belle	.05
60	Lee Smith	.05
61	Frank Thomas	.05
62	Roger Clemens	.60
63	Bobby Bonilla	.05
64	Paul Molitor	.40
65	Chuck Knoblauch	.05
66	Steve Finley	.05
67	Craig Biggio	.05
68	Ramon Martinez	.05
69	Jason Isringhausen	.05
70	Mark Wohlers	.05
71	Vinny Castilla	.05
72	Ron Gant	.05
73	Juan Gonzalez	.20
74	Mark McGwire	1.00
75	Jeff King	.05
76	Pedro Martinez	.40
77	Chad Curtis	.05
78	John Olerud	.05
79	Greg Maddux	.05
80	Derek Jeter	1.50
81	Mike Mussina	.25
82	Gregg Jefferies	.05
83	Jim Edmonds	.05
84	Carlos Perez	.05
85	Mo Vaughn	.05
86	Todd Hundley	.05
87	Roberto Hernandez	.05
88	Derek Bell	.05
89	Andres Galarraga	.05
90	Brian McRae	.05
91	Joe Carter	.05
92	Orlando Merced	.05
93	Cecil Fielder	.05
94	Dean Palmer	.05
95	Randy Johnson	.40
96	Chipper Jones	.50
97	Barry Larkin	.05
98	Hideo Nomo	.25
99	Gary Gaetti	.05
100	Edgar Martinez	.05
101	John Wetteland	.05
102	Rafael Palmeiro	.35
103	Chuck Finley	.05
104	Ivan Rodriguez	.35
105	Shawn Green	.10
106	Manny Ramirez	.40
107	Lance Johnson	.05
108	Jose Canseco	.20
109	Fred McGriff	.05
110	David Segui	.05
111	Tim Salmon	.05
112	Hal Morris	.05
113	Tino Martinez	.05
114	Bret Saberhagen	.05
115	Brian Jordan	.05
116	David Justice	.05
117	Jack McDowell	.05
118	Barry Bonds	1.50
119	Mark Langston	.05
120	John Valentin	.05
121	Raul Mondesi	.05
122	Quilvio Veras	.05
123	Randy Myers	.05
124	Tony Gwynn	.50
125	Johnny Damon	.20
126	Doug Drabek	.05
127	Bill Pulsipher	.05
128	Paul O'Neill	.05
129	Rickey Henderson	.40
130	Deion Sanders	.10
131	Orel Hershiser	.05
132	Gary Sheffield	.20

1996 Bazooka Mickey Mantle 1959 Reprint

Continuing its tribute to the late Mickey Mantle across all of its product lines, Topps produced a special reprint of the 1959 Bazooka Mantle card exclusively for inclusion in factory sets of its 1996 Bazooka cards. While the original '59 Mantle was printed in nearly 3" x 5" size on the bottom of gum boxes, the reprint is in the current 2-1/2" x 3-1/2" size.

	NM/M
Mickey Mantle	7.50

1992 Ben's Bakery Super Hitters Discs

Ben's Bakery, a small eastern Canadian bakery, inserted promotional discs in its hot dog and hamburger buns in 1992. As in the case of 1991, which was the company's first year in the promotion, the 1992 set contained 20 different players, including many of the top stars in the country. Twenty of the game's top hitters, with a special emphasis on Blue Jays players, are featured in this regional issue by a small Eastern Canada bakery. The 2-3/4" diameter discs were packaged in the company's hot dog and hamburger buns. Fronts feature a color photo on which team logos have been airbrushed away. The bakery logo is flanked by a red "Super Hitters" in the white border at top. The player's name appears in white on an orange banner beneath the photo, with his team and position in blue at bottom. Backs are printed in black and include a few biographical details and 1991 stats, along with a card number and appropriate logos and copyright notices.

	NM/M
Complete Set (20):	15.00
Common Player:	.75

1	Cecil Fielder	.75
2	Joe Carter	.75
3	Roberto Alomar	1.00
4	Devon White	.75
5	Kelly Gruber	.75
6	Cal Ripken, Jr.	3.50
7	Kirby Puckett	2.00
8	Paul Molitor	1.50
9	Julio Franco	.75
10	Ken Griffey Jr.	3.00
11	Frank Thomas	1.50
12	Jose Canseco	1.25
13	Danny Tartabull	.75
14	Terry Pendleton	.75
15	Tony Gwynn	2.00
16	Howard Johnson	.75
17	Will Clark	.75
18	Barry Bonds	3.50

19	Ryne Sandberg	2.00
20	Bobby Bonilla	.75

1993 Ben's Bakery Super Pitchers Discs

An emphasis on Toronto's pitchers is noted in the checklist for this regional bakery issue. The 2-3/4" diameter discs were packed with hot dog and hamburger buns and follow a 1991 issue by the company featuring super hitters. A color player portrait at center has had the uniform logos airbrushed away. "Super Pitchers" in red flanks the bakery logo in the white border above the photo. The player's name appears in white in an orange banner beneath the photo, with his team and position in blue at bottom. Backs are printed in black and include minimal biographical data, a card number, 1992 stats and copyright information.

		NM/M
Complete Set (20):		10.00
Common Player:		.45
1	Dennis Eckersley	1.50
2	Chris Bosio	.45
3	Jack Morris	.45
4	Greg Maddux	2.50
5	Dennis Martinez	.45
6	Tom Glavine	.75
7	Doug Drabek	.45
8	John Smoltz	.45
9	Randy Myers	.45
10	Jack McDowell	.45
11	John Wetteland	.45
12	Roger Clemens	3.00
13	Mike Mussina	.75
14	Juan Guzman	.45
15	Jose Rijo	.45
16	Tom Henke	.45
17	Gregg Olson	.45
18	Jim Abbott	.45
19	Jimmy Key	.45
20	Rheal Cormier	.45

1987 David Berg Hot Dogs Cubs

(8) ANDRE DAWSON, OF

Changing sponsors from Gatorade to David Berg Pure Beef Hot Dogs, the Chicago Cubs handed out a 26-card set of baseball cards to fans attending the July 29th game at Wrigley Field. The cards are printed in full-color on white stock and measure 2-7/8" x 4-1/4" in size. The set is numbered by the players' uniform numbers. The card backs contain player personal and statistical information, plus a full-color picture of a David Berg hot dog in a bun with all the garnishings. The set marked the sixth consecutive year the Cubs held a baseball card giveaway promotion.

		NM/M
Complete Set (26):		10.00
Common Player:		.40
1	Dave Martinez	.40
4	Gene Michael	.40
7	Keith Moreland	.40
7	Jody Davis	.40
8	Andre Dawson	1.00
10	Leon Durham	.40
11	Jim Sundberg	.40
12	Shawon Dunston	.40
19	Manny Trillo	.40
20	Bob Dernier	.40
21	Scott Sanderson	.40
22	Jerry Mumphrey	.40
23	Ryne Sandberg	5.00
29	Brian Dayett	.40
29	Chico Walker	.40
31	Greg Maddux	5.00
33	Frank DiPino	.40
34	Steve Trout	.40
37	Gary Matthews	.40
37	Ed Lynch	.40
39	Ron Davis	.40
46	Rick Sutcliffe	.40
46	Lee Smith	.40
49	Dickie Noles	.40
49	Jamie Moyer	.40
---	The Coaching Staff (Johnny Oates, Jim Snyder, Herm Starrette, John Vukovich, Billy Williams)	.40

1988 David Berg Hot Dogs Cubs

(17) MARK GRACE, IF

This oversized (2-7/8" x 4-1/2") set of 26 cards was distributed to fans at Wrigley Field on August 24th. The set includes cards for the manager and coaching staff, as well as players. Full-color action photos are framed in red and blue on a white background. The backs feature small black and white player close-ups, colorful team logos, statistics and sponsor logos (David Berg Hot Dogs and Venture Store Restaurants). The numbers in the following checklist refer to players' uniforms.

		NM/M
Complete Set (27):		17.50
Common Player:		.40
2	Vance Law	.40
4	Don Zimmer	.40
7	Jody Davis	.40
8	Andre Dawson	1.00
9	Damon Berryhill	.40
12	Shawon Dunston	.40
17	Mark Grace	1.00
18	Angel Salazar	.40
19	Manny Trillo	.40
22	Scott Sanderson	.40
22	Jerry Mumphrey	.40
23	Ryne Sandberg	4.00
24	Gary Varsho	.40
25	Rafael Palmeiro	2.50
28	Mitch Webster	.40
30	Darrin Jackson	.40
31	Greg Maddux	4.00
32	Calvin Schiraldi	.40
33	Frank DiPino	.40
37	Pat Perry	.40
40	Rick Sutcliffe	.40
43	Jeff Pico	.40
45	Al Nipper	.40
49	Jamie Moyer	.40
50	Les Lancaster	.40
54	Rich Gossage	.40
---	The Coaching Staff (Joe Altobelli, Chuck Cottier, Larry Cox, Jose Martinez, Dick Pole)	.40

1994 Big Apple 1969 Mets Discs

Big Apple Collector, Inc. released the "1969 World

Champion Miracle Mets Commemorative Cap Sheet," which has likenesses of each of the 31 members of the squad captured in oil paintings by sports artist Ron Lewis. The player's likeness is centered in a 1-5/8" diameter round commemorative cap which is die cut but remains in place on the sheet. Each cap is gold foil accented, and each 11" x 14" sheet is produced in full color on 48-point card stock. The sheet has a suggested retail price of $39.95.

		NM/M
Complete Set (31):		12.00
Common Player:		.25
		.00
(1)	Gil Hodges	1.50
(2)	Rube Walker	.25
(3)	Yogi Berra	1.50
(4)	Joe Pignatano	.25
(5)	Ed Yost	.25
(6)	Tommie Agee	.25
(7)	Ken Boswell	.25
(8)	Don Cardwell	.25
(9)	Ed Charles	.25
(10)	Donn Clendenon	.25
(11)	Jack DiLauro	.25
(12)	Duffy Dyer	.25
(13)	Wayne Garrett	.25
(14)	Rod Gaspar	.25
(15)	Gary Gentry	.25
(16)	Jerry Grote	.25
(17)	Bud Harrelson	.30
(18)	Cleon Jones	.25
(19)	Cal Koonce	.25
(20)	Jerry Koosman	.30
(21)	Ed Kranepool	.25
(22)	J.C. Martin	.25
(23)	Jim McAndrew	.25
(24)	Tug McGraw	.40
(25)	Bob Pfeil	.25
(26)	Nolan Ryan	4.00
(27)	Tom Seaver	2.00
(28)	Art Shamsky	.25
(29)	Ron Swoboda	.25
(30)	Ron Taylor	.25
(31)	Al Weis	.25

2001 The Big Book of Jewish Baseball

HY COHEN

To promote its book on Jewish ballplayers, S.P.I. Books of Ft. Lee, N.J., issued a nine-card sheet. The sheet measures 8-1/2" x 12". At top on a purple background are nine cards which, if cut out on the yellow dotted lines, would each measure 2-11/16" x 3-3/8". Card #1 pictures the book's cover with its picture of Sandy Koufax. The other cards have color photos or colorized photos of some of the players featured in the book. Black-and-white backs have minimal player data and stats. At the bottom of the sheet is a coupon for ordering the book.

		NM/M
Sheet:		6.00
Complete Set (9):		6.00
Common Player:		.50

(1980s Big League Cards card shown)

BOBBY LOANE
OUTFIELDER
1939-1940

(1)	Book Cover (Sandy Koufax)	2.00
2	Lipman Pike	1.00
3	Moe Berg	2.00
4	Jesse Levis	.50
5	Harry Shuman	.50
6	Hank Greenberg	1.00
7	Harry Danning	.50
8	Cy Malis	.50
9	Hy Cohen	.50

1980s Big League Cards

Former major league pitcher and author Jim Bouton was a principal in the most successful of many "vanity" card manufacturers which sprang up in the 1980s and 1990s. For a price, anybody could send a picture to the New Jersey company and have it placed on a run of baseball cards. Persons could, and did, also send photos of ballplayers to create fantasy cards and at least several ballplayers who never appeared on cards contemporary with their careers had cards made up for themselves retroactively. Fronts have black, blue and red graphics. Backs are printed in blue on white with personal data, stats and other information provided by person ordering the cards. Unlike most other contemporary vanity cards, the Big League Cards are printed on thick quality similar to vintage baseball cards. There is no way to document the individual issue of these cards.

(Collector value indeterminable.)

1986 Big League Chew

HOME RUN LEGENDS

1945

OUTFIELDER
MEL OTT

The 1986 Big League Chew set consists of 12 cards featuring the players who have hit 500 or more career home runs. The cards, which measure 2-1/2" x 3-1/2", were inserted in specially marked packages of Big League Chew, the shredded bubble gum developed by former major leaguer Jim Bouton. The set is entitled "Home Run Legends" and was available through a write-in offer on the package. Recent-day players in the set are shown in color photos, while the older sluggers are pictured in black and white.

		NM/M
Complete Set (12):		10.00
Common Player:		1.00

1	Hank Aaron	2.00
2	Babe Ruth	3.00
3	Willie Mays	2.00
4	Frank Robinson	1.00
5	Harmon Killebrew	1.00
6	Mickey Mantle	4.00
7	Jimmie Foxx	1.00
8	Ted Williams	2.00
9	Ernie Banks	1.00
10	Eddie Mathews	1.00
11	Mel Ott	1.00
12	500-HR Group Card	.50

1997 Big League Chew Alumni

JUAN MARICHAL

Autographed cards of three Hall of Famers were available through a mail-in offer by Big League Chew shredded bubble gum. Cards could be obtained by sending in proofs of purchase from pouches with the players' photos on them. Each card comes with a certificate of authenticity from Major League Baseball Players Alumni, which licensed the issue. Because the cards are not licensed by Major League Baseball, uniform logos have been removed from the color photos. Cards have a green, orange and white color scheme on front and back and are standard 2-1/2" x 3-1/2". Backs include career highlights and lifetime stats.

		NM/M
Complete Set (3):		20.00
Common Player:		7.50
(1)	Juan Marichal	7.50
(2)	Brooks Robinson	7.50
(3)	Billy Williams	7.50

1982 Big League Collectibles Diamond Classics, Series 1

Attempting to recapture the flavor of vintage baseball cards, this collectors set presents former stars in a 2-1/2" x 3-3/4" format on thick white cardboard stock. Fronts have a painted player portrait in color with no other graphic elements. Backs are in black and blue and include in-depth biographical sketches and career stats. The edition was limited to 10,000 sets.

		NM/M
Complete Set (56):		30.00
Common Player:		.60
1	Joe DiMaggio	5.00
2	Enos Slaughter	.60

3	Smokey Joe Wood (Smoky)	.60
4	Roy Campanella	1.25
5	Charlie Gehringer	.60
6	Carl Hubbell	.60
7	Rogers Hornsby	.60
8	Arky Vaughan	.60
9	Al Simmons	.60
10	Wally Berger	.60
11	Sam Rice	.60
12	Dizzy Dean	.60
13	Babe Ruth	5.00
14	Frankie Frisch	.60
15	George Kell	.60
16	Pee Wee Reese	.60
17	Earl Averill	.60
18	Willie Mays	2.50
19	Frank Baker	.60
20	Hack Wilson	.60
21	Ted Williams	3.00
22	Chuck Klein	.60
23	Bill Dickey	.60
24	Johnny Mize	.60
25	Luke Appling	.60
26	Duke Snider	.60
27	Wahoo Sam Crawford	.60
28	Waite Hoyt	.60
29	Eddie Collins	.60
30	Warren Spahn	.60
31	Satchel Paige	1.25
32	Ernie Lombardi	.60
33	Dom DiMaggio	.60
34	Joe Garagiola	.60
35	Lou Gehrig	2.50
36	Burleigh Grimes	.60
37	Walter Johnson	.60
38	Bill Terry	.60
39	Ty Cobb	2.50
40	Pie Traynor	.60
41	Ted Lyons	.60
42	Richie Ashburn	.60
43	Lefty Grove	.60
44	Edd Roush	.60
45	Phil Rizzuto	.60
46	Stan Musial	2.00
47	Bob Feller	.60
48	Jackie Robinson	2.50
49	Hank Greenberg	1.25
50	Mel Ott	.60
51	Joe Cronin	.60
52	Lefty O'Doul	.60
53	Indian Bob Johnson	.60
54	Kiki Cuyler	.60
55	Mickey Mantle	7.50
---	Checklist	.10

1983 Big League Collectibles Diamond Classics, Series 2

A second series of cards featuring past greats was issued by Big League Collectibles in 1983. Again at 55 cards, the set featured painted portraits of the players on front, devoid of any other graphics. Backs are in red and black and include a lengthy career summary along with innovative stats and a few biographical bits. The 2-1/2" x 3-3/4" cards are printed on a heavy white cardboard stock. The series was produced in an edition of 10,000 sets.

		NM/M
Complete Set (56):		20.00
Common Player:		.60
56	Ernie Banks	1.50
57	Stan Coveleski	.60
58	Vince DiMaggio	.60
59	Sunny Jim Bottomley	.60
60	Sandy Koufax	4.00
61	Doc Cramer	.60
62	Ted Kluszewski	.60
63	Zeke Bonura	.60
64	Spud Davis	.60
65	Jackie Jensen	.60
66	Honus Wagner	.75
67	Brooks Robinson	.60

68	Dazzy Vance	.60
69	George Uhle	.60
70	Juan Marichal	.60
71	Bobo Newsom	.60
72	Billy Herman	.60
73	Al Rosen	.60
74	Roberto Clemente	4.00
75	George Case	.60
76	Bill Nicholson	.60
77	Tommy Bridges	.60
78	Rabbit Maranville	.60
79	Bob Lemon	.60
80	Heinie Groh	.60
81	Tris Speaker	.60
82	Hank Aaron	4.00
83	Whitey Ford	1.25
84a	Guy Bush (Ernie Banks back.)	.60
84b	Guy Bush (Correct back.)	.60
85	Jimmie Foxx	.60
86	Marty Marion	.60
87a	Hal Newhouser (Charlie Grimm back.)	.60
87b	Hal Newhouser (Correct back.)	.60
88	George Kelley (Kelly)	.60
89	Harmon Killebrew	.60
90	Willie McCovey	.60
91	Mel Harder	.60
92	Vada Pinson	.60
93	Luis Aparicio	.60
94	Grover Alexander	.60
95	Joe Kuhel	.60
96	Casey Stengel	.60
97	Joe Sewell	.60
98	Red Lucas	.60
99	Luke Sewell	.60
100	Charlie Grimm	.60
101	Cecil Travis	.60
102	Travis Jackson	.60
103	Lou Boudreau	.60
104	Nap Rucker	.60
105	Chief Bender	.60
106	Riggs Stephenson	.60
107	Red Ruffing	.60
108	Robin Roberts	.60
109	Harland Clift (Harland)	.60
110	Ralph Kiner	.60
---	Checklist	.10

1983 Big League Collectibles Original All-Stars

Players in the first modern All-Star Game, staged in conjunction with the Chicago World's Fair in 1933, are featured in this collectors issue. The 2-1/2" x 3-3/4" cards feature pastel paintings of the players on front. A circled baseball at lower-left has player and set identification. Backs are printed in blue and black and include All-Star Game and overall 1933 season performance.

		NM/M
Complete Set (40):		20.00
Common Player:		.50
American League		
2	Connie Mack	.50
3	Alvin Crowder	.50
4	Lefty Gomez	.50
5	Jimmy Dykes	.50
6	Earl Averill	.50
7	Charlie Gehringer	.50
8	Lefty Grove	.50
9	Lou Gehrig	2.00
10	Al Simmons	.50
11	Ben Chapman	.50
12	Jimmie Foxx	.75
13	Oral Hildebrand	.50
14	Joe Cronin	.50
15	Bill Dickey	.50
16	Sam West	.50
17	Rick Ferrell	.50
18	Tony Lazzeri	.50
19	Wes Ferrell	.50
20	Babe Ruth	2.50
National League		
22	John McGraw	.50
23	Pepper Martin	.50
24	Woody English	.50
25	Paul Waner	.50
26	Lefty O'Doul	.50
27	Chuck Klein	.50
28	Tony Cuccinello	.50
29	Frankie Frisch	.50
30	Gabby Hartnett	.50
31	Carl Hubbell	.50
32	Chick Hafey	.50
33	Dick Bartell	.50
34	Bill Hallahan	.50
35	Hal Schumacher	.50
36	Lon Warneke	.50
37	Wally Berger	.50
38	Bill Terry	.50
39	Jimmy Wilson	.50
40	Pie Traynor	.50

1985 Big League Collectibles National Pastime 1930-1939

SYLVESTER W. JOHNSON Pit-N P

Major league baseball in the 1930s is chronicled in this boxed collectors set. In 2-1/8" x 3-1/8" format (the same size as the 1951-52 Bowmans), the cards feature painted player portraits on front with identification in the white border at bottom. Backs are in black and red on thick white cardboard stock and feature in-depth career summaries and unique stats. The edition was limited to 5,000 sets, with a serially numbered header card.

		NM/M
Complete Set (90):		45.00
Common Player:		.60
1	Header card	.10
2	William H. Walters	.60
3	Montgomery M. Pearson	.60
4	Stanley C. Hack	.60
5	Joseph E. Cronin	.60
6	Leo E. Durocher	.60
7	Max F. Bishop	.60
8	Frank O'Donnell Hurst	.60
9	W. Barney McCosky	.60
10	Remy P. Kremer	.60
11	Julius J. Solters	.60
12	Daniel K. MacFayden	.60
13	Gordon S. Cochrane	.60
14	Ethan N. Allen	.60
15	Luzerne A. Blue	.60
16	John R. Mize	.60
17	Joseph P. DiMaggio	3.50
18	George F. Grantham	.60
19	William E. Kamm	.60
20	Charles A. Root	.60
21	Morris Berg	2.00
22	Floyd C. Herman	.60
23	Henry E. Manush	.60
24	Adolf L. Camilli	.60
25	Rudolph P. York	.60
26	Truett B. Sewell	.60
27	Richard B. Ferrell	.60
28	Arthur C. Whitney	.60
29	Edmund J. Miller	.60
30	August R. Mancuso	.60
31	John B. Conlan	.60
32	Joseph M. Medwick	.60
33	John T. Allen	.60
34	John S. Vander Meer	.60
35	H. Earl Averill	.60
36	Taylor L. Douthit	.60
37	Charles S. Myer	.60
38	Van Lingle Mungo	.60
39	Smead P. Jolley	.60
40	C. Flint Rhem	.60
41	Leon A. Goslin	.60
42	Adam A. Comorosky	.60
43	Jack I. Burns	.60
44	Edward A. Brandt	.60
45	Robert L. Johnson	.60
46	Melvin T. Ott	.60
47	Monty F.P. Stratton	.60
48	Paul D. Dean	.60
49	H. Louis Gehrig	3.50
50	Frank A. McCormick	.60
51	J. Geoffrey Heath	.60
52	Charles L. Hartnett	.60
53	Oswald L. Bluege	.60
54	George H. Ruth	6.00
55	Robert P. Doerr	.60
56	Virgil L. Davis	.60
57	D. Dale Alexander	.60
58	James A. Tobin	.60
59	Joseph F. Vosmik	.60
60	Alfonso R. Lopez	.60
61	James E. Foxx	.60
62	Frederick L. Fitzsimmons	.60
63	Robert R. Fothergill	.60
64	Morton C. Cooper	.60
65	George A. Selkirk	.60
66	Burton E. Shotton	.60
67	Robert W.A. Feller	.60
68	Lawrence H. French	.60
69	Joseph I. Judge	.60
70	Clyde L. Sukeforth	.60
71	James R. Tabor	.60
72	Silas K. Johnson	.60
73	W. Earl Webb	.60
74	Charles F. Lucas	.60
75	Ralph Kress	.60
76	Charles D. Stengel	.60
77	George W. Haas	.60
78	Joe G. Moore	.60
79	Carl N. Reynolds	.60
80	James O. Carleton	.60
81	John J. Murphy	.60
82	Paul Derringer	.60
83	Harold A. Trosky, Sr.	.60
84	Fred C. Lindstrom	.60
85	Jack E. Russell	.60
86	Stanley G. Bordagaray	.60
87	Roy C. Johnson	.60
88	Sylvester W. Johnson	.60
89	Michael F. Higgins	.60
90	J. Floyd Vaughan	.60

1989 Bimbo Cookies Super Stars Discs

A dozen Hispanic players are featured in this set of 2-3/4" diameter discs distributed in Puerto Rico in boxes of cookies. Color portrait photos at center have cap logos removed because the discs are licensed only by the players' union, not MLB; typical for issues from Michael Schechter Associates. The Bimbo bear logo is at top-center, with the player name in a yellow strip at bottom; team and position are in blue in the white border beneath that. Yellow stars, blue baseballs and red words "SUPER STARS" flank the player photo. Backs are printed in blue and have a few biographical details, 1988 card year stats, card number and appropriate logos.

		NM/M
Complete Set (12):		15.00
Common Player:		1.50
1	Carmelo Martinez	1.50
2	Candy Maldonado	1.50
3	Benito Santiago	1.50
4	Rey Quinones	1.50
5	Jose Oquendo	1.50
6	Ruben Sierra	1.50
7	Jose Lind	1.50
8	Juan Beniquez	1.50
9	Willie Hernandez	1.50
10	Juan Nieves	1.50
11	Jose Guzman	1.50
12	Roberto Alomar (Photo actually Sandy Alomar Jr.)	3.50

1991-1992 Bleachers Promos

To introduce its 1992 lineup of single-player 23-Karat gold trimmed card sets, Bleachers produced a series of promo cards. Fronts have color portraits of the players. Backs have another picture of the player and information about ordering and coming releases. The Nolan Ryan card, showing him winding up in a tuxedo, is known in several variations with different card show names stamped on front in gold, representing venues at which sample cards were given away.

		NM/M
Complete Set (3):		3.00
(1)	Ken Griffey Jr.	1.00
(2)	David Justice	.50
(3)	Nolan Ryan	2.00

1991 Bleachers Frank Thomas

This limited edition three-card set features 23-Karat gold cards. The photos feature Frank Thomas at different stages of his baseball career before the big leagues. Production was limited to 10,000 sets and 1,500 uncut strips. All are numbered and feature a gold facsimile autograph on the back.

		NM/M
Complete Set (3):		4.00
Common Card:		2.00
1	Frank Thomas (Auburn Tigers)	2.00
2	Frank Thomas (Sarasota White Sox)	2.00
3	Frank Thomas (Birmingham Barons)	2.00

1992 Bleachers Ken Griffey, Jr.

KEN GRIFFEY, JR. MOELLER HIGH SCHOOL - OF

Young superstar Ken Griffey, Jr. is honored in this three-card set featuring him at different stages of his baseball career. The 23-Karat gold cards feature full-color photos and a facsimile autograph on the back. Production was limited to 10,000 cut sets and 1,500 uncut strips.

		NM/M
Complete Set (3):		10.00
Common Card:		3.00
1	Ken Griffey Jr. (Moeller High School)	4.00
2	Ken Griffey Jr. (Bellingham Mariners)	4.00
3	Ken Griffey Jr. (San Bernadino Spirit)	4.00

1992 Bleachers David Justice

Atlanta Brave slugger David Justice is the subject of this three card 23-Karat gold set. The cards depict Justice at different stages of his baseball career. Like the other Bleachers issues, production was limited to 10,000 cut card sets and 1,500 uncut strips.

		NM/M
Complete Set (3):		6.00
Common Card:		2.50
1	David Justice (Durham Bulls)	2.50
2	David Justice (Greenville Braves)	2.50
3	David Justice (Richmond Braves)	2.50

1992 Bleachers Nolan Ryan

Three stops along Ryan's minor league trail are recalled in this collectors issue. The 2-1/2" x 3-1/2" cards have photos of Ryan at center with different colored borders and trim on each card. "23KT," his name and team are gold-foil stamped on front. Backs have career information and highlights, along with a serial number from within an edition of 10,000. Cards with silver prismatic foil on front rather than gold were random inserts in sets. Three-card uncut strips were made available in an edition of 1,500.

		NM/M
Complete Set (3):		6.00
Common Card:		2.00
Silver-foil:		2X
1	Nolan Ryan (Marion Mets)	2.00
2	Nolan Ryan (Greenville Mets)	2.00
3	Nolan Ryan (Jacksonville Suns)	2.00

1993 Bleachers Promos

To introduce its 1993 issues, Bleachers distributed large quantities of promo cards within the hobby to dealers and to the public at several large card shows. Most of the '93 promos can be found with several different show logos overprinted in gold foil on the front. All cards carry a 1993 copyright date on back, except the plain Ryan/tuxedo card, which has a 1992 date on back, but 1993 card-show indicia on front.

		NM/M
Common Card:		1.00
(1)	Barry Bonds (Arizona State)	2.00
(2)	Ken Griffey Jr. (Moeller High School uniform.)	2.00
(3)	Nolan Ryan (Triple-exposure pitching.)	2.00
(4)	Nolan Ryan (Tuxedo, '92 copyright.)	2.00
(5)	Nolan Ryan (Tuxedo, gold background.)	2.00
(6)	Nolan Ryan (Tuxedo, silver speckled background.)	2.00
(7)	Nolan Ryan (Tuxedo, wavy silver background.)	2.00
(8)	Nolan Ryan (Western clothing.)	2.00
(9)	Nolan Ryan (W/glove and ball in Bleachers cap.)	2.00
(10)	Nolan Ryan (With Yellow Lab puppy.)	2.00
(11)	Ryne Sandberg (3-sport high school photos.)	1.00

1993 Bleachers Barry Bonds

The pre-major league career of Barry Bonds is featured on this trio of collectors cards. Fronts have color photos of Bonds within a gold border. His name, team and the notation "23KT" are printed in gold foil. Backs have career data and highlights, along with a serial number. It was reported that 10,000 sets and 1,500 three-card strips were issued. Cards found with silver prismatic borders on front are random inserts in sets.

		NM/M
Complete Set (3):		9.00
Common Card:		3.00
Silver:		2X
1	Barry Bonds (Arizona State University)	4.00
2	Barry Bonds (Price Williams Pirates)	4.00
3	Barry Bonds (Hawaii Islanders)	4.00

1993 Bleachers Nolan Ryan

Nolan Ryan's career is recapped in this set of collectors issues. Fronts have prismatic foil borders around color or colorized photos. Information on front is stamped in gold foil. Backs have a photo of a young

Ryan along with career data and stats, and a serial number from within an announced edition of 10,000 sets and 1,500 three-card uncut strips.

		NM/M
Complete Set (6):		15.00
Common Card:		3.00
1	Nolan Ryan (Little League)	3.00
2	Nolan Ryan (High school.)	3.00
3	Nolan Ryan (Minor league highlights.)	3.00
4	Nolan Ryan (Minor league stats.)	3.00
5	Nolan Ryan (Strikeout record.)	3.00
6	Nolan Ryan (Career highlights.)	3.00

1993 Bleachers Nolan Ryan 23KT

"The Express" is pictured with each of his four major league teams in this collectors issue. Each 2-1/2" x 3-1/2" card has a color photo of Ryan at center with variously colored borders and gold-foil graphic highlights. Backs have his stats with that team, a facsimile autograph and a serial number from within an edition of 10,000 sets. Uncut strips were also issued, numbered to 1,500.

		NM/M
Complete Set (4):		15.00
Uncut Strip:		20.00
Common Card:		4.00
1	Nolan Ryan/Mets	4.00
2	Nolan Ryan/Angels	4.00
3	Nolan Ryan/Astros	4.00
4	Nolan Ryan/Rangers	4.00

1993 Bleachers Ryne Sandberg

Ryno's pre-major league career is featured on this trio of collectors cards. Fronts have color photos of Sandberg within a gold border. His name, team and the notation "23KT" are printed in gold foil. Backs have career data and highlights, along with a serial number. It was reported that 10,000 sets and 1,500 three-card, gold highlighted strips were issued. Cards found with silver prismatic borders on front are random inserts in sets.

	NM/M
Complete Set (3):	9.00
Common Card:	3.00
Gold Strip:	12.00
Silver:	3X

1	Ryne Sandberg (North Central H.S.)	3.00
2	Ryne Sandberg (Helena Phillies)	3.00
3	Ryne Sandberg (Reading Phillies)	3.00

1992 Blockbuster Video Pin/Cards

Given away at special promotional games, these combination collectibles feature a 2-3/4" x 4" card, beneath which is a perforated tab of 2-3/4" x 1-9/16". The card has a borderless photo with the player name and his uniform number. The tab has a sponsor's logo. Attached to the tab is an enameled pin, about 1-1/4" square, which has a representation of the player's jersey. The black-and-white back has a portrait photo, player biographical details and career highlights. On back of the tab is a list of the Blockbuster locations participating in the promotion.

		NM/M
Common Player:		3.00
3	Jay Bell	3.00
6	Orlando Merced	3.00
15	Doug Drabek	3.00
24	Barry Bonds	15.00

1988 Blue Cross/Blue Shield Bob Uecker Reprint

Issued as a fund-raiser and sold for $3 to benefit Bob Uecker's Ride for the Arts bicycling event in 1988, this 2-1/2" x 3-1/2" card features on its front a reprint of Uecker's card from the 1963 Topps set. Back has history and details of the fund-raiser and the logos of Blue Cross and Blue Shield.

		NM/M
(1)	Bob Uecker	6.00

1987 Bluegrass State Games

Athletes with ties to Kentucky and public figures from the state are featured on this set issued in conjunction with the 1987 Bluegrass State

Games. Fronts have color photos on a blue background with white borders. Beneath the photo are the logos of Champions Against Drugs and sponsors Coke and Valvoline. Backs have an anti-drug message from the pictured celebrity. Cards were handed out over the period May 25-October 19 by law enforcement officers. Only the baseball-related cards are listed here.

		NM/M
Complete Set (24):		50.00
Common Player:		.50
5	Doug Flynn	1.00
13	Pee Wee Reese	5.00
22	A.B. (Happy) Chandler	1.00

1987 Boardwalk and Baseball All Time Record Holders

This boxed set was a repackaging of the cards produced by Topps for Woolworth stores in 1985. Fronts have "framed" black-and-white or color photos with player identification in a "plaque" at bottom. Blue-on-orange backs have brief biographical data, a listing of the player's record and career highlights, and lifetime stats.

(See 1985 Woolworth for checklist and values.)

1987 Boardwalk and Baseball Top Run Makers

Created by Topps for distribution at the Boardwalk and Baseball theme park near Orlando, Fla., the cards are standard size with a thin, pink border around a color action photo. The backs are printed in black and light red, with the Topps and B/B logos at the bottom. There are 33-cards in the "Top Run Makers" boxed set, all hitters. A checklist appears on the back panel of the box. A much scarcer version of each card can be found with no slash between the "B"s on front.

		NM/M
Complete Set (33):		4.00
Common Player:		.10
No Slash:		3X
1	Mike Schmidt	1.00
2	Eddie Murray	.45
3	Dale Murphy	.25
4	Dave Winfield	.45
5	Jim Rice	.25
6	Cecil Cooper	.10
7	Dwight Evans	.10
8	Rickey Henderson	.45
9	Robin Yount	.45
10	Andre Dawson	.25
11	Gary Carter	.45
12	Keith Hernandez	.10
13	George Brett	1.00
14	Bill Buckner	.10
15	Tony Armas	.10
16	Harold Baines	.10
17	Don Baylor	.10
18	Steve Garvey	.10
19	Lance Parrish	.10
20	Dave Parker	.10
21	Buddy Bell	.10
22	Cal Ripken, Jr.	1.50
23	Bob Horner	.10
24	Tim Raines	.10
25	Jack Clark	.10
26	Leon Durham	.10
27	Pedro Guerrero	.10
28	Kent Hrbek	.10
29	Kirk Gibson	.10
30	Ryne Sandberg	.60
31	Wade Boggs	.60
32	Don Mattingly	.75
33	Darryl Strawberry	.10

1987 Bohemian Hearth Bread Padres

Bohemian Hearth Bread of San Diego issued this Padres team set. Produced in conjunction with Mike Schechter Associates, the cards are 2-1/2" x 3-1/2". Fronts have a color portrait photo encompassed by a yellow border. The Bohemian Hearth logo is located in the upper-left corner. Card backs are printed in light brown on a cream stock and carry player personal and statistical information, along with a facsimile autograph.

		NM/M
Complete Set (22):		20.00
Common Player:		.50
1	Garry Templeton	.50
4	Jose Cora	.50
5	Randy Ready	.50
6	Steve Garvey	3.00
7	Kevin Mitchell	.50
8	John Kruk	.65
9	Benito Santiago	.75
10	Larry Bowa	.50
11	Tim Flannery	.50
14	Carmelo Martinez	.50
16	Marvell Wynne	.50
19	Tony Gwynn	15.00
21	James Steels	.50
22	Stan Jefferson	.50
30	Eric Show	.50
31	Ed Whitson	.50
34	Storm Davis	.50
37	Craig Lefferts	.50
40	Andy Hawkins	.50
41	Lance McCullers	.50
43	Dave Dravecky	.50
54	Rich Gossage	.50

1984 Borden's Reds Stickers

This regional set of eight Reds stickers was issued by Borden Dairy in the Cincinnati area in 1984. Originally issued in two perforated sheets of four stickers each, the individual stickers measure 2-1/2" x 3-7/8", while a full sheet measures 5-1/2" x 8". The colorful stickers feature a player photo surrounded by a bright red border with the Reds logo and the Borden logo in the corners. The backs display coupons for Borden dairy products. The set is numbered according to the players' uniform numbers.

		NM/M
Complete Panel Set (2):		8.00
Complete Singles Set (8):		8.00
Common Player:		.50
	PANEL (1)	5.00
2	Gary Redus	.50
20	Eddie Milner	.50
24	Tony Perez	3.00
46	Jeff Russell	.50
	PANEL (2)	3.00
16	Ron Oester	.50
36	Mario Soto	.50
39	Dave Parker	.60
44	Eric Davis	1.00

1983 Boston Herald Sox Stamps

Current and former Red Sox stars are featured in this set of stamps issued by one of Boston's daily newspapers. Coupons in the paper could be redeemed for packets of stamps which could be mounted on a large (34" x 22") colorful wallchart. Persons completing the set could enter a contest for various prizes. Stamps #1-26 and 39-42 are in color and feature portrait photos of the '83 team. They measure 1" x 1-3/4". Stamps #27-38 and 43-50 are 1" x 1-1/8" and may have either color or black-and-white photos of current and former players. Values shown are for unused stamps.

		NM/M
Complete Set (50):		30.00
Common Player:		.50
Wallchart:		15.00
1	Jerry Remy	.50
2	Glenn Hoffman	.50
3	Luis Aponte	.50
4	Jim Rice	1.00
5	Mark Clear	.50
6	Reid Nichols	.50
7	Wade Boggs	5.00
8	Dennis Eckersley	2.00
9	Jeff Newman	.50
10	Bob Ojeda	.50
11	Ed Jurak	.50
12	Rick Miller	.50
13	Carl Yastrzemski	7.50
14	Mike Brown	.50
15	Bob Stanley	.50
16	John Tudor	.50
17	Gary Allenson	.50
18	Rich Gedman	.50
19	Tony Armas	.75
20	Doug Bird	.50
21	Bruce Hurst	.50
22	Dave Stapleton	.50
23	Dwight Evans	1.00
24	Julio Valdez	.50
25	John Henry Johnson	.50
26	Ralph Houk	.50
27	George Scott	.75
28	Bobby Doerr	.60
29	Frank Malzone	.50
30	Rico Petrocelli	.75
31	Carl Yastrzemski	5.00
32	Ted Williams	7.50
33	Dwight Evans	.75
34	Carlton Fisk	4.00
35	Dick Radatz	.50
36	Luis Tiant	.75
37	Mel Parnell	.50
38	Jim Rice	.75
39	Dennis Boyd	.60
40	Marty Barrett	.50
41	Brian Denman	.50
42	Steve Crawford	.50
43	Cy Young	.75
44	Jimmy Collins	.50
45	Tris Speaker	.75
46	Harry Hooper	.50
47	Lefty Grove	.60
48	Joe Cronin	.50
49	Jimmie Foxx	.75
50	Ted Williams	7.50

1982 Boston Red Sox Favorites

No issuer is identified on this collectors set, though some attribute it to the Boston Globe newspaper. The 2-1/2" x 3-1/2" cards are black-and-white with rather wide white borders on front. There is no player identification on front. Backs are roughly in the style of 1955 Bowmans and have player identification, personal data, stats, career highlights and a trivia question.

		NM/M
Complete Set (128):		35.00
Common Player:		.25
1	Harry Agganis	2.00
2	Ken Aspromonte	.25
3	Bobby Avila	.25
4	Frank Baumann	.25
5	Lou Berberet	.25
6	Milt Bolling	.25
7	Lou Boudreau	.50
8	Ted Bowsfield	.25
9	Tom Brewer	.25
10	Don Buddin	.25
11	Jerry Casale	.25
12	Billy Consolo	.25
13	Pete Daley	.25
14	Ike Delock	.25
15	Dom DiMaggio	1.00
16	Bobby Doerr	.50
17	Walt Dropo	.50
18	Arnold Earley	.25
19	Hoot Evers	.25
20	Mike Fornieles	.25
21	Gary Geiger	.25
22	Don Gile	.25
23	Joe Ginsberg	.25
24	Billy Goodman	.25
25	Pumpsie Green	.35
26	Grady Hatten	.25
27	Mike Higgins	.25
28	Jackie Jensen	.50
29	George Kell	.50
30	Marty Keough	.25
31	Leo Kiely	.25
32	Ellis Kinder	.25
33	Billy Klaus	.25
34	Don Lenhardt	.25
35	Ted Lepcio	.25
36	Frank Malzone	.35
37	Gene Mauch	.25

38	Maury McDermott	.25
39	Bill Monbouquette	.25
40	Chet Nichols	.25
41	Willard Nixon	.25
42	Jim Pagliaroni	.25
43	Mel Parnell	.25
44	Johnny Pesky	.25
45	Jimmy Piersall	.50
46	Bob Porterfield	.25
47	Pete Runnels	.25
48	Dave Sisler	.25
49	Riverboat Smith	.25
50	Gene Stephens	.25
51	Vern Stephens	.25
52	Chuck Stobbs	.25
53	Dean Stone	.25
54	Frank Sullivan	.25
55	Haywood Sullivan	.25
56	Birdie Tebbetts	.25
57	Mickey Vernon	.35
58	Vic Wertz	.25
59	Sammy White	.25
60	Ted Williams	6.00
61	Ted Wills	.25
62	Earl Wilson	.25
63	Al Zarilla	.25
64	Norm Zauchin	.25
65	Ted Williams, Carl Yastrzemski	4.00
66	Jim Lonborg, George Scott, Dick Williams, Carl Yastrzemski	2.00
67	Billy Conigliaro, Tony Conigliaro	.75
68	Jerry Adair	.25
69	Mike Andrews	.25
70	Gary Bell	.25
71	Dennis Bennett	.25
72	Ed Bressoud	.25
73	Ken Brett	.25
74	Lu Clinton	.25
75	Tony Conigliaro	1.00
76	Billy Conigliaro	.25
77	Gene Conley	.25
78	Ray Culp	.25
79	Dick Ellsworth	.25
80	Joe Foy	.25
81	Russ Gibson	.25
82	Jim Gosger	.25
83	Lennie Green	.25
84	Ken Harrelson	.25
85	Tony Horton	.35
86	Elston Howard	.35
87	Dalton Jones	.25
88	Eddie Kasko	.25
89	Joe Lahoud	.25
90	Jack Lamabe	.25
91	Jim Lonborg	.50
92	Sparky Lyle	.50
93	Felix Mantilla	.25
94	Roman Mejias	.25
95	Don McMahon	.25
96	Dave Morehead	.25
97	Gerry Moses	.25
98	Mike Nagy	.25
99	Russ Nixon	.25
100	Gene Oliver	.25
101	Dan Osinski	.25
102	Rico Petrocelli	.50
103	Juan Pizzaro	.25
104	Dick Radatz	.25
105	Vicente Romo	.25
106	Mike Ryan	.25
107	Jose Santiago	.25
108	Chuck Schilling	.35
109	Dick Schofield	.25
110	Don Schwall	.25
111	George Scott	.35
112	Norm Siebern	.25
113	Sonny Siebert	.25
114	Reggie Smith	.35
115	Bill Spanswick	.25
116	Tracy Stallard	.25
117	Lee Stange	.25
118	Jerry Stephenson	.25
119	Dick Stuart	.25
120	Tom Sturdivant	.25
121	Jose Tartabull	.25
122	George Thomas	.25
123	Lee Thomas	.25
124	Bob Tillman	.25
125	Gary Waslewski	.25
126	Dick Williams	.25
127	John Wyatt	.25
128	Carl Yastrzemski	4.00

1993 Boston Red Sox Police

This police set was issued by the police department and local sponsors around the Red Sox spring training base in Florida. Card fronts have studio poses of the players. The Winter Haven P.D. and Police Athletic League logos are at top, while the Red Sox logo, player ID and uniform number are beneath the portrait. Backs have a little personal data,

some stats, a safety message and the names of sponsoring businesses.

		NM/M
Complete Set (28):		10.00
Common Player:		.50
1	Checklist	.10
2	Scott Bankhead	.50
3	Danny Darwin	.50
4	Andre Dawson	.75
5	Scott Fletcher	.50
6	Billy Hatcher	.50
7	Jack Clark	.50
8	Roger Clemens	5.00
9	Scott Cooper	.50
10	John Dopson	.50
11	Paul Quantrill	.50
12	Mike Greenwell	.50
13	Greg A. Harris	.50
14	Joe Hesketh	.50
15	Peter Hoy	.50
16	Daryl Irvine	.50
17	John Marzano	.50
18	Jeff McNeeley	.50
19	Tim Naehring	.50
20	Matt Young	.50
21	Jeff Plympton	.50
22	Bob Melvin	.50
23	Tony Pena	.50
24	Luis Rivera	.50
25	Scott Taylor	.50
26	John Valentin	.50
27	Mo Vaughn	.50
28	Frank Viola	.50

2001 Boston Red Sox 100 Seasons

This limited edition card set was issued by the team as part of its 100 seasons anniversary. One card was designated as a give-away at each of 16 home games during spring training. The first 4,000 fans at each game received that day's card. An additional 1,000 sets was reserved for team use. The 2-1/2" x 3-1/2" cards have sepia photos on front, along with a 100 seasons logo and the years the player was with the Red Sox. Backs have a Grapefruit League logo, a few career highlights and the logos of the sponsors, Aramark and gulf-coasting.com.

		NM/M
Complete Set (16):		25.00
Common Player:		1.00
1	Jimmy Collins	1.00
2	Cy Young	2.00
3	Tris Speaker	1.50
4	Babe Ruth	7.50
5	Lefty Grove	1.00
6	Joe Cronin	1.00
7	Jimmie Foxx	1.50
8	Bobby Doerr	1.00
9	Ted Williams	6.00
10	Dom DiMaggio	1.00
11	Johnny Pesky	1.00
12	Carl Yastrzemski	4.00
13	Carlton Fisk	3.00
14	Jim Rice	1.50
15	Nomar Garciaparra	4.50
16	Pedro Martinez	2.50

1987 Bowery Bank Joe DiMaggio

These cards were issued to promote the New York City bank's relationship with spokesman Joe DiMaggio. The 2-1/2" x 3-1/2" cards have a posed color photo on front. The back has biographical data, career highlights and stats printed in black and red.

| | NM/M |
| Joe DiMaggio | 17.50 |

1989 Bowman

Topps, which purchased Bowman in 1955, revived the brand name in 1989, issuing a 484-card set. The 2-1/2" x 3-3/4" cards are slightly taller than current standard. Fronts contain a full-color player photo, with facsimile autograph and the Bowman logo in an upper corner. Backs include a breakdown of the player's stats against each team in his league. A series of "Hot Rookie Stars" highlights the set. The cards were distributed in both wax packs and rack packs. Each pack included a special reproduction of a classic Bowman card with a sweepstakes on the back.

		NM/M
Unopened Fact. Set (484):		20.00
Complete Set (484):		15.00
Common Player:		.05
Wax Pack (12+1):		.75
Wax Box (36):		15.00
Rack Pack (40):		1.00
Rack Box (24):		20.00
1	Oswald Peraza	.05
2	Brian Holton	.05
3	Jose Bautista	.05
4	Pete Harnisch RC	.10
5	Dave Schmidt	.05
6	Gregg Olson	.05
7	Jeff Ballard	.05
8	Bob Melvin	.05
9	Cal Ripken, Jr.	.75
10	Randy Milligan	.05
11	Juan Bell RC	.05
12	Billy Ripken	.05
13	Jim Trabor	.05
14	Pete Stanicek	.05
15	Steve Finley RC	.25
16	Larry Sheets	.05
17	Phil Bradley	.05
18	Brady Anderson	.05
19	Lee Smith	.05
20	Tom Fischer	.05
21	Mike Boddicker	.05
22	Rob Murphy	.05
23	Wes Gardner	.05
24	John Dopson	.05
25	Bob Stanley	.05
26	Roger Clemens	.60
27	Rich Gedman	.05
28	Marty Barrett	.05
29	Luis Rivera	.05
30	Jody Reed	.05
31	Nick Esasky	.05
32	Wade Boggs	.50
33	Jim Rice	.20
34	Mike Greenwell	.05
35	Dwight Evans	.05
36	Ellis Burks	.05
37	Chuck Finley	.05
38	Kirk McCaskill	.05
39	Jim Abbott	.05
40	Bryan Harvey RC	.05
41	Bert Blyleven	.05
42	Mike Witt	.05
43	Bob McClure	.05
44	Bill Schroeder	.05
45	Lance Parrish	.05
46	Dick Schofield	.05
47	Wally Joyner	.05
48	Jack Howell	.05
49	Johnny Ray	.05
50	Chili Davis	.05
51	Tony Armas	.05
52	Claudell Washington	.05
53	Brian Downing	.05
54	Devon White	.05
55	Bobby Thigpen	.05
56	Bill Long	.05
57	Jerry Reuss	.05
58	Shawn Hillegas	.05
59	Melido Perez	.05
60	Jeff Bittiger	.05
61	Jack McDowell	.05
62	Carlton Fisk	.40
63	Steve Lyons	.05
64	Ozzie Guillen	.05
65	Robin Ventura	.05
66	Fred Manrique	.05
67	Dan Pasqua	.05
68	Ivan Calderon	.05
69	Ron Kittle	.05
70	Daryl Boston	.05
71	Dave Gallagher	.05
72	Harold Baines	.05
73	Charles Nagy RC	.15
74	John Farrell	.05
75	Kevin Wickander	.05
76	Greg Swindell	.05
77	Mike Walker	.05
78	Doug Jones	.05
79	Rich Yett	.05
80	Tom Candiotti	.05
81	Jesse Orosco	.05
82	Bud Black	.05
83	Andy Allanson	.05
84	Pete O'Brien	.05
85	Jerry Browne	.05
86	Brook Jacoby	.05
87	Mark Lewis RC	.05
88	Luis Aguayo	.05
89	Cory Snyder	.05
90	Oddibe McDowell	.05
91	Joe Carter	.05
92	Frank Tanana	.05
93	Jack Morris	.05
94	Doyle Alexander	.05
95	Steve Searcy	.05
96	Randy Bockus	.05
97	Jeff Robinson	.05
98	Mike Henneman	.05
99	Paul Gibson	.05
100	Frank Williams	.05
101	Matt Nokes	.05
102	Rico Brogna	.05
103	Lou Whitaker	.05
104	Al Pedrique	.05
105	Alan Trammell	.05
106	Chris Brown	.05
107	Pat Sheridan	.05
108	Gary Pettis	.05
109	Keith Moreland	.05
110	Mel Stottlemyre, Jr.	.05
111	Bret Saberhagen	.05
112	Floyd Bannister	.05
113	Jeff Montgomery	.05
114	Steve Farr	.05
115	Tom Gordon	.05
116	Charlie Leibrandt	.05
117	Mark Gubicza	.05
118	Mike MacFarlane	.05
119	Bob Boone	.05
120	Kurt Stillwell	.05
121	George Brett	.60
122	Frank White	.05
123	Kevin Seitzer	.05
124	Willie Wilson	.05
125	Pat Tabler	.05
126	Bo Jackson	.10
127	Hugh Walker	.05
128	Danny Tartabull	.05
129	Teddy Higuera	.05
130	Don August	.05
131	Juan Nieves	.05
132	Mike Birkbeck	.05
133	Dan Plesac	.05
134	Chris Bosio	.05
135	Bill Wegman	.05
136	Chuck Crim	.05
137	B.J. Surhoff	.05
138	Joey Meyer	.05
139	Dale Sveum	.05
140	Paul Molitor	.40
141	Jim Gantner	.05
142	Gary Sheffield RC	.75
143	Greg Brock	.05
144	Robin Yount	.40
145	Glenn Braggs	.05
146	Rob Deer	.05
147	Fred Toliver	.05
148	Jeff Reardon	.05
149	Allan Anderson	.05
150	Frank Viola	.05
151	Shane Rawley	.05
152	Juan Berenguer	.05
153	Johnny Ard	.05
154	Tim Laudner	.05
155	Brian Harper	.05
156	Al Newman	.05
157	Kent Hrbek	.05
158	Gary Gaetti	.05
159	Wally Backman	.05
160	Gene Larkin	.05
161	Greg Gagne	.05
162	Kirby Puckett	.50
163	Danny Gladden	.05
164	Randy Bush	.05
165	Dave LaPoint	.05
166	Andy Hawkins	.05
167	Dave Righetti	.05
168	Lance McCullers	.05
169	Jimmy Jones	.05
170	Al Leiter	.05
171	John Candelaria	.05
172	Don Slaught	.05
173	Jamie Quirk	.05
174	Rafael Santana	.05
175	Mike Pagliarulo	.05
176	Don Mattingly	.60
177	Ken Phelps	.05
178	Steve Sax	.05
179	Dave Winfield	.40
180	Stan Jefferson	.05
181	Rickey Henderson	.40
182	Bob Brower	.05
183	Roberto Kelly	.05
184	Curt Young	.05
185	Gene Nelson	.05
186	Bob Welch	.05
187	Rick Honeycutt	.05
188	Dave Stewart	.05
189	Mike Moore	.05
190	Dennis Eckersley	.35
191	Eric Plunk	.05
192	Storm Davis	.05
193	Terry Steinbach	.05
194	Ron Hassey	.05
195	Stan Royer	.05
196	Walt Weiss	.05
197	Mark McGwire	.65
198	Carney Lansford	.05
199	Glenn Hubbard	.05
200	Dave Henderson	.05
201	Jose Canseco	.30
202	Dave Parker	.05
203	Scott Bankhead	.05
204	Tom Niedenfuer	.05
205	Mark Langston	.05
206	Erik Hanson RC	.05
207	Mike Jackson	.05
208	Dave Valle	.05
209	Scott Bradley	.05
210	Harold Reynolds	.05
211	Tino Martinez	.05
212	Rich Renteria	.05
213	Rey Quinones	.05
214	Jim Presley	.05
215	Alvin Davis	.05
216	Edgar Martinez	.05
217	Darnell Coles	.05
218	Jeffrey Leonard	.05
219	Jay Buhner	.05
220	Ken Griffey Jr. RC	6.00
221	Drew Hall	.05
222	Bobby Witt	.05
223	Jamie Moyer	.05
224	Charlie Hough	.05
225	Nolan Ryan	.75
226	Jeff Russell	.05
227	Jim Sundberg	.05
228	Julio Franco	.05
229	Buddy Bell	.05
230	Scott Fletcher	.05
231	Jeff Kunkel	.05
232	Steve Buechele	.05
233	Monty Fariss	.05
234	Rick Leach	.05
235	Ruben Sierra	.05
236	Cecil Espy	.05
237	Rafael Palmeiro	.35
238	Pete Incaviglia	.05
239	Dave Steib	.05
240	Jeff Musselman	.05
241	Mike Flanagan	.05
242	Todd Stottlemyre	.05
243	Jimmy Key	.05
244	Tony Castillo	.05
245	Alex Sanchez	.05
246	Tom Henke	.05
247	John Cerutti	.05
248	Ernie Whitt	.05
249	Bob Brenly	.05
250	Rance Mulliniks	.05
251	Kelly Gruber	.05
252	Ed Sprague	.05
253	Fred McGriff	.05
254	Tony Fernandez	.05
255	Tom Lawless	.05
256	George Bell	.05
257	Jesse Barfield	.05
258	Sandy Alomar, Sr.	.05
259	Ken Griffey (With Ken Griffey Jr.)	.30
260	Cal Ripken, Sr.	.05
261	Mel Stottlemyre, Sr.	.05
262	Zane Smith	.05
263	Charlie Puleo	.05
264	Derek Lilliquist	.05
265	Paul Assenmacher	.05
266	John Smoltz	.05
267	Tom Glavine	.25
268	Steve Avery RC	.05
269	Pete Smith RC	.05
270	Jody Davis	.05
271	Bruce Benedict	.05
272	Andres Thomas	.05
273	Gerald Perry	.05
274	Ron Gant	.05
275	Darrell Evans	.05
276	Dale Murphy	.25
277	Dion James	.05
278	Lonnie Smith	.05
279	Geronimo Berroa	.05
280	Steve Wilson	.05
281	Rick Suctcliffe	.05
282	Kevin Coffman	.05
283	Mitch Williams	.05
284	Greg Maddux	.50
285	Paul Kilgus	.05
286	Mike Harkey	.05
287	Lloyd McClendon	.05
288	Damon Berryhill	.05
289	Ty Griffin	.05
290	Ryne Sandberg	.50
291	Mark Grace	.05
292	Curt Wilkerson	.05
293	Vance Law	.05
294	Shawon Dunston	.05
295	Jerome Walton	.05
296	Mitch Webster	.05
297	Dwight Smith	.05
298	Andre Dawson	.25
299	Jeff Sellers	.05
300	Jose Rijo	.05
301	John Franco	.05
302	Rick Mahler	.05
303	Ron Robinson	.05
304	Danny Jackson	.05
305	Rob Dibble	.05
306	Tom Browning	.05
307	Bo Diaz	.05
308	Manny Trillo	.05
309	Chris Sabo (RC)	.05
310	Ron Oester	.05
311	Barry Larkin	.05
312	Todd Benzinger	.05
313	Paul O'Neill	.05
314	Kal Daniels	.05
315	Joel Youngblood	.05
316	Eric Davis	.05
317	Dave Smith	.05
318	Mark Portugal	.05
319	Brian Meyer	.05
320	Jim Deshaies	.05
321	Juan Agosto	.05
322	Mike Scott	.05
323	Rick Rhoden	.05
324	Jim Clancy	.05
325	Larry Andersen	.05
326	Alex Trevino	.05
327	Alan Ashby	.05
328	Craig Reynolds	.05
329	Bill Doran	.05
330	Rafael Ramirez	.05
331	Glenn Davis	.05
332	Willie Ansley RC	.05
333	Gerald Young	.05
334	Cameron Drew	.05
335	Jay Howell	.05
336	Tim Belcher	.05
337	Fernando Valenzuela	.05
338	Ricky Horton	.05
339	Tim Leary	.05
340	Bill Bene	.05
341	Orel Hershiser	.05
342	Mike Scioscia	.05
343	Rick Dempsey	.05
344	Willie Randolph	.05
345	Alfredo Griffin	.05
346	Eddie Murray	.40
347	Mickey Hatcher	.05
348	Mike Sharperson	.05
349	John Shelby	.05
350	Mike Marshall	.05
351	Kirk Gibson	.05
352	Mike Davis	.05
353	Bryn Smith	.05
354	Pascual Perez	.05
355	Kevin Gross	.05
356	Andy McGaffigan	.05
357	Brian Holman	.05
358	Dave Wainhouse	.05
359	Denny Martinez	.05
360	Tim Burke	.05
361	Nelson Santovenia	.05
362	Tim Wallach	.05
363	Spike Owen	.05
364	Rex Hudler	.05
365	Andres Galarraga	.05
366	Otis Nixon	.05
367	Hubie Brooks	.05
368	Mike Aldrete	.05
369	Rock Raines	.05
370	Dave Martinez	.05
371	Bob Ojeda	.05
372	Ron Darling	.05
373	Wally Whitehurst	.05
374	Randy Myers	.05
375	David Cone	.05
376	Dwight Gooden	.05
377	Sid Fernandez	.05

378	Dave Proctor	.05
379	Gary Carter	.40
380	Keith Miller	.05
381	Gregg Jefferies	.05
382	Tim Teufel	.05
383	Kevin Elster	.05
384	Dave Magadan	.05
385	Keith Hernandez	.05
386	Mookie Wilson	.05
387	Darryl Strawberry	.05
388	Kevin McReynolds	.05
389	Mark Carreon	.05
390	Jeff Parrett	.05
391	Mike Maddux	.05
392	Don Carman	.05
393	Bruce Ruffin	.05
394	Ken Howell	.05
395	Steve Bedrosian	.05
396	Floyd Youmans	.05
397	Larry McWilliams	.05
398	Pat Combs	.05
399	Steve Lake	.05
400	Dickie Thon	.05
401	Ricky Jordan	.05
402	Mike Schmidt	.60
403	Tom Herr	.05
404	Chris James	.05
405	Juan Samuel	.05
406	Von Hayes	.05
407	Ron Jones	.05
408	Curt Ford	.05
409	Bob Walk	.05
410	Jeff Robinson	.05
411	Jim Gott	.05
412	Scott Medvin	.05
413	John Smiley	.05
414	Bob Kipper	.05
415	Brian Fisher	.05
416	Doug Drabek	.05
417	Mike Lavalliere	.05
418	Ken Oberkfell	.05
419	Sid Bream	.05
420	Austin Manahan	.05
421	Jose Lind	.05
422	Bobby Bonilla	.05
423	Glenn Wilson	.05
424	Andy Van Slyke	.05
425	Gary Redus	.05
426	Barry Bonds	.75
427	Don Heinkel	.05
428	Ken Dayley	.05
429	Todd Worrell	.05
430	Brad DuVall	.05
431	Jose DeLeon	.05
432	Joe Magrane	.05
433	John Ericks	.05
434	Frank DiPino	.05
435	Tony Pena	.05
436	Ozzie Smith	.50
437	Terry Pendleton	.05
438	Jose Oquendo	.05
439	Tim Jones	.05
440	Pedro Guerrero	.05
441	Milt Thompson	.05
442	Willie McGee	.05
443	Vince Coleman	.05
444	Tom Brunansky	.05
445	Walt Terrell	.05
446	Eric Show	.05
447	Mark Davis	.05
448	Andy Benes **RC**	.10
449	Eddie Whitson	.05
450	Dennis Rasmussen	.05
451	Bruce Hurst	.05
452	Pat Clements	.05
453	Benito Santiago	.05
454	Sandy Alomar, Jr.	.05
455	Garry Templeton	.05
456	Jack Clark	.05
457	Tim Flannery	.05
458	Roberto Alomar	.25
459	Camelo Martinez	.05
460	John Kruk	.05
461	Tony Gwynn	.50
462	Jerald Clark	.05
463	Don Robinson	.05
464	Craig Lefferts	.05
465	Kelly Downs	.05
466	Rick Rueschel	.05
467	Scott Garrelts	.05
468	Wil Tejada	.05
469	Kirt Manwaring	.05
470	Terry Kennedy	.05
471	Jose Uribe	.05
472	Royce Clayton **RC**	.10
473	Robby Thompson	.05
474	Kevin Mitchell	.05
475	Ernie Riles	.05
476	Will Clark	.05
477	Donnell Nixon	.05
478	Candy Maldonado	.05
479	Tracy Jones	.05
480	Brett Butler	.05
481	Checklist 1-121	.05
482	Checklist 122-242	.05
483	Checklist 243-363	.05
484	Checklist 364-484	.05

Tiffany

A special collectors' version of the revitalized Bowman cards was produced in 1989, differing from the regular-issue cards in the application of a high-gloss finish to the front and the use of a white cardboard stock. The "Tiffany" version (as the glossies are known to collectors), was sold only in complete boxed sets, with an estimated production of 6,000 sets.

	NM/M
Unopened Set (495):	165.00
Complete Set (495):	100.00
Common Player:	.25

(Star/rookie cards valued at 4-5X regular-issue 1989 Bowman.)

Inserts

Bowman inserted sweepstakes cards in its 1989 packs. Each sweepstakes card reproduces a classic Bowman card on the front, with a prominent "REPRINT" notice. With one card in each pack, they are by no means scarce. A "Tiffany" version of the reprints was produced for inclusion in the factory set of 1989 Bowman cards. The glossy-front inserts are valued at 10X the standard version.

		NM/M
Complete Set (11):		3.50
Common Player:		.10
(1)	Richie Ashburn	.10
(2)	Yogi Berra	.10
(3)	Whitey Ford	.10
(4)	Gil Hodges	.10
(5)	Mickey Mantle/1951	2.00
(6)	Mickey Mantle/1953	1.50
(7)	Willie Mays	.50
(8)	Satchel Paige	.25
(9)	Jackie Robinson	1.00
(10)	Duke Snider	.10
(11)	Ted Williams	1.00

1990 Bowman

Bowman followed its 1989 rebirth with a 528-card set in 1990. The 1990 cards follow the classic Bowman style featuring a full-color photo bordered in white. The Bowman logo appears in the upper-left corner. The player's team nickname and name appear on the bottom border of the card photo. Unlike the 1989 set, the 1990 cards are standard 2-1/2" x 3-1/2". Backs are horizontal and display the player's statistics against the teams in his league.

	NM/M
Unopened Factory Set (528):	20.00
Complete Set (528):	15.00
Common Player:	.05
Wax Pack (15):	.75
Wax Box (36):	15.00
Jumbo Pack (31):	1.00
Jumbo Box (24):	15.00
Rack Pack (39):	1.50
Rack Box (24):	20.00

1	Tommy Greene **RC**	.05
2	Tom Glavine	.30
3	Andy Nezelek	.05
4	Mike Stanton	.05
5	Rick Lueken	.05
6	Kent Mercker	.05
7	Derek Lilliquist	.05
8	Charlie Liebrandt	.05
9	Steve Avery	.05
10	John Smoltz	.05
11	Mark Lemke	.05
12	Lonnie Smith	.05
13	Oddibe McDowell	.05
14	Tyler Houston **RC**	.05
15	Jeff Blauser	.05
16	Ernie Whitt	.05
17	Alexis Infante	.05
18	Jim Presley	.05
19	Dale Murphy	.25
20	Nick Esasky	.05
21	Rick Sutcliffe	.05
22	Mike Bielecki	.05
23	Steve Wilson	.05
24	Kevin Blankenship	.05
25	Mitch Williams	.05
26	Dean Wilkins	.05
27	Greg Maddux	.05
28	Mike Harkey	.05
29	Mark Grace	.05
30	Ryne Sandberg	.50
31	Greg Smith	.05
32	Dwight Smith	.05
33	Damon Berryhill	.05
34	Earl Cunningham	.05
35	Jerome Walton	.05
36	Lloyd McClendon	.05
37	Ty Griffin	.05
38	Shawon Dunston	.05
39	Andre Dawson	.25
40	Luis Salazar	.05
41	Tim Layana	.05
42	Rob Dibble	.05
43	Tom Browning	.05
44	Danny Jackson	.05
45	Jose Rijo	.05
46	Scott Scudder	.05
47	Randy Myers	.05
48	Brian Lane	.05
49	Paul O'Neill	.05
50	Barry Larkin	.05
51	Reggie Jefferson	.05
52	Jeff Branson	.05
53	Chris Sabo	.05
54	Joe Oliver	.05
55	Todd Benzinger	.05
56	Rolando Roomes	.05
57	Hal Morris	.05
58	Eric Davis	.05
59	Scott Bryant	.05
60	Ken Griffey	.05
61	Darryl Kile **RC**	.05
62	Dave Smith	.05
63	Mark Portugal	.05
64	Jeff Juden **RC**	.05
65	Bill Gullickson	.05
66	Danny Darwin	.05
67	Larry Andersen	.05
68	Jose Cano	.05
69	Dan Schatzeder	.05
70	Jim Deshaies	.05
71	Mike Scott	.05
72	Gerald Young	.05
73	Ken Caminiti	.05
74	Ken Oberkfell	.05
75	Dave Rhode	.05
76	Bill Doran	.05
77	Andujar Cedeno	.05
78	Craig Biggio	.05
79	Karl Rhodes	.05
80	Glenn Davis	.05
81	Eric Anthony **RC**	.05
82	John Wetteland	.05
83	Jay Howell	.05
84	Orel Hershiser	.05
85	Tim Belcher	.05
86	Kiki Jones	.05
87	Mike Hartley	.05
88	Ramon Martinez	.05
89	Mike Scioscia	.05
90	Willie Randolph	.05
91	Juan Samuel	.05
92	Jose Offerman **RC**	.05
93	Dave Hansen	.05
94	Jeff Hamilton	.05
95	Alfredo Griffin	.05
96	Tom Goodwin	.05
97	Kirk Gibson	.05
98	Jose Vizcaino	.05
99	Kal Daniels	.05
100	Hubie Brooks	.05
101	Eddie Murray	.40
102	Dennis Boyd	.05
103	Tim Burke	.05
104	Bill Sampen	.05
105	Brett Gideon	.05
106	Mark Gardner	.05
107	Howard Farmer	.05
108	Mel Rojas	.05
109	Kevin Gross	.05
110	Dave Schmidt	.05
111	Denny Martinez	.05
112	Jerry Goff	.05
113	Andres Galarraga	.05
114	Tim Welch	.05
115	Marquis Grissom **RC**	.25
116	Spike Owen	.05
117	Larry Walker **RC**	1.00
118	Rock Raines	.05
119	Delino DeShields **RC**	.10
120	Tom Foley	.05
121	Dave Martinez	.05
122	Frank Viola	.05
123	Julio Valera	.05
124	Alejandro Pena	.05
125	David Cone	.05
126	Dwight Gooden	.05
127	Kevin Brown	.05
128	John Franco	.05
129	Terry Bross	.05
130	Blaine Beatty	.05
131	Sid Fernandez	.05
132	Mike Marshall	.05
133	Howard Johnson	.05
134	Jaime Roseboro	.05
135	Alan Zinter	.05
136	Keith Miller	.05
137	Kevin Elster	.05
138	Kevin McReynolds	.05
139	Barry Lyons	.05
140	Gregg Jefferies	.05
141	Darryl Strawberry	.05
142	Todd Hundley **RC**	.10
143	Scott Service	.05
144	Chuck Malone	.05
145	Steve Ontiveros	.05
146	Roger McDowell	.05
147	Ken Howell	.05
148	Pat Combs	.05
149	Jeff Parrett	.05
150	Chuck McElroy	.05
151	Jason Grimsley	.05
152	Len Dykstra	.05
153	Mickey Morandini	.05
154	John Kruk	.05
155	Dickie Thon	.05
156	Ricky Jordan	.05
157	Jeff Jackson	.05
158	Darren Daulton	.05
159	Tom Herr	.05
160	Von Hayes	.05
161	Dave Hollins **RC**	.05
162	Carmelo Martinez	.05
163	Bob Walk	.05
164	Doug Drabek	.05
165	Walt Terrell	.05
166	Bill Landrum	.05
167	Scott Ruskin	.05
168	Bob Patterson	.05
169	Bobby Bonilla	.05
170	Jose Lind	.05
171	Andy Van Slyke	.05
172	Mike LaValliere	.05
173	Willie Greene **RC**	.05
174	Jay Bell	.05
175	Sid Bream	.05
176	Tom Prince	.05
177	Wally Backman	.05
178	Moises Alou **RC**	.25
179	Steve Carter	.05
180	Gary Redus	.05
181	Barry Bonds	1.00
182	Don Slaught	.05
183	Joe Magrane	.05
184	Bryn Smith	.05
185	Todd Worrell	.05
186	Jose Deleon	.05
187	Frank DiPino	.05
188	John Tudor	.05
189	Howard Hilton	.05
190	John Ericks	.05
191	Ken Dayley	.05
192	Ray Lankford **RC**	.10
193	Todd Zeile	.05
194	Willie McGee	.05
195	Ozzie Smith	.50
196	Milt Thompson	.05
197	Terry Pendleton	.05
198	Vince Coleman	.05
199	Paul Coleman	.05
200	Jose Oquendo	.05
201	Pedro Guerrero	.05
202	Tom Brunansky	.05
203	Roger Smithberg	.05
204	Eddie Whitson	.05
205	Dennis Rasmussen	.05
206	Craig Lefferts	.05
207	Andy Benes	.05
208	Bruce Hurst	.05
209	Eric Show	.05
210	Rafael Valdez	.05
211	Joey Cora	.05
212	Thomas Howard	.05
213	Rob Nelson	.05
214	Jack Clark	.05
215	Garry Templeton	.05
216	Fred Lynn	.05
217	Tony Gwynn	.50
218	Benny Santiago	.05
219	Mike Pagliarulo	.05
220	Joe Carter	.05
221	Roberto Alomar	.25
222	Bip Roberts	.05
223	Rick Reuschel	.05
224	Russ Swan	.05
225	Eric Gunderson	.05
226	Steve Bedrosian	.05
227	Mike Remlinger	.05
228	Scott Garrelts	.05
229	Ernie Camacho	.05
230	Andres Santana	.05
231	Will Clark	.05
232	Kevin Mitchell	.05
233	Robby Thompson	.05
234	Bill Bathe	.05
235	Tony Perezchica	.05
236	Gary Carter	.40
237	Brett Butler	.05
238	Matt Williams	.05
239	Ernie Riles	.05
240	Kevin Bass	.05
241	Terry Kennedy	.05
242	Steve Hosey **RC**	.05
243	Ben McDonald **RC**	.15
244	Jeff Ballard	.05
245	Joe Price	.05
246	Curt Schilling	.30
247	Pete Harnisch	.05
248	Mark Williamson	.05
249	Gregg Olson	.05
250	Chris Myers	.05
251a	David Segui (No bio. data on back.)	3.50
251b	David Segui (Bio. data on back.)	.05
252	Joe Orsulak	.05
253	Craig Worthington	.05
254	Mickey Tettleton	.05
255	Cal Ripken, Jr.	1.00
256	Billy Ripken	.05
257	Randy Milligan	.05
258	Brady Anderson	.05
259	Chris Hoiles **RC**	.05
260	Mike Devereaux	.05
261	Phil Bradley	.05
262	Leo Gomez **RC**	.05
263	Lee Smith	.05
264	Mike Rochford	.05
265	Jeff Reardon	.05
266	Wes Gardner	.05
267	Mike Boddicker	.05
268	Roger Clemens	.60
269	Rob Murphy	.05
270	Mickey Pina	.05
271	Tony Pena	.05
272	Jody Reed	.05
273	Kevin Romine	.05
274	Mike Greenwell	.05
275	Mo Vaughn **RC**	.60
276	Danny Heep	.05
277	Scott Cooper	.05
278	Greg Blosser **RC**	.05
279	Dwight Evans	.05
280	Ellis Burks	.05
281	Wade Boggs	.50
282	Marty Barrett	.05
283	Kirk McCaskill	.05
284	Mark Langston	.05
285	Bert Blyleven	.05
286	Mike Fetters	.05
287	Kyle Abbott	.05
288	Jim Abbott	.05
289	Chuck Finley	.05
290	Gary DiSarcina	.05
291	Dick Schofield	.05
292	Devon White	.05
293	Bobby Rose	.05
294	Brian Downing	.05
295	Lance Parrish	.05
296	Jack Howell	.05
297	Claudell Washington	.05
298	John Orton	.05
299	Wally Joyner	.05
300	Lee Stevens	.05
301	Chili Davis	.05
302	Johnny Ray	.05
303	Greg Hibbard	.05
304	Eric King	.05
305	Jack McDowell	.05
306	Bobby Thigpen	.05
307	Adam Peterson	.05
308	Scott Radinsky **RC**	.05
309	Wayne Edwards	.05
310	Melido Perez	.05
311	Robin Ventura	.05
312	Sammy Sosa **RC**	5.00
313	Dan Pasqua	.05
314	Carlton Fisk	.40
315	Ozzie Guillen	.05
316	Ivan Calderon	.05
317	Daryl Boston	.05
318	Craig Grebeck	.05
319	Scott Fletcher	.05
320	Frank Thomas **RC**	2.00
321	Steve Lyons	.05
322	Carlos Martinez	.05
323	Joe Skalski	.05
324	Tom Candiotti	.05
325	Greg Swindell	.05
326	Steve Olin	.05
327	Kevin Wickander	.05
328	Doug Jones	.05
329	Jeff Shaw	.05
330	Kevin Bearse	.05
331	Dion James	.05
332	Jerry Browne	.05
333	Albert Belle	.05
334	Felix Fermin	.05
335	Candy Maldonado	.05
336	Cory Snyder	.05
337	Sandy Alomar	.05
338	Mark Lewis	.05
339	Carlos Baerga **RC**	.10
340	Chris James	.05
341	Brook Jacoby	.05
342	Keith Hernandez	.05
343	Frank Tanana	.05
344	Scott Aldred	.05
345	Mike Henneman	.05
346	Steve Wapnick	.05
347	Greg Gohr	.05
348	Eric Stone	.05
349	Brian DuBois	.05
350	Kevin Ritz	.05
351	Rico Brogna	.05
352	Mike Heath	.05
353	Alan Trammell	.05
354	Chet Lemon	.05
355	Dave Bergman	.05
356	Lou Whitaker	.05
357	Cecil Fielder	.05
358	Milt Cuyler	.05
359	Tony Phillips	.05
360	Travis Fryman **RC**	.10
361	Ed Romero	.05
362	Lloyd Moseby	.05
363	Mark Gubicza	.05
364	Bret Saberhagen	.05
365	Tom Gordon	.05
366	Steve Farr	.05
367	Kevin Appier	.05
368	Storm Davis	.05
369	Mark Davis	.05
370	Jeff Montgomery	.05
371	Frank White	.05
372	Brent Mayne	.05
373	Bob Boone	.05
374	Jim Eisenreich	.05
375	Danny Tartabull	.05
376	Kurt Stillwell	.05
377	Bill Pecota	.05
378	Bo Jackson	.10
379	Bob Hamelin **RC**	.05
380	Kevin Seitzer	.05
381	Rey Palacios	.05
382	George Brett	.60
383	Gerald Perry	.05
384	Teddy Higuera	.05
385	Tom Filer	.05
386	Dan Plesac	.05
387	Cal Eldred **RC**	.05
388	Jaime Navarro	.05
389	Chris Bosio	.05
390	Randy Veres	.05
391	Gary Sheffield	.25
392	George Canale	.05
393	B.J. Surhoff	.05
394	Tim McIntosh	.05
395	Greg Brock	.05
396	Greg Vaughn	.05
397	Darryl Hamilton	.05
398	Dave Parker	.05
399	Paul Molitor	.40
400	Jim Gantner	.05
401	Rob Deer	.05
402	Billy Spiers	.05
403	Glenn Braggs	.05
404	Robin Yount	.40
405	Rick Aguilera	.05
406	Johnny Ard	.05
407	Kevin Tapani **RC**	.10
408	Park Pittman	.05
409	Allan Anderson	.05
410	Juan Berenguer	.05
411	Willie Banks	.05
412	Rich Yett	.05
413	Dave West	.05
414	Greg Gagne	.05
415	Chuck Knoblauch **RC**	.50
416	Randy Bush	.05
417	Gary Gaetti	.05
418	Kent Hrbek	.05
419	Al Newman	.05
420	Danny Gladden	.05
421	Paul Sorrento	.05
422	Derek Parks	.05
423	Scott Leius	.05
424	Kirby Puckett	.50
425	Willie Smith	.05
426	Dave Righetti	.05
427	Jeff Robinson	.05
428	Alan Mills	.05
429	Tim Leary	.05
430	Pascual Perez	.05
431	Alvaro Espinoza	.05
432	Dave Winfield	.40
433	Jesse Barfield	.05
434	Randy Velarde	.05
435	Rick Cerone	.05
436	Steve Balboni	.05
437	Mel Hall	.05
438	Bob Geren	.05
439	Bernie Williams **RC**	1.00
440	Kevin Maas	.05
441	Mike Blowers	.05
442	Steve Sax	.05
443	Don Mattingly	.60
444	Roberto Kelly	.05
445	Mike Moore	.05
446	Reggie Harris	.05
447	Scott Sanderson	.05
448	Dave Otto	.05
449	Dave Stewart	.05
450	Rick Honeycutt	.05
451	Dennis Eckersley	.35
452	Carney Lansford	.05
453	Scott Hemond	.05
454	Mark McGwire	.75
455	Felix Jose	.05
456	Terry Steinbach	.05
457	Rickey Henderson	.40
458	Dave Henderson	.05
459	Mike Gallego	.05
460	Jose Canseco	.30
461	Walt Weiss	.05
462	Ken Phelps	.05
463	Darren Lewis **RC**	.05
464	Ron Hassey	.05
465	Roger Salkeld **RC**	.05
466	Scott Bankhead	.05
467	Keith Comstock	.05

468	Randy Johnson	.40
469	Erik Hanson	.05
470	Mike Schooler	.05
471	Gary Eave	.05
472	Jeffrey Leonard	.05
473	Dave Valle	.05
474	Omar Vizquel	.05
475	Pete O'Brien	.05
476	Henry Cotto	.05
477	Jay Buhner	.05
478	Harold Reynolds	.05
479	Alvin Davis	.05
480	Darnell Coles	.05
481	Ken Griffey Jr.	.65
482	Greg Briley	.05
483	Scott Bradley	.05
484	Tino Martinez	.05
485	Jeff Russell	.05
486	Nolan Ryan	1.00
487	Robb Nen	.05
488	Kevin Brown	.05
489	Brian Bohanon	.05
490	Ruben Sierra	.05
491	Pete Incaviglia	.05
492	Juan Gonzalez RC	1.50
493	Steve Buechele	.05
494	Scott Coolbaugh	.05
495	Geno Petralli	.05
496	Rafael Palmeiro	.35
497	Julio Franco	.05
498	Gary Pettis	.05
499	Donald Harris	.05
500	Monty Fariss	.05
501	Harold Baines	.05
502	Cecil Espy	.05
503	Jack Daugherty	.05
504	Willie Blair	.05
505	Dave Steib	.05
506	Tom Henke	.05
507	John Cerutti	.05
508	Paul Kilgus	.05
509	Jimmy Key	.05
510	John Olerud RC	.75
511	Ed Sprague	.05
512	Manny Lee	.05
513	Fred McGriff	.05
514	Glenallen Hill	.05
515	George Bell	.05
516	Mookie Wilson	.05
517	Luis Sojo	.05
518	Nelson Liriano	.05
519	Kelly Gruber	.05
520	Greg Myers	.05
521	Pat Borders	.05
522	Junior Felix	.05
523	Eddie Zosky	.05
524	Tony Fernandez	.05
525	Checklist	.05
526	Checklist	.05
527	Checklist	.05
528	Checklist	.05

Tiffany

Reported production of fewer than 10,000 sets has created a significant premium for these glossy "Tiffany" versions of Bowman's 1990 baseball card set. The use of white cardboard stock and high-gloss front finish distinguishes these cards from regular-issue Bowmans.

	NM/M
Unopened Set (539):	200.00
Complete Set (539):	60.00
Common Player:	.25

(Star/rookie cards valued about 4-5X regular-issue 1990 Bowman.)

Inserts

Bowman inserted sweepstakes cards in its 1990 packs, much like in 1989. This 11-card set features current players displayed in drawings by Craig Pursley.

	NM/M
Complete Set (11):	1.00
Common Player:	.05
(1) Will Clark	.05
(2) Mark Davis	.05
(3) Dwight Gooden	.05
(4) Bo Jackson	.10
(5) Don Mattingly	.40
(6) Kevin Mitchell	.05
(7) Gregg Olson	.05
(8) Nolan Ryan	.50
(9) Bret Saberhagen	.05
(10) Jerome Walton	.05
(11) Robin Yount	.25

Lithographs

The paintings which were the basis for the sweepstakes insert cards in 1990 Bowman were also used in the creation of a set of 11" x 14" lithographs. The lithographs were offered as a prize in the sweepstakes or could be purchased from hobby dealers for a retail price in the $400-450 range.

	NM/M
Complete Set (11):	250.00
Common Player:	10.00
(1) Will Clark	10.00
(2) Mark Davis	10.00
(3) Dwight Gooden	10.00
(4) Bo Jackson	20.00
(5) Don Mattingly	50.00
(6) Kevin Mitchell	10.00
(7) Gregg Olson	10.00
(8) Nolan Ryan	100.00
(9) Bret Saberhagen	10.00
(10) Jerome Walton	10.00
(11) Robin Yount	25.00

1991 Bowman

The 1991 Bowman set features 704 cards compared to 528 cards in the 1990 issue. The cards imitate the 1953 Bowman style. Special Rod Carew cards and gold foil-stamped cards are included. The set is numbered by teams. Like the 1989 and 1990 issues, the card backs feature a breakdown of performance against each other team in the league.

	NM/M
Unopened Factory Set (704):	30.00
Complete Set (704):	20.00
Common Player:	.05
Wax Pack (14):	.75
Wax Box (36):	17.50
Cello Pack (29):	1.50
Cello Box (24):	25.00

1	Rod Carew-I	.10
2	Rod Carew-II	.10
3	Rod Carew-III	.10
4	Rod Carew-IV	.10
5	Rod Carew-V	.10
6	Willie Fraser	.05
7	John Olerud	.05
8	William Suero	.05
9	Roberto Alomar	.20
10	Todd Stottlemyre	.05
11	Joe Carter	.05
12	Steve Karsay RC	.10
13	Mark Whiten	.05
14	Pat Borders	.05
15	Mike Timlin	.05
16	Tom Henke	.05
17	Eddie Zosky	.05
18	Kelly Gruber	.05
19	Jimmy Key	.05
20	Jerry Schunk	.05
21	Manny Lee	.05
22	Dave Steib	.05
23	Pat Hentgen	.05
24	Glenallen Hill	.05
25	Rene Gonzales	.05
26	Ed Sprague	.05
27	Ken Dayley	.05
28	Pat Tabler	.05
29	Denis Boucher RC	.05
30	Devon White	.05
31	Dante Bichette	.05
32	Paul Molitor	.40
33	Greg Vaughn	.05
34	Dan Plesac	.05
35	Chris George	.05
36	Tim McIntosh	.05
37	Franklin Stubbs	.05
38	Bo Dodson	.05
39	Ron Robinson	.05
40	Ed Nunez	.05
41	Greg Brock	.05
42	Jaime Navarro	.05
43	Chris Bosio	.05
44	B.J. Surhoff	.05
45	Chris Johnson	.05
46	Willie Randolph	.05
47	Narciso Elvira	.05
48	Jim Gantner	.05
49	Kevin Brown	.05
50	Julio Machado	.05
51	Chuck Crim	.05
52	Gary Sheffield	.30
53	Angel Miranda	.05
54	Teddy Higuera	.05
55	Robin Yount	.40
56	Cal Eldred	.05
57	Sandy Alomar	.05
58	Greg Swindell	.05
59	Brook Jacoby	.05
60	Efrain Valdez	.05
61	Ever Magallanes	.05
62	Tom Candiotti	.05
63	Eric King	.05
64	Alex Cole	.05
65	Charles Nagy	.05
66	Mitch Webster	.05
67	Chris James	.05
68	Jim Thome RC	3.00
69	Carlos Baerga	.05
70	Mark Lewis	.05
71	Jerry Browne	.05
72	Jesse Orosco	.05
73	Mike Huff	.05
74	Jose Escobar	.05
75	Jeff Manto	.05
76	Turner Ward RC	.05
77	Doug Jones	.05
78	Bruce Egloff RC	.05
79	Tim Costo	.05
80	Beau Allred	.05
81	Albert Belle	.05
82	John Farrell	.05
83	Glenn Davis	.05
84	Joe Orsulak	.05
85	Mark Williamson	.05
86	Ben McDonald	.05
87	Billy Ripken	.05
88	Leo Gomez	.05
89	Bob Melvin	.05
90	Jeff Robinson	.05
91	Jose Mesa	.05
92	Gregg Olson	.05
93	Mike Devereaux	.05
94	Luis Mercedes	.05
95	Arthur Rhodes RC	.10
96	Juan Bell	.05
97	Mike Mussina RC	3.00
98	Jeff Ballard	.05
99	Chris Hoiles	.05
100	Brady Anderson	.05
101	Bob Milacki	.05
102	David Segui	.05
103	Dwight Evans	.05
104	Cal Ripken, Jr.	1.00
105	Mike Linskey	.05
106	Jeff Tackett RC	.05
107	Jeff Reardon	.05
108	Dana Kiecker	.05
109	Ellis Burks	.05
110	Dave Owen	.05
111	Danny Darwin	.05
112	Mo Vaughn	.05
113	Jeff McNeely	.05
114	Tom Bolton	.05
115	Greg Blosser	.05
116	Mike Greenwell	.05
117	Phil Plantier RC	.05
118	Roger Clemens	.60
119	John Marzano	.05
120	Jody Reed	.05
121	Scott Taylor	.05
122	Jack Clark	.05
123	Derek Livernois	.05
124	Tony Pena	.05
125	Tom Brunansky	.05
126	Carlos Quintana	.05
127	Tom Naehring	.05
128	Matt Young	.05
129	Wade Boggs	.50
130	Kevin Morton	.05
131	Pete Incaviglia	.05
132	Rob Deer	.05
133	Bill Gullickson	.05
134	Rico Brogna	.05
135	Lloyd Moseby	.05
136	Cecil Fielder	.05
137	Tony Phillips	.05
138	Mark Leiter	.05
139	John Cerutti	.05
140	Mickey Tettleton	.05
141	Milt Cuyler	.05
142	Greg Gohr	.05
143	Tony Bernazard	.05
144	Dan Gakeler	.05
145	Travis Fryman	.05
146	Dan Petry	.05
147	Scott Aldred	.05
148	John DeSilva	.05
149	Rusty Meacham	.05
150	Lou Whitaker	.05
151	Dave Haas	.05
152	Luis de los Santos	.05
153	Ivan Cruz	.05
154	Alan Trammell	.05
155	Pat Kelly	.05
156	Carl Everett RC	.25
157	Greg Cadaret	.05
158	Kevin Maas	.05
159	Jeff Johnson	.05
160	Willie Smith	.05
161	Gerald Williams	.05
162	Mike Humphreys	.05
163	Alvaro Espinoza	.05
164	Matt Nokes	.05
165	Wade Taylor	.05
166	Roberto Kelly	.05
167	John Habyan	.05
168	Steve Farr	.05
169	Jesse Barfield	.05
170	Steve Sax	.05
171	Jim Leyritz	.05
172	Robert Eenhoorn	.05
173	Bernie Williams	.05
174	Scott Lusader	.05
175	Torey Lovullo	.05
176	Chuck Cary	.05
177	Scott Sanderson	.05
178	Don Mattingly	.60
179	Mel Hall	.05
180	Juan Gonzalez	.30
181	Hensley Meulens	.05
182	Jose Offerman	.05
183	Jeff Bagwell RC	2.50
184	Jeff Conine RC	.25
185	Henry Rodriguez RC	.05
186	Jimmie Reese	.05
187	Kyle Abbott	.05
188	Lance Parrish	.05
189	Rafael Montalvo	.05
190	Floyd Bannister	.05
191	Dick Schofield	.05
192	Scott Lewis	.05
193	Jeff Robinson	.05
194	Kent Anderson	.05
195	Wally Joyner	.05
196	Chuck Finley	.05
197	Luis Sojo	.05
198	Jeff Richardson	.05
199	Dave Parker	.05
200	Jim Abbott	.05
201	Junior Felix	.05
202	Mark Langston	.05
203	Tim Salmon RC	1.00
204	Cliff Young	.05
205	Scott Bailes	.05
206	Bobby Rose	.05
207	Gary Gaetti	.05
208	Ruben Amaro	.05
209	Luis Polonia	.05
210	Dave Winfield	.40
211	Bryan Harvey	.05
212	Mike Moore	.05
213	Rickey Henderson	.40
214	Steve Chitren	.05
215	Bob Welch	.05
216	Terry Steinbach	.05
217	Ernie Riles	.05
218	Todd Van Poppel RC	.10
219	Mike Gallego	.05
220	Curt Young	.05
221	Todd Burns	.05
222	Vance Law	.05
223	Eric Show	.05
224	Don Peters	.05
225	Dave Stewart	.05
226	Dave Henderson	.05
227	Jose Canseco	.30
228	Walt Weiss	.05
229	Dann Howitt	.05
230	Willie Wilson	.05
231	Harold Baines	.05
232	Scott Hemond	.05
233	Joe Slusarski	.05
234	Mark McGwire	.75
235	Kirk Dressendorfer RC	.05
236	Craig Paquette RC	.05
237	Dennis Eckersley	.35
238	Dana Allison	.05
239	Scott Bradley	.05
240	Brian Holman	.05
241	Mike Schooler	.05
242	Rich Delucia	.05
243	Edgar Martinez	.05
244	Henry Cotto	.05
245	Omar Vizquel	.05
246a	Ken Griffey Jr.	.65
246b	Ken Griffey Sr. (Should be #255.)	.10
247	Jay Buhner	.05
248	Bill Krueger	.05
249	Dave Fleming RC	.05
250	Patrick Lennon RC	.05
251	Dave Valle	.05
252	Harold Reynolds	.05
253	Randy Johnson	.40
254	Scott Bankhead	.05
255	(Not issued, see #246b.)	
256	Greg Briley	.05
257	Tino Martinez	.05
258	Alvin Davis	.05
259	Pete O'Brien	.05
260	Erik Hanson	.05
261	Bret Boone RC	.50
262	Roger Salkeld	.05
263	Dave Burba	.05
264	Kerry Woodson RC	.05
265	Julio Franco	.05
266	Dan Peltier	.05
267	Jeff Russell	.05
268	Steve Buechele	.05
269	Donald Harris	.05
270	Robb Nen	.05
271	Rich Gossage	.05
272	Ivan Rodriguez RC	3.00
273	Jeff Huson	.05
274	Kevin Brown	.05
275	Dan Smith RC	.05
276	Gary Pettis	.05
277	Jack Daugherty	.05
278	Mike Jeffcoat	.05
279	Brad Arnsberg	.05
280	Nolan Ryan	1.00
281	Eric McCray	.05
282	Scott Chiamparino	.05
283	Ruben Sierra	.05
284	Geno Petralli	.05
285	Monty Fariss	.05
286	Rafael Palmeiro	.35
287	Bobby Witt	.05
288	Dean Palmer	.05
289	Tony Scruggs	.05
290	Kenny Rogers	.05
291	Bret Saberhagen	.05
292	Brian McRae RC	.05
293	Storm Davis	.05
294	Danny Tartabull	.05
295	David Howard	.05
296	Mike Boddicker	.05
297	Joel Johnston	.05
298	Tim Spehr	.05
299	Hector Wagner	.05
300	George Brett	.60
301	Mike Macfarlane	.05
302	Kirk Gibson	.05
303	Harvey Pulliam	.05
304	Jim Eisenreich	.05
305	Kevin Seitzer	.05
306	Mark Davis	.05
307	Kurt Stillwell	.05
308	Jeff Montgomery	.05
309	Kevin Appier	.05
310	Bob Hamelin	.05
311	Tom Gordon	.05
312	Kerwin Moore RC	.05
313	Hugh Walker	.05
314	Terry Shumpert	.05
315	Warren Cromartie	.05
316	Gary Thurman	.05
317	Steve Bedrosian	.05
318	Danny Gladden	.05
319	Jack Morris	.05
320	Kirby Puckett	.50
321	Kent Hrbek	.05
322	Kevin Tapani	.05
323	Denny Neagle	.05
324	Rich Garces	.05
325	Larry Casian	.05
326	Shane Mack	.05
327	Allan Anderson	.05
328	Junior Ortiz	.05
329	Paul Abbott RC	.05
330	Chuck Knoblauch	.05
331	Chili Davis	.05
332	Todd Ritchie RC	.05
333	Brian Harper	.05
334	Rick Aguilera	.05
335	Scott Erickson	.05
336	Pedro Munoz	.05
337	Scott Leuis	.05
338	Greg Gagne	.05
339	Mike Pagliarulo	.05
340	Terry Leach	.05
341	Willie Banks	.05
342	Bobby Thigpen	.05
343	Roberto Hernandez RC	.10
344	Melido Perez	.05
345	Carlton Fisk	.40
346	Norberto Martin RC	.05
347	Johnny Ruffin RC	.05
348	Jeff Carter RC	.05
349	Lance Johnson	.05
350	Sammy Sosa	.50
351	Alex Fernandez	.05
352	Jack McDowell	.05
353	Bob Wickman	.05
354	Wilson Alvarez	.05
355	Charlie Hough	.05
356	Ozzie Guillen	.05
357	Cory Snyder	.05
358	Robin Ventura	.05
359	Scott Fletcher	.05
360	Cesar Bernhardt	.05
361	Dan Pasqua	.05
362	Tim Raines	.05
363	Brian Drahman	.05
364	Wayne Edwards	.05
365	Scott Radinsky	.05
366	Frank Thomas	.40
367	Cecil Fielder	.05
368	Julio Franco	.05
369	Kelly Gruber	.05
370	Alan Trammell	.05
371	Rickey Henderson	.30
372	Jose Canseco	.15
373	Ellis Burks	.05
374	Lance Parrish	.05
375	Dave Parker	.05
376	Eddie Murray	.30
377	Ryne Sandberg	.35
378	Matt Williams	.05
379	Barry Larkin	.05
380	Barry Bonds	.75
381	Bobby Bonilla	.05
382	Darryl Strawberry	.05
383	Benny Santiago	.05
384	Don Robinson	.05
385	Paul Coleman	.05
386	Milt Thompson	.05
387	Lee Smith	.05
388	Ray Lankford	.05
389	Tom Pagnozzi	.05
390	Ken Hill	.05
391	Jamie Moyer	.05
392	Greg Carmona RC	.05
393	John Ericks	.05
394	Bob Tewksbury	.05
395	Jose Oquendo	.05
396	Rheal Cormier	.05
397	Mike Milchin RC	.05
398	Ozzie Smith	.50
399	Aaron Holbert RC	.05
400	Jose DeLeon	.05
401	Felix Jose	.05
402	Juan Agosto	.05
403	Pedro Guerrero	.05
404	Todd Zeile	.05
405	Gerald Perry	.05
407	Bryn Smith	.05
408	Bernard Gilkey	.05
409	Rex Hudler	.05
410a	Ralph Branca, Bobby Thomson	.10
410b	Donovan Osborne	.05
411	Lance Dickson	.05
412	Danny Jackson	.05
413	Jerome Walton	.05
414	Sean Cheetham	.05
415	Joe Girardi	.05
416	Ryne Sandberg	.50
417	Mike Harkey	.05
418	George Bell	.05
419	Rick Wilkins RC	.05
420	Earl Cunningham	.05
421	Heathcliff Slocumb	.05
422	Mike Bielecki	.05
423	Jessie Hollins RC	.05
424	Shawon Dunston	.05
425	Dave Smith	.05
426	Greg Maddux	.50
427	Jose Vizcaino	.05
428	Luis Salazar	.05
429	Andre Dawson	.25
430	Rick Sutcliffe	.05
431	Paul Assenmacher	.05
432	Erik Pappas	.05
433	Mark Grace	.05
434	Denny Martinez	.05
435	Marquis Grissom	.05
436	Wil Cordero RC	.05
437	Tim Wallach	.05
438	Brian Barnes RC	.05
439	Barry Jones	.05
440	Ivan Calderon	.05
441	Stan Spencer RC	.05
442	Larry Walker	.05
443	Chris Haney RC	.05
444	Hector Rivera	.05
445	Delino DeShields	.05
446	Andres Galarraga	.05
447	Gilberto Reyes	.05
448	Willie Greene	.05
449	Greg Colbrunn	.05
450	Rondell White RC	.25
451	Steve Frey	.05
452	Shane Andrews RC	.10
453	Mike Fitzgerald	.05
454	Spike Owen	.05
455	Dave Martinez	.05
456	Dennis Boyd	.05
457	Eric Bullock	.05
458	Reid Cornelius RC	.05
459	Chris Nabholz	.05
460	David Cone	.05
461	Hubie Brooks	.05
462	Sid Fernandez	.05
463	Doug Simons RC	.05
464	Howard Johnson	.05
465	Chris Donnels	.05
466	Anthony Young	.05
467	Todd Hundley	.05
468	Rick Cerone	.05
469	Kevin Elster	.05
470	Wally Whitehurst	.05
471	Vince Coleman	.05
472	Dwight Gooden	.05
473	Charlie O'Brien	.05
474	Jeromy Burnitz RC	.50
475	John Franco	.05
476	Daryl Boston	.05
477	Frank Viola	.05
478	D.J. Dozier	.05
479	Kevin McReynolds	.05
480	Tom Herr	.05
481	Gregg Jefferies	.05
482	Pete Schourek	.05
483	Ron Darling	.05
484	Dave Magadan	.05

485 Andy Ashby RC .05
486 Dale Murphy .20
487 Von Hayes .05
488 Kim Batiste RC .05
489 Tony Longmire RC .05
490 Wally Backman .05
491 Jeff Jackson .05
492 Mickey Morandini .05
493 Darrel Akerfelds .05
494 Ricky Jordan .05
495 Randy Ready .05
496 Darrin Fletcher .05
497 Chuck Malone .05
498 Pat Combs .05
499 Dickie Thon .05
500 Roger McDowell .05
501 Len Dykstra .05
502 Joe Boever .05
503 John Kruk .05
504 Terry Mulholland .05
505 Wes Chamberlain .05
506 Mike Lieberthal RC .75
507 Darren Daulton .05
508 Charlie Hayes .05
509 John Smiley .05
510 Gary Varsho .05
511 Curt Wilkerson .05
512 Orlando Merced RC .05
513 Barry Bonds 1.00
514 Mike Lavalliere .05
515 Doug Drabek .05
516 Gary Redus .05
517 William Pennyfeather RC .05
518 Randy Tomlin RC .05
519 Mike Zimmerman RC .05
520 Jeff King .05
521 Kurt Miller RC .05
522 Jay Bell .05
523 Bill Landrum .05
524 Zane Smith .05
525 Bobby Bonilla .05
526 Bob Walk .05
527 Austin Manahan .05
528 Joe Ausanio RC .05
529 Andy Van Slyke .05
530 Jose Lind .05
531 Carlos Garcia RC .05
532 Don Slaught .05
533 Colin Powell .25
534 Frank Bolick RC .05
535 Gary Scott RC .05
536 Nikco Riesgo .05
537 Reggie Sanders RC .25
538 Tim Howard RC .05
539 Ryan Bowen RC .05
540 Eric Anthony .05
541 Jim Deshaies .05
542 Tom Nevers .05
543 Ken Caminiti .05
544 Karl Rhodes .05
545 Xavier Hernandez .05
546 Mike Scott .05
547 Jeff Juden .05
548 Darryl Kile .05
549 Willie Ansley .05
550 Luis Gonzalez RC 1.00
551 Mike Simms RC .05
552 Mark Portugal .05
553 Jimmy Jones .05
554 Jim Clancy .05
555 Pete Harnisch .05
556 Craig Biggio .05
557 Eric Yelding .05
558 Dave Rohde .05
559 Casey Candaele .05
560 Curt Schilling .25
561 Steve Finley .05
562 Javier Ortiz .05
563 Andujar Cedeno .05
564 Rafael Ramirez .05
565 Kenny Lofton RC .50
566 Steve Avery .05
567 Lonnie Smith .05
568 Kent Mercker .05
569 Chipper Jones RC 3.00
570 Terry Pendleton .05
571 Otis Nixon .05
572 Juan Berenguer .05
573 Charlie Leibrandt .05
574 Dave Justice .05
575 Keith Mitchell .05
576 Tom Glavine .25
577 Greg Olson .05
578 Rafael Belliard .05
579 Ben Rivera .05
580 John Smoltz .05
581 Tyler Houston .05
582 Mark Wohlers RC .05
583 Ron Gant .05
584 Ramon Caraballo .05
585 Sid Bream .05
586 Jeff Treadway .05
587 Javier Lopez RC .05
588 Deion Sanders .10
589 Mike Heath .05
590 Ryan Klesko RC .20
591 Bob Ojeda .05
592 Alfredo Griffin .05
593 Raul Mondesi RC .25
594 Greg Smith .05
595 Orel Hershiser .05
596 Juan Samuel .05
597 Brett Butler .05
598 Gary Carter .40
599 Stan Javier .05
600 Kal Daniels .05
601 Jamie McAndrew RC .05

602 Mike Sharperson .05
603 Jay Howell .05
604 Eric Karros RC .25
605 Tim Belcher .05
606 Dan Opperman .05
607 Lenny Harris .05
608 Tom Goodwin .05
609 Darryl Strawberry .05
610 Ramon Martinez .05
611 Kevin Gross .05
612 Zakary Shinall .05
613 Mike Scioscia .05
614 Eddie Murray .40
615 Ronnie Walden .05
616 Will Clark .05
617 Adam Hyzdu .05
618 Matt Williams .05
619 Don Robinson .05
620 Jeff Brantley .05
621 Greg Litton .05
622 Steve Decker .05
623 Robby Thompson .05
624 Mark Leonard .05
625 Kevin Bass .05
626 Scott Garrelts .05
627 Jose Uribe .05
628 Eric Gunderson .05
629 Steve Hosey .05
630 Trevor Wilson .05
631 Terry Kennedy .05
632 Dave Righetti .05
633 Kelly Downs .05
634 Johnny Ard .05
635 Eric Christopherson RC .05
636 Kevin Mitchell .05
637 John Burkett .05
638 Kevin Rogers RC .05
639 Bud Black .05
640 Willie McGee .05
641 Royce Clayton .05
642 Tony Fernandez .05
643 Ricky Bones .05
644 Thomas Howard .05
645 Dave Staton .05
646 Jim Presley .05
647 Tony Gwynn .50
648 Marty Barrett .05
649 Scott Coolbaugh .05
650 Craig Lefferts .05
651 Eddie Whitson .05
652 Oscar Azocar .05
653 Wes Gardner .05
654 Bip Roberts .05
655 Robbie Beckett RC .05
656 Benny Santiago .05
657 Greg W. Harris .05
658 Jerald Clark .05
659 Fred McGriff .05
660 Larry Andersen .05
661 Bruce Hurst .05
662 Steve Martin .05
663 Rafael Valdez .05
664 Paul Faries RC .05
665 Andy Benes .05
666 Randy Myers .05
667 Rob Dibble .05
668 Glenn Sutko .05
669 Glenn Braggs .05
670 Billy Hatcher .05
671 Joe Oliver .05
672 Freddie Benavides .05
673 Barry Larkin .05
674 Chris Sabo .05
675 Mariano Duncan .05
676 Chris Jones RC .05
677 Gino Minutelli RC .05
678 Reggie Jefferson .05
679 Jack Armstrong .05
680 Chris Hammond .05
681 Jose Rijo .05
682 Bill Doran .05
683 Terry Lee .05
684 Tom Browning .05
685 Paul O'Neill .05
686 Eric Davis .05
687 Dan Wilson RC .05
688 Ted Power .05
689 Tim Layana .05
690 Norm Charlton .05
691 Hal Morris .05
692 Rickey Henderson .35
693 Sam Militello RC .05
694 Matt Mieske RC .05
695 Paul Russo RC .05
696 Domingo Mota RC .05
697 Todd Guggiana RC .05
698 Marc Newfield .05
699 Checklist .05
700 Checklist .05
701 Checklist .05
702 Checklist .05
703 Checklist .05
704 Checklist .05

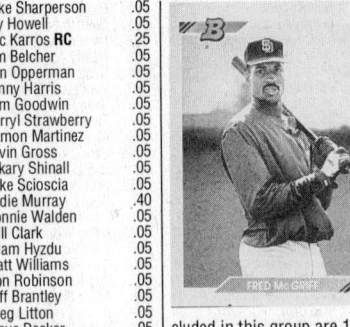

FRED McGRIFF

cluded in this group are 1991 MVP's of the minor leagues and first round draft choices. Eighteen of the gold-foil enchanced cards have been identified as short-prints (designated SP in the listings), printed in quantities one-half the other foils.

	NM/M
Complete Set (705):	90.00
Common Player:	.10
Pack (15):	4.00
Wax Box (36):	135.00
Jumbo Pack (25):	8.00
Jumbo Box (36):	200.00

1 Ivan Rodriguez 1.25
2 Kirk McCaskill .10
3 Scott Livingstone .10
4 Salomon Torres RC .10
5 Carlos Hernandez .10
6 Dave Hollins .10
7 Scott Fletcher .10
8 Jorge Fabregas .10
9 Andujar Cedeno .10
10 Howard Johnson .10
11 Trevor Hoffman RC 2.00
12 Roberto Kelly .10
13 Gregg Jefferies .10
14 Marquis Grissom .10
15 Mike Ignasiak .10
16 Jack Morris .10
17 William Pennyfeather .10
18 Todd Stottlemyre .10
19 Chito Martinez .10
20 Roberto Alomar .30
21 Sam Militello .10
22 Hector Fajardo .10
23 Paul Quantrill RC .10
24 Chuck Knoblauch .10
25 Reggie Jefferson .10
26 Jeremy McGarity .10
27 Jerome Walton .10
28 Chipper Jones 3.00
29 Brian Barber RC .10
30 Ron Darling .10
31 Roberto Petagine RC .10
32 Chuck Finley .10
33 Edgar Martinez .10
34 Napolean Robinson .10
35 Andy Van Slyke .10
36 Bobby Thigpen .10
37 Travis Fryman .10
38 Eric Christopherson .10
39 Terry Mulholland .10
40 Darryl Strawberry .10
41 Manny Alexander RC .10
42 Tracey Sanders RC .10
43 Pete Incaviglia .10
44 Kim Batiste .10
45 Frank Rodriguez .10
46 Greg Swindell .10
47 Delino DeShields .10
48 John Ericks .10
49 Franklin Stubbs .10
50 Tony Gwynn 2.00
51 Clifton Garrett RC .10
52 Mike Gardella .10
53 Scott Erickson .10
54 Gary Caballo .10
55 Jose Oliva RC .10
56 Brook Fordyce .10
57 Mark Whiten .10
58 Joe Slusarski .10
59 J.R. Phillips RC .10

1992 Bowman

Topps introduced several changes with the release of its 1992 Bowman set. The 705-card set features 45 special insert cards stamped with gold foil. The cards are printed with a premium UV coated glossy card stock. Several players without major league experience are featured in the set. In-

60 Barry Bonds 4.00
61 Bob Milacki .10
62 Keith Mitchell .10
63 Angel Miranda .10
64 Raul Mondesi .10
65 Brian Koelling .10
66 Brian McRae .10
67 John Patterson .10
68 John Wetteland .10
69 Wilson Alvarez .10
70 Wade Boggs 2.00
71 Darryl Ratliff .10
72 Jeff Jackson .10
73 Jeremy Hernandez .10
74 Darryl Hamilton .10
75 Rafael Belliard .10
76 Ricky Trlicek .10
77 Felipe Crespo RC .10
78 Carney Lansford .10
79 Ryan Long .10
80 Kirby Puckett 2.00
81 Earl Cunningham .10
82 Pedro Martinez 1.50
83 Scott Hatteberg .10
84 Juan Gonzalez .75
85 Robert Nutting .10
86 Calvin Reese RC .50
87 Dave Silvestri .10
88 Scott Ruffcorn RC .10
89 Rick Aguilera .10
90 Cecil Fielder .10
91 Kirk Dressendorfer .10
92 Jerry DiPoto .10
93 Mike Felder .10
94 Craig Paquette .10
95 Elvin Paulino .10
96 Donovan Osborne .10
97 Hubie Brooks .10
98 Derek Lowe 4.00
99 David Zancanaro .10
100 Ken Griffey Jr. 2.75
101 Todd Hundley .10
102 Mike Trombley .10
103 Ricky Gutierrez RC .10
104 Braulio Castillo .10
105 Craig Lefferts .10
106 Rick Sutcliffe .10
107 Dean Palmer .10
108 Henry Rodriguez .10
109 Mark Clark RC .10
110 Kenny Lofton .10
111 Mark Carreon .10
112 J.T. Bruett RC .10
113 Gerald Williams .10
114 Frank Thomas 1.50
115 Kevin Reimer .10
116 Sammy Sosa 2.00
117 Mickey Tettleton .10
118 Reggie Sanders .10
119 Trevor Wilson .10
120 Cliff Brantley .10
121 Spike Owen .10
122 Jeff Montgomery .10
123 Alex Sutherland .10
124 Brien Taylor RC .10
125 Brian Williams .10
126 Kevin Seitzer .10
127 Carlos Delgado RC 15.00
128 Gary Scott .10
129 Scott Cooper .10
130 Domingo Jean RC .10
131 Pat Mahomes RC .10
132 Mike Boddicker .10
133 Roberto Hernandez .10
134 Dave Valle .10
135 Kurt Stillwell .10
136 Brad Pennington RC .10
137 Jermaine Swifton .10
138 Ryan Hawblitzel .10
139 Tito Navarro .10
140 Sandy Alomar .10
141 Todd Benzinger .10
142 Danny Jackson .10
143 Melvin Nieves RC .25
144 Jim Campanis .10
145 Luis Gonzalez .10
146 Dave Doorneweerd .10
147 Charlie Hayes .10
148 Greg Maddux 2.00
149 Brian Harper .10
150 Brent Miller .10
151 Shawn Estes RC .75
152 Mike Williams .10
153 Charlie Hough .10
154 Randy Myers .10
155 Kevin Young RC .10
156 Rick Wilkins .10
157 Terry Schumpert .10
158 Steve Karsay .10
159 Gary DiSarcina .10
160 Deion Sanders .10
161 Tom Browning .10
162 Dickie Thon .10
163 Luis Mercedes .10
164 Ricardo Ingram .10
165 Tavo Alavarez RC .10
166 Rickey Henderson 1.50
167 Jaime Navarro .10
168 Billy Ashley RC .10
169 Phil Dauphin .10
170 Ivan Cruz .10
171 Harold Baines .10
172 Bryan Harvey .10
173 Alex Cole .10
174 Curtis Shaw .10
175 Matt Williams .10
176 Felix Jose .10
177 Sam Horn .10
178 Randy Johnson 1.50
179 Ivan Calderon .10
180 Steve Avery .10
181 William Suero .10
182 Bill Swift .10
183 Howard Battle RC .10
184 Ruben Amaro .10
185 Jim Abbott .10
186 Mike Fitzgerald .10
187 Bruce Hurst .10
188 Jeff Juden .10
189 Jeromy Burnitz .10
190 Dave Burba .10
191 Kevin Brown .10
192 Patrick Lennon .10
193 Jeffrey McNeely .10
194 Wil Cordero .10
195 Chili Davis .10
196 Milt Cuyler .10
197 Von Hayes .10

198 Todd Revening RC .10
199 Joel Johnson .10
200 Jeff Bagwell 1.50
201 Alex Fernandez .10
202 Todd Jones .10
203 Charles Nagy .10
204 Tim Raines .10
205 Kevin Maas .10
206 Julio Franco .10
207 Randy Velarde .10
208 Lance Johnson .10
209 Scott Leius .10
210 Derek Lee .10
211 Joe Sondrini .10
212 Royce Clayton .10
213 Chris George .10
214 Gary Sheffield .60
215 Mark Gubicza .10
216 Mike Moore .10
217 Rick Huisman .10
218 Jeff Russell .10
219 D.J. Dozier .10
220 Dave Martinez .10
221 Al Newman .10
222 Nolan Ryan 4.00
223 Teddy Higuera .10
224 Damon Buford RC .10
225 Ruben Sierra .10
226 Tom Nevers .10
227 Tommy Greene .10
228 Nigel Wilson RC .10
229 John DeSilva .10
230 Bobby Witt .10
231 Greg Cadaret .10
232 John VanderWal .10
233 Jack Clark .10
234 Bill Doran .10
235 Bobby Bonilla .10
236 Steve Olin .10
237 Derek Bell .10
238 David Cone .10
239 Victor Cole .10
240 Rod Bolton .10
241 Tom Pagnozzi .10
242 Rob Dibble .10
243 Michael Carter .10
244 Don Peters .10
245 Mike LaValliere .10
246 Joe Perona .10
247 Mitch Williams .10
248 Jay Buhner .10
249 Andy Benes .10
250 Alex Ochoa RC .10
251 Greg Blosser .10
252 Jack Armstrong .10
253 Juan Samuel .10
254 Terry Pendleton .10
255 Ramon Martinez .10
256 Rico Brogna .10
257 John Smiley .10
258 Carl Everett .10
259 Tim Salmon .10
260 Will Clark .10
261 Ugueth Urbina RC .40
262 Jason Wood .10
263 Dave Magadan .10
264 Dante Bichette .10
265 Jose DeLeon .10
266 Mike Neill RC .10
267 Paul O'Neill .10
268 Anthony Young .10
269 Greg Harris .10
270 Todd Van Poppel .10
271 Pete Castellano .10
272 Tony Phillips .10
273 Mike Gallego .10
274 Steve Cooke RC .10
275 Robin Ventura .10
276 Kevin Mitchell .10
277 Doug Linton .10
278 Robert Eenhorn .10
279 Gabe White RC .10
280 Dave Stewart .10
281 Mo Sanford .10
282 Greg Perschke .10
283 Kevin Flora .10
284 Jeff Williams .10
285 Keith Miller .10
286 Andy Ashby .10
287 Doug Dascenzo .10
288 Eric Karros .10
289 Glenn Murray RC .10
290 Troy Percival RC .75
291 Orlando Merced .10
292 Peter Hoy .10
293 Tony Fernandez .10
294 Juan Guzman .10
295 Jesse Barfield .10
296 Sid Fernandez .10
297 Scott Cepicky .10
298 Garret Anderson RC 6.00
299 Cal Eldred .10
300 Ryne Sandberg 2.00
301 Jim Gantner .10
302 Mariano Rivera RC 25.00
303 Ron Lockett .10
304 Jose Offerman .10
305 Denny Martinez .10
306 Luis Ortiz RC .10
307 David Howard .10
308 Russ Springer .10
309 Chris Howard .10
310 Kyle Abbott .10
311 Aaron Sele RC 1.00
312 Dave Justice .10
313 Pete O'Brien .10
314 Greg Hansell .10
315 Dave Winfield 1.50

316 Lance Dickson .10
317 Eric King .10
318 Vaughn Eshelman .10
319 Tim Belcher .10
320 Andres Galarraga .10
321 Scott Bullett .10
322 Doug Strange .10
323 Jerald Clark .10
324 Dave Righetti .10
325 Greg Hibbard .10
326 Eric Dillman .10
327 Shane Reynolds RC .25
328 Chris Hammond .10
329 Albert Belle .10
330 Rich Becker RC .10
331 Eddie Williams .10
332 Donald Harris .10
333 Dave Smith .10
334 Steve Fireovid .10
335 Steve Buechele .10
336 Mike Schooler .10
337 Kevin McReynolds .10
338 Hensley Meulens .10
339 Benji Gil RC .10
340 Don Mattingly 2.50
341 Alvin Davis .10
342 Alan Mills .10
343 Kelly Downs .10
344 Leo Gomez .10
345 Tarrik Brock RC .10
346 Ryan Turner .10
347 John Smoltz .10
348 Bill Sampen .10
349 Paul Byrd .10
350 Mike Bordick .10
351 Jose Lind .10
352 David Wells .10
353 Barry Larkin .10
354 Bruce Ruffin .10
355 Luis Rivera .10
356 Sid Bream .10
357 Julian Vasquez .10
358 Jason Bere RC .10
359 Ben McDonald .10
360 Scott Stahoviak .10
361 Kirt Manwaring .10
362 Jeff Johnson .10
363 Rob Deer .10
364 Tony Pena .10
365 Melido Perez .10
366 Clay Parker .10
367 Dale Sveum .10
368 Mike Scioscia .10
369 Roger Salkeld .10
370 Mike Stanley .10
371 Jack McDowell .10
372 Tim Wallach .10
373 Billy Ripken .10
374 Mike Christopher .10
375 Paul Molitor 1.50
376 Dave Stieb .10
377 Pedro Guerrero .10
378 Russ Swan .10
379 Bob Ojeda .10
380 Donn Pall .10
381 Eddie Zosky .10
382 Darnell Coles .10
383 Tom Smith .10
384 Mark McGwire 3.00
385 Gary Carter 1.50
386 Rich Amaral .10
387 Alan Embree .10
388 Jonathan Hurst .10
389 Bobby Jones RC .10
390 Rico Rossy .10
391 Dan Smith .10
392 Terry Steinbach .10
393 Jon Farrell .10
394 Dave Anderson .10
395 Benito Santiago .10
396 Mark Wohlers .10
397 Mo Vaughn .10
398 Randy Kramer .10
399 John Jaha RC .10
400 Cal Ripken, Jr. 4.00
401 Ryan Bowen .10
402 Tim McIntosh .10
403 Bernard Gilkey .10
404 Junior Felix .10
405 Cris Colon .10
406 Marc Newfield .10
407 Bernie Williams .10
408 Jay Howell .10
409 Zane Smith .10
410 Jeff Shaw .10
411 Kerry Woodson .10
412 Wes Chamberlain .10
413 Dave Mlicki .10
414 Benny Distefano .10
415 Kevin Rogers .10
416 Tim Naehring .10
417 Clemente Nunez .10
418 Luis Sojo .10
419 Kevin Ritz .10
420 Omar Oliveras .10
421 Manuel Lee .10
422 Julio Valera .10
423 Omar Vizquel .10
424 Darren Burton .10
425 Mel Hall .10
426 Dennis Powell .10
427 Lee Stevens .10
428 Glenn Davis .10
429 Willie Greene .10
430 Kevin Wickander .10
431 Dennis Eckersley 1.25
432 Joe Orsulak .10
433 Eddie Murray 1.50

434	Matt Stairs RC	.10
435	Wally Joyner	.10
436	Rondell White	.10
437	Rob Mauer	.10
438	Joe Redfield	.10
439	Mark Lewis	.10
440	Darren Daulton	.10
441	Mike Henneman	.10
442	John Cangelosi	.10
443	Vince Moore	.10
444	John Wehner	.10
445	Kent Hrbek	.10
446	Mark McLemore	.10
447	Bill Wegman	.10
448	Robby Thompson	.10
449	Mark Anthony	.10
450	Archi Cianfrocco	.10
451	Johnny Ruffin	.10
452	Javier Lopez	.10
453	Greg Gohr	.10
454	Tim Scott	.10
455	Stan Belinda	.10
456	Darrin Jackson	.10
457	Chris Gardner	.10
458	Esteban Beltre	.10
459	Phil Plantier	.10
460	Jim Thome	1.25
461	Mike Piazza RC	25.00
462	Matt Sinatro	.10
463	Scott Servais	.10
464	Brian Jordan	.75
465	Doug Drabek	.10
466	Carl Willis	.10
467	Bret Barbarie	.10
468	Hal Morris	.10
469	Steve Sax	.10
470	Jerry Willard	.10
471	Dan Wilson	.10
472	Chris Hoiles	.10
473	Rheal Cormier	.10
474	John Morris	.10
475	Jeff Reardon	.10
476	Mark Leiter	.10
477	Tom Gordon	.10
478	Kent Bottenfield RC	.10
479	Gene Larkin	.10
480	Dwight Gooden	.10
481	B.J. Surhoff	.10
482	Andy Stankiewicz	.10
483	Tino Martinez	.10
484	Craig Biggio	.10
485	Denny Neagle	.10
486	Rusty Meacham	.10
487	Kal Daniels	.10
488	Dave Henderson	.10
489	Tim Costo	.10
490	Doug Davis	.10
491	Frank Viola	.10
492	Cory Snyder	.10
493	Chris Martin	.10
494	Dion James	.10
495	Randy Tomlin	.10
496	Greg Vaughn	.10
497	Dennis Cook	.10
498	Rosario Rodriguez	.10
499	Dave Staton	.10
500	George Brett	2.50
501	Brian Barnes	.10
502	Butch Henry	.10
503	Harold Reynolds	.10
504	David Nied RC	.10
505	Lee Smith	.10
506	Steve Chitren	.10
507	Ken Hill	.10
508	Robbie Beckett	.10
509	Troy Afenir	.10
510	Kelly Gruber	.10
511	Bret Boone	.10
512	Jeff Branson	.10
513	Mike Jackson	.10
514	Pete Harnisch	.10
515	Chad Kreuter	.10
516	Joe Vitko	.10
517	Orel Hershiser	.10
518	John Doherty RC	.10
519	Jay Bell	.10
520	Mark Langston	.10
521	Dann Howitt	.10
522	Bobby Reed	.10
523	Roberto Munoz	.10
524	Todd Ritchie	.10
525	Bip Roberts	.10
526	Pat Listach	.10
527	Scott Brosius RC	.10
528	John Roper RC	.10
529	Phil Hiatt RC	.10
530	Denny Walling	.10
531	Carlos Baerga	.10
532	Manny Ramirez	20.00
533	Pat Clements	.10
534	Ron Gant	.10
535	Pat Kelly	.10
536	Billy Spiers	.10
537	Darren Reed	.10
538	Ken Caminiti	.10
539	Butch Huskey RC	.10
540	Matt Nokes	.10
541	John Kruk	.10
542	John Jaha/SP (Foil)	.35
543	Justin Thompson RC	.10
544	Steve Hosey	.10
545	Joe Kmak	.10
546	John Franco	.10
547	Devon White	.10
548	Elston Hansen/SP (Foil)	.35
549	Ryan Klesko	.10
550	Danny Tartabull	.10

551	Frank Thomas/SP (Foil)	1.50
552	Kevin Tapani	.10
553a	Willie Banks	.10
553b	Pat Clements	.10
554	B.J. Wallace/SP RC (Foil)	.35
555	Orlando Miller RC	.10
556	Mark Smith RC	.10
557	Tim Wallach (Foil)	.10
558	Bill Gullickson	.10
559	Derek Bell (Foil)	.10
560	Joe Randa (Foil)	.10
561	Frank Seminara	.10
562	Mark Gardner	.10
563	Rick Greene (Foil)	.10
564	Gary Gaetti	.10
565	Ozzie Guillen	.10
566	Charles Nagy (Foil)	.10
567	Mike Milchin	.10
568	Ben Shelton (Foil)	.10
569	Chris Roberts (Foil)	.10
570	Ellis Burks	.10
571	Scott Scudder	.10
572	Jim Abbott (Foil)	.10
573	Joe Carter	.10
574	Steve Finley	.10
575	Jim Olander (Foil)	.10
576	Carlos Garcia	.10
577	Greg Olson	.10
578	Greg Swindell (Foil)	.10
579	Matt Williams (Foil)	.10
580	Mark Grace	.10
581	Howard House (Foil)	.10
582	Luis Polonia	.10
583	Erik Hanson	.10
584	Salomon Torres (Foil)	.10
585	Carlton Fisk	1.50
586	Bret Saberhagen	.10
587	Chad McDonnell RC (Foil)	.10
588	Jimmy Key	.10
589	Mike MacFarlane	.10
590	Barry Bonds (Foil)	3.50
591	Jamie McAndrew	.10
592	Shane Mack	.10
593	Kerwin Moore	.10
594	Joe Oliver	.10
595	Chris Sabo	.10
596	Alex Gonzalez RC	.50
597	Brett Butler	.10
598	Mark Hutton	.10
599	Andy Benes (Foil)	.10
600	Jose Canseco	.60
601	Darryl Kile	.10
602	Matt Stairs/SP (Foil)	.35
603	Rob Butler (Foil)	.10
604	Willie McGee	.10
605	Jack McDowell	.10
606	Tom Candiotti	.10
607	Ed Martel	.10
608	Matt Mieske (Foil)	.10
609	Darrin Fletcher	.10
610	Rafael Palmeiro	1.25
611	Bill Swift (Foil)	.10
612	Mike Mussina	.65
613	Vince Coleman	.10
614	Scott Cepicky (Foil)	.10
615	Mike Greenwell	.10
616	Kevin McGehee	.10
617	Jeffrey Hammonds (Foil)	.10
618	Scott Taylor	.10
619	Dave Otto	.10
620	Mark McGwire (Foil)	3.00
621	Kevin Tatar	.10
622	Steve Farr	.10
623	Ryan Klesko (Foil)	.10
625	Andre Dawson	.40
626	Tino Martinez/SP (Foil)	.10
627	Chad Curtis RC	.50
628	Mickey Morandini	.10
629	Gregg Olson/SP (Foil)	.35
630	Lou Whitaker	.10
631	Arthur Rhodes	.10
632	Brandon Wilson	.10
633	Lance Jennings RC	.10
634	Allen Watson RC	.10
635	Len Dykstra	.10
636	Joe Girardi	.10
637	Kiki Hernandez/SP (Foil)	.35
638	Mike Hampton RC	1.00
639	Al Osuna	.10
640	Kevin Appier	.10
641	Rick Helling/SP (Foil)	.35
642	Jody Reed	.10
643	Ray Lankford	.10
644	John Olerud	.10
645	Paul Molitor/SP (Foil)	1.50
646	Pat Borders	.10
647	Mike Morgan	.10
648	Larry Walker	.10
649	Pete Castellano/SP (Foil)	.35
650	Fred McGriff	.10
651	Walt Weiss	.10
652	Calvin Murray/SP RC (Foil)	.35
653	Dave Nilsson	.10
654	Greg Pirkl	.10

655	Robin Ventura/SP (Foil)	.35
656	Mark Portugal	.10
657	Roger McDowell	.10
658	Rick Hirtensteiner/SP (Foil)	.35
659	Glenallen Hill	.10
660	Greg Gagne	.10
661	Charles Johnson/SP (Foil)	.35
662	Brian Hunter	.10
663	Mark Lemke	.10
664	Tim Belcher/SP (Foil)	.35
665	Rich DeLucia	.10
666	Bob Walk	.10
667	Joe Carter/SP (Foil)	.35
668	Jose Guzman	.10
669	Otis Nixon	.10
670	Phil Nevin (Foil)	.10
671	Eric Davis	.10
672	Damion Easley RC	.25
673	Will Clark (Foil)	.10
674	Mark Kiefer	.10
675	Ozzie Smith	2.00
676	Manny Ramirez (Foil)	6.00
677	Gregg Olson	.10
678	Cliff Floyd RC	1.00
679	Duane Singleton	.10
680	Jose Rijo	.10
681	Willie Randolph	.10
682	Michael Tucker RC (Foil)	.25
683	Darren Lewis	.10
684	Dale Murphy	.35
685	Mike Pagliarulo	.10
686	Paul Miller	.10
687	Mike Patterson	.10
688	Mike Devereaux	.10
689	Pedro Astacio	.10
690	Alan Trammell	.10
691	Roger Clemens	2.50
692	Bud Black	.10
693	Turk Wendell	.10
694	Barry Larkin/SP (Foil)	.35
695	Todd Zeile	.10
696	Pat Hentgen	.10
697	Eddie Taubensee RC	.10
698	Guillermo Vasquez	.10
699	Tom Glavine	.30
700	Robin Yount	1.50
701	Checklist	.10
702	Checklist	.10
703	Checklist	.10
704	Checklist	.10
705	Checklist	.10

1993 Bowman

Bowman's 708-card 1993 set once again features a premium UV-coated glossy stock. There are also 48 special insert cards, with gold foil stamping, randomly inserted one per pack or two per jumbo pack. The foil cards, numbered 339-374 and 693-704, feature top prospects and rookie-of-the-year candidates, as do several regular cards in the set. Cards are standard size.

	NM/M
Complete Set (708):	35.00
Common Player:	.10
Pack (15):	1.50
Wax Box (24):	35.00
Jumbo Pack (22):	2.50
Jumbo Box (20):	40.00

1	Glenn Davis	.10
2	Hector Roa RC	.10
3	Ken Ryan RC	.10
4	Derek Wallace RC	.10
5	Jorge Fabregas	.10
6	Joe Oliver	.10
7	Brandon Wilson	.10
8	Mark Thompson RC	.10
9	Tracy Sanders	.10
10	Rich Renteria	.10
11	Lou Whitaker	.10
12	Brian Hunter RC	.10
13	Joe Vitiello	.10
14	Eric Karros	.10
15	Joe Kmak	.10
16	Tavo Alvarez	.10
17	Steve Dunn RC	.10
18	Tony Fernandez	.10

ABBREVIATIONS

SP - Short Print

19	Melido Perez	.10
20	Mike Lieberthal	.10
21	Terry Steinbach	.10
22	Stan Belinda	.10
23	Jay Buhner	.10
24	Allen Watson	.10
25	Glenallen Hill	.10
26	Ray McDavid RC	.10
27	Shawn Green	.30
28	Bud Black	.10
29	Sherman Obando RC	.10
30	Mike Hostetler RC	.10
31	Nate Hinchey RC	.10
32	Randy Myers	.10
33	Brian Grebeck RC	.10
34	John Roper	.10
35	Larry Thomas	.10
36	Alex Cole	.10
37	Tom Kramer RC	.10
38	Matt Whisenant RC	.10
39	Chris Gomez RC	.10
40	Luis Gonzalez	.10
41	Kevin Appier	.10
42	Omar Daal RC	.10
43	Duane Singleton RC	.10
44	Bill Risley	.10
45	Pat Meares RC	.10
46	Butch Huskey	.10
47	Bobby Munoz	.10
48	Juan Bell	.10
49	Scott Lydy RC	.10
50	Dennis Moeller	.10
51	Marc Newfield	.10
52	Tripp Cromer RC	.10
53	Kurt Miller	.10
54	Jim Pena	.10
55	Juan Guzman	.10
56	Matt Williams	.10
57	Harold Reynolds	.10
58	Donnie Elliott RC	.10
59	Jon Shave RC	.10
60	Kevin Roberson RC	.10
61	Hilly Hathaway RC	.10
62	Jose Rijo	.10
63	Kerry Taylor RC	.10
64	Ryan Hawblitzel	.10
65	Glenallen Hill	.10
66	Ramon D. Martinez RC	.10
67	Travis Fryman	.10
68	Tom Nevers	.10
69	Phil Hiatt	.10
70	Tim Wallach	.10
71	B.J. Surhoff	.10
72	Rondell White	.10
73	Denny Hocking RC	.10
74	Mike Oquist RC	.10
75	Paul O'Neill	.10
76	Willie Banks	.10
77	Bob Welch	.10
78	Jose Sandoval RC	.10
79	Bill Haselman	.10
80	Rheal Cormier	.10
81	Dean Palmer	.10
82	Pat Gomez RC	.10
83	Steve Karsay	.10
84	Carl Hanselman RC	.10
85	T.R. Lewis RC	.10
86	Chipper Jones	2.00
87	Scott Hatteberg RC	.10
88	Greg Hibbard	.10
89	Lance Painter RC	.10
90	Chad Mottola RC	.10
91	Jason Bere	.10
92	Dante Bichette	.10
93	Sandy Alomar	.10
94	Carl Everett	.10
95	Danny Bautista RC	.10
96	Steve Finley	.10
97	David Cone	.10
98	Todd Hollandsworth RC	.10
99	Matt Mieske	.10
100	Larry Walker	.10
101	Shane Mack	.10
102	Aaron Ledesma RC	.10
103	Andy Pettitte RC	4.00
104	Kevin Stocker RC	.10
105	Mike Mobler	.10
106	Tony Menedez	.10
107	Derek Lowe RC	.10
108	Basil Shabazz RC	.10
109	Dan Smith	.10
110	Scott Sanders RC	.10
111	Todd Stottlemyre	.10
112	Benji Sikonton RC	.10
113	Rick Sutcliffe	.10
114	Lee Heath RC	.10
115	Jeff Russell	.10
116	Dave Stevens RC	.10
117	Mark Holzemer RC	.10
118	Tim Belcher	.10
119	Bobby Thigpen	.10
120	Roger Bailey RC	.10
121	Tony Mitchell RC	.10
122	Junior Felix	.10
123	Rich Robertson RC	.10
124	Andy Cook RC	.10
125	Brian Bevil RC	.10
126	Darryl Strawberry	.10
127	Cal Eldred	.10
128	Cliff Floyd	.10
129	Alan Newman	.10
130	Howard Johnson	.10
131	Jim Abbott	.10
132	Chad McConnell	.10
133	Miguel Jimenez RC	.10
134	Brett Backlund RC	.10
135	John Cummings RC	.10
136	Brian Barber	.10

137	Rafael Palmeiro	1.25
138	Tim Worrell RC	.10
139	Jose Pett RC	.10
140	Barry Bonds	4.00
141	Damon Buford	.10
142	Jeff Blauser	.10
143	Frankie Rodriguez	.10
144	Mike Morgan	.10
145	Gary DeSarcina	.10
146	Calvin Reese	.10
147	Johnny Ruffin	.10
148	David Nied	.10
149	Charles Nagy	.10
150	Mike Myers RC	.10
151	Kenny Carlyle RC	.10
152	Eric Anthony	.10
153	Jose Lind	.10
154	Pedro Martinez	1.50
155	Mark Kiefer	.10
156	Tim Laker RC	.10
157	Pat Mahomes	.10
158	Bobby Bonilla	.10
159	Domingo Jean	.10
160	Darren Daulton	.10
161	Mark McGwire	3.50
162	Jason Kendall RC	1.00
163	Desi Relaford	.10
164	Ozzie Canseco	.10
165	Rick Helling	.10
166	Steve Pegues RC	.10
167	Paul Molitor	1.50
168	Larry Carter RC	.10
169	Arthur Rhodes	.10
170	Damon Hollins RC	.10
171	Frank Viola	.10
172	Steve Trachsel RC	.25
173	J.T. Snow RC	.50
174	Keith Gordon RC	.10
175	Carlton Fisk	1.50
176	Jason Bates RC	.10
177	Mike Crosby RC	.10
178	Benny Santiago	.10
179	Mike Moore	.10
180	Jeff Juden	.10
181	Darren Burton	.10
182	Todd Williams RC	.10
183	John Jaha	.10
184	Mike Lansing RC	.50
185	Pedro Grifol RC	.10
186	Vince Coleman	.10
187	Pat Kelly	.10
188	Clemente Alvarez RC	.10
189	Ron Darling	.10
190	Orlando Merced	.10
191	Chris Bosio	.10
192	Steve Dixon RC	.10
193	Doug Dascenzo	.10
194	Ray Holbert RC	.10
195	Howard Battle	.10
196	Willie McGee	.10
197	John O'Donoghue RC	.10
198	Steve Avery	.10
199	Greg Blosser	.10
200	Ryne Sandberg	2.00
201	Joe Grahe	.10
202	Dan Wilson	.10
203	Domingo Martinez RC	.10
204	Andres Galarraga	.10
205	Jamie Taylor RC	.10
206	Darrell Whitmore RC	.10
207	Ben Blomdahl RC	.10
208	Doug Drabek	.10
209	Keith Miller	.10
210	Billy Ashley	.10
211	Mike Farrell RC	.10
212	John Wetteland	.10
213	Randy Tomlin	.10
214	Sid Fernandez	.10
215	Quilvio Veras RC	.10
216	Dave Hollins	.10
217	Mike Neill	.10
218	Andy Van Slyke	.10
219	Bret Boone	.10
220	Tom Pagnozzi	.10
221	Mike Welch RC	.10
222	Frank Seminara	.10
223	Ron Villone	.10
224	D.J. Thielen RC	.10
225	Cal Ripken, Jr.	4.00
226	Pedro Borbon RC	.10
227	Carlos Quintana	.10
228	Tommy Shields RC	.10
229	Tim Salmon	.10
230	John Smiley	.10
231	Ellis Burks	.10
232	Pedro Castellano	.10
233	Paul Byrd	.10
234	Bryan Harvey	.10
235	Scott Livingstone	.10
236	James Mouton RC	.10
237	Joe Randa	.10
238	Pedro Astacio	.10
239	Darryl Hamilton	.10
240	Joey Eischen RC	.10
241	Edgar Herrera RC	.10
242	Dwight Gooden	.10
243	Sam Militello	.10
244	Ron Blazier RC	.10
245	Ruben Sierra	.10
246	Al Martin	.10
247	Mike Felder	.10
248	Bob Tewksbury	.10
249	Craig Lefferts	.10
250	Luis Lopez	.10
251	Devon White	.10
252	Will Clark	.10
253	Mark Smith	.10
254	Terry Pendleton	.10

255	Aaron Sele	.10
256	Jose Viera RC	.10
257	Damion Easley	.10
258	Rod Lofton RC	.10
259	Chris Snopek RC	.10
260	Quinton McCracken RC	.10
261	Mike Matthews RC	.10
262	Hector Carrasco RC	.10
263	Rick Greene	.10
264	Chris Bolt RC	.10
265	George Brett	2.50
266	Rick Gorecki RC	.10
267	Francisco Gamez RC	.10
268	Marquis Grissom	.10
269	Kevin Tapani	.10
270	Ryan Thompson	.10
271	Gerald Williams	.10
272	Paul Fletcher RC	.10
273	Lance Blankenship	.10
274	Marty Heff RC	.10
275	Shawn Estes	.10
276	Rene Arocha RC	.10
277	Scott Evre RC	.10
278	Phil Plantier	.10
279	Paul Spoljaric RC	.10
280	Chris Gahbs	.10
281	Harold Baines	.10
282	Jose Oliva RC	.10
283	Matt Whiteside	.10
284	Brant Brown RC	.10
285	Russ Springer	.10
286	Chris Sabo	.10
287	Ozzie Guillen	.10
288	Marcus Moore RC	.10
289	Chad Ogea	.10
290	Walt Weiss	.10
291	Brian Edmondson	.10
292	Jimmy Gonzalez	.10
293	Danny Miceli RC	.10
294	Jose Offerman	.10
295	Greg Vaughn	.10
296	Frank Bolick	.10
297	Mike Maksudian RC	.10
298	John Franco	.10
299	Danny Tartabull	.10
300	Len Dykstra	.10
301	Bobby Witt	.10
302	Trey Beamon RC	.10
303	Tino Martinez	.10
304	Aaron Holbert	.10
305	Juan Gonzalez	.75
306	Billy Hall RC	.10
307	Duane Ward	.10
308	Rod Beck	.10
309	Jose Mercedes RC	.10
310	Otis Nixon	.10
311	Gettys Glaze RC	.10
312	Candy Maldonado	.10
313	Chad Curtis	.10
314	Tim Costo	.10
315	Mike Robertson	.10
316	Nigel Wilson	.10
317	Greg McMichael RC	.10
318	Scott Pose RC	.10
319	Ivan Cruz	.10
320	Greg Swindell	.10
321	Kevin McReynolds	.10
322	Tom Candiotti	.10
323	Bob Wishnevski RC	.10
324	Ken Hill	.10
325	Kirby Puckett	2.00
326	Tim Bogar RC	.10
327	Mariano Rivera RC	.30
328	Mitch Williams	.10
329	Craig Paquette	.10
330	Jay Bell	.10
331	Jose Martinez RC	.10
332	Rob Deer	.10
333	Brook Fordyce	.10
334	Matt Nokes	.10
335	Derek Lee	.10
336	Paul Ellis RC	.10
337	Desi Wilson RC	.10
338	Roberto Alomar	.30
339	Jim Tatum (Foil)	.10
340	J.T. Snow (Foil)	.10
341	Tim Salmon (Foil)	.10
342	Russ Davis RC (Foil)	.25
343	Javier Lopez (Foil)	.10
344	Troy O'Leary RC (Foil)	.10
345	Marty Cordova (Foil)	.60
346	Bubba Smith RC (Foil)	.10
347	Chipper Jones (Foil)	1.50
348	Jessie Hollins RC (Foil)	.10
349	Willie Greene (Foil)	.10
350	Mark Thompson (Foil)	.10
351	Nigel Wilson (Foil)	.10
352	Todd Jones (Foil)	.10
353	Raul Mondesi (Foil)	.10
354	Cliff Floyd (Foil)	.10
355	Bobby Jones (Foil)	.10
356	Kevin Stocker (Foil)	.10
357	Midre Cummings (Foil)	.10
358	Allen Watson (Foil)	.10
359	Ray McDavid (Foil)	.10
360	Steve Hosey (Foil)	.10
361	Brad Pennington (Foil)	.10
362	Frankie Rodriguez (Foil)	.10
363	Troy Percival (Foil)	.10
364	Jason Bere (Foil)	.10
365	Manny Ramirez (Foil)	.75
366	Justin Thompson (Foil)	.10
367	Joe Vitiello (Foil)	.10
368	Tyrone Hill (Foil)	.10
369	David McCarty (Foil)	.10
370	Brien Taylor (Foil)	.10
371	Todd Van Poppel (Foil)	.10

372 Marc Newfield (Foil)	.10
373 Terrell Lowery RC (Foil)	.10
374 Alex Gonzalez (Foil)	.10
375 Ken Griffey Jr.	3.00
376 Donovan Osborne	.10
377 Ritchie Moody RC	.10
378 Shane Andrews	.10
379 Carlos Delgado	.65
380 Bill Swift	.10
381 Leo Gomez	.10
382 Ron Gant	.10
383 Scott Fletcher	.10
384 Matt Walbeck RC	.10
385 Chuck Finley	.10
386 Kevin Mitchell	.10
387 Wilson Alvarez	.10
388 John Burke RC	.10
389 Alan Embree	.10
390 Trevor Hoffman	.10
391 Alan Trammell	.10
392 Todd Jones	.10
393 Felix Jose	.10
394 Orel Hershiser	.10
395 Pat Listach	.10
396 Gabe White	.10
397 Dan Serafini RC	.10
398 Todd Hundley	.10
399 Wade Boggs	2.00
400 Tyler Green	.10
401 Mike Bordick	.10
402 Scott Bullett	.10
403 Lagrande Russell RC	.10
404 Ray Lankford	.10
405 Nolan Ryan	4.00
406 Robbie Beckett	.10
407 Brent Bowers RC	.10
408 Adell Davenport RC	.10
409 Brady Anderson	.10
410 Tom Glavine	.35
411 Doug Hecker RC	.10
412 Jose Guzman	.10
413 Luis Polonia	.10
414 Brian Williams	.10
415 Bo Jackson	.15
416 Eric Young	.10
417 Kenny Lofton	.10
418 Orestes Destrade	.10
419 Tony Phillips	.10
420 Jeff Bagwell	1.50
421 Hark Gardner	.10
422 Brett Butler	.10
423 Graeme Lloyd RC	.10
424 Delino DeShields	.10
425 Scott Erickson	.10
426 Jeff Kent	.10
427 Jimmy Key	.10
428 Mickey Morandini	.10
429 Marcos Arkas RC	.10
430 Don Slaught	.10
431 Randy Johnson	1.50
432 Omar Olivares	.10
433 Charlie Leibrandt	.10
434 Kurt Stillwell	.10
435 Scott Brow RC	.10
436 Robby Thompson	.10
437 Ben McDonald	.10
438 Deion Sanders	.10
439 Tony Pena	.10
440 Mark Grace	.10
441 Eduardo Perez	.10
442 Tim Pugh RC	.10
443 Scott Ruffcorn	.10
444 Jay Gainer RC	.10
445 Albert Belle	.10
446 Bret Barberie	.10
447 Justin Mashore	.10
448 Pete Harnisch	.10
449 Greg Gagne	.10
450 Eric Davis	.10
451 Dave Mlicki	.10
452 Moises Alou	.10
453 Rick Aguilera	.10
454 Eddie Murray	1.50
455 Bob Wickman	.10
456 Wes Chamberlain	.10
457 Brent Gates	.10
458 Paul Weber	.10
459 Mike Hampton	.10
460 Ozzie Smith	2.00
461 Tom Henke	.10
462 Ricky Gutuerrez	.10
463 Jack Morris	.10
464 Joel Chimelis RC	.10
465 Gregg Olson	.10
466 Javier Lopez	.10
467 Scott Cooper	.10
468 Willie Wilson	.10
469 Mark Langston	.10
470 Barry Larkin	.10
471 Rod Bolton	.10
472 Freddie Benavides	.10
473 Ken Ramos RC	.10
474 Chuck Carr	.10
475 Cecil Fielder	.10
476 Eddie Taubensee	.10
477 Chris Eddy RC	.10
478 Greg Hansell	.10
479 Kevin Reimer	.10
480 Denny Martinez	.10
481 Chuck Knoblauch	.10
482 Mike Draper	.10
483 Spike Owen	.10
484 Terry Mulholland	.10
485 Dennis Eckersley	1.25
486 Blas Minor	.10
487 Dave Fleming	.10
488 Dan Cholonsky RC	.10
489 Ivan Rodriguez	1.25

490 Gary Sheffield	.45
491 Ed Sprague	.10
492 Steve Hosey	.10
493 Jimmy Haynes RC	.10
494 John Smoltz	.10
495 Andre Dawson	.35
496 Rey Sanchez	.10
497 Ty Van Burkleo RC	.10
498 Bobby Ayala RC	.10
499 Tim Raines	.10
500 Charlie Hayes	.10
501 Paul Sorrento	.10
502 Richie Lewis RC	.10
503 Jason Pfaff RC	.10
504 Ken Caminiti	.10
505 Mike Macfarlane	.10
506 Jody Reed	.10
507 Bobby Hughes RC	.10
508 Wil Cordero	.10
509 George Tsanis RC	.10
510 Bret Saberhagen	.10
511 Derek Jeter RC	20.00
512 Gene Schall	.10
513 Curtis Shaw	.10
514 Steve Cooke	.10
515 Edgar Martinez	.10
516 Mike Milchin	.10
517 Billy Ripken	.10
518 Andy Benes	.10
519 Juan de la Rosa RC	.10
520 John Burkett	.10
521 Alex Ochoa	.10
522 Tony Tarasco RC	.10
523 Luis Ortiz	.10
524 Rick Williams	.10
525 Chris Turner RC	.10
526 Rob Dibble	.10
527 Jack McDowell	.10
528 Daryl Boston	.10
529 Bill Wertz RC	.10
530 Charlie Hough	.10
531 Sean Bergman	.10
532 Doug Jones	.10
533 Jeff Montgomery	.10
534 Roger Cedeno RC	.25
535 Robin Yount	1.50
536 Mo Vaughn	.10
537 Brian Harper	.10
538 Juan Castillo	.10
539 Steve Farr	.10
540 John Kruk	.10
541 Troy Neel	.10
542 Danny Clyburn RC	.10
543 Jim Converse RC	.10
544 Gregg Jefferies	.10
545 Jose Canseco	.40
546 Julio Bruno RC	.10
547 Rob Butler	.10
548 Royce Clayton	.10
549 Chris Hoiles	.10
550 Greg Maddux	2.00
551 Joe Ciccarella RC	.10
552 Ozzie Timmons	.10
553 Chili Davis	.10
554 Brian Koelling	.10
555 Frank Thomas	1.50
556 Vinny Castilla	.10
557 Reggie Jefferson	.10
558 Rob Natal	.10
559 Mike Henneman	.10
560 Craig Biggio	.10
561 Billy Brewer RC	.10
562 Dan Melendez	.10
563 Kenny Felder RC	.10
564 Miguel Batista RC	.10
565 Dave Winfield	1.50
566 Al Shirley	.10
567 Robert Eenhoorn	.10
568 Mike Williams	.10
569 Tanyon Sturtze RC	.10
570 Tim Wakefield	.10
571 Greg Pirkl	.10
572 Sean Lowe RC	.25
573 Terry Burows RC	.10
574 Kevin Higgins RC	.10
575 Joe Carter	.10
576 Kevin Rogers	.10
577 Manny Alexander	.10
578 Dave Justice	.10
579 Brian Conroy RC	.10
580 Jessie Hollins RC	.10
581 Ron Watson RC	.10
582 Bip Roberts	.10
583 Tom Urbani RC	.10
584 Jason Hutchins RC	.10
585 Carlos Baerga	.10
586 Jeff Mutis	.10
587 Justin Thompson	.10
588 Orlando Miller	.10
589 Brian McRae	.10
590 Ramon Martinez	.10
591 Dave Nilsson	.10
592 Jose Vidro RC	1.50
593 Rich Becker	.10
594 Preston Wilson RC	1.50
595 Don Mattingly	2.50
596 Tony Longmire	.10
597 Kevin Seitzer	.10
598 Midre Cummings RC	.10
599 Omar Vizquel	.10
600 Lee Smith	.10
601 David Hulse RC	.10
602 Darrell Sherman RC	.10
603 Alex Gonzalez	.10
604 Geronimo Pena	.10
605 Mike Devereaux	.10
606 Sterling Hitchcock RC	.25
607 Mike Greenwell	.10

608 Steve Buechele	.10
609 Troy Percival	.10
610 Bobby Kelly	.10
611 James Haynes RC	.10
612 Jerald Clark	.10
613 Albie Lopez RC	.10
614 Dave Magadan	.10
615 Mickey Tettleton	.10
616 Sean Runyan RC	.10
617 Bob Hamelin	.10
618 Raul Mondesi	.10
619 Tyrone Hill	.10
620 Darrin Fletcher	.10
621 Mike Trombley	.10
622 Jeromy Burnitz	.10
623 Bernie Williams	.10
624 Mike Farmer RC	.10
625 Rickey Henderson	1.50
626 Carlos Garcia	.10
627 Jeff Darwin RC	.10
628 Todd Zeile	.10
629 Benji Gil	.10
630 Tony Gwynn	2.00
631 Aaron Small RC	.10
632 Joe Rosselli RC	.10
633 Mike Mussina	1.00
634 Ryan Klesko	.10
635 Roger Clemens	2.50
636 Sammy Sosa	2.00
637 Orlando Palmeiro RC	.10
638 Willie Greene	.10
639 George Bell	.10
640 Garvin Alston RC	.10
641 Pete Janicki RC	.10
642 Chris Sheff RC	.10
643 Felipe Lira RC	.10
644 Roberto Petagine RC	.10
645 Wally Joyner	.10
646 Mike Piazza	3.00
647 Jaime Navarro	.10
648 Jeff Hartsock RC	.10
649 David McCarty	.10
650 Bobby Jones	.10
651 Mark Hutton	.10
652 Kyle Abbott	.10
653 Steve Cox RC	.10
654 Jeff King	.10
655 Norm Charlton	.10
656 Mike Gulan RC	.10
657 Julio Franco	.10
658 Cameron Cairncross RC	.10
659 John Olerud	.10
660 Salomon Torres	.10
661 Brad Pennington	.10
662 Melvin Nieves	.10
663 Ivan Calderon	.10
664 Turk Wendell	.10
665 Chris Pritchett	.10
666 Reggie Sanders	.10
667 Robin Ventura	.10
668 Joe Girardi	.10
669 Manny Ramirez	1.50
670 Jeff Conine	.10
671 Greg Gohr	.10
672 Andujar Cedeno	.10
673 Les Norman RC	.10
674 Mike James RC	.10
675 Marshall Boze RC	.10
676 B.J. Wallace	.10
677 Kent Hrbek	.10
678 Jack Voight	.10
679 Brien Taylor	.10
680 Curt Schilling	.35
681 Todd Van Poppel	.10
682 Kevin Young	.10
683 Tommy Adams	.10
684 Bernard Gilkey	.10
685 Kevin Brown	.10
686 Fred McGriff	.10
687 Pat Borders	.10
688 Kirt Manwaring	.10
689 Sid Bream	.10
690 John Valentin	.10
691 Steve Olsen RC	.10
692 Roberto Mejia RC	.10
693 Carlos Delgado (Foil)	.50
694 Steve Gibralter RC (Foil)	.10
695 Gary Mota (Foil)	.10
696 Jose Malave RC (Foil)	.10
697 Larry Sutton RC (Foil)	.10
698 Dan Frye RC (Foil)	.10
699 Tim Clark RC (Foil)	.10
700 Brian Rupp RC (Foil)	.10
701 Felipe Alou, Moises Alou (Foil)	.10
702 Bobby Bonds, Barry Bonds (Foil)	1.00
703 Ken Griffey Sr., Ken Griffey Jr. (Foil)	1.00
704 Hal McRae, Brian McRae (Foil)	.10
705 Checklist 1	.10
706 Checklist 2	.10
707 Checklist 3	.10
708 Checklist 4	.10

1994 Bowman Previews

Bowman Preview cards were randomly inserted into Stadium Club 1994 Baseball Series II at a rate of one every 24 packs. This 10-card set featured several proven major

league stars, as well as minor league players. Card number 10, James Mouton, is designed as a special MVP foil card.

	NM/M
Complete Set (10):	7.00
Common Player:	.50
1 Frank Thomas	1.50
2 Mike Piazza	3.00
3 Albert Belle	.50
4 Javier Lopez	.50
5 Cliff Floyd	.50
6 Alex Gonzalez	.50
7 Ricky Bottalico	.50
8 Tony Clark	.50
9 Mac Suzuki	.50
10 James Mouton (Foil)	.50

1994 Bowman

Bowman baseball for 1994 was a 682-card set issued all in one series, including a 52-card foil subset. There were 11 regular cards plus one foil card in each pack, with a suggested retail price of $2. The cards have a full-bleed design, with gold-foil stamping on every card. As in the past, the set includes numerous rookies and prospects, along with the game's biggest stars. The 52-card foil subset features 28 Top Prospects, with the player's team logo in the background; 17 Minor League MVPs, with a stadium in the background; and seven Diamonds in the Rough, with, you guessed it, a diamond as a backdrop.

	NM/M
Complete Set (682):	40.00
Common Player:	.10
Pack (12):	1.50
Wax Box (24):	30.00
1 Joe Carter	.10
2 Marcus Moore	.10
3 Doug Creek RC	.10
4 Pedro Martinez	1.50
5 Ken Griffey Jr.	3.00
6 Greg Swindell	.10
7 J.J. Johnson	.10
8 Homer Bush RC	.10
9 Arquimedez Pozo RC	.10
10 Bryan Harvey	.10
11 J.T. Snow	.10
12 Alan Benes RC	.10
13 Chad Kreuter	.10
14 Eric Karros	.10
15 Frank Thomas	1.50
16 Bret Saberhagen	.10
17 Terrell Lowery	.10
18 Rod Bolton	.10
19 Harold Baines	.10
20 Matt Walbeck	.10
21 Tom Glavine	.30
22 Todd Jones	.10
23 Alberto Castillo	.10
24 Ruben Sierra	.10
25 Don Mattingly	2.50
26 Mike Morgan	.10

27 Jim Musselwhite RC	.10
28 Matt Brunson RC	.10
29 Adam Meinershagen RC	.10
30 Joe Girardi	.10
31 Shane Halter	.10
32 Jose Paniagua RC	.10
33 Paul Perkins	.10
34 John Hudek RC	.10
35 Frank Viola	.10
36 David Lamb RC	.10
37 Marshall Boze	.10
38 Jorge Posada RC	5.00
39 Brian Anderson	.25
40 Mark Whiten	.10
41 Sean Bergman	.10
42 Jose Parra RC	.10
43 Mike Robertson	.10
44 Pete Walker RC	.10
45 Juan Gonzalez	.75
46 Cleveland Ladell RC	.10
47 Mark Smith	.10
48 Kevin Jarvis RC	.10
49 Amaury Telemaco RC	.10
50 Andy Van Slyke	.10
51 Rikkert Faneyte RC	.10
52 Curtis Shaw	.10
53 Matt Drews RC	.10
54 Wilson Alvarez	.10
55 Manny Ramirez	1.50
56 Bobby Munoz	.10
57 Ed Sprague	.10
58 Jamey Wright RC	.10
59 Jeff Montgomery	.10
60 Kirk Rueter	.10
61 Edgar Martinez	.10
62 Luis Gonzalez	.10
63 Tim Vanegmond RC	.10
64 Bip Roberts	.10
65 John Jaha	.10
66 Chuck Carr	.10
67 Chuck Finley	.10
68 Aaron Holbert RC	.10
69 Cecil Fielder	.10
70 Tom Engle RC	.10
71 Ron Karkovice	.10
72 Joe Orsulak	.10
73 Duff Brumley RC	.10
74 Craig Clayton RC	.10
75 Cal Ripken, Jr.	4.00
76 Brad Fullmer RC	.50
77 Tony Tarasco	.10
78 Terry Farrar RC	.10
79 Matt Williams	.10
80 Rickey Henderson	1.50
81 Terry Mulholland	.10
82 Sammy Sosa	2.00
83 Paul Sorrento	.10
84 Pete Incaviglia	.10
85 Darren Hall RC	.10
86 Scott Klingenbeck RC	.10
87 Dario Perez RC	.10
88 Ugueth Urbina RC	.10
89 Dave Vanhof RC	.10
90 Domingo Jean	.10
91 Otis Nixon	.10
92 Andres Berumen RC	.10
93 Jose Valentin	.10
94 Edgar Renteria RC	5.00
95 Chris Turner	.10
96 Ray Lankford	.10
97 Danny Bautista	.10
98 Chan Ho Park RC	1.00
99 Glenn DiSarcina RC	.10
100 Butch Huskey	.10
101 Ivan Rodriguez	1.00
102 Johnny Ruffin	.10
103 Alex Ochoa	.10
104 Torii Hunter RC	6.00
105 Ryan Klesko	.10
106 Jay Bell	.10
107 Kurt Peltzer RC	.10
108 Miguel Jimenez	.10
109 Russ Davis	.10
110 Derek Wallace	.10
111 Keith Lockhart RC	.10
112 Mike Lieberthal	.10
113 Dave Stewart	.10
114 Tom Schmidt RC	.10
115 Brian McRae	.10
116 Moises Alou	.10
117 Dave Fleming	.10
118 Jeff Bagwell	1.50
119 Luis Ortiz	.10
120 Tony Gwynn	2.00
121 Jaime Navarro	.10
122 Benny Santiago	.10
123 Darrel Whitmore	.10
124 John Mabry RC	.15
125 Mickey Tettleton	.10
126 Tom Candiotti	.10
127 Tim Raines	.10
128 Bobby Bonilla	.10
129 John Dettmer RC	.10
130 Hector Carrasco	.10
131 Chris Hoiles	.10
132 Rick Aguilera	.10
133 Dave Justice	.10
134 Esteban Loaiza RC	1.50
135 Barry Bonds	4.00
136 Bob Welch	.10
137 Mike Stanley	.10
138 Roberto Hernandez	.10
139 Sandy Alomar	.10
140 Darren Daulton	.10
141 Angel Martinez RC	.10
142 Howard Johnson	.10
143 Bob Hamelin	.10

144 J.J. Thobe RC	.10
145 Roger Salkeld	.10
146 Orlando Miller	.10
147 Dmitri Young	.10
148 Tim Hyers RC	.10
149 Mark Loretta RC	3.00
150 Chris Hammond	.10
151 Joel Moore RC	.10
152 Todd Zeile	.10
153 Wil Cordero	.10
154 Chris Smith	.10
155 James Baldwin	.10
156 Edgardo Alfonzo RC	1.00
157 Kym Ashworth RC	.10
158 Paul Bako RC	.10
159 Rick Krivda RC	.10
160 Pat Mahomes	.10
161 Damon Hollins	.10
162 Felix Martinez RC	.10
163 Jason Myers RC	.10
164 Izzy Molina RC	.10
165 Brien Taylor	.10
166 Kevin Orie RC	.10
167 Casey Whitten RC	.10
168 Tony Longmire	.10
169 John Olerud	.10
170 Mark Thompson	.10
171 Jorge Fabregas	.10
172 John Wetteland	.10
173 Dan Wilson	.10
174 Doug Drabek	.10
175 Jeffrey McNeely	.10
176 Melvin Nieves	.10
177 Doug Glanville RC	.10
178 Javier De La Hoya RC	.10
179 Chad Curtis	.10
180 Brian Barber	.10
181 Mike Henneman	.10
182 Jose Offerman	.10
183 Robert Ellis RC	.10
184 John Franco	.10
185 Benji Gil	.10
186 Hal Morris	.10
187 Chris Sabo	.10
188 Blaise Ilsley RC	.10
189 Steve Avery	.10
190 Rick White RC	.10
191 Rod Beck	.10
(192) Mark McGwire (No card number.)	3.00
193 Jim Abbott	.10
194 Randy Myers	.10
195 Kenny Lofton	.10
196 Mariano Duncan	.10
197 Lee Daniels RC	.10
198 Armando Reynoso	.10
199 Joe Randa	.10
200 Cliff Floyd	.10
201 Tim Harkrider RC	.10
202 Kevin Gallaher RC	.10
203 Scott Cooper	.10
204 Phil Stidham RC	.10
205 Jeff D'Amico RC	.25
206 Matt Whisenant	.10
207 De Shawn Warren RC	.10
208 Rene Arocha	.10
209 Tony Clark RC	.50
210 Jason Jacome RC	.10
211 Scott Christman RC	.10
212 Bill Pulsipher	.10
213 Dean Palmer	.10
214 Chad Mottola	.10
215 Manny Alexander	.10
216 Rich Becker	.10
217 Andre King RC	.10
218 Carlos Garcia	.10
219 Ron Pezzoni RC	.10
220 Steve Karsay	.10
221 Jose Musset RC	.10
222 Karl Rhodes	.10
223 Frank Cimorelli RC	.10
224 Kevin Jordan RC	.10
225 Duane Ward	.10
226 John Burke	.10
227 Mike MacFarlane	.10
228 Mike Lansing	.10
229 Chuck Knoblauch	.10
230 Ken Caminiti	.10
231 Gar Finnvold RC	.10
232 Derrek Lee RC	12.00
233 Brady Anderson	.10
234 Vic Darensbourg RC	.10
235 Mark Langston	.10
236 T.J. Mathews RC	.10
237 Lou Whitaker	.10
238 Roger Cedeno	.10
239 Alex Fernandez	.10
240 Ryan Thompson	.10
241 Kerry Lacy RC	.10
242 Reggie Sanders	.10
243 Brad Pennington	.10
244 Bryan Eversgerd RC	.10
245 Greg Maddux	2.00
246 Jason Kendall	.10
247 J.R. Phillips	.10
248 Bobby Witt	.10
249 Paul O'Neil	.10
250 Ryne Sandberg	2.00
251 Charles Nagy	.10
252 Kevin Stocker	.10
253 Shawn Green	.30
254 Charlie Hayes	.10
255 Donnie Elliott	.10
256 Rob Fitzpatrick RC	.10
257 Tim Davis	.10
258 James Mouton	.10
259 Mike Greenwell	.10
260 Ray McDavid	.10

#	Player	Price
261	Mike Kelly	.10
262	Andy Larkin RC	.10
(263)	Marquis Riley (No card number.)	.10
264	Bob Tewksbury	.10
265	Brian Edmondson	.10
266	Eduardo Lantigua RC	.10
267	Brandon Wilson	.10
268	Mike Welch	.10
269	Tom Henke	.10
270	Calvin Reese	.85
271	Gregg Zaun RC	.10
272	Todd Ritchie	.10
273	Javier Lopez	.10
274	Kevin Young	.10
275	Kirt Manwaring	.10
276	Bill Taylor RC	.10
277	Robert Eenhoorn	.10
278	Jessie Hollins	.10
279	Julian Tavarez RC	.10
280	Gene Schall	.10
281	Paul Molitor	1.50
282	Neifi Perez RC	.10
283	Greg Gagne	.10
284	Marquis Grissom	.10
285	Randy Johnson	1.50
286	Pete Harnisch	.10
287	Joel Bennett RC	.10
288	Derek Bell	.10
289	Darryl Hamilton	.10
290	Gary Sheffield	.40
291	Eduardo Perez	.10
292	Basil Shabazz	.10
293	Eric Davis	.10
294	Pedro Astacio	.10
295	Robin Ventura	.10
296	Jeff Kent	.10
297	Rick Helling	.10
298	Joe Oliver	.10
299	Lee Smith	.10
300	Dave Winfield	1.50
301	Deion Sanders	.10
302	Ravelo Manzanillo RC	.10
303	Mark Portugal	.10
304	Brent Gates	.10
305	Wade Boggs	2.00
306	Rick Wilkins	.10
307	Carlos Baerga	.10
308	Curt Schilling	.35
309	Shannon Stewart	.10
310	Darren Holmes	.10
311	Robert Toth RC	.10
312	Gabe White	.10
313	Mac Suzuki RC	.10
314	Alvin Morman RC	.10
315	Mo Vaughn	.10
316	Bryce Florie RC	.10
317	Gabby Martinez RC	.10
318	Carl Everett	.10
319	Kerwin Moore	.10
320	Tom Pagnozzi	.10
321	Chris Gomez	.10
322	Todd Williams	.10
323	Pat Hentgen	.10
324	Kirk Presley RC	.10
325	Kevin Brown	.10
326	Jason Isringhausen RC	.25
327	Rick Forney RC	.10
328	Carlos Pulido RC	.10
329	Terrell Wade RC	.10
330	Al Martin	.10
331	Dan Carlson RC	.10
332	Mark Acre RC	.10
333	Sterling Hitchcock	.10
334	Jon Ratliff RC	.10
335	Alex Ramirez RC	.10
336	Phil Geisler RC	.10
337	Eddie Zambrano RC (Foil)	.10
338	Jim Thome (Foil)	.60
339	James Mouton (Foil)	.10
340	Cliff Floyd (Foil)	.10
341	Carlos Delgado (Foil)	.40
342	Roberto Petagine (Foil)	.10
343	Tim Clark (Foil)	.10
344	Bubba Smith (Foil)	.10
345	Randy Curtis RC (Foil)	.10
346	Joe Biasucci RC (Foil)	.10
347	D.J. Boston RC (Foil)	.10
348	Ruben Rivera RC (Foil)	.75
349	Bryan Link RC (Foil)	.10
350	Mike Bell RC (Foil)	.25
351	Marty Watson RC (Foil)	.10
352	Jason Myers (Foil)	.10
353	Chipper Jones (Foil)	1.25
354	Brooks Kieschnick (Foil)	.10
355	Calvin Reese (Foil)	.10
356	John Burke (Foil)	.10
357	Kurt Miller (Foil)	.10
358	Orlando Miller (Foil)	.10
359	Todd Hollandsworth (Foil)	.10
360	Rondell White (Foil)	.10
361	Bill Pulsipher (Foil)	.10
362	Tyler Green (Foil)	.10
363	Midre Cummings (Foil)	.10
364	Brian Barber (Foil)	.10
365	Melvin Nieves (Foil)	.10
366	Salomon Torres (Foil)	.10
367	Alex Ochoa (Foil)	.10
368	Frank Rodriguez (Foil)	.10
369	Brian Anderson (Foil)	.10
370	James Baldwin (Foil)	.10
371	Manny Ramirez (Foil)	.75
372	Justin Thompson (Foil)	.10
373	Johnny Damon (Foil)	.50
374	Jeff D'Amico (Foil)	.10
375	Rich Becker (Foil)	.10
376	Derek Jeter (Foil)	3.00
377	Steve Karsay (Foil)	.10
378	Mac Suzuki (Foil)	.10
379	Benji Gil (Foil)	.10
380	Alex Gonzalez (Foil)	.10
381	Jason Bere (Foil)	.10
382	Brett Butler (Foil)	.10
383	Jeff Conine (Foil)	.10
384	Darren Daulton (Foil)	.10
385	Jeff Kent (Foil)	.10
386	Don Mattingly (Foil)	1.50
387	Mike Piazza (Foil)	2.00
388	Ryne Sandberg (Foil)	1.25
389	Rich Amaral (Foil)	.10
390	Craig Biggio (Foil)	.10
391	Jeff Suppan RC	.35
392	Andy Benes	.10
393	Cal Eldred	.10
394	Jeff Conine	.10
395	Tim Salmon	.10
396	Ray Suplee RC	.10
397	Tony Phillips	.10
398	Ramon Martinez	.10
399	Julio Franco	.10
400	Dwight Gooden	.10
401	Kevin Lomon RC	.10
402	Jose Rijo	.10
403	Mike Devereaux	.10
404	Mike Zolecki RC	.10
405	Fred McGriff	.10
406	Danny Clyburn	.10
407	Robby Thompson	.10
408	Terry Steinbach	.10
409	Luis Polonia	.10
410	Mark Grace	.10
411	Albert Belle	.10
412	John Kruk	.10
413	Scott Spiezio RC	.25
414	Ellis Burks	.10
415	Joe Vitiello	.10
416	Tim Costo	.10
417	Marc Newfield	.10
418	Oscar Henriquez RC	.10
419	Matt Perisho RC	.10
420	Julio Bruno	.10
421	Kenny Felder	.10
422	Tyler Green	.10
423	Jim Edmonds	.10
424	Ozzie Smith	2.00
425	Rick Greene	.10
426	Todd Hollandsworth	.10
427	Eddie Pearson RC	.10
428	Quilvio Veras	.10
429	Kenny Rogers	.10
430	Willie Greene	.10
431	Vaughn Eshelman	.10
432	Pat Meares	.10
433	Jermaine Dye RC	8.00
434	Steve Cooke	.10
435	Bill Swift	.10
436	Fausto Cruz RC	.10
437	Mark Hutton	.10
438	Brooks Kieschnick RC	.10
439	Yorkis Perez	.10
440	Len Dykstra	.10
441	Pat Borders	.10
442	Doug Walls RC	.10
443	Wally Joyner	.10
444	Ken Hill	.10
445	Eric Anthony	.10
446	Mitch Williams	.10
447	Cory Bailey RC	.10
448	Dave Staton	.10
449	Greg Vaughn	.10
450	Dave Magadan	.10
451	Chili Davis	.10
452	Gerald Santos RC	.10
453	Joe Perona	.10
454	Delino DeShields	.10
455	Jack McDowell	.10
456	Todd Hundley	.10
457	Ritchie Moody	.10
458	Bret Boone	.10
459	Ben McDonald	.10
460	Kirby Puckett	2.00
461	Gregg Olson	.10
462	Rich Aude RC	.10
463	John Burkett	.10
464	Troy Neel	.10
465	Jimmy Key	.10
466	Ozzie Timmons	.10
467	Eddie Murray	1.50
468	Mark Tranberg RC	.10
469	Alex Gonzalez	.10
470	David Nied	.10
471	Barry Larkin	.10
472	Brian Looney RC	.10
473	Shawn Estes	.10
474	A.J. Sager RC	.10
475	Roger Clemens	2.50
476	Vince Moore	.10
477	Scott Karl RC	.10
478	Kurt Miller	.10
479	Garret Anderson	.10
480	Allen Watson	.10
481	Jose Lima RC	.10
482	Rick Gorecki	.10
483	Jimmy Hurst RC	.10
484	Preston Wilson	.10
485	Will Clark	.10
486	Mike Ferry RC	.10
487	Curtis Goodwin RC	.10
488	Mike Myers	.10
489	Chipper Jones	2.00
490	Jeff King	.10
491	Bill Van Landingham RC	.10
492	Carlos Reyes RC	.10
493	Andy Pettitte	.30
494	Brant Brown	.10
495	Daron Kirkreit	.10
496	Ricky Bottalico RC	.25
497	Devon White	.10
498	Jason Johnson RC	.10
499	Vince Coleman	.10
500	Bobby Ayala	.10
501	Steve Finley	.10
502	Scott Fletcher	.10
503	Brad Ausmus	.10
504	Scott Talanoa RC	.10
505	Orestes Destrade	.10
506	Gary DiSarcina	.10
507	Willie Smith RC	.10
508	Alan Trammell	.10
509	Mike Piazza	3.00
510	Ozzie Guillen	.10
511	Jeromy Burnitz	.10
512	Darren Oliver	.10
513	Kevin Mitchell	.10
514	Rafael Palmeiro	1.00
515	David McCarty	.10
516	Jeff Blauser	.10
517	Trey Beamon	.10
518	Royce Clayton	.10
519	Dennis Eckersley	1.00
520	Bernie Williams	.10
521	Steve Buechele	.10
522	Denny Martinez	.10
523	Dave Hollins	.10
524	Joey Hamilton	.10
525	Andres Galarraga	.10
526	Jeff Granger	.10
527	Joey Eischen	.10
528	Desi Relaford	.10
529	Roberto Petagine	.10
530	Andre Dawson	.30
531	Ray Holbert	.10
532	Duane Singleton	.10
533	Kurt Abbott RC	.20
534	Bo Jackson	.20
535	Gregg Jefferies	.10
536	David Mysel	.10
537	Raul Mondesi	.10
538	Chris Snopek	.10
539	Brook Fordyce	.10
540	Ron Frazier RC	.10
541	Brian Koelling	.10
542	Jimmy Haynes	.10
543	Marty Cordova	.10
544	Jason Green RC	.10
545	Orlando Merced	.10
546	Lou Pote RC	.10
547	Todd Van Poppel	.10
548	Pat Kelly	.10
549	Turk Wendell	.10
550	Herb Perry RC	.10
551	Ryan Karp RC	.10
552	Juan Guzman	.10
553	Bryan Rekar RC	.10
554	Kevin Appier	.10
555	Chris Schwab RC	.10
556	Jay Buhner	.10
557	Andujar Cedeno	.10
558	Ryan McGuire RC	.10
559	Ricky Gutierrez	.10
560	Keith Kimsey RC	.10
561	Tim Clark	.10
562	Damon Easley	.10
563	Clint Davis RC	.10
564	Clint Davis RC	.10
565	Mike Moore	.10
566	Orel Hershiser	.10
567	Jason Bere	.10
568	Kevin McReynolds	.10
569	Leland Macon RC	.10
570	John Courtright RC	.10
571	Sid Fernandez	.10
572	Chad Roper	.10
573	Terry Pendleton	.10
574	Danny Miceli	.10
575	Joe Rosselli	.10
576	Mike Bordick	.10
577	Danny Tartabull	.10
578	Jose Guzman	.10
579	Omar Vizquel	.10
580	Tommy Greene	.10
581	Paul Spoljaric	.10
582	Walt Weiss	.10
583	Oscar Jimenez RC	.10
584	Rod Henderson	.10
585	Derek Lowe	.10
586	Richard Hidalgo RC	1.00
587	Shayne Bennett RC	.10
588	Tim Belk RC	.10
589	Matt Mieske	.10
590	Nigel Wilson	.10
591	Jeff Knox RC	.10
592	Bernard Gilkey	.10
593	David Cone	.10
594	Paul LoDuca RC	5.00
595	Scott Ruffcorn	.10
596	Chris Roberts	.10
597	Oscar Munoz RC	.10
598	Scott Sullivan RC	.10
599	Matt Jarvis RC	.10
600	Jose Canseco	.35
601	Tony Graffanino RC	.10
602	Don Slaught	.10
603	Brett King RC	.10
604	Jose Herrera RC	.10
605	Melido Perez	.10
606	Mike Hubbard RC	.10
607	Chad Ogea	.10
608	Wayne Gomes RC	.10
609	Roberto Alomar	.25
610	Angel Echevarria RC	.10
611	Jose Lind	.10
612	Darrin Fletcher	.10
613	Chris Bosio	.10
614	Darryl Kile	.10
615	Frank Rodriguez	.10
616	Phil Plantier	.10
617	Pat Listach	.10
618	Charlie Hough	.10
619	Ryan Hancock RC	.10
620	Darrel Deak RC	.10
621	Travis Fryman	.10
622	Brett Butler	.10
623	Lance Johnson	.10
624	Pete Smith	.10
625	James Hurst	.10
626	Roberto Kelly	.10
627	Mike Mussina	.50
628	Kevin Tapani	.10
629	John Smoltz	.10
630	Midre Cummings	.10
631	Salomon Torres	.10
632	Willie Adams	.10
633	Derek Jeter	4.00
634	Steve Trachsel	.10
635	Albie Lopez	.10
636	Jason Moler	.10
637	Carlos Delgado	.50
638	Roberto Mejia	.10
639	Darren Burton	.10
640	B.J. Wallace	.10
641	Brad Clontz RC	.10
642	Billy Wagner RC	1.00
643	Aaron Sele	.10
644	Cameron Cairncross	.10
645	Brian Harper	.10
(646)	Marc Valdes (No card number.)	.10
647	Mark Ratekin	.10
648	Terry Bradshaw RC	.10
649	Justin Thompson	.10
650	Mike Busch RC	.10
651	Joe Hall RC	.10
652	Bobby Jones	.10
653	Kelly Stinnett RC	.10
654	Rod Steph RC	.10
655	Jay Powell RC	.10
(656)	Keith Garagozzo RC (No card number.)	.10
657	Todd Dunn	.10
658	Charles Peterson RC	.10
659	Darren Lewis	.10
660	John Wasdin RC	.10
661	Tate Seefried RC	.10
662	Hector Trinidad RC	.10
663	John Carter RC	.10
664	Larry Mitchell	.10
665	David Catlett RC	.10
666	Dante Bichette	.10
667	Felix Jose	.10
668	Rondell White	.10
669	Tino Martinez	.10
670	Brian Hunter	.10
671	Jose Malave	.10
672	Archi Cianfrocco	.10
673	Mike Matheny RC	.15
674	Bret Barberie	.10
675	Andrew Lorraine RC	.10
676	Brian Jordan	.10
677	Tim Belcher	.10
678	Antonio Osuna RC	.10
679	Checklist I	.10
680	Checklist II	.10
681	Checklist III	.10
682	Checklist IV	.10

Superstar Sampler

As an insert in 1994 Topps retail factory sets, three-card cello packs of "Superstar Sampler" cards were included. The packs contained special versions of the same player's 1994 Bowman, Finest and Stadium Club cards. Forty-five of the game's top stars are represented in the issue. The Bowman cards in this issue are identical to the cards in the regular set except for the appearance of a round "Topps Superstar Sampler" logo on back.

		NM/M
Complete Set (45):		275.00
Common Player:		2.00
1	Joe Carter	2.00
5	Ken Griffey Jr.	20.00
15	Frank Thomas	10.00
21	Tom Glavine	3.00
25	Don Mattingly	17.50
45	Juan Gonzalez	6.00
50	Andy Van Slyke	2.00

#	Player	Price
55	Manny Ramirez	10.00
69	Cecil Fielder	2.00
75	Cal Ripken Jr.	35.00
79	Matt Williams	2.00
118	Jeff Bagwell	10.00
120	Tony Gwynn	15.00
128	Bobby Bonilla	2.00
133	Dave Justice	2.00
135	Barry Bonds	35.00
140	Darren Daulton	2.00
169	John Olerud	2.00
200	Cliff Floyd	2.00
245	Greg Maddux	15.00
250	Ryne Sandberg	15.00
281	Paul Molitor	10.00
284	Marquis Grissom	2.00
285	Randy Johnson	10.00
290	Gary Sheffield	4.00
307	Carlos Baerga	2.00
315	Mo Vaughn	2.00
395	Tim Salmon	2.00
405	Fred McGriff	2.00
410	Mark Grace	2.00
411	Albert Belle	2.00
440	Len Dykstra	2.00
455	Jack McDowell	2.00
460	Kirby Puckett	15.00
471	Barry Larkin	2.00
475	Roger Clemens	17.50
485	Will Clark	2.00
500	Larry Walker	2.00
510	Mike Piazza	20.00
515	Rafael Palmeiro	9.00
526	Andres Galarraga	2.00
536	Gregg Jefferies	2.00
538	Raul Mondesi	2.00
600	Jose Canseco	2.00
609	Roberto Alomar	4.00

1994 Bowman's Best

The debut Bowman's Best consists of 90 red cards (largely veterans), 90 blue cards (rookies and young players) and 20 Mirror Images combining veteran and young stars by position. Utilizing Topps Finest technology, cards are full-color front and back with high-gloss surfaces. Cards were sold in eight-card foil packs with one Mirror Image card in each pack. A 200-card parallel version officially called "Special Effects," uses Topps refractor technology. Red and Blue sets each contain cards numbered 1-90, while the Mirror Image cards are numbered 91-110.

	NM/M
Complete Set (200):	30.00
Red Set (90):	10.00
Blue Set (90):	20.00
Common Player:	.15
Pack (8):	1.50
Wax Box (24):	30.00

RED SET

#	Player	Price
1	Paul Molitor	1.50
2	Eddie Murray	1.50
3	Ozzie Smith	2.00
4	Rickey Henderson	1.50
5	Lee Smith	.15
6	Dave Winfield	1.50
7	Roberto Alomar	.30
8	Matt Williams	.15
9	Mark Grace	.15
10	Lance Johnson	.15
11	Darren Daulton	.15
12	Tom Glavine	.35
13	Gary Sheffield	.40
14	Rod Beck	.15
15	Fred McGriff	.15
16	Joe Carter	.15
17	Dante Bichette	.15
18	Danny Tartabull	.15
19	Juan Gonzalez	.75
20	Steve Avery	.15
21	John Wetteland	.15
22	Ben McDonald	.15
23	Jack McDowell	.15
24	Jose Canseco	.65
25	Tim Salmon	.15
26	Wilson Alvarez	.15
27	Gregg Jefferies	.15
28	John Burkett	.15
29	Greg Vaughn	.15
30	Robin Ventura	.15
31	Paul O'Neill	.15
32	Cecil Fielder	.15
33	Kevin Mitchell	.15
34	Jeff Conine	.15
35	Carlos Baerga	.15
36	Greg Maddux	2.00
37	Roger Clemens	2.25
38	Deion Sanders	.15
39	Delino DeShields	.15
40	Ken Griffey Jr.	2.50
41	Albert Belle	1.50
42	Wade Boggs	2.00
43	Andres Galarraga	.15
44	Aaron Sele	.15
45	Don Mattingly	2.25
46	David Cone	.15
47	Lenny Dykstra	.15
48	Brett Butler	.15
49	Bill Swift	.15
50	Bobby Bonilla	.15
51	Rafael Palmeiro	1.25
52	Moises Alou	.15
53	Jeff Bagwell	1.50
54	Mike Mussina	.50
55	Frank Thomas	1.50
56	Jose Rijo	.15
57	Ruben Sierra	.15
58	Randy Myers	.15
59	Barry Bonds	4.00
60	Jimmy Key	.15
61	Travis Fryman	.15
62	John Olerud	.15
63	David Justice	.15
64	Ray Lankford	.15
65	Bob Tewksbury	.15
66	Chuck Carr	.15
67	Jay Buhner	.15
68	Kenny Lofton	.15
69	Marquis Grissom	.15
70	Sammy Sosa	2.00
71	Cal Ripken Jr.	4.00
72	Ellis Burks	.15
73	Jeff Montgomery	.15
74	Julio Franco	.15
75	Kirby Puckett	2.00
76	Larry Walker	.15
77	Andy Van Slyke	.15
78	Tony Gwynn	2.00
79	Will Clark	.15
80	Mo Vaughn	.15
81	Mike Piazza	2.50
82	James Mouton	.15
83	Carlos Delgado	.60
84	Ryan Klesko	.15
85	Javy Lopez	.15
86	Raul Mondesi	.15
87	Cliff Floyd	.15
88	Manny Ramirez	1.50
89	Hector Carrasco	.15
90	Jeff Granger	.15

BLUE SET

#	Player	Price
1	Chipper Jones	2.00
2	Derek Jeter	4.00
3	Bill Pulsipher	.15
4	James Baldwin	.15
5	Brooks Kieschnick RC	.50
6	Justin Thompson	.15
7	Midre Cummings	.15
8	Joey Hamilton	.15
9	Calvin Reese	.15
10	Brian Barber	.15
11	John Burke	.15
12	De Shawn Warren	.15
13	Edgardo Alfonzo RC	.75
14	Eddie Pearson RC	.15
15	Jimmy Haynes	.15
16	Danny Bautista	.15
17	Roger Cedeno	.15
18	Jon Lieber	.15
19	Billy Wagner RC	.75
20	Tate Seefried RC	.15
21	Chad Mottola	.15
22	Jose Malave	.15
23	Terrell Wade RC	.15
24	Shane Andrews	.15
25	Chan Ho Park RC	.15
26	Kirk Presley RC	.15
27	Robbie Beckett	.15
28	Orlando Miller	.15
29	Jorge Posada RC	6.00
30	Frank Rodriguez	.15
31	Brian Hunter	.15
32	Billy Ashley	.15
33	Rondell White	.15
34	John Roper	.15
35	Marc Valdes	.15
36	Scott Ruffcorn	.15
37	Rod Henderson	.15
38	Curt Goodwin	.15
39	Russ Davis	.15
40	Rick Gorecki	.15
41	Johnny Damon	.60
42	Roberto Petagine	.15
43	Chris Snopek	.15
44	Mark Acre	.15
45	Todd Hollandsworth	.15
46	Shawn Green	.35
47	John Carter	.15
48	Jim Pittsley	.15
49	John Wasdin RC	.15
50	D.J. Boston	.15
51	Tim Clark	.15

52 Alex Ochoa .15
53 Chad Roper .15
54 Mike Kelly .15
55 Brad Fullmer RC .50
56 Carl Everett .15
57 Tim Belk RC .15
58 Jimmy Hurst RC .15
59 Mac Suzuki RC .15
60 Michael Moore .15
61 Alan Benes RC .15
62 Tony Clark RC 1.00
63 Edgar Renteria RC 8.00
64 Trey Beamon .15
65 LaTroy Hawkins RC .15
66 Wayne Gomes RC .15
67 Ray McDavid .15
68 John Dettmer .15
69 Willie Greene .15
70 Dave Stevens .15
71 Kevin Orie RC .15
72 Chad Ogea .15
73 Ben Van Ryn .15
74 Kym Ashworth .15
75 Dmitri Young .15
76 Herb Perry .15
77 Joey Eischen .15
78 Arquimedez Pozo RC .15
79 Ugueth Urbina .15
80 Keith Williams .15
81 John Frascatore RC .15
82 Garey Ingram .15
83 Aaron Small .15
84 Olmedo Saenz RC .15
85 Jesus Tavarez .15
86 Jose Silva RC .15
87 Gerald Witasick Jr. RC .15
88 Jay Maldonado .15
89 Keith Heberling .15
90 Rusty Greer RC .50

MIRROR IMAGES

91 Frank Thomas, Kevin Young .60
92 Fred McGriff, Brooks Kieschnick RC .15
93 Matt Williams, Shane Andrews .15
94 Cal Ripken Jr., Kevin Orie RC 1.50
95 Barry Larkin, Derek Jeter 1.50
96 Ken Griffey Jr., Johnny Damon 1.50
97 Barry Bonds, Rondell White 1.50
98 Albert Belle, Jimmy Hurst RC .15
99 Raul Mondesi, Ruben Rivera RC .15
100 Roger Clemens, Scott Ruffcorn 1.00
101 Greg Maddux, John Wasdin RC .75
102 Tim Salmon, Chad Mottola .15
103 Carlos Baerga, Arquimedez Pozo RC .15
104 Mike Piazza, Bobby Hughes 1.00
105 Carlos Delgado, Melvin Nieves .50
106 Javy Lopez, Jorge Posada RC 2.00
107 Manny Ramirez, Jose Malave .65
108 Travis Fryman, Chipper Jones .75
109 Steve Avery, Bill Pulsipher .15
110 John Olerud, Shawn Green .50

Best Refractors

This 200-card parallel set, officially titled "Special Effects," uses Topps' refractor technology. The refractors were packed at the rate of three per wax box of Bowman's Best, but are very difficult to differentiate from the regular high-tech cards.

Superstars: 8-10X
Stars: 4-8X

(See 1994 Bowman's Best for checklist and base card values.)

1995 Bowman

Large numbers of rookie cards and a lengthy run of etched-foil cards distinguishes the 1995 Bowman set. The set's basic cards share a design with a large color photo flanked at left by a severely horizontally compressed mirror image in green, and at bottom by a similar version in brown. Most of the bottom image is covered by the player's last name printed in silver (cards #1-220, rookies) or gold (cards #275-439, veterans) foil. A color team logo is in the lower-left corner of all cards, and the Bowman logo is in red foil at top. In between the foil-etched subsets of "Minor League MVPs," "1st Impressions," and "Prime Prospects." Each of these cards, seeded one per regular pack and two per jumbo, has the player photo set against a background of textured color foil, with a prismatic silver border. Each of the foil cards can also be found in a gold-toned version, in a ratio of six silver to one gold. Backs of the rookies' cards have a portrait photo at right and a scouting report at left. Veterans' cards have either a scouting report for younger players, or a chart of stats versus each team played in 1994. Backs of all the foil cards have a scouting report.

	NM/M
Complete Set (439):	150.00
Common Player:	.10
Pack (10):	6.00
Wax Box (24):	125.00
Rack Pack (15):	5.00
Rack Box (24):	125.00

1 Billy Wagner .10
2 Chris Widger .10
3 Brent Bowers .10
4 Bob Abreu RC 10.00
5 Lou Collier RC .10
6 Juan Acevedo RC .25
7 Jason Kelley RC .10
8 Brian Sackinsky .10
9 Scott Christman .10
10 Damon Hollins .10
11 Willis Otanez RC .10
12 Jason Ryan RC .10
13 Jason Giambi .75
14 Andy Taulbee RC .10
15 Mark Thompson .10
16 Hugo Pivaral RC .10
17 Brien Taylor .10
18 Antonio Osuna .10
19 Edgardo Alfonzo .10
20 Carl Everett .10
21 Matt Drews .10
22 Bartolo Colon RC 4.00
23 Andruw Jones RC 30.00
24 Robert Person RC .40
25 Derrek Lee RC .75
26 John Ambrose RC .10
27 Eric Knowles RC .10
28 Chris Roberts .10
29 Don Wengert RC .10
30 Marcus Jensen RC .10
31 Brian Barber .10
32 Kevin Brown .10
33 Benji Gil .10
34 Mike Hubbard .10
35 Bart Evans RC .10
36 Enrique Wilson RC .50
37 Brian Buchanan RC .10
38 Ken Ray RC .10
39 Micah Franklin RC .10
40 Ricky Otero RC .10
41 Jason Kendall .10
42 Jimmy Hurst .10
43 Jerry Wolak RC .10
44 Jayson Peterson RC .10
45 Allen Battle RC .10
46 Scott Stahoviak .10
47 Steve Schrenk RC .10
48 Travis Miller RC .25
49 Eddie Rios RC .10
50 Mike Hampton .10
51 Chad Frontera RC .10
52 Tom Evans RC .10
53 C.J. Nitkowski RC .10
54 Clay Caruthers RC .10
55 Shannon Stewart .10
56 Jorge Posada .50
57 Aaron Holbert .10
58 Harry Berrios RC .10
59 Steve Rodriguez .10
60 Shane Andrews .10
61 Will Cunnane RC .10
62 Richard Hidalgo .10
63 Bill Selby RC .10
64 Jay Cranford RC .10
65 Jeff Suppan RC .10
66 Curtis Goodwin .10
67 John Thomson RC .10
68 Justin Thompson .10
69 Troy Percival RC .10
70 Matt Wagner RC .10
71 Terry Bradshaw RC .10
72 Greg Hansell .10
73 John Burke .10
74 Jeff D'Amico RC .10
75 Ernie Young .10
76 Jason Bates .10
77 Chris Stynes .10
78 Cade Gaspar RC .10
79 Melvin Nieves .10
80 Rick Gorecki .10
81 Felix Rodriguez RC .50
82 Ryan Hancock .10
83 Chris Carpenter RC 6.00
84 Ray McDavid .10
85 Chris Wimmer .10
86 Doug Glanville .10
87 DeShawn Warren RC .10
88 Damian Moss RC .50
89 Rafael Orellano RC .10
90 Vladimir Guerrero RC 50.00
91 Raul Casanova RC .40
92 Karim Garcia RC .75
93 Bryce Florie .10
94 Kevin Orie .10
95 Ryan Nye RC .10
96 Matt Sachse RC .10
97 Ivan Arteaga RC .10
98 Glenn Murray .10
99 Stacy Hollins RC .10
100 Jim Pittsley .10
101 Craig Mattson RC .10
102 Neifi Perez .10
103 Keith Williams .10
104 Roger Cedeno .10
105 Tony Terry RC .10
106 Jose Malave .10
107 Joe Rosselli .10
108 Kevin Jordan .10
109 Sid Roberson RC .10
110 Alan Embree .10
111 Terrell Wade .10
112 Bob Wolcott .10
113 Carlos Perez RC .10
114 Mike Bovee RC .10
115 Tommy Davis RC .10
116 Jeremey Kendall RC .10
117 Rich Aude .10
118 Rick Huisman .10
119 Tim Belk .10
120 Edgar Renteria .25
121 Calvin Maduro RC .10
122 Jerry Martin RC .10
123 Ramon Fermin RC .10
124 Kimera Bartee RC .10
125 Mark Farris .10
126 Frank Rodriguez .10
127 Bobby Higginson RC .50
128 Bret Wagner .10
129 Edwin Diaz RC .10
130 Jimmy Haynes .10
131 Chris Weinke RC .75
132 Damian Jackson RC .10
133 Felix Martinez .10
134 Edwin Hurtado RC .25
135 Matt Raleigh RC .10
136 Paul Wilson .10
137 Ron Villone .10
138 Eric Stuckenschneider RC .10
139 Tate Seefried .10
140 Rey Ordonez RC .75
141 Eddie Pearson .10
142 Kevin Gallaher .10
143 Torii Hunter RC .25
144 Daron Kirkreit .10
145 Craig Wilson .10
146 Ugueth Urbina .10
147 Chris Snopek .10
148 Kym Ashworth .10
149 Wayne Gomes .10
150 Mark Loretta .10
151 Ramon Morel RC .10
152 Trot Nixon .10
153 Desi Relaford .10
154 Scott Sullivan RC .10
155 Marc Barcelo .10
156 Willie Adams .10
157 Derrick Gibson RC .10
158 Brian Meadows RC .10
159 Julian Tavarez .10
160 Bryan Rekar .10
161 Steve Gibralter .10
162 Esteban Loaiza .10
163 John Wasdin .10
164 Kirk Presley .10
165 Mariano Rivera .50
166 Andy Larkin .10
167 Sean Whiteside RC .10
168 Matt Apana RC .10
169 Shawn Senior RC .10
170 Scott Gentile .10
171 Quilvio Veras .10
172 Elieser Marrero RC 1.00
173 Mendy Lopez RC .10
174 Homer Bush .10
175 Brian Stephenson RC .10
176 Jon Nunnally .10
177 Jose Herrera .10
178 Corey Avrard RC .10
179 David Bell .10
180 Jason Isringhausen .10
181 Jamey Wright .10
182 Lonell Roberts RC .10
183 Marty Cordova .10
185 Amaury Telemaco .10
185 John Mabry .10
186 Andrew Vessel RC .10
187 Jim Cole RC .10
188 Marquis Riley .10
189 Todd Dunn .10
190 John Carter .10
191 Donnie Sadler RC .25
192 Mike Bell .10
193 Chris Cumberland RC .10
194 Jason Schmidt .25
195 Matt Brunson .10
196 James Baldwin .10
197 Bill Simas .10
198 Gus Gandarillas .10
199 Mac Suzuki .10
200 Rick Holifield RC .10
201 Fernando Lunar RC .10
202 Kevin Jarvis .10
203 Everett Stull RC .10
204 Steve Wojciechowski .10
205 Shawn Estes .10
206 Jermaine Dye .10
207 Marc Kroon .10
208 Peter Munro RC .10
209 Pat Watkins .10
210 Matt Smith .10
211 Joe Vitiello .10
212 Gerald Witasick Jr. .10
213 Freddy Garcia RC .10
214 Glenn Dishman RC .10
215 Jay Canizaro RC .10
216 Angel Martinez .10
217 Yamil Benitez RC .10
218 Fausto Macey RC .10
219 Eric Owens .10
220 Checklist .10
221 Dwayne Hosey RC (Minor League MVPs) .10
222 Brad Woodall (Minor League MVPs) .25
223 Billy Ashley (Minor League MVPs) .10
224 Mark Grudzielanek RC (Minor League MVPs) 2.00
225 Mark Johnson RC (Minor League MVPs) .10
226 Tim Unroe RC (Minor League MVPs) .10
227 Todd Greene (Minor League MVPs) .10
228 Larry Sutton (Minor League MVPs) .10
229 Derek Jeter (Minor League MVPs) 3.00
230 Sal Fasano RC (Minor League MVPs) .10
231 Ruben Rivera (Minor League MVPs) .10
232 Chris Truby RC (Minor League MVPs) .10
233 John Donati (Minor League MVPs) .10
234 Decomba Conner RC (Minor League MVPs) .10
235 Sergio Nunez RC (Minor League MVPs) .10
236 Ray Brown RC (Minor League MVPs) .10
237 Juan Melo RC (Minor League MVPs) .10
238 Hideo Nomo RC (First Impressions) 4.00
239 Jaime Bluma RC (First Impressions) .10
240 Jay Payton RC (First Impressions) 1.50
241 Paul Konerko RC (First Impressions) .75
242 Scott Elarton RC (First Impressions) .50
243 Jeff Abbott RC (First Impressions) .25
244 Jim Brower RC (First Impressions) .10
245 Geoff Blum RC (First Impressions) .40
246 Aaron Boone RC (First Impressions) 1.00
247 J.R. Phillips (Top Prospects) .10
248 Alex Ochoa (Top Prospects) .10
249 Nomar Garciaparra (Top Prospects) 5.00
250 Garret Anderson (Top Prospects) .25
251 Ray Durham (Top Prospects) .10
252 Paul Shuey (Top Prospects) .10
253 Tony Clark (Top Prospects) .10
254 Johnny Damon (Top Prospects) 1.00
255 Duane Singleton (Top Prospects) .10
256 LaTroy Hawkins (Top Prospects) .10
257 Andy Pettitte (Top Prospects) .40
258 Ben Grieve (Top Prospects) .10
259 Marc Newfield (Top Prospects) .10
260 Terrell Lowery (Top Prospects) .10
261 Shawn Green (Top Prospects) .40
262 Chipper Jones (Top Prospects) 1.50
263 Brooks Kieschnick (Top Prospects) .10
264 Calvin Reese (Top Prospects) .10
265 Doug Million (Top Prospects) .10
266 Marc Valdes (Top Prospects) .10
267 Brian Hunter (Top Prospects) .10
268 Todd Hollandsworth (Top Prospects) .10
269 Rod Henderson (Top Prospects) .10
270 Bill Pulsipher (Top Prospects) .10
271 Scott Rolen RC (Top Prospects) 15.00
272 Trey Beamon (Top Prospects) .10
273 Alan Benes (Top Prospects) .10
274 Dustin Hermanson (Top Prospects) .10
275 Ricky Bottalico RC .10
276 Albert Belle .10
277 Deion Sanders .25
278 Matt Williams .10
279 Jeff Bagwell .75
280 Kirby Puckett 1.50
281 Dave Hollins .10
282 Don Mattingly 1.50
283 Joey Hamilton .10
284 Bobby Bonilla .10
285 Moises Alou .25
286 Tom Glavine .25
287 Brett Butler .10
288 Chris Hoiles .10
289 Kenny Rogers .10
290 Larry Walker .25
291 Tim Raines .10
292 Kevin Appier .10
293 Roger Clemens 2.00
294a Chuck Carr .10
294b Cliff Floyd (Should be #394.) .10
295 Randy Myers .10
296 Dave Nilsson .10
297 Joe Carter .10
298 Chuck Finley .10
299 Ray Lankford .10
300 Roberto Kelly .10
301 Jon Lieber .10
302 Travis Fryman .10
303 Mark McGwire 1.50
304 Tony Gwynn 1.00
305 Kenny Lofton .10
306 Mark Whiten .10
307 Doug Drabek .10
308 Terry Steinbach .10
309 Ryan Klesko .10
310 Mike Piazza 1.50
311 Ben McDonald .10
312 Reggie Sanders .10
313 Alex Fernandez .10
314 Aaron Sele .10
315 Gregg Jefferies .10
316 Rickey Henderson .75
317 Brian Anderson .10
318 Jose Valentin .10
319 Rod Beck .10
320 Marquis Grissom .10
321 Ken Griffey Jr. 2.00
322 Bret Saberhagen .10
323 Juan Gonzalez .50
324 Paul Molitor .75
325 Gary Sheffield .40
326 Darren Daulton .10
327 Bill Swift .10
328 Brian McRae .10
329 Robin Ventura .10
330 Lee Smith .10
331 Fred McGriff .20
332 Delino DeShields .10
333 Edgar Martinez .10
334 Mike Mussina .50
335 Orlando Merced .10
336 Carlos Baerga .10
337 Wil Cordero .10
338 Tom Pagnozzi .10
339 Pat Hentgen .10
340 Chad Curtis .10
341 Darren Lewis .10
342 Jeff Kent .20
343 Bip Roberts .10
344 Ivan Rodriguez .50
345 Jeff Montgomery .10
346 Hal Morris .10
347 Danny Tartabull .10
348 Raul Mondesi .10
349 Ken Hill .10
350 Pedro Martinez 1.00
351 Frank Thomas .75
352 Manny Ramirez 1.00
353 Tim Salmon .10
354 William Van Landingham .10
355 Andres Galarraga .10
356 Paul O'Neill .25
357 Brady Anderson .10
358 Ramon Martinez .10
359 John Olerud .10
360 Ruben Sierra .10
361 Cal Eldred .10
362 Jay Buhner .10
363 Jay Bell .10
364 Wally Joyner .10
365 Chuck Knoblauch .10
366 Len Dykstra .10
367 John Wetteland .10
368 Roberto Alomar .25
369 Craig Biggio .25
370 Ozzie Smith 1.50
371 Terry Pendleton .10
372 Sammy Sosa 1.00
373 Carlos Garcia .10
374 Jose Rijo .10
375 Chris Gomez .10
376 Barry Bonds 2.00
377 Steve Avery .10
378 Rick Wilkins .10
379 Pete Harnisch .10
380 Dean Palmer .10
381 Bob Hamelin .10
382 Jason Bere .10
383 Jimmy Key .10
384 Dante Bichette .10
385 Rafael Palmeiro .50
386 David Justice .10
387 Chili Davis .10
388 Mike Greenwell .10
389 Todd Zeile .10
390 Jeff Conine .10
391 Rick Aguilera .10
392 Eddie Murray .50
393 Mike Stanley .10
394 (NOT ISSUED, SEE #294.)
395 Randy Johnson 1.00
396 David Nied .10
397 Devon White .10
398 Royce Clayton .10
399 Andy Benes .10
400 John Hudek .10
401 Bobby Jones .10
402 Eric Karros .10
403 Will Clark .25
404 Mark Langston .10
405 Kevin Brown .10
406 Greg Maddux 1.50
407 David Cone .10
408 Wade Boggs .75
409 Steve Trachsel .10
410 Greg Vaughn .10
411 Mo Vaughn .10
412 Wilson Alvarez .10
413 Cal Ripken Jr. 3.00
414 Rico Brogna .10
415 Barry Larkin .40
416 Cecil Fielder .10
417 Jose Canseco .50
418 Jack McDowell .10
419 Mike Lieberthal .10
420 Andrew Lorraine .10
421 Rich Becker .10
422 Tony Phillips .10
423 Scott Ruffcorn .10
424 Jeff Granger .10
425 Greg Pirkl .10
426 Dennis Eckersley .50
427 Jose Lima .10
428 Russ Davis .10
429 Armando Benitez .10
430 Alex Gonzalez .10
431 Carlos Delgado .75
432 Chan Ho Park .10
433 Mickey Tettleton .10
434 Dave Winfield .75
435 John Burkett .10
436 Orlando Miller .10
437 Jose Oliva .10
438 Jose Oliva .10
439 Checklist .10

Gold

The only chase cards in the '95 Bowman set are gold versions of the foil-etched "Minor League MVPs," "1st Impressions," and "Prime Prospects." The gold cards are

TREY BEAMON
PRIME PROSPECT

found in every 6th (regular) or 12th (jumbo) pack, on average, in place of the silver versions.

	NM/M
Complete Set (54):	100.00
Common Player:	.50
Stars/RC's:	2.5X

(See 1995 Bowman #221-274 for checklist and base card values.)

1995 Bowman's Best

Actually made up of three subsets, all cards feature a player photo set against a silver foil background. The 90 veterans' cards have a broad red-foil stripe in the background beneath the team logo; the 90 rookies' cards have a similar stripe in tones of blue. All of those cards are printed in Topps' Finest technology. The 15 Mirror Image cards are in horizontal format, printed more conventionally on metallic foil, and have a rookie and veteran sharing the card. Backs of each card continue the color theme, have '94 and career stats and a highlight or two. Standard packaging was seven-card foil packs with inserts consisting of higher-tech parallel sets of the regular issue.

	NM/M
Complete Set (195):	200.00
Common Player:	.25
Pack (7):	12.00
Wax Box (24):	275.00
Complete Set Red (90):	45.00

1	Randy Johnson	1.50
2	Joe Carter	.25
3	Chili Davis	.25
4	Moises Alou	.25
5	Gary Sheffield	.40
6	Kevin Appier	.25
7	Denny Neagle	.25
8	Ruben Sierra	.25
9	Darren Daulton	.25
10	Cal Ripken Jr.	4.00
11	Bobby Bonilla	.25
12	Manny Ramirez	1.50
13	Barry Bonds	4.00
14	Eric Karros	.25
15	Greg Maddux	2.00
16	Jeff Bagwell	1.50
17	Paul Molitor	1.50
18	Ray Lankford	.25
19	Mark Grace	.25
20	Kenny Lofton	.25
21	Tony Gwynn	2.00
22	Will Clark	.25
23	Roger Clemens	2.25
24	Dante Bichette	.25
25	Barry Larkin	.25
26	Wade Boggs	2.00
27	Kirby Puckett	2.00
28	Cecil Fielder	.25
29	Jose Canseco	.50
30	Juan Gonzalez	.75
31	David Cone	.25

32	Craig Biggio	.25
33	Tim Salmon	.25
34	David Justice	.25
35	Sammy Sosa	2.00
36	Mike Piazza	2.50
37	Carlos Baerga	.25
38	Jeff Conine	.25
39	Rafael Palmeiro	1.25
40	Bret Saberhagen	.25
41	Len Dykstra	.25
42	Mo Vaughn	.25
43	Wally Joyner	.25
44	Chuck Knoblauch	.25
45	Robin Ventura	.25
46	Don Mattingly	2.25
47	Dave Hollins	.25
48	Andy Benes	.25
49	Ken Griffey Jr.	2.50
50	Albert Belle	.25
51	Matt Williams	.25
52	Rondell White	.25
53	Raul Mondesi	.25
54	Brian Jordan	.25
55	Greg Vaughn	.25
56	Fred McGriff	.25
57	Roberto Alomar	.40
58	Dennis Eckersley	1.25
59	Lee Smith	.25
60	Eddie Murray	1.50
61	Kenny Rogers	.25
62	Ron Gant	.25
63	Larry Walker	.25
64	Chad Curtis	.25
65	Frank Thomas	1.50
66	Paul O'Neill	.25
67	Kevin Seitzer	.25
68	Marquis Grissom	.25
69	Mark McGwire	3.00
70	Travis Fryman	.25
71	Andres Galarraga	.25
72	Carlos Perez RC	.25
73	Tyler Green	.25
74	Marty Cordova	.25
75	Shawn Green	.40
76	Vaughn Eshelman	.25
77	John Mabry	.25
78	Jason Bates	.25
79	Jon Nunnally	.25
80	Ray Durham	.25
81	Edgardo Alfonzo	.25
82	Esteban Loaiza	.25
83	Hideo Nomo RC	10.00
84	Orlando Miller	.25
85	Alex Gonzalez	.25
86	Mark Grudzielanek RC	.65
87	Julian Tavarez	.25
88	Benji Gil	.25
89	Quilvio Veras	.25
90	Ricky Bottalico	.25
Complete Set Blue (90):		**150.00**
1	Derek Jeter	3.00
2	Vladimir Guerrero RC	80.00
3	Bob Abreu RC	25.00
4	Chan Ho Park	.25
5	Paul Wilson	.25
6	Chad Ogea	.25
7	Andruw Jones RC	50.00
8	Brian Barber	.25
9	Andy Larkin	.25
10	Richie Sexson RC	10.00
11	Everett Stull RC	.25
12	Brooks Kieschnick	.25
13	Matt Murray	.25
14	John Wasdin	.25
15	Shannon Stewart	.25
16	Luis Ortiz	.25
17	Marc Kroon	.25
18	Todd Greene	.25
19	Juan Acevedo	.25
20	Tony Clark	.25
21	Jermaine Dye	.25
22	Derrek Lee	1.00
23	Pat Watkins	.25
24	Calvin Reese	.25
25	Brian Grieve	.25
26	Julio Santana RC	.25
27	Felix Rodriguez RC	.50
28	Paul Konerko	2.00
29	Nomar Garciaparra	2.00
30	Pat Ahearne	.25
31	Jason Schmidt	.25
32	Billy Wagner	.25
33	Rey Ordonez RC	1.00
34	Curtis Goodwin	.25
35	Sergio Nunez RC	.25
36	Tim Belk	.25
37	Scott Elarton RC	1.00
38	Jason Isringhausen	.25
39	Trot Nixon	.35
40	Sid Roberson	.25
41	Ron Villone	.25
42	Ruben Rivera	.25
43	Rick Huisman	.25
44	Todd Hollandsworth	.25
45	Johnny Damon	1.00
46	Garret Anderson	.25
47	Jeff D'Amico	.25
48	Dustin Hermanson	.25
49	Juan Encarnacion RC	4.00
50	Andy Pettitte	.50
51	Chris Stynes	.25
52	Troy Percival	.25
53	LaTroy Hawkins	.25
54	Roger Cedeno	.25
55	Alan Benes	.25
56	Karim Garcia RC	1.50
57	Andrew Lorraine	.25

58	Gary Rath RC	.25
59	Bret Wagner	.25
60	Jeff Suppan	.25
61	Bill Pulsipher	.25
62	Jay Payton RC	3.00
63	Alex Ochoa	.25
64	Ugueth Urbina	.25
65	Armando Benitez	.25
66	George Arias	.25
67	Raul Casanova RC	.50
68	Matt Drews	.25
69	Jimmy Haynes	.25
70	Jimmy Hurst	.25
71	C.J. Nitkowski	.25
72	Tommy Davis RC	.25
73	Bartolo Colon RC	5.00
74	Chris Carpenter RC	10.00
75	Trey Beamon	.25
76	Bryan Rekar	.25
77	James Baldwin	.25
78	Marc Valdes	.25
79	Tom Fordham RC	.25
80	Marc Newfield	.25
81	Angel Martinez	.25
82	Brian Hunter	.25
83	Jose Herrera	.25
84	Glenn Dishman RC	.25
85	Jacob Cruz RC	.25
86	Paul Shuey	.25
87	Scott Rolen RC	25.00
88	Doug Million	.25
89	Desi Relaford	.25
90	Michael Tucker	.25
Mirror Image:		**.50**
1	Ben Davis RC,	
	Ivan Rodriguez	1.00
2	Mark Redman RC,	
	Manny Ramirez	1.50
3	Reggie Taylor RC,	
	Deion Sanders	.50
4	Ryan Jaroncyk,	
	Shawn Green	.50
5	Juan LeBron,	
	Juan Gonzalez	1.00
6	Toby McKnight,	
	Craig Biggio	.50
7	Michael Barrett RC,	
	Travis Fryman	1.00
8	Corey Jenkins,	
	Mo Vaughn	.50
9	Ruben Rivera,	
	Frank Thomas	1.50
10	Curtis Goodwin,	
	Kenny Lofton	.50
11	Brian Hunter,	
	Tony Gwynn	1.75
12	Todd Greene,	
	Ken Griffey Jr.	2.50
13	Karim Garcia,	
	Matt Williams	.75
14	Billy Wagner,	
	Randy Johnson	1.50
15	Pat Watkins,	
	Jeff Bagwell	1.50

Refractors

The large volume of silver foil in the background of the red and blue subsets in '95 Best make the Refractor technology much easier to see than in past issues. The chase cards, found one per six packs on average, also have a small "REFRACTOR" printed near the lower-left corner on back. The 15-card Mirror Image subset was not paralleled in Refractor technology, but in a process Topps calls "diffraction-foil" which creates a strong vertical-stripe rainbow effect in the background. Cards #72 (Carlos Perez) and 84 (Orlando Miller) can be found both with and without the "REFRACTOR" notice on back; neither version commands a premium.

	NM/M
Common Player:	1.00
Stars:	3-6X
Rookies:	2-3X

(See 1995 Bowman's Best for checklist and base card values.)

Refractors - Jumbo

These super-size versions of Bowman's Best Refractors were produced exclusively for inclusion as a one-per-box insert in retail boxes of the product distributed by ANCO to large retail chains. The 4-1/4" x 5-3/4" cards are identical in all ways except size to the regular refractors. The jumbo inserts were not produced in equal quantities, with the most popular players printed in greater numbers.

		NM/M
Complete Set (10):		35.00
Common Player:		2.00
10	Cal Ripken Jr.	10.00
15	Greg Maddux	4.00
21	Tony Gwynn	4.00
35	Sammy Sosa	5.00
36	Mike Piazza	6.00
42	Mo Vaughn	2.00
49	Ken Griffey Jr.	6.00
50	Albert Belle	2.00
65	Frank Thomas	3.50
83	Hideo Nomo	3.00

1996 Bowman

KATSUHIRO MAEDA

In a "Guaranteed Value Program," Topps stated it would pay $100 for this set in 1999, if collectors mail in a request form (one per three packs), a $5 fee and the complete set in numerical order (only one per person). Every set redeemed was destroyed. The 385-card set has 110 veteran stars and 275 prospects. Backs of the prospects' cards provide a detailed scouting report. A "1st Bowman Card" gold-foil stamped logo was included on the card front for 156 players making their first appearance in a Bowman set. Insert sets include Bowman's Best Previews (along with Refractor and Atomic Refractor versions), a 1952 Mickey Mantle Bowman reprint (1 in 48 packs) and Minor League Player of the Year candidates. A 385-card parallel version of the entire base set was also produced on 18-point foilboard; seeded one per pack.

	NM/M
Complete Set (385):	50.00
Common Player:	.10
Foils:	1.5X
Pack (11):	2.00
Wax Box (24):	40.00

1	Cal Ripken Jr.	2.00
2	Ray Durham	.10
3	Ivan Rodriguez	.50
4	Fred McGriff	.20
5	Hideo Nomo	.50
6	Troy Percival	.10
7	Moises Alou	.20
8	Mike Stanley	.10
9	Jay Buhner	.10
10	Shawn Green	.25
11	Ryan Klesko	.25
12	Andres Galarraga	.10
13	Dean Palmer	.10
14	Jeff Conine	.10
15	Brian Hunter	.10
16	J.T. Snow	.10
17	Larry Walker	.25
18	Barry Larkin	.40
19	Alex Gonzalez	.10
20	Edgar Martinez	.25
21	Mo Vaughn	.10
22	Mark McGwire	1.50
23	Jose Canseco	.50
24	Jack McDowell	.10
25	Dante Bichette	.25
26	Wade Boggs	.50
27	Mike Piazza	1.00
28	Ray Lankford	.10
29	Craig Biggio	.25
30	Rafael Palmeiro	.50
31	Ron Gant	.10
32	Javy Lopez	.10
33	Brian Jordan	.10
34	Paul O'Neill	.20
35	Mark Grace	.25
36	Matt Williams	.20
37	Pedro Martinez	.75
38	Rickey Henderson	.25
39	Bobby Bonilla	.10
40	Todd Hollandsworth	.10
41	Jim Thome	.75
42	Gary Sheffield	.40
43	Tim Salmon	.10
44	Gregg Jefferies	.10
45	Roberto Alomar	.25
45p	Roberto Alomar	
	(Unmarked promo	
	card, fielding photo	
	on front.)	3.00
46	Carlos Baerga	.10
47	Mark Grudzielanek	.10
48	Randy Johnson	.75
49	Tino Martinez	.25
50	Robin Ventura	.10
51	Ryne Sandberg	1.50
52	Jay Bell	.10
53	Jason Schmidt	.10
54	Frank Thomas	1.50
55	Kenny Lofton	.10
56	Ariel Prieto	.10
57	David Cone	.10
58	Reggie Sanders	.10
59	Michael Tucker	.10
60	Vinny Castilla	.10
61	Lenny Dykstra	.10
62	Todd Hundley	.10
63	Brian McRae	.10
64	Dennis Eckersley	.40
65	Rondell White	.10
66	Eric Karros	.10
67	Greg Maddux	1.50
68	Kevin Appier	.10
69	Eddie Murray	.50
70	John Olerud	.10
71	Tony Gwynn	.75
72	David Justice	.10
73	Ken Caminiti	.10
74	Terry Steinbach	.10
75	Alan Benes	.10
76	Chipper Jones	1.00
77	Jeff Bagwell	.50
77p	Jeff Bagwell	
	(Unmarked promo card,	
	name in gold.)	6.00
78	Barry Bonds	2.00
79	Ken Griffey Jr.	1.50
80	Roger Cedeno	.10
81	Joe Carter	.10
82	Henry Rodriguez	.10
83	Jason Isringhausen	.10
84	Chuck Knoblauch	.25
85	Manny Ramirez	.75
86	Tom Glavine	.30
87	Jeffrey Hammonds	.10
88	Paul Molitor	.75
89	Roger Clemens	2.00
90	Greg Vaughn	.10
91	Marty Cordova	.10
92	Albert Belle	.10
93	Mike Mussina	.40
94	Garret Anderson	.10
95	Juan Gonzalez	.10
96	John Valentin	.10
97	Jason Giambi	.10
98	Kirby Puckett	1.50
99	Jim Edmonds	.25
100	Cecil Fielder	.10
101	Mike Aldrete	.10
102	Marquis Grissom	.10
103	Derek Bell	.10
104	Raul Mondesi	.10
105	Sammy Sosa	1.00
106	Travis Fryman	.10
107	Rico Brogna	.10
108	Will Clark	.25
109	Bernie Williams	.40
110	Brady Anderson	.10
111	Torii Hunter	.10
112	Derek Jeter	2.00
113	Mike Kusiewicz RC	.10
114	Scott Rolen	1.00
115	Ramon Castro	.10

116	Jose Guillen RC	2.50
117	Wade Walker RC	.10
118	Shawn Senior	.10
119	Onan Masaoka RC	.10
120	Marlon Anderson RC	.75
121	Katsuhiro Maeda RC	.25
122	Garrett Stephenson RC	.25
123	Butch Huskey	.10
124	D'Angelo Jimenez RC	.10
125	Tony Mounce RC	.20
126	Jay Canizaro	.10
127	Juan Melo	.10
128	Steve Gibralter	.10
129	Freddy Garcia	.10
130	Julio Santana	.10
131	Richard Hidalgo	.10
132	Jermaine Dye	.10
133	Willie Adams	.10
134	Everett Stull	.10
135	Ramon Morel	.10
136	Chan Ho Park	.10
137	Jamey Wright	.10
138	Luis Garcia RC	.10
139	Dan Serafini	.10
140	Ryan Dempster RC	.50
141	Tate Seefried	.10
142	Jimmy Hurst	.10
143	Travis Miller	.10
144	Curtis Goodwin	.10
145	Rocky Coppinger RC	.10
146	Enrique Wilson	.10
147	Jaime Bluma	.10
148	Andrew Vessel	.10
149	Damian Moss	.10
150	Shawn Gallagher RC	.10
151	Pat Watkins	.10
152	Jose Paniagua	.10
153	Danny Graves	.10
154	Bryon Gainey RC	.10
155	Steve Soderstrom	.10
156	Cliff Brumbaugh RC	.10
157	Eugene Kingsale RC	.10
158	Lou Collier	.10
159	Todd Walker	.10
160	Kris Detmers RC	.10
161	Josh Booty RC	.25
162	Greg Whiteman RC	.10
163	Damian Jackson	.10
164	Tony Clark	.10
165	Jeff D'Amico	.10
166	Johnny Damon	.50
167	Rafael Orellano	.10
168	Ruben Rivera	.10
169	Alex Ochoa	.10
170	Jay Powell	.10
171	Tom Evans	.10
172	Ron Villone	.10
173	Shawn Estes	.10
174	John Wasdin	.10
175	Bill Simas	.10
176	Kevin Brown	.10
177	Shannon Stewart	.10
178	Todd Greene	.10
179	Bob Wolcott	.10
180	Chris Snopek	.10
181	Nomar Garciaparra	1.00
182	Cameron Smith RC	.10
183	Matt Drews	.10
184	Jimmy Haynes	.10
185	Chris Carpenter	.25
186	Desi Relaford	.10
187	Ben Grieve	.10
188	Mike Bell	.10
189	Luis Castillo RC	.75
190	Ugueth Urbina	.10
191	Paul Wilson	.10
191p	Paul Wilson	
	(Unmarked promo card,	
	name in gold.)	1.00
192	Andruw Jones	.75
193	Wayne Gomes	.10
194	Craig Counsell RC	.75
195	Jim Cole	.10
196	Brooks Kieshnick	.10
197	Trey Beamon	.10
198	Marino Santana RC	.10
199	Bob Abreu	.25
200	Calvin Reese	.10
201	Dante Powell	.10
202	George Arias	.10
202p	George Arias	
	(Unmarked promo card,	
	name in gold.)	1.00
203	Jorge Velandia RC	.10
204	George Lombard RC	.10
205	Byron Browne RC	.10
206	John Frascatore	.10
207	Terry Adams	.10
208	Wilson Delgado RC	.10
209	Billy McMillon	.10
210	Jeff Abbott	.10
211	Trot Nixon	.10
212	Amaury Telemaco	.10
213	Scott Sullivan	.10
214	Justin Thompson	.10
215	Decomba Conner	.10
216	Ryan McGuire	.10
217	Matt Luke RC	.10
218	Doug Million	.10
219	Jason Dickson RC	.25
220	Ramon Hernandez RC	.50
221	Mark Bellhorn RC	.25
222	Eric Ludwick RC	.10
223	Luke Wilcox RC	.10
224	Marty Malloy RC	.10
225	Gary Coffee RC	.10
226	Wendell Magee RC	.10
227	Brett Tomko RC	.25

#	Player		Price
228	Derek Lowe		.10
229	Jose Rosado	RC	.10
230	Steve Bourgeois	RC	.10
231	Neil Weber	RC	.10
232	Jeff Ware		.10
233	Edwin Diaz		.10
234	Greg Norton		.10
235	Aaron Boone		.10
236	Jeff Suppan		.10
237	Bret Wagner		.10
238	Elieser Marrero		.10
239	Will Cunnane		.10
240	Brian Barkley	RC	.10
241	Jay Payton		.10
242	Marcus Jensen		.10
243	Ryan Nye		.10
244	Chad Mottola		.10
245	Scott McClain	RC	.10
246	Jesse Ibarra	RC	.10
247	Mike Darr	RC	.10
248	Bobby Estalella	RC	.50
249	Michael Barrett		.10
250	Jamie Lopiccolo	RC	.10
251	Shane Spencer	RC	.40
252	Ben Petrick	RC	.50
253	Jason Bell	RC	.10
254	Arnold Gooch	RC	.10
255	T.J. Mathews		.10
256	Jason Ryan		.10
257	Pat Cline	RC	.10
258	Rafael Carmona	RC	.10
259	Carl Pavano	RC	1.00
260	Ben Davis		.10
261	Matt Lawton	RC	1.00
262	Kevin Sefcik	RC	.10
263	Chris Fussell	RC	.10
264	Mike Cameron	RC	1.50
265	Marty Janzen	RC	.10
266	Livan Hernandez	RC	1.00
267	Raul Ibanez	RC	1.50
268	Juan Encarnacion		.10
269	David Yocum	RC	.10
270	Jonathan Johnson	RC	.10
271	Reggie Taylor		.10
272	Danny Buxbaum	RC	.10
273	Jacob Cruz		.10
274	Bobby Morris	RC	.10
275	Andy Fox	RC	.10
276	Greg Keagle		.10
277	Charles Peterson		.10
278	Derrek Lee		.50
279	Bryant Nelson	RC	.10
280	Antone Williamson		.10
281	Scott Elarton		.10
282	Shad Williams	RC	.10
283	Rich Hunter	RC	.10
284	Chris Sheff		.10
285	Derrick Gibson		.10
286	Felix Rodriguez		.10
287	Brian Banks	RC	.10
288	Jason McDonald		.10
289	Glendon Rusch	RC	.50
290	Gary Rath		.10
291	Peter Munro		.10
292	Tom Fordham		.10
293	Jason Kendall		.10
294	Russ Johnson		.10
295	Joe Long		.10
296	Robert Smith	RC	.10
297	Jarrod Washburn	RC	.75
298	Dave Coggin	RC	.10
299	Jeff Yoder	RC	.10
300	Jed Hansen	RC	.10
301	Matt Morris	RC	1.00
302	Josh Bishop	RC	.10
303	Dustin Hermanson		.10
304	Mike Gulan		.10
305	Felipe Crespo		.10
306	Quinton McCracken	RC	.10
307	Jim Bonnici	RC	.10
308	Sal Fasano		.10
309	Gabe Alvarez	RC	.10
310	Heath Murray	RC	.10
311	Jose Valentin	RC	.10
312	Bartolo Colon		.10
313	Olmedo Saenz		.10
314	Norm Hutchins	RC	.10
315	Chris Holt	RC	.10
316	David Doster	RC	.10
317	Robert Person		.10
318	Donne Wall	RC	.10
319	Adam Riggs	RC	.10
320	Homer Bush		.10
321	Brad Rigby	RC	.10
322	Lou Merloni	RC	.25
323	Neifi Perez		.10
324	Chris Cumberland		.10
325	Alvie Shepherd	RC	.10
326	Jarrod Patterson	RC	.10
327	Ray Ricken	RC	.10
328	Danny Klassen	RC	.10
329	David Miller	RC	.10
330	Chad Alexander	RC	.10
331	Matt Beaumont		.10
332	Damon Hollins		.10
333	Todd Dunn		.10
334	Mike Sweeney	RC	1.50
335	Richie Sexson		.40
336	Billy Wagner		.10
337	Ron Wright	RC	.10
338	Paul Konerko		.25
339	Tommy Phelps	RC	.10
340	Karim Garcia		.10
341	Mike Grace	RC	.10
342	Russell Branyan	RC	.40
343	Randy Winn	RC	.10
344	A.J. Pierzynski	RC	1.50
345	Mike Busby	RC	.10

#	Player		Price
346	Matt Beech	RC	.10
347	Jose Cepeda	RC	.10
348	Brian Stephenson		.10
349	Rey Ordonez		.10
350	Rich Aurilia	RC	1.00
351	Edgard Velazquez	RC	.25
352	Raul Casanova		.10
353	Carlos Guillen	RC	1.00
354	Bruce Aven	RC	.10
355	Ryan Jones	RC	.10
356	Derek Aucoin	RC	.10
357	Brian Rose	RC	.10
358	Richard Almanzar	RC	.10
359	Fletcher Bates	RC	.10
360	Russ Ortiz	RC	.75
361	Wilton Guerrero	RC	.10
362	Geoff Jenkins	RC	1.00
363	Pete Janicki		.10
364	Yamil Benitez		.10
365	Aaron Holbert		.10
366	Tim Belk		.10
367	Terrell Wade		.10
368	Terrence Long		.10
369	Brad Fullmer		.10
370	Matt Wagner		.10
371	Craig Wilson		.10
372	Mark Loretta		.10
373	Eric Owens		.10
374	Vladimir Guerrero		1.00
375	Tommy Davis		.10
376	Donnie Sadler		.10
377	Edgar Renteria		.25
378	Todd Helton		.50
379	Ralph Milliard	RC	.10
380	Darin Blood	RC	.10
381	Shayne Bennett		.10
382	Mark Redman		.10
383	Felix Martinez		.10
384	Sean Watkins	RC	.10
385	Oscar Henriquez		.10

Minor League Player of the Year

Fifteen prospects who were candidates for Minor League Player of the Year are featured in this 1996 Bowman baseball insert set. Cards were seeded one per every 12 packs.

		NM/M
Complete Set (15):		12.50
Common Player:		.50
1	Andruw Jones	4.00
2	Derrick Gibson	.50
3	Bob Abreu	.75
4	Todd Walker	.50
5	Jamey Wright	.50
6	Wes Helms	.50
7	Karim Garcia	.75
8	Bartolo Colon	2.00
9	Alex Ochoa	.50
10	Mike Sweeney	2.00
11	Ruben Rivera	.50
12	Gabe Alvarez	.50
13	Billy Wagner	.50
14	Vladimir Guerrero	4.00
15	Edgard Velazquez	.50

1952 Mickey Mantle Reprints

Reprints of Mickey Mantle's 1952 Bowman baseball card were created for insertion in Bowman and Bowman's

Best products for 1996. The 2-1/2" x 3-1/2" card can be found in regular (gold seal on front), Finest, Finest Refractor and Atomic Refractor versions.

		NM/M
Complete Set (4):		20.00
Common Card:		2.50
20	Mickey Mantle/ Reprint	2.50
20	Mickey Mantle/Finest	5.00
20	Mickey Mantle/ Refractor	7.50
20	Mickey Mantle/ Atomic Refractor	10.00

Best Preview

NOMAR GARCIAPARRA

These cards use Topps' Finest technology. The cards were seeded one per every 12 packs of 1996 Bowman baseball. Fifteen veterans and 15 prospects are featured in the set. Refractor versions are found one per 24 packs, with Atomic Refractors a 1:48 pick.

		NM/M
Complete Set (30):		18.50
Common Player:		.20
Refractors:		1.5X
Atomic Refractors:		2X
1	Chipper Jones	1.50
2	Alan Benes	.25
3	Brooks Kieschnick	.25
4	Barry Bonds	3.00
5	Rey Ordonez	.25
6	Tim Salmon	.25
7	Mike Piazza	2.00
8	Billy Wagner	.25
9	Andruw Jones	1.00
10	Tony Gwynn	1.50
11	Paul Wilson	.25
12	Calvin Reese	.25
13	Frank Thomas	1.00
14	Greg Maddux	1.50
15	Derek Jeter	3.00
16	Jeff Bagwell	1.00
17	Barry Larkin	.25
18	Todd Greene	.25
19	Ruben Rivera	.25
20	Richard Hidalgo	.25
21	Larry Walker	.25
22	Carlos Baerga	.25
23	Derrick Gibson	.25
24	Richie Sexson	.25
25	Mo Vaughn	.50
26	Hideo Nomo	.50
27	Nomar Garciaparra	1.50
28	Cal Ripken Jr.	3.00
29	Karim Garcia	.25
30	Ken Griffey Jr.	2.00

Best

CHUCK KNOBLAUCH

Bowman's Best returns in its traditional format of 180 cards: 90 established stars and 90 up-and-coming prospects and rookies. Three types of insert sets are found in Bowman's Best: Mirror Image, Bowman's Best Cuts and the 1952 Bowman Mickey

Mantle reprints. There are also parallel sets of Refractors and Atomic Refractors randomly seeded in packs. Refractors are found on average of one per 12 packs; Atomic Refractors are seeded one per 48 packs. Mirror Image Refractors are found one per 96 packs, while Mirror Image Atomic Refractors are seeded one per 192 packs. Refractor versions of the Mantle reprint are seeded one per every 96 packs; Atomic Refractor Mantle reprints are seeded in every 192nd pack.

		NM/M
Complete Set (180):		30.00
Common Player:		.25
Refractors:		2X
Atomics:		15X
1952 Mickey Mantle:		2.50
1952 Mantle Finest:		5.00
1952 Mantle Refractor:		7.50
1952 Mantle Atomic:		10.00
Pack (6):		2.50
Wax Box (24):		40.00
1	Hideo Nomo	.75
2	Edgar Martinez	.25
3	Cal Ripken Jr.	4.00
4	Wade Boggs	1.00
5	Cecil Fielder	.25
6	Albert Belle	.25
7	Chipper Jones	1.50
8	Ryne Sandberg	2.00
9	Tim Salmon	.25
10	Barry Bonds	3.00
11	Ken Caminiti	.25
12	Ron Gant	.25
13	Frank Thomas	1.00
14	Dante Bichette	.25
15	Jason Kendall	.25
16	Mo Vaughn	.25
17	Rey Ordonez	.25
18	Henry Rodriguez	.25
19	Ryan Klesko	.25
20	Jeff Bagwell	1.00
21	Randy Johnson	1.50
22	Jim Edmonds	.25
23	Kenny Lofton	.25
24	Andy Pettitte	.50
25	Brady Anderson	.25
26	Mike Piazza	2.50
27	Greg Vaughn	.25
28	Joe Carter	.25
29	Jason Giambi	1.00
30	Ivan Rodriguez	1.00
31	Jeff Conine	.25
32	Rafael Palmeiro	.75
33	Roger Clemens	3.00
34	Chuck Knoblauch	.25
35	Reggie Sanders	.25
36	Andres Galarraga	.25
37	Paul O'Neill	.25
38	Tony Gwynn	2.00
39	Paul Wilson	.25
40	Garret Anderson	.25
41	David Justice	.25
42	Eddie Murray	1.00
43	Mike Grace	RC	.25
44	Marty Cordova	.25
45	Kevin Appier	.25
46	Raul Mondesi	.25
47	Jim Thome	1.00
48	Sammy Sosa	2.00
49	Craig Biggio	.50
50	Marquis Grissom	.25
51	Alan Benes	.25
52	Manny Ramirez	1.50
53	Gary Sheffield	.75
54	Mike Mussina	.50
55	Robin Ventura	.25
56	Johnny Damon	1.00
57	Jose Canseco	.75
58	Juan Gonzalez	.75
59	Tino Martinez	.25
60	Brian Hunter	.25
61	Fred McGriff	.25
62	Jay Buhner	.25
63	Carlos Delgado	.75
64	Moises Alou	.25
65	Roberto Alomar	.50
66	Barry Larkin	.50
67	Vinny Castilla	.25
68	Ray Durham	.25
69	Travis Fryman	.25
70	Jason Isringhausen	.25
71	Ken Griffey Jr.	2.50
72	John Smoltz	.50
73	Matt Williams	.25
74	Chan Ho Park	.25
75	Mark McGwire	2.50
76	Jeffrey Hammonds	.25
77	Will Clark	.25
78	Kirby Puckett	2.00
79	Derek Jeter	4.00
80	Derek Bell	.25
81	Eric Karros	.25
82	Lenny Dykstra	.25
83	Larry Walker	.50
84	Mark Grudzielanek	.25
85	Greg Maddux	2.50
86	Carlos Baerga	.25
87	Paul Molitor	1.00
88	John Valentin	.25
89	Mark Grace	.50
90	Ray Lankford	.25
91	Andruw Jones	1.50
92	Nomar Garciaparra	2.00
93	Alex Ochoa	.25
94	Derrick Gibson	.25
95	Jeff D'Amico	.25
96	Ruben Rivera	.25
97	Vladimir Guerrero	1.50
98	Calvin Reese	.25
99	Richard Hidalgo	.25
100	Bartolo Colon	.25
101	Karim Garcia	.25
102	Ben Davis	.25
103	Jay Powell	.25
104	Chris Snopek	.25
105	Glendon Rusch	RC	1.00
106	Enrique Wilson	.25
107	Antonio Alfonseca	RC	.75
108	Wilton Guerrero	RC	.50
109	Jose Guillen	RC	3.00
110	Miguel Mejia	RC	.25
111	Jay Payton	.25
112	Scott Elarton	.25
113	Brooks Kieschnick	.25
114	Dustin Hermanson	.25
115	Roger Cedeno	.25
116	Matt Wagner	.25
117	Lee Daniels	.25
118	Ben Grieve	.25
119	Ugueth Urbina	.25
120	Danny Graves	.25
121	Dan Donato	RC	.25
122	Matt Ruebel	RC	.25
123	Mark Sievert	RC	.25
124	Chris Stynes	.25
125	Jeff Abbott	.25
126	Rocky Coppinger	RC	.25
127	Jermaine Dye	.25
128	Todd Greene	.15
129	Chris Carpenter	1.00
130	Edgar Renteria	.50
131	Matt Drews	.25
132	Edgard Velazquez	RC	.50
133	Casey Whitten	.25
134	Ryan Jones	RC	.25
135	Todd Walker	.20
136	Geoff Jenkins	RC	2.00
137	Matt Morris	RC	2.00
138	Richie Sexson	.75
139	Todd Dunwoody	RC	.50
140	Gabe Alvarez	RC	.50
141	J.J. Johnson	.25
142	Shannon Stewart	.25
143	Brad Fullmer	.25
144	Julio Santana	.25
145	Scott Rolen	1.00
146	Amaury Telemaco	.25
147	Trey Beamon	.25
148	Billy Wagner	.25
149	Todd Hollandsworth	.25
150	Doug Million	.25
151	Jose Valentin	RC	.25
152	Wes Helms	RC	.50
153	Jeff Suppan	.25
154	Luis Castillo	RC	1.50
155	Bob Abreu	.50
156	Paul Konerko	.50
157	Jamey Wright	.25
158	Eddie Pearson	.25
159	Jimmy Haynes	.25
160	Derrek Lee	.75
161	Damian Moss	.15
162	Carlos Guillen	RC	2.00
163	Chris Fussell	RC	.25
164	Mike Sweeney	RC	3.00
165	Donnie Sadler	.15
166	Desi Relaford	.25
167	Steve Gibralter	.25
168	Neifi Perez	.25
169	Antone Williamson	.25
170	Marty Janzen	RC	.25
171	Todd Helton	1.00
172	Raul Ibanez	RC	2.00
173	Bill Selby	.25
174	Shane Monahan	RC	.35
175	Robin Jennings	RC	.25
176	Bobby Chouinard	RC	.25
177	Einar Diaz	.25
178	Jason Thompson	.15
179	Rafael Medina	RC	.25
180	Kevin Orie	.25

Best Cuts

KEN GRIFFEY JR.

Bowman's Best Cuts gave collectors the first die-cut chromium cards in a 15-card set of top stars. The cards were seeded one per 24 packs. Refractor versions are inserted on average of one per 48 packs; Atomic Refractor versions are found one per 96 packs.

		NM/M
Complete Set (15):		15.00
Common Player:		.25
Refractors:		1.5X
Atomic Refractors:		2X
1	Ken Griffey Jr.	2.50
2	Jason Isringhausen	.25
3	Derek Jeter	4.00
4	Andruw Jones	1.00
5	Chipper Jones	2.00
6	Ryan Klesko	.25
7	Raul Mondesi	.25
8	Hideo Nomo	.50
9	Mike Piazza	2.50
10	Manny Ramirez	1.00
11	Cal Ripken Jr.	4.00
12	Ruben Rivera	.25
13	Tim Salmon	.25
14	Frank Thomas	1.00
15	Jim Thome	.75

Best Mirror Image

Mirror Image inserts feature four top players at 10 different positions, pairing an American League veteran and a prospect on one side and a National League veteran and prospect on the other. These cards are seeded one per every 48 packs. Mirror Image Refractors (one in every 96 packs) and Mirror Image Atomic Refractors (one in every 192 packs) were also produced.

		NM/M
Complete Set (10):		24.00
Common Card:		1.50
Refractors:		1.5X
Atomics:		2X
1	Jeff Bagwell, Todd Helton, Frank Thomas, Richie Sexson	3.00
2	Craig Biggio, Luis Castillo, Roberto Alomar, Desi Relaford	1.50
3	Chipper Jones, Scott Rolen, Wade Boggs, George Arias	3.50
4	Barry Larkin, Neifi Perez, Cal Ripken Jr., Mark Bellhorn	6.00
5	Larry Walker, Karim Garcia, Albert Belle, Ruben Rivera	1.50
6	Barry Bonds, Andruw Jones, Kenny Lofton, Donnie Sadler	6.00
7	Tony Gwynn, Vladimir Guerrero, Ken Griffey Jr., Ben Grieve	4.50
8	Mike Piazza, Ben Davis, Ivan Rodriguez, Jose Valentin	4.50
9	Greg Maddux, Jamey Wright, Mike Mussina, Bartolo Colon	3.50
10	Tom Glavine, Billy Wagner, Randy Johnson, Jarrod Washburn	1.50

1997 Bowman Pre-Production

The format for 1997 Bowman's base set was previewed in this sample issue distributed to card dealers and the hobby press. The samples are virtually identical to the issued versions of the same players' cards, except they carry a "PP" prefix to the number on back.

		NM/M
Complete Set (4):		9.00
Common Player:		1.50
PP1	Jose Cruz, Jr.	1.50
PP2	Andruw Jones	2.00
PP3	Derek Jeter	4.50
PP4	Sammy Sosa	3.00

1997 Bowman

The 1997 Bowman set consists of 440 base cards, an increase of 55 cards from the '96 set. Fronts have a player photo within a red or blue frame with black borders. Backs feature another color photo, along with 1996 statistics broken down by opponent. Players making their first appearance in a Bowman set have a "1st Bowman Card" designation on the card. Prospects' cards have red foil on front; veterans have blue. Inserts include International parallels, Certified Autographs, Scout's Honor Roll and Bowman's Best Previews. Cards were sold in 10-card packs with a suggested retail price of $2.50. Topps offered collectors a $125 guarantee on the value of the set through the year 2000.

		NM/M
Complete Set (440):		50.00
Complete Series 1 (221):		25.00
Complete Series 2 (219):		25.00
Common Player:		.10
Series 1 Pack (10):		2.00
Series 1 Wax Box (24):		35.00
Series 2 Pack (10):		2.00
Series 2 Wax Box (24):		35.00
1	Derek Jeter	2.00
2	Edgar Renteria	.10
3	Chipper Jones	1.00
4	Hideo Nomo	.40
5	Tim Salmon	.10
6	Jason Giambi	.50
7	Robin Ventura	.10
8	Tony Clark	.25
9	Barry Larkin	.25
10	Paul Molitor	.75
11	Bernard Gilkey	.10
12	Jack McDowell	.10
13	Andy Benes	.10
14	Ryan Klesko	.10
15	Mark McGwire	1.50
16	Ken Griffey Jr.	1.50
17	Robb Nen	.10
18	Cal Ripken Jr.	2.00
19	John Valentin	.10
20	Ricky Bottalico	.10
21	Mike Lansing	.10
22	Ryne Sandberg	1.00
23	Carlos Delgado	.50
24	Craig Biggio	.25
25	Eric Karros	.10
26	Kevin Appier	.10
27	Mariano Rivera	.10
28	Vinny Castilla	.10
29	Juan Gonzalez	.40
30	Al Martin	.10
31	Jeff Cirillo	.10
32	Eddie Murray	.75
33	Ray Lankford	.10
34	Manny Ramirez	.75
35	Roberto Alomar	.25
36	Will Clark	.25
37	Chuck Knoblauch	.10
38	Harold Baines	.10
39	Trevor Hoffman	.10
40	Edgar Martinez	.10
41	Geronimo Berroa	.10
42	Rey Ordonez	.10
43	Mike Stanley	.10
44	Mike Mussina	.40
45	Kevin Brown	.10
46	Dennis Eckersley	.50
47	Henry Rodriguez	.10
48	Tino Martinez	.10
49	Eric Young	.10
50	Bret Boone	.10
51	Raul Mondesi	.10
52	Sammy Sosa	1.00
53	John Smoltz	.25
54	Billy Wagner	.10
55	Jeff D'Amico	.10
56	Ken Caminiti	.10
57	Jason Kendall	.10
58	Wade Boggs	.75
59	Andres Galarraga	.10
60	Jeff Brantley	.10
61	Mel Rojas	.10
62	Brian Hunter	.10
63	Bobby Bonilla	.10
64	Roger Clemens	1.50
65	Jeff Kent	.20
66	Matt Williams	.10
67	Albert Belle	.10
68	Jeff King	.10
69	John Wetteland	.10
70	Deion Sanders	.25
71	Bubba Trammell RC	.25
72	Felix Heredia RC	.25
73	Billy Koch RC	.25
74	Sidney Ponson RC	.25
75	Ricky Ledee RC	.25
76	Brett Tomko	.10
77	Braden Looper RC	.25
78	Damian Jackson	.10
79	Jason Dickson	.10
80	Chad Green RC	.10
81	R.A. Dickey RC	.10
82	Jeff Liefer	.10
83	Matt Wagner	.10
84	Richard Hidalgo	.10
85	Adam Riggs	.10
86	Robert Smith	.10
87	Chad Hermansen RC	.10
88	Felix Martinez	.10
89	J.J. Johnson	.10
90	Todd Dunwoody	.10
91	Katsuhiro Maeda	.10
92	Darin Erstad	.25
93	Elieser Marrero	.10
94	Bartolo Colon	.10
95	Chris Fussell	.10
96	Ugueth Urbina	.10
97	Josh Paul RC	.10
98	Jaime Bluma	.10
99	Seth Greisinger RC	.10
100	Jose Cruz RC	.25
101	Todd Dunn	.10
102	Joe Young RC	.10
103	Jonathan Johnson	.10
104	Justin Towle RC	.10
105	Brian Rose	.10
106	Jose Guillen	.10
107	Andruw Jones	.75
108	Mark Kotsay RC	1.00
109	Wilton Guerrero	.10
110	Jacob Cruz	.10
111	Mike Sweeney	.10
112	Julio Mosquera	.10
113	Matt Morris	.10
114	Wendell Magee	.10
115	John Thomson	.10
116	Javier Valentin RC	.10
117	Tom Fordham	.10
118	Ruben Rivera	.10
119	Mike Drumright RC	.10
120	Chris Holt	.10
121	Sean Maloney RC	.10
122	Michael Barrett	.10
123	Tony Saunders RC	.10
124	Kevin Brown	.10
125	Richard Almanzar	.10
126	Mark Redman	.10
127	Anthony Sanders RC	.10
128	Jeff Abbott	.10
129	Eugene Kingsale	.10
130	Paul Konerko	.40
131	Randall Simon RC	.25
132	Andy Larkin	.10
133	Rafael Medina	.10
134	Mendy Lopez	.10
135	Freddy Garcia	.10
136	Karim Garcia	.15
137	Larry Rodriguez RC	.10
138	Carlos Guillen	.10
139	Aaron Boone	.10
140	Donnie Sadler	.10
141	Brooks Kieschnick	.10
142	Scott Spiezio	.10
143	Everett Stull	.10
144	Enrique Wilson	.10
145	Milton Bradley RC	1.50
146	Kevin Orie	.10
147	Derek Wallace	.10
148	Russ Johnson	.10
149	Joe Lagarde RC	.10
150	Luis Castillo	.10
151	Jay Payton	.10
152	Joe Long	.10
153	Livan Hernandez	.10
154	Vladimir Nunez RC	.15
155	Not issued	.00
156a	George Arias	.10
156b	Calvin Reese (Should be #155.)	.10
157	Homer Bush	.10
158	Not issued	.00
159a	Eric Milton RC	.50
159b	Chris Carpenter (Should be #158.)	.50
160	Richie Sexson	.40
161	Carl Pavano	.10
162	Chris Gissell RC	.10
163	Mac Suzuki	.10
164	Pat Cline	.10
165	Ron Wright	.10
166	Dante Powell	.10
167	Mark Bellhorn	.10
168	George Lombard	.10
169	Pee Wee Lopez RC	.10
170	Paul Wilder RC	.10
171	Brad Fullmer	.10
172	Willie Martinez RC	.10
173	Dario Veras RC	.10
174	Dave Coggin	.10
175	Kris Benson	1.00
176	Torii Hunter	.25
177	D.T. Cromer RC	.10
178	Nelson Figueroa RC	.10
179	Hiram Bocachica RC	.15
180	Shane Monahan	.10
181	Jimmy Anderson RC	.10
182	Juan Melo	.10
183	Pablo Ortega RC	.10
184	Calvin Pickering RC	.50
185	Reggie Taylor	.10
186	Jeff Farnsworth RC	.10
187	Terrence Long	.10
188	Geoff Jenkins	.10
189	Steve Rain RC	.10
190	Nerio Rodriguez RC	.10
191	Derrick Gibson	.10
192	Darin Blood	.10
193	Ben Davis	.10
194	Adrian Beltre RC	2.00
195	Damian Sapp RC	.10
196	Kerry Wood RC	3.00
197	Nate Rolison RC	.10
198	Fernando Tatis RC	.25
199	Brad Penny RC	2.00
200	Jake Westbrook RC	.15
201	Edwin Diaz	.10
202	Joe Fontenot RC	.10
203	Matt Halloran RC	.10
204	Blake Stein RC	.10
205	Onan Masaoka	.10
206	Ben Petrick	.10
207	Matt Clement RC	1.00
208	Todd Greene	.10
209	Ray Ricken	.10
210	Eric Chavez RC	3.00
211	Edgard Velazquez	.10
212	Bruce Chen RC	.10
213	Danny Patterson RC	.10
214	Jeff Yoder	.10
215	Luis Ordaz RC	.10
216	Chris Widger	.10
217	Jason Brester	.10
218	Carlton Loewer	.10
219	Chris Reitsma RC	.10
220	Neifi Perez	.10
221	Hideki Irabu RC	.25
222	Ellis Burks	.10
223	Pedro Martinez	.75
224	Kenny Lofton	.10
225	Randy Johnson	.75
226	Terry Steinbach	.10
227	Bernie Williams	.25
228	Dean Palmer	.10
229	Alan Benes	.10
230	Marquis Grissom	.10
231	Gary Sheffield	.40
232	Curt Schilling	.10
233	Reggie Sanders	.10
234	Bobby Higginson	.10
235	Moises Alou	.20
236	Tom Glavine	.25
237	Mark Grace	.25
238	Ramon Martinez	.10
239	Rafael Palmeiro	.50
240	John Olerud	.10
241	Dante Bichette	.10
242	Greg Vaughn	.10
243	Jeff Bagwell	.50
244	Barry Bonds	2.00
245	Pat Hentgen	.10
246	Jim Thome	.50
247	Jermaine Allensworth	.10
248	Andy Pettitte	.25
249	Jay Bell	.10
250	John Jaha	.10
251	Jim Edmonds	.25
252	Ron Gant	.10
253	David Cone	.10
254	Jose Canseco	.40
255	Jay Buhner	.10
256	Greg Maddux	1.50
257	Brian McRae	.10
258	Lance Johnson	.10
259	Travis Fryman	.10
260	Paul O'Neill	.20
261	Ivan Rodriguez	.50
262	Gregg Jefferies	.10
263	Fred McGriff	.20
264	Derek Bell	.10
265	Jeff Conine	.10
266	Mike Piazza	1.50
267	Mark Grudzielanek	.10
268	Brady Anderson	.10
269	Marty Cordova	.10
270	Ray Durham	.10
271	Joe Carter	.10
272	Brian Jordan	.10
273	David Justice	.10
274	Tony Gwynn	1.00
275	Larry Walker	.20
276	Cecil Fielder	.10
277	Mo Vaughn	.10
278	Alex Fernandez	.10
279	Michael Tucker	.10
280	Jose Valentin	.10
281	Sandy Alomar	.10
282	Todd Hollandsworth	.10
283	Rico Brogna	.10
284	Rusty Greer	.10
285	Roberto Hernandez	.10
286	Hal Morris	.10
287	Johnny Damon	.75
288	Todd Hundley	.10
289	Rondell White	.10
290	Frank Thomas	.75
291	Don Denbow RC	.10
292	Derrek Lee	.50
293	Todd Walker	.10
294	Scott Rolen	.50
295	Wes Helms	.10
296	Bob Abreu	.25
297	John Patterson RC	1.50
298	Alex Gonzalez RC	.25
299	Grant Roberts RC	.10
300	Jeff Suppan	.10
301	Luke Wilcox	.10
302	Marlon Anderson	.10
303	Ray Brown	.10
304	Mike Caruso RC	.10
305	Sam Marsonek RC	.10
306	Brady Raggio RC	.10
307	Kevin McGlinchy RC	.10
308	Roy Halladay	3.00
309	Jeremi Gonzalez RC	.25
310	Aramis Ramirez RC	4.00
311	Dermal Brown RC	.10
312	Justin Thompson	.10
313	Jay Tessmer RC	.10
314	Mike Johnson	.10
315	Danny Clyburn	.10
316	Bruce Aven	.10
317	Keith Foulke RC	1.50
318	Jimmy Osting RC	.10
319	Valerio De Los Santos RC	.10
320	Shannon Stewart	.10
321	Willie Adams	.10
322	Larry Barnes	.10
323	Mark Johnson	.10
324	Chris Stowers RC	.10
325	Brandon Reed	.10
326	Randy Winn	.10
327	Steven Chavez	.10
328	Nomar Garciaparra	1.00
329	Jacque Jones RC	.10
330	Chris Clemons	.10
331	Todd Helton	.50
332	Ryan Brannan RC	.10
333	Alex Sanchez RC	.25
334	Arnold Gooch	.10
335	Russell Branyan	.10
336	Daryle Ward	.10
337	John LeRoy RC	.10
338	Steve Cox	.10
339	Kevin Witt	.10
340	Norm Hutchins	.10
341	Gabby Martinez	.10
342	Kris Detmers	.10
343	Mike Villano RC	.10
344	Preston Wilson	.10
345	Jim Manias RC	.10
346	Deivi Cruz RC	.25
347	Donzell McDonald RC	.10
348	Rod Myers RC	.10
349	Shawn Chacon RC	.25
350	Elvin Hernandez RC	.10
351	Orlando Cabrera RC	1.00
352	Brian Banks	.10
353	Robbie Bell	.10
354	Brad Rigby	.10
355	Scott Elarton	.10
356	Kevin Sweeney RC	.10
357	Steve Soderstrom	.10
358	Ryan Nye	.10
359	Marlon Allen RC	.10
360	Donny Leon RC	.10
361	Garrett Neubart RC	.10
362	Abraham Nunez RC	.25
363	Adam Eaton RC	.50
364	Octavio Dotel RC	.40
365	Dean Crow RC	.10
366	Jason Baker RC	.10
367	Sean Casey	.10
368	Joe Lawrence RC	.10
369	Adam Johnson RC	.10
370	Scott Schoeneweis RC	.25
371	Gerald Witasick Jr.	.10
372	Ronnie Belliard RC	.10
373	Russ Ortiz	.10
374	Robert Stratton RC	.10
375	Bobby Estalella	.10
376	Corey Lee RC	.10
377	Carlos Beltran	.50
378	Mike Cameron	.10
379	Scott Randall RC	.10
380	Corey Erickson RC	.10
381	Ian Canizaro	.10
382	Kerry Robinson RC	.10
383	Todd Noel RC	.10
384	A.J. Zapp RC	.10
385	Jarrod Washburn	.10
386	Ben Grieve	.10
387	Javier Vazquez RC	1.50
388	Tony Graffanino	.10
389	Travis Lee RC	.50
390	DaRond Stovall	.10
391	Dennis Reyes RC	.25
392	Danny Buxbaum	.10
393	Marc Lewis RC	.10
394	Kelvim Escobar RC	.25
395	Danny Klassen	.10
396	Ken Cloude RC	.25
397	Gabe Alvarez	.10
398	Jaret Wright RC	.50
399	Raul Casanova	.10
400	Clayton Brunner RC	.10
401	Jason Marquis RC	.50
402	Marc Kroon	.10
403	Jamey Wright	.10
404	Matt Snyder RC	.10
405	Josh Garrett RC	.10
406	Juan Encarnacion	.10
407	Heath Murray	.10
408	Brett Herbison RC	.10
409	Brent Butler RC	.25
410	Danny Peoples RC	.10
411	Miguel Tejada RC	10.00
412	Damian Moss	.10
413	Jim Pittsley	.10
414	Dmitri Young	.10
415	Glendon Rusch	.10
416	Vladimir Guerrero	.75
417	Cole Liniak RC	.10
418	Ramon Hernandez	.10
419	Cliff Politte RC	.25
420	Mel Rosario RC	.10
421	Jorge Carrion RC	.10
422	John Barnes RC	.10
423	Chris Stowe RC	.10
424	Vernon Wells RC	4.00
425	Brett Caradonna RC	.10
426	Scott Hodges RC	.10
427	Jon Garland RC	1.50
428	Nathan Haynes RC	.25
429	Geoff Goetz RC	.25
430	Adam Kennedy RC	.10
431	T.J. Tucker RC	.10
432	Aaron Akin RC	.10
433	Jayson Werth RC	.50
434	Glenn Davis RC	.10
435	Mark Mangum RC	.10
436	Troy Cameron RC	.10
437	J.J. Davis RC	.10
438	Lance Berkman RC	4.00
439	Jason Standridge RC	.25
440	Jason Dellaero RC	.10
441	Hideki Irabu RC	.25

Certified Autographs

Ninety players signed autographs for inclusion in Series 1 and 2 packs. Each autograph card features a gold-foil Certified Autograph stamp on front and can be found in one of three versions: Blue, 1:96 packs; black, 1:503 packs and gold, 1:1,509 packs. Derek Jeter's card can also be found in a green-ink autographed version, inserted one per 1,928 packs. Card numbers have a "CA" prefix.

		NM/M
Common Blue:		2.00
Black:		1.5X
Gold:		4X
Derek Jeter Green:		1.5X
1	Jeff Abbott	2.00
2	Bob Abreu	40.00
3	Willie Adams	2.00
4	Brian Banks	2.00
5	Kris Benson	15.00
6	Darin Blood	2.00
7	Jaime Bluma	2.00
8	Kevin Brown	5.00
9	Ray Brown	2.00
10	Homer Bush	2.00
11	Mike Cameron	8.00
12	Jay Canizaro	3.00
13	Luis Castillo	2.00
14	Dave Coggin	2.00
15	Bartolo Colon	15.00
16	Rocky Coppinger	3.00
17	Jacob Cruz	5.00
18	Jose Cruz	8.00
19	Jeff D'Amico	5.00
20	Ben Davis	5.00
21	Mike Drumbright	5.00
22	Scott Elarton	5.00
23	Darin Erstad	10.00
24	Bobby Estalella	5.00
25	Joe Fontenot	4.00
26	Tom Fordham	2.00
27	Brad Fullmer	5.00
28	Chris Fussell	2.00
29	Karim Garcia	5.00
30	Kris Detmers	2.00
31	Todd Greene	4.00
32	Ben Grieve	5.00
33	Vladimir Guerrero	75.00
34	Jose Guillen	15.00
35	Roy Halladay	65.00
36	Wes Helms	5.00
37	Chad Hermansen	3.00
38	Richard Hidalgo	8.00
39	Todd Hollandsworth	3.00
40	Damian Jackson	3.00
41	Derek Jeter	120.00
42	Andruw Jones	40.00
43	Brooks Kieschnick	3.00
44	Eugene Kingsale	5.00
45	Paul Konerko	15.00
46	Marc Kroon	2.00
47	Derrek Lee	40.00
48	Travis Lee	5.00
49	Terrence Long	4.00
50	Curt Lyons	2.00
51	Elieser Marrero	3.00
52	Rafael Medina	2.00
53	Juan Melo	3.00
54	Shane Monahan	2.00
55	Julio Mosquera	2.00
56	Heath Murray	2.00
57	Ryan Nye	2.00
58	Kevin Orie	4.00
59	Russ Ortiz	5.00
60	Carl Pavano	30.00
61	Jay Payton	5.00
62	Neifi Perez	3.00
63	Sidney Ponson	10.00
64	Calvin Reese	8.00
65	Ray Ricken	3.00
66	Brad Rigby	3.00
67	Adam Riggs	3.00
68	Ruben Rivera	4.00
69	J.J. Johnson	2.00
70	Scott Rolen	40.00
71	Tony Saunders	3.00
72	Donnie Sadler	5.00
73	Richie Sexson	15.00
74	Scott Spiezio	6.00
75	Everett Stull	2.00
76	Mike Sweeney	15.00
77	Fernando Tatis	4.00
78	Miguel Tejada	120.00
79	Justin Thompson	5.00
80	Justin Towle	6.00
81	Billy Wagner	20.00
82	Todd Walker	5.00
83	Luke Wilcox	2.00
84	Paul Wilder	4.00
85	Enrique Wilson	5.00
86	Kerry Wood	60.00
87	Jamey Wright	5.00
88	Ron Wright	5.00
89	Dmitri Young	10.00
90	Nelson Figueroa	2.00

International

Inserted at the rate of one per pack, the International parallel set replaces the regular photo background on front and back with the flag of the player's native land. Card #441 from the regular-issue version does not exist as an International parallel.

	NM/M
Complete Set (440):	75.00
Complete Series 1 (221):	40.00
Complete Series 2 (219):	40.00
Common Player:	.25
Stars and Rookies:	1.5X

(See 1997 Bowman for checklist and base card values.)

International Best

This Series 2 insert set features a flag design in the background of each card front depicting the player's country of origin. On back is another color photo, player personal data, a record of his best season and colored flags representing 14 nations which have sent players to the major leagues. One International Best card was inserted in every second series pack. Card numbers carry a "BBI" prefix. Refractor versions are a 1:48 parallel with Atomic Refractors found 1:96.

		NM/M
Complete Set (20):		20.00
Common Player:		.60
Refractors:		1.5X
Atomic Refractors:		2X
1	Frank Thomas	1.50
2	Ken Griffey Jr.	2.50
3	Juan Gonzalez	1.50
4	Bernie Williams	.60
5	Hideo Nomo	1.50
6	Sammy Sosa	3.50
7	Larry Walker	.60
8	Vinny Castilla	.75
9	Mariano Rivera	.75
10	Rafael Palmeiro	1.00
11	Nomar Garciaparra	3.50
12	Todd Walker	.60
13	Andruw Jones	1.50
14	Vladimir Guerrero	1.50
15	Ruben Rivera	.60
16	Bob Abreu	.75
17	Karim Garcia	.75
18	Katsuhiro Maeda	.60
19	Jose Cruz Jr.	1.00
20	Damian Moss	.60

Rookie of the Year Candidates

This 15-card insert was inserted in one per 12 packs of Bowman Series 2. Fronts feature a color shot of the player over a textured foil background, with the player's name across the bottom and the words "Rookie of the Year Favorites" across the top with the word "Rookie" in large script letters. Card numbers have a "ROY" prefix.

		NM/M
Complete Set (15):		9.00
Common Player:		.50
1	Jeff Abbott	.50
2	Karim Garcia	.50
3	Todd Helton	2.50
4	Richard Hidalgo	.50
5	Geoff Jenkins	.50
6	Russ Johnson	.50
7	Paul Konerko	.75
8	Mark Kotsay	.50
9	Ricky Ledee	.50
10	Travis Lee	.75
11	Derrek Lee	1.50
12	Elieser Marrero	.50
13	Juan Melo	.50
14	Brian Rose	.50
15	Fernando Tatis	.50

Scout's Honor Roll

This insert features 15 prospects deemed to have the most potential by Topps' scouts. Each card features a double-etched foil design and is inserted 1:12 packs.

		NM/M
Complete Set (15):		12.50
Common Player:		.50
1	Dmitri Young	.50
2	Bob Abreu	.75
3	Vladimir Guerrero	2.00
4	Paul Konerko	.75
5	Kevin Orie	.50
6	Todd Walker	.50
7	Ben Grieve	.50
8	Darin Erstad	1.00
9	Derrek Lee	1.00
10	Jose Cruz	.50
11	Scott Rolen	1.00
12	Travis Lee	.75
13	Andruw Jones	2.00
14	Wilton Guerrero	.50
15	Nomar Garciaparra	2.50

Best Preview

NOMAR GARCIAPARRA

This 20-card set, featuring 10 veterans and 10 prospects, is a preview of the format used in the Bowman's Best product. Three different versions of the Preview cards were available: Regular (1:12 packs), Refractors (1:48) and Atomic Refractors (1:96).

		NM/M
Complete Set (20):		30.00
Common Player:		.75
Refractors:		1.5X
Atomic Refractors:		2X
1	Frank Thomas	1.50
2	Ken Griffey Jr.	3.00
3	Barry Bonds	5.00
4	Derek Jeter	5.00
5	Chipper Jones	2.00
6	Mark McGwire	4.00
7	Cal Ripken Jr.	5.00
8	Kenny Lofton	.75
9	Gary Sheffield	.75
10	Jeff Bagwell	1.50
11	Wilton Guerrero	.75
12	Scott Rolen	1.00
13	Todd Walker	.75
14	Ruben Rivera	.75
15	Andruw Jones	1.50
16	Nomar Garciaparra	2.00
17	Vladimir Guerrero	1.00
18	Miguel Tejada	1.00
19	Bartolo Colon	.75
20	Katsuhiro Maeda	.75

1997 Bowman Chrome

DEREK JETER

Bowman Chrome was released in one 300-card series following the conclusion of the 1997 season. Four-card foil packs carried an SRP of $3. Each card reprints one of the regular Bowman set, utilizing chromium technology on front. Inserts include: In-

ternational parallels, Rookie of the Year Favorites and Scout's Honor Roll.

		NM/M
Complete Set (300):		150.00
Common Player:		.25
Pack (3):		5.00
Wax Box (24):		100.00
1	Derek Jeter	4.00
2	Chipper Jones	2.00
3	Hideo Nomo	.75
4	Tim Salmon	.25
5	Robin Ventura	.25
6	Tony Clark	.25
7	Barry Larkin	.50
8	Paul Molitor	1.00
9	Andy Benes	.25
10	Ryan Klesko	.25
11	Mark McGwire	3.00
12	Ken Griffey Jr.	2.50
13	Robb Nen	.25
14	Cal Ripken Jr.	4.00
15	John Valentin	.25
16	Ricky Bottalico	.25
17	Mike Lansing	.25
18	Ryne Sandberg	2.00
19	Carlos Delgado	1.00
20	Craig Biggio	.50
21	Eric Karros	.25
22	Kevin Appier	.25
23	Mariano Rivera	.75
24	Vinny Castilla	.25
25	Juan Gonzalez	.50
26	Al Martin	.25
27	Jeff Cirillo	.25
28	Ray Lankford	.25
29	Manny Ramirez	1.50
30	Roberto Alomar	.40
31	Will Clark	.50
32	Chuck Knoblauch	.25
33	Harold Baines	.25
34	Edgar Martinez	.25
35	Mike Mussina	.50
36	Kevin Brown	.25
37	Dennis Eckersley	.75
38	Tino Martinez	.25
39	Raul Mondesi	.25
40	Sammy Sosa	1.50
41	John Smoltz	.75
42	Billy Wagner	.25
43	Ken Caminiti	.25
44	Wade Boggs	1.50
45	Andres Galarraga	.25
46	Roger Clemens	3.00
47	Matt Williams	.25
48	Albert Belle	.25
49	Jeff King	.25
50	John Wetteland	.25
51	Deion Sanders	.50
52	Ellis Burks	.25
53	Pedro Martinez	1.50
54	Kenny Lofton	.50
55	Randy Johnson	1.50
56	Bernie Williams	.50
57	Marquis Grissom	.25
58	Gary Sheffield	.50
59	Curt Schilling	1.00
60	Reggie Sanders	.25
61	Bobby Higginson	.25
62	Moises Alou	.25
63	Tom Glavine	.50
64	Mark Grace	.50
65	Rafael Palmeiro	1.00
66	John Olerud	.25
67	Dante Bichette	.25
68	Jeff Bagwell	1.00
69	Barry Bonds	3.00
70	Pat Hentgen	.25
71	Jim Thome	1.00
72	Andy Pettitte	.25
73	Jay Bell	.25
74	Jim Edmonds	.25
75	Ron Gant	.25
76	David Cone	.25
77	Jose Canseco	.75
78	Jay Buhner	.25
79	Greg Maddux	2.50
80	Lance Johnson	.25
81	Travis Fryman	.25
82	Paul O'Neill	.25
83	Ivan Rodriguez	1.00
84	Fred McGriff	.25
85	Mike Piazza	2.50
86	Brady Anderson	.25
87	Marty Cordova	.25
88	Joe Carter	.25
89	Brian Jordan	.25
90	David Justice	.25
91	Tony Gwynn	2.00
92	Larry Walker	.40
93	Mo Vaughn	.25
94	Sandy Alomar	.25
95	Rusty Greer	.25
96	Roberto Hernandez	.25
97	Hal Morris	.25
98	Todd Hundley	.25
99	Rondell White	.25
100	Frank Thomas	1.50
101	Bubba Trammell RC	.25
102	Sidney Ponson RC	1.50
103	Ricky Ledee RC	.50
104	Brett Tomko	.25
105	Braden Looper RC	.50
106	Jason Dickson	.25
107	Chad Green RC	.25
108	R.A. Dickey RC	.25
109	Jeff Liefer	.25
110	Richard Hidalgo	.25
111	Chad Hermansen RC	.50
112	Felix Martinez	.25
113	J.J. Johnson	.25
114	Todd Dunwoody	.25
115	Katsuhiro Maeda	.25
116	Darin Erstad	.50
117	Elieser Marrero	.25
118	Bartolo Colon	.25
119	Ugueth Urbina	.25
120	Jaime Bluma	.25
121	Seth Greisinger RC	.50
122	Jose Cruz Jr. RC	1.50
123	Todd Dunn	.25
124	Justin Towle RC	.25
125	Brian Rose	.25
126	Jose Guillen	.25
127	Andruw Jones	1.50
128	Mark Kotsay RC	2.50
129	Wilton Guerrero	.25
130	Jacob Cruz	.25
131	Mike Sweeney	.25
132	Matt Morris	.25
133	John Thomson	.25
134	Javier Valentin RC	.25
135	Mike Drumright RC	.25
136	Michael Barrett	.25
137	Tony Saunders RC	.25
138	Kevin Brown	.25
139	Anthony Sanders RC	.25
140	Jeff Abbott	.25
141	Eugene Kingsale	.25
142	Paul Konerko	.50
143	Randall Simon RC	.50
144	Freddy Garcia	.25
145	Karim Garcia	.25
146	Carlos Guillen	.25
147	Aaron Boone	.25
148	Donnie Sadler	.25
149	Brooks Kieschnick	.25
150	Scott Spiezio	.25
151	Kevin Orie	.25
152	Russ Johnson	.25
153	Livan Hernandez	.25
154	Vladimir Nunez RC	.75
155	Calvin Reese	.25
156	Chris Carpenter	.25
157	Eric Milton RC	1.50
158	Richie Sexson	.50
159	Carl Pavano	.25
160	Pat Cline	.25
161	Ron Wright	.25
162	Dante Powell	.25
163	Mark Bellhorn	.25
164	George Lombard	.25
165	Paul Wilder	.25
166	Brad Fullmer	.25
167	Kris Benson	2.00
168	Torii Hunter	.50
169	D.T. Cromer	.25
170	Nelson Figueroa RC	.50
171	Hiram Bocachica RC	.50
172	Shane Monahan	.25
173	Juan Melo	.25
174	Calvin Pickering RC	1.50
175	Reggie Taylor	.25
176	Geoff Jenkins	.25
177	Steve Rain RC	.25
178	Nerio Rodriguez	.25
179	Derrick Gibson	.25
180	Darin Blood	.25
181	Ben Davis	.25
182	Adrian Beltre RC	8.00
183	Kerry Wood RC	8.00
184	Nate Rolison	.25
185	Fernando Tatis RC	.50
186	Jake Westbrook RC	2.00
187	Edwin Diaz	.25
188	Joe Fontenot RC	.50
189	Matt Halloran RC	.25
190	Matt Clement RC	3.00
191	Todd Greene	.25
192	Eric Chavez RC	10.00
193	Edgard Velazquez	.25
194	Bruce Chen RC	.25
195	Jason Brester	.25
196	Chris Reitsma RC	.50
197	Neifi Perez	.25
198	Hideki Irabu RC	.50
199	Don Denbow RC	.25
200	Derrek Lee	.75
201	Todd Walker	.25
202	Scott Rolen	1.00
203	Wes Helms	.25
204	Bob Abreu	.50
205	John Patterson RC	2.00
206	Alex Gonzalez RC	1.00
207	Grant Roberts RC	.50
208	Jeff Suppan	.25
209	Luke Wilcox	.25
210	Marlon Anderson	.25
211	Mike Caruso RC	.75
212	Roy Halladay RC	8.00
213	Jeremi Gonzalez RC	.50
214	Aramis Ramirez RC	10.00
215	Dermal Brown RC	.25
216	Justin Thompson	.25
217	Danny Clyburn	.25
218	Bruce Aven	.25
219	Keith Foulke RC	2.00
220	Shannon Stewart	.25
221	Larry Barnes	.25
222	Mark Johnson RC	.25
223	Randy Winn	.25
224	Nomar Garciaparra	2.00
225	Jacque Jones RC	4.00
226	Chris Clemons	.25
227	Todd Helton	1.00
228	Ryan Brannan RC	.25
229	Alex Sanchez RC	.50
230	Russell Branyan	.25
231	Daryle Ward	.25
232	Kevin Witt	.25
233	Gabby Martinez	.25
234	Preston Wilson	.25
235	Donzell McDonald RC	.25
236	Orlando Cabrera RC	5.00
237	Brian Banks	.25
238	Robbie Bell	.25
239	Brad Rigby	.25
240	Scott Elarton	.25
241	Donny Leon RC	.25
242	Abraham Nunez RC	1.00
243	Adam Eaton RC	2.00
244	Octavio Dotel RC	1.00
245	Sean Casey	.35
246	Joe Lawrence RC	.50
247	Adam Johnson RC	.25
248	Ronnie Belliard RC	1.00
249	Bobby Estalella	.25
250	Corey Lee RC	.25
251	Mike Cameron	.25
252	Kerry Robinson RC	.25
253	A.J. Zapp RC	.25
254	Jarrod Washburn RC	.25
255	Ben Grieve	.25
256	Javier Vazquez RC	3.00
257	Travis Lee RC	1.00
258	Dennis Reyes RC	.50
259	Danny Buxbaum	.25
260	Kelvim Escobar RC	1.00
261	Danny Klassen	.25
262	Ken Cloude RC	.50
263	Gabe Alvarez	.25
264	Clayton Brunner RC	.25
265	Jason Marquis RC	1.50
266	Jamey Wright	.25
267	Matt Snyder RC	.25
268	Josh Garrett RC	.25
269	Juan Encarnacion	.25
270	Heath Murray	.25
271	Brent Butler RC	1.00
272	Danny Peoples RC	.50
273	Miguel Tejada RC	30.00
274	Jim Pittsley	.25
275	Dmitri Young	.25
276	Vladimir Guerrero	1.50
277	Cole Liniak RC	.25
278	Ramon Hernandez	.25
279	Cliff Politte RC	.25
280	Mel Rosario RC	.25
281	Jorge Carrion RC	.25
282	John Barnes RC	.25
283	Chris Stowe RC	.25
284	Vernon Wells RC	15.00
285	Brett Caradonna RC	.25
286	Scott Hodges RC	.25
287	Jon Garland RC	4.00
288	Nathan Haynes RC	.50
289	Geoff Goetz RC	.50
290	Adam Kennedy RC	1.00
291	T.J. Tucker RC	.25
292	Aaron Akin RC	.25
293	Jayson Werth RC	2.50
294	Glenn Davis RC	.25
295	Mark Mangum RC	.25
296	Troy Cameron RC	.25
297	J.J. Davis RC	.25
298	Lance Berkman RC	15.00
299	Jason Standridge RC	.75
300	Jason Dellaero RC	.25

Refractors

All 300 cards in Bowman Chrome were reprinted in Refractor versions and inserted one per 12 packs. The cards are very similar to the base cards, but feature a refractive foil finish on front.

	NM/M
Common Player:	1.00
Stars:	4X

(See 1997 Bowman Chrome for checklist and base card values.)

International

Internationals paralleled all 300 cards in the base set with a flag from the player's native country in the background. These inserts were seeded one per four packs.

	NM/M
Common Player:	1.00
Stars:	3X

Inserted 1:4
(See 1997 Bowman Chrome for checklist and base card values.)

International Refractors

Each International parallel card was also reprinted in a Refractor version. International Refractors were seeded one per 24 packs.

	NM/M
Common Player:	2.00

Stars: 6X
(See 1997 Bowman Chrome for checklist and base card values.)

ROY Candidates

MARK KOTSAY

This 15-card insert set features color action photos of 1998 Rookie of the Year candidates printed on chromium finish cards. Card backs are numbered with a "ROY" prefix and were inserted one per 24 packs of Bowman Chrome. Refractor versions are seeded one per 72 packs.

		NM/M
Complete Set (15):		9.00
Common Player:		.50
Refractors:		1.5X
1	Jeff Abbott	.50
2	Karim Garcia	.75
3	Todd Helton	2.50
4	Richard Hidalgo	.50
5	Geoff Jenkins	.50
6	Russ Johnson	.50
7	Paul Konerko	1.00
8	Mark Kotsay	.50
9	Ricky Ledee	.50
10	Travis Lee	.75
11	Derrek Lee	1.50
12	Elieser Marrero	.50
13	Juan Melo	.50
14	Brian Rose	.50
15	Fernando Tatis	.50

Scout's Honor Roll

TODD WALKER

This 15-card set features top prospects and rookies as selected by the Topps' scouts. These chromium cards are numbered with a "SHR" prefix and are inserted one per 12 packs, while Refractor versions are seeded one per 36 packs.

		NM/M
Complete Set (15):		12.00
Common Player:		.50
Refractors:		1.5X
1	Dmitri Young	.50
2	Bob Abreu	.75
3	Vladimir Guerrero	2.00
4	Paul Konerko	.75
5	Kevin Orie	.50
6	Todd Walker	.50
7	Ben Grieve	.50
8	Darin Erstad	1.00
9	Derrek Lee	1.00
10	Jose Cruz, Jr.	.50
11	Scott Rolen	1.00
12	Travis Lee	.50
13	Andruw Jones	2.00
14	Wilton Guerrero	.50
15	Nomar Garciaparra	2.50

1997 Bowman's Best

The 200-card base set is divided into a 100-card subset featuring current stars on a gold-chromium stock, and 100 cards of top prospects in silver

DEION SANDERS

chromium. Packs contain six cards and were issued with a suggested retail price of $5. Autographed cards of 10 different players were randomly inserted into packs, with each player signing regular, Refractor and Atomic Refractor versions of their cards. Bowman's Best Laser Cuts and Mirror Image are the two other inserts, each with Refractor and Atomic Refractor editions.

		NM/M
Complete Set (200):		25.00
Common Player:		.25
Star Refractors:		4X
Star Atomics:		6X
Pack (6):		2.00
Wax Box (24):		40.00
1	Ken Griffey Jr.	1.50
2	Cecil Fielder	.25
3	Albert Belle	.25
4	Todd Hundley	.25
5	Mike Piazza	1.00
6	Matt Williams	.25
7	Mo Vaughn	.25
8	Ryne Sandberg	1.50
9	Chipper Jones	1.00
10	Edgar Martinez	.25
11	Kenny Lofton	.25
12	Ron Gant	.25
13	Moises Alou	.25
14	Pat Hentgen	.25
15	Steve Finley	.25
16	Mark Grace	.25
17	Jay Buhner	.25
18	Jeff Conine	.25
19	Jim Edmonds	.25
20	Todd Hollandsworth	.25
21	Andy Pettitte	.50
22	Jim Thome	.75
23	Eric Young	.25
24	Ray Lankford	.25
25	Marquis Grissom	.25
26	Tony Clark	.25
27	Jermaine Allensworth	.25
28	Ellis Burks	.25
29	Tony Gwynn	1.50
30	Barry Larkin	.25
31	John Olerud	.25
32	Mariano Rivera	.40
33	Paul Molitor	1.00
34	Ken Caminiti	.25
35	Gary Sheffield	.45
36	Al Martin	.25
37	John Valentin	.25
38	Frank Thomas	.75
39	John Jaha	.25
40	Greg Maddux	1.50
41	Alex Fernandez	.25
42	Dean Palmer	.25
43	Bernie Williams	.25
44	Deion Sanders	.25
45	Mark McGwire	2.00
46	Brian Jordan	.25
47	Bernard Gilkey	.25
48	Will Clark	.25
49	Kevin Appier	.25
50	Tom Glavine	.40
51	Chuck Knoblauch	.25
52	Rondell White	.25
53	Greg Vaughn	.25
54	Mike Mussina	.50
55	Brian McRae	.25
56	Chili Davis	.25
57	Wade Boggs	1.50
58	Jeff Bagwell	.75
59	Roberto Alomar	.35
60	Dennis Eckersley	.50
61	Ryan Klesko	.25
62	Manny Ramirez	1.00
63	John Wetteland	.25
64	Cal Ripken Jr.	2.00
65	Edgar Renteria	.25
66	Tino Martinez	.25
67	Larry Walker	.25
68	Gregg Jefferies	.25
69	Lance Johnson	.25
70	Carlos Delgado	.50
71	Craig Biggio	.25
72	Jose Canseco	.50
73	Barry Bonds	2.00
74	Juan Gonzalez	.50
75	Eric Karros	.25

76	Reggie Sanders	.25
77	Robin Ventura	.25
78	Hideo Nomo	.50
79	David Justice	.25
80	Vinny Castilla	.25
81	Travis Fryman	.25
82	Derek Jeter	2.00
83	Sammy Sosa	1.50
84	Ivan Rodriguez	.75
85	Rafael Palmeiro	.75
86	Roger Clemens	2.00
87	Jason Giambi	.50
88	Andres Galarraga	.25
89	Jermaine Dye	.25
90	Joe Carter	.25
91	Brady Anderson	.25
92	Derek Bell	.25
93	Randy Johnson	1.00
94	Fred McGriff	.25
95	John Smoltz	.25
96	Harold Baines	.25
97	Raul Mondesi	.25
98	Tim Salmon	.25
99	Carlos Baerga	.25
100	Dante Bichette	.25
101	Vladimir Guerrero	1.00
102	Richard Hidalgo	.25
103	Paul Konerko	.25
104	Alex Gonzalez RC	.50
105	Jason Dickson	.25
106	Jose Rosado	.25
107	Todd Walker	.25
108	Seth Greisinger RC	.40
109	Todd Helton	.75
110	Ben Davis	.25
111	Bartolo Colon	.25
112	Elieser Marrero	.25
113	Jeff D'Amico	.25
114	Miguel Tejada RC	8.00
115	Darin Erstad	.50
116	Kris Benson RC	1.00
117	Adrian Beltre RC	2.00
118	Neifi Perez	.25
119	Calvin Reese	.25
120	Carl Pavano	.25
121	Juan Melo	.25
122	Kevin McGlinchy RC	.50
123	Pat Cline	.25
124	Felix Heredia RC	.40
125	Aaron Boone	.25
126	Glendon Rusch	.25
127	Mike Cameron	.25
128	Justin Thompson	.25
129	Chad Hermansen RC	.25
130	Sidney Ponson RC	1.00
131	Willie Martinez	.25
132	Paul Wilder RC	.25
133	Geoff Jenkins	.25
134	Roy Halladay RC	2.00
135	Carlos Guillen	.25
136	Tony Batista	.25
137	Todd Greene	.25
138	Luis Castillo	.25
139	Jimmy Anderson RC	.25
140	Edgard Velazquez	.25
141	Chris Snopek	.25
142	Ruben Rivera	.25
143	Javier Valentin RC	.25
144	Brian Rose	.25
145	Fernando Tatis RC	.50
146	Dean Crow RC	.25
147	Karim Garcia	.25
148	Dante Powell	.25
149	Hideki Irabu RC	.40
150	Matt Morris	.25
151	Wes Helms	.25
152	Russ Johnson	.25
153	Jarrod Washburn	.25
154	Kerry Wood RC	4.00
155	Joe Fontenot RC	.25
156	Eugene Kingsale	.25
157	Terrence Long	.25
158	Calvin Maduro	.25
159	Jeff Suppan	.25
160	DaRond Stovall	.25
161	Mark Redman	.25
162	Ken Cloude RC	.25
163	Bobby Estalella	.25
164	Abraham Nunez RC	.75
165	Derrick Gibson	.25
166	Mike Drumright RC	.25
167	Katsuhiro Maeda	.25
168	Jeff Liefer	.25
169	Ben Grieve	.25
170	Bob Abreu	.25
171	Shannon Stewart	.25
172	Braden Looper RC	.40
173	Brant Brown	.25
174	Marlon Anderson	.25
175	Brad Fullmer	.25
176	Carlos Beltran	.25
177	Nomar Garciaparra	1.50
178	Derrek Lee	.75
179	Valerio De Los Santos RC	.25
180	Dmitri Young	.25
181	Jamey Wright	.25
182	Hiram Bocachica RC	.25
183	Wilton Guerrero	.25
184	Chris Carpenter	.25
185	Scott Spiezio	.25
186	Andruw Jones	1.00
187	Travis Lee RC	.75
188	Jose Cruz Jr.	1.00
189	Jose Guillen	.25
190	Jeff Abbott	.25
191	Ricky Ledee RC	.40
192	Mike Sweeney	.25
193	Donnie Sadler	.25
194	Scott Rolen	.75
195	Kevin Orie	.25
196	Jason Conti RC	.25
197	Mark Kotsay RC	.75
198	Eric Milton RC	1.00
199	Russell Branyan	.25
200	Alex Sanchez RC	.50

Autographs

SCOTT SPIEZIO

Ten different players each signed 10 regular versions of their respective Bowman's Best cards (1:170 packs), 10 of their Bowman's Best Refractors (1:2,036 packs) and 10 of their Bowman's Best Atomic Refractors (1:6,107 packs). Each autograph card features a special Certified Autograph stamp on the front.

		NM/M
Complete Set (10):		150.00
Common Player:		5.00
Refractors:		1.5X
Atomics:		2X
29	Tony Gwynn	30.00
33	Paul Molitor	20.00
82	Derek Jeter	100.00
91	Brady Anderson	7.50
98	Tim Salmon	10.00
107	Todd Walker	5.00
183	Wilton Guerrero	5.00
185	Scott Spiezio	5.00
188	Jose Cruz Jr.	6.00
194	Scott Rolen	20.00

Cuts

MARK McGWIRE

Each of these 20-card inserts features a laser-cut pattern in the chromium stock. Backs have another color photo and list several of the player's career "Bests." Three different versions of each card are available: Regular (1:24 packs), Refractor (1:48) and Atomic Refractor (1:96). Cards are numbered with a "BC" prefix.

		NM/M
Complete Set (20):		20.00
Common Player:		.35
Refractors:		1.5X
Atomic Refractors:		2X
1	Derek Jeter	4.00
2	Chipper Jones	1.50
3	Frank Thomas	1.00
4	Cal Ripken Jr.	4.00
5	Mark McGwire	3.00
6	Ken Griffey Jr.	2.00
7	Jeff Bagwell	1.00
8	Mike Piazza	2.00
9	Ken Caminiti	.35
10	Albert Belle	.35
11	Jose Cruz Jr.	.35
12	Wilton Guerrero	.35
13	Darin Erstad	.50
14	Andruw Jones	1.00
15	Scott Rolen	.75
16	Jose Guillen	.35
17	Bob Abreu	.35
18	Vladimir Guerrero	1.00
19	Todd Walker	.35
20	Nomar Garciaparra	1.50

Mirror Image

MIRROR IMAGE

RICHARD HIDALGO OF

This 10-card insert features four players on each double-sided card - two veterans and two rookies - utilizing Finest technology. Regular Mirror Image cards are found 1:48 packs, while Refractor versions are seeded 1:96 packs and Atomic Refractors are found 1:192 packs. Cards are numbered with an "MI" prefix.

		NM/M
Complete Set (10):		35.00
Common Card:		2.00
Refractors:		1.5X
Atomic Refractors:		2X
1	Nomar Garciaparra, Derek Jeter, Hiram Bocachica, Barry Larkin	7.50
2	Travis Lee, Frank Thomas, Derek Lee, Jeff Bagwell	3.50
3	Kerry Wood, Greg Maddux, Kris Benson, John Smoltz	3.50
4	Kevin Brown, Ivan Rodriguez, Elieser Marrero, Mike Piazza	5.00
5	Jose Cruz Jr., Ken Griffey Jr., Andruw Jones, Barry Bonds	7.50
6	Jose Guillen, Juan Gonzalez, Richard Hidalgo, Gary Sheffield	2.00
7	Paul Konerko, Mark McGwire, Todd Helton, Rafael Palmeiro	6.00
8	Wilton Guerrero, Craig Biggio, Donnie Sadler, Chuck Knoblauch	2.00
9	Russell Branyan, Matt Williams, Adrian Beltre, Chipper Jones	3.50
10	Bob Abreu, Kenny Lofton, Vladimir Guerrero, Albert Belle	3.00

Jumbos

MIKE PIAZZA

This large-format (4" x 5-5/8") version of 1997 Bowman's Best features 16 of the season's top stars and hottest rookies. Utilizing chromium, Refractor and Atomic Refractor technologies, the cards are identical in every way except size to the regular-issue Bowman's Best. The jumbos are sold only through Topps Stadium Club. Each of the sets consists of 12 chromium cards,

plus three randomly packaged Refractors and one Atomic Refractor. About 900 sets were produced according to Topps sales literature, which breaks down to 700 regular cards, 170 Refractors and 60 Atomic Refractors of each player.

		NM/M
Complete Set (16):		90.00
Common Player:		4.50
Refractor:		1.5X
Atomic Refractor:		2X
1	Ken Griffey Jr.	7.50
5	Mike Piazza	7.50
9	Chipper Jones	6.00
11	Kenny Lofton	4.50
29	Tony Gwynn	6.00
33	Paul Molitor	5.00
38	Frank Thomas	5.00
45	Mark McGwire	9.00
64	Cal Ripken Jr.	12.00
73	Barry Bonds	12.00
74	Juan Gonzalez	4.50
82	Derek Jeter	12.00
101	Vladimir Guerrero	5.00
177	Nomar Garciaparra	6.00
186	Andruw Jones	5.00
188	Jose Cruz, Jr.	4.50

1998 Bowman

ROBIN VENTURA

Bowman was a 441-card set released in a pair of 220-card series in 1998 (Orlando Hernandez, #221, was a late Series 1 addition.) Within each series are 150 prospects printed in a silver and blue design and 70 veterans printed in silver and red. Cards feature a Bowman seal, and in cases of a player's first Bowman card, a "Bowman Rookie Card" stamp is applied. The player's facsimile signature from his first contract runs down the side. The entire set was paralleled twice in Bowman International (one per pack) and Golden Anniversary (serially numbered to 50). Inserts in Series 1 include Autographs, Scout's Choice, and Japanese Rookies. Inserts in Series 2 include Autographs, 1999 Rookie of the Year Favorites, Minor League MVPs and Japanese Rookies.

		NM/M
Complete Set (441):		40.00
Series 1 (221):		20.00
Series 2 (220):		20.00
Common Player:		.10
Internationals:		1.5X
Inserted 1:1		
Series 1 Pack (10):		2.00
Series 1 Wax Box (24):		30.00
Series 2 Pack (10):		1.50
Series 2 Wax Box (24):		25.00
1	Nomar Garciaparra	1.50
2	Scott Rolen	.75
3	Andy Pettitte	.30
4	Ivan Rodriguez	.65
5	Mark McGwire	2.50
6	Jason Dickson	.10
7	Jose Cruz Jr.	.10
8	Jeff Kent	.10
9	Mike Mussina	.30
10	Jason Kendall	.10
11	Brett Tomko	.10
12	Jeff King	.10
13	Brad Radke	.10
14	Robin Ventura	.10
15	Jeff Bagwell	1.00
16	Greg Maddux	1.50
17	John Jaha	.10
18	Mike Piazza	2.00
19	Edgar Martinez	.10
20	David Justice	.10
21	Todd Hundley	.10
22	Tony Gwynn	1.50
23	Larry Walker	.10
24	Bernie Williams	.10

25	Edgar Renteria	.10
26	Rafael Palmeiro	.75
27	Tim Salmon	.10
28	Matt Morris	.10
29	Shawn Estes	.10
30	Vladimir Guerrero	1.00
31	Fernando Tatis	.10
32	Justin Thompson	.10
33	Ken Griffey Jr.	2.00
34	Edgardo Alfonzo	.10
35	Mo Vaughn	.10
36	Marty Cordova	.10
37	Craig Biggio	.10
38	Roger Clemens	1.75
39	Mark Grace	.10
40	Ken Caminiti	.10
41	Tony Womack	.10
42	Albert Belle	.10
43	Tino Martinez	.10
44	Sandy Alomar	.10
45	Jeff Cirillo	.10
46	Jason Giambi	.50
47	Darin Erstad	.25
48	Livan Hernandez	.10
49	Mark Grudzielanek	.10
50	Sammy Sosa	1.50
51	Curt Schilling	.30
52	Brian Hunter	.10
53	Neifi Perez	.10
54	Todd Walker	.10
55	Jose Guillen	.10
56	Jim Thome	.10
57	Tom Glavine	.30
58	Todd Greene	.10
59	Rondell White	.10
60	Roberto Alomar	.25
61	Tony Clark	.10
62	Vinny Castilla	.10
63	Barry Larkin	.10
64	Hideki Irabu	.10
65	Johnny Damon	.35
66	Juan Gonzalez	.50
67	John Olerud	.10
68	Gary Sheffield	.25
69	Raul Mondesi	.10
70	Chipper Jones	1.50
71	David Ortiz	.50
72	Warren Morris RC	.50
73	Alex Gonzalez	.10
74	Nick Bierbrodt	.10
75	Roy Halladay	.10
76	Danny Buxbaum	.10
77	Adam Kennedy	.10
78	Jared Sandberg RC	.75
79	Michael Barrett	.10
80	Gil Meche	.10
81	Jayson Werth	.10
82	Abraham Nunez	.10
83	Ben Petrick	.10
84	Brett Caradonna	.10
85	Mike Lowell RC	2.00
86	Clay Bruner RC	.10
87	John Curtice RC	.10
88	Bobby Estalella	.10
89	Juan Melo	.10
90	Arnold Gooch	.10
91	Kevin Millwood RC	1.00
92	Richie Sexson	.10
93	Orlando Cabrera	.10
94	Pat Cline	.10
95	Anthony Sanders	.10
96	Russ Johnson	.10
97	Ben Grieve	.10
98	Kevin McGlinchy	.10
99	Paul Wilder	.10
100	Russ Ortiz	.10
101	Ryan Jackson RC	.10
102	Heath Murray	.10
103	Brian Rose	.10
104	Ryan Radmanovich RC	.10
105	Ricky Ledee	.10
106	Jeff Wallace RC	.10
107	Ryan Minor RC	.10
108	Dennis Reyes	.10
109	James Manias RC	.10
110	Chris Carpenter	.10
111	Daryle Ward	.10
112	Vernon Wells	.10
113	Chad Green	.10
114	Mike Stoner RC	.10
115	Brad Fullmer	.10
116	Adam Eaton	.10
117	Jeff Liefer	.10
118	Corey Koskie RC	1.00
119	Todd Helton	.75
120	Jaime Jones RC	.10
121	Mel Rosario	.10
122	Geoff Goetz	.10
123	Adrian Beltre	.40
124	Jason Dellaero	.10
125	Gabe Kapler RC	.50
126	Scott Schoeneweis	.10
127	Ryan Brannan	.10
128	Aaron Akin	.10
129	Ryan Anderson RC	.25
130	Brad Penny	.10
131	Bruce Chen	.10
132	Eli Marrero	.10
133	Eric Chavez	.10
134	Troy Glaus RC	4.00
135	Troy Cameron	.10
136	Brian Sikorski RC	.10
137	Mike Kinkade RC	.25
138	Braden Looper	.10
139	Mark Mangum	.10
140	Danny Peoples	.10
141	J.J. Davis	.10
142	Ben Davis	.10

#	Player	Price	#	Player	Price	#	Player	Price
143	Jacque Jones	.10	261	Jose Valentin	.10	379	Julio Ramirez RC	.10
144	Derrick Gibson	.10	262	Andruw Jones	1.00	380	Seth Greisinger	.10
145	Bronson Arroyo	.10	263	Kenny Rogers	.10	381	Mike Judd RC	.10
146	Cristian Guzman RC	.50	264	Moises Alou	.10	382	Ben Ford RC	.10
147	Jeff Abbott	.10	265	Denny Neagle	.10	383	Tom Bennett	.10
148	Mike Cuddyer RC	1.00	266	Ugueth Urbina	.10	384	Adam Butler RC	.10
149	Jason Romano	.10	267	Derrek Lee	.45	385	Wade Miller RC	.75
150	Shane Monahan	.10	268	Ellis Burks	.10	386	Kyle Peterson RC	.10
151	Ntema Ndungidi RC	.10	269	Mariano Rivera	.30	387	Tommy Peterman RC	.10
152	Alex Sanchez	.10	270	Dean Palmer	.10	388	Onan Masaoka	.10
153	Jack Cust RC	.50	271	Eddie Taubensee	.10	389	Jason Rakers RC	.10
154	Brent Butler	.10	272	Brady Anderson	.10	390	Rafael Medina	.10
155	Ramon Hernandez	.10	273	Brian Giles	.10	391	Luis Lopez	.10
156	Norm Hutchins	.10	274	Quinton McCracken	.10	392	Jeff Yoder	.10
157	Jason Marquis	.10	275	Henry Rodriguez	.10	393	Vance Wilson RC	.25
158	Jacob Cruz	.10	276	Andres Galarraga	.10	394	Fernando Seguignol RC	.25
159	Rob Burger RC	.10	277	Jose Canseco	.45	395	Ron Wright	.10
160	Eric Milton	.10	278	David Segui	.10	396	Ruben Mateo RC	.40
161	Preston Wilson	.10	279	Bret Saberhagen	.10	397	Steve Lomasney RC	.25
162	Jason Fitzgerald RC	.10	280	Kevin Brown	.10	398	Damian Jackson	.10
163	Dan Serafini	.10	281	Chuck Knoblauch	.10	399	Mike Jerzembeck RC	.10
164	Peter Munro	.10	282	Jeromy Burnitz	.10	400	Luis Rivas RC	.25
165	Trot Nixon	.10	283	Jay Bell	.10	401	Kevin Burford RC	.10
166	Homer Bush	.10	284	Manny Ramirez	1.00	402	Glenn Davis	.10
167	Dermal Brown	.10	285	Rick Helling	.10	403	Robert Luce RC	.10
168	Chad Hermansen	.10	286	Francisco Cordova	.10	404	Cole Liniak	.10
169	Julio Moreno	.20	287	Bob Abreu	.20	405	Matthew LeCroy RC	.20
170	John Roskos RC	.10	288	J.T. Snow Jr.	.10	406	Jeremy Giambi RC	.40
171	Grant Roberts	.10	289	Hideo Nomo	.50	407	Shawn Chacon	.10
172	Ken Cloude	.10	290	Brian Jordan	.10	408	Dewayne Wise RC	.10
173	Jason Brester	.10	291	Javy Lopez	.10	409	Steve Woodard RC	.10
174	Jason Conti	.10	292	Travis Lee	.10	410	Francisco Cordero RC	.25
175	Jon Garland	.10	293	Russell Branyan	.10	411	Damon Minor RC	.20
176	Robbie Bell	.10	294	Paul Konerko	.10	412	Lou Collier	.10
177	Nathan Haynes	.10	295	Masato Yoshii RC	.50	413	Justin Towle	.10
178	Ramon Ortiz RC	.50	296	Kris Benson	.10	414	Juan LeBron	.10
179	Shannon Stewart	.10	297	Juan Encarnacion	.10	415	Michael Coleman	.10
180	Pablo Ortega	.10	298	Eric Milton	.10	416	Felix Rodriguez	.10
181	Jimmy Rollins RC	2.50	299	Mike Caruso	.10	417	Paul Ah Yat RC	.10
182	Sean Casey	.30	300	Ricardo Aramboles RC	.10	418	Kevin Barker RC	.10
183	Ted Lilly RC	.25	301	Bobby Smith	.10	419	Brian Meadows	.10
184	Chris Enochs RC	.10	302	Billy Koch	.10	420	Darnell McDonald RC	.20
185	Magglio Ordonez RC	3.00	303	Richard Hidalgo	.10	421	Matt Kinney RC	.25
186	Mike Drumright	.10	304	Justin Baughman RC	.10	422	Mike Vavrek RC	.10
187	Aaron Boone	.10	305	Chris Gissell	.10	423	Courtney Duncan RC	.10
188	Matt Clement	.10	306	Donnie Bridges RC	.10	424	Kevin Millar RC	.50
189	Todd Dunwoody	.10	307	Nelson Lara RC	.10	425	Ruben Rivera	.10
190	Larry Rodriguez	.10	308	Randy Wolf RC	1.00	426	Steve Shoemaker RC	.10
191	Todd Noel	.10	309	Jason LaRue RC	.25	427	Dan Reichert RC	.10
192	Geoff Jenkins	.10	310	Jason Gooding RC	.10	428	Carlos Lee RC	2.00
193	George Lombard	.10	311	Edgar Clemente RC	.10	429	Rod Barajas	.10
194	Lance Berkman	.10	312	Andrew Vessel	.10	430	Pablo Ozuna RC	.20
195	Marcus McCain RC	.10	313	Chris Reitsma	.10	431	Todd Belitz RC	.10
196	Ryan McGuire	.10	314	Jesus Sanchez RC	.10	432	Sidney Ponson	.10
197	Jhensy Sandoval RC	.10	315	Buddy Carlyle RC	.10	433	Steve Carver RC	.10
198	Corey Lee	.10	316	Randy Winn	.10	434	Esteban Yan	.10
199	Mario Valdez	.10	317	Luis Rivera	.10	435	Cedrick Bowers RC	.10
200	Robert Fick RC	.20	318	Marcus Thames RC	1.50	436	Marlon Anderson	.10
201	Donnie Sadler	.10	319	A.J. Pierzynski	.10	437	Carl Pavano	.10
202	Marc Kroon	.10	320	Scott Randall	.10	438	Jae Weong Seo RC	.50
203	David Miller	.10	321	Damian Sapp	.10	439	Jose Taveras RC	.10
204	Jarrod Washburn	.10	322	Eddie Yarnell RC	.10	440	Matt Anderson RC	.25
205	Miguel Tejada	.30	323	Luke Allen RC	.10	441	Darron Ingram RC	.10
206	Raul Ibanez	.10	324	J.D. Smart	.10			
207	John Patterson	.10	325	Willie Martinez	.10			
208	Calvin Pickering	.10	326	Alex Ramirez	.10			
209	Felix Martinez	.10	327	Eric DuBose RC	.10			
210	Mark Redman	.10	328	Kevin Witt	.10			
211	Scott Elarton	.10	329	Dan McKinley RC	.10			
212	Jose Amado RC	.10	330	Cliff Politte	.10			
213	Kerry Wood	.40	331	Vladimir Nunez	.10			
214	Dante Powell	.10	332	John Halama RC	.25			
215	Aramis Ramirez	.10	333	Nerio Rodriguez	.10			
216	A.J. Hinch	.10	334	Desi Relaford	.10			
217	Dustin Carr RC	.10	335	Robinson Checo	.10			
218	Mark Kotsay	.10	336	John Nicholson RC	.10			
219	Jason Standridge	.10	337	Tom LaRosa RC	.10			
220	Luis Ordaz	.10	338	Kevin Nicholson RC	.10			
221	Orlando Hernandez RC	.50	339	Javier Vazquez	.10			
222	Cal Ripken Jr.	3.00	340	A.J. Zapp	.10			
223	Paul Molitor	1.00	341	Tom Evans	.10			
224	Derek Jeter	3.00	342	Kerry Robinson	.10			
225	Barry Bonds	3.00	343	Gabe Gonzalez RC	.10			
226	Jim Edmonds	.10	344	Ralph Milliard	.10			
227	John Smoltz	.10	345	Enrique Wilson	.10			
228	Eric Karros	.10	346	Elvin Hernandez	.10			
229	Ray Lankford	.10	347	Mike Lincoln RC	.10			
230	Rey Ordonez	.10	348	Cesar King RC	.10			
231	Kenny Lofton	.10	349	Cristian Guzman RC	1.00			
232	Alex Rodriguez	2.50	350	Donzell McDonald	.10			
233	Dante Bichette	.10	351	Jim Parque RC	.10			
234	Pedro Martinez	1.00	352	Mike Saipe RC	.10			
235	Carlos Delgado	.45	353	Carlos Febles RC	.40			
236	Rod Beck	.10	354	Dernell Stenson RC	.25			
237	Matt Williams	.10	355	Mark Osborne RC	.10			
238	Charles Johnson	.10	356	Odalis Perez RC	.40			
239	Rico Brogna	.10	357	Jason Dewey RC	.10			
240	Frank Thomas	1.00	358	Joe Fontenot	.10			
241	Paul O'Neill	.10	359	Jason Grilli RC	.10			
242	Jaret Wright	.10	360	Kevin Haverbusch RC	.25			
243	Brant Brown	.10	361	Jay Yennaco RC	.10			
244	Ryan Klesko	.10	362	Brian Buchanan	.10			
245	Chuck Finley	.10	363	John Barnes	.10			
246	Derek Bell	.10	364	Chris Fussell	.10			
247	Delino DeShields	.10	365	Kevin Gibbs RC	.10			
248	Chan Ho Park	.10	366	Joe Lawrence	.10			
249	Wade Boggs	1.50	367	DaRond Stovall	.10			
250	Jay Buhner	.10	368	Brian Fuentes RC	.10			
251	Butch Huskey	.10	369	Jimmy Anderson	.10			
252	Steve Finley	.10	370	Laril Gonzalez RC	.10			
253	Will Clark	.10	371	Scott Williamson RC	.40			
254	John Valentin	.10	372	Milton Bradley	.10			
255	Bobby Higginson	.10	373	Jason Halper RC	.10			
256	Darryl Strawberry	.10	374	Brent Billingsley RC	.10			
257	Randy Johnson	1.00	375	Joe DePastino RC	.10			
258	Al Martin	.10	376	Jake Westbrook	.10			
259	Travis Fryman	.10	377	Octavio Dotel	.10			
260	Fred McGriff	.10	378	Jason Williams RC	.10			

Golden Anniversary

This 441-card parallel set celebrates Bowman's 50th anniversary with a gold, rather than black, facsimile autograph on each card. Golden Anniversary cards were inserted in both Series 1 (1:237) and Series 2 (1:194) packs and are sequentially numbered to 50.

	NM/M
Common Player:	4.00
Veteran Stars:	15-30X
Young Stars:	5-10X
Rookie Cards:	5-10X

(See 1998 Bowman for checklist and base card values.)

International

All 441 cards in Bowman Series 1 and 2 are paralleled in an International version, with the player's native country highlighted. Background map designs and vital information were translated into the player's native language on these one per pack parallel cards.

	NM/M
Common Player:	.25
Stars:	1.5X
Inserted 1:1	

(See 1998 Bowman for checklist and base card values.)

Autographs

Nomar Garciaparra

Rookies and prospects are featured on the certified autograph cards found as '98 Bowman inserts. Each player signed cards in blue, silver and gold ink. The front of each autographed card bears a certification seal. Relative values in the current market come nowhere near reflecting those scarcities.

	NM/M
Common Player:	3.00
Inserted 1:149	
Silvers (1:992):	1.5-2.5X
Golds (1:2,976):	2-4X
1 Adrian Beltre	15.00
2 Brad Fullmer	5.00
3 Ricky Ledee	5.00
4 David Ortiz	35.00
5 Fernando Tatis	3.00
6 Kerry Wood	20.00
7 Mel Rosario	3.00
8 Cole Liniak	3.00
9 A.J. Hinch	5.00
10 Jhensy Sandoval	3.00
11 Jose Cruz Jr.	5.00
12 Richard Hidalgo	6.00
13 Geoff Jenkins	8.00
14 Carl Pavano	10.00
15 Richie Sexson	12.00
16 Tony Womack	3.00
17 Scott Rolen	20.00
18 Ryan Minor	5.00
19 Elieser Marrero	3.00
20 Jason Marquis	5.00
21 Mike Lowell	5.00
22 Todd Helton	20.00
23 Chad Green	3.00
24 Scott Elarton	5.00
25 Russell Branyan	5.00
26 Mike Drumright	3.00
27 Ben Grieve	5.00
28 Jacque Jones	8.00
29 Jared Sandberg	5.00
30 Grant Roberts	5.00
31 Mike Stoner	3.00
32 Brian Rose	3.00
33 Randy Winn	5.00
34 Justin Towle	3.00
35 Anthony Sanders	3.00
36 Rafael Medina	3.00
37 Corey Lee	3.00
38 Mike Kinkade	5.00
39 Norm Hutchins	3.00
40 Jason Brester	3.00
41 Ben Davis	5.00
42 Nomar Garciaparra	75.00
43 Jeff Liefer	3.00
44 Eric Milton	6.00
45 Preston Wilson	8.00
46 Miguel Tejada	30.00
47 Luis Ordaz	3.00
48 Travis Lee	5.00
49 Kris Benson	6.00
50 Jacob Cruz	3.00
51 Dermal Brown	3.00
52 Marc Kroon	3.00
53 Chad Hermansen	15.00
54 Roy Halladay	5.00
55 Eric Chavez	10.00
56 Jason Conti	3.00
57 Juan Encarnacion	5.00
58 Paul Wilder	3.00
59 Aramis Ramirez	15.00
60 Cliff Politte	3.00
61 Todd Dunwoody	5.00
62 Paul Konerko	10.00
63 Shane Monahan	3.00
64 Alex Sanchez	3.00
65 Jeff Abbott	3.00
66 John Patterson	3.00
67 Peter Munro	3.00
68 Jarrod Washburn	5.00
69 Derrek Lee	20.00
70 Ramon Hernandez	5.00

Japanese Rookies

Hideo Nomo (P) 11

Bowman offered collectors a chance to receive original 1991 BBM-brand Japanese rookie cards of three players. Series 1 had rookie cards of Hideo Nomo and Shigetoshi Hasegawa inserted in one per 2,685 packs, while Series 2 offered Hideki Irabu seeded one per 4,411 packs. Card numbers have a "BBM" prefix.

	NM/M
Complete Set (3):	15.00
Common Player:	5.00
11 Hideo Nomo	10.00
17 Shigetosi Hasegawa	5.00
Hideki Irabu	5.00

Minor League MVP

1990 Minor League MVP

This 11-card insert set features players who are former Minor League MVPs who had graduated to the majors. Minor League MVPs are seeded one per 12 packs of Series 2 and are numbered with a "MVP" prefix.

	NM/M
Complete Set (11):	9.00
Common Player:	.50
1 Jeff Bagwell	1.00
2 Andres Galarraga	.50
3 Juan Gonzalez	.60
4 Tony Gwynn	1.50
5 Vladimir Guerrero	1.00
6 Derek Jeter	3.00
7 Andruw Jones	1.00
8 Tino Martinez	.50
9 Manny Ramirez	1.00
10 Gary Sheffield	.60
11 Jim Thome	.65

Rookie of the Year Favorites

Rookie of the Year Favorites displays 10 players who had a legitimate shot at the 1999 ROY award in the opinion of the Bowman scouts. The insert was seeded one per 12 packs of Series 2 and numbered with an "ROY" prefix.

	NM/M
Complete Set (10):	6.00
Common Player:	.50
1 Adrian Beltre	.75
2 Troy Glaus	3.00
3 Chad Hermansen	.50
4 Matt Clement	.50
5 Eric Chavez	.75
6 Kris Benson	.50
7 Richie Sexson	.50
8 Randy Wolf	.50
9 Ryan Minor	.50
10 Alex Gonzalez	.50

Scout's Choice

Abraham Nunez

This Series 1 insert has players with potential for Major League stardom. Fronts have action photos with gold-foil highlights. Backs have a portrait photo and an assessment of the player's skills in the traditional five areas of raw talent. Cards are numbered with an "SC" prefix.

	NM/M
Complete Set (21):	8.00
Common Player:	.25
Inserted 1:12	
1 Paul Konerko	.50
2 Richard Hidalgo	.25
3 Mark Kotsay	.25
4 Ben Grieve	.25
5 Chad Hermansen	.25
6 Matt Clement	.25
7 Brad Fullmer	.25
8 Eli Marrero	.25
9 Kerry Wood	1.50
10 Adrian Beltre	1.50
11 Ricky Ledee	.25
12 Travis Lee	.25
13 Abraham Nunez	.25
14 Ryan Anderson	.25
15 Dermal Brown	.25
16 Juan Encarnacion	.25
17 Aramis Ramirez	.25
18 Todd Helton	2.50
19 Kris Benson	.25
20 Russell Branyan	.25
21 Mike Stoner	.25

1998 Bowman Chrome

Nomar Garciaparra

All 441 cards in Bowman 1 and 2 were reprinted with a chromium finish for Bowman Chrome. Chrome contains International and Golden Anniversary parallels, like Bowman. Internationals are seeded one per four packs, with Refractor versions every 24 packs. Golden Anniversary parallels are exclusive to hobby packs and inserted one per 164 packs and sequentially numbered to 50 sets. Refractor versions are seeded one per 1,279 packs and numbered to just five sets. In addition, 50 Bowman Chrome Reprints were inserted with 25 in each series.

		NM/M
Complete Set (441):		100.00
Complete Series 1 (221):		60.00
Complete Series 2 (220):		50.00
Common Player:		.20
Series 1 Pack (4):		2.50
Series 2 Pack (4):		2.00
Series 1 Box (24):		45.00
Series 2 Box (24):		35.00
1	Nomar Garciaparra	1.00
2	Scott Rolen	.75
3	Andy Pettitte	.40
4	Ivan Rodriguez	.75
5	Mark McGwire	2.50
6	Jason Dickson	.20
7	Jose Cruz Jr.	.20
8	Jeff Kent	.20
9	Mike Mussina	.50
10	Jason Kendall	.20
11	Brett Tomko	.20
12	Jeff King	.20
13	Brad Radke	.20
14	Robin Ventura	.20
15	Jeff Bagwell	1.00
16	Greg Maddux	1.50
17	John Jaha	.20
18	Mike Piazza	2.00
19	Edgar Martinez	.20
20	David Justice	.20
21	Todd Hundley	.20
22	Tony Gwynn	1.50
23	Larry Walker	.20
24	Bernie Williams	.20
25	Edgar Renteria	.20
26	Rafael Palmeiro	.75
27	Tim Salmon	.20
28	Matt Morris	.20
29	Shawn Estes	.20
30	Vladimir Guerrero	1.00
31	Fernando Tatis	.20
32	Justin Thompson	.20
33	Ken Griffey Jr.	2.00
34	Edgardo Alfonzo	.20
35	Mo Vaughn	.20
36	Marty Cordova	.20
37	Craig Biggio	.20
38	Roger Clemens	2.00
39	Mark Grace	.20
40	Ken Caminiti	.20
41	Tony Womack	.20
42	Albert Belle	.20
43	Tino Martinez	.20
44	Sandy Alomar	.20
45	Jeff Cirillo	.20
46	Jason Giambi	.50
47	Darin Erstad	.45
48	Livan Hernandez	.20
49	Mark Grudzielanek	.20
50	Sammy Sosa	1.50
51	Curt Schilling	.50
52	Brian Hunter	.20
53	Neifi Perez	.20
54	Todd Walker	.20
55	Jose Guillen	.20
56	Jim Thome	.50
57	Tom Glavine	.40
58	Todd Greene	.20
59	Rondell White	.20
60	Roberto Alomar	.35
61	Tony Clark	.20
62	Vinny Castilla	.20
63	Barry Larkin	.20
64	Hideki Irabu	.20
65	Johnny Damon	.60
66	Juan Gonzalez	.50
67	John Olerud	.20
68	Gary Sheffield	.45
69	Raul Mondesi	.20
70	Chipper Jones	1.50
71	David Ortiz	.75
72	Warren Morris RC	.50
73	Alex Gonzalez	.20
74	Nick Bierbrodt	.20
75	Roy Halladay	.20
76	Danny Buxbaum	.20
77	Adam Kennedy	.20
78	Jared Sandberg RC	.50
79	Michael Barrett	.20
80	Gil Meche	.20
81	Jayson Werth	.20
82	Abraham Nunez	.20
83	Ben Petrick	.20
84	Brett Caradonna	.20
85	Mike Lowell RC	4.00
86	Clay Bruner RC	.20
87	John Curtice RC	.20
88	Bobby Estalella	.20
89	Juan Melo	.20
90	Arnold Gooch	.20
91	Kevin Millwood RC	4.00
92	Richie Sexson	.20
93	Orlando Cabrera	.20
94	Pat Cline	.20
95	Anthony Sanders	.20
96	Russ Johnson	.20
97	Ben Grieve	.50

98	Kevin McGlinchy	.20
99	Paul Wilder	.20
100	Russ Ortiz	.20
101	Ryan Jackson RC	.50
102	Heath Murray	.20
103	Brian Rose	.20
104	Ryan Radmanovich RC	.20
105	Ricky Ledee	.20
106	Jeff Wallace RC	.20
107	Ryan Minor RC	.45
108	Dennis Reyes	.20
109	James Manias RC	.20
110	Chris Carpenter	.20
111	Daryle Ward	.20
112	Vernon Wells	.20
113	Chad Green	.20
114	Mike Stoner RC	.20
115	Brad Fullmer	.20
116	Adam Eaton	.20
117	Jeff Liefer	.20
118	Corey Koskie RC	1.50
119	Todd Helton	.75
120	Jaime Jones RC	.20
121	Mel Rosario	.20
122	Geoff Goetz	.20
123	Adrian Beltre	.40
124	Jason Dellaero	.20
125	Gabe Kapler RC	1.00
126	Scott Schoeneweis	.20
127	Ryan Brannan	.20
128	Aaron Akin	.20
129	Ryan Anderson RC	.50
130	Brad Penny	.20
131	Bruce Chen	.20
132	Eli Marrero	.20
133	Eric Chavez	.35
134	Troy Glaus RC	10.00
135	Troy Cameron	.20
136	Brian Sikorski RC	.20
137	Mike Kinkade RC	.50
138	Braden Looper	.20
139	Mark Mangum	.20
140	Danny Peoples	.20
141	J.J. Davis	.20
142	Ben Davis	.20
143	Jacque Jones	.20
144	Derrick Gibson	.20
145	Bronson Arroyo	.20
146	Luis De Los Santos RC	.20
147	Jeff Abbott	.20
148	Mike Cuddyer RC	1.50
149	Jason Romano	.20
150	Shane Monahan	.20
151	Ntema Ndungidi RC	.20
152	Alex Sanchez	.20
153	Jack Cust RC	.50
154	Brent Butler	.20
155	Ramon Hernandez	.20
156	Norm Hutchins	.20
157	Jason Marquis	.20
158	Jacob Cruz	.20
159	Rob Burger RC	.20
160	Eric Milton	.20
161	Preston Wilson	.20
162	Jason Fitzgerald RC	.20
163	Dan Serafini	.20
164	Peter Munro	.20
165	Trot Nixon	.40
166	Homer Bush	.20
167	Dermal Brown	.20
168	Chad Hermansen	.20
169	Julio Moreno	.20
170	John Roskos RC	.20
171	Grant Roberts	.20
172	Ken Cloude	.20
173	Jason Brester	.20
174	Jason Conti	.20
175	Jon Garland	.20
176	Robbie Bell	.20
177	Nathan Haynes	.20
178	Ramon Ortiz RC	.50
179	Shannon Stewart	.20
180	Pablo Ortega	.20
181	Jimmy Rollins RC	8.00
182	Sean Casey	.45
183	Ted Lilly RC	.20
184	Chris Enochs RC	.20
185	Magglio Ordonez RC	3.00
186	Mike Drumright	.20
187	Aaron Boone	.20
188	Matt Clement	.20
189	Todd Dunwoody	.20
190	Larry Rodriguez	.20
191	Todd Noel	.20
192	Geoff Jenkins	.20
193	George Lombard	.20
194	Lance Berkman	.20
195	Marcus McCain RC	.20
196	Ryan McGuire	.20
197	Jhensy Sandoval RC	.20
198	Corey Lee	.20
199	Mario Valdez	.20
200	Robert Fick RC	.20
201	Donnie Sadler	.20
202	Marc Kroon	.20
203	David Miller	.20
204	Jarrod Washburn	.20
205	Miguel Tejada	.40
206	Raul Ibanez	.20
207	John Patterson	.20
208	Calvin Pickering	.20
209	Felix Martinez	.20
210	Mark Redman	.20
211	Scott Elarton	.20
212	Jose Amado RC	.20
213	Kerry Wood	.50
214	Dante Powell	.20
215	Aramis Ramirez	.20

216	A.J. Hinch	.20
217	Dustin Carr RC	.20
218	Mark Kotsay	.20
219	Jason Standridge RC	.20
220	Luis Ordaz	.20
221	Orlando Hernandez RC	3.00
222	Cal Ripken Jr.	3.00
223	Paul Molitor	1.00
224	Derek Jeter	3.00
225	Barry Bonds	3.00
226	Jim Edmonds	.20
227	John Smoltz	.20
228	Eric Karros	.20
229	Ray Lankford	.20
230	Rey Ordonez	.20
231	Kenny Lofton	.20
232	Alex Rodriguez	2.50
233	Dante Bichette	.20
234	Pedro Martinez	1.00
235	Carlos Delgado	.50
236	Rod Beck	.20
237	Matt Williams	.20
238	Charles Johnson	.20
239	Rico Brogna	.20
240	Frank Thomas	1.00
241	Paul O'Neill	.20
242	Jaret Wright	.20
243	Brant Brown	.20
244	Ryan Klesko	.20
245	Chuck Finley	.20
246	Derek Bell	.20
247	Delino DeShields	.20
248	Chan Ho Park	.20
249	Wade Boggs	1.50
250	Jay Buhner	.20
251	Butch Huskey	.20
252	Steve Finley	.20
253	Will Clark	.20
254	John Valentin	.20
255	Bobby Higginson	.20
256	Darryl Strawberry	.20
257	Randy Johnson	1.00
258	Al Martin	.20
259	Travis Fryman	.20
260	Fred McGriff	.20
261	Jose Valentin	.20
262	Andruw Jones	1.00
263	Kenny Rogers	.20
264	Moises Alou	.20
265	Denny Neagle	.20
266	Ugueth Urbina	.20
267	Derrek Lee	.50
268	Ellis Burks	.20
269	Mariano Rivera	.40
270	Dean Palmer	.20
271	Eddie Taubensee	.20
272	Brady Anderson	.20
273	Brian Giles	.20
274	Quinton McCracken	.20
275	Henry Rodriguez	.20
276	Andres Galarraga	.20
277	Jose Canseco	.40
278	David Segui	.20
279	Bret Saberhagen	.20
280	Kevin Brown	.20
281	Chuck Knoblauch	.20
282	Jeromy Burnitz	.20
283	Jay Bell	.20
284	Manny Ramirez	1.00
285	Rick Helling	.20
286	Francisco Cordova	.20
287	Bob Abreu	.30
288	J.T. Snow Jr.	.20
289	Hideo Nomo	.50
290	Brian Jordan	.20
291	Javy Lopez	.20
292	Aaron Akin RC	.20
293	Russell Branyan	.20
294	Paul Konerko	.20
295	Masato Yoshii RC	1.00
296	Kris Benson	.20
297	Juan Encarnacion	.20
298	Eric Milton	.20
299	Mike Caruso	.20
300	Ricardo Aramboles RC	.20
301	Bobby Smith	.20
302	Billy Koch	.20
303	Richard Hidalgo	.20
304	Justin Baughman RC	.20
305	Chris Gissell	.20
306	Donnie Bridges RC	.20
307	Nelson Lara RC	.20
308	Randy Wolf RC	1.00
309	Jason LaRue	.50
310	Jason Gooding RC	.20
311	Edgar Clemente RC	.20
312	Andrew Vessel	.20
313	Chris Reitsma	.20
314	Jesus Sanchez RC	.20
315	Buddy Carlyle RC	.20
316	Randy Winn	.20
317	Luis Rivera	.20
318	Marcus Thames RC	5.00
319	A.J. Pierzynski	.20
320	Scott Randall	.20
321	Damian Sapp	.20
322	Eddie Yarnell RC	.20
323	Luke Allen RC	.20
324	J.D. Smart	.20
325	Willie Martinez	.20
326	Alex Ramirez	.20
327	Eric DuBose RC	.20
328	Kevin Witt	.20
329	Dan McKinley RC	.20
330	Cliff Politte	.20
331	Vladimir Nunez	.20
332	John Halama RC	.50

333	Nerio Rodriguez	.20
334	Desi Relaford	.20
335	Robinson Checo	.20
336	John Nicholson RC	.20
337	Tom LaRosa RC	.20
338	Kevin Nicholson RC	.20
339	Javier Vazquez	.20
340	A.J. Zapp	.20
341	Tom Evans	.20
342	Kerry Robinson	.20
343	Gabe Gonzalez RC	.20
344	Ralph Milliard	.20
345	Enrique Wilson	.20
346	Elvin Hernandez	.20
347	Mike Lincoln RC	.35
348	Cesar King RC	.20
349	Cristian Guzman RC	.50
350	Donzell McDonald	.20
351	Jim Parque RC	.20
352	Mike Saipe RC	.20
353	Carlos Febles RC	.50
354	Dernell Stenson RC	.20
355	Mark Osborne RC	.20
356	Odalis Perez RC	2.00
357	Jason Dewey RC	.20
358	Joe Fontenot	.20
359	Jason Grilli RC	.40
360	Kevin Haverbusch RC	.20
361	Jay Yennaco RC	.20
362	Brian Buchanan	.20
363	John Barnes	.20
364	Chris Fussell	.20
365	Kevin Gibbs RC	.20
366	Joe Lawrence	.20
367	DaRond Stovall	.20
368	Brian Fuentes RC	.20
369	Jimmy Anderson	.20
370	Laril Gonzalez RC	.20
371	Scott Williamson RC	1.00
372	Milton Bradley	.20
373	Jason Halper RC	.20
374	Brent Billingsley RC	.20
375	Joe DePastino RC	.20
376	Jake Westbrook	.20
377	Octavio Dotel	.20
378	Jason Williams RC	.20
379	Julio Ramirez RC	.20
380	Seth Greisinger	.20
381	Mike Judd RC	.20
382	Ben Ford RC	.20
383	Tom Bennett RC	.20
384	Adam Butler RC	.20
385	Wade Miller RC	1.50
386	Kyle Peterson RC	.20
387	Tommy Peterman RC	.20
388	Onan Masaoka	.20
389	Jason Rakers RC	.20
390	Rafael Medina	.20
391	Luis Lopez	.20
392	Jeff Yoder	.20
393	Vance Wilson RC	.20
394	Fernando Seguignol RC	.35
395	Ron Wright	.20
396	Ruben Mateo RC	1.00
397	Steve Lomasney RC	.50
398	Damian Jackson	.20
399	Mike Jerzembeck RC	.20
400	Luis Rivas RC	.50
401	Kevin Burford RC	.20
402	Glenn Davis	.20
403	Robert Luce RC	.20
404	Cole Liniak	.20
405	Matthew LeCroy RC	.20
406	Jeremy Giambi RC	.50
407	Shawn Chacon	.20
408	Dewayne Wise RC	.20
409	Steve Woodard RC	.50
410	Francisco Cordero RC	.20
411	Damon Minor RC	.20
412	Lou Collier	.20
413	Justin Towle	.20
414	Juan LeBron	.20
415	Michael Coleman	.20
416	Felix Rodriguez	.20
417	Paul Ah Yat RC	.20
418	Kevin Barker RC	.20
419	Brian Meadows	.20
420	Darnell McDonald RC	.40
421	Matt Kinney RC	.20
422	Mike Vavrek RC	.20
423	Courtney Duncan RC	.20
424	Kevin Millar RC	1.50
425	Ruben Rivera	.20
426	Steve Shoemaker RC	.20
427	Dan Reichert RC	.20
428	Carlos Lee RC	6.00
429	Rod Barajas RC	.20
430	Pablo Ozuna RC	.50
431	Todd Belitz RC	.20
432	Sidney Ponson	.20
433	Steve Carver RC	.20
434	Esteban Yan RC	.20
435	Cedrick Bowers RC	.20
436	Marlon Anderson	.20
437	Carl Pavano	.20
438	Jae Weong Seo RC	1.00
439	Jose Taveras RC	.20
440	Matt Anderson RC	.50
441	Darron Ingram RC	.20

"Refractor" on the back in black letters directly under the card number.

	NM/M
Common Player:	2.00
Stars:	3X
Inserted 1:12	
Int'l Refractors:	6X
Inserted 1:24	

(See 1998 Bowman Chrome for checklist and base card values.)

Golden Anniversary

Golden Anniversary parallels were printed for all 441 cards in Bowman Chrome. They are exclusive to hobby packs, seeded one per 164 packs and sequentially numbered to 50 sets. Refractor versions were also available, numbered to just five sets and inserted one per 1,279 packs.

	NM/M
Common Player:	5.00
Stars:	20X
Common Refractor:	20.00

(See 1998 Bowman Chrome for checklist and base card values.)

International

All 441 cards throughout Bowman Chrome Series 1 and 2 were paralleled in International versions. Cards fronts have the regular background replaced by a map denoting the player's birthplace. Backs are written in the player's native language.

	NM/M
Common Player:	.50
Stars and Rookies:	1.5X
Inserted 1:4	

(See 1998 Bowman Chrome for checklist and base card values.)

Reprints

Bowman Chrome Reprints showcase 50 of the most popular rookie cards to appear in the brand since 1948. The 25 odd-numbered cards are found in Series 1; the evens in Series 2. The Reprints are numbered with a "BC" prefix.

		NM/M
Complete Set (50):		20.00
Common Player:		.25
Inserted 1:12		
Refractors:		1.5X
Inserted 1:36		
1	Yogi Berra	.50
2	Jackie Robinson	2.00
3	Don Newcombe	.25
4	Satchel Paige	.50
5	Willie Mays	2.00
6	Gil McDougald	.25

Refractors

Refractor versions for all 441 cards in Bowman Chrome Series 1 and 2 were created. The cards contained the word

7	Don Larsen	.25
8	Elston Howard	.25
9	Robin Ventura	.25
10	Brady Anderson	.25
11	Gary Sheffield	.35
12	Tino Martinez	.25
13	Ken Griffey Jr.	1.25
14	John Smoltz	.25
15	Sandy Alomar Jr.	.25
16	Larry Walker	.25
17	Todd Hundley	.25
18	Mo Vaughn	.25
19	Sammy Sosa	1.00
20	Frank Thomas	.50
21	Chuck Knoblauch	.25
22	Bernie Williams	.25
23	Juan Gonzalez	.40
24	Mike Mussina	.25
25	Jeff Bagwell	.50
26	Tim Salmon	.25
27	Ivan Rodriguez	.35
28	Kenny Lofton	.25
29	Chipper Jones	1.00
30	Javier Lopez	.25
31	Ryan Klesko	.25
32	Raul Mondesi	.25
33	Jim Thome	.35
34	Carlos Delgado	.25
35	Mike Piazza	1.25
36	Manny Ramirez	.50
37	Andy Pettitte	.35
38	Derek Jeter	2.00
39	Brad Fullmer	.25
40	Richard Hidalgo	.25
41	Tony Clark	.25
42	Andruw Jones	.50
43	Vladimir Guerrero	.50
44	Nomar Garciaparra	1.00
45	Paul Konerko	.25
46	Ben Grieve	.35
47	Hideo Nomo	.40
48	Scott Rolen	.40
49	Jose Guillen	.25
50	Livan Hernandez	.25

1998 Bowman's Best

Bowman's Best was issued in a single 200-card series comprised of 100 prospects and 100 veterans. Prospects are shown on a silver background, while the veterans are showcased on gold. The set was paralleled twice: A Refractor version is seeded one per 20 packs and sequentially numbered to 400, while an Atomic Refractor version is a 1:82 find and numbered to 100 sets. Inserts include regular, Refractor and Atomic Refractor versions of: Autographs, Mirror Image and Performers.

		NM/M
Complete Set (200):		30.00
Common Player:		.25
Refractors:		8X
Production 400 Sets		
Atomic Refractors:		12X
Production 100 Sets		
Pack (6):		2.50
Wax Box (24):		35.00
1	Mark McGwire	2.00
2	Hideo Nomo	.50
3	Barry Bonds	3.00
4	Dante Bichette	.25
5	Chipper Jones	1.50
6	Frank Thomas	1.00
7	Kevin Brown	.25
8	Juan Gonzalez	.50
9	Jay Buhner	.25
10	Chuck Knoblauch	.25
11	Cal Ripken Jr.	3.00
12	Matt Williams	.25
13	Jim Edmonds	.25
14	Manny Ramirez	1.00
15	Tony Clark	.25
16	Mo Vaughn	.25
17	Bernie Williams	.25
18	Scott Rolen	.75
19	Gary Sheffield	.40
20	Albert Belle	.25
21	Mike Piazza	2.00

22	John Olerud	.25
23	Tony Gwynn	1.50
24	Jay Bell	.25
25	Jose Cruz Jr.	.25
26	Justin Thompson	.25
27	Ken Griffey Jr.	2.00
28	Sandy Alomar	.25
29	Mark Grudzielanek	.25
30	Mark Grace	.25
31	Ron Gant	.25
32	Javy Lopez	.25
33	Jeff Bagwell	1.00
34	Fred McGriff	.25
35	Rafael Palmeiro	.75
36	Vinny Castilla	.25
37	Andy Benes	.25
38	Pedro Martinez	1.00
39	Andy Pettitte	.40
40	Marty Cordova	.25
41	Rusty Greer	.25
42	Kevin Orie	.25
43	Chan Ho Park	.25
44	Ryan Klesko	.25
45	Alex Rodriguez	2.50
46	Travis Fryman	.25
47	Jeff King	.25
48	Roger Clemens	2.00
49	Darin Erstad	.50
50	Brady Anderson	.25
51	Jason Kendall	.25
52	John Valentin	.25
53	Ellis Burks	.25
54	Brian Hunter	.25
55	Paul O'Neill	.25
56	Ken Caminiti	.25
57	David Justice	.25
58	Eric Karros	.25
59	Pat Hentgen	.25
60	Greg Maddux	1.50
61	Craig Biggio	.25
62	Edgar Martinez	.25
63	Mike Mussina	.50
64	Larry Walker	.25
65	Tino Martinez	.25
66	Jim Thome	.60
67	Tom Glavine	.40
68	Raul Mondesi	.25
69	Marquis Grissom	.25
70	Randy Johnson	1.00
71	Steve Finley	.25
72	Jose Guillen	.25
73	Nomar Garciaparra	1.50
74	Wade Boggs	1.50
75	Bobby Higginson	.25
76	Robin Ventura	.25
77	Derek Jeter	3.00
78	Andruw Jones	1.00
79	Ray Lankford	.25
80	Vladimir Guerrero	1.00
81	Kenny Lofton	.25
82	Ivan Rodriguez	.75
83	Neifi Perez	.25
84	John Smoltz	.25
85	Tim Salmon	.25
86	Carlos Delgado	.50
87	Sammy Sosa	1.50
88	Jaret Wright	.25
89	Roberto Alomar	.25
90	Paul Molitor	1.00
91	Dean Palmer	.25
92	Barry Larkin	.25
93	Jason Giambi	.50
94	Curt Schilling	.40
95	Eric Young	.25
96	Denny Neagle	.25
97	Moises Alou	.25
98	Livan Hernandez	.25
99	Todd Hundley	.25
100	Andres Galarraga	.25
101	Travis Lee	.25
102	Lance Berkman	.25
103	Orlando Cabrera	.25
104	Mike Lowell RC	2.00
105	Ben Grieve	.25
106	Jae Weong Seo RC	.50
107	Richie Sexson	.25
108	Eli Marrero	.25
109	Aramis Ramirez	.25
110	Paul Konerko	.25
111	Carl Pavano	.25
112	Brad Fullmer	.25
113	Matt Clement	.25
114	Donzell McDonald	.25
115	Todd Helton	.75
116	Mike Caruso	.25
117	Donnie Sadler	.25
118	Bruce Chen	.25
119	Jarrod Washburn	.25
120	Adrian Beltre	.40
121	Ryan Jackson RC	.50
122	Kevin Millar RC	1.50
123	Corey Koskie RC	.50
124	Dermal Brown	.25
125	Kerry Wood	.50
126	Juan Melo	.25
127	Ramon Hernandez	.25
128	Roy Halladay	.25
129	Ron Wright	.25
130	Darnell McDonald RC	.25
131	Odalis Perez RC	.75
132	Alex Cora RC	.25
133	Justin Towle	.25
134	Juan Encarnacion	.25
135	Brian Rose	.25
136	Russell Branyan RC	.25
137	Cesar King RC	.25
138	Ruben Rivera	.25
139	Ricky Ledee	.25
140	Vernon Wells	.25
141	Luis Rivas RC	.50
142	Brent Butler	.25
143	Karim Garcia	.25
144	George Lombard	.25
145	Masato Yoshii RC	.50
146	Braden Looper	.25
147	Alex Sanchez	.25
148	Kris Benson	.25
149	Mark Kotsay	.25
150	Richard Hidalgo	.25
151	Scott Elarton	.25
152	Ryan Minor RC	.25
153	Troy Glaus RC	5.00
154	Carlos Lee RC	2.00
155	Michael Coleman	.25
156	Jason Grilli RC	.50
157	Julio Ramirez RC	.50
158	Randy Wolf RC	.75
159	Ryan Brannan	.25
160	Edgar Clemente RC	.50
161	Miguel Tejada	.40
162	Chad Hermansen	.25
163	Ryan Anderson RC	.50
164	Ben Petrick	.25
165	Alex Gonzalez	.25
166	Ben Davis	.25
167	John Patterson	.25
168	Cliff Politte	.25
169	Randall Simon	.25
170	Javier Vazquez	.25
171	Kevin Witt	.25
172	Geoff Jenkins	.25
173	David Ortiz	.60
174	Derrick Gibson	.25
175	Abraham Nunez	.25
176	A.J. Hinch	.25
177	Ruben Mateo RC	.75
178	Magglio Ordonez RC	2.50
179	Todd Dunwoody	.25
180	Daryle Ward	.25
181	Mike Kinkade RC	.50
182	Willie Martinez	.25
183	Orlando Hernandez RC	1.50
184	Eric Milton	.25
185	Eric Chavez	.50
186	Damian Jackson	.25
187	Jim Parque	.25
188	Dan Reichert RC	.25
189	Mike Drumright	.25
190	Todd Walker	.25
191	Shane Monahan	.25
192	Derrek Lee	.65
193	Jeremy Giambi RC	.50
194	Dan McKinley RC	.25
195	Tony Armas RC	.75
196	Matt Anderson RC	.50
197	Jim Chamblee RC	.25
198	Francisco Cordero RC	.25
199	Calvin Pickering	.25
200	Reggie Taylor	.25

Refractors

Refractor versions for all 200 cards in Bowman's Best were available. Fronts featured a reflective finish, while backs were numbered to 400 and inserted one per 20 packs.

	NM/M
Common Player:	4.00
Stars:	8X

Production 400 Sets
(See 1998 Bowman's Best for checklist and base card values.)

Atomic Refractors

Atomic Refractor versions were available for all 200 cards in Bowman's Best. The cards were printed in a prismatic foil on the front, sequentially numbered to 100 sets on the back and inserted one per 82 packs.

	NM/M
Common Player:	6.00
Stars:	12X

Production 100 Sets
(See 1998 Bowman's Best for checklist and base card values.)

Autographs

This 10-card set offers autographs from five prospects and five veteran stars. Each card has on front the Topps "Certified Autograph Issue" logo for authentication.

	NM/M
Complete Set (10):	65.00
Common Player:	5.00
Inserted 1:180	
Refractors:	1.5X
Inserted 1:2,158	
Atomics:	2X
Inserted 1:6,437	
5 Chipper Jones	30.00
10 Chuck Knoblauch	5.00
15 Tony Clark	5.00
20 Albert Belle	8.00
25 Jose Cruz Jr.	5.00

105	Ben Grieve	5.00
110	Paul Konerko	15.00
115	Todd Helton	15.00
120	Adrian Beltre	15.00
125	Kerry Wood	20.00

Mirror Image Fusion

This 20-card die-cut insert features a veteran star on one side and a young player at the same position on the other. Regular versions are seeded one per 12 packs, while Refractors are found 1:809 packs and numbered within an edition of 100, and Atomic Refractors are a 1:3,237 find numbered to 25. All have a "MI" prefix to the card number.

	NM/M
Complete Set (20):	35.00
Common Player (1:12):	.50
Refractor (1:809):	6X
Atomic Refractor (1:3,237):	12X
1 Frank Thomas, David Ortiz	2.00
2 Chuck Knoblauch, Enrique Wilson	.50
3 Nomar Garciaparra, Miguel Tejada	2.50
4 Alex Rodriguez, Mike Caruso	3.50
5 Cal Ripken Jr., Ryan Minor	4.50
6 Ken Griffey Jr., Ben Grieve	3.00
7 Juan Gonzalez, Juan Encarnacion	.75
8 Jose Cruz Jr., Ruben Mateo	.50
9 Randy Johnson, Ryan Anderson	1.50
10 Ivan Rodriguez, A.J. Hinch	1.25
11 Jeff Bagwell, Paul Konerko	1.50
12 Mark McGwire, Travis Lee	3.50
13 Craig Biggio, Chad Hermanson	.50
14 Mark Grudzielanek, Alex Gonzalez	.50
15 Chipper Jones, Adrian Beltre	2.50
16 Larry Walker, Mark Kotsay	.50
17 Tony Gwynn, Preston Wilson	2.50
18 Barry Bonds, Richard Hidalgo	4.50
19 Greg Maddux, Kerry Wood	2.50
20 Mike Piazza, Ben Petrick	3.00

Performers

Performers are 10 players who had the best minor league seasons in 1997. Regular versions were inserted one per six packs, while Refractors are seeded 1:809 and serially numbered to 200, and Atomic Refractors are 1:3,237 and numbered to 50 sets. All versions have card numbers with a "BP" prefix.

	NM/M
Complete Set (10):	4.00
Common Player:	.35
Refractor (1:309):	3X
Atomic Refractor (1:3,237):	5X
1 Ben Grieve	.35
2 Travis Lee	.35
3 Ryan Minor	.35
4 Todd Helton	2.00
5 Brad Fullmer	.35
6 Paul Konerko	.50
7 Adrian Beltre	.75
8 Richie Sexson	.35
9 Aramis Ramirez	.35
10 Russell Branyan	.35

1999 Bowman Pre-Production

Bowman's 1999 issue was introduced with this group of sample cards. Format is nearly identical to the issued cards, except for the use of a "PP" prefix to the card number on back.

	NM/M
Complete Set (6):	4.00
Common Player:	.60
1 Andres Galarraga	.60
2 Raul Mondesi	.60
3 Vinny Castilla	.60
4 Corey Koskie	2.00
5 Octavio Dotel	.60
6 Dernell Stenson	.60

1999 Bowman

The set was issued in two 220-card series, each comprised of 70 veterans and 150 rookies and prospects. Rookie/prospect cards have blue metallic foil highlights; veteran cards are highlighted with red foil. On each card is the player's facsimile autograph, reproduced from their initial Topps contract.

	NM/M
Complete Set (440):	60.00
Complete Series 1 (220):	30.00
Complete Series 2 (220):	35.00
Common Player:	.10
Series 1 Pack (10):	2.00
Series 1 Box (24):	35.00
Series 2 Pack (10):	3.00
Series 2 Box (24):	50.00
1 Ben Grieve	.10
2 Kerry Wood	.40
3 Ruben Rivera	.10
4 Sandy Alomar	.10
5 Cal Ripken Jr.	2.00
6 Mark McGwire	1.75
7 Vladimir Guerrero	.75
8 Moises Alou	.10
9 Jim Edmonds	.10
10 Greg Maddux	1.00
11 Gary Sheffield	.40

12	John Valentin	.10
13	Chuck Knoblauch	.10
14	Tony Clark	.10
15	Rusty Greer	.10
16	Al Leiter	.10
17	Travis Lee	.10
18	Jose Cruz Jr.	.10
19	Pedro Martinez	.75
20	Paul O'Neill	.10
21	Todd Walker	.10
22	Vinny Castilla	.10
23	Barry Larkin	.10
24	Curt Schilling	.40
25	Jason Kendall	.10
26	Scott Erickson	.10
27	Andres Galarraga	.10
28	Jeff Shaw	.10
29	John Olerud	.10
30	Orlando Hernandez	.10
31	Larry Walker	.10
32	Andruw Jones	.75
33	Jeff Cirillo	.10
34	Barry Bonds	2.00
35	Manny Ramirez	.75
36	Mark Kotsay	.10
37	Ivan Rodriguez	.60
38	Jeff King	.10
39	Brian Hunter	.10
40	Ray Durham	.10
41	Bernie Williams	.10
42	Darin Erstad	.30
43	Chipper Jones	1.00
44	Pat Hentgen	.10
45	Eric Young	.10
46	Jaret Wright	.10
47	Juan Guzman	.10
48	Jorge Posada	.10
49	Bobby Higginson	.10
50	Jose Guillen	.10
51	Trevor Hoffman	.10
52	Ken Griffey Jr.	1.50
53	David Justice	.10
54	Matt Williams	.10
55	Eric Karros	.10
56	Derek Bell	.10
57	Ray Lankford	.10
58	Mariano Rivera	.25
59	Brett Tomko	.10
60	Mike Mussina	.40
61	Kenny Lofton	.10
62	Chuck Finley	.10
63	Alex Gonzalez	.10
64	Mark Grace	.10
65	Raul Mondesi	.10
66	David Cone	.10
67	Brad Fullmer	.10
68	Andy Benes	.10
69	John Smoltz	.10
70	Shane Reynolds	.10
71	Bruce Chen	.10
72	Adam Kennedy	.10
73	Jack Cust	.10
74	Matt Clement	.10
75	Derrick Gibson	.10
76	Darnell McDonald	.10
77	Adam Everett RC	.50
78	Ricardo Aramboles	.10
79	Mark Quinn RC	.25
80	Jason Rakers	.10
81	Seth Etherton RC	.35
82	Jeff Urban RC	.25
83	Manny Aybar	.10
84	Mike Nannini RC	.25
85	Onan Masaoka	.10
86	Rod Barajas	.10
87	Mike Frank	.10
88	Scott Randall	.10
89	Justin Bowles RC	.25
90	Chris Haas	.10
91	Arturo McDowell RC	.25
92	Matt Belisle RC	.35
93	Scott Elarton	.10
94	Vernon Wells	.25
95	Pat Cline	.10
96	Ryan Anderson	.10
97	Kevin Barker	.10
98	Ruben Mateo	.10
99	Robert Fick	.10
100	Corey Koskie	.10
101	Ricky Ledee	.10
102	Rick Elder RC	.25
103	Jack Cressend RC	.10
104	Joe Lawrence	.10
105	Mike Lincoln	.10
106	Kit Pellow RC	.35
107	Matt Burch RC	.25
108	Brent Butler	.10
109	Jason Dewey	.10
110	Cesar King	.10
111	Julio Ramirez	.10
112	Jake Westbrook	.10
113	Eric Valent RC	.35
114	Roosevelt Brown RC	.35
115	Choo Freeman RC	.50
116	Juan Melo	.10
117	Jason Grilli	.10
118	Jared Sandberg	.10
119	Glenn Davis	.10
120	David Riske RC	.25
121	Jacque Jones	.10
122	Corey Lee	.10
123	Michael Barrett	.10
124	Lariel Gonzalez	.10
125	Mitch Meluskey	.10
126	Freddy Garcia	.10
127	Tony Torcato RC	.25
128	Jeff Liefer	.10
129	Ntema Ndungidi	.10
130	Andy Brown RC	.35
131	Ryan Mills RC	.25
132	Andy Abad RC	.25
133	Carlos Febles	.10
134	Jason Tyner RC	.25
135	Mark Osborne	.10
136	Phil Norton	.10
137	Nathan Haynes	.10
138	Roy Halladay	.10
139	Juan Encarnacion	.10
140	Brad Penny	.10
141	Grant Roberts	.10
142	Aramis Ramirez	.10
143	Cristian Guzman	.10
144	Mamon Tucker RC	.25
145	Ryan Bradley	.10
146	Brian Simmons	.10
147	Dan Reichert	.10
148	Russ Branyon	.10
149	Victor Valencia RC	.25
150	Scott Schoeneweis	.10
151	Sean Spencer RC	.25
152	Odalis Perez	.10
153	Joe Fontenot	.10
154	Milton Bradley	.10
155	Josh McKinley RC	.25
156	Terrence Long	.10
157	Danny Klassen	.10
158	Paul Hoover RC	.25
159	Ron Belliard	.10
160	Armando Rios	.10
161	Ramon Hernandez	.10
162	Jason Conti	.10
163	Chad Hermansen	.10
164	Jason Standridge	.10
165	Jason Dellaero	.10
166	John Curtice	.10
167	Clayton Andrews RC	.25
168	Jeremy Giambi	.10
169	Alex Ramirez	.10
170	Gabe Molina RC	.25
171	Mario Encarnacion RC	.25
172	Mike Zywica RC	.25
173	Chip Ambres	.10
174	Trot Nixon	.10
175	Pat Burrell RC	2.00
176	Jeff Yoder	.10
177	Chris Jones RC	.25
178	Kevin Witt	.10
179	Keith Luuloa RC	.25
180	Billy Koch	.10
181	Damaso Marte RC	.25
182	Ryan Glynn RC	.25
183	Calvin Pickering	.10
184	Michael Cuddyer	.10
185	Nick Johnson RC	.75
186	Doug Mientkiewicz RC	1.00
187	Nate Cornejo RC	.35
188	Octavio Dotel	.10
189	Wes Helms	.10
190	Nelson Lara	.10
191	Chuck Abbott RC	.25
192	Tony Armas Jr.	.10
193	Gil Meche	.10
194	Ben Petrick	.10
195	Chris George RC	.25
196	Scott Hunter RC	.25
197	Ryan Brannan	.10
198	Amaury Garcia RC	.25
199	Chris Gissell	.10
200	Austin Kearns RC	1.50
201	Alex Gonzalez	.10
202	Wade Miller	.10
203	Scott Williamson	.10
204	Chris Enochs	.10
205	Fernando Seguignol	.10
206	Marlon Anderson	.10
207	Todd Sears RC	.25
208	Nate Bump RC	.10
209	J.M. Gold RC	.25
210	Matt LeCroy	.10
211	Alex Hernandez	.10
212	Luis Rivera	.10
213	Troy Cameron	.10
214	Alex Escobar RC	.50
215	Jason LaRue	.10
216	Kyle Peterson	.10
217	Brent Butler	.10
218	Dernell Stenson	.10
219	Adrian Beltre	.40
220	Daryle Ward	.10
----	Series 1 Checklist Folder	.10
221	Jim Thome	.60
222	Cliff Floyd	.10
223	Rickey Henderson	.75
224	Garret Anderson	.10
225	Ken Caminiti	.10
226	Bret Boone	.10
227	Jeromy Burnitz	.10
228	Steve Finley	.10
229	Miguel Tejada	.40
230	Greg Vaughn	.10
231	Jose Offerman	.10
232	Andy Ashby	.10
233	Albert Belle	.10
234	Fernando Tatis	.10
235	Todd Helton	.65
236	Sean Casey	.10
237	Brian Giles	.10
238	Andy Pettitte	.25
239	Fred McGriff	.10
240	Roberto Alomar	.30
241	Edgar Martinez	.10
242	Lee Stevens	.10
243	Shawn Green	.25
244	Ryan Klesko	.10
245	Sammy Sosa	1.00

246	Todd Hundley	.10
247	Shannon Stewart	.10
248	Randy Johnson	.75
249	Rondell White	.10
250	Mike Piazza	1.50
251	Craig Biggio	.10
252	David Wells	.10
253	Brian Jordan	.10
254	Edgar Renteria	.10
255	Bartolo Colon	.10
256	Frank Thomas	.75
257	Will Clark	.10
258	Dean Palmer	.10
259	Dmitri Young	.10
260	Scott Rolen	.60
261	Jeff Kent	.10
262	Dante Bichette	.10
263	Nomar Garciaparra	1.00
264	Tony Gwynn	1.00
265	Alex Rodriguez	1.75
266	Jose Canseco	.45
267	Jason Giambi	.40
268	Jeff Bagwell	.75
269	Carlos Delgado	.40
270	Tom Glavine	.40
271	Eric Davis	.10
272	Edgardo Alfonzo	.10
273	Tim Salmon	.10
274	Johnny Damon	.35
275	Rafael Palmeiro	.65
276	Denny Neagle	.10
277	Neifi Perez	.10
278	Roger Clemens	1.25
279	Brant Brown	.10
280	Kevin Brown	.10
281	Jay Bell	.10
282	Jay Buhner	.10
283	Matt Lawton	.10
284	Robin Ventura	.10
285	Juan Gonzalez	.35
286	Mo Vaughn	.10
287	Kevin Millwood	.10
288	Tino Martinez	.10
289	Justin Thompson	.10
290	Derek Jeter	2.00
291	Ben Davis	.10
292	Mike Lowell	.10
293	Joe Crede **RC**	.75
294	Micah Bowie **RC**	.25
295	Lance Berkman	.10
296	Jason Marquis	.10
297	Chad Green	.10
298	Dee Brown	.10
299	Jerry Hairston Jr.	.10
300	Gabe Kapler	.10
301	Brent Stentz **RC**	.25
302	Scott Mullen **RC**	.25
303	Brandon Reed	.10
304	Shea Hillenbrand **RC**	.50
305	J.D. Closser **RC**	.50
306	Gary Matthews Jr.	.10
307	Toby Hall **RC**	.25
308	Jason Phillips **RC**	.25
309	Jose Macias **RC**	.25
310	Jung Bong **RC**	.25
311	Ramon Soler **RC**	.25
312	Kelly Dransfeldt **RC**	.25
313	Carlos Hernandez **RC**	.25
314	Kevin Haverbusch	.10
315	Aaron Myette **RC**	.25
316	Chad Harville **RC**	.35
317	Kyle Farnsworth **RC**	.50
318	Travis Dawkins **RC**	.50
319	Willie Martinez	.10
320	Carlos Lee	.10
321	Carlos Pena **RC**	.50
322	Peter Bergeron **RC**	.25
323	A.J. Burnett **RC**	.50
324	Bucky Jacobsen **RC**	.25
325	Mo Bruce **RC**	.25
326	Reggie Taylor	.10
327	Jackie Rexrode	.10
328	Alvin Morrow **RC**	.25
329	Carlos Beltran	.40
330	Eric Chavez	.25
331	John Patterson	.10
332	Jayson Werth	.10
333	Richie Sexson	.10
334	Randy Wolf	.10
335	Eli Marrero	.10
336	Paul LoDuca	.10
337	J.D. Smart	.10
338	Ryan Minor	.10
339	Kris Benson	.10
340	George Lombard	.10
341	Troy Glaus	.75
342	Eddie Yarnell	.10
343	Kip Wells **RC**	.50
344	C.C. Sabathia **RC**	1.00
345	Sean Burroughs **RC**	.50
346	Felipe Lopez **RC**	1.50
347	Ryan Rupe **RC**	.25
348	Orber Moreno **RC**	.25
349	Rafael Roque **RC**	.25
350	Alfonso Soriano **RC**	5.00
351	Pablo Ozuna	.10
352	Corey Patterson **RC**	1.00
353	Braden Looper	.10
354	Robbie Bell	.10
355	Mark Mulder **RC**	2.00
356	Angel Pena	.10
357	Kevin McGlinchy **RC**	.10
358	Michael Restovich **RC**	.35
359	Eric DuBose	.10
360	Geoff Jenkins	.10
361	Mark Harriger **RC**	.25
362	Junior Herndon **RC**	.25
363	Tim Raines Jr. **RC**	.25

364	Rafael Furcal **RC**	.75
365	Marcus Giles **RC**	1.00
366	Ted Lilly	.10
367	Jorge Toca **RC**	.25
368	David Kelton **RC**	.35
369	Adam Dunn **RC**	5.00
370	Guillermo Mota **RC**	.35
371	Brett Laxton **RC**	.25
372	Travis Harper **RC**	.25
373	Tom Davey **RC**	.25
374	Darren Blakely **RC**	.25
375	Tim Hudson **RC**	3.00
376	Jason Romano	.10
377	Dan Reichert	.10
378	Julio Lugo **RC**	.75
379	Jose Garcia **RC**	.25
380	Erubiel Durazo **RC**	.25
381	Jose Jimenez	.10
382	Chris Fussell	.10
383	Steve Lomasney	.25
384	Juan Pena **RC**	.25
385	Allen Levrault **RC**	.25
386	Juan Rivera **RC**	.25
387	Steve Colyer **RC**	.25
388	Joe Nathan **RC**	.25
389	Ron Walker **RC**	.10
390	Nick Bierbrodt	.10
391	Luke Prokopec **RC**	.25
392	Dave Roberts **RC**	.40
393	Mike Darr	.10
394	Abraham Nunez **RC**	.35
395	Giuseppe Chiaramonte **RC**	.25
396	Jermaine Van Buren **RC**	.10
397	Mike Kusiewicz	.10
398	Matt Wise **RC**	.25
399	Joe McEwing **RC**	.40
400	Matt Holliday **RC**	3.00
401	Willi Mo Pena **RC**	1.50
402	Ruben Quevedo **RC**	.25
403	Rob Ryan **RC**	.25
404	Freddy Garcia **RC**	1.00
405	Kevin Eberwein **RC**	.25
406	Jesus Colome **RC**	.25
407	Chris Singleton **RC**	.25
408	Bubba Crosby **RC**	.50
409	Jesus Cordero **RC**	.25
410	Donny Leon	.10
411	Goefrey Tomlinson **RC**	.10
412	Jeff Winchester **RC**	.25
413	Adam Piatt **RC**	.50
414	Robert Stratton	.10
415	T.J. Tucker	.10
416	Ryan Langerhans **RC**	.25
417	Anthony Shumaker **RC**	.25
418	Matt Miller **RC**	.25
419	Doug Clark **RC**	.25
420	Kory DeHaan **RC**	.25
421	David Eckstein **RC**	.75
422	Brian Cooper **RC**	.25
423	Brady Clark **RC**	.25
424	Chris Magruder **RC**	.25
425	Bobby Seay **RC**	.25
426	Aubrey Huff **RC**	1.00
427	Mike Jerzembeck	.10
428	Matt Blank **RC**	.25
429	Benny Agbayani **RC**	.25
430	Kevin Beirne **RC**	.25
431	Josh Hamilton **RC**	4.00
432	Josh Girdley **RC**	.25
433	Kyle Snyder **RC**	.25
434	Mike Paradis **RC**	.25
435	Jason Jennings **RC**	.25
436	David Walling **RC**	.25
437	Omar Ortiz **RC**	.25
438	Jay Gehrke **RC**	.25
439	Casey Burns **RC**	.25
440	Carl Crawford **RC**	2.50

Gold

Gold, rather than black, ink for the facsimile autograph, Bowman logo and player name on front, and a serial number on back from within an edition of 99, designate these parallels. Stated odds of finding the Gold cards were one per 111 packs of Series 1, and 1:59 in Series 2.

	NM/M
Common Player:	3.00
Gold Stars:	10X

(See 1999 Bowman for checklist and base card values.)

International

ALEX RAMIREZ

International parallels are a one-per-pack insert. Fronts are printed in metallic silver on which the photo's background has been replaced with a scenic picture supposed to be indicative of the player's native land. That location is spelled out at the lower-left corner of the photo. Backs of the Internationals are printed in the player's native language.

	NM/M
Common Player:	.25
Int'l Stars:	1.5X

(See 1999 Bowman for checklist and base card values.)

Autographs

Bruce Chen

Autographs were randomly seeded in Series 1 and 2 packs, with each card bearing a Topps Certified Autograph seal on the front and numbered with a "BA" prefix on back. Levels of scarcity are color coded by the metallic-foil highlights on front: Golds are the most difficult to find at 1:1,941 Series 1 packs and 1:1,024 Series 2. Silvers and gold are seeded 1:485 in Series 1, 1:256 Series 2. Blues are found at an average rate of 1:162 in first series and 1:85 in second series.

	NM/M
Common Player:	3.00

Blues inserted 1:162 or 1:85
Silvers inserted 1:485 or 1:256
Golds inserted 1:1,954 or 1:1,024

1	Ruben Mateo B	5.00
2	Troy Glaus G	40.00
3	Ben Davis G	5.00
4	Jayson Werth B	5.00
5	Jerry Hairston Jr. S	4.00
6	Darnell McDonald B	4.00
7	Calvin Pickering S	8.00
8	Ryan Minor S	4.00
9	Alex Escobar B	6.00
10	Grant Roberts B	5.00
11	Carlos Guillen B	10.00
12	Ryan Anderson S	6.00
13	Gil Meche S	5.00
14	Russell Branyan S	5.00
15	Alex Ramirez S	5.00
16	Jason Rakers S	5.00
17	Eddie Yarnall B	4.00
18	Freddy Garcia B	20.00
19	Jason Conti B	3.00
20	Corey Koskie B	5.00
21	Roosevelt Brown B	5.00
22	Willie Martinez B	3.00
23	Mike Jerzembeck B	3.00
24	Lariel Gonzalez B	3.00
25	Fernando Seguignol B	3.00
26	Robert Fick S	5.00
27	J.D. Smart B	3.00
28	Ryan Mills B	3.00
29	Chad Hermansen G	6.00
30	Jason Grilli B	3.00

31	Michael Cuddyer B	5.00
32	Jacque Jones S	10.00
33	Reggie Taylor B	3.00
34	Richie Sexson G	15.00
35	Michael Barrett B	8.00
36	Paul LoDuca B	8.00
37	Adrian Beltre G	30.00
38	Peter Bergeron B	4.00
39	Joe Fontenot B	3.00
40	Randy Wolf B	6.00
41	Nick Johnson B	12.00
42	Ryan Bradley B	4.00
43	Mike Lowell S	10.00
44	Ricky Ledee B	5.00
45	Mike Lincoln S	4.00
46	Jeremy Giambi B	5.00
47	Dermal Brown S	3.00
48	Derrick Gibson B	3.00
49	Scott Randall B	3.00
50	Ben Petrick S	3.00
51	Jason LaRue B	3.00
52	Cole Liniak B	3.00
53	John Curtice B	3.00
54	Jackie Rexrode B	3.00
55	John Patterson B	3.00
56	Brad Penny S	6.00
57	Jared Sandberg B	3.00
58	Kerry Wood G	20.00
59	Eli Marrero B	5.00
60	Jason Marquis B	8.00
61	George Lombard S	5.00
62	Bruce Chen S	3.00
63	Kevin Witt S	5.00
64	Vernon Wells B	15.00
65	Billy Koch B	3.00
66	Roy Halladay B	20.00
67	Nathan Haynes B	3.00
68	Ben Grieve G	8.00
69	Eric Chavez G	10.00
70	Lance Berkman S	15.00

Early Risers

MIKE PIAZZA C

This insert set features 11 current baseball superstars who have already won a Rookie of the Year award and who continue to excel. Cards have an "ER" prefix to the number on back.

		NM/M
Complete Set (11):		8.00
Common Player:		.25
Inserted 1:12		
1	Mike Piazza	1.00
2	Cal Ripken Jr.	2.00
3	Jeff Bagwell	.50
4	Ben Grieve	.25
5	Kerry Wood	.40
6	Mark McGwire	1.50
7	Nomar Garciaparra	.75
8	Derek Jeter	2.00
9	Scott Rolen	.50
10	Jose Canseco	.45
11	Raul Mondesi	.25

Late Bloomers

This 10-card set features late-round picks from previous drafts who have emerged as bona fide stars. These inserts are numbered with an "LB" prefix.

	NM/M
Complete Set (10):	4.00
Common Player:	.25

Scout's Choice

Scout's Choice inserts were randomly inserted in Series 1 packs and feature a borderless, double-etched design. The 21-card set focuses on prospects who have potential to win a future Rookie of the Year award.

		NM/M
Complete Set (21):		12.00
Common Player:		.40
Inserted 1:12		
SC1	Ruben Mateo	.40
SC2	Ryan Anderson	.40
SC3	Pat Burrell	3.00
SC4	Troy Glaus	4.00
SC5	Eric Chavez	1.00
SC6	Adrian Beltre	1.00
SC7	Bruce Chen	.40
SC8	Carlos Beltran	1.00
SC9	Alex Gonzalez	.40
SC10	Carlos Lee	.40
SC11	George Lombard	.40
SC12	Matt Clement	.40
SC13	Calvin Pickering	.40
SC14	Marlon Anderson	.40
SC15	Chad Hermansen	.40
SC16	Russell Branyan	.40
SC17	Jeremy Giambi	.40
SC18	Ricky Ledee	.40
SC19	John Patterson	.40
SC20	Roy Halladay	.75
SC21	Michael Barrett	.40

2000 Rookie of the Year

PAT BURRELL

Randomly inserted in Series 2 packs, these cards have a borderless, double-etched foil design. The 10-card set focuses on players that have potential to win the 2000 Rookie of the Year award.

		NM/M
Complete Set (10):		7.00
Common Player:		.50
Inserted 1:12		
1	Ryan Anderson	.50
2	Pat Burrell	2.50
3	A.J. Burnett	.50
4	Ruben Mateo	.50
5	Alex Escobar	.50
6	Pablo Ozuna	.50
7	Mark Mulder	1.00
8	Corey Patterson	1.00
9	George Lombard	.50
10	Nick Johnson	1.00

1999 Bowman Chrome

JUAN GONZALEZ

Bowman Chrome was released in two 220-card series as an upscale chromium parallel version of Bowman Baseball. Like Bowman, each series has 150 prospect cards with blue foil, while 70 veteran cards have red foil. Packs contain four cards with an original SRP of $3.

	NM/M
Complete Set (440):	175.00
Complete Series 1 (220):	65.00
Complete Series 2 (220):	125.00
Common Player:	.25
Series 1 Pack (4):	4.00
Series 1 Wax Box (24):	65.00
Series 2 Pack (4):	6.50
Series 2 Wax Box (24):	120.00

1	Ben Grieve	.25
2	Kerry Wood	.45
3	Ruben Rivera	.25
4	Sandy Alomar	.25
5	Cal Ripken Jr.	3.00
6	Mark McGwire	2.50
7	Vladimir Guerrero	1.00
8	Moises Alou	.25
9	Jim Edmonds	.25
10	Greg Maddux	1.50
11	Gary Sheffield	.50
12	John Valentin	.25
13	Chuck Knoblauch	.25
14	Tony Clark	.25
15	Rusty Greer	.25
16	Al Leiter	.25
17	Travis Lee	.25
18	Jose Cruz Jr.	.25
19	Pedro Martinez	1.00
20	Paul O'Neill	.25
21	Todd Walker	.25
22	Vinny Castilla	.25
23	Barry Larkin	.25
24	Curt Schilling	.40
25	Jason Kendall	.25
26	Scott Erickson	.25
27	Andres Galarraga	.25
28	Jeff Shaw	.25
29	John Olerud	.25
30	Orlando Hernandez	.40
31	Larry Walker	.25
32	Andruw Jones	1.00
33	Jeff Cirillo	.25
34	Barry Bonds	3.00
35	Manny Ramirez	1.00
36	Mark Kotsay	.25
37	Ivan Rodriguez	.75
38	Jeff King	.25
39	Brian Hunter	.25
40	Ray Durham	.25
41	Bernie Williams	.50
42	Darin Erstad	.50
43	Chipper Jones	1.50
44	Pat Hentgen	.25
45	Eric Young	.25
46	Jaret Wright	.25
47	Juan Guzman	.25
48	Jorge Posada	.25
49	Bobby Higginson	.25
50	Jose Guillen	.25
51	Trevor Hoffman	.25
52	Ken Griffey Jr.	2.00
53	David Justice	.25
54	Matt Williams	.25
55	Eric Karros	.25
56	Derek Bell	.25
57	Ray Lankford	.25
58	Mariano Rivera	.40
59	Brett Tomko	.25
60	Mike Mussina	.50
61	Kenny Lofton	.25
62	Chuck Finley	.25
63	Alex Gonzalez	.25
64	Mark Grace	.25
65	Raul Mondesi	.25
66	David Cone	.25
67	Brad Fullmer	.25
68	Andy Benes	.25
69	John Smoltz	.25
70	Shane Reynolds	.25
71	Bruce Chen	.25
72	Adam Kennedy	.25
73	Jack Cust	.25

Veteran checklist (LB):

LB1	Mike Piazza	2.00
LB2	Jim Thome	.75
LB3	Larry Walker	.25
LB4	Vinny Castilla	.25
LB5	Andy Pettitte	.50
LB6	Jim Edmonds	.25
LB7	Kenny Lofton	.25
LB8	John Smoltz	.25
LB9	Mark Grace	.25
LB10	Trevor Hoffman	.25

No.	Player	Price
74	Matt Clement	.25
75	Derrick Gibson	.25
76	Darnell McDonald	.25
77	Adam Everett RC	.75
78	Ricardo Aramboles	.25
79	Mark Quinn RC	.50
80	Jason Rakers	.25
81	Seth Etherton RC	.50
82	Jeff Urban RC	.25
83	Manny Aybar	.25
84	Mike Nannini RC	.25
85	Onan Masaoka	.25
86	Rod Barajas	.25
87	Mike Frank	.25
88	Scott Randall	.25
89	Justin Bowles RC	.25
90	Chris Haas	.25
91	Arturo McDowell RC	.25
92	Matt Belisle RC	.50
93	Scott Elarton	.25
94	Vernon Wells	.25
95	Pat Cline	.25
96	Ryan Anderson	.25
97	Kevin Barker	.25
98	Ruben Mateo	.25
99	Robert Fick	.25
100	Corey Koskie	.25
101	Ricky Ledee	.25
102	Rick Elder RC	.35
103	Jack Cressend RC	.25
104	Joe Lawrence	.25
105	Mike Lincoln	.25
106	Kit Pellow RC	.50
107	Matt Burch RC	.35
108	Brent Butler	.25
109	Jason Dewey	.25
110	Cesar King	.25
111	Julio Ramirez	.25
112	Jake Westbrook	.25
113	Eric Valent RC	1.00
114	Roosevelt Brown RC	.25
115	Choo Freeman RC	1.50
116	Juan Melo	.25
117	Jason Grilli	.25
118	Jared Sandberg	.25
119	Glenn Davis	.25
120	David Riske RC	.35
121	Jacque Jones	.25
122	Corey Lee	.25
123	Michael Barrett	.25
124	Lariel Gonzalez	.25
125	Mitch Meluskey	.25
126	Freddy Garcia RC	.35
127	Tony Torcato RC	.35
128	Jeff Liefer	.25
129	Ntema Ndungidi RC	.25
130	Andy Brown RC	.50
131	Ryan Mills RC	.25
132	Andy Abad RC	.25
133	Carlos Febles	.25
134	Jason Tyner RC	.50
135	Mark Osborne	.25
136	Phil Norton RC	.25
137	Nathan Haynes	.25
138	Roy Halladay RC	.35
139	Juan Encarnacion	.25
140	Brad Penny	.25
141	Grant Roberts	.25
142	Aramis Ramirez	.25
143	Cristian Guzman	.25
144	Mamon Tucker RC	.35
145	Ryan Bradley	.25
146	Brian Simmons	.25
147	Dan Reichert	.25
148	Russ Branyon	.25
149	Victor Valencia RC	.35
150	Scott Schoeneweis	.25
151	Sean Spencer RC	.35
152	Odalis Perez	.25
153	Joe Fontenot	.25
154	Milton Bradley	.25
155	Josh McKinley RC	.25
156	Terrence Long	.25
157	Danny Klassen	.25
158	Paul Hoover RC	.35
159	Ron Belliard	.25
160	Armando Rios	.25
161	Ramon Hernandez	.25
162	Jason Conti	.25
163	Chad Hermansen	.25
164	Jason Standridge	.25
165	Jason Dellaero	.25
166	John Curtice	.25
167	Clayton Andrews RC	.35
168	Jeremy Giambi	.25
169	Alex Ramirez	.25
170	Gabe Molina RC	.35
171	Mario Encarnacion RC	.35
172	Mike Zywica RC	.35
173	Chip Ambres RC	.35
174	Trot Nixon	.25
175	Pat Burrell RC	10.00
176	Jeff Yoder	.25
177	Chris Jones RC	.25
178	Kevin Witt	.25
179	Keith Luuloa RC	.35
180	Billy Koch	.25
181	Damaso Marte RC	.35
182	Ryan Glynn RC	.25
183	Calvin Pickering	.25
184	Michael Cuddyer	.25
185	Nick Johnson RC	6.00
186	Doug Mientkiewicz RC	2.00
187	Nate Cornejo RC	1.00
188	Octavio Dotel	.25
189	Wes Helms	.25
190	Nelson Lara	.25
191	Chuck Abbott RC	.25
192	Tony Armas Jr.	.25
193	Gil Meche	.25
194	Ben Petrick	.25
195	Chris George RC	.35
196	Scott Hunter RC	.35
197	Ryan Brannan	.25
198	Amaury Garcia RC	.35
199	Chris Gissell	.25
200	Austin Kearns RC	6.00
201	Alex Gonzalez	.25
202	Wade Miller	.25
203	Scott Williamson	.25
204	Chris Enochs	.25
205	Fernando Seguignol	.25
206	Marlon Anderson	.25
207	Todd Sears RC	.35
208	Nate Bump RC	.35
209	J.M. Gold RC	.50
210	Matt LeCroy RC	.35
211	Alex Hernandez	.25
212	Luis Rivera	.25
213	Troy Cameron	.25
214	Alex Escobar RC	1.00
215	Jason LaRue	.25
216	Kyle Peterson	.25
217	Brent Butler	.25
218	Dernell Stenson	.25
219	Adrian Beltre	.40
220	Daryle Ward	.25
221	Jim Thome	.65
222	Cliff Floyd	.25
223	Rickey Henderson	1.00
224	Garret Anderson	.25
225	Ken Caminiti	.25
226	Bret Boone	.25
227	Jeromy Burnitz	.25
228	Steve Finley	.25
229	Miguel Tejada	.40
230	Greg Vaughn	.25
231	Jose Offerman	.25
232	Andy Ashby	.25
233	Albert Belle	.25
234	Fernando Tatis	.25
235	Todd Helton	.75
236	Sean Casey	.40
237	Brian Giles	.40
238	Andy Pettitte	.40
239	Fred McGriff	.25
240	Roberto Alomar	.40
241	Edgar Martinez	.25
242	Lee Stevens	.25
243	Shawn Green	.40
244	Ryan Klesko	.25
245	Sammy Sosa	1.50
246	Todd Hundley	.25
247	Shannon Stewart	.25
248	Randy Johnson	1.00
249	Rondell White	.25
250	Mike Piazza	2.00
251	Craig Biggio	.25
252	David Wells	.25
253	Brian Jordan	.25
254	Edgar Renteria	.25
255	Bartolo Colon	.25
256	Frank Thomas	1.00
257	Will Clark	.25
258	Dean Palmer	.25
259	Dmitri Young	.25
260	Scott Rolen	.65
261	Jeff Kent	.25
262	Dante Bichette	.25
263	Nomar Garciaparra	1.50
264	Tony Gwynn	1.50
265	Alex Rodriguez	2.00
266	Jose Canseco	.50
267	Jason Giambi	.25
268	Jeff Bagwell	1.00
269	Carlos Delgado	.65
270	Tom Glavine	.50
271	Eric Davis	.25
272	Edgardo Alfonzo	.25
273	Tim Salmon	.25
274	Johnny Damon	.50
275	Rafael Palmeiro	.25
276	Denny Neagle	.25
277	Neifi Perez	.25
278	Roger Clemens	1.75
279	Brant Brown	.25
280	Kevin Brown	.25
281	Jay Bell	.25
282	Jay Buhner	.25
283	Matt Lawton	.25
284	Robin Ventura	.25
285	Juan Gonzalez	.50
286	Mo Vaughn	.25
287	Kevin Millwood	.25
288	Tino Martinez	.25
289	Justin Thompson	.25
290	Derek Jeter	3.00
291	Ben Davis	.25
292	Mike Lowell	.25
293	Joe Crede RC	3.00
294	Micah Bowie RC	.50
295	Lance Berkman	.25
296	Jason Marquis	.25
297	Chad Green	.25
298	Dee Brown	.25
299	Jerry Hairston Jr.	.25
300	Gabe Kapler	.25
301	Brent Stentz RC	.35
302	Scott Mullen RC	.35
303	Brandon Reed	.25
304	Shea Hillenbrand RC	2.50
305	J.D. Closser RC	1.00
306	Gary Matthews Jr.	.25
307	Toby Hall RC	1.00
308	Jason Phillips RC	.35
309	Jose Macias RC	.50
310	Jung Bong RC	.35
311	Ramon Soler RC	.35
312	Kelly Dransfeldt RC	.35
313	Carlos Hernandez RC	.50
314	Kevin Haverbusch	.25
315	Aaron Myette RC	.75
316	Chad Harville RC	.75
317	Kyle Farnsworth RC	1.00
318	Travis Dawkins RC	.75
319	Willie Martinez	.25
320	Carlos Lee	.35
321	Carlos Pena RC	1.50
322	Peter Bergeron RC	.50
323	A.J. Burnett RC	4.00
324	Bucky Jacobsen RC	1.00
325	Mo Bruce RC	.35
326	Reggie Taylor	.25
327	Jackie Rexrode	.25
328	Alvin Morrow RC	.25
329	Carlos Beltran	.50
330	Eric Chavez	.50
331	John Patterson	.25
332	Jayson Werth	.25
333	Richie Sexson	.25
334	Randy Wolf	.25
335	Eli Marrero	.25
336	Paul LoDuca	.25
337	J.D. Smart	.25
338	Ryan Minor	.25
339	Kris Benson	.25
340	George Lombard	.25
341	Troy Glaus	.75
342	Eddie Yarnell	.25
343	Kip Wells RC	1.00
344	C.C. Sabathia RC	4.00
345	Sean Burroughs RC	1.00
346	Felipe Lopez RC	6.00
347	Ryan Rupe RC	.75
348	Orber Moreno RC	.50
349	Rafael Roque RC	.35
350	Alfonso Soriano RC	25.00
351	Pablo Ozuna	.25
352	Corey Patterson RC	3.00
353	Braden Looper	.25
354	Robbie Bell	.25
355	Mark Mulder RC	5.00
356	Angel Pena	.25
357	Kevin McGlinchy	.25
358	Michael Restovich RC	1.00
359	Eric DuBose	.25
360	Geoff Jenkins	.25
361	Mark Harriger RC	.35
362	Junior Herndon RC	.35
363	Tim Raines Jr. RC	.35
364	Rafael Furcal RC	3.00
365	Marcus Giles RC	2.00
366	Ted Lilly	.25
367	Jorge Toca RC	.35
368	David Kelton RC	1.50
369	Adam Dunn RC	25.00
370	Guillermo Mota RC	.35
371	Brett Laxton RC	.35
372	Travis Harper RC	.35
373	Tom Davey RC	.35
374	Darren Blakely RC	.35
375	Tim Hudson RC	10.00
376	Jason Romano	.25
377	Dan Reichert	.25
378	Julio Lugo RC	.35
379	Jose Garcia RC	.35
380	Erubiel Durazo RC	1.50
381	Jose Jimenez	.25
382	Chris Fussell	.25
383	Steve Lomasney	.25
384	Juan Pena RC	.75
385	Allen Levrault RC	.35
386	Juan Rivera RC	.35
387	Steve Colyer RC	.35
388	Joe Nathan RC	1.50
389	Ron Walker RC	.35
390	Nick Bierbrodt	.25
391	Luke Prokopec RC	.35
392	Dave Roberts RC	.35
393	Mike Darr	.25
394	Abraham Nunez RC	1.00
395	Giuseppe Chiaramonte RC	.35
396	Jermaine Van Buren RC	.35
397	Mike Kusiewicz	.25
398	Matt Wise RC	.35
399	Joe McEwing RC	.50
400	Matt Holliday RC	10.00
401	Willi Mo Pena RC	4.00
402	Ruben Quevedo RC	.35
403	Rob Ryan RC	.35
404	Freddy Garcia RC	3.00
405	Kevin Eberwein RC	.35
406	Jesus Colome RC	.35
407	Chris Singleton RC	.35
408	Bubba Crosby RC	1.50
409	Jesus Cordero RC	.35
410	Donny Leon	.25
411	Goefrey Tomlinson RC	.35
412	Jeff Winchester RC	.35
413	Adam Piatt RC	.50
414	Robert Stratton	.25
415	T.J. Tucker	.25
416	Ryan Langerhans RC	1.50
417	Chris Wakeland RC	.35
418	Matt Miller RC	.35
419	Doug Clark RC	.35
420	Kory DeHaan RC	.35
421	David Eckstein RC	2.00
422	Brian Cooper RC	.35
423	Brady Clark RC	1.50
424	Chris Magruder RC	.35
425	Bobby Seay RC	.50
426	Aubrey Huff RC	8.00
427	Mike Jerzembeck	.25
428	Matt Blank RC	.35
429	Benny Agbayani RC	.35
430	Kevin Beirne RC	.35
431	Josh Hamilton RC	15.00
432	Josh Girdley RC	.35
433	Kyle Snyder RC	.35
434	Mike Paradis RC	.35
435	Jason Jennings RC	.75
436	David Walling RC	.35
437	Omar Ortiz RC	.35
438	Jay Gehrke RC	.35
439	Casey Burns RC	.35
440	Carl Crawford RC	12.00

Refractors

Refractor versions of all Bowman Chrome base cards and inserts were also created. Base card Refractors are found at the average rate of one per 12 packs. Scout's Choice Refractors are a 1:48 find; International Refractors (serially numbered within an edition of 100 each) are 1:76 and Diamond Aces Refractors are 1:84.

	NM/M
Common Player:	1.00
Refractor Stars:	5X

(See 1999 Bowman Chrome for checklist and base card values.)

Gold

A gold, rather than black, facsimile signature differentiates this parallel from the base-card issue. At an average insertion rate of 1:12, the Series 1 Golds are twice as easy as the Series 2 (1:24). Conversely, a Refractor version which is limited to 25 serially numbered sets, is an easier pull in Series 2 (1:200) than in Series 1 (1:305).

	NM/M
Common Player, Series 1:	1.50
Common Player, Series 2:	2.00
Stars:	3X
Gold Refractors:	30X

(See 1999 Bowman Chrome for checklist and base card values.)

International

Replacing the regular-card background with a scene from the player's native land gives this parallel an international flavor. For the geographically challenged, the place of birth is spelled out in the lower-left corner of the photo. In addition, the card backs are printed in the player's native language. Series 1 Internationals are found on the average of one per four packs, while the scarcer Series 2 Internationals are a 1:12 pick. Conversely, the Refractor version, individually numbered within an edition of 100 each is scarcer in Series 1 (1:76) than in Series 2 (1:50).

	NM/M
Common Player, Series 1:	.25
Common Player, Series 2:	.50
Stars:	1.5X
Common Refractor:	5.00
Refractors:	12X

(See 1999 Bowman Chrome for checklist and base card values.)

Diamond Aces

This 18-card set features nine emerging stars along with nine proven veterans. The cards have a prismatic look with "Diamond Aces" across the top. They are inserted in Series 1 packs. A parallel Refractor version is also randomly inserted.

	NM/M
Complete Set (18):	24.00
Common Player:	.50
Inserted 1:21	
Refractors:	1.5X
Inserted 1:84	

No.	Player	Price
DA1	Troy Glaus	1.50
DA2	Eric Chavez	.75
DA3	Fernando Seguignol	.50
DA4	Ryan Anderson	.50
DA5	Ruben Mateo	.50
DA6	Carlos Beltran	1.00
DA7	Adrian Beltre	.75
DA8	Bruce Chen	.50
DA9	Pat Burrell	2.00
DA10	Mike Piazza	3.00
DA11	Ken Griffey Jr.	3.00
DA12	Chipper Jones	2.00
DA13	Derek Jeter	4.00
DA14	Mark McGwire	3.50
DA15	Nomar Garciaparra	2.00
DA16	Sammy Sosa	2.00
DA17	Juan Gonzalez	.75
DA18	Alex Rodriguez	3.50

Early Impact

The checklist of this Series 2 insert mixes a dozen youngsters - labeled "Early Impact" on front - who are already making a mark in the majors with eight veteran stars, whose cards are labeled "Lasting Impact." A Refractor version is a parallel.

	NM/M
Complete Set (20):	35.00
Common Player:	.75
Inserted 1:15	
Refractor:	1.5X
Inserted 1:75	

No.	Player	Price
1	Alfonso Soriano	2.00
2	Pat Burrell	2.00
3	Ruben Mateo	.75
4	A.J. Burnett	.75
5	Corey Patterson	1.00
6	Daryle Ward	.75
7	Eric Chavez	.75
8	Troy Glaus	2.00
9	Sean Casey	1.00
10	Joe McEwing	.75
11	Gabe Kapler	.75
12	Michael Barrett	.75
13	Sammy Sosa	2.50
14	Alex Rodriguez	3.00
15	Mark McGwire	4.00
16	Derek Jeter	5.00
17	Nomar Garciaparra	2.50
18	Mike Piazza	3.00
19	Chipper Jones	2.50
20	Ken Griffey Jr.	3.00

Scout's Choice

This is a chromium parallel of the inserts found in Series 1 Bowman. The 21-card set showcases prospects that have potential to win a future Rookie of the Year award. Refractor parallels are also randomly inserted.

	NM/M
Complete Set (21):	20.00
Common Player:	.75
Inserted 1:12	
Refractors:	1.5X
Inserted 1:48	

No.	Player	Price
SC1	Ruben Mateo	.75
SC2	Ryan Anderson	.75
SC3	Pat Burrell	3.00
SC4	Troy Glaus	4.00
SC5	Eric Chavez	2.00
SC6	Adrian Beltre	1.50
SC7	Bruce Chen	.75
SC8	Carlos Beltran	2.50
SC9	Alex Gonzalez	.75
SC10	Carlos Lee	1.00
SC11	George Lombard	.75
SC12	Matt Clement	.75
SC13	Calvin Pickering	.75
SC14	Marlon Anderson	.75
SC15	Chad Hermansen	.75
SC16	Russell Branyan	.75
SC17	Jeremy Giambi	.75
SC18	Ricky Ledee	.75
SC19	John Patterson	.75
SC20	Roy Halladay	1.00
SC21	Michael Barrett	.75

2000 Rookie of the Year

This is a chromium parallel of the inserts found in Series 2 Bowman. The 10-card set is inserted in Series 2 Chrome packs and showcases prospects that have potential to win the 2000 Rookie of the Year award. Refractor parallels are also randomly inserted.

	NM/M
Complete Set (10):	12.00
Common Player:	1.00
Inserted 1:20	
Refractors:	1.5-3X
Inserted 1:100	

No.	Player	Price
1	Ryan Anderson	1.00
2	Pat Burrell	4.00
3	A.J. Burnett	1.00
4	Ruben Mateo	1.00
5	Alex Escobar	1.00
6	Pablo Ozuna	1.00
7	Mark Mulder	1.50
8	Corey Patterson	2.00
9	George Lombard	1.00
10	Nick Johnson	2.00

1999 Bowman's Best Pre-Production

These cards were issued to draw interest to the '99 Bowman's Best issue. The promos are virtually identical to the issued version of each player's card except for the card number which is preceeded by a "PP" prefix.

	NM/M
Complete Set (3):	3.00
Common Player:	2.00
PP1 Javy Lopez	1.00
PP2 Marlon Anderson	1.00
PP3 J.M. Gold	1.00

1999 Bowman's Best

Bowman's Best consists of 200 cards printed on thick 27-point stock. Within the base set are 85 veteran stars printed on gold foil, 15 Best Performers on bronze foil, 50 Prospects on silver foil and 50 rookies on blue foil. The rookies are seeded one per pack. There are also two parallel versions: Refractors and Atomic Refractors. Refractors are inserted 1:15 packs and are sequentially numbered to 400, while Atomic Refractors are found 1:62 packs and are sequentially numbered to 100.

		NM/M
Complete Set (200):		30.00
Common Player:		.25
Pack (6):		2.00
Wax Box (24):		40.00
1	Chipper Jones	1.50
2	Brian Jordan	.25
3	David Justice	.25
4	Jason Kendall	.25
5	Mo Vaughn	.25
6	Jim Edmonds	.25
7	Wade Boggs	1.50
8	Jeromy Burnitz	.25
9	Todd Hundley	.25
10	Rondell White	.25
11	Cliff Floyd	.25
12	Sean Casey	.40
13	Bernie Williams	.25
14	Dante Bichette	.25
15	Greg Vaughn	.25
16	Andres Galarraga	.25
17	Ray Durham	.25
18	Jim Thome	.60
19	Gary Sheffield	.45
20	Frank Thomas	1.00
21	Orlando Hernandez	.35
22	Ivan Rodriguez	.75
23	Jose Cruz Jr.	.25
24	Jason Giambi	.50
25	Craig Biggio	.25
26	Kerry Wood	.45
27	Manny Ramirez	1.00
28	Curt Schilling	.45
29	Mike Mussina	.45
30	Tim Salmon	.25
31	Mike Piazza	2.00
32	Roberto Alomar	.40
33	Larry Walker	.25
34	Barry Larkin	.25
35	Nomar Garciaparra	1.50
36	Paul O'Neill	.25
37	Todd Walker	.25
38	Eric Karros	.25

39	Brad Fullmer	.25
40	John Olerud	.25
41	Todd Helton	.75
42	Raul Mondesi	.25
43	Jose Canseco	.50
44	Matt Williams	.25
45	Ray Lankford	.25
46	Carlos Delgado	.50
47	Darin Erstad	.50
48	Vladimir Guerrero	1.00
49	Robin Ventura	.25
50	Alex Rodriguez	2.50
51	Vinny Castilla	.25
52	Tony Clark	.25
53	Pedro Martinez	1.00
54	Rafael Palmeiro	.65
55	Scott Rolen	.65
56	Tino Martinez	.25
57	Tony Gwynn	1.50
58	Barry Bonds	3.00
59	Kenny Lofton	.25
60	Javy Lopez	.25
61	Mark Grace	.25
62	Travis Lee	.25
63	Kevin Brown	.25
64	Al Leiter	.25
65	Albert Belle	.25
66	Sammy Sosa	1.50
67	Greg Maddux	1.50
68	Mark Kotsay	.25
69	Dmitri Young	.25
70	Mark McGwire	2.50
71	Juan Gonzalez	.50
72	Andruw Jones	1.00
73	Derek Jeter	3.00
74	Randy Johnson	1.00
75	Cal Ripken Jr.	3.00
76	Shawn Green	.35
77	Moises Alou	.25
78	Tom Glavine	.45
79	Sandy Alomar	.25
80	Ken Griffey Jr.	2.00
81	Ryan Klesko	.25
82	Jeff Bagwell	1.00
83	Ben Grieve	.25
84	John Smoltz	.25
85	Roger Clemens	1.75
86	Ken Griffey Jr.	1.00
87	Roger Clemens	.85
88	Derek Jeter	1.50
89	Nomar Garciaparra	.75
90	Mark McGwire	1.25
91	Sammy Sosa	.75
92	Alex Rodriguez	1.25
93	Greg Maddux	.75
94	Vladimir Guerrero	1.00
95	Chipper Jones	.75
96	Kerry Wood	.30
97	Ben Grieve	.25
98	Tony Gwynn	.75
99	Juan Gonzalez	.30
100	Mike Piazza	1.00
101	Eric Chavez	.40
102	Billy Koch	.25
103	Dernell Stenson	.25
104	Marlon Anderson	.25
105	Ron Belliard	.25
106	Bruce Chen	.25
107	Carlos Beltran	.40
108	Chad Hermansen	.25
109	Ryan Anderson	.25
110	Michael Barrett	.25
111	Matt Clement	.25
112	Ben Davis	.25
113	Calvin Pickering	.25
114	Brad Penny	.25
115	Paul Konerko	.35
116	Alex Gonzalez	.25
117	George Lombard	.25
118	John Patterson	.25
119	Rob Bell	.25
120	Ruben Mateo	.25
121	Troy Glaus	.75
122	Ryan Bradley	.25
123	Carlos Lee	.35
124	Gabe Kapler	.25
125	Ramon Hernandez	.25
126	Carlos Febles	.25
127	Mitch Meluskey	.25
128	Michael Cuddyer	.25
129	Pablo Ozuna	.25
130	Jayson Werth	.25
131	Ricky Ledee	.25
132	Jeremy Giambi	.25
133	Danny Klassen	.25
134	Mark DeRosa	.25
135	Randy Wolf	.25
136	Roy Halladay	.35
137	Derrick Gibson	.25
138	Ben Petrick	.25
139	Warren Morris	.25
140	Lance Berkman	.25
141	Russell Branyan	.25
142	Adrian Beltre	.40
143	Juan Encarnacion	.25
144	Fernando Seguignol	.25
145	Corey Koskie	.25
146	Preston Wilson	.25
147	Homer Bush	.25
148	Daryle Ward	.25
149	Joe McEwing RC	.50
150	Peter Bergeron RC	.50
151	Pat Burrell RC	3.00
152	Choo Freeman RC	.50
153	Matt Belisle RC	.50
154	Carlos Pena RC	.75
155	A.J. Burnett RC	.75
156	Doug Mientkiewicz RC	.75

157	Sean Burroughs RC	.50
158	Mike Zywica RC	.35
159	Corey Patterson RC	1.50
160	Austin Kearns RC	2.00
161	Chip Ambres RC	.35
162	Kelly Dransfeldt RC	.35
163	Mike Nannini RC	.35
164	Mark Mulder RC	2.00
165	Jason Tyner RC	.50
166	Bobby Seay RC	.50
167	Alex Escobar RC	.75
168	Nick Johnson RC	1.00
169	Alfonso Soriano RC	4.00
170	Clayton Andrews RC	.35
171	C.C. Sabathia RC	1.00
172	Matt Holliday RC	3.00
173	Brad Lidge RC	1.00
174	Kit Pellow RC	.50
175	J.M. Gold RC	.50
176	Roosevelt Brown RC	.50
177	Eric Valent RC	.50
178	Adam Everett RC	.75
179	Jorge Toca RC	.35
180	Matt Roney RC	.35
181	Andy Brown RC	.35
182	Phil Norton RC	.35
183	Mickey Lopez RC	.35
184	Chris George RC	.35
185	Arturo McDowell RC	.35
186	Jose Fernandez RC	.35
187	Seth Etherton RC	.50
188	Josh McKinley RC	.50
189	Nate Cornejo RC	.50
190	Giuseppe Chiaramonte RC	.35
191	Mamon Tucker RC	.35
192	Ryan Mills RC	.50
193	Chad Moeller RC	.50
194	Tony Torcato RC	.35
195	Jeff Winchester RC	.35
196	Rick Elder RC	.35
197	Matt Burch RC	.35
198	Jeff Urban RC	.35
199	Chris Jones RC	.35
200	Masao Kida RC	.50

Refractors

Inserted at an average rate of about one per 15 packs, Best Refractor's are so marked on the back in the card-number box at upper-right. Also found on back is a serial numbered stamped in gold-foil from within an edition of 400.

	NM/M
Complete Set (200):	250.00
Common Player:	1.00
Stars:	6X
Production 400 Sets	

(See 1999 Bowman's Best for checklist and base card values.)

Atomic Refractors

The vibrant refractive background on front announces these parallels which are found on average of about once per 62 packs. Backs identify the variation in the card-number box at upper-right and with a serial number from within an edition of 100 per card.

	NM/M
Common Player:	3.00
Stars:	12X
Production 100 Sets	

(See 1999 Bowman's Best for checklist and base card values.)

Franchise Best

Ten league leaders are featured in this insert set on three different technologies: Mach I, Mach II and Mach III. Mach I features die-cut Serillusion stock and is numbered to 3,000. Mach II features die-cut refractive styrene stock, numbered to 1,000; and, Mach III features die-cut polycarbonate stock and is limited to 500 numbered sets. All cards numbers have an "FB" prefix.

		NM/M
Complete Set (10):		15.00
Common Player:		.75
Production 3,000 Sets		
Mach II (1,000):		1.5X
Mach III (500):		2.5X
1	Mark McGwire	2.50
2	Ken Griffey Jr.	1.50
3	Sammy Sosa	1.25
4	Nomar Garciaparra	1.25
5	Alex Rodriguez	2.50
6	Derek Jeter	3.50
7	Mike Piazza	1.50
8	Frank Thomas	1.00
9	Chipper Jones	1.25
10	Juan Gonzalez	.75

Franchise Favorites

This six-card set features retired legends and current stars in three versions. Version A features a current star, Version B features a retired player and Version C pairs the current star with the retired player. Cards have an "FR" prefix to the number on back.

		NM/M
Complete Set (6):		12.00
Common Player:		.50
Inserted 1:75		
1A	Derek Jeter	5.00
1B	Don Mattingly	2.00
1C	Derek Jeter, Don Mattingly	5.00
2A	Scott Rolen	.50
2B	Mike Schmidt	1.50
2C	Scott Rolen, Mike Schmidt	1.00

Franchise Favorites Autographs

This is a parallel autographed version of the regular Franchise Favorites inserts.

	NM/M
Common Player:	15.00
Version A & B 1:1,548	

		NM/M
Version C 1:6,191		
1A	Derek Jeter	100.00
1B	Don Mattingly	60.00
1C	Derek Jeter, Don Mattingly	300.00
2A	Scott Rolen	20.00
2B	Mike Schmidt	50.00
2C	Scott Rolen, Mike Schmidt	100.00

Future Foundations

Ten up-and-coming players are featured in this set that has the same technologies as the Franchise Best inserts and broken down the same way. The insert rates are 1:41 packs for Mach I, 1:124 for Mach II and 1:248 for Mach III.

		NM/M
Complete Set (10):		16.00
Common Player:		.75
Production 3,000 Sets		
Mach II (1,000):		1.5X
Mach III (500):		2.5X
1	Ruben Mateo	.75
2	Troy Glaus	4.00
3	Eric Chavez	1.50
4	Pat Burrell	4.00
5	Adrian Beltre	1.50
6	Ryan Anderson	.75
7	Alfonso Soriano	3.00
8	Brad Penny	.75
9	Derrick Gibson	.75
10	Bruce Chen	.75

Mirror Image

These inserts feature a veteran player on one side and a prospect on the other side for a total of 10 double-sided cards featuring 20 players. There are also parallel Refractor and Atomic Refractor versions.

		NM/M
Complete Set (10):		20.00
Common Player:		1.50
Inserted 1:24		
Refractors (1:96):		1.5X
Atomic Refractors (1:192):		2X
1	Alex Rodriguez, Alex Gonzalez	2.50
2	Ken Griffey Jr., Ruben Mateo	2.00
3	Derek Jeter, Alfonso Soriano	4.00
4	Sammy Sosa, Corey Patterson	1.50
5	Greg Maddux, Bruce Chen	1.50
6	Chipper Jones, Eric Chavez	1.50
7	Vladimir Guerrero, Carlos Beltran	1.50
8	Frank Thomas, Nick Johnson	1.50
9	Nomar Garciaparra, Pablo Ozuna	1.50
10	Mark McGwire, Pat Burrell	3.00

Rookie Locker Room Autographs

This five-card set features autographs of baseball's current hot prospects. Each card is branded with a "Topps Certified Autograph Issue" stamp.

		NM/M
Common Player:		4.00
Inserted 1:248		
1	Pat Burrell	10.00
2	Michael Barrett	4.00
3	Troy Glaus	10.00
4	Gabe Kapler	4.00
5	Eric Chavez	7.50

Rookie Locker Room Game-Worn Jerseys

This four-card set spotlights hot prospects and has a swatch of game-used jersey from the featured player embedded into the card.

		NM/M
Complete Set (4):		12.00
Common Player:		3.00
Inserted 1:270		
1	Richie Sexson	3.00
2	Michael Barrett	3.00
3	Troy Glaus	7.50
4	Eric Chavez	4.50

Rookie Locker Room Game-Used Lumber

This six-card set features actual pieces of each player's game-used bat embedded into the cards.

		NM/M
Complete Set (6):		35.00
Common Player:		4.00
Inserted 1:258		
1	Pat Burrell	10.00
2	Michael Barrett	4.00
3	Troy Glaus	10.00
4	Gabe Kapler	4.00
5	Eric Chavez	7.50
6	Richie Sexson	5.00

Rookie of the Year

This set salutes 1998 AL and NL Rookie of Year award winners Kerry Wood and Ben Grieve. They are inserted 1:95 packs and are numbered with a ROY prefix. Ben Grieve also autographed some of the inserts which feature a "Topps Certified Autograph Issue" stamp. Autographs are seeded 1:1,241 packs.

	NM/M
Complete Set (2):	4.00

No	Player	Price
1	Ben Grieve	2.00
2	Kerry Wood	4.00
A1	Ben Grieve/Auto.	6.00

2000 Bowman

Released in one 440-card series. The card fronts are foil stamped to differentiate Veterans (gold foil) from Rookies and Prospects (silver). All card fronts feature facsimile signatures from the players' original Topps contracts. All bona fide rookie cards also exhibit the "Bowman Rookie Card" stamped under the 2000 Bowman logo.

		NM/M
Complete Set (440):		65.00
Common Player:		.15
Common Rookie:		.25
Pack (10):		2.50
Box (24):		40.00
1	Vladimir Guerrero	.75
2	Chipper Jones	.75
3	Todd Walker	.15
4	Barry Larkin	.25
5	Bernie Williams	.40
6	Todd Helton	.75
7	Jermaine Dye	.15
8	Brian Giles	.15
9	Freddy Garcia	.15
10	Greg Vaughn	.15
11	Alex Gonzalez	.15
12	Luis Gonzalez	.25
13	Ron Belliard	.15
14	Ben Grieve	.15
15	Carlos Delgado	.50
16	Brian Jordan	.15
17	Fernando Tatis	.15
18	Ryan Rupe	.15
19	Miguel Tejada	.50
20	Mark Grace	.30
21	Kenny Lofton	.15
22	Eric Karros	.15
23	Cliff Floyd	.15
24	John Halama	.15
25	Cristian Guzman	.15
26	Scott Williamson	.15
27	Mike Lieberthal	.15
28	Tim Hudson	.40
29	Warren Morris	.15
30	Pedro Martinez	1.00
31	John Smoltz	.15
32	Ray Durham	.15
33	Chad Allen	.15
34	Tony Clark	.15
35	Tino Martinez	.15
36	J.T. Snow Jr.	.15
37	Kevin Brown	.25
38	Bartolo Colon	.15
39	Rey Ordonez	.15
40	Jeff Bagwell	.50
41	Ivan Rodriguez	.50
42	Eric Chavez	.25
43	Eric Milton	.15
44	Jose Canseco	.50
45	Shawn Green	.25
46	Rich Aurilia	.15
47	Roberto Alomar	.40
48	Brian Daubach	.15
49	Magglio Ordonez	.25
50	Derek Jeter	2.00
51	Kris Benson	.15
52	Albert Belle	.15
53	Rondell White	.15
54	Justin Thompson	.15
55	Nomar Garciaparra	.75
56	Chuck Finley	.15
57	Omar Vizquel	.15
58	Luis Castillo	.15
59	Richard Hidalgo	.15
60	Barry Bonds	2.00
61	Craig Biggio	.15
62	Doug Glanville	.15
63	Gabe Kapler	.15
64	Johnny Damon	.15
65	Pokey Reese	.15
66	Andy Pettitte	.25
67	B.J. Surhoff	.15
68	Richie Sexson	.40
69	Javy Lopez	.15
70	Raul Mondesi	.15
71	Darin Erstad	.25
72	Kevin Millwood	.15
73	Ricky Ledee	.15
74	John Olerud	.15
75	Sean Casey	.25
76	Carlos Febles	.15
77	Paul O'Neill	.25
78	Bob Abreu	.15
79	Neifi Perez	.15
80	Tony Gwynn	.75
81	Russ Ortiz	.15
82	Matt Williams	.15
83	Chris Carpenter	.15
84	Roger Cedeno	.15
85	Tim Salmon	.30
86	Billy Koch	.15
87	Jeromy Burnitz	.15
88	Edgardo Alfonzo	.15
89	Jay Bell	.15
90	Manny Ramirez	.75
91	Frank Thomas	.75
92	Mike Mussina	.50
93	J.D. Drew	.25
94	Adrian Beltre	.25
95	Alex Rodriguez	2.00
96	Larry Walker	.15
97	Juan Encarnacion	.15
98	Mike Sweeney	.15
99	Rusty Greer	.15
100	Randy Johnson	.75
101	Jose Vidro	.15
102	Preston Wilson	.15
103	Greg Maddux	1.50
104	Jason Giambi	.50
105	Cal Ripken Jr.	3.00
106	Carlos Beltran	.50
107	Vinny Castilla	.15
108	Mariano Rivera	.25
109	Mo Vaughn	.25
110	Rafael Palmeiro	.50
111	Shannon Stewart	.15
112	Mike Hampton	.15
113	Joe Nathan	.15
114	Ben Davis	.15
115	Andruw Jones	.50
116	Robin Ventura	.15
117	Damion Easley	.15
118	Jeff Cirillo	.15
119	Kerry Wood	.25
120	Scott Rolen	.75
121	Sammy Sosa	.75
122	Ken Griffey Jr.	2.00
123	Shane Reynolds	.15
124	Troy Glaus	.40
125	Tom Glavine	.35
126	Michael Barrett	.15
127	Al Leiter	.15
128	Jason Kendall	.15
129	Roger Clemens	2.00
130	Juan Gonzalez	.40
131	Corey Koskie	.15
132	Curt Schilling	.15
133	Mike Piazza	1.00
134	Gary Sheffield	.40
135	Jim Thome	.40
136	Orlando Hernandez	.25
137	Ray Lankford	.15
138	Geoff Jenkins	.15
139	Jose Lima	.15
140	Mark McGwire	1.50
141	Adam Piatt	.15
142	Pat Manning RC	.25
143	Marcos Castillo RC	.25
144	Lesli Brea RC	.25
145	Humberto Cota RC	.25
146	Ben Petrick	.15
147	Kip Wells	.15
148	Willi Mo Pena RC	.25
149	Chris Wakeland	.15
150	Brad Baker RC	.15
151	Robbie Morrison RC	.50
152	Reggie Taylor	.15
153	Brian Cole RC	.25
154	Peter Bergeron	.15
155	Roosevelt Brown	.15
156	Matt Cepicky RC	.25
157	Ramon Castro	.15
158	Brad Baisley RC	.25
159	Jeff Goldbach RC	.50
160	Mitch Meluskey	.15
161	Chad Harville	.15
162	Brian Cooper	.15
163	Marcus Giles	.15
164	Jim Morris	.50
165	Geoff Goetz	.15
166	Bobby Bradley RC	.50
167	Rob Bell	.15
168	Joe Crede	.15
169	Michael Restovich RC	.15
170	Quincy Foster RC	.50
171	Enrique Cruz RC	.15
172	Mark Quinn	.15
173	Nick Johnson	.15
174	Jeff Liefer	.15
175	Kevin Mench RC	1.50
176	Steve Lomasney	.15
177	Jayson Werth	.15
178	Tim Drew	.15
179	Chip Ambres	.15
180	Ryan Anderson	.15
181	Matt Blank	.15
182	Giuseppe Chiaramonte	.15
183	Corey Myers RC	.50
184	Jeff Yoder	.15
185	Craig Dingman RC	.15
186	Jon Hamilton RC	.25
187	Toby Hall	.15
188	Russell Branyan	.15
189	Brian Falkenborg RC	.25
190	Aaron Harang RC	.50
191	Juan Pena	.15
192	Travis Thompson RC	.15
193	Alfonso Soriano	.50
194	Alejandro Diaz RC	.25
195	Carlos Pena	.15
196	Kevin Nicholson	.15
197	Mo Bruce	.15
198	C.C. Sabathia	.15
199	Carl Crawford	.25
200	Rafael Furcal	.15
201	Andrew Beinbrink RC	.25
202	Jimmy Osting	.15
203	Aaron McNeal RC	.50
204	Brett Laxton	.15
205	Chris George	.15
206	Felipe Lopez	.15
207	Ben Sheets RC	2.00
208	Mike Meyers RC	.40
209	Jason Conti	.15
210	Milton Bradley	.15
211	Chris Mears RC	.25
212	Carlos Hernandez RC	.50
213	Jason Romano	.15
214	Goefrey Tomlinson	.15
215	Jimmy Rollins	.40
216	Pablo Ozuna	.15
217	Steve Cox	.15
218	Terrence Long	.15
219	Jeff DaVanon RC	.40
220	Rick Ankiel	.25
221	Jason Standridge	.15
222	Tony Armas	.15
223	Jason Tyner	.15
224	Ramon Ortiz	.15
225	Daryle Ward	.15
226	Enger Veras RC	.15
227	Chris Jones RC	.50
228	Eric Cammack RC	.25
229	Ruben Mateo	.15
230	Ken Harvey RC	1.00
231	Jake Westbrook	.15
232	Rob Purvis RC	.15
233	Choo Freeman	.15
234	Aramis Ramirez	.15
235	A.J. Burnett	.15
236	Kevin Barker	.15
237	Chance Caple RC	.50
238	Jarrod Washburn	.15
239	Lance Berkman	.15
240	Michael Wenner RC	.25
241	Alex Sanchez	.15
242	Jake Esteves RC	.25
243	Grant Roberts	.15
244	Mark Ellis RC	.50
245	Donny Leon	.15
246	David Eckstein	.15
247	Dicky Gonzalez RC	.25
248	John Patterson	.15
249	Chad Green	.15
250	Scot Shields RC	.25
251	Troy Cameron	.15
252	Jose Molina	.15
253	Rob Pugmire RC	.25
254	Rick Elder	.15
255	Sean Burroughs	.25
256	Josh Kalinowski RC	.25
257	Matt LeCroy	.15
258	Alex Graman RC	.50
259	Tomokazu Ohka RC	.50
260	Brady Clark	.15
261	Rico Washington RC	.25
262	Gary Matthews Jr.	.15
263	Matt Wise	.15
264	Keith Reed RC	.15
265	Santiago Ramirez RC	.25
266	Ben Broussard RC	.50
267	Ryan Langerhans	.15
268	Juan Rivera	.15
269	Shawn Gallagher	.15
270	Jorge Toca	.15
271	Brad Lidge	.15
272	Leo Estrella RC	.25
273	Ruben Quevedo	.15
274	Jack Cust	.15
275	T.J. Tucker	.15
276	Mike Colangelo	.15
277	Brian Schneider	.15
278	Calvin Murray	.15
279	Josh Girdley	.15
280	Mike Paradis	.15
281	Chad Hermansen	.15
282	Ty Howington RC	.50
283	Aaron Myette	.15
284	D'Angelo Jimenez	.15
285	Dernell Stenson	.15
286	Jerry Hairston Jr.	.15
287	Gary Majewski RC	.25
288	Derrin Ebert RC	.25
289	Steve Fish RC	.25
290	Carlos Hernandez	.15
291	Allen Levrault	.15
292	Sean McNally RC	.25
293	Randey Dorame RC	.25
294	Wes Anderson RC	.50
295	B.J. Ryan	.15
296	Alan Webb RC	.15
297	Brandon Inge RC	.75
298	David Walling	.15
299	Sun-Woo Kim RC	.40
300	Pat Burrell	.25
301	Rick Guttormson RC	.25
302	Gil Meche	.15
303	Carlos Zambrano RC	3.00
304	Eric Byrnes RC (Photo actually Bo Porter.)	1.00
305	Robb Quinlan RC	.25
306	Jackie Rexrode	.15
307	Nate Bump	.15
308	Sean DePaula RC	.25
309	Matt Riley	.15
310	Ryan Minor	.15
311	J.J. Davis	.15
312	Randy Wolf	.15
313	Jason Jennings	.15
314	Scott Seabol RC	.25
315	Doug Davis	.15
316	Todd Moser RC	.15
317	Rob Ryan	.15
318	Bubba Crosby	.15
319	Lyle Overbay RC	1.00
320	Mario Encarnacion	.15
321	Francisco Rodriguez RC	2.00
322	Michael Cuddyer	.15
323	Eddie Yarnall	.15
324	Cesar Saba RC	.15
325	Travis Dawkins	.15
326	Alex Escobar	.15
327	Julio Zuleta	.40
328	Josh Hamilton	.25
329	Nick Neugebauer RC	.25
330	Matt Belisle	.15
331	Kurt Ainsworth RC	.50
332	Tim Raines Jr.	.15
333	Eric Munson	.15
334	Donzell McDonald	.15
335	Larry Bigbie RC	.25
336	Matt Watson	.15
337	Aubrey Huff	.15
338	Julio Ramirez	.15
339	Jason Grabowski RC	.25
340	Jon Garland	.15
341	Austin Kearns	.25
342	Josh Pressley	.15
343	Miguel Olivo RC	.25
344	Julio Lugo	.15
345	Roberto Vaz	.15
346	Ramon Soler	.15
347	Brandon Phillips RC	1.00
348	Vince Faison RC	.25
349	Mike Venafro	.15
350	Rick Asadoorian RC	.25
351	B.J. Garbe RC	.25
352	Dan Reichert	.15
353	Jason Stumm RC	.25
354	Ruben Salazar RC	.15
355	Francisco Cordero	.15
356	Juan Guzman RC	.25
357	Mike Bacsik RC	.15
358	Jared Sandberg	.15
359	Rod Barajas	.15
360	Junior Brignac RC	.25
361	J.M. Gold	.15
362	Octavio Dotel	.15
363	David Kelton	.15
364	Scott Morgan RC	.25
365	Wascar Serrano RC	.25
366	Wilton Veras	.15
367	Eugene Kingsale	.15
368	Ted Lilly	.15
369	George Lombard	.15
370	Chris Haas	.15
371	Wilton Pena RC	.50
372	Vernon Wells	.15
373	Jason Royer RC	.25
374	Jeff Heaverlo RC	.25
375	Calvin Pickering	.15
376	Mike Lamb	.40
377	Kyle Snyder	.15
378	Javier Cardona RC	.15
379	Aaron Rowand RC	1.00
380	Dee Brown	.15
381	Brett Myers RC	1.00
382	Abraham Nunez	.20
383	Eric Valent	.15
384	Jody Gerut RC	.25
385	Adam Dunn	.50
386	Jay Gehrke	.15
387	Omar Ortiz	.15
388	Darnell McDonald	.15
389	Chad Alexander	.15
390	J.D. Closser	.15
391	Ben Christensen	.15
392	Adam Kennedy	.15
393	Nick Green RC	.25
394	Ramon Hernandez	.15
395	Roy Oswalt RC	4.00
396	Andy Tracy RC	.50
397	Eric Gagne	.15
398	Michael Tejera RC	.25
399	Adam Everett	.15
400	Corey Patterson	.25
401	Gary Knotts RC	.25
402	Ryan Christianson RC	.50
403	Eric Ireland RC	.25
404	Andrew Good RC	.25
405	Brad Penny	.15
406	Jason LaRue	.15
407	Kit Pellow	.15
408	Kevin Beirne	.15
409	Kelly Dransfeldt	.15
410	Jason Grilli	.15
411	Scott Downs RC	.25
412	Jesus Colome	.15
413	John Sneed RC	.25
414	Tony McKnight RC	.25
415	Luis Rivera	.15
416	Adam Eaton	.15
417	Mike MacDougal RC	.50
418	Mike Nannini	.15
419	Barry Zito RC	2.50
420	Dewayne Wise	.15
421	Jason Dellaero	.15
422	Chad Moeller	.15
423	Jason Marquis	.15
424	Tim Redding RC	.50
425	Mark Mulder	.15
426	Josh Paul	.15
427	Chris Enochs	.15
428	Wilfredo Rodriguez RC	.50
429	Kevin Witt	.15
430	Scott Sobkowiak RC	.25
431	McKay Christensen	.15
432	Jung Bong	.15
433	Kevin Evans RC	.25
434	Garry Maddox Jr.	.15
435	Ramon Santiago RC	.50
436	Alex Cora	.15
437	Carlos Lee	.15
438	Jason Repko RC	.15
439	Matt Burch	.15
440	Shawn Sonnier RC	.25

Gold

Golds are a 440-card parallel to the base set and are highlighted by gold-stamped facsimile autographs on the card front. Golds are limited to 99 serial numbered sets.

Stars: 10-20X
Rookies: 4-8X
Production 99 Sets
(See 2000 Bowman for checklist and base card values.)

Retro/Future

These inserts are a parallel to the 440-card base set. The foiled card fronts have a horizontal format and a design reminiscent of the 1955 Bowman "television set" design. They were seeded one per pack.

	NM/M
Common Player:	.25
Stars:	2-3X
Rookies:	.75-2X
Inserted 1:1	

(See 2000 Bowman for checklist and base card values.)

Autographs

Jose Vidro

This set consists of 40 players with card rarity differentiated by either a Blue, Silver or Gold foil Topps "Certified Autograph Issue" stamp. Card backs are numbered using the player initials and have a Topps serial numbered foil hologram to ensure the authenticity of the autograph.

		NM/M
Common Autograph:		5.00
Blue Inserted 1:144		
Silver 1:312		
Gold 1:1,604		
CA	Chip Ambres/B	5.00
RA	Rick Ankiel/G	10.00
CB	Carlos Beltran/G	40.00
LB	Lance Berkman/S	20.00
DB	Dee Brown/S	8.00
SB	Sean Burroughs/S	8.00
JDC	J.D. Closser/B	5.00
SC	Steve Cox/B	5.00
MC	Michael Cuddyer/S	10.00
JC	Jack Cust/S	5.00
SD	Scott Downs/S	10.00
JDD	J.D. Drew/G	25.00
AD	Adam Dunn/B	25.00
CF	Choo Freeman/S	5.00
RF	Rafael Furcal/S	15.00
AH	Aubrey Huff/B	8.00
JJ	Jason Jennings/B	8.00
NJ	Nick Johnson/S	10.00
AK	Austin Kearns/B	15.00
DK	David Kelton/B	5.00
RM	Ruben Mateo/G	15.00
MM	Mike Meyers/B	5.00
CP	Corey Patterson/S	20.00
BWP	Brad Penny/G	10.00
BP	Ben Petrick/G	10.00
AP	Adam Piatt/S	8.00
MQ	Mark Quinn/S	8.00
MR	Mike Restovich/B	8.00
MR	Matt Riley/S	8.00
JR	Jason Romano/B	5.00
BS	Ben Sheets/B	30.00
AS	Alfonso Soriano/S	40.00
EV	Eric Valent/B	5.00
JV	Jose Vidro/S	10.00
VW	Vernon Wells/G	20.00
SW	Scott Williamson/G	10.00
KJW	Kevin Witt/S	10.00
KLW	Kerry Wood/S	25.00
EY	Eddie Yarnall/S	5.00
JZ	Julio Zuleta/B	5.00

Bowman's Best Previews

DEREK JETER

This 10-card insert set is identical in design to 2000 Bowman's Best. The card fronts have a Refractor like sheen and the card backs are numbered with a "BBP" prefix.

		NM/M
Complete Set (10):		15.00
Common Player:		.50
Inserted 1:18		
1	Derek Jeter	4.00
2	Ken Griffey Jr.	3.00
3	Nomar Garciaparra	2.00
4	Mike Piazza	2.00
5	Alex Rodriguez	4.00
6	Sammy Sosa	2.00
7	Mark McGwire	3.00
8	Pat Burrell	1.00
9	Josh Hamilton	1.00
10	Adam Piatt	.50

Early Indications

This 10-card set has a blue foiled card front with red foil stamping. Card backs are numbered with an "E" prefix.

		NM/M
Complete Set (10):		18.00
Common Player:		1.00
Inserted 1:24		
1	Nomar Garciaparra	1.50
2	Cal Ripken Jr.	4.00
3	Derek Jeter	4.00
4	Mark McGwire	3.00
5	Alex Rodriguez	3.00
6	Chipper Jones	1.50
7	Todd Helton	1.00
8	Vladimir Guerrero	1.50
9	Mike Piazza	1.50
10	Jose Canseco	1.00

Major Power

This 10-card set spotlights the top home run hitters. Card fronts have a red border on a full foiled card front. These are

Major Power

numbered with an "MP" prefix on the card back.

		NM/M
Complete Set (10):		20.00
Common Player:		1.00
Inserted 1:24		
1	Mark McGwire	4.00
2	Chipper Jones	2.50
3	Alex Rodriguez	4.00
4	Sammy Sosa	3.00
5	Rafael Palmeiro	1.00
6	Ken Griffey Jr.	3.00
7	Nomar Garciaparra	3.00
8	Barry Bonds	5.00
9	Derek Jeter	5.00
10	Jeff Bagwell	1.50

Tool Time

This 20-card set focuses on the top minor league Prospects in five different categories: batting, power, speed, arm strength and defense. These are seeded 1:8 packs. Backs are numbered with a "TT" prefix.

		NM/M
Complete Set (20):		8.00
Common Player:		.40
Inserted 1:8		
1	Pat Burrell	1.00
2	Aaron Rowand	.40
3	Chris Wakeland	.40
4	Ruben Mateo	.40
5	Pat Burrell	1.00
6	Adam Piatt	.50
7	Nick Johnson	1.00
8	Jack Cust	.40
9	Rafael Furcal	.40
10	Julio Ramirez	.40
11	Travis Dawkins	.40
12	Corey Patterson	1.00
13	Ruben Mateo	.40
14	Jason Dellaero	.40
15	Sean Burroughs	1.00
16	Ryan Langerhans	.40
17	D'Angelo Jimenez	.40
18	Corey Patterson	1.00
19	Troy Cameron	.40
20	Michael Cuddyer	.50

2000 Bowman Chrome

Released as a single series 440-card set, Bowman

Chrome is identical in design to 2000 Bowman besides the Chromium finish on all cards. Foil highlights differentiate rookies and prospects (blue) from veterans (red). Three parallels to the base set are randomly seeded: Refractors, Retro/Future and Retro/Future Refractors.

		NM/M
Complete Set (440):		120.00
Common Player:		.25
Common Rookie:		.50
Pack (4):		3.00
Box (24):		60.00
1	Vladimir Guerrero	1.00
2	Chipper Jones	1.00
3	Todd Walker	.25
4	Barry Larkin	.25
5	Bernie Williams	.50
6	Todd Helton	.75
7	Jermaine Dye	.25
8	Brian Giles	.25
9	Freddy Garcia	.25
10	Greg Vaughn	.25
11	Alex Gonzalez	.25
12	Luis Gonzalez	.25
13	Ron Belliard	.25
14	Ben Grieve	.25
15	Carlos Delgado	.75
16	Brian Jordan	.25
17	Fernando Tatis	.25
18	Ryan Rupe	.25
19	Miguel Tejada	.40
20	Mark Grace	.35
21	Kenny Lofton	.25
22	Eric Karros	.25
23	Cliff Floyd	.25
24	John Halama	.25
25	Cristian Guzman	.25
26	Scott Williamson	.25
27	Mike Lieberthal	.25
28	Tim Hudson	.40
29	Warren Morris	.25
30	Pedro Martinez	1.00
31	John Smoltz	.25
32	Ray Durham	.25
33	Chad Allen	.25
34	Tony Clark	.25
35	Tino Martinez	.25
36	J.T. Snow Jr.	.25
37	Kevin Brown	.40
38	Bartolo Colon	.25
39	Rey Ordonez	.25
40	Jeff Bagwell	.50
41	Ivan Rodriguez	.75
42	Eric Chavez	.50
43	Eric Milton	.25
44	Jose Canseco	.50
45	Shawn Green	.50
46	Rich Aurilia	.25
47	Roberto Alomar	.50
48	Brian Daubach	.25
49	Magglio Ordonez	.50
50	Derek Jeter	2.00
51	Kris Benson	.25
52	Albert Belle	.25
53	Rondell White	.25
54	Justin Thompson	.25
55	Nomar Garciaparra	1.00
56	Chuck Finley	.25
57	Omar Vizquel	.25
58	Luis Castillo	.25
59	Richard Hidalgo	.25
60	Barry Bonds	2.00
61	Craig Biggio	.25
62	Doug Glanville	.25
63	Gabe Kapler	.25
64	Johnny Damon	.40
65	Pokey Reese	.25
66	Jason Pettitte	.50
67	B.J. Surhoff	.25
68	Richie Sexson	.50
69	Javy Lopez	.25
70	Raul Mondesi	.25
71	Darin Erstad	.40
72	Kevin Millwood	.40
73	Ricky Ledee	.25
74	John Olerud	.25
75	Sean Casey	.25
76	Carlos Febles	.25
77	Paul O'Neill	.25
78	Bob Abreu	.25
79	Neifi Perez	.25
80	Tony Gwynn	1.00
81	Russ Ortiz	.25
82	Matt Williams	.25
83	Chris Carpenter	.25
84	Roger Cedeno	.25
85	Tim Salmon	.35
86	Billy Koch	.25
87	Jeromy Burnitz	.25
88	Edgardo Alfonzo	.25
89	Jay Bell	.15
90	Manny Ramirez	.75
91	Frank Thomas	.75
92	Mike Mussina	.50
93	J.D. Drew	.40
94	Adrian Beltre	.25
95	Alex Rodriguez	2.00
96	Larry Walker	.25
97	Juan Encarnacion	.25
98	Mike Sweeney	.25
99	Rusty Greer	.25
100	Randy Johnson	.75
101	Jose Vidro	.25
102	Preston Wilson	.25
103	Greg Maddux	1.50
104	Jason Giambi	.75
105	Cal Ripken Jr.	3.00
106	Carlos Beltran	.25
107	Vinny Castilla	.25
108	Mariano Rivera	.35
109	Mo Vaughn	.25
110	Rafael Palmeiro	.50
111	Shannon Stewart	.25
112	Mike Hampton	.25
113	Joe Nathan	.25
114	Ben Davis	.25
115	Andruw Jones	.75
116	Robin Ventura	.25
117	Damian Easley	.25
118	Jeff Cirillo	.25
119	Kerry Wood	.40
120	Scott Rolen	.75
121	Sammy Sosa	1.00
122	Ken Griffey Jr.	2.00
123	Shane Reynolds	.25
124	Troy Glaus	.50
125	Tom Glavine	.40
126	Michael Barrett	.25
127	Al Leiter	.25
128	Jason Kendall	.25
129	Roger Clemens	2.00
130	Juan Gonzalez	.50
131	Corey Koskie	.25
132	Curt Schilling	.75
133	Mike Piazza	1.00
134	Gary Sheffield	.50
135	Jim Thome	.50
136	Orlando Hernandez	.40
137	Ray Lankford	.25
138	Geoff Jenkins	.25
139	Jose Lima	.25
140	Mark McGwire	1.50
141	Adam Piatt	.25
142	Pat Manning	.25
143	Marcos Castillo RC	.50
144	Lesli Brea RC	.50
145	Humberto Cota RC	.50
146	Ben Petrick	.25
147	Kip Wells	.25
148	Willi Mo Pena	.40
149	Chris Wakeland	.25
150	Brad Baker RC	.50
151	Robbie Morrison RC	.50
152	Reggie Taylor	.25
153	Matt Ginter RC	.50
154	Peter Bergeron	.25
155	Roosevelt Brown	.25
156	Matt Cepicky RC	.50
157	Ramon Castro	.25
158	Brad Baisley RC	.50
159	Jason Hart RC	1.00
160	Mitch Meluskey	.25
161	Chad Harville	.25
162	Brian Cooper	.25
163	Marcus Giles	.25
164	Jim Morris	.50
165	Geoff Goetz	.25
166	Bobby Bradley RC	.50
167	Rob Bell	.25
168	Joe Crede	.25
169	Michael Restovich	.25
170	Quincy Foster RC	.50
171	Enrique Cruz RC	.50
172	Mark Quinn	.25
173	Nick Johnson	.40
174	Jeff Liefer	.25
175	Kevin Mench RC	5.00
176	Steve Lomasney	.25
177	Jayson Werth	.25
178	Tim Drew	.25
179	Chip Ambres	.25
180	Ryan Anderson	.25
181	Matt Blank	.25
182	Giuseppe Chiaramonte	.25
183	Corey Myers RC	.50
184	Jeff Yoder	.25
185	Craig Dingman RC	.50
186	Jon Hamilton RC	.50
187	Toby Hall	.25
188	Russell Branyan	.25
189	Brian Falkenborg RC	.50
190	Aaron Harang RC	2.00
191	Juan Pena	.25
192	Chin-Hui Tsao RC	3.00
193	Alfonso Soriano	.25
194	Alejandro Diaz RC	.50
195	Carlos Pena	.25
196	Kevin Nicholson	.25
197	Mo Bruce	.25
198	C.C. Sabathia	.25
199	Carl Crawford	.50
200	Rafael Furcal	.50
201	Andrew Beinbrink RC	.50
202	Jimmy Osting	.25
203	Aaron McNeal RC	.50
204	Brett Laxton	.25
205	Chris George	.25
206	Felipe Lopez	.25
207	Ben Sheets RC	6.00
208	Mike Meyers RC	.50
209	Jason Conti	.25
210	Milton Bradley	.25
211	Chris Mears RC	.50
212	Carlos Hernandez RC	.50
213	Jason Romano	.25
214	Goefrey Tomlinson	.25
215	Jimmy Rollins	.75
216	Pablo Ozuna	.25
217	Steve Cox	.25
218	Terrence Long	.25
219	Jeff DaVanon RC	.50
220	Rick Ankiel	.25
221	Jason Standridge	.25
222	Tony Armas	.25
223	Jason Tyner	.25
224	Ramon Ortiz	.25
225	Daryle Ward	.25
226	Enger Veras RC	.50
227	Chris Jones RC	.50
228	Eric Cammack RC	.50
229	Ruben Mateo	.25
230	Ken Harvey RC	1.00
231	Jake Westbrook	.50
232	Rob Purvis RC	.50
233	Choo Freeman	.25
234	Aramis Ramirez	.25
235	A.J. Burnett	.25
236	Kevin Barker	.25
237	Chance Caple RC	.50
238	Jarrod Washburn	.25
239	Lance Berkman	.50
240	Michael Wenner RC	.50
241	Alex Sanchez	.25
242	Jake Esteves RC	.50
243	Grant Roberts	.25
244	Mark Ellis RC	.50
245	Donny Leon	.25
246	David Eckstein	.25
247	Dicky Gonzalez RC	.50
248	John Patterson	.25
249	Chad Green	.25
250	Scot Shields RC	.50
251	Troy Cameron	.25
252	Jose Molina	.25
253	Rob Pugmire RC	.50
254	Rick Elder	.25
255	Sean Burroughs	.50
256	Josh Kalinowski RC	.50
257	Matt LeCroy	.25
258	Alex Graman RC	.50
259	Juan Silvestre RC	.50
260	Brady Clark	.25
261	Rico Washington RC	.50
262	Gary Matthews Jr.	.25
263	Matt Wise	.25
264	Keith Reed RC	.50
265	Santiago Ramirez RC	.50
266	Ben Broussard RC	.50
267	Ryan Langerhans	.50
268	Juan Rivera	.50
269	Shawn Gallagher	.25
270	Jorge Toca	.25
271	Brad Lidge	.25
272	Leo Estrella RC	.50
273	Ruben Quevedo	.25
274	Jack Cust	.25
275	T.J. Tucker	.25
276	Mike Colangelo	.25
277	Brian Schneider	.25
278	Calvin Murray	.25
279	Josh Girdley	.25
280	Mike Paradis	.25
281	Chad Hermansen	.25
282	Ty Howington RC	.50
283	Aaron Myette	.25
284	D'Angelo Jimenez	.25
285	Dernell Stenson	.25
286	Jerry Hairston Jr.	.25
287	Gary Majewski RC	.50
288	Derrin Ebert RC	.50
289	Steve Fish RC	.50
290	Carlos Hernandez	.25
291	Allen Levrault	.25
292	Sean McNally RC	.50
293	Randey Dorame RC	.50
294	Wes Anderson RC	.50
295	B.J. Ryan	.25
296	Alan Webb RC	.50
297	Brandon Inge RC	2.00
298	David Walling	.25
299	Sun-Woo Kim RC	1.00
300	Pat Burrell	.50
301	Rick Guttormson RC	.50
302	Gil Meche	.25
303	Carlos Zambrano RC	10.00
304	Eric Byrnes RC (Photo actually Bo Porter.)	2.00
305	Robb Quinlan RC	.50
306	Jackie Rexrode RC	.50
307	Nate Bump	.25
308	Sean DePaula RC	.50
309	Matt Riley	.25
310	Ryan Minor	.25
311	J.J. Davis	.25
312	Randy Wolf	.25
313	Jason Jennings	.25
314	Scott Seabol RC	.50
315	Doug Davis	.25
316	Todd Moser RC	.50
317	Rob Ryan	.25
318	Bubba Crosby	.25
319	Lyle Overbay RC	2.50
320	Mario Encarnacion	.25
321	Francisco Rodriguez RC	6.00
322	Michael Cuddyer	.25
323	Eddie Yarnall	.25
324	Cesar Saba RC	.50
325	Travis Dawkins	.25
326	Alex Escobar	.25
327	Julio Zuleta RC	.50
328	Josh Hairston RC	.50
329	Carlos Urquiola RC	.50
330	Matt Belisle	.25
331	Kurt Ainsworth RC	1.00
332	Tim Raines Jr.	.25
333	Eric Munson	.25
334	Donzell McDonald	.25
335	Larry Bigbie RC	.50
336	Matt Watson	.25
337	Aubrey Huff	.25
338	Julio Ramirez	.25
339	Jason Grabowski RC	.50
340	Jon Garland	.25
341	Austin Kearns	.50
342	Josh Pressley	.25
343	Miguel Olivo RC	.50
344	Julio Lugo	.25
345	Roberto Vaz	.25
346	Ramon Soler	.25
347	Brandon Phillips RC	3.00
348	Vince Faison RC	.50
349	Mike Venafro	.25
350	Rick Asadoorian RC	.50
351	B.J. Garbe RC	.50
352	Dan Reichert	.25
353	Jason Stumm RC	.50
354	Ruben Salazar RC	.50
355	Francisco Cordero	.25
356	Juan Guzman RC	.50
357	Mike Bacsik RC	.50
358	Jared Sandberg	.25
359	Rod Barajas	.25
360	Junior Brignac RC	.50
361	J.M. Gold	.25
362	Octavio Dotel	.25
363	David Kelton	.25
364	Scott Morgan RC	.50
365	Wascar Serrano RC	.50
366	Wilton Veras	.25
367	Eugene Kingsale	.25
368	Ted Lilly	.25
369	George Lombard	.25
370	Chris Haas	.25
371	Wilton Pena RC	.50
372	Vernon Wells	.25
373	Keith Ginter RC	.50
374	Jeff Heaverlo RC	.50
375	Calvin Pickering	.25
376	Mike Lamb RC	.50
377	Kyle Snyder	.25
378	Javier Cardona RC	.50
379	Aaron Rowand RC	3.00
380	Dee Brown	.25
381	Brett Myers RC	4.00
382	Abraham Nunez	.25
383	Eric Valent	.25
384	Jody Gerut RC	.50
385	Adam Dunn	.50
386	Jay Gehrke	.25
387	Omar Ortiz	.25
388	Darnell McDonald	.25
389	Chad Alexander	.25
390	J.D. Closser	.25
391	Ben Christensen RC	.50
392	Adam Kennedy	.25
393	Nick Green RC	.50
394	Ramon Hernandez	.25
395	Roy Oswalt RC	20.00
396	Andy Tracy RC	1.00
397	Eric Gagne	.25
398	Michael Tejera RC	.50
399	Adam Everett	.25
400	Corey Patterson	.25
401	Gary Knotts RC	.50
402	Ryan Christianson RC	.50
403	Eric Ireland RC	.50
404	Andrew Good RC	.50
405	Brad Penny	.25
406	Jason LaRue	.25
407	Kit Pellow	.25
408	Kevin Beirne	.25
409	Kelly Dransfeldt	.25
410	Jason Grilli	.25
411	Scott Downs RC	.50
412	Jesus Colome	.25
413	John Sneed RC	.50
414	Tony McKnight RC	.50
415	Luis Rivera	.25
416	Adam Eaton	.25
417	Mike MacDougal RC	1.00
418	Mike Nannini	.25
419	Barry Zito RC	6.00
420	Dewayne Wise	.25
421	Jason Dellaero	.25
422	Chad Moeller	.25
423	Jason Marquis	.25
424	Tim Redding RC	.50
425	Mark Mulder	.25
426	Josh Paul	.25
427	Chris Enochs	.25
428	Wilfredo Rodriguez RC	.50
429	Kevin Witt	.25
430	Scott Sobkowiak RC	.50
431	McKay Christensen	.25
432	Jung Bong	.25
433	Keith Evans RC	.50
434	Garry Maddox Jr.	.25
435	Ramon Santiago RC	.50
436	Alex Cora	.25
437	Carlos Lee	.25
438	Jason Repko RC	.50
439	Matt Burch	.25
440	Shawn Sonnier RC	1.00

number on the back. These were seeded 1:12 packs.

Stars:	4-8X
Rookies:	2-4X

Inserted 1:12
(See 2000 Bowman Chrome for checklist and base card values.)

Retro/Future

This 440-card parallel to the base set is modeled after the 1955 Bowman "television set" design and are seeded 1:6 packs, with Refractors seeded 1:60 packs.

Stars:	1.5-3X
Rookies:	.75X
Inserted 1:6	
Refractors:	6-8X
Rookies:	1-3X

Inserted 1:60
(See 2000 Bowman Chrome for checklist and base values.)

Bidding for the Call

Top minor league prospects are highlighted on a design with gold foil background on an all chromium finish. Card backs are numbered with a "BC" prefix. A Refractor parallel version was also produced.

		NM/M
Complete Set (15):		10.00
Common Player:		.50
Inserted 1:16		
Refractors:		2-4X
Inserted 1:160		
1	Adam Piatt	.50
2	Pat Burrell	1.00
3	Mark Mulder	1.00
4	Nick Johnson	1.00
5	Alfonso Soriano	2.00
6	Chin-Feng Chen	2.50
7	Scott Sobkowiak	.50
8	Corey Patterson	1.00
9	Jack Cust	.50
10	Sean Burroughs	.50
11	Josh Hamilton	.50
12	Corey Myers	.50
13	Eric Munson	.50
14	Wes Anderson	.50
15	Lyle Overbay	1.00

Refractors

A parallel to the 440-card base set, these inserts have a mirror like sheen to them on the card front and are listed Refractor underneath the card

Meteoric Rise

This 10-card set spotlights players who all made their first All-Star team within their first two years. Card fronts have a futuristic background, with the player in an intergalactic setting. Card backs are numbered with a "MR" prefix. A Refractor parallel version also exists.

		NM/M
Complete Set (10):		20.00
Common Player:		1.50
Inserted 1:24		
Refractors:		2-4X
Inserted 1:240		
1	Nomar Garciaparra	3.00
2	Mark McGwire	4.00
3	Ken Griffey Jr.	3.00
4	Chipper Jones	2.50
5	Manny Ramirez	2.00
6	Mike Piazza	3.00
7	Cal Ripken Jr.	5.00
8	Ivan Rodriguez	1.00
9	Greg Maddux	3.00
10	Randy Johnson	2.00

Oversize

		NM/M
Complete Set (8):		8.00
Common Player:		.75
Inserted 1:Box		
1	Pat Burrell	2.00
2	Josh Hamilton	1.00
3	Rafael Furcal	1.00
4	Corey Patterson	1.50
5	A.J. Burnett	.75
6	Eric Munson	.75
7	Nick Johnson	1.00
8	Alfonso Soriano	2.00

Rookie Class 2000

This set highlighted 10 prospects who were thought to contend for the 2000 Rookie of the Year awards. Backs are numbered with a "RC" prefix. A Refractor parallel version was also issued.

		NM/M
Complete Set (10):		8.00
Common Player:		1.50
Inserted 1:24		
Refractors:		2-4X
Inserted 1:240		
1	Pat Burrell	2.00
2	Rick Ankiel	.75
3	Ruben Mateo	.75
4	Vernon Wells	1.50
5	Mark Mulder	1.50
6	A.J. Burnett	.75
7	Chad Hermansen	.75
8	Corey Patterson	1.50
9	Rafael Furcal	1.00
10	Mike Lamb	.75

Teen Idols

This 15-card set highlights top teenagers who are predicted to emerge as major league standouts.

		NM/M
Complete Set (15):		15.00
Common Player:		1.50
Inserted 1:16		
Refractors:		2-4X
Inserted 1:160		
1	Alex Rodriguez	5.00

2	Andruw Jones	1.50
3	Juan Gonzalez	1.00
4	Ivan Rodriguez	1.50
5	Ken Griffey Jr.	3.00
6	Bobby Bradley	.75
7	Brett Myers	.75
8	C.C. Sabathia	.75
9	Ty Howington	.75
10	Brandon Phillips	1.00
11	Rick Asadoorian	1.00
12	Wily Pena	1.00
13	Sean Burroughs	.75
14	Josh Hamilton	1.00
15	Rafael Furcal	1.00

2000 Bowman Draft Picks and Prospects

		NM/M
Complete Set (110):		40.00
Common Player:		.15
1	Pat Burrell	.25
2	Rafael Furcal	.15
3	Grant Roberts	.25
4	Barry Zito	.50
5	Julio Zuleta	.15
6	Mark Mulder	.25
7	Rob Bell	.15
8	Adam Piatt	.15
9	Mike Lamb	.15
10	Pablo Ozuna	.15
11	Jason Tyner	.15
12	Jason Marquis	.15
13	Eric Munson	.15
14	Seth Etherton	.15
15	Milton Bradley	.15
16	Nick Green	.15
17	Chin-Feng Chen RC	1.00
18	Matt Boone RC	.25
19	Kevin Gregg RC	.25
20	Eddy Garabito RC	.25
21	Aaron Capista RC	.25
22	Esteban German RC	.25
23	Derek Thompson RC	.25
24	Phil Merrell RC	.25
25	Brian O'Connor RC	.25
26	Yamid Haad	.15
27	Hector Mercado RC	.25
28	Jason Woolf RC	.25
29	Eddie Furniss RC	.25
30	Cha Sueng Baek RC	.25
31	Colby Lewis RC	.25
32	Pasqual Coco RC	.25
33	Jorge Cantu RC	1.50
34	Erasmo Ramirez RC	.25
35	Bobby Kielty RC	.50
36	Joaquin Benoit RC	.25
37	Brian Esposito RC	.25
38	Michael Wenner	.15
39	Juan Rincon RC	.25
40	Yorvit Torrealba RC	.25
41	Chad Durham RC	.25
42	Jim Mann RC	.25
43	Shane Loux RC	.25
44	Luis Rivas	.15
45	Ken Chenard RC	.25
46	Mike Lockwood RC	.25
47	Yovanny Lara RC	.25
48	Bubba Carpenter RC	.25
49	Jeremy Griffiths RC	.25
50	John Stephens RC	.25
51	Pedro Feliz RC	.75
52	Kenny Kelly RC	.25
53	Neil Jenkins RC	.25
54	Mike Glendenning RC	.15
55	Bo Porter	.15

56	Eric Byrnes	.15
57	Tony Alvarez RC	.25
58	Kazuhiro Sasaki RC	.25
59	Chad Durbin RC	.25
60	Mike Bynum RC	.25
61	Travis Wilson RC	.25
62	Jose Leon RC	.25
63	Bill Ortega RC	.25
64	Geraldo Guzman RC	.25
65	Craig Anderson RC	.25
66	Carlos Silva RC	.50
67	Brad Thomas RC	.25
68	Chin-Hui Tsao RC	.75
69	Mark Buehrle RC	2.00
70	Juan Salas RC	.25
71	Denny Abreu RC	.25
72	Keith McDonald RC	.25
73	Chris Richard RC	.25
74	Tomas de la Rosa RC	.25
75	Vicente Padilla	.50
76	Justin Brunette RC	.25
77	Scott Linebrink RC	.25
78	Jeff Sparks RC	.25
79	Tike Redman RC	.25
80	John Lackey RC	1.50
81	Joe Strong RC	.25
82	Brian Tollberg RC	.25
83	Steve Sisco RC	.25
84	Chris Clapinski	.15
85	Augie Ojeda RC	.25
86	Adrian Gonzalez RC (Draft Picks)	2.50
87	Mike Stodolka RC (Draft Picks)	
88	Adam Johnson RC (Draft Picks)	
89	Matt Wheatland RC (Draft Picks)	.25
90	Corey Smith RC (Draft Picks)	.25
91	Rocco Baldelli RC (Draft Picks)	3.00
92	Keith Bucktrot RC (Draft Picks)	
93	Adam Wainwright RC (Draft Picks)	2.00
94	Blaine Boyer RC (Draft Picks)	
95	Aaron Herr RC (Draft Picks)	
96	Scott Thorman RC (Draft Picks)	1.50
97	Brian Digby RC (Draft Picks)	.25
98	Josh Shortslef RC (Draft Picks)	.25
99	Sean Smith RC (Draft Picks)	.25
100	Alex Cruz RC (Draft Picks)	.25
101	Marc Love RC (Draft Picks)	.25
102	Kevin Lee RC (Draft Picks)	.25
103	Victor Ramos RC (Draft Picks)	.25
104	Jason Kanoi RC (Draft Picks)	.25
105	Luis Escobar RC (Draft Picks)	.25
106	Tripper Johnson RC (Draft Picks)	.25
107	Phil Dumatrait RC (Draft Picks)	.25
108	Bryan Edwards RC (Draft Picks)	.25
109	Grady Sizemore RC (Draft Picks)	20.00
110	Thomas Mitchell RC (Draft Picks)	.25

Autograph

Pat Burrell

		NM/M
Common Autograph:		5.00
Inserted 1:Set		
1	Pat Burrell	20.00
2	Rafael Furcal	15.00
3	Grant Roberts	5.00
4	Barry Zito	40.00
5	Julio Zuleta	5.00
6	Mark Mulder	15.00
7	Bob Bell	5.00
8	Adam Piatt	8.00
9	Mike Lamb	5.00
10	Pablo Ozuna	5.00
11	Jason Tyner	5.00
12	Jason Marquis	5.00

13	Eric Munson	6.00
14	Seth Etherton	5.00
15	Milton Bradley	15.00
16	NOT ISSUED	
17	Michael Wenner	5.00
18	Mike Glendenning	5.00
19	Tony Alvarez	5.00
20	Adrian Gonzalez	90.00
21	Corey Smith	10.00
22	Matt Wheatland	5.00
23	Adam Johnson	8.00
24	Mike Stodolka	5.00
25	Rocco Baldelli	50.00
26	Juan Rincon	5.00
27	Chad Durbin	5.00
28	Yorvit Torrealba	5.00
29	Nick Green	10.00
30	Derek Thompson	5.00
31	John Lackey	30.00
32	NOT ISSUED	.00
33	Kevin Gregg	5.00
34	NOT ISSUED	
35	Denny Abreu	5.00
36	Brian Tollberg	5.00
37	Yamid Haad	5.00
38	Grady Sizemore	450.00
39	Carlos Silva	10.00
40	Jorge Cantu	60.00
41	Bobby Kielty	8.00
42	Scott Thorman	50.00
43	Juan Salas	10.00
44	Phil Dumatrait	5.00
45	NOT ISSUED	
46	Mike Lockwood	5.00
47	Yovanny Lara	5.00
48	Tripper Johnson	10.00
49	Colby Lewis	5.00
50	Neil Jenkins	5.00
51	Keith Bucktrot	5.00
52	Eric Byrnes	10.00
53	Aaron Herr	5.00
54	Erasmo Ramirez	5.00
55	Chris Richard	5.00
56	NOT ISSUED	
57	Mike Bynum	5.00
58	Brian Esposito	5.00
59	Chris Clapinski	5.00
60	Augie Ojeda	5.00

2000 Bowman Chrome Draft Picks and Prospects

Jon Rauch

		NM/M
Complete Set (110):		50.00
Common Player:		.25
1	Pat Burrell	.50
2	Rafael Furcal	.50
3	Grant Roberts	.25
4	Barry Zito	2.00
5	Julio Zuleta	.50
6	Mark Mulder	.25
7	Rob Bell	.25
8	Adam Piatt	.25
9	Mike Lamb	.25
10	Pablo Ozuna	.25
11	Jason Tyner	.25
12	Jason Marquis	.25
13	Eric Munson	.25
14	Seth Etherton	.25
15	Milton Bradley	.25
16	Nick Green	.25
17	Chin-Feng Chen RC	2.00
18	Matt Boone RC	.50
19	Kevin Gregg RC	.50
20	Eddy Garabito RC	.50
21	Aaron Capista RC	.50
22	Esteban German RC	.50
23	Derek Thompson RC	.50
24	Phil Merrell RC	.50
25	Brian O'Connor RC	.50
26	Yamid Haad	.25
27	Hector Mercado RC	.50
28	Jason Woolf RC	.50
29	Eddie Furniss RC	.50
30	Cha Sueng Baek RC	.50
31	Colby Lewis RC	.50
32	Pasqual Coco RC	.50
33	Jorge Cantu RC	4.00
34	Erasmo Ramirez RC	.50
35	Bobby Kielty RC	1.00
36	Joaquin Benoit RC	.50
37	Brian Esposito RC	.50
38	Michael Wenner	.25
39	Juan Rincon RC	.50
40	Yorvit Torrealba RC	.50

41	Chad Durham RC	.50
42	Jim Mann RC	.50
43	Shane Loux RC	.50
44	Luis Rivas	.25
45	Ken Chenard RC	.50
46	Mike Lockwood RC	.50
47	Giovanni Lara RC	.50
48	Bubba Carpenter RC	.50
49	Ryan Dittfurth RC	.50
50	John Stephens RC	.50
51	Pedro Feliz RC	2.00
52	Kenny Kelly RC	.50
53	Neil Jenkins RC	.50
54	Mike Glendenning RC	.50
55	Bo Porter	.25
56	Eric Byrnes	.25
57	Tony Alvarez RC	.50
58	Kazuhiro Sasaki RC	1.00
59	Chad Durbin RC	.50
60	Mike Bynum RC	.50
61	Travis Wilson RC	.50
62	Jose Leon RC	.50
63	Ryan Vogelsong RC	.50
64	Geraldo Guzman RC	.50
65	Craig Anderson RC	.50
66	Carlos Silva RC	1.00
67	Brad Thomas RC	.50
68	Chin-Hui Tsao	1.50
69	Mark Buehrle RC	6.00
70	Juan Salas RC	.50
71	Denny Abreu RC	.50
72	Keith McDonald RC	.50
73	Chris Richard RC	.50
74	Tomas de la Rosa RC	.50
75	Vicente Padilla	1.00
76	Justin Brunette RC	.50
77	Scott Linebrink RC	.50
78	Jeff Sparks RC	.50
79	Tike Redman RC	.50
80	John Lackey RC	3.00
81	Joe Strong RC	.50
82	Brian Tollberg RC	.50
83	Steve Sisco RC	.50
84	Chris Clapinski	.25
85	Augie Ojeda RC	.50
86	Adrian Gonzalez RC (Draft Picks)	8.00
87	Mike Stodolka RC (Draft Picks)	
88	Adam Johnson RC (Draft Picks)	.50
89	Matt Wheatland RC (Draft Picks)	.50
90	Corey Smith RC (Draft Picks)	.50
91	Rocco Baldelli RC (Draft Picks)	4.00
92	Keith Bucktrot RC (Draft Picks)	.50
93	Adam Wainwright RC (Draft Picks)	8.00
94	Blaine Boyer RC (Draft Picks)	
95	Aaron Herr RC (Draft Picks)	.50
96	Scott Thorman RC (Draft Picks)	3.00
97	Brian Digby RC (Draft Picks)	.50
98	Josh Shortslef RC (Draft Picks)	.50
99	Sean Smith RC (Draft Picks)	.50
100	Alex Cruz RC (Draft Picks)	.50
101	Marc Love RC (Draft Picks)	.50
102	Kevin Lee RC (Draft Picks)	.50
103	Timoniel Perez RC (Draft Picks)	.50
104	Alex Cabrera RC (Draft Picks)	1.00
105	Shane Heams RC (Draft Picks)	.50
106	Tripper Johnson RC (Draft Picks)	.50
107	Brent Abernathy RC (Draft Picks)	.50
108	John Cotton RC (Draft Picks)	.50
109	Brad Wilkerson RC (Draft Picks)	3.00
110	Jon Rauch RC (Draft Picks)	.50

2000 Bowman's Best Pre-Production

BRETT MYERS

Three-card cello packs of promotional cards introduced the Bowman's Best issue for 2000. The cards are virtually identical to the regularly issued version except for the numbering on the back which includes a "PP" prefix.

		NM/M
Complete Set (3):		6.00
Common Player:		2.00
PP1	Larry Walker	2.00
PP2	Adam Dunn	2.00
PP3	Brett Myers	2.00

2000 Bowman's Best

JUAN GONZALEZ

The base set consists of 200-cards on a mirror like sheen, reminiscent of Refractors. Veteran cards have gold highlights while rookies and prospects have blue highlights. There are three subsets: Best Performers (86-100), Prospects (101-150) and Rookies (151-200). Rookies are serially numbered to 2,999 on the card back and are randomly inserted on the average of 1:7 packs.

		NM/M
Complete Set (200):		275.00
Common Player:		.20
Common Rookie (151-200):		5.00
Production 2,999 Sets		
Pack (4):		4.00
Box (24):		75.00
1	Nomar Garciaparra	2.00
2	Chipper Jones	1.50
3	Damion Easley	.20
4	Bernie Williams	.40
5	Barry Bonds	3.00
6	Jermaine Dye	.20
7	John Olerud	.20
8	Mike Hampton	.20
9	Cal Ripken Jr.	3.00
10	Jeff Bagwell	1.00
11	Troy Glaus	1.00
12	J.D. Drew	.40
13	Jeromy Burnitz	.20
14	Carlos Delgado	.75
15	Shawn Green	.40
16	Kevin Millwood	.40
17	Rondell White	.20
18	Scott Rolen	.75
19	Jeff Cirillo	.20
20	Barry Larkin	.20
21	Brian Giles	.20
22	Roger Clemens	1.75
23	Manny Ramirez	1.00
24	Alex Gonzalez	.20
25	Mark Grace	.35
26	Fernando Tatis	.20
27	Randy Johnson	1.00
28	Roger Cedeno	.20
29	Brian Jordan	.20
30	Kevin Brown	.40
31	Greg Vaughn	.20
32	Roberto Alomar	.50
33	Larry Walker	.20
34	Rafael Palmeiro	.75
35	Curt Schilling	.50
36	Orlando Hernandez	.20
37	Todd Walker	.20
38	Juan Gonzalez	1.00
39	Sean Casey	.35
40	Tony Gwynn	1.50
41	Albert Belle	.20
42	Gary Sheffield	.40
43	Michael Barrett	.20
44	Preston Wilson	.20
45	Jim Thome	.40
46	Shannon Stewart	.20
47	Mo Vaughn	.20
48	Ben Grieve	.20
49	Adrian Beltre	.35
50	Sammy Sosa	2.00
51	Bob Abreu	.20
52	Edgardo Alfonzo	.20
53	Carlos Febles	.20
54	Frank Thomas	1.00
55	Alex Rodriguez	2.50

56	Cliff Floyd	.20
57	Jose Canseco	.40
58	Erubiel Durazo	.20
59	Tim Hudson	.50
60	Craig Biggio	.20
61	Eric Karros	.20
62	Mike Mussina	.50
63	Robin Ventura	.20
64	Carlos Beltran	.50
65	Pedro Martinez	1.00
66	Gabe Kapler	.20
67	Jason Kendall	.20
68	Derek Jeter	3.00
69	Magglio Ordonez	.50
70	Mike Piazza	2.00
71	Mike Lieberthal	.20
72	Andres Galarraga	.20
73	Raul Mondesi	.20
74	Eric Chavez	.40
75	Greg Maddux	1.50
76	Matt Williams	.30
77	Kris Benson	.20
78	Ivan Rodriguez	.50
79	Pokey Reese	.20
80	Vladimir Guerrero	1.00
81	Mark McGwire	2.50
82	Vinny Castilla	.20
83	Todd Helton	1.00
84	Andruw Jones	.75
85	Ken Griffey Jr.	2.00
86	Mark McGwire (Best Performers)	1.25
87	Derek Jeter (Best Performers)	1.50
88	Chipper Jones (Best Performers)	.75
89	Nomar Garciaparra (Best Performers)	1.00
90	Sammy Sosa (Best Performers)	.75
91	Cal Ripken Jr. (Best Performers)	1.50
92	Juan Gonzalez (Best Performers)	.50
93	Alex Rodriguez (Best Performers)	1.25
94	Barry Bonds (Best Performers)	1.50
95	Sean Casey (Best Performers)	.25
96	Vladimir Guerrero (Best Performers)	.50
97	Mike Piazza (Best Performers)	1.00
98	Shawn Green (Best Performers)	.25
99	Jeff Bagwell (Best Performers)	.50
100	Ken Griffey Jr. (Best Performers)	1.00
101	Rick Ankiel (Prospects)	.35
102	John Patterson (Prospects)	.20
103	David Walling (Prospects)	.20
104	Michael Restovich (Prospects)	.20
105	A.J. Burnett (Prospects)	.20
106	Matt Riley (Prospects)	.20
107	Chad Hermansen (Prospects)	.20
108	Choo Freeman (Prospects)	.20
109	Mark Quinn (Prospects)	.20
110	Corey Patterson (Prospects)	.20
111	Ramon Ortiz (Prospects)	.20
112	Vernon Wells (Prospects)	.40
113	Milton Bradley (Prospects)	.20
114	Travis Dawkins (Prospects)	.20
115	Sean Burroughs (Prospects)	.35
116	Willi Mo Pena (Prospects)	.40
117	Dee Brown (Prospects)	.20
118	C.C. Sabathia (Prospects)	.20
119	Larry Bigbie RC (Prospects)	.20
120	Octavio Dotel (Prospects)	.20
121	Kip Wells (Prospects)	.20
122	Ben Petrick (Prospects)	.20
123	Mark Mulder (Prospects)	.40
124	Jason Standridge (Prospects)	.20
125	Adam Piatt (Prospects)	.20
126	Steve Lomasney (Prospects)	.20
127	Jayson Werth (Prospects)	.20
128	Alex Escobar (Prospects)	.20
129	Ryan Anderson (Prospects)	.20
130	Adam Dunn (Prospects)	.50
131	Omar Ortiz (Prospects)	.20
132	Brad Penny (Prospects)	.20
133	Daryle Ward (Prospects)	.20

134	Eric Munson (Prospects)	.20
135	Nick Johnson (Prospects)	.50
136	Jason Jennings (Prospects)	.20
137	Tim Raines Jr. (Prospects)	.20
138	Ruben Mateo (Prospects)	.20
139	Jack Cust (Prospects)	.20
140	Rafael Furcal (Prospects)	.20
141	Eric Gagne (Prospects)	.35
142	Tony Armas (Prospects)	.20
143	Mike Paradis (Prospects)	.20
144	Chris George (Prospects)	.20
145	Alfonso Soriano (Prospects)	.75
146	Josh Hamilton (Prospects)	.50
147	Michael Cuddyer (Prospects)	.35
148	Jay Gehrke (Prospects)	.20
149	Josh Girdley (Prospects)	.20
150	Pat Burrell (Prospects)	.75
151	Brett Myers RC	15.00
152	Scott Seabol RC	5.00
153	Keith Reed RC	5.00
154	Francisco Rodriguez RC	20.00
155	Barry Zito RC	25.00
156	Pat Manning RC	5.00
157	Ben Christensen RC	5.00
158	Corey Myers RC	5.00
159	Wascar Serrano RC	5.00
160	Wes Anderson RC	5.00
161	Andy Tracy RC	5.00
162	Cesar Saba RC	5.00
163	Mike Lamb RC	5.00
164	Bobby Bradley RC	5.00
165	Vince Faison RC	5.00
166	Ty Howington RC	8.00
167	Ken Harvey RC	5.00
168	Josh Kalinowski RC	5.00
169	Ruben Salazar RC	5.00
170	Aaron Rowand RC	10.00
171	Ramon Santiago RC	5.00
172	Scott Sobkowiak RC	5.00
173	Lyle Overbay RC	10.00
174	Rico Washington RC	5.00
175	Rick Asadoorian RC	5.00
176	Matt Ginter RC	5.00
177	Jason Stumm RC	5.00
178	B.J. Garbe RC	5.00
179	Mike MacDougal RC	5.00
180	Ryan Christianson RC	5.00
181	Kurt Ainsworth RC	5.00
182	Brad Baisley RC	5.00
183	Ben Broussard RC	5.00
184	Aaron McNeal RC	5.00
185	John Sneed RC	5.00
186	Junior Brignac RC	5.00
187	Chance Caple RC	5.00
188	Scott Downs RC	5.00
189	Matt Cepicky RC	5.00
190	Chin-Feng Chen RC	25.00
191	Johan Santana RC	75.00
192	Brad Baker RC	5.00
193	Jason Repko RC	5.00
194	Craig Dingman RC	5.00
195	Chris Wakeland RC	5.00
196	Rogelio Arias RC	5.00
197	Luis Matos RC	8.00
198	Robert Ramsay RC	5.00
199	Willie Bloomquist RC	20.00
200	Tony Pena Jr. RC	5.00

Franchise Favorites

Two current players and two retired stars are featured in this six-card set. Card backs are numbered with a "FR" prefix.

		NM/M
	Complete Set (6):	15.00
	Common Player:	1.00
	Inserted 1:17	
1A	Sean Casey	1.00
1B	Johnny Bench	3.00
1C	Sean Casey, Johnny Bench	3.00
2A	Cal Ripken Jr.	5.00
2B	Brooks Robinson	2.00
2C	Cal Ripken Jr., Brooks Robinson	5.00

Franchise Favorites Autograph

These autographs are seeded 1:1,291 packs, while the two dual autographed versions are inserted 1:5,153 packs.

		NM/M
	Common Player:	20.00
	Version A & B 1:1,291	
	Version C 1:5,153	
1A	Sean Casey	20.00
1B	Johnny Bench	50.00
1C	Sean Casey, Johnny Bench	100.00
2A	Cal Ripken Jr.	125.00
2B	Brooks Robinson	50.00
2C	Cal Ripken Jr., Brooks Robinson	250.00

Bets

This 10-card set high-lighted prospects who had the best chance of making the big league. The upper left corner and bottom right corner are die-cut. A small action photo is superimposed over a larger background shot of the fea-tured player. Backs are num-bered with a "BBB" prefix.

		NM/M
	Complete Set (10):	10.00

Franchise 2000

Each of the 25-cards in this set have rounded corners on a holographic silver design. Backs are numbered with a "F" prefix.

		NM/M
	Complete Set (25):	60.00
	Common Player:	1.00
	Inserted 1:18	
1	Cal Ripken Jr.	8.00
2	Nomar Garciaparra	6.00
3	Frank Thomas	2.00
4	Manny Ramirez	1.50

	Common Player:	.75
	Inserted 1:15	
1	Pat Burrell	2.00
2	Alfonso Soriano	2.00
3	Corey Patterson	1.50
4	Eric Munson	.75
5	Sean Burroughs	1.00
6	Rafael Furcal	.75
7	Rick Ankiel	1.00
8	Nick Johnson	1.50
9	Ruben Mateo	.75
10	Josh Hamilton	1.00

5	Juan Gonzalez	1.50
6	Carlos Beltran	2.00
7	Derek Jeter	8.00
8	Alex Rodriguez	6.00
9	Ben Grieve	1.00
10	Jose Canseco	1.50
11	Ivan Rodriguez	1.50
12	Mo Vaughn	1.00
13	Randy Johnson	3.00
14	Chipper Jones	4.00
15	Sammy Sosa	5.00
16	Ken Griffey Jr.	5.00
17	Larry Walker	1.00
18	Preston Wilson	1.00
19	Jeff Bagwell	2.00
20	Shawn Green	1.00
21	Vladimir Guerrero	2.00
22	Mike Piazza	5.00
23	Scott Rolen	2.00
24	Tony Gwynn	3.50
25	Barry Bonds	8.00

Locker Room Collection Autographs

Part of the Locker Room Collection, these autographs feature 19 players. Backs are numbered with a "LRCA" prefix.

		NM/M
	Common Player:	8.00
	Inserted 1:57	
1	Carlos Beltran	25.00
2	Rick Ankiel	8.00
3	Vernon Wells	12.00
4	Ruben Mateo	8.00
5	Ben Petrick	8.00
6	Adam Piatt	8.00
7	Eric Munson	8.00
8	Alfonso Soriano	40.00
9	Kerry Wood	25.00
10	Jack Cust	8.00
11	Rafael Furcal	15.00
12	Josh Hamilton	10.00
13	Brad Penny	8.00
14	Dee Brown	8.00
15	Milton Bradley	12.00
16	Ryan Anderson	8.00
17	John Patterson	8.00
18	Nick Johnson	10.00
19	Peter Bergeron	8.00

Locker Room Collection Jerseys

These inserts have a piece of game-worn jersey embed-ded into them and are num-bered with a "LRCJ" prefix.

		NM/M
	Common Player:	4.00
	Inserted 1:206	
1	Carlos Beltran	12.00
2	Rick Ankiel	5.00
3	Adam Kennedy	4.00
4	Ben Petrick	4.00
5	Adam Piatt	4.00

Locker Room Collection Lumber

These inserts have a piece of game-used bat embedded into them. They are numbered with a "LRCL" prefix on the back.

		NM/M
	Common Player:	5.00
	Inserted 1:376	
1	Carlos Beltran	15.00
2	Rick Ankiel	5.00
3	Vernon Wells	10.00
4	Adam Kennedy	5.00
5	Ben Petrick	5.00
6	Adam Piatt	5.00
7	Eric Munson	5.00
8	Rafael Furcal	8.00
9	J.D. Drew	8.00
10	Pat Burrell	10.00

Rookie Signed Baseballs

Redemption inserts, re-deemable for Rookie Signed Baseballs, were randomly insert-ed. Signed baseball displays the Bowman "Rookie Autograph" logo and the Topps "Genuine Is-sue" sticker.

		NM/M
	Complete Set (5):	75.00
	Common Player:	10.00
	Inserted 1:688	
1	Josh Hamilton	30.00
2	Rick Ankiel	15.00
3	Alfonso Soriano	50.00
4	Nick Johnson	30.00
5	Corey Patterson	20.00

Selections

This 15-card set is printed on a luminescent, die-cut de-sign. The set features former Rookies of the Year and former No. 1 overall Draft Picks. These are seeded 1:30 packs. Backs are numbered with a "BBS" prefix.

		NM/M
	Complete Set (15):	50.00
	Common Player:	1.00
	Inserted 1:30	
1	Alex Rodriguez	7.50
2	Ken Griffey Jr.	6.00
3	Pat Burrell	2.00
4	Mark McGwire	7.50
5	Derek Jeter	10.00
6	Nomar Garciaparra	6.00
7	Mike Piazza	6.00
8	Josh Hamilton	1.00
9	Cal Ripken Jr.	10.00
10	Jeff Bagwell	2.50
11	Chipper Jones	4.50
12	Jose Canseco	1.50
13	Carlos Beltran	2.00
14	Kerry Wood	2.00
15	Ben Grieve	1.00

Year By Year

This 10-card set highlights 10 duos who began their careers in the same year. They have a horizontal format on a mirror foiled card front. Backs are num-bered with a "YY" prefix.

		NM/M
	Complete Set (10):	25.00
	Common Card:	1.50
	Inserted 1:23	
1	Sammy Sosa, Ken Griffey Jr.	4.00
2	Nomar Garciaparra, Vladimir Guerrero	4.00
3	Alex Rodriguez, Jeff Cirillo	5.00
4	Mike Piazza, Pedro Martinez	4.00
5	Derek Jeter, Edgardo Alfonzo	6.00
6	Alfonso Soriano, Rick Ankiel	2.00
7	Mark McGwire, Barry Bonds	6.00
8	Juan Gonzalez, Larry Walker	1.50
9	Ivan Rodriguez, Jeff Bagwell	1.50
10	Shawn Green, Manny Ramirez	1.50

2001 Bowman

LUIS MONTANEZ • SS
CHICAGO CUBS

		NM/M
	Complete Set (440):	140.00
	Common Player:	.15
	Common Rookie:	.25
	Golds:	1-2X
	Inserted 1:1	
	Pack (10):	10.00
	Box (24):	200.00
1	Jason Giambi	.40
2	Rafael Furcal	.15
3	Rick Ankiel	.15
4	Freddy Garcia	.15
5	Magglio Ordonez	.25
6	Bernie Williams	.40
7	Kenny Lofton	.15
8	Al Leiter	.15
9	Albert Belle	.15
10	Craig Biggio	.15
11	Mark Mulder	.15
12	Carlos Delgado	.40
13	Darin Erstad	.25
14	Richie Sexson	.15
15	Randy Johnson	.75
16	Greg Maddux	1.50
17	Cliff Floyd	.15
18	Mark Buehrle	.15
19	Chris Singleton	.15
20	Orlando Hernandez	.20
21	Javier Vazquez	.15
22	Jeff Kent	.15
23	Jim Thome	.50
24	John Olerud	.15
25	Jason Kendall	.15
26	Scott Rolen	.50
27	Tony Gwynn	.75
28	Edgardo Alfonzo	.15
29	Pokey Reese	.15
30	Todd Helton	.50
31	Mark Quinn	.15
32	Dan Tosca RC	.25
33	Dean Palmer	.15
34	Jacque Jones	.15
35	Ray Durham	.15
36	Rafael Palmeiro	.50
37	Carl Everett	.15
38	Ryan Dempster	.15
39	Randy Wolf	.15
40	Vladimir Guerrero	.75
41	Livan Hernandez	.15
42	Mo Vaughn	.15
43	Shannon Stewart	.15
44	Preston Wilson	.15
45	Jose Vidro	.15
46	Fred McGriff	.15
47	Kevin Brown	.25
48	Peter Bergeron	.15
49	Miguel Tejada	.50
50	Chipper Jones	.75
51	Edgar Martinez	.15
52	Tony Batista	.15
53	Jorge Posada	.40
54	Ricky Ledee	.15
55	Sammy Sosa	1.00
56	Steve Cox	.15
57	Tony Armas Jr.	.15
58	Gary Sheffield	.40
59	Bartolo Colon	.15
60	Pat Burrell	.40
61	Jay Payton	.15
62	Sean Casey	.25
63	Larry Walker	.15
64	Mike Mussina	.40
65	Nomar Garciaparra	1.00
66	Darren Dreifort	.15
67	Richard Hidalgo	.15
68	Troy Glaus	.40
69	Ben Grieve	.15
70	Jim Edmonds	.40
71	Raul Mondesi	.15
72	Andruw Jones	.50
73	Luis Castillo	.15
74	Mike Sweeney	.15
75	Derek Jeter	2.00
76	Ruben Mateo	.15
77	Carlos Lee	.15
78	Cristian Guzman	.15
79	Mike Hampton	.25
80	J.D. Drew	.25
81	Matt Lawton	.15
82	Moises Alou	.15
83	Terrence Long	.15
84	Geoff Jenkins	.15
85	Manny Ramirez	.75
86	Johnny Damon	.15
87	Barry Larkin	.15
88	Pedro Martinez	.75

89	Juan Gonzalez	.40
90	Roger Clemens	2.00
91	Carlos Beltran	.50
92	Brad Radke	.15
93	Orlando Cabrera	.15
94	Roberto Alomar	.50
95	Barry Bonds	2.00
96	Tim Hudson	.25
97	Tom Glavine	.25
98	Jeromy Burnitz	.15
99	Adrian Beltre	.15
100	Mike Piazza	1.00
101	Kerry Wood	.40
102	Steve Finley	.15
103	Alex Cora	.15
104	Bob Abreu	.15
105	Neifi Perez	.15
106	Mark Redman	.15
107	Paul Konerko	.15
108	Jermaine Dye	.15
109	Brian Giles	.15
110	Ivan Rodriguez	.50
111	Vinny Castilla	.15
112	Adam Kennedy	.15
113	Eric Chavez	.25
114	Billy Koch	.15
115	Shawn Green	.15
116	Matt Williams	.15
117	Greg Vaughn	.15
118	Gabe Kapler	.15
119	Jeff Cirillo	.15
120	Frank Thomas	.50
121	David Justice	.15
122	Cal Ripken Jr.	3.00
123	Rich Aurilia	.15
124	Curt Schilling	.40
125	Barry Zito	.25
126	Brian Jordan	.15
127	Chan Ho Park	.15
128	J.T. Snow Jr.	.15
129	Kazuhiro Sasaki	.15
130	Alex Rodriguez	2.00
131	Mariano Rivera	.25
132	Eric Milton	.15
133	Andy Pettitte	.25
134	Scott Elarton	.15
135	Ken Griffey Jr.	1.50
136	Bengie Molina	.15
137	Jeff Bagwell	.50
138	Kevin Millwood	.15
139	Tino Martinez	.15
140	Mark McGwire	1.50
141	Larry Barnes	.15
142	John Buck	.25
143	Freddie Bynum RC	.25
144	Abraham Nunez	.15
145	Felix Diaz	.25
146	Horatio Estrada RC	.25
147	Ben Diggins	.25
148	Tsuyoshi Shinjo RC	.50
149	Rocco Baldelli	.15
150	Rod Barajas	.15
151	Luis Terrero	.15
152	Milton Bradley	.15
153	Kurt Ainsworth	.15
154	Russell Branyan	.15
155	Ryan Anderson	.15
156	Mitch Jones RC	.25
157	Chip Ambres	.15
158	Steve Bennett RC	.25
159	Ivanon Coffie	.15
160	Sean Burroughs	.25
161	Keith Bucktrot	.15
162	Tony Alvarez	.15
163	Joaquin Benoit	.15
164	Rick Asadoorian	.15
165	Ben Broussard	.15
166	Ryan Madson RC	1.50
167	Dee Brown	.15
168	Sergio Contreras RC	.25
169	John Barnes	.15
170	Ben Washburn RC	.50
171	Erick Almonte RC	.25
172	Shawn Fagan RC	.25
173	Gary Johnson RC	.25
174	Brady Clark	.15
175	Grant Roberts	.15
176	Tony Torcato	.15
177	Ramon Castro	.15
178	Esteban German	.15
179	Joe Hamer RC	.15
180	Nick Neugebauer	.25
181	Dernell Stenson	.25
182	Yhency Brazoban RC	.40
183	Aaron Myette	.15
184	Juan Sosa	.15
185	Brandon Inge	.15
186	Domingo Guante RC	.15
187	Adrian Brown	.15
188	Deivi Mendez RC	.15
189	Luis Matos	.15
190	Pedro Liriano RC	.15
191	Donnie Bridges	.15
192	Alex Cintron	.15
193	Jace Brewer	.15
194	Ron Davenport RC	.50
195	Jason Belcher RC	.15
196	Adrian Hernandez RC	.25
197	Bobby Kielty	.15
198	Reggie Griggs RC	.15
199	Reggie Abercrombie RC	1.00
200	Troy Farnsworth RC	.50
201	Matt Belisle	.15
202	Miguel Villilo RC	.50
203	Adam Everett	.15
204	John Lackey	.15
205	Pasqual Coco	.15

206	Adam Wainwright	.25
207	Matt White RC	.25
208	Chin-Feng Chen	.25
209	Jeff Andra	.25
210	Willie Bloomquist	.15
211	Wes Anderson	.15
212	Enrique Cruz	.15
213	Jerry Hairston Jr.	.15
214	Mike Bynum	.15
215	Brian Hitchcox RC	.25
216	Ryan Christianson	.15
217	J.J. Davis	.15
218	Jovanny Cedeno	.15
219	Elvin Nina	.15
220	Alex Graman	.15
221	Arturo McDowell	.25
222	Deivi Santos RC	.25
223	Jody Gerut	.15
224	Sun-Woo Kim	.15
225	Jimmy Rollins	.25
226	Pappy Ndungidi	.15
227	Ruben Salazar	.15
228	Josh Girdley	.15
229	Carl Crawford	.45
230	Luis Montanez RC	.50
231	Ramon Carvajal RC	.25
232	Matt Riley	.15
233	Ben Davis	.15
234	Jason Grabowski	.15
235	Chris George	.15
236	Hank Blalock RC	5.00
237	Roy Oswalt	.25
238	Eric Reynolds RC	.15
239	Brian Cole	.15
240	Denny Bautista RC	.75
241	Hector Garcia RC	.25
242	Joe Thurston RC	.25
243	Brad Cresse	.15
244	Corey Patterson	.25
245	Brett Evert RC	.25
246	Elpidio Guzman RC	.15
247	Vernon Wells	.15
248	Roberto Miniel RC	.25
249	Brian Bass RC	.50
250	Mark Burnett RC	.25
251	Juan Silvestre	.15
252	Pablo Ozuna	.15
253	Jayson Werth	.25
254	Russ Jacobsen RC	.25
255	Chad Hermansen	.15
256	Travis Hafner RC	8.00
257	Bradley Baker	.15
258	Gookie Dawkins	.15
259	Michael Cuddyer	.15
260	Mark Buehrle	.15
261	Ricardo Aramboles	.15
262	Esix Snead RC	.25
263	Wilson Betemit RC	.50
264	Albert Pujols RC	85.00
265	Joe Lawrence	.15
266	Ramon Ortiz	.15
267	Ben Sheets	.50
268	Luke Lockwood RC	.25
269	Toby Hall	.15
270	Jack Cust	.15
271	Pedro Feliz	.15
272	Noel Devarez RC	.25
273	Josh Beckett	.15
274	Alex Escobar	.15
275	Doug Gredvig RC	.25
276	Marcus Giles	.15
277	Jon Rauch	.15
278	Brian Schmitt RC	.25
279	Seung Song RC	.50
280	Kevin Mench	.15
281	Adam Eaton	.15
282	Shawn Sonnier	.15
283	Andy Van Hekken RC	.25
284	Aaron Rowand	.15
285	Tony Blanco RC	.25
286	Ryan Kohlmeier	.15
287	C.C. Sabathia	.15
288	Bubba Crosby	.15
289	Josh Hamilton	.25
290	Dee Haynes RC	.25
291	Jason Marquis	.15
292	Julio Zuleta	.15
293	Carlos Hernandez	.15
294	Matt LeCroy	.15
295	Andy Beal RC	.25
296	Carlos Pena	.15
297	Reggie Taylor	.15
298	Bob Keppel RC	.25
299	Miguel Cabrera (Photo actually Manuel Esquivia.)	.75
300	Ryan Franklin	.15
301	Brandon Phillips	.15
302	Victor Hall RC	.25
303	Tony Pena Jr.	.15
304	Jim Journell RC	.25
305	Cristian Guerrero	.25
306	Miguel Olivo	.15
307	Jin Ho Cho	.15
308	Choo Freeman	.15
309	Danny Borrell RC	.25
310	Doug Mientkiewicz	.15
311	Aaron Herr	.15
312	Keith Ginter	.15
313	Felipe Lopez	.25
314	Jeff Goldbach RC	.25
315	Travis Harper	.15
316	Paul LoDuca	.25
317	Joe Torres	.15
318	Eric Byrnes	.15
319	George Lombard	.15
320	David Krynzel	.15
321	Ben Christensen	.15

322	Aubrey Huff	.15
323	Lyle Overbay	.15
324	Sean McGowan	.15
325	Jeff Heaverlo	.15
326	Timo Perez	.15
327	Octavio Martinez RC	.25
328	Vince Faison	.15
329	David Parrish RC	.25
330	Bobby Bradley	.15
331	Jason Miller RC	.25
332	Corey Spencer RC	.25
333	Craig House	.15
334	Maxim St. Pierre RC	.25
335	Adam Johnson	.15
336	Joe Crede	.25
337	Greg Nash RC	.25
338	Chad Durbin	.15
339	Pat Magness RC	.25
340	Matt Wheatland	.15
341	Julio Lugo	.15
342	Grady Sizemore	.50
343	Adrian Gonzalez	.25
344	Tim Raines Jr.	.15
345	Rainier Olmedo RC	.25
346	Phil Dumatrait	.15
347	Brandon Mims RC	.25
348	Jason Jennings	.15
349	Phil Wilson RC	.25
350	Jason Hart	.15
351	Cesar Izturis	.15
352	Matt Butler RC	.25
353	David Kelton	.15
354	Luke Prokopec	.15
355	Corey Smith	.15
356	Joel Pineiro RC	.75
357	Ken Chenard	.15
358	Keith Reed	.15
359	David Walling	.15
360	Alexis Gomez RC	.50
361	Justin Morneau RC	10.00
362	Josh Fogg RC	.50
363	J.R. House	.15
364	Andy Tracy	.15
365	Kenny Kelly	.15
366	Aaron McNeal	.15
367	Nick Johnson	.25
368	Brian Esposito	.15
369	Charles Frazier RC	.25
370	Scott Heard	.15
371	Patrick Strange	.15
372	Mike Meyers	.15
373	Ryan Ludwick RC	.50
374	Brad Wilkerson	.15
375	Allen Levrault	.15
376	Seth McClung RC	.40
377	Joe Nathan	.15
378	Rafael Soriano RC	.75
379	Chris Richard	.15
380	Xavier Nady	.15
381	Tike Redman	.15
382	Adam Dunn	.15
383	Jared Abruzzo RC	.25
384	Jason Richardson RC	.15
385	Matt Holliday	.15
386	Darwin Cubillian RC	.25
387	Mike Nannini	.15
388	Blake Williams RC	.25
389	Valentino Pascucci RC	.25
390	Jon Garland	.15
391	Josh Pressley	.15
392	Jose Ortiz	.15
393	Ryan Hannaman RC	.25
394	Steve Smyth RC	.25
395	John Patterson	.15
396	Chad Petty RC	.25
397	Jake Peavy RC	10.00
398	Onix Mercado RC	.25
399	Jason Romano	.15
400	Luis Torres RC	.25
401	Casey Fossum RC	.25
402	Eduardo Figueroa RC	.25
403	Bryan Barnowski RC	.25
404	Tim Redding	.15
405	Jason Standridge	.15
406	Marvin Seale RC	.25
407	Todd Moser	.15
408	Alex Gordon	.15
409	Steve Smitherman RC	.75
410	Ben Petrick	.15
411	Eric Munson	.15
412	Luis Rivas	.15
413	Matt Ginter	.15
414	Alfonso Soriano	.50
415	Rafael Boitel RC	.25
416	Dany Morban RC	.25
417	Justin Woodrowc RC	.25
418	Wilfredo Rodriguez	.15
419	Derrick Van Dusen RC	.25
420	Josh Spoerl RC	.25
421	Juan Pierre	.15
422	J.C. Romero	.15
423	Ed Rogers RC	.25
424	Tomokazu Ohka	.15
425	Ben Hendrickson RC	.25
426	Carlos Zambrano	.15
427	Brett Myers	.25
428	Scott Seabol	.15
429	Thomas Mitchell	.15
430	Jose Reyes RC	30.00
431	Kip Wells	.15
432	Willi Mo Pena	.15
433	Adam Pettyjohn RC	.25
434	Austin Kearns	.15
435	Rico Washington	.15
436	Doug Nickle RC	.25
437	Steve Lomasney	.15
438	Jason Jones RC	.25
439	Bobby Seay	.15
440	Justin Wayne RC	.50

Autographs

JOSH PRESSLEY

		NM/M
	Common Autograph: Inserted 1:74	5.00
BB	Brian Barnowski	5.00
WB	Wilson Betemit	8.00
JB	Jason Botts	15.00
SB	Sean Burroughs	5.00
FB	Freddie Bynum	5.00
ND	Noel Devarez	5.00
JD	Jose Diaz	5.00
BD	Ben Diggins	5.00
AE	Alex Escobar	8.00
RF	Rafael Furcal	10.00
AG	Adrian Gonzalez	15.00
AKG	Alex Gordon	5.00
AJG	Alex Graman	5.00
CG	Cristian Guerrero	5.00
TH	Travis Hafner	100.00
JH	Josh Hamilton	30.00
JWH	Jason Hart	5.00
JRH	J.R. House	5.00
RJ	Russ Jacobson	5.00
TJ	Tripper Johnson	5.00
DWK	David Kelton	5.00
DK	David Krynzel	5.00
PR	Pedro Liriano	5.00
SM	Sean McGowan	5.00
KM	Kevin Mench	5.00
LM	Luis Montanez	8.00
JM	Justin Morneau	125.00
LO	Lyle Overbay	12.00
ADP	Adam Piatt	8.00
JP	Josh Pressley	6.00
AP	Albert Pujols	650.00
BS	Ben Sheets	20.00
SDS	Steve Smyth	5.00
SS	Shawn Sonnier	5.00
SU	Sixto Urena	5.00
MV	Miguel Villilo	5.00
BW	Brad Wilkerson	10.00
BZ	Barry Zito	25.00

Autoproofs

	Common Player:	
	Inserted 1:18,259H	
	Inserted 1:8,306HTA	
	Redemption Expired 4/30/03	
	Values Undetermined	

Futures Game-Worn Jersey

2000 All-Star Futures Game

		NM/M
	Common Player: Inserted 1:82	5.00
KA	Kurt Ainsworth	6.00
CA	Craig Anderson	5.00
RA	Ryan Anderson	5.00
BB	Bobby Bradley	5.00
MB	Mike Bynum	5.00
RC	Ramon Castro	5.00
CC	Chin-Feng Chen	25.00
JC	Jack Cust	5.00
TD	Travis Dawkins	5.00
RD	Randey Dorame	5.00
AE	Alex Escobar	5.00
CG	Chris George	5.00
MG	Marcus Giles	6.00
JH	Josh Hamilton	8.00
CH	Carlos Hernandez	5.00
SK	Sun-Woo Kim	5.00
FL	Felipe Lopez	5.00
EM	Eric Munson	5.00
AM	Aaron Myette	5.00
NN	Ntema Ndungidi	5.00
TO	Tomokazu Ohka	5.00
RO	Ramon Ortiz	5.00
DCP	Corey Patterson	8.00
CP	Carlos Pena	5.00
BP	Ben Petrick	5.00
GR	Grant Roberts	5.00
JR	Jason Romano	5.00
BS	Ben Sheets	6.00
CT	Chin-Hui Tsao	15.00

VW	Vernon Wells	8.00
BW	Brad Wilkerson	5.00
TW	Travis Wilson	5.00
BZ	Barry Zito	15.00
JZ	Julio Zuleta	5.00

Futures Game Three-Piece Game-Used

		NM/M
	Common Player:	20.00
RC	Ramon Castro	20.00
CC	Chin-Feng Chen	80.00
JC	Jack Cust	20.00
TD	Travis Dawkins	20.00
AE	Alex Escobar	20.00
MG	Marcus Giles	20.00
JH	Josh Hamilton	20.00
FL	Felipe Lopez	20.00
EM	Eric Munson	25.00
NN	Ntema Ndungidi	20.00
DCP	Corey Patterson	25.00
CP	Carlos Pena	20.00
BP	Ben Petrick	20.00
JR	Jason Romano	20.00
VW	Vernon Wells	80.00
BW	Brad Wilkerson	20.00
TW	Travis Wilson	20.00
JZ	Julio Zuleta	20.00

Autographed Three-Piece Game-Used

No pricing due to scarcity.

Rookie of the Year Dual Jersey

	NM/M
Inserted 1:2,202	
ROYR Kazuhiro Sasaki, Rafael Furcal	30.00

Rookie Reprints

WILLIE MAYS

		NM/M
	Complete Set (25):	50.00
	Common Player:	1.50
	Inserted 1:12	
1	Yogi Berra	5.00
2	Ralph Kiner	2.50
3	Stan Musial	6.00
4	Warren Spahn	4.00
5	Roy Campanella	4.00
6	Bob Lemon	1.50
7	Robin Roberts	2.00
8	Duke Snider	4.00
9	Early Wynn	1.50
10	Richie Ashburn	1.50
11	Gil Hodges	2.00
12	Hank Bauer	2.00
13	Don Newcombe	1.50
14	Al Rosen	1.50
15	Willie Mays	8.00
16	Joe Garagiola	2.00
17	Whitey Ford	4.00
18	Lew Burdette	1.50
19	Gil McDougald	1.50
20	Minnie Minoso	1.50
21	Eddie Mathews	4.00
22	Harvey Kuenn	2.00
23	Don Larsen	3.00
24	Elston Howard	2.00
25	Don Zimmer	1.50

Autographed Rookie Reprints

Willie Mays illustration

		NM/M
	Common Autograph:	20.00
	Inserted 1:2,467	
1	Yogi Berra	70.00
2	Willie Mays	200.00
3	Stan Musial	100.00
4	Duke Snider	35.00
5	Warren Spahn	50.00
6	Ralph Kiner	25.00
8	Don Larsen	30.00
9	Don Zimmer	20.00
10	Minnie Minoso	20.00

Game-Used Bat Rookie Reprints

		NM/M
	Common Player:	10.00
	Inserted 1:1,954	
1	Willie Mays	60.00
2	Duke Snider	25.00
3	Minnie Minoso	10.00
4	Hank Bauer	10.00
5	Al Rosen	10.00

Autographed Game-Used Bat Rookie Reprints

Inserted 1:18,259
No pricing due to scarcity.

2001 Bowman Chrome

RAFAEL PALMEIRO • 1B
TEXAS RANGERS

		NM/M
	Complete Set (351):	
	Common (1-110, 201-310):	.20
	Common Ref.	
	(111-200, 311-330):	4.00
	Inserted 1:4	
	Common Ref. Auto.	
	(331-350):	25.00
	Production 500	
	Pack (4):	20.00
	Box (24):	475.00
1	Jason Giambi	.60
2	Rafael Furcal	.40
3	Bernie Williams	.50
4	Kenny Lofton	.20
5	Al Leiter	.20
6	Albert Belle	.20
7	Craig Biggio	.40
8	Mark Mulder	.40
9	Carlos Delgado	.75
10	Darin Erstad	.75
11	Richie Sexson	.20
12	Randy Johnson	1.00
13	Greg Maddux	1.50
14	Orlando Hernandez	.40
15	Javier Vazquez	.20
16	Jeff Kent	.40
17	Jim Thome	.50
18	John Olerud	.20
19	Jason Kendall	.20
20	Scott Rolen	.75
21	Tony Gwynn	1.00
22	Edgardo Alfonzo	.20
23	Pokey Reese	.20
24	Todd Helton	.75
25	Mark Quinn	.20
26	Dean Palmer	.20
27	Ray Durham	.20
28	Rafael Palmeiro	.75
29	Carl Everett	.20
30	Vladimir Guerrero	1.00
31	Livan Hernandez	.20
32	Preston Wilson	.20
33	Jose Vidro	.20
34	Fred McGriff	.40
35	Kevin Brown	.20
36	Miguel Tejada	.40
37	Chipper Jones	1.00
38	Edgar Martinez	.20
39	Tony Batista	.20
40	Jorge Posada	.50
41	Sammy Sosa	1.00
42	Gary Sheffield	.50
43	Bartolo Colon	.20
44	Pat Burrell	.50

45	Jay Payton	.20
46	Mike Mussina	.60
47	Nomar Garciaparra	1.00
48	Darren Dreifort	.20
49	Richard Hidalgo	.20
50	Troy Glaus	.50
51	Ben Grieve	.20
52	Jim Edmonds	.40
53	Raul Mondesi	.20
54	Andruw Jones	.75
55	Mike Sweeney	.20
56	Derek Jeter	3.00
57	Ruben Mateo	.20
58	Cristian Guzman	.20
59	Mike Hampton	.20
60	J.D. Drew	.20
61	Matt Lawton	.20
62	Moises Alou	.40
63	Terrence Long	.20
64	Geoff Jenkins	.20
65	Manny Ramirez	1.00
66	Johnny Damon	1.00
67	Pedro Martinez	1.00
68	Juan Gonzalez	.50
69	Roger Clemens	2.00
70	Carlos Beltran	.75
71	Roberto Alomar	.50
72	Barry Bonds	3.00
73	Tim Hudson	.50
74	Tom Glavine	.50
75	Jeromy Burnitz	.20
76	Adrian Beltre	.20
77	Mike Piazza	1.00
78	Kerry Wood	.40
79	Steve Finley	.20
80	Bobby Abreu	.40
81	Neifi Perez	.20
82	Mark Redman	.20
83	Paul Konerko	.40
84	Jermaine Dye	.20
85	Brian Giles	.20
86	Ivan Rodriguez	.75
87	Adam Kennedy	.20
88	Eric Chavez	.40
89	Billy Koch	.20
90	Shawn Green	.40
91	Matt Williams	.20
92	Greg Vaughn	.20
93	Jeff Cirillo	.20
94	Frank Thomas	.75
95	David Justice	.20
96	Cal Ripken Jr.	3.00
97	Curt Schilling	.75
98	Barry Zito	.40
99	Brian Jordan	.20
100	Chan Ho Park	.20
101	J.T. Snow Jr.	.20
102	Kazuhiro Sasaki	.20
103	Alex Rodriguez	2.50
104	Mariano Rivera	.50
105	Eric Milton	.20
106	Andy Pettitte	.50
107	Ken Griffey Jr.	2.00
108	Bengie Molina	.20
109	Jeff Bagwell	.75
110	Mark McGwire	2.00
111	Dan Tosca RC	4.00
112	Sergio Contreras RC	4.00
113	Mitch Jones RC	4.00
114	Ramon Carvajal RC	4.00
115	Ryan Madson RC	12.00
116	Hank Blalock RC	40.00
117	Ben Washburn RC	4.00
118	Erick Almonte RC	4.00
119	Shawn Fagan RC	4.00
120	Gary Johnson RC	4.00
121	Brett Evert RC	4.00
122	Joe Hamer RC	4.00
123	Yhency Brazoban RC	6.00
124	Domingo Guante RC	4.00
125	Deivi Mendez RC	4.00
126	Adrian Hernandez RC	4.00
127	Reggie Abercrombie RC	8.00
128	Steve Bennett RC	4.00
129	Matt White RC	4.00
130	Brian Hitchcox RC	4.00
131	Deivis Santos RC	4.00
132	Luis Montanez RC	4.00
133	Eric Reynolds RC	4.00
134	Denny Bautista RC	8.00
135	Hector Garcia RC	4.00
136	Joe Thurston RC	4.00
137	Tsuyoshi Shinjo RC	8.00
138	Elpidio Guzman RC	4.00
139	Brian Bass RC	4.00
140	Mark Burnett RC	4.00
141	Russ Jacobsen RC	4.00
142	Travis Hafner RC	65.00
143	Wilson Betemit RC	12.00
144	Luke Lockwood RC	4.00
145	Noel Devarez RC	4.00
146	Doug Gredvig RC	4.00
147	Seung Jun Song RC	6.00
148	Andy Van Hekken RC	4.00
149	Ryan Kohlmeier RC	4.00
150	Dee Haynes RC	6.00
151	Jim Journell RC	6.00
152	Chad Petty RC	4.00
153	Danny Borrell RC	4.00
154	David Krynzel RC	4.00
155	Octavio Martinez RC	4.00
156	David Parrish RC	4.00
157	Jason Miller RC	4.00
158	Corey Spencer RC	4.00
159	Maxim St. Pierre RC	4.00
160	Pat Magness RC	4.00
161	Rainier Olmedo RC	4.00

162	Brandon Mims RC	4.00
163	Phil Wilson RC	4.00
164	Jose Reyes RC	200.00
165	Matt Butler RC	4.00
166	Joel Pineiro RC	4.00
167	Ken Chenard RC	4.00
168	Alexis Gomez RC	6.00
169	Justin Morneau RC	75.00
170	Josh Fogg RC	5.00
171	Charles Frazier RC	4.00
172	Ryan Ludwick RC	6.00
173	Seth McClung RC	6.00
174	Justin Wayne RC	6.00
175	Rafael Soriano RC	6.00
176	Jared Abruzzo RC	4.00
177	Jason Richardson RC	4.00
178	Darwin Cubillan RC	4.00
179	Blake Williams RC	4.00
180	Valentino Pascucci RC	4.00
181	Ryan Hannaman RC	4.00
182	Steve Smyth RC	4.00
183	Jake Peavy RC	40.00
184	Onix Mercado RC	4.00
185	Luis Torres RC	4.00
186	Casey Fossum RC	6.00
187	Eduardo Figueroa RC	4.00
188	Bryan Barnowski RC	4.00
189	Jason Standridge RC	4.00
190	Marvin Seale RC	4.00
191	Steve Smitherman RC	8.00
192	Rafael Boitel RC	4.00
193	Dany Morban RC	4.00
194	Justin Woodrow RC	4.00
195	Ed Rogers RC	4.00
196	Ben Hendrickson RC	4.00
197	Thomas Mitchell RC	4.00
198	Adam Pettyjohn RC	4.00
199	Doug Nickle RC	4.00
200	Jason Jones RC	4.00
201	Larry Barnes	.20
202	Ben Diggins	.20
203	Dee Brown	.20
204	Rocco Baldelli	1.00
205	Luis Terrero	.20
206	Milton Bradley	.20
207	Kurt Ainsworth	.20
208	Sean Burroughs	.20
209	Rick Asadoorian	.20
210	Ramon Castro	.20
211	Nick Neugebauer	.20
212	Aaron Myette	.20
213	Luis Matos	.20
214	Donnie Bridges	.20
215	Alex Cintron	.20
216	Bobby Kielty	.20
217	Matt Belisle	.20
218	Adam Everett	.20
219	John Lackey	.20
220	Adam Wainwright	.50
221	Jerry Hairston Jr.	.20
222	Mike Bynum	.20
223	Ryan Christianson	.20
224	J.J. Davis	.20
225	Alex Graman	.20
226	Abraham Nunez	.20
227	Sun-Woo Kim	.20
228	Jimmy Rollins	.50
229	Ruben Salazar	.20
230	Josh Girdley	.20
231	Carl Crawford	.20
232	Ben Davis	.20
233	Jason Grabowski	.20
234	Chris George	.20
235	Roy Oswalt	.75
236	Brian Cole	.20
237	Corey Patterson	.40
238	Vernon Wells	.20
239	Bradley Baker	.20
240	Gookie Dawkins	.20
241	Michael Cuddyer	.20
242	Ricardo Aramboles	.20
243	Ben Sheets	.50
244	Toby Hall	.20
245	Jack Cust	.20
246	Pedro Feliz	.20
247	Josh Beckett	.50
248	Alex Escobar	.20
249	Marcus Giles	.20
250	Jon Rauch	.20
251	Kevin Mench	.20
252	Shawn Sonnier	.20
253	Aaron Rowand	.20
254	C.C. Sabathia	.20
255	Bubba Crosby	.20
256	Josh Hamilton	.20
257	Carlos Hernandez	.25
258	Carlos Pena	.20
259	Miguel Cabrera (Photo actually Manuel Esquivia.)	2.50
260	Brandon Phillips	.20
261	Tony Pena Jr.	.20
262	Cristian Guerrero	.20
263	Jin Ho Cho	.20
264	Aaron Herr	.20
265	Keith Ginter	.20
266	Felipe Lopez	.20
267	Travis Harper	.20
268	Joe Torres	.20
269	Eric Byrnes	.20
270	Ben Christensen	.20
271	Aubrey Huff	.20
272	Lyle Overbay	.20
273	Vince Faison	.20
274	Bobby Bradley	.20
275	Joe Crede	.20
276	Matt Wheatland	.20
277	Grady Sizemore	1.50

278	Adrian Gonzalez	.50
279	Timothy Raines Jr.	.20
280	Phil Dumatrait	.20
281	Jason Hart	.20
282	David Kelton	.20
283	David Walling	.20
284	J.R. House	.50
285	Kenny Kelly	.20
286	Aaron McNeal	.20
287	Nick Johnson	.20
288	Scott Heard	.20
289	Brad Wilkerson	.20
290	Allen Levrault	.20
291	Chris Richard	.20
292	Jared Sandberg	.20
293	Tike Redman	.20
294	Adam Dunn	.75
295	Josh Pressley	.20
296	Jose Ortiz	.20
297	Jason Romano	.20
298	Tim Redding	.20
299	Alex Gordon	.20
300	Ben Petrick	.20
301	Eric Munson	.20
302	Luis Rivas	.20
303	Matt Ginter	.20
304	Alfonso Soriano	.75
305	Wilfredo Rodriguez	.20
306	Brett Myers	.20
307	Scott Seabol	.20
308	Tony Alvarez	.20
309	Donzell McDonald	.20
310	Austin Kearns	.20
311	Will Ohman RC	4.00
312	Ryan Soules RC	4.00
313	Cody Ross RC	4.00
314	Bill Whitecotton RC	4.00
315	Mike Burns RC	4.00
316	Manuel Acosta RC	4.00
317	Lance Niekro RC	10.00
318	Travis Thompson RC	4.00
319	Zach Sorensen RC	4.00
320	Austin Evans RC	4.00
321	Brad Stiles RC	4.00
322	Joe Kennedy RC	4.00
323	Luke Martin RC	4.00
324	Juan Diaz RC	4.00
325	Pat Hallmark RC	4.00
326	Christian Parker RC	4.00
327	Ronny Corona RC	4.00
328	Jermaine Clark RC	4.00
329	Scott Dunn RC	4.00
330	Scott Chiasson RC	4.00
331	Greg Nash/Auto. RC	25.00
332	Brad Cresse/Auto.	25.00
333	John Buck/Auto. RC	60.00
334	Freddie Bynum/Auto. RC	25.00
335	Felix Diaz/Auto. RC	25.00
336	Jason Belcher/Auto. RC	25.00
337	Troy Farnsworth RC	25.00
338	Roberto Miniel RC	25.00
339	Esix Snead RC	25.00
340	Albert Pujols RC	2,800.
341	Jeff Andra RC	25.00
342	Victor Hall RC	25.00
343	Pedro Liriano RC	25.00
344	Andy Beal RC	25.00
345	Bob Keppel RC	40.00
346	Brian Schmitt RC	25.00
347	Ron Davenport RC	150.00
348	Tony Blanco RC	50.00
349	Reggie Griggs RC	50.00
350	Derrick Van Dusen RC	25.00
351a	Ichiro Suzuki Eng. RC	80.00
351b	Ichiro Suzuki Japanese RC	80.00

Gold Refractors

BRIAN BASS • P
KANSAS CITY ROYALS

Stars: 8-15X
Rookies: 1.5-3X
Production 99 Sets
(See 2001 Bowman Chrome for checklist and base card values.)

X-Fractors

RICHIE SEXSON OF

Stars: 4-8X
Rookies: .75-1.5X
Inserted 1:23
(See 2001 Bowman Chrome for checklist and base card values.)

Futures Game Memorabilia

		NM/M
	Common Player:	6.00
	Inserted 1:460	
KA	Kurt Ainsworth	8.00
CA	Craig Anderson	6.00
RA	Ryan Anderson	6.00
BB	Bobby Bradley	6.00
MB	Mike Bynum	6.00
RC	Ramon Castro	6.00
CC	Chin-Feng Chen	30.00
JC	Jack Cust	6.00
RD	Randey Dorame	6.00
AE	Alex Escobar	6.00
CG	Chris George	6.00
MG	Marcus Giles	6.00
JH	Josh Hamilton	8.00
CH	Carlos Hernandez	6.00
SK	Sun-Woo Kim	6.00
FL	Felipe Lopez	8.00
EM	Eric Munson	6.00
AM	Aaron Myette	6.00
NN	Ntema Ndungidi	6.00
TO	Tomokazu Ohka	6.00
DCP	Corey Patterson	10.00
CP	Carlos Pena	6.00
BP	Ben Petrick	6.00
JR	Jason Romano	6.00
BS	Ben Sheets	8.00
CT	Chin-Hui Tsao	40.00
BW	Brad Wilkerson	6.00
TW	Travis Wilson	6.00
BZ	Barry Zito	15.00
JZ	Julio Zuleta	6.00

Rookie Reprints

Don James Larsen

	NM/M
Complete Set (25):	50.00
Common Player:	2.00
Inserted 1:12	
Refractors:	2-3X
Production 299 Sets	

1	Yogi Berra	5.00
2	Ralph Kiner	3.00
3	Stan Musial	6.00
4	Warren Spahn	4.00
5	Roy Campanella	4.00
6	Bob Lemon	2.00
7	Robin Roberts	3.00
8	Duke Snider	4.00
9	Early Wynn	2.00
10	Richie Ashburn	3.00
11	Gil Hodges	3.00
12	Hank Bauer	2.00
13	Don Newcombe	2.00
14	Al Rosen	2.00
15	Willie Mays	8.00
16	Joe Garagiola	3.00
17	Whitey Ford	4.00
18	Lew Burdette	2.00
19	Gil McDougald	2.00
20	Minnie Minoso	2.00
21	Eddie Mathews	4.00
22	Harvey Kuenn	2.00
23	Don Larsen	3.00
24	Elston Howard	2.00
25	Don Zimmer	2.00

Rookie Reprint Relics

		NM/M
	Common Player:	8.00
	Inserted 1:244	
1	David Justice	8.00
2	Richie Sexson	12.00
3	Sean Casey	8.00
4	Mike Piazza	50.00
5	Carlos Delgado	8.00
6	Chipper Jones	25.00

2001 Bowman Draft Picks & Prospects

ICHIRO • OF
SEATTLE MARINERS

		NM/M
Complete Set (110):		35.00
Complete Factory Set (112):		40.00
Common Player:		.10
1	Alfredo Amezaga RC	.10
2	Andrew Good	.10
3	Kelly Johnson RC	3.00
4	Larry Bigbie	.10
5	Matt Thompson RC	.40
6	Wilton Chavez RC	.40
7	Joe Borchard RC	.50
8	David Espinosa	.10
9	Zach Day	.50
10	Brad Hawpe RC	3.00
11	Nate Cornejo	.10
12	Jim Kavourias RC	.25
13	Brad Judge	.10
14	Angel Berroa RC	.75
15	Lamont Matthews RC	.25
16	Jose Garcia	.10
17	Grant Balfour RC	.25
18	Ron Chiavacci RC	.25
19	Jae Seo	.10
20	Juan Rivera	.10
21	D'Angelo Jimenez	.10
22	Aaron Harang	.10
23	Marlon Byrd RC	.50
24	Sean Burnett	.10
25	Josh Pearce RC	.25
26	Brandon Duckworth RC	.25
27	Jack Taschner RC	.25
28	Bo Robinson RC	.25
29	Brent Abernathy	.10
30	David Elder RC	.25
31	Scott Cassidy RC	.25
32	Dennis Tankersley RC	.25
33	Denny Stark	.10
34	Dave Williams RC	.10
35	Boof Bonser RC	1.00
36	Kris Foster RC	.25
37	Neal Musser RC	.25
38	Shawn Chacon	.10
39	Mike Rivera RC	.25
40	Will Smith RC	.25
41	Morgan Ensberg RC	1.50
42	Ken Harvey RC	.10
43	Ricardo Rodriguez RC	.25
44	Jose Mieses RC	.25
45	Luis Maza RC	.25
46	Julio Perez RC	.25
47	Billy Traber RC	.25
48	David Martinez RC	.25
49	Covelli Crisp RC	2.00
50	Mario Ramos RC	.25
51	Matt Thornton RC	.25
52	Xavier Nady	.10
53	Ryan Vogelsong RC	.25
54	Jim Magrane RC	.25
55	Domingo Valdez RC	.25
56	Brent Butler	.10

57	Brian Tallet RC	.25
58	Brian Reith RC	.25
59	Mario Valenzuela RC	.25
60	Bobby Hill RC	.50
61	Rich Rundles RC	.25
62	Rick Elder	.10
63	J.D. Closser	.10
64	Scot Shields RC	.10
65	Miguel Olivo	.10
66	Stubby Clapp RC	.25
67	Jerome Williams RC	.40
68	Jason Lane RC	.75
69	Chase Utley RC	20.00
70	Erik Bedard RC	4.00
71	Alex Herrera RC	.20
72	Juan Cruz RC	.40
73	Billy Martin RC	.20
74	Ronnie Merrill RC	.20
75	Jason Kinchen RC	.20
76	Wilken Ruan RC	.20
77	Cody Ransom RC	.25
78	Bud Smith RC	.25
79	Wily Mo Pena RC	.10
80	Jeff Nettles RC	.20
81	Jamal Strong RC	.25
82	Bill Ortega	.10
83	Junior Zamora	.10
84	Ichiro Suzuki RC	10.00
85	Fernando Rodney RC	.25
86	Chris Smith RC	.40
87	John Van Benschoten RC	.50
88	Bobby Crosby RC	3.00
89	Kenny Baugh RC	.25
90	Jake Gautreau RC	.40
91	Gabe Gross RC	.75
92	Kris Honel RC	.25
93	Daniel Denham RC	.25
94	Aaron Heilman RC	1.00
95	Irvin Guzman RC	5.00
96	Mike Jones RC	.50
97	John-Ford Griffin RC	.50
98	Macay McBride RC	.50
99	John Rheineckar RC	.50
100	Bronson Sardinha RC	.25
101	Jason Weintraub RC	.25
102	J.D. Martin RC	.25
103	Jayson Nix RC	.25
104	Noah Lowry RC	3.00
105	Richard Lewis RC	.25
106	Brad Hennessey RC	.40
107	Jeff Mathis RC	.75
108	Jon Skaggs RC	.25
109	Justin Pope RC	.25
110	Josh Burrus RC	.25

Autographs

KEARNS 75

Thirteen players on the original checklist from Bowman were never issued.

		NM/M
	Common Autograph:	5.00
	Inserted 1:Set	
JA	Jared Abruzzo	5.00
AA	Alfredo Amezaga	10.00
GA	Garrett Atkins	50.00
BB	Bobby Bradley	5.00
ANC	Antoine Cameron	5.00
ROC	Ramon Carvajal	5.00
RC	Ryan Church	15.00
AC	Alex Cintron	5.00
RD	Ryan Dittfurth	5.00
AE	Adam Everett	5.00
AF	Alex Fernandez	5.00
AG	Alexis Gomez	10.00
CG	Cristian Guerrero	5.00
BH	Beau Hale	5.00
SH	Scott Heard	5.00
AH	Aaron Herr	5.00
CI	Cesar Izturis	5.00
GJ	Gary Johnson	5.00
NJ	Nick Johnson	10.00
AK	Austin Kearns	15.00
JK	Joe Kennedy	5.00
JL	John Lackey	12.00
FL	Felipe Lopez	8.00
RI	Ryan Ludwick	10.00
RMM	Ryan Madson	15.00
TO	Tomo Ohka	8.00
RO	Roy Oswalt	35.00
CP	Christian Parra	5.00
BP	Brandon Phillips	10.00
JP	Joel Pineiro	15.00
NR	Nick Regilio	5.00
ER	Ed Rogers	5.00
SS	Scott Seabol	5.00

BS	Bud Smith	5.00
BJS	Brian Specht	5.00
JT	Joe Torres	5.00
JMW	Justin Wayne	8.00

Draft Pick Relics

		NM/M
Common Player:		4.00
One per factory set.		
CI	Cesar Izturis	4.00
GJ	Gary Johnson	4.00
NR	Nick Regilio	4.00
RC	Ryan Church	4.00
BJS	Brian Specht	4.00
JRH	J.R. House	4.00

Futures Game Relics

		NM/M
Common Player:		4.00
One per factory set.		
AA	Alfredo Amezaga	4.00
AD	Adam Dunn	10.00
AG	Adrian Gonzalez	8.00
AH	Alex Herrera	4.00
BM	Brett Myers	8.00
CD	Cody Ransom	4.00
CG	Chris George	4.00
CH	Carlos Hernandez	5.00
CU	Chase Utley	25.00
EB	Eric Bedard	12.00
GB	Grant Balfour	4.00
HB	Hank Blalock	18.00
JB	Joe Borchard	10.00
JC	Juan Cruz	5.00
JP	Josh Pearce	4.00
JR	Juan Rivera	4.00
LG	Luis Garcia	4.00
MC	Miguel Cabrera	10.00
MR	Mike Rivera	4.00
RR	Ricardo Rodriguez	4.00
SC	Scott Chiasson	4.00
SS	Seung Jun Song	6.00
TB	Toby Hall	4.00
WB	Wilson Betemit	4.00
WP	Wily Mo Pena	5.00
JAP	Juan Pena	4.00

2001 Bowman Heritage Promos

To introduce its Heritage issue, Topps produced this five-card promo set for distribution at the National Sports Collectors Convention in Cleveland, June 28 through July 1. The three Indians cards were available from the PSA booth, the Pujols card from the Beckett booth and the McGwire card from the SCD booth. Only 500 of each card were produced. Styled after the 1948 Bowman cards with black-and-white photos on front and gray cardboard backs, the promos are in the standard 2-1/2" x 3-1/2" size and were given away in a cello pack with a cello-wrapped piece of bubblegum.

	NM/M
Complete Set (5):	60.00

2001 Bowman Heritage

Common Player:		6.00
1	Roberto Alomar	6.00
2	Albert Pujols	50.00
3	C.C. Sabathia	6.00
4	Mark McGwire	12.50
5	Juan Gonzalez	6.00

2001 Bowman Heritage

		NM/M
Complete Set (440):		200.00
Common Player:		.15
Common (331-440):		1.00
Inserted 1:2		
Pack (10):		7.00
Box (24):		140.00
1	Chipper Jones	1.25
2	Pete Harnisch	.15
3	Brian Giles	.15
4	J.T. Snow	.15
5	Bartolo Colon	.15
6	Jorge Posada	.25
7	Shawn Green	.25
8	Derek Jeter	2.50
9	Benito Santiago	.15
10	Ramon Hernandez	.15
11	Bernie Williams	.40
12	Greg Maddux	1.50
13	Barry Bonds	2.50
14	Roger Clemens	2.00
15	Miguel Tejada	.50
16	Pedro Feliz	.15
17	Jim Edmonds	.40
18	Tom Glavine	.40
19	David Justice	.25
20	Rich Aurilia	.15
21	Jason Giambi	.75
22	Orlando Hernandez	.25
23	Shawn Estes	.15
24	Nelson Figueroa	.15
25	Terrence Long	.25
26	Mike Mussina	.50
27	Eric Davis	.15
28	Jimmy Rollins	.50
29	Andy Pettitte	.50
30	Shawon Dunston	.15
31	Tim Hudson	.40
32	Jeff Kent	.25
33	Scott Brosius	.15
34	Livan Hernandez	.15
35	Alfonso Soriano	1.00
36	Mark McGwire	1.50
37	Russ Ortiz	.15
38	Fernando Vina	.15
39	Ken Griffey Jr.	1.50
40	Edgar Renteria	.15
41	Kevin Brown	.15
42	Robb Nen	.15
43	Paul LoDuca	.15
44	Bobby Abreu	.25
45	Adam Dunn	.50
46	Osvaldo Fernandez	.15
47	Marvin Benard	.15
48	Mark Gardner	.15
49	Alex Rodriguez	2.00
50	Preston Wilson	.15
51	Roberto Alomar	.40
52	Ben Davis	.15
53	Derek Bell	.15
54	Ken Caminiti	.15
55	Barry Zito	.40
56	Scott Rolen	.75
57	Geoff Jenkins	.15
58	Mike Cameron	.15
59	Ben Grieve	.15
60	Chuck Knoblauch	.15
61	Matt Lawton	.15
62	Chan Ho Park	.15
63	Lance Berkman	.40
64	Carlos Beltran	.50
65	Dean Palmer	.15
66	Alex Gonzalez	.15
67	Larry Walker	.25
68	Magglio Ordonez	.25
69	Ellis Burks	.15
70	Mark Mulder	.25
71	Randy Johnson	.75
72	John Smoltz	.40
73	Jerry Hairston Jr.	.15
74	Pedro Martinez	.75
75	Fred McGriff	.15
76	Sean Casey	.25
77	C.C. Sabathia	.15
78	Todd Helton	.40
79	Brad Penny	.15
80	Mike Sweeney	.15
81	Billy Wagner	.15
82	Mark Buehrle	.25
83	Cristian Guzman	.15
84	Jose Vidro	.15
85	Pat Burrell	.40
86	Jermaine Dye	.15
87	Brandon Inge	.15
88	David Wells	.15
89	Mike Piazza	1.00
90	Jose Cabrera	.15
91	Cliff Floyd	.15
92	Matt Morris	.15
93	Raul Mondesi	.15
94	Joe Kennedy	.50
95	Jack Wilson RC	1.00
96	Andruw Jones	.75
97	Mariano Rivera	.50
98	Mike Hampton	.15
99	Roger Cedeno	.15
100	Jose Cruz	.15
101	Mike Lowell	.15
102	Pedro Astacio	.15
103	Joe Mays	.15
104	John Franco	.15
105	Tim Redding	.15
106	Sandy Alomar	.15
107	Bret Boone	.15
108	Josh Towers RC	.50
109	Matt Stairs	.15
110	Chris Truby	.15
111	Jeff Suppan	.15
112	J.C. Romero	.15
113	Felipe Lopez	.15
114	Ben Sheets	.40
115	Frank Thomas	.75
116	A.J. Burnett	.15
117	Tony Clark	.15
118	Mac Suzuki	.15
119	Brad Radke	.15
120	Jeff Shaw	.15
121	Nick Neugebauer	.15
122	Kenny Lofton	.15
123	Jacque Jones	.15
124	Brent Mayne	.15
125	Carlos Hernandez	.15
126	Shane Spencer	.15
127	John Lackey	.15
128	Sterling Hitchcock	.15
129	Darren Dreifort	.15
130	Rusty Greer	.15
131	Michael Cuddyer	.15
132	Tyler Houston	.15
133	Chin-Feng Chen	.15
134	Ken Harvey	.15
135	Marquis Grissom	.15
136	Russell Branyan	.15
137	Eric Karros	.15
138	Josh Beckett	.25
139	Todd Zeile	.15
140	Corey Koskie	.15
141	Steve Sparks	.15
142	Bobby Seay	.15
143	Tim Raines	.15
144	Julio Zuleta	.15
145	Jose Lima	.15
146	Dante Bichette	.15
147	Randy Keisler	.15
148	Brent Butler	.15
149	Antonio Alfonseca	.15
150	Bryan Rekar	.15
151	Jeffrey Hammonds	.15
152	Larry Bigbie	.15
153	Blake Stein	.15
154	Robin Ventura	.15
155	Rondell White	.15
156	Juan Silvestre	.15
157	Marcus Thames	.15
158	Sidney Ponson	.15
159	Juan Pena	.15
160	Charles Johnson	.15
161	Adam Everett	.15
162	Eric Munson	.15
163	Jason Isringhausen	.15
164	Brad Fullmer	.15
165	Miguel Olivo	.15
166	Fernando Tatis	.15
167	Freddy Garcia	.15
168	Tom Goodwin	.15
169	Armando Benitez	.15
170	Paul Konerko	.40
171	Jeff Cirillo	.15
172	Shane Reynolds	.15
173	Kevin Tapani	.15
174	Joe Crede	.25
175	Omar Infante RC	.50
176	Jake Peavy RC	5.00
177	Corey Patterson	.25
178	Alfredo Amezaga RC	.25
179	Jeromy Burnitz	.15
180	David Segui	.15
181	Marcus Giles	.15
182	Paul O'Neill	.25
183	John Olerud	.15
184	Andy Benes	.15
185	Brad Cresse RC	.15
186	Ricky Ledee	.15
187	Allen Levrault	.15
188	Royce Clayton	.15
189	Kelly Johnson RC	4.00
190	Quilvio Veras	.15
191	Mike Williams	.15
192	Jason Lane RC	1.00
193	Rick Helling	.15
194	Tim Wakefield	.15
195	James Baldwin	.15
196	Cody Ransom RC	.15
197	Bobby Kielty	.15
198	Bobby Jones	.15
199	Steve Cox	.15
200	Jamal Strong RC	.25
201	Steve Lomasney	.15
202	Bill Ortega	.15
203	Mike Matheny	.15
204	Jeff Randazzo RC	.25
205	Aubrey Huff	.15
206	Chuck Finley	.15
207	Denny Bautista RC	1.50
208	Terry Mulholland	.15
209	Rey Ordonez	.15
210	Jason Belcher RC	.15
211	Orlando Cabrera	.15
212	Juan Encarnacion	.15
213	Dustin Hermanson	.15
214	Luis Rivas	.15
215	Mark Quinn	.15
216	Randy Velarde	.15
217	Billy Koch	.15
218	Ryan Rupe	.15
219	Keith Ginter	.15
220	Woody Williams	.15
221	Blake Williams RC	.25
222	Aaron Myette	.15
223	Joe Borchard RC	.75
224	Nate Cornejo	.15
225	Julian Tavarez	.15
226	Kevin Millwood	.15
227	Travis Hafner RC	5.00
228	Charles Nagy	.15
229	Mike Lieberthal	.15
230	Jeff Nelson	.15
231	Ryan Dempster	.15
232	Andres Galarraga	.15
233	Chad Durbin	.15
234	Timoniel Perez	.15
235	Troy O'Leary	.15
236	Kevin Young	.15
237	Gabe Kapler	.15
238	Juan Cruz RC	.15
239	Masato Yoshii	.15
240	Aramis Ramirez	.40
241	Matt Cooper	.15
242	Randy Flores RC	.25
243	Rafael Furcal	.15
244	David Eckstein	.15
245	Matt Clement	.15
246	Craig Biggio	.40
247	Rick Reed	.15
248	Jose Macias	.15
249	Alex Escobar	.15
250	Roberto Hernandez	.15
251	Andy Ashby	.15
252	Tony Armas	.15
253	Jamie Moyer	.15
254	Jason Tyner	.15
255	Ryan Ludwick RC	.50
256	Jeff Conine	.15
257	Francisco Cordova	.15
258	Ted Lilly	.15
259	Joe Randa	.15
260	Jeff D'Amico	.15
261	Albie Lopez	.15
262	Kevin Appier	.15
263	Richard Hidalgo	.15
264	Omar Daal	.15
265	Ricky Gutierrez	.15
266	John Rocker	.15
267	Ray Lankford	.15
268	Beau Hale RC	.25
269	Tony Blanco RC	.25
270	Derrek Lee	.75
271	Jamey Wright	.15
272	Alex Gordon	.15
273	Jeff Weaver	.15
274	Jaret Wright	.15
275	Jose Hernandez	.15
276	Bruce Chen	.15
277	Todd Hollandsworth	.15
278	Wade Miller	.15
279	Luke Prokopec	.15
280	Rafael Soriano RC	.75
281	Damian Easley	.15
282	Darren Oliver	.15
283	Brandon Duckworth RC	.50
284	Aaron Herr	.15
285	Ray Durham	.15
286	Adrian Hernandez RC	.40
287	Ugueth Urbina	.15
288	Scott Seabol	.15
289	Lance Niekro RC	1.00
290	Trot Nixon	.15
291	Adam Kennedy	.15
292	Brian Schmitt RC	.25
293	Grant Roberts	.15
294	Benny Agbayani	.15
295	Travis Lee	.15
296	Erick Almonte RC	.40
297	Jim Thome	.50
298	Eric Young	.15
299	Daniel Denham RC	.25
300	Boof Bonser RC	2.00
301	Denny Neagle	.15
302	Kenny Rogers	.15
303	J.D. Closser	.15
304	Chase Utley RC	15.00
305	Rey Sanchez	.15
306	Sean McGowan	.15
307	Justin Pope RC	.25
308	Torii Hunter	.40
309	B.J. Surhoff	.15
310	Aaron Heilman RC	.50
311	Gabe Gross RC	.75
312	Lee Stevens	.15
313	Todd Hundley	.15
314	Macay McBride RC	.50
315	Edgar Martinez	.15
316	Omar Vizquel	.15
317	Reggie Sanders	.15
318	John-Ford Griffin RC	.50
319	Tim Salmon (Photo actually Troy Glaus.)	.50
320	Pokey Reese	.15
321	Jay Payton	.15
322	Doug Glanville	.15
323	Greg Vaughn	.15
324	Ruben Sierra	.15
325	Kip Wells	.15
326	Carl Everett	.15
327	Garret Anderson	.15
328	Jay Bell	.15
329	Barry Larkin	.15
330	Jeff Mathis RC	.75
331	Adrian Gonzalez	2.00
332	Juan Rivera	1.00
333	Tony Alvarez	1.00
334	Xavier Nady	1.00
335	Josh Hamilton	1.00
336	Will Smith RC	1.50
337	Israel Alcantara	1.00
338	Chris George	1.00
339	Sean Burroughs	1.00
340	Jack Cust	1.00
341	Eric Byrnes	1.00
342	Carlos Pena	1.00
343	J.R. House	1.00
344	Carlos Silva	1.00
345	Mike Rivera RC	1.00
346	Adam Johnson	1.00
347	Scott Heard	1.00
348	Alex Cintron	1.00
349	Miguel Cabrera	3.00
350	Nick Johnson	1.00
351	Albert Pujols RC	80.00
352	Ichiro Suzuki RC	35.00
353	Carlos Delgado	1.50
354	Troy Glaus	2.00
355	Sammy Sosa	2.00
356	Ivan Rodriguez	2.00
357	Vladimir Guerrero	2.00
358	Manny Ramirez	2.00
359	Luis Gonzalez	1.00
360	Roy Oswalt	1.50
361	Moises Alou	1.00
362	Juan Gonzalez	1.50
363	Tony Gwynn	2.00
364	Hideo Nomo	1.00
365	Tsuyoshi Shinjo RC	1.00
366	Kazuhiro Sasaki	1.00
367	Cal Ripken Jr.	8.00
368	Rafael Palmeiro	2.00
369	J.D. Drew	1.00
370	Doug Mientkiewicz	1.00
371	Jeff Bagwell	2.00
372	Darin Erstad	2.00
373	Tom Gordon	1.00
374	Ben Petrick	1.00
375	Eric Milton	1.00
376	Nomar Garciaparra	3.00
377	Julio Lugo	1.00
378	Tino Martinez	1.50
379	Javier Vazquez	1.00
380	Jeremy Giambi	1.00
381	Marty Cordova	1.00
382	Adrian Beltre	1.50
383	John Burkett	1.00
384	Aaron Boone	1.00
385	Eric Chavez	1.00
386	Curt Schilling	1.50
387	Cory Lidle	1.00
388	Jason Schmidt	1.00
389	Johnny Damon	3.00
390	Steve Finley	1.00
391	Edgardo Alfonzo	1.00
392	Jose Valentin	1.00
393	Jose Canseco	1.50
394	Ryan Klesko	1.00
395	David Cone	1.00
396	Jason Kendall	1.00
397	Placido Polanco	1.00
398	Glendon Rusch	1.00
399	Aaron Sele	1.00
400	D'Angelo Jimenez	1.00
401	Mark Grace	1.50
402	Al Leiter	1.00
403	Brian Jordan	1.00
404	Phil Nevin	1.00
405	Brent Abernathy	1.00
406	Kerry Wood	1.00
407	Alex Gonzalez	1.00
408	Robert Fick	1.00
409	Dmitri Young	1.00
410	Wes Helms	1.00
411	Trevor Hoffman	1.00
412	Rickey Henderson	2.00
413	Bobby Higginson	1.00
414	Gary Sheffield	1.50
415	Darryl Kile	1.00
416	Richie Sexson	1.50
417	Frank Menechino	1.00
418	Javy Lopez	1.00
419	Carlos Lee	1.00
420	Jon Lieber	1.00
421	Hank Blalock RC	6.00
422	Marlon Byrd RC	1.50
423	Jason Kinchen RC	1.00
424	Morgan Ensberg RC	5.00
425	Greg "Toe" Nash RC	1.00
426	Dennis Tankersley RC	1.00
427	Joel Pineiro	1.00
428	Chris Smith RC	1.00
429	Jake Gautreau RC	1.00
430	John Van Benschoten RC	1.50
431	Travis Thompson	1.00
432	Orlando Hudson RC	2.50
433	Jerome Williams RC	2.00
434	Kevin Reese	1.00
435	Ed Rogers RC	1.00
436	Grant Balfour RC	1.00
437	Adam Pettyjohn RC	1.00
438	Hee Seop Choi RC	2.00
439	Justin Morneau RC	20.00
440	Mitch Jones RC	1.00

Autographs

		NM/M
Common Player:		90.00
BB	Barry Bonds	180.00
RC	Roger Clemens	120.00
AR	Alex Rodriguez	90.00

Team Topps Legends Autographs

		NM/M
Common Autograph:		30.00
Inserted 1:332		
TT13F	Warren Spahn/1965	40.00
TT21R	Bob Feller/1952	30.00

1948 Bowman Reprints

		NM/M
Complete Set (13):		10.00
Common Player:		.75
Inserted 1:2		
1	Ralph Kiner	.75
2	Johnny Mize	.75
3	Bobby Thomson	.75
4	Yogi Berra	1.50
5	Phil Rizzuto	1.00
6	Bob Feller	1.00
7	Enos Slaughter	.75
8	Stan Musial	2.00
9	Hank Sauer	.75
10	Ferris Fain	.75
11	Red Schoendienst	.75
12	Allie Reynolds	.75
13	Johnny Sain	.75

1948 Bowman Reprint Autographs

		NM/M
1	Warren Spahn	40.00
2	Bob Feller	40.00

1948 Reprint Relics

	NM/M
Common Player:	8.00
Inserted 1:44	

ORIGINAL SHIBE PARK SEAT

YB1	Yogi Berra	20.00
YB2	Yogi Berra	35.00
FF	Ferris Fain	8.00
BF	Bob Feller	12.00
RK	Ralph Kiner	15.00
JM	Johnny Mize	15.00
SM1	Stan Musial	30.00
PR	Phil Rizzuto	15.00
HS	Hank Sauer	8.00
RS	Red Schoendienst	10.00
ES	Enos Slaughter	10.00
BT	Bobby Thomson	8.00

Chrome

Stars: 4-8X
SP's: 2-4X
Inserted 1:12
(See 2001 Bowman Heritage for checklist and base card values.)

2001 Bowman's Best Pre-Production

TIM HUDSON

The flashy new look for Bowman's Best in 2001 was debuted in this three-card sample set. Identical in format to the issued cards, they have textured foil printing on front and a matte back.

		NM/M
Complete Set (3):		6.00
Common Player:		2.00
PP1	Todd Helton	3.00
PP2	Tim Hudson	2.00
PP3	Vernon Wells	2.00

2001 Bowman's Best

		NM/M
Complete Set (200):		
Common Player:		.20
Common SP (151-200):		5.00
Production 2,999		
Pack (5):		10.00
Box (24):		200.00
1	Vladimir Guerrero	1.00
2	Miguel Tejada	.50
3	Geoff Jenkins	.20
4	Jeff Bagwell	.75
5	Todd Helton	.75
6	Ken Griffey Jr.	2.00
7	Nomar Garciaparra	1.00
8	Chipper Jones	1.00
9	Darin Erstad	.40
10	Frank Thomas	

JASON GIAMBI

11	Jim Thome	.50
12	Preston Wison	.20
13	Kevin Brown	.20
14	Derek Jeter	3.00
15	Scott Rolen	1.00
16	Ryan Klesko	.20
17	Jeff Kent	.40
18	Raul Mondesi	.20
19	Greg Vaughn	.20
20	Bernie Williams	.40
21	Mike Piazza	1.00
22	Richard Hidalgo	.20
23	Dean Palmer	.20
24	Roberto Alomar	.40
25	Sammy Sosa	1.00
26	Randy Johnson	1.00
27	Manny Ramirez	1.00
28	Roger Clemens	2.00
29	Terrence Long	.20
30	Jason Kendall	.20
31	Richie Sexson	.40
32	David Wells	.20
33	Andruw Jones	1.00
34	Pokey Reese	.20
35	Juan Gonzalez	.50
36	Carlos Beltran	.75
37	Shawn Green	.40
38	Mariano Rivera	.50
39	John Olerud	.20
40	Jim Edmonds	.40
41	Andres Galarraga	.20
42	Carlos Delgado	.75
43	Kris Benson	.20
44	Andy Pettitte	.40
45	Jeff Cirillo	.20
46	Magglio Ordonez	.40
47	Tom Glavine	.40
48	Garret Anderson	.20
49	Cal Ripken Jr.	3.00
50	Pedro Martinez	1.00
51	Barry Bonds	3.00
52	Alex Rodriguez	2.50
53	Ben Grieve	.20
54	Edgar Martinez	.20
55	Jason Giambi	.75
56	Jeromy Burnitz	.20
57	Mike Mussina	.75
58	Moises Alou	.40
59	Sean Casey	.40
60	Greg Maddux	1.50
61	Tim Hudson	.50
62	Mark McGwire	2.00
63	Rafael Palmeiro	.75
64	Tony Batista	.20
65	Kazuhiro Sasaki	.40
66	Jorge Posada	.50
67	Johnny Damon	1.00
68	Brian Giles	.20
69	Jose Vidro	.20
70	Jermaine Dye	.20
71	Craig Biggio	.40
72	Larry Walker	.40
73	Eric Chavez	.40
74	David Segui	.20
75	Tim Salmon	.40
76	Javy Lopez	.20
77	Paul Konerko	.40
78	Barry Larkin	.40
79	Mike Hampton	.20
80	Bobby Higginson	.20
81	Mark Mulder	.40
82	Pat Burrell	.50
83	Kerry Wood	.50
84	J.T. Snow	.20
85	Ivan Rodriguez	.75
86	Edgardo Alfonzo	.20
87	Orlando Hernandez	.20
88	Gary Sheffield	.50
89	Mike Sweeney	.20
90	Carlos Lee	.20
91	Rafael Furcal	.40
92	Troy Glaus	.50
93	Bartolo Colon	.20
94	Cliff Floyd	.20
95	Barry Zito	.50
96	J.D. Drew	.40
97	Eric Karros	.20
98	Jose Valentin	.20
99	Ellis Burks	.20
100	David Justice	.20
101	Larry Barnes	.20
102	Rod Barajas	.20
103	Tony Pena	.20
104	Jerry Hairston Jr.	.20
105	Keith Ginter	.20
106	Corey Patterson	.40
107	Aaron Rowand	.20
108	Miguel Olivo	.20

109	Gookie Dawkins	.20
110	C.C. Sabathia	.20
111	Ben Petrick	.20
112	Eric Munson	.20
113	Ramon Castro	.20
114	Alex Escobar	.20
115	Josh Hamilton	.40
116	Jason Marquis	.20
117	Ben Davis	.20
118	Alex Cintron	.20
119	Julio Zuleta	.20
120	Ben Broussard	.20
121	Adam Everett	.20
122	Ramon Carvajal RC	.75
123	Felipe Lopez	.20
124	Alfonso Soriano	1.00
125	Jayson Werth	.20
126	Donzell McDonald	.20
127	Jason Hart	.25
128	Joe Crede	.50
129	Sean Burroughs	.20
130	Jack Cust	.20
131	Corey Smith	.20
132	Adrian Gonzalez	.40
133	J.R. House	.20
134	Steve Lomasney	.20
135	Tim Raines Jr.	.20
136	Tony Alvarez	.20
137	Doug Mientkiewicz	.20
138	Rocco Baldelli	.75
139	Jason Romano	.20
140	Vernon Wells	.40
141	Mike Bynum	.20
142	Xavier Nady	.20
143	Brad Wilkerson	.20
144	Ben Diggins	.20
145	Aubrey Huff	.20
146	Eric Byrnes	.20
147	Alex Gordon	.20
148	Roy Oswalt	.50
149	Brian Esposito	.20
150	Scott Seabol	.20
151	Erick Almonte RC	5.00
152	Gary Johnson RC	5.00
153	Pedro Liriano RC	5.00
154	Matt White RC	5.00
155	Luis Montanez RC	5.00
156	Brad Cresse RC	5.00
157	Wilson Betemit RC	6.00
158	Octavio Martinez RC	5.00
159	Adam Pettyjohn RC	5.00
160	Corey Spencer RC	5.00
161	Mark Burnett RC	5.00
162	Ichiro Suzuki RC	60.00
163	Alexis Gomez RC	5.00
164	Greg "Toe" Nash RC	5.00
165	Roberto Miniel RC	5.00
166	Justin Morneau RC	40.00
167	Ben Washburn RC	5.00
168	Bob Keppel RC	5.00
169	Deivi Mendez RC	5.00
170	Tsuyoshi Shinjo RC	5.00
171	Jared Abruzzo RC	5.00
172	Derrick Van Dusen RC	5.00
173	Hee Seop Choi RC	8.00
174	Albert Pujols RC	300.00
175	Travis Hafner RC	35.00
176	Ron Davenport RC	6.00
177	Luis Torres RC	5.00
178	Jake Peavy RC	25.00
179	Elvis Corporan RC	5.00
180	David Krynzel RC	5.00
181	Tony Blanco RC	5.00
182	Elpidio Guzman RC	5.00
183	Matt Butler RC	5.00
184	Joe Thurston RC	5.00
185	Andy Beal RC	5.00
186	Kevin Nulton RC	5.00
187	Sneideer Santos RC	5.00
188	Joe Dillon RC	5.00
189	Jeremy Blevins RC	5.00
190	Chris Amador RC	5.00
191	Mark Hendrickson RC	5.00
192	Willy Aybar RC	10.00
193	Antoine Cameron RC	5.00
194	Jonathan Johnson RC	5.00
195	Ryan Ketchner RC	5.00
196	Bjorn Ivy RC	5.00
197	Josh Kroeger RC	5.00
198	Ty Wigginton RC	5.00
199	Stubby Clapp RC	5.00
200	Jerrod Riggan RC	5.00

Autographs

ADRIAN GONZALEZ
FLORIDA MARLINS

	NM/M
Common Player:	8.00
Inserted 1:95	

SB	Sean Burroughs	8.00
BC	Brad Cresse	8.00
AG	Adrian Gonzalez	15.00
JH	Josh Hamilton	30.00
JRH	J.R. House	8.00
TL	Terrence Long	8.00
JR	Jon Rauch	8.00

Exclusive Rookie Autographs

JONATHAN JOHNSON
CHICAGO CUBS

		NM/M
Common Player:		6.00
Inserted 1:50		
WA	Willy Aybar	25.00
SC	Stubby Clapp	6.00
BI	Bjorn Ivy	6.00
JJ	Jonathan Johnson	6.00
TW	Ty Wigginton	6.00
JR	Jerrod Riggan	6.00
SS	Sneideer Santos	6.00
JB	Jeremy Blevins	6.00
MH	Mark Hendrickson	6.00

Franchise Favorites

		NM/M
Complete Set (8):		30.00
Common Player:		1.50
Inserted 1:16		
DM	Don Mattingly	6.00
AR	Alex Rodriguez	6.00
DE	Darin Erstad	1.50
DW	Dave Winfield	1.50
NR	Nolan Ryan	8.00
RJ	Reggie Jackson	2.00
MW	Don Mattingly, Dave Winfield	4.00
RR	Nolan Ryan, Alex Rodriguez	8.00
EJ	Darin Erstad, Reggie Jackson	2.00

Franchise Favorites Autographs

ALEX RODRIGUEZ

		NM/M
Common Player:		25.00
Inserted 1:556		
Combo 1:4,436		
DE	Darin Erstad	20.00
RJ	Reggie Jackson	40.00
EJ	Darin Erstad, Reggie Jackson	65.00
DM	Don Mattingly	60.00
MW	Don Mattingly, Dave Winfield	150.00
AR	Alex Rodriguez	80.00
NR	Nolan Ryan	80.00
RR	Nolan Ryan, Alex Rodriguez	300.00
DW	Dave Winfield	25.00

Franchise Favorites Relics

NOLAN RYAN

	NM/M
Common Player:	6.00

Jersey 1:139		
Pants 1:307		
Combo Relic 1:1,114		
JB	Jeff Bagwell	10.00
CB	Craig Biggio	6.00
BB	Craig Biggio, Jeff Bagwell	25.00
DE	Darin Erstad	6.00
RJ	Reggie Jackson	10.00
EJ	Reggie Jackson, Darin Erstad	25.00
DM	Don Mattingly	30.00
MW	Don Mattingly, Dave Winfield	65.00
AR	Alex Rodriguez	20.00
NR	Nolan Ryan	40.00
RR	Nolan Ryan, Alex Rodriguez	60.00
DW	Dave Winfield	8.00

Franchise Futures

		NM/M
Complete Set (12):		15.00
Common Player:		1.00
Inserted 1:24		
FF1	Josh Hamilton	1.00
FF2	Wes Helms	1.00
FF3	Alfonso Soriano	4.00
FF4	Nick Johnson	1.50
FF5	Jose Ortiz	1.00
FF6	Ben Sheets	1.50
FF7	Sean Burroughs	1.50
FF8	Ben Petrick	1.00
FF9	Corey Patterson	1.50
FF10	J.R. House	1.00
FF11	Alex Escobar	1.00
FF12	Travis Hafner	1.50

Game-Used Bats

PAT BURRELL

		NM/M
Common Player:		5.00
Inserted 1:267		
PB	Pat Burrell	10.00
SB	Sean Burroughs	5.00
AG	Adrian Gonzalez	10.00
EM	Eric Munson	5.00
CP	Corey Patterson	8.00

Game-Worn Jerseys

ERIC CHAVEZ

		NM/M
Common Player:		5.00
Inserted 1:133		
EC	Eric Chavez	8.00
MM	Mark Mulder	8.00
JP	Jay Payton	5.00
PR	Pokey Reese	5.00
PW	Preston Wilson	5.00

Impact Players

		NM/M
Complete Set (20):		15.00
Common Player:		.50
Inserted 1:7		
IP1	Mark McGwire	3.00
IP2	Sammy Sosa	2.00
IP3	Manny Ramirez	1.00
IP4	Troy Glaus	1.00
IP5	Ken Griffey Jr.	2.00
IP6	Gary Sheffield	.75
IP7	Vladimir Guerrero	1.00
IP8	Carlos Delgado	.75
IP9	Jason Giambi	.75
IP10	Frank Thomas	1.50

KEITH GINTER

IP11	Vernon Wells	.60
IP12	Carlos Pena	.50
IP13	Joe Crede	.50
IP14	Keith Ginter	.50
IP15	Aubrey Huff	.50
IP16	Brad Cresse	.50
IP17	Austin Kearns	.75
IP18	Nick Johnson	.50
IP19	Josh Hamilton	.50
IP20	Corey Patterson	.60

Rookie Fever

		NM/M
Complete Set (10):		10.00
Common Player:		.50
Inserted 1:10		
RF1	Chipper Jones	2.00
RF2	Preston Wilson	.50
RF3	Todd Helton	1.00
RF4	Jay Payton	.50
RF5	Ivan Rodriguez	.75
RF6	Manny Ramirez	1.00
RF7	Derek Jeter	4.00
RF8	Orlando Hernandez	.50
RF9	Marcus Quinn	.50
RF10	Terrence Long	.50

Team Topps

LUIS TIANT
INDIANS

		NM/M
Common Player:		10.00
Overall odds 1:71.		
13R	Warren Spahn/1952	40.00
37R	Tug McGraw/1965	10.00
48R	Bobby Richardson/1957	15.00
25R	Luis Tiant/1965 + Exchange	10.00
31R	Clete Boyer/1957	15.00
23R	Gil McDougald/1952	15.00
27R	Andy Pafko/1952	15.00
28R	Herb Score/1956	15.00
18R	Bob Gibson/1959	40.00
29R	Moose Skowron/1954	15.00
37F	Tug McGraw/1985	15.00
28F	Herb Score/1962	15.00

2002 Bowman

		NM/M
Complete Set (440):		70.00
Common Player:		.15
Common Rookie:		.40
Pack (10):		4.50
Box (24):		90.00
1	Adam Dunn	.50
2	Derek Jeter	2.00
3	Alex Rodriguez	1.50

#	Player	Price
4	Miguel Tejada	.50
5	Nomar Garciaparra	1.00
6	Toby Hall	.15
7	Brandon Duckworth	.15
8	Paul LoDuca	.15
9	Brian Giles	.15
10	C.C. Sabathia	.15
11	Curt Schilling	.75
12	Tsuyoshi Shinjo	.15
13	Ramon Hernandez	.15
14	Jose Cruz Jr.	.15
15	Albert Pujols	2.00
16	Joe Mays	.15
17	Javy Lopez	.15
18	J.T. Snow	.15
19	David Segui	.15
20	Jorge Posada	.40
21	Doug Mientkiewicz	.15
22	Jerry Hairston Jr.	.15
23	Bernie Williams	.40
24	Mike Sweeney	.15
25	Jason Giambi	.50
26	Ryan Dempster	.15
27	Ryan Klesko	.15
28	Mark Quinn	.15
29	Jeff Kent	.25
30	Eric Chavez	.30
31	Adrian Beltre	.25
32	Andruw Jones	.50
33	Alfonso Soriano	1.00
34	Aramis Ramirez	.40
35	Greg Maddux	1.00
36	Andy Pettitte	.50
37	Bartolo Colon	.15
38	Ben Sheets	.40
39	Bobby Higginson	.15
40	Ivan Rodriguez	.50
41	Brad Penny	.15
42	Carlos Lee	.25
43	Damion Easley	.15
44	Preston Wilson	.15
45	Jeff Bagwell	.50
46	Eric Milton	.15
47	Rafael Palmeiro	.50
48	Gary Sheffield	.40
49	J.D. Drew	.25
50	Jim Thome	.50
51	Ichiro Suzuki	1.50
52	Bud Smith	.15
53	Chan Ho Park	.15
54	D'Angelo Jimenez	.15
55	Ken Griffey Jr.	1.50
56	Wade Miller	.15
57	Vladimir Guerrero	.50
58	Troy Glaus	.40
59	Shawn Green	.40
60	Kerry Wood	.40
61	Jack Wilson	.15
62	Kevin Brown	.25
63	Marcus Giles	.15
64	Pat Burrell	.40
65	Larry Walker	.25
66	Sammy Sosa	.75
67	Raul Mondesi	.15
68	Tim Hudson	.25
69	Lance Berkman	.40
70	Mike Mussina	.40
71	Barry Zito	.40
72	Jimmy Rollins	.15
73	Barry Bonds	2.00
74	Craig Biggio	.40
75	Todd Helton	.50
76	Roger Clemens	1.50
77	Frank Catalanotto	.15
78	Josh Towers	.15
79	Roy Oswalt	.40
80	Chipper Jones	1.00
81	Cristian Guzman	.15
82	Darin Erstad	.40
83	Freddy Garcia	.15
84	Jason Tyner	.15
85	Carlos Delgado	.40
86	Jon Lieber	.15
87	Juan Pierre	.15
88	Matt Morris	.15
89	Phil Nevin	.15
90	Jim Edmonds	.40
91	Magglio Ordonez	.25
92	Mike Hampton	.15
93	Rafael Furcal	.25
94	Richie Sexson	.40
95	Luis Gonzalez	.25
96	Scott Rolen	.50
97	Tim Redding	.15
98	Moises Alou	.25
99	Jose Vidro	.15
100	Mike Piazza	1.00
101	Pedro Martinez	.75
102	Geoff Jenkins	.15
103	Johnny Damon	.75
104	Mike Cameron	.15
105	Randy Johnson	.75
106	David Eckstein	.15
107	Javier Vazquez	.15
108	Mark Mulder	.25
109	Robert Fick	.15
110	Roberto Alomar	.40
111	Wilson Betemit	.15
112	Chris Tritle RC	.50
113	Ed Rogers	.15
114	Juan Pena	.15
115	Josh Beckett	.50
116	Juan Cruz	.15
117	Noochie Varner RC	.50
118	Taylor Buchholz RC	.15
119	Mike Rivera	.15
120	Hank Blalock	.40
121	Hansel Izquierdo RC	.15
122	Orlando Hudson	.15
123	Bill Hall	.15
124	Jose Reyes	.50
125	Juan Rivera	.15
126	Eric Valent	.15
127	Scotty Layfield RC	.40
128	Austin Kearns	.50
129	Nic Jackson RC	.50
130	Chris Baker RC	.50
131	Chad Qualls RC	.40
132	Marcus Thames	.15
133	Nathan Haynes	.15
134	Brett Evert	.15
135	Joe Borchard	.40
136	Ryan Christianson	.15
137	Josh Hamilton	.15
138	Corey Patterson	.15
139	Travis Wilson	.15
140	Alex Escobar	.15
141	Alexis Gomez	.15
142	Nick Johnson	.15
143	Kenny Kelly	.15
144	Marlon Byrd	.15
145	Kory DeHaan	.15
146	Matt Belisle	.15
147	Carlos Hernandez	.15
148	Sean Burroughs	.15
149	Angel Berroa	.15
150	Aubrey Huff	.15
151	Travis Hafner	.40
152	Brandon Berger	.15
153	David Krynzel	.15
154	Ruben Salazar	.15
155	J.R. House	.15
156	Juan Silvestre	.15
157	Dewon Brazelton	.15
158	Jayson Werth	.15
159	Larry Barnes	.15
160	Elvis Pena	.15
161	Ruben Gotay RC	.40
162	Tommy Marx RC	.40
163	John Suomi RC	.40
164	Javier Colina	.15
165	Greg Sain RC	.40
166	Robert Cosby RC	.40
167	Angel Pagan RC	2.00
168	Ralph Santana RC	.40
169	Joe Orloski RC	.40
170	Shayne Wright RC	.40
171	Jay Caligiuri RC	.25
172	Greg Montalbano RC	.50
173	Rich Harden RC	3.00
174	Rich Thompson RC	.40
175	Fred Bastardo RC	.40
176	Alejandro Giron RC	.40
177	Jesus Medrano RC	.15
178	Kevin Deaton RC	.40
179	Mike Rosamond RC	.50
180	Jon Guzman RC	.40
181	Gerard Oakes RC	.40
182	Francisco Liriano RC	10.00
183	Matt Allegra RC	.40
184	Mike Snyder RC	.40
185	James Shanks RC	.40
186	Anderson Hernandez RC	.40
187	Dan Trumble RC	.40
188	Luis DePaula RC	.40
189	Randall Shelley RC	.40
190	Richard Lane RC	.40
191	Antwon Rollins RC	.50
192	Ryan Bukvich RC	.40
193	Derrick Lewis	.15
194	Eric Miller RC	.40
195	Justin Schuda RC	.40
196	Brian West RC	.40
197	Adam Roller RC	.40
198	Neal Frendling RC	.40
199	Jeremy Hill RC	.40
200	James Barrett RC	.50
201	Brett Kay RC	.50
202	Ryan Mottl RC	.50
203	Brad Nelson RC	.40
204	Juan Gonzalez	.15
205	Curtis Legendre RC	.40
206	Ronald Acuna RC	.40
207	Chris Flinn RC	.40
208	Nick Alvarez RC	.40
209	Jason Ellison RC	.40
210	Blake McGinley RC	.50
211	Dan Phillips RC	.50
212	Demetrius Heath RC	.40
213	Eric Bruntlett RC	.40
214	Joe Jiannetti RC	.40
215	Mike Hill RC	.40
216	Ricardo Cordova RC	.40
217	Mark Hamilton RC	.50
218	David Mattox RC	.40
219	Jose Morban RC	.50
220	Scott Wiggins RC	.50
221	Steve Green	.15
222	Brian Rogers	.15
223	Chin-Hui Tsao	.40
224	Kenny Baugh	.15
225	Nate Teut	.15
226	Josh Wilson RC	.40
227	Christian Parker	.15
228	Tim Raines Jr.	.15
229	Anastacio Martinez RC	.40
230	Richard Lewis	.15
231	Tim Kalita RC	.15
232	Edwin Almonte RC	.40
233	Hee Seop Choi	.25
234	Ty Howington	.15
235	Victor Alvarez RC	.15
236	Morgan Ensberg	.15
237	Jeff Austin	.40
238	Luis Terrero	.15
239	Adam Wainwright	.15
240	Clint Weibl RC	.40
241	Eric Cyr RC	.40
242	Marlyn Tisdale RC	.40
243	John VanBenschoten	.15
244	Ryan Raburn RC	.40
245	Miguel Cabrera	.75
246	Jung Bong	.15
247	Raul Chavez RC	.40
248	Erik Bedard	.15
249	Chris Snelling RC	.40
250	Joe Rogers RC	.40
251	Nate Field RC	.40
252	Matt Herges	.15
253	Matt Childers RC	.50
254	Erick Almonte	.15
255	Nick Neugebauer	.15
256	Ron Calloway RC	.15
257	Seung Jun Song	.15
258	Brandon Phillips	.15
259	Cole Barthel	.25
260	Jason Lane	.15
261	Jae Weong Seo	.15
262	Randy Flores	.15
263	Scott Chiasson	.15
264	Chase Utley	1.00
265	Tony Alvarez	.15
266	Ben Howard RC	.40
267	Nelson Castro RC	.40
268	Mark Lukasiewicz	.15
269	Eric Glaser RC	.40
270	Rob Henkel RC	.40
271	Jose Valverde RC	.40
272	Ricardo Rodriguez	.15
273	Chris Smith	.15
274	Mark Prior	.75
275	Miguel Olivo	.15
276	Ben Broussard	.15
277	Zach Sorensen	.15
278	Brian Mallette RC	.40
279	Brad Wilkerson	.15
280	Carl Crawford	.15
281	Chone Figgins RC	.40
282	Jimmy Alvarez RC	.40
283	Gavin Floyd	1.50
284	Josh Bonifay RC	.50
285	Garrett Guzman RC	.50
286	Blake Williams	.15
287	Matt Holliday	.15
288	Ryan Madson	.15
289	Luis Torres	.40
290	Jeff Verplancke RC	.40
291	Nate Espy RC	.40
292	Jeff Lincoln RC	.40
293	Ryan Snare RC	.40
294	Jose Ortiz	.15
295	Eric Munson	.15
296	Denny Bautista	.15
297	Willy Aybar	.15
298	Kelly Johnson	.15
299	Justin Morneau	.50
300	Derrick Van Dusen	.15
301	Chad Petty	.15
302	Mike Restovich	.15
303	Shawn Fagan	.15
304	Yurendell DeCaster RC	.40
305	Justin Wayne	.15
306	Mike Peeples	.40
307	Joel Guzman RC	.75
308	Ryan Vogelsong	.15
309	Jorge Padilla RC	.50
310	Grady Sizemore	.50
311	Joe Jester RC	.40
312	Jim Journell	.15
313	Bobby Seay	.15
314	Ryan Church RC	1.00
315	Grant Balfour	.15
316	Mitch Jones	.15
317	Travis Foley	.15
318	Bobby Crosby	.40
319	Adrian Gonzalez	.40
320	Ronnie Merrill	.15
321	Joel Pineiro	.15
322	John-Ford Griffin	.15
323	Brian Forystek RC	.40
324	Sean Douglass	.15
325	Manny Delcarmen RC	.40
326	Donnie Bridges	.15
327	Jim Kavourias	.15
328	Gabe Gross	.15
329	Greg "Toe" Nash	.15
330	Bill Ortega	.15
331	Joey Hammond RC	.40
332	Ramon Moreta RC	.40
333	Ron Davenport	.15
334	Brett Myers	.15
335	Carlos Pena	.15
336	Ezequiel Astacio RC	.40
337	Edwin Yan RC	.50
338	Josh Girdley	.15
339	Shaun Boyd	.15
340	Juan Rincon	.15
341	Chris Duffy RC	.50
342	Jason Kinchen	.15
343	Brad Thomas	.15
344	David Kelton	.15
345	Rafael Soriano	.15
346	Colin Young RC	.50
347	Eric Byrnes	.15
348	Chris Narveson RC	.50
349	John Rheinecker RC	.40
350	Mike Wilson RC	.40
351	Justin Sherrod RC	.50
352	Deivi Mendez	.15
353	Wily Mo Pena	.40
354	Brett Roneberg RC	.50
355	Trey Lunsford RC	.40
356	Jimmy Gobble RC	.40
357	Brent Butler	.15
358	Aaron Heilman	.15
359	Wilkin Ruan	.15
360	Brian Wolfe RC	.40
361	Cody Ransom	.40
362	Koyie Hill	.40
363	Scott Cassidy	.15
364	Tony Fontana RC	.50
365	Mark Teixeira	.40
366	Doug Sessions RC	.40
367	Victor Hall	.15
368	Josh Cisneros RC	.40
369	Kevin Mench	.15
370	Tike Redman	.15
371	Jeff Heaverlo	.15
372	Carlos Brackley RC	.40
373	Brad Hawpe	.50
374	Jesus Colome	.15
375	David Espinosa	.15
376	Jesse Foppert	.75
377	Ross Peeples RC	.40
378	Alexander Requena RC	.40
379	Joe Mauer RC	12.00
380	Carlos Silva	.15
381	David Wright	40.00
382	Craig Kuzmic RC	.50
383	Peter Zamora RC	.40
384	Matt Parker RC	.50
385	Ricardo Rodriguez	.15
386	Gary Cates Jr. RC	.40
387	Justin Reid RC	.50
388	Jake Mauer RC	.50
389	John-Ford Griffin	.15
390	Josh Barfield	2.00
391	Luis Maza	.15
392	Henry Pichardo RC	.40
393	Michael Floyd RC	.40
394	Clint Nageotte RC	.75
395	Jim Warden	.15
396	Mauricio Lara RC	.50
397	Alejandro Cadena RC	.40
398	Jonny Gomes RC	3.00
399	Jason Bulger RC	.50
400	Bobby Jenks RC	1.00
401	David Gil	.40
402	Joel Crump RC	.40
403	Kazuhisa Ishii RC	.75
404	So Taguchi RC	.75
405	Ryan Doumit RC	1.00
406	Macay McBride	.15
407	Brandon Claussen	.15
408	Chin-Feng Chen	.15
409	Josh Phelps	.25
410	Freddie Money RC	.40
411	Clifford Bartosh RC	.40
412	Josh Pearce	.15
413	Lyle Overbay	.15
414	Ryan Anderson	.15
415	Terrance Hill RC	.40
416	John Rodriguez RC	.40
417	Richard Stahl	.15
418	Brian Specht	.15
419	Chris Latham RC	.50
420	Carlos Cabrera RC	.40
421	Jose Bautista RC	.50
422	Kevin Frederick RC	.40
423	Jerome Williams	.40
424	Napoleon Calzado RC	.50
425	Benito Baez	.15
426	Xavier Nady	.15
427	Jason Botts RC	.50
428	Steve Bechler RC	.50
429	Reed Johnson RC	.50
430	Mark Outlaw RC	.40
431	Billy Sylvester	.15
432	Luke Lockwood	.15
433	Jake Peavy	.40
434	Alfredo Amezaga	.15
435	Aaron Cook RC	.40
436	Josh Shaffer RC	.40
437	Dan Wright	.40
438	Ryan Gripp RC	.50
439	Alex Herrera	.15
440	Jason Bay RC	4.00

Gold

Stars:	1-2.5X
Rookies:	1-2X
Inserted 1:1	

Uncirculated

	NM/M
Common Player:	4.00
Production 1,000 Sets	
112	Chris Tritle	6.00
113	Ed Rogers	4.00
114	Juan Pena	4.00
115	Josh Beckett	8.00
116	Juan Cruz	4.00
117	Noochie Varner	6.00
118	Taylor Buchholz	4.00
119	Mike Rivera	4.00
120	Hank Blalock	4.00
121	Hansel Izquierdo	4.00
122	Orlando Hudson	4.00
123	Bill Hall	4.00
124	Jose Reyes	8.00
125	Juan Rivera	4.00
126	Eric Valent	4.00
127	Scotty Layfield	4.00
128	Austin Kearns	8.00
129	Nic Jackson	4.00
130	Chris Baker	4.00
131	Chad Qualls	4.00

Autographs

	NM/M
Common Autograph:	5.00
Inserted 1:37	
AA	Alfredo Amezaga	5.00
GA	Garrett Atkins	20.00
JB	Josh Beckett	25.00
WB	Wilson Betemit	5.00
LB	Larry Bigbie	5.00
HB	Hank Blalock	20.00
TB	Tony Blanco	5.00
JAB	Jason Botts	5.00
MB	Marlon Byrd	10.00
BDC	Brian Cardwell	5.00
BC	Ben Christensen	5.00
BAC	Brandon Claussen	8.00
JD	Jeff Davanon	5.00
MD	Manny Delcarmen	8.00
RF	Randy Flores	5.00
RF	Ryan Franklin	5.00
KG	Keith Ginter	5.00
TH	Toby Hall	5.00
AH	Aubrey Huff	10.00
GJ	Gary Johnson	5.00
NJ	Nick Johnson	10.00
CK	Charles Kegley	5.00
JL	Jason Lane	10.00
NN	Nick Neugebauer	5.00
RO	Roy Oswalt	15.00
JP	Juan Pena	5.00
MP	Mark Prior	20.00
CR	Cody Ransom	5.00
JS	Juan Silvestre	5.00
TS	Termel Sledge	8.00
BS	Bud Smith	5.00
CS	Chris Smith	5.00
WS	Will Smith	5.00
BJS	Brian Specht	5.00
CT	Chris Tritle	8.00
CU	Chase Utley	75.00
DV	Domingo Valdez	5.00
NV	Noochie Varner	5.00
RV	Ryan Vogelsong	5.00
JLW	Jerome Williams	8.00
DW	Dan Wright	5.00

Futures Game Game-Used Base

	NM/M
Randomly Inserted	
TB	Toby Hall	15.00

Futures Game Game-Worn Jersey

	NM/M
Common Player:	15.00
Inserted 1:193	
WB	Wilson Betemit	15.00
CH	Carlos Hernandez	15.00
JRH	J.R. House	15.00
NJ	Nick Johnson	20.00
RL	Ryan Ludwick	15.00
CP	Carlos Pena	15.00
DT	Dennis Tankersley	15.00
JW	Jerome Williams	15.00

Game-Used Relics

	NM/M
Common Player:	4.00
Inserted 1:165	
JA1	Jared Abruzzo	4.00
JA2	Jared Abruzzo	4.00
GA	Garrett Atkins	8.00
AB	Angel Berroa	6.00
AC	Antoine Cameron	4.00
RC	Ryan Church	6.00

ALC	Alex Cintron	4.00
NC	Nate Cornejo	4.00
RD	Ryan Dittfurth	4.00
AE	Adam Everett	4.00
AF1	Alex Fernandez	4.00
AF2	Alex Fernandez	4.00
AG	Alexis Gomez	4.00
CG	Cristian Guerrero	4.00
CI	Cesar Izturis	4.00
DJ	D'Angelo Jimenez	4.00
FJ	Forrest Johnson	4.00
AK	Austin Kearns	6.00
JL	Jason Lane	4.00
RM	Ryan Madson	4.00
NN	Nick Neugebauer	4.00
CP	Corey Patterson	6.00
RS	Ruben Salazar	4.00
RST	Richard Stahl	4.00
JS	Jamal Strong	4.00
CY	Colin Young	4.00

2002 Bowman Chrome

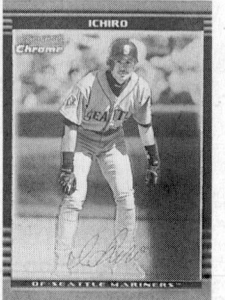

	NM/M
Complete Set (405):	
Common Player:	.25
Common SP:	3.00
Inserted 1:3	
Common Auto.	
(384-402,405)	10.00
Inserted 1:18	
Pack (4):	15.00
Box (18):	250.00
1	Adam Dunn	.50
2	Derek Jeter	3.00
3	Alex Rodriguez	2.50
4	Miguel Tejada	1.00
5	Nomar Garciaparra	1.00
6	Toby Hall	.25
7	Brandon Duckworth	.25
8	Paul LoDuca	.25
9	Brian Giles	.25
10	C.C. Sabathia	.25
11	Curt Schilling	.75
12	Tsuyoshi Shinjo	.25
13	Ramon Hernandez	.25
14	Jose Cruz Jr.	.25
15	Albert Pujols	3.00
16	Joe Mays	.25
17	Javy Lopez	.25
18	J.T. Snow	.25
19	David Segui	.25
20	Jorge Posada	.50
21	Doug Mientkiewicz	.25
22	Jerry Hairston Jr.	.25
23	Bernie Williams	.50
24	Mike Sweeney	.25
25	Jason Giambi	.75
26	Ryan Dempster	.25
27	Ryan Klesko	.25
28	Mark Quinn	.25
29	Jeff Kent	.25
30	Eric Chavez	.25
31	Adrian Beltre	.40
32	Andruw Jones	1.00
33	Alfonso Soriano	1.00
34	Aramis Ramirez	.25
35	Greg Maddux	1.50
36	Andy Pettitte	.50
37	Bartolo Colon	.25
38	Ben Sheets	.40
39	Bobby Higginson	.25
40	Ivan Rodriguez	.60
41	Brad Penny	.25
42	Carlos Lee	.40
43	Damion Easley	.25
44	Preston Wilson	.25

#	Player	Price
45	Jeff Bagwell	1.00
46	Eric Milton	.25
47	Rafael Palmeiro	.75
48	Gary Sheffield	.50
49	J.D. Drew	.40
50	Jim Thome	.75
51	Ichiro Suzuki	2.00
52	Bud Smith	.25
53	Chan Ho Park	.25
54	D'Angelo Jimenez	.25
55	Ken Griffey Jr.	2.00
56	Wade Miller	.25
57	Vladimir Guerrero	1.00
58	Troy Glaus	.50
59	Shawn Green	.40
60	Kerry Wood	.50
61	Jack Wilson	.25
62	Kevin Brown	.25
63	Marcus Giles	.25
64	Pat Burrell	.50
65	Larry Walker	.40
66	Sammy Sosa	1.00
67	Raul Mondesi	.25
68	Tim Hudson	.40
69	Lance Berkman	.50
70	Mike Mussina	.50
71	Barry Zito	.50
72	Jimmy Rollins	.75
73	Barry Bonds	3.00
74	Craig Biggio	.40
75	Todd Helton	.75
76	Roger Clemens	2.00
77	Frank Catalanotto	.25
78	Josh Towers	.25
79	Roy Oswalt	.40
80	Chipper Jones	1.00
81	Cristian Guzman	.25
82	Darin Erstad	.60
83	Freddy Garcia	.25
84	Jason Tyner	.25
85	Carlos Delgado	.50
86	Jon Lieber	.25
87	Juan Pierre	.25
88	Matt Morris	.25
89	Phil Nevin	.25
90	Jim Edmonds	.40
91	Magglio Ordonez	.40
92	Mike Hampton	.25
93	Rafael Furcal	.40
94	Richie Sexson	.40
95	Luis Gonzalez	.40
96	Scott Rolen	.75
97	Tim Redding	.25
98	Moises Alou	.40
99	Jose Vidro	.25
100	Mike Piazza	1.50
101	Pedro Martinez	1.00
102	Geoff Jenkins	.25
103	Johnny Damon	1.00
104	Mike Cameron	.25
105	Randy Johnson	1.00
106	David Eckstein	.25
107	Javier Vazquez	.25
108	Mark Mulder	.40
109	Robert Fick	.25
110	Roberto Alomar	.40
111	Wilson Betemit	.25
112	Chris Tritle/SP RC	4.00
113	Ed Rogers	.25
114	Juan Pena	.25
115	Josh Beckett	.50
116	Juan Cruz	.25
117	Noochie Varner/ SP RC	6.00
118	Blake Williams	.25
119	Mike Rivera	.25
120	Hank Blalock	.50
121	Hansel Izquierdo/ SP RC	4.00
122	Orlando Hudson	.25
123	Bill Hall	.25
124	Jose Reyes	1.00
125	Juan Rivera	.25
126	Eric Valent	.25
127	Scotty Layfield/SP RC	3.00
128	Austin Kearns	.50
129	Nic Jackson/SP RC	5.00
130	Scott Chiasson	.25
131	Chad Qualls/SP RC	4.00
132	Marcus Thames	.25
133	Nathan Haynes	.25
134	Joe Borchard	.25
135	Josh Hamilton	.25
136	Corey Patterson	.25
137	Travis Wilson	.25
138	Alex Escobar	.25
139	Alexis Gomez	.25
140	Nick Johnson	.25
141	Marlon Byrd	.25
142	Kory DeHaan	.25
143	Carlos Hernandez	.25
144	Sean Burroughs	.25
145	Angel Berroa	.25
146	Aubrey Huff	.25
147	Travis Hafner	.75
148	Brandon Berger	.25
149	J.R. House	.25
150	Dewon Brazelton	.25
151	Jayson Werth	.25
152	Larry Barnes	.25
153	Ruben Gotay/SP	6.00
154	Tommy Marx/SP RC	3.00
155	John Suomi/SP RC	4.00
156	Javier Colina/SP	3.00
157	Greg Sain/SP RC	3.00
158	Robert Cosby/SP RC	3.00
159	Angel Pagan/SP RC	10.00
160	Ralph Santana RC	2.00

#	Player	Price
161	Joe Orloski RC	2.00
162	Shayne Wright/SP	3.00
163	Jay Caligiuri/SP RC	3.00
164	Greg Montalbano/ SP RC	5.00
165	Rich Harden/SP RC	25.00
166	Rich Thompson/ SP RC	3.00
167	Fred Bastardo/SP RC	3.00
168	Alejandro Giron/ SP RC	3.00
169	Jesus Medrano/SP RC	3.00
170	Kevin Deaton/SP RC	4.00
171	Mike Rosamond RC	2.00
172	Jon Guzman/SP	3.00
173	Gerard Oakes/SP RC	4.00
174	Francisco Liriano/ SP RC	50.00
175	Matt Allegra/SP RC	4.00
176	Mike Snyder/SP RC	4.00
177	James Shanks/SP RC	3.00
178	Anderson Hernandez/ SP RC	5.00
179	Dan Trumble/SP RC	3.00
180	Luis DePaula/SP RC	4.00
181	Randall Shelley/SP RC	5.00
182	Richard Lane/SP RC	4.00
183	Antwon Rollins/SP RC	5.00
184	Ryan Bukvich/SP RC	5.00
185	Derrick Lewis/SP	3.00
186	Eric Miller/SP RC	3.00
187	Justin Schuda/SP RC	3.00
188	Brian West/SP RC	4.00
189	Brad Wilkerson	.25
190	Neal Frendling/SP RC	3.00
191	Jeremy Hill/SP RC	3.00
192	James Barrett/SP RC	5.00
193	Brett Kay/SP RC	4.00
194	Ryan Mottl/SP RC	4.00
195	Brad Nelson/SP RC	5.00
196	Juan Gonzalez/SP	.25
197	Curtis Legendre/ SP RC	3.00
198	Ronald Acuna/SP RC	3.00
199	Chris Flinn/SP RC	3.00
200	Nick Alvarez/SP RC	3.00
201	Jason Ellison/SP RC	3.00
202	Blake McGinley/SP RC	3.00
203	Dan Phillips/SP RC	3.00
204	Demetrius Heath/ SP RC	3.00
205	Eric Bruntlett/SP RC	3.00
206	Joe Jiannetti/SP RC	3.00
207	Mike Hill/SP RC	3.00
208	Ricardo Cordova/ SP RC	3.00
209	Mark Hamilton/SP RC	3.00
210	David Mattox/SP RC	3.00
211	Jose Morban/SP RC	5.00
212	Scott Wiggins/SP RC	3.00
213	Steve Green	.25
214	Brian Rogers/SP	3.00
215	Kenny Baugh	.25
216	Anastacio Martinez/ SP RC	3.00
217	Richard Lewis	.25
218	Tim Kalita/SP RC	3.00
219	Edwin Almonte/SP RC	3.00
220	Hee Seop Choi	.25
221	Ty Howington	.25
222	Victor Alvarez/SP RC	3.00
223	Morgan Ensberg	.25
224	Jeff Austin/SP RC	3.00
225	Clint Weibl/SP RC	4.00
226	Eric Cyr RC	1.00
227	Marlyn Tisdale/SP RC	3.00
228	John VanBenschoten	.25
229	Ruben Salazar	.25
230	Raul Chavez/SP RC	3.00
231	Brett Evert	.25
232	Joe Rogers/SP RC	3.00
233	Adam Wainwright	.25
234	Matt Herges	.25
235	Matt Childers/SP RC	4.00
236	Nick Neugebauer	.25
237	Carl Crawford	.25
238	Seung Jun Song	.25
239	Randy Flores	.25
240	Jason Lane	.25
241	Chase Utley	1.00
242	Ben Howard/SP RC	3.00
243	Eric Glaser/SP RC	3.00
244	Josh Wilson RC	1.00
245	Jose Valverde/SP RC	3.00
246	Chris Smith	.25
247	Mark Prior	3.00
248	Brian Mallette/SP RC	3.00
249	Chone Figgins/SP RC	8.00
250	Jimmy Alvarez/SP RC	3.00
251	Luis Terrero	.25
252	Josh Bonifay/SP RC	4.00
253	Garrett Guzman/ SP RC	3.00
254	Jeff Verplancke/ SP RC	3.00
255	Nate Espy/SP RC	4.00
256	Jeff Lincoln/SP RC	3.00
257	Ryan Snare/SP RC	4.00
258	Jose Ortiz	.25
259	Denny Bautista	.25
260	Willy Aybar	.25
261	Kelly Johnson	.25
262	Shawn Fagan	.25
263	Yurendell DeCaster/ SP RC	3.00
264	Mike Peeples/SP RC	3.00
265	Joel Guzman/SP RC	3.00
266	Ryan Vogelsong	.25

#	Player	Price
267	Jorge Padilla/SP RC	3.00
268	Joe Jester/SP RC	3.00
269	Ryan Church/SP RC	10.00
270	Mitch Jones	.25
271	Travis Foley/SP	3.00
272	Bobby Crosby	2.00
273	Adrian Gonzalez	.25
274	Ronnie Merrill	.25
275	Joel Pineiro	.25
276	John-Ford Griffin	.25
277	Brian Forystek/SP RC	3.00
278	Sean Douglass	.25
279	Manny Delcarmen/ SP RC	3.00
280	Jim Kavourias/SP	3.00
281	Gabe Gross	.25
282	Bill Ortega	.25
283	Joey Hammond /SP RC	3.00
284	Brett Myers	.25
285	Carlos Pena	.25
286	Ezequiel Astacio/ SP RC	3.00
287	Edwin Yan/SP RC	3.00
288	Chris Duffy/SP RC	6.00
289	Jason Kinchen	.25
290	Rafael Soriano	.25
291	Colin Young	.50
292	Eric Byrnes	.25
293	Chris Narveson/ SP RC	5.00
294	John Rheinecker RC	1.00
295	Mike Wilson/SP RC	3.00
296	Justin Sherrod/SP RC	5.00
297	Deivi Mendez	.25
298	Wily Mo Pena	.25
299	Brett Roneberg/SP RC	4.00
300	Trey Lunsford/SP RC	3.00
301	Christian Parker	.25
302	Brent Butler	.25
303	Aaron Heilman	.25
304	Wilkin Ruan	.25
305	Kenny Kelly	.25
306	Cody Ransom	.25
307	Koyie Hill/SP	3.00
308	Tony Fontana/SP RC	3.00
309	Mark Teixeira	.75
310	Doug Sessions/ SP RC	3.00
311	Josh Cisneros/SP RC	3.00
312	Carlos Brackley/ SP RC	3.00
313	Tim Raines Jr.	.25
314	Ross Peeples/SP RC	5.00
315	Alexander Requena/ SP RC	5.00
316	Chin-Hui Tsao	.25
317	Tony Alvarez	.25
318	Craig Kuzmic/SP RC	3.00
319	Peter Zamora/SP RC	3.00
320	Matt Parker/SP RC	3.00
321	Keith Ginter	.25
322	Gary Cates Jr./SP RC	3.00
323	Matt Belisle	.25
324	Ben Broussard	.25
325	Jake Mauer/auto RC	10.00
326	Dennis Tankersley	.25
327	Juan Silvestre	.25
328	Henry Pichardo/ SP RC	3.00
329	Michael Floyd/SP RC	3.00
330	Clint Nageotte/SP RC	10.00
331	Raymond Cabrera/ SP RC	3.00
332	Mauricio Lara/SP RC	4.00
333	Alejandro Cadena/ SP RC	3.00
334	Jonny Gomes/SP RC	15.00
335	Jason Bulger/SP RC	4.00
336	Nate Teut	.25
337	David Gil/SP RC	3.00
338	Joel Crump/SP RC	3.00
339	Brandon Phillips	.25
340	Macay McBride	.25
341	Brandon Claussen	1.00
342	Josh Phelps	.25
343	Freddie Money/SP RC	4.00
344	Terrance Hill/SP RC	3.00
345	John Rodriguez/ SP RC	4.00
346	Chris Latham/SP RC	3.00
347	Carlos Cabrera/SP RC	3.00
348	Jose Bautista/SP RC	5.00
349	Kevin Frederick/ SP RC	3.00
350	Jerome Williams	.75
351	Napoleon Calzado/ SP RC	3.00
352	Benito Baez/SP	3.00
353	Xavier Nady	.25
354	Jason Botts/SP RC	3.00
355	Steve Bechler/SP RC	4.00
356	Reed Johnson/SP RC	8.00
357	Mark Outlaw/SP RC	3.00
358	Jake Peavy	.25
359	Josh Shaffer/SP RC	3.00
360	Dan Wright/SP	.25
361	Ryan Gripp/SP RC	3.00
362	Nelson Castro/SP RC	3.00
363	Jason Bay/SP RC	3.00
364	Franklin German/ SP RC	3.00
365	Corwin Malone/SP	3.00
366	Kelly Ramos/SP RC	3.00
367	John Ennis/SP RC	3.00
368	George Perez/SP	3.00

#	Player	Price
369	Rene Reyes/SP RC	3.00
370	Rolando Viera/SP RC	3.00
371	Earl Snyder/SP RC	4.00
372	Kyle Kane/SP RC	3.00
373	Mario Ramos/SP	3.00
374	Tyler Yates/SP RC	3.00
375	Jason Young/SP RC	5.00
376	Chris Bootcheck/ SP RC	5.00
377	Jesus Cota/SP RC	5.00
378	Corky Miller/SP	.25
379	Matt Erickson/SP RC	3.00
380	Justin Huber/SP RC	3.00
381	Felix Escalona/SP RC	3.00
382	Kevin Cash/SP RC	3.00
383	J.J. Putz/SP RC	3.00
384	Chris Snelling RC	20.00
385	David Wright	500.00
386	Brian Wolfe RC	10.00
387	Justin Reid RC	10.00
389	Ryan Raburn RC	10.00
390	Josh Barfield	50.00
391	Joe Mauer RC	180.00
392	Bobby Jenks RC	25.00
393	Rob Henkel RC	10.00
394	Jimmy Gobble RC	10.00
395	Jesse Foppert RC	15.00
396	Gavin Floyd	25.00
397	Nate Field RC	10.00
398	Ryan Doumit RC	25.00
399	Ron Calloway RC	10.00
400	Taylor Buchholz RC	10.00
401	Adam Roller RC	10.00
402	Cole Barthel	10.00
403	Kazuhisa Ishii/SP RC	6.00
404	So Taguchi/SP RC	10.00
405	Chris Baker RC	10.00

Common Player: 1.00
Inserted 1:6
Refractors: 1.5-2X
Inserted 1:18

	Player	Price
JB	Jeff Bagwell	1.50
BC	Bartolo Colon	1.00
CD	Carlos Delgado	1.00
JG	Juan Gonzalez	1.50
LG	Luis Gonzalez	1.00
KG	Ken Griffey Jr.	3.00
VG	Vladimir Guerrero	2.00
DJ	Derek Jeter	5.00
AJ.	Andruw Jones	1.50
CJ	Chipper Jones	2.50
JK	Jason Kendall	1.00
MP	Mike Piazza	3.00
JP	Jorge Posada	1.00
IR	Ivan Rodriguez	1.00
SR	Scott Rolen	1.00
GS	Gary Sheffield	1.00
MS	Mike Sweeney	1.00
FT	Frank Thomas	1.50
LW	Larry Walker	1.00
BW	Bernie Williams	1.00

2002 Bowman Draft Picks & Prospects

Refractors

	NM/M
Complete Set (165):	35.00
Common Player:	.15
Common RC:	.15
Pack: (4 + 2 Chrome):	10.00
Box: (24):	200.00

#	Player	Price
BDP1	Clint Everts RC	.75
BDP2	Fred Lewis RC	.40
BDP3	Jonathan Broxton RC	.75
BDP4	Jason Anderson RC	.25
BDP5	Mike Eusebio RC	.25
BDP6	Zack Greinke RC	5.00
BDP7	Joe Blanton RC	2.00
BDP8	Sergio Santos RC	.50
BDP9	Jason Cooper RC	.50
BDP10	Delwyn Young RC	1.00
BDP11	Jeremy Hermida RC	5.00

Star Refractors (1-220): 2-3X
SP Refractors: .5-1.5X
Production 500
X-Refractors (1-220): 3-5X
SP X-Refractors: .75-2X
Production 250:
Gold Refractors (1-220): 8-15X
SP Gold Refractors: 2-4X
Production 50
Refractor Autos.
(384-402,405): .75-1.5X
Production 500
X-Fractor Autos.: .75-2X
Production 250
Gold Autographs: 2-4X
Production 50

Uncirculated

Cards: 1-3X
Production 350
Autos. 10 cards of each player.
No Pricing

Ishii & Taguchi Autographs

	NM/M
Refractors:	.75-1.5X
Production 100	
X-Fractors:	2-4X
Production 50	
Golds: Production 10	
403 Kazuhisa Ishii	50.00
404 So Taguchi	25.00

Rookie Reprints

	NM/M
Complete Set (20):	25.00

#	Player	Price
BDP12	Dan Ortmeyer RC	.40
BDP13	Kevin Jepsen RC	.25
BDP14	Russ Adams RC	1.00
BDP15	Mike Nixon RC	.25
BDP16	Nick Swisher RC	5.00
BDP17	Cole Hamels RC	10.00
BDP18	Brian Dopirak RC	1.00
BDP19	James Loney RC	4.00
BDP20	Denard Span RC	.25
BDP21	Billy Petrick RC	.25
BDP22	Jared Doyle RC	.25
BDP23	Jeff Francoeur RC	15.00
BDP24	Nick Bourgeois RC	.25
BDP25	Matt Cain RC	8.00
BDP26	John McCurdy RC	.40
BDP27	Mark Kiger RC	.25
BDP28	Bill Murphy RC	.40
BDP29	Matt Craig RC	.25
BDP30	Mike Megrew RC	.50
BDP31	Ben Crockett RC	.25
BDP32	Luke Hagerty RC	.50
BDP33	Matt Whitney RC	.50
BDP34	Dan Meyer RC	1.00
BDP35	Jeremy Brown RC	.50
BDP36	Doug Johnson RC	.25
BDP37	Steve Obenchain RC	.25
BDP38	Matt Clanton RC	.40
BDP39	Mark Teahen RC	1.50
BDP40	Thomas Carrow RC	.25
BDP41	Micah Schilling RC	.25
BDP42	Blair Johnson RC	.25
BDP43	Jason Pridie RC	.25
BDP44	Joey Votto RC	2.50
BDP45	Taber Lee RC	.25
BDP46	Adam Peterson RC	.25
BDP47	Adam Donachie RC	.40
BDP48	Josh Murray RC	.25
BDP49	Brent Clevlen RC	1.50
BDP50	Chad Pleiness RC	.25
BDP51	Zach Hammes RC	.50
BDP52	Chris Snyder RC	.50
BDP53	Chris Smith	.25
BDP54	Justin Maureau RC	.25
BDP55	David Bush RC	1.00
BDP56	Tim Gilhooly RC	.25
BDP57	Blair Barbier RC	.25
BDP58	Zach Segovia RC	.25
BDP59	Jeremy Reed RC	2.00
BDP60	Matt Pender RC	.25
BDP61	Eric Thomas RC	.25
BDP62	Justin Jones RC	1.00

#	Player	Price
BDP63	Brian Slocum RC	.40
BDP64	Larry Broadway RC	1.00
BDP65	Bo Flowers RC	.25
BDP66	Scott White RC	.75
BDP67	Steve Stanley RC	.25
BDP68	Alex Merricks RC	.25
BDP69	Josh Womack RC	.40
BDP70	Dave Jensen RC	.25
BDP71	Curtis Granderson RC	2.50
BDP72	Pat Osborn RC	.40
BDP73	Nic Carter RC	.25
BDP74	Mitch Talbot RC	.25
BDP75	Don Murphy RC	.25
BDP76	Val Majewski RC	.50
BDP77	Javy Rodriguez RC	.25
BDP78	Fernando Pacheco RC	.40
BDP79	Steve Russell RC	.25
BDP80	Jon Slack RC	.25
BDP81	John Baker RC	.25
BDP82	Aaron Coonrod RC	.25
BDP83	Josh Johnson RC	3.00
BDP84	Jake Blalock RC	.75
BDP85	Alex Hart RC	.50
BDP86	Wes Bankston RC	1.50
BDP87	Josh Rupe RC	.40
BDP88	Dan Cevette RC	.25
BDP89	Kiel Fisher RC	.50
BDP90	Alan Rick RC	.25
BDP91	Charlie Morton RC	.50
BDP92	Chad Spann RC	.50
BDP93	Kyle Boyer RC	.25
BDP94	Bob Malek RC	.25
BDP95	Ryan Rodriguez RC	.25
BDP96	Jordan Renz RC	.25
BDP97	Randy Frye RC	.25
BDP98	Rich Hill RC	3.00
BDP99	B.J. Upton RC	5.00
BDP100	Dan Christensen RC	.50
BDP101	Casey Kotchman	1.00
BDP102	Eric Good RC	.25
BDP103	Mike Fontenot	.50
BDP104	John Webb RC	.25
BDP105	Jason Dubois	.75
BDP106	Ryan Kibler RC	.25
BDP107	Jhonny Peralta RC	2.50
BDP108	Kirk Saarloos	.75
BDP109	Rhett Parrott RC	.25
BDP110	Jason Grove RC	.25
BDP111	Colt Griffin	.50
BDP112	Dallas McPherson	1.00
BDP113	Oliver Perez	1.50
BDP114	Marshall McDougall RC	.25
BDP115	Mike Wood RC	.40
BDP116	Scott Hairston	1.00
BDP117	Jason Simontacchi RC	.50
BDP118	Taggert Bozied RC	1.00
BDP119	Shelly Duncan	.15
BDP120	Dontrelle Willis RC	6.00
BDP121	Sean Burnett	.25
BDP122	Aaron Cook RC	.25
BPD123	Brett Evert	.15
BDP124	Jimmy Journell	.15
BDP125	Brett Myers	.15
BDP126	Brad Baker	.15
BDP127	Billy Traber	.50
BDP128	Adam Wainwright	.25
BDP129	Jason Young	.40
BDP130	John Buck	.25
BDP131	Kevin Cash RC	.25
BDP132	Jason Stokes RC	.50
BDP133	Drew Henson	.25
BDP134	Chad Tracy RC	1.50
BDP135	Orlando Hudson	.25
BDP136	Brandon Phillips	.15
BDP137	Joe Borchard	.15
BDP138	Marlon Byrd	.15
BDP139	Carl Crawford	.15
BDP140	Michael Restovich	.25
BDP141	Corey Hart RC	1.00
BDP142	Edwin Almonte	.15
BDP143	Francis Beltran RC	.25
BDP144	Jorge De La Rosa RC	.50
BDP145	Gerardo Garcia RC	.25
BDP146	Franklyn German RC	.25
BDP147	Francisco Liriano RC	4.00
BDP148	Francisco Rodriguez	.50
BDP149	Ricardo Rodriguez	.15
BDP150	Seung Jun Song	.15
BDP151	John Stephens	.15
BDP152	Justin Huber RC	1.00
BDP153	Victor Martinez	.50
BDP154	Hee Seop Choi	.15
BDP155	Justin Morneau	.50
BDP156	Miguel Cabrera	.75
BDP157	Victor Diaz RC	.50
BDP158	Jose Reyes	.50
BDP159	Omar Infante RC	.25
BDP160	Angel Berroa	.15
BDP161	Tony Alvarez	.25
BDP162	Shin-Soo Choo RC	1.00
BDP163	Wily Mo Pena	.15
BDP164	Andres Torres	.15
BDP165	Jose Lopez RC	2.00

Gold

Rookies: .75-1.5X
Inserted 1:1

Fabric of Future

	NM/M
Common Player:	4.00
Inserted 1:55	
EA Edwin Almonte	4.00

TA	Tony Alvarez	4.00
FB	Francis Beltran	4.00
AB	Angel Berroa	5.00
SB	Sean Burnett	4.00
KC	Kevin Cash	4.00
HC	Hee Seop Choi	5.00
SC	Shin-Soo Choo	10.00
CC	Carl Crawford	4.00
JR	Jorge de la Rosa	4.00
VD	Victor Diaz	6.00
GG	Gerardo Garcia	4.00
FG	Franklyn German	6.00
CH	Corey Hart	6.00
DH	Drew Henson	6.00
JH	Justin Huber	6.00
JK	Josh Karp	4.00
FL	Francisco Liriano	15.00
JL	Jose Lopez	8.00
BM	Brett Meyers	6.00
WP	Wily Mo Pena	6.00
MR	Michael Restovich	4.00
JS	John Stephens	4.00
JS	Jason Stokes	5.00
AT	Andres Torres	4.00
BT	Billy Traber	4.00
CT	Chad Tracy	4.00
AW	Adam Wainwright	10.00

Freshman Fiber

NM/M

Common Player: 4.00
Bat inserted 1:605
Jersey 1:45

BA	Brent Abernathy	4.00
DB	Dewon Brazelton	4.00
MB	Marlon Byrd/Bat	4.00
TH	Toby Hall	4.00
JH	Josh Hamilton	8.00
AH	Aubrey Huff	6.00
AK	Austin Kearns/Bat	4.00
JK	Joe Kennedy	4.00
JS	Jared Sandberg	4.00
JWS	Jason Standridge	4.00
MT	Mark Teixeira/Bat	10.00
JV	John Van Benschoten	4.00

Signs of the Future

NM/M

Common Autograph: 5.00

EB	Erik Bedard	25.00
LB	Larry Bigbie	5.00
TB	Taylor Buchholz	5.00
DD	Daniel Denham	5.00
ME	Morgan Ensberg	10.00
MF	Mike Fontenot	8.00
KH	Kris Honel	8.00
BI	Brandon Inge	8.00
NJ	Nic Jackson	5.00
MJ	Mitch Jones	8.00
BK	Bob Keppel	5.00
TL	Todd Linden	5.00
JM	Jake Mauer	8.00
JEM	Justin Morneau	25.00
LN	Lance Niekro	5.00
CP	Christian Parra	5.00
BP	Brandon Phillips	8.00
JR	Juan Rivera	5.00
BS	Bud Smith	5.00
AT	Chad Tracy	15.00
JW	Jerome Williams	8.00

2002 Bowman Chrome Draft Picks & Prospects

DONTRELLE WILLIS
P FLORIDA MARLINS

NM/M

Complete Set (175): 275.00
Common Player: .25
Common RC: .75
1-165 two per pack.
Common Auto. (166-175): 10.00
Auto.'s inserted 1:45

BDP1	Clint Everts RC	2.00
BDP2	Fred Lewis RC	1.00
BDP3	Jonathan Broxton RC	2.00
BDP4	Jason Anderson RC	.75
BDP5	Mike Eusebio RC	.75
BDP6	Zack Greinke RC	5.00
BDP7	Joe Blanton RC	5.00
BDP8	Sergio Santos RC	2.00
BDP9	Jason Cooper RC	1.50
BDP10	Delwyn Young RC	3.00
BDP11	Jeremy Hermida RC	15.00
BDP12	Dan Ortmeyer RC	1.50
BDP13	Kevin Jepsen RC	2.00
BDP14	Russ Adams RC	2.00
BDP15	Mike Nixon RC	.75
BDP16	Nick Swisher RC	15.00
BDP17	Cole Hamels RC	30.00
BDP18	Brian Dopirak RC	3.00
BDP19	James Loney RC	15.00
BDP20	Denard Span RC	.75
BDP21	Billy Petrick RC	.75
BDP22	Jared Doyle RC	.75
BDP23	Jeff Francoeur RC	50.00
BDP24	Nick Bourgeois RC	.75
BDP25	Matt Cain RC	30.00
BDP26	John McCurdy RC	.75
BDP27	Mark Kiger RC	.75
BDP28	Bill Murphy RC	1.00
BDP29	Matt Craig RC	1.00
BDP30	Mike Megrew RC	.75
BDP31	Ben Crockett RC	.75
BDP32	Luke Hagerty RC	1.50
BDP33	Matt Whitney RC	2.00
BDP34	Dan Meyer RC	1.00
BDP35	Jeremy Brown RC	1.00
BDP36	Doug Johnson RC	.75
BDP37	Steve Obenchain RC	.75
BDP38	Matt Clanton RC	1.00
BDP39	Mark Teahen RC	3.00
BDP40	Thomas Carrow RC	.75
BDP41	Micah Schilling RC	.75
BDP42	Blair Johnson RC	.75
BDP43	Jason Pridie RC	1.50
BDP44	Joey Votto RC	10.00
BDP45	Taber Lee RC	.75
BDP46	Adam Peterson RC	.75
BDP47	Adam Donachie RC	1.00
BDP48	Josh Murray RC	.75
BDP49	Brent Clevlen RC	4.00
BDP50	Chad Pleiness RC	.75
BDP51	Zach Hammes RC	1.50
BDP52	Chris Snyder RC	2.00
BDP53	Chris Smith RC	.50
BDP54	Justin Maureau RC	.75
BDP55	David Bush RC	3.00
BDP56	Tim Gilhooly RC	.75
BDP57	Blair Barbier RC	.75
BDP58	Zach Segovia RC	1.00
BDP59	Jeremy Reed RC	4.00
BDP60	Matt Pender RC	.75
BDP61	Eric Thomas RC	.75
BDP62	Justin Jones RC	1.50
BDP63	Brian Slocum RC	1.00
BDP64	Larry Broadway RC	1.50
BDP65	Bo Flowers RC	.75
BDP66	Scott White RC	1.00
BDP67	Steve Stanley RC	.75
BDP68	Alex Merricks RC	.75
BDP69	Josh Womack RC	.75
BDP70	Dave Jensen RC	.75
BDP71	Curtis Granderson RC	8.00
BDP72	Pat Osborn RC	1.50
BDP73	Nic Carter RC	.75
BDP74	Mitch Talbot RC	.75
BDP75	Don Murphy RC	.75
BDP76	Val Majewski RC	1.50
BDP77	Javy Rodriguez RC	.75
BDP78	Fernando Pacheco RC	1.00
BDP79	Steve Russell RC	.75
BDP80	Jon Slack RC	.75
BDP81	John Baker RC	.75
BDP82	Aaron Coonrod RC	.75
BDP83	Josh Johnson RC	10.00
BDP84	Jake Blalock RC	1.50
BDP85	Alex Hart RC	1.50
BDP86	Wes Bankston RC	5.00
BDP87	Josh Rupe RC	1.00
BDP88	Dan Cevette RC	.75
BDP89	Kiel Fisher RC	1.00
BDP90	Alan Rick RC	.75
BDP91	Charlie Morton RC	.75
BDP92	Chad Spann RC	2.00
BDP93	Kyle Boyer RC	1.00
BDP94	Bob Malek RC	.75
BDP95	Ryan Rodriguez RC	.75
BDP96	Jordan Renz RC	.75
BDP97	Randy Frye RC	.75
BDP98	Rich Hill RC	10.00
BDP99	B.J. Upton RC	15.00
BDP100	Dan Christensen RC	1.00
BDP101	Casey Kotchman RC	3.00
BDP102	Eric Good RC	.75
BDP103	Mike Fontenot RC	1.50
BDP104	John Webb RC	.75
BDP105	Jason Dubois RC	1.50
BDP106	Ryan Kibler RC	.75
BDP107	Jhonny Peralta RC	8.00
BDP108	Kirk Saarloos RC	1.50
BDP109	Rhett Parrott RC	.75
BDP110	Jason Grove RC	.75
BDP111	Colt Griffin RC	1.00
BDP112	Dallas McPherson RC	2.50
BDP113	Oliver Perez RC	2.00
BDP114	Marshall McDougall RC	.75
BDP115	Mike Wood RC	1.00
BDP116	Scott Hairston RC	1.50
BDP117	Jason Simontacchi RC	1.00
BDP118	Taggert Bozied RC	1.50
BDP119	Shelly Duncan RC	.75
BDP120	Dontrelle Willis RC	15.00
BDP121	Sean Burnett RC	.25
BDP122	Aaron Cook RC	.75
BPD123	Brett Evert RC	.25
BDP124	Jimmy Journell RC	.25
BDP125	Brett Myers RC	.25
BDP126	Brad Baker	.25
BDP127	Billy Traber	1.50
BDP128	Adam Wainwright	.25
BDP129	Jason Young	1.00
BDP130	John Buck	.25
BDP131	Kevin Cash	.25
BDP132	Jason Stokes RC	1.50
BDP133	Drew Henson	.50
BDP134	Chad Tracy RC	4.00
BDP135	Orlando Hudson	.50
BDP136	Brandon Phillips	.25
BDP137	Joe Borchard	.25
BDP138	Marlon Byrd	.25
BDP139	Carl Crawford	.25
BDP140	Michael Restovich	.25
BDP141	Corey Hart RC	5.00
BDP142	Angel Berroa	.25
BDP143	Francis Beltran RC	1.00
BDP144	Jorge De La Rosa RC	.75
BDP145	Gerardo Garcia RC	.75
BDP146	Franklyn German RC	.75
BDP147	Francisco Liriano	10.00
BDP148	Francisco Rodriguez	.50
BDP149	Ricardo Rodriguez	.25
BDP150	Seung Jun Song	.25
BDP151	John Stephens	.25
BDP152	Justin Huber	2.00
BDP153	Victor Martinez	.40
BDP154	Hee Seop Choi	.25
BDP155	Justin Morneau	.75
BDP156	Miguel Cabrera	2.00
BDP157	Victor Diaz RC	2.00
BDP158	Jose Reyes	.75
BDP159	Omar Infante RC	.75
BDP160	Angel Berroa	.25
BDP161	Tony Alvarez	.25
BDP162	Shin-Soo Choo RC	4.00
BDP163	Wily Mo Pena	.25
BDP164	Andres Torres	.25
BDP165	Jose Lopez RC	4.00
BDP166	Scott Moore/Auto. RC	15.00
BDP167	Chris Gruler/Auto. RC	15.00
BDP168	Joe Saunders/Auto. RC	20.00
BDP169	Jeff Francis/Auto. RC	30.00
BDP170	Royce Ring/Auto. RC	10.00
BDP171	Greg Miller/Auto.	20.00
BDP172	Brandon Weeden/Auto. RC	10.00
BDP173	Drew Meyer/Auto. RC	10.00
BDP174	Khalil Greene/Auto. RC	50.00
BDP175	Mark Schramek/Auto. RC	10.00

Refractor

Cards 1-165:	2-4X
Rookies 1-175:	2-3X

1-165 Production 300 Sets
166-175 inserted 1:154

Gold Refractor

Cards 1-165:	8-15X
Rookies 1-165:	5-10X

1-165 Production 50 Sets

166-175:	No Pricing

X-Fractor

JUSTIN SHERROD

Cards 1-165:	2-5X
Rookies 1-165:	3-4X
Rookies 166-175:	.75-1.5X

1-165 Production 150 Sets
166-175 Inserted 1:309

2002 Bowman Heritage

NM/M

Complete Set (439):	190.00
Common Player:	.25
Common SP:	1.00

Inserted 1:2

Black Box Variations:	2-3X

Inserted 1:2

Pack (10):	4.00
Box (24):	75.00

1	Brent Abernathy	.25
2	Jermaine Dye	.25
3	James Shanks RC	.40
4	Chris Flinn RC	.40

Roy Oswalt

5	Mike Peeples/SP RC	1.50
6	Gary Sheffield	.50
7	Livan Hernandez/SP	1.00
8	Jeff Austin RC	.40
9	Jeremy Giambi	.25
10	Adam Roller RC	.50
11	Sandy Alomar Jr./SP	.25
12	Matt Williams/SP	1.00
13	Hee Seop Choi	.25
14	Jose Offerman	.25
15	Robin Ventura	.25
16	Craig Biggio	.50
17	David Wells	.40
18	Rob Henkel RC	.40
19	Edgar Martinez	.25
20	Matt Morris/SP	2.00
21	Jose Valentin	.25
22	Barry Bonds	2.50
23	Justin Schuda RC	.50
24	Josh Phelps	.25
25	John Rodriguez RC	.50
26	Angel Pagan RC	1.50
27	Aramis Ramirez	.50
28	Jack Wilson	.25
29	Roger Clemens	2.00
30	Kazuhisa Ishii RC	1.50
31	Carlos Beltran	.75
32	Drew Henson/SP	1.50
33	Kevin Young/SP	1.00
34	Juan Cruz	.25
35	Curtis Legendre RC	.40
36	Jose Morban RC	.50
37	Ricardo Cordova/SP RC	1.50
38	Adam Everett	.25
39	Mark Prior	.75
40	Jose Bautista RC	.75
41	Travis Foley	.25
42	Kerry Wood	.50
43	B.J. Surhoff	.25
44	Moises Alou	.40
45	Joey Hammond RC	.50
46	Eric Bruntlett RC	.50
47	Carlos Guillen	.25
48	Joe Crede	.40
49	Dan Phillips RC	.25
50	Jason LaRue	.25
51	Javy Lopez	.25
52	Larry Bigbie/SP	1.00
53	Chris Baker RC	.75
54	Marty Cordova	.25
55	C.C. Sabathia	.25
56	Mike Piazza	1.00
57	Brian Giles	.25
58	Mike Bordick/SP	1.00
59	Tyler Houston/SP	1.00
60	Gabe Kapler	.25
61	Ben Broussard	.25
62	Steve Finley/SP	1.50
63	Koyie Hill	.25
64	Jeff D'Amico	.25
65	Edwin Almonte RC	.50
66	Pedro J. Martinez	1.00
67	Travis Fryman/SP	1.50
68	Brady Clark	.25
69	Reed Johnson/SP RC	4.00
70	Mark Grace/SP	4.00
71	Tony Batista/SP	1.00
72	Roy Oswalt	.50
73	Pat Burrell	.50
74	Dennis Tankersley	.25
75	Ramon Ortiz	.25
76	Neal Frendling/SP RC	1.50
77	Omar Vizquel/SP	2.00
78	Hideo Nomo	.50
79	Orlando Hernandez/SP	1.50
80	Andy Pettitte	.50
81	Cole Barthel	.25
82	Bret Boone	.25
83	Alfonso Soriano	1.00
84	Brandon Duckworth	.25
85	Ben Grieve	.25
86	Mike Rosamond/SP RC	1.50
87	Luke Prokopec	.25
88	Chone Figgins RC	1.50
89	Rick Ankiel/SP	.50
90	David Eckstein	.25
91	Corey Koskie	.25
92	David Justice	.25
93	Jimmy Alvarez RC	.40
94	Jason Schmidt	.25
95	Reggie Sanders	.25
96	Victor Alvarez RC	.40
97	Brett Roneberg RC	.40
98	D'Angelo Jimenez	.25
99	Hank Blalock	.50
100	Juan Rivera	.25
101	Mark Buehrle/SP	1.50
102	Juan Uribe	.25
103	Royce Clayton/SP	1.00
104	Brett Kay RC	.50
105	John Olerud	.25
106	Richie Sexson	.40
107	Chipper Jones	1.00
108	Adam Dunn	.75
109	Tim Salmon/SP	1.50
110	Eric Karros	.25
111	Jose Vidro	.25
112	Jerry Hairston Jr.	.25
113	Anastacio Martinez RC	.50
114	Robert Fick/SP	1.50
115	Randy Johnson	1.00
116	Trot Nixon/SP	2.00
117	Nick Bierbrodt/SP	1.00
118	Jim Edmonds	.40
119	Rafael Palmeiro	.25
120	Jose Macias	.25
121	Josh Beckett	.50
122	Sean Douglass	.25
123	Jeff Kent	.25
124	Tim Redding	.25
125	Xavier Nady	.25
126	Carl Everett	.25
127	Joe Randa	.25
128	Luke Hudson/SP	1.00
129	Eric Miller RC	.40
130	Melvin Mora	.25
131	Adrian Gonzalez	.25
132	Larry Walker/SP	1.50
133	Nic Jackson/SP RC	2.00
134	Mike Lowell/SP	1.00
135	Jim Thome	.50
136	Eric Milton	.25
137	Rich Thompson/SP RC	1.50
138	Placido Polanco/SP	1.00
139	Juan Pierre	.25
140	David Segui	.25
141	Chuck Finley	.25
142	Felipe Lopez	.25
143	Toby Hall	.25
144	Fred Bastardo RC	.50
145	Troy Glaus	.50
146	Todd Helton	.75
147	Ruben Gotay/SP RC	1.50
148	Darin Erstad	.40
149	Ryan Gripp/SP RC	1.50
150	Orlando Cabrera	.25
151	Jason Young RC	.50
152	Sterling Hitchcock/SP	1.00
153	Miguel Tejada	.25
154	Al Leiter	.25
155	Taylor Buchholz RC	.75
156	Juan Gonzalez	.50
157	Damion Easley	.25
158	Jimmy Gobble RC	1.00
159	Dennis Ulacia/SP	1.00
160	Shane Reynolds/SP	1.00
161	Javier Colina	.25
162	Frank Thomas	1.00
163	Chuck Knoblauch	.25
164	Sean Burroughs	.25
165	Greg Maddux	1.50
166	Jason Ellison RC	.50
167	Tony Womack	.25
168	Randall Shelley/SP RC	1.50
169	Jason Marquis	.25
170	Brian Jordan	.25
171	Darryl Kile	.25
172	Barry Zito	.50
173	Matt Allegra/SP RC	.50
174	Ralph Santana/SP RC	1.50
175	Carlos Lee	.40
176	Richard Hidalgo/SP	1.50
177	Kevin Deaton RC	.50
178	Juan Encarnacion	.25
179	Mark Quinn	.25
180	Rafael Furcal	.40
181	Garret Anderson	.50
182	David Wright	25.00
183	Jose Reyes	.50
184	Mario Ramos/SP	1.00
185	J.D. Drew	.50
186	Juan Gonzalez	.50
187	Nick Neugebauer	.25
188	Alejandro Giron RC	.25
189	John Burkett	.25
190	Ben Sheets	.25
191	Vinny Castilla/SP	1.00
192	Cory Lidle	.25
193	Fernando Vina	.25
194	Russell Branyan/SP	1.00
195	Ben Davis	.25
196	Angel Berroa	.25
197	Alex Gonzalez	.25
198	Jared Sandberg	.25
199	Travis Lee/SP	1.00
200	Luis DePaula/SP RC	1.50
201	Ramon Hernandez/SP	1.00
202	Brandon Inge	.25
203	Aubrey Huff	.25
204	Mike Rivera	.25
205	Brad Nelson/SP	.50
206	Colt Griffin/SP	2.00
207	Joel Pineiro	.25
208	Adam Pettyjohn	.25
209	Mark Redman	.25
210	Roberto Alomar/SP	3.00
211	Denny Neagle	.25
212	Adam Kennedy	.25
213	Jason Arnold/SP	2.00
214	Jamie Moyer	.25
215	Aaron Boone	.25
216	Doug Glanville	.25
217	Nick Johnson/SP	1.00
218	Mike Cameron/SP	1.50
219	Tim Wakefield/SP	1.50
220	Todd Stottlemyre/SP	1.00
221	Mo Vaughn	.25
222	Vladimir Guerrero	.25
223	Bill Ortega	.25
224	Kevin Brown	.25
225	Peter Bergeron/SP	1.00
226	Shannon Stewart/SP	1.50
227	Eric Chavez	.25
228	Clint Weibl RC	.40
229	Todd Hollandsworth/SP	1.00
230	Jeff Bagwell	.75
231	Chad Qualls RC	.40
232	Ben Howard RC	.40
233	Rondell White/SP	1.50
234	Fred McGriff	.20
235	Steve Cox/SP	.25
236	Chris Tritle RC	1.50
237	Eric Valent	.25
238	Joe Mauer RC	12.00
239	Shawn Green	.40
240	Jimmy Rollins	.25
241	Edgar Renteria	.25
242	Edwin Yan RC	.40
243	Noochie Varner RC	.40
244	Kris Benson/SP	1.50
245	Mike Hampton	.25
246	So Taguchi RC	1.00
247	Sammy Sosa	1.00
248	Terrence Long	.25
249	Jason Bay RC	5.00
250	Kevin Millar/SP	1.00
251	Albert Pujols	2.50
252	Chris Latham RC	.25
253	Eric Byrnes	.25
254	Napoleon Calzado/SP RC	1.50
255	Bobby Higginson	.25
256	Ben Molina	.25
257	Torii Hunter/SP	3.00
258	Jason Giambi	.25
259	Bartolo Colon	.25
260	Benito Baez	.25
261	Ichiro Suzuki	2.00
262	Mike Sweeney	.25
263	Brian West RC	.40
264	Brad Penny	.25
265	Kevin Millwood/SP	2.00
266	Orlando Hudson	.25
267	Doug Mientkiewicz	.25
268	Luis Gonzalez/SP	1.50
269	Jay Caligiuri RC	.40
270	Nate Cornejo/SP	1.00
271	Lee Stevens	.25
272	Eric Hinske	.25
273	Antwon Rollins RC	.25
274	Bobby Jenks RC	1.00
275	Joe Mays	.25
276	Josh Shaffer RC	.25
277	Jonny Gomes RC	3.00
278	Bernie Williams	.50
279	Ed Rogers	.25
280	Carlos Delgado	.25
281	Raul Mondesi/SP	1.50
282	Jose Ortiz	.25
283	Cesar Izturis	.25
284	Ryan Dempster/SP	1.00
285	Brian Daubach	.25
286	Hansel Izquierdo RC	1.00
287	Mike Lieberthal/SP	1.00
288	Marcus Thames	.25
289	Nomar Garciaparra	.75
290	Brad Fullmer	.25
291	Tino Martinez	.25
292	James Barrett RC	.40
293	Jacque Jones	.25
294	Nick Alvarez/SP RC	1.50
295	Jason Grove/SP RC	1.50
296	Mike Wilson/SP RC	1.50
297	J.T. Snow	.25
298	Cliff Floyd	.25
299	Todd Hundley/SP	1.00
300	Tony Clark/SP	1.00
301	Demetrius Heath RC	.40
302	Morgan Ensberg	.25
303	Cristian Guzman	.25
304	Frank Catalanotto	.25
305	Jeff Weaver	.25
306	Tim Hudson	.25
307	Scott Wiggins/SP RC	1.50
308	Shea Hillenbrand/SP	2.00
309	Todd Walker/SP	1.00
310	Tsuyoshi Shinjo	.25
311	Adrian Beltre	.25
312	Craig Kuzmic RC	.40
313	Paul Konerko	.40
314	Scott Hairston	1.50
315	Chan Ho Park	.25
316	Jorge Posada	.40
317	Chris Snelling RC	.75
318	Keith Foulke	.25
319	John Smoltz	.50
320	Ryan Church/SP RC	3.00
321	Mike Mussina	.75
322	Tony Armas Jr/SP	1.00
323	Craig Counsell	.25
324	Marcus Giles	.25
325	Greg Vaughn	.25
326	Curt Schilling	.75
327	Jeromy Burnitz	.25
328	Eric Byrnes	.25
329	Johnny Damon	.25
330	Michael Floyd/SP RC	1.50
331	Edgardo Alfonzo	.25
332	Jeremy Hill RC	.25
333	Josh Bonifay RC	.40

#	Player	Price
334	Byung-Hyun Kim	.25
335	Keith Ginter	.25
336	Ronald Acuna/SP RC	1.50
337	Mike Hill/SP RC	1.50
338	Sean Casey	.25
339	Matt Anderson/SP	1.00
340	Dan Wright	.25
341	Ben Petrick	.25
342	Mike Sirotka/SP	1.00
343	Alex Rodriguez	2.50
344	Einar Diaz	.25
345	Derek Jeter	2.50
346	Jeff Conine	.25
347	Ray Durham/SP	1.00
348	Wilson Betemit/SP	1.00
349	Jeffrey Hammonds	.25
350	Dan Trumble RC	.40
351	Phil Nevin/SP	1.50
352	A.J. Burnett	.25
353	Bill Mueller	.25
354	Charles Nagy	.25
355	Rusty Greer/SP	1.00
356	Jason Botts RC	.25
357	Magglio Ordonez	.50
358	Kevin Appier	.25
359	Brad Radke	.25
360	Chris George	.25
361	Chris Piersoll RC	.25
362	Ivan Rodriguez	.75
363	Jim Kavourias	.25
364	Rick Helling/SP	1.00
365	Dean Palmer	.25
366	Rich Aurilia/SP	1.00
367	Ryan Vogelsong	.25
368	Matt Lawton	.25
369	Wade Miller	.25
370	Dustin Hermanson	.25
371	Craig Wilson	.25
372	Todd Zeile/SP	1.00
373	Jon Guzman RC	.40
374	Ellis Burks	.25
375	Robert Cosby/SP RC	1.50
376	Jason Kendall	.25
377	Scott Rolen/SP	4.00
378	Andruw Jones	1.00
379	Greg Sain RC	.25
380	Paul LoDuca	.25
381	Scotty Layfield RC	.25
382	Drew Henson	.50
383	Garrett Guzman RC	.40
384	Jack Cust	.25
385	Shayne Wright RC	.40
386	Derrek Lee	.75
387	Jesus Medrano RC	.40
388	Javier Vazquez	.25
389	Preston Wilson/SP	1.50
390	Gavin Floyd	1.00
391	Sidney Ponson/SP	1.00
392	Jose Hernandez	.25
393	Scott Erickson/SP	1.00
394	Jose Valverde RC	.40
395	Mark Hamilton/SP RC	1.50
396	Brad Cresse	.25
397	Danny Bautista	.25
398	Ray Lankford/SP	1.00
399	Miguel Batista/SP	1.00
400	Brent Butler	.25
401	Manny Delcarmen/SP RC	1.50
402	Kyle Farnsworth/SP	1.00
403	Freddy Garcia	.25
404	Joe Jiannetti RC	.40
405	Josh Barfield	2.00
406	Corey Patterson	.25
407	Josh Towers	.25
408	Carlos Pena	.25
409	Jeff Cirillo	.25
410	Jon Lieber	.25
411	Woody Williams/SP	1.00
412	Richard Lane/SP RC	1.50
413	Alex Gonzalez	.25
414	Wilkin Ruan	.25
415	Geoff Jenkins	.25
416	Carlos Hernandez	.25
417	Matt Clement/SP	1.00
418	Jose Cruz Jr.	.25
419	Jake Mauer RC	.50
420	Matt Childers RC	.50
421	Tom Glavine/SP	1.00
422	Ken Griffey Jr.	2.00
423	Anderson Hernandez RC	.40
424	John Suomi RC	.40
425	Doug Sessions RC	.40
426	Jaret Wright	.25
427	Rolando Viera/SP RC	1.50
428	Aaron Sele	.25
429	Dmitri Young	.25
430	Ryan Klesko	.25
431	Kevin Tapani/SP	1.00
432	Joe Kennedy	.25
433	Austin Kearns	.40
434	Roger Cedeno	.25
435	Lance Berkman	.50
436	Frank Menechino	.25
437	Brett Myers	.25
438	Bobby Abreu	.50
439	Shawn Estes	.25

Relics

NM/M
Common Player: 4.00
Inserted 1:47

	Player	Price
EA	Edgardo Alfonzo	4.00
JB	Josh Beckett	8.00
BB	Barry Bonds	20.00
EC	Eric Chavez	6.00

DARIN ERSTAD

	Player	Price
CD	Carlos Delgado	6.00
JE	Jim Edmonds	8.00
DE	Darin Erstad	4.00
NG	Nomar Garciaparra	15.00
TG	Tony Gwynn	10.00
TH	Todd Helton	8.00
CJ	Chipper Jones	10.00
PK	Paul Konerko	8.00
GM	Greg Maddux	15.00
EM	Edgar Martinez	8.00
MP	Mike Piazza	10.00
AP	Albert Pujols	20.00
MR	Mariano Rivera	8.00
IR	Ivan Rodriguez	8.00
SR	Scott Rolen	10.00
TS	Tim Salmon	5.00
KS	Kazuhiro Sasaki	4.00
JS	John Smoltz	8.00
FT	Frank Thomas	8.00
JT	Jim Thome	8.00
LW	Larry Walker	4.00
PW	Preston Wilson	4.00

Autographs

NM/M
Common Player: 8.00
Inserted 1:45

	Player	Price
LB	Lance Berkman	20.00
HB	Hank Blalock	20.00
KG	Keith Ginter	8.00
TH	Toby Hall	8.00
DH	Drew Henson	15.00
KI	Kazuhiro Ishii	25.00
CI	Cesar Izturis	10.00
PL	Paul LoDuca	15.00
JM	Joe Mauer	75.00
RO	Roy Oswalt	15.00
MP	Mark Prior	30.00
AP	Albert Pujols	250.00
JR	Juan Rivera	8.00

1954 Bowman Reprints

NM/M
Complete Set (20): 40.00
Common Player: 2.00
Inserted 1:12

	Player	Price
RA	Richie Ashburn	2.00
YB	Yogi Berra	4.00
DC	Del Crandell	2.00
BF	Bob Feller	2.50
WF	Whitey Ford	4.00
NF	Nellie Fox	2.00
CL	Clem Labine	2.00
DL	Don Larsen	3.00
JL	Johnny Logan	2.00
WM	Willie Mays	6.00
GM	Gil McDougald	2.00
DM	Don Mueller	2.00
JP	Jimmy Piersall	2.00
AR	Allie Reynolds	2.00
PR	Phil Rizzuto	3.00
ES	Enos Slaughter	2.00
DS	Duke Snider	4.00
WW	Wes Westrum	2.00
HW	Hoyt Wilhelm	2.00
DW	Davey Williams	2.00

1954 Bowman Reprint Autographs

NM/M
Common Player: 10.00
Inserted 1:118

	Player	Price
YB	Yogi Berra	50.00
DC	Del Crandell	15.00
CL	Clem Labine	15.00
JL	Johnny Logan	12.00
DM	Don Mueller	10.00
DW	Davey Williams	10.00

Team Topps Legends Autographs

NM/M
Common Player: 8.00

Player	Price
Gil McDougald	8.00
Joe Pepitone	8.00
Bobby Richardson	8.00
Robin Roberts	12.00
Warren Spahn	30.00
Luis Tiant	8.00
Carl Yastrzemski	40.00

Chrome Refractor

Stars: 3-6X
SP's: 1-2X
Inserted 1:16
Gold Refractors: 4-8X
SP's: 2-3X
Inserted 1:32

2002 Bowman's Best

Casey Kotchman

NM/M
Complete Set (181):
Common Player: .40
Common (91-181): 4.00
Inserted 1:Pack
Blue (1-90): 1-2X
Production 300
Red (1-90): 1-2X
Production 200
Gold (1-90): 3-6X
Production 50
Blue (91-181): .75-1X
Production 500
Red (91-181): 1-1.5X
Production 150
Gold (91-181): 1-2X
Production 50
Pack (5): 20.00
Box (10): 180.00

#	Player	Price
1	Josh Beckett	.75
2	Derek Jeter	4.00
3	Alex Rodriguez	3.00
4	Miguel Tejada	1.50
5	Nomar Garciaparra	1.50
6	Aramis Ramirez	.75
7	Jeremy Giambi	.40
8	Bernie Williams	.50
9	Juan Pierre	.40
10	Chipper Jones	1.50
11	Jimmy Rollins	.75
12	Alfonso Soriano	1.00
13	Daryle Ward	.40
14	Paul Konerko	.75
15	Tim Hudson	.75
16	Doug Mientkiewicz	.40
17	Todd Helton	1.00
18	Moises Alou	.75
19	Juan Gonzalez	.75
20	Jorge Posada	.75
21	Jeff Kent	.50
22	Roger Clemens	3.00
23	Phil Nevin	.40
24	Brian Giles	.40
25	Carlos Delgado	1.00
26	Jason Giambi	1.00
27	Vladimir Guerrero	1.50
28	Cliff Floyd	.40
29	Shea Hillenbrand	.40
30	Ken Griffey Jr.	2.50
31	Mike Piazza	1.50
32	Carlos Pena	.40
33	Larry Walker	.50
34	Magglio Ordonez	.50
35	Mike Mussina	.75
36	Andruw Jones	1.00
37	Mark Teixeira	.75
38	Curt Schilling	1.00
39	Eric Chavez	.60
40	Bartolo Colon	.40
41	Eric Hinske	.40
42	Sean Burroughs	.40
43	Randy Johnson	1.00
44	Adam Dunn	.75
45	Pedro Martinez	1.50
46	Garret Anderson	.40
47	Jim Thome	1.00
48	Gary Sheffield	1.00
49	Tsuyoshi Shinjo	.40
50	Albert Pujols	4.00
51	Ichiro Suzuki	3.00
52	C.C. Sabathia	.40
53	Bobby Abreu	.75
54	Ivan Rodriguez	.75
55	J.D. Drew	.50
56	Jacque Jones	.40
57	Jason Kendall	.40
58	Javier Vazquez	.40
59	Jeff Bagwell	.75
60	Greg Maddux	2.50
61	Jim Edmonds	.50
62	Austin Kearns	.50
63	Jose Vidro	.40
64	Kevin Brown	.40
65	Preston Wilson	.40
66	Sammy Sosa	1.50
67	Lance Berkman	.75
68	Mark Mulder	.60
69	Marty Cordova	.40
70	Frank Thomas	1.00
71	Mike Cameron	.40
72	Mike Sweeney	.40
73	Barry Bonds	4.00
74	Troy Glaus	.75
75	Barry Zito	.75
76	Pat Burrell	.50
77	Paul LoDuca	.40
78	Rafael Palmeiro	.75
79	Mark Prior	1.00
80	Darin Erstad	.50
81	Richie Sexson	.75
82	Roberto Alomar	.75
83	Roy Oswalt	.75
84	Ryan Klesko	.40
85	Luis Gonzalez	.50
86	Scott Rolen	1.00
87	Shannon Stewart	.40
88	Shawn Green	.60
89	Toby Hall	.40
90	Bret Boone	.40
91	Casey Kotchman/Bat	10.00
92	Jose Valverde/Auto. RC	8.00
93	Cole Barthel/Bat	4.00
94	Brad Nelson/Auto. RC	8.00
95	Mauricio Lara/Auto. RC	8.00
96	Ryan Gripp/Bat RC	4.00
97	Brian West/Auto. RC	8.00
98	Chris Piersoll/Auto. RC	8.00
99	Ryan Church/Auto. RC	15.00
100	Javier Colina/Auto.	8.00
101	Juan Gonzalez/Auto.	8.00
102	Benito Baez/Auto.	8.00
103	Mike Hill RC	4.00
104	Jason Grove/Auto. RC	8.00
105	Koyie Hill/Auto	8.00
106	Mark Outlaw/Auto. RC	8.00
107	Jason Bay/Bat RC	20.00
108	Jorge Padilla/Auto. RC	8.00
109	Peter Zamora/Auto. RC	8.00
110	Joe Mauer/Auto RC	80.00
111	Franklyn German/Auto. RC	8.00
112	Chris Flinn/Auto. RC	8.00
113	David Wright/Bat	80.00
114	Anastacio Martinez/Auto. RC	8.00
115	Nic Jackson/Bat RC	8.00
116	Rene Reyes/Auto. RC	8.00
117	Colin Young/Auto. RC	8.00
118	Joe Orloski/Auto. RC	8.00
119	Mike Wilson/Auto. RC	8.00
120	Rich Thompson/Auto. RC	8.00
121	Jake Mauer/Auto. RC	8.00
122	Mario Ramos/Auto.	8.00
123	Doug Sessions/Auto. RC	8.00
124	Doug DeVore/Bat RC	4.00
125	Travis Foley/Auto.	10.00
126	Chris Baker/Auto. RC	8.00
127	Michael Floyd/Auto. RC	8.00
128	Josh Barfield/Bat	15.00
129	Jose Bautista/Bat RC	6.00
130	Gavin Floyd/Auto.	15.00
131	Jason Botts/Bat RC	8.00
132	Clint Nageotte/Auto. RC	10.00
133	Jesus Cota/Auto. RC	10.00
134	Ron Calloway/Bat RC	4.00
135	Kevin Cash/Bat RC	4.00
136	Jonny Gomes/Auto. RC	25.00
137	Dennis Ulacia/Auto.	8.00
138	Ryan Snare/Auto. RC	8.00
139	Kevin Deaton/Auto. RC	8.00
140	Bobby Jenks/Auto. RC	15.00
141	Casey Kotchman/Auto.	20.00
142	Adam Walker/Auto. RC	8.00
143	Mike Gonzalez/Auto. RC	8.00
144	Ruben Gotay/Bat RC	6.00
145	Jason Grove/Bat RC	6.00
146	Freddy Sanchez/Auto. RC	25.00
147	Jason Arnold/Auto.	10.00
148	Scott Hairston/Auto.	10.00
149	Jason St. Clair/Auto. RC	8.00
150	Chris Tritle/Bat RC	4.00
151	Edwin Yan/Bat RC	4.00
152	Freddy Sanchez/Bat RC	10.00
153	Greg Sain/Bat RC	4.00
154	Yurendell DeCaster/Bat RC	6.00
155	Noochie Varner/Bat RC	6.00
156	Nelson Castro/Auto. RC	8.00
157	Randall Shelley/Bat RC	6.00
158	Reed Johnson/Bat RC	10.00
159	Ryan Raburn/Auto. RC	8.00
160	Jose Morban/Bat RC	5.00
161	Justin Schuda/Auto. RC	8.00
162	Henry Pichardo/Auto. RC	8.00
163	Josh Bard/Auto. RC	10.00
164	Josh Bonifay/Auto. RC	8.00
165	Brandon League/Auto.	8.00
166	Julio DePaula/Auto. RC	10.00
167	Todd Linden/Auto. RC	10.00
168	Francisco Liriano/Auto. RC	120.00
169	Chris Snelling/Auto. RC	15.00
170	Blake McGinley/Auto. RC	8.00
171	Cody McKay/Auto. RC	8.00
172	Jason Stanford/Auto. RC	8.00
173	Lenny Dinardo/Auto. RC	8.00
174	Greg Montalbano/Auto. RC	8.00
175	Earl Snyder/Auto. RC	8.00
176	Justin Huber/Auto. RC	10.00
177	Chris Narveson/Auto. RC	8.00
178	Jon Switzer/Auto.	8.00
179	Ronald Acuna/Auto. RC	8.00
180	Chris Duffy/Bat RC	8.00
181	Kazuhisa Ishii/Bat RC	8.00

2003 Bowman

JOEY GOMES OF

NM/M
Complete Set (330): 75.00
Common Player: .15
Common Rookie: .40
Pack (10): 3.00
Box (24): 60.00

#	Player	Price
1	Garret Anderson	.15
2	Derek Jeter	2.00
3	Gary Sheffield	.40
4	Matt Morris	.25
5	Derek Lowe	.15
6	Andy Van Hekken	.15
7	Sammy Sosa	1.00
8	Ken Griffey Jr.	1.50
9	Omar Vizquel	.15
10	Jorge Posada	.40
11	Lance Berkman	.40
12	Mike Sweeney	.15
13	Adrian Beltre	.25
14	Richie Sexson	.25
15	A.J. Pierzynski	.15
16	Bartolo Colon	.15
17	Mike Mussina	.40
18	Paul Byrd	.15
19	Bobby Abreu	.40
20	Miguel Tejada	.50
21	Aramis Ramirez	.40
22	Edgardo Alfonzo	.15
23	Edgar Martinez	.25
24	Albert Pujols	2.00
25	Carl Crawford	.25
26	Eric Hinske	.15
27	Tim Salmon	.25
28	Luis Gonzalez	.25
29	Jay Gibbons	.15
30	John Smoltz	.40
31	Tim Wakefield	.15
32	Mark Prior	.75
33	Magglio Ordonez	.25
34	Adam Dunn	.25
35	Larry Walker	.25
36	Luis Castillo	.15
37	Wade Miller	.15
38	Carlos Beltran	.50
39	Odalis Perez	.15
40	Alex Sanchez	.15
41	Torii Hunter	.25
42	Cliff Floyd	.15
43	Andy Pettitte	.25
44	Francisco Rodriguez	.15
45	Eric Chavez	.40
46	Kevin Millwood	.25
47	Dennis Tankersley	.15
48	Hideo Nomo	.25
49	Freddy Garcia	.15
50	Randy Johnson	.75
51	Aubrey Huff	.15
52	Carlos Delgado	.25
53	Troy Glaus	.50
54	Junior Spivey	.15
55	Mike Hampton	.15
56	Sidney Ponson	.15
57	Aaron Boone	.15
58	Kerry Wood	.40
59	Willie Harris	.15
60	Nomar Garciaparra	1.00
61	Todd Helton	.50
62	Mike Lowell	.15
63	Roy Oswalt	.40
64	Raul Ibanez	.15
65	Brian Jordan	.15
66	Geoff Jenkins	.15
67	Jermaine Dye	.15
68	Tom Glavine	.25
69	Bernie Williams	.40
70	Vladimir Guerrero	.75
71	Mark Mulder	.25
72	Jimmy Rollins	.40
73	Oliver Perez	.15
74	Rich Aurilia	.15
75	Joel Pineiro	.15
76	J.D. Drew	.25
77	Ivan Rodriguez	.50
78	Josh Phelps	.15
79	Darin Erstad	.40
80	Curt Schilling	.40
81	Paul LoDuca	.15
82	Marty Cordova	.15
83	Manny Ramirez	.75
84	Bobby Hill	.15
85	Paul Konerko	.40
86	Austin Kearns	.25
87	Jason Jennings	.15
88	Brad Penny	.15
89	Jeff Bagwell	.75
90	Shawn Green	.40
91	Jason Schmidt	.40
92	Doug Mientkiewicz	.15
93	Jose Vidro	.15
94	Bret Boone	.15
95	Jason Giambi	.50
96	Barry Zito	.40
97	Roy Halliday	.40
98	Pat Burrell	.40
99	Sean Burroughs	.15
100	Barry Bonds	2.00
101	Kazuhiro Sasaki	.15
102	Fernando Vina	.15
103	Chan Ho Park	.15
104	Andruw Jones	.75
105	Adam Kennedy	.15
106	Shea Hillenbrand	.15
107	Greg Maddux	1.50
108	Jim Edmonds	.25
109	Pedro J. Martinez	1.00
110	Moises Alou	.25
111	Jeff Weaver	.25
112	C.C. Sabathia	.15
113	Robert Fick	.15
114	A.J. Burnett	.25
115	Jeff Kent	.25
116	Kevin Brown	.25
117	Rafael Furcal	.15
118	Cristian Guzman	.15
119	Brad Wilkerson	.15
120	Mike Piazza	1.00
121	Alfonso Soriano	.75
122	Mark Ellis	.15
123	Vicente Padilla	.15
124	Eric Gagne	.25
125	Ryan Klesko	.25
126	Ichiro Suzuki	1.50
127	Tony Batista	.15
128	Roberto Alomar	.40
129	Alex Rodriguez	2.00
130	Jim Thome	.75

131 Jarrod Washburn .15
132 Orlando Hudson .15
133 Chipper Jones 1.00
134 Rodrigo Lopez .15
135 Johnny Damon .75
136 Matt Clement .15
137 Frank Thomas .75
138 Ellis Burks .15
139 Carlos Pena .15
140 Josh Beckett .15
141 Joe Randa .15
142 Brian Giles .25
143 Kazuhisa Ishii .15
144 Corey Koskie .15
145 Orlando Cabrera .15
146 Mark Buehrle .25
147 Roger Clemens 2.00
148 Tim Hudson .40
149 Randy Wolf .15
150 Josh Fogg .15
151 Phil Nevin .15
152 John Olerud .15
153 Scott Rolen .75
154 Joe Kennedy .15
155 Rafael Palmeiro .75
156 Chad Hutchinson .40
157 Quincy Carter .15
158 Hee Seop Choi .15
159 Joe Borchard .15
160 Brandon Phillips .15
161 Wily Mo Pena .15
162 Victor Martinez .25
163 Jason Stokes .15
164 Ken Harvey .15
165 Juan Rivera .15
166 Jose Contreras RC 1.00
167 Dan Haren .75
168 Michel Hernandez RC .40
169 Eider Torres RC .40
170 Chris De La Cruz RC .50
171 Ramon A. Martinez RC .40
172 Mike Adams RC .40
173 Justin Arneson RC .40
174 Jamie Athas RC .40
175 Dwaine Bacon RC .40
176 Clint Barmes RC 1.00
177 B.J. Barns RC .40
178 Tyler Johnson RC .40
179 Bobby Basham RC .50
180 T.J. Bohn RC .50
181 J.D. Durbin RC .50
182 Brandon Bowe RC .40
183 Craig Brazell RC .50
184 Dusty Brown RC .50
185 Brian Bruney RC .40
186 Greg Bruso RC .40
187 Jaime Bubela RC .40
188 Bryan Bullington RC .50
189 Brian Burgamy RC .40
190 Eny Cabreja RC .50
191 Daniel Cabrera RC 1.00
192 Ryan Cameron RC .40
193 Lance Caraccioli RC .50
194 David Cash RC .40
195 Bernie Castro RC .40
196 Ismael Castro RC .40
197 Daryl Clark RC .50
198 Jeff Clark RC .40
199 Chris Colton RC .40
200 Dexter Cooper RC .40
201 Callix Crabbe RC .40
202 Chien-Ming Wang RC 5.00
203 Eric Crozier RC .40
204 Nook Logan RC .40
205 David DeJesus RC .75
206 Matt DeMarco RC .40
207 Chris Duncan RC 3.00
208 Eric Eckenstahler RC .40
209 Willie Eyre RC .40
210 Evel Bastida-Martinez RC .40
211 Chris Fallon RC .75
212 Mike Flannery RC .40
213 Mike O'Keefe RC .40
214 Ben Francisco RC .50
215 Kason Gabbard RC .40
216 Mike Gallo RC .40
217 Jairo Garcia RC .40
218 Angel Garcia RC .40
219 Michael Garciaparra RC .50
220 Joey Gomes RC .40
221 Dusty Gomon RC .40
222 Bryan Grace RC .40
223 Tyson Graham RC .40
224 Henry Guerrero RC .40
225 Franklin Gutierrez RC .50
226 Carlos Guzman RC .40
227 Matthew Hagen RC .40
228 Josh Hall RC .50
229 Rob Hammock RC .50
230 Brendan Harris RC .50
231 Gary Harris RC .40
232 Clay Hensley RC .75
233 Michael Hinckley RC .40
234 Luis Hodge RC .40
235 Donnie Hood RC .50
236 Travis Ishikawa RC .50
237 Edwin Jackson RC .50
238 Ardley Jansen RC .50
239 Ferenc Jongejan RC .40
240 Matt Kata RC .50
241 Kazuhiro Takeoka RC .40
242 Beau Kemp RC .40
243 Il Kim RC .50
244 Brennan King RC .40
245 Cris Kroski RC .40
246 Jason Kubel RC 2.00
247 Pete LaForest RC .40

248 Wilfredo Ledezma RC .40
249 Jeremy Bonderman 3.00
250 Gonzalo Lopez RC .40
251 Brian Luderer RC .50
252 Ruddy Lugo RC .40
253 Wayne Lydon RC .40
254 Mark Malaska RC .40
255 Andy Marte RC 2.50
256 Tyler Martin RC .40
257 Branden Florence RC .40
258 Aneudis Mateo RC .40
259 Derell McCall RC .40
260 Brian McCann 5.00
261 Mike McNutt RC .40
262 Jacabo Meque RC .40
263 Derek Michaelis RC .50
264 Aaron Miles RC 1.00
265 Jose Morales .40
266 Dustin Moseley RC .40
267 Adrian Myers RC .40
268 Dan Neil RC .40
269 Jon Nelson RC .50
270 Mike Neu RC .40
271 Leigh Neuage RC .40
272 Weston O'Brien RC .40
273 Trent Oeltjen RC .40
274 Tim Olson RC .40
275 David Pahucki RC .40
276 Nathan Panther RC .50
277 Arnie Munoz RC .40
278 David Pember RC .40
279 Jason Perry RC .40
280 Matthew Peterson RC .40
281 Ryan Shealy RC 1.50
282 Jorge Piedra RC .40
283 Simon Pond RC .40
284 Aaron Rakers RC .40
285 Hanley Ramirez RC 4.00
286 Manuel Ramirez RC .40
287 Kevin Randel RC .50
288 Darrell Rasner RC .40
289 Prentice Redman RC .50
290 Eric Reed RC .50
291 Wilton Reynolds RC .40
292 Eric Riggs RC .40
293 Carlos Rijo RC .40
294 Rajai Davis RC .50
295 Aron Weston RC .50
296 Arturo Rivas RC .50
297 Kyle Roat RC .40
298 Bubba Nelson RC .40
299 Levi Robinson RC .40
300 Ray Sadler RC .40
301 Gary Schneidmiller RC .50
302 Jon Schuerholz RC .75
303 Corey Shafer RC .40
304 Brian Shackelford RC .40
305 Bill Simon RC .40
306 Haj Turay RC .40
307 Sean Smith RC .40
308 Ryan Spataro RC .40
309 Jemel Spearman RC .50
310 Keith Stamler RC .40
311 Luke Steidlmayer RC .50
312 Adam Stern RC .50
313 Jay Sitzman RC .40
314 Thomari Story-Harden RC .50
315 Terry Tiffee RC .50
316 Nick Trzesniak RC .50
317 Denny Tussen RC .50
318 Scott Tyler RC .40
319 Shane Victorino RC .40
320 Doug Waechter RC .50
321 Brandon Watson RC .50
322 Todd Wellemeyer RC .50
323 Eli Whiteside RC .50
324 Josh Willingham RC 1.00
325 Travis Wong RC .40
326 Brian Wright RC .40
327 Kevin Youkilis RC 2.00
328 Andy Sisco RC .50
329 Dustin Yount RC .40
330 Andrew Dominique RC .40

Gold

Stars (1-165): 1-2X
Rookies (166-330): 1-2X
Inserted 1:1

Uncirculated

Stars (1-165): 3-5X
Rookies (166-330): 2-4X
Production 250 Sets

Future Fiber Relics

NM/M
Common Player: 4.00
RB Rocco Baldelli 10.00
WB Wilson Betemit 6.00
HB Hank Blalock 10.00
JB Jason Botts 5.00
SB Sean Burroughs 8.00
KC Kevin Cash 4.00
KD Kory DeHaan 5.00
CD Chris Duffy 5.00
PF Pedro Feliz 5.00
AG Adrian Gonzalez 5.00
JG Jason Grove 5.00
JH Josh Hamilton 8.00
NH Nathan Haynes 5.00
DH Drew Henson 8.00
AH Aubrey Huff 6.00
RJ Reed Johnson 6.00
AK Austin Kearns 5.00
CK Casey Kotchman 8.00

RK Ryan Langerhans 5.00
JDM Jake Mauer 6.00
JM Joe Mauer 15.00
XN Xavier Nady 6.00
MR Michael Restovich 6.00
WR Wilkin Ruan 6.00
FS Freddy Sanchez 8.00
RS Randall Shelley 4.00
BS Bud Smith 4.00
ES Esix Snead 4.00
ST So Taguchi 8.00
JW Justin Wayne 5.00
TW Travis Wilson 6.00
DW David Wright 15.00
EY Edwin Yan 4.00

Futures Game Gear Relics

NM/M
Common Player: 4.00
Inserted 1:26
EA Edwin Almonte 4.00
TA Tony Alvarez 4.00
BB Brad Baker 4.00
FB Francis Beltran 4.00
JEB Joe Borchard 4.00
JB John Buck 4.00
SB Sean Burnett 6.00
MB Marlon Byrd 4.00
MC Miguel Cabrera 10.00
KC Kevin Cash 4.00
HC Hee Seop Choi 5.00
SC Shin-Soo Choo 6.00
AC Aaron Cook 5.00
CC Carl Crawford 5.00
JDR Jorge De La Rosa 4.00
VD Victor Diaz 4.00
RD Ryan Dittfurth 4.00
BE Brett Evert 4.00
GG Gerardo Garcia 4.00
BH Bill Hall 4.00
CH Corey Hart 4.00
DH Drew Henson 8.00
JH Justin Huber 6.00
OH Orlando Hudson 4.00
OI Omar Infante 4.00
JJ Jimmy Journell 4.00
JK Josh Karp 4.00
FL Francisco Liriano 4.00
JL Jose Lopez 4.00
VM Victor Martinez 8.00
JM Justin Morneau 10.00
BM Brett Myers 6.00
LO Lyle Overbay 6.00
WP Wily Mo Pena 6.00
BP Brandon Phillips 6.00
MR Mike Restovich 8.00
JR Jose Reyes 10.00
FR Francisco Rodriguez 4.00
RR Ricardo Rodriguez 4.00
SS Seung Jun Song 4.00
JMS John Stephens 4.00
JS Jason Stokes 8.00
BT Billy Traber 5.00
CT Chad Tracey 4.00
AW Adam Wainwright 10.00
JY Jason Young 4.00

Futures Game MVP Autograph

NM/M
Complete Set (1):
JR Jose Reyes 40.00

ROY Dual Relic

NM/M
Inserted 1:765
JH Eric Hinske, Jason Jennings 10.00

Signs of the Future

NM/M
Common Autograph: 5.00
Red Autographs: 1-2.5X
Production 50 Sets

JA Jason Arnold 8.00
JB John Buck 5.00
BB Bryan Bullington 10.00
QC Quincy Carter 10.00
NC Nelson Castro 8.00
RC Ryan Church 10.00
JC Jesus Cota 5.00
JOG Jonny Gomes 20.00
DG Doug Gredvig 5.00
KG Khalil Greene 25.00
ZG Zack Greinke 10.00
JG Jason Grove 5.00
JGU Jeremy Guthrie 10.00
CH Cole Hamels 75.00
JRH Joel Hanrahan 8.00
CJH Corey Hart 15.00
KH Koyie Hill 8.00
CMH Chad Hutchinson 10.00
BJ Bobby Jenks 12.00
BK Ben Kozlowski 5.00
BL Brandon League 5.00
DL Donald Levinski 5.00
FL Fred Lewis 5.00
TL Todd Linden 5.00
JL James Loney 30.00
VM Val Majewski 8.00
DHM Dustin McGowan 5.00
CP Chris Piersoll 8.00
HR Hanley Ramirez 30.00
PR Prentice Redman 8.00
JR Jose Reyes 40.00
JSC Jason St. Clair 6.00
FS Freddy Sanchez 15.00
ZS Zach Segovia 8.00
DS Doug Sessions 5.00
BS Brian Slocum 5.00
RS Ryan Snare 8.00
MT Mitch Talbot 5.00
AT Andres Torres 5.00
AV Andy Van Hekken 5.00
OV Oscar Villarreal 5.00

Dual Signs of the Future Autograph

NM/M
Inserted 1:9,220
CH Quincy Carter, Chad Hutchinson 85.00

2003 Bowman Chrome

NM/M
Complete Set (351): 400.00
Common Player: .25
Common Rookie: 1.00
Common RC Auto. (331-350): 10.00
Pack (4): 7.50
Box (18): 125.00
1 Garret Anderson .50
2 Derek Jeter 3.00
3 Gary Sheffield .50
4 Matt Morris .35
5 Derek Lowe .25
6 Andy Van Hekken .25
7 Sammy Sosa 1.00
8 Ken Griffey Jr. 2.00
9 Omar Vizquel .40
10 Jorge Posada .50
11 Lance Berkman .50
12 Mike Sweeney .50
13 Adrian Beltre .50
14 Richie Sexson .50
15 A.J. Pierzynski .25
16 Bartolo Colon .25
17 Mike Mussina .75
18 Paul Byrd .25
19 Bobby Abreu .50
20 Miguel Tejada .75
21 Aramis Ramirez .25
22 Edgardo Alfonzo .25
23 Edgar Martinez .40
24 Albert Pujols 3.00
25 Carl Crawford .40
26 Eric Hinske .25
27 Tim Salmon .40
28 Luis Gonzalez .25
29 Jay Gibbons .25
30 John Smoltz .50
31 Tim Wakefield .25
32 Mark Prior 1.00
33 Magglio Ordonez .40
34 Adam Dunn .75
35 Larry Walker .40
36 Luis Castillo .25
37 Wade Miller .25

38 Carlos Beltran .75
39 Odalis Perez .25
40 Alex Sanchez .25
41 Torii Hunter .50
42 Cliff Floyd .25
43 Andy Pettitte .50
44 Francisco Rodriguez .50
45 Eric Chavez .50
46 Kevin Millwood .40
47 Dennis Tankersley .25
48 Hideo Nomo .50
49 Freddy Garcia .25
50 Randy Johnson 1.00
51 Aubrey Huff .25
52 Carlos Delgado .50
53 Troy Glaus .50
54 Junior Spivey .25
55 Mike Hampton .25
56 Sidney Ponson .25
57 Aaron Boone .25
58 Kerry Wood .50
59 Willie Harris .25
60 Nomar Garciaparra 1.00
61 Todd Helton .75
62 Mike Lowell .25
63 Roy Oswalt .25
64 Raul Ibanez .25
65 Brian Jordan .25
66 Geoff Jenkins .25
67 Jermaine Dye .25
68 Tom Glavine .50
69 Bernie Williams .50
70 Vladimir Guerrero 1.00
71 Mark Mulder .40
72 Jimmy Rollins .25
73 Oliver Perez .25
74 Rich Aurilia .25
75 Joel Pineiro .25
76 J.D. Drew .25
77 Ivan Rodriguez .75
78 Josh Phelps .25
79 Darin Erstad .40
80 Curt Schilling 1.00
81 Paul LoDuca .25
82 Marty Cordova .25
83 Manny Ramirez 1.00
84 Bobby Hill .25
85 Paul Konerko .25
86 Austin Kearns .40
87 Jason Jennings .25
88 Brad Penny .25
89 Jeff Bagwell .75
90 Shawn Green .25
91 Jason Schmidt .25
92 Doug Mientkiewicz .25
93 Jose Vidro .25
94 Bret Boone .25
95 Jason Giambi .75
96 Barry Zito .50
97 Roy Halliday .50
98 Pat Burrell .50
99 Sean Burroughs .25
100 Barry Bonds 3.00
101 Kazuhiro Sasaki .25
102 Fernando Vina .25
103 Chan Ho Park .25
104 Andruw Jones 1.00
105 Adam Kennedy .25
106 Shea Hillenbrand .25
107 Greg Maddux 2.00
108 Jim Edmonds .50
109 Pedro J. Martinez 1.00
110 Moises Alou .40
111 Jeff Weaver .25
112 C.C. Sabathia .25
113 Robert Fick .25
114 A.J. Burnett .25
115 Jeff Kent .40
116 Kevin Brown .25
117 Rafael Furcal .40
118 Cristian Guzman .25
119 Brad Wilkerson .25
120 Mike Piazza .75
121 Alfonso Soriano 1.00
122 Mark Ellis .25
123 Vicente Padilla .25
124 Eric Gagne .50
125 Ryan Klesko .25
126 Ichiro Suzuki 2.00
127 Tony Batista .25
128 Roberto Alomar .50
129 Alex Rodriguez 2.50
130 Jim Thome .75
131 Jarrod Washburn .25
132 Orlando Hudson .25
133 Chipper Jones 1.00
134 Rodrigo Lopez .25
135 Johnny Damon 1.00
136 Matt Clement .25
137 Frank Thomas 1.00
138 Ellis Burks .25
139 Carlos Pena .25
140 Josh Beckett .25
141 Joe Randa .25
142 Brian Giles .25
143 Kazuhisa Ishii .25
144 Corey Koskie .25
145 Orlando Cabrera .25
146 Mark Buehrle .25
147 Roger Clemens 2.00
148 Tim Hudson .50
149 Randy Wolf .25
150 Josh Fogg .25
151 Phil Nevin .25
152 John Olerud .25
153 Scott Rolen 1.00
154 Joe Kennedy .25
155 Rafael Palmeiro .75

156 Chad Hutchinson .50
157 Quincy Carter .50
158 Hee Seop Choi .40
159 Joe Borchard .25
160 Brandon Phillips .25
161 Wily Mo Pena .25
162 Victor Martinez .25
163 Jason Stokes .25
164 Ken Harvey .25
165 Juan Rivera .25
166 Joe Valentine RC 1.50
167 Dan Haren 3.00
168 Michel Hernandez RC 1.00
169 Eider Torres RC 1.00
170 Chris De La Cruz RC 1.00
171 Ramon A. Martinez RC 1.50
172 Mike Adams RC 1.00
173 Justin Arneson RC 1.00
174 Jamie Athas RC 1.00
175 Dwaine Bacon RC 1.00
176 Clint Barmes RC 3.00
177 B.J. Barns RC 1.00
178 Tyler Johnson RC 1.00
179 Brandon Webb RC 8.00
180 T.J. Bohn RC 1.00
181 Ozzie Chavez RC 1.50
182 Brandon Bowe RC 1.00
183 Craig Brazell RC 1.00
184 Dusty Brown RC 1.00
185 Brian Bruney RC 1.00
186 Greg Bruso RC 1.00
187 Jaime Bubela RC 1.00
188 Matt Diaz RC 1.50
189 Brian Burgamy RC 1.00
190 Eny Cabreja RC 1.00
191 Daniel Cabrera RC 3.00
192 Ryan Cameron RC 1.00
193 Lance Caraccioli RC 1.50
194 David Cash RC 1.00
195 Bernie Castro RC 1.00
196 Ismael Castro RC 1.00
197 Cory Doyne RC 2.00
198 Jeff Clark RC 1.00
199 Chris Colton RC 1.50
200 Dexter Cooper RC 1.00
201 Callix Crabbe RC 1.00
202 Chien-Ming Wang RC 15.00
203 Eric Crozier RC 1.50
204 Nook Logan RC 1.50
205 David DeJesus RC 4.00
206 Matt DeMarco RC 1.00
207 Chris Duncan RC 10.00
208 Eric Eckenstahler RC 1.00
209 Willie Eyre RC 1.00
210 Evel Bastida-Martinez RC 1.00
211 Chris Fallon RC 1.50
212 Mike Flannery RC 1.00
213 Mike O'Keefe RC 1.00
214 Lew Ford RC 2.00
215 Kason Gabbard RC 1.00
216 Mike Gallo RC 1.00
217 Jairo Garcia RC 1.00
218 Angel Garcia RC 1.00
219 Michael Garciaparra RC 1.50
220 Jeremy Griffiths RC 1.00
221 Dusty Gomon RC 1.00
222 Bryan Grace RC 1.00
223 Tyson Graham RC 1.00
224 Henry Guerrero RC 1.00
225 Franklin Gutierrez RC 4.00
226 Carlos Guzman RC 1.00
227 Matthew Hagen RC 2.00
228 Josh Hall RC 1.00
229 Rob Hammock RC 1.00
230 Brendan Harris RC 1.50
231 Gary Harris RC 1.00
232 Clay Hensley RC 1.50
233 Michael Hinckley RC 1.00
234 Luis Hodge RC 1.00
235 Donnie Hood RC 1.00
236 Matt Hensley RC 1.00
237 Edwin Jackson RC 1.50
238 Ardley Jansen RC 2.00
239 Ferenc Jongejan RC 1.00
240 Matt Kata RC 1.50
241 Kazuhiro Takeoka RC 1.00
242 Charlie Manning RC 1.00
243 Il Kim RC 1.00
244 Brennan King RC 1.00
245 Cris Kroski RC 1.00
246 David Martinez RC 1.00
247 Pete LaForest RC 1.00
248 Wilfredo Ledezma RC 1.00
249 Jeremy Bonderman 12.00
250 Gonzalo Lopez RC 1.00
251 Brian Luderer RC 1.00
252 Ruddy Lugo RC 1.00
253 Wayne Lydon RC 1.00
254 Mark Malaska RC 1.00
255 Andy Marte RC 10.00
256 Tyler Martin RC 1.00
257 Branden Florence RC 1.00
258 Aneudis Mateo RC 1.00
259 Derell McCall RC 1.00
260 Elizardo Ramirez RC 2.00
261 Mike McNutt RC 1.00
262 Jacabo Meque RC 1.00
263 Derek Michaelis RC 1.00
264 Aaron Miles RC 2.00
265 Jose Morales 1.00
266 Dustin Moseley RC 1.00
267 Adrian Myers RC 1.00
268 Dan Neil RC 1.00
269 Jon Nelson RC 2.00
270 Mike Neu RC 1.00
271 Leigh Neuage RC 1.00
272 Weston O'Brien RC 1.00

#	Player		Price
273	Trent Oeltjen	RC	2.00
274	Tim Olson	RC	2.00
275	David Pahucki	RC	1.00
276	Nathan Panther	RC	1.50
277	Arnie Munoz	RC	1.00
278	David Pember	RC	1.00
279	Jason Perry	RC	2.00
280	Matthew Peterson	RC	1.00
281	Greg Aquino	RC	1.50
282	Jorge Piedra	RC	1.00
283	Simon Pond	RC	2.00
284	Aaron Rakers	RC	1.00
285	Felix Sanchez	RC	1.50
286	Manuel Ramirez	RC	1.00
287	Kevin Randel	RC	1.00
288	Kelly Shoppach	RC	3.00
289	Prentice Redman	RC	2.00
290	Eric Reed	RC	2.00
291	Wilton Reynolds	RC	1.00
292	Eric Riggs	RC	1.00
293	Carlos Rijo	RC	1.00
294	Tyler Adamczyk	RC	2.00
295	Jon-Mark Sprowl	RC	2.00
296	Arturo Rivas	RC	1.00
297	Kyle Roat	RC	1.00
298	Bubba Nelson	RC	1.00
299	Levi Robinson	RC	1.00
300	Ray Sadler	RC	1.00
301	Rylan Reed	RC	1.00
302	Jon Schuerholz	RC	1.00
303	Nobuaki Yoshida	RC	1.50
304	Brian Shackelford	RC	1.00
305	Bill Simon	RC	1.00
306	Haj Turay	RC	1.00
307	Sean Smith		1.00
308	Ryan Spataro	RC	1.00
309	Jemel Spearman	RC	1.50
310	Keith Stamler	RC	1.00
311	Luke Steidlmayer	RC	1.00
312	Adam Stern		1.00
313	Jay Sitzman	RC	1.00
314	Mike Wodnicki	RC	1.50
315	Terry Tiffee	RC	1.00
316	Nick Trzesniak	RC	1.00
317	Denny Tussen	RC	1.00
318	Scott Tyler		1.00
319	Shane Victorino	RC	2.00
320	Doug Waechter	RC	1.50
321	Brandon Watson	RC	1.50
322	Todd Wellemeyer	RC	1.50
323	Eli Whiteside	RC	1.00
324	Josh Willingham	RC	4.00
325	Travis Wong	RC	1.50
326	Brian Wright	RC	1.00
327	Felix Pie	RC	12.00
328	Andy Sisco	RC	1.00
329	Dustin Yount	RC	2.00
330	Andrew Dominique RC		1.50
331	Brian McCann	RC	100.00
332	Jose Contreras	RC	150.00
333	Corey Shafer	RC	10.00
334	Hanley Ramirez	RC	80.00
335	Ryan Shealy	RC	40.00
336	Kevin Youkilis	RC	40.00
337	Jason Kubel	RC	30.00
338	Aron Weston	RC	10.00
339	J.D. Durbin	RC	15.00
340	Gary Schneidmiller RC		15.00
341	Travis Ishikawa	RC	15.00
342	Ben Francisco	RC	10.00
343	Bobby Basham	RC	10.00
344	Joey Gomes	RC	10.00
345	Beau Kemp	RC	10.00
346	Thomari Story-Harden RC		10.00
347	Daryl Clark	RC	10.00
348	Bryan Bullington	RC	15.00
349	Rajai Davis	RC	10.00
350	Darrell Rasner	RC	10.00
351	Willie Mays		3.00

Refractors

TOM GLAVINE · P

Stars (1-165, 351): 2-4X
Rookies (166-350): .5-1.5X
X-Fractors (1-165, 351): 3-6X
X-Fractors (166-350): 1-2X
Uncirc.Gold Refractors (1-165): 5-10X
Gold Refractors (166-350): 2-3X
Production 170 Sets
Gold Refractors (331-350): 1-3X

Willie Mays Autograph

NM/M
Production 150
351AU Willie Mays 220.00

2003 Bowman Draft Picks & Prospects

GRADY SIZEMORE · OF

		NM/M
Complete Set (165):		35.00
Common Player:		.15
Common Rookie:		.25
Pack (5 + 2 Chrome):		12.00
Box (24):		240.00
BDP1	Dontrelle Willis	.40
BDP2	Freddy Sanchez	.15
BDP3	Miguel Cabrera	.50
BDP4	Ryan Ludwick	.15
BDP5	Ty Wigginton	.15
BDP6	Mark Teixeira	.50
BDP7	Trey Hodges	.15
BDP8	Laynce Nix	.15
BDP9	Antonio Perez	.15
BDP10	Jody Gerut	.15
BDP11	Jae Weong Seo	.15
BDP12	Erick Almonte	.15
BDP13	Lyle Overbay	.15
BDP14	Billy Traber	.15
BDP15	Andres Torres	.15
BDP16	Jose Valverde	.15
BDP17	Aaron Heilman	.15
BDP18	Brandon Larson	.15
BDP19	Jung Bong	.15
BDP20	Jesse Foppert	.15
BDP21	Angel Berroa	.15
BDP22	Jeff DaVanon	.15
BDP23	Kurt Ainsworth	.15
BDP24	Brandon Claussen	.15
BDP25	Xavier Nady	.15
BDP26	Travis Hafner	.40
BDP27	Jerome Williams	.15
BDP28	Jose Reyes	.40
BDP29	Sergio Mitre RC	.25
BDP30	Bo Hart RC	.75
BDP31	Adam Miller RC	4.00
BDP32	Brian Finch RC	.25
BDP33	Taylor Mattingly RC	.75
BDP34	Daric Barton RC	3.00
BDP35	Chris Ray RC	.25
BDP36	Jarrod Saltalamacchia RC	4.00
BDP37	Dennis Dove RC	.25
BDP38	James Houser RC	.50
BDP39	Clinton King RC	.50
BDP40	Lou Palmisano RC	.50
BDP41	Dan Moore RC	.50
BDP42	Craig Stansberry RC	.50
BDP43	Jo Jo Reyes RC	.75
BDP44	Jake Stevens RC	.75
BDP45	Tom Gorzelanny RC	.75
BDP46	Brian Marshall RC	.25
BDP47	Scott Beerer RC	.25
BDP48	Javi Herrera RC	.25
BDP49	Steve Lerud RC	.75
BDP50	Josh Banks RC	.75
BDP51	Jonathan Papelbon RC	10.00
BDP52	Juan Valdes RC	.50
BDP53	Beau Vaghan RC	.50
BDP54	Matt Chico RC	.50
BDP55	Todd Jennings RC	.25
BDP56	Tony Gwynn Jr. RC	1.00
BDP57	Matt Harrison RC	.25
BDP58	Aaron Mardsen RC	.25
BDP59	Casey Abrams RC	.25
BDP60	Cory Stuart RC	.25
BDP61	Mike Wagner RC	.25
BDP62	Jordan Pratt RC	.50
BDP63	Andre Randolph RC	.25
BDP64	Blake Balkcom RC	.25
BDP65	Josh Muecke RC	.25
BDP66	Jamie D'Antona RC	1.00
BDP67	Cole Seifrig RC	.50
BDP68	Josh Anderson RC	.25
BDP69	Matt Lorenzo RC	.25
BDP70	Nate Spears RC	.25
BDP71	Chris Goodman RC	.25
BDP72	Brian McFall RC	.25
BDP73	Billy Hogan RC	.25
BDP74	Jamie Romak RC	.25
BDP75	Jeff Cook RC	.50
BDP76	Brooks McNiven RC	.50
BDP77	Xavier Paul RC	1.00
BDP78	Bob Zimmerman RC	.25
BDP79	Mickey Hall RC	.25
BDP80	Shaun Marcum RC	.25
BDP81	Matt Nachreiner RC	.25
BDP82	Chris Kinsey RC	.25
BDP83	Jonathan Fulton RC	.50
BDP84	Edgardo Baez RC	.50
BDP85	Robert Valido RC	.75
BDP86	Kenny Lewis RC	.50
BDP87	Trent Peterson RC	.25
BDP88	Johnny Woodard RC	.25
BDP89	Wes Littleton RC	.50
BDP90	Sean Rodriguez RC	1.00
BDP91	Kyle Pearson RC	.25
BDP92	Josh Rainwater RC	.75
BDP93	Travis Schlichting RC	.50
BDP94	Tim Battle RC	.75
BDP95	Aaron Hill RC	.75
BDP96	Bob McCrory RC	.25
BDP97	Rick Guarno RC	.25
BDP98	Brandon Yarbrough RC	.25
BDP99	Peter Stonard RC	.50
BDP100	Darin Downs RC	.50
BDP101	Matt Bruback RC	.25
BDP102	Danny Garcia RC	.25
BDP103	Cory Stewart RC	.25
BDP104	Ferdin Tejeda RC	.50
BDP105	Kade Johnson RC	.25
BDP106	Andrew Brown RC	.25
BDP107	Aquilino Lopez RC	.25
BDP108	Stephen Randolph RC	.25
BDP109	Dave Matranga RC	.25
BDP110	Dustin McGowan RC	.75
BDP111	Juan Camacho RC	.50
BDP112	Cliff Lee	.15
BDP113	Jeff Duncan RC	.50
BDP114	C.J. Wilson	.25
BDP115	Brandon Roberson RC	.25
BDP116	David Corrente RC	.25
BDP117	Kevin Beavers RC	.25
BDP118	Anthony Webster RC	.50
BDP119	Oscar Villarreal RC	.25
BDP120	Hong-Chih Kuo RC	2.00
BDP121	Josh Barfield RC	.15
BDP122	Denny Bautista RC	.15
BDP123	Chris Burke	.75
BDP124	Robinson Cano RC	10.00
BDP125	Jose Castillo	.15
BDP126	Neal Cotts	.15
BDP127	Jorge De La Rosa	.15
BDP128	J.D. Durbin	.15
BDP129	Edwin Encarnacion	.50
BDP130	Gavin Floyd	.15
BDP131	Alexis Gomez	.15
BDP132	Edgar Gonzalez RC	.25
BDP133	Khalil Greene	.25
BDP134	Zack Greinke	.15
BDP135	Franklin Gutierrez	.15
BDP136	Rich Harden	.15
BDP137	J.J. Hardy	1.50
BDP138	Ryan Howard	25.00
BDP139	Justin Huber	.15
BDP140	David Kelton	.15
BDP141	David Krynzel	.15
BDP142	Pete LaForest	.15
BDP143	Adam LaRoche	.15
BDP144	Preston Larrison	.15
BDP145	John Maine RC	2.00
BDP146	Andy Marte	1.00
BDP147	Jeff Mathis	.15
BDP148	Joe Mauer	.50
BDP149	Clint Nageotte	.15
BDP150	Chris Narveson	.15
BDP151	Ramon Nivar RC	.50
BDP152	Felix Pie RC	4.00
BDP153	Guillermo Quiroz RC	.50
BDP154	Rene Reyes	.15
BDP155	Royce Ring	.15
BDP156	Alexis Rios	.75
BDP157	Grady Sizemore	.75
BDP158	Stephen Smitherman	.15
BDP159	Seung Jun Song	.15
BDP160	Scott Thorman	.15
BDP161	Chad Tracy	.15
BDP162	Chin-Hui Tsao	.15
BDP163	John Van Benschoten RC	.25
BDP164	Kevin Youkilis	1.00
BDP165	Chien-Ming Wang	3.00

Gold

JEFF COOK · OF

Cards (1-165): 1-2X
Inserted 1:1

Fabric of Future

		NM/M
Common Player:		4.00
JB	Josh Barfield	6.00
RC	Robinson Cano	25.00

fabric of... FUTURES — Adam LaRoche

JD	J.D. Durbin	4.00
GF	Gavin Floyd	4.00
EG	Edgar Gonzalez	4.00
KG	Khalil Greene	8.00
ZG	Zack Greinke	4.00
FG	Franklin Gutierrez	4.00
RH	Rich Harden	4.00
RJH	Ryan Howard	50.00
JH	Justin Huber	5.00
AL	Adam LaRoche	8.00
AM	Andy Marte	8.00
JSM	Jeff Mathis	6.00
JM	Joe Mauer	10.00
CN	Chris Narveson	4.00
FP	Felix Pie	15.00
RR	Rene Reyes	4.00
RRR	Royce Ring	4.00
GS	Grady Sizemore	10.00

Prospect Premiums

		NM/M
Common Player:		4.00
RB	Rocco Baldelli	6.00
HB	Hank Blalock	6.00
CC	Carl Crawford	5.00
TH	Travis Hafner	8.00
BH	Brendan Harris	4.00
NH	Nathan Haynes	4.00
JM	Justin Morneau	8.00
CS	Chris Snelling	4.00
JT	Joe Thurston	4.00
CU	Chase Utley	10.00

Signs of the Future

		NM/M
Common Player:		5.00
JA	Jason Arnold	5.00
ZG	Zack Greinke	15.00
CS	Cory Stewart	5.00
DT	Dennis Tankersley	5.00
AT	Andres Torres	8.00

2003 Bowman Chrome Draft Picks & Prospects

BO HART · 2B

		NM/M
Complete Set (176):		500.00
Common Player:		.25
Common Rookie:		1.00
Common RK Autograph (166-176):		10.00
BDP1	Dontrelle Willis	.75
BDP2	Freddy Sanchez	.75
BDP3	Miguel Cabrera	.75
BDP4	Ryan Ludwick	.25
BDP5	Ty Wigginton	.25
BDP6	Mark Teixeira	.75
BDP7	Trey Hodges	.25
BDP8	Laynce Nix	.25
BDP9	Antonio Perez	.25
BDP10	Jody Gerut	.25
BDP11	Jae Weong Seo	.25
BDP12	Erick Almonte	.25
BDP13	Lyle Overbay	.25
BDP14	Billy Traber	.25
BDP15	Andres Torres	.25
BDP16	Jose Valverde	.25
BDP17	Aaron Heilman	.25
BDP18	Brandon Larson	.25
BDP19	Jung Bong	.25
BDP20	Jesse Foppert	.25
BDP21	Angel Berroa	.25
BDP22	Jeff DaVanon	.25
BDP23	Kurt Ainsworth	.25
BDP24	Brandon Claussen	.25
BDP25	Xavier Nady	.25
BDP26	Travis Hafner	.75
BDP27	Jerome Williams	.25
BDP28	Jose Reyes	.50
BDP29	Sergio Mitre RC	1.00
BDP30	Bo Hart RC	1.00
BDP31	Adam Miller RC	12.00
BDP32	Brian Finch RC	1.00
BDP33	Taylor Mattingly RC	2.00
BDP34	Daric Barton RC	10.00
BDP35	Chris Ray RC	2.00
BDP36	Jarrod Saltalamacchia RC	15.00
BDP37	Dennis Dove RC	1.00
BDP38	James Houser RC	1.50
BDP39	Clinton King RC	1.00
BDP40	Lou Palmisano RC	1.00
BDP41	Dan Moore RC	1.00
BDP42	Craig Stansberry RC	1.50
BDP43	Jo Jo Reyes RC	2.00
BDP44	Jake Stevens RC	1.00
BDP45	Tom Gorzelanny RC	3.00
BDP46	Brian Marshall RC	1.50
BDP47	Scott Beerer RC	1.00
BDP48	Javi Herrera RC	1.50
BDP49	Steve Lerud RC	2.00
BDP50	Josh Banks RC	2.00
BDP51	Jonathan Papelbon RC	30.00
BDP52	Juan Valdes RC	1.50
BDP53	Beau Vaghan RC	1.50
BDP54	Matt Chico RC	2.00
BDP55	Todd Jennings RC	1.50
BDP56	Tony Gwynn Jr. RC	2.50
BDP57	Matt Harrison RC	2.00
BDP58	Aaron Mardsen RC	1.50
BDP59	Casey Abrams RC	1.50
BDP60	Cory Stuart RC	1.50
BDP61	Mike Wagner RC	1.00
BDP62	Jordan Pratt RC	1.50
BDP63	Andre Randolph RC	1.00
BDP64	Blake Balkcom RC	1.00
BDP65	Josh Muecke RC	1.00
BDP66	Jamie D'Antona RC	4.00
BDP67	Cole Seifrig RC	2.50
BDP68	Josh Anderson RC	2.00
BDP69	Matt Lorenzo RC	1.50
BDP70	Nate Spears RC	1.50
BDP71	Chris Goodman RC	1.50
BDP72	Brian McFall RC	1.50
BDP73	Billy Hogan RC	1.50
BDP74	Jamie Romak RC	1.50
BDP75	Jeff Cook RC	1.50
BDP76	Brooks McNiven RC	1.00
BDP77	Xavier Paul RC	2.00
BDP78	Bob Zimmerman RC	1.00
BDP79	Mickey Hall RC	1.00
BDP80	Shaun Marcum RC	1.00
BDP81	Matt Nachreiner RC	1.00
BDP82	Chris Kinsey RC	1.00
BDP83	Jonathan Fulton RC	1.50
BDP84	Edgardo Baez RC	1.50
BDP85	Robert Valido RC	2.00
BDP86	Kenny Lewis RC	1.50
BDP87	Trent Peterson RC	1.00
BDP88	Johnny Woodard RC	1.00
BDP89	Wes Littleton RC	1.00
BDP90	Sean Rodriguez RC	4.00
BDP91	Kyle Pearson RC	1.00
BDP92	Josh Rainwater RC	2.50
BDP93	Travis Schlichting RC	1.00
BDP94	Tim Battle RC	2.00
BDP95	Aaron Hill RC	2.50
BDP96	Bob McCrory RC	1.00
BDP97	Rick Guarno RC	1.00
BDP98	Brandon Yarbrough RC	1.00
BDP99	Peter Stonard RC	1.50
BDP100	Darin Downs RC	1.50
BDP101	Matt Bruback RC	1.00
BDP102	Danny Garcia RC	1.00
BDP103	Cory Stewart RC	1.50
BDP104	Ferdin Tejeda RC	1.50
BDP105	Kade Johnson RC	1.00
BDP106	Andrew Brown RC	2.00
BDP107	Aquilino Lopez RC	1.00
BDP108	Stephen Randolph RC	1.00
BDP109	Dave Matranga RC	1.50
BDP110	Dustin McGowan RC	1.50
BDP111	Juan Camacho RC	1.50
BDP112	Cliff Lee	.15
BDP113	Jeff Duncan RC	1.00
BDP114	C.J. Wilson	.50
BDP115	Brandon Roberson RC	1.00
BDP116	David Corrente RC	1.00
BDP117	Kevin Beavers RC	1.00
BDP118	Anthony Webster RC	1.50
BDP119	Oscar Villarreal RC	1.00
BDP120	Hong-Chih Kuo RC	6.00
BDP121	Josh Barfield	.15
BDP122	Denny Bautista	.15
BDP123	Chris Burke	4.00
BDP124	Robinson Cano RC	30.00
BDP125	Jose Castillo	.15
BDP126	Neal Cotts	.15
BDP127	Jorge De La Rosa	.15
BDP128	J.D. Durbin	.15
BDP129	Edwin Encarnacion	2.00
BDP130	Gavin Floyd	.15
BDP131	Alexis Gomez	.15
BDP132	Edgar Gonzalez RC	1.00
BDP133	Khalil Greene	.50
BDP134	Zack Greinke	.50
BDP135	Franklin Gutierrez	2.00
BDP136	Rich Harden	.15
BDP137	J.J. Hardy	5.00
BDP138	Ryan Howard	75.00
BDP139	Justin Huber	.15
BDP140	David Kelton	.15
BDP141	David Krynzel	.15
BDP142	Pete LaForest	.15
BDP143	Adam LaRoche	.15
BDP144	Preston Larrison	.15
BDP145	John Maine RC	8.00
BDP146	Andy Marte	5.00
BDP147	Jeff Mathis	.15
BDP148	Joe Mauer	1.00
BDP149	Clint Nageotte	.15
BDP150	Chris Narveson	.15
BDP151	Ramon Nivar RC	.15
BDP152	Felix Pie	8.00
BDP153	Guillermo Quiroz RC	.15
BDP154	Rene Reyes	.15
BDP155	Royce Ring	.15
BDP156	Alexis Rios	2.50
BDP157	Grady Sizemore	1.00
BDP158	Stephen Smitherman	.15
BDP159	Seung Jun Song	.15
BDP160	Scott Thorman	.15
BDP161	Chad Tracy	.15
BDP162	Chin-Hui Tsao	.15
BDP163	John Van Benschoten RC	1.00
BDP164	Kevin Youkilis	3.00
BDP165	Chien-Ming Wang	6.00
BDP166	Chris Lubanski/ Auto. RC	40.00
BDP167	Ryan Harvey/ Auto.	30.00
BDP168	Matt Murton/ Auto. RC	30.00
BDP169	Jay Sborz/ Auto. RC	10.00
BDP170	Brandon Wood/ Auto. RC	100.00
BDP171	Nicholas Markakis/ Auto.	85.00
BDP172	Rickie Weeks/ Auto. RC	60.00
BDP173	Eric Duncan/ Auto.	35.00
BDP174	Chad Billingsley/ Auto.	50.00
BDP175	Ryan Wagner/ Auto. RC	10.00
BDP176	Delmon Young/ Auto. RC	200.00

Refractor

JOHN MAINE · P

Rookies (29-165): 2-4X
Inserted 1:11
Autos. (166-176): .75-1.5X
Inserted 1:196

Gold Refractor

Rookies (29-165): 3-5X
Production 50 Sets
Autos. (166-176): No Pricing
Inserted 1:1,479

X-Fractor

BROOKS McNIVEN · P

Rookies (29-165): 2-4X
Production 130 Sets
Autos. (166-176): .75-2X
Inserted 1:393

2003 Bowman Heritage

	NM/M
Complete Set (280):	60.00

MIGUEL CABRERA • Third Base • MARLINS

Common Player: .25
Cards 171-180 have 3 versions.
Pack (8): 4.00
Box (24): 80.00

1	Jorge Posada	.50
2	Todd Helton	.75
3	Marcus Giles	.25
4	Eric Chavez	.40
5	Edgar Martinez	.25
6	Luis Gonzalez	.40
7	Corey Patterson	.25
8	Preston Wilson	.25
9	Ryan Klesko	.25
10	Randy Johnson	1.00
11	Eric Byrnes	.25
12	Carlos Lee	.40
13	Steve Finley	.25
14	A.J. Pierzynski	.25
15	Troy Glaus	.50
16	Darin Erstad	.40
17	Moises Alou	.40
18	Torii Hunter	.50
19	Marlon Byrd	.25
20	Mark Prior	.75
21	Shannon Stewart	.25
22	Craig Biggio	.40
23	Johnny Damon	.75
24	Robert Fick	.25
25	Jason Giambi	.75
26	Fernando Vina	.25
27	Aubrey Huff	.25
28	Benito Santiago	.25
29	Jay Gibbons	.25
30	Ken Griffey Jr.	2.00
31	Rocco Baldelli	.50
32	Pat Burrell	.50
33	A.J. Burnett	.25
34	Omar Vizquel	.25
35	Greg Maddux	1.50
36	Jae Weong Seo	.25
37	C.C. Sabathia	.25
38	Geoff Jenkins	.25
39	Ty Wigginton	.25
40	Jeff Kent	.40
41	Orlando Hudson	.25
42	Edgardo Alfonzo	.25
43	Greg Myers	.25
44	Melvin Mora	.25
45	Sammy Sosa	1.00
46	Russ Ortiz	.25
47	Josh Beckett	.50
48	David Wells	.25
49	Woody Williams	.25
50	Alex Rodriguez	2.00
51	Randy Wolf	.25
52	Carlos Beltran	.75
53	Austin Kearns	.40
54	Trot Nixon	.25
55	Ivan Rodriguez	.75
56	Shea Hillenbrand	.25
57	Roberto Alomar	.40
58	John Olerud	.25
59	Michael Young	.25
60	Garret Anderson	.25
61	Mike Lieberthal	.25
62	Adam Dunn	.50
63	Raul Ibanez	.25
64	Kenny Lofton	.25
65	Ichiro Suzuki	1.50
66	Jarrod Washburn	.25
67	Shawn Chacon	.25
68	Alex Gonzalez	.25
69	Roy Halladay	.40
70	Vladimir Guerrero	1.00
71	Hee Seop Choi	.25
72	Brandon Phillips	.25
73	Ray Durham	.25
74	Mark Teixeira	.75
75	Hank Blalock	.40
76	Jerry Hairston Jr.	.25
77	Erubiel Durazo	.25
78	Frank Catalanotto	.25
79	Jacque Jones	.25
80	Bobby Abreu	.50
81	Mike Hampton	.25
82	Zach Day	.25
83	Jimmy Rollins	.50
84	Joel Pineiro	.25
85	Brett Myers	.25
86	Frank Thomas	.75
87	Aramis Ramirez	.40
88	Paul LoDuca	.25
89	Bobby Higginson	.25
90	Brian Giles	.25
91	Jose Cruz Jr.	.25
92	Derek Lowe	.25
93	Mark Buehrle	.25
94	Wade Miller	.25
95	Derek Jeter	2.00
96	Bret Boone	.25
97	Tony Batista	.25
98	Sean Casey	.25
99	Eric Hinske	.25
100	Albert Pujols	2.00
101	Runelvys Hernandez	.25
102	Vernon Wells	.40
103	Kerry Wood	.25
104	Lance Berkman	.50
105	Alfonso Soriano	1.00
106	Ken Harvey	.25
107	Bartolo Colon	.25
108	Andy Pettitte	.40
109	Rafael Furcal	.40
110	Dontrelle Willis	.40
111	Carl Crawford	.40
112	Scott Rolen	.75
113	Chipper Jones	1.00
114	Magglio Ordonez	.50
115	Bernie Williams	.50
116	Roy Oswalt	.50
117	Kevin Brown	.35
118	Cristian Guzman	.25
119	Kazuhisa Ishii	.25
120	Larry Walker	.40
121	Miguel Tejada	.50
122	Manny Ramirez	1.00
123	Mike Mussina	.50
124	Mike Lowell	.40
125	Barry Bonds	2.00
126	Aaron Boone	.25
127	Carlos Delgado	.60
128	Jose Vidro	.25
129	Brad Radke	.25
130	Rafael Palmeiro	.75
131	Mark Mulder	.40
132	Jason Schmidt	.40
133	Gary Sheffield	.50
134	Richie Sexson	.40
135	Barry Zito	.50
136	Tom Glavine	.40
137	Jim Edmonds	.40
138	Andruw Jones	.75
139	Pedro J. Martinez	1.00
140	Curt Schilling	.75
141	Joe Kennedy	.25
142	Nomar Garciaparra	1.00
143	Vicente Padilla	.25
144	Kevin Millwood	.40
145	Shawn Green	.40
146	Jeff Bagwell	.75
147	Hideo Nomo	.50
148	Fred McGriff	.50
149	Matt Morris	.25
150	Roger Clemens	2.00
151	Damian Moss	.25
152	Orlando Cabrera	.25
153	Tim Hudson	.40
154	Mike Sweeney	.25
155	Jim Thome	.75
156	Rich Aurilia	.25
157	Mike Piazza	1.00
158	Edgar Renteria	.25
159	Javy Lopez	.25
160	Jamie Moyer	.25
161	Miguel Cabrera	.75
162	Adam Loewen RC	1.00
163	Jose Reyes	.50
164	Zack Greinke	.25
165	Cole Hamels	.25
166	Jeremy Guthrie	.25
167	Victor Martinez	.40
168	Rich Harden	.25
169	Joe Mauer	.75
170	Khalil Greene	.25
171	Willie Mays	2.00
172	Phil Rizzuto	.50
173	Al Kaline	1.00
174	Warren Spahn	1.00
175	Jimmy Piersall	.50
176	Luis Aparicio	.50
177	Whitey Ford	1.00
178	Harmon Killebrew	1.00
179	Duke Snider	1.00
180	Bobby Richardson	.50
181	David Martinez	.25
182	Felix Pie RC	3.00
183	Kevin Correia RC	.50
184	Brandon Webb RC	2.50
185	Matt Diaz RC	.50
186	Lew Ford RC	.50
187	Jeremy Griffiths	.50
188	Matt Hensley RC	.75
189	Danny Garcia RC	.50
190	Elizardo Ramirez RC	.50
191	Greg Aquino RC	.50
192	Felix Sanchez RC	.50
193	Kelly Shoppach RC	.75
194	Bubba Nelson RC	.50
195	Mike O'Keefe RC	.50
196	Hanley Ramirez RC	4.00
197	Todd Wellemeyer RC	.50
198	Dustin Moseley RC	.75
199	Eric Crozier RC	.50
200	Ryan Shealy RC	1.50
201	Jeremy Bonderman	2.00
202	Bo Hart RC	.50
203	Dusty Brown RC	.50
204	Rob Hammock RC	.50
205	Jorge Piedra RC	.50
206	Jason Kubel RC	.50
207	Stephen Randolph RC	.50
208	Andy Sisco RC	.50
209	Matt Kata RC	.50
210	Robinson Cano RC	12.00
211	Ben Francisco RC	.50
212	Arnie Munoz RC	.50
213	Ozzie Chavez RC	.50
214	Beau Kemp RC	.50
215	Travis Wong RC	.50
216	Brian McCann RC	5.00
217	Aquilino Lopez RC	.50
218	Bobby Basham RC	.50
219	Tim Olson RC	.50
220	Nathan Panther RC	.50
221	Wilfredo Ledezma RC	.50
222	Josh Willingham RC	1.00
223	David Cash RC	.50
224	Oscar Villarreal RC	.50
225	Jeff Duncan RC	.75
226	Dan Haren RC	.50
227	Michel Hernandez RC	.50
228	Matt Murton RC	1.50
229	Clay Hensley RC	.75
230	Tyler Johnson RC	.50
231	Tyler Martin RC	.50
232	J.D. Durbin RC	.75
233	Shane Victorino RC	.50
234	Rajai Davis RC	.50
235	Chien-Ming Wang RC	6.00
236	Travis Ishikawa RC	.50
237	Eric Eckenstahler	.25
238	Dustin McGowan RC	.50
239	Prentice Redman RC	.50
240	Haj Turay RC	.50
241	Matt DeMarco RC	.50
242	Lou Palmisano RC	.50
243	Eric Reed RC	.50
244	Willie Eyre RC	.50
245	Ferdin Tejeda RC	.75
246	Michael Garciaparra RC	.50
247	Michael Hinckley RC	.50
248	Branden Florence RC	.50
249	Trent Oeltjen RC	.50
250	Mike Neu RC	.75
251	Chris Lubanski RC	1.50
252	Brandon Wood RC	8.00
253	Delmon Young RC	5.00
253	Delmon Young/ Auto. RC	130.00
254	Matt Harrison RC	.50
255	Chad Billingsley RC	2.00
256	Josh Anderson RC	.50
257	Brian McFall RC	.50
258	Ryan Wagner RC	.50
259	Billy Hogan RC	.50
260	Nate Spears RC	.50
261	Ryan Harvey RC	2.00
262	Wes Littleton RC	.50
263	Xavier Paul RC	.75
264	Sean Rodriguez RC	1.50
265	Brian Finch RC	.50
266	Josh Rainwater RC	.50
267	Brian Snyder RC	.75
268	Eric Duncan RC	1.50
269	Rickie Weeks RC	2.00
270	Tim Battle RC	.50
271	Scott Beerer RC	.50
272	Aaron Hill RC	.75
273	Casey Abrams RC	.50
274	Jonathan Fulton RC	.50
275	Todd Jennings RC	.50
276	Jordan Pratt RC	.50
277	Tom Gorzelanny RC	1.00
278	Matt Lorenzo RC	.75
279	Jarrod Saltalamacchia RC	3.00
280	Mike Wagner RC	.50

Diamond Cuts

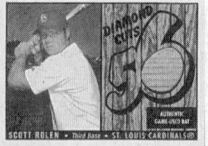

SCOTT ROLEN • Third Base • ST. LOUIS CARDINALS

		NM/M
Common Player:		4.00
Red:		1-2X
Production 56 Sets		
JA	Jeremy Affeldt	4.00
MA	Moises Alou	5.00
TA	Tony Armas Jr.	4.00
JB	Jeff Bagwell	6.00
CB	Craig Biggio	6.00
HB	Hank Blalock	6.00
BB	Bret Boone	4.00
EC	Eric Chavez	4.00
JE	Jim Edmonds	6.00
JG	Jason Giambi	8.00
TG	Troy Glaus	6.00
MG	Mark Grace	6.00
VG	Vladimir Guerrero	8.00
CG	Cristian Guzman	4.00
TH	Todd Helton	8.00
RH	Rickey Henderson	12.00
JJ	Jason Jennings	4.00
AJ	Andruw Jones	6.00
CJ1	Chipper Jones/Jsy	8.00
CJ2	Chipper Jones/Bat	8.00
AK	Austin Kearns	4.00
PL	Paul LoDuca	4.00
JL	Javy Lopez	4.00
PM	Pedro J. Martinez	4.00
KM	Kevin Millwood	4.00
MM	Mark Mulder	4.00
BM	Brett Myers	4.00
HN	Hideo Nomo	8.00
RP1	Rafael Palmeiro/Jsy	8.00
RP2	Rafael Palmeiro/Bat	8.00
JLP	Josh Phelps	4.00
AP	Albert Pujols	15.00
JR	Jose Reyes	8.00
AR1	Alex Rodriguez/Jsy	10.00
AR2	Alex Rodriguez/Bat	10.00
SR1	Scott Rolen/Jsy	8.00
SR2	Scott Rolen/Bat	10.00
KI	Kazuhiro Sasaki	4.00
GS	Gary Sheffield	6.00
AS	Alfonso Soriano	8.00
SS1	Sammy Sosa/Jsy	10.00
SS2	Sammy Sosa/Bat	10.00
MS	Mike Sweeney	4.00
MT	Miguel Tejada	6.00
JV	Javier Vazquez	4.00
JW	Jarrod Washburn	4.00
VW	Vernon Wells	4.00
BW	Bernie Williams	6.00
KW	Kerry Wood	5.00
BZ	Barry Zito	6.00

Keith Olbermann Autograph

KEITH OLBERMANN

		NM/M
Inserted 1:1,421		
KO	Keith Olbermann	50.00

Signs of Greatness

		NM/M
Common Player:		6.00
Inserted 1:30		
Red Ink:		No Pricing
Production One Set		
CB	Chad Billingsley	25.00
RC	Robinson Cano	200.00
JD	Jeff Duncan	8.00
BF	Brian Finch	8.00
TG	Tom Gorzelanny	15.00
RH	Rich Harden	20.00
MM	Matt Murton	20.00
FP	Felix Pie	30.00
BS	Brian Snyder	8.00
RW	Rickie Weeks	25.00
DW	Dontrelle Willis	25.00
KY	Kevin Youkilis	25.00

2003 Bowman's Best

DAN HAREN

		NM/M
Complete Set:		
Common Player:		.50
Pack (5):		50.00
Box (10):		450.00
Veterans		
GJA	Garret Anderson	.50
LB	Lance Berkman	.75
BLB	Barry Bonds	
PB	Pat Burrell	.50
WRC	Roger Clemens	
NG	Nomar Garciaparra	1.50
JGG	Jason Giambi	1.00
BSG	Brian Giles	
SG	Shawn Green	.50
KG	Ken Griffey Jr.	2.50
VG	Vladimir Guerrero	1.50
TH	Todd Helton	1.00
TKH	Torii Hunter	.75
DJ	Derek Jeter	4.00
RJ	Randy Johnson	1.50
CJ	Chipper Jones	1.50
AK	Austin Kearns	.50
JFK	Jeff Kent	.50
GM	Greg Maddux	1.50
PM	Pedro J. Martinez	1.50
MOR	Magglio Ordonez	1.00
MJP	Mike Piazza	1.50
MP	Mark Prior	1.50
AP	Albert Pujols	4.00
MR	Manny Ramirez	1.50
AR	Alex Rodriguez	1.50
CMS	Curt Schilling	1.50
AS	Alfonso Soriano	1.50
SS	Sammy Sosa	2.50
IS	Ichiro Suzuki	2.50
MS	Mike Sweeney	1.00
MT	Miguel Tejada	1.00
JT	Jim Thome	1.00
LW	Larry Walker	.50
BZ	Barry Zito	.75
First-Year Players		
JB	Jeremy Bonderman	4.00
TJB	T.J. Bohn	1.00
MB	Matt Bruback	1.00
BC	Bernie Castro RC	1.00
JC	Jose Contreras RC	2.00
MD	Matt Diaz	2.00
BJH	Bo Hart	1.00
RM	Ramon Martinez	1.00
MO	Mike O'Keefe	1.00
JMS	Jon-Mark Sprowl RC	1.00
TT	Terry Tiffee	1.00
HT	Haj Turay	2.00
SV	Shane Victorino RC	3.00
CW	Chien-Ming Wang RC	15.00
DY	Dustin Yount RC	2.00
First-Year Player Autographs		
Common Auto.:		8.00
Inserted 1:1		
TA	Tyler Adamczyk RC	8.00
GA	Greg Aquino RC	8.00
BWB	Bobby Basham RC	8.00
GB	Gregor Blanco RC	10.00
AB	Andrew Brown RC	8.00
BB	Bryan Bullington RC	15.00
RC	Ryan Cameron RC	8.00
DC	David Cash RC	8.00
OC	Ozzie Chavez RC	8.00
RD	Rajai Davis RC	8.00
CDC	Chris De La Cruz RC	10.00
MD	Matt Diaz RC	8.00
CAD	Carlos Duran RC	10.00
JDD	J.D. Durbin RC	10.00
WE	Willie Eyre RC	8.00
BF	Branden Florence RC	10.00
LF	Lew Ford RC	8.00
BLF	Ben Francisco RC	10.00
JG	Joey Gomes	10.00
JRG	Jeremy Griffiths	10.00
MNH	Matt Hagen RC	10.00
RWH	Robby Hammock RC	10.00
DH	Dan Haren	20.00
BH	Brendan Harris RC	8.00
MDH	Matt Hensley RC	8.00
MH	Michel Hernandez	
MHI	Michael Hinckley RC	10.00
RH	Ryan Howard	600.00
TI	Travis Ishikawa RC	8.00
KJ	Kade Johnson RC	8.00
TJ	Tyler Johnson RC	8.00
MK	Matt Kata RC	8.00
BK	Beau Kemp RC	8.00
JK	Jason Kubel RC	25.00
PL	Pete LaForest RC	10.00
WL	Wilfredo Ledezma RC	10.00
NL	Nook Logan RC	10.00
MDM	Mark Malaska RC	8.00
CM	Charlie Manning RC	10.00
DM	David Martinez	10.00
AM	Aneudis Mateo RC	8.00
BM	Brian McCann	90.00
DMM	Dustin McGowan RC	10.00
JM	Jose Morales	10.00
DAM	Dustin Moseley RC	10.00
TO	Tim Olson RC	10.00
FP	Felix Pie RC	100.00
ER	Elizardo Ramirez RC	10.00
HR	Hanley Ramirez RC	65.00
DR	Darrell Rasner RC	8.00
PR	Prentice Redman RC	10.00
FS	Felix Sanchez RC	10.00
GS	Gary Schneidmiller RC	8.00
CSS	Corey Shafer RC	8.00
RS	Ryan Shealy RC	20.00
KS	Kelly Shoppach RC	15.00
CS	Cory Stewart RC	10.00
TSH	Thomari Story-Harden RC	8.00
FT	Ferdin Tejeda RC	10.00
ET	Eider Torres RC	10.00
ST	Scott Tyler	10.00
JV	Joe Valentine RC	8.00
OV	Oscar Villarreal RC	10.00
DW	Doug Waechter RC	10.00
AW	Aron Weston RC	8.00
JW	Josh Willingham RC	30.00
CJW	C.J. Wilson	10.00
KY	Kevin Youkilis RC	25.00
CW	Chien-Ming Wang RC	300.00

Blue

Blue Autographs: 1-1.5X
Inserted 1:32
Blue Base Card: 3-5X
Blue Rookies: 1-2X
Production 100

Red

Red Autographs: 2-4X
Inserted 1:63
Red Base Card: 4-8X
Red Rookies: 2-3X
Production 50

Double Play

		NM/M
Common Card:		20.00
Inserted 1:55		
EB	Elizardo Ramirez, Bryan Bullington	25.00
GK	Joey Gomes, Jason Kubel	50.00
SR	Felix Sanchez, Darrell Rasner	15.00
YS	Kevin Youkilis, Kelly Shoppach	40.00
HV	Dan Haren, Joe Valentine	15.00
GM	Jeremy Griffiths, David Martinez	15.00
HM	Michael Hinckley, Brian McCann	15.00
RS	Prentice Redman, Gary Schneidmiller	15.00
LL	Nook Logan, Wilfredo Ledezma	25.00
SB	Corey Shafer, Gregor Blanco	25.00

Triple Play

		NM/M
Inserted 1:219		
DRS	Rajai Davis, Hanley Ramirez, Ryan Shealy	85.00
BCS	Andrew Brown, David Cash, Cory Stewart	30.00

First-Year Player Relics

		NM/M
Common Player:		5.00
RLD	Rajai Davis	5.00
JLF	Lew Ford	8.00
JGG	Joey Gomes	5.00
RJH	Ryan Howard	100.00
JJK	Jason Kubel	8.00
HRB	Hanley Ramirez	15.00
RNS	Ryan Shealy	10.00
KBS	Kelly Shoppach	8.00
KEY	Kevin Youkilis	10.00

2004 Bowman

ROGER CLEMENS • P

		NM/M
Complete Set (330):		70.00
Common Player:		.15
Common Rookie:		.50
Pack (10):		3.00
Box (24):		60.00
1	Garret Anderson	.15
2	Larry Walker	.15
3	Derek Jeter	2.00
4	Curt Schilling	.75
5	Carlos Zambrano	.40
6	Shawn Green	.25
7	Manny Ramirez	.75
8	Randy Johnson	.75
9	Jeremy Bonderman	.25
10	Alfonso Soriano	.75
11	Scott Rolen	.75
12	Kerry Wood	.25
13	Eric Gagne	.25
14	Ryan Klesko	.15
15	Kevin Millar	.15
16	Ty Wigginton	.15
17	David Ortiz	.75
18	Luis Castillo	.15
19	Bernie Williams	.25
20	Edgar Renteria	.25
21	Matt Kata	.15
22	Bartolo Colon	.25
23	Derrek Lee	.50
24	Gary Sheffield	.50

#	Player	Price
25	Nomar Garciaparra	.75
26	Kevin Millwood	.25
27	Corey Patterson	.25
28	Carlos Beltran	.50
29	Mike Lieberthal	.15
30	Troy Glaus	.40
31	Preston Wilson	.15
32	Jorge Posada	.40
33	Bo Hart	.15
34	Mark Prior	.40
35	Hideo Nomo	.25
36	Jason Kendall	.15
37	Shea Hillenbrand	.15
38	Dmitri Young	.15
39	Aaron Boone	.15
40	Jim Edmonds	.40
41	Ryan Ludwick	.15
42	Brandon Webb	.25
43	Todd Helton	.50
44	Jacque Jones	.15
45	Xavier Nady	.15
46	Tim Salmon	.25
47	Kelvim Escobar	.15
48	Tony Batista	.15
49	Nick Johnson	.15
50	Jim Thome	.50
51	Casey Blake	.25
52	Trot Nixon	.25
53	Luis Gonzalez	.25
54	Dontrelle Willis	.25
55	Mike Mussina	.40
56	Carl Crawford	.25
57	Mark Buehrle	.25
58	Scott Podsednik	.25
59	Brian Giles	.15
60	Rafael Furcal	.25
61	Miguel Cabrera	.75
62	Rich Harden	.15
63	Mark Teixeira	.50
64	Frank Thomas	.75
65	Johan Santana	.50
66	Jason Schmidt	.25
67	Aramis Ramirez	.40
68	Jose Reyes	.75
69	Magglio Ordonez	.15
70	Mike Sweeney	.15
71	Eric Chavez	.25
72	Rocco Baldelli	.25
73	Jerry Hairston	.15
74	Javy Lopez	.25
75	Roy Oswalt	.25
76	Raul Ibanez	.15
77	Ivan Rodriguez	.50
78	Jerome Williams	.15
79	Carlos Lee	.25
80	Geoff Jenkins	.15
81	Sean Burroughs	.15
82	Marcus Giles	.15
83	Mike Lowell	.15
84	Barry Zito	.40
85	Aubrey Huff	.15
86	Esteban Loaiza	.15
87	Torii Hunter	.25
88	Phil Nevin	.15
89	Andruw Jones	.50
90	Josh Beckett	.40
91	Mark Mulder	.25
92	Hank Blalock	.15
93	Jason Phillips	.15
94	Russ Ortiz	.15
95	Juan Pierre	.15
96	Tom Glavine	.25
97	Gil Meche	.15
98	Ramon Ortiz	.15
99	Richie Sexson	.40
100	Albert Pujols	2.00
101	Javier Vazquez	.15
102	Johnny Damon	.75
103	Alex Rodriguez	1.50
104	Omar Vizquel	.25
105	Chipper Jones	.75
106	Lance Berkman	.40
107	Tim Hudson	.40
108	Carlos Delgado	.40
109	Austin Kearns	.25
110	Orlando Cabrera	.25
111	Edgar Martinez	.25
112	Melvin Mora	.15
113	Jeff Bagwell	.50
114	Marlon Byrd	.15
115	Vernon Wells	.25
116	C.C. Sabathia	3.00
117	Cliff Floyd	.15
118	Ichiro Suzuki	1.00
119	Miguel Olivo	.15
120	Mike Piazza	.75
121	Adam Dunn	.40
122	Paul Lo Duca	.15
123	Brett Myers	.15
124	Michael Young	.25
125	Larry Bigbie	.15
126	Greg Maddux	1.00
127	Vladimir Guerrero	.75
128	Miguel Tejada	.40
129	Andy Pettitte	.40
130	Jose Cruz	.15
131	Ken Griffey Jr.	1.50
132	Shannon Stewart	.15
133	Joel Pineiro	.15
134	Luis Matos	.15
135	Jeff Kent	.25
136	Randy Wolf	.15
137	Chris Woodward	.15
138	Jody Gerut	.15
139	Jose Vidro	.15
140	Bret Boone	.15
141	Bill Mueller	.15
142	Angel Berroa	.15

#	Player	Price
143	Bobby Abreu	.25
144	Roy Halladay	.25
145	Delmon Young	.50
146	Jonny Gomes	.15
147	Rickie Weeks	.40
148	Edwin Jackson	.15
149	Neal Cotts	.15
150	Jason Bay	.40
151	Khalil Greene	.25
152	Joe Mauer	.40
153	Bobby Jenks	.15
154	Chin-Feng Chen	.15
154	Chin-Feng Chen/Jsy	10.00
155	Chien-Ming Wang	.75
155	Chien-Ming Wang/Jsy	25.00
156	Mickey Hall	.15
156	Mickey Hall/Jsy	5.00
157	James Houser	.15
157	James Houser/Jsy	5.00
158	Jay Sborz	.15
158	Jay Sborz/Jsy	5.00
159	Jonathan Fulton	.15
159	Jonathan Fulton/Jsy	5.00
160	Steve Lerud	.15
160	Steve Lerud/Jsy	5.00
161	Grady Sizemore	.50
161	Grady Sizemore/Auto.	40.00
162	Felix Pie	.50
162	Felix Pie/Auto.	15.00
163	Dustin McGowan	.15
163	Dustin McGowan/Auto.	10.00
164	Chris Lubanski	.15
164	Chris Lubanski/Auto.	10.00
164	Chris Lubanski/Jsy	5.00
165	Tom Gorzelanny	.15
165	Tom Gorzelanny/Auto.	15.00
166	Rudy Guillen RC	1.00
166	Rudy Guillen/Auto.	10.00
167	Bobby Brownlie RC	1.00
167	Bobby Brownlie/Auto.	10.00
168	Conor Jackson	1.50
168	Conor Jackson/Auto.	30.00
169	Matt Moses	1.00
169	Matt Moses/Auto.	20.00
170	Ervin Santana	1.50
170	Ervin Santana/Auto.	20.00
171	Merkin Valdez RC	.50
171	Merkin Valdez/Auto.	10.00
172	Erick Aybar RC	1.00
172	Erick Aybar/Auto.	15.00
173	Brad Sullivan	.50
173	Brad Sullivan/Auto.	10.00
174	David Aardsma	.50
174	David Aardsma/Auto.	10.00
175	Brad Snyder	.75
175	Brad Snyder/Auto.	10.00
176	Alberto Callaspo RC	.50
177	Brandon Medders RC	.50
178	Zach Miner RC	1.00
179	Charlie Zink RC	.40
180	Adam Greenberg	.75
181	Kevin Howard RC	.50
182	Wanell Severino RC	.50
183	Kevin Kouzmanoff	2.00
184	Joel Zumaya RC	4.00
185	Skip Schumaker RC	.50
186	Nic Ungs RC	.50
187	Todd Self RC	.50
188	Brian Steffek RC	.50
189	Brock Peterson RC	.50
190	Greg Thissen RC	.50
191	Frank Brooks RC	.50
192	Estee Harris RC	.50
192	Estee Harris/Jsy RC	5.00
193	Chris Mabeus RC	.50
194	Daniel Giese RC	.50
195	Jared Wells RC	.50
196	Carlos Sosa RC	.50
197	Bobby Madritsch RC	.50
198	Calvin Hayes RC	.75
199	Omar Quintanilla RC	.50
200	Chris O'Riordan RC	.50
201	Tim Hutting RC	.50
202	Carlos Quentin	3.00
203	Brayan Pena RC	.50
204	Jeff Salazar RC	1.00
205	David Murphy	1.00
206	Alberto Garcia RC	.50
207	Ramon Ramirez RC	.50
208	Luis Bolivar RC	.50
209	Rodney Choy Foo RC	.50
210	Kyle Sleeth	.50
211	Anthony Acevedo RC	.50
212	Chad Santos RC	.50
213	Jason Frasor RC	.75
214	Jesse Roman RC	.50
215	James Tomlin RC	.50
216	Josh Labandeira RC	.75
217	Joaquin Arias RC	.50
218	Don Sutton RC (Photo actually Nick Swisher.)	1.50
219	Danny Gonzalez RC	.50
220	Javier Guzman RC	.50
221	Anthony Lerew RC	.50
221	Anthony Lerew/Jsy RC	5.00
222	Jon Knott RC	.50
223	Jesse English RC	.50
224	Felix Hernandez RC	8.00
225	Travis Hanson	.50

#	Player	Price
226	Jesse Floyd RC	.50
227	Nick Gorneault RC	.50
228	Craig Ansman RC	.50
229	Wardell Starling RC	.50
230	Carl Loadenthal RC	.50
231	David Crouthers RC	.50
232	Harvey Garcia RC	.50
233	Casey Kopitzke RC	.50
234	Ricky Nolasco RC	1.00
235	Miguel Perez RC	.50
236	Ryan Mulhern RC	.50
237	Chris Aguila RC	.50
238	Brooks Conrad RC	.50
239	Damaso Espino RC	.50
240	Jereme Milons RC	.50
241	Luke Hughes RC	.50
242	Kory Casto RC	.50
243	Jose Valdez RC	.50
244	J.T. Stotts	.50
245	Lee Gwaltney RC	.50
246	Yoann Torrealba RC	.50
247	Omar Falcon RC	.50
248	Jon Coutlangus RC	.50
249	George Sherrill RC	.50
250	John Santor RC	.50
251	Tony Richie RC	.50
252	Kevin Richardson RC	.50
253	Tim Bittner RC	.50
254	Dustin Nippert RC	1.00
255	Jose Capellan RC	.50
256	Donald Levinski	.50
257	Jerome Gamble RC	.50
258	Jeff Keppinger RC	.50
259	Jason Szuminski RC	.50
260	Akinori Otsuka RC	.50
261	Ryan Budde	.50
262	Shingo Takatsu RC	.75
263	Jeffrey Allison	.40
264	Hector Gimenez RC	.50
265	Tim Frend RC	.50
266	Tom Farmer RC	.50
267	Shawn Hill RC	.50
268	Lastings Milledge	5.00
269	Scott Proctor RC	.75
270	Jorge Mejia RC	.50
271	Terry Jones RC	.50
272	Zachary Duke RC	1.50
273	Tim Stauffer	.75
274	Luke Anderson RC	.50
275	Hunter Brown RC	.50
276	Matt Lemanczyk RC	.50
277	Fernando Cortez RC	.50
278	Vince Perkins RC	.50
279	Tommy Murphy RC	.50
280	Mike Gosling RC	.50
281	Paul Bacot RC	.50
282	Matt Capps RC	.75
283	Juan Gutierrez RC	.50
284	Teodoro Encarnacion RC	.50
285	Juan Cedeno RC	.50
286	Matt Creighton RC	.50
287	Ryan Hankins RC	.50
288	Leo Nunez RC	.50
289	Dave Wallace RC	.50
290	Rob Tejeda RC	.75
291	Lincoln Holdzkom RC	.50
292	Jason Hirsh	1.50
293	Tydus Meadows RC	.50
294	Khalid Ballouli RC	.50
295	Benji DeQuin RC	.50
296	Tyler Davidson RC	1.00
297	Brent Colamarino RC	.50
298	Marcus McBeth RC	.50
299	Brad Eldred RC	.75
300	David Pauley RC	.50
301	Yadier Molina RC	1.00
302	Chris Shelton RC	1.00
303	Travis Blackley RC	.50
304	Jon DeVries RC	.50
305	Sheldon Fulse RC	.50
306	Vito Chiaravalloti RC	.50
307	Warner Madrigal RC	.75
308	Reid Gorecki RC	.50
309	Sung Jung RC	.50
310	Peter Shier RC	.50
311	Michael Mooney RC	.50
312	Kenny Perez RC	.50
313	Mike Mallory RC	.50
314	Ben Himes RC	.50
315	Ivan Ochoa RC	.50
316	Donald Kelly RC	.50
317	Logan Kensing RC	.50
318	Kevin Davidson RC	.50
319	Brian Pilkington RC	.50
320	Alex Romero RC	.50
321	Chad Chop RC	.50
322	Dioner Navarro RC	.75
323	Casey Myers RC	.50
324	Mike Rouse	.50
325	Sergio Silva RC	.50
326	J.J. Furmaniak RC	.75
327	Brad Vericker RC	.50
328	Blake Hawksworth RC	1.00
329	Brock Jacobsen RC	.50
330	Alec Zumwalt RC	.50

Gold

Stars:	1-2X
Rookies:	1-2X

Inserted 1:1

Stars:	4-8X
Rookies:	3-5X
Production 245 Sets	

1st Edition

	NM/M
Stars:	3-5X
Rookies:	1-2X
HTA Exclusive	
Pack (10):	4.00
Box (20):	75.00

Base of the Future Autographed Relic

	NM/M
HTA Exclusive	
GS Grady Sizemore	40.00

Futures Game Gear

	NM/M
Common Player:	4.00
DB Denny Bautista	6.00
CB Chris Burke	6.00
JC Jose Castillo	4.00
NC Neal Cotts	5.00
JD Jorge De La Rosa	4.00
EE Edwin Encarnacion	8.00
SH Shawn Hill	4.00
EJ Edwin Jackson	4.00
DK David Kelton	4.00
DBK David Krynzel	4.00
PL Pete LaForest	4.00
JM John Maine	10.00
CN Clint Nageotte	6.00
RN Ramon Nivar	4.00
GQ Guillermo Quiroz	4.00
AR Alexis Rios	8.00
ES Ervin Santana	4.00
SS Stephen Smitherman	4.00
SJS Seung Jun Song	4.00
CT Chad Tracy	8.00
ST Scott Thorman	8.00
MV Merkin Valdez	4.00
JV John VanBenschoten	6.00
CW Chien-Ming Wang	40.00
KY Kevin Youkilis	10.00

Rookie of the Year Dual Relic

	NM/M
Inserted 1:829	
BW Angel Berroa, Dontrelle Willis	15.00

Signs of Future

	NM/M
Common Autograph:	8.00
Red Ink:	No Pricing
Production 25 Sets	
JB Justin Backsmeyer	10.00
IC Ismael Castro	8.00

BC Brent Clevelen	20.00
ED Eric Duncan	15.00
BF Brian Finch	8.00
RH Ryan Harvey	15.00
AH Aaron Hill	12.00
JH James Houser	8.00
TJ Tyler Johnson	8.00
TL Todd Linden	8.00
NM Nicholas Markakis	30.00
BM Brandon Medders	8.00
MM Matt Murton	12.00
CS Corey Shafer	8.00
GS Grady Sizemore	40.00
BS Brian Snyder	8.00
DS Denard Span	8.00
JV Joey Votto	30.00
BW Brandon Wood	35.00

2004 Bowman Chrome

	NM/M
Complete Set (350):	
Common Player:	.25
Common Rookie:	1.00
Common Rookie Auto. (331-350):	10.00
Inserted 1:18	
Pack (4):	7.00
Box (18):	120.00

#	Player	Price
1	Garret Anderson	.50
2	Larry Walker	.50
3	Derek Jeter	2.50
4	Curt Schilling	.75
5	Carlos Zambrano	.50
6	Shawn Green	.50
7	Manny Ramirez	1.00
8	Randy Johnson	1.00
9	Jeremy Bonderman	.50
10	Alfonso Soriano	.50
11	Scott Rolen	1.00
12	Kerry Wood	.50
13	Eric Gagne	.50
14	Ryan Klesko	.25
15	Kevin Millar	.25
16	Ty Wigginton	.25
17	David Ortiz	1.50
18	Luis Castillo	.25
19	Bernie Williams	.50
20	Edgar Renteria	.25
21	Matt Kata	.25
22	Bartolo Colon	.25
23	Derrek Lee	.75
24	Gary Sheffield	.50
25	Nomar Garciaparra	1.00
26	Kevin Millwood	.25
27	Corey Patterson	.50
28	Carlos Beltran	.75
29	Mike Lieberthal	.25
30	Troy Glaus	.50
31	Preston Wilson	.25
32	Jorge Posada	.50
33	Bo Hart	.25
34	Mark Prior	.75
35	Hideo Nomo	.50
36	Jason Kendall	.25
37	Roger Clemens	2.50
38	Dmitri Young	.25
39	Jason Giambi	.75
40	Jim Edmonds	.75
41	Ryan Ludwick	.25
42	Brandon Webb	.50
43	Todd Helton	.75
44	Jacque Jones	.25
45	Jamie Moyer	.25
46	Tim Salmon	.50
47	Kelvim Escobar	.25
48	Tony Batista	.25
49	Nick Johnson	.25
50	Jim Thome	1.00
51	Casey Blake	.25
52	Trot Nixon	.50
53	Luis Gonzalez	.50
54	Dontrelle Willis	.50
55	Mike Mussina	.50
56	Carl Crawford	.50
57	Mark Buehrle	.50
58	Scott Podsednik	.50
59	Brian Giles	.50
60	Rafael Furcal	.50
61	Miguel Cabrera	1.00
62	Rich Harden	.50
63	Mark Teixeira	.75
64	Frank Thomas	.75
65	Johan Santana	.75
66	Jason Schmidt	.50
67	Aramis Ramirez	.50
68	Jose Reyes	.75

#	Player	Price
69	Magglio Ordonez	.50
70	Mike Sweeney	.25
71	Eric Chavez	.50
72	Rocco Baldelli	.50
73	Sammy Sosa	.75
74	Javy Lopez	.50
75	Roy Oswalt	.50
76	Raul Ibanez	.25
77	Ivan Rodriguez	.75
78	Jerome Williams	.50
79	Carlos Lee	.50
80	Geoff Jenkins	.25
81	Sean Burroughs	.25
82	Marcus Giles	.25
83	Mike Lowell	.25
84	Barry Zito	.50
85	Aubrey Huff	.25
86	Esteban Loaiza	.25
87	Torii Hunter	.50
88	Phil Nevin	.25
89	Andruw Jones	.75
90	Josh Beckett	.50
91	Mark Mulder	.50
92	Hank Blalock	.50
93	Jason Phillips	.25
94	Russ Ortiz	.25
95	Juan Pierre	.25
96	Tom Glavine	.50
97	Gil Meche	.25
98	Ramon Ortiz	.25
99	Richie Sexson	.25
100	Albert Pujols	2.50
101	Javier Vazquez	.25
102	Johnny Damon	1.00
103	Alex Rodriguez	2.50
104	Omar Vizquel	.50
105	Chipper Jones	1.00
106	Lance Berkman	.50
107	Tim Hudson	.50
108	Carlos Delgado	.50
109	Austin Kearns	.40
110	Orlando Cabrera	.25
111	Edgar Martinez	.25
112	Melvin Mora	.25
113	Jeff Bagwell	.75
114	Marlon Byrd	.25
115	Vernon Wells	.50
116	C.C. Sabathia	.50
117	Cliff Floyd	.25
118	Ichiro Suzuki	2.00
119	Miguel Olivo	.25
120	Mike Piazza	1.00
121	Adam Dunn	.75
122	Paul Lo Duca	.25
123	Brett Myers	.50
124	Michael Young	.50
125	Sidney Ponson	.25
126	Greg Maddux	1.00
127	Vladimir Guerrero	1.00
128	Miguel Tejada	.50
129	Andy Pettitte	.50
130	Rafael Palmeiro	.75
131	Ken Griffey Jr.	2.00
132	Shannon Stewart	.25
133	Joel Pineiro	.25
134	Luis Matos	.25
135	Jeff Kent	.50
136	Randy Wolf	.25
137	Chris Woodward	.25
138	Jody Gerut	.25
139	Jose Vidro	.25
140	Bret Boone	.25
141	Bill Mueller	.25
142	Angel Berroa	.25
143	Bobby Abreu	.50
144	Roy Halladay	.50
145	Delmon Young	.50
146	Jonny Gomes	.25
147	Rickie Weeks	.50
148	Edwin Jackson	.25
149	Neal Cotts	.25
150	Jason Bay	.50
151	Khalil Greene	.50
152	Joe Mauer	.50
153	Bobby Jenks	.25
154	Chin-Feng Chen	.25
155	Chien-Ming Wang	.75
156	Mickey Hall	.25
157	James Houser	.25
158	Jay Sborz	.25
159	Jonathan Fulton	.25
160	Steve Lerud	.25
161	Grady Sizemore	.75
162	Felix Pie	.50
163	Dustin McGowan	.25
164	Chris Lubanski	.50
165	Tom Gorzelanny	.50
166	Rudy Guillen RC	3.00
167	Aarom Baldiris RC	2.00
168	Conor Jackson	8.00
169	Matt Moses	4.00
170	Ervin Santana RC	5.00
171	Merkin Valdez RC	3.00
172	Erick Aybar RC	3.00
173	Brad Sullivan	3.00
174	Joey Gathright RC	3.00
175	Brad Snyder	3.00
176	Alberto Callaspo RC	3.00
177	Brandon Medders RC	3.00
178	Zach Miner RC	4.00
179	Charlie Zink RC	1.50
180	Adam Greenberg	2.50
181	Kevin Howard RC	1.00
182	Wanell Severino RC	1.00
183	Chin-Lung Hu RC	3.00
184	Joel Zumaya RC	10.00
185	Skip Schumaker RC	1.00
186	Nic Ungs RC	1.00

2004 Bowman Chrome Uncirculated

187 Todd Self RC 2.00
188 Brian Steffek RC 1.00
189 Brock Peterson RC 2.00
190 Greg Thissen RC 1.00
191 Frank Brooks RC 1.00
192 Scott Olsen RC 4.00
193 Chris Mabeus RC 1.00
194 Daniel Giese RC 1.00
195 Jared Wells RC 1.00
196 Carlos Sosa RC 2.00
197 Bobby Madritsch RC 1.00
198 Calvin Hayes RC 1.50
199 Omar Quintanilla RC 2.00
200 Chris O'Riordan RC 1.00
201 Tim Hutting RC 1.00
202 Carlos Quentin RC 10.00
203 Brayan Pena RC 1.00
204 Jeff Salazar RC 4.00
205 David Murphy 3.00
206 Alberto Garcia RC 2.00
207 Ramon Ramirez RC 2.00
208 Luis Bolivar RC 1.00
209 Rodney Choy Foo RC 1.00
210 Fausto Carmona RC 4.00
211 Anthony Acevedo RC 2.00
212 Chad Santos RC 1.00
213 Jason Frasor RC 1.50
214 Jesse Roman RC 1.00
215 James Tomlin RC 1.00
216 Josh Labandeira RC 1.00
217 Ryan Meaux RC 1.00
218 Don Sutton RC 3.00
219 Danny Gonzalez RC 1.00
220 Javier Guzman RC 2.00
221 Anthony Lerew RC 2.00
222 Jon Connolly RC 4.00
223 Jesse English RC 1.00
224 Hector Made RC 2.50
225 Travis Hanson RC 1.50
226 Jesse Floyd RC 1.00
227 Nick Gorneault RC 1.00
228 Craig Ansman RC 1.00
229 Paul McAnulty RC 2.50
230 Carl Loadenthal RC 1.50
231 David Crouthers RC 1.00
232 Harvey Garcia RC 1.00
233 Casey Kopitzke RC 1.00
234 Ricky Nolasco RC 4.00
235 Miguel Perez RC 1.00
236 Ryan Mulhern RC 1.00
237 Chris Aguila RC 1.00
238 Brooks Conrad RC 1.00
239 Damaso Espino RC 1.00
240 Jereme Milons RC 1.50
241 Luke Hughes RC 1.00
242 Kory Casto RC 1.50
243 Jose Valdez RC 1.00
244 J.T. Stotts RC 1.50
245 Lee Gwaltney RC 1.00
246 Yoann Torrealba RC 1.00
247 Omar Falcon RC 1.00
248 Jon Coutlangus RC 1.00
249 George Sherrill RC 2.00
250 John Santor RC 1.00
251 Tony Richie RC 1.00
252 Kevin Richardson RC 1.00
253 Tim Bittner RC 1.00
254 Chris Saenz RC 1.50
255 Jose Capellan RC 2.00
256 Donald Levinski RC 1.00
257 Jerome Gamble RC 1.00
258 Jeff Keppinger RC 1.00
259 Jason Szuminski RC 1.00
260 Akinori Otsuka RC 1.50
261 Ryan Budde RC 1.00
262 Marland Williams RC 2.00
263 Jeffrey Allison RC 1.00
264 Hector Gimenez RC 1.00
265 Tim Frend RC 1.00
266 Tom Farmer RC 1.00
267 Shawn Hill RC 1.00
268 Mike Huggins RC 2.00
269 Scott Proctor RC 1.50
270 Jorge Mejia RC 1.00
271 Terry Jones RC 1.50
272 Zachary Duke RC 6.00
273 Jesse Crain 3.00
274 Luke Anderson RC 1.50
275 Hunter Brown RC 1.00
276 Matt Lemanczyk RC 1.00
277 Fernando Cortez RC 1.00
278 Vince Perkins RC 1.00
279 Tommy Murphy RC 1.00
280 Mike Gosling RC 1.00
281 Paul Bacot 1.50
282 Matt Capps RC 2.00
283 Juan Gutierrez RC 1.00
284 Teodoro Encarnacion RC 2.00
285 Chad Bentz RC 1.50
286 Kazuo Matsui RC 1.50
287 Ryan Hankins RC 1.00
288 Leo Nunez RC 1.00
289 Dave Wallace RC 1.00
290 Rob Tejeda RC 2.50
291 Paul Maholm RC 3.00
292 Casey Daigle RC 1.00
293 Tydus Meadows RC 1.00
294 Khalid Ballouli RC 1.00
295 Benji DeQuin RC 2.00
296 Tyler Davidson RC 2.00
297 Brent Colamarino RC 3.00
298 Marcus McBeth RC 1.00
299 Brad Eldred RC 2.50
300 David Pauley RC 3.00
301 Yadier Molina RC 4.00
302 Chris Shelton RC 4.00
303 Nyjer Morgan RC 1.00

304 Jon DeVries 1.00
305 Sheldon Fulse RC 1.00
306 Vito Chiaravalloti RC 1.50
307 Warner Madrigal RC 3.00
308 Reid Gorecki RC 1.00
309 Sung Jung RC 1.00
310 Peter Shier RC 1.00
311 Michael Mooney RC 1.00
312 Kenny Perez RC 1.00
313 Mike Mallory RC 1.00
314 Ben Himes RC 1.00
315 Ivan Ochoa RC 1.00
316 Donald Kelly RC 1.00
317 Tom Mastny RC 1.00
318 Kevin Davidson RC 1.50
319 Brian Pilkington 1.00
320 Alex Romero RC 1.00
321 Chad Chop RC 1.00
322 Kody Kirkland RC 2.50
323 Casey Myers RC 1.00
324 Mike Rouse 1.00
325 Sergio Silva RC 1.00
326 J.J. Furmaniak RC 3.00
327 Brad Vericker RC 1.00
328 Blake Hawksworth RC 2.00
329 Brock Jacobsen RC 1.00
330 Alec Zumwalt RC 1.00
331 Wardell Starling RC 10.00
332 Estee Harris RC 10.00
333 Kyle Sleeth RC 15.00
334 Dioner Navarro RC 15.00
335 Logan Kensing RC 10.00
336 Travis Blackley RC 10.00
337 Lincoln Holdzkom RC 10.00
338 Jason Hirsh 25.00
339 Juan Cedeno RC 10.00
340 Matt Creighton RC 15.00
341 Tim Stauffer RC 15.00
342 Shingo Takatsu RC 15.00
343 Lastings Milledge RC 75.00
344 Dustin Nippert RC 15.00
345 Felix Hernandez RC 175.00
346 Joaquin Arias RC 20.00
347 Kevin Kouzmanoff 40.00
348 Bobby Brownlie RC 15.00
349 David Aardsma RC 15.00
350 Jon Knott RC 15.00

Refractor
Stars (1-165): 2-4X
Rookies (166-330): 1-2X
Inserted 1:4
Autograph (331-350): 1-2X
Inserted 1:100

Gold Refractor
Stars (1-165): 4-8X
Rookies (166-330): 3-5X
Production 50
Autograph (331-350): No Pricing
Inserted 1:1,003

X-Fractor

LANCE BERKMAN OF

Stars (1-165): 3-5X
Rookies (166-330): 2-4X
Production 173
Autograph (331-350): No Pricing
Inserted 1:200

Stars Of The Future
NM/M
Inserted 1:600
YSS Delmon Young, Kyle Sleeth, Tim Stauffer 70.00
LHC Chris Lubanski, Ryan Harvey, Chad Cordero 50.00
MHD Nicholas Markakis, Aaron Hill, Eric Duncan 50.00

2004 Bowman Draft Picks & Prospects
NM/M
Complete Set (1-165): 30.00
Common Player: .15
Common Rookie: .25
Pack
(5 Bowman + 2 Chrome): 7.00
Box (24): 140.00
BDP1 Lyle Overbay .25

FIRST BOWMAN YEAR
JOSE CAPELLAN P

BDP2 David Newhan .15
BDP3 J.R. House .15
BDP4 Chad Tracy .15
BDP5 Humberto Quintero .15
BDP6 David Bush .15
BDP7 Scott Hairston .15
BDP8 Mike Wood .15
BDP9 Alexis Rios .25
BDP10 Sean Burnett .15
BDP11 Wilson Valdez .15
BDP12 Lew Ford .15
BDP13 Freddy Thon RC .15
BDP14 Zack Greinke .15
BDP15 Bucky Jacobsen .15
BDP16 Kevin Youkilis .15
BDP17 Grady Sizemore .25
BDP18 Denny Bautista .15
BDP19 David DeJesus .15
BDP20 Casey Kotchman .15
BDP21 David Kelton .15
BDP22 Charles Thomas RC .25
BDP23 Kazuhito Tadano RC .50
BDP24 Justin Leone RC .25
BDP25 Eduardo Villacis .25
BDP26 Brian Dallimore .25
BDP27 Nick Green .25
BDP28 Sam McConnell .25
BDP29 Brad Halsey RC .25
BDP30 Roman Colon RC .25
BDP31 Josh Fields RC 2.00
BDP32 Cody Bunkelman .50
BDP33 Jay Rainville RC 1.00
BDP34 Richie Robnett RC 1.00
BDP35 Jon Poterson RC .75
BDP36 Huston Street RC 1.00
BDP37 Erick San Pedro RC 1.00
BDP38 Cory Dunlap 1.00
BDP39 Kurt Suzuki RC .75
BDP40 Anthony Swarzak .50
BDP41 Ian Desmond RC .50
BDP42 Chris Covington .40
BDP43 Christian Garcia .40
BDP44 Gaby Hernandez RC 1.00
BDP45 Steven Register .25
BDP46 Eduardo Morlan .25
BDP47 Collin Balester .50
48 Nathan Phillips .25
49 Dan Schwartzbauer .25
50 Rafael Gonzalez .25
51 K.C. Herren RC .25
52 William Susdorf .25
53 Rob Johnson .25
54 Louis Marson .50
55 Joe Koshansky RC 1.50
56 Jamar Walton 1.00
57 Mark Lowe .75
58 Matt Macri .75
59 Donny Lucy .25
60 Mike Ferris .50
61 Mike Nickeas .50
62 Eric Hurley RC .75
63 Scott Elbert RC 1.50
64 Blake DeWitt RC 1.50
65 Danny Putnam RC .75
66 J.P. Howell RC .75
67 John Wiggins .25
68 Justin Orenduff RC .50
69 Ray Liotta RC .75
70 Billy Buckner RC .25
71 Eric Campbell RC 2.00
72 Olin Wick .25
73 Sean Gamble .40
74 Seth Smith 1.00
75 Wade Davis RC 1.00
76 Joe Jacobitz .25
77 J.A. Happ .50
78 Eric Ridener .25
79 Matt Tuiasosopo RC 1.00
80 Bradley Bergesen .25
81 Javy Guerra RC .50
82 Buck Shaw .50
83 Paul Janish .50
84 Sean Kazmar .50
85 Josh Johnson RC .50
86 Angel Salome .75
87 Jordan Parraz .50
88 Kelvin Vazquez .25
89 Grant Hansen .25
90 Matt Fox RC .25
91 Trevor Plouffe RC 1.50
92 Wes Whisler .50
93 Curtis Thigpen .50
94 Donnie Smith RC .25
95 Luis Rivera .40
96 Jesse Hoover .25
97 Jason Vargas RC 1.00
98 Clary Carlsen .25
99 Mark Robinson .25

100 J.C. Holt RC .40
101 Chad Blackwell .25
102 Daryl Jones RC .75
103 Jonathan Tierce .25
104 Patrick Bryant .25
105 Eddie Prasch .40
106 Mitch Einertson RC .75
107 Kyle Waldrop RC .75
108 Jeff Marquez RC .50
109 Zach Jackson RC .50
110 Josh Wahpepah .25
111 Adam Lind RC 3.00
112 Kyle Bloom .25
113 Ben Harrison .25
114 Taylor Tankersley RC .75
115 Steven Jackson .25
116 David Purcey RC .50
117 Jacob McGee 1.00
118 Lucas Harrell RC .25
119 Brandon Allen .75
120 Van Pope .50
121 Jeff Francis .25
122 Joe Blanton .25
123 Wilfredo Ledezma .15
124 Bryan Bullington .15
125 Jairo Garcia .15
126 Matt Cain .40
127 Arnie Munoz .15
128 Clint Everts .15
129 Jesus Cota .15
130 Gavin Floyd .15
131 Edwin Encarnacion .15
132 Koyie Hill .15
133 Ruben Gotay .15
134 Jeff Mathis .15
135 Andy Marte .15
136 Dallas McPherson .15
137 Justin Morneau .40
138 Rickie Weeks .25
139 Joel Guzman .15
140 Shin-Soo Choo .15
141 Yusmeiro Petit RC 2.00
142 Jorge Cortes .15
143 Val Majewski .15
144 Felix Pie .15
145 Aaron Hill .15
146 Jose Capellan .25
147 Dioner Navarro RC .25
148 Fausto Carmona RC .50
149 Robinson Diaz .25
150 Felix Hernandez 3.00
151 Andres Blanco .25
152 Jason Kubel .15
153 Willy Taveras RC .25
154 Merkin Valdez .40
155 Robinson Cano .50
156 Bill Murphy .15
157 Chris Burke .15
158 Kyle Sleeth .25
159 B.J. Upton .25
160 Tim Stauffer .25
161 David Wright 1.00
162 Conor Jackson .25
163 Brad Thompson RC .25
164 Delmon Young .40
165 Jeremy Reed .15

Gold

Rookies: .75-1.5X
Inserted 1:1

Red
No Pricing
Production One Set

AFLAC All-Americans
Complete Set (40):
Common Player

Printing Plates
No Pricing
Production one for each color.

Prospect Premiums
NM/M
Common Player: 4.00
AB Angel Berroa 4.00
KC Kevin Cash 4.00
RH Ryan Harvey 6.00
CJ Conor Jackson 10.00
EJ Edwin Jackson 4.00
LM Lastings Milledge 15.00
DN Dioner Navarro 4.00
CQ Carlos Quentin 8.00

JR Jeremy Reed 6.00
NS Nick Swisher 8.00
BU B.J. Upton 8.00
DY Delmon Young 8.00

Signs of the Future
NM/M
Common Player:
CC Chad Cordero 10.00
JH James Houser 8.00
AL Adam Loewen 15.00
PM Paul Maholm 8.00
TP Tyler Pelland 8.00
TT Terry Tiffee 8.00

2004 Bowman Chrome Draft Picks & Prospects

PHILIP HUGHES

NM/M
Complete Set (175):
Common Player: .25
Common Rookie: 1.00
Common RC Auto.
(166-175): 15.00
Inserted 1:60
BDP1 Lyle Overbay .50
BDP2 David Newhan .25
BDP3 J.R. House .25
BDP4 Chad Tracy .25
BDP5 Humberto Quintero .25
BDP6 David Bush .25
BDP7 Scott Hairston .25
BDP8 Mike Wood .25
BDP9 Alexis Rios .50
BDP10 Sean Burnett .25
BDP11 Wilson Valdez .25
BDP12 Lew Ford .25
BDP13 Freddy Thon RC 1.00
BDP14 Zack Greinke .25
BDP15 Bucky Jacobsen .25
BDP16 Kevin Youkilis .40
BDP17 Grady Sizemore .25
BDP18 Denny Bautista .25
BDP19 David DeJesus .25
BDP20 Casey Kotchman .25
BDP21 David Kelton .25
BDP22 Charles Thomas RC 1.00
BDP23 Kazuhito Tadano RC 1.50
BDP24 Justin Leone RC 1.00
BDP25 Eduardo Villacis RC 1.00
BDP26 Brian Dallimore RC 1.00
BDP27 Nick Green RC 1.00
BDP28 Sam McConnell RC 1.00
BDP29 Brad Halsey RC 1.00
BDP30 Roman Colon RC 1.00
BDP31 Josh Fields RC 6.00
BDP32 Cody Bunkelman RC 1.00
BDP33 Jay Rainville RC 4.00
BDP34 Richie Robnett RC 3.00
BDP35 Jon Poterson RC 2.50
BDP36 Huston Street RC 3.00
BDP37 Erick San Pedro RC 1.00
BDP38 Cory Dunlap RC 1.00
BDP39 Kurt Suzuki RC 3.00
BDP40 Anthony Swarzak RC 2.00
BDP41 Ian Desmond RC 3.00
BDP42 Chris Covington RC 1.50
BDP43 Christian Garcia RC 1.50
BDP44 Gaby Hernandez RC 5.00
BDP45 Steven Register RC 1.00
BDP46 Eduardo Morlan RC 2.50
BDP47 Collin Balester RC 2.00
BDP48 Nathan Phillips RC 1.00
BDP49 Dan Schwartzbauer RC 1.00
BDP50 Rafael Gonzalez RC 2.00
BDP51 K.C. Herren RC 2.00
BDP52 William Susdorf RC 1.00
BDP53 Rob Johnson RC 1.00
BDP54 Louis Marson RC 2.00
BDP55 Joe Koshansky RC 3.00
BDP56 Jamar Walton RC 3.00
BDP57 Mark Lowe RC 3.00
BDP58 Matt Macri RC 3.00
BDP59 Donny Lucy RC 1.00
BDP60 Mike Ferris RC 1.50
BDP61 Mike Nickeas RC 1.50
BDP62 Eric Hurley RC 2.00
BDP63 Scott Elbert RC 4.00
BDP64 Blake DeWitt RC 2.00
BDP65 Danny Putnam RC 2.00
BDP66 J.P. Howell RC 3.00
BDP67 John Wiggins RC 1.00
BDP68 Justin Orenduff RC 2.00

BDP69 Ray Liotta RC 2.00
BDP70 Billy Buckner RC 1.00
BDP71 Eric Campbell RC 6.00
BDP72 Olin Wick RC 2.00
BDP73 Sean Gamble RC 1.50
BDP74 Seth Smith RC 2.00
BDP75 Wade Davis RC 4.00
BDP76 Joe Jacobitz RC 1.00
BDP77 J.A. Happ RC 2.00
BDP78 Eric Ridener RC 1.00
BDP79 Matt Tuiasosopo RC 3.00
BDP80 Bradley Bergesen RC 3.00
BDP81 Javy Guerra RC 1.50
BDP82 Buck Shaw RC 2.00
BDP83 Paul Janish RC 1.00
BDP84 Sean Kazmar RC 1.00
BDP85 Josh Johnson RC 1.50
BDP86 Angel Salome RC 1.00
BDP87 Jordan Parraz RC 1.00
BDP88 Kelvin Vazquez RC 1.00
BDP89 Grant Hansen RC 1.00
BDP90 Matt Fox RC 1.00
BDP91 Trevor Plouffe RC 4.00
BDP92 Wes Whisler RC 1.00
BDP93 Curtis Thigpen RC 2.00
BDP94 Donnie Smith RC 1.00
BDP95 Luis Rivera RC 1.50
BDP96 Jesse Hoover RC 1.00
BDP97 Jason Vargas RC 4.00
BDP98 Clary Carlsen RC 1.00
BDP99 Mark Robinson RC 1.00
BDP100 J.C. Holt RC 1.50
BDP101 Chad Blackwell RC 1.00
BDP102 Daryl Jones RC 1.00
BDP103 Jonathan Tierce RC 1.00
BDP104 Patrick Bryant RC 1.00
BDP105 Eddie Prasch RC 1.50
BDP106 Mitch Einertson RC 1.00
BDP107 Kyle Waldrop RC 4.00
BDP108 Jeff Marquez RC 2.00
BDP109 Zach Jackson RC 2.00
BDP110 Josh Wahpepah RC 1.00
BDP111 Adam Lind RC 10.00
BDP112 Kyle Bloom RC 1.00
BDP113 Ben Harrison RC 1.00
BDP114 Taylor Tankersley RC 2.00
BDP115 Steven Jackson RC 1.00
BDP116 David Purcey RC 1.50
BDP117 Jacob McGee RC 3.00
BDP118 Lucas Harrell RC 1.00
BDP119 Brandon Allen RC 2.50
BDP120 Van Pope RC 1.50
BDP121 Jeff Francis .25
BDP122 Joe Blanton .25
BDP123 Wilfredo Ledezma .25
BDP124 Bryan Bullington .25
BDP125 Jairo Garcia .25
BDP126 Matt Cain .75
BDP127 Arnie Munoz .25
BDP128 Clint Everts .25
BDP129 Jesus Cota .25
BDP130 Gavin Floyd .25
BDP131 Edwin Encarnacion .25
BDP132 Koyie Hill .25
BDP133 Ruben Gotay .25
BDP134 Jeff Mathis .25
BDP135 Andy Marte .50
BDP136 Dallas McPherson .50
BDP137 Justin Morneau .50
BDP138 Rickie Weeks .40
BDP139 Joel Guzman .25
BDP140 Shin-Soo Choo .25
BDP141 Yusmeiro Petit RC 6.00
BDP142 Jorge Cortes 1.00
BDP143 Val Majewski .50
BDP144 Felix Pie .50
BDP145 Aaron Hill .50
BDP146 Jose Capellan .25
BDP147 Dioner Navarro RC 1.00
BDP148 Fausto Carmona 1.00
BDP149 Robinzon Diaz RC 1.00
BDP150 Felix Hernandez 8.00
BDP151 Andres Blanco RC 1.00
BDP152 Jason Kubel .25
BDP153 Willy Taveras RC 2.50
BDP154 Merkin Valdez 1.00
BDP155 Robinson Cano 1.00
BDP156 Bill Murphy .50
BDP157 Chris Burke .25
BDP158 Kyle Sleeth .75
BDP159 B.J. Upton .75
BDP160 Tim Stauffer 1.00
BDP161 David Wright 3.00
BDP162 Conor Jackson 3.00
BDP163 Brad Thompson RC 2.00
BDP164 Delmon Young .50
BDP165 Jeremy Reed .75
BDP166 Matt Bush RC 25.00
BDP167 Mark Rogers RC 25.00
BDP168 Thomas Diamond RC 20.00
BDP169 Greg Golson RC 25.00
BDP170 Homer Bailey RC 120.00
BDP171 Chris Lambert RC 35.00
BDP172 Neil Walker RC 35.00
BDP173 Bill Bray RC 15.00
BDP174 Phillip Hughes RC 200.00
BDP175 Gio Gonzalez RC 40.00

Refractor
Rookies: 2-4X
Inserted 1:11
Rookie Autos. (166-175): .75-1.5X
Inserted 1:204

Gold Refractor

Rookies: 10-20X
Production 50
Rookie Autos. (166-175): 3-5X
Inserted 1:2,045

X-Fractor

Rookies: 3-6X
Production 125
Rookie Autos. (166-175): 1-2X
Inserted 1:407

2004 Bowman Heritage

	NM/M
Complete Set (347):	
Common Player:	.15
Common SP:	4.00
Common SP Rookie:	4.00
SP's Inserted 1:3	
Pack (8):	6.00
Box (24):	120.00
1 Tom Glavine	.40
2 Mike Piazza/SP	8.00
3 Sidney Ponson	.15
4 Jerry Hairston Jr.	.15
5 Jermaine Dye	.25
6 Bobby Crosby	.15
7 Carlos Zambrano	.25
8 Moises Alou	.25
9 Alex Rodriguez/SP	10.00
10 Derek Jeter	2.00
11 Rafael Furcal	.25
12 J.D. Drew	.25
13 Joe Mauer/SP	6.00
14 Brad Radke	.15
15 Johnny Damon	.75
16 Derek Lowe	.15
17 Pat Burrell	.25
18 Mike Lieberthal	.15
19 Cliff Lee	.15
20 Ronnie Belliard	.15
21 Eric Gagne/SP	4.00
22 Brad Penny	.15
23 Al Kaline	.50
24 Mike Maroth	.15
25 Magglio Ordonez/SP	4.00
26 Mark Buehrle	.25
27 Jack Wilson	.15
28 Oliver Perez	.15
29 Al "Red" Schoendienst	.15
30 Yadier Molina RC	1.50
31 Ryan Freel	.15
32 Adam Dunn	.50
33 Paul Konerko	.40
34 Esteban Loaiza	.15
35 Ivan Rodriguez	.50
36 Carlos Guillen	.15
37 Adrian Beltre	.25
38 C.C. Sabathia	.25
39 Hideo Nomo	.40
40 Victor Martinez/SP	4.00
41 Bobby Abreu	.25
42 Randy Wolf	.15
43 Johnny Estrada	.15
44 Russ Ortiz	.15
45 Kenny Rogers	.15
46 Hank Blalock/SP	4.00
47 David Ortiz	1.00
48 Pedro Martinez/SP	6.00
49 Austin Kearns	.25
50 Ken Griffey Jr./SP	6.00
51 Mark Prior	.50
52 Kerry Wood	.40
53 Eric Chavez	.25
54 Tim Hudson	.25
55 Rafael Palmeiro/SP	5.00
56 Javy Lopez	.15
57 Jason Bay	.40
58 Craig Wilson	.15
59 Ed "Whitey" Ford	.50
60 Jason Giambi	.50
61 Scott Rolen/SP	6.00
62 Matt Morris	.15
63 Javier Vazquez	.15
64 Jim Thome	.50
65 Don Zimmer	.25
66 Shawn Green	.25
67 Don Larsen	.50
68 Gary Sheffield	.40
69 Jorge Posada	.50
70 Bernie Williams	.40
71 Chipper Jones	.75
72 Andruw Jones	.50
73 John Thomson	.15
74 Jim Edmonds	.40
75 Albert Pujols	2.00
76 Chris Carpenter	.50
77 Aubrey Huff/SP	4.00
78 Carl Crawford	.40
79 Victor Zambrano	.15
80 Alfonso Soriano/SP	5.00
81 Lance Berkman	.40
82 Mike Sweeney	.15
83 Ken Harvey	.15
84 Angel Berroa	.15
85 A.J. Burnett	.15
86 Mike Lowell	.15
87 Miguel Cabrera/SP	5.00
88 Preston Wilson	.15
89 Todd Helton/SP	4.00
90 Larry Walker	.25
91 Vladimir Guerrero	.75
92 Garret Anderson	.15
93 Bartolo Colon	.15
94 Scott Hairston	.15
95 Richie Sexson/SP	4.00
96 Sean Casey	.25
97 Johnny Podres	.40
98 Andy Pettitte	.40
99 Roy Oswalt	.25
100 Roger Clemens/SP	8.00
101 Scott Podsednik	.25
102 Ben Sheets	.25
103 Lyle Overbay	.15
104 Nick Johnson/SP	4.00
105 Zach Day	.15
106 Jose Reyes	.75
107 Khalil Greene	.25
108 Sean Burroughs	.15
109 David Wells/SP	4.00
110 Jason Schmidt	.25
111 Neifi Perez	.15
112 Edgar Renteria	.15
113 Rich Aurilia	.15
114 Edgar Martinez	.15
115 Joel Pineiro	.15
116 Mark Teixeira	.40
117 Michael Young	.25
118 Ricardo Rodriguez	.15
119 Carlos Delgado	.50
120 Roy Halladay	.25
121 Jose Guillen	.15
122 Troy Glaus	.40
123 Shea Hillenbrand	.15
124 Luis Gonzalez	.25
125 Horacio Ramirez	.15
126 Melvin Mora	.15
127 Miguel Tejada/SP	4.00
128 Manny Ramirez	.75
129 Tim Wakefield	.15
130 Curt Schilling/SP	5.00
131 Aramis Ramirez	.40
132 Sammy Sosa/SP	8.00
133 Matt Clement	.15
134 Juan Uribe	.15
135 Dontrelle Willis	.25
136 Paul LoDuca	.15
137 Juan Pierre	.15
138 Kevin Brown	.15
139 Brian Giles, Marcus Giles	.15
140 Brian Giles	.15
141 Nomar Garciaparra/SP	8.00
142 Cesar Izturis	.15
143 Don Newcombe	.15
144 Craig Biggio	.25
145 Carlos Beltran	.50
146 Torii Hunter	.25
147 Livan Hernandez	.15
148 Cliff Floyd	.15
149 Barry Zito	.40
150 Mark Mulder	.25
151 Rocco Baldelli	.25
152 Bret Boone	.15
153 Jamie Moyer	.15
154 Ichiro Suzuki	1.50
155 Brett Myers	.25
156 Carl Pavano	.15
157 Josh Beckett	.25
158 Randy Johnson	.75
159 Trot Nixon	.15
160 Dmitri Young	.15
161 Jacque Jones	.15
162 Lew Ford	.15
163 Jose Vidro	.15
164 Mark Kotsay	.15
165 A.J. Pierzynski	.15
166 Dewon Brazelton	.15
167 Jeromy Burnitz	.15
168 Johan Santana	.50
169 Greg Maddux	1.00
170 Carl Erskine	.15
171 Robin Roberts	.15
172 Freddy Garcia	.15
173 Carlos Lee	.25
174 Jeff Bagwell	.40
175 Jeff Kent	.25
176 Kazuhisa Ishii	.15
177 Orlando Cabrera	.25
178 Shannon Stewart	.15
179 Mike Cameron	.15
180 Mike Mussina	.40
181 Frank Thomas	.75
182 Jaret Wright	.15
183 Alex Gonzalez/SP	4.00
184 Matt Lawton	.15
185 Derrek Lee	.50
186 Omar Vizquel	.25
187 Jeremy Bonderman	.25
188 Jake Westbrook	.15
189 Zack Greinke/SP	.15
190 Chad Tracy	.15
191 Rondell White	.15
192 Alex Gonzalez	.15
193 Geoff Jenkins	.15
194 Ralph Kiner	.40
195 Al Leiter	.15
196 Kevin Millwood	.15
197 Jason Kendall	.15
198 Kris Benson	.15
199 Ryan Klesko	.15
200 Mark Loretta	.15
201 Richard Hidalgo	.15
202 Reed Johnson	.15
203 Luis Castillo	.15
204 Jon Zeringue/SP RC	6.00
205 Matt Bush RC	2.00
206 Kurt Suzuki/SP RC	5.00
207 Mark Rogers RC	2.00
208 Jason Vargas/SP RC	5.00
209 Homer Bailey RC	6.00
210 Ray Liotta/SP RC	5.00
211 Eric Campbell RC	2.50
212 Thomas Diamond RC	2.00
213 Gaby Hernandez/SP RC	8.00
214 Neil Walker RC	2.00
215 Bill Bray RC	1.00
216 Wade Davis/SP RC	5.00
217 David Purcey RC	2.00
218 Scott Elbert RC	2.00
219 Josh Fields RC	3.00
220 Josh Johnson/SP	4.00
221 Chris Lambert RC	2.00
222 Trevor Plouffe RC	3.00
223 Bruce Froemming	.15
224 Matt Macri/SP RC	5.00
225 Greg Golson RC	2.00
226 Phillip Hughes RC	15.00
227 Kyle Waldrop RC	2.00
228 Matt Tuiasosopo/SP RC	5.00
229 Richie Robnett RC	2.00
230 Taylor Tankersley RC	1.50
231 Blake DeWitt RC	2.50
232 Charlie Reliford	.15
233 Eric Hurley RC	1.00
234 Jordan Parraz/SP RC	4.00
235 J.P. Howell RC	2.00
236 Dana DeMuth	.15
237 Zach Jackson RC	1.00
238 Justin Orenduff RC	1.00
239 Brad Thompson RC	1.00
240 J.C. Holt/SP RC	5.00
241 Matt Fox RC	1.00
242 Danny Putnam RC	1.00
243 Daryl Jones/SP RC	5.00
244 Jon Poterson RC	1.00
245 Gio Gonzalez RC	5.00
246 Lucas Harrell/SP RC	5.00
247 Jerry Crawford	.15
248 Jay Rainville RC	2.00
249 Donnie Smith/SP RC	5.00
250 Huston Street RC	2.00
251 Jeff Marquez RC	1.00
252 Reid Brignac RC	3.00
253 Yusmeiro Petit RC	1.00
254 K.C. Herren RC	1.00
255 Dale Scott	.15
256 Erick San Pedro RC	1.00
257 Ed Montague	.15
258 Billy Buckner RC	1.00
259 Mitch Einertson/SP RC	4.00
260 Aarom Baldiris RC	1.00
261 Conor Jackson RC	2.00
262 Rick Reed	.15
263 Ervin Santana RC	2.00
264 Gerry Davis	.15
265 Merkin Valdez RC	1.00
266 Joey Gathright RC	1.00
267 Alberto Callaspo RC	.75
268 Carlos Quentin/SP	8.00
269 Gary Darling	.15
270 Jeff Salazar/SP RC	4.00
271 Akinori Otsuka/SP RC	4.00
272 Joe Brinkman	.15
273 Omar Quintanilla	.50
274 Brian Runge	.15
275 Tom Mastny RC	.50
276 John Hirschbeck	.15
277 Warner Madrigal RC	.50
278 Joe West	.15
279 Paul Maholm RC	1.00
280 Larry Young	.15
281 Mike Reilly	.15
282 Kazuo Matsui/SP RC	4.00
283 Randy Marsh	.15
284 Frank Francisco RC	.50
285 Zachary Duke RC	2.00
286 Tim McClelland	.15
287 Jesse Crain	.75
288 Hector Gimenez RC	.50
289 Marland Williams RC	.50
290 Brian Gorman	.15
291 Jose Capellan/SP RC	4.00
292 Tim Welke	.15
293 Javier Guzman RC	.50
294 Paul McAnulty RC	.50
295 Hector Made RC	.50
296 Jon Connolly RC	.50
297 Don Sutton RC	1.00
298 Fausto Carmona RC	.50
299 Ramon Ramirez RC	.50
300 Brad Snyder RC	.50
301 Chin-Lung Hu RC	1.00
302 Rudy Guillen RC	.50
303 Matt Moses RC	1.00
304 Brad Halsey/SP RC	.40
305 Erick Aybar RC	1.50
306 Brad Sullivan RC	1.00
307 Nick Gorneault RC	1.00
308 Craig Ansman RC	1.00
309 Ricky Nolasco RC	1.00
310 Luke Hughes RC	1.00
311 Danny Gonzalez RC	1.00
312 Josh Labandeira RC	.50
313 Donald Levinski RC	.50
314 Vince Perkins RC	.50
315 Tommy Murphy RC	.50
316 Chad Bentz RC	.50
317 Chris Shelton RC	2.00
318 Nyjer Morgan/SP RC	4.00
319 Kody Kirkland RC	.50
320 Blake Hawksworth RC	.50
321 Alex Romero RC	.50
322 Mike Gosling RC	.50
323 Ryan Budde RC	.50
324 Kevin Howard RC	.50
325 Wanell Macia RC	.50
326 Travis Blackley RC	.50
327 Kazuhito Tadano/SP RC	4.00
328 Shingo Takatsu RC	1.00
329 Joaquin Arias RC	.50
330 Juan Cedeno RC	.75
331 Bobby Brownlie RC	1.00
332 Lastings Milledge RC	.75
333 Estee Harris RC	.75
334 Tim Stauffer/SP RC	.50
335 Jon Knott RC	.50
336 David Aardsma RC	.50
337 Wardell Starling RC	.50
338 Dioner Navarro RC	1.00
339 Logan Kensing RC	.50
340 Jason Hirsh RC	1.50
341 Matt Creighton RC	.50
342 Felix Hernandez/SP RC	20.00
343 Kyle Sleeth RC	.50
344 Dustin Nippert RC	.50
345 Anthony Lerew RC	.50
346 Chris Saenz RC	.50
347 Steve Palermo	.15
348 Barry Bonds	20.00

Black & White

Stars: 2X
SP Stars: .5-1X
Rookies: 1-2X
SP Rookies: .5-.75X
Inserted 1:1

Mohagany

Stars: 15-25X
SP Stars: 3-4X
Rookies: 4-8X
SP Rookies: 3-5X
Production 25 Sets

Printing Plates

No Pricing
Production One Set

Commissioner's Cut

Production One
FF Ford Frick

Signs of Authority

	NM/M
Common Autograph:	15.00
Inserted 1:49	
Red Ink:	1.5-2X
Production 55 Sets	
JB Joe Brinkman	15.00
JC Jerry Crawford	15.00
GDA Gary Darling	15.00
GD Gerry Davis	15.00
DD Dana DeMuth	15.00
BF Bruce Froemming	20.00
BG Brian Gorman	15.00
JH John Hirschbeck	15.00
RM Randy Marsh	15.00
TM Tim McClelland	15.00
EM Ed Montague	15.00
SP Steve Palermo	15.00
ER Rick Reed	15.00
MR Mike Reilly	15.00
CM Charlie Reliford	15.00
BR Brian Runge	15.00
DS Dale Scott	20.00
TW Tim Welke	15.00
JW Joe West	20.00
LY Larry Young	15.00

Signs of Glory

	NM/M
Common Autograph:	25.00
Inserted 1:246	
Red Ink:	2X
Production 55 Sets	
GK George Kell	25.00
BK Bob Kuzava	25.00
PR Elwin "Preacher Roe	30.00
BS Bobby Shantz	25.00
MS Bill "Moose" Skowron	30.00

Signs of Greatness

	NM/M
Common Autograph:	10.00
Inserted 1:57	
Red Ink:	2-4X
Production 55 Sets	
BB Bill Bray	
MB Matt Bush	15.00
TD Thomas Diamond	15.00
GG Greg Golson	15.00
PH Phillip Hughes	120.00
CL Chris Lambert	10.00
JM Jeff Marquez	10.00
TP Trevor Plouffe	15.00
JR Jay Rainville	15.00
MR Mark Rogers	15.00
TT Taylor Tankersley	
NW Neil Walker	20.00

Threads of Greatness

	NM/M
Common Player:	4.00
Inserted 1:12	
Gold:	2-3X
Production 55 Sets	
MA Moises Alou	5.00
JB Jeff Bagwell	8.00
JB2 Jeff Bagwell	8.00
RB Rocco Baldelli	4.00
TB Tony Batista	4.00
JB Josh Beckett	4.00
JB2 Josh Beckett	4.00
AB Adrian Beltre	6.00
AGB Armando Benitez	4.00
LB Lance Berkman	6.00
LB2 Lance Berkman	6.00
AMB Angel Berroa	4.00
HB Hank Blalock	6.00
HB2 Hank Blalock	6.00
WB3 Wade Boggs	8.00
BB Bret Boone	4.00
BB2 Bret Boone	4.00
PB Pat Burrell	4.00
MC Miguel Cabrera	8.00
EC Eric Chavez	4.00
EC2 Eric Chavez	4.00
RC Roger Clemens	10.00
BC Bobby Cox	4.00
JD Johnny Damon	15.00
CE Carl Everett	4.00
NG Nomar Garciaparra	8.00
JG Jason Giambi	6.00
JG2 Jason Giambi	6.00
JAG Jason Gonzalez	6.00
RH Roy Halladay	6.00
TH Todd Helton	6.00
AJ Andruw Jones	6.00
DJ David Justice	4.00
PL Paul LoDuca	4.00
JL Javy Lopez	4.00
ML Mike Lowell	4.00
JM Joe Mauer	10.00
MCD Mike McDougal	4.00
KM Kevin Millwood	4.00
MM Mark Mulder	4.00
MM2 Mark Mulder	4.00
HN Hideo Nomo	8.00
JO John Olerud	4.00
JO2 John Olerud	4.00
AEP Andy Pettitte	4.00
MP Mike Piazza	10.00
MP2 Mike Piazza	10.00
AP Albert Pujols	15.00
AP2 Albert Pujols	15.00
MR Manny Ramirez	8.00
MR2 Manny Ramirez	8.00
JR Jose Reyes	10.00
AR Alex Rodriguez	15.00
CS C.C. Sabathia	6.00
JDS Jason Schmidt	6.00
GS Gary Sheffield	6.00
RS Robin Sierra	4.00
JS John Smoltz	6.00
JS2 John Smoltz	6.00
AS Alfonso Soriano	8.00
SS Sammy Sosa	8.00
SS2 Sammy Sosa	8.00
SS3 Sammy Sosa	8.00
MS Mike Sweeney	4.00
MCT Mark Teixeira	6.00
MT Miguel Tejada	6.00
MT2 Miguel Tejada	6.00
MT3 Miguel Tejada	6.00
FT Frank Thomas	8.00
JT Jim Thome	8.00
JT2 Jim Thome	8.00
OV Omar Vizquel	4.00
JW Jarrod Washburn	4.00
VW Vernon Wells	6.00
BW Bernie Williams	6.00
DW Dontrelle Willis	6.00
KW Kerry Wood	4.00
KW2 Kerry Wood	4.00
MY Michael Young	4.00
BZ Barry Zito	4.00

2004 Bowman Sterling

	NM/M
Common Rookie:	5.00
Pack (5):	60.00
Box (6):	325.00
ABA Aarom Baldiris RC	5.00
BBR Bill Bray RC	5.00
RBR Reid Brignac RC	15.00
BBU Billy Buckner RC	5.00
JC Jose Capellan RC	5.00
FC Fausto Carmona RC	8.00
JCR Jesse Crain RC	6.00
TD Thomas Diamond RC	10.00
ZD Zachary Duke RC	10.00
ME Mitch Einertson RC	5.00
BE Brad Eldred RC	5.00
MF Mike Ferris RC	5.00
JFI Josh Fields RC	15.00
MFO Matt Fox RC	5.00
JG Joey Gathright RC	5.00
GG Greg Golson RC	8.00
GIG Gio Gonzalez RC	10.00
FG Freddy Guzman RC	5.00
GH Gaby Hernandez RC	5.00
FH Felix Hernandez RC	35.00
KCH K.C. Herren RC	5.00
JH Jesse Hoover RC	5.00
JPH J.P. Howell RC	5.00
PH Phillip Hughes RC	35.00
EH Eric Hurley RC	5.00
CJ Conor Jackson RC	15.00
ZJ Zach Jackson RC	5.00
CLA Chris Lambert RC	5.00
CH Chin-Lung Hu RC	10.00
MMC Matt Macri RC	5.00
HM Hector Made RC	5.00
PGM Paul Maholm RC	6.00
NM Nyjer Morgan RC	5.00
CN Chris Nelson RC	5.00
JO Justin Orenduff RC	5.00
YP Yusmeiro Petit RC	15.00
DPU David Purcey RC	5.00
OQ Omar Quintanilla RC	5.00
MRO Mark Rogers RC	10.00
ESP Erick San Pedro RC	5.00
NS Nate Schierholtz RC	5.00
SSM Seth Smith RC	10.00
KS Kurt Suzuki RC	8.00
KT Kazuhito Tadano RC	5.00
CT Curtis Thigpen RC	5.00
BT Brad Thompson RC	5.00
NW Neil Walker RC	10.00
AWH Anthony Whittington RC	5.00
MW Marland Williams RC	5.00
JZ Jon Zeringue RC	5.00

Rookie Relic Autographs

HB Homer Bailey RC	60.00
BB Brian Bixler RC	10.00
MB Matt Bush RC	20.00
BD Blake DeWitt RC	20.00
CG Christian Garcia RC	10.00
SK Scott Kazmir RC	40.00
JM Jeff Marquez RC	10.00
SO Scott Olsen RC	25.00
TP Trevor Plouffe RC	20.00
DP Danny Putnam RC	10.00
HS Huston Street RC	25.00
TT Taylor Tankersley RC	10.00
MT Matt Tuiasosopo RC	30.00
KWA Kyle Waldrop RC	20.00

Prospect Relic Autographs

RC Robinson Cano	60.00
CC Chad Cordero	15.00
DD David DeJesus	20.00
RH Ryan Harvey	15.00
CL Chris Lubanski	15.00
FP Felix Pie	30.00
BU B.J. Upton	25.00
AW Adam Wainwright	35.00

DW	David Wright	75.00
DY	Delmon Young	40.00

Rookie Autographs:

CA	Chris Aguila RC	8.00
AC	Alberto Callaspo RC	20.00
HG	Hector Gimenez RC	10.00
BH	Blake Hawksworth RC	15.00
LH	Lincoln Holdzkom RC	10.00
RM	Ryan Meaux RC	8.00
MM	Matt Moses RC	20.00
VP	Vince Perkins RC	8.00
CQ	Carlos Quentin RC	40.00
JR	Jay Rainville RC	15.00
AR	Alex Romero RC	
MR	Mike Rouse	
JS	Jeremy Sowers RC	30.00
AZ	Alec Zumwalt RC	8.00

Relics:

MA	Moises Alou	5.00
JB	Jeff Bagwell	8.00
RB	Rocco Baldelli	5.00
CIB	Carlos Beltran	10.00
LB	Lance Berkman	5.00
AB	Angel Berroa	5.00
CB	Craig Biggio	5.00
HJB	Hank Blalock	5.00
MC	Miguel Cabrera	8.00
LC	Luis Castillo	5.00
HC	Hee Seop Choi	5.00
BC2	Bobby Crosby	5.00
JD	Johnny Damon	10.00
AD	Adam Dunn	8.00
JE	Johnny Estrada	5.00
EG	Eric Gagne	5.00
TG	Troy Glaus	5.00
TMG	Tom Glavine	5.00
VG	Vladimir Guerrero	10.00
TLH	Todd Helton	8.00
RJH	Richard Hidalgo	5.00
NJ	Nick Johnson	5.00
AJ	Andruw Jones	8.00
AK	Austin Kearns	5.00
JK	Jason Kendall	5.00
PL	Paul LoDuca	5.00
TM	Tino Martinez	5.00
MAM	Mark Mulder	5.00
LN	Laynce Nix	5.00
RO	Russ Ortiz	5.00
RP	Rafael Palmeiro	6.00
MJP	Mike Piazza	10.00
JP	Juan Pierre	5.00
MP	Mark Prior	8.00
AP	Albert Pujols	20.00
ANR	Aramis Ramirez	8.00
MAR	Manny Ramirez	8.00
PR	Pokey Reese	5.00
AER	Alex Rodriguez	15.00
IR	Ivan Rodriguez	8.00
GS	Gary Sheffield	8.00
SS	Sammy Sosa	10.00
MCT	Mark Teixeira	8.00
MT1	Miguel Tejada/bat	8.00
MT2	Miguel Tejada/jsy	8.00
FT	Frank Thomas	10.00
BW	Bernie Williams	8.00
DWW	Dontrelle Willis	5.00
KW	Kerry Wood	5.00
MY	Michael Young	5.00

Refractors

Regular Rookies:	1.5-2X
Rookie Relic Autos.:	1-2X
Rookie Autos.:	1-2X
Prospect Relic Autos.:	1-2X
Relics:	1-2X
Production 199 Sets	

Black Refractors
No Pricing
Production 25 Sets

Red Refractor
No Pricing
Production One Set

Uncirculated

No Pricing
Production 16 Sets

Autographed Originals

Complete Set (51):	
Common Player	

2004 Bowman's Best

NM/M

Complete Set:	
Common Player:	.25
Pack (5):	14.00
Box (12):	100.00

Veterans

GA	Garret Anderson	.25
CB	Carlos Beltran	.75
HB	Hank Blalock	.50
MTC	Miguel Cabrera	1.00
EC	Eric Chavez	.50
RC	Roger Clemens	2.50
CD	Carlos Delgado	.50
NAG	Nomar Garciaparra	1.00
JGG	Jason Giambi	.75
BG	Brian Giles	.25
VG	Vladimir Guerrero	1.00
TLH	Todd Helton	.75
RJ	Randy Johnson	1.00
LWJ	Chipper Jones	1.00
JLO	Javy Lopez	.25
MO	Magglio Ordonez	.25
LO	Lyle Overbay	.25
MJP	Mike Piazza	1.50
JP	Jorge Posada	.50
MWP	Mark Prior	.75
AP	Albert Pujols	3.00
MAR	Manny Ramirez	1.00
AER	Alex Rodriguez	2.50
IR	Ivan Rodriguez	.75
SR	Scott Rolen	1.00
CMS	Curt Schilling	1.00
JDS	Jason Schmidt	.50
RS	Richie Sexson	.50
AS	Alfonso Soriano	1.00
SS	Sammy Sosa	1.00
IS	Ichiro Suzuki	2.00
MT	Miguel Tejada	.50
JT	Jim Thome	.75
JAV	Jose Vidro	.25
MY	Michael Young	.25

First-Year Players

	Common Rookie:	2.00
JJC	Jon Connolly RC	2.00
JRG	Joey Gathright RC	2.00
DG	Danny Gonzalez RC	1.50
NG	Nick Gorneault RC	2.00
MG	Mike Gosling	1.50
CH	Chin-Lung Hu RC	2.00
TJ	Terry Jones	1.50
AL	Anthony Lerew RC	1.50
HM	Hector Made RC	
WM	Warner Madrigal RC	2.00
PMM	Paul McAnulty RC	2.00
AO	Akinori Otsuka RC	2.00
TS	Todd Self RC	1.50
KS	Kyle Sleeth	2.00
DS	Don Sutton	3.00

First-Year Player Autographs

	Common Autograph:	8.00
DA	David Aardsma	10.00
CMA	Craig Ansman RC	10.00
JA	Joaquin Arias RC	10.00
EA	Erick Aybar RC	20.00
BB	Bobby Brownlie RC	10.00
RB	Ryan Budde	10.00
KC	Kory Casto RC	10.00
JC	Juan Cedeno RC	10.00
VC	Vito Chiaravalloti RC	10.00
MDC	Matt Creighton RC	8.00
DC	David Crouthers	10.00
TD	Tyler Davidson	10.00
ZD	Zachary Duke RC	30.00
JE	Jesse English RC	10.00
AG	Adam Greenberg	10.00
RG	Rudy Guillen RC	10.00
TOH	Travis Hanson	10.00
EH	Estee Harris RC	10.00
FH	Felix Hernandez RC	85.00
SH	Shawn Hill	10.00
JH	Jason Hirsh	20.00
LTH	Luke Hughes RC	8.00
CJ	Conor Jackson RC	30.00
LK	Logan Kensing RC	10.00
JK	Jon Knott RC	10.00
KK	Kevin Kouzmanoff RC	25.00
JL	Josh Labandeira RC	8.00
DL	Donald Levinski RC	10.00
PM	Paul Maholm RC	20.00
TRM	Tom Mastny RC	10.00
BEM	Brandon Medders RC	8.00
LM	Lastings Milledge RC	50.00
YM	Yadier Molina RC	25.00
DM	David Murphy	15.00
DN	Dioner Navarro RC	10.00

DDN	Dustin Nippert RC	10.00
RN	Ricky Nolasco RC	20.00
BP	Brayan Pena RC	8.00
QQ	Omar Quintanilla RC	10.00
RR	Ramon Ramirez RC	10.00
JS	Jeff Salazar RC	10.00
ES	Ervin Santana RC	30.00
BMS	Brad Snyder RC	15.00
WS	Wardell Starling RC	10.00
TJS	Tim Stauffer RC	10.00
BS	Brad Sullivan RC	10.00
JSZ	Jason Szuminski RC	10.00
RT	Rob Tejeda RC	10.00
NU	Nic Ungs RC	10.00
MV	Merkin Valdez RC	10.00
CZ	Charlie Zink RC	10.00

First-Year Player Relics

TB	Travis Blackley RC	5.00
KRK	Kody Kirkland RC	6.00
KM	Kazuo Matsui RC	6.00
KT	Kazuhito Tadano RC	6.00
ST	Shingo Takatsu RC	8.00

Green

Green Stars:	4-8X
Green Non-Auto. RC's:	1.5-3X
Production 100	
Green RC Autos.:	1-2X

Red

Red Stars:	No Pricing
Production 20	
Red Non-Auto. RC's:	No Pricing
Red RC Autos.:	No Pricing

Double Play Autographs

NM/M

	Common Duo:	20.00
	Inserted 1:33	
MH	Lastings Milledge, Estee Harris	40.00
QS	Omar Quintanilla, Brad Snyder	20.00
SC	Tim Stauffer, Vito Chiaravalloti	20.00
HJ	Travis Hanson, Conor Jackson	25.00
MN	Brandon Medders, Dustin Nippert	20.00
UK	Nic Ungs, Kevin Kouzmanoff	25.00
CC	Matt Creighton, David Crouthers	20.00
EN	Jesse English, Ricky Nolasco	20.00
SV	Ervin Santana, Merkin Valdez	30.00
SK	Jeff Salazar, Jon Knott	20.00

Triple Play Autographs

NM/M

	Common Trio:	30.00
	Inserted 1:109	
CBA	Juan Cedeno, Bobby Brownlie, Joaquin Arias	30.00
ALS	David Aardsma, Donald Levinski, Brad Sullivan	25.00
SSV	Tim Stauffer, Ervin Santana, Merkin Valdez	50.00

2005 Bowman

NM/M

Complete Set (330):	60.00
Common Player:	.15
Common Rookie:	.50
Pack (10):	3.00
Box (24):	60.00

1	Gavin Floyd	.25
2	Eric Chavez	.25
3	Miguel Tejada	.25
4	Dmitri Young	.15
5	Hank Blalock	.25
6	Kerry Wood	.25
7	Andy Pettitte	.40
8	Pat Burrell	.15
9	Johnny Estrada	.15
10	Frank Thomas	.75
11	Juan Pierre	.25
12	Tom Glavine	.40

13	Lyle Overbay	.25
14	Jim Edmonds	.40
15	Steve Finley	.15
16	Jermaine Dye	.25
17	Omar Vizquel	.15
18	Nick Johnson	.15
19	Brian Giles	.25
20	Justin Morneau	.50
21	Preston Wilson	.15
22	Wily Mo Pena	.15
23	Rafael Palmeiro	.50
24	Scott Kazmir	.25
25	Derek Jeter	2.00
26	Barry Zito	.25
27	Mike Lowell	.15
28	Jason Bay	.25
29	Ken Harvey	.15
30	Nomar Garciaparra	.75
31	Roy Halladay	.25
32	Todd Helton	.50
33	Mark Kotsay	.15
34	Jake Peavy	.40
35	David Wright	1.00
36	Dontrelle Willis	.40
37	Marcus Giles	.15
38	Chone Figgins	.15
39	Sidney Ponson	.15
40	Randy Johnson	.75
41	John Smoltz	.25
42	Kevin Millar	.15
43	Mark Teixeira	.50
44	Alex Rios	.25
45	Mike Piazza	1.00
46	Victor Martinez	.25
47	Jeff Bagwell	.50
48	Shawn Green	.25
49	Ivan Rodriguez	.50
50	Alex Rodriguez	1.50
51	Kazuo Matsui	.15
52	Mark Mulder	.40
53	Michael Young	.25
54	Javy Lopez	.15
55	Johnny Damon	.75
56	Jeff Francis	.25
57	Rich Harden	.25
58	Bobby Abreu	.40
59	Mark Loretta	.15
60	Gary Sheffield	.40
61	Jamie Moyer	.15
62	Garret Anderson	.25
63	Vernon Wells	.25
64	Orlando Cabrera	.25
65	Magglio Ordonez	.25
66	Ronnie Belliard	.15
67	Carlos Lee	.25
68	Carl Pavano	.25
69	Jon Lieber	.15
70	Aubrey Huff	.15
71	Rocco Baldelli	.25
72	Jason Schmidt	.25
73	Bernie Williams	.40
74	Hideki Matsui	1.50
75	Ken Griffey Jr.	1.50
76	Josh Beckett	.25
77	Mark Buehrle	.25
78	David Ortiz	.75
79	Luis Gonzalez	.25
80	Scott Rolen	.75
81	Joe Mauer	.50
82	Jose Reyes	.50
83	Adam Dunn	.50
84	Greg Maddux	1.00
85	Bartolo Colon	.25
86	Bret Boone	.15
87	Mike Mussina	.50
88	Ben Sheets	.40
89	Lance Berkman	.40
90	Miguel Cabrera	.75
91	C.C. Sabathia	.25
92	Mike Maroth	.15
93	Andruw Jones	.40
94	Jack Wilson	.15
95	Ichiro Suzuki	1.50
96	Geoff Jenkins	.15
97	Zack Greinke	.15
98	Jorge Posada	.40
99	Travis Hafner	.40
100	Barry Bonds	2.00
101	Aaron Rowand	.15
102	Aramis Ramirez	.40
103	Curt Schilling	.50
104	Melvin Mora	.15
105	Albert Pujols	2.00
106	Austin Kearns	.25
107	Shannon Stewart	.15
108	Carl Crawford	.40
109	Carlos Zambrano	.40
110	Roger Clemens	2.00
111	Javier Vazquez	.15
112	Randy Wolf	.15
113	Chipper Jones	.75
114	Larry Walker	.25
115	Alfonso Soriano	.25
116	Brad Wilkerson	.15
117	Bobby Crosby	.25
118	Jim Thome	.75
119	Oliver Perez	.25
120	Vladimir Guerrero	.75
121	Roy Oswalt	.40
122	Torii Hunter	.25
123	Rafael Furcal	.25
124	Luis Castillo	.15
125	Carlos Beltran	.50
126	Mike Sweeney	.25
127	Johan Santana	.50
128	Tim Hudson	.40
129	Troy Glaus	.40
130	Manny Ramirez	.75

131	Jeff Kent	.25
132	Jose Vidro	.15
133	Edgar Renteria	.25
134	Russ Ortiz	.15
135	Sammy Sosa	.75
136	Carlos Delgado	.40
137	Richie Sexson	.25
138	Pedro Martinez	.75
139	Adrian Beltre	.25
140	Mark Prior	.40
141	Omar Quintanilla	.25
142	Carlos Quentin	.25
143	Dan Johnson	.15
144	Jake Stevens	.15
145	Nate Schierholtz	.15
146	Neil Walker	.15
147	Bill Bray	.15
148	Taylor Tankersley	.15
149	Trevor Plouffe	.15
150	Felix Hernandez	.50
151	Phillip Hughes	.50
152	James Houser	.15
153	David Murphy	.15
154	Ervin Santana	.15
155	Anthony Whittington	.15
156	Chris Lambert	.15
157	Jeremy Sowers	.15
158	Gio Gonzalez	.15
159	Blake DeWitt	.15
160	Thomas Diamond	.15
161	Greg Golson	.15
162	David Aardsma	.15
163	Paul Maholm	.15
164	Mark Rogers	.15
165	Homer Bailey	.50
166	Chip Cannon RC	1.00
167	Tony Giarratano RC	.50
168	Darren Fenster RC	.50
169	Elvys Quezada RC	.75
170	Glen Perkins RC	1.00
171	Ian Kinsler RC	4.00
172	Michael Bourn RC	.75
173	Jeremy West RC	.75
174	Justin Verlander RC	3.00
175	Kevin West RC	.50
176	Luis Hernandez RC	1.00
177	Matt Campbell RC	.75
178	Nate McLouth RC	.50
179	Ryan Goleski RC	.50
180	Matt Lindstrom RC	.50
181	Matt DeSalvo RC	.50
182	Kole Strayhorn RC	.50
183	Jose Vaquedano RC	.50
184	James Jurries RC	.50
185	Ian Bladergroen RC	.75
186	Eric Nielsen RC	.50
187	Chris Vines RC	1.00
188	Chris Denorfia RC	.50
189	Kevin Melillo RC	.50
190	Melky Cabrera RC	2.00
191	Ryan Sweeney RC	1.50
192	Sean Marshall RC	.50
193	Andy LaRoche RC	3.00
194	Tyler Pelland RC	1.50
195	Mike Morse RC	.75
196	Wes Swackhamer RC	.50
197	Wade Robinson RC	.50
198	Dan Santin RC	.50
199	Steven Doetsch RC	.50
200	Shane Costa RC	.50
201	Scott Mathieson RC	.75
202	Ben Jones RC	.75
203	Michael Rogers RC	.50
204	Matt Rogelstad RC	.50
205	Luis Ramirez RC	1.00
206	Landon Powell RC	.75
207	Erik Cordier RC	.50
208	Chris Seddon RC	.50
209	Chris Roberson RC	.75
210	Tom Oldham RC	.50
211	Dana Eveland RC	1.00
212	Cody Haerther RC	.50
213	Danny Core RC	.50
214	Craig Tatum RC	.50
215	Elliot Johnson RC	.75
216	Ender Chavez RC	.75
217	Errol Simonitsch RC	.50
218	Matt Van Der Bosch RC	.75
219	Eulogio de la Cruz RC	.50
220	C.J. Smith RC	.50
221	Adam Boeve RC	.75
222	Adam Harben RC	.75
223	Baltazar Lopez RC	.75
224	Russ Martin RC	1.00
225	Brian Bannister RC	1.00
226	Brian Miller RC	.50
227	Casey McGehee RC	.50
228	Humberto Sanchez RC	1.50
229	Javon Moran RC	.50
230	Brandon McCarthy RC	2.00
231	Danny Zell RC	.50
232	Jake Postlewait RC	.50
233	Juan Tejeda RC	.50
234	Keith Ramsey RC	.50
235	Lorenzo Scott RC	.50
236	Wladimir Balentien RC	1.50
237	Martin Prado RC	.50
238	Matt Albers RC	.50
239	Brian Schweiger RC	.50
240	Brian Stavisky RC	.50
241	Pat Misch RC	.50
242	Pat Osborn RC	.50
243	Ryan Feierabend RC	1.00
244	Shaun Marcum	.50
245	Kevin Collins RC	.50
246	Stuart Pomeranz RC	.50
247	Tetsu Yofu RC	.50
248	Hernan Iribarren RC	1.00

249	Mike Spiegel RC	.50
250	Tony Arnerich RC	.50
251	Manny Parra RC	.75
252	Drew Anderson RC	.75
253	T.J. Beam RC	1.00
254	Pedro Lopez RC	.75
255	Andy Sides RC	.75
256	Bear Bay RC	.50
257	Bill McCarthy RC	.75
258	Daniel Haigwood RC	1.50
259	Brian Sprout RC	.75
260	Bryan Triplett RC	.75
261	Steve Bondurant RC	.50
262	Darwinson Salazar RC	.50
263	David Shepard RC	.50
264	Johan Silva RC	.75
265	J.B. Thurmond RC	.50
266	Brandon Moorhead RC	.50
267	Kyle Nichols RC	.50
268	Jonathan Sanchez RC	1.00
269	Mike Esposito RC	.50
270	Erik Schindewolf RC	.75
271	Peeter Ramos RC	.50
272	Juan Senreiso RC	.50
273	Matthew Kemp RC	3.00
274	Vinny Rottino RC	.50
275	Micah Furtado RC	.50
276	George Kottaras RC	.75
277	Billy Butler RC	4.00
278	Buck Coats RC	.50
279	Ken Durost RC	.50
280	Nic Touchstone RC	.50
281	Jerry Owens RC	1.00
282	Stefan Bailie	.50
283	Jesse Gutierrez RC	.50
284	Chuck Tiffany RC	1.00
285	Brendan Ryan RC	.50
286	Hayden Penn RC	2.00
287	Shawn Bowman RC	.50
288	Alexander Smit RC	.50
289	Micah Schnurstein RC	.75
290	Jared Gothreaux RC	.50
291	Jair Jurrjens RC	1.50
292	Bobby Livingston RC	.75
293	Ryan Speier RC	.50
294	Zachary Parker RC	.50
295	Christian Colonel RC	.50
296	Scott Mitchinson RC	.50
297	Neil Wilson RC	.50
298	Chuck James RC	2.50
299	Heath Totten RC	.50
300	Sean Tracey RC	.75
301	Ismael Ramirez RC	.50
302	Matt Brown RC	.50
303	Franklin Morales RC	1.00
304	Brandon Sing RC	.50
305	D.J. Houlton RC	.50
306	Jayce Tingler RC	.50
307	Mitchell Arnold RC	.50
308	Jim Burt RC	.75
309	Jason Motte RC	.50
310	David Gassner RC	.50
311	Andy Santana RC	.50
312	Kelvin Pichardo RC	.50
313	Carlos Carrasco RC	1.00
314	Willy Mota RC	.50
315	Frank Mata RC	.50
316	Carlos Gonzalez RC	2.50
317	Jeff Niemann RC	1.00
318	Chris Young RC	2.00
319	Billy Sadler RC	.50
320	Ricky Barrett RC	.50
321	Benjamin Harrison RC	.50
322	Steve Nelson RC	.50
323	Daryl Thompson RC	.75
324	Philip Humber RC	1.50
325	Jeremy Harts RC	.50
326	Nick Masset RC	.50
327	Mike Rodriguez RC	.50
328	Mike Garber RC	.50
329	Kennard Bibbs RC	.50
330	Ryan Garko RC	1.50

Gold

Stars:	1-2X
Rookies:	1-2X
Inserted 1:1	

White

Stars:	3-6X
Rookies:	3-6X
Production 240 Sets	

1st Edition

NM/M

Stars:	3-5X
Rookies:	1-2X

A-Rod Throwbacks

	HTA Exclusive	
	Pack (10):	3.50
	Box (20):	60.00

		NM/M
	Complete Set (4):	6.00
	Common A-Rod:	2.00
94-AR	Alex Rodriguez	2.00
95-AR	Alex Rodriguez	2.00
96-AR	Alex Rodriguez	2.00
97-AR	Alex Rodriguez	2.00

A-Rod Throwbacks Autographs

		NM/M
	Production 1-225	
96A-AR	Alex Rodriguez/99	150.00
97A-AR	Alex Rodriguez/225	150.00

A-Rod Throwbacks Relic

		NM/M
	Quantity produced listed	
96R-AR	Alex Rodriguez/99	20.00
97R-AR	Alex Rodriguez/800	15.00

Autographed Base Card Variations

		NM/M
	Inserted 1:1,599	
141	Omar Quintanilla	8.00
142	Carlos Quentin	20.00
143	Dan Johnson	10.00
144	Jake Stevens	10.00
145	Nate Schierholtz	10.00
146	Neil Walker	15.00
147	Bill Bray	8.00
148	Taylor Tankersley	10.00
149	Trevor Plouffe	12.00
150	Felix Hernandez	30.00
151	Phillip Hughes	40.00
152	James Houser	15.00
153	David Murphy	15.00
154	Ervin Santana	15.00
155	Anthony Whittington	8.00
156	Chris Lambert	12.00
157	Jeremy Sowers	15.00
158	Gio Gonzalez	15.00
159	Blake DeWitt	25.00
160	Thomas Diamond	15.00
161	Greg Golson	12.00
162	David Aardsma	10.00
163	Paul Maholm	12.00
164	Mark Rogers	15.00
165	Homer Bailey	30.00

Dual Rookie of the Year Relic

		NM/M
	Inserted 1:668	
ROY-BC	Jason Bay, Bobby Crosby	15.00

Futures Game Gear

		NM/M
JB	Joe Blanton	5.00
BB	Bryan Bullington	5.00
MC	Matt Cain	5.00
SC	Shin-Soo Choo	6.00

JCO	Jorge Cortes	5.00
JC	Jesus Cota	5.00
EE	Edwin Encarnacion	5.00
CE	Clint Everts	5.00
GF	Gavin Floyd	5.00
JF	Jeff Francis	5.00
JG	Jairo Garcia	5.00
RG	Ruben Gotay	5.00
JGU	Joel Guzman	5.00
AH	Aaron Hill	5.00
KH	Koyie Hill	5.00
WL	Wilfredo Ledezma	5.00
VM	Val Majewski	5.00
AMA	Andy Marte	8.00
JM	Jeff Mathis	5.00
DM	Dallas McPherson	8.00
JMO	Justin Morneau	8.00
AM	Arnie Munoz	5.00
YP	Yusmeiro Petit	8.00
FP	Felix Pie	8.00
RW	Rickie Weeks	8.00

Printing Plates

No Pricing
Production One Set

Relic Base Card Variations

		NM/M
	Inserted 1:50	
2	Eric Chavez	5.00
5	Hank Blalock	8.00
23	Rafael Palmeiro	8.00
43	Mark Teixeira	8.00
49	Ivan Rodriguez	8.00
50	Alex Rodriguez	15.00
60	Gary Sheffield	8.00
65	Magglio Ordonez	5.00
78	David Ortiz	10.00
83	Adam Dunn	8.00
90	Miguel Cabrera	8.00
93	Andruw Jones	5.00
100	Barry Bonds	25.00
104	Melvin Mora	5.00
105	Albert Pujols	20.00
115	Alfonso Soriano	8.00
120	Vladimir Guerrero	8.00
125	Carlos Beltran	10.00
130	Manny Ramirez	8.00
135	Sammy Sosa	12.00

Signs of the Future

		NM/M
BB	Brian Bixler	10.00
MC	Melky Cabrera	25.00
RC	Robinson Cano	45.00
CC	Chad Cordero	10.00
BC	Bobby Crosby	15.00
BD	Blake DeWitt	20.00
CG	Christian Garcia	10.00
TG	Tom Gorzelanny	10.00
PH	Phillip Hughes	40.00
TH	Tim Hutting	10.00
SK	Scott Kazmir	15.00
AL	Adam Loewen	10.00
PM	Paul Maholm	10.00
DM	Dallas McPherson	10.00
SO	Scott Olson	10.00
TP	Trevor Plouffe	15.00
DP	Dan Putnam	15.00
JR	Jay Rainville	15.00
RR	Richie Robnett	15.00
ES	Ervin Santana	15.00
JS	Jay Sborz	10.00
BMS	Brad Snyder	10.00
HS	Huston Street	25.00
BS	Brad Sullivan	10.00
TT	Taylor Tankersley	12.00
RW	Ryan Wagner	10.00
KW	Kyle Waldrop	10.00
AW	Anthony Whittington	10.00
DW	David Wright	70.00

Two of a Kind Autograph

No Pricing
Production 13

2005 Bowman Chrome

		NM/M
	Complete Set (352):	
	Common Player:	.25

	Common Rookie:	1.00
	Common RC Auto.	
	(331-352):	10.00
	Pack (4):	7.00
	Box (18):	100.00
1	Gavin Floyd	.25
2	Eric Chavez	.50
3	Miguel Tejada	.75
4	Dmitri Young	.25
5	Hank Blalock	.50
6	Kerry Wood	.50
7	Andy Pettitte	.50
8	Pat Burrell	.50
9	Johnny Estrada	.25
10	Frank Thomas	.75
11	Juan Pierre	.25
12	Tom Glavine	.50
13	Lyle Overbay	.25
14	Jim Edmonds	.50
15	Steve Finley	.25
16	Jermaine Dye	.25
17	Omar Vizquel	.25
18	Nick Johnson	.25
19	Brian Giles	.25
20	Justin Morneau	.50
21	Preston Wilson	.25
22	Wily Mo Pena	.25
23	Rafael Palmeiro	.75
24	Scott Kazmir	1.00
25	Derek Jeter	3.00
26	Barry Zito	.50
27	Mike Lowell	.25
28	Jason Bay	.50
29	Ken Harvey	.25
30	Nomar Garciaparra	1.00
31	Roy Halladay	.50
32	Todd Helton	.75
33	Mark Kotsay	.25
34	Jake Peavy	.50
35	David Wright	1.00
36	Dontrelle Willis	.50
37	Marcus Giles	.25
38	Chone Figgins	.25
39	Sidney Ponson	.25
40	Randy Johnson	1.00
41	John Smoltz	.50
42	Kevin Millar	.25
43	Mark Teixeira	.75
44	Alex Rios	.25
45	Mike Piazza	1.00
46	Victor Martinez	.50
47	Jeff Bagwell	.75
48	Shawn Green	.50
49	Ivan Rodriguez	.75
50	Alex Rodriguez	2.50
51	Kazuo Matsui	.25
52	Mark Mulder	.50
53	Michael Young	.50
54	Javy Lopez	.25
55	Johnny Damon	1.00
56	Jeff Francis	.25
57	Rich Harden	.50
58	Bobby Abreu	.50
59	Mark Loretta	.25
60	Gary Sheffield	.50
61	Jamie Moyer	.25
62	Garret Anderson	.50
63	Vernon Wells	.50
64	Orlando Cabrera	.25
65	Magglio Ordonez	.25
66	Ronnie Belliard	.25
67	Carlos Lee	.50
68	Carl Pavano	.25
69	Jon Lieber	.25
70	Aubrey Huff	.25
71	Rocco Baldelli	.25
72	Jason Schmidt	.50
73	Bernie Williams	.50
74	Hideki Matsui	2.00
75	Ken Griffey Jr.	2.00
76	Josh Beckett	.50
77	Mark Buehrle	.40
78	David Ortiz	1.00
79	Luis Gonzalez	.25
80	Scott Rolen	1.00
81	Joe Mauer	.75
82	Jose Reyes	.75
83	Adam Dunn	.75
84	Greg Maddux	2.00
85	Bartolo Colon	.40
86	Bret Boone	.25
87	Mike Mussina	.50
88	Ben Sheets	.50
89	Lance Berkman	.50
90	Miguel Cabrera	1.00
91	C.C. Sabathia	.25
92	Mike Maroth	.25
93	Andruw Jones	.50

94	Jack Wilson	.25
95	Ichiro Suzuki	2.00
96	Geoff Jenkins	.25
97	Zack Greinke	.25
98	Jorge Posada	.50
99	Travis Hafner	.50
100	Barry Bonds	3.00
101	Aaron Rowand	.25
102	Aramis Ramirez	.50
103	Curt Schilling	.50
104	Melvin Mora	.25
105	Albert Pujols	3.00
106	Austin Kearns	.40
107	Shannon Stewart	.25
108	Carl Crawford	.25
109	Carlos Zambrano	.50
110	Roger Clemens	3.00
111	Javier Vazquez	.25
112	Randy Wolf	.25
113	Chipper Jones	1.00
114	Larry Walker	.50
115	Alfonso Soriano	1.00
116	Brad Wilkerson	.25
117	Bobby Crosby	.25
118	Jim Thome	.75
119	Oliver Perez	.25
120	Vladimir Guerrero	1.00
121	Roy Oswalt	.50
122	Torii Hunter	.50
123	Rafael Furcal	.25
124	Luis Castillo	.25
125	Carlos Beltran	.75
126	Mike Sweeney	.25
127	Johan Santana	.75
128	Tim Hudson	.50
129	Troy Glaus	.50
130	Manny Ramirez	1.00
131	Jeff Kent	.40
132	Jose Vidro	.25
133	Edgar Renteria	.40
134	Russ Ortiz	.25
135	Sammy Sosa	1.00
136	Carlos Delgado	.50
137	Richie Sexson	.50
138	Pedro Martinez	1.00
139	Adrian Beltre	.50
140	Mark Prior	.75
141	Omar Quintanilla	.25
142	Carlos Quentin	.25
143	Dan Johnson	.25
144	Jake Stevens	.25
145	Nate Schierholtz	.25
146	Neil Walker	.25
147	Bill Bray	.25
148	Taylor Tankersley	.25
149	Trevor Plouffe	.25
150	Felix Hernandez	1.00
151	Phillip Hughes	.50
152	James Houser	.25
153	David Murphy	.25
154	Ervin Santana	.25
155	Anthony Whittington	.25
156	Chris Lambert	.25
157	Jeremy Sowers	.40
158	Gio Gonzalez	.25
159	Blake DeWitt	.25
160	Thomas Diamond	.25
161	Greg Golson	.25
162	David Aardsma	.25
163	Paul Maholm	.25
164	Mark Rogers	.25
165	Homer Bailey	.50
166	Elvin Puello RC	1.00
167	Tony Giarratano RC	1.50
168	Darren Fenster RC	1.00
169	Elvys Quezada RC	1.00
170	Glen Perkins RC	2.50
171	Ian Kinsler RC	15.00
172	Adam Bostick RC	1.00
173	Jeremy West RC	2.00
174	Brett Harper RC	2.00
175	Kevin West RC	1.00
176	Luis Hernandez RC	1.00
177	Matt Campbell RC	1.00
178	Nate McLouth RC	1.50
179	Ryan Goleski RC	2.00
180	Matt Lindstrom RC	1.00
181	Matt DeSalvo RC	1.50
182	Kole Strayhorn RC	1.00
183	Jose Vaquedano RC	1.00
184	James Jurries RC	1.50
185	Ian Bladergroen RC	2.50
186	Kila Kaaihue RC	4.00
187	Luke Scott RC	4.00
188	Chris Denorfia RC	3.00
189	Jai Miller RC	1.50
190	Melky Cabrera RC	6.00
191	Ryan Sweeney RC	5.00
192	Sean Marshall RC	3.00
193	Eric Abreu RC	2.00
194	Tyler Pelland RC	1.50
195	Cole Armstrong RC	1.50
196	John Hudgins RC	1.00
197	Wade Robinson RC	1.00
198	Dan Santin RC	1.00
199	Steven Doetsch RC	1.50
200	Shane Costa RC	1.00
201	Scott Mathieson RC	2.00
202	Ben Jones RC	2.00
203	Michael Rogers RC	1.50
204	Matt Rogelstad RC	1.50
205	Luis Ramirez RC	1.00
206	Landon Powell RC	2.00
207	Erik Cordier RC	1.50
208	Chris Seddon RC	1.00
209	Chris Roberson RC	1.50
210	Tom Oldham RC	1.00
211	Dana Eveland RC	2.50

212	Cody Haerther RC	1.00
213	Danny Core RC	1.00
214	Craig Tatum RC	1.00
215	Elliot Johnson RC	2.50
216	Ender Chavez RC	1.00
217	Errol Simonitsch RC	1.50
218	Matt Van Der Bosch RC	6.00
219	Eulogio de la Cruz RC	1.00
220	Drew Toussaint RC	1.00
221	Adam Boeve RC	2.00
222	Adam Harben RC	1.50
223	Baltazar Lopez RC	1.00
224	Russell Martin RC	4.00
225	Brian Bannister RC	2.00
226	Chris Walker RC	1.00
227	Casey McGehee RC	1.50
228	Humberto Sanchez RC	6.00
229	Javon Moran RC	1.00
230	Brandon McCarthy RC	5.00
231	Danny Zell RC	1.00
232	Kevin Barry RC	1.00
233	Juan Tejeda RC	1.50
234	Keith Ramsey RC	1.00
235	Lorenzo Scott RC	1.00
236	Jonathan Barratt RC	1.00
237	Martin Prado RC	2.00
238	Matt Albers RC	3.00
239	Brian Schweiger RC	1.00
240	Raul Tablado RC	1.00
241	Pat Misch RC	1.00
242	Pat Osborn RC	1.00
243	Ryan Feierabend RC	1.00
244	Shaun Marcum RC	1.00
245	Kevin Collins RC	1.00
246	Stuart Pomeranz RC	1.00
247	Tetsu Yofu RC	1.00
248	Hernan Iribarren RC	3.00
249	Michael Spidale RC	1.00
250	Tony Americh RC	1.00
251	Manny Parra RC	1.00
252	Drew Anderson RC	1.00
253	T.J. Beam RC	3.00
254	Claudio Arias RC	2.00
255	Andy Sides RC	1.00
256	Bear Bay RC	2.00
257	Bill McCarthy RC	1.00
258	Daniel Haigwood RC	3.00
259	Brian Sprout RC	1.00
260	Bryan Triplett RC	1.00
261	Steve Bondurant RC	1.00
262	Darwinson Salazar RC	1.00
263	David Shepard RC	1.00
264	Johan Silva RC	1.50
265	J.B. Thurmond RC	1.00
266	Brandon Moorhead RC	1.00
267	Kyle Nichols RC	2.00
268	Jonathan Sanchez RC	4.00
269	Mike Esposito RC	1.00
270	Erik Schindewolf RC	2.00
271	Peeter Ramos RC	1.00
272	Juan Senreiso RC	1.00
273	Travis Chick RC	2.00
274	Vinny Rottino RC	1.00
276	Micah Furtado RC	1.00
276	George Kottaras RC	2.00
277	Abel Gomez RC	1.50
278	Buck Coats RC	1.00
279	Ken Durost RC	1.00
280	Nick Touchstone RC	1.00
281	Jerry Owens RC	2.00
282	Stefan Bailie RC	1.00
283	Jesse Gutierrez RC	1.00
284	Chuck Tiffany RC	3.00
285	Brendan Ryan RC	1.00
286	Julio Pimentel RC	1.00
287	Shawn Bowman RC	1.50
288	Alexander Smit RC	1.50
289	Micah Schnurstein RC	1.50
290	Jared Gothreaux RC	1.00
291	Jair Jurrjens RC	2.00
292	Bobby Livingston RC	1.00
293	Ryan Speier RC	1.00
294	Zachary Parker RC	1.00
295	Christian Colonel RC	1.00
296	Scott Mitchinson RC	1.00
297	Neil Wilson RC	1.00
298	Chuck James RC	6.00
299	Heath Totten RC	1.00
300	Sean Tracey RC	1.00
301	Tadahito Iguchi RC	2.50
302	Matt Brown RC	1.00
303	Franklin Morales RC	4.00
304	Brandon Sing RC	3.00
305	D.J. Houlton RC	1.50
306	Jayce Tingler RC	1.00
307	Mitchell Arnold RC	1.00
308	Jim Burt RC	1.00
309	Jason Motte RC	1.00
310	David Gassner RC	1.00
311	Andy Santana RC	1.00
312	Kelvin Pichardo RC	1.00
313	Carlos Carrasco RC	4.00
314	Willy Mota RC	1.00
315	Frank Mata RC	1.00
316	Carlos Gonzalez RC	15.00
317	Jesse Floyd RC	1.00
318	Chris Young RC	6.00
319	Billy Sadler RC	1.00
320	Ricky Barrett RC	1.00
321	Benjamin Harrison RC	1.00
322	Steve Nelson RC	1.00
323	Daryl Thompson RC	1.00
324	Davis Romero RC	1.00
325	Jeremy Harts RC	1.00
326	Nick Masset RC	1.00

327	Thomas Pauly RC	1.00
328	Mike Garber RC	1.00
329	Kennard Bibbs RC	1.00
330	Colter Bean RC	1.00
331	Justin Verlander RC	85.00
332	Chip Cannon RC	40.00
333	Kevin Melillo RC	15.00
334	Jake Postlewait RC	10.00
335	Wes Swackhamer RC	15.00
336	Mike Rodriguez RC	15.00
337	Philip Humber RC	40.00
338	Jeff Niemann RC	30.00
339	Brian Miller RC	10.00
340	Chris Vines RC	10.00
341	Andy LaRoche RC	75.00
342	Michael Bourn RC	20.00
343	Eric Nielsen RC	15.00
344	Wladimir Balentien RC	30.00
345	Ismael Ramirez RC	15.00
346	Pedro Lopez RC	10.00
347	Shawn Bowman RC	15.00
348	Hayden Penn RC	25.00
349	Matthew Kemp RC	80.00
350	Brian Stavisky RC	10.00
351	C.J. Smith RC	10.00
352	Mike Morse RC	20.00
353	Billy Butler RC	100.00

Refractor

Stars (1-165):	2-4X
Rookies (166-330):	1-2X
Inserted 1:4	
Autograph (331-353):	1-2X
Production 500	

Blue Refractor

Stars (1-165):	3-5X
Rookies (166-330):	3-5X
Autograph (331-353):	1-2.5X
Production 150 Sets	

Gold Refractor

Stars (1-165):	8-15X
Rookies (166-330):	15-25X
Autograph (331-353):	3-6X
Production 50 Sets	

Red Refractor

No Pricing
Production 5 Sets

Superfractor

No Pricing
Production One Set

X-Fractor

Stars (1-165):	3-5X
Rookies (166-330):	2-5X
Autograph (331-353):	1-2.5X
Production 225 Sets	

Printing Plates

No Pricing
Production one set per color.

A-Rod Throwback

		NM/M
	Complete Set (4):	6.00
	Common A-Rod	2.00
	Inserted 1:9	
	Refractor:	2-3X
	Production 499 Sets	
	X-Fractor:	3-5X
	Production 99 Sets	
	Superfractor:	No Pricing
	Production One Set	
94AR	Alex Rodriguez	2.00
95AR	Alex Rodriguez	2.00
96AR	Alex Rodriguez	2.00
97AR	Alex Rodriguez	2.00

A-Rod Throwback Autograph

		NM/M
	Quantity produced listed	
94AR	Alex Rodriguez/1	
95AR	Alex Rodriguez/25	
96AR	Alex Rodriguez/50	160.00
97AR	Alex Rodriguez/99	150.00

One Of A Kind Autograph

No Pricing
Production 13

2005 Bowman Draft Picks & Prospects

		NM/M
Complete Set (165):		30.00
Commmon Player:		.15
Common Rookie		.25
Pack (5 + 2 Chrome):		6.00
Box (24):		120.00
BDP1	Rickie Weeks	.15
BDP2	Kyle Davies	.15
BDP3	Garrett Atkins	.15
BDP4	Chien-Ming Wang	.50
BDP5	Dallas McPherson	.15
BDP6	Dan Johnson	.15
BDP7	Andy Sisco	.15
BDP8	Ryan Doumit	.15
BDP9	J.P. Howell	.15
BDP10	Tim Stauffer	.15
BDP11	Willy Taveras	.15
BDP12	Aaron Hill	.15
BDP13	Victor Diaz	.15
BDP14	Wilson Betemit	.15
BDP15	Ervin Santana	.15
BDP16	Mike Morse	.15
BDP17	Yadier Molina	.15
BDP18	Kelly Johnson	.15
BDP19	Clint Barmes	.15
BDP20	Robinson Cano	.40
BDP21	Brad Thompson	.15
BDP22	Jorge Cantu	.15
BDP23	Brad Halsey	.15
BDP24	Lance Niekro	.15
BDP25	D.J. Houlton	.15
BDP26	Ryan Church	.15
BDP27	Hayden Penn	.15
BDP28	Chris Young	.15
BDP29	Chad Orvella	.15
BDP30	Mark Teahen	.15
BDP31	Mark McCormick RC	.25
BDP32	Jay Bruce RC	3.00
BDP33	Beau Jones RC	.75
BDP34	Tyler Greene RC	.40
BDP35	Zach Ward RC	.75
BDP36	Josh Bell RC	1.00
BDP37	Josh Wall RC	.50
BDP38	Nick Webber RC	.25
BDP39	Travis Buck RC	1.00
BDP40	Kyle Winters RC	.25
BDP41	Mitch Boggs RC	.25
BDP42	Tommy Mendoza RC	.25
BDP43	Brad Corley RC	.40
BDP44	Drew Butera RC	.25
BDP45	Ryan Mount RC	.40
BDP46	Tyler Herron RC	.25
BDP47	Nick Weglarz RC	1.00
BDP48	Brandon Erbe RC	1.00
BDP49	Cody Allen RC	.25
BDP50	Eric Fowler RC	.25
BDP51	James Boone RC	.50
BDP52	Josh Flores RC	.75
BDP53	Brandon Monk RC	.50
BDP54	Kieron Pope RC	.75
BDP55	Kyle Cofield RC	.40
BDP56	Brent Lillibridge RC	.40
BDP57	Daryl Jones RC	.50
BDP58	Eli Iorg RC	.50
BDP59	Brett Hayes RC	.25
BDP60	Mike Durant RC	.75
BDP61	Michael Bowden RC	.50
BDP62	Paul Kelly RC	.50
BDP63	Andrew McCutchen RC	1.50
BDP64	Travis Wood RC	.75
BDP65	Cesar Ramos RC	.25
BDP66	Chaz Roe RC	.40
BDP67	Matt Torra RC	.50
BDP68	Kevin Slowey RC	1.50
BDP69	Trayvon Robinson RC	.40
BDP70	Reid Engel RC	.40
BDP71	Kris Harvey RC	.50
BDP72	Craig Italiano RC	.50
BDP73	Matt Maloney RC	.75
BDP74	Sean West RC	1.00
BDP75	Henry Sanchez RC	.50
BDP76	Scott Blue RC	.25
BDP77	Jordan Schafer RC	.50
BDP78	Chris Robinson RC	.25
BDP79	Chris Hobdy RC	.25
BDP80	Brandon Durden RC	.25
BDP81	Clay Buchholz RC	1.00
BDP82	Josh Geer RC	.25
BDP83	Sam LeCure RC	.25
BDP84	Justin Thomas RC	.25
BDP85	Brett Gardner RC	.50
BDP86	Tommy Manzella RC	.25
BDP87	Matt Green RC	.25
BDP88	Yunel Escobar RC	.75
BDP89	Mike Costanzo RC	.75
BDP90	Nick Hundley RC	.25
BDP91	Zach Simons RC	.25
BDP92	Jacob Marceaux RC	.25
BDP93	Jed Lowrie RC	.40
BDP94	Brandon Snyder RC	1.00
BDP95	Matt Goyen RC	.25
BDP96	Jon Egan RC	.40
BDP97	Drew Thompson RC	.25
BDP98	Bryan Anderson RC	1.00
BDP99	Clayton Richard RC	.25
BDP100	Jimmy Shull RC	.25
BDP101	Mark Pawelek RC	1.00
BDP102	P.J. Phillips RC	.40
BDP103	John Drennen RC	.75
BDP104	Nolan Reimold RC	1.50
BDP105	Troy Tulowitzki RC	2.50
BDP106	Kevin Whelan RC	.25
BDP107	Wade Townsend RC	.50
BDP108	Micah Owings RC	1.50
BDP109	Ryan Tucker RC	.40
BDP110	Jeff Clement RC	1.50
BDP111	Josh Sullivan RC	.25
BDP112	Jeff Lyman RC	.25
BDP113	Brian Bogusevic RC	.40
BDP114	Trevor Bell RC	.50
BDP115	Brent Cox RC	.75
BDP116	Michael Billek RC	.25
BDP117	Garrett Olson RC	.40
BDP118	Steven Johnson RC	.25
BDP119	Chase Headley RC	.75
BDP120	Daniel Carte RC	.50
BDP121	Francisco Liriano RC	.75
BDP122	Fausto Carmona RC	.15
BDP123	Zach Jackson RC	.15
BDP124	Adam Loewen RC	.15
BDP125	Chris Lambert RC	.15
BDP126	Scott Mathieson RC	.15
BDP127	Paul Maholm RC	.15
BDP128	Fernando Nieve RC	.15
BDP129	Justin Verlander RC	.75
BDP130	Yusmeiro Petit RC	.40
BDP131	Joel Zumaya RC	.15
BDP132	Merkin Valdez	.15
BDP133	Ryan Garko RC	.75
BDP134	Edinson Volquez RC	.75
BDP135	Russell Martin RC	.50
BDP136	Conor Jackson	.25
BDP137	Miguel Montero RC	.50
BDP138	Josh Barfield	.15
BDP139	Delmon Young	.25
BDP140	Andy LaRoche RC	.75
BDP141	William Bergolla	.15
BDP142	B.J. Upton	.15
BDP143	Hernan Iribarren RC	.25
BDP144	Brandon Wood	.40
BDP145	Jose Bautista	.15
BDP146	Edwin Encarnacion	.15
BDP147	Javier Herrera RC	1.00
BDP148	Jeremy Hermida	.25
BDP149	Frank Diaz RC	.25
BDP150	Chris Young	.50
BDP151	Shin-Soo Choo	.15
BDP152	Kevin Thompson	.15
BDP153	Hanley Ramirez	.25
BDP154	Lastings Milledge	.25
BDP155	Luis Montanez	.15
BDP156	Justin Huber	.15
BDP157	Zachary Duke	.15
BDP158	Jeff Francoeur	.25
BDP159	Melky Cabrera	1.00
BDP160	Bobby Jenks	.15
BDP161	Ian Snell	.15
BDP162	Fernando Cabrera	.15
BDP163	Troy Patton	.50
BDP164	Anthony Lerew	.15
BDP165	Nelson Cruz	.75

White

Rookies: 3-5X
Production 225 Sets

Red

No Pricing
Production One Set

Base Relic Variation

		NM/M
Common Player:		4.00
BDP121	Francisco Liriano	8.00
BDP122	Fausto Carmona	4.00
BDP123	Zach Jackson	4.00
BDP124	Adam Loewen	4.00
BDP125	Chris Lambert	4.00
BDP126	Scott Mathieson	4.00
BDP127	Paul Maholm	4.00
BDP128	Fernando Nieve	4.00
BDP129	Justin Verlander	8.00
BDP130	Yusmeiro Petit	6.00
BDP131	Joel Zumaya	10.00
BDP132	Merkin Valdez	4.00
BDP133	Ryan Garko	6.00
BDP134	Edinson Volquez	6.00
BDP135	Russell Martin	6.00
BDP136	Conor Jackson	6.00
BDP137	Miguel Montero	6.00
BDP138	Josh Barfield	4.00
BDP139	Delmon Young	6.00
BDP140	Andy LaRoche	6.00
BDP141	William Bergolla	4.00
BDP142	B.J. Upton	4.00
BDP143	Hernan Iribarren	4.00
BDP144	Brandon Wood	10.00
BDP145	Jose Bautista	4.00
BDP146	Edwin Encarnacion	4.00
BDP147	Javier Herrera	6.00
BDP148	Jeremy Hermida	6.00
BDP149	Frank Diaz	4.00
BDP150	Chris Young	6.00

Signs of the Future

		NM/M
Common Player:		8.00
HB	Homer Bailey	25.00
BB	Bill Bray	8.00
JF	Jeff Frazier	8.00
GG	Greg Golson	8.00
AG	Angel Guzman	10.00
JH	Justin Hoyman	8.00
JJ	Justin Jones	8.00
DL	Donald Lucey	8.00
TL	Tyler Lumsden	8.00
DM	David Murphy	10.00
JP	Jonathan Poterson	8.00
DP	David Purcey	8.00
RR	Richie Robnett	8.00
JS	Jeremy Sowers	10.00

2005 Bowman Chrome Draft Picks & Prospects

		NM/M
Complete Set (180):		
Common Player:		.25
Common Rookie:		1.00
Common RK Auto.		
(166-180):		15.00
BDP1	Rickie Weeks	.40
BDP2	Kyle Davies	.25
BDP3	Garrett Atkins	.25
BDP4	Chien-Ming Wang	.75
BDP5	Dallas McPherson	.25
BDP6	Dan Johnson	.25
BDP7	Andy Sisco	.25
BDP8	Ryan Doumit	.25
BDP9	J.P. Howell	.25
BDP10	Tim Stauffer	.25
BDP11	Willy Taveras	.25
BDP12	Aaron Hill	.25
BDP13	Victor Diaz	.25
BDP14	Wilson Betemit	.25
BDP15	Ervin Santana	.25
BDP16	Mike Morse	.25
BDP17	Yadier Molina	.25
BDP18	Kelly Johnson	.25
BDP19	Clint Barmes	.25
BDP20	Robinson Cano	.75
BDP21	Brad Thompson	.25
BDP22	Jorge Cantu	.25
BDP23	Brad Halsey	.25
BDP24	Lance Niekro	.25
BDP25	D.J. Houlton	.25
BDP26	Ryan Church	.25
BDP27	Hayden Penn	.25
BDP28	Chris Young	.25
BDP29	Chad Orvella	.50
BDP30	Mark Teahen	.25
BDP31	Mark McCormick RC	1.00
BDP32	Jay Bruce RC	10.00
BDP33	Beau Jones RC	2.50
BDP34	Tyler Greene RC	1.50
BDP35	Zach Ward RC	2.50
BDP36	Josh Bell RC	4.00
BDP37	Josh Wall RC	2.00
BDP38	Nick Webber RC	1.00
BDP39	Travis Buck RC	3.00
BDP40	Kyle Winters RC	1.00
BDP41	Mitch Boggs RC	1.00
BDP42	Tommy Mendoza RC	2.00
BDP43	Brad Corley RC	1.50
BDP44	Drew Butera RC	1.00
BDP45	Ryan Mount RC	1.50
BDP46	Tyler Herron RC	1.00
BDP47	Nick Weglarz RC	4.00
BDP48	Brandon Erbe RC	4.00
BDP49	Cody Allen RC	1.00
BDP50	Eric Fowler RC	1.00
BDP51	James Boone RC	1.50
BDP52	Josh Flores RC	3.00
BDP53	Brandon Monk RC	2.00
BDP54	Kieron Pope RC	2.50
BDP55	Kyle Cofield RC	1.50
BDP56	Brent Lillibridge RC	2.00
BDP57	Daryl Jones RC	1.50
BDP58	Eli Iorg RC	2.00
BDP59	Brett Hayes RC	1.00
BDP60	Mike Durant RC	3.00
BDP61	Michael Bowden RC	4.00
BDP62	Paul Kelly RC	4.00
BDP63	Andrew McCutchen RC	8.00
BDP64	Travis Wood RC	3.00
BDP65	Cesar Ramos RC	1.00
BDP66	Chaz Roe RC	1.50
BDP67	Matt Torra RC	2.00
BDP68	Kevin Slowey RC	6.00
BDP69	Trayvon Robinson RC	1.50
BDP70	Reid Engel RC	1.50
BDP71	Kris Harvey RC	2.00
BDP72	Craig Italiano RC	2.50
BDP73	Matt Maloney RC	2.50
BDP74	Sean West RC	4.00
BDP75	Henry Sanchez RC	2.50
BDP76	Scott Blue RC	1.00
BDP77	Jordan Schafer RC	2.00
BDP78	Chris Robinson RC	1.00
BDP79	Chris Hobdy RC	1.00
BDP80	Brandon Durden RC	1.00
BDP81	Clay Buchholz RC	4.00
BDP82	Josh Geer RC	1.00
BDP83	Sam LeCure RC	1.00
BDP84	Justin Thomas RC	1.00
BDP85	Brett Gardner RC	1.50
BDP86	Tommy Manzella RC	1.00
BDP87	Matt Green RC	1.00
BDP88	Yunel Escobar RC	3.00
BDP89	Mike Costanzo RC	3.00
BDP90	Nick Hundley RC	1.00
BDP91	Zach Simons RC	1.00
BDP92	Jacob Marceaux RC	1.00
BDP93	Jed Lowrie RC	2.00
BDP94	Brandon Snyder RC	4.00
BDP95	Matt Goyen RC	1.00
BDP96	Jon Egan RC	1.50
BDP97	Drew Thompson RC	1.50
BDP98	Bryan Anderson RC	4.00
BDP99	Clayton Richard RC	1.00
BDP100	Jimmy Shull RC	1.00
BDP101	Mark Pawelek RC	5.00
BDP102	P.J. Phillips RC	1.50
BDP103	John Drennen RC	2.00
BDP104	Nolan Reimold RC	5.00
BDP105	Troy Tulowitzki RC	10.00
BDP106	Kevin Whelan RC	1.00
BDP107	Wade Townsend RC	2.00
BDP108	Micah Owings RC	4.00
BDP109	Ryan Tucker RC	1.50
BDP110	Jeff Clement RC	6.00
BDP111	Josh Sullivan RC	1.00
BDP112	Jeff Lyman RC	1.00
BDP113	Brian Bogusevic RC	1.00
BDP114	Trevor Bell RC	2.00
BDP115	Brent Cox RC	1.50
BDP116	Michael Billek RC	1.00
BDP117	Garrett Olson RC	1.50
BDP118	Steven Johnson RC	1.00
BDP119	Chase Headley RC	3.00
BDP120	Daniel Carte RC	2.00
BDP121	Francisco Liriano RC	1.50
BDP122	Fausto Carmona	.25
BDP123	Zach Jackson	.25
BDP124	Adam Loewen	.25
BDP125	Chris Lambert	.25
BDP126	Scott Mathieson RC	1.00
BDP127	Paul Maholm	.25
BDP128	Fernando Nieve	.25
BDP129	Justin Verlander	3.00
BDP130	Yusmeiro Petit	.25
BDP131	Joel Zumaya	1.00
BDP132	Merkin Valdez	.25
BDP133	Ryan Garko	4.00
BDP134	Edinson Volquez RC	2.00
BDP135	Russell Martin	2.00
BDP136	Conor Jackson	.25
BDP137	Miguel Montero RC	3.00
BDP138	Josh Barfield	.50
BDP139	Delmon Young	.50
BDP140	Andy LaRoche	2.00
BDP141	William Bergolla	.25
BDP142	B.J. Upton	.25
BDP143	Hernan Iribarren	1.00
BDP144	Brandon Wood	1.00
BDP145	Jose Bautista	.25
BDP146	Edwin Encarnacion	.25
BDP147	Javier Herrera RC	4.00
BDP148	Jeremy Hermida	.25
BDP149	Frank Diaz RC	1.00
BDP150	Chris Young	2.00
BDP151	Shin-Soo Choo	.25
BDP152	Kevin Thompson	.25
BDP153	Hanley Ramirez	.50
BDP154	Lastings Milledge	.50
BDP155	Luis Montanez	.25
BDP156	Justin Huber	.25
BDP157	Zachary Duke	.25
BDP158	Jeff Francoeur	.50
BDP159	Melky Cabrera	3.00
BDP160	Bobby Jenks	.25
BDP161	Ian Snell	.25
BDP162	Fernando Cabrera	.25
BDP163	Troy Patton	2.00
BDP164	Anthony Lerew	.25
BDP165	Nelson Cruz	3.00
BDP166	Stephen Drew RC	120.00
BDP167	Jered Weaver RC	100.00
BDP168	Ryan Braun RC	90.00
BDP169	John Mayberry Jr. RC	30.00
BDP170	Aaron Thompson RC	15.00
BDP171	Cesar Carrillo RC	25.00
BDP172	Jacoby Ellsbury RC	50.00
BDP173	Matt Garza RC	60.00
BDP174	Cliff Pennington RC	10.00
BDP175	Colby Rasmus RC	60.00
BDP176	Chris Volstad RC	25.00
BDP177	Ricky Romero RC	15.00
BDP178	Ryan Zimmerman RC	125.00
BDP179	C.J. Henry RC	30.00
BDP180	Eddy Martinez RC	25.00

Refractor

Rookies: 2-4X
Inserted 1:11
RK Autos. (166-180): 1-1.5X
Production 500

Blue Refractor

Rookies: 4-6X
RK Autos. (166-180): 1.5-3X
Production 150 Sets

Gold Refractor

Rookies: 8-15X
RK Autos. (166-180): 4-6X
Production 50 Sets

Red Refractor

No Pricing
Production One Set

SuperFractor

No Pricing
Production One Set

X-Fractor

Rookies: 4-6X
RK Autos. (166-180): 1-2X
Production 250 Sets

2005 Bowman Heritage

		NM/M
Complete Set (349):		
Common Player (1-300):		.15
Common SP (301-349):		3.00
Inserted 1:3		
Draft Pick Variations		
(325-349):		1-1.5X
One DPV pack per hobby box.		
Pack (8):		4.00
Box (24):		75.00
1	Steven White RC	.75
2	Jorge Posada	.25
3	Brett Myers	.15
4	Pat Burrell	.25
5	Grady Sizemore	.50
6	Jeff Weaver	.15
7	Jeff Kent	.25
8	Mark Kotsay	.15
9	Nick Swisher	.15
10	Scott Rolen	.50
11	Matt Morris	.15
12	Luis Castillo	.15
13	Pedro Feliz	.15
14	Omar Vizquel	.15
15	Edgar Renteria	.25
16	David Wells	.15
17	Chad Cordero	.15
18	Brad Wilkerson	.15
19	Kelly Johnson	.15
20	Johnny Estrada	.15
21	Brian Roberts	.25
22	Jeremy Burnitz	.15
23	Maggio Ordonez	.25
24	Adam Dunn	.50
25	Randy Johnson	1.50
26	Derek Jeter	2.00
27	Jon Lieber	.15
28	Jim Thome	.50
29	Ronnie Belliard	.15
30	Jake Westbrook	.15
31	Bengie Molina	.15
32	J.D. Drew	.25
33	Rich Harden	.25
34	David Eckstein	.15
35	Scott Podsednik	.25
36	Mark Buehrle	.25
37	Barry Bonds	2.00
38	Brian Schneider	.15
39	Tim Wakefield	.15
40	Craig Wilson	.15
41	Jose Vidro	.15
42	Jacque Jones	.15
43	Felix Hernandez	.50
44	Nomar Garciaparra	.75
45	Neifi Perez	.15
46	Brandon Inge	.15
47	Felipe Lopez	.15
48	Ken Griffey Jr.	1.50
49	Robinson Cano	.40
50	Jason Giambi	.50
51	Mike Lieberthal	.15
52	Bobby Abreu	.25
53	C.C. Sabathia	.15
54	Aaron Boone	.15
55	Milton Bradley	.15
56	Derek Lowe	.15
57	Barry Zito	.25
58	Jim Edmonds	.40
59	Jon Garland	.15
60	Tadahito Iguchi RC	1.50
61	Jason Schmidt	.15
62	David Ortiz	.75
63	Matt Lawton	.15
64	Zachary Duke	.25
65	Gary Sheffield	.40
66	Chipper Jones	.75
67	Sammy Sosa	.75
68	Rafael Palmeiro	.50
69	Carlos Zambrano	.25
70	Aramis Ramirez	.15
71	Chris Shelton	.15
72	Wily Mo Pena	.15
73	Mike Mussina	.25
74	Chien-Ming Wang	.50
75	Randy Wolf	.15
76	Jimmy Rollins	.25
77	Chase Utley	.25
78	Kevin Millwood	.15
79	Victor Martinez	.25
80	Morgan Ensberg	.15
81	Bartolo Colon	.25
82	Bobby Crosby	.25
83	Dan Johnson	.15
84	Danny Haren	.15
85	Yadier Molina	.15
86	Mark Mulder	.25
87	Russell Branyan	.15
88	Lyle Overbay	.15
89	Edgardo Alfonzo	.15
90	Mike Matheny	.15
91	J.T. Snow	.15
92	Curt Schilling	.75
93	Oliver Perez	.15
94	Mark Redman	.15
95	Esteban Loaiza	.15
96	Livan Hernandez	.15
97	Ryan Church	.15
98	Kyle Davies	.15
99	Mike Hampton	.15
100	Jeff Francoeur	.25
101	Javy Lopez	.25
102	Mark Prior	.75
103	Kerry Wood	.25
104	Carlos Guillen	.25
105	Dmitri Young	.15
106	David Wright	1.00
107	Cliff Floyd	.15
108	Carlos Beltran	.50
109	Melky Cabrera RC	2.00
110	Carl Pavano	.15
111	Jamie Moyer	.15
112	Joel Pineiro	.15
113	Adrian Beltre	.25
114	Jhonny Peralta	.15
115	Travis Hafner	.40
116	Cesar Izturis	.15
117	Brad Penny	.15
118	Garret Anderson	.15
119	Scott Kazmir	.25
120	Aubrey Huff	.15
121	Larry Walker	.25
122	Albert Pujols	2.00
123	Paul Konerko	.25
124	Frank Thomas	.50
125	Phil Nevin	.15
126	Brian Giles	.15
127	Ramon Hernandez	.15
128	Johnny Damon	.75
129	Trot Nixon	.15
130	Rocco Baldelli	.15
131	Carl Crawford	.25
132	Alfonso Soriano	.50
133	Mark Teixeira	.50
134	Gustavo Chacin	.15
135	Vernon Wells	.25
136	Erik Bedard	.15
137	Daniel Cabrera	.15
138	Michael Barrett	.15
139	Greg Maddux	1.00
140	Javier Vazquez	.15
141	Chad Tracy	.15
142	Michael Young	.25
143	Kenny Rogers	.15
144	Mike Piazza	.75
145	Jose Reyes	.40
146	Geoff Jenkins	.15
147	Carlos Lee	.25
148	Brady Clark	.15
149	Torii Hunter	.25
150	Johan Santana	.75
151	Steve Finley	.15

#	Player	Price
152	Darin Erstad	.25
153	Jake Peavy	.25
154	Xavier Nady	.15
155	Ryan Klesko	.15
156	Ichiro Suzuki	1.50
157	Richie Sexson	.40
158	Raul Ibanez	.15
159	Freddy Garcia	.15
160	Brad Hawpe	.15
161	Jeff Francis	.15
162	Todd Helton	.40
163	Clint Barmes	.15
164	Rodrigo Lopez	.15
165	Melvin Mora	.15
166	Brandon Webb	.15
167	Shawn Green	.25
168	Moises Alou	.25
169	Matt Clement	.25
170	John Smoltz	.40
171	Rafael Furcal	.25
172	Jeff Bagwell	.25
173	Roger Clemens	2.00
174	Dontrelle Willis	.40
175	Paul LoDuca	.15
176	Zack Greinke	.15
177	David DeJesus	.15
178	Mike Sweeney	.15
179	Ben Sheets	.25
180	Doug Davis	.15
181	Mike Cameron	.15
182	Lance Berkman	.40
183	Craig Biggio	.25
184	Shannon Stewart	.15
185	Joe Mauer	.50
186	Justin Morneau	.25
187	Mike Maroth	.15
188	Ivan Rodriguez	.50
189	Luis Gonzalez	.15
190	Troy Glaus	.25
191	Adam Eaton	.15
192	Khalil Greene	.25
193	Mike Lowell	.15
194	Miguel Cabrera	.75
195	Roy Halladay	.25
196	Ted Lilly	.15
197	Alex Rios	.25
198	Josh Beckett	.25
199	A.J. Burnett	.15
200	Juan Pierre	.15
201	Marcus Giles	.15
202	Craig Tatum RC	.50
203	Hayden Penn RC	.50
204	C.J. Smith RC	.25
205	Matt Albers RC	1.00
206	Jared Gothreaux RC	.25
207	Mike Rodriguez RC	.25
208	Hernan Iribarren RC	.25
209	Manny Parra RC	.25
210	Kevin Collins RC	.25
211	Buck Coats RC	.50
212	Jeremy West RC	.50
213	Ian Bladergroen RC	.25
214	Chuck Tiffany RC	1.50
215	Andy LaRoche RC	2.00
216	Frank Diaz RC	.25
217	Jai Miller RC	.25
218	Tony Giarratano RC	.50
219	Danny Zell RC	.25
220	Justin Verlander RC	4.00
221	Ryan Sweeney RC	1.00
222	Brandon McCarthy RC	1.00
223	Jerry Owens RC	.25
224	Glen Perkins RC	.50
225	Kevin West RC	.25
226	Billy Butler RC	3.00
227	Shane Costa RC	.50
228	Erik Schindewolf RC	.50
229	Miguel Montero RC	.75
230	Stephen Drew RC	4.00
231	Matt DeSalvo RC	.25
232	Ben Jones RC	.75
233	Bill McCarthy RC	.25
234	Chuck James RC	2.00
235	Brandon Sing RC	.75
236	Andy Santana RC	.75
237	Brendan Ryan RC	.50
238	Wes Swackhamer RC	.50
239	Jeff Niemann RC	1.00
240	Ian Kinsler RC	4.00
241	Micah Furtado RC	.50
242	Ryan Mount RC	1.00
243	P.J. Phillips RC	.50
244	Trevor Bell RC	1.00
245	Jered Weaver RC	4.00
246	Eddy Martinez-Esteve RC	.75
247	Brian Bannister RC	1.00
248	Philip Humber RC	1.00
249	Michael Rogers RC	.50
250	Landon Powell RC	.50
251	Kennard Bibbs RC	.50
252	Nelson Cruz RC	1.00
253	Paul Kelly RC	.75
254	Kevin Slowey RC	1.50
255	Brandon Snyder RC	1.00
256	Nolan Reimold RC	1.50
257	Brian Stavisky RC	.25
258	Javier Herrera RC	1.50
259	Russell Martin RC	1.00
260	Matthew Kemp RC	3.00
261	Wade Townsend RC	.75
262	Nick Touchstone RC	.50
263	Ryan Feierabend RC	.50
264	Bobby Livingston RC	.50
265	Wladimir Balentien RC	.75
266	Keiichi Yabu RC	1.00

#	Player	Price
267	Craig Italiano RC	.50
268	Ryan Goleski RC	.50
269	Ryan Garko RC	.75
270	Michael Bourn RC	.75
271	Scott Mathieson RC	.75
272	Scott Mitchinson RC	.75
273	Tyler Greene RC	1.00
274	Mark McCormick RC	.50
275	Daryl Jones RC	.50
276	Travis Chick RC	.50
277	Luis Hernandez RC	.25
278	Steven Doetsch RC	.25
279	Chris Vines RC	.25
280	Mike Costanzo RC	1.00
281	Matt Maloney RC	1.00
282	Matt Goyen RC	.25
283	Jacob Marceaux RC	.25
284	David Gassner RC	.50
285	Ricky Barrett RC	.50
286	Jon Egan RC	.50
287	Scott Blue RC	.50
288	Steve Bondurant RC	.50
289	Kevin Melillo RC	.50
290	Brad Corley RC	.50
291	Brent Lillibridge RC	1.00
292	Mike Morse RC	.25
293	Justin Thomas RC	.50
294	Nick Webber RC	.50
295	Mitch Boggs RC	.50
296	Jeff Lyman RC	.50
297	Jordan Schafer RC	.50
298	Ismael Ramirez RC	.25
299	Chris Young RC	2.00
300	Brian Miller RC	.50
301	Jason Bay	4.00
302	Tim Hudson	3.00
303	Miguel Tejada	4.00
304	Jeremy Bonderman	3.00
305	Alex Rodriguez	8.00
306	Rickie Weeks	3.00
307	Manny Ramirez	6.00
308	Nick Johnson	3.00
309	Andruw Jones	4.00
310	Hideki Matsui	6.00
311	Jeremy Reed	5.00
312	Dallas McPherson	3.00
313	Vladimir Guerrero	5.00
314	Eric Chavez	3.00
315	Chris Carpenter	4.00
316	Aaron Hill	3.00
317	Derrek Lee	5.00
318	Mark Loretta	3.00
319	Garrett Atkins	3.00
320	Hank Blalock	3.00
321	Chris Young	5.00
322	Roy Oswalt	3.00
323	Carlos Delgado	4.00
324	Pedro Martinez	5.00
325	Jeff Clement RC	6.00
326	Jimmy Shull RC	4.00
327	Daniel Carte RC	4.00
328	Travis Buck RC	4.00
329	Chris Volstad RC	3.00
330	Andrew McCutchen RC	8.00
331	Cliff Pennington RC	4.00
332	John Mayberry Jr. RC	4.00
333	C.J. Henry RC	6.00
334	Ricky Romero RC	4.00
335	Aaron Thompson RC	5.00
336	Cesar Carrillo RC	4.00
337	Jacoby Ellsbury RC	6.00
338	Matt Garza RC	8.00
339	Colby Rasmus RC	6.00
340	Ryan Zimmerman RC	12.00
341	Ryan Braun RC	8.00
342	Brent Lillibridge RC	3.00
343	Jay Bruce RC	8.00
344	Matt Green RC	4.00
345	Brent Cox RC	6.00
346	Jed Lowrie RC	4.00
347	Beau Jones RC	3.00
348	Eli Iorg RC	4.00
349	Chaz Roe RC	4.00

Mahogany

Stars (1-300):	1-2X
SP's (301-349):	.5-1X
Inserted 1:1	

Mini

Stars (1-300):	1-2X
SP's (301-349):	.5-1X
Inserted 1:1	

Red

No Pricing
Production One Set

ABBREVIATIONS

AS - All-Star
HL - Hit List
PC - Promo Card
RC - Rookie Class
RR - Rated Rookie
SP - Short Print
TP - Top Performers

Draft Pick Variation

NM/M

Variations (325-349): 1-1.5X base
One DPV pack per hobby box.

#	Player	Price
325	Jeff Clement	10.00
326	Jimmy Shull	6.00
327	Daniel Carte	6.00
328	Travis Buck	5.00
329	Chris Volstad	5.00
330	Andrew McCutchen	12.00
331	Cliff Pennington	6.00
332	John Mayberry Jr.	6.00
333	C.J. Henry	8.00
334	Ricky Romero	6.00
335	Aaron Thompson	6.00
336	Cesar Carrillo	6.00
337	Jacoby Ellsbury	10.00
338	Matt Garza	10.00
339	Colby Rasmus	10.00
340	Ryan Zimmerman	15.00
341	Ryan Braun	10.00
342	Brent Lillibridge	6.00
343	Jay Bruce	10.00
344	Matt Green	6.00
345	Brent Cox	6.00
346	Jed Lowrie	6.00
347	Beau Jones	5.00
348	Eli Iorg	6.00
349	Chaz Roe	6.00

Future Greatness

NM/M

	Player	Price
	Common Player:	4.00
TB	Tony Blanco	4.00
JB	Joe Blanton	4.00
BB	Bryan Bullington	4.00
MC	Matt Cain	8.00
FC	Fausto Carmona	4.00
SC	Shin-Soo Choo	4.00
JC	Jorge Cortes	4.00
JCO	Jesus Cota	4.00
EE	Edwin Encarnacion	4.00
CE	Clint Everts	4.00
GF	Gavin Floyd	4.00
JF	Jeff Francis	4.00
JGA	Jairo Garcia	4.00
RG	Ruben Gotay	4.00
JG	Joel Guzman	4.00
AH	Aaron Hill	3.00
KH	Koyie Hill	4.00
JK	Jason Kubel	4.00
WL	Wilfredo Ledezma	4.00
VM	Val Majewski	4.00
AMA	Andy Marte	8.00
JMA	Jeff Mathis	8.00
DM	Dallas McPherson	8.00
JM	Justin Morneau	8.00
AM	Arnie Munoz	4.00
JP	Juan Perez	4.00
YP	Yusmeiro Petit	4.00
FP	Felix Pie	6.00
BT	Brad Thompson	15.00
RW	Rickie Weeks	6.00
DY	Delmon Young	8.00

Pieces of Greatness

NM/M

	Player	Price
	Common Player:	4.00
JB	Josh Beckett	4.00
CB	Carlos Beltran	6.00
BB	Barry Bonds	20.00
MC	Miguel Cabrera	8.00
EC	Eric Chavez	4.00
RC	Roger Clemens	10.00
BC	Bobby Crosby	4.00
JD	Johnny Damon	8.00
CD	Carlos Delgado	6.00
AD	Adam Dunn	8.00
JG	Josh Gibson	15.00
TG	Troy Glaus	4.00
RH	Rich Harden	4.00
TH	Todd Helton	6.00
JK	Jeff Kent	4.00
PK	Paul Konerko	6.00
PM	Pedro Martinez	8.00
MMO	Melvin Mora	4.00
MM	Mark Mulder	4.00
BM	Brett Myers	4.00
AP	Albert Pujols	20.00
MR	Manny Ramirez	8.00
BR	Brian Roberts	4.00
AR	Alex Rodriguez	15.00
JS	John Smoltz	8.00
IS	Ichiro Suzuki	15.00
MT	Miguel Tejada	6.00
JT	Jim Thome	6.00
DW	Dontrelle Willis	6.00
DWR	David Wright	15.00
BZ	Barry Zito	4.00

Printing Plates

No Pricing
Production one set per color.

Signs of Greatness

NM/M

	Player	Price
	Common Player:	8.00
RB	Ryan Braun	30.00
JB	Jay Bruce	40.00
PB	Patrick Bryant	10.00
MB	Matt Bush	15.00
TC	Travis Chick	6.00
TD	Thomas Diamond	10.00
SE	Scott Elbert	15.00
MG	Matt Green	8.00
AG	Angel Guzman	8.00
JH	J.P. Howell	8.00
PH	Philip Humber	20.00
ZJ	Zach Jackson	8.00
JJ	Jason Jaramillo	10.00
DJ	Dan Johnson	8.00
BL	Brent Lillibridge	10.00
DL	Donald Lucey	8.00
EM	Eddy Martinez-Esteve	8.00
JM	John Mayberry Jr.	20.00
AM	Andrew McCutchen	35.00
JP	Jonathan Papelbon	50.00
DP	David Purcey	8.00
RR	Ricky Romero	10.00
HS	Huston Street	20.00
CT	Curtis Thigpen	10.00
WW	Wes Whisler	10.00
JZ	Jon Zeringue	8.00
RZ	Ryan Zimmerman	60.00

51 Topps Heritage Blue Back

NM/M

	Player	Price
	Common Player:	1.00
1	Adam Dunn	3.00
2	Zachary Duke	1.50
3	Alex Rodriguez	8.00
4	Vladimir Guerrero	3.00
5	Andruw Jones	2.00
6	Travis Chick	2.00
7	Alfonso Soriano	2.00
8	Scott Rolen	3.00
9	Brian Bannister	2.00
10	Randy Johnson	3.00
11	Barry Bonds	8.00
12	Pat Burrell	1.50
13	Barry Zito	1.50
14	Nomar Garciaparra	3.00
15	C.C. Sabathia	1.00
16	Miguel Tejada	2.00
17	Hideki Matsui	6.00
18	John Smoltz	2.00
19	Ken Griffey Jr.	5.00
20	Chris Carpenter	1.50
21	Ian Kinsler	4.00
22	Chuck Tiffany	1.50
23	Gary Sheffield	2.00
24	Mark Mulder	1.50
25	Ichiro Suzuki	5.00
26	Kerry Wood	1.50
27	Jose Reyes	1.00
28	Derrek Lee	2.00
29	Justin Verlander	2.00
30	Johnny Damon	3.00
31	Chris Volstad	1.00
32	Jeremy Bonderman	1.00
33	David Ortiz	3.00
34	Morgan Ensberg	1.00
35	Mark Buehrle	1.00
36	Chuck James	2.00
37	Miguel Cabrera	2.00
38	Magglio Ordonez	1.50
39	Michael Young	1.00
40	Carlos Beltran	2.00
41	Nick Johnson	1.00
42	Billy Butler	2.00
43	Brian Giles	1.00
44	Paul Konerko	1.50
45	Roy Oswalt	1.50
46	Bobby Abreu	1.50
47	Sammy Sosa	3.00
48	Aramis Ramirez	1.50
49	Torii Hunter	1.50
50	Aubrey Huff	1.00
51	Vernon Wells	1.00
52	Joe Mauer	1.50

51 Topps Heritage Red Back

NM/M

	Player	Price
	Common Player:	1.00
1	Andy LaRoche	3.00
2	Mike Piazza	4.00
3	Pedro Martinez	3.00
4	Wladimir Balentien	2.00
5	Tim Hudson	1.50
6	Richie Sexson	1.50
7	Carlos Delgado	1.00
8	Derek Jeter	8.00
9	Ryan Zimmerman	6.00
10	Mark Teixeira	2.00
11	David Wright	3.00
12	Jake Peavy	1.50
13	Jose Vidro	1.00
14	Jim Thome	2.00
15	Carlos Zambrano	1.50
16	Hank Blalock	1.50
17	Johan Santana	2.00
18	Cliff Pennington	1.00
19	Rafael Palmeiro	1.50
20	Curt Schilling	2.00
21	Brandon McCarthy	2.00
22	Stephen Drew	8.00
23	Jeff Niemann	2.00
24	Eric Chavez	1.00
25	Hernan Iribarren	1.00
26	Jered Weaver	5.00

#	Player	Price
27	Edgar Renteria	1.00
28	Travis Hafner	1.00
29	Frank Thomas	1.50
30	Brian Roberts	1.00
31	Anthony Reyes	1.00
32	Scott Kazmir	1.00
33	Carlos Lee	1.00
34	Jimmy Rollins	1.00
35	Garret Anderson	1.00
36	Jason Schmidt	1.00
37	Jon Garland	1.00
38	Dontrelle Willis	1.50
39	C.J. Henry	3.00
40	Greg Maddux	4.00
41	Todd Helton	2.00
42	Ivan Rodriguez	3.00
43	Chipper Jones	3.00
44	Rich Harden	1.50
45	Mark Prior	2.00
46	Roy Halladay	1.50
47	Albert Pujols	8.00
48	Roger Clemens	8.00
49	Andrew McCutchen	6.00
50	Scott Podsednik	1.50
51	Manny Ramirez	2.00
52	Carl Crawford	1.00
53	Jim Edmonds	1.50
54	Wily Mo Pena	1.00

2005 Bowman Sterling

NM/M

Pack (5):	50.00
Box (6):	280.00

First Year Autographs

	Player	Price
MA	Matt Albers RC	20.00
RB	Ryan Braun RC	50.00
TC	Travis Chick RC	10.00
MG	Matt Green RC	10.00
CH	C.J. Henry RC	20.00
GK	George Kottaras RC	20.00
EM	Eddy Martinez-Esteve RC	15.00
JM	John Mayberry Jr. RC	20.00
GO	Garrett Olson RC	20.00
CP	Cliff Pennington RC	10.00
HS	Humberto Sanchez RC	35.00
BS	Brandon Sing RC	15.00
AT	Aaron Thompson RC	15.00
CV	Chris Volstad RC	15.00
SW	Steven White RC	10.00

Autographed First Year Relics

	Player	Price
TB	Trevor Bell RC	15.00
MB	Michael Bowden RC	30.00
JB	Jay Bruce RC	60.00
MC	Mike Conroy RC	15.00
BC	J. Brent Cox RC	15.00
JE	Jacoby Ellsbury RC	40.00
JG	Josh Geer RC	15.00
PH	Philip Humber RC	30.00
EI	Eli Iorg RC	15.00
BJ	Beau Jones RC	15.00
BL	Bobby Livingston RC	15.00
JL	Jeff Lyman RC	20.00
SM	Steve Marek RC	15.00
RM	Russell Martin RC	25.00
BM	Brandon McCarthy RC	25.00
AM	Andrew McCutchen RC	25.00
TM	Tyler Minges RC	15.00
JCN	John Nelson RC	15.00
JN	Jeff Niemann RC	20.00
JO	Jon Nelson RC	10.00
CPP	Carmen Pignatiello RC	15.00
CR	Colby Rasmus RC	50.00
CRO	Chaz Roe RC	20.00
CS	C.J. Smith RC	10.00
RT	Raul Tablado RC	15.00
JV	Justin Verlander RC	65.00

Autographed Prospect Base Relics

	Player	Price
BB	Billy Buckner	15.00
SE	Scott Elbert	15.00
BE	Brad Eldred	20.00
JF	Josh Fields	20.00
AL	Adam Lind	25.00
CN	Chris Nelson	15.00
DP	Dustin Pedroia	25.00
CT	Curtis Thigpen	15.00

First Year Base Cards

	Player	Price
BA	Brian Anderson	6.00
BRB	Brian Bogusevic RC	4.00
CBU	Clay Buchholz RC	15.00
TBU	Travis Buck RC	4.00
BBU	Billy Butler RC	15.00
CC	Cesar Carrillo RC	4.00
DC	Daniel Carte RC	6.00
JC	Jeff Clement RC	20.00
MCO	Mike Constanzo RC	6.00
BCR	Brad Corley RC	4.00
JDR	John Drennen RC	4.00
SD	Stephen Drew RC	20.00
JEG	Jon Egan RC	4.00
YE	Yunel Escobar RC	6.00
MGA	Matt Garza RC	12.00
TG	Tyler Greene RC	4.00
BH	Brett Hayes RC	4.00
CHE	Chase Headley RC	4.00
THE	Tyler Herron RC	4.00
NH	Nick Hundley RC	4.00
TI	Tadahito Iguchi RC	6.00
HI	Hernan Iribarren RC	4.00
CI	Craig Italiano RC	6.00
CJ	Chuck James RC	12.00
PK	Paul Kelly RC	8.00
ACL	Andy LaRoche RC	10.00
JLY	Jeff Lyman RC	4.00
MAM	Matt Maloney RC	8.00
JMA	Jacob Marceaux RC	4.00
MMC	Mark McCormick RC	4.00
RMO	Ryan Mount RC	6.00
PP	P.J. Phillips RC	4.00
CRA	Cesar Ramos RC	4.00
NR	Nolan Reimold RC	8.00
RR	Ricky Romero RC	6.00
HAS	Henry Sanchez RC	6.00
ZS	Zach Simons RC	4.00
KS	Kevin Slowey RC	12.00
BSN	Brandon Snyder RC	6.00
DT	Drew Thompson RC	4.00
CLT	Chuck Tiffany RC	6.00
MTO	Matt Torra RC	6.00
WT	Wade Townsend RC	6.00
TT	Troy Tulowitzki RC	15.00
JW	Josh Wall RC	4.00
JWE	Jered Weaver RC	20.00
NW	Nick Webber RC	4.00
KW	Kevin Whelan RC	4.00
TW	Travis Wood RC	4.00
RZ	Ryan Zimmerman RC	25.00

Refractors

Rookies:	1.5-2X
Rookie Auto.:	1-2X
Rookie Relic Auto.:	1-2X
Production 199 Sets	

Black Refractors

No Pricing
Production 25 Sets

Red Refractor

No Pricing
Production One Set

MLB Logo Patch

No Pricing
Production One Set

Original Autographs

NM/M

Production 1-160

	Player	Price
AJ4	Andruw Jones 02 B/122	25.00
AJ6	Andruw Jones 03 B/112	25.00
AJ8	Andruw Jones 04 B/71	25.00
DL1	Derrek Lee 95 B/37	25.00
DL2	Derrek Lee 96 B/29	25.00
DL5	Derrek Lee 98 B/22	25.00
DL6	Derrek Lee 04 B/92	20.00
DL7	Derrek Lee 04 BC/26	25.00
DW1	David Wright 04 BD/98	85.00

Values shown are for cards that have not been authenticated and/or graded by an independent certification company. Because the standards and reputations of such companies vary widely, prices listed here cannot be correlated to values for "slabbed" cards.

DW3	David Wright 05 B/139	85.00
GA1	Garret Anderson 04 BC/36	20.00
GA2	Garret Anderson 05 B/48	20.00
JR1	Jeremy Reed 04 BD/82	15.00
JR2	Jeremy Reed 04 BCD/48	20.00
MC2	Miguel Cabrera 02 BD/26	50.00
MC4	Miguel Cabrera 03 BD/27	50.00
MC5	Miguel Cabrera 03 BCD/25	50.00
MC6	Miguel Cabrera 04 B/127	25.00
MC7	Miguel Cabrera 04 BC/25	50.00
MC8	Miguel Cabrera 05 B/154	25.00
MC9	Miguel Cabrera 05 BC/25	50.00
MK3	Mark Kotsay 98 B/56	15.00
MK5	Mark Kotsay 99 B/75	15.00
MK7	Mark Kotsay 05 B/160	10.00
MK8	Mark Kotsay 05 BC/46	15.00
MY1	Michael Young 04 B/148	15.00
MY2	Michael Young 04 BC/64	15.00
MY3	Michael Young 05 B/92	15.00

Relics

		NM/M
Common Player:		4.00
Refractor:		1-1.5X
Production 199 Sets		
Black Refractor:		2-4X
Production 25 Sets		
JBE	Josh Beckett	4.00
RBE	Ronnie Belliard	4.00
CB	Carlos Beltran	6.00
HB	Hank Blalock	4.00
BLB	Barry Bonds	20.00
MCA	Miguel Cabrera	8.00
EC	Eric Chavez	4.00
JD	Johnny Damon	8.00
CD	Carlos Delgado	4.00
JPE	Jim Edmonds	6.00
RF	Rafael Furcal	4.00
JGI	Josh Gibson	15.00
MGI	Marcus Giles	4.00
KG	Khalil Greene	6.00
VG	Vladimir Guerrero	8.00
TLH	Todd Helton	6.00
THU	Tim Hudson	4.00
TH	Torii Hunter	4.00
LWJ	Chipper Jones	8.00
DL	Derrek Lee	6.00
PL	Paul LoDuca	4.00
GM	Greg Maddux	10.00
PM	Pedro Martinez	8.00
TM	Tino Martinez	4.00
VM	Victor Martinez	4.00
HM	Hideki Matsui	15.00
KM	Kevin Millar	4.00
BMU	Bill Mueller	4.00
MM	Mark Mulder	4.00
TN	Trot Nixon	4.00
DO	David Ortiz	10.00
MP	Mike Piazza	8.00
JP	Jorge Posada	6.00
MPR	Mark Prior	6.00
AP	Albert Pujols	20.00
ARA	Aramis Ramirez	4.00
MR	Manny Ramirez	8.00
AR	Alex Rodriguez	20.00
IR	Ivan Rodriguez	6.00
SR	Scott Rolen	8.00
CSU	Curt Schilling	6.00
GS	Gary Sheffield	6.00
JS	John Smoltz	6.00
AS	Alfonso Soriano	6.00
SS	Sammy Sosa	8.00
MTE	Mark Teixeira	8.00
MT	Miguel Tejada	6.00
DW	Dontrelle Willis	6.00
MY	Michael Young	4.00
BZ	Barry Zito	4.00

2005 Bowman's Best

	NM/M
Common Player:	.25
Common Rookie:	1.00
Common Rookie Auto. (101-143):	10.00
Production 974	
Pack (5):	14.00
Box (10):	120.00

1	Jose Vidro	.25
2	Adam Dunn	.50
3	Manny Ramirez	.75
4	Miguel Tejada	.50
5	Ken Griffey Jr.	1.00
6	Pedro Martinez	1.00
7	Alex Rodriguez	1.50
8	Ichiro Suzuki	1.50
9	Alfonso Soriano	.75
10	Brian Giles	.25
11	Roger Clemens	2.00
12	Todd Helton	.50
13	Ivan Rodriguez	.50
14	David Ortiz	.75
15	Sammy Sosa	1.00
16	Chipper Jones	.75
17	Mark Buehrle	.50
18	Miguel Cabrera	.75
19	Johan Santana	.75
20	Randy Johnson	.75
21	Jim Thome	.50
22	Vladimir Guerrero	.75
23	Dontrelle Willis	.50
24	Nomar Garciaparra	.75
25	Barry Bonds	2.00
26	Curt Schilling	.75
27	Carlos Beltran	.50
28	Albert Pujols	2.00
29	Mark Prior	.75
30	Derek Jeter	2.00
31	Ryan Garko RC	4.00
32	Eulogio de la Cruz RC	1.00
33	Luke Scott RC	3.00
34	Shane Costa RC	1.00
35	Casey McGehee RC	1.00
36	Jered Weaver RC	12.00
37	Kevin Melillo RC	2.00
38	D.J. Houlton RC	2.00
39	Brandon Moorhead RC	1.00
40	Jerry Owens RC	1.00
41	Elliot Johnson RC	1.50
42	Kevin West RC	2.00
43	Hernan Iribarren RC	1.00
44	Miguel Montero RC	6.00
45	Craig Tatum RC	1.00
46	Ryan Sweeney RC	2.00
47	Micah Furtado RC	1.00
48	Cody Haerther RC	1.00
49	Erik Abreu RC	1.00
50	Chuck Tiffany RC	2.00
51	Tadahito Iguchi RC	4.00
52	Frank Diaz RC	3.00
53	Errol Simonitsch RC	1.00
54	Wade Robinson RC	2.00
55	Adam Boeve RC	1.00
56	Steve Bondurant RC	1.00
57	Jason Motte RC	1.00
58	Juan Senreiso RC	1.00
59	Vinny Rottino RC	1.00
60	Jai Miller RC	1.00
61	Thomas Pauly RC	1.00
62	Tony Giarratano RC	1.00
63	Alexander Smit RC	1.00
64	Keiichi Yabu RC	1.00
65	Brian Bannister RC	2.50
66	Kennard Bibbs RC	1.00
67	Anthony Reyes RC	6.00
68	Tom Oldham RC	1.00
69	Benjamin Harrison RC	1.00
70	Daryl Thompson RC	1.00
71	Kevin Collins RC	1.00
72	Wes Swackhamer RC	1.50
73	Landon Powell RC	1.50
74	Matt Brown RC	1.00
75	Russell Martin RC	3.00
76	Nick Touchstone RC	1.00
77	Steven White RC	1.00
78	Ian Bladergroen RC	1.00
79	Sean Marshall RC	2.00
80	Nick Masset RC	1.00
81	Ryan Goleski RC	1.50
82	Matt Campbell RC	1.00
83	Manny Parra RC	1.00
84	Melky Cabrera RC	5.00
85	Ryan Feierabend RC	1.50
86	Nate McLouth RC	1.50
87	Glen Perkins RC	2.50
88	Kila Kaaihue RC	1.50
89	Dana Eveland RC	1.50
90	Tyler Pelland RC	1.00
91	Matt Van Der Bosch RC	1.00
92	Andy Santana RC	1.00
93	Eric Nielsen RC	1.00
94	Brendan Ryan RC	1.00
95	Ian Kinsler RC	6.00
96	Matthew Kemp RC	8.00
97	Stephen Drew RC	12.00
98	Peeter Ramos RC	2.00
99	Chris Seddon RC	2.00
100	Chuck James RC	6.00
101	Travis Chick RC	10.00
102	Justin Verlander RC	60.00
103	Billy Butler RC	50.00
104	Chris Young RC	80.00
105	Jake Postlewait RC	10.00
106	C.J. Smith RC	10.00
107	Mike Rodriguez RC	12.00
108	Philip Humber RC	25.00
109	Jeff Niemann RC	20.00
110	Brian Miller RC	10.00
111	Chris Vines RC	10.00
112	Andy LaRoche RC	40.00
113	Mike Bourn RC	12.00
114	Wladimir Balentien RC	15.00
115	Ismael Ramirez RC	10.00
116	Hayden Penn RC	15.00
117	Pedro Lopez RC	10.00
118	Shawn Bowman RC	15.00
119	Chad Orvella RC	10.00
120	Sean Tracey RC	10.00
121	Bobby Livingston RC	10.00
122	Michael Rogers RC	10.00
123	Willy Mota RC	15.00
124	Brandon McCarthy RC	20.00
125	Mike Morse RC	10.00
126	Matt Lindstrom RC	10.00
127	Brian Stavisky RC	10.00
128	Rich Gardner RC	10.00
129	Scott Mitchinson RC	10.00
130	Billy McCarthy RC	10.00
131	Brandon Sing RC	15.00
132	Matt Albers RC	12.00
133	George Kottaras RC	15.00
134	Luis Hernandez RC	10.00
135	Humberto Sanchez RC	35.00
136	Buck Coats RC	12.00
137	Jonathan Barratt RC	10.00
138	Raul Tablado RC	12.00
139	Jake Mullinax RC	15.00
140	Edgar Varela RC	12.00
141	Ryan Garko RC	25.00
142	Nate McLouth RC	10.00
143	Shane Costa RC	10.00

Green Refractor

Stars:	2-3X
Rookies:	1-2X
Production 899	
Rookie Autos.:	1-1.5X
Production 399	

Blue Refractor

Stars:	2-4X
Rookies:	1-2X
Production 499	
Rookie Autos.:	1-1.5X
Production 299	

Red Refractor

Stars:	3-5X
Rookies:	2-3X
Rookie Autos.:	1.5-2X
Production 199 Sets	

Silver Refractor

Stars:	4-6X
Rookies:	2-3X
Rookie Autos.:	1.5-3X
Production 99 Sets	

Gold Refractor

No Pricing
Production 25 Sets

Printing Plates

No Pricing
Production one set for each color.

Printing Plates Autograph

No Pricing
Production one set for each color.

A-Rod Throwback Autograph

		NM/M
Production 100		
AR	Alex Rodriguez	150.00
Production 100		
AR	Alex Rodriguez	150.00

Bowman's Best Shortstops

Production 25

Mirror Image Spokesmen

Production 10

Mirror Image Throwback

		NM/M
Production 50		
RR	Cal Ripken Jr., Alex Rodriguez	450.00

2006 Bowman

	NM/M
Complete Set (231):	
Common Player (1-200):	.15
Common RC (201-220):	.25
Common Auto. (219-231):	10.00
Pack (10):	4.00
Box (24):	85.00

1	Nick Swisher	.15
2	Ted Lilly	.15
3	John Smoltz	.25
4	Lyle Overbay	.15
5	Alfonso Soriano	.50
6	Javier Vazquez	.15
7	Ronnie Belliard	.15
8	Jose Reyes	.50
9	Brian Roberts	.25
10	Curt Schilling	.75
11	Adam Dunn	.50
12	Zack Greinke	.25
13	Carlos Guillen	.15
14	Jon Garland	.15
15	Robinson Cano	.25
16	Chris Burke	.15
17	Barry Zito	.25
18	Russ Adams	.15
19	Chris Capuano	.15
20	Scott Rolen	.50
21	Kerry Wood	.25
22	Scott Kazmir	.25
23	Brandon Webb	.25
24	Jeff Kent	.25
25	Albert Pujols	2.00
26	C.C. Sabathia	.15
27	Adrian Beltre	.15
28	Brad Wilkerson	.15
29	Randy Wolf	.15
30	Jason Bay	.25
31	Austin Kearns	.15
32	Clint Barmes	.15
33	Mike Sweeney	.15
34	Justin Verlander (RC)	.25
35	Justin Morneau	.25
36	Scott Podsednik	.25
37	Jason Giambi	.25
38	Steve Finley	.15
39	Morgan Ensberg	.25
40	Eric Chavez	.25
41	Roy Halladay	.25
42	Horacio Ramirez	.15
43	Ben Sheets	.25
44	Chris Carpenter	.40
45	Andruw Jones	.25
46	Carlos Zambrano	.25
47	Jonny Gomes	.25
48	Shawn Green	.15
49	Moises Alou	.25
50	Ichiro Suzuki	1.50
51	Juan Pierre	.15
52	Grady Sizemore	.40
53	Kazuo Matsui	.15
54	Jose Vidro	.15
55	Jake Peavy	.25
56	Dallas McPherson	.15
57	Ryan Howard	1.00
58	Zachary Duke	.15
59	Michael Young	.15
60	Todd Helton	.50
61	David DeJesus	.15
62	Ivan Rodriguez	.50
63	Johan Santana	.50
64	Danny Haren	.15
65	Derek Jeter	2.00
66	Greg Maddux	1.00
67	Jorge Cantu	.15
68	Conor Jackson (RC)	.15
69	Victor Martinez	.25
70	David Wright	1.00
71	Ryan Church	.15
72	Khalil Greene	.15
73	Jimmy Rollins	.25
74	Hank Blalock	.25
75	Pedro Martinez	.75
76	Jonathan Papelbon (RC)	3.00
77	Felipe Lopez	.15
78	Jeff Francis	.15
79	Andrew Sisco	.15
80	Hideki Matsui	1.50
81	Ken Griffey Jr.	1.50
82	Nomar Garciaparra	.75
83	Kevin Millwood	.25
84	Paul Konerko	.25
85	A.J. Burnett	.15
86	Mike Piazza	.75
87	Brian Giles	.25
88	Johnny Damon	.75
89	Jim Thome	.50
90	Roger Clemens	2.00
91	Aaron Rowand	.15
92	Rafael Furcal	.25
93	Gary Sheffield	.50
94	Mike Cameron	.15
95	Carlos Delgado	.50
96	Jorge Posada	.40
97	Denny Bautista	.15
98	Mike Maroth	.15
99	Brad Radke	.15
100	Alex Rodriguez	2.00
101	Freddy Garcia	.15
102	Oliver Perez	.15
103	Jon Lieber	.15
104	Melvin Mora	.25
105	Travis Hafner	.40
106	Matt Cain (RC)	.25
107	Derek Lowe	.15
108	Luis Castillo	.15
109	Livan Hernandez	.15
110	Tadahito Iguchi	.25
111	Shawn Chacon	.15
112	Frank Thomas	.40
113	Josh Beckett	.25
114	Aubrey Huff	.15
115	Derrek Lee	.50
116	Chien-Ming Wang	.25
117	Joe Crede	.15
118	Torii Hunter	.25
119	J.D. Drew	.25
120	Troy Glaus	.40
121	Sean Casey	.15
122	Edgar Renteria	.25
123	Craig Wilson	.15
124	Adam Eaton	.15
125	Jeff Francoeur	.50
126	Bruce Chen	.15
127	Cliff Floyd	.15
128	Jeremy Reed	.15
129	Jarrod Washburn	.15
130	Wily Mo Pena	.15
131	Toby Hall	.15
132	David Ortiz	.75
133	David Eckstein	.15
134	Brady Clark	.15
135	Marcus Giles	.15
136	Aaron Hill	.15
137	Mark Kotsay	.15
138	Carlos Lee	.25
139	Roy Oswalt	.40
140	Chone Figgins	.15
141	Mike Mussina	.50
142	Orlando Hernandez	.15
143	Magglio Ordonez	.15
144	Jim Edmonds	.40
145	Bobby Abreu	.40
146	Nick Johnson	.15
147	Carlos Beltran	.50
148	Jhonny Peralta	.15
149	Pedro Feliz	.15
150	Miguel Tejada	.50
151	Luis Gonzalez	.25
152	Carl Crawford	.25
153	Yadier Molina	.15
154	Rich Harden	.25
155	Tim Wakefield	.15
156	Rickie Weeks	.25
157	Johnny Estrada	.15
158	Gustavo Chacin	.15
159	Dan Johnson	.15
160	Willy Taveras	.15
161	Garret Anderson	.25
162	Randy Johnson	.50
163	Jermaine Dye	.15
164	Joe Mauer	.50
165	Ervin Santana	.15
166	Jeremy Bonderman	.15
167	Garrett Atkins	.25
168	Manny Ramirez	.75
169	Brad Eldred	.15
170	Chase Utley	.25
171	Mark Loretta	.15
172	John Patterson	.15
173	Tom Glavine	.40
174	Dontrelle Willis	.25
175	Mark Teixeira	.50
176	Felix Hernandez	.50
177	Cliff Lee	.15
178	Jason Schmidt	.25
179	Chad Tracy	.15
180	Rocco Baldelli	.15
181	Aramis Ramirez	.25
182	Andy Pettitte	.25
183	Mark Mulder	.25
184	Geoff Jenkins	.15
185	Chipper Jones	.75
186	Vernon Wells	.25
187	Bobby Crosby	.15
188	Lance Berkman	.40
189	Vladimir Guerrero	.75
190	Jose Capellan (RC)	.15
191	Brad Penny	.15
192	Jose Guillen	.15
193	Brett Myers	.15
194	Miguel Cabrera	.75
195	Bartolo Colon	.15
196	Craig Biggio	.25
197	Tim Hudson	.25
198	Mark Prior	.50
199	Mark Buehrle	.25
200	Barry Bonds	2.00
201	Anderson Hernandez (RC)	.25
202	Charlton Jimerson (RC)	.25
203	Jeremy Accardo RC	.50
204	Hanley Ramirez (RC)	.50
205	Matt Capps (RC)	.25
206	John-Ford Griffin (RC)	.25
207	Chuck James (RC)	.25
208	Jaime Bubela (RC)	.25
209	Mark Woodyard (RC)	.25
210	Jason Botts (RC)	.25
211	Chris Demaria RC	.75
212	Miguel Perez (RC)	.25
213	Tom Gorzelanny (RC)	.25
214	Adam Wainwright (RC)	.25
215	Ryan Garko (RC)	.25
216	Jason Bergmann RC	1.00
217	J.J. Furmaniak (RC)	.25
218	Francisco Liriano (RC)	.50
219	Kenji Johjima RC	2.50
219	Kenji Johjima/ Auto.	100.00
220	Craig Hansen RC	1.50
220	Craig Hansen/ Auto.	50.00
221	Ryan Zimmerman/ Auto.	50.00
222	Joey Devine/ Auto.	10.00
223	Scott Olsen/ Auto.	15.00
224	Darrell Rasner/ Auto.	10.00
225	Craig Breslow/ Auto.	10.00
226	Reggie Abercrombie/ Auto. (RC)	15.00
227	Dan Uggla/ Auto. (RC)	35.00
228	Willie Eyre/ Auto. (RC)	10.00
229	Joel Zumaya/ Auto. (RC)	35.00
230	Ricky Nolasco/ Auto. (RC)	15.00
231	Ian Kinsler/ Auto. (RC)	15.00

White

Stars:	3-6X
Rookies (201-220):	3-6X
RC Auto. (219-231):	1-2X
Production 120 Sets	

Blue

Stars:	2-4X
Rookies (201-220):	2-4X
RC Auto. (219-231):	1-1.5X
Production 500 Sets	

Gold

Stars:	1-2X
Rookies (201-220):	1-2X
Inserted 1:1	

Red

No Pricing
Production One Set

Base of the Future

		NM/M
JH	Justin Huber	20.00

Prospects

		NM/M
Common Player:		.25
B1	Alex Gordon	10.00
B2	Jonathan George	.25

B3 Scott Walter .25
B4 Brian Holliday .25
B5 Ben Copeland .50
B6 Bobby Wilson .50
B7 Mayker Sandoval .50
B8 Alejandro de Aza .25
B9 David Munoz .25
B10 Josh LeBlanc .50
B11 Philippe Valiquette .50
B12 Edwin Bellorin .50
B13 Jason Quarles .50
B14 Mark Trumbo .75
B15 Steve Kelly .25
B16 Jamie Hoffman .25
B17 Joseph Bauserman .25
B18 Nick Adenhart 2.50
B19 Mike Butia .25
B20 Jon Weber .25
B21 Luis Valdez .50
B22 Rafael Rodriguez .75
B23 Wyatt Toregas .75
B24 John Vanden Berg .25
B25 Mike Connolly .25
B26 Mike O'Connor 1.00
B27 Garrett Mock .25
B28 Bill Layman .25
B29 Luis Pena .25
B30 Billy Killian .50
B31 Ross Ohlendorf .25
B32 Mark Kaiser .25
B33 Ryan Costello .25
B34 Dale Thayer .25
B35 Steve Garrabrants .25
B36 Samuel Deduno .25
B37 Juan Portes 1.00
B38 Javier Martinez .25
B39 Clint Sammons .25
B40 Andrew Kown .75
B41 Matt Tolbert .25
B42 Michael Ekstrom .25
B43 Shawn Norris .25
B44 Diory Hernandez .25
B45 Chris Maples .25
B46 Aaron Hathaway .50
B47 Steven Baker .25
B48 Greg Creek .50
B49 Collin Mahoney .25
B50 Corey Ragsdale .50
B51 Ariel Nunez .25
B52 Max Ramirez 1.50
B53 Eric Rodland .50
B54 Dante Brinkley .50
B55 Casey Craig .50
B56 Ryan Spilborghs 1.00
B57 Fredy Deza .25
B58 Jeff Frazier .25
B59 Vince Cordova .25
B60 Oswaldo Navarro .75
B61 Jarod Rine .25
B62 Jordan Tata .25
B63 Ben Julianel .25
B64 Yung-Chi Chen 1.50
B65 Carlos Torres .50
B66 Juan Francia .50
B67 Brett Smith .50
B68 Francisco Leandro .50
B69 Chris Turner 1.00
B70 Matt Joyce .50
B71 Jason Jones .25
B72 Jose Diaz .25
B73 Kevin Ool .25
B74 Nate Bumstead .25
B75 Omir Santos .25
B76 Shawn Riggans .25
B77 Ofilio Castro .25
B78 Mike Rozier .75
B79 Wilkin Ramirez .75
B80 Yobal Duenas .50
B81 Adam Bourassa .25
B82 Tony Granadillo .25
B83 Brad McCann 1.50
B84 Dustin Majewski .50
B85 Kelvin Jimenez .25
B86 Mark Reed 1.50
B87 Asdrubal Cabrera 1.00
B88 James Barthmaier .25
B89 Brandon Boggs .25
B90 Raul Valdez .25
B91 Jose Campusano .50
B92 Henry Owens .25
B93 Tug Hulett .50
B94 Nate Gold .25
B95 Lee Mitchell .25
B96 John Hardy .25
B97 Aaron Wideman .25
B98 Brandon Roberts .50
B99 Lou Santangelo .50
B100 Kyle Kendrick .50

B101 Michael Collins .75
B102 Camilo Vazquez .25
B103 Mark McLemore .25
B104 Alexander Peralta .25
B105 Josh Whitesell .50
B106 Carlos Guevara .25
B107 Michael Aubrey .50
B108 Brandon Chaves .25
B109 Leonard Davis .25
B110 Kendry Morales 1.50
B111 Koby Clemens 40.00
B112 Lance Broadway 30.00
B113 Cameron Maybin 100.00
B114 Mike Aviles 15.00
B115 Kyle Blanks 30.00
B116 Chris Dickerson 15.00
B117 Sean Gallagher 30.00
B118 Jamar Hill 20.00
B119 Garrett Mock 15.00
B120 Kendry Morales 25.00
B121 Russel Rohlicek 20.00
B122 Clete Thomas 15.00
B123 Josh Kinney 20.00
B124 Justin Huber 15.00

Prospects White
White: 4-6X
White Autos.: 1.5-2X
Production 120 Sets

Prospects Blue
Blue: 2-3X
Blue Autos.: 1.5X
Production 500 Sets

Prospects Gold
Gold: 1-1.5X
Inserted 1:1

2006 Bowman Chrome Prospects

NM/M
Common Prospect: .50
BC1 Alex Gordon 25.00
BC2 Jonathan George .50
BC3 Scott Walter .50
BC4 Brian Holliday .50
BC5 Ben Copeland 1.00
BC6 Bobby Wilson 1.50
BC7 Mayker Sandoval 1.50
BC8 Alejandro de Aza .75
BC9 David Munoz .75
BC10 Josh LeBlanc 1.00
BC11 Philippe Valiquette 1.00
BC12 Edwin Bellorin 1.00
BC13 Jason Quarles 1.00
BC14 Mark Trumbo 2.00
BC15 Steve Kelly .75
BC16 Jamie Hoffman .75
BC17 Joseph Bauserman .75
BC18 Nick Adenhart 8.00
BC19 Mike Butia .75
BC20 Jon Weber .75
BC21 Luis Valdez 1.00
BC22 Rafael Rodriguez 1.50
BC23 Wyatt Toregas 1.50
BC24 John Vanden Berg .75
BC25 Mike Connolly .75
BC26 Mike O'Connor 3.00
BC27 Garrett Mock .75
BC28 Bill Layman .75
BC29 Luis Pena .75
BC30 Billy Killian 1.00
BC31 Ross Ohlendorf .50
BC32 Mark Kaiser .75
BC33 Ryan Costello .75
BC34 Dale Thayer .50
BC35 Steve Garrabrants .75
BC36 Samuel Deduno .75
BC37 Juan Portes 3.00
BC38 Javier Martinez .75
BC39 Clint Sammons 1.00
BC40 Andrew Kown 1.50
BC41 Matt Tolbert .50
BC42 Michael Ekstrom .75
BC43 Shawn Norris .75
BC44 Diory Hernandez .75
BC45 Chris Maples .75
BC46 Aaron Hathaway 1.00
BC47 Steven Baker .75
BC48 Greg Creek 1.00
BC49 Collin Mahoney .75
BC50 Corey Ragsdale 1.50
BC51 Ariel Nunez .75
BC52 Max Ramirez 4.00
BC53 Eric Rodland 1.50

BC54 Dante Brinkley 1.00
BC55 Casey Craig 1.00
BC56 Ryan Spilborghs 2.50
BC57 Fredy Deza .75
BC58 Jeff Frazier .50
BC59 Vince Cordova .50
BC60 Oswaldo Navarro 1.50
BC61 Jarod Rine .75
BC62 Jordan Tata 1.50
BC63 Ben Julianel 1.00
BC64 Yung-Chi Chen 4.00
BC65 Carlos Torres 1.00
BC66 Juan Francia 1.50
BC67 Brett Smith 1.00
BC68 Francisco Leandro 1.00
BC69 Chris Turner 3.00
BC70 Matt Joyce 1.50
BC71 Jason Jones 1.00
BC72 Jose Diaz .50
BC73 Kevin Ool .75
BC74 Nate Bumstead 1.00
BC75 Omir Santos 1.00
BC76 Shawn Riggans 1.00
BC77 Ofilio Castro 1.00
BC78 Mike Rozier 1.50
BC79 Wilkin Ramirez 2.00
BC80 Yobal Duenas 1.00
BC81 Adam Bourassa 1.00
BC82 Tony Granadillo 1.00
BC83 Brad McCann 4.00
BC84 Dustin Majewski 1.00
BC85 Kelvin Jimenez .50
BC86 Mark Reed 4.00
BC87 Asdrubal Cabrera 3.50
BC88 James Barthmaier 1.00
BC89 Brandon Boggs .75
BC90 Raul Valdez .50
BC91 Jose Campusano 1.50
BC92 Henry Owens 1.00
BC93 Tug Hulett 1.00
BC94 Nate Gold 1.00
BC95 Lee Mitchell 1.00
BC96 John Hardy .75
BC97 Aaron Wideman .75
BC98 Brandon Roberts 1.50
BC99 Lou Santangelo .50
BC100 Kyle Kendrick 1.50
BC101 Michael Collins 2.00
BC102 Camilo Vazquez .75
BC103 Mark McLemore .50
BC104 Alexander Peralta .75
BC105 Josh Whitesell 1.00
BC106 Carlos Guevara .50
BC107 Michael Aubrey 1.50
BC108 Brandon Chaves 1.00
BC109 Leonard Davis 1.00
BC110 Kendry Morales 4.00

Refractor
Refractor (1-110): 2-4X
Production 500 Sets

X-Fractor
X-Fractor (1-110): 3-6X
Production 250 Sets

Red Refractor
No Pricing
Production Five Sets

Gold Refractor
Gold Refractor (1-110): 8-15X
Production 50 Sets

Blue Refractor
Blue Refractor (1-110): 4-6X
Production 150 Sets

Orange Refractor
No Pricing
Production 25 Sets

Signs of the Future
NM/M
BB Brian Bogusevic 15.00
MB Michael Bowden 20.00
RB Ryan Braun 20.00
TB Travis Buck 15.00
JC Jeff Clement 25.00
BC Ben Copeland 15.00
MC Mike Costanzo 20.00
TC Trevor Crowe 20.00
JD John Drennen 20.00
JE Jacoby Ellsbury 20.00
YE Yunel Escobar 15.00
JM John Mayberry Jr. 20.00
GO Garrett Olson 20.00
CR Cesar Ramos 15.00
RR Ricky Romero 15.00
HS Henry Sanchez 20.00
DS Denard Span 15.00
AT Aaron Thompson 20.00
RT Ryan Tucker 15.00
TT Troy Tulowitzki 25.00
SW Sean West 20.00

2006 Bowman Chrome
NM/M
Complete Set (224):
Common Player: .25
Common Rookie (201-220): .50
Pack (4): 8.00
Box (18): 125.00

1 Nick Swisher .25
2 Ted Lilly .25
3 John Smoltz .50
4 Lyle Overbay .25
5 Alfonso Soriano .75
6 Javier Vazquez .25
7 Ronnie Belliard .25
8 Jose Reyes .75
9 Brian Roberts .25
10 Curt Schilling .75
11 Adam Dunn .50
12 Zack Greinke .25
13 Carlos Guillen .25
14 Jon Garland .25
15 Robinson Cano .50
16 Chris Burke .25
17 Barry Zito .50
18 Russ Adams .25
19 Chris Capuano .25
20 Scott Rolen .75
21 Kerry Wood .50
22 Scott Kazmir .50
23 Brandon Webb .50
24 Jeff Kent .40
25 Albert Pujols 2.50
26 C.C. Sabathia .25
27 Adrian Beltre .25
28 Brad Wilkerson .25
29 Randy Wolf .25
30 Jason Bay .50
31 Austin Kearns .25
32 Clint Barmes .25
33 Mike Sweeney .25
34 Kevin Youkilis .50
35 Justin Morneau .50
36 Scott Podsednik .40
37 Jason Giambi .75
38 Steve Finley .25
39 Morgan Ensberg .25
40 Eric Chavez .40
41 Roy Halladay .25
42 Horacio Ramirez .25
43 Ben Sheets .40
44 Chris Carpenter .50
45 Andruw Jones .75
46 Carlos Zambrano .40
47 Jonny Gomes .40
48 Shawn Green .40
49 Moises Alou .40
50 Ichiro Suzuki 1.50
51 Juan Pierre .25
52 Grady Sizemore .75
53 Kazuo Matsui .25
54 Jose Vidro .25
55 Jake Peavy .25
56 Dallas McPherson .25
57 Ryan Howard 2.00
58 Zachary Duke .25
59 Michael Young .75
60 Todd Helton .75
61 David DeJesus .25
62 Ivan Rodriguez .75
63 Johan Santana .75
64 Danny Haren .25
65 Derek Jeter 2.50
66 Greg Maddux 1.50
67 Jorge Cantu .25
68 J.J. Hardy .25
69 Victor Martinez .50
70 David Wright 1.50
71 Ryan Church .25
72 Khalil Greene .25
73 Jimmy Rollins .50
74 Hank Blalock .40
75 Pedro Martinez 1.00
76 Chris Shelton .25
77 Felipe Lopez .25
78 Jeff Francis .25
79 Andrew Sisco .25
80 Hideki Matsui 1.50
81 Ken Griffey Jr. 1.50
82 Nomar Garciaparra .75
83 Kevin Millwood .25
84 Paul Konerko .50
85 A.J. Burnett .25
86 Mike Piazza 1.00
87 Brian Giles .40
88 Johnny Damon .75
89 Jim Thome .75
90 Roger Clemens 2.50
91 Aaron Rowand .25
92 Rafael Furcal .40
93 Gary Sheffield .50
94 Mike Cameron .25
95 Carlos Delgado .50
96 Jorge Posada .50
97 Denny Bautista .25
98 Mike Maroth .25

99 Brad Radke .25
100 Alex Rodriguez 2.50
101 Freddy Garcia .25
102 Oliver Perez .25
103 Jon Lieber .25
104 Melvin Mora .25
105 Travis Hafner .50
106 Alex Rios .25
107 Derek Lowe .25
108 Luis Castillo .25
109 Livan Hernandez .25
110 Tadahito Iguchi .25
111 Shawn Chacon .25
112 Frank Thomas .75
113 Josh Beckett .50
114 Aubrey Huff .25
115 Derrek Lee .75
116 Chien-Ming Wang .50
117 Joe Crede .50
118 Torii Hunter .50
119 J.D. Drew .40
120 Troy Glaus .50
121 Sean Casey .50
122 Edgar Renteria .40
123 Craig Wilson .25
124 Adam Eaton .25
125 Jeff Francoeur .40
126 Bruce Chen .25
127 Cliff Floyd .25
128 Jeremy Reed .25
129 Jake Westbrook .25
130 Wily Mo Pena .25
131 Toby Hall .25
132 David Ortiz 1.00
133 David Eckstein .25
134 Brady Clark .25
135 Marcus Giles .25
136 Aaron Hill .25
137 Mark Kotsay .25
138 Carlos Lee .50
139 Roy Oswalt .50
140 Chone Figgins .25
141 Mike Mussina .75
142 Orlando Hernandez .25
143 Magglio Ordonez .40
144 Jim Edmonds .50
145 Bobby Abreu .50
146 Nick Johnson .25
147 Carlos Beltran .75
148 Jhonny Peralta .25
149 Pedro Feliz .25
150 Miguel Tejada .50
151 Luis Gonzalez .40
152 Carl Crawford .50
153 Yadier Molina .25
154 Rich Harden .40
155 Tim Wakefield .25
156 Rickie Weeks .50
157 Johnny Estrada .25
158 Gustavo Chacin .25
159 Dan Johnson .25
160 Willy Taveras .25
161 Garret Anderson .40
162 Randy Johnson 1.00
163 Jermaine Dye .25
164 Joe Mauer .75
165 Ervin Santana .25
166 Jeremy Bonderman .50
167 Garrett Atkins .25
168 Manny Ramirez 1.00
169 Brad Eldred .25
170 Chase Utley .75
171 Mark Loretta .25
172 John Patterson .25
173 Tom Glavine .50
174 Dontrelle Willis .50
175 Mark Teixeira .50
176 Felix Hernandez .50
177 Cliff Lee .25
178 Jason Schmidt .40
179 Chad Tracy .25
180 Rocco Baldelli .25
181 Aramis Ramirez .40
182 Andy Pettitte .50
183 Mark Mulder .40
184 Geoff Jenkins .25
185 Chipper Jones .75
186 Vernon Wells .50
187 Bobby Crosby .25
188 Lance Berkman .50
189 Vladimir Guerrero .75
190 Coco Crisp .25
191 Brad Penny .25
192 Jose Guillen .25
193 Brett Myers .25
194 Miguel Cabrera .75
195 Bartolo Colon .25
196 Craig Biggio .50
197 Tim Hudson .50
198 Mark Prior .50
199 Mark Buehrle .40
200 Barry Bonds 2.50
201 Anderson Hernandez (RC) .50
202 Jose Capellan (RC) .50
203 Jeremy Accardo RC 1.00
204 Hanley Ramirez (RC) 1.00
205 Matt Capps (RC) .50
206 Jonathan Papelbon (RC) .50
207 Chuck James (RC) .50
208 Matt Cain (RC) .50
209 Cole Hamels (RC) 1.00
210 Jason Botts (RC) .50
211 Lastings Milledge (RC) .50
212 Conor Jackson (RC) .50
213 Yusmeiro Petit (RC) .50
214 Alay Soler RC 2.00

215 Willy Aybar (RC) .50
216 Adam Loewen (RC) .50
217 Justin Verlander (RC) 1.00
218 Francisco Liriano (RC) 5.00
219 Kenji Johjima RC 4.00
219 Kenji Johjima/ Auto. RC 100.00
220 Craig Hansen RC 3.00
221 Prince Fielder (RC) 50.00
222 Josh Barfield (RC) 15.00
223 Fausto Carmona (RC) 15.00
224 James Loney (RC) 20.00

2006 Bowman Chrome Refractor
Refractor (1-200): 2-4X
Refractor (201-220): 2-3X
Inserted 1:4
Autograph (219, 221-224): 1-1.5X
Production 500

X-Fractor
X-Refractor (1-200): 3-5X
X-Refractor (201-220): 3-5X
Production 250
X-Fractor Auto.
(219, 221-224): 1-2X
Production 225

Blue Refractor
Blue Refractor (1-200): 3-6X
Blue Refractor (201-220): 4-6X
Production 150
Blue Ref. Auto.
(219, 221-224): 1-2.5X
Production 150

Gold Refractor
Gold Refractor (1-200): 8-15X
Gold Refractor (201-220): 8-15X
Production 50
Gold Ref. Auto.
(219, 221-224): 3-5X
Production 50

Orange Refractor
Orange Refractor (1-200): 15-25X
Orange Refractor (201-220): 15-25X
Production 25
Orange Ref. Auto.
(221-224): No Pricing
Production 25

Red Refractor
No Pricing
Production Five Sets

Super Fractor
No Pricing
Production One Set

Printing Plates
No Pricing
Production One Set

Bowman Chrome Prospects

NM/M
Common Prospect: .50
BC111 Koby Clemens 3.00
BC112 Lance Broadway 1.50
BC113 Cameron Maybin 15.00
BC114 Mike Aviles .50
BC115 Kyle Blanks 2.00
BC116 Chris Dickerson 1.00
BC117 Sean Gallagher 2.50
BC118 Jamar Hill .50
BC119 Garrett Mock .75
BC120 Russel Rohlicek .50
BC121 Clete Thomas 1.00
BC122 Elvis Andrus 8.00
BC123 Brandon Moss .75
BC124 Mark Holliman 1.00
BC125 Jose Tabata 15.00
BC126 Corey Wimberly 1.50
BC127 Bobby Wilson .50
BC128 Edward Mujica 1.50
BC129 Hunter Pence 6.00
BC130 Adam Heether .50
BC131 Andy Wilson .50
BC132 Radhames Liz 4.00
BC133 Garrett Patterson .50

Card	Player	Price
BC134	Carlos Gomez	10.00
BC135	Jared Lansford	1.00
BC136	Jose Arredondo	2.00
BC137	Renee Cortez	1.00
BC138	Francisco Rosario	.50
BC139	Brian Stokes	.50
BC140	Will Thompson	.50
BC141	Ernesto Frieri	1.00
BC142	Jose Mijares	1.00
BC143	Jeremy Slayden	2.00
BC144	Brandon Fahey	1.00
BC145	Jason Windsor	1.50
BC146	Shawn Nottingham	1.00
BC147	Dallas Trahern	1.00
BC148	Jon Niese	2.00
BC149	A.J. Shappi	.50
BC150	Jordan Pals	.50
BC151	Tim Moss	.50
BC152	Stephen Marek	1.00
BC153	Mat Gamel	2.00
BC154	Sean Henn	.50
BC155	Matt Guillory	.50
BC156	Brandon Jones	2.00
BC157	Gary Galvez	1.00
BC158	Shane Lindsay	1.50
BC159	Jesus Reina	.50
BC160	Lorenzo Cain	6.00
BC161	Chris Britton	1.00
BC162	Yovani Gallardo	3.00
BC163	Matt Walker	1.00
BC164	Shaun Cumberland	1.00
BC165	Ryan Patterson	2.00
BC166	Michael Hollimon	1.00
BC167	Eude Brito	.50
BC168	John Bowker	.50
BC169	James Avery	.50
BC170	Juan Bannister	.50
BC171	Juan Ciriaco	.50
BC172	Manuel Corpas	1.00
BC173	Leo Rosales	.50
BC174	Tim Kennelly	.50
BC175	Adam Russell	.50
BC176	Jeremy Hellickson	3.00
BC177	Ryan Klosterman	.50
BC178	Evan Meek	1.00
BC179	Steve Murphy	2.00
BC180	Scott Feldman	.50
BC181	Pablo Sandoval	2.00
BC182	Dexter Fowler	2.00
BC183	Jairo Cuevas	1.50
BC184	Andrew Pinckney	1.00
BC185	Marino Salas	.50
BC186	Justin Christian	.50
BC187	Ching-Lung Lo	3.00
BC188	Randy Roth	2.00
BC189	Andrew Sonnanstine	3.00
BC190	Josh Outman	2.50
BC191	Yuber A. Rodriguez	1.00
BC192	Hainley Statia	2.00
BC193	Kevin Estrada	1.50
BC194	Jeff Karstens	1.00
BC195	Corey Coles	1.00
BC196	Gustavo Espinoza	1.00
BC197	Brian Horwitz	1.00
BC198	Landon Jacobsen	.50
BC199	Ben Krosschell	1.00
BC200	Jason Jaramillo	1.00
BC201	Josh Wilson	.50
BC202	Jason Ray	.50
BC203	Brent Dlugach	1.00
BC204	Cesar Jimenez	1.00
BC205	Eric Haberer	.50
BC206	Felipe Paulino	.50
BC207	Alcides Escobar	2.00
BC208	Jose Ascanio	1.00
BC209	Yoel Hernandez	1.00
BC210	Geoff Vandel	1.00
BC211	Travis Denker	1.50
BC212	Ramon Alvarado	1.00
BC213	Welinson Baez	1.50
BC214	Chris Kolkhorst	1.00
BC215	Emiliano Fruto	1.00
BC216	Luis Cota	1.00
BC217	Mark Worrell	.50
BC218	Cla Meredith	1.50
BC219	Emmanuel Garcia	1.50
BC220	B.J. Szymanski	1.00
BC221	Alex Gordon	240.00
BC222	Mark Pawelek	25.00
BC223	Justin Upton	150.00
BC224	Sean West	20.00
BC225	Tyler Greene	20.00
BC226	Josh Kinney	25.00
BC227	Pedro Lopez	15.00
BC228	Troy Patton	25.00
BC229	Chris Iannetta	50.00
BC230	Jared Wells	15.00
BC231	Brandon Wood	35.00
BC232	Josh Geer	20.00
BC233	Cesar Carrillo	20.00
BC234	Franklin Gutierrez	25.00
BC235	Matt Garza	30.00
BC236	Eli Iorg	20.00
BC237	Trevor Bell	20.00
BC238	Jeff Lyman	20.00
BC239	Jon Lester	60.00
BC240	Kendry Morales	30.00
BC241	J. Brent Cox	20.00
BC242	Jose Bautista	20.00
BC243	Josh Sullivan	20.00
BC244	Brandon Snyder	20.00
BC245	Elvin Puello	20.00
BC246	Henry Sanchez	20.00
BC247	Jacob Marceaux	20.00

Prospects Refractors
Refractor (111-220): 2-4X
Refractor Auto. (221-247): 1-1.5X
Production 500 Sets

Prospects X-Fractors
X-Refractor (111-220): 3-5X
Production 250
X-Refractor Auto. (221-247): 1-2X
Production 225

Prospects Blue Refractors
Blue Refractor (111-220): 4-6X
Blue Refractor Auto. (221-247): 1-2.5X
Production 150 Sets

Prospects Gold Refractors
Gold Refractor (111-220): 8-15X
Gold Refractor Auto. (221-247): 3-5X
Production 50 Sets

Prospects Orange Refractors
Orange Refractor (111-220): 15-25X
Orange Refractor Auto. (221-247): 4-6X
Production 25 Sets

Prospects Red Refractors
No Pricing
Production Five Sets

Prospects Super Fractors
No Pricing
Production One Set

2006 Bowman Chrome Draft
Complete Set (55): 25.00
Common Player: NM/M

#	Player	Price
1	Matthew Kemp (RC)	1.00
2	Taylor Tankersley (RC)	.50
3	Michael Napoli RC	.50
4	Brian Bannister (RC)	.50
5	Melky Cabrera (RC)	.50
6	Bill Bray (RC)	.50
7	Brian Anderson (RC)	.50
8	Jered Weaver (RC)	1.50
9	Chris Duncan (RC)	.50
10	Boof Bonser (RC)	1.00
11	Mike Rouse (RC)	.50
12	David Pauley (RC)	.50
13	Russell Martin (RC)	.50
14	Jeremy Sowers (RC)	.50
15	Kevin Reese (RC)	.50
16	John Rheinecker (RC)	.50
17	Tommy Murphy (RC)	.50
18	Sean Marshall (RC)	.50
19	Jason Kubel (RC)	.50
20	Chad Billingsley (RC)	1.50
21	Kendry Morales (RC)	1.00
22	Jon Lester (RC)	2.00
23	Brandon Fahey RC	.50
24	Josh Johnson (RC)	.50
25	Kevin Frandsen (RC)	.50
26	Casey Janssen RC	.50
27	Scott Thorman (RC)	.50
28	Scott Mathieson (RC)	.50
29	Jeremy Hermida (RC)	.50
30	Dustin Nippert (RC)	.50
31	Kevin Thompson (RC)	.50
32	Bobby Livingston (RC)	.50
33	Travis Ishikawa (RC)	.50
34	Jeff Mathis (RC)	.50
35	Charlie Haeger RC	1.00
36	Josh Willingham (RC)	.50
37	Taylor Buchholz (RC)	.50
38	Joel Guzman (RC)	.50
39	Zach Jackson (RC)	.50
40	Howie Kendrick (RC)	1.00
41	T.J. Beam (RC)	1.00
42	Ty Taubenheim RC	1.00
43	Erick Aybar (RC)	1.00
44	Anibal Sanchez (RC)	1.00
45	Mike Pelfrey RC	6.00
46	Shawn Hill (RC)	.50
47	Chris Roberson (RC)	.50
48	Carlos Villanueva RC	.50
49	Andre Ethier (RC)	1.50
50	Anthony Reyes (RC)	1.00
51	Franklin Gutierrez (RC)	.50
52	Angel Guzman (RC)	.50
53	Michael O'Connor RC	.50
54	James Shields RC	1.50
55	Nate McLouth (RC)	.50

SuperFractor
No Pricing
Production One Set

Red Refractor
No Pricing
Production Five Sets

Orange Refractor
Orange Refractor (1-55): 15-25X
Production 25 Sets

Gold Refractor
Gold Refractor (1-55): 8-15X
Production 50 Sets

Blue Refractor
Blue Refractor (1-55): 4-8X
Production 199 Sets

X-Fractor
X-Fractor (1-55): 3-6X
Production 299 Sets

Refractor
Refractor (1-55): 2-4X

Draft Picks
NM/M
Complete Set (90):
Common Draft Pick (1-65): 1.00
Common Auto. (66-90): 20.00

#	Player	Price
1	Tyler Colvin	3.00
2	Chris Marrero	4.00
3	Hank Conger	4.00
4	Chris Parmelee	4.00
5	Jason Place	5.00
6	Billy Rowell	5.00
7	Travis Snider	8.00
8	Colton Willems	3.00
9	Chase Fontaine	2.00
10	Jon Jay	2.00
11	Wade Leblanc	2.00
12	Justin Masterson	2.00
13	Gary Daley	1.50
14	Justin Edwards	1.00
15	Charlie Yarbrough	1.50
16	Cyle Hankerd	4.00
17	Zach McAllister	1.50
18	Tyler Robertson	1.00
19	Joe Smith	1.00
20	Nate Culp	1.00
21	John Holdzkom	1.00
22	Patrick Bresnahan	1.00
23	Chad Lee	1.00
24	Ryan Morris	1.00
25	D'Arby Myers	2.50
26	Garrett Olson	2.00
27	Jon Still	1.50
28	Brandon Rice	1.00
29	Chris Davis	2.00
30	Zack Daeges	1.50
31	Bobby Henson	1.50
32	George Kontos	1.00
33	Jermaine Mitchell	2.50
34	Adam Coe	2.00
35	Dustin Richardson	1.00
36	Allen Craig	1.00
37	Austin McClune	1.50
38	Doug Fister	1.00
39	Corey Madden	1.00
40	Justin Jacobs	1.50
41	Jim Negrych	1.00
42	Tyler Norrick	1.00
43	Adam Davis	1.00
44	Brett Logan	1.00
45	Brian Omogrosso	1.00
46	Kyle Drabek	4.00
47	Jamie Ortiz	2.00
48	Alex Presley	2.00
49	Terrance Warren	2.00
50	David Christensen	2.00
51	Helder Velazquez	1.00
52	Matt McBride	1.50
53	Quintin Berry	1.00
54	Michael Eisenberg	1.00
55	Dan Garcia	1.00
56	Scott Cousins	1.00
57	Sean Land	1.00
58	Kristopher Medlen	1.00
59	Tyler Reves	1.00
60	John Shelby	1.50
61	Jordan Newton	1.50
62	Ricky Orta	1.00
63	Jason Donald	1.50
64	David Huff	1.50
65	Brett Sinkbeil	1.00
66	Evan Longoria/Auto.	120.00
67	Cody Johnson/Auto.	40.00
68	Kris Johnson/Auto.	25.00
69	Kasey Kiker/Auto.	25.00
70	Ronny Bourquin/Auto.	20.00
71	Adrian Cardenas/Auto.	35.00
72	Matt Antonelli/Auto.	30.00
73	Brooks Brown/Auto.	20.00
74	Steven Evarts/Auto.	25.00
75	Joshua Butler/Auto.	20.00
76	Chad Huffman/Auto.	30.00
77	Steven Wright/Auto.	20.00
78	Cory Rasmus/Auto.	25.00
79	Brad Furnish/Auto.	20.00
80	Andrew Carpenter/Auto.	20.00
81	Dustin Evans/Auto.	20.00
82	Tommy Hickman/Auto.	25.00
83	Matt Long/Auto.	20.00
84	Clayton Kershaw/Auto.	75.00
85	Kyle McCulloch/Auto.	25.00
86	Pedro Beato/Auto.	25.00
87	Kyler Burke/Auto.	25.00
88	Stephen Englund/Auto.	25.00
89	Michael Felix/Auto.	20.00
90	Sean Watson/Auto.	20.00

Draft Picks X-Fractor
X-Fractor (1-65): 3-6X
Production 299 Sets
X-Fractor Auto. (66-90): 1-2X
Production 225 Sets

Draft Picks Refractor
Refractor (1-65): 2-4X
Refractor Auto. (66-90): 1-1.5X
Production 500 for #'s 66-90

Draft Picks SuperFractor
No Pricing
Production One Set

Draft Picks Red Refractor
No Pricing
Production Five Sets

Draft Picks Orange Refractor
Orange Refractor (1-65): 15-25X
Production 25 Sets
Orange Auto. (66-90): No Pricing
Production 25 Sets

Draft Picks Gold Refractor
Gold Refractor (1-65): 8-15X
Production 50 Sets
Gold Auto. (66-90): 3-5X
Production 50 Sets

Draft Picks Blue Refractor
Blue Refractor (1-65): 4-8X
Production 199 Sets
Blue Auto. (66-90): 1-2.5X
Production 150 Sets

Draft Future's Game Prospects
NM/M
Complete Set (45): 20.00
Common Player: .50

#	Player	Price
1	Nick Adenhart	1.00
2	Joel Guzman	.50
3	Ryan Braun	.50
4	Carlos Carrasco	.50
5	Neil Walker	.50
6	Pablo Sandoval	.50
7	Gio Gonzalez	.50
8	Joey Votto	.50
9	Luis Cruz	.50
10	Nolan Reimold	.50
11	Juan Salas	.50
12	Josh Fields	1.00
13	Yovani Gallardo	1.00
14	Radhames Liz	.50
15	Eric Patterson	.50
16	Cameron Maybin	2.50
17	Edgar Martinez	.50
18	Hunter Pence	1.50
19	Phillip Hughes	2.00
20	Trent Oeltjen	.50
21	Nick Pereira	.50
22	Wladimir Balentien	.50
23	Stephen Drew	1.50
24	Davis Romero	.50
25	Joe Koshansky	.50
26	Chin-Lung Hu	2.00
27	Jason Hirsh	.50
28	Jose Tabata	2.00
29	Eric Hurley	.50
30	Yung-Chi Chen	2.50
31	Howie Kendrick	1.00
32	Humberto Sanchez	1.00
33	Alex Gordon	4.00
34	Yunel Escobar	.50
35	Travis Buck	.75
36	Billy Butler	.50
37	Homer Bailey	1.00
38	George Kottaras	.50
39	Kurt Suzuki	.50
40	Joaquin Arias	.50
41	Matt Lindstrom	.50
42	Sean Smith	.50
43	Carlos Gonzalez	.50
44	Jaime Garcia	1.00
45	Jose Garcia	1.00

Draft Future's Game Red Refractor
No Pricing
Production Five Sets

Draft Future's Game Orange Refractor
Orange (1-45): 15-30X
Production 25 Sets

Draft Future's Game Gold Refractor
Gold (1-45): 8-15X
Production 50 Sets

Draft Future's Game Blue Refractor
Blue (1-45): 4-8X
Production 199 Sets

Draft Future's Game X-Fractor
X-Fractor (1-45): 3-6X
Production 299 Sets

Draft Future's Game Refractor
Refractor (1-45): 2-4X

Draft Head of the Class Dual Auto.
NM/M
Production 174
Refractor: 1-1.5X
Production 50
Gold Refractor: No Pricing
Production 25
RU Alex Rodriguez, Justin Upton 150.00

2006 Bowman Draft
NM/M
Complete Set (55): 10.00
Common Player: .25
Pack (5 + 2 Chrome): 3.50
Box (24): 75.00

#	Player	Price
1	Matthew Kemp (RC)	.50
2	Taylor Tankersley (RC)	.25
3	Michael Napoli RC	.25
4	Brian Bannister (RC)	.25
5	Melky Cabrera (RC)	.25
6	Bill Bray (RC)	.25
7	Brian Anderson (RC)	.25
8	Jered Weaver (RC)	.75
9	Chris Duncan (RC)	.25
10	Boof Bonser (RC)	.25
11	Mike Rouse (RC)	.25
12	David Pauley (RC)	.25
13	Russell Martin (RC)	.25
14	Jeremy Sowers (RC)	.25
15	Kevin Reese (RC)	.25
16	John Rheinecker (RC)	.25
17	Tommy Murphy (RC)	.25
18	Sean Marshall (RC)	.25
19	Jason Kubel (RC)	.25
20	Chad Billingsley (RC)	.75
21	Kendry Morales (RC)	.50
22	Jon Lester (RC)	.75
23	Brandon Fahey RC	.25
24	Josh Johnson (RC)	.25
25	Kevin Frandsen (RC)	.25
26	Casey Janssen RC	.25
27	Scott Thorman (RC)	.25
28	Scott Mathieson (RC)	.25
29	Jeremy Hermida (RC)	.25
30	Dustin Nippert (RC)	.25
31	Kevin Thompson (RC)	.25
32	Bobby Livingston (RC)	.25
33	Travis Ishikawa (RC)	.25
34	Jeff Mathis (RC)	.25
35	Charlie Haeger RC	.50
36	Josh Willingham (RC)	.25
37	Taylor Buchholz (RC)	.25
38	Joel Guzman (RC)	.25
39	Zach Jackson (RC)	.25
40	Howie Kendrick (RC)	.50
41	T.J. Beam (RC)	.50
42	Ty Taubenheim RC	.50
43	Erick Aybar (RC)	.50
44	Anibal Sanchez (RC)	.50
45	Mike Pelfrey RC	2.00
46	Shawn Hill (RC)	.25
47	Chris Roberson (RC)	.25
48	Carlos Villanueva RC	.25
49	Andre Ethier (RC)	.50
50	Anthony Reyes (RC)	.25
51	Franklin Gutierrez (RC)	.25
52	Angel Guzman (RC)	.25
53	Michael O'Connor RC	.25
54	James Shields RC	.50
55	Nate McLouth (RC)	.25

Future's Game Prospects
NM/M
Complete Set (45): 10.00
Common Player: .25

#	Player	Price
1	Nick Adenhart	.50
2	Joel Guzman	.25
3	Ryan Braun	.25
4	Carlos Carrasco	.25
5	Neil Walker	.25
6	Pablo Sandoval	.25
7	Gio Gonzalez	.25
8	Joey Votto	.25
9	Luis Cruz	.25
10	Nolan Reimold	.25
11	Juan Salas	.25
12	Josh Fields	.50
13	Yovani Gallardo	.50
14	Radhames Liz	.25
15	Eric Patterson	.25
16	Cameron Maybin	1.00
17	Edgar Martinez	.25
18	Hunter Pence	.75
19	Phillip Hughes	.75
20	Trent Oeltjen	.25
21	Nick Pereira	.25
22	Wladimir Balentien	.25
23	Stephen Drew	.75
24	Davis Romero	.25
25	Joe Koshansky	.25
26	Chin-Lung Hu	.50
27	Jason Hirsh	.25
28	Jose Tabata	.50
29	Eric Hurley	.25
30	Yung-Chi Chen	.75
31	Howie Kendrick	.50
32	Humberto Sanchez	.50
33	Alex Gordon	1.50
34	Yunel Escobar	.25
35	Travis Buck	.25
36	Billy Butler	.25
37	Homer Bailey	.50
38	George Kottaras	.25
39	Kurt Suzuki	.25
40	Joaquin Arias	.25
41	Matt Lindstrom	.25
42	Sean Smith	.25
43	Carlos Gonzalez	.25
44	Jaime Garcia	.50
45	Jose Garcia	.50

Draft Picks
NM/M
Complete Set (65): 20.00

Future's Game Prospects Relics

		NM/M
	Common Player:	4.00
1	Nick Adenhart	8.00
2	Joel Guzman	4.00
3	Ryan Braun	6.00
4	Carlos Carrasco	4.00
5	Neil Walker	4.00
6	Pablo Sandoval	6.00
7	Gio Gonzalez	4.00
8	Joey Votto	6.00
9	Luis Cruz	4.00
10	Nolan Reimold	4.00
11	Juan Salas	4.00
12	Josh Fields	6.00
13	Yovani Gallardo	4.00
14	Radhames Liz	4.00
15	Eric Patterson	6.00
16	Cameron Maybin	10.00
17	Edgar Martinez	4.00
18	Hunter Pence	8.00
19	Phillip Hughes	20.00
20	Trent Oeltjen	4.00
21	Nick Pereira	4.00
22	Wladimir Balentien	4.00
23	Stephen Drew	8.00
24	Davis Romero	4.00
25	Joe Koshansky	4.00
26	Chin-Lung Hu	25.00
27	Jason Hirsh	4.00
28	Jose Tabata	15.00
29	Eric Hurley	4.00
30	Yung-Chi Chen	35.00
31	Howie Kendrick	8.00
32	Humberto Sanchez	4.00
33	Alex Gordon	20.00
34	Yunel Escobar	4.00
35	Travis Buck	6.00
36	Billy Butler	8.00
37	Homer Bailey	10.00
38	George Kottaras	4.00
39	Kurt Suzuki	4.00
40	Joaquin Arias	4.00
41	Matt Lindstrom	4.00
42	Sean Smith	4.00
43	Carlos Gonzalez	4.00
44	Jaime Garcia	4.00
45	Jose Garcia	4.00

Gold
Gold (1-55): 1-2X
Inserted 1:1

Printing Plates
No Pricing
Production one set per color.

Red
No Pricing
Production One Set

Signs of the Future

		NM/M
	Common Autograph:	6.00
BS	Brandon Snyder	8.00
KC	Koby Clemens	20.00
AG	Alex Gordon	80.00
CI	Chris Iannetta	15.00
MO	Micah Owings	10.00
JC	Jeff Clement	15.00
CR	Clayton Richard	8.00
TB	Travis Buck	15.00
BJ	Beau Jones	15.00
DJ	Daryl Jones	8.00
CDR	Chaz Roe	8.00
JM	Jacob Marceaux	8.00
CTI	Craig Italiano	6.00
JB	Jay Bruce	20.00
WT	Wade Townsend	8.00
MM	Mark McCormick	8.00
HS	Henry Sanchez	8.00
MC	Mike Costanzo	8.00
CRA	Cesar Ramos	8.00

White
White (1-55): 2-5X
Production 225 Sets

2006 Bowman Heritage

		NM/M
	Complete Set (300):	.15
	Common SP (1-200):	.15
	Common SP (even #'s 202-300):	3.00
	Inserted 1:3	
	Pack (8):	3.50
	Box (24):	70.00
1	David Wright	1.00
2	Andruw Jones	.50
3	Ryan Howard	1.50
4	Jason Bay	.25
5	Paul Konerko	.25
6	Jake Peavy	.25
7	Todd Jones	.15
8	Troy Glaus	.25
9	Rocco Baldelli	.15
10	Rafael Furcal	.25
11	Freddy Sanchez	.15
12	Jermaine Dye	.15
13	A.J. Burnett	.15
14	Michael Cuddyer	.25
15	Barry Zito	.25
16	Chipper Jones	.75
17	Paul LoDuca	.15
18	Mark Mulder	.15
19	Raul Ibanez	.15
20	Carlos Delgado	.40
21	Marcus Giles	.15
22	Danny Haren	.15
23	Justin Morneau	.40
24	Livan Hernandez	.15
25	Ken Griffey Jr.	1.50
26	Aaron Hill	.15
27	Tadahito Iguchi	.15
28	Nate Robertson	.15
29	Kevin Millwood	.15
30	Jim Thome	.50
31	Aubrey Huff	.15
32	Dontrelle Willis	.25
33	Khalil Greene	.25
34	Doug Davis	.15
35	Ivan Rodriguez	.50
36	Rickie Weeks	.25
37	Jhonny Peralta	.15
38	Yadier Molina	.15
39	Eric Chavez	.25
40	Alfonso Soriano	.75
41	Pat Burrell	.25
42	B.J. Ryan	.15
43	Carl Crawford	.25
44	Preston Wilson	.15
45	Jorge Posada	.40
46	Carlos Zambrano	.25
47	Mark Teahen	.15
48	Nick Johnson	.15
49	Mark Kotsay	.15
50	Derek Jeter	2.00
51	Moises Alou	.25
52	Ryan Freel	.15
53	Shannon Stewart	.15
54	Casey Blake	.15
55	Edgar Renteria	.15
56	Frank Thomas	.50
57	Ty Wigginton	.15
58	Jeff Kent	.25
59	Chien-Ming Wang	.50
60	Josh Beckett	.25
61	Chase Utley	.40
62	Gary Matthews	.15
63	Torii Hunter	.25
64	Bobby Jenks	.15
65	Wilson Betemit	.15
66	Jeremy Bonderman	.25
67	Scott Rolen	.75
68	Brad Penny	.15
69	Jacque Jones	.15
70	Jose Reyes	.50
71	Brian Roberts	.15
72	John Smoltz	.25
73	Johnny Estrada	.15
74	Ronnie Belliard	.15
75	Vladimir Guerrero	.75
76	A.J. Pierzynski	.15
77	Garrett Atkins	.15
78	Adam LaRoche	.15
79	Mark Loretta	.15
80	Todd Helton	.50
81	Jose Vidro	.15
82	Carlos Guillen	.15
83	Michael Barrett	.15
84	Lyle Overbay	.15
85	Travis Hafner	.25
86	Shea Hillenbrand	.15
87	Julio Lugo	.25
88	Tim Hudson	.25
89	Scott Podsednik	.15
90	Roy Halladay	.15
91	Bartolo Colon	.15
92	Ryan Langerhans	.15
93	Tom Glavine	.15
94	Ken Rogers	.15
95	Robinson Cano	.50
96	Mark Prior	.50
97	Jason Schmidt	.25
98	Bengie Molina	.15
99	Jon Lieber	.15
100	Alex Rodriguez	2.00
101	Scott Kazmir	.25
102	Jeff Francoeur	.25
103	Chris Carpenter	.40
104	Juan Uribe	.15
105	Mariano Rivera	.40
106	Rich Harden	.15
107	Jack Wilson	.15
108	Austin Kearns	.15
109	Marcus Thames	.15
110	Miguel Tejada	.25
111	Chone Figgins	.15
112	Bronson Arroyo	.15
113	Chad Cordero	.15
114	Bill Hall	.15
115	Curt Schilling	.50
116	David Eckstein	.15
117	Ramon Hernandez	.15
118	Eric Byrnes	.15
119	Clint Barmes	.15
120	Bobby Abreu	.15
121	Joe Crede	.25
122	Derek Lowe	.15
123	Jason Marquis	.15
124	Erik Bedard	.15
125	Derrek Lee	.50
126	Brian McCann	.25
127	Magglio Ordonez	.25
128	Ben Sheets	.25
129	Brandon Inge	.15
130	Miguel Cabrera	.75
131	Jim Edmonds	.25
132	John Lackey	.15
133	Kevin Mench	.15
134	Adrian Beltre	.25
135	Curtis Granderson	.15
136	Shawn Green	.25
137	Jose Contreras	.15
138	Joe Nathan	.15
139	Bobby Crosby	.15
140	Johnny Damon	.50
141	Brad Hawpe	.15
142	Brandon Phillips	.15
143	Victor Martinez	.15
144	Jimmy Rollins	.50
145	Corey Patterson	.15
146	Grady Sizemore	.40
147	Placido Polanco	.15
148	Mike Lowell	.15
149	Francisco Rodriguez	.15
150	Ichiro Suzuki	1.50
151	Kris Benson	.15
152	Scott Hatteberg	.15
153	Akinori Otsuka	.15
154	Cesar Izturis	.15
155	Roger Clemens	2.00
156	Kerry Wood	.25
157	Tom Gordon	.15
158	Sean Casey	.15
159	Jose Lopez	.15
160	Orlando Hernandez	.15
161	Aramis Ramirez	.25
162	J.D. Drew	.25
163	David DeJesus	.15
164	Craig Biggio	.25
165	Brad Myers	.15
166	C.C. Sabathia	.15
167	Zachary Duke	.15
168	Luis Castillo	.15
169	Hideki Matsui	1.00
170	Brian Giles	.15
171	Coco Crisp	.15
172	Richie Sexson	.25
173	Nomar Garciaparra	.75
174	Roy Oswalt	.25
175	David Ortiz	.75
176	Matt Morris	.15
177	Felipe Lopez	.15
178	Garret Anderson	.15
179	Kevin Youkilis	.25
180	Alex Rios	.15
181	John Garland	.15
182	Luis Gonzalez	.15
183	Cliff Floyd	.15
184	Juan Encarnacion	.15
185	Nick Swisher	.25
186	Mike Cameron	.15
187	Jose Castillo	.15
188	Ray Durham	.15
189	Jorge Cantu	.15
190	Andy Pettitte	.25
191	Chad Tracy	.15
192	Adrian Gonzalez	.15
193	Jose Valentin	.15
194	Mark Buehrle	.25
195	Huston Street	.15
196	Chris Capuano	.15
197	Aaron Rowand	.15
198	Billy Wagner	.15
199	Orlando Cabrera	.15
200	Albert Pujols	2.00
201	Dan Uggla RC	.50
202	Alay Soler RC	3.00
203	Matthew Kemp (RC)	1.00
204	Michael Napoli RC	3.00
205	Joel Zumaya (RC)	3.00
206	Mike Pelfrey RC	6.00
207	Ian Kinsler (RC)	.50
208	Josh Willingham (RC)	3.00
209	Erick Aybar (RC)	1.00
210	Willie Eyre (RC)	3.00
211	Kendry Morales (RC)	1.00
212	Scott Thorman (RC)	3.00
213	Hanley Ramirez (RC)	1.00
214	Boof Bonser (RC)	4.00
215	Anthony Reyes (RC)	.50
216	Justin Huber (RC)	3.00
217	Yusmeiro Petit (RC)	.50
218	Jason Bartlett (RC)	3.00
219	Shin-Soo Choo (RC)	1.00
220	Francisco Liriano (RC)	5.00
221	Craig Hansen RC	3.00
222	Ricky Nolasco (RC)	3.00
223	Adam Loewen (RC)	.50
224	Scott Olsen (RC)	3.00
225	Cole Hamels (RC)	3.00
226	Martin Prado (RC)	3.00
227	James Loney (RC)	1.00
228	Kevin Thompson (RC)	3.00
229	Adam Jones (RC)	3.00
230	Josh Johnson (RC)	3.00
231	Anderson Hernandez (RC)	1.00
232	Tony Gwynn Jr. (RC)	3.00
233	Casey Janssen RC	1.00
234	Taylor Tankersley (RC)	3.00
235	Mike Thompson RC	1.00
236	Jeremy Sowers (RC)	4.00
237	Anibal Sanchez (RC)	.50
238	Adam Wainwright (RC)	4.00
239	Rich Hill (RC)	.50
240	Russell Martin (RC)	3.00
241	Joe Inglett (RC)	3.00
242	Tony Pena (RC)	3.00
243	Joshua Sharpless RC	1.00
244	Darrell Rasner (RC)	3.00
245	Joe Saunders (RC)	3.00
246	Jon Lester (RC)	6.00
247	Jeremy Hermida (RC)	1.00
248	Chad Billingsley (RC)	4.00
249	Bobby Livingston (RC)	.50
250	Justin Verlander (RC)	5.00
251	Mickey Mantle	12.00
252	Hank Blalock	3.00
253	Manny Ramirez	1.00
254	Mike Mussina	5.00
255	Greg Maddux	2.00
256	Jason Giambi	4.00
257	Mark Teixeira	1.00
258	Carlos Beltran	4.00
259	Matt Holliday	.50
260	Pedro Martinez	1.00
261	Joe Mauer	4.00
262	Melvin Mora	3.00
263	Mike Piazza	1.50
264	B.J. Upton	4.00
265	Vernon Wells	.75
266	Gary Sheffield	4.00
267	Randy Johnson	1.00
268	Ryan Zimmerman	4.00
269	Lance Berkman	.75
270	Johan Santana	4.00
271	Carlos Lee	.50
272	Brandon Webb	3.00
273	Adam Dunn	.75
274	Michael Young	3.00
275	Barry Bonds	2.00
276	Jonathan Papelbon (RC)	5.00
277	Howie Kendrick (RC)	1.00
278	Melky Cabrera (RC)	3.00
279	Jered Weaver (RC)	3.00
280	Josh Barfield (RC)	3.00
281	Chuck James (RC)	1.00
282	Lastings Milledge (RC)	5.00
283	Nicholas Markakis (RC)	1.50
284	Jose Capellan (RC)	3.00
285	Prince Fielder (RC)	4.00
286	Jason Botts (RC)	3.00
287	Eliezer Alfonzo RC	.50
288	Sean Marshall (RC)	3.00
289	Ryan Garko (RC)	.75
290	Stephen Drew (RC)	5.00
291	Joel Guzman (RC)	3.00
292	Hong-Chih Kuo (RC)	3.00
293	Zach Miner (RC)	.50
294	Angel Guzman (RC)	3.00
295	Andre Ethier (RC)	3.00
296	Fausto Carmona (RC)	3.00
297	Ronny Paulino (RC)	.75
298	Matt Cain (RC)	3.00
299	Carlos Quentin (RC)	.75
300	Kenji Johjima RC	6.00

Mini
Mini (1-300): 1-2X
Mini (301-350): .5-1X
Inserted 1:1

Foil
Foil (1-300): 1-2X
Foil (301-350): .5-1X
Inserted 1:1

Black
No Pricing
Production One Set

Printing Plates
No Pricing
Production One Set

Signs of Greatness

		NM/M
	Common Autograph:	10.00
	White:	No Pricing
	Production 5 Sets	
	Black:	No Pricing
	Production One Set	
BB	Brian Bogusevic	10.00
LB	Lance Broadway	15.00
KC	Koby Clemens	40.00
JCL	Jeff Clement	25.00
JC	Jesus Cota	15.00
TC	Trevor Crowe	20.00
JD	John Drennen	15.00
SG	Sean Gallagher	15.00
AG	Alex Gordon	85.00
JH	Justin Huber	15.00
CI	Craig Italiano	15.00
SL	Sam LeCure	10.00
MM	Matt Maloney	30.00
CM	Cameron Maybin	60.00
JS	Jarrod Saltalamacchia	25.00
BS	Brandon Snyder	25.00
ST	Steve Tolleson	15.00
WT	Wade Townsend	15.00
RT	Ryan Tucker	15.00
JU	Justin Upton	80.00
KW	Kevin Whelan	15.00
BW	Brandon Wood	25.00

Pieces of Greatness

		NM/M
	Common Player:	5.00
	Inserted 1:12	
	White:	1.5-3X
	Production 49 Sets	
	Black:	No Pricing
	Production One Set	

PIECES OF GREATNESS
AUTHENTIC GAME-WORN JERSEY

LB	Lance Berkman	5.00
CB	Craig Biggio	8.00
HB	Hank Blalock	5.00
BB	Barry Bonds	25.00
MB	Milton Bradley	5.00
RC	Robinson Cano	20.00
AD	Adam Dunn	5.00
JD	Jermaine Dye	5.00
DE	David Eckstein	15.00
EE	Edwin Encarnacion	5.00
ME	Morgan Ensberg	5.00
CF	Cliff Floyd	5.00
JF	Jeff Francoeur	10.00
RF	Rafael Furcal	5.00
VG	Vladimir Guerrero	10.00
THE	Todd Helton	8.00
RH	Ryan Howard	25.00
TH	Torii Hunter	5.00
AJ	Andruw Jones	8.00
AJ2	Andruw Jones	8.00
CJ	Chipper Jones	8.00
CJ2	Chipper Jones	8.00
NJ	Nick Johnson	5.00
JK	Jeff Kent	5.00
AL	Adam LaRoche	5.00
DL	Derrek Lee	8.00
JL	Jay Lopez	5.00
ML	Mike Lowell	5.00
GM	Greg Maddux	10.00
VM	Victor Martinez	5.00
XN	Xavier Nady	5.00
MO	Magglio Ordonez	5.00
DO	David Ortiz	15.00
AJP	A.J. Pierzynski	5.00
SP	Scott Podsednik	10.00
AP	Albert Pujols	25.00
AP2	Albert Pujols	25.00
ARA	Aramis Ramirez	5.00
MR	Manny Ramirez	8.00
BR	Brian Roberts	5.00
AR	Alex Rodriguez	20.00
CS	Curt Schilling	8.00
GS	Gary Sheffield	8.00
NS	Nick Swisher	8.00
JT	Jim Thome	8.00
CU	Chase Utley	8.00
BW	Brad Wilkerson	5.00
DW	Dontrelle Willis	5.00
MY	Michael Young	5.00
BZ	Barry Zito	5.00

Prospects

		NM/M
	Common Prospect:	.50
	Inserted 2:Pack	
	Black:	No Pricing
	Production One Set	
BHP1	Justin Upton	5.00
BHP2	Koby Clemens	6.00
BHP3	Lance Broadway	1.00
BHP4	Cameron Maybin	8.00
BHP5	Garrett Mock	1.00
BHP6	Alex Gordon	6.00
BHP7	Ben Copeland	1.00
BHP8	Nick Adenhart	2.00
BHP9	Yung-Chi Chen	3.00
BHP10	Tim Moss	.50
BHP11	Francisco Leandro	.50
BHP12	Brad McCann	1.00
BHP13	Dallas Trahern	1.00
BHP14	Dustin Majewski	2.00
BHP15	James Barthmaier	1.00
BHP16	Nate Gold	1.00
BHP17	John Hardy	.50
BHP18	Mark McLemore	.50
BHP19	Michael Aubrey	1.00
BHP20	Mark Holliman	2.00
BHP21	Bobby Wilson	.50
BHP22	Radhames Liz	1.00
BHP23	Jose Tabata	8.00
BHP24	Jared Lansford	.50
BHP25	Brent Dlugach	1.00
BHP26	Steve Garrabrants	.50
BHP27	Eric Haberer	.50
BHP28	Chris Dickerson	.50
BHP29	Welinson Baez	1.00
BHP30	Chris Kolkhorst	.50
BHP31	Brandon Moss	2.00
BHP32	Corey Wimberly	.50
BHP33	Ryan Patterson	2.00
BHP34	Michael Hollimon	.50
BHP35	John Bannister	.50
BHP36	Pablo Sandoval	.50
BHP37	Dexter Fowler	.50
BHP38	Elvis Andrus	2.00
BHP39	Jason Windsor	1.00
BHP40	B.J. Szymanski	1.00
BHP41	Yovani Gallardo	4.00
BHP42	John Bowker	.50
BHP43	Justin Christian	2.00
BHP44	Andrew Sonnanstine	2.00
BHP45	Jeremy Slayden	.50
BHP46	Brandon Jones	.50
BHP47	Travis Denker	.50
BHP48	Emmanuel Garcia	3.00
BHP49	Landon Jacobsen	6.00
BHP50	Kevin Estrada	.50
BHP51	Ross Ohlendorf	.50
BHP52	Wyatt Toregas	.50
BHP53	Andrew Kown	1.00
BHP54	Steve Kelly	.50
BHP55	Mike Butia	.50
BHP56	Mike Connolly	.50
BHP57	Brian Horwitz	.50
BHP58	Dale Thayer	.50
BHP59	Diory Hernandez	1.00
BHP60	Samuel Deduno	.50
BHP61	Jamie Hoffman	.50
BHP62	Matt Tolbert	3.00
BHP63	Michael Ekstrom	.50
BHP64	Chris Maples	.50
BHP65	Adam Coe	1.00
BHP66	Max Ramirez	.50
BHP67	Evan MacLane	.50
BHP68	Jose Campusano	.50
BHP69	Lou Santangelo	1.00
BHP70	Shawn Riggans	1.00
BHP71	Kyle Kendrick	.50
BHP72	Oswaldo Navarro	.50
BHP73	Eric Rodland	1.00
BHP74	Omir Santos	2.00
BHP75	Kyle McCulloch	.50
BHP76	Evan Longoria	5.00
BHP77	Adrian Cardenas	1.00
BHP78	Steven Wright	.50
BHP79	Andrew Carpenter	2.00
BHP80	Dustin Evans	1.50
BHP81	Chad Tracy	.50
BHP82	Matthew Sulentic	4.00
BHP83	Adam Ottavino	.50
BHP84	Matt Long	.50
BHP85	Clayton Kershaw	3.00
BHP86	Matt Antonelli	2.00
BHP87	Chris Parmelee	.50
BHP88	Billy Rowell	3.00
BHP89	Chase Fontaine	1.00
BHP90	Chris Murrero	2.00
BHP91	Jamie Ortiz	.50
BHP92	Sean Watson	1.00
BHP93	Brooks Brown	1.00
BHP94	Brad Furnish	2.00
BHP95	Chad Huffman	2.00
BHP96	Pedro Beato	3.00
BHP97	Kyler Burke	1.00
BHP98	Stephen Englund	1.00
BHP99	Tyler Norrick	.50
BHP100	Brent Sinkbeil	.50

Draft Pick Variations
One five card pack per box.

		NM/M
BHP76	Evan Longoria	5.00
BHP77	Adrian Cardenas	1.00
BHP78	Steven Wright	1.00
BHP79	Andrew Carpenter	2.00
BHP80	Dustin Evans	2.00
BHP81	Chad Tracy	1.00
BHP82	Matthew Sulentic	4.00
BHP83	Adam Ottavino	2.00
BHP84	Matt Long	2.00
BHP85	Clayton Kershaw	3.00
BHP86	Matt Antonelli	2.00
BHP87	Chris Parmelee	2.00
BHP88	Billy Rowell	3.00
BHP89	Chase Fontaine	2.00
BHP90	Chris Murrero	1.00
BHP91	Jamie Ortiz	1.00
BHP92	Sean Watson	1.00
BHP93	Brooks Brown	1.00
BHP94	Brad Furnish	3.00
BHP95	Chad Huffman	3.00
BHP96	Pedro Beato	3.00
BHP97	Kyler Burke	1.00
BHP99	Stephen Englund	1.00
BHP99	Tyler Norrick	1.00
BHP100	Brent Sinkbeil	1.00

2006 Bowman Originals

		NM/M
	Complete Set (55):	50.00
	Common Player (1-35):	.50
	Common Player (36-55):	2.00
	Pack (7):	60.00
	Box (6):	350.00
1	David Wright	3.00
2	Derek Jeter	5.00
3	Eric Chavez	1.00
4	Ken Griffey Jr.	4.00
5	Albert Pujols	5.00
6	Ryan Howard	5.00
7	Joe Mauer	1.50
8	Andruw Jones	1.50
9	Nomar Garciaparra	1.00
10	Michael Young	1.00
11	Miguel Tejada	1.50
12	Alfonso Soriano	2.00
13	Alex Rodriguez	2.00
14	Paul Konerko	1.50
15	Carl Crawford	1.00
16	Nick Johnson	1.00

17	Jim Thome	1.50
18	Ivan Rodriguez	1.50
19	Chipper Jones	2.00
20	Pedro Martinez	2.00
21	Carlos Delgado	1.50
22	Roger Clemens	5.00
23	Mark Teixeira	1.50
24	Manny Ramirez	2.00
25	Barry Bonds	5.00
26	Vernon Wells	1.00
27	Vladimir Guerrero	2.00
28	Miguel Cabrera	2.00
29	Victor Martinez	1.00
30	Derrek Lee	1.50
31	Carlos Lee	1.00
32	Ichiro Suzuki	3.00
33	Johan Santana	1.50
34	David Ortiz	2.00
35	Jason Bay	1.50
36	Kendry Morales (RC)	3.00
37	Nicholas Markakis (RC)	
38	Conor Jackson (RC)	2.00
39	Justin Verlander (RC)	5.00
40	Ryan Zimmerman (RC)	5.00
41	Jeremy Hermida (RC)	2.00
42	Dan Uggla (RC)	3.00
43	Matthew Kemp (RC)	3.00
44	Lastings Milledge (RC)	
45	Kenji Johjima RC	5.00
46	Ian Kinsler (RC)	3.00
47	Hanley Ramirez (RC)	3.00
48	Melky Cabrera (RC)	3.00
49	Willy Aybar (RC)	2.00
50	Jonathan Papelbon (RC)	6.00
51	Prince Fielder (RC)	4.00
52	Cole Hamels (RC)	5.00
53	Josh Barfield (RC)	2.00
54	Alay Soler RC	3.00
55	Russell Martin (RC)	3.00

Blue
Blue (1-55): 2-3X
Production 249 Sets

Black
Black (1-55): 3-5X
Production 99 Sets

Red
No Pricing
Production One Set

Printing Plates
No Pricing
Production one set per color.

Buyback Autographs
NM/M

Adam Loewen/68	15.00
Adam Loewen/719	10.00
Adam Loewen/198	15.00
Adrian Gonzalez/976	20.00
Albert Pujols/44	250.00
Albert Pujols/50	250.00
Alex Gordon/49	250.00
Alex Gordon/32	260.00
Andrew McCutchen/391	40.00
Andrew McCutchen/33	60.00
Andrew McCutchen/561	35.00
Andruw Jones/34	50.00
Andruw Jones/22	60.00
Andruw Jones/24	60.00
Andruw Jones/28	60.00
Andruw Jones/48	50.00
Andy LaRoche/109	40.00
Andy LaRoche/60	40.00
Andy LaRoche/66	40.00
Andy LaRoche/734	25.00
Alex Rodriguez/21	150.00
Alex Rodriguez/22	150.00
B.J. Upton/58	30.00
B.J. Upton/136	25.00
B.J. Upton/667	20.00
B.J. Upton/120	25.00
Beau Jones/576	15.00
Beau Jones/63	30.00
Beau Jones/329	20.00
Beau Jones/33	30.00
Billy Buckner/99	25.00
Billy Buckner/432	20.00
Billy Buckner/182	20.00
Billy Buckner/33	30.00
Billy Wagner/56	30.00
Billy Wagner/47	30.00
Billy Wagner/64	25.00
Billy Wagner/90	30.00
Billy Wagner/99	30.00
Billy Wagner/37	30.00
Billy Wagner/38	30.00
Brandon Phillips/46	15.00
Brandon Phillips/26	20.00
Brandon Phillips/67	10.00
Brandon Phillips/28	20.00
Brandon Phillips/32	15.00
Brandon Phillips/140	10.00
Brandon Phillips/35	15.00
Brandon Phillips/335	10.00

Brandon Phillips/257	10.00
Brandon Snyder/461	15.00
Brandon Wood/70	30.00
Brandon Wood/100	30.00
Brandon Wood/627	20.00
Brandon Wood/239	30.00
Brent Cox/240	15.00
Brent Cox/66	20.00
Brent Cox/688	15.00
Carl Crawford/37	25.00
Carl Crawford/40	25.00
Carl Crawford/20	30.00
Carl Crawford/30	25.00
Carl Crawford/71	20.00
Carl Crawford/71	20.00
Carl Crawford/334	15.00
Carl Crawford/279	15.00
Carlos Silva/996	10.00
Cesar Ramos/25	25.00
Cesar Ramos/76	25.00
Cesar Ramos/161	15.00
Cesar Ramos/732	15.00
Chase Utley/23	75.00
Chase Utley/150	40.00
Chase Utley/303	40.00
Chase Utley/23	75.00
Chaz Roe/73	15.00
Chaz Roe/774	10.00
Chaz Roe/132	10.00
Chien-Ming Wang/25	500.00
Chien-Ming Wang/25	600.00
Chien-Ming Wang/25	500.00
Chien-Ming Wang/25	600.00
Chipper Jones/20	80.00
Chipper Jones/20	80.00
Chipper Jones/20	80.00
Chipper Jones/20	80.00
Chris Young/70	20.00
Chris Young/772	20.00
Chris Young/146	20.00
Chris Young/211	20.00
Chris Young/44	75.00
Chris Young/88	40.00
Chris Young/81	40.00
Chris Young/558	25.00
Clint Barmes/61	20.00
Clint Barmes/113	15.00
Clint Barmes/375	10.00
Clint Barmes/430	15.00
Conor Jackson/70	30.00
Conor Jackson/78	50.00
Conor Jackson/457	20.00
Conor Jackson/360	20.00
Craig Italiano/160	15.00
Craig Italiano/658	10.00
Craig Italiano/163	15.00
Dan Johnson/276	15.00
Dan Johnson/575	15.00
Dan Johnson/101	15.00
Dan Johnson/29	20.00
David Wright/543	60.00
David Wright/264	150.00
David Wright/45	80.00
David Wright/64	80.00
Derrek Lee/61	20.00
Dontrelle Willis/147	20.00
Dontrelle Willis/55	25.00
Dontrelle Willis/525	20.00
Dontrelle Willis/79	25.00
Dontrelle Willis/78	25.00
Dontrelle Willis/24	25.00
Dontrelle Willis/36	25.00
Eli Iorg/167	15.00
Eli Iorg/151	15.00
Eli Iorg/672	15.00
Eric Chavez/34	20.00
Eric Chavez/301	15.00
Eric Chavez/25	20.00
Eric Chavez/70	20.00
Eric Chavez/62	20.00
Ervin Santana/369	15.00
Ervin Santana/544	15.00
Ervin Santana/51	20.00
Ervin Santana/109	20.00
Ervin Santana/76	20.00
Ervin Santana/67	20.00
Ervin Santana/62	50.00
Fausto Carmona/131	10.00
Fausto Carmona/56	15.00
Fausto Carmona/263	10.00
Francisco Cordero/64	10.00
Francisco Cordero/87	10.00
Francisco Cordero/49	10.00
Francisco Cordero/138	10.00
Francisco Cordero/140	10.00
Francisco Liriano/142	35.00
FFrancisco Liriano/63	40.00
Francisco Liriano/47	35.00
Francisco Liriano/222	30.00
Francisco Liriano/350	25.00
Francisco Liriano/212	65.00
Garrett Atkins/121	15.00
Garrett Atkins/27	20.00

Garrett Atkins/209	15.00
Garrett Atkins/581	15.00
Garrett Atkins/38	15.00
Hanley Ramirez/435	20.00
Hanley Ramirez/98	25.00
Hanley Ramirez/466	20.00
Jason Bay/24	30.00
Jason Bay/298	25.00
Jason Bay/50	25.00
Jason Bay/58	25.00
Jason Bay/66	25.00
Jason Botts/29	15.00
Jason Botts/31	15.00
Jason Botts/269	10.00
Jason Botts/46	15.00
Jason Botts/59	15.00
Jason Botts/577	10.00
Jason Kubel/232	15.00
Jason Kubel/25	25.00
Jason Kubel/77	20.00
Jason Marquis/944	8.00
Jason Marquis/26	15.00
Jay Bruce/66	80.00
Jay Bruce/434	50.00
Jed Lowrie/123	15.00
Jed Lowrie/141	15.00
Jed Lowrie/716	15.00
Jeff Mathis/127	15.00
Jeff Mathis/185	15.00
Jeff Mathis/97	15.00
Jerome Williams/292	8.00
Jerome Williams/48	10.00
Jerome Williams/45	10.00
Jerome Williams/97	8.00
Joel Guzman/274	15.00
Joel Guzman/54	20.00
Joel Guzman/53	20.00
Joel Zumaya/233	50.00
Joel Zumaya/57	50.00
Joel Zumaya/96	40.00
Joel Zumaya/582	40.00
Joel Zumaya/163	50.00
John Drennen/78	30.00
John Drennen/387	15.00
John Van Benschoten/51	15.00
John Van Benschoten/24	20.00
John Van Benschoten/130	15.00
John Van Benschoten/272	10.00
Jonny Gomes/341	15.00
Jonny Gomes/27	50.00
Jonny Gomes/175	15.00
Jonny Gomes/363	10.00
Josh Barfield/158	20.00
Josh Barfield/557	15.00
Josh Barfield/178	30.00
Josh Geer/343	15.00
Josh Geer/138	15.00
Justin Huber/32	15.00
Justin Huber/99	15.00
Justin Huber/572	15.00
Justin Huber/212	15.00
Justin Huber/26	20.00
Justin Huber/37	15.00
Justin Upton/1000	90.00
Kevin Gregg/988	10.00
Lastings Milledge/166	35.00
Lastings Milledge/166	35.00
Lastings Milledge/632	25.00
Mark Mulder/20	25.00
Mark Mulder/20	25.00
Mark Mulder/20	25.00
Mark Mulder/20	25.00
Matt Cain/36	30.00
Matt Cain/389	25.00
Matt Maloney/350	25.00
Matt Maloney/60	50.00
Matt Maloney/20	75.00
Matt Maloney/60	60.00
Matt Torra/456	15.00
Matt Torra/37	15.00
Melky Cabrera/606	30.00
Melky Cabrera/191	35.00
Melky Cabrera/60	50.00
Melky Cabrera/24	70.00
Melky Cabrera/495	40.00
Melky Cabrera/12	12.00
Merkin Valdez/14	15.00
Merkin Valdez/325	8.00
Merkin Valdez/70	15.00
Merkin Valdez/66	15.00
Micah Owings/138	30.00
Micah Owings/648	20.00
Michael Bowden/27	40.00
Michael Bowden/24	40.00
Michael Bowden/449	20.00
Miguel Cabrera/70	30.00
Miguel Cabrera/70	30.00
Miguel Cabrera/69	30.00
Miguel Cabrera/98	30.00
Miguel Cabrera/63	30.00
Miguel Cabrera/130	40.00
Mike Costanzo/466	15.00
Mike Lamb/993	15.00
Morgan Ensberg/74	15.00
Morgan Ensberg/334	10.00
Morgan Ensberg/64	15.00
Nick Swisher/342	20.00
Nick Swisher/73	25.00
Nick Swisher/31	25.00

Nolan Reimold/41	60.00
Nolan Reimold/419	20.00
Nolan Reimold/30	60.00
Rich Harden/87	20.00
Rich Harden/82	20.00
Rich Harden/70	20.00
Rich Harden/68	30.00
Ricky Nolasco/52	15.00
Ricky Nolasco/256	15.00
Ricky Nolasco/148	15.00
Robinson Cano/90	50.00
Robinson Cano/72	50.00
Robinson Cano/101	50.00
Robinson Cano/222	40.00
Roy Oswalt/96	25.00
Roy Oswalt/42	30.00
Roy Oswalt/61	30.00
Roy Oswalt/63	40.00
Roy Oswalt/25	50.00
Roy Oswalt/199	25.00
Russell Martin/33	30.00
Russell Martin/96	25.00
Russell Martin/577	20.00
Russell Martin/252	20.00
Ryan Howard/50	350.00
Scott Elbert/79	50.00
Scott Elbert/330	35.00
Scott Elbert/50	50.00
Scott Kazmir/99	25.00
Scott Kazmir/36	30.00
Scott Kazmir/153	20.00
Scott Kazmir/26	30.00
Scott Kazmir/661	20.00
Scott Mathieson/472	8.00
Scott Mathieson/108	20.00
Scott Mathieson/72	25.00
Scott Thorman/980	10.00
Sean West/394	20.00
Sean West/70	30.00
Shaun Marcum/133	15.00
Shaun Marcum/26	20.00
Shaun Marcum/138	20.00
Shaun Marcum/153	20.00
Shaun Marcum/33	25.00
Travis Buck/60	40.00
Travis Buck/44	60.00
Travis Buck/747	25.00
Travis Hafner/114	20.00
Travis Hafner/96	20.00
Travis Hafner/386	20.00
Travis Hafner/45	25.00
Travis Hafner/280	25.00
Trevor Bell/146	15.00
Trevor Bell/28	15.00
Trevor Bell/689	15.00
Troy Patton/121	15.00
Troy Patton/50	30.00
Troy Patton/736	15.00
Vernon Wells/52	25.00
Vernon Wells/100	25.00
Vernon Wells/96	25.00
Vernon Wells/68	25.00
Vernon Wells/56	25.00
Vernon Wells/40	40.00
Vernon Wells/29	40.00
Vernon Wells/426	20.00
Vladimir Guerrero/21	80.00
Vladimir Guerrero/45	60.00
Vladimir Guerrero/20	80.00
Wade Townsend/423	15.00
Wade Townsend/53	20.00
Wily Mo Pena/79	20.00
Wily Mo Pena/70	20.00
Wily Mo Pena/134	20.00
Wily Mo Pena/62	20.00
Xavier Nady/105	20.00
Xavier Nady/72	20.00
Xavier Nady/192	15.00
Xavier Nady/213	20.00
Xavier Nady/294	15.00
Xavier Nady/41	20.00
Yunel Escobar/69	30.00
Yunel Escobar/395	20.00
Yusmeiro Petit/68	20.00
Yusmeiro Petit/160	15.00
Yusmeiro Petit/630	15.00

Prospects
NM/M

Common Player:		2.00
Blue:		1.5-2X
Production 249 Sets		
Black:		2-4X
Production 99 Sets		
Red:		No Pricing
Production One Set		
1	Cameron Maybin	15.00
2	Koby Clemens	5.00
3	Lance Broadway	2.00
4	Chris Dickerson	2.00
5	Garrett Mock	2.00
6	Ben Copeland	2.00
7	Nick Adenhart	2.00
8	Brad McCann	3.00
9	Dustin Majewski	2.00
10	Jimmy Barthmaier	2.00
11	Michael Aubrey	2.00
12	Evan Longoria	20.00
13	Clayton Kershaw	8.00
14	Juan Francia	2.00
15	Elvis Andrus	6.00
16	Mark Trumbo	2.00
17	Shawn Riggans	2.00
18	Asdrubal Cabrera	2.00
19	Mark McLemore	2.00
20	Radhames Liz	2.00
21	Mat Gamel	2.00
22	Wilkin Ramirez	2.00
23	Jared Lansford	2.00
24	Hunter Pence	4.00
25	Justin Upton	12.00
26	Brent Dlugach	2.00
27	B.J. Szymanski	2.00
28	Stephen Marek	4.00
29	Shaun Cumberland	2.00
30	Yovani Gallardo	4.00
31	Will Venable	2.00
32	A.J. Shappi	2.00
33	Dallas Trahern	2.00
34	Jason Jaramillo	2.00
35	Jose Tabata	5.00
36	Jose Campusano	2.00
37	Ryan Patterson	2.00
38	Andrew Pinckney	2.00
39	Dexter Fowler	2.00
40	Cody Johnson	3.00
41	Steve Murphy	2.00
42	Mark Reed	2.00
43	Chris Iannetta	4.00
44	Michael Hollimon	4.00
45	Omir Santos	2.00
46	Diory Hernandez	2.00
47	Matt Tolbert	4.00
48	Jeff Frazier	2.00
49	Max Ramirez	3.00
50	Alex Gordon	20.00
51	Steve Garrabrants	2.00
52	Steven Baker	2.00
53	Ryan Klosterman	2.00
54	Michael Collins	2.00
55	Corey Wimberly	2.00

2006 Bowman Sterling
NM/M

Common Relic:		5.00
Pack (5):		50.00
Box (6):		260.00
CB	Carlos Beltran	8.00
CB2	Carlos Beltran	8.00
LB	Lance Berkman	5.00
HB	Hank Blalock	5.00
BLB	Barry Bonds	20.00
MC	Miguel Cabrera	10.00
MC2	Miguel Cabrera	10.00
RC	Robinson Cano	15.00
CC	Chris Carpenter	8.00
EC	Eric Chavez	5.00
JDD	Johnny Damon	8.00
AD	Adam Dunn	5.00
ME	Morgan Ensberg	5.00
VG	Vladimir Guerrero	10.00
JRH	Rich Harden	5.00
TH	Todd Helton	8.00
RH	Ryan Howard	25.00
AJ	Andruw Jones	8.00
LWJ	Chipper Jones	8.00
PK	Paul Konerko	8.00
MCM	Mickey Mantle	120.00
PM	Pedro Martinez	8.00
HM	Hideki Matsui	20.00
MM	Mark Mulder	5.00
DO	David Ortiz	10.00
MJP	Mike Piazza	10.00
AP	Albert Pujols	25.00
AP2	Albert Pujols	25.00
AR	Aramis Ramirez	8.00
MR	Manny Ramirez	10.00
MR2	Manny Ramirez	10.00
BR	Brian Roberts	5.00
AER	Alex Rodriguez	20.00
IR	Ivan Rodriguez	8.00
SR	Scott Rolen	8.00
JAS	Johan Santana	8.00
CS	Curt Schilling	8.00
GS	Grady Sizemore	8.00
APS	Alfonso Soriano	10.00
IS	Ichiro Suzuki	25.00
MCT	Mark Teixeira	8.00
MT	Miguel Tejada	8.00
JHT	Jim Thome	8.00
DWW	Dontrelle Willis	8.00
DW	David Wright	20.00

Common Rookie:		4.00
BA	Brian Anderson (RC)	4.00
WA	Willy Aybar (RC)	4.00
BB	Brian Bannister (RC)	4.00
CRB	Chad Billingsley (RC)	10.00
BON	Boof Bonser (RC)	6.00
MCC	Melky Cabrera (RC)	6.00
JD	Joey Devine RC	4.00
SD	Stephen Drew (RC)	10.00
KF	Kevin Frandsen (RC)	4.00
RK	Ryan Garko (RC)	4.00
DG	David Gassner (RC)	4.00
EG	Enrique Gonzalez	
FG	Franklin Gutierrez (RC)	4.00
TGJ	Tony Gwynn Jr. (RC)	6.00
CRH	Craig Hansen RC	4.00
CJ	Conor Jackson (RC)	4.00
CHJ	Chuck James (RC)	4.00
CJJ	Casey Janssen RC	4.00
KJ	Kenji Johjima RC	10.00
JJ	Josh Johnson (RC)	6.00
JK	Jeff Karstens RC	6.00
MK	Matthew Kemp (RC)	6.00
HK	Howie Kendrick (RC)	6.00
FL	Francisco Liriano (RC)	12.00
JL	James Loney (RC)	6.00
NM	Nicholas Markakis (RC)	8.00
RM	Russell Martin (RC)	4.00
SM	Scott Mathieson (RC)	6.00
JM	Jeff Mathis (RC)	6.00
KM	Kendry Morales (RC)	6.00
SO	Scott Olsen (RC)	4.00
JP	Jonathan Papelbon (RC)	10.00
DP	David Pauley (RC)	6.00
MPP	Mike Pelfrey RC	20.00
HP	Hayden Penn (RC)	4.00
CQ	Carlos Quentin (RC)	4.00
HR	Hanley Ramirez (RC)	6.00
AS	Anibal Sanchez (RC)	4.00
JS	James Shields RC	6.00
MS	Matt Smith (RC)	4.00
ALS	Alay Soler RC	6.00
JBS	Jeremy Sowers (RC)	4.00
TT	Taylor Tankersley	
JTA	Jordan Tata RC	4.00
DU	Dan Uggla (RC)	6.00
JV	Justin Verlander (RC)	10.00
JW	Jered Weaver (RC)	8.00
RZ	Ryan Zimmerman (RC)	20.00
BZ	Benjamin Zobrist (RC)	6.00
JZ	Joel Zumaya (RC)	6.00

Common Rookie Autograph:		
JLB	Josh Barfield (RC)	15.00
JCB	Jason Botts (RC)	25.00
AE	Andre Ethier (RC)	25.00
JI	Joe Inglett RC	
IK	Ian Kinsler (RC)	15.00
LM	Lastings Milledge (RC)	25.00
ZM	Zach Miner (RC)	15.00
RN	Ricky Nolasco (RC)	15.00

Common Rookie Relic Auto.:		
JB	Jason Bulger (RC)	
PF	Prince Fielder (RC)	40.00
CI	Chris Iannetta (RC)	40.00
CH	Cole Hamels (RC)	40.00
HK	Howie Kendrick (RC)	40.00
JTL	Jon Lester (RC)	30.00
BL	Bobby Livingston (RC)	15.00
MN	Erik Naposki RC	20.00
RP	Ronny Paulino (RC)	20.00
YP	Yusmeiro Petit (RC)	20.00
MP	Martin Prado (RC)	25.00
ALR	Anthony Reyes (RC)	25.00
JT	Jack Taschner (RC)	15.00
ST	Scott Thorman (RC)	15.00

Refractors
Rookies:	1.5-2X
Rookie Auto.:	1-2X
Rookie Relic Auto.:	1-2X
Relics:	1-2X
Prospects:	1.5-2X
Prospect Auto.:	1-2X
Production 199 Sets	

Black Refractors
No Pricing
Production 25 Sets

Printing Plates
No Pricing
Production One Set

Red Refractors
No Pricing
Production One Set

Gold Refractors
No Pricing
Production 10 Sets

Prospect Autographs
NM/M

BA	Brandon Allen	8.00
MAA	Matt Antonelli	20.00
MA	Mike Aviles	15.00
PB	Pedro Beato	20.00
RB	Ronny Bourquin	20.00
BB	Brooks Brown	15.00
TB	Travis Buck	15.00
KB	Kyler Burke	15.00
JBU	Joshua Butler	15.00
AC	Adrian Cardenas	30.00
KC	Koby Clemens	20.00
JC	Jeff Clement	25.00
TC	Tyler Colvin	35.00
HC	Hank Conger	50.00
TC	Trevor Crowe	20.00
CD	Chris Dickerson	20.00
KD	Kyle Drabek	35.00
DE	Dustin Evans	15.00
SE	Steven Evarts	15.00
MF	Michael Felix	15.00
BF	Brad Furnish	15.00
AG	Alex Gordon	100.00
DH	Daniel Haigwood	15.00
BH	Brett Hayes	15.00
CH	Chase Headley	20.00
LH	Luke Hochevar	50.00

DHU	David Huff	20.00
CHH	Chad Huffman	20.00
JJ	Jeremy Jeffress	25.00
CJ	Cody Johnson	30.00
KJ	Kris Johnson	20.00
CK	Clayton Kershaw	40.00
KK	Kasey Kiker	20.00
EL	Evan Longoria	80.00
PL	Pedro Lopez	8.00
CM	Cameron Maybin	80.00
MM	Mark McCormick	15.00
KM	Kyle McCulloch	20.00
GM	Garrett Mock	15.00
BM	Brandon Moss	20.00
JN	Jason Neighborgall	10.00
AO	Adam Ottavino	20.00
MO	Micah Owings	20.00
CP	Chris Parmelee	35.00
TP	Troy Patton	20.00
EP	Elvin Puello	10.00
CR	Cory Rasmus	15.00
JR	Joshua Rodriguez	15.00
BR	Billy Rowell	60.00
JS	Jarrod Saltalamacchia	20.00
BSI	Brett Sinkbeil	20.00
BS	Brandon Snyder	15.00
WT	Wade Townsend	15.00
CT	Chad Tracy	15.00
JU	Justin Upton	80.00
SWA	Sean Watson	15.00
JW	Johnny Whittleman	20.00
CW	Colten Willems	20.00
BW	Brandon Wood	25.00
SW	Steven Wright	15.00

Prospect

		NM/M
NA	Nick Adenhart	5.00
EA	Elvis Andrus	15.00
MRA	Michael Aubrey	5.00
JRB	Jimmy Barthmaier	5.00
AJC	Asdrubal Cabrera	5.00
JAC	Jose Campusano	5.00
YC	Yung-Chi Chen	20.00
ADC	Adam Coe	8.00
MC	Michael Collins	8.00
BC	Ben Copeland	5.00
SC	Shaun Cumberland	5.00
CD	Chris Dickerson	5.00
BD	Brent Dlugach	5.00
DF	Dexter Fowler	6.00
JF	Juan Francia	5.00
JKF	Jeff Frazier	5.00
YG	Yovani Gallardo	8.00
MG	Mat Gamel	5.00
SGG	Steve Garrabrants	8.00
DIH	Diory Hernandez	5.00
MH	Michael Hollimon	5.00
JJ	Jason Jaramillo	5.00
BJ	Brandon Jones	5.00
RK	Ryan Klosterman	8.00
JTL	Jared Lansford	5.00
RL	Radhames Liz	8.00
EM	Evan MacLane	5.00
DM	Dustin Majewski	6.00
SM	Stephen Marek	5.00
BWM	Brad McCann	5.00
MSM	Mark McLemore	5.00
GLM	Garrett Mock	5.00
SMM	Steve Murphy	5.00
ON	Oswaldo Navarro	5.00
RP	Ryan Patterson	6.00
HP	Hunter Pence	5.00
AP	Andrew Pinckney	8.00
MRR	Max Ramirez	6.00
WR	Wilkin Ramirez	5.00
MR	Mark Reed	5.00
SR	Shawn Riggans	5.00
OS	Omir Santos	5.00
AS	A.J. Shappi	5.00
BJS	B.J. Szymanski	5.00
JT	Jose Tabata	25.00
CMT	Matt Tolbert	8.00
DT	Dallas Trahern	5.00
MT	Mark Trumbo	6.00
WV	Will Venable	5.00
CW	Corey Wimberly	5.00

1992-2004 Boy Scouts of America Atlanta Braves

In 1992 the Atlanta-area Boy Scouts of America began a "Collector's Edition" series of commemorative baseball cards featuring Braves players. The 2-1/2" x 3-1/2" cards have a variety of designs with color photos, usually game-action. Red, white and blue backs have player information and stats and logos of the team, sponsor(s), and/or BSA.

		NM/M
Complete Set (13):		50.00
Common Player:		2.00
(1)	Jeff Treadway/1992	2.00
(2)	Dale Murphy/1993	15.00
(3)	Deion Sanders/1994	8.00
(4)	Gregory McMichael/1995	3.00
(5)	Ryan Klesko/1996	3.00
(6)	Jeff Blauser/1997	3.00
(7)	Greg Maddux/1998	12.00
(8)	John Rocker/1999	5.00
(9)	John Smoltz/2000	3.00
(10)	Tom Glavine/2001	3.00
(11)	Kevin Millwood/2002	2.00
(12)	Marcus Giles/2003	2.00
(13)	Russ Ortiz/2004	2.00

1998 Bryan Braves Team Photo Set

After a one-year absence and a change of stadium hot dog vendors, the Braves again distributed a team photo foldout in 1998. The 10-5/8" x 31-3/8" three-panel perforated sheet has a large team photo and individual 2-1/8" x 3-1/8" cards of 35 players and staff. The player cards have a portrait photo on a background of brown baseballs and faded red "A"s. The player name is in gold at the bottom; his position vertically in a blue strip at left. A red Bryan logo is at top-left. Backs are in red, white and blue with biographical and career notes and stats. The unnumbered cards are checklisted here in alpabetically.

		NM/M
Complete Foldout Set:		8.00
Common Player:		.10
(1)	Danny Bautista	.10
(2)	Jim Beauchamp	.10
(3)	Rafael Belliard	.10
(4)	Adam Butler	.10
(5)	Norm Charlton	.10
(6)	Greg Colbrunn	.10
(7)	Pat Corrales	.10
(8)	Bobby Cox	.10
(9)	Bobby Dews	.10
(10)	Frank Fultz	.10
(11)	Andres Galarraga	.10
(12)	Tom Glavine	1.00
(13)	Tony Graffanino	.10
(14)	Ozzie Guillen	.10
(15)	Andruw Jones	1.50
(16)	Chipper Jones	3.00
(17)	Clarence Jones	.10
(18)	Ryan Klesko	.10
(19)	Kerry Ligtenberg	.10
(20)	Keith Lockhart	.10
(21)	Javy Lopez	.10
(22)	Greg Maddux	2.00
(23)	Dennis Martinez	.10
(24)	Leo Mazzone	.10
(25)	Kevin Millwood	.50
(26)	Denny Neagle	.10
(27)	Eddie Perez	.10
(28)	John Rocker	.10
(29)	Rudy Seanez	.10
(30)	John Smoltz	1.00
(31)	Russ Springer	.10
(32)	Michael Tucker	.10
(33)	Walt Weiss	.10
(34)	Gerald Williams	.10
(35)	Ned Yost	.10
(36)	Team Photo	.50

1999 Bryan Braves

These Tuesday-night homestand give-away cards were sponsored by the team's hot dog vendor and given away three players at a time to children only. Completion of a set is thus a challenge. The cards of Hernandez, Mulholland and Myers were late-season additions and differ from the rest of the set in that the player names in gold vertically at left are in upper- and lower-case type, while most cards have the name in all-caps. The 2-1/2" x 3-1/2" cards have player portraits bordered in blue at left and bottom. The position is in gold at bottom; the uniform number in gold at top. A red Bryan logo is at lower-left. Black, white and blue backs have minimal player vitae and full professional stats. The unnumbered cards are checklisted here in alphabetical order.

		NM/M
Complete Set (30):		32.50
Common Player:		1.00
(1)	Don Baylor	1.00
(2)	Bret Boone	1.00
(3)	Pat Corrales	1.00
(4)	Bobby Cox	1.00
(5)	Bobby Dews	1.00
(6)	Tom Glavine	1.50
(7)	Ozzie Guillen	1.00
(8)	Jose Hernandez	1.00
(9)	Glenn Hubbard	1.00
(10)	Brian Hunter	1.00
(11)	Andruw Jones	2.50
(12)	Chipper Jones	4.00
(13)	Brian Jordan	1.00
(14)	Ryan Klesko	1.00
(15)	Keith Lockhart	1.00
(16)	Javy Lopez	1.00
(17)	Greg Maddux	3.00
(18)	Leo Mazzone	1.00
(19)	Kevin Millwood	1.00
(20)	Terry Mulholland	1.00
(21)	Greg Myers	1.00
(22)	Otis Nixon	1.00
(23)	Eddie Perez	1.00
(24)	Odalis Perez	1.00
(25)	Mike Remlinger	1.00
(26)	John Rocker	1.00
(27)	Rudy Seanez	1.00
(28)	John Smoltz	1.50
(29)	Walt Weiss	1.00
(30)	Ned Yost	1.00

Team Photo Set

Children visiting Turner Field for a late-season game received this foldout sponsored by the team's hot dog vendor. The 10-5/8" x 31-3/8" three-panel perforated sheet has a large team photo and individual 2-1/8" x 3-1/8" cards

2000 Bryan Braves

For the first time since the Braves hot dog concessionaires began issuing annual stadium give-away card sets in 1989, the number of Tuesday home games in 2000 dictated that some players be issued in more than one variation to allow for three cards to be given away each date. The 2-1/2" x 3-1/2" cards have game-action photos vignetted with blue borders. The player's full name and position are in red at left, and his last name in white at right. His uniform number is at top. A red Bryan logo is at bottom. Black, white and blue backs have a few bits of personal data and complete minor and major league stats. The unnumbered cards are checklisted here alphabetically.

		NM/M
Complete Set (39):		45.00
Common Player:		1.00
(1)	Andy Ashby	1.00
(2)	Bobby Bonilla	1.00
(3)	John Burkett	1.00
(4)	Pat Corrales	1.00
(5)	Bobby Cox	1.00
(6)	Bobby Dews	1.00
(7)	Rafael Furcal	1.50
(8)	Andres Galarraga/Btg	1.00
(9)	Andres Galarraga/Fielding	1.00
(10)	Tom Glavine	2.00
(11)	Glenn Hubbard	1.00

of 35 players and staff. The player cards have a portrait photo on a baseball background. The player name and position are at left. A large red Bryan logo is at top-right. Backs are in red, white and black with biographical and career notes and stats. The unnumbered cards are checklisted here alphabetically.

		NM/M
Complete Foldout Set:		8.00
Common Player:		.10
(1)	Don Baylor	.10
(2)	Bret Boone	.25
(3)	Bruce Chen	.10
(4)	Pat Corrales	.10
(5)	Bobby Cox	.10
(6)	Bobby Dews	.10
(7)	Frank Fultz	.10
(8)	Tom Glavine	1.00
(9)	Ozzie Guillen	.10
(10)	Jose Hernandez	.10
(11)	Glenn Hubbard	.10
(12)	Brian Hunter	.10
(13)	Andruw Jones	1.50
(14)	Chipper Jones	3.00
(15)	Brian Jordan	.10
(16)	Ryan Klesko	.10
(17)	Keith Lockhart	.10
(18)	Javy Lopez	.10
(19)	Greg Maddux	2.00
(20)	Leo Mazzone	.10
(21)	Kevin McGlinchy	.10
(22)	Kevin Millwood	.50
(23)	Terry Mulholland	.10
(24)	Greg Myers	.10
(25)	Otis Nixon	.10
(26)	Eddie Perez	.10
(27)	Mike Remlinger	.10
(28)	John Rocker	.10
(29)	Rudy Seanez	.10
(30)	Randall Simon	.10
(31)	John Smoltz	1.00
(32)	Russ Springer	.10
(33)	Walt Weiss	.10
(34)	Gerald Williams	.10
(35)	Ned Yost	.10
(36)	Team photo	.50

(12)	Andruw Jones (Batting stance.)	2.50
(13)	Andruw Jones (Follow-through.)	2.50
(14)	Chipper Jones (Back turned.)	4.00
(15)	Chipper Jones/Fielding	4.00
(16)	Brian Jordan/Btg	1.00
(17)	Brian Jordan/Portrait	1.00
(18)	Wally Joyner	1.00
(19)	Kerry Ligtenberg	1.00
(20)	Keith Lockhart	1.00
(21)	Javy Lopez/Btg	1.00
(22)	Javy Lopez/Catching	1.00
(23)	Greg Maddux	3.00
(24)	Leo Mazzone	1.00
(25)	Kevin McGlinchy	1.00
(26)	Kevin Millwood	1.00
(27)	Terry Mulholland	1.00
(28)	Eddie Perez	1.00
(29)	Odalis Perez	1.00
(30)	Mike Remlinger	1.00
(31)	Merv Rettenmund	1.00
(32)	John Rocker	1.00
(33)	Reggie Sanders	1.00
(34)	Rudy Seanez	1.00
(35)	John Smoltz	2.00
(36)	B.J. Surhoff	1.00
(37)	Quilvio Veras	1.00
(38)	Walt Weiss	1.00
(39)	Ned Yost	1.00

Team Photo Set

Children visiting Turner Field for a late-season game received this foldout sponsored by the team's hot dog vendor. The 10-5/8" x 31-3/8" three-panel perforated sheet has a large team photo and individual 2-1/8" x 3-1/8" cards of 35 players and staff. The staff cards have a portrait photo on a blue background. The player cards have game-action photos. All cards are bordered in brown with a nameplate design at bottom with identification and a Bryan logo. Backs are in red, white and black with biographical and career notes and stats. The unnumbered cards are checklisted here alphabetically.

		NM/M
Complete Foldout Set:		8.00
Common Player:		.10
(1)	Andy Ashby	.10
(2)	Bobby Bonilla	.10
(3)	John Burkett	.10
(4)	Bobby Cox	.10
(5)	Pat Corrales	.10
(6)	Bobby Dews	.10
(7)	Frank Fultz	.10
(8)	Rafael Furcal	.75
(9)	Andres Galarraga	.10
(10)	Tom Glavine	1.00
(11)	Glenn Hubbard	.10
(12)	Andruw Jones	1.00
(13)	Chipper Jones	3.00
(14)	Brian Jordan	.10
(15)	Wally Joyner	.10
(16)	Kerry Ligtenberg	.10
(17)	Keith Lockhart	.10
(18)	Javy Lopez	.10
(19)	Greg Maddux	1.50
(20)	Leo Mazzone	.10
(21)	Kevin McGlinchy	.10
(22)	Kevin Millwood	.10
(23)	Terry Mulholland	.10
(24)	Eddie Perez	.10
(25)	Odalis Perez	.10
(26)	Mike Remlinger	.10
(27)	Merv Rettenmund	.10
(28)	John Rocker	.10
(29)	Reggie Sanders	.10
(30)	Rudy Seanez	.10
(31)	John Smoltz	1.00
(32)	B.J. Surhoff	.10
(33)	Quilvio Veras	.10
(34)	Walt Weiss	.10
(35)	Ned Yost	.10

2001 Bryan Braves

Three cards were given out at each Tuesday home game to children 12 and under from this set sponsored by Turner Field's hot dog vendor. The 2-1/2" x 3-1/2" cards have game-action photos with a team logo at top, a sponsor's logo at bottom, a trio of ghost-image baseballs at left and the player name and position at right. Black, white and blue backs have minimal player personal data and complete pro stats. The unnumbered cards are checklisted here in alphabetical order. Due to the manner of their distribution, assembly of a complete set is difficult.

		NM/M
Complete Set (29):		30.00
Common Player:		1.00
(1)	Rico Brogna	1.00
(2)	John Burkett	1.00
(3)	Jose Cabrera	1.00
(4)	Ken Caminiti	1.00
(5)	Bobby Cox	1.00
(6)	Mark DeRosa	1.00
(7)	Bobby Dews	1.00
(8)	Rafael Furcal	1.50
(9)	Marcus Giles	1.00
(10)	Tom Glavine	2.00
(11)	Wes Helms	1.00
(12)	Andruw Jones	2.50
(13)	Chipper Jones	4.00
(14)	Brian Jordan	1.00
(15)	Kerry Ligtenberg	1.00
(16)	Keith Lockhart	1.00
(17)	George Lombard	1.00
(18)	Javy Lopez	1.00
(19)	Greg Maddux	3.00
(20)	Jason Marquis	1.00
(21)	Dave Martinez	1.00
(22)	Leo Mazzone	1.00
(23)	Kevin Millwood	1.50
(24)	Odalis Perez	1.00
(25)	Mike Remlinger	1.00
(26)	John Rocker	1.00
(27)	John Smoltz	2.00
(28)	B.J. Surhoff	1.00
(29)	Quilvio Veras	1.00

Team Photo Set

Children visiting Turner Field for a late-season game received this foldout sponsored by the team's hot dog vendor. The 10-5/8" x 31-3/8" three-panel perforated sheet has a large team photo and individual 2-1/8" x 3-1/8" cards of 35 players and staff. The staff cards have a portrait photo; the player cards have game-action photos. All photos are in the "sweet spot" on a baseball background with name and position in red at left and a large Bryan logo at lower-right. Backs are in red, white and black with biographical and career notes and stats on a ghost image of the front photo. The unnumbered cards are checklisted here alpabetically.

	NM/M
Complete Foldout Set:	8.00
Common Player:	.10
(1) Paul Bako	.10
(2) John Burkett	.10
(3) Jose Cabrera	.10
(4) Ken Caminiti	.10
(5) Pat Corrales	.10
(6) Bobby Cox	.10
(7) Mark DeRosa	.10
(8) Bobby Dews	.10
(9) Frank Fultz	.10
(10) Marcus Giles	.10
(11) Bernard Gilkey	.10
(12) Tom Glavine	.75
(13) Wes Helms	.10
(14) Glenn Hubbard	.10
(15) Andruw Jones	1.00
(16) Chipper Jones	3.00
(17) Brian Jordan	.10
(18) Steve Karsay	.10
(19) Kerry Ligtenberg	.10
(20) Keith Lockhart	.10
(21) George Lombard	.10
(22) Javy Lopez	.10
(23) Greg Maddux	2.00
(24) Jason Marquis	.10
(25) Dave Martinez	.10
(26) Leo Mazzone	.10
(27) Kevin Millwood	.35
(28) Odalis Perez	.10
(29) Steve Reed	.10
(30) Mike Remlinger	.10
(31) Merv Rettenmund	.10
(32) Rey Sanchez	.10
(33) John Smoltz	.75
(34) B.J. Surhoff	.10
(35) Ned Yost	.10
(36) Team photo	.50

2002 Bryan Braves Team Photo Set

Children visiting Turner Field for a September game received this foldout sponsored by the team's hot dog vendor. The 10-5/8" x 31-3/8" three-panel perforated sheet has a large team photo and individual 2-1/8" x 3-1/8" cards of 35 players and staff. The staff cards have a portrait photo; the player cards have game-action photos. All photos are framed in blue and bordered in white. Name and position are at bottom, a red "A" at top and a large Bryan logo at lower-left. Backs are in blue, white and black with biographical and career notes and stats on a ghost image of the front photo. The unnumbered cards are checklisted here alpabetically.

	NM/M
Complete Foldout Set:	8.00
Common Player:	.10
(1) Henry Blanco	.10
(2) Darren Bragg	.10
(3) Vinny Castilla	.10
(4) Pat Corrales	.10
(5) Bobby Cox	.10
(6) Mark DeRosa	.10
(7) Bobby Dews	.10
(8) Julio Franco	.10
(9) Matt Franco	.10
(10) Frank Fultz	.10
(11) Rafael Furcal	.10
(12) Jesse Garcia	.10
(13) Marcus Giles	.10
(14) Tom Glavine	1.00
(15) Chris Hammond	.10
(16) Wes Helms	.10

(17) Darren Holmes	.10
(18) Glenn Hubbard	.10
(19) Andruw Jones	1.00
(20) Chipper Jones	3.00
(21) Kerry Ligtenberg	.10
(22) Keith Lockhart	.10
(23) Albie Lopez	.10
(24) Javy Lopez	.10
(25) Greg Maddux	2.00
(26) Jason Marquis	.10
(27) Leo Mazzone	.10
(28) Kevin Millwood	.35
(29) Damian Moss	.25
(30) Terry Pendleton	.10
(31) Mike Remlinger	.10
(32) Gary Sheffield	.35
(33) John Smoltz	1.00
(34) Tim Spooneybarger	.10
(35) Ned Yost	.10
(36) Team Photo	.50

1982 Builders Emporium Los Angeles Dodgers

Shoppers at this chain of building supply stores in Southern California were able to receive one of this seven-card set with each visit. Cards are printed in black-and-white in 11" x 8-1/2" format with blank backs. Fronts of the player cards have both portrait and action photos, the manager's card has only a portrait. Team and sponsors' logos are at bottom-right. The unnumbered cards are checklisted here in alphabetical order.

	NM/M
Complete Set (7):	35.00
Common Player:	6.00
(1) Dusty Baker	6.00
(2) Ron Cey	6.00
(3) Steve Garvey	9.00
(4) Pedro Guerrero	6.00
(5) Tommy Lasorda	6.00
(6) Jerry Reuss	6.00
(7) Steve Sax	6.00

1982 Burger King Braves

A set consisting of 27 "Collector Lids" featuring the Atlanta Braves was issued by Burger King restaurants in 1982. The plastic lids, 3-5/8" in diameter, were placed on a special Coca-Cola cup which listed the scores of the Braves' season-opening 13-game win streak. A black-and-white photo plus the player's name, position, height, weight, and 1981 statistics are found on the lid front. The unnumbered, blank-backed lids also contain logos for Burger King, Coca-Cola, and the Major League Baseball Players Association.

	NM/M
Complete Set (27):	20.00
Common Player:	1.00
(1) Steve Bedrosian	1.00
(2) Bruce Benedict	1.00
(3) Tommy Boggs	1.00
(4) Brett Butler	1.50
(5) Rick Camp	1.00
(6) Chris Chambliss	1.00
(7) Ken Dayley	1.00
(8) Gene Garber	1.00
(9) Preston Hanna	1.00
(10) Terry Harper	1.00

(11) Bob Horner	1.50
(12) Al Hrabosky	1.00
(13) Glenn Hubbard	1.00
(14) Randy Johnson	1.00
(15) Rufino Linares	1.00
(16) Rick Mahler	1.00
(17) Larry McWilliams	1.00
(18) Dale Murphy	12.50
(19) Phil Niekro	1.00
(20) Biff Pocoroba	1.00
(21) Rafael Ramirez	1.00
(22) Jerry Royster	1.00
(23) Ken Smith	1.00
(24) Bob Walk	1.00
(25) Claudell Washington	1.00
(26) Bob Watson	1.00
(27) Larry Whisenton	1.00

1982 Burger King Indians

This set was sponsored by WUAB-TV and Burger Kings in the Cleveland vicinity. The cards' green borders encompass a large yellow area which contains a black-and-white photo plus a baseball tip. Manager Dave Garcia and his coaches provide the baseball hints. The cards, which measure 3" x 5", are unnumbered and blank-backed.

	NM/M
Complete Set (12):	7.00
Common Player:	.75
(1) Dave Garcia (Be In The Game)	.75
(2) Dave Garcia (Sportsmanship)	.75
(3) Johnny Goryl (Rounding The Bases)	.75
(4) Johnny Goryl (3rd Base Running)	.75
(5) Tom McCraw (Follow Thru)	.75
(6) Tom McCraw (Selecting A Bat)	.75
(7) Tom McCraw (Watch The Ball)	.75
(8) Mel Queen (Master One Pitch)	.75
(9) Mel Queen (Warm Up)	.75
(10) Dennis Sommers (Get Down On A Ground Ball)	.75
(11) Dennis Sommers (Protect Your Fingers)	.75
(12) Dennis Sommers (Tagging First Base)	.75

1986 Burger King

Burger King restaurants in the Pennsylvania and New Jersey areas issued a set entitled "All-Pro Series." Cards were issued with the purchase of a Whopper sandwich and came in folded panels of two cards each, along with a coupon

card. Fronts feature a color photo and identification plus the Burger King logo. Due to a lack of MLB licensing, team insignias on the players' uniforms were airbrushed away. Backs are in black-and-white and contain brief biographical and statistical information.

	NM/M
Complete Panel Set (10):	3.00
Complete Singles Set (20):	3.00
Common Panel:	.25
Common Single Player:	.05
PANEL (1)	.40
1 Tony Pena	.05
2 Dave Winfield	.20
PANEL (2)	1.00
3 Fernando Valenzuela	.05
4 Pete Rose	.45
PANEL (3)	1.00
5 Mike Schmidt	.20
6 Steve Carlton	.20
PANEL (4)	.25
7 Glenn Wilson	.05
8 Jim Rice	.15
PANEL (5)	.50
9 Wade Boggs	.25
10 Juan Samuel	.05
PANEL (6)	.50
11 Dale Murphy	.10
12 Reggie Jackson	.35
PANEL (7)	.40
13 Kirk Gibson	.05
14 Eddie Murray	.20
PANEL (8)	1.00
15 Cal Ripken Jr.	.50
16 Willie McGee	.05
PANEL (9)	.40
17 Dwight Gooden	.05
18 Steve Garvey	.10
PANEL (10)	1.00
19 Don Mattingly	.40
20 George Brett	.40

1987 Burger King

The 1987 "All-Pro 2nd Edition Series" set was part of a giveaway promotion at participating Burger King restaurants. The set is comprised of 20 players on ten different panels. Cards measure 2-1/2" x 3-1/2" each with a three-card panel (includes a coupon card) measuring 7-5/8" x 3-1/2". Fronts feature a full-color photo and Burger King logo surrounded by a blue stars-and-stripes border. Backs are black-and-white with a brief biography and 1986/Career statistics. The set was produced by Mike Schecter Associates and, as with many MSA issues, all team insignias were airbrushed away.

	NM/M
Complete Panel Set (10):	3.00
Complete Singles Set (20):	3.00
Common Panel:	.30
Common Single Player:	.05
PANEL (1)	.75
1 Wade Boggs	.40
2 Gary Carter	.30
PANEL (2)	.75
3 Will Clark	.05
4 Roger Clemens	.40
PANEL (3)	.40
5 Steve Garvey	.20
6 Ron Darling	.05
PANEL (4)	.30
7 Pedro Guerrero	.05
8 Von Hayes	.05
PANEL (5)	.50
9 Rickey Henderson	.30
10 Keith Hernandez	.05
PANEL (6)	.40
11 Wally Joyner	.05
12 Mike Krukow	.05
PANEL (7)	1.00
13 Don Mattingly	.50
14 Ozzie Smith	.40

PANEL (8)	.30
15 Tony Pena	.05
16 Jim Rice	.20
PANEL (9)	1.00
17 Ryne Sandberg	.40
18 Mike Schmidt	.50
PANEL (10)	.30
19 Darryl Strawberry	.05
20 Fernando Valenzuela	.05

1994 Burger King Cal Ripken Jr.

Although the cards themselves do not indicate it, this issue was co-sponsored by Burger King and Coke, and distributed in BK restaurants in the Baltimore-Washington area. Cards were available in three-card packs for 25 cents with the purchase of a Coke product. Each pack contains two regular cards and a gold card. Each of the nine cards could be found in a regular and gold version. Cards feature color photos with a semi-circular black border at top or left. "Score '94" appears in orange in one of the upper corners, along with an Orioles logo. Cal Ripken, Jr.'s name appears at the bottom. On the gold premium version, there is a gold-foil circle around the Orioles logo and Ripken's name appears in gold, rather than white. Backs have a smaller color photo, again meeting at a semi-circular edge with the black border at left and bottom. In the black are another Score logo, a card number, an Orioles logo, a headline and a few career details and/or stats. Cards are UV coated on each side. Several hundred of the cards were personally autographed by Ripken and distributed in a drawing.

	NM/M
Complete Set (9):	5.00
Complete Set, Gold (9):	9.00
Common Card:	.75
Common Card, Gold:	1.25
Autographed Card:	185.00
1 Double Honors	.75
1a Double Honors/Gold	1.25
2 Perennial All-Star	.75
2a Perennial All-Star/Gold	1.25
3 Peerless Power	.75
3a Peerless Power/Gold	1.25
4 Fitness Fan	.75
4a Fitness Fan/Gold	1.25
5 Prime Concerns	.75
5a Prime Concerns/Gold	1.25
6 Home Run Club	.75
6a Home Run Club/Gold	1.25
7 The Iron Man	.75
7a The Iron Man/Gold	1.25
8 Heavy Hitter	.75
8a Heavy Hitter/Gold	1.25
9 Gold Glover	.75
9a Gold Glover/Gold	1.25

1997 Burger King Cal Ripken Jr.

Three years after its 1994 tribute, Burger King in 1997 created an eight-card set honoring the future Hall of Famer. Participating BK outlets in Maryland, the District of Columbia, Delaware, Pennsylvania, Virginia and West Virginia offered the cards for 99¢ with a meal purchase or $1.15 without. Each card was produced

in two forms: with and without a gold holographic foil facsimile autograph and "1 of 10,000" notation. The 2-1/2" x 3-1/2" cards have action photos of Ripken on front with muted backgrounds. His name, uniform number and team logo also appear. Backs, numbered "X/8" have another color photo with ghosted background and a paragraph of a career highlight. Autographed cards were part of a prize structure explained on information cards accompanying the Ripken card in each pack.

	NM/M
Complete Set (8):	5.00
Complete Gold Set (8):	10.00
Common Card:	1.00
Common Gold Card:	2.00
Autographed Card:	185.00
1-8 Cal Ripken Jr.	1.00
-- Autograph information card	.25

1999 Burger King N.Y. Yankees

Members of the World Champion 1998 N.Y. Yankees are featured on this three-sheet set of cards sold by metropolitan New York Burger King restaurants in April-May, 1999. The 12-1/2" x 10-1/2" perforated sheets each include nine standard-size cards. Fronts feature action photos with the Yankees and Fleer logos. Backs have the same photo along with season and career stats and highlights, printed on a ghosted background of a Yankees pin-striped jersey. The Fleer and team logos appear on back, as do those of the players' union and the restaurant chain. On the sheet along with the player cards are a checklist, team schedule, mention of the BK Cancer Foundation of New York and a kids' club offer.

	NM/M
Complete Sheet Set (3):	7.50
Complete Singles Set (27):	7.50
Common Player:	.25
SHEET 1	6.00
1 Derek Jeter	4.00
2 Paul O'Neill	.25
3 Scott Brosius	.25
4 Mariano Rivera	.50
5 Chuck Knoblauch	.25
6 Graeme Lloyd	.25
7 Joe Girardi	.25
8 Orlando Hernandez	.25
9 Tim Raines	.25
SHEET 2	3.50
10 Bernie Williams	.45
11 Tino Martinez	.25
12 Andy Pettitte	.40
13 Hideki Irabu	.25
14 Ramiro Mendoza	.25
15 Jeff Nelson	.25
16 Homer Bush	.25

17	Darren Holmes	.25
18	Yankees Championship History	.25
	SHEET 3	**3.50**
19	David Cone	.25
20	David Wells	.25
21	Chili Davis	.25
22	Darryl Strawberry	.25
23	Ricky Ledee	.25
24	Jorge Posada	.25
25	Luis Sojo	.25
26	Chad Curtis	.25
27	Mike Stanton	.25

C

1989 Cadaco All-Star Baseball Discs

This set of player discs was sold with and intended for use in a board game. Fronts of the 3-1/2" diameter position players' discs have a yellow border sectioned with numbers from 1 to 14, indicating that player's likelihood of performing a specific baseball result based on career stats. At center is a color player photo from which the uniform details have been airbrushed. Logos of the game's producer and the Major League Players Association flank the portrait. The player's name, team and position are below the photo. Backs have up to five years of recent stats and lifetime totals, along with a few biographical data. Several of the discs have player names misspelled. Each disc can be found either with or without the team name and league on back. Four error discs from the initial print run (with team, league on back) were corrected. The unnumbered discs are checklisted alphabetically.

		NM/M
Complete Set (63):		20.00
Common Player:		.25
(1)	Harold Baines	.25
(2)	Wade Boggs	2.00
(3)	Bobby Bonilla	2.50
(4)	George Brett	2.50
(5)	Jose Canseco	1.00
(6)	Gary Carter	1.50
(7)	Joe Carter	.25
(8)	Will Clark	.25
(9a)	Rodger Clemens (First name misspelled.)	3.00
(9b)	Roger Clemens (corrected)	3.00
(10)	Vince Coleman	.25
(11)	David Cone	.25
(12)	Alvin Davis	.25
(13)	Eric Davis	.25
(14)	Glenn Davis	.25
(15)	Andre Dawson	.65
(16)	Shawon Dunston	.25
(17)	Dennis Eckersley	.60
(18)	Carlton Fisk	1.50
(19)	Scott Fletcher	.25
(20a)	John Frannko (Last name misspelled.)	.35
(20b)	John Franco (Corrected)	.25
(21)	Julio Franko (Franco)	.25
(22)	Gary Gaetti	.25
(23)	Andres Galarraga	.25
(24)	Kirk Gibson	.25
(25)	Mike Greenwell	.25
(26)	Mark Gubicza	.25
(27)	Pedro Guerrero	.25
(28)	Tony Gwynn	2.00
(29)	Rickey Henderson	1.50
(30)	Orel Hershiser	.25
(31)	Kent Hrbek	.25
(32)	Danny Jackson	.25
(33a)	Barry Larkin (Wrong photo.)	.65
(33b)	Barry Larkin (Corrected)	.25
(34)	Greg Maddux	2.00
(35)	Don Mattingly	2.50
(36a)	Mark McGuire (Last name misspelled.)	4.50
(36b)	Mark McGwire (Corrected)	4.50
(37)	Fred McGriff	.25
(38)	Paul Molitor	1.50
(39)	Tony Pena	.25
(40)	Gerald Perry	.25
(41)	Dan Plesac	.25
(42)	Kirby Puckett	2.00
(43)	Johnny Ray	.25
(44)	Jeff Reardon	.25
(45)	Cal Ripken, Jr.	4.50
(46)	Babe Ruth	3.50
(47)	Nolan Ryan	4.50
(48)	Juan Samuel	.25
(49)	Ryne Sandberg	2.00
(50)	Benito Santiago	.25
(51)	Steve Sax	.25
(52)	Mike Schmidt	2.25
(53)	Kevin Seitzer	.25
(54)	Ozzie Smith	2.00
(55)	Terry Steinbach	.25
(56)	Dave Stewart	.25
(57)	Darryl Strawberry	.25
(58)	Andres Thomas	.25
(59)	Alan Trammell (Trammell)	.25
(60)	Andy Van Slyke	.25
(61)	Frank Viola	.25
(62)	Dave Winfield	1.50
(63)	Todd Worrell	.25

1990 Cadaco All-Star Baseball Discs

This set of player discs was sold with and intended for use in a board game. Fronts of the 3-1/2" diameter position players' discs have a border sectioned with numbers from 1 to 14, indicating the player's likelihood of performing a specific baseball result based on career stats. At center is a color player photo from which the uniform details have been airbrushed. Logos of the game's producer and the Major League Players Association flank the portrait. The player's name, team and position are below the photo. Backs have up to five years of recent stats and lifetime totals, along with brief biographical data. A handful of the game's past greats were included among the contemporary players which make up the bulk of the disc set. The unnumbered discs are checklisted alphabetically.

		NM/M
Complete Set (63):		20.00
Common Player:		.25
(1)	Harold Baines	.25
(2)	Damon Berryhill	.25
(3)	Craig Biggio	.25
(4)	Wade Boggs	2.00
(5)	Bobby Bonilla	1.00
(6)	Jose Canseco	1.00
(7)	Will Clark	.25
(8)	Roger Clemens	2.50
(9)	Roberto Clemente	4.00
(10)	Ty Cobb	2.50
(11)	Vince Coleman	.25
(12)	Eric Davis	.25
(13)	Glenn Davis	.25
(14)	Andre Dawson	.65
(15)	Shawon Dunston	.25
(16)	Tony Fernandez	.25
(17)	Carlton Fisk	1.50
(18)	Julio Franco	.25
(19)	Gary Gaetti	.25
(20)	Lou Gehrig	4.00
(21)	Kirk Gibson	.25
(22)	Mark Grace	.25
(23)	Ken Griffey Jr.	3.00
(24)	Pedro Guerrero	.25
(25)	Tony Gwynn	2.00
(26)	Rickey Henderson	1.50
(27)	Orel Hershiser	.25
(28)	Bo Jackson	.60
(29)	Howard Johnson	.25
(30)	Carney Lansford	.25
(31)	Barry Larkin	.25
(32)	Greg Maddux	2.00
(33)	Don Mattingly	2.50
(34)	Fred McGriff	.25
(35)	Mark McGwire	3.50
(36)	Kevin Mitchell	.25
(37)	Tony Pena	.25
(38)	Kirby Puckett	2.00
(39)	Willie Randolph	.25
(40)	Cal Ripken Jr.	4.50
(41)	Babe Ruth	4.00
(42)	Nolan Ryan	4.50
(43)	Bret Saberhagen	.25
(44)	Chris Sabo	.25
(45)	Ryne Sandberg	2.00
(46)	Benito Santiago	.25
(47)	Steve Sax	.25
(48)	Mike Scott	.25
(49)	Kevin Seitzer	.25
(50)	Ruben Sierra	.25
(51)	Ozzie Smith	2.00
(52)	Terry Steinbach	.25
(53)	Dave Stewart	.25
(54)	Mickey Tettleton	.25
(55)	Robby Thompson	.25
(56)	Alan Trammell	.25
(57)	Jose Uribe	.25
(58)	Andy Van Slyke	.25
(59)	Honus Wagner	1.50
(60)	Jerome Walton	.25
(61)	Lou Whitaker	.25
(62)	Matt Williams	.25
(63)	Robin Yount	1.50

1991 Cadaco All-Star Baseball Discs

This set of player discs was sold with and intended for use in a board game. Fronts of the 3-1/2" diameter discs have a yellow border sectioned with numbers from 1 to 14, indicating that player's likelihood of performing a specific baseball result based on career stats. At center is a color player photo from which the uniform details have been airbrushed. Logos of the game's producer and the Major League Players Association flank the portrait. The player's name, team and position are below the photo. Backs have up to five years of recent stats and lifetime totals, along with a few biographical data. The unnumbered discs are checklisted alphabetically.

		NM/M
Complete Set (62):		20.00
Common Player:		.25
(1)	Roberto Alomar	.35
(2)	Harold Baines	.25
(3)	Craig Biggio	.25
(4)	Wade Boggs	2.00
(5)	Barry Bonds	4.50
(6)	Bobby Bonilla	.25
(7)	Jose Canseco	.75
(8)	Will Clark	.25
(9)	Roger Clemens	2.50
(10)	Roberto Clemente	4.00
(11)	Ty Cobb	2.50
(12)	Vince Coleman	.25
(13)	Eric Davis	.25
(14)	Glenn Davis	.25
(15)	Andre Dawson	.65
(16)	Delino DeShields	.25
(17)	Shawon Dunston	.25
(18)	Tony Fernandez	.25
(19)	Cecil Fielder	.25
(20)	Carlton Fisk	1.50
(21)	Julio Franco	.25
(22)	Gary Gaetti	.25
(23)	Lou Gehrig	3.00
(24)	Kirk Gibson	.25
(25)	Mark Grace	.25
(26)	Ken Griffey Jr.	3.00
(27)	Kelly Gruber	.25
(28)	Tony Gwynn	2.00
(29)	Rickey Henderson	1.50
(30)	Orel Hershiser	.25
(31)	David Justice	.25
(32)	Bo Jackson	.50
(33)	Howard Johnson	.25
(34)	Barry Larkin	.25
(35)	Ramon Martinez	.25
(36)	Don Mattingly	2.50
(37)	Fred McGriff	.25
(38)	Mark McGwire	3.50
(39)	Kevin Mitchell	.25
(40)	Lance Parrish	.25
(41)	Tony Pena	.25
(42)	Kirby Puckett	2.00
(43)	Cal Ripken Jr.	4.50
(44)	Babe Ruth	4.00
(45)	Nolan Ryan	4.50
(46)	Bret Saberhagen	.25
(47)	Chris Sabo	.25
(48)	Ryne Sandberg	2.00
(49)	Benito Santiago	.25
(50)	Steve Sax	.25
(51)	Gary Sheffield	.75
(52)	Ruben Sierra	.25
(53)	Ozzie Smith	2.00
(54)	Terry Steinbach	.25
(55)	Dave Stewart	.25
(56)	Mickey Tettleton	.25
(57)	Alan Trammell	.25
(58)	Jose Uribe	.25
(59)	Honus Wagner	1.50
(60)	Lou Whitaker	.25
(61)	Matt Williams	.25
(62)	Robin Yount	1.50

1993 Cadaco All-Star Baseball Discs

This set of player discs was sold with and intended for use in a board game. Fronts of the 3-1/2" diameter discs have a yellow border sectioned with numbers from 1 to 14, indicating that player's likelihood of performing a specific baseball result based on career stats. At center is a color player photo from which the uniform details have been airbrushed. Logos of the game's producer and the Major League Players Association flank the portrait. The player's name, team and position are below the photo. Backs have up to five years of recent stats and lifetime totals, along with a few biographical data. The unnumbered discs are checklisted alphabetically.

		NM/M
Complete Set (62):		20.00
Common Player:		.25
(1)	Kevin Appier	.25
(2)	Carlos Baerga	.25
(3)	Harold Baines	.25
(4)	Derek Bell	.25
(5)	George Bell	.25
(6)	Jay Bell	.25
(7)	Mike Boddicker	.25
(8)	Wade Boggs	2.00
(9)	Hubie Brooks	.25
(10)	Jose Canseco	.75
(11)	Roger Clemens	2.50
(12)	Roberto Clemente	4.00
(13)	Ty Cobb	2.50
(14)	Alex Cole	.25
(15)	Jeff Conine	.25
(16)	Andre Dawson	.65
(17)	Shawon Dunston	.25
(18)	Lenny Dykstra	.25
(19)	Carlton Fisk	1.50
(20)	Darrin Fletcher	.25
(21)	Gary Gaetti	.25
(22)	Greg Gagne	.25
(23)	Mike Gallego	.25
(24)	Lou Gehrig	4.00
(25)	Kirk Gibson	.25
(26)	Tom Glavine	.50
(27)	Mark Grace	.25
(28)	Ken Griffey Jr.	3.00
(29)	Tony Gwynn	2.00
(30)	Charlie Hayes	.25
(31)	Rickey Henderson	1.50
(32)	Orel Hershiser	.25
(33)	Bo Jackson	.50
(34)	Howard Johnson	.25
(35)	Randy Johnson	1.50
(36)	Ricky Jordan	.25
(37)	David Justice	.25
(38)	Ray Lankford	.25
(39)	Ramon Martinez	.25
(40)	Don Mattingly	2.50
(41)	Mark McGwire	3.50
(42)	Brian McRae	.25
(43)	Joe Oliver	.25
(44)	Tony Pena	.25
(45)	Kirby Puckett	2.00
(46)	Cal Ripken Jr.	4.50
(47)	Babe Ruth	4.00
(48)	Nolan Ryan	4.50
(49)	Bret Saberhagen	.25
(50)	Chris Sabo	.25
(51)	Ryne Sandberg	2.00
(52)	Benito Santiago	.25
(53)	Steve Sax	.25
(54)	Gary Sheffield	.75
(55)	Ozzie Smith	2.00
(56)	Dave Stewart	.25
(57)	Darryl Strawberry	.25
(58)	Frank Thomas	1.50
(59)	Robin Ventura	.25
(60)	Hector Villanueva	.25
(61)	Honus Wagner	1.50
(62)	Lou Whitaker	.25

1985 Cain's Potato Chips Tigers

This set commemorating the 1984 World Champion Tigers were issued in bags of Cain's Potato Chips in the Michigan area in 1985. The yellow-bordered, unnumbered cards measure 2-3/4" in diameter and feature full-color oval photos inside a diamond. The word "Cain's" appears in the upper left corner, while the player's name appears in the lower left with his position directly below the photo. The words "1984 World Champions" are printed in the upper right corner. Backs include 1984 statistics.

		NM/M
Complete Set (20):		10.00
Common Player:		.50
(1)	Doug Bair	.50
(2)	Juan Berenguer	.50
(3)	Dave Bergman	.50
(4)	Tom Brookens	.50
(5)	Marty Castillo	.50
(6)	Darrell Evans	1.00
(7)	Barbaro Garbey	.50
(8)	Kirk Gibson	1.00
(9)	John Grubb	.50
(10)	Willie Hernandez	.50
(11)	Larry Herndon	.50
(12)	Chet Lemon	.50
(13)	Aurelio Lopez	.50
(14)	Jack Morris	1.00
(15)	Lance Parrish	1.00
(16)	Dan Petry	.50
(17)	Bill Scherrer	.50
(18)	Alan Trammell	2.50
(19)	Lou Whitaker	1.50
(20)	Milt Wilcox	.50

1986 Cain's Potato Chips Tigers

For the second year in a row, player discs of the Detroit Tigers were found in boxes of Cain's Potato Chips sold in the Detroit area. Twenty discs make up the set which is branded as a "1986 Annual Collectors' Edition." Discs, measuring 2-3/4" in diameter, have fronts which contain a color photo plus the player's name, team and position. The Cain's logo and the Major League Baseball Players Association's logo also appear. The backs, which display black print on white stock, contain player information plus the card number.

		NM/M
Complete Set (20):		7.50
Common Player:		.50
1	Tom Brookens	.50
2	Willie Hernandez	.50
3	Dave Bergman	.50
4	Lou Whitaker	1.25
5	Dave LaPoint	.50
6	Lance Parrish	.75
7	Randy O'Neal	.50
8	Nelson Simmons	.50
9	Larry Herndon	.50
10	Doug Flynn	.50
11	Jack Morris	.75
12	Dan Petry	.50
13	Walt Terrell	.50
14	Chet Lemon	.50
15	Frank Tanana	.50
16	Kirk Gibson	.75
17	Darrell Evans	.75
18	Dave Collins	.50
19	John Grubb	.50
20	Alan Trammell	2.00

1987 Cain's Potato Chips Tigers

Player discs of the Detroit Tigers were inserted in boxes of Cain's Potato Chips for the third consecutive year. The 1987 edition is made up of cards each measuring 2-3/4" in diameter. The discs, which were packaged in a cellophane wrapper, feature a full-color photo surrounded by an orange border. Backs are printed in red on white stock. The set was produced by Mike Schechter and Associates.

		NM/M
Complete Set (20):		12.50
Common Player:		.60
1	Tom Brookens	.60
2	Darnell Coles	.60
3	Mike Heath	.60
4	Dave Bergman	.60
5	Dwight Lowry	.60
6	Darrell Evans	1.00
7	Alan Trammell	2.50
8	Lou Whitaker	1.75
9	Kirk Gibson	1.00
10	Chet Lemon	.60
11	Larry Herndon	.60
12	John Grubb	.60
13	Willie Hernandez	.60
14	Jack Morris	1.00
15	Dan Petry	.60
16	Walt Terrell	.60
17	Mark Thurmond	.60
18	Pat Sheridan	.60
19	Eric King	.60
20	Frank Tanana	.60

1984 California Angels Fire Safety

This 32-card set was distributed at a June home game to fans 14 and under. Cards measure 2-1/2" x 3-1/2". Fronts have full-color action photos along a portrait of Smokey the Bear and U.S. and California Forest Service logos commemorating Smokey's 40th birthday. Black-and-white backs have minimal player data and stats and a tip for preventing forest fires.

	NM/M
Complete Set (32):	4.00

Common Player: .25
(1)	Don Aase	.25
(2)	Juan Beniquez	.25
(3)	Bob Boone	.45
(4)	Rick Burleson	.25
(5)	Rod Carew	1.50
(6)	John Curtis	.25
(7)	Doug DeCinces	.25
(8)	Brian Downing	.25
(9)	Ken Forsch	.25
(10)	Bobby Grich	.25
(11)	Reggie Jackson	2.00
(12)	Ron Jackson	.25
(13)	Tommy John	.50
(14)	Curt Kaufman	.25
(15)	Bruce Kison	.25
(16)	Frank LaCorte	.25
(17)	Fred Lynn	.45
(18)	John McNamara	.25
(19)	Jerry Narron	.25
(20)	Gary Pettis	.25
(21)	Robert Picciolo	.25
(22)	Ron Romanick	.25
(23)	Luis Sanchez	.25
(24)	Dick Schofield	.25
(25)	Daryl Sconiers	.25
(26)	Jim Slaton	.25
(27)	Ellis Valentine	.25
(28)	Robert Wilfong	.25
(29)	Mike Witt	.25
(30)	Geoff Zahn	.25
---	Forestry Dept. Logo Card	.10
---	Smokey Logo Card	.10

1985 California Angels Fire Safety

This full-color set of large-format cards was given to fans attending the July 14 game at Anaheim Stadium. Fronts feature player photos with their last name at the top above the picture. In the bottom border are a portrait of Smokey the Bear, and logos of the Angels, California Forestry Service and U.S. Forestry Service. Cards measure 4-1/4" x 6". On back, printed in black-and-white, are personal data, a few stats and a wildfire safety tip.

NM/M
Complete Set (24): 5.00
Common Player: .25
1	Mike Witt	.25
2	Reggie Jackson	1.50
3	Bob Boone	.45
4	Mike Brown	.25
5	Rod Carew	1.00
6	Doug DeCinces	.25
7	Brian Downing	.25
8	Ken Forsch	.25
9	Gary Pettis	.25
10	Jerry Narron	.25
11	Ron Romanick	.25
12	Bobby Grich	.25
13	Dick Schofield	.25
14	Juan Beniquez	.25
15	Geoff Zahn	.25
16	Luis Sanchez	.25
17	Jim Slaton	.25
18	Doug Corbett	.25
19	Ruppert Jones	.25
20	Rob Wilfong	.25
21	Donnie Moore	.25
22	Pat Clements	.25
23	Tommy John	.50
24	Gene Mauch	.25

1986 California Angels Fire Safety

The Angels, in conjuction with the U.S. and California Forestry Services, issued this set promoting Wildfire Prevention. Cards measure 4-1/4" x 6" and offer a full-color front with the player's picture in an oval frame. Backs have player stats with a drawing and fire safety tip. The sets were given out August 9 at the game in Anaheim Stadium.

NM/M
Complete Set (24): 5.00
Common Player: .25
1	Mike Witt	.25
2	Reggie Jackson	1.50
3	Bob Boone	.40
4	Don Sutton	1.00
5	Kirk McCaskill	.25
6	Doug DeCinces	.25
7	Brian Downing	.25
8	Doug Corbett	.25
9	Gary Pettis	.25
10	Jerry Narron	.25
11	Ron Romanick	.25
12	Bobby Grich	.25
13	Dick Schofield	.25
14	George Hendrick	.25
15	Rick Burleson	.25
16	John Candelaria	.25
17	Jim Slaton	.25
18	Darrell Miller	.25
19	Ruppert Jones	.25
20	Rob Wilfong	.25
21	Donnie Moore	.25
22	Wally Joyner	1.00
23	Terry Forster	.25
24	Gene Mauch	.25

1987 California Angels Fire Safety

The U.S. Forestry Service distributed this set to 25,000 fans in attendance at Anaheim Stadium on August 1. The full-color cards measure 4" x 6". Fronts carry a design of baseballs and bats framing the player photo. Only the player's last name is given. At bottom is a Smokey Bear portrait and team logo. Backs contain the player's name, position and personal data along with a Smokey Bear caution fire prevention tip and sponsors' logos.

NM/M
Complete Set (24): 5.00
Common Player: .25
1	John Candelaria	.25
2	Don Sutton	1.00
3	Mike Witt	.25
4	Gary Lucas	.25
5	Kirk McCaskill	.25
6	Chuck Finley	.25
7	Willie Fraser	.25
8	Donnie Moore	.25
9	Urbano Lugo	.25
10	Butch Wynegar	.25
11	Darrell Miller	.25
12	Wally Joyner	.75
13	Mark McLemore	.25
14	Mark Ryal	.25
15	Dick Schofield	.25
16	Jack Howell	.25
17	Doug DeCinces	.25
18	Gus Polidor	.25
19	Brian Downing	.25
20	Gary Pettis	.25
21	Ruppert Jones	.25
22	George Hendrick	.25
23	Devon White	.25
---	Smokey Bear Logo Card/Checklist	.10

1988 California Angels Fire Safety

These borderless full-color cards (2-1/2" x 3-1/2") are highlighted by a thin white outline on front. The player name, team logo and a Smokey Bear picture logo appear in the photo's lower-right corner. Backs are black-and-white and include personal information and a large cartoon fire prevention tip. Part of the U.S. Forest Service fire prevention campaign, the cards were distributed in three separate in-stadium giveaways during August and September games.

NM/M
Complete Set (25): 4.50
Common Player: .25
1	Cookie Rojas	.25
2	Johnny Ray	.25
3	Jack Howell	.25
4	Mike Witt	.25
5	Tony Armas	.25
6	Gus Polidor	.25
7	DeWayne Buice	.25
8	Dan Petry	.25
9	Bob Boone	.50
10	Chili Davis	.25
11	Greg Minton	.25
12	Kirk McCaskill	.25
13	Devon White	.25
14	Willie Fraser	.25
15	Chuck Finley	.25
16	Dick Schofield	.25
17	Wally Joyner	.50
18	Brian Downing	.25
19	Stewart Cliburn	.25
20	Donnie Moore	.25
21	Bryan Harvey	.25
22	Mark McLemore	.25
23	Butch Wynegar	.25
24	George Hendrick	.25
---	Team Logo/Checklist	.10

1989 California Angels All-Stars Fire Safety

The U.S. Forest Service, in conjunction with the California Angels, issued this all-time team set. The 2-1/2" x 3-1/2" cards have a silver border with the player photo outlined in red. Beneath the photo a banner across homeplate reads "Angels All-Stars," along with the player's name and position, which are flanked by Smokey Bear on the left and the Angels 1989 All-Star Game logo on the right. Card backs highlight the

player's career with the Angels and include an illustrated fire prevention tip.

NM/M
Complete Set (20): 6.00
Common Player: .25
1	Bill Rigney	.25
2	Dean Chance	.40
3	Jim Fregosi	.25
4	Bobby Knoop	.25
5	Don Mincher	.25
6	Clyde Wright	.25
7	Nolan Ryan	4.00
8	Frank Robinson	1.00
9	Frank Tanana	.25
10	Rod Carew	1.00
11	Bobby Grich	.25
12	Brian Downing	.25
13	Don Baylor	.25
14	Fred Lynn	.35
15	Reggie Jackson	1.50
16	Doug DeCinces	.25
17	Bob Boone	.35
18	Wally Joyner	.50
19	Mike Witt	.25
20	Johnny Ray	.25

1990 California Angels Fire Safety

This set was released by the U.S. Forestry Service in conjunction with the California Angels. The sets were distributed at the May 27 home game. The 2-1/2" x 3-1/2" cards feature full-color action photos surrounded by metallic silver borders. Team and Smokey Bear logos appear on front. Backs contain player data and a cartoon Smokey Bear message urging the prevention of forest fires.

NM/M
Complete Set (20): 5.00
Common Player: .25
1	Jim Abbott	.25
2	Bert Blyleven	.50
3	Chili Davis	.25
4	Brian Downing	.25
5	Chuck Finley	.25
6	Willie Fraser	.25
7	Bryan Harvey	.25
8	Jack Howell	.25
9	Wally Joyner	.50
10	Mark Langston	.25
11	Kirk McCaskill	.25
12	Mark McLemore	.25
13	Lance Parrish	.25
14	Johnny Ray	.25
15	Dick Schofield	.25
16	Mike Witt	.25
17	Claudell Washington	.25
18	Devon White	.25
19	Scott Bailes	.25
20	Bob McClure	.25

1991 California Angels Fire Safety

This set was sponsored by the California Department

of Forestry. Front of the 2-1/2" x 3-1/2" cards features gray borders surrounding full-color action photos. The flip sides feature a fire safety cartoon and biographical information, along with sponsor logos, printed in blue and red on white.

NM/M
Complete Set (20): 6.00
Common Player: .25
1	Luis Polonia	.25
2	Junior Felix	.25
3	Dave Winfield	2.00
4	Dave Parker	.25
5	Lance Parrish	.25
6	Wally Joyner	.35
7	Jim Abbott	.45
8	Mark Langston	.25
9	Dick Schofield	.25
10	Kirk McCaskill	.25
11	Jack Howell	.25
12	Donnie Hill	.25
13	Gary Gaetti	.25
14	Chuck Finley	.25
15	Luis Sojo	.25
16	Mark Eichhorn	.25
17	Bryan Harvey	.25
18	Jeff Robinson	.25
19	Scott Lewis	.25
20	John Orton	.25

1992 California Angels Police

This safety set was sponsored by Carl's Jr. fast food restaurants and distributed by the Orange County Sheriff's Deputy Single cards were distributed to children over the course of the season and complete sets were handed out at the Angels' September 19 game. Fronts have color player action photos on a star-studded red, white and blue border. Backs have a small black-and-white portrait photo, stats, career highlights, an anti-drug message and sponsors' logos.

NM/M
Complete Set (18): 8.00
Common Player: .50
1	Jim Abbott	.60
2	Gene Autry	1.00
3	Bert Blyleven	.75
4	Hubie Brooks	.50
5	Chad Curtis	.50
6	Alvin Davis	.50
7	Gary DiSarcina	.50
8	Junior Felix	.50
9	Chuck Finley	.50
10	Gary Gaetti	.50
11	Rene Gonzalez	.50
12	Von Hayes	.50
13	Carl Karcher	.50
14	Mark Langston	.50
15	Luis Polonia	.50
16	Bobby Rose	.50
17	Lee Stevens	.50
18	Happy Star/Mascot	.50

1993 California Angels Police

Sponsored by the Carl's Jr. hamburger restaurant chain and distributed through the California Chiefs & Sheriffs Association, it was reported that 20,000-25,000 sets were produced. The 2-1/2" x 3-1/2" cards have a player action photo on front. Backs are printed in blue

and black and include a portrait photo, career highlights, stats and an anti-drug message.

NM/M
Complete Set (21): 16.00
Common Player: .50
1	Gene Autry	1.00
2	Carl Karcher	.50
3	Buck Rodgers	.50
4	Rod Carew	3.50
5	Kelly Gruber	.50
6	Chili Davis	.50
7	Chad Curtis	.50
8	Mark Langston	.50
9	Scott Sanderson	.50
10	J.T. Snow	2.00
11	Rene Gonzalez	.50
12	Jimmie Reese	.50
13	Damion Easley	.50
14	Julio Valera	.50
15	Luis Polonia	.50
16	John Orton	.50
17	Gary DiSarcina	.50
18	Greg Myers	.50
19	Chuck Finley	.50
20	Tim Salmon	2.50
21	Happy Star/Mascot	.50

1995 California Angels Police

The California Highway Patrol sponsored this safety set to coincide with the Angels 35th anniversary. Cards have action photos bordered in gray and dark blue. The team's anniversary logo and CHP logo appear in opposite corners. Black-and-white backs have a few bit of player data and a safety tip.

NM/M
Complete Set (16): 20.00
Common Player: 1.00
1	Tim Salmon	2.00
2	Chuck Finley	1.00
3	Mark Langston	1.00
4	Gary Disarcina	1.00
5	Damion Easley	1.00
6	Spike Owen	1.00
7	Troy Percival	1.00
8	Chili Davis	1.00
9	Jim Edmonds	2.00
10	Rex Hudler	1.00
11	Greg Myers	1.00
12	Brian Anderson	1.00
13	J.T. Snow	1.50
14	Tony Phillips	1.00
15	Lee Smith	1.50
16	Marcel Lachemann, Don Watkins (Chief, CHP)	1.00

2004 California Angels Card Deck

This stadium giveaway was sponsored by Coast Plaza Doctors Hospital and Redio Disney. Cards are 2-1/4" x 3-7/16" with rounded corners. Red backs have team and sponsors' logos. Each player appears four times in the deck, with an identical portrait photo on the same value card in each suit. Two Rally Monkey jokers complete the boxed set.

		NM/M
Complete Set (54):		10.00
Common Player:		.25
2	Adam Kennedy	.25
3	Garret Anderson	.25
4	Bartolo Colon	.25
5	David Eckstein	.25
6	Jose Guillen	.35
7	Darin Erstad	.25
8	Kelvim Escobar	.25
9	Tim Salmon	.25
10	Bengie Molina	.25
J	Troy Percival	.25
Q	Troy Glaus	.40
K	Vladimir Guerrero	.50
A	Mike Scioscia	.25
Joker	Rally Monkey	.25

1992-93 Canadian Card News Repli-cards

Krause Publications short-lived attempt to service the Canadian card collecting market with a newsstand magazine included the use of repli-card panels of five in each of the magazine's five issues. The cards feature a mix of hockey players, CFL stars and Blue Jays and Expos. Only the baseball players are listed here.

		NM/M
Complete (Baseball) Set (12):		6.50
Common Player:		.50
2	Kelly Gruber	.50
3	Roberto Alomar	.75
5	Larry Walker, Marquis Grissom, Delino DeShields	.50
8	Dave Winfield	2.00
14	Ken Hill	.50
16	Jimmy Key	.50
17	Pat Borders	.50
21	Joe Carter	.50
22	Larry Walker	.75
23	Delino DeShields	.50
24	Derek Bell	.50
25	Wil Cordero	.50

1996 Canadian Club Classic Stars of the Game

A promotion for Canadian Club's Classic 12 whisky offered a series of autographed Hall of Famer cards. One card was included in a special folder attached to bottles. An offer sheet inside gave details for ordering other cards for $5 each

---

plus proof of purchase. Also in the bottle-hanger was a certificate of authenticity for the enclosed signed card. In standard 2-1/2" x 3-1/2" format, cards feature vintage color player photos on which uniform logos have been deleted. Cards have a black border, are highlighted in gold foil and have an authentic autograph on front. Backs have career stats and summary. Cards #1-4 were labeled as Series I, cards #5-6 are Series II.

		NM/M
Complete Set (6):		60.00
Common Player:		6.00
1	Brooks Robinson	12.00
2	Billy Williams	6.00
3	Willie Stargell	13.50
4	Ernie Banks	17.50
5	Frank Robinson	15.00
6	Rollie Fingers	6.00

2000 CaP Cure Home Run Challenge

JASON GIAMBI

As part of its fund-raising "Home Run Challenge" promotion June 15-20, 2000, the Association for the Cure of Cancer of the Prostate issued a nine-card perforated sheet of 2-1/2" x 3-1/2" cards. Fronts have an action photo with black borders. At top-left is the CaP Cure logo, at lower-right is the MLBPA logo. Backs have messages promoting the cause, along with contact information for the organization.

		NM/M
Complete Sheet:		20.00
Complete Set (9):		20.00
Common Player:		2.00
(1)	Jason Giambi	2.00
(2)	Ken Griffey Jr.	3.00
(3)	Tony Gwynn	2.50
(4)	Derek Jeter	5.00
(5)	Mark McGwire	4.00
(6)	Alex Rodriguez	4.00
(7)	Sammy Sosa	2.50
(8)	Robin Ventura	1.00
(9)	Header Card	.25

2001 CaP Cure Home Run Challenge

As part of its fund-raising "Home Run Challenge" promotion, the Association for the Cure of Cancer of the Prostate issued a nine-card perforated sheet of 2-1/2" x 3-1/2" cards. Each card has two fronts, with each side having an action photo which is bor-

---

derless at top, bottom and right. The CaP Cure logo is at lower-right, the player name and uniform number in a colored strip at right and the MLB Players Choice logo at top-left. The association phone number is at left. The center card on the sheet offers a contest to win autographed baseballs, utilizing the individual serial number on the back.

		NM/M
Complete Sheet:		15.00
Common Player:		1.50
(1)	Jeff Bagwell, Carlos Delgado	1.50
(2)	Jay Bell, Alex Rodriguez	3.00
(3)	Nomar Garciaparra, Sammy Sosa	2.00
(4)	Jason Giambi, Mark McGwire	2.50
(5)	Ken Griffey Jr., Robin Ventura	2.25
(6)	Tony Gwynn, Ivan Rodriguez	2.00
(7)	Derek Jeter, Mike Sweeney	3.00
(8)	Chipper Jones, Jim Thome	2.00
(9)	Contest Card	.25

2002 CaP Cure Home Run Challenge

JASON GIAMBI

In its third season, the Association for the Cure of Cancer of the Prostate reduced the number of cards to four and the size of the cards to 1-5/8" x 2-3/4". Cards have action photos on front, which are repeated in ghost-image form on back. A Q-and-A about prostate cancer is presented on back.

		NM/M
Complete Set (4):		8.00
Common Player:		1.50
(1)	Derek Jeter	3.50
(2)	Jason Giambi	1.50
(3)	Ken Griffey Jr.	2.50
(4)	Sammy Sosa	2.00

1994 Capital Cards 1969 Mets Postcards

Capital Cards produced a 32-card postcard set of members of the 1969 World Champion New York Mets from Ron Lewis paintings, limited to 25,000 sets. Capital

---

Cards also produced 5,000 uncut sheets that are individually numbered and carried a suggested retail price of $99.95. The boxed postcard set retailed for $39.95. The cards could also be purchased with autographs.

		NM/M
Complete Sheet:		15.00
Common Player:		.35
Uncut Sheet:		15.00
1	Logo Card	.35
2	Gil Hodges	2.00
3	Rube Walker	.35
4	Yogi Berra	2.00
5	Joe Pignatano	.35
6	Ed Yost	.35
7	Tommie Agee	.35
8	Ken Boswell	.35
9	Don Cardwell	.35
10	Ed Charles	.35
11	Donn Clendenon	.35
12	Jack DiLauro	.35
13	Duffy Dyer	.35
14	Wayne Garrett	.35
15	Rod Gaspar	.35
16	Gary Gentry	.35
17	Jerry Grote	.35
18	Bud Harrelson	.50
19	Cleon Jones	.50
20	Cal Koonce	.35
21	Jerry Koosman	.50
22	Ed Kranepool	.35
23	J.C. Martin	.35
24	Jim McAndrew	.35
25	Tug McGraw	.50
26	Bob Pfeil	.35
27	Nolan Ryan	6.00
28	Tom Seaver	3.00
29	Art Shamsky	.35
30	Ron Swoboda	.35
31	Ron Taylor	.35
32	Al Weis	.35

1989 Cap'n Crunch

This 22-card set was produced by Topps for Cap'n Crunch cereal boxes. Two cards and a stick of gum were included in each cereal box while the offer was active. The fronts of these 2-1/2" x 3-1/2" cards feature red, white and blue borders. The card backs are horizontal and feature lifetime statistics. The set was not offered in any complete set deal.

		NM/M
Complete Set (22):		5.00
Common Player:		.10
1	Jose Canseco	.40
2	Kirk Gibson	.10
3	Orel Hershiser	.10
4	Frank Viola	.10
5	Tony Gwynn	.65
6	Cal Ripken	1.50
7	Darryl Strawberry	.10
8	Don Mattingly	.75
9	George Brett	.75
10	Andre Dawson	.25

11	Dale Murphy	.25
12	Alan Trammell	.10
13	Eric Davis	.10
14	Jack Clark	.10
15	Eddie Murray	.50
16	Mike Schmidt	.75
17	Dwight Gooden	.10
18	Roger Clemens	.75
19	Will Clark	.10
20	Kirby Puckett	.65
21	Robin Yount	.50
22	Mark McGwire	1.00

1995 Cardtoons

Just about everything related to baseball comes in for the jab in this set of parody cards. Players, teams, attitudes, owners, mascots, Hall of Famers, announcers and the business of baseball are all panned. Besides a base set of 95 cards, there are several insert issues and send-away prizes. Cards are standard 2-1/2" x 3-1/2" with easily identifiable caricatures on front and sophomoric humor on the back. The cards make a point of stating they are parodies and not licensed either by the players or Major League Baseball. While they carry a 1993 copyright date, the cards were not issued until 1995.

		NM/M
Complete Set (95):		10.00
Common Card:		.25
1	Hey Abbott	.25
2	Robin Adventura	.25
3	Roberto Alamode	.30
4	Don Battingly	1.25
5	Cow Belle	.25
6	Jay Bellhop	.25
7	Fowl Boggs	1.00
8	Treasury Bonds	2.50
9	True Brett	1.25
10	Wild Pitch Mitch	.25
11	Balou's Brothers (Felipe Balou, Moises Balou)	.25
12	Charlie Bustle	2.00
13	Brett Butter	.25
14	Rambo Canseco	.40
15	Roberto Cementie	2.50
16	Roger Clemency	1.25
17	Will Clock	.25
18	David Clone	.25
19	Tom Clowning	.25
20	Mr. Club	1.00
21	Joe Crater	.25
22	Doolin' Daulton	.25
23	Chili Dog Davis	.25
24	Doug Drawback	.25
25	Dennis Excellency	.65
26	Silly Fanatic	.25
27	Wand Gonzalez	.40
28	Amazing Grace	.25
29	Tom Grapevine	.25
30	Marquis Gruesome	.25
31	Homerin' Hank	2.00
32	Kevin Happier	.25
33	Pete Harness	.25
34	Charlie Haze	.25
35	Egotisticky Henderson	.75
36	Sayanora Infielder	.25
37	Snoozin' Ted & Tarzan Jane	.25
38	Cloud Johnson	.75
39	Sandy K-Fax	2.00
40	The Say What Kid	2.00
41	Tommy Lasagna	.25
42	Greg Maddogs	1.00
43	Stamp the Man	.25
44	Mark McBash	2.00
45	Fred McGruff	.25
46	Mount Mick	3.00
47	Pat Moustache	.25
48	Ozzie Myth	.25
49	Bob Nukesbury	.25
50	Reggie October	1.00
51	Doctor OK	.25
52	Rafael Palmist	.65
53	Lose Piniella	.25

54	Vince Poleman	.25
55	Charlie Puff	.25
56	Rob Quibble	.25
57	Darryl Razzberry	.25
58	Cal Ripkenwinkle	2.50
59	Budge Rodriguez	.65
60	Ryne Sandbox	1.00
61	Steve Saxophone	.25
62	Harry Scary	.25
63	Scary Sheffield	.45
64	Ruben Siesta	.25
65	Dennis Smartiendz	.25
66	Lee Smite	.25
67	Ken Spiffey Jr.	1.50
68	Nails Spikestra	.25
69	The Splendid Spinner	2.00
70	Toad Stottlemyre	.25
71	Raging Tartabull	.25
72	Robbery Thompson	.25
73	Alan Trampoline	.25
74	Monster Truk	.25
75	Shawon Tungsten	.25
76	Tony Twynn	1.00
77	Andy Van Tyke	.25
78	Derrick Ventriloquist	.25
79	Frank Violin	.25
80	Rap Winfielder	.75
81	Robinhood Yount	.75
82	Swift Justice	.25
83	Brat Saberhagen	.25
84	Mike Pizazz	1.50
85	Andres Colorado	.25
86	Money Bagswell	.75
87	Video Nomo	.40
88	Out of the Park	.25
89	Tim Wallet	.25
90	Checklist	.10
91	Greenback Jack	.25
92	Mighty Matt	.25
	Power Hitter	.25
93	Frankenthomas	.75
94	Neon Peon Slanders	.35
95	Just Air Jordan	2.50
---	Replacement Card No. 1 (Redeemable for "Cardtoons Annual Awards" set with payment of $26.95.)	.10
---	Replacement Card No. 2 (Redeemable for Cardtoons binder and plastic sheets with payment of $18.95.)	.13
---	Replacement card No. 3 (Redeemable for Cardtoons phone card set of four with payment of $39.95.)	.13

Awards Replacement Set

This set was available via a mail-in offer for $26.95.

		NM/M
Complete Set (8):		6.25
Common Card:		1.00
R1	No Ball Peace Prize	1.00
R2	Forrest Grump	1.00
R3	Most Virtous Player	1.00
R4	Golden Glove Award	1.00
R5	Comdown Player of the Year	1.00
R6	Corkville Slugger	1.00
R7	Can't Get No Relief	1.00
R8	1994 World Series Champ	1.00

Big Bang Bucks

This insert set lampoons baseball's top 20 salaried players. Fronts resemble U.S. currency overprinted with gold foil in denominations of five, six and seven million. A player caricature portrait is in color at center of the 3-1/2" x 2-1/2" card. Backs give the player's salary history and rationale for his being overpaid. A statement on back says the cards are intended to be a parody and that they are not licensed by MLB or the players' union. The cards are numbered with the "BB" prefix.

		NM/M
Complete Set (20):		20.00
Common Card:		1.00
1	Treasury Bonds	4.00
2	Sayanora Infielder	1.00
3	Cal Ripkenwinkle	4.00
4	Bobby Bonus	1.00
5	Joe Crater	1.00
6	Kirby Plunkit	2.00
7	David Clone	1.00
8	Ken Spiffey Jr.	3.00
9	Ruben Siesta	1.00
10	Greg Maddogs	2.00
11	Mark McBash	3.50
12	Rafael Palmist	1.50
13	Roberto Alamode	1.00
14	Greenback Jack	1.00
15	Raging Tartabull	1.00
16	Jimmy Kiwi	1.00
17	Roger Clemency	2.25
18	Rambo Canseco	1.25
19	Tom Grapevine	1.00
20	John Smileyface	1.00

Field of Greed Puzzle Set

These nine-cards are inserts which form a "Field of Greed" picture when the individual cards are aligned. Fronts have 1/9th of the cartoon puzzle, backs have a history of baseball's recent labor problems. Cards have an "FOG" prefix to their number.

		NM/M
Complete Set (9):		1.50
Common Card:		.20
1	1972 Strike	.25
2	1973 Lockout	.25
3	1976 Lockout	.25
4	1980 Strike	.25
5	1981 Strike	.25
6	1985 Strike	.25
7	1990 Lockout	.25
8	1994 Strike	.25
9	Future Problems	.25

Grand Slam Foils

This insert set utilizes foil printing technology to give a high-tech look to the caricatures of major leaguers. Fronts have cartoon parodies of the players, backs attempt to be humorous. A note on back says the cards are not licensed by either the players or Major League Baseball. Cards are numbered with a "F" prefix.

		NM/M
Complete Set (10):		12.00
Common Player:		1.00
1	Bo Action	1.50
2	Andre Awesome	1.25
3	Bobby Bonus	1.00
4	Steve Bravery	1.00
5	Carlton Fist	2.00
6	E.T. McGee	1.00
7	Kirby Plunkit	4.00
8	Jose Rheostat	1.00
9	Sir Noble Ryan	6.00
10	Day-Glo Sabo	1.00

Politics in Baseball

This insert set takes a poke at the perceived problems of baseball during the 1994-95 strike. Fronts have cartoons, backs have pointed commentary. Cards are numbered with the "S" prefix.

		NM/M
Complete Set (11):		3.00
Common Card:		.15
1	Pledge of Allegiance	.15
2	The Wave	.15
3	Slick Willie	1.50
4	Umpires Convention	.15
5	The Slide	.15
6	SH-H-H-H-H-H-H	.15
7	Throwing Out the First Contract	.15
8	Babe Rush	1.00
9	Hot Prospect	.15
10	Let's Play Ball	.15
11	Role Model	.15

1992 Carl's Jr. Padres

For the fifth consecutive year the San Diego Padres issued a card set in conjunction with the Jr. Padres program. Carl's Jr., a fast food chain, began sponsoring the set in 1991. The set contains 25 cards and was available in either nine-card perforated sheets or precut. At 2-9/16" x 3-9/16" the cards are slightly larger than current standard. Player photos feature an All-Star Game logo in the lower-right corner. On the white border, the player's name and position are printed in dark blue beneath the photo. The team name is in light brown above the photo. On back, the player's stats, career highlights and biographical data are printed in dark blue. The unnumbered cards are checklisted here in alphabetical order.

		NM/M
Complete Set (25):		6.00
Common Player:		.25
(1)	Larry Anderson	.25
(2)	Oscar Azocar	.25
(3)	Andy Benes	.25

(4)	Dann Bilardello	.25
(5)	Jerald Clark	.25
(6)	Tony Fernandez	.25
(7)	Tony Gwynn	4.00
(8)	Greg Harris	.25
(9)	Bruce Hurst	.25
(10)	Darrin Jackson	.25
(11)	Craig Lefferts	.25
(12)	Mike Maddux	.25
(13)	Fred McGriff	1.00
(14)	Jose Melendez	.25
(15)	Randy Myers	.25
(16)	Greg Riddoch	.25
(17)	Rich Rodriguez	.25
(18)	Benito Santiago	.25
(19)	Gary Sheffield	.50
(20)	Craig Shipley	.25
(21)	Kurt Stillwell	.25
(22)	Tim Teufel	.25
(23)	Kevin Ward	.25
(24)	Ed Whitson	.25
(25)	All-Star logo	.25

2003 Carl's Jr. San Diego Padres

Marking the team's 35th anniversary, the fast-food chain sponsored a card giveaway at Qualcomm on September 6. A baker's dozen past and current Padres stars are featured in the set, in several designs in 2-1/2" x 3-1/2" format on thin cardboard. Fronts have game-action color photos. On a two-toned blue background on back stats for the player's tenure with the Pads, printed in white, along with team and sponsor logos are presented. The unnumbered cards are listed here in alphabetical order.

		NM/M
Complete Set (13):		8.00
Common Player:		.25
(1)	Roberto Alomar	.40
(2)	Bruce Bochy	.25
(3)	Kevin Brown	.25
(4)	Ken Caminiti	.25
(5)	Steve Finley	.25
(6)	Steve Garvey	.50
(7)	Tony Gwynn	3.00
(8)	Trevor Hoffman	.25
(9)	Randy Jones	.25
(10)	Gaylord Perry	.50
(11)	Benito Santiago	.25
(12)	Ozzie Smith	3.00
(13)	Dave Winfield	2.00

1992 Carlson Travel 1982 Brewers

The team's American League Championship season of 1982 was commemorated a decade later with this card set given away at a Brewers promotional date. The cards were sponsored by Carlson Travel and United Airlines, whose logos appear on the front of the cards, along with

Channel 6 television, whose logo is on the back. Fronts feature game-action photos of the '82 Brewers, borderless at top and sides. Beneath the photo is a thin gold stripe, then a blue stripe with the player's name and position in white. A red, white and blue 1982 World Series logo appears in the lower-left corner. Backs are printed in blue, and include 1982 stats and a summary of the player's season. Player cards are numbered by uniform number in the upper-left.

		NM/M
Complete Set (31):		12.00
Common Player:		.25
4	Paul Molitor	5.00
5	Ned Yost	.25
7	Don Money	.25
10	Bob McClure	.25
11	Ed Romero	.25
13	Roy Howell	.25
15	Cecil Cooper	.25
16	Marshall Edwards	.25
17	Jim Gantner	.25
19	Robin Yount	5.00
20	Gorman Thomas	.25
21	Don Sutton	1.00
22	Charlie Moore	.25
23	Ted Simmons	.25
24	Ben Oglivie	.25
27	Pete Ladd	.25
29	Mark Brouhard	.25
30	Moose Haas	.25
32	Harvey Kuenn	.25
33	Doc Medich	.25
34	Rollie Fingers	1.00
41	Jim Slaton	.25
46	Jerry Augustine	.25
47	Dwight Bernard	.25
48	Mike Caldwell	.25
50	Pete Vuckovich	.25
---	Coaches (Pat Dobson, Larry Haney, Ron Hansen, Cal McLish, Harry Warner)	.25
---	Team Card	.25
---	Bernie Brewer/Mascot	.25
---	Post-season Rally	.25
---	$50 travel coupon	.25

1985 CBS Radio Game of the Week

To promote its Game of the Week radio broadcasts, CBS issued a six-card set picturing network announcers, including Hall of Famer Johnny Bench. The cards, standard 2-1/2" x 3-1/2" format, were sent to CBS affiliate stations only. Fronts of the full-color cards picture the announcers in CBS Radio Sports baseball-style uniforms.

		NM/M
Complete Set (6):		55.00
Common Player:		3.00
(1)	Johnny Bench	35.00
(2)	Brent Musburger	15.00
(3)	Lindsey Nelson	7.50
(4)	John Rooney	3.00
(5)	Dick Stockton	4.50
(6)	Bill White	7.50

1986 CBS Radio Game of the Week

For the second consecutive year, CBS Radio Sports issued a five-card set featuring announcers used by the network for the Game of the Week and post-season broadcasts. The cards, packaged in a custom-designed wax wrapper,

were sent to CBS radio affiliates as a promotion. The color cards measure 2-1/2" x 3-1/2".

		NM/M
Complete Set (5):		35.00
Common Player:		3.00
(1)	Sparky Anderson	15.00
(2)	Jack Buck	10.00
(3)	Howard David	3.00
(4)	Ernie Harwell	10.00
(5)	Ted Robinson	3.00

1987 Champion Phillies

This four card set is interesting in that the players are not identified on the card fronts or backs. The full-color cards, which measure 2-3/4"x 4-5/16", were produced by the Champion Spark Plug Co. as part of a contest held at participating Big A, Car Quest and Pep Boys auto parts stores. Entrants were advised to return the scratch-off coupon portion of the card for a chance to win a Blackbird Racer. Each card contains a scratch-off portion which may have contained an instant prize. Each card can be found with either a Big A, Car Quest or Pep Boys logo in the lower left corner on the card front. The contest was also sponsored in part by the Philadelphia Phillies and radio station WIP.

		NM/M
Complete Set (4):		15.00
Common Player:		1.00
(1)	Von Hayes (Glove on knee.)	1.00
(2)	Steve Jeltz (#30 on uniform.)	1.00
(3)	Juan Samuel (Laying on base.)	1.00
(4)	Mike Schmidt (Making throw.)	12.00

1981 Champions of American Sport

From June 1981, through June 1982, Phillip Morris and Miller Beer sponsored a traveling exhibition of sporting art and artifacts from The National Portrait Gallery and the Smithsonian Institution. In conjunction with the exhibitions in Washington, D.C., Chicago, Los Angeles and New York, an 18-card souvenir set was issued featuring many of the top athletes featured in the exhibits. The set was released in the

form of an 8" x 11" eight-page booklet. Inside were two sheets of nine cards each. The perforated cards could be separated into individual cards of 2-1/2" x 3-3/4" dimensions. Fronts featured colored photos or artwork, backs had quotes about the athlete and stats. The unnumbered cards are checklisted here alphabetically.

		NM/M
Complete Set, Booklet:		60.00
Complete Set, Singles (18):		40.00
Common Player:		2.00
(1)	Muhammad Ali	6.00
(2)	Arthur Ashe	2.00
(3)	Peggy Fleming	2.00
(4)	A.J. Foyt	2.00
(5)	Eric Heiden	2.00
(6)	Bobby Hull	4.00
(7)	Sandy Koufax	6.00
(8)	Joe Louis	3.00
(9)	Bob Mathias	2.00
(10)	Willie Mays	6.00
(11)	Joe Namath	5.00
(12)	Jack Nicklaus	5.00
(13)	Knute Rockne	2.00
(14)	Bill Russell	5.00
(15)	Jim Ryun	2.00
(16)	Willie Shoemaker	2.00
(17)	Casey Stengel	2.00
(18)	Johnny Unitas	2.00

1988 Chef Boyardee

This uncut sheet features 12 each American and National League players. Color player portraits are printed beneath a red, white and blue "1988 1st Annual Collector's Edition" header. The player name, team and position appear beneath his photo. Card backs are printed in blue on red and include biographical information, stats and career highlights. The set was produced by American Home Food Products for distribution via a mail-in offer involving proofs of purchase from the company's Chef Boyardee products. Photos, licensed only by the players' union, have had uniform logos airbrushed off.

		NM/M
Complete Set, Sheet:		6.00
Complete Set, Singles (24):		6.00
Common Player:		.10
1	Mark McGwire	1.00
2	Eric Davis	.10
3	Jack Morris	.10
4	George Bell	.10
5	Ozzie Smith	.60
6	Tony Gwynn	.60
7	Cal Ripken, Jr.	1.50
8	Todd Worrell	.10

9	Larry Parrish	.10
10	Gary Carter	.50
11	Ryne Sandberg	.60
12	Keith Hernandez	.10
13	Kirby Puckett	.60
14	Mike Schmidt	.75
15	Frank Viola	.10
16	Don Mattingly	.75
17	Dale Murphy	.25
18a	Andre Dawson	
	(1987 team is Expos)	.25
18b	Andre Dawson	
	(1987 team is Cubs)	.25
19	Mike Scott	.10
20	Rickey Henderson	.50
21	Jim Rice	.25
22	Wade Boggs	.60
23	Roger Clemens	.75
24	Fernando Valenzuela	.10

1996 Chevrolet/ Geo Pirates Team Sheet

Western Pennsylvania Chevy/Geo dealers sponsored this issue of a team card set given away at the May 12 game vs. the Giants. The individual 2-1/4" x 3-1/4" cards are perforated for removal from the sheet. Individual cards have a color player photo at center with team name and '96 logo at top in a red stripe and the player name and Chev logo at bottom in an orange stripe. Backs are in black-and-white. The cards are checklisted here in alphabetical order.

		NM/M
Complete Set, Uncut Sheet:		9.00
Complete Set, Singles (30):		7.00
Common Player:		.25
(1)	Jay Bell	.25
(2)	Cam Bonifay	.25
(3)	Jacob Brumfield	.25
(4)	Jason Christiansen	.25
(5)	Dave Clark	.25
(6)	Steve Cooke	.25
(7)	Francisco Cordova	.25
(8)	Danny Darwin	.25
(9)	John Ericks	.25
(10)	Carlos Garcia	.25
(11)	Lee Hancock	.25
(12)	Charlie Hayes	.25
(13)	Mark Johnson	.25
(14)	Jason Kendall	.75
(15)	Jim Leyland	.25
(16)	Jeff King	.25
(17)	Mike Kingery	.25
(18)	Nelson Liriano	.25
(19)	Jon Lieber	.25
(20)	Al Martin	.25
(21)	Orlando Merced	.25
(22)	Dan Miceli	.25
(23)	Denny Neagle	.25
(24)	Keith Osik	.25
(25)	Steve Parris	.25
(26)	Dan Plesac	.25
(27)	Zane Smith	.25
(28)	Paul Wagner	.25
(29)	John Wehner	.25
(30)	Pirate Parrot/Mascot	.25

1992 Chevron Giants Hall of Fame Pins

This series of card/pin combinations was distributed by Chevron gas stations honoring San Francisco Giants enshrined in baseball's Hall of Fame. Fronts of the 2-1/2" x 5" cards have a color player photo in an oval frame with an orange border. The player name and team logo are in a large white strip at bottom. Black-and-white backs have a

---

Willie Mays

small player portrait photo, some personal data, career highlights and pictures of the pins in the set. An enameled pin, about 1-1/8" x 1-1/4", with a representation of the player in action, is attached at the bottom of the card.

		NM/M
Complete Set (3):		15.00
Common Player:		4.00
24	Willie Mays	7.50
36	Gaylord Perry	4.00
44	Willie McCovey	4.00

2004 Chevron Clean Outta' Here

This premium set was regionally marketed with customers receiving a one-card pack with each $8 fuel purchase. Fronts have game-action photos and a Chevron "Clean Outta' Here" logo. Red, white and blue backs have stats, player data and career highlights. Printed on thin cardboard, the cards were produced by Upper Deck.

		NM/M
Complete Set (12):		3.00
Common Player:		.25
1	Andruw Jones	.50
2	Hank Blalock	.35
3	Jeff Bagwell	.50
4	Vladimir Guerrero	.50
5	Shawn Green	.35
6	Mike Lowell	.25
7	Aubrey Huff	.25
8	Richie Sexson	.25
9	Brian Giles	.25
10	Bret Boone	.25
11	A.J. Pierzynski	.25
12	Eric Chavez	.25

1985 Chicago Cubs Playing Cards

A regular 52-card deck plus two jokers comprise this set produced by long-time Cubs broadcaster Jack Brickhouse, whose photo and trademark phrase "Hey Hey!" are featured on the back of each card. Card fronts have a black-and-white photo with player(s) names and a date beneath. Traditional suit and value marking of a playing card deck are included in the corners of the 2-1/2" x 3-1/2"

---

round-cornered cards. The cards are arranged in roughly chronological order.

		NM/M
Complete Set (54):		10.00
Common Player:		.25
AH	Jack Brickhouse	.25
2H	1876 Champions (Team composite photo.)	.25
3H	Cap Anson	.25
4H	Joe Tinker, Johnny Evers, Frank Chance, Harry Steinfeldt	2.00
5H	Ed Reulbach	.25
6H	Mordecai Brown	.25
7H	Jim Vaughn	.25
8H	Joe McCarthy	.25
9H	Jimmy Cooney	.25
10H	Rogers Hornsby	.50
JH	Hack Wilson	.25
QH	"Homers Row" (Hack Wilson, Babe Ruth, Lou Gehrig)	.50
KH	Babe Ruth ("Called the Shot")	4.00
AC	Lon Warneke	.25
2C	Augie Galan	.25
3C	1935 Pennant Winning Cubs (Team photo.)	.25
4C	Dizzy Dean	.50
5C	Gabby Hartnett	.25
6C	Billy Herman	.25
7C	Charlie Root	.25
8C	Charlie Grimm	.25
9C	Andy Pafko	.25
10C	Stan Hack	.25
JC	Phil Cavarretta	.25
QC	National League Champs 1945 (Team photo.)	.25
KC	Bill Nicholson	.25
KD	Hank Sauer	.25
QD	Ernie Banks	4.00
JD	Sam Jones	.25
10D	Dale Long	.25
9D	Lou Boudreau	.30
8D	Don Cardwell	.25
7D	Ken Hubbs	.50
6D	Billy Williams	.30
5D	1969 Cubs - The Team That Almost Made It (Composite photo.)	.25
4D	Ken Holtzman	.25
3D	Ron Santo	.30
2D	Fergie Jenkins	.40
AD	Burt Hooten (Hooton)	.25
KS	Milt Pappas	.25
QS	Rick Reuschel	.25
JS	Bill Madlock	.25
10S	Dallas Green	.25
9S	Jody Davis	.25
8S	Rick Sutcliffe	.25
7S	Jim Frey	.25
6S	Ryne Sandberg	4.00
5S	Eastern Division Champs 1984 (Team photo.)	.25
4S	Bob Dernier	.25
3S	Gary Matthews	.25
2S	Keith Moreland	.25
AS	Leon Durham	.25
Joker	Ron Cey	.25
Joker	Hey Hey! and Holy Cow! (Jack Brickhouse, Harry Caray.)	.25

1988 Chicago Cubs Fire Safety

Vance Law
Infielder

This set of four oversize (approximately 3-7/8" x 5-1/2") cards was produced on a single perforated sheet for distribution to fans as part of a U.S. Forest Service fire prevention campaign. Card fronts feature color player photos framed with vertical blue and pink borders and the player's name in light blue at bottom. Team and Smokey logos flank the name while the team name is printed in red above the photo. Backs have a bit of player biography and a large cartoon fire safety message.

		NM/M
Complete Set (4):		7.00
Common Card:		1.00
1	Vance Law (With Smokey.)	2.00
2	Vance Law/Fielding	2.00
3	Vance Law/Btg	2.00
4	Smokey Bear	1.00

1992 Chicago White Sox 1917 Team Issue Reprints

FRED McMULLEN
THIRD BASE

Card dealer Greg Manning, who purchased the unique original set of 1917 White Sox team-issue cards in 1991 issued a collectors' reprint set a year later. The reprints are in 2" x 3" format, slightly larger than the originals. The cards of the banned "Black Sox" have had a black frame added around the picture and have career information and 1919 stats on back. The other cards have blank backs. A second, colorized card of Joe Jackson was added to the reprint set. The unnumbered cards are checklisted here in alphabetical order.

		NM/M
Complete Set (26):		9.00
Common Player:		.25
(1)	Joe Benz	.25
(2)	Eddie Cicotte	1.00
(3)	Eddie Collins	.25
(4)	Shano Collins	.25
(5)	Charles Comiskey	.25
(6)	Dave Danforth	.25
(7)	Red Faber	.25
(8)	Happy Felsch	.25
(9)	Chick Gandil	1.00
(10)	Kid Gleason	.25
(11)	Joe Jackson (Black-and-white.)	3.00
(12)	Joe Jackson (Colorized)	3.00
(12)	Joe Jenkins	.25
(13)	Ted Jourdan	.25
(14)	Nemo Leibold	.25
(15)	Byrd Lynn	.25
(16)	Fred McMullin	.50
(17)	Eddie Murphy	.25
(18)	Swede Risberg	.50
(19)	Pants Rowland	.25
(20)	Reb Russell	.25
(21)	Ray Schalk	.25
(22)	James Scott	.25
(23)	Buck Weaver	1.00
(24)	Lefty Williams	.50
(25)	Mellie Wolfgang	.25

2005 Chicago White Sox Carlton Fisk

This oversize (8-1/2" x 11") card was a Comiskey Park

---

stadium giveaway on August 7 when the Hall of Famer's uniform number was retired by the White Sox. Sponsored by Nike, the back of the card has personal data and career stats.

		NM/M
	Carlton Fisk	7.50

1994 Churchs Chicken Hometown Stars

Produced by Pinnacle Brands for distribution in the fried chicken restaurant chain, the cards were distributed in packs of four with the purchase of a nine-piece family meal or were sold separately for 69 cents. Each foil pack contained three regular cards and one card with gold foil instead of regular printing on the player's name and "Hometown Stars." Every fourth pack contains one of 10 "Show Stoppers" Dufex-process chase cards. In standard 2-1/2" x 3-1/2", the cards featured full-bleed front action photos with the Churchs logo at lower-left and the player's name at lower-right. "Hometown Stars" is printed vertically at top-left. Backs have a portrait photo at left, a career summary and 1993 and career stats. Because the cards were licensed by the Major League Baseball Players Association, but not Major League Baseball, both the front and the back photos on each card have had the uniform logos airbrushed away.

		NM/M
Complete Set (28):		7.00
Complete Set (Gold) (28):		15.00
Common Player:		.10
Common Player (Gold):		.25
1	Brian McRae	.10
1a	Brian McRae/Gold	.25
2	Dwight Gooden	.10
2a	Dwight Gooden/Gold	.25
3	Ruben Sierra	.10
3a	Ruben Sierra/Gold	.25
4	Greg Maddux	1.00
4a	Greg Maddux/Gold	1.50
5	Kirby Puckett	1.00
5a	Kirby Puckett/Gold	1.50
6	Jeff Bagwell	.75
6a	Jeff Bagwell/Gold	1.00
7	Cal Ripken, Jr.	1.50
7a	Cal Ripken, Jr./Gold	2.50
8	Lenny Dykstra	.10
8a	Lenny Dykstra/Gold	.25
9	Tim Salmon	.10
9a	Tim Salmon/Gold	.25
10	Matt Williams	.10
10a	Matt Williams/Gold	.25
11	Roberto Alomar	.30
11a	Roberto Alomar/Gold	.45
12	Barry Larkin	.10

12a	Barry Larkin/Gold	.25
13	Roger Clemens	1.00
13a	Roger Clemens/Gold	1.75
14	Mike Piazza	1.25
14a	Mike Piazza/Gold	2.00
15	Travis Fryman	.10
15a	Travis Fryman/Gold	.25
16	Ryne Sandberg	1.00
16a	Ryne Sandberg/Gold	1.50
17	Robin Ventura	.10
17a	Robin Ventura/Gold	.25
18	Gary Sheffield	.35
18a	Gary Sheffield/Gold	.50
19	Carlos Baerga	.25
19a	Carlos Baerga/Gold	.25
20	Jay Bell	.10
20a	Jay Bell/Gold	.25
21	Edgar Martinez	.25
21a	Edgar Martinez/Gold	.25
22	Phil Plantier	.10
22a	Phil Plantier/Gold	.25
23	Danny Tartabull	.10
23a	Danny Tartabull/Gold	.25
24	Marquis Grissom	.10
24a	Marquis Grissom/Gold	.25
25	Robin Yount	.75
25a	Robin Yount/Gold	1.00
26	Ozzie Smith	.75
26a	Ozzie Smith/Gold	1.50
27	Ivan Rodriguez	.60
27a	Ivan Rodriguez/Gold	.75
28	Dante Bichette	.10
28a	Dante Bichette/Gold	.25

Show Stoppers

Ten of baseball's top home-run hitters are featured in this insert set. Found approximately once every four packs in the four-card packs distributed by the fried chicken chain, the cards were produced by Pinnacle Brands using its foil-printing Dufex process. A player action photo is depicted inside a home-plate shaped frame at right. "Show Stoppers" is printed vertically at left in red and yellow tones. The background merges from green at left to purple at right, with the player's name in black in a yellow-to-red rainbow effect box beneath the photo. The Churchs logo is at bottom-left. On back is a portrait photo in a light blue box. There is a description of the player's home run prowess along with gold boxes showing his 1993 homers, slugging percentage and at bat/home run ratio. The border mirrors the front's green-to-purple effect. Because the cards are not licensed by Major League Baseball, the uniform logos have been removed from both the front and back photos.

		NM/M
Complete Set (10):		7.50
Common Player:		.50
1	Juan Gonzalez	.75
2	Barry Bonds	2.50
3	Ken Griffey Jr.	2.00
4	David Justice	.50
5	Frank Thomas	1.50
6	Fred McGriff	.50
7	Albert Belle	.50
8	Joe Carter	.50
9	Cecil Fielder	.50
10	Mickey Tettleton	.50

1998 CHW San Francisco Giants

At four special Senior Citizens Days at 3Com Park Giants home games, cards of four Hall of Famers were given away. The promotion was

willie mays

sponsored by Catholic Health-care West, whose logo and name appear at top-left on the cards' fronts. Fronts combine vintage action photos with recent portrait shots and include a facsimile autograph. Backs provide a tip for healthy living and the phone numbers of various health care providers.

		NM/M
Complete Set (4):		20.00
Common Player:		4.00
(1)	Orlando Cepeda	4.00
(2)	Juan Marichal	4.00
(3)	Willie Mays	12.00
(4)	Willie McCovey	4.00

1982 Cincinnati Reds Yearbook Cards

In 1982 the Reds began a series of yearbook inserts consisting of two nine-card sheets. The 16-3/4" x 10-7/8" sheet contains 18 perforated 2-5/8" x 3-3/4" cards. Fronts have color photos with red graphics and a white border. Backs are in black-and-white and include complete major and minor league stats. The cards are checklisted here by uniform number.

		NM/M
Complete Set, Sheet:		7.50
Complete Set, Singles (18):		6.00
Common Player:		.25
3	John McNamara	.25
5	Johnny Bench	3.00
13	Dave Concepcion	.25
16	Ron Oester	.25
21	Paul Householder	.25
22	Dan Driessen	.25
28	Cesar Cedeno	.25
29	Alex Trevino	.25
30	Clint Hurdle	.25
35	Frank Pastore	.25
36	Mario Soto	.25
38	Bruce Berenyi	.25
41	Tom Seaver	2.00
47	Tom Hume	.25
49	Joe Price	.25
51	Mike LaCoss	.25
---	Best in Baseball	.25
---	Riverfront Stadium	.25

1983 Cincinnati Reds Yearbook Cards

This 16-3/4" x 10-7/8" cardboard sheet was stapled into the Reds 1983 yearbook. The sheet contains 18 2-5/8" x 3-3/4" cards perforated for removal. Fronts have color game-action photos with red graphics. Backs are in black-and-white and in-clude complete career stats. Cards are checklisted here by uniform number.

		NM/M
Complete Set, Sheet:		6.00
Complete Set, Singles (18):		5.00
Common Player:		.25
2	Gary Redus	.25
5	Johnny Bench	3.00
7	Russ Nixon	.25
13	Dave Concepcion	.25
16	Ron Oester	.25
20	Eddie Milner	.25
21	Paul Householder	.25
22	Dan Driessen	.25
28	Charlie Puleo	.25
28	Cesar Cedeno	.25
29	Alex Trevino	.25
32	Rich Gale	.25
35	Frank Pastore	.25
36	Mario Soto	.25
38	Bruce Berenyi	.25
47	Tom Hume	.25
49	Joe Price	.25
---	Riverfront Stadium	.25

1984 Cincinnati Reds Yearbook Cards

Once again in 1984 the Reds inserted a 16-3/4" x 11" cardboard panel into their yearbook. The sheet contains 18 cards, 2-5/8" x 3-3/4", perforated for removal. Fronts have color photos with a large red frame and white borders. Backs are in black-and-white with complete major and minor league stats. Cards are checklisted here by uniform number.

		NM/M
Complete Set, Sheet:		5.00
Complete Set, Singles (18):		3.00
Common Player:		.25
2	Gary Redus	.25
9	Vern Rapp	.25
11	Dann Bilardello	.25
12	Nick Esasky	.25
13	Dave Concepcion	.25
16	Ron Oester	.25
20	Eddie Milner	.25
22	Dan Driessen	.25
24	Tony Perez	1.00
26	Duane Walker	.25
34	Bill Scherrer	.25
35	Frank Pastore	.25
36	Mario Soto	.25
38	Bruce Berenyi	.25
39	Dave Parker	.35
47	Tom Hume	.25
49	Joe Price	.25
---	Bob Howsam/ President	.25

1985 Cincinnati Reds Yearbook Cards

Once again in 1985 the Reds inserted a 16-3/4" x 11" cardboard panel into their

yearbook. The sheet contains 18 cards, 2-5/8" x 3-3/4", perforated for removal. Fronts have color photos with red and white graphics. Backs are in black-and-white with complete major and minor league stats. Cards are checklisted here alphabetically.

		NM/M
Complete Sheet:		6.00
Complete Set (18):		5.00
Common Player:		.25
(1)	Cesar Cedeno	.25
(2)	Dave Concepcion	.25
(3)	Eric Davis	.75
(4)	Nick Esasky	.25
(5)	Tom Foley	.25
(6)	John Franco	.25
(7)	Brad Gulden	.25
(8)	Wayne Krenchicki	.25
(9)	Eddie Milner	.25
(10)	Ron Oester	.25
(11)	Dave Parker	.25
(12)	Ted Power	.25
(13)	Joe Price	.25
(14)	Pete Rose	3.00
(15)	Jeff Russell	.25
(16)	Mario Soto	.25
(17)	Jay Tibbs	.25
(18)	Duane Walker	.25

2003 Cincinnati Reds Scratch-Offs

The first 10,000 fans entering the newly opened Great American Ball Park for a trio of promotional dates received a special scratch-off card. The card has a game-action borderless photo on front. At top left is the sponsor's (Klosterman or Kroger) logo, with a silver box beneath. Scratching off the box revealed whether the fan won one of 500 player-autographed balls which were given away that day. The team's 2003 logo is at bottom-right. The back has the same logos, along with a career summary and an ink-jetted serial number.

		NM/M
Complete Set (3):		4.00
Common Player:		1.00
(1)	Johnny Bench	2.00
(2)	Aaron Boone	1.00
(3)	Adam Dunn	1.50

1996 Circa

This hobby-exclusive product was limited to 2,000 sequentially numbered cases. The regular-issue set has 196 player cards, including 18 top prospects and four prospects. Circa also has a 200-card parallel set called Rave which is limited to 150 sets. Each Rave

card is sequentially numbered from 1-150. Two other insert sets were also produced - Access and Boss.

		NM/M
Complete Set (200):		15.00
Common Player:		.10
Raves: 30X		
Pack (8):		1.50
Wax Box (24):		25.00
1	Roberto Alomar	.25
2	Brady Anderson	.10
3	Rocky Coppinger **RC**	.10
4	Eddie Murray	.75
5	Mike Mussina	.35
6	Randy Myers	.10
7	Rafael Palmeiro	.65
8	Cal Ripken Jr.	2.00
9	Jose Canseco	.50
10	Roger Clemens	1.00
11	Mike Greenwell	.10
12	Tim Naehring	.10
13	John Valentin	.10
14	Mo Vaughn	.25
15	Tim Wakefield	.10
16	Jim Abbott	.10
17	Garret Anderson	.10
18	Jim Edmonds	.10
19	Darin Erstad **RC**	2.00
20	Chuck Finley	.10
21	Troy Percival	.10
22	Tim Salmon	.10
23	J.T. Snow	.10
24	Wilson Alvarez	.10
25	Harold Baines	.10
26	Ray Durham	.10
27	Alex Fernandez	.10
28	Tony Phillips	.10
29	Frank Thomas	.75
30	Robin Ventura	.10
31	Sandy Alomar Jr.	.10
32	Albert Belle	.10
33	Kenny Lofton	.10
34	Dennis Martinez	.10
35	Jose Mesa	.10
36	Charles Nagy	.10
37	Manny Ramirez	.75
37p	Manny Ramire/OPS	2.00
38	Jim Thome	.60
39	Travis Fryman	.10
40	Bob Higginson	.10
41	Melvin Nieves	.10
42	Alan Trammell	.10
43	Kevin Appier	.10
44	Johnny Damon	.30
45	Keith Lockhart	.10
46	Jeff Montgomery	.10
47	Joe Randa	.10
48	Bip Roberts	.10
49	Ricky Bones	.10
50	Jeff Cirillo	.10
51	Marc Newfield	.10
52	Dave Nilsson	.10
53	Kevin Seitzer	.10
54	Ron Coomer	.10
55	Marty Cordova	.10
56	Roberto Kelly	.10
57	Chuck Knoblauch	.10
58	Paul Molitor	.75
59	Kirby Puckett	1.00
60	Scott Stahoviak	.10
61	Wade Boggs	1.00
62	David Cone	.10
63	Cecil Fielder	.10
64	Dwight Gooden	.10
65	Derek Jeter	2.00
66	Tino Martinez	.10
67	Paul O'Neill	.10
68	Andy Pettitte	.35
69	Ruben Rivera	.10
70	Bernie Williams	.10
71	Geronimo Berroa	.10
72	Jason Giambi	.45
73	Mark McGwire	1.50
74	Terry Steinbach	.10
75	Todd Van Poppel	.10
76	Jay Buhner	.10
77	Norm Charlton	.10
78	Ken Griffey Jr.	1.25
79	Randy Johnson	.75
80	Edgar Martinez	.10
81	Alex Rodriguez	1.50
82	Paul Sorrento	.10
83	Dan Wilson	.10
84	Will Clark	.10
85	Kevin Elster	.10
86	Juan Gonzalez	.40
87	Rusty Greer	.10
88	Ken Hill	.10
89	Mark McLemore	.10
90	Dean Palmer	.10
91	Roger Pavlik	.10
92	Ivan Rodriguez	.65
93	Joe Carter	.10
94	Carlos Delgado	.35
95	Juan Guzman	.10
96	John Olerud	.10
97	Ed Sprague	.10
98	Jermaine Dye	.10
99	Tom Glavine	.30
100	Marquis Grissom	.10
101	Andruw Jones	.75
102	Chipper Jones	1.00
103	David Justice	.10
104	Ryan Klesko	.10
105	Greg Maddux	1.00
106	Fred McGriff	.10
107	John Smoltz	.10
108	Brant Brown	.10
109	Mark Grace	.10
110	Brian McRae	.10
111	Ryne Sandberg	1.00
112	Sammy Sosa	1.00
113	Steve Trachsel	.10
114	Bret Boone	.10
115	Eric Davis	.10
116	Steve Gibralter	.10
117	Barry Larkin	.10
118	Reggie Sanders	.10
119	John Smiley	.10
120	Dante Bichette	.10
121	Ellis Burks	.10
122	Vinny Castilla	.10
123	Andres Galarraga	.10
124	Larry Walker	.10
125	Eric Young	.10
126	Kevin Brown	.10
127	Greg Colbrunn	.10
128	Jeff Conine	.10
129	Charles Johnson	.10
130	Al Leiter	.10
131	Gary Sheffield	.50
132	Devon White	.10
133	Jeff Bagwell	.75
134	Derek Bell	.10
135	Craig Biggio	.10
136	Doug Drabek	.10
137	Brian Hunter	.10
138	Darryl Kile	.10
139	Shane Reynolds	.10
140	Brett Butler	.10
141	Eric Karros	.10
142	Ramon Martinez	.10
143	Raul Mondesi	.10
144	Hideo Nomo	.40
145	Chan Ho Park	.10
146	Mike Piazza	1.25
147	Moises Alou	.10
148	Yamil Benitez	.10
149	Mark Grudzielanek	.10
150	Pedro Martinez	.75
151	Henry Rodriguez	.10
152	David Segui	.10
153	Rondell White	.10
154	Carlos Baerga	.10
155	John Franco	.10
156	Bernard Gilkey	.10
157	Todd Hundley	.10
158	Jason Isringhausen	.10
159	Lance Johnson	.10
160	Alex Ochoa	.10
161	Rey Ordonez	.10
162	Paul Wilson	.10
163	Ron Blazier	.10
164	Ricky Bottalico	.10
165	Jim Eisenreich	.10
166	Pete Incaviglia	.10
167	Mickey Morandini	.10
168	Ricky Otero	.10
169	Curt Schilling	.25
170	Jay Bell	.10
171	Charlie Hayes	.10
172	Jason Kendall	.10
173	Jeff King	.10
174	Al Martin	.10
175	Alan Benes	.10
176	Royce Clayton	.10
177	Brian Jordan	.10
178	Ray Lankford	.10
179	John Mabry	.10
180	Willie McGee	.10
181	Ozzie Smith	1.00
182	Todd Stottlemyre	.10
183	Andy Ashby	.10
184	Ken Caminiti	.10
185	Steve Finley	.10
186	Tony Gwynn	1.00
187	Rickey Henderson	.75
188	Wally Joyner	.10
189	Fernando Valenzuela	.10
190	Greg Vaughn	.10
191	Rod Beck	.10
192	Barry Bonds	2.00
193	Shawon Dunston	.10
194	Chris Singleton	.10
195	Robby Thompson	.10
196	Matt Williams	.10
197	Checklist (Barry Bonds)	.75
198	Checklist (Ken Griffey Jr.)	.65
199	Checklist (Cal Ripken Jr.)	.75
200	Checklist (Frank Thomas)	.40

Rave

Rainbow metallic foil highlights on front and a serial number on back from within an edition of 150 of each card differentiate this parallel issue from the Circa base cards. Announced insertion rate for Raves was one per 60 packs.

	NM/M
Common Player:	2.00
Stars:	30X

Access

This 1996 Fleer Circa insert set highlights 30 players on a three-panel foldout design that includes multiple photographs, personal information and statistics. The cards were seeded about one every 12 packs.

		NM/M
Complete Set (30):		50.00
Common Player:		.60
1	Cal Ripken Jr.	6.00
2	Mo Vaughn	.60
3	Tim Salmon	.75
4	Frank Thomas	2.00
5	Albert Belle	.75
6	Kenny Lofton	.60
7	Manny Ramirez	2.00
8	Paul Molitor	2.00
9	Kirby Puckett	3.00
10	Paul O'Neill	.60
11	Mark McGwire	5.00
12	Ken Griffey Jr.	4.00
13	Randy Johnson	2.00
14	Greg Maddux	3.00
15	John Smoltz	.60
16	Sammy Sosa	4.00
17	Barry Larkin	.60
18	Gary Sheffield	1.00
19	Jeff Bagwell	2.00
20	Hideo Nomo	2.00
21	Mike Piazza	4.00
22	Moises Alou	.60
23	Henry Rodriguez	.60
24	Rey Ordonez	.60
25	Jay Bell	.60
26	Ozzie Smith	3.00
27	Tony Gwynn	3.00
28	Rickey Henderson	2.00
29	Barry Bonds	6.00
30	Matt Williams	.60
30p	Matt Williams/OPS	1.00

Boss

This insert set showcases the game's top stars on an embossed design. Cards were seeded one per six packs.

	NM/M
Complete Set (50):	50.00
Common Player:	.45

ABBREVIATIONS

OPS - Overprinted "Promotional Sample"

#	Player	Price
1	Roberto Alomar	1.00
2	Cal Ripken Jr.	5.00
2p	Cal Ripken Jr./OPS	3.00
3	Jose Canseco	1.50
4	Mo Vaughn	.45
5	Tim Salmon	.60
6	Frank Thomas	2.00
7	Robin Ventura	.45
8	Albert Belle	.60
9	Kenny Lofton	.45
10	Manny Ramirez	2.00
11	Dave Nilsson	.45
12	Chuck Knoblauch	.45
13	Paul Molitor	2.00
14	Kirby Puckett	3.00
15	Wade Boggs	3.00
16	Dwight Gooden	.45
17	Paul O'Neill	.45
18	Mark McGwire	4.00
19	Jay Buhner	.45
20	Ken Griffey Jr.	3.50
21	Randy Johnson	2.00
22	Will Clark	.60
23	Juan Gonzalez	2.00
24	Joe Carter	.45
25	Tom Glavine	.45
26	Ryan Klesko	.45
27	Greg Maddux	3.00
28	John Smoltz	.45
29	Ryne Sandberg	3.00
30	Sammy Sosa	3.50
31	Barry Larkin	.45
32	Reggie Sanders	.45
33	Dante Bichette	.45
34	Andres Galarraga	.45
35	Charles Johnson	.45
36	Gary Sheffield	1.50
37	Jeff Bagwell	2.00
38	Hideo Nomo	2.00
39	Mike Piazza	3.50
40	Moises Alou	.45
41	Henry Rodriguez	.45
42	Rey Ordonez	.45
43	Ricky Otero	.45
44	Jay Bell	.45
45	Royce Clayton	.45
46	Ozzie Smith	3.00
47	Tony Gwynn	3.00
48	Rickey Henderson	2.00
49	Barry Bonds	5.00
50	Matt Williams	.45

1997 Circa

Circa baseball returned for the second year in 1997, with a 400-card set, including 393 player cards and seven checklists. Cards feature action photos on a dynamic graphic arts background, and arrived in eight-card packs. The set was paralleled in a Rave insert and was accompanied by five inserts: Boss, Fast Track, Icons, Limited Access and Rave Reviews.

	NM/M
Complete Set (400):	15.00
Common Player:	.10
Pack (8):	1.00
Retail Wax Box (18):	15.00
Hobby Wax Box (36):	30.00

#	Player	Price
1	Kenny Lofton	.10
2	Ray Durham	.10
3	Mariano Rivera	.20
4	Jon Lieber	.10
5	Tim Salmon	.10
6	Mark Grudzielanek	.10
7	Neifi Perez	.10
8	Cal Ripken Jr.	3.00
9	John Olerud	.10
10	Edgar Renteria	.10
11	Jose Rosado	.10
12	Mickey Morandini	.10
13	Orlando Miller	.10
14	Ben McDonald	.10
15	Hideo Nomo	.40

ABBREVIATIONS

OPS - Overprinted "Promotional Sample"

#	Player	Price
16	Fred McGriff	.10
17	Sean Berry	.10
18	Roger Pavlik	.10
19	Aaron Sele	.10
20	Joey Hamilton	.10
21	Roger Clemens	1.25
22	Jose Herrera	.10
23	Ryne Sandberg	1.00
24	Ken Griffey Jr.	1.50
25	Barry Bonds	3.00
26	Dan Naulty	.10
27	Wade Boggs	1.00
28	Ray Lankford	.10
29	Rico Brogna	.10
30	Wally Joyner	.10
31	F.P. Santangelo	.10
32	Vinny Castilla	.10
33	Eddie Murray	.75
34	Kevin Elster	.10
35	Mike Macfarlane	.10
36	Jeff Kent	.10
37	Orlando Merced	.10
38	Jason Isringhausen	.10
39	Chad Ogea	.10
40	Greg Gagne	.10
41	Curt Lyons	.10
42	Mo Vaughn	.10
43	Rusty Greer	.10
44	Shane Reynolds	.10
45	Frank Thomas	.75
46	Chris Hoiles	.10
47	Scott Sanders	.10
48	Mark Lemke	.10
49	Fernando Vina	.10
50	Mark McGwire	2.00
51	Bernie Williams	.10
52	Bobby Higginson	.10
53	Kevin Tapani	.10
54	Rich Becker	.10
55	Felix Heredia RC	.30
56	Delino DeShields	.10
57	Rick Wilkins	.10
58	Edgardo Alfonzo	.10
59	Brett Butler	.10
60	Ed Sprague	.10
61	Joe Randa	.10
62	Ugueth Urbina	.10
63	Todd Greene	.10
64	Devon White	.10
65	Bruce Ruffin	.10
66	Mark Gardner	.10
67	Omar Vizquel	.10
68	Luis Gonzalez	.10
69	Tom Glavine	.25
70	Cal Eldred	.10
71	William Van Landingham	.10
72	Jay Buhner	.10
73	James Baldwin	.10
74	Robin Jennings	.10
75	Terry Steinbach	.10
76	Billy Taylor	.10
77	Armando Benitez	.10
78	Joe Girardi	.10
79	Jay Bell	.10
80	Damon Buford	.10
81	Deion Sanders	.15
82	Bill Haselman	.10
83	John Flaherty	.10
84	Todd Stottlemyre	.10
85	J.T. Snow	.10
86	Felipe Lira	.10
87	Steve Avery	.10
88	Trey Beamon	.10
89	Alex Gonzalez	.10
90	Mark Clark	.10
91	Shane Andrews	.10
92	Randy Myers	.10
93	Gary Gaetti	.10
94	Jeff Blauser	.10
95	Tony Batista	.10
96	Todd Worrell	.10
97	Jim Edmonds	.10
98	Eric Young	.10
99	Roberto Kelly	.10
100	Alex Rodriguez	2.00
100p	Alex Rodriguez/OPS	2.00
101	Julio Franco	.10
102	Jeff Bagwell	.75
103	Bobby Witt	.10
104	Tino Martinez	.10
105	Shannon Stewart	.10
106	Brian Banks	.10
107	Eddie Taubensee	.10
108	Terry Mulholland	.10
109	Lyle Mouton	.10
110	Jeff Conine	.10
111	Johnny Damon	.30
112	Quilvio Veras	.10
113	Wilton Guerrero	.10
114	Dmitri Young	.10
115	Garret Anderson	.10
116	Bill Pulsipher	.10
117	Jacob Brumfield	.10
118	Mike Lansing	.10
119	Jose Canseco	.50
120	Mike Bordick	.10
121	Kevin Stocker	.10
122	Frank Rodriguez	.10
123	Mike Cameron	.10
124	Tony Womack RC	.25
125	Bret Boone	.10
126	Moises Alou	.10
127	Tim Naehring	.10
128	Brant Brown	.10
129	Todd Zeile	.10
130	Dave Nilsson	.10
131	Donne Wall	.10
132	Jose Mesa	.10
133	Mark McLemore	.10
134	Mike Stanton	.10
135	Dan Wilson	.10
136	Jose Offerman	.10
137	David Justice	.10
138	Kirt Manwaring	.10
139	Raul Casanova	.10
140	Ron Coomer	.10
141	Dave Hollins	.10
142	Shawn Estes	.10
143	Darren Daulton	.10
144	Turk Wendell	.10
145	Darrin Fletcher	.10
146	Marquis Grissom	.10
147	Andy Benes	.10
148	Nomar Garciaparra	1.00
149	Andy Pettitte	.30
150	Tony Gwynn	1.00
151	Robb Nen	.10
152	Kevin Seitzer	.10
153	Ariel Prieto	.10
154	Scott Karl	.10
155	Carlos Baerga	.10
156	Wilson Alvarez	.10
157	Thomas Howard	.10
158	Kevin Appier	.10
159	Russ Davis	.10
160	Justin Thompson	.10
161	Pete Schourek	.10
162	John Burkett	.10
163	Roberto Alomar	.25
164	Darren Holmes	.10
165	Travis Miller	.10
166	Mark Langston	.10
167	Juan Guzman	.10
168	Pedro Astacio	.10
169	Mark Johnson	.10
170	Mark Leiter	.10
171	Heathcliff Slocumb	.10
172	Dante Bichette	.10
173	Brian Giles RC	1.00
174	Paul Wilson	.10
175	Eric Davis	.10
176	Charles Johnson	.10
177	Willie Greene	.10
178	Geronimo Berroa	.10
179	Mariano Duncan	.10
180	Robert Person	.10
181	David Segui	.10
182	Ozzie Guillen	.10
183	Osvaldo Fernandez	.10
184	Dean Palmer	.10
185	Bob Wickman	.10
186	Eric Karros	.10
187	Travis Fryman	.10
188	Andy Ashby	.10
189	Scott Stahoviak	.10
190	Norm Charlton	.10
191	Craig Paquette	.10
192	John Smoltz	.10
193	Orel Hershiser	.10
194	Glenallen Hill	.10
195	George Arias	.10
196	Brian Jordan	.10
197	Greg Vaughn	.10
198	Rafael Palmeiro	.60
199	Darryl Kile	.10
200	Derek Jeter	3.00
201	Jose Vizcaino	.10
202	Rick Aguilera	.10
203	Jason Schmidt	.10
204	Trot Nixon	.10
205	Tom Pagnozzi	.10
206	Mark Wohlers	.10
207	Lance Johnson	.10
208	Carlos Delgado	.40
209	Cliff Floyd	.10
210	Kent Mercker	.10
211	Matt Mieske	.10
212	Ismael Valdes	.10
213	Shawon Dunston	.10
214	Melvin Nieves	.10
215	Tony Phillips	.10
216	Scott Spiezio	.10
217	Michael Tucker	.10
218	Matt Williams	.10
219	Ricky Otero	.10
220	Kevin Ritz	.10
221	Darryl Strawberry	.10
222	Troy Percival	.10
223	Eugene Kingsale	.10
224	Julian Tavarez	.10
225	Jermaine Dye	.10
226	Jason Kendall	.10
227	Sterling Hitchcock	.10
228	Jeff Cirillo	.10
229	Roberto Hernandez	.10
230	Ricky Bottalico	.10
231	Bobby Bonilla	.10
232	Edgar Martinez	.10
233	John Valentin	.10
234	Ellis Burks	.10
235	Benito Santiago	.10
236	Terrell Wade	.10
237	Armando Reynoso	.10
238	Danny Graves	.10
239	Ken Hill	.10
240	Dennis Eckersley	.65
241	Darin Erstad	.25
242	Lee Smith	.10
243	Cecil Fielder	.10
244	Tony Clark	.10
245	Scott Erickson	.10
246	Bob Abreu	.10
247	Ruben Sierra	.10
248	Chili Davis	.10
249	Darryl Hamilton	.10
250	Albert Belle	.10
251	Todd Hollandsworth	.10
252	Terry Adams	.10
253	Rey Ordonez	.10
254	Steve Finley	.10
255	Jose Valentin	.10
256	Royce Clayton	.10
257	Sandy Alomar	.10
258	Mike Lieberthal	.10
259	Ivan Rodriguez	.65
260	Rod Beck	.10
261	Ron Karkovice	.10
262	Mark Gubicza	.10
263	Chris Holt	.10
264	Jaime Bluma	.10
265	Francisco Cordova	.10
266	Javy Lopez	.10
267	Reggie Jefferson	.10
268	Kevin Brown	.10
269	Scott Brosius	.10
270	Dwight Gooden	.10
271	Marty Cordova	.10
272	Jeff Brantley	.10
273	Joe Carter	.10
274	Todd Jones	.10
275	Sammy Sosa	1.00
276	Randy Johnson	.75
277	B.J. Surhoff	.10
278	Chan Ho Park	.10
279	Jamey Wright	.10
280	Manny Ramirez	.75
281	John Franco	.10
282	Tim Worrell	.10
283	Scott Rolen	.60
284	Reggie Sanders	.10
285	Mike Fetters	.10
286	Tim Wakefield	.10
287	Trevor Hoffman	.10
288	Donovan Osborne	.10
289	Phil Nevin	.10
290	Jermaine Allensworth	.10
291	Rocky Coppinger	.10
292	Tim Raines	.10
293	Henry Rodriguez	.10
294	Paul Sorrento	.10
295	Tom Goodwin	.10
296	Raul Mondesi	.10
297	Allen Watson	.10
298	Derek Bell	.10
299	Gary Sheffield	.45
300	Paul Molitor	.75
301	Shawn Green	.15
302	Darren Oliver	.10
303	Jack McDowell	.10
304	Denny Neagle	.10
305	Doug Drabek	.10
306	Mel Rojas	.10
307	Andres Galarraga	.10
308	Alex Ochoa	.10
309	Gary DiSarcina	.10
310	Ron Gant	.10
311	Gregg Jefferies	.10
312	Ruben Rivera	.10
313	Vladimir Guerrero	.75
314	Willie Adams	.10
315	Bip Roberts	.10
326	Mark Grace	.10
316	Bernard Gilkey	.10
318	Marc Newfield	.10
319	Al Leiter	.10
320	Otis Nixon	.10
321	Tom Candiotti	.10
322	Mike Stanley	.10
323	Jeff Fassero	.10
324	Billy Wagner	.10
325	Todd Walker	.10
327	Chad Curtis	.10
328	Quinton McCracken	.10
329	Will Clark	.10
330	Andruw Jones	.75
331	Robin Ventura	.10
332	Curtis Pride	.10
333	Barry Larkin	.10
334	Jimmy Key	.10
335	David Wells	.10
336	Mike Holtz	.10
337	Paul Wagner	.10
338	Greg Maddux	1.00
339	Curt Schilling	.35
340	Steve Trachsel	.10
341	John Wetteland	.10
342	Rickey Henderson	.75
343	Ernie Young	.10
344	Harold Baines	.10
345	Bobby Jones	.10
346	Jeff D'Amico	.10
347	John Mabry	.10
348	Pedro Martinez	.75
349	Mark Lewis	.10
350	Dan Miceli	.10
351	Chuck Knoblauch	.10
352	John Smiley	.10
353	Brady Anderson	.10
354	Jim Leyritz	.10
355	Al Martin	.10
356	Pat Hentgen	.10
357	Mike Piazza	1.50
358	Charles Nagy	.10
359	Luis Castillo	.10
360	Paul O'Neill	.10
361	Steve Reed	.10
362	Tom Gordon	.10
363	Craig Biggio	.10
364	Jeff Montgomery	.10
365	Jamie Moyer	.10
366	Ryan Klesko	.10
367	Bobby Estalella	.10
368	Jason Giambi	.50
369	Brian Hunter	.10
370	Ramon Martinez	.10
371	Carlos Garcia	.10
372	Hal Morris	.10
373	Juan Gonzalez	.40
374	Brian McRae	.10
375	Mike Mussina	.40
376	John Ericks	.10
377	Larry Walker	.10
378	Chris Gomez	.10
379	John Jaha	.10
380	Rondell White	.10
381	Chipper Jones	1.00
382	David Cone	.10
383	Alan Benes	.10
384	Troy O'Leary	.10
385	Ken Caminiti	.10
386	Jeff King	.10
387	Mike Hampton	.10
388	Jaime Navarro	.10
389	Brad Radke	.10
390	Joey Cora	.10
391	Jim Thome	.60
392	Alex Fernandez	.10
393	Chuck Finley	.10
394	Andruw Jones Checklist	.35
395	Ken Griffey Jr. Checklist	.60
396	Frank Thomas Checklist	.35
397	Alex Rodriguez Checklist	.75
398	Cal Ripken Jr. Checklist	1.00
399	Mike Piazza Checklist	.60
400	Greg Maddux Checklist	.45

Rave

In its second year, Circa Rave parallel inserts were limited to inclusion only in hobby packs at the stated rate of one card per "30 to 40" packs. Raves are distinguished from regular-edition Circa cards by the use of purple metallic foil for the brand name and player identification on front. Rave backs carry a silver-foil serial number detailing its position within a production of 150 for each card.

	NM/M
Common Player:	3.00
Stars/Rookies:	10-15X

Boss

Boss was Circa's most common insert series. Twenty embossed cards were seeded one per six packs, displaying some of baseball's best players. A Super Boss parallel insert features metallic-foil background and graphics on front, and is inserted at a rate of one per 36 packs.

	NM/M
Complete Set (20):	10.00
Common Player:	.15
Super Boss:	2X
1 Jeff Bagwell	.60

#	Player	Price
2	Albert Belle	.15
3	Barry Bonds	2.00
4	Ken Caminiti	.15
5	Juan Gonzalez	.30
6	Ken Griffey Jr.	.75
7	Tony Gwynn	.75
8	Derek Jeter	2.00
9	Andruw Jones	.60
10	Chipper Jones	.75
11	Greg Maddux	.75
12	Mark McGwire	1.50
13	Mike Piazza	1.00
14	Manny Ramirez	.60
15	Cal Ripken Jr.	2.00
16	Alex Rodriguez	1.50
17	John Smoltz	.15
18	Frank Thomas	.60
19	Mo Vaughn	.15
20	Bernie Williams	.15

Emerald Autograph Redemption Cards

These box-topper cards were a hobby exclusive redeemable until May 31, 1998, for autographed special cards of six young stars. Fronts have a green-foil enhanced player action photo. Backs provide details of the redemption program.

	NM/M
Complete Set (6):	6.50
Common Player:	.50
(1) Darin Erstad	1.25
(2) Todd Hollandsworth	.50
(3) Alex Ochoa	.50
(4) Alex Rodriguez	6.00
(5) Scott Rolen	1.50
(6) Todd Walker	.50

Emerald Autographs

Special green-foil enhanced cards of six top young stars were available via a mail-in redemption. The cards feature authentic player signatures on front and an embossed authentication seal. Backs are identical to the regular card of each featured player.

	NM/M
Complete Set (6):	100.00
Common Player:	7.50
100 Alex Rodriguez	75.00
241 Darin Erstad	9.00
251 Todd Hollandsworth	6.00
283 Scott Rolen	12.00
308 Alex Ochoa	6.00
325 Todd Walker	6.00

Fast Track

Fast Track highlights 10 top rookies and young stars on a flocked background simulating grass. Cards were inserted every 24 packs.

	NM/M
Complete Set (10):	12.00
Common Player:	.50

FAST TRACK — SCOTT ROLEN

1	Vladimir Guerrero	1.50
2	Todd Hollandsworth	.50
3	Derek Jeter	4.00
4	Andruw Jones	1.50
5	Chipper Jones	2.50
6	Andy Pettitte	1.00
7	Mariano Rivera	.75
8	Alex Rodriguez	3.00
9	Scott Rolen	1.25
10	Todd Walker	.50

Icons

mike piazza

Twelve of baseball's top sluggers were displayed on 100-percent holofoil cards in Icons. Icons were found at a rate of one per 36 packs.

		NM/M
Complete Set (12):		25.00
Common Player:		.50
1	Juan Gonzalez	.75
2	Ken Griffey Jr.	3.00
3	Tony Gwynn	2.00
4	Derek Jeter	5.00
5	Chipper Jones	2.00
6	Greg Maddux	2.00
7	Mark McGwire	4.00
8	Mike Piazza	3.00
9	Cal Ripken Jr.	5.00
10	Alex Rodriguez	4.00
11	Frank Thomas	1.50
12	Matt Williams	.50

Limited Access

Limited Access was a retail-only insert found every 18 packs. Cards feature an in-depth, statistical analysis including the player's favorite pitcher to hit and each pitcher's least favorite hitter to face. Limited Access is formatted as a die-cut, bi-fold design resembling a book.

		NM/M
Complete Set (15):		30.00
Common Player:		1.25
1	Jeff Bagwell	2.00
2	Albert Belle	1.25
3	Barry Bonds	5.00
4	Juan Gonzalez	1.50
5	Ken Griffey Jr.	3.25
6	Tony Gwynn	2.50

7	Derek Jeter	5.00
8	Chipper Jones	2.50
9	Greg Maddux	2.50
10	Mark McGwire	4.00
11	Mike Piazza	3.50
12	Cal Ripken Jr.	5.00
13	Alex Rodriguez	4.00
14	Frank Thomas	2.00
15	Mo Vaughn	1.25

Rave Reviews

Juan gonzalez

Hitters that continually put up great numbers were selected for Rave Reviews. The insert was found every 288 packs and was printed on 100-percent holofoil.

		NM/M
Complete Set (12):		75.00
Common Player:		3.00
1	Albert Belle	3.00
2	Barry Bonds	12.00
3	Juan Gonzalez	3.00
4	Ken Griffey Jr.	7.50
5	Tony Gwynn	6.00
6	Greg Maddux	6.00
7	Mark McGwire	9.00
8	Eddie Murray	4.00
9	Mike Piazza	7.50
10	Cal Ripken Jr.	12.00
11	Alex Rodriguez	9.00
12	Frank Thomas	4.50

1998 Circa Thunder

Circa Thunder was issued as one series of 300 cards, sold in packs of eight for $1.59. The set marked Sky-Box's brand transition from Circa to Thunder so the cards are labeled with both names. Inserts include: Rave and Super Rave parallels, Boss, Fast Track, Quick Strike, Limited Access, Rave Review and Thunder Boomers.

		NM/M
Complete Set (300):		10.00
Common Player:		.10
Pack (8):		1.00
Wax Box (36):		20.00
1	Ben Grieve	.10
2	Derek Jeter	2.50
3	Alex Rodriguez	2.00
4	Paul Molitor	.75
5	Nomar Garciaparra	1.00
6	Fred McGriff	.10
7	Kenny Lofton	.10
8a	Cal Ripken Jr.	2.50
8b	Marquis Grissom (Should be #280.)	.10
8s	Cal Ripken Jr./OPS	2.50
9	Matt Williams	.10
10	Chipper Jones	1.00
11	Barry Larkin	.10
12	Steve Finley	.10
13	Billy Wagner	.10
14	Rico Brogna	.10
15	Tim Salmon	.10
16	Hideo Nomo	.40
17	Tony Clark	.10
18	Jason Kendall	.10
19	Juan Gonzalez	.40

20	Jeromy Burnitz	.10
21	Roger Clemens	1.25
22	Mark Grace	.10
23	Robin Ventura	.10
24	Manny Ramirez	.75
25	Mark McGwire	2.00
26	Gary Sheffield	.50
27	Vladimir Guerrero	.75
28	Butch Huskey	.10
29	Cecil Fielder	.10
30	Roderick Myers	.10
31	Greg Maddux	1.00
32	Bill Mueller	.10
33	Larry Walker	.10
34	Henry Rodriguez	.10
35	Mike Mussina	.35
36	Ricky Ledee	.10
37	Bobby Bonilla	.10
38	Curt Schilling	.35
39	Luis Gonzalez	.10
40	Troy Percival	.10
41	Eric Milton	.10
42	Mo Vaughn	.35
43	Raul Mondesi	.10
44	Kenny Rogers	.10
45	Frank Thomas	.75
46	Jose Canseco	.10
47	Tom Glavine	.35
48	Rich Butler RC	.10
49	Jay Buhner	.10
50	Jose Cruz Jr.	.10
51	Bernie Williams	.10
52	Doug Glanville	.10
53	Travis Fryman	.10
54	Rey Ordonez	.10
55	Jeff Conine	.10
56	Trevor Hoffman	.10
57	Kirk Rueter	.10
58	Ron Gant	.10
59	Carl Everett	.10
60	Joe Carter	.10
61	Livan Hernandez	.10
62	John Jaha	.10
63	Ivan Rodriguez	.65
64	Willie Blair	.10
65	Todd Helton	.65
66	Kevin Young	.10
67	Mike Caruso	.10
68	Steve Trachsel	.10
69	Marty Cordova	.10
70	Alex Fernandez	.10
71	Eric Karros	.10
72	Reggie Sanders	.10
73	Russ Davis	.10
74	Roberto Hernandez	.10
75	Barry Bonds	2.50
76	Alex Gonzalez	.10
77	Roberto Alomar	.25
78	Troy O'Leary	.10
79	Bernard Gilkey	.10
80	Ismael Valdes	.10
81	Travis Lee	.10
82	Brant Brown	.10
83	Gary DiSarcina	.10
84	Joe Randa	.10
85	Jaret Wright	.10
86	Quilvio Veras	.10
87	Rickey Henderson	.75
88	Randall Simon	.10
89	Mariano Rivera	.25
90	Ugueth Urbina	.10
91	Fernando Vina	.10
92	Alan Benes	.10
93	Dante Bichette	.10
94	Karim Garcia	.10
95	A.J. Hinch	.10
96	Shane Reynolds	.10
97	Kevin Stocker	.10
98	John Wetteland	.10
99	Terry Steinbach	.10
100	Ken Griffey Jr.	1.50
101	Mike Cameron	.10
102	Damion Easley	.10
103	Randy Myers	.10
104	Jason Schmidt	.10
105	Jeff King	.10
106	Gregg Jefferies	.10
107	Sean Casey	.15
108	Mark Kotsay	.10
109	Brad Fullmer	.10
110	Wilson Alvarez	.10
111	Sandy Alomar Jr.	.10
112	Walt Weiss	.10
113	Doug Jones	.10
114	Andy Benes	.10
115	Paul O'Neill	.10
116	Dennis Eckersley	.65
117	Todd Greene	.10
118	Bobby Jones	.10
119	Darrin Fletcher	.10
120	Eric Young	.10
121	Jeffrey Hammonds	.10
122	Mickey Morandini	.10
123	Chuck Knoblauch	.10
124	Moises Alou	.10
125	Miguel Tejada	.15
126	Brian Anderson	.10
127	Edgar Renteria	.10
128	Mike Lansing	.10
129	Quinton McCracken	.10
130	Ray Lankford	.10
131	Andy Ashby	.10
132	Kelvim Escobar	.10
133	Mike Lowell RC	.40
134	Randy Johnson	.75
135	Andres Galarraga	.10
136	Armando Benitez	.10
137	Rusty Greer	.10

138	Jose Guillen	.10
139	Paul Konerko	.15
140	Edgardo Alfonzo	.10
141	Jim Leyritz	.10
142	Mark Clark	.10
143	Brian Johnson	.10
144	Scott Rolen	.60
145	David Cone	.10
146	Jeff Shaw	.10
147	Shannon Stewart	.10
148	Brian Hunter	.10
149	Garret Anderson	.10
150	Jeff Bagwell	.75
151	James Baldwin	.10
152	Devon White	.10
153	Jim Thome	.60
154	Wally Joyner	.10
155	Mark Wohlers	.10
156	Jeff Cirillo	.10
157	Jason Giambi	.60
158	Royce Clayton	.10
159	Dennis Reyes	.10
160	Raul Casanova	.10
161	Pedro Astacio	.10
162	Todd Dunwoody	.10
163	Sammy Sosa	1.00
164	Todd Hundley	.10
165	Wade Boggs	1.00
166	Robb Nen	.10
167	Dan Wilson	.10
168	Hideki Irabu	.10
169	B.J. Surhoff	.10
170	Carlos Delgado	.40
171	Fernando Tatis	.10
172	Bob Abreu	.15
173	David Ortiz	.50
174	Tony Womack	.10
175	Magglio Ordonez RC	1.00
176	Aaron Boone	.10
177	Brian Giles	.10
178	Kevin Appier	.10
179	Chuck Finley	.10
180	Brian Rose	.10
181	Ryan Klesko	.10
182	Mike Stanley	.10
183	Dave Nilsson	.10
184	Carlos Perez	.10
185	Jeff Blauser	.10
186	Richard Hidalgo	.10
187	Charles Johnson	.10
188	Vinny Castilla	.10
189	Joey Hamilton	.10
190	Bubba Trammell	.10
191	Eli Marrero	.10
192	Scott Erickson	.10
193	Pat Hentgen	.10
194	Jorge Fabregas	.10
195	Tino Martinez	.10
196	Bobby Higginson	.10
197	Dave Hollins	.10
198	Rolando Arrojo RC	.25
199	Joey Cora	.10
200	Mike Piazza	1.50
201	Reggie Jefferson	.10
202	John Smoltz	.10
203	Bobby Smith	.10
204	Tom Goodwin	.10
205	Omar Vizquel	.10
206	John Olerud	.10
207	Matt Stairs	.10
208	Bobby Estalella	.10
209	Miguel Cairo	.10
210	Shawn Green	.20
211	Jon Nunnally	.10
212	Al Leiter	.10
213	Matt Lawton	.10
214	Brady Anderson	.10
215	Jeff Kent	.10
216	Ray Durham	.10
217	Al Martin	.10
218	Jeff D'Amico	.10
219	Kevin Tapani	.10
220	Jim Edmonds	.10
221	Jose Vizcaino	.10
222	Jay Bell	.10
223	Ken Caminiti	.10
224	Craig Biggio	.10
225	Bartolo Colon	.10
226	Neifi Perez	.10
227	Delino DeShields	.10
228	Javier Lopez	.10
229	David Wells	.10
230	Brad Rigby	.10
231	John Franco	.10
232	Michael Coleman	.10
233	Edgar Martinez	.10
234	Francisco Cordova	.10
235	Johnny Damon	.30
236	Deivi Cruz	.10
237	J.T. Snow	.10
238	Enrique Wilson	.10
239	Rondell White	.10
240	Aaron Sele	.10
241	Tony Saunders	.10
242	Ricky Bottalico	.10
243	Cliff Floyd	.10
244	Chili Davis	.10
245	Brian McRae	.10
246	Brad Radke	.10
247	Chan Ho Park	.10
248	Lance Johnson	.10
249	Rafael Palmeiro	.65
250	Tony Gwynn	1.00
251	Denny Neagle	.10
252	Dean Palmer	.10
253	Jose Valentin	.10
254	Matt Morris	.10
255	Ellis Burks	.10

256	Jeff Suppan	.10
257	Jimmy Key	.10
258	Justin Thompson	.10
259	Brett Tomko	.10
260	Mark Grudzielanek	.10
261	Mike Hampton	.10
262	Jeff Fassero	.10
263	Charles Nagy	.10
264	Pedro Martinez	.75
265	Todd Zeile	.10
266	Will Clark	.10
267	Abraham Nunez	.10
268	Dave Martinez	.10
269	Jason Dickson	.10
270	Eric Davis	.10
271	Kevin Orie	.10
272	Derrek Lee	.50
273	Andruw Jones	.75
274	Juan Encarnacion	.10
275	Carlos Baerga	.10
276	Andy Pettitte	.35
277	Brent Brede	.10
278	Paul Sorrento	.10
279	Mike Lieberthal	.10
280	(Not issued, see #8)	
281	Darin Erstad	.25
282	Willie Greene	.10
283	Derek Bell	.10
284	Scott Spiezio	.10
285	David Segui	.10
286	Albert Belle	.10
287	Ramon Martinez	.10
288	Jeremi Gonzalez	.10
289	Shawn Estes	.10
290	Ron Coomer	.10
291	John Valentin	.10
292	Kevin Brown	.10
293	Michael Tucker	.10
294	Brian Jordan	.10
295	Darryl Kile	.10
296	David Justice	.10
297	Jose Cruz Jr. Checklist	.10
298	Alex Rodriguez Checklist	1.00
299	Ken Griffey Jr. Checklist	.75
300	Frank Thomas Checklist	.65

Rave

Javier Lopez - C

Rave parallels each card in Circa Thunder except for the four checklist cards. A special silver sparkling foil is used on the player's name and the Thunder logo on front. This 296-card set was inserted approximately one per 36 packs and sequentially numbered to 150 sets on the back.

	NM/M
Common Player:	2.00
Stars:	15X

Super Rave

Only 25 Super Rave parallel sets were printed and they were inserted approximately one per 216 packs. The set contains 296 player cards (no checklist cards). Fronts are identified by sparkling gold foil on the player's name and the Thunder logo, with sequential numbering on the back to 25.

	NM/M
Common Player:	6.00
Stars:	40X

Boss

This insert set has cards embossed with the player's last name in large letters across the top.

		NM/M
Complete Set (20):		10.00
Common Player:		.25
Inserted 1:6		
1B	Jeff Bagwell	.75

JETER — BOSS98

2B	Barry Bonds	2.00
3B	Roger Clemens	1.00
4B	Jose Cruz Jr.	.25
5B	Nomar Garciaparra	1.00
6B	Juan Gonzalez	.40
7B	Ken Griffey Jr.	1.25
8B	Tony Gwynn	1.00
9B	Derek Jeter	2.00
10B	Chipper Jones	1.00
11B	Travis Lee	.25
12B	Greg Maddux	1.00
13B	Pedro Martinez	.75
14B	Mark McGwire	1.50
15B	Mike Piazza	1.25
16B	Cal Ripken Jr.	2.00
17B	Alex Rodriguez	1.50
18B	Scott Rolen	.65
19B	Frank Thomas	.75
20B	Larry Walker	.25

Fast Track

FAST TRACK JUAN ENCARNACION — Detroit Tigers

This 10-card insert showcases some of the top young stars in baseball. Fronts picture the player over a closeup of a gold foil baseball on the left. The right side has smaller head shots of all 10 players with the featured player's head in gold foil.

		NM/M
Complete Set (10):		8.00
Common Player:		.25
Inserted 1:24		
1FT	Jose Cruz Jr.	.25
2FT	Juan Encarnacion	.25
3FT	Brad Fullmer	.25
4FT	Nomar Garciaparra	4.00
5FT	Todd Helton	2.50
6FT	Livan Hernandez	.25
7FT	Travis Lee	.25
8FT	Neifi Perez	.25
9FT	Scott Rolen	1.50
10FT	Jaret Wright	.25

Limited Access

LIMITED ACCESS

These retail-exclusive insert cards are bi-fold and die-cut with foil stamping on front. The theme of the insert was to provide an in-depth statistical scouting analysis of each player.

	NM/M
Complete Set (15):	17.50

		NM/M
Common Player:		.50
Inserted 1:18		
1LA	Jeff Bagwell	1.25
2LA	Roger Clemens	1.75
3LA	Jose Cruz Jr.	.50
4LA	Nomar Garciaparra	1.50
5LA	Juan Gonzalez	1.00
6LA	Ken Griffey Jr.	2.00
7LA	Tony Gwynn	1.50
8LA	Derek Jeter	3.00
9LA	Greg Maddux	1.50
10LA	Pedro Martinez	1.25
11LA	Mark McGwire	2.50
12LA	Mike Piazza	2.00
13LA	Alex Rodriguez	2.50
14LA	Frank Thomas	1.25
15LA	Larry Walker	.50

Quick Strike

This insert pictures players over a colorful die-cut foil-board front.

		NM/M
Complete Set (12):		20.00
Common Player:		.50
Inserted 1:36		
1QS	Jeff Bagwell	2.00
2QS	Roger Clemens	2.75
3QS	Jose Cruz Jr.	.50
4QS	Nomar Garciaparra	2.50
5QS	Ken Griffey Jr.	3.00
6QS	Greg Maddux	2.50
7QS	Pedro Martinez	2.00
8QS	Mark McGwire	4.00
9QS	Mike Piazza	3.00
10QS	Alex Rodriguez	4.00
11QS	Frank Thomas	2.00
12QS	Larry Walker	.50

Rave Reviews

Rave Reviews cards are die-cut in a horizontal design with bronze foil etching and the image of a ballfield in the background.

		NM/M
Complete Set (15):		100.00
Common Player:		2.00
Inserted 1:288		
1RR	Jeff Bagwell	5.00
2RR	Barry Bonds	15.00
3RR	Roger Clemens	7.50
4RR	Jose Cruz Jr.	2.00
5RR	Nomar Garciaparra	6.00
6RR	Juan Gonzalez	3.50
7RR	Ken Griffey Jr.	10.00
8RR	Tony Gwynn	6.00
9RR	Derek Jeter	15.00
10RR	Greg Maddux	6.00
11RR	Mark McGwire	12.50
12RR	Mike Piazza	10.00
13RR	Alex Rodriguez	12.50
14RR	Frank Thomas	5.00
15RR	Larry Walker	2.00

Thunder Boomers

Thunder Boomers feature top power hitters imposed over a see-through cloud-like plastic center with the imagery of a wooden fence with a large hole blasted through the middle of it.

		NM/M
Complete Set (12):		50.00
Common Player:		1.50
Inserted 1:96		
1TB	Jeff Bagwell	6.00
2TB	Barry Bonds	10.00
3TB	Jay Buhner	1.50
4TB	Andres Galarraga	1.50
5TB	Juan Gonzalez	3.00
6TB	Ken Griffey Jr.	7.50
7TB	Tino Martinez	1.50
8TB	Mark McGwire	9.00
9TB	Mike Piazza	7.50
10TB	Frank Thomas	6.00
11TB	Jim Thome	4.50
12TB	Larry Walker	1.50

1985 Circle K

Produced by Topps for Circle K stores, this set is titled "Baseball All Time Home Run Kings." The 2-1/2" x 3-1/2" cards are numbered on the back according to the player's position on the all-time career home run list. Joe DiMaggio, who ranked 31st, was not included in the set. Glossy card fronts generally feature a color photo, although black-and-whites were utilized for a few of the homer kings who played before 1960. Backs have blue and red print on white stock and contain the player's career batting statistics. The set was issued in a specially designed box.

		NM/M
Complete Set (33):		5.00
Common Player:		.10
1	Hank Aaron	1.25
2	Babe Ruth	2.00
3	Willie Mays	1.25
4	Frank Robinson	.15
5	Harmon Killebrew	.15
6	Mickey Mantle	2.50
7	Jimmie Foxx	.15
8	Willie McCovey	.15
9	Ted Williams	1.25
10	Ernie Banks	.30
11	Eddie Mathews	.15
12	Mel Ott	.15
13	Reggie Jackson	.60
14	Lou Gehrig	1.25
15	Stan Musial	.75
16	Willie Stargell	.15
17	Carl Yastrzemski	.25
18	Billy Williams	.15
19	Mike Schmidt	.60
20	Duke Snider	.30
21	Al Kaline	.25
22	Johnny Bench	.25
23	Frank Howard	.15
24	Orlando Cepeda	.15
25	Norm Cash	.15
26	Dave Kingman	.15
27	Rocky Colavito	.15
28	Tony Perez	.15
29	Gil Hodges	.30
30	Ralph Kiner	.15
32	Johnny Mize	.15
33	Yogi Berra	.30
34	Lee May	.15

1993 City Pride Roberto Clemente

To assist in the building of the statue of Roberto Clemente which was unveiled at Three Rivers Stadium during All-Star festivities in 1994, Pittsburgh's City Pride bakery contributed a portion of

Roberto Clemente

sales proceeds from a special run of bread loaves featuring Roberto Clemente cards. The cards came in a special plastic pouch within the bread wrapper to protect them from stains. The wrapper itself included a portrait of Clemente and details of the statue project. The 2-1/2" x 3-1/2" cards featured sepia-toned or color photos of Clemente inside black and gold borders. A color team logo appears in the lower-right corner with his name in an orange stripe at the bottom of the photo. Backs are in black-and-white and contain a narrative of Clemente's career, with one card containing his lifetime stats. The unnumbered cards are checklisted here in chronological order.

		NM/M
Complete Set (6):		6.00
Common Card:		1.50
(1)	Roberto Clemente/Btg (1934-1958, sepia photo)	1.50
(2)	Roberto Clemente/Bth (1960-1966, color photo)	1.50
(3)	Roberto Clemente/Running (1971-1972, to first base)	1.50
(4)	Roberto Clemente/Portrait (1972-1973)	1.50
(5)	Roberto Clemente (Fielding records, kneeling with one bat.)	1.50
(6)	Roberto Clemente (Batting record, kneeling with five bats.)	1.50

1993 Clark Candy Reggie Jackson

The reintroduction of the "Reggie" candy bar by the Clark company was accompanied by a three-card set highlighting his career produced by Upper Deck. One card was found in each candy bar. Cards have a color photo of Jackson on front, on which uniform logos have been removed. Backs have an equipment montage and a paragraph about the slugger. Clark and UD logos appear on front, with an UD logo on back. A limited number (200) of autographed cards were randomly inserted.

	NM/M
Complete Set (3):	3.00
Common Player:	1.00
Autographed Card:	75.00

		NM/M
C1	Reggie Jackson (Hall of Fame, 1993)	1.00
C2	Reggie Jackson (Mr. October, 1977)	1.00
C3	Reggie Jackson (A.L. MVP, 1973)	1.00

1987 Classic Major League Baseball Game

Pete Rose

The "Classic Major League Baseball Board Game" set consists of 100 full-color cards used to play the game in which participants answer trivia questions found on the card backs. Cards measure 2-1/2" x 3-1/2" and are printed on semi-gloss stock. Backs carry the player's career stats besides the trivia questions. The game was produced by Game Time, Ltd. of Marietta, Ga., and sold for $19.95 in most retail outlets. In 1991-92 the set was selling for $200 or more, with the Bo Jackson card advertised as high as $80.

		NM/M
Complete Boxed Set:		25.00
Complete Set (100):		20.00
Common Player:		.05
1	Pete Rose	2.00
2	Len Dykstra	.05
3	Darryl Strawberry	.05
4	Keith Hernandez	.05
5	Gary Carter	.65
6	Wally Joyner	.05
7	Andres Thomas	.05
8	Pat Dodson	.05
9	Kirk Gibson	.05
10	Don Mattingly	1.00
11	Dave Winfield	.65
12	Rickey Henderson	.65
13	Dan Pasqua	.05
14	Don Baylor	.05
15	Bo Jackson	2.50
16	Pete Incaviglia	.05
17	Kevin Bass	.05
18	Barry Larkin	.05
19	Dave Magadan	.05
20	Steve Sax	.05
21	Eric Davis	.05
22	Mike Pagliarulo	.05
23	Fred Lynn	.05
24	Reggie Jackson	1.00
25	Larry Parrish	.05
26	Tony Gwynn	.75
27	Steve Garvey	.20
28	Glenn Davis	.05
29	Tim Raines	.05
30	Vince Coleman	.05
31	Willie McGee	.05
32	Ozzie Smith	.75
33	Dave Parker	.05
34	Tony Pena	.05
35	Ryne Sandberg	.75
36	Brett Butler	.05
37	Dale Murphy	.25
38	Bob Horner	.05
39	Pedro Guerrero	.05
40	Brook Jacoby	.05
41	Carlton Fisk	.65
42	Harold Baines	.05
43	Rob Deer	.05
44	Robin Yount	.65
45	Paul Molitor	.65
46	Jose Canseco	.50
47	George Brett	1.00
48	Jim Presley	.05
49	Rich Gedman	.05
50	Lance Parrish	.05
51	Eddie Murray	.65
52	Cal Ripken, Jr.	3.00
53	Kent Hrbek	.05
54	Gary Gaetti	.05
55	Kirby Puckett	.75
56	George Bell	.05
57	Tony Fernandez	.05
58	Jesse Barfield	.05
59	Jim Rice	.25
60	Wade Boggs	.75
61	Marty Barrett	.05

		NM/M
62	Mike Schmidt	1.00
63	Von Hayes	.05
64	Jeff Leonard	.05
65	Chris Brown	.05
66	Dave Smith	.05
67	Mike Krukow	.05
68	Ron Guidry	.05
69	Rob Woodward (Photo actually Pat Dodson.)	
70	Rob Murphy	.05
71	Andres Galarraga	.05
72	Dwight Gooden	.05
73	Bob Ojeda	.05
74	Sid Fernandez	.05
75	Jesse Orosco	.05
76	Roger McDowell	.05
77	John Tutor (Tudor)	.05
78	Tom Browning	.05
79	Rick Aguilera	.05
80	Lance McCullers	.05
81	Mike Scott	.05
82	Nolan Ryan	3.00
83	Bruce Hurst	.05
84	Roger Clemens	1.00
85	Oil Can Boyd	.05
86	Dave Righetti	.05
87	Dennis Rasmussen	.05
88	Bret Saberhagen (Saberhagen)	.05
89	Mark Langston	.05
90	Jack Morris	.05
91	Fernando Valenzuela	.05
92	Orel Hershiser	.05
93	Rick Honeycutt	.05
94	Jeff Reardon	.05
95	John Habyan	.05
96	Goose Gossage	.05
97	Todd Worrell	.05
98	Floyd Youmans	.05
99	Don Aase	.05
100	John Franco	.05

Travel Update (Yellow)

B.J. Surhoff

Game Time, Ltd. of Marietta, Ga., issued as an update to its Classic Baseball Board Game a 50-card set entitled "Travel Edition." Cards measure 2-1/2" x 3-1/2" in the same format as the first release, though with yellow, rather than green, borders. Numbered from 101 to 150, the "Travel Edition," besides updating player trades and showcasing rookies, offers several highlights from the 1987 season. All new trivia questions are found on the card backs. It was reported that about 50,000 of the set's 150,000 press run was mistakenly printed with green, rather than yellow backs; the green-back errors sell for a premium.

	NM/M
Complete Set (50):	15.00
Common Player:	.05
Green-backs:	1.5X
101	Mike Schmidt	.75
102	Eric Davis	.05
103	Pete Rose	1.50
104	Don Mattingly	.75
105	Wade Boggs	.60
106	Dale Murphy	.20
107	Glenn Davis	.05
108	Wally Joyner	.05
109	Bo Jackson	.15
110	Cory Snyder	.05
111	Jim Lindeman	.05
112	Kirby Puckett	.60
113	Barry Bonds	10.00
114	Roger Clemens	.75
115	Oddibe McDowell	.05
116	Bret Saberhagen	.05
117	Joe Magrane	.05
118	Scott Fletcher	.05
119	Mark McLemore	.05
120	Who Me? (Joe Niekro)	.25
121	Mark McGwire	2.00
122	Darryl Strawberry	.05
123	Mike Scott	.05

		NM/M
124	Andre Dawson	.20
125	Jose Canseco	.50
126	Kevin McReynolds	.05
127	Joe Carter	.05
128	Casey Candaele	.05
129	Matt Nokes	.05
130	Kal Daniels	.05
131	Pete Incaviglia	.05
132	Benito Santiago	.05
133	Barry Larkin	.05
134	Gary Pettis	.05
135	B.J. Surhoff	.05
136	Juan Nieves	.05
137	Jim Deshaies	.05
138	Pete O'Brien	.05
139	Kevin Seitzer	.05
140	Devon White	.05
141	Rob Deer	.05
142	Kurt Stillwell	.05
143	Edwin Correa	.05
144	Dion James	.05
145	Danny Tartabull	.05
146	Jerry Browne	.05
147	Ted Higuera	.05
148	Jack Clark	.05
149	Ruben Sierra	.05
150	Mark McGwire, Eric Davis	.60

1988 Classic Travel Update 1 (Red)

Phil Niekro

This set was produced for use with the travel edition of Game Time's Classic Baseball Board Game. Special cards in the set include a McGwire/Mattingly, an instruction card with McGwire/Canseco and three different cards featuring Phil Niekro (in different uniforms). Update I card fronts have red borders, a yellow Classic logo in the upper-left corner and a black and beige name banner beneath the photo. Backs are printed in red and pink on white and include the player name, personal info., major league records, a baseball question and space for the player autograph. Classic card series sold via hobby dealers and retail toy stores nationwide. Game Time Ltd., the set's producer, was purchased by Scoreboard of Cherry Hill, N.J. in 1988.

		NM/M
Complete Set (50):		4.00
Common Player:		.05
151	Don Mattingly, Mark McGwire	.45
152	Don Mattingly	.65
153	Mark McGwire	1.00
154	Eric Davis	.05
155	Wade Boggs	.50
156	Dale Murphy	.15
157	Andre Dawson	.15
158	Roger Clemens	.65
159	Kevin Seitzer	.05
160	Benito Santiago	.05
161	Kal Daniels	.05
162	John Kruk	.05
163	Bill Ripken	.05
164	Kirby Puckett	.50
165	Jose Canseco	.30
166	Matt Nokes	.05
167	Mike Schmidt	.60
168	Tim Raines	.05
169	Ryne Sandberg	.50
170	Dave Winfield	.40
171	Dwight Gooden	.05
172	Bret Saberhagen	.05
173	Willie McGee	.05
174	Jack Morris	.05
175	Jeff Leonard	.05
176	Cal Ripken, Jr.	1.50
177	Pete Incaviglia	.05
178	Devon White	.05
179	Nolan Ryan	1.50
180	Ruben Sierra	.05
181	Todd Worrell	.05

182	Glenn Davis	.05
183	Frank Viola	.05
184	Cory Snyder	.05
185	Tracy Jones	.05
186	Terry Steinbach	.05
187	Julio Franco	.05
188	Larry Sheets	.05
189	John Marzano	.05
190	Kevin Elster	.05
191	Vincente Palacios	.05
192	Kent Hrbek	.05
193	Eric Bell	.05
194	Kelly Downs	.05
195	Jose Lind	.05
196	Dave Stewart	.05
197	Jose Canseco, Mark McGwire	.45
198	Phil Niekro	.10
199	Phil Niekro	.10
200	Phil Niekro	.10

Update 2 (Blue)

Darryl Strawberry

This set was produced for use with the travel edition of Game Time's Classic Baseball Board Game. Fronts have blue borders, a yellow Classic logo in the upper-left corner and a black and beige name banner beneath the photo. Backs are printed in blue on white and include the player name, personal info, major league records, a baseball question and space for the player autograph. Classic card series are sold via hobby dealers and retail toy stores nationwide. Game Time Ltd., the set's producer, was purchased by Scoreboard of Cherry Hill, N.J. in 1988.

		NM/M
Complete Set (50):		4.00
Common Player:		.05
201	Dale Murphy, Eric Davis	.10
202	B.J. Surhoff	.05
203	John Kruk	.05
204	Sam Horn	.05
205	Jack Clark	.25
206	Wally Joyner	.05
207	Matt Nokes	.05
208	Bo Jackson	.10
209	Darryl Strawberry	.05
210	Ozzie Smith	.60
211	Don Mattingly	.75
212	Mark McGwire	1.50
213	Eric Davis	.05
214	Wade Boggs	.60
215	Dale Murphy	.25
216	Andre Dawson	.25
217	Roger Clemens	.75
218	Kevin Seitzer	.05
219	Benito Santiago	.05
220	Tony Gwynn	.60
221	Mike Scott	.05
222	Steve Bedrosian	.05
223	Vince Coleman	.05
224	Rick Sutcliffe	.05
225	Will Clark	.05
226	Pete Rose	1.00
227	Mike Greenwell	.05
228	Ken Caminiti	.05
229	Ellis Burks	.05
230	Dave Magadan	.05
231	Alan Trammell	.05
232	Paul Molitor	.50
233	Gary Gaetti	.05
234	Rickey Henderson	.50
235	Danny Tartabull	.05
236	Bobby Bonilla	.05
237	Mike Dunne	.05
238	Al Leiter	.05
239	John Farrell	.05
240	Joe Magrane	.05
241	Mike Henneman	.05
242	George Bell	.05
243	Gregg Jefferies	.10
244	Jay Buhner	.05
245	Todd Benzinger	.05
246	Matt Williams	.05
(247)	Don Mattingly, Mark McGwire (No card number on back.)	.50
248	George Brett	.75
249	Jimmy Key	.05
250	Mark Langston	.05

1989 Classic

David Cone

This 100-card set was released by The Score Board to accompany trivia board games. Fronts have a wide border which graduates from pink at the top to blue at the bottom. Card backs are printed in blue. The flip side includes personal information, and major league record in a boxed area. Another boxed area below the record presents five trivia questions. The lower border on back provides an autograph space. The Classic card series was sold by retail stores and hobby dealers nationwide.

		NM/M
Complete Set (100):		6.00
Common Player:		.05
1	Orel Hershiser	.05
2	Wade Boggs	.50
3	Jose Canseco	.30
4	Mark McGwire	1.00
5	Don Mattingly	.60
6	Gregg Jefferies	.05
7	Dwight Gooden	.05
8	Darryl Strawberry	.05
9	Eric Davis	.05
10	Joey Meyer	.05
11	Joe Carter	.05
12	Paul Molitor	.40
13	Mark Grace	.05
14	Kurt Stillwell	.05
15	Kirby Puckett	.50
16	Keith Miller	.05
17	Glenn Davis	.05
18	Will Clark	.05
19	Cory Snyder	.05
20	Jose Lind	.05
21	Andres Thomas	.05
22	Dave Smith	.05
23	Mike Scott	.05
24	Kevin McReynolds	.05
25	B.J. Surhoff	.05
26	Mackey Sasser	.05
27	Chad Kreuter	.05
28	Hal Morris	.05
29	Wally Joyner	.05
30	Tony Gwynn	.05
31	Kevin Mitchell	.05
32	Dave Winfield	.40
33	Billy Bean	.05
34	Steve Bedrosian	.05
35	Ron Gant	.05
36	Len Dykstra	.05
37	Andre Dawson	.25
38	Brett Butler	.05
39	Rob Deer	.05
40	Tommy John	.05
41	Gary Gaetti	.05
42	Tim Raines	.05
43	George Bell	.05
44	Dwight Evans	.05
45	Denny Martinez	.05
46	Andres Galarraga	.05
47	George Brett	.60
48	Mike Schmidt	.60
49	Dave Steib	.05
50	Rickey Henderson	.40
51	Craig Biggio	.05
52	Mark Lemke	.05
53	Chris Sabo	.05
54	Jeff Treadway	.05
55	Kent Hrbek	.05
56	Cal Ripken, Jr.	1.50
57	Tim Belcher	.05
58	Ozzie Smith	.05
59	Keith Hernandez	.05
60	Pedro Guerrero	.05
61	Greg Swindell	.05
62	Bret Saberhagen	.05
63	John Tudor	.05
64	Gary Carter	.40
65	Kevin Seitzer	.05
66	Jesse Barfield	.05
67	Luis Medina	.05
68	Walt Weiss	.05
69	Terry Steinbach	.05
70	Barry Larkin	.05
71	Pete Rose	.75
72	Luis Salazar	.05
73	Benito Santiago	.05
74	Kal Daniels	.05
75	Kevin Elster	.05
76	Rob Dibble	.05
77	Bobby Witt	.05
78	Steve Searcy	.05
79	Sandy Alomar (Photo is Roberto Alomar.)	.05
80	Chili Davis	.05
81	Alvin Davis	.05
82	Charlie Leibrandt	.05
83	Robin Yount	.40
84	Mark Carreon	.05
85	Pascual Perez	.05
86	Dennis Rasmussen	.05
87	Ernie Riles	.05
88	Melido Perez	.05
89	Doug Jones	.05
90	Dennis Eckersley	.35
91	Bob Welch	.05
92	Bob Milacki	.05
93	Jeff Robinson	.05
94	Mike Henneman	.05
95	Randy Johnson	1.00
96	Ron Jones	.05
97	Jack Armstrong	.05
98	Willie McGee	.05
99	Ryne Sandberg	.50
100	David Cone, Danny Jackson	.05

Travel Update 1 (Orange)

Roberto Alomar

Sold only as a 50-card complete set under the official name of "Travel Update I," these cards are identical in format to the 1989 Classic 100-card set with the exception that the borders are orange at the top, graduating to maroon at the bottom. Backs are maroon.

		NM/M
Complete Set (50):		5.00
Common Player:		.05
101	Gary Sheffield	.25
102	Wade Boggs	.50
103	Jose Canseco	.30
104	Mark McGwire	1.00
105	Orel Hershiser	.05
106	Don Mattingly	.60
107	Dwight Gooden	.05
108	Darryl Strawberry	.05
109	Eric Davis	.05
110	Bam Bam Meulens	.05
111	Andy Van Slyke	.05
112	Al Leiter	.05
113	Matt Nokes	.05
114	Mike Krukow	.05
115	Tony Fernandez	.05
116	Fred McGriff	.05
117	Barry Bonds	1.50
118	Gerald Perry	.05
119	Roger Clemens	.60
120	Kirk Gibson	.05
121	Greg Maddux	.50
122	Bo Jackson	.10
123	Danny Jackson	.05
124	Dale Murphy	.20
125	David Cone	.05
126	Tom Browning	.05
127	Roberto Alomar	.25
128	Alan Trammell	.05
129	Ricky Jordan	.05
130	Ramon Martinez	.05
131	Ken Griffey Jr.	3.00
132	Gregg Olson	.05
133	Carlos Quintana	.05
134	Dave West	.05
135	Cameron Drew	.05
136	Ted Higuera	.05
137	Sil Campusano	.05
138	Mark Gubicza	.05
139	Mike Boddicker	.05
140	Paul Gibson	.05
141	Jose Rijo	.05
142	John Costello	.05
143	Cecil Espy	.05
144	Frank Viola	.05
145	Erik Hanson	.05
146	Juan Samuel	.05
147	Harold Reynolds	.05
148	Joe Magrane	.05
149	Mike Greenwell	.05
150	Darryl Strawberry, Will Clark	.05

Travel Update 2 (Purple)

Jerome Walton

Numbered from 151-200, this set features rookies and traded players with their new teams. The cards are purple and gray and were sold as part of a board game with baseball trivia questions.

		NM/M
Complete Set (50):		5.00
Common Player:		.05
151	Jim Abbott	.05
152	Ellis Burks	.05
153	Mike Schmidt	.75
154	Gregg Jefferies	.05
155	Mark Grace	.05
156	Jerome Walton	.05
157	Bo Jackson	.10
158	Jack Clark	.05
159	Tom Glavine	.20
160	Eddie Murray	.45
161	John Dopson	.05
162	Ruben Sierra	.05
163	Rafael Palmeiro	.40
164	Nolan Ryan	1.50
165	Barry Larkin	.05
166	Tommy Herr	.05
167	Roberto Kelly	.05
168	Glenn Davis	.05
169	Glenn Braggs	.05
170	Juan Bell	.05
171	Todd Burns	.05
172	Derek Lilliquist	.05
173	Orel Hershiser	.05
174	John Smoltz	.05
175	Ozzie Guillen, Ellis Burks	.05
176	Kirby Puckett	.60
177	Robin Ventura	.05
178	Allan Anderson	.05
179	Steve Sax	.05
180	Will Clark	.05
181	Mike Devereaux	.05
182	Tom Gordon	.05
183	Rob Murphy	.05
184	Pete O'Brien	.05
185	Cris Carpenter	.05
186	Tom Brunansky	.05
187	Bob Boone	.05
188	Lou Whitaker	.05
189	Dwight Gooden	.05
190	Mark McGwire	1.00
191	John Smiley	.05
192	Tommy Gregg	.05
193	Ken Griffey Jr.	3.00
194	Bruce Hurst	.05
195	Greg Swindell	.05
196	Nelson Liriano	.05
197	Randy Myers	.05
198	Kevin Mitchell	.05
199	Dante Bichette	.05
200	Deion Sanders	.10

1990 Classic

Ozzie Smith

Classic baseball returned in 1990 with a 150-card set. Cards have a blue border on front, with splashes of pink. The cards were again sold as part of a baseball trivia game.

		NM/M
Complete Set (150):		4.00
Common Player:		.05
1	Nolan Ryan	1.00
2	Bo Jackson	.10
3	Gregg Olson	.05
4	Tom Gordon	.05
5	Robin Ventura	.05
6	Will Clark	.05
7	Ruben Sierra	.05
8	Mark Grace	.05
9	Luis de los Santos	.05
10	Bernie Williams	.05
11	Eric Davis	.05
12	Carney Lansford	.05
13	John Smoltz	.05
14	Gary Sheffield	.20
15	Kent Merker	.05
16	Don Mattingly	.60
17	Tony Gwynn	.50
18	Ozzie Smith	.50
19	Fred McGriff	.05
20	Ken Griffey Jr.	.65
21a	Deion Sanders ("Prime Time")	.30
21b	Deion Sanders (Deion "Prime Time" Sanders)	.15
22	Jose Canseco	.25
23	Mitch Williams	.05
24	Cal Ripken, Jr.	1.00
25	Bob Geren	.05
26	Wade Boggs	.50
27	Ryne Sandberg	.50
28	Kirby Puckett	.50
29	Mike Scott	.05
30	Dwight Smith	.05
31	Craig Worthington	.05
32	Ricky Jordan	.05
33	Darryl Strawberry	.05
34	Jerome Walton	.05
35	John Olerud	.05
36	Tom Glavine	.15
37	Rickey Henderson	.30
38	Rolando Roomes	.05
39	Mickey Tettleton	.05
40	Jim Abbott	.05
41	Dave Righetti	.05
42	Mike LaValliere	.05
43	Rob Dibble	.05
44	Pete Harnisch	.05
45	Jose Offerman	.05
46	Walt Weiss	.05
47	Mike Greenwell	.05
48	Barry Larkin	.05
49	Dave Gallagher	.05
50	Junior Felix	.05
51	Roger Clemens	.60
52	Lonnie Smith	.05
53	Jerry Browne	.05
54	Greg Briley	.05
55	Delino DeShields	.05
56	Carmelo Martinez	.05
57	Craig Biggio	.05
58	Dwight Gooden	.05
59a	Bo, Ruben, Mark (Bo Jackson, Ruben Sierra, Mark McGwire)	.25
59b	A.L. Fence Busters (Bo Jackson, Ruben Sierra, Mark McGwire)	.15
60	Greg Vaughn	.05
61	Roberto Alomar	.20
62	Steve Bedrosian	.05
63	Devon White	.05
64	Kevin Mitchell	.05
65	Marquis Grissom	.05
66	Brian Holman	.05
67	Julio Franco	.05
68	Dave West	.05
69	Harold Baines	.05
70	Eric Anthony	.05
71	Glenn Davis	.05
72	Mark Langston	.05
73	Matt Williams	.05
74	Rafael Palmeiro	.25
75	Pete Rose, Jr.	.25
76	Ramon Martinez	.05
77	Dwight Evans	.05
78	Mackey Sasser	.05
79	Mike Schooler	.05
80	Dennis Cook	.05
81	Orel Hershiser	.05
82	Barry Bonds	1.00
83	Geronimo Berroa	.05
84	George Bell	.05
85	Andre Dawson	.25
86	John Franco	.05
87a	Clark/Gwynn (Will Clark, Tony Gwynn)	.25
87b	N.L. Hit Kings (Will Clark, Tony Gwynn)	.15
88	Glenallen Hill	.05
89	Jeff Ballard	.05
90	Todd Zeile	.05
91	Frank Viola	.05
92	Ozzie Guillen	.05
93	Jeff Leonard	.05
94	Dave Smith	.05
95	Dave Parker	.05
96	Jose Gonzalez	.05
97	Dave Steib	.05
98	Charlie Hayes	.05
99	Jesse Barfield	.05
100	Joey Belle	.15
101	Jeff Reardon	.05
102	Bruce Hurst	.05
103	Luis Medina	.05
104	Mike Moore	.05
105	Vince Coleman	.05
106	Alan Trammell	.05
107	Randy Myers	.05
108	Frank Tanana	.05
109	Craig Lefferts	.05
110	John Wetteland	.05
111	Chris Gwynn	.05
112	Mark Carreon	.05
113	Von Hayes	.05
114	Doug Jones	.05
115	Andres Galarraga	.05
116	Carlton Fisk	.30
117	Paul O'Neill	.05
118	Tim Raines	.05
119	Tom Brunansky	.05
120	Andy Benes	.05
121	Mark Portugal	.05
122	Willie Randolph	.05
123	Jeff Blauser	.05
124	Don August	.05
125	Chuck Cary	.05
126	John Smiley	.05
127	Terry Mullholland	.05
128	Harold Reynolds	.05
129	Hubie Brooks	.05
130	Ben McDonald	.05
131	Kevin Ritz	.05
132	Luis Quinones	.05
133a	Bam Bam Muelens (Last name incorrect.)	.25
133b	Bam Bam Meulens (Last name correct.)	.05
134	Bill Spiers	.05
135	Andy Hawkins	.05
136	Alvin Davis	.05
137	Lee Smith	.05
138	Joe Carter	.05
139	Bret Saberhagen	.05
140	Sammy Sosa	1.00
141	Matt Nokes	.05
142	Bert Blyleven	.05
143	Bobby Bonilla	.05
144	Howard Johnson	.05
145	Joe Magrane	.05
146	Pedro Guerrero	.05
147	Robin Yount	.30
148	Dan Gladden	.05
149	Steve Sax	.05
150a	Clark/Mitchell (Will Clark, Kevin Mitchell)	.25
150b	Bay Bombers (Will Clark, Kevin Mitchell)	.25

Series 2

Juan Gonzalez

As in previous years, Classic released a 50-card second series set for use with its trivia board game. Unlike earlier update sets, the 1990 Series II set is numbered 1-50 with a "T" designation accompanying the card number. Cards measure 2-1/2" x 3-1/2" and share the format of the original 1990 Classic cards; Series III cards have pink borders with blue highlights. The cards were issued only in complete set form.

		NM/M
Complete Set (50):		3.00
Common Player:		.05
1	Gregg Jefferies	.05
2	Steve Adkins	.05
3	Sandy Alomar, Jr.	.05
4	Steve Avery	.05
5	Mike Blowers	.05
6	George Brett	.75
7	Tom Browning	.05
8	Ellis Burks	.05
9	Joe Carter	.05
10	Jerald Clark	.05
11	"Hot Corners" (Matt Williams, Will Clark)	.10
12	Pat Combs	.05
13	Scott Cooper	.05
14	Mark Davis	.05
15	Storm Davis	.05

16 Larry Walker .05
17 Brian DuBois .05
18 Len Dykstra .05
19 John Franco .05
20 Kirk Gibson .05
21 Juan Gonzalez .20
22 Tommy Greene .05
23 Kent Hrbek .05
24 Mike Huff .05
25 Bo Jackson .10
26 Nolan Knows Bo
 (Bo Jackson,
 Nolan Ryan) 1.50
27 Roberto Kelly .05
28 Mark Langston .05
29 Ray Lankford .05
30 Kevin Maas .05
31 Julio Machado .05
32 Greg Maddux .60
33 Mark McGwire 1.00
34 Paul Molitor .40
35 Hal Morris .05
36 Dale Murphy .20
37 Eddie Murray .40
38 Jaime Navarro .05
39 Dean Palmer .05
40 Derek Parks .05
41 Bobby Rose .05
42 Wally Joyner .05
43 Chris Sabo .05
44 Benito Santiago .05
45 Mike Stanton .05
46 Terry Steinbach .05
47 Dave Stewart .05
48 Greg Swindell .05
49 Jose Vizcaino .05
---- "Royal Flush"
 (Bret Saberhagen,
 Mark Davis) .05

Series 3

Scott Coolbaugh

Classic's third series of 1990 features the same format as the previous two releases. Series 3 borders are yellow with blue accents. The cards have trivia questions on back and are numbered 1T-100T. No card 51T or 57T exists. Two cards in the set are unnumbered. Like other Classic issues, the cards are designed for use with the trivia board game and were sold only as complete sets.

NM/M
Complete Set (100): 4.00
Common Player: .05
1 Ken Griffey Jr. .75
2 John Tudor .05
3 John Kruk .05
4 Mark Gardner .05
5 Scott Radinsky .05
6 John Burkett .05
7 Will Clark .05
8 Gary Carter .40
9 Ted Higuera .05
10 Dave Parker .05
11 Dante Bichette .05
12 Don Mattingly .60
13 Greg Harris .05
14 David Hollins .05
15 Matt Nokes .05
16 Kevin Tapani .05
17 Shane Mack .05
18 Randy Myers .05
19 Greg Olson .05
20 Shawn Abner .05
21 Jim Presley .05
22 Randy Johnson .40
23 Edgar Martinez .05
24 Scott Coolbaugh .05
25 Jeff Treadway .05
26 Joe Klink .05
27 Rickey Henderson .40
28 Sam Horn .05
29 Kurt Stillwell .05
30 Andy Van Slyke .05
31 Willie Banks .05
32 Jose Canseco .35
33 Felix Jose .05
34 Candy Maldonado .05
35 Carlos Baerga .05
36 Keith Hernandez .05
37 Frank Viola .05

38 Pete O'Brien .05
39 Pat Borders .05
40 Mike Heath .05
41 Kevin Brown .05
42 Chris Bosio .05
43 Shawn Boskie .05
44 Carlos Quintana .05
45 Juan Samuel .05
46 Tim Layana .05
47 Mike Harkey .05
48 Gerald Perry .05
49 Mike Witt .05
50 Joe Orsulak .05
52 Willie Blair .05
53 Gene Larkin .05
54 Jody Reed .05
55 Jeff Reardon .05
56 Kevin McReynolds .05
58 Eric Yelding .05
59 Fred Lynn .05
60 Jim Leyritz .05
61 John Orton .05
62 Mike Lieberthal .05
63 Mike Hartley .05
64 Kal Daniels .05
65 Terry Shumpert .05
66 Sil Campusano .05
67 Tony Pena .05
68 Barry Bonds 1.00
69 Oddibe McDowell .05
70 Kelly Gruber .05
71 Willie Randolph .05
72 Rick Parker .05
73 Bobby Bonilla .05
74 Jack Armstrong .05
75 Hubie Brooks .05
76 Sandy Alomar, Jr. .05
77 Ruben Sierra .05
78 Erik Hanson .05
79 Tony Phillips .05
80 Rondell White .05
81 Bobby Thigpen .05
82 Ron Walden .05
83 Don Peters .05
84 #6 (Nolan Ryan) 1.00
85 Lance Dickson .05
86 Ryne Sandberg .60
87 Eric Christopherson .05
88 Shane Andrews .05
89 Marc Newfield .05
90 Adam Hyzdu .05
91 "Texas Heat" (Nolan Ryan,
 Reid Ryan) 1.00
92 Chipper Jones .75
93 Frank Thomas .75
94 Cecil Fielder .05
95 Delino DeShields .05
96 John Olerud .05
97 Dave Justice .05
98 Joe Oliver .05
99 Alex Fernandez .05
100 Todd Hundley .05
--- Mike Marshall (Game
 instructions on back.) .05
--- 4 in 1 (Frank Viola,
 Nolan/Reid Ryan,
 Chipper Jones,
 Don Mattingly) .50

1991 Classic

Kirby Puckett

Top rookies and draft picks highlight this set from Classic. The cards come with a trivia board game and accessories. Fronts have fading blue borders with a touch of red. A blank-back "4-in-1" micro-player card is included with each game set.

NM/M
Complete Set (99): 4.00
Common Player: .05
1 John Olerud .05
2 Tino Martinez .05
3 Ken Griffey Jr. .65
4 Jeromy Burnitz .05
5 Ron Gant .05
6 Mike Benjamin .05
7 Steve Decker .05
8 Matt Williams .05
9 Rafael Novoa .05
10 Kevin Mitchell .05
11 Dave Justice .05
12 Leo Gomez .05
13 Chris Hoiles .05
14 Ben McDonald .05

15 David Segui .05
16 Anthony Telford .05
17 Mike Mussina .30
18 Roger Clemens .60
19 Wade Boggs .50
20 Tim Naehring .05
21 Joe Carter .05
22 Phil Plantier .05
23 Rob Dibble .05
24 Mo Vaughn .05
25 Lee Stevens .05
26 Chris Sabo .05
27 Mark Grace .05
28 Derrick May .05
29 Ryne Sandberg .50
30 Matt Stark .05
31 Bobby Thigpen .05
32 Frank Thomas .40
33 Don Mattingly .60
34 Eric Davis .05
35 Reggie Jefferson .05
36 Alex Cole .05
37 Mark Lewis .05
38 Tim Costo .05
39 Sandy Alomar, Jr. .05
40 Travis Fryman .05
41 Cecil Fielder .05
42 Milt Cuyler .05
43 Andujar Cedeno .05
44 Danny Darwin .05
45 Randy Henis .05
46 George Brett .60
47 Jeff Conine .05
48 Bo Jackson .10
49 Brian McRae .05
50 Brent Mayne .05
51 Eddie Murray .40
52 Ramon Martinez .05
53 Jim Neidlinger .05
54 Jim Poole .05
55 Tim McIntosh .05
56 Randy Veres .05
57 Kirby Puckett .50
58 Todd Ritchie .05
59 Rich Garces .05
60 Moises Alou .05
61 Delino DeShields .05
62 Oscar Azocar .05
63 Kevin Maas .05
64 Alan Mills .05
65 John Franco .05
66 Chris Jelic .05
67 Dave Magadan .05
68 Darryl Strawberry .05
69 Hensley Meulens .05
70 Juan Gonzalez .20
71 Reggie Harris .05
72 Rickey Henderson .40
73 Mark McGwire .75
74 Willie McGee .05
75 Todd Van Poppel .05
76 Bob Welch .05
77 "Future Aces"
 (Todd Van Poppel,
 Don Peters,
 David Zancanaro,
 Kirk Dressendorfer) .05
78 Lenny Dykstra .05
79 Mickey Morandini .05
80 Wes Chamberlain .05
81 Barry Bonds 1.00
82 Doug Drabek .05
83 Randy Tomlin .05
84 Scott Chiamparino .05
85 Rafael Palmeiro .35
86 Nolan Ryan 1.00
87 Bobby Witt .05
88 Fred McGriff .05
89 Dave Steib .05
90 Ed Sprague .05
91 Vince Coleman .05
92 Rod Brewer .05
93 Bernard Gilkey .05
94 Roberto Alomar .20
95 Chuck Finley .05
96 Dale Murphy .20
97 Jose Rijo .05
98 Hal Morris .05
99 "Friendly Foes"
 (Dwight Gooden,
 Darryl Strawberry) .05
--- John Olerud,
 Dwight Gooden,
 Jose Canseco,
 Darryl Strawberry .10

Series 2

Tim Raines

Classic released a 100-card second series in 1991. Cards feature the same format as the first series, with the exception of border color; Series II features maroon borders. The cards are designed for trivia game use. Series II includes several players with new teams and top rookies. Special Four-In-One, 300 Game Winner and Strikeout Kings cards are included with each set.

NM/M
Complete Set (100): 4.50
Common Player: .05
1 Ken Griffey Jr. .75
2 Wilfredo Cordero .05
3 Cal Ripken, Jr. 1.00
4 D.J. Dozier .05
5 Darrin Fletcher .05
6 Glenn Davis .05
7 Alex Fernandez .05
8 Cory Snyder .05
9 Tim Raines .05
10 Greg Swindell .05
11 Mark Lewis .05
12 Rico Brogna .05
13 Gary Sheffield .30
14 Paul Molitor .50
15 Kent Hrbek .05
16 Scott Erickson .05
17 Steve Sax .05
18 Dennis Eckersley .40
19 Jose Canseco .30
20 Kirk Dressendorfer .05
21 Ken Griffey Sr. .05
22 Erik Hanson .05
23 Dan Peltier .05
24 John Olerud .05
25 Eddie Zosky .05
26 Steve Avery .05
27 John Smoltz .05
28 Frank Thomas .50
29 Jerome Walton .05
30 George Bell .05
31 Jose Rijo .05
32 Randy Myers .05
33 Barry Larkin .05
34 Eric Anthony .05
35 Dave Hansen .05
36 Eric Karros .05
37 Jose Offerman .05
38 Marquis Grissom .05
39 Dwight Gooden .05
40 Gregg Jefferies .05
41 Pat Combs .05
42 Todd Zeile .05
43 Benito Santiago .05
44 Dave Staton .05
45 Tony Fernandez .05
46 Fred McGriff .05
47 Jeff Brantley .05
48 Junior Felix .05
49 Jack Morris .05
50 Chris George .05
51 Henry Rodriguez .05
52 Paul Marak .05
53 Ryan Klesko .05
54 Darren Lewis .05
55 Lance Dickson .05
56 Anthony Young .05
57 Willie Banks .05
58 Mike Bordick .05
59 Roger Salkeld .05
60 Steve Karsay .05
61 Bernie Williams .05
62 Mickey Tettleton .05
63 Dave Justice .05
64 Steve Decker .05
65 Roger Clemens .65
66 Phil Plantier .05
67 Ryne Sandberg .60
68 Sandy Alomar, Jr. .05
69 Cecil Fielder .05
70 George Brett .65
71 Delino DeShields .05
72 Dave Magadan .05
73 Darryl Strawberry .05
74 Juan Gonzalez .25
75 Rickey Henderson .50
76 Willie McGee .05
77 Todd Van Poppel .05
78 Barry Bonds 1.00
79 Doug Drabek .05
80 Nolan Ryan
 (300 games) 1.00
81 Roberto Alomar .20
82 Ivan Rodriguez .50
83 Dan Opperman .05
84 Jeff Bagwell .50
85 Braulio Castillo .05
86 Doug Simons .05
87 Wade Taylor .05
88 Gary Scott .05
89 Dave Stewart .05
90 Mike Simms .05
91 Luis Gonzalez .05
92 Bobby Bonilla .05
93 Tony Gwynn .60
94 Will Clark .05
95 Rich Rowland .05
96 Alan Trammell .05

97 "Strikeout Kings"
 (Nolan Ryan,
 Roger Clemens) .50
98 Joe Carter .05
99 Jack Clark .05
100 Four-In-One .20

Series 3

Tim Salmon

Green borders highlight Classic's third series of cards for 1991. The set includes a gameboard and player cards featuring trivia questions on the back. Statistics and biographical information are also found on back.

NM/M
Complete Set (100): 4.50
Common Player: .05
1 Jim Abbott .05
2 Craig Biggio .05
3 Wade Boggs .45
4 Bobby Bonilla .05
5 Ivan Calderon .05
6 Jose Canseco .25
7 Andy Benes .05
8 Wes Chamberlain .05
9 Will Clark .05
10 Royce Clayton .05
11 Gerald Alexander .05
12 Chili Davis .05
13 Eric Davis .05
14 Andre Dawson .25
15 Rob Dibble .05
16 Chris Donnels .05
17 Scott Erickson .05
18 Monty Fariss .05
19 Ruben Amaro Jr. .05
20 Chuck Finley .05
21 Carlton Fisk .35
22 Carlos Baerga .05
23 Ron Gant .05
24 Dave Justice, Ron Gant .05
25 Mike Gardiner .05
26 Tom Glavine .15
27 Joe Grahe .05
28 Derek Bell .05
29 Mike Greenwell .05
30 Ken Griffey Jr. .75
31 Leo Gomez .05
32 Tom Goodwin .05
33 Tony Gwynn .45
34 Mel Hall .05
35 Brian Harper .05
36 Dave Henderson .05
37 Albert Belle .05
38 Orel Hershiser .05
39 Brian Hunter .05
40 Howard Johnson .05
41 Felix Jose .05
42 Wally Joyner .05
43 Jeff Juden .05
44 Pat Kelly .05
45 Jimmy Key .05
46 Chuck Knoblauch .05
47 John Kruk .05
48 Ray Lankford .05
49 Ced Landrum .05
50 Scott Livingstone .05
51 Kevin Maas .05
52 Greg Maddux .45
53 Dennis Martinez .05
54 Edgar Martinez .05
55 Pedro Martinez .50
56 Don Mattingly .50
57 Orlando Merced .05
58 Keith Mitchell .05
59 Kevin Mitchell .05
60 Paul Molitor .35
61 Jack Morris .05
62 Hal Morris .05
63 Kevin Morton .05
64 Pedro Munoz .05
65 Eddie Murray .35
66 Jack McDowell .05
67 Jeff McNeely .05
68 Brian McRae .05
69 Kevin McReynolds .05
70 Gregg Olson .05
71 Rafael Palmeiro .30
72 Dean Palmer .05
73 Tony Phillips .05
74 Kirby Puckett .45
75 Carlos Quintana .05
76 Pat Rice .05

77 Cal Ripken, Jr. 1.00
78 Ivan Rodriguez .30
79 Nolan Ryan 1.00
80 Bret Saberhagen .05
81 Tim Salmon .05
82 Juan Samuel .05
83 Ruben Sierra .05
84 Heathcliff Slocumb .05
85 Joe Slusarski .05
86 John Smiley .05
87 Dave Smith .05
88 Ed Sprague .05
89 Todd Stottlemyre .05
90 Mike Timlin .05
91 Greg Vaughn .05
92 Frank Viola .05
93 John Wehner .05
94 Devon White .05
95 Matt Williams .05
96 Rick Wilkins .05
97 Bernie Williams .05
98 Starter & Stopper
 (Goose Gossage,
 Nolan Ryan) .20
99 Gerald Williams .05
---- 4-in-1 (Bobby Bonilla,
 Will Clark, Cal Ripken Jr.,
 Scott Erickson) .25

Collector's Edition

Cal Ripken, Jr.

The Classic Collector's edition made its debut in 1991. This package includes a board game, trivia baseball player cards, a baseball tips booklet and a certificate of authenticity, all packaged in a collector's edition box. Each box is individually and sequentially numbered on the outside, with a reported 100,000 available.

NM/M
Complete Set (200): 7.50
Common Player: .05
1 Frank Viola .05
2 Tim Wallach .05
3 Lou Whitaker .05
4 Brett Butler .05
5 Jim Abbott .05
6 Jack Armstrong .05
7 Craig Biggio .05
8 Brian Barnes .05
9 Dennis "Oil Can" Boyd .05
10 Tom Browning .05
11 Tom Brunansky .05
12 Ellis Burks .05
13 Harold Baines .05
14 Kal Daniels .05
15 Mark Davis .05
16 Storm Davis .05
17 Tom Glavine .25
18 Mike Greenwell .05
19 Kelly Gruber .05
20 Mark Gubicza .05
21 Pedro Guerrero .05
22 Mike Harkey .05
23 Orel Hershiser .05
24 Ted Higuera .05
25 Von Hayes .05
26 Andre Dawson .25
27 Shawon Dunston .05
28 Roberto Kelly .05
29 Joe Magrane .05
30 Dennis Martinez .05
31 Kevin McReynolds .05
32 Matt Nokes .05
33 Dan Plesac .05
34 Dave Parker .05
35 Randy Johnson .40
36 Bret Saberhagen .05
37 Mackey Sasser .05
38 Mike Scott .05
39 Ozzie Smith .50
40 Kevin Seitzer .05
41 Ruben Sierra .05
42 Kevin Tapani .05
43 Danny Tartabull .05
44 Robby Thompson .05
45 Andy Van Slyke .05
46 Greg Vaughn .05
47 Harold Reynolds .05
48 Will Clark .05
49 Gary Gaetti .05
50 Joe Grahe .05
51 Carlton Fisk .40

52 Robin Ventura .05
53 Ozzie Guillen .05
54 Tom Candiotti .05
55 Doug Jones .05
56 Eric King .05
57 Kirk Gibson .05
58 Tim Costo .05
59 Robin Yount .40
60 Sammy Sosa .50
61 Jesse Barfield .05
62 Marc Newfield .05
63 Jimmy Key .05
64 Felix Jose .05
65 Mark Whiten .05
66 Tommy Greene .05
67 Kent Mercker .05
68 Greg Maddux .50
69 Danny Jackson .05
70 Reggie Sanders .05
71 Eric Yelding .05
72 Karl Rhodes .05
73 Fernando Valenzuela .05
74 Chris Nabholz .05
75 Andres Galarraga .05
76 Howard Johnson .05
77 Hubie Brooks .05
78 Terry Mulholland .05
79 Paul Molitor .40
80 Roger McDowell .05
81 Darren Daulton .05
82 Zane Smith .05
83 Ray Lankford .05
84 Bruce Hurst .05
85 Andy Benes .05
86 John Burkett .05
87 Dave Righetti .05
88 Steve Karsay .05
89 D.J. Dozier .05
90 Jeff Bagwell .40
91 Joe Carter .05
92 Wes Chamberlain .05
93 Vince Coleman .05
94 Pat Combs .05
95 Jerome Walton .05
96 Jeff Conine .05
97 Alan Trammell .05
98 Don Mattingly .55
99 Ramon Martinez .05
100 Dave Magadan .05
101 Greg Swindell .05
102 Dave Stewart .05
103 Gary Sheffield .30
104 George Bell .05
105 Mark Grace .05
106 Steve Sax .05
107 Ryne Sandberg .50
108 Chris Sabo .05
109 Jose Rijo .05
110 Cal Ripken, Jr. 1.00
111 Kirby Puckett .50
112 Eddie Murray .40
113 Roberto Alomar .20
114 Randy Myers .05
115 Rafael Palmeiro .35
116 John Olerud .05
117 Gregg Jefferies .05
118 Kent Hrbek .05
119 Marquis Grissom .05
120 Ken Griffey Jr. .60
121 Dwight Gooden .05
122 Juan Gonzalez .20
123 Ron Gant .05
124 Travis Fryman .05
125 John Franco .05
126 Dennis Eckersley .35
127 Cecil Fielder .05
128 Phil Plantier .05
129 Kevin Mitchell .05
130 Kevin Maas .05
131 Mark McGwire .75
132 Ben McDonald .05
133 Lenny Dykstra .05
134 Delino DeShields .05
135 Jose Canseco .30
136 Eric Davis .05
137 George Brett .55
138 Steve Avery .05
139 Eric Anthony .05
140 Bobby Thigpen .05
141 Ken Griffey Sr. .05
142 Barry Larkin .05
143 Jeff Brantley .05
144 Bobby Bonilla .05
145 Jose Offerman .05
146 Mike Mussina .30
147 Erik Hanson .05
148 Dale Murphy .15
149 Roger Clemens .55
150 Tino Martinez .05
151 Todd Van Poppel .05
152 Mo Vaughn .05
153 Derrick May .05
154 Jack Clark .05
155 Dave Hansen .05
156 Tony Gwynn .05
157 Brian McRae .05
158 Matt Williams .05
159 Kirk Dressendorfer .05
160 Scott Erickson .05
161 Tony Fernandez .05
162 Willie McGee .05
163 Fred McGriff .05
164 Leo Gomez .05
165 Bernard Gilkey .05
166 Bobby Witt .05
167 Doug Drabek .05
168 Rob Dibble .05
169 Glenn Davis .05

170 Danny Darwin .05
171 Eric Karros .05
172 Eddie Zosky .05
173 Todd Zeile .05
174 Tim Raines .05
175 Benito Santiago .05
176 Dan Peltier .05
177 Darryl Strawberry .05
178 Hal Morris .05
179 Hensley Meulens .05
180 John Smoltz .05
181 Frank Thomas .40
182 Dave Staton .05
183 Scott Chiamparino .05
184 Alex Fernandez .05
185 Mark Lewis .05
186 Bo Jackson .10
187 Mickey Morandini
(Photo actually
Darren Daulton.) .05
188 Cory Snyder .05
189 Rickey Henderson .40
190 Junior Felix .05
191 Milt Cuyler .05
192 Wade Boggs .50
193 "Justice Prevails"
(David Justice) .05
194 Sandy Alomar, Jr. .05
195 Barry Bonds 1.00
196 Nolan Ryan 1.00
197 Rico Brogna .05
198 Steve Decker .05
199 Bob Welch .05
200 Andujar Cedeno .05

1991 Classic/ American Collectables Nolan Ryan

This set of Nolan Ryan highlights was produced by Classic for American Collectables and sold as a limited-edition issue. The cards feature color photos of Ryan bordered in a garish green and yellow design. Backs have personal data and stats printed in black on green, along with a color MLB logo.

NM/M
Complete Set (10): 7.50
Common Card: 1.00
1 Nolan Ryan
(Mets '66-'71) 1.00
2 Nolan Ryan
(Angels '72-'79) 1.00
3 Nolan Ryan
(Astros '80-'88) 1.00
4 Nolan Ryan
(Rangers '89-'90) 1.00
5 Nolan Ryan
(5000 K's) 1.00
6 Nolan Ryan
(6th No-No) 1.00
7 Nolan Ryan
(Angels '72-'79) 1.00
8 Nolan Ryan
(Astros '80-'88) 1.00
9 Nolan Ryan
(Rangers '89-'90) 1.00
10 Nolan Ryan
(300 Wins) 1.00

1992 Classic Series 1

Classic introduced an innovative design with the release of its 1992 set. Fronts feature full-color photos bordered in white, while backs feature statistics, biographical information and trivia questions accented by a fading stadium shot. The cards were released with a gameboard and are numbered on back with a "T" prefix.

NM/M
Complete Set (100): 4.50

CHITO MARTINEZ

Common Player: .05
1 Jim Abbott .05
2 Kyle Abbott .05
3 Scott Aldred .05
4 Roberto Alomar .20
5 Wilson Alvarez .05
6 Andy Ashby .05
7 Steve Avery .05
8 Jeff Bagwell .40
9 Bret Barberie .05
10 Kim Batiste .05
11 Derek Bell .05
12 Jay Bell .05
13 Albert Belle .05
14 Andy Benes .05
15 Sean Berry .05
16 Barry Bonds 1.00
17 Ryan Bowen .05
18 Trifecta (Alejandro Pena,
Mark Wohlers,
Kent Mercker) .05
19 Scott Brosius .05
20 Jay Buhner .05
21 David Burba .05
22 Jose Canseco .35
23 Andujar Cedeno .05
24 Will Clark .05
25 Royce Clayton .05
26 Roger Clemens .50
27 David Cone .05
28 Scott Cooper .05
29 Chris Cron .05
30 Len Dykstra .05
31 Cal Eldred .05
32 Hector Fajardo .05
33 Cecil Fielder .05
34 Dave Fleming .05
35 Steve Foster .05
36 Julio Franco .05
37 Carlos Garcia .05
38 Tom Glavine .15
39 Tom Goodwin .05
40 Ken Griffey Jr. .65
41 Chris Haney .05
42 Bryan Harvey .05
43 Rickey Henderson .40
44 Carlos Hernandez .05
45 Roberto Hernandez .05
46 Brook Jacoby .05
47 Howard Johnson .05
48 Pat Kelly .05
49 Darryl Kile .05
50 Chuck Knoblauch .05
51 Ray Lankford .05
52 Mark Leiter .05
53 Darren Lewis .05
54 Scott Livingstone .05
55 Shane Mack .05
56 Chito Martinez .05
57 Dennis Martinez .05
58 Don Mattingly .50
59 Paul McClellan .05
60 Chuck McElroy .05
61 Fred McGriff .05
62 Orlando Merced .05
63 Luis Mercedes .05
64 Kevin Mitchell .05
65 Hal Morris .05
66 Jack Morris .05
67 Mike Mussina .30
68 Denny Neagle .05
69 Tom Pagnozzi .05
70 Terry Pendleton .05
71 Phil Plantier .05
72 Kirby Puckett .45
73 Carlos Quintana .05
74 Willie Randolph .05
75 Arthur Rhodes .05
76 Cal Ripken 1.00
77 Ivan Rodriguez .35
78 Nolan Ryan 1.00
79 Ryne Sandberg .05
80 Deion Sanders .10
81 Reggie Sanders .05
82 Mo Sanford .05
83 Terry Shumpert .05
84 Tim Spehr .05
85 Lee Stevens .05
86 Darryl Strawberry .05
87 Kevin Tapani .05
88 Danny Tartabull .05
89 Frank Thomas .30
90 Todd Van Poppel .30
91 Andy Van Slyke .05
92 John Wehner .05
93 John Wetteland .05
94 Devon White .05

96 Brian Williams .05
97 Mark Wohlers .05
98 Robin Yount .40
99 Eddie Zosky .05
--- 4-in-1 (Barry Bonds,
Roger Clemens, Steve
Avery, Nolan Ryan) .50

Series 2

JIM ABBOTT

The 100-cards in Classic's 1992 Series II came packaged with a gameboard and spinner. In a completely different format from Classic's other '92 issues, Series II features player photos bordered at left and right with red or blue color bars which fade toward top and bottom. Backs have biographical data, previous-year and career statistics and five trivia questions, along with a color representation of the team's uniform. Cards, except the 4-In-1, are numbered with a "T" prefix.

NM/M
Complete Set (100): 4.50
Common Player: .05
1 Jim Abbott .05
2 Jeff Bagwell .40
3 Jose Canseco .30
4 Julio Valera .05
5 Scott Brosius .05
6 Mark Langston .05
7 Andy Stankiewicz .05
8 Gary DiSarcina .05
9 Pete Harnisch .05
10 Mark McGwire .75
11 Ricky Bones .05
12 Steve Avery .05
13 Deion Sanders .10
14 Mike Mussina .25
15 Dave Justice .05
16 Pat Hentgen .05
17 Tom Glavine .20
18 Juan Guzman .05
19 Ron Gant .05
20 Kelly Gruber .05
21 Eric Karros .05
22 Derrick May .05
23 Dave Hansen .05
24 Andre Dawson .25
25 Eric Davis .05
26 Ozzie Smith .45
27 Sammy Sosa .05
28 Lee Smith .05
29 Ryne Sandberg .45
30 Robin Yount .40
31 Matt Williams .05
32 John Vander Wal .05
33 Bill Swift .05
34 Delino DeShields .05
35 Royce Clayton .05
36 Moises Alou .05
37 Will Clark .05
38 Darryl Strawberry .05
39 Larry Walker .05
40 Ramon Martinez .05
41 Howard Johnson .05
42 Tino Martinez .05
43 Dwight Gooden .05
44 Ken Griffey Jr. .60
45 David Cone .05
46 Kenny Lofton .05
47 Bobby Bonilla .05
48 Carlos Baerga .05
49 Don Mattingly .50
50 Sandy Alomar, Jr. .05
51 Lenny Dykstra .05
52 Tony Gwynn .45
53 Felix Jose .05
54 Rick Sutcliffe .05
55 Wes Chamberlain .05
56 Cal Ripken, Jr. 1.00
57 Kyle Abbott .05
58 Leo Gomez .05
59 Gary Sheffield .20
60 Anthony Young .05
61 Roger Clemens .50
62 Rafael Palmeiro .35
63 Wade Boggs .45
64 Andy Van Slyke .05
65 Ruben Sierra .05

66 Denny Neagle .05
67 Nolan Ryan 1.00
68 Doug Drabek .05
69 Ivan Rodriguez .35
70 Barry Bonds 1.00
71 Chuck Knoblauch .05
72 Reggie Sanders .05
73 Cecil Fielder .05
74 Barry Larkin .05
75 Scott Aldred .05
76 Rob Dibble .05
77 Brian McRae .05
78 Tim Belcher .05
79 George Brett .50
80 Frank Viola .05
81 Roberto Kelly .05
82 Jack McDowell .05
83 Mel Hall .05
84 Esteban Beltre .05
85 Robin Ventura .05
86 George Bell .05
87 Frank Thomas .40
88 John Smiley .05
89 Bobby Thigpen .05
90 Kirby Puckett .45
91 Kevin Mitchell .05
92 Peter Hoy .05
93 Russ Springer .05
94 Donovan Osborne .05
95 Dave Silvestri .05
96 Chad Curtis .05
97 Pat Mahomes .05
98 Danny Tartabull .05
99 John Doherty .05
--- 4-in-1 (Ryne Sandberg,
Mike Mussina,
Reggie Sanders,
Jose Canseco) .25

Collector's Edition

TIM RAINES

The second annual 200-card "Collector's Edition" set was packaged with a gameboard, spinner, generic player pieces, a mechanical scoreboard and a book of tips from star players. The UV-coated card fronts feature color player photos against a deep purple border. Backs have a few biographical details, previous season and career stats, plus five trivia questions in case anyone actually wanted to play the game.

NM/M
Complete Set (200): 9.00
Common Player: .05
1 Chuck Finley .05
2 Craig Biggio .05
3 Luis Gonzalez .05
4 Pete Harnisch .05
5 Jeff Juden .05
6 Harold Baines .05
7 Kirk Dressendorfer .05
8 Dennis Eckersley .35
9 Dave Henderson .05
10 Dave Stewart .05
11 Joe Carter .05
12 Juan Guzman .05
13 Dave Stieb .05
14 Todd Stottlemyre .05
15 Ron Gant .05
16 Brian Hunter .05
17 Dave Justice .05
18 John Smoltz .05
19 Mike Stanton .05
20 Chris George .05
21 Paul Molitor .40
22 Omar Olivares .05
23 Lee Smith .05
24 Ozzie Smith .50
25 Todd Zeile .05
26 George Bell .05
27 Andre Dawson .25
28 Shawon Dunston .05
29 Mark Grace .05
30 Greg Maddux .50
31 Dave Smith .05
32 Brett Butler .05
33 Orel Hershiser .05
34 Eric Karros .05
35 Ramon Martinez .05
36 Jose Offerman .05

37 Juan Samuel .05
38 Delino DeShields .05
39 Marquis Grissom .05
40 Tim Wallach .05
41 Eric Gunderson .05
42 Willie McGee .05
43 Dave Righetti .05
44 Robby Thompson .05
45 Matt Williams .05
46 Sandy Alomar, Jr. .05
47 Reggie Jefferson .05
48 Mark Lewis .05
49 Robin Ventura .05
50 Tino Martinez .05
51 Roberto Kelly .05
52 Vince Coleman .05
53 Dwight Gooden .05
54 Todd Hundley .05
55 Kevin Maas .05
56 Wade Taylor .05
57 Bryan Harvey .05
58 Leo Gomez .05
59 Ben McDonald .05
60 Ricky Bones .05
61 Tony Gwynn .50
62 Benito Santiago .05
63 Wes Chamberlain .05
64 Tommy Greene .05
65 Dale Murphy .15
66 Steve Buechele .05
67 Doug Drabek .05
68 Joe Grahe .05
69 Rafael Palmeiro .35
70 Wade Boggs .50
71 Ellis Burks .05
72 Mike Greenwell .05
73 Mo Vaughn .05
74 Derek Bell .05
75 Rob Dibble .05
76 Barry Larkin .05
77 Jose Rijo .05
78 Doug Henry .05
79 Chris Sabo .05
80 Pedro Guerrero .05
81 George Brett .60
82 Tom Gordon .05
83 Mark Gubicza .05
84 Mark Whiten .05
85 Brian McRae .05
86 Danny Jackson .05
87 Milt Cuyler .05
88 Travis Fryman .05
89 Mickey Tettleton .05
90 Alan Trammell .05
91 Lou Whitaker .05
92 Chili Davis .05
93 Scott Erickson .05
94 Kent Hrbek .05
95 Alex Fernandez .05
96 Carlton Fisk .40
97 Ramon Garcia .05
98 Ozzie Guillen .05
99 Tim Raines .05
100 Bobby Thigpen .05
101 Kirby Puckett .50
102 Bernie Williams .05
103 Dave Hansen .05
104 Kevin Tapani .05
105 Don Mattingly .60
106 Frank Thomas .40
107 Monty Fariss .05
108 Bo Jackson .10
109 Jim Abbott .05
110 Jose Canseco .25
111 Phil Plantier .05
112 Brian Williams .05
113 Mark Langston .05
114 Wilson Alvarez .05
115 Roberto Hernandez .05
116 Darryl Kile .05
117 Ryan Bowen .05
118 Rickey Henderson .40
119 Mark McGwire 1.00
120 Devon White .05
121 Roberto Alomar .20
122 Kelly Gruber .05
123 Eddie Zosky .05
124 Tom Glavine .25
125 Kal Daniels .05
126 Cal Eldred .05
127 Deion Sanders .10
128 Robin Yount .05
129 Cecil Fielder .05
130 Ray Lankford .05
131 Ryne Sandberg .05
132 Darryl Strawberry .05
133 Chris Haney .05
134 Dennis Martinez .05
135 Bryan Hickerson .05
136 Will Clark .05
137 Hal Morris .05
138 Charles Nagy .05
139 Jim Thome .35
140 Albert Belle .05
141 Reggie Sanders .05
142 Scott Cooper .05
143 David Cone .05
144 Anthony Young .05
145 Howard Johnson .05
146 Arthur Rhodes .05
147 Scott Aldred .05
148 Mike Mussina .25
149 Fred McGriff .05
150 Andy Benes .05
151 Ruben Sierra .05
152 Len Dykstra .05
153 Andy Van Slyke .05
154 Orlando Merced .05

155	Barry Bonds	1.50
156	John Smiley	.05
157	Julio Franco	.05
158	Juan Gonzalez	.20
159	Ivan Rodriguez	.35
160	Willie Banks	.05
161	Eric Davis	.05
162	Eddie Murray	.40
163	Dave Fleming	.05
164	Wally Joyner	.05
165	Kevin Mitchell	.05
166	Ed Taubensee	.05
167	Danny Tartabull	.05
168	Ken Hill	.05
169	Willie Randolph	.05
170	Kevin McReynolds	.05
171	Gregg Jefferies	.05
172	Patrick Lennon	.05
173	Luis Mercedes	.05
174	Glenn Davis	.05
175	Bret Saberhagen	.05
176	Bobby Bonilla	.05
177	Kenny Lofton	.05
178	Jose Lind	.05
179	Royce Clayton	.05
180	Scott Scudder	.05
181	Chuck Knoblauch	.05
182	Terry Pendleton	.05
183	Nolan Ryan	1.50
184	Rob Maurer	.05
185	Brian Bohanon	.05
186	Ken Griffey Jr.	.75
187	Jeff Bagwell	.40
188	Steve Avery	.05
189	Roger Clemens	.60
190	Cal Ripken, Jr.	1.50
191	Kim Batiste	.05
192	Bip Roberts	.05
193	Greg Swindell	.05
194	Dave Winfield	.40
195	Steve Sax	.05
196	Frank Viola	.05
197	Mo Sanford	.05
198	Kyle Abbott	.05
199	Jack Morris	.05
200	Andy Ashby	.05

1993 Classic

A 100-card travel edition of Classic's baseball trivia cards was produced for 1993. Cards feature game-action player photos with dark blue borders. Backs have previous season and career stats along with five trivia questions. Card numbers have a "T" prefix.

		NM/M
Complete Set (100):		4.00
Common Player:		.05
1	Jim Abbott	.05
2	Roberto Alomar	.20
3	Moises Alou	.05
4	Brady Anderson	.05
5	Eric Anthony	.05
6	Alex Arias	.05
7	Pedro Astacio	.05
8	Steve Avery	.05
9	Carlos Baerga	.05
10	Jeff Bagwell	.40
11	George Bell	.05
12	Albert Belle	.05
13	Craig Biggio	.05
14	Barry Bonds	1.00
15	Bobby Bonilla	.05
16	Mike Bordick	.05
17	George Brett	.55
18	Jose Canseco	.30
19	Joe Carter	.05
20	Royce Clayton	.05
21	Roger Clemens	.55
22	Greg Colbrunn	.05
23	David Cone	.05
24	Darren Daulton	.05
25	Delino DeShields	.05
26	Rob Dibble	.05
27	Dennis Eckersley	.35
28	Cal Eldred	.05
29	Scott Erickson	.05
30	Junior Felix	.05
31	Tony Fernandez	.05
32	Cecil Fielder	.05
33	Steve Finley	.05
34	Dave Fleming	.05
35	Travis Fryman	.05

36	Tom Glavine	.25
37	Juan Gonzalez	.20
38	Ken Griffey Jr.	.60
39	Marquis Grissom	.05
40	Juan Guzman	.05
41	Tony Gwynn	.50
42	Rickey Henderson	.40
43	Felix Jose	.05
44	Wally Joyner	.05
45	David Justice	.05
46	Eric Karros	.05
47	Roberto Kelly	.05
48	Ryan Klesko	.05
49	Chuck Knoblauch	.05
50	John Kruk	.05
51	Ray Lankford	.05
52	Barry Larkin	.05
53	Pat Listach	.05
54	Kenny Lofton	.05
55	Shane Mack	.05
56	Greg Maddux	.50
57	Dave Magadan	.05
58	Edgar Martinez	.05
59	Don Mattingly	.55
60	Ben McDonald	.05
61	Jack McDowell	.05
62	Fred McGriff	.05
63	Mark McGwire	.75
64	Kevin McReynolds	.05
65	Sam Militello	.05
66	Paul Molitor	.40
67	Jeff Montgomery	.05
68	Jack Morris	.05
69	Eddie Murray	.40
70	Mike Mussina	.30
71	Otis Nixon	.05
72	Donovan Osborne	.05
73	Terry Pendleton	.05
74	Mike Piazza	.60
75	Kirby Puckett	.50
76	Cal Ripken, Jr.	1.00
77	Bip Roberts	.05
78	Ivan Rodriguez	.35
79	Nolan Ryan	1.00
80	Ryne Sandberg	.50
81	Deion Sanders	.10
82	Reggie Sanders	.05
83	Frank Seminara	.05
84	Gary Sheffield	.30
85	Ruben Sierra	.05
86	John Smiley	.05
87	Lee Smith	.05
88	Ozzie Smith	.50
89	John Smoltz	.05
90	Danny Tartabull	.05
91	Bob Tewksbury	.05
92	Frank Thomas	.40
93	Andy Van Slyke	.05
94	Mo Vaughn	.05
95	Robin Ventura	.05
96	Tim Wakefield	.05
97	Larry Walker	.05
98	Dave Winfield	.05
99	Robin Yount	.40
---	4-in-1 (Mark McGwire, Sam Militello, Ryan Klesko, Greg Maddux)	.50

1996 Classic/ Metallic Impressions Nolan Ryan

Nolan Ryan's career is traced in this set of 2-5/8" x 3-5/8" embossed metal cards produced for Classic by Metallic Impressions. The center of each card's front is a raised color photo which continues in muted tones of yellow and orange to the edges. The Classic and The Metal Edge logos are embossed, as well. Horizontal backs are identical in design with a color portrait of Ryan at left and a paragraph describing a highlight or milestone at right. Classic and Cooperstown Collection logos are in opposite corners. Each of 14,950 sets was sold

with a numbered certificate of authenticity in an embossed lithographed metal box.

		NM/M
Complete Boxed Set (10):		7.50
Single Card:		1.00
1	Nolan Ryan (Career ends with Rangers.)	1.00
2	Nolan Ryan (1970s, California Angels.)	1.00
3	Nolan Ryan (Major League debut.)	1.00
4	Nolan Ryan (Over-40 no-hitters.)	1.00
5	Nolan Ryan (Rangers no-hitters.)	1.00
6	Nolan Ryan (Mets trade Ryan.)	1.00
7	Nolan Ryan (Joins Astros.)	1.00
8	Nolan Ryan (Career records.)	1.00
9	Nolan Ryan (Lean years in Houston.)	1.00
10	Nolan Ryan ("Ryan Express" returns to A.L.)	1.00

1989 Cleveland Indians Team Issue

(28) Cory Snyder, OF

The Cleveland Indians released this oversized (2-3/4" x 4-1/2") set in 1989. Cards feature a full-color player photo on front with the "Tribe" logo in the upper left corner. Card backs include major and minor league statistics and a facsimile autograph.

		NM/M
Complete Set (28):		6.00
Common Player:		.25
(1)	Doc Edwards	.25
(2)	Joel Skinner	.25
(3)	Andy Allanson	.25
(4)	Tom Candiotti	.25
(5)	Doug Jones	.25
(6)	Keith Atherton	.25
(7)	Rich Yett	.25
(8)	John Farrell	.25
(9)	Rod Nichols	.25
(10)	Joe Skalski	.25
(11)	Pete O'Brien	.25
(12)	Jerry Browne	.25
(13)	Brook Jacoby	.25
(14)	Felix Fermin	.25
(15)	Bud Black	.25
(16)	Brad Havens	.25
(17)	Greg Swindell	.25
(18)	Scott Bailes	.25
(19)	Jesse Orosco	.25
(20)	Oddibe McDowell	.25
(21)	Joe Carter	.50
(22)	Cory Snyder	.25
(23)	Louie Medina	.25
(24)	Dave Clark	.25
(25)	Brad Komminsk	.25
(26)	Luis Aguayo	.25
(27)	Pat Keedy	.25
(28)	Tribe Coaches	.25

1990 Cleveland Indians Team Issue

The Cleveland Indians released this oversized (2-7/8" x 4-1/4") set in 1990. Cards feature a full-color portrait photo on front with the "Tribe" logo in the top-left corner. Player name, uniform number and position are in the bottom border. Backs are blank.

		NM/M
Complete Set (46):		12.00
Common Player:		.25
(1)	Beau Allred	.25
(2)	Sandy Alomar Jr.	.50
(3)	Carlos Baerga	.25
(4)	Kevin Bearse	.25

(17) Keith Hernandez, 1B

(5)	Joey (Albert) Belle	2.00
(6)	Bud Black	.25
(7)	Tom Brookens	.25
(8)	Jerry Browne	.25
(9)	Tom Candiotti	.25
(10)	Colin Charland	.25
(11)	Rich Dauer	.25
(12)	John Farrell	.25
(13)	Felix Fermin	.25
(14)	Cecilio Guante	.25
(15)	Mike Hargrove	.35
(16)	Keith Hernandez	.40
(17)	Luis Isaac	.25
(18)	Brook Jacoby	.25
(19)	Chris James	.25
(20)	Dion James	.25
(21)	Doug Jones	.25
(22)	Carl Kelipuleole	.25
(23)	Tom Lampkin	.25
(24)	Tom Magrann	.25
(25)	Candy Maldonado	.25
(26)	Jeff Manto	.25
(27)	John McNamara	.25
(28)	Jose Morales	.25
(29)	Rod Nichols	.25
(30)	Al Nipper	.25
(31)	Steve Olin	.25
(32)	Jesse Orosco	.25
(33)	Doug Robertson	.25
(34)	Rudy Seanez	.25
(35)	Jeff Shaw	.25
(36)	Doug Sisk	.25
(37)	Joe Skalski	.25
(38)	Joel Skinner	.25
(39)	Cory Snyder	.25
(40)	Greg Swindell	.25
(41)	Sergio Valdez	.25
(42)	Mike Walker	.25
(43)	Mitch Webster	.25
(44)	Kevin Wickander	.25
(45)	Mark Wiley	.25
(46)	Billy Williams	.25

1993 Cleveland Indians Team Issue

(8) Albert Belle

Only the mascot's card carries the logo of the television station which sponsored this team set. In 2-1/2" x 3-1/2" format printed on thin cardboard, the fronts feature color game-action photos with borders of red, white and blue. The player's uniform number appears in the lower-left corner. Backs are in black-and-white with major league career stats and a log commemorating the team's 61 years at Municipal Stadium. The set is checklisted here alphabetically.

		NM/M
Complete Set (34):		12.00
Common Player:		.25
(1)	Sandy Alomar Jr.	.50
(2)	Carlos Baerga	.25
(3)	Albert Belle	1.00
(4)	Mike Bielecki	.25
(5)	Mike Christopher	.25
(6)	Mark Clark	.25
(7)	Dennis Cook	.25
(8)	Alvaro Espinoza	.25
(9)	Felix Fermin	.25

(10)	Mike Hargrove	.25
(11)	Glenallen Hill	.25
(12)	Thomas Howard	.25
(13)	Reggie Jefferson	.25
(14)	Wayne Kirby	.25
(15)	Tom Kramer	.25
(16)	Mark Lewis	.25
(17)	Derek Lilliquist	.25
(18)	Kenny Lofton	.35
(19)	Carlos Martinez	.25
(20)	Jose Mesa	.25
(21)	Jeff Mutis	.25
(22)	Charles Nagy	.25
(23)	Bob Ojeda	.25
(24)	Junior Ortiz	.25
(25)	Eric Plunk	.25
(26)	Ted Power	.25
(27)	Scott Scudder	.25
(28)	Joel Skinner	.25
(29)	Paul Sorrento	.25
(30)	Jim Thome	2.00
(31)	Jeff Treadway	.25
(32)	Kevin Wickander	.25
(33)	Indians coaches (Rick Adair, Ken Bolke, Dom Chiti, Ron Clark, Jose Morales, Dave Nelson, Jeff Newman)	.25
(34)	Slider/Mascot	.25

2005 Cloverdale Meats Seattle Mariners

Ryan Franklin

Cloverdale Mets sponsored a kids' trading card stadium giveaway on June 16, distributing 27-card packs to fans 14 and under. Each pack contained 20 different cards and seven duplicates to trade in an effort to complete the set. Fronts of the 2-1/2" x 3-1/2" cards have game-action photos. Full-color backs have a portrait photo, player data and trivia, and team and sponsor's logos.

		NM/M
Complete Set (27):		10.00
Common Player:		.35
1	Mike Hargrove	.35
2	Adrian Beltre	.75
3	Willie Bloomquist	.35
4	Bret Boone	.35
5	Ryan Franklin	.35
6	Eddie Guardado	.35
7	Shigetoshi Hasegawa	.35
8	Raul Ibanez	.35
9	Bobby Madritsch	.35
10	Julio Mateo	.35
11	Gil Meche	.35
12	Jamie Moyer	.35
13	Jeff Nelson	.35
14	Miguel Olivo	.35
15	Joel Pineiro	.35
16	J.J. Putz	.35
17	Jeremy Reed	.75
18	Pokey Reese	.35
19	Aaron Sele	.35
20	Richie Sexson	.35
21	Scott Spiezio	.35
22	Ichiro Suzuki	3.00
23	Matt Thornton	.35
24	Wilson Valdez	.35
25	Ron Villone	.35
26	Dan Wilson	.35
27	Randy Winn	.35

1992 Clovis Police Department Mark's Moments

Highlights of Mark McGwire's career to that point are shown and/or described in this set of police cards from the Clovis, Calif., P.D. Cards have color photos framed in gold with green borders. The city seal is at upper-left, the

MARK McGWIRE

Oakland description of a "Moment," a safety tip, the description of the "Moment" on front, a safety tip, the logo of the Clovis P.D., another team logo and sponsors' credits.

	NM/M
Complete Set (24):	35.00
Common Card:	1.50

1981 Coca-Cola

JOHNNY BENCH

In 1981 Topps produced for Coca-Cola 12-card sets for 11 American and National League teams. The sets include 11 player cards and one unnumbered header card. The 2-1/2" x 3-1/2" cards are identical in format to the 1981 Topps regular issue with an added Coca-Cola logo. Backs differ from the '81 Topps regular set in that they are numbered 1-11 and carry the Coca-Cola trademark and copyright line. The header cards contain an offer for 132-card uncut sheets of 1981 Topps baseball cards. Some New York Yankees' cards were prepared, but never issued; to date, only three of the players are known.

		NM/M
Complete Set (No Yankees) (132):		20.00
Common Player:		.05
Boston Red Sox Team Set		3.00
1	Tom Burgmeier	.10
2	Dennis Eckersley	.35
3	Dwight Evans	.20
4	Bob Stanley	.10
5	Glenn Hoffman	.10
6	Carney Lansford	.10
7	Frank Tanana	.10
8	Tony Perez	.75
9	Jim Rice	.50
10	Dave Stapleton	.10
11	Carl Yastrzemski	2.00
----	Red Sox header card	.05
Chicago Cubs Team Set		1.25
1	Tim Blackwell	.10
2	Bill Buckner	.35
3	Ivan DeJesus	.10
4	Leon Durham	.10
5	Steve Henderson	.10
6	Mike Krukow	.10
7	Ken Reitz	.10
8	Rick Reuschel	.10
9	Scot Thompson	.10
10	Dick Tidrow	.10
11	Mike Tyson	.10
----	Cubs header card	.05
Chicago White Sox Team Set		1.00
1	Britt Burns	.10
2	Todd Cruz	.10
3	Rich Dotson	.10
4	Jim Essian	.10
5	Ed Farmer	.10
6	Lamar Johnson	.10
7	Ron LeFlore	.10

8	Chet Lemon	.10
9	Bob Molinaro	.10
10	Jim Morrison	.10
11	Wayne Nordhagen	.10
----	White Sox header card	.05

Cincinnati Reds Team Set 3.50
1	Johnny Bench	2.75
2	Dave Collins	.20
3	Dave Concepcion	.20
4	Dan Driessen	.10
5	George Foster	.20
6	Ken Griffey	.20
7	Tom Hume	.10
8	Ray Knight	.20
9	Ron Oester	.10
10	Tom Seaver	1.75
11	Mario Soto	.10
----	Reds header card	.05

Detroit Tigers Team Set 2.25
1	Champ Summers	.10
2	Al Cowens	.10
3	Rich Hebner	.10
4	Steve Kemp	.10
5	Aurelio Lopez	.10
6	Jack Morris	.20
7	Lance Parrish	.35
8	Johnny Wockenfuss	.10
9	Alan Trammell	.75
10	Lou Whitaker	.35
11	Kirk Gibson	.35
----	Tigers header card	.05

Houston Astros Team Set 5.00
1a	Alan Ashby	.10
1b	Nolan Ryan	25.00
2	Cesar Cedeno	.10
3	Jose Cruz	.10
4	Art Howe	.10
5	Rafael Landestoy	.10
6	Joe Niekro	.20
7	Terry Puhl	.10
8	J.R. Richard	.20
9	Nolan Ryan	4.00
10	Joe Sambito	.10
11	Don Sutton	.75
----	Astros Header Card	.05

Kansas City Royals Team Set 3.00
1	Willie Aikens	.10
2	George Brett	2.00
3	Larry Gura	.10
4	Dennis Leonard	.10
5	Hal McRae	.10
6	Amos Otis	.10
7	Dan Quisenberry	.10
8	U.L. Washington	.10
9	John Wathan	.10
10	Frank White	.10
11	Willie Wilson	.20
----	Royals header card	.05

New York Mets Team Set 1.25
1	Neil Allen	.10
2	Doug Flynn	.10
3	Dave Kingman	.35
4	Randy Jones	.10
5	Pat Zachry	.10
6	Lee Mazzilli	.10
7	Rusty Staub	.20
8	Craig Swan	.10
9	Frank Taveras	.10
10	Alex Trevino	.10
11	Joel Youngblood	.10
----	Mets Header Card	.05

New York Yankees Team Set 75.00
1	Rich Gossage	15.00
2	Reggie Jackson	60.00
3	Rick Cerone	12.50
----	Yankees Header Card	4.00

Philadelphia Phillies Team Set 6.00
1	Bob Boone	.35
2	Larry Bowa	.20
3	Steve Carlton	1.25
4	Greg Luzinski	.10
5	Garry Maddox	.10
6	Bake McBride	.10
7	Tug McGraw	.10
8	Pete Rose	2.75
9	Mike Schmidt	2.75
10	Lonnie Smith	.10
11	Manny Trillo	.10
----	Phillies header card	.05

Pittsburgh Pirates Team Set 3.00
1	Jim Bibby	.10
2	John Candelaria	.10
3	Mike Easler	.10
4	Tim Foli	.10
5	Phil Garner	.10
6	Bill Madlock	.20
7	Omar Moreno	.10
8	Ed Ott	.10
9	Dave Parker	.30
10	Willie Stargell	2.00
11	Kent Tekulve	.10
----	Pirates header card	.05

St. Louis Cardinals Team Set 1.25
1	Bob Forsch	.10
2	George Hendrick	.10
3	Keith Hernandez	.20
4	Tom Herr	.10
5	Sixto Lezcano	.10
6	Ken Oberkfell	.10
7	Darrell Porter	.10
8	Tony Scott	.10
9	Lary Sorensen	.10
10	Bruce Sutter	.50
11	Garry Templeton	.10
----	Cardinals Header Card	.05

Brigham's Red Sox Ad Signs

These 6" x 17-1/2" blank-back cardboard ad pieces were designed to be folded into a countertop tent card, identical on each side. The color player photos on the ad pieces are different than those found on the issued cards.

NM/M
Complete Set (11):		35.00
Common Player:		2.00
(1)	Tom Burgmeier	2.00
(2)	Dennis Eckersley	4.00
(3)	Dwight Evans	3.00
(4)	Bob Stanley	2.00
(5)	Glenn Hoffman	2.00
(6)	Carney Lansford	2.00
(7)	Frank Tanana	2.00
(8)	Tony Perez	6.00
(9)	Jim Rice	8.00
(10)	Dave Stapleton	2.00
(11)	Carl Yastrzemski	15.00

1982 Coca-Cola Brigham's Red Sox

Coca-Cola, in conjunction with Brigham's Ice Cream stores, issued a 23-card set in the Boston area featuring Red Sox players. The Topps-produced cards, 2-1/2" x 3-1/2", are identical in format to the regular 1982 Topps set but contain the Coca-Cola and Brigham's logos in the corners. The cards were distributed in three-card cello packs, including an unnumbered header card.

NM/M
Complete Set (23):		5.00
Common Player:		.25
1	Gary Allenson	.25
2	Tom Burgmeier	.25
3	Mark Clear	.25
4	Steve Crawford	.25
5	Dennis Eckersley	1.50
6	Dwight Evans	.35
7	Rich Gedman	.25
8	Garry Hancock	.25
9	Glen Hoffman (Glenn)	.25
10	Carney Lansford	.25
11	Rick Miller	.25
12	Reid Nichols	.25
13	Bob Ojeda	.25
14	Tony Perez	1.50
15	Chuck Rainey	.25
16	Jerry Remy	.25
17	Jim Rice	1.00
18	Bob Stanley	.25
19	Dave Stapleton	.25
20	Mike Torrez	.25
21	John Tudor	.25
22	Carl Yastrzemski	3.00
----	Header Card	.10

Reds

Produced by Topps for Coca-Cola, the set consists of 23 cards featuring the Cincinnati Reds and was distributed in the Cincinnati area. The cards, which are 2-1/2" x 3-1/2" in size, are identical in design to the regular 1982 Topps set but have a Coca-Cola logo on the front and red backs. An unnumbered header card is included in the set.

NM/M
Complete Set (23):		3.00
Common Player:		.25
1	Johnny Bench	2.00
2	Bruce Berenyi	.25
3	Larry Biittner	.25
4	Cesar Cedeno	.35
5	Dave Concepcion	.35
6	Dan Driessen	.25
7	Greg Harris	.25
8	Paul Householder	.25
9	Tom Hume	.25
10	Clint Hurdle	.25
11	Jim Kern	.25
12	Wayne Krenchicki	.25
13	Rafael Landestoy	.25
14	Charlie Leibrandt	.25
15	Mike O'Berry	.25
16	Ron Oester	.25
17	Frank Pastore	.25
18	Joe Price	.25
19	Tom Seaver	1.00
20	Mario Soto	.25
21	Alex Trevino	.25
22	Mike Vail	.25
----	Header Card	.05

1985 Coca-Cola Dodgers Photocards

The first of two annual player photocard sets sponsored by Coke, these 3-1/2" x 5-1/2" cards feature color player action photos on front, surrounded by a white border. Below the photo is a 1985 copyright notice; the player's name is at bottom. Backs have a Coca-Cola logo in the lower-right corner, and may be found both with and without a printed message. The unnumbered cards are checklisted here in alphabetical order.

NM/M
Complete Set (34):		15.00
Common Player:		.50
(1)	Joe Amalfitano	.50
(2)	Dave Anderson	.50
(3)	Bob Bailor	.50
(4)	Monty Basgall	.50
(5)	Tom Brennan	.50
(6)	Greg Brock	.50
(7)	Bobby Castillo	.50
(8)	Mark Cresse	.50
(9)	Carlos Diaz	.50
(10)	Mariano Duncan	.60
(11)	Pedro Guerrero	.50
(12)	Orel Hershiser	2.00
(13)	Rick Honeycutt	.50
(14)	Steve Howe	.60
(15)	Ken Howell	.50
(16)	Jay Johnstone	.50
(17)	Ken Landreaux	.50
(18)	Tommy Lasorda	.75
(19)	Candy Maldonado	.50
(20)	Mike Marshall	.50
(21)	Manny Mota	.50
(22)	Tom Niedenfuer	.50
(23)	Al Oliver	.60
(24)	Alejandro Pena	.50
(25)	Ron Perranoski	.50
(26)	Jerry Reuss	.50
(27)	R.J. Reynolds	.50
(28)	Bill Russell	.50
(29)	Steve Sax	.50
(30)	Mike Scioscia	.50
(31)	Fernando Valenzuela	.75
(32)	Bob Welch	.50
(33)	Terry Whitfield	.50
(34)	Steve Yeager	.50

Pirates

13 Steve Kemp OF

A companion set to the cards issued in the 1985 Pirates yearbook, this set was given away to the first 10,000 youngsters attending May 18 and July 13 home games. The card of Kent Tekulve was withdrawn after his trade to the Phillies, making it quite scarce. The 2-1/2" x 3-1/2" cards have a color photo at center, surrounded by black and gold borders. A white panel at bottom has the player's name, position and uniform number. Backs are in black-and-white and feature complete major and minor league stats, plus the Cameron/Coca-Cola sponsors' logos.

NM/M
Complete Set (29) (No Tekulve):		12.00
Complete Set (30) (W/ Tekulve):		20.00
Common Player:		.50
2	Jim Morrison	.50
3	Johnny Ray	.50
5	Bill Madlock	1.00
6	Tony Pena	.60
7	Chuck Tanner	.50
10	Tim Foli	.50
11	Joe Orsulak	.50
12	Bill Almon	.50
13	Steve Kemp	.50
14	George Hendrick	.50
15	Lee Mazzilli	.50
16	Jerry Dybzinski	.50
19	Rod Scurry	.50
22	Lee Tunnell	.50
25	Jose DeLeon	.50
27	Kent Tekulve	7.50
28	Sixto Lezcano	.50
29	Rick Rhoden	.50
30	Jason Thompson	.50
34	Mike Bielecki	.50
35	Al Holland	.50
36	Marvell Wynne	.50
37	Rafael Belliard	.50
43	Don Robinson	.50
45	John Candelaria	.50
47	Cecilio Guante	.50
48	Larry McWilliams	.50
51	Doug Frobel	.50
--	Pirates coaches	.50

White Sox

Featuring past and present White Sox players, the cards in this set were given out on Tuesday night home games. The 2-5/8" x 4-1/8" cards contain a color photo of a current Sox member. A red box at the bottom of the card carries the team logo, player name, uniform number and position, plus a small oval portrait of a past Sox player. Backs contain the Coca-Cola logo and lifetime stats for the current and past player. The set is listed here by the player's uniform number with the last three cards being unnumbered. Complete sets were available through a fan club offer found in White Sox programs.

NM/M
Complete Set (30):		7.50
Common Player:		.25
0	Oscar Gamble, Zeke Bonura	.25
1	Scott Fletcher, Luke Appling	.60
3	Harold Baines, Bill Melton	.75
5	Luis Salazar, Chico Carrasquel	.25
7	Marc Hill, Sherman Lollar	.25
8	Daryl Boston, Jim Landis	.25
10	Tony LaRussa, Al Lopez	.75
12	Julio Cruz, Nellie Fox	1.50
13	Ozzie Guillen, Luis Aparicio	2.00
17	Jerry Hairston Sr., Smoky Burgess	.50
20	Joe DeSa, Carlos May	.25
22	Joel Skinner, J.C. Martin	.25
23	Rudy Law, Bill Skowron	.50
24	Floyd Bannister, Red Faber	.25
29	Greg Walker, Dick Allen	1.00
30	Gene Nelson, Early Wynn	.50
32	Tim Hulett, Pete Ward	.25
34	Richard Dotson, Ed Walsh	.25
37	Dan Spillner, Thornton Lee	.25
40	Britt Burns, Gary Peters	.25
41	Tom Seaver, Ted Lyons	2.00
42	Ron Kittle, Minnie Minoso	1.00
43	Bob James, Hoyt Wilhelm	1.00
44	Tom Paciorek, Eddie Collins	.25
46	Tim Lollar, Billy Pierce	.25
50	Juan Agosto, Wilbur Wood	.25
72	Carlton Fisk, Ray Schalk	1.50
---	Comiskey Park	.50
---	Ribbie and Roobarb/Mascots	.25
---	Nancy Faust/Organist	.25

1986 Coca-Cola Dodgers Photocards

For a second year Coke sponsored this set of 3-1/2" x 5-1/2" color cards. Fronts feature an action photo with white borders. Beneath the photo is a 1986 copyright line; the player's name is at bottom.

Backs have a red Coca-Cola logo in the lower-right corner, and can be found either otherwise blank or with a message to fans from the pictured player, along with a facsimile autograph. The unnumbered cards are checklisted here alphabetically.

NM/M
Complete Set (34):		15.00
Common Player:		.50
(1)	Joe Amalfitano	.50
(2)	Dave Anderson	.50
(3)	Monty Basgall	.50
(4)	Greg Brock	.50
(5)	Enos Cabell	.50
(6)	Cesar Cedeno	.50
(7)	Mark Cresse	.50
(8)	Carlos Diaz	.50
(9)	Mariano Duncan	.50
(10)	Pedro Guerrero	.50
(11)	Orel Hershiser	1.00
(12)	Ben Hines	.50
(13)	Rick Honeycutt	.50
(14)	Ken Howell	.50
(15)	Ken Landreaux	.50
(16)	Tom Lasorda	.75
(17)	Bill Madlock	.50
(18)	Mike Marshall	.50
(19)	Len Matuszek	.50
(20)	Manny Mota	.50
(21)	Tom Niedenfuer	.50
(22)	Alejandro Pena	.50
(23)	Ron Perranoski	.50
(24)	Dennis Powell	.50
(25)	Jerry Reuss	.50
(26)	Bill Russell	.50
(27)	Steve Sax	.50
(28)	Mike Scioscia	.50
(29)	Franklin Stubbs	.50
(30)	Alex Trevino	.50
(31)	Fernando Valenzuela	.75
(32)	Ed Vande Berg	.50
(33)	Bob Welch	.50
(34)	Terry Whitfield	.50

White Sox

For the second year in a row, Coca-Cola, in conjunction with the Chicago White Sox, issued a 30-card set. As in 1985, cards were given out at the park on Tuesday night games. Full sets were available through a fan club offer found in the White Sox program. The 2-5/8" x 4-1/8" cards feature 25 players plus other team personnel. Fronts have a color photo (a game-action shot in most instances) and a white bar at the bottom. A black and white bat with "SOX" shown on the barrel is located within the white bar, along with the player's name, position and uniform number.

The white and gray backs with black print include the Coca-Cola trademark. Lifetime statistics are shown on all player cards, but there is no personal information such as height, weight or age. The non-player cards are blank-backed save for the name and logo at the top. The cards in the checklist that follows are numbered by the players' uniform numbers, with the last five cards of the set being unnumbered.

		NM/M
Complete Set (30):		12.00
Common Player:		.25
1	Wayne Tolleson	.25
3	Harold Baines	.75
7	Marc Hill	.25
8	Daryl Boston	.25
12	Julio Cruz	.25
13	Ozzie Guillen	.50
17	Jerry Hairston Sr.	.25
19	Floyd Bannister	.25
20	Reid Nichols	.25
22	Joel Skinner	.25
24	Dave Schmidt	.25
26	Bobby Bonilla	1.00
29	Greg Walker	.25
30	Gene Nelson	.25
32	Tim Hulett	.25
33	Neil Allen	.25
34	Richard Dotson	.25
40	Joe Cowley	.25
41	Tom Seaver	3.00
42	Ron Kittle	.35
43	Bob James	.25
44	John Cangelosi	.25
50	Juan Agosto	.25
52	Joel Davis	.25
72	Carlton Fisk	3.00
---	Ribbie & Roobarb/ Mascots	.25
---	Nancy Faust/Organist	.25
---	Ken "Hawk" Harrelson	.35
---	Tony LaRussa	.60
---	Minnie Minoso	1.50

1987 Coca-Cola Tigers

Pat Sheridan
DETROIT TIGERS OUTFIELD

Coca-Cola and S. Abraham & Sons, Inc. issued a set of 18 baseball cards featuring members of the Detroit Tigers. The set is comprised of six four-part folding panels. Each panel includes three player cards (each 2-1/2" x 3-1/2") and one team logo card. A bright yellow border surrounds the full-color photo. The backs are designed on a vertical format and contain personal data and career statistics. The set was produced by Mike Schecter and Associates.

		NM/M
Complete Panel Set (6):		4.00
Complete Singles Set (18):		2.00
Common Panel:		.50
Common Player:		.05
Panel		.85
1	Kirk Gibson	.30
2	Larry Herndon	.05
3	Walt Terrell	.05
Panel		1.50
4	Alan Trammell	.50
5	Frank Tanana	.05
6	Pat Sheridan	.05
Panel		.85
7	Jack Morris	.30
8	Mike Heath	.05
9	Dave Bergman	.05
Panel		.50
10	Chet Lemon	.05
11	Dwight Lowry	.05
12	Dan Petry	.05
Panel		.85
13	Darrell Evans	.25

14	Darnell Coles	.05
15	Willie Hernandez	.05
Panel		1.00
16	Lou Whitaker	.25
17	Tom Brookens	.05
18	John Grubb	.05

White Sox

3 Harold Baines, OF

The Chicago White Sox Fan Club, in conjunction with Coca-Cola, offered members a set of 30 trading cards. For the $10 membership fee, fans received the set plus additional fan club gifts and privileges. The cards, 2-5/8" x 4", feature full-color photos inside a blue and red border. Backs include the player's name, position, uniform number and statistics, plus the Coca-Cola logo. Cards are checklisted here by uniform number.

		NM/M
Complete Set (30):		7.50
Common Player:		.25
1	Jerry Royster	.25
3	Harold Baines	.50
5	Ron Karkovice	.25
8	Daryl Boston	.25
10	Fred Manrique	.25
12	Steve Lyons	.25
13	Ozzie Guillen	.50
14	Russ Morman	.25
16	Donnie Hill	.25
16	Jim Fregosi	.25
17	Jerry Hairston Sr.	.25
19	Floyd Bannister	.25
21	Gary Redus	.25
22	Ivan Calderon	.25
25	Ron Hassey	.25
26	Jose DeLeon	.25
29	Greg Walker	.25
32	Tim Hulett	.25
33	Neil Allen	.25
34	Rich Dotson	.25
36	Ray Searage	.25
37	Bobby Thigpen	.25
39	Jim Winn	.25
43	Bob James	.25
50	Joel McKeon	.25
52	Joel Davis	.25
72	Carlton Fisk	3.00
---	Ribbie & Roobarb/ Mascots	.25
---	Nancy Faust/Organist	.25
---	Minnie Minoso	.75

1988 Coca-Cola Padres

LARRY BOWA
#10 Manager

A 20-card set sponsored by Coca-Cola was designed as part of the San Diego Padres Junior Fan Club promotion for 1988. This set was distributed as a nine-card starter sheet, with 11 additional single cards handed out during various home games. The standard-size cards feature full-color player photos framed by a black and orange border. The player's name is printed above the photo; uniform number and position appear at lower-right. A large Padres logo curves upward from the lower-left corner. Backs are brown on white and include the Padres logo at upper-left opposite the player's name and personal information. Career highlights and 1987 stats appear in the center of the card back above the Coca-Cola and Junior Padres Fan Club logos.

		NM/M
Complete Set (21):		20.00
Common Player:		.50
Panel		
1	Garry Templeton	.60
5	Randy Ready	.50
10	Larry Bowa	.60
11	Tim Flannery	.50
35	Chris Brown	.50
45	Jimmy Jones	.50
48	Mark Davis	.50
55	Mark Grant	.50
---	20th Anniversary Logo Card	.10
Singles		
7	Keith Moreland	1.00
8	John Kruk	2.00
9	Benito Santiago	2.00
14	Carmelo Martinez	1.00
15	Jack McKeon	1.00
19	Tony Gwynn	6.00
22	Stan Jefferson	1.00
27	Mark Parent	1.00
30	Eric Show	1.00
31	Ed Whitson	1.00
41	Lance McCullers	1.00
51	Greg Booker	1.00

White Sox

Part of a fan club membership package, this unnumbered 30-card set features full-color photos of 27 players, the team mascot, team organist and Comiskey Park. Cards have a bright red border, with team logo in the photo's lower-left corner. The player name fills the bottom border. Backs are printed in black on gray and white and include player name, personal info and career summary. The set was included in the $10 membership package, with a portion of the cost going to the ChiSox Kids Charity.

		NM/M
Complete Set (30):		5.00
Common Player:		.25
(1)	Harold Baines	.50
(2)	Daryl Boston	.25
(3)	Ivan Calderon	.25
(4)	John Davis	.25
(5)	Jim Fregosi	.25
(6)	Carlton Fisk	2.50
(7)	Ozzie Guillen	.50
(8)	Donnie Hill	.25
(9)	Rick Horton	.25
(10)	Lance Johnson	.25
(11)	Dave LaPoint	.25
(12)	Bill Long	.25
(13)	Steve Lyons	.25
(14)	Jack McDowell	.30
(15)	Fred Manrique	.25
(16)	Minnie Minoso	.75
(17)	Dan Pasqua	.25
(18)	John Pawlowski	.25
(19)	Melido Perez	.25
(20)	Billy Pierce	.25
(21)	Gary Redus	.25
(22)	Jerry Reuss	.25
(23)	Mark Salas	.25
(24)	Jose Segura	.25
(25)	Bobby Thigpen	.25

---

(26)	Greg Walker	.25
(27)	Kenny Williams	.25
(28)	Nancy Faust/Organist	.25
(29)	Ribbie & Roobarb/ Mascots	.25
(30)	Comiskey Park	.40

1989 Coca-Cola Padres

#25 First Base
JACK CLARK

This 20-card set is part of the Junior Padres Fan Club membership package. Members receive a nine-card starter set printed on one large perforated sheet. Additional cards are distributed to kids at specially designated games (free admission for kids). Fronts feature an orange-and-brown double border, with a bright orange Padres logo printed at lower-left. Uniform number and position are printed diagonally across the upper-left corner, with the player's name in large block letters along the bottom border.

		NM/M
Complete Set (21):		26.00
Common Player:		.50
Panel		
1	Garry Templeton	.60
5	Randy Ready	.50
12	Roberto Alomar	4.50
14	Carmelo Martinez	.50
15	Jack McKeon	.50
30	Eric Show	.50
31	Ed Whitson	.50
43	Dennis Rasmussen	.50
---	Logo card	.10
Singles		
6	Luis Salazar	1.00
9	Benito Santiago	1.00
10	Leon Roberts	1.00
11	Tim Flannery	1.00
18	Chris James	1.00
19	Tony Gwynn	8.00
23	Jack Clark	1.00
27	Mark Parent	1.00
35	Walt Terrell	1.00
47	Bruce Hurst	1.00
48	Mark Davis	1.00
55	Mark Grant	1.00

White Sox

Chicago White Sox American Pastime
Steve Lyons • 2B

For the fifth straight year, Coca-Cola sponsored a set of cards featuring the Chicago White Sox. The 30-card set was distributed to fans attending a special promotional game at Comiskey Park and was also available by mail to members of the ChiSox fan club. Card fronts feature blue borders with red and white graphics and a pair of crossed bats. Horizontal backs include player biographies, personal data and the Coca-Cola logo. Cards measure 2-5/8" x 3-1/2".

		NM/M
Complete Set (30):		5.00
Common Player:		.20
1	New Comiskey Park, 1991	.40
2	Comiskey Park	.40
3	Jeff Torborg	.20
4	Coaching staff (Dave LaRoche, Terry Bevington, Walt Hriniak, Sammy Ellis, Glenn Rosenbaum, Ron Clark)	.20
5	Harold Baines	.45
6	Daryl Boston	.20
7	Ivan Calderon	.20
8	Carlton Fisk	2.50
9	Dave Gallagher	.20
10	Ozzie Guillen	.20
11	Shawn Hillegas	.20
12	Barry Jones	.20
13	Ron Karkovice	.20
14	Eric King	.20
15	Ron Kittle	.20
16	Bill Long	.20
17	Steve Lyons	.20
18	Donn Pall	.20
19	Dan Pasqua	.20
20	Ken Patterson	.20
21	Melido Perez	.20
22	Jerry Reuss	.20
23	Billy Jo Robidoux	.20
24	Steve Rosenberg	.20
25	Jeff Schaefer	.20
26	Bobby Thigpen	.20
27	Greg Walker	.20
28	Eddie Williams	.20
29	Nancy Faust/Organist	.20
30	Minnie Minoso	.75

1990 Coca-Cola Padres

PADRES
TONY GWYNN

This set was designed for members of the Junior Padres Club sponsored by Coca-Cola. Each member received an eight-card panel and then received two different single cards at every Junior Padres Club game attended. Card fronts feature full-color photos with the Padres logo in the upper-right corner of the card. Backs feature statistics, career highlights and a red Coca-Cola logo. The cards are numbered by the player's uniform number.

		NM/M
Complete Set (21):		16.00
Common Player:		.35
Panel		
10	Bip Roberts	.35
15	Jack McKeon	.35
30	Eric Show	.35
31	Ed Whitson	.35
40	Andy Benes	.75
43	Dennis Rasmussen	.35
55	Mark Grant	.35
---	Logo card	.35
Singles		
1	Garry Templeton	.50
8	Fred Lynn	.75
9	Benito Santiago	1.00
11	Craig Lefferts	.50
12	Mike Pagliarulo	.50
17	Joe Carter	1.00
19	Tony Gwynn	6.00
25	Jack Clark	.50
27	Mark Parent	.50
38	Calvin Schiraldi	.50
46	Greg Harris	.50
47	Bruce Hurst	.50

Garry Templeton

Coca-Cola, Vons stores and the Padres joined forces to release this special pin/Baseball card collectible in honor of Garry Templeton becoming the club's all-time leader in games

---

MOST GAMES PLAYED
THE CAPTAIN
PADRES
TEMPLETON

played. The card front features a full-color photo of Templeton and displays "Most Games Played" and "The Captain" in orange at the top of the photo. "Templeton" appears vertically in white along the left border. The Coca-Cola and Padre logos also appear on the card front. The bottom of the card features a perforated edge where the pin is attached as an extension of the card. The card back is printed in black and white and displays biographical information, career highlights and career statistics.

		NM/M
Card/Pin Combination:		1.50
(1)	Most Games Played Card (Garry Templeton)	.50
(2)	Most Games Played Pin (Garry Templeton)	1.00

Tigers

Detroit Tigers

(9) LARRY SHEETS
Outfielder

Once again utilizing the larger 2-7/8" x 4-1/4" format, this set was jointly sponsored by Coke and Kroger grocery stores and distributed at the July 14 game. Cards feature color action photos on front, surrounded by green borders. Backs have a black-and-white portrait photo, the appropriate logos and complete minor and major league stats. The player's uniform number appears in the upper-left corner.

		NM/M
Complete Set (28):		6.00
Common Player:		.15
(1)	Sparky Anderson	.50
(2)	Dave Bergman	.15
(3)	Brian DuBois	.15
(4)	Cecil Fielder	.25
(5)	Paul Gibson	.15
(6)	Jerry D. Gleaton	.15
(7)	Mike Heath	.15
(8)	Mike Henneman	.15
(9)	Tracy Jones	.15
(10)	Chet Lemon	.15
(11)	Urbano Lugo	.15
(12)	Jack Morris	.20
(13)	Lloyd Moseby	.15
(14)	Matt Nokes	.15
(15)	Edwin Nunez	.15
(16)	Dan Petry	.15
(17)	Tony Phillips	.15
(18)	Kevin Ritz	.15
(19)	Jeff Robinson	.15
(20)	Ed Romero	.15
(21)	Mark Salas	.15

(22) Larry Sheets .15
(23) Frank Tanana .15
(24) Alan Trammell .75
(25) Gary Ward .15
(26) Lou Whitaker .40
(27) Ken Williams .15
(28) Coaches (Billy Consolo, Alex Grammas, Billy Muffett, Vada Pinson, Dick Tracewski) .15

White Sox

An attractive "Comiskey Park 1910-1990" logo is featured on the front of each card in this set. Fronts also feature full-color photos with a thin white inner border. The cards are numbered according to uniform number, with the exception of four special cards including Top Prospect Frank Thomas. Horizontal card backs feature black print on white and gray stock; 1989 statistics and career highlights are provided. The 1990 set marks the sixth straight year that Coca-Cola sponsored a White Sox set.

		NM/M
Complete Set (30):		80.00
Common Player:		.25
1	Lance Johnson	.25
7	Scott Fletcher	.25
10	Jeff Torborg	.25
12	Steve Lyons	.25
13	Ozzie Guillen	.50
14	Craig Grebeck	.25
17	Dave Gallagher	.25
20	Ron Karkovice	.25
22	Ivan Calderon	.25
23	Robin Ventura	1.00
24	Carlos Martinez	.25
25	Sammy Sosa	65.00
27	Greg Hibbard	.25
29	Jack McDowell	.25
30	Donn Pall	.25
31	Scott Radinsky	.25
33	Melido Perez	.25
34	Ken Patterson	.25
36	Eric King	.25
37	Bobby Thigpen	.25
42	Ron Kittle	.25
44	Dan Pasqua	.25
45	Wayne Edwards	.25
50	Barry Jones	.25
52	Jerry Kutzler	.25
72	Carlton Fisk	5.00
---	Top Prospect (Frank Thomas)	15.00
---	White Sox manager, coaches (Jeff Torborg)	.25
---	Captains (Ozzie Guillen, Carlton Fisk)	1.00
---	Rookies (Wayne Edwards, Craig Greback, Jerry Kutzler, Scott Radinsky, Robin Ventura)	.35

1991 Coca-Cola Don Mattingly

Though sponsored by Coca-Cola, the manner of distribution of this issue is unclear. The "Mattingly's 23" logo on each side of the card suggests a connection to his Evansville, Ind., restaurant. Fronts of the 2-1/2" x 3-1/2" cards have photos in black-and-white or color, or artwork. The border is white with blue pinstripes. The year of the picture is at top of the photo and there is a Coke logo at bottom. Backs are printed in red and blue and contain career highlights and stats, along with a card number and logos.

		NM/M
Complete Set (15):		10.00
Common Card:		1.00
1	Don Mattingly/1978	1.00
2	Don Mattingly/1979	1.00
3	Don Mattingly/1980	1.00
4	Don Mattingly/1981	1.00
5	Don Mattingly/1982	1.00
6	Don Mattingly/1983	1.00
7	Don Mattingly/'83-'84	1.00
8	Don Mattingly/1984	1.00
9	Don Mattingly/1985	1.00
10	Don Mattingly/1986	1.00
11	Don Mattingly/1987	1.00
12	Don Mattingly/1990	1.00
13	Don Mattingly/1991 (Photo)	1.00
14	Don Mattingly/1991 (Artwork)	1.00
15	Don Mattingly/1991 (Coca-Cola logo.)	1.00

Tigers

This set was sponsored by Coca-Cola and Kroger, whose logos appear on the red, white and blue backs. The oversize (2-7/8" x 4-1/4") cards feature game-action or portrait color photos on front along with the player's name vertically printed on the right border and the Tigers logo in the lower-left corner. Backs are printed horizontally and feature complete minor and major league statistics. The set is numbered according to uniform number, which appears in an orange triangle on front.

		NM/M
Complete Set (28):		7.00
Common Player:		.35
1	Lou Whitaker	.75
3	Alan Trammell	1.00
4	Tony Phillips	.35
10	Andy Allanson	.35
11	Sparky Anderson	.75
14	Dave Bergman	.35
15	Lloyd Moseby	.35
19	Jerry Don Gleaton	.35
20	Mickey Tettleton	.35
22	Milt Cuyler	.35
23	Mark Leiter	.35
24	Travis Fryman	.35
25	John Shelby	.35
26	Frank Tanana	.35
27	Mark Salas	.35
29	Pete Incaviglia	.35
31	Kevin Ritz	.35
35	Walt Terrell	.35
36	Bill Gullickson	.35
39	Mike Henneman	.35
42	Mike Dalton	.35
44	Rob Deer	.35
45	Cecil Fielder	.50
46	Dan Petry	.35
48	Paul Gibson	.35
49	Steve Searcy	.35
55	John Cerutti	.35

Tigers Coaches (Billy Consolo, Jim Davenport, Alex Grammas, Billy Muffett, Vada Pinson, Dick Tracewski) .35

1992 Coca-Cola Nolan Ryan Career Series

This 26-card set was produced by Donruss in conjunction with Coca-Cola to honor Nolan Ryan's 26 major league seasons. One Nolan Ryan card was packaged with three regular 1992 Donruss cards in special 12-packs of Coke. Complete sets, in a black, red and gold box, were available through a mail-in offer. The 2-1/2" x 3-1/2" cards have a full-color photo on front, framed by a gold border. Ryan's name is printed in gold toward the bottom, above a blue bar which presents a team and year. The Coke logo is at upper right. On back there are details of Ryan's performance in the indicated year, the card number, and team and Coke logos. An 18" x 12" color poster picturing the cards and a photo of a Ryan-autographed ball was issued as a point-of-purchase display.

		NM/M
Complete Set (26):		7.50
Common Card:		.50
Display Poster:		15.00
1	1966 Breaking In	.50
2	1968 Record-Setting Rookie	.50
3	1969 World Champions	.50
4	1970 Growing Pains	.50
5	1971 Traded	.50
6	1972 Fitted for a Halo	.50
7	1973 First Two No-Nos and a Record	.50
8	1974 No-Hitter No. 3/Another K Record	.50
9	1975 Tying Koufax	.50
10	1976 Back on Track	.50
11	1977 Carrying the Load	.50
12	1978 A Year of Injuries	.50
13	1979 California Farewell	.50
14	1980 Coming Home	.50
15	1981 A Gusher in Houston	.50
16	1982 Mounting 'Em Up	.50
17	1983 Passing the Big Train	.50
18	1984 Misleading Signs of Age	.50
19	1985 Another Milestone/ A New Contract	.50
20	1986 The Elbow Flares Up Again	.50
21	1987 Another ERA/Strikeout Crown at 40	.50
22	1988 Leaving Home Again	.50
23	1989 5,000 Strikeouts	.50
24	1990 Win No. 300, No-Hitter No. 6	.50
25	1991 No-Hitter No. 7	.50
26	1992 Man of Records	.50

Tigers

This set of large-format (2-7/8" x 4-1/4") cards features central photos of the Bengals in action. Dark blue stripes at top and bottom have the team name in white, while the player name, uniform number and position are printed in black on an orange

stripe directly beneath the photo. A color team logo in the upper-right completes the front design. Backs have complete major and minor league stats, a few personal data and color logos of Coke and the Kroger grocery chain.

		NM/M
Complete Set (28):		5.00
Common Player:		.15
1	Lou Whitaker	.35
3	Alan Trammell	.75
7	Tony Phillips	.15
9	Scott Livingstone	.15
11	Skeeter Barnes	.15
11	Sparky Anderson	.50
14	Dave Bergman	.15
15	Mark Carreon	.15
18	Gary Pettis	.15
19	Chad Kreuter	.15
20	Mickey Tettleton	.15
22	Milt Cuyler	.15
23	Mark Leiter	.15
24	Travis Fryman	.25
26	Frank Tanana	.15
27	Kurt Knudsen	.15
28	Rob Deer	.15
31	Kevin Ritz	.15
32	Dan Gladden	.15
35	Walt Terrell	.15
36	Bill Gullickson	.15
39	Mike Henneman	.15
43	Mike Munoz	.15
44	John Doherty	.15
45	Cecil Fielder	.25
46	John Kiely	.15
48	Les Lancaster	.15
---	Tigers coaches (Billy Consolo, Gene Roof, Larry Herndon, Dick Tracewksi, Billy Muffett, Dan Whitmer)	.15

1992 Coca-Cola/ Hardees Major League Line-Up Discs

This set of 3" diameter "Major League Line-Up" cardboard discs was a regional give-away sponsored by Coca-Cola and distributed by Hardee's restaurants. The glossy discs have player photos at center with position and uniform numbers at the sides. Backs are in black-and-white with a few stats and career highlights and various logos. A checklist disc was also distributed.

		NM/M
Complete Set (24):		12.00
Common Player:		.50
1	Roger Clemens	2.50
2	Sandy Alomar Jr.	.50
3	Rafael Palmeiro	1.25
4	Roberto Alomar	.75
5	Kelly Gruber	.50
6	Ozzie Guillen	.50
7	Devon White	.50
8	David Henderson	.50
9	Robin Yount	1.50
10	Chili Davis	.50
11	Chuck Knoblauch	.50

Caption: (1) Lou Whitaker IF

12	Paul Molitor	1.50
13	Tom Glavine	.75
14	Benito Santiago	.50
15	Hal Morris	.50
16	Delino DeShields	.50
17	Matt Williams	.50
18	Ozzie Smith	2.00
19	Andy Van Slyke	.50
20	Andre Dawson	.75
21	Ron Gant	.50
22	Jeff Bagwell	1.50
23	Terry Pendleton	.50
24	Brett Butler	.50

1993 Coca-Cola Commanders of the Hill

Coca-Cola and Topps teamed up to print a 30-card Commanders of the Hill set in 1993. The cards were available in five-card packages with soft-drink purchases on military bases at base exchange food court concessions. The set was divided into three areas: Cy Young Winners, Strikeout Leaders and Team ERA Leaders, with the National League player's names in yellow on a red background and the American League in red on yellow.

		NM/M
Complete Set (30):		5.00
Common Player:		.10
1	Dennis Eckersley	.50
2	Mike Mussina	.40
3	Roger Clemens	1.00
4	Jim Abbott	.10
5	Jack McDowell	.10
6	Charles Nagy	.10
7	Bill Gullickson	.10
8	Kevin Appier	.10
9	Bill Wegman	.10
10	John Smiley	.10
11	Melido Perez	.10
12	Dave Stewart	.10
13	Dave Fleming	.10
14	Kevin Brown	.10
15	Juan Guzman	.10
16	Randy Johnson	.60
17	Greg Maddux	.75
18	Tom Glavine	.35
19	Greg Maddux	.75
20	Jose Rijo	.10
21	Pete Harnisch	.10
22	Tom Candiotti	.10
23	Denny Martinez	.10
24	Sid Fernandez	.10
25	Curt Schilling	.35
26	Doug Drabek	.10
27	Bob Tewksbury	.10
28	Andy Benes	.10
29	Bill Swift	.10
30	John Smoltz	.10

1995 Coca-Cola Minnesota Twins POGs

Over the course of three games in July 1995, the Twins issued a three-sheet series of POGs, 15,000 at each game. The souvenir measures about 10-1/4" x 9-1/2" and features a

large color game photo, around and above which are POGs, about 1-1/8" diameter, of players, coaches and sponsors. The POGs are die-cut for removal from the sheets. Each sheet has 11 players or coaches, and each has the same four sponsors' POGs. Fronts have player portrait photos while backs have a repeating Coca-Cola logo. The POGs are un-numbered and listed here alphabetically by sheet. The players are not identified on the POGs themselves.

		NM/M
Complete Set, Sheets (3):		12.00
Complete Set, Singles (33):		9.00
Common Player:		.25
	Series 1, July 1	4.00
(1)	Rick Aguilera	.25
(2)	Rich Becker	.25
(3)	Marty Cordova	.25
(4)	Terry Crowley	.25
(5)	Eddie Guardado	.25
(6)	Jeff Reboulet	.25
(7)	Rich Robertson	.25
(8)	Scott Stahoviak	.25
(9)	Dick Such	.25
(10)	Kevin Tapani	.25
(11)	Matt Walbeck	.25
	Series 2, July 17	3.00
(12)	Alex Cole	.25
(13)	Scott Erickson	.25
(14)	Ron Gardenhire	.25
(15)	Chip Hale	.25
(16)	Chuck Knoblauch	.25
(17)	Scott Leius	.25
(18)	Pat Mahomes	.25
(19)	Pedro Munoz	.25
(20)	Erik Schullstrom	.25
(21)	Dave Stevens	.25
(22)	Scott Ullger	.25
	Series 3, July 28	5.00
(23)	Jerald Clark	.25
(24)	Mark Guthrie	.25
(25)	Tom Kelly	.25
(26)	Kevin Maas	.25
(27)	Pat Meares	.25
(28)	Matt Merullo	.25
(29)	Kirby Puckett	3.50
(30)	Brad Radke	.25
(31)	Rick Stelmaszek	.25
(32)	Mike Trombley	.25
(33)	Jerry White	.25
---	Coca-Cola	.05
---	Fox 29 TV	.05
---	Minnesota Twins logo	.10
---	Nestle	.05

Pittsburgh Pirates POGs

To celebrate the 25th anniversary of Three Rivers Stadium, Coca-Cola and the Pirates issued a set of POGs marking the 25 greatest baseball moments at the stadium. The POGs were issued nine apiece on heavy 6" x 8" cardboard panels. Individual POGs measure about 1-3/4" diameter and are perforated at the edge so they can be removed from the panel. Most fronts have a border of team-color orange and black, with central photos in black-and-white or color. Backs of #1-8 have a green Fruitopia ad; backs of #10-18 have an ad for Sprite in green, while #9, 19-25 have a red Coca-Cola ad on back.

		NM/M
Complete Set Panels (3):		15.00
Complete Set Singles (27):		9.00
Common POG:		.25
1	1994 All-Star Game (All-Star logo.)	.25
2	Roberto Clemente (3,000th Hit)	2.00
3	Roberto Clemente (Uniform #21 retired.)	2.00

		NM/M
4	Pirates Win 1979 N.L. Pennant (We Are Family logo.)	.25
5	John Candelaria (No-Hitss Dodgers)	.25
6	Willie Stargell (Uniform #8 retired.)	.50
7	Mike Schmidt (500th Home Run)	.75
8	Kent Tekulve (First Game, 7/16/70)	.25
---	Coke/Fruitopia logos	.05
9	First World Series Night Game	.25
10	Nellie Briles (1971 World Series 2-Hitter)	.25
11	Pirates Win 1971 N.L. Pennant	.25
12	Pirates Clinch N.L. East, 1979	.25
13	Pirates Clinch N.L. East, 1992 (Jim Leyland)	.25
14	Bob Gibson (No-Hits Pirates 8/14/71)	.40
15	1979 World Series Game 5 (Jim Rooker)	.25
16	Pirates Clinch N.L. East, 1971	.25
17	Beat Braves in NLCS Game 5, 1992	.25
18	John Milner (Grand Slam Beats Phillis 8/5/79)	.25
19	Barry Bonds (11th Inning HR Beats St. Louis 8/12/91)	.75
20	Jeff King (5 Runs in 9th to Beat Dodgers, 5/28/90)	.25
21	Danny Murtaugh (Murtaugh, Joe L. Brown Retire)	.25
22	"Gunner" Returns to Broadcast Booth	.25
23	Sweep Phillies in 9/29/78 Doubleheader	.25
24	Jim Leyland (Makes Pittsburgh Debut)	.25
25	1974 All-Star Game (Program)	.25
---	Coke logos	.05

1995 Coca-Cola/ Publix Florida Marlins

Coca-Cola and the Publix grocery store chain sponsored this team set issue. Fronts of the standard-size (2-1/2" x 3-1/2") cards have color player action photos on a large background of the team logo. Backs have a color portrait photo and stats. Cards are checklisted here by uniform number.

		NM/M
Complete Set (27):		7.50
Common Player:		.50
3	Quilvio Veras	.50
4	Greg Colbrunn	.50
6	Tommy Gregg	.50
7	Kurt Abbott	.50
8	Andre Dawson	2.50
9	Terry Pendleton	.50
10	Gary Sheffield	2.50
11	Chris Hammond	.50
14	Jerry Browne	.50
15	Marcel Lacheman	.50
17	Darrell Whitmore	.50
21	Chuck Carr	.50
23	Charles Johnson	.50
26	Alex Arias	.50
28	Mark Gardner	.50
30	Mario Diaz	.50
31	Robb Nen	.50
33	John Burkett	.50
34	Bryan Harvey	.50
35	David Weathers	.50
42	Jeremy Hernandez	.50
48	Pat Rapp	.50
51	Terry Mathews	.50
52	Randy Veres	.50
58	Yorkis Perez	.50
---	Coaches	.50
---	Billy the Marlin/Mascot	.50

1996 Coca-Cola/ Kroger Nolan Ryan Card/Pin

Culminating activities during Nolan Ryan Appreciation Week at Arlington, September 12-15, fans attending the September 15 game, during which Ryan's uniform number was retired by the Rangers, received a baseball card/pin combination sponsored by Coca-Cola and Kroger grocers. The giveaway is a 2-1/2" x 5-1/2" cardboard panel. At top is a 2-1/2" x 3-7/8" card separated by perforations from the bottom panel on which the 1-1/8" x 1-1/2" enameled jersey pin is affixed. The front has a spring-training game-action color photo of Ryan. The back is in black-and-white with a career summary, sponsor' logos and a picture of the pin.

	NM/M
Card/Pin Combination:	7.00

1998 Coca-Cola Chipper Jones

This 2-1/2" x 3-1/2" card was an Atlanta-area exclusive. The front shows the Braves' star enjoying a Coke. On back is a coupon for a free 20 ounce Coca-Cola.

	NM/M
Chipper Jones	10.00

2002 Coca-Cola S.F. Giants

Each of the 12-card single-player sets produced by photographer Barry Colla in 1990 was preceded by a

A dozen of the most popular Giants are pictured in game-action photos on the fronts of these regionally issued cards. Two-card cello packs were inserted in each specially marked 24-can case of Coke, making acquisition of the set an expensive proposition. The glossy fronts have red borders with Coca-Cola and team logos in the lower corners. Backs have a portrait photo, a few bits of personal data and stats, and a host of appropriate logos.

		NM/M
Complete Set (12):		20.00
Common Player:		1.00
1	Jeff Kent	1.00
2	Rich Aurilia	1.00
3	J.T. Snow	1.00
4	Marvin Benard	1.00
5	Pedro Feliz	1.00
6	Shawon Dunston	1.00
7	Robb Nen	1.00
8	Felix Rodriguez	1.00
9	Russ Ortiz	1.00
10	Kirk Reuter	1.00
11	Livan Hernandez	1.00
12	Barry Bonds	12.00

1989 Barry Colla Postcards

In 1989, California baseball photographer Barry Colla began a series of player postcard sets. Each set contains eight postcards of the player and was sold in a white paper envelope with the team logo. The postcards are identical in format, measuring 3-1/2" x 5-1/2". Fronts feature borderless color photos on high-gloss stock. Backs are printed in black-and-white and feature a team logo at center. The player's name, uniform number, team and position are printed in the upper-left. A card number appears at top-center.

		NM/M
1-8	Will Clark	3.00
1-8	Jose Canseco	4.00
1-8	Andre Dawson	4.00
1-8	Mike Greenwell	3.00
1-8	Don Mattingly	5.00
1-8	Mark McGwire	6.00
1-8	Kevin Mitchell	3.00
1-8	Ozzie Smith	4.50

1990 Barry Colla Promos

Barry Colla continued his series of single-player postcard sets 1990. The basic format continued unchanged. The 3-1/2" x 5-1/2" card feature borderless color game-action and posed photos on high-gloss stock. Black-and-white backs feature a team logo at center, a card number at top and, in the upper-left, the player's name, uniform number, team and position. Sets were sold in white paper envelopes with color team logos on the front.

		NM/M
1-8	Mark Grace	3.00

1991 Barry Colla Promos

Each of the eight 12-card single-player sets produced by California photographer

promo card. The promos feature the same borderless color photography as the issued cards. Backs have information on date and size of the limited-edition issues and ordering information printed in black and white. Checklist of the unnumbered cards is presented here in alphabetical order.

		NM/M
Complete Set (4):		6.00
Common Player:		1.00
(1)	Jose Canseco	2.00
(2)	Will Clark	1.00
(3)	Kevin Maas	1.00
(4)	Don Mattingly	3.00

1990 Barry Colla

In 1990 baseball photographer Barry Colla began production of a series of single-player card sets. In standard 2-1/2" x 3-1/2" size, the cards featured high-gloss borderless photos on front, with no extraneous graphics. Backs feature stats, career notes, personal data and team logos. The 12-card sets were sold in small decorative cardboard boxes. Production figures are noted in parentheses.

		NM/M
1-12	Jose Canseco/20,000	3.00
1-12	Will Clark/15,000	2.00
1-12	Kevin Maas/7,500	2.00
1-12	Don Mattingly/15,000	7.50

1991 Barry Colla

In 1991, baseball photographer Barry Colla continued production of a series of single-player card sets. In standard 2-1/2" x 3-1/2" size, the cards featured high-gloss borderless photos on front, with no extraneous graphics. Backs feature stats, career notes, personal data and team logos. The 12-card sets were sold in small decorative cardboard boxes. Production figures are noted in parentheses.

		NM/M
1-12	Roberto Alomar/ 7,500	2.00
1-12	Barry Bonds/7,500	12.00
1-12	Joe Carter/7,500	1.50
1-12	Dwight Gooden/ 15,000	1.50
1-12	Ken Griffey Jr./15,000	6.00
1-12	David Justice/15,000	1.50
1-12	Ryne Sandberg/ 15,000	4.00
1-12	Darryl Strawberry/ 15,000	1.50

Postcards

Only one single-player postcard set was produced by Barry Colla in 1991: Ryne Sandberg. The eight-card set, like the 1989-90 issues, features full-color game-action and posed photos presented on a borderless, high-gloss 3-1/2" x 5-1/2" format. Back design was changed for the

Barry Colla in 1991 was preceded by the issue of a promo card. Identical in format, the promos feature high quality borderless photos on glossy stock. Backs are printed in black-and-white and include information on the size and release date of the limited-edition set, along with ordering information and appropriate logos. The checklist of the unnumbered promo cards is presented here alphabetically.

		NM/M
Complete Set (10):		12.00
Common Player:		1.00
(1a)	Roberto Alomar	1.25
(1b)	Roberto Alomar (French)	1.50
(2)	Barry Bonds	4.00
(3a)	Joe Carter	1.00
(3b)	Joe Carter (French)	1.00
(4)	Dwight Gooden	1.00
(5)	Ken Griffey Jr.	3.00
(6)	Dave Justice	1.00
(7)	Ryne Sandberg	2.50
(8)	Darryl Strawberry	1.00

1992 Barry Colla

1991 issue. The team logo now appears in the upper-left corner with the player's name at top and his uniform number, team and position beneath. Sets were sold in a white paper envelope featuring a color Cubs logo.

		NM/M
1-8	Ryne Sandberg	5.00

1992 Barry Colla Promos

Each of the seven card sets produced by California photographer Barry Colla in 1992 was preceded by a promo card. In standard 2-1/2" x 3-1/2" size, the promos follow the format of the regular-issue cards with a borderless color photo on high-gloss stock. All of the card backs are printed in black-and-white and feature ordering information about the sets, expected release date and issue size and appropriate logos. Some promo cards feature checklists of all existing Colla Collection card sets. The unnumbered promo cards are checklisted here alphabetically.

		NM/M
Complete Set (7):		7.50
Common Player:		1.00
(1)	All-Star Set (Juan Guzman)	1.00
(2)	Steve Avery	1.00
(3)	Jeff Bagwell	1.50
(4)	Tony Gwynn	1.50
(5)	Mark McGwire	2.00
(6)	Frank Thomas	1.50
(7)	Nolan Ryan	2.50

1992 Barry Colla

In 1992, photographer Barry Colla continued production of a series of single-player card sets. In standard 2-1/2" x 3-1/2" size, the cards featured high-gloss borderless photos on front, with no extraneous graphics. Backs feature stats, career notes, personal data, team logos and/or a cartoon. Card #1 in each set was serially numbered on the back. The 12-card sets were sold in small decorative cardboard boxes. Production figures are noted in parentheses. One in every 125 Mark McGwire sets contained an autographed card numbered from an edition of 200, but since the cards are not otherwise marked, caution should be exercised in paying a significant premium for such a set.

		NM/M
1-12	Steve Avery/7,500	2.00
1-12	Jeff Bagwell/25,000	4.00
1-12	Tony Gwynn/7,500	2.00
1-12	Mark McGwire/15,000	6.00
1-12	Mark McGwire (Autographed edition.)	300.00
1-12	Nolan Ryan/25,000	6.00
1-12	Frank Thomas/25,000	4.00

All-Stars

The 1992 Colla All-Star set consists of 24 players from the All-Star game in San Diego that year, packaged in a collector's box. Limited to 25,000 sets, the first card in each set is numbered and collectors had the opportunity to win numbered and autographed Roberto Alomar cards. Two hundred autographed Frank Thomas cards were also created for use as a premium, but he did not play in the 1992 All-Star Game due to injury.

		NM/M
Complete Set (24):		7.00
Common Player:		.25
1	Mark McGwire	1.50
2	Will Clark	.25
3	Roberto Alomar	.35
3a	Roberto Alomar/Auto.	10.00
4	Ryne Sandberg	1.00
5	Cal Ripken, Jr.	2.00
6	Ozzie Smith	1.00
7	Wade Boggs	1.00
8	Terry Pendleton	.25
9	Kirby Puckett	1.00
10	Chuck Knoblauch	.25
11	Ken Griffey Jr.	1.25
12	Joe Carter	.25
13	Sandy Alomar, Jr.	.25
14	Benito Santiago	.25
15	Mike Mussina	.35
16	Fred McGriff	.25
17	Dennis Eckersley	.75
18	Tony Gwynn	1.00
19	Roger Clemens	1.00
20	Gary Sheffield	.35
21	Jose Canseco	.35
22	Barry Bonds	2.00
23	Ivan Rodriguez	.75
24	Tony Fernandez	.25
---	Frank Thomas/Auto.	25.00

Postcards

Only one single-player postcard set was produced by Barry Colla in 1992: Ivan Rodriguez. The four-card set, like the 1989-91 issues, features full-color game-action and posed photos presented on a borderless, high-gloss 3-1/2 x 5-1/2 format. Besides the I-Rod set, Colla also produced at least one one-card "set," apparently on special order. These cards are in the same format as his other issues and

KEN GRIFFEY, JR.

are individually serially numbered on back from within an edition of 4,000.

		NM/M
1-4	Ivan Rodriguez	4.00
6492	Ken Griffey Jr.	6.00

1993 Barry Colla All-Stars

MATT WILLIAMS
THIRD BASE

For the second year in 1993 California photographer Barry Colla produced a 24-card All-Star set commemorating the game played in Baltimore on July 13. The specially boxed collector's edition includes an unnumbered All-Star logo/checklist card. Cards feature black borders on the UV-coated front, featuring game-action or posed photos. Team logos are centered beneath the photo, with the player's name and position in white at bottom. Backs are also bordered in black and include another player color photo, league and All-Star logos and information and stats on prior All-Star Game appearances.

		NM/M
Complete Set (25):		4.00
Common Player:		.15
1	Roberto Alomar	.30
2	Barry Bonds	.75
3	Ken Griffey Jr.	.50
4	John Kruk	.15
5	Kirby Puckett	.45
6	Darren Daulton	.15
7	Wade Boggs	.45
8	Matt Williams	.15
9	Cal Ripken, Jr.	.75
10	Ryne Sandberg	.45
11	Ivan Rodriguez	.30
12	Andy Van Slyke	.15
13	John Olerud	.15
14	Tom Glavine	.25
15	Juan Gonzalez	.30
16	David Justice	.15
17	Mike Mussina	.25
18	Tony Gwynn	.45
19	Joe Carter	.15
20	Barry Larkin	.15
21	Brian Harper	.15
22	Ozzie Smith	.45
23	Mark McGwire	.60
24	Mike Piazza	.50
---	Checklist	.05

Postcards

Following a one-year lay-off, Barry Colla continued his single-player, eight-card postcard series in 1993 with a pair of sets. Like the earlier issues, the cards are 3-1/2 x 5-1/2 and feature high-gloss fronts

with borderless game-action and posed photos. Black-and-white backs have a more traditional postcard format than earlier issues. The sets were sold in white paper envelopes with color team logos on front. A version of each set was made with an embossed gold-foil team logo on front; they are valued about 5X the regular issue.

		NM/M
1-8	Mike Piazza	3.50
1-8	Cal Ripken Jr.	6.00

1994 Collector's Choice Promos

Promotional Use Only

Upper Deck used a pair of promo cards to preview its new 1994 Collector's Choice brand. Ken Griffey Jr. was featured on the promos, though the photos differ from those which appear on his regular-issue card, as does the card number. "For Promotional Use Only" is printed diagonally in black on both the front and back of the regular-size card. The 5" x 7-3/8" promo card uses the same front photo as the smaller promo and has advertising on the back describing the Collector's Choice issue.

		NM/M
50	Ken Griffey Jr.	5.00
---	Ken Griffey Jr. (Jumbo)	5.00

1994 Collector's Choice

This base-brand set, released in two series, was more widely available than the regular 1994 Upper Deck issue. Cards feature UD production

staples such as UV coating and hologram and have large photos with a narrow pinstripe border. Backs have stats and a color photo. Series 1 has 320 cards and subsets titled Rookie Class, Draft Picks and Top Performers. Series 2 subsets are Up Close and Personal, Future Foundation and Rookie Class. Each of the set's player cards can also be found with either a gold- (1 in 36 packs) or silver-foil replica-autograph card; one silver-signature card appears in every pack. Factory sets include five randomly selected gold-signature cards.

		NM/M
Unopened Fact. Set (675):		25.00
Complete Set (670):		20.00
Common Player:		.05
Silver Signature:		2.5X
Gold Signature:		15X
Series 1 Pack (12):		.35
Series 1 Box (36):		8.00
Series 2 Pack (12):		.75
Series 2 Box (36):		17.50
1	Rich Becker RC	.05
2	Greg Blosser	.05
3	Midre Cummings	.05
4	Carlos Delgado	.30
5	Steve Dreyer RC	.05
6	Carl Everett RC	.50
7	Cliff Floyd	.05
8	Alex Gonzalez	.05
9	Shawn Green	.10
10	Butch Huskey	.05
11	Mark Hutton	.05
12	Miguel Jimenez	.05
13	Steve Karsay	.05
14	Marc Newfield	.05
15	Luis Ortiz	.05
16	Manny Ramirez	.60
17	Johnny Ruffin	.05
18	Scott Stahoviak RC	.05
19	Salomon Torres	.05
20	Gabe White RC	.10
21	Brian Anderson RC	.05
22	Wayne Gomes RC	.05
23	Jeff Granger	.05
24	Steve Soderstrom RC	.05
25	Trot Nixon RC	.50
26	Kirk Presley RC	.05
27	Matt Brunson RC	.05
28	Brooks Kieschnick RC	.05
29	Billy Wagner RC	.50
30	Matt Drews RC	.05
31	Kurt Abbott RC	.05
32	Luis Alicea	.05
33	Roberto Alomar	.20
34	Sandy Alomar Jr.	.05
35	Moises Alou	.05
36	Wilson Alvarez	.05
37	Rich Amaral	.05
38	Eric Anthony	.05
39	Luis Aquino	.05
40	Jack Armstrong	.05
41	Rene Arocha	.05
42	Rich Aude RC	.05
43	Brad Ausmus	.05
44	Steve Avery	.05
45	Bob Ayrault	.05
46	Willie Banks	.05
47	Bret Barberie	.05
48	Kim Batiste	.05
49	Rod Beck	.05
50	Jason Bere	.05
51	Sean Berry	.05
52	Dante Bichette	.05
53	Jeff Blauser	.05
54	Mike Blowers	.05
55	Tim Bogar	.05
56	Tom Bolton	.05
57	Ricky Bones	.05
58	Bobby Bonilla	.05
59	Bret Boone	.05
60	Pat Borders	.05
61	Mike Bordick	.05
62	Daryl Boston	.05
63	Ryan Bowen	.05
64	Jeff Branson	.05
65	George Brett	.85
66	Steve Buechele	.05
67	Dave Burba	.05
68	John Burkett	.05
69	Jeromy Burnitz	.05
70	Brett Butler	.05
71	Rob Butler	.05
72	Ken Caminiti	.05
73	Cris Carpenter	.05
74	Vinny Castilla	.05
75	Andujar Cedeno	.05
76	Wes Chamberlain	.05
77	Archi Cianfrocco	.05
78	Dave Clark	.05
79	Jerald Clark	.05
80	Royce Clayton	.05
81	David Cone	.05
82	Jeff Conine	.05
83	Steve Cooke	.05
84	Scott Cooper	.05
85	Joey Cora	.05

		NM/M
86	Tim Costa	.05
87	Chad Curtis	.05
88	Ron Darling	.05
89	Danny Darwin	.05
90	Rob Deer	.05
91	Jim Deshaies	.05
92	Delino DeShields	.05
93	Rob Dibble	.05
94	Gary DiSarcina	.05
95	Doug Drabek	.05
96	Scott Erickson	.05
97	Rikkert Faneyte RC	.05
98	Jeff Fassero	.05
99	Alex Fernandez	.05
100	Cecil Fielder	.05
101	Dave Fleming	.05
102	Darrin Fletcher	.05
103	Scott Fletcher	.05
104	Mike Gallego	.05
105	Carlos Garcia	.05
106	Jeff Gardner	.05
107	Brent Gates	.05
108	Benji Gil	.05
109	Bernard Gilkey	.05
110	Chris Gomez	.05
111	Luis Gonzalez	.05
112	Tom Gordon	.05
113	Jim Gott	.05
114	Mark Grace	.05
115	Tommy Greene	.05
116	Willie Greene	.05
117	Ken Griffey Jr.	1.00
118	Bill Gullickson	.05
119	Ricky Gutierrez	.05
120	Juan Guzman	.05
121	Chris Gwynn	.05
122	Tony Gwynn	.75
123	Jeffrey Hammonds	.05
124	Erik Hanson	.05
125	Gene Harris	.05
126	Greg Harris	.05
127	Bryan Harvey	.05
128	Billy Hatcher	.05
129	Hilly Hathaway	.05
130	Charlie Hayes	.05
131	Rickey Henderson	.60
132	Mike Henneman	.05
133	Pat Hentgen	.05
134	Roberto Hernandez	.05
135	Orel Hershiser	.05
136	Phil Hiatt	.05
137	Glenallen Hill	.05
138	Ken Hill	.05
139	Eric Hillman	.05
140	Chris Hoiles	.05
141	Dave Hollins	.05
142	David Hulse	.05
143	Todd Hundley	.05
144	Pete Incaviglia	.05
145	Danny Jackson	.05
146	John Jaha	.05
147	Domingo Jean	.05
148	Gregg Jefferies	.05
149	Reggie Jefferson	.05
150	Lance Johnson	.05
151	Bobby Jones	.05
152	Chipper Jones	.75
153	Todd Jones	.05
154	Brian Jordan	.05
155	Wally Joyner	.05
156	Dave Justice	.05
157	Ron Karkovice	.05
158	Eric Karros	.05
159	Jeff Kent	.05
160	Jimmy Key	.05
161	Mark Kiefer	.05
162	Darryl Kile	.05
163	Jeff King	.05
164	Wayne Kirby	.05
165	Ryan Klesko	.05
166	Chuck Knoblauch	.05
167	Chad Kreuter	.05
168	John Kruk	.05
169	Mark Langston	.05
170	Mike Lansing	.05
171	Barry Larkin	.05
172	Manuel Lee	.05
173	Phil Leftwich RC	.05
174	Darren Lewis	.05
175	Derek Lilliquist	.05
176	Jose Lind	.05
177	Albie Lopez	.05
178	Javier Lopez	.05
179	Torey Lovullo	.05
180	Scott Lydy	.05
181	Mike Macfarlane	.05
182	Shane Mack	.05
183	Greg Maddux	.75
184	Dave Magadan	.05
185	Joe Magrane	.05
186	Kirt Manwaring	.05
187	Al Martin	.05
188	Pedro A. Martinez RC	.05
189	Pedro Martinez	.60
190	Ramon Martinez	.05
191	Tino Martinez	.05
192	Don Mattingly	.85
193	Derrick May	.05
194	David McCarty	.05
195	Ben McDonald	.05
196	Roger McDowell	.05
197	Fred McGriff	.05
198	Mark McLemore	.05
199	Greg McMichael	.05
200	Jeff McNeely	.05
201	Brian McRae	.05
202	Pat Meares	.05
203	Roberto Mejia	.05

		NM/M
204	Orlando Merced	.05
205	Jose Mesa	.05
206	Blas Minor	.05
207	Angel Miranda	.05
208	Paul Molitor	.60
209	Raul Mondesi	.05
210	Jeff Montgomery	.05
211	Mickey Morandini	.05
212	Mike Morgan	.05
213	Jamie Moyer	.05
214	Bobby Munoz	.05
215	Troy Neel	.05
216	Dave Nilsson	.05
217	John O'Donoghue	.05
218	Paul O'Neill	.05
219	Jose Offerman	.05
220	Joe Oliver	.05
221	Greg Olson	.05
222	Donovan Osborne	.05
223	Jayhawk Owens	.05
224	Mike Pagliarulo	.05
225	Craig Paquette	.05
226	Roger Pavlik	.05
227	Brad Pennington	.05
228	Eduardo Perez	.05
229	Mike Perez	.05
230	Tony Phillips	.05
231	Hipolito Pichardo	.05
232	Phil Plantier	.05
233	Curtis Pride RC	.05
234	Tim Pugh	.05
235	Scott Radinsky	.05
236	Pat Rapp	.05
237	Kevin Reimer	.05
238	Armando Reynoso	.05
239	Jose Rijo	.05
240	Cal Ripken, Jr.	2.00
241	Kevin Roberson	.05
242	Kenny Rogers	.05
243	Kevin Rogers	.05
244	Mel Rojas	.05
245	John Roper	.05
246	Kirk Rueter	.05
247	Scott Ruffcorn	.05
248	Ken Ryan	.05
249	Nolan Ryan	2.00
250	Bret Saberhagen	.05
251	Tim Salmon	.05
252	Reggie Sanders	.05
253	Curt Schilling	.20
254	David Segui	.05
255	Aaron Sele	.05
256	Scott Servais	.05
257	Gary Sheffield	.30
258	Ruben Sierra	.05
259	Don Slaught	.05
260	Lee Smith	.05
261	Cory Snyder	.05
262	Paul Sorrento	.05
263	Sammy Sosa	.75
264	Bill Spiers	.05
265	Mike Stanley	.05
266	Dave Staton	.05
267	Terry Steinbach	.05
268	Kevin Stocker	.05
269	Todd Stottlemyre	.05
270	Doug Strange	.05
271	Bill Swift	.05
272	Kevin Tapani	.05
273	Tony Tarasco	.05
274	Julian Tavarez RC	.05
275	Mickey Tettleton	.05
276	Ryan Thompson	.05
277	Chris Turner	.05
278	John Valentin	.05
279	Todd Van Poppel	.05
280	Andy Van Slyke	.05
281	Mo Vaughn	.05
282	Robin Ventura	.05
283	Frank Viola	.05
284	Jose Vizcaino	.05
285	Omar Vizquel	.05
286	Larry Walker	.05
287	Duane Ware	.05
288	Allen Watson	.05
289	Bill Wegman	.05
290	Turk Wendell	.05
291	Lou Whitaker	.05
292	Devon White	.05
293	Rondell White	.05
294	Mark Whiten	.05
295	Darrell Whitmore	.05
296	Bob Wickman	.05
297	Rick Wilkins	.05
298	Bernie Williams	.05
299	Matt Williams	.05
300	Woody Williams	.05
301	Nigel Wilson	.05
302	Dave Winfield	.60
303	Anthony Young	.05
304	Eric Young	.05
305	Todd Zeile	.05
306	Jack McDowell, John Burkett, Tom Glavine/TP	.05
307	Randy Johnson/TP	.25
308	Randy Myers/TP	.05
309	Jack McDowell/TP	.05
310	Mike Piazza/TP	.40
311	Barry Bonds/TP	.60
312	Andres Galarraga/TP	.05

ABBREVIATIONS

TP - Top Performers

#	Player	Price
313	Juan Gonzalez, Barry Bonds/TP	.45
314	Albert Belle/TP	.05
315	Kenny Lofton/TP	.05
316	Checklist 1-64 (Barry Bonds)	.50
317	Checklist 65-128 (Ken Griffey Jr.)	.35
318	Checklist 129-192 (Mike Piazza)	.35
319	Checklist 193-256 (Kirby Puckett)	.25
320	Checklist 257-320 (Nolan Ryan)	.50
321	Checklist 321-370 (Roberto Alomar)	.10
322	Checklist 371-420 (Roger Clemens)	.30
323	Checklist 421-470 (Juan Gonzalez)	.10
324	Checklist 471-520 (Ken Griffey Jr.)	.35
325	Checklist 521-570 (David Justice)	.05
326	Checklist 571-620 (John Kruk)	.05
327	Checklist 621-670 (Frank Thomas)	.20
328	Angels Checklist (Tim Salmon)	.05
329	Astros Checklist (Jeff Bagwell)	.20
330	Athletics Checklist (Mark McGwire)	.45
331	Blue Jays Checklist (Roberto Alomar)	.10
332	Braves Checklist (David Justice)	.05
333	Brewers Checklist (Pat Listach)	.05
334	Cardinals Checklist (Ozzie Smith)	.25
335	Cubs Checklist (Ryne Sandberg)	.25
336	Dodgers Checklist (Mike Piazza)	.35
337	Expos Checklist (Cliff Floyd)	.05
338	Giants Checklist (Barry Bonds)	.50
339	Indians Checklist (Albert Belle)	.05
340	Mariners Checklist (Ken Griffey Jr.)	.35
341	Marlins Checklist (Gary Sheffield)	.10
342	Mets Checklist (Dwight Gooden)	.05
343	Orioles Checklist (Cal Ripken, Jr.)	.50
344	Padres Checklist (Tony Gwynn)	.25
345	Phillies Checklist (Lenny Dykstra)	.05
346	Pirates Checklists (Andy Van Slyke)	.05
347	Rangers Checklist (Juan Gonzalez)	.10
348	Red Sox Checklist (Roger Clemens)	.30
349	Reds Checklist (Barry Larkin)	.05
350	Rockies Checklist (Andres Galarraga)	.05
351	Royals Checklist (Kevin Appier)	.05
352	Tigers Checklist (Cecil Fielder)	.05
353	Twins Checklist (Kirby Puckett)	.25
354	White Sox Checklist (Frank Thomas)	.20
355	Yankees Checklist (Don Mattingly)	.30
356	Bo Jackson	.10
357	Randy Johnson	.60
358	Darren Daulton	.05
359	Charlie Hough	.05
360	Andres Galarraga	.05
361	Mike Felder	.05
362	Chris Hammond	.05
363	Shawon Dunston	.05
364	Junior Felix	.05
365	Ray Lankford	.05
366	Darryl Strawberry	.05
367	Dave Magadan	.05
368	Gregg Olson	.05
369	Len Dykstra	.05
370	Darrin Jackson	.05
371	Dave Stewart	.05
372	Terry Pendleton	.05
373	Arthur Rhodes	.05
374	Benito Santiago	.05
375	Travis Fryman	.05
376	Scott Brosius	.05
377	Stan Belinda	.05
378	Derek Parks	.05
379	Kevin Seitzer	.05
380	Wade Boggs	.75
381	Wally Whitehurst	.05
382	Scott Leius	.05
383	Danny Tartabull	.05
384	Harold Reynolds	.05
385	Tim Raines	.05
386	Darryl Hamilton	.05
387	Felix Fermin	.05
388	Jim Eisenreich	.05
389	Kurt Abbott	.05
390	Kevin Appier	.05
391	Chris Bosio	.05
392	Randy Tomlin	.05
393	Bob Hamelin	.05
394	Kevin Gross	.05
395	Wil Cordero	.05
396	Joe Girardi	.05
397	Orestes Destrade	.05
398	Chris Haney	.05
399	Xavier Hernandez	.05
400	Mike Piazza	1.00
401	Alex Arias	.05
402	Tom Candiotti	.05
403	Kirk Gibson	.05
404	Chuck Carr	.05
405	Brady Anderson	.05
406	Greg Gagne	.05
407	Bruce Ruffin	.05
408	Scott Hemond	.05
409	Keith Miller	.05
410	John Wetteland	.05
411	Eric Anthony	.05
412	Andre Dawson	.25
413	Doug Henry	.05
414	John Franco	.05
415	Julio Franco	.05
416	Dave Hansen	.05
417	Mike Harkey	.05
418	Jack Armstrong	.05
419	Joe Orsulak	.05
420	John Smoltz	.05
421	Scott Livingstone	.05
422	Darren Holmes	.05
423	Ed Sprague	.05
424	Jay Buhner	.05
425	Kirby Puckett	.75
426	Phil Clark	.05
427	Anthony Young	.05
428	Reggie Jefferson	.05
429	Mariano Duncan	.05
430	Tom Glavine	.20
431	Dave Henderson	.05
432	Melido Perez	.05
433	Paul Wagner	.05
434	Tim Worrell	.05
435	Ozzie Guillen	.05
436	Mike Butcher	.05
437	Jim Deshaies	.05
438	Kevin Young	.05
439	Tom Browning	.05
440	Mike Greenwell	.05
441	Mike Stanton	.05
442	John Doherty	.05
443	John Dopson	.05
444	Carlos Baerga	.05
445	Jack McDowell	.05
446	Kent Mercker	.05
447	Ricky Jordan	.05
448	Jerry Browne	.05
449	Fernando Vina	.05
450	Jim Abbott	.05
451	Teddy Higuera	.05
452	Tim Naehring	.05
453	Jim Leyritz	.05
454	Frank Castillo	.05
455	Joe Carter	.05
456	Craig Biggio	.05
457	Geronimo Pena	.05
458	Alejandro Pena	.05
459	Mike Moore	.05
460	Randy Myers	.05
461	Greg Myers	.05
462	Greg Hibbard	.05
463	Jose Guzman	.05
464	Tom Pagnozzi	.05
465	Marquis Grissom	.05
466	Tim Wallach	.05
467	Joe Grahe	.05
468	Bob Tewksbury	.05
469	B.J. Surhoff	.05
470	Kevin Mitchell	.05
471	Bobby Witt	.05
472	Milt Thompson	.05
473	John Smiley	.05
474	Alan Trammell	.05
475	Mike Mussina	.30
476	Rick Aguilera	.05
477	Jose Valentin	.05
478	Harold Baines	.05
479	Bip Roberts	.05
480	Edgar Martinez	.05
481	Rheal Cormier	.05
482	Hal Morris	.05
483	Pat Kelly	.05
484	Roberto Kelly	.05
485	Chris Sabo	.05
486	Kent Hrbek	.05
487	Scott Kamieniecki	.05
488	Walt Weiss	.05
489	Karl Rhodes	.05
490	Derek Bell	.05
491	Chili Davis	.05
492	Brian Harper	.05
493	Felix Jose	.05
494	Trevor Hoffman	.05
495	Dennis Eckersley	.50
496	Pedro Astacio	.05
497	Jay Bell	.05
498	Randy Velarde	.05
499	David Wells	.05
500	Frank Thomas	.60
501	Mark Lemke	.05
502	Mike Devereaux	.05
503	Chuck McElroy	.05
504	Luis Polonia	.05
505	Damion Easley	.05
506	Greg A. Harris	.05
507	Chris James	.05
508	Terry Mulholland	.05
509	Pete Smith	.05
510	Rickey Henderson	.60
511	Sid Fernandez	.05
512	Al Leiter	.05
513	Doug Jones	.05
514	Steve Farr	.05
515	Chuck Finley	.05
516	Bobby Thigpen	.05
517	Jim Edmonds	.05
518	Graeme Lloyd	.05
519	Dwight Gooden	.05
520	Pat Listach	.05
521	Kevin Bass	.05
522	Willie Banks	.05
523	Steve Finley	.05
524	Delino DeShields	.05
525	Mark McGwire	1.50
526	Greg Swindell	.05
527	Chris Nabholz	.05
528	Scott Sanders	.05
529	David Segui	.05
530	Howard Johnson	.05
531	Jaime Navarro	.05
532	Jose Vizcaino	.05
533	Mark Lewis	.05
534	Pete Harnisch	.05
535	Robby Thompson	.05
536	Marcus Moore	.05
537	Kevin Brown	.05
538	Mark Clark	.05
539	Sterling Hitchcock	.05
540	Will Clark	.05
541	Denis Boucher	.05
542	Jack Morris	.05
543	Pedro Munoz	.05
544	Bret Boone	.05
545	Ozzie Smith	.75
546	Dennis Martinez	.05
547	Dan Wilson	.05
548	Rick Sutcliffe	.05
549	Kevin McReynolds	.05
550	Roger Clemens	.85
551	Todd Benzinger	.05
552	Bill Haselman	.05
553	Bobby Munoz	.05
554	Ellis Burks	.05
555	Ryne Sandberg	.75
556	Lee Smith	.05
557	Danny Bautista	.05
558	Rey Sanchez	.05
559	Norm Charlton	.05
560	Jose Canseco	.35
561	Tim Belcher	.05
562	Denny Neagle	.05
563	Eric Davis	.05
564	Jody Reed	.05
565	Kenny Lofton	.05
566	Gary Gaetti	.05
567	Todd Worrell	.05
568	Mark Portugal	.05
569	Dick Schofield	.05
570	Andy Benes	.05
571	Zane Smith	.05
572	Bobby Ayala	.05
573	Chip Hale	.05
574	Bob Welch	.05
575	Deion Sanders	.10
576	Dave Nied	.05
577	Pat Mahomes	.05
578	Charles Nagy	.05
579	Otis Nixon	.05
580	Dean Palmer	.05
581	Roberto Petagine	.05
582	Dwight Smith	.05
583	Jeff Russell	.05
584	Mark Dewey	.05
585	Greg Vaughn	.05
586	Brian Hunter	.05
587	Willie McGee	.05
588	Pedro J. Martinez	.60
589	Roger Salkeld	.05
590	Jeff Bagwell	.60
591	Spike Owen	.05
592	Jeff Reardon	.05
593	Erik Pappas	.05
594	Brian Williams	.05
595	Eddie Murray	.60
596	Henry Rodriguez	.05
597	Erik Hanson	.05
598	Stan Javier	.05
599	Mitch Williams	.05
600	John Olerud	.05
601	Vince Coleman	.05
602	Damon Berryhill	.05
603	Tom Brunansky	.05
604	Robb Nen	.05
605	Rafael Palmeiro	.50
606	Cal Eldred	.05
607	Jeff Brantley	.05
608	Alan Mills	.05
609	Jeff Nelson	.05
610	Barry Bonds	2.00
611	Carlos Pulido RC	.05
612	Tim Hyers RC	.05
613	Steve Howe	.05
614	Brian Turang RC	.05
615	Leo Gomez	.05
616	Jesse Orosco	.05
617	Dan Pasqua	.05
618	Marvin Freeman	.05
619	Tony Fernandez	.05
620	Albert Belle	.50
621	Eddie Taubensee	.05
622	Mike Jackson	.05
623	Jose Bautista	.05
624	Jim Thome	.40
625	Ivan Rodriguez	.50
626	Ben Rivera	.05
627	Dave Valle	.05
628	Tom Henke	.05
629	Omar Vizquel	.05
630	Juan Gonzalez	.30
631	Roberto Alomar (Up Close)	.10
632	Barry Bonds (Up Close)	.60
633	Juan Gonzalez (Up Close)	.15
634	Ken Griffey Jr. (Up Close)	.50
635	Michael Jordan (Up Close)	1.50
636	Dave Justice (Up Close)	.05
637	Mike Piazza (Up Close)	.50
638	Kirby Puckett (Up Close)	.25
639	Tim Salmon (Up Close)	.05
640	Frank Thomas (Up Close)	.35
641	Alan Benes/FF RC	.35
642	Johnny Damon/FF	.35
643	Brad Fullmer/FF RC	.35
644	Derek Jeter/FF	2.00
645	Derrek Lee/FF RC	.75
646	Alex Ochoa/FF	.05
647	Alex Rodriguez/FF RC	5.00
648	Jose Silva/FF RC	.05
649	Terrell Wade/FF RC	.05
650	Preston Wilson/FF	.05
651	Shane Andrews/RC	.05
652	James Baldwin/RC	.05
653	Ricky Bottalico/RC RC	.10
654	Tavo Alvarez/RC	.05
655	Donnie Elliott/RC	.05
656	Joey Eischen/RC	.05
657	Jason Giambi/RC	.50
658	Todd Hollandsworth/ RC	.05
659	Brian Hunter/RC	.05
660	Charles Johnson/RC	.05
661	Michael Jordan/RC RC	3.00
662	Jeff Juden/RC	.05
663	Mike Kelly/RC	.05
664	James Mouton/RC	.05
665	Ray Holbert/RC	.05
666	Pokey Reese/RC	.05
667	Ruben Santana/RC RC	.05
668	Paul Spoljaric/RC	.05
669	Luis Lopez/RC	.05
670	Matt Walbeck/RC	.05

1994 Collector's Choice Silver Signature

Each of the cards in the debut edition of Upper Deck's Collector's Choice brand was also issued in a parallel edition bearing a facsimile silver-foil signature on front. The silver-signature cards were inserted at a one-per-pack rate in the set's foil packs, and proportionally in other types of packaging.

	NM/M
Common Player:	.15
Stars:	2.5X
647	Alex Rodriguez (White Letters. Some A-Rod Silver Signature parallels were mistakenly printed on base cards with his name and other details on front and back printed in white, rather than gray.) 100.00

1994 Collector's Choice Gold Signature

A super-scarce parallel set of the premiere-issue Collec-

ABBREVIATIONS

FF - Future Foundation
RC - Rookie Class

tor's Choice in 1994 was the gold-signature version found on average of only once per 36 foil packs. In addition to a gold-foil facsimile signature on the card front, this edition features gold-colored borders on the regular player cards.

	NM/M
Common Player:	2.00
Stars:	15X

Home Run All-Stars

Among the most attractive of the 1994 chase cards, the perceived high production (over a million sets according to stated odds of winning) of this set keeps it affordable. Sets were available by a mail-in offer to persons who found a winner card in Series 1 foil packs (about one per box). Cards feature a combination of brick-bordered hologram and color player photo on front, along with a gold-foil facsimile autograph. On back the brick border is repeated, as is the photo on the hologram, though this time in full color. There is a stadium photo in the background, over which is printed a description of the player's home run prowess. A numbering error resulted in two cards numbered HA4 and no card with the HA5 number.

	NM/M
Complete Set (8):	4.00
Common Player:	.25
1HA	Juan Gonzalez	.50
2HA	Ken Griffey Jr.	1.50
3HA	Barry Bonds	2.50
4HAa	Bobby Bonilla	.25
4HAb	Cecil Fielder	.25
6HA	Albert Belle	.25
7HA	David Justice	.25
8HA	Mike Piazza	1.50

Team vs. Team Scratchoff

Team vs. Team scratch-offs are a 15-card set, with one game card being inserted into every pack of Collector's Choice 1994 baseball. Each card allowed two persons to play a nine-inning baseball game. Game cards also double as a prize card in the "You Crash The Deck" contest.

	NM/M
Complete Set (15):	4.50
Common Card:	.25
1	Blue Jays-White Sox (Roberto Alomar, Frank Thomas)	.30
2	Phillies-Braves (Lenny Dykstra, David Justice)	.25
3	Mariners-Rangers (Ken Griffey Jr., Juan Gonzalez)	.50
4	Dodgers-Giants (Mike Piazza, Barry Bonds)	.75
5	Red Sox-Yankees (Roger Clemens, Don Mattingly)	.45
6	Reds-Astros (Barry Larkin, Jeff Bagwell)	.25
7	Orioles-Tigers (Cal Ripken Jr., Cecil Fielder)	.75
8	Cubs-Cardinals (Ryne Sandberg, Ozzie Smith)	.35
9	Athletics-Angels (Mark McGwire, Tim Salmon)	.60
10	Pirates-Expos (Andy Van Slyke, Cliff Floyd)	.25
11	Brewers-Indians (Pat Listach, Albert Belle)	.25
12	Rockies-Padres (Andres Galarraga, Tony Gwynn)	.35
13	Twins-Royals (Kirby Puckett, Brian McRae)	.35
14	Mets-Marlins (Dwight Gooden, Gary Sheffield)	.25
15	N.L. All-Stars-A.L. All-Stars (Barry Bonds, Ken Griffey Jr.)	.75

1995 Collector's Choice

Issued in a single series, Upper Deck's base-brand baseball series features a number of subsets within the main body of the issue, as well as several insert sets. Basic cards feature large photos on front and back, with the back having full major league stats. The set opens with a 27-card Rookie Class subset featuring front photos on which the background has been rendered in hot pink tones. Backs have a lime-green box with a scouting report on the player and a box featuring 1994 minor and major league stats. The next 18 cards are Future Foundation cards which have the prospects pictured with a posterized background on front, with backs similar to the Rookie Class cards. Career finale cards of five retired superstars follow, then a run of Best of the '90s cards honoring record-setting achievements, followed by cards depicting major award winners of the previous season. Each of the last three named subsets features borderless color photos on front, with backs similar to the regular cards. Immediately preceding the regular cards, which are arranged in team-set order, is a five-card What's the Call? subset featuring cartoon representations of the players. A set of five checklist cards marking career highlights ends the set.

NM/M

Unopened Fact. Set (545): 17.50
Complete Set (530): 12.50
Common Player: .05
Silver Stars: 2X
Gold Stars: 6X
Pack (12): 1.00
Wax Box (36): 20.00

1 Charles Johnson/RC .05
2 Scott Ruffcorn/RC .05
3 Ray Durham/RC .05
4 Armando Benitez/RC .05
5 Alex Rodriguez/RC 1.25
6 Julian Tavarez/RC .05
7 Chad Ogea/RC .05
8 Quilvio Veras/RC .05
9 Phil Nevin/RC .05
10 Michael Tucker/RC .05
11 Mark Thompson/RC .05
12 Rod Henderson/RC .05
13 Andrew Lorraine/RC .05
14 Joe Randa/RC .05
15 Derek Jeter/RC 1.50
16 Tony Clark/RC .05
17 Juan Castillo/RC .05
18 Mark Acre/RC .05
19 Orlando Miller/RC .05
20 Paul Wilson/RC .05
21 John Mabry/RC .05
22 Garey Ingram/RC .05
23 Garret Anderson/RC .05
24 Dave Stevens/RC .05
25 Dustin Hermanson/RC .05
26 Paul Shuey/RC .05
27 J.R. Phillips/RC .05
28 Ruben Rivera/FF .05
29 Nomar Garciaparra/FF .75
30 John Wasdin/FF .05
31 Jim Pittsley/FF .05
32 Scott Elarton/FF **RC** .15
33 Raul Casanova/FF **RC** .05
34 Todd Greene/FF .05
35 Bill Pulsipher/FF .05
36 Trey Beamon/FF .05
37 Curtis Goodwin/FF .05
38 Doug Million/FF .05
39 Karim Garcia/FF **RC** 1.00
40 Ben Grieve/FF .05
41 Mark Farris/FF .05
42 Juan Acevedo/FF **RC** .05
43 C.J. Nitkowski/FF .05
44 Travis Miller/FF **RC** .10
45 Reid Ryan/FF .10
46 Nolan Ryan 1.50
47 Robin Yount .50
48 Ryne Sandberg .75
49 George Brett .85
50 Mike Schmidt .85
51 Cecil Fielder (Best of the 90's) .05
52 Nolan Ryan (Best of the 90's) .75
53 Rickey Henderson (Best of the 90's) .20
54 George Brett, Robin Yount, Dave Winfield (Best of the 90's) .25
55 Sid Bream (Best of the 90's) .05
56 Carlos Baerga (Best of the 90's) .05
57 Lee Smith (Best of the 90's) .05
58 Mark Whiten (Best of the 90's) .05
59 Joe Carter (Best of the 90's) .05
60 Barry Bonds (Best of the 90's) .75
61 Tony Gwynn (Best of the 90's) .40
62 Ken Griffey Jr. (Best of the 90's) .50
63 Greg Maddux (Best of the 90's) .40
64 Frank Thomas (Best of the 90's) .35
65 Dennis Martinez, Kenny Rogers (Best of the 90's) .05
66 David Cone (Cy Young) .05
67 Greg Maddux (Cy Young) .75
68 Jimmy Key (Most Victories) .05
69 Fred McGriff (All-Star MVP) .05
70 Ken Griffey Jr. (HR Champ) 1.00
71 Matt Williams (HR Champ) .05
72 Paul O'Neill (Batting Title) .05
73 Tony Gwynn (Batting Title) .40
74 Randy Johnson (Ks Leader) .60
75 Frank Thomas/MVP .60
76 Jeff Bagwell/MVP .60
77 Kirby Puckett (RBI leader) .75
78 Bob Hamelin (ROY) .05
79 Raul Mondesi (ROY) .05
80 Mike Piazza/AS 1.00
81 Kenny Lofton (SB Leader) .05

82 Barry Bonds (Gold Glove) 1.50
83 Albert Belle/AS .05
84 Juan Gonzalez (HR Champ) .30
85 Cal Ripken Jr. (2,000 Straight Games) 1.50
86 Barry Bonds (What's the Call?) .75
87 Mike Piazza (What's the Call?) .60
88 Ken Griffey Jr. (What's the Call?) .50
89 Frank Thomas (What's the Call?) .35
90 Juan Gonzalez (What's the Call?) .10
91 Jorge Fabregas .05
92 J.T. Snow .05
93 Spike Owen .05
94 Eduardo Perez .05
95 Bo Jackson .10
96 Damion Easley .05
97 Gary DiSarcina .05
98 Jim Edmonds .05
99 Chad Curtis .05
100 Tim Salmon .05
101 Chili Davis .05
102 Chuck Finley .05
103 Mark Langston .05
104 Brian Anderson .05
105 Lee Smith .05
106 Phil Leftwich .05
107 Chris Donnels .05
108 John Hudek .05
109 Craig Biggio .05
110 Luis Gonzalez .05
111 Brian L. Hunter .05
112 James Mouton .05
113 Scott Servais .05
114 Tony Eusebio .05
115 Derek Bell .05
116 Doug Drabek .05
117 Shane Reynolds .05
118 Darryl Kile .05
119 Greg Swindell .05
120 Phil Plantier .05
121 Todd Jones .05
122 Steve Ontiveros .05
123 Bobby Witt .05
124 Brent Gates .05
125 Rickey Henderson .60
126 Scott Brosius .05
127 Mike Bordick .05
128 Fausto Cruz .05
129 Stan Javier .05
130 Mark McGwire 1.25
131 Geronimo Berroa .05
132 Terry Steinbach .05
133 Steve Karsay .05
134 Dennis Eckersley .50
135 Ruben Sierra .05
136 Ron Darling .05
137 Todd Van Poppel .05
138 Alex Gonzalez .20
139 John Olerud .05
140 Roberto Alomar .20
141 Darren Hall .05
142 Ed Sprague .05
143 Devon White .05
144 Shawn Green .20
145 Paul Molitor .60
146 Pat Borders .05
147 Carlos Delgado .35
148 Juan Guzman .05
149 Pat Hentgen .05
150 Joe Carter .05
151 Dave Stewart .05
152 Todd Stottlemyre .05
153 Dick Schofield .05
154 Chipper Jones .75
155 Ryan Klesko .05
156 Dave Justice .05
157 Mike Kelly .05
158 Roberto Kelly .05
159 Tony Tarasco .05
160 Javier Lopez .05
161 Steve Avery .05
162 Greg McMichael .05
163 Kent Mercker .05
164 Mark Lemke .05
165 Tom Glavine .20
166 Jose Oliva .05
167 John Smoltz .05
168 Jeff Blauser .05
169 Troy O'Leary .05
170 Greg Vaughn .05
171 Jody Reed .05
172 Kevin Seitzer .05
173 Jeff Cirillo .05
174 B.J. Surhoff .05
175 Cal Eldred .05
176 Jose Valentin .05
177 Turner Ward .05
178 Darryl Hamilton .05
179 Pat Listach .05
180 Matt Mieske .05
181 Brian Harper .05
182 Dave Nilsson .05

ABBREVIATIONS

FF - Future Foundation
RC - Rookie Class
AS - All-Star

183 Mike Fetters .05
184 John Jaha .05
185 Ricky Bones .05
186 Geronimo Pena .05
187 Bob Tewksbury .05
188 Todd Zeile .05
189 Danny Jackson .05
190 Ray Lankford .05
191 Bernard Gilkey .05
192 Brian Jordan .05
193 Tom Pagnozzi .05
194 Rick Sutcliffe .05
195 Mark Whiten .05
196 Tom Henke .05
197 Rene Arocha .05
198 Allen Watson .05
199 Mike Perez .05
200 Ozzie Smith .75
201 Anthony Young .05
202 Rey Sanchez .05
203 Steve Buechele .05
204 Shawon Dunston .05
205 Mark Grace .05
206 Glenallen Hill .05
207 Eddie Zambrano .05
208 Rick Wilkins .05
209 Derrick May .05
210 Sammy Sosa .75
211 Kevin Roberson .05
212 Steve Trachsel .05
213 Willie Banks .05
214 Kevin Foster .05
215 Randy Myers .05
216 Mike Morgan .05
217 Rafael Bournigal .05
218 Delino DeShields .05
219 Tim Wallach .05
220 Eric Karros .05
221 Jose Offerman .05
222 Tom Candiotti .05
223 Ismael Valdes .05
224 Henry Rodriguez .05
225 Billy Ashley .05
226 Darren Dreifort .05
227 Ramon Martinez .05
228 Pedro Astacio .05
229 Orel Hershiser .05
230 Brett Butler .05
231 Todd Hollandsworth .05
232 Chan Ho Park .05
233 Mike Lansing .05
234 Sean Berry .05
235 Rondell White .05
236 Ken Hill .05
237 Marquis Grissom .05
238 Larry Walker .05
239 John Wetteland .05
240 Cliff Floyd .05
241 Joey Eischen .05
242 Lou Frazier .05
243 Darrin Fletcher .05
244 Pedro J. Martinez .60
245 Wil Cordero .05
246 Jeff Fassero .05
247 Butch Henry .05
248 Mel Rojas .05
249 Kirk Rueter .05
250 Moises Alou .05
251 Rod Beck .05
252 John Patterson .05
253 Robby Thompson .05
254 Royce Clayton .05
255 William Van Landingham .05
256 Darren Lewis .05
257 Kirt Manwaring .05
258 Mark Portugal .05
259 Bill Swift .05
260 Rikkert Faneyte .05
261 Mike Jackson .05
262 Todd Benzinger .05
263 Bud Black .05
264 Salomon Torres .05
265 Eddie Murray .60
266 Mark Clark .05
267 Paul Sorrento .05
268 Jim Thome .45
269 Omar Vizquel .05
270 Carlos Baerga .05
271 Jeff Russell .05
272 Herbert Perry .05
273 Sandy Alomar Jr. .05
274 Dennis Martinez .05
275 Manny Ramirez .60
276 Wayne Kirby .05
277 Charles Nagy .05
278 Albie Lopez .05
279 Jeromy Burnitz .05
280 Dave Winfield .60
281 Tim Davis .05
282 Marc Newfield .05
283 Tino Martinez .05
284 Mike Blowers .05
285 Goose Gossage .05
286 Luis Sojo .05
287 Edgar Martinez .05
288 Rich Amaral .05
289 Felix Fermin .05
290 Jay Buhner .05
291 Dan Wilson .05
292 Bobby Ayala .05
293 Dave Fleming .05
294 Greg Pirkl .05
295 Reggie Jefferson .05
296 Greg Hibbard .05
297 Yorkis Perez .05
298 Kurt Miller .05
299 Chuck Carr .05

300 Gary Sheffield .30
301 Jerry Browne .05
302 Dave Magadan .05
303 Kurt Abbott .05
304 Pat Rapp .05
305 Jeff Conine .05
306 Benito Santiago .05
307 Dave Weathers .05
308 Robb Nen .05
309 Chris Hammond .05
310 Bryan Harvey .05
311 Charlie Hough .05
312 Greg Colbrunn .05
313 David Segui .05
314 Rico Brogna .05
315 Jeff Kent .05
316 Jose Vizcaino .05
317 Jim Lindeman .05
318 Carl Everett .05
319 Ryan Thompson .05
320 Bobby Bonilla .05
321 Joe Orsulak .05
322 Pete Harnisch .05
323 Doug Linton .05
324 Todd Hundley .05
325 Bret Saberhagen .05
326 Kelly Stinnett .05
327 Jason Jacome .05
328 Bobby Jones .05
329 John Franco .05
330 Rafael Palmeiro .50
331 Chris Hoiles .05
332 Leo Gomez .05
333 Chris Sabo .05
334 Brady Anderson .05
335 Jeffrey Hammonds .05
336 Dwight Smith .05
337 Jack Voigt .05
338 Harold Baines .05
339 Ben McDonald .05
340 Mike Mussina .30
341 Bret Barberie .05
342 Jamie Moyer .05
343 Mike Oquist .05
344 Sid Fernandez .05
345 Eddie Williams .05
346 Joey Hamilton .05
347 Brian Williams .05
348 Luis Lopez .05
349 Steve Finley .05
350 Andy Benes .05
351 Andujar Cedeno .05
352 Bip Roberts .05
353 Ray McDavid .05
354 Ken Caminiti .05
355 Trevor Hoffman .05
356 Mel Nieves .05
357 Brad Ausmus .05
358 Andy Ashby .05
359 Scott Sanders .05
360 Gregg Jefferies .05
361 Mariano Duncan .05
362 Dave Hollins .05
363 Kevin Stocker .05
364 Fernando Valenzuela .05
365 Lenny Dykstra .05
366 Jim Eisenreich .05
367 Ricky Bottalico .05
368 Doug Jones .05
369 Ricky Jordan .05
370 Darren Daulton .05
371 Mike Lieberthal .05
372 Bobby Munoz .05
373 John Kruk .05
374 Curt Schilling .20
375 Orlando Merced .05
376 Carlos Garcia .05
377 Lance Parrish .05
378 Steve Cooke .05
379 Jeff King .05
380 Jay Bell .05
381 Al Martin .05
382 Paul Wagner .05
383 Rick White .05
384 Midre Cummings .05
385 Jon Lieber .05
386 Dave Clark .05
387 Don Slaught .05
388 Denny Neagle .05
389 Zane Smith .05
390 Andy Van Slyke .05
391 Ivan Rodriguez .50
392 David Hulse .05
393 John Burkett .05
394 Kevin Brown .05
395 Dean Palmer .05
396 Otis Nixon .05
397 Rick Helling .05
398 Kenny Rogers .05
399 Darren Oliver .05
400 Will Clark .05
401 Jeff Frye .05
402 Kevin Gross .05
403 John Dettmer .05
404 Manny Lee .05
405 Rusty Greer .05
406 Aaron Sele .05
407 Carlos Rodriguez .05
408 Scott Cooper .05
409 John Valentin .05
410 Roger Clemens .05
411 Mike Greenwell .05
412 Tim Vanegmond .05
413 Tom Brunansky .05
414 Steve Farr .05
415 Jose Canseco .35
416 Joe Hesketh .05
417 Ken Ryan .05

418 Tim Naehring .05
419 Frank Viola .05
420 Andre Dawson .25
421 Mo Vaughn .05
422 Jeff Brantley .05
423 Pete Schourek .05
424 Hal Morris .05
425 Deion Sanders .10
426 Brian L. Hunter .05
427 Bret Boone .05
428 Willie Greene .05
429 Ron Gant .05
430 Barry Larkin .05
431 Reggie Sanders .05
432 Eddie Taubensee .05
433 Jack Morris .05
434 Jose Rijo .05
435 Johnny Ruffin .05
436 John Smiley .05
437 John Roper .05
438 David Nied .05
439 Roberto Mejia .05
440 Andres Galarraga .05
441 Mike Kingery .05
442 Curt Leskanic .05
443 Walt Weiss .05
444 Marvin Freeman .05
445 Charlie Hayes .05
446 Eric Young .05
447 Ellis Burks .05
448 Joe Girardi .05
449 Lance Painter .05
450 Dante Bichette .05
451 Bruce Ruffin .05
452 Jeff Granger .05
453 Wally Joyner .05
454 Jose Lind .05
455 Jeff Montgomery .05
456 Gary Gaetti .05
457 Greg Gagne .05
458 Vince Coleman .05
459 Mike Macfarlane .05
460 Brian McRae .05
461 Tom Gordon .05
462 Kevin Appier .05
463 Billy Brewer .05
464 Mark Gubicza .05
465 Travis Fryman .05
466 Danny Bautista .05
467 Sean Bergman .05
468 Mike Henneman .05
469 Mike Moore .05
470 Cecil Fielder .05
471 Alan Trammell .05
472 Kirk Gibson .05
473 Tony Phillips .05
474 Mickey Tettleton .05
475 Lou Whitaker .05
476 Chris Gomez .05
477 John Doherty .05
478 Greg Gohr .05
479 Bill Gullickson .05
480 Rick Aguilera .05
481 Matt Walbeck .05
482 Kevin Tapani .05
483 Scott Erickson .05
484 Steve Dunn .05
485 David McCarty .05
486 Scott Leius .05
487 Pat Meares .05
488 Jeff Reboulet .05
489 Pedro Munoz .05
490 Chuck Knoblauch .05
491 Rich Becker .05
492 Alex Cole .05
493 Pat Mahomes .05
494 Ozzie Guillen .05
495 Tim Raines .05
496 Kirk McCaskill .05
497 Olmedo Saenz .05
498 Scott Sanderson .05
499 Lance Johnson .05
500 Michael Jordan 1.50
501 Warren Newson .05
502 Ron Karkovice .05
503 Wilson Alvarez .05
504 Jason Bere .05
505 Robin Ventura .05
506 Alex Fernandez .05
507 Roberto Hernandez .05
508 Norberto Martin .05
509 Bob Wickman .05
510 Don Mattingly .85
511 Melido Perez .05
512 Pat Kelly .05
513 Randy Velarde .05
514 Tony Fernandez .05
515 Jack McDowell .05
516 Luis Polonia .05
517 Bernie Williams .05
518 Danny Tartabull .05
519 Mike Stanley .05
520 Wade Boggs .75
521 Jim Leyritz .05
522 Steve Howe .05
523 Scott Kamieniecki .05
524 Russ Davis .05
525 Jim Abbott .05
526 Checklist 1-106 (Eddie Murray) .20
527 Checklist 107-212 (Alex Rodriguez) .40
528 Checklist 213-318 (Jeff Bagwell) .20
529 Checklist 319-424 (Joe Carter) .05
530 Checklist 425-530 (Fred McGriff) .05

--- National Packtime offer card .05

Silver Signature

A silver-foil facsimile autograph added to the card front is the only difference between these chase cards and regular-issue Collector's Choice cards. The silver-signature inserts are found one per pack in regular foil packs, and two per pack in retail jumbo packs.

NM/M
Common Player: .10
Stars: 2X

Gold Signature

The top-of-the-line chase card in 1995 Collector's Choice is the Gold Signature parallel set. Each of the 530 cards in the set was created in a special gold version that was found on average only one per box of foil packs. Other than the addition of a gold-foil facsimile autograph on front, the cards are identical to regular-issue Collector's Choice.

NM/M
Common Player: .50
Stars: 6X

Trade Cards

A series of five mail-in redemption cards was included as inserts into UD Collector's Choice, at the rate of approximately one per 11 packs. The cards could be sent in with $2 to receive 11 Collector's Choice Update cards, as specified on the front of the card. The trade offer expired on Feb. 1, 1996. Cards are numbered with the "TC" prefix.

NM/M
Complete Set (5): 1.00
Common Player: .25

1	Larry Walker (#531-541)	.25
2	David Cone (#542-552)	.25
3	Marquis Grissom (#553-563)	.25
4	Terry Pendleton (#564-574)	.25
5	Fernando Valenzuela (#575-585)	.25

Redemption Cards

These update cards were available only via a mail-in offer involving trade cards found in foil packs. Each trade card was redeemable for a specific 11-card set of players shown in their new uniforms as a result of rookie call-ups, trades and free agent signings. The cards are in the same format as the regular 1995 Collector's Choice issue. The update redemption cards are numbered by team nickname from Angels through Yankees, the numbers running contiguously from the body of the CC set.

		NM/M
Complete Set (55):		2.50
Common Player:		.10
531	Tony Phillips	.10
532	Dave Magadan	.10
533	Mike Gallego	.10
534	Dave Stewart	.10
535	Todd Stottlemyre	.10
536	David Cone	.10
537	Marquis Grissom	.10
538	Derrick May	.10
539	Joe Oliver	.10
540	Scott Cooper	.10
541	Ken Hill	.10
542	Howard Johnson	.10
543	Brian McRae	.10
544	Jaime Navarro	.10
545	Ozzie Timmons	.10
546	Roberto Kelly	.10
547	Hideo Nomo	1.50
548	Shane Andrews	.10
549	Mark Grudzielanek	.10
550	Carlos Perez	.10
551	Henry Rodriguez	.10
552	Tony Tarasco	.10
553	Glenallen Hill	.10
554	Terry Mulholland	.10
555	Orel Hershiser	.10
556	Darren Bragg	.10
557	John Burkett	.10
558	Bobby Witt	.10
559	Terry Pendleton	.10
560	Andre Dawson	.50
561	Brett Butler	.10
562	Kevin Brown	.10
563	Doug Jones	.10
564	Andy Van Slyke	.10
565	Jody Reed	.10
566	Fernando Valenzuela	.10
567	Charlie Hayes	.10
568	Benji Gil	.10
569	Mark McLemore	.10
570	Mickey Tettleton	.10
571	Bob Tewksbury	.10
572	Rheal Cormier	.10
573	Vaughn Eshelman	.10
574	Mike Macfarlane	.10
575	Mark Whiten	.10
576	Benito Santiago	.10
577	Jason Bates	.10
578	Bill Swift	.10
579	Larry Walker	.10
580	Chad Curtis	.10
581	Bobby Higginson	.10
582	Marty Cordova	.10
583	Mike Devereaux	.10
584	John Kruk	.10
585	John Wetteland	.10

Crash the Game

These insert cards gave collectors a reason to follow box scores around the major leagues between June 18-Octo-ber 1. Each of 20 noted home run hitters can be found with three different dates foil-stamped on the card front. If the player hit a home run on that day, the card could be redeemed for a set of 20 special prize cards. Stated odds of finding a You Crash the Game card were one in five packs. Most of the inserts are silver-foil enhanced, with about one in eight being found with gold foil. Winning cards are much scarcer than the others since they had to be mailed in for redemption.

		NM/M
Complete Set, Silver (20):		5.00
Common Player, Silver:		.15
Complete Set, Gold (20):		12.00
Common Player, Gold:		.35
CG1	Jeff Bagwell (July 30)	.25
CG1	Jeff Bagwell (Aug. 13)	.25
CG1	Jeff Bagwell (Sept. 28)	.25
CG2	Albert Belle (June 18)	.15
CG2	Albert Belle (Aug. 26)	.15
CG2	Albert Belle (Sept. 20)	.15
CG3	Barry Bonds (June 28)	1.00
CG3	Barry Bonds (July 9)	1.00
CG3	Barry Bonds (Sept. 6)	1.00
CG4	Jose Canseco/Winner (June 30)	1.00
CG4	Jose Canseco/Winner (July 30)	1.00
CG4	Jose Canseco (Sept. 3)	.35
CG5	Joe Carter (July 14)	.15
CG5	Joe Carter (Aug. 9)	.15
CG5	Joe Carter (Sept. 23)	.15
CG6	Cecil Fielder (July 4)	.15
CG6	Cecil Fielder (Aug. 2)	.15
CG6	Cecil Fielder (Oct. 1)	.15
CG7	Juan Gonzalez (June 29)	.30
CG7	Juan Gonzalez (Aug. 13)	.30
CG7	Juan Gonzalez/Winner (Sept. 3)	1.00
CG8	Ken Griffey Jr. (July 2)	.60
CG8	Ken Griffey Jr./Winner (Aug. 24)	2.50
CG8	Ken Griffey Jr. (Sept. 15)	.60
CG9	Bob Hamelin (July 23)	.15
CG9	Bob Hamelin (Aug. 1)	.15
CG9	Bob Hamelin (Sept. 29)	.15
CG10	David Justice (June 24)	.15
CG10	David Justice (July 25)	.15
CG10	David Justice (Sept. 17)	.15
CG11	Ryan Klesko (July 13)	.15
CG11	Ryan Klesko (Aug. 20)	.15
CG11	Ryan Klesko (Sept. 10)	.15
CG12	Fred McGriff (Aug. 25)	.15
CG12	Fred McGriff (Sept. 8)	.15
CG12	Fred McGriff (Sept. 24)	.15
CG13	Mark McGwire (July 23)	2.00
CG13	Mark McGwire/Winner (Aug. 3)	4.00
CG13	Mark McGwire (Sept. 27)	2.00
CG14	Raul Mondesi/Winner (July 27)	1.25
CG14	Raul Mondesi (Aug. 13)	.45
CG14	Raul Mondesi/Winner (Sept. 15)	1.25
CG15	Mike Piazza/Winner (July 23)	3.00
CG15	Mike Piazza/Winner (Aug. 27)	3.00
CG15	Mike Piazza (Sept. 19)	1.00
CG16	Manny Ramirez (June 21)	.75
CG16	Manny Ramirez (Aug. 13)	.75
CG16	Manny Ramirez (Sept. 26)	.75
CG17	Alex Rodriguez (Sept. 10)	1.00
CG17	Alex Rodriguez (Sept. 18)	1.00
CG17	Alex Rodriguez (Sept. 24)	1.00
CG18	Gary Sheffield (July 5)	.75
CG18	Gary Sheffield (Aug. 13)	.75
CG18	Gary Sheffield (Sept. 4)(winner)	2.00
CG19	Frank Thomas (July 26)	.65
CG19	Frank Thomas (Aug. 17)	.65
CG19	Frank Thomas (Sept. 23)	.65
CG20	Matt Williams (July 29)	.45
CG20	Matt Williams (Aug. 12)	.45
CG20	Matt Williams (Sept. 19)	.45

Crash Winners

These 20-card sets were awarded to collectors who redeemed "You Crash the Game" winners cards. A silver-foil enhanced set was sent to winners with silver redemption cards, a gold version was sent to gold winners. A $3 redemption fee was required. Fronts are similar to the game cards, except for the foil printing down the left side in the place of the game date. Instead of redemption

CG18	Gary Sheffield (Aug. 13)	.30
CG18	Gary Sheffield/Winner (Sept. 4)	1.00
CG19	Frank Thomas (July 26)	.50
CG19	Frank Thomas (Aug. 17)	.50
CG19	Frank Thomas (Sept. 23)	.50
CG20	Matt Williams (July 29)	.15
CG20	Matt Williams (Aug. 12)	.15
CG20	Matt Williams (Sept. 19)	.15
CG1	Jeff Bagwell (July 30)	.75
CG1	Jeff Bagwell (Aug. 13)	.75
CG1	Jeff Bagwell (Sept. 28)	.75
CG2	Albert Belle (June 18)	.35
CG2	Albert Belle (Aug. 26)	.35
CG2	Albert Belle (Sept. 20)	.35
CG3	Barry Bonds (June 28)	2.50
CG3	Barry Bonds (July 9)	2.50
CG3	Barry Bonds (Sept. 6)	2.50
CG4	Jose Canseco/Winner (June 30)	2.00
CG4	Jose Canseco/Winner (July 30)	2.00
CG4	Jose Canseco (Sept. 3)	.75
CG5	Joe Carter (July 14)	.35
CG5	Joe Carter (Aug. 9)	.35
CG5	Joe Carter (Sept. 23)	.35
CG6	Cecil Fielder (July 4)	.35
CG6	Cecil Fielder (Aug. 2)	.35
CG6	Cecil Fielder (Oct. 1)	.35
CG7	Juan Gonzalez (June 29)	.45
CG7	Juan Gonzalez (Aug. 13)	.45
CG7	Juan Gonzalez/Winner (Sept. 3)	1.50
CG8	Ken Griffey Jr. (July 2)	1.50
CG8	Ken Griffey Jr./Winner (Aug. 24)	3.00
CG8	Ken Griffey Jr. (Sept. 15)	1.50
CG9	Bob Hamelin (July 23)	.35
CG9	Bob Hamelin (Aug. 1)	.35
CG9	Bob Hamelin (Sept. 29)	.35
CG10	David Justice (June 24)	.35
CG10	David Justice (July 25)	.35
CG10	David Justice (Sept. 17)	.35
CG11	Ryan Klesko (July 13)	.35
CG11	Ryan Klesko (Aug. 20)	.35
CG11	Ryan Klesko (Sept. 10)	.35
CG12	Fred McGriff (Aug. 25)	.35
CG12	Fred McGriff (Sept. 8)	.35
CG12	Fred McGriff (Sept. 24)	.35
CG13	Mark McGwire (July 23)	2.00
CG13	Mark McGwire/Winner (Aug. 3)	4.00
CG13	Mark McGwire (Sept. 27)	2.00
CG14	Raul Mondesi/Winner (July 27)	1.25
CG14	Raul Mondesi (Aug. 13)	.45
CG14	Raul Mondesi/Winner (Sept. 15)	1.25
CG15	Mike Piazza/Winner (July 23)	3.00
CG15	Mike Piazza/Winner (Aug. 27)	3.00
CG15	Mike Piazza (Sept. 19)	1.00
CG16	Manny Ramirez (June 21)	.75
CG16	Manny Ramirez (Aug. 13)	.75
CG16	Manny Ramirez (Sept. 26)	.75
CG17	Alex Rodriguez (Sept. 10)	1.00
CG17	Alex Rodriguez (Sept. 18)	1.00
CG17	Alex Rodriguez (Sept. 24)	1.00
CG18	Gary Sheffield (July 5)	.75

---

rules on the back of award cards there are career highlights at left and a panel at right with the names of the players in the set.

		NM/M
Complete Set, Silver (20):		6.00
Complete Set, Gold (20):		25.00
Common Player, Silver:		.25
Common Player, Gold:		1.00
CR1	Jeff Bagwell	.60
CR2	Albert Belle	.25
CR3	Barry Bonds	2.50
CR4	Jose Canseco	.50
CR5	Joe Carter	.25
CR6	Cecil Fielder	.25
CR7	Juan Gonzalez	.50
CR8	Ken Griffey Jr.	1.50
CR9	Bob Hamelin	.25
CR10	Dave Justice	.25
CR11	Ryan Klesko	.25
CR12	Fred McGriff	.25
CR13	Mark McGwire	2.00
CR14	Raul Mondesi	.25
CR15	Mike Piazza	1.50
CR16	Manny Ramirez	.60
CR17	Alex Rodriguez	2.00
CR18	Gary Sheffield	.50
CR19	Frank Thomas	.60
CR20	Matt Williams	.25
CR1	Jeff Bagwell	2.00
CR2	Albert Belle	1.00
CR3	Barry Bonds	4.00
CR4	Jose Canseco	1.50
CR5	Joe Carter	1.00
CR6	Cecil Fielder	1.00
CR7	Juan Gonzalez	1.50
CR8	Ken Griffey Jr.	3.00
CR9	Bob Hamelin	1.00
CR10	Dave Justice	1.00
CR11	Ryan Klesko	1.00
CR12	Fred McGriff	1.00
CR13	Mark McGwire	3.00
CR14	Raul Mondesi	1.00
CR15	Mike Piazza	3.00
CR16	Manny Ramirez	1.00
CR17	Alex Rodriguez	3.50
CR18	Gary Sheffield	1.50
CR19	Frank Thomas	1.00
CR20	Matt Williams	1.00

1995 Collector's Choice Michael Jordan Jumbo

A limited edition of 10,000 of these 3" x 5" cards was produced for direct sales to consumers. The card is in the format of the 1995 Collector's Choice Rookie Class subset and includes a silver foil facsimile of Jordan's autograph on front. Back includes a serial number in the lower-right corner.

		NM/M
661	Michael Jordan	15.00

1995 Collector's Choice Ichiro Suzuki

This card was part of a set produced by Upper Deck's Collector's Choice brand in conjunction with a series of NBA games held in Japan. The cards were made for various members of the media, sports dignitaries, etc., to be used as personal business cards. Cards are in standard 2-1/2" x 3-1/2" format.

		NM/M
59	Ichiro Suzuki	1,000

1995 Collector's Choice/SE

The first Upper Deck baseball card issue for 1995 was this 265-card set which uses blue borders and a blue foil "Special Edition" trapezoidal logo to impart a premium look. The set opens with a Rookie Class subset of 25 cards on which the background has been rendered in orange hues. A series of six Record Pace cards, horizontal with blue and yellow backgrounds, immediately precedes the regular cards. Base cards in the set are arranged in team-alpha order. Front and back have large color photos, while backs offer complete major league stats. Interspersed within the teams are special cards with borderless front designs honoring players who won significant awards in the 1994 season. Another subset, Stat Leaders, pictures various players in a silver dollar-sized circle at the center of the card and lists the 1994 leaders in that category on the back. A dozen-card Fantasy Team subset near the end of the set lists on back the top-rated players at each position, picturing one of them on front, with a giant blue baseball. The set closes with five checklists honoring career highlights from the '94 season.

		NM/M
Complete Set (265):		17.50
Common Player:		.05
Silver Stars:		1.5X
Gold Stars:		8X
Pack (12):		1.25
Wax Box (36):		25.00

1	Alex Rodriguez	1.50
2	Derek Jeter	2.00
3	Dustin Hermanson	.05
4	Bill Pulsipher	.05
5	Terrell Wade	.05
6	Darren Dreifort	.05
7	LaTroy Hawkins	.05
8	Alex Ochoa	.05
9	Paul Wilson	.05
10	Ernie Young	.05
11	Alan Benes	.05
12	Garret Anderson	.05
13	Armando Benitez	.05
14	Robert Perez	.05
15	Herbert Perry	.05
16	Jose Silva	.05
17	Orlando Miller	.05
18	Russ Davis	.05
19	Jason Isringhausen	.05
20	Ray McDavid	.05
21	Duane Singleton	.05
22	Paul Shuey	.05
23	Steve Dunn	.05
24	Mike Lieberthal	.05
25	Chan Ho Park	.05
26	Ken Griffey Jr. (Record Pace)	.65
27	Tony Gwynn (Record Pace)	.40
28	Chuck Knoblauch (Record Pace)	.05
29	Frank Thomas (Record Pace)	.35
30	Matt Williams (Record Pace)	.05
31	Chili Davis	.05
32	Chad Curtis	.05
33	Brian Anderson	.05
34	Chuck Finley	.05
35	Tim Salmon	.05
36	Bo Jackson	.10
37	Doug Drabek	.05
38	Craig Biggio	.05
39	Ken Caminiti	.05
40	Jeff Bagwell	.65
41	Darryl Kile	.05
42	John Hudek	.05
43	Brian L. Hunter	.05
44	Dennis Eckersley	.60
45	Mark McGwire	1.50
46	Brent Gates	.05
47	Steve Karsay	.05
48	Rickey Henderson	.65
49	Terry Steinbach	.05
50	Ruben Sierra	.05
51	Roberto Alomar	.25
52	Carlos Delgado	.25
53	Alex Gonzalez	.05
54	Joe Carter	.25
55	Paul Molitor	.65
56	Juan Guzman	.05
57	John Olerud	.05
58	Shawn Green	.25
59	Tom Glavine	.25
60	Greg Maddux	.75
61	Roberto Kelly	.05
62	Ryan Klesko	.05
63	Javier Lopez	.05
64	Jose Oliva	.05
65	Fred McGriff	.25
66	Steve Avery	.05
67	Dave Justice	.25
68	Ricky Bones	.05
69	Cal Eldred	.05
70	Greg Vaughn	.05
71	Dave Nilsson	.05
72	Jose Valentin	.05
73	Matt Mieske	.05
74	Todd Zeile	.05
75	Ozzie Smith	.75
76	Bernard Gilkey	.05
77	Ray Lankford	.05
78	Bob Tewksbury	.05
79	Mark Whiten	.05
80	Gregg Jefferies	.05
81	Randy Myers	.05
82	Shawon Dunston	.05
83	Mark Grace	.25
84	Derrick May	.05
85	Sammy Sosa	.75
86	Steve Trachsel	.05
87	Brett Butler	.05
88	Delino DeShields	.05
89	Orel Hershiser	.05
90	Mike Piazza	1.00
91	Todd Hollandsworth	.05
92	Eric Karros	.05
93	Ramon Martinez	.05
94	Tim Wallach	.05
95	Raul Mondesi	.05
96	Larry Walker	.05
97	Wil Cordero	.05
98	Marquis Grissom	.05
99	Ken Hill	.05
100	Cliff Floyd	.05
101	Pedro J. Martinez	.65
102	John Wetteland	.05
103	Rondell White	.05
104	Moises Alou	.05
105	Barry Bonds	2.00
106	Darren Lewis	.05
107	Mark Portugal	.05
108	Matt Williams	.05
109	William Van Landingham	.05
110	Bill Swift	.05
111	Robby Thompson	.05
112	Rod Beck	.05

#	Player	Price
113	Darryl Strawberry	.05
114	Jim Thome	.50
115	Dave Winfield	.65
116	Eddie Murray	.65
117	Manny Ramirez	.65
118	Carlos Baerga	.05
119	Kenny Lofton	.05
120	Albert Belle	.05
121	Mark Clark	.05
122	Dennis Martinez	.05
123	Randy Johnson	.65
124	Jay Buhner	.05
125	Ken Griffey Jr.	1.00
125a	Ken Griffey Jr./OPS	1.50
126	Rich Gossage	.05
127	Tino Martinez	.05
128	Reggie Jefferson	.05
129	Edgar Martinez	.05
130	Gary Sheffield	.30
131	Pat Rapp	.05
132	Bret Barberie	.05
133	Chuck Carr	.05
134	Jeff Conine	.05
135	Charles Johnson	.05
136	Benito Santiago	.05
137	Matt Williams (Stat Leaders)	.05
138	Jeff Bagwell (Stat Leaders)	.35
139	Kenny Lofton (Stat Leaders)	.05
140	Tony Gwynn (Stat Leaders)	.40
141	Jimmy Key (Stat Leaders)	.05
142	Greg Maddux (Stat Leaders)	.40
143	Randy Johnson (Stat Leaders)	.25
144	Lee Smith (Stat Leaders)	.05
145	Bobby Bonilla	.05
146	Jason Jacome	.05
147	Jeff Kent	.05
148	Ryan Thompson	.05
149	Bobby Jones	.05
150	Bret Saberhagen	.05
151	John Franco	.05
152	Lee Smith	.05
153	Rafael Palmeiro	.60
154	Brady Anderson	.05
155	Cal Ripken Jr.	2.00
156	Jeffrey Hammonds	.05
157	Mike Mussina	.35
158	Chris Hoiles	.05
159	Ben McDonald	.05
160	Tony Gwynn	.75
161	Joey Hamilton	.05
162	Andy Benes	.05
163	Trevor Hoffman	.05
164	Phil Plantier	.05
165	Derek Bell	.05
166	Bip Roberts	.05
167	Eddie Williams	.05
168	Fernando Valenzuela	.05
169	Mariano Duncan	.05
170	Lenny Dykstra	.05
171	Darren Daulton	.05
172	Danny Jackson	.05
173	Bobby Munoz	.05
174	Doug Jones	.05
175	Jay Bell	.05
176	Zane Smith	.05
177	Jon Lieber	.05
178	Carlos Garcia	.05
179	Orlando Merced	.05
180	Andy Van Slyke	.05
181	Rick Helling	.05
182	Rusty Greer	.05
183	Kenny Rogers	.05
184	Will Clark	.05
185	Jose Canseco	.40
186	Juan Gonzalez	.35
187	Dean Palmer	.05
188	Ivan Rodriguez	.60
189	John Valentin	.05
190	Roger Clemens	.85
191	Aaron Sele	.05
192	Scott Cooper	.05
193	Mike Greenwell	.05
194	Mo Vaughn	.25
195	Andre Dawson	.05
196	Ron Gant	.05
197	Jose Rijo	.05
198	Bret Boone	.05
199	Deion Sanders	.10
200	Barry Larkin	.05
201	Hal Morris	.05
202	Reggie Sanders	.05
203	Kevin Mitchell	.05
204	Marvin Freeman	.05
205	Andres Galarraga	.05
206	Walt Weiss	.05
207	Charlie Hayes	.05
208	David Nied	.05
209	Dante Bichette	.05
210	David Cone	.05
211	Jeff Montgomery	.05
212	Felix Jose	.05
213	Mike Macfarlane	.05
214	Wally Joyner	.05
215	Bob Hamelin	.05
216	Brian McRae	.05
217	Kirk Gibson	.05
218	Lou Whitaker	.05
219	Chris Gomez	.05
220	Cecil Fielder	.05
221	Mickey Tettleton	.05
222	Travis Fryman	.05
223	Tony Phillips	.05
224	Rick Aguilera	.05
225	Scott Erickson	.05
226	Chuck Knoblauch	.05
227	Kent Hrbek	.05
228	Shane Mack	.05
229	Kevin Tapani	.05
230	Kirby Puckett	.75
231	Julio Franco	.05
232	Jack McDowell	.05
233	Jason Bere	.05
234	Alex Fernandez	.05
235	Frank Thomas	.65
236	Ozzie Guillen	.05
237	Robin Ventura	.05
238	Michael Jordan	2.00
239	Wilson Alvarez	.05
240	Don Mattingly	.85
241	Jim Abbott	.05
242	Jim Leyritz	.05
243	Paul O'Neill	.05
244	Melido Perez	.05
245	Wade Boggs	.75
246	Mike Stanley	.05
247	Danny Tartabull	.05
248	Jimmy Key	.05
249	Greg Maddux (Fantasy Team)	.40
250	Randy Johnson (Fantasy Team)	.20
251	Bret Saberhagen (Fantasy Team)	.05
252	John Wetteland (Fantasy Team)	.05
253	Mike Piazza (Fantasy Team)	.50
254	Jeff Bagwell (Fantasy Team)	.35
255	Craig Biggio (Fantasy Team)	.05
256	Matt Williams (Fantasy Team)	.05
257	Wil Cordero (Fantasy Team)	.05
258	Kenny Lofton (Fantasy Team)	.05
259	Barry Bonds (Fantasy Team)	.75
260	Dante Bichette (Fantasy Team)	.05
261	Checklist 1-53 (Ken Griffey Jr.)	.35
262	Checklist 54-106 (Goose Gossage)	.05
263	Checklist 107-159 (Cal Ripken Jr.)	.45
264	Checklist 160-212 (Kenny Rogers)	.05
265	Checklist 213-265 (John Valentin)	.05

SE Silver

The cards in this parallel edition feature the addition of a silver-foil facsimile autograph on the card front. Also, the blue SE logo and card borders have been replaced with silver on the chase cards, which are found on average of one per pack.

NM/M
Common Player: .15
Stars: 1.5X

SE Gold

Each of the cards in the SE issue can be found in a premium chase card version which replaces the blue border and SE logo with gold, and adds a gold-foil facsimile autograph to the front of the card. The gold-version SE inserts are found on average of one per 36 packs.

NM/M
Common Player: 1.00
Stars: 8X

1996 Collector's Choice Promo

To introduce its base-brand set, Upper Deck issued a promotional sample card of Ken Griffey, Jr. numbered 100 (he's #310 in the issued set), the back is overprinted "For Promotional Use Only."

NM/M
100 Ken Griffey Jr. 4.00

1996 Collector's Choice

The third year for Collector's Choice includes 730 cards in two series with packs formatted in retail and hobby versions. The 280 regular player cards are joined by subsets of Rookie Class, International Flavor, Traditional Threads, Fantasy Team, Stat Leaders, Season Highlights, First Class, Arizona Fall League, Awards and Checklists. Packs feature a number of different insert sets including silver and gold signature parallel sets, interactive "You Make the Play" cards, four cards from the cross-brand Cal Ripken Collection and three postseason trade cards redeemable for 10-card sets recalling the League Championships and World Series. An additional 30 cards (#761-790) featuring traded players in their new uniforms was issued only in factory sets.

NM/M
Unopened Fact. Set (790): 17.50
Complete Set: (760): 12.50
Traded Set (366T-395T): 3.00
Common Player: .05
Series 1 Pack (12): .75
Series 1 Wax Box (36): 22.50
Series 2 Pack (14): 1.00
Series 2 Wax Box (40): 25.00

#	Player	Price
1	Cal Ripken Jr.	2.00
2	Edgar Martinez, Tony Gwynn (1995 Stat Leaders)	.05
3	Albert Belle, Dante Bichette (1995 Stat Leaders)	.05
4	Albert Belle, Mo Vaughn, Dante Bichette (1995 Stat Leaders)	.05
5	Kenny Lofton, Quilvio Veras (1995 Stat Leaders)	.05
6	Mike Mussina, Greg Maddux (1995 Stat Leaders)	.40
7	Randy Johnson, Hideo Nomo (1995 Stat Leaders)	.25
8	Randy Johnson, Greg Maddux (1995 Stat Leaders)	.40
9	Jose Mesa, Randy Myers (1995 Stat Leaders)	.05
10	Johnny Damon/RC	.35
11	Rick Krivda/RC	.05
12	Roger Cedeno/RC	.05
13	Angel Martinez/RC	.05
14	Ariel Prieto/RC	.05
15	John Wasdin/RC	.05
16	Edwin Hurtado/RC	.05
17	Lyle Mouton/RC	.05
18	Chris Snopek/RC	.05
19	Mariano Rivera/RC	.15
20	Ruben Rivera/RC	.05
21	Juan Castro/RC RC	.05
22	Jimmy Haynes/RC	.05
23	Bob Wolcott/RC	.05
24	Brian Barber/RC	.05
25	Frank Rodriguez/RC	.05
26	Jesus Tavarez/RC	.05
27	Glenn Dishman/RC	.05
28	Jose Herrera/RC	.05
29	Chan Ho Park/RC	.05
30	Jason Isringhausen/RC	.05
31	Doug Johns/RC	.05
32	Gene Schall/RC	.05
33	Kevin Jordan/RC	.05
34	Matt Lawton/RC RC	.10
35	Karim Garcia/RC	.05
36	George Williams/RC	.05
37	Orlando Palmeiro/RC	.05
38	Jamie Brewington/RC	.05
39	Robert Person/RC	.05
40	Greg Maddux	.75
41	Marquis Grissom	.05
42	Chipper Jones	.75
43	David Justice	.05
44	Mark Lemke	.05
45	Fred McGriff	.05
46	Javy Lopez	.05
47	Mark Wohlers	.05
48	Jason Schmidt	.05
49	John Smoltz	.05
50	Curtis Goodwin	.05
51	Gregg Zaun	.05
52	Armando Benitez	.05
53	Manny Alexander	.05
54	Chris Hoiles	.05
55	Harold Baines	.05
56	Ben McDonald	.05
57	Scott Erickson	.05
58	Jeff Manto	.05
59	Luis Alicea	.05
60	Roger Clemens	.85
61	Rheal Cormier	.05
62	Vaughn Eshelman	.05
63	Zane Smith	.05
64	Mike Macfarlane	.05
65	Erik Hanson	.05
66	Tim Naehring	.05
67	Lee Tinsley	.05
68	Troy O'Leary	.05
69	Garret Anderson	.05
70	Chili Davis	.05
71	Jim Edmonds	.05
72	Troy Percival	.05
73	Mark Langston	.05
74	Spike Owen	.05
75	Tim Salmon	.05
76	Brian Anderson	.05
77	Lee Smith	.05
78	Jim Abbott	.05
79	Jim Bullinger	.05
80	Mark Grace	.05
81	Todd Zeile	.05
82	Kevin Foster	.05
83	Howard Johnson	.05
84	Brian McRae	.05
85	Randy Myers	.05
86	Jaime Navarro	.05
87	Luis Gonzalez	.05
88	Ozzie Timmons	.05
89	Wilson Alvarez	.05
90	Frank Thomas	.60
91	James Baldwin	.05
92	Ray Durham	.05
93	Alex Fernandez	.05
94	Ozzie Guillen	.05
95	Tim Raines	.05
96	Roberto Hernandez	.05
97	Lance Johnson	.05
98	John Kruk	.05
99	Mark Portugal	.05
100	Don Mattingly (Traditional Threads)	.65
101	Jose Canseco (Traditional Threads)	.15
102	Raul Mondesi (Traditional Threads)	.05
103	Cecil Fielder (Traditional Threads)	.05
104	Ozzie Smith (Traditional Threads)	.40
105	Frank Thomas (Traditional Threads)	.45
106	Sammy Sosa (Traditional Threads)	.50
107	Fred McGriff (Traditional Threads)	.05
108	Barry Bonds (Traditional Threads)	1.00
109	Thomas Howard	.05
110	Ron Gant	.05
111	Eddie Taubensee	.05
112	Hal Morris	.05
113	Jose Rijo	.05
114	Pete Schourek	.05
115	Reggie Sanders	.05
116	Benito Santiago	.05
117	Jeff Brantley	.05
118	Julian Tavarez	.05
119	Carlos Baerga	.05
120	Jim Thome	.40
121	Jose Mesa	.05
122	Dennis Martinez	.05
123	Dave Winfield	.60
124	Eddie Murray	.60
125	Manny Ramirez	.60
126	Paul Sorrento	.05
127	Kenny Lofton	.05
128	Eric Young	.05
129	Jason Bates	.05
130	Bret Saberhagen	.05
131	Andres Galarraga	.05
132	Joe Girardi	.05
133	John Vander Wal	.05
134	David Nied	.05
135	Dante Bichette	.05
136	Vinny Castilla	.05
137	Kevin Ritz	.05
138	Felipe Lira	.05
139	Joe Boever	.05
140	Cecil Fielder	.05
141	John Flaherty	.05
142	Kirk Gibson	.05
143	Brian Maxcy	.05
144	Lou Whitaker	.05
145	Alan Trammell	.05
146	Bobby Higginson	.05
147	Chad Curtis	.05
148	Quilvio Veras	.05
149	Jerry Browne	.05
150	Andre Dawson	.25
151	Robb Nen	.05
152	Greg Colbrunn	.05
153	Chris Hammond	.05
154	Kurt Abbott	.05
155	Charles Johnson	.05
156	Terry Pendleton	.05
157	Dave Weathers	.05
158	Mike Hampton	.05
159	Craig Biggio	.05
160	Jeff Bagwell	.60
161	Brian L. Hunter	.05
162	Mike Henneman	.05
163	Dave Magadan	.05
164	Shane Reynolds	.05
165	Derek Bell	.05
166	Orlando Miller	.05
167	James Mouton	.05
168	Melvin Bunch	.05
169	Tom Gordon	.05
170	Kevin Appier	.05
171	Tom Goodwin	.05
172	Greg Gagne	.05
173	Gary Gaetti	.05
174	Jeff Montgomery	.05
175	Jon Nunnally	.05
176	Michael Tucker	.05
177	Joe Vitiello	.05
178	Billy Ashley	.05
179	Tom Candiotti	.05
180	Hideo Nomo	.30
181	Chad Fonville	.05
182	Todd Hollandsworth	.05
183	Eric Karros	.05
184	Roberto Kelly	.05
185	Mike Piazza	1.00
186	Ramon Martinez	.05
187	Tim Wallach	.05
188	Jeff Cirillo	.05
189	Sid Roberson	.05
190	Kevin Seitzer	.05
191	Mike Fetters	.05
192	Steve Sparks	.05
193	Matt Mieske	.05
194	Joe Oliver	.05
195	B.J. Surhoff	.05
196	Alberto Reyes	.05
197	Fernando Vina	.05
198	LaTroy Hawkins	.05
199	Marty Cordova	.05
200	Kirby Puckett	.75
201	Brad Radke	.05
202	Pedro Munoz	.05
203	Scott Klingenbeck	.05
204	Pat Meares	.05
205	Chuck Knoblauch	.05
206	Scott Stahoviak	.05
207	Dave Stevens	.05
208	Shane Andrews	.05
209	Moises Alou	.05
210	David Segui	.05
211	Cliff Floyd	.05
212	Carlos Perez	.05
213	Mark Grudzielanek	.05
214	Butch Henry	.05
215	Rondell White	.05
216	Mel Rojas	.05
217	Ugueth Urbina	.05
218	Edgardo Alfonzo	.05
219	Carl Everett	.05
220	John Franco	.05
221	Todd Hundley	.05
222	Bobby Jones	.05
223	Bill Pulsipher	.05
224	Rico Brogna	.05
225	Jeff Kent	.05
226	Chris Jones	.05
227	Butch Huskey	.05
228	Robert Eenhoorn	.05
229	Sterling Hitchcock	.05
230	Wade Boggs	.75
231	Derek Jeter	2.00
232	Tony Fernandez	.05
233	Jack McDowell	.05
234	Andy Pettitte	.35
235	David Cone	.05
236	Mike Stanley	.05
237	Don Mattingly	.85
238	Geronimo Berroa	.05
239	Scott Brosius	.05
240	Rickey Henderson	.60
241	Terry Steinbach	.05
242	Mike Gallego	.05
243	Jason Giambi	.40
244	Steve Ontiveros	.05
245	Dennis Eckersley	.50
246	Dave Stewart	.05
247	Don Wengert	.05
248	Paul Quantrill	.05
249	Ricky Bottalico	.05
250	Kevin Stocker	.05
251	Lenny Dykstra	.05
252	Tony Longmire	.05
253	Tyler Green	.05
254	Mike Mimbs	.05
255	Charlie Hayes	.05
256	Mickey Morandini	.05
257	Heathcliff Slocumb	.05
258	Jeff King	.05
259	Midre Cummings	.05
260	Mark Johnson	.05
261	Freddy Garcia	.05
262	Jon Lieber	.05
263	Esteban Loaiza	.05
264	Danny Miceli	.05
265	Orlando Merced	.05
266	Denny Neagle	.05
267	Steve Parris	.05
268	Fantasy Team '95 (Greg Maddux)	.35
269	Fantasy Team '95 (Randy Johnson)	.20
270	Fantasy Team '95 (Hideo Nomo)	.15
271	Fantasy Team '95 (Jose Mesa)	.05
272	Fantasy Team '95 (Mike Piazza)	.60
273	Fantasy Team '95 (Mo Vaughn)	.05
274	Fantasy Team '95 (Craig Biggio)	.05
275	Fantasy Team '95 (Edgar Martinez)	.05
276	Fantasy Team '95 (Barry Larkin)	.05
277	Fantasy Team '95 (Sammy Sosa)	.50
278	Fantasy Team '95 (Dante Bichette)	.05
279	Fantasy Team '95 (Albert Belle)	.05
280	Ozzie Smith	.75
281	Mark Sweeney	.05
282	Terry Bradshaw	.05
283	Allen Battle	.05
284	Danny Jackson	.05
285	Tom Henke	.05
286	Scott Cooper	.05
287	Tripp Cromer	.05
288	Bernard Gilkey	.05
289	Brian Jordan	.05
290	Tony Gwynn	.75
291	Brad Ausmus	.05
292	Bryce Florie	.05
293	Andres Berumen	.05
294	Ken Caminiti	.05
295	Bip Roberts	.05
296	Trevor Hoffman	.05
297	Roberto Petagine	.05
298	Jody Reed	.05
299	Fernando Valenzuela	.05
300	Barry Bonds	2.00
301	Mark Leiter	.05
302	Mark Carreon	.05
303	Royce Clayton	.05
304	Kirt Manwaring	.05
305	Glenallen Hill	.05
306	Deion Sanders	.10
307	Joe Rosselli	.05
308	Robby Thompson	.05
309	William Van Landingham	.05
310	Ken Griffey Jr.	1.00
311	Bobby Ayala	.05
312	Joey Cora	.05
313	Mike Blowers	.05
314	Darren Bragg	.05
315	Randy Johnson	.60
316	Alex Rodriguez	1.50
317	Andy Benes	.05
318	Tino Martinez	.05
319	Dan Wilson	.05

320	Will Clark	.05
321	Jeff Frye	.05
322	Benji Gil	.05
323	Rick Helling	.05
324	Mark McLemore	.05
325	Dave Nilsson (International Flavor)	.05
326	Larry Walker (International Flavor)	.05
327	Jose Canseco (International Flavor)	.15
328	Raul Mondesi (International Flavor)	.05
329	Manny Ramirez (International Flavor)	.30
330	Robert Eenhoorn (International Flavor)	.05
331	Chili Davis (International Flavor)	.05
332	Hideo Nomo (International Flavor)	.15
333	Benji Gil (International Flavor)	.05
334	Fernando Valenzuela (International Flavor)	.05
335	Dennis Martinez (International Flavor)	.05
336	Roberto Kelly (International Flavor)	.05
337	Carlos Baerga (International Flavor)	.05
338	Juan Gonzalez (International Flavor)	.15
339	Roberto Alomar (International Flavor)	.10
340	Chan Ho Park (International Flavor)	.05
341	Andres Galarraga (International Flavor)	.05
342	Midre Cummings (International Flavor)	.05
343	Otis Nixon	.05
344	Jeff Russell	.05
345	Ivan Rodriguez	.50
346	Mickey Tettleton	.05
347	Bob Tewksbury	.05
348	Domingo Cedeno	.05
349	Lance Parrish	.05
350	Joe Carter	.05
351	Devon White	.05
352	Carlos Delgado	.35
353	Alex Gonzalez	.05
354	Darren Hall	.05
355	Paul Molitor	.60
356	Al Leiter	.05
357	Randy Knorr	.05
358	Checklist 1-46 (12-player Astros-Padres trade)	.05
359	Checklist 47-92 (Hideo Nomo)	.15
360	Checklist 93-138 (Ramon Martinez)	.05
361	Checklist 139-184 (Robin Ventura)	.05
362	Checklist 185-230 (Cal Ripken Jr.)	.30
363	Checklist 231-275 (Ken Caminiti)	.05
364	Checklist 276-320 (Eddie Murray)	.20
365	Checklist 321-365 (Randy Johnson)	.15
366	A.L. Divisional Series (Tony Pena)	.10
367	A.L. Divisional Series (Jim Thome)	.25
368	A.L. Divisional Series (Don Mattingly)	.60
369	A.L. Divisional Series (Jim Leyritz)	.10
370	A.L. Divisional Series (Ken Griffey Jr.)	.60
371	N.L. Divisional Series (Edgar Martinez)	.10
372	N.L. Divisional Series (Pete Schourek)	.10
373	N.L. Divisional Series (Mark Lewis)	.10
374	N.L. Divisional Series (Chipper Jones)	.50
375	N.L. Divisonal Series (Fred McGriff)	.10
376	N.L. Championship Series (Javy Lopez)	.10
377	N.L. Championship Series (Fred McGriff)	.10
378	N.L. Championship Series (Charlie O'Brien)	.10
379	N.L. Championship Series (Mike Devereaux)	.10
380	N.L. Championship Series (Mark Wohlers)	.10
381	A.L. Championship Series (Bob Wolcott)	.10
382	A.L. Championship Series (Manny Ramirez)	.25
383	A.L. Championship Series (Jay Buhner)	.10
384	A.L. Championship Series (Orel Hershiser)	.10
385	A.L. Championship Series (Kenny Lofton)	.10
386	World Series (Greg Maddux)	.50
387	World Series (Javy Lopez)	.10
388	World Series (Kenny Lofton)	.10
389	World Series (Eddie Murray)	.10
390	World Series (Luis Polonia)	.10
391	World Series (Pedro Borbon)	.10
392	World Series (Jim Thome)	.25
393	World Series (Orel Hershiser)	.10
394	World Series (David Justice)	.10
395	World Series (Tom Glavine)	.10
396	Braves Team Checklist (Greg Maddux)	.25
397	Mets Team Checklist (Brett Butler)	.05
398	Phillies Team Checklist (Darren Daulton)	.05
399	Marlins Team Checklist (Gary Sheffield)	.05
400	Expos Team Checklist (Moises Alou)	.05
401	Reds Team Checklist (Barry Larkin)	.05
402	Astros Team Checklist (Jeff Bagwell)	.20
403	Cubs Team Checklist (Sammy Sosa)	.35
404	Cardinals Team Checklist (Ozzie Smith)	.25
405	Pirates Team Checklist (Jeff King)	.05
406	Dodgers Team Checklist (Mike Piazza)	.50
407	Rockies Team Checklist (Dante Bichette)	.05
408	Padres Team Checklist (Tony Gwynn)	.25
409	Giants Team Checklist (Barry Bonds)	.45
410	Indians Team Checklist (Kenny Lofton)	.05
411	Royals Team Checklist (Jon Nunnally)	.05
412	White Sox Team Checklist (Frank Thomas)	.20
413	Brewers Team Checklist (Greg Vaughn)	.05
414	Twins Team Checklist (Paul Molitor)	.20
415	Mariners Team Checklist (Ken Griffey Jr.)	.35
416	Angels Team Checklist (Jim Edmonds)	.05
417	Rangers Team Checklist (Juan Gonzalez)	.15
418	Athletics Team Checklist (Mark McGwire)	.75
419	Red Sox Team Checklist (Roger Clemens)	.30
420	Yankees Team Checklist (Wade Boggs)	.35
421	Orioles Team Checklist (Cal Ripken Jr.)	.40
422	Tigers Team Checklist (Cecil Fielder)	.05
423	Blue Jays Team Checklist (Joe Carter)	.05
424	Osvaldo Fernandez RC (Rookie Class)	.15
425	Billy Wagner/RC	.05
426	George Arias/RC	.05
427	Mendy Lopez/RC	.05
428	Jeff Suppan/RC	.05
429	Rey Ordonez/RC	.05
430	Brooks Kieschnick/RC	.05
431	Raul Ibanez RC/RC	.05
432	Livan Hernandez/RC RC	.05
433	Shannon Stewart/RC	.05
434	Steve Cox/RC	.05
435	Trey Beamon/RC	.05
436	Sergio Nunez/RC	.05
437	Jermaine Dye/RC	.05
438	Mike Sweeney/RC RC	.45
439	Richard Hidalgo/RC	.05
440	Todd Greene/RC	.05
441	Robert Smith/RC RC	.05
442	Rafael Orellano/RC	.05
443	Wilton Guerrero/RC RC	.05
444	David Doster/RC RC	.05
445	Jason Kendall/RC	.05
446	Edgar Renteria/RC	.05
447	Scott Spiezio/RC	.05
448	Jay Canizaro/RC	.05
449	Enrique Wilson/RC	.05
450	Bob Abreu/RC	.10
451	Dwight Smith	.05
452	Jeff Blauser	.05
453	Steve Avery	.05
454	Brad Clontz	.05
455	Tom Glavine	.20
456	Mike Mordecai	.05
457	Rafael Belliard	.05
458	Greg McMichael	.05
459	Pedro Borbon	.05
460	Ryan Klesko	.05
461	Terrell Wade	.05
462	Brady Anderson	.05
463	Roberto Alomar	.20
464	Bobby Bonilla	.05
465	Mike Mussina	.40
466	Cesar Devarez RC	.05
467	Jeffrey Hammonds	.05
468	Mike Devereaux	.05
469	B.J. Surhoff	.05
470	Rafael Palmeiro	.50
471	John Valentin	.05
472	Mike Greenwell	.05
473	Dwayne Hosey	.05
474	Tim Wakefield	.05
475	Jose Canseco	.35
476	Aaron Sele	.05
477	Stan Belinda	.05
478	Mike Stanley	.05
479	Jamie Moyer	.05
480	Mo Vaughn	.05
481	Randy Velarde	.05
482	Gary DiSarcina	.05
483	Jorge Fabregas	.05
484	Rex Hudler	.05
485	Chuck Finley	.05
486	Tim Wallach	.05
487	Eduardo Perez	.05
488	Scott Sanderson	.05
489	J.T. Snow	.05
490	Sammy Sosa	.75
491	Terry Adams	.05
492	Matt Franco	.05
493	Scott Servais	.05
494	Frank Castillo	.05
495	Ryne Sandberg	.75
496	Rey Sanchez	.05
497	Steve Trachsel	.05
498	Jose Hernandez	.05
499	Dave Martinez	.05
500	Babe Ruth (First Class)	1.00
501	Ty Cobb (First Class)	.50
502	Walter Johnson (First Class)	.10
503	Christy Mathewson (First Class)	.10
504	Honus Wagner (First Class)	.25
505	Robin Ventura	.05
506	Jason Bere	.05
507	Mike Cameron RC	.25
508	Ron Karkovice	.05
509	Matt Karchner	.05
510	Harold Baines	.05
511	Kirk McCaskill	.05
512	Larry Thomas	.05
513	Danny Tartabull	.05
514	Steve Gibralter	.05
515	Bret Boone	.05
516	Jeff Branson	.05
517	Kevin Jarvis	.05
518	Xavier Hernandez	.05
519	Eric Owens	.05
520	Barry Larkin	.05
521	Dave Burba	.05
522	John Smiley	.05
523	Paul Assenmacher	.05
524	Chad Ogea	.05
525	Orel Hershiser	.05
526	Alan Embree	.05
527	Tony Pena	.05
528	Omar Vizquel	.05
529	Mark Clark	.05
530	Albert Belle	.05
531	Charles Nagy	.05
532	Herbert Perry	.05
533	Darren Holmes	.05
534	Ellis Burks	.05
535	Bill Swift	.05
536	Armando Reynoso	.05
537	Curtis Leskanic	.05
538	Quinton McCracken	.05
539	Steve Reed	.05
540	Larry Walker	.05
541	Walt Weiss	.05
542	Bryan Rekar	.05
543	Tony Clark	.05
544	Steve Rodriguez	.05
545	C.J. Nitkowski	.05
546	Todd Steverson	.05
547	Jose Lima	.05
548	Phil Nevin	.05
549	Chris Gomez	.05
550	Travis Fryman	.05
551	Mark Lewis	.05
552	Alex Arias	.05
553	Marc Valdes	.05
554	Kevin Brown	.05
555	Jeff Conine	.05
556	John Burkett	.05
557	Devon White	.05
558	Pat Rapp	.05
559	Jay Powell	.05
560	Gary Sheffield	.30
561	Jim Dougherty	.05
562	Todd Jones	.05
563	Tony Eusebio	.05
564	Darryl Kile	.05
565	Doug Drabek	.05
566	Mike Simms	.05
567	Derrick May	.05
568	Donne Wall RC	.05
569	Greg Swindell	.05
570	Jim Pittsley	.05
571	Bob Hamelin	.05
572	Mark Gubicza	.05
573	Chris Haney	.05
574	Keith Lockhart	.05
575	Mike Macfarlane	.05
576	Les Norman	.05
577	Joe Randa	.05
578	Chris Stynes	.05
579	Greg Gagne	.05
580	Raul Mondesi	.05
581	Delino DeShields	.05
582	Pedro Astacio	.05
583	Antonio Osuna	.05
584	Brett Butler	.05
585	Todd Worrell	.05
586	Mike Blowers	.05
587	Felix Rodriguez	.05
588	Ismael Valdes	.05
589	Ricky Bones	.05
590	Greg Vaughn	.05
591	Mark Loretta	.05
592	Cal Eldred	.05
593	Chuck Carr	.05
594	Dave Nilsson	.05
595	John Jaha	.05
596	Scott Karl	.05
597	Pat Listach	.05
598	Jose Valentin RC	.05
599	Mike Trombley	.05
600	Paul Molitor	.60
601	Dave Hollins	.05
602	Ron Coomer	.05
603	Matt Walbeck	.05
604	Roberto Kelly	.05
605	Rick Aguilera	.05
606	Pat Mahomes	.05
607	Jeff Reboulet	.05
608	Rich Becker	.05
609	Tim Scott	.05
610	Pedro J. Martinez	.60
611	Kirk Rueter	.05
612	Tavo Alvarez	.05
613	Yamil Benitez	.05
614	Darrin Fletcher	.05
615	Mike Lansing	.05
616	Henry Rodriguez	.05
617	Tony Tarasco	.05
618	Alex Ochoa	.05
619	Tim Bogar	.05
620	Bernard Gilkey	.05
621	Dave Mlicki	.05
622	Brent Mayne	.05
623	Ryan Thompson	.05
624	Pete Harnisch	.05
625	Lance Johnson	.05
626	Jose Vizcaino	.05
627	Doug Henry	.05
628	Scott Kamieniecki	.05
629	Jim Leyritz	.05
630	Ruben Sierra	.05
631	Pat Kelly	.05
632	Joe Girardi	.05
633	John Wetteland	.05
634	Melido Perez	.05
635	Paul O'Neill	.05
636	Jorge Posada	.05
637	Bernie Williams	.05
638	Mark Acre	.05
639	Mike Bordick	.05
640	Mark McGwire	1.50
641	Fausto Cruz	.05
642	Ernie Young	.05
643	Todd Van Poppel	.05
644	Craig Paquette	.05
645	Brent Gates	.05
646	Pedro Munoz	.05
647	Andrew Lorraine	.05
648	Sid Fernandez	.05
649	Jim Eisenreich	.05
650	Johnny Damon (Arizona Fall League)	.30
651	Dustin Hermanson (Arizona Fall League)	.05
652	Joe Randa (Arizona Fall League)	.05
653	Michael Tucker (Arizona Fall League)	.05
654	Alan Benes (Arizona Fall League)	.05
655	Chad Fonville (Arizona Fall League)	.05
656	David Bell (Arizona Fall League)	.05
657	Jon Nunnally (Arizona Fall League)	.05
658	Chan Ho Park (Arizona Fall League)	.05
659	LaTroy Hawkins (Arizona Fall League)	.05
660	Jamie Brewington (Arizona Fall League)	.05
661	Quinton McCracken (Arizona Fall League)	.05
662	Tim Unroe (Arizona Fall League)	.05
663	Jeff Ware (Arizona Fall League)	.05
664	Todd Greene (Arizona Fall League)	.05
665	Andrew Lorraine (Arizona Fall League)	.05
666	Ernie Young (Arizona Fall League)	.05
667	Toby Borland	.05
668	Lenny Webster	.05
669	Benito Santiago	.05
670	Gregg Jefferies	.05
671	Darren Daulton	.05
672	Curt Schilling	.25
673	Mark Whiten	.05
674	Todd Zeile	.05
675	Jay Bell	.05
676	Paul Wagner	.05
677	Dave Clark	.05
678	Nelson Liriano	.05
679	Ramon Morel	.05
680	Charlie Hayes	.05
681	Angelo Encarnacion	.05
682	Al Martin	.05
683	Jacob Brumfield	.05
684	Mike Kingery	.05
685	Carlos Garcia	.05
686	Tom Pagnozzi	.05
687	David Bell	.05
688	Todd Stottlemyre	.05
689	Jose Oliva	.05
690	Ray Lankford	.05
691	Mike Morgan	.05
692	John Frascatore	.05
693	John Mabry	.05
694	Mark Petkovsek	.05
695	Alan Benes	.05
696	Steve Finley	.05
697	Marc Newfield	.05
698	Andy Ashby	.05
699	Marc Kroon	.05
700	Wally Joyner	.05
701	Joey Hamilton	.05
702	Dustin Hermanson	.05
703	Scott Sanders	.05
704	Marty Cordova (Award Win.-ROY)	.05
705	Hideo Nomo (Award Win.-ROY)	.15
706	Mo Vaughn (Award Win.-MVP)	.05
707	Barry Larkin (Award Win.-MVP)	.05
708	Randy Johnson (Award Win.-CY)	.20
709	Greg Maddux (Award Win.-CY)	.35
710	Mark McGwire (Award-Comeback)	.75
711	Ron Gant (Award-Comeback)	.05
712	Andujar Cedeno	.05
713	Brian Johnson	.05
714	J.R. Phillips	.05
715	Rod Beck	.05
716	Sergio Valdez	.05
717	Marvin Benard RC	.25
718	Steve Scarsone	.05
719	Rich Aurilia RC	.10
720	Matt Williams	.05
721	John Patterson	.05
722	Shawn Estes	.05
723	Russ Davis	.05
724	Rich Amaral	.05
725	Edgar Martinez	.05
726	Norm Charlton	.05
727	Paul Sorrento	.05
728	Luis Sojo	.05
729	Arquimedez Pozo	.05
730	Jay Buhner	.05
731	Chris Bosio	.05
732	Chris Widger	.05
733	Kevin Gross	.05
734	Darren Oliver	.05
735	Dean Palmer	.05
736	Matt Whiteside	.05
737	Luis Ortiz	.05
738	Roger Pavlik	.05
739	Damon Buford	.05
740	Juan Gonzalez	.30
741	Rusty Greer	.05
742	Lou Frazier	.05
743	Pat Hentgen	.05
744	Tomas Perez	.05
745	Juan Guzman	.05
746	Otis Nixon	.05
747	Robert Perez	.05
748	Ed Sprague	.05
749	Tony Castillo	.05
750	John Olerud	.05
751	Shawn Green	.05
752	Jeff Ware	.05
753	Checklist 396-441/Blake St. Bombers (Dante Bichette, Larry Walker, Andres Galarraga, Vinny Castilla)	.05
754	Checklist 442-487 (Greg Maddux)	.25
755	Checklist 488-533 (Marty Cordova)	.05
756	Checklist 534-579 (Ozzie Smith)	.35
757	Checklist 580-625 (John Vander Wal)	.05
758	Checklist 626-670 (Andres Galarraga)	.05
759	Checklist 671-715 (Frank Thomas)	.20
760	Checklist 716-760 (Tony Gwynn)	.25
761	Randy Myers	.10
762	Kent Mercker	.10
763	David Wells	.10
764	Tom Gordon	.10
765	Wil Cordero	.10
766	Dave Magadan	.10
767	Doug Jones	.10
768	Kevin Tapani	.10
769	Curtis Goodwin	.10
770	Julio Franco	.10
771	Jack McDowell	.10
772	Al Leiter	.10
773	Sean Berry	.10
774	Bip Roberts	.10
775	Jose Offerman	.10
776	Ben McDonald	.10
777	Dan Serafini	.10
778	Ryan McGuire	.10
779	Tim Raines	.10
780	Tino Martinez	.10
781	Kenny Rogers	.10
782	Bob Tewksbury	.10
783	Rickey Henderson	.60
784	Ron Gant	.10
785	Gary Gaetti	.10
786	Andy Benes	.10
787	Royce Clayton	.10
788	Darryl Hamilton	.10
789	Ken Hill	.10
790	Erik Hanson	.10

Silver Signature

A silver border instead of white, and a facsimile autograph in silver ink on the card front differentiate these parallel insert cards from the regular-issue Collector's Choice. The inserts are seeded at the rate of one per pack.

	NM/M
Common Player:	.10
Stars:	1.5X

Gold Signature

This insert set parallels each card in the regular Collector's Choice set. Found on average of one per 35 packs, the cards are nearly identical to the regular version except for the presence of a facsimile autograph in gold ink on the front and gold, instead of white, borders.

	NM/M
Common Player:	1.00
Stars:	10X

A Cut Above

This 10-card set highlights the career of Ken Griffey Jr. The front has a color photo with "The Griffey Years" printed in the left border and a title in the right border. Die-cut gold-foil tops have "A CUT ABOVE" in black. Backs have a portrait photo on a marbled border and a narrative. This set was inserted one per six-card Wal-Mart exclusive pack.

	NM/M
Complete Set (10):	8.00
Common Card:	1.00
CA1	Ken Griffey Jr. (Teenage Rookie)	1.00
CA2	Ken Griffey Jr. (Great Defense)	1.00
CA3	Ken Griffey Jr. (Fun-Loving)	1.00

CA4	Ken Griffey Jr. (All-Star Games)	1.00
CA5	Ken Griffey Jr. ('93 Season)	1.00
CA6	Ken Griffey Jr. ('94 HR Records)	1.00
CA7	Ken Griffey Jr. ('94 Season)	1.00
CA8	Ken Griffey Jr. ('95 Season)	1.00
CA9	Ken Griffey Jr. ('95 Postseason)	1.00
CA10	Ken Griffey Jr. ('96: A Look Ahead)	1.00

Crash the Game

For a second season, UD continued its interactive chase card series, "You Crash the Game." At a ratio of about one per five packs for a silver version and one per 49 packs for a gold version, cards of the game's top sluggers can be found bearing one of three date ranges representing a three- or four-game series in which that player was scheduled to play during the 1996 season. If the player hit a home run during the series shown on the card, the card could be redeemed (for $1.75) by mail for a "Super Premium" wood-and-plastic card of the player. Both silver and gold Crash cards feature silver and red prismatic foil behind the player action photo. Silver versions have the Crash logo, series dates and player ID in silver foil on front; those details are in gold foil on the gold cards. Backs have contest rules printed on a gray (silver) or yellow (gold) background. Card numbers are preceded by a "CG" prefix. Cards were redeemable only until Nov. 25, 1996. Winning cards are indicated with an asterisk; they would be in shorter supply than those which could not be redeemed.

		NM/M
	Complete Set (90):	75.00
	Common Silver Player:	.50
	Golds:	2X
1a	Chipper Jones (July 11-14*)	2.50
1b	Chipper Jones (Aug. 27-29*)	2.50
1c	Chipper Jones (Sept. 19-23)	1.50
2a	Fred McGriff (July 1-3)	.50
2b	Fred McGriff (Aug. 30-Sept. 1)	.50
2c	Fred McGriff (Sept. 10-12*)	1.00
3a	Rafael Palmeiro (July 4-7*)	1.75
3b	Rafael Palmeiro (Aug. 29-Sept. 1)	.75
3c	Rafael Palmeiro (Sept. 26-29)	.75
4a	Cal Ripken Jr. (June 27-30)	2.50
4b	Cal Ripken Jr. (July 25-28*)	5.00
4c	Cal Ripken Jr. (Sept. 2-4)	2.50
5a	Jose Canseco (June 27-30)	.65
5b	Jose Canseco (July 11-14*)	1.50
5c	Jose Canseco (Aug. 23-25)	.65
6a	Mo Vaughn (June 21-23*)	1.00
6b	Mo Vaughn (July 18-21*)	1.05

6c	Mo Vaughn (Sept. 20-22)	.50
7a	Jim Edmonds (July 18-21*)	1.00
7b	Jim Edmonds (Aug. 16-18*)	1.00
7c	Jim Edmonds (Sept. 20-22)	.50
8a	Tim Salmon (June 20-23)	.50
8b	Tim Salmon (July 30-Aug. 1)	.50
8c	Tim Salmon (Sept. 9-12)	.50
9a	Sammy Sosa (July 4-7*)	2.50
9b	Sammy Sosa (Aug. 1-4*)	2.50
9c	Sammy Sosa (Sept. 2-4)	1.50
10a	Frank Thomas (June 27-30)	1.00
10b	Frank Thomas (July 4-7)	1.00
10c	Frank Thomas (Sept. 2-4*)	2.00
11a	Albert Belle (June 25-26)	.50
11b	Albert Belle (Aug. 2-5*)	1.00
11c	Albert Belle (Sept. 6-8)	.50
12a	Manny Ramirez (July 18-21*)	2.00
12b	Manny Ramirez (Aug. 26-28)	1.00
12c	Manny Ramirez (Sept. 9-12*)	2.00
13a	Jim Thome (June 27-30)	.75
13b	Jim Thome (July 4-7*)	1.25
13c	Jim Thome (Sept. 23-25)	.75
14a	Dante Bichette (July 11-14*)	1.00
14b	Dante Bichette (Aug. 9-11)	.50
14c	Dante Bichette (Sept. 9-12)	.50
15a	Vinny Castilla (July 1-3)	.50
15b	Vinny Castilla (Aug. 23-25*)	1.00
15c	Vinny Castilla (Sept. 13-15*)	1.00
16a	Larry Walker (June 24-26)	.50
16b	Larry Walker (July 18-21)	.50
16c	Larry Walker (Sept. 27-29)	.50
17a	Cecil Fielder (June 27-30)	.50
17b	Cecil Fielder (July 30-Aug. 1*)	1.00
17c	Cecil Fielder (Sept. 17-19*)	1.00
18a	Gary Sheffield (July 4-7)	.65
18b	Gary Sheffield (Aug. 2-4)	.65
18c	Gary Sheffield (Sept. 5-8*)	1.50
19a	Jeff Bagwell (July 4-7*)	2.00
19b	Jeff Bagwell (Aug. 16-18)	1.00
19c	Jeff Bagwell (Sept. 13-15)	1.00
20a	Eric Karros (July 4-7*)	1.00
20b	Eric Karros (Aug. 13-15*)	1.00
20c	Eric Karros (Sept. 16-18)	.50
21a	Mike Piazza (June 27-30*)	3.00
21b	Mike Piazza (July 26-28)	1.75
21c	Mike Piazza (Sept. 12-15*)	3.00
22a	Ken Caminiti (July 11-14*)	1.00
22b	Ken Caminiti (Aug. 16-18*)	1.00
22c	Ken Caminiti (Sept. 19-22*)	1.00
23a	Barry Bonds (June 27-30*)	5.00
23b	Barry Bonds (July 22-24)	2.50
23c	Barry Bonds (Sept. 24-26)	2.50
24a	Matt Williams (July 11-14*)	1.00
24b	Matt Williams (Aug. 19-21)	.50
24c	Matt Williams (Sept. 27-29)	.50
25a	Jay Buhner (June 20-23)	.50
25b	Jay Buhner (July 25-28)	.50
25c	Jay Buhner (Aug. 29-Sept. 1*)	1.00
26a	Ken Griffey Jr. (July 18-21*)	3.00

26b	Ken Griffey Jr. (Aug. 16-18*)	3.00
26c	Ken Griffey Jr. (Sept. 20-22*)	3.00
27a	Ron Gant (June 24-27*)	1.00
27b	Ron Gant (July 11-14*)	1.00
27c	Ron Gant (Sept. 27-29*)	1.00
28a	Juan Gonzalez (June 28-30*)	1.25
28b	Juan Gonzalez (July 15-17*)	1.25
28c	Juan Gonzalez (Aug. 6-8)	.60
29a	Mickey Tettleton (July 4-7*)	1.00
29b	Mickey Tettleton (Aug. 6-8)	.50
29c	Mickey Tettleton (Sept. 6-8*)	1.00
30a	Joe Carter (June 25-27)	.50
30b	Joe Carter (Aug. 5-8)	.50
30c	Joe Carter (Sept. 23-25)	.50

Crash Winners

Collectors who held "You Crash The Game" insert cards with date ranges on which the pictured player hit a home run could redeem them (for $1.75 per card) for a premium card of that player. The redemption cards have a layer of clear plastic bonded to a wood-laminate front. Within a starburst cutout at center is the player photo with a red background. Cards have a Crash/Game logo in the lower-right corner, in either silver or gold, depending on which winning card was submitted for exchange. Backs have 1995 and career stats along with licensing and copyright data. There were no winning cards of Tim Salmon, Larry Walker or Joe Carter.

		NM/M
	Complete Set (27):	35.00
	Common Player:	1.00
	Golds:	2X
CR1	Chipper Jones	2.50
CR2	Fred McGriff	1.00
CR3	Rafael Palmeiro	1.75
CR4	Cal Ripken Jr.	4.00
CR5	Jose Canseco	1.50
CR6	Mo Vaughn	1.00
CR7	Jim Edmonds	1.00
CR8	Sammy Sosa	2.50
CR9	Frank Thomas	2.00
CR10	Albert Belle	1.00
CR11	Manny Ramirez	2.00
CR12	Jim Thome	1.00
CR13	Dante Bichette	1.00
CR14	Vinny Castilla	1.00
CR15	Cecil Fielder	1.00
CR16	Gary Sheffield	1.00
CR17	Jeff Bagwell	2.00
CR18	Eric Karros	1.00
CR19	Mike Piazza	3.00
CR20	Ken Caminiti	1.00
CR21	Barry Bonds	4.00
CR22	Matt Williams	1.00
CR23	Jay Buhner	1.00
CR24	Ken Griffey Jr.	3.00
CR25	Ron Gant	1.00
CR26	Juan Gonzalez	1.50
CR27	Mickey Tettleton	1.00

Nomo Scrapbook

The five-card, regular-sized set was randomly inserted in 1996 Collector's Choice baseball. Fronts depict the Dodgers pitcher in action with his name in atypical lower-case type up the right border.

Backs feature in-depth text below Nomo's name. A version featuring Japanese text was issued in Japan.

	NM/M
Complete Set (5):	10.00
Common Card:	2.00
Japanese:	3X
1-5 Hideo Nomo	2.00

Ripken Collection

The 23-card, regular-sized Cal Ripken Collection was randomly inserted in various Upper Deck baseball releases in 1996. Cards #1-4 were found in Series 1 Collector's Choice; cards 5-8 were found in Upper Deck Series 1; cards 9-12 in Collector's Choice Series 2; cards 13-17 in Upper Deck Series 2; cards 18-22 in SP baseball and the header card in Collector's Choice.

	NM/M
Complete Set (1-4, 9-12)	15.00
Common Card:	2.50
Header Card:	2.00

Cal Ripken Jr. Jumbo

This 5" x 3-1/2" card is a virtual parallel to the #1 card in the multi-brand Ripken set which was issued to mark his career to the point of his 2,131st consecutive game. This version, however, was sold only through a television shopping program. The front has a silver facsimile autograph. On back is a "Limited Edition" seal and a serial number within an edition of 21,310.

		NM/M
1	Cal Ripken Jr.	5.00

You Make the Play

This insert series of interactive game cards was packaged with Series 1 Collector's Choice. Each player's card can be found with one of two play outcomes printed thereon, which are then used to play a baseball card game utilizing a playing field and scorecard

found on box bottoms. Regular versions of the cards are seeded one per pack, while gold-signature versions are found one per 36 packs.

		NM/M
	Complete Set (45):	60.00
	Common Player:	.50
	Gold:	4X
1a	Kevin Appier (Strike out)	.50
1b	Kevin Appier (Pick off.)	.50
2a	Carlos Baerga (Home run.)	.50
2b	Carlos Baerga (Ground out.)	.50
3a	Jeff Bagwell (Walk)	1.00
3b	Jeff Bagwell (Strike out.)	1.00
4a	Jay Bell (Sacrifice)	.50
4b	Jay Bell (Walk)	.50
5a	Albert Belle (Fly out)	.50
5b	Albert Belle (Home run.)	.50
6a	Craig Biggio (Single)	.50
6b	Craig Biggio (Strike out.)	.50
7a	Wade Boggs (Single)	1.50
7b	Wade Boggs (Ground out.)	1.50
8a	Barry Bonds (Strike out.)	3.00
8b	Barry Bonds (Reach on error.)	3.00
9a	Bobby Bonilla (Walk)	.50
9b	Bobby Bonilla (Strike out.)	.50
10a	Jose Canseco (Strike out.)	.75
10b	Jose Canseco (Double)	.75
11a	Joe Carter (Double)	.50
11b	Joe Carter (Fly out)	.50
12a	Darren Daulton (Ground out.)	.50
12b	Darren Daulton (Catcher's interference.)	.50
13a	Cecil Fielder (Stolen base.)	.50
13b	Cecil Fielder (Home run.)	.50
14a	Ron Gant (Home run.)	.50
14b	Ron Gant (Fly out)	.50
15a	Juan Gonzalez (Double)	.65
15b	Juan Gonzalez (Fly out)	.65
16a	Ken Griffey Jr. (Home run.)	2.00
16b	Ken Griffey Jr. (Hit by pitch.)	2.00
17a	Tony Gwynn (Single)	1.50
17b	Tony Gwynn (Ground out.)	1.50
18a	Randy Johnson (Strike out.)	1.00
18b	Randy Johnson (K - reach on wild pitch.)	1.00
19a	Chipper Jones (Walk)	1.50
19b	Chipper Jones (Strike out.)	1.50
20a	Barry Larkin (Ground out.)	.50
20b	Barry Larkin (Stolen base.)	.50
21a	Kenny Lofton (Triple)	.50
21b	Kenny Lofton (Stolen base.)	.50
22a	Greg Maddux (Single)	1.50
22b	Greg Maddux (Strike out.)	1.50
23a	Don Mattingly (Fly out.)	1.75
23b	Don Mattingly (Double)	1.75
24a	Fred McGriff (Double)	.50
24b	Fred McGriff (Home run.)	.50
25a	Mark McGwire (Strike out.)	2.50
25b	Mark McGwire (Home run.)	2.50
26a	Paul Molitor (Ground out.)	1.00
26b	Paul Molitor (Single)	1.00
27a	Raul Mondesi (Single)	.50
27b	Raul Mondesi (Fly out.)	.50
28a	Eddie Murray (Sacrifice fly.)	1.00

28b	Eddie Murray (Ground out.)	1.00
29a	Hideo Nomo (Strike out)	.65
29b	Hideo Nomo (Balk)	.65
30a	Jon Nunnally (Single)	.50
30b	Jon Nunnally (Error)	.50
31a	Mike Piazza (Strike out)	2.00
31b	Mike Piazza (Single)	2.00
32a	Kirby Puckett (Walk)	1.50
32b	Kirby Puckett (Ground out.)	1.50
33a	Cal Ripken Jr. (Home run.)	3.00
33b	Cal Ripken Jr. (Double)	3.00
34a	Alex Rodriguez (Strike out.)	2.50
34b	Alex Rodriguez (Triple)	2.50
35a	Tim Salmon (Sacrifice fly.)	.50
35b	Tim Salmon (Strike out.)	.50
36a	Gary Sheffield (Fly out.)	.65
36b	Gary Sheffield (Single)	.65
37a	Lee Smith (Strike out.)	.50
37b	Lee Smith (Pick off of lead runner.)	.50
38a	Ozzie Smith (Ground out.)	1.50
38b	Ozzie Smith (Single)	1.50
39a	Sammy Sosa (Stolen base.)	1.50
39b	Sammy Sosa (Single)	1.50
40a	Frank Thomas (Walk)	1.00
40b	Frank Thomas (Home run.)	1.00
41a	Greg Vaughn (Sacrifice fly.)	.50
41b	Greg Vaughn (Strike out.)	.50
42a	Mo Vaughn (Hit by Pitch.)	.50
42b	Mo Vaughn (Stolen base.)	.50
43a	Larry Walker (Strike out.)	.50
43b	Larry Walker (Walk)	.50
44a	Rondell White (Triple)	.50
44b	Rondell White (Fly out.)	.50
45a	Matt Williams (Home run.)	.50
45b	Matt Williams (Single)	.50

1997 Collector's Choice

The 506-card, standard-size set contains five subsets: Rookie Class (1-27), Leaders (56-63), Postseason (218-224), Ken Griffey Jr. Checklists (244-249) and Griffey Hot List (325-334). Insert sets are: All-Star Connection, Big Shots, Stick'Ums, Premier Power, Clearly Dominant, The Big Show, Toast of the Town and New Frontier. Basic card fronts feature a color action shot with the player's name appearing on the bottom edge. The team logo is located in the lower-left corner and each card features a white border. Backs contain another action shot on the upper half with biography and career/season stats. The cards were issued in 12-card packs retailing for 99 cents. A factory set was issued that includes 10 Premier Power jumbo cards.

		NM/M
	Factory Set (516):	16.00
	Complete Set (506):	12.00
	Common Player:	.05
	Pack (12):	1.00
	Wax Box (36):	20.00
1	Andruw Jones/RC	1.00
2	Rocky Coppinger/RC	.05
3	Jeff D'Amico/RC	.05

#	Player	Price
4	Dmitri Young/RC	.05
5	Darin Erstad/RC	.75
6	Jermaine Allensworth/RC	.05
7	Damian Jackson/RC	.05
8	Bill Mueller/RC	.05
9	Jacob Cruz/RC	.05
10	Vladimir Guerrero/RC	1.00
11	Marty Janzen/RC	.05
12	Kevin L. Brown/RC	.05
13	Willie Adams/RC	.05
14	Wendell Magee/RC	.05
15	Scott Rolen/RC	.65
16	Matt Beech/RC	.05
17	Neifi Perez/RC	.05
18	Jamey Wright/RC	.05
19	Jose Paniagua/RC	.05
20	Todd Walker/RC	.05
21	Justin Thompson/RC	.05
22	Robin Jennings/RC	.05
23	Dario Veras/RC **RC**	.05
24	Brian Lesher/RC	.05
25	Nomar Garciaparra/RC	1.25
26	Luis Castillo/RC	.05
27	Brian Giles/RC **RC**	.75
28	Jermaine Dye	.05
29	Terrell Wade	.05
30	Fred McGriff	.05
31	Marquis Grissom	.05
32	Ryan Klesko	.05
33	Javier Lopez	.05
34	Mark Wohlers	.05
35	Tom Glavine	.05
36	Denny Neagle	.05
37	Scott Erickson	.05
38	Chris Hoiles	.05
39	Roberto Alomar	.25
40	Eddie Murray	.75
41	Cal Ripken Jr.	2.00
42	Randy Myers	.05
43	B.J. Surhoff	.05
44	Rick Krivda	.05
45	Jose Canseco	.50
46	Heathcliff Slocumb	.05
47	Jeff Suppan	.05
48	Tom Gordon	.05
49	Aaron Sele	.05
50	Mo Vaughn	.05
51	Darren Bragg	.05
52	Wil Cordero	.05
53	Scott Bullett	.05
54	Terry Adams	.05
55	Jackie Robinson	.35
56	Tony Gwynn, Alex Rodriguez (Batting Leaders)	.35
57	Andres Galarraga, Mark McGwire (Homer Leaders)	.50
58	Andres Galarraga, Albert Belle (RBI Leaders)	.05
59	Eric Young, Kenny Lofton (SB Leaders)	.05
60	John Smoltz, Andy Pettitte (Victory Leaders)	.05
61	John Smoltz, Roger Clemens (Strikout Leaders)	.20
62	Kevin Brown, Juan Guzman (ERA Leaders)	.05
63	John Wetteland, Todd Worrell, Jeff Brantley (Save Leaders)	.05
64	Scott Servais	.05
65	Sammy Sosa	1.00
66	Ryne Sandberg	1.00
67	Frank Castillo	.05
68	Rey Sanchez	.05
69	Steve Trachsel	.05
70	Robin Ventura	.05
71	Wilson Alvarez	.05
72	Tony Phillips	.05
73	Lyle Mouton	.05
74	Mike Cameron	.05
75	Harold Baines	.05
76	Albert Belle	.05
77	Chris Snopek	.05
78	Reggie Sanders	.05
79	Jeff Brantley	.05
80	Barry Larkin	.05
81	Kevin Jarvis	.05
82	John Smiley	.05
83	Pete Schourek	.05
84	Thomas Howard	.05
85	Lee Smith	.05
86	Omar Vizquel	.05
87	Julio Franco	.05
88	Orel Hershiser	.05
89	Charles Nagy	.05
90	Matt Williams	.05
91	Dennis Martinez	.05
92	Jose Mesa	.05
93	Sandy Alomar Jr.	.05
94	Jim Thome	.50
95	Vinny Castilla	.05
96	Armando Reynoso	.05
97	Kevin Ritz	.05
98	Larry Walker	.05
99	Eric Young	.05
100	Dante Bichette	.05
101	Quinton McCracken	.05
102	John Vander Wal	.05
103	Phil Nevin	.05
104	Tony Clark	.05
105	Alan Trammell	.05
106	Felipe Lira	.05
107	Curtis Pride	.05
108	Bobby Higginson	.05
109	Mark Lewis	.05
110	Travis Fryman	.05
111	Al Leiter	.05
112	Devon White	.05
113	Jeff Conine	.05
114	Charles Johnson	.05
115	Andre Dawson	.25
116	Edgar Renteria	.05
117	Robb Nen	.05
118	Kevin Brown	.05
119	Derek Bell	.05
120	Bob Abreu	.10
121	Mike Hampton	.05
122	Todd Jones	.05
123	Billy Wagner	.05
124	Shane Reynolds	.05
125	Jeff Bagwell	.75
126	Brian L. Hunter	.05
127	Jeff Montgomery	.05
128	Rod Myers **RC**	.05
129	Tim Belcher	.05
130	Kevin Appier	.05
131	Mike Sweeney	.05
132	Craig Paquette	.05
133	Joe Randa	.05
134	Michael Tucker	.05
135	Raul Mondesi	.05
136	Tim Wallach	.05
137	Brett Butler	.05
138	Karim Garcia	.10
139	Todd Hollandsworth	.05
140	Eric Karros	.05
141	Hideo Nomo	.40
142	Ismael Valdes	.05
143	Cal Eldred	.05
144	Scott Karl	.05
145	Matt Mieske	.05
146	Mike Fetters	.05
147	Mark Loretta	.05
148	Fernando Vina	.05
149	Jeff Cirillo	.05
150	Dave Nilsson	.05
151	Kirby Puckett	1.00
152	Rich Becker	.05
153	Chuck Knoblauch	.05
154	Marty Cordova	.05
155	Paul Molitor	.75
156	Rick Aguilera	.05
157	Pat Meares	.05
158	Frank Rodriguez	.05
159	David Segui	.05
160	Henry Rodriguez	.05
161	Shane Andrews	.05
162	Pedro J. Martinez	.05
163	Mark Grudzielanek	.05
164	Mike Lansing	.05
165	Rondell White	.05
166	Ugueth Urbina	.05
167	Rey Ordonez	.05
168	Robert Person	.05
169	Carlos Baerga	.05
170	Bernard Gilkey	.05
171	John Franco	.05
172	Pete Harnisch	.05
173	Butch Huskey	.05
174	Paul Wilson	.05
175	Bernie Williams	.05
176	Dwight Gooden	.05
177	Wade Boggs	1.00
178	Ruben Rivera	.05
179	Jim Leyritz	.05
180	Derek Jeter	2.00
181	Tino Martinez	.05
182	Tim Raines	.05
183	Scott Brosius	.05
184	Jason Giambi	.60
185	Geronimo Berroa	.05
186	Ariel Prieto	.05
187	Scott Spiezio	.05
188	John Wasdin	.05
189	Ernie Young	.05
190	Mark McGwire	1.50
191	Jim Eisenreich	.05
192	Ricky Bottalico	.05
193	Darren Daulton	.05
194	David Doster	.05
195	Gregg Jefferies	.05
196	Lenny Dykstra	.05
197	Curt Schilling	.20
198	Todd Stottlemyre	.05
199	Willie McGee	.05
200	Ozzie Smith	1.00
201	Dennis Eckersley	.65
202	Ray Lankford	.05
203	John Mabry	.05
204	Alan Benes	.05
205	Ron Gant	.05
206	Archi Cianfrocco	.05
207	Fernando Valenzuela	.05
208	Greg Vaughn	.05
209	Steve Finley	.05
210	Tony Gwynn	1.00
211	Rickey Henderson	.75
212	Trevor Hoffman	.05
213	Jason Thompson	.05
214	Osvaldo Fernandez	.05
215	Glenallen Hill	.05
216	William Van Landingham	.05
217	Marvin Benard	.05
218	Juan Gonzalez (Postseason)	.10
219	Roberto Alomar (Postseason)	.05
220	Brian Jordan (Postseason)	.05
221	John Smoltz (Postseason)	.05
222	Javy Lopez (Postseason)	.05
223	Bernie Williams (Postseason)	.05
224	Jim Leyritz, John Wetteland (Postseason)	.05
225	Barry Bonds	2.00
226	Rich Aurilia	.05
227	Jay Canizaro	.05
228	Dan Wilson	.05
229	Bob Wolcott	.05
230	Ken Griffey Jr.	1.25
231	Sterling Hitchcock	.05
232	Edgar Martinez	.05
233	Joey Cora	.05
234	Norm Charlton	.05
235	Alex Rodriguez	1.50
236	Bobby Witt	.05
237	Darren Oliver	.05
238	Kevin Elster	.05
239	Rusty Greer	.05
240	Juan Gonzalez	.40
241	Will Clark	.05
242	Dean Palmer	.05
243	Ivan Rodriguez	.65
244	Checklist (Ken Griffey Jr.)	.25
245	Checklist (Ken Griffey Jr.)	.25
246	Checklist (Ken Griffey Jr.)	.25
247	Checklist (Ken Griffey Jr.)	.25
248	Checklist (Ken Griffey Jr.)	.25
249	Checklist (Ken Griffey Jr.)	.25
250	Eddie Murray	.75
251	Troy Percival	.05
252	Garret Anderson	.05
253	Allen Watson	.05
254	Jason Dickson	.05
255	Jim Edmonds	.05
256	Chuck Finley	.05
257	Randy Velarde	.05
258	Shigetosi Hasegawa	.05
259	Todd Greene	.05
260	Tim Salmon	.05
261	Mark Langston	.05
262	Dave Hollins	.05
263	Gary DiSarcina	.05
264	Kenny Lofton	.05
265	John Smoltz	.05
266	Greg Maddux	1.00
267	Jeff Blauser	.05
268	Alan Embree	.05
269	Mark Lemke	.05
270	Chipper Jones	1.00
271	Mike Mussina	.65
272	Rafael Palmeiro	.65
273	Jimmy Key	.05
274	Mike Bordick	.05
275	Brady Anderson	.05
276	Eric Davis	.05
277	Jeffrey Hammonds	.05
278	Reggie Jefferson	.05
279	Tim Naehring	.05
280	John Valentin	.05
281	Troy O'Leary	.05
282	Shane Mack	.05
283	Mike Stanley	.05
284	Tim Wakefield	.05
285	Brian McRae	.05
286	Brooks Kieschnick	.05
287	Shawon Dunston	.05
288	Kevin Foster	.05
289	Mel Rojas	.05
290	Mark Grace	.05
291	Brant Brown	.05
292	Amaury Telemaco	.05
293	Dave Martinez	.05
294	Jaime Navarro	.05
295	Ray Durham	.05
296	Ozzie Guillen	.05
297	Roberto Hernandez	.05
298	Ron Karkovice	.05
299	James Baldwin	.05
300	Frank Thomas	.75
301	Eddie Taubensee	.05
302	Bret Boone	.05
303	Willie Greene	.05
304	Dave Burba	.05
305	Deion Sanders	.10
306	Reggie Sanders	.05
307	Hal Morris	.05
308	Pokey Reese	.05
309	Tony Fernandez	.05
310	Manny Ramirez	.75
311	Chad Ogea	.05
312	Jack McDowell	.05
313	Kevin Mitchell	.05
314	Chad Curtis	.05
315	Steve Kline	.05
316	Kevin Seitzer	.05
317	Kirt Manwaring	.05
318	Bill Swift	.05
319	Ellis Burks	.05
320	Andres Galarraga	.05
321	Bruce Ruffin	.05
322	Mark Thompson	.05
323	Walt Weiss	.05
324	Todd Jones	.05
325	Andruw Jones (Griffey Hot List)	.50
326	Chipper Jones (Griffey Hot List)	.65
327	Mo Vaughn (Griffey Hot List)	.05
328	Frank Thomas (Griffey Hot List)	.50
329	Albert Belle (Griffey Hot List)	.10
330	Mark McGwire (Griffey Hot List)	1.00
331	Derek Jeter (Griffey Hot List)	1.50
332	Alex Rodriguez (Griffey Hot List)	1.00
333	Jay Buhner (Griffey Hot List)	.05
334	Ken Griffey Jr. (Griffey Hot List)	.75
335	Brian L. Hunter	.05
336	Brian Johnson	.05
337	Omar Olivares	.05
338	Deivi Cruz **RC**	.05
339	Damion Easley	.05
340	Melvin Nieves	.05
341	Moises Alou	.05
342	Jim Eisenreich	.05
343	Mark Hutton	.05
344	Alex Fernandez	.05
345	Gary Sheffield	.35
346	Pat Rapp	.05
347	Brad Ausmus	.05
348	Sean Berry	.05
349	Darryl Kile	.05
350	Craig Biggio	.05
351	Chris Holt	.05
352	Luis Gonzalez	.05
353	Pat Listach	.05
354	Jose Rosado	.05
355	Mike Macfarlane	.05
356	Tom Goodwin	.05
357	Chris Haney	.05
358	Chili Davis	.05
359	Jose Offerman	.05
360	Johnny Damon	.30
361	Bip Roberts	.05
362	Ramon Martinez	.05
363	Pedro Astacio	.05
364	Todd Zeile	.05
365	Mike Piazza	1.25
366	Greg Gagne	.05
367	Chan Ho Park	.05
368	Wilton Guerrero	.05
369	Todd Worrell	.05
370	John Jaha	.05
371	Steve Sparks	.05
372	Mike Matheny	.05
373	Marc Newfield	.05
374	Jeromy Burnitz	.05
375	Jose Valentin	.05
376	Ben McDonald	.05
377	Roberto Kelly	.05
378	Bob Tewksbury	.05
379	Ron Coomer	.05
380	Brad Radke	.05
381	Matt Lawton	.05
382	Dan Naulty	.05
383	Scott Stahoviak	.05
384	Matt Wagner	.05
385	Jim Bullinger	.05
386	Carlos Perez	.05
387	Darrin Fletcher	.05
388	Chris Widger	.05
389	F.P. Santangelo	.05
390	Lee Smith	.05
391	Bobby Jones	.05
392	John Olerud	.05
393	Mark Clark	.05
394	Jason Isringhausen	.05
395	Todd Hundley	.05
396	Lance Johnson	.05
397	Edgardo Alfonzo	.05
398	Alex Ochoa	.05
399	Darryl Strawberry	.05
400	David Cone	.05
401	Paul O'Neill	.05
402	Joe Girardi	.05
403	Charlie Hayes	.05
404	Andy Pettitte	.25
405	Mariano Rivera	.05
406	Mariano Duncan	.05
407	Kenny Rogers	.05
408	Cecil Fielder	.05
409	George Williams	.05
410	Jose Canseco	.35
411	Tony Batista	.05
412	Steve Karsay	.05
413	Dave Telgheder	.05
414	Billy Taylor	.05
415	Mickey Morandini	.05
416	Calvin Maduro	.05
417	Mark Leiter	.05
418	Kevin Stocker	.05
419	Mike Lieberthal	.05
420	Rico Brogna	.05
421	Mark Portugal	.05
422	Rex Hudler	.05
423	Mark Johnson	.05
424	Esteban Loiaza	.05
425	Lou Collier	.05
426	Kevin Elster	.05
427	Francisco Cordova	.05
428	Marc Wilkins	.05
429	Joe Randa	.05
430	Jason Kendall	.05
431	Jon Lieber	.05
432	Steve Cooke	.05
433	Emil Brown **RC**	.05
434	Tony Womack **RC**	.25
435	Al Martin	.05
436	Jason Schmidt	.05
437	Andy Benes	.05
438	Delino DeShields	.05
439	Royce Clayton	.05
440	Brian Jordan	.05
441	Donovan Osborne	.05
442	Gary Gaetti	.05
443	Tom Pagnozzi	.05
444	Joey Hamilton	.05
445	Wally Joyner	.05
446	John Flaherty	.05
447	Chris Gomez	.05
448	Sterling Hitchcock	.05
449	Andy Ashby	.05
450	Ken Caminiti	.05
451	Tim Worrell	.05
452	Jose Vizcaino	.05
453	Rod Beck	.05
454	Wilson Delgado	.05
455	Darryl Hamilton	.05
456	Mark Lewis	.05
457	Mark Gardner	.05
458	Rick Wilkins	.05
459	Scott Sanders	.05
460	Kevin Orie	.05
461	Glendon Rusch	.05
462	Juan Melo	.05
463	Richie Sexson	.05
464	Bartolo Colon	.05
465	Jose Guillen	.05
466	Heath Murray	.05
467	Aaron Boone	.05
468	Bubba Trammell **RC**	.05
469	Jeff Abbott	.05
470	Derrick Gibson	.05
471	Matt Morris	.05
472	Ryan Jones	.05
473	Pat Cline	.05
474	Adam Riggs	.05
475	Jay Payton	.05
476	Derek Lee	.50
477	Elieser Marrero	.05
478	Lee Tinsley	.05
479	Jamie Moyer	.05
480	Jay Buhner	.05
481	Bob Wells	.05
482	Jeff Fassero	.05
483	Paul Sorrento	.05
484	Russ Davis	.05
485	Randy Johnson	.75
486	Roger Pavlik	.05
487	Damon Buford	.05
488	Julio Santana	.05
489	Mark McLemore	.05
490	Mickey Tettleton	.05
491	Ken Hill	.05
492	Benji Gil	.05
493	Ed Sprague	.05
494	Mike Timlin	.05
495	Pat Hentgen	.05
496	Orlando Merced	.05
497	Carlos Garcia	.05
498	Carlos Delgado	.35
499	Juan Guzman	.05
500	Roger Clemens	1.00
501	Erik Hanson	.05
502	Otis Nixon	.05
503	Shawn Green	.10
504	Charlie O'Brien	.05
505	Joe Carter	.05
506	Alex Gonzalez	.05
13	Cal Ripken Jr.	1.50
14	Juan Gonzalez	.25
15	Manny Ramirez	.50
16	Bernie Williams	.10
17	Terry Steinbach	.10
18	Andy Pettitte	.25
19	Jeff Bagwell	.50
20	Craig Biggio	.10
21	Ken Caminiti	.10
22	Barry Larkin	.10
23	Tony Gwynn	.50
24	Barry Bonds	1.50
25	Kenny Lofton	.10
26	Mike Piazza	.75
27	John Smoltz	.10
28	Andres Galarraga	.10
29	Ryne Sandberg	.60
30	Chipper Jones	.60
31	Mark Grudzielanek	.10
32	Sammy Sosa	.60
33	Steve Finley	.10
34	Gary Sheffield	.25
35	Todd Hundley	.10
36	Greg Maddux	.60
37	Mo Vaughn	.10
38	Eric Young	.10
39	Vinny Castilla	.10
40	Derek Jeter	1.50
41	Lance Johnson	.10
42	Ellis Burks	.10
43	Dante Bichette	.10
44	Javy Lopez	.10
45	Hideo Nomo	.25

Big Shots

This 20-card insert depicts the game's top stars in unique photos. Cards were inserted 1:12 packs. Gold Signature Editions, featuring a gold foil-stamped facsimile autograph, were inserted 1:144 packs. Fronts are highlighted in silver foil. Backs repeat a portion of the front photo, have a picture of the photographer and his comments about the picture.

		NM/M
Complete Set (19):		15.00
Common Player:		.25
Gold Signature Edition:		2X
1	Ken Griffey Jr.	2.00
2	Nomar Garciaparra	1.50
3	Brian Jordan	.25
4	Scott Rolen	.75
5	Alex Rodriguez	2.50
6	Larry Walker	.25
7	Mariano Rivera	.35
8	Cal Ripken Jr.	3.00
9	Deion Sanders	.25
10	Frank Thomas	1.00
11	Dean Palmer	.25
12	Ken Caminiti	.25
13	Derek Jeter	3.00
14	Barry Bonds	3.00
15	Chipper Jones	1.50
16	Mo Vaughn	.25
17	Jay Buhner	.25
18	Mike Piazza	2.00
19	Tony Gwynn	1.50

All-Star Connection

This 45-card insert from Series 2 highlights All-Star caliber players. Cards feature a large starburst pattern on a metallic-foil background behind the player's photo. They were inserted one per pack.

		NM/M
Complete Set (45):		10.00
Common Player:		.10
1	Mark McGwire	1.00
2	Chuck Knoblauch	.35
3	Jim Thome	.35
4	Alex Rodriguez	1.00
5	Ken Griffey Jr.	.75
6	Brady Anderson	.40
7	Albert Belle	.50
8	Ivan Rodriguez	.40
9	Pat Hentgen	.10
10	Frank Thomas	.50
11	Roberto Alomar	.25
12	Robin Ventura	.10

1997 Collector's Choice Big Show

The 45-card, regular-sized set was inserted one per pack of Series 1. Backs feature player comments written by ESPN SportsCenter hosts Keith Olbermann and Dan Patrick, whose portraits appear both front and back. On front, printed on metallic foil, is an action shot of the player, with his name printed along the left border of the horizontal cards. The cards are numbered "X/45." A parallel set to this chase-card series carries a gold-foil "World Headquarters Edition" seal at lower-right and was a 1:35 insert.

	NM/M
Complete Set (45):	7.00
Common Player:	.10
World Headquarters:	8X
1 Greg Maddux	.50
2 Chipper Jones	.50
3 Andruw Jones	.40
4 John Smoltz	.10
5 Cal Ripken Jr.	1.00
6 Roberto Alomar	.25
7 Rafael Palmeiro	.35
8 Eddie Murray	.40
9 Jose Canseco	.30
10 Roger Clemens	.55
11 Mo Vaughn	.40
12 Jim Edmonds	.10
13 Tim Salmon	.10
14 Sammy Sosa	.50
15 Albert Belle	.40
16 Frank Thomas	.40
17 Barry Larkin	.10
18 Kenny Lofton	.10
19 Manny Ramirez	.40
20 Matt Williams	.10
21 Dante Bichette	.10
22 Gary Sheffield	.30
23 Craig Biggio	.10
24 Jeff Bagwell	.40
25 Todd Hollandsworth	.10
26 Raul Mondesi	.10
27 Hideo Nomo	.60
28 Mike Piazza	.60
29 Paul Molitor	.40
30 Kirby Puckett	.50
31 Rondell White	.10
32 Rey Ordonez	.10
33 Paul Wilson	.10
34 Derek Jeter	1.00
35 Andy Pettitte	.25
36 Mark McGwire	.75
37 Jason Kendall	.10
38 Ozzie Smith	.50
39 Tony Gwynn	.50
40 Barry Bonds	1.00
41 Alex Rodriguez	.75
42 Jay Buhner	.10
43 Ken Griffey Jr.	.60
44 Randy Johnson	.40
45 Juan Gonzalez	.25

World Headquarters

The 45-card chase set in Series 2 is also found in a special parallel version which carries a "World Headquarters Edition" gold-foil seal on front at the lower-right.

	NM/M
Complete Set (45):	50.00
Common Player:	1.50
Stars:	8X

1997 Collector's Choice Clearly Dominant

The five-card, regular-sized set features Seattle outfielder Ken Griffey Jr. on each card and was inserted every 144 packs of 1997 Collector's Choice baseball.

	NM/M
Complete Set (5):	16.00
Common Card:	4.00
CD1 Ken Griffey Jr.	4.00
CD2 Ken Griffey Jr.	4.00
CD3 Ken Griffey Jr.	4.00
CD4 Ken Griffey Jr.	4.00
CD5 Ken Griffey Jr.	4.00

Jumbos

Each of the five Ken Griffey Jr. cards from the Collector's Choice insert set was also produced in a special retail-only 5" x 3-1/2" jumbo version. The supersize Clearly Dominant cards were packaged in a special collectors' kit which also included a Griffey stand-up figure and eight packs of CC cards, retailing for about $15. The cards could also be purchased as a complete set for $10. Cards are numbered with a "CD" prefix.

	NM/M
Complete Set (5):	10.00
Common Card:	2.00
1 Ken Griffey Jr.	2.00
2 Ken Griffey Jr.	2.00
3 Ken Griffey Jr.	2.00
4 Ken Griffey Jr.	2.00
5 Ken Griffey Jr.	2.00

Hot List Jumbos

These 5" x 7" versions of the "Ken Griffey Jr.'s Hot List" subset from Series 2 are an exclusive box-topper in certain retail packaging of Collector's Choice. Other than size, the jumbos are identical to the regular Hot List cards, including foil background printing on front.

	NM/M
Complete Set (10):	15.00
Common Player:	.50
325 Andruw Jones	1.50
326 Chipper Jones	2.00
327 Mo Vaughn	.50
328 Frank Thomas	1.50
329 Albert Belle	.50
330 Mark McGwire	3.00
331 Derek Jeter	4.00
332 Alex Rodriguez	3.00
333 Jay Buhner	.50
334 Ken Griffey Jr.	2.50

New Frontier

This is a 40-card Series 2 insert highlighting anticipated interleague matchups. Cards were designed with each player's action photo superimposed on a metallic-foil background depicting half of a ballfield. Pairs could then be

displayed side-by-side. Cards were inserted 1:69 packs. They are numbered and carry a "NF" prefix.

	NM/M
Complete Set (40):	75.00
Common Player:	1.00
1 Alex Rodriguez	5.00
2 Tony Gwynn	3.00
3 Jose Canseco	1.25
4 Hideo Nomo	1.25
5 Mark McGwire	5.00
6 Barry Bonds	6.00
7 Juan Gonzalez	1.25
8 Ken Caminiti	1.00
9 Tim Salmon	1.00
10 Mike Piazza	4.00
11 Ken Griffey Jr.	4.00
12 Andres Galarraga	1.00
13 Jay Buhner	1.00
14 Dante Bichette	1.00
15 Frank Thomas	2.00
16 Ryne Sandberg	3.00
17 Roger Clemens	3.50
18 Andruw Jones	2.00
19 Jim Thome	1.50
20 Sammy Sosa	3.00
21 David Justice	1.00
22 Deion Sanders	1.00
23 Todd Walker	1.00
24 Kevin Orie	1.00
25 Albert Belle	1.00
26 Jeff Bagwell	2.00
27 Manny Ramirez	2.00
28 Brian Jordan	1.00
29 Derek Jeter	6.00
30 Chipper Jones	3.00
31 Mo Vaughn	1.00
32 Gary Sheffield	1.50
33 Carlos Delgado	1.50
34 Vladimir Guerrero	2.00
35 Cal Ripken Jr.	6.00
36 Greg Maddux	3.00
37 Cecil Fielder	1.00
38 Todd Hundley	1.00
39 Mike Mussina	1.25
40 Scott Rolen	1.50

1997 Collector's Choice Premier Power

The 20-card, regular-sized set was included one per 15 packs of Series 1. Fronts feature an action photo with the "Premier Power" logo in silver foil in the lower half and "spotlights" aiming out toward the sides. The bottom portion of the card is transparent red. Backs are bordered in red with the same card front shot appearing in black-and-white above a brief description and "Power Facts." The cards are numbered with a "PP" prefix. A parallel gold-foil version was available every 69 packs.

	NM/M
Complete Set (20):	20.00
Common Player:	.40
Gold:	2X
1 Mark McGwire	3.00
2 Brady Anderson	.40
3 Ken Griffey Jr.	2.50
4 Albert Belle	.40
5 Juan Gonzalez	.60
6 Andres Galarraga	.40
7 Jay Buhner	.40
8 Mo Vaughn	.40
9 Barry Bonds	3.50
10 Gary Sheffield	.75
11 Todd Hundley	.40
12 Frank Thomas	1.50
13 Sammy Sosa	2.00
14 Ken Caminiti	.40
15 Vinny Castilla	.40
16 Ellis Burks	.40
17 Rafael Palmeiro	1.00
18 Alex Rodriguez	3.00

19 Mike Piazza	2.50
20 Eddie Murray	1.50

Jumbo

Each factory set of 1997 Collector's Choice included 10 super-size (3" x 5") versions of the Premier Power inserts. Besides the size, the jumbos differ from the insert version in the addition of a metallic facsimile autograph on front.

	NM/M
Complete Set (20):	15.00
Common Player:	.50
1 Mark McGwire	2.50
2 Brady Anderson	.50
3 Ken Griffey Jr.	2.00
4 Albert Belle	.50
5 Juan Gonzalez	.75
6 Andres Galarraga	.50
7 Jay Buhner	.50
8 Mo Vaughn	.50
9 Barry Bonds	3.00
10 Gary Sheffield	.65
11 Todd Hundley	.50
12 Frank Thomas	1.00
13 Sammy Sosa	1.50
14 Ken Caminiti	.50
15 Vinny Castilla	.50
16 Ellis Burks	.50
17 Rafael Palmeiro	.75
18 Alex Rodriguez	2.50
19 Mike Piazza	2.00
20 Eddie Murray	1.00

Stick'Ums

The 30-piece 2-1/2" x 3-1/2" sticker set was inserted one per three packs of Series 1 Collector's Choice. Fronts feature a bright background color and include five different peel-off stickers: An action shot of the player, a pennant in team colors featuring the player's name, a team logo, an Upper Deck Collector's Choice logo and a "Super Action Stick'Ums" decal. Backs feature the player checklist in black ink over a gray background. An unnumbered version of the stickers (without Smith and Puckett) was sold in a special retail-only package.

	NM/M
Complete Set (30):	5.00
Common Player:	.05
1 Ozzie Smith	.50
2 Andruw Jones	.40
3 Alex Rodriguez	.75
4 Paul Molitor	.40
5 Jeff Bagwell	.40
6 Manny Ramirez	.40
7 Kenny Lofton	.05
8 Albert Belle	.40
9 Jay Buhner	.05
10 Chipper Jones	.50
11 Barry Larkin	.05
12 Dante Bichette	.05
13 Mike Piazza	.60
14 Andres Galarraga	.05
15 Barry Bonds	1.00
16 Brady Anderson	.05
17 Gary Sheffield	.20
18 Jim Thome	.35
19 Tony Gwynn	.40
20 Cal Ripken Jr.	1.00
21 Sammy Sosa	.50
22 Juan Gonzalez	.50
23 Greg Maddux	.50
24 Ken Griffey Jr.	.60
25 Mark McGwire	.75
26 Kirby Puckett	.50
27 Mo Vaughn	.05
28 Vladimir Guerrero	.40
29 Ken Caminiti	.05
30 Frank Thomas	.40

Toast of the Town

This 30-card Series 2 insert features top stars on foil-enhanced cards. Odds of finding one are 1:35 packs. Cards are numbered with a "T" prefix.

	NM/M
Complete Set (30):	40.00
Common Player:	.30
1 Andruw Jones	2.00
2 Chipper Jones	2.50
3 Greg Maddux	2.50
4 John Smoltz	.30
5 Kenny Lofton	.30
6 Brady Anderson	.30
7 Cal Ripken Jr.	6.00
8 Mo Vaughn	.30
9 Sammy Sosa	2.50
10 Albert Belle	.50
11 Frank Thomas	2.00
12 Barry Larkin	.30
13 Manny Ramirez	2.00
14 Jeff Bagwell	2.00
15 Mike Piazza	4.00
16 Paul Molitor	2.00
17 Vladimir Guerrero	.30
18 Todd Hundley	.30
19 Derek Jeter	6.00
20 Andy Pettitte	.45
21 Bernie Williams	.30
22 Mark McGwire	5.00
23 Scott Rolen	1.00
24 Ken Caminiti	.30
25 Tony Gwynn	2.50
26 Barry Bonds	4.00
27 Ken Griffey Jr.	4.00
28 Alex Rodriguez	5.00
29 Juan Gonzalez	.75
30 Roger Clemens	3.00

Update

This update set was offered via a mail-in redemption offer. Traded players in their new uniforms and 1997 rookies are the focus of the set. Fronts are color photos which are borderless at top and sides. Beneath each photo the player's name and team logo appear in a red (A.L.) or blue (N.L.) baseball design. Backs have another photo, major and minor league career stats and a trivia question. Cards are numbered with a "U" prefix.

	NM/M
Complete Set (30):	2.00
Common Player:	.10
1 Jim Leyritz	.10
2 Matt Perisho	.10
3 Michael Tucker	.10
4 Mike Johnson	.10
5 Jaime Navarro	.10
6 Doug Drabek	.10
7 Terry Mulholland	.10
8 Brett Tomko	.10
9 Marquis Grissom	.10
10 David Justice	.50
11 Brian Moehler	.10
12 Bobby Bonilla	.10
13 Todd Dunwoody	.10
14 Tony Saunders	.10

15 Jay Bell	.10
16 Jeff King	.10
17 Terry Steinbach	.10
18 Steve Bieser	.10
19 Takashi Kashiwada RC	.10
20 Hideki Irabu	.50
21 Damon Mashore	.10
22 Quilvio Veras	.10
23 Will Cunnane	.10
24 Jeff Kent	.50
25 J.T. Snow	.50
26 Dante Powell	.10
17 Jose Cruz Jr.	1.00
28 John Burkett	.10
29 John Wetteland	.10
30 Benito Santiago	.10

1997 Collector's Choice You Crash the Game

A 30-player interactive set found in Series 2 packs features the game's top home run hitters. Cards were inserted 1:5 packs. Fronts feature a red-foil Crash logo and a range of game dates. Those holding cards of players who homered in that span could (for $2 per card handling fee) redeem them for high-tech versions. Instant winner cards (seeded 1:721) were redeemable for complete 30-card upgrade sets. Winning cards are marked with an asterisk; theoretically they would be scarcer than losing cards because many were redeemed. The contest cards expired on Sept. 8, 1997. Cards are numbered with a "CG" prefix.

	NM/M
Complete Set (90):	65.00
Common Player:	.25
July 28-30	.25
August 8-11	.25
Sept. 19-21	.25
August 15-17	1.00
August 29-31	1.00
Sept. 12-14	1.00
August 22-24*	1.50
Sept. 1-3	.75
Sept. 19-22	.75
July 31-Aug. 3*	.50
Sept. 4-7	.25
Sept. 19-22	.25
July 29-30	.60
Aug. 29-31	.60
Sept. 26-28	.60
August 8-10*	4.00
Sept. 1-3*	4.00
Sept. 11-14	2.00
August 14-17	.25
August 29-31*	.50
Sept. 23-25*	.50
August 1-3*	2.00
August 29-31	1.00
Sept. 19-21*	2.00
August 7-10	.25
Sept. 11-14	.25
Sept. 19-21*	.50
August 29-31	.75
Sept. 1-3	.75
Sept. 23-25*	1.50
August 12-14*	1.50
August 29-31	.75
Sept. 11-14*	1.50
July 28-30	.50
August 15-18*	1.00
Sept. 19-22	.50
August 4-5	.25
Sept. 1-3*	.25
Sept. 23-25	.25
July 24-27*	.50
August 28-29	.25
Sept. 26-28*	.50
August 12-13	.25
Sept. 4-7*	.25
Sept. 19-21	.25
Sept. 11-14	.50
August 8-10*	.50
August 30-31	.25
Sept. 12-14	.25
August 1-3*	.75
Sept. 1-3*	.75
Sept. 12-14*	.75
Sept. 9-10	.25
Sept. 19-22*	1.50
Sept. 23-25*	1.50
August 1-3	.25
August 15-17	.25

Sept. 25-28*	.50
August 11-12	1.25
Sept. 5-8*	2.50
Sept. 19-21*	2.50
August 22-24	.75
August 29-31	.75
Sept. 19-22	.75
August 29-31	.25
Sept. 4-7	.25
Sept. 26-28*	.50
August 22-24	.35
Sept. 12-14	.35
Sept. 26-28	.35
July 31-Aug. 3	1.50
August 30-31	1.50
Sept. 19-22*	3.00
August 8-10	.25
Sept. 4-7	.25
Sept. 17-18*	.50
August 5-7	2.00
Sept. 4-7*	4.00
Sept. 23-24*	4.00
August 7-10	.25
August 28-29	.25
Sept. 1-3	.25
August 22-24*	2.50
August 28-29	1.25
Sept. 19-22*	2.50
July 29-31	1.50
August 30-31	1.50
Sept. 12-15	1.50
August 11-13*	.75
August 30-31	.40
Sept. 19-21*	.75

Winners

These are the prize cards from CC's interactive "You Crash the Game" cards in Series 2. Persons who redeemed a Crash card with the correct date(s) on which the pictured player homered received (for a $2 handling fee) this high-end version of the Crash card. The redemption cards have the same basic design as the contest cards, but use different player photos with fronts printed on metallic-foil stock, and a team logo in place of the Crash foil logo. Where the contest cards have game rules on back, the redemption cards have another photo of the player and career highlights. Complete redemption sets were available upon redeeming an instant winner card, found on average of one per 721 packs. Because some cards were only available in complete redemption sets (marked with an "SP" here), and others might have been available for more than one date range, some cards will be scarcer than others.

	NM/M
Complete Set (30):	55.00
Common Player:	.50
CG1 Ryan Klesko/SP	1.25
CG2 Chipper Jones/SP	12.00
CG3 Andruw Jones	.75
CG4 Brady Anderson	.50
CG5 Rafael Palmeiro/SP	2.50
CG6 Cal Ripken Jr.	10.00
CG7 Mo Vaughn	.50
CG8 Sammy Sosa	3.00
CG9 Albert Belle	.50
CG10 Frank Thomas	1.00
CG11 Manny Ramirez	.75
CG12 Jim Thome	.65
CG13 Matt Williams	.50
CG14 Dante Bichette	.50
CG15 Vinny Castilla	.50
CG16 Andres Galarraga	.50
CG17 Gary Sheffield	.65
CG18 Jeff Bagwell	.75
CG19 Eric Karros	.50
CG20 Mike Piazza	2.50
CG21 Vladimir Guerrero/SP	3.00
CG22 Cecil Fielder/SP	1.25
CG23 Jose Canseco/SP	2.00

ABBREVIATIONS

SP - Short Print
RC - Rookie Class

CG24 Mark McGwire	7.50
CG25 Ken Caminiti	.50
CG26 Barry Bonds	10.00
CG27 Jay Buhner/SP	1.25
CG28 Ken Griffey Jr.	2.50
CG29 Alex Rodriguez/SP	9.00
CG30 Juan Gonzalez	.60

Instant Winner

Found on average of one per 721 packs, these Instant Winner cards could be redeemed (with a $2 handling fee) for a complete set of You Crash the Game exchange cards - the only way eight of the Crash winner cards could be obtained. These special cards have a red foil "instant winner!" logo on front and a congratulatory message on back, along with instructions for redemption prior to the Dec., 8 1997 deadline.

	NM/M
Complete Set (30):	300.00
Common Player:	2.00

Team Sets

A special version of Collector's Choice cards for several popular major league teams was produced in two retail packages by Upper Deck. In one version, blister packs containing 13 player cards and a metallic-foil team logo/checklist card was sold for a suggested retail price of $1.99. The second version, exclusive to Wal-Mart, is a hard plastic blister pack containing two cellowrapped packages. One holds a random assortment of 15 Series 1 Collector's Choice cards. The other has 13 player cards and a foil logo/checklist card for a specific team. The team-set cards are identical to the regular-issue cards, from either Series 1 or Series 2, except each of the team-set cards has a number on back which differs from the regular edition. Packaged with the Wal-Mart version is a 3-1/2"x5" "Home Team Heroes" card, listed seperately.

	NM/M
Common Player:	.10

Atlanta Braves

Team Set:	3.00
AB Team logo/checklist	.10
AB1 Andruw Jones	.60
AB2 Kenny Lofton	.10
AB3 Fred McGriff	.10
AB4 Michael Tucker	.10
AB5 Ryan Klesko	.10
AB6 Javy Lopez	.10
AB7 Mark Wohlers	.10
AB8 Tom Glavine	.25
AB9 Denny Neagle	.10
AB10 Chipper Jones	.75
AB11 Jeff Blauser	.10
AB12 Greg Maddux	.75
AB13 John Smoltz	.10

Baltimore Orioles

Team Set:	2.00
BO Team logo/checklist	.10
BO1 Rocky Coppinger	.10
BO2 Scott Erickson	.10
BO3 Chris Hoiles	.10
BO4 Roberto Alomar	.30
BO5 Cal Ripken Jr.	1.50
BO6 Randy Myers	.10
BO7 B.J. Surhoff	.10
BO8 Mike Mussina	.40
BO9 Rafael Palmeiro	.50
BO10 Jimmy Key	.10
BO11 Mike Bordick	.10
BO12 Brady Anderson	.10
BO13 Eric Davis	.10

Chicago White Sox

Team Set:	2.50
CW Team logo/checklist	.10
CW1 Robin Ventura	.10
CW2 Wilson Alvarez	.10
CW3 Tony Phillips	.10
CW4 Lyle Mouton	.10
CW5 James Baldwin	.10
CW6 Harold Baines	.10
CW7 Albert Belle	.10
CW8 Chris Snopek	.10
CW9 Ray Durham	.10
CW10 Frank Thomas	.60
CW11 Ozzie Guillen	.10
CW12 Roberto Hernandez	.10
CW13 Jaime Navarro	.10

Cleveland Indians

Team Set:	1.50
CI Team logo/checklist	.10
CI1 Brian Giles	.10
CI2 Omar Vizquel	.10
CI3 Julio Franco	.10
CI4 Orel Hershiser	.10
CI5 Charles Nagy	.10
CI6 Matt Williams	.10
CI7 Jose Mesa	.10
CI8 Sandy Alomar	.10
CI9 Jim Thome	.50
CI10 David Justice	.10
CI11 Marquis Grissom	.10
CI12 Chad Ogea	.10
CI13 Manny Ramirez	.60

Colorado Rockies

Team Set:	1.25
CR Team logo/checklist	.10
CR1 Dante Bichette	.10
CR2 Vinny Castilla	.10
CR3 Kevin Ritz	.10
CR4 Larry Walker	.10
CR5 Eric Young	.10
CR6 Quinton McCracken	.10
CR7 John Vander Wal	.10
CR8 Jamey Wright	.10
CR9 Mark Thompson	.10
CR10 Andres Galarraga	.10
CR11 Ellis Burks	.10
CR12 Kirt Manwaring	.10
CR13 Walt Weiss	.10

Florida Marlins

Team Set:	2.00
FM Team logo/checklist	.10
FM1 Luis Castillo	.10
FM2 Al Leiter	.10
FM3 Devon White	.10
FM4 Jeff Conine	.10
FM5 Charles Johnson	.10
FM6 Edgar Renteria	.10
FM7 Robb Nen	.10
FM8 Kevin Brown	.10
FM9 Gary Sheffield	.45
FM10 Alex Fernandez	.10
FM11 Pat Rapp	.10
FM12 Moises Alou	.10
FM13 Bobby Bonilla	.10

L.A. Dodgers

Team Set:	3.00
LA Team logo/checklist	.10
LA1 Raul Mondesi	.10
LA2 Brett Butler	.10
LA3 Todd Hollandsworth	.10
LA4 Eric Karros	.10
LA5 Hideo Nomo	.30
LA6 Ismael Valdes	.10
LA7 Wilton Guerrero	.10
LA8 Ramon Martinez	.10
LA9 Greg Gagne	.10
LA10 Mike Piazza	1.00
LA11 Chan Ho Park	.10
LA12 Todd Worrell	.10
LA13 Todd Zeile	.10

New York Yankees

Team Set:	3.00
NY Team logo/checklist	.10
NY1 Bernie Williams	.10
NY2 Dwight Gooden	.10
NY3 Wade Boggs	.75
NY4 Ruben Rivera	.10
NY5 Derek Jeter	1.50
NY6 Tino Martinez	.10
NY7 Tim Raines	.10
NY8 Joe Girardi	.10
NY9 Charlie Hayes	.10
NY10 Andy Pettitte	.30
NY11 Cecil Fielder	.10
NY12 Paul O'Neill	.10
NY13 David Cone	.10

Seattle Mariners

Team Set:	3.00
SM Team logo/checklist	.10
SM1 Dan Wilson	.10
SM2 Ken Griffey Jr.	1.00
SM3 Edgar Martinez	.10
SM4 Joey Cora	.10
SM5 Norm Charlton	.10
SM6 Alex Rodriguez	1.25
SM7 Randy Johnson	.60
SM8 Paul Sorrento	.10
SM9 Jamie Moyer	.10
SM10 Jay Buhner	.10
SM11 Russ Davis	.10
SM12 Jeff Fassero	.10
SM13 Bob Wells	.10

Texas Rangers

Team Set:	3.00
TR Team logo/checklist	.10
TR1 Bobby Witt	.10
TR2 Darren Oliver	.10
TR3 Rusty Greer	.10
TR4 Juan Gonzalez	.30
TR5 Will Clark	.10
TR6 Dean Palmer	.10
TR7 Ivan Rodriguez	.50
TR8 John Wetteland	.10
TR9 Mark McLemore	.10
TR10 John Burkett	.10
TR11 Benji Gil	.10
TR12 Ken Hill	.10
TR13 Mickey Tettleton	.10

1998 Collector's Choice

The 530-card Collectors Choice set was issued in two 265-card series. Series 1 features 197 regular cards, five checklists and four subsets: Cover Story features 18 of the leagues' top stars, Rookie Class has 27 young players, the nine-card Top of the Charts subset honors 1997's statistical leaders and Masked Marauders is a nine-card subset. Inserts in Series 1 are Super Action Stick-Ums, Evolution Revolution and StarQuest. Series 2 has 233 regular cards, five checklist cards, an 18-card Rookie Class subset and the nine-card Golden Jubilee subset. Inserts in Series 2 include Mini Bobbing Head Cards, You Crash the Game and StarQuest. Factory sets include a random assortment of 10 StarQuest cards.

	NM/M
Unopened Fact. Set (540):	15.00
Complete Set (530):	10.00
Common Player:	.05
Pack (14):	1.00
Wax Box (36):	15.00
1 Nomar Garciaparra (Cover Glory)	.50
2 Roger Clemens (Cover Glory)	.50
3 Larry Walker (Cover Glory)	.05
4 Mike Piazza (Cover Glory)	.60
5 Mark McGwire (Cover Glory)	.75
6 Tony Gwynn (Cover Glory)	.45
7 Jose Cruz Jr. (Cover Glory)	.40
8 Frank Thomas (Cover Glory)	.40
9 Tino Martinez (Cover Glory)	.05
10 Ken Griffey Jr. (Cover Glory)	.60
11 Barry Bonds (Cover Glory)	.85
12 Scott Rolen (Cover Glory)	.30
13 Randy Johnson (Cover Glory)	.15
14 Ryne Sandberg (Cover Glory)	.35
15 Eddie Murray (Cover Glory)	.15
16 Kevin Brown (Cover Glory)	.05
17 Greg Maddux (Cover Glory)	.35
18 Sandy Alomar Jr. (Cover Glory)	.05
19 Checklist (Ken Griffey Jr., Adam Riggs)	.40
20 Checklist (Nomar Garciaparra, Charlie O'Brien)	.10
21 Checklist (Ben Grieve, Ken Griffey Jr., Larry Walker, Mark McGwire)	.50
22 Checklist (Mark McGwire, Cal Ripken Jr.)	.50
23 Checklist (Tino Martinez)	.05
24 Jason Dickson	.05
25 Darin Erstad	.25
26 Todd Greene	.05
27 Chuck Finley	.05
28 Garret Anderson	.05
29 Dave Hollins	.05
30 Rickey Henderson	.60
31 John Smoltz	.05
32 Michael Tucker	.05
33 Jeff Blauser	.05
34 Javier Lopez	.05
35 Andruw Jones	.60
36 Denny Neagle	.05
37 Randall Simon	.05
38 Mark Wohlers	.05
39 Harold Baines	.05
40 Cal Ripken Jr.	1.50
41 Mike Bordick	.05
42 Jimmy Key	.05
43 Armando Benitez	.05
44 Scott Erickson	.05
45 Eric Davis	.05
46 Bret Saberhagen	.05
47 Darren Bragg	.05
48 Steve Avery	.05
49 Jeff Frye	.05
50 Aaron Sele	.05
51 Scott Hatteberg	.05
52 Tom Gordon	.05
53 Kevin Orie	.05
54 Kevin Foster	.05
55 Ryne Sandberg	.75
56 Doug Glanville	.05
57 Tyler Houston	.05
58 Steve Trachsel	.05
59 Mark Grace	.05
60 Frank Thomas	.60
61 Scott Eyre RC	.05
62 Jeff Abbott	.05
63 Chris Clemons	.05
64 Jorge Fabregas	.05
65 Robin Ventura	.05
66 Matt Karchner	.05
67 Jon Nunnally	.05
68 Aaron Boone	.05
69 Pokey Reese	.05
70 Deion Sanders	.10
71 Jeff Shaw	.05
72 Eduardo Perez	.05
73 Brett Tomko	.05
74 Bartolo Colon	.05
75 Manny Ramirez	.60
76 Jose Mesa	.05
77 Brian Giles	.05
78 Richie Sexson	.05
79 Orel Hershiser	.05
80 Matt Williams	.05
81 Walt Weiss	.05
82 Jerry DiPoto	.05
83 Quinton McCracken	.05
84 Neifi Perez	.05
85 Vinny Castilla	.05
86 Ellis Burks	.05
87 John Thomson	.05
88 Willie Blair	.05
89 Bob Hamelin	.05
90 Tony Clark	.05
91 Todd Jones	.05
92 Deivi Cruz	.05
93 Frank Catalanotto RC	.15
94 Justin Thompson	.05
95 Gary Sheffield	.25
96 Kevin Brown	.05
97 Charles Johnson	.05
98 Bobby Bonilla	.05
99 Livan Hernandez	.05
100 Paul Konerko/RC	.10
101 Craig Counsell/RC	.05
102 Magglio Ordonez/RC RC	1.00
103 Garrett Stephenson/RC	.05
104 Ken Cloude/RC	.05
105 Miguel Tejada/RC	.25
106 Juan Encarnacion/RC	.05
107 Dennis Reyes/RC	.05
108 Orlando Cabrera/RC	.05
109 Kelvim Escobar/RC	.05
110 Ben Grieve/RC	.50
111 Brian Rose/RC	.05
112 Fernando Tatis/RC	.05
113 Tom Evans/RC	.05
114 Tom Fordham/RC	.05
115 Mark Kotsay/RC	.05
116 Mario Valdez/RC	.05
117 Jeremi Gonzalez/RC	.05
118 Todd Dunwoody/RC	.05
119 Javier Valentin/RC	.05
120 Todd Helton/RC	.50
121 Jason Varitek/RC	.50
122 Chris Carpenter/RC	.05
123 Kevin Millwood/RC RC	.75
124 Brad Fullmer/RC	.05
125 Jaret Wright/RC	.05
126 Brad Rigby/RC	.05
127 Edgar Renteria	.05
128 Robb Nen	.05
129 Tony Pena	.05
130 Craig Biggio	.05
131 Brad Ausmus	.05
132 Shane Reynolds	.05
133 Mike Hampton	.05
134 Billy Wagner	.05
135 Richard Hidalgo	.05
136 Jose Rosado	.05
137 Yamil Benitez	.05
138 Felix Martinez	.05
139 Jeff King	.05
140 Jose Offerman	.05
141 Joe Vitiello	.05
142 Tim Belcher	.05
143 Brett Butler	.05
144 Greg Gagne	.05
145 Mike Piazza	1.00
146 Ramon Martinez	.05
147 Raul Mondesi	.05
148 Adam Riggs	.05
149 Eddie Murray	.50
150 Jeff Cirillo	.05
151 Scott Karl	.05
152 Mike Fetters	.05
153 Dave Nilsson	.05
154 Antone Williamson	.05
155 Jeff D'Amico	.05
156 Jose Valentin	.05
157 Brad Radke	.05
158 Torii Hunter	.05
159 Chuck Knoblauch	.05
160 Paul Molitor	.60
161 Travis Miller	.05
162 Rich Robertson	.05
163 Ron Coomer	.05
164 Mark Grudzielanek	.05
165 Lee Smith	.05
166 Vladimir Guerrero	.60
167 Dustin Hermanson	.05
168 Ugueth Urbina	.05
169 F.P. Santangelo	.05
170 Rondell White	.05
171 Bobby Jones	.05
172 Edgardo Alfonzo	.05
173 John Franco	.05
174 Carlos Baerga	.05
175 Butch Huskey	.05
176 Rey Ordonez	.05
177 Matt Franco	.05
178 Dwight Gooden	.05
179 Chad Curtis	.05
180 Tino Martinez	.05
181 Charlie O'Brien (Masked Marauders)	.05
182 Sandy Alomar Jr. (Masked Marauders)	.05
183 Raul Casanova (Masked Marauders)	.05
184 Jim Leyritz (Masked Marauders)	.05
185 Mike Piazza (Masked Marauders)	.60
186 Ivan Rodriguez (Masked Marauders)	.25
187 Charles Johnson (Masked Marauders)	.05
188 Brad Ausmus (Masked Marauders)	.05
189 Brian Johnson (Masked Marauders)	.05
190 Wade Boggs	.75
191 David Wells	.05
192 Tim Raines	.05
193 Ramiro Mendoza	.05
194 Willie Adams	.05
195 Matt Stairs	.05
196 Jason McDonald	.05
197 Dave Magadan	.05
198 Mark Bellhorn	.05
199 Ariel Prieto	.05
200 Jose Canseco	.05
201 Bobby Estalella	.05
202 Tony Barron RC	.05
203 Midre Cummings	.05
204 Ricky Bottalico	.05
205 Mike Grace	.05
206 Rico Brogna	.05
207 Mickey Morandini	.05
208 Lou Collier	.05
209 Kevin Polcovich RC	.05
210 Kevin Young	.05
211 Jose Guillen	.05
212 Esteban Loaiza	.05
213 Marc Wilkins	.05
214 Jason Schmidt	.05
215 Gary Gaetti	.05
216 Fernando Valenzuela	.05
217 Willie McGee	.05
218 Alan Benes	.05
219 Eli Marrero	.05
220 Mark McGwire	1.25
221 Matt Morris	.05
222 Trevor Hoffman	.05
223 Will Cunnane	.05
224 Joey Hamilton	.05
225 Ken Caminiti	.05
226 Derrek Lee	.35
227 Mark Sweeney	.05
228 Carlos Hernandez	.05
229 Brian Johnson	.05
230 Jeff Kent	.05
231 Kirk Rueter	.05
232 Bill Mueller	.05
233 Dante Powell	.05
234 J.T. Snow	.05
235 Shawn Estes	.05
236 Dennis Martinez	.05

237	Jamie Moyer	.05
238	Dan Wilson	.05
239	Joey Cora	.05
240	Ken Griffey Jr.	1.00
241	Paul Sorrento	.05
242	Jay Buhner	.05
243	Hanley Frias RC	.05
244	John Burkett	.05
245	Juan Gonzalez	.30
246	Rick Helling	.05
247	Darren Oliver	.05
248	Mickey Tettleton	.05
249	Ivan Rodriguez	.45
250	Joe Carter	.05
251	Pat Hentgen	.05
252	Marty Janzen	.05
253	Frank Thomas, Tony Gwynn (Top of the Charts)	.25
254	Mark McGwire, Ken Griffey Jr., Larry Walker (Top of the Charts)	.50
255	Ken Griffey Jr., Andres Galarraga (Top of the Charts)	.40
256	Brian Hunter, Tony Womack (Top of the Charts)	.05
257	Roger Clemens, Denny Neagle (Top of the Charts)	.10
258	Roger Clemens, Curt Schilling (Top of the Charts)	.30
259	Roger Clemens, Pedro J. Martinez (Top of the Charts)	.25
260	Randy Myers, Jeff Shaw (Top of the Charts)	.05
261	Nomar Garciaparra, Scott Rolen (Top of the Charts)	.25
262	Charlie O'Brien	.05
263	Shannon Stewart	.05
264	Robert Person	.05
265	Carlos Delgado	.25
266	Checklist (Matt Williams, Travis Lee)	.05
267	Checklist (Nomar Garciaparra, Cal Ripken Jr.)	.50
268	Checklist (Mark McGwire, Mike Piazza)	.50
269	Checklist (Tony Gwynn, Ken Griffey Jr.)	.40
270	Checklist (Fred McGriff, Jose Cruz Jr.)	.05
271	Andruw Jones (Golden Jubilee)	.25
272	Alex Rodriguez (Golden Jubilee)	.65
273	Juan Gonzalez (Golden Jubilee)	.15
274	Nomar Garciaparra (Golden Jubilee)	.50
275	Ken Griffey Jr. (Golden Jubilee)	.60
276	Tino Martinez (Golden Jubilee)	.05
277	Roger Clemens (Golden Jubilee)	.40
278	Barry Bonds (Golden Jubilee)	.85
279	Mike Piazza (Golden Jubilee)	.60
280	Tim Salmon (Golden Jubilee)	.05
281	Gary DiSarcina	.05
282	Cecil Fielder	.05
283	Ken Hill	.05
284	Troy Percival	.05
285	Jim Edmonds	.05
286	Allen Watson	.05
287	Brian Anderson	.05
288	Jay Bell	.05
289	Jorge Fabregas	.05
290	Devon White	.05
291	Yamil Benitez	.05
292	Jeff Suppan	.05
293	Tony Batista	.05
294	Brent Brede	.05
295	Andy Benes	.05
296	Felix Rodriguez	.05
297	Karim Garcia	.05
298	Omar Daal	.05
299	Andy Stankiewicz	.05
300	Matt Williams	.05
301	Willie Blair	.05
302	Ryan Klesko	.05
303	Tom Glavine	.25
304	Walt Weiss	.05
305	Greg Maddux	.75
306	Chipper Jones	.75
307	Keith Lockhart	.05
308	Andres Galarraga	.05
309	Chris Hoiles	.05
310	Roberto Alomar	.25
311	Joe Carter	.05
312	Doug Drabek	.05
313	Jeffrey Hammonds	.05
314	Rafael Palmeiro	.40
315	Mike Mussina	.40
316	Brady Anderson	.05
317	B.J. Surhoff	.05
318	Dennis Eckersley	.45
319	Jim Leyritz	.05
320	Mo Vaughn	.05
321	Nomar Garciaparra	.75
322	Reggie Jefferson	.05
323	Tim Naehring	.05
324	Troy O'Leary	.05
325	Pedro J. Martinez	.50
326	John Valentin	.05
327	Mark Clark	.05
328	Rod Beck	.05
329	Mickey Morandini	.05
330	Sammy Sosa	.75
331	Jeff Blauser	.05
332	Lance Johnson	.05
333	Scott Servais	.05
334	Kevin Tapani	.05
335	Henry Rodriguez	.05
336	Jaime Navarro	.05
337	Benji Gil	.05
338	James Baldwin	.05
339	Mike Cameron	.05
340	Ray Durham	.05
341	Chris Snopek	.05
342	Eddie Taubensee	.05
343	Bret Boone	.05
344	Willie Greene	.05
345	Barry Larkin	.05
346	Chris Stynes	.05
347	Pete Harnisch	.05
348	Dave Burba	.05
349	Sandy Alomar Jr.	.05
350	Kenny Lofton	.25
351	Geronimo Berroa	.05
352	Omar Vizquel	.05
353	Travis Fryman	.05
354	Dwight Gooden	.05
355	Jim Thome	.40
356	David Justice	.05
357	Charles Nagy	.05
358	Chad Ogea	.05
359	Pedro Astacio	.05
360	Larry Walker	.05
361	Mike Lansing	.05
362	Kirt Manwaring	.05
363	Dante Bichette	.05
364	Jamey Wright	.05
365	Darryl Kile	.05
366	Luis Gonzalez	.05
367	Joe Randa	.05
368	Raul Casanova	.05
369	Damion Easley	.05
370	Brian L. Hunter	.05
371	Bobby Higginson	.05
372	Brian Moehler	.05
373	Scott Sanders	.05
374	Jim Eisenreich	.05
375	Derrek Lee	.35
376	Jay Powell	.05
377	Cliff Floyd	.05
378	Alex Fernandez	.05
379	Felix Heredia	.05
380	Jeff Bagwell	.60
381	Bill Spiers	.05
382	Chris Holt	.05
383	Carl Everett	.05
384	Derek Bell	.05
385	Moises Alou	.05
386	Ramon Garcia	.05
387	Mike Sweeney	.05
388	Glendon Rusch	.05
389	Kevin Appier	.05
390	Dean Palmer	.05
391	Jeff Conine	.05
392	Johnny Damon	.25
393	Jose Vizcaino	.05
394	Todd Hollandsworth	.05
395	Eric Karros	.05
396	Todd Zeile	.05
397	Chan Ho Park	.25
398	Ismael Valdes	.05
399	Eric Young	.05
400	Hideo Nomo	.25
401	Mark Loretta	.05
402	Doug Jones	.05
403	Jeromy Burnitz	.05
404	John Jaha	.05
405	Marquis Grissom	.05
406	Mike Matheny	.05
407	Todd Walker	.05
408	Marty Cordova	.05
409	Matt Lawton	.05
410	Terry Steinbach	.05
411	Pat Meares	.05
412	Rick Aguilera	.05
413	Otis Nixon	.05
414	Derrick May	.05
415	Carl Pavano/RC	.05
416	A.J. Hinch/RC	.05
417	David Dellucci/RC RC	.10
418	Bruce Chen/RC	.05
419	Darron Ingram/RC RC	.05
420	Sean Casey/RC	.20
421	Mark L. Johnson/RC	.05
422	Gabe Alvarez/RC	.05
423	Alex Gonzalez/RC	.05
424	Daryle Ward/RC	.05
425	Russell Branyan/RC	.05
426	Mike Caruso/RC)	.05
427	Mike Kinkade/RC RC	.20
428	Ramon Hernandez/RC	.05
429	Matt Clement/RC	.05
430	Travis Lee/RC	.05
431	Shane Monahan/RC RC	.05
432	Rich Butler/RC RC	.05
433	Chris Widger	.05
434	Jose Vidro	.05
435	Carlos Perez	.05
436	Ryan McGuire	.05
437	Brian McRae	.05
438	Al Leiter	.05
439	Rich Becker	.05
440	Todd Hundley	.05
441	Dave Mlicki	.05
442	Bernard Gilkey	.05
443	John Olerud	.05
444	Paul O'Neill	.05
445	Andy Pettitte	.30
446	David Cone	.05
447	Chili Davis	.05
448	Bernie Williams	.05
449	Joe Girardi	.05
450	Derek Jeter	1.50
451	Mariano Rivera	.20
452	George Williams	.05
453	Kenny Rogers	.05
454	Tom Candiotti	.05
455	Rickey Henderson	.60
456	Jason Giambi	.40
457	Scott Spiezio	.05
458	Doug Glanville	.05
459	Desi Relaford	.05
460	Curt Schilling	.20
461	Bob Abreu	.10
462	Gregg Jefferies	.05
463	Scott Rolen	.40
464	Mike Lieberthal	.05
465	Tony Womack	.05
466	Jermaine Allensworth	.05
467	Francisco Cordova	.05
468	Jon Lieber	.05
469	Al Martin	.05
470	Jason Kendall	.05
471	Todd Stottlemyre	.05
472	Royce Clayton	.05
473	Brian Jordan	.05
474	John Mabry	.05
475	Ray Lankford	.05
476	Delino DeShields	.05
477	Ron Gant	.05
478	Mark Langston	.05
479	Steve Finley	.05
480	Tony Gwynn	.75
481	Andy Ashby	.05
482	Wally Joyner	.05
483	Greg Vaughn	.05
484	Sterling Hitchcock	.05
485	J. Kevin Brown	.05
486	Orel Hershiser	.05
487	Charlie Hayes	.05
488	Darryl Hamilton	.05
489	Mark Gardner	.05
490	Barry Bonds	1.50
491	Robb Nen	.05
492	Kirk Rueter	.05
493	Randy Johnson	.50
494	Jeff Fassero	.05
495	Alex Rodriguez	1.25
496	David Segui	.05
497	Rich Amaral	.05
498	Russ Davis	.05
499	Bubba Trammell	.05
500	Wade Boggs	.75
501	Roberto Hernandez	.05
502	Dave Martinez	.05
503	Dennis Springer	.05
504	Paul Sorrento	.05
505	Wilson Alvarez	.05
506	Mike Kelly	.05
507	Albie Lopez	.05
508	Tony Saunders	.05
509	John Flaherty	.05
510	Fred McGriff	.05
511	Quinton McCracken	.05
512	Terrell Wade	.05
513	Kevin Stocker	.05
514	Kevin Elster	.05
515	Will Clark	.05
516	Bobby Witt	.05
517	Tom Goodwin	.05
518	Aaron Sele	.05
519	Lee Stevens	.05
520	Rusty Greer	.05
521	John Wetteland	.05
522	Darrin Fletcher	.05
523	Jose Canseco	.35
524	Randy Myers	.05
525	Jose Cruz Jr.	.05
526	Shawn Green	.15
527	Tony Fernandez	.05
528	Alex Gonzalez	.05
529	Ed Sprague	.05
530	Roger Clemens	.85

1	Nomar Garciaparra	1.50
2	Roger Clemens	2.00
3	Larry Walker	1.00
4	Mike Piazza	2.50
5	Mark McGwire	3.00
6	Tony Gwynn	1.50
7	Jose Cruz Jr.	1.00
8	Frank Thomas	1.25
9	Tino Martinez	1.00
10	Ken Griffey Jr.	2.50

Evolution Revolution

This 28-card insert features one player from each Major League team. The fronts picture the team jersey and open to reveal the player's top 1997 accomplishment. Evolution Revolution was inserted in Series 1 packs. Cards are numbered with an "ER" prefix.

		NM/M
Complete Set (28):		36.00
Common Player:		.40
Inserted 1:13		
1	Tim Salmon	.40
2	Greg Maddux	2.50
3	Cal Ripken Jr.	6.00
4	Mo Vaughn	.40
5	Sammy Sosa	2.50
6	Frank Thomas	1.50
7	Barry Larkin	.40
8	Jim Thome	.65
9	Larry Walker	.40
10	Travis Fryman	.40
11	Gary Sheffield	.65
12	Jeff Bagwell	1.50
13	Johnny Damon	.65
14	Mike Piazza	4.00
15	Jeff Cirillo	.40
16	Paul Molitor	1.50
17	Vladimir Guerrero	1.50
18	Todd Hundley	.40
19	Tino Martinez	.40
20	Jose Canseco	.65
21	Scott Rolen	.75
22	Al Martin	.40
23	Mark McGwire	5.00
24	Tony Gwynn	2.50
25	Barry Bonds	6.00
26	Ken Griffey Jr.	4.00
27	Juan Gonzalez	.75
28	Roger Clemens	3.00

Golden Jubilee Jumbos

The Golden Jubilee subset cards from Series 2 C.C. were reproduced in 4X (5" x 7") size as one-per-box inserts in special versions of retail packaging.

		NM/M
Complete Set (9):		17.50
Common Player:		1.00
271	Andruw Jones	1.50
272	Alex Rodriguez	4.00
273	Juan Gonzalez	1.00
274	Nomar Garciaparra	2.00
275	Ken Griffey Jr.	3.00
276	Tino Martinez	1.00

Cover Glory 5x7

	NM/M
Complete Set (10):	10.00
Common Player:	1.00

277	Roger Clemens	2.00
278	Barry Bonds	5.00
279	Mike Piazza	3.00

Jumbos (3.5x5)

These double-size versions of various Series 1 cards were available one per special blister pack of Collector's Choice sold in retail chains.

		NM/M
Complete Set (15):		17.50
Common Player:		1.00
35	Andruw Jones	1.50
40	Cal Ripken Jr.	3.00
60	Ryne Sandberg	1.75
95	Frank Thomas	1.50
97	Gary Sheffield	1.25
145	Mike Piazza	2.00
160	Paul Molitor	1.50
180	Tino Martinez	1.00
220	Mark McGwire	2.50
225	Ken Caminiti	1.00
240	Ken Griffey Jr.	2.00
242	Jay Buhner	1.00
245	Juan Gonzalez	1.25
249	Ivan Rodriguez	1.25

Jumbos (5x7)

These super-size (5" x 7") cards were one-per-box inserts in Series 2 retail packaging. Besides being four times the size of a normal card, the 5x7s are identical to the regular versions.

		NM/M
Complete Set (10):		15.00
Common Player:		1.00
306	Chipper Jones	2.00
321	Nomar Garciaparra	2.00
360	Larry Walker	1.00
450	Derek Jeter	4.00
463	Scott Rolen	1.25
480	Tony Gwynn	2.00
490	Barry Bonds	4.00
495	Alex Rodriguez	3.00
525	Jose Cruz Jr.	1.00
530	Roger Clemens	2.50

Mini Bobbing Heads

The cards in this 30-card insert series can be punched out and assembled into a stand-up figure with a removable bobbing head. They are a Series 2 insert.

	NM/M
Complete Set (30):	20.00

Common Player:		.25
Inserted 1:3		
1	Tim Salmon	.25
2	Travis Lee	.25
3	Matt Williams	.25
4	Chipper Jones	1.00
5	Greg Maddux	1.00
6	Cal Ripken Jr.	2.50
7	Nomar Garciaparra	1.00
8	Mo Vaughn	.25
9	Sammy Sosa	1.00
10	Frank Thomas	.75
11	Kenny Lofton	.25
12	Jaret Wright	.25
13	Larry Walker	.25
14	Tony Clark	.25
15	Edgar Renteria	.25
16	Jeff Bagwell	.75
17	Mike Piazza	1.50
18	Vladimir Guerrero	.75
19	Derek Jeter	2.50
20	Ben Grieve	.25
21	Scott Rolen	.50
22	Mark McGwire	2.00
23	Tony Gwynn	1.00
24	Barry Bonds	2.50
25	Ken Griffey Jr.	1.50
26	Alex Rodriguez	2.00
27	Fred McGriff	.25
28	Juan Gonzalez	.40
29	Roger Clemens	1.25
30	Jose Cruz Jr.	.25

Rookie Class: Prime Choice

This 18-card set is a parallel of the Rookie Class subset. Each card is foil-stamped with the words "Prime Choice Reserve." This hobby-only set is sequentially numbered to 500 and was inserted in Series 2 packs.

		NM/M
Complete Set (18):		30.00
Common Player:		2.00
415	Carl Pavano	2.00
416	A.J. Hinch	2.00
417	David Dellucci	2.00
418	Bruce Chen	2.00
419	Darron Ingram	2.00
420	Sean Casey	5.00
421	Mark L. Johnson	2.00
422	Gabe Alvarez	2.00
423	Alex Gonzalez	2.00
424	Daryle Ward	2.00
425	Russell Branyan	2.00
426	Mike Caruso	2.00
427	Mike Kinkade	2.00
428	Ramon Hernandez	2.00
429	Matt Clement	2.00
430	Travis Lee	2.50
431	Shane Monahan	2.00
432	Rich Butler	2.00

StarQuest - Series 1

The StarQuest insert in Series 1 consists of 90 cards within four tiers. The tiers are designated by the number of stars found on front, the more the better: Special Delivery (#1-45, one star), Students of the Game (two stars, #46-65), Super Powers (three stars, #66-80) and Super Star Domain (four stars, #81-90). All cards are numbered with a "SQ" prefix.

	NM/M
Complete Set (90):	185.00
Common Special Delivery (1-45):	.25
Inserted 1:1	
Common Student of the Game (46-65):	.75
Inserted 1:21	
Common Super Power (66-80):	2.00
Inserted 1:71	
Common Superstar Domain (81-90):	3.00
Inserted 1:145	
1 Nomar Garciaparra	1.50
2 Scott Rolen	.75
3 Jason Dickson	.25
4 Jaret Wright	.25
5 Kevin Orie	.25
6 Jose Guillen	.25
7 Matt Morris	.25
8 Mike Cameron	.25
9 Kevin Polcovich	.25
10 Jose Cruz Jr.	.25
11 Miguel Tejada	.40
12 Fernando Tatis	.25
13 Todd Helton	.65
14 Ken Cloude	.25
15 Ben Grieve	.25
16 Dante Powell	.25
17 Bubba Trammell	.25
18 Juan Encarnacion	.25
19 Derrek Lee	.25
20 Paul Konerko	.35
21 Richard Hidalgo	.25
22 Denny Neagle	.25
23 David Justice	.25
24 Pedro J. Martinez	1.00
25 Greg Maddux	1.50
26 Edgar Martinez	.25
27 Cal Ripken Jr.	2.50
28 Tim Salmon	.25
29 Shawn Estes	.25
30 Ken Griffey Jr.	2.00
31 Brad Radke	.25
32 Andy Pettitte	.40
33 Curt Schilling	.50
34 Raul Mondesi	.25
35 Alex Rodriguez	2.25
36 Jeff Kent	.25
37 Jeff Bagwell	1.00
38 Juan Gonzalez	.50
39 Barry Bonds	2.50
40 Mark McGwire	2.00
41 Frank Thomas	1.00
42 Ray Lankford	.25
43 Tony Gwynn	1.50
44 Mike Piazza	1.75
45 Tino Martinez	.25
46 Nomar Garciaparra	3.00
47 Paul Molitor	1.50
48 Chuck Knoblauch	.75
49 Rusty Greer	.75
50 Cal Ripken Jr.	6.00
51 Roberto Alomar	1.00
52 Scott Rolen	1.00
53 Derek Jeter	6.00
54 Mark Grace	.75
55 Randy Johnson	1.50
56 Craig Biggio	.75
57 Kenny Lofton	.75
58 Eddie Murray	1.50
59 Ryne Sandberg	2.00
60 Rickey Henderson	1.50
61 Darin Erstad	1.00
62 Jim Edmonds	.75
63 Ken Caminiti	.75
64 Ivan Rodriguez	1.25
65 Tony Gwynn	2.00
66 Tony Clark	2.00
67 Andres Galarraga	2.00
68 Rafael Palmeiro	3.00
69 Manny Ramirez	6.00
70 Albert Belle	2.00
71 Jay Buhner	2.00
72 Mo Vaughn	2.00
73 Barry Bonds	15.00
74 Chipper Jones	7.50
75 Jeff Bagwell	6.00
76 Jim Thome	3.00
77 Sammy Sosa	7.50
78 Todd Hundley	2.00
79 Matt Williams	2.00
80 Vinny Castilla	2.00
81 Jose Cruz Jr.	3.00
82 Frank Thomas	7.50
83 Juan Gonzalez	7.50
84 Mike Piazza	15.00
85 Alex Rodriguez	20.00
86 Larry Walker	3.00
87 Tino Martinez	3.00
88 Greg Maddux	12.50
89 Mark McGwire	20.00
90 Ken Griffey Jr.	15.00

StarQuest - Series 2

The 30-card StarQuest insert was included in Series 2 packs. The insert has four parallel tiers - Single, Double, Triple and Home Run - designated by the number of baseball diamond icons on the card front. Single cards were inserted 1:1, Doubles 1:21, Triples 1:71 and Home Runs are sequentially numbered to 100. The second series SQ cards feature a front design with the letters "QSUTEASRT" in color blocks vertically at left.

	NM/M
Complete Set (30):	17.50
Common Player:	.25
Singles 1:1	
Doubles 1:21	2X
Triples 1:71	6X
Home Runs	15X
1 Ken Griffey Jr.	1.25
2 Jose Cruz Jr.	.25
3 Cal Ripken Jr.	2.00
4 Roger Clemens	1.00
5 Frank Thomas	.75
6 Derek Jeter	2.00
7 Alex Rodriguez	1.50
8 Andruw Jones	.75
9 Vladimir Guerrero	.75
10 Mark McGwire	1.50
11 Kenny Lofton	.25
12 Pedro J. Martinez	.25
13 Greg Maddux	1.00
14 Larry Walker	.25
15 Barry Bonds	2.00
16 Chipper Jones	1.00
17 Jeff Bagwell	.75
18 Juan Gonzalez	.75
19 Tony Gwynn	1.00
20 Mike Piazza	1.25
21 Tino Martinez	.25
22 Mo Vaughn	.20
23 Ben Grieve	.25
24 Scott Rolen	.60
25 Nomar Garciaparra	1.00
26 Paul Konerko	.35
27 Jaret Wright	.25
28 Gary Sheffield	.50
29 Travis Lee	.25
30 Todd Helton	.65

StarQuest Super Powers Jumbos

This enlarged (3-1/2" x 5") version of the StarQuest Super Powers cards from Series 1 were a retail-only variation found one per blister pack of specially marked Collector's Choice product.

	NM/M
Complete Set (10):	17.50
Common Player:	1.00
SQ67 Andres Galarraga	1.00
SQ68 Rafael Palmeiro	2.00
SQ69 Manny Ramirez	2.50
SQ70 Albert Belle	1.00
SQ71 Jay Buhner	1.00
SQ72 Mo Vaughn	1.00
SQ73 Barry Bonds	5.00
SQ74 Chipper Jones	3.00
SQ75 Jeff Bagwell	2.50
SQ76 Jim Thome	1.50

Stickums

This 30-card insert was seeded 1:3 Series 1 packs. The stickers can be peeled off the card and reused.

	NM/M
Complete Set (30):	7.00
Common Player:	.10
Inserted 1:3	
1 Andruw Jones	.35
2 Chipper Jones	.45
3 Cal Ripken Jr.	1.00
4 Nomar Garciaparra	.45
5 Mo Vaughn	.10
6 Ryne Sandberg	.45
7 Sammy Sosa	.45
8 Frank Thomas	.35
9 Albert Belle	.10
10 Jim Thome	.30
11 Manny Ramirez	.35
12 Larry Walker	.10
13 Gary Sheffield	.20
14 Jeff Bagwell	.35
15 Mike Piazza	.60
16 Paul Molitor	.35
17 Pedro J. Martinez	.35
18 Todd Hundley	.10
19 Derek Jeter	1.00
20 Tino Martinez	.10
21 Curt Schilling	.25
22 Mark McGwire	.75
23 Tony Gwynn	.45
24 Barry Bonds	1.00
25 Ken Griffey Jr.	.60
26 Alex Rodriguez	.75
27 Juan Gonzalez	.20
28 Ivan Rodriguez	.30
29 Roger Clemens	.50
30 Jose Cruz Jr.	.10

1998 Collector's Choice You Crash the Game

These 90 game cards were inserted one per five Series 2 packs. Each card features a player and a list of dates. If the pictured player hit a home run on one of those days, collectors with the card could mail it in for a graphically enhanced prize version. Instant Winner cards of each player were also inserted at the rate of 1:721 and could be exchanged for the complete 30-card prize set. Deadline for exchange of all winning cards was Dec. 1, 1998. Winning cards are designated here with an asterisk and can be expected to be somewhat scarcer than non-winning dates.

	NM/M
Complete Set (90):	75.00
Common Player:	.50
Instant Winner:	8X
Inserted 1:5	
CG1 Ken Griffey Jr. (June 26-28*)	3.00
CG1 Ken Griffey Jr. (July 7)	1.25
CG1 Ken Griffey Jr. (Sept. 21-24*)	3.00
CG2 Travis Lee (July 27-30)	.50
CG2 Travis Lee (Aug. 27-30)	.50
CG2 Travis Lee (Sept. 17-20)	.50
CG3 Larry Walker (July 17-19)	.50
CG3 Larry Walker (Aug. 27-30*)	1.00
CG3 Larry Walker (Sept. 25-27*)	1.00
CG4 Tony Clark (July 9-12*)	1.00
CG4 Tony Clark (June 30-July 2)	.50
CG4 Tony Clark (Sept. 4-6)	.50
CG5 Cal Ripken Jr. (June 22-25*)	4.00
CG5 Cal Ripken Jr. (July 7)	2.00
CG5 Cal Ripken Jr. (Sept. 4-6)	2.00
CG6 Tim Salmon (June 22-25)	.50
CG6 Tim Salmon (Aug. 28-30)	.50
CG6 Tim Salmon (Sept. 14-15)	.50
CG7 Vinny Castilla (June 30-July 2*)	1.00
CG7 Vinny Castilla (Aug. 27-30*)	1.00
CG7 Vinny Castilla (Sept. 7-10*)	1.00
CG8 Fred McGriff (June 22-25)	.50
CG8 Fred McGriff (July 3-5)	.50
CG8 Fred McGriff (Sept. 18-20*)	1.00
CG9 Matt Williams (July 17-29)	.50
CG9 Matt Williams (Sept. 14-16*)	1.00
CG9 Matt Williams (Sept. 18-20)	.50
CG10 Mark McGwire (July 7)	1.50
CG10 Mark McGwire (July 24-26*)	3.50
CG10 Mark McGwire (Aug. 18-19*)	3.50
CG11 Albert Belle (July 3-5)	.50
CG11 Albert Belle (Aug. 21-23*)	1.00
CG11 Albert Belle (Sept. 11-13)	1.00
CG12 Jay Buhner (July 9-12*)	1.00
CG12 Jay Buhner (Aug. 6-9)	.50
CG12 Jay Buhner (Sept. 25-27)	1.00
CG13 Vladimir Guerrero (June 22-25)	.75
CG13 Vladimir Guerrero (Aug. 10-12*)	1.50
CG13 Vladimir Guerrero (Sept. 14-16*)	1.50
CG14 Andruw Jones (July 16-19*)	1.50
CG14 Andruw Jones (Aug. 27-30*)	1.50
CG14 Andruw Jones (Sept. 17-20)	.75
CG15 Nomar Garciaparra (July 9-12)	1.00
CG15 Nomar Garciaparra (Aug. 13-16*)	2.50
CG15 Nomar Garciaparra (Sept. 24-27)	1.00
CG16 Ken Caminiti (June 26-28*)	1.00
CG16 Ken Caminiti (July 13-15*)	1.00
CG16 Ken Caminiti (Sept. 10-13)	.50
CG17 Sammy Sosa (July 9-12*)	2.50
CG17 Sammy Sosa (Aug. 27-30*)	2.50
CG17 Sammy Sosa (Sept. 18-20)	1.00
CG18 Ben Grieve (June 30-July 2*)	1.00
CG18 Ben Grieve (Aug. 14-16)	.50
CG18 Ben Grieve (Sept. 24-27)	.50
CG19 Mo Vaughn (July 7)	.50
CG19 Mo Vaughn (Sept. 7-9)	.50
CG19 Mo Vaughn (Sept. 24-27*)	1.00
CG20 Frank Thomas (July 7)	.75
CG20 Frank Thomas (July 17-19*)	1.50
CG20 Frank Thomas (Sept. 4-6)	.75
CG21 Manny Ramirez (July 9-12)	.75
CG21 Manny Ramirez (Aug. 13-16*)	1.50
CG21 Manny Ramirez (Sept. 18-20*)	1.50
CG22 Jeff Bagwell (July 7)	.75
CG22 Jeff Bagwell (Aug. 28-30*)	1.50
CG22 Jeff Bagwell (Sept. 4-6*)	1.50
CG23 Jose Cruz Jr. (July 9-12)	.50
CG23 Jose Cruz Jr. (Aug. 13-16)	.50
CG23 Jose Cruz Jr. (Sept. 18-20)	.50
CG24 Alex Rodriguez (July 7*)	3.50
CG24 Alex Rodriguez (Aug. 6-9*)	3.50
CG24 Alex Rodriguez (Sept. 21-23*)	3.50
CG25 Mike Piazza (June 22-25*)	3.00
CG25 Mike Piazza (July 7)	1.25
CG25 Mike Piazza (Sept. 10-13*)	3.00
CG26 Tino Martinez (June 26-28*)	1.00
CG26 Tino Martinez (July 9-12)	.50
CG26 Tino Martinez (Aug. 13-16)	.50
CG27 Chipper Jones (July 3-5)	1.00
CG27 Chipper Jones (Aug. 27-30)	1.00
CG27 Chipper Jones (Sept. 17-20)	1.00
CG28 Juan Gonzalez (July 7)	.60
CG28 Juan Gonzalez (Aug. 6-9*)	1.25
CG28 Juan Gonzalez (Sept. 11-13*)	1.25
CG29 Jim Thome (June 22-23)	.60
CG29 Jim Thome (July 23-26*)	1.25
CG29 Jim Thome (Sept. 24-27)	.60
CG30 Barry Bonds (July 7*)	4.00
CG30 Barry Bonds (Sept. 4-6)	4.00
CG30 Barry Bonds (Sept. 18-20*)	4.00

Winners

Collectors who redeemed winning "Crash" cards prior to the Dec. 1, 1998 deadline received an upgraded version of that player's card. Similar in format, the winners' cards have an action photo on front (different than the game card), with a metallic foil background. Instead of dates in the three circles at bottom are the letters "W I N." Backs have a career summary and stats, instead of the redemption instructions found on the game cards. The cards are numbered with a "CG" prefix. Cards of players who didn't homer during their designated dates were available only by redeeming a scarce (1:721 packs) Instant Win card. They are indicated here by "SP."

	NM/M
Complete Set (30):	9.00
Common Player:	.25
CG1 Ken Griffey Jr.	1.00
CG2 Travis Lee/SP	.75
CG3 Larry Walker	.25
CG4 Tony Clark	.25
CG5 Cal Ripken Jr.	1.50
CG6 Tim Salmon/SP	.60
CG7 Vinny Castilla	.25
CG8 Fred McGriff	.25
CG9 Matt Williams	.25
CG10 Mark McGwire	1.25
CG11 Albert Belle	.25
CG12 Jay Buhner	.25
CG13 Vladimir Guerrero	.50
CG14 Andruw Jones	.50
CG15 Nomar Garciaparra	.75
CG16 Ken Caminiti	.25
CG17 Sammy Sosa	.75
CG18 Ben Grieve	.25
CG19 Mo Vaughn	.25
CG20 Frank Thomas	.50
CG21 Manny Ramirez	.50
CG22 Jeff Bagwell	.50
CG23 Jose Cruz Jr./SP	.60
CG24 Alex Rodriguez	1.25
CG25 Mike Piazza	1.00
CG26 Tino Martinez	.25
CG27 Chipper Jones /SP	1.50
CG28 Juan Gonzalez	.35
CG29 Jim Thome	.35
CG30 Barry Bonds	1.50

Instant Winner

Found on average of one per 721 packs, these Instant Winner cards could be redeemed (with a $2 handling fee) for a complete set of You Crash the Game exchange cards - the only way Crash winner cards of Travis Lee, Jose Cruz Jr. and Chipper Jones could be obtained. These special cards have an instant winner logo on front in place of game dates, and a congratulatory message on back along with instructions for redemption prior to the Dec. 1, 1998 deadline.

	NM/M
Complete Set (30):	250.00
Common Player:	4.00

1995 Collector's Edge Ball Park Franks Baseball Legends

"Baseball Legends" Yogi Berra and Brooks Robinson are featured in this hot dog promotional set. Sunday newspapers on March 5 featured a coupon used to obtain the pair of autographed cards for eight proofs-of-purchase, or $2.50 with four UPCs or $5 with two UPCs. Cards have color photos, with uniform logos removed, and marbled borders. An authentic autograph is across the front of the card. Backs have a portrait photo and career summary. Each card was accompanied by a card-like certificate of authenticity.

	NM/M
Complete Set (2):	20.00
(1) Yogi Berra	16.00
(2) Frank Robinson	8.00

1993 Colorado Fever Rockies

In its inaugural issue, a fan magazine titled "Colorado Fever" issued a sheet of nine baseball cards in both its "Regional" and "Metro" editions. Stapled into the center of the magazine is an 8-3/8" x 11" cardboard insert. One panel has nine Rockies cards which are not perforated and would measure about 2-5/8" x 3-5/8" if cut from the sheet. Cards from the Metro edition feature players in uniform; most of the cards from the Regional edition show the players in street clothes. It is not known whether future editions of the announced twice-annual magazine were ever published or if they contained baseball card inserts.

	NM/M
Complete Set (18):	8.00
Common Player:	.50
1M David Nied	.50
2M Charlie Hayes	.50
3M Andy Ashby	.50
4M Joe Girardi	.50
5M Don Baylor	.60
6M Andres Galarraga	.50
7M Jim Tatum	.50

8M	Eric Young	.50
9M	Dante Bichette	.50
1R	Alex Cole	.50
2R	Don Baylor	.60
3R	Dante Bichette	.50
4R	Jeff Parrett	.50
5R	David Nied	.50
6R	Butch Henry	.50
7R	Andres Galarraga	.50
8R	Daryl Boston	.50
9R	Joe Girardi	.50

1994 Colorado Rockies Police

Howard Johnson
Outfield

The Rockies' premiere police set is an oversized (2-5/8" x 4") effort with posed and action player photos on a yellow and purple background on front. Team logo and name are above the photo, while ID and uniform number are beneath the photo. Backs are printed in purple with a few bits of personal data and stats, a safety message and sponsors' logos. The cards are checklisted here in alphabetical order.

		NM/M
Complete Set (27):		6.00
Common Player:		.50
(1)	Don Baylor	.75
(2)	Dante Bichette	.75
(3)	Willie Blair	.50
(4)	Kent Bottenfield	.50
(5)	Ellis Burks	.50
(6)	Vinny Castilla	.50
(7)	Marvin Freeman	.50
(8)	Andres Galarraga	.75
(9)	Andres Galarraga (Batting champion.)	.75
(10)	Joe Girardi	.50
(11)	Mike Harkey	.50
(12)	Greg Harris	.50
(13)	Charlie Hayes	.50
(14)	Darren Holmes	.50
(15)	Howard Johnson	.50
(16)	Nelson Liriano	.50
(17)	Roberto Mejia	.50
(18)	Mike Munoz	.50
(19)	David Nied	.50
(20)	Steve Reed	.50
(21)	Armando Reynoso	.50
(22)	Bruce Ruffin	.50
(23)	Danny Sheaffer	.50
(24)	Darrell Sherman	.50
(25)	Walt Weiss	.50
(26)	Eric Young	.50
(27)	Rockies coaches (Larry Bearnarth, Dwight Evans, Gene Glynn, Ron Hassey, Bill Plummer, Don Zimmer)	.50

1995 Colorado Rockies Police

Castilla • 1995

With only a dozen players included, this is one of the smallest safety sets of the

genre. The 2-5/8" x 4" cards have color player action photos on front, bordered in black with the team logo in the lower-right corner. The player's last name and year appear in orange in the upper-right. Backs are in black-and-white and include a safety message or cartoon, and a few biographical data and stats. Cards are checklisted by uniform number.

		NM/M
Complete Set (12):		5.00
Common Player:		.50
6	Jason Bates	.50
7	Joe Girardi	.50
9	Vinny Castilla	.50
10	Dante Bichette	.50
12	Mike Kingery	.50
14	Andres Galarraga	.75
20	Bill Swift	.50
21	Eric Young	.50
22	Walt Weiss	.50
25	Don Baylor	.75
26	Ellis Burks	.50
33	Larry Walker	1.50

1996 Colorado Rockies Police

Painter • 28

The Rockies third annual safety set is the team's largest, at 27 cards. The set's format is 2-5/8" x 4" and is sponsored by Kansas City Life Insurance. Fronts have game-action photos, with the team logo, player last name and uniform number at bottom. Backs are printed in purple and feature a safety-message cartoon. The set was initially distributed to fans attending an April game. The set is checklisted here by uniform number. A Spanish-language version of the set was also issued.

		NM/M
Complete Set (27):		5.00
Common Player:		.25
Spanish:		2X
1	Trenidad Hubbard	.25
3	Quinton McCracken	.25
6	Jason Bates	.25
9	Vinny Castilla	.25
10	Dante Bichette	.50
14	Andres Galarraga	.50
16	Curtis Leskanic	.25
18	Bruce Ruffin	.25
20	Bill Swift	.25
21	Eric Young	.25
22	Walt Weiss	.25
23	Bryan Rekar	.25
25	Don Baylor	.35
26	Ellis Burks	.25
28	Lance Painter	.25
30	Kevin Ritz	.25
31	Bret Saberhagen	.35
32	Mark Thompson	.25
33	Larry Walker	1.00
34	Jayhawk Owens	.25
35	John Vander Wal	.25
38	Roger Bailey	.25
39	Steve Reed	.25
40	Darren Holmes	.25
42	Armando Reynoso	.25
43	Mike Munoz	.25
44	Marvin Freeman	.25

1997 Colorado Rockies Police

In conjunction with the Colorado Association of Chiefs of Police, the Rockies handed out this safety set at a designated home game early

in the season. It is the team's fourth annual safety set. The 2-1/2" x 3-1/2" cards feature game-action photos on front surrounded by a white border. The team logo is at upper-left; player identification is in purple and gray stripes diagonally at bottom. Backs are in black-and-white and have some player personal data, a career-best stat lines and a safety message. Cards are numbered by uniform number in a baseball at upper-right.

		NM/M
Complete Set (12):		5.00
Common Player:		.60
3	Quinton McCracken	.60
6	Kirt Manwaring	.60
9	Vinny Castilla	.60
10	Dante Bichette	.60
14	Andres Galarraga	.75
20	Bill Swift	.60
21	Eric Young	.60
22	Walt Weiss	.60
25	Don Baylor	.75
26	Ellis Burks	.60
33	Larry Walker	1.50
00	Dinger (mascot)	.60

1998 Colorado Rockies Police

Dante BICHETTE OF

Children attending a May 31 promotional game at Coors Field received this set of Rockies cards. Game-action color photos are featured on front, borderless at top, bottom and left. At right is a vertical gray stripe with the player's name and position; team logo and name are at bottom. On back is a player portrait photo, identification, biographical details, an inspirational message and logos of the sponsoring organizations.

		NM/M
Complete Set (12):		6.00
Common Player:		.35
3	Mike Lansing	.50
5	Neifi Perez	.50
8	Kirt Manwaring	.50
9	Vinny Castilla	.50
10	Dante Bichette	.50
17	Todd Helton	4.00
25	Don Baylor	.60
26	Ellis Burks	.50
33	Larry Walker	1.00
34	Pedro Astacio	.50
57	Darryl Kile	.50
00	Dinger/Mascot	.50

1999 Colorado Rockies Police

Children attending a promotional game at Coors Field received this set of Rockies cards. Borderless game-ac-

tion color photos are featured on front. At right is a vertical strip with the team name; the player name and position are at bottom. On back is a player portrait photo, identification, biographical details, a safety message and logos of the sponsoring organizations.

		NM/M
Complete Set (12):		6.00
Common Player:		1.00
(1)	Dante Bichette	1.00
(2)	Vinny Castilla	1.00
(3)	Dinger/Mascot	1.00
(4)	Jerry DiPoto	1.00
(5)	Darryl Hamilton	1.00
(6)	Todd Helton	2.50
(7)	Darryl Kile	1.00
(8)	Mike Lansing	1.00
(9)	Jim Leyland	1.00
(10)	Kirt Manwaring	1.00
(11)	Neifi Perez	1.00
(12)	Larry Walker	1.50

2000 Colorado Rockies Police

Todd Helton Infield

Children attending a May 28 promotional game at Coors Field received this set of Rockies cards. Borderless game-action color photos are featured on front. On back is a player portrait, identification, biographical details, an inspirational message and a credit line for the Colorado Association of Chiefs of Police.

		NM/M
Complete Set (12):		6.00
Common Player:		.75
3	Mike Lansing	.75
4	Jeffrey Hammonds	.75
5	Neifi Perez	.75
7	Jeff Cirillo	.75
8	Brent Mayne	.75
17	Todd Helton	3.00
24	Tom Goodwin	.75
25	Buddy Bell	.75
30	Rolando Arrojo	.75
33	Larry Walker	1.50
00	Dinger/Mascot	.75
---	Coors Field	.75

2002 Colorado Rockies Police

The Rockies hot dog vendor sponsored this stadium give-away safety set featuring the manager and 11 popular players. The 2-1/2" x 3-1/2" cards have game-action photos vignetted on front with white borders. A 10-year team anniversary logo is lower-left. Horizontal backs have a portrait photo in the top-right corner and a ghosted image of the

front photo at left, which is overprinted with player data, 2001 stats, career highlights and a safety or inspirational message in English or Spanish. The sponsor and team logos are at right.

		NM/M
Complete Set (12):		6.00
Common Player:		.50
2	Jose Ortiz	.50
4	Juan Uribe	.50
9	Juan Pierre	1.50
10	Mike Hampton	.50
12	Todd Zeile	.50
13	Clint Hurdle	.50
15	Denny Neagle	.50
17	Todd Helton	2.50
27	Todd Hollandsworth	.50
29	Gary Bennett	.50
33	Larry Walker	1.00
00	Dinger/Mascot	.50

2005 Comcast Oakland A's

JASON KENDALL c

Sponsored by Comcast, 15,000 of these team sets were given away at the September 24 game. Fronts have a gold border. Green-and-gold backs have player personal data.

		NM/M
Complete Set (32):		10.00
Common Player:		.25
(1)	Team Photo/Checklist	.25
2	Ken Macha	.25
4	Eric Chavez	.75
5	Mark Kotsay	.25
6	Rich Harden	.75
7	Jason Kendall	.25
8	Bobby Crosby	1.00
9	Jay Payton	.25
10	Scott Hatteberg	.25
11	Huston Street	1.00
12	Mark Ellis	.25
13	Dan Haren	.75
15	Nick Swisher	.25
16	Joe Blanton	.75
17	Marco Scutaro	.25
17	Kirk Saarloos	.25
18	Dan Johnson	.75
19	Kiko Calero	.25
20	Bobby Kielty	.25
21	Justin Duchscherer	.25
22	Adam Melhuse	.25
23	Ricardo Rincon	.25
24	Joe Kennedy	.25
25	Keiichi Yabu	.25
26	Erubiel Durazo	.25
27	Juan Cruz	.25
28	Keith Ginter	.25
29	Octavio Dotel	.25
30	Charles Thomas	.25
31	Jay Witasick	.25
32	Coaching Staff (Brad Fischer, Bob Geren, Dave Hudgens, Rene Lachemann, Curt Young, Ron Washington)	.25

1995 Comic Images National Pastime Promo

This unnumbered card was issued to promote Comic Images' set of baseball history cards. The 2-1/2" x 3-1/2" card has a familiar color photo of company spokesman Phil Rizzuto on front, done up in chromium technology and with the Yankees team logos removed from the uniform. The back advertises the forthcoming card set.

	NM/M
Phil Rizzuto	3.00

1995 Comic Images The National Pastime

This set is principally made up of 19th Century baseball images done up in 20th Century chromium card technology to detail the history of baseball from the 1860s through the 1950s. As might be expected, there was little positive reaction from collectors. Photos of old baseball collectibles, including a few vintage baseball cards are scattered throughout the set as are a few actual player photos. Hall of Famer Phil Rizzuto was tapped to promote the issue, but his name was misspelled on the cards' box. A number of special inserts including Rizzuto autographed cards were part of the issue.

		NM/M
Complete Set (90):		8.00
Common Card:		.10
Autographed Rizzuto Card:		35.00
MagnaChrome Rizzuto Career Card (6):		2.00
MagnaChrome Diamond Cover (3):		1.00
Medallion Card:		2.00
Six-card Case-Topper Sheet:		6.00
1	Sportsman's Park	.10
2	Harper's Weekly, August, 1913	.10
3	Shibe Park	.10
4	Polo Grounds Print	.10
5	Forbes Field	.10
6	Hall of Fame (Phil Rizzuto)	.25
7	League Park	.10
8	Highlander Park	.10
9	South Side Park	.10
10	Catchers' Mitt	.10
11	Baseball Trophy	.10
12	Baseball Plate	.10
13	Bisque Figure	.10
14	Beanbag	.10
15	Tobacco Carved Figure	.10

16	Sunday Magazine	.10
17	Street & Smith Sport	.10
18	Collier's	.10
19	Bluebook	.10
20	Chadwick's	.10
21	Harper's Weekly	.10
22	American Magazine	.10
23	Crazy Baseball Stories	.10
24	New York Giants, 1892	.10
25	Cincinnati American Association, 1882	.10
26	Chicago White Stockings, 1885	.10
27	Baltimore Blues, 1890	.10
28	Chicago & All-Americans, 1889	.10
29	Philadelphia Baseball Team, 1910	.10
30	1887 Goodwin & Co. Champions	.25
31	John McGraw	.15
32	Home Run (1885 trade card)	.10
33	Lorillard Chicago BBC	.10
34	Boston BBC	.10
35	Out at First (Trade card)	.10
36	"Coffee Cards"	.10
37	Uncut Sheet - Detail	.10
38	Tobin Lithographers	.10
39	Uncut Sheet - Die Cut	.10
40	Patsy Dougherty (T207)	.10
41	A Regular Corker (1885 trade card)	.10
42	Barker's Advertising Book	.10
43	Toledo BBC Tobacco Poster	.10
44	Shredded Wheat Advertisement	.10
45	BVD Advertisement	.10
46	Police Gazette Poster	.10
47	Japanese Poster	.10
48	Safe Hit Vegetable Crate Label	.10
49	Slide, Kelly, Slide Poster	.10
50	Peck & Snyder Hat Advertisement	.10
51	Reach Gloves Catalog	.10
52	New York Giants Scorecard	.10
53	Game Card	.10
54	Wright & Ditson Guide	.10
55	1933 All-Star Game Program	.10
56	Stadium Scene	.10
57	Currier & Ives Print	.10
58	Scorecard Artwork	.10
59	Folk Art	.10
60	Batter (Wrong front, belongs to #73.)	.10
61	Cartoon	.10
62	Teddy Roosevelt Cartoon	.10
63	Uncle Sam Cartoon	.10
64	Casey at the Bat	.15
65	Seymour Church Print	.10
66	Valentine Card	.10
67	Pinup Book	.10
68	Uncle Sam WWI Sheet Music	.10
69	Baseball Sheet Music	.10
70	Saturday Globe	.10
71	Ft. Wayne Woman Player	.15
72	Spalding Baseball Guide	.10
73	Rally Day Postcard (Wrong front, belongs to #60.)	.10
74	Spalding Advertisement Die Cut	.10
75	Our Baseball Club Cover	.10
76	Jake Beckley	.15
77	Cap Anson (Allen & Ginter album page.)	.25
78	St. Louis Player	.10
79	Sam Thompson (Scrap's Die Cut)	.10
80	Bobby Wallace (Turkey Red Cabinet)	.15
81	Fogarty & McGuire Jim Fogarty, Deacon McGuire (1887 Kalamazoo Bats detail.)	.15
82	Yank Robinson (1887 die-cut game card.)	.15
83	Charles Comiskey (1887 Scrap's tobacco die-cut.)	.15
84	Picked Off! (Action photo.)	.10
85	Error (Action photo.)	.10
86	Third Base (Action photo.)	.10
87	Safe at Home (Action photo.)	.10
88	Baseball Action (Action photo.)	.10
89	Great Fielding (action photo.)	.10
90	Checklist	

1991 Conlon Collection Prototypes

The cards which previewed the debut set of Conlon Collection cards in the 1990s can generally be identified by the lack of Major League Baseball logo and Curtis Management copyright information on back. Except for the colorized Babe Ruth card, they are not otherwise marked as prototypes. While most of the 1991 Conlon prototypes were distributed in relatively small quantities, reportedly 2,940, the colorized Ty Cobbs was an edition of 60,000 and the colorized Babe Ruth card was produced for the 12th National Sports Collectors Convention in Anaheim, Calif., to the tune of 225,000 cards.

		NM/M
	Complete Set (6):	9.00
	Common Player:	2.00
13	Ty Cobb (Colorized edition of 60,000.)	4.50
34	Dizzy Dean	2.00
111	Lou Gehrig	3.50
145	Babe Ruth	4.50
145	Babe Ruth (Colorized, edition of 225,000.)	3.00
250	Ty Cobb	3.00

1991 Conlon Collection

This 330-card set features the photography of Charles Martin Conlon, who was active from before 1910 through the early 1940s. Black-and-white photos are set against black borders on the UV-coated card fronts. Megacards worked with The Sporting News (owners of the Conlon photos) to release the set. Several subsets are featured such as Hall of Famers, 1927 New York Yankees, MVPs and more. The backs feature statistics and career highlights and can be found either with or without the MLB logo.

		NM/M
	Complete Factory Set (330):	13.50
	Factory Set w/Autographed Feller:	16.00
	Complete Set (330):	9.00
	Common Player:	.10
	Wax Pack (18):	.50
	Wax Box (36):	15.00
1	Rogers Hornsby	.25
2	James E. Foxx	.25
3	Jay H. Dean	.25
4	Walter J.V. Maranville	.10
5	Paul G. Waner	.10
6	Lloyd J. Waner	.10
7	Melvin T. Ott	.15
8	John P. Wagner	.30
9	Walter P. Johnson	.25
10	Carl O. Hubbell	.15
11	Frank F. Frisch	.15
12	Hazen S. Cuyler	.10
13	Charles H. Ruffing	.10
14	Henry B. Greenberg	.15
15	John J. Evers	.10
16	Hugh A. Jennings	.10
17	David J. Bancroft	.10
18	Joseph M. Medwick	.10
19	Theodore A. Lyons	.10
20	Charles A. Bender	.10
21	Edward T. Collins	.10
22	James L. Bottomley	.10
23	Robert M. Grove	.15
24	Max Carey	.10
25	Burleigh A. Grimes	.10
26	Ross M. Youngs	.10
27	Ernest N. Lombardi	.10
28	Joseph V. McCarthy	.10
29	Lewis R. Wilson	.10
30	Charles H. Klein	.10
31	Howard E. Averill Sr.	.10
32	Grover C. Alexander	.15
33	Charles J. Hafey	.10
34	William B. McKechnie	.10
35	Robert W.A. Feller	.15
36	Harold J. Traynor	.10
37	Charles D. Stengel	.15
38	Joseph F. Vaughan	.10
39	Eppa Rixey	.10
40	Joseph W. Sewell	.10
41	Urban C. Faber	.10
42	Travis C. Jackson	.10
43	Jesse J. Haines	.10
44	Tristram E. Speaker	.25
45	Cornelius Mack	.10
46	Cornelius Mack	.10
47	Cornelius Mack	.10
48	Raymond W. Schalk	.10
49	Aloysius H. Simmons	.10
50	Joseph E. Cronin	.10
51	Gordon S. Cochrane	.10
52	Harry E. Heilmann	.10
53	John R. Mize	.15
54	Edgar C. Rice	.10
55	Edd J. Roush	.10
56	Enos B. Slaughter	.10
57	Christopher Mathewson	.25
58	Fred C. Lindstrom	.10
59	Charles L. Hartnett	.10
60	George L. Kelly	.10
61	Stanley R. Harris	.10
62	Leon A. Goslin	.10
63	Henry E. Manush	.10
64	William H. Terry	.10
65	John J. McGraw	.10
66	George H. Sisler	.10
67	Vernon L. Gomez	.10
68	Joseph I. Judge	.10
69	Thomas J. Thevenow	.10
70	Charles M. Gelbert	.10
71	Minter C. Hayes	.10
72	Robert R. Fothergill	.10
73	Adam A. Comorosky	.10
74	Earl S. Smith	.10
75	Samuel D. Gray	.10
76	Peter W. Appleton	.10
77	Eugene Moore Jr.	.10
78	Arndt L. Jorgens	.10
79	William H. Knickerbocker	.10
80	Carl N. Reynolds	.10
81	Oscar D. Melillo	.10
82	John H. Burnett	.10
83	Alvin J. Powell	.10
84	John J. Murphy	.10
85	Leroy E. Parmelee	.10
86	James A. Ripple	.10
87	Gerald H. Walker	.10
88	George L. Earnshaw	.10
89	William H. Southworth	.10
90	Wallace Moses	.10
91	George E. Walberg	.10
92	James J. Dykes	.10
93	Charles H. Root	.10
94	John W. Cooney	.10
95	Charles J. Grimm	.10
96	Robert L. Johnson	.10
97	John W. Scott	.10
98	Raymond A. Radcliff	.10
99	Frederick R. Ostermueller	.10
100	Julian V. Wera	.10
101	Miller J. Huggins	.10
102	Raymond A. Morehart	.10
103	Bernard O. Bengough	.10
104	Walter H. Ruether	.10
105	Earle B. Combs	.10
106	Myles L. Thomas	.10
107	Benjamin E. Paschal	.10
108	Cedric M. Durst	.10
109	William M. Moore	.10
110	George H. Ruth	1.00
111	Louis H. Gehrig	.50
112	Joseph A. Dugan	.10
113	Anthony M. Lazzeri	.10
114	Urban J. Shocker	.10
115	Waite C. Hoyt	.10
116	Charles T. O'Leary	.10
117	Arthur Fletcher	.10
118	Tharon L. Collins	.10
119	Joseph O. Giard	.10
120	Herbert J. Pennock	.10
121	Michael Gazella	.10
122	Robert W. Meusel	.10
123	George W. Pipgras	.10
124	John P. Grabowski	.10
125	Mark A. Koenig	.10
126	Stanley C. Hack	.10
127	Earl O. Whitehill	.10
128	William C. Lee	.10
129	Frank O. Mancuso	.10
130	Francis R. Blades	.10
131	John I. Burns	.10
132	Clinton H. Brown	.10
133	William J. Dietrich	.10
134	Darrell E. Blanton	.10
135	Harry B. Hooper	.10
136	Charles H. Shorten	.10
137	Clarence W. Walker	.10
138	George Foster	.10
139	John J. Barry	.10
140	Samuel P. Jones	.10
141	Ernest G. Shore	.10
142	Hubert B. Leonard	.10
143	Herbert J. Pennock	.10
144	Harold C. Janvrin	.10
145	George H. Ruth	1.00
146	George E. Lewis	.10
147	William L. Gardner	.10
148	Richard C. Hoblitzel	.10
149	Lewis E. Scott	.10
150	Carl W. Mays	.10
151	John A. Niehoff	.10
152	Burton E. Shotton	.10
153	Leon K. Ames	.10
154	Fred Williams	.10
155	William W. Hinchman	.10
156	James R. Shawkey	.10
157	Walter C. Pipp	.10
158	George J. Burns	.10
159	Robert H. Veach	.10
160	Harold H. Chase	.10
161	Thomas L. Hughes	.10
162	Derrill B. Pratt	.10
163	Henry K. Groh	.10
164	Zachariah D. Wheat	.10
165	Francis J. O'Doul	.10
166	William E. Kamm	.10
167	Paul G. Waner	.10
168	Fred C. Snodgrass	.10
169	Floyd C. Herman	.10
170	Albert H. Bridwell	.10
171	John T. Meyers	.10
172	John B. Lobert	.10
173	Raymond B. Bressler	.10
174	Samuel P. Jones	.10
175	Robert A. O'Farrell	.10
176	George Toporcer	.10
177	George E. McNeely	.10
178	John H. Knott	.10
179	Clarence F. Mueller	.10
180	Thomas J.D. Bridges	.10
181	Lloyd A. Brown	.10
182	Lawrence J. Benton	.10
183	Max F. Bishop	.10
184	Morris Berg	.20
185	Ralph F. Perkins	.10
186	Stephen F. O'Neill	.10
187	Glenn C. Myatt	.10
188	Joseph A. Kuhel	.10
189	Martin J. McManus	.10
190	Charles F. Lucas	.10
191	John P. McInnis	.10
192	Edmund J. Miller	.10
193	James L. Sewell	.10
194	William H. Sherdel	.10
195	Harold J. Rhyne	.10
196	Guy T. Bush	.10
197	Ervin Fox	.10
198	Wesley C. Ferrell	.10
199	Roy C. Johnson	.10
200	William Wambsganss	.10
201	George H. Burns	.10
202	Clarence E. Mitchell	.10
203	Cornelius Ball	.10
204	John H. Neun	.10
205	Homer W. Summa	.10
206	Ernest K. Padgett	.10
207	Walter H. Holke	.10
208	Forrest G. Wright	.10
209	Henry M. Gowdy	.10
210	James W. Taylor	.10
211	Benjamin C. Cantwell	.10
212	Joseph F. Demaree	.10
213	Samuel P. Derringer	.10
214	William A. Hallahan	.10
215	Daniel K. MacFayden	.10
216	Harry F. Rice	.10
217	Robert Eldridge Smith	.10
218	Jackson R. Stephenson	.10
219	Perce L. Malone	.10
220	Henry B. Tate	.10
221	Joseph F. Vosmik	.10
222	George A. Watkins	.10
223	James Wilson	.10
224	George E. Uhle	.10
225	Melvin T. Ott	.15
226	Nicholas Altrock	.10
227	Charles H. Ruffing	.10
228	Joseph V.L. Krakauskas	.10
229	Walter A. Berger	.10
230	Norman L. Newsom	.10
231	Lonnie Warneke	.10
232	Frank E. Snyder	.10
233	Myril O. Hoag	.10
234	Baldomero M. Almada	.10
235	Ivy B. Wingo	.10
236	James P. Austin	.10
237	Henry J. Bonura	.10
238	Russell G. Wrightstone	.10
239	Alfred C. Todd	.10
240	Harold B. Warstler	.10
241	Samuel F. West	.10
242	Arthur C. Reinhart	.10
243	Walter C. Stewart	.10
244	John B. Gooch	.10
245	Eugene F. Hargrave	.10
246	George W. Harper	.10
247	George W. Connally	.10
248	Edgar G. Braxton	.10
249	Walter H. Schang	.10
250	Tyrus R. Cobb	.50
251	Rogers Hornsby	.15
252	Richard W. Marquard	.10
253	Carl O. Hubbell	.15
254	Joe Wood	.10
255	Robert M. Grove	.15
256	Lynwood T. Rowe	.10
257	Alvin F. Crowder	.10
258	Walter P. Johnson	.10
259	Charles J. Hafey	.10
260	Frederick L. Fitzsimmons	.10
261	William E. Webb	.10
262	Earle B. Combs	.10
263	Edward J. Konetchy	.10
264	Taylor L. Douthit	.10
265	Lloyd J. Waner	.10
266	Gordon S. Cochrane	.10
267	John O. Wilson	.10
268	Harold J. Traynor	.10
269	Virgil L. Davis	.10
270	Henry E. Manush	.10
271	Michael F. Higgins	.10
272	Adrian Joss	.10
273	Edward Augustine Walsh	.10
274	Johnny L.R. Martin	.10
275	Joseph W. Sewell	.10
276	Hubert B. Leonard	.10
277	Clifford C. Cravath	.10
278	Oral C. Hildebrand	.10
279	Remy P. Kremer	.10
280	Frank A. Pytlak	.10
281	Samuel D. Byrd	.10
282	Curtis B. Davis	.10
283	Lewis A. Fonseca	.10
284	Herold D. Ruel	.10
285	Julius J. Solters	.10
286	Fred W. Schulte	.10
287	John P. Quinn	.10
288	Arthur C. Whitney	.10
289	Jonathon T. Stone	.10
290	Hugh M. Critz	.10
291	Ira J. Flagstead	.10
292	George F. Grantham	.10
293	Samuel D. Hale	.10
294	James F. Hogan	.10
295	Oswald L. Bluege	.10
296	Debs Garms	.10
297	Augistaf B. Friberg	.10
298	Edward A. Brandt	.10
299	Ralston B. Hemsley	.10
300	Charles H. Klein	.10
301	Morton C. Cooper	.10
302	James L. Bottomley	.10
303	James E. Foxx	.15
304	Frank Schulte	.10
305	Frank F. Frisch	.15
306	Frank A. McCormick	.10
307	Jacob E. Daubert	.10
308	Roger T. Peckinpaugh	.10
309	George H. Burns	.10
310	Louis H. Gehrig	.50
311	Aloysius H. Simmons	.10
312	Edward T. Collins	.10
313	Charles L. Hartnett	.10
314	Joseph E. Cronin	.10
315	Paul G. Waner	.10
316	Robert A. O'Farrell	.10
317	Lawrence J. Doyle	.10
318	Lynford H. Lary	.10
319	Frank S. May	.10
320	Roy H. Spencer	.10
321	Samuel R. Coffman	.10
322	Peter J. Donohue	.10
323	George W. Haas	.10
324	Edward S. Farrell	.10
325	Charles F. Rhem	.10
326	Frederick Marberry	.10
327	Charles Martin Conlon	.10
328	Checklist 1-110	.10
329	Checklist 111-220	.10
330	Checklist 221-330	.10

1992 Conlon Collection Prototypes

Along with the 1991 Babe Ruth prototype card, these five cards were distributed at the Anaheim National Sports Collectors Convention in 1991. The announced distribution was 20,000 of each card except the Joe Jackson, which had a press run of 67,000. Except for card 331, all the prototypes have different numbers than the same card in the regular-issue Conlon set. Each of the

JOE JACKSON
CLEVELAND INDIANS – OUTFIELD 1913

1992 cards has a gray "PROTOTYPE" overprinted diagonally on the back.

		NM/M
	Complete Set (6):	9.00
	Common Player:	.50
14	Joe Jackson (Colorized, edition of 60,000.)	3.00
331	Christy Mathewson	1.50
400	Joe Jackson	2.50
450	Hughie Jennings	.50
500	Ty Cobb	2.00
520	Goose Goslin	.50

1992 Conlon Collection

ALLEN SOTHORON
ST. LOUIS BROWNS – PITCHER 1917

In their second season, the 330 cards of the Conlon Collection were numbered consecutively where the 1991 premiere issue ended. Cards 331-660 also maintained the high-gloss black-and-white format of the previous year. Many subsets within the issue carry special designations on the card fronts. Subsets included no-hitters, Triple Crown winners, "Great Stories," nicknames and more.

		NM/M
	Factory Set (330):	25.00
	Complete Set (330):	15.00
	Common Player:	.10
	Wax Pack:	.50
	Wax Box (36):	15.00
331	Christopher Mathewson	.15
332	George L. Wiltse	.10
333	George N. Rucker	.10
334	Leon K. Ames	.10
335	Charles A. Bender	.10
336	Joe Wood	.10
337	Edward Augustine Walsh	.10
338	George J. Mullin	.10
339	Earl A. Hamilton	.10
340	Charles M Tesreau	.10
341	James Scott	.10
342	Richard W. Marquard	.10
343	Claude R. Hendrix	.10
344	James S. Lavender	.10
345	Leslie A. Bush	.10
346	Hubert B. Leonard	.10
347	Fred A. Toney	.10
348	James L. Vaughn	.10
349	Ernest G. Koob	.10
350	Robert Groom	.10
351	Ernest G. Shore	.10
352	Horace O. Eller	.10
353	Walter P. Johnson	.15
354	Charles C. Robertson	.10
355	Jesse L. Barnes	.10
356	Samuel P. Jones	.10
357	Howard J. Ehmke	.10
358	Jesse J. Haines	.10
359	Theodore A. Lyons	.10
360	Carl O. Hubbell	.15
361	Wesley C. Ferrell	.10
362	Robert J. Burke	.10
363	Paul D. Dean	.10
364	Norman L. Newsom	.10
365	Lloyd V. Kennedy	.10

366	William J. Dietrich	.10
367	John S. Vander Meer	.10
368	John S. Vander Meer	.10
369	Montgomery M. Pearson	.10
370	Robert W.A. Feller	.15
371	Lonnie Warneke	.10
372	James A. Tobin	.10
373	Earl A. Moore	.10
374	William H. Dineen	.10
375	Malcolm W. Eason	.10
376	George A. Mogridge	.10
377	Clarence A. Vance	.10
378	James O. Carleton	.10
379	Clyde M. Shoun	.10
380	Franklin W. Hayes	.10
381	Benjamin R. Frey	.10
382	Henry W. Johnson	.10
383	Ralph Kress	.10
384	John T. Allen	.10
385	Harold A. Trosky Sr.	.10
386	Eugene E. Robertson	.10
387	Lemuel F. Young	.10
388	George A. Selkirk	.10
389	Edwin L. Wells	.10
390	James D. Weaver	.10
391	George H. McQuinn	.10
392	John B. Lobert	.10
393	Ernest E. Swanson	.10
394	Ernest A. Nevers	.10
395	James J. Levey	.10
396	Hugo F. Bezdek	.10
397	Walter E. French	.10
398	Charles F. Berry	.10
399	Franklin T. Grube	.10
400	Charles W. Dressen	.10
401	Alfred E. Neale	.10
402	Henry A. Vick	.10
403	James F. Thorpe	.50
404	Walter J. Gilbert	.10
405	John L. Urban	.10
406	Everett V. Purdy	.10
407	Albert O. Wright	.10
408	William M. Urbanski	.10
409	Charles W. Fischer	.10
410	John R. Warner	.10
411	Chalmer W. Cissell	.10
412	Mervin D.J. Shea	.10
413	Adolfo Luque	.10
414	John L. Bassler	.10
415	Arvel O. Hale	.10
416	Lawrence R. French	.10
417	William C. Walker	.10
418	Allen L. Cooke	.10
419	Philip J. Todt	.10
420	Ivy P. Andrews	.10
421	William J. Herman	.10
422	Tristram E. Speaker	.15
423	Aloysius H. Simmons	.10
424	Lewis R. Wilson	.10
425	Tyrus R. Cobb	.40
426	George H. Ruth	.50
427	Ernest N. Lombardi	.15
428	Jay H. Dean	.15
429	Lloyd J. Waner	.15
430	Henry B. Greenberg	.15
431	Robert M. Grove	.15
432	Gordon S. Cochrane	.15
433	Burleigh A. Grimes	.10
434	Harold J. Traynor	.10
435	John R. Mize	.15
436	Edgar C. Rice	.15
437	Leon A. Goslin	.15
438	Charles H. Klein	.10
439	Cornelius Mack	.15
440	James L. Bottomley	.10
441	Jackson R. Stephenson	.10
442	Kenneth Williams	.10
443	Charles B. Adams	.10
444	Joseph J. Jackson	.50
445	Harold Newhouser	.10
446	Wesley C. Ferrell	.10
447	Francis J. O'Doul	.15
448	Walter H. Schang	.10
449	Sherwood R. Magee	.15
450	Michael J. Donlin	.10
451	Roger M. Cramer	.10
452	Richard W. Bartell	.10
453	Earle T. Mack	.15
454	Walter G. Brown	.10
455	John A. Heving	.10
456	Percy L. Jones	.10
457	Theodore Blankenship	.10
458	Absalom H. Wingo	.10
459	Roger P. Bresnahan	.15
460	William J. Klem	.10
461	Charles L. Gehringer	.15
462	Stanley A. Coveleski	.10
463	Edward S. Plank	.10
464	Clark C.F. Griffith	.10
465	Herbert J. Pennock	.10
466	Earle B. Combs	.10
467	Robert P. Doerr	.10
468	Waite C. Hoyt	.10
469	Thomas H. Connolly	.10
470	Harry B. Hooper	.10
471	Richard B. Ferrell	.10
472	William G. Evans	.10
473	William J. Herman	.10
474	William M. Dickey	.15
475	Lucius B. Appling	.15
476	Ralph A. Pinelli	.10
477	Donald E. McNair	.10
478	John F. Blake	.10
479	Valentine J. Picinich	.10
480	Fred A. Heimach	.10
481	John G. Graney	.10
482	Ewell A. Russell	.10

483	Urban C. Faber	.10
484	Benjamin M. Kauff	.10
485	Clarence L. Rowland	.10
486	Robert H. Veach	.10
487	James C. Bagby	.10
488	William D. Perritt	.10
489	Charles L. Herzog	.10
490	Arthur Fletcher	.10
491	Walter H. Holke	.10
492	Arthur N. Nehf	.10
493	Lafayette F. Thompson	.10
494	James D. Welsh	.10
495	Oscar J. Vitt	.10
496	Owen T. Carroll	.10
497	James K. O'Dea	.10
498	Fredrick M. Frankhouse	.10
499	Jewel W. Ens	.10
500	Morris Arnovich	.10
501	Walter Gerber	.10
502	George W. Davis	.10
503	Charles S. Myer	.10
504	Samuel A. Leslie	.10
505	William C. Bolton	.10
506	Fred Walker	.10
507	John W. Smith	.10
508	Irving D. Hadley	.10
509	Clyde E. Crouse	.10
510	Joseph C. Glenn	.10
511	Clyde E. Kimsey	.10
512	Louis K. Finney	.10
513	Alfred V. Lawson	.10
514	Charles P. Fullis	.10
515	Earl H. Sheely	.10
516	George Gibson	.10
517	John J. Broaca	.10
518	Bibb A. Falk	.10
519	Frank O. Hurst	.10
520	Grover A. Hartley	.10
521	Donald H. Heffner	.10
522	Harvey L. Hendrick	.10
523	Allen S. Sothoron	.10
524	Anthony F. Piet	.10
525	Tyrus R. Cobb	.40
526	James E. Foxx	.15
527	Rogers Hornsby	.15
528	Napoleon LaJoie	.15
529	Louis H. Gehrig	.40
530	Henry Zimmerman	.10
531	Charles H. Klein	.10
532	Hugh Duffy	.10
533	Robert M. Grove	.15
534	Grover C. Alexander	.15
535	Amos W. Rusie	.10
536	Vernon L. Gomez	.10
537	William H. Walters	.10
538	Urban J. Hodapp	.10
539	Bruce D. Campbell	.10
540	Horace M. Lisenbee	.10
541	John F. Fournier	.10
542	James R. Tabor	.10
543	John H. Burnett	.10
544	Roy A. Hartzell	.10
545	Walter P. Gautreau	.10
546	Emil O. Yde	.10
547	Robert L. Johnson	.10
548	Joseph J. Hauser	.10
549	Edward M. Reulbach	.10
550	Baldomero M. Almada	.10
551	Gordon S. Cochrane	.15
552	Carl O. Hubbell	.15
553	Charles L. Gehringer	.10
554	Aloysius H. Simmons	.10
555	Mordecai P.C. Brown	.10
556	Hugh A. Jennings	.10
557	Norman A. Elberfeld	.10
558	Charles D. Stengel	.10
559	Alexander Schacht	.10
560	James E. Foxx	.15
561	George L. Kelly	.10
562	Lloyd J. Waner	.10
563	Paul G. Waner	.10
564	Walter P. Johnson	.15
565	John Franklin Baker	.10
566	Roy J. Hughes	.10
567	Lewis S. Riggs	.10
568	John H. Whitehead	.10
569	Elam R. Vangilder	.10
570	William A. Zitzmann	.10
571	Walter J. Schmidt	.10
572	John A. Tavener	.10
573	Joseph E. Genewich	.10
574	John A. Marcum	.10
575	Fred Hofmann	.10
576	Robert A. Rolfe	.10
577	Victor G. Sorrell	.10
578	Floyd J. Scott	.10
579	Alphonse Thomas	.10
580	Alfred J. Smith	.10
581	Walter J. Henline	.10
582	Edward T. Collins	.10
583	Earle B. Combs	.10
584	John J. McGraw	.10
585	Lewis R. Wilson	.10
586	Charles L. Hartnett	.10
587	Hazen S. Cuyler	.10
588	William H. Terry	.10
589	Joseph V. McCarthy	.10
590	Henry B. Greenberg	.10
591	Tristram E. Speaker	.10
592	William B. McKechnie	.10
593	Stanley R. Harris	.10
594	Herbert J. Pennock	.10
595	George H. Sisler	.10
596	Fred C. Lindstrom	.10
597	Howard E. Averill Sr.	.10
598	David J. Bancroft	.10
599	Cornelius Mack	.10
600	Joseph E. Cronin	.10

601	Kenneth L. Ash	.10
602	Alfred R. Spohrer	.10
603	Lee R. Mahaffey	.10
604	James F. O'Rourke	.10
605	Ulysses S.G. Stoner	.10
606	Frank H. Gabler	.10
607	Thomas F. Padden	.10
608	Charles A. Shires	.10
609	Sherrod M. Smith	.10
610	Philip Weintraub	.10
611	Russell Van Atta	.10
612	Joyner C. White	.10
613	Clifford G. Melton	.10
614	James J. Ring	.10
615	John H. Sand	.10
616	David D. Alexander	.10
617	Kent Greenfield	.10
618	Edwin H. Dyer	.10
619	William H. Sherdel	.10
620	Hubert M. Lanier	.10
621	Robert A. O'Farrell	.10
622	Rogers Hornsby	.15
623	William A. Beckman	.10
624	Morton C. Cooper	.10
625	William P. Delancey	.10
626	Martin W. Marion	.10
627	William H. Southworth	.10
628	John R. Mize	.10
629	Joseph M. Medwick	.10
630	Grover C. Alexander	.10
631	Paul D. Dean	.10
632	Herman S. Bell	.10
633	William W. Cooper	.10
634	Frank F. Frisch	.10
635	Jay H. Dean	.10
636	Donald J. Gutteridge	.10
637	Johnny L.R. Martin	.10
638	Edward J. Konetchy	.10
639	William A. Hallahan	.10
640	Lonnie Warneke	.10
641	Terry B. Moore	.10
642	Enos B. Slaughter	.10
643	Clarence F. Mueller	.10
644	George Toporcer	.10
645	James L. Bottomely	.10
646	Francis R. Blades	.10
647	Jesse J. Haines	.10
648	Andrew A. High	.10
649	Miller J. Huggins	.10
650	Ernesto R. Orsatti	.10
651	Lester R. Bell	.10
652	Charles E. Street	.10
653	Walter H. Roettger	.10
654	Sylvester W. Johnson	.10
655	Miguel A. Gonzalez	.10
656	James A. Collins	.10
657	Charles J. Hafey	.10
658	Checklist 331-440	.10
659	Checklist 441-550	.10
660	Checklist 551-660	.10

1992-94 Conlon Collection Gold

FRANKIE FRISCH
NATIONAL LEAGUE - 2ND BASE 1933

Four of the heroes of the inaugural All-Star Game of 1933 were featured in a pop-up ad in the program for the 1992 Game in San Diego. One card was inserted into each of the programs printed for distribution at the game and by mail order. Each card was reported printed in an edition of 34,000. Cards are similar in format to the regular Conlon Collection issues except for the gold-foil border around the player photo on front and the use of a "G" suffix to the card number. A banner at top front reads, "Game of the Century." On back is a summary of the player's 1933 All-Star performance and his stats. Gold editions of other Conlon cards were also issued in several different venues in 1993-94. Six cards (#665-880) were included in 1992 Conlon factory sets in editions of up to 90,000. The Johnson-Ryan gold card was available only in

packaging sold in Eckerd stores, while the 1994 Cobb gold card was only available at Toys R Us. Cards are numbered with a "G" suffix.

		NM/M
Complete Set (12):		50.00
Common Player:		2.00
661	Bill Terry	2.00
662	Lefty Gomez	2.00
663	Babe Ruth	12.00
664	Frankie Frisch	2.00
665	Carl Hubbell	2.00
667	Charlie Gehringer (Edition of 20,000.)	4.00
730	Luke Appling (Edition of 20,000.)	4.00
770	Tommy Henrich	2.00
820	John McGraw	2.00
880	Gabby Hartnett	2.00
934	Walter Johnson, Nolan Ryan (Edition of 100,000.)	12.00
1000	Ty Cobb (Edition of 100,000.)	6.00

1992 Conlon Collection 13th National

These samples of the 1993 Conlon Collection series were distributed at the National Sports Collectors Convention in Atlanta in 1992. Other than the Joe Jackson card, they carry the same numbers as the regularly issued versions. Designs are also identical except for the overprint on back in outline letters, "13TH NATIONAL."

		NM/M
Complete Set (4):		4.00
Common Player:		.50
14	Joe Jackson	1.00
663	George H. Ruth	2.00
775	John T. Meyers	.50
800	James L. Vaughn	.50

1993 Conlon Collection Prototypes

RED FABER
CHICAGO WHITE SOX - PITCHER 1932

The cards in this issue were produced to preview the basic set and various subsets of the 1993 Conlon Collection issue. Cards are similar to the regular-issue set with the exception that the word "PROTOTYPE" is printed in gray diagonally on back. Production of most of the black-and-white cards was 60,000, though Gomez and Frisch were limited to 10,000 apiece. Three of the cards can be found with "All Star FanFest" notations on back, having been distributed as samples there.

		NM/M
Complete Set (8):		3.00
Common Player:		1.00
661	Bill Terry	1.00
661	Bill Terry (All Star FanFest)	2.00
662	Lefty Gomez	1.00
663	Babe Ruth	6.00
664	Frankie Frisch	1.00
710	Red Faber	1.00
710	Red Faber (All Star FanFest)	2.00
775	Chief Meyers	1.00
800	Hippo Vaughn	1.00
888	Babe Ruth (Colorized, edition of 52,000.)	5.00
905	Lena Blackburne	1.00

905	Lena Blackbourne (All Star FanFest)	2.00
934	Walter Johnson, Nolan Ryan (Colorized edition of 52,000.)	4.00

1993 Conlon Collection

WALTER JOHNSON
HURLER OF THE UNSEEN FASTBALL 1927

The third annual Conlon Collection issue of 330 cards is numbered 661-990, a continuation of the series produced in 1991-92. The format of black-and-white photos produced 50-90 years ago by Charles Martin Conlon and surrounded by a wide black border and UV coating was continued. As with earlier issues, card backs contain brief biographical data, a few stats and well-written career highlights. The 1993 set also featured many subsets arranged by topic, such as spitballers, native Americans, players who overcame handicaps, etc. One subset compared Nolan Ryan with star pitchers in baseball history and included a fantasy photo of Ryan shaking hands in the dugout with Walter Johnson (card #934).

		NM/M
Complete Set in Commemorative Tin:		20.00
Complete Set (330):		15.00
Common Player:		.10
Wax Pack:		.50
Wax Box (36):		15.00
661	William H. Terry	.10
662	Vernon L. Gomez	.10
663	George H. Ruth	.50
664	Frank F. Frisch	.10
665	Carl O. Hubbell	.10
666	Aloysius H. Simmons	.15
667	Charles L. Gehringer	.15
668	Howard E. Averill Sr.	.15
669	Robert M. Grove	.15
670	Harold J. Traynor	.15
671	Charles H. Klein	.15
672	Paul G. Waner	.15
673	Louis H. Gehrig	.40
674	Richard B. Ferrell	.10
675	Charles L. Hartnett	.10
676	Joseph E. Cronin	.15
677	Charles J. Hafey	.10
678	James J. Dykes	.10
679	Samuel F. West	.10
680	Johnny L.R. Martin	.10
681	Francis J. O'Doul	.10
682	Alvin F. Crowder	.10
683	James Wilson	.10
684	Richard W. Bartell	.10
685	William A. Hallahan	.10
686	Walter A. Berger	.10
687	Lonnie Warneke	.10
688	William B. Chapman	.10
689	Elwood G. English	.10
690	James H. Reese	.10
691	Roscoe A. Holm	.10
692	Charles D. Jamieson	.10
693	Jonathan T.W. Zachary	.10
694	John C. Ryan	.10
695	Earl J. Adams	.10
696	William E. Hunnefield	.10
697	Henry L. Meadows	.10
698	Thomas F. Carey	.10
699	John W. Rawlings	.10
700	Kenneth E. Holloway	.10
701	Lance C. Richbourg	.10
702	Raymond L. Fisher	.10
703	Edward Augustine Walsh	.10
704	Richard Rudolph	.10
705	Raymond B. Caldwell	.10
706	Burleigh A. Grimes	.10
707	Stanley A. Coveleski	.10
708	George A. Hildebrand	.10
709	John P. Quinn	.10
710	Urban C. Faber	.10
711	Urban J. Shocker	.10

712	Hubert B. Leonard	.10
713	Louis L. Koupal	.10
714	James C. Wasdell	.10
715	John H. Lindell	.10
716	Don W. Padgett	.10
717	Nelson T. Potter	.10
718	Lynwood T. Rowe	.10
719	David C. Danforth	.10
720	Claude W. Passeau	.10
721	Harry L. Kelley	.10
722	John T. Allen	.10
723	Thomas J.D. Bridges	.10
724	William C. Lee	.10
725	Fredrick M. Frankhouse	.10
726	John J. McCarthy	.10
727	Glen D. Russell	.10
728	Emory E. Rigney	.10
729	Howard S. Shanks	.10
730	Lucius B. Appling	.10
731	William J. Byron	.10
732	Earle B. Combs	.10
733	Henry B. Greenberg	.15
734	Walter W. Beck	.10
735	Hollis J. Thurston	.10
736	Lewis R. Wilson	.10
737	William A. McGowan	.10
738	Henry J. Bonura	.10
739	Thomas C. Baker	.10
740	William C. Jacobson	.10
741	Hazen S. Cuyler	.10
742	George F. Blaeholder	.10
743	Wilson D. Miles	.10
744	Lee E. Handley	.10
745	John F. Collins	.10
746	Wilfred P. Ryan	.10
747	Aaron L. Ward	.10
748	Montgomery M. Pearson	.10
749	Jacob W. Early	.10
750	William F. Atwood	.10
751	Mark A. Koenig	.10
752	John A. Hassett	.10
753	David J. Jones	.10
754	John P. Wagner	.25
755	William M. Dickey	.15
756	Albert M. Butcher	.10
757	Waite C. Hoyt	.10
758	Walter P. Johnson	.15
759	Howard J. Ehmke	.10
760	Norman L. Newsom	.10
761	Anthony M. Lazzeri	.10
762	Anthony M. Lazzeri	.10
763	Spurgeon F. Chandler	.10
764	Walter K. Higbe	.10
765	Paul R. Richards	.10
766	Rogers Hornsby	.15
767	Joseph F. Vosmik	.10
768	Jesse J. Haines	.10
769	William H. Walters	.10
770	Thomas D. Henrich	.10
771	James F. Thorpe	.40
772	Euel W. Moore	.10
773	Rudolph P. York	.10
774	Charles A. Bender	.10
775	John T. Meyers	.10
776	Robert L. Johnson	.10
777	Roy C. Johnson	.10
778	Richard T. Porter	.10
779	Ethan N. Allen	.10
780	Harry F. Sallee	.10
781	Roy C. Bell	.10
782	Arnold J. Statz	.10
783	Frank J. Henry	.10
784	Charles L. Woodall	.10
785	Philip E. Collins	.10
786	Joseph W. Sewell	.10
787	William J. Herman	.10
788	Rueben H. Oldring	.10
789	William H. Walker	.10
790	Joseph C. Schultz	.10
791	Fred E. Maguire	.10
792	Claude W. Willoughby	.10
793	James A. Ferguson	.10
794	John D. Morrison	.10
795	Tristram E. Speaker	.15
796	Tyrus R. Cobb	.40
797	Max Carey	.10
798	George H. Sisler	.10
799	Charles J. Hollocher	.10
800	James L. Vaughn	.10
801	Samuel P. Jones	.10
802	Harry B. Hooper	.10
803	Clifford C. Cravath	.10
804	Walter P. Johnson	.15
805	Jacob E. Daubert	.10
806	Jesse C. Milan	.10
807	Hugh A. McQuillan	.10
808	George F. Brickell	.10
809	Joseph V. Stripp	.10
810	Urban J. Hodapp	.10
811	John L. Vergez	.10
812	Linus R. Frey	.10
813	William W. Regan	.10
814	Norman R. Young	.10
815	Charles C. Robertson	.10
816	Walter F. Judnich	.10
817	Joseph B. Tinker	.15
818	John Evers	.15
819	Frank L. Chance	.15
820	John J. McGraw	.10
821	Charles J. Grimm	.10
822	Ted Lyons	.10
823	Joe McCarthy	.10
824	Connie Mack	.10
825	George Gibson	.10
826	Steve O'Neill	.10
827	Tristram E. Speaker	.15
828	William F. Carrigan	.10

829	Charles D. Stengel	.15
830	Miller J. Huggins	.10
831	William B. McKechnie	.10
832	Charles W. Dressen	.10
833	Charles E. Street	.10
834	Melvin T. Ott	.15
835	Frank F. Frisch	.10
836	George H. Sisler	.10
837	Napoleon LaJoie	.10
838	Tyrus R. Cobb	.40
839	William H. Southworth	.10
840	Clark C.F. Griffith	.10
841	William H. Terry	.10
842	Rogers Hornsby	.10
843	Joseph E. Cronin	.10
844	Alfonso R. Lopez	.10
845	Stanley R. Harris	.10
846	Wilbert Robinson	.10
847	Hugh A. Jennings	.10
848	James J. Dykes	.10
849	Roy J. Cullenbine	.10
850	Graham E. Moore	.10
851	John H. Rothrock	.10
852	William H. Lamar	.10
853	Monte Weaver	.10
854	Ival R. Goodman	.10
855	Henry L. Severeid	.10
856	Fred G. Haney	.10
857	Joseph B. Shaute	.10
858	Smead P. Jolley	.10
859	Edwin D. Williams	.10
860	Bernard O. Bengough	.10
861	Richard B. Ferrell	.10
862	Robert A. O'Farrell	.10
863	Virgil L. Davis	.10
864	Franklin W. Hayes	.10
865	Herold D. Ruel	.10
866	Gordon S. Cochrane	.10
867	John Kling	.10
868	Ivy B. Wingo	.10
869	William M. Dickey	.15
870	Frank E. Snyder	.10
871	Roger P. Bresnahan	.10
872	Walter H. Schang	.10
873	Alfonso R. Lopez	.10
874	James Wilson	.10
875	Valentine J. Picinich	.10
876	Stephen F. O'Neill	.10
877	Ernest N. Lombardi	.10
878	John L. Bassler	.10
879	Raymond W. Schalk	.10
880	Charles L. Hartnett	.10
881	Bruce D. Campbell	.10
882	Charles H. Ruffing	.10
883	Mordecai P.C. Brown	.10
884	Peter J. Archer	.10
885	David E. Keefe	.10
886	Nathan H. Andrews	.10
887	Edgar C. Rice	.10
888	George H. Ruth	.50
889	Charles J. Hafey	.10
890	Oscar D. Melillo	.10
891	Joe Wood	.10
892	John J. Evers	.10
893	George Toporcer	.10
894	Myril O. Hoag	.10
895	Robert G. Weiland	.10
896	Joseph A. Marty	.10
897	Sherwood R. Magee	.10
898	Daniel T. Taylor	.10
899	William E. Kamm	.10
900	Samuel J.T. Sheckard	.10
901	Sylvester W. Johnson	.10
902	Stephen R. Sundra	.10
903	Roger M. Cramer	.10
904	Hubert S. Pruett	.10
905	Russell A. Blackburne	.10
906	Eppa Rixey	.10
907	Leon A. Goslin	.10
908	George L. Kelly	.10
909	James L. Bottomley	.10
910	Christopher Mathewson	.15
911	Anthony M. Lazzeri	.10
912	John A. Mostil	.10
913	Robert P. Doerr	.10
914	Walter J.V. Maranville	.10
915	Harry E. Heilmann	.10
916	Rodrick J. Wallace	.10
917	James E. Foxx	.15
918	John R. Mize	.10
919	John N. Bentley	.10
920	Alexander Schacht	.10
921	Parke E. Coleman	.10
922	George H. Paskert	.10
923	Horace H. Ford	.10
924	Randolph E. Moore	.10
925	Milburn J. Shoffner	.10
926	Richard W. Siebert	.10
927	Anthony C. Kaufmann	.10
928	Jay H. Dean, Nolan Ryan	.25
929	Clarence A. Vance, Nolan Ryan	.25
930	Robert M. Grove, Nolan Ryan	.25
931	George E. Waddell, Nolan Ryan	.25
932	Grover C. Alexander, Nolan Ryan	.25
933	Robert W.A. Feller, Nolan Ryan	.50
934	Walter P. Johnson, Nolan Ryan	.50
935	Theodore A. Lyons, Nolan Ryan	.25
936	James C. Bagby	.10
937	Joseph Sugden	.10
938	Robert E. Grace	.10

939	John G. Heath	.10
940	Kenneth Williams	.10
941	Marvin J. Owen	.10
942	Cyril R. Weatherly	.10
943	Edward C. Morgan	.10
944	John C. Rizzo	.10
945	Archie R. McKain	.10
946	Robert M. Garbark	.10
947	John B. Osborn	.10
948	John S. Podgajny	.10
949	Joseph P. Evans	.10
950	George A. Rensa	.10
951	John H. Humphries	.10
952	Merritt P. Cain	.10
953	Roy E. Hansen	.10
954	John A. Niggeling	.10
955	Harold J. Wiltse	.10
956	Alejandro A.A.E. Carrasquel	.10
957	George A. Grant	.10
958	Philip W. Weinert	.10
959	Ervin B. Brame	.10
960	Raymond J. Harrell	.10
961	Edward K. Linke	.10
962	Samuel B. Gibson	.10
963	John C. Watwood	.10
964	James T. Prothro	.10
965	Julio G. Bonetti	.10
966	Howard R. Mills	.10
967	Clarence E. Galloway	.10
968	Harold J. Kelleher	.10
969	Elon C. Hogsett	.10
970	Edward B. Heusser	.10
971	Edward J. Baecht	.10
972	Otto H. Saltzgaver	.10
973	Leroy G. Herrmann	.10
974	Beveric B. Bean	.10
975	Harry Seibold	.10
976	Howard V. Keen	.10
977	William J. Barrett	.10
978	Patrick H. McNulty	.10
979	George E. Turbeville	.10
980	Edward D. Phillips	.10
981	Garland M. Buckeye	.10
982	Victor P. Frasier	.10
983	John G. Rhodes	.10
984	Emile D. Barnes	.10
985	James C. Edwards	.10
986	Herschel E. Bennett	.10
987	Carmen P. Hill	.10
988	Checklist 661-770	.10
989	Checklist 771-880	.10
990	Checklist 881-990	.10

1993-95 Conlon Collection Color

The cards in this set were previously released in black-and-white in regular 1991-94 Conlon sets. Cards 1-12 were issued as bonus cards in Megacards accessory items; 250,000 of each were produced. Cards 13-20 were randomly inserted in 1993 Conlon counter and blister packs; 100,000 of those were produced. Cards 21-22, in an edition of 75,000, were only available through a send-away offer. Card 23 was available exclusively as an insert in the 7th Edition SCD Baseball Card Price Guide, in an edition of 60,000. Cards 24-39 were issued in 1994. Numbers 24-28 were random inserts printed to the number of 84,000 apiece. Cards 29-30 were a send-away premium; #31-33 were hobby foil inserts. All were issued in quantities of 12,000. Cards 34-37 - 48,000 of each - were a Toys R Us exclusive insert. Cards 38-39 were special-offer premiums. A special printing of 24,000 of #28 were issued with a "Conlon Collection Day" overprint

on back and were distributed at the Sept. 11, 1994, St. Louis Cardinals game.

		NM/M
Complete Set (47):		100.00
Common Player:		2.00
1	Sunny Jim Bottomley	2.00
2	Lefty Grove	10.00
3	Lou Gehrig	10.00
4	Babe Ruth	10.00
5	Casey Stengel	3.00
6	Rube Marquard	3.00
7	Walter Johnson	3.00
8	Lou Gehrig	5.00
9	Christy Mathewson	3.00
10	Ty Cobb	5.00
11	Mel Ott	2.00
12	Carl Hubbell	2.00
13	Al Simmons	2.00
14	Connie Mack	2.00
15	Grover C. Alexander	2.00
16	Jimmie Foxx	3.00
17	Lloyd Waner	2.00
18	Tris Speaker	4.00
19	Dizzy Dean	5.00
20	Rogers Hornsby	3.00
21	Shoeless Joe Jackson	7.50
22	Jim Thorpe	7.50
23	Bob Feller	8.00
24	Hal Newhouser	2.00
25	Hughie Jennings	2.00
26	Red Faber	2.00
27	Enos Slaughter	2.00
28	Johnny Mize	2.00
28CCD	Johnny Mize	4.00
29	Pie Traynor	2.00
30	Walter Johnson, Nolan Ryan	4.00
31	Lou Gehrig	2.00
32	Benny Bengough	2.00
33	Babe Ruth	2.00
34	Charlie Gehringer	2.00
35	Babe Ruth	2.00
36	Bill Dickey	2.00
37	Mordecai Brown	2.00
38	Ray Schalk	4.00
39	Home Run Baker	5.00
40	Frank Frisch	2.00
41	Hack Wilson	2.00
42	Ty Cobb	6.00
43	Honus Wagner	4.00
44	John McGraw	2.00
45	Reds vs. Giants	2.00
46	Indians vs. Yanks	2.00
47	Babe Ruth	12.00

1993 Conlon Collection Master Series

"The Best There Was" was the subtitle on this portfolio of oversized (10" x 8") cards produced from the photos of Charles Martin Conlon. On the high-gloss card fronts, a wide black border surrounds the black-and-white photo, with a gold-foil pinstripe border between the two. The player's name appears in gold at the bottom. Backs are printed in black-and-white and feature a large player portrait, complete major league stats and a career summary. A serial numbered certificate placing the set within an edition of 25,000 was included with the set; a deluxe portfolio album to house the collection was available for $10.

		NM/M
Complete Set (9):		15.00
Common Player:		1.50
1	Title card	.50
2	Babe Ruth	6.00
3	Lou Gehrig, Walter Johnson	4.00
4	Honus Wagner	3.00
5	Mickey Cochrane	1.50
6	Tris Speaker	1.50
7	Ty Cobb	4.00
8	Rogers Hornsby	1.50
9	Pie Traynor	1.50

1993 Conlon Collection Color Masters

Some of the premier photography of Charles Martin Conlon was computer color-enhanced and placed on these oversized (10" x 8") cards in a special edition of 25,000. High-gloss fronts feature the colorized photos separated by a thin white pinstripe from the dark blue background. Backs are printed in black and blue on white and feature a career summary or other historical data, along with a description of the front photo. A serially numbered certificate of authenticity accompanied the set and could be redeemed, along with $10, for a deluxe portfolio to house the collection.

		NM/M
Complete Set (9):		15.00
Common Player:		1.50
1	Title card	.50
2	Napoleon Lajoie	1.50
3	Walter Johnson, Nolan Ryan (Fantasy photo.)	6.00
4	Action at Hilltop Park	.50
5	Babe Ruth	6.00
6	Frank Baker	1.50
7	John McGraw	1.50
8	John McGraw, Wilbert Robinson, Christy Mathewson	1.50
9	Hughie Jennings	1.50

1994 Conlon Collection Prototypes

A large gray "PROTOTYPE" overprint on back identifies these cards as sample of the fourth annual edition of Conlon Collection cards by Megacards. Cards carry the same number as issued versions. It was reported that 26,000 prototypes were issued of Martin, Traynor, Hubbell, Klem and Koenig; while 52,000 each were issued of Jackson and the Deans.

		NM/M
Complete Set (8):		8.00
Common Player		1.00
991	Pepper Martin	1.00
1030	Joe Jackson	3.00
1050	Pie Traynor	1.00
1105	Carl Hubbell	1.00
1140	Lefty Grove	1.00
1170	Dizzy Dean, Paul Dean	1.50
1190	Bill Klem	1.00
1230	Mark Koenig	1.00

1994 Conlon Collection

DAFFY & DIZZY DEAN

The production of "old-timers" cards based on the baseball photography of Charles M. Conlon from the

1910s through the 1930s continued into a fourth year in 1994 with another 330-card series, numbered 991-1320. Once again the format of previous years was continued. Subsets included the 1919 Chicago White Sox, major league brothers and action photos.

		NM/M
Complete Set in Commemorative Tin:		40.00
Complete Set (330):		30.00
Common Player:		.10
Wax Box (36):		40.00
991	Johnny L.R. Martin	.10
992	Joseph W. Sewell	.10
993	Edd J. Roush	.10
994	Richard B. Ferrell	.10
995	John J. Broaca	.10
996	James L. Sewell	.10
997	Burleigh A. Grimes	.10
998	Lewis R. Wilson	.10
999	Robert M. Grove	.15
1000	Tyrus R. Cobb	.40
1001	John J. McGraw	.10
1002	Edward S. Plank	.10
1003	Samuel P. Jones	.10
1004	James L. Bottomley	.10
1005	Henry B. Greenberg	.15
1006	Lloyd J. Waner	.10
1007	William W. Moore	.10
1008	Lucius B. Appling	.10
1009	Harold Newhouser	.10
1010	Alfonso R. Lopez	.10
1011	Tyrus R. Cobb	.40
1012	Charles A. Nichols	.10
1013	Edward Augustine Walsh	.10
1014	Hugh Duffy	.10
1015	Richard W. Marquard	.10
1016	Adrian Joss	.10
1017	Rodrick J. Wallace	.10
1018	William H. Keeler	.10
1019	Jacob E. Daubert	.10
1020	Harry F. Sallee	.10
1021	Adolfo Luque	.10
1022	Ivy B. Wingo	.10
1023	Edd J. Roush	.10
1024	William A. Rariden	.10
1025	Sherwood R. Magee	.10
1026	Louis B. Duncan	.10
1027	Horace O. Eller	.10
1028	Alfred E. Neale	.10
1029	George D. Weaver	.10
1030	Joseph J. Jackson	.50
1031	Arnold Gandil	.10
1032	Charles A. Risberg	.10
1033	Raymond W. Schalk	.10
1034	Edward V. Cicotte	.10
1035	William H. James	.10
1036	Harry L. Leibold	.10
1037	Richard H. Kerr	.10
1038	William J. Jackson	.10
1039	Frederick W. McMullin (Middle initial actually "D.")	.10
1040	Edward T. Collins	.10
1041	Sox Pitchers (Lefty Williams, Bill James, Ed Cicotte, Dicky Kerr)	.10
1042	Sox Outfielders (Nemo Leibold, Happy Felsch, Shano Collins)	.10
1043	Kenneth F. Keltner	.10
1044	Charles F. Berry	.10
1045	Walter J. Lutzke	.10
1046	John C. Schulte	.10
1047	John V. Welch	.10
1048	Jack E. Russell	.10
1049	John J. Murray	.10
1050	Harold J. Traynor	.10
1051	Michael J. Donlin	.10
1052	Charles L. Hartnett	.10
1053	Anthony M. Lazzeri	.10
1054	Lawrence H. Miller	.10
1055	Clarence A. Vance	.10
1056	Williams F. Carrigan	.10
1057	John J. Murphy	.10
1058	Clifton E Heathcote	.10
1059	Joseph A. Dugan	.10
1060	Walter J.V. Maranville	.10
1061	Thomas D. Henrich	.10
1062	Leroy E. Parmelee	.10
1063	Vernon L. Gomez	.10
1064	Ernest N. Lombardi	.10
1065	David J. Bancroft	.10
1066	William B. McKechnie	.10
1067	John A. Hassett	.10
1068	Spurgeon F. Chandler	.10
1069	Roy J. Hughes	.10
1070	George A. Dauss	.10
1071	Joseph J. Hauser	.10
1072	Virgil L. Davis	.10
1073	Albert M. Butcher	.10
1074	Louis P. Chiozza	.10
1075	Center Field Bleachers	.10
1076	Charles L. Gehringer	.10
1077	Henry E. Manush	.10
1078	Charles H. Ruffing	.10
1079	Melvin H. Harder	.10
1080	George H. Ruth	.50
1081	William B. Chapman	.10
1082	Louis H. Gehrig	.40

1083	James E. Foxx	.15
1084	Aloysius H. Simmons	.10
1085	Joseph E. Cronin	.10
1086	William M. Dickey	.15
1087	Gordon S. Cochrane	.10
1088	Vernon L. Gomez	.10
1089	Howard E. Averill Sr.	.10
1090	Samuel F. West	.10
1091	Frank F. Frisch	.10
1092	William J. Herman	.10
1093	Harold J. Traynor	.10
1094	Joseph M. Medwick	.10
1095	Charles H. Klein	.10
1096	Hazen S. Cuyler	.10
1097	Melvin T. Ott	.15
1098	Walter T. Berger	.10
1099	Paul G. Waner	.10
1100	William H. Terry	.10
1101	Travis C. Jackson	.10
1102	Joseph F. Vaughan	.10
1103	Charles L. Hartnett	.10
1104	Alfonso R. Lopez	.10
1105	Carl O. Hubbell	.15
1106	Lonnie Warneke	.10
1107	Van L. Mungo	.10
1108	Johnny J.R. Martin	.10
1109	Jay H. Dean	.15
1110	Fredrick M. Frankhouse	.10
1111	Giullaedeau Spink Heydler	
1112	JG Taylor Spink/ Mrs. Spink	.10
1113	Hirchman, Keller	.10
1114	Victor E. Aldridge	.10
1115	Michael F. Higgins	.10
1116	Harold E. Carlson	.10
1117	Frederick L. Fitzsimmons	
1118	William H. Walters	.10
1119	Nicholas Altrock	.10
1120	Charles W. Dressen	.10
1121	Mark A. Koenig	.10
1122	Charles L. Gehringer	.10
1123	Lloyd V. Kennedy	.10
1124	Harlond B. Clift	.10
1125	Ernest G. Phelps	.10
1126	John R. Mize	.15
1127	Harold H. Schumacher	.10
1128	Ethan N. Allen	.10
1129	William A. Wambsganss	.10
1130	Frederick Leach	.10
1131	John W. Clancy	.10
1132	John F. Stewart	.10
1133	Wilbur L. Brubaker	.10
1134	Leslie Mann	.10
1135	Howard J. Ehmke	.10
1136	Aloysius H. Simmons	.10
1137	George L. Earnshaw	.10
1138	George W. Haas	.10
1139	Edmund J. Miller	.10
1140	Robert M. Grove	.15
1141	John P. Boley	.10
1142	Edward T. Collins Sr.	.10
1143	Walter E. French	.10
1144	Donald E. McNair	.10
1145	William D. Shores	.10
1146	Gordon S. Cochrane	.10
1147	Homer W. Summa	.10
1148	John P. Quinn	.10
1149	Max F. Bishop	.10
1150	James J. Dykes	.10
1151	George E. Walberg	.10
1152	James E. Foxx	.15
1153	George H. Burns	.10
1154	Roger M. Cramer	.10
1155	Samuel D. Hale	.10
1156	Edwin A. Rommel	.10
1157	Ralph F. Perkins	.10
1158	James J. Cronin	.10
1159	Cornelius Mack	.10
1160	Raymond C. Kolp	.10
1161	Clyde J. Manion	.10
1162	Franklin T. Grube	.10
1163	Stephen A. Swetonic	.10
1164	Joseph B. Tinker	.10
1165	John J. Evers	.10
1166	Frank L. Chance	.10
1167	Emerson Dickman	.10
1168	John T. Tobin	.10
1169	Wesley C. Ferrell	.10
1170	Jay H. Dean	.15
1171	Tony & Al Cuccinello (Tony Cuccinello, Al Cuccinello)	.10
1172	Harry Coveleski, Stan Coveleski	
1173	Bob Johnson, Roy Johnson	
1174	Andy & Hugh High	.10
1175	Joe Sewell, Luke Sewell	
1176	Joe Heving, John Heving	
1177	Ab & Ivy Wingo	.10
1178	Wade Killefer, Bill Killefer	.10
1179	Bubbles Hargrave, Pinky Hargrave	
1180	Paul Waner, Lloyd Waner	
1181	John S. Vander Meer	.10
1182	Joe G. Moore	.10
1183	Robert J. Burke	.10
1184	John F. Moore	.10
1185	John J. Egan	.10
1186	Thomas H. Connolly	.15
1187	Frank H. O'Loughlin	.10

1188	John E. Reardon	.10
1189	Charles B. Moran	.10
1190	William J. Klem	.10
1191	Albert D. Stark	.10
1192	Albert L. Orth	.10
1193	William E. Bransfield	.10
1194	Roy Van Graflan	.10
1195	Eugene F. Hart	.10
1196	John B. Conlan	.10
1197	Ralph A. Pinelli	.10
1198	John F. Sheridan	.10
1199	Richard F. Nallin	.10
1200	William H. Dineen	.10
1201	Henry F. O'Day	.10
1202	Charles Rigler	.10
1203	Robert D. Emslie	.10
1204	Charles H. Pfirman	.10
1205	Harry C. Geisel	.10
1206	Ernest C. Quigley	.10
1207	Emmett T. Ormsby	.10
1208	George A. Hildebrand	.10
1209	George J. Moriarty	.10
1210	William G. Evans	.10
1211	Clarence B. Owens	.10
1212	William A. McGowan	.10
1213	Walter K. Higbe	.10
1214	Taylor L. Douthit	.10
1215	Delmar D. Baker	.10
1216	Albert W. Demaree	.10
1217	Cornelius Mack	.10
1218	Napoleon Lajoie	.15
1219	John P. Wagner	.25
1220	Christopher Mathewson	.15
1221	Samuel E. Crawford	.10
1222	Tristram E. Speaker	.15
1223	Grover C. Alexander	.15
1224	Joseph E. Bowman	.10
1225	John D. Rigney	.10
1226	William E. Webb	.10
1227	Lloyd A. Moore	.10
1228	Bruce D. Campbell	.10
1229	Luzerne A. Blue	.10
1230	Mark A. Koenig	.10
1231	Walter H. Schang	.10
1232	Max Carey	.10
1233	Frank F. Frisch	.10
1234	Owen J. Bush	.10
1235	Goerge S. Davis	.10
1236	William G. Rogell	.10
1237	James A. Collins	.10
1238	Mauricel L. Burrus	.10
1239	Ernest E. Swanson	.10
1240	Elwood G. English	.10
1241	Joseph Harris	.10
1242	Harry H. McCurdy	.10
1243	Richard W. Bartell	.10
1244	Rupert L. Thompson	.10
1245	Charles B. Adams	.10
1246	Arthur N. Nehf	.10
1247	John G. Graney	.10
1248	Theodore A. Lyons	.10
1249	Louis H. Gehrig	.40
1250	Michael F. Welch	.10
1251	Urban C. Faber	.10
1252	Joseph J. McGinnity	.10
1253	Rogers Hornsby	.15
1254	Melvin T. Ott	.15
1255	Walter P. Johnson	.15
1256	Edgar C. Rice	.10
1257	James A. Tobin	.10
1258	Roger T. Peckinpaugh	.10
1259	George T. Stovall	.10
1260	Fredrick C. Merkle	.10
1261	Harry W. Collins	.10
1262	Henry C. Lind	.10
1263	George N. Rucker	.10
1264	Hollis J. Thurston	.10
1265	Alexander Metzler	.10
1266	Charles Martin Conlon	.10
1267	McCarty Gets Magee (Lew McCarty, Lee Magee)	.10
1268	Sliding Home	.10
1269	Kauff Safe at 3rd (Benny Kauff)	.10
1270	Groh Out at 3rd (Heine Groh)	.10
1271	Mollwitz Out at the Plate (Fred Mollwitz)	.10
1272	Burns Safe at Home	.10
1273	Lee Magee Out Stealing 3rd (Lee Magee)	.10
1274	Killefer Out at Plate (Bill Killefer)	.10
1275	John M. Warhop	.10
1276	Emil J. Leonard	.10
1277	Alvin F. Crowder	.10
1278	Chester P. Laabs	.10
1279	Leslie A. Bush	.10
1280	Raymond B. Bréssler	.10
1281	Robret M. Brown	.10
1282	Bernard Deviveiros	.10
1283	Leslie W. Tietje	.10
1284	Charles Devens	.10
1285	Elliott A. Bigelow	.10
1286	John O. Dickshot	.10
1287	Charles L. Chatham	.10
1288	Walter E. Beall	.10
1289	Richard D. Attreau	.10
1290	Anthony V. Brief	.10
1291	James J. Gleason	.10
1292	Walter D. Shaner	.10
1293	Clifford R. Crawford	.10
1294	Manuel Salvo	.10
1295	Calvin L. Dorsett	.10
1296	Russell D. Peters	.10
1297	John D. Couch	.10

1298	Frank W. Ulrich	.10
1299	James M. Bivin	.10
1300	Paul E. Strand	.10
1301	John Y. Lanning	.10
1302	William R. Brenzel	.10
1303	Don Songer	.10
1304	Emil H. Levsen	.10
1305	Otto A. Bluege	.10
1306	Fabian S. Gaffke	.10
1307	Maurice J. Archdeacon	.10
1308	James B. Chaplin	.10
1309	Lawrence J. Rosenthal	.10
1310	William M. Bagwell	.10
1311	Ralph F. Dawson	.10
1312	John P.J. Sturm	.10
1313	Haskell C. Billings	.10
1314	Vernon S. Wilshere	.10
1315	Robert A. Asbjornson	.10
1316	Henry J. Steinbacher	.10
1317	Stanwood F. Baumgartner	.10
1318	Checklist 991-1100	.10
1319	Checklist 1101-1210	.10
1320	Checklist 1211-1320	.10

1994 Conlon Collection Burgundy

A parallel version of the 1994 Conlon series with burgundy, rather than black, borders was issued as a one-per-pack insert.

	NM/M
Complete Set (330):	30.00
Common Player:	.50

1995 Conlon Collection Prototypes

LOU GEHRIG — NEW YORK YANKEES — 1ST BASE — 1935

Megacards issued this 10-card series of prototypes to introduce its basic series for 1995. Cards are similar to the issued versions except that they lack the gold-foil enhancements on front and have different card numbers on some of the card backs. Cards have "PROMOTIONAL" printed diagonally on the back. Prototypes are listed here alphabetically.

		NM/M
Complete Set (10):		12.00
Common Player:		2.00
(1)	Lou Boudreau	2.00
(2)	Ray Chapman	2.00
(3)	Charles Comiskey	2.00
(4)	Bill Dickey	2.00
(5)	Bob Feller	2.00
(6)	Lou Gehrig	3.00
(7)	Charles L. Hartnett	2.00
(8)	Walter J.V. Maranville	2.00
(9)	Babe Ruth	4.00
(10)	Tris Speaker	2.00

1995 Conlon Collection

ANDY COHEN — NEW YORK GIANTS — 2ND BASE — 1926

Gold-foil enhanced printing was a first for the Conlon Collection in 1995. For the first time, each regular card in the issue featured gold frames around the black-and-white photos, and a gold Conlon Collection seal at lower-right. Background for the 1995 cards is in dark green, with typography in white. Backs are black-and-white and feature an in-depth historical vignette. In its fifth year, numbers for Conlon Collection cards continued from previous years, beginning at #1321. The first series, cards 1321-1430, were issued in February, a second series, #1431-1540, was announced for August release but was never issued. A special Babe Ruth 100th birthday anniversary card was included with the issue, bearing a combined Topps/Conlon Collection logo and paralleling card #3 in the 1995 Topps issue. Conlon cards for 1995 were issued in plastic clam-shell packaging of 22, 55 or 110 cards. Once again, many of the cards in the set were grouped into themes such as "Baseball Goes to War," "Nicknames" and "Beating the Odds."

		NM/M
Complete Set, Commemorative Tin:		100.00
Complete Set (111):		80.00
Common Player:		1.00
1321	Grover Alexander	1.00
1322	Christy Mathewson	1.50
1323	Eddie Grant	1.00
1324	Gabby Street	1.00
1325	Hank Gowdy	1.00
1326	Jack Bentley	1.00
1327	Eppa Rixey	1.00
1328	Bob Shawkey	1.00
1329	Rabbit Maranville	1.00
1330	Casey Stengel	1.00
1331	Herb Pennock	1.00
1332	Eddie Collins	1.00
1333	Buddy Hassett	1.00
1334	Andy Cohen	1.00
1335	Hank Greenberg	1.50
1336	Andy High	1.00
1337	Bob Feller	1.00
1338	George Earnshaw	1.00
1339	Jack Knott	1.00
1340	Larry French	1.00
1341	Skippy Roberge	1.00
1342	Boze Berger	1.00
1343	Bill Posedel	1.00
1344	Kirby Higbe	1.00
1345	Bob Neighbors	1.00
1346	Hugh Mulcahy	1.00
1347	Harry Walker	1.00
1348	Buddy Lewis	1.00
1349	Cecil Travis	1.00
1350	Moe Berg	2.00
1351	Nixey Callahan	1.00
1352	Heinie Peitz	1.00
1353	Doc White	1.00
1354	Smokey Joe Wood	1.00
1355	Larry Gardner	1.00
1356	Steve O'Neill	1.00
1357	Tris Speaker	1.00
1358	Bill Wambsganss	1.00
1359	Geo. H. Burns	1.00
1360	Charlie Jamieson	1.00
1361	Les Nunamaker	1.00
1362	Stan Coveleski	1.00
1363	Joe Sewell	1.00
1364	Jim Bagby	1.00
1365	Duster Mails	1.00
1366	Jack Graney	1.00
1367	Elmer Smith	1.00
1368	Tommy Leach	1.00
1369	Russ Ford	1.00
1370	Harry Wolter	1.00
1371	Dazzy Vance	1.00
1372	Germany Schaefer	1.00
1373	Elbie Fletcher	1.00
1374	Clark Griffith	1.00
1375	Al Simmons	1.00
1376	Billy Jurges	1.00
1377	Earl Averill	1.00
1378	Bill Klem	1.00
1379	Armando Marsans	1.00
1380	Mike Gonzalez	1.00
1381	Jacques Fournier	1.00
1382	Ol' Stubblebeard (Burleigh Grimes)	1.00
1383	Freshest Man on Earth (Arlie Latham)	1.00
1384	Cracker (Ray Schalk)	1.00
1385	Goose (Goose Goslin)	1.00
1386	Unser Choe (Joe Hauser)	1.00
1387	The People's Cherce (Dixie Walker)	1.00

1388	The Crab (Jesse Burkett)	1.00
1389	Mountain Music (Cliff Melton)	1.00
1390	Gee (Gee Walker)	1.00
1391	Tony Cuccinello	1.00
1392	Vern Kennedy	1.00
1393	Tuck Stainback	1.00
1394	Ed Barrow	1.00
1395	Ford Frick	1.00
1396	Ban Johnson	1.00
1397	Charles Comiskey	1.00
1398	Jacob Ruppert	1.00
1399	Branch Rickey	1.00
1400	Jack Kieran	1.00
1401	Mike Ryba	1.00
1402	Stan Spence	1.00
1403	Red Barrett	1.00
1404	Gabby Hartnett	1.00
1405	Babe Ruth	3.00
1406	Fred Merkle	1.00
1407	Claude Passeau	1.00
1408	Smokey Joe Wood	1.00
1409	Cliff Heathcote	1.00
1410	Walt Cruise	1.00
1411	Cookie Lavagetto	1.00
1412	Tony Lazzari	1.00
1413	Atley Donald	1.00
1414	Ken Raffensberger	1.00
1415	Dizzy Trout	1.00
1416	Augie Galan	1.00
1417	Monty Stratton	1.00
1418	Claude Passeau	1.00
1419	Oscar Grimes Jr.	1.00
1420	Rollie Hemsley	1.00
1421	Lou Gehrig	2.00
1422	Tom Sunkel	1.00
1423	Tris Speaker	1.00
1424	Chick Fewster	1.00
1425	Lou Boudreau	1.00
1426	Hank Leiber	1.00
1427	Eddie Mayo	1.00
1428	Charley Gelbert	1.00
1429	Jackie Hayes	1.00
1430	Checklist 1321-1430	1.00
3C	Babe Ruth (100th Birthday)	4.00

In the Zone

KEN GRIFFEY JR. — THE ZONE — WITH TY COBB

An eight-card set comparing Ken Griffey Jr. with superstars of the past was randomly inserted into 1995 Conlon Collection packs. Fronts feature a colorized background photo of the player with whom Griffey is being compared. A smaller color photo of Griffey is in the foreground. An "In the Zone" logo is at lower-left. Backs share a background photo of Griffey and have a black-and-white portrait of the comparison player in the upper-left. Narrative describes how the two players compare. A card number is at upper-right in the Zone logo. Megacard and Cooperstown Collection logos are at bottom. The first six cards of the series coould be found in Conlon Collection packs, cards 7 and 8 were available only through a mail-in offer for $2 plus five proofs-of-purchase. The print run was announced as no more than 50,000 sets.

		NM/M
Complete Set (8):		12.00
Common Card:		2.00
1	Ken Griffey Jr., Babe Ruth	3.50
2	Ken Griffey Jr., Lou Gehrig	2.00
3	Ken Griffey Jr., Ty Cobb	3.00
4	Ken Griffey Jr., Jimmie Foxx	2.00
5	Ken Griffey Jr., Mel Ott	2.00
6	Ken Griffey Jr., Joe Jackson	3.00

7	Ken Griffey Jr., Tris Speaker	2.00
8	Ken Griffey Jr., Jim Bottomley	2.00

1979-83 Coral-Lee Postcards

A number of baseball subjects were among a series of sports postcards published by Coral-Lee of California. Two formats are seen, standard postcard size of 3-1/2" x 5-1/2", and a larger 4" x 6" style seen on cards numbered 14 or higher. The standard-size cards have borderless color portrait photos on front, with no identification. Postcard style backs have the player's id, along with publisher, printer and copyright information in black-and-white. Most are dated. The larger cards have action photos on front, with backs similar to the smaller type. This list may not be complete as far as baseball-related cards within the series.

		NM/M
Common Player:		.25
1	Pete Rose	3.00
2	Davey Lopes	.25
3	Dave Winfield	1.50
4	Billy Martin	1.00
5	George Steinbrenner, Billy Martin, Reggie Jackson, Thurman Munson	1.50
6	Reggie Jackson	1.50
7	Bruce Kison	.25
9	Bobby Grich	.25
9	Rod Carew	.50
11	Tommy John	.25
12	Dick Howser	.25
12	George Brett	1.00
14-C	Cal Ripken Jr.	2.00
15-C	Carl Yastrzemski	1.00
16-C	Joe Morgan	.50
18-C	Graig Nettles	.25
69	Willie Mays, Ronald Reagan, Edward Stack	1.00
81	Fernando Valenzuela, Jose Lopez Portillo	1.00

1988-93 Costacos Brothers Ad Cards

KIRBY PUCKETT — PUCKETT WRECKING CO. — THE WRECKING BALL

During the hey-day of sports hero personality posters in the late 1980s and early 1990s, one of the industry's major players, Costacos Brothers, issued a series of 4" x 6" cards to advertise their poster offerings. Card fronts duplicate the issued poster, while backs contain an ad for the poster company. Players in many sports were included in the series but only the baseball players are listed here.

		NM/M
Complete Set (31):		125.00
Common Player:		4.00
(1)	Barry Bonds (License to Thrill)	10.00
(2)	Bobby Bonilla (Bobby Bo)	4.00
(3)	Will Clark (Thriller)	4.00
(4)	Will Clark (Willpower)	4.00
(5)	Roger Clemens (The Rocket)	8.00
(6)	Darren Daulton (D-Day)	4.00
(7)	Glenn Davis (The Big Bopper)	4.00
(8)	Andre Dawson (Class for All Seasons) (w/Jordan, Payton)	4.00
(9)	Lenny Dykstra (Nails)	4.00
(10)	Dennis Eckersley (Cy of Relief)	5.00
(11)	Andres Galarraga (The Big Cat)	4.00
(12)	Kirk Gibson (Big Game Hunter)	4.00
(13)	Dwight Gooden (Doc)	4.00
(14)	Tom Gordon (Flash)	4.00
(15)	Mike Greenwell (Gator Tough)	4.00
(16)	Ken Griffey Sr., Ken Griffey Jr. (The Next Generation)	8.00
(17)	Ken Griffey Jr. (In Jr. We Trust)	9.00
(18)	Derek Jeter (Jeter Airways)	9.00
(19)	Howard Johnson (HoJo)	4.00
(20)	Eric Karros (The Artful Dodger)	4.00
(21)	Barry Larkin (Red Hot)	4.00
(22)	Don Mattingly (The Man With The Golden Glove)	7.50
(23)	Fred McGriff (Blue Thunder)	4.00
(24)	Kevin Mitchell (Bat Man)	4.00
(25)	Kirby Puckett (The Wrecking Ball)	7.50
(26)	Tim Raines (Steal Wheels)	4.00
(27)	Harold Reynolds (Turning Point)	4.00
(28)	Benito Santiago (Thou Shalt Not Steal!)	4.00
(29)	Steve Sax (Sax Appeal)	4.00
(30)	Darryl Strawberry (Straw-Some)	4.00
(31)	Greg Swindell, Pete Harnisch, Doug Drabek (Shooting Stars)	4.00

1991 Country Hearth Mariners

KEN GRIFFEY JR. — outfield — Seattle Mariners

This 29-card set was inserted in loaves of bread and also given away at a Mariner home game. The card fronts feature full-color glossy photos, while the flip sides feature statistics.

		NM/M
Complete Set (29):		15.00
Common Player:		.50
1	Jim Lefebvre	.50
2	Jeff Schaefer	.50
3	Harold Reynolds	.75
4	Greg Briley	.50
5	Scott Bradley	.50
6	Dave Valle	.50
7	Edgar Martinez	1.00
8	Pete O'Brien	.50
9	Omar Vizquel	1.00
10	Tino Martinez	1.00
11	Scott Bankhead	.50
12	Bill Swift	.50
13	Jay Buhner	1.00
14	Alvin Davis	.50
15	Ken Griffey, Jr.	10.00
16	Tracy Jones	.50
17	Brent Knackert	.50
18	Henry Cotto	.50
19	Ken Griffey Sr.	.50
20	Keith Comstock	.50

21	Brian Holman	.50
22	Russ Swan	.50
23	Mike Jackson	.50
24	Erik Hanson	.50
25	Mike Schooler	.50
26	Randy Johnson	3.00
27	Rich DeLucia	.50
28	The Griffeys (Ken Griffey Jr., Ken Griffey Sr.)	2.00
29	Mascot	.50

1993 Country Time Brooks Robinson

Sponsored by Country Time drink mix, this set honors the career of the Orioles' Hall of Fame third baseman. The 2-1/2" x 3-5/8" cards feature color and colorized action photos with pale yellow frames, black diamond and textured green backgrounds and red and black borders. "Country Time Legends" and MLB logos appear in one of the bottom corners. Backs are printed in black, green and yellow about some phase of Robinson's career. The cards are not numbered.

		NM/M
Complete Set (8):		7.00
Common Card:		1.00
(1)	Title Card	.25
(2)	Brooks Robinson/Btg (Back view.)	1.00
(3)	Brooks Robinson/Btg (Front view.)	1.00
(4)	Brooks Robinson/Btg (Horizontal.)	1.00
(5)	Brooks Robinson/Fielding (Horizontal white jersey.)	1.00
(6)	Brooks Robinson/Fielding (Horizontal orange jersey.)	1.00
(7)	Brooks Robinson/Fielding (Vertical.)	1.00
(8)	Brooks Robinson (Saluting crowd.)	1.00

1982 Cracker Jack

The Topps-produced 1982 Cracker Jack set was issued to promote the first "Old Timers Baseball Classic," held in Washington, D.C. The set was issued in two sheets of eight player cards, plus an advertising card located in the center. Individual cards are 2-1/2" x 3-1/2", with the complete sheets measuring 7-1/2" x 10-1/2". Cards #1-8 feature American League players with #9-16 being former National League stars. Fronts feature a full-color photo inside a Cracker Jack border. Backs contain the

sponsor's logo plus a short player biography and his lifetime pitching or batting record. Complete sheets were available through a write-in offer.

Complete Panel Set (2):		12.00
Complete Singles Set (17):		10.00
Common Single Player:		.50
A.L. Panel		6.00
1	Larry Doby	.50
2	Bob Feller	.50
3	Whitey Ford	.50
4	Al Kaline	.50
5	Harmon Killebrew	.50
6	Mickey Mantle	5.00
7	Tony Oliva	.50
8	Brooks Robinson	.50
---	Advertising card	.05
N.L. Panel		4.00
9	Hank Aaron	2.00
10	Ernie Banks	.50
11	Ralph Kiner	.50
12	Eddie Mathews	.50
13	Willie Mays	2.00
14	Robin Roberts	.50
15	Duke Snider	.50
16	Warren Spahn	.50
---	Advertising card	.05

1991 Cracker Jack Topps 1st Series

In their first issue in almost 10 years, Cracker Jack inserted miniature cards (1-1/4" x 1-3/4") as the toy surprise in packages of the famous snack. The company produced two 36-card series, portraying many of the top stars in the game. Card fronts are identical to the corresponding regular-issue Topps cards, but the backs are significantly different because of the small amount of space available for statistics. The Cracker Jack sailor logo appears on the bright red backs, along with copyright information listing Borden, Cracker Jack's parent company. These are sometimes found on 2-1/2" x 3-1/2" cards bearing four different of the mini-cards; these were cut from sheets illegally removed from the printer.

		NM/M
Complete Set (36):		10.00
Common Player:		.25
1	Nolan Ryan	3.00
2	Paul Molitor	.60
3	Tim Raines	.25
4	Frank Viola	.25
5	Sandy Alomar Jr.	.25
6	Ryne Sandberg	.75
7	Don Mattingly	1.00
8	Pedro Guerrero	.25
9	Jose Rijo	.25
10	Jose Canseco	.40
11	Dave Parker	.25
12	Doug Drabek	.25
13	Cal Ripken	3.00
14	Dave Justice	.25
15	George Brett	1.00
16	Eric Davis	.25
17	Mark Langston	.25
18	Rickey Henderson	.60
19	Barry Bonds	3.00
20	Kevin Maas	.25
21	Len Dykstra	.25
22	Roger Clemens	1.00
23	Robin Yount	.60
24	Mark Grace	.25
25	Bo Jackson	.40
26	Tony Gwynn	.75
27	Mark McGwire	2.00
28	Dwight Gooden	.25
29	Wade Boggs	.75
30	Kevin Mitchell	.25
31	Cecil Fielder	.25
32	Bobby Thigpen	.25
33	Benito Santiago	.25
34	Kirby Puckett	.75
35	Will Clark	.25
36	Ken Griffey Jr.	1.50

2nd Series

A second series of 36 micro cards was found in Cracker Jack boxes later in the 1991 season. Again numbered from 1-18, the 1-1/4" x 1-3/4" cards carry a "2nd Series" designation on the back above the card number. Like the first series, these cards replicate the front of the 1991 Topps issue and have modified back design which includes the "Sailor Jack" logo of the candy company. Four-card panels, believed to have been cut from sheets illegally removed from the printer, are known.

		NM/M
Complete Set (36):		5.00
Common Player:		.35
1	Eddie Murray	.75
2	Carlton Fisk	.75
3	Eric Anthony	.40
4	Kelly Gruber	.40
5	Von Hayes	.40
6	Ben McDonald	.40
7	Andre Dawson	.60
8	Ellis Burks	.40
9	Matt Williams	.40
10	Dave Stewart	.40
11	Barry Larkin	.40
12	Chuck Finley	.40
13	Shane Andrews	.40
14	Bret Saberhagen	.40
15	Bobby Bonilla	.40
16	Roberto Kelly	.40
17	Orel Hershiser	.40
18	Ruben Sierra	.40
19	Ron Gant	.40
20	Frank Thomas	1.00
21	Tim Wallach	.40
22	Gregg Olson	.40
23	Shawon Dunston	.40
24	Kent Hrbek	.40
25	Ramon Martinez	.40
26	Alan Trammell	.40
27	Ozzie Smith	2.00
28	Bob Welch	.40
29	Chris Sabo	.40
30	Steve Sax	.40
31	Bip Roberts	.40
32	Dave Steib	.40
33	Howard Johnson	.40
34	Mike Greenwell	.40
35	Delino DeShields	.40
36	Alex Fernandez	.40

1992 Cracker Jack Donruss Series 1

In 1992, Cracker Jack turned to Donruss to produce the cards for the surprise in their packages. The first series of micro cards (1-1/4" x 1-3/4") was numbered 1-36 and features many top players. Card fronts are identical to the regular-issue '92 Donruss, but the backs have a different format and much less information because of the tiny space available. The backs have a blue border, with some spot red printing and the Cracker Jack sailor logo in the lower-left corner.

		NM/M
Complete Set (36):		20.00
Common Player:		.50
Album:		10.00
1	Dennis Eckersley	1.00
2	Jeff Bagwell	1.25
3	Jim Abbott	.50
4	Steve Avery	.50
5	Kelly Gruber	.50
6	Ozzie Smith	1.50
7	Lance Dickson	.50
8	Robin Yount	1.25
9	Brett Butler	.50
10	Sandy Alomar Jr.	.50
11	Travis Fryman	.50
12	Ken Griffey Jr.	2.00
13	Cal Ripken, Jr.	4.00
14	Will Clark	.50
15	Nolan Ryan	4.00
16	Tony Gwynn	1.50
17	Roger Clemens	1.75
18	Wes Chamberlain	.50
19	Barry Larkin	.50
20	Brian McRae	.50
21	Marquis Grissom	.50
22	Cecil Fielder	.50
23	Dwight Gooden	.50
24	Chuck Knoblauch	.50
25	Jose Canseco	.65
26	Terry Pendleton	.50
27	Ivan Rodriguez	1.00
28	Ryne Sandberg	1.50
29	Kent Hrbek	.50
30	Ramon Martinez	.50
31	Todd Zeile	.50
32	Hal Morris	.50
33	Robin Ventura	.50
34	Doug Drabek	.50
35	Frank Thomas	1.25
36	Don Mattingly	1.75

Series 2

The Second Series of the 1992 Crack Jack Donruss set is almost identical to the first series, with the only change being different players and red border on the back instead of blue. The micro cards are numbered 1-36, just as in the first series.

		NM/M
Complete Set (36):		15.00
Common Player:		.50
1	Craig Biggio	.50
2	Tom Glavine	.65
3	David Justice	.50
4	Lee Smith	.50
5	Mark Grace	.50
6	George Bell	.50
7	Darryl Strawberry	.50
8	Eric Davis	.50
9	Ivan Calderon	.50
10	Royce Clayton	.50
11	Matt Williams	.50
12	Fred McGriff	.50
13	Len Dykstra	.50
14	Barry Bonds	3.00
15	Reggie Sanders	.50
16	Chris Sabo	.50
17	Howard Johnson	.50
18	Bobby Bonilla	.50
19	Rickey Henderson	.75
20	Mark Langston	.50
21	Joe Carter	.50
22	Paul Molitor	.75
23	Glenallen Hill	.50
24	Edgar Martinez	.50
25	Gregg Olson	.50
26	Ruben Sierra	.50
27	Julio Franco	.50
28	Phil Plantier	.50
29	Wade Boggs	1.00
30	George Brett	1.25
31	Alan Trammell	.50
32	Kirby Puckett	1.00
33	Scott Erickson	.50
34	Matt Nokes	.50
35	Danny Tartabull	.50
36	Jack McDowell	.50

1993 Cracker Jack Anniversary

In 1993, as part of the company's 100th anniversary celebration, Cracker Jack issued a 24-card set of mini replicas of its famous 1915 cards. The cards, 1-1/4" x 1-3/4", were included in specially-marked packages of the famous snack. The set features Hall of Famers

CRACKER JACK BALL PLAYERS

WHEAT, BROOKLYN - NATIONALS

such as Cobb, Mathewson, Walter Johnson and others, plus the Joe Jackson card. A red plastic album, with color pictures of the replicas inside, was also available.

		NM/M
Complete Set (24):		10.00
Common Player:		.50
Album:		5.00
1	Ty Cobb	1.50
2	Joe Jackson	3.00
3	Honus Wagner	1.00
4	Christy Mathewson	.75
5	Walter Johnson	.75
6	Tris Speaker	.50
7	Grover Alexander	.50
8	Nap Lajoie	.50
9	Rube Marquard	.50
10	Connie Mack	.50
11	Johnny Evers	.50
12	Branch Rickey	.50
13	Fred Clarke	.50
14	Harry Hooper	.50
15	Zack Wheat	.50
16	Joe Tinker	.50
17	Eddie Collins	.50
18	Mordecai Brown	.50
19	Eddie Plank	.50
20	Rabbit Maranville	.50
21	John McGraw	.50
22	Miller Huggins	.50
23	Ed Walsh	.50
24	Leslie Bush	.50

1997 Cracker Jack All Stars

DEREK JETER

After an hiatus of three years, Cracker Jack resumed the use of baseball cards as premiums in 1997 with a 20-card All Stars set. Like the other CJ issues of the 1990s, this set features miniature (1-5/16" x 1-3/4") cards. Cards feature player action photos on front along with a Cracker Jack All Stars logo. Photos have uniform logos removed as the set is licensed only by the Players Association and not Major League Baseball. Backs are printed in red and blue with Cracker Jack and MLBPA logos, a few stats and personal data. Cards were also distributed as prizes in various promotional contests conducted by American Sports Classics, which inserted a logo card within the regular Cracker Jack prize wrapping.

		NM/M
Complete Set (20):		15.00
Common Player:		.50
1	Jeff Bagwell	1.00
2	Chuck Knoblauch	.50
3	Cal Ripken Jr.	3.00
4	Chipper Jones	1.50
5	Derek Jeter	3.00
6	Barry Larkin	.50
7	Bernie Williams	.50
8	Barry Bonds	3.00
9	Kenny Lofton	.50
10	Gary Sheffield	.65
11	Sammy Sosa	1.50
12	Paul Molitor	1.00
13	Andres Galarraga	.50
14	Ivan Rodriguez	.75
15	Mike Piazza	2.00
16	Andy Pettitte	.65
17	Tom Glavine	.65
18	Albert Belle	.50
19	Mark McGwire	2.50
20	Mo Vaughn	.50
Album:		2.00

1999 Cracker Jack Mac Stickers

In conjunction with its season-long promotion with Rawlings in which various Big Mac equipment items were given away, individual boxes of the snack could be found bearing one of 10 different McGwire stickers. The 1-1/2" x 2-1/8" stickers each include some type of interactive play element. Values shown are for opened, but complete, prize booklets. The color photos of McGwire on the stickers have had uniform logos removed.

	NM/M
Complete Set (10):	5.00
Common Sticker:	.50

1999 Cracker Jack Mark McGwire Home Run Record

One of several premiums which were part of a Rawlings promotion in boxes of Cracker Jack and related mail-in offers, this card marks McGwire's 70-HR season of 1998. The front is optical-variable, offering an image of McGwire in his home run-followthrough and, with a change in viewing angle, tipping his helmet to the crowd. Back has the date and distance of each of his 1998 homers, along with Rawling and Cracker Jack logos. The card is in standard 2-1/2" x 3-1/2" format.

	NM/M
Mark McGwire	10.00

1999 Cracker Jack Mark McGwire Spinners

"Home Run Around" is the name given to these spinner discs found as prizes in Cracker Jack boxes. The 1-5/8" plastic discs have a "magic motion" picture of McGwire on front with a large "70." Around the front rim are segments with other numbers. Instructions on back are to spin the disc and stop it to see if the player can hit more homers than McGwire. A raised spot at center allow the disc to be spun. While the Rawlings logo appears on front and back, Cardinals uniform logos have been deleted from the photos.

	NM/M
Complete Set (5):	10.00
Common Disc:	2.00

2002 Cracker Jack All-Stars

After skipping four years, Cracker Jack resumed the use of baseball cards as premiums in 2002 with a 30-card All-Stars set produced by Topps. Like the CJ issues of the 1990s, this set features miniature (1-5/8" x 2-1/8") cards with player action photos on front along with a Cracker Jack All-Stars logo. The checklist shows one player from each team. Backs are printed in color with Cracker Jack, Topps and MLB/MLBPA logos, a few stats and personal data. Complete sets in a customer holder were available by mail for $9.99.

		NM/M
Complete Set (30):		12.00
Common Player:		.25
1	Roger Clemens	.75
2	Pedro Martinez	.50
3	Carlos Delgado	.35
4	Jeff Conine	.25
5	Greg Vaughn	.25
6	Jim Thome	.40
7	Brad Radke	.25
8	Frank Thomas	.50
9	Steve Sparks	.25
10	Carlos Beltran	.35
11	Ichiro	2.00
12	Mark Mulder	.25
13	Troy Glaus	.25
14	Alex Rodriguez	1.50
15	Chipper Jones	.65
16	Bobby Abreu	.25
17	Mike Piazza	1.00
18	Cliff Floyd	.25
19	Vladimir Guerrero	.50
20	Jeff Bagwell	.50
21	Albert Pujols	1.50
22	Sammy Sosa	.65
23	Richie Sexson	.25
24	Sean Casey	.25
25	Brian Giles	.25
26	Randy Johnson	.50
27	Barry Bonds	2.00
28	Kevin Brown	.25
29	Phil Nevin	.25
30	Todd Helton	.40

2003 Cracker Jack All-Stars

The baseball cards inserted in boxes of Cracker Jack for 2003 were an entirely new for-

mat, printed on round-cornered 1-5/8" x 1-5/8" plastic squares. The printing is formatted to give the cards a diamond shape. Fronts have a player portrait in the upper half with personal data below. Team and sponsor logos also appear. Backs have team and sponsor logos, along with those of the licensors. The unnumbered cards are checklisted here alphabetically. Besides product insertion, the complete set was available by mail, along with a color 10-1/2" x 21" poster in which the cards could be displayed, for about $12.

		NM/M
Complete Set (32):		12.00
Common Player:		.50
Poster:		5.00
(1)	Roberto Alomar	.60
(2)	Jeff Bagwell	.75
(3)	Tony Batista	.50
(4)	Carlos Beltran	.60
(5)	Bret Boone	.50
(6)	Ellis Burks	.50
(7)	A.J. Burnett	.50
(8)	Pat Burrell	.50
(9)	Sean Casey	.50
(10)	Carlos Delgado	.65
(11)	Damion Easley	.50
(12)	Jason Giambi	.65
(13)	Brian Giles	.65
(14)	Troy Glaus	.65
(15)	Shawn Green	.60
(16)	Ben Grieve	.50
(17)	Vladimir Guerrero	.75
(18)	Todd Helton	.65
(19)	Torii Hunter	.50
(20)	Randy Johnson	.75
(21)	Chipper Jones	1.00
(22)	Ryan Klesko	.50
(23)	Paul Konerko	.60
(24)	Pedro Martinez	.75
(25)	Mark Mulder	.50
(26)	Robb Nen	.50
(27)	Rafael Palmeiro	.65
(28)	Albert Pujols	2.00
(29)	Ben Sheets	.50
(30)	Sammy Sosa	1.00
(31)	All-Star Game logo	.15
(32)	Cracker Jack logo	.15

2004 Cracker Jack Baseball History

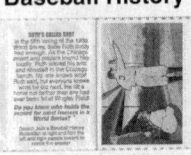

Illustrations of great moments in baseball history are reproduced in this set of Cracker Jack prize inserts. When opened, each 2" x 2-1/2" prize wrapper has the illustration on one side and narrative on the other. If detached and folded, the illustration reveals the answer to a trivia question.

		NM/M
Complete Set (10):		10.00
Common Player:		.50
(1)	Aaron Hits #715 (Hank Aaron)	1.00
(2)	Back to Back (Johnny Vander Meer)	.50
(3)	Jackie Robinson	1.00
(4)	Joe DiMaggio/ The Streak	1.00
(5)	Larsen's Perfect Game (Don Larsen)	.50
(6)	Pete Gray	.50
(7)	Roberto Clemente	2.00
(8)	Ruth's Called Shot (Babe Ruth)	2.00
(9)	Shot Heard Round the World (Bobby Thomson)	.50
(10)	The Catch (Willie Mays)	1.00

2005 Cracker Jack Ballpark Legends

THURMAN MUNSON

A set of 10 small booklets featuring past stars was produced for inclusion in 99-cent packages of Cracker Jack. The prize was in the form of a small (about 1-1/2" x 2-1/8" booklet about the individual player, with a baseball card in the center. The booklet has a career summary and checklist. The card has a heavily retouched photo with uniform details removed, "BALLPARK LEGENDS" at top and the player name between stars at bottom. Backs have biographical data, career highlights and lifetime stats.

Complete Set, Booklets (10)
Common Player Booklet
Unattached Cards: 50%

1980-83 Cramer Baseball Legends

JOE McCARTHY

Consecutively numbered, this set was issued over a period of four years by Cramer Sports Promotions, the forerunner of today's Pacific card company. Sold in wax packs and measuring the standard 2-1/2" x 3-1/2", the cards have a sepia-toned photo on front with a black frame. In the background is a weathered wooden slat design with the player's name on a hanging board beneath. The borders are dull yellow. Backs are printed in brown and include a few personal data, career stats and a career summary. Cards 1-30 were issued in 1980; #31-60 in 1981; #61-90 in 1982 and #90-124 in 1983. Cards #121-124 were issued on the 1983 wax box.

		NM/M
Complete Set (124):		45.00
Complete Set (120):		40.00
Common Player:		.25
1980		
1	Babe Ruth	3.00
2	Heinie Manush	.25
3	Rabbit Maranville	.25
4	Earl Averill	.25
5	Joe DiMaggio	2.00
6	Mickey Mantle	3.00
7	Hank Aaron	1.50
8	Stan Musial	1.25
9	Bill Terry	.25
10	Sandy Koufax	1.50
11	Ernie Lombardi	.25
12	Dizzy Dean	.25
13	Lou Gehrig	2.00
14	Walter Alston	.25
15a	Jackie Robinson/ Portrait	4.00
15b	Jackie Robinson/Btg	1.00
16	Jimmie Foxx	.25
17	Billy Southworth	.25
18	Honus Wagner	.50
19	Duke Snider	.25
20	Rogers Hornsby	.25
21	Paul Waner	.25
22	Luke Appling	.25
23	Billy Herman	.25
24	Lloyd Waner	.25
25	Fred Hutchinson	.25
26	Eddie Collins	.25
27	Lefty Grove	.25
28	Chuck Connors	.25
29	Lefty O'Doul	.25
30	Hank Greenberg	.25
1981		
31	Ty Cobb	2.50
32	Enos Slaughter	.25
33	Ernie Banks	.45
34	Christy Mathewson	.35
35	Mel Ott	.25
36	Pie Traynor	.25
37	Clark Griffith	.25
38	Mickey Cochrane	.25
39	Joe Cronin	.25
40	Leo Durocher	.25
41	Frank Baker	.25
42	Joe Tinker	.25
43	John McGraw	.25
44	Bill Dickey	.25
45	Walter Johnson	.35
46	Frankie Frisch	.25
47	Casey Stengel	.25
48	Willie Mays	2.00
49	Johnny Mize	.25
50	Roberto Clemente	4.00
51	Burleigh Grimes	.25
52	Pee Wee Reese	.25
53	Bob Feller	.25
54	Brooks Robinson	.25
55	Sam Crawford	.25
56	Robin Roberts	.25
57	Warren Spahn	.25
58	Joe McCarthy	.25
59	Jocko Conlan	.25
60	Satchel Paige	.75
1982		
61	Ted Williams	3.00
62	George Kelly	.25
63	Gil Hodges	.25
64	Jim Bottomley	.25
65	Al Kaline	.25
66	Harvey Kuenn	.25
67	Yogi Berra	.25
68	Nellie Fox	.25
69	Harmon Killebrew	.25
70	Edd Roush	.25
71	Mordecai Brown	.25
72	Gabby Hartnett	.25
73	Early Wynn	.25
74	Nap Lajoie	.25
75	Charlie Grimm	.25
76	Joe Garagiola	.25
77	Ted Lyons	.25
78	Mickey Vernon	.25
79	Lou Boudreau	.25
80	Al Dark	.25
81	Ralph Kiner	.25
82	Phil Rizzuto	.25
83	Stan Hack	.25
84	Frank Chance	.25
85	Ray Schalk	.25
86	Bill McKechnie	.25
87	Travis Jackson	.25
88	Pete Reiser	.25
89	Carl Hubbell	.25
90	Roy Campanella	.25
1983		
91	Cy Young	.25
92	Kiki Cuyler	.25
93	Chief Bender	.25
94	Richie Ashburn	.25
95	Riggs Stephenson	.25
96	Minnie Minoso	.25
97	Hack Wilson	.25
98	Al Lopez	.25
99	Willie Keeler	.25
100	Fred Lindstrom	.25
101	Roger Maris	.25
102	Roger Bresnahan	.25
103	Monty Stratton	.25
104	Goose Goslin	.25
105	Earle Combs	.25
106	Pepper Martin	.25
107	Joe Jackson	3.00
108	George Sisler	.25
109	Red Ruffing	.25
110	Johnny Vander Meer	.25
111	Herb Pennock	.25
112	Chuck Klein	.25
113	Paul Derringer	.25
114	Addie Joss	.25
115	Bobby Thomson	.25
116	Chick Hafey	.25
117	Lefty Gomez	.25
118	George Kell	.25
119	Al Simmons	.25
120	Bob Lemon	.25
121	Hoyt Wilhelm	1.00
122	Arky Vaughan	1.00
123	Frank Robinson	1.50
124	Grover Alexander	1.50

1991 Crown/ Coke Orioles

FRANK ZUPO-C

Claiming to include every player for the modern (1954-1991) Baltimore Orioles, this 501-card set was issued in four series. The first three series contain 120 cards each in a format of a dozen perforated cards on each of 10 sheets. Those series were given away at May 17, June 28 and August 11 home games. The fourth series, 12 sheets of 12 cards each, including three blank cards, was available only at participating Crown gas stations, which also sold the first three series following the giveaway days at the ballpark. Cards measure 2-1/2" x 3-3/16" and are perforated on two, three or four sides, depending on their position on the sheet. All players are featured in sepia-toned head shots, virtually all in Orioles' uniform. Around the photos are borders of, successively, green, orange, black and white. The player's name and position appear in a black banner above the photo. In the lower-left corner is a 1954-1991 Memorial Stadium "Season to Remember" logo. That logo is repeated at bottom-center of the black-and-white backs, flanked by the logos of Coca-Cola and Crown. A card number appears in the lower-right. Most cards were numbered alphabetically. Backs include stats for the player's major league career and time with the Orioles.

		NM/M
Complete Set (501):		30.00
Common Player:		.15
1	Don Aase	.15
2	Cal Abrams	.15
3	Jerry Adair	.15
4	Bobby Adams	.15
5	Mike Adamson	.15
6	Jay Aldrich	.15
7	Bob Alexander	.15
8	Doyle Alexander	.15
9	Brady Anderson	.40
10	John Anderson	.15
11	Mike Anderson	.15
12	Luis Aparicio	1.25
13	Tony Arnold	.15
14	Bobby Avila	.15
15	Benny Ayala	.15
16	Bob Bailor	.15
17	Frank Baker	.15
18	Jeff Ballard	.15
19	George Bamberger	.15
20	Steve Barber	.15
21	Ray "Buddy" Barker	.15
22	Ed Barnowski	.15
23	Jose Bautista	.15
24	Don Baylor	.40
25	Charlie Beamon	.15
26	Fred Beene	.15
27	Mark Belanger	.25
28	Eric Bell	.15
29	Juan Bell	.15
30	Juan Beniquez	.15
31	Neil Berry	.15
32	Frank Bertaina	.15
33	Fred Besana	.15
34	Vern Bickford	.15
35	Babe Birrer	.15
36	Paul Blair	.15
37	Curt Blefary	.15
38	Mike Blyzka	.15
39	Mike Boddicker	.15
40	Juan Bonilla	.15
41	Bob Bonner	.15
42	Dan Boone	.15
43	Rich Bordi	.15
44	Dave Boswell	.15
45	Sam Bowens	.15
46	Bob Boyd	.15
47	Gene Brabender	.15
48	Phil Bradley	.15
49	Jackie Brandt	.15
50	Marv Breeding	.15
51	Jim Brideweser	.15
52	Nellie Briles	.15
53	Dick Brown	.15
54	Hal Brown	.15
55	Larry Brown	.15
56	Mark Brown	.15
57	Marty Brown	.15
58	George Brunet	.15
59	Don Buford	.25
60	Al Bumbry	.15
61	Wally Bunker	.15
62	Leo Burke	.15
63	Rick Burleson	.15
64	Pete Burnside	.15
65	Jim Busby	.15
66	John Buzhardt	.15
67	Harry Byrd	.15
68	Enos Cabell	.15
69	Chico Carrasquel	.15
70	Camilo Carreon	.15
71	Foster Castleman	.15
72	Wayne Causey	.15
73	Art Ceccarelli	.15
74	Bob Chakales	.15
75	Tony Chevez	.15
76	Tom Chism	.15
77	Gino Cimoli	.15
78	Gil Coan	.15
79	Rich Coggins	.15
80	Joe Coleman	.15
81	Rip Coleman	.15
82	Fritz Connally	.15
83	Sandy Consuegra	.15
84	Doug Corbett	.15
85	Mark Corey	.15
86	Clint Courtney	.15
87	Billy Cox	.15
88	Dave Criscione	.15
89	Terry Crowley	.15
90	Todd Cruz	.15
91	Mike Cuellar	.30
92	Angie Dagres	.15
93	Clay Dalrymple	.15
94	Rich Dauer	.15
95	Jerry DaVanon	.15
96	Butch Davis	.15
97	Storm Davis	.15
98	Tommy Davis	.15
99	Doug DeCinces	.25
100	Luis DeLeon	.15
101	Ike Delock	.15
102	Rick Dempsey	.25
103	Mike Devereaux	.15
104	Chuck Diering	.15
105	Gordon Dillard	.15
106	Bill Dillman	.15
107	Mike Dimmel	.15
108	Ken Dixon	.15
109	Pat Dobson	.15
110	Tom Dodd	.15
111	Harry Dorish	.15
112	Moe Drabowsky	.15
113	Dick Drago	.15
114	Walt Dropo	.15
115	Tom Dukes	.15
116	Dave Duncan	.15
117	Ryne Duren	.15
118	Joe Durham	.15
119	Jim Dwyer	.15
120	Jim Dyck	.15
121	Mike Epstein	.15
122	Chuck Essegian	.15
123	Chuck Estrada	.15
124	Andy Etchebarren	.15
125	Hoot Evers	.15
126	Ed Farmer	.15
127	Chico Fernandez	.15
128	Don Ferrarese	.15
129	Jim Finigan	.15
130	Steve Finley	.15
131	Mike Fiore	.15
132	Eddie Fisher	.15
133	Jack Fisher	.15
134	Tom Fisher	.15
135	Mike Flanagan	.15
136	John Flinn	.15
137	Bobby Floyd	.15
138	Hank Foiles	.15
139	Dan Ford	.15
140	Dave Ford	.15
141	Mike Fornieles	.15
142	Howie Fox	.15
143	Tito Francona	.15
144	Joe Frazier	.15
145	Roger Freed	.15
146	Jim Fridley	.15
147	Jim Fuller	.15
148	Joe Gaines	.15
149	Vinicio "Chico" Garcia	.15
150	Kiko Garcia	.15
151	Billy Gardner	.15
152	Wayne Garland	.15
153	Tommy Gastall	.15
154	Jim Gentile	.15
155	Ken Gerhart	.15
156	Paul Gilliford	.15
157	Joe Ginsberg	.15
158	Leo Gomez	.15
159	Rene Gonzales	.15
160	Billy Goodman	.15
161	Dan Graham	.15

#	Player	Value
162	Ted Gray	.15
163	Gene Green	.15
164	Lenny Green	.15
165	Bobby Grich	.30
166	Mike Griffin	.15
167	Ross Grimsley	.15
168	Wayne Gross	.15
169	Glenn Gulliver	.15
170	Jackie Gutierrez	.15
171	John Habyan	.15
172	Harvey Haddix	.15
173	Bob Hale	.15
174	Djck Hall	.15
175	Bert Hamric	.15
176	Larry Haney	.15
177	Ron Hansen	.15
178	Jim Hardin	.15
179	Larry Harlow	.15
180	Pete Harnisch	.15
181	Tommy Harper	.15
182	Bob Harrison	.15
183	Roric Harrison	.15
184	Jack Harshman	.15
185	Mike Hart	.15
186	Paul Hartzell	.15
187	Grady Hatton	.15
188	Brad Havens	.15
189	Drungo Hazewood	.15
190	Jehosie Heard	.15
191	Mel Held	.15
192	Woodie Held	.15
193	Ellie Hendricks	.25
194	Leo Hernandez	.15
195	Whitey Herzog	.15
196	Kevin Hickey	.15
197	Billy Hoeft	.15
198	Chris Hoiles	.15
199	Fred Holdsworth	.15
200	Brian Holton	.15
201	Ken Holtzman	.15
202	Don Hood	.15
203	Sam Horn	.15
204	Art Houtteman	.15
205	Bruce Howard	.15
206	Rex Hudler	.15
207	Phil Huffman	.15
208	Keith Hughes	.15
209	Mark Huismann	.15
210	Tim Hulett	.15
211	Billy Hunter	.15
212	Dave Huppert	.15
213	Jim Hutto	.15
214	Dick Hyde	.15
215	Grant Jackson	.15
216	Lou Jackson	.15
217	Reggie Jackson	5.00
218	Ron Jackson	.15
219	Jesse Jefferson	.15
220	Stan Jefferson	.15
221	Bob Johnson	.15
222	Connie Johnson	.15
223	Darrell Johnson	.15
224	Dave Johnson	.15
225	Davey Johnson	.25
226	David Johnson	.15
227	Don Johnson	.15
228	Ernie Johnson	.15
229	Gordon Jones	.15
230	Ricky Jones	.15
231	O'Dell Jones	.15
232	Sam Jones	.15
233	George Kell	.75
234	Frank Kellert	.15
235	Pat Kelly	.15
236	Bob Kennedy	.15
237	Terry Kennedy	.15
238	Joe Kerrigan	.15
239	Mike Kinnunen	.15
240	Willie Kirkland	.15
241	Ron Kittle	.15
242	Billy Klaus	.15
243	Ray Knight	.25
244	Darold Knowles	.15
245	Dick Kokos	.15
246	Brad Komminsk	.15
247	Dave Koslo	.15
248	Wayne Krenchicki	.15
249	Lou Kretlow	.15
250	Dick Kryhoski	.15
251	Bob Kuzava	.15
252	Lee Lacy	.15
253	Hobie Landrith	.15
254	Tito Landrum	.15
255	Don Larsen	.25
256	Charlie Lau	.25
257	Jim Lehew	.15
258	Ken Lehman	.15
259	Don Lenhardt	.15
260	Dave Leonhard	.15
261	Don Leppert	.15
262	Dick Littlefield	.15
263	Charlie Locke	.15
264	Whitey Lockman	.15
265	Billy Loes	.15
266	Ed Lopat	.15
267	Carlos Lopez	.15
268	Marcelino Lopez	.15
269	John Lowenstein	.15
270	Steve Luebber	.15
271	Dick Luebke	.15
272	Fred Lynn	.45
273	Bobby Mabe	.15
274	Elliott Maddox	.15
275	Hank Majeski	.15
276	Roger Marquis	.15
277	Freddie Marsh	.15
278	Jim Marshall	.15
279	Morrie Martin	.15

#	Player	Value
280	Dennis Martinez	.25
281	Tippy Martinez	.25
282	Tom Matchick	.15
283	Charlie Maxwell	.15
284	Dave May	.15
285	Lee May	.15
286	Rudy May	.15
287	Mike McCormick	.15
288	Ben McDonald	.15
289	Jim McDonald	.15
290	Scott McGregor	.25
291	Mickey McGuire	.15
292	Jeff McKnight	.15
293	Dave McNally	.25
294	Sam Mele	.15
295	Francisco Melendez	.15
296	Bob Melvin	.15
297	Jose Mesa	.15
298	Eddie Miksis	.15
299	Bob Milacki	.15
300	Bill Miller	.15
301	Dyar Miller	.15
302	John Miller	.15
303	Randy Miller	.15
304	Stu Miller	.15
305	Randy Milligan	.15
306	Paul Mirabella	.15
307	Willy Miranda	.15
308	John Mitchell	.15
309	Paul Mitchell	.15
310	Ron Moeller	.15
311	Bob Molinaro	.15
312	Ray Moore	.15
313	Andres Mora	.15
314	Jose Morales	.15
315	Keith Moreland	.15
316	Mike Morgan	.15
317	Dan Morogiello	.15
318	John Morris	.15
319	Les Moss	.15
320	Curt Motton	.15
321	Eddie Murray	1.50
322	Ray Murray	.15
323	Tony Muser	.15
324	Buster Narum	.15
325	Bob Nelson	.15
326	Roger Nelson	.15
327	Carl Nichols	.15
328	Dave Nicholson	.15
329	Tom Niedenfuer	.15
330	Bob Nieman	.15
331	Donell Nixon	.15
332	Joe Nolan	.15
333	Dickie Noles	.15
334	Tim Nordbrook	.15
335	Jim Northrup	.15
336	Jack O'Connor	.15
337	Billy O'Dell	.15
338	John O'Donoghue	.15
339	Tom O'Malley	.15
340	Johnny Oates	.15
341	Chuck Oertel	.15
342	Bob Oliver	.15
343	Gregg Olson	.15
344	John Orsino	.15
345	Joe Orsulak	.15
346	John Pacella	.15
347	Dave Pagan	.15
348	Erv Palica	.15
349	Jim Palmer	1.50
350	John Papa	.15
351	Milt Pappas	.15
352	Al Pardo	.15
353	Kelly Paris	.15
354	Mike Parrott	.15
355	Tom Patton	.15
356	Albie Pearson	.15
357	Orlando Pena	.15
358	Oswaldo Peraza	.15
359	Buddy Peterson	.15
360	Dave Philley	.15
361	Tom Phoebus	.15
362	Al Pilarcik	.15
363	Duane Pillette	.15
364	Lou Piniella	.25
365	Dave Pope	.15
366	Arnie Portocarrero	.15
367	Boog Powell	1.00
368	Johnny Powers	.15
369	Carl Powis	.15
370	Joe Price	.15
371	Jim Pyburn	.15
372	Art Quirk	.15
373	Jamie Quirk	.15
374	Allan Ramirez	.15
375	Floyd Rayford	.15
376	Mike Reinbach	.15
377	Merv Rettenmund	.15
378	Bob Reynolds	.15
379	Del Rice	.15
380	Pete Richert	.15
381	Jeff Rineer	.15
382	Bill Ripken	.15
383	Cal Ripken	9.00
384	Robin Roberts	1.25
385	Brooks Robinson	4.00
386	Earl Robinson	.15
387	Eddie Robinson	.15
388	Frank Robinson	3.00
389	Sergio Robles	.15
390	Aurelio Rodriguez	.15
391	Vic Rodriguez	.15
392	Gary Roenicke	.15
393	Saul Rogovin	.15
394	Wade Rowdon	.15
395	Ken Rowe	.15
396	Willie Royster	.15
397	Vic Roznovsky	.15

#	Player	Value
398	Ken Rudolph	.15
399	Lenn Sakata	.15
400	Chico Salmon	.15
401	Orlando Sanchez	.15
402	Bob Saverine	.15
403	Art Schallock	.15
404	Bill Scherrer	.15
405	Curt Schilling	.75
406	Dave Schmidt	.15
407	Johnny Schmitz	.15
408	Jeff Schneider	.15
409	Rick Schu	.15
410	Mickey Scott	.15
411	Kal Segrist	.15
412	David Segui	.15
413	Al Severinsen	.15
414	Larry Sheets	.15
415	John Shelby	.15
416	Barry Shetrone	.15
417	Tom Shopay	.15
418	Bill Short	.15
419	Norm Siebern	.15
420	Nelson Simmons	.15
421	Ken Singleton	.25
422	Doug Sisk	.15
423	Dave Skaggs	.15
424	Lou Sleater	.15
425	Al Smith	.15
426	Billy Smith	.15
427	Hal Smith	.15
428	"Texas" Mike Smith	.15
429	Nate Smith	.15
430	Nate Snell	.15
431	Russ Snyder	.15
432	Don Stanhouse	.15
433	Pete Stanicek	.15
434	Herm Starrette	.15
435	John Stefero	.15
436	Gene Stephens	.15
437	Vern Stephens	.15
438	Earl Stephenson	.15
439	Sammy Stewart	.15
440	Royle Stillman	.15
441	Wes Stock	.15
442	Tim Stoddard	.15
443	Dean Stone	.15
444	Jeff Stone	.15
445	Steve Stone	.25
446	Marlin Stuart	.15
447	Gordie Sundin	.15
448	Bill Swaggerty	.15
449	Willie Tasby	.15
450	Joe Taylor	.15
451	Dorn Taylor	.15
452	Anthony Telford	.15
453	Johnny Temple	.15
454	Mickey Tettleton	.15
455	Valmy Thomas	.15
456	Bobby Thomson	.25
457	Marv Thorneberry	.15
458	Mark Thurmond	.15
459	Jay Tibbs	.15
460	Mike Torrez	.15
461	Jim Traber	.15
462	Gus Triandos	.15
463	Paul "Dizzy" Trout	.15
464	Bob Turley	.15
465	Tom Underwood	.15
466	Fred Valentine	.15
467	Dave Van Gorder	.15
468	Dave Vineyard	.15
469	Ozzie Virgil	.15
470	Eddie Waitkus	.15
471	Greg Walker	.15
472	Jerry Walker	.15
473	Pete Ward	.15
474	Carl Warwick	.15
475	Ron Washington	.15
476	Eddie Watt	.15
477	Don Welchel	.15
478	George Werley	.15
479	Vic Wertz	.15
480	Wally Westlake	.15
481	Mickey Weston	.15
482	Alan Wiggins	.15
483	Bill Wight	.15
484	Hoyt Wilhelm	.50
485	Dallas Williams	.15
486	Dick Williams	.15
487	Earl Williams	.15
488	Mark Williamson	.15
489	Jim Wilson	.15
490	Gene Woodling	.15
491	Craig Worthington	.15
492	Bobby Young	.15
493	Mike Young	.15
494	Frank Zupo	.15
495	George Zuverink	.15
496	Glenn Davis	.15
497	Dwight Evans	.25
498	Dave Gallagher	.15
499	Paul Kilgus	.15
500	Jeff Robinson	.15
501	Ernie Whitt	.15

1992 Crown Orioles Action Standups

Crown Petroleum released a set of standup cards in 1992 of 12 Oriole greats, most retired, that was sold at service stations in three series. The 4-1/4" x 9" cards have color photos on a white background

on front; backs have black-and-white stats, logos, and career highlights. Cal Ripken, Jr. and Tippy Martinez were the only active players portrayed in the set. Suggested retail price at issue was $4 per series; about $2 with a gasoline purchase. A collector's album could also be purchased.

	NM/M
Complete Set (12):	20.00
Common Player:	1.00

SET 1 — 10.00

(1)	Frank Robinson	3.00
(2)	Brooks Robinson	4.00
(3)	Jim Palmer	3.00
(4)	Rick Dempsey	1.00

SET 2 — 12.00

(5)	Cal Ripken Jr.	10.00
(6)	Tippy Martinez	1.00
(7)	Bobby Grich	1.00
(8)	Earl Weaver	1.00

SET 3 — 4.00

(9)	Boog Powell	1.50
(10)	Paul Blair	1.00
(11)	Terry Crowley	1.00
(12)	Ken Singleton	1.00

1998 CyberAction

During the 1998 National Sports Collectors Convention in Chicago, CyberAction gave away samples of its product. The cards are printed on flimsy cardboard in standard 2-1/2" x 3-1/2" format. Fronts have a blue-bordered action photo at center. In the background is a large team logo. The firm's website address is at top; its logo at bottom. Backs have details on winning a World Series trip.

	NM/M
Complete Set (6):	11.00
Common Player:	1.50

1	Ken Griffey Jr.	2.25
2	Mark McGwire	2.50
3	Barry Bonds	3.00
4	Derek Jeter	3.00
5	Greg Maddux	2.00
6	Larry Walker	1.50

D

1992 Dairy Queen Team USA

In 1992, in conjunction with the Dairy Queen Team

USA Sundae-in-a-Helmet promotion, customers received a four-card pack of Team USA cards, part of a 33-card set manufactured by Topps for the company. Included in the set are Team USA players from the 1984 and 1988 Olympics, many of whom have gone on to major league stardom. The set also has 15 Team USA Prospects, a 1988 Gold Medal team celebration card and a card of 1992 coach Ron Fraser. Fronts feature each player in their Team USA uniform and the backs include statistics from amateur, Team USA and professional competition.

	NM/M
Complete Set (33):	13.50
Common Player:	.25

1	Mark McGwire/1984	4.00
2	Will Clark/1984	1.00
3	John Marzano/1984	.25
4	Barry Larkin/1984	1.00
5	Bobby Witt/1984	.25
6	Scott Bankhead/1984	.25
7	B.J. Surhoff/1984	.25
8	Shane Mack/1984	.25
9	Jim Abbott/1988	.35
10	Ben McDonald/1988	.25
11	Robin Ventura/1988	.50
12	Charles Nagy/1988	.25
13	Andy Benes/1988	.25
14	Joe Slusarski/1988	.25
15	Ed Sprague/1988	.25
16	Bret Barberie/1988	.25
17	Gold Medal - 1988/1988	.25
18	Jeff Granger/1992	.25
19	John Dettmer/1992	.25
20	Todd Greene/1992	.25
21	Jeffrey Hammonds/1992	.25
22	Dan Melendez/1992	.25
23	Kennie Steenstra/1992	.25
24	Todd Johnson/1992	.25
25	Chris Roberts/1992	.25
26	Steve Rodriguez/1992	.25
27	Charles Johnson/1992	.25
28	Chris Wimmer/1992	.25
29	Tony Phillips/1992	.25
30	Craig Wilson/1992	.25
31	Jason Giambi/1992	6.00
32	Paul Shuey/1992	.25
33	Ron Fraser/1992 coach	.25

1993 Dairy Queen Magic Mariner Moments Pin/Cards

1992 Crown Orioles Action Standups

	NM/M
Common Player:	2.00

1	Randy Johnson ('92 AL K King)	3.25
2	Edgar Martinez ('92 AL Batting Champ)	2.00
3	Chris Bosio (No-Hitter)	2.00
4	Ken Griffey Jr. ('92 All-Star MVP)	4.00

1994 Dairy Queen Ken Griffey, Jr.

Distributed by Dairy Queen stores in the Pacific Northwest, this set was issued in two different versions, with green borders and with gold borders. All cards feature a "Ken Griffey Jr. Golden Moments" logo in the upper-left corner. His name and the DQ logo appear at the bottom. Backs have another photo of Griffey along with a description of the career highlight depicted on front, sponsors' logos and a card number. Values shown here are for green-bordered cards; gold-bordered cards sell for about twice those figures.

	NM/M
Complete Set (10):	7.50
Common Player:	.75
Gold:	2X

1	Ken Griffey Jr. ("The Spider Man Catch")	.75
2	Ken Griffey Jr. ("Back to Back Homeruns")	.75
3	Ken Griffey Jr. (Hit .327 in 1991)	.75
4	Ken Griffey Jr. (1992 All-Star MVP)	.75
5	Ken Griffey Jr. ("Dialing Long Distance")	.75
6	Ken Griffey Jr. ("8 Straight Homeruns")	.75
7	Ken Griffey Jr. (4-Time Golden Glove Winner)	.75
8	Ken Griffey Jr. (45 Homeruns in 1993)	.75
9	Ken Griffey Jr. (Major League Career Hitting Record)	.75
10	Ken Griffey Jr. ("Looking to 1994")	.75

1996-2003 Danbury Mint 22kt Gold Cooperstown Collection

A series of embossed 22kt. gold-foil cards was offered by the private mint beginning in 1996. Each month two cards were sent to subscribers. The standard-size cards have a player picture on front with team logo and player identification at bottom. Backs have career stats. Each card was sealed in acrylic. An

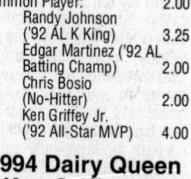

album for the set has identification labels with name in both printed and facsimile autograph form. Only persons who completed Set 1 were allowed to purchase subsequent sets. While each card is numbered, they are checklisted here alphabetically within series. Because the Babe Ruth card was used as a free promotional give-away, it is more common than the others.

	NM/M
Complete Set (200):	750.00
Common Player (1-50):	5.00
Common Player (51-100):	6.00
Common Player (101-150):	7.50
Common Player (151-200):	7.50
(1) Richie Allen	4.00
(2) Paul Blair	3.00
(3) Vida Blue	3.00
(4) Bert Blyleven	3.00
(5) Roy Campanella	6.00
(6) Bert Campaneris	3.00
(7) Gary Carter	4.00
(8) Cesar Cedeno	3.00
(9) Orlando Cepeda	4.00
(10) Ty Cobb	7.50
(11) Mickey Cochrane	3.00
(12) Eddie Collins	3.00
(13) Dizzy Dean	5.00
(14) Bob Feller	4.00
(15) George Foster	3.00
(16) Steve Garvey	3.00
(17) Lou Gehrig	7.50
(18) Lefty Gomez	3.00
(19) Gil Hodges	4.00
(20) Carl Hubbell	3.00
(21) Walter Johnson	5.00
(22) Jim Kaat	3.00
(23) Don Kessinger	3.00
(24) Harmon Killebrew	4.00
(25) Jerry Koosman	3.00
(26) Mickey Lolich	3.00
(27) Sparky Lyle	3.00
(28) Fred Lynn	3.00
(29) Bill Mazeroski	4.00
(30) Minnie Minoso	3.00
(31) Johnny Mize	3.00
(32) Thurman Munson	5.00
(33) Graig Nettles	3.00
(34) Phil Niekro	3.00
(35) Tony Oliva	3.00
(36) Al Oliver	3.00
(37) Satchel Paige	7.50
(38) Jim Palmer	3.00
(39) Herb Pennock	3.00
(40) Tony Perez	3.00
(41) Boog Powell	3.00
(42) Brooks Robinson	4.00
(43) Babe Ruth	2.50
(44) Duke Snider	3.00
(45) Tris Speaker	3.00
(46) Willie Stargell	3.00
(47) Luis Tiant	3.00
(48) Honus Wagner	5.00
(49) Maury Wills	3.00
(50) Cy Young	5.00
(51) Grover Alexander	6.00
(52) Sandy Alomar Jr.	6.00
(53) Jeff Bagwell	9.00
(54) Dusty Baker	6.00
(55) Albert Belle	6.00
(56) Wade Boggs	10.00
(57) Barry Bonds	17.50
(58) Joe Carter	6.00
(59) Will Clark	6.00
(60) Roger Clemens	12.00
(61) Dwight Evans	6.00
(62) Jim Fregosi	6.00
(63) Andres Galarraga	6.00
(64) Bob Gibson	6.00
(65) Ken Griffey Jr.	13.50
(66) Tony Gwynn	10.00
(67) Rogers Hornsby	6.00
(68) Catfish Hunter	6.00
(69) Joe Jackson	17.50
(70) Ferguson Jenkins	6.00
(71) Derek Jeter	17.50
(72) Randy Johnson	9.00
(73) Jimmy Key	6.00
(74) Ralph Kiner	6.00
(75) Don Larsen	6.00
(76) Greg Maddux	10.00
(77) Juan Marichal	6.00
(78) Eddie Mathews	7.50
(79) Christy Mathewson	9.00
(80) Fred McGriff	6.00
(81) Mark McGwire	15.00
(82) Dave McNally	6.00
(83) Bobby Murcer	6.00
(84) Dale Murphy	7.50
(85) Gaylord Perry	6.00
(86) Rico Petrocelli	6.00
(87) Andy Pettitte	7.50
(88) Mike Piazza	13.50
(89) Cal Ripken Jr.	17.50
(90) Alex Rodriguez	15.00
(91) Joe Rudi	6.00
(92) Ron Santo	6.00
(93) Gary Sheffield	6.00
(94) John Smoltz	6.00
(95) Sammy Sosa	10.00
(96) Warren Spahn	6.00
(97) Billy Williams	6.00
(98) Bobby Thomson	6.00
(99) Mo Vaughn	6.00
(100) Hoyt Wilhelm	6.00
(101) Brady Anderson	7.50
(102) Luis Aparicio	7.50
(103) Kevin Appier	7.50
(104) Richie Ashburn	9.00
(105) Lou Boudreau	7.50
(106) Lou Brock	7.50
(107) Kevin Brown	7.50
(108) Jim Bunning	9.00
(109) Jose Canseco	9.00
(110) David Cone	7.50
(111) Rollie Fingers	7.50
(112) Chuck Finley	7.50
(113) Curt Flood	7.50
(114) Jimmie Foxx	10.00
(115) Nomar Garciaparra	12.00
(116) Tom Glavine	7.50
(117) Juan Gonzalez	7.50
(118) Luis Gonzalez	7.50
(119) Mark Grace	7.50
(120) Shawn Green	7.50
(121) Burleigh Grimes	7.50
(122) Lefty Grove	7.50
(123) Al Hrabosky	7.50
(124) Chipper Jones	12.00
(125) Al Kaline	9.00
(126) Tony Lazzeri	7.50
(127) Bill Lee	7.50
(128) Jose Lima	7.50
(129) Bill Madlock	7.50
(130) Roger Maris	9.00
(131) Pedro Martinez	10.00
(132) Tino Martinez	7.50
(133) Tug McGraw	7.50
(134) Kevin Millwood	7.50
(135) Joe Morgan	7.50
(136) Charles Nagy	7.50
(137) Mel Ott	7.50
(138) Rafael Palmeiro	7.50
(139) Manny Ramirez	9.00
(140) Jim Rice	7.50
(141) Ivan Rodriguez	7.50
(142) Edd Roush	7.50
(143) Manny Sanguillen	7.50
(144) Curt Schilling	7.50
(145) Ron Swoboda	7.50
(146) Greg Vaughn	7.50
(147) Larry Walker	7.50
(148) Zack Wheat	7.50
(149) Bernie Williams	7.50
(150) Jim Wynn	7.50
(151) Bobby Abreu	7.50
(152) Roberto Alomar	7.50
(153) Moises Alou	7.50
(154) Carlos Beltran	7.50
(155) Armando Benitez	7.50
(156) Lance Berkman	7.50
(157) Bret Boone	7.50
(158) Ellis Burks	7.50
(159) Sean Casey	7.50
(160) Carlos Delgado	10.00
(161) J.D. Drew	10.00
(162) Jim Edmonds	7.50
(163) Cliff Floyd	7.50
(164) Freddy Garcia	7.50
(165) Jason Giambi	10.00
(166) Brian Giles	7.50
(167) Troy Glaus	10.00
(168) Vladimir Guerrero	12.50
(169) Mike Hampton	7.50
(170) Todd Helton	10.00
(171) Trevor Hoffman	7.50
(172) Tim Hudson	10.00
(173) Andruw Jones	12.50
(174) Jeff Kent	7.50
(175) Ryan Klesko	7.50
(176) Al Leiter	7.50
(177) Edgar Martinez	7.50
(178) Raul Mondesi	7.50
(179) Matt Morris	7.50
(180) Jamie Moyer	7.50
(181) Mark Mulder	7.50
(182) Mike Mussina	9.00
(183) Robb Nen	7.50
(184) Phil Nevin	7.50
(185) John Olerud	7.50
(186) Magglio Ordonez	7.50
(187) Roy Oswalt	7.50
(188) Chan Ho Park	7.50
(189) Troy Percival	7.50
(190) Albert Pujols	15.00
(191) Brad Radke	7.50
(192) Mariano Rivera	7.50
(193) Kazuhiro Sasaki	7.50
(194) Jeff Shaw	7.50
(195) Alfonso Soriano	9.00
(196) Frank Thomas	12.50
(197) Jim Thome	7.50
(198) Billy Wagner	7.50
(199) Kerry Wood	9.00
(200) Barry Zito	7.50

1991 Jimmy Dean

Baseball cards were inserted into packages of Jimmy Dean sausages in 1991. The complete set consists of 25 star players' cards. Red and yellow borders surround color player photos on the card fronts. No team logos appear on the cards. The card backs

feature statistics, biographical information and a facsimile autograph. The set is entitled the "Signature Edition." An uncut sheet was also available via special offer.

	NM/M
Complete Set (25):	5.00
Common Player:	.15
Uncut Sheet:	6.00
1 Will Clark	.15
2 Ken Griffey Jr.	.75
3 Dale Murphy	.25
4 Barry Bonds	1.00
5 Darryl Strawberry	.15
6 Ryne Sandberg	.25
7 Gary Sheffield	.25
8 Sandy Alomar, Jr.	.15
9 Frank Thomas	.45
10 Barry Larkin	.15
11 Kirby Puckett	.50
12 George Brett	.60
13 Kevin Mitchell	.15
14 Dave Justice	.15
15 Cal Ripken, Jr.	1.00
16 Craig Biggio	.15
17 Rickey Henderson	.45
18 Roger Clemens	.60
19 Jose Canseco	.25
20 Ozzie Smith	.50
21 Cecil Fielder	.15
22 Dave Winfield	.45
23 Kevin Maas	.15
24 Nolan Ryan	1.00
25 Dwight Gooden	.15

1992 Jimmy Dean

For the second year in a row, baseball cards were inserted into packages of Jimmy Dean sausage in 1992. Featuring 18 star players, the set portrays the player's name on a vertical panel at the left of the card, along with his team name and position. The Jimmy Dean logo appears in the lower-right corner. Major League team logos have been eliminated from the photos.

	NM/M
Complete Set (18):	5.00
Common Player:	.15
1 Jim Abbott	.15
2 Barry Bonds	1.50
3 Jeff Bagwell	.45
4 Frank Thomas	.45
5 Steve Avery	.15
6 Chris Sabo	.15
7 Will Clark	.15
8 Don Mattingly	.60
9 Darryl Strawberry	.15
10 Roger Clemens	.60
11 Ken Griffey Jr.	1.00
12 Chuck Knoblauch	.15
13 Tony Gwynn	.50
14 Juan Gonzalez	.30
15 Cecil Fielder	.15
16 Bobby Bonilla	.15
17 Wes Chamberlain	.15
18 Ryne Sandberg	.50

1992 Jimmy Dean Living Legends

Approximately 100,000 of these six-card sets were made available via a mail-in offer for $1 and proofs of purchase from the company's breakfast meats. Color photos on front have had uniform logos removed and are overprinted with a gold-foil facsimile autograph. Other gold foil highlights the player, team and sponsor names on front. Backs are printed in black and yellow and include a few biographical details, career highlights and summary statistics.

	NM/M
Complete Set (6):	8.00
Common Player:	.15
1 George Brett	2.00
2 Carlton Fisk	1.00
3 Ozzie Smith	1.50
4 Robin Yount	1.00
5 Cal Ripken, Jr.	1.00
6 Nolan Ryan	3.00

Rookie Stars

Nine of 1992's hottest rookies were featured in this set issued as inserts into various Jimmy Dean meat products. Cards feature full-bleed photos on which uniform logos have been airbrushed away. A 1992 Rookie Star logo appears at upper-left, atop a black vertical strip containing the player's name, team and position. A white strip at bottom has the Jimmy Dean logo. On back, personal data and minor and major league stats are featured in a center panel, surrounded by a light blue border.

	NM/M
Complete Set (9):	3.00
Common Player:	.50
1 Andy Stankiewicz	.50
2 Pat Listach	.50
3 Brian Jordan	.50
4 Eric Karros	.50
5 Reggie Sanders	.50
6 Dave Fleming	.50
7 Donovan Osborne	.50
8 Kenny Lofton	.50
9 Moises Alou	.50

1993 Jimmy Dean

Issued in the company's meat products and via a mail-in offer, this set once again features player photos on which the uniform logos have been airbrushed away, due to lack of a license from Major League

Baseball. A pair of horizontal color bars in one of the lower corners contains a Jimmy Dean logo and the player's name. Backs have a line drawing portrait of the player, along with stats, personal data and logos.

	NM/M
Complete Set (28):	6.00
Common Player:	.15
1 Frank Thomas	.50
2 Barry Larkin	.15
3 Cal Ripken	1.25
4 Andy Van Slyke	.15
5 Darren Daulton	.15
6 Don Mattingly	.65
7 Roger Clemens	.65
8 Juan Gonzalez	.35
9 Mark Langston	.15
10 Barry Bonds	1.25
11 Ken Griffey Jr.	.75
12 Cecil Fielder	.15
13 Kirby Puckett	.60
14 Tom Glavine	.25
15 George Brett	.65
16 Nolan Ryan	1.25
17 Eddie Murray	.50
18 Gary Sheffield	.35
19 Doug Drabek	.15
20 Ray Lankford	.15
21 Benito Santiago	.15
22 Mark McGwire	1.00
23 Kenny Lofton	.15
24 Eric Karros	.15
25 Ryne Sandberg	.60
26 Charlie Hayes	.15
27 Mike Mussina	.25
28 Pat Listach	.15

Rookie Cards

Jimmy Dean Foods issued a Rookie Stars baseball card set in 1993. The nine-card set features promising rookies, with players highlighted against a marblized background with color photos on both sides of the cards. The cards were distributed randomly in three-card sets in specially-marked packages of Jimmy Dean products.

	NM/M
Complete Set (9):	3.00
Common Player:	.10
(1) Rich Amaral	.10
(2) Vinny Castilla	.15
(3) Jeff Conine	.25
(4) Brent Gates	.10
(5) Wayne Kirby	.10
(6) Mike Lansing	.25
(7) David Nied	.10
(8) Mike Piazza	2.00
(9) Tim Salmon	.75

1995 Jimmy Dean All Time Greats

Six Hall of Famers are featured in this promotion for the country singer's breakfast meats. Besides inclusion of

regular cards in food packages, a send-away deal offered autographed cards of three of the players for proofs of purchase and $7 apiece. Cards feature action photos on which team uniform logos have been removed; while the cards are licensed by the Major League Baseball Players Alumni, they are not sanctioned by MLB. A large "1995 All Time Greats Collectors Set" logo appears in the upper-right corner on front, while the Jimmy Dean logo and player name are in the lower-left. Full-color backs offer a career summary and lifetime stats, along with a ghost image of the front photo.

	NM/M
Complete Set (6):	5.00
Common Player:	.50
1 Rod Carew	.50
2 Jim "Catfish" Hunter	.50
2a Jim "Catfish" Hunter/ Auto.	15.00
3 Al Kaline	1.50
3a Al Kaline/Auto.	8.00
4 Mike Schmidt	1.50
5 Billy Williams	.50
5a Billy Williams/Auto.	8.00
6 Carl Yastrzemski	1.50

1997 Jimmy Dean Great Moments

These two-card sets were available via a mail-in offer for $12.95 apiece plus proofs of purchase. Each set consists of an autographed "Great Moments in Baseball" card with an action photo and a "Great Baseball Stadiums" card featuring a player photo set against the stadium background. All pictures are sepia toned with uniform logos removed. Cards have player or stadium information on the backs and came with a certificate of authenticity.

	NM/M
Complete Set (4):	35.00
(1) Yogi Berra/Auto.	20.00
(2) Yogi Berra (Yankee Stadium)	5.00
(3) Brooks Robinson/ Auto.	10.00
(4) Brooks Robinson (Memorial Stadium)	3.00

1984 Decathlon Negro League Baseball Stars

According to contemporary advertising, this set was produced in conjunction with the Negro Baseball Hall of History in Kentucky, to a total of 2,000 sets and 300 uncut sheets. The cards and checklist are identical to the 1986 issue by Larry Fritsch Cards,

Negro League Baseball Stars — Ray Dandridge

which purchased rights to the set, except for the copyright line at bottom on back.

	NM/M
Complete Set (119):	35.00
Common Player:	.30
Stars:	3X

1985 Decathlon Ultimate Baseball Card Set

MAYSVILLE

Originally intended to be a six-series, 90-card issue, this collectors' set was cut short after the first series. The large-format (4" x 5-5/8") cards feature on front color artwork by former Topps artist Gerry Dvorak. The portraits are surrounded by a white border. Black-and-white backs have a career capsule. Announced as an edition of 10,000 sets, original issue price was about $11.

	NM/M
Complete Set (15):	20.00
Common Player:	1.00
1 Ty Cobb	3.00
2 Honus Wagner	3.00
3 Babe Ruth	4.00
4 Lou Gehrig	4.00
5 Frank Baker	1.00
6 Casey Stengel	1.00
7 Moses Walker	1.00
8 Cy Young	1.00
9 Joe DiMaggio	4.00
10 John McGraw	1.00
11 Josh Gibson	1.00
12 Johnny Mize	1.00
13 Walter Johnson	1.00
14 Walter Alston	1.00
15 Enos Slaughter	1.00

1993 Dempster's Blue Jays

One of several Canadian baseball card issues marking the 1992 World Series victory of the Toronto Blue Jays, the Dempster's stores set is a 25-card issue in standard 2-1/2"

x 3-1/2", UV-coatd on both sides. Fronts have a large dark blue border with white horizontal white pinstripes. An action photo is at center, with the player's name and position below. The Jays World Championship logo and Players Association logo are at top; the sponsor's logo at lower-right. A baseball at bottom center has the card number. Backs feature a large portrait photo at top, against a dark blue background. Color bars carry the player's '92 and career stats. A facsimile autograph appears beneath the team logo at right.

	NM/M
Complete Set (25):	6.50
Common Player:	.25
1 Juan Guzman	.25
2 Roberto Alomar	.75
3 Danny Cox	.25
4 Paul Molitor	4.00
5 Todd Stottlemyre	.25
6 Joe Carter	.50
7 Jack Morris	.35
8 Ed Sprague	.25
9 Turner Ward	.25
10 John Olerud	.75
11 Duane Ward	.25
12 Alfredo Griffin	.25
13 Cito Gaston	.25
14 Dave Stewart	.25
15 Mark Eichhorn	.25
16 Darnell Coles	.25
17 Randy Knorr	.25
18 Al Leiter	.25
19 Pat Hentgen	.25
20 Devon White	.25
21 Pat Borders	.25
22 Darrin Jackson	.25
23 Dick Schofield	.25
24 Luis Sojo	.25
25 Mike Timlin	.25

1991 Denny's Grand Slam

This 26-card set was produced by Upper Deck and features one player from each Major League team. One hologram card was distributed with the purchase of a Grand Slam meal. The cards are numbered on the front and are 3-D. The card backs describe grand slams hit by the featured player.

	NM/M
Complete Set (26):	12.50
Common Player:	.50
1 Ellis Burks	.50
2 Cecil Fielder	.50
3 Will Clark	.50
4 Eric Davis	.50
5 Dave Parker	.50
6 Kelly Gruber	.50
7 Kent Hrbek	.50
8 Don Mattingly	1.50
9 Brook Jacoby	.50
10 Mark McGwire	2.00
11 Howard Johnson	.50
12 Tim Wallach	.50
13 Ricky Jordan	.50
14 Andre Dawson	.75
15 Eddie Murray	1.00
16 Danny Tartabull	.50
17 Bobby Bonilla	.50
18 Benito Santiago	.50
19 Alvin Davis	.50
20 Cal Ripken	2.50
21 Ruben Sierra	.50
22 Pedro Guerrero	.50
23 Wally Joyner	.50
24 Craig Biggio	.50
25 Dave Justice	.50
26 Tim Raines	.50

1992 Denny's Grand Slam

The second year of the Denny's Gland Slam promotion featured one power hitter from each major league team, portrayed on a hologram in front of a scene from his team's city. As in the first year, the cards were produced by Upper Deck and given away, one at a time, with a Denny's purchase during the middle of the summer. An album with plastic pages holding four cards each was also available.

	NM/M
Complete Set (26):	7.50
Common Player:	.25
Album:	3.00
1 Marquis Grissom	.25
2 Ken Caminiti	.25
3 Fred McGriff	.25
4 Felix Jose	.25
5 Jack Clark	.25
6 Albert Belle	.25
7 Sid Bream	.25
8 Robin Ventura	.25
9 Cal Ripken, Jr.	2.00
10 Ryne Sandberg	1.00
11 Paul O'Neill	.25
12 Luis Polonia	.25
13 Cecil Fielder	.25
14 Kal Daniels	.25
15 Brian McRae	.25
16 Howard Johnson	.25
17 Greg Vaughn	.25
18 Dale Murphy	.60
19 Kent Hrbek	.25
20 Barry Bonds	2.00
21 Matt Nokes	.25
22 Jose Canseco	.50
23 Jay Buhner	.25
24 Will Clark	.25
25 Ruben Sierra	.25
26 Joe Carter	.25

1993 Denny's Grand Slam

The 1993 Denny's Grand Slam set expanded to 28 cards with the addition of the Florida and Colorado expansion teams. The featured color photos of one grand slam slugger for each team superimposed over the player's grand slam background. The reverse of each card gives anecdotes about the player's grand slams along with his career total. The cards were distributed at participating Denny's restaurants during mid-summer.

	NM/M
Complete Set (28):	7.50
Common Player:	.25
1 Chili Davis	.25
2 Eric Anthony	.25
3 Rickey Henderson	.60

4 Joe Carter	.25
5 Terry Pendleton	.25
6 Robin Yount	.60
7 Ray Lankford	.25
8 Ryne Sandberg	.75
9 Darryl Strawberry	.25
10 Marquis Grissom	.25
11 Will Clark	.25
12 Albert Belle	.25
13 Edgar Martinez	.25
14 Benito Santiago	.25
15 Eddie Murray	.60
16 Cal Ripken, Jr.	2.00
17 Gary Sheffield	.45
18 Dave Hollins	.25
19 Andy Van Slyke	.25
20 Juan Gonzalez	.45
21 John Valentin	.25
22 Joe Oliver	.25
23 Dante Bichette	.25
24 Wally Joyner	.25
25 Cecil Fielder	.25
26 Kirby Puckett	.75
27 Robin Ventura	.25
28 Danny Tartabull	.25

1994 Denny's Grand Slam

For its fourth annual hologram card promotion, Denny's chose a horizontal format with portrait and action photos of one player from each major league team. Designated the "Anniversary Edition," the set features the 125th year logo at bottom center, with the player's name at left; Upper Deck and Denny's logos are at top. On back the same two photos are conventionally printed along with a brief player biography, appropriate logos and copyright notices. The cards are numbered alphabetically. Cards were available with certain menu items from July 1 through August 31. Each restaurant received one special boxed set for use as a contest prize. These sets include a special Reggie Jackson "Route to Cooperstown" hologram card; the edition was limited to about 1,500.

	NM/M
Complete Set (28 / no Jackson):	7.50
Common Player:	.25
1 Jim Abbott	.25
2 Roberto Alomar	.35
3 Kevin Appier	.25
4 Jeff Bagwell	.60
5 Albert Belle	.25
6 Barry Bonds	2.00
7 Bobby Bonilla	.25
8 Lenny Dykstra	.25
9 Cal Eldred	.25
10 Cecil Fielder	.25
11 Andres Galarraga	.25
12 Juan Gonzalez	.40
13 Ken Griffey Jr.	1.00
14 Tony Gwynn	.75
15 Rickey Henderson	.60
16 Kent Hrbek	.25
17 David Justice	.25
18 Mike Piazza	1.50
19 Jose Rijo	.25
20 Cal Ripken, Jr.	2.00
21 Tim Salmon	.25
22 Ryne Sandberg	.75
23 Gary Sheffield	.35
24 Ozzie Smith	.75
25 Frank Thomas	.60
26 Andy Van Slyke	.25
27 Mo Vaughn	.25
28 Larry Walker	.25
--- Reggie Jackson	60.00

1995 Denny's Classic Hits

	NM/M
Complete Set (28):	5.00

For the fifth consecutive year, this August 1-September 30 promotion offered a hologram baseball card with the purchase of selected items from the restaurant's "Classic Hits" menu. The cards were produced for Denny's by Upper Deck and combine photographic and holographic images of the player on the horizontal-format front. Backs have another color photo, career highlights, and past-season/lifetime stats. Each Major League team is represented in the set by one player card. According to advertisements for the promotion, a total of 8,000,000 cards was produced - about 286,000 of each player.

	NM/M
Complete Set (28):	6.00
Common Player:	.15
1 Roberto Alomar	.30
2 Moises Alou	.15
3 Jeff Bagwell	.35
4 Albert Belle	.15
5 Jason Bere	.15
6 Roger Clemens	.15
7 Darren Daulton	.15
8 Cecil Fielder	.15
9 Andres Galarraga	.15
10 Juan Gonzalez	.35
11 Ken Griffey Jr.	.75
12 Tony Gwynn	.50
13 Barry Larkin	.15
14 Greg Maddux	.50
15 Don Mattingly	.50
16 Mark McGwire	1.00
17 Orlando Merced	.15
18 Jeff Montgomery	.15
19 Rafael Palmeiro	.35
20 Mike Piazza	1.00
21 Kirby Puckett	.50
22 Bret Saberhagen	.15
23 Tim Salmon	.15
24 Gary Sheffield	.30
25 Ozzie Smith	.50
26 Sammy Sosa	.50
27 Greg Vaughn	.15
28 Matt Williams	.15

1996 Denny's Instant Replay Holograms

Pinnacle, in its first year as supplier for Denny's annual baseball card promotion, attempted breakthrough technology that didn't quite hit the mark. The hologram portion of the card front was supposed to show as much as four seconds of on-field action, but unless viewed at exactly the right distance and angle, and under exacting light requirements, the action is little more than a silver-foil streak. Card fronts also included a color player photo. Another color photo appears on the back, along with a description of the action on front for those who couldn't master the "Full Motion" hologram. Cards were sold in single-card foil packs for 49 cents (limit two) with a qualifying purchase. Besides the hologram card, each pack includes a card explaining "How To View a Full Motion Hologram." Besides the regular cards, two "Grand Slam" chase sets were issued along with instant winner cards for complete card sets or trips to the World Series. Stated odds on the chase cards would indicate about 750,000 of each regular card were produced. One player from each team is represented in the checklist.

	NM/M
Complete Set (28):	5.00

Common Player:	.15
1 Greg Maddux	.50
2 Cal Ripken Jr.	1.00
3 Frank Thomas	.45
4 Albert Belle	.15
5 Mo Vaughn	.15
6 Jeff Bagwell	.45
7 Jay Buhner	.15
8 Barry Bonds	1.00
9 Ryne Sandberg	.50
10 Hideo Nomo	.35
11 Kirby Puckett	.50
12 Gary Sheffield	.30
13 Barry Larkin	.50
14 Wade Boggs	.50
15 Tony Gwynn	.50
16 Tim Salmon	.15
17 Jason Isringhausen	.15
18 Cecil Fielder	.15
19 Dante Bichette	.15
20 Ozzie Smith	.50
21 Ivan Rodriguez	.35
22 Kevin Appier	.15
23 Joe Carter	.15
24 Moises Alou	.15
25 Mark McGwire	.75
26 Kevin Seitzer	.15
27 Darren Daulton	.15
28 Jay Bell	.15

1996 Denny's Grand Slam

Exploding fireworks in the background are an allegory for the firepower brought to the plate by the sluggers featured in this chase set from Denny's annual baseball card promotion. A Grand Slam card is randomly substituted for the standard hologram card about once every 56 packs.

	NM/M
Complete Set (10):	13.50
Common Player:	1.00
1 Cal Ripken Jr.	2.50
2 Frank Thomas	1.50
3 Mike Piazza	2.25
4 Tony Gwynn	2.00
5 Sammy Sosa	2.00
6 Barry Bonds	2.50
7 Jeff Bagwell	1.50
8 Albert Belle	1.00
9 Mo Vaughn	1.00
10 Kirby Puckett	2.00

Artist's Proofs

A specially marked Artist's Proof version of the Grand Slam chase cards are substituted for the standard hologram card in about every 360 packs, according to stated odds.

	NM/M
Complete Set (10):	50.00
Common Player:	2.00
1 Cal Ripken Jr.	10.00
2 Frank Thomas	5.00
3 Mike Piazza	7.50
4 Tony Gwynn	6.00
5 Sammy Sosa	6.00
6 Barry Bonds	10.00
7 Jeff Bagwell	5.00
8 Albert Belle	2.00
9 Mo Vaughn	2.00
10 Kirby Puckett	6.00

1997 Denny's 3-D Holograms

Denny's seventh annual baseball card issue was produced by Pinnacle and showcases two popular card technologies. Fronts of the 3-1/2" x 2-1/2" horizontal cards feature a deep 3D look. Backs have a player portrait hologram at the right. A partial baseball at left is the background for player data and stats along with sponsor and licensor logos. Cards were distributed one per pack for 59 cents from June 26-Sept. 3, with 10 cents from the sale of each card being donated to children's charities. The set features one player from each major league team, plus a Jackie Robinson tribute card.

		NM/M
Complete Set (29):		8.00
Common Player:		.20
1	Tim Salmon	.20
2	Rafael Palmeiro	.45
3	Mo Vaughn	.20
4	Frank Thomas	.50
5	David Justice	.20
6	Travis Fryman	.20
7	Johnny Damon	.35
8	John Jaha	.20
9	Chuck Knoblauch	.20
10	Mark McGwire	1.00
11	Alex Rodriguez	1.00
12	Juan Gonzalez	.35
13	Roger Clemens	.65
14	Derek Jeter	1.50
15	Andruw Jones	.50
16	Sammy Sosa	.60
17	Barry Larkin	.20
18	Dante Bichette	.20
19	Jeff Bagwell	.50
20	Mike Piazza	.75
21	Gary Sheffield	.35
22	Vladimir Guerrero	.50
23	Todd Hundley	.20
24	Jason Kendall	.20
25	Ray Lankford	.20
26	Ken Caminiti	.20
27	Barry Bonds	1.50
28	Scott Rolen	.40
29	Jackie Robinson (50th Anniversary Commemorative)	1.50

1997 Denny's Larry Doby

In the same format as the restaurant chain's regular set of 1997, this card honors the first black player to appear in the American League. The card was available only at the All-Star FanFest and All-Star Game in Cleveland in early July. Fronts have a black-and-white 3-D image; backs have a color hologram at right and a 50th anniversary logo at upper-left. Personal data, career highlights and stats are included, as well as appropriate logos.

		NM/M
1	Larry Doby	6.00

1981 Detroit News Tigers Centennial

The 100th anniversary of professional baseball in Detroit was marked by "The Detroit News" with the issue of this set honoring "The Boys of Summer." The 2-1/2" x 3-1/2" cards have black-and-white photos on front, over a mock

sports page. Cards can be found either with or without a red border on front, though the relative scarcity of each version is not known. Black-and-white backs have player data, career summary and stats, or a description of the front photo/highlight.

		NM/M
Complete Set (135):		30.00
Common Player:		.25
1	Detroit Boys of Summer 100th Anniversary	.25
2	Charles W. Bennett	.25
3	Mickey Cochrane	.25
4	Harry Heilmann	.25
5	Walter O. Briggs	.25
6	Mark Fidrych	.75
7	1887 Tigers	.25
8	Tiger Stadium	.25
9	Rudy York	.25
10	George Kell	.25
11	Steve O'Neill	.25
12	John Hiller	.25
13	1934 Tigers	.25
14	Charlie Gehringer	.45
15	Denny McLain	.60
16	Billy Rogell	.25
17	Ty Cobb	5.00
18	Sparky Anderson	.60
19	Davy Jones	.25
20	Kirk Gibson	.45
21	Pat Mullin	.25
22	1972 Tigers	.25
23	What a Night	.25
24	"Doc" Cramer	.25
25	Mickey Stanley	.25
26	Johnny Lipon	.25
27	Jo Jo White	.25
28	Recreation Park	.25
29	Wild Bill Donovan	.25
30	Ray Oyler	.25
31	Earl Whitehill	.25
32	Billy Hoeft	.25
33	Johnny Groth	.25
34	Hughie Jennings	.25
35	Mayo Smith	.25
36	Bennett Park	.25
37	Tigers Win	.25
38	Donie Bush	.25
39	Harry Coveleski	.25
40	Paul Richards	.25
41	Jonathan Stone	.25
42	Bill Swift	.25
43	Roy Cullenbine	.25
44	Hoot Evers	.25
45	Tigers Win Series	.25
46	Art Houtteman	.25
47	Aurelio Rodriguez	.25
48	Fred Hutchinson	.25
49	Don Mossi	.25
50	Gehrig's Streak Ends in Detroit (Lou Gehrig)	2.50
51	Earl Wilson	.25
52	Jim Northrup	.25
53	1907 Tigers	.25
54	Greenberg's Two Homers Ties Ruth (Hank Greenberg)	.45
55	Mickey Lolich	.45
56	Tommy Bridges	.25
57	Al Benton	.25
58	Del Baker	.25
59	Lou Whitaker	.45
60	Navin Field	.25
61	1945 Tigers	.25
62	Ernie Harwell	.25
63	League Champs	.25
64	Bobo Newsom	.25
65	Don Wert	.25
66	Ed Summers	.25
67	Billy Martin	.45
68	Alan Trammell	1.50
69	Dale Alexander	.25
70	Ed Brinkman	.25
71	Right Man in Right Place Wins (Ted Williams)	2.00
72	Bill Freehan	.25
73	Norm Cash	.60
74	George Dauss	.25
75	Aurelio Lopez	.25
76	Charlie Maxwell	.25
77	Ed Barrow	.25
78	Willie Horton	.25
79	Denny Sets Record (Denny McLain)	.45
80	Dan Brouthers	.25
81	John E. Fetzer	.25
82	Heinie Manush	.25
83	1935 Tigers	.25
84	Ray Boone	.25
85	Bob Fothergill	.25
86	Steve Kemp	.25
87	Ed Killian	.25
88	Giebell is Ineligible (Floyd Giebell)	.25
89	Pinky Higgins	.25
90	Lance Parrish	.25
91	Eldon Auker	.25
92	Birdie Tebbetts	.25
93	Schoolboy Rowe	.25
94	McLain Wins 30th (Denny McLain)	.45
95	1909 Tigers	.25

96	Harvey Kuenn	.40
97	Jim Bunning	.60
98	1940 Tigers	.25
99	Rocky Colavito	2.50
100	Kaline Enters Hall of Fame (Al Kaline)	1.00
101	Billy Bruton	.25
102	Germany Schaefer	.25
103	Frank Bolling	.25
104	Briggs Stadium	.25
105	Bucky Harris	.25
106	Gates Brown	.25
107	Martin Made the Difference (Billy Martin)	.25
108	1908 Tigers	.25
109	"Gee" Walker	.25
110	Pete Fox	.25
111	Virgil Trucks	.25
112	1968 Tigers	1.50
113	Dizzy Trout	.25
114	Barney McCosky	.25
115	Lu Blue	.25
116	Hal Newhouser	.25
117	Tigers are Home for Series	.25
118	Bobby Veach	.25
119	George Mullins (Mullin)	.25
120	Reggie's Super Homer (Reggie Jackson)	.60
121	Sam Crawford	.25
122	Hank Aguirre	.25
123	Vic Wertz	.25
124	Goose Goslin	.25
125	Frank Lary	.25
126	Joe Coleman	.25
127	Ed Katalinas	.25
128	Jack Morris	.25
129	3 Time AL Leaders	.25
130	James A. Campbell	.25
131	Ted Gray	.25
132	Al Kaline	5.00
133	Hank Greenberg	2.50
134	Dick McAuliffe	.25
135	Ozzie Virgil	.25

1988 Detroit Tigers Police

This unnumbered issue, sponsored by the Michigan State Police features 13 players and manager Sparky Anderson in full-color standard-size (2-1/2" x 3-1/2") cards. Player photos are framed by a blue border, with the Detroit logo upper left and a large name block that lists the player's name, position batting/throwing preference, height, weight and birthday beneath the photo. The backs carry an anti-drug or anti-crime message.

		NM/M
Complete Set (14):		7.00
Common Player:		.50
(1)	Doyle Alexander	.50
(2)	Sparky Anderson	1.00
(3)	Dave Bergman	.50
(4)	Tom Brookens	.50
(5)	Darrell Evans	.60
(6)	Larry Herndon	.50
(7)	Chet Lemon	.50
(8)	Jack Morris	.60
(9)	Matt Nokes	.50
(10)	Jeff Robinson	.50
(11)	Frank Tanana	.50
(12)	Walt Terrell	.50
(13)	Alan Trammell	1.00
(14)	Lou Whitaker	.75

1989 Detroit Tigers Police

This unnumbered issue, distributed and sponsored by the Michigan State Police Department features 14 full-color 2-1/2" x 3-1/2" cards. Player photos are framed by a blue and orange border,

(21) GUILLERMO HERNANDEZ—P
B-L T-L HT: 6'2", WT: 185, BORN: 11-14-54

with the team logo in the upper left and biographical information below the photo. The card backs feature anti-drug or anti-crime messages.

		NM/M
Complete Set (14):		4.00
Common Player:		.25
(1)	Doyle Alexander	.25
(2)	Sparky Anderson	.75
(3)	Dave Bergman	.25
(4)	Mike Henneman	.25
(5)	Guillermo Hernandez	.25
(6)	Chet Lemon	.25
(7)	Fred Lynn	.25
(8)	Jack Morris	.35
(9)	Matt Nokes	.25
(10)	Jeff Robinson	.25
(11)	Pat Sheridan	.25
(12)	Frank Tanana	.25
(13)	Alan Trammell	.75
(14)	Lou Whitaker	.50

1991 Detroit Tigers Police

One of the scarcer safety issues is this Tigers team issue. Cards have a color player action photo on front with orange and blue team-color graphics. Backs have a safety message and the logos of sponsors HSP and Team Michigan, along with the Michigan State Police. The unnumbered cards are checklisted here alphabetically.

		NM/M
Complete Set (14):		7.00
Common Player:		.50
(1)	Sparky Anderson	.75
(2)	Dave Bergman	.50
(3)	Cecil Fielder	.75
(4)	Travis Fryman	.50
(5)	Paul Gibson	.50
(6)	Jerry Don Gleaton	.50
(7)	Lloyd Moseby	.50
(8)	Dan Petry	.50
(9)	Tony Phillips	.50
(10)	Mark Salas	.50
(11)	John Shelby	.50
(12)	Frank Tanana	.50
(13)	Alan Trammell	.75
(14)	Lou Whitaker	.75

1993 Diamond Marks Prototypes

In the same format as the regular-issue DiamondMark cards, these promos were produced to preview the concept for dealers and collectors. The promo cards feature

different photos than those used on the issued version. The unnumbered cards are listed here alphabetically. On the back of the promos, the phrase "1993 PROTOTYPE" appears vertically at left.

		NM/M
Complete Set (8):		40.00
Common Player:		3.00
(1)	Roberto Alomar	4.00
(2)	Will Clark	3.00
(3)	Dennis Eckersley	5.00
(4)	Juan Gonzalez	4.00
(5)	Ken Griffey Jr.	10.00
(6)	Kirby Puckett	7.50
(7)	Ryne Sandberg	6.00
(8)	Frank Thomas	6.00

1993 Diamond Marks

While they look like baseball cards and were sold in foil packs like baseball cards, DaimondMarks were licensed as book marks. Issued by Barry Colla Productions, the 2-1/2" x 5" cards feature Barry Colla's trademark high-quality player photos on front and back. The UV-coated fronts feature black borders with the player's name in white above the photo and a color team logo beneath. Backs, also bordered in black, feature two color player photos in an open book design. There is a portrait photo on the left and a head-and-shoulders reproduction of the front photo at right. A bookmark with team logo is incorporated in the design. The 120-card set is unnumbered and is arranged in the checklist below alphabetically within league and team.

		NM/M
Complete Set (120):		12.00
Common Player:		.15
Wax Box (48):		20.00
Atlanta Braves		
(1)	Steve Avery	.15
(2)	Ron Gant	.15
(3)	Tom Glavine	.35
(4)	David Justice	.15
(5)	Terry Pendleton	.15
(6)	Deion Sanders	.25
(7)	John Smoltz	.15
Chicago Cubs		
(8)	Mark Grace	.15
(9)	Randy Myers	.15
(10)	Ryne Sandberg	.75
(11)	Jose Vizcaino	.15
Cincinnati Reds		
(12)	Bobby Kelly	.15
(13)	Barry Larkin	.15
(14)	Kevin Mitchell	.15
(15)	Jose Rijo	.15
(16)	Reggie Sanders	.15
Colorado Rockies		
(17)	Dante Bichette	.15
(18)	Daryl Boston	.15
(19)	Andres Galarraga	.15
(20)	Charlie Hayes	.15
Florida Marlins		
(21)	Orestes Destrade	.15
(22)	Benito Santiago	.15
(23)	Gary Sheffield	.35
(24)	Walt Weiss	.15

Houston Astros		
(25)	Jeff Bagwell	.60
(26)	Craig Biggio	.15
(27)	Ken Caminiti	.15
(28)	Luis Gonzalez	.15
Los Angeles Dodgers		
(29)	Brett Butler	.15
(30)	Eric Davis	.15
(31)	Orel Hershiser	.15
(32)	Eric Karros	.15
(33)	Ramon Martinez	.15
(34)	Mike Piazza	1.50
(35)	Darryl Strawberry	.15
Montreal Expos		
(36)	Moises Alou	.15
(37)	Delino DeShields	.15
(38)	Marquis Grissom	.15
(39)	Dennis Martinez	.15
(40)	Larry Walker	.15
New York Mets		
(41)	Bobby Bonilla	.15
(42)	Dwight Gooden	.15
(43)	Howard Johnson	.15
(44)	Eddie Murray	.60
Philadelphia Phillies		
(45)	Darren Daulton	.15
(46)	Lenny Dykstra	.15
(47)	Dave Hollins	.15
(48)	John Kruk	.15
Pittsburgh Pirates		
(49)	Jay Bell	.15
(50)	Al Martin	.15
(51)	Orlando Merced	.15
(52)	Andy Van Slyke	.15
St. Louis Cardinals		
(53)	Gregg Jefferies	.15
(54)	Tom Pagnozzi	.15
(55)	Ozzie Smith	.75
(56)	Todd Zeile	.15
San Diego Padres		
(57)	Derek Bell	.15
(58)	Tony Gwynn	.75
(59)	Fred McGriff	.15
San Francisco Giants		
(60)	Barry Bonds	2.00
(61)	John Burkett	.15
(62)	Will Clark	.15
(63)	Matt Williams	.15
Baltimore Orioles		
(64)	Brady Anderson	.15
(65)	Mike Mussina	.30
(66)	Cal Ripken, Jr.	2.00
Boston Red Sox		
(67)	Roger Clemens	1.00
(68)	Andre Dawson	.30
(69)	Mike Greenwell	.15
(70)	Mo Vaughn	.15
Detroit Tigers		
(71)	Cecil Fielder	.15
(72)	Tony Phillips	.15
(73)	Mickey Tettleton	.15
(74)	Alan Trammell	.15
Cleveland Indians		
(75)	Sandy Alomar Jr.	.15
(76)	Carlos Baerga	.15
(77)	Albert Belle	.15
(78)	Kenny Lofton	.15
Chicago White Sox		
(79)	Bo Jackson	.25
(80)	Frank Thomas	.60
(81)	Robin Ventura	.15
California Angels		
(82)	Chad Curtis	.15
(83)	Gary DiSarcina	.15
(84)	Tim Salmon	.15
(85)	J.T. Snow	.15
Kansas City Royals		
(86)	George Brett	1.00
(87)	Wally Joyner	.15
(88)	Mike MacFarlane	.15
(89)	Brian McRae	.15
Milwaukee Brewers		
(90)	Darryl Hamilton	.15
(91)	Pat Listach	.15
(92)	B.J. Surhoff	.15
(93)	Robin Yount	.60
Minnesota Twins		
(94)	Kent Hrbek	.15
(95)	Chuck Knoblauch	.15
(96)	Kirby Puckett	.75
(97)	Dave Winfield	.60
New York Yankees		
(98)	Wade Boggs	.75
(99)	Don Mattingly	1.00
(100)	Danny Tartabull	.15
Oakland Athletics		
(101)	Dennis Eckersley	.50
(102)	Rickey Henderson	.60
(103)	Mark McGwire	1.50
(104)	Ruben Sierra	.15
(105)	Terry Steinbach	.15
Seattle Mariners		
(106)	Ken Griffey Jr.	1.50
(107)	Edgar Martinez	.15
(108)	Pete O'Brien	.15
(109)	David Valle	.15
Texas Rangers		
(110)	Jose Canseco	.35
(111)	Juan Gonzalez	.35
(112)	Ivan Rodriguez	.50
(113)	Nolan Ryan	2.00
Toronto Blue Jays		
(114)	Roberto Alomar	.30
(115)	Pat Borders	.15
(116)	Joe Carter	.15
(117)	Juan Guzman	.15
(118)	Paul Molitor	.60
(119)	John Olerud	.15
(120)	Dave Stewart	.15

Inserts

KEN GRIFFEY, JR.

Randomly inserted into packs of DiamondMarks cards at the rate of one per 48-pack carton was a series of eight cards featuring the baseball artwork of Terry Smith. The inserts are the same 2-1/2" x 5" size as the regular issue and carry on with the basic black bordered design, though the inserts are UV-coated both front and back. Beneath the fantasy-design player art on the front is the player's name. On back the open book design is seen again, with a short player profile on the left and a Barry Colla photo portrait on the right, along with the appropriate team logo.

		NM/M
Complete Set (8):		50.00
Common Player:		5.00
(1)	Roberto Alomar	6.00
(2)	Barry Bonds	15.00
(3)	Ken Griffey Jr.	10.00
(4)	David Justice	5.00
(5)	John Olerud	5.00
(6)	Nolan Ryan	15.00
(7)	Frank Thomas	7.50
(8)	Robin Yount	7.50

1981 Diamond Stars Extension Set

About 1980, an uncut sheet of artwork apparently intended for use in the original Diamond Stars series (1934-36) was discovered. The art was used to create a collectors' issue "extension" set by Den's Collectors Den of Maryland. The new cards were printed in the same 2-3/8" x 2-7/8" format as the 1930s issue with the player name on front. Backs are printed in blue with a career summary, biographical details and a 1981 copyright line. The set was sold in a heavy paper wrapper patterned after the original.

		NM/M
Complete Set (12):		5.00
Uncut Sheet:		25.00
Common Player:		.25
109	Benny Frey	.25
110	Pete Fox	.25
111	Phil Cavarretta	.35
112	Leon Goslin	.50
113	Mel Harder	.35
114	Roger Cramer	.35
115	Gene Moore	.25

116	Rip Collins	.35
117	Linus Frey	.25
118	Vernon Gomez	1.00
119	Jim Bottomley, Rogers Hornsby	1.50
120	Lon Warneke	.25

1993 Diamond Stars Extension Set

In the style of the 1934-36 Diamond Stars bubblegum cards from National Chicle Co., this collectors' issue features colorful painting of players from the mid-1930s. Cards measure about 2-3/8" x 2-7/8" with white borders on front with no player identification or other graphics. The artwork is by D'Augst Roth Martin. Backs have player id, personal data and a career summary purporting to have been written by Travis Lake in August, 1936, the man who wrote the backs for the original cards. A copyright line at bottom identifies the "Extended Edition" as a 1993 issue of "The Chicle Fantasy Co." According to the set's producer, 4,166 were printed with 1,936 cut into hand-numbered sets which were originally sold at $19.95. Promo versions of each card in the set have a red rubber-stamped ad on back.

		NM/M
Complete Set, Uncut Sheet:		15.00
Complete Set (36):		10.00
Common Player:		.25
121	Moe Berg	2.00
122	Harlond Clift	.25
123	Joe Cronin	.50
124	Dizzy Dean	1.00
125	Paul Dean	.50
126	Joe DiMaggio	3.00
127	Leo Durocher	.50
128	Bob Feller	1.00
129	Carl Fisher	.25
130	Lou Gehrig	2.00
131	Bump Hadley	.25
132	Jesse Haines	.25
133	Bad News Hale	.25
134	Gabby Hartnett	.25
135	Babe Herman	.25
136	Billy Herman	.25
137	Waite Hoyt	.25
138	Bob Johnson	.25
139	Chuck Klein	.50
140	Mike Kreevich	.25
141	Fred Lindstrom	.25
142	Connie Mack	.50
143	Joe McCarthy	.25
144	Bill McKechnie	.25
145	Johnny Mize	.60
146	Johnny Moore	.25
147	Hugh Mulcahy	.25
148	Buck Newsom	.25
149	Al Smith	.25
150	Casey Stengel	1.00
151	Arky Vaughan	.25
152	Gee Walker	.25
153	Kenesaw M. Landis	.25
	Cool Papa Bell	.25
	Josh Gibson	.50
	Satchel Paige	1.00
	Title card	.10

1992 Diet Pepsi Collector Series

This Canadian issue includes 30 top stars, with a slight emphasis on the two Canadian teams. Because the set is licensed only by the players' association, and not Major League Baseball, all photos had team logos eliminated. Fronts feature action photo with Diet Pepsi logos in a strip

---

1992 COLLECTOR SERIES
SÉRIE DE COLLECTION

DIET PEPSI · Dwight Gooden · DIET PEPSI

below. Backs have a portrait photo, recent stats and a facsimile autograph. Card number 5 of Tom Glavine can be found showing him pitching right-handed (error) or left-handed (right). Cards are UV coated on both sides. A poster picturing all 30 cards was also issued. Cards were issued in three-card packs.

		NM/M
Complete Set (30):		7.00
Poster:		7.50
Common Player:		.15
1	Roger Clemens	.60
2	Dwight Gooden	.15
3	Tom Henke	.15
4	Dennis Martinez	.15
5a	Tom Glavine (Pitching right-handed.)	.25
5b	Tom Glavine (Pitching left-handed.)	.75
6	Jack Morris	.15
7	Dennis Eckersley	.35
8	Jeff Reardon	.15
9	Bryan Harvey	.15
10	Sandy Alomar Jr.	.15
11	Carlton Fisk	.40
12	Gary Carter	.40
13	Cecil Fielder	.15
14	Will Clark	.15
15	Roberto Alomar	.30
16	Ryne Sandberg	.50
17	Cal Ripken Jr.	1.50
18	Barry Larkin	.15
19	Ozzie Smith	.50
20	Kelly Gruber	.15
21	Wade Boggs	.50
22	Tim Wallach	.15
23	Howard Johnson	.15
24	Jose Canseco	.30
25	Joe Carter	.15
26	Ken Griffey Jr.	.65
27	Kirby Puckett	.40
28	Rickey Henderson	.40
29	Barry Bonds	1.50
30	Dave Winfield	.40

2002 Disabled American Veterans

In conjunction with its "DAV at the Ballpark" program, the vets' service organization and many Major League teams had special promotions during the 2002 season. Baseball cards featuring one or more members of the home team were distributed to fans. Cards share a format of standard 2-1/2" x 3-1/2" size with glossy coating on both sides. Fronts have action pictures against a ghosted image of the home ballpark. A small portrait photo also appears, along with team and DAV logos and a card number.

		NM/M
Complete Set (42):		30.00
Common Player:		1.00
1	Robby Hammock	1.00
	Austin Kearns	2.00

Backs have information about the DAV and contact data. This checklist is not complete.

		NM/M
Common Player:		1.00
2	Ben Sheets	1.00
5	Trevor Hoffman	1.00
8	Steve Cox	1.00
13	Jay Gibbons	1.00
14	Rusty Greer	1.00
15	Danny Graves	1.00
16	Todd Helton	1.50
17	Eddie Guardado	1.00
20	Kazuhiro Sasaki	1.00
21	Ichiro Suzuki	2.50
22	Mike Cameron, Mark McLemore	1.00
23	Mike Scioscia	1.00

2003 Disabled American Veterans

DAV
Richie SEXSON
Brewers

In conjunction with its "DAV at the Ballpark" program, the vets' service organization and several Major League teams had special promotions during the 2003 season. Baseball cards featuring one or more members of the home team were distributed to fans. Cards share a format of standard 2-1/2" x 3-1/2" size with glossy coating on both sides. Fronts have action pictures against a ghosted image of the home ballpark. A team and DAV logo also appear, along with uniform and "Limited Edition" card numbers. Backs have information about the DAV and contact data. This checklist is not complete.

		NM/M
Common Player:		1.00
3	Richie Sexson	1.00
9	Rocco Baldelli	1.50
12	Edgar Martinez	1.00
16	Preston Wilson	1.00
26	Adam Dunn	1.00

2004 Disabled American Veterans

SHEETS

In conjunction with its "DAV at the Ballpark" program, the vets' service organization and several Major League teams had special promotions during the 2004 season. Baseball cards featuring one or more members of the home team were distributed to fans. Cards share a format of standard 2-1/2" x 3-1/2" size with glossy coating on both sides. Fronts have a large portrait photo and smaller action photo. A team logo and uniform number are at top, at bottom is "Limited Edition" and a card number. Backs have information about the DAV and contact data.

Common Player:

3	Larry Bigbie	1.00
4	Wes Helms	1.00
5	Scott Podsednik	2.00
6	Ben Sheets	1.00
7	Brian Giles	1.00
8	Joel Pineiro	1.50
9	Dan Wilson	1.00
10	Ron Gardenhire	1.00
11	Eddie Guardado	1.00
12	Raul Ibanez	1.00
13	Hank Blalock	4.00
14	Mark Teixeira	2.00
15	Michael Young	1.00
16	Danys Baez	1.00
17	Jose Cruz Jr.	1.00
18	Robert Fick	1.00
19	Toby Hall	1.00
20	Tino Martinez	1.00
21	Mike Maroth	1.00
22	Lou Piniella	1.00
23	Damian Rolls	1.00
24	Doug Waechter	1.00
25	Don Zimmer	1.00
27	J.D. Drew	3.00
28	Horacio Ramirez	1.00
29	Jeff Kent	1.00
30	John Thomson	1.00
31	John Estrada	1.00
32	Rafael Furcal	1.00
33	John Smoltz	1.00
34	Chipper Jones	5.00
35	Marcus Giles	1.00
36	Andruw Jones	4.00
37	Josh Beckett	2.00
38	Miguel Cabrera	1.50
39	Hee Seop Choi	1.00
40	Brad Penny	1.00
41	Juan Pierre	1.50
42	Dontrelle Willis	1.00

2005 Disabled American Veterans

DAV
ICHIRO SUZUKI

These cards were issued by vets' service organization and several Major League teams in special promotions during the 2005 season. Baseball cards featuring one or more members of the home team were distributed to fans. Cards share a format of standard 2-1/2" x 3-1/2" size with glossy coating on both sides. Fronts have an action photo on a ball-and-glove background with team logo. At bottom is "Limited Edition" and a card number. Backs have information about the DAV and contact data.

Common Player:

1988 Domino's Pizza Tigers

DOMINO'S PIZZA SALUTES THE 1968 WORLD CHAMPION DETROIT TIGERS

Denny McLain

Domino's Pizza produced a 28-card set commemorating the 20th anniversary of the 1968 World Champion Detroit Tigers. The cards were given away at an Old Timers Game

---

at Tiger Stadium in 1988. The cards, which measure 2-1/2" x 3-1/2", feature black and white photos semi-surrounded by a two-stripe band. The stripes on the card's left side are the same color (red and light blue) as the Domino's Pizza logo in the upper corner. The stripes on the card's right side match the colors of the Tigers logo (red and dark blue). The backs of all the cards (except for Ernie Harwell) contain a brief summary of the Tigers' 1968 season. Located at the bottom on the card backs are the players' major league records through 1968 plus their 1968 World Series statistics.

		NM/M
Complete Set (29):		8.00
Common Player:		.25
(1)	Gates Brown	.25
(2)	Norm Cash	1.00
(3)	Wayne Comer	.25
(4)	Pat Dobson	.25
(5)	Bill Freehan	.60
(6)	John Hiller	.25
(7)	Ernie Harwell (Announcer)	.30
(8)	Willie Horton	.40
(9a)	Al Kaline/Btg	3.00
(9b)	Al Kaline (In outfield.)	3.00
(10)	Fred Lasher	.25
(11)	Mickey Lolich	.75
(12)	Tom Matchick	.25
(13)	Ed Mathews	1.25
(14)	Dick McAuliff (McAuliffe)	.25
(15)	Denny McLain	.75
(16)	Don McMahon	.25
(17)	Jim Northrup	.25
(18)	Ray Oyler	.25
(19)	Daryl Patterson	.25
(20)	Jim Price	.25
(21)	Joe Sparma	.25
(22)	Mickey Stanley	.25
(23)	Dick Tracewski	.25
(24)	Jon Warden	.25
(25)	Don Wert	.25
(26)	Earl Wilson	.25
(27)	Header Card	.05
(28)	Coupon Card	.05

1980 Donruss Prototypes

YANKEES
REGGIE JACKSON

When it became apparent that Topps' monopoly on baseball card production was going to be ended by the courts, Memphis-based Donruss began work to produce a bubblegum card set for 1981. As part of its research, Donruss created a three-card prototype panel in three different sizes to test collector preference. Two of the prototypes have player pictures, the third does not. Backs are blank.

	NM/M
Small Panel (about 6" x 2-3/4"):	75.00
Regular Panel (about 7-1/2" x 3-1/2"):	75.00
Large Panel (about 10-1/2" x 4-3/4"):	75.00
George Brett (2" x 2-3/4")	35.00
George Brett (2-1/2" x 3-1/2")	35.00
George Brett (3-1/2" x 4-3/4")	30.00
Reggie Jackson (2" x 2-3/4")	35.00
Reggie Jackson (2-1/2" x 3-1/2")	35.00

Reggie Jackson (3-1/2" x 4-3/4")	30.00
No Player Pictured (2" x 2-3/4")	7.50
No Player Pictured (2-1/2" x 3-1/2")	5.00
No Player Pictured (3-1/2" x 4-3/4")	5.00

1981 Donruss Promo Sheet

Rookie sensation Joe Charbonneau was the featured attraction when this sample sheet was issued to introduce Donruss' debut baseball card issue. The 10" x 7" sheet is comprised of eight of the cards which appeared in the set.

	NM/M
Complete Sheet:	35.00

1981 Donruss

TOM SEAVER PITCHER

The Donruss Co. of Memphis, Tenn., produced its premiere baseball card issue in 1981 with a set that consisted of 600 numbered cards and five unnumbered checklists. The cards, which measure 2-1/2" x 3-1/2", are printed on thin stock. The card fronts contain the Donruss logo plus the year of issue. The card backs are designed on a vertical format and have black print on red and white. The set, entitled "First Edition Collector Series," contains nearly 40 variations, those being first-printing errors that were corrected in a subsequent print run. The cards were sold in wax packs with bubblegum. The complete set price does not include the higher priced variations.

	NM/M
Complete Set (605):	25.00
Uncut Sheet Set (5):	65.00
Common Player:	.10
Wax Pack (18):	2.00
Wax Box (36):	60.00

1	Ozzie Smith	2.00
2	Rollie Fingers	1.00
3	Rick Wise	.10
4	Gene Richards	.10
5	Alan Trammell	1.00
6	Tom Brookens	.10
7a	Duffy Dyer (1980 Avg. .185)	.25
7b	Duffy Dyer (1980 Avg. 185)	.10
8	Mark Fidrych	.15
9	Dave Rozema	.10
10	Ricky Peters	.10
11	Mike Schmidt	3.00
12	Willie Stargell	1.25
13	Tim Foli	.10
14	Manny Sanguillen	.10
15	Grant Jackson	.10
16	Eddie Solomon	.10
17	Omar Moreno	.10
18	Joe Morgan	1.25
19	Rafael Landestoy	.10
20	Bruce Bochy	.10
21	Joe Sambito	.10
22	Manny Trillo	.10
23a	Dave Smith RC (Incomplete box around stats.)	.10
23b	Dave Smith RC (Complete box around stats.)	.15
24	Terry Puhl	.10
25	Bump Wills	.10
26a	John Ellis (Danny Walton photo - with bat.)	.30
26b	John Ellis (John Ellis photo - with glove.)	.10
27	Jim Kern	.10
28	Richie Zisk	.10
29	John Mayberry	.10
30	Bob Davis	.10
31	Jackson Todd	.10
32	Al Woods	.10
33	Steve Carlton	1.50
34	Lee Mazzilli	.10
35	John Stearns	.10
36	Roy Jackson	.10
37	Mike Scott	.10
38	Lamar Johnson	.10
39	Kevin Bell	.10
40	Ed Farmer	.10
41	Ross Baumgarten	.10
42	Leo Sutherland	.10
43	Dan Meyer	.10
44	Ron Reed	.10
45	Mario Mendoza	.10
46	Rick Honeycutt	.10
47	Glenn Abbott	.10
48	Leon Roberts	.10
49	Rod Carew	1.50
50	Bert Campaneris	.10
51a	Tom Donahue (Incorrect spelling.)	.25
51b	Tom Donohue (Donohue on front.)	.10
52	Dave Frost	.10
53	Ed Halicki	.10
54	Dan Ford	.10
55	Garry Maddox	.10
56a	Steve Garvey (Surpassed 25 HR..)	1.25
56b	Steve Garvey (Surpassed 21 HR..)	.60
57	Bill Russell	.10
58	Don Sutton	1.00
59	Reggie Smith	.10
60	Rick Monday	.10
61	Ray Knight	.10
62	Johnny Bench	1.50
63	Mario Soto	.10
64	Doug Bair	.10
65	George Foster	.10
66	Jeff Burroughs	.10
67	Keith Hernandez	.10
68	Tom Herr	.10
69	Bob Forsch	.10
70	John Fulgham	.10
71a	Bobby Bonds (lifetime HR 986)	.35
71b	Bobby Bonds (lifetime HR 326)	.15
72a	Rennie Stennett ("...breaking broke leg..." on back)	.25
72b	Rennie Stennett ("...breaking leg..." on back)	.10
73	Joe Strain	.10
74	Ed Whitson	.10
75	Tom Griffin	.10
76	Bill North	.10
77	Gene Garber	.10
78	Mike Hargrove	.10
79	Dave Rosello	.10
80	Ron Hassey	.10
81	Sid Monge	.10
82a	Joe Charboneau RC ("For some reason, Phillies..." on back.)	2.00
82b	Joe Charboneau RC ("Phillies..." on back.)	.25
83	Cecil Cooper	.10
84	Sal Bando	.10
85	Moose Haas	.10
86	Mike Caldwell	.10
87a	Larry Hisle ("...Twins with 28 RBI." on back.)	.25
87b	Larry Hisle ("...Twins with 28 HR" on back.)	.10
88	Luis Gomez	.10
89	Larry Parrish	.10
90	Gary Carter	1.25
91	Bill Gullickson RC	.15
92	Fred Norman	.10
93	Tommy Hutton	.10
94	Carl Yastrzemski	1.50
95	Glenn Hoffman	.10
96	Dennis Eckersley	1.25
97a	Tom Burgmeier (Throws: Right)	.25
97b	Tom Burgmeier (Throws: Left)	.10
98	Win Remmerswaal	.10
99	Bob Horner	.10
100	George Brett	3.00
101	Dave Chalk	.10
102	Dennis Leonard	.10
103	Renie Martin	.10
104	Amos Otis	.10
105	Graig Nettles	.10
106	Eric Soderholm	.10
107	Tommy John	.10
108	Tom Underwood	.10
109	Lou Piniella	.15
110	Mickey Klutts	.10
111	Bobby Murcer	.10
112	Eddie Murray	1.50

113	Rick Dempsey	.10
114	Scott McGregor	.10
115	Ken Singleton	.10
116	Gary Roenicke	.10
117	Dave Revering	.10
118	Mike Norris	.10
119	Rickey Henderson	2.00
120	Mike Heath	.10
121	Dave Cash	.10
122	Randy Jones	.10
123	Eric Rasmussen	.10
124	Jerry Mumphrey	.10
125	Richie Hebner	.10
126	Mark Wagner	.10
127	Jack Morris	.10
128	Dan Petry	.10
129	Bruce Robbins	.10
130	Champ Summers	.10
131a	Pete Rose ("See card 251" on back.)	2.00
131b	Pete Rose ("See card 371" on back.)	2.00
132	Willie Stargell	1.25
133	Ed Ott	.10
134	Jim Bibby	.10
135	Bert Blyleven	.10
136	Dave Parker	.10
137	Bill Robinson	.10
138	Enos Cabell	.10
139	Dave Bergman	.10
140	J.R. Richard	.10
141	Ken Forsch	.10
142	Larry Bowa	.10
143	Frank LaCorte (Photo actually Randy Niemann.)	.10
144	Dennis Walling	.10
145	Buddy Bell	.10
146	Fergie Jenkins	1.00
147	Danny Darwin	.10
148	John Grubb	.10
149	Alfredo Griffin	.10
150	Jerry Garvin	.10
151	Paul Mirabella RC	.10
152	Rick Bosetti	.10
153	Dick Ruthven	.10
154	Frank Taveras	.10
155	Craig Swan	.10
156	Jeff Reardon RC	1.00
157	Steve Henderson	.10
158	Jim Morrison	.10
159	Glenn Borgmann	.10
160	Lamarr Hoyt (LaMarr) RC	.10
161	Rich Wortham	.10
162	Thad Bosley	.10
163	Julio Cruz	.10
164a	Del Unser (No 3B in stat heads.)	.25
164b	Del Unser (3B in stat heads)	.10
165	Jim Anderson	.10
166	Jim Beattie	.10
167	Shane Rawley	.10
168	Joe Simpson	.10
169	Rod Carew	1.50
170	Fred Patek	.10
171	Frank Tanana	.10
172	Alfredo Martinez	.10
173	Chris Knapp	.10
174	Joe Rudi	.10
175	Greg Luzinski	.10
176	Steve Garvey	.60
177	Joe Ferguson	.10
178	Bob Welch	.10
179	Dusty Baker	.10
180	Rudy Law	.10
181	Dave Concepcion	.10
182	Johnny Bench	1.50
183	Mike LaCoss	.10
184	Ken Griffey	.10
185	Dave Collins	.10
186	Brian Asselstine	.10
187	Garry Templeton	.10
188	Mike Phillips	.10
189	Pete Vukovich	.10
190	John Urrea	.10
191	Tony Scott	.10
192	Darrell Evans	.10
193	Milt May	.10
194	Bob Knepper	.10
195	Randy Moffitt	.10
196	Larry Herndon	.10
197	Rick Camp	.10
198	Andre Thornton	.10
199	Tom Veryzer	.10
200	Gary Alexander	.10
201	Rick Waits	.10
202	Rick Manning	.10
203	Paul Molitor	1.25
204	Jim Gantner	.10
205	Paul Mitchell	.10
206	Reggie Cleveland	.10
207	Sixto Lezcano	.10
208	Bruce Benedict	.10
209	Rodney Scott	.10
210	John Tamargo	.10
211	Bill Lee	.10
212	Andre Dawson	.75
213	Rowland Office	.10
214	Carl Yastrzemski	1.50
215	Jerry Remy	.10
216	Mike Torrez	.10
217	Skip Lockwood	.10
218	Fred Lynn	.10
219	Chris Chambliss	.10
220	Willie Aikens	.10
221	John Wathan	.10

222	Dan Quisenberry	.10
223	Willie Wilson	.10
224	Clint Hurdle	.10
225	Bob Watson	.10
226	Jim Spencer	.10
227	Ron Guidry	.15
228	Reggie Jackson	2.00
229	Oscar Gamble	.10
230	Jeff Cox	.10
231	Luis Tiant	.10
232	Rich Dauer	.10
233	Dan Graham	.10
234	Mike Flanagan	.10
235	John Lowenstein	.10
236	Benny Ayala	.10
237	Wayne Gross	.10
238	Rick Langford	.10
239	Tony Armas	.10
240a	Bob Lacy (Incorrect spelling.)	.25
240b	Bob Lacey (Correct spelling.)	.10
241	Gene Tenace	.10
242	Bob Shirley	.10
243	Gary Lucas	.10
244	Jerry Turner	.10
245	John Wockenfuss	.10
246	Stan Papi	.10
247	Milt Wilcox	.10
248	Dan Schatzeder	.10
249	Steve Kemp	.10
250	Jim Lentine	.10
251	Pete Rose	2.00
252	Bill Madlock	.10
253	Dale Berra	.10
254	Kent Tekulve	.10
255	Enrique Romo	.10
256	Mike Easler	.10
257	Chuck Tanner	.10
258	Art Howe	.10
259	Alan Ashby	.10
260	Nolan Ryan	5.00
261a	Vern Ruhle (Ken Forsch photo - head shot.)	.25
261b	Vern Ruhle (Vern Ruhle photo - waist to head shot.)	.10
262	Bob Boone	.10
263	Cesar Cedeno	.10
264	Jeff Leonard	.10
265	Pat Putnam	.10
266	Jon Matlack	.10
267	Dave Rajsich	.10
268	Billy Sample	.10
269	Damaso Garcia RC	.10
270	Tom Buskey	.10
271	Joey McLaughlin	.10
272	Barry Bonnell	.10
273	Tug McGraw	.10
274	Mike Jorgensen	.10
275	Pat Zachry	.10
276	Neil Allen	.10
277	Joel Youngblood	.10
278	Greg Pryor	.10
279	Britt Burns RC	.10
280	Rich Dotson RC	.25
281	Chet Lemon	.10
282	Rusty Kuntz	.10
283	Ted Cox	.10
284	Sparky Lyle	.10
285	Larry Cox	.10
286	Floyd Bannister	.10
287	Byron McLaughlin	.10
288	Rodney Craig	.10
289	Bobby Grich	.10
290	Dickie Thon	.10
291	Mark Clear	.10
292	Dave Lemanczyk	.10
293	Jason Thompson	.10
294	Rick Miller	.10
295	Lonnie Smith	.10
296	Ron Cey	.10
297	Steve Yeager	.10
298	Bobby Castillo	.10
299	Manny Mota	.10
300	Jay Johnstone	.10
301	Dan Driessen	.10
302	Joe Nolan	.10
303	Paul Householder	.10
304	Harry Spilman	.10
305	Cesar Geronimo	.10
306a	Gary Mathews (Mathews on front.)	.35
306b	Gary Matthews (Matthews on front.)	.10
307	Ken Reitz	.10
308	Ted Simmons	.10
309	John Littlefield	.10
310	George Frazier	.10
311	Dane Iorg	.10
312	Mike Ivie	.10
313	Dennis Littlejohn	.10
314	Gary LaVelle (Lavelle)	.10
315	Jack Clark	.10
316	Jim Wohlford	.10
317	Rick Matula	.10
318	Toby Harrah	.10
319a	Dwane Kuiper (Dwane on front.)	.25
319b	Duane Kuiper (Duane on front.)	.10
320	Len Barker	.10
321	Victor Cruz	.10
322	Dell Alston	.10
323	Robin Yount	1.25
324	Charlie Moore	.10
325	Lary Sorensen	.10

326a	Gorman Thomas ("...30-HR mark 4th..." on back)	.25
326b	Gorman Thomas ("...30-HR mark 3rd..." on back)	.10
327	Bob Rodgers	.10
328	Phil Niekro	1.00
329	Chris Speier	.10
330a	Steve Rodgers (Rodgers on front.)	.25
330b	Steve Rogers (Rogers on front.)	.10
331	Woodie Fryman	.10
332	Warren Cromartie	.10
333	Jerry White	.10
334	Tony Perez	1.25
335	Carlton Fisk	1.25
336	Dick Drago	.10
337	Steve Renko	.10
338	Jim Rice	.75
339	Jerry Royster	.10
340	Frank White	.10
341	Jamie Quirk	.10
342a	Paul Spittorff (Spittorff on front.)	.25
342b	Paul Splittorff (Splittorff on front.)	.10
343	Marty Pattin	.10
344	Pete LaCock	.10
345	Willie Randolph	.10
346	Rick Cerone	.10
347	Rich Gossage	.10
348	Reggie Jackson	2.00
349	Ruppert Jones	.10
350	Dave McKay	.10
351	Yogi Berra	.50
352	Doug Decinces (DeCinces)	.10
353	Jim Palmer	1.25
354	Tippy Martinez	.10
355	Al Bumbry	.10
356	Earl Weaver	.50
357a	Bob Picciolo (Bob on front.)	.25
357b	Rob Picciolo (Rob on front.)	.10
358	Matt Keough	.10
359	Dwayne Murphy	.10
360	Brian Kingman	.10
361	Bill Fahey	.10
362	Steve Mura	.10
363	Dennis Kinney	.10
364	Dave Winfield	1.25
365	Lou Whitaker	.10
366	Lance Parrish	.10
367	Tim Corcoran	.10
368	Pat Underwood	.10
369	Al Cowens	.10
370	Sparky Anderson	.50
371	Pete Rose	3.00
372	Phil Garner	.10
373	Steve Nicosia	.10
374	John Candelaria	.10
375	Don Robinson	.10
376	Lee Lacy	.10
377	John Milner	.10
378	Craig Reynolds	.10
379a	Luis Pujols (Pujols on front.)	.25
379b	Luis Pujols (Pujols on front.)	.10
380	Joe Niekro	.10
381	Joaquin Andujar	.10
382	Keith Moreland RC	.15
383	Jose Cruz	.10
384	Bill Virdon	.10
385	Jim Sundberg	.10
386	Doc Medich	.10
387	Al Oliver	.10
388	Jim Norris	.10
389	Bob Bailor	.10
390	Ernie Whitt	.10
391	Otto Velez	.10
392	Roy Howell	.10
393	Bob Walk RC	.10
394	Doug Flynn	.10
395	Pete Falcone	.10
396	Tom Hausman	.10
397	Elliott Maddox	.10
398	Mike Squires	.10
399	Marvis Foley	.10
400	Steve Trout	.10
401	Wayne Nordhagen	.10
402	Tony Larussa (LaRussa)	.10
403	Bruce Bochte	.10
404	Bake McBride	.10
405	Jerry Narron	.10
406	Rob Dressler	.10
407	Dave Heaverlo	.10
408	Tom Paciorek	.10
409	Carney Lansford	.10
410	Brian Downing	.10
411	Don Aase	.10
412	Jim Barr	.10
413	Don Baylor	.10
414	Jim Fregosi	.10
415	Dallas Green	.10
416	Dave Lopes	.10
417	Jerry Reuss	.10
418	Rick Sutcliffe	.10
419	Derrel Thomas	.10
420	Tommy LaSorda (Lasorda)	.50
421	Charlie Leibrandt RC	.25
422	Tom Seaver	1.50
423	Ron Oester	.10
424	Junior Kennedy	.10
425	Tom Seaver	1.50

426	Bobby Cox	.10
427	Leon Durham RC	.20
428	Terry Kennedy	.10
429	Silvio Martinez	.10
430	George Hendrick	.10
431	Red Schoendienst	.50
432	John LeMaster	.10
433	Vida Blue	.10
434	John Montefusco	.10
435	Terry Whitfield	.10
436	Dave Bristol	.10
437	Dale Murphy	.75
438	Jerry Dybzinski	.10
439	Jorge Orta	.10
440	Wayne Garland	.10
441	Miguel Dilone	.10
442	Dave Garcia	.10
443	Don Money	.10
444a	Buck Martinez (Photo reversed.)	.35
444b	Buck Martinez (Photo correct.)	.10
445	Jerry Augustine	.10
446	Ben Oglivie	.10
447	Jim Slaton	.10
448	Doyle Alexander	.10
449	Tony Bernazard	.10
450	Scott Sanderson	.10
451	Dave Palmer	.10
452	Stan Bahnsen	.10
453	Dick Williams	.10
454	Rick Burleson	.10
455	Gary Allenson	.10
456	Bob Stanley	.10
457a	John Tudor RC (Lifetime W/L 9.7.)	.40
457b	John Tudor RC (Lifetime W/L 9-7.)	.20
458	Dwight Evans	.10
459	Glenn Hubbard	.10
460	U L Washington	.10
461	Larry Gura	.10
462	Rich Gale	.10
463	Hal McRae	.10
464	Jim Frey	.10
465	Bucky Dent	.10
466	Dennis Werth	.10
467	Ron Davis	.10
468	Reggie Jackson	2.50
469	Bobby Brown	.10
470	Mike Davis RC	.10
471	Gaylord Perry	1.25
472	Mark Belanger	.10
473	Jim Palmer	1.25
474	Sammy Stewart	.10
475	Tim Stoddard	.10
476	Steve Stone	.10
477	Jeff Newman	.10
478	Steve McCatty	.10
479	Billy Martin	.10
480	Mitchell Page	.10
481	Steve Carlton/CY	.40
482	Bill Buckner	.10
483a	Ivan DeJesus (Lifetime hits 702.)	.25
483b	Ivan DeJesus (Lifetime hits 642.)	.10
484	Cliff Johnson	.10
485	Lenny Randle	.10
486	Larry Milbourne	.10
487	Roy Smalley	.10
488	John Castino	.10
489	Ron Jackson	.10
490a	Dave Roberts (1980 highlights begins "Showed pop...")	.25
490b	Dave Roberts (1980 highlights begins "Declared himself...")	.10
491	George Brett/MVP	1.50
492	Mike Cubbage	.10
493	Rob Wilfong	.10
494	Danny Goodwin	.10
495	Jose Morales	.10
496	Mickey Rivers	.10
497	Mike Edwards	.10
498	Mike Sadek	.10
499	Lenn Sakata	.10
500	Gene Michael	.10
501	Dave Roberts	.10
502	Steve Dillard	.10
503	Jim Essian	.10
504	Rance Mulliniks	.10
505	Darrell Porter	.10
506	Joe Torre	.50
507	Terry Crowley	.10
508	Bill Travers	.10
509	Nelson Norman	.10
510	Bob McClure	.10
511	Steve Howe RC	.15
512	Dave Rader	.10
513	Mick Kelleher	.10
514	Kiko Garcia	.10
515	Larry Biittner	.10
516a	Willie Norwood (1980 highlights begins "Spent most...")	.25
516b	Willie Norwood (1980 highlights begins "Traded to...")	.10
517	Bo Diaz	.10
518	Juan Beniquez	.10
519	Scot Thompson	.10
520	Jim Tracy	.10
521	Carlos Lezcano	.10
522	Joe Amalfitano	.10
523	Preston Hanna	.10

No.	Player	Price
524a	Ray Burris (1980 highlights begins "Went on...")	.25
524b	Ray Burris (1980 highlights begins "Drafted by...")	.15
525	Broderick Perkins	.10
526	Mickey Hatcher	.10
527	John Goryl	.10
528	Dick Davis	.10
529	Butch Wynegar	.10
530	Sal Butera	.10
531	Jerry Koosman	.10
532a	Jeff (Geoff) Zahn (1980 highlights begins "Was 2nd in...")	.25
532b	Jeff (Geoff) Zahn (1980 highlights begins "Signed a 3 year ...")	.25
533	Dennis Martinez	.10
534	Gary Thomasson	.10
535	Steve Macko	.10
536	Jim Kaat	.15
537	Best Hitters (George Brett, Rod Carew)	1.50
538	Tim Raines RC	3.00
539	Keith Smith	.10
540	Ken Macha	.10
541	Burt Hooton	.10
542	Butch Hobson	.10
543	Bill Stein	.10
544	Dave Stapleton	.10
545	Bob Pate	.10
546	Doug Corbett	.10
547	Darrell Jackson	.10
548	Pete Redfern	.10
549	Roger Erickson	.10
550	Al Hrabosky	.10
551	Dick Tidrow	.10
552	Dave Ford	.10
553	Dave Kingman	.10
554a	Mike Vail (1980 highlights begins "After...")	.25
554b	Mike Vail (1980 highlights begins "Traded...")	.10
555a	Jerry Martin (1980 highlights begins "Overcame...")	.25
555b	Jerry Martin (1980 highlights begins "Traded...")	.10
556a	Jesus Figueroa (1980 highlights begins "Had...")	.25
556b	Jesus Figueroa (1980 highlights begins "Traded...")	.10
557	Don Stanhouse	.10
558	Barry Foote	.10
559	Tim Blackwell	.10
560	Bruce Sutter	1.25
561	Rick Reuschel	.10
562	Lynn McGlothen	.10
563a	Bob Owchinko (1980 highlights begins "Traded...")	.25
563b	Bob Owchinko (1980 highlights begins "Involved...")	.10
564	John Verhoeven	.10
565	Ken Landreaux	.10
566a	Glen Adams (Glen on front.)	.25
566b	Glenn Adams (Glenn on front.)	.10
567	Hosken Powell	.10
568	Dick Noles	.10
569	Danny Ainge RC	2.00
570	Bobby Mattick	.10
571	Joe LeFebvre (Lefebvre)	.10
572	Bobby Clark	.10
573	Dennis Lamp	.10
574	Randy Lerch	.10
575	Mookie Wilson RC	.30
576	Ron LeFlore	.10
577	Jim Dwyer	.10
578	Bill Castro	.10
579	Greg Minton	.10
580	Mark Littell	.10
581	Andy Hassler	.10
582	Dave Stieb	.10
583	Ken Oberkfell	.10
584	Larry Bradford	.10
585	Fred Stanley	.10
586	Bill Caudill	.10
587	Doug Capilla	.10
588	George Riley	.10
589	Willie Hernandez	.10
590	Mike Schmidt/MVP	1.50
591	Steve Stone (Cy Young 1980.)	.10
592	Rick Sofield	.10
593	Bombo Rivera	.10
594	Gary Ward	.10
595a	Dave Edwards (1980 highlights begins "Sidelined...")	.25
595b	Dave Edwards (1980 highlights begins "Traded...")	.10
596	Mike Proly	.10
597	Tommy Boggs	.10
598	Greg Gross	.10
599	Elias Sosa	.10
600	Pat Kelly	.10
----	Checklist 1-120 (51 Tom Donahue)	.25
----	Checklist 1-120 (51 Tom Donahue)	.10
----	Checklist 121-240	.10
----	Checklist 241-360 (306 Gary Mathews)	.25
----	Checklist 241-360 (306 Gary Matthews)	.10
----	Checklist 361-480 (379 Luis Pujois)	.25
----	Checklist 361-480 (379 Luis Pujols)	.10
----	Checklist 481-600 (566 Glen Adams)	.25
----	Checklist 481-600 (566 Glenn Adams)	.10

1982 Donruss

Brewers — CECIL COOPER 1B

Using card stock thicker than the previous year, Donruss issued a 660-card set which includes 653 numbered cards and seven unnumbered checklists. The cards were sold with puzzle pieces rather than gum as a result of a lawsuit by Topps. The puzzle pieces (three pieces on one card per pack) feature Babe Ruth. The first 26 cards of the set, entitled Diamond Kings, showcase the artwork of Dick Perez. Card fronts display the Donruss logo and the year of issue. Backs have black and blue ink on white stock and include the player's career highlights. The complete set price does not include the higher priced variations.

	NM/M
Unopened Fact. Set (660):	50.00
Complete Set (660):	45.00
Complete Set, Uncut Sheets (5):	175.00
Common Player:	.10
Babe Ruth Puzzle:	1.00
Wax Pack (15):	2.50
Wax Box (36):	80.00

No.	Player	Price
1	Pete Rose/DK	4.00
2	Gary Carter/DK	1.25
3	Steve Garvey/DK	.45
4	Vida Blue/DK	.10
5a	Alan Trammel/DK (Last name incorrect.)	1.00
5b	Alan Trammell/DK (Corrected)	.30
6	Len Barker/DK	.10
7	Dwight Evans/DK	.45
8	Rod Carew/DK	1.25
9	George Hendrick/DK	.10
10	Phil Niekro/DK	1.00
11	Richie Zisk/DK	.10
12	Dave Parker/DK	.10
13	Nolan Ryan/DK	5.00
14	Ivan DeJesus/DK	.10
15	George Brett/DK	2.00
16	Tom Seaver/DK	1.25
17	Dave Kingman/DK	.15
18	Dave Winfield/DK	1.25
19	Mike Norris/DK	.10
20	Carlton Fisk/DK	1.25
21	Ozzie Smith/DK	1.50
22	Roy Smalley/DK	.10
23	Buddy Bell/DK	.10
24	Ken Singleton/DK	.10
25	John Mayberry/DK	.10
26	Gorman Thomas/DK	.10
27	Earl Weaver	.50
28	Rollie Fingers	1.00
29	Sparky Anderson	.50
30	Dennis Eckersley	1.25
31	Dave Winfield	1.25
32	Burt Hooton	.10
33	Rick Waits	.10
34	George Brett	2.00
35	Steve McCatty	.10
36	Steve Rogers	.10
37	Bill Stein	.10
38	Steve Renko	.10

ABBREVIATIONS

DK - Diamond King

No.	Player	Price
39	Mike Squires	.10
40	George Hendrick	.10
41	Bob Knepper	.10
42	Steve Carlton	1.25
43	Larry Biittner	.10
44	Chris Welsh	.10
45	Steve Nicosia	.10
46	Jack Clark	.10
47	Chris Chambliss	.10
48	Ivan DeJesus	.10
49	Lee Mazzilli	.10
50	Julio Cruz	.10
51	Pete Redfern	.10
52	Dave Stieb	.10
53	Doug Corbett	.10
54	George Bell RC	.50
55	Joe Simpson	.10
56	Rusty Staub	.10
57	Hector Cruz	.10
58	Claudell Washington RC	.10
59	Enrique Romo	.10
60	Gary Lavelle	.10
61	Tim Flannery	.10
62	Joe Nolan	.10
63	Larry Bowa	.10
64	Sixto Lezcano	.10
65	Joe Sambito	.10
66	Bruce Kison	.10
67	Wayne Nordhagen	.10
68	Woodie Fryman	.10
69	Billy Sample	.10
70	Amos Otis	.10
71	Matt Keough	.10
72	Toby Harrah	.10
73	Dave Righetti RC	.30
74	Carl Yastrzemski	1.50
75	Bob Welch	.10
76a	Alan Trammel (Last name misspelled.)	1.00
76b	Alan Trammell (Corrected)	.10
77	Rick Dempsey	.10
78	Paul Molitor	1.25
79	Dennis Martinez	.10
80	Jim Slaton	.10
81	Champ Summers	.10
82	Carney Lansford	.10
83	Barry Foote	.10
84	Steve Garvey	.45
85	Rick Manning	.10
86	John Wathan	.10
87	Brian Kingman	.10
88	Andre Dawson	.50
89	Jim Kern	.10
90	Bobby Grich	.10
91	Bob Forsch	.10
92	Art Howe	.10
93	Marty Bystrom	.10
94	Ozzie Smith	1.50
95	Dave Parker	.10
96	Doyle Alexander	.10
97	Al Hrabosky	.10
98	Frank Taveras	.10
99	Tim Blackwell	.10
100	Floyd Bannister	.10
101	Alfredo Griffin	.10
102	Dave Engle	.10
103	Mario Soto	.10
104	Ross Baumgarten	.10
105	Ken Singleton	.10
106	Ted Simmons	.10
107	Jack Morris	.10
108	Bob Watson	.10
109	Dwight Evans	.10
110	Tom Lasorda	.50
111	Bert Blyleven	.10
112	Dan Quisenberry	.10
113	Rickey Henderson	1.25
114	Gary Carter	1.25
115	Brian Downing	.10
116	Al Oliver	.10
117	LaMarr Hoyt	.10
118	Cesar Cedeno	.10
119	Keith Moreland	.10
120	Bob Shirley	.10
121	Terry Kennedy	.10
122	Frank Pastore	.10
123	Gene Garber	.10
124	Tony Pena RC	.10
125	Allen Ripley	.10
126	Randy Martz	.10
127	Richie Zisk	.10
128	Mike Scott	.10
129	Lloyd Moseby RC	.10
130	Rob Wilfong	.10
131	Tim Stoddard	.10
132	Gorman Thomas	.10
133	Dan Petry	.10
134	Bob Stanley	.10
135	Lou Piniella	.15
136	Pedro Guerrero RC	.10
137	Len Barker	.10
138	Richard Gale	.10
139	Wayne Gross	.10
140	Tim Wallach RC	.50
141	Gene Mauch	.10
142	Doc Medich	.10
143	Tony Bernazard	.10
144	Bill Virdon	.10
145	John Littlefield	.10
146	Dave Bergman	.10
147	Dick Davis	.10
148	Tom Seaver	1.50
149	Matt Sinatro	.10
150	Chuck Tanner	.10
151	Leon Durham	.10
152	Gene Tenace	.10
153	Al Bumbry	.10
154	Mark Brouhard	.10
155	Rick Peters	.10
156	Jerry Remy	.10
157	Rick Reuschel	.10
158	Steve Howe	.10
159	Alan Bannister	.10
160	U L Washington	.10
161	Rick Langford	.10
162	Bill Gullickson	.10
163	Mark Wagner	.10
164	Geoff Zahn	.10
165	Ron LeFlore	.10
166	Dane Iorg	.10
167	Joe Niekro	.10
168	Pete Rose	3.00
169	Dave Collins	.10
170	Rick Wise	.10
171	Jim Bibby	.10
172	Larry Herndon	.10
173	Bob Horner	.10
174	Steve Dillard	.10
175	Mookie Wilson	.10
176	Dan Meyer	.10
177	Fernando Arroyo	.10
178	Jackson Todd	.10
179	Darrell Jackson	.10
180	Al Woods	.10
181	Jim Anderson	.10
182	Dave Kingman	.10
183	Steve Henderson	.10
184	Brian Asselstine	.10
185	Rod Scurry	.10
186	Fred Breining	.10
187	Danny Boone	.10
188	Junior Kennedy	.10
189	Sparky Lyle	.10
190	Whitey Herzog	.10
191	Dave Smith	.10
192	Ed Ott	.10
193	Greg Luzinski	.10
194	Bill Lee	.10
195	Don Zimmer	.10
196	Hal McRae	.10
197	Mike Norris	.10
198	Duane Kuiper	.10
199	Rick Cerone	.10
200	Jim Rice	.45
201	Steve Yeager	.10
202	Tom Brookens	.10
203	Jose Morales	.10
204	Roy Howell	.10
205	Tippy Martinez	.10
206	Moose Haas	.10
207	Al Cowens	.10
208	Dave Stapleton	.10
209	Bucky Dent	.10
210	Ron Cey	.10
211	Jorge Orta	.10
212	Jamie Quirk	.10
213	Jeff Jones	.10
214	Tim Raines	.25
215	Jon Matlack	.10
216	Rod Carew	1.50
217	Jim Kaat	.15
218	Joe Pittman	.10
219	Larry Christenson	.10
220	Juan Bonilla	.10
221	Mike Easler	.10
222	Vida Blue	.10
223	Rick Camp	.10
224	Mike Jorgensen	.10
225	Jody Davis RC	.15
226	Mike Parrott	.10
227	Jim Clancy	.10
228	Hosken Powell	.10
229	Tom Hume	.10
230	Britt Burns	.10
231	Jim Palmer	1.25
232	Bob Rodgers	.10
233	Milt Wilcox	.10
234	Dave Revering	.10
235	Mike Torrez	.10
236	Robert Castillo	.10
237	Von Hayes RC	.25
238	Renie Martin	.10
239	Dwayne Murphy	.10
240	Rodney Scott	.10
241	Fred Patek	.10
242	Mickey Rivers	.10
243	Steve Trout	.10
244	Jose Cruz	.10
245	Manny Trillo	.10
246	Lary Sorensen	.10
247	Dave Edwards	.10
248	Dan Driessen	.10
249	Tommy Boggs	.10
250	Dale Berra	.10
251	Ed Whitson	.10
252	Lee Smith RC	4.00
253	Tom Paciorek	.10
254	Pat Zachry	.10
255	Luis Leal	.10
256	John Castino	.10
257	Rich Dauer	.10
258	Cecil Cooper	.10
259	Dave Rozema	.10
260	John Tudor	.10
261	Jerry Mumphrey	.10
262	Jay Johnstone	.10
263	Bo Diaz	.10
264	Dennis Leonard	.10
265	Jim Spencer	.10
266	Jim Milner	.10
267	Don Aase	.10
268	Jim Sundberg	.10
269	Lamar Johnson	.10
270	Frank LaCorte	.10
271	Barry Evans	.10
272	Enos Cabell	.10
273	Del Unser	.10
274	George Foster	.10
275	Brett Butler RC	.50
276	Lee Lacy	.10
277	Ken Reitz	.10
278	Keith Hernandez	.10
279	Doug DeCinces	.10
280	Charlie Moore	.10
281	Lance Parrish	.10
282	Ralph Houk	.10
283	Rich Gossage	.10
284	Jerry Reuss	.10
285	Mike Stanton	.10
286	Frank White	.10
287	Bob Owchinko	.10
288	Scott Sanderson	.10
289	Bump Wills	.10
290	Dave Frost	.10
291	Chet Lemon	.10
292	Tito Landrum	.10
293	Vern Ruhle	.10
294	Mike Schmidt	2.00
295	Sam Mejias	.10
296	Gary Lucas	.10
297	John Candelaria	.10
298	Jerry Martin	.10
299	Dale Murphy	.50
300	Mike Lum	.10
301	Tom Hausman	.10
302	Glenn Abbott	.10
303	Roger Erickson	.10
304	Otto Velez	.10
305	Danny Goodwin	.10
306	John Mayberry	.10
307	Lenny Randle	.10
308	Bob Bailor	.10
309	Jerry Morales	.10
310	Rufino Linares	.10
311	Kent Tekulve	.10
312	Joe Morgan	1.25
313	John Urrea	.10
314	Paul Householder	.10
315	Garry Maddox	.10
316	Mike Ramsey	.10
317	Alan Ashby	.10
318	Bob Clark	.10
319	Tony LaRussa	.15
320	Charlie Lea	.10
321	Danny Darwin	.10
322	Cesar Geronimo	.10
323	Tom Underwood	.10
324	Andre Thornton	.10
325	Rudy May	.10
326	Frank Tanana	.10
327	Davey Lopes	.10
328	Richie Hebner	.10
329	Mike Flanagan	.10
330	Mike Caldwell	.10
331	Scott McGregor	.10
332	Jerry Augustine	.10
333	Stan Papi	.10
334	Rick Miller	.10
335	Graig Nettles	.15
336	Dusty Baker	.10
337	Dave Garcia	.10
338	Larry Gura	.10
339	Cliff Johnson	.10
340	Warren Cromartie	.10
341	Steve Comer	.10
342	Rick Burleson	.10
343	John Martin	.10
344	Craig Reynolds	.10
345	Mike Proly	.10
346	Ruppert Jones	.10
347	Omar Moreno	.10
348	Greg Minton	.10
349	Rick Mahler RC	.10
350	Alex Trevino	.10
351	Mike Krukow	.10
352a	Shane Rawley (Jim Anderson photo - shaking hands.)	.50
352b	Shane Rawley (Correct photo - kneeling.)	.15
353	Garth Iorg	.10
354	Pete Mackanin	.10
355	Paul Moskau	.10
356	Richard Dotson	.10
357	Steve Stone	.10
358	Larry Hisle	.10
359	Aurelio Lopez	.10
360	Oscar Gamble	.10
361	Tom Burgmeier	.10
362	Terry Forster	.10
363	Joe Charboneau	.25
364	Ken Brett	.10
365	Tony Armas	.10
366	Chris Speier	.10
367	Fred Lynn	.10
368	Buddy Bell	.10
369	Jim Essian	.10
370	Terry Puhl	.10
371	Greg Gross	.10
372	Bruce Sutter	1.25
373	Joe Lefebvre	.10
374	Ray Knight	.10
375	Bruce Benedict	.10
376	Tim Foli	.10
377	Al Holland	.10
378	Ken Kravec	.10
379	Jeff Burroughs	.10
380	Pete Falcone	.10
381	Ernie Whitt	.10
382	Brad Havens	.10
383	Terry Crowley	.10
384	Don Money	.10
385	Dan Schatzeder	.10
386	Gary Allenson	.10
387	Yogi Berra	.50
388	Ken Landreaux	.10
389	Mike Hargrove	.10
390	Darryl Motley	.10
391	Dave McKay	.10
392	Stan Bahnsen	.10
393	Ken Forsch	.10
394	Mario Mendoza	.10
395	Jim Morrison	.10
396	Mike Ivie	.10
397	Broderick Perkins	.10
398	Darrell Evans	.10
399	Ron Reed	.10
400	Johnny Bench	1.50
401	Steve Bedrosian RC	.20
402	Bill Robinson	.10
403	Bill Buckner	.10
404	Ken Oberkfell	.10
405	Cal Ripken, Jr. RC	35.00
406	Jim Gantner	.10
407	Kirk Gibson RC	.10
408	Tony Perez	1.00
409	Tommy John	.10
410	Dave Stewart RC	2.50
411	Dan Spillner	.10
412	Willie Aikens	.10
413	Mike Heath	.10
414	Ray Burris	.10
415	Leon Roberts	.10
416	Mike Witt RC	.15
417	Bobby Molinaro	.10
418	Steve Braun	.10
419	Nolan Ryan	4.00
420	Tug McGraw	.10
421	Dave Concepcion	.10
422a	Juan Eichelberger (Gary Lucas photo - white player.)	.50
422b	Juan Eichelberger (Correct photo - black player.)	.10
423	Rick Rhoden	.10
424	Frank Robinson	.50
425	Eddie Miller	.10
426	Bill Caudill	.10
427	Doug Flynn	.10
428	Larry Anderson (Andersen)	.10
429	Al Williams	.10
430	Jerry Garvin	.10
431	Glenn Adams	.10
432	Barry Bonnell	.10
433	Jerry Narron	.10
434	John Stearns	.10
435	Mike Tyson	.10
436	Glenn Hubbard	.10
437	Eddie Solomon	.10
438	Jeff Leonard	.10
439	Randy Bass	.10
440	Mike LaCoss	.10
441	Gary Matthews	.10
442	Mark Littell	.10
443	Don Sutton	1.00
444	John Harris	.10
445	Vada Pinson	.10
446	Elias Sosa	.10
447	Charlie Hough	.10
448	Willie Wilson	.10
449	Fred Stanley	.10
450	Tom Veryzer	.10
451	Ron Davis	.10
452	Mark Clear	.10
453	Bill Russell	.10
454	Lou Whitaker	.10
455	Dan Graham	.10
456	Reggie Cleveland	.10
457	Sammy Stewart	.10
458	Pete Vuckovich	.10
459	John Wockenfuss	.10
460	Glenn Hoffman	.10
461	Willie Randolph	.10
462	Fernando Valenzuela	.10
463	Ron Hassey	.10
464	Paul Splittorff	.10
465	Rob Picciolo	.10
466	Larry Parrish	.10
467	Johnny Grubb	.10
468	Dan Ford	.10
469	Silvio Martinez	.10
470	Kiko Garcia	.10
471	Bob Boone	.10
472	Luis Salazar	.10
473	Randy Niemann	.10
474	Tom Griffin	.10
475	Phil Niekro	1.00
476	Hubie Brooks RC	.10
477	Dick Tidrow	.10
478	Jim Beattie	.10
479	Damaso Garcia	.10
480	Mickey Hatcher	.10
481	Joe Price	.10
482	Ed Farmer	.10
483	Eddie Murray	1.25
484	Ben Oglivie	.10
485	Kevin Saucier	.10
486	Bobby Murcer	.10
487	Bill Campbell	.10
488	Reggie Smith	.10
489	Wayne Garland	.10
490	Jim Wright	.10
491	Billy Martin	.10
492	Jim Fanning	.10
493	Don Baylor	.10
494	Rick Honeycutt	.10
495	Carlton Fisk	1.25
496	Denny Walling	.10
497	Bake McBride	.10

No.	Player	Price
498	Darrell Porter	.10
499	Gene Richards	.10
500	Ron Oester	.10
501	Ken Dayley RC	.10
502	Jason Thompson	.10
503	Milt May	.10
504	Doug Bird	.10
505	Bruce Bochte	.10
506	Neil Allen	.10
507	Joey McLaughlin	.10
508	Butch Wynegar	.10
509	Gary Roenicke	.10
510	Robin Yount	1.25
511	Dave Tobik	.10
512	Rich Gedman RC	.15
513	Gene Nelson RC	.10
514	Rick Monday	.10
515	Miguel Dilone	.10
516	Clint Hurdle	.10
517	Jeff Newman	.10
518	Grant Jackson	.10
519	Andy Hassler	.10
520	Pat Putnam	.10
521	Greg Pryor	.10
522	Tony Scott	.10
523	Steve Mura	.10
524	Johnnie LeMaster	.10
525	Dick Ruthven	.10
526	John McNamara	.10
527	Larry McWilliams	.10
528	Johnny Ray RC	.15
529	Pat Tabler RC	.15
530	Tom Herr	.10
531a	San Diego Chicken (W/trademark symbol.)	.75
531b	San Diego Chicken (No trademark symbol.)	.50
532	Sal Butera	.10
533	Mike Griffin	.10
534	Kelvin Moore	.10
535	Reggie Jackson	2.00
536	Ed Romero	.10
537	Derrel Thomas	.10
538	Mike O'Berry	.10
539	Jack O'Connor	.10
540	Bob Ojeda RC	.25
541	Roy Lee Jackson	.10
542	Lynn Jones	.10
543	Gaylord Perry	1.00
544a	Phil Garner (Photo reversed.)	.50
544b	Phil Garner (Photo correct.)	.10
545	Garry Templeton	.10
546	Rafael Ramirez RC	.10
547	Jeff Reardon	.10
548	Ron Guidry	.10
549	Tim Laudner RC	.15
550	John Henry Johnson	.10
551	Chris Bando	.10
552	Bobby Brown	.10
553	Larry Bradford	.10
554	Scott Fletcher RC	.20
555	Jerry Royster	.10
556	Shooty Babbitt	.10
557	Kent Hrbek RC	2.00
558	Yankee Winners (Ron Guidry, Tommy John)	.15
559	Mark Bomback	.10
560	Julio Valdez	.10
561	Buck Martinez	.10
562	Mike Marshall RC	.15
563	Rennie Stennett	.10
564	Steve Crawford	.10
565	Bob Babcock	.10
566	Johnny Podres	.10
567	Paul Serna	.10
568	Harold Baines RC	1.00
569	Dave LaRoche	.10
570	Lee May	.10
571	Gary Ward RC	.10
572	John Denny	.10
573	Roy Smalley	.10
574	Bob Brenly RC	.20
575	Bronx Bombers (Reggie Jackson, Dave Winfield)	1.50
576	Luis Pujols	.10
577	Butch Hobson	.10
578	Harvey Kuenn	.10
579	Cal Ripken, Sr.	.10
580	Juan Berenguer	.10
581	Benny Ayala	.10
582	Vance Law RC	.10
583	Rick Leach RC	.15
584	George Frazier	.10
585	Phillies Finest (Pete Rose, Mike Schmidt)	1.00
586	Joe Rudi	.10
587	Juan Beniquez	.10
588	Luis DeLeon RC	.10
589	Craig Swan	.10
590	Dave Chalk	.10
591	Billy Gardner	.10
592	Sal Bando	.10
593	Bert Campaneris	.10
594	Steve Kemp	.10
595a	Randy Lerch/Braves	.10
595b	Randy Lerch/Brewers	.10
596	Bryan Clark	.10
597	Dave Ford	.10
598	Mike Scioscia RC	.10
599	John Lowenstein	.10
600	Rene Lachmann (Lachemann)	.10
601	Mick Kelleher	.10
602	Ron Jackson	.10
603	Jerry Koosman	.10
604	Dave Goltz	.10
605	Ellis Valentine	.10
606	Lonnie Smith	.10
607	Joaquin Andujar	.10
608	Garry Hancock	.10
609	Jerry Turner	.10
610	Bob Bonner	.10
611	Jim Dwyer	.10
612	Terry Bulling	.10
613	Joel Youngblood	.10
614	Larry Milbourne	.10
615	Phil Roof (Photo actually Gene Roof.)	.10
616	Keith Drumright	.10
617	Dave Rosello	.10
618	Rickey Keeton	.10
619	Dennis Lamp	.10
620	Sid Monge	.10
621	Jerry White	.10
622	Luis Aguayo RC	.10
623	Jamie Easterly	.10
624	Steve Sax RC	.50
625	Dave Roberts	.10
626	Rick Bosetti	.10
627	Terry Francona RC	.15
628	Pride of the Reds (Johnny Bench, Tom Seaver)	1.00
629	Paul Mirabella	.10
630	Rance Mulliniks	.10
631	Kevin Hickey	.10
632	Reid Nichols	.10
633	Dave Geisel	.10
634	Ken Griffey	.10
635	Bob Lemon	.15
636	Orlando Sanchez	.10
637	Bill Almon	.10
638	Danny Ainge	1.00
639	Willie Stargell	1.25
640	Bob Sykes	.10
641	Ed Lynch	.10
642	John Ellis	.10
643	Fergie Jenkins	1.00
644	Lenn Sakata	.10
645	Julio Gonzales	.10
646	Jesse Orosco RC	.10
647	Jerry Dybzinski	.10
648	Tommy Davis	.10
649	Ron Gardenhire	.10
650	Felipe Alou	.10
651	Harvey Haddix	.10
652	Willie Upshaw RC	.10
653	Bill Madlock	.10
----	Checklist 1-26 DK (5 Trammel)	.25
----	Checklist 1-26 DK (5 Trammell)	.10
----	Checklist 27-130	.10
----	Checklist 131-234	.10
----	Checklist 235-338	.10
----	Checklist 339-442	.10
----	Checklist 443-544	.10
----	Checklist 545-653	.10

1982-89 Donruss Puzzle Promo Sheets

Part of the advertising materials which Donruss issued each year was a series of approximately 8" x 10-7/8" color glossy sheets picturing the Dick Perez art which appear on the Diamond Kings puzzle pieces inserted into card packs.

		NM/M
	Complete Set (10):	20.00
	Common Player:	2.50
(1)	Babe Ruth/1982	2.50
(2)	Ty Cobb/1983	2.50
(3)	Mickey Mantle/1983	2.50
(4)	Duke Snider/1984	2.50
(5)	Ted Williams/1984	2.50
(6)	Lou Gehrig/1985	2.50
(7)	Hank Aaron/1986	2.50
(8)	Roberto Clemente/1987	2.50
(9)	Stan Musial/1988	2.50
(10)	Warren Spahn/1989	2.50

1983 Donruss Promo Sheet

To debut its 1983 card design for dealers, Donruss prepared this eight-card sheet, including one Diamond Stars card. Card fronts are identical to the issued versions. Backs of most cards differ in the Career Highlights write-up. The sheet measures 10" x 7".

	NM/M
Uncut Sheet:	10.00

1983 Donruss

The 1983 Donruss set consists of 653 numbered cards plus seven unnumbered checklists. The 2-1/2" x 3-1/2" cards were issued with puzzle pieces (three pieces on one card per pack) that feature Ty Cobb. The first 26 cards in the set were once again the Diamond Kings series. The card fronts display the Donruss logo and the year of issue. The card backs have black print on yellow and white and include statistics, career highlights, and the player's contract status. (DK) in the checklist below indicates cards which belong to the Diamond Kings series.

		NM/M
	Unopened Fact. Set (660):	50.00
	Complete Set (660):	40.00
	Common Player:	.10
	Ty Cobb Puzzle:	2.50
	Wax Pack (15):	2.50
	Wax Box (36):	80.00
1	Fernando Valenzuela/DK	.15
2	Rollie Fingers/DK	.75
3	Reggie Jackson/DK	2.50
4	Jim Palmer/DK	1.00
5	Jack Morris/DK	.15
6	George Foster/DK	.15
7	Jim Sundberg/DK	.10
8	Willie Stargell/DK	1.00
9	Dave Stieb/DK	.15
10	Joe Niekro/DK	.15
11	Rickey Henderson/DK	1.25
12	Dale Murphy/DK	.50
13	Toby Harrah/DK	.10
14	Bill Buckner/DK	.15
15	Willie Wilson/DK	.10
16	Steve Carlton/DK	1.25
17	Ron Guidry/DK	.15
18	Steve Rogers/DK	.10
19	Kent Hrbek/DK	.15
20	Keith Hernandez/DK	.10
21	Floyd Bannister/DK	.10
22	Johnny Bench/DK	2.00
23	Britt Burns/DK	.10
24	Joe Morgan/DK	1.25
25	Carl Yastrzemski/DK	2.00
26	Terry Kennedy/DK	.10
27	Gary Roenicke	.10
28	Dwight Bernard	.10
29	Pat Underwood	.10
30	Gary Allenson	.10
31	Ron Guidry	.10
32	Burt Hooton	.10

ABBREVIATIONS
DK - Diamond King

No.	Player	Price
33	Chris Bando	.10
34	Vida Blue	.10
35	Rickey Henderson	1.25
36	Ray Burris	.10
37	John Butcher	.10
38	Don Aase	.10
39	Jerry Koosman	.10
40	Bruce Sutter	1.00
41	Jose Cruz	.10
42	Pete Rose	3.00
43	Cesar Cedeno	.10
44	Floyd Chiffer	.10
45	Larry McWilliams	.10
46	Alan Fowlkes	.10
47	Dale Murphy	.50
48	Doug Bird	.10
49	Hubie Brooks	.10
50	Floyd Bannister	.10
51	Jack O'Connor	.10
52	Steve Senteney	.10
53	Gary Gaetti RC	1.00
54	Damaso Garcia	.10
55	Gene Nelson	.10
56	Mookie Wilson	.10
57	Allen Ripley	.10
58	Bob Horner	.10
59	Tony Pena	.10
60	Gary Lavelle	.10
61	Tim Lollar	.10
62	Frank Pastore	.10
63	Garry Maddox	.10
64	Bob Forsch	.10
65	Harry Spilman	.10
66	Geoff Zahn	.10
67	Salome Barojas	.10
68	David Palmer	.10
69	Charlie Hough	.10
70	Dan Quisenberry	.10
71	Tony Armas	.10
72	Rick Sutcliffe	.10
73	Steve Balboni RC	.10
74	Jerry Remy	.10
75	Mike Scioscia	.10
76	John Wockenfuss	.10
77	Jim Palmer	1.00
78	Rollie Fingers	.75
79	Joe Nolan	.10
80	Pete Vuckovich	.10
81	Rick Leach	.10
82	Rick Miller	.10
83	Graig Nettles	.15
84	Ron Cey	.10
85	Miguel Dilone	.10
86	John Wathan	.10
87	Kelvin Moore	.10
88a	Byrn Smith (First name incorrect.)	.35
88b	Bryn Smith (First name correct.)	.10
89	Dave Hostetler	.10
90	Rod Carew	1.50
91	Lonnie Smith	.10
92	Bob Knepper	.10
93	Marty Bystrom	.10
94	Chris Welsh	.10
95	Jason Thompson	.10
96	Tom O'Malley	.10
97	Phil Niekro	.75
98	Neil Allen	.10
99	Bill Buckner	.10
100	Ed Vande Berg RC	.10
101	Jim Clancy	.10
102	Robert Castillo	.10
103	Bruce Berenyi	.10
104	Carlton Fisk	1.25
105	Mike Flanagan	.10
106	Cecil Cooper	.10
107	Jack Morris	.10
108	Mike Morgan RC	.10
109	Luis Aponte	.10
110	Pedro Guerrero	.10
111	Len Barker	.10
112	Willie Wilson	.10
113	Dave Beard	.10
114	Mike Gates	.10
115	Reggie Jackson	2.50
116	George Wright	.10
117	Vance Law	.10
118	Nolan Ryan	4.00
119	Mike Krukow	.10
120	Ozzie Smith	2.00
121	Broderick Perkins	.10
122	Tom Seaver	1.50
123	Chris Chambliss	.10
124	Chuck Tanner	.10
125	Johnnie LeMaster	.10
126	Mel Hall RC	.15
127	Bruce Bochte	.10
128	Charlie Puleo RC	.10
129	Luis Leal	.10
130	John Pacella	.10
131	Glenn Gulliver	.10
132	Don Money	.10
133	Dave Rozema	.10
134	Bruce Hurst RC	.10
135	Rudy May	.10
136	Tom LaSorda (Lasorda)	.40
137	Dan Spillner (Photo actually Ed Whitson.)	.10
138	Jerry Martin	.10
139	Mike Norris	.10
140	Al Oliver	.10
141	Daryl Sconiers	.10
142	Lamar Johnson	.10
143	Harold Baines	.10
144	Alan Ashby	.10
145	Garry Templeton	.10
146	Al Holland	.10
147	Bo Diaz	.10
148	Dave Concepcion	.10
149	Rick Camp	.10
150	Jim Morrison	.10
151	Randy Martz	.10
152	Keith Hernandez	.10
153	John Lowenstein	.10
154	Mike Caldwell	.10
155	Milt Wilcox	.10
156	Rich Gedman	.10
157	Rich Gossage	.20
158	Jerry Reuss	.10
159	Ron Hassey	.10
160	Larry Gura	.10
161	Dwayne Murphy	.10
162	Woodie Fryman	.10
163	Steve Comer	.10
164	Ken Forsch	.10
165	Dennis Lamp	.10
166	David Green	.10
167	Terry Puhl	.10
168	Mike Schmidt	2.50
169	Eddie Milner RC	.10
170	John Curtis	.10
171	Don Robinson	.10
172	Richard Gale	.10
173	Steve Bedrosian	.10
174	Willie Hernandez	.10
175	Ron Gardenhire	.10
176	Jim Beattie	.10
177	Tim Laudner	.10
178	Buck Martinez	.10
179	Kent Hrbek	.10
180	Alfredo Griffin	.10
181	Larry Andersen	.10
182	Pete Falcone	.10
183	Jody Davis	.10
184	Glenn Hubbard	.10
185	Dale Berra	.10
186	Greg Minton	.10
187	Gary Lucas	.10
188	Dave Van Gorder	.10
189	Bob Dernier RC	.10
190	Willie McGee RC	1.50
191	Dickie Thon	.10
192	Bob Boone	.10
193	Britt Burns	.10
194	Jeff Reardon	.10
195	Jon Matlack	.10
196	Don Slaught RC	.15
197	Fred Stanley	.10
198	Rick Manning	.10
199	Dave Righetti	.10
200	Dave Stapleton	.10
201	Steve Yeager	.10
202	Enos Cabell	.10
203	Sammy Stewart	.10
204	Moose Haas	.10
205	Lenn Sakata	.10
206	Charlie Moore	.10
207	Alan Trammell	.10
208	Jim Rice	.40
209	Roy Smalley	.10
210	Bill Russell	.10
211	Andre Thornton	.10
212	Willie Aikens	.10
213	Dave McKay	.10
214	Tim Blackwell	.10
215	Buddy Bell	.10
216	Doug DeCinces	.10
217	Tom Herr	.10
218	Frank LaCorte	.10
219	Steve Carlton	1.25
220	Terry Kennedy	.10
221	Mike Easler	.10
222	Jack Clark	.10
223	Gene Garber	.10
224	Scott Holman	.10
225	Mike Proly	.10
226	Terry Bulling	.10
227	Jerry Garvin	.10
228	Ron Davis	.10
229	Tom Hume	.10
230	Marc Hill	.10
231	Dennis Martinez	.10
232	Jim Gantner	.10
233	Larry Pashnick	.10
234	Dave Collins	.10
235	Tom Burgmeier	.10
236	Ken Landreaux	.10
237	John Denny	.10
238	Hal McRae	.10
239	Matt Keough	.10
240	Doug Flynn	.10
241	Fred Lynn	.10
242	Billy Sample	.10
243	Tom Paciorek	.10
244	Joe Sambito	.10
245	Sid Monge	.10
246	Ken Oberkfell	.10
247	Joe Pittman (Photo actually Juan Eichelberger.)	.10
248	Mario Soto	.10
249	Claudell Washington	.10
250	Rick Rhoden	.10
251	Darrell Evans	.10
252	Steve Henderson	.10
253	Manny Castillo	.10
254	Craig Swan	.10
255	Joey McLaughlin	.10
256	Pete Redfern	.10
257	Ken Singleton	.10
258	Robin Yount	1.25
259	Elias Sosa	.10
260	Bob Ojeda	.10
261	Bobby Murcer	.10
262	Candy Maldonado RC	.10
263	Rick Waits	.10
264	Greg Pryor	.10
265	Bob Owchinko	.10
266	Chris Speier	.10
267	Bruce Kison	.10
268	Mark Wagner	.10
269	Steve Kemp	.10
270	Phil Garner	.10
271	Gene Richards	.10
272	Renie Martin	.10
273	Dave Roberts	.10
274	Dan Driessen	.10
275	Rufino Linares	.10
276	Lee Lacy	.10
277	Ryne Sandberg RC	12.50
278	Darrell Porter	.10
279	Cal Ripken, Jr.	4.00
280	Jamie Easterly	.10
281	Bill Fahey	.10
282	Glenn Hoffman	.10
283	Willie Randolph	.10
284	Fernando Valenzuela	.10
285	Alan Bannister	.10
286	Paul Splittorff	.10
287	Joe Rudi	.10
288	Bill Gullickson	.10
289	Danny Darwin	.10
290	Andy Hassler	.10
291	Ernesto Escarrega	.10
292	Steve Mura	.10
293	Tony Scott	.10
294	Manny Trillo	.10
295	Greg Harris RC	.10
296	Luis DeLeon	.10
297	Kent Tekulve	.10
298	Atlee Hammaker RC	.10
299	Bruce Benedict	.10
300	Fergie Jenkins	.75
301	Dave Kingman	.10
302	Bill Caudill	.10
303	John Castino	.10
304	Ernie Whitt	.10
305	Randy S. Johnson	.10
306	Garth Iorg	.10
307	Gaylord Perry	.75
308	Ed Lynch	.10
309	Keith Moreland	.10
310	Rafael Ramirez	.10
311	Bill Madlock	.10
312	Milt May	.10
313	John Montefusco	.10
314	Wayne Krenchicki	.10
315	George Vukovich	.10
316	Joaquin Andujar	.10
317	Craig Reynolds	.10
318	Rick Burleson	.10
319	Richard Dotson	.10
320	Steve Rogers	.10
321	Dave Schmidt RC	.10
322	Bud Black RC	.10
323	Jeff Burroughs	.10
324	Von Hayes	.10
325	Butch Wynegar	.10
326	Carl Yastrzemski	1.50
327	Ron Roenicke	.10
328	Howard Johnson RC	1.00
329	Rick Dempsey	.10
330a	Jim Slaton (One yellow box on back.)	.25
330b	Jim Slaton (Two yellow boxes on back.)	.10
331	Benny Ayala	.10
332	Ted Simmons	.10
333	Lou Whitaker	.10
334	Chuck Rainey	.10
335	Lou Piniella	.15
336	Steve Sax	.10
337	Toby Harrah	.10
338	George Brett	2.50
339	Davey Lopes	.10
340	Gary Carter	1.25
341	John Grubb	.10
342	Tim Foli	.10
343	Jim Kaat	.15
344	Mike LaCoss	.10
345	Larry Christenson	.10
346	Juan Bonilla	.10
347	Omar Moreno	.10
348	Chili Davis	.10
349	Tommy Boggs	.10
350	Rusty Staub	.15
351	Bump Wills	.10
352	Rick Sweet	.10
353	Jim Gott RC	.15
354	Terry Felton	.10
355	Jim Kern	.10
356	Bill Almon	.10
357	Tippy Martinez	.10
358	Roy Howell	.10
359	Dan Petry	.10
360	Jerry Mumphrey	.10
361	Mark Clear	.10
362	Mike Marshall	.10
363	Lary Sorensen	.10
364	Amos Otis	.10
365	Rick Langford	.10
366	Brad Mills	.10
367	Brian Downing	.10
368	Mike Richardt	.10
369	Aurelio Rodriguez	.10
370	Dave Smith	.10
371	Tug McGraw	.10
372	Doug Bair	.10
373	Ruppert Jones	.10
374	Alex Trevino	.10
375	Bob Ojeda	.10
376	Rod Scurry	.10
377	Bob Brenly RC	.10

#	Player	Price
378	Scot Thompson	.10
379	Julio Cruz	.10
380	John Stearns	.10
381	Dale Murray	.10
382	Frank Viola RC	1.50
383	Al Bumbry	.10
384	Ben Oglivie	.10
385	Dave Tobik	.10
386	Bob Stanley	.10
387	Andre Robertson	.10
388	Jorge Orta	.10
389	Ed Whitson	.10
390	Don Hood	.10
391	Tom Underwood	.10
392	Tim Wallach	.10
393	Steve Renko	.10
394	Mickey Rivers	.10
395	Greg Luzinski	.10
396	Art Howe	.10
397	Alan Wiggins	.10
398	Jim Barr	.10
399	Ivan DeJesus	.10
400	Tom Lawless RC	.10
401	Bob Walk	.10
402	Jimmy Smith	.10
403	Lee Smith	.20
404	George Hendrick	.10
405	Eddie Murray	1.25
406	Marshall Edwards	.10
407	Lance Parrish	.10
408	Carney Lansford	.10
409	Dave Winfield	1.25
410	Bob Welch	.10
411	Larry Milbourne	.10
412	Dennis Leonard	.10
413	Dan Meyer	.10
414	Charlie Lea	.10
415	Rick Honeycutt	.10
416	Mike Witt	.10
417	Steve Trout	.10
418	Glenn Brummer	.10
419	Denny Walling	.10
420	Gary Matthews	.10
421	Charlie Liebrandt (Leibrandt)	.10
422	Juan Eichelberger	.10
423	Matt Guante (Cecilio) RC	.10
424	Bill Laskey	.10
425	Jerry Royster	.10
426	Dickie Noles	.10
427	George Foster	.10
428	Mike Moore RC	.25
429	Gary Ward	.10
430	Barry Bonnell	.10
431	Ron Washington	.10
432	Rance Mulliniks	.10
433	Mike Stanton	.10
434	Jesse Orosco	.10
435	Larry Bowa	.10
436	Biff Pocoroba	.10
437	Johnny Ray	.10
438	Joe Morgan	1.25
439	Eric Show RC	.15
440	Larry Biittner	.10
441	Greg Gross	.10
442	Gene Tenace	.10
443	Danny Heep	.10
444	Bobby Clark	.10
445	Kevin Hickey	.10
446	Scott Sanderson	.10
447	Frank Tanana	.10
448	Cesar Geronimo	.10
449	Jimmy Sexton	.10
450	Mike Hargrove	.10
451	Doyle Alexander	.10
452	Dwight Evans	.10
453	Terry Forster	.10
454	Tom Brookens	.10
455	Rich Dauer	.10
456	Rob Picciolo	.10
457	Terry Crowley	.10
458	Ned Yost	.10
459	Kirk Gibson	.10
460	Reid Nichols	.10
461	Oscar Gamble	.10
462	Dusty Baker	.10
463	Jack Perconte	.10
464	Frank White	.10
465	Mickey Klutts	.10
466	Warren Cromartie	.10
467	Larry Parrish	.10
468	Bobby Grich	.10
469	Dane Iorg	.10
470	Joe Niekro	.10
471	Ed Farmer	.10
472	Tim Flannery	.10
473	Dave Parker	.10
474	Jeff Leonard	.10
475	Al Hrabosky	.10
476	Ron Hodges	.10
477	Leon Durham	.10
478	Jim Essian	.10
479	Roy Lee Jackson	.10
480	Brad Havens	.10
481	Joe Price	.10
482	Tony Bernazard	.10
483	Scott McGregor	.10
484	Paul Molitor	1.25
485	Mike Ivie	.10
486	Ken Griffey	.10
487	Dennis Eckersley	1.00
488	Steve Garvey	.40
489	Mike Fischlin	.10
490	U.L. Washington	.10
491	Steve McCatty	.10
492	Roy Johnson	.10
493	Don Baylor	.10
494	Bobby Johnson	.10
495	Mike Squires	.10
496	Bert Roberge	.10
497	Dick Ruthven	.10
498	Tito Landrum	.10
499	Sixto Lezcano	.10
500	Johnny Bench	1.50
501	Larry Whisenton	.10
502	Manny Sarmiento	.10
503	Fred Breining	.10
504	Bill Campbell	.10
505	Todd Cruz	.10
506	Bob Bailor	.10
507	Dave Stieb	.10
508	Al Williams	.10
509	Dan Ford	.10
510	Gorman Thomas	.10
511	Chet Lemon	.10
512	Mike Torrez	.10
513	Shane Rawley	.10
514	Mark Belanger	.10
515	Rodney Craig	.10
516	Onix Concepcion	.10
517	Mike Heath	.10
518	Andre Dawson	.50
519	Luis Sanchez	.10
520	Terry Bogener	.10
521	Rudy Law	.10
522	Ray Knight	.10
523	Joe Lefebvre	.10
524	Jim Wohlford	.10
525	Julio Franco RC	2.00
526	Ron Oester	.10
527	Rick Mahler	.10
528	Steve Nicosia	.10
529	Junior Kennedy	.10
530a	Whitey Herzog (One yellow box on back.)	.25
530b	Whitey Herzog (Two yellow boxes on back.)	.15
531a	Don Sutton (Blue frame.)	.75
531b	Don Sutton (Green frame.)	.75
532	Mark Brouhard	.10
533a	Sparky Anderson (One yellow box on back.)	.50
533b	Sparky Anderson (Two yellow boxes on back.)	.50
534	Roger LaFrancois	.10
535	George Frazier	.10
536	Tom Niedenfuer	.10
537	Ed Glynn	.10
538	Lee May	.10
539	Bob Kearney	.10
540	Tim Raines	.10
541	Paul Mirabella	.10
542	Luis Tiant	.10
543	Ron LeFlore	.10
544	Dave LaPoint RC	.15
545	Randy Moffitt	.10
546	Luis Aguayo	.10
547	Brad Lesley	.10
548	Luis Salazar	.10
549	John Candelaria	.10
550	Dave Bergman	.10
551	Bob Watson	.10
552	Pat Tabler	.10
553	Brent Gaff	.10
554	Al Cowens	.10
555	Tom Brunansky RC	.10
556	Lloyd Moseby	.10
557a	Pascual Perez/Twins	.25
557b	Pascual Perez/Braves	.10
558	Willie Upshaw	.10
559	Richie Zisk	.10
560	Pat Zachry	.10
561	Jay Johnstone	.10
562	Carlos Diaz	.10
563	John Tudor	.10
564	Frank Robinson	.50
565	Dave Edwards	.10
566	Paul Householder	.10
567	Ron Reed	.10
568	Mike Ramsey	.10
569	Kiko Garcia	.10
570	Tommy John	.10
571	Tony LaRussa	.10
572	Joel Youngblood	.10
573	Wayne Tolleson RC	.10
574	Keith Creel	.10
575	Billy Martin	.10
576	Jerry Dybzinski	.10
577	Rick Cerone	.10
578	Tony Perez	1.00
579	Greg Brock RC	.10
580	Glen Wilson (Glenn)	.10
581	Tim Stoddard	.10
582	Bob McClure	.10
583	Jim Dwyer	.10
584	Ed Romero	.10
585	Larry Herndon	.10
586	Wade Boggs RC	10.00
587	Jay Howell RC	.10
588	Dave Stewart	.10
589	Bert Blyleven	.10
590	Dick Howser	.10
591	Wayne Gross	.10
592	Terry Francona	.10
593	Don Werner	.10
594	Bill Stein	.10
595	Jesse Barfield	.10
596	Bobby Molinaro	.10
597	Mike Vail	.10
598	Tony Gwynn RC	10.00
599	Gary Rajsich	.10
600	Jerry Ujdur	.10
601	Cliff Johnson	.10
602	Jerry White	.10
603	Bryan Clark	.10
604	Joe Ferguson	.10
605	Guy Sularz	.10
606a	Ozzie Virgil RC (Green frame around photo.)	.25
606b	Ozzie Virgil RC (Orange frame around photo.)	.10
607	Terry Harper RC	.10
608	Harvey Kuenn	.10
609	Jim Sundberg	.10
610	Willie Stargell	1.25
611	Reggie Smith	.10
612	Rob Wilfong	.10
613	Niekro Brothers (Joe Niekro, Phil Niekro)	.25
614	Lee Elia	.10
615	Mickey Hatcher	.10
616	Jerry Hairston Sr.	.10
617	John Martin	.10
618	Wally Backman RC	.10
619	Storm Davis RC	.15
620	Alan Knicely	.10
621	John Stuper	.10
622	Matt Sinatro	.10
623	Gene Petralli RC	.10
624	Duane Walker	.10
625	Dick Williams	.10
626	Pat Corrales	.10
627	Vern Ruhle	.10
628	Joe Torre	.10
629	Anthony Johnson	.10
630	Steve Howe	.10
631	Gary Woods	.10
632	Lamarr Hoyt (LaMarr)	.10
633	Steve Swisher	.10
634	Terry Leach RC	.10
635	Jeff Newman	.10
636	Brett Butler	.10
637	Gary Gray	.10
638	Lee Mazzilli	.10
639a	Ron Jackson/A's	2.50
639b	Ron Jackson (Angels - green frame around photo.)	.25
639c	Ron Jackson (Angels - red frame around photo.)	.15
640	Juan Beniquez	.10
641	Dave Rucker	.10
642	Luis Pujols	.10
643	Rick Monday	.10
644	Hosken Powell	.10
645	San Diego Chicken	.20
646	Dave Engle	.10
647	Dick Davis	.10
648	MVP's (Vida Blue, Joe Morgan, Frank Robinson)	.15
649	Al Chambers	.10
650	Jesus Vega	.10
651	Jeff Jones	.10
652	Marvis Foley	.10
653	Ty Cobb (Puzzle)	.10
----	DK checklist Dick Perez (No word "Checklist" on back.)	.25
----	DK Checklist Dick Perez (Word "Checklist" on back.)	.10
----	Checklist 27-130	.10
----	Checklist 131-234	.10
----	Checklist 235-338	.10
----	Checklist 339-442	.10
----	Checklist 443-546	.10
----	Checklist 547-653	.10

1983 Donruss Action All-Stars Promo Sheet

To introduce its series of large-format star cards, Donruss issued this sample sheet with four players on a 10" x 7" format.

	NM/M
Complete Sheet:	15.00

1983 Donruss Action All-Stars

The cards in this 60-card set are designed on a horizontal format and contain a large close-up photo of the player on the left and a smaller action photo on the right. The 5" x 3-1/2" cards have deep red borders and contain the Donruss logo and the year of issue. Backs are printed in black on red and white and contain statistical and biographical information. The cards were sold with puzzle pieces (three pieces on one card per pack) that feature Mickey Mantle.

	NM/M
Complete Set (60):	6.00
Common Player:	.05
Mickey Mantle puzzle:	6.00
Cello Pack (3):	.35
Cello Box (36):	8.00
1 Eddie Murray	.30
2 Dwight Evans	.05
3a Reggie Jackson (Red covers part of statistics on back.)	.50
3b Reggie Jackson (Red does not cover any statistics on back.)	.50
4 Greg Luzinski	.05
5 Larry Herndon	.05
6 Al Oliver	.05
7 Bill Buckner	.05
8 Jason Thompson	.05
9 Andre Dawson	.20
10 Greg Minton	.05
11 Terry Kennedy	.05
12 Phil Niekro	.05
13 Willie Wilson	.05
14 Johnny Bench	.45
15 Ron Guidry	.05
16 Hal McRae	.05
17 Damaso Garcia	.05
18 Gary Ward	.05
19 Cecil Cooper	.05
20 Keith Hernandez	.05
21 Ron Cey	.05
22 Rickey Henderson	.30
23 Nolan Ryan	2.00
24 Steve Carlton	.30
25 John Stearns	.05
26 Jim Sundberg	.05
27 Joaquin Andujar	.05
28 Gaylord Perry	.25
29 Jack Clark	.05
30 Bill Madlock	.05
31 Pete Rose	1.00
32 Mookie Wilson	.05
33 Rollie Fingers	.25
34 Lonnie Smith	.05
35 Tony Pena	.05
36 Dave Winfield	.30
37 Tim Lollar	.05
38 Rod Carew	.30
39 Toby Harrah	.05
40 Buddy Bell	.05
41 Bruce Sutter	.25
42 George Brett	.75
43 Carlton Fisk	.30
44 Carl Yastrzemski	.45
45 Dale Murphy	.20
46 Bob Horner	.05
47 Dave Concepcion	.05
48 Dave Stieb	.05
49 Kent Hrbek	.05
50 Lance Parrish	.05
51 Joe Niekro	.05
52 Cal Ripken, Jr.	2.00
53 Fernando Valenzuela	.05
54 Rickie Zisk	.05
55 Leon Durham	.05
56 Robin Yount	.30
57 Mike Schmidt	.75
58 Gary Carter	.30
59 Fred Lynn	.05
60 Checklist	.05

1983 Donruss Hall of Fame Heroes Promo Sheet

To introduce its series of former star Perez-Steele art cards, Donruss issued this sample sheet which reproduces four of the cards in a 5" x 7" format.

	NM/M
Complete Sheet:	10.00

1983 Donruss Hall of Fame Heroes

The artwork of Dick Perez is featured in the 44-card Hall of Fame Heroes set issued in 1983. The 2-1/2" x 3-1/2" cards were available in wax packs that contained eight cards plus a Mickey Mantle puzzle piece card (three pieces on one card). Backs display red and blue print on white stock and contain a short biographical sketch.

	NM/M
Complete Set (44):	5.00
Common Player:	.10
Mickey Mantle Puzzle:	6.00
Wax Pack (8):	.75
Wax Box (36):	15.00
1 Ty Cobb	.75
2 Walter Johnson	.15
3 Christy Mathewson	.15
4 Josh Gibson	.15
5 Honus Wagner	.35
6 Jackie Robinson	.75
7 Mickey Mantle	2.00
8 Luke Appling	.10
9 Ted Williams	.75
10 Johnny Mize	.10
11 Satchel Paige	.35
12 Lou Boudreau	.10
13 Jimmie Foxx	.10
14 Duke Snider	.25
15 Monte Irvin	.10
16 Hank Greenberg	.25
17 Roberto Clemente	1.00
18 Al Kaline	.15
19 Frank Robinson	.15
20 Joe Cronin	.10
21 Burleigh Grimes	.10
22 The Waner Brothers (Lloyd Waner, Paul Waner)	.10
23 Grover Alexander	.10
24 Yogi Berra	.25
25 James Bell	.10
26 Bill Dickey	.10
27 Cy Young	.15
28 Charlie Gehringer	.10
29 Dizzy Dean	.15
30 Bob Lemon	.10
31 Red Ruffing	.10
32 Stan Musial	.60
33 Carl Hubbell	.10
34 Hank Aaron	.75
35 John McGraw	.10
36 Bob Feller	.15
37 Casey Stengel	.10
38 Ralph Kiner	.10
39 Roy Campanella	.25
40 Mel Ott	.10
41 Robin Roberts	.10
42 Early Wynn	.10
43 Mickey Mantle Puzzle Card	.25
--- Checklist	.05

1984 Donruss Promo Sheet

The front designs of nine 1984 Donruss baseball cards were printed on this glossy paper sheet to introduce the company's design for 1994. The 7-1/2" x 10-1/2" sheets are blank-backed. Players are listed here alphabetically.

	NM/M
Complete Sheet:	15.00

1984 Donruss

The 1984 Donruss set consists of 651 numbered cards, seven unnumbered checklists and two "Living Legends" cards (designated A and B). The A and B cards were issued only in wax packs and were not available to hobby dealers purchasing factory sets. The card fronts differ in style from the previous years, however the Donruss logo and year of issue are still included. Backs have black print on green and white and are identical in format to the preceding year. The 2-1/2" x 3-1/2" cards were issued in packs with three pieces of a 63-piece puzzle of Duke Snider. The complete set price in the checklist that follows does not include the higher priced variations. Cards marked with (DK) or (RR) in the checklist refer to the Diamond Kings and Rated Rookies subsets. Each of the Diamond Kings cards and the DK checklist can be found in two varieties. The more common has Frank Steele's name misspelled "Steel" in the credit line at the bottom-right corner on the back. The error was later corrected.

	NM/M
Unopened Fact. Set (658):	150.00
Complete Set (660):	75.00
Common Player:	.15
Duke Snider Puzzle:	2.00
Wax Pack (15):	4.50
Wax Box (36):	150.00
Rack Pack (45):	15.00
A Living Legends (Rollie Fingers, Gaylord Perry)	1.50
B Living Legends (Johnny Bench, Carl Yastrzemski)	4.00
1a Robin Yount/DK (Steel)	2.50
1b Robin Yount/DK (Steele)	3.00
2a Dave Concepcion/DK (Steel)	.25
2b Dave Concepcion/DK (Steele)	.35
3a Dwayne Murphy/DK (Steel)	.25
3b Dwayne Murphy/DK (Steele)	.35
4a John Castino/DK (Steel)	.25
4b John Castino/DK (Steele)	.35
5a Leon Durham/DK (Steel)	.25
5b Leon Durham/DK (Steele)	.35
6a Rusty Staub/DK (Steel)	.30

ABBREVIATIONS

DK - Diamond King

#	Player	Price
6b	Rusty Staub/DK (Steele)	.45
7a	Jack Clark/DK (Steel)	.25
7b	Jack Clark/DK (Steel)	.35
8a	Dave Dravecky/DK (Steele)	.25
8b	Dave Dravecky/DK (Steele)	.35
9a	Al Oliver/DK (Steel)	.35
9b	Al Oliver/DK (Steele)	.50
10a	Dave Righetti/DK (Steele)	.25
10b	Dave Righetti/DK (Steele)	.35
11a	Hal McRae/DK (Steel)	.35
11b	Hal McRae/DK (Steele)	.35
12a	Ray Knight/DK (Steel)	.35
12b	Ray Knight/DK (Steel)	.35
13a	Bruce Sutter/DK (Steel)	2.50
13b	Bruce Sutter/DK (Steele)	.35
14a	Bob Horner/DK (Steel)	3.00
14b	Bob Horner/DK (Steele)	.35
15a	Lance Parrish/DK (Steel)	.25
15b	Lance Parrish/DK (Steele)	.35
16a	Matt Young/DK (Steel)	.25
16b	Matt Young/DK (Steele)	.35
17a	Fred Lynn/DK (Steel)	.35
17b	Fred Lynn/DK (Steel)	.50
18a	Ron Kittle/DK (Steel)	.25
18b	Ron Kittle/DK (Steele)	.25
19a	Jim Clancy/DK (Steel)	.25
19b	Jim Clancy/DK (Steele)	.25
20a	Bill Madlock/DK (Steel)	.25
20b	Bill Madlock/DK (Steele)	.35
21a	Larry Parrish/DK (Steel)	.25
21b	Larry Parrish/DK (Steele)	.35
22a	Eddie Murray/DK (Steel)	2.50
22b	Eddie Murray/DK (Steele)	3.00
23a	Mike Schmidt/DK (Steel)	3.00
23b	Mike Schmidt/DK (Steele)	4.00
24a	Pedro Guerrero/DK (Steel)	.25
24b	Pedro Guerrero/DK (Steele)	.35
25a	Andre Thornton/DK (Steel)	.25
25b	Andre Thornton/DK (Steele)	.35
26a	Wade Boggs/DK (Steel)	3.00
26b	Wade Boggs/DK (Steele)	3.00
27	Joel Skinner/RR RC	.15
28	Tom Dunbar/RR	.15
29a	Mike Stenhouse/RR (No number on back.)	.15
29b	Mike Stenhouse/RR (29 on back.)	1.00
30a	Ron Darling/RR RC (No number on back.)	1.50
30b	Ron Darling/RR RC (30 on back.)	2.50
31	Dion James/RR RC	
32	Tony Fernandez/RR RC	3.00
33	Angel Salazar/RR	.15
34	Kevin McReynolds/RR RC	1.50
35	Dick Schofield/RR RC	.20
36	Brad Komminsk/RR RC	.15
37	Tim Teufel/RR RC	.25
38	Doug Frobel/RR	.15
39	Greg Gagne/RR RC	1.00
40	Mike Fuentes/RR	.15
41	Joe Carter/RR RC	8.00
42	Mike Brown/RR	.15
43	Mike Jeffcoat/RR	.15
44	Sid Fernandez/RR RC	2.00
45	Brian Dayett/RR	.15
46	Chris Smith/RR	.15
47	Eddie Murray	3.00
48	Robin Yount	3.00
49	Lance Parrish	.15
50	Jim Rice	1.00
51	Dave Winfield	3.00
52	Fernando Valenzuela	.15
53	George Brett	5.00
54	Rickey Henderson	3.00
55	Gary Carter	3.00
56	Buddy Bell	.15
57	Reggie Jackson	5.00
58	Harold Baines	.15
59	Ozzie Smith	4.00
60	Nolan Ryan	8.00
61	Pete Rose	7.50
62	Ron Oester	.15
63	Steve Garvey	.75
64	Jason Thompson	.15
65	Jack Clark	.15
66	Dale Murphy	1.50
67	Leon Durham	.15
68	Darryl Strawberry	2.00
69	Richie Zisk	.15
70	Kent Hrbek	.15
71	Dave Stieb	.15
72	Ken Schrom	.15
73	George Bell	.15
74	John Moses	.15
75	Ed Lynch	.15
76	Chuck Rainey	.15
77	Biff Pocoroba	.15
78	Cecilio Guante	.15
79	Jim Barr	.15
80	Kurt Bevacqua	.15
81	Tom Foley	.15
82	Joe Lefebvre	.15
83	Andy Van Slyke RC	2.00
84	Bob Lillis	.15
85	Rick Adams	.15
86	Jerry Hairston Sr.	.15
87	Bob James	.15
88	Joe Altobelli	.15
89	Ed Romero	.15
90	John Grubb	.15
91	John Henry Johnson	.15
92	Juan Espino	.15
93	Candy Maldonado	.15
94	Andre Thornton	.15
95	Onix Concepcion	.15
96	Don Hill RC	.15
97	Andre Dawson	1.50
98	Frank Tanana	.15
99	Curt Wilkerson RC	.15
100	Larry Gura	.15
101	Dwayne Murphy	.15
102	Tom Brennan	.15
103	Dave Righetti	.15
104	Steve Sax	.15
105	Dan Petry	.15
106	Cal Ripken, Jr.	8.00
107	Paul Molitor	3.00
108	Fred Lynn	.15
109	Neil Allen	.15
110	Joe Niekro	.15
111	Steve Carlton	3.00
112	Terry Kennedy	.15
113	Bill Madlock	.15
114	Chili Davis	.15
115	Jim Gantner	.15
116	Tom Seaver	4.00
117	Bill Buckner	.15
118	Bill Caudill	.15
119	Jim Clancy	.15
120	John Castino	.15
121	Dave Concepcion	.15
122	Greg Luzinski	.15
123	Mike Boddicker RC	.15
124	Pete Ladd	.15
125	Juan Berenguer	.15
126	John Montefusco	.15
127	Ed Jurak	.15
128	Tom Niedenfuer	.15
129	Bert Blyleven	.25
130	Bud Black	.15
131	Gorman Heimueller	.15
132	Dan Schatzeder	.15
133	Ron Jackson	.15
134	Tom Henke RC	1.00
135	Kevin Hickey	.15
136	Mike Scott	.15
137	Bo Diaz	.15
138	Glenn Brummer	.15
139	Sid Monge	.15
140	Rich Gale	.15
141	Brett Butler	.15
142	Brian Harper	.15
143	John Rabb	.15
144	Gary Woods	.15
145	Pat Putnam	.15
146	Jim Acker RC	.15
147	Mickey Hatcher	.15
148	Todd Cruz	.15
149	Tom Tellmann	.15
150	John Wockenfuss	.15
151	Wade Boggs	5.00
152	Don Baylor	.15
153	Bob Welch	.15
154	Alan Bannister	.15
155	Willie Aikens	.15
156	Jeff Burroughs	.15
157	Bryan Little	.15
158	Bob Boone	.15
159	Dave Hostetler	.15
160	Jerry Dybzinski	.15
161	Mike Madden	.15
162	Luis DeLeon	.15
163	Willie Hernandez	.15
164	Frank Pastore	.15
165	Rick Camp	.15
166	Lee Mazzilli	.15
167	Scot Thompson	.15
168	Bob Forsch	.15
169	Mike Flanagan	.15
170	Rick Manning	.15
171	Chet Lemon	.15
172	Jerry Remy	.15
173	Ron Guidry	.20
174	Pedro Guerrero	.15
175	Willie Wilson	.15
176	Carney Lansford	.15
177	Al Oliver	.15
178	Jim Sundberg	.15
179	Bobby Grich	.15
180	Richard Dotson	.15
181	Joaquin Andujar	.15
182	Jose Cruz	.15
183	Mike Schmidt	5.00
184	Gary Redus RC	.15
185	Garry Templeton	.15
186	Tony Pena	.15
187	Greg Minton	.15
188	Phil Niekro	1.50
189	Fergie Jenkins	1.50
190	Mookie Wilson	.15
191	Jim Beattie	.15
192	Gary Ward	.15
193	Jesse Barfield	.15
194	Pete Filson	.15
195	Roy Lee Jackson	.15
196	Rick Sweet	.15
197	Jesse Orosco	.15
198	Steve Lake RC	.15
199	Ken Dayley	.15
200	Manny Sarmiento	.15
201	Mark Davis RC	.15
202	Tim Flannery	.15
203	Bill Scherrer	.15
204	Al Holland	.15
205	David Von Ohlen	.15
206	Mike LaCoss	.15
207	Juan Beniquez	.15
208	Juan Agosto RC	.15
209	Bobby Ramos	.15
210	Al Bumbry	.15
211	Mark Brouhard	.15
212	Howard Bailey	.15
213	Bruce Hurst	.15
214	Bob Shirley	.15
215	Pat Zachry	.15
216	Julio Franco	.15
217	Mike Armstrong	.15
218	Dave Beard	.15
219	Steve Rogers	.15
220	John Butcher	.15
221	Mike Smithson RC	.15
222	Frank White	.15
223	Mike Heath	.15
224	Chris Bando	.15
225	Roy Smalley	.15
226	Dusty Baker	.15
227	Lou Whitaker	.15
228	John Lowenstein	.15
229	Ben Oglivie	.15
230	Doug DeCinces	.15
231	Lonnie Smith	.15
232	Ray Knight	.15
233	Gary Matthews	.15
234	Juan Bonilla	.15
235	Rod Scurry	.15
236	Atlee Hammaker	.15
237	Mike Caldwell	.15
238	Keith Hernandez	.15
239	Larry Bowa	.15
240	Tony Bernazard	.15
241	Damaso Garcia	.15
242	Tom Brunansky	.15
243	Dan Driessen	.15
244	Ron Kittle RC	.15
245	Tim Stoddard	.15
246	Bob L. Gibson	.15
247	Marty Castillo	.15
248	Don Mattingly RC	25.00
249	Jeff Newman	.15
250	Alejandro Pena RC	.15
251	Toby Harrah	.15
252	Cesar Geronimo	.15
253	Tom Underwood	.15
254	Doug Flynn	.15
255	Andy Hassler	.15
256	Odell Jones	.15
257	Rudy Law	.15
258	Harry Spilman	.15
259	Marty Bystrom	.15
260	Dave Rucker	.15
261	Ruppert Jones	.15
262	Jeff Jones	.15
263	Gerald Perry RC	.15
264	Gene Tenace	.15
265	Brad Wellman	.15
266	Dickie Noles	.15
267	Jamie Allen	.15
268	Jim Gott	.15
269	Ron Davis	.15
270	Benny Ayala	.15
271	Ned Yost	.15
272	Dave Rozema	.15
273	Dave Stapleton	.15
274	Lou Piniella	.25
275	Jose Morales	.15
276	Brod Perkins	.15
277	Butch Davis	.15
278	Tony Phillips	.15
279	Jeff Reardon	.15
280	Ken Forsch	.15
281	Pete O'Brien RC	.15
282	Tom Paciorek	.15
283	Frank LaCorte	.15
284	Tim Lollar	.15
285	Greg Gross	.15
286	Alex Trevino	.15
287	Gene Garber	.15
288	Dave Parker	.15
289	Lee Smith	.25
290	Dave LaPoint	.15
291	John Shelby RC	.15
292	Charlie Moore	.15
293	Alan Trammell	.15
294	Tony Armas	.15
295	Shane Rawley	.15
296	Greg Brock	.15
297	Hal McRae	.15
298	Mike Davis	.15
299	Tim Raines	.15
300	Bucky Dent	.15
301	Tommy John	.35
302	Carlton Fisk	3.00
303	Darrell Porter	.15
304	Dickie Thon	.15
305	Garry Maddox	.15
306	Cesar Cedeno	.15
307	Gary Lucas	.15
308	Johnny Ray	.15
309	Andy McGaffigan	.15
310	Claudell Washington	.15
311	Ryne Sandberg	5.00
312	George Foster	.15
313	Spike Owen	.25
314	Gary Gaetti	.15
315	Willie Upshaw	.15
316	Al Williams	.15
317	Jorge Orta	.15
318	Orlando Mercado	.15
319	Junior Ortiz RC	.15
320	Mike Proly	.15
321	Randy S. Johnson	.15
322	Jim Morrison	.15
323	Max Venable	.15
324	Tony Gwynn	5.00
325	Duane Walker	.15
326	Ozzie Virgil	.15
327	Jeff Lahti	.15
328	Bill Dawley RC	.15
329	Rob Wilfong	.15
330	Marc Hill	.15
331	Ray Burris	.15
332	Allan Ramirez	.15
333	Chuck Porter	.15
334	Wayne Krenchicki	.15
335	Gary Allenson	.15
336	Bob Meacham RC	.15
337	Joe Beckwith	.15
338	Rick Sutcliffe	.15
339	Mark Huismann RC	.15
340	Tim Conroy RC	.15
341	Scott Sanderson	.15
342	Larry Biittner	.15
343	Dave Stewart	.15
344	Darryl Motley	.15
345	Chris Codiroli RC	.15
346	Rick Behenna	.15
347	Andre Robertson	.15
348	Mike Marshall	.15
349	Larry Herndon	.15
350	Rich Dauer	.15
351	Cecil Cooper	.15
352	Rod Carew	3.00
353	Willie McGee	.15
354	Phil Garner	.15
355	Joe Morgan	3.00
356	Luis Salazar	.15
357	John Candelaria	.15
358	Bill Laskey	.15
359	Bob McClure	.15
360	Dave Kingman	.15
361	Ron Cey	.15
362	Matt Young RC	.15
363	Lloyd Moseby	.15
364	Frank Viola	.15
365	Eddie Milner	.15
366	Floyd Bannister	.15
367	Dan Ford	.15
368	Moose Haas	.15
369	Doug Bair	.15
370	Ray Fontenot RC	.15
371	Luis Aponte	.15
372	Jack Fimple	.15
373	Neal Heaton RC	.15
374	Greg Pryor	.15
375	Wayne Gross	.15
376	Charlie Lea	.15
377	Steve Lubratich	.15
378	Jon Matlack	.15
379	Julio Cruz	.15
380	John Mizerock	.15
381	Kevin Gross RC	.15
382	Mike Ramsey	.15
383	Doug Gwosdz	.15
384	Kelly Paris	.15
385	Pete Falcone	.15
386	Milt May	.15
387	Fred Breining	.15
388	Craig Lefferts RC	.25
389	Steve Henderson	.15
390	Randy Moffitt	.15
391	Ron Washington	.15
392	Gary Roenicke	.15
393	Tom Candiotti RC	.75
394	Larry Pashnick	.15
395	Dwight Evans	.15
396	Goose Gossage	.25
397	Derrel Thomas	.15
398	Juan Eichelberger	.15
399	Leon Roberts	.15
400	Davey Lopes	.15
401	Bill Gullickson	.15
402	Geoff Zahn	.15
403	Billy Sample	.15
404	Mike Squires	.15
405	Craig Reynolds	.15
406	Eric Show	.15
407	John Denny	.15
408	Dann Bilardello	.15
409	Bruce Benedict	.15
410	Kent Tekulve	.15
411	Mel Hall	.15
412	John Stuper	.15
413	Rick Dempsey	.15
414	Don Sutton	1.50
415	Jack Morris	.15
416	John Tudor	.15
417	Willie Randolph	.15
418	Jerry Reuss	.15
419	Don Slaught RC	.15
420	Steve McCatty	.15
421	Tim Wallach	.15
422	Larry Parrish	.15
423	Brian Downing	.15
424	Britt Burns	.15
425	David Green	.15
426	Jerry Mumphrey	.15
427	Ivan DeJesus	.15
428	Mario Soto	.15
429	Gene Richards	.15
430	Dale Berra	.15
431	Darrell Evans	.15
432	Glenn Hubbard	.15
433	Jody Davis	.15
434	Danny Heep	.15
435	Ed Nunez RC	.15
436	Bobby Castillo	.15
437	Ernie Whitt	.15
438	Scott Ullger	.15
439	Doyle Alexander	.15
440	Domingo Ramos	.15
441	Craig Swan	.15
442	Warren Brusstar	.15
443	Len Barker	.15
444	Mike Easler	.15
445	Renie Martin	.15
446	Dennis Rasmussen RC	.25
447	Ted Power RC	.15
448	Charlie Hudson RC	.15
449	Danny Cox RC	.15
450	Kevin Bass RC	.15
451	Daryl Sconiers	.15
452	Scott Fletcher	.15
453	Bryn Smith	.15
454	Jim Dwyer	.15
455	Rob Picciolo	.15
456	Enos Cabell	.15
457	Dennis Boyd RC	.20
458	Butch Wynegar	.15
459	Burt Hooton	.15
460	Ron Hassey	.15
461	Danny Jackson RC	.15
462	Bob Kearney	.15
463	Terry Francona	.15
464	Wayne Tolleson	.15
465	Mickey Rivers	.15
466	John Wathan	.15
467	Bill Almon	.15
468	George Vukovich	.15
469	Steve Kemp	.15
470	Ken Landreaux	.15
471	Milt Wilcox	.15
472	Tippy Martinez	.15
473	Ted Simmons	.15
474	Tim Foli	.15
475	George Hendrick	.15
476	Terry Puhl	.15
477	Von Hayes	.15
478	Bobby Brown	.15
479	Lee Lacy	.15
480	Joel Youngblood	.15
481	Jim Slaton	.15
482	Mike Fitzgerald RC	.15
483	Keith Moreland	.15
484	Ron Roenicke	.15
485	Luis Leal	.15
486	Bryan Oelkers	.15
487	Bruce Berenyi	.15
488	LaMarr Hoyt	.15
489	Joe Nolan	.15
490	Marshall Edwards	.15
491	Mike Laga RC	.15
492	Rick Cerone	.15
493	Mike Miller (Rick)	.15
494	Rick Honeycutt	.15
495	Mike Hargrove	.15
496	Joe Simpson	.15
497	Keith Atherton RC	.15
498	Chris Welsh	.15
499	Bruce Kison	.15
500	Bob Johnson	.15
501	Jerry Koosman	.15
502	Frank DiPino	.15
503	Tony Perez	2.00
504	Ken Oberkfell	.15
505	Mark Thurmond RC	.15
506	Joe Price	.15
507	Pascual Perez	.15
508	Marvell Wynne RC	.15
509	Mike Krukow	.15
510	Dick Ruthven	.15
511	Al Cowens	.15
512	Cliff Johnson	.15
513	Randy Bush RC	.15
514	Sammy Stewart	.15
515	Bill Schroeder RC	.15
516	Aurelio Lopez	.15
517	Mike Brown	.15
518	Graig Nettles	.25
519	Dave Sax	.15
520	Gerry Willard	.15
521	Paul Splittorff	.15
522	Tom Burgmeier	.15
523	Chris Speier	.15
524	Bobby Clark	.15
525	George Wright	.15
526	Dennis Lamp	.15
527	Tony Scott	.15
528	Ed Whitson	.15
529	Ron Reed	.15
530	Charlie Puleo	.15
531	Jerry Royster	.15
532	Don Robinson	.15
533	Steve Trout	.15
534	Bruce Sutter	2.50
535	Bob Horner	.15
536	Pat Tabler	.15
537	Chris Chambliss	.15
538	Bob Ojeda	.15
539	Alan Ashby	.15
540	Jay Johnstone	.15
541	Bob Dernier	.15
542	Brook Jacoby RC	.15
543	U.L. Washington	.15
544	Danny Darwin	.15
545	Kiko Garcia	.15
546	Vance Law	.15
547	Tug McGraw	.15
548	Dave Smith	.15
549	Len Matuszek	.15
550	Tom Hume	.15
551	Dave Dravecky	.15
552	Rick Rhoden	.15
553	Duane Kuiper	.15
554	Rusty Staub	.20
555	Bill Campbell	.15
556	Mike Torrez	.15
557	Dave Henderson RC	.15
558	Len Whitehouse	.15
559	Barry Bonnell	.15
560	Rick Lysander	.15
561	Garth Iorg	.15
562	Bryan Clark	.15
563	Brian Giles	.15
564	Vern Ruhle	.15
565	Steve Bedrosian	.15
566	Larry McWilliams	.15
567	Jeff Leonard	.15
568	Alan Wiggins	.15
569	Jeff Russell RC	.15
570	Salome Barojas	.15
571	Dane Iorg	.15
572	Bob Knepper	.15
573	Gary Lavelle	.15
574	Gorman Thomas	.15
575	Manny Trillo	.15
576	Jim Palmer	3.00
577	Dale Murray	.15
578	Tom Brookens	.15
579	Rich Gedman	.15
580	Bill Doran RC	.25
581	Steve Yeager	.15
582	Dan Spillner	.15
583	Dan Quisenberry	.15
584	Rance Mulliniks	.15
585	Storm Davis	.15
586	Dave Schmidt	.15
587	Bill Russell	.15
588	Pat Sheridan RC	.15
589	Rafael Ramirez	.15
590	Bud Anderson	.15
591	George Frazier	.15
592	Lee Tunnell RC	.15
593	Kirk Gibson	.15
594	Scott McGregor	.15
595	Bob Bailor	.15
596	Tom Herr	.15
597	Luis Sanchez	.15
598	Dave Engle	.15
599	Craig McMurtry RC	.15
600	Carlos Diaz	.15
601	Tom O'Malley	.15
602	Nick Esasky RC	.15
603	Ron Hodges	.15
604	Ed Vande Berg	.15
605	Alfredo Griffin	.15
606	Glenn Hoffman	.15
607	Hubie Brooks	.15
608	Richard Barnes (Photo actually Neal Heaton.)	.15
609	Greg Walker RC	.15
610	Ken Singleton	.15
611	Mark Clear	.15
612	Buck Martinez	.15
613	Ken Griffey	.20
614	Reid Nichols	.15
615	Doug Sisk RC	.15
616	Bob Brenly	.15
617	Joey McLaughlin	.15
618	Glenn Wilson	.15
619	Bob Stoddard	.15
620	Len Sakata (Lenn)	.15
621	Mike Young RC	.15
622	John Stefero	.15
623	Carmelo Martinez RC	.15
624	Dave Bergman	.15
625	Runnin' Reds (David Green, Willie McGee, Lonnie Smith, Ozzie Smith)	.75
626	Rudy May	.15
627	Matt Keough	.15
628	Jose DeLeon RC	.15
629	Jim Essian	.15
630	Darnell Coles RC	.15
631	Mike Warren	.15
632	Del Crandall	.15
633	Dennis Martinez	.15
634	Mike Moore	.15
635	Lary Sorensen	.15
636	Ricky Nelson	.15
637	Omar Moreno	.15
638	Charlie Hough	.15
639	Dennis Eckersley	2.50
640	Walt Terrell RC	.15
641	Denny Walling	.15
642	Dave Anderson RC	.15
643	Jose Oquendo RC	.15
644	Bob Stanley	.15
645	Dave Geisel	.15
646	Scott Garrelts RC	.15
647	Gary Pettis RC	.15
648	Duke Snider Puzzle Card	
649	Johnnie LeMaster	.15
650	Dave Collins	.15
651	San Diego Chicken	.25
----	Checklist 1-26 DK (Perez-Steel on back.)	
----	Checklist 1-26 DK (Perez-Steele on back.)	.15
----	Checklist 27-130	.15
----	Checklist 131-234	.15
----	Checklist 235-338	.15
----	Checklist 339-442	.15
----	Checklist 443-546	.15
----	Checklist 547-651	.15

Action All-Stars

Full-color photos on the card fronts and backs make the 1984 Donruss Action All-Stars set somewhat unusual. Fronts contain a large action photo plus the Donruss logo and year of issue inside a deep red border. The top half of the backs features a close-up photo with the bottom portion containing biographical and statistical information. The 3-1/2"x5" cards were sold with Ted Williams puzzle pieces.

		NM/M
Complete Set (60):		4.00
Common Player:		.05
Ted Williams Puzzle:		2.50
Cello Pack (5):		.75
Cello Box (36):		12.50
1	Gary Lavelle	.05
2	Willie McGee	.05
3	Tony Pena	.05
4	Lou Whitaker	.05
5	Robin Yount	.40
6	Doug DeCinces	.05
7	John Castino	.05
8	Terry Kennedy	.05
9	Rickey Henderson	.40
10	Bob Horner	.05
11	Harold Baines	.05
12	Buddy Bell	.05
13	Fernando Valenzuela	.05
14	Nolan Ryan	1.00
15	Andre Thornton	.05
16	Gary Redus	.05
17	Pedro Guerrero	.05
18	Andre Dawson	.25
19	Dave Stieb	.05
20	Cal Ripken, Jr.	1.00
21	Ken Griffey	.05
22	Wade Boggs	.50
23	Keith Hernandez	.10
24	Steve Carlton	.40
25	Hal McRae	.05
26	John Lowenstein	.05
27	Fred Lynn	.05
28	Bill Buckner	.05
29	Chris Chambliss	.05
30	Richie Zisk	.05
31	Jack Clark	.05
32	George Hendrick	.05
33	Bill Madlock	.05
34	Lance Parrish	.05
35	Paul Molitor	.40
36	Reggie Jackson	.60
37	Kent Hrbek	.15
38	Steve Garvey	.15
39	Carney Lansford	.05
40	Dale Murphy	.15
41	Greg Luzinski	.05
42	Larry Parrish	.05
43	Ryne Sandberg	.50
44	Dickie Thon	.05
45	Bert Blyleven	.05
46	Ron Oester	.05
47	Dusty Baker	.05
48	Steve Rogers	.05
49	Jim Clancy	.05
50	Eddie Murray	.40
51	Ron Guidry	.05
52	Jim Rice	.20
53	Tom Seaver	.40
54	Pete Rose	.75
55	George Brett	.65
56	Dan Quisenberry	.05
57	Mike Schmidt	.60
58	Ted Simmons	.05
59	Dave Righetti	.05
60	Checklist	.05

Champions

The Champions set includes 10 Hall of Famers, 49 current players and a numbered checklist. Hall of Famers' cards (called Grand Champions) feature the artwork of Dick Perez, while cards of the current players (called Champions) are color photos. All cards measure

3-1/2" x 5". The Grand Champions represent hallmarks of excellence in various statistical categories, while the Champions are the leaders among then-active players in each category. The cards were issued with Duke Snider puzzle pieces.

		NM/M
Complete Set (60):		4.00
Common Player:		.10
Duke Snider Puzzle:		2.00
Pack (5):		.75
Box (36):		12.50
1	Babe Ruth	1.25
2	George Foster	.10
3	Dave Kingman	.10
4	Jim Rice	.25
5	Gorman Thomas	.10
6	Ben Oglivie	.10
7	Jeff Burroughs	.10
8	Hank Aaron	.75
9	Reggie Jackson	.60
10	Carl Yastrzemski	.50
11	Mike Schmidt	.60
12	Graig Nettles	.10
13	Greg Luzinski	.10
14	Ted Williams	.75
15	George Brett	.50
16	Wade Boggs	.50
17	Hal McRae	.10
18	Bill Buckner	.10
19	Eddie Murray	.35
20	Rogers Hornsby	.35
21	Rod Carew	.35
22	Bill Madlock	.10
23	Lonnie Smith	.10
24	Cecil Cooper	.10
25	Ken Griffey	.10
26	Ty Cobb	.60
27	Pete Rose	.75
28	Rusty Staub	.15
29	Tony Perez	.15
30	Al Oliver	.15
31	Cy Young	.25
32	Gaylord Perry	.15
33	Ferguson Jenkins	.15
34	Phil Niekro	.15
35	Jim Palmer	.15
36	Tommy John	.15
37	Walter Johnson	.25
38	Steve Carlton	.35
39	Nolan Ryan	1.25
40	Tom Seaver	.35
41	Don Sutton	.15
42	Bert Blyleven	.15
43	Frank Robinson	.35
44	Joe Morgan	.35
45	Rollie Fingers	.15
46	Keith Hernandez	.10
47	Robin Yount	.35
48	Cal Ripken, Jr.	1.25
49	Dale Murphy	.15
50	Mickey Mantle	1.50
51	Johnny Bench	.35
52	Carlton Fisk	.35
53	Tug McGraw	.10
54	Paul Molitor	.35
55	Carl Hubbell	.10
56	Steve Garvey	.15
57	Dave Parker	.10
58	Gary Carter	.35
59	Fred Lynn	.15
60	Checklist	.05

1985 Donruss Promo Sheet

To introduce its design for 1985, Donruss distributed this 8-1/2" x 11" paper sample sheet to dealers. The blank-back sheet has examples of nine Donruss cards from the '85 set. Players are listed here in alphabetical order.

	NM/M
Complete Sheet:	8.00

1985 Donruss

The black-bordered 1985 Donruss set includes 653 numbered cards and seven unnumbered checklists. Displaying the artwork of Dick Perez for the fourth consecutive year, cards #1-26 feature the Diamond Kings series. Donruss, reacting to the hobby craze over rookie cards, included a Rated Rookies subset (cards #27-46). The cards, in standard 2-1/2" x 3-1/2", were issued with a Lou Gehrig puzzle. Backs repeat the format of previous years with black print on yellow and white. The complete set price does not include the higher priced variations. /DK and /RR refer to the Diamond Kings and Rated Rookies subsets.

		NM/M
Unopened Fact. Set (660):		75.00
Complete Set (660):		50.00
Common Player:		.10
Lou Gehrig Puzzle:		3.00
Wax Pack (15):		4.00
Wax Box (36):		120.00
Rack Pack (45):		7.00
1	Ryne Sandberg/DK	2.50
2	Doug DeCinces/DK	.10
3	Rich Dotson/DK	.10
4	Bert Blyleven/DK	.25
5	Lou Whitaker/DK	.25
6	Dan Quisenberry/DK	.10
7	Don Mattingly/DK	4.00
8	Carney Lansford/DK	.10
9	Frank Tanana/DK	.10
10	Willie Upshaw/DK	.10
11	Claudell Washington/DK	.10
12	Mike Marshall/DK	.10
13	Joaquin Andujar/DK	.10
14	Cal Ripken, Jr./DK	6.00
15	Jim Rice/DK	.75
16	Don Sutton/DK	1.00
17	Frank Viola/DK	.50
18	Alvin Davis/DK	.10
19	Mario Soto/DK	.10
20	Jose Cruz/DK	.10
21	Charlie Lea/DK	.10
22	Jesse Orosco/DK	.10
23	Juan Samuel/DK **RC**	.10
24	Tony Pena/DK	.10
25	Tony Gwynn/DK	2.50
26	Bob Brenly/DK	.10
27	Danny Tartabull/RR **RC**	1.50
28	Mike Bielecki/RR **RC**	.10
29	Steve Lyons/RR **RC**	.25
30	Jeff Reed/RR **RC**	.10
31	Tony Brewer/RR	.10
32	John Morris/RR **RC**	.10
33	Daryl Boston/RR **RC**	.15
34	Alfonso Pulido/RR	.10
35	Steve Kiefer/RR **RC**	.10
36	Larry Sheets/RR **RC**	.10
37	Scott Bradley/RR **RC**	.10
38	Calvin Schiraldi/RR **RC**	.10
39	Shawon Dunston/RR **RC**	1.50
40	Charlie Mitchell/RR	.10
41	Billy Hatcher/RR **RC**	.15
42	Russ Stephans/RR	.10
43	Alejandro Sanchez/RR	.10
44	Steve Jeltz /RR **RC**	.10
45	Jim Traber/RR **RC**	.10
46	Doug Loman/RR	.10
47	Eddie Murray	2.00
48	Robin Yount	2.00
49	Lance Parrish	.10
50	Jim Rice	.75
51	Dave Winfield	2.00
52	Fernando Valenzuela	.10
53	George Brett	3.00
54	Dave Kingman	.10
55	Gary Carter	2.00
56	Buddy Bell	.10
57	Reggie Jackson	3.00
58	Harold Baines	.10
59	Ozzie Smith	2.00
60	Nolan Ryan	6.00
61	Mike Schmidt	3.00
62	Dave Parker	.10
63	Tony Gwynn	2.50
64	Tony Pena	.10
65	Jack Clark	.10
66	Dale Murphy	.60
67	Ryne Sandberg	2.50
68	Keith Hernandez	.10
69	Alvin Davis	.10
70	Kent Hrbek	.10
71	Willie Upshaw	.10
72	Dave Engle	.10
73	Alfredo Griffin	.10
74a	Jack Perconte (Last line of highlights begins "Batted .346...")	.10
74b	Jack Perconte (Last line of highlights begins "Led the ...")	.15
75	Jesse Orosco	.10
76	Jody Davis	.10
77	Bob Horner	.15
78	Larry McWilliams	.10
79	Joel Youngblood	.10
80	Alan Wiggins	.10
81	Ron Oester	.10
82	Ozzie Virgil	.10
83	Ricky Horton **RC**	.10
84	Bill Doran	.10
85	Rod Carew	2.00
86	LaMarr Hoyt	.10
87	Tim Wallach	.10
88	Mike Flanagan	.10
89	Jim Sundberg	.10
90	Chet Lemon	.10
91	Bob Stanley	.10
92	Willie Randolph	.10
93	Bill Russell	.10
94	Julio Franco	.10
95	Dan Quisenberry	.10
96	Bill Caudill	.10
97	Bill Gullickson	.10
98	Danny Darwin	.10
99	Curtis Wilkerson	.10
100	Bud Black	.10
101	Tony Phillips	.10
102	Tony Bernazard	.10
103	Jay Howell	.10
104	Burt Hooton	.10
105	Milt Wilcox	.10
106	Rich Dauer	.10
107	Don Sutton	1.00
108	Mike Witt	.10
109	Bruce Sutter	1.50
110	Enos Cabell	.10
111	John Denny	.10
112	Dave Dravecky	.10
113	Marvell Wynne	.10
114	Johnnie LeMaster	.10
115	Chuck Porter	.10
116	John Gibbons	.10
117	Keith Moreland	.10
118	Darnell Coles	.10
119	Dennis Lamp	.10
120	Ron Davis	.10
121	Nick Esasky	.10
122	Vance Law	.10
123	Gary Roenicke	.10
124	Bill Schroeder	.10
125	Dave Rozema	.10
126	Bobby Meacham	.10
127	Marty Barrett **RC**	.10
128	R.J. Reynolds **RC**	.15
129	Ernie Camacho	.10
130	Jorge Orta	.10
131	Lary Sorensen	.10
132	Terry Francona	.10
133	Fred Lynn	.10
134	Bobby Jones	.10
135	Jerry Hairston Sr.	.10
136	Kevin Bass	.10
137	Garry Maddox	.10
138	Dave LaPoint	.10
139	Kevin McReynolds	.10
140	Wayne Krenchicki	.10
141	Rafael Ramirez	.10
142	Rod Scurry	.10
143	Greg Minton	.10
144	Tim Stoddard	.10
145	Steve Henderson	.10
146	George Bell	.10
147	Dave Meier	.10
148	Sammy Stewart	.10
149	Mark Brouhard	.10
150	Larry Herndon	.10
151	Oil Can Boyd	.10
152	Brian Dayett	.10
153	Tom Niedenfuer	.10
154	Brook Jacoby	.10
155	Onix Concepcion	.10
156	Tim Conroy	.10
157	Joe Hesketh **RC**	.15
158	Brian Downing	.10
159	Tommy Dunbar	.10
160	Marc Hill	.10
161	Phil Garner	.10
162	Jerry Davis	.10
163	Bill Campbell	.10
164	John Franco **RC**	1.50
165	Len Barker	.10
166	Benny Distefano **RC**	.10
167	George Frazier	.10
168	Tito Landrum	.10
169	Cal Ripken, Jr.	6.00
170	Cecil Cooper	.10
171	Alan Trammell	.10
172	Wade Boggs	2.50
173	Don Baylor	.10
174	Pedro Guerrero	.10
175	Frank White	.10
176	Rickey Henderson	2.00
177	Charlie Lea	.10
178	Pete O'Brien	.10
179	Doug DeCinces	.10
180	Ron Kittle	.10
181	George Hendrick	.10
182	Joe Niekro	.10
183	Juan Samuel **RC**	.10
184	Mario Soto	.10
185	Goose Gossage	.15
186	Johnny Ray	.10
187	Bob Brenly	.10
188	Craig McMurtry	.10
189	Leon Durham	.10
190	Dwight Gooden	.25
191	Barry Bonnell	.10
192	Tim Teufel	.10
193	Dave Stieb	.10
194	Mickey Hatcher	.10
195	Jesse Barfield	.10
196	Al Cowens	.10
197	Hubie Brooks	.10
198	Steve Trout	.10
199	Glenn Hubbard	.10
200	Bill Madlock	.10
201	Jeff Robinson **RC**	.10
202	Eric Show	.10
203	Dave Concepcion	.10
204	Ivan DeJesus	.10
205	Neil Allen	.10
206	Jerry Mumphrey	.10
207	Mike Brown	.10
208	Carlton Fisk	2.00
209	Bryn Smith	.10
210	Tippy Martinez	.10
211	Dion James	.10
212	Willie Hernandez	.10
213	Mike Easler	.10
214	Ron Guidry	.10
215	Rick Honeycutt	.10
216	Brett Butler	.10
217	Larry Gura	.10
218	Ray Burris	.10
219	Steve Rogers	.10
220	Frank Tanana	.10
221	Ned Yost	.10
222	Bret Saberhagen **RC**	.35
223	Mike Davis	.10
224	Bert Blyleven	.10
225	Steve Kemp	.10
226	Jerry Reuss	.10
227	Darrell Evans	.10
228	Wayne Gross	.10
229	Jim Gantner	.10
230	Bob Boone	.10
231	Lonnie Smith	.10
232	Frank DiPino	.10
233	Jerry Koosman	.10
234	Graig Nettles	.15
235a	John Tudor	.10
236	John Rabb	.10
237	Rick Manning	.10
238	Mike Fitzgerald	.10
239	Gary Matthews	.10
240	Jim Presley **RC**	.10
241	Dave Collins	.10
242	Gary Gaetti	.10
243	Dann Bilardello	.10
244	Rudy Law	.10
245	John Lowenstein	.10
246	Tom Tellmann	.10
247	Howard Johnson	.10
248	Ray Fontenot	.10
249	Tony Armas	.10
250	Candy Maldonado	.10
251	Mike Jeffcoat **RC**	.10
252	Dane Iorg	.10
253	Bruce Bochte	.10
254	Pete Rose	5.00
255	Don Aase	.10
256	George Wright	.10
257	Britt Burns	.10
258	Mike Scott	.10
259	Len Matuszek	.10
260	Dave Rucker	.10
261	Craig Lefferts	.10
262	Jay Tibbs **RC**	.10
263	Bruce Benedict	.10
264	Don Robinson	.10
265	Gary Lavelle	.10
266	Scott Sanderson	.10
267	Matt Young	.10
268	Ernie Whitt	.10
269	Houston Jimenez	.10
270	Ken Dixon **RC**	.10
271	Peter Ladd	.10
272	Juan Berenguer	.10
273	Roger Clemens	35.00
274	Rick Cerone	.10
275	Dave Anderson	.10
276	George Vukovich	.10
277	Greg Pryor	.10
278	Mike Warren	.10
279	Bob James	.10
280	Bobby Grich	.10
281	Mike Mason **RC**	.10
282	Ron Reed	.10
283	Alan Ashby	.10
284	Mark Thurmond	.10
285	Joe Lefebvre	.10
286	Ted Power	.10
287	Chris Chambliss	.10
288	Lee Tunnell	.10
289	Rich Bordi	.10
290	Glenn Brummer	.10
291	Mike Boddicker	.10
292	Rollie Fingers	1.00
293	Lou Whitaker	.10
294	Dwight Evans	.10
295	Don Mattingly	5.00
296	Mike Marshall	.10
297	Willie Wilson	.10
298	Mike Heath	.10
299	Tim Raines	.10
300	Larry Parrish	.10
301	Geoff Zahn	.10
302	Rich Dotson	.10
303	David Green	.10
304	Jose Cruz	.10
305	Steve Carlton	2.00
306	Gary Redus	.10
307	Steve Garvey	.40
308	Jose DeLeon	.10
309	Randy Lerch	.10
310	Claudell Washington	.10
311	Lee Smith	.25
312	Darryl Strawberry	.50
313	Jim Beattie	.10
314	John Butcher	.10
315	Damaso Garcia	.10
316	Mike Smithson	.10
317	Luis Leal	.10
318	Ken Phelps **RC**	.10
319	Wally Backman	.10
320	Ron Cey	.10
321	Brad Komminsk	.10
322	Jason Thompson	.10
323	Frank Williams **RC**	.10
324	Tim Lollar	.10
325	Eric Davis **RC**	1.50
326	Von Hayes	.10
327	Andy Van Slyke	.10
328	Craig Reynolds	.10
329	Dick Schofield	.10
330	Scott Fletcher	.10
331	Jeff Reardon	.10
332	Rick Dempsey	.10
333	Ben Oglivie	.10
334	Dan Petry	.10
335	Jackie Gutierrez	.10
336	Dave Righetti	.10
337	Alejandro Pena	.10
338	Mel Hall	.10
339	Pat Sheridan	.10
340	Keith Atherton	.10
341	David Palmer	.10
342	Gary Ward	.10
343	Dave Stewart	.10
344	Mark Gubicza **RC**	.50
345	Carney Lansford	.10
346	Jerry Willard	.10
347	Ken Griffey	.10
348	Franklin Stubbs **RC**	.10
349	Aurelio Lopez	.10
350	Al Bumbry	.10
351	Charlie Moore	.10
352	Luis Sanchez	.10
353	Darrell Porter	.10
354	Bill Dawley	.10
355	Charlie Hudson	.10
356	Garry Templeton	.10
357	Cecilio Guante	.10
358	Jeff Leonard	.10
359	Paul Molitor	2.00
360	Ron Gardenhire	.10
361	Larry Bowa	.10
362	Bob Kearney	.10
363	Garth Iorg	.10
364	Tom Brunansky	.10
365	Brad Gulden	.10
366	Greg Walker	.10
367	Mike Young	.10
368	Rick Waits	.10
369	Doug Bair	.10
370	Bob Shirley	.10
371	Bob Ojeda	.10
372	Bob Welch	.10
373	Neal Heaton	.10
374	Danny Jackson (Photo actually Steve Farr.)	.10
375	Donnie Hill	.10
376	Mike Stenhouse	.10
377	Bruce Kison	.10
378	Wayne Tolleson	.10
379	Floyd Bannister	.10
380	Vern Ruhle	.10
381	Tim Corcoran	.10
382	Kurt Kepshire	.10
383	Bobby Brown	.10
384	Dave Van Gorder	.10
385	Rick Mahler	.10
386	Lee Mazzilli	.10
387	Bill Laskey	.10

Abbreviations

DK - Diamond King
RR - Rated Rookie

#	Player	Price
388	Thad Bosley	.10
389	Al Chambers	.10
390	Tony Fernandez	.10
391	Ron Washington	.10
392	Bill Swaggerty	.10
393	Bob L. Gibson	.10
394	Marty Castillo	.10
395	Steve Crawford	.10
396	Clay Christiansen	.10
397	Bob Bailor	.10
398	Mike Hargrove	.10
399	Charlie Leibrandt	.10
400	Tom Burgmeier	.10
401	Razor Shines	.10
402	Rob Wilfong	.10
403	Tom Henke	.10
404	Al Jones	.10
405	Mike LaCoss	.10
406	Luis DeLeon	.10
407	Greg Gross	.10
408	Tom Hume	.10
409	Rick Camp	.10
410	Milt May	.10
411	Henry Cotto **RC**	.10
412	Dave Von Ohlen	.10
413	Scott McGregor	.10
414	Ted Simmons	.10
415	Jack Morris	.10
416	Bill Buckner	.10
417	Butch Wynegar	.10
418	Steve Sax	.10
419	Steve Balboni	.10
420	Dwayne Murphy	.10
421	Andre Dawson	.65
422	Charlie Hough	.10
423	Tommy John	.15
424a	Tom Seaver (Floyd Bannister photo, left-hander.)	2.00
424b	Tom Seaver (Correct photo.)	7.50
425	Tom Herr	.10
426	Terry Puhl	.10
427	Al Holland	.10
428	Eddie Milner	.10
429	Terry Kennedy	.10
430	John Candelaria	.10
431	Manny Trillo	.10
432	Ken Oberkfell	.10
433	Rick Sutcliffe	.10
434	Ron Darling	.10
435	Spike Owen	.10
436	Frank Viola	.10
437	Lloyd Moseby	.10
438	Kirby Puckett	8.00
439	Jim Clancy	.10
440	Mike Moore	.10
441	Doug Sisk	.10
442	Dennis Eckersley	1.50
443	Gerald Perry	.10
444	Dale Berra	.10
445	Dusty Baker	.10
446	Ed Whitson	.10
447	Cesar Cedeno	.10
448	Rick Schu **RC**	.10
449	Joaquin Andujar	.10
450	Mark Bailey **RC**	.10
451	Ron Romanick **RC**	.10
452	Julio Cruz	.10
453	Miguel Dilone	.10
454	Storm Davis	.10
455	Jaime Cocanower	.10
456	Barbaro Garbey	.10
457	Rich Gedman	.10
458	Phil Niekro	1.00
459	Mike Scioscia	.10
460	Pat Tabler	.10
461	Darryl Motley	.10
462	Chris Codiroli (Codiroli)	.10
463	Doug Flynn	.10
464	Billy Sample	.10
465	Mickey Rivers	.10
466	John Wathan	.10
467	Bill Krueger	.10
468	Andre Thornton	.10
469	Rex Hudler	.10
470	Sid Bream **RC**	.25
471	Kirk Gibson	.10
472	John Shelby	.10
473	Moose Haas	.10
474	Doug Corbett	.10
475	Willie McGee	.10
476	Bob Knepper	.10
477	Kevin Gross	.10
478	Carmelo Martinez	.10
479	Kent Tekulve	.10
480	Chili Davis	.10
481	Bobby Clark	.10
482	Mookie Wilson	.10
483	Dave Owen	.10
484	Ed Nunez	.10
485	Rance Mulliniks	.10
486	Ken Schrom	.10
487	Jeff Russell	.10
488	Tom Paciorek	.10
489	Dan Ford	.10
490	Mike Caldwell	.10
491	Scottie Earl	.10
492	Jose Rijo	.10
493	Bruce Hurst	.10
494	Ken Landreaux	.10
495	Mike Fischlin	.10
496	Don Slaught	.10
497	Steve McCatty	.10
498	Gary Lucas	.10
499	Gary Pettis	.10
500	Marvis Foley	.10

#	Player	Price
501	Mike Squires	.10
502	Jim Pankovitz **RC**	.10
503	Luis Aguayo	.10
504	Ralph Citarella	.10
505	Bruce Bochy	.10
506	Bob Owchinko	.10
507	Pascual Perez	.10
508	Lee Lacy	.10
509	Atlee Hammaker	.10
510	Bob Dernier	.10
511	Ed Vande Berg	.10
512	Cliff Johnson	.10
513	Len Whitehouse	.10
514	Dennis Martinez	.10
515	Ed Romero	.10
516	Rusty Kuntz	.10
517	Rick Miller	.10
518	Dennis Rasmussen	.10
519	Steve Yeager	.10
520	Chris Bando	.10
521	U.L. Washington	.10
522	Curt Young **RC**	.10
523	Angel Salazar	.10
524	Curt Kaufman	.10
525	Odell Jones	.10
526	Juan Agosto	.10
527	Denny Walling	.10
528	Andy Hawkins **RC**	.10
529	Sixto Lezcano	.10
530	Skeeter Barnes	.10
531	Randy S. Johnson	.10
532	Jim Morrison	.10
533	Warren Brusstar	.10
534a	Jeff Pendleton **RC** (Error)	1.00
534b	Terry Pendleton **RC** (Correct)	4.50
535	Vic Rodriguez	.10
536	Bob McClure	.10
537	Dave Bergman	.10
538	Mark Clear	.10
539	Mike Pagliarulo **RC**	.25
540	Terry Whitfield	.10
541	Joe Beckwith	.10
542	Jeff Burroughs	.10
543	Dan Schatzeder	.10
544	Donnie Scott	.10
545	Jim Slaton	.10
546	Greg Luzinski	.10
547	Mark Salas **RC**	.10
548	Dave Smith	.10
549	John Wockenfuss	.10
550	Frank Pastore	.10
551	Tim Flannery	.10
552	Rick Rhoden	.10
553	Mark Davis	.10
554	Jeff Dedmon **RC**	.15
555	Gary Woods	.10
556	Danny Heep	.10
557	Mark Langston	.10
558	Darrell Brown	.10
559	Jimmy Key	.10
560	Rick Lysander	.10
561	Doyle Alexander	.10
562	Mike Stanton	.10
563	Sid Fernandez	.10
564	Richie Hebner	.10
565	Alex Trevino	.10
566	Brian Harper	.10
567	Dan Gladden **RC**	.25
568	Luis Salazar	.10
569	Tom Foley	.10
570	Larry Andersen	.10
571	Danny Cox	.10
572	Joe Sambito	.10
573	Juan Beniquez	.10
574	Joel Skinner	.10
575	Randy St. Claire **RC**	.10
576	Floyd Rayford	.10
577	Roy Howell	.10
578	John Grubb	.10
579	Ed Jurak	.10
580	John Montefusco	.10
581	Orel Hershiser **RC**	3.00
582	Tom Waddell **RC**	.10
583	Mark Huismann	.10
584	Joe Morgan	2.00
585	Jim Wohlford	.10
586	Dave Schmidt	.10
587	Jeff Kunkel **RC**	.10
588	Hal McRae	.10
589	Bill Almon	.10
590	Carmen Castillo **RC**	.10
591	Omar Moreno	.10
592	Ken Howell **RC**	.10
593	Tom Brookens	.10
594	Joe Nolan	.10
595	Willie Lozado	.10
596	Tom Nieto **RC**	.10
597	Walt Terrell	.10
598	Al Oliver	.10
599	Shane Rawley	.10
600	Denny Gonzalez **RC**	.10
601	Mark Grant **RC**	.10
602	Mike Armstrong	.10
603	George Foster	.10
604	Davey Lopes	.10
605	Salome Barojas	.10
606	Roy Lee Jackson	.10
607	Pete Filson	.10
608	Duane Walker	.10
609	Glenn Wilson	.10
610	Rafael Santana **RC**	.10
611	Roy Smith	.10
612	Ruppert Jones	.10
613	Joe Cowley **RC**	.10
614	Al Nipper **RC** (Photo actually Mike Brown.)	.15

#	Player	Price
615	Gene Nelson	.10
616	Joe Carter	.10
617	Ray Knight	.10
618	Chuck Rainey	.10
619	Dan Driessen	.10
620	Daryl Sconiers	.10
621	Bill Stein	.10
622	Roy Smalley	.10
623	Ed Lynch	.10
624	Jeff Stone **RC**	.10
625	Bruce Berenyi	.10
626	Kelvin Chapman	.10
627	Joe Price	.10
628	Steve Bedrosian	.10
629	Vic Mata	.10
630	Mike Krukow	.10
631	Phil Bradley **RC**	.15
632	Jim Gott	.10
633	Randy Bush	.10
634	Tom Browning **RC**	.25
635	Lou Gehrig Puzzle Card	.10
636	Reid Nichols	.10
637	Dan Pasqua **RC**	.25
638	German Rivera	.10
639	Don Schulze **RC**	.10
640a	Mike Jones (Last line of highlights begins "Was 11- 7...")	
640b	Mike Jones (Last line of highlights begins "Spent some ...")	.15
641	Pete Rose	4.00
642	Wade Rowdon **RC**	.10
643	Jerry Narron	.10
644	Darrell Miller **RC**	.10
645	Tim Hulett **RC**	.10
646	Andy McGaffigan	.10
647	Kurt Bevacqua	.10
648	John Russell **RC**	.10
649	Ron Robinson **RC**	.10
650	Donnie Moore **RC**	.10
651a	Two for the Title Don Mattingly, Dave Winfield (Yellow letters)	3.00
651b	Two for the Title Don Mattingly, Dave Winfield (White letters)	4.50
652	Tim Laudner	.10
653	Steve Farr **RC**	.10
----	Checklist 1-26 DK	.10
----	Checklist 27-130	.10
----	Checklist 131-234	.10
----	Checklist 235-338	.10
----	Checklist 339-442	.10
----	Checklist 443-546	.10
----	Checklist 547-653	.10

Box Panels

In 1985, Donruss placed on the bottoms of its wax pack boxes a four-card panel which included three player cards and a Lou Gehrig puzzle card. The player cards, numbered PC1 through PC3, have backs identical to the regular 1985 Donruss issue. The card fronts are identical in design to the regular issue, but carry different photos.

		NM/M
Complete Panel:		2.50
Complete Singles Set (4):		2.50
Common Player:		.10
PC1	Dwight Gooden	.25
PC2	Ryne Sandberg	2.50
PC3	Ron Kittle	.10
---	Lou Gehrig (Puzzle card.)	.10

Action All-Stars

In 1985, Donruss issued an Action All-Stars set for the third consecutive year. Card fronts feature an action photo with an inset portrait of the player inside a black border with grey boxes through it. The card backs have black print on blue and white and include sta-

tistical and biographical information. The cards were issued with a Lou Gehrig puzzle.

		NM/M
Complete Set (60):		4.00
Common Player:		.05
Lou Gehrig Puzzle:		3.00
Cello Pack (3):		.50
Cello Box (36):		9.00
1	Tim Raines	.05
2	Jim Gantner	.05
3	Mario Soto	.05
4	Spike Owen	.05
5	Lloyd Moseby	.05
6	Damaso Garcia	.05
7	Cal Ripken, Jr.	1.00
8	Dan Quisenberry	.05
9	Eddie Murray	.50
10	Tony Pena	.05
11	Buddy Bell	.05
12	Dave Winfield	.50
13	Ron Kittle	.05
14	Rich Gossage	.10
15	Dwight Evans	.10
16	Al Davis	.05
17	Mike Schmidt	.75
18	Pascual Perez	.05
19	Tony Gwynn	.60
20	Nolan Ryan	1.00
21	Robin Yount	.50
22	Mike Marshall	.05
23	Brett Butler	.05
24	Ryne Sandberg	.60
25	Dale Murphy	.20
26	George Brett	.75
27	Jim Rice	.25
28	Ozzie Smith	.60
29	Larry Parrish	.05
30	Jack Clark	.05
31	Manny Trillo	.05
32	Dave Kingman	.05
33	Geoff Zahn	.05
34	Pedro Guerrero	.05
35	Dave Parker	.05
36	Rollie Fingers	.35
37	Fernando Valenzuela	.05
38	Wade Boggs	.60
39	Reggie Jackson	.75
40	Kent Hrbek	.05
41	Keith Hernandez	.05
42	Lou Whitaker	.05
43	Tom Herr	.05
44	Alan Trammell	.05
45	Butch Wynegar	.05
46	Leon Durham	.05
47	Dwight Gooden	.20
48	Don Mattingly	.75
49	Phil Niekro	.25
50	Johnny Ray	.05
51	Doug DeCinces	.05
52	Willie Upshaw	.05
53	Lance Parrish	.05
54	Jody Davis	.05
55	Steve Carlton	.50
56	Juan Samuel	.05
57	Gary Carter	.50
58	Harold Baines	.05
59	Eric Show	.05
60	Checklist	.04

Diamond Kings Supers

The 1985 Donruss Diamond Kings Supers are enlarged versions of the Diamond Kings cards in the regular 1985 Donruss set. The cards measure 4-15/16" x 6-3/4". The Diamond Kings series features the artwork of Dick Perez. Twenty-eight cards make up the Super set - 26 DK cards, an unnumbered checklist, and an unnumbered Dick Perez card. The back of the Perez card contains a brief history of Dick Perez and the Perez-Steele Galleries. The set could be obtained through a mail-in offer found on wax pack wrappers.

		NM/M
Complete Set (28):		5.00
Common Player:		.10
1	Ryne Sandberg	1.00
2	Doug DeCinces	.10
3	Richard Dotson	.10
4	Bert Blyleven	.10
5	Lou Whitaker	.10
6	Dan Quisenberry	.10
7	Don Mattingly	1.50
8	Carney Lansford	.10
9	Frank Tanana	.10
10	Willie Upshaw	.10
11	Claudell Washington	.10
12	Mike Marshall	.10
13	Joaquin Andujar	.10
14	Cal Ripken, Jr.	2.00
15	Jim Rice	.25
16	Don Sutton	.50
17	Frank Viola	.10
18	Alvin Davis	.10
19	Mario Soto	.10
20	Jose Cruz	.10
21	Charlie Lea	.10
22	Jesse Orosco	.10
23	Juan Samuel	.10
24	Tony Pena	.10
25	Tony Gwynn	1.00
26	Bob Brenly	.10
	Checklist	.03
	Dick Perez (DK artist)	.10

Highlights

Designed in the style of the regular 1985 Donruss set, this issue features the Player of the Month in the major leagues plus highlight cards of special baseball events and milestones of the 1985 season. Fifty-six cards, including an unnumbered checklist, comprise the set which was available only through hobby dealers. The cards measure 2-1/2" x 3-1/2" and have glossy fronts. The last two cards in the set feature Donruss' picks for the A.L. and N.L. Rookies of the Year. The set was issued in a specially designed box.

		NM/M
Complete Set (56):		3.00
Common Player:		.05
1	Sets Opening Day Record (Tom Seaver)	.10
2	Establishes A.L. Save Mark (Rollie Fingers)	.10
3	A.L. Player of the Month - April (Mike Davis)	.05
4	A.L. Pitcher of the Month - April (Charlie Leibrandt)	.05
5	N.L. Player of the Month - April (Dale Murphy)	.10
6	N.L. Pitcher of the Month - April (Fernando Valenzuela)	.05
7	N.L. Shortstop Record (Larry Bowa)	.05
8	Joins Reds 2000 Hit Club (Dave Concepcion)	.05
9	Eldest Grand Slammer (Tony Perez)	.05
10	N.L. Career Run Leader (Pete Rose)	.50
11	A.L. Player of the Month - May (George Brett)	.25
12	A.L. Pitcher of the Month - May (Dave Stieb)	.05
13	N.L. Player of the Month - May (Dave Parker)	.05
14	N.L. Pitcher of the Month - May (Andy Hawkins)	.05
15	Records 11th Straight Win (Andy Hawkins)	.05
16	Two Homers In First Inning (Von Hayes)	.05
17	A.L. Player of the Month - June (Rickey Henderson)	.15
18	A.L. Pitcher of the Month - June (Jay Howell)	.05
19	N.L. Player of the Month - June (Pedro Guerrero)	.05
20	N.L. Pitcher of the Month - June (John Tudor)	.05
21	Marathon Game Iron Men (Gary Carter, Keith Hernandez)	.05
22	Records 4000th K (Nolan Ryan)	.50
23	All-Star Game MVP (LaMarr Hoyt)	.05
24	1st Ranger To Hit For Cycle (Oddibe McDowell)	.05
25	A.L. Player of the Month - July (George Brett)	.25
26	A.L. Pitcher of the Month - July (Bret Saberhagen)	.05
27	N.L. Player of the Month - July (Keith Hernandez)	.05
28	N.L. Pitcher of the Month - July (Fernando Valenzuela)	.05
29	Record Setting Base Stealers (Vince Coleman, Willie McGee)	.05
30	Notches 300th Career Win (Tom Seaver)	.10
31	Strokes 3000th Hit (Rod Carew)	.10
32	Establishes Met Record (Dwight Gooden)	.05
33	Achieves Strikeout Milestone (Dwight Gooden)	.05
34	Explodes For 9 RBI (Eddie Murray)	.10
35	A.L. Career Hbp Leader (Don Baylor)	.05
36	A.L. Player of the Month - August (Don Mattingly)	.50
37	A.L. Pitcher of the Month - August (Dave Righetti)	.05
38	N.L. Player of the Month - August (Willie McGee)	.05
39	N.L. Pitcher of the Month - August (Shane Rawley)	.05
40	Ty-Breaking Hit (Pete Rose)	.50
41	Hits 3 HRs, Drives In 8 Runs (Andre Dawson)	.05
42	Sets Yankee Theft Mark (Rickey Henderson)	.15
43	20 Wins In Rookie Season (Tom Browning)	.05
44	Yankee Milestone For Hits (Don Mattingly)	.50
45	A.L. Player of the Month - September (Don Mattingly)	.50
46	A.L. Pitcher of the Month - September (Charlie Leibrandt)	.05
47	N.L. Player of the Month - September (Gary Carter)	.05
48	N.L. Pitcher of the Month - September (Dwight Gooden)	.05
49	Major League Record Setter (Wade Boggs)	.05
50	Hurls Shutout For 300th Win (Phil Niekro)	.05
51	Venerable HR King (Darrell Evans)	.05
52	N.L. Switch-hitting Record (Willie McGee)	.05
53	Equals DiMaggio Feat (Dave Winfield)	.10
54	Donruss N.L. Rookie of the Year (Vince Coleman)	.10
55	Donruss A.L. Rookie of the Year (Ozzie Guillen)	.05
----	Checklist	.05

Sluggers of The Hall of Fame

In much the same manner as the 1959-71 Bazooka cards were issued, this eight-player set consists of cards printed on the bottom panel of a box of bubble gum. When cut off the box, cards measure 3-1/2" x 6-1/2", with blank backs. Players are pictured on the cards in paintings done by

Dick Perez. Cards were issued on blue Color Bubbles brand boxes and on red Super Bubble boxes, each numbered on a tab at top or bottom; this checklist is arranged by the number on the card front.

	NM/M
Complete Set (8):	6.00
Common Player:	.30
1 Babe Ruth	2.00
2 Ted Williams	1.00
3 Lou Gehrig	1.00
4 Johnny Mize	.30
5 Stan Musial	.60
6 Mickey Mantle	2.50
7 Hank Aaron	.75
8 Frank Robinson	.45

1986 Donruss

In 1986, Donruss issued a 660-card set which included 653 numbered cards and seven unnumbered checklists. The 2-1/2" x 3-1/2" cards have fronts that feature blue borders and backs that have black print on blue and white. For the fifth year in a row, the first 26 cards in the set are Diamond Kings. The Rated Rookies subset (#27-46) appears once again. The cards were distributed with a Hank Aaron puzzle. The complete set price does not include the higher priced variations. In the checklist that follows, (DK) and (RR) refer to the Diamond Kings and Rated Rookies series.

	NM/M
Unopened Factory Set (660):	35.00
Complete Set (660):	30.00
Common Player:	.05
Hank Aaron Puzzle:	3.00
Wax Pack (15):	1.25
Wax Box (36):	35.00
Rack Pack (45):	2.50
1 Kirk Gibson/DK	.15
2 Goose Gossage/DK	.10
3 Willie McGee/DK	.10
4 George Bell/DK	.10
5 Tony Armas/DK	.05
6 Chili Davis/DK	.05
7 Cecil Cooper/DK	.05
8 Mike Boddicker/DK	.05
9 Davey Lopes/DK	.05
10 Bill Doran/DK	.05
11 Bret Saberhagen/DK	.10
12 Brett Butler/DK	.10
13 Harold Baines/DK	.15
14 Mike Davis/DK	.05
15 Tony Perez/DK	1.00

ABBREVIATIONS

DK - Diamond King
RR - Rated Rookie

16 Willie Randolph/DK	.05
17 Bob Boone/DK	.10
18 Orel Hershiser/DK	.10
19 Johnny Ray/DK	.05
20 Gary Ward/DK	.05
21 Rick Mahler/DK	.05
22 Phil Bradley/DK	.05
23 Jerry Koosman/DK	.10
24 Tom Brunansky/DK	.05
25 Andre Dawson/DK	.50
26 Dwight Gooden/DK	.10
27 Kal Daniels/RR **RC**	.15
28 Fred McGriff/RR **RC**	4.00
29 Cory Snyder/RR **RC**	.10
30 Jose Guzman/RR **RC**	.05
31 Ty Gainey/RR **RC**	.05
32 Johnny Abrego/RR **RC**	.05
33a Andres Galarraga/RR **RC** (Accent mark over e of Andres on back.)	2.00
33b Andres Galarraga/RR **RC** (No accent mark.)	2.00
34 Dave Shipanoff/RR **RC**	.05
35 Mark McLemore/RR **RC**	.50
36 Marty Clary/RR **RC**	.50
37 Paul O'Neill/RR **RC**	2.00
38 Danny Tartabull/RR **RC**	.50
39 Jose Canseco/RR **RC**	6.00
40 Juan Nieves/RR **RC**	.05
41 Lance McCullers/RR **RC**	.05
42 Rick Surhoff/RR **RC**	.05
43 Todd Worrell/RR **RC**	.25
44 Bob Kipper/RR **RC**	.05
45 John Habyan/RR **RC**	.05
46 Mike Woodard/RR **RC**	.05
47 Mike Boddicker	.05
48 Robin Yount	1.50
49 Lou Whitaker	.05
50 Dennis Boyd	.05
51 Rickey Henderson	1.50
52 Mike Marshall	.05
53 George Brett	2.50
54 Dave Kingman	.05
55 Hubie Brooks	.05
56 Oddibe McDowell **RC**	.15
57 Doug DeCinces	.05
58 Britt Burns	.05
59 Ozzie Smith	2.00
60 Jose Cruz	.05
61 Mike Schmidt	2.50
62 Pete Rose	3.00
63 Steve Garvey	.40
64 Tony Pena	.05
65 Chili Davis	.05
66 Dale Murphy	.40
67 Ryne Sandberg	2.00
68 Gary Carter	1.50
69 Alvin Davis	.05
70 Kent Hrbek	.05
71 George Bell	.05
72 Kirby Puckett	2.00
73 Lloyd Moseby	.05
74 Bob Kearney	.05
75 Dwight Gooden	.05
76 Gary Matthews	.05
77 Rick Mahler	.05
78 Benny Distefano	.05
79 Jeff Leonard	.05
80 Kevin McReynolds	.05
81 Ron Oester	.05
82 John Russell	.05
83 Tommy Herr	.05
84 Jerry Mumphrey	.05
85 Ron Romanick	.05
86 Daryl Boston	.05
87 Andre Dawson	.50
88 Eddie Murray	1.50
89 Dion James	.05
90 Chet Lemon	.05
91 Bob Stanley	.05
92 Willie Randolph	.05
93 Mike Scioscia	.05
94 Tom Waddell	.05
95 Danny Jackson	.05
96 Mike Davis	.05
97 Mike Fitzgerald	.05
98 Gary Ward	.05
99 Pete O'Brien	.05
100 Bret Saberhagen	.05
101 Alfredo Griffin	.05
102 Brett Butler	.05
103 Ron Guidry	.15
104 Jerry Reuss	.05
105 Jack Morris	.05
106 Rick Dempsey	.05
107 Ray Burris	.05
108 Brian Downing	.05
109 Willie McGee	.05
110 Bill Doran	.05
111 Kent Tekulve	.05
112 Tony Gwynn	2.00
113 Marvell Wynne	.05
114 David Green	.05
115 Jim Gantner	.05
116 George Foster	.05
117 Steve Trout	.05
118 Mark Langston	.05
119 Tony Fernandez	.05

120 John Butcher	.05
121 Ron Robinson	.05
122 Dan Spillner	.05
123 Mike Young	.05
124 Paul Molitor	1.50
125 Kirk Gibson	.05
126 Ken Griffey	.05
127 Tony Armas	.05
128 Mariano Duncan **RC**	.15
129 Pat Tabler (Mr. Clutch)	.05
130 Frank White	.05
131 Carney Lansford	.05
132 Vance Law	.05
133 Dick Schofield	.05
134 Wayne Tolleson	.05
135 Greg Walker	.05
136 Denny Walling	.05
137 Ozzie Virgil	.05
138 Ricky Horton	.05
139 LaMarr Hoyt	.05
140 Wayne Krenchicki	.05
141 Glenn Hubbard	.05
142 Cecilio Guante	.05
143 Mike Krukow	.05
144 Lee Smith	.15
145 Edwin Nunez	.05
146 Dave Stieb	.05
147 Mike Smithson	.05
148 Ken Dixon	.05
149 Danny Darwin	.05
150 Chris Pittaro	.05
151 Bill Buckner	.05
152 Mike Pagliarulo	.05
153 Bill Russell	.05
154 Brook Jacoby	.05
155 Pat Sheridan	.05
156 Mike Gallego **RC**	.05
157 Jim Wohlford	.05
158 Gary Pettis	.05
159 Toby Harrah	.05
160 Richard Dotson	.05
161 Bob Knepper	.05
162 Dave Dravecky	.05
163 Greg Gross	.05
164 Eric Davis	.05
165 Gerald Perry	.05
166 Rick Rhoden	.05
167 Keith Moreland	.05
168 Jack Clark	.05
169 Storm Davis	.05
170 Cecil Cooper	.05
171 Alan Trammell	.05
172 Roger Clemens	2.50
173 Don Mattingly	2.50
174 Pedro Guerrero	.05
175 Willie Wilson	.05
176 Dwayne Murphy	.05
177 Tim Raines	.05
178 Larry Parrish	.05
179 Mike Witt	.05
180 Harold Baines	.05
181 Vince Coleman **RC**	.35
182 Jeff Heathcock **RC**	.05
183 Steve Carlton	1.50
184 Mario Soto	.05
185 Goose Gossage	.10
186 Johnny Ray	.05
187 Dan Gladden	.05
188 Bob Horner	.05
189 Rick Sutcliffe	.05
190 Keith Hernandez	.05
191 Phil Bradley	.05
192 Tom Brunansky	.05
193 Jesse Barfield	.05
194 Frank Viola	.05
195 Willie Upshaw	.05
196 Jim Beattie	.05
197 Darryl Strawberry	.05
198 Ron Cey	.05
199 Steve Bedrosian	.05
200 Steve Kemp	.05
201 Manny Trillo	.05
202 Garry Templeton	.05
203 Dave Parker	.05
204 John Denny	.05
205 Terry Pendleton	.05
206 Terry Puhl	.05
207 Bobby Grich	.05
208 Ozzie Guillen **RC**	2.00
209 Jeff Reardon	.05
210 Cal Ripken, Jr.	3.00
211 Bill Schroeder	.05
212 Dan Petry	.05
213 Jim Rice	.50
214 Dave Righetti	.05
215 Fernando Valenzuela	.05
216 Julio Franco	.05
217 Darryl Motley	.05
218 Dave Collins	.05
219 Tim Wallach	.05
220 George Wright	.05
221 Tommy Dunbar	.05
222 Steve Balboni	.05
223 Jay Howell	.05
224 Joe Carter	.05
225 Ed Whitson	.05
226 Orel Hershiser	.05
227 Willie Hernandez	.05
228 Lee Lacy	.05
229 Rollie Fingers	1.00
230 Bob Boone	.05
231 Joaquin Andujar	.05
232 Craig Reynolds	.05
233 Shane Rawley	.05
234 Eric Show	.05
235 Jose DeLeon	.05
236 Jose Uribe **RC**	.05
237 Moose Haas	.05

238 Wally Backman	.05
239 Dennis Eckersley	1.25
240 Mike Moore	.05
241 Damaso Garcia	.05
242 Tim Teufel	.05
243 Dave Concepcion	.05
244 Floyd Bannister	.05
245 Fred Lynn	.05
246 Charlie Moore	.05
247 Walt Terrell	.05
248 Dave Winfield	1.50
249 Dwight Evans	.05
250 Dennis Powell **RC**	.05
251 Andre Thornton	.05
252 Onix Concepcion	.05
253 Mike Heath	.05
254a David Palmer (2B on front)	.05
254b David Palmer (P on front)	.15
255 Donnie Moore	.05
256 Curtis Wilkerson	.05
257 Julio Cruz	.05
258 Nolan Ryan	3.00
259 Jeff Stone	.05
260a John Tudor (1981 Games is .18)	.05
260b John Tudor (1981 Games is 18)	.15
261 Mark Thurmond	.05
262 Jay Tibbs	.05
263 Rafael Ramirez	.05
264 Larry McWilliams	.05
265 Mark Davis	.05
266 Bob Dernier	.05
267 Matt Young	.05
268 Jim Clancy	.05
269 Mickey Hatcher	.05
270 Sammy Stewart	.05
271 Bob L. Gibson	.05
272 Nelson Simmons	.05
273 Rich Gedman	.05
274 Butch Wynegar	.05
275 Ken Howell	.05
276 Mel Hall	.05
277 Jim Sundberg	.05
278 Chris Codiroli	.05
279 Herman Winningham **RC**	.05
280 Rod Carew	1.50
281 Don Slaught	.05
282 Scott Fletcher	.05
283 Bill Dawley	.05
284 Andy Hawkins	.05
285 Glenn Wilson	.05
286 Nick Esasky	.05
287 Claudell Washington	.05
288 Lee Mazzilli	.05
289 Jody Davis	.05
290 Darrell Porter	.05
291 Scott McGregor	.05
292 Ted Simmons	.05
293 Aurelio Lopez	.05
294 Marty Barrett	.05
295 Dale Berra	.05
296 Greg Brock	.05
297 Charlie Leibrandt	.05
298 Bill Krueger	.05
299 Bryn Smith	.05
300 Burt Hooton	.05
301 Stu Cliburn **RC**	.05
302 Luis Salazar	.05
303 Ken Dayley	.05
304 Frank DiPino	.05
305 Von Hayes	.05
306a Gary Redus (1983 2B is .20)	.05
306b Gary Redus (1983 2B is 20)	.15
307 Craig Lefferts	.05
308 Sam Khalifa	.05
309 Scott Garrelts	.05
310 Rick Cerone	.05
311 Shawon Dunston	.05
312 Howard Johnson	.05
313 Jim Presley	.05
314 Gary Gaetti	.05
315 Luis Leal	.05
316 Mark Salas	.05
317 Bill Caudill	.05
318 Dave Henderson	.05
319 Rafael Santana	.05
320 Leon Durham	.05
321 Bruce Sutter	1.25
322 Jason Thompson	.05
323 Bob Brenly	.05
324 Carmelo Martinez	.05
325 Eddie Milner	.05
326 Juan Samuel	.05
327 Tom Nieto	.05
328 Dave Smith	.05
329 Urbano Lugo **RC**	.05
330 Joel Skinner	.05
331 Bill Gullickson	.05
332 Floyd Rayford	.05
333 Ben Oglivie	.05
334 Lance Parrish	.05
335 Jackie Gutierrez	.05
336 Dennis Rasmussen	.05
337 Terry Whitfield	.05
338 Neal Heaton	.05
339 Jorge Orta	.05
340 Donnie Hill	.05
341 Joe Hesketh	.05
342 Charlie Hough	.05
343 Dave Rozema	.05
344 Greg Pryor	.05
345 Mickey Tettleton	.05

346 George Vukovich	.05
347 Don Baylor	.05
348 Carlos Diaz	.05
349 Barbaro Garbey	.05
350 Larry Sheets	.05
351 Ted Higuera **RC**	.10
352 Juan Beniquez	.05
353 Bob Forsch	.05
354 Mark Bailey	.05
355 Larry Andersen	.05
356 Terry Kennedy	.05
357 Don Robinson	.05
358 Jim Gott	.05
359 Earnest Riles **RC**	.05
360 John Christensen **RC**	.05
361 Ray Fontenot	.05
362 Spike Owen	.05
363 Jim Acker	.05
364a Ron Davis (Last line in highlights ends with "...in May.")	.05
364b Ron Davis (Last line in highlights ends with "...relievers (9).")	.15
365 Tom Hume	.05
366 Carlton Fisk	1.50
367 Nate Snell	.05
368 Rick Manning	.05
369 Darrell Evans	.05
370 Ron Hassey	.05
371 Wade Boggs	2.00
372 Rick Honeycutt	.05
373 Chris Bando	.05
374 Bud Black	.05
375 Steve Henderson	.05
376 Charlie Lea	.05
377 Reggie Jackson	2.50
378 Dave Schmidt	.05
379 Bob James	.05
380 Glenn Davis **RC**	.05
381 Tim Corcoran	.05
382 Danny Cox	.05
383 Tim Flannery	.05
384 Tom Browning	.05
385 Rick Camp	.05
386 Jim Morrison	.05
387 Dave LaPoint	.05
388 Davey Lopes	.05
389 Al Cowens	.05
390 Doyle Alexander	.05
391 Tim Laudner	.05
392 Don Aase	.05
393 Jaime Cocanower	.05
394 Randy O'Neal **RC**	.05
395 Mike Easler	.05
396 Scott Bradley	.05
397 Tom Niedenfuer	.05
398 Jerry Willard	.05
399 Lonnie Smith	.05
400 Bruce Bochte	.05
401 Terry Francona	.05
402 Jim Slaton	.05
403 Bill Stein	.05
404 Tim Hulett	.05
405 Alan Ashby	.05
406 Tim Stoddard	.05
407 Garry Maddox	.05
408 Ted Power	.05
409 Len Barker	.05
410 Denny Gonzalez	.05
411 George Frazier	.05
412 Andy Van Slyke	.05
413 Jim Dwyer	.05
414 Paul Householder	.05
415 Alejandro Sanchez	.05
416 Steve Crawford	.05
417 Dan Pasqua	.05
418 Enos Cabell	.05
419 Mike Jones	.05
420 Steve Kiefer	.05
421 Tim Burke **RC**	.05
422 Mike Mason	.05
423 Ruppert Jones	.05
424 Jerry Hairston Sr.	.05
425 Tito Landrum	.05
426 Jeff Calhoun	.05
427 Don Carman **RC**	.05
428 Tony Perez	1.00
429 Jerry Davis	.05
430 Bob Walk	.05
431 Brad Wellman	.05
432 Terry Forster	.05
433 Billy Hatcher	.05
434 Clint Hurdle	.05
435 Ivan Calderon **RC**	.05
436 Pete Filson	.05
437 Tom Henke	.05
438 Dave Engle	.05
439 Tom Filer	.05
440 Gorman Thomas	.05
441 Rick Aguilera **RC**	.25
442 Scott Sanderson	.05
443 Jeff Dedmon	.05
444 Joe Orsulak **RC**	.10
445 Atlee Hammaker	.05
446 Jerry Royster	.05
447 Buddy Bell	.05
448 Dave Rucker	.05
449 Ivan DeJesus	.05
450 Jim Pankovits	.05
451 Jerry Narron	.05
452 Bryan Little	.05
453 Gary Lucas	.05
454 Dennis Martinez	.05
455 Ed Romero	.05
456 Bob Melvin **RC**	.05
457 Glenn Hoffman	.05
458 Bob Shirley	.05

459 Bob Welch	.05
460 Carmen Castillo	.05
461 Dave Leeper	.05
462 Tim Birtsas **RC**	.05
463 Randy St. Claire	.05
464 Chris Welsh	.05
465 Greg Harris	.05
466 Lynn Jones	.05
467 Dusty Baker	.05
468 Roy Smith	.05
469 Andre Robertson	.05
470 Ken Landreaux	.05
471 Dave Bergman	.05
472 Gary Roenicke	.05
473 Pete Vuckovich	.05
474 Kirk McCaskill **RC**	.10
475 Jeff Lahti	.05
476 Mike Scott	.05
477 Darren Daulton **RC**	1.50
478 Graig Nettles	.15
479 Bill Almon	.05
480 Greg Minton	.05
481 Randy Ready **RC**	.05
482 Len Dykstra **RC**	1.50
483 Thad Bosley	.05
484 Harold Reynolds **RC**	1.00
485 Al Oliver	.05
486 Roy Smalley	.05
487 John Franco	.05
488 Juan Agosto	.05
489 Al Pardo	.05
490 Bill Wegman **RC**	.05
491 Frank Tanana	.05
492 Brian Fisher **RC**	.05
493 Mark Clear	.05
494 Len Matuszek	.05
495 Ramon Romero	.05
496 John Wathan	.05
497 Rob Picciolo	.05
498 U.L. Washington	.05
499 John Candelaria	.05
500 Duane Walker	.05
501 Gene Nelson	.05
502 John Mizerock	.05
503 Luis Aguayo	.05
504 Kurt Kepshire	.05
505 Ed Wojna	.05
506 Joe Price	.05
507 Milt Thompson **RC**	.05
508 Junior Ortiz	.05
509 Vida Blue	.05
510 Steve Engel	.05
511 Karl Best	.05
512 Cecil Fielder **RC**	2.00
513 Frank Eufemia	.05
514 Tippy Martinez	.05
515 Billy Robidoux **RC**	.05
516 Bill Scherrer	.05
517 Bruce Hurst	.05
518 Rich Bordi	.05
519 Steve Yeager	.05
520 Tony Bernazard	.05
521 Hal McRae	.05
522 Jose Rijo	.05
523 Mitch Webster **RC**	.05
524 Jack Howell **RC**	.05
525 Alan Bannister	.05
526 Ron Kittle	.05
527 Phil Garner	.05
528 Kurt Bevacqua	.05
529 Kevin Gross	.05
530 Bo Diaz	.05
531 Ken Oberkfell	.05
532 Rick Reuschel	.05
533 Ron Meridith	.05
534 Steve Braun	.05
535 Wayne Gross	.05
536 Ray Searage	.05
537 Tom Brookens	.05
538 Al Nipper	.05
539 Billy Sample	.05
540 Steve Sax	.05
541 Dan Quisenberry	.05
542 Tony Phillips	.05
543 Floyd Youmans **RC**	.05
544 Steve Buechele **RC**	.05
545 Craig Gerber	.05
546 Joe DeSa	.05
547 Brian Harper	.05
548 Kevin Bass	.05
549 Tom Foley	.05
550 Dave Van Gorder	.05
551 Bruce Bochy	.05
552 R.J. Reynolds	.05
553 Chris Brown **RC**	.05
554 Bruce Benedict	.05
555 Warren Brusstar	.05
556 Danny Heep	.05
557 Darnell Coles	.05
558 Greg Gagne	.05
559 Ernie Whitt	.05
560 Ron Washington	.05
561 Jimmy Key	.05
562 Billy Swift	.05
563 Ron Darling	.05
564 Dick Ruthven	.05
565 Zane Smith	.05
566 Sid Bream	.05
567a Joel Youngblood (P on front)	.05
567b Joel Youngblood (IF on front)	.15
568 Mario Ramirez	.05
569 Tom Runnells	.05
570 Rick Schu	.05
571 Bill Campbell	.05
572 Dickie Thon	.05
573 Al Holland	.05

574	Reid Nichols	.05
575	Bert Roberge	.05
576	Mike Flanagan	.05
577	Tim Leary RC	.05
578	Mike Laga	.05
579	Steve Lyons	.05
580	Phil Niekro	1.00
581	Gilberto Reyes	.05
582	Jamie Easterly	.05
583	Mark Gubicza	.05
584	Stan Javier RC	.15
585	Bill Laskey	.05
586	Jeff Russell	.05
587	Dickie Noles	.05
588	Steve Farr	.05
589	Steve Ontiveros RC	.05
590	Mike Hargrove	.05
591	Marty Bystrom	.05
592	Franklin Stubbs	.05
593	Larry Herndon	.05
594	Bill Swaggerty	.05
595	Carlos Ponce	.05
596	Pat Perry RC	.05
597	Ray Knight	.05
598	Steve Lombardozzi RC	.05
599	Brad Havens	.05
600	Pat Clements RC	.05
601	Joe Niekro	.05
602	Hank Aaron Puzzle Card	.05
603	Dwayne Henry RC	.05
604	Mookie Wilson	.05
605	Buddy Biancalana	.05
606	Rance Mulliniks	.05
607	Alan Wiggins	.05
608	Joe Cowley	.05
609a	Tom Seaver (Green stripes around name.)	1.50
609b	Tom Seaver (Yellow stripes around name.)	2.00
610	Neil Allen	.05
611	Don Sutton	1.00
612	Fred Toliver RC	.05
613	Jay Baller	.05
614	Marc Sullivan	.05
615	John Grubb	.05
616	Bruce Kison	.05
617	Bill Madlock	.05
618	Chris Chambliss	.05
619	Dave Stewart	.05
620	Tim Lollar	.05
621	Gary Lavelle	.05
622	Charles Hudson	.05
623	Joel Davis RC	.05
624	Joe Johnson RC	.05
625	Sid Fernandez	.05
626	Dennis Lamp	.05
627	Terry Harper	.05
628	Jack Lazorko	.05
629	Roger McDowell RC	.25
630	Mark Funderburk	.05
631	Ed Lynch	.05
632	Rudy Law	.05
633	Roger Mason RC	.05
634	Mike Felder RC	.05
635	Ken Schrom	.05
636	Bob Ojeda	.05
637	Ed Vande Berg	.05
638	Bobby Meacham	.05
639	Cliff Johnson	.05
640	Garth Iorg	.05
641	Dan Driessen	.05
642	Mike Brown	.05
643	John Shelby	.05
644	Pete Rose/RB	.50
645	Knuckle Brothers (Joe Niekro, Phil Niekro)	.25
646	Jesse Orosco	.05
647	Billy Beane RC	.05
648	Cesar Cedeno	.05
649	Bert Blyleven	.15
650	Max Venable	.05
651	Fleet Feet (Vince Coleman, Willie McGee)	.25
652	Calvin Schiraldi	.05
653	King of Kings (Pete Rose)	3.00
----	Checklist 1-26 DK	.05
----	Checklist 27-130 (45 is Beane)	.05
----	Checklist 27-130 (45 is Habyan)	.05
----	Checklist 131-234	.05
----	Checklist 235-338	.05
----	Checklist 339-442	.05
----	Checklist 443-546	.05
----	Checklist 547-653	.05

Box Panels

For the second year in a row, Donruss placed baseball cards on the bottom of its wax and cello pack boxes. The cards, printed four to a panel, are standard 2-1/2" x 3-1/2". With numbering that begins where Donruss left off in 1985, cards PC4 through PC6 were found on boxes of regular Donruss issue wax packs. Cards PC7 through PC9 were found on boxes of the 1986 All-Star/Pop-up packs. An unnumbered Hank Aaron puzzle card was included on each box.

		NM/M
Complete Panel Set (2):		3.00
Complete Singles Set (8):		3.00
Common Single Player:		.15
Panel		.50
PC4	Kirk Gibson	.15
PC5	Willie Hernandez	.15
PC6	Doug DeCinces	.05
---	Aaron Puzzle Card	.05
Panel		2.00
PC7	Wade Boggs	1.50
PC8	Lee Smith	.20
PC9	Cecil Cooper	.15
---	Aaron Puzzle Card	.05

All-Stars

Issued in conjunction with the 1986 Donruss Pop-Ups set, the All-Stars consist of 60 cards in 3-1/2" x 5" format. Fifty-nine players involved in the 1985 All-Star game plus an unnumbered checklist comprise the set. Card fronts have the same blue border found on the regular 1986 Donruss issue. Retail packs included one Pop-up card, three All-Star cards and one Hank Aaron puzzle-piece card.

		NM/M
Complete Set (60):		6.00
Common Player:		.05
Hank Aaron puzzle:		3.00
Cello Pack (3):		.50
Cello Box (36):		6.00
1	Tony Gwynn	.40
2	Tommy Herr	.05
3	Steve Garvey	.20
4	Dale Murphy	.20
5	Darryl Strawberry	.40
6	Graig Nettles	.05
7	Terry Kennedy	.05
8	Ozzie Smith	.05
9	LaMarr Hoyt	.05
10	Rickey Henderson	.35
11	Lou Whitaker	.05
12	George Brett	.75
13	Eddie Murray	.40
14	Cal Ripken, Jr.	1.50
15	Dave Winfield	.40
16	Jim Rice	.25
17	Carlton Fisk	.40
18	Jack Morris	.05
19	Jose Cruz	.05
20	Tim Raines	.05
21	Nolan Ryan	1.50
22	Tony Pena	.05
23	Jack Clark	.05
24	Dave Parker	.05
25	Tim Wallach	.05
26	Ozzie Virgil	.05
27	Fernando Valenzuela	.05
28	Dwight Gooden	.05
29	Glenn Wilson	.05
30	Garry Templeton	.05
31	Goose Gossage	.05
32	Ryne Sandberg	.50
33	Jeff Reardon	.05
34	Pete Rose	1.00
35	Scott Garrelts	.05
36	Willie McGee	.05
37	Ron Darling	.05
38	Dick Williams	.05
39	Paul Molitor	.40
40	Damaso Garcia	.05
41	Phil Bradley	.05
42	Dan Petry	.05
43	Willie Hernandez	.05
44	Tom Brunansky	.05
45	Alan Trammell	.05
46	Donnie Moore	.05
47	Wade Boggs	.50
48	Ernie Whitt	.05
49	Harold Baines	.05
50	Don Mattingly	.75
51	Gary Ward	.05
52	Bert Blyleven	.05
53	Jimmy Key	.05
54	Cecil Cooper	.05
55	Dave Stieb	.05
56	Rich Gedman	.05
57	Jay Howell	.05
58	Sparky Anderson	.05
59	Minneapolis Metrodome	.05
---	Checklist	.03

Diamond Kings Supers

Donruss produced a set of large-format Diamond Kings in 1986 for the second year in a row. The 4-11/16" x 6-3/4" cards are enlarged versions of the 26 Diamond Kings cards found in the regular 1986 Donruss set, plus an unnumbered checklist and an unnumbered Pete Rose "King of Kings" card.

		NM/M
Complete Set (28):		6.00
Common Player:		.25
1	Kirk Gibson	.25
2	Goose Gossage	.25
3	Willie McGee	.25
4	George Bell	.25
5	Tony Armas	.25
6	Chili Davis	.25
7	Cecil Cooper	.25
8	Mike Boddicker	.25
9	Davey Lopes	.25
10	Bill Doran	.25
11	Bret Saberhagen	.25
12	Brett Butler	.25
13	Harold Baines	.25
14	Mike Davis	.25
15	Tony Perez	.75
16	Willie Randolph	.25
17	Orel Hershiser	.25
18	Johnny Ray	.25
19	Gary Ward	.25
20	Rick Mahler	.25
21	Phil Bradley	.25
22	Jerry Koosman	.25
23	Tom Brunansky	.25
24	Andre Dawson	.50
25	Dwight Gooden	.25
26	Checklist	.05
---	King of Kings (Pete Rose)	4.00

Highlights

Donruss, for the second year in a row, issued a 56-card highlights set featuring cards of each league's Player of the Month plus significant events of the 1986 season. The cards, 2-1/2" x 3-1/2," are similar in design to the regular 1986 Donruss set but have a gold border instead of blue. A yellow "Highlights" logo appears in the lower-left corner of each card front. Backs are designed on a vertical format and feature black print on a yellow background. As in 1985, the set includes Donruss' picks for the Rookies of the Year. A new feature was three cards honoring the 1986 Hall of Fame inductees. The set, available only through hobby dealers, was issued in a specially designed box. Each card can also be found with the word "Highlights" in the logo in white, a much scarcer variation that sometimes attracts significant premiums from single-player specialist collectors.

		NM/M
Complete Set (56):		3.00
Common Player:		.05
White "Highlights":		20X
1	Homers In First At-Bat (Will Clark)	.05
2	Oakland Milestone For Strikeouts (Jose Rijo)	.05
3	Royals' All-Time Hit Man (George Brett)	.50
4	Phillies RBI Leader (Mike Schmidt)	.50
5	KKKKKKKKKKKKKKK KKKKKK (Roger Clemens)	.50
6	A.L. Pitcher of the Month-April (Roger Clemens)	.50
7	A.L. Player of the Month-April (Kirby Puckett)	.25
8	N.L. Pitcher of the Month-April (Dwight Gooden)	.05
9	N.L. Player of the Month-April (Johnny Ray)	.05
10	Eclipses Mantle HR Record (Reggie Jackson)	.50
11	First Five Hit Game of Career (Wade Boggs)	.25
12	A.L. Pitcher of the Month-May (Don Aase)	.05
13	A.L. Player of the Month-May (Wade Boggs)	.25
14	N.L. Pitcher of the Month-May (Jeff Reardon)	.05
15	N.L. Player of the Month-May (Hubie Brooks)	.05
16	Notches 300th Career Win (Don Sutton)	.05
17	Starts Season 14-0 (Roger Clemens)	.50
18	A.L. Pitcher of the Month-June (Roger Clemens)	.50
19	A.L. Player of the Month-June (Kent Hrbek)	.05
20	N.L. Pitcher of the Month-June (Rick Rhoden)	.05
21	N.L. Player of the Month-June (Kevin Bass)	.05
22	Blasts 4 HRS in 1 Game (Bob Horner)	.05
23	Starting All Star Rookie (Wally Joyner)	.05
24	Starts 3rd Straight All Star Game (Darryl Strawberry)	.05
25	Ties All Star Game Record (Fernando Valenzuela)	.05
26	All Star Game MVP (Roger Clemens)	.50
27	A.L. Pitcher of the Month-July (Jack Morris)	.05
28	A.L. Player of the Month-July (Scott Fletcher)	.05
29	N.L. Pitcher of the Month-July (Todd Worrell)	.05
30	N.L. PLayer of the Month-July (Eric Davis)	.05
31	Records 3000th Strikeout (Bert Blyleven)	.05
32	1986 Hall of Fame Inductee (Bobby Doerr)	.05
33	1986 Hall of Fame Inductee (Ernie Lombardi)	.05
34	1986 Hall of Fame Inductee (Willie McCovey)	.05
35	Notches 4000th K (Steve Carlton)	.25
36	Surpasses DiMaggio Record (Mike Schmidt)	.50
37	Records 3rd "Quadruple Double" (Juan Samuel)	.05
38	A.L. Pitcher of the Month-August (Mike Witt)	.05
39	A.L. Player of the Month-August (Doug DeCinces)	.05
40	N.L. Pitcher of the Month-August (Bill Gullickson)	.05
41	N.L. Player of the Month-August (Dale Murphy)	.15
42	Sets Tribe Offensive Record (Joe Carter)	.05
43	Longest HR In Royals Stadium (Bo Jackson)	.15
44	Majors 1st No-Hitter In 2 Years (Joe Cowley)	.05
45	Sets M.L. Strikeout Record (Jim Deshaies)	.05
46	No Hitter Clinches Division (Mike Scott)	.05
47	A.L. Pitcher of the Month-September (Bruce Hurst)	.05
48	A.L. Player of the Month-September (Don Mattingly)	.50
49	N.L. Pitcher of the Month-September (Mike Krukow)	.05
50	N.L. Player of the Month-September (Steve Sax)	.05
51	A.L. Record For Steals By A Rookie (John Cangelosi)	.05
52	Shatters M.L. Save Mark (Dave Righetti)	.05
53	Yankee Record For Hits & Doubles (Don Mattingly)	.50
54	Donruss N.L. Rookie of the Year (Todd Worrell)	.05
55	Donruss A.L. Rookie of the Year (Jose Canseco)	.50
56	Highlight Checklist	.05

Pop-Ups

Issued in conjunction with the 1986 Donruss All-Stars set, the Pop-Ups (18 unnumbered cards) feature the 1985 All-Star Game starting lineups. The cards, 2-1/2" x 5", are die-cut and fold out to form a three-dimensional stand-up card. The background for the cards is the Minneapolis Metrodome, site of the 1985 All-Star Game. Retail packs included one Pop-Up card, three All-Star cards and one Hank Aaron puzzle card.

		NM/M
Complete Set (18):		4.00
Common Player:		.05
Hank Aaron Puzzle:		3.00
Cello Pack (3):		.50
Cello Box (36):		6.00
(1)	George Brett	.75
(2)	Carlton Fisk	.40
(3)	Steve Garvey	.20
(4)	Tony Gwynn	.50
(5)	Rickey Henderson	.40
(6)	Tommy Herr	.05
(7)	LaMarr Hoyt	.05
(8)	Terry Kennedy	.05
(9)	Jack Morris	.05
(10)	Dale Murphy	.25
(11)	Eddie Murray	.40
(12)	Graig Nettles	.05
(13)	Jim Rice	.25
(14)	Cal Ripken, Jr.	1.00
(15)	Ozzie Smith	.50
(16)	Darryl Strawberry	.05
(17)	Lou Whitaker	.05
(18)	Dave Winfield	.40

Rookies

Entitled "The Rookies," this 56-card set includes the top 55 rookies of 1986 plus an unnumbered checklist. The cards are similar in format to the 1986 Donruss regular issue, except that the borders

are green rather than blue. Several of the rookies who had cards in the regular 1986 Donruss set appear again in "The Rookies" set. The sets, which were only available through hobby dealers, came in a specially designed box.

		NM/M
Unopened Set (56):		35.00
Opened Set (56):		30.00
Common Player:		.05
1	Wally Joyner RC	.50
2	Tracy Jones RC	.05
3	Allan Anderson RC	.05
4	Ed Correa RC	.05
5	Reggie Williams	.05
6	Charlie Kerfeld RC	.05
7	Andres Galarraga	.15
8	Bob Tewksbury RC	.05
9	Al Newman	.05
10	Andres Thomas RC	.05
11	Barry Bonds RC	20.00
12	Juan Nieves	.05
13	Mark Eichhorn RC	.05
14	Dan Plesac RC	.05
15	Cory Snyder	.05
16	Kelly Gruber	.05
17	Kevin Mitchell RC	.25
18	Steve Lombardozzi	.05
19	Mitch Williams	.05
20	John Cerutti	.05
21	Todd Worrell	.05
22	Jose Canseco	2.00
23	Pete Incaviglia RC	.15
24	Jose Guzman	.05
25	Scott Bailes RC	.05
26	Greg Mathews RC	.05
27	Eric King RC	.05
28	Paul Assenmacher	.05
29	Jeff Sellers	.05
30	Bobby Bonilla RC	.25
31	Doug Drabek RC	.25
32	Will Clark RC	1.00
33	Bip Roberts	.05
34	Jim Deshaies RC	.05
35	Mike LaValliere RC	.05
36	Scott Bankhead RC	.05
37	Dale Sveum RC	.05
38	Bo Jackson RC	2.00
39	Rob Thompson RC	.05
40	Eric Plunk RC	.05
41	Bill Bathe	.05
42	John Kruk RC	.25
43	Andy Allanson RC	.05
44	Mark Portugal	.05
45	Danny Tartabull	.25
46	Bob Kipper	.05
47	Gene Walter	.05
48	Rey Quinonez	.05
49	Bobby Witt RC	.05
50	Bill Mooneyham	.05
51	John Cangelosi RC	.05
52	Ruben Sierra RC	.25
53	Rob Woodward	.05
54	Ed Hearn	.05
55	Joel McKeon	.05
56	Checklist 1-56	.05

1987 Donruss

The 1987 Donruss set consists of 660 numbered cards, each measuring 2-1/2" x 3-1/2". Color photos are surrounded by a bold black border separated by two narrow bands of yellow which enclose a brown area filled with baseballs. The player's name, team and team logo appear on the card fronts along with the words "Donruss '87." The card backs are designed on a horizontal format and contain black print on a yellow and white background. The backs are very similar to those in previous years' sets. Backs of cards issued in wax and rack packs face to the left when turned over, while those issued in factory sets face to the right. Cards were sold with Roberto Clemente puzzle pieces in each pack. Cards checklisted with a (DK) suffix are Diamond Kings; cards with an (RR) suffix are Rated Rookies.

	NM/M
Unopened Fact. Set (660):	40.00
Complete Set (660):	30.00
Common Player:	.05
Roberto Clemente Puzzle:	2.50
Wax Pack (15):	1.25
Wax Box (36):	35.00
Rack Pack (45):	3.00
Jumbo Rack (75):	4.00

No.	Player	Price
1	Wally Joyner/DK	.25
2	Roger Clemens/DK	1.00
3	Dale Murphy/DK	.25
4	Darryl Strawberry/DK	.10
5	Ozzie Smith/DK	.75
6	Jose Canseco/DK	.40
7	Charlie Hough/DK	.05
8	Brook Jacoby/DK	.05
9	Fred Lynn/DK	.10
10	Rick Rhoden/DK	.05
11	Chris Brown/DK	.05
12	Von Hayes/DK	.05
13	Jack Morris/DK	.10
14a	Kevin McReynolds/DK (No yellow stripe on back.)	.25
14b	Kevin McReynolds/DK (Yellow stripe on back.)	.25
15	George Brett/DK	1.00
16	Ted Higuera/DK	.05
17	Hubie Brooks/DK	.05
18	Mike Scott/DK	.05
19	Kirby Puckett/DK	.75
20	Dave Winfield/DK	.60
21	Lloyd Moseby/DK	.05
22a	Eric Davis/DK (No yellow stripe on back.)	.25
22b	Eric Davis/DK (Yellow stripe on back.)	.15
23	Jim Presley/DK	.05
24	Keith Moreland/DK	.05
25a	Greg Walker/DK (No yellow stripe on back.)	.25
25b	Greg Walker/DK (Yellow stripe on back.)	.10
26	Steve Sax/DK	.10
27	Checklist 1-27	.05
28	B.J. Surhoff/RR RC	.30
29	Randy Myers/RR RC	.50
30	Ken Gerhart/RR RC	.05
31	Benito Santiago/RR	.15
32	Greg Swindell/RR RC	.15
33	Mike Birkbeck/RR RC	.05
34	Terry Steinbach/RR RC	.25
35	Bo Jackson/RR	1.50
36	Greg Maddux/RR RC	6.00
37	Jim Lindeman/RR RC	.05
38	Devon White/RR RC	.75
39	Eric Bell/RR RC	.05
40	Will Fraser/RR RC	.05
41	Jerry Browne/RR RC	.05
42	Chris James/RR RC	.05
43	Rafael Palmeiro/RR RC	4.00
44	Pat Dodson/RR RC	.05
45	Duane Ward/RR RC	.10
46	Mark McGwire/RR RC	6.00
47	Bruce Fields/RR RC (Photo actually Darnell Coles.)	.05
48	Eddie Murray	.60
49	Ted Higuera	.05
50	Kirk Gibson	.05
51	Oil Can Boyd	.05
52	Don Mattingly	1.00
53	Pedro Guerrero	.05
54	George Brett	1.00
55	Jose Rijo	.05
56	Tim Raines	.05
57	Ed Correa RC	.05
58	Mike Witt	.05
59	Greg Walker	.05
60	Ozzie Smith	.75
61	Glenn Davis	.05
62	Glenn Wilson	.05
63	Tom Browning	.05
64	Tony Gwynn	.75
65	R.J. Reynolds	.05
66	Will Clark	.25
67	Ozzie Virgil	.05
68	Rick Sutcliffe	.05
69	Gary Carter	.60
70	Mike Moore	.05
71	Bert Blyleven	.10
72	Tony Fernandez	.05
73	Kent Hrbek	.05
74	Lloyd Moseby	.05
75	Alvin Davis	.05
76	Keith Hernandez	.05
77	Ryne Sandberg	.75
78	Dale Murphy	.40
79	Sid Bream	.05
80	Chris Brown	.05
81	Steve Garvey	.25
82	Mario Soto	.05
83	Shane Rawley	.05
84	Willie McGee	.05
85	Jose Cruz	.05
86	Brian Downing	.05
87	Ozzie Guillen	.05
88	Hubie Brooks	.05
89	Cal Ripken, Jr.	2.50
90	Juan Nieves	.05
91	Lance Parrish	.05
92	Jim Rice	.05
93	Ron Guidry	.10
94	Fernando Valenzuela	.05
95	Andy Allanson RC	.05
96	Willie Wilson	.05
97	Jose Canseco	.40
98	Jeff Reardon	.05
99	Bobby Witt RC	.20
100	Checklist 28-133	.05
101	Jose Guzman	.05
102	Steve Balboni	.05
103	Tony Phillips	.05
104	Brook Jacoby	.05
105	Dave Winfield	.60
106	Orel Hershiser	.05
107	Lou Whitaker	.05
108	Fred Lynn	.05
109	Bill Wegman	.05
110	Donnie Moore	.05
111	Jack Clark	.05
112	Bob Knepper	.05
113	Von Hayes	.05
114	Bip Roberts RC	.25
115	Tony Pena	.05
116	Scott Garrelts	.05
117	Paul Molitor	.60
118	Darryl Strawberry	.05
119	Shawon Dunston	.05
120	Jim Presley	.05
121	Jesse Barfield	.05
122	Gary Gaetti	.05
123	Kurt Stillwell RC	.10
124	Joel Davis	.05
125	Mike Boddicker	.05
126	Robin Yount	.60
127	Alan Trammell	.05
128	Dave Righetti	.05
129	Dwight Evans	.05
130	Mike Scioscia	.05
131	Julio Franco	.05
132	Bret Saberhagen	.05
133	Mike Davis	.05
134	Joe Hesketh	.05
135	Wally Joyner	.05
136	Don Slaught	.05
137	Daryl Boston	.05
138	Nolan Ryan	2.50
139	Mike Schmidt	1.00
140	Tommy Herr	.05
141	Garry Templeton	.05
142	Kal Daniels	.05
143	Billy Sample	.05
144	Johnny Ray	.05
145	Rob Thompson RC	.10
146	Bob Dernier	.05
147	Danny Tartabull	.05
148	Ernie Whitt	.05
149	Kirby Puckett	.75
150	Mike Young	.05
151	Ernest Riles	.05
152	Frank Tanana	.05
153	Rich Gedman	.05
154	Willie Randolph	.05
155a	Bill Madlock (Name in brown band.)	.10
155b	Bill Madlock (Name in red band.)	.25
156a	Joe Carter (Name in brown band.)	.10
156b	Joe Carter (Name in red band.)	.25
157	Danny Jackson	.05
158	Carney Lansford	.05
159	Bryn Smith	.05
160	Gary Pettis	.05
161	Oddibe McDowell	.05
162	John Cangelosi RC	.10
163	Mike Scott	.05
164	Eric Show	.05
165	Juan Samuel	.05
166	Nick Esasky	.05
167	Zane Smith	.05
168	Mike Brown	.05
169	Keith Moreland	.05
170	John Tudor	.05
171	Ken Dixon	.05
172	Jim Gantner	.05
173	Jack Morris	.05
174	Bruce Hurst	.05
175	Dennis Rasmussen	.05
176	Mike Marshall	.05
177	Dan Quisenberry	.05
178	Eric Plunk RC	.05
179	Tim Wallach	.05
180	Steve Buechele	.05
181	Don Sutton	.50
182	Dave Schmidt	.05
183	Terry Pendleton	.05
184	Jim Deshaies RC	.05
185	Steve Bedrosian	.05
186	Pete Rose	2.00
187	Dave Dravecky	.05
188	Rick Reuschel	.05
189	Dan Gladden	.05
190	Rick Mahler	.05
191	Thad Bosley	.05
192	Ron Darling	.05
193	Matt Young	.05
194	Tom Brunansky	.05
195	Dave Stieb	.05
196	Frank Viola	.05
197	Tom Henke	.05
198	Karl Best	.05
199	Dwight Gooden	.05
200	Checklist 134-239	.05
201	Steve Trout	.05
202	Rafael Ramirez	.05
203	Bob Walk	.05
204	Roger Mason	.05
205	Terry Kennedy	.05
206	Ron Oester	.05
207	John Russell	.05
208	Greg Mathews RC	.05
209	Charlie Kerfeld	.05
210	Reggie Jackson	1.00
211	Floyd Bannister	.05
212	Vance Law	.05
213	Rich Bordi	.05
214	Dan Plesac RC	.10
215	Dave Collins	.05
216	Bob Stanley	.05
217	Joe Niekro	.05
218	Tom Niedenfuer	.05
219	Brett Butler	.05
220	Charlie Leibrandt	.05
221	Steve Ontiveros	.05
222	Tim Burke	.05
223	Curtis Wilkerson	.05
224	Pete Incaviglia RC	.10
225	Lonnie Smith	.05
226	Chris Codiroli	.05
227	Scott Bailes RC	.05
228	Rickey Henderson	.60
229	Ken Howell	.05
230	Darnell Coles	.05
231	Don Aase	.05
232	Tim Leary	.05
233	Bob Boone	.05
234	Ricky Horton	.05
235	Mark Bailey	.05
236	Kevin Gross	.05
237	Lance McCullers	.05
238	Cecilio Guante	.05
239	Bob Melvin	.05
240	Billy Jo Robidoux	.05
241	Roger McDowell	.05
242	Leon Durham	.05
243	Ed Nunez	.05
244	Jimmy Key	.05
245	Mike Smithson	.05
246	Bo Diaz	.05
247	Carlton Fisk	.60
248	Larry Sheets	.05
249	Juan Castillo RC	.05
250	Eric King RC	.05
251	Doug Drabek	.05
252	Wade Boggs	.75
253	Mariano Duncan	.05
254	Pat Tabler	.05
255	Frank White	.05
256	Alfredo Griffin	.05
257	Floyd Youmans	.05
258	Rob Wilfong	.05
259	Pete O'Brien	.05
260	Tim Hulett	.05
261	Dickie Thon	.05
262	Darren Daulton	.05
263	Vince Coleman	.05
264	Andy Hawkins	.05
265	Eric Davis	.05
266	Andres Thomas RC	.05
267	Mike Diaz RC	.05
268	Chili Davis	.05
269	Jody Davis	.05
270	Phil Bradley	.05
271	George Bell	.05
272	Keith Atherton	.05
273	Storm Davis	.05
274	Rob Deer RC	.05
275	Walt Terrell	.05
276	Roger Clemens	1.00
277	Mike Easler	.05
278	Steve Sax	.05
279	Andre Thornton	.05
280	Jim Sundberg	.05
281	Bill Schroeder	.05
282	Jay Tibbs	.05
283	Dick Schofield	.05
284	Mike Mason	.05
285	Jerry Hairston Sr.	.05
286	Bill Doran	.05
287	Tim Flannery	.05
288	Gary Redus	.05
289	John Franco	.05
290	Paul Assenmacher RC	.10
291	Joe Orsulak	.05
292	Lee Smith	.10
293	Mike Laga	.05
294	Rick Dempsey	.05
295	Mike Felder	.05
296	Tom Brookens	.05
297	Al Nipper	.05
298	Mike Pagliarulo	.05
299	Franklin Stubbs	.05
300	Checklist 240-345	.05
301	Steve Farr	.05
302	Bill Mooneyham RC	.05
303	Andres Galarraga	.05
304	Scott Fletcher	.05
305	Jack Howell	.05
306	Russ Morman RC	.05
307	Todd Worrell	.05
308	Dave Smith	.05
309	Jeff Stone	.05
310	Ron Robinson	.05
311	Bruce Bochy	.05
312	Jim Winn	.05
313	Mark Davis	.05
314	Jeff Dedmon	.05
315	Jamie Moyer RC	.10
316	Wally Backman	.05
317	Ken Phelps	.05
318	Steve Lombardozzi	.05
319	Rance Mulliniks	.05
320	Tim Laudner	.05
321	Mark Eichhorn RC	.10
322	Lee Guetterman RC	.05
323	Sid Fernandez	.05
324	Jerry Mumphrey	.05
325	David Palmer	.05
326	Bill Almon	.05
327	Candy Maldonado	.05
328	John Kruk	.05
329	John Denny	.05
330	Milt Thompson	.05
331	Mike LaValliere RC	.10
332	Alan Ashby	.05
333	Doug Corbett	.05
334	Ron Karkovice RC	.05
335	Mitch Webster	.05
336	Lee Lacy	.05
337	Glenn Braggs RC	.05
338	Dwight Lowry	.05
339	Don Baylor	.05
340	Brian Fisher	.05
341	Reggie Williams RC	.05
342	Tom Candiotti	.05
343	Rudy Law	.05
344	Curt Young	.05
345	Mike Fitzgerald	.05
346	Ruben Sierra	.05
347	Mitch Williams RC	.25
348	Jorge Orta	.05
349	Mickey Tettleton	.05
350	Ernie Camacho	.05
351	Ron Kittle	.05
352	Ken Landreaux	.05
353	Chet Lemon	.05
354	John Shelby	.05
355	Mark Clear	.05
356	Doug DeCinces	.05
357	Ken Dayley	.05
358	Phil Garner	.05
359	Steve Jeltz	.05
360	Ed Whitson	.05
361	Barry Bonds	10.00
362	Vida Blue	.05
363	Cecil Cooper	.05
364	Bob Ojeda	.05
365	Dennis Eckersley	.50
366	Mike Morgan	.05
367	Willie Upshaw	.05
368	Allan Anderson RC	.05
369	Bill Gullickson	.05
370	Bobby Thigpen RC	.10
371	Juan Beniquez	.05
372	Charlie Moore	.05
373	Dan Petry	.05
374	Rod Scurry	.05
375	Tom Seaver	.75
376	Ed Vande Berg	.05
377	Tony Bernazard	.05
378	Greg Pryor	.05
379	Dwayne Murphy	.05
380	Andy McGaffigan	.05
381	Kirk McCaskill	.05
382	Greg Harris	.05
383	Rich Dotson	.05
384	Craig Reynolds	.05
385	Greg Gross	.05
386	Tito Landrum	.05
387	Craig Lefferts	.05
388	Dave Parker	.05
389	Bob Horner	.05
390	Pat Clements	.05
391	Jeff Leonard	.05
392	Chris Speier	.05
393	John Moses	.05
394	Garth Iorg	.05
395	Greg Gagne	.05
396	Nate Snell	.05
397	Bryan Clutterbuck RC	.05
398	Darrell Evans	.05
399	Steve Crawford	.05
400	Checklist 346-451	.05
401	Phil Lombardi RC	.05
402	Rick Honeycutt	.05
403	Ken Schrom	.05
404	Bud Black	.05
405	Donnie Hill	.05
406	Wayne Krenchicki	.05
407	Chuck Finley RC	.35
408	Toby Harrah	.05
409	Steve Lyons	.05
410	Kevin Bass	.05
411	Marvell Wynne	.05
412	Ron Roenicke	.05
413	Tracy Jones RC	.05
414	Gene Garber	.05
415	Mike Bielecki	.05
416	Frank DiPino	.05
417	Andy Van Slyke	.05
418	Jim Dwyer	.05
419	Ben Oglivie	.05
420	Dave Bergman	.05
421	Joe Sambito	.05
422	Bob Tewksbury RC	.30
423	Len Matuszek	.05
424	Mike Kingery RC	.05
425	Dave Kingman	.05
426	Al Newman RC	.05
427	Gary Ward	.05
428	Ruppert Jones	.05
429	Harold Baines	.05
430	Pat Perry	.05
431	Terry Puhl	.05
432	Don Carman	.05
433	Eddie Milner	.05
434	LaMarr Hoyt	.05
435	Rick Rhoden	.05
436	Jose Uribe	.05
437	Ken Oberkfell	.05
438	Ron Davis	.05
439	Jesse Orosco	.05
440	Scott Bradley	.05
441	Randy Bush	.05
442	John Cerutti RC	.05
443	Roy Smalley	.05
444	Kelly Gruber	.05
445	Bob Kearney	.05
446	Ed Hearn RC	.05
447	Scott Sanderson	.05
448	Bruce Benedict	.05
449	Junior Ortiz	.05
450	Mike Aldrete RC	.05
451	Kevin McReynolds	.05
452	Rob Murphy RC	.05
453	Kent Tekulve	.05
454	Curt Ford RC	.05
455	Davey Lopes	.05
456	Bobby Grich	.05
457	Jose DeLeon	.05
458	Andre Dawson	.35
459	Mike Flanagan	.05
460	Joey Meyer RC	.05
461	Chuck Cary RC	.05
462	Bill Buckner	.05
463	Bob Shirley	.05
464	Jeff Hamilton RC	.05
465	Phil Niekro	.50
466	Mark Gubicza	.05
467	Jerry Willard	.05
468	Bob Sebra RC	.05
469	Larry Parrish	.05
470	Charlie Hough	.05
471	Hal McRae	.05
472	Dave Leiper RC	.05
473	Mel Hall	.05
474	Dan Pasqua	.05
475	Bob Welch	.05
476	Johnny Grubb	.05
477	Jim Traber	.05
478	Chris Bosio RC	.05
479	Mark McLemore	.05
480	John Morris	.05
481	Billy Hatcher	.05
482	Dan Schatzeder	.05
483	Rich Gossage	.10
484	Jim Morrison	.05
485	Bob Brenly	.05
486	Bill Schroeder	.05
487	Mookie Wilson	.05
488	Dave Martinez RC	.10
489	Harold Reynolds	.05
490	Jeff Hearron	.05
491	Mickey Hatcher	.05
492	Barry Larkin RC	2.00
493	Bob James	.05
494	John Habyan	.05
495	Jim Adduci RC	.05
496	Mike Heath	.05
497	Tim Stoddard	.05
498	Tony Armas	.05
499	Dennis Powell	.05
500	Checklist 452-557	.05
501	Chris Bando	.05
502	David Cone RC	2.00
503	Jay Howell	.05
504	Tom Foley	.05
505	Ray Chadwick RC	.05
506	Mike Loynd RC	.05
507	Neil Allen	.05
508	Danny Darwin	.05
509	Rick Schu	.05
510	Jose Oquendo	.05
511	Gene Walter	.05
512	Terry McGriff RC	.05
513	Ken Griffey	.05
514	Benny Distefano	.05
515	Terry Mulholland RC	.25
516	Ed Lynch	.05
517	Bill Swift	.05
518	Manny Lee RC	.05
519	Andre David	.05
520	Scott McGregor	.05
521	Rick Manning	.05
522	Willie Hernandez	.05
523	Marty Barrett	.05
524	Wayne Tolleson	.05
525	Jose Gonzalez RC	.05
526	Cory Snyder	.05
527	Buddy Biancalana	.05
528	Moose Haas	.05
529	Wilfredo Tejada RC	.05
530	Stu Cliburn	.05
531	Dale Mohorcic RC	.05
532	Ron Hassey	.05
533	Ty Gainey	.05
534	Jerry Royster	.05
535	Mike Maddux RC	.05
536	Ted Power	.05
537	Ted Simmons	.05
538	Rafael Belliard RC	.05
539	Chico Walker	.05
540	Bob Forsch	.05
541	John Stefero	.05
542	Dale Sveum RC	.05
543	Mark Thurmond	.05
544	Jeff Sellers RC	.05
545	Joel Skinner	.05
546	Alex Trevino	.05
547	Randy Kutcher RC	.05
548	Joaquin Andujar	.05
549	Casey Candaele RC	.10
550	Jeff Russell	.05
551	John Candelaria	.05
552	Joe Cowley	.05
553	Danny Cox	.05
554	Denny Walling	.05
555	Bruce Ruffin RC	.10
556	Buddy Bell	.05
557	Jimmy Jones RC	.05
558	Bobby Bonilla	.05
559	Jeff Robinson	.05
560	Ed Olwine	.05
561	Glenallen Hill RC	.25
562	Lee Mazzilli	.05
563	Mike Brown	.05
564	George Frazier	.05
565	Mike Sharperson RC	.10
566	Mark Portugal RC	.05
567	Rick Leach	.05
568	Mark Langston	.05
569	Rafael Santana	.05
570	Manny Trillo	.05
571	Cliff Speck	.05
572	Bob Kipper	.05
573	Kelly Downs RC	.05
574	Randy Asadoor RC	.05
575	Dave Magadan RC	.25
576	Marvin Freeman RC	.05
577	Jeff Lahti	.05
578	Jeff Calhoun	.05
579	Gus Polidor RC	.05
580	Gene Nelson	.05
581	Tim Teufel	.05
582	Odell Jones	.05
583	Mark Ryal	.05
584	Randy O'Neal	.05
585	Mike Greenwell RC	.50
586	Ray Knight	.05
587	Ralph Bryant RC	.05
588	Carmen Castillo	.05
589	Ed Wojna	.05
590	Stan Javier	.05
591	Jeff Musselman RC	.05
592	Mike Stanley RC	.05
593	Darrell Porter	.05
594	Drew Hall RC	.05
595	Rob Nelson RC	.05
596	Bryan Oelkers	.05
597	Scott Nielsen RC	.05
598	Brian Holton RC	.05
599	Kevin Mitchell	.05
600	Checklist 558-660	.05
601	Jackie Gutierrez	.05
602	Barry Jones RC	.05
603	Jerry Narron	.05
604	Steve Lake	.05
605	Jim Pankovits	.05
606	Ed Romero	.05
607	Dave LaPoint	.05
608	Don Robinson	.05
609	Mike Krukow	.05
610	Dave Valle RC	.05
611	Len Dykstra	.05
612	Roberto Clemente Puzzle Card	.25
613	Mike Trujillo RC	.05
614	Damaso Garcia	.05
615	Neal Heaton	.05
616	Juan Berenguer	.05
617	Steve Carlton	.75
618	Gary Lucas	.05
619	Geno Petralli	.05
620	Rick Aguilera	.05
621	Fred McGriff	.05
622	Dave Henderson	.05
623	Dave Clark RC	.05
624	Angel Salazar	.05
625	Randy Hunt	.05
626	John Gibbons	.05
627	Kevin Brown RC	2.00
628	Bill Dawley	.05
629	Aurelio Lopez	.05
630	Charlie Hudson	.05
631	Ray Soff	.05
632	Ray Hayward RC	.05
633	Spike Owen	.05
634	Glenn Hubbard	.05
635	Kevin Elster RC	.10
636	Mike LaCoss	.05
637	Dwayne Henry	.05
638	Rey Quinones RC	.05
639	Jim Clancy	.05
640	Larry Andersen	.05
641	Calvin Schiraldi	.05
642	Stan Jefferson RC	.05
643	Marc Sullivan	.05
644	Mark Grant	.05
645	Cliff Johnson	.05
646	Howard Johnson	.05

ABBREVIATIONS

DK - Diamond King
RR - Rated Rookie

647	Dave Sax	.05
648	Dave Stewart	.05
649	Danny Heep	.05
650	Joe Johnson	.05
651	Bob Brower **RC**	.05
652	Rob Woodward	.05
653	John Mizerock	.05
654	Tim Pyznarski **RC**	.05
655	Luis Aquino **RC**	.05
656	Mickey Brantley **RC**	.05
657	Doyle Alexander	.05
658	Sammy Stewart	.05
659	Jim Acker	.05
660	Pete Ladd	.05

Box Panels

Continuing with an idea they initiated in 1985, Donruss once again placed baseball cards on the bottoms of their retail boxes. The cards, which are 2-1/2" x 3-1/2" in size, come four to a panel with each panel containing an unnumbered Roberto Clemente puzzle card. With numbering that begins where Donruss left off in 1986, cards PC 10 through PC 12 were found on boxes of Donruss regular issue wax packs. Cards PC 13 through PC 15 were located on boxes of the 1987 All-Star/Pop-Up packs.

		NM/M
Complete Panel Set (2):		4.00
Complete Singles Set (8):		4.00
Common Single Player:		.15
Panel		1.50
10	Dale Murphy	.40
11	Jeff Reardon	.15
12	Jose Canseco	.60
----	Roberto Clemente Puzzle Card	.15
Panel		3.00
13	Mike Scott	.15
14	Roger Clemens	2.00
15	Mike Krukow	.15
----	Roberto Clemente Puzzle Card	.15

All-Stars

Issued in conjunction with the Donruss Pop-Ups set for the second consecutive year, the 1987 Donruss All-Stars consist of 59 players (plus a checklist) who were selected to the 1986 All-Star Game. Measuring 3-1/2" x 5" in size, the card fronts feature black borders and American or National League logos. Included on back are the player's career highlights and All-Star Game statistics. Retail packs included one Pop-Up card, three All-Star cards and one Roberto Clemente puzzle card.

		NM/M
Complete Set (60):		4.00
Common Player:		.05
1	Wally Joyner	.05
2	Dave Winfield	.40
3	Lou Whitaker	.05
4	Kirby Puckett	.50
5	Cal Ripken, Jr.	1.00
6	Rickey Henderson	.40
7	Wade Boggs	.50
8	Roger Clemens	.65
9	Lance Parrish	.05
10	Dick Howser	.05
11	Keith Hernandez	.05
12	Darryl Strawberry	.05
13	Ryne Sandberg	.50
14	Dale Murphy	.25
15	Ozzie Smith	.05
16	Tony Gwynn	.50
17	Mike Schmidt	.65
18	Dwight Gooden	.05
19	Gary Carter	.40
20	Whitey Herzog	.05
21	Jose Canseco	.25
22	John Franco	.05
23	Jesse Barfield	.05
24	Rick Rhoden	.05
25	Harold Baines	.05
26	Sid Fernandez	.05
27	George Brett	.65
28	Steve Sax	.05
29	Jim Presley	.05
30	Dave Smith	.05
31	Eddie Murray	.40
32	Mike Scott	.05
33	Don Mattingly	.65
34	Dave Parker	.05
35	Tony Fernandez	.05
36	Tim Raines	.05
37	Brook Jacoby	.05
38	Chili Davis	.05
39	Rich Gedman	.05
40	Kevin Bass	.05
41	Frank White	.05
42	Glenn Davis	.05
43	Willie Hernandez	.05
44	Chris Brown	.05
45	Jim Rice	.25
46	Tony Pena	.05
47	Don Aase	.05
48	Hubie Brooks	.05
49	Charlie Hough	.05
50	Jody Davis	.05
51	Mike Witt	.05
52	Jeff Reardon	.05
53	Ken Schrom	.05
54	Fernando Valenzuela	.05
55	Dave Righetti	.05
56	Shane Rawley	.05
57	Ted Higuera	.05
58	Mike Krukow	.05
59	Lloyd Moseby	.05
60	Checklist	.05

Diamond Kings Supers

For a third season, Donruss produced a set of enlarged Diamond Kings, measuring 4-11/16" x 6-3/4". The 28-cards feature the artwork of Dick Perez, and contain 26 player cards, a checklist and a Roberto Clemente puzzle card. The set was available through a mail-in offer for $9.50 plus three wrappers.

		NM/M
Complete Set (28):		5.00
Common Player:		.15
1	Wally Joyner	.15
2	Roger Clemens	1.50
3	Dale Murphy	.30
4	Darryl Strawberry	.15
5	Ozzie Smith	1.00
6	Jose Canseco	.30
7	Charlie Hough	.15
8	Brook Jacoby	.15
9	Fred Lynn	.15
10	Rick Rhoden	.15
11	Chris Brown	.15
12	Von Hayes	.15
13	Jack Morris	.15
14	Kevin McReynolds	.15
15	George Brett	1.50

16	Ted Higuera	.15
17	Hubie Brooks	.15
18	Mike Scott	.15
19	Kirby Puckett	1.00
20	Dave Winfield	.60
21	Lloyd Moseby	.15
22	Eric Davis	.15
23	Jim Presley	.15
24	Keith Moreland	.15
25	Greg Walker	.15
26	Steve Sax	.15
27	Checklist	.05
---	Roberto Clemente Puzzle Card	.50

Highlights

For a third consecutive year, Donruss produced a 56-card set which highlighted the special events of the 1987 baseball season. The 2-1/2" x 3-1/2" cards have a front design similar to the regular 1987 Donruss set. A blue border and the "Highlights" logo are the significant differences. The backs feature black print on a white background and include the date the event took place plus the particulars. As in the past, the set includes Donruss' picks for the A.L. and N.L. Rookies of the Year. The set was issued in a specially designed box and was available only through hobby dealers.

		NM/M
Complete Set (56):		3.00
Common Player:		.05
1	First No-Hitter For Brewers (Juan Nieves)	.05
2	Hits 500th Homer (Mike Schmidt)	.35
3	N.L. Player of the Month - April (Eric Davis)	.05
4	N.L. Pitcher of the Month - April (Sid Fernandez)	.05
5	A.L. Player of the Month - April (Brian Downing)	.05
6	A.L. Pitcher of the Month - April (Bret Saberhagen)	.05
7	Free Agent Holdout Returns (Tim Raines)	.05
8	N.L. Player of the Month - May (Eric Davis)	.05
9	N.L. Pitcher of the Month - May (Steve Bedrosian)	.05
10	A.L. Player of the Month - May (Larry Parrish)	.05
11	A.L. Pitcher of the Month - May (Jim Clancy)	.05
12	N.L. Player of the Month - June (Tony Gwynn)	.25
13	N.L. Pitcher of the Month - June (Orel Hershiser)	.05
14	A.L. Player of the Month - June (Wade Boggs)	.25
15	A.L. Pitcher of the Month - June (Steve Ontiveros)	.05
16	All Star Game Hero (Tim Raines)	.05
17	Consecutive Game Homer Streak (Don Mattingly)	.35
18	1987 Hall of Fame Inductee (Jim "Catfish" Hunter)	.10
19	1987 Hall of Fame Inductee (Ray Dandridge)	.05
20	1987 Hall of Fame Inductee (Billy Williams)	.10
21	N.L. Player of the Month - July (Bo Diaz)	.05
22	N.L. Pitcher of the Month - July (Floyd Youmans)	.05
23	A.L. Player of the Month - July (Don Mattingly)	.35
24	A.L. Pitcher of the Month - July (Frank Viola)	.05
25	Strikes Out 4 Batters In 1 Inning (Bobby Witt)	.05
26	Ties A.L. 9-Inning Game Hit Mark (Kevin Seitzer)	.05

27	Sets Rookie Home Run Record (Mark McGwire)	.50
28	Sets Cubs' 1st Year Homer Mark (Andre Dawson)	.05
29	Hits In 39 Straight Games (Paul Molitor)	.15
30	Record Weekend (Kirby Puckett)	.15
31	N.L. Player of the Month - August (Andre Dawson)	.05
32	N.L. Pitcher of the Month - August (Doug Drabek)	.05
33	A.L. Player of the Month - August (Dwight Evans)	.05
34	A.L. Pitcher of the Month - August (Mark Langston)	.05
35	100 RBI In 1st 2 Major League Seasons (Wally Joyner)	.05
36	100 SB In 1st 3 Major League Seasons (Vince Coleman)	.05
37	Orioles' All Time Homer King (Eddie Murray)	.15
38	Ends Consecutive Innings Streak (Cal Ripken)	.50
39	Blue Jays Hit Record 10 Homers In 1 Game (Rob Ducey, Fred McGriff, Ernie Whitt)	.05
40	Equal A's RBI Marks (Jose Canseco, Mark McGwire)	.35
41	Sets All-Time Catching Record (Bob Boone)	.05
42	Sets Mets' One-Season HR Mark (Darryl Strawberry)	.05
43	N.L.'s All-Time Switch Hit HR King (Howard Johnson)	.05
44	Five Straight 200-Hit Seasons (Wade Boggs)	.25
45	Eclipses Rookie Game Hitting Streak (Benito Santiago)	.05
46	Eclipses Jackson's A's HR Record (Mark McGwire)	.45
47	13th Rookie To Collect 200 Hits (Kevin Seitzer)	.05
48	Sets Slam Record (Don Mattingly)	.35
49	N.L. Player of the Month - September (Darryl Strawberry)	.05
50	N.L. Pitcher of the Month - September (Pascual Perez)	.05
51	A.L. Player of the Month - September (Alan Trammell)	.05
52	A.L. Pitcher of the Month - September (Doyle Alexander)	.05
53	Strikeout King - Again (Nolan Ryan)	.50
54	Donruss A.L. Rookie of the Year (Mark McGwire)	.50
55	Donruss N.L. Rookie of the Year (Benito Santiago)	.05
56	Highlight Checklist	.05

Opening Day

The Donruss Opening Day set includes all players in major league baseball's starting lineups on the opening day of the 1987 baseball season. Cards in the 272-piece set measure 2-1/2" x 3-1/2" and have a glossy coating. The fronts are identical in design to the regular Donruss set, but new photos were utilized along with maroon borders as opposed to black. The backs carry black printing on white and yellow and offer a brief player biography plus the player's career statistics.

The set was packaged in a sturdy 15" by 5" by 2" box with a clear acetate lid.

		NM/M
Unopened Fact. Set (272):		25.00
Complete Set (272):		12.00
Common Player:		.10
1	Doug DeCinces	.10
2	Mike Witt	.10
3	George Hendrick	.10
4	Dick Schofield	.10
5	Devon White	.10
6	Butch Wynegar	.10
7	Wally Joyner	.10
8	Mark McLemore	.10
9	Brian Downing	.10
10	Gary Pettis	.10
11	Bill Doran	.10
12	Phil Garner	.10
13	Jose Cruz	.10
14	Kevin Bass	.10
15	Mike Scott	.10
16	Glenn Davis	.10
17	Alan Ashby	.10
18	Billy Hatcher	.10
19	Craig Reynolds	.10
20	Carney Lansford	.10
21	Mike Davis	.10
22	Reggie Jackson	.75
23	Mickey Tettleton	.10
24	Jose Canseco	.35
25	Rob Nelson	.10
26	Tony Phillips	.10
27	Dwayne Murphy	.10
28	Alfredo Griffin	.10
29	Curt Young	.10
30	Willie Upshaw	.10
31	Mike Sharperson	.10
32	Rance Mulliniks	.10
33	Ernie Whitt	.10
34	Jesse Barfield	.10
35	Tony Fernandez	.10
36	Lloyd Moseby	.10
37	Jimmy Key	.10
38	Fred McGriff	.10
39	George Bell	.10
40	Dale Murphy	.25
41	Rick Mahler	.10
42	Ken Griffey	.10
43	Andres Thomas	.10
44	Dion James	.10
45	Ozzie Virgil	.10
46	Ken Oberkfell	.10
47	Gary Roenicke	.10
48	Glenn Hubbard	.10
49	Bill Schroeder	.10
50	Greg Brock	.10
51	Billy Jo Robidoux	.10
52	Glenn Braggs	.10
53	Jim Gantner	.10
54	Paul Molitor	.50
55	Dale Sveum	.10
56	Ted Higuera	.10
57	Rob Deer	.10
58	Robin Yount	.50
59	Jim Lindeman	.10
60	Vince Coleman	.10
61	Tommy Herr	.10
62	Terry Pendleton	.10
63	John Tudor	.10
64	Tony Pena	.10
65	Ozzie Smith	.60
66	Tito Landrum	.10
67	Jack Clark	.10
68	Bob Dernier	.10
69	Rick Sutcliffe	.10
70	Andre Dawson	.30
71	Keith Moreland	.10
72	Jody Davis	.10
73	Brian Dayett	.10
74	Leon Durham	.10
75	Ryne Sandberg	.60
76	Shawon Dunston	.10
77	Mike Marshall	.10
78	Bill Madlock	.10
79	Orel Hershiser	.10
80	Mike Ramsey	.10
81	Ken Landreaux	.10
82	Mike Scioscia	.10
83	Franklin Stubbs	.10
84	Mariano Duncan	.10
85	Steve Sax	.10
86	Mitch Webster	.10
87	Reid Nichols	.10
88	Tim Wallach	.10
89	Floyd Youmans	.10
90	Andres Galarraga	.10
91	Hubie Brooks	.10
92	Jeff Reed	.10
93	Alonzo Powell	.10
94	Vance Law	.10
95	Bob Brenly	.10
96	Will Clark	.60
97	Chili Davis	.10
98	Mike Krukow	.10
99	Jose Uribe	.10
100	Chris Brown	.10
101	Rob Thompson	.10
102	Candy Maldonado	.10
103	Jeff Leonard	.10
104	Tom Candiotti	.10
105	Chris Bando	.10
106	Cory Snyder	.10
107	Pat Tabler	.10
108	Andre Thornton	.10
109	Joe Carter	.10

110	Tony Bernazard	.10
111	Julio Franco	.10
112	Brook Jacoby	.10
113	Brett Butler	.10
114	Donnell Nixon	.10
115	Alvin Davis	.10
116	Mark Langston	.10
117	Harold Reynolds	.10
118	Ken Phelps	.10
119	Mike Kingery	.10
120	Dave Valle	.10
121	Rey Quinones	.10
122	Phil Bradley	.10
123	Jim Presley	.10
124	Keith Hernandez	.10
125	Kevin McReynolds	.10
126	Rafael Santana	.10
127	Bob Ojeda	.10
128	Darryl Strawberry	.10
129	Mookie Wilson	.10
130	Gary Carter	.50
131	Tim Teufel	.10
132	Howard Johnson	.10
133	Cal Ripken, Jr.	2.00
134	Rick Burleson	.10
135	Fred Lynn	.10
136	Eddie Murray	.50
137	Ray Knight	.10
138	Alan Wiggins	.10
139	John Shelby	.10
140	Mike Boddicker	.10
141	Ken Gerhart	.10
142	Terry Kennedy	.10
143	Steve Garvey	.25
144	Marvell Wynne	.10
145	Kevin Mitchell	.60
146	Tony Gwynn	.60
147	Joey Cora	.10
148	Benito Santiago	.10
149	Eric Show	.10
150	Garry Templeton	.10
151	Carmelo Martinez	.10
152	Von Hayes	.10
153	Lance Parrish	.10
154	Milt Thompson	.10
155	Mike Easler	.10
156	Juan Samuel	.10
157	Steve Jeltz	.10
158	Glenn Wilson	.10
159	Shane Rawley	.10
160	Mike Schmidt	.75
161	Andy Van Slyke	.10
162	Johnny Ray	.10
163a	Barry Bonds (Dark jersey, photo actually Johnny Ray.)	600.00
163b	Barry Bonds (White jersey, correct photo.)	9.00
164	Junior Ortiz	.10
165	Rafael Belliard	.10
166	Bob Patterson	.10
167	Bobby Bonilla	.10
168	Sid Bream	.10
169	Jim Morrison	.10
170	Jerry Browne	.10
171	Scott Fletcher	.10
172	Ruben Sierra	.10
173	Larry Parrish	.10
174	Pete O'Brien	.10
175	Pete Incaviglia	.10
176	Don Slaught	.10
177	Oddibe McDowell	.10
178	Charlie Hough	.10
179	Steve Buechele	.10
180	Bob Stanley	.10
181	Wade Boggs	.60
182	Jim Rice	.30
183	Bill Buckner	.10
184	Dwight Evans	.10
185	Spike Owen	.10
186	Don Baylor	.10
187	Marc Sullivan	.10
188	Marty Barrett	.10
189	Dave Henderson	.10
190	Bo Diaz	.10
191	Barry Larkin	.10
192	Kal Daniels	.10
193	Terry Francona	.10
194	Tom Browning	.10
195	Ron Oester	.10
196	Buddy Bell	.10
197	Eric Davis	.10
198	Dave Parker	.10
199	Steve Balboni	.10
200	Danny Tartabull	.10
201	Ed Hearn	.10
202	Buddy Biancalana	.10
203	Danny Jackson	.10
204	Frank White	.10
205	Bo Jackson	.25
206	George Brett	.75
207	Kevin Seitzer	.10
208	Willie Wilson	.10
209	Orlando Mercado	.10
210	Darrell Evans	.10
211	Larry Herndon	.10
212	Jack Morris	.10
213	Chet Lemon	.10
214	Mike Heath	.10
215	Darnell Coles	.10
216	Alan Trammell	.10
217	Terry Harper	.10
218	Lou Whitaker	.10
219	Gary Gaetti	.10
220	Tom Nieto	.10
221	Kirby Puckett	.60
222	Tom Brunansky	.10
223	Greg Gagne	.10

Wax related listings (top of column 2):

Roberto Clemente Puzzle:		2.50
Wax Pack:		.35
Wax Box (48):		5.00
1	Wally Joyner	.05
2	Dave Winfield	.40
3	Lou Whitaker	.05
4	Kirby Puckett	.50
5	Cal Ripken, Jr.	1.00
6	Rickey Henderson	.40
7	Wade Boggs	.50
8	Roger Clemens	.65
9	Lance Parrish	.05
10	Dick Howser	.05
11	Keith Hernandez	.05
12	Darryl Strawberry	.05
13	Ryne Sandberg	.50
14	Dale Murphy	.25
15	Ozzie Smith	.05

224	Dan Gladden	.10
225	Mark Davidson	.10
226	Bert Blyleven	.10
227	Steve Lombardozzi	.10
228	Kent Hrbek	.10
229	Gary Redus	.10
230	Ivan Calderon	.10
231	Tim Hulett	.10
232	Carlton Fisk	.50
233	Greg Walker	.10
234	Ron Karkovice	.10
235	Ozzie Guillen	.10
236	Harold Baines	.10
237	Donnie Hill	.10
238	Rich Dotson	.10
239	Mike Pagliarulo	.10
240	Joel Skinner	.10
241	Don Mattingly	.75
242	Gary Ward	.10
243	Dave Winfield	.50
244	Dan Pasqua	.10
245	Wayne Tolleson	.10
246	Willie Randolph	.10
247	Dennis Rasmussen	.10
248	Rickey Henderson	.50
249	Angels Checklist	.05
250	Astros Checklist	.05
251	Athletics Checklist	.05
252	Blue Jays Checklist	.05
253	Braves Checklist	.05
254	Brewers Checklist	.05
255	Cardinals Checklist	.05
256	Dodgers Checklist	.05
257	Expos Checklist	.05
258	Giants Checklist	.05
259	Indians Checklist	.05
260	Mariners Checklist	.05
261	Orioles Checklist	.05
262	Padres Checklist	.05
263	Phillies Checklist	.05
264	Pirates Checklist	.05
265	Rangers Checklist	.05
266	Red Sox Checklist	.05
267	Reds Checklist	.05
268	Royals Checklist	.05
269	Tigers Checklist	.05
270	Twins Checklist	.05
271	White Sox/Cubs Checklist	.05
272	Yankees/Mets Checklist	.05

Pop-Ups

For the second straight year, Donruss released in conjunction with its All-Stars issue a set of cards designed to fold out to form a three-dimensional stand-up card. Consisting of 20 cards, as opposed to the previous year's 18, the 1987 Donruss Pop-Ups set contains players selected to the 1986 All-Star Game. Background for the 2-1/2" x 5" cards is the Houston Astrodome, site of the 1986 midsummer classic. Retail packs included one Pop-Up card, three All-Star cards and one Roberto Clemente puzzle card.

		NM/M
Complete Set (20):		3.00
Common Player:		.10
Roberto Clemente Puzzle:		2.50
Wax Pack:		.35
Wax Box (48):		5.00
(1)	Wade Boggs	.50
(2)	Gary Carter	.40
(3)	Roger Clemens	.60
(4)	Dwight Gooden	.10
(5)	Tony Gwynn	.50
(6)	Rickey Henderson	.40
(7)	Keith Hernandez	.10
(8)	Whitey Herzog	.10
(9)	Dick Howser	.10
(10)	Wally Joyner	.10
(11)	Dale Murphy	.25
(12)	Lance Parrish	.10
(13)	Kirby Puckett	.50
(14)	Cal Ripken, Jr.	.75
(15)	Ryne Sandberg	.50
(16)	Mike Schmidt	.60
(17)	Ozzie Smith	.50
(18)	Darryl Strawberry	.10
(19)	Lou Whitaker	.10
(20)	Dave Winfield	.40

Rookies

As they did in 1986, Donruss issued a 56-card set highlighting the major leagues' most promising rookies. The cards are standard 2-1/2" x 3-1/2" and are identical in design to the regular Donruss issue. The card fronts have green borders as opposed to the black found in the regular issue and carry the words "The Rookies" in the lower-left portion of the card. The set came housed in a specially designed box and was available only through hobby dealers.

		NM/M
Unopened Fact. Set (56):		15.00
Complete Set (56):		10.00
Common Player:		.05
1	Mark McGwire	6.00
2	Eric Bell	.05
3	Mark Williamson RC	.05
4	Mike Greenwell	.05
5	Ellis Burks	.05
6	DeWayne Buice RC	.05
7	Mark Mclemore (McLemore)	.05
8	Devon White	.05
9	Willie Fraser	.05
10	Lester Lancaster RC	.05
11	Ken Williams RC	.05
12	Matt Nokes	.05
13	Jeff Robinson RC	.05
14	Bo Jackson	.25
15	Kevin Seitzer RC	.05
16	Billy Ripken RC	.05
17	B.J. Surhoff	.05
18	Chuck Crim RC	.05
19	Mike Birbeck	.05
20	Chris Bosio	.05
21	Les Straker RC	.05
22	Mark Davidson RC	.05
23	Gene Larkin RC	.05
24	Ken Gerhart	.05
25	Luis Polonia RC	.05
26	Terry Steinbach	.05
27	Mickey Brantley	.05
28	Mike Stanley	.05
29	Jerry Browne	.05
30	Todd Benzinger RC	.05
31	Fred McGriff	.25
32	Mike Henneman RC	.05
33	Casey Candaele	.05
34	Dave Magadan	.05
35	David Cone	.05
36	Mike Jackson RC	.05
37	John Mitchell RC	.05
38	Mike Dunne RC	.05
39	John Smiley	.05
40	Joe Magrane RC	.05
41	Jim Lindeman	.05
42	Shane Mack RC	.05
43	Stan Jefferson	.05
44	Benito Santiago	.05
45	Matt Williams RC	1.50
46	Dave Meads RC	.05
47	Rafael Palmeiro	4.00
48	Bill Long RC	.05
49	Bob Brower	.05
50	James Steels RC	.05
51	Paul Noce RC	.05
52	Greg Maddux	5.00
53	Jeff Musselman	.05
54	Brian Holton	.05
55	Chuck Jackson RC	.05
56	Checklist 1-56	.03

1988 Donruss Promo Sheet

The full effect of the 1988 Donruss border design of black, blue and red geometric patterns was previewed on this promo sheet. Printed on glossy paper with blank-back, eight regular cards (all pitchers!) and a Diamond King are showcased on the 7-1/2" x 10-1/2" sheet.

	NM/M
Uncut Sheet:	7.50

1988 Donruss

The 1988 Donruss set consists of 660 cards, each measuring 2-1/2" x 3-1/2". Fronts feature a full-color photo surrounded by a colorful border - alternating stripes of black, red, black, blue, black, blue, black, red and black (in that order) - separated by soft-focus edges and airbrushed fades. The player's name and position appear in a red band at the bottom of the card. The Donruss logo is situated in the upper-left corner, while the team logo is located in the lower-right. For the seventh consecutive season, Donruss included a subset of "Diamond Kings" cards (#1-27) in the issue. And for the fifth straight year, Donruss incorporated the popular "Rated Rookies" (card #28-47) with the set. Twenty-six of the cards between #603-660 were short-printed to accommodate the printing of the 26 MVP insert cards.

		NM/M
Unopened Fact. Set (660):		10.00
Complete Set (660):		8.00
Common Player:		.05
Stan Musial Puzzle:		1.00
Wax Pack (15):		.40
Wax Box (36):		10.00
Cello Pack (36):		.75
Cello Box (24):		12.00
Rack Pack (45):		.05
1	Mark McGwire/DK	.75
2	Tim Raines/DK	.05
3	Benito Santiago/DK	.05
4	Alan Trammell/DK	.05
5	Danny Tartabull/DK	.05
6	Ron Darling/DK	.05
7	Paul Molitor /DK	.40
8	Devon White/DK	.05
9	Andre Dawson/DK	.25
10	Julio Franco/DK	.05

ABBREVIATIONS

DK - Diamond King
RR - Rated Rookie

11	Scott Fletcher /DK	.05
12	Tony Fernandez/DK	.05
13	Shane Rawley/DK	.05
14	Kal Daniels/DK	.05
15	Jack Clark/DK	.05
16	Dwight Evans/DK	.05
17	Tommy John/DK	.05
18	Andy Van Slyke/DK	.05
19	Gary Gaetti/DK	.05
20	Mark Langston/DK	.05
21	Will Clark/DK	.05
22	Glenn Hubbard/DK	.05
23	Billy Hatcher/DK	.05
24	Bob Welch/DK	.05
25	Ivan Calderon/DK	.05
26	Cal Ripken, Jr./DK	1.00
27	Checklist 1-27	.05
28	Mackey Sasser/RR RC	.05
29	Jeff Treadway/RR RC	.05
30	Mike Campbell/RR RC	.05
31	Lance Johnson/RR RC	.15
32	Nelson Liriano/RR RC	.05
33	Shawn Abner/RR RC	.05
34	Roberto Alomar/RR RC	1.00
35	Shawn Hillegas/RR RC	.05
36	Joey Meyer/RR	.05
37	Kevin Elster/RR	.05
38	Jose Lind/RR	.05
39	Kirt Manwaring/RR RC	.05
40	Mark Grace/RR RC	.50
41	Jody Reed/RR RC	.10
42	John Farrell/RR RC	.05
43	Al Leiter/RR RC	.20
44	Gary Thurman/RR RC	.05
45	Vicente Palacios/RR RC	.05
46	Eddie Williams/RR RC	.05
47	Jack McDowell/RR RC	.20
48	Ken Dixon	.05
49	Mike Birkbeck	.05
50	Eric King	.05
51	Roger Clemens	.60
52	Pat Clements	.05
53	Fernando Valenzuela	.05
54	Mark Gubicza	.05
55	Jay Howell	.05
56	Floyd Youmans	.05
57	Ed Correa	.05
58	DeWayne Buice RC	.05
59	Jose DeLeon	.05
60	Danny Cox	.05
61	Nolan Ryan	1.00
62	Steve Bedrosian	.05
63	Tom Browning	.05
64	Mark Davis	.05
65	R.J. Reynolds	.05
66	Kevin Mitchell	.05
67	Ken Oberkfell	.05
68	Rick Sutcliffe	.05
69	Dwight Gooden	.05
70	Scott Bankhead	.05
71	Bert Blyleven	.10
72	Jimmy Key	.05
73	Les Straker RC	.05
74	Jim Clancy	.05
75	Mike Moore	.05
76	Ron Darling	.05
77	Ed Lynch	.05
78	Dale Murphy	.20
79	Doug Drabek	.05
80	Scott Garrelts	.05
81	Ed Whitson	.05
82	Rob Murphy	.05
83	Shane Rawley	.05
84	Greg Mathews	.05
85	Jim Deshaies	.05
86	Mike Witt	.05
87	Donnie Hill	.05
88	Jeff Reed	.05
89	Mike Boddicker	.05
90	Ted Higuera	.05
91	Walt Terrell	.05
92	Bob Stanley	.05
93	Dave Righetti	.05
94	Orel Hershiser	.05
95	Chris Bando	.05
96	Bret Saberhagen	.05
97	Curt Young	.05
98	Tim Burke	.05
99	Charlie Hough	.05
100a	Checklist 28-137	.05
100b	Checklist 28-133	.05
101	Bobby Witt	.05
102	George Brett	.60
103	Mickey Tettleton	.05
104	Scott Bailes	.05
105	Mike Pagliarulo	.05
106	Mike Scioscia	.05
107	Tom Brookens	.05
108	Ray Knight	.05
109	Dan Plesac	.05
110	Wally Joyner	.05
111	Bob Forsch	.05
112	Mike Scott	.05
113	Kevin Gross	.05
114	Benito Santiago	.05
115	Bob Kipper	.05
116	Mike Krukow	.05
117	Chris Bosio	.05
118	Sid Fernandez	.05
119	Jody Davis	.05
120	Mike Morgan	.05
121	Mark Eichhorn	.05
122	Jeff Reardon	.05
123	John Franco	.05
124	Richard Dotson	.05
125	Eric Bell	.05
126	Juan Nieves	.05
127	Jack Morris	.05
128	Rick Rhoden	.05
129	Rich Gedman	.05
130	Ken Howell	.05
131	Brook Jacoby	.05
132	Danny Jackson	.05
133	Gene Nelson	.05
134	Neal Heaton	.05
135	Willie Fraser	.05
136	Jose Guzman	.05
137	Ozzie Guillen	.05
138	Bob Knepper	.05
139	Mike Jackson RC	.05
140	Joe Magrane RC	.05
141	Jimmy Jones	.05
142	Ted Power	.05
143	Ozzie Virgil	.05
144	Felix Fermin RC	.05
145	Kelly Downs	.05
146	Shawon Dunston	.05
147	Scott Bradley	.05
148	Dave Stieb	.05
149	Frank Viola	.05
150	Terry Kennedy	.05
151	Bill Wegman	.05
152	Matt Nokes RC	.10
153	Wade Boggs	.50
154	Wayne Tolleson	.05
155	Mariano Duncan	.05
156	Julio Franco	.05
157	Charlie Leibrandt	.05
158	Terry Steinbach	.05
159	Mike Fitzgerald	.05
160	Jack Lazorko	.05
161	Mitch Williams	.05
162	Greg Walker	.05
163	Alan Ashby	.05
164	Tony Gwynn	.05
165	Bruce Ruffin	.05
166	Ron Robinson	.05
167	Zane Smith	.05
168	Junior Ortiz	.05
169	Jamie Moyer	.05
170	Tony Pena	.05
171	Cal Ripken, Jr.	1.00
172	B.J. Surhoff	.05
173	Lou Whitaker	.05
174	Ellis Burks RC	.20
175	Ron Guidry	.10
176	Steve Sax	.05
177	Danny Tartabull	.05
178	Carney Lansford	.05
179	Casey Candaele	.05
180	Scott Fletcher	.05
181	Mark McLemore	.05
182	Ivan Calderon	.05
183	Jack Clark	.05
184	Glenn Davis	.05
185	Luis Aguayo	.05
186	Bo Diaz	.05
187	Stan Jefferson	.05
188	Sid Bream	.05
189	Bob Brenly	.05
190	Dion James	.05
191	Leon Durham	.05
192	Jesse Orosco	.05
193	Alvin Davis	.05
194	Gary Gaetti	.05
195	Fred McGriff	.05
196	Steve Lombardozzi	.05
197	Rance Mulliniks	.05
198	Rey Quinones	.05
199	Gary Carter	.40
200a	Checklist 138-247	.05
200b	Checklist 134-239	.05
201	Keith Moreland	.05
202	Ken Griffey	.05
203	Tommy Gregg RC	.05
204	Will Clark	.05
205	John Kruk	.05
206	Buddy Bell	.05
207	Von Hayes	.05
208	Tommy Herr	.05
209	Craig Reynolds	.05
210	Gary Pettis	.05
211	Harold Baines	.05
212	Vance Law	.05
213	Ken Gerhart	.05
214	Jim Gantner	.05
215	Chet Lemon	.05
216	Dwight Evans	.05
217	Don Mattingly	.60
218	Franklin Stubbs	.05
219	Pat Tabler	.05
220	Bo Jackson	.10
221	Tony Phillips	.05
222	Tim Wallach	.05
223	Ruben Sierra	.05
224	Steve Buechele	.05
225	Frank White	.05
226	Alfredo Griffin	.05
227	Greg Swindell	.05
228	Willie Randolph	.05
229	Mike Marshall	.05
230	Alan Trammell	.05
231	Eddie Murray	.40
232	Dale Sveum	.05
233	Dick Schofield	.05
234	Jose Oquendo	.05
235	Bill Doran	.05
236	Milt Thompson	.05
237	Marvell Wynne	.05
238	Bobby Bonilla	.05
239	Chris Speier	.05
240	Glenn Braggs	.05
241	Wally Backman	.05
242	Ryne Sandberg	.50
243	Phil Bradley	.05
244	Kelly Gruber	.05
245	Tom Brunansky	.05
246	Ron Oester	.05
247	Bobby Thigpen	.05
248	Fred Lynn	.40
249	Paul Molitor	.05
250	Darrell Evans	.05
251	Gary Ward	.05
252	Bruce Hurst	.05
253	Bob Welch	.05
254	Joe Carter	.05
255	Willie Wilson	.05
256	Mark McGwire	.75
257	Mitch Webster	.05
258	Brian Downing	.05
259	Mike Stanley	.05
260	Carlton Fisk	.40
261	Billy Hatcher	.05
262	Glenn Wilson	.05
263	Ozzie Smith	.50
264	Randy Ready	.05
265	Kurt Stillwell	.05
266	David Palmer	.05
267	Mike Diaz	.05
268	Rob Thompson	.05
269	Andre Dawson	.25
270	Lee Guetterman	.05
271	Willie Upshaw	.05
272	Randy Bush	.05
273	Larry Sheets	.05
274	Rob Deer	.05
275	Kirk Gibson	.05
276	Marty Barrett	.05
277	Rickey Henderson	.40
278	Pedro Guerrero	.05
279	Brett Butler	.05
280	Kevin Seitzer	.05
281	Mike Davis	.05
282	Andres Galarraga	.05
283	Devon White	.05
284	Pete O'Brien	.05
285	Jerry Hairston Sr.	.05
286	Kevin Bass	.05
287	Carmelo Martinez	.05
288	Juan Samuel	.05
289	Kal Daniels	.05
290	Albert Hall	.05
291	Andy Van Slyke	.05
292	Lee Smith	.10
293	Vince Coleman	.05
294	Tom Niedenfuer	.05
295	Robin Yount	.40
296	Jeff Robinson RC	.05
297	Todd Benzinger RC	.10
298	Dave Winfield	.40
299	Mickey Hatcher	.05
300a	Checklist 248-357	.05
300b	Checklist 240-345	.05
301	Bud Black	.05
302	Jose Canseco	.25
303	Tom Foley	.05
304	Pete Incaviglia	.05
305	Bob Boone	.05
306	Bill Long RC	.05
307	Willie McGee	.05
308	Ken Caminiti RC	.20
309	Darren Daulton	.05
310	Tracy Jones	.05
311	Greg Booker	.05
312	Mike LaValliere	.05
313	Chili Davis	.05
314	Glenn Hubbard	.05
315	Paul Noce RC	.05
316	Keith Hernandez	.05
317	Mark Langston	.05
318	Keith Atherton	.05
319	Tony Fernandez	.05
320	Kent Hrbek	.05
321	John Cerutti	.05
322	Mike Kingery	.05
323	Dave Magadan	.05
324	Rafael Palmeiro	.35
325	Jeff Dedmon	.05
326	Barry Bonds	1.00
327	Jeffrey Leonard	.05
328	Tim Flannery	.05
329	Dave Concepcion	.05
330	Mike Schmidt	.60
331	Bill Dawley	.05
332	Larry Andersen	.05
333	Jack Howell	.05
334	Ken Williams RC	.05
335	Bryn Smith	.05
336	Billy Ripken RC	.10
337	Greg Brock	.05
338	Mike Heath	.05
339	Mike Greenwell	.05
340	Claudell Washington	.05
341	Jose Gonzalez	.05
342	Mel Hall	.05
343	Jim Eisenreich	.05
344	Tony Bernazard	.05
345	Tim Raines	.05
346	Bob Brower	.05
347	Larry Parrish	.05
348	Thad Bosley	.05
349	Dennis Eckersley	.35
350	Cory Snyder	.05
351	Rick Cerone	.05
352	John Shelby	.05
353	Larry Herndon	.05
354	John Habyan	.05
355	Chuck Crim RC	.05
356	Gus Polidor	.05
357	Ken Dayley	.05
358	Danny Darwin	.05
359	Lance Parrish	.05
360	James Steels RC	.05

#	Player	Price
361	Al Pedrique RC	.05
362	Mike Aldrete	.05
363	Juan Castillo	.05
364	Len Dykstra	.05
365	Luis Quinones	.05
366	Jim Presley	.05
367	Lloyd Moseby	.05
368	Kirby Puckett	.50
369	Eric Davis	.05
370	Gary Redus	.05
371	Dave Schmidt	.05
372	Mark Clear	.05
373	Dave Bergman	.05
374	Charles Hudson	.05
375	Calvin Schiraldi	.05
376	Alex Trevino	.05
377	Tom Candiotti	.05
378	Steve Farr	.05
379	Mike Gallego	.05
380	Andy McGaffigan	.05
381	Kirk McCaskill	.05
382	Oddibe McDowell	.05
383	Floyd Bannister	.05
384	Denny Walling	.05
385	Don Carman	.05
386	Todd Worrell	.05
387	Eric Show	.05
388	Dave Parker	.05
389	Rick Mahler	.05
390	Mike Dunne RC	.10
391	Candy Maldonado	.05
392	Bob Dernier	.05
393	Dave Valle	.05
394	Ernie Whitt	.05
395	Juan Berenguer	.05
396	Mike Young	.05
397	Mike Felder	.05
398	Willie Hernandez	.05
399	Jim Rice	.25
400a	Checklist 358-467	.05
400b	Checklist 346-451	.05
401	Tommy John	.10
402	Brian Holton	.05
403	Carmen Castillo	.05
404	Jamie Quirk	.05
405	Dwayne Murphy	.05
406	Jeff Parrett RC	.05
407	Don Sutton	.35
408	Jerry Browne	.05
409	Jim Winn	.05
410	Dave Smith	.05
411	Shane Mack RC	.05
412	Greg Gross	.05
413	Nick Esasky	.05
414	Damaso Garcia	.05
415	Brian Fisher	.05
416	Brian Dayett	.05
417	Curt Ford	.05
418	Mark Williamson RC	.05
419	Bill Schroeder	.05
420	Mike Henneman RC	.10
421	John Marzano RC	.05
422	Ron Kittle	.05
423	Matt Young	.05
424	Steve Balboni	.05
425	Luis Polonia RC	.05
426	Randy St. Claire	.05
427	Greg Harris	.05
428	Johnny Ray	.05
429	Ray Searage	.05
430	Ricky Horton	.05
431	Gerald Young RC	.05
432	Rick Schu	.05
433	Paul O'Neill	.05
434	Rich Gossage	.10
435	John Cangelosi	.05
436	Mike LaCoss	.05
437	Gerald Perry	.05
438	Dave Martinez	.05
439	Darryl Strawberry	.05
440	John Moses	.05
441	Greg Gagne	.05
442	Jesse Barfield	.05
443	George Frazier	.05
444	Garth Iorg	.05
445	Ed Nunez	.05
446	Rick Aguilera	.05
447	Jerry Mumphrey	.05
448	Rafael Ramirez	.05
449	John Smiley RC	.10
450	Atlee Hammaker	.05
451	Lance McCullers	.05
452	Guy Hoffman RC	.05
453	Chris James	.05
454	Terry Pendleton	.05
455	Dave Meads RC	.05
456	Bill Buckner	.05
457	John Pawlowski RC	.05
458	Bob Sebra	.05
459	Jim Dwyer	.05
460	Jay Aldrich RC	.05
461	Frank Tanana	.05
462	Oil Can Boyd	.05
463	Dan Pasqua	.05
464	Tim Crews RC	.10
465	Andy Allanson	.05
466	Bill Pecota RC	.05
467	Steve Ontiveros	.05
468	Hubie Brooks	.05
469	Paul Kilgus RC	.05
470	Dale Mohorcic	.05
471	Dan Quisenberry	.05
472	Dave Stewart	.05
473	Dave Clark	.05
474	Joel Skinner	.05
475	Dave Anderson	.05
476	Dan Petry	.05
477	Carl Nichols RC	.05
478	Ernest Riles	.05
479	George Hendrick	.05
480	John Morris	.05
481	Manny Hernandez RC	.05
482	Jeff Stone	.05
483	Chris Brown	.05
484	Mike Bielecki	.05
485	Dave Dravecky	.05
486	Rick Manning	.05
487	Bill Almon	.05
488	Jim Sundberg	.05
489	Ken Phelps	.05
490	Tom Henke	.05
491	Dan Gladden	.05
492	Barry Larkin	.05
493	Fred Manrique RC	.05
494	Mike Griffin	.05
495	Mark Knudson RC	.05
496	Bill Madlock	.05
497	Tim Stoddard	.05
498	Sam Horn RC	.05
499	Tracy Woodson RC	.05
500a	Checklist 468-577	.05
500b	Checklist 452-557	.05
501	Ken Schrom	.05
502	Angel Salazar	.05
503	Eric Plunk	.05
504	Joe Hesketh	.05
505	Greg Minton	.05
506	Geno Petralli	.05
507	Bob James	.05
508	Robbie Wine RC	.05
509	Jeff Calhoun	.05
510	Steve Lake	.05
511	Mark Grant	.05
512	Frank Williams	.05
513	Jeff Blauser RC	.10
514	Bob Walk	.05
515	Craig Lefferts	.05
516	Manny Trillo	.05
517	Jerry Reed	.05
518	Rick Leach	.05
519	Mark Davidson RC	.05
520	Jeff Ballard RC	.05
521	Dave Stapleton RC	.05
522	Pat Sheridan	.05
523	Al Nipper	.05
524	Steve Trout	.05
525	Jeff Hamilton	.05
526	Tommy Hinzo RC	.05
527	Lonnie Smith	.05
528	Greg Cadaret RC	.05
529	Rob McClure (Bob)	.05
530	Chuck Finley	.05
531	Jeff Russell	.05
532	Steve Lyons	.05
533	Terry Puhl	.05
534	Eric Nolte RC	.05
535	Kent Tekulve	.05
536	Pat Pacillo RC	.05
537	Charlie Puleo	.05
538	Tom Prince RC	.05
539	Greg Maddux	.50
540	Jim Lindeman	.05
541	Pete Stanicek RC	.05
542	Steve Kiefer	.05
543	Jim Morrison	.05
544	Spike Owen	.05
545	Jay Buhner RC	.50
546	Mike Devereaux RC	.10
547	Jerry Don Gleaton	.05
548	Jose Rijo	.05
549	Dennis Martinez	.05
550	Mike Loynd	.05
551	Darrell Miller	.05
552	Dave LaPoint	.05
553	John Tudor	.05
554	Rocky Childress RC	.05
555	Wally Ritchie RC	.05
556	Terry McGriff	.05
557	Dave Leiper	.05
558	Jeff Robinson	.05
559	Jose Uribe	.05
560	Ted Simmons	.05
561	Lester Lancaster RC	.10
562	Keith Miller RC	.05
563	Harold Reynolds	.05
564	Gene Larkin RC	.05
565	Cecil Fielder	.05
566	Roy Smalley	.05
567	Duane Ward	.05
568	Bill Wilkinson RC	.05
569	Howard Johnson	.05
570	Frank DiPino	.05
571	Pete Smith RC	.05
572	Darnell Coles	.05
573	Don Robinson	.05
574	Rob Nelson	.05
575	Dennis Rasmussen	.05
576	Steve Jeltz (Photo actually Juan Samuel.)	.05
577	Tom Pagnozzi RC	.05
578	Ty Gainey	.05
579	Gary Lucas	.05
580	Ron Hassey	.05
581	Herm Winningham	.05
582	Rene Gonzales RC	.05
583	Brad Komminsk	.05
584	Doyle Alexander	.05
585	Jeff Sellers	.05
586	Bill Gullickson	.05
587	Tim Belcher RC	.05
588	Doug Jones RC	.05
589	Melido Perez RC	.05
590	Rick Honeycutt	.05
591	Pascual Perez	.05
592	Curt Wilkerson	.05
593	Steve Howe	.05
594	John Davis RC	.05
595	Storm Davis	.05
596	Sammy Stewart	.05
597	Neil Allen	.05
598	Alejandro Pena	.05
599	Mark Thurmond	.05
600a	Checklist 578-BC26	.05
600b	Checklist 558-660	.05
601	Jose Mesa RC	.10
602	Don August RC	.05
603	Terry Leach/SP	.10
604	Tom Newell RC	.05
605	Randall Byers/SP RC	.10
606	Jim Gott	.05
607	Harry Spilman	.05
608	John Candelaria	.05
609	Mike Brumley RC	.05
610	Mickey Brantley	.05
611	Jose Nunez/SP RC	.10
612	Tom Nieto	.05
613	Rick Reuschel	.05
614	Lee Mazzilli/SP	.10
615	Scott Lusader RC	.05
616	Bobby Meacham	.05
617	Kevin McReynolds/SP	.10
618	Gene Garber	.05
619	Barry Lyons/SP RC	.10
620	Randy Myers	.05
621	Donnie Moore	.05
622	Domingo Ramos	.05
623	Ed Romero	.05
624	Greg Myers RC	.10
625	Ripken Baseball Family (Billy Ripken, Cal Ripken, Jr., Cal Ripken, Sr.)	.40
626	Pat Perry	.05
627	Andres Thomas/SP	.10
628	Matt Williams/SP	.15
629	Dave Hengel RC	.10
630	Jeff Musselman/SP	.10
631	Tim Laudner	.05
632	Bob Ojeda/SP	.10
633	Rafael Santana	.05
634	Wes Gardner RC	.05
635	Roberto Kelly/SP RC	.15
636	Mike Flanagan/SP	.05
637	Jay Bell RC	.35
638	Bob Melvin	.05
639	Damon Berryhill RC	.05
640	David Wells/SP RC	.40
641	Stan Musial Puzzle Card	.05
642	Doug Sisk	.05
643	Keith Hughes RC	.05
644	Tom Glavine RC	1.00
645	Al Newman	.05
646	Scott Sanderson	.05
647	Scott Terry	.05
648	Tim Teufel/SP	.10
649	Garry Templeton/SP	.10
650	Manny Lee/SP	.10
651	Roger McDowell/SP	.10
652	Mookie Wilson/SP	.10
653	David Cone/SP	.10
654	Ron Gant/SP RC	.20
655	Joe Price/SP	.05
656	George Bell/SP	.05
657	Gregg Jefferies/SP RC	.25
658	Todd Stottlemyre/SP RC	.25
659	Geronimo Berroa/SP RC	.20
660	Jerry Royster/SP	.10

carry the same basic red-blue-black border design as the 1988 Donruss basic issue. Backs are the same as the regular issue, except for the numbering system.

		NM/M
Complete Set (26):		3.00
Common Player:		.10
1	Cal Ripken, Jr.	1.00
2	Eric Davis	.10
3	Paul Molitor	.40
4	Mike Schmidt	.60
5	Ivan Calderon	.10
6	Tony Gwynn	.50
7	Wade Boggs	.50
8	Andy Van Slyke	.10
9	Joe Carter	.10
10	Andre Dawson	.25
11	Alan Trammell	.10
12	Mike Scott	.10
13	Wally Joyner	.10
14	Dale Murphy	.20
15	Kirby Puckett	.50
16	Pedro Guerrero	.10
17	Kevin Seitzer	.10
18	Tim Raines	.10
19	George Bell	.10
20	Darryl Strawberry	.10
21	Don Mattingly	.60
22	Ozzie Smith	.50
23	Mark McGwire	.75
24	Will Clark	.50
25	Alvin Davis	.10
26	Ruben Sierra	.10

All-Stars

For the third consecutive year, this set of 64 cards was marketed in conjunction with Donruss Pop-Ups. The 1988 issue included a major change - the cards were reduced in size from 3-1/2" x 5" to a standard 2-1/2" x 3-1/2". The set features players from the 1987 All-Star Game starting lineup. Card fronts feature full-color photos, framed in blue, black and white, with a Donruss logo at upper-left. Player name and position appear in a red banner below the photo, along with the appropriate National or American League logo. Backs include player stats and All-Star Game record. In 1988, All-Stars cards were distributed in individual packages containing three All-Stars, one Pop-Up and three Stan Musial puzzle pieces.

		NM/M
Complete Set (64):		5.00
Common Player:		.05
Stan Musial Puzzle:		1.00
Wax Pack:		.50
Wax Box (48):		10.00
1	Don Mattingly	.60
2	Dave Winfield	.40
3	Willie Randolph	.05
4	Rickey Henderson	.40
5	Cal Ripken, Jr.	1.00
6	George Bell	.05
7	Wade Boggs	.50
8	Bret Saberhagen	.05
9	Terry Kennedy	.05
10	John McNamara	.05
11	Jay Howell	.05
12	Harold Baines	.05
13	Harold Reynolds	.05
14	Bruce Hurst	.05
15	Kirby Puckett	.50
16	Matt Nokes	.05
17	Pat Tabler	.05
18	Dan Plesac	.05
19	Mark McGwire	.75
20	Mike Witt	.05
21	Larry Parrish	.05
22	Alan Trammell	.05
23	Dwight Evans	.05
24	Jack Morris	.05

MVP

Dale Murphy OF

This 26-card set of standard-size player cards replaced the Donruss box-bottom cards in 1988. The bonus cards (numbered BC1 - BC26) were randomly inserted in Donruss wax or rack packs. Cards feature the company's choice of Most Valuable Player for each major league team and are titled "Donruss MVP." The MVP cards were not included in the factory-collated sets. Fronts

ABBREVIATIONS
SP - Short Print

25	Tony Fernandez	.05
26	Mark Langston	.05
27	Kevin Seitzer	.05
28	Tom Henke	.05
29	Dave Righetti	.05
30	Oakland Coliseum	.05
31	Wade Boggs (Top Vote Getter)	.25
32	Checklist 1-32	.05
33	Jack Clark	.05
34	Darryl Strawberry	.05
35	Ryne Sandberg	.50
36	Andre Dawson	.05
37	Ozzie Smith	.50
38	Eric Davis	.05
39	Mike Schmidt	.60
40	Mike Scott	.05
41	Gary Carter	.40
42	Davey Johnson	.05
43	Rick Sutcliffe	.05
44	Willie McGee	.05
45	Hubie Brooks	.05
46	Dale Murphy	.20
47	Bo Diaz	.05
48	Pedro Guerrero	.05
49	Keith Hernandez	.05
50	Ozzie Virgil	.05
51	Tony Gwynn	.50
52	Rick Reuschel	.05
53	John Franco	.05
54	Jeffrey Leonard	.05
55	Juan Samuel	.05
56	Orel Hershiser	.05
57	Tim Raines	.05
58	Sid Fernandez	.05
59	Tim Wallach	.05
60	Lee Smith	.05
61	Steve Bedrosian	.05
62	Tim Raines/MVP	.05
63	Ozzie Smith (Top Vote Getter)	.25
64	Checklist 33-64	.05

Baseball's Best

The design of this 336-card set is similar to the regular 1988 Donruss issue with the exception of the borders which are orange, instead of blue. Player photos on the glossy front are framed by the Donruss logo upper-left, team logo lower-right and a bright red and white player name that spans the bottom margin. Backs are black and white, framed by a yellow border, and include personal information, year-by-year stats and major league totals. This set was packaged in a bright red cardboard box containing six individually shrink-wrapped packs of 56 cards. Donruss marketed the set via retail chain outlets with a suggested retail price of $21.95.

		NM/M
Complete Set (336):		10.00
Common Player:		.05
1	Don Mattingly	.75
2	Ron Gant	.05
3	Bob Boone	.05
4	Mark Grace	.15
5	Andy Allanson	.05
6	Kal Daniels	.05
7	Floyd Bannister	.05
8	Alan Ashby	.05
9	Marty Barrett	.05
10	Tim Belcher	.05
11	Harold Baines	.05
12	Hubie Brooks	.05
13	Doyle Alexander	.05
14	Gary Carter	.50
15	Glenn Braggs	.05
16	Steve Bedrosian	.05
17	Barry Bonds	1.50
18	Bert Blyleven	.10
19	Tom Brunansky	.05
20	John Candelaria	.05
21	Shawn Abner	.05
22	Jose Canseco	.30
23	Brett Butler	.05
24	Scott Bradley	.05
25	Ivan Calderon	.05
26	Rich Gossage	.05
27	Brian Downing	.05
28	Jim Rice	.25
29	Dion James	.05
30	Terry Kennedy	.05
31	George Bell	.05
32	Scott Fletcher	.05
33	Bobby Bonilla	.05
34	Tim Burke	.05
35	Darrell Evans	.05
36	Mike Davis	.05
37	Shawon Dunston	.05
38	Kevin Bass	.05
39	George Brett	.75
40	David Cone	.05
41	Ron Darling	.05
42	Roberto Alomar	.60
43	Dennis Eckersley	.40
44	Vince Coleman	.05
45	Sid Bream	.05
46	Gary Gaetti	.05
47	Phil Bradley	.05
48	Jim Clancy	.05
49	Jack Clark	.05
50	Mike Krukow	.05
51	Henry Cotto	.05
52	Rich Dotson	.05
53	Jim Gantner	.05
54	John Franco	.05
55	Pete Incaviglia	.05
56	Joe Carter	.05
57	Roger Clemens	.75
58	Gerald Perry	.05
59	Jack Howell	.05
60	Vance Law	.05
61	Jay Bell	.05
62	Eric Davis	.05
63	Gene Garber	.05
64	Glenn Davis	.05
65	Wade Boggs	.60
66	Kirk Gibson	.05
67	Carlton Fisk	.50
68	Casey Candaele	.05
69	Mike Heath	.05
70	Kevin Elster	.05
71	Greg Brock	.05
72	Don Carman	.05
73	Doug Drabek	.05
74	Greg Gagne	.05
75	Danny Cox	.05
76	Rickey Henderson	.50
77	Chris Brown	.05
78	Terry Steinbach	.05
79	Will Clark	.05
80	Mickey Brantley	.05
81	Ozzie Guillen	.05
82	Greg Maddux	.60
83	Kirk McCaskill	.05
84	Dwight Evans	.05
85	Ozzie Virgil	.05
86	Mike Morgan	.05
87	Tony Fernandez	.05
88	Jose Guzman	.05
89	Mike Dunne	.05
90	Andres Galarraga	.05
91	Mike Henneman	.05
92	Alfredo Griffin	.05
93	Rafael Palmeiro	.40
94	Jim Deshaies	.05
95	Mark Gubicza	.05
96	Dwight Gooden	.05
97	Howard Johnson	.05
98	Mark Davis	.05
99	Dave Stewart	.05
100	Joe Magrane	.05
101	Brian Fisher	.05
102	Kent Hrbek	.05
103	Kevin Gross	.05
104	Tom Henke	.05
105	Mike Pagliarulo	.05
106	Kelly Downs	.05
107	Alvin Davis	.05
108	Willie Randolph	.05
109	Rob Deer	.05
110	Bo Diaz	.05
111	Paul Kilgus	.05
112	Tom Candiotti	.05
113	Dale Murphy	.20
114	Rick Mahler	.05
115	Wally Joyner	.05
116	Ryne Sandberg	.60
117	John Farrell	.05
118	Nick Esasky	.05
119	Bo Jackson	.10
120	Bill Doran	.05
121	Ellis Burks	.05
122	Pedro Guerrero	.05
123	Dave LaPoint	.05
124	Neal Heaton	.05
125	Willie Hernandez	.05
126	Roger McDowell	.05
127	Ted Higuera	.05
128	Von Hayes	.05
129	Mike LaValliere	.05
130	Dan Gladden	.05
131	Willie McGee	.05
132	Al Leiter	.05
133	Mark Grant	.05
134	Bob Welch	.05
135	Dave Dravecky	.05
136	Mark Langston	.05
137	Dan Pasqua	.05
138	Rick Sutcliffe	.05
139	Dan Petry	.05
140	Rich Gedman	.05
141	Ken Griffey	.05

142	Eddie Murray	.50
143	Jimmy Key	.05
144	Dale Mohorcic	.05
145	Jose Lind	.05
146	Dennis Martinez	.05
147	Chet Lemon	.05
148	Orel Hershiser	.05
149	Dave Martinez	.05
150	Billy Hatcher	.05
151	Charlie Leibrandt	.05
152	Keith Hernandez	.05
153	Kevin McReynolds	.05
154	Tony Gwynn	.60
155	Stan Javier	.05
156	Tony Pena	.05
157	Andy Van Slyke	.05
158	Gene Larkin	.05
159	Chris James	.05
160	Fred McGriff	.05
161	Rick Rhoden	.05
162	Scott Garrelts	.05
163	Mike Campbell	.05
164	Dave Righetti	.05
165	Paul Molitor	.50
166	Danny Jackson	.05
167	Pete O'Brien	.05
168	Julio Franco	.05
169	Mark McGwire	1.00
170	Zane Smith	.05
171	Johnny Ray	.05
172	Lester Lancaster	.05
173	Mel Hall	.05
174	Tracy Jones	.05
175	Kevin Seitzer	.05
176	Bob Knepper	.05
177	Mike Greenwell	.05
178	Mike Marshall	.05
179	Melido Perez	.05
180	Tim Raines	.05
181	Jack Morris	.05
182	Darryl Strawberry	.05
183	Robin Yount	.50
184	Lance Parrish	.05
185	Darnell Coles	.05
186	Kirby Puckett	.60
187	Terry Pendleton	.05
188	Don Slaught	.05
189	Jimmy Jones	.05
190	Dave Parker	.05
191	Mike Aldrete	.05
192	Mike Moore	.05
193	Greg Walker	.05
194	Calvin Schiraldi	.05
195	Dick Schofield	.05
196	Jody Reed	.05
197	Pete Smith	.05
198	Cal Ripken, Jr.	1.50
199	Lloyd Moseby	.05
200	Ruben Sierra	.05
201	R.J. Reynolds	.05
202	Bryn Smith	.05
203	Gary Pettis	.05
204	Steve Sax	.05
205	Frank DiPino	.05
206	Mike Scott	.05
207	Kurt Stillwell	.05
208	Mookie Wilson	.05
209	Lee Mazzilli	.05
210	Lance McCullers	.05
211	Rick Honeycutt	.05
212	John Tudor	.05
213	Jim Gott	.05
214	Frank Viola	.05
215	Juan Samuel	.05
216	Jesse Barfield	.05
217	Claudell Washington	.05
218	Rick Reuschel	.05
219	Jim Presley	.05
220	Tommy John	.05
221	Dan Plesac	.05
222	Barry Larkin	.05
223	Mike Stanley	.05
224	Cory Snyder	.05
225	Andre Dawson	.25
226	Ken Oberkfell	.05
227	Devon White	.05
228	Jamie Moyer	.05
229	Brook Jacoby	.05
230	Rob Murphy	.05
231	Bret Saberhagen	.05
232	Nolan Ryan	1.50
233	Bruce Hurst	.05
234	Jesse Orosco	.05
235	Bobby Thigpen	.05
236	Pascual Perez	.05
237	Matt Nokes	.05
238	Bob Ojeda	.05
239	Joey Meyer	.05
240	Shane Rawley	.05
241	Jeff Robinson	.05
242	Jeff Reardon	.05
243	Ozzie Smith	.60
244	Dave Winfield	.50
245	John Kruk	.05
246	Carney Lansford	.05
247	Candy Maldonado	.05
248	Ken Phelps	.05
249	Ken Williams	.05
250	Al Nipper	.05
251	Mark McLemore	.05
252	Lee Smith	.05
253	Albert Hall	.05
254	Billy Ripken	.05
255	Kelly Gruber	.05
256	Charlie Hough	.05
257	John Smiley	.05
258	Tim Wallach	.05
259	Frank Tanana	.05

260	Mike Scioscia	.05
261	Damon Berryhill	.05
262	Dave Smith	.05
263	Willie Wilson	.05
264	Len Dykstra	.05
265	Randy Myers	.05
266	Keith Moreland	.05
267	Eric Plunk	.05
268	Todd Worrell	.05
269	Bob Walk	.05
270	Keith Atherton	.05
271	Mike Schmidt	.75
272	Mike Flanagan	.05
273	Rafael Santana	.05
274	Rob Thompson	.05
275	Rey Quinones	.05
276	Cecilio Guante	.05
277	B.J. Surhoff	.05
278	Chris Sabo	.05
279	Mitch Williams	.05
280	Greg Swindell	.05
281	Alan Trammell	.05
282	Storm Davis	.05
283	Chuck Finley	.05
284	Dave Stieb	.05
285	Scott Bailes	.05
286	Larry Sheets	.05
287	Danny Tartabull	.05
288	Checklist	.05
289	Todd Benzinger	.05
290	John Shelby	.05
291	Steve Lyons	.05
292	Mitch Webster	.06
293	Walt Terrell	.05
294	Pete Stanicek	.05
295	Chris Bosio	.05
296	Milt Thompson	.05
297	Fred Lynn	.05
298	Juan Berenguer	.05
299	Ken Dayley	.05
300	Joel Skinner	.05
301	Benito Santiago	.05
302	Ron Hassey	.05
303	Jose Uribe	.05
304	Harold Reynolds	.05
305	Dale Sveum	.05
306	Glenn Wilson	.05
307	Mike Witt	.05
308	Ron Robinson	.05
309	Denny Walling	.05
310	Joe Orsulak	.05
311	David Wells	.05
312	Steve Buechele	.05
313	Jose Oquendo	.05
314	Floyd Youmans	.05
315	Lou Whitaker	.05
316	Fernando Valenzuela	.05
317	Mike Boddicker	.05
318	Gerald Young	.05
319	Frank White	.05
320	Bill Wegman	.05
321	Tom Niedenfuer	.05
322	Ed Whitson	.05
323	Curt Young	.05
324	Greg Mathews	.05
325	Doug Jones	.05
326	Tommy Herr	.05
327	Kent Tekulve	.05
328	Rance Mulliniks	.05
329	Checklist	.05
330	Craig Lefferts	.05
331	Franklin Stubbs	.05
332	Rick Cerone	.05
333	Dave Schmidt	.05
334	Larry Parrish	.05
335	Tom Browning	.05
336	Checklist	.05

Diamond Kings Supers

TOMMY JOHN

This 28-card set (including the checklist) marks the fourth edition of Donruss' super-size (5" x 7") set. These cards are exact duplicates of the 1988 Diamond Kings that feature player portraits by Dick Perez. A 12-piece Stan Musial puzzle was also included with the purchase of the super-size set which was marketed via a mail-in offer printed on Donruss wrappers.

	NM/M
Complete Set (28):	5.00

Rookies

For the third consecutive year, Donruss issued a 56-card boxed set highlighting current rookies. The complete set includes a checklist and a 15-piece Stan Musial Diamond Kings puzzle. As in previous years, the set is similar to the company's basic issue, with the exception of the logo and border color. Card fronts fea-

Common Player:		.10
1	Mark McGwire	2.00
2	Tim Raines	.10
3	Benito Santiago	.10
4	Alan Trammell	.10
5	Danny Tartabull	.10
6	Ron Darling	.10
7	Paul Molitor	1.00
8	Devon White	.10
9	Andre Dawson	.25
10	Julio Franco	.10
11	Scott Fletcher	.10
12	Tony Fernandez	.10
13	Shane Rawley	.10
14	Kal Daniels	.10
15	Jack Clark	.10
16	Dwight Evans	.10
17	Tommy John	.15
18	Andy Van Slyke	.10
19	Gary Gaetti	.10
20	Mark Langston	.10
21	Will Clark	.10
22	Glenn Hubbard	.10
23	Billy Hatcher	.10
24	Bob Welch	.10
25	Ivan Calderon	.10
26	Cal Ripken, Jr.	3.00
27	Checklist	.05
641	Stan Musial Puzzle Card	

Pop-Ups

WADE BOGGS
RED SOX · 3B

Donruss' 1988 Pop-Up cards were reduced to the standard 2-1/2" x 3-1/2". The set includes 20 cards that fold out so that the upper portion of the player stands upright, giving a three-dimensional effect. Pop-Ups feature players from the All-Star Game starting lineup. Fronts have the player's name, team and position printed in black on a yellow banner near the bottom. As in previous issues, backs contain only the player's name, team and position and a Leaf copyright. Pop-Ups were distributed in individual packages containing one Pop-Up, five Stan Musial puzzle pieces and three All-Star cards.

	NM/M
Complete Set (20):	4.00
Common Player:	.05
Stan Musial Puzzle:	1.00
Wax Pack:	.50
Wax Box (48):	10.00

(1)	George Bell	.05
(2)	Wade Boggs	.50
(3)	Gary Carter	.40
(4)	Jack Clark	.05
(5)	Eric Davis	.05
(6)	Andre Dawson	.25
(7)	Rickey Henderson	.40
(8)	Davey Johnson	.05
(9)	Don Mattingly	.65
(10)	Terry Kennedy	.05
(11)	John McNamara	.05
(12)	Willie Randolph	.05
(13)	Cal Ripken, Jr.	1.00
(14)	Bret Saberhagen	.05
(15)	Ryne Sandberg	.50
(16)	Mike Schmidt	.65
(17)	Mike Scott	.05
(18)	Ozzie Smith	.50
(19)	Darryl Strawberry	.05
(20)	Dave Winfield	.40

Team Books

DONRUSS
1988 Puzzle & Cards
The New York Yankees
TEAM COLLECTION
N.Y. Yankees

Mark Grace 13

ture red, green and black-striped borders, with a red-and-white player name printed in the lower-left corner beneath the photo. "The Rookies" logo is printed in red, white and black in the lower-right corner. Backs are printed in black on bright aqua and include personal data, recent performance stats and major league totals, as well as 1984-88 minor league stats. The cards are the standard 2-1/2" x 3-1/2".

	NM/M
Complete Set (56):	4.00
Common Player:	.05

1	Mark Grace	.25
2	Mike Campbell	.05
3	Todd Frohwirth RC	.05
4	Dave Stapleton	.05
5	Shawn Abner	.05
6	Jose Cecena RC	.05
7	Dave Gallagher RC	.05
8	Mark Parent RC	.05
9	Cecil Espy RC	.05
10	Pete Smith	.05
11	Jay Buhner	.25
12	Pat Borders RC	.05
13	Doug Jennings RC	.05
14	Brady Anderson RC	1.00
15	Pete Stanicek	.05
16	Roberto Kelly	.05
17	Jeff Treadway	.05
18	Walt Weiss RC	.05
19	Paul Gibson RC	.05
20	Tim Crews	.05
21	Melido Perez	.05
22	Steve Peters RC	.05
23	Craig Worthington RC	.05
24	John Trautwein RC	.05
25	DeWayne Vaughn RC	.05
26	David Wells	.15
27	Al Leiter	.15
28	Tim Belcher	.05
29	Johnny Paredes RC	.05
30	Chris Sabo RC	.05
31	Damon Berryhill	.05
32	Randy Milligan	.05
33	Gary Thurman	.05
34	Kevin Elster	.05
35	Roberto Alomar	1.50
36	Edgar Martinez RC (Photo actually Edwin Nunez.)	1.50
37	Todd Stottlemyre	.05
38	Joey Meyer	.05
39	Carl Nichols	.05
40	Jack McDowell	.05
41	Jose Bautista RC	.05
42	Sil Campusano RC	.05
43	John Dopson RC	.05
44	Jody Reed	.05
45	Darrin Jackson RC	.05
46	Mike Capel RC	.05
47	Ron Gant	.05
48	John Davis	.05
49	Kevin Coffman RC	.05
50	Cris Carpenter RC	.05
51	Mackey Sasser	.05
52	Luis Alicea RC	.05
53	Bryan Harvey RC	.05
54	Steve Ellsworth RC	.05
55	Mike Macfarlane RC	.05
56	Checklist 1-56	.05

Three pages of nine cards each and a Stan Musial puzzle highlight these special team collection books. The cards feature the same design as the regular 1988 Donruss cards, but contain a 1988 copyright date instead of 1987 like the regular set. The cards are numbered like the regular issue with the exception of new cards of traded players and rookies produced especially for the team collection books. Books are commonly found complete with the cards and puzzle. The puzzle pieces are perforated for removal, but the card sheets are not.

	NM/M
Complete Set, Books (5):	12.00
Common Player:	.05

	Boston Red Sox	
	Team Book:	3.00
NEW	Brady Anderson	.50
NEW	Rick Cerone	.05
NEW	Steve Ellsworth	.05
NEW	Dennis Lamp	.05
NEW	Kevin Romine	.05
NEW	Lee Smith	.25
NEW	Mike Smithson	.05
NEW	John Trautwein	.05
41	Jody Reed	.05
51	Roger Clemens	.75
92	Bob Stanley	.05
129	Rich Gedman	.05
153	Wade Boggs	.65
174	Ellis Burks	.05
216	Dwight Evans	.05
252	Bruce Hurst	.05
276	Marty Barrett	.05
297	Todd Benzinger	.05
339	Mike Greenwell	.05
399	Jim Rice	.25
421	John Marzano	.05
462	Oil Can Boyd	.05
498	Sam Horn	.05
544	Spike Owen	.05
585	Jeff Sellers	.05
623	Ed Romero	.05
634	Wes Gardner	.05
	Chicago Cubs	
	Team Book:	3.00
NEW	Mike Bielecki	.05
NEW	Rich Gossage	.25
NEW	Drew Hall	.05
NEW	Darrin Jackson	.05
NEW	Vance Law	.05
NEW	Al Nipper	.05
NEW	Angel Salazar	.05
NEW	Calvin Schiraldi	.05
40	Mark Grace	.50
68	Rick Sutcliffe	.05
119	Jody Davis	.05
146	Shawon Dunston	.05
169	Jamie Moyer	.05
191	Leon Durham	.05
242	Ryne Sandberg	.65
269	Andre Dawson	.25
315	Paul Noce	.05
324	Rafael Palmeiro	.40
438	Dave Martinez	.05
447	Jerry Mumphrey	.05
488	Jim Sundberg	.05
516	Manny Trillo	.05
539	Greg Maddux	.65
561	Les Lancaster	.05
570	Frank DiPino	.05
639	Damon Berryhill	.05
646	Scott Sanderson	.05
	N.Y. Mets Team Book:	3.00
NEW	Jeff Innis	.05
NEW	Mackey Sasser	.05
NEW	Gene Walter	.05
37	Kevin Elster	.05
69	Dwight Gooden	.05
76	Ron Darling	.05
118	Sid Fernandez	.05
199	Gary Carter	.50
241	Wally Backman	.05
316	Keith Hernandez	.05
323	Dave Magadan	.05
364	Len Dykstra	.05
439	Darryl Strawberry	.05
446	Rick Aguilera	.05
562	Keith Miller	.05
569	Howard Johnson	.05
603	Terry Leach	.05
614	Lee Mazzilli	.05
617	Kevin McReynolds	.05
619	Barry Lyons	.05
620	Randy Myers	.05
632	Bob Ojeda	.05
648	Tim Teufel	.05
651	Roger McDowell	.05
652	Mookie Wilson	.05
653	David Cone	.05
657	Gregg Jefferies	.35
	N.Y. Yankees Team Book:	3.00
NEW	John Candelaria	.05
NEW	Jack Clark	.05
NEW	Jose Cruz	.05
NEW	Richard Dotson	.05

NEW	Cecilio Guante	.05
NEW	Lee Guetterman	.05
NEW	Rafael Santana	.05
NEW	Steve Shields	.05
NEW	Don Slaught	.15
43	Al Leiter	.05
93	Dave Righetti	.05
105	Mike Pagliarulo	.05
128	Rick Rhoden	.05
175	Ron Guidry	.05
217	Don Mattingly	.75
228	Willie Randolph	.05
251	Gary Ward	.05
277	Rickey Henderson	.50
278	Dave Winfield	.50
340	Claudell Washington	.05
374	Charles Hudson	.05
401	Tommy John	.10
474	Joel Skinner	.05
497	Tim Stoddard	.05
545	Jay Buhner	.10
635	Roberto Kelly	.05
	Oakland A's	
	Team Book:	3.00
NEW	Don Baylor	.25
NEW	Ron Hassey	.05
NEW	Dave Henderson	.05
NEW	Glenn Hubbard	.05
NEW	Stan Javier	.05
NEW	Doug Jennings	.05
NEW	Ed Jurak	.05
NEW	Dave Parker	.15
NEW	Walt Weiss	.05
NEW	Bob Welch	.05
NEW	Matt Young	.05
97	Curt Young	.05
133	Gene Nelson	.05
158	Terry Steinbach	.05
178	Carney Lansford	.05
221	Tony Phillips	.05
256	Mark McGwire	1.00
302	Jose Canseco	.30
349	Dennis Eckersley	.40
379	Mike Gallego	.05
425	Luis Polonia	.05
467	Steve Ontiveros	.05
472	Dave Stewart	.05
503	Eric Plunk	.05
528	Greg Cadaret	.05
590	Rick Honeycutt	.05
595	Storm Davis	.05

1989 Donruss Promo Sheet

To introduce its card design for 1989, Donruss produced this sheet. Printed on semi-gloss paper, the 7-1/2" x 10-1/2" blank-back sheet has images of seven regular cards, a Diamond King and an MVP.

	NM/M
Complete Sheet:	10.00

1989 Donruss

Fred McGriff 1B

This basic annual issue consists of 660 2-1/2" x 3-1/2" cards, including 26 Diamond Kings (DK) portrait cards and 20 Rated Rookies (RR) cards. Top and bottom borders of the cards are printed in a variety of colors that fade from dark to light. A white-lettered player name is printed across the top margin. The team logo appears upper-right and the Donruss logo lower-left. A black outer stripe varnish gives faintly visible film-strip texture to the border. Backs are in orange and black, similar to the 1988 design, with personal info, recent stats and major league totals. Team logo sticker cards (22 total) and Warren Spahn puzzle cards (63 total) are included in individual wax packs of cards. Each regular player card can be found with a back variation in the header line above the stats: i.e., "*Denotes" or "*Denotes*." Neither version carries a premium.

	NM/M
Unopened Fact. Set (660):	17.50
Complete Set (660):	15.00
Common Player:	.05
Warren Spahn Puzzle:	.50
Wax Pack (15):	.75
Wax Box (36):	15.00
Cello Pack (32):	1.00
Cello Box (24):	15.00
Rack Pack (45):	.75

#	Player	Price
1	Mike Greenwell/DK	.05
2	Bobby Bonilla/DK	.05
3	Pete Incaviglia/DK	.05
4	Chris Sabo/DK	.05
5	Robin Yount/DK	.40
6	Tony Gwynn/DK	.50
7	Carlton Fisk/DK	.40
8	Cory Snyder/DK	.05
9	David Cone/DK	.05
10	Kevin Seitzer/DK	.05
11	Rick Reuschel/DK	.05
12	Johnny Ray/DK	.05
13	Dave Schmidt/DK	.05
14	Andres Galarraga/DK	.05
15	Kirk Gibson/DK	.05
16	Fred McGriff/DK	.05
17	Mark Grace/DK	.15
18	Jeff Robinson/DK	.05
19	Vince Coleman/DK	.05
20	Dave Henderson/DK	.05
21	Harold Reynolds/DK	.05
22	Gerald Perry/DK	.05
23	Frank Viola/DK	.05
24	Steve Bedrosian/DK	.05
25	Glenn Davis/DK	.05
26	Don Mattingly/DK	.60
27	Checklist 1-27	.05
28	Sandy Alomar, Jr./RR RC	.35
29	Steve Searcy/RR RC	
30	Cameron Drew/RR RC	
31	Gary Sheffield/RR RC	1.00
32	Erik Hanson/RR RC	.05
33	Ken Griffey Jr./RR RC	6.00
34	Greg Harris/RR RC	
35	Gregg Jefferies/RR	.05
36	Luis Medina/RR RC	.05
37	Carlos Quintana/RR RC	.05
38	Felix Jose/RR RC	
39	Cris Carpenter/RR RC	.05
40	Ron Jones/RR RC	.05
41	Dave West/RR RC	
42	Randy Johnson/RR RC	3.00
43	Mike Harkey/RR RC	
44	Pete Harnisch/RR RC	.10
45	Tom Gordon/RR RC	.25
46	Gregg Olson/RR RC	.10
47	Alex Sanchez/RR RC	.05
48	Ruben Sierra	.05
49	Rafael Palmeiro	.35
50	Ron Gant	.05
51	Cal Ripken, Jr.	1.00
52	Wally Joyner	.05
53	Gary Carter	.40
54	Andy Van Slyke	.05
55	Robin Yount	.40
56	Pete Incaviglia	.05
57	Greg Brock	.05
58	Melido Perez	.05
59	Craig Lefferts	.05
60	Gary Pettis	.05
61	Danny Tartabull	.05
62	Guillermo Hernandez	.05
63	Ozzie Smith	.50
64	Gary Gaetti	.05
65	Mark Davis	.05
66	Lee Smith	.05
67	Dennis Eckersley	.35
68	Wade Boggs	.50
69	Mike Scott	.05
70	Fred McGriff	.05
71	Tom Browning	.05
72	Claudell Washington	.05
73	Mel Hall	.05
74	Don Mattingly	.60
75	Steve Bedrosian	.05
76	Juan Samuel	.05
77	Mike Scioscia	.05
78	Dave Righetti	.05
79	Alfredo Griffin	.05
80	Eric Davis	.05
81	Juan Berenguer	.05
82	Todd Worrell	.05
83	Joe Carter	.05
84	Steve Sax	.05
85	Frank White	.05
86	John Kruk	.05
87	Rance Mulliniks	.05
88	Alan Ashby	.05
89	Charlie Leibrandt	.05
90	Frank Tanana	.05
91	Jose Canseco	.50
92	Barry Bonds	1.00
93	Harold Reynolds	.05
94	Mark McLemore	.05
95	Mark McGwire	.75
96	Eddie Murray	.40
97	Tim Raines	.05
98	Rob Thompson	.05
99	Kevin McReynolds	.05
100	Checklist 28-137	.05
101	Carlton Fisk	.40
102	Dave Martinez	.05
103	Glenn Braggs	.05
104	Dale Murphy	.15
105	Ryne Sandberg	.50
106	Dennis Martinez	.05
107	Pete O'Brien	.05
108	Dick Schofield	.05
109	Henry Cotto	.05
110	Mike Marshall	.05
111	Keith Moreland	.05
112	Tom Brunansky	.05
113	Kelly Gruber	.05
114	Brook Jacoby	.05
115	Keith Brown RC	.05
116	Matt Nokes	.05
117	Keith Hernandez	.05
118	Bob Forsch	.05
119	Bert Blyleven	.10
120	Willie Wilson	.05
121	Tommy Gregg	.05
122	Jim Rice	.25
123	Bob Knepper	.05
124	Danny Jackson	.05
125	Eric Plunk	.05
126	Brian Fisher	.05
127	Mike Pagliarulo	.05
128	Tony Gwynn	.50
129	Lance McCullers	.05
130	Andres Galarraga	.05
131	Jose Uribe	.05
132	Kirk Gibson	.05
133	David Palmer	.05
134	R.J. Reynolds	.05
135	Greg Walker	.05
136	Kirk McCaskill	.05
137	Shawon Dunston	.05
138	Andy Allanson	.05
139	Rob Murphy	.05
140	Mike Aldrete	.05
141	Terry Kennedy	.05
142	Scott Fletcher	.05
143	Steve Balboni	.05
144	Bret Saberhagen	.05
145	Ozzie Virgil	.05
146	Dale Sveum	.05
147	Darryl Strawberry	.05
148	Harold Baines	.10
149	George Bell	.05
150	Dave Parker	.05
151	Bobby Bonilla	.05
152	Mookie Wilson	.05
153	Ted Power	.05
154	Nolan Ryan	1.00
155	Jeff Reardon	.05
156	Tim Wallach	.05
157	Jamie Moyer	.05
158	Rich Gossage	.10
159	Dave Winfield	.40
160	Von Hayes	.05
161	Willie McGee	.05
162	Rich Gedman	.05
163	Tony Pena	.05
164	Mike Morgan	.05
165	Charlie Hough	.05
166	Mike Stanley	.05
167	Andre Dawson	.20
168	Joe Boever RC	.05
169	Pete Stanicek	.05
170	Bob Boone	.05
171	Ron Darling	.05
172	Bob Walk	.05
173	Rob Deer	.05
174	Steve Buechele	.05
175	Ted Higuera	.05
176	Ozzie Guillen	.05
177	Candy Maldonado	.05
178	Doyle Alexander	.05
179	Mark Gubicza	.05
180	Alan Trammell	.05
181	Vince Coleman	.05
182	Kirby Puckett	.50
183	Chris Brown	.05
184	Marty Barrett	.05
185	Stan Javier	.05
186	Mike Greenwell	.05
187	Billy Hatcher	.05
188	Jimmy Key	.05
189	Nick Esasky	.05
190	Don Slaught	.05
191	Cory Snyder	.05
192	John Candelaria	.05
193	Mike Schmidt	.60
194	Kevin Gross	.05
195	John Tudor	.05
196	Neil Allen	.05
197	Orel Hershiser	.05
198	Kal Daniels	.05
199	Kent Hrbek	.05
200	Checklist 138-247	.05
201	Joe Magrane	.05
202	Scott Bailes	.05
203	Tim Belcher	.05
204	George Brett	.60
205	Benito Santiago	.05
206	Tony Fernandez	.05
207	Gerald Young	.05
208	Bo Jackson	.10
209	Chet Lemon	.05
210	Storm Davis	.05
211	Doug Drabek	.05
212	Mickey Brantley (Photo actually Nelson Simmons.)	.05
213	Devon White	.05
214	Dave Stewart	.05
215	Dave Schmidt	.05
216	Bryn Smith	.05
217	Brett Butler	.05
218	Bob Ojeda	.05
219	Steve Rosenberg RC	.05
220	Hubie Brooks	.05
221	B.J. Surhoff	.05
222	Rick Mahler	.05
223	Rick Sutcliffe	.05
224	Neal Heaton	.05
225	Mitch Williams	.05
226	Chuck Finley	.05
227	Mark Langston	.05
228	Jesse Orosco	.05
229	Ed Whitson	.05
230	Terry Pendleton	.05
231	Lloyd Moseby	.05
232	Greg Swindell	.05
233	John Franco	.05
234	Jack Morris	.05
235	Howard Johnson	.05
236	Glenn Davis	.05
237	Frank Viola	.05
238	Kevin Seitzer	.05
239	Gerald Perry	.05
240	Dwight Evans	.05
241	Jim Deshaies	.05
242	Bo Diaz	.05
243	Carney Lansford	.05
244	Mike LaValliere	.05
245	Rickey Henderson	.40
246	Roberto Alomar	.20
247	Jimmy Jones	.05
248	Pascual Perez	.05
249	Will Clark	.05
250	Fernando Valenzuela	.05
251	Shane Rawley	.05
252	Sid Bream	.05
253	Steve Lyons	.05
254	Brian Downing	.05
255	Mark Grace	.50
256	Tom Candiotti	.05
257	Barry Larkin	.05
258	Mike Krukow	.05
259	Billy Ripken	.05
260	Cecilio Guante	.05
261	Scott Bradley	.05
262	Floyd Bannister	.05
263	Pete Smith	.05
264	Jim Gantner	.05
265	Roger McDowell	.05
266	Bobby Thigpen	.05
267	Jim Clancy	.05
268	Terry Steinbach	.05
269	Mike Dunne	.05
270	Dwight Gooden	.05
271	Mike Heath	.05
272	Dave Smith	.05
273	Keith Atherton	.05
274	Tim Burke	.05
275	Damon Berryhill	.05
276	Vance Law	.05
277	Rich Dotson	.05
278	Lance Parrish	.05
279	Geronimo Berroa	.05
280	Roger Clemens	.60
281	Greg Mathews	.05
282	Tom Niedenfuer	.05
283	Paul Kilgus	.05
284	Jose Guzman	.05
285	Calvin Schiraldi	.05
286	Charlie Puleo	.05
287	Joe Orsulak	.05
288	Jack Howell	.05
289	Kevin Elster	.05
290	Jose Lind	.05
291	Paul Molitor	.40
292	Cecil Espy	.05
293	Bill Wegman	.05
294	Dan Pasqua	.05
295	Scott Garrelts	.05
296	Walt Terrell	.05
297	Ed Hearn	.05
298	Lou Whitaker	.05
299	Ken Dayley	.05
300	Checklist 248-357	.05
301	Tommy Herr	.05
302	Mike Brumley	.05
303	Ellis Burks	.05
304	Curt Young	.05
305	Jody Reed	.05
306	Bill Doran	.05
307	David Wells	.05
308	Ron Robinson	.05
309	Rafael Santana	.05
310	Julio Franco	.05
311	Jack Clark	.05
312	Chris James	.05
313	Milt Thompson	.05
314	John Shelby	.05
315	Al Leiter	.05
316	Mike Davis	.05
317	Chris Sabo RC	.15
318	Greg Gagne	.05
319	Jose Oquendo	.05
320	John Farrell	.05
321	Franklin Stubbs	.05
322	Kurt Stillwell	.05
323	Shawn Abner	.05
324	Mike Flanagan	.05
325	Kevin Bass	.05
326	Pat Tabler	.05
327	Mike Henneman	.05
328	Rick Honeycutt	.05
329	John Smiley	.05
330	Rey Quinones	.05
331	Johnny Ray	.05
332	Bob Welch	.05
333	Larry Sheets	.05
334	Jeff Parrett	.05
335	Rick Reuschel	.05
336	Randy Myers	.05
337	Ken Williams	.05
338	Andy McGaffigan	.05
339	Joey Meyer	.05
340	Dion James	.05
341	Les Lancaster	.05
342	Tom Foley	.05
343	Geno Petralli	.05
344	Dan Petry	.05
345	Alvin Davis	.05
346	Mickey Hatcher	.05
347	Marvell Wynne	.05
348	Danny Cox	.05
349	Dave Stieb	.05
350	Jay Bell	.05
351	Jeff Treadway	.05
352	Luis Salazar	.05
353	Len Dykstra	.05
354	Juan Agosto	.05
355	Gene Larkin	.05
356	Steve Farr	.05
357	Paul Assenmacher	.05
358	Todd Benzinger	.05
359	Larry Andersen	.05
360	Paul O'Neill	.05
361	Ron Hassey	.05
362	Jim Gott	.05
363	Ken Phelps	.05
364	Tim Flannery	.05
365	Randy Ready	.05
366	Nelson Santovenia RC	.05
367	Kelly Downs	.05
368	Danny Heep	.05
369	Phil Bradley	.05
370	Jeff Robinson	.05
371	Ivan Calderon	.05
372	Mike Witt	.05
373	Greg Maddux	.50
374	Carmen Castillo	.05
375	Jose Rijo	.05
376	Joe Price	.05
377	R.C. Gonzalez	.05
378	Oddibe McDowell	.05
379	Jim Presley	.05
380	Brad Wellman	.05
381	Tom Glavine	.20
382	Dan Plesac	.05
383	Wally Backman	.05
384	Dave Gallagher RC	.05
385	Tom Henke	.05
386	Luis Polonia	.05
387	Junior Ortiz	.05
388	David Cone	.05
389	Dave Bergman	.05
390	Danny Darwin	.05
391	Dan Gladden	.05
392	John Dopson RC	.05
393	Frank DiPino	.05
394	Al Nipper	.05
395	Willie Randolph	.05
396	Don Carman	.05
397	Scott Terry	.05
398	Rick Cerone	.05
399	Tom Pagnozzi	.05
400	Checklist 358-467	.05
401	Mickey Tettleton	.05
402	Curtis Wilkerson	.05
403	Jeff Russell	.05
404	Pat Perry	.05
405	Jose Alvarez RC	.05
406	Rick Schu	.05
407	Sherman Corbett RC	.05
408	Dave Magadan	.05
409	Bob Kipper	.05
410	Don August	.05
411	Bob Brower	.05
412	Chris Bosio	.05
413	Jerry Reuss	.05
414	Atlee Hammaker	.05
415	Jim Walewander RC	.05
416	Mike Macfarlane RC	.10
417	Pat Sheridan	.05
418	Pedro Guerrero	.05
419	Allan Anderson	.05
420	Mark Parent RC	.05
421	Bob Stanley	.05
422	Mike Gallego	.05
423	Bruce Hurst	.05
424	Dave Meads	.05
425	Jesse Barfield	.05
426	Rob Dibble RC	.15
427	Joel Skinner	.05
428	Ron Kittle	.05
429	Rick Rhoden	.05
430	Bob Dernier	.05
431	Steve Jeltz	.05
432	Rick Dempsey	.05
433	Roberto Kelly	.05
434	Dave Anderson	.05
435	Herm Winningham	.05
436	Al Newman	.05
437	Jose DeLeon	.05
438	Doug Jones	.05
439	Brian Holton	.05
440	Jeff Montgomery RC	.05
441	Dickie Thon	.05
442	Cecil Fielder	.05
443	John Fishel RC	.05
444	Jerry Don Gleaton	.05
445	Paul Gibson RC	.05
446	Walt Weiss	.05
447	Glenn Wilson	.05
448	Mike Moore	.05
449	Chili Davis	.05
450	Dave Henderson	.05
451	Jose Bautista RC	.05
452	Rex Hudler	.05
453	Bob Brenly	.05
454	Mackey Sasser	.05
455	Daryl Boston	.05
456	Mike Fitzgerald	.05
457	Jeffery Leonard	.05
458	Bruce Sutter	.35
459	Mitch Webster	.05
460	Joe Hesketh	.05
461	Bobby Witt	.05
462	Stew Cliburn	.05
463	Scott Bankhead	.05
464	Ramon Martinez RC	.25
465	Dave Leiper	.05
466	Luis Alicea RC	.05
467	John Cerutti	.05
468	Ron Washington	.05
469	Jeff Reed	.05
470	Jeff Robinson	.05
471	Sid Fernandez	.05
472	Terry Puhl	.05
473	Charlie Lea	.05
474	Israel Sanchez RC	.05
475	Bruce Benedict	.05
476	Oil Can Boyd	.05
477	Craig Reynolds	.05
478	Frank Williams	.05
479	Greg Cadaret	.05
480	Randy Kramer RC	.05
481	Dave Eiland RC	.05
482	Eric Show	.05
483	Garry Templeton	.05
484	Wallace Johnson RC	.05
485	Kevin Mitchell	.05
486	Tim Crews	.05
487	Mike Maddux	.05
488	Dave LaPoint	.05
489	Fred Manrique	.05
490	Greg Minton	.05
491	Doug Dascenzo RC	.05
492	Willie Upshaw	.05
493	Jack Armstrong RC	.05
494	Kirt Manwaring	.05
495	Jeff Ballard	.05
496	Jeff Kunkel	.05
497	Mike Campbell	.05
498	Gary Thurman	.05
499	Zane Smith	.05
500	Checklist 468-577	.05
501	Mike Birkbeck	.05
502	Terry Leach	.05
503	Shawn Hillegas	.05
504	Manny Lee	.05
505	Doug Jennings RC	.05
506	Ken Oberkfell	.05
507	Tim Teufel	.05
508	Tom Brookens	.05
509	Rafael Ramirez	.05
510	Fred Toliver	.05
511	Brian Holman RC	.05
512	Mike Bielecki	.05
513	Jeff Pico RC	.05
514	Charles Hudson	.05
515	Bruce Ruffin	.05
516	Larry McWilliams	.05
517	Jeff Sellers	.05
518	John Costello RC	.05
519	Brady Anderson	.05
520	Craig McMurtry	.05
521	Ray Hayward	.05
522	Drew Hall	.05
523	Mark Lemke RC	.05
524	Oswald Peraza RC	.05
525	Bryan Harvey RC	.05
526	Rick Aguilera	.05
527	Tom Prince	.05
528	Mark Clear	.05
529	Jerry Browne	.05
530	Juan Castillo	.05
531	Jack McDowell	.05
532	Chris Speier	.05
533	Darrell Evans	.05
534	Luis Aquino	.05
535	Eric King	.05
536	Ken Hill RC	.05
537	Randy Bush	.05
538	Shane Mack	.05
539	Tom Bolton RC	.05
540	Gene Nelson	.05
541	Wes Gardner	.05
542	Ken Caminiti	.05
543	Duane Ward	.05
544	Norm Charlton RC	.10
545	Hal Morris RC	.25
546	Rich Yett RC	.05
547	Hensley Meulens RC	.10
548	Greg Harris	.05
549	Darren Daulton	.05
550	Jeff Hamilton	.05
551	Luis Aguayo	.05
552	Tim Leary	.05
553	Ron Oester	.05
554	Steve Lombardozzi	.05
555	Tim Jones	.05
556	Bud Black	.05
557	Alejandro Pena	.05
558	Jose DeJesus RC	.05
559	Dennis Rasmussen	.05
560	Pat Borders	.25
561	Craig Biggio	.05
562	Luis de los Santos RC	.05
563	Fred Lynn	.05
564	Todd Burns RC	.05
565	Felix Fermin	.05
566	Darnell Coles	.05
567	Willie Fraser	.05
568	Glenn Hubbard	.05
569	Craig Worthington RC	.05
570	Johnny Paredes RC	.05
571	Don Robinson	.05
572	Barry Lyons	.05
573	Bill Long	.05
574	Tracy Jones	.05
575	Juan Nieves	.05
576	Andres Thomas	.05
577	Rolando Roomes RC	.05
578	Luis Rivera RC	.05
579	Chad Kreuter RC	.10
580	Tony Armas	.05
581	Jay Buhner	.05
582	Ricky Horton	.05
583	Andy Hawkins	.05
584	Sil Campusano RC	.05
585	Dave Clark	.05
586	Van Snider RC	.05
587	Todd Frohwirth RC	.05
588	Warren Spahn Puzzle Card	.05
589	William Brennan RC	.05
590	German Gonzalez RC	.05
591	Ernie Whitt	.05
592	Jeff Blauser	.05
593	Spike Owen	.05
594	Matt Williams	.05
595	Lloyd McClendon RC	.05
596	Steve Ontiveros	.05
597	Scott Medvin RC	.05
598	Hipolito Pena RC	.05
599	Jerald Clark RC	.05
600a	Checklist 578-BC26 (#635 is Kurt Schilling)	.10
600b	Checklist 578-BC26 (#635 is Curt Schilling)	.05
601	Carmelo Martinez	.05
602	Mike LaCoss	.05
603	Mike Devereaux	.05
604	Alex Madrid RC	.05
605	Gary Redus	.05
606	Lance Johnson	.05
607	Terry Clark RC	.05
608	Manny Trillo	.05
609	Scott Jordan RC	.05
610	Jay Howell	.05
611	Francisco Melendez RC	.05
612	Mike Boddicker	.05
613	Kevin Brown	.05
614	Dave Valle	.05
615	Tim Laudner	.05
616	Andy Nezelek RC	.05
617	Chuck Crim	.05
618	Jack Savage RC	.05
619	Adam Peterson RC	.05
620	Todd Stottlemyre	.05
621	Lance Blankenship RC	.05
622	Miguel Garcia RC	.05
623	Keith Miller	.05
624	Ricky Jordan RC	.05
625	Ernest Riles	.05
626	John Moses	.05
627	Nelson Liriano	.05
628	Mike Smithson	.05
629	Scott Sanderson	.05
630	Dale Mohorcic	.05
631	Marvin Freeman	.05
632	Mike Young	.05
633	Dennis Lamp	.05
634	Dante Bichette RC	.25
635	Curt Schilling RC	3.00
636	Scott May RC	.05
637	Mike Schooler RC	.05
638	Rick Leach	.05
639	Tom Lampkin RC	.05
640	Brian Meyer RC	.05
641	Brian Harper	.05
642	John Smoltz	.05
643	Jose Canseco (40/40)	.15
644	Bill Schroeder	.05
645	Edgar Martinez RC	.10
646	Dennis Cook RC	.05
647	Barry Jones	.05
648	Orel Hershiser (59 and Counting)	.05
649	Rod Nichols RC	.05
650	Jody Davis	.05
651	Bob Milacki RC	.05
652	Mike Jackson	.05
653	Derek Lilliquist RC	.05
654	Paul Mirabella	.05
655	Mike Diaz	.05
656	Jeff Musselman	.05
657	Jerry Reed	.05

#	Player	Price
658	Kevin Blankenship RC	.05
659	Wayne Tolleson	.05
660	Eric Hetzel RC	.05

Grand Slammers

Walt Weiss SS

One card from this 12-card set was included in each Donruss cello pack. The complete insert set was included in factory sets. The featured players all hit grand slams in 1988. The 2-1/2" x 3-1/2" cards feature full color action photos. Backs tell the story of the player's grand slam. As many as five border-color variations on the front of each card have been discovered, but the prices are not affected.

		NM/M
Complete Set (12):		2.00
Common Player:		.25
1	Jose Canseco	.35
2	Mike Marshall	.25
3	Walt Weiss	.25
4	Kevin McReynolds	.25
5	Mike Greenwell	.25
6	Dave Winfield	.50
7	Mark McGwire	1.50
8	Keith Hernandez	.25
9	Franklin Stubbs	.25
10	Danny Tartabull	.25
11	Jesse Barfield	.25
12	Ellis Burks	.25

MVP

Will Clark 1B — MVP

This set, numbered BC1-BC26, was randomly inserted in Donruss wax packs, but not included in factory sets or other card packs. Players highlighted were selected by Donruss, one player per team. MVP cards feature a variation of the design in the basic Donruss issue, with multi-color upper and lower borders and black side borders. The "MVP" designation in large, bright letters serves as a backdrop for the full-color player photo. The cards measure 2-1/2" x 3-1/2".

		NM/M
Complete Set (26):		2.00
Common Player:		.05
1	Kirby Puckett	.40
2	Mike Scott	.05
3	Joe Carter	.05
4	Orel Hershiser	.05
5	Jose Canseco	.25
6	Darryl Strawberry	.05
7	George Brett	.50
8	Andre Dawson	.20
9	Paul Molitor	.30
10	Andy Van Slyke	.30
11	Dave Winfield	.30
12	Kevin Gross	.05
13	Mike Greenwell	.05
14	Ozzie Smith	.40
15	Cal Ripken	1.00
16	Andres Galarraga	.05
17	Alan Trammell	.05
18	Kal Daniels	.05
19	Fred McGriff	.05
20	Tony Gwynn	.40
21	Wally Joyner	.05
22	Will Clark	.40
23	Ozzie Guillen	.05
24	Gerald Perry	.05
25	Alvin Davis	.05
26	Ruben Sierra	.05

All-Stars

Jose Canseco

For the fourth consecutive year Donruss featured a 64-card set with players from the 1988 All-Star Game. The card fronts include a red-to-gold fade or gold-to-red fade border and blue vertical side borders. The top border features the player's name and position along with the "Donruss '89" logo. Each full-color player photo is highlighted by a thin white line and includes a league logo in the lower right corner. Card backs reveal an orange-gold border and black and white printing. The player's ID and personal information is displayed with a gold star on both sides. The star in the left corner includes the card number, 1988 All-Star game statistics and run totals follow along with a career highlights feature surrounded by the team, All-Star Game MLB, MLBPA, and Leaf Inc. logos. The All-Stars were distributed in wax packages containing five All-Stars, one Pop-Up, and one three-piece Warren Spahn puzzle card.

		NM/M
Complete Set (64):		4.00
Common Player:		.10
Warren Spahn Puzzle:		.50
Wax Pack (5+1):		.30
Wax Box (48):		10.00
1	Mark McGwire	.75
2	Jose Canseco	.25
3	Paul Molitor	.40
4	Rickey Henderson	.40
5	Cal Ripken, Jr.	1.00
6	Dave Winfield	.40
7	Wade Boggs	.50
8	Frank Viola	.10
9	Terry Steinbach	.10
10	Tom Kelly	.10
11	George Brett	.65
12	Doyle Alexander	.10
13	Gary Gaetti	.10
14	Roger Clemens	.65
15	Mike Greenwell	.40
16	Dennis Eckersley	.40
17	Carney Lansford	.10
18	Mark Gubicza	.10
19	Tim Laudner	.10
20	Doug Jones	.10
21	Dan Plesac	.10
22	Dan Plesac	.10
23	Kirby Puckett	.50
24	Jeff Reardon	.10
25	Johnny Ray	.10
26	Jeff Russell	.10
27	Harold Reynolds	.10
28	Dave Stieb	.10
29	Kurt Stillwell	.10
30	Jose Canseco	.25
31	Terry Steinbach	.10
32	A.L. Checklist	.05
33	Will Clark	.10
34	Darryl Strawberry	.50
35	Ryne Sandberg	.50
36	Andre Dawson	.25
37	Ozzie Smith	.50
38	Vince Coleman	.10
39	Bobby Bonilla	.10
40	Dwight Gooden	.10
41	Gary Carter	.40
42	Whitey Herzog	.05
43	Shawon Dunston	.10
44	David Cone	.10
45	Andres Galarraga	.10
46	Mark Davis	.10
47	Barry Larkin	.10
48	Kevin Gross	.10
49	Vance Law	.10
50	Orel Hershiser	.10
51	Willie McGee	.10
52	Danny Jackson	.10
53	Rafael Palmeiro	.35
54	Bob Knepper	.10
55	Lance Parrish	.10
56	Greg Maddux	.50
57	Gerald Perry	.10
58	Bob Walk	.10
59	Chris Sabo	.10
60	Todd Worrell	.10
61	Andy Van Slyke	.10
62	Ozzie Smith	.50
63	Riverfront Stadium	.10
64	N.L. Checklist	.05

Baseball's Best

Mattingly 1B

For the second consecutive year, Donruss issued a "Baseball's Best" set in 1989 to highlight the game's top players. The special 336-card set was packaged in a special box and was sold at various retail chains nationwide following the conclusion of the 1989 baseball season. The cards are styled after the regular 1989 Donruss set with green borders and a glossy finish. The set included a Warren Spahn puzzle.

		NM/M
Unopened Set (336):		30.00
Complete Set (336):		25.00
Common Player:		.05
1	Don Mattingly	.75
2	Tom Glavine	.25
3	Bert Blyleven	.10
4	Andre Dawson	.25
5	Pete O'Brien	.05
6	Eric Davis	.05
7	George Brett	.75
8	Glenn Davis	.05
9	Ellis Burks	.05
10	Kirk Gibson	.05
11	Carlton Fisk	.50
12	Andres Galarraga	.05
13	Alan Trammell	.05
14	Dwight Gooden	.05
15	Paul Molitor	.50
16	Roger McDowell	.05
17	Doug Drabek	.05
18	Kent Hrbek	.05
19	Vince Coleman	.05
20	Steve Sax	.05
21	Roberto Alomar	.20
22	Carney Lansford	.05
23	Will Clark	.05
24	Alvin Davis	.05
25	Bobby Thigpen	.05
26	Ryne Sandberg	.60
27	Devon White	.05
28	Mike Greenwell	.05
29	Dale Murphy	.20
30	Jeff Ballard	.05
31	Kelly Gruber	.05
32	Julio Franco	.05
33	Bobby Bonilla	.25
34	Tim Wallach	.05
35	Lou Whitaker	.05
36	Jay Howell	.05
37	Greg Maddux	.60
38	Bill Doran	.05
39	Danny Tartabull	.05
40	Darryl Strawberry	.25
41	Ron Darling	.05
42	Tony Gwynn	.60
43	Mark McGwire	1.00
44	Ozzie Smith	.60
45	Andy Van Slyke	.05
46	Juan Berenguer	.05
47	Von Hayes	.05
48	Tony Fernandez	.05
49	Eric Plunk	.05
50	Ernest Riles	.05
51	Harold Reynolds	.05
52	Andy Hawkins	.05
53	Robin Yount	.50
54	Danny Jackson	.05
55	Nolan Ryan	1.50
56	Joe Carter	.05
57	Jose Canseco	.35
58	Jody Davis	.05
59	Lance Parrish	.05
60	Mitch Williams	.05
61	Brook Jacoby	.05
62	Tom Browning	.05
63	Kurt Stillwell	.05
64	Rafael Ramirez	.05
65	Roger Clemens	.75
66	Mike Scioscia	.05
67	Dave Gallagher	.05
68	Mark Langston	.05
69	Chet Lemon	.05
70	Kevin McReynolds	.05
71	Rob Deer	.05
72	Tommy Herr	.05
73	Barry Bonds	1.50
74	Frank Viola	.05
75	Pedro Guerrero	.05
76	Dave Righetti	.05
77	Bruce Hurst	.05
78	Rickey Henderson	.50
79	Robby Thompson	.05
80	Randy Johnson	6.00
81	Harold Baines	.05
82	Calvin Schiraldi	.05
83	Kirk McCaskill	.05
84	Lee Smith	.05
85	John Smoltz	1.00
86	Mickey Tettleton	.05
87	Jimmy Key	.05
88	Rafael Palmeiro	.45
89	Sid Bream	.05
90	Dennis Martinez	.05
91	Frank Tanana	.05
92	Eddie Murray	.50
93	Shawon Dunston	.05
94	Mike Scott	.05
95	Bret Saberhagen	.05
96	David Cone	.05
97	Kevin Elster	.05
98	Jack Clark	.05
99	Dave Stewart	.05
100	Jose Oquendo	.05
101	Jose Lind	.05
102	Gary Gaetti	.05
103	Ricky Jordan	.05
104	Fred McGriff	.05
105	Don Slaught	.05
106	Jose Uribe	.05
107	Jeffrey Leonard	.05
108	Lee Guetterman	.05
109	Chris Bosio	.05
110	Barry Larkin	.05
111	Ruben Sierra	.05
112	Greg Swindell	.05
113	Gary Sheffield	1.00
114	Lonnie Smith	.05
115	Chili Davis	.05
116	Damon Berryhill	.05
117	Tom Candiotti	.05
118	Kal Daniels	.05
119	Mark Gubicza	.05
120	Jim Deshaies	.05
121	Dwight Evans	.05
122	Mike Morgan	.05
123	Dan Pasqua	.05
124	Bryn Smith	.05
125	Doyle Alexander	.05
126	Howard Johnson	.05
127	Chuck Crim	.05
128	Darren Daulton	.05
129	Jeff Robinson	.05
130	Kirby Puckett	.60
131	Joe Magrane	.05
132	Jesse Barfield	.05
133	Mark Davis (Photo actually Dave Leiper)	.05
134	Dennis Eckersley	.45
135	Mike Krukow	.05
136	Jay Buhner	.05
137	Ozzie Guillen	.05
138	Rick Sutcliffe	.05
139	Wally Joyner	.05
140	Wade Boggs	.60
141	Jeff Treadway	.05
142	Cal Ripken	1.50
143	Dave Steib	.05
144	Pete Incaviglia	.05
145	Bob Walk	.05
146	Nelson Santovenia	.05
147	Mike Heath	.05
148	Willie Randolph	.05
149	Paul Kilgus	.05
150	Billy Hatcher	.05
151	Steve Farr	.05
152	Gregg Jefferies	.05
153	Randy Myers	.05
154	Garry Templeton	.05
155	Walt Weiss	.05
156	Terry Pendleton	.05
157	John Smiley	.05
158	Greg Gagne	.05
159	Lenny Dykstra	.05
160	Nelson Liriano	.05
161	Alvaro Espinoza	.05
162	Rick Reuschel	.05
163	Omar Vizquel	.05
164	Clay Parker	.05
165	Dan Plesac	.05
166	John Franco	.05
167	Scott Fletcher	.05
168	Cory Snyder	.05
169	Bo Jackson	.10
170	Tommy Gregg	.05
171	Jim Abbott	.05
172	Jerome Walton	.05
173	Doug Jones	.05
174	Todd Benzinger	.05
175	Frank White	.05
176	Craig Biggio	.50
177	John Dopson	.05
178	Alfredo Griffin	.05
179	Melido Perez	.05
180	Tim Burke	.05
181	Matt Nokes	.05
182	Gary Carter	.50
183	Ted Higuera	.05
184	Ken Howell	.05
185	Rey Quinones	.05
186	Wally Backman	.05
187	Tom Brunansky	.05
188	Steve Balboni	.05
189	Marvell Wynne	.05
190	Dave Henderson	.05
191	Don Robinson	.05
192	Ken Griffey Jr.	9.00
193	Ivan Calderon	.05
194	Mike Bielecki	.05
195	Johnny Ray	.05
196	Rob Murphy	.05
197	Andres Thomas	.05
198	Phil Bradley	.05
199	Junior Felix	.05
200	Jeff Russell	.05
201	Mike LaValliere	.05
202	Kevin Gross	.05
203	Keith Moreland	.05
204	Mike Marshall	.05
205	Dwight Smith	.05
206	Jim Clancy	.05
207	Kevin Seitzer	.05
208	Keith Hernandez	.05
209	Bob Ojeda	.05
210	Ed Whitson	.05
211	Tony Phillips	.05
212	Milt Thompson	.05
213	Randy Kramer	.05
214	Randy Bush	.05
215	Randy Ready	.05
216	Duane Ward	.05
217	Jimmy Jones	.05
218	Scott Garrelts	.05
219	Scott Bankhead	.05
220	Lance McCullers	.05
221	B.J. Surhoff	.05
222	Chris Sabo	.05
223	Steve Buechele	.05
224	Joel Skinner	.05
225	Orel Hershiser	.05
226	Derek Lilliquist	.05
227	Claudell Washington	.05
228	Lloyd McClendon	.05
229	Felix Fermin	.05
230	Paul O'Neill	.05
231	Charlie Leibrandt	.05
232	Dave Smith	.05
233	Bob Stanley	.05
234	Tim Belcher	.05
235	Eric King	.05
236	Spike Owen	.05
237	Mike Henneman	.05
238	Juan Samuel	.05
239	Greg Brock	.05
240	John Kruk	.05
241	Glenn Wilson	.05
242	Jeff Reardon	.05
243	Todd Worrell	.05
244	Dave LaPoint	.05
245	Walt Terrell	.05
246	Mike Moore	.05
247	Kelly Downs	.05
248	Dave Valle	.05
249	Ron Kittle	.05
250	Steve Wilson	.05
251	Dick Schofield	.05
252	Marty Barrett	.05
253	Dion James	.05
254	Bob Milacki	.05
255	Ernie Whitt	.05
256	Kevin Brown	.05
257	R.J. Reynolds	.05
258	Tim Raines	.05
259	Frank Williams	.05
260	Jose Gonzalez	.05
261	Mitch Webster	.05
262	Ken Caminiti	.05
263	Bob Boone	.05
264	Dave Magadan	.05
265	Rick Aguilera	.05
266	Chris James	.05
267	Bob Welch	.05
268	Ken Dayley	.05
269	Junior Ortiz	.05
270	Allan Anderson	.05
271	Steve Jeltz	.05
272	George Bell	.05
273	Roberto Kelly	.05
274	Brett Butler	.05
275	Mike Schooler	.05
276	Ken Phelps	.05
277	Glenn Braggs	.05
278	Jose Rijo	.05
279	Bobby Witt	.05
280	Jerry Browne	.05
281	Kevin Mitchell	.05
282	Craig Worthington	.05
283	Greg Minton	.05
284	Nick Esasky	.05
285	John Farrell	.05
286	Rick Mahler	.05
287	Tom Gordon	.05
288	Gerald Young	.05
289	Jody Reed	.05
290	Jeff Hamilton	.05
291	Gerald Perry	.05
292	Hubie Brooks	.05
293	Bo Diaz	.05
294	Terry Puhl	.05
295	Jim Gantner	.05
296	Jeff Parrett	.05
297	Mike Boddicker	.05
298	Dan Gladden	.05
299	Tony Pena	.05
300	Checklist	.05
301	Tom Henke	.05
302	Pascual Perez	.05
303	Steve Bedrosian	.05
304	Ken Hill	.05
305	Jerry Reuss	.05
306	Jim Eisenreich	.05
307	Jack Howell	.05
308	Rick Cerone	.05
309	Tim Leary	.05
310	Joe Orsulak	.05
311	Jim Dwyer	.05
312	Geno Petralli	.05
313	Rick Honeycutt	.05
314	Tom Foley	.05
315	Kenny Rogers	.05
316	Mike Flanagan	.05
317	Bryan Harvey	.05
318	Billy Ripken	.05
319	Jeff Montgomery	.05
320	Erik Hanson	.05
321	Brian Downing	.05
322	Gregg Olson	.05
323	Terry Steinbach	.05
324	Sammy Sosa	12.00
325	Gene Harris	.05
326	Mike Devereaux	.05
327	Dennis Cook	.05
328	David Wells	.05
329	Checklist	.05
330	Kirt Manwaring	.05
331	Jim Presley	.05
332	Checklist	.05
333	Chuck Finley	.05
334	Rob Dibble	.05
335	Cecil Espy	.05
336	Dave Parker	.05

Diamond King Supers

CHRIS SABO

Once again for 1989, collectors could acquire a 4-3/4" x 6-3/4" version of the Diamond King subset via a wrapper mail-in offer. Other than size, cards are identical to the DKs in the regular issue.

		NM/M
Complete Set (27):		5.00
Common Player:		.25
1	Mike Greenwell	.25
2	Bobby Bonilla	.25
3	Pete Incaviglia	.25
4	Chris Sabo	.25
5	Robin Yount	1.00
6	Tony Gwynn	1.50
7	Carlton Fisk	1.00
8	Cory Snyder	.25
9	David Cone	.25
10	Kevin Seitzer	.25
11	Rick Reuschel	.25
12	Johnny Ray	.25
13	Dave Schmidt	.25
14	Andres Galarraga	.25
15	Kirk Gibson	.25
16	Fred McGriff	.25
17	Mark Grace	.25
18	Jeff Robinson	.25
19	Vince Coleman	.25
20	Dave Henderson	.25
21	Harold Reynolds	.25
22	Gerald Perry	.25
23	Frank Viola	.25
24	Steve Bedrosian	.25
25	Glenn Davis	.25
26	Don Mattingly	2.00
27	Checklist	.05

Pop-Ups

DWIGHT GOODEN
METS - P

This set features the eighteen starters from the 1988 Major League All-Star game. The cards are designed with a perforated outline so each player can be popped up to stand upright. The flip side features a red, white, and blue "Cincinnati Reds All-Star Game" logo at the top, a league designation, and the player's name and position. The lower portion displays instructions for creating the base of the Pop-Up. The Pop-Ups were marketed in packs with five All-Star cards and Warren Spahn puzzle-piece cards.

	NM/M
Complete Set (20):	2.00
Common Player:	.10
Warren Spahn Puzzle:	.50
Wax Pack (5+1):	.30
Wax Box (48):	10.00
(1) Mark McGwire	.45
(2) Jose Canseco	.20
(3) Paul Molitor	.25
(4) Rickey Henderson	.25
(5) Cal Ripken, Jr.	.50
(6) Dave Winfield	.35
(7) Wade Boggs	.35
(8) Frank Viola	.10
(9) Terry Steinbach	.10
(10) Tom Kelly	.10
(11) Will Clark	.10
(12) Darryl Strawberry	.10
(13) Ryne Sandberg	.35
(14) Andre Dawson	.10
(15) Ozzie Smith	.35
(16) Vince Coleman	.10
(17) Bobby Bonilla	.10
(18) Dwight Gooden	.10
(19) Gary Carter	.25
(20) Whitey Herzog	.10

Rookies

Ramon Martinez P

For the fourth straight year, Donruss issued a 56-card "Rookies" set in 1989. As in previous years, the set is similar in design to the regular Donruss set, except for a new "The Rookies" logo and a green and black border.

	NM/M
Complete Set (56):	8.00
Common Player:	.05
1 Gary Sheffield	.75
2 Gregg Jefferies	.05
3 Ken Griffey Jr.	5.00
4 Tom Gordon	.05
5 Billy Spiers RC	.05
6 Deion Sanders RC	.50
7 Donn Pall RC	.05
8 Steve Carter RC	.05
9 Francisco Oliveras RC	.05
10 Steve Wilson RC	.05
11 Bob Geren RC	.05
12 Tony Castillo RC	.05
13 Kenny Rogers RC	.05
14 Carlos Martinez RC	.05

15	Edgar Martinez	.05
16	Jim Abbott RC	.05
17	Torey Lovullo RC	.05
18	Mark Carreon RC	.05
19	Geronimo Berroa	.05
20	Luis Medina	.05
21	Sandy Alomar, Jr.	.05
22	Bob Milacki	.05
23	Joe Girardi RC	.10
24	German Gonzalez	.05
25	Craig Worthington	.05
26	Jerome Walton RC	.05
27	Gary Wayne RC	.05
28	Tim Jones	.05
29	Dante Bichette	.05
30	Alexis Infante RC	.05
31	Ken Hill	.05
32	Dwight Smith RC	.05
33	Luis de los Santos	.05
34	Eric Yelding RC	.05
35	Gregg Olson	.05
36	Phil Stephenson RC	.05
37	Ken Patterson RC	.05
38	Rick Wrona RC	.05
39	Mike Brumley	.05
40	Cris Carpenter	.05
41	Jeff Brantley RC	.05
42	Ron Jones	.05
43	Randy Johnson	2.00
44	Kevin Brown	.05
45	Ramon Martinez	.05
46	Greg Harris	.05
47	Steve Finley	.05
48	Randy Kramer	.05
49	Erik Hanson	.05
50	Matt Merullo RC	.05
51	Mike Devereaux	.05
52	Clay Parker RC	.05
53	Omar Vizquel RC	.05
54	Derek Lilliquist	.05
55	Junior Felix RC	.05
56	Checklist	.05

Traded

Rafael Palmeiro OF
RANGERS

Donruss issued its first "Traded" set in 1989, releasing a 56-card boxed set designed in the same style as the regular 1989 Donruss set. The set included a Stan Musial puzzle card and a checklist.

	NM/M
Complete Set (56):	2.00
Common Player:	.05
1 Jeffrey Leonard	.05
2 Jack Clark	.05
3 Kevin Gross	.05
4 Tommy Herr	.05
5 Bob Boone	.05
6 Rafael Palmeiro	.30
7 John Dopson	.05
8 Willie Randolph	.05
9 Chris Brown	.05
10 Wally Backman	.05
11 Steve Ontiveros	.05
12 Eddie Murray	.45
13 Lance McCullers	.05
14 Spike Owen	.05
15 Rob Murphy	.05
16 Pete O'Brien	.05
17 Ken Williams	.05
18 Nick Esasky	.05
19 Nolan Ryan	1.50
20 Brian Holton	.05
21 Mike Moore	.05
22 Joel Skinner	.05
23 Steve Sax	.05
24 Rick Mahler	.05
25 Mike Aldrete	.05
26 Jesse Orosco	.05
27 Dave LaPoint	.05
28 Walt Terrell	.05
29 Eddie Williams	.05
30 Mike Devereaux	.05
31 Julio Franco	.05
32 Jim Clancy	.05
33 Felix Fermin	.05
34 Curtis Wilkerson	.05
35 Bert Blyleven	.05
36 Mel Hall	.05
37 Eric King	.05
38 Mitch Williams	.05
39 Jamie Moyer	.05
40 Rick Rhoden	.05
41 Phil Bradley	.05
42 Paul Kilgus	.05

43	Milt Thompson	.05
44	Jerry Browne	.05
45	Bruce Hurst	.05
46	Claudell Washington	.05
47	Todd Benzinger	.05
48	Steve Balboni	.05
49	Oddibe McDowell	.05
50	Charles Hudson	.05
51	Ron Kittle	.05
52	Andy Hawkins	.05
53	Tom Brookens	.05
54	Tom Niedenfuer	.05
55	Jeff Parrett	.05
56	Checklist	.05

1990 Donruss Previews

1990 PREVIEW CARDS
No. 10 of 12
JEROME WALTON
OUTFIELDER
CAREER HIGHLIGHTS

To introduce its 1990 baseball issue, Donruss sent two preview cards from a set of 12 to each member of its dealers' network. Though the photos are different than those used on the issued versions, the front format was the same. Backs are printed in black on white and contain career highlights, but no stats. Issued at the dawn of the "promo card" craze, and succeeding the relatively valueless sample sheets used by most companies in earlier years, little value was attached to these preview cards initially. Today they are among the scarcest of the early-1990s promos.

	NM/M
Complete Set (12):	85.00
Common Player:	3.00
1 Todd Zeile	3.00
2 Ben McDonald	3.00
3 Bo Jackson	7.50
4 Will Clark	3.00
5 Dave Stewart	3.00
6 Kevin Mitchell	3.00
7 Nolan Ryan	50.00
8 Howard Johnson	3.00
9 Tony Gwynn	25.00
10 Jerome Walton	3.00
11 Wade Boggs	25.00
12 Kirby Puckett	25.00

1990 Donruss

Donruss marked its 10th anniversary in the baseball card hobby with a 715-card set in 1990, up from previous 660-card sets. The standard-size cards feature bright red borders with the player's name in script at the top. The set includes 26 "Diamond Kings" (DK) in the checklist, 20 "Rated Rookies" (RR) and a Carl Yastrzemski puzzle. Each All-Star card back has two variations. The more common has the stats box headed "All-Star Performance." Slightly scarcer versions say "Recent Major League Performance", and are worth about twice the value of the correct version.

	NM/M
Unopened Factory Set (716):	9.00
Complete Set (716):	7.50
Common Player:	.05

Carl Yastrzemski Puzzle:	1.00		
Wax Pack (16):	.50		
Wax Box (36):	10.00		
Rack Pack (48):	1.00		
Blister Rack (78):	1.50		
1	Bo Jackson/DK	.05	
2	Steve Sax/DK	.05	
3a	Ruben Sierra/DK		
	(No vertical black line at top-right on back.)	.25	
3b	Ruben Sierra/DK		
	(Vertical line at top-right on back.)	.05	
4	Ken Griffey Jr./DK	.65	
5	Mickey Tettleton/DK	.05	
6	Dave Stewart/DK	.05	
7	Jim Deshaies/DK	.05	
8	John Smoltz/DK	.05	
9	Mike Bielecki/DK	.05	
10a	Brian Downing/DK		
	(Reversed negative.)	.25	
10b	Brian Downing/DK		
	(Corrected)	.05	
11	Kevin Mitchell/DK	.05	
12	Kelly Gruber/DK	.05	
13	Joe Magrane/DK	.05	
14	John Franco/DK	.05	
15	Ozzie Guillen/DK	.05	
16	Lou Whitaker/DK	.05	
17	John Smiley/DK	.05	
18	Howard Johnson/DK	.05	
19	Willie Randolph/DK	.05	
20	Chris Bosio/DK	.05	
21	Tommy Herr/DK	.05	
22	Dan Gladden/DK	.05	
23	Ellis Burks/DK	.05	
24	Pete O'Brien/DK	.05	
25	Bryn Smith/DK	.05	
26	Ed Whitson/DK	.05	
27	Checklist 1-27	.05	
28	Robin Ventura/RR	.05	
29	Todd Zeile/RR RC	.15	
30	Sandy Alomar, Jr./RR	.05	
31	Kent Mercker/RR RC	.05	
32	Ben McDonald/RR RC	.25	
33a	Juan Gonzalez/RR (Reversed negative.) RC	2.00	
33b	Juan Gonzalez/RR RC (Corrected)	1.50	
34	Eric Anthony/RR RC	.05	
35	Mike Fetter/RRs RC	.05	
36	Marquis Grissom/RR RC	.50	
37	Greg Vaughn/RR RC	.25	
38	Brian Dubois/RR RC	.05	
39	Steve Avery/RR RC	.10	
40	Mark Gardner/RR RC	.05	
41	Andy Benes/RR	.05	
42	Delino DeShields/RR RC	.15	
43	Scott Coolbaugh/RR RC	.05	
44	Pat Combs/RR RC	.10	
45	Alex Sanchez/RR RC	.05	
46	Kelly Mann/RR RC	.05	
47	Julio Machado/RR RC	.05	
48	Pete Incaviglia	.05	
49	Shawon Dunston	.05	
50	Jeff Treadway	.05	
51	Jeff Ballard	.05	
52	Claudell Washington	.05	
53	Juan Samuel	.05	
54	John Smiley	.05	
55	Rob Deer	.05	
56	Geno Petralli	.05	
57	Chris Bosio	.05	
58	Carlton Fisk	.40	
59	Kirt Manwaring	.05	
60	Chet Lemon	.05	
61	Bo Jackson	.05	
62	Doyle Alexander	.05	
63	Pedro Guerrero	.05	
64	Allan Anderson	.05	
65	Greg Harris	.05	
66	Mike Greenwell	.05	
67	Walt Weiss	.05	
68	Wade Boggs	.50	
69	Jim Clancy	.05	
70	Junior Felix RC	.05	
71	Barry Larkin	.25	
72	Dave LaPoint	.05	
73	Joel Skinner	.05	
74	Jesse Barfield	.05	
75	Tommy Herr	.05	
76	Ricky Jordan	.05	
77	Eddie Murray	.40	
78	Steve Sax	.05	
79	Tim Belcher	.05	
80	Danny Jackson	.05	
81	Kent Hrbek	.05	
82	Milt Thompson	.05	
83	Brook Jacoby	.05	
84	Mike Marshall	.05	
85	Kevin Seitzer	.05	
86	Tony Gwynn	.50	
87	Dave Steib	.05	
88	Dave Smith	.05	
89	Bret Saberhagen	.05	
90	Alan Trammell	.05	

91	Tony Phillips	.05	
92	Doug Drabek	.05	
93	Jeffrey Leonard	.05	
94	Wally Joyner	.05	
95	Carney Lansford	.05	
96	Cal Ripken, Jr.	1.00	
97	Andres Galarraga	.05	
98	Kevin Mitchell	.05	
99	Howard Johnson	.05	
100a	Checklist 28-129	.05	
100b	Checklist 28-125	.05	
101	Melido Perez	.05	
102	Spike Owen	.05	
103	Paul Molitor	.40	
104	Geronimo Berroa	.05	
105	Ryne Sandberg	.50	
106	Bryn Smith	.05	
107	Steve Buechele	.05	
108	Jim Abbott	.05	
109	Alvin Davis	.05	
110	Lee Smith	.05	
111	Roberto Alomar	.20	
112	Rick Reuschel	.05	
113a	Kelly Gruber (Born 2/22)	.05	
113b	Kelly Gruber (Born 2/26)	.20	
114	Joe Carter	.05	
115	Jose Rijo	.05	
116	Greg Minton	.05	
117	Bob Ojeda	.05	
118	Glenn Davis	.05	
119	Jeff Reardon	.05	
120	Kurt Stillwell	.05	
121	John Smoltz	.05	
122	Dwight Evans	.05	
123	Eric Yelding	.05	
124	John Franco	.05	
125	Jose Canseco	.20	
126	Barry Bonds	1.00	
127	Lee Guetterman	.05	
128	Jack Clark	.05	
129	Dave Valle	.05	
130	Hubie Brooks	.05	
131	Ernest Riles	.05	
132	Mike Morgan	.05	
133	Steve Jeltz	.05	
134	Jeff Robinson	.05	
135	Ozzie Guillen	.05	
136	Chili Davis	.05	
137	Mitch Webster	.05	
138	Jerry Browne	.05	
139	Bo Diaz	.05	
140	Robby Thompson	.05	
141	Craig Worthington	.05	
142	Julio Franco	.05	
143	Brian Holman	.05	
144	George Brett	.60	
145	Tom Glavine	.20	
146	Robin Yount	.40	
147	Gary Carter	.40	
148	Ron Kittle	.05	
149	Tony Fernandez	.05	
150	Dave Stewart	.05	
151	Gary Gaetti	.05	
152	Kevin Elster	.05	
153	Gerald Perry	.05	
154	Jesse Orosco	.05	
155	Wally Backman	.05	
156	Dennis Martinez	.05	
157	Rick Sutcliffe	.05	
158	Greg Maddux	.50	
159	Andy Hawkins	.05	
160	John Kruk	.05	
161	Jose Oquendo	.05	
162	John Dopson	.05	
163	Joe Magrane	.05	
164	Billy Ripken	.05	
165	Fred Manrique	.05	
166	Nolan Ryan	1.00	
167	Damon Berryhill	.05	
168	Dale Murphy	.20	
169	Mickey Tettleton	.05	
170a	Kirk McCaskill (Born 4/19)	.05	
170b	Kirk McCaskill (Born 4/9)	.10	
171	Dwight Gooden	.05	
172	Jose Lind	.05	
173	B.J. Surhoff	.05	
174	Ruben Sierra	.05	
175	Dan Plesac	.05	
176	Dan Pasqua	.05	
177	Kelly Downs	.05	
178	Matt Nokes	.05	
179	Luis Aquino	.05	
180	Frank Tanana	.05	
181	Tony Pena	.05	
182	Dan Gladden	.05	
183	Bruce Hurst	.05	
184	Roger Clemens	.60	
185	Mark McGwire	.75	
186	Rob Murphy	.05	
187	Jim Deshaies	.05	
188	Fred McGriff	.05	
189	Rob Dibble	.05	
190	Don Mattingly	.60	
191	Felix Fermin	.05	
192	Roberto Kelly	.05	
193	Dennis Cook	.05	
194	Darren Daulton	.05	
195	Alfredo Griffin	.05	
196	Eric Plunk	.05	
197	Orel Hershiser	.05	
198	Paul O'Neill	.05	
199	Randy Bush	.05	
200a	Checklist 130-231	.05	
200b	Checklist 126-223	.05	

201	Ozzie Smith	.50	
202	Pete O'Brien	.05	
203	Jay Howell	.05	
204	Mark Gubicza	.05	
205	Ed Whitson	.05	
206	George Bell	.05	
207	Mike Scott	.05	
208	Charlie Leibrandt	.05	
209	Mike Heath	.05	
210	Dennis Eckersley	.35	
211	Mike LaValliere	.05	
212	Darnell Coles	.05	
213	Lance Parrish	.05	
214	Mike Moore	.05	
215	Steve Finley RC	.20	
216	Tim Raines	.05	
217a	Scott Garrelts (Born 10/20)	.05	
217b	Scott Garrelts (Born 10/30)	.10	
218	Kevin McReynolds	.05	
219	Dave Gallagher	.05	
220	Tim Wallach	.05	
221	Chuck Crim	.05	
222	Lonnie Smith	.05	
223	Andre Dawson	.20	
224	Nelson Santovenia	.05	
225	Rafael Palmeiro	.35	
226	Devon White	.05	
227	Harold Reynolds	.05	
228	Ellis Burks	.05	
229	Mark Parent	.05	
230	Will Clark	.05	
231	Jimmy Key	.05	
232	John Farrell	.05	
233	Eric Davis	.05	
234	Johnny Ray	.05	
235	Darryl Strawberry	.05	
236	Bill Doran	.05	
237	Greg Gagne	.05	
238	Jim Eisenreich	.05	
239	Tommy Gregg	.05	
240	Marty Barrett	.05	
241	Rafael Ramirez	.05	
242	Chris Sabo	.05	
243	Dave Henderson	.05	
244	Andy Van Slyke	.05	
245	Alvaro Espinoza	.05	
246	Garry Templeton	.05	
247	Gene Harris	.05	
248	Kevin Gross	.05	
249	Brett Butler	.05	
250	Willie Randolph	.05	
251	Roger McDowell	.05	
252	Rafael Belliard	.05	
253	Steve Rosenberg	.05	
254	Jack Howell	.05	
255	Marvell Wynne	.05	
256	Tom Candiotti	.05	
257	Todd Benzinger	.05	
258	Don Robinson	.05	
259	Phil Bradley	.05	
260	Cecil Espy	.05	
261	Scott Bankhead	.05	
262	Frank White	.05	
263	Andres Thomas	.05	
264	Glenn Braggs	.05	
265	David Cone	.05	
266	Bobby Thigpen	.05	
267	Nelson Liriano	.05	
268	Terry Steinbach	.05	
269	Kirby Puckett	.50	
270	Gregg Jefferies	.05	
271	Jeff Blauser	.05	
272	Cory Snyder	.05	
273	Roy Smith	.05	
274	Tom Foley	.05	
275	Mitch Williams	.05	
276	Paul Kilgus	.05	
277	Don Slaught	.05	
278	Von Hayes	.05	
279	Vince Coleman	.05	
280	Mike Boddicker	.05	
281	Ken Dayley	.05	
282	Mike Devereaux	.05	
283	Kenny Rogers RC	.05	
284	Jeff Russell	.05	
285	Jerome Walton RC	.10	
286	Derek Lilliquist	.05	
287	Joe Orsulak	.05	
288	Dick Schofield	.05	
289	Ron Darling	.05	
290	Bobby Bonilla	.05	
291	Jim Gantner	.05	
292	Bobby Witt	.05	
293	Greg Brock	.05	
294	Ivan Calderon	.05	
295	Steve Bedrosian	.05	
296	Mike Henneman	.05	
297	Tom Gordon	.05	
298	Lou Whitaker	.05	
299	Terry Pendleton	.05	
300a	Checklist 232-333	.05	
300b	Checklist 224-321	.05	
301	Juan Berenguer	.05	
302	Mark Davis	.05	
303	Nick Esasky	.05	
304	Rickey Henderson	.40	
305	Rick Cerone	.05	
306	Craig Biggio	.05	
307	Duane Ward	.05	
308	Tom Browning	.05	
309	Walt Terrell	.05	
310	Greg Swindell	.05	
311	Dave Righetti	.05	
312	Mike Maddux	.05	
313	Len Dykstra	.05	
314	Jose Gonzalez	.05	

ABBREVIATIONS

DK - Diamond King
RR - Rated Rookie

315 Steve Balboni .05
316 Mike Scioscia .05
317 Ron Oester .05
318 Gary Wayne RC .05
319 Todd Worrell .05
320 Doug Jones .05
321 Jeff Hamilton .05
322 Danny Tartabull .05
323 Chris James .05
324 Mike Flanagan .05
325 Gerald Young .05
326 Bob Boone .05
327 Frank Williams .05
328 Dave Parker .05
329 Sid Bream .05
330 Mike Schooler .05
331 Bert Blyleven .10
332 Bob Welch .05
333 Bob Milacki .05
334 Tim Burke .05
335 Jose Uribe .05
336 Randy Myers .05
337 Eric King .05
338 Mark Langston .05
339 Ted Higuera .05
340 Oddibe McDowell .05
341 Lloyd McClendon .05
342 Pascual Perez .05
343 Kevin Brown .05
344 Chuck Finley .05
345 Erik Hanson .05
346 Rich Gedman .05
347 Bip Roberts .05
348 Matt Williams .05
349 Tom Henke .05
350 Brad Komminsk .05
351 Jeff Reed .05
352 Brian Downing .05
353 Frank Viola .05
354 Terry Puhl .05
355 Brian Harper .05
356 Steve Farr .05
357 Joe Boever .05
358 Danny Heep .05
359 Larry Andersen .05
360 Rolando Roomes .05
361 Mike Gallego .05
362 Bob Kipper .05
363 Clay Parker .05
364 Mike Pagliarulo .05
365 Ken Griffey Jr. .65
366 Rex Hudler .05
367 Pat Sheridan .05
368a Kirk Gibson (May 25 birthdate.) .05
368b Kirk Gibson (May 28 birthdate.) .05
369 Jeff Parrett .05
370 Bob Walk .05
371 Ken Patterson .05
372 Bryan Harvey .05
373 Mike Bielecki .05
374 Tom Magrann RC .05
375 Rick Mahler .05
376 Craig Lefferts .05
377 Gregg Olson .05
378 Jamie Moyer .05
379 Randy Johnson .40
380 Jeff Montgomery .05
381 Marty Clary .05
382 Bill Spiers RC .05
383 Dave Magadan .05
384 Greg Hibbard RC .05
385 Ernie Whitt .05
386 Rick Honeycutt .05
387 Dave West .05
388 Keith Hernandez .05
389 Jose Alvarez .05
390 Albert Belle .20
391 Rick Aguilera .05
392 Mike Fitzgerald .05
393 Dwight Smith RC .05
394 Steve Wilson RC .05
395 Bob Geren RC .05
396 Randy Ready .05
397 Ken Hill .05
398 Jody Reed .05
399 Tom Brunansky .05
400a Checklist 334-435 .05
400b Checklist 322-419 .05
401 Rene Gonzales .05
402 Harold Baines .05
403 Cecilio Guante .05
404 Joe Girardi .05
405a Sergio Valdez RC (Black line crosses S in Sergio.) .10
405b Sergio Valdez (Corrected) .05
406 Mark Williamson .05
407 Glenn Hoffman .05
408 Jeff Innis RC .05
409 Randy Kramer .05
410 Charlie O'Brien RC .05
411 Charlie Hough .05
412 Gus Polidor .05
413 Ron Karkovice .05
414 Trevor Wilson RC .05
415 Kevin Ritz RC .05
416 Gary Thurman .05
417 Jeff Robinson .05
418 Scott Terry .05
419 Tim Laudner .05
420 Dennis Rasmussen .05
421 Luis Rivera .05
422 Jim Corsi RC .05
423 Dennis Lamp .05
424 Ken Caminiti .05

425 David Wells .05
426 Norm Charlton .05
427 Deion Sanders .05
428 Dion James .05
429 Chuck Cary .05
430 Ken Howell .05
431 Steve Lake .05
432 Kal Daniels .05
433 Lance McCullers .05
434 Lenny Harris RC .05
435 Scott Scudder RC .05
436 Gene Larkin .05
437 Dan Quisenberry .05
438 Steve Olin RC .05
439 Mickey Hatcher .05
440 Willie Wilson .05
441 Mark Grant .05
442 Mookie Wilson .05
443 Alex Trevino .05
444 Pat Tabler .05
445 Dave Bergman .05
446 Todd Burns .05
447 R.J. Reynolds .05
448 Jay Buhner .05
449 Lee Stevens RC .05
450 Ron Hassey .05
451 Bob Melvin .05
452 Dave Martinez .05
453 Greg Litton RC .05
454 Mark Carreon .05
455 Scott Fletcher .05
456 Otis Nixon .05
457 Tony Fossas RC .05
458 John Russell .05
459 Paul Assenmacher .05
460 Zane Smith .05
461 Jack Daugherty RC .05
462 Rich Monteleone RC .05
463 Greg Briley RC .05
464 Mike Smithson .05
465 Benito Santiago .05
466 Jeff Brantley RC .05
467 Jose Nunez .05
468 Scott Bailes .05
469 Ken Griffey .05
470 Bob McClure .05
471 Mackey Sasser .05
472 Glenn Wilson .05
473 Kevin Tapani RC .10
474 Bill Buckner .05
475 Ron Gant .05
476 Kevin Romine RC .05
477 Juan Agosto .05
478 Herm Winningham .05
479 Storm Davis .05
480 Jeff King RC .05
481 Kevin Mmahat RC .05
482 Carmelo Martinez .05
483 Omar Vizquel .05
484 Jim Dwyer .05
485 Bob Knepper .05
486 Dave Anderson .05
487 Ron Jones .05
488 Jay Bell .05
489 Sammy Sosa RC 3.00
490 Kent Anderson RC .05
491 Domingo Ramos .05
492 Dave Clark .05
493 Tim Birtsas .05
494 Ken Oberkfell .05
495 Larry Sheets .05
496 Jeff Kunkel .05
497 Jim Presley .05
498 Mike Macfarlane .05
499 Pete Smith .05
500a Checklist 436-537 .05
500b Checklist 420-517 .05
501 Gary Sheffield .20
502 Terry Bross RC .05
503 Jerry Kutzler RC .05
504 Lloyd Moseby .05
505 Curt Young .05
506 Al Newman .05
507 Keith Miller .05
508 Mike Stanton RC .20
509 Rich Yett .05
510 Tim Drummond RC .05
511 Joe Hesketh .05
512 Rick Wrona RC .05
513 Luis Salazar .05
514 Hal Morris .05
515 Terry Mulholland .05
516 John Morris .05
517 Carlos Quintana .05
518 Frank DiPino .05
519 Randy Milligan .05
520 Chad Kreuter .05
521 Mike Jeffcoat .05
522 Mike Harkey .05
523a Andy Nezelek (Born 1985.) .05
523b Andy Nezelek (Born 1965.) .05
524 Dave Schmidt .05
525 Tony Armas .05
526 Barry Lyons .05
527 Rick Reed RC .05
528 Jerry Reuss .05
529 Dean Palmer RC .10
530 Jeff Peterek RC .05
531 Carlos Martinez RC .05
532 Atlee Hammaker .05
533 Mike Brumley .05
534 Terry Leach .05
535 Doug Strange RC .05
536 Jose DeLeon .05
537 Shane Rawley .05
538 Joey Cora RC .05

539 Eric Hetzel .05
540 Gene Nelson .05
541 Wes Gardner .05
542 Mark Portugal .05
543 Al Leiter .05
544 Jack Armstrong .05
545 Greg Cadaret .05
546 Rod Nichols .05
547 Luis Polonia .05
548 Charlie Hayes .05
549 Dickie Thon .05
550 Tim Crews .05
551 Dave Winfield .40
552 Mike Davis .05
553 Ron Robinson .05
554 Carmen Castillo .05
555 John Costello .05
556 Bud Black .05
557 Rick Dempsey .05
558 Jim Acker .05
559 Eric Show .05
560 Pat Borders .05
561 Danny Darwin .05
562 Rick Luecken RC .05
563 Edwin Nunez .05
564 Felix Jose .05
565 John Cangelosi .05
566 Billy Swift .05
567 Bill Schroeder .05
568 Stan Javier .05
569 Jim Traber .05
570 Wallace Johnson .05
571 Donell Nixon .05
572 Sid Fernandez .05
573 Lance Johnson .05
574 Andy McGaffigan .05
575 Mark Knudson .05
576 Tommy Greene RC .05
577 Mark Grace .05
578 Larry Walker RC 1.00
579 Mike Stanley .05
580 Mike Witt .05
581 Scott Bradley .05
582 Greg Harris .05
583a Kevin Hickey (Black stripe over top of "K" vertical stroke.) .05
583b Kevin Hickey (Black stripe under "K.") .05
584 Lee Mazzilli .05
585 Jeff Pico .05
586 Joe Oliver RC .05
587 Willie Fraser .05
588 Puzzle card (Carl Yastrzemski) .05
589 Kevin Bass .05
590 John Moses .05
591 Tom Pagnozzi .05
592 Tony Castillo RC .05
593 Jerald Clark .05
594 Dan Schatzeder .05
595 Luis Quinones .05
596 Pete Harnisch .05
597 Gary Redus .05
598 Mel Hall .05
599 Rick Schu .05
600a Checklist 538-639 .05
600b Checklist 518-617 .05
601 Mike Kingery .05
602 Terry Kennedy .05
603 Mike Sharperson .05
604 Don Carman .05
605 Jim Gott .05
606 Donn Pall .05
607 Rance Mulliniks .05
608 Curt Wilkerson .05
609 Mike Felder .05
610 Guillermo Hernandez .05
611 Candy Maldonado .05
612 Mark Thurmond .05
613 Rick Leach .05
614 Jerry Reed .05
615 Franklin Stubbs .05
616 Billy Hatcher .05
617 Don August .05
618 Tim Teufel .05
619 Shawn Hillegas .05
620 Manny Lee .05
621 Gary Ward .05
622 Mark Guthrie RC .05
623 Jeff Musselman .05
624 Mark Lemke .05
625 Fernando Valenzuela .05
626 Paul Sorrento RC .05
627 Glenallen Hill .05
628 Les Lancaster .05
629 Vance Law .05
630 Randy Velarde RC .05
631 Todd Frohwirth .05
632 Willie McGee .05
633 Oil Can Boyd .05
634 Cris Carpenter .05
635 Brian Holton .05
636 Tracy Jones .05
637 Terry Steinbach/AS .05
638 Brady Anderson .05
639a Jack Morris (Black line crosses J of Jack.) .10
639b Jack Morris (Corrected) .05

640 Jaime Navarro RC .05
641 Darrin Jackson .05
642 Mike Dyer RC .05
643 Mike Schmidt .60
644 Henry Cotto .05
645 John Cerutti .05
646 Francisco Cabrera RC .05
647 Scott Sanderson .05
648 Brian Meyer .05
649 Ray Searage .05
650 Bo Jackson/AS .15
651 Steve Lyons .05
652 Mike LaCoss .05
653 Ted Power .05
654 Howard Johnson/AS .05
655 Mauro Gozzo RC .05
656 Mike Blowers RC .05
657 Paul Gibson .05
658 Neal Heaton .05
659a Nolan Ryan 5,000 K's (King of Kings (#665) back.) 1.50
659b Nolan Ryan 5,000 K's (Correct back.) .60
660a Harold Baines/AS (Black line through star on front, Recent Major League Performance on back.) .25
660b Harold Baines/AS (Black line through star on front, All-Star Game Performance on back.) .25
660c Harold Baines/AS (Black line behind star on front, Recent Major League Performance on back.) .25
660d Harold Baines/AS (Black line behind star on front, All-Star Game Performance on back.) .10
661 Gary Pettis .05
662 Clint Zavaras RC .05
663 Rick Reuschel/AS .05
664 Alejandro Pena .05
665a Nolan Ryan (King of Kings) 5,000 K's (#659 back.) 1.50
665b Nolan Ryan (King of Kings) (Correct back.) 1.00
665c Nolan Ryan (King of Kings) (No number on back.) 1.00
666 Ricky Horton .05
667 Curt Schilling .05
668 Bill Landrum RC .05
669 Todd Stottlemyre .05
670 Tim Leary .05
671 John Wetteland RC .25
672 Calvin Schiraldi .05
673 Ruben Sierra/AS .05
674 Pedro Guerrero/AS .05
675 Ken Phelps .05
676 Cal Ripken/AS .50
677 Denny Walling .05
678 Goose Gossage .05
679 Gary Mielke RC .05
680 Bill Bathe .05
681 Tom Lawless .05
682 Xavier Hernandez RC .05
683 Kirby Puckett/AS .25
684 Mariano Duncan .05
685 Ramon Martinez .05
686 Tim Jones .05
687 Tim Filer .05
688 Steve Lombardozzi .05
689 Bernie Williams RC 1.00
690 Chip Hale RC .05
691 Beau Allred RC .05
692 Ryne Sandberg/AS .05
693 Jeff Huson RC .05
694 Curt Ford .05
695 Eric Davis/AS .05
696 Scott Lusader .05
697 Mark McGwire/AS .40
698 Steve Cummings RC .05
699 George Canale RC .05
700a Checklist 640-715/ BC1-BC26 .05
700b Checklist 640-716/ BC1-BC26 .05
700c Checklist 618-716 .05
701 Julio Franco/AS .05
702 Dave Johnson RC .05
703 Dave Stewart/AS .05
704 Dave Justice RC .50
705 Tony Gwynn/AS .25
706 Greg Myers .05
707 Will Clark/AS .05
708 Benito Santiago/AS .05
709 Larry McWilliams .05
710 Ozzie Smith/AS .05
711 John Olerud RC .50
712 Wade Boggs/AS .25
713 Gary Eave RC .05
714 Bob Tewksbury .05
715 Kevin Mitchell/AS .05
716 A. Bartlett Giamatti .25

Grand Slammers

For the second consecutive year Donruss produced a set in honor of players who hit grand slams in the previous season. The cards are styled after the 1990 Donruss regular issue. The cards were inserted into 1990 Donruss factory sets, and one card per cello pack. Each card can be found

ABBREVIATIONS

AS - All-Star
DK - Diamond King
RR - Rated Rookie

1990 Donruss Aqueous Test

Little is known about this mystery issue which few hob-

byists had ever heard of prior to 1999. The cards appear in all major respects to be regular 1990 Donruss cards, but on back have the words "AQUE-OUS TEST" printed. The test cards also lack the period after "INC" in the copyright line at upper-right. Approximately 2,000-2,500 cards in total are known, with only part of the '90D checklist represented in the test issue. As few as one specimen each are known for some cards, while a half-dozen or more of others are recorded. Because of limited supply, prices can be volatile depending on the activity of single-player specialist collectors at any given time. It is possible the checklist here is not complete. The cards may have been produced to test a semi-gloss coating known in the printing trade as aqueous.

		NM/M
Complete Set (12):		2.00
Common Player:		.10
1	Matt Williams	.10
2	Jeffrey Leonard	.10
3	Chris James	.10
4	Mark McGwire	1.50
5	Dwight Evans	.10
6	Will Clark	.10
7	Mike Scioscia	.10
8	Todd Benzinger	.10
9	Fred McGriff	.10
10	Kevin Bass	.10
11	Jack Clark	.10
12	Bo Jackson	.25

MVP

This special 26-card set includes one player from each Major League team. Numbered BC-1 (the "BC" stands for "Bonus Card") through BC-26, the cards from this set were randomly packed in 1990 Donruss wax packs and were not available in factory sets or other types of packaging. The red-bordered cards are similar in design to the regular 1990 Donruss set, except the player photos are set against a special background made up of the "MVP" logo.

		NM/M
Complete Set (26):		1.25
Common Player:		.10
1	Bo Jackson	.20
2	Howard Johnson	.10
3	Dave Stewart	.10
4	Tony Gwynn	.35
5	Orel Hershiser	.10
6	Pedro Guerrero	.10
7	Tim Raines	.10
8	Kirby Puckett	.35
9	Alvin Davis	.10
10	Ryne Sandberg	.35
11	Kevin Mitchell	.10
12a	John Smoltz (Photo of Tom Glavine.)	1.50
12b	John Smoltz (Corrected)	.30
13	George Bell	.10
14	Julio Franco	.10
15	Paul Molitor	.25
16	Bobby Bonilla	.10
17	Mike Greenwell	.10
18	Cal Ripken	.50
19	Carlton Fisk	.25
20	Chili Davis	.10
21	Glenn Davis	.10
22	Steve Sax	.10
23	Eric Davis	.10
24	Greg Swindell	.10
25	Von Hayes	.10
26	Alan Trammell	.10

1990 Donruss Aqueous Test

		NM/M
Common Player:		5.00
1	Bo Jackson/DK	17.50
3	Ruben Sierra/DK	5.00
6	Dave Stewart/DK	6.50
8	Mike Bielecki/DK	5.00
9	Mike Bielecki/DK	5.00
16	Lou Whitaker/DK	5.00
18	Howard Johnson/DK	5.00
22	Dan Gladden/DK	5.00
24	Pete O'Brien/DK	5.00
28	Robin Ventura/RR	15.00
29	Todd Zeile/RR	15.00
30	Sandy Alomar Jr./RR	15.00
31	Kent Mercker/RR	5.00
32	Ben McDonald/RR	7.50
33	Juan Gonzalez/RR (Reversed negatives.)	75.00
34	Eric Anthony/RR	5.00
35	Mike Fetters/RR	5.00
48	Pete Incaviglia	5.00
51	Jeff Ballard	5.00
52	Claudell Washington	5.00
55	Rob Deer	5.00
56	Geno Petralli	5.00
59	Chris Bosio	5.00
60	Chet Lemon	5.00
61	Bo Jackson	25.00
63	Pedro Guerrero	5.00
64	Allan Anderson	5.00
65	Greg Harris	5.00
66	Mike Greenwell	5.00
68	Wade Boggs	60.00
70	Junior Felix	5.00
71	Barry Larkin	5.00
72	Dave LaPoint	5.00
74	Jesse Barfield	5.00
77	Eddie Murray	45.00
78	Steve Sax	5.00
79	Tim Belcher	5.00
80	Danny Jackson	5.00
82	Kent Hrbek	5.00
83	Brook Jacoby	5.00
84	Mike Marshall	5.00
85	Kevin Seitzer	5.00
86	Tony Gwynn	60.00
87	Dave Steib	5.00
89	Bret Saberhagen	5.00
90	Alan Trammell	5.00
91	Tony Phillips	5.00
93	Jeff Leonard	5.00
94	Wally Joyner	5.00
95	Carney Lansford	5.00
96	Cal Ripken	100.00
97	Andres Galarraga	5.00
98	Kevin Mitchell	5.00
100	Checklist 28-129	2.50
101	Spike Owen	5.00
102	Paul Molitor	45.00
105	Ryne Sandberg	60.00
107	Steve Buechele	5.00
108	Jim Abbott	5.00
109	Alvin Davis	5.00
110	Lee Smith	5.00
111	Roberto Alomar	15.00
112	Rick Reuschel	5.00
113	Kelly Gruber	5.00
114	Joe Carter	5.00
115	Jose Rijo	5.00
116	Bobby Ojeda	5.00
117	Glenn Davis	5.00
118	Jeff Reardon	5.00
119	Jeff Reardon	5.00
120	Kurt Stillwell	5.00
122	Dwight Evans	5.00
123	John Franco	5.00
125	Jose Canseco	35.00
126	Barry Bonds	100.00

No.	Player	Price		No.	Player	Price
127	Lee Guetterman	5.00		259	Phil Bradley	5.00
128	Jack Clark	5.00		260	Cecil Espy	5.00
129	Dave Valle	5.00		261	Scott Bankhead	5.00
132	Mike Morgan	5.00		262	Frank White	5.00
133	Steve Jeltz	5.00		263	Andre Thomas	5.00
134	Jeff Robinson	5.00		264	Glenn Braggs	5.00
139	Bo Diaz	5.00		265	David Cone	5.00
140	Robby Thompson	5.00		266	Bobby Thigpen	5.00
141	Craig Worthington	5.00		267	Nelson Liriano	5.00
144	George Brett	75.00		268	Terry Steinbach	5.00
145	Tom Glavine	15.00		269	Kirby Puckett	60.00
146	Robin Yount	45.00		270	Gregg Jefferies	5.00
147	Gary Carter	45.00		271	Jeff Blauser	5.00
148	Ron Kittle	5.00		272	Cory Snyder	5.00
149	Tony Fernandez	5.00		273	Roy Smith	5.00
150	Dave Stewart	5.00		274	Tom Foley	5.00
151	Gary Gaetti	5.00		275	Mitch Williams	5.00
154	Jesse Orosco	5.00		276	Paul Kilgus	5.00
155	Wally Backman	5.00		277	Don Slaught	5.00
156	Dennis Martinez	5.00		278	Von Hayes	5.00
157	Rick Sutcliffe	6.50		279	Vince Coleman	5.00
158	Greg Maddux	60.00		280	Mike Boddicker	5.00
160	John Kruk	5.00		281	Ken Dayley	5.00
162	John Dopson	5.00		282	Mike Devereaux	5.00
164	Billy Ripken	5.00		283	Kenny Rogers	5.00
165	Fred Manrique	5.00		BC-1	Bo Jackson/MVP	15.00
166	Nolan Ryan	100.00		BC-2	Howard Johnson/MVP	5.00
167	Damon Berryhill	5.00		BC-3	Dave Stewart/MVP	5.00
168	Dale Murphy	35.00		BC-4	Tony Gwynn/MVP	45.00
169	Mickey Tettleton	5.00		BC-5	Orel Hershiser/MVP	5.00
170	Kirk McCaskill	5.00		BC-6	Pedro Guerrero/MVP	5.00
171	Dwight Gooden	5.00		BC-7	Tim Raines/MVP	6.50
172	Jose Lind	5.00		BC-8	Kirby Puckett/MVP	45.00
173	B.J. Surhoff	5.00		BC-9	Alvin Davis	5.00
174	Ruben Sierra	5.00				
175	Dan Plesac	5.00				
176	Dan Pasqua	5.00				
177	Kelly Downs	5.00				
178	Matt Nokes	5.00				
179	Luis Aquino	5.00				
180	Frank Tanana	5.00				
181	Tony Pena	5.00				
182	Dan Gladden	5.00				
183	Bruce Hurst	5.00				
184	Roger Clemens	75.00				
185	Mark McGwire	85.00				
186	Rob Murphy	5.00				
187	Jim Deshaies	5.00				
188	Fred McGriff	5.00				
189	Rob Dibble	5.00				
190	Don Mattingly	75.00				
191	Felix Fermin	5.00				
192	Roberto Kelly	5.00				
193	Dennis Cook	5.00				
194	Darren Daulton	5.00				
195	Alfredo Griffin	5.00				
196	Eric Plunk	5.00				
197	Orel Hershiser	5.00				
198	Paul O'Neill	5.00				
199	Randy Bush	5.00				
201	Ozzie Smith	60.00				
202	Pete O'Brien	5.00				
203	Jay Howell	5.00				
204	Mark Gubicza	5.00				
205	Ed Whitson	5.00				
206	George Bell	5.00				
207	Mike Scott	5.00				
208	Charlie Leibrandt	5.00				
209	Mike Heath	5.00				
210	Dennis Eckersley	45.00				
211	Mike LaValliere	5.00				
212	Darnell Coles	5.00				
213	Lance Parrish	5.00				
214	Mike Moore	5.00				
215	Steve Finley	5.00				
216	Tim Raines	5.00				
217	Scott Garrelts	5.00				
218	Kevin McReynolds	5.00				
219	Dave Gallagher	5.00				
220	Tim Wallach	5.00				
221	Chuck Crim	5.00				
222	Lonnie Smith	5.00				
223	Andre Dawson	15.00				
224	Nelson Santovenia	5.00				
225	Rafael Palmeiro	45.00				
226	Devon White	5.00				
227	Harold Reynolds	6.50				
228	Ellis Burks	5.00				
229	Mark Parent	5.00				
230	Will Clark	6.50				
231	Jimmy Key	5.00				
232	John Farrell	5.00				
233	Eric Davis	5.00				
234	Johnny Ray	5.00				
235	Darryl Strawberry	5.00				
236	Bill Doran	5.00				
237	Greg Gagne	5.00				
238	Jim Eisenreich	5.00				
239	Tommy Gregg	5.00				
240	Marty Barrett	5.00				
241	Rafael Ramirez	5.00				
242	Chris Sabo	5.00				
243	Dave Henderson	5.00				
244	Andy Van Slyke	5.00				
245	Alvaro Espinoza	5.00				
246	Garry Templeton	5.00				
247	Gene Harris	5.00				
248	Kevin Gross	5.00				
249	Brett Butler	5.00				
250	Willie Randolph	5.00				
251	Roger McDowell	5.00				
252	Rafael Belliard	5.00				
253	Steve Rosenberg	5.00				
254	Jack Howell	5.00				
255	Marvell Wynne	5.00				
256	Tom Candiotti	5.00				
257	Todd Benzinger	5.00				
258	Don Robinson	5.00				

1990 Donruss Blue/White Test Issue

Relatively few examples of this test printing have found their way into the hobby. The cards are "two-headed" with the fronts of two different cards printed back-to-back. The cards use the same photos found on the issued versions and differ only in the border colors. Each card can be found with one side bordered in blue and the other bordered in white. The blue side of the card has a glossier finish than the white. The number of different players' cards which can be found in this version is unknown.

Best A.L.

This 144-card set features the top players of the American League. The 2-1/2" x 3-1/2" cards feature the same front design as the regular Donruss set, exception with blue borders instead of red. Backs feature a yellow frame with complete statistics and biographical information provided. This marks the first year that Donruss divided its baseball-best issue into two sets designated by league.

		NM/M
Complete Set (144):		10.00
Common Player:		.05
1	Ken Griffey Jr.	1.00
2	Bob Milacki	.05
3	Mike Boddicker	.05
4	Bert Blyleven	.05
5	Carlton Fisk	.50
6	Greg Swindell	.05
7	Alan Trammell	.05
8	Mark Davis	.05
9	Chris Bosio	.05
10	Gary Gaetti	.05
11	Matt Nokes	.05
12	Dennis Eckersley	.45
13	Kevin Brown	.05
14	Tom Henke	.05
15	Mickey Tettleton	.05
16	Jody Reed	.05
17	Mark Langston	.05
18	Melido Perez	.05
19	John Farrell	.05
20	Tony Phillips	.05
21	Bret Saberhagen	.05
22	Robin Yount	.60
23	Kirby Puckett	.60
24	Steve Sax	.05
25	Dave Stewart	.05
26	Alvin Davis	.05
27	Geno Petralli	.05
28	Mookie Wilson	.05
29	Jeff Ballard	.05
30	Ellis Burks	.05
31	Wally Joyner	.05
32	Bobby Thigpen	.05
33	Keith Hernandez	.05
34	Jack Morris	.05
35	George Brett	.75
36	Dan Plesac	.05
37	Brian Harper	.05
38	Don Mattingly	.75
39	Dave Henderson	.05
40	Scott Bankhead	.05
41	Rafael Palmeiro	.45
42	Jimmy Key	.05
43	Gregg Olson	.05
44	Tony Pena	.05
45	Jack Howell	.05
46	Eric King	.05
47	Cory Snyder	.05
48	Frank Tanana	.05
49	Nolan Ryan	2.00
50	Bob Boone	.05
51	Dave Parker	.05
52	Allan Anderson	.05
53	Tim Leary	.05
54	Mark McGwire	1.50
55	Dave Valle	.05
56	Fred McGriff	.05
57	Cal Ripken	2.00
58	Roger Clemens	.75
59	Lance Parrish	.05
60	Robin Ventura	.05
61	Doug Jones	.05
62	Lloyd Moseby	.05
63	Bo Jackson	.15
64	Paul Molitor	.50
65	Kent Hrbek	.05
66	Mel Hall	.05
67	Bob Welch	.05
68	Erik Hanson	.05
69	Harold Baines	.05
70	Junior Felix	.05
71	Craig Worthington	.05
72	Jeff Reardon	.05
73	Johnny Ray	.05
74	Ozzie Guillen	.05
75	Brook Jacoby	.05
76	Chet Lemon	.05
77	Mark Gubicza	.05
78	B.J. Surhoff	.05
79	Rick Aguilera	.05
80	Pascual Perez	.05
81	Jose Canseco	.30
82	Mike Schooler	.05
83	Jeff Huson	.05
84	Kelly Gruber	.05
85	Randy Milligan	.05
86	Wade Boggs	.60
87	Dave Winfield	.50
88	Scott Fletcher	.05
89	Tom Candiotti	.05
90	Mike Heath	.05
91	Kevin Seitzer	.05
92	Ted Higuera	.05
93	Kevin Tapani	.05
94	Roberto Kelly	.05
95	Walt Weiss	.05
96	Checklist	.05
97	Sandy Alomar	.05
98	Pete O'Brien	.05
99	Jeff Russell	.05
100	John Olerud	.05
101	Pete Harnisch	.05
102	Dwight Evans	.05
103	Chuck Finley	.05
104	Sammy Sosa	6.00
105	Mike Henneman	.05
106	Kurt Stillwell	.05
107	Greg Vaughn	.05
108	Dan Gladden	.05
109	Jesse Barfield	.05
110	Willie Randolph	.05
111	Randy Johnson	.50
112	Julio Franco	.05
113	Tony Fernandez	.05
114	Ben McDonald	.05
115	Mike Greenwell	.05
116	Luis Polonia	.05
117	Carney Lansford	.05
118	Bud Black	.05
119	Lou Whitaker	.05
120	Jim Eisenreich	.05
121	Gary Sheffield	.20
122	Shane Mack	.05
123	Alvaro Espinoza	.05
124	Rickey Henderson	.50
125	Jeffrey Leonard	.05
126	Gary Pettis	.05
127	Dave Steib	.05
128	Danny Tartabull	.05
129	Joe Orsulak	.05
130	Tom Brunansky	.05
131	Dick Schofield	.05
132	Candy Maldonado	.05
133	Cecil Fielder	.05
134	Terry Shumpert	.05
135	Greg Gagne	.05
136	Dave Righetti	.05
137	Terry Steinbach	.05
138	Harold Reynolds	.05
139	George Bell	.05
140	Carlos Quintana	.05
141	Ivan Calderon	.05
142	Greg Brock	.05
143	Ruben Sierra	.05
144	Checklist	.05

Best N.L.

This 144-card set features the top players in the National League for 1990. The 2-1/2" x 3-1/2" cards feature the same design as the regular 1990 Donruss cards, except they have blue, rather than red borders. Traded players are featured with their new teams. This set, along with the A.L. Best set, was available at select retail stores and within the hobby.

		NM/M
Complete Set (144):		7.50
Common Player:		.05
1	Eric Davis	.05
2	Tom Glavine	.20
3	Mike Bielecki	.05
4	Jim Deshaies	.05
5	Mike Scioscia	.05
6	Spike Owen	.05
7	Dwight Gooden	.05
8	Ricky Jordan	.05
9	Doug Drabek	.05
10	Bryn Smith	.05
11	Tony Gwynn	.75
12	John Burkett	.05
13	Nick Esasky	.05
14	Greg Maddux	.75
15	Joe Oliver	.05
16	Mike Scott	.05
17	Tim Belcher	.05
18	Kevin Gross	.05
19	Howard Johnson	.05
20	Darren Daulton	.05
21	John Smiley	.05
22	Ken Dayley	.05
23	Craig Lefferts	.05
24	Will Clark	.05
25	Greg Olson	.05
26	Ryne Sandberg	.75
27	Tom Browning	.05
28	Eric Anthony	.05
29	Juan Samuel	.05
30	Dennis Martinez	.05
31	Kevin Elster	.05
32	Tom Herr	.05
33	Sid Bream	.05
34	Terry Pendleton	.05
35	Roberto Alomar	.20
36	Kevin Bass	.05
37	Jim Presley	.05
38	Les Lancaster	.05
39	Paul O'Neill	.05
40	Dave Smith	.05
41	Kirk Gibson	.05
42	Tim Burke	.05
43	David Cone	.05
44	Ken Howell	.05
45	Barry Bonds	6.00
46	Joe Magrane	.05
47	Andy Benes	.05
48	Gary Carter	.50
49	Pat Combs	.05
50	John Smoltz	.05
51	Mark Grace	.05
52	Barry Larkin	.05
53	Danny Darwin	.05
54	Orel Hershiser	.05
55	Tim Wallach	.05
56	Dave Magadan	.05
57	Roger McDowell	.05
58	Bill Landrum	.05
59	Jose DeLeon	.05
60	Bip Roberts	.05
61	Matt Williams	.05
62	Dale Murphy	.20
63	Dwight Smith	.05
64	Chris Sabo	.05
65	Glenn Davis	.05
66	Jay Howell	.05
67	Andres Galarraga	.05
68	Frank Viola	.05
69	John Kruk	.05
70	Bobby Bonilla	.05
71	Todd Zeile	.05
72	Joe Carter	.05
73	Robby Thompson	.05
74	Jeff Blauser	.05
75	Mitch Williams	.05
76	Rob Dibble	.05
77	Rafael Ramirez	.05
78	Eddie Murray	.50
79	Dave Martinez	.05
80	Darryl Strawberry	.05
81	Dickie Thon	.05
82	Jose Lind	.05
83	Ozzie Smith	.75
84	Bruce Hurst	.05
85	Kevin Mitchell	.05
86	Lonnie Smith	.05
87	Joe Girardi	.05
88	Randy Myers	.05
89	Craig Biggio	.05
90	Fernando Valenzuela	.05
91	Larry Walker	.05
92	John Franco	.05
93	Dennis Cook	.05
94	Bob Walk	.05
95	Pedro Guerrero	.05
96	Checklist	.05
97	Andre Dawson	.25
98	Ed Whitson	.05
99	Steve Bedrosian	.05
100	Oddibe McDowell	.05
101	Todd Benzinger	.05
102	Bill Doran	.05
103	Alfredo Griffin	.05
104	Tim Raines	.05
105	Sid Fernandez	.05
106	Charlie Hayes	.05
107	Mike LaValliere	.05
108	Jose Oquendo	.05
109	Jack Clark	.05
110	Scott Garrelts	.05
111	Ron Gant	.05
112	Shawon Dunston	.05
113	Mariano Duncan	.05
114	Eric Yelding	.05
115	Hubie Brooks	.05
116	Delino DeShields	.05
117	Gregg Jefferies	.05
118	Len Dykstra	.05
119	Andy Van Slyke	.05
120	Lee Smith	.05
121	Benito Santiago	.05
122	Jose Uribe	.05
123	Jeff Treadway	.05
124	Jerome Walton	.05
125	Billy Hatcher	.05
126	Ken Caminiti	.05
127	Kal Daniels	.05
128	Marquis Grissom	.05
129	Kevin McReynolds	.05
130	Wally Backman	.05
131	Willie McGee	.05
132	Terry Kennedy	.05
133	Garry Templeton	.05
134	Lloyd McClendon	.05
135	Daryl Boston	.05
136	Jay Bell	.05
137	Mike Pagliarulo	.05
138	Vince Coleman	.05
139	Brett Butler	.05
140	Von Hayes	.05
141	Ramon Martinez	.05
142	Jack Armstrong	.05
143	Franklin Stubbs	.05
144	Checklist	.05

Diamond Kings Supers

Donruss made this set available through a mail-in offer. Three wrappers, $10 and $2 for postage were necessary to obtain this set. The cards are exactly the same design as the regular Donruss Diamond Kings except they measure approximately 5"x 6-3/4" in size. The artwork of Dick Perez is featured.

		NM/M
Complete Set (26):		5.00
Common Player:		.10

Learning Series

Cards from this 55-card set were released as part of an educational package available to schools. The cards are styled like the regular-issue 1990 Donruss cards, but feature a special "learning series" logo on the front. The backs feature career highlights, statistics and card numbers. The cards were not released directly to the hobby.

		NM/M
Complete Set (55):		25.00
Common Player:		.10
1	George Brett/DK	3.00
2	Kevin Mitchell	.10
3	Andy Van Slyke	.10
4	Benito Santiago	.10
5	Gary Carter	1.00
6	Jose Canseco	.50
7	Rickey Henderson	1.00
8	Ken Griffey Jr.	4.00
9	Ozzie Smith	2.00
10	Dwight Gooden	.10
11	Ryne Sandberg/DK	2.00
12	Don Mattingly	2.50
13	Ozzie Guillen	.10
14	Dave Righetti	.10
15	Rick Dempsey	.10
16	Tom Herr	.10
17	Julio Franco	.10
18	Von Hayes	.10
19	Cal Ripken	6.00
20	Alan Trammell	.10
21	Wade Boggs	2.00
22	Glenn Davis	.10
23	Will Clark	.10
24	Nolan Ryan	6.00
25	George Bell	.10
26	Cecil Fielder	.10
27	Gregg Olson	.10
28	Tim Wallach	.10
29	Ron Darling	.10
30	Kelly Gruber	.10
31	Shawn Boskie	.10
32	Mike Greenwell	.10
33	Dave Parker	.10
34	Joe Magrane	.10
35	Dave Stewart	.10
36	Kent Hrbek	.10
37	Robin Yount	1.00
38	Bo Jackson	.15
39	Fernando Valenzuela	.10
40	Sandy Alomar, Jr.	.10
41	Lance Parrish	.10
42	Candy Maldonado	.10
43	Mike LaValliere	.10
44	Jim Abbott	.10
45	Edgar Martinez	.10
46	Kirby Puckett	2.00
47	Delino DeShields	.10
48	Tony Gwynn	2.00
49	Carlton Fisk	1.00
50	Mike Scott	.10
51	Barry Larkin	.10
52	Andre Dawson	.35

Learning Series numbers 1–26 (separate listing):

No.	Player	Price
1	Bo Jackson	.25
2	Steve Sax	.10
3	Ruben Sierra	.10
4	Ken Griffey Jr.	4.00
5	Mickey Tettleton	.10
6	Dave Stewart	.10
7	Jim Deshaies	.10
8	John Smoltz	.10
9	Mike Bielecki	.10
10	Brian Downing	.10
11	Kevin Mitchell	.10
12	Kelly Gruber	.10
13	Joe Magrane	.10
14	John Franco	.10
15	Ozzie Guillen	.10
16	Lou Whitaker	.10
17	John Smiley	.10
18	Howard Johnson	.10
19	Willie Randolph	.10
20	Chris Bosio	.10
21	Tommy Herr	.10
22	Dan Gladden	.10
23	Ellis Burks	.10
24	Pete O'Brien	.10
25	Bryn Smith	.10
26	Ed Whitson	.10

53 Tom Glavine .50
54 Tom Browning .10
55 Checklist .05

Rookies

For the fifth straight year, Donruss issued a 56-card "Rookies" set in 1990. As in previous years, the set is similar in design to the regular Donruss set, except for a new "The Rookies" logo and green borders instead of red. The set is packaged in a special box and includes a Carl Yastrzemski puzzle card.

NM/M
Complete Set (56): 1.00
Common Player: .05
1 Sandy Alomar .05
2 John Olerud .40
3 Pat Combs .05
4 Brian Dubois .05
5 Felix Jose .05
6 Delino DeShields .05
7 Mike Stanton .05
8 Mike Munoz RC .05
9 Craig Grebeck RC .05
10 Joe Kraemer RC .05
11 Jeff Huson .05
12 Bill Sampen RC .05
13 Brian Bohanon RC .05
14 Dave Justice .40
15 Robin Ventura .05
16 Greg Vaughn .05
17 Wayne Edwards RC .05
18 Shawn Boskie .05
19 Carlos Baerga RC .20
20 Mark Gardner .05
21 Kevin Appier RC .05
22 Mike Harkey .05
23 Tim Layana RC .05
24 Glenallen Hill .05
25 Jerry Kutzler .05
26 Mike Blowers .05
27 Scott Ruskin RC .05
28 Dana Kiecker RC .05
29 Willie Blair RC .05
30 Ben McDonald .05
31 Todd Zeile .05
32 Scott Coolbaugh .05
33 Xavier Hernandez .05
34 Mike Hartley RC .05
35 Kevin Tapani .05
36 Kevin Wickander RC .05
37 Carlos Hernandez RC .05
38 Brian Traxler RC .05
39 Marty Brown RC .05
40 Scott Radinsky RC .05
41 Julio Machado .05
42 Steve Avery .05
43 Mark Lemke .05
44 Alan Mills RC .05
45 Marquis Grissom .05
46 Greg Olson RC .05
47 Dave Hollins RC .05
48 Jerald Clark .05
49 Eric Anthony .05
50 Tim Drummond .05
51 John Burkett RC .05
52 Brent Knackert RC .05
53 Jeff Shaw RC .05
54 John Orton RC .05
55 Terry Shumpert RC .05
56 Checklist .05

1991 Donruss Previews

Once again in late 1990 Donruss distributed individual cards from a 12-card preview issue to its dealer network as an introduction to its 1991 issue. Like the previous year's preview cards, the '91 samples utilized the format which would follow on the regular-issue cards, but the photos were different. This has helped create demand for these cards from superstar collectors. Backs are printed in black-

and-white and have little more than a player name, card number and MLB logos.

NM/M
Complete Set (12): 135.00
Common Player: 2.50
1 Dave Justice 2.50
2 Doug Drabek 2.50
3 Scott Chiamparino 2.50
4 Ken Griffey Jr. 35.00
5 Bob Welch 2.50
6 Tino Martinez 2.50
7 Nolan Ryan 45.00
8 Dwight Gooden 2.50
9 Ryne Sandberg 17.50
10 Barry Bonds 45.00
11 Jose Canseco 7.50
12 Eddie Murray 12.00

1991 Donruss

Donruss used a two-series format in 1991. The first series was released in December 1990, and the second in February 1991. The 1991 design is somewhat reminiscent of the 1986 set, with blue borders on Series I cards; green on Series II. Limited edition cards including an autographed Ryne Sandberg card (5,000) were randomly inserted in wax packs. Other features of the set include 40 Rated Rookies, (RR) in the checklist, Legends and Elite insert series, and another Diamond King (DK) subset. Cards were distributed in packs with Willie Stargell puzzle pieces.

NM/M
Factory Set w/Previews (788): 12.00
Factory Collector's Set (792): 12.00
Complete Set (770): 8.00
Common Player: .05
Willie Stargell Puzzle: .50
Series 1 or 2 Pack (15): .50
Series 1 or 2 Wax Box (36): 12.50
1 Dave Steib/DK .05
2 Craig Biggio/DK .05
3 Cecil Fielder/DK .05
4 Barry Bonds/DK 1.00
5 Barry Larkin/DK .05
6 Dave Parker/DK .05
7 Len Dykstra/DK .05
8 Bobby Thigpen/DK .05
9 Roger Clemens/DK .60
10 Ron Gant/DK .05
11 Delino DeShields/DK .05
12 Roberto Alomar/DK .20
13 Sandy Alomar/DK .05

Abbreviations
DK - Diamond King
RR - Rated Rookie
AS - All-Star

14 Ryne Sandberg/DK .50
15 Ramon Martinez/DK .05
16 Edgar Martinez/DK .05
17 Dave Magadan/DK .05
18 Matt Williams/DK .05
19 Rafael Palmeiro/DK .40
20 Bob Welch/DK .05
21 Dave Righetti/DK .05
22 Brian Harper/DK .05
23 Gregg Olson/DK .05
24 Kurt Stillwell/DK .05
25 Pedro Guerrero/DK .05
26 Chuck Finley/DK .05
27 Diamond King checklist .05
28 Tino Martinez/RR .05
29 Mark Lewis/RR .05
30 Bernard Gilkey/RR RC .10
31 Hensley Meulens/RR .05
32 Derek Bell/RR RC .30
33 Jose Offerman/RR .05
34 Terry Bross/RR .05
35 Leo Gomez/RR RC .05
36 Derrick May/RR .05
37 Kevin Morton/RR RC .05
38 Moises Alou/RR .05
39 Julio Valera/RR .05
40 Milt Cuyler/RR RC .05
41 Phil Plantier/RR RC .10
42 Scott Chiamparino/RR RC .05
43 Ray Lankford/RR RC .20
44 Mickey Morandini/RR RC .10
45 Dave Hansen/RR RC .05
46 Kevin Belcher/RR RC .05
47 Darrin Fletcher/RR RC .05
48 Steve Sax/AS .05
49 Ken Griffey Jr./AS .30
50a Jose Canseco/AS (A's in stat line on back.) .10
50b Jose Canseco/AS (AL in stat line on back.) .25
51 Sandy Alomar/AS .05
52 Cal Ripken, Jr./AS .20
53 Rickey Henderson/AS .50
54 Bob Welch/AS .05
55 Wade Boggs/AS .25
56 Mark McGwire/AS .50
57a Jack McDowell (Career Games 30) .05
57b Jack McDowell (Career Games 63) .25
58 Jose Lind .05
59 Alex Fernandez .05
60 Pat Combs .05
61 Mike Walker RC .05
62 Juan Samuel .05
63 Mike Blowers .05
64 Mark Guthrie .05
65 Mark Salas .05
66 Tim Jones .05
67 Tim Leary .05
68 Andres Galarraga .05
69 Bob Milacki .05
70 Tim Belcher .05
71 Todd Zeile .05
72 Jerome Walton .05
73 Kevin Seitzer .05
74 Jerald Clark .05
75 John Smoltz .05
76 Mike Henneman .05
77 Ken Griffey Jr. .65
78 Jim Abbott .05
79 Gregg Jefferies .05
80 Kevin Reimer RC .05
81 Roger Clemens .60
82 Mike Fitzgerald .05
83 Bruce Hurst .05
84 Eric Davis .05
85 Paul Molitor .40
86 Will Clark .05
87 Mike Bielecki .05
88 Bret Saberhagen .05
89 Nolan Ryan 1.00
90 Bobby Thigpen .05
91 Dickie Thon .05
92 Duane Ward .05
93 Luis Polonia .05
94 Terry Kennedy .05
95 Kent Hrbek .05
96 Danny Jackson .05
97 Sid Fernandez .05
98 Jimmy Key .05
99 Franklin Stubbs .05
100 Checklist 28-103 .05
101 R.J. Reynolds .05
102 Dave Stewart .05
103 Dan Pasqua .05
104 Dan Plesac .05
105 Mark McGwire .75
106 John Farrell .05
107 Don Mattingly .60
108 Carlton Fisk .40
109 Ken Oberkfell .05
110 Darrel Akerfelds .05
111 Gregg Olson .05
112 Mike Scioscia .05
113 Bryn Smith .05
114 Bob Geren .05
115 Tom Candiotti .05
116 Kevin Tapani .05
117 Jeff Treadway .05
118 Alan Trammell .05
119 Pete O'Brien .05
120 Joel Skinner .05
121 Mike LaValliere .05
122 Dwight Evans .05

123 Jody Reed .05
124 Lee Guetterman .05
125 Tim Burke .05
126 Dave Johnson .05
127 Fernando Valenzuela .05
128 Jose DeLeon .05
129 Andre Dawson .20
130 Gerald Perry .05
131 Greg Harris .05
132 Tom Glavine .25
133 Lance McCullers .05
134 Randy Johnson .40
135 Lance Parrish .05
136 Mackey Sasser .05
137 Geno Petralli .05
138 Dennis Lamp .05
139 Dennis Martinez .05
140 Mike Pagliarulo .05
141 Hal Morris .05
142 Dave Parker .05
143 Brett Butler .05
144 Paul Assenmacher .05
145 Mark Gubicza .05
146 Charlie Hough .05
147 Sammy Sosa .50
148 Randy Ready .05
149 Kelly Gruber .05
150 Devon White .05
151 Gary Carter .40
152 Gene Larkin .05
153 Chris Sabo .05
154 David Cone .05
155 Todd Stottlemyre .05
156 Glenn Wilson .05
157 Bob Walk .05
158 Mike Gallego .05
159 Greg Hibbard .05
160 Chris Bosio .05
161 Mike Moore .05
162 Jerry Browne .05
163 Steve Sax .05
164 Melido Perez .05
165 Danny Darwin .05
166 Roger McDowell .05
167 Bill Ripken .05
168 Mike Sharperson .05
169 Lee Smith .05
170 Matt Nokes .05
171 Jesse Orosco .05
172 Rick Aguilera .05
173 Jim Presley .05
174 Lou Whitaker .05
175 Harold Reynolds .05
176 Brook Jacoby .05
177 Wally Backman .05
178 Wade Boggs .50
179 Chuck Cary .05
180 Tom Foley .05
181 Pete Harnisch .05
182 Mike Morgan .05
183 Bob Tewksbury .05
184 Joe Girardi .05
185 Storm Davis .05
186 Ed Whitson .05
187 Steve Avery .05
188 Lloyd Moseby .05
189 Scott Bankhead .05
190 Mark Langston .05
191 Kevin McReynolds .05
192 Julio Franco .05
193 John Dopson .05
194 Oil Can Boyd .05
195 Bip Roberts .05
196 Billy Hatcher .05
197 Edgar Diaz RC .05
198 Greg Litton .05
199 Mark Grace .05
200 Checklist 104-179 .05
201 George Brett .60
202 Jeff Russell .05
203 Ivan Calderon .05
204 Ken Howell .05
205 Tom Henke .05
206 Bryan Harvey .05
207 Steve Bedrosian .05
208 Al Newman .05
209 Randy Myers .05
210 Daryl Boston .05
211 Manny Lee .05
212 Dave Smith .05
213 Don Slaught .05
214 Walt Weiss .05
215 Donn Pall .05
216 Jamie Navarro .05
217 Willie Randolph .05
218 Rudy Seanez RC .05
219 Jim Leyritz RC .15
220 Ron Karkovice .05
221 Ken Caminiti .05
222a Von Hayes (Traded players' first names included in How Acquired on back.) .05
222b Von Hayes (No first names.) .05
223 Cal Ripken, Jr. 1.00
224 Lenny Harris .05
225 Milt Thompson .05
226 Alvaro Espinoza .05
227 Chris James .05
228 Dan Gladden .05
229 Jeff Blauser .05
230 Mike Heath .05
231 Omar Vizquel .05
232 Doug Jones .05
233 Jeff King .05
234 Luis Rivera .05
235 Ellis Burks .05
236 Greg Cadaret .05

237 Dave Martinez .05
238 Mark Williamson .05
239 Stan Javier .05
240 Ozzie Smith .50
241 Shawn Boskie RC .05
242 Tom Gordon .05
243 Tony Gwynn .50
244 Tommy Gregg .05
245 Jeff Robinson .05
246 Keith Comstock .05
247 Jack Howell .05
248 Keith Miller .05
249 Bobby Witt .05
250 Rob Murphy .05
251 Spike Owen .05
252 Garry Templeton .05
253 Glenn Braggs .05
254 Ron Robinson .05
255 Kevin Mitchell .05
256 Les Lancaster .05
257 Mel Stottlemyre RC .10
258 Kenny Rogers .05
259 Lance Johnson .05
260 John Kruk .05
261 Fred McGriff .05
262 Dick Schofield .05
263 Trevor Wilson .05
264 David West .05
265 Scott Scudder .05
266 Dwight Gooden .05
267 Willie Blair RC .05
268 Mark Portugal .05
269 Doug Drabek .05
270 Dennis Eckersley .35
271 Eric King .05
272 Robin Yount .40
273 Carney Lansford .05
274 Carlos Baerga .05
275 Dave Righetti .05
276 Scott Fletcher .05
277 Eric Yelding .05
278 Charlie Hayes .05
279 Jeff Ballard .05
280 Orel Hershiser .05
281 Jose Oquendo .05
282 Mike Witt .05
283 Mitch Webster .05
284 Greg Gagne .05
285 Greg Olson RC .05
286 Tony Phillips .05
287 Scott Bradley .05
288 Cory Snyder .05
289 Jay Bell .05
290 Kevin Romine .05
291 Jeff Robinson .05
292 Steve Frey RC .05
293 Craig Worthington .05
294 Tim Crews .05
295 Joe Magrane .05
296 Hector Villanueva RC .05
297 Terry Shumpert RC .05
298 Joe Carter .05
299 Kent Mercker .05
300 Checklist 180-255 .05
301 Chet Lemon .05
302 Mike Schooler .05
303 Dante Bichette .05
304 Kevin Elster .05
305 Jeff Huson .05
306 Greg Harris .05
307 Marquis Grissom .05
308 Calvin Schiraldi .05
309 Mariano Duncan .05
310 Bill Spiers .05
311 Scott Garrelts .05
312 Mitch Williams .05
313 Mike Macfarlane .05
314 Kevin Brown .05
315 Robin Ventura .05
316 Darren Daulton .05
317 Pat Borders .05
318 Mark Eichhorn .05
319 Jeff Brantley .05
320 Shane Mack .05
321 Rob Dibble .05
322 John Franco .05
323 Junior Felix .05
324 Casey Candaele .05
325 Bobby Bonilla .05
326 Dave Henderson .05
327 Wayne Edwards .05
328 Mark Knudson .05
329 Terry Steinbach .05
330 Colby Ward RC .05
331 Oscar Azocar RC .05
332 Scott Radinsky RC .10
333 Eric Anthony .05
334 Steve Lake .05
335 Bob Melvin .05
336 Kal Daniels .05
337 Tom Pagozzi .05
338 Alan Mills RC .05
339 Steve Olin .05
340 Juan Berenguer .05
341 Francisco Cabrera .05
342 Dave Bergman .05
343 Henry Cotto .05
344 Sergio Valdez .05
345 Bob Patterson .05
346 John Marzano .05
347 Dana Kiecker RC .05
348 Dion James .05
349 Hubie Brooks .05
350 Bill Landrum .05
351 Bill Sampen RC .05
352 Greg Briley .05
353 Paul Gibson .05
354 Dave Eiland .05

355 Steve Finley .05
356 Bob Boone .05
357 Steve Buechele .05
358 Chris Hoiles .05
359 Larry Walker .05
360 Frank DiPino .05
361 Mark Grant .05
362 Dave Magadan .05
363 Robby Thompson .05
364 Lonnie Smith .05
365 Steve Farr .05
366 Dave Valle .05
367 Tim Naehring RC .05
368 Jim Acker .05
369 Jeff Reardon .05
370 Tim Teufel .05
371 Juan Gonzalez .20
372 Luis Salazar .05
373 Rick Honeycutt .05
374 Greg Maddux .50
375 Jose Uribe .05
376 Donnie Hill .05
377 Don Carman .05
378 Craig Grebeck RC .05
379 Willie Fraser .05
380 Glenallen Hill .05
381 Joe Oliver .05
382 Randy Bush .05
383 Alex Cole RC .05
384 Norm Charlton .05
385 Gene Nelson .05
386a Checklist 256-331 (Blue borders.) .05
386b Checklist 256-331 (Green borders.) .05
387 Rickey Henderson/MVP .20
388 Lance Parrish/MVP .05
389 Fred McGriff/MVP .05
390 Dave Parker/MVP .05
391 Candy Maldonado/MVP .05
392 Ken Griffey Jr./MVP .50
393 Gregg Olson/MVP .05
394 Rafael Palmeiro/MVP .05
395 Roger Clemens/MVP .30
396 George Brett/MVP .30
397 Cecil Fielder/MVP .05
398 Brian Harper/MVP .05
399 Bobby Thigpen/MVP .05
400 Roberto Kelly/MVP .05
401 Danny Darwin/MVP .05
402 Dave Justice/MVP .05
403 Lee Smith/MVP .05
404 Ryne Sandberg/MVP .25
405 Eddie Murray/MVP .20
406 Tim Wallach/MVP .05
407 Kevin Mitchell/MVP .05
408 Darryl Strawberry/MVP .05
409 Joe Carter/MVP .05
410 Len Dykstra/MVP .05
411 Doug Drabek/MVP .05
412 Chris Sabo/MVP .05
413 Paul Marak/RR RC .05
414 Tim McIntosh/RR RC .05
415 Brian Barnes/RR RC .05
416 Eric Gunderson/RR RC .05
417 Mike Gardiner/RR RC .05
418 Steve Carter/RR .05
419 Gerald Alexander/RR RC .05
420 Rich Garces/RR RC .05
421 Chuck Knoblauch/RR RC .50
422 Scott Aldred/RR RC .05
423 Wes Chamberlain/RR RC .05
424 Lance Dickson/RR RC .05
425 Greg Colbrunn/RR RC .10
426 Rich Delucia/RR RC .05
427 Jeff Conine/RR RC .50
428 Steve Decker/RR RC .05
429 Turner Ward/RR RC .05
430 Mo Vaughn/RR .05
431 Steve Chitren/RR RC .05
432 Mike Benjamin/RR RC .05
433 Ryne Sandberg/AS .25
434 Len Dykstra/AS .15
435 Andre Dawson/AS .15
436 Mike Scioscia/AS .05
437 Ozzie Smith/AS .25
438 Kevin Mitchell/AS .05
439 Jack Armstrong/AS .05
440 Chris Sabo/AS .05
441 Will Clark/AS .05
442 Mel Hall .05
443 Mark Gardner .05
444 Mike Devereaux .05
445 Kirk Gibson .05
446 Terry Pendleton .05
447 Mike Harkey .05
448 Jim Eisenreich .05
449 Benito Santiago .05
450 Oddibe McDowell .05
451 Cecil Fielder .05
452 Ken Griffey Sr. .05
453 Bert Blyleven .10
454 Howard Johnson .05
455 Monty Farris RC .05
456 Tony Pena .05
457 Tim Raines .05
458 Dennis Rasmussen .05
459 Luis Quinones .05
460 B.J. Surhoff .05
461 Ernest Riles .05
462 Rick Sutcliffe .05
463 Danny Tartabull .05
464 Pete Incaviglia .05
465 Carlos Martinez .05
466 Ricky Jordan .05

467 John Cerutti	.05
468 Dave Winfield	.40
469 Francisco Oliveras	.05
470 Roy Smith	.05
471 Barry Larkin	.05
472 Ron Darling	.05
473 David Wells	.05
474 Glenn Davis	.05
475 Neal Heaton	.05
476 Ron Hassey	.05
477 Frank Thomas	.40
478 Greg Vaughn	.05
479 Todd Burns	.05
480 Candy Maldonado	.05
481 Dave LaPoint	.05
482 Alvin Davis	.05
483 Mike Scott	.05
484 Dale Murphy	.20
485 Ben McDonald	.05
486 Jay Howell	.05
487 Vince Coleman	.05
488 Alfredo Griffin	.05
489 Sandy Alomar	.05
490 Kirby Puckett	.50
491 Andres Thomas	.05
492 Jack Morris	.05
493 Matt Young	.05
494 Greg Myers	.05
495 Barry Bonds	1.00
496 Scott Cooper	.05
497 Dan Schatzeder	.05
498 Jesse Barfield	.05
499 Jerry Goff RC	.05
500 Checklist 332-408	.05
501 Anthony Telford RC	.05
502 Eddie Murray	.40
503 Omar Olivares RC	.05
504 Ryne Sandberg	.50
505 Jeff Montgomery	.05
506 Mark Parent	.05
507 Ron Gant	.05
508 Frank Tanana	.05
509 Jay Buhner	.05
510 Max Venable	.05
511 Wally Whitehurst	.05
512 Gary Pettis	.05
513 Tom Brunansky	.05
514 Tim Wallach	.05
515 Craig Lefferts RC	.05
516 Tim Layana RC	.05
517 Darryl Hamilton	.05
518 Rick Reuschel	.05
519 Steve Wilson	.05
520 Kurt Stillwell	.05
521 Rafael Palmeiro	.30
522 Ken Patterson	.05
523 Len Dykstra	.05
524 Tony Fernandez	.05
525 Kent Anderson	.05
526 Mark Leonard RC	.05
527 Allan Anderson	.05
528 Tom Browning	.05
529 Frank Viola	.05
530 John Olerud	.05
531 Juan Agosto	.05
532 Zane Smith	.05
533 Scott Sanderson	.05
534 Barry Jones	.05
535 Mike Felder	.05
536 Jose Canseco	.20
537 Felix Fermin	.05
538 Roberto Kelly	.05
539 Brian Holman	.05
540 Mark Davidson	.05
541 Terry Mulholland	.05
542 Randy Milligan	.05
543 Jose Gonzalez	.05
544 Craig Wilson RC	.05
545 Mike Hartley	.05
546 Greg Swindell	.05
547 Gary Gaetti	.05
548 Dave Justice	.05
549 Steve Searcy	.05
550 Erik Hanson	.05
551 Dave Stieb	.05
552 Andy Van Slyke	.05
553 Mike Greenwell	.05
554 Kevin Maas	.05
555 Delino Deshields	.05
556 Curt Schilling	.20
557 Ramon Martinez	.05
558 Pedro Guerrero	.05
559 Dwight Smith	.05
560 Mark Davis	.05
561 Shawn Abner	.05
562 Charlie Leibrandt	.05
563 John Shelby	.05
564 Bill Swift	.05
565 Mike Fetters	.05
566 Alejandro Pena	.05
567 Ruben Sierra	.05
568 Carlos Quintana	.05
569 Kevin Gross	.05
570 Derek Lilliquist	.05
571 Jack Armstrong	.05
572 Greg Brock	.05
573 Mike Kingery	.05
574 Greg Smith RC	.05
575 Brian McRae RC	.05
576 Jack Daugherty	.05
577 Ozzie Guillen	.05
578 Joe Boever	.05
579 Luis Sojo	.05
580 Chili Davis	.05
581 Don Robinson	.05
582 Brian Harper	.05
583 Paul O'Neill	.05
584 Bob Ojeda	.05

585 Mookie Wilson	.05
586 Rafael Ramirez	.05
587 Gary Redus	.05
588 Jamie Quirk	.05
589 Shawn Hilligas	.05
590 Tom Edens RC	.05
591 Joe Klink RC	.05
592 Charles Nagy	.05
593 Eric Plunk	.05
594 Tracy Jones	.05
595 Craig Biggio	.05
596 Jose DeJesus	.05
597 Mickey Tettleton	.05
598 Chris Gwynn	.05
599 Rex Hudler	.05
600 Checklist 409-506	.05
601 Jim Gott	.05
602 Jeff Manto RC	.05
603 Nelson Liriano	.05
604 Mark Lemke	.05
605 Clay Parker	.05
606 Edgar Martinez	.05
607 Mark Whiten RC	.10
608 Ted Power	.05
609 Tom Bolton	.05
610 Tom Herr	.05
611 Andy Hawkins	.05
612 Scott Ruskin	.05
613 Ron Kittle	.05
614 John Wetteland	.05
615 Mike Perez RC	.05
616 Dave Clark	.05
617 Brent Mayne RC	.05
618 Jack Clark	.05
619 Marvin Freeman	.05
620 Edwin Nunez	.05
621 Russ Swan RC	.05
622 Johnny Ray	.05
623 Charlie O'Brien	.05
624 Joe Bitker RC	.05
625 Mike Marshall	.05
626 Otis Nixon	.05
627 Andy Benes	.05
628 Ron Oester	.05
629 Ted Higuera	.05
630 Kevin Bass	.05
631 Damon Berryhill	.05
632 Bo Jackson	.10
633 Brad Arnsberg	.05
634 Jerry Willard	.05
635 Tommy Greene	.05
636 Bob MacDonald RC	.05
637 Kirk McCaskill	.05
638 John Burkett	.05
639 Paul Abbott RC	.05
640 Todd Benzinger	.05
641 Todd Hundley RC	.05
642 George Bell	.05
643 Javier Ortiz RC	.05
644 Sid Bream	.05
645 Bob Welch	.05
646 Phil Bradley	.05
647 Bill Krueger	.05
648 Rickey Henderson	.40
649 Kevin Wickander	.05
650 Steve Balboni	.05
651 Gene Harris	.05
652 Jim Deshaies	.05
653 Jason Grimsley	.05
654 Joe Orsulak	.05
655 Jimmy Poole RC	.05
656 Felix Jose	.05
657 Dennis Cook	.05
658 Tom Brookens	.05
659 Junior Ortiz	.05
660 Jeff Parrett	.05
661 Jerry Don Gleaton	.05
662 Brent Knackert	.05
663 Rance Mulliniks	.05
664 John Smiley	.05
665 Larry Andersen	.05
666 Willie McGee	.05
667 Chris Nabholz RC	.05
668 Brady Anderson	.05
669 Darren Holmes RC	.10
670 Ken Hill	.05
671 Gary Varsho	.05
672 Bill Pecota	.05
673 Fred Lynn	.05
674 Kevin D. Brown RC	.05
675 Dan Petry	.05
676 Mike Jackson	.05
677 Wally Joyner	.05
678 Danny Jackson	.05
679 Bill Haselman RC	.05
680 Mike Boddicker	.05
681 Mel Rojas RC	.05
682 Roberto Alomar	.20
683 Dave Justice (R.O.Y.)	.05
684 Chuck Crim	.05
685a Matt Williams (Last line of Career Highlights ends, "most DP's in.")	.10
685b Matt Williams (Last line ends "8/24-27/87.")	.25
686 Shawon Dunston	.05
687 Jeff Schulz RC	.05
688 John Barfield RC	.05
689 Gerald Young	.05
690 Luis Gonzalez RC	.75
691 Frank Wills	.05
692 Chuck Finley	.05
693 Sandy Alomar (R.O.Y.)	.05
694 Tim Drummond	.05
695 Herm Winningham	.05
696 Darryl Strawberry	.05
697 Al Leiter	.05
698 Karl Rhodes RC	.05

699 Stan Belinda RC	.05
700 Checklist 507-604	.05
701 Lance Blankenship	.05
702 Willie Stargell (Puzzle Card)	.05
703 Jim Gantner	.05
704 Reggie Harris RC	.05
705 Rob Ducey	.05
706 Tim Hulett	.05
707 Atlee Hammaker	.05
708 Xavier Hernandez	.05
709 Chuck McElroy RC	.05
710 John Mitchell	.05
711 Carlos Hernandez	.05
712 Geronimo Pena RC	.05
713 Jim Neidlinger RC	.05
714 John Orton	.05
715 Terry Leach	.05
716 Mike Stanton	.05
717 Walt Terrell	.05
718 Luis Aquino	.05
719 Bud Black	.05
720 Bob Kipper	.05
721 Jeff Gray RC	.05
722 Jose Rijo	.05
723 Curt Young	.05
724 Jose Vizcaino RC	.05
725 Randy Tomlin RC	.05
726 Junior Noboa	.05
727 Bob Welch (Award Winner)	.05
728 Gary Ward	.05
729 Rob Deer	.05
730 David Segui RC	.05
731 Mark Carreon	.05
732 Vicente Palacios	.05
733 Sam Horn	.05
734 Howard Farmer RC	.05
735 Ken Dayley	.05
736 Kelly Mann	.05
737 Joe Grahe RC	.05
738 Kelly Downs	.05
739 Jimmy Kremers RC	.05
740 Kevin Appier	.05
741 Jeff Reed	.05
742 Jose Rijo (World Series)	.05
743 Dave Rohde RC	.05
744 Dr. Dirt/Mr. Clean (Len Dykstra, Dale Murphy)	.10
745 Paul Sorrento	.05
746 Thomas Howard RC	.05
747 Matt Stark RC	.05
748 Harold Baines	.05
749 Doug Dascenzo	.05
750 Doug Drabek (Award Winner)	.05
751 Gary Sheffield	.20
752 Terry Lee RC	.05
753 Jim Vatcher RC	.05
754 Lee Stevens	.05
755 Randy Veres RC	.05
756 Bill Doran	.05
757 Gary Wayne	.05
758 Pedro Munoz RC	.05
759 Chris Hammond RC	.05
760 Checklist 605-702	.05
761 Rickey Henderson/MVP	.20
762 Barry Bonds/MVP	.50
763 Billy Hatcher (World Series)	.05
764 Julio Machado	.05
765 Jose Mesa	.05
766 Willie Randolph (World Series)	.05
767 Scott Erickson RC	.10
768 Travis Fryman	.05
769 Rich Rodriguez RC	.05
770 Checklist 703-770; BC1-BC22	.05

	NM/M
Complete Set (10):	250.00
Common Player:	15.00
1 Barry Bonds	60.00
2 George Brett	40.00
3 Jose Canseco	25.00
4 Andre Dawson	15.00
5 Doug Drabek	7.50
6 Cecil Fielder	7.50
7 Rickey Henderson	25.00
8 Matt Williams	7.50
--- Nolan Ryan (Legend)	65.00
--- Ryne Sandberg (Signature)	100.00

Grand Slammers

This set features players who hit grand slams in 1990. The cards are styled after the 1991 Donruss regular-issue cards. The featured player is showcased with a star in the background. The set was included in factory sets and randomly in jumbo packs.

	NM/M
Complete Set (14):	2.00
Common Player:	.10
1 Joe Carter	.10
2 Bobby Bonilla	.10
3 Kal Daniels	.10
4 Jose Canseco	.30
5 Barry Bonds	1.00
6 Jay Buhner	.10
7 Cecil Fielder	.10
8 Matt Williams	.10
9 Andres Galarraga	.10
10 Luis Polonia	.10
11 Mark McGwire	.75
12 Ron Karkovice	.10
13 Darryl Strawberry	.10
14 Mike Greenwell	.10

Highlights

These inserts feature highlights from the 1990 season. Cards have a "BC" (Bonus Card) prefix to the number and are styled after the 1991 regular-issue Donruss cards. Cards 1-10 feature blue borders due to their release with Series 1 cards. Cards 11-22 feature green borders and were released with Series 2 cards. A highlight logo appears on the front of the card. Each highlight is explained in depth on the card back.

Elite

Donruss released a series of special inserts in 1991. Ten thousand of each Elite card was released, while 7,500 Legend cards and 5,000 Signature cards were issued. Cards were inserted in wax packs and feature marble borders. The Legend card features a Dick Perez drawing. Each card is designated with a serial number on the back.

	NM/M
Complete Set (22):	3.00
Common Player:	
1 Mark Langston, Mike Witt (No-Hit Mariners)	.10
2 Randy Johnson (No-Hits Tigers)	.25
3 Nolan Ryan (No-Hits A's)	.50
4 Dave Stewart (No-Hits Blue Jays)	.10
5 Cecil Fielder (50 Homer Club)	.10
6 Carlton Fisk (Record Home Run)	.20
7 Ryne Sandberg (Sets Fielding Records)	.25
8 Gary Carter (Breaks Catching Mark)	.20
9 Mark McGwire (Home Run Milestone)	.45
10 Bo Jackson (4 Consecutive HRs)	.15
11 Fernando Valenzuela (No-Hits Cardinals)	.10
12a Andy Hawkins (PITCHER)	2.50
12b Andy Hawkins (No-Hits White Sox)	.10
13 Melido Perez (No-Hits Yankees)	.10
14 Terry Mulholland (No-Hits Giants)	.10
15 Nolan Ryan (300th Win)	.50
16 Delino DeShields (4 Hits In Debut)	.10
17 Cal Ripken (Errorless Games)	.10
18 Eddie Murray (Switch Hit Homers)	.20
19 George Brett (3 Decade Champ)	.30
20 Bobby Thigpen (Shatters Save Mark)	.10
21 Dave Stieb (No-Hits Indians)	.10
22 Willie McGee e (NL Batting Champ)	.10

Diamond Kings Supers

Donruss made this set available through a mail-in offer. Three wrappers, $12 and postage were necessary to obtain this set. The cards are exactly the same design as the regular Donruss Diamond Kings except they measure approximately 5" x 6-3/4" in size. The artwork of Dick Perez is featured.

	NM/M
Complete Set (26):	8.00
Common Player:	.25
1 Dave Steib	.25
2 Craig Biggio	.25
3 Cecil Fielder	.25
4 Barry Bonds	4.50
5 Barry Larkin	.25
6 Dave Parker	.25
7 Len Dykstra	.25
8 Bobby Thigpen	.25
9 Roger Clemens	2.50
10 Ron Gant	.25
11 Delino DeShields	.25
12 Roberto Alomar	.40
13 Sandy Alomar	.25
14 Ryne Sandberg	1.50
15 Ramon Martinez	.25
16 Edgar Martinez	.25
17 Dave Magadan	.25
18 Matt Williams	.25
19 Rafael Palmeiro	1.00
20 Bob Welch	.25
21 Dave Righetti	.25
22 Brian Harper	.25
23 Gregg Olson	.25
24 Kurt Stillwell	.25
25 Pedro Guerrero	.25
26 Chuck Finley	.25

Rookies

Red borders highlight the 1991 Donruss Rookies cards. This set marks the sixth year that Donruss produced such an issue. As in past years, "The Rookies" logo appears on the card fronts. The set is packaged in a special box and includes a Willie Stargell puzzle card.

	NM/M
Complete Set (56):	4.00
Common Player:	.05
1 Pat Kelly RC	.05
2 Rich DeLucia	.05
3 Wes Chamberlain	.05
4 Scott Leius RC	.05
5 Darryl Kile RC	.05
6 Milt Cuyler	.05
7 Todd Van Poppel	.05
8 Ray Lankford	.05
9 Brian Hunter	.05
10 Tony Perezchica	.05
11 Ced Landrum RC	.05
12 Dave Burba RC	.05
13 Ramon Garcia	.05
14 Ed Sprague RC	.05
15 Warren Newson RC	.05
16 Paul Faries RC	.05
17 Luis Gonzalez	.15
18 Charles Nagy	.05
19 Chris Hammond	.05
20 Frank Castillo	.05
21 Pedro Munoz	.05
22 Orlando Merced	.05
23 Jose Melendez RC	.05
24 Kirk Dressendorfer	.05
25 Heathcliff Slocumb RC	.05
26 Doug Simons RC	.05
27 Mike Timlin RC	.05
28 Jeff Fassero	.05
29 Mark Leiter RC	.05
30 Jeff Bagwell RC	2.50
31 Brian McRae	.05
32 Mark Whiten	.05
33 Ivan Rodriguez RC	1.50
34 Wade Taylor RC	.05
35 Darren Lewis	.05
36 Mo Vaughn	.25
37 Mike Remlinger RC	.05
38 Rick Wilkins	.05
39 Chuck Knoblauch	.05
40 Kevin Morton	.05
41 Carlos Rodriguez RC	.05
42 Mark Lewis	.05
43 Brent Mayne	.05
44 Chris Haney RC	.05
45 Denis Boucher RC	.05
46 Mike Gardiner	.05
47 Jeff Johnson RC	.05
48 Dean Palmer	.05
49 Chuck McElroy	.05
50 Chris Jones RC	.05
51 Scott Kamieniecki RC	.05
52 Al Osuna RC	.05
53 Rusty Meacham RC	.05
54 Chito Martinez	.05
55 Reggie Jefferson	.05
56 Checklist	.05

1992 Donruss Previews

Four-card cello packs distributed to members of the Donruss dealers' network previewed the forthcoming 1992 baseball card issue. The preview cards have the same format, front and back photos as their counterparts in the regular set. Only the card number, the security underprinting, "Donruss Preview Card," and the stats, complete only through 1990, differ.

	NM/M
Complete Set (12):	25.00
Common Player:	.50
1 Wade Boggs	2.50
2 Barry Bonds	7.50
3 Will Clark	.50
4 Andre Dawson	.75
5 Dennis Eckersley	1.50
6 Robin Ventura	.50
7 Ken Griffey Jr.	4.00
8 Kelly Gruber	.50
9 Ryan Klesko/RR	.50
10 Cal Ripken, Jr.	7.50
11 Nolan Ryan (Highlight)	7.50
12 Todd Van Poppel	.50

1992 Donruss

For the second consecutive year, Donruss released its card set in two series. The 1992 cards feature improved stock, an anti-counterfeit feature and include both front and back photos. Once again Rated Rookies and All-Stars are included in the set. Special highlight cards also can be found in the 1992 Donruss set. Production was reduced in 1992 compared to 1988-1991. Retail factory sets include four 1992 Leaf preview cards.

	NM/M
Unopened Retail Set (788):	15.00
Unopened Hobby Set (784):	12.50
Unopened "Coca-Cola" Set (784):	25.00
Complete Set (784):	12.00
Common Player:	.05
Rod Carew Puzzle:	.50
Series 1 or 2 Pack (15):	.50
Series 1 or 2 Wax Box (36):	15.00
Blister Rack (92):	1.50

1	Mark Wohlers/RR **RC**	.05
2	Wil Cordero/RR	.05
3	Kyle Abbott/RR	.05
4	Dave Nilsson/RR **RC**	.05
5	Kenny Lofton/RR	.15
6	Luis Mercedes/RR **RC**	.05
7	Roger Salkeld/RR	.05
8	Eddie Zosky/RR **RC**	.05
9	Todd Van Poppel/RR **RC**	.10
10	Frank Seminara/RR **RC**	.05
11	Andy Ashby/RR **RC**	.10
12	Reggie Jefferson/RR **RC**	.05
13	Ryan Klesko/RR	.05
14	Carlos Garcia/RR **RC**	.10
15	John Ramos/RR **RC**	.05
16	Eric Karros/RR	.05
17	Pat Lennon/RR **RC**	.05
18	Eddie Taubensee/RR **RC**	.05
19	Roberto Hernandez/RR **RC**	.05
20	D.J. Dozier/RC **RC**	.05
21	Dave Henderson/AS	.05
22	Cal Ripken, Jr./AS	.50
23	Wade Boggs/AS	.25
24	Ken Griffey Jr./AS	.35
25	Jack Morris/AS	.05
26	Danny Tartabull/AS	.05
27	Cecil Fielder/AS	.05
28	Roberto Alomar/AS	.10
29	Sandy Alomar/AS	.05
30	Rickey Henderson/AS	.25
31	Ken Hill	.05
32	John Habyan	.05
33	Otis Nixon (Highlight)	.05
34	Tim Wallach	.05
35	Cal Ripken, Jr.	1.00
36	Gary Carter	.35
37	Juan Agosto	.05
38	Doug Dascenzo	.05
39	Kirk Gibson	.05
40	Benito Santiago	.05
41	Otis Nixon	.05
42	Andy Allanson	.05
43	Brian Holman	.05
44	Dick Schofield	.05
45	Dave Magadan	.05
46	Rafael Palmeiro	.35
47	Jody Reed	.05
48	Ivan Calderon	.05
49	Greg Harris	.05
50	Chris Sabo	.05
51	Paul Molitor	.35
52	Robby Thompson	.05
53	Dave Smith	.05
54	Mark Davis	.05
55	Kevin Brown	.05
56	Donn Pall	.05
57	Len Dykstra	.05
58	Roberto Alomar	.15
59	Jeff Robinson	.05
60	Willie McGee	.05
61	Jay Buhner	.05
62	Mike Pagliarulo	.05
63	Paul O'Neill	.05
64	Hubie Brooks	.05
65	Kelly Gruber	.05
66	Ken Caminiti	.05
67	Gary Redus	.05
68	Harold Baines	.05
69	Charlie Hough	.05
70	B.J. Surhoff	.05
71	Walt Weiss	.05
72	Shawn Hillegas	.05
73	Roberto Kelly	.05
74	Jeff Ballard	.05
75	Craig Biggio	.05
76	Pat Combs	.05
77	Jeff Robinson	.05
78	Tim Belcher	.05
79	Cris Carpenter	.05
80	Checklist 1-79	.05
81	Steve Avery	.05
82	Chris James	.05
83	Brian Harper	.05
84	Charlie Leibrandt	.05
85	Mickey Tettleton	.05
86	Pete O'Brien	.05
87	Danny Darwin	.05
88	Bob Walk	.05
89	Jeff Reardon	.05
90	Bobby Rose	.05
91	Danny Jackson	.05
92	John Morris	.05
93	Bud Black	.05
94	Tommy Greene (Highlight)	.05
95	Rick Aguilera	.05
96	Gary Gaetti	.05
97	David Cone	.05
98	John Olerud	.05
99	Joel Skinner	.05
100	Jay Bell	.05
101	Bob Milacki	.05
102	Norm Charlton	.05
103	Chuck Crim	.05
104	Terry Steinbach	.05
105	Juan Samuel	.05
106	Steve Howe	.05
107	Rafael Belliard	.05
108	Joey Cora	.05
109	Tommy Greene	.05
110	Gregg Olson	.05
111	Frank Tanana	.05
112	Lee Smith	.05
113	Greg Harris	.05
114	Dwayne Henry	.05
115	Chili Davis	.05
116	Kent Mercker	.05
117	Brian Barnes	.05
118	Rich DeLucia	.05
119	Andre Dawson	.20
120	Carlos Baerga	.05
121	Mike LaValliere	.05
122	Jeff Gray	.05
123	Bruce Hurst	.05
124	Alvin Davis	.05
125	John Candelaria	.05
126	Matt Nokes	.05
127	George Bell	.05
128	Bret Saberhagen	.05
129	Jeff Russell	.05
130	Jim Abbott	.05
131	Bill Gullickson	.05
132	Todd Zeile	.05
133	Dave Winfield	.35
134	Wally Whitehurst	.05
135	Matt Williams	.05
136	Tom Browning	.05
137	Marquis Grissom	.05
138	Erik Hanson	.05
139	Rob Dibble	.05
140	Don August	.05
141	Tom Henke	.05
142	Dan Pasqua	.05
143	George Brett	.60
144	Jerald Clark	.05
145	Robin Ventura	.05
146	Dale Murphy	.20
147	Dennis Eckersley	.30
148	Eric Yelding	.05
149	Mario Diaz	.05
150	Casey Candaele	.05
151	Steve Olin	.05
152	Luis Salazar	.05
153	Kevin Maas	.05
154	Nolan Ryan (Highlight)	.50
155	Barry Jones	.05
156	Chris Hoiles	.05
157	Bobby Ojeda	.05
158	Pedro Guerrero	.05
159	Paul Assenmacher	.05
160	Checklist 80-157	.05
161	Mike Macfarlane	.05
162	Craig Lefferts	.05
163	Brian Hunter **RC**	.05
164	Alan Trammell	.05
165	Ken Griffey Jr.	.65
166	Lance Parrish	.05
167	Brian Downing	.05
168	John Barfield	.05
169	Jack Clark	.05
170	Chris Nabholz	.05
171	Tim Teufel	.05
172	Chris Hammond	.05
173	Robin Yount	.35
174	Dave Righetti	.05
175	Joe Girardi	.05
176	Mike Boddicker	.05
177	Dean Palmer	.05
178	Greg Hibbard	.05
179	Randy Ready	.05
180	Devon White	.05
181	Mark Eichhorn	.05
182	Mike Felder	.05
183	Joe Klink	.05
184	Steve Bedrosian	.05
185	Barry Larkin	.05
186	John Franco	.05
187	Ed Sprague **RC**	.05
188	Mark Portugal	.05
189	Jose Lind	.05
190	Bob Welch	.05
191	Alex Fernandez	.05
192	Gary Sheffield	.20
193	Rickey Henderson	.35
194	Rod Nichols	.05
195	Scott Kamieniecki **RC**	.05
196	Mike Flanagan	.05
197	Steve Finley	.05
198	Darren Daulton	.05
199	Leo Gomez	.05
200	Mike Morgan	.05
201	Bob Tewksbury	.05
202	Sid Bream	.05
203	Sandy Alomar	.05
204	Greg Gagne	.05
205	Juan Berenguer	.05
206	Cecil Fielder	.05
207	Randy Johnson	.35
208	Tony Pena	.05
209	Doug Drabek	.05
210	Wade Boggs	.45
211	Bryan Harvey	.05
212	Jose Vizcaino	.05
213	Alonzo Powell **RC**	.05
214	Will Clark	.05
215	Rickey Henderson (Highlight)	.20
216	Jack Morris	.05
217	Junior Felix	.05
218	Vince Coleman	.05
219	Jimmy Key	.05
220	Alex Cole	.05
221	Bill Landrum	.05
222	Randy Milligan	.05
223	Jose Rijo	.05
224	Greg Vaughn	.05
225	Dave Stewart	.05
226	Lenny Harris	.05
227	Scott Sanderson	.05
228	Jeff Blauser	.05
229	Ozzie Guillen	.05
230	John Kruk	.05
231	Bob Melvin	.05
232	Milt Cuyler	.05
233	Felix Jose	.05
234	Ellis Burks	.05
235	Pete Harnisch	.05
236	Kevin Tapani	.05
237	Terry Pendleton	.05
238	Mark Gardner	.05
239	Harold Reynolds	.05
240	Checklist 158-237	.05
241	Mike Harkey	.05
242	Felix Fermin	.05
243	Barry Bonds	1.00
244	Roger Clemens	.60
245	Dennis Rasmussen	.05
246	Jose DeLeon	.05
247	Orel Hershiser	.05
248	Mel Hall	.05
249	Rick Wilkins **RC**	.05
250	Tom Gordon	.05
251	Kevin Reimer	.05
252	Luis Polonia	.05
253	Mike Henneman	.05
254	Tom Pagnozzi	.05
255	Chuck Finley	.05
256	Mackey Sasser	.05
257	John Burkett	.05
258	Hal Morris	.05
259	Larry Walker	.05
260	Billy Swift	.05
261	Joe Oliver	.05
262	Julio Machado	.05
263	Todd Stottlemyre	.05
264	Matt Merullo	.05
265	Brent Mayne	.05
266	Thomas Howard	.05
267	Lance Johnson	.05
268	Terry Mulholland	.05
269	Rick Honeycutt	.05
270	Luis Gonzalez	.05
271	Jose Guzman	.05
272	Jimmy Jones	.05
273	Mark Lewis	.05
274	Rene Gonzales	.05
275	Jeff Johnson **RC**	.05
276	Dennis Martinez (Highlight)	.05
277	Delino DeShields	.05
278	Sam Horn	.05
279	Kevin Gross	.05
280	Jose Oquendo	.05
281	Mark Grace	.05
282	Mark Gubicza	.05
283	Fred McGriff	.05
284	Ron Gant	.05
285	Lou Whitaker	.05
286	Edgar Martinez	.05
287	Ron Tingley	.05
288	Kevin McReynolds	.05
289	Ivan Rodriguez	.30
290	Mike Gardiner	.05
291	Chris Haney **RC**	.05
292	Darrin Jackson	.05
293	Bill Doran	.05
294	Ted Higuera	.05
295	Jeff Brantley	.05
296	Les Lancaster	.05
297	Jim Eisenreich	.05
298	Ruben Sierra	.05
299	Scott Radinsky	.05
300	Jose DeJesus	.05
301	Mike Timlin **RC**	.05
302	Luis Sojo	.05
303	Kelly Downs	.05
304	Scott Bankhead	.05
305	Pedro Munoz	.05
306	Scott Scudder	.05
307	Kevin Elster	.05
308	Duane Ward	.05
309	Darryl Kile **RC**	.10
310	Orlando Merced	.05
311	Dave Henderson	.05
312	Tim Raines	.05
313	Mark Lee **RC**	.05
314	Mike Gallego	.05
315	Charles Nagy	.05
316	Jesse Barfield	.05
317	Todd Frohwirth	.05
318	Al Osuna	.05
319	Darrin Fletcher	.05
320	Checklist 238-316	.05
321	David Segui	.05
322	Stan Javier	.05
323	Bryn Smith	.05
324	Jeff Treadway	.05
325	Mark Whiten	.05
326	Kent Hrbek	.05
327	Dave Justice	.05
328	Tony Phillips	.05
329	Rob Murphy	.05
330	Kevin Morton	.05
331	John Smiley	.05
332	Luis Rivera	.05
333	Wally Joyner	.05
334	Heathcliff Slocumb **RC**	.05
335	Rick Cerone	.05
336	Mike Remlinger **RC**	.05
337	Mike Moore	.05
338	Lloyd McClendon	.05
339	Al Newman	.05
340	Kirk McCaskill	.05
341	Howard Johnson	.05
342	Greg Myers	.05
343	Kal Daniels	.05
344	Bernie Williams	.05
345	Shane Mack	.05
346	Gary Thurman	.05
347	Dante Bichette	.05
348	Mark McGwire	.75
349	Travis Fryman	.05
350	Ray Lankford	.05
351	Mike Jeffcoat	.05
352	Jack McDowell	.05
353	Mitch Williams	.05
354	Mike Devereaux	.05
355	Andres Galarraga	.05
356	Henry Cotto	.05
357	Scott Bailes	.05
358	Jeff Bagwell	.35
359	Scott Leius	.05
360	Zane Smith	.05
361	Bill Pecota	.05
362	Tony Fernandez	.05
363	Glenn Braggs	.05
364	Bill Spiers	.05
365	Vicente Palacios	.05
366	Tim Burke	.05
367	Randy Tomlin	.05
368	Kenny Rogers	.05
369	Brett Butler	.05
370	Pat Kelly	.05
371	Bip Roberts	.05
372	Gregg Jefferies	.05
373	Kevin Bass	.05
374	Ron Karkovice	.05
375	Paul Gibson	.05
376	Bernard Gilkey	.05
377	Dave Gallagher	.05
378	Bill Wegman	.05
379	Pat Borders	.05
380	Ed Whitson	.05
381	Gilberto Reyes	.05
382	Russ Swan	.05
383	Andy Van Slyke	.05
384	Wes Chamberlain	.05
385	Steve Chitren	.05
386	Greg Olson	.05
387	Brian McRae	.05
388	Rich Rodriguez	.05
389	Steve Decker	.05
390	Chuck Knoblauch	.05
391	Bobby Witt	.05
392	Eddie Murray	.35
393	Juan Gonzalez	.20
394	Scott Ruskin	.05
395	Jay Howell	.05
396	Checklist 317-396	.05
397	Royce Clayton/RR **RC**	.05
398	John Jaha/RR **RC**	.05
399	Dan Wilson/RR **RC**	.05
400	Archie Corbin/RR **RC**	.05
401	Barry Manuel/RR **RC**	.05
402	Kim Batiste/RR **RC**	.05
403	Pat Mahomes/RR **RC**	.05
404	Dave Fleming/RR **RC**	.05
405	Jeff Juden/RR **RC**	.05
406	Jim Thome/RR	.40
407	Sam Militello/RR **RC**	.05
408	Jeff Nelson/RR **RC**	.05
409	Anthony Young/RR	.05
410	Tino Martinez/RR	.05
411	Jeff Mutis/RR **RC**	.05
412	Rey Sanchez/RR **RC**	.05
413	Chris Gardner/RR **RC**	.05
414	John Vander Wal/RR **RC**	.10
415	Reggie Sanders/RR	.05
416	Brian Williams/RR **RC**	.05
417	Mo Sanford/RR **RC**	.05
418	David Weathers/RR **RC**	.05
419	Hector Fajardo/RR **RC**	.05
420	Steve Foster/RR **RC**	.05
421	Lance Dickson/RR	.05
422	Andre Dawson/AS	.15
423	Ozzie Smith/AS	.25
424	Chris Sabo/AS	.05
425	Tony Gwynn/AS	.25
426	Tom Glavine/AS	.05
427	Bobby Bonilla/AS	.05
428	Will Clark/AS	.05
429	Ryne Sandberg/AS	.25
430	Benito Santiago/AS	.05
431	Ivan Calderon/AS	.05
432	Ozzie Smith	.45
433	Tim Leary	.05
434	Bret Saberhagen (Highlight)	.05
435	Mel Rojas	.05
436	Ben McDonald	.05
437	Tim Crews	.05
438	Rex Hudler	.05
439	Chico Walker	.05
440	Kurt Stillwell	.05
441	Tony Gwynn	.45
442	John Smoltz	.05
443	Lloyd Moseby	.05
444	Mike Schooler	.05
445	Joe Grahe	.05
446	Dwight Gooden	.05
447	Oil Can Boyd	.05
448	John Marzano	.05
449	Bret Barberie	.05
450	Mike Maddux	.05
451	Jeff Reed	.05
452	Dale Sveum	.05
453	Jose Uribe	.05
454	Bob Scanlan	.05
455	Kevin Appier	.05
456	Jeff Huson	.05
457	Ken Patterson	.05
458	Ricky Jordan	.05
459	Tom Candiotti	.05
460	Lee Stevens	.05
461	Rod Beck **RC**	.10
462	Dave Valle	.05
463	Scott Erickson	.05
464	Chris Jones	.05
465	Mark Carreon	.05
466	Rob Ducey	.05
467	Jim Corsi	.05
468	Jeff King	.05
469	Curt Young	.05
470	Bo Jackson	.15
471	Chris Bosio	.05
472	Jamie Quirk	.05
473	Jesse Orosco	.05
474	Alvaro Espinoza	.05
475	Joe Orsulak	.05
476	Checklist 397-477	.05
477	Gerald Young	.05
478	Wally Backman	.05
479	Juan Bell	.05
480	Mike Scioscia	.05
481	Omar Olivares	.05
482	Francisco Cabrera	.05
483	Greg Swindell	.05
484	Terry Leach	.05
485	Tommy Gregg	.05
486	Scott Aldred	.05
487	Greg Briley	.05
488	Phil Plantier	.05
489	Curtis Wilkerson	.05
490	Tom Brunansky	.05
491	Mike Fetters	.05
492	Frank Castillo	.05
493	Joe Boever	.05
494	Kirt Manwaring	.05
495	Wilson Alvarez (Highlight)	.05
496	Gene Larkin	.05
497	Gary DiSarcina	.05
498	Frank Viola	.05
499	Manuel Lee	.05
500	Albert Belle	.05
501	Stan Belinda	.05
502	Dwight Evans	.05
503	Eric Davis	.05
504	Darren Holmes	.05
505	Mike Bordick	.05
506	Dave Hansen	.05
507	Lee Guetterman	.05
508	Keith Mitchell **RC**	.05
509	Melido Perez	.05
510	Dickie Thon	.05
511	Mark Williamson	.05
512	Mark Salas	.05
513	Milt Thompson	.05
514	Mo Vaughn	.05
515	Jim Deshaies	.05
516	Rich Garces	.05
517	Lonnie Smith	.05
518	Spike Owen	.05
519	Tracy Jones	.05
520	Greg Maddux	.45
521	Carlos Martinez	.05
522	Neal Heaton	.05
523	Mike Greenwell	.05
524	Andy Benes	.05
525	Jeff Schaefer	.05
526	Mike Sharperson	.05
527	Wade Taylor	.05
528	Jerome Walton	.05
529	Storm Davis	.05
530	Jose Hernandez **RC**	.05
531	Mark Langston	.05
532	Rob Deer	.05
533	Geronimo Pena	.05
534	Juan Guzman **RC**	.10
535	Pete Schourek	.05
536	Todd Benzinger	.05
537	Billy Hatcher	.05
538	Tom Foley	.05
539	Dave Cochrane	.05
540	Mariano Duncan	.05
541	Edwin Nunez	.05
542	Rance Mulliniks	.05
543	Carlton Fisk	.35
544	Luis Aquino	.05
545	Ricky Bones	.05
546	Craig Grebeck	.05
547	Charlie Hayes	.05
548	Jose Canseco	.25
549	Andujar Cedeno	.05
550	Geno Petralli	.05
551	Javier Ortiz	.05
552	Rudy Seanez	.05
553	Rich Gedman	.05
554	Eric Plunk	.05
555	Nolan Ryan, Rich Gossage (Highlight)	.25
556	Checklist 478-555	.05
557	Greg Colbrunn	.05
558	Chito Martinez **RC**	.05
559	Darryl Strawberry	.05
560	Luis Alicea	.05
561	Dwight Smith	.05
562	Terry Shumpert	.05
563	Jim Vatcher	.05
564	Deion Sanders	.10
565	Walt Terrell	.05
566	Dave Burba	.05
567	Dave Howard	.05
568	Todd Hundley	.05
569	Jack Daugherty	.05
570	Scott Cooper	.05
571	Bill Sampen	.05
572	Jose Melendez	.05
573	Freddie Benavides	.05
574	Jim Gantner	.05
575	Trevor Wilson	.05
576	Ryne Sandberg	.45
577	Kevin Seitzer	.05
578	Gerald Alexander	.05
579	Mike Huff	.05
580	Von Hayes	.05
581	Derek Bell	.05
582	Mike Stanley	.05
583	Kevin Mitchell	.05
584	Mike Jackson	.05
585	Dan Gladden	.05
586	Ted Power	.05
587	Jeff Innis	.05
588	Bob MacDonald	.05
589	Jose Tolentino **RC**	.05
590	Bob Patterson	.05
591	Scott Brosius **RC**	.10
592	Frank Thomas	.35
593	Darryl Hamilton	.05
594	Kirk Dressendorfer	.05
595	Jeff Shaw	.05
596	Don Mattingly	.60
597	Glenn Davis	.05
598	Andy Mota	.05
599	Jason Grimsley	.05
600	Jimmy Poole	.05
601	Jim Gott	.05
602	Stan Royer	.05
603	Marvin Freeman	.05
604	Denis Boucher	.05
605	Denny Neagle	.05
606	Mark Lemke	.05
607	Jerry Don Gleaton	.05
608	Brent Knackert	.05
609	Carlos Quintana	.05
610	Bobby Bonilla	.05
611	Joe Hesketh	.05
612	Daryl Boston	.05
613	Shawon Dunston	.05
614	Danny Cox	.05
615	Darren Lewis	.05
616	Alejandro Pena, Kent Mercker, Mark Wohlers (Highlight)	.05
617	Kirby Puckett	.45
618	Franklin Stubbs	.05
619	Chris Donnels	.05
620	David Wells	.05
621	Mike Aldrete	.05
622	Bob Kipper	.05
623	Anthony Telford	.05
624	Randy Myers	.05
625	Willie Randolph	.05
626	Joe Slusarski	.05
627	John Wetteland	.05
628	Greg Cadaret	.05
629	Tom Glavine	.20
630	Wilson Alvarez	.05
631	Wally Ritchie	.05
632	Mike Mussina	.25
633	Mark Leiter	.05
634	Gerald Perry	.05
635	Matt Young	.05
636	Checklist 556-635	.05

ABBREVIATIONS

AS - All-Star
RR - Rated Rookie

No.	Player	Price
637	Scott Hemond	.05
638	David West	.05
639	Jim Clancy	.05
640	Doug Piatt RC	.05
641	Omar Vizquel	.05
642	Rick Sutcliffe	.05
643	Glenallen Hill	.05
644	Gary Varsho	.05
645	Tony Fossas	.05
646	Jack Howell	.05
647	Jim Campanis RC	.05
648	Chris Gwynn	.05
649	Jim Leyritz	.05
650	Chuck McElroy	.05
651	Sean Berry RC	.05
652	Donald Harris RC	.05
653	Don Slaught	.05
654	Rusty Meacham RC	.05
655	Scott Terry	.05
656	Ramon Martinez	.05
657	Keith Miller	.05
658	Ramon Garcia RC	.05
659	Milt Hill RC	.05
660	Steve Frey	.05
661	Bob McClure	.05
662	Ced Landrum RC	.05
663	Doug Henry RC	.05
664	Candy Maldonado	.05
665	Carl Willis	.05
666	Jeff Montgomery	.05
667	Craig Shipley RC	.05
668	Warren Newson RC	.05
669	Mickey Morandini	.05
670	Brook Jacoby	.05
671	Ryan Bowen RC	.05
672	Bill Krueger	.05
673	Rob Mallicoat	.05
674	Doug Jones	.05
675	Scott Livingstone	.05
676	Danny Tartabull	.05
677	Joe Carter (Highlight)	.05
678	Cecil Espy	.05
679	Randy Velarde	.05
680	Bruce Ruffin	.05
681	Ted Wood RC	.05
682	Dan Plesac	.05
683	Eric Bullock	.05
684	Junior Ortiz	.05
685	Dave Hollins	.05
686	Dennis Martinez	.05
687	Larry Andersen	.05
688	Doug Simons	.05
689	Tim Spehr RC	.05
690	Calvin Jones RC	.05
691	Mark Guthrie	.05
692	Alfredo Griffin	.05
693	Joe Carter	.05
694	Terry Mathews RC	.05
695	Pascual Perez	.05
696	Gene Nelson	.05
697	Gerald Williams	.05
698	Chris Cron RC	.05
699	Steve Buechele	.05
700	Paul McClellan RC	.05
701	Jim Lindeman	.05
702	Francisco Oliveras	.05
703	Rob Maurer RC	.05
704	Pat Hentgen RC	.15
705	Jaime Navarro	.05
706	Mike Magnante RC	.05
707	Nolan Ryan	1.00
708	Bobby Thigpen	.05
709	John Cerutti	.05
710	Steve Wilson	.05
711	Hensley Meulens	.05
712	Rheal Cormier RC	.05
713	Scott Bradley	.05
714	Mitch Webster	.05
715	Roger Mason	.05
716	Checklist 636-716	.05
717	Jeff Fassero RC	.05
718	Cal Eldred RC	.05
719	Sid Fernandez	.05
720	Bob Zupcic RC	.05
721	Jose Offerman	.05
722	Cliff Brantley RC	.05
723	Ron Darling	.05
724	Dave Stieb	.05
725	Hector Villanueva	.05
726	Mike Hartley	.05
727	Arthur Rhodes RC	.05
728	Randy Bush	.05
729	Steve Sax	.05
730	Dave Otto	.05
731	John Wehner RC	.05
732	Dave Martinez	.05
733	Ruben Amaro RC	.05
734	Billy Ripken	.05
735	Steve Farr	.05
736	Shawn Abner	.05
737	Gil Heredia RC	.05
738	Ron Jones	.05
739	Tony Castillo	.05
740	Sammy Sosa	.45
741	Julio Franco	.05
742	Tim Naehring	.05
743	Steve Wapnick RC	.05
744	Craig Wilson RC	.05
745	Darrin Chapin RC	.05
746	Chris George RC	.05
747	Mike Simms	.05
748	Rosario Rodriguez	.05
749	Skeeter Barnes	.05
750	Roger McDowell	.05
751	Dann Howitt	.05
752	Paul Sorrento	.05
753	Braulio Castillo RC	.05
754	Yorkis Perez RC	.05
755	Willie Fraser	.05
756	Jeremy Hernandez RC	.05
757	Curt Schilling	.20
758	Steve Lyons	.05
759	Dave Anderson	.05
760	Willie Banks	.05
761	Mark Leonard	.05
762	Jack Armstrong	.05
763	Scott Servais	.05
764	Ray Stephens	.05
765	Junior Noboa	.05
766	Jim Olander RC	.05
767	Joe Magrane	.05
768	Lance Blankenship	.05
769	Mike Humphreys RC	.05
770	Jarvis Brown RC	.05
771	Damon Berryhill	.05
772	Alejandro Pena	.05
773	Jose Mesa	.05
774	Gary Cooper RC	.05
775	Carney Lansford	.05
776	Mike Bielecki	.05
777	Charlie O'Brien	.05
778	Carlos Hernandez	.05
779	Howard Farmer	.05
780	Mike Stanton	.05
781	Reggie Harris	.05
782	Xavier Hernandez	.05
783	Bryan Hickerson RC	.05
784	Checklist 717-BC8	.05

Bonus Cards

The eight bonus cards were randomly inserted in 1992 foil packs and are numbered with a "BC" prefix. Both leagues' MVPs, Cy Young and Rookie of the Year award winners are featured, as are logo cards for the expansion Colorado Rockies and Florida Marlins. Cards are standard size in a format similar to the regular issue.

		NM/M
Complete Set (8):		5.00
Common Player:		.25
1	Cal Ripken, Jr./MVP	2.50
2	Terry Pendleton/MVP	.25
3	Roger Clemens (Cy Young)	2.00
4	Tom Glavine (Cy Young)	.40
5	Chuck Knoblauch (Rookie of the Year)	.25
6	Jeff Bagwell (Rookie of the Year)	1.50
7	Colorado Rockies	.25
8	Florida Marlins	.25

1992 Donruss Diamond Kings

Donruss changed its Diamond Kings style and distribution in 1992. The cards still feature the art of Dick Perez, but quality was improved from past years. The cards were randomly inserted in foil packs. One player from each team is featured. Card numbers have a "DK" prefix.

		NM/M
Complete Set (27):		17.50
Common Player:		.40
1	Paul Molitor	2.00
2	Will Clark	.50
3	Joe Carter	.50
4	Julio Franco	.50
5	Cal Ripken, Jr.	6.00
6	Dave Justice	.50
7	George Bell	.50
8	Frank Thomas	2.00
9	Wade Boggs	4.00
10	Scott Sanderson	.50
11	Jeff Bagwell	2.00
12	John Kruk	.50
13	Felix Jose	.50
14	Harold Baines	.50
15	Dwight Gooden	.50
16	Brian McRae	.50
17	Jay Bell	.50
18	Brett Butler	.50
19	Hal Morris	.50
20	Mark Langston	.50
21	Scott Erickson	.50
22	Randy Johnson	2.00
23	Greg Swindell	.50
24	Dennis Martinez	.50
25	Tony Phillips	.50
26	Fred McGriff	.50
27	Checklist	.10

Supers

Produced in very limited numbers, possibly as a prototype for use in a sales presentation to a major retail chain, these 4-7/8" x 6-3/4" cards are identical in virtually everything but size to the regular 1992 DK inserts. Both front and back feature a high-gloss finish.

		NM/M
Complete Set (27):		900.00
Common Player:		15.00
1	Paul Molitor	95.00
2	Will Clark	15.00
3	Joe Carter	15.00
4	Julio Franco	15.00
5	Cal Ripken, Jr.	335.00
6	Dave Justice	15.00
7	George Bell	15.00
8	Frank Thomas	100.00
9	Wade Boggs	125.00
10	Scott Sanderson	15.00
11	Jeff Bagwell	95.00
12	John Kruk	15.00
13	Felix Jose	15.00
14	Harold Baines	15.00
15	Dwight Gooden	15.00
16	Brian McRae	15.00
17	Jay Bell	15.00
18	Brett Butler	15.00
19	Hal Morris	15.00
20	Mark Langston	15.00
21	Scott Erickson	15.00
22	Randy Johnson	75.00
23	Greg Swindell	15.00
24	Dennis Martinez	15.00
25	Tony Phillips	15.00
26	Fred McGriff	15.00
27	Checklist (Dick Perez)	5.00

Elite

Donruss continued its Elite series in 1992 by inserting cards in foil packs. Each card was released in the same quantity as the 1991 inserts - 10,000 Elite, 7,500 Legend and 5,000 Signature. The Elite cards, now featuring a prismatic border, are numbered as a continuation of the 1991 issue.

		NM/M
Complete Set (12):		300.00
Common Player:		7.50
9	Wade Boggs	15.00
10	Joe Carter	7.50
11	Will Clark	7.50
12	Dwight Gooden	7.50
13	Ken Griffey Jr.	30.00
14	Tony Gwynn	15.00
15	Howard Johnson	7.50
16	Terry Pendleton	7.50
17	Kirby Puckett	15.00
18	Frank Thomas	15.00
---	Rickey Henderson (Legend)	20.00
---	Cal Ripken, Jr. (Signature)	250.00

Rookies

Donruss increased the size of its Rookies set in 1992 to include 132 cards. In the past the cards were released only in boxed set form, but the 1992 cards were available in packs. Special "Phenoms" cards were randomly inserted into Rookies packs. The Phenoms cards feature black borders, while the Rookies cards are styled after the regular 1992 Donruss issue. The cards are numbered alphabetically.

		NM/M
Complete Set (132):		6.00
Common Player:		.05
Pack (12):		.50
Wax Box (36):		10.00
1	Kyle Abbott	.05
2	Troy Afenir	.05
3	Rich Amaral RC	.05
4	Ruben Amaro RC	.05
5	Billy Ashley RC	.05
6	Pedro Astacio RC	.05
7	Jim Austin RC	.05
8	Robert Ayrault RC	.05
9	Kevin Baez RC	.05
10	Estaban Beltre RC	.05
11	Brian Bohanon RC	.05
12	Kent Bottenfield RC	.05
13	Jeff Branson RC	.05
14	Brad Brink RC	.05
15	John Briscoe RC	.05
16	Doug Brocail RC	.05
17	Rico Brogna RC	.05
18	J.T. Bruett RC	.05
19	Jacob Brumfield	.05
20	Jim Bullinger RC	.05
21	Kevin Campbell RC	.05
22	Pedro Castellano RC	.05
23	Mike Christopher RC	.05
24	Archi Cianfrocco RC	.05
25	Mark Clark RC	.05
26	Craig Colbert RC	.05
27	Victor Cole RC	.05
28	Steve Cooke RC	.05
29	Tim Costo RC	.05
30	Chad Curtis RC	.05
31	Doug Davis RC	.05
32	Gary DiSarcina	.05
33	John Doherty RC	.05
34	Mike Draper RC	.05
35	Monty Fariss	.05
36	Bien Figueroa RC	.05
37	John Flaherty RC	.05
38	Tim Fortugno RC	.05
39	Eric Fox RC	.05
40	Jeff Frye RC	.05
41	Ramon Garcia RC	.05
42	Brent Gates RC	.05
43	Tom Goodwin RC	.05
44	Buddy Groom RC	.05
45	Jeff Grotewold RC	.05
46	Juan Guerrero RC	.05
47	Johnny Guzman RC	.05
48	Shawn Hare RC	.05
49	Ryan Hawblitzel RC	.05
50	Bert Heffernan RC	.05
51	Butch Henry RC	.05
52	Cesar Hernandez RC	.05
53	Vince Horsman RC	.05
54	Steve Hosey RC	.05
55	Pat Howell RC	.05
56	Peter Hoy RC	.05
57	Jon Hurst RC	.05
58	Mark Hutton RC	.05
59	Shawn Jeter RC	.05
60	Joel Johnston RC	.05
61	Jeff Kent RC	1.00
62	Kurt Knudsen RC	.05
63	Kevin Koslofski RC	.05
64	Danny Leon RC	.05
65	Jesse Levis RC	.05
66	Tom Marsh RC	.05
67	Ed Martel RC	.05
68	Al Martin RC	.05
69	Pedro Martinez RC	2.00
70	Derrick May	.05
71	Matt Maysey RC	.05
72	Russ McGinnis RC	.05
73	Tim McIntosh	.05
74	Jim McNamara RC	.05
75	Jeff McNeely RC	.05
76	Rusty Meacham	.05
77	Tony Melendez RC	.05
78	Henry Mercedes RC	.05
79	Paul Miller RC	.05
80	Joe Millette RC	.05
81	Blas Minor RC	.05
82	Dennis Moeller RC	.05
83	Raul Mondesi RC	.25
84	Rob Natal RC	.05
85	Troy Neel RC	.05
86	David Nied RC	.05
87	Jerry Nielsen RC	.05
88	Donovan Osborne	.05
89	John Patterson RC	.05
90	Roger Pavlik RC	.05
91	Dan Peltier RC	.05
92	Jim Pena RC	.05
93	William Pennyfeather RC	.05
94	Mike Perez	.05
95	Hipolito Pichardo RC	.05
96	Greg Pirkl RC	.05
97	Harvey Pulliam RC	.05
98	Manny Ramirez RC	3.00
99	Pat Rapp RC	.05
100	Jeff Reboulet RC	.05
101	Darren Reed RC	.05
102	Shane Reynolds RC	.05
103	Bill Risley RC	.05
104	Ben Rivera RC	.05
105	Henry Rodriguez RC	.05
106	Rico Rossy RC	.05
107	Johnny Ruffin RC	.05
108	Steve Scarsone RC	.05
109	Tim Scott RC	.05
110	Steve Shifflett RC	.05
111	Dave Silvestri RC	.05
112	Matt Stairs RC	.05
113	William Suero RC	.05
114	Jeff Tackett RC	.05
115	Eddie Taubensee RC	.05
116	Rick Trlicek RC	.05
117	Scooter Tucker RC	.05
118	Shane Turner RC	.05
119	Julio Valera RC	.05
120	Paul Wagner RC	.05
121	Tim Wakefield RC	.05
122	Mike Walker RC	.05
123	Bruce Walton RC	.05
124	Lenny Webster	.05
125	Bob Wickman RC	.05
126	Mike Williams RC	.05
127	Kerry Woodson RC	.05
128	Eric Young RC	.05
129	Kevin Young RC	.05
130	Pete Young RC	.05
131	Checklist	.05
132	Checklist	.05

Rookie Phenoms

The first 12 cards in this insert set were available in Donruss Rookies foil packs. Cards 13-20 were found randomly packed in jumbo packs. Predominantly black on both front and back, the borders are highlighted with gold. A gold-foil "Phenoms" appears at top front.

		NM/M
Complete Set (20):		12.50
Common Player:		.25
1	Moises Alou	.50
2	Bret Boone	.50
3	Jeff Conine	.25
4	Dave Fleming	.25
5	Tyler Green	.25
6	Eric Karros	.25
7	Pat Listach	.25
8	Kenny Lofton	.25
9	Mike Piazza	10.00
10	Tim Salmon	.50
11	Andy Stankiewicz	.25
12	Dan Walters	.25
13	Ramon Caraballo	.25
14	Brian Jordan	.25
15	Ryan Klesko	.25
16	Sam Militello	.25
17	Frank Seminara	.25
18	Salomon Torres	.25
19	John Valentin	.25
20	Wil Cordero	.25

Update

Each retail factory set of 1992 Donruss cards contained a cello-wrapped four-card selection from this 22-card Update set. The cards feature the same basic format as the regular '92 Donruss, except they carry a "U" prefix to the card number on back. The cards feature rookies, highlights and traded players from the 1992 season.

		NM/M
Complete Set (22):		15.00
Common Player:		.50
1	Pat Listach/RR	.50
2	Andy Stankiewicz/RR	.50
3	Brian Jordan/RR	.50
4	Dan Walters/RR	.50
5	Chad Curtis/RR	.50
6	Kenny Lofton/RR	1.50
7	Mark McGwire (Highlight)	8.00
8	Eddie Murray (Highlight)	1.00
9	Jeff Reardon (Highlight)	.50
10	Frank Viola	.50
11	Gary Sheffield	.75
12	George Bell	.50
13	Rick Sutcliffe	.50
14	Wally Joyner	.50
15	Kevin Seitzer	.50
16	Bill Krueger	.50
17	Danny Tartabull	.50
18	Dave Winfield	2.00
19	Gary Carter	1.50
20	Bobby Bonilla	.50
21	Cory Snyder	.50
22	Bill Swift	.50

1992 Donruss/ Durivage Montreal Expos

Green borders and posed portrait photos are featured in this custom-published team set which Donruss produced for the Quebec bakery Durivage. Bilingual backs have personal data, recent major league stats and appropriate logos on a gray pinstriped background. Roster changes are reflected in the assignment of the same number to different players in several cases.

	NM/M
Complete Set (26):	50.00
Common Player:	2.00
Album:	5.00
1 Bret Barberie	2.00
2a Chris Haney	2.00
2b Brian Barnes	2.00
3a Bill Sampen	2.00
3b Phil Bradley	2.00
4 Ivan Calderon	2.00
5 Gary Carter	10.00
6 Delino DeShields	2.00
7 Jeff Fassero	2.00
8 Darrin Fletcher	2.00
9 Mark Gardner	2.00
10 Marquis Grissom	2.00
11 Ken Hill	2.00
12 Dennis Martinez	2.00
13 Chris Nabholz	2.00
14 Spike Owen	2.00
15a Tom Runnells	2.00
15b Felipe Alou	3.00
16a John Vander Wal	2.00
16b Matt Stairs	2.00
17a Bill Landrum	2.00
17b Dave Wainhouse	2.00
18 Larry Walker	10.00
19 Tim Wallach	2.00
20 John Wetteland	2.00
--- Checklist	1.00

1993 Donruss Previews

Twenty-two of the game's biggest stars were selected for inclusion in the preview version of Donruss' 1993 baseball card set. The previews follow the same basic format of the regular-issue 1993 except for the addition of the word "PREVIEW" above the card number in the home plate on back. Front photos are different between the preview and issued versions.

	NM/M
Complete Set (22):	60.00
Common Player:	1.50
1 Tom Glavine	2.00
2 Ryne Sandberg	5.00
3 Barry Larkin	1.50
4 Jeff Bagwell	4.00
5 Eric Karros	1.50
6 Larry Walker	1.50
7 Eddie Murray	4.00
8 Darren Daulton	1.50
9 Andy Van Slyke	1.50
10 Gary Sheffield	2.00
11 Will Clark	1.50
12 Cal Ripken Jr.	9.00
13 Roger Clemens	6.00
14 Frank Thomas	4.00
15 Cecil Fielder	1.50
16 George Brett	6.00
17 Robin Yount	4.00
18 Don Mattingly	6.00
19 Dennis Eckersley	3.50
20 Ken Griffey Jr.	7.50
21 Jose Canseco	2.50
22 Roberto Alomar	2.00

1993 Donruss

Rated Rookies and a randomly inserted Diamond Kings subset once again are featured in the 1993 Donruss

set. Series I of the set includes 396 cards. Card fronts feature white borders surrounding a full-color player photo. The flip sides feature an additional photo, biographical information and career statistics. The cards are numbered on the back and the card's series is given with the number. The cards are UV coated. Series II contains a subset of players labeled with an "Expansion Draft" headline over their Marlins or Rockies team logo on front, even though the player photos are in the uniform of their previous team.

	NM/M
Complete Set (792):	10.00
Common Player:	.05
Series 1 or 2 Pack (14):	.50
Series 1 or 2 Box (36):	10.00
1 Craig Lefferts	.05
2 Kent Mercker	.05
3 Phil Plantier	.05
4 Alex Arias RC	.05
5 Julio Valera	.05
6 Dan Wilson RC	.05
7 Frank Thomas	.50
8 Eric Anthony	.05
9 Derek Lilliquist	.05
10 Rafael Bournigal RC	.05
11 Manny Alexander/RR RC	.05
12 Bret Barberie	.05
13 Mickey Tettleton	.05
14 Anthony Young	.05
15 Tim Spehr	.05
16 Bob Ayrault RC	.05
17 Bill Wegman	.05
18 Jay Bell	.05
19 Rick Aguilera	.05
20 Todd Zeile	.05
21 Steve Farr	.05
22 Andy Benes	.05
23 Lance Blankenship	.05
24 Ted Wood	.05
25 Omar Vizquel	.05
26 Steve Avery	.05
27 Brian Bohanon	.05
28 Rick Wilkins	.05
29 Devon White	.05
30 Bobby Ayala RC	.05
31 Leo Gomez	.05
32 Mike Simms	.05
33 Ellis Burks	.05
34 Steve Wilson	.05
35 Jim Abbott	.05
36 Tim Wallach	.05
37 Wilson Alvarez	.05
38 Daryl Boston	.05
39 Sandy Alomar, Jr.	.05
40 Mitch Williams	.05
41 Rico Brogna	.05
42 Gary Varsho	.05
43 Kevin Appier	.05
44 Eric Wedge/RR RC	.05
45 Dante Bichette	.05
46 Jose Oquendo	.05
47 Mike Trombley RC	.05
48 Dan Walters	.05
49 Gerald Williams	.05
50 Bud Black	.05
51 Bobby Witt	.05
52 Mark Davis	.05
53 Shawn Barton RC	.05
54 Paul Assenmacher	.05
55 Kevin Reimer	.05
56 Billy Ashley/RR RC	.05
57 Eddie Zosky	.05
58 Chris Sabo	.05
59 Billy Ripken	.05
60 Scooter Tucker RC	.05
61 Tim Wakefield/RR RC	.10
62 Mitch Webster	.05
63 Jack Clark	.05
64 Mark Gardner	.05
65 Lee Stevens	.05
66 Todd Hundley	.05
67 Bobby Thigpen	.05
68 Dave Hollins	.05
69 Jack Armstrong	.05
70 Alex Cole	.05

71 Mark Carreon	.05
72 Todd Worrell	.05
73 Steve Shifflett RC	.05
74 Jerald Clark	.05
75 Paul Molitor	.50
76 Larry Carter RC	.05
77 Rich Rowland RC	.05
78 Damon Berryhill	.05
79 Willie Banks	.05
80 Hector Villanueva	.05
81 Mike Gallego	.05
82 Tim Belcher	.05
83 Mike Bordick	.05
84 Craig Biggio	.05
85 Lance Parrish	.05
86 Brett Butler	.05
87 Mike Timlin	.05
88 Brian Barnes	.05
89 Brady Anderson	.05
90 D.J. Dozier	.05
91 Frank Viola	.05
92 Darren Daulton	.05
93 Chad Curtis	.05
94 Zane Smith	.05
95 George Bell	.05
96 Rex Hudler	.05
97 Mark Whiten	.05
98 Tim Teufel	.05
99 Kevin Ritz	.05
100 Jeff Brantley	.05
101 Jeff Conine	.05
102 Vinny Castilla	.05
103 Greg Vaughn	.05
104 Steve Buechele	.05
105 Darren Reed	.05
106 Bip Roberts	.05
107 John Habyan	.05
108 Scott Servais	.05
109 Walt Weiss	.05
110 J.T. Snow/RR RC	.50
111 Jay Buhner	.05
112 Darryl Strawberry	.05
113 Roger Pavlik RC	.05
114 Chris Nabholz	.05
115 Pat Borders	.05
116 Pat Howell RC	.05
117 Gregg Olson	.05
118 Curt Schilling	.25
119 Roger Clemens	.65
120 Victor Cole RC	.05
121 Gary DiSarcina	.05
122 Checklist 1-80	.05
123 Steve Sax	.05
124 Chuck Carr RC	.05
125 Mark Lewis	.05
126 Tony Gwynn	.60
127 Travis Fryman	.05
128 Dave Burba	.05
129 Wally Joyner	.05
130 John Smoltz	.05
131 Cal Eldred	.05
132 Checklist 81-159	.05
133 Arthur Rhodes	.05
134 Jeff Blauser	.05
135 Scott Cooper	.05
136 Doug Strange	.05
137 Luis Sojo	.05
138 Jeff Branson RC	.05
139 Alex Fernandez	.05
140 Ken Caminiti	.05
141 Charles Nagy	.05
142 Tom Candiotti	.05
143 Willie Green/RR	.05
144 John Vander Wal	.05
145 Kurt Knudsen RC	.05
146 John Franco	.05
147 Eddie Pierce RC	.05
148 Kim Batiste	.05
149 Darren Holmes	.05
150 Steve Cooke RC	.05
151 Terry Jorgensen	.05
152 Mark Clark RC	.05
153 Randy Velarde	.05
154 Greg Harris	.05
155 Kevin Campbell RC	.05
156 John Burkett	.05
157 Kevin Mitchell	.05
158 Deion Sanders	.05
159 Jose Canseco	.25
160 Jeff Hartsock RC	.05
161 Tom Quinlan RC	.05
162 Tim Pugh RC	.05
163 Glenn Davis	.05
164 Shane Reynolds RC	.10
165 Jody Reed	.05
166 Mike Sharperson	.05
167 Scott Lewis	.05
168 Dennis Martinez	.05
169 Scott Radinsky	.05
170 Dave Gallagher	.05
171 Jim Thome	.45
172 Terry Mulholland	.05
173 Milt Cuyler	.05
174 Bob Patterson	.05
175 Jeff Montgomery	.05
176 Tim Salmon/RR	.25
177 Franklin Stubbs	.05
178 Donovan Osborne	.05
179 Jeff Reboulet RC	.05
180 Jeremy Hernandez	.05
181 Charlie Hayes	.05

182 Matt Williams	.05
183 Mike Raczka	.05
184 Francisco Cabrera	.05
185 Rich DeLucia	.05
186 Sammy Sosa	.60
187 Ivan Rodriguez	.45
188 Bret Boone/RR	.15
189 Juan Guzman	.05
190 Tom Browning	.05
191 Randy Milligan	.05
192 Steve Finley	.05
193 John Patterson/RR	.05
194 Kip Gross	.05
195 Tony Fossas	.05
196 Ivan Calderon	.05
197 Junior Felix	.05
198 Pete Schourek	.05
199 Craig Grebeck	.05
200 Juan Bell	.05
201 Glenallen Hill	.05
202 Danny Jackson	.05
203 John Kiely	.05
204 Bob Tewksbury	.05
205 Kevin Koslofski RC	.05
206 Craig Shipley	.05
207 John Jaha RC	.05
208 Royce Clayton	.05
209 Mike Piazza/RR	2.00
210 Ron Gant	.05
211 Scott Erickson	.05
212 Doug Dascenzo	.05
213 Andy Stankiewicz RC	.05
214 Geronimo Berroa	.05
215 Dennis Eckersley	.45
216 Al Osuna	.05
217 Tino Martinez	.05
218 Henry Rodriguez RC	.05
219 Ed Sprague	.05
220 Ken Hill	.05
221 Chito Martinez	.05
222 Bret Saberhagen	.05
223 Mike Greenwell	.05
224 Mickey Morandini	.05
225 Chuck Finley	.05
226 Denny Neagle	.05
227 Kirk McCaskill	.05
228 Rheal Cormier	.05
229 Paul Sorrento	.05
230 Darrin Jackson	.05
231 Rob Deer	.05
232 Bill Swift	.05
233 Kevin McReynolds	.05
234 Terry Pendleton	.05
235 Dave Nilsson	.05
236 Chuck McElroy	.05
237 Derek Parks	.05
238 Norm Charlton	.05
239 Matt Nokes	.05
240 Juan Guerrero RC	.05
241 Jeff Parrett	.05
242 Ryan Thompson/RR	.05
243 Dave Fleming	.05
244 Dave Hansen	.05
245 Monty Fariss	.05
246 Archi Cianfrocco RC	.05
247 Pat Hentgen	.05
248 Bill Pecota	.05
249 Ben McDonald	.05
250 Cliff Brantley	.05
251 John Valentin RC	.05
252 Jeff King	.05
253 Reggie Williams RC	.05
254 Checklist 160-238	.05
255 Ozzie Guillen	.05
256 Mike Perez	.05
257 Thomas Howard	.05
258 Kurt Stillwell	.05
259 Mike Henneman	.05
260 Steve Decker	.05
261 Brent Mayne	.05
262 Otis Nixon	.05
263 Mark Keifer RC	.05
264 Checklist 239-317	.05
265 Richie Lewis RC	.05
266 Pat Gomez RC	.05
267 Scott Taylor RC	.05
268 Shawon Dunston	.05
269 Greg Myers	.05
270 Tim Costo	.05
271 Greg Hibbard	.05
272 Pete Harnisch	.05
273 Dave Mlicki RC	.05
274 Orel Hershiser	.05
275 Sean Berry/RR	.05
276 Doug Simons	.05
277 John Doherty RC	.05
278 Eddie Murray	.50
279 Chris Haney	.05
280 Stan Javier	.05
281 Jaime Navarro	.05
282 Orlando Merced	.05
283 Kent Hrbek	.05
284 Bernard Gilkey	.05
285 Russ Springer	.05
286 Mike Maddux	.05
287 Eric Fox RC	.05
288 Mark Leonard	.05
289 Tim Leary	.05
290 Brian Hunter	.05
291 Donald Harris	.05
292 Bob Scanlan	.05
293 Turner Ward	.05
294 Hal Morris	.05
295 Jimmy Poole	.05
296 Doug Jones	.05
297 Tony Pena	.05
298 Ramon Martinez	.05
299 Tim Fortugno RC	.05

300 Marquis Grissom	.05
301 Lance Johnson	.05
302 Jeff Kent RC	1.00
303 Reggie Jefferson	.05
304 Wes Chamberlain	.05
305 Shawn Hare RC	.05
306 Mike LaValliere	.05
307 Gregg Jefferies	.05
308 Troy Neel/RR RC	.05
309 Pat Listach	.05
310 Geronimo Pena	.05
311 Pedro Munoz	.05
312 Guillermo Velasquez RC	.05
313 Roberto Kelly	.05
314 Mike Jackson	.05
315 Rickey Henderson	.50
316 Mark Lemke	.05
317 Erik Hanson	.05
318 Derrick May	.05
319 Geno Petralli	.05
320 Melvin Nieves/RR	.05
321 Doug Linton RC	.05
322 Rob Dibble	.05
323 Chris Hoiles	.05
324 Jimmy Jones	.05
325 Dave Staton/RR	.05
326 Pedro Martinez	.05
327 Paul Quantrill RC	.05
328 Greg Colbrunn	.05
329 Hilly Hathaway RC	.05
330 Jeff Innis	.05
331 Ron Karkovice	.05
332 Keith Shepherd RC	.05
333 Alan Embree RC	.05
334 Paul Wagner RC	.05
335 Dave Haas RC	.05
336 Ozzie Canseco	.05
337 Bill Sampen	.05
338 Rich Rodriguez	.05
339 Dean Palmer	.05
340 Greg Litton	.05
341 Jim Tatum/RR	.05
342 Todd Haney RC	.05
343 Larry Casian	.05
344 Ryne Sandberg	.60
345 Sterling Hitchcock RC	.10
346 Chris Hammond	.05
347 Vince Horsman RC	.05
348 Butch Henry RC	.05
349 Dann Howitt	.05
350 Roger McDowell	.05
351 Jack Morris	.05
352 Bill Krueger	.05
353 Cris Colon RC	.05
354 Joe Vitko RC	.05
355 Willie McGee	.05
356 Jay Baller	.05
357 Pat Mahomes	.05
358 Roger Mason	.05
359 Jerry Nielsen RC	.05
360 Tom Pagnozzi	.05
361 Kevin Baez RC	.05
362 Tim Scott RC	.05
363 Domingo Martinez RC	.05
364 Kirt Manwaring	.05
365 Rafael Palmeiro	.45
366 Ray Lankford	.05
367 Tim McIntosh	.05
368 Jessie Hollins RC	.05
369 Scott Leius	.05
370 Bill Doran	.05
371 Sam Militello RC	.05
372 Ryan Bowen	.05
373 Dave Henderson	.05
374 Dan Smith/RR RC	.05
375 Steve Reed RC	.05
376 Jose Offerman	.05
377 Kevin Brown	.05
378 Darrin Fletcher	.05
379 Duane Ward	.05
380 Wayne Kirby/RR RC	.05
381 Steve Scarsone RC	.05
382 Mariano Duncan	.05
383 Ken Ryan RC	.05
384 Lloyd McClendon	.05
385 Brian Holman	.05
386 Braulio Castillo	.05
387 Danny Leon RC	.05
388 Omar Olivares	.05
389 Kevin Wickander	.05
390 Fred McGriff	.05
391 Phil Clark RC	.05
392 Darren Lewis	.05
393 Phil Hiatt RC	.10
394 Mike Morgan	.05
395 Shane Mack	.05
396 Checklist 318-396	.05
397 David Segui	.05
398 Rafael Belliard	.05
399 Tim Naehring	.05
400 Frank Castillo	.05
401 Joe Grahe	.05
402 Reggie Sanders	.05
403 Roberto Hernandez	.05
404 Luis Gonzalez	.05
405 Carlos Baerga	.05
406 Carlos Hernandez	.05
407 Pedro Astacio/RR	.05
408 Mel Rojas	.05
409 Scott Livingstone	.05
410 Chico Walker	.05
411 Brian McRae	.05
412 Ben Rivera	.05
413 Ricky Bones	.05
414 Andy Van Slyke	.05
415 Chuck Knoblauch	.05
416 Luis Alicea	.05
417 Bob Wickman	.05

418 Doug Brocail	.05
419 Scott Brosius	.05
420 Rod Beck	.05
421 Edgar Martinez	.05
422 Ryan Klesko	.05
423 Nolan Ryan	1.50
424 Rey Sanchez	.05
425 Roberto Alomar	.20
426 Barry Larkin	.05
427 Mike Mussina	.30
428 Jeff Bagwell	.05
429 Mo Vaughn	.05
430 Eric Karros	.05
431 John Orton	.05
432 Wil Cordero	.05
433 Jack McDowell	.05
434 Howard Johnson	.05
435 Albert Belle	.05
436 John Kruk	.05
437 Skeeter Barnes	.05
438 Don Slaught	.05
439 Rusty Meacham	.05
440 Tim Laker/RR	.05
441 Robin Yount	.50
442 Brian Jordan	.05
443 Kevin Tapani	.05
444 Gary Sheffield	.25
445 Rich Monteleone	.05
446 Will Clark	.05
447 Jerry Browne	.05
448 Jeff Treadway	.05
449 Mike Schooler	.05
450 Mike Harkey	.05
451 Julio Franco	.05
452 Kevin Young/RR	.05
453 Kelly Gruber	.05
454 Jose Rijo	.05
455 Mike Devereaux	.05
456 Andujar Cedeno	.05
457 Damion Easley/RR	.05
458 Kevin Gross	.05
459 Matt Young	.05
460 Matt Stairs	.05
461 Luis Polonia	.05
462 Dwight Gooden	.05
463 Warren Newson	.05
464 Jose DeLeon	.05
465 Jose Mesa	.05
466 Danny Cox	.05
467 Dan Gladden	.05
468 Gerald Perry	.05
469 Mike Boddicker	.05
470 Jeff Gardner	.05
471 Doug Henry	.05
472 Mike Benajmin	.05
473 Dan Peltier/RR	.05
474 Mike Stanton	.05
475 John Smiley	.05
476 Dwight Smith	.05
477 Jim Leyritz	.05
478 Dwayne Henry	.05
479 Mark McGwire	1.00
480 Pete Incaviglia	.05
481 Dave Cochrane	.05
482 Eric Davis	.05
483 John Olerud	.05
484 Ken Bottenfield	.05
485 Mark McLemore	.05
486 Dave Magadan	.05
487 John Marzano	.05
488 Ruben Amaro	.05
489 Rob Ducey	.05
490 Stan Belinda	.05
491 Dan Pasqua	.05
492 Joe Magrane	.05
493 Brook Jacoby	.05
494 Gene Harris	.05
495 Mark Leiter	.05
496 Bryan Hickerson	.05
497 Tom Gordon	.05
498 Pete Smith	.05
499 Chris Bosio	.05
500 Shawn Boskie	.05
501 Dave West	.05
502 Milt Hill	.05
503 Pat Kelly	.05
504 Joe Boever	.05
505 Terry Steinbach	.05
506 Butch Huskey/RR	.05
507 David Valle	.05
508 Mike Scioscia	.05
509 Kenny Rogers	.05
510 Moises Alou	.05
511 David Wells	.05
512 Mackey Sasser	.05
513 Todd Frohwirth	.05
514 Ricky Jordan	.05
515 Mike Gardiner	.05
516 Gary Redus	.05
517 Gary Gaetti	.05
518 Checklist 397-476	.05
519 Carlton Fisk	.50
520 Ozzie Smith	.60
521 Rod Nichols	.05
522 Benito Santiago	.05
523 Bill Gullickson	.05
524 Robby Thompson	.05
525 Mike Macfarlane	.05
526 Sid Bream	.05
527 Darryl Hamilton	.05
528 Checklist 477-555	.05
529 Jeff Tackett	.05
530 Greg Olson	.05
531 Bob Zupcic	.05
532 Mark Grace	.05
533 Steve Frey	.05
534 Dave Martinez	.05
535 Robin Ventura	.05

ABBREVIATIONS

RR - Rated Rookie

#	Player	Price
536	Casey Candaele	.05
537	Kenny Lofton	.05
538	Jay Howell	.05
539	Fernando Ramsey/RR	.05
540	Larry Walker	.05
541	Cecil Fielder	.05
542	Lee Guetterman	.05
543	Keith Miller	.05
544	Len Dykstra	.05
545	B.J. Surhoff	.05
546	Bob Walk	.05
547	Brian Harper	.05
548	Lee Smith	.05
549	Danny Tartabull	.05
550	Frank Seminara	.05
551	Henry Mercedes	.05
552	Dave Righetti	.05
553	Ken Griffey Jr.	.75
554	Tom Glavine	.25
555	Juan Gonzalez	.25
556	Jim Bullinger	.05
557	Derek Bell	.05
558	Cesar Hernandez	.05
559	Cal Ripken, Jr.	1.50
560	Eddie Taubensee	.05
561	John Flaherty	.05
562	Todd Benzinger	.05
563	Hubie Brooks	.05
564	Delino DeShields	.05
565	Tim Raines	.05
566	Sid Fernandez	.05
567	Steve Olin	.05
568	Tommy Greene	.05
569	Buddy Groom	.05
570	Randy Tomlin	.05
571	Hipolito Pichardo	.05
572	Rene Arocha/RR	.05
573	Mike Fetters	.05
574	Felix Jose	.05
575	Gene Larkin	.05
576	Bruce Hurst	.05
577	Bernie Williams	.05
578	Trevor Wilson	.05
579	Bob Welch	.05
580	Dave Justice	.05
581	Randy Johnson	.50
582	Jose Vizcaino	.05
583	Jeff Huson	.05
584	Rob Maurer/RR	.05
585	Todd Stottlemyre	.05
586	Joe Oliver	.05
587	Bob Milacki	.05
588	Rob Murphy	.05
589	Greg Pirkl/RR	.05
590	Lenny Harris	.05
591	Luis Rivera	.05
592	John Wetteland	.05
593	Mark Langston	.05
594	Bobby Bonilla	.05
595	Esteban Beltre	.05
596	Mike Hartley	.05
597	Felix Fermin	.05
598	Carlos Garcia	.05
599	Frank Tanana	.05
600	Pedro Guerrero	.05
601	Terry Shumpert	.05
602	Wally Whitehurst	.05
603	Kevin Seitzer	.05
604	Chris James	.05
605	Greg Gohr/RR	.05
606	Mark Wohlers	.05
607	Kirby Puckett	.60
608	Greg Maddux	.60
609	Don Mattingly	.05
610	Greg Cadaret	.05
611	Dave Stewart	.05
612	Mark Portugal	.05
613	Pete O'Brien	.05
614	Bobby Ojeda	.05
615	Joe Carter	.05
616	Pete Young	.05
617	Sam Horn	.05
618	Vince Coleman	.05
619	Wade Boggs	.60
620	Todd Pratt RC	.05
621	Ron Tingley	.05
622	Doug Drabek	.05
623	Scott Hemond	.05
624	Tim Jones	.05
625	Dennis Cook	.05
626	Jose Melendez	.05
627	Mike Munoz	.05
628	Jim Pena	.05
629	Gary Thurman	.05
630	Charlie Leibrandt	.05
631	Scott Fletcher	.05
632	Andre Dawson	.25
633	Greg Gagne	.05
634	Greg Swindell	.05
635	Kevin Maas	.05
636	Xavier Hernandez	.05
637	Ruben Sierra	.05
638	Dimitri Young/RR	.05
639	Harold Reynolds	.05
640	Tom Goodwin	.05
641	Todd Burns	.05
642	Jeff Fassero	.05
643	Dave Winfield	.50
644	Willie Randolph	.05
645	Luis Mercedes	.05
646	Dale Murphy	.20
647	Danny Darwin	.05
648	Dennis Moeller	.05
649	Chuck Crim	.05
650	Checklist 556-634	.05
651	Shawn Abner	.05
652	Tracy Woodson	.05
653	Scott Scudder	.05
654	Tom Lampkin	.05
655	Alan Trammell	.05
656	Cory Snyder	.05
657	Chris Gwynn	.05
658	Lonnie Smith	.05
659	Jim Austin	.05
660	Checklist 635-713	.05
661	Tim Hulett	.05
662	Marvin Freeman	.05
663	Greg Harris	.05
664	Heathcliff Slocumb	.05
665	Mike Butcher	.05
666	Steve Foster	.05
667	Donn Pall	.05
668	Darryl Kile	.05
669	Jesse Levis	.05
670	Jim Gott	.05
671	Mark Hutton RC	.05
672	Brian Drahman	.05
673	Chad Kreuter	.05
674	Tony Fernandez	.05
675	Jose Lind	.05
676	Kyle Abbott	.05
677	Dan Plesac	.05
678	Barry Bonds	1.50
679	Chili Davis	.05
680	Stan Royer	.05
681	Scott Kamieniecki	.05
682	Carlos Martinez	.05
683	Mike Moore	.05
684	Candy Maldonado	.05
685	Jeff Nelson	.05
686	Lou Whitaker	.05
687	Jose Guzman	.05
688	Manuel Lee	.05
689	Bob MacDonald	.05
690	Scott Bankhead	.05
691	Alan Mills	.05
692	Brian Williams	.05
693	Tom Brunansky	.05
694	Lenny Webster	.05
695	Greg Briley	.05
696	Paul O'Neill	.05
697	Joey Cora	.05
698	Charlie O'Brien	.05
699	Junior Ortiz	.05
700	Ron Darling	.05
701	Tony Phillips	.05
702	William Pennyweather	.05
703	Mark Gubicza	.05
704	Steve Hosey/RR	.05
705	Henry Cotto	.05
706	David Hulse RC	.05
707	Mike Pagliarulo	.05
708	Dave Stieb	.05
709	Melido Perez	.05
710	Jimmy Key	.05
711	Jeff Russell	.05
712	David Cone	.05
713	Russ Swan	.05
714	Mark Guthrie	.05
715	Checklist 714-792	.05
716	Al Martin/RR	.05
717	Randy Knorr	.05
718	Mike Stanley	.05
719	Rick Sutcliffe	.05
720	Terry Leach	.05
721	Chipper Jones/RR	1.00
722	Jim Eisenreich	.05
723	Tom Henke	.05
724	Jeff Frye	.05
725	Harold Baines	.05
726	Scott Sanderson	.05
727	Tom Foley	.05
728	Bryan Harvey/ED	.05
729	Tom Edens	.05
730	Eric Young/ED	.05
731	Dave Weathers/ED	.05
732	Spike Owen	.05
733	Scott Aldred/ED	.05
734	Cris Carpenter/ED	.05
735	Dion James	.05
736	Joe Girardi/ED	.05
737	Nigel Wilson/ED	.05
738	Scott Chiamparino/ED	.05
739	Jeff Reardon	.05
740	Willie Blair/ED	.05
741	Jim Corsi/ED	.05
742	Ken Patterson	.05
743	Andy Ashby/ED	.05
744	Rob Natal/ED	.05
745	Kevin Bass	.05
746	Freddie Benavides/ED	.05
747	Chris Donnels/ED	.05
748	Kerry Woodson RC	.05
749	Calvin Jones/ED	.05
750	Gary Scott	.05
751	Joe Orsulak	.05
752	Armando Reynoso/ED	.05
753	Monty Farriss/ED	.05
754	Billy Hatcher	.05
755	Denis Boucher/ED	.05
756	Walt Weiss	.05
757	Mike Fitzgerald	.05
758	Rudy Seanez	.05
759	Bret Barberie/ED	.05
760	Mo Sanford/ED	.05
761	Pedro Castellano/ED RC	.05
762	Chuck Carr/ED	.05
763	Steve Howe	.05
764	Andres Galarraga	.05
765	Jeff Conine/ED	.05
766	Ted Power	.05
767	Butch Henry/ED	.05
768	Steve Decker/ED	.05
769	Storm Davis	.05
770	Vinny Castilla/ED	.05
771	Junior Felix/ED	.05
772	Walt Terrell	.05
773	Brad Ausmus/ED	.05
774	Jamie McAndrew/ED	.05
775	Milt Thompson	.05
776	Charlie Hayes/ED	.05
777	Jack Armstrong/ED	.05
778	Dennis Rasmussen/ED	.05
779	Darren Holmes/ED	.05
780	Alex Arias RC	.05
781	Randy Bush	.05
782	Javier Lopez/RR	.05
783	Dante Bichette	.05
784	John Johnstone/ED	.05
785	Rene Gonzales	.05
786	Alex Cole/ED	.05
787	Jeromy Burnitz/RR	.05
788	Michael Huff	.05
789	Anthony Telford	.05
790	Jerald Clark/ED	.05
791	Joel Johnston	.05
792	David Nied/RR	.05

Diamond Kings

The traditional Donruss Diamond Kings cards were again used as an insert in Series 2 and Series 2 foil packs in 1993. The first 15 cards were found in Series 1 packs, while cards 16-31 were available in the second series packs.

		NM/M
Complete Set (31):		17.50
Common Player:		.25
1	Ken Griffey Jr.	4.00
2	Ryne Sandberg	3.00
3	Roger Clemens	3.50
4	Kirby Puckett	3.00
5	Bill Swift	.25
6	Larry Walker	.25
7	Juan Gonzalez	.75
8	Wally Joyner	.25
9	Andy Van Slyke	.25
10	Robin Ventura	.25
11	Bip Roberts	.25
12	Roberto Kelly	.25
13	Carlos Baerga	.25
14	Orel Hershiser	.25
15	Cecil Fielder	.25
16	Robin Yount	1.50
17	Darren Daulton	.25
18	Mark McGwire	4.00
19	Tom Glavine	.25
20	Roberto Alomar	.50
21	Gary Sheffield	.75
22	Bob Tewksbury	.25
23	Brady Anderson	.25
24	Craig Biggio	.25
25	Eddie Murray	1.50
26	Luis Polonia	.25
27	Nigel Wilson	.25
28	David Nied	.25
29	Pat Listach	.25
30	Eric Karros	.25
31	Checklist	.05

1993 Donruss Elite

Continuing the card numbering from the 1992 Elite set, the Elite '93 inserts utilized a silver-foil prismatic front border with blue back printing. Each card is serial numbered as one of 10,000; this identified production number helping to make the Elites among the more valuable of insert cards.

		NM/M
Complete Set (20):		150.00
Common Player:		10.00
19	Fred McGriff	10.00
20	Ryne Sandberg	20.00
21	Eddie Murray	15.00
22	Paul Molitor	15.00
23	Barry Larkin	10.00
24	Don Mattingly	25.00
25	Dennis Eckersley	15.00
26	Roberto Alomar	12.50
27	Edgar Martinez	10.00
28	Gary Sheffield	12.50
29	Darren Daulton	10.00
30	Larry Walker	10.00
31	Barry Bonds	30.00
32	Andy Van Slyke	25.00
33	Mark McGwire	25.00
34	Cecil Fielder	10.00
35	Dave Winfield	15.00
36	Juan Gonzalez	12.50
---	Robin Yount (Legend)	17.50
---	Will Clark (Signature)	40.00

Elite Supers

A Wal-Mart exclusive, Donruss produced 3-1/2" x 5" versions of its 1993 Elite inserts, added Nolan Ryan and Frank Thomas and a new card of Barry Bonds in his Giants uniform and packaged them one per shrink-wrapped box with Series 1 Donruss leftovers. Each super-size card features a color player photo and silver-foil prismatic borders on front. Backs are printed in blue and include a serial number identifying each of the cards from an edition of 5,000.

		NM/M
Complete Set (20):		150.00
Common Player:		5.00
1	Fred McGriff	5.00
2	Ryne Sandberg	17.50
3	Eddie Murray	10.00
4	Paul Molitor	10.00
5	Barry Larkin	5.00
6	Don Mattingly	20.00
7	Dennis Eckersley	10.00
8	Roberto Alomar	6.50
9	Edgar Martinez	5.00
10	Gary Sheffield	6.50
11	Darren Daulton	5.00
12	Larry Walker	5.00
13	Barry Bonds	25.00
14	Andy Van Slyke	5.00
15	Mark McGwire	25.00
16	Cecil Fielder	5.00
17	Dave Winfield	10.00
18	Juan Gonzalez	7.50
19	Frank Thomas	15.00
20	Nolan Ryan	40.00

Long Ball Leaders

Carrying a prefix of "LL" before the card number, these inserts were released in Series 1 (#1-9) and Series 2 (#10-18) jumbo packs, detailing mammoth home runs of the previous season.

	NM/M
Complete Set (18):	5.00
Common Player:	.10

ALBERT BELLE · Indians

MVPs

This set was inserted in jumbo packs of both Series 1 and Series 2. Cards carry a MVP prefix to the card number.

		NM/M
Complete Set (26):		10.00
Common Player:		.10
1	Luis Polonia	.10
2	Frank Thomas	.60
3	George Brett	.75
4	Paul Molitor	.60
5	Don Mattingly	.75
6	Roberto Alomar	.25
7	Terry Pendleton	.10
8	Eric Karros	.10
9	Larry Walker	.10
10	Eddie Murray	.60
11	Darren Daulton	.10
12	Ray Lankford	.10
13	Will Clark	.10
14	Cal Ripken, Jr.	2.00
15	Roger Clemens	.75
16	Carlos Baerga	.10
17	Cecil Fielder	.10
18	Kirby Puckett	.65
19	Mark McGwire	1.50
20	Ken Griffey Jr.	1.25
21	Juan Gonzalez	.30
22	Ryne Sandberg	.65
23	Bip Roberts	.10
24	Jeff Bagwell	.60
25	Barry Bonds	2.00
26	Gary Sheffield	.25

Spirit of the Game

Series 1 and Series 2 foil and jumbo packs could be found with these cards randomly inserted. Several multi-player cards are included in the set. Card numbers bear an SG prefix.

		NM/M
Complete Set (20):		5.00
Common Player:		.25
1	Turning Two (Dave Winfield, Mike Bordick)	.35
2	Play at the Plate (David Justice)	.25
3	In There (Roberto Alomar)	.30
4	Pumped (Dennis Eckersley)	.60
5	Dynamic Duo (Juan Gonzalez, Jose Canseco)	.50
6	Gone (Frank Thomas, George Bell)	.60
7	Safe or Out? (Wade Boggs)	.75
8	The Thrill (Will Clark)	.30
9	Safe at Home (Damon Berryhill, Bip Roberts, Glenn Braggs)	.25
10	Thirty X 31 (Cecil Fielder, Mickey Tettleton, Rob Deer)	.25
11	Bag Bandit (Kenny Lofton)	.25
12	Back to Back (Fred McGriff, Gary Sheffield)	.30
13	Range Rovers (Greg Gagne, Barry Larkin)	.25
14	The Ball Stops Here (Ryne Sandberg)	.75
15	Over the Top (Carlos Baerga, Gary Gaetti)	.25
16	At the Wall (Danny Tartabull)	.25
17	Head First (Brady Anderson)	.25
18	Big Hurt (Frank Thomas)	.65
19	No-Hitter (Kevin Gross)	.25
20	3,000 (Robin Yount)	.65

Dominators

Created as a premium to move left-over boxes of its 1993 product on a home shopping network at $100 apiece, this special edition was produced in standard 2-1/2" x 3-1/2" size in a format similar to the 1991-93 Donruss Elite chase cards. Cards feature green prismatic borders, liberal use of foil stamping, etc. Only 5,000 of each card were produced, and each card is serially numbered on the back. Half of the cards of Nolan Ryan, Juan Gonzalez, Don Mattingly and Paul Molitor were personally autographed by the player.

		NM/M
Complete Set (20):		135.00
Common Player:		3.00
1	Ryne Sandberg	10.00
2	Fred McGriff	3.00
3	Greg Maddux	10.00
4	Ron Gant	3.00
5	Dave Justice	3.00
6	Don Mattingly	12.00
7	Tim Salmon	3.00
8	Mike Piazza	12.00
9	John Olerud	3.00
10	Nolan Ryan	20.00
11	Juan Gonzalez	5.00
12	Ken Griffey Jr.	12.00
13	Frank Thomas	7.50
14	Tom Glavine	4.50
15	George Brett	12.00

16	Barry Bonds	20.00
17	Albert Belle	3.00
18	Paul Molitor	7.50
19	Cal Ripken, Jr.	20.00
20	Roberto Alomar	5.00

Autographed Cards:

6	Don Mattingly	35.00
10	Nolan Ryan	65.00
11	Juan Gonzalez	20.00
18	Paul Molitor	20.00

Masters of the Game

Donruss issued a series of "Masters of the Game" art cards that were available only at Wal-Mart stores. The oversized cards (3-1/2" x 5") feature the artwork of Dick Perez, creator of the Diamond Kings cards for the same company. The cards came issued one to a pack, along with a foil pack of 1993 Donruss cards for a retail price of about $3.

NM/M

Complete Set (16):		15.00
Common Player:		1.00
1	Frank Thomas	1.50
2	Nolan Ryan	3.00
3	Gary Sheffield	1.25
4	Fred McGriff	1.00
5	Ryne Sandberg	1.75
6	Cal Ripken, Jr.	3.00
7	Jose Canseco	1.25
8	Ken Griffey Jr.	2.50
9	Will Clark	1.00
10	Roberto Alomar	1.00
11	Juan Gonzalez	1.25
12	David Justice	1.00
13	Kirby Puckett	1.75
14	Barry Bonds	3.00
15	Robin Yount	1.50
16	Deion Sanders	1.00

1993 Donruss 1992 Blue Jays Commemorative Set

Issued only as a special gold-boxed set, this series commemorates the Toronto Blue Jays 1992 World Championship. Each player on the Jays '92 roster has a card. There are also special cards recalling each game of the Series and a SkyDome card. The World Series highlights cards have a bunting design at top and a gold-foil World Series logo on front. Player cards feature borderless photos; a Blue Jays "Commemorative Set" logo is at lower-left. Backs feature a player photo at top and a stat box at bottom with season, career and 1992 LCS and World Series numbers.

NM/M

Complete Set (54):		5.00
Common Card:		.15
1	Checklist/Logo card	.15
2	Roberto Alomar	.45
3	Derek Bell	.15
4	Pat Borders	.15
5	Joe Carter	.45
6	Alfredo Griffin	.15
7	Kelly Gruber	.15
8	Manuel Lee	.15
9	Candy Maldonado	.15
10	John Olerud	.45
11	Ed Sprague	.15
12	Pat Tabler	.15
13	Devon White	.15
14	Dave Winfield	1.00
15	David Cone	.25
16	Mark Eichhorn	.15
17	Juan Guzman	.15
18	Tom Henke	.15
19	Jimmy Key	.15
20	Jack Morris	.25
21	Todd Stottlemyre	.15
22	Mike Timlin	.15
23	Duane Ward	.15
24	David Wells	.40
25	Randy Knorr	.15
26	Rance Mulliniks	.15
27	Tom Quinlan	.15
28	Cito Gaston	.15
29	Dave Steib	.15
30	Ken Dayley	.15
31	Turner Ward	.15
32	Eddie Zosky	.15
33	Pat Hentgen	.15
34	Al Leiter	.15
35	Doug Linton	.15
36	Bob MacDonald	.15
37	Rick Trlicek	.15
38	Domingo Martinez	.15
39	Mike Maksudian	.15
40	Rob Ducey	.15
41	Jeff Kent	.60
42	Greg Myers	.15
43	Dave Weathers	.15
44	Skydome	.15
45	Trophy Presentation (Jim Kaat, Cito Gaston, Paul Beeston, Bobby Brown)	.15
	World Series Highlights	.10
1WS	Series Opener (Blue Jays vs. Braves)	.10
2WS	Game 1 - Carter Homers in 4th	.25
3WS	Homer	.10
4WS	Game 3 - Maldonado Drives in Game-Winner	.10
5WS	Game 4 - Key's Win Puts Jays Up 3-1	.10
6WS	Game 5 - Olerud Scores Both Jays Runs	.10
7WS	Game 6 - Winfield's Double in 11th Wins	.25
8WS	Pat Border Series MVP	.10
9WS	World Champs Celebration	.10

1994 Donruss Promotional Samples

To introduce both its regular 1994 issue and the "Special Edition" gold cards, Donruss produced this 12-card promo set for distribution to its dealer network. The promos are virtually identical in format to the regular cards except for the large gray diagonal overprint "PROMOTIONAL SAMPLE" on both front and back. Card numbers also differ on the promos.

NM/M

Complete Set (12):		10.00
Common Player:		.50
1	Barry Bonds	2.00
2	Darren Daulton	.50
3	John Olerud	.50
4	Frank Thomas	1.00
5	Mike Piazza	1.50
6	Tim Salmon	.50
7	Ken Griffey Jr.	1.50
8	Fred McGriff	.50
9	Don Mattingly	1.25
10	Gary Sheffield	.75

Special Edition Gold:

| 1G | Barry Bonds (Special Edition Gold) | 2.50 |
| 4G | Frank Thomas (Special Edition Gold) | 1.00 |

1994 Donruss

Donruss released its 1994 set in two 330-card series. Each series also includes, 50 Special Edition gold cards and several insert sets. Regular cards have full-bleed photos and are UV coated and foil stamped. Special Edition cards are gold-foil stamped on both sides and are included in each pack. Insert sets titled Spirit of the Game and Decade Dominators were produced in regular and super (3-1/2" x 5") formats. Other inserts were MVPs and Long Ball Leaders in regular size and super-size Award Winners. An Elite series of cards, continuing from previous years with #37-48, was also issued as inserts. A 10th Anniversary insert set features 10 popular 1984 Donruss cards in gold-foil enhanced reprint versions.

NM/M

Complete Set (660):		15.00
Common Player:		.05
Series 1 or 2 Pack (13):		.50
Series 1 or 2 Box (36):		12.50
1	Nolan Ryan (Career Salute 27 Years.)	2.00
2	Mike Piazza	1.00
3	Moises Alou	.05
4	Ken Griffey Jr.	1.00
5	Gary Sheffield	.25
6	Roberto Alomar	.20
7	John Kruk	.05
8	Gregg Olson	.05
9	Gregg Jefferies	.05
10	Tony Gwynn	.65
11	Chad Curtis	.05
12	Craig Biggio	.05
13	John Burkett	.05
14	Carlos Baerga	.05
15	Robin Yount	.60
16	Dennis Eckersley	.50
17	Dwight Gooden	.05
18	Ryne Sandberg	.65
19	Rickey Henderson	.60
20	Jack McDowell	.05
21	Jay Bell	.05
22	Kevin Brown	.05
23	Robin Ventura	.05
24	Paul Molitor	.60
25	Dave Justice	.05
26	Rafael Palmeiro	.50
27	Cecil Fielder	.05
28	Chuck Knoblauch	.05
29	Dave Hollins	.05
30	Jimmy Key	.05
31	Mark Langston	.05
32	Darryl Kile	.05
33	Ruben Sierra	.05
34	Ron Gant	.05
35	Ozzie Smith	.65
36	Wade Boggs	.65
37	Marquis Grissom	.05
38	Will Clark	.05
39	Kenny Lofton	.05
40	Cal Ripken, Jr.	2.00
41	Steve Avery	.05
42	Mo Vaughn	.05
43	Brian McRae	.05
44	Mickey Tettleton	.05
45	Barry Larkin	.05
46	Charlie Hayes	.05
47	Kevin Appier	.05
48	Robby Thompson	.05
49	Juan Gonzalez	.30
50	Paul O'Neill	.05
51	Marcos Armas	.05
52	Mike Butcher	.05
53	Ken Caminiti	.05
54	Pat Borders	.05
55	Pedro Munoz	.05
56	Tim Belcher	.05
57	Paul Assenmacher	.05
58	Damon Berryhill	.05
59	Ricky Bones	.05
60	Rene Arocha	.05
61	Shawn Boskie	.05
62	Pedro Astacio	.05
63	Frank Bolick	.05
64	Bud Black	.05
65	Sandy Alomar, Jr.	.05
66	Rich Amaral	.05
67	Luis Aquino	.05
68	Kevin Baez	.05
69	Mike Devereaux	.05
70	Andy Ashby	.05
71	Larry Andersen	.05
72	Steve Cooke	.05
73	Mario Diaz	.05
74	Rob Deer	.05
75	Bobby Ayala	.05
76	Freddie Benavides	.05
77	Stan Belinda	.05
78	John Doherty	.05
79	Willie Banks	.05
80	Spike Owen	.05
81	Mike Bordick	.05
82	Chili Davis	.05
83	Luis Gonzalez	.05
84	Ed Sprague	.05
85	Jeff Reboulet	.05
86	Jason Bere	.05
87	Mark Hutton	.05
88	Jeff Blauser	.05
89	Cal Eldred	.05
90	Bernard Gilkey	.05
91	Frank Castillo	.05
92	Jim Gott	.05
93	Greg Colbrunn	.05
94	Jeff Brantley	.05
95	Jeremy Hernandez	.05
96	Norm Charlton	.05
97	Alex Arias	.05
98	John Franco	.05
99	Chris Hoiles	.05
100	Brad Ausmus	.05
101	Wes Chamberlain	.05
102	Mark Dewey	.05
103	Benji Gil/RR	.05
104	John Dopson	.05
105	John Smiley	.05
106	David Nied	.05
107	George Brett (Career Salute 21 Years.)	.75
108	Kirk Gibson	.05
109	Larry Casian	.05
110	Checklist (Ryne Sandberg 2,000 Hits)	.25
111	Brent Gates	.05
112	Damion Easley	.05
113	Pete Harnisch	.05
114	Danny Cox	.05
115	Kevin Tapani	.05
116	Roberto Hernandez	.05
117	Domingo Jean	.05
118	Sid Bream	.05
119	Doug Henry	.05
120	Omar Olivares	.05
121	Mike Harkey	.05
122	Carlos Hernandez	.05
123	Jeff Fassero	.05
124	Dave Burba	.05
125	Wayne Kirby	.05
126	John Cummings	.05
127	Bret Barberie	.05
128	Todd Hundley	.05
129	Tim Hulett	.05
130	Phil Clark	.05
131	Danny Jackson	.05
132	Tom Foley	.05
133	Donald Harris	.05
134	Scott Fletcher	.05
135	Johnny Ruffin/RR	.05
136	Jerald Clark	.05
137	Billy Brewer	.05
138	Dan Gladden	.05
139	Eddie Guardado	.05
140	Checklist (Cal Ripken, Jr. 2,000 Hits)	.35
141	Scott Hemond	.05
142	Steve Frey	.05
143	Xavier Hernandez	.05
144	Mark Eichhorn	.05
145	Ellis Burks	.05
146	Jim Leyritz	.05
147	Mark Lemke	.05
148	Pat Listach	.05
149	Donovan Osborne	.05
150	Glenallen Hill	.05
151	Orel Hershiser	.05
152	Darrin Fletcher	.05
153	Royce Clayton	.05
154	Derek Lilliquist	.05
155	Mike Felder	.05
156	Jeff Conine	.05
157	Ryan Thompson	.05
158	Ben McDonald	.05
159	Ricky Gutierrez	.05
160	Terry Mulholland	.05
161	Carlos Garcia	.05
162	Tom Henke	.05
163	Mike Greenwell	.05
164	Thomas Howard	.05
165	Joe Girardi	.05
166	Hubie Brooks	.05
167	Greg Gohr	.05
168	Chip Hale	.05
169	Rick Honeycutt	.05
170	Hilly Hathaway	.05
171	Todd Jones	.05
172	Tony Fernandez	.05
173	Bo Jackson	.10
174	Bobby Munoz	.05
175	Greg McMichael	.05
176	Graeme Lloyd	.05
177	Tom Pagnozzi	.05
178	Derrick May	.05
179	Pedro Martinez	.60
180	Ken Hill	.05
181	Bryan Hickerson	.05
182	Jose Mesa	.05
183	Dave Fleming	.05
184	Henry Cotto	.05
185	Jeff Kent	.05
186	Mark McLemore	.05
187	Trevor Hoffman	.05
188	Todd Pratt	.05
189	Blas Minor	.05
190	Charlie Leibrandt	.05
191	Tony Pena	.05
192	Larry Luebbers RC	.05
193	Greg Harris	.05
194	David Cone	.05
195	Bill Gullickson	.05
196	Brian Harper	.05
197	Steve Karsay/RR	.05
198	Greg Myers	.05
199	Mark Portugal	.05
200	Pat Hentgen	.05
201	Mike La Valliere	.05
202	Mike Stanley	.05
203	Kent Mercker	.05
204	Dave Nilsson	.05
205	Erik Pappas	.05
206	Mike Morgan	.05
207	Roger McDowell	.05
208	Mike Lansing	.05
209	Kirt Manwaring	.05
210	Randy Milligan	.05
211	Erik Hanson	.05
212	Orestes Destrade	.05
213	Mike Maddux	.05
214	Alan Mills	.05
215	Tim Mauser	.05
216	Ben Rivera	.05
217	Don Slaught	.05
218	Bob Patterson	.05
219	Carlos Quintana	.05
220	Checklist (Tim Raines 2,000 Hits)	.05
221	Hal Morris	.05
222	Darren Holmes	.05
223	Chris Gwynn	.05
224	Chad Kreuter	.05
225	Mike Hartley	.05
226	Scott Lydy	.05
227	Eduardo Perez	.05
228	Greg Swindell	.05
229	Al Leiter	.05
230	Scott Radinsky	.05
231	Bob Wickman	.05
232	Otis Nixon	.05
233	Kevin Reimer	.05
234	Geronimo Pena	.05
235	Kevin Roberson/RR	.05
236	Jody Reed	.05
237	Kirk Rueter/RR	.05
238	Willie McGee	.05
239	Charles Nagy	.05
240	Tim Leary	.05
241	Carl Everett	.05
242	Charlie O'Brien	.05
243	Mike Pagliarulo	.05
244	Kerry Taylor	.05
245	Kevin Stocker	.05
246	Joel Johnston	.05
247	Geno Petralli	.05
248	Jeff Russell	.05
249	Joe Oliver	.05
250	Robert Mejia	.05
251	Chris Haney	.05
252	Bill Krueger	.05
253	Shane Mack	.05
254	Terry Steinbach	.05
255	Luis Polonia	.05
256	Eddie Taubensee	.05
257	Dave Stewart	.05
258	Tim Raines	.05
259	Bernie Williams	.05
260	John Smoltz	.05
261	Kevin Seitzer	.05
262	Bob Tewksbury	.05
263	Bob Scanlan	.05
264	Henry Rodriguez	.05
265	Tim Scott	.05
266	Scott Sanderson	.05
267	Eric Plunk	.05
268	Edgar Martinez	.05
269	Charlie Hough	.05
270	Joe Orsulak	.05
271	Harold Reynolds	.05
272	Tim Teufel	.05
273	Bobby Thigpen	.05
274	Randy Tomlin	.05
275	Gary Redus	.05
276	Ken Ryan	.05
277	Tim Pugh	.05
278	Jayhawk Owens	.05
279	Phil Hiatt/RR	.05
280	Alan Trammell	.05
281	Dave McCarty/RR	.05
282	Bob Welch	.05
283	J.T. Snow	.05
284	Brian Williams	.05
285	Devon White	.05
286	Steve Sax	.05
287	Tony Tarasco	.05
288	Bill Spiers	.05
289	Allen Watson	.05
290	Checklist (Rickey Henderson 2,000 Hits)	.05
291	Joe Vizcaino	.05
292	Darryl Strawberry	.05
293	John Wetteland	.05
294	Bill Swift	.05
295	Jeff Treadway	.05
296	Tino Martinez	.05
297	Richie Lewis	.05
298	Bret Saberhagen	.05
299	Arthur Rhodes	.05
300	Guillermo Velasquez	.05
301	Milt Thompson	.05
302	Doug Strange	.05
303	Aaron Sele	.05
304	Bip Roberts	.05
305	Bruce Ruffin	.05
306	Jose Lind	.05
307	David Wells	.05
308	Bobby Witt	.05
309	Mark Wohlers	.05
310	B.J. Surhoff	.05
311	Mark Whiten	.05
312	Turk Wendell	.05
313	Raul Mondesi	.05
314	Brian Turang RC	.05
315	Chris Hammond	.05
316	Tim Bogar	.05
317	Brad Pennington	.05
318	Tim Worrell	.05
319	Mitch Williams	.05
320	Rondell White/RR	.05
321	Frank Viola	.05
322	Manny Ramirez	.75
323	Gary Wayne	.05
324	Mike Macfarlane	.05
325	Russ Springer	.05
326	Tim Wallach	.05
327	Salomon Torres/RR	.05
328	Omar Vizquel	.05
329	Andy Tomberlin RC	.05
330	Chris Sabo	.05
331	Mike Mussina	.30
332	Andy Benes	.05
333	Darren Daulton	.05
334	Orlando Merced	.05
335	Mark McGwire	1.50
336	Dave Winfield	.60
337	Sammy Sosa	.65
338	Eric Karros	.05
339	Greg Vaughn	.05
340	Don Mattingly	.75
341	Frank Thomas	.60
342	Fred McGriff	.05
343	Kirby Puckett	.65
344	Roberto Kelly	.05
345	Wally Joyner	.05
346	Andres Galarraga	.05
347	Bobby Bonilla	.05
348	Benito Santiago	.05
349	Barry Bonds	2.00
350	Delino DeShields	.05
351	Albert Belle	.05
352	Randy Johnson	.60
353	Tim Salmon	.05
354	John Olerud	.05
355	Dean Palmer	.05
356	Roger Clemens	.75
357	Jim Abbott	.05
358	Mark Grace	.05
359	Ozzie Guillen	.05
360	Lou Whitaker	.05
361	Jose Rijo	.05
362	Jeff Montgomery	.05
363	Chuck Finley	.05
364	Tom Glavine	.25
365	Jeff Bagwell	.60
366	Joe Carter	.05
367	Ray Lankford	.05
368	Ramon Martinez	.05
369	Jay Buhner	.05
370	Matt Williams	.05
371	Larry Walker	.05
372	Jose Canseco	.30
373	Len Dykstra	.05
374	Bryan Harvey	.05
375	Andy Van Slyke	.05
376	Ivan Rodriguez	.50
377	Kevin Mitchell	.05
378	Travis Fryman	.05
379	Duane Ward	.05
380	Greg Maddux	.65
381	Scott Servais	.05
382	Greg Olson	.05
383	Rey Sanchez	.05
384	Tom Kramer	.05
385	David Valle	.05
386	Eddie Murray	.60
387	Kevin Higgins	.05
388	Dan Wilson	.05
389	Todd Frohwirth	.05
390	Gerald Williams	.05
391	Hipolito Pichardo	.05
392	Pat Meares	.05
393	Luis Lopez	.05
394	Ricky Jordan	.05
395	Bob Walk	.05
396	Sid Fernandez	.05
397	Todd Worrell	.05
398	Darryl Hamilton	.05
399	Randy Myers	.05
400	Rod Brewer	.05
401	Lance Blankenship	.05
402	Steve Finley	.05
403	Phil Leftwich RC	.05
404	Juan Guzman	.05
405	Anthony Young	.05

406	Jeff Gardner	.05
407	Ryan Bowen	.05
408	Fernando Valenzuela	.05
409	David West	.05
410	Kenny Rogers	.05
411	Bob Zupcic	.05
412	Eric Young	.05
413	Bret Boone	.05
414	Danny Tartabull	.05
415	Bob MacDonald	.05
416	Ron Karkovice	.05
417	Scott Cooper	.05
418	Dante Bichette	.05
419	Tripp Cromer	.05
420	Billy Ashley	.05
421	Roger Smithberg	.05
422	Dennis Martinez	.05
423	Mike Blowers	.05
424	Darren Lewis	.05
425	Junior Ortiz	.05
426	Butch Huskey	.05
427	Jimmy Poole	.05
428	Walt Weiss	.05
429	Scott Bankhead	.05
430	Deion Sanders	.05
431	Scott Bullett	.05
432	Jeff Huson	.05
433	Tyler Green	.05
434	Billy Hatcher	.05
435	Bob Hamelin	.05
436	Reggie Sanders	.05
437	Scott Erickson	.05
438	Steve Reed	.05
439	Randy Velarde	.05
440	Checklist (Tony Gwynn 2,000 Hits)	.15
441	Terry Leach	.05
442	Danny Bautista	.05
443	Kent Hrbek	.05
444	Rick Wilkins	.05
445	Tony Phillips	.05
446	Dion James	.05
447	Joey Cora	.05
448	Andre Dawson	.15
449	Pedro Castellano	.05
450	Tom Gordon	.05
451	Rob Dibble	.05
452	Ron Darling	.05
453	Chipper Jones	.65
454	Joe Grahe	.05
455	Domingo Cedeno	.05
456	Tom Edens	.05
457	Mitch Webster	.05
458	Jose Bautista	.05
459	Troy O'Leary	.05
460	Todd Zeile	.05
461	Sean Berry	.05
462	Brad Holman RC	.05
463	Dave Martinez	.05
464	Mark Lewis	.05
465	Paul Carey	.05
466	Jack Armstrong	.05
467	David Telgheder	.05
468	Gene Harris	.05
469	Danny Darwin	.05
470	Kim Batiste	.05
471	Tim Wakefield	.05
472	Craig Lefferts	.05
473	Jacob Brumfield	.05
474	Lance Painter	.05
475	Milt Cuyler	.05
476	Melido Perez	.05
477	Derek Parks	.05
478	Gary DiSarcina	.05
479	Steve Bedrosian	.05
480	Eric Anthony	.05
481	Julio Franco	.05
482	Tommy Greene	.05
483	Pat Kelly	.05
484	Nate Minchey/RR	.05
485	William Pennyfeather	.05
486	Harold Baines	.05
487	Howard Johnson	.05
488	Angel Miranda	.05
489	Scott Sanders	.05
490	Shawon Dunston	.05
491	Mel Rojas	.05
492	Jeff Nelson	.05
493	Archi Cianfrocco	.05
494	Al Martin	.05
495	Mike Gallego	.05
496	Mike Henneman	.05
497	Armando Reynoso	.05
498	Mickey Morandini	.05
499	Rick Renteria	.05
500	Rick Sutcliffe	.05
501	Bobby Jones/RR	.05
502	Gary Gaetti	.05
503	Rick Aguilera	.05
504	Todd Stottlemyre	.05
505	Mike Mohler	.05
506	Mike Stanton	.05
507	Jose Guzman	.05
508	Kevin Rogers	.05
509	Chuck Carr	.05
510	Chris Jones	.05
511	Brent Mayne	.05
512	Greg Harris	.05
513	Dave Henderson	.05
514	Eric Hillman	.05
515	Dan Peltier	.05
516	Craig Shipley	.05
517	John Valentin	.05
518	Wilson Alvarez	.05
519	Andujar Cedeno	.05
520	Troy Neel	.05
521	Tom Candiotti	.05
522	Matt Mieske	.05

523	Jim Thome	.50
524	Lou Frazier	.05
525	Mike Jackson	.05
526	Pedro Martinez	.05
527	Roger Pavlik	.05
528	Kent Bottenfield	.05
529	Felix Jose	.05
530	Mark Guthrie	.05
531	Steve Farr	.05
532	Craig Paquette	.05
533	Doug Jones	.05
534	Luis Alicea	.05
535	Cory Snyder	.05
536	Paul Sorrento	.05
537	Nigel Wilson	.05
538	Jeff King	.05
539	Willie Green	.05
540	Kirk McCaskill	.05
541	Al Osuna	.05
542	Greg Hibbard	.05
543	Brett Butler	.05
544	Jose Valentin	.05
545	Wil Cordero	.05
546	Chris Bosio	.05
547	Jamie Moyer	.05
548	Jim Eisenreich	.05
549	Vinny Castilla	.05
550	Checklist (Dave Winfield 3,000 Hits)	.05
551	John Roper	.05
552	Lance Johnson	.05
553	Scott Kamieniecki	.05
554	Mike Moore	.05
555	Steve Buechele	.05
556	Terry Pendleton	.05
557	Todd Van Poppel	.05
558	Rob Butler	.05
559	Zane Smith	.05
560	David Hulse	.05
561	Tim Costo	.05
562	John Habyan	.05
563	Terry Jorgensen	.05
564	Matt Nokes	.05
565	Kevin McReynolds	.05
566	Phil Plantier	.05
567	Chris Turner	.05
568	Carlos Delgado	.40
569	John Jaha	.05
570	Dwight Smith	.05
571	John Vander Wal	.05
572	Trevor Wilson	.05
573	Felix Fermin	.05
574	Marc Newfield/RR	.05
575	Jeromy Burnitz	.05
576	Leo Gomez	.05
577	Curt Schilling	.25
578	Kevin Young	.05
579	Jerry Spradlin RC	.05
580	Curt Leskanic	.05
581	Carl Willis	.05
582	Alex Fernandez	.05
583	Mark Holzemer	.05
584	Domingo Martinez	.05
585	Pete Smith	.05
586	Brian Jordan	.05
587	Kevin Gross	.05
588	J.R. Phillips/RR	.05
589	Chris Nabholz	.05
590	Bill Wertz	.05
591	Derek Bell	.05
592	Brady Anderson	.05
593	Matt Turner	.05
594	Pete Incaviglia	.05
595	Greg Gagne	.05
596	John Flaherty	.05
597	Scott Livingstone	.05
598	Rod Bolton	.05
599	Mike Perez	.05
600	Checklist (Roger Clemens 2,000 Strikeouts)	.25
601	Tony Castillo	.05
602	Henry Mercedes	.05
603	Mike Fetters	.05
604	Rod Beck	.05
605	Damon Buford	.05
606	Matt Whiteside	.05
607	Shawn Green	.05
608	Midre Cummings/RR	.05
609	Jeff McNeeley	.05
610	Danny Sheaffer	.05
611	Paul Wagner	.05
612	Torey Lovullo	.05
613	Javier Lopez	.05
614	Mariano Duncan	.05
615	Doug Brocail	.05
616	Dave Hansen	.05
617	Ryan Klesko	.05
618	Eric Davis	.05
619	Scott Ruffcorn/RR	.05
620	Mike Trombley	.05
621	Jaime Navarro	.05
622	Rheal Cormier	.05
623	Jose Offerman	.05
624	David Segui	.05
625	Robb Nen/RR	.05
626	Dave Gallagher	.05
627	Julian Tavarez RC	.05
628	Chris Gomez	.05
629	Jeffrey Hammonds/RR	.05
630	Scott Brosius	.05
631	Willie Blair	.05
632	Doug Drabek	.05
633	Bill Wegman	.05
634	Jeff McKnight	.05
635	Rich Rodriguez	.05
636	Steve Trachsel	.05
637	Buddy Groom	.05
638	Sterling Hitchcock	.05

639	Chuck McElroy	.05
640	Rene Gonzales	.05
641	Dan Plesac	.05
642	Jeff Branson	.05
643	Darrell Whitmore	.05
644	Paul Quantrill	.05
645	Rich Rowland	.05
646	Curtis Pride RC	.05
647	Erik Plantenberg	.05
648	Albie Lopez	.05
649	Rich Batchelor RC	.05
650	Lee Smith	.05
651	Cliff Floyd	.05
652	Pete Schourek	.05
653	Reggie Jefferson	.05
654	Bill Haselman	.05
655	Steve Hosey	.05
656	Mark Clark	.05
657	Mark Davis	.05
658	Dave Magadan	.05
659	Candy Maldonado	.05
660	Checklist (Mark Langston 2,000 Strikeouts)	.05

Special Edition - Gold

In 1994 Donruss added a Special Edition subset of 100 of the game's top players. Fifty cards each were included one or two per pack in all types of Donruss' Series 1 and 2 packaging. The cards use the same photos and format as the regular-issue version, but have special gold-foil stamping on front in the area of the team logo and player name, and on back in a "Special Edition" number box in the upper-left corner.

		NM/M
Complete Set (100):		7.50
Common Player:		.10
1	Nolan Ryan	1.50
2	Mike Piazza	1.00
3	Moises Alou	.10
4	Ken Griffey Jr.	1.00
5	Gary Sheffield	.25
6	Roberto Alomar	.20
7	John Kruk	.10
8	Gregg Olson	.10
9	Gregg Jefferies	.10
10	Tony Gwynn	.65
11	Chad Curtis	.10
12	Craig Biggio	.10
13	John Burkett	.10
14	Carlos Baerga	.10
15	Robin Yount	.60
16	Dennis Eckersley	.50
17	Dwight Gooden	.10
18	Ryne Sandberg	.65
19	Rickey Henderson	.60
20	Jack McDowell	.10
21	Jay Bell	.10
22	Kevin Brown	.10
23	Robin Ventura	.10
24	Paul Molitor	.60
25	David Justice	.25
26	Rafael Palmeiro	.50
27	Cecil Fielder	.10
28	Chuck Knoblauch	.10
29	Dave Hollins	.10
30	Jimmy Key	.10
31	Mark Langston	.10
32	Darryl Kile	.10
33	Ruben Sierra	.10
34	Ron Gant	.10
35	Ozzie Smith	.65
36	Wade Boggs	.65
37	Marquis Grissom	.10
38	Will Clark	.10
39	Kenny Lofton	.10
40	Cal Ripken, Jr.	1.50
41	Steve Avery	.10
42	Mo Vaughn	.10
43	Brian McRae	.10
44	Mickey Tettleton	.10
45	Barry Larkin	.10
46	Charlie Hayes	.10
47	Kevin Appier	.10
48	Robby Thompson	.10
49	Juan Gonzalez	.30
50	Paul O'Neill	.10
51	Mike Mussina	.40
52	Andy Benes	.10
53	Darren Daulton	.10
54	Orlando Merced	.10
55	Mark McGwire	1.25
56	Dave Winfield	.60
57	Sammy Sosa	.65
58	Eric Karros	.10
59	Greg Vaughn	.10
60	Don Mattingly	.75
61	Frank Thomas	.60
62	Fred McGriff	.10
63	Kirby Puckett	.65
64	Roberto Kelly	.10
65	Wally Joyner	.10
66	Andres Galarraga	.10
67	Bobby Bonilla	.10
68	Benito Santiago	.10
69	Barry Bonds	1.50
70	Delino DeShields	.10
71	Albert Belle	.10
72	Randy Johnson	.60
73	Tim Salmon	.10
74	John Olerud	.10
75	Dean Palmer	.10
76	Roger Clemens	.75
77	Jim Abbott	.10
78	Mark Grace	.10
79	Ozzie Guillen	.10
80	Lou Whitaker	.10
81	Jose Rijo	.10
82	Jeff Montgomery	.10
83	Chuck Finley	.10
84	Tom Glavine	.25
85	Jeff Bagwell	.60
86	Joe Carter	.10
87	Ray Lankford	.10
88	Ramon Martinez	.10
89	Jay Buhner	.10
90	Matt Williams	.10
91	Larry Walker	.10
92	Jose Canseco	.25
93	Len Dykstra	.10
94	Bryan Harvey	.10
95	Andy Van Slyke	.10
96	Ivan Rodriguez	.50
97	Kevin Mitchell	.10
98	Travis Fryman	.10
99	Duane Ward	.10
100	Greg Maddux	.65

Anniversary-1984

RICKEY HENDERSON OF

This set commemorates and features 10 of the most popular cards from Donruss' 1984 set. The cards, inserted in Series I hobby foil packs only, are "holographically enhanced" with foil stamping and UV coating.

		NM/M
Complete Set (10):		20.00
Common Player:		1.00
1	Joe Carter	1.00
2	Robin Yount	1.50
3	George Brett	2.50
4	Rickey Henderson	1.50
5	Nolan Ryan	6.00
6	Cal Ripken, Jr.	6.00
7	Wade Boggs	2.00
8	Don Mattingly	2.50
9	Ryne Sandberg	2.00
10	Tony Gwynn	2.00

Award Winners Supers

Major award winners of the 1993 season are honored in this super-size (3-1/2" x 5") insert set. One card was packaged in each box of U.S. jumbo packs and in each Canadian foil-pack box. On a gold-tone background, the card backs have another player photo, a description of his award winning performance

and a white strip with a serial number identifying the card's place in an edition of 10,000.

		NM/M
Complete Set (10):		25.00
Common Player:		1.25
1	Barry Bonds (N.L. MVP)	5.00
2	Greg Maddux (N.L. Cy Young)	2.50
3	Mike Piazza (N.L. ROY)	3.50
4	Barry Bonds (N.L. HR Champ)	5.00
5	Kirby Puckett (All-Star MVP)	2.50
6	Frank Thomas (A.L. MVP)	2.00
7	Jack McDowell (A.L. Cy Young)	1.25
8	Tim Salmon (A.L. ROY)	1.25
9	Juan Gonzalez (A.L. HR Champ)	1.50
10	Paul Molitor (World Series MVP)	2.00

1994 Donruss Decade Dominators

DOMINATORS

CECIL FIELDER HOMERUNS

Donruss selected 10 top home run hitters (Series I) and 10 RBI leaders of the 1990s for this insert set. Cards were issued in all types of Series I and II packs. Full-bleed UV-coated cards were gold-foil enhanced on the front. Backs featured another full-color player photo and charted information on his 1990s home run or RBI output and ranking.

		NM/M
Complete Set (20):		15.00
Common Player:		.35
Series 1		
1	Cecil Fielder	.35
2	Barry Bonds	2.50
3	Fred McGriff	.35
4	Matt Williams	.35
5	Joe Carter	.35
6	Juan Gonzalez	.40
7	Jose Canseco	.50
8	Ron Gant	.35
9	Ken Griffey Jr.	1.50
10	Mark McGwire	2.00
Series 2		
1	Tony Gwynn	1.00
2	Frank Thomas	.75
3	Paul Molitor	.75
4	Edgar Martinez	.35
5	Kirby Puckett	1.00
6	Ken Griffey, Jr.	1.50
7	Barry Bonds	2.50
8	Willie McGee	.35
9	Len Dykstra	1.50
10	John Kruk	.35

Supers

Super-size (3-1/2" x 5") versions of the 1994 Donruss Decade Dominators insert

cards were produced as a premium, one card being packaged in a paper checklist envelope in each hobby box of Donruss foil packs. The supers are identical in format to the regular-size cards with the exception of a white serial number strip on the back, identifying each card's position in an edition of 10,000.

90's DOMINATORS

		NM/M
Complete Set (20):		25.00
Common Player:		1.00
Series 1		
1	Cecil Fielder	1.00
2	Barry Bonds	2.50
3	Fred McGriff	1.00
4	Matt Williams	1.00
5	Joe Carter	1.00
6	Juan Gonzalez	1.25
7	Jose Canseco	1.25
8	Ron Gant	1.00
9	Ken Griffey Jr.	2.00
10	Mark McGwire	2.00
Series 2		
1	Tony Gwynn	2.00
2	Frank Thomas	1.50
3	Paul Molitor	1.50
4	Edgar Martinez	1.00
5	Kirby Puckett	2.00
6	Ken Griffey, Jr.	2.25
7	Barry Bonds	2.50
8	Willie McGee	1.00
9	Lenny Dykstra	2.00
10	John Kruk	1.00

1994 Donruss Diamond Kings

The artwork of Dick Perez is again featured on this insert set included in foil packs. Player art is set against garish color backgrounds with a red-and-silver "Diamond Kings" foil logo above, and the player's name in script at bottom. Backs are printed in red on pale yellow and feature a 1993 season summary. Cards have a DK preface to the number. Cards #1-14 and #29, Dave Winfield, were included in Series 1 packs; cards #15-28 were found in Series 2, along with the checklist card (#30), featuring a Dick Perez self-portrait.

		NM/M
Complete Set (30):		12.00
Common Player:		.25
1	Barry Bonds	2.50
2	Mo Vaughn	.25
3	Steve Avery	.25
4	Tim Salmon	.25
5	Rick Wilkins	.25
6	Brian Harper	.25
7	Andres Galarraga	.25
8	Albert Belle	.25
9	John Kruk	.25
10	Ivan Rodriguez	.75
11	Tony Gwynn	1.25

12	Brian McRae	.25
13	Bobby Bonilla	.25
14	Ken Griffey Jr.	2.00
15	Mike Piazza	2.00
16	Don Mattingly	1.50
17	Barry Larkin	.25
18	Ruben Sierra	.25
19	Orlando Merced	.25
20	Greg Vaughn	.25
21	Gregg Jefferies	.25
22	Cecil Fielder	.25
23	Moises Alou	.25
24	John Olerud	.25
25	Gary Sheffield	.25
26	Mike Mussina	.60
27	Jeff Bagwell	1.00
28	Frank Thomas	1.00
29	Dave Winfield (King of Kings)	1.00
30	Dick Perez (Checklist)	.25

Supers

Each retail box of 1994 Donruss foil packs contains one super-size (4-7/8" x 6-13/16") version of the Diamond Kings inserts. Series 1 boxes offer cards #1-14, while #15-28 are found in Series 2 boxes. A 29th card, honoring Dave Winfield, was also produced. Super DKs are identical in format to the regular-size inserts, with the exception of a white serial number strip on the back which identifies the card within an edition of 10,000.

		NM/M
Complete Set (29):		70.00
Common Player:		2.00
1	Barry Bonds	7.50
2	Mo Vaughn	2.00
3	Steve Avery	2.00
4	Tim Salmon	2.00
5	Rick Wilkins	2.00
6	Brian Harper	2.00
7	Andres Galarraga	2.00
8	Albert Belle	2.00
9	John Kruk	2.00
10	Ivan Rodriguez	3.50
11	Tony Gwynn	5.00
12	Brian McRae	2.00
13	Bobby Bonilla	2.00
14	Ken Griffey Jr.	6.50
15	Mike Piazza	6.50
16	Don Mattingly	6.00
17	Barry Larkin	2.00
18	Ruben Sierra	2.00
19	Orlando Merced	2.00
20	Greg Vaughn	2.00
21	Gregg Jefferies	2.00
22	Cecil Fielder	2.00
23	Moises Alou	2.00
24	John Olerud	2.00
25	Gary Sheffield	3.00
26	Mike Mussina	3.00
27	Jeff Bagwell	4.00
28	Frank Thomas	4.00
29	Dave Winfield (King of Kings)	4.00

Elite

Donruss continued its popular Elite Series with 12 more players in 1994. The cards, numbered #37-48, were inserted in foil packs only. The cards feature the player in a diamond on the front; the back offers an opinion of why the player is considered an elite and is serially numbered to 10,000.

		NM/M
Complete Set (12):		50.00
Common Player:		4.00
37	Frank Thomas	6.00
38	Tony Gwynn	7.50
39	Tim Salmon	4.00
40	Albert Belle	4.00
41	John Kruk	4.00
42	Juan Gonzalez	5.00
43	John Olerud	4.00
44	Barry Bonds	12.00
45	Ken Griffey Jr.	9.00
46	Mike Piazza	9.00
47	Jack McDowell	4.00
48	Andres Galarraga	4.00

Long Ball Leaders

The "Tale of the Tape" for the 1993 season is chronicled in this Series II hobby-only foil-pack insert. Silver prismatic foil highlights the typography on the front of the card which includes the "Long Ball Leaders" logos (complete with embossed baseball). The player's last name and the distance of his blast. Cards backs have another player photo superimposed on the venue in which the home run was hit. The distance is repeated in silver over the ballpark photo. In a wide silver box at bottom is data about the home run.

		NM/M
Complete Set (10):		6.00
Common Player:		.30
1	Cecil Fielder	.30
2	Dean Palmer	.30
3	Andres Galarraga	.30
4	Bo Jackson	.40
5	Ken Griffey Jr.	1.50
6	Dave Justice	.30
7	Mike Piazza	1.50
8	Frank Thomas	1.00
9	Barry Bonds	3.00
10	Juan Gonzalez	.50

MVPs

These inserts were included in 1994 jumbo packs only. The fronts have a large metallic blue MVP logo, beneath which is a red stripe with the player's name and position in white. Backs have a portrait photo, stats for 1993 and a summary of why the player was selected as team MVP.

		NM/M
Complete Set (28):		20.00
Common Player:		.25
1	Dave Justice	.25
2	Mark Grace	.25
3	Jose Rijo	.25
4	Andres Galarraga	.25
5	Bryan Harvey	.25
6	Jeff Bagwell	1.00
7	Mike Piazza	2.50
8	Moises Alou	.25
9	Bobby Bonilla	.25
10	Len Dykstra	.25
11	Jeff King	.25
12	Gregg Jefferies	.25
13	Tony Gwynn	1.50
14	Barry Bonds	4.00
15	Cal Ripken, Jr.	4.00
16	Mo Vaughn	.25
17	Tim Salmon	.25
18	Frank Thomas	1.00
19	Albert Belle	.25
20	Cecil Fielder	.25
21	Wally Joyner	.25
22	Greg Vaughn	.25
23	Kirby Puckett	1.50
24	Don Mattingly	2.00
25	Ruben Sierra	.25
26	Ken Griffey Jr.	2.50
27	Juan Gonzalez	.50
28	John Olerud	.25

1994 Donruss Spirit of the Game

Ten players are featured in this insert set, packaged exclusively in retail boxes. Horizontal in format, fronts feature a color player action photo set against a gold-tone background which has the appearance of a multiple-exposure photo. On back a player portrait photo is set against a backdrop of red, white and blue bunting. There is a short previous-season write-up at right. Cards #1-5 were included with Series I, cards 6-10 were in Series II packs.

		NM/M
Complete Set (10):		10.00
Common Player:		.70
1	John Olerud	.50
2	Barry Bonds	2.50
3	Ken Griffey Jr.	2.00
4	Mike Piazza	2.00
5	Juan Gonzalez	.60
6	Frank Thomas	1.00
7	Tim Salmon	.50
8	Dave Justice	.50
9	Don Mattingly	1.50
10	Len Dykstra	.50

Supers

Virtually identical in format to the regular-size "Spirit of the Game" cards, these 3-1/2" x 5" versions have gold-foil, rather than holographic printing on the front, and have a serial number on back identifying it from an edition of 10,000. One super card was inserted in each specially designated retail box.

		NM/M
Complete Set (10):		20.00
Common Player:		1.50
1	John Olerud	1.50
2	Barry Bonds	4.00
3	Ken Griffey Jr.	3.50
4	Mike Piazza	3.50
5	Juan Gonzalez	2.00
6	Frank Thomas	2.50
7	Tim Salmon	1.50
8	Dave Justice	1.50
9	Don Mattingly	3.00
10	Len Dykstra	1.50

1995 Donruss Samples

The cards in this preview release of Donruss' 1995 baseball issue are virtually identical to the issued versions of the same players' cards except for slight picture cropping differences. They are unmakred as to sample status.

		NM/M
Complete Set (7):		10.00
Common Player:		1.00
5	Mike Piazza	2.00
8	Barry Bonds	3.00
20	Jeff Bagwell	1.50
42	Juan Gonzalez	1.00
55	Don Mattingly	2.00
275	Frank Thomas	1.50
331	Greg Maddux	1.50

1995 Donruss

A pair of player photos on the front of each card and silver-foil highlights are featured on the 1995 Donruss set. Besides the main action photo on front, each card has a second photo in a home plate picture frame at lower-left. A silver-foil ribbon beneath has the player's team and name embossed. Above the small photo is the player's position, with a half-circle of stars over all; both elements in silver foil. Completing the silver-foil highlights is the Donruss logo at upper-left. Full-bleed backs have yet another action photo at center, with a large team logo at left and five years' worth of stats plus career numbers at bottom. Donruss was issued in retail and hobby 12-card packs, magazine distributor packs of 16 and jumbo packs of 20 cards. New to Donruss in 1995 were Super Packs. These were packs that contained complete insert sets and were seeded every 90 packs.

		NM/M
Complete Set (550):		20.00
Common Player:		.05
Press Proofs:		15X
Series 1 or 2 Pack (12):		.75
Series 1 or 2 Wax Box (36):		20.00
1	Dave Justice	.05
2	Rene Arocha	.05
3	Sandy Alomar Jr.	.05
4	Luis Lopez	.05
5	Mike Piazza	1.50
6	Bobby Jones	.05
7	Damion Easley	.05
8	Barry Bonds	2.50
9	Mike Mussina	.40
10	Kevin Seitzer	.05
11	John Smiley	.05
12	W. Van Landingham	.05
13	Ron Darling	.05
14	Walt Weiss	.05
15	Mike Lansing	.05
16	Allen Watson	.05
17	Aaron Sele	.05
18	Randy Johnson	.65
19	Dean Palmer	.05
20	Jeff Bagwell	.65
21	Curt Schilling	.25
22	Darrell Whitmore	.05
23	Steve Trachsel	.05
24	Dan Wilson	.05
25	Steve Finley	.05
26	Bret Boone	.05
27	Charles Johnson	.05
28	Mike Stanton	.05
29	Ismael Valdes	.05
30	Salomon Torres	.05
31	Eric Anthony	.05
32	Spike Owen	.05
33	Joey Cora	.05
34	Robert Eenhoorn	.05
35	Rick White	.05
36	Omar Vizquel	.05
37	Carlos Delgado	.45
38	Eddie Williams	.05
39	Shawon Dunston	.05
40	Darrin Fletcher	.05
41	Leo Gomez	.05
42	Juan Gonzalez	.40
43	Luis Alicea	.05
44	Ken Ryan	.05
45	Lou Whitaker	.05
46	Mike Blowers	.05
47	Willie Blair	.05
48	Todd Van Poppel	.05
49	Roberto Alomar	.25
50	Ozzie Smith	.75
51	Sterling Hitchcock	.05
52	Mo Vaughn	.05
53	Rick Aguilera	.05
54	Kent Mercker	.05
55	Don Mattingly	1.00
56	Bob Scanlan	.05
57	Wilson Alvarez	.05
58	Jose Mesa	.05
59	Scott Kamieniecki	.05
60	Todd Jones	.05
61	John Kruk	.05
62	Mike Stanley	.05
63	Tino Martinez	.05
64	Eddie Zambrano	.05
65	Todd Hundley	.05
66	Jamie Moyer	.05
67	Rich Amaral	.05
68	Jose Valentin	.05
69	Alex Gonzalez	.05
70	Kurt Abbott	.05
71	Delino DeShields	.05
72	Brian Anderson	.05
73	John Vander Wal	.05
74	Turner Ward	.05
75	Tim Raines	.05
76	Mark Acre	.05
77	Jose Offerman	.05
78	Jimmy Key	.05
79	Mark Whiten	.05
80	Mark Gubicza	.05
81	Darren Hall	.05
82	Travis Fryman	.05
83	Cal Ripken, Jr.	2.50
84	Geronimo Berroa	.05
85	Bret Barberie	.05
86	Andy Ashby	.05
87	Steve Avery	.05
88	Rich Becker	.05
89	John Valentin	.05
90	Glenallen Hill	.05
91	Carlos Garcia	.05
92	Dennis Martinez	.05
93	Pat Kelly	.05
94	Orlando Miller	.05
95	Felix Jose	.05
96	Mike Kingery	.05
97	Jeff Kent	.05
98	Pete Incaviglia	.05
99	Chad Curtis	.05
100	Thomas Howard	.05
101	Hector Carrasco	.05
102	Tom Pagnozzi	.05
103	Danny Tartabull	.05
104	Donnie Elliott	.05
105	Danny Jackson	.05
106	Steve Dunn	.05
107	Roger Salkeld	.05
108	Jeff King	.05
109	Cecil Fielder	.05
110	Checklist	.05
111	Denny Neagle	.05
112	Troy Neel	.05
113	Rod Beck	.05
114	Alex Rodriguez	2.00
115	Joey Eischen	.05
116	Tom Candiotti	.05
117	Ray McDavid	.05
118	Vince Coleman	.05
119	Pete Harnisch	.05
120	David Nied	.05
121	Pat Rapp	.05
122	Sammy Sosa	.75
123	Steve Reed	.05
124	Jose Oliva	.05
125	Rick Bottalico	.05
126	Jose DeLeon	.05
127	Pat Hentgen	.05
128	Will Clark	.05
129	Mark Dewey	.05
130	Greg Vaughn	.05
131	Darren Dreifort	.05
132	Ed Sprague	.05
133	Lee Smith	.05
134	Charles Nagy	.05
135	Phil Plantier	.05
136	Jason Jacome	.05
137	Jose Lima	.05
138	J.R. Phillips	.05
139	J.T. Snow	.05
140	Mike Huff	.05
141	Billy Brewer	.05
142	Jeromy Burnitz	.05
143	Ricky Bones	.05
144	Carlos Rodriguez	.05
145	Luis Gonzalez	.05
146	Mark Lemke	.05
147	Al Martin	.05
148	Mike Bordick	.05
149	Robb Nen	.05
150	Wil Cordero	.05
151	Edgar Martinez	.05
152	Gerald Williams	.05
153	Esteban Beltre	.05
154	Mike Moore	.05
155	Mark Langston	.05
156	Mark Clark	.05
157	Bobby Ayala	.05
158	Rick Wilkins	.05
159	Bobby Munoz	.05
160	Checklist	.05
161	Scott Erickson	.05
162	Paul Molitor	.65
163	Jon Lieber	.05
164	Jason Grimsley	.05
165	Norberto Martin	.05
166	Javier Lopez	.05
167	Brian McRae	.05
168	Gary Sheffield	.40
169	Marcus Moore	.05
170	John Hudek	.05
171	Kelly Stinett	.05
172	Chris Gomez	.05
173	Rey Sanchez	.05
174	Juan Guzman	.05
175	Chan Ho Park	.05
176	Terry Shumpert	.05
177	Steve Ontiveros	.05
178	Brad Ausmus	.05
179	Tim Davis	.05
180	Billy Ashley	.05
181	Vinny Castilla	.05
182	Bill Spiers	.05
183	Randy Knorr	.05
184	Brian Hunter	.05
185	Pat Meares	.05
186	Steve Buechele	.05
187	Kirt Manwaring	.05
188	Tim Naehring	.05
189	Matt Mieske	.05
190	Josias Manzanillo	.05
191	Greg McMichael	.05
192	Chuck Carr	.05
193	Midre Cummings	.05
194	Darryl Strawberry	.05
195	Greg Gagne	.05
196	Steve Cooke	.05
197	Woody Williams	.05
198	Ron Karkovice	.05
199	Phil Leftwich	.05
200	Jim Thome	.50
201	Brady Anderson	.05
202	Pedro Martinez	.65
203	Steve Karsay	.05
204	Reggie Sanders	.05
205	Bill Risley	.05
206	Jay Bell	.05
207	Kevin Brown	.05
208	Tim Scott	.05
209	Len Dykstra	.05
210	Willie Greene	.05
211	Jim Eisenreich	.05
212	Cliff Floyd	.05
213	Otis Nixon	.05
214	Eduardo Perez	.05
215	Manuel Lee	.05
216	Armando Benitez **RC**	.10
217	Dave McCarty	.05
218	Scott Livingstone	.05
219	Chad Kreuter	.05
220	Checklist	.05
221	Brian Jordan	.05
222	Matt Whiteside	.05
223	Jim Edmonds	.05
224	Tony Gwynn	.75
225	Jose Lind	.05
226	Marvin Freeman	.05
227	Ken Hill	.05
228	David Hulse	.05
229	Joe Hesketh	.05
230	Roberto Petagine	.05
231	Jeffrey Hammonds	.05
232	John Jaha	.05
233	John Burkett	.05
234	Hal Morris	.05
235	Tony Castillo	.05
236	Ryan Bowen	.05
237	Wayne Kirby	.05
238	Brent Mayne	.05
239	Jim Bullinger	.05
240	Mike Lieberthal	.05
241	Barry Larkin	.05
242	David Segui	.05
243	Jose Bautista	.05
244	Hector Fajardo	.05
245	Orel Hershiser	.05
246	James Mouton	.05
247	Scott Leius	.05
248	Tom Glavine	.05
249	Danny Bautista	.05
250	Jose Mercedes	.05
251	Marquis Grissom	.05
252	Charlie Hayes	.05
253	Ryan Klesko	.05
254	Vicente Palacios	.05
255	Matias Carillo	.05
256	Gary DiSarcina	.05
257	Kirk Gibson	.05
258	Garey Ingram	.05
259	Alex Fernandez	.05
260	John Mabry	.05
261	Chris Howard	.05
262	Miguel Jimenez	.05
263	Heath Slocumb	.05
264	Albert Belle	.05
265	Dave Clark	.05

266	Joe Orsulak	.05
267	Joey Hamilton	.05
268	Mark Portugal	.05
269	Kevin Tapani	.05
270	Sid Fernandez	.05
271	Steve Dreyer	.05
272	Denny Hocking	.05
273	Troy O'Leary	.05
274	Milt Cuyler	.05
275	Frank Thomas	.65
276	Jorge Fabregas	.05
277	Mike Gallego	.05
278	Mickey Morandini	.05
279	Johnny Ruffin	.05
280	Henry Rodriguez	.05
281	Garret Anderson	.05
282	Bob Wickman	.05
283	Gar Finnvold	.05
284	Paul O'Neill	.05
285	Royce Clayton	.05
286	Chuck Knoblauch	.05
287	Johnny Ruffin	.05
288	Dave Nilsson	.05
289	David Cone	.05
290	Chuck McElroy	.05
291	Kevin Stocker	.05
292	Jose Rijo	.05
293	Sean Berry	.05
294	Ozzie Guillen	.05
295	Chris Hoiles	.05
296	Kevin Foster	.05
297	Jeff Frye	.05
298	Lance Johnson	.05
299	Mike Kelly	.05
300	Ellis Burks	.05
301	Roberto Kelly	.05
302	Dante Bichette	.05
303	Alvaro Espinoza	.05
304	Alex Cole	.05
305	Rickey Henderson	.65
306	Dave Weathers	.05
307	Shane Reynolds	.05
308	Bobby Bonilla	.05
309	Junior Felix	.05
310	Jeff Fassero	.05
311	Darren Lewis	.05
312	John Doherty	.05
313	Scott Servais	.05
314	Rick Helling	.05
315	Pedro Martinez	.65
316	Wes Chamberlain	.05
317	Bryan Eversgerd	.05
318	Trevor Hoffman	.05
319	John Patterson	.05
320	Matt Walbeck	.05
321	Jeff Montgomery	.05
322	Mel Rojas	.05
323	Eddie Taubensee	.05
324	Ray Lankford	.05
325	Jose Vizcaino	.05
326	Carlos Baerga	.05
327	Jack Voigt	.05
328	Julio Franco	.05
329	Brent Gates	.05
330	Checklist	.05
331	Greg Maddux	.75
332	Jason Bere	.05
333	Bill Wegman	.05
334	Tuffy Rhodes	.05
335	Kevin Young	.05
336	Andy Benes	.05
337	Pedro Astacio	.05
338	Reggie Jefferson	.05
339	Tim Belcher	.05
340	Ken Griffey Jr.	1.50
341	Mariano Duncan	.05
342	Andres Galarraga	.05
343	Rondell White	.05
344	Cory Bailey	.05
345	Bryan Harvey	.05
346	John Franco	.05
347	Greg Swindell	.05
348	David West	.05
349	Fred McGriff	.05
350	Jose Canseco	.35
351	Orlando Merced	.05
352	Rheal Cormier	.05
353	Carlos Pulido	.05
354	Terry Steinbach	.05
355	Wade Boggs	.75
356	B.J. Surhoff	.05
357	Rafael Palmeiro	.60
358	Anthony Young	.05
359	Tom Brunansky	.05
360	Todd Stottlemyre	.05
361	Chris Turner	.05
362	Joe Boever	.05
363	Jeff Blauser	.05
364	Derek Bell	.05
365	Matt Williams	.05
366	Jeremy Hernandez	.05
367	Joe Girardi	.05
368	Mike Devereaux	.05
369	Jim Abbott	.05
370	Manny Ramirez	.05
371	Kenny Lofton	.05
372	Mark Smith	.05
373	Dave Fleming	.05
374	Dave Stewart	.05
375	Roger Pavlik	.05
376	Hipolito Pichardo	.05
377	Bill Taylor	.05
378	Robin Ventura	.05
379	Bernard Gilkey	.05
380	Kirby Puckett	.75
381	Steve Howe	.05
382	Devon White	.05
383	Roberto Mejia	.05

384	Darrin Jackson	.05
385	Mike Morgan	.05
386	Rusty Meacham	.05
387	Bill Swift	.05
388	Lou Frazier	.05
389	Andy Van Slyke	.05
390	Brett Butler	.05
391	Bobby Witt	.05
392	Jeff Conine	.05
393	Tim Hyers	.05
394	Terry Pendleton	.05
395	Ricky Jordan	.05
396	Eric Plunk	.05
397	Melido Perez	.05
398	Darryl Kile	.05
399	Mark McLemore	.05
400	Greg Harris	.05
401	Jim Leyritz	.05
402	Doug Strange	.05
403	Tim Salmon	.05
404	Terry Mulholland	.05
405	Robby Thompson	.05
406	Ruben Sierra	.05
407	Tony Phillips	.05
408	Moises Alou	.05
409	Felix Fermin	.05
410	Pat Listach	.05
411	Kevin Bass	.05
412	Ben McDonald	.05
413	Scott Cooper	.05
414	Jody Reed	.05
415	Deion Sanders	.05
416	Ricky Gutierrez	.05
417	Gregg Jefferies	.05
418	Jack McDowell	.05
419	Al Leiter	.05
420	Tony Longmire	.05
421	Paul Wagner	.05
422	Geronimo Pena	.05
423	Ivan Rodriguez	.60
424	Kevin Gross	.05
425	Kirk McCaskill	.05
426	Greg Myers	.05
427	Roger Clemens	1.00
428	Chris Hammond	.05
429	Randy Myers	.05
430	Roger Mason	.05
431	Bret Saberhagen	.05
432	Jeff Reboulet	.05
433	John Olerud	.05
434	Bill Gullickson	.05
435	Eddie Murray	.65
436	Pedro Munoz	.05
437	Charlie O'Brien	.05
438	Jeff Nelson	.05
439	Mike Macfarlane	.05
440	Checklist	.05
441	Derrick May	.05
442	John Roper	.05
443	Darryl Hamilton	.05
444	Dan Miceli	.05
445	Tony Eusebio	.05
446	Jerry Browne	.05
447	Wally Joyner	.05
448	Brian Harper	.05
449	Scott Fletcher	.05
450	Bip Roberts	.05
451	Pete Smith	.05
452	Chili Davis	.05
453	Dave Hollins	.05
454	Tony Pena	.05
455	Butch Henry	.05
456	Craig Biggio	.05
457	Zane Smith	.05
458	Ryan Thompson	.05
459	Mike Jackson	.05
460	Mark McGwire	2.00
461	John Smoltz	.05
462	Steve Scarsone	.05
463	Greg Colbrunn	.05
464	Shawn Green	.25
465	David Wells	.05
466	Jose Hernandez	.05
467	Chip Hale	.05
468	Tony Tarasco	.05
469	Kevin Mitchell	.05
470	Billy Hatcher	.05
471	Jay Buhner	.05
472	Ken Caminiti	.05
473	Tom Henke	.05
474	Todd Worrell	.05
475	Mark Eichhorn	.05
476	Bruce Ruffin	.05
477	Chuck Finley	.05
478	Marc Newfield	.05
479	Paul Shuey	.05
480	Bob Tewksbury	.05
481	Ramon Martinez	.05
482	Melvin Nieves	.05
483	Todd Zeile	.05
484	Benito Santiago	.05
485	Stan Javier	.05
486	Kirk Rueter	.05
487	Andre Dawson	.25
488	Eric Karros	.05
489	Dave Magadan	.05
490	Checklist	.05
491	Randy Velarde	.05
492	Larry Walker	.05
493	Cris Carpenter	.05
494	Tom Gordon	.05
495	Dave Burba	.05
496	Darren Bragg	.05
497	Darren Daulton	.05
498	Don Slaught	.05
499	Pat Borders	.05
500	Lenny Harris	.05
501	Joe Ausanio	.05

502	Alan Trammell	.05
503	Mike Fetters	.05
504	Scott Ruffcorn	.05
505	Rich Rowland	.05
506	Juan Samuel	.05
507	Bo Jackson	.10
508	Jeff Branson	.05
509	Bernie Williams	.05
510	Paul Sorrento	.05
511	Dennis Eckersley	.60
512	Pat Mahomes	.05
513	Rusty Greer	.05
514	Luis Polonia	.05
515	Willie Banks	.05
516	John Wetteland	.05
517	Mike LaValliere	.05
518	Tommy Greene	.05
519	Mark Grace	.05
520	Bob Hamelin	.05
521	Scott Sanderson	.05
522	Joe Carter	.05
523	Jeff Brantley	.05
524	Andrew Lorraine	.05
525	Rico Brogna	.05
526	Shane Mack	.05
527	Mark Wohlers	.05
528	Scott Sanders	.05
529	Chris Bosio	.05
530	Andujar Cedeno	.05
531	Kenny Rogers	.05
532	Doug Drabek	.05
533	Curt Leskanic	.05
534	Craig Shipley	.05
535	Craig Grebeck	.05
536	Cal Eldred	.05
537	Mickey Tettleton	.05
538	Harold Baines	.05
539	Tim Wallach	.05
540	Damon Buford	.05
541	Lenny Webster	.05
542	Kevin Appier	.05
543	Raul Mondesi	.05
544	Eric Young	.05
545	Russ Davis	.05
546	Mike Benjamin	.05
547	Mike Greenwell	.05
548	Scott Brosius	.05
549	Brian Dorsett	.05
550	Checklist	.05

Press Proofs

Designated as Press Proofs, the first 2,000 cards of each player in the '95 Donruss set were enhanced with gold, rather than silver, foil and inserted into packs at an average rate of one per 20 packs.

	NM/M
Complete Set (550):	150.00
Common Player:	1.00
Stars:	15X

All-Stars

Exclusive to Wal-Mart jumbo packs were Donruss All-Stars. Nine cards featuring American Leaguers were inserted into Series 1, while nine National League All-Stars were inserted into Series 2 jumbos.

	NM/M
Complete Set (18):	26.00

Common Player:		.40
AL1	Jimmy Key	.40
AL2	Ivan Rodriguez	1.25
AL3	Frank Thomas	1.50
AL4	Roberto Alomar	.60
AL5	Wade Boggs	2.00
AL6	Cal Ripken, Jr.	4.50
AL7	Joe Carter	.40
AL8	Ken Griffey Jr.	3.00
AL9	Kirby Puckett	2.00
NL1	Greg Maddux	2.00
NL2	Mike Piazza	3.00
NL3	Gregg Jefferies	.40
NL4	Mariano Duncan	.40
NL5	Matt Williams	.40
NL6	Ozzie Smith	2.00
NL7	Barry Bonds	4.50
NL8	Tony Gwynn	2.00
NL9	Dave Justice	.40

Bomb Squad

Bomb Squad features the top six home run hitters in each league on double-sided cards. These cards were only inserted into Series I retail and magazine distributor packs at a rate of one per 24 retail packs and one per 16 magazine distributor packs.

		NM/M
Complete Set (6):		3.00
Common Player:		.50
1	Ken Griffey Jr., Matt Williams	1.00
2	Frank Thomas, Jeff Bagwell	.75
3	Albert Belle, Barry Bonds	1.50
4	Jose Canseco, Fred McGriff	.60
5	Cecil Fielder, Andres Galarraga	.50
6	Joe Carter, Kevin Mitchell	.50

Diamond Kings

Continuing a tradition begun in 1982, artist Dick Perez painted a series of 28 water colors to produce insert cards of the game's best; 14 in each series. A portrait of the player appears on a party-colored background, with Diamond Kings in gold across the top. DKs were inserted in Series 1 and 2 packs at a rate of one per 10.

		NM/M
Complete Set (29):		35.00
Common Player:		.75
1	Frank Thomas	3.00
2	Jeff Bagwell	3.00
3	Chili Davis	.75
4	Dante Bichette	.75
5	Ruben Sierra	.75
6	Jeff Conine	.75
7	Paul O'Neill	.75
8	Bobby Bonilla	.75
9	Joe Carter	.75
10	Moises Alou	.75
11	Kenny Lofton	.75
12	Matt Williams	.75
13	Kevin Seitzer	.75
14	Sammy Sosa	3.50
15	Scott Cooper	.75
16	Raul Mondesi	.75
17	Will Clark	.75
18	Lenny Dykstra	.75
19	Kirby Puckett	3.50
20	Hal Morris	.75
21	Travis Fryman	.75
22	Greg Maddux	3.50
23	Rafael Palmeiro	2.50
24	Tony Gwynn	3.50
25	David Cone	.75
26	Al Martin	.75
27	Ken Griffey Jr.	5.00
28	Gregg Jefferies	.75
29	Checklist	.10

Dominators

Dominators is a nine-card chase set inserted into hobby packs of Series II Donruss baseball at a rate of one per 24 packs. These acetate cards feature three of the top players at each position on a horizontal format.

		NM/M
Complete Set (9):		7.50
Common Player:		.50
1	David Cone, Mike Mussina, Greg Maddux	1.00
2	Ivan Rodriguez, Mike Piazza, Darren Daulton	2.00
3	Fred McGriff, Frank Thomas, Jeff Bagwell	1.50
4	Roberto Alomar, Carlos Baerga, Craig Biggio	.75
5	Robin Ventura, Travis Fryman, Matt Williams	.50
6	Cal Ripken Jr., Barry Larkin, Wil Cordero	2.50
7	Albert Belle, Barry Bonds, Moises Alou	2.50
8	Ken Griffey Jr., Kenny Lofton, Marquis Grissom	2.00
9	Kirby Puckett, Paul O'Neill, Tony Gwynn	2.00

Elite

Another Donruss insert tradition continues with the fifth annual presentation of the Elite series. Each of the 12 cards (six each Series 1 and 2) is produced in a numbered edition of 10,000 and inserted into all types of packaging at the rate of one per 210 packs.

		NM/M
Complete Set (12):		100.00
Common Player:		6.00
49	Jeff Bagwell	12.00
50	Paul O'Neill	6.00
51	Greg Maddux	15.00
52	Mike Piazza	17.50
53	Matt Williams	6.00
54	Ken Griffey Jr.	17.50
55	Frank Thomas	12.00
56	Barry Bonds	20.00
57	Kirby Puckett	15.00
58	Fred McGriff	6.00
59	Jose Canseco	9.00
60	Albert Belle	6.00

Long Ball Leaders

Exclusive to Series 1 hobby packs, these cards feature the top long-distance home runs of 1994 in an eye-popping holo-

graphic foil presentation. Stated odds of picking one from a hobby pack are one in 24.

		NM/M
Complete Set (8):		7.50
Common Player:		.50
1	Frank Thomas	1.50
2	Fred McGriff	.50
3	Ken Griffey Jr.	2.00
4	Matt Williams	.50
5	Mike Piazza	2.00
6	Jose Canseco	.75
7	Barry Bonds	2.50
8	Jeff Bagwell	1.50

Mound Marvels

Mound Marvels is an eight-card insert set containing some of the best pitchers in baseball. Cards were inserted into one per 18 retail and magazine packs of Donruss Series II. Each card features a two-way mirror that allows collectors to see the players' face through the mirror.

		NM/M
Complete Set (8):		7.50
Common Player:		1.00
1	Greg Maddux	4.00
2	David Cone	1.00
3	Mike Mussina	2.00
4	Bret Saberhagen	1.00
5	Jimmy Key	1.00
6	Doug Drabek	1.00
7	Randy Johnson	3.00
8	Jason Bere	1.00

Top of the Order Card Game

In one of the earliest efforts to wed the play factor and collectibility that had made various fantasy card games so successful in 1994-95, Donruss created the interactive Top of the Order baseball card game. Printed on playing card stock with rounded corners and semi-gloss surface, the player cards feature color action photos and all manners of game-action indicators. Backs of each card are printed primarily in green with Donruss logos. Cards were sold in several types of packaging, including 80- and 160-card boxed sets, and 12-card foil "booster" packs. Stars' cards were printed in lesser quantities than those of journeyman players, resulting in values higher than would be the case based on player popularity alone if all cards were printed in equal quantities. The unnumbered cards are checklisted here in alphabetical order within team and league.

		NM/M
Complete Set (360):		125.00
Common Player:		.10
Starter Deck (80):		6.00
Starter Deck (160):		12.00
Wax Pack (12):		1.00
Wax Box (36):		20.00
(1)	Brady Anderson	.10
(2)	Harold Baines	.10
(3)	Bret Barberie	.10
(4)	Armando Benitez	.10
(5)	Bobby Bonilla	.10
(6)	Scott Erickson	.10
(7)	Leo Gomez	.10
(8)	Curtis Goodwin	.10
(9)	Jeffrey Hammonds	.10
(10)	Chris Hoiles	.10
(11)	Doug Jones	.10
(12)	Ben McDonald	.10
(13)	Mike Mussina	1.50
(14)	Rafael Palmeiro	2.50
(15)	Cal Ripken Jr.	10.00
(16)	Rick Aguilera	.10
(17)	Luis Alicea	.10
(18)	Jose Canseco	1.50
(19)	Roger Clemens	5.00
(20)	Mike Greenwell	.10
(21)	Erik Hanson	.10
(22)	Mike Macfarlane	.10
(23)	Tim Naehring	.10
(24)	Troy O'Leary	.10
(25)	Ken Ryan	.10
(26)	Aaron Sele	.10
(27)	Lee Tinsley	.10
(28)	John Valentin	.10
(29)	Mo Vaughn	.10
(30)	Jim Abbott	.10
(31)	Mike Butcher	.10
(32)	Chili Davis	.10
(33)	Gary DiSarcina	.10
(34)	Damion Easley	.10
(35)	Jim Edmonds	.10
(36)	Chuck Finley	.10
(37)	Mark Langston	.10
(38)	Greg Myers	.10
(39)	Spike Owen	.10
(40)	Troy Percival	.10
(41)	Tony Phillips	.10
(42)	Tim Salmon	.10
(43)	Lee Smith	.10
(44)	J.T. Snow	.10
(45)	Jason Bere	.10
(46)	Mike Devereaux	.10
(47)	Ray Durham	.10
(48)	Alex Fernandez	.10
(49)	Ozzie Guillen	.10
(50)	Roberto Hernandez	.10
(51)	Lance Johnson	.10
(52)	Ron Karkovice	.10
(53)	Tim Raines	.10
(54)	Frank Thomas	3.00
(55)	Robin Ventura	.10
(56)	Sandy Alomar Jr.	.10
(57)	Carlos Baerga	.10
(58)	Albert Belle	.10
(59)	Kenny Lofton	.10
(60)	Dennis Martinez	.10
(61)	Jose Mesa	.10
(62)	Eddie Murray	3.00
(63)	Charles Nagy	.10
(64)	Tony Pena	.10
(65)	Eric Plunk	.10
(66)	Manny Ramirez	3.00
(67)	Paul Sorrento	.10
(68)	Jim Thome	2.00
(69)	Omar Vizquel	.10
(70)	Danny Bautista	.10
(71)	Joe Boever	.10
(72)	Chad Curtis	.10
(73)	Cecil Fielder	.10
(74)	John Flaherty	.10
(75)	Travis Fryman	.10
(76)	Kirk Gibson	.10
(77)	Chris Gomez	.10
(78)	Mike Henneman	.10
(79)	Bob Higginson	.10
(80)	Alan Trammell	.10
(81)	Lou Whitaker	.10
(82)	Kevin Appier	.10
(83)	Billy Brewer	.10
(84)	Vince Coleman	.10
(85)	Gary Gaetti	.10
(86)	Greg Gagne	.10
(87)	Tom Goodwin	.10
(88)	Tom Gordon	.10
(89)	Mark Gubicza	.10
(90)	Bob Hamelin	.10
(91)	Phil Hiatt	.10
(92)	Wally Joyner	.10
(93)	Brent Mayne	.10
(94)	Jeff Montgomery	.10
(95)	Ricky Bones	.10
(96)	Mike Fetters	.10
(97)	Darryl Hamilton	.10
(98)	Pat Listach	.10

(99)	Matt Mieske	.10
(100)	Dave Nilsson	.10
(101)	Joe Oliver	.10
(102)	Kevin Seitzer	.10
(103)	B.J. Surhoff	.10
(104)	Jose Valentin	.10
(105)	Greg Vaughn	.10
(106)	Bill Wegman	.10
(107)	Alex Cole	.10
(108)	Marty Cordova	.10
(109)	Chuck Knoblauch	.10
(110)	Scott Leius	.10
(111)	Pat Meares	.10
(112)	Pedro Munoz	.10
(113)	Kirby Puckett	4.00
(114)	Scott Stahoviak	.10
(115)	Mike Trombley	.10
(116)	Matt Walbeck	.10
(117)	Wade Boggs	4.00
(118)	David Cone	.10
(119)	Tony Fernandez	.10
(120)	Don Mattingly	5.00
(121)	Jack McDowell	.10
(122)	Paul O'Neill	.10
(123)	Melido Perez	.10
(124)	Luis Polonia	.10
(125)	Ruben Sierra	.10
(126)	Mike Stanley	.10
(127)	Randy Velarde	.10
(128)	John Wetteland	.10
(129)	Bob Wickman	.10
(130)	Bernie Williams	.10
(131)	Gerald Williams	.10
(132)	Geronimo Berroa	.10
(133)	Mike Bordick	.10
(134)	Scott Brosius	.10
(135)	Dennis Eckersley	.10
(136)	Brent Gates	.10
(137)	Rickey Henderson	3.00
(138)	Stan Javier	.10
(139)	Mark McGwire	8.00
(140)	Steve Ontiveros	.10
(141)	Terry Steinbach	.10
(142)	Todd Stottlemyre	.10
(143)	Danny Tartabull	.10
(144)	Bobby Ayala	.10
(145)	Andy Benes	.10
(146)	Mike Blowers	.10
(147)	Jay Buhner	.10
(148)	Joey Cora	.10
(149)	Alex Diaz	.10
(150)	Ken Griffey Jr.	6.00
(151)	Randy Johnson	3.00
(152)	Edgar Martinez	.10
(153)	Tino Martinez	.10
(154)	Bill Risley	.10
(155)	Alex Rodriguez	8.00
(156)	Dan Wilson	.10
(157)	Will Clark	.10
(158)	Jeff Frye	.10
(159)	Benji Gil	.10
(160)	Juan Gonzalez	1.50
(161)	Rusty Greer	.10
(162)	Mark McLemore	.10
(163)	Otis Nixon	.10
(164)	Dean Palmer	.10
(165)	Ivan Rodriguez	2.50
(166)	Kenny Rogers	.10
(167)	Jeff Russell	.10
(168)	Mickey Tettleton	.10
(169)	Bob Tewksbury	.10
(170)	Bobby Witt	.10
(171)	Roberto Alomar	.30
(172)	Joe Carter	.10
(173)	Alex Gonzalez	.10
(174)	Candy Maldonado	.10
(175)	Paul Molitor	3.00
(176)	John Olerud	.10
(177)	Lance Parrish	.10
(178)	Ed Sprague	.10
(179)	Devon White	.10
(180)	Woody Williams	.10
(181)	Steve Avery	.10
(182)	Jeff Blauser	.10
(183)	Tom Glavine	.50
(184)	Marquis Grissom	.10
(185)	Chipper Jones	4.00
(186)	Dave Justice	.10
(187)	Ryan Klesko	.10
(188)	Mark Lemke	.10
(189)	Javier Lopez	.10
(190)	Greg Maddux	4.00
(191)	Fred McGriff	.10
(192)	Greg McMichael	.10
(193)	John Smoltz	.10
(194)	Mark Wohlers	.10
(195)	Jim Bullinger	.10
(196)	Shawon Dunston	.10
(197)	Kevin Foster	.10
(198)	Luis Gonzalez	.10
(199)	Mark Grace	.10
(200)	Brian McRae	.10
(201)	Randy Myers	.10
(202)	Jaime Navarro	.10
(203)	Rey Sanchez	.10
(204)	Scott Servais	.10
(205)	Sammy Sosa	4.00
(206)	Steve Trachsel	.10
(207)	Todd Zeile	.10
(208)	Bret Boone	.10
(209)	Jeff Branson	.10
(210)	Jeff Brantley	.10
(211)	Hector Carrasco	.10
(212)	Ron Gant	.10
(213)	Lenny Harris	.10
(214)	Barry Larkin	.10
(215)	Darren Lewis	.10
(216)	Hal Morris	.10

(217)	Mark Portugal	.10
(218)	Jose Rijo	.10
(219)	Reggie Sanders	.10
(220)	Pete Schourek	.10
(221)	John Smiley	.10
(222)	Eddie Taubensee	.10
(223)	Dave Wells	.10
(224)	Jason Bates	.10
(225)	Dante Bichette	.10
(226)	Vinny Castilla	.10
(227)	Andres Galarraga	.10
(228)	Joe Girardi	.10
(229)	Mike Kingery	.10
(230)	Steve Reed	.10
(231)	Bruce Ruffin	.10
(232)	Bret Saberhagen	.10
(233)	Bill Swift	.10
(234)	Larry Walker	.10
(235)	Walt Weiss	.10
(236)	Eric Young	.10
(237)	Kurt Abbott	.10
(238)	John Burkett	.10
(239)	Chuck Carr	.10
(240)	Greg Colbrunn	.10
(241)	Jeff Conine	.10
(242)	Andre Dawson	.35
(243)	Chris Hammond	.10
(244)	Charles Johnson	.10
(245)	Robb Nen	.10
(246)	Terry Pendleton	.10
(247)	Gary Sheffield	.50
(248)	Quilvio Veras	.10
(249)	Jeff Bagwell	3.00
(250)	Derek Bell	.10
(251)	Craig Biggio	.10
(252)	Doug Drabek	.10
(253)	Tony Eusebio	.10
(254)	John Hudek	.10
(255)	Brian Hunter	.10
(256)	Todd Jones	.10
(257)	Dave Magadan	.10
(258)	Orlando Miller	.10
(259)	James Mouton	.10
(260)	Shane Reynolds	.10
(261)	Greg Swindell	.10
(262)	Billy Ashley	.10
(263)	Tom Candiotti	.10
(264)	Delino DeShields	.10
(265)	Eric Karros	.10
(266)	Roberto Kelly	.10
(267)	Ramon Martinez	.10
(268)	Raul Mondesi	.10
(269)	Hideo Nomo	1.50
(270)	Jose Offerman	.10
(271)	Mike Piazza	6.00
(272)	Kevin Tapani	.10
(273)	Ismael Valdes	.10
(274)	Tim Wallach	.10
(275)	Todd Worrell	.10
(276)	Moises Alou	.10
(277)	Sean Berry	.10
(278)	Wil Cordero	.10
(279)	Jeff Fassero	.10
(280)	Darrin Fletcher	.10
(281)	Mike Lansing	.10
(282)	Pedro J. Martinez	3.00
(283)	Carlos Perez	.10
(284)	Mel Rojas	.10
(285)	Tim Scott	.10
(286)	David Segui	.10
(287)	Tony Tarasco	.10
(288)	Rondell White	.10
(289)	Rico Brogna	.10
(290)	Brett Butler	.10
(291)	John Franco	.10
(292)	Pete Harnisch	.10
(293)	Todd Hundley	.10
(294)	Bobby Jones	.10
(295)	Jeff Kent	.10
(296)	Joe Orsulak	.10
(297)	Ryan Thompson	.10
(298)	Jose Vizcaino	.10
(299)	Ricky Bottalico	.10
(300)	Darren Daulton	.10
(301)	Mariano Duncan	.10
(302)	Lenny Dykstra	.10
(303)	Jim Eisenreich	.10
(304)	Tyler Green	.10
(305)	Charlie Hayes	.10
(306)	Dave Hollins	.10
(307)	Gregg Jefferies	.10
(308)	Mickey Morandini	.10
(309)	Curt Schilling	.50
(310)	Heathcliff Slocumb	.10
(311)	Kevin Stocker	.10
(312)	Jay Bell	.10
(313)	Jacob Brumfield	.10
(314)	Dave Clark	.10
(315)	Carlos Garcia	.10
(316)	Mark Johnson	.10
(317)	Jeff King	.10
(318)	Nelson Liriano	.10
(319)	Al Martin	.10
(320)	Orlando Merced	.10
(321)	Dan Miceli	.10
(322)	Denny Neagle	.10
(323)	Mark Parent	.10
(324)	Dan Plesac	.10
(325)	Scott Cooper	.10
(326)	Bernard Gilkey	.10
(327)	Tom Henke	.10
(328)	Ken Hill	.10
(329)	Danny Jackson	.10
(330)	Brian Jordan	.10
(331)	Ray Lankford	.10
(332)	John Mabry	.10
(333)	Jose Oquendo	.10
(334)	Tom Pagnozzi	.10

(335)	Ozzie Smith	4.00
(336)	Andy Ashby	.10
(337)	Brad Ausmus	.10
(338)	Ken Caminiti	.10
(339)	Andujar Cedeno	.10
(340)	Steve Finley	.10
(341)	Tony Gwynn	4.00
(342)	Joey Hamilton	.10
(343)	Trevor Hoffman	.10
(344)	Jody Reed	.10
(345)	Bip Roberts	.10
(346)	Eddie Williams	.10
(347)	Rod Beck	.10
(348)	Mike Benjamin	.10
(349)	Barry Bonds	10.00
(350)	Royce Clayton	.10
(351)	Glenallen Hill	.10
(352)	Kirt Manwaring	.10
(353)	Terry Mulholland	.10
(354)	John Patterson	.10
(355)	J.R. Phillips	.10
(356)	Deion Sanders	.25
(357)	Steve Scarsone	.10
(358)	Robby Thompson	.10
(359)	William Van Landingham	.10
(360)	Matt Williams	.10

1996 Donruss Samples

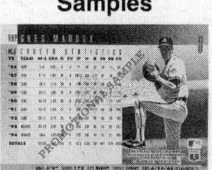

To introduce its 1996 series to dealers and the hobby press, Donruss issued an eight-card sample set. Identical in format to the issued version, the samples are numbered differently from the same players' cards in the regular issue (except #1, Frank Thomas). The samples also differ in that they lack 1995 stats on back, may have slightly different wording in the career highlights, and have printed on front and back a diagonal gray "PROMOTIONAL SAMPLE."

		NM/M
Complete Set (8):		9.00
Common Player:		1.00
1	Frank Thomas	1.00
2	Barry Bonds	2.50
3	Hideo Nomo	1.00
4	Ken Griffey Jr.	1.50
5	Cal Ripken Jr.	2.50
6	Manny Ramirez	1.00
7	Mike Piazza	1.50
8	Greg Maddux	1.25

1996 Donruss

A clean, borderless look marks the 1996 Donruss regular-issue cards. Besides the player name in white inside a fading team-color stripe at top-right, the only graphic enhancement on front is a 7/8" square foil box at bottom-center with the company and team name, team logo, player position and uniform number. The foil box is enhanced with team colors, which are carried over to the horizontal backs. Backs also feature a color action photo, a large gray team logo, stats and career highlights. Basic packaging was 12-card foil packs with a suggested retail

price of $1.79. Several types of insert cards were offered, each at a virtually unprecedented rate of scarcity. The set was issued in two series; Series 1 with 330 cards, Series 2 with 220 cards.

		NM/M
Complete Set (550):		20.00
Complete Series 1 (330):		12.00
Complete Series 2 (220):		10.00
Common Player:		.05
Press Proofs:		7X
Series 1 Pack (12):		1.00
Series 1 Wax Box (36):		20.00
Series 2 Pack (12):		1.00
Series 2 Wax Box (18):		12.50
1	Frank Thomas	1.00
2	Jason Bates	.05
3	Steve Sparks	.05
4	Scott Servais	.05
5	Angelo Encarnacion	.05
6	Scott Sanders	.05
7	Billy Ashley	.05
8	Alex Rodriguez	2.00
9	Sean Bergman	.05
10	Brad Radke	.05
11	Andy Van Slyke	.05
12	Joe Girardi	.05
13	Mark Grudzielanek	.05
14	Rick Aguilera	.05
15	Randy Veres	.05
16	Tim Bogar	.05
17	Dave Veres	.05
18	Kevin Stocker	.05
19	Marquis Grissom	.05
20	Will Clark	.05
21	Jay Bell	.05
22	Allen Battle	.05
23	Frank Rodriguez	.05
24	Terry Steinbach	.05
25	Gerald Williams	.05
26	Sid Roberson	.05
27	Gregg Zaun	.05
28	Ozzie Timmons	.05
29	Vaughn Eshelman	.05
30	Ed Sprague	.05
31	Gary DiSarcina	.05
32	Joe Boever	.05
33	Steve Avery	.05
34	Brad Ausmus	.05
35	Kirt Manwaring	.05
36	Gary Sheffield	.25
37	Jason Bere	.05
38	Jeff Manto	.05
39	David Cone	.05
40	Manny Ramirez	1.00
41	Sandy Alomar	.05
42	Curtis Goodwin/RR	.05
43	Tino Martinez	.05
44	Woody Williams	.05
45	Dean Palmer	.05
46	Hipolito Pichardo	.05
47	Jason Giambi	.60
48	Lance Johnson	.05
49	Bernard Gilkey	.05
50	Kirby Puckett	1.25
51	Tony Fernandez	.05
52	Alex Gonzalez	.05
53	Bret Saberhagen	.05
54	Lyle Mouton/RR	.05
55	Brian McRae	.05
56	Mark Gubicza	.05
57	Sergio Valdez	.05
58	Darrin Fletcher	.05
59	Steve Parris	.05
60	Johnny Damon/RR	.35
61	Rickey Henderson	1.00
62	Darrell Whitmore	.05
63	Roberto Petagine	.05
64	Trenidad Hubbard	.05
65	Heathcliff Slocumb	.05
66	Steve Finley	.05
67	Mariano Rivera	.25
68	Brian Hunter	.05
69	Jamie Moyer	.05
70	Ellis Burks	.05
71	Pat Kelly	.05
72	Mickey Tettleton	.05
73	Garret Anderson	.05
74	Andy Pettitte/RR	.75
75	Glenallen Hill	.05
76	Brent Gates	.05
77	Lou Whitaker	.05
78	David Segui	.05
79	Dan Wilson	.05
80	Pat Listach	.05
81	Jeff Bagwell	1.00
82	Ben McDonald	.05
83	John Valentin	.05
84	John Jaha	.05
85	Pete Schourek	.05
86	Bryce Florie	.05
87	Brian Jordan	.05
88	Ron Karkovice	.05
89	Al Leiter	.05
90	Tony Longmire	.05
91	Nelson Liriano	.05
92	David Bell	.05
93	Kevin Gross	.05
94	Tom Candiotti	.05
95	Dave Martinez	.05
96	Greg Myers	.05
97	Rheal Cormier	.05
98	Chris Hammond	.05
99	Randy Myers	.05

100	Bill Pulsipher/RR	.05
101	Jason Isringhausen/ RR.05	
102	Dave Stevens	.05
103	Roberto Alomar	.20
104	Bob Higginson/RR	.05
105	Eddie Murray	1.00
106	Matt Walbeck	.05
107	Mark Wohlers	.05
108	Jeff Nelson	.05
109	Tom Goodwin	.05
110	Checklist 1-83	
	(Cal Ripken Jr. (2,131 Consecutive Games))	1.25
111	Rey Sanchez	.05
112	Hector Carrasco	.05
113	B.J. Surhoff	.05
114	Dan Miceli	.05
115	Dean Hartgraves	.05
116	John Burkett	.05
117	Gary Gaetti	.05
118	Ricky Bones	.05
119	Mike Macfarlane	.05
120	Bip Roberts	.05
121	Dave Mlicki	.05
122	Chili Davis	.05
123	Mark Whiten	.05
124	Herbert Perry	.05
125	Butch Henry	.05
126	Derek Bell	.05
127	Al Martin	.05
128	John Franco	.05
129	William Van Landingham	.05
130	Mike Bordick	.05
131	Mike Mordecai	.05
132	Robby Thompson	.05
133	Greg Colbrunn	.05
134	Domingo Cedeno	.05
135	Chad Curtis	.05
136	Jose Hernandez	.05
137	Scott Klingenbeck	.05
138	Ryan Klesko	.05
139	John Smiley	.05
140	Charlie Hayes	.05
141	Jay Buhner	.05
142	Doug Drabek	.05
143	Roger Pavlik	.05
144	Todd Worrell	.05
145	Cal Ripken Jr.	2.50
146	Steve Reed	.05
147	Chuck Finley	.05
148	Mike Blowers	.05
149	Orel Hershiser	.05
150	Allen Watson	.05
151	Ramon Martinez	.05
152	Melvin Nieves	.05
153	Tripp Cromer	.05
154	Yorkis Perez	.05
155	Stan Javier	.05
156	Mel Rojas	.05
157	Aaron Sele	.05
158	Eric Karros	.05
159	Robb Nen	.05
160	Raul Mondesi	.05
161	John Wetteland	.05
162	Tim Scott	.05
163	Kenny Rogers	.05
164	Melvin Bunch	.05
165	Rod Beck	.05
166	Andy Benes	.05
167	Lenny Dykstra	.05
168	Orlando Merced	.05
169	Tomas Perez	.05
170	Xavier Hernandez	.05
171	Ruben Sierra	.05
172	Alan Trammell	.05
173	Mike Fetters	.05
174	Wilson Alvarez	.05
175	Erik Hanson	.05
176	Travis Fryman	.05
177	Jim Abbott	.05
178	Bret Boone	.05
179	Sterling Hitchcock	.05
180	Pat Mahomes	.05
181	Mark Acre	.05
182	Charles Nagy	.05
183	Rusty Greer	.05
184	Mike Stanley	.05
185	Jim Bullinger	.05
186	Shane Andrews	.05
187	Brian Keyser	.05
188	Tyler Green	.05
189	Mark Grace	.05
190	Bob Hamelin	.05
191	Luis Ortiz	.05
192	Joe Carter	.05
193	Eddie Taubensee	.05
194	Brian Anderson	.05
195	Edgardo Alfonzo	.05
196	Pedro Munoz	.05
197	David Justice	.05
198	Trevor Hoffman	.05
199	Bobby Ayala	.05
200	Tony Eusebio	.05
201	Jeff Russell	.05
202	Mike Hampton	.05
203	Walt Weiss	.05
204	Joey Hamilton	.05
205	Roberto Hernandez	.05
206	Greg Vaughn	.05
207	Felipe Lira	.05
208	Harold Baines	.05
209	Tim Wallach	.05
210	Manny Alexander	.05
211	Tim Laker	.05
212	Chris Haney	.05
213	Brian Maxcy	.05
214	Eric Young	.05

215 Darryl Strawberry .05
216 Barry Bonds 2.50
217 Tim Naehring .05
218 Scott Brosius .05
219 Reggie Sanders .05
220 Checklist 84-166
Eddie Murray
(3,000 Career Hits) .35
221 Luis Alicea .05
222 Albert Belle .05
223 Benji Gil .05
224 Dante Bichette .05
225 Bobby Bonilla .05
226 Todd Stottlemyre .05
227 Jim Edmonds .05
228 Todd Jones .05
229 Shawn Green .25
230 Javy Lopez .05
231 Ariel Prieto .05
232 Tony Phillips .05
233 James Mouton .05
234 Jose Oquendo .05
235 Royce Clayton .05
236 Chuck Carr .05
237 Doug Jones .05
238 Mark Mclemore
(McLemore) .05
239 Bill Swift .05
240 Scott Leius .05
241 Russ Davis .05
242 Ray Durham/RR .05
243 Matt Mieske .05
244 Brent Mayne .05
245 Thomas Howard .05
246 Troy O'Leary .05
247 Jacob Brumfield .05
248 Mickey Morandini .05
249 Todd Hundley .05
250 Chris Bosio .05
251 Omar Vizquel .05
252 Mike Lansing .05
253 John Mabry .05
254 Mike Perez .05
255 Delino DeShields .05
256 Wil Cordero .05
257 Mike James .05
258 Todd Van Poppel .05
259 Joey Cora .05
260 Andre Dawson .25
261 Jerry DiPoto .05
262 Rick Krivda .05
263 Glenn Dishman .05
264 Mike Mimbs .05
265 John Ericks .05
266 Jose Canseco .35
267 Jeff Branson .05
268 Curt Leskanic .05
269 Jon Nunnally .05
270 Scott Stahoviak .05
271 Jeff Montgomery .05
272 Hal Morris .05
273 Esteban Loaiza .05
274 Rico Brogna .05
275 Dave Winfield 1.00
276 J.R. Phillips .05
277 Todd Zeile .05
278 Tom Pagnozzi .05
279 Mark Lemke .05
280 Dave Magadan .05
281 Greg McMichael .05
282 Mike Morgan .05
283 Moises Alou .05
284 Dennis Martinez .05
285 Jeff Kent .05
286 Mark Johnson .05
287 Darren Lewis .05
288 Brad Clontz .05
289 Chad Fonville/RR .05
290 Paul Sorrento .05
291 Lee Smith .05
292 Tom Glavine .25
293 Antonio Osuna .05
294 Kevin Foster .05
295 Sandy Martinez RC .05
296 Mark Leiter .05
297 Julian Tavarez .05
298 Mike Kelly .05
299 Joe Oliver .05
300 John Flaherty .05
301 Don Mattingly 1.50
302 Pat Meares .05
303 John Doherty .05
304 Joe Vitiello .05
305 Vinny Castilla .05
306 Jeff Brantley .05
307 Mike Greenwell .05
308 Midre Cummings .05
309 Curt Schilling .25
310 Ken Caminiti .05
311 Scott Erickson .05
312 Carl Everett .05
313 Charles Johnson .05
314 Alex Diaz .05
315 Jose Mesa .05
316 Mark Carreon .05
317 Carlos Perez/RR .05
318 Ismael Valdes .05
319 Frank Castillo .05
320 Tom Henke .05
321 Spike Owen .05
322 Joe Orsulak .05
323 Paul Menhart .05
324 Pedro Borbon .05
325 Checklist 167-249
Paul Molitor
(1,000 Career RBI) .35
326 Jeff Cirillo .05
327 Edwin Hurtado .05

328 Orlando Miller .05
329 Steve Ontiveros .05
330 Checklist 250-330
Kirby Puckett
(1,000 Career RBI) .75
331 Scott Bullett .05
332 Andres Galarraga .05
333 Cal Eldred .05
334 Sammy Sosa 1.25
335 Don Slaught .05
336 Jody Reed .05
337 Roger Cedeno .05
338 Ken Griffey Jr. 1.75
339 Todd Hollandsworth .05
340 Mike Trombley .05
341 Gregg Jefferies .05
342 Larry Walker .05
343 Pedro Martinez .05
344 Dwayne Hosey .05
345 Terry Pendleton .05
346 Pete Harnisch .05
347 Tony Castillo .05
348 Paul Quantrill .05
349 Fred McGriff .05
350 Ivan Rodriguez .65
351 Butch Huskey .05
352 Ozzie Smith 1.25
353 Marty Cordova .05
354 John Wasdin .05
355 Wade Boggs 1.25
356 Dave Nilsson .05
357 Rafael Palmeiro .65
358 Luis Gonzalez .05
359 Reggie Jefferson .05
360 Carlos Delgado .60
361 Orlando Palmeiro .05
362 Chris Gomez .05
363 John Smoltz .05
364 Marc Newfield .05
365 Matt Williams .05
366 Jesus Tavarez .05
367 Bruce Ruffin .05
368 Sean Berry .05
369 Randy Velarde .05
370 Tony Pena .05
371 Jim Thome .60
372 Jeffrey Hammonds .05
373 Bob Wolcott .05
374 Juan Guzman .05
375 Juan Gonzalez .50
376 Michael Tucker .05
377 Doug Johns .05
378 Mike Cameron RC .75
379 Ray Lankford .05
380 Jose Parra .05
381 Jimmy Key .05
382 John Olerud .05
383 Kevin Ritz .05
384 Tim Raines .05
385 Rich Amaral .05
386 Keith Lockhart .05
387 Steve Scarsone .05
388 Cliff Floyd .05
389 Rich Aude .05
390 Hideo Nomo .50
391 Geronimo Berroa .05
392 Pat Rapp .05
393 Dustin Hermanson .05
394 Greg Maddux 1.25
395 Darren Daulton .05
396 Kenny Lofton .05
397 Ruben Rivera .05
398 Billy Wagner .05
399 Kevin Brown .05
400 Mike Kingery .05
401 Bernie Williams .05
402 Otis Nixon .05
403 Damian Easley .05
404 Paul O'Neill .05
405 Deion Sanders .05
406 Dennis Eckersley 1.00
407 Tony Clark .05
408 Rondell White .05
409 Luis Sojo .05
410 David Hulse .05
411 Shane Reynolds .05
412 Chris Hoiles .05
413 Lee Tinsley .05
414 Scott Karl .05
415 Ron Gant .05
416 Brian Johnson .05
417 Jose Oliva .05
418 Jack McDowell .05
419 Paul Molitor 1.00
420 Ricky Bottalico .05
421 Paul Wagner .05
422 Terry Bradshaw .05
423 Bob Tewksbury .05
424 Bill Risley .05
425 Luis Andujar RC .05
426 Mark Langston .05
427 Stan Belinda .05
428 Kurt Abbott .05
429 Shawon Dunston .05
430 Bobby Jones .05
431 Jose Vizcaino .05
432 Matt Lawton RC .05
433 Pat Hentgen .05
434 Cecil Fielder .05
435 Carlos Baerga .05
436 Rich Becker .05
437 Chipper Jones 1.25
438 Bill Risley .05
439 Kevin Appier .05
440 Checklist .05
441 Jaime Navarro .05
442 Barry Larkin .05
443 Jose Valentin RC .05

444 Bryan Rekar .05
445 Rick Wilkins .05
446 Quilvio Veras .05
447 Greg Gagne .05
448 Mark Kiefer .05
449 Bobby Witt .05
450 Andy Ashby .05
451 Alex Ochoa .05
452 Jorge Fabregas .05
453 Gene Schall .05
454 Ken Hill .05
455 Tony Tarasco .05
456 Donnie Wall .05
457 Carlos Garcia .05
458 Ryan Thompson .05
459 Marvin Benard RC .05
460 Jose Herrera .05
461 Jeff Blauser .05
462 Chris Hook .05
463 Jeff Conine .05
464 Devon White .05
465 Danny Bautista .05
466 Steve Trachsel .05
467 C.J. Nitkowski .05
468 Mike Devereaux .05
469 David Wells .05
470 Jim Eisenreich .05
471 Edgar Martinez .05
472 Craig Biggio .05
473 Jeff Frye .05
474 Karim Garcia .05
475 Jimmy Haynes .05
476 Darren Holmes .05
477 Tim Salmon .05
478 Randy Johnson 1.00
479 Eric Plunk .05
480 Scott Cooper .05
481 Chan Ho Park .05
482 Ray McDavid .05
483 Mark Petkovsek .05
484 Greg Swindell .05
485 George Williams .05
486 Yamil Benitez .05
487 Tim Wakefield .05
488 Kevin Tapani .05
489 Derrick May .05
490 Checklist
(Ken Griffey Jr.) 1.00
491 Derek Jeter 2.50
492 Jeff Fassero .05
493 Benito Santiago .05
494 Tom Gordon .05
495 Jamie Brewington .05
496 Vince Coleman .05
497 Kevin Jordan .05
498 Jeff King .05
499 Mike Simms .05
500 Jose Rijo .05
501 Denny Neagle .05
502 Jose Lima .05
503 Kevin Seitzer .05
504 Alex Fernandez .05
505 Mo Vaughn .05
506 Phil Nevin .05
507 J.T. Snow .05
508 Andujar Cedeno .05
509 Ozzie Guillen .05
510 Mark Clark .05
511 Mark McGwire 2.00
512 Jeff Reboulet .05
513 Armando Benitez .05
514 LaTroy Hawkins .05
515 Brett Butler .05
516 Tavo Alvarez .05
517 Chris Snopek .05
518 Mike Mussina .50
519 Darryl Kile .05
520 Wally Joyner .05
521 Willie McGee .05
522 Kent Mercker .05
523 Mike Jackson .05
524 Troy Percival .05
525 Tony Gwynn 1.25
526 Ron Coomer .05
527 Darryl Hamilton .05
528 Phil Plantier .05
529 Norm Charlton .05
530 Craig Paquette .05
531 Dave Burba .05
532 Mike Henneman .05
533 Terrell Wade .05
534 Eddie Williams .05
535 Robin Ventura .05
536 Chuck Knoblauch .05
537 Les Norman .05
538 Brady Anderson .05
539 Roger Clemens 1.50
540 Mark Portugal .05
541 Mike Matheny .05
542 Jeff Parrett .05
543 Roberto Kelly .05
544 Damon Buford .05
545 Chad Ogea .05
546 Jose Offerman .05
547 Brian Barber .05
548 Danny Tartabull .05
549 Duane Singleton .05
550 Checklist
(Tony Gwynn) .75

stamped along the right side. As opposed to regular-issue cards which have silver-and-black card numbers and personal data strip at bottom, the Press Proof cards have those elements printed in black-on-gold. Stated odds of finding a Press Proof are one per 12 packs in Series 1, one per 10 packs in Series 2, on average.

	NM/M
Complete Set (550):	150.00
Common Player:	.50

Diamond Kings

The most "common" of the '96 Donruss inserts are the popular Diamond Kings, featuring the portraits of Dick Perez on a black background within a mottled gold-foil frame. Once again, the DKs feature one player from each team, with 14 issued in each of Series 1 and 2. Like all '96 Donruss inserts, the DKs are numbered on back, within an edition of 10,000. Also on back are color action photos and career highlights. Diamond Kings are inserted at the rate of one per 60 foil packs (Series 1), and one per 30 packs (Series 2), on average.

		NM/M
Complete Set (31):		160.00
Common Player:		2.25
1	Frank Thomas	7.50
2	Mo Vaughn	2.50
3	Manny Ramirez	2.50
4	Mark McGwire	13.50
5	Juan Gonzalez	4.00
6	Roberto Alomar	3.00
7	Tim Salmon	2.50
8	Barry Bonds	15.00
9	Tony Gwynn	10.00
10	Reggie Sanders	2.50
11	Larry Walker	2.50
12	Pedro Martinez	2.50
13	Jeff King	2.50
14	Mark Grace	2.50
15	Greg Maddux	10.00
16	Don Mattingly	12.50
17	Gregg Jefferies	2.50
18	Chad Curtis	2.50
19	Jason Isringhausen	2.50
20	B.J. Surhoff	2.50
21	Jeff Conine	2.50
22	Kirby Puckett	10.00
23	Derek Bell	2.50
24	Wally Joyner	2.50
25	Brian Jordan	2.50
26	Edgar Martinez	2.50
27	Hideo Nomo	4.00
28	Mike Mussina	7.50
29	Eddie Murray	7.50
30	Cal Ripken Jr.	15.00
31	Checklist	.25

Press Proofs

The first 2,000 of each regular card issued in the 1996 Donruss set are distinguished by the addition of a gold-foil "PRESS PROOF"

Elite

The Elite series continued as a Donruss insert in 1996, and they are the elite of the chase cards, being found on average only once per 140 packs (Series 1) or once per 75 packs (Series 2). The '96 Elite cards have a classic look bespeaking value. Player action photos at top center are framed in mottled silver foil and bordered in bright silver. Backs have another action photo, a few words about the player and a serial number from within an edition of 10,000 cards each. As usual, card numbering continues from the previous year.

		NM/M
Complete Set (12):		55.00
Complete Series 1 (61-66):		27.50
Complete Series 2 (67-72):		32.50
Common Player Series 1:		2.50
Common Player Series 2:		1.75
61	Cal Ripken Jr.	12.00
62	Hideo Nomo	3.00
63	Reggie Sanders	2.50
64	Mo Vaughn	2.50
65	Tim Salmon	2.50
66	Chipper Jones	9.00
67	Manny Ramirez	6.00
68	Greg Maddux	7.50
69	Frank Thomas	6.00
70	Ken Griffey Jr.	10.00
71	Dante Bichette	1.75
72	Tony Gwynn	7.50

Freeze Frame

One of two insert sets exclusive to Series 2 Donruss is the Freeze Frame issue. Printed on heavy, round-cornered cardboard stock, the inserts feature multiple photos of the player on both front and back. Fronts combine matte and glossy finish plus a gold-foil Donruss logo. Backs are conventionally printed, include 1995 season highlights and a serial number from within the edition of 5,000. Stated odds of pulling a Freeze Frame insert are one per 60 packs.

		NM/M
Complete Set (8):		16.00
Common Player:		1.00
1	Frank Thomas	2.00
2	Ken Griffey Jr.	3.00
3	Cal Ripken Jr.	4.00
4	Hideo Nomo	1.50
5	Greg Maddux	2.50
6	Albert Belle	1.00
7	Chipper Jones	2.50
8	Mike Piazza	3.00

Hit List

Printed on metallic foil with gold-foil graphic highlights, players who hit for high average with power or who collected milestone hits are featured in this insert set. Eight inserts were included in each of Series 1 and 2. Backs

have a color action photo, a description of the player's batting prowess and a serial number from an edition of 10,000 cards each. Hit List inserts are found at an average rate of once per 106 foil packs in Series 1 and once per 60 packs in Series 2.

		NM/M
Complete Set (16):		30.00
Common Player:		.60
1	Tony Gwynn	3.00
2	Ken Griffey Jr.	5.00
3	Will Clark	.60
4	Mike Piazza	5.00
5	Carlos Baerga	.60
6	Mo Vaughn	.60
7	Mark Grace	.60
8	Kirby Puckett	3.00
9	Frank Thomas	2.00
10	Barry Bonds	6.00
11	Jeff Bagwell	2.00
12	Edgar Martinez	.60
13	Tim Salmon	.60
14	Wade Boggs	3.00
15	Don Mattingly	4.00
16	Eddie Murray	2.00

Long Ball Leaders

Once again the previous season's longest home runs are recalled in this retail-only insert set, found at an average rate of once per 96 packs in Series 1 only. Fronts are bordered and trimmed in bright silver foil and feature the player in his home run stroke against a black background. The date, location and distance of his tape-measure shot are in an arc across the card front. Backs feature another batting action photo, further details of the home run and a serial number within an edition of 5,000.

		NM/M
Complete Set (8):		45.00
Common Player:		1.50
1	Barry Bonds	15.00
2	Ryan Klesko	1.50
3	Mark McGwire	15.00
4	Raul Mondesi	1.50
5	Cecil Fielder	1.50
6	Ken Griffey Jr.	12.00
7	Larry Walker	1.50
8	Frank Thomas	6.00

Power Alley

Among the most visually dazzling of 1996's inserts is this hobby-only chase set featuring baseball's top sluggers. Action batting photos are found within several layers of prismatic foil in geometric patterns on front.

Backs are horizontally formatted, feature portrait photos at left and power stats at right and bottom. In the lower-left corner is an individual serial number from within an edition of 5,000 cards each. The first 500 of each player's cards are specially die-cut at left- and right-center. Found only in Series 1 hobby foil packs, Power Alley inserts are a one per 92 pack pick.

	NM/M
Complete Set (10):	30.00
Common Player	2.00
Die-Cut:	2X
1 Frank Thomas	4.00
2 Barry Bonds	7.50
3 Reggie Sanders	2.00
4 Albert Belle	2.00
5 Tim Salmon	2.00
6 Dante Bichette	2.00
7 Mo Vaughn	2.00
8 Jim Edmonds	2.00
9 Manny Ramirez	4.00
10 Ken Griffey Jr.	6.00

Pure Power

These cards were random inserts found only in Series 2 retail packs. Fronts are printed on foil backgrounds and at bottom have a die-cut hole giving the impression a baseball has been batted through the card. On back the inserts are individually serial numbered within an edition of 5,000.

	NM/M
Complete Set (8):	25.00
Common Player:	2.25
1 Raul Mondesi	2.25
2 Barry Bonds	10.00
3 Albert Belle	2.25
4 Frank Thomas	4.50
5 Mike Piazza	7.50
6 Dante Bichette	2.25
7 Manny Ramirez	4.50
8 Mo Vaughn	2.25

Round Trippers

An embossed white home plate design bearing the player's 1995 dinger output is featured on this Series 2 insert set. The entire background has been rendered in gold-flecked sepia tones. Typography on front is in bronze foil. Backs repeat the sepia background photo and include a month-by-month bar graph of the player's 1995 and career homers. Within the white home plate frame is the card's unique serial number from within an edition of 5,000. Odds of finding a Round Trippers card are stated at one per 55 packs, in hobby packs only.

	NM/M
Complete Set (10):	35.00
Common Player:	2.50
1 Albert Belle	2.50
2 Barry Bonds	7.50
3 Jeff Bagwell	4.00
4 Tim Salmon	2.50
5 Mo Vaughn	2.50
6 Ken Griffey Jr.	5.00
7 Mike Piazza	5.00
8 Cal Ripken Jr.	7.50
9 Frank Thomas	4.00
9p Frank Thomas (Promo)	2.50
10 Dante Bichette	2.50

Showdown

Baseball's top hitters and pitchers are matched on a silver and black foil background in this insert set. Gold-foil graphic highlights complete the horizontal front design. Backs are printed on a black and gold background with color action photos and write-ups about each player. At top is a serial number from within an edition of 10,000 cards each. Showdown inserts are found at an average rate of one per Series 1 foil packs.

	NM/M
Complete Set (8):	22.50
Common Player:	.75
1 Frank Thomas, Hideo Nomo	3.00
2 Barry Bonds, Randy Johnson	6.00
3 Greg Maddux, Ken Griffey Jr.	5.00
4 Roger Clemens, Tony Gwynn	4.50
5 Mike Piazza, Mike Mussina	5.00
6 Cal Ripken Jr., Pedro Martinez	6.00
7 Tim Wakefield, Matt Williams	.75
8 Manny Ramirez, Carlos Perez	2.50

1997 Donruss

Donruss' 1997 Series 1 features 270 base cards with a full-bleed color action photo on the front. Horizontal backs have a photo, career statistics, a brief player profile and bio-graphical tidbits. A Press Proofs parallel was made of the base cards in an edition of 2,000 each. Other Series 1 inserts include the annual Diamond Kings, Elites, Armed and Dangerous cards, Longball Leaders and Rocket Launchers. A 180-card Update set was released later as a follow-up to the regular '97 Donruss series. The Updates are numbered contiguously, #271-450, from the first series. Press Proofs and Gold Press Proof parallel inserts were available; other Update inserts include Dominators, Franchise Futures, Power Alley, Rookie Diamond Kings and a special Cal Ripken Jr. set.

	NM/M
Complete Set (450):	20.00
Series 1 Set (270):	10.00
Update Set (180):	10.00
Common Player:	.05
Press Proof Set (450):	250.00
Common Press Proof:	.50
Press Proof Stars:	5X
Press Proof Gold Set (450):	600.00
Common Press Proof Gold:	2.00
Press Proof Gold Stars:	10X
Wax Pack (10):	1.50
Hobby Wax Box (18):	25.00
Retail Wax Box (36):	40.00
Magazine Pack (13):	1.50
Magazine Box (24):	20.00
Update Pack (10):	1.50
Update Wax Box (24):	30.00
1 Juan Gonzalez	.40
2 Jim Edmonds	.05
3 Tony Gwynn	1.00
4 Andres Galarraga	.05
5 Joe Carter	.05
6 Raul Mondesi	.05
7 Greg Maddux	1.00
8 Travis Fryman	.05
9 Brian Jordan	.05
10 Henry Rodriguez	.05
11 Manny Ramirez	.75
12 Mark McGwire	1.75
13 Marc Newfield	.05
14 Craig Biggio	.05
15 Sammy Sosa	1.00
16 Brady Anderson	.05
17 Wade Boggs	1.00
18 Charles Johnson	.05
19 Matt Williams	.05
20 Denny Neagle	.05
21 Ken Griffey Jr.	1.50
22 Robin Ventura	.05
23 Barry Larkin	.05
24 Todd Zeile	.05
25 Chuck Knoblauch	.05
26 Todd Hundley	.05
27 Roger Clemens	1.25
28 Michael Tucker	.05
29 Rondell White	.05
30 Osvaldo Fernandez	.05
31 Ivan Rodriguez	.65
32 Alex Fernandez	.05
33 Jason Isringhausen	.05
34 Chipper Jones	1.00
35 Paul O'Neill	.05
36 Hideo Nomo	.40
37 Roberto Alomar	.20
38 Derek Bell	.05
39 Paul Molitor	.75
40 Andy Benes	.05
41 Steve Trachsel	.05
42 J.T. Snow	.05
43 Jason Kendall	.05
44 Alex Rodriguez	1.75
45 Joey Hamilton	.05
46 Carlos Delgado	.50
47 Jason Giambi	.50
48 Larry Walker	.50
49 Derek Jeter	2.00
50 Kenny Lofton	.05
51 Devon White	.05
52 Matt Mieske	.05
53 Melvin Nieves	.05
54 Jose Canseco	.40
55 Tino Martinez	.05
56 Rafael Palmeiro	.65
57 Edgardo Alfonzo	.05
58 Jay Buhner	.05
59 Shane Reynolds	.05
60 Steve Finley	.05
61 Bobby Higginson	.05
62 Dean Palmer	.05
63 Terry Pendleton	.05
64 Marquis Grissom	.05
65 Mike Stanley	.05
66 Moises Alou	.05
67 Ray Lankford	.05
68 Marty Cordova	.05
69 John Olerud	.05
70 David Cone	.05
71 Benito Santiago	.05
72 Ryne Sandberg	1.00
73 Rickey Henderson	.75
74 Roger Cedeno	.05
75 Wilson Alvarez	.05
76 Tim Salmon	.05
77 Orlando Merced	.05
78 Vinny Castilla	.05
79 Ismael Valdes	.05
80 Dante Bichette	.05
81 Kevin Brown	.05
82 Andy Pettitte	.40
83 Scott Stahoviak	.05
84 Mickey Tettleton	.05
85 Jack McDowell	.05
86 Tom Glavine	.30
87 Gregg Jefferies	.05
88 Chili Davis	.05
89 Randy Johnson	.75
90 John Mabry	.05
91 Billy Wagner	.05
92 Jeff Cirillo	.05
93 Trevor Hoffman	.05
94 Juan Guzman	.05
95 Geronimo Berroa	.05
96 Bernard Gilkey	.05
97 Danny Tartabull	.05
98 Johnny Damon	.35
99 Charlie Hayes	.05
100 Reggie Sanders	.05
101 Robby Thompson	.05
102 Bobby Bonilla	.05
103 Reggie Jefferson	.05
104 John Smoltz	.05
105 Jim Thome	.60
106 Ruben Rivera	.05
107 Darren Oliver	.05
108 Mo Vaughn	.05
109 Roger Pavlik	.05
110 Terry Steinbach	.05
111 Jermaine Dye	.05
112 Mark Grudzielanek	.05
113 Rick Aguilera	.05
114 Jamey Wright	.05
115 Eddie Murray	.75
116 Brian Hunter	.05
117 Hal Morris	.05
118 Tom Pagnozzi	.05
119 Mike Mussina	.40
120 Mark Grace	.05
121 Cal Ripken Jr.	2.00
122 Tom Goodwin	.05
123 Paul Sorrento	.05
124 Jay Bell	.05
125 Todd Hollandsworth	.05
126 Edgar Martinez	.05
127 George Arias	.05
128 Greg Vaughn	.05
129 Roberto Hernandez	.05
130 Delino DeShields	.05
131 Bill Pulsipher	.05
132 Joey Cora	.05
133 Mariano Rivera	.15
134 Mike Piazza	1.50
135 Carlos Baerga	.05
136 Jose Mesa	.05
137 Will Clark	.05
138 Frank Thomas	.75
139 John Wetteland	.05
140 Shawn Estes	.05
141 Garret Anderson	.05
142 Andre Dawson	.25
143 Eddie Taubensee	.05
144 Ryan Klesko	.05
145 Rocky Coppinger	.05
146 Jeff Bagwell	.75
147 Donovan Osborne	.05
148 Greg Myers	.05
149 Brant Brown	.05
150 Kevin Elster	.05
151 Bob Wells	.05
152 Wally Joyner	.05
153 Rico Brogna	.05
154 Dwight Gooden	.05
155 Jermaine Allensworth	.05
156 Ray Durham	.05
157 Cecil Fielder	.05
158 Ryan Hancock	.05
159 Gary Sheffield	.30
160 Albert Belle	.05
161 Tomas Perez	.05
162 David Doster	.05
163 John Valentin	.05
164 Danny Graves	.05
165 Jose Paniagua	.05
166 Brian Giles **RC**	.50
167 Barry Bonds	2.00
168 Sterling Hitchcock	.05
169 Bernie Williams	.05
170 Fred McGriff	.05
171 George Williams	.05
172 Amaury Telemaco	.05
173 Ken Caminiti	.05
174 Ron Gant	.05
175 David Justice	.05
176 James Baldwin	.05
177 Pat Hentgen	.05
178 Ben McDonald	.05
179 Tim Naehring	.05
180 Jim Eisenreich	.05
181 Ken Hill	.05
182 Paul Wilson	.05
183 Marvin Benard	.05
184 Alan Benes	.05
185 Ellis Burks	.05
186 Scott Servais	.05
187 David Segui	.05
188 Scott Brosius	.05
189 Jose Offerman	.05
190 Eric Davis	.05
191 Brett Butler	.05
192 Curtis Pride	.05
193 Yamil Benitez	.05
194 Chan Ho Park	.05
195 Bret Boone	.05
196 Omar Vizquel	.05
197 Orlando Miller	.05
198 Ramon Martinez	.05
199 Harold Baines	.05
200 Eric Young	.05
201 Fernando Vina	.05
202 Alex Gonzalez	.05
203 Fernando Valenzuela	.05
204 Steve Avery	.05
205 Ernie Young	.05
206 Kevin Appier	.05
207 Randy Myers	.05
208 Jeff Suppan	.05
209 James Mouton	.05
210 Russ Davis	.05
211 Al Martin	.05
212 Troy Percival	.05
213 Al Leiter	.05
214 Dennis Eckersley	.65
215 Mark Johnson	.05
216 Eric Karros	.05
217 Royce Clayton	.05
218 Tony Phillips	.05
219 Tim Wakefield	.05
220 Alan Trammell	.05
221 Eduardo Perez	.05
222 Butch Huskey	.05
223 Tim Belcher	.05
224 Jamie Moyer	.05
225 F.P. Santangelo	.05
226 Rusty Greer	.05
227 Jeff Brantley	.05
228 Mark Langston	.05
229 Ray Montgomery	.05
230 Rich Becker	.05
231 Ozzie Smith	1.00
232 Rey Ordonez	.05
233 Ricky Otero	.05
234 Mike Cameron	.05
235 Mike Sweeney	.05
236 Mark Lewis	.05
237 Luis Gonzalez	.05
238 Marcus Jensen	.05
239 Ed Sprague	.05
240 Jose Valentin	.05
241 Jeff Frye	.05
242 Charles Nagy	.05
243 Carlos Garcia	.05
244 Mike Hampton	.05
245 B.J. Surhoff	.05
246 Wilton Guerrero	.05
247 Frank Rodriguez	.05
248 Gary Gaetti	.05
249 Lance Johnson	.05
250 Darren Bragg	.05
251 Darryl Hamilton	.05
252 John Jaha	.05
253 Craig Paquette	.05
254 Jaime Navarro	.05
255 Shawon Dunston	.05
256 Ron Wright	.05
257 Tim Belk	.05
258 Jeff Darwin	.05
259 Ruben Sierra	.05
260 Chuck Finley	.05
261 Darryl Strawberry	.05
262 Shannon Stewart	.05
263 Pedro Martinez	.05
264 Neifi Perez	.05
265 Jeff Conine	.05
266 Orel Hershiser	.05
267 Checklist 1-90 Eddie Murray (500 Career HR)	.05
268 Checklist 91-180 Paul Molitor (3,000 Career Hits)	.05
269 Checklist 181-270 Barry Bonds (300 Career HR)	.90
270 Checklist - inserts Mark McGwire (300 Career HR)	.75
271 Matt Williams	.05
272 Todd Zeile	.05
273 Roger Clemens	1.25
274 Michael Tucker	.05
275 J.T. Snow	.05
276 Kenny Lofton	.05
277 Jose Canseco	.40
278 Marquis Grissom	.05
279 Moises Alou	.05
280 Benito Santiago	.05
281 Willie McGee	.05
282 Chili Davis	.05
283 Ron Coomer	.05
284 Orlando Merced	.05
285 Delino DeShields	.05
286 John Wetteland	.05
287 Darren Daulton	.05
288 Lee Stevens	.05
289 Albert Belle	.05
290 Sterling Hitchcock	.05
291 David Justice	.05
292 Eric Davis	.05
293 Brian Hunter	.05
294 Darryl Hamilton	.05
295 Steve Avery	.05
296 Joe Vitiello	.05
297 Jaime Navarro	.05
298 Eddie Murray	.75
299 Randy Myers	.05
300 Francisco Cordova	.05
301 Javier Lopez	.05
302 Geronimo Berroa	.05
303 Jeffrey Hammonds	.05
304 Deion Sanders	.05
305 Jeff Fassero	.05
306 Curt Schilling	.25
307 Robb Nen	.05
308 Mark McLemore	.05
309 Jimmy Key	.05
310 Quilvio Veras	.05
311 Bip Roberts	.05
312 Esteban Loaiza	.05
313 Andy Ashby	.05
314 Sandy Alomar Jr.	.05
315 Shawn Green	.20
316 Luis Castillo	.05
317 Benji Gil	.05
318 Otis Nixon	.05
319 Aaron Sele	.05
320 Brad Ausmus	.05
321 Troy O'Leary	.05
322 Terrell Wade	.05
323 Jeff King	.05
324 Kevin Seitzer	.05
325 Mark Wohlers	.05
326 Edgar Renteria	.05
327 Dan Wilson	.05
328 Brian McRae	.05
329 Rod Beck	.05
330 Julio Franco	.05
331 Dave Nilsson	.05
332 Glenallen Hill	.05
333 Kevin Elster	.05
334 Joe Girardi	.05
335 David Wells	.05
336 Jeff Blauser	.05
337 Darryl Kile	.05
338 Jeff Kent	.05
339 Jim Leyritz	.05
340 Todd Stottlemyre	.05
341 Tony Clark	.05
342 Chris Hoiles	.05
343 Mike Lieberthal	.05
344 Matt Lawton	.05
345 Alex Ochoa	.05
346 Chris Snopek	.05
347 Rudy Pemberton	.05
348 Eric Owens	.05
349 Joe Randa	.05
350 John Olerud	.05
351 Steve Karsay	.05
352 Mark Whiten	.05
353 Bob Abreu	.10
354 Bartolo Colon	.05
355 Vladimir Guerrero	.75
356 Darin Erstad	.30
357 Scott Rolen	.60
358 Andruw Jones	.75
359 Scott Spiezio	.05
360 Karim Garcia	.05
361 Hideki Irabu **RC**	.25
362 Nomar Garciaparra	1.00
363 Dmitri Young	.05
364 Bubba Trammell **RC**	.25
365 Kevin Orie	.05
366 Jose Rosado	.05
367 Jose Guillen	.05
368 Brooks Kieschnick	.05
369 Pokey Reese	.05
370 Glendon Rusch	.05
371 Jason Dickson	.05
372 Todd Walker	.05
373 Justin Thompson	.05
374 Todd Greene	.05
375 Jeff Suppan	.05
376 Trey Beamon	.05
377 Damon Mashore	.05
378 Wendell Magee	.05
379 Shigetosi Hasegawa	.05
380 Bill Mueller	.05
381 Chris Widger	.05
382 Tony Grafannino	.05
383 Derrek Lee	.50
384 Brian Moehler	.05
385 Quinton McCracken	.05
386 Matt Morris	.05
387 Marvin Benard	.05
388 Deivi Cruz **RC**	.25
389 Javier Valentin **RC**	.05
390 Todd Dunwoody	.05
391 Derrick Gibson	.05
392 Raul Casanova	.05
393 George Arias	.05
394 Tony Womack **RC**	.25
395 Antone Williamson	.05
396 Jose Cruz Jr. **RC**	.50
397 Desi Relaford	.05
398 Frank Thomas/HL	.40
399 Ken Griffey Jr./HL	.65
400 Cal Ripken Jr./HL	1.00
401 Chipper Jones/HL	.50
402 Mike Piazza/HL	.65
403 Gary Sheffield/HL	.15
404 Alex Rodriguez/HL	.75
405 Wade Boggs/HL	.50
406 Juan Gonzalez/HL	.20
407 Tony Gwynn/HL	.50
408 Edgar Martinez/HL	.05
409 Jeff Bagwell/HL	.40
410 Larry Walker/HL	.05
411 Kenny Lofton/HL	.05
412 Manny Ramirez/HL	.40

ABBREVIATIONS

HL - Hit List

413	Mark McGwire/HL	.75
414	Roberto Alomar/HL	.10
415	Derek Jeter/HL	1.00
416	Brady Anderson/HL	.05
417	Paul Molitor/HL	.35
418	Dante Bichette/HL	.05
419	Jim Edmonds/HL	.05
420	Mo Vaughn/HL	.05
421	Barry Bonds/HL	.90
422	Rusty Greer/HL	.05
423	Greg Maddux (King of the Hill)	.50
424	Andy Pettitte (King of the Hill)	.15
425	John Smoltz (King of the Hill)	.05
426	Randy Johnson (King of the Hill)	.40
427	Hideo Nomo (King of the Hill)	.20
428	Roger Clemens (King of the Hill)	.60
429	Tom Glavine (King of the Hill)	.15
430	Pat Hentgen (King of the Hill)	.05
431	Kevin Brown (King of the Hill)	.05
432	Mike Mussina (King of the Hill)	.20
433	Alex Fernandez (King of the Hill)	.05
434	Kevin Appier (King of the Hill)	.05
435	David Cone (King of the Hill)	.05
436	Jeff Fassero (King of the Hill)	.05
437	John Wetteland (King of the Hill)	.05
438	Barry Bonds, Ivan Rodriguez/IS	.90
439	Ken Griffey Jr., Andres Galarraga/IS	.65
440	Fred McGriff, Rafael Palmeiro/IS	.05
441	Barry Larkin, Jim Thome/IS	.05
442	Sammy Sosa, Albert Belle/IS	.50
443	Bernie Williams, Todd Hundley/IS	.05
444	Chuck Knoblauch, Brian Jordan/IS	.05
445	Mo Vaughn, Jeff Conine/IS	.05
446	Ken Caminiti, Jason Giambi/IS	.25
447	Raul Mondesi, Tim Salmon/IS	.05
448	Checklist (Cal Ripken Jr.)	.75
449	Checklist (Greg Maddux)	.60
450	Checklist (Ken Griffey Jr.)	.50

Press Proofs

Each of the 450 cards in the Donruss base set was also produced in a Press Proof parallel edition of 2,000 cards. Virtually identical in design to the regular cards, the Press Proofs are printed on a metallic background with silver-foil highlights. Most Press Proof backs carry the notation "1 of 2000." Stated odds of finding a press proof are one per eight packs. A special "gold" press proof chase set features cards with gold-foil highlights, die-cut at top and bottom and the note "1 of 500" on back. Gold press proofs are found on average of once per 32 packs.

	NM/M
Complete Set (270):	150.00
Common Player:	.50
Stars/Rookies:	5X
Complete Gold Set (270):	350.00
Common Gold Player:	2.00
Gold Stars/Rookies:	10X

Armed and Dangerous

These 15 cards are numbered up to 5,000. They were inserted in 1997 Donruss Series 1 retail packs only.

		NM/M
Complete Set (15):		35.00
Common Player:		1.00
1	Ken Griffey Jr.	4.00
2	Raul Mondesi	1.00
3	Chipper Jones	3.00
4	Ivan Rodriguez	1.50
5	Alex Rodriguez	5.00
6	Larry Walker	1.00
7	Cal Ripken Jr.	6.00
8	Kenny Lofton	1.00
9	Derek Jeter	6.00
10	Barry Bonds	6.00
11	Charles Johnson	1.00
12	Greg Maddux	3.00
13	Roberto Alomar	1.00
14	Barry Larkin	1.00

Diamond Kings

Diamond Kings for 1997 are sequentially numbered from 1 to 10,000. To celebrate 15 years of this popular insert set, Donruss offered collectors a one-of-a-kind piece of artwork if they find one of the 10 cards with the serial number 1,982 (1982 was the first year of the Diamond Kings). Those who find these cards can redeem them for an original artwork provided by artist Dan Gardiner. In addition, Donruss printed the first 500 of each card on canvas stock.

		NM/M
Complete Set (10):		35.00
Common Player:		.70
Canvas (1st 500):		2X
1	Ken Griffey Jr.	6.00
2	Cal Ripken Jr.	9.00
3	Mo Vaughn	.75
4	Chuck Knoblauch	.75
5	Jeff Bagwell	3.00
6	Henry Rodriguez	.75
7	Mike Piazza	6.00
8	Ivan Rodriguez	2.50
9	Frank Thomas	3.00
10	Chipper Jones	4.50

Elite Inserts

There were 2,500 sets of these insert cards made. The cards were randomly included in 1997 Donruss Series I packs. Fronts have a white marbled border and are graphically enhanced with silver foil, including a large script "E." On back is another photo, a career summary and a serial number

from within the edition limit of 2,500. A promo card version of each card also exists.

		NM/M
Complete Set (12):		100.00
Common Player:		3.00
Promos: 50%		
1	Frank Thomas	7.50
2	Paul Molitor	7.50
3	Sammy Sosa	10.00
4	Barry Bonds	20.00
5	Chipper Jones	10.00
6	Alex Rodriguez	15.00
7	Ken Griffey Jr.	12.50
8	Jeff Bagwell	7.50
9	Cal Ripken Jr.	20.00
10	Mo Vaughn	3.00
11	Mike Piazza	12.50
12	Juan Gonzalez	4.50

Longball Leaders

These 1997 Donruss Series 1 inserts have an action photo printed on a metallic foil background. Printed on the gold-foil border is a gauge with the player's 1996 home run total indicated. Horizontal backs have a player photo and record of career HRs by season. Each card is serially numbered within an edition of 5,000. The set was seeded in retail packs only.

		NM/M
Complete Set (15):		20.00
Common Player:		.50
1	Frank Thomas	2.00
2	Albert Belle	.50
3	Mo Vaughn	.50
4	Brady Anderson	.50
5	Greg Vaughn	.50
6	Ken Griffey Jr.	3.00
7	Jay Buhner	.50
8	Juan Gonzalez	.75
9	Mike Piazza	3.00
10	Jeff Bagwell	2.00
11	Sammy Sosa	2.50
12	Mark McGwire	4.00
13	Cecil Fielder	.50
14	Ryan Klesko	.50
15	Jose Canseco	.85

Rated Rookies

Although numbered more like an insert set, Rated Rookies are part of the regular-issue set. Cards are numbered 1-30, with no ratio given on packs. The cards are differentiated by a large silver-foil strip on the top right side with the words Rated Rookie.

		NM/M
Complete Set (30):		10.00
Common Player:		.50
1	Jason Thompson	.50
2	LaTroy Hawkins	.50
3	Scott Rolen	1.50
4	Trey Beamon	.50
5	Kimera Bartee	.50
6	Nerio Rodriguez	.50
7	Jeff D'Amico	.50
8	Quinton McCracken	.50
9	John Wasdin	.50
10	Robin Jennings	.50
11	Steve Gibralter	.50
12	Tyler Houston	.50
13	Tony Clark	.50
14	Ugueth Urbina	.50
15	Billy McMillon	.50
16	Raul Casanova	.50
17	Brooks Kieschnick	.50
18	Luis Castillo	.50
19	Edgar Renteria	.50
20	Andruw Jones	2.00
21	Chad Mottola	.50
22	Makoto Suzuki	.50
23	Justin Thompson	.50
24	Darin Erstad	1.00
25	Todd Walker	.50
26	Todd Greene	.50
27	Vladimir Guerrero	2.00
28	Darren Dreifort	.50
29	John Burke	.50
30	Damon Mashore	.50

Jackie Robinson Rookie Reprint

In conjunction with its program of special issues and giveaways honoring the 50th anniversary of Robinson's major league debut, Donruss issued this "Commemorative Rookie Card." Printed in the same size as the 1949 Leaf Robinson, and on heavier, coarser stock than modern cards, the card carries a reprint notice and is serially numbered on back in gold foil from within an edition of 1,948.

		NM/M
79	Jackie Robinson	10.00

Jackie Robinson Sweepstakes Scratch-Off

This pack insert features inside a scratch-off contest in which genuine vintage 1948-49 Leaf Jackie Robinson cards were awarded. The 2-3/8" x 2-7/8" folder has a color photo of the Leaf Robinson rookie card on front. On back is information on ordering numbered lithographs

of the Robinson card; an edition of 1,000 selling for $199 apiece, an edition of 500 autographed by his widow selling for $299 apiece.

		NM/M
	Jackie Robinson	.50

Rocket Launchers

These 1997 Donruss Series 1 inserts are limited to 5,000 each. They were only included in magazine packs.

		NM/M
Complete Set (15):		25.00
Common Player:		.75
1	Frank Thomas	2.50
2	Albert Belle	.75
3	Chipper Jones	3.00
4	Mike Piazza	4.00
5	Mo Vaughn	.75
6	Juan Gonzalez	1.00
7	Fred McGriff	.75
8	Jeff Bagwell	2.50
9	Matt Williams	.75
10	Gary Sheffield	1.00
11	Barry Bonds	5.00
12	Manny Ramirez	2.00
13	Henry Rodriguez	.75
14	Jason Giambi	1.50
15	Cal Ripken Jr.	5.00

Update Dominators

This 20-card insert highlights players known for being able to "take over a game." Each card features silver-foil highlights on front and stats on back.

		NM/M
Complete Set (20):		22.50
Common Player:		.50
1	Frank Thomas	1.25
2	Ken Griffey Jr.	2.25
3	Greg Maddux	1.50
4	Cal Ripken Jr.	3.00
5	Alex Rodriguez	2.50
6	Albert Belle	.50
7	Mark McGwire	2.50
8	Juan Gonzalez	.65
9	Chipper Jones	1.50
10	Hideo Nomo	.65
11	Roger Clemens	2.00
12	John Smoltz	.50
13	Mike Piazza	2.25
14	Sammy Sosa	1.50
15	Matt Williams	.50
16	Kenny Lofton	.50
17	Barry Larkin	.50
18	Rafael Palmeiro	1.00
19	Ken Caminiti	.50
20	Gary Sheffield	.75

Update Franchise Features

This hobby-exclusive insert consists of 15 cards designed with a movie poster theme. The double-front design highlights a top veteran player on one side with an up-

and-coming rookie on the other. The side featuring the veteran has the designation "Now Playing," while the rookie side carries the banner "Coming Attraction." Each card is printed on an all-foil stock and numbered to 3,000.

		NM/M
Complete Set (15):		45.00
Common Player:		2.00
1	Ken Griffey Jr., Andruw Jones	4.00
2	Frank Thomas, Darin Erstad	2.50
3	Alex Rodriguez, Nomar Garciaparra	5.00
4	Chuck Knoblauch, Wilton Guerrero	2.00
5	Juan Gonzalez, Bubba Trammell	2.00
6	Chipper Jones, Todd Walker	3.00
7	Barry Bonds, Vladimir Guerrero	6.00
8	Mark McGwire, Dmitri Young	5.00
9	Mike Piazza, Mike Sweeney	4.00
10	Mo Vaughn, Tony Clark	2.00
11	Gary Sheffield, Jose Guillen	2.00
12	Kenny Lofton, Shannon Stewart	2.00
13	Cal Ripken Jr., Scott Rolen	6.00
14	Derek Jeter, Pokey Reese	6.00
15	Tony Gwynn, Bob Abreu	3.00

Update Power Alley

This 24-card insert is fractured into three different styles: Gold, Blue and Green. Each card is micro-etched and printed on holographic foil board. All cards are sequentially numbered, with the first 250 cards in each level being die-cut. Twelve players' cards feature a green finish and are numbered to 4,000. Eight players are printed on blue cards that are numbered to 2,000. Four players are found on gold cards numbered to 1,000.

		NM/M
Complete Set (24):		100.00
Common Gold:		7.50
Common Blue:		3.00
Common Green:		1.50
Die-Cut:		3X
1	Frank Thomas/G	7.50
2	Ken Griffey Jr./G	10.00
3	Cal Ripken Jr./G	15.00
4	Jeff Bagwell/B	5.00
5	Mike Piazza/B	7.50
6	Andruw Jones/GR	3.50
7	Alex Rodriguez/G	12.50
8	Albert Belle/GR	1.50
9	Mo Vaughn/GR	1.50
10	Chipper Jones/B	6.00

#	Player	NM/M
11	Juan Gonzalez/B	3.00
12	Ken Caminiti/GR	1.50
13	Manny Ramirez/GR	3.50
14	Mark McGwire/GR	6.00
15	Kenny Lofton/B	3.00
16	Barry Bonds/GR	7.50
17	Gary Sheffield/GR	1.50
18	Tony Gwynn/GR	4.50
19	Vladimir Guerrero/B	5.00
20	Ivan Rodriguez/B	3.50
21	Paul Molitor/B	5.00
22	Sammy Sosa/GR	4.50
23	Matt Williams/GR	1.50
24	Derek Jeter/GR	7.50

Update Press Proofs

This 180-card parallel set is printed on an all-foil stock with bright foil accents. Each card is numbered "1 of 2,000." Special die-cut gold versions are numbered as "1 of 500."

	NM/M
Complete Set (180):	200.00
Common Player:	.50
Stars:	7X
Complete Set, Gold (180):	400.00
Common Player, Gold:	2.00
Gold Stars:	15X

Update Cal Ripken

This 10-card set salutes Cal Ripken Jr. and is printed on an all-foil stock with foil highlights. Photos and text are taken from Ripken's autobiography, "The Only Way I Know." The first nine cards of the set were randomly inserted into packs. The 10th card was only available inside the book. Each card found within packs was numbered to 5,000.

		NM/M
Complete Set (10):		75.00
Common Card:		10.00
1-9	Cal Ripken Jr.	10.00
10	Cal Ripken Jr. (Book insert.)	10.00

Update Rookie Diamond Kings

This popular Donruss Update insert set features a new twist - all 10 cards feature promising rookies. Each card is sequentially numbered to 10,000, with the first 500 cards of each player printed on actual canvas.

#	Player	NM/M
	Complete Set (10):	20.00
	Common Player:	1.50
	Canvas:	1.5X
1	Andruw Jones	4.00
2	Vladimir Guerrero	10.00
3	Scott Rolen	2.00
4	Todd Walker	1.50
5	Bartolo Colon	2.00
6	Jose Guillen	1.50
7	Nomar Garciaparra	6.00
8	Darin Erstad	2.00
9	Dmitri Young	1.50
10	Wilton Guerrero	1.50

Team Sets

A total of 163 cards were part of the Donruss Team Set issue. Packs consisted solely of players from one of 11 different teams. In addition, a full 163-card parallel set called Pennant Edition was available, featuring red and gold foil and a special "Pennant Edition" logo. Cards were sold in five-card packs for $1.99 each. The Angels and Indians set were sold only at their teams' souvenir outlets. Cards #131 Bernie Williams and #144 Russ Davis were never issued. The Team Set cards utilize team-color foil highlights and the numbers on back differ from the regular-issue version.

#	Player	NM/M
	Comp. Angels Set (1-15):	1.25
	Comp. Braves Set (16-30):	3.00
	Comp. Orioles Set (31-45):	2.50
	Comp. Red Sox Set (46-60):	1.50
	Comp. White Sox Set (61-75):	
	Comp. Indians Set (76-90):	1.50
	Comp. Rockies Set (91-105):	1.50
	Comp. Dodgers Set (106-120):	2.25
	Comp. Yankees Set (121-135):	4.50
	Comp. Mariners Set (136-150):	4.50
	Comp. Cardinals Set (151-165):	2.00
	Common Player:	.05
	Pennant Edition Stars:	3X
1	Jim Edmonds	.05
2	Tim Salmon	.05
3	Tony Phillips	.05
4	Garret Anderson	.05
5	Troy Percival	.05
6	Mark Langston	.05
7	Chuck Finley	.05
8	Eddie Murray	.75
9	Jim Leyritz	.05
10	Darin Erstad	.30
11	Jason Dickson	.05
12	Allen Watson	.05
13	Shigetosi Hasegawa	.05
14	Dave Hollins	.05
15	Gary DiSarcina	.05
16	Greg Maddux	1.00
17	Denny Neagle	.05
18	Chipper Jones	1.00
19	Tom Glavine	.25
20	John Smoltz	.05
21	Ryan Klesko	.05
22	Fred McGriff	.05
23	Michael Tucker	.05
24	Kenny Lofton	.05
25	Javier Lopez	.05
26	Mark Wohlers	.05
27	Jeff Blauser	.05
28	Andruw Jones	.75
29	Tony Graffanino	.05
30	Terrell Wade	.05
31	Brady Anderson	.05
32	Roberto Alomar	.15
33	Rafael Palmeiro	.65
34	Mike Mussina	.35
35	Cal Ripken Jr.	2.00
36	Rocky Coppinger	.05
37	Randy Myers	.05
38	B.J. Surhoff	.05
39	Eric Davis	.05
40	Armando Benitez	.05
41	Jeffrey Hammonds	.05
42	Jimmy Key	.05
43	Chris Hoiles	.05
44	Mike Bordick	.05
45	Pete Incaviglia	.05
46	Mike Stanley	.05
47	Reggie Jefferson	.05
48	Mo Vaughn	.05
49	John Valentin	.05
50	Tim Naehring	.05
51	Jeff Suppan	.05
52	Tim Wakefield	.05
53	Jeff Frye	.05
54	Darren Bragg	.05
55	Steve Avery	.05
56	Shane Mack	.05
57	Aaron Sele	.05
58	Troy O'Leary	.05
59	Rudy Pemberton	.05
60	Nomar Garciaparra	1.00
61	Robin Ventura	.05
62	Wilson Alvarez	.05
63	Roberto Hernandez	.05
64	Frank Thomas	.75
65	Ray Durham	.05
66	James Baldwin	.05
67	Harold Baines	.05
68	Doug Drabek	.05
69	Mike Cameron	.05
70	Albert Belle	.05
71	Jaime Navarro	.05
72	Chris Snopek	.05
73	Lyle Mouton	.05
74	Dave Martinez	.05
75	Ozzie Guillen	.05
76	Manny Ramirez	.75
77	Jack McDowell	.05
78	Jim Thome	.50
79	Jose Mesa	.05
80	Brian Giles	.05
81	Omar Vizquel	.05
82	Charles Nagy	.05
83	Orel Hershiser	.05
84	Matt Williams	.05
85	Marquis Grissom	.05
86	David Justice	.05
87	Sandy Alomar	.05
88	Kevin Seitzer	.05
89	Julio Franco	.05
90	Bartolo Colon	.05
91	Andres Galarraga	.05
92	Larry Walker	.05
93	Vinny Castilla	.05
94	Dante Bichette	.05
95	Jamey Wright	.05
96	Ellis Burks	.05
97	Eric Young	.05
98	Neifi Perez	.05
99	Quinton McCracken	.05
100	Bruce Ruffin	.05
101	Walt Weiss	.05
102	Roger Bailey	.05
103	Jeff Reed	.05
104	Bill Swift	.05
105	Kirt Manwaring	.05
106	Raul Mondesi	.05
107	Hideo Nomo	.35
108	Roger Cedeno	.05
109	Ismael Valdes	.05
110	Todd Hollandsworth	.05
111	Mike Piazza	1.50
112	Brett Butler	.05
113	Chan Ho Park	.05
114	Ramon Martinez	.05
115	Eric Karros	.05
116	Wilton Guerrero	.05
117	Todd Zeile	.05
118	Karim Garcia	.05
119	Greg Gagne	.05
120	Darren Dreifort	.05
121	Wade Boggs	1.00
122	Paul O'Neill	.05
123	Derek Jeter	2.00
124	Tino Martinez	.05
125	David Cone	.05
126	Andy Pettitte	.25
127	Charlie Hayes	.05
128	Mariano Rivera	.15
129	Dwight Gooden	.05
130	Cecil Fielder	.05
132	Darryl Strawberry	.05
133	Joe Girardi	.05
134	David Wells	.05
135	Hideki Irabu	.05
136	Ken Griffey Jr.	1.25
137	Alex Rodriguez	1.50
138	Jay Buhner	.05
139	Randy Johnson	.75
140	Paul Sorrento	.05
141	Edgar Martinez	.05
142	Joey Cora	.05
143	Bob Wells	.05
145	Jamie Moyer	.05
146	Jeff Fassero	.05
147	Dan Wilson	.05
148	Jose Cruz, Jr.	.05
149	Scott Sanders	.05
150	Rich Amaral	.05
151	Brian Jordan	.05
152	Andy Benes	.05
153	Ray Lankford	.05
154	John Mabry	.05
155	Tom Pagnozzi	.05
156	Ron Gant	.05
157	Alan Benes	.05
158	Dennis Eckersley	.65
159	Royce Clayton	.05
160	Todd Stottlemyre	.05
161	Gary Gaetti	.05
162	Willie McGee	.05
163	Delino DeShields	.05
164	Dmitri Young	.05
165	Matt Morris	.05

Team Sets MVP

The top players at each position were available in this 18-card insert set. Each card is sequentially numbered to 1,000. Fronts are printed with a textured foil background and holographic foil highlights. Backs have a portrait photo.

#	Player	NM/M
	Complete Set (18):	45.00
	Common Player:	.50
1	Ivan Rodriguez	1.50
2	Mike Piazza	5.50
3	Frank Thomas	2.50
4	Jeff Bagwell	2.50
5	Chuck Knoblauch	.50
6	Eric Young	.50
7	Alex Rodriguez	6.00
8	Barry Larkin	.50
9	Cal Ripken Jr.	7.50
10	Chipper Jones	4.00
11	Albert Belle	.50
12	Barry Bonds	7.50
13	Ken Griffey Jr.	5.50
14	Kenny Lofton	.50
15	Juan Gonzalez	1.00
16	Larry Walker	.50
17	Roger Clemens	5.00
18	Greg Maddux	4.00

1997 Donruss Elite

Donruss Elite Baseball is a 150-card, single-series set distributed as a hobby-only product. The regular-issue cards feature a silver border around the entire card, with a marblized frame around a color player photo at center. Backs feature a color player photo and minimal statistics and personal data. Elite was accompanied by an Elite Stars parallel set and three inserts: Leather and Lumber, Passing the Torch and Turn of the Century.

#	Player	NM/M
	Complete Set (150):	10.00
	Common Player:	.10
	Complete Elite Star Set (150):	60.00
	Common Elite Star:	.50
	Elite Stars Stars/RC's:	4X
	Pack (6):	2.50
	Wax Box (18):	35.00
1	Juan Gonzalez	.40
2	Alex Rodriguez	2.00
3	Frank Thomas	.75
4	Greg Maddux	1.00
5	Ken Griffey Jr.	1.50
6	Cal Ripken Jr.	2.50
7	Mike Piazza	1.50
8	Chipper Jones	1.00
9	Albert Belle	.10
10	Andruw Jones	.75
11	Vladimir Guerrero	.75
12	Mo Vaughn	.10
13	Ivan Rodriguez	.65
14	Andy Pettitte	.40
15	Tony Gwynn	1.00
16	Barry Bonds	2.50
17	Jeff Bagwell	.75
18	Manny Ramirez	.75
19	Kenny Lofton	.10
20	Roberto Alomar	.20
21	Mark McGwire	2.00
22	Ryan Klesko	.10
23	Tim Salmon	.10
24	Derek Jeter	2.50
25	Eddie Murray	.75
26	Jermaine Dye	.10
27	Ruben Rivera	.10
28	Jim Edmonds	.10
29	Mike Mussina	.40
30	Randy Johnson	.75
31	Sammy Sosa	1.00
32	Hideo Nomo	.40
33	Chuck Knoblauch	.10
34	Paul Molitor	.75
35	Rafael Palmeiro	.75
36	Brady Anderson	.10
37	Will Clark	.10
38	Craig Biggio	.10
39	Jason Giambi	.10
40	Roger Clemens	1.25
41	Jay Buhner	.10
42	Edgar Martinez	.10
43	Gary Sheffield	.35
44	Fred McGriff	.10
45	Bobby Bonilla	.10
46	Tom Glavine	.25
47	Wade Boggs	1.00
48	Jeff Conine	.10
49	John Smoltz	.10
50	Jim Thome	.60
51	Billy Wagner	.10
52	Jose Canseco	.40
53	Javy Lopez	.10
54	Cecil Fielder	.10
55	Garret Anderson	.10
56	Alex Ochoa	.10
57	Scott Rolen	.60
58	Darin Erstad	.30
59	Rey Ordonez	.10
60	Dante Bichette	.10
61	Joe Carter	.10
62	Moises Alou	.10
63	Jason Isringhausen	.10
64	Karim Garcia	.10
65	Brian Jordan	.10
66	Ruben Sierra	.10
67	Todd Hollandsworth	.10
68	Paul Wilson	.10
69	Ernie Young	.10
70	Ryne Sandberg	1.00
71	Raul Mondesi	.10
72	George Arias	.10
73	Ray Durham	.10
74	Dean Palmer	.10
75	Shawn Green	.30
76	Eric Young	.10
77	Jason Kendall	.10
78	Greg Vaughn	.10
79	Terrell Wade	.10
80	Bill Pulsipher	.10
81	Bobby Higginson	.10
82	Mark Grudzielanek	.10
83	Ken Caminiti	.10
84	Todd Greene	.10
85	Carlos Delgado	.50
86	Mark Grace	.10
87	Rondell White	.10
88	Barry Larkin	.10
89	J.T. Snow	.10
90	Alex Gonzalez	.10
91	Raul Casanova	.10
92	Marc Newfield	.10
93	Jermaine Allensworth	.10
94	John Mabry	.10
95	Kirby Puckett	1.00
96	Travis Fryman	.10
97	Kevin Brown	.15
98	Andres Galarraga	.10
99	Marty Cordova	.10
100	Henry Rodriguez	.10
101	Sterling Hitchcock	.10
102	Trey Beamon	.10
103	Brett Butler	.10
104	Rickey Henderson	.75
105	Tino Martinez	.10
106	Kevin Appier	.10
107	Brian Hunter	.10
108	Eric Karros	.10
109	Andre Dawson	.10
110	Darryl Strawberry	.10
111	James Baldwin	.10
112	Chad Mottola	.10
113	Dave Nilsson	.10
114	Carlos Baerga	.10
115	Chan Ho Park	.10
116	John Jaha	.10
117	Alan Benes	.10
118	Mariano Rivera	.20
119	Ellis Burks	.10
120	Tony Clark	.10
121	Todd Walker	.10
122	Dwight Gooden	.10
123	Ugueth Urbina	.10
124	David Cone	.10
125	Ozzie Smith	1.00
126	Kimera Bartee	.10
127	Rusty Greer	.10
128	Pat Hentgen	.10
129	Charles Johnson	.10
130	Quinton McCracken	.10
131	Troy Percival	.10
132	Shane Reynolds	.10
133	Charles Nagy	.10
134	Tom Goodwin	.10
135	Ron Gant	.10
136	Dan Wilson	.10
137	Matt Williams	.10
138	LaTroy Hawkins	.10
139	Kevin Seitzer	.10
140	Michael Tucker	.10
141	Todd Hundley	.10
142	Alex Fernandez	.10
143	Marquis Grissom	.10
144	Steve Finley	.10
145	Curtis Pride	.10
146	Derek Bell	.10
147	Butch Huskey	.10
148	Dwight Gooden	.10
149	Al Leiter	.10
150	Hideo Nomo	.40

Stars

Gold, rather than silver, foil differentiates the parallel set of Elite Stars from the regular-issue versions of each of the base cards in the Elite set. The parallels also have a small "Elite Stars" printed at top, flanking the position. Stated odds of finding a Stars insert are about one per five packs.

	NM/M
Complete Set (150):	60.00
Common Player:	1.00

Leather & Lumber

Leather and Lumber is a 10-card insert set filled with veterans. Genuine leather is featured on one side of the card, while wood card stock is on the other. There were 500 sequentially numbered sets produced.

#	Player	NM/M
	Complete Set (10):	140.00
	Common Player:	4.00
1	Ken Griffey Jr.	20.00
2	Alex Rodriguez	25.00
3	Frank Thomas	9.00
4	Chipper Jones	12.50
5	Ivan Rodriguez	7.50
6	Cal Ripken Jr.	35.00
7	Barry Bonds	35.00
8	Chuck Knoblauch	4.00
9	Manny Ramirez	9.00
10	Mark McGwire	25.00

Passing the Torch

Passing the Torch is a 12-card insert limited to 1,500 individually numbered sets. It features eight differ ent stars, each with their own cards and then featured on a double-sided card with another player from the set.

		NM/M
Complete Set (12):		110.00
Common Player:		4.50
1	Cal Ripken Jr.	20.00
2	Alex Rodriguez	15.00
3	Cal Ripken Jr., Alex Rodriguez	17.50
4	Kirby Puckett	10.00
5	Andruw Jones	7.50
6	Kirby Puckett, Andruw Jones	7.50
7	Cecil Fielder	4.50
8	Frank Thomas	7.50
9	Cecil Fielder, Frank Thomas	6.00
10	Ozzie Smith	10.00
11	Derek Jeter	20.00
12	Ozzie Smith, Derek Jeter	12.00

Passing the Torch Autographs

The first 150 individually numbered sets of the Passing the Torch insert were autographed. This means that cards 3, 6, 9 and 12 are dual-autographed on their double-sided format.

		NM/M
Common Card:		15.00
1	Cal Ripken Jr.	200.00
2	Alex Rodriguez	275.00
3	Cal Ripken Jr., Alex Rodriguez	750.00
4	Kirby Puckett	80.00
5	Andruw Jones	40.00
6	Kirby Puckett, Andruw Jones	140.00
7	Cecil Fielder	45.00
8	Frank Thomas	75.00
9	Cecil Fielder, Frank Thomas	125.00
10	Ozzie Smith	120.00
11	Derek Jeter	160.00
12	Ozzie Smith, Derek Jeter	325.00

Turn of the Century

Turn of the Century includes 20 potential year 2000 superstars on an insert set numbered to 3,500. The first 500 of these sets feature an external die-cut design. Cards feature the player over a framed background image on silver foil board, with black strips down each side. Backs have a color photo, a few words about the player and the serial number. Each card can also be found in an overprinted "SAMPLE" version.

		NM/M
Complete Set (20):		55.00
Common Player:		1.00
Die-Cut:		3X
Samples:		1X
1	Alex Rodriguez	10.00
2	Andruw Jones	6.00
3	Chipper Jones	7.50
4	Todd Walker	1.00
5	Scott Rolen	4.00
6	Trey Beamon	1.00
7	Derek Jeter	12.50
8	Darin Erstad	3.00
9	Tony Clark	1.00
10	Todd Greene	1.00
11	Jason Giambi	3.00
12	Justin Thompson	1.00
13	Ernie Young	1.00
14	Jason Kendall	1.00
15	Alex Ochoa	1.00
16	Brooks Kieschnick	1.00
17	Bobby Higginson	1.00
18	Ruben Rivera	1.00
19	Chan Ho Park	1.00
20	Chad Mottola	1.00

1997 Donruss Limited

Each of the 200 base cards in this set features a double-front design showcasing an action photo on each side. The set is divided into four subsets. Counterparts (100 cards) highlights two different players from the same position; Double Team (40 cards) features some of the majors' top teammate duos; Star Factor (40 cards) consists of two photos of some of the hobby's favorite players; and Unlimited Potential/Talent (20 cards) combines a top veteran with a top prospect. The issue also includes a Limited Exposure parallel set and a multi-tiered insert called Fabric of the Game. Odds of finding any insert card were 1:5 packs. Less than 1,100 base sets were available. Cards were sold in five-card packs for $4.99.

		NM/M
Complete Set (200):		450.00
Common Counterpart:		.20
Common Double Team:		.75
Common Star Factor:		1.50
Common Unlimited Potential:		1.25
Pack (5):		2.00
Wax Box (24):		45.00
1	Ken Griffey Jr., Rondell White (Counterparts)	1.00
2	Greg Maddux, David Cone (Counterparts)	.75
3	Gary Sheffield, Moises Alou/DT	1.25
4	Frank Thomas/SF	10.00
5	Cal Ripken Jr., Kevin Orie (Counterparts)	2.00
6	Vladimir Guerrero, Barry Bonds/UPT	20.00
7	Eddie Murray, Reggie Jefferson (Counterparts)	.60
8	Manny Ramirez, Marquis Grissom/DT	2.50
9	Mike Piazza/SF	15.00
10	Barry Larkin, Rey Ordonez (Counterparts)	.20
11	Jeff Bagwell, Eric Karros (Counterparts)	.60
12	Chuck Knoblauch, Ray Durham (Counterparts)	.20
13	Alex Rodriguez, Edgar Renteria (Counterparts)	1.50
14	Matt Williams, Vinny Castilla (Counterparts)	.20
15	Todd Hollandsworth, Bob Abreu (Counterparts)	.20
16	John Smoltz, Pedro Martinez (Counterparts)	.60
17	Jose Canseco, Chili Davis (Counterparts)	.40
18	Jose Cruz, Jr., Ken Griffey Jr./UPT	15.00
19	Ken Griffey Jr./SF	15.00
20	Paul Molitor, John Olerud (Counterparts)	.60
21	Roberto Alomar, Luis Castillo (Counterparts)	.35
22	Derek Jeter, Lou Collier (Counterparts)	2.00
23	Chipper Jones, Robin Ventura (Counterparts)	.75
24	Gary Sheffield, Ron Gant (Counterparts)	.25
25	Ramon Martinez, Bobby Jones (Counterparts)	.20
26	Mike Piazza, Raul Mondesi/DT	7.50
27	Darin Erstad, Jeff Bagwell/UPT	7.50
28	Ivan Rodriguez/SF	7.50
29	J.T. Snow, Kevin Young (Counterparts)	.20
30	Ryne Sandberg, Julio Franco (Counterparts)	.75
31	Travis Fryman, Chris Snopek (Counterparts)	.20
32	Wade Boggs, Russ Davis (Counterparts)	.75
33	Brooks Kieschnick, Marty Cordova (Counterparts)	.20
34	Andy Pettitte, Denny Neagle (Counterparts)	.35
35	Paul Molitor, Matt Lawton (Double Team)	2.50
36	Scott Rolen, Cal Ripken Jr./UPT	20.00
37	Cal Ripken Jr./SF	20.00
38	Jim Thome, Dave Nilsson (Counterparts)	.50
39	Tony Womack RC, Carlos Baerga (Counterparts)	.20
40	Nomar Garciaparra, Mark Grudzielanek (Counterparts)	.75
41	Todd Greene, Chris Widger (Counterparts)	.20
42	Deion Sanders, Bernard Gilkey (Counterparts)	.20
43	Hideo Nomo, Charles Nagy (Counterparts)	.50
44	Ivan Rodriguez, Rusty Greer/DT	2.00
45	Todd Walker, Chipper Jones/UPT	10.00
46	Greg Maddux/SF	12.00
47	Mo Vaughn, Cecil Fielder (Counterparts)	.20
48	Craig Biggio, Scott Spiezio (Counterparts)	.20
49	Pokey Reese, Jeff Blauser (Counterparts)	.20
50	Ken Caminiti, Joe Randa (Counterparts)	.20
51	Albert Belle, Shawn Green (Counterparts)	.20
52	Randy Johnson, Jason Dickson (Counterparts)	.60
53	Hideo Nomo, Chan Ho Park/DT	2.00
54	Scott Spiezio, Chuck Knoblauch/UPT	1.25
55	Chipper Jones/SF	12.00
56	Tino Martinez, Ryan McGuire (Counterparts)	.20
57	Eric Young, Wilton Guerrero (Counterparts)	.20
58	Ron Coomer, Dave Hollins (Counterparts)	.20
59	Sammy Sosa, Angel Echevarria (Counterparts)	.75
60	Dennis Reyes RC, Jimmy Key (Counterparts)	.20
61	Barry Larkin, Deion Sanders/DT	.75
62	Wilton Guerrero, Roberto Alomar/UPT	2.00
63	Albert Belle/SF	1.50
64	Mark McGwire, Andres Galarraga (Counterparts)	1.50
65	Edgar Martinez, Todd Walker (Counterparts)	.20
66	Steve Finley, Rich Becker (Counterparts)	.20
67	Tom Glavine, Andy Ashby (Counterparts)	.30
68	Sammy Sosa, Ryne Sandberg/DT	5.00
69	Nomar Garciaparra, Alex Rodriguez/UPT	15.00
70	Jeff Bagwell/SF	10.00
71	Darin Erstad, Mark Grace (Counterparts)	.40
72	Scott Rolen, Edgardo Alfonzo (Counterparts)	.50
73	Kenny Lofton, Lance Johnson (Counterparts)	.20
74	Joey Hamilton, Brett Tomko (Counterparts)	.20
75	Eddie Murray, Tim Salmon/DT	2.50
76	Dmitri Young, Mo Vaughn/UPT	1.25
77	Juan Gonzalez/SF	3.00
78	Frank Thomas, Tony Clark (Counterparts)	.60
79	Shannon Stewart, Bip Roberts (Counterparts)	.20
80	Shawn Estes, Alex Fernandez (Counterparts)	.20
81	John Smoltz, Javier Lopez (Double Team)	.75
82	Todd Greene, Mike Piazza/UPT	15.00
83	Derek Jeter/SF	20.00
84	Dmitri Young, Antone Williamson (Counterparts)	.20
85	Rickey Henderson, Darryl Hamilton (Counterparts)	.60
86	Billy Wagner, Dennis Eckersley (Counterparts)	.60
87	Larry Walker, Eric Young/DT	.75
88	Mark Kotsay, Juan Gonzalez/UPT	3.00
89	Barry Bonds/SF	20.00
90	Will Clark, Jeff Conine (Counterparts)	.20
91	Tony Gwynn, Brett Butler (Counterparts)	.75
92	John Wetteland, Rod Beck (Counterparts)	.20
93	Bernie Williams, Tino Martinez/DT	1.25
94	Andruw Jones, Kenny Lofton/UPT	7.50
95	Mo Vaughn/SF	1.50
96	Joe Carter, Derrek Lee (Counterparts)	.50
97	John Mabry, F.P. Santangelo (Counterparts)	.20
98	Esteban Loaiza, Wilson Alvarez (Counterparts)	.20
99	Matt Williams, David Justice/DT	.75
100	Derrek Lee, Frank Thomas/UPT	7.50
101	Mark McGwire/SF	7.50
102	Fred McGriff, Paul Sorrento (Counterparts)	.20
103	Jermaine Allensworth, Bernie Williams (Counterparts)	.20
104	Ismael Valdes, Chris Holt (Counterparts)	.20
105	Fred McGriff, Ryan Klesko (Double Team)	.75
106	Tony Clark, Mark McGwire/UPT	17.50
107	Tony Gwynn/SF	12.00
108	Jeffrey Hammonds, Ellis Burks (Counterparts)	.20
109	Shane Reynolds, Andy Benes (Counterparts)	.20
110	Roger Clemens, Carlos Delgado/DT	10.00
111	Karim Garcia, Albert Belle/UPT	1.25
112	Paul Molitor/SF	10.00
113	Trey Beamon, Eric Owens (Counterparts)	.20
114	Curt Schilling, Darryl Kile (Counterparts)	.30
115	Tom Glavine, Michael Tucker/DT	.75
116	Pokey Reese, Derek Jeter/UPT	20.00
117	Manny Ramirez/SF	10.00
118	Juan Gonzalez, Brant Brown (Counterparts)	.40
119	Juan Guzman, Francisco Cordova (Counterparts)	.20
120	Randy Johnson, Edgar Martinez/DT	2.50
121	Hideki Irabu, Greg Maddux/UPT	10.00
122	Alex Rodriguez/SF	17.50
123	Barry Bonds, Quinton McCracken (Counterparts)	2.00
124	Roger Clemens, Alan Benes (Counterparts)	.85
125	Wade Boggs, Paul O'Neill/DT	1.75
126	Mike Cameron, Larry Walker/UPT	1.25
127	Gary Sheffield/SF	2.50
128	Andruw Jones, Raul Mondesi (Counterparts)	.60
129	Brian Anderson, Terrell Wade (Counterparts)	.20
130	Brady Anderson, Rafael Palmeiro/DT	2.00
131	Neifi Perez, Barry Larkin/UPT	1.25
132	Ken Caminiti/SF	1.50
133	Larry Walker, Rusty Greer (Counterparts)	.20
134	Mariano Rivera, Mark Wohlers (Counterparts)	.30
135	Hideki Irabu, Andy Pettitte (Double Team)	1.50
136	Jose Guillen, Tony Gwynn/UPT	10.00
137	Hideo Nomo/SF	3.00
138	Vladimir Guerrero, Jim Edmonds (Counterparts)	.60
139	Justin Thompson, Dwight Gooden (Counterparts)	.20
140	Andres Galarraga, Dante Bichette/DT	.75
141	Kenny Lofton/SF	1.50
142	Tim Salmon, Manny Ramirez (Counterparts)	.60
143	Kevin Brown, Matt Morris (Counterparts)	.20
144	Craig Biggio, Bob Abreu/DT	.75
145	Roberto Alomar/SF	2.00
146	Jose Guillen, Brian Jordan (Counterparts)	.20
147	Bartolo Colon, Kevin Appier (Counterparts)	.20
148	Ray Lankford, Brian Jordan (Double Team)	.75
149	Chuck Knoblauch/SF	1.50
150	Henry Rodriguez, Ray Lankford (Counterparts)	.20
151	Jaret Wright RC, Ben McDonald (Counterparts)	.20
152	Bobby Bonilla, Kevin Brown/DT	.75
153	Barry Larkin/SF	1.50
154	David Justice, Reggie Sanders (Counterparts)	.20
155	Mike Mussina, Ken Hill (Counterparts)	.40
156	Mark Grace, Brooks Kieschnick/DT	.75
157	Jim Thome/SF	2.50
158	Michael Tucker, Curtis Goodwin (Counterparts)	.20
159	Jeff Suppan, Jeff Fassero (Counterparts)	.20
160	Mike Mussina, Jeffrey Hammonds/DT	1.00
161	John Smoltz/SF	1.50
162	Moises Alou, Eric Davis (Counterparts)	.20
163	Sandy Alomar Jr., Dan Wilson (Counterparts)	.20
164	Rondell White, Henry Rodriguez/DT	.75
165	Roger Clemens/SF	12.50
166	Brady Anderson, Al Martin (Counterparts)	.20
167	Jason Kendall, Charles Johnson (Counterparts)	.20
168	Jason Giambi, Jose Canseco/DT	2.00
169	Larry Walker/SF	1.50
170	Jay Buhner, Geronimo Berroa (Counterparts)	.20
171	Ivan Rodriguez, Mike Sweeney (Counterparts)	.50
172	Kevin Appier, Jose Rosado/DT	.75
173	Bernie Williams/SF	1.50
174	Todd Dunwoody, Brian Giles RC (Counterparts)	.40
175	Javier Lopez, Scott Hatteberg (Counterparts)	.20
176	John Jaha, Jeff Cirillo/DT	.75
177	Andy Pettitte/SF	2.00
178	Dante Bichette, Butch Huskey (Counterparts)	.20
179	Raul Casanova, Todd Hundley (Counterparts)	.20
180	Jim Edmonds, Garret Anderson/DT	.75
181	Deion Sanders/SF	1.50
182	Ryan Klesko, Paul O'Neill (Counterparts)	.20
183	Joe Carter, Pat Hentgen/DT	.75
184	Brady Anderson/SF	1.50
185	Carlos Delgado, Wally Joyner (Counterparts)	.50
186	Jermaine Dye, Johnny Damon/DT	1.00
187	Randy Johnson/SF	7.50
188	Todd Hundley, Carlos Baerga/DT	.75
189	Tom Glavine/SF	2.50
190	Damon Mashore, Jason McDonald/DT	.75
191	Wade Boggs/SF	12.00
192	Al Martin, Jason Kendall/DT	.75
193	Matt Williams/SF	1.50
194	Will Clark, Dean Palmer/DT	.75
195	Sammy Sosa/SF	12.00
196	Jose Cruz, Jr., Jay Buhner/DT	.75
197	Eddie Murray/SF	10.00
198	Darin Erstad, Jason Dickson/DT	1.00
199	Fred McGriff/SF	1.50
200	Bubba Trammell, Bobby Higginson/DT	.75

ABBREVIATIONS

DT - Double Team

SF - Star Factor

UPT - Unlimited Potential/Talent

Exposure

A complete 200-card parallel set printed with Holographic Poly-Chromium technology on both sides and featuring a special "Limited Exposure" stamp. Less than 40 sets of the Star Factor Limited Exposures are thought to exist.

	NM/M
Complete Set (200):	1,200
Common Counterparts:	.75
Common Double Team:	3.00
Common Star Factor:	6.50
Common Unlimited:	4.50
Stars:	4X

Exposure Non-Glossy

In error, half (100 cards) of the Limited Exposure parallels were produced in regular technology (non-chrome) on regular (non-glossy) cardboard stock. These cards do not carry the Limited Exposure identification in the card-number box on back, but do not carry the correct cards' higher values. No checklist of which 100 cards were involved in the error is available.

	NM/M
Common Non-Glossy:	.50
Stars: 25%	

Fabric of the Game

This fractured insert set consists of 69 different cards highlighting three different technologies representing three statistical categories: Canvas (stolen bases), Leather (doubles) and Wood (home runs). Each of the 23 cards in each category are found in varying levels of scarcity: Legendary Material (one card per theme; numbered to 100), Hall of Fame Material (four cards numbered to 250), Superstar Material (five cards numbered to 500), Star Material (six cards numbered to 750), and Major League Material (seven cards numbered to 1,000).

	NM/M
Complete Set: (69)	275.00
Common Player:	1.50
Complete Canvas Set (23)	80.00
Rickey Henderson/100	12.00
Barry Bonds/250	15.00
Kenny Lofton/250	2.50
Roberto Alomar/250	4.50
Ryne Sandberg/250	12.00
Tony Gwynn/500	7.50
Barry Larkin/500	2.00
Brady Anderson/500	2.00
Chuck Knoblauch/500	2.00
Craig Biggio/500	2.00
Sammy Sosa/500	7.50
Gary Sheffield/750	2.00
Eric Young/750	1.50
Larry Walker/750	1.50
Ken Griffey Jr./750	10.00
Deion Sanders/750	1.50
Raul Mondesi/1,000	1.50
Rondell White/1,000	1.50
Derek Jeter/1,000	10.00
Nomar Garciaparra/1,000	6.00
Wilton Guerrero/1,000	1.50
Pokey Reese/1,000	1.50
Darin Erstad/1,000	2.00
Complete Leather Set (23)	90.00
Paul Molitor/100	15.00
Wade Boggs/250	12.00
Cal Ripken Jr./250	20.00
Tony Gwynn/250	12.00
Joe Carter/250	2.50
Rafael Palmeiro/500	5.00
Mark Grace/500	1.50
Bobby Bonilla/500	1.50
Andres Galarraga/500	1.50
Edgar Martinez/500	1.50
Ken Caminiti/750	1.50
Ivan Rodriguez/750	6.00
Frank Thomas/750	6.00
Jeff Bagwell/750	6.00
Albert Belle/750	1.50
Bernie Williams/750	1.50
Chipper Jones/1,000	7.50
Rusty Greer/1,000	1.50
Todd Walker/1,000	1.50
Scott Rolen/1,000	3.00
Bob Abreu/1,000	1.50
Jose Guillen/1,000	1.50
Jose Cruz Jr./1,000	1.50
Complete Wood Set (23)	110.00
Eddie Murray/100	12.00
Cal Ripken Jr./250	20.00
Barry Bonds/250	20.00
Mark McGwire/250	17.50
Fred McGriff/250	2.00
Ken Griffey Jr./500	7.50
Albert Belle/500	2.00
Frank Thomas/500	6.50
Juan Gonzalez/500	5.00
Matt Williams/500	2.00
Mike Piazza/750	7.50
Jeff Bagwell/750	6.00
Mo Vaughn/750	1.50
Gary Sheffield/750	2.00
Tim Salmon/750	1.50
David Justice/750	1.50
Manny Ramirez/1,000	5.00
Jim Thome/1,000	2.50

1997 Donruss Preferred

Each of the 200 base cards is printed on all-foil microetched stock. Conventional backs have a color player photo and a few stats. The set is fractured into four increasingly scarce levels: 100 Bronze cards, 70 Silver, 20 Gold and 10 Platinum. Instead of traditional packs, cards were sold in five-card collectible tins. Four different inserts were included with the product: Staremaster, X-Ponential Power, Cut to The Chase (a die-cut parallel) and Precious Metals. Odds of finding any insert were 1:4 packs.

	NM/M
Complete Set (200):	225.00
Common Bronze:	.10
Common Silver:	.60
Common Gold:	1.25
Common Platinum:	6.00
Cut to the Chase:	1.5X
Tin Pack (5):	2.50
Tin Box (24):	40.00
1 Frank Thomas/P	7.50
2 Ken Griffey Jr./P	12.50
3 Cecil Fielder/B	.10
4 Chuck Knoblauch/G	1.25
5 Garret Anderson/B	.10
6 Greg Maddux/P	10.00
7 Matt Williams/B	.60
8 Marquis Grissom/S	.60
9 Jason Isringhausen/B	.10
10 Larry Walker/S	.60
11 Charles Nagy/B	.10
12 Dan Wilson/B	.10
13 Albert Belle/G	1.25
14 Javier Lopez/B	.10
15 David Cone/B	.10
16 Bernard Gilkey/B	.10
17 Andres Galarraga/S	.60
18 Bill Pulsipher/B	.10
19 Alex Fernandez/B	.10
20 Andy Pettitte/S	1.25
21 Mark Grudzielanek/B	.10
22 Juan Gonzalez/P	6.00
23 Reggie Sanders/B	.10
24 Kenny Lofton/G	1.25
25 Andy Ashby/B	.10
26 John Wetteland/B	.10
27 Bobby Bonilla/B	.10
28 Hideo Nomo/G	2.50
29 Joe Carter/B	.10
30 Jose Canseco/B	.40
31 Ellis Burks/B	.10
32 Edgar Martinez/S	.60
33 Chan Ho Park/B	.10
34 David Justice/B	.10
35 Carlos Delgado/S	.50
36 Jeff Cirillo/B	.10
37 Charles Johnson/B	.10
38 Manny Ramirez/G	4.50
39 Greg Vaughn/B	.10
40 Henry Rodriguez/B	.10
41 Darryl Strawberry/B	.10
42 Jim Thome/B	2.50
43 Ryan Klesko/S	.60
44 Jermaine Allensworth/B	.10
45 Brian Jordan/B	1.25
46 Tony Gwynn/P	10.00
47 Rafael Palmeiro/S	3.50
48 Dante Bichette/B	.60
49 Ivan Rodriguez/S	3.50
50 Mark McGwire/G	8.00
51 Tim Salmon/B	.10
52 Roger Clemens/B	1.50
53 Matt Lawton/B	.10
54 Wade Boggs/S	3.50
55 Travis Fryman/B	.10
56 Bobby Higginson/B	.60
57 John Jaha/S	.60
58 Rondell White/S	.60
59 Tom Glavine/S	1.25
60 Eddie Murray/S	2.50
61 Vinny Castilla/B	.10
62 Todd Hundley/S	.10
63 Jay Buhner/S	.60
64 Paul O'Neill/B	.60
65 Steve Finley/B	.10
66 Kevin Appier/B	.10
67 Ray Durham/B	.10
68 Dave Nilsson/B	.10
69 Jeff Bagwell/S	4.50
70 Al Martin/S	.60
71 Paul Molitor/S	4.50
72 Kevin Brown/S	.60
73 Ron Gant/S	.10
74 Dwight Gooden/B	.10
75 Quinton McCracken/B	.10
76 Rusty Greer/S	.60
77 Juan Guzman/B	.10
78 Fred McGriff/S	.60
79 Tino Martinez/S	.10
80 Ray Lankford/B	.10
81 Ken Caminiti/S	1.25
82 James Baldwin/S	.10
83 Jermaine Dye/S	1.25
84 Mark Grace/S	.60
85 Pat Hentgen/S	.10
86 Jason Giambi/S	1.50
87 Brian Hunter/B	.10
88 Andy Benes/B	.10
89 Jose Rosado/B	.10
90 Shawn Green/B	.25
91 Jason Kendall/B	.10
92 Alex Rodriguez/P	15.00
93 Chipper Jones/P	10.00
94 Barry Bonds/G	9.00
95 Brady Anderson/G	1.25
96 Ryne Sandberg/S	3.50
97 Lance Johnson/B	.10
98 Cal Ripken Jr./P	17.50
99 Craig Biggio/S	.60
100 Dean Palmer/S	.10
101 Gary Sheffield/G	1.50
102 Johnny Damon/S	.35
103 Mo Vaughn/G	1.25
104 Randy Johnson/S	2.50
105 Raul Mondesi/S	.60
106 Roberto Alomar/G	2.00
107 Mike Piazza/P	12.50
108 Rey Ordonez/B	.10
109 Barry Larkin/G	1.25
110 Tony Clark/S	.60
111 Bernie Williams/S	.60
112 John Smoltz/S	1.25
113 Moises Alou/B	.10
114 Will Clark/B	.10
115 Sammy Sosa/G	6.00
116 Jim Edmonds/B	.60
117 Jeff Conine/B	.10
118 Joey Hamilton/B	.10
119 Todd Hollandsworth/B	.10
120 Troy Percival/B	.10
121 Paul Wilson/B	.10
122 Ken Hill/B	.10
123 Mariano Rivera/S	.75
124 Eric Karros/B	.10
125 Derek Jeter/G	10.00
126 Eric Young/S	.60
127 John Mabry/B	.10
128 Gregg Jefferies/B	.10
129 Ismael Valdes/S	.60
130 Marty Cordova/B	.10
131 Omar Vizquel/B	.10
132 Mike Mussina/S	1.25
133 Darin Erstad/S	.30
134 Edgar Renteria/S	.60
135 Billy Wagner/S	.10
136 Alex Ochoa/B	.10
137 Luis Castillo/B	.10
138 Rocky Coppinger/B	.10
139 Mike Sweeney/B	.10
140 Michael Tucker/B	.10
141 Chris Snopek/B	.10
142 Dmitri Young/S	.60
143 Andruw Jones/P	7.50
144 Mike Cameron/B	.60
145 Brant Brown/B	.10
146 Todd Walker/G	1.25
147 Nomar Garciaparra/G	6.00
148 Glendon Rusch/B	.10
149 Karim Garcia/S	.60
150 Bubba Trammell/S **RC**	.60
151 Todd Greene/B	.10
152 Wilton Guerrero/G	1.25
153 Scott Spiezio/B	.10
154 Brooks Kieschnick/B	.10
155 Vladimir Guerrero/S	4.50
156 Brian Giles/S **RC**	1.50
157 Pokey Reese/S	.10
158 Jason Dickson/G	1.25
159 Kevin Orie/S	.60
160 Scott Rolen/G	3.00
161 Bartolo Colon/S	.60
162 Shannon Stewart/S	1.25
163 Wendell Magee/B	.10
164 Jose Guillen/S	.60
165 Bob Abreu/B	.60
166 Deivi Cruz/B **RC**	.25
167 Alex Rodriguez/B	
(National Treasures)	3.00
168 Frank Thomas/B	
(National Treasures)	.75
169 Cal Ripken Jr./B	
(National Treasures)	4.00
170 Chipper Jones/B	
(National Treasures)	1.25
171 Mike Piazza/B	
(National Treasures)	2.50
172 Tony Gwynn/S	
(National Treasures)	3.50
173 Juan Gonzalez/B	
(National Treasures)	.40
174 Kenny Lofton/S	
(National Treasures)	.60
175 Ken Griffey Jr./S	
(National Treasures)	2.50
176 Mark McGwire/S	
(National Treasures)	3.00
177 Jeff Bagwell/B	
(National Treasures)	.75
178 Paul Molitor/S	
(National Treasures)	2.50
179 Andruw Jones/B	
(National Treasures)	.75
180 Manny Ramirez/S	
(National Treasures)	2.50
181 Ken Caminiti/S	
(National Treasures)	.60
182 Barry Bonds/S	
(National Treasures)	4.00
183 Mo Vaughn/B	
(National Treasures)	.10
184 Derek Jeter/B	
(National Treasures)	4.00
185 Barry Larkin/S	
(National Treasures)	.60
186 Ivan Rodriguez/S	
(National Treasures)	.65
187 Albert Belle/S	
(National Treasures)	.60
188 John Smoltz/S	
(National Treasures)	.60
189 Chuck Knoblauch/S	
(National Treasures)	.60
190 Brian Jordan/S	
(National Treasures)	.60
191 Gary Sheffield/S	
(National Treasures)	1.00
192 Jim Thome/S	
(National Treasures)	2.00
193 Brady Anderson/S	
(National Treasures)	.60
194 Hideo Nomo/S	
(National Treasures)	1.50
195 Sammy Sosa/S	
(National Treasures)	3.50
196 Greg Maddux/S	
(National Treasures)	1.25
197 Checklist	
(Vladimir Guerrero/B)	.40
198 Checklist	
(Scott Rolen/B)	.15
199 Checklist	
(Todd Walker/B)	.10
200 Checklist	
(Nomar Garciaparra/B)	.60

Cut To The Chase

Each of the cards in the Donruss Preferred series can also be found in this parallel set with die-cut borders, in the same bronze, silver, gold and platinum finishes. Multiplier values of the die-cuts are inverse to that usually found, with platinum cards the lowest, followed by gold, silver and bronze. Besides die-cutting, the chase cards feature a "CUT TO THE CHASE" designation at bottom.

Typical Value:	1.5X

Precious Metals

This 25-card partial parallel set features cards printed on actual silver, gold and platinum stock. Only 100 of each card were produced.

	NM/M
Common Player:	7.50
1 Frank Thomas/P	45.00
2 Ken Griffey Jr./P	75.00
3 Greg Maddux/P	60.00
4 Albert Belle/G	7.50
5 Juan Gonzalez/P	25.00
6 Kenny Lofton/G	7.50
7 Tony Gwynn/P	60.00
8 Ivan Rodriguez/G	30.00
9 Mark McGwire/G	90.00
10 Matt Williams/S	7.50
11 Wade Boggs/S	60.00
12 Eddie Murray/S	45.00
13 Jeff Bagwell/G	45.00
14 Ken Caminiti/S	7.50
15 Alex Rodriguez/P	90.00
16 Chipper Jones/P	60.00
17 Barry Bonds/S	125.00
18 Cal Ripken Jr./P	125.00
19 Mo Vaughn/G	7.50
20 Mike Piazza/P	75.00
21 Derek Jeter/G	125.00
22 Bernie Williams/S	7.50
23 Andruw Jones/P	45.00
24 Vladimir Guerrero/G	45.00
25 Jose Guillen/S	7.50

Staremasters

A 20-card insert printed on foil stock and accented with holographic foil, Staremasters is designed to show upclose "game-face" photography. Each card is sequentially numbered to 1,500. Each of the Staremasters inserts can also be found in a version overprinted with a large diagonal black "SAMPLE" on front and back. These were distributed to dealers and the media. The sample cards have a "PROMO/1500" on back in place of a serial number.

	NM/M
Complete Set: (20)	55.00
Common Player:	1.00
Samples: 50%	
1 Alex Rodriguez	6.00
2 Frank Thomas	3.00
3 Chipper Jones	4.00
4 Cal Ripken Jr.	7.50
5 Mike Piazza	4.50
6 Juan Gonzalez	2.25
7 Derek Jeter	7.50
8 Jeff Bagwell	3.00
9 Ken Griffey Jr.	4.50
10 Tony Gwynn	4.00
11 Barry Bonds	7.50
12 Albert Belle	1.00
13 Greg Maddux	4.00
14 Mark McGwire	6.00
15 Ken Caminiti	1.00
16 Hideo Nomo	2.25
17 Gary Sheffield	1.50
18 Andruw Jones	3.00
19 Mo Vaughn	1.00
20 Ivan Rodriguez	2.25

X-Ponential Power

This 20-card die-cut insert contains two top hitters from 10 different teams. Placing the cards of teammates together forms an "X" shape. Cards are printed on thick plastic stock and gold holographic foil stamping and are sequentially numbered to 3,000.

	NM/M
Complete Set (20):	50.00
Common Player:	1.00
1A Manny Ramirez	3.50

		NM/M
1B	Jim Thome	2.00
2A	Paul Molitor	3.50
2B	Chuck Knoblauch	1.00
3A	Ivan Rodriguez	2.50
3B	Juan Gonzalez	2.00
4A	Albert Belle	1.00
4B	Frank Thomas	3.50
5A	Roberto Alomar	1.25
5B	Cal Ripken Jr.	9.00
6A	Tim Salmon	1.00
6B	Jim Edmonds	1.00
7A	Ken Griffey Jr.	6.00
7B	Alex Rodriguez	7.50
8A	Chipper Jones	4.50
8B	Andruw Jones	3.50
9A	Mike Piazza	6.00
9B	Raul Mondesi	4.50
10A	Tony Gwynn	4.50
10B	Ken Caminiti	1.00

Tins

Twenty-five different players are featured on the lithographed steel tins which were the "packs" of Donruss Preferred baseball. The 3" x 4-1/2" x 5/8" tins are hinged along the left side and were produced in two versions. Predominantly blue tins are the standard package. A premium parallel version is gold-colored and serially numbered within an edition of 1,200. Gold tins were packed one per 24-pack box of Preferred. Values shown are for opened tins. Shrink-wrapped unopened tins are valued about 1.5-3X the figures shown.

		NM/M
Complete Set, Blue (25):		10.00
Common Tin:		.25
Gold:		10X
1	Frank Thomas	.40
2	Ken Griffey Jr.	.60
3	Andruw Jones	.40
4	Cal Ripken Jr.	1.00
5	Mike Piazza	.60
6	Chipper Jones	.50
7	Alex Rodriguez	.75
8	Derek Jeter	1.00
9	Juan Gonzalez	.30
10	Albert Belle	.25
11	Tony Gwynn	.50
12	Greg Maddux	.50
13	Jeff Bagwell	.50
14	Roger Clemens	.55
15	Mark McGwire	.75
16	Gary Sheffield	.30
17	Manny Ramirez	.40
18	Hideo Nomo	.30
19	Kenny Lofton	.25
20	Mo Vaughn	.25
21	Ryne Sandberg	.50
22	Barry Bonds	1.00
23	Sammy Sosa	.50
24	John Smoltz	.25
25	Ivan Rodriguez	.35

Tin Boxes

Twenty-five different players are featured on the lithographed steel boxes in which the "packs" of Donruss Preferred baseball were sold. Boxes measure about 5-1/4" x 9-1/4" x 5-3/8". Inside the removable lid is a serial number from within an edition of 1,200 (blue) or 299 (gold). The gold versions were a later, hobby-only release.

		NM/M
Complete Set, Blue (25):		70.00
Common Box:		2.00
Gold:		4X
1	Frank Thomas	3.00
2	Ken Griffey Jr.	5.00
3	Andruw Jones	3.00
4	Cal Ripken Jr.	7.50
5	Mike Piazza	5.00
6	Chipper Jones	4.00
7	Alex Rodriguez	6.00
8	Derek Jeter	7.50
9	Juan Gonzalez	2.50
10	Albert Belle	2.00
11	Tony Gwynn	4.00
12	Greg Maddux	4.00
13	Jeff Bagwell	3.00
14	Roger Clemens	4.50
15	Mark McGwire	6.00
16	Gary Sheffield	2.50
17	Manny Ramirez	3.00
18	Hideo Nomo	2.50
19	Kenny Lofton	2.00
20	Mo Vaughn	2.00
21	Ryne Sandberg	4.00
22	Barry Bonds	7.50
23	Sammy Sosa	4.00
24	John Smoltz	2.00
25	Ivan Rodriguez	2.50

1997 Donruss Signature

Donruss ventured in the autograph-per-pack market with this series featuring 100 base cards (unsigned) and various types and versions of authentically autographed cards. The suggested retail price for each five-card pack was $14.99. Base cards have textured silver-foil borders and highlights on front. Backs have a second photo and lengthy stats. A parallel insert edition of each base card was also issued. labeled "Platinum Press Proof." the parallels have blue metallic foil on front and are designated "1 of 150" on the back.

	NM/M
Complete Set (100):	15.00
Common Player:	.10
Platinum Stars/RC's:	12X
Pack (5):	7.50
Wax Box (12):	80.00
1	Mark McGwire	1.25
2	Kenny Lofton	.10
3	Tony Gwynn	.75
4	Tony Clark	.10
5	Tim Salmon	.10
6	Ken Griffey Jr.	1.00
7	Mike Piazza	1.00
8	Greg Maddux	.75
9	Roberto Alomar	.20
10	Andres Galarraga	.10
11	Roger Clemens	.90

12	Bernie Williams	.10
13	Rondell White	.10
14	Kevin Appier	.10
15	Ray Lankford	.10
16	Frank Thomas	.65
17	Will Clark	.10
18	Chipper Jones	.75
19	Jeff Bagwell	.65
20	Manny Ramirez	.65
21	Ryne Sandberg	.75
22	Paul Molitor	.65
23	Gary Sheffield	.10
24	Jim Edmonds	.10
25	Barry Larkin	.10
26	Rafael Palmeiro	.60
27	Alan Benes	.10
28	David Justice	.10
29	Randy Johnson	.65
30	Barry Bonds	1.50
31	Mo Vaughn	.10
32	Michael Tucker	.10
33	Larry Walker	.10
34	Tino Martinez	.10
35	Jose Guillen	.10
36	Carlos Delgado	.40
37	Jason Dickson	.10
38	Tom Glavine	.25
39	Raul Mondesi	.10
40	Jose Cruz Jr. RC	.50
41	Johnny Damon	.20
42	Mark Grace	.35
43	Juan Gonzalez	.35
44	Vladimir Guerrero	.65
45	Kevin Brown	.10
46	Justin Thompson	.10
47	Eric Young	.10
48	Ron Coomer	.10
49	Mark Kotsay	.10
50	Scott Rolen	.60
51	Derek Jeter	1.50
52	Jim Thome	.50
53	Fred McGriff	.10
54	Albert Belle	.10
55	Garret Anderson	.10
56	Wilton Guerrero	.10
57	Jose Canseco	.40
58	Cal Ripken Jr.	1.50
59	Sammy Sosa	.75
60	Dmitri Young	.10
61	Alex Rodriguez	1.25
62	Javier Lopez	.10
63	Sandy Alomar Jr.	.10
64	Joe Carter	.10
65	Dante Bichette	.10
66	Al Martin	.10
67	Darin Erstad	.30
68	Pokey Reese	.10
69	Brady Anderson	.10
70	Andruw Jones	.65
71	Ivan Rodriguez	.50
72	Nomar Garciaparra	.75
73	Moises Alou	.10
74	Andy Pettitte	.35
75	Jay Buhner	.10
76	Craig Biggio	.10
77	Wade Boggs	.75
78	Shawn Estes	.10
79	Neifi Perez	.10
80	Rusty Greer	.10
81	Pedro Martinez	.60
82	Mike Mussina	.40
83	Jason Giambi	.40
84	Hideo Nomo	.35
85	Todd Hundley	.10
86	Deion Sanders	.10
87	Mike Cameron	.10
88	Bobby Bonilla	.10
89	Todd Greene	.10
90	Kevin Orie	.10
91	Ken Caminiti	.10
92	Chuck Knoblauch	.10
93	Matt Morris	.10
94	Matt Williams	.10
95	Pat Hentgen	.10
96	John Smoltz	.10
97	Edgar Martinez	.10
98	Jason Kendall	.10
99	Checklist (Ken Griffey Jr.)	.50
100	Checklist (Frank Thomas)	.30

Platinum Press Proofs

This parallel insert set features metallic blue borders and graphics on front and has a "1 of 150" notation on back.

	NM/M
Common Player:	2.00
Stars:	12X

Autographs Promo

The "autograph" on the front of this promo card is a facsimile signature, rather than hand-penned. The sample is identical in format to the common red base level autographs in the set, but Thomas does not appear in that format.

	NM/M
Frank Thomas	6.00

Autographs (Red)

The basic level of authentically autographed cards found one per ($15) pack in Donruss Signature is the unnumbered "red" version. Cards have the background of the front photo printed only in red. For most players, 3,900 cards of the red version were autographed for insertion. Some players, however, signed fewer reds. Exchange cards had to be issued for Raul Mondesi and Edgar Renteria, whose signed cards were not ready when the set was first issued. It has been reported that Mondesi never signed any of the red version autograph cards. Cards are checklisted here in alphabetical order, in concordance with the larger Millenium checklist. The reported number of red cards signed appears in parentheses. This list differs significantly from the original list announced by Donruss in November 1997 due to last minute additions and deletions. Players signed in black and/or blue ink. Some players also added personal touches to some or all of their signatures, such as Bible verse citations, uniform numbers, etc.

		NM/M
Complete Set (116):		700.00
Common Player:		2.00
(1)	Jeff Abbott/3900	2.00
(2)	Bob Abreu/3900	8.00
(3)	Edgardo Alfonzo/3900	3.00
(4)	Roberto Alomar/150	50.00
(5)	Sandy Alomar Jr./1400	6.00
(6)	Moises Alou/900	10.00
(7)	Garret Anderson/3900	7.00
(8)	Andy Ashby/3900	3.00
(10)	Trey Beamon/3900	2.00
(12)	Alan Benes/3900	2.00
(13)	Geronimo Berroa/3900	2.00
(14)	Wade Boggs/150	175.00
(18)	Kevin L. Brown/3900	2.00
(19)	Brett Butler/1400	3.50
(21)	Mike Cameron/3900	7.00
(22)	Giovanni Carrara/2900	2.00
(23)	Luis Castillo/3900	4.00
(24)	Tony Clark/3900	3.00
(25)	Will Clark/1400	12.00
(27)	Lou Collier/3900	2.00
(28)	Bartolo Colon/3900	12.50
(29)	Ron Coomer/3900	2.00
(30)	Marty Cordova/3900	3.00
(31)	Jacob Cruz/3900	2.00
(32)	Jose Cruz Jr./900	8.00
(33)	Russ Davis/3900	3.00
(34)	Jason Dickson/3900	2.00
(35)	Todd Dunwoody/3900	2.00
(36)	Jermaine Dye/3900	3.00
(37)	Jim Edmonds/3900	12.00
(38)	Darin Erstad/900	8.00
(39)	Bobby Estalella/3900	3.00
(40)	Shawn Estes/3900	3.00
(41)	Jeff Fassero/3900	2.00
(42)	Andres Galarraga/900	6.00
(44)	Karim Garcia/3900	3.00
(45)	Derrick Gibson/3900	2.00
(46)	Brian Giles/3900	8.00
(47)	Tom Glavine/150	50.00
(49)	Rick Gorecki/900	4.50
(50)	Shawn Green/1900	15.00
(51)	Todd Greene/3900	3.00
(52)	Rusty Greer/3900	3.00
(53)	Ben Grieve/3900	3.00
(54)	Mark Grudzielanek/3900	3.00
(55)	Vladimir Guerrero/1900	20.00
(56)	Wilton Guerrero/2150	3.00
(57)	Jose Guillen/2900	8.00
(59)	Jeffrey Hammonds/2150	3.50
(60)	Todd Helton/1400	16.00
(61)	Todd Hollandsworth/2900	3.00
(62)	Trenidad Hubbard/900	4.00
(63)	Todd Hundley/1400	3.00
(66)	Bobby Jones/3900	3.00
(68)	Brian Jordan/1400	4.00
(69)	David Justice/900	10.00
(70)	Eric Karros/650	4.50
(71)	Jason Kendall/3900	6.00
(72)	Jimmy Key /3900	5.00
(73)	Brooks Kieschnick/3900	2.00
(74)	Ryan Klesko/225	10.00
(76)	Paul Konerko/3900	10.00
(77)	Mark Kotsay/2400	3.00
(78)	Ray Lankford/3900	4.00
(79)	Barry Larkin/150	35.00
(80)	Derrek Lee/3900	10.00
(81)	Esteban Loaiza/3900	3.00
(82)	Javier Lopez/1400	10.00
(84)	Edgar Martinez/150	50.00
(85)	Pedro Martinez/900	35.00
(87)	Rafael Medina/3900	2.00
(88)	Raul Mondesi (Exchange Card)	
(89)	Matt Morris/3900	10.00
(92)	Paul O'Neill/900	15.00
(93)	Kevin Orie/3900	2.00
(94)	David Ortiz/3900	50.00
(95)	Rafael Palmeiro/900	30.00
(96)	Jay Payton/3900	2.50
(97)	Neifi Perez/3900	2.00
(99)	Manny Ramirez/900	40.00
(100)	Joe Randa/3900	2.00
(101)	Calvin Reese/3900	3.00
(102)	Edgar Renteria (?)	20.00
(102)	Edgar Renteria (Exchange Card.)	3.00
(103)	Dennis Reyes/3900	2.00
(106)	Henry Rodriguez/3900	2.00
(108)	Scott Rolen/1900	25.00
(109)	Kirk Rueter/2900	3.00
(110)	Ryne Sandberg/400	60.00
(112)	Dwight Smith/2900	3.00
(113)	J.T. Snow/3900	4.00
(114)	Scott Spiezio/3900	3.00
(115)	Shannon Stewart/2900	3.00
(116)	Jeff Suppan/1900	3.00
(117)	Mike Sweeney/3900	6.00
(118)	Miguel Tejada/3900	6.00
(121)	Justin Thompson/2400	3.00
(122)	Brett Tomko/3900	3.00
(123)	Bubba Trammell/3900	2.50
(124)	Michael Tucker/3900	2.00
(125)	Javier Valentin/3900	2.00
(126)	Mo Vaughn/150	12.00
(127)	Robin Ventura/3900	8.00
(128)	Terrell Wade/3900	2.00
(129)	Billy Wagner/3900	12.00
(130)	Larry Walker/900	25.00
(131)	Todd Walker/2400	3.00
(132)	Rondell White/3900	6.00
(133)	Kevin Wickander/900	4.00
(134)	Chris Widger/3900	2.00
(136)	Matt Williams/150	25.00
(137)	Antone Williamson/3900	2.00
(138)	Dan Wilson/3900	2.00
(139)	Tony Womack/3900	5.00
(140)	Jaret Wright/3900	12.00
(141)	Dmitri Young/3900	8.00
(142)	Eric Young/3900	2.50
(143)	Kevin Young/3900	2.50

Century Marks (Blue)

Virtually identical to the more common red and green (Millenium) versions, the Century Marks are identifiable at first glance by the use of blue ink in the background of the front photo and the "Century Marks" designation at top. On back, the cards are numbered from 0001 through 0100 in metallic foil at center. Several players initially had to be represented in the set by exchange cards. The unnumbered cards are checklisted here alphabetically.

		NM/M
Common Player:		20.00
(1)	Jeff Abbott	20.00
(2)	Bob Abreu	30.00
(3)	Edgardo Alfonzo	20.00
(4)	Roberto Alomar	75.00
(5)	Sandy Alomar Jr.	25.00
(6)	Moises Alou	35.00
(7)	Garret Anderson	60.00
(8)	Andy Ashby	20.00
(9)	Jeff Bagwell	80.00
(10)	Trey Beamon	20.00
(11)	Albert Belle	30.00
(12)	Alan Benes	20.00
(13)	Geronimo Berroa	20.00
(14)	Wade Boggs	100.00
(15)	Barry Bonds	300.00
(16)	Bobby Bonilla	20.00
(17)	Kevin Brown	75.00
(18)	Kevin L. Brown	20.00
(19)	Jay Buhner	30.00
(20)	Brett Butler	30.00
(21)	Mike Cameron	25.00
(22)	Giovanni Carrara	20.00
(23)	Luis Castillo	20.00
(24)	Tony Clark	20.00
(25)	Will Clark	100.00
(26)	Roger Clemens	200.00
(27)	Lou Collier	20.00
(28)	Bartolo Colon	30.00
(29)	Ron Coomer	20.00
(30)	Marty Cordova	20.00
(31)	Jacob Cruz	20.00
(32)	Jose Cruz Jr.	30.00
(33)	Russ Davis	20.00
(34)	Jason Dickson	25.00
(35)	Todd Dunwoody	20.00
(36)	Jermaine Dye	20.00
(37)	Jim Edmonds	60.00
(38)	Darin Erstad	40.00
(39)	Bobby Estalella	20.00
(40)	Shawn Estes	20.00
(41)	Jeff Fassero	20.00
(42)	Andres Galarraga	30.00
(43)	Karim Garcia	20.00
(44)	Nomar Garciaparra (SP/62)	225.00
(45)	Derrick Gibson	20.00
(46)	Brian Giles	30.00
(47)	Tom Glavine	100.00
(48)	Juan Gonzalez	55.00
(49)	Rick Gorecki	20.00
(50)	Shawn Green	90.00
(51)	Todd Greene	20.00
(52)	Rusty Greer	20.00
(53)	Ben Grieve	20.00
(54)	Mark Grudzielanek	20.00
(55)	Vladimir Guerrero	100.00
(56)	Wilton Guerrero	20.00
(57)	Jose Guillen	30.00
(58)	Tony Gwynn	95.00
(59)	Jeffrey Hammonds	20.00
(60)	Todd Helton	60.00
(61)	Todd Hollandsworth	20.00
(62)	Trenidad Hubbard	20.00
(63)	Todd Hundley	25.00
(64)	Derek Jeter	200.00
(65)	Andruw Jones	50.00
(66)	Bobby Jones	20.00
(67)	Chipper Jones	100.00
(68)	Brian Jordan	35.00
(69)	David Justice	30.00
(70)	Eric Karros	25.00
(71)	Jason Kendall	30.00
(72)	Jimmy Key	50.00
(73)	Brooks Kieschnick	20.00
(74)	Ryan Klesko	25.00
(75)	Chuck Knoblauch	25.00
(76)	Paul Konerko	25.00
(77)	Mark Kotsay	25.00
(78)	Ray Lankford	20.00
(79)	Barry Larkin	60.00
(80)	Derrek Lee	40.00
(81)	Esteban Loaiza	20.00
(82)	Javy Lopez	45.00
(83)	Greg Maddux	175.00
(84)	Edgar Martinez	50.00
(85)	Pedro Martinez	100.00
(86)	Tino Martinez	50.00
(87)	Rafael Medina	20.00
(88)	Raul Mondesi	35.00
(88)	Raul Mondesi (Exchange card)	5.00
(89)	Matt Morris	40.00
(90)	Eddie Murray	75.00
(91)	Mike Mussina	80.00
(92)	Paul O'Neill	40.00
(93)	Kevin Orie	20.00
(94)	David Ortiz	100.00
(95)	Rafael Palmeiro	80.00
(96)	Jay Payton	20.00
(97)	Neifi Perez	20.00
(98)	Andy Petitte	50.00
(99)	Manny Ramirez	100.00
(100)	Joe Randa	20.00
(101)	Calvin Reese	20.00
(102)	Edgar Renteria	50.00
(102)	Edgar Renteria (Exchange card)	5.00
(103)	Dennis Reyes	20.00
(104)	Cal Ripken Jr.	225.00
(105)	Alex Rodriguez	180.00
(106)	Henry Rodriguez	20.00
(107)	Ivan Rodriguez	75.00
(108)	Scott Rolen	75.00
(109)	Kirk Rueter	20.00
(110)	Ryne Sandberg	125.00
(111)	Gary Sheffield	50.00
(112)	Dwight Smith	20.00
(113)	J.T. Snow	25.00
(114)	Scott Spiezio	20.00
(115)	Shannon Stewart	25.00
(116)	Jeff Suppan	20.00
(117)	Mike Sweeney	20.00
(118)	Miguel Tejada	120.00
(119)	Frank Thomas	80.00
(120)	Jim Thome	75.00
(120)	Jim Thome (Exchange card)	5.00
(121)	Justin Thompson	20.00
(122)	Brett Tomko	20.00
(123)	Bubba Trammell	20.00
(124)	Michael Tucker	20.00
(125)	Javier Valentin	20.00
(126)	Mo Vaughn	25.00
(127)	Robin Ventura	30.00
(128)	Terrell Wade	20.00
(129)	Billy Wagner	40.00
(130)	Larry Walker	80.00
(131)	Todd Walker	25.00
(132)	Rondell White	25.00
(133)	Kevin Wickander	20.00
(134)	Chris Widger	20.00
(135)	Bernie Williams	75.00
(136)	Matt Williams	30.00
(137)	Antone Williamson	20.00
(138)	Dan Wilson	20.00
(139)	Tony Womack	25.00
(140)	Jaret Wright	35.00
(141)	Dmitri Young	30.00
(142)	Eric Young	30.00
(143)	Kevin Young	20.00

Millennium Marks (Green)

One thousand cards of most of the players who signed Signature Autographs are found in an edition marked on front as "Millenium Marks." These cards are also distinguished by the use of green ink in the background of the front photo. On back, the cards have a silver-foil serial number between (generally) 0101-1,000. Some cards as noted in the alphabetical checklist here were produced in lower numbers. The MM autographs were a random insert among the one-per-pack autographed cards found in $15 packs of Donruss Signature. Packs carried exchange cards redeemable for autographed cards of Raul Mondesi, Edgar Renteria and Jim Thome. This checklist differs significantly from that released in November 1997 by Donruss due to the last-minute addition, deletion and substitution of players. It is possible that cards exist of players not shown here.

		NM/M
Complete Set (143):		1,450
Common Player:		2.00
(1)	Jeff Abbott	2.00
(2)	Bob Abreu	8.00
(3)	Edgardo Alfonzo	5.00
(4)	Roberto Alomar	20.00
(5)	Sandy Alomar Jr.	8.00
(6)	Moises Alou	15.00
(7)	Garret Anderson	10.00
(8)	Andy Ashby	5.00
(9)	Jeff Bagwell/400	75.00
(10)	Trey Beamon	2.00
(11)	Albert Belle/400	12.50
(12)	Alan Benes	5.00
(13)	Geronimo Berroa	2.00
(14)	Wade Boggs	30.00
(15)	Barry Bonds/400	200.00
(16)	Bobby Bonilla/900	7.50
(17)	Kevin Brown/900	12.00
(18)	Kevin L. Brown	2.00
(19)	Jay Buhner/900	10.00
(20)	Brett Butler	6.00
(21)	Mike Cameron	4.00
(22)	Giovanni Carrara	2.00
(23)	Luis Castillo	5.00
(24)	Tony Clark	5.00
(25)	Will Clark	12.00
(26)	Roger Clemens/400	120.00
(27)	Lou Collier	2.00
(28)	Bartolo Colon	8.00
(29)	Ron Coomer	2.00
(30)	Marty Cordova	2.00
(31)	Jacob Cruz	2.00
(32)	Jose Cruz Jr.	6.00
(33)	Russ Davis	2.00
(34)	Jason Dickson	5.00
(35)	Todd Dunwoody	5.00
(36)	Jermaine Dye	5.00
(37)	Jim Edmonds	30.00
(38)	Darin Erstad	10.00
(39)	Bobby Estalella	3.00
(40)	Shawn Estes	5.00
(41)	Jeff Fassero	4.00
(42)	Andres Galarraga	10.00
(43)	Karim Garcia	3.50
(44)	Nomar Garciaparra/650	75.00
(45)	Derrick Gibson	4.00
(46)	Brian Giles	5.00
(47)	Tom Glavine	25.00
(48)	Juan Gonzalez/900	25.00
(49)	Rick Gorecki	2.00
(50)	Shawn Green	20.00
(51)	Todd Greene	7.50
(52)	Rusty Greer	7.50
(53)	Ben Grieve	5.00
(54)	Mark Grudzielanek	2.00
(55)	Vladimir Guerrero	25.00
(56)	Wilton Guerrero	2.00
(57)	Jose Guillen	6.00
(58)	Tony Gwynn/900	30.00
(59)	Jeffrey Hammonds	2.00
(60)	Todd Helton	30.00
(61)	Todd Hollandsworth	2.00
(62)	Trenidad Hubbard	2.00
(63)	Todd Hundley	6.00
(64)	Derek Jeter/400	100.00
(65)	Andruw Jones	15.00
(66)	Bobby Jones	2.00
(67)	Chipper Jones	30.00
(68)	Brian Jordan	7.50
(69)	David Justice	10.00
(70)	Eric Karros	6.00
(71)	Jason Kendall	8.00
(72)	Jimmy Key	2.00
(73)	Brooks Kieschnick	4.00
(74)	Ryan Klesko	8.00
(75)	Chuck Knoblauch/900	5.00
(76)	Paul Konerko	5.00
(77)	Mark Kotsay	6.00
(78)	Ray Lankford	2.00
(79)	Barry Larkin	30.00
(80)	Derek Lee	20.00
(81)	Esteban Loaiza	2.00
(82)	Javy Lopez	8.00
(83)	Greg Maddux/400	80.00
(84)	Edgar Martinez	25.00
(85)	Pedro Martinez	40.00
(86)	Tino Martinez/900	15.00
(87)	Rafael Medina	2.00
(88)	Raul Mondesi	10.00
(88)	Raul Mondesi (Exchange Card.)	2.00
(89)	Matt Morris	15.00
(90)	Eddie Murray/900	27.50
(91)	Mike Mussina	20.00
(92)	Paul O'Neill	12.50
(93)	Kevin Orie	2.00
(94)	David Ortiz	40.00
(95)	Rafael Palmeiro	30.00
(96)	Jay Payton	5.00
(97)	Neifi Perez	2.00
(98)	Andy Petitte/900	25.00
(99)	Manny Ramirez	30.00
(100)	Joe Randa	2.00
(101)	Calvin Reese	2.00
(102)	Edgar Renteria	30.00
(102)	Edgar Renteria (Exchange Card.)	2.00
(103)	Dennis Reyes	3.00
(104)	Cal Ripken Jr./400	135.00
(105)	Alex Rodriguez/400	100.00
(106)	Henry Rodriguez	3.00
(107)	Ivan Rodriguez/900	20.00
(108)	Scott Rolen	25.00
(109)	Kirk Rueter	2.00
(110)	Ryne Sandberg	40.00
(111)	Gary Sheffield/400	25.00
(112)	Dwight Smith	2.00
(113)	J.T. Snow	7.50
(114)	Scott Spiezio	5.00
(115)	Shannon Stewart	2.00
(116)	Jeff Suppan	2.00
(117)	Mike Sweeney	5.00
(118)	Miguel Tejada	40.00
(119)	Frank Thomas/400	50.00
(120)	Jim Thome/900	30.00
(120)	Jim Thome (Exchange Card.)	2.00
(121)	Justin Thompson	2.00
(122)	Brett Tomko	2.00
(123)	Bubba Trammell	4.00
(124)	Michael Tucker	2.00
(125)	Javier Valentin	2.00
(126)	Mo Vaughn	8.00
(127)	Robin Ventura	8.00
(128)	Terrell Wade	2.00
(129)	Billy Wagner	10.00
(130)	Larry Walker	20.00
(131)	Todd Walker	6.00
(132)	Rondell White	6.00
(133)	Kevin Wickander	2.00
(134)	Chris Widger	2.00
(135)	Bernie Williams/400	60.00
(136)	Matt Williams	8.00
(137)	Antone Williamson	2.00
(138)	Dan Wilson	2.00
(139)	Tony Womack	2.00
(140)	Jaret Wright	15.00
(141)	Dmitri Young	5.00
(142)	Eric Young	5.00
(143)	Kevin Young	2.00

Notable Nicknames

Current and former players whose nicknames are instantly recognized are featured in this Signature Series insert. The autographs are generally enhanced by the appearance of those nicknames, though Roger Clemens omitted "The Rocket" from many of his cards. Backs have a serial number from within an edition of 200 of each card.

		NM/M
Common Player:		20.00
(1)	Ernie Banks (Mr. Cub)	150.00
(2)	Tony Clark (The Tiger)	20.00
(3)	Roger Clemens (The Rocket)	300.00
(4)	Reggie Jackson (Mr. October)	125.00
(5)	Randy Johnson (Big Unit)	300.00
(6)	Stan Musial (The Man)	180.00
(7)	Ivan Rodriguez (Pudge)	100.00
(8)	Frank Thomas (The Big Hurt)	125.00

(9)	Mo Vaughn (Hit Dog)	20.00
(10)	Billy Wagner (The Kid)	40.00

Significant Signatures

Retired superstars from the early 1960s through the mid 1990s are featured in this insert series. Cards are horizontal in format with color photos on front and back. Generally autographed on front, each card is serially numbered on back from within an edition of 2,000. The unnumbered cards are listed here in alphabetical order.

		NM/M
Common Player:		15.00
(1)	Ernie Banks	25.00
(2)	Johnny Bench	30.00
(3)	Yogi Berra	30.00
(4)	George Brett	40.00
(5)	Lou Brock	25.00
(6)	Rod Carew	25.00
(7)	Steve Carlton	20.00
(8)	Larry Doby	35.00
(9)	Carlton Fisk	30.00
(10)	Bob Gibson	25.00
(11)	Reggie Jackson	25.00
(12)	Al Kaline	25.00
(13)	Harmon Killebrew	30.00
(14)	Don Mattingly	40.00
(15)	Stan Musial	45.00
(16)	Jim Palmer	15.00
(17)	Brooks Robinson	25.00
(18)	Frank Robinson	15.00
(19)	Mike Schmidt	35.00
(20)	Tom Seaver	20.00
(21)	Duke Snider	20.00
(22)	Carl Yastrzemski	40.00

Frank Thomas The Big Heart

In one of several specialty card charitable endeavors, Thomas and Donruss teamed up to issue this set as a fund raiser for "The Big Hurt's" charitable foundation. Each of the cards was available in an edition limited to 2,500 for a $20 donation. Cards are standard 2-1/2" x 3-1/2" with posed photos on front and "THE BIG HEART,"cd a play on his nickname. Backs have information on the foundation, a second photo and a gold-foil serial number.

		NM/M
Complete Set (4):		20.00
Common Player:		5.00
1	Frank Thomas, Rod Carew	5.00
2	Frank Thomas	5.00
3	Frank Thomas	5.00
4	Frank Thomas	5.00

1997 Donruss VXP 1.0

This set was issued to accompany the hobby's first major effort to bring baseball cards into the computer age. The standard-format cards have motion-variable portrait and action pho-

tos on front and another photo on back. Cards were sold in packs of 10 with one of six CD ROMs for about $10.

		NM/M
Complete Set (50):		17.50
Common Player:		.25
1	Darin Erstad	.40
2	Jim Thome	.50
3	Alex Rodriguez	1.50
4	Greg Maddux	1.00
5	Scott Rolen	.65
6	Roberto Alomar	.30
7	Tony Clark	.25
8	Randy Johnson	.75
9	Sammy Sosa	1.00
10	Jose Guillen	.25
11	Cal Ripken Jr.	2.00
12	Paul Molitor	.75
13	Jose Cruz Jr.	.20
14	Barry Larkin	.25
15	Ken Caminiti	.25
16	Rafael Palmeiro	.65
17	Chuck Knoblauch	.25
18	Juan Gonzalez	.40
19	Larry Walker	.25
20	Tony Gwynn	1.00
21	Brady Anderson	.25
22	Derek Jeter	2.00
23	Rusty Greer	.25
24	Gary Sheffield	.35
25	Barry Bonds	2.00
26	Mo Vaughn	.20
27	Tino Martinez	.25
28	Ivan Rodriguez	.65
29	Jeff Bagwell	.75
30	Tim Salmon	.25
31	Nomar Garciaparra	1.00
32	Bernie Williams	.25
33	Kenny Lofton	.25
34	Mike Piazza	1.25
35	Jim Edmonds	.25
36	Frank Thomas	.75
37	Andy Pettitte	.35
38	Andruw Jones	.75
39	Raul Mondesi	.25
40	John Smoltz	.25
41	Albert Belle	.25
42	Mark McGwire	1.50
43	Chipper Jones	1.00
44	Hideo Nomo	.40
45	David Justice	.25
46	Manny Ramirez	.75
47	Ken Griffey Jr.	1.25
48	Roger Clemens	1.00
49	Vladimir Guerrero	.75
50	Ryne Sandberg	1.00

CDs

One of the earliest attempts to bring baseball cards into the computer age was Donruss "VXP 1.0 CD ROM" trading cards. Retailed, with 10 special-series player cards for about $10, the 4" x 2-3/4" "card" is a CD with player portrait and action photos on front. The CD was sold in a cardboard folder with the player's picture on front and instructions for use inside. CDs feature player stats, action footage and other interactive elements.

		NM/M
Complete Set (6):		12.00
Common Player:		2.00
(1)	Ken Griffey Jr.	2.25
(2)	Greg Maddux	2.00
(3)	Mike Piazza	2.25
(4)	Cal Ripken Jr.	3.00
(5)	Alex Rodriguez	2.50
(6)	Frank Thomas	2.50

1998 Donruss

This 170-card set includes 155 regular player cards, the 10-card Fan Club subset and five checklists. The cards have color photos and the player's name listed at the bottom. The backs have a horizontal layout with stats and a biography on the left and another photo on the right. The base set is paralleled twice. Silver Press Proofs is a silver foil and die-cut parallel numbered "1 of 1,500." Gold Press Proofs is die-cut, has gold foil and is numbered "1 of 500." The inserts are Crusade, Diamond Kings, Longball Leaders, Production Line and Rated Rookies.

		NM/M
Complete Set (420):		30.00
Complete Series 1 (170):		10.00
Complete Update 2 (250):		15.00
Common Player:		.05
Silver Press Proofs:		3X
Production 1,500 Sets		
Gold Press Proofs:		8X
Production 500 Sets		
Pack (10):		1.00
Wax Box (24):		16.00
1	Paul Molitor	.75
2	Juan Gonzalez	.40
3	Darryl Kile	.05
4	Randy Johnson	.75
5	Tom Glavine	.25
6	Pat Hentgen	.05
7	David Justice	.05
8	Kevin Brown	.05
9	Mike Mussina	.45
10	Ken Caminiti	.05
11	Todd Hundley	.05
12	Frank Thomas	.75
13	Ray Lankford	.05
14	Justin Thompson	.05
15	Jason Dickson	.05
16	Kenny Lofton	.25
17	Ivan Rodriguez	.65
18	Pedro Martinez	.75
19	Brady Anderson	.05
20	Barry Larkin	.05
21	Chipper Jones	1.50
22	Tony Gwynn	1.50
23	Roger Clemens	1.50
24	Sandy Alomar Jr.	.05
25	Tino Martinez	.05
26	Jeff Bagwell	.75
27	Shawn Estes	.05
28	Ken Griffey Jr.	1.75
29	Javier Lopez	.05
30	Denny Neagle	.05
31	Mike Piazza	1.75
32	Andres Galarraga	.05
33	Larry Walker	.05
34	Alex Rodriguez	2.00
35	Greg Maddux	1.50
36	Albert Belle	.05
37	Barry Bonds	2.50
38	Mo Vaughn	.05
39	Kevin Appier	.05
40	Wade Boggs	1.50
41	Garret Anderson	.05
42	Jeffrey Hammonds	.05
43	Marquis Grissom	.05
44	Jim Edmonds	.05
45	Brian Jordan	.05
46	Raul Mondesi	.05
47	John Valentin	.05
48	Brad Radke	.05
49	Ismael Valdes	.05
50	Matt Stairs	.05
51	Matt Williams	.05
52	Reggie Jefferson	.05
53	Alan Benes	.05
54	Charles Johnson	.05
55	Chuck Knoblauch	.05
56	Edgar Martinez	.05
57	Nomar Garciaparra	1.50
58	Craig Biggio	.05
59	Bernie Williams	.05
60	David Cone	.05
61	Cal Ripken Jr.	2.50
62	Mark McGwire	2.00
63	Roberto Alomar	.20
64	Fred McGriff	.05
65	Eric Karros	.05
66	Robin Ventura	.05
67	Darin Erstad	.30
68	Michael Tucker	.05
69	Jim Thome	.60
70	Mark Grace	.05
71	Lou Collier	.05
72	Karim Garcia	.05
73	Alex Fernandez	.05
74	J.T. Snow	.05
75	Reggie Sanders	.05
76	John Smoltz	.05
77	Tim Salmon	.05
78	Paul O'Neill	.05
79	Vinny Castilla	.05
80	Rafael Palmeiro	.65
81	Jaret Wright	.05
82	Jay Buhner	.05
83	Brett Butler	.05
84	Todd Greene	.05
85	Scott Rolen	.65
86	Sammy Sosa	1.50
87	Jason Giambi	.50
88	Carlos Delgado	.05
89	Deion Sanders	.05
90	Wilton Guerrero	.05
91	Andy Pettitte	.30
92	Brian Giles	.05
93	Dmitri Young	.05
94	Ron Coomer	.05
95	Mike Cameron	.05
96	Edgardo Alfonzo	.05
97	Jimmy Key	.05
98	Ryan Klesko	.05
99	Andy Benes	.05
100	Derek Jeter	2.50
101	Jeff Fassero	.05
102	Neifi Perez	.05
103	Hideo Nomo	.40
104	Andruw Jones	.75
105	Todd Helton	.50
106	Livan Hernandez	.05
107	Brett Tomko	.05
108	Shannon Stewart	.05
109	Bartolo Colon	.05
110	Matt Morris	.05
111	Miguel Tejada	.20
112	Pokey Reese	.05
113	Fernando Tatis	.05
114	Todd Dunwoody	.05
115	Jose Cruz Jr.	.05
116	Chan Ho Park	.05
117	Kevin Young	.05
118	Rickey Henderson	.75
119	Hideki Irabu	.05
120	Francisco Cordova	.05
121	Al Martin	.05
122	Tony Clark	.25
123	Curt Schilling	.25
124	Rusty Greer	.05
125	Jose Canseco	.40
126	Edgar Renteria	.05
127	Todd Walker	.05
128	Wally Joyner	.05
129	Bill Mueller	.05
130	Jose Guillen	.05
131	Manny Ramirez	.75
132	Bobby Higginson	.05
133	Kevin Orie	.05
134	Will Clark	.05
135	Dave Nilsson	.05
136	Jason Kendall	.05
137	Ivan Cruz	.05
138	Gary Sheffield	.25
139	Bubba Trammell	.05
140	Vladimir Guerrero	.75
141	Dennis Reyes	.05
142	Bobby Bonilla	.05
143	Ruben Rivera	.05
144	Ben Grieve	.05
145	Moises Alou	.05
146	Tony Womack	.05
147	Eric Young	.05
148	Paul Konerko	.10
149	Dante Bichette	.05
150	Joe Carter	.05
151	Rondell White	.05
152	Chris Holt	.05
153	Shawn Green	.20
154	Mark Grudzielanek	.05
155	Jermaine Dye	.05
156	Ken Griffey Jr. (Fan Club)	.90
157	Frank Thomas (Fan Club)	.50
158	Chipper Jones (Fan Club)	.75
159	Mike Piazza (Fan Club)	.90
160	Cal Ripken Jr. (Fan Club)	1.25
161	Greg Maddux (Fan Club)	.75
162	Juan Gonzalez (Fan Club)	.20
163	Alex Rodriguez (Fan Club)	1.00
164	Mark McGwire (Fan Club)	1.00
165	Derek Jeter (Fan Club)	1.25
166	Checklist (Larry Walker)	.05
167	Checklist (Tony Gwynn)	.60
168	Checklist (Tino Martinez)	.05

#	Player	NM/M
169	Checklist (Scott Rolen)	.15
170	Checklist (Nomar Garciaparra)	.60
171	Mike Sweeney	.05
172	Dustin Hermanson	.05
173	Darren Dreifort	.05
174	Ron Gant	.05
175	Todd Hollandsworth	.05
176	John Jaha	.05
177	Kerry Wood	.30
178	Chris Stynes	.05
179	Kevin Elster	.05
180	Derek Bell	.05
181	Darryl Strawberry	.05
182	Damion Easley	.05
183	Jeff Cirillo	.05
184	John Thomson	.05
185	Dan Wilson	.05
186	Jay Bell	.05
187	Bernard Gilkey	.05
188	Marc Valdes	.05
189	Ramon Martinez	.05
190	Charles Nagy	.05
191	Derek Lowe	.05
192	Andy Benes	.05
193	Delino DeShields	.05
194	Ryan Jackson RC	.05
195	Kenny Lofton	.05
196	Chuck Knoblauch	.05
197	Andres Galarraga	.05
198	Jose Canseco	.50
199	John Olerud	.05
200	Lance Johnson	.05
201	Darryl Kile	.05
202	Luis Castillo	.05
203	Joe Carter	.05
204	Dennis Eckersley	.65
205	Steve Finley	.05
206	Esteban Loaiza	.05
207	Ryan Christenson RC	.05
208	Deivi Cruz	.05
209	Mariano Rivera	.15
210	Mike Judd RC	.05
211	Billy Wagner	.05
212	Scott Spiezio	.05
213	Russ Davis	.05
214	Jeff Suppan	.05
215	Doug Glanville	.05
216	Dmitri Young	.05
217	Rey Ordonez	.05
218	Cecil Fielder	.05
219	Masato Yoshii RC	.10
220	Raul Casanova	.05
221	Rolando Arrojo RC	.20
222	Ellis Burks	.05
223	Butch Huskey	.05
224	Brian Hunter	.05
225	Marquis Grissom	.05
226	Kevin Brown	.05
227	Joe Randa	.05
228	Henry Rodriguez	.05
229	Omar Vizquel	.05
230	Fred McGriff	.05
231	Matt Williams	.05
232	Moises Alou	.05
233	Travis Fryman	.05
234	Wade Boggs	1.50
235	Pedro Martinez	.75
236	Rickey Henderson	.75
237	Bubba Trammell	.05
238	Mike Caruso	.05
239	Wilson Alvarez	.05
240	Geronimo Berroa	.05
241	Eric Milton	.05
242	Scott Erickson	.05
243	Todd Erdos RC	.05
244	Bobby Hughes	.05
245	Dave Hollins	.05
246	Dean Palmer	.05
247	Carlos Baerga	.05
248	Jose Silva	.05
249	Jose Cabrera RC	.05
250	Tom Evans	.05
251	Marty Cordova	.05
252	Hanley Frias RC	.05
253	Javier Valentin	.05
254	Mario Valdez	.05
255	Joey Cora	.05
256	Mike Lansing	.05
257	Jeff Kent	.05
258	David Dellucci RC	.10
259	Curtis King RC	.05
260	David Segui	.05
261	Royce Clayton	.05
262	Jeff Blauser	.05
263	Manny Aybar RC	.05
264	Mike Cather RC	.05
265	Todd Zeile	.05
266	Richard Hidalgo	.05
267	Dante Powell	.05
268	Mike DeJean RC	.05
269	Ken Cloude	.05
270	Danny Klassen RC	.05
271	Sean Casey	.15
272	A.J. Hinch	.05
273	Rich Butler RC	.05
274	Ben Ford RC	.05
275	Billy McMillon	.05
276	Wilson Delgado	.05
277	Orlando Cabrera	.05
278	Geoff Jenkins	.05
279	Enrique Wilson	.05
280	Derek Lee	.60
281	Marc Pisciotta RC	.05
282	Abraham Nunez	.05
283	Aaron Boone	.05
284	Brad Fullmer	.05
285	Rob Stanifer RC	.05
286	Preston Wilson	.05
287	Greg Norton	.05
288	Bobby Smith	.05
289	Josh Booty	.05
290	Russell Branyan	.05
291	Jeremi Gonzalez	.05
292	Michael Coleman	.05
293	Cliff Politte	.05
294	Eric Ludwick	.05
295	Rafael Medina	.05
296	Jason Varitek	.05
297	Ron Wright	.05
298	Mark Kotsay	.05
299	David Ortiz	.50
300	Frank Catalanotto RC	.20
301	Robinson Checo	.05
302	Kevin Millwood RC	.75
303	Jacob Cruz	.05
304	Javier Vazquez	.05
305	Magglio Ordonez RC	1.50
306	Kevin Witt	.05
307	Derrick Gibson	.05
308	Shane Monahan	.05
309	Brian Rose	.05
310	Bobby Estalella	.05
311	Desi Relaford	.05
312	Esteban Yan RC	.05
313	Ricky Ledee	.05
314	Steve Woodard RC	.05
315	Pat Watkins	.05
316	Damian Moss	.05
317	Bob Abreu	.05
318	Jeff Abbott	.05
319	Miguel Cairo	.05
320	Rigo Beltran RC	.05
321	Tony Saunders	.05
322	Randall Simon	.05
323	Hiram Bocachica	.05
324	Richie Sexson	.05
325	Karim Garcia	.05
326	Mike Lowell RC	.50
327	Pat Cline	.05
328	Matt Clement	.05
329	Scott Elarton	.05
330	Manuel Barrios RC	.05
331	Bruce Chen	.05
332	Juan Encarnacion	.05
333	Travis Lee	.05
334	Wes Helms	.05
335	Chad Fox RC	.05
336	Donnie Sadler	.05
337	Carlos Mendoza RC	.05
338	Damian Jackson	.05
339	Julio Ramirez RC	.05
340	John Halama RC	.05
341	Felix Heredia	.05
342	Edwin Diaz	.05
343	Felix Martinez	.05
344	Eli Marrero	.05
345	Carl Pavano	.05
346	Vladimir Guerrero/HL	.40
347	Barry Bonds/HL	1.25
348	Darin Erstad/HL	.10
349	Albert Belle/HL	.05
350	Kenny Lofton/HL	.05
351	Mo Vaughn/HL	.05
352	Jose Cruz Jr./HL	.05
353	Tony Clark/HL	.05
354	Roberto Alomar/HL	.10
355	Manny Ramirez/HL	.40
356	Paul Molitor/HL	.40
357	Jim Thome/HL	.40
358	Tino Martinez/HL	.05
359	Tim Salmon/HL	.05
360	David Justice/HL	.05
361	Raul Mondesi/HL	.05
362	Mark Grace/HL	.05
363	Craig Biggio/HL	.05
364	Larry Walker/HL	.05
365	Mark McGwire/HL	1.00
366	Juan Gonzalez/HL	.20
367	Derek Jeter/HL	1.25
368	Chipper Jones/HL	.75
369	Frank Thomas/HL	.50
370	Alex Rodriguez/HL	1.00
371	Mike Piazza/HL	.90
372	Tony Gwynn/HL	.75
373	Jeff Bagwell/HL	.40
374	Nomar Garciaparra/HL	.40
375	Ken Griffey Jr./HL	.90
376	Livan Hernandez (Untouchables)	
377	Chan Ho Park (Untouchables)	
378	Mike Mussina (Untouchables)	
379	Andy Pettitte (Untouchables)	.05
380	Greg Maddux (Untouchables)	.75
381	Hideo Nomo (Untouchables)	.20
382	Roger Clemens (Untouchables)	.80
383	Randy Johnson (Untouchables)	
384	Pedro Martinez (Untouchables)	
385	Jaret Wright (Untouchables)	.05
386	Ken Griffey Jr. (Spirit of the Game)	.90
387	Todd Helton (Spirit of the Game)	.05
388	Paul Konerko (Spirit of the Game)	.05
389	Cal Ripken Jr. (Spirit of the Game)	1.25
390	Larry Walker (Spirit of the Game)	.05
391	Ken Caminiti (Spirit of the Game)	.05
392	Jose Guillen (Spirit of the Game)	.05
393	Jim Edmonds (Spirit of the Game)	.05
394	Barry Larkin (Spirit of the Game)	.05
395	Bernie Williams (Spirit of the Game)	.05
396	Tony Clark (Spirit of the Game)	.05
397	Jose Cruz Jr. (Spirit of the Game)	.05
398	Ivan Rodriguez (Spirit of the Game)	.30
399	Darin Erstad (Spirit of the Game)	.10
400	Scott Rolen (Spirit of the Game)	.15
401	Mark McGwire (Spirit of the Game)	1.00
402	Andruw Jones (Spirit of the Game)	.40
403	Juan Gonzalez (Spirit of the Game)	.20
404	Derek Jeter (Spirit of the Game)	1.25
405	Chipper Jones (Spirit of the Game)	.75
406	Greg Maddux (Spirit of the Game)	.75
407	Frank Thomas (Spirit of the Game)	.50
408	Alex Rodriguez (Spirit of the Game)	1.00
409	Mike Piazza (Spirit of the Game)	.90
410	Tony Gwynn (Spirit of the Game)	.75
411	Jeff Bagwell (Spirit of the Game)	.40
412	Nomar Garciaparra (Spirit of the Game)	.75
413	Hideo Nomo (Spirit of the Game)	.20
414	Barry Bonds (Spirit of the Game)	1.25
415	Ben Grieve (Spirit of the Game)	.05
416	Checklist (Barry Bonds)	1.25
417	Checklist (Mark McGwire)	1.00
418	Checklist (Roger Clemens)	.65
419	Checklist (Livan Hernandez)	.05
420	Checklist (Ken Griffey Jr.)	.75

Silver Press Proofs

Silver Press Proofs paralleled all 420 cards in the Donruss and Donruss Update Baseball. Cards featured silver foil stamping and a die-cut top right corner. Backs had a silver tint and were numbered "1 of 1500" in the bottom left corner.

	NM/M
Complete Set (420):	150.00
Common Player:	.50
Stars/RC's:	2X
Production 1,500 Sets	

Gold Press Proofs

All 420 cards in Donruss and Donruss Update were also issued in Gold Press Proofs. These cards were die-cut on the top right corner and contained gold foil stamping.

Backs featured a gold tint and "1 of 500" was printed in black in the bottom-left corner.

	NM/M
Complete Set (420):	300.00
Common Player:	1.00
Stars/RC's:	6X
Production 500 Sets	

Crusade

This 100-card insert was included in 1998 Donruss (40 cards), Leaf (30) and Donruss Update (30). The cards use refractive technology and the background features heraldic-style lions. The cards are sequentially numbered to 250. Crusade Purple (numbered to 100) and Red (25) parallels were also inserted in the three products.

	NM/M
Complete Set, Green (40):	425.00
Common Player:	6.00
Production 250 Sets	
Purples (100 Sets):	3X
Reds (25 Sets):	12X
5 Jason Dickson	6.00
6 Todd Greene	6.00
7 Roberto Alomar	7.50
8 Cal Ripken Jr.	60.00
12 Mo Vaughn	6.00
13 Nomar Garciaparra	30.00
16 Mike Cameron	6.00
20 Sandy Alomar Jr.	6.00
21 David Justice	6.00
25 Justin Thompson	6.00
27 Kevin Appier	6.00
33 Tino Martinez	6.00
36 Hideki Irabu	6.00
37 Jose Canseco	10.00
39 Ken Griffey Jr.	40.00
42 Edgar Martinez	6.00
45 Will Clark	6.00
47 Rusty Greer	6.00
50 Shawn Green	9.00
51 Jose Cruz Jr.	6.00
52 Kenny Lofton	6.00
53 Chipper Jones	30.00
62 Kevin Orie	6.00
65 Deion Sanders	6.00
67 Larry Walker	6.00
68 Dante Bichette	6.00
71 Todd Helton	15.00
74 Bobby Bonilla	6.00
75 Kevin Brown	6.00
78 Craig Biggio	6.00
82 Wilton Guerrero	6.00
85 Pedro Martinez	20.00
86 Edgardo Alfonzo	6.00
88 Scott Rolen	15.00
89 Francisco Cordova	6.00
90 Jose Guillen	6.00
92 Ray Lankford	6.00
93 Mark McGwire	45.00
94 Matt Morris	6.00
100 Shawn Estes	6.00

Days

Similar in design, but featuring heavier stock, a metallic foil background and gold-foil graphic highlights on front, these cards were part of a ballpark promotion conducted by Donruss during the 1998 baseball season. Fans were given exchange cards at selected ballparks which could be traded at specially designated card shops in those locations for one of these premium star cards. Production was reportedly fewer than 10,000 of each card. Backs are numbered "X of 14," but are otherwise identical to the regular-issue version.

	NM/M
Complete Set (14):	16.00
Common Player:	.50
1 Frank Thomas	1.00
2 Tony Clark	.50
3 Ivan Rodriguez	.65
4 David Justice	.50
5 Nomar Garciaparra	1.50
6 Mark McGwire	2.50
7 Travis Lee	.50
8 Cal Ripken Jr.	3.00
9 Jeff Bagwell	1.00
10 Barry Bonds	3.00
11 Ken Griffey Jr.	2.00
12 Derek Jeter	3.00
13 Raul Mondesi	.50
14 Greg Maddux	1.50

Diamond Kings

Diamond Kings is a 20-card insert featuring a painted portrait by Dan Gardiner. Backs have a ghosted image of the portrait with a player biography and the card's number overprinted. A total of 10,000 sets were produced with the first 500 of each card printed on canvas. A Frank Thomas sample card was also created.

	NM/M
Complete Set (20):	65.00
Common Player:	2.00
Production 9,500 Sets	
Canvas (1st 500 Sets):	2X
1 Cal Ripken Jr.	9.00
2 Greg Maddux	4.50
3 Ivan Rodriguez	2.50
4 Tony Gwynn	4.50
5 Paul Molitor	3.00
6 Kenny Lofton	2.00
7 Andy Pettitte	2.00
8 Darin Erstad	2.00
9 Randy Johnson	3.00
10 Derek Jeter	9.00
11 Hideo Nomo	2.50
12 David Justice	2.00
13 Bernie Williams	2.00
14 Roger Clemens	5.00
15 Barry Larkin	2.00
16 Andruw Jones	3.00
17 Mike Piazza	6.50
18 Frank Thomas	3.00
18s Frank Thomas (Sample)	3.00
19 Alex Rodriguez	7.50
20 Ken Griffey Jr.	6.50

Longball Leaders

Longball Leaders features 24 top home run hitters. The right border features a home run meter with zero at the bottom, 61 at the top and the player's 1997 home run total marked. Each card is sequentially numbered to 5,000.

	NM/M
Complete Set (24):	50.00
Common Player:	1.00
Production 5,000 Sets	
1 Ken Griffey Jr.	5.00
2 Mark McGwire	6.00
3 Tino Martinez	1.00
4 Barry Bonds	7.50
5 Frank Thomas	3.00
6 Albert Belle	1.00
7 Mike Piazza	5.00
8 Chipper Jones	4.00
9 Vladimir Guerrero	3.00
10 Matt Williams	1.00
11 Sammy Sosa	4.00
12 Tim Salmon	1.00
13 Raul Mondesi	1.00
14 Jeff Bagwell	3.00
15 Mo Vaughn	1.00
16 Manny Ramirez	3.00
17 Jim Thome	2.00
18 Jim Edmonds	1.00
19 Tony Clark	1.00
20 Nomar Garciaparra	4.00
21 Juan Gonzalez	1.50
22 Scott Rolen	2.00
23 Larry Walker	1.00
24 Andres Galarraga	1.00

Production Line-ob

This 20-card insert is printed on holographic foil board. Inserted in magazine packs, this insert features player's with a high on-base percentage in 1997. Each player's card is sequentially numbered to his on-base percentage from that season. The card back has a player photo and a list of the 20 players with their stat.

	NM/M
Complete Set (20):	85.00
Common Player:	1.50
1 Frank Thomas/456	1.50
2 Edgar Martinez/456	1.50
3 Roberto Alomar/390	1.50
4 Chuck Knoblauch/390	1.50
5 Mike Piazza/431	10.00
6 Barry Larkin/440	1.50
7 Kenny Lofton/409	1.50
8 Jeff Bagwell/425	6.00
9 Barry Bonds/446	15.00
10 Rusty Greer/405	1.50
11 Gary Sheffield/424	2.00
12 Mark McGwire/393	12.00
13 Chipper Jones/371	8.00
14 Tony Gwynn/409	8.00
15 Craig Biggio/415	1.50
16 Mo Vaughn/420	1.50
17 Bernie Williams/408	1.50
18 Ken Griffey Jr./382	10.00

		NM/M
19	Brady Anderson/393	1.50
20	Derek Jeter/370	15.00

Production Line-pi

This 20-card insert was printed on holographic board. The set features players with a high power index from 1997. Each card is sequentially numbered to that player's power index from that season.

		NM/M
Complete Set (20):		85.00
Common Player:		1.50
1	Frank Thomas/1067	5.00
2	Mark McGwire/1039	12.00
3	Barry Bonds/1031	12.50
4	Jeff Bagwell/1017	5.00
5	Ken Griffey Jr./1028	10.00
6	Alex Rodriguez/846	12.00
7	Chipper Jones/850	7.00
8	Mike Piazza/1070	10.00
9	Mo Vaughn/980	1.50
10	Brady Anderson/863	1.50
11	Manny Ramirez/953	1.50
12	Albert Belle/823	1.50
13	Jim Thome/1001	1.50
14	Bernie Williams/952	1.50
15	Scott Rolen/846	2.00
16	Vladimir Guerrero/833	5.00
17	Larry Walker/1172	1.50
18	David Justice/1013	1.50
19	Tino Martinez/948	1.50
20	Tony Gwynn/957	7.00

Production Line-sg

This 20-card insert was printed on holographic board. It featured players with high slugging percentages in 1997. Each card is sequentially numbered to the player's slugging percentage from that season.

		NM/M
Complete Set (20):		135.00
Common Player:		3.00
1	Mark McGwire/646	20.00
2	Ken Griffey Jr./646	12.50
3	Andres Galarraga/585	3.00
4	Barry Bonds/585	22.50
5	Juan Gonzalez/589	4.50
6	Mike Piazza/638	12.50
7	Jeff Bagwell/592	7.50
8	Manny Ramirez/538	7.50
9	Jim Thome/579	4.50
10	Mo Vaughn/560	3.00
11	Larry Walker/720	3.00
12	Tino Martinez/577	3.00
13	Frank Thomas/611	7.50
14	Tim Salmon/517	3.00
15	Raul Mondesi/541	3.00
16	Alex Rodriguez/496	15.00
17	Nomar Garciaparra/534	10.00
18	Jose Cruz Jr./499	3.00
19	Tony Clark/500	3.00
20	Cal Ripken Jr./402	25.00

Rated Rookies

This 30-card insert features top young players. The fronts have a color player photo in front of a stars and stripes background, with "Rated Rookies" and the player's name printed on the right. The backs have another photo, basic player information and career highlights. A rare (250 each) Medalist version is micro-etched in gold holographic foil.

		NM/M
Complete Set (30):		32.50
Common Player:		1.00
Medalists (250 Sets):		6X
1	Mark Kotsay	1.00
2	Neifi Perez	1.00
3	Paul Konerko	1.50
4	Jose Cruz Jr.	1.00
5	Hideki Irabu	1.00
6	Mike Cameron	1.00
7	Jeff Suppan	1.00
8	Kevin Orie	1.00
9	Pokey Reese	1.00
10	Todd Dunwoody	1.00
11	Miguel Tejada	1.50
12	Jose Guillen	1.00
13	Bartolo Colon	1.50
14	Derrek Lee	2.50
15	Antone Williamson	1.00
16	Wilton Guerrero	1.00
17	Jaret Wright	1.00
18	Todd Helton	4.00
19	Shannon Stewart	1.00
20	Nomar Garciaparra	6.00
21	Brett Tomko	1.00
22	Fernando Tatis	1.00
23	Raul Ibanez	1.00
24	Dennis Reyes	1.00
25	Bobby Estalella	1.00
26	Lou Collier	1.00
27	Bubba Trammell	1.00
28	Ben Grieve	1.00
29	Ivan Cruz	1.00
30	Karim Garcia	1.00

Update Crusade

This 30-card insert is continued from 1998 Donruss and Leaf baseball sets. Each card features a color action photo in front of a Medieval background. The player's name and background are green and each card is serial numbered to 250. Purple (numbered to 100) and Red (25) parallel versions were also created. Crusade is a 130-card cross-brand insert with 40 cards included in 1998 Donruss and 30 each in 1998 Leaf and Leaf Rookies & Stars.

		NM/M
Complete Set, Green (30):		325.00
Common Player:		6.00
Production 250 Sets		
Purples (100 Sets):		3X
Reds (25 Sets):		10X
1	Tim Salmon	6.00
2	Garret Anderson	6.00
9	Rafael Palmeiro	15.00
10	Brady Anderson	6.00
14	Frank Thomas	15.00
17	Robin Ventura	6.00
22	Matt Williams	6.00
23	Tony Clark	6.00
29	Chuck Knoblauch	6.00
31	Bernie Williams	6.00
32	Derek Jeter	50.00
38	Jason Giambi	10.00
43	Jay Buhner	6.00
44	Juan Gonzalez	7.50
49	Carlos Delgado	9.00
55	Greg Maddux	20.00
57	Tom Glavine	9.00
58	Mark Grace	6.00
61	Sammy Sosa	20.00
63	Barry Larkin	6.00
69	Neifi Perez	6.00
72	Gary Sheffield	7.50
77	Jeff Bagwell	15.00
80	Raul Mondesi	6.00
81	Hideo Nomo	7.50
83	Rondell White	6.00

84	Vladimir Guerrero	15.00
87	Todd Hundley	6.00
96	Brian Jordan	6.00
99	Barry Bonds	50.00

Update Dominators

This 30-card insert features color player photos and holographic foil.

		NM/M
Complete Set (30):		25.00
Common Player:		.25
Approx: 1:12		
1	Roger Clemens	1.50
2	Tony Clark	.25
3	Darin Erstad	.50
4	Jeff Bagwell	1.00
5	Ken Griffey Jr.	1.75
6	Andruw Jones	1.00
7	Juan Gonzalez	.50
8	Ivan Rodriguez	.75
9	Randy Johnson	1.00
10	Tino Martinez	.25
11	Mark McGwire	2.00
12	Chuck Knoblauch	.25
13	Jim Thome	.65
14	Alex Rodriguez	2.00
15	Hideo Nomo	.50
16	Jose Cruz Jr.	.25
17	Chipper Jones	1.50
18	Tony Gwynn	1.50
19	Barry Bonds	2.00
20	Mo Vaughn	.25
21	Cal Ripken Jr.	2.50
22	Greg Maddux	1.50
23	Manny Ramirez	1.00
24	Andres Galarraga	.25
25	Vladimir Guerrero	1.00
26	Albert Belle	.25
27	Nomar Garciaparra	1.50
28	Kenny Lofton	.25
29	Mike Piazza	1.75
30	Frank Thomas	1.00

Update Elite

This 20-card insert features color player photos in a diamond-shaped border at the top with the Elite Series logo and player's name at the bottom. The fronts have a cream-colored border.

		NM/M
Complete Set (20):		115.00
Common Player:		3.00
Production 2,500 Sets		
1	Jeff Bagwell	4.50
2	Andruw Jones	4.50
3	Ken Griffey Jr.	7.50
4	Derek Jeter	15.00
5	Juan Gonzalez	3.50
6	Mark McGwire	10.00
7	Ivan Rodriguez	4.50
8	Paul Molitor	4.50
9	Hideo Nomo	3.50
10	Mo Vaughn	3.00
11	Chipper Jones	6.00
12	Nomar Garciaparra	6.00
13	Mike Piazza	7.50
14	Frank Thomas	4.50
15	Greg Maddux	6.00
16	Cal Ripken Jr.	15.00
17	Alex Rodriguez	10.00
18	Scott Rolen	3.50

Update FANtasy Team

This 20-card set features the top vote getters from the Donruss online Fan Club ballot box. The top ten make up the 1st Team FANtasy Team and are sequentially numbered to 2,000. The other players are included in the 2nd Team FANtasy Team and are numbered to 4,000. The first 250 cards of each player are die-cut. The front of the cards feature a color photo inside a stars and stripes border.

		NM/M
Complete Set (20):		35.00
Common Player (1-10)		
(1,750 Sets):		1.50
Common Player (11-20)		
(3,750 Sets):		1.00
Die-Cut (250 Each):		2X
1	Frank Thomas	2.00
2	Ken Griffey Jr.	3.50
3	Cal Ripken Jr.	5.00
4	Jose Cruz Jr.	1.00
5	Travis Lee	1.00
6	Greg Maddux	2.50
7	Alex Rodriguez	4.00
8	Mark McGwire	4.00
9	Chipper Jones	2.50
10	Andruw Jones	2.00
11	Mike Piazza	3.50
12	Tony Gwynn	2.50
13	Larry Walker	1.00
14	Nomar Garciaparra	3.00
15	Jaret Wright	1.00
16	Livan Hernandez	1.00
17	Roger Clemens	2.75
18	Derek Jeter	5.00
19	Scott Rolen	1.25
20	Jeff Bagwell	1.50

Update Rookie Diamond Kings

The Rookie Diamond Kings insert features color portraits by artist Dan Gardiner of young players inside a golden border. Player identification and Rookie Diamond Kings logo are at the bottom. Each card is sequentially numbered to 10,000 with the first 500 printed on canvas.

		NM/M
Complete Set (12):		20.00
Common Player:		2.00
Production 9,500 Sets		
Canvas (500 Sets):		2X
1	Travis Lee	2.00
2	Fernando Tatis	2.00
3	Livan Hernandez	2.00
4	Todd Helton	5.00
5	Derrek Lee	3.50
6	Jaret Wright	2.00
7	Ben Grieve	2.00

19	Barry Bonds	15.00
20	Tony Gwynn	6.00

8	Paul Konerko	2.50
9	Jose Cruz Jr.	2.00
10	Mark Kotsay	2.00
11	Todd Greene	2.00
12	Brad Fullmer	2.00

Update Sony MLB 99

This 20-card set promotes the MLB '99 game for Sony PlayStation systems. The card front has a color player photo with a red border on two sides. The Donruss, PlayStation and MLB '99 logos appear on the front as well. The backs have a MLB '99 Tip and instructions on entering the PlayStation ML '99 Sweepstakes.

		NM/M
Complete Set (20):		3.00
Common Player:		.05
1	Cal Ripken Jr.	.75
2	Nomar Garciaparra	.40
3	Barry Bonds	.75
4	Mike Mussina	.20
5	Pedro Martinez	.25
6	Derek Jeter	.75
7	Andruw Jones	.25
8	Kenny Lofton	.05
9	Gary Sheffield	.15
10	Raul Mondesi	.05
11	Jeff Bagwell	.25
12	Tim Salmon	.05
13	Tom Glavine	.15
14	Ben Grieve	.05
15	Matt Williams	.05
16	Juan Gonzalez	.15
17	Mark McGwire	.50
18	Bernie Williams	.05
19	Andres Galarraga	.05
20	Jose Cruz Jr.	.05

Collections

Collections consists of a 750-card base set made up of cards from the Donruss (200 cards), Leaf (200), Donruss Elite (150) and Donruss Preferred (200) sets. The cards were reproduced with a chromium finish and have the scripted word "Collections" vertically at left-front. The Collections logo is repeated on back and each card has a second number within the 750-piece set. The Donruss and Leaf cards were inserted two per pack, Elite was inserted one per pack and Preferred cards had a production run of less than 1,400, averaging one card per two packs. The 200 Collections versions of Donruss cards can be found with a large black "SAMPLE" overprint value on back.

		NM/M
Complete Set (750):		1,000

Complete Donruss Set (200):	135.00
Complete Leaf Set (200):	165.00
Complete Elite Set (150):	155.00
Complete Preferred Set (200):	600.00
Prized Collections Parallel:	2X
Pack (5):	6.00
Wax Box (20):	100.00
Samples:	6X
1	Paul Molitor	
2	Juan Gonzalez	1.00
3	Darryl Kile	.25
4	Randy Johnson	2.00
5	Tom Glavine	.50
6	Pat Hentgen	.25
7	David Justice	.25
8	Kevin Brown	.25
9	Mike Mussina	.50
10	Ken Caminiti	.25
11	Todd Hundley	.25
12	Frank Thomas	2.00
13	Ray Lankford	.25
14	Justin Thompson	.25
15	Jason Dickson	.25
16	Kenny Lofton	.25
17	Ivan Rodriguez	1.50
18	Pedro Martinez	2.00
19	Brady Anderson	.25
20	Barry Larkin	.25
21	Chipper Jones	3.00
22	Tony Gwynn	3.00
23	Roger Clemens	3.25
24	Sandy Alomar Jr.	.25
25	Tino Martinez	.25
26	Jeff Bagwell	2.00
27	Shawn Estes	.25
28	Ken Griffey Jr.	3.50
29	Javier Lopez	.25
30	Denny Neagle	.25
31	Mike Piazza	3.50
32	Andres Galarraga	.25
33	Larry Walker	.25
34	Alex Rodriguez	4.50
35	Greg Maddux	3.00
36	Albert Belle	.25
37	Barry Bonds	6.00
38	Mo Vaughn	.25
39	Kevin Appier	.25
40	Wade Boggs	3.00
41	Garret Anderson	.25
42	Jeffrey Hammonds	.25
43	Marquis Grissom	.25
44	Jim Edmonds	.25
45	Brian Jordan	.25
46	Raul Mondesi	.25
47	John Valentin	.25
48	Brad Radke	.25
49	Ismael Valdes	.25
50	Matt Stairs	.25
51	Matt Williams	.25
52	Reggie Jefferson	.25
53	Alan Benes	.25
54	Charles Johnson	.25
55	Chuck Knoblauch	.25
56	Edgar Martinez	.25
57	Nomar Garciaparra	3.00
58	Craig Biggio	.25
59	Bernie Williams	.50
60	David Cone	.25
61	Cal Ripken Jr.	6.00
62	Mark McGwire	4.50
63	Roberto Alomar	.50
64	Fred McGriff	.25
65	Eric Karros	.25
66	Robin Ventura	.25
67	Darin Erstad	.50
68	Michael Tucker	.25
69	Jim Thome	1.00
70	Mark Grace	.25
71	Lou Collier	.25
72	Karim Garcia	.25
73	Alex Fernandez	.25
74	J.T. Snow	.25
75	Reggie Sanders	.25
76	John Smoltz	.25
77	Tim Salmon	.25
78	Paul O'Neill	.25
79	Vinny Castilla	.25
80	Rafael Palmeiro	1.50
81	Jaret Wright	.25
82	Jay Buhner	.25
83	Brett Butler	.25
84	Todd Greene	.25
85	Scott Rolen	1.50
86	Sammy Sosa	3.00
87	Jason Giambi	1.00
88	Carlos Delgado	.75
89	Deion Sanders	.25
90	Wilton Guerrero	.25
91	Andy Pettitte	.45
92	Brian Giles	.25
93	Dmitri Young	.25
94	Ron Coomer	.25
95	Mike Cameron	.25
96	Edgardo Alfonzo	.25
97	Jimmy Key	.25
98	Ryan Klesko	.25
99	Andy Benes	.25
100	Derek Jeter	6.00
101	Jeff Fassero	.25
102	Neifi Perez	.25
103	Hideo Nomo	1.00
104	Andruw Jones	2.00
105	Todd Helton	1.50
106	Livan Hernandez	.25
107	Brett Tomko	.25
108	Shannon Stewart	.25

#	Player	Price
109	Bartolo Colon	.25
110	Matt Morris	.25
111	Miguel Tejada	.40
112	Pokey Reese	.25
113	Fernando Tatis	.25
114	Todd Dunwoody	.25
115	Jose Cruz Jr.	.25
116	Chan Ho Park	.25
117	Kevin Young	.25
118	Rickey Henderson	2.00
119	Hideki Irabu	.25
120	Francisco Cordova	.25
121	Al Martin	.25
122	Tony Clark	.25
123	Curt Schilling	.40
124	Rusty Greer	.25
125	Jose Canseco	.60
126	Edgar Renteria	.25
127	Todd Walker	.25
128	Wally Joyner	.25
129	Bill Mueller	.25
130	Jose Guillen	.25
131	Manny Ramirez	2.00
132	Bobby Higginson	.25
133	Kevin Orie	.25
134	Will Clark	.25
135	Dave Nilsson	.25
136	Jason Kendall	.25
137	Ivan Cruz	.25
138	Gary Sheffield	.40
139	Bubba Trammell	.25
140	Vladimir Guerrero	2.00
141	Dennis Reyes	.25
142	Bobby Bonilla	.25
143	Ruben Rivera	.25
144	Ben Grieve	.25
145	Moises Alou	.25
146	Tony Womack	.25
147	Eric Young	.25
148	Paul Konerko	.35
149	Dante Bichette	.25
150	Joe Carter	.25
151	Rondell White	.25
152	Chris Holt	.25
153	Shawn Green	.40
154	Mark Grudzielanek	.25
155	Jermaine Dye	.25
156	Ken Griffey Jr. (Fan Club)	1.75
157	Frank Thomas (Fan Club)	1.00
158	Chipper Jones (Fan Club)	1.50
159	Mike Piazza (Fan Club)	1.75
160	Cal Ripken Jr. (Fan Club)	3.00
161	Greg Maddux (Fan Club)	1.50
162	Juan Gonzalez (Fan Club)	.50
163	Alex Rodriguez (Fan Club)	2.25
164	Mark McGwire (Fan Club)	2.25
165	Derek Jeter (Fan Club)	3.00
166	Larry Walker (Checklist)	.25
167	Tony Gwynn (Checklist)	.75
168	Tino Martinez (Checklist)	.25
169	Scott Rolen (Checklist)	.40
170	Nomar Garciaparra (Checklist)	.75
1	Mark Kotsay	.50
2	Neifi Perez	.50
3	Paul Konerko	1.00
4	Jose Cruz Jr.	.50
5	Hideki Irabu	.50
6	Mike Cameron	.50
7	Jeff Suppan	.50
8	Kevin Orie	.50
9	Pokey Reese	.50
10	Todd Dunwoody	.50
11	Miguel Tejada	1.00
12	Jose Guillen	.50
13	Bartolo Colon	.50
14	Derek Lee	.75
15	Antone Williamson	.50
16	Wilton Guerrero	.50
17	Jaret Wright	.50
18	Todd Helton	2.00
19	Shannon Stewart	.50
20	Nomar Garciaparra	3.00
21	Brett Tomko	.50
22	Fernando Tatis	.50
23	Raul Ibanez	.50
24	Dennis Reyes	.50
25	Bobby Estalella	.50
26	Lou Collier	.50
27	Bubba Trammell	.50
28	Ben Grieve	.50
29	Ivan Cruz	.50
30	Karim Garcia	.50
1	Rusty Greer	.25
2	Tino Martinez	.25
3	Bobby Bonilla	.25
4	Jason Giambi	.65
5	Matt Morris	.25
6	Craig Counsell	.25
7	Reggie Jefferson	.25
8	Brian Rose	.25
9	Ruben Rivera	.25
10	Shawn Estes	.25
11	Tony Gwynn	3.00
12	Jeff Abbott	.25
13	Jose Cruz Jr.	.25
14	Francisco Cordova	.25
15	Ryan Klesko	.25
16	Tim Salmon	.25
17	Brett Tomko	.25
18	Matt Williams	.25
19	Joe Carter	.25
20	Harold Baines	.25
21	Gary Sheffield	.40
22	Charles Johnson	.25
23	Aaron Boone	.35
24	Eddie Murray	2.00
25	Matt Stairs	.25
26	David Cone	.25
27	Jon Nunnally	.25
28	Chris Stynes	.25
29	Enrique Wilson	.25
30	Randy Johnson	2.00
31	Garret Anderson	.25
32	Manny Ramirez	2.00
33	Jeff Suppan	.25
34	Rickey Henderson	2.00
35	Scott Spiezio	.25
36	Rondell White	.25
37	Todd Greene	.25
38	Delino DeShields	.25
39	Kevin Brown	.25
40	Chili Davis	.25
41	Jimmy Key	.25
43	Mike Mussina	1.00
44	Joe Randa	.25
45	Chan Ho Park	.25
46	Brad Radke	.25
47	Geronimo Berroa	.25
48	Wade Boggs	3.00
49	Kevin Appier	.25
50	Moises Alou	.25
51	David Justice	.25
52	Ivan Rodriguez	1.50
53	J.T. Snow	.25
54	Brian Giles	.25
55	Will Clark	.25
56	Justin Thompson	.25
57	Javier Lopez	.25
58	Hideki Irabu	.25
59	Mark Grudzielanek	.25
60	Abraham Nunez	.25
61	Todd Hollandsworth	.25
62	Jay Bell	.25
63	Nomar Garciaparra	3.00
64	Vinny Castilla	.25
65	Lou Collier	.25
66	Kevin Orie	.25
67	John Valentin	.25
68	Robin Ventura	.25
69	Denny Neagle	.25
70	Tony Womack	.25
71	Dennis Reyes	.25
72	Wally Joyner	.25
73	Kevin Brown	.35
74	Ray Durham	.25
75	Mike Cameron	.25
76	Dante Bichette	.25
77	Jose Guillen	.25
78	Carlos Delgado	.60
79	Paul Molitor	2.00
80	Jason Kendall	.25
81	Mark Belhorn	.25
82	Damian Jackson	.25
83	Bill Mueller	.25
84	Kevin Young	.25
85	Curt Schilling	.50
86	Jeffrey Hammonds	.25
87	Sandy Alomar Jr.	.25
88	Bartolo Colon	.25
89	Wilton Guerrero	.25
90	Bernie Williams	.25
91	Deion Sanders	.25
92	Mike Piazza	3.50
93	Butch Huskey	.25
94	Edgardo Alfonzo	.25
95	Alan Benes	.25
96	Craig Biggio	.25
97	Mark Grace	.25
98	Shawn Green	.40
99	Derek Lee	1.00
100	Ken Griffey Jr.	3.50
101	Tim Raines	.25
102	Pokey Reese	.25
103	Lee Stevens	.25
104	Shannon Stewart	.25
105	John Smoltz	.25
106	Frank Thomas	2.00
107	Jeff Fassero	.25
108	Jay Buhner	.25
109	Jose Canseco	.45
110	Omar Vizquel	.25
111	Travis Fryman	.25
112	Dave Nilsson	.25
113	John Olerud	.25
114	Larry Walker	.25
115	Jim Edmonds	.25
116	Bobby Higginson	.25
117	Todd Hundley	.25
118	Paul O'Neill	.25
119	Bip Roberts	.25
120	Ismael Valdes	.25
121	Pedro Martinez	2.00
122	Jeff Cirillo	.25
123	Andy Benes	.25
124	Bobby Jones	.25
125	Brian Hunter	.25
126	Darryl Kile	.25
127	Pat Hentgen	.25
128	Marquis Grissom	.25
129	Eric Davis	.25
130	Chipper Jones	3.00
131	Edgar Martinez	.25
132	Andy Pettitte	.50
133	Cal Ripken Jr.	6.00
134	Scott Rolen	1.50
135	Ron Coomer	.25
136	Luis Castillo	.25
137	Fred McGriff	.25
138	Neifi Perez	.25
139	Eric Karros	.25
140	Alex Fernandez	.25
141	Jason Dickson	.25
142	Lance Johnson	.25
143	Ray Lankford	.25
144	Sammy Sosa	3.00
145	Eric Young	.25
146	Bubba Trammell	.25
147	Todd Walker	.25
148	Mo Vaughn/CC	.25
149	Jeff Bagwell/CC	2.00
150	Kenny Lofton/CC	.25
151	Raul Mondesi/CC	.25
152	Mike Piazza/CC	3.50
153	Chipper Jones/CC	3.00
154	Larry Walker/CC	.25
155	Greg Maddux/CC	3.00
156	Ken Griffey Jr./CC	3.50
157	Frank Thomas/CC	2.00
158	Darin Erstad/GLS	.25
159	Roberto Alomar/GLS	1.50
160	Albert Belle/GLS	1.00
161	Jim Thome/GLS	2.00
162	Tony Clark/GLS	1.00
163	Chuck Knoblauch/GLS	1.00
164	Derek Jeter/GLS	12.00
165	Alex Rodriguez/GLS	8.00
166	Tony Gwynn/GLS	6.00
167	Roger Clemens/GLS	7.00
168	Barry Larkin/GLS	1.00
169	Andres Galarraga/GLS	1.00
170	Vladimir Guerrero/GLS	4.50
171	Mark McGwire/GLS	8.00
172	Barry Bonds/GLS	12.00
173	Juan Gonzalez/GLS	2.50
174	Andruw Jones/GLS	4.50
175	Paul Molitor/GLS	4.50
176	Hideo Nomo/GLS	2.50
177	Cal Ripken Jr./GLS	12.50
178	Brad Fullmer/GLR	1.00
179	Jaret Wright/GLR	1.00
180	Bobby Estalella/GLR	1.00
181	Ben Grieve/GLR	1.00
182	Paul Konerko/GLR	1.50
183	David Ortiz/GLR	3.00
184	Todd Helton/GLR	3.00
185	Juan Encarnacion/GLR	1.00
186	Miguel Tejada/GLR	1.50
187	Jacob Cruz/GLR	1.00
188	Mark Kotsay/GLR	1.00
189	Fernando Tatis/GLR	1.00
190	Ricky Ledee/GLR	1.00
191	Richard Hidalgo/GLR	1.00
192	Richie Sexson/GLR	1.00
193	Luis Ordaz/GLR	1.00
194	Eli Marrero/GLR	1.00
195	Livan Hernandez/GLR	1.00
196	Homer Bush/GLR	1.00
197	Raul Ibanez/GLR	1.00
198	Checklist (Nomar Garciaparra)	1.00
199	Checklist (Scott Rolen)	.75
200	Checklist (Jose Cruz Jr.)	.25
201	Al Martin	.25
1	Ken Griffey Jr.	4.00
2	Frank Thomas	2.50
3	Alex Rodriguez	6.00
4	Mike Piazza	4.00
5	Greg Maddux	3.00
6	Cal Ripken Jr.	7.00
7	Chipper Jones	3.00
8	Derek Jeter	7.00
9	Tony Gwynn	3.00
10	Andruw Jones	2.50
11	Juan Gonzalez	1.25
12	Jeff Bagwell	2.50
13	Mark McGwire	6.00
14	Roger Clemens	3.00
15	Albert Belle	.50
16	Barry Bonds	7.00
17	Kenny Lofton	.50
18	Ivan Rodriguez	2.00
19	Manny Ramirez	2.50
20	Jim Thome	1.50
21	Chuck Knoblauch	.50
22	Paul Molitor	2.50
23	Barry Larkin	.50
24	Andy Pettitte	1.00
25	John Smoltz	.50
26	Randy Johnson	2.50
27	Bernie Williams	.50
28	Larry Walker	.50
29	Mo Vaughn	.50
30	Bobby Higginson	.50
31	Edgardo Alfonzo	.50
32	Justin Thompson	.50
33	Jeff Suppan	.50
34	Roberto Alomar	1.00
35	Hideo Nomo	1.25
36	Rusty Greer	.50
37	Tim Salmon	.50
38	Jim Edmonds	.50
39	Gary Sheffield	.75
40	Ken Caminiti	.50
41	Sammy Sosa	3.00
42	Tony Womack	.50
43	Matt Williams	.50
44	Andres Galarraga	.50
45	Garret Anderson	.50
46	Rafael Palmeiro	2.00
47	Mike Mussina	1.00
48	Craig Biggio	.50
49	Wade Boggs	3.00
50	Tom Glavine	.75
51	Jason Giambi	1.00
52	Will Clark	.50
53	David Justice	.50
54	Sandy Alomar Jr.	.50
55	Edgar Martinez	.50
56	Brady Anderson	.50
57	Eric Young	.50
58	Ray Lankford	.50
59	Kevin Brown	.60
60	Raul Mondesi	.50
61	Bobby Bonilla	.50
62	Javier Lopez	.50
63	Fred McGriff	.50
64	Rondell White	.50
65	Todd Hundley	.50
66	Mark Grace	.50
67	Alan Benes	.50
68	Jeff Abbott	.50
69	Bob Abreu	.50
70	Deion Sanders	.50
71	Tino Martinez	.50
72	Shannon Stewart	.50
73	Homer Bush	.50
74	Carlos Delgado	1.50
75	Raul Ibanez	.50
76	Hideki Irabu	.50
77	Jose Cruz Jr.	.50
78	Tony Clark	.50
79	Wilton Guerrero	.50
80	Vladimir Guerrero	2.50
81	Scott Rolen	2.25
82	Nomar Garciaparra	3.00
83	Darin Erstad	1.00
84	Chan Ho Park	.50
85	Mike Cameron	.50
86	Todd Walker	.50
87	Todd Dunwoody	.50
88	Neifi Perez	.50
89	Brett Tomko	.50
90	Jose Guillen	.50
91	Matt Morris	.50
92	Bartolo Colon	.50
93	Jaret Wright	.50
94	Shawn Estes	.50
95	Livan Hernandez	.50
96	Bobby Estalella	.50
97	Ben Grieve	.50
98	Paul Konerko	.75
99	David Ortiz	1.00
100	Todd Helton	2.00
101	Juan Encarnacion	.50
102	Bubba Trammell	.50
103	Miguel Tejada	1.00
104	Jacob Cruz	.50
105	Todd Greene	.50
106	Kevin Orie	.50
107	Mark Kotsay	.50
108	Fernando Tatis	.50
109	Jay Payton	.50
110	Pokey Reese	.50
111	Derrek Lee	1.50
112	Richard Hidalgo	.50
113	Ricky Ledee	.50
114	Lou Collier	.50
115	Ruben Rivera	.50
116	Shawn Green	1.00
117	Moises Alou	.50
118	Ken Griffey Jr. (Generations)	2.00
119	Frank Thomas (Generations)	1.25
120	Alex Rodriguez (Generations)	3.00
121	Mike Piazza (Generations)	2.00
122	Greg Maddux (Generations)	1.75
123	Cal Ripken Jr. (Generations)	3.50
124	Chipper Jones (Generations)	1.75
125	Derek Jeter (Generations)	3.50
126	Tony Gwynn (Generations)	1.75
127	Andruw Jones (Generations)	1.25
128	Juan Gonzalez (Generations)	.75
129	Jeff Bagwell (Generations)	1.25
130	Mark McGwire (Generations)	
131	Roger Clemens (Generations)	1.75
132	Albert Belle (Generations)	.50
133	Barry Bonds (Generations)	3.50
134	Kenny Lofton (Generations)	.50
135	Ivan Rodriguez (Generations)	1.00
136	Manny Ramirez (Generations)	1.25
137	Jim Thome (Generations)	1.00
138	Chuck Knoblauch (Generations)	.50
139	Paul Molitor (Generations)	1.25
140	Barry Larkin (Generations)	.50
141	Mo Vaughn (Generations)	.50
142	Hideki Irabu (Generations)	.50
143	Jose Cruz Jr. (Generations)	.50
144	Tony Clark (Generations)	.50
145	Vladimir Guerrero (Generations)	1.25
146	Scott Rolen (Generations)	1.00
147	Nomar Garciaparra (Generations)	2.00
148	Checklist (Nomar Garciaparra)	1.00
149	Checklist (Larry Walker)	.50
150	Checklist (Tino Martinez)	.50
1	Ken Griffey Jr./EX	12.00
2	Frank Thomas/EX	7.50
3	Cal Ripken Jr./EX	17.50
4	Alex Rodriguez/EX	15.00
5	Greg Maddux/EX	10.00
6	Mike Piazza/EX	12.00
7	Chipper Jones/EX	10.00
8	Tony Gwynn/EX	10.00
9	Derek Jeter/FB	17.50
10	Jeff Bagwell/EX	7.50
11	Juan Gonzalez/EX	4.00
12	Nomar Garciaparra/EX	10.00
13	Andruw Jones/FB	7.50
14	Hideo Nomo/FB	2.00
15	Roger Clemens/FB	13.50
16	Mark McGwire/FB	15.00
17	Scott Rolen/FB	4.00
18	Vladimir Guerrero/FB	7.50
19	Barry Bonds/FB	17.50
20	Darin Erstad/FB	4.00
21	Albert Belle/FB	2.00
22	Kenny Lofton/FB	2.00
23	Mo Vaughn/FB	2.00
24	Tony Clark/FB	2.00
25	Ivan Rodriguez/FB	6.00
26	Larry Walker/CL	2.00
27	Eddie Murray/CL	7.50
28	Andy Pettitte/CL	4.00
29	Roberto Alomar/CL	2.00
30	Randy Johnson/CL	7.50
31	Manny Ramirez/CL	2.00
32	Paul Molitor/FB	7.50
33	Mike Mussina/CL	4.00
34	Jim Thome/FB	2.00
35	Tino Martinez/CL	2.00
36	Gary Sheffield/CL	3.00
37	Chuck Knoblauch/CL	2.00
38	Bernie Williams/CL	2.00
39	Tim Salmon/CL	2.00
40	Sammy Sosa/CL	10.00
41	Wade Boggs/MZ	10.00
42	Will Clark/GS	2.00
43	Andres Galarraga/CL	2.00
44	Raul Mondesi/CL	2.00
45	Rickey Henderson/GS	6.50
46	Jose Canseco/CL	4.00
47	Pedro Martinez/GS	6.50
48	Jay Buhner/GS	2.00
49	Ryan Klesko/GS	2.00
50	Barry Larkin/CL	2.00
51	Charles Johnson/GS	2.00
52	Tom Glavine/GS	3.00
53	Edgar Martinez/CL	2.00
54	Fred McGriff/GS	2.00
55	Moises Alou/MZ	2.00
56	Dante Bichette/GS	2.00
57	Jim Edmonds/CL	2.00
58	Mark Grace/MZ	2.00
59	Chan Ho Park/MZ	2.00
60	Justin Thompson/MZ	2.00
61	John Smoltz/MZ	2.00
62	Craig Biggio/CL	2.00
63	Ken Caminiti/MZ	2.00
64	Deion Sanders/MZ	2.00
65	Carlos Delgado/GS	4.00
66	David Justice/MZ	2.00
67	J.T. Snow/GS	2.00
68	Jason Giambi/MZ	2.00
69	Garret Anderson/MZ	2.00
70	Rondell White/MZ	2.00
71	Matt Williams/MZ	2.00
72	Brady Anderson/MZ	2.00
73	Eric Karros/GS	2.00
74	Javier Lopez/GS	2.00
75	Pat Hentgen/GS	2.00
76	Todd Hundley/MZ	2.00
77	Ray Lankford/GS	2.00
78	Denny Neagle/MZ	2.00
79	Henry Rodriguez/GS	2.00
80	Sandy Alomar Jr./MZ	2.00
81	Rafael Palmeiro/MZ	5.00
82	Robin Ventura/GS	2.00
83	John Olerud/GS	2.00
84	Omar Vizquel/MZ	2.00
85	Joe Randa/GS	2.00
86	Lance Johnson/GS	2.00
87	Kevin Brown/GS	2.00
88	Curt Schilling/GS	4.00
89	Ismael Valdes/GS	2.00
90	Francisco Cordova/GS	2.00
91	David Cone/GS	2.00
92	Paul O'Neill/GS	2.00
93	Jimmy Key/GS	2.00
94	Brad Radke/GS	2.00
95	Kevin Appier/GS	2.00
96	Al Martin/GS	2.00
97	Rusty Greer/MZ	2.00
98	Reggie Jefferson/GS	2.00
99	Ron Coomer/GS	2.00
100	Vinny Castilla/GS	2.00
101	Bobby Bonilla/MZ	2.00
102	Eric Young/GS	2.00
103	Tony Womack/GS	2.00
104	Jason Kendall/GS	2.00
105	Jeff Suppan/GS	2.00
106	Shawn Estes/MZ	2.00
107	Shawn Green/GS	2.00
108	Edgardo Alfonzo/MZ	2.00
109	Alan Benes/MZ	2.00
110	Bobby Higginson/GS	2.00
111	Mark Grudzielanek/GS	2.00
112	Wilton Guerrero/GS	2.00
113	Todd Greene/MZ	2.00
114	Pokey Reese/GS	2.00
115	Jose Guillen CL	2.00
116	Neifi Perez/MZ	2.00
117	Luis Castillo/GS	2.00
118	Edgar Renteria/GS	2.00
119	Karim Garcia/GS	2.00
120	Butch Huskey/GS	2.00
121	Michael Tucker/GS	2.00
122	Jason Dickson/GS	2.00
123	Todd Walker/MZ	2.00
124	Brian Jordan/GS	2.00
125	Joe Carter/GS	2.00
126	Matt Morris/MZ	2.00
127	Brett Tomko/MZ	2.00
128	Mike Cameron/CL	2.00
129	Russ Davis/GS	2.00
130	Shannon Stewart/MZ	2.00
131	Kevin Orie/GS	2.00
132	Scott Spiezio/GS	2.00
133	Brian Giles/GS	2.00
134	Raul Casanova/GS	2.00
135	Jose Cruz Jr./CL	2.00
136	Hideki Irabu/GS	2.00
137	Bubba Trammell/GS	2.00
138	Richard Hidalgo/CL	2.00
139	Paul Konerko/GS	2.50
140	Todd Helton/FB	5.00
141	Miguel Tejada/CL	3.00
142	Fernando Tatis/MZ	2.00
143	Ben Grieve/FB	2.00
144	Travis Lee/FB	2.00
145	Mark Kotsay/CL	2.00
146	Eli Marrero/MZ	2.00
147	David Ortiz/MZ	4.00
148	Juan Encarnacion/MZ	2.00
149	Jaret Wright/MZ	2.00
150	Livan Hernandez/CL	2.00
151	Ruben Rivera/GS	2.00
152	Brad Fullmer/MZ	2.00
153	Dennis Reyes/GS	2.00
154	Enrique Wilson/MZ	2.00
155	Todd Dunwoody/MZ	2.00
156	Derrick Gibson/MZ	2.00
157	Aaron Boone/MZ	2.00
158	Ron Wright/MZ	2.00
159	Preston Wilson/MZ	2.00
160	Abraham Nunez/GS	2.00
161	Shane Monahan/GS	2.00
162	Carl Pavano/GS	2.00
163	Derrek Lee	4.00
164	Jeff Abbott/GS	2.00
165	Wes Helms/MZ	2.00
166	Brian Rose/GS	2.00
167	Bobby Estalella/GS	2.00
168	Ken Griffey Jr./GS	9.00
169	Frank Thomas/GS	5.00
170	Cal Ripken Jr./GS	15.00
171	Alex Rodriguez/GS	12.00
172	Greg Maddux/GS	7.50
173	Mike Piazza/GS	9.00
174	Chipper Jones/GS	7.50
175	Tony Gwynn/GS	7.50
176	Derek Jeter/GS	15.00
177	Jeff Bagwell/GS	6.00
178	Juan Gonzalez/GS	3.00
179	Nomar Garciaparra/GS	7.50
180	Andruw Jones/GS	6.00
181	Hideo Nomo/GS	3.00
182	Roger Clemens/GS	7.50
183	Mark McGwire/GS	12.00
184	Scott Rolen/GS	3.00
185	Barry Bonds/GS	7.50
186	Darin Erstad/GS	3.00
187	Mo Vaughn/GS	3.00
188	Ivan Rodriguez/GS	5.00
189	Larry Walker/MZ	2.00
190	Andy Pettitte/GS	2.00
191	Randy Johnson/MZ	6.00
192	Paul Molitor/GS	6.00
193	Jim Thome/MZ	4.00
194	Tino Martinez/MZ	3.00
195	Gary Sheffield/MZ	3.00
196	Albert Belle/GS	2.00
197	Jose Cruz Jr./GS	2.00
198	Todd Helton/GS	5.00
199	Ben Grieve/GS	2.00
200	Paul Konerko/GS	2.50

ABBREVIATIONS

CC - Curtain Calls
GLS - Gold Leaf Stars
GLR - Gold Leaf Rookies

1998 Donruss Elite

Donruss Elite consists of a 150-card base set with two parallels and five inserts. The base cards feature a foil background with player photo on front. Another photo is on the back with stats and basic player information. The Aspirations parallel is numbered to 750 and the Status parallel is numbered to 100. The base set also includes the 30-card Generations subset and three checklists. The inserts are Back to the Future, Back to the Future Autographs, Craftsmen, Prime Numbers and Prime Numbers Die-Cuts.

	NM/M
Complete Set (150):	15.00
Common Player:	.10
Aspirations (750 Sets):	2.5X
Status (100 Sets):	15X
Pack (5):	2.50
Wax Box (18):	40.00
1 Ken Griffey Jr.	1.50
2 Frank Thomas	.75
3 Alex Rodriguez	2.00
4 Mike Piazza	1.50
5 Greg Maddux	1.00
6 Cal Ripken Jr.	2.50
7 Chipper Jones	1.00
8 Derek Jeter	2.50
9 Tony Gwynn	1.00
10 Andruw Jones	.75
11 Juan Gonzalez	.40
12 Jeff Bagwell	.75
13 Mark McGwire	2.00
14 Roger Clemens	1.25
15 Albert Belle	.10
16 Barry Bonds	2.50
17 Kenny Lofton	.10
18 Ivan Rodriguez	.65
19 Manny Ramirez	.75
20 Jim Thome	.50
21 Chuck Knoblauch	.10
22 Paul Molitor	.75
23 Barry Larkin	.10
24 Andy Pettitte	.40
25 John Smoltz	.10
26 Randy Johnson	.75
27 Bernie Williams	.10
28 Larry Walker	.10
29 Mo Vaughn	.10
30 Bobby Higginson	.10
31 Edgardo Alfonzo	.10
32 Justin Thompson	.10
33 Jeff Suppan	.10
34 Roberto Alomar	.30
35 Hideo Nomo	.40
36 Rusty Greer	.10
37 Tim Salmon	.10
38 Jim Edmonds	.10
39 Gary Sheffield	.25
40 Ken Caminiti	.10
41 Sammy Sosa	1.00
42 Tony Womack	.10
43 Matt Williams	.10
44 Andres Galarraga	.10
45 Garret Anderson	.10
46 Rafael Palmeiro	.65
47 Mike Mussina	.40
48 Craig Biggio	.10
49 Wade Boggs	1.00
50 Tom Glavine	.25
51 Jason Giambi	.50
52 Will Clark	.10
53 David Justice	.10
54 Sandy Alomar Jr.	.10
55 Edgar Martinez	.10
56 Brady Anderson	.10
57 Eric Young	.10
58 Ray Lankford	.10
59 Kevin Brown	.10
60 Raul Mondesi	.10
61 Bobby Bonilla	.10
62 Javier Lopez	.10
63 Fred McGriff	.10
64 Rondell White	.10
65 Todd Hundley	.10
66 Mark Grace	.10
67 Alan Benes	.10
68 Jeff Abbott	.10
69 Bob Abreu	.10
70 Deion Sanders	.10
71 Tino Martinez	.10
72 Shannon Stewart	.10
73 Homer Bush	.10
74 Carlos Delgado	.50
75 Raul Ibanez	.10
76 Hideki Irabu	.10
77 Jose Cruz Jr.	.10
78 Tony Clark	.10
79 Wilton Guerrero	.10
80 Vladimir Guerrero	.75
81 Scott Rolen	.60
82 Nomar Garciaparra	1.00
83 Darin Erstad	.30
84 Chan Ho Park	.10
85 Mike Cameron	.10
86 Todd Walker	.10
87 Todd Dunwoody	.10
88 Neifi Perez	.10
89 Brett Tomko	.10
90 Jose Guillen	.10
91 Matt Morris	.10
92 Bartolo Colon	.10
93 Jaret Wright	.10
94 Shawn Estes	.10
95 Livan Hernandez	.10
96 Bobby Estalella	.10
97 Ben Grieve	.15
98 Paul Konerko	.15
99 David Ortiz	.40
100 Todd Helton	.65
101 Juan Encarnacion	.10
102 Bubba Trammell	.10
103 Miguel Tejada	.25
104 Jacob Cruz	.10
105 Todd Greene	.10
106 Kevin Orie	.10
107 Mark Kotsay	.10
108 Fernando Tatis	.10
109 Jay Payton	.10
110 Pokey Reese	.10
111 Derrek Lee	.10
112 Richard Hidalgo	.10
113 Ricky Ledee	.10
114 Lou Collier	.10
115 Ruben Rivera	.10
116 Shawn Green	.20
117 Moises Alou	.10
118 Ken Griffey Jr. (Generations)	.65
119 Frank Thomas (Generations)	.40
120 Alex Rodriguez (Generations)	.75
121 Mike Piazza (Generations)	.65
122 Greg Maddux (Generations)	.50
123 Cal Ripken Jr. (Generations)	1.00
124 Chipper Jones (Generations)	.50
125 Derek Jeter (Generations)	1.00
126 Tony Gwynn (Generations)	.50
127 Andruw Jones (Generations)	.40
128 Juan Gonzalez (Generations)	.20
129 Jeff Bagwell (Generations)	.40
130 Mark McGwire (Generations)	.75
131 Roger Clemens (Generations)	.65
132 Albert Belle (Generations)	
133 Barry Bonds (Generations)	1.00
134 Kenny Lofton (Generations)	.10
135 Ivan Rodriguez (Generations)	.25
136 Manny Ramirez (Generations)	.40
137 Jim Thome (Generations)	.25
138 Chuck Knoblauch (Generations)	.10
139 Paul Molitor (Generations)	.40
140 Barry Larkin (Generations)	.10
141 Mo Vaughn (Generations)	.10
142 Hideki Irabu (Generations)	.10
143 Jose Cruz Jr. (Generations)	.10
144 Tony Clark (Generations)	.10
145 Vladimir Guerrero (Generations)	.40
146 Scott Rolen (Generations)	.20
147 Nomar Garciaparra (Generations)	.50
148 Checklist Nomar Garciaparra (Hit Streaks)	
149 Checklist Larry Walker (Long HR-Coors)	.10
150 Checklist Tino Martinez (3 HR in game)	.10

Aspirations

A parallel edition of 750 of each player are found in this die-cut set. Cards have a scalloped treatment cut into the top and sides and red, rather than silver metallic borders. The word "ASPIRATIONS" is printed on front at bottom-right. Backs have the notation "1 of 750."

	NM/M
Complete Set (150):	60.00
Common Player:	.50
Stars/Rookies:	2.5X

Status

Just 100 serially numbered cards of each player are found in this die-cut parallel set. Cards have a scalloped treatment cut into the top and sides and red, rather than silver metallic borders.

	NM/M
Complete Set (150):	350.00
Common Player:	1.50
Stars/Rookies:	15X

Back to the Future

These double-front cards feature a veteran or retired star on one side and a young player on the other. Each player's name, team and "Back to the Future" are printed in the border. The cards are numbered to 1,500, with the first 100 of each card signed by both players. Exceptions are cards #1 and #6. Ripken and Konerko did not sign the same cards and Frank Thomas did not sign his Back to the Future card. Thomas instead signed 100 copies of his Elite base set card which was specially marked.

	NM/M
Complete Set (8):	40.00
Common Player:	2.50

Production 1,400 Sets
1	Cal Ripken Jr., Paul Konerko	9.00
2	Jeff Bagwell, Todd Helton	4.50
3	Eddie Mathews, Chipper Jones	5.00
4	Juan Gonzalez, Ben Grieve	2.50
5	Hank Aaron, Jose Cruz Jr.	7.50
6	Frank Thomas, David Ortiz	4.50
7	Nolan Ryan, Greg Maddux	9.00
8	Alex Rodriguez, Nomar Garciaparra	9.00

Back to the Future Autographs

The first 100 of each card in the Back to the Future insert was autographed by both players. Exceptions are cards #1 and #6. Ripken and Konerko did not sign the same cards and Frank Thomas did not sign his Back to the Future card. Thomas instead signed 100 specially marked copies of his Elite base-set card.

		NM/M
Production 100 Sets		
1a	Paul Konerko	30.00
1b	Cal Ripken Jr.	150.00
2	Jeff Bagwell, Todd Helton	120.00
3	Eddie Mathews, Chipper Jones	200.00
4	Juan Gonzalez, Ben Grieve	30.00
5	Hank Aaron, Jose Cruz Jr.	180.00
7	Nolan Ryan, Greg Maddux	850.00
8	Alex Rodriguez, Nomar Garciaparra	450.00
	Frank Thomas (Specially autographed Elite.)	45.00

Craftsmen

This 30-card insert has color player photos on front and back. The set is sequentially numbered to 3,500. The Master Craftsmen parallel is numbered to 100.

	NM/M
Complete Set (30):	40.00
Common Player:	.50
Production 3,500 Sets	
Master Craftsman (100 Sets):	10X
1 Ken Griffey Jr.	3.00
2 Frank Thomas	1.50
3 Alex Rodriguez	4.00
4 Cal Ripken Jr.	5.00
5 Greg Maddux	2.00
6 Mike Piazza	3.00
7 Chipper Jones	2.00
8 Derek Jeter	5.00
9 Tony Gwynn	2.00
10 Nomar Garciaparra	2.00
11 Scott Rolen	1.25
12 Jose Cruz Jr.	.50
13 Tony Clark	.50
14 Vladimir Guerrero	1.50
15 Todd Helton	1.25
16 Ben Grieve	.50
17 Andruw Jones	1.50
18 Jeff Bagwell	1.50
19 Mark McGwire	4.00
20 Juan Gonzalez	.75
21 Roger Clemens	2.50
22 Albert Belle	.50
23 Barry Bonds	5.00
24 Kenny Lofton	.50
25 Ivan Rodriguez	1.25
26 Paul Molitor	1.50
27 Barry Larkin (Incorrect "CARDINALS" on front.)	.50

Prime Numbers

This 36-card insert includes three cards for each of 12 players. Each card has a single number in the background. The three numbers for each player represent a key statistic for the player (ex. Mark McGwire's cards are 3-8-7; his career home run total at the time was 387). Each card in the set is sequentially numbered. The total is dependent upon the player's statistic. Promo versions with no serial number and a large "SAMPLE" on back exist for each card.

		NM/M
Common Card:		5.00
Samples: 50% Player's Common		
1A	Ken Griffey Jr. 2/94	25.00
1B	Ken Griffey Jr. 9/204	20.00
1C	Ken Griffey Jr. 4/290	17.50
2A	Frank Thomas 4/56	25.00
2B	Frank Thomas 5/406	7.50
2C	Frank Thomas 6/450	7.50
3A	Mark McGwire 3/87	30.00
3B	Mark McGwire 8/307	20.00
3C	Mark McGwire 7/380	20.00
4A	Cal Ripken Jr. 5/17	135.00
4B	Cal Ripken Jr. 1/507	13.50
4C	Cal Ripken Jr. 7/510	13.50
5A	Mike Piazza 5/76	30.00
5B	Mike Piazza 7/506	12.00
5C	Mike Piazza 6/570	12.00
6A	Chipper Jones 4/89	25.00
6B	Chipper Jones 8/409	9.00
6C	Chipper Jones 9/480	9.00
7A	Tony Gwynn 3/72	25.00
7B	Tony Gwynn 7/702	9.00
7C	Tony Gwynn 2/370	9.00
8A	Barry Bonds 3/74	45.00
8B	Barry Bonds 7/304	12.00
8C	Barry Bonds 4/370	12.00
9A	Jeff Bagwell 4/25	25.00
9B	Jeff Bagwell 2/405	7.50
9C	Jeff Bagwell 5/420	7.50
10A	Juan Gonzalez 5/89	9.00
10B	Juan Gonzalez 8/509	6.00
10C	Juan Gonzalez 9/580	6.00
11A	Alex Rodriguez 5/34	55.00
11B	Alex Rodriguez 3/504	12.00
11C	Alex Rodriguez 4/530	12.00
12A	Kenny Lofton 3/54	15.00
12B	Kenny Lofton 5/304	5.00
12C	Kenny Lofton 4/350	5.00

Prime Numbers Die-Cuts

This set is a die-cut parallel of the Prime Numbers insert. Each card is sequentially numbered. The production run for each player is the number featured on his first card times 100, his second card times 10 and his third card is sequentially numbered to the number featured on the card.

		NM/M
Common Player:		4.00
1A	Ken Griffey Jr. 2/200	20.00
1B	Ken Griffey Jr. 9/90	35.00
1C	Ken Griffey Jr. 4/4	130.00
2A	Frank Thomas 4/400	6.00
2B	Frank Thomas 5/50	20.00
2C	Frank Thomas 6/6	60.00
3A	Mark McGwire 3/300	17.50
3B	Mark McGwire 8/80	50.00
3C	Mark McGwire 7/7	110.00
4A	Cal Ripken Jr. 5/500	12.50
4B	Cal Ripken Jr. 1/10	95.00
4C	Cal Ripken Jr. 7/7	120.00
5A	Mike Piazza 5/500	10.00
5B	Mike Piazza 7/70	30.00
5C	Mike Piazza 6/6	75.00
6A	Chipper Jones 4/400	7.50
6B	Chipper Jones 8/80	25.00
6C	Chipper Jones 9/9	55.00
7A	Tony Gwynn 3/300	9.00
7B	Tony Gwynn 7/70	25.00
7C	Tony Gwynn 2/2	160.00
8A	Barry Bonds 3/300	10.00
8B	Barry Bonds 7/70	35.00
8C	Barry Bonds 4/4	160.00
9A	Jeff Bagwell 4/400	4.00
9B	Jeff Bagwell 2/20	25.00
9C	Jeff Bagwell 5/5	55.00
10A	Juan Gonzalez 5/500	4.00
10B	Juan Gonzalez 8/80	15.00
10C	Juan Gonzalez 9/9	55.00
11A	Alex Rodriguez 5/500	8.00
11B	Alex Rodriguez 3/30	60.00
11C	Alex Rodriguez 4/4	160.00
12A	Kenny Lofton 3/300	7.50
12B	Kenny Lofton 5/50	7.50
12C	Kenny Lofton 4/4	30.00

1998 Donruss Preferred

The Donruss Preferred 200-card base set is broken down into five subsets: 100 Grand Stand cards (5:1), 40 Mezzanine (1:6), 30 Club Level (1:12), 20 Field Box (1:23) and 10 Executive Suite (1:65). The base set is paralleled in the Preferred Seating set. Each subset has a different die-cut in the parallel. Inserts in this product include Great X-Pectations, Precious Metals and Title Waves.

	NM/M
Complete Set (200):	90.00
Common Grand Stand (5:1):	.10
Common Mezzanine (1:6):	.20
Common Club Level (1:12):	.30
Common Field Box: (1:23)	.40
Common Executive Suite (1:65):	1.50
Tin Pack (5):	3.00
Tin Box (24):	40.00
1 Ken Griffey Jr./EX	4.00
2 Frank Thomas/EX	2.50
3 Cal Ripken Jr./EX	7.50
4 Alex Rodriguez/EX	5.00
5 Greg Maddux/EX	3.00
6 Mike Piazza/EX	4.00
7 Chipper Jones/EX	3.00
8 Tony Gwynn/FB	2.50
9 Derek Jeter/FB	6.00
10 Jeff Bagwell/EX	2.50
11 Juan Gonzalez/EX	1.50
12 Nomar Garciaparra/EX	3.00
13 Andruw Jones/FB	2.00
14 Hideo Nomo/FB	.65
15 Roger Clemens/FB	3.00
16 Mark McGwire/FB	5.00
17 Scott Rolen/FB	.75
18 Vladimir Guerrero/FB	2.00
19 Barry Bonds/FB	6.00
20 Darin Erstad/FB	.60
21 Albert Belle/FB	.40
22 Kenny Lofton/FB	.40
23 Mo Vaughn/FB	.40
24 Tony Clark/FB	.40
25 Ivan Rodriguez/FB	1.50
26 Larry Walker/CL	.30
27 Eddie Murray/CL	1.00
28 Andy Pettitte/CL	.45
29 Roberto Alomar/CL	.40
30 Randy Johnson/CL	1.00
31 Manny Ramirez/CL	1.00
32 Paul Molitor/FB	2.00
33 Mike Mussina/CL	.50
34 Jim Thome/FB	.75
35 Tino Martinez/CL	.30
36 Gary Sheffield/CL	.45
37 Chuck Knoblauch/CL	.30
38 Bernie Williams/CL	.30
39 Tim Salmon/CL	.30
40 Sammy Sosa/CL	1.50
41 Wade Boggs/MZ	.75
42 Will Clark/GS	.30
43 Andres Galarraga/CL	.30

44	Raul Mondesi/CL	.30
45	Rickey Henderson/GS	.50
46	Jose Canseco/GS	.35
47	Pedro Martinez/GS	.50
48	Jay Buhner/GS	.10
49	Ryan Klesko/GS	.30
50	Barry Larkin/CL	.30
51	Charles Johnson/GS	.10
52	Tom Glavine/GS	.25
53	Edgar Martinez/CL	.30
54	Fred McGriff/GS	.30
55	Moises Alou/GS	.20
56	Dante Bichette/GS	.20
57	Jim Edmonds/CL	.30
58	Mark Grace/MZ	.30
59	Chan Ho Park/MZ	.20
60	Justin Thompson/MZ	.20
61	John Smoltz/MZ	.20
62	Craig Biggio/CL	.30
63	Ken Caminiti/MZ	.20
64	Deion Sanders/GS	.20
65	Carlos Delgado/GS	.20
66	David Justice/CL	.30
67	J.T. Snow/GS	.10
68	Jason Giambi/CL	.50
69	Garret Anderson/MZ	.20
70	Rondell White/MZ	.20
71	Matt Williams/MZ	.20
72	Brady Anderson/MZ	.20
73	Eric Karros/GS	.10
74	Javier Lopez/GS	.10
75	Pat Hentgen/GS	.10
76	Todd Hundley/GS	.10
77	Ray Lankford/GS	.10
78	Denny Neagle/GS	.10
79	Henry Rodriguez/GS	.10
80	Sandy Alomar Jr./MZ	.20
81	Rafael Palmeiro/MZ	.50
82	Robin Ventura/GS	.10
83	John Olerud/GS	.10
84	Omar Vizquel/GS	.10
85	Joe Randa/GS	.10
86	Lance Johnson/GS	.10
87	Kevin Brown/GS	.10
88	Curt Schilling/GS	.25
89	Ismael Valdes/GS	.10
90	Francisco Cordova/GS	.10
91	David Cone/GS	.10
92	Paul O'Neill/GS	.10
93	Jimmy Key/GS	.10
94	Brad Radke/GS	.10
95	Kevin Appier/GS	.10
96	Al Martin/GS	.10
97	Rusty Greer/MZ	.20
98	Reggie Jefferson/GS	.10
99	Ron Coomer/GS	.10
100	Vinny Castilla/GS	.10
101	Bobby Bonilla/MZ	.20
102	Eric Young/GS	.10
103	Tony Womack/GS	.10
104	Jason Kendall/GS	.10
105	Jeff Suppan/GS	.10
106	Shawn Estes/MZ	.20
107	Shawn Green/GS	.25
108	Edgardo Alfonzo/MZ	.20
109	Alan Benes/MZ	.20
110	Bobby Higginson/GS	.10
111	Mark Grudzielanek/GS	.10
112	Wilton Guerrero/GS	.10
113	Todd Greene/MZ	.20
114	Pokey Reese/GS	.10
115	Jose Guillen/CL	.30
116	Neifi Perez/MZ	.20
117	Luis Castillo/GS	.10
118	Edgar Renteria/GS	.10
119	Karim Garcia/GS	.10
120	Butch Huskey/GS	.10
121	Michael Tucker/GS	.10
122	Jason Dickson/GS	.10
123	Todd Walker/MZ	.20
124	Brian Jordan/GS	.10
125	Joe Carter/GS	.10
126	Matt Morris/MZ	.20
127	Brett Tomko/MZ	.20
128	Mike Cameron/CL	.30
129	Russ Davis/GS	.10
130	Shannon Stewart/MZ	.20
131	Kevin Orie/GS	.10
132	Scott Spiezio/GS	.10
133	Brian Giles/GS	.10
134	Raul Casanova/GS	.10
135	Jose Cruz Jr./CL	.30
136	Hideki Irabu/GS	.10
137	Bubba Trammell/GS	.10
138	Richard Hidalgo/CL	.30
139	Paul Konerko/CL	.35
140	Todd Helton/FB	1.00
141	Miguel Tejada/CL	.40
142	Fernando Tatis/MZ	.20
143	Ben Grieve/FB	.40
144	Travis Lee/FB	.65
145	Mark Kotsay/CL	.30
146	Eli Marrero/MZ	.20
147	David Ortiz/CL	.20
148	Juan Encarnacion/MZ	.20
149	Jaret Wright/MZ	.20
150	Livan Hernandez/CL	.20
151	Ruben Rivera/MZ	.20
152	Brad Fullmer/MZ	.20
153	Dennis Reyes/GS	.20
154	Enrique Wilson/MZ	.20
155	Todd Dunwoody/MZ	.20
156	Derrick Gibson/MZ	.20
157	Aaron Boone/MZ	.20
158	Ron Wright/MZ	.20
159	Preston Wilson/MZ	.20
160	Abraham Nunez/GS	.10
161	Shane Monahan/MZ	.20
162	Carl Pavano/GS	.10
163	Derrek Lee/GS	.35
164	Jeff Abbott/GS	.10
165	Wes Helms/MZ	.20
166	Brian Rose/GS	.10
167	Bobby Estalella/GS	.10
168	Ken Griffey Jr./GS	.75
169	Frank Thomas/GS	.50
170	Cal Ripken Jr./GS	1.50
171	Alex Rodriguez/GS	1.00
172	Greg Maddux/GS	.60
173	Mike Piazza/GS	.75
174	Chipper Jones/GS	.60
175	Tony Gwynn/GS	.50
176	Derek Jeter/GS	1.50
177	Jeff Bagwell/GS	.50
178	Juan Gonzalez/GS	.30
179	Nomar Garciaparra/GS	.60
180	Andruw Jones/GS	.50
181	Hideo Nomo/GS	.30
182	Roger Clemens/GS	.65
183	Mark McGwire/GS	1.00
184	Scott Rolen/GS	.35
185	Barry Bonds/GS	1.50
186	Darin Erstad/GS	.25
187	Mo Vaughn/GS	.10
188	Ivan Rodriguez/GS	.40
189	Larry Walker/MZ	.20
190	Andy Pettitte/GS	.30
191	Randy Johnson/MZ	.60
192	Paul Molitor/GS	.50
193	Jim Thome/GS	.35
194	Tino Martinez/MZ	.20
195	Gary Sheffield/GS	.30
196	Albert Belle/GS	.10
197	Jose Cruz Jr./GS	.10
198	Todd Helton/GS	.40
199	Ben Grieve/GS	.10
200	Paul Konerko/GS	.20

Seating

Preferred Seating is a die-cut parallel of the base set. Each section of the base set has a different die-cut.

	NM/M
Common Grand Stand:	.50
Stars and Rookies:	4X
Common Mezzanine:	.50
Stars and Rookies:	2X
Common Club Level:	.50
Stars and Rookies:	2X
Common Field Box:	.50
Stars and Rookies:	1.5X
Common Executive Suite:	2.50
Stars and Rookies:	1X

Great X-pectations

This 26-card insert features a veteran player on one side and a young player on the other. A large "GX" appears in the background on each side. The cards are sequentially numbered to 2,700, with the first 300 of each die-cut around the "GX."

	NM/M
Complete Set (26):	35.00
Common Player:	.75
Die-Cut:	3X
Samples:	1X
1 Jeff Bagwell, Travis Lee	1.25
2 Jose Cruz Jr., Ken Griffey Jr.	2.00
3 Larry Walker, Ben Grieve	.75
4 Frank Thomas, Todd Helton	1.25
5 Jim Thome, Paul Konerko	1.00
6 Alex Rodriguez, Miguel Tejada	2.50
7 Greg Maddux, Livan Hernandez	1.75
8 Roger Clemens, Jaret Wright	1.75
9 Albert Belle, Juan Encarnacion	.75
10 Mo Vaughn, David Ortiz	1.00
11 Manny Ramirez, Mark Kotsay	1.25
12 Tim Salmon, Brad Fullmer	.75
13 Cal Ripken Jr., Fernando Tatis	3.50
14 Hideo Nomo, Hideki Irabu	1.50
15 Mike Piazza, Todd Greene	2.00
16 Gary Sheffield, Richard Hidalgo	.75
17 Paul Molitor, Darin Erstad	1.25
18 Ivan Rodriguez, Eli Marrero	1.00
19 Ken Caminiti, Todd Walker	.75
20 Tony Gwynn, Jose Guillen	1.75
21 Derek Jeter, Nomar Garciaparra	3.50
22 Chipper Jones, Scott Rolen	1.75
23 Juan Gonzalez, Andruw Jones	1.25
24 Barry Bonds, Vladimir Guerrero	3.50
25 Mark McGwire, Tony Clark	2.50
26 Bernie Williams, Mike Cameron	.75

Precious Metals

Precious Metals is a 30-card partial parallel of the Preferred base set. Each card was printed on stock using real silver, gold or platinum. Fifty complete sets were produced.

	NM/M
Complete Set (30):	850.00
Common Player:	7.50
1 Ken Griffey Jr.	50.00
2 Frank Thomas	35.00
3 Cal Ripken Jr.	75.00
4 Alex Rodriguez	60.00
5 Greg Maddux	45.00
6 Mike Piazza	50.00
7 Chipper Jones	45.00
8 Tony Gwynn	45.00
9 Derek Jeter	75.00
10 Jeff Bagwell	35.00
11 Juan Gonzalez	15.00
12 Nomar Garciaparra	45.00
13 Andruw Jones	35.00
14 Hideo Nomo	15.00
15 Roger Clemens	45.00
16 Mark McGwire	60.00
17 Scott Rolen	25.00
18 Barry Bonds	75.00
19 Darin Erstad	15.00
20 Kenny Lofton	7.50
21 Mo Vaughn	7.50
22 Ivan Rodriguez	25.00
23 Randy Johnson	35.00
24 Paul Molitor	35.00
25 Jose Cruz Jr.	7.50
26 Paul Konerko	7.50
27 Todd Helton	25.00
28 Ben Grieve	7.50
29 Travis Lee	7.50
30 Mark Kotsay	7.50

Title Waves

This 30-card set features players who won awards or titles between 1993-1997.

Printed on plastic stock, each card is sequentially numbered to the year the player won the award. The card fronts feature the Title Waves logo, a color player photo in front of a background of fans and the name of the award the player won.

	NM/M
Complete Set (30):	100.00
Common Player:	1.00
1 Nomar Garciaparra	5.00
2 Scott Rolen	2.50
3 Roger Clemens	5.50
4 Gary Sheffield	1.50
5 Jeff Bagwell	3.50
6 Cal Ripken Jr.	10.00
7 Frank Thomas	3.50
8 Ken Griffey Jr.	6.00
9 Larry Walker	1.00
10 Derek Jeter	10.00
11 Juan Gonzalez	2.00
12 Bernie Williams	1.00
13 Andruw Jones	3.50
14 Andy Pettitte	1.50
15 Ivan Rodriguez	2.50
16 Alex Rodriguez	8.00
17 Mark McGwire	8.00
18 Andres Galarraga	1.00
19 Hideo Nomo	2.00
20 Mo Vaughn	1.00
21 Randy Johnson	3.50
22 Chipper Jones	5.00
23 Greg Maddux	5.00
24 Manny Ramirez	3.50
25 Tony Gwynn	5.00
26 Albert Belle	1.00
27 Kenny Lofton	1.00
28 Mike Piazza	6.00
29 Paul Molitor	3.50
30 Barry Bonds	10.00

Tins

Donruss Preferred was packaged in collectible tins. Each tin contained five cards and featured one of 24 players on the top. Silver (numbered to 999) and gold (199) parallel tins were also produced and included in hobby-only boxes. The values shown are for empty tins.

	NM/M
Complete Set (24):	17.50
Common Player:	.25
Gold Tins (199):	3X
Silver Tins (999):	1.5X
1 Todd Helton	.65
2 Ben Grieve	.25
3 Cal Ripken Jr.	2.50
4 Alex Rodriguez	2.00
5 Greg Maddux	1.00
6 Mike Piazza	1.50
7 Chipper Jones	1.00
8 Travis Lee	.25
9 Derek Jeter	2.50
10 Jeff Bagwell	.75
11 Juan Gonzalez	.50
12 Mark McGwire	2.00
13 Hideo Nomo	.50
14 Roger Clemens	1.25
15 Andruw Jones	.75
16 Paul Molitor	.75
17 Vladimir Guerrero	.75
18 Jose Cruz Jr.	.25
19 Nomar Garciaparra	1.00
20 Scott Rolen	.65
21 Ken Griffey Jr.	1.50
22 Larry Walker	.25
23 Frank Thomas	.75
24 Tony Gwynn	1.00

Double-Wide Tins

Double-wide flip-top tins of Donruss Preferred cards were a reail exclusive with a price tag of about $6. The double-wide retail tins use the same player checklist and photo as the green hobby-version single tins, but have predominantly blue color. Values shown are for opened tins.

	NM/M
Complete Set (12):	12.00
Common Tin:	.65
1 Todd Helton, Ben Grieve	.65
2 Cal Ripken Jr., Alex Rodriguez	2.00
3 Greg Maddux, Mike Piazza	1.25
4 Chipper Jones, Travis Lee	1.00
5 Derek Jeter, Jeff Bagwell	2.00
6 Juan Gonzalez, Mark McGwire	1.50
7 Hideo Nomo, Roger Clemens	1.00
8 Andruw Jones, Paul Molitor	.75
9 Vladimir Guerrero, Jose Cruz Jr.	.75
10 Nomar Garciaparra, Scott Rolen	1.00
11 Ken Griffey Jr., Larry Walker	1.25
12 Tony Gwynn, Frank Thomas	1.00

Tin Boxes

The boxes for 1998 Donruss Preferred consisted of a lithographed steel lidded box which contained 24 tin packs. The basic tin box was green in color and individually serial numbered to 999. A parallel gold box issue was randomly inserted in Preferred cases and had boxes numbered to 199. Values shown are for empty boxes.

	NM/M
Complete Set (24):	85.00
Common Player:	1.00
Gold:	1.5X
1 Todd Helton	2.50
2 Ben Grieve	1.00
3 Cal Ripken Jr.	10.00
4 Alex Rodriguez	7.50
5 Greg Maddux	5.00
6 Mike Piazza	6.00
7 Chipper Jones	5.00
8 Travis Lee	1.00
9 Derek Jeter	10.00
10 Jeff Bagwell	3.00
11 Juan Gonzalez	1.50
12 Mark McGwire	7.50
13 Hideo Nomo	1.50
14 Roger Clemens	5.50
15 Andruw Jones	3.00
16 Paul Molitor	3.00
17 Vladimir Guerrero	3.00
18 Jose Cruz Jr.	1.00
19 Nomar Garciaparra	5.00
20 Scott Rolen	2.00
21 Ken Griffey Jr.	6.00
22 Larry Walker	1.00
23 Frank Thomas	3.00
24 Tony Gwynn	5.00

1998 Donruss Signature Series Preview Autographs

This insert was a surprise addition to Donruss Update. The set features autographs

from top rookies and stars. The number of cards produced varies for each player. The card fronts have a color player photo in front of a gold checkered border with the signature in a white area near the bottom. Cards of a number of players (Alou, Casey, Jenkins, Wilson, etc.) were never officially released, having been returned too late by the players; specimens, have, however made their way into the hobby market in unknown numbers.

	NM/M
Common Player:	10.00
(1) Sandy Alomar Jr./96	30.00
(2) Moises Alou	50.00
(3) Andy Benes/135	15.00
(4) Russell Branyan/188	15.00
(5) Sean Casey	85.00
(6) Tony Clark/188	20.00
(7) Juan Encarnacion/193	15.00
(8) Brad Fullmer/396	10.00
(9) Juan Gonzalez/108	115.00
(10) Ben Grieve/100	35.00
(11) Todd Helton/101	50.00
(12) Richard Hidalgo/380	10.00
(13) A.J. Hinch/400	10.00
(14) Damian Jackson/15	65.00
(15) Geoff Jenkins	185.00
(16) Derek Jeter	1,225
(17) Chipper Jones/112	125.00
(18) Chuck Knoblauch/98	50.00
(19) Travis Lee/101	20.00
(20) Mike Lowell/450	15.00
(21) Greg Maddux/92	165.00
(22) Kevin Millwood/395	30.00
(23) Magglio Ordonez/420	50.00
(24) David Ortiz/393	75.00
(25) Rafael Palmeiro/107	50.00
(26) Cal Ripken Jr./22	850.00
(27) Alex Rodriguez/23	1,150
(28) Curt Schilling/100	100.00
(29) Randall Simon/380	10.00
(30) Fernando Tatis/400	10.00
(31) Miguel Tejada/375	40.00
(32) Robin Ventura/95	30.00
(33) Dan Wilson	85.00
(34) Kerry Wood/373	40.00

1998 Donruss Signature Series

The 140-card base set has a white border encasing the player photo with the logo stamped with silver foil. Card backs have a small photo and complete year-by-year statistics. Signature Proofs are a parallel to the base set utilizing holo-foil treatment and "Signature Proof" written down the left edge of the card front. Each card is numbered "1 of 150" on the card back.

	NM/M
Complete Set (140):	30.00

Common Player:		.10
Signature Proofs:		12X
Pack (5):		12.50
Wax Box (12):		150.00
1	David Justice	.10
2	Derek Jeter	2.50
3	Nomar Garciaparra	1.00
4	Ryan Klesko	.10
5	Jeff Bagwell	.75
6	Dante Bichette	.10
7	Ivan Rodriguez	.65
8	Albert Belle	.10
9	Cal Ripken Jr.	2.50
10	Craig Biggio	.10
11	Barry Larkin	.10
12	Jose Guillen	.10
13	Will Clark	.10
14	J.T. Snow	.10
15	Chuck Knoblauch	.10
16	Todd Walker	.10
17	Scott Rolen	.60
18	Rickey Henderson	.75
19	Juan Gonzalez	.40
20	Justin Thompson	.10
21	Roger Clemens	1.25
22	Ray Lankford	.10
23	Jose Cruz Jr.	.10
24	Ken Griffey Jr.	1.50
25	Andruw Jones	.75
26	Darin Erstad	.30
27	Jim Thome	.50
28	Wade Boggs	1.00
29	Ken Caminiti	.10
30	Todd Hundley	.10
31	Mike Piazza	1.50
32	Sammy Sosa	1.00
33	Larry Walker	.10
34	Matt Williams	.10
35	Frank Thomas	.75
36	Gary Sheffield	.30
37	Alex Rodriguez	2.00
38	Hideo Nomo	.40
39	Kenny Lofton	.10
40	John Smoltz	.10
41	Mo Vaughn	.10
42	Edgar Martinez	.10
43	Paul Molitor	.75
44	Rafael Palmeiro	.65
45	Barry Bonds	2.50
46	Vladimir Guerrero	.75
47	Carlos Delgado	.50
48	Bobby Higginson	.10
49	Greg Maddux	2.00
50	Jim Edmonds	.10
51	Randy Johnson	.75
52	Mark McGwire	2.00
53	Rondell White	.10
54	Raul Mondesi	.10
55	Manny Ramirez	.75
56	Pedro Martinez	.75
57	Tim Salmon	.10
58	Moises Alou	.10
59	Fred McGriff	.10
60	Garret Anderson	.10
61	Sandy Alomar Jr.	.10
62	Chan Ho Park	.10
63	Mark Kotsay	.10
64	Mike Mussina	.50
65	Tom Glavine	.25
66	Tony Clark	.10
67	Mark Grace	.10
68	Tony Gwynn	1.00
69	Tino Martinez	.10
70	Kevin Brown	.10
71	Todd Greene	.10
72	Andy Pettitte	.30
73	Livan Hernandez	.10
74	Curt Schilling	.25
75	Andres Galarraga	.10
76	Rusty Greer	.10
77	Jay Buhner	.10
78	Bobby Bonilla	.10
79	Chipper Jones	1.00
80	Eric Young	.10
81	Jason Giambi	.50
82	Javy Lopez	.10
83	Roberto Alomar	.25
84	Bernie Williams	.10
85	A.J. Hinch	.10
86	Kerry Wood	.40
87	Juan Encarnacion	.10
88	Brad Fullmer	.10
89	Ben Grieve	.10
90	Magglio Ordonez RC	2.00
91	Todd Helton	.65
92	Richard Hidalgo	.15
93	Paul Konerko	.15
94	Aramis Ramirez	.10
95	Ricky Ledee	.10
96	Derrek Lee	.50
97	Travis Lee	.15
98	Matt Anderson RC	.10
99	Jaret Wright	.10
100	David Ortiz	.35
101	Carl Pavano	.10
102	Orlando Hernandez RC	.50
103	Fernando Tatis	.10
104	Miguel Tejada	.30
105	Rolando Arrojo RC	.50
106	Kevin Millwood RC	.10
107	Ken Griffey Jr. (Checklist)	.50
108	Frank Thomas (Checklist)	.30
109	Cal Ripken Jr. (Checklist)	.75
110	Greg Maddux (Checklist)	.40

111	John Olerud	.10
112	David Cone	.10
113	Vinny Castilla	.10
114	Jason Kendall	.10
115	Brian Jordan	.10
116	Hideki Irabu	.10
117	Bartolo Colon	.10
118	Greg Vaughn	.10
119	David Segui	.10
120	Bruce Chen	.10
121	Julio Ramirez RC	.10
122	Troy Glaus RC	4.00
123	Jeremy Giambi RC	.50
124	Ryan Minor RC	.15
125	Richie Sexson	.10
126	Dermal Brown	.10
127	Adrian Beltre	.15
128	Eric Chavez	.30
129	J.D. Drew RC	4.00
130	Gabe Kapler RC	.15
131	Masato Yoshii RC	.25
132	Mike Lowell RC	1.00
133	Jim Parque RC	.25
134	Roy Halladay	.10
135	Carlos Lee RC	1.00
136	Jin Ho Cho RC	.25
137	Michael Barrett	.10
138	Fernando Seguignol RC	.40
139	Odalis Perez RC	.50
140	Mark McGwire (Checklist)	.65

Proofs

This parallel set differs from the regular issue Signature Series base cards in the presence at left-front of a vertical stack of gold refractive foil strips on which "SIGNATURE PROOF" is spelled out. Also, backs of the proofs have a gold, rather than white, background.

	NM/M
Complete Set (140):	450.00
Common Player:	1.00
Stars/Rookies:	12X

Autographs Samples

An unknown number of cards can be found with facsimile signatures on front and a "SAMPLE" overprint on back.

	NM/M
Adrian Beltre (Century)	12.50
Will Clark (Century)	12.50
Travis Lee/Red	3.00

Autographs (Red)

Autographs were inserted one per pack and feature the player photo over a silver and red foil background. The featured player's autograph appears on the bottom portion of front with the Donruss logo stamped in gold foil. Autographs are un-numbered. The first 100 cards signed by each

player are blue, sequentially numbered and designated as "Century Marks." The next 1,000 signed are green, sequentially numbered and designated as "Millennium Marks." Greg Maddux signed only 12 regular Donruss Signature Autographs.

		NM/M
Common Player:		2.50
(1)	Roberto Alomar/150	35.00
(2)	Sandy Alomar Jr./700	10.00
(3)	Moises Alou/900	15.00
(4)	Gabe Alvarez/2,900	2.50
(5)	Wilson Alvarez/1,600	4.00
(6)	Jay Bell/1,500	4.00
(7)	Adrian Beltre/1,900	25.00
(8)	Andy Benes/2,600	4.00
(9)	Aaron Boone/3,400	10.00
(10)	Russell Branyan/1,650	4.00
(11)	Orlando Cabrera/3,100	8.00
(12)	Mike Cameron/1,150	6.00
(13)	Joe Carter/400	12.00
(14)	Sean Casey/2,275	4.00
(15)	Bruce Chen/150	5.00
(16)	Tony Clark/2,275	7.00
(17)	Will Clark/1,400	15.00
(18)	Matt Clement/1,400	4.00
(19)	Pat Cline/400	6.00
(20)	Ken Cloude/3,400	2.50
(21)	Michael Coleman/2,800	2.50
(22)	David Cone/25	50.00
(23)	Jeff Conine/1,400	5.00
(24)	Jacob Cruz/3,200	2.50
(25)	Russ Davis/3,500	4.00
(26)	Jason Dickson/1,400	4.00
(27)	Todd Dunwoody/3,500	2.50
(28)	Juan Encarnacion/3,400	5.00
(29)	Darin Erstad/700	15.00
(30)	Bobby Estalella/3,400	4.00
(31)	Jeff Fassero/3,400	2.50
(32)	John Franco/1,80	2.50
(33)	Brad Fullmer/3,100	5.00
(34)	Jason Giambi/3,100	15.00
(35)	Derrick Gibson/1,200	5.00
(36)	Todd Greene/1,400	5.00
(37)	Ben Grieve/1,400	6.00
(38)	Mark Grudzielanek/3,200	4.00
(39)	Vladimir Guerrero/2,100	25.00
(40)	Wilton Guerrero/1,900	4.00
(41)	Jose Guillen/2,400	5.00
(42)	Todd Helton/1,300	20.00
(43)	Richard Hidalgo/3,400	4.00
(44)	A.J. Hinch/2,900	4.00
(45)	Butch Huskey/1,900	4.00
(46)	Raul Ibanez/3,300	2.50
(47)	Damian Jackson/900	2.50
(48)	Geoff Jenkins/3,100	6.00
(49)	Eric Karros/650	10.00
(50)	Ryan Klesko/400	10.00
(51)	Mark Kotsay/3,600	5.00
(52)	Ricky Ledee/2,200	5.00
(53)	Derrek Lee/3,400	15.00
(54)	Travis Lee/150	25.00
(54s)	Travis Lee (Facsimile autograph, "SAMPLE" on back.)	3.00
(55)	Javier Lopez/650	8.00
(56)	Mike Lowell/3,500	8.00
(57)	Greg Maddux/12	625.00
(58)	Eli Marrero/3,500	4.00
(59)	Al Martin/1,300	4.00
(60)	Rafael Medina/1,400	2.50
(61)	Scott Morgan/900	4.50
(62)	Abraham Nunez/3,500	2.50
(63)	Paul O'Neill/1,000	20.00
(64)	Luis Ordaz/2,700	2.50
(65)	Magglio Ordonez/3,200	15.00
(66)	Kevin Orie/1,350	5.00
(67)	David Ortiz/3,400	25.00
(68)	Rafael Palmeiro/1,000	25.00
(69)	Carl Pavano/2,600	8.00
(70)	Neifi Perez/3,050	2.50
(71)	Dante Powell/3,050	2.50

(72)	Aramis Ramirez/2,800	10.00
(73)	Mariano Rivera/900	35.00
(74)	Felix Rodriguez/1,400	3.00
(75)	Henry Rodriguez/3,400	3.00
(76)	Scott Rolen/1,900	30.00
(77)	Brian Rose/1,400	3.00
(78)	Curt Schilling/900	30.00
(79)	Richie Sexson/3,500	8.00
(80)	Randall Simon/3,500	3.00
(81)	J.T. Snow/400	10.00
(82)	Jeff Suppan/1,400	5.00
(83)	Fernando Tatis/3,900	3.00
(84)	Miguel Tejada/3,900	15.00
(85)	Brett Tomko/3,400	2.50
(86)	Bubba Trammell/3,900	2.50
(87)	Ismael Valdez/1,900	5.00
(88)	Robin Ventura/1,400	7.00
(89)	Billy Wagner/3,900	10.00
(90)	Todd Walker/1,900	5.00
(91)	Daryle Ward/400	4.00
(92)	Rondell White/3,400	5.00
(93)	Antone Williamson/3,350	2.50
(94)	Dan Wilson/2,400	4.00
(95)	Enrique Wilson/3,400	2.50
(96)	Preston Wilson/2,100	5.00
(97)	Tony Womack/3,500	2.50
(98)	Kerry Wood/3,400	20.00

Century Marks (Blue)

This 121-card set is a serially numbered, blue-foil parallel of the Autographs insert set and limited to 100 cards signed by each featured player (unless otherwise shown in the checklist). Jason Kendall's cards were never signed or returned to Donruss for packaging. A few have made their way into the hobby.

		NM/M
Common Player:		10.00
(1)	Roberto Alomar	60.00
(2)	Sandy Alomar Jr.	15.00
(3)	Moises Alou	40.00
(4)	Gabe Alvarez	10.00
(5)	Wilson Alvarez	10.00
(6)	Brady Anderson	20.00
(7)	Jay Bell	20.00
(8)	Albert Belle	20.00
(9)	Adrian Beltre	60.00
(10)	Andy Benes	10.00
(11)	Wade Boggs	60.00
(12)	Barry Bonds	250.00
(13)	Aaron Boone	40.00
(14)	Russell Branyan	10.00
(15)	Jay Buhner	10.00
(16)	Ellis Burks	10.00
(17)	Orlando Cabrera	20.00
(18)	Mike Cameron	10.00
(19)	Ken Caminiti	25.00
(20)	Joe Carter	20.00
(21)	Sean Casey	15.00
(22)	Bruce Chen	10.00
(23)	Tony Clark	10.00
(24)	Will Clark	60.00
(25)	Roger Clemens	200.00
(26)	Matt Clement	20.00
(27)	Pat Cline	10.00
(28)	Ken Cloude	10.00
(29)	Michael Coleman	10.00
(30)	David Cone	25.00
(31)	Jeff Conine	10.00
(32)	Jacob Cruz	10.00
(33)	Jose Cruz Jr.	15.00
(34)	Russ Davis	10.00
(35)	Jason Dickson	10.00
(36)	Todd Dunwoody	10.00
(37)	Scott Elarton	10.00
(38)	Darin Erstad	25.00
(39)	Bobby Estalella	10.00
(40)	Jeff Fassero	10.00
(41)	John Franco	10.00
(42)	Brad Fullmer	10.00
(43)	Andres Galarraga	15.00
(44)	Nomar Garciaparra	100.00
(45)	Jason Giambi	10.00
(46)	Derrick Gibson	10.00
(47)	Tom Glavine	75.00
(48)	Juan Gonzalez	75.00
(49)	Todd Greene	10.00

(50)	Ben Grieve	10.00
(51)	Mark Grudzielanek	10.00
(52)	Vladimir Guerrero	75.00
(53)	Wilton Guerrero	10.00
(54)	Jose Guillen	10.00
(55)	Tony Gwynn	100.00
(56)	Todd Helton	60.00
(57)	Richard Hidalgo	10.00
(58)	A.J. Hinch	10.00
(59)	Butch Huskey	10.00
(60)	Raul Ibanez	10.00
(61)	Damian Jackson	10.00
(62)	Geoff Jenkins	10.00
(63)	Derek Jeter	220.00
(64)	Randy Johnson	150.00
(65)	Chipper Jones	100.00
(66)	Eric Karros/50	15.00
(67)	Jason Kendall (Unsigned)	20.00
(68)	Ryan Klesko	10.00
(69)	Chuck Knoblauch	10.00
(70)	Mark Kotsay	10.00
(71)	Ricky Ledee	10.00
(72)	Derrek Lee	25.00
(73)	Travis Lee	15.00
(74)	Javier Lopez	15.00
(75)	Mike Lowell	30.00
(76)	Greg Maddux	150.00
(77)	Eli Marrero	10.00
(78)	Al Martin	10.00
(79)	Rafael Medina	10.00
(80)	Paul Molitor	50.00
(81)	Scott Morgan	10.00
(82)	Mike Mussina	80.00
(83)	Abraham Nunez	15.00
(84)	Paul O'Neill	40.00
(85)	Luis Ordaz	10.00
(86)	Magglio Ordonez	30.00
(87)	Kevin Orie	10.00
(88)	David Ortiz	10.00
(89)	Rafael Palmeiro	85.00
(90)	Carl Pavano	25.00
(91)	Neifi Perez	10.00
(92)	Andy Pettitte	50.00
(93)	Aramis Ramirez	25.00
(94)	Cal Ripken Jr.	225.00
(95)	Mariano Rivera	75.00
(96)	Alex Rodriguez	200.00
(97)	Felix Rodriguez	70.00
(98)	Henry Rodriguez	10.00
(99)	Scott Rolen	70.00
(100)	Brian Rose	10.00
(101)	Curt Schilling	50.00
(102)	Richie Sexson	20.00
(103)	Randall Simon	10.00
(104)	J.T. Snow	10.00
(105)	Darryl Strawberry	45.00
(106)	Jeff Suppan	10.00
(107)	Fernando Tatis	10.00
(108)	Brett Tomko	10.00
(109)	Bubba Trammell	10.00
(110)	Ismael Valdez	10.00
(111)	Robin Ventura	20.00
(112)	Billy Wagner	40.00
(113)	Todd Walker	15.00
(114)	Daryle Ward	10.00
(115)	Rondell White	20.00
(116)	Matt Williams/80	35.00
(117)	Antone Williamson	10.00
(118)	Dan Wilson	15.00
(119)	Enrique Wilson	10.00
(120)	Preston Wilson	25.00
(121)	Tony Womack	10.00
(122)	Kerry Wood	60.00

Millennium Marks (Green)

This is a green-foil parallel version of the Autographs insert set and features 1,000 cards signed by the featured player (unless otherwise shown in the checklist). Cards are not numbered.

		NM/M
Common Player:		3.00
(1)	Roberto Alomar	5.00
(2)	Sandy Alomar Jr.	3.00
(3)	Moises Alou	3.00
(4)	Gabe Alvarez	3.00
(5)	Wilson Alvarez	3.00
(6)	Brady Anderson/800	3.00
(7)	Jay Bell	3.00
(8)	Albert Belle/400	9.00
(9)	Adrian Beltre	15.00

(10)	Andy Benes	3.00
(11)	Wade Boggs/900	20.00
(12)	Barry Bonds/400	150.00
(13)	Aaron Boone	4.00
(14)	Russell Branyan	3.00
(15)	Jay Buhner/400	15.00
(16)	Ellis Burks/900	6.00
(17)	Orlando Cabrera	6.00
(18)	Mike Cameron	5.00
(19)	Ken Caminiti/900	22.50
(20)	Joe Carter	7.50
(21)	Sean Casey	8.00
(22)	Bruce Chen	3.00
(23)	Tony Clark	5.00
(24)	Will Clark	25.00
(25)	Roger Clemens/400	75.00
(26)	Matt Clement/900	8.00
(27)	Pat Cline	3.00
(28)	Ken Cloude	3.00
(29)	Michael Coleman	10.00
(30)	David Cone	10.00
(31)	Jeff Conine	3.00
(32)	Jacob Cruz	3.00
(33)	Jose Cruz Jr./850	5.00
(34)	Russ Davis/950	3.00
(35)	Jason Dickson/950	3.00
(36)	Todd Dunwoody	3.00
(37)	Scott Elarton/900	3.00
(38)	Juan Encarnacion	5.00
(39)	Darin Erstad	7.00
(40)	Bobby Estalella	3.00
(41)	Jeff Fassero	3.00
(42)	John Franco/950	7.00
(43)	Brad Fullmer	3.00
(44)	Andres Galarraga/900	10.00
(45)	Nomar Garciaparra/400	60.00
(46)	Jason Giambi	20.00
(47)	Derrick Gibson	3.00
(48)	Tom Glavine/700	25.00
(49)	Juan Gonzalez	25.00
(50)	Todd Greene	3.00
(51)	Ben Grieve	4.00
(52)	Mark Grudzielanek	3.00
(53)	Vladimir Guerrero	30.00
(54)	Wilton Guerrero	3.00
(55)	Jose Guillen	3.00
(56)	Tony Gwynn/900	30.00
(57)	Todd Helton	20.00
(58)	Richard Hidalgo	3.00
(59)	A.J. Hinch	3.00
(60)	Butch Huskey	3.00
(61)	Raul Ibanez	3.00
(62)	Damian Jackson	3.00
(63)	Geoff Jenkins	3.00
(64)	Derek Jeter/400	100.00
(65)	Randy Johnson/800	50.00
(66)	Chipper Jones/900	30.00
(67)	Eric Karros	7.00
(68)	Ryan Klesko	6.00
(69)	Chuck Knoblauch/900	10.00
(70)	Mark Kotsay	5.00
(71)	Ricky Ledee	3.00
(72)	Derrek Lee	20.00
(73)	Travis Lee	20.00
(74)	Javier-Lopez/800	10.00
(75)	Mike Lowell	10.00
(76)	Greg Maddux/400	85.00
(77)	Eli Marrero	3.00
(78)	Al Martin/950	3.00
(79)	Rafael Medina/850	3.00
(80)	Paul Molitor/900	17.50
(81)	Scott Morgan	3.00
(82)	Mike Mussina/900	17.50
(83)	Abraham Nunez	3.00
(84)	Paul O'Neill/900	20.00
(85)	Luis Ordaz	3.00
(86)	Magglio Ordonez	15.00
(87)	Kevin Orie	3.00
(88)	David Ortiz	3.00
(89)	Rafael Palmeiro/900	30.00
(90)	Carl Pavano	10.00
(91)	Neifi Perez	3.00
(92)	Andy Pettitte/900	20.00
(93)	Dante Powell/950	3.00
(94)	Aramis Ramirez	3.00
(95)	Cal Ripken Jr./375	100.00
(96)	Mariano Rivera	30.00
(97)	Alex Rodriguez/350	75.00
(98)	Felix Rodriguez	6.00
(99)	Henry Rodriguez	3.00
(100)	Scott Rolen	20.00
(101)	Brian Rose	3.00
(102)	Curt Schilling	8.00
(103)	Richie Sexson	8.00
(104)	Randall Simon	3.00
(105)	J.T. Snow	4.00
(106)	Darryl Strawberry/900	40.00
(107)	Jeff Suppan	3.00
(108)	Fernando Tatis	6.00
(109)	Miguel Tejada	40.00
(110)	Brett Tomko	3.00
(111)	Bubba Trammell	3.00
(112)	Ismael Valdes	3.00
(113)	Robin Ventura	6.00
(114)	Billy Wagner/900	3.00
(115)	Todd Walker	4.00
(116)	Daryle Ward	3.00
(117)	Rondell White	6.00
(118)	Matt Williams/820	8.00
(119)	Antone Williamson	3.00
(120)	Dan Wilson	3.00
(121)	Enrique Wilson	3.00
(122)	Preston Wilson/400	10.00
(123)	Tony Womack	3.00
(124)	Kerry Wood	25.00

Significant Signatures

This 18-card autographed set features some of baseball's all-time great players. Each card is sequentially numbered to 2,000. The Sandy Koufax autographs weren't received in time prior to release and was redeemable by sending in the Billy Williams autograph, the collector would then receive both the Williams and Koufax back. Exchange cards were also initially released for Nolan Ryan and Ozzie Smith. Early in the 2000s, a large quantity of the Koufax cards found its way into the hobby market.

		NM/M
Complete Set (18):		425.00
Common Player:		10.00
	Ernie Banks	25.00
	Yogi Berra	25.00
	George Brett	40.00
	Catfish Hunter	35.00
	Al Kaline	25.00
	Harmon Killebrew	25.00
	Ralph Kiner	10.00
	Sandy Koufax	100.00
	Eddie Mathews	25.00
	Don Mattingly	50.00
	Willie McCovey	25.00
	Stan Musial	40.00
	Phil Rizzuto	
	(Edition of 1,000.)	20.00
	Nolan Ryan	60.00
	Nolan Ryan	
	(Exchange Card)	5.00
	Ozzie Smith	20.00
	Ozzie Smith	
	(Exchange Card)	5.00
	Duke Snider	25.00
	Don Sutton	12.00
	Billy Williams	12.00

Redemption Baseballs

Redemption cards for authentically autographed baseballs were randomly inserted in Donruss Signature Series packs. Baseballs are laser burned with a Donruss seal to ensure authenticity. Every ball, except Ben Grieve's, is serial numbered within the edition limit shown. Signing Bonus redemption cards, no longer valid, are valued about 10 percent of the corresponding ball.

		NM/M
Common Autographed Ball:		15.00
Redemption Card: 10%		
(1)	Roberto Alomar/60	35.00
(2)	Sandy Alomar Jr./60	20.00
(3)	Ernie Banks/12	85.00
(4)	Ken Caminiti/60	20.00
(5)	Tony Clark/60	20.00
(6)	Jacob Cruz/12	20.00
(7)	Russ Davis/60	15.00
(8)	Juan Encarnacion/ 60	20.00
(9)	Bobby Estalella/60	15.00
(10)	Jeff Fassero/60	15.00
(11)	Mark Grudzielanek/ 60	15.00
(12)	Ben Grieve/30	20.00
(13)	Jose Guillen/120	20.00
(14)	Tony Gwynn/60	100.00
(15)	Al Kaline/12	75.00
(16)	Paul Konerko/100	15.00
(17)	Travis Lee/100	20.00
(18)	Mike Lowell/60	15.00
(19)	Eli Marrero/60	15.00
(20)	Eddie Mathews/12	80.00
(21)	Paul Molitor/60	65.00
(22)	Stan Musial/12	125.00
(23)	Abraham Nunez/12	20.00
(24)	Luis Ordaz/12	20.00
(25)	Magglio Ordonez/12	50.00
(26)	Scott Rolen/60	45.00
(27)	Bubba Trammell/24	25.00
(28)	Robin Ventura/60	20.00
(29)	Billy Wagner/60	20.00
(30)	Rondell White/60	20.00
(31)	Antone Williamson/ 12	15.00
(32)	Tony Womack/60	15.00

2001 Donruss

		NM/M
Complete Set (220):		
Common Player:		.15
Common Rated Rookie (151-200):		4.00
Production 2001		
Hobby Pack (5):		6.00
Hobby Box (24):		120.00
The Rookies Coupon:		1.00
Inserted 1:72		
Baseball's Best Coupon:		1.00
Inserted 1:720		
Exchange Deadline 11/01/01		
1	Alex Rodriguez	2.00
2	Barry Bonds	2.50
3	Cal Ripken Jr.	2.50
4	Chipper Jones	1.00
5	Derek Jeter	2.50
6	Troy Glaus	.50
7	Frank Thomas	.75
8	Greg Maddux	1.00
9	Ivan Rodriguez	.50
10	Jeff Bagwell	.50
11	Jose Canseco	.40
12	Todd Helton	.50
13	Ken Griffey Jr.	1.50
14	Manny Ramirez	.75
15	Mark McGwire	2.00
16	Mike Piazza	1.50
17	Nomar Garciaparra	1.00
18	Pedro Martinez	1.00
19	Randy Johnson	.75
20	Rick Ankiel	.15
21	Ricky Henderson	.75
22	Roger Clemens	2.00
23	Sammy Sosa	1.00
24	Tony Gwynn	1.00
25	Vladimir Guerrero	.75
26	Eric Davis	.15
27	Roberto Alomar	.25
28	Mark Mulder	.25
29	Pat Burrell	.40
30	Harold Baines	.15
31	Carlos Delgado	.40
32	J.D. Drew	.25
33	Jim Edmonds	.40
34	Darin Erstad	.25
35	Jason Giambi	.50
36	Tom Glavine	.30
37	Juan Gonzalez	.35
38	Mark Grace	.25
39	Shawn Green	.25
40	Tim Hudson	.25
41	Andruw Jones	.75
42	David Justice	.15
43	Jeff Kent	.25
44	Barry Larkin	.25
45	Pokey Reese	.15
46	Mike Mussina	.40
47	Hideo Nomo	.35
48	Rafael Palmeiro	.50
49	Adam Piatt	.15
50	Scott Rolen	.75
51	Gary Sheffield	.40
52	Bernie Williams	.25
53	Bob Abreu	.25
54	Edgardo Alfonzo	.15
55	Jermaine Clark **RC**	.15
56	Albert Belle	.15
57	Craig Biggio	.25
58	Andres Galarraga	.15
59	Edgar Martinez	.15
60	Fred McGriff	.15
61	Magglio Ordonez	.15
62	Jim Thome	.50
63	Matt Williams	.15
64	Kerry Wood	.25
65	Moises Alou	.25
66	Brady Anderson	.15
67	Garret Anderson	.15
68	Tony Armas Jr.	.15
69	Tony Batista	.15
70	Jose Cruz Jr.	.15
71	Carlos Beltran	.50
72	Adrian Beltre	.25
73	Kris Benson	.15
74	Lance Berkman	.40
75	Kevin Brown	.15
76	Jay Buhner	.15
77	Jeromy Burnitz	.15
78	Ken Caminiti	.15
79	Sean Casey	.25
80	Luis Castillo	.15
81	Eric Chavez	.25
82	Jeff Cirillo	.15
83	Bartolo Colon	.15
84	David Cone	.15
85	Freddy Garcia	.15
86	Johnny Damon	.50
87	Ray Durham	.15
88	Jermaine Dye	.15
89	Juan Encarnacion	.15
90	Terrence Long	.15
91	Carl Everett	.15
92	Steve Finley	.15
93	Cliff Floyd	.15
94	Brad Fullmer	.15
95	Brian Giles	.15
96	Luis Gonzalez	.15
97	Rusty Greer	.15
98	Jeffrey Hammonds	.15
99	Mike Hampton	.15
100	Orlando Hernandez	.15
101	Richard Hidalgo	.15
102	Geoff Jenkins	.15
103	Jacque Jones	.15
104	Brian Jordan	.15
105	Gabe Kapler	.15
106	Eric Karros	.15
107	Jason Kendall	.15
108	Adam Kennedy	.15
109	Byung-Hyun Kim	.15
110	Ryan Klesko	.15
111	Chuck Knoblauch	.15
112	Paul Konerko	.40
113	Carlos Lee	.25
114	Kenny Lofton	.15
115	Javy Lopez	.15
116	Tino Martinez	.15
117	Ruben Mateo	.15
118	Kevin Millwood	.15
119	Ben Molina	.15
120	Raul Mondesi	.15
121	Trot Nixon	.15
122	John Olerud	.15
123	Paul O'Neill	.15
124	Chan Ho Park	.15
125	Andy Pettitte	.25
126	Jorge Posada	.25
127	Mark Quinn	.15
128	Aramis Ramirez	.40
129	Mariano Rivera	.25
130	Tim Salmon	.15
131	Curt Schilling	.75
132	Richie Sexson	.40
133	John Smoltz	.25
134	J.T. Snow	.15
135	Jay Payton	.15
136	Shannon Stewart	.15
137	B.J. Surhoff	.15
138	Mike Sweeney	.15
139	Fernando Tatis	.15
140	Miguel Tejada	.40
141	Jason Varitek	.40
142	Greg Vaughn	.15
143	Mo Vaughn	.15
144	Robin Ventura	.15
145	Jose Vidro	.15
146	Omar Vizquel	.15
147	Larry Walker	.15
148	David Wells	.15
149	Rondell White	.15
150	Preston Wilson	.15
151	Brent Abernathy	4.00
152	Cory Aldridge **RC**	4.00
153	Gene Altman **RC**	4.00
154	Josh Beckett	4.00
155	Wilson Betemit **RC**	8.00
156	Albert Pujols/ 500 **RC**	275.00
157	Joe Crede	8.00
158	Jack Cust	4.00
159	Ben Sheets/500	40.00
160	Alex Escobar	4.00
161	Adrian Hernandez **RC**	4.00
162	Pedro Feliz	4.00
163	Nate Frese **RC**	4.00
164	Carlos Garcia **RC**	4.00
165	Marcus Giles	4.00
166	Alexis Gomez **RC**	4.00
167	Jason Hart	4.00
168	Eric Hinske **RC**	8.00
169	Cesar Izturis	4.00
170	Nick Johnson	4.00
171	Mike Young	4.00
172	Brian Lawrence **RC**	6.00
173	Steve Lomasney	4.00
174	Nick Maness **RC**	4.00
175	Jose Mieses **RC**	4.00
176	Greg Miller **RC**	4.00
177	Eric Munson	4.00
178	Xavier Nady	4.00
179	Blaine Neal **RC**	4.00
180	Abraham Nunez	4.00
181	Jose Ortiz	4.00
182	Jeremy Owens **RC**	4.00
183	Pablo Ozuna	4.00
184	Corey Patterson	4.00
185	Carlos Pena	4.00
186	Wily Mo Pena	4.00
187	Timo Perez	4.00
188	Adam Pettyjohn **RC**	4.00
189	Luis Rivas	4.00
190	Jackson Melian **RC**	4.00
191	Wilken Ruan **RC**	4.00
192	Duaner Sanchez **RC**	4.00
193	Alfonso Soriano	5.00
194	Rafael Soriano **RC**	6.00
195	Ichiro Suzuki **RC**	60.00
196	Billy Sylvester **RC**	4.00
197	Juan Uribe **RC**	4.00
198	Eric Valent	4.00
199	Carlos Valderrama **RC**	4.00
200	Matt White **RC**	4.00
201	Alex Rodriguez	2.50
202	Barry Bonds	3.00
203	Cal Ripken Jr.	3.00
204	Chipper Jones	1.00
205	Derek Jeter	2.50
206	Troy Glaus	.50
207	Frank Thomas	.75
208	Greg Maddux	1.50
209	Ivan Rodriguez	.50
210	Jeff Bagwell	.50
211	Todd Helton	.50
212	Ken Griffey Jr.	1.50
213	Manny Ramirez	.75
214	Mark McGwire	1.50
215	Mike Piazza	1.50
216	Pedro Martinez	.75
217	Sammy Sosa	1.50
218	Tony Gwynn	1.00
219	Vladimir Guerrero	1.00
220	Nomar Garciaparra	1.00

Baseball's Best

This up-scale version of 2001 Donruss was available to those who not only beat the 1:720 pack insertion odds, but also paid $105 to redeem the "winning" coupon. The boxed set contains 330 cards comprised of the 220-card '01 Donruss base set, the 105-card The Rookies set and the five Rookies Diamond King cards. The cards are printed on a thicker, glossy stock and have a "Baseball's Best" logo foil stamped on front in either bronze, silver or gold. Those redeeming coupons had an apparently random chance of receiving one of 999 bronze sets, 499 silver sets or 99 gold sets. Coupons expired in January 2002.

	NM/M
Complete Set, Bronze (330):	100.00
999 produced	
Stars:	2-3X
Complete Set, Silver (330):	300.00
499 produced	
Stars:	2-4X
Complete Set, Gold (330):	550.00
99 produced	
Stars:	4-8X

2001 Donruss All-Time Diamond Kings

	NM/M
Complete Set (10):	150.00
Common Player:	8.00
Production 2,500 Sets	

Studio Series

		2-3X
Studio Series:		
Production 250		
#9 undetermined redemp.		
1a	Frank Robinson	8.00
1b	Willie Mays (Should have been ATDK-9.)	25.00
2	Harmon Killebrew	8.00
3	Mike Schmidt	20.00
4	Reggie Jackson	8.00
5	Nolan Ryan	35.00
6	George Brett	25.00
7	Tom Seaver	10.00
8	Hank Aaron	25.00
10	Stan Musial	20.00

Autograph

		NM/M
Production 50 Sets		
1	Frank Robinson	100.00
1	Willie Mays	200.00
2	Harmon Killebrew	80.00
3	Mike Schmidt	200.00
4	Reggie Jackson	80.00
5	Nolan Ryan	250.00
6	George Brett	225.00
7	Tom Seaver	85.00
8	Hank Aaron	200.00
10	Stan Musial	120.00

2001 Donruss Bat Kings

		NM/M
Common Card:		20.00
Production 250 Sets		
1	Ivan Rodriguez	20.00
2	Tony Gwynn	35.00
3	Barry Bonds	75.00
4	Todd Helton	20.00
5	Troy Glaus	20.00
6	Mike Schmidt	50.00
7	Reggie Jackson	20.00
8	Harmon Killebrew	20.00
9	Frank Robinson	20.00
10	Hank Aaron	75.00

Autograph

		NM/M
Production 50 Sets		
1	Ivan Rodriguez	75.00
2	Tony Gwynn	120.00
3	Barry Bonds/ No Auto.	50.00
4	Todd Helton	65.00
5	Troy Glaus	65.00
6	Mike Schmidt	150.00
7	Reggie Jackson	100.00
8	Harmon Killebrew	100.00
9	Frank Robinson	85.00
10	Hank Aaron	200.00

2001 Donruss Diamond Kings Hawaii Promo

The first look at the resurrected Donruss brand under Playoff ownership was provided at the 2001 Hawaii trade show where a special promotional Diamond King card was distributed in two versions. The cards feature a Dan Gardiner artwork portrait with gold-foil graphic highlights on front, including a "HAWAII 2001" logo. Cards have a color photo on back. A special autographed version of the card was also created, signed on front and numbered in gold-foil on back from within an edition of 100.

		NM/M
HDK-1	Alex Rodriguez	3.00
HDK-1	Alex Rodriguez/ Auto.	150.00

2001 Donruss 2001 Diamond Kings

		NM/M
Complete Set (20):		150.00
Common Player:		5.00
Production 2,500 Sets		
Studio Canvas Parallel:		1-2X
Production 250		
1	Alex Rodriguez	12.50
2	Cal Ripken Jr.	15.00
3	Mark McGwire	12.50
4	Ken Griffey Jr.	10.00
5	Derek Jeter	10.00
6	Nomar Garciaparra	10.00
7	Mike Piazza	10.00
8	Roger Clemens	9.00
9	Greg Maddux	8.00
10	Chipper Jones	8.00
11	Tony Gwynn	8.00
12	Barry Bonds	15.00
13	Sammy Sosa	10.00
14	Vladimir Guerrero	6.00
15	Frank Thomas	6.00
16	Troy Glaus	6.00
17	Todd Helton	6.00
18	Ivan Rodriguez	5.00
19	Pedro Martinez	5.00
20	Carlos Delgado	5.00

Studio Series Autograph

		NM/M
Common Autograph:		50.00
Production 50 Sets		
1	Alex Rodriguez	180.00
2	Cal Ripken Jr.	250.00
8	Roger Clemens	150.00
9	Greg Maddux	150.00
10	Chipper Jones	85.00
11	Tony Gwynn	80.00
14	Vladimir Guerrero	100.00
16	Troy Glaus	50.00
17	Todd Helton	60.00
18	Ivan Rodriguez	60.00

Reprints

		NM/M
Complete Set (20):		160.00
Common Player:		5.00
#'d to yr. produced		
1	Rod Carew	5.00
2	Nolan Ryan	25.00
3	Tom Seaver	10.00
4	Carlton Fisk	10.00
5	Reggie Jackson	12.00
6	Steve Carlton	5.00
7	Johnny Bench	10.00
8	Joe Morgan	5.00
9	Mike Schmidt	20.00
10	Wade Boggs	15.00
11	Cal Ripken Jr.	25.00

12	Tony Gwynn	15.00
13	Andre Dawson	5.00
14	Ozzie Smith	15.00
15	George Brett	20.00
16	Dave Winfield	5.00
17	Paul Molitor	10.00
18	Will Clark	5.00
19	Robin Yount	10.00
20	Ken Griffey Jr.	17.50

Reprints Autograph

NM/M
Common Player:

DKR1	Rod Carew/82	40.00
DKR2	Nolan Ryan/82	150.00
DKR3	Tom SeaveR/82	75.00
DKR4	Carlton Fisk/82	65.00
DKR5	Reggie Jackson/83	60.00
DKR6	Steve Carlton/83	80.00
DKR7	Johnny Bench/83	80.00
DKR8	Joe Morgan/83	30.00
DKR9	Mike Schmidt/84	120.00
DKR10	Wade Boggs/84	60.00
DKR11	Cal Ripken Jr./85	180.00
DKR12	Tony Gwynn/86	75.00
DKR13	Andre Dawson/86	35.00
DKR14	Ozzie Smith/87	50.00
DKR15	George Brett/87	120.00
DKR16	Dave Winfield/87	60.00
DKR17	Paul Molitor/88	60.00
DKR18	Will Clark/88	75.00
DKR19	Robin Yount/89	80.00
DKR20	Ken Griffey Jr./89/No Auto.	25.00

Elite Series

NM/M
Complete Set (20): 75.00
Common Player: 2.00
Production 2,500 Sets
Dominators: 5-8X
Production 25 Sets

1	Vladimir Guerrero	4.00
2	Cal Ripken Jr.	10.00
3	Greg Maddux	5.00
4	Alex Rodriguez	8.00
5	Barry Bonds	10.00
6	Chipper Jones	5.00
7	Derek Jeter	10.00
8	Ivan Rodriguez	2.50
9	Ken Griffey Jr.	7.00
10	Mark McGwire	8.00
11	Mike Piazza	7.00
12	Nomar Garciaparra	7.00
13	Pedro Martinez	4.00
14	Randy Johnson	4.00
15	Roger Clemens	6.00
16	Sammy Sosa	7.00
17	Tony Gwynn	5.00
18	Darin Erstad	3.00
19	Andruw Jones	4.00
20	Bernie Williams	2.00

Jersey Kings

NM/M
Common Card: 25.00

Production 250 Sets

1	Vladimir Guerrero	20.00
2	Cal Ripken Jr.	80.00
3	Greg Maddux	40.00
4	Chipper Jones	25.00
5	Roger Clemens	40.00
6	George Brett	50.00
7	Tom Seaver	20.00
8	Nolan Ryan	85.00
9	Stan Musial	45.00

Autographs

NM/M
Production 50 Sets

1	Vladimir Guerrero	90.00
2	Cal Ripken Jr.	225.00
3	Greg Maddux	150.00
4	Chipper Jones	85.00
5	Roger Clemens	175.00
6	George Brett	200.00
7	Tom Seaver	75.00
8	Nolan Ryan	200.00
9	Stan Musial	120.00
10	Ozzie Smith	100.00

Longball Leaders

NM/M
Complete Set (20): 50.00
Common Player: 1.00
Production 1,000 Sets
Die-Cut Parallel: 3-5X
#'d to '00 HR Total

1	Vladimir Guerrero	4.00
2	Alex Rodriguez	8.00
3	Barry Bonds	10.00
4	Troy Glaus	4.00
5	Frank Thomas	4.00
6	Jeff Bagwell	4.00
7	Todd Helton	4.00
8	Ken Griffey Jr.	6.00
9	Manny Ramirez	4.00
10	Mike Piazza	6.00
11	Sammy Sosa	6.00
12	Carlos Delgado	2.00
13	Jim Edmonds	1.00
14	Jason Giambi	3.00
15	David Justice	1.00
16	Rafael Palmeiro	3.00
17	Gary Sheffield	2.00
18	Jim Thome	1.00
19	Tony Batista	1.00
20	Richard Hidalgo	1.00

Production Line

NM/M
Complete Set (60): 150.00
Common Player: .50
Die-Cut OBP (1-20): 1-2X
Die-Cut SLG (21-40): 1-2.5X
Die-Cut PI (41-60): 1.5-3X
Production 100 Sets

1	Jason Giambi/476	3.00
2	Carlos Delgado/470	2.00
3	Todd Helton/463	3.00
4	Manny Ramirez/457	3.00
5	Barry Bonds/440	15.00
6	Gary Sheffield/438	2.00
7	Frank Thomas/436	3.00
8	Nomar Garciaparra/434	10.00
9	Brian Giles/432	.50
10	Edgardo Alfonzo/425	.50
11	Jeff Kent/424	.75
12	Jeff Bagwell/424	3.00
13	Edgar Martinez/423	.75
14	Alex Rodriguez/420	10.00
15	Luis Castillo/418	.50
16	Will Clark/418	2.50
17	Jorge Posada/417	2.00
18	Derek Jeter/416	7.00
19	Bob Abreu/416	1.00
20	Moises Alou/416	.75
21	Todd Helton/698	3.00
22	Manny Ramirez/697	3.00
23	Barry Bonds/688	15.00
24	Carlos Delgado/664	2.00
25	Vladimir Guerrero/664	3.00
26	Jason Giambi/647	3.00
27	Gary Sheffield/643	2.00
28	Richard Hidalgo/636	.50
29	Sammy Sosa/634	8.00
30	Frank Thomas/625	3.00
31	Moises Alou/623	.75
32	Jeff Bagwell/615	3.00
33	Mike Piazza/614	8.00
34	Alex Rodriguez/606	10.00
35	Troy Glaus/604	3.00
36	Nomar Garciaparra/599	10.00
37	Jeff Kent/596	.75
38	Brian Giles/594	.75
39	Geoff Jenkins/588	.50
40	Carl Everett/587	.50
41	Todd Helton/1161	3.00
42	Manny Ramirez/1154	3.00
43	Carlos Delgado/1134	2.00
44	Barry Bonds/1128	12.00
45	Jason Giambi/1123	3.00
46	Gary Sheffield/1081	2.00
47	Vladimir Guerrero/1074	3.00
48	Frank Thomas/1061	3.00
49	Sammy Sosa/1040	8.00
50	Moises Alou/1039	1.00
51	Jeff Bagwell/1039	3.00
52	Nomar Garciaparra/1033	10.00
53	Richard Hidalgo/1027	.50
54	Alex Rodriguez/1026	10.00
55	Brian Giles/1026	1.00
56	Jeff Kent/1020	1.00
57	Mike Piazza/1012	8.00
58	Troy Glaus/1008	3.00
59	Edgar Martinez/1002	1.00
60	Jim Edmonds/994	1.00

Rookie Reprints

NM/M
Complete Set (40): 200.00
Common Player: 3.00
#'d to Original Yr. issued

1	Cal Ripken Jr.	20.00
2	Wade Boggs	10.00
3	Tony Gwynn	10.00
4	Ryne Sandberg	10.00
5	Don Mattingly	12.00
6	Joe Carter	3.00
7	Roger Clemens	12.00
8	Kirby Puckett	10.00
9	Orel Hershiser	3.00
10	Andres Galarraga	3.00
11	Jose Canseco	3.00
12	Fred McGriff	3.00
13	Paul O'Neill	3.00
14	Mark McGwire	15.00
15	Barry Bonds	20.00
16	Kevin Brown	3.00
17	David Cone	3.00
18	Rafael Palmeiro	8.00
19	Barry Larkin	3.00
20	Bo Jackson	4.00
21	Greg Maddux	10.00
22	Roberto Alomar	4.00
23	Mark Grace	3.00
24	David Wells	3.00
25	Tom Glavine	4.00
26	Matt Williams	4.00
27	Ken Griffey Jr.	12.00
28	Randy Johnson	4.00
29	Gary Sheffield	4.00
30	Craig Biggio	4.00
31	Curt Schilling	4.00
32	Larry Walker	3.00
33	Bernie Williams	4.00
34	Sammy Sosa	12.00
35	Juan Gonzalez	8.00
36	David Justice	6.00
37	Ivan Rodriguez	6.00
38	Jeff Bagwell	8.00
39	Jeff Kent	3.00
40	Manny Ramirez	8.00

Autographs

NM/M
Common Player:
#'d to last 2 digits of yr. issued

1	Cal Ripken/82	150.00
2	Wade Boggs/83	40.00
3	Tony Gwynn/83	75.00
4	Ryne Sandberg/83	100.00
5	Don Mattingly/84	100.00
6	Joe Carter/84	20.00
7	Roger Clemens/85	200.00
8	Kirby Puckett/85	60.00
9	Orel Hershiser/85	25.00
10	Andres Galarraga/86	30.00
15	Barry Bonds/87	200.00
16	Kevin Brown/87	30.00
17	David Cone/87	30.00
18	Rafael Palmeiro/87	50.00
20	Bo Jackson/87	85.00
21	Greg Maddux/87	150.00
22	Roberto Alomar/88	40.00
24	David Wells/88	25.00
25	Tom Glavine/88	40.00
28	Randy Johnson/89	100.00
29	Gary Sheffield/89	50.00
31	Curt Schilling/89	75.00
35	Juan Gonzalez/90	40.00
36	David Justice/90	40.00
37	Ivan Rodriguez/92	40.00
39	Manny Ramirez/92	100.00

2001 Donruss Stat Line Career

NM/M
Cards #1-150 print run

251-400:	3-6X
1-150 p/r 201-250:	4-8X
1-150 p/r 151-200:	4-8X
1-150 p/r 101-150:	5-10X
1-150 p/r 61-100:	10-20X
1-150 p/r 41-60:	20-30X
1-150 p/r 21-40:	25-40X
1-150 p/r 15-20:	30-60X
Common (151-200) p/r 251-400:	1.00
Common (151-200) p/r 151-250:	1.00
Common (151-200) p/r 101-150:	2.00
Common (151-200) p/r 76-100:	2.00
Common (151-200) p/r 31-75:	4.00
Common (151-200) p/r 20-30:	6.00
cards 201-220 p/r 201-400:	1-2X
201-220 p/r 101-200:	2-4X
201-220 p/r 75-100:	3-5X
201-220 p/r 40-74:	4-8X
156 Albert Pujols/154	150.00
190 Jackson Melian/26	50.00
195 Ichiro Suzuki/106	200.00

Line Season

NM/M
Cards #1-150 print run

151-200:	4-8X
1-150 p/r 101-150:	4-8X
1-150 p/r 76-100:	10-20X
1-150 p/r 51-75:	10-20X
1-150 p/r 36-50:	15-25X
1-150 p/r 21-35:	20-40X
Common (151-200) p/r 151-200:	1.00
Common (151-200) p/r 101-150:	1.00
Common (151-200) p/r 101-150:	1.00
Common (151-200) p/r 76-100:	2.00
Common (151-200) p/r 31-75:	3.00
Common (151-200) p/r 20-30:	6.00
cards 201-220 p/r 151-200:	1-3X
201-220 p/r 101-150:	2-4X
201-220 p/r 75-100:	3-5X
201-220 p/r 40-74:	4-8X
156 Albert Pujols/17	400.00
190 Jackson Melian/73	40.00
195 Ichiro Suzuki/153	150.00

2001 Donruss 1999 Retro

NM/M
Complete Set (100): 200.00
Common Player: .25
Inserted 1:Hobby Pack
Common (81-100): 3.00
Production 1,999

1	Ken Griffey Jr.	2.00
2	Nomar Garciaparra	2.00
3	Alex Rodriguez	2.50
4	Mark McGwire	2.50
5	Sammy Sosa	2.00
6	Chipper Jones	1.50
7	Mike Piazza	2.00
8	Barry Larkin	.25
9	Andruw Jones	1.00
10	Albert Belle	.25
11	Jeff Bagwell	1.00
12	Tony Gwynn	1.50
13	Manny Ramirez	1.00
14	Mo Vaughn	.25
15	Barry Bonds	3.00
16	Frank Thomas	2.00
17	Vladimir Guerrero	1.00
18	Derek Jeter	3.00
19	Randy Johnson	1.00
20	Greg Maddux	1.50
21	Pedro Martinez	1.00
22	Cal Ripken Jr.	3.00
23	Ivan Rodriguez	.75
24	Matt Williams	.25
25	Javy Lopez	.25
26	Tim Salmon	.25
27	Raul Mondesi	.25
28	Todd Helton	1.00
29	Magglio Ordonez	.40
30	Sean Casey	.25
31	Jeromy Burnitz	.25
32	Jeff Kent	.25
33	Jim Edmonds	.25
34	Jim Thome	.25
35	Dante Bichette	.25
36	Larry Walker	.25
37	Will Clark	.35
38	Omar Vizquel	.25
39	Mike Mussina	.50
40	Eric Karros	.25
41	Kenny Lofton	.25
42	David Justice	.25
43	Craig Biggio	.25
44	J.D. Drew	.25
45	Rickey Henderson	1.00
46	Bernie Williams	.45
47	Brian Giles	.25
48	Paul O'Neill	.25
49	Orlando Hernandez	.25
50	Jason Giambi	.50
51	Curt Schilling	.45
52	Scott Rolen	1.00
53	Mark Grace	.35
54	Moises Alou	.25
55	Jason Kendall	.25
56	Ray Lankford	.25
57	Kerry Wood	.50
58	Gary Sheffield	.50
59	Ruben Mateo	.25
60	Darin Erstad	.65
61	Troy Glaus	1.00
62	Jose Canseco	.50
63	Wade Boggs	1.50
64	Tom Glavine	.50
65	Gabe Kapler	.25
66	Juan Gonzalez	1.00
67	Rafael Palmeiro	.75
68	Richie Sexson	.25
69	Carl Everett	.25
70	David Wells	.25
71	Carlos Delgado	.75
72	Eric Davis	.25
73	Shawn Green	.40
74	Andres Galarraga	.25
75	Edgar Martinez	.25
76	Roberto Alomar	.50
77	John Olerud	.25
78	Luis Gonzalez	.25
79	Kevin Brown	.25
80	Roger Clemens	1.75
81	Josh Beckett	5.00
82	Alfonso Soriano	8.00
83	Alex Escobar	3.00
84	Pat Burrell	4.00
85	Eric Chavez	4.00
86	Erubiel Durazo	3.00
87	Abraham Nunez	3.00
88	Carlos Pena	3.00
89	Nick Johnson	4.00
90	Eric Munson	3.00
91	Corey Patterson	4.00
92	Wily Mo Pena	3.00
93	Rafael Furcal	3.00
94	Eric Valent	3.00
95	Mark Mulder	4.00
96	Chad Hutchinson	3.00
97	Freddy Garcia	3.00
98	Tim Hudson	5.00
99	Rick Ankiel	3.00
100	Kip Wells	3.00

2001 Donruss 1999 Diamond Kings

NM/M
Complete Set (5): 40.00
Common Player: 8.00
Production 2,500 Sets

1	Scott Rolen	8.00
2	Sammy Sosa	10.00
3	Juan Gonzalez	8.00
4	Ken Griffey Jr.	10.00
5	Derek Jeter	20.00

2001 Donruss 1999 Retro Stat Line Career

NM/M
Cards #1-80 print run

251-400:	2-3X
(1-80) p/r 151-250:	2-4X
(1-80) p/r 101-150:	3-6X
(1-80) p/r 76-100:	4-8X
(1-80) p/r 51-75:	5-10X
(1-80) p/r 30-50:	8-15X

1	Ken Griffey Jr./350	20.00
2	Nomar Garciaparra/309	20.00
3	Alex Rodriguez/313	20.00
4	Mark McGwire/219	25.00
5	Sammy Sosa/273	12.00
6	Chipper Jones/297	15.00
7	Mike Piazza/333	20.00
8	Barry Larkin/305	5.00
9	Andruw Jones/273	6.00
10	Albert Belle/321	2.50
11	Jeff Bagwell/304	8.00
12	Tony Gwynn/339	12.00
13	Manny Ramirez/154	15.00
14	Mo Vaughn/304	2.50
15	Barry Bonds/290	12.00
16	Frank Thomas/286	10.00

17	Vladimir Guerrero/305	10.00
18	Derek Jeter/308	25.00
19	Randy Johnson/336	8.00
20	Greg Maddux/202	20.00
21	Pedro Martinez/298	10.00
22	Cal Ripken Jr./276	25.00
23	Ivan Rodriguez/232	8.00
24	Matt Williams/299	8.00
25	Javy Lopez/333	2.50
26	Tim Salmon/179	2.50
27	Raul Mondesi/295	2.50
28	Todd Helton/310	8.00
30	Magglio Ordonez/173	4.00
30	Sean Casey/269	2.50
31	Jeromy Burnitz/294	2.50
32	Jeff Kent/193	5.00
33	Jim Edmonds/294	5.00
34	Jim Thome/163	4.00
35	Dante Bichette/300	2.50
36	Larry Walker/225	5.00
37	Will Clark/302	6.00
38	Omar Vizquel/196	4.00
39	Mike Mussina/118	10.00
40	Eric Karros/177	4.00
41	Kenny Lofton/311	2.50
42	David Justice/214	5.00
43	Craig Biggio/318	2.50
44	J.D. Drew/35	25.00
45	Rickey Henderson/283	6.00
46	Bernie Williams/213	4.00
47	Brian Giles/157	4.00
48	Paul O'Neill/223	5.00
49	Orlando Hernandez/313	6.00
50	Jason Giambi/73	15.00
51	Curt Schilling/336	2.50
52	Scott Rolen/220	5.00
53	Mark Grace/310	6.00
54	Moises Alou/201	3.00
55	Jason Kendall/308	2.50
56	Ray Lankford/225	3.00
57	Kerry Wood/233	5.00
58	Gary Sheffield/202	5.00
59	Ruben Mateo/384	2.50
60	Darin Erstad/179	8.00
61	Troy Glaus/218	10.00
62	Jose Canseco/296	5.00
63	Wade Boggs/329	8.00
64	Tom Glavine/331	5.00
66	Juan Gonzalez/301	8.00
67	Rafael Palmeiro/314	5.00
68	Richie Sexson/308	2.50
69	Carl Everett/209	3.00
70	David Wells/124	6.00
71	Carlos Delgado/333	6.00
72	Eric Davis/342	2.50
73	Shawn Green/77	15.00
74	Andres Galarraga/364	4.00
76	Edgar Martinez/318	4.00
76	Roberto Alomar/302	6.00
77	John Olerud/301	2.50
78	Luis Gonzalez/237	3.00
79	Kevin Brown/330	2.50
80	Roger Clemens/295	12.00
82	Alfonso Soriano/113	15.00
83	Alex Escobar/181	10.00
84	Pat Burrell/303	12.00
85	Eric Chavez/314	5.00
86	Erubiel Durazo/147	5.00
87	Abraham Nunez/106	15.00
88	Carlos Pena/46	25.00
89	Nick Johnson/259	6.00
90	Eric Munson/392	6.00
91	Corey Patterson/117	15.00
92	Wily Mo Pena/247	8.00
93	Rafael Furcal/137	10.00
94	Eric Valent/53	10.00
95	Mark Mulder/340	4.00
97	Freddy Garcia/397	3.00
98	Tim Hudson/17	50.00
99	Rick Ankiel/222	10.00
100	Kip Wells/371	2.50

Season

		NM/M
Cards #1-80 print run		
251-400:		2-3X
(1-80) p/r 151-250:		2-4X
(1-80) p/r 101-150:		3-6X
(1-80) p/r 76-100:		4-8X
(1-80) p/r 51-75:		5-10X
(1-80) p/r 30-50:		8-15X
1	Ken Griffey Jr./56	70.00
2	Nomar Garciaparra/35	100.00

3	Alex Rodriguez/42	100.00
4	Mark McGwire/70	80.00
5	Sammy Sosa/66	40.00
6	Chipper Jones/123	30.00
7	Mike Piazza/111	50.00
8	Barry Larkin/166	8.00
9	Andruw Jones/31	30.00
10	Albert Belle/49	8.00
11	Jeff Bagwell/164	12.00
12	Tony Gwynn/148	25.00
13	Manny Ramirez/145	20.00
14	Mo Vaughn/40	10.00
15	Barry Bonds/120	25.00
16	Frank Thomas/155	15.00
17	Vladimir Guerrero/38	40.00
18	Derek Jeter/127	60.00
19	Randy Johnson/19	75.00
21	Pedro Martinez/19	80.00
22	Cal Ripken Jr./163	40.00
23	Ivan Rodriguez/186	12.00
24	Matt Williams/136	8.00
25	Javy Lopez/106	6.00
26	Tim Salmon/139	8.00
27	Raul Mondesi/162	4.00
28	Todd Helton/25	60.00
29	Magglio Ordonez/151	4.00
30	Sean Casey/82	8.00
31	Jeromy Burnitz/125	5.00
32	Jeff Kent/128	8.00
33	Jim Edmonds/115	12.00
34	Jim Thome/129	6.00
35	Dante Bichette/122	6.00
36	Larry Walker/113	15.00
37	Will Clark/169	10.00
38	Omar Vizquel/166	4.00
39	Mike Mussina/175	10.00
40	Eric Karros/150	5.00
41	Kenny Lofton/54	10.00
42	David Justice/151	5.00
43	Craig Biggio/51	10.00
45	Rickey Henderson/66	25.00
46	Bernie Williams/26	30.00
47	Brian Giles/94	5.00
48	Paul O'Neill/116	10.00
49	Orlando Hernandez/12	35.00
50	Jason Giambi/166	4.00
51	Curt Schilling/15	40.00
52	Scott Rolen/31	30.00
53	Mark Grace/92	15.00
54	Moises Alou/124	5.00
55	Jason Kendall/175	4.00
56	Ray Lankford/156	4.00
57	Kerry Wood/13	50.00
58	Gary Sheffield/132	5.00
59	Ruben Mateo/134	5.00
60	Darin Erstad/159	5.00
62	Jose Canseco/46	30.00
63	Wade Boggs/122	15.00
64	Tom Glavine/20	50.00
65	Gabe Kapler/25	20.00
66	Juan Gonzalez/50	30.00
69	Rafael Palmeiro/121	10.00
70	Carl Everett/138	5.00
71	David Wells/163	4.00
72	Carlos Delgado/155	10.00
73	Eric Davis/148	5.00
74	Shawn Green/100	12.00
75	Andres Galarraga/44	20.00
76	Edgar Martinez/102	10.00
77	Roberto Alomar/166	15.00
78	John Olerud/22	20.00
79	Luis Gonzalez/146	5.00
80	Kevin Brown/18	25.00
81	Roger Clemens/20	120.00
82	Josh Beckett/178	10.00
83	Alex Escobar/27	40.00
85	Eric Chavez/33	15.00
86	Erubiel Durazo/19	20.00
87	Abraham Nunez/95	10.00
88	Carlos Pena/319	6.00
89	Nick Johnson/31	50.00
90	Eric Munson/16	40.00
91	Corey Patterson/22	40.00
93	Rafael Furcal/88	20.00
95	Mark Mulder/113	6.00
96	Chad Hutchinson/51	6.00
98	Tim Hudson/152	15.00
99	Rick Ankiel/12	40.00
100	Kip Wells/135	2.50

2001 Donruss 2000 Retro

		NM/M
Complete Set (100):		90.00
Common Player:		.25

Common (81-100):		3.00
Production 2,000		
1	Vladimir Guerrero	.75
2	Alex Rodriguez	2.00
3	Ken Griffey Jr.	1.50
4	Nomar Garciaparra	1.50
5	Mike Piazza	1.50
6	Mark McGwire	2.00
7	Sammy Sosa	1.50
8	Chipper Jones	1.00
9	Jim Edmonds	.25
10	Tony Gwynn	1.00
11	Andruw Jones	.75
12	Albert Belle	.75
13	Jeff Bagwell	.75
14	Manny Ramirez	.75
15	Mo Vaughn	.25
16	Barry Bonds	2.50
17	Frank Thomas	.75
18	Ivan Rodriguez	.65
19	Derek Jeter	2.50
20	Randy Johnson	.75
21	Greg Maddux	1.00
22	Pedro Martinez	.75
23	Cal Ripken Jr.	2.50
24	Mark Grace	.35
25	Javy Lopez	.25
26	Ray Durham	.25
27	Todd Helton	.75
28	Magglio Ordonez	.25
29	Sean Casey	.25
30	Darin Erstad	.65
31	Barry Larkin	.25
32	Will Clark	.35
33	Jim Thome	.25
34	Dante Bichette	.25
35	Larry Walker	.25
36	Ken Caminiti	.25
37	Omar Vizquel	.25
38	Miguel Tejada	.40
39	Eric Karros	.25
40	Gary Sheffield	.40
41	Jeff Cirillo	.25
42	Rondell White	.25
43	Rickey Henderson	.75
44	Bernie Williams	.40
45	Brian Giles	.25
46	Paul O'Neill	.25
47	Orlando Hernandez	.25
48	Ben Grieve	.25
49	Jason Giambi	.50
50	Curt Schilling	.40
51	Scott Rolen	.75
52	Bobby Abreu	.25
53	Jason Kendall	.25
54	Fernando Tatis	.25
55	Jeff Kent	.25
56	Mike Mussina	.40
57	Troy Glaus	.75
58	Jose Canseco	.45
59	Wade Boggs	1.00
60	Fred McGriff	.25
61	Juan Gonzalez	.75
62	Rafael Palmeiro	.65
63	Rusty Greer	.25
64	Carl Everett	.25
65	David Wells	.25
66	Carlos Delgado	.50
67	Shawn Green	.40
68	David Justice	.25
69	Edgar Martinez	.25
70	Andres Galarraga	.25
71	Roberto Alomar	.50
72	Jermaine Dye	.25
73	John Olerud	.25
74	Luis Gonzalez	.35
75	Craig Biggio	.25
76	Kevin Millwood	.25
77	Kevin Brown	.35
78	John Smoltz	.25
79	Roger Clemens	1.25
80	Mike Hampton	.25
81	Tomas De La Rosa	3.00
82	C.C. Sabathia	3.00
83	Ryan Christenson	3.00
84	Pedro Feliz	3.00
85	Jose Ortiz	3.00
86	Xavier Nady	3.00
87	Julio Zuleta	3.00
88	Jason Hart	3.00
89	Keith Ginter	3.00
90	Brent Abernathy	3.00
91	Timo Perez	3.00
92	Juan Pierre	3.00
93	Tike Redman	3.00
94	Mike Lamb	3.00
95	Ben Sheets	5.00
96	Kazuhiro Sasaki	4.00
97	Barry Zito	8.00
98	Adam Bernero	3.00
99	Chad Durbin	3.00
100	Matt Ginter	3.00

2001 Donruss 2000 Diamond Kings

		NM/M
Complete Set (5):		35.00
Common Player:		8.00
Production 2,500 Sets		
Studio:		1-2X
Production 250 Sets		
1	Frank Thomas	8.00
2	Greg Maddux	9.00
3	Alex Rodriguez	10.00
4	Jeff Bagwell	8.00
5	Manny Ramirez	8.00

2001 Donruss 2000 Retro Stat Line Career

		NM/M
Cards #1-80 print run		
251-400:		2-3X
1-80 p/r 151-250:		2-4X
1-80 p/r 101-150:		3-6X
1-80 p/r 76-100:		4-8X
1-80 p/r 51-75:		5-10X
1-80 p/r 31-50:		8-15X
1-80 p/r 21-30:		15-25X
Common (81-100) p/r 251-400:		1.00
Common (81-100) p/r 151-250:		1.00
Common (81-100) p/r 101-150:		2.00
Common (81-100) p/r 76-100:		2.00
Common (81-100) p/r 31-75		3.00

Season

		NM/M
Cards #1-80 print run		
251-400:		2-3X
1-80 p/r 151-250:		2-4X
1-80 p/r 101-150:		3-6X
1-80 p/r 76-100:		4-8X
1-80 p/r 51-75:		5-10X
1-80 p/r 31-50:		8-15X
1-80 p/r 21-30:		15-25X
Common (81-100) p/r 151-200:		1.00
Common (81-100) p/r 81-150:		2.00
Common (81-100) p/r 51-80:		2.00

2001 Donruss Classics

		NM/M
Common Player:		.50
Common SP (101-150):		5.00
Production 585		
Common SP (151-200):		3.00
Production 1,755		
Pack (6):		12.00
Box (18):		180.00
1	Alex Rodriguez	3.00
2	Barry Bonds	3.00
3	Cal Ripken Jr.	4.00
4	Chipper Jones	2.00
5	Derek Jeter	3.00
6	Troy Glaus	.75
7	Frank Thomas	1.00
8	Greg Maddux	2.00
9	Ivan Rodriguez	1.00
10	Jeff Bagwell	1.00
11	Cliff Floyd	.50
12	Todd Helton	1.00
13	Ken Griffey Jr.	2.00
14	Manny Ramirez	1.00
15	Mark McGwire	3.00
16	Mike Piazza	2.00
17	Nomar Garciaparra	3.00
18	Pedro Martinez	1.50
19	Randy Johnson	1.50
20	Rick Ankiel	.50
21	Rickey Henderson	.75
22	Roger Clemens	3.00
23	Sammy Sosa	2.50
24	Tony Gwynn	1.50
25	Vladimir Guerrero	1.50
26	Kazuhiro Sasaki	.50
27	Roberto Alomar	.75
28	Barry Zito	.75
29	Pat Burrell	.75
30	Harold Baines	.50
31	Carlos Delgado	.75
32	J.D. Drew	.50
33	Jim Edmonds	.75
34	Darin Erstad	.75
35	Jason Giambi	1.00
36	Tom Glavine	.75
37	Juan Gonzalez	1.00
38	Mark Grace	.75
39	Shawn Green	.75
40	Tim Hudson	.75
41	Andruw Jones	.75
42	Jeff Kent	.50
43	Barry Larkin	.75
44	Rafael Furcal	.75
45	Mike Mussina	.75
46	Hideo Nomo	.75
47	Rafael Palmeiro	.75

48	Scott Rolen	1.00
49	Gary Sheffield	.75
50	Bernie Williams	.75
51	Bob Abreu	.50
52	Edgardo Alfonzo	.50
53	Edgar Martinez	.50
54	Magglio Ordonez	.75
55	Kerry Wood	.50
56	Adrian Beltre	.50
57	Lance Berkman	.75
58	Kevin Brown	.75
59	Sean Casey	.75
60	Eric Chavez	.75
61	Bartolo Colon	.50
62	Johnny Damon	.50
63	Jermaine Dye	.50
64	Juan Encarnacion	.50
65	Carl Everett	.50
66	Brian Giles	.50
67	Mike Hampton	.50
68	Richard Hidalgo	.50
69	Geoff Jenkins	.50
70	Jacque Jones	.50
71	Jason Kendall	.50
72	Ryan Klesko	.75
73	Chan Ho Park	.50
74	Richie Sexson	.75
75	Mike Sweeney	.50
76	Fernando Tatis	.50
77	Miguel Tejada	.75
78	Jose Vidro	.50
79	Larry Walker	.75
80	Preston Wilson	.50
81	Craig Biggio	.75
82	Fred McGriff	.75
83	Jim Thome	1.00
84	Garret Anderson	.75
85	Russell Branyan	.50
86	Tony Batista	.50
87	Terrence Long	.50
88	Brad Fullmer	.50
89	Rusty Greer	.50
90	Orlando Hernandez	.50
91	Gabe Kapler	.50
92	Paul Konerko	.50
93	Carlos Lee	.50
94	Kenny Lofton	.50
95	Raul Mondesi	.50
96	Jorge Posada	.75
97	Tim Salmon	.50
98	Greg Vaughn	.50
99	Mo Vaughn	.50
100	Omar Vizquel	.50
101	Aubrey Huff	5.00
102	Jimmy Rollins	5.00
103	Cory Aldridge RC	5.00
104	Wilmy Caceres RC	5.00
105	Josh Beckett	6.00
106	Wilson Betemit RC	5.00
107	Timo Perez	5.00
108	Albert Pujols RC	240.00
109	Bud Smith RC	5.00
110	Jack Wilson RC	10.00
111	Alex Escobar	5.00
112	Johnny Estrada RC	10.00
113	Pedro Feliz	5.00
114	Nate Frese RC	5.00
115	Carlos Garcia RC	5.00
116	Brandon Larson RC	5.00
117	Alexis Gomez RC	5.00
118	Jason Hart	5.00
119	Adam Dunn	5.00
120	Marcus Giles	5.00
121	Christian Parker RC	5.00
122	Jackson Melian RC	5.00
123	Eric Chavez	5.00
124	Adrian Hernandez RC	5.00
125	Joe Kennedy RC	5.00
126	Jose Mieses RC	5.00
127	C.C. Sabathia	5.00
128	Eric Munson	5.00
129	Xavier Nady	5.00
130	Horacio Ramirez RC	10.00
131	Abraham Nunez	5.00
132	Jose Ortiz	5.00
133	Jeremy Owens RC	5.00
134	Claudio Vargas RC	5.00
135	Corey Patterson	5.00
136	Audres Torres RC	5.00
137	Ben Sheets	5.00
138	Joe Crede	5.00
139	Adam Pettyjohn RC	5.00
140	Elpidio Guzman RC	5.00
141	Jay Gibbons RC	10.00
142	Wilkin Ruan RC	5.00
143	Tsuyoshi Shinjo RC	10.00
144	Alfonso Soriano	5.00
145	Nick Johnson	5.00
146	Ichiro Suzuki RC	80.00
147	Juan Uribe RC	8.00
148	Jack Cust	5.00
149	Carlos Valderrama RC	5.00
150	Matt White RC	5.00
151	Hank Aaron	10.00
152	Ernie Banks	4.00
153	Johnny Bench	6.00
154	George Brett	10.00
155	Lou Brock	3.00
156	Rod Carew	4.00
157	Steve Carlton	3.00
158	Bob Feller	3.00
159	Bob Gibson	5.00
160	Reggie Jackson	5.00
161	Al Kaline	6.00
162	Sandy Koufax	600.00
163	Don Mattingly	10.00
164	Willie Mays	10.00
165	Willie McCovey	3.00

166	Joe Morgan	3.00
167	Stan Musial	8.00
168	Jim Palmer	3.00
169	Brooks Robinson	5.00
170	Frank Robinson	3.00
171	Nolan Ryan	15.00
172	Mike Schmidt	10.00
173	Tom Seaver	4.00
174	Warren Spahn	4.00
175	Robin Yount	4.00
176	Wade Boggs	4.00
177	Ty Cobb	10.00
178	Lou Gehrig	10.00
179	Luis Aparicio	3.00
180	Babe Ruth	15.00
181	Ryne Sandberg	10.00
182	Yogi Berra	5.00
183	Roberto Clemente	10.00
184	Eddie Murray	5.00
185	Robin Roberts	3.00
186	Duke Snider	5.00
187	Orlando Cepeda	3.00
188	Billy Williams	3.00
189	Juan Marichal	3.00
190	Harmon Killebrew	5.00
191	Kirby Puckett	8.00
192	Carlton Fisk	4.00
193	Dave Winfield	4.00
194	Whitey Ford	4.00
195	Paul Molitor	4.00
196	Tony Perez	3.00
197	Ozzie Smith	6.00
198	Ralph Kiner	3.00
199	Fergie Jenkins	3.00
200	Phil Rizzuto	4.00

Timeless Tributes

Stars (1-100):		4-8X
SP's (101-150):		1-1.5X
SP's (151-200):		1-2.5X
Production 100 Sets		

Benchmarks

		NM/M
Common Player:		5.00
Inserted 1:18		
1	Todd Helton	5.00
2	Roberto Clemente	40.00
3	Mark McGwire	30.00
4	Barry Bonds	40.00
5	Bob Gibson	10.00
6	Ken Griffey Jr.	20.00
7	Frank Robinson	8.00
8	Greg Maddux	15.00
9	Reggie Jackson	10.00
10	Sammy Sosa	20.00
11	Willie Stargell	8.00
12	Vladimir Guerrero	8.00
13	Johnny Bench	15.00
14	Tony Gwynn	10.00
15	Mike Schmidt	17.50
16	Ivan Rodriguez	6.00
17	Jeff Bagwell	10.00
18	Cal Ripken Jr.	40.00
19	Kirby Puckett	15.00
21	Frank Thomas	8.00
22	Joe Morgan	5.00
23	Mike Piazza	20.00
25	Andruw Jones	5.00

Benchmarks Autographs

		NM/M
5	Bob Gibson	60.00
7	Frank Robinson	50.00
9	Reggie Jackson	100.00
15	Mike Schmidt	100.00
22	Joe Morgan	50.00
25	Andruw Jones	60.00

Classic Combos

		NM/M
Common Card:		20.00
1	Roberto Clemente	125.00

2 Willie Stargell 25.00
3 Babe Ruth 450.00
4 Lou Gehrig 300.00
5 Hank Aaron 100.00
6 Eddie Mathews 30.00
7 Johnny Bench 40.00
8 Joe Morgan 20.00
9 Robin Yount 40.00
10 Paul Molitor 35.00
11 Steve Carlton 25.00
12 Mike Schmidt 75.00
13 Stan Musial 75.00
14 Lou Brock 20.00
15 Yogi Berra 30.00
16 Phil Rizzuto 25.00
17 Ernie Banks 40.00
18 Billy Williams 20.00
19 Don Mattingly 70.00
21 Jackie Robinson 100.00
22 Duke Snider 30.00
23 Frank Robinson 25.00
24 Brooks Robinson 40.00
26 Willie McCovey 30.00
27 Ryne Sandberg 60.00
29 Harmon Killebrew 40.00
30 Rod Carew 40.00
31 Roberto Clemente, Willie Stargell 200.00
32 Babe Ruth, Lou Gehrig 1,000
33 Hank Aaron, Eddie Mathews 200.00
34 Johnny Bench, Joe Morgan 80.00
35 Robin Yount, Paul Molitor 100.00
36 Steve Carlton, Mike Schmidt 200.00
37 Stan Musial, Lou Brock 150.00
38 Phil Rizzuto, Yogi Berra 100.00
41 Jackie Robinson, Duke Snider 150.00
42 Brooks Robinson, Frank Robinson 75.00
43 Willie McCovey, Orlando Cepeda 60.00
45 Harmon Killebrew, Rod Carew 100.00

Classic Combos Autographs
No pricing due to scarcity.

Legendary Lumberjacks

NM/M
Common Player: 5.00
Inserted 1:18
1 Hack Wilson/244 75.00
2 Chipper Jones 10.00
3 Rogers Hornsby/SP/301 85.00
4 Nellie Fox 75.00
5 Ivan Rodriguez 10.00
6 Jimmie Foxx/300 120.00
7 Hank Aaron 40.00
8 Yogi Berra 15.00
9 Ernie Banks/SP/300 50.00
10 George Brett 25.00
11 Ty Cobb/SP/100 150.00
12 Roberto Clemente 125.00
13 Carlton Fisk 5.00
14 Reggie Jackson 10.00
15 Al Kaline 15.00
16 Harmon Killebrew 15.00
17 Ralph Kiner 5.00
18 Roger Maris/SP/275 120.00
19 Eddie Mathews 25.00
20 Ted Williams/SP/300 125.00
21 Willie McCovey 5.00
22 Eddie Murray 5.00
23 Joe Morgan/SP/268 20.00
24 Frank Robinson 10.00
25 Tony Perez 5.00
26 Mike Schmidt 20.00
27 Ryne Sandberg 15.00
28 Duke Snider/SP/300 25.00
30 Billy Williams 5.00
31 Dave Winfield 8.00
32 Robin Yount 10.00
33 Barry Bonds 30.00

ABBREVIATIONS
SP - Short Print

34 Stan Musial/SP/300 35.00
35 Johnny Bench/SP/300 20.00
36 Orlando Cepeda 5.00
37 Jeff Bagwell 8.00
38 Frank Thomas 8.00
39 Juan Gonzalez 8.00
40 Cal Ripken Jr. 40.00
41 Rafael Palmeiro 8.00
42 Troy Glaus/SP/100 15.00
43 Manny Ramirez 8.00
44 Paul Molitor 15.00
45 Tony Gwynn 8.00
46 Rod Carew 8.00
47 Lou Brock 8.00
48 Wade Boggs 5.00
49 Babe Ruth/SP 225.00
50 Lou Gehrig/SP 150.00

Legendary Lumberjacks Autographs
NM/M
No pricing due to scarcity.
LL24 Frank Robinson 200.00

Significant Signatures

NM/M
Common Autograph: 5.00
Inserted 1:18
101 Aubrey Huff 6.00
103 Cory Aldridge 5.00
105 Josh Beckett/SP 25.00
106 Wilson Betemit 5.00
107 Timo Perez 5.00
108 Albert Pujols 600.00
110 Jack Wilson 5.00
111 Alex Escobar 5.00
112 Johnny Estrada 20.00
113 Pedro Feliz 5.00
114 Nate Frese 5.00
115 Carlos Garcia 5.00
116 Brandon Larson 8.00
118 Jason Hart 5.00
119 Adam Dunn/SP 25.00
120 Marcus Giles 8.00
121 Christian Parker 5.00
126 Jose Mieses 5.00
127 C.C. Sabathia 10.00
129 Xavier Nady 8.00
130 Horacio Ramirez 10.00
131 Abraham Nunez 5.00
132 Jose Ortiz 5.00
133 Jeremy Owens 5.00
134 Claudio Vargas 5.00
135 Corey Patterson/SP 20.00
136 Andres Torres 5.00
137 Ben Sheets/SP 25.00
138 Joe Crede 8.00
139 Adam Pettyjohn 5.00
141 Elpidio Guzman 5.00
142 Wilkin Ruan 5.00
144 Alfonso Soriano/SP 40.00
145 Nick Johnson 10.00
147 Juan Uribe 10.00
149 Carlos Valderrama 5.00
151 Hank Aaron/SP 200.00
152 Ernie Banks 35.00
153 Johnny Bench/SP 100.00
154 George Brett/SP 150.00
155 Lou Brock 15.00
156 Rod Carew 25.00
157 Steve Carlton 25.00
158 Bob Feller 15.00
159 Bob Gibson 25.00
160 Reggie Jackson/SP 65.00
161 Al Kaline 40.00
162 Nolan Ryan/SP 150.00
163 Don Mattingly 80.00
164 Willie Mays/SP 160.00
165 Willie McCovey 20.00
166 Joe Morgan 10.00
167 Stan Musial/SP 85.00
168 Jim Palmer 15.00
169 Brooks Robinson 40.00
170 Frank Robinson 40.00
171 Nolan Ryan/SP 150.00

172 Mike Schmidt 75.00
173 Tom Seaver 30.00
174 Warren Spahn 40.00
175 Robin Yount/SP 100.00
176 Wade Boggs/SP 50.00
179 Luis Aparicio 10.00
181 Ryne Sandberg 75.00
182 Yogi Berra 30.00
184 Eddie Murray 50.00
185 Ron Santo 25.00
186 Duke Snider 25.00
187 Orlando Cepeda 10.00
188 Billy Williams 10.00
189 Juan Marichal 15.00
190 Harmon Killebrew 40.00
191 Kirby Puckett/SP 60.00
192 Carlton Fisk 15.00
193 Dave Winfield/SP 50.00
194 Whitey Ford 25.00
195 Paul Molitor/SP 50.00
196 Tony Perez 15.00
197 Ozzie Smith/SP 80.00
198 Ralph Kiner 25.00
199 Fergie Jenkins 10.00
200 Phil Rizzuto 40.00

Stadium Stars

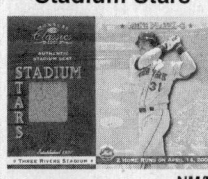

NM/M
Common Player: 4.00
Inserted 1:18
1 Babe Ruth 40.00
2 Cal Ripken Jr. 20.00
3 Brooks Robinson 8.00
4 Tony Gwynn 10.00
5 Ty Cobb 25.00
6 Vladimir Guerrero 8.00
7 Lou Gehrig 35.00
8 Nomar Garciaparra 12.00
9 Sammy Sosa 12.00
10 Reggie Jackson 8.00
11 Alex Rodriguez 12.00
12 Derek Jeter 20.00
13 Willie McCovey 4.00
14 Mark McGwire 15.00
15 Chipper Jones 10.00
16 Honus Wagner 10.00
17 Ken Griffey Jr. 12.00
18 Frank Robinson 8.00
19 Barry Bonds 20.00
20 Yogi Berra 8.00
21 Mike Piazza 12.00
22 Roger Clemens 10.00
23 Duke Snider 8.00
24 Frank Thomas 8.00
25 Andruw Jones 8.00

Stadium Stars Autographs
Common Autograph:

Timeless Treasures

NM/M
Inserted 1:420
1 Mark McGwire/Ball 200.00
2 Babe Ruth/Seat 60.00
3 Harmon Killebrew/Bat 30.00
4 Derek Jeter/Base 25.00
5 Barry Bonds/Ball 85.00

2001 Donruss Class of 2001 Samples

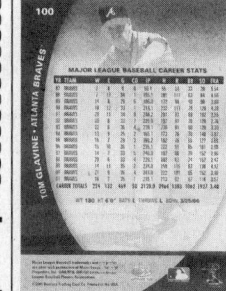

Each February, 2002, issue of Beckett Baseball Card Monthly included a sample Donruss Class of 2001 card rubber-cemented inside. The cards differ from the issued version only in the appearance on back of a (usually) silver-foil "SAMPLE" notation. Some cards were produced with the overprint in gold-foil, in much more limited quantities. The number of different players' cards involved in the promotion is unknown.

NM/M
Common Player: .10
Stars: 1.5-2X
Gold: 20X

2001 Donruss Class of 2001

NM/M
Complete Set (300):
Common Player: .20
Common (101-200): 3.00
Production 1,875
Common (201-300):
Production 625
Pack (3): 6.00
Box (24 + bobble head): 125.00
1 Alex Rodriguez 2.00
2 Barry Bonds 2.50
3 Vladimir Guerrero .75
4 Jim Edmonds .20
5 Derek Jeter 2.50
6 Jose Canseco .40
7 Rafael Furcal .20
8 Cal Ripken Jr. 2.50
9 Brad Radke .20
10 Miguel Tejada .40
11 Pat Burrell .50
12 Ken Griffey Jr. 1.50
13 Cliff Floyd .20
14 Luis Gonzalez .20
15 Frank Thomas .75
16 Mike Sweeney .20
17 Paul LoDuca .20
18 Lance Berkman .20
19 Tony Gwynn 1.00
20 Chipper Jones 1.00
21 Eric Chavez .40
22 Kerry Wood .35
23 Jorge Posada .20
24 J.D. Drew .50
25 Garret Anderson .20
26 Mike Piazza 1.50
27 Kenny Lofton .20
28 Mike Mussina .40
29 Paul Konerko .20
30 Bernie Williams .20
31 Eric Milton .20
32 Shawn Green .40
33 Paul O'Neill .20
34 Juan Gonzalez .35
35 Andres Galarraga .20
36 Gary Sheffield .40
37 Ben Grieve .20
38 Scott Rolen .60
39 Mark Grace .20
40 Hideo Nomo .35
41 Barry Zito .50
42 Edgar Martinez .20
43 Jarrod Washburn .20
44 Greg Maddux 1.00
45 Mark Buehrle .20
46 Larry Walker .20
47 Trot Nixon .20
48 Nomar Garciaparra 1.50
49 Robert Fick .20
50 Sean Casey .40
51 Joe Mays .20
52 Roger Clemens 1.25
53 Chan Ho Park .20
54 Carlos Delgado .50
55 Phil Nevin .20
56 Jason Giambi .20
57 Raul Mondesi .20
58 Roberto Alomar .35
59 Ryan Klesko .20
60 Andruw Jones .75
61 Gabe Kapler .20
62 Darin Erstad .35
63 Cristian Guzman .20

64 Kazuhiro Sasaki .20
65 Doug Mientkiewicz .20
66 Sammy Sosa 1.50
67 Mike Hampton .20
68 Rickey Henderson .75
69 Mark Mulder .30
70 Mark McGwire 2.00
72 Freddy Garcia .20
73 Ivan Rodriguez .60
73 Terrence Long .20
74 Jeff Bagwell .75
75 Moises Alou .20
76 Todd Helton .65
77 Preston Wilson .20
78 Pedro Martinez .75
79 Bobby Abreu .20
80 Manny Ramirez .75
81 Jose Vidro .20
82 Randy Johnson .75
83 Richie Sexson .20
84 Troy Glaus .65
85 Kevin Brown .20
86 Carlos Lee .20
87 Adrian Beltre .30
88 Brian Giles .20
89 Jermaine Dye .20
90 Craig Biggio .20
91 Richard Hidalgo .20
92 Magglio Ordonez .20
93 Aramis Ramirez .20
94 Jeff Kent .20
95 Curt Schilling .50
96 Tim Hudson .40
97 Fred McGriff .20
98 Barry Larkin .20
99 Jim Thome .60
100 Tom Glavine .40
101 Sean Douglass RC 3.00
102 Rob Mackowiak RC 3.00
103 Jeremy Fikac RC 3.00
104 Henry Mateo RC 3.00
105 Geronimo Gil RC 3.00
106 Ramon Vazquez RC 5.00
107 Pedro Santana RC 3.00
108 Ryan Jensen RC 3.00
109 Paul Phillips RC 3.00
110 Saul Rivera RC 3.00
111 Larry Bigbie RC 3.00
112 Josh Phelps RC 3.00
113 Justin Kaye RC 3.00
114 Kris Keller RC 3.00
115 Adam Bernero RC 3.00
116 Victor Zambrano RC 3.00
117 Felipe Lopez RC 3.00
118 Brian Roberts RC 8.00
119 Kurt Ainsworth RC 3.00
120 George Perez RC 3.00
121 Wilson Guzman RC 3.00
122 Derrick Lewis RC 3.00
123 Nate Teut RC 3.00
124 Martin Vargas RC 3.00
125 Brandon Inge RC 3.00
126 Travis Phelps RC 3.00
127 Les Walrond RC 3.00
128 Justin Atchley RC 3.00
129 Stubby Clapp RC 3.00
130 Bret Prinz RC 3.00
131 Bert Snow RC 3.00
132 Joe Crede RC 3.00
133 Nick Punto RC 3.00
134 Carlos Hernandez RC 3.00
135 Ken Vining RC 3.00
136 Luis Pineda RC 3.00
137 Winston Abreu RC 3.00
138 Matt Ginter RC 3.00
139 Jason Smith RC 3.00
140 Gene Altman RC 3.00
141 Brian Rogers RC 3.00
142 Michael Cuddyer RC 3.00
143 Mike Penney RC 3.00
144 Scott Podsednik RC 10.00
145 Esix Snead RC 3.00
146 Steve Watkins RC 3.00
147 Orlando Woodards RC 3.00
148 Mike Young RC 3.00
149 Chris George RC 3.00
150 Blaine Neal RC 3.00
151 Ben Sheets RC 3.00
152 Scott Stewart RC 3.00
153 Mike Koplove RC 3.00
154 Kyle Lohse RC 8.00
155 Dee Brown RC 3.00
156 Aubrey Huff RC 3.00
157 Pablo Ozuna RC 3.00
158 Bill Ortega RC 3.00
159 Toby Hall RC 3.00
160 Kevin Olsen RC 3.00
161 Will Ohman RC 3.00
162 Nate Cornejo RC 3.00
163 Jack Cust RC 3.00
164 Juan Rivera RC 3.00
165 Jerrod Riggan RC 3.00
166 Dustan Mohr RC 3.00
167 Doug Nickle RC 3.00
168 Craig Monroe RC 3.00
169 Jason Jennings RC 3.00
170 Bart Miadich RC 3.00
171 Luis Rivas RC 3.00
172 Tim Christman RC 3.00
173 Luke Hudson RC 3.00
174 Brett Jodie RC 3.00
175 Jorge Julio RC 4.00
176 David Espinosa RC 3.00
177 Mike Maroth RC 3.00
178 Keith Ginter RC 3.00
179 Juan Moreno RC 3.00
180 Brandon Knight RC 3.00
181 Steve Lomasney RC 3.00

182 John Grabow RC 3.00
183 Steve Green RC 3.00
184 Jason Karnuth RC 3.00
185 Bob File RC 3.00
186 Brent Abernathy RC 3.00
187 Morgan Ensberg RC 12.00
188 Wily Mo Pena RC 3.00
189 Ken Harvey RC 3.00
190 Josh Pearce RC 3.00
191 Cesar Izturis RC 3.00
192 Eric Hinske RC 5.00
193 Joe Beimel RC 3.00
194 Timo Perez RC 3.00
195 Troy Mattes RC 3.00
196 Eric Valent RC 3.00
197 Ed Rogers RC 3.00
198 Grant Balfour RC 3.00
199 Benito Baez RC 3.00
200 Vernon Wells RC 3.00
201 Joe Kennedy RC 4.00
202 Wilson Betemit RC 8.00
203 Christian Parker RC 3.00
204 Jay Gibbons RC 10.00
205 Carlos Garcia RC 4.00
206 Jack Wilson RC 4.00
207 Johnny Estrada RC 10.00
208 Wilkin Ruan RC 3.00
209 Brandon Duckworth RC 5.00
210 Willie Harris RC 3.00
211 Marlon Byrd RC 10.00
212 C.C. Sabathia RC 3.00
213 Dennis Tankersley RC 5.00
214 Brandon Larson RC 5.00
215 Alexis Gomez RC 3.00
216 Bill Hall RC 15.00
217 Antonio Perez RC 4.00
218 Jeremy Affeldt RC 4.00
219 Junior Spivey RC 8.00
220 Casey Fossum RC 8.00
221 Brandon Lyon RC 4.00
222 Angel Santos RC 3.00
223 Lance Davis RC 3.00
224 Zach Day RC 4.00
225 David Williams RC 3.00
226 Cesar Crespo RC 3.00
227 Jose Acevedo RC 3.00
228 Travis Hafner RC 20.00
229 Orlando Hudson RC 10.00
230 Jose Mieses RC 3.00
231 Ricardo Rodriguez RC 3.00
232 Alfonso Soriano 3.00
233 Jason Hart 3.00
234 Endy Chavez RC 3.00
235 Delvin James RC 3.00
236 Ryan Drese RC 3.00
237 Jeremy Owens RC 3.00
238 Brad Voyles RC 3.00
239 Nate Frese 3.00
240 Josh Beckett 3.00
241 Roy Oswalt 3.00
242 Juan Uribe RC 3.00
243 Cory Aldridge RC 3.00
244 Adam Dunn 3.00
245 Bud Smith RC 3.00
246 Adrian Hernandez RC 3.00
247 Matt Guerrier RC 3.00
248 Jimmy Rollins 3.00
249 Wilmy Caceres RC 3.00
250 Jason Michaels RC 3.00
251 Ichiro Suzuki RC 60.00
252 John Buck RC 3.00
253 Andres Torres RC 3.00
254 Alfredo Amezaga RC 3.00
255 Corky Miller RC 3.00
256 Rafael Soriano RC 10.00
257 Donaldo Mendez RC 3.00
258 Victor Martinez RC 60.00
259 Corey Patterson 3.00
260 Horacio Ramirez RC 8.00
261 Elpidio Guzman RC 3.00
262 Juan Diaz RC 3.00
263 Mike Rivera RC 3.00
264 Brian Lawrence RC 3.00
265 Josue Perez RC 3.00
266 Jose Nunez 3.00
267 Erik Bedard RC 20.00
268 Albert Pujols RC 200.00
269 Duaner Sanchez RC 3.00
270 Cody Ransom RC 3.00
271 Greg Miller RC 3.00
272 Adam Pettyjohn RC 3.00
273 Tsuyoshi Shinjo RC 3.00
274 Claudio Vargas RC 3.00
275 Justin Duchscherer RC 5.00
276 Tim Spooneybarger RC 3.00
277 Rick Bauer RC 3.00
278 Josh Fogg RC 5.00
279 Brian Reith RC 3.00
280 Scott MacRae RC 3.00
281 Ryan Ludwick RC 5.00
282 Erick Almonte RC 3.00
283 Josh Towers RC 8.00
284 Juan Pena 3.00
285 David Brous RC 3.00
286 Erik Hiljus RC 3.00
287 Nick Neugebauer RC 3.00
288 Jackson Melian RC 3.00
289 Billy Sylvester RC 3.00
290 Carlos Valderrama RC 3.00
291 Jose Cueto RC 3.00
292 Matt White RC 3.00
293 Nick Maness RC 3.00
294 Jason Lane RC 10.00
295 Brandon Berger RC 3.00

296	Angel Berroa RC	6.00
297	Juan Cruz RC	4.00
298	Dewon Brazelton RC	3.00
299	Mark Prior RC	25.00
300	Mark Teixeira RC	40.00

First Class

Stars (1-100): 5-10X
Production 100
SP's (101-300): 1-3X
Production 50

First Class Autographs

NM/M
Common Player:

10	Miguel Tejada/75	50.00
17	Paul LoDuca/100	8.00
21	Eric Chavez/100	20.00
41	Barry Zito/100	30.00
45	Mark Buehrle/100	25.00
49	Robert Fick/100	15.00
50	Sean Casey/100	25.00
51	Joe Mays/100	15.00
59	Ryan Klesko/50	25.00
69	Mark Mulder/100	25.00
73	Terrence Long/100	15.00
81	Jose Vidro/100	15.00
83	Richie Sexson/100	25.00
84	Troy Glaus/100	25.00
89	Jermaine Dye/100	20.00
91	Richard Hidalgo/100	15.00
93	Aramis Ramirez/100	20.00
96	Tim Hudson/100	15.00

Rookie Autographs

NM/M
Common Autograph: 8.00

109	Paul Phillips/250	8.00
114	Kris Keller/250	8.00
115	Adam Bernero/250	8.00
120	George Perez/250	8.00
123	Nate Teut/250	8.00
124	Martin Vargas/250	8.00
127	Les Walrond/250	8.00
132	Joe Crede/250	10.00
137	Winston Abreu/250	8.00
138	Matt Ginter/250	8.00
140	Gene Altman/250	8.00
142	Michael Cuddyer/250	8.00
143	Mike Penney/250	8.00
145	Esix Snead/250	8.00
147	Orlando Woodards/250	
148	Jeff Deardorff/100	8.00
150	Blaine Neal/250	8.00
156	Aubrey Huff/250	10.00
157	Pablo Ozuna/250	8.00

158	Bill Ortega/250	8.00
160	Kevin Olsen/250	8.00
161	Will Ohman/250	8.00
163	Jack Cust/250	8.00
168	Craig Monroe/250	8.00
169	Jason Jennings/250	8.00
171	Luis Rivas/250	8.00
173	Luke Hudson/250	12.00
176	David Espinosa/250	8.00
177	Mike Maroth/250	8.00
178	Keith Ginter/250	8.00
181	Steve Lomasney/250	8.00
182	John Grabow/250	8.00
184	Jason Karnuth/250	8.00
186	Brent Abernathy/250	8.00
188	Wily Mo Pena/250	15.00
191	Cesar Izturis/250	8.00
192	Eric Hinske/250	10.00
194	Timo Perez/100	8.00
196	Eric Valent/250	8.00
201	Joe Kennedy/100	8.00
202	Wilson Betemit/100	15.00
203	Christian Parker/100	8.00
204	Jay Gibbons/100	20.00
205	Carlos Garcia/200	8.00
206	Jack Wilson/100	15.00
207	Johnny Estrada/200	20.00
208	Wilkin Ruan/200	8.00
209	Brandon Duckworth/100	8.00
211	Marlon Byrd/100	20.00
213	Dennis Tankersley/100	10.00
214	Brandon Larson/200	8.00
215	Alexis Gomez/200	10.00
216	Bill Hall/100	50.00
217	Antonio Perez/100	8.00
218	Jeremy Affeldt/200	10.00
220	Casey Fossum/200	10.00
224	Zach Day/200	8.00
225	David Williams/200	8.00
227	Jose Acevedo/200	8.00
229	Orlando Hudson/100	25.00
230	Jose Mieses/200	8.00
231	Ric Rodriguez/200	8.00
232	Alfonso Soriano/200	40.00
233	Jason Hart/100	8.00
234	Endy Chavez/200	8.00
235	Delvin James/100	8.00
237	Jeremy Owens/200	8.00
238	Brad Voyles/200	8.00
239	Nate Frese/200	8.00
240	Josh Beckett/25	60.00
241	Roy Oswalt/100	25.00
242	Juan Uribe/150	10.00
243	Cory Aldridge/200	8.00
244	Adam Dunn/100	30.00
246	Bud Smith/100	8.00
246	Adrian Hernandez/100	8.00
249	Wilmy Caceres/200	8.00
250	Jason Michaels/200	8.00
252	John Buck/100	15.00
253	Andres Torres/100	8.00
255	Corky Miller/100	8.00
256	Rafael Soriano/200	10.00
257	Donaldo Mendez/200	8.00
258	Corey Patterson/100	15.00
260	Horacio Ramirez/200	10.00
261	Elpidio Guzman/200	8.00
262	Juan Diaz/200	8.00
264	Brian Lawrence/200	10.00
265	Josue Perez/200	8.00
266	Jose Nunez/200	8.00
268	Albert Pujols/100	500.00
269	Duaner Sanchez/200	8.00
270	Greg Miller/200	8.00
272	Adam Pettyjohn/200	8.00
274	Claudio Vargas/200	8.00
279	Brian Reith/200	8.00
283	Josh Towers/100	8.00
285	David Brous/200	8.00
287	Nick Neugebauer/100	8.00
289	Billy Sylvester/200	8.00
290	Carlos Valderrama/200	8.00
292	Matt White/200	8.00
293	Nick Maness/200	8.00
296	Angel Berroa/100	15.00
297	Juan Cruz/100	8.00
298	Dewon Brazelton/100	8.00
299	Mark Prior/100	150.00
300	Mark Teixeira/100	275.00

Aces

NM/M
Complete Set (20): 70.00
Common Player: 3.00

Inserted 1:30

1	Roger Clemens	12.00
2	Randy Johnson	7.50
3	Freddy Garcia	3.00
4	Greg Maddux	10.00
5	Tim Hudson	5.00
6	Curt Schilling	5.00
7	Mark Buehrle	3.00
8	Matt Morris	3.00
9	Joe Mays	3.00
10	Javier Vazquez	3.00
11	Mark Mulder	4.00
12	Wade Miller	3.00
13	Barry Zito	5.00
14	Pedro Martinez	7.50
15	Al Leiter	3.00
16	Chan Ho Park	3.00
17	John Burkett	3.00
18	C.C. Sabathia	3.00
19	Jamie Moyer	3.00
20	Mike Mussina	5.00

Diamond Aces

NM/M
Common Player: 5.00
Varying quantities produced

1	Roger Clemens/200	30.00
2	Randy Johnson/750	10.00
3	Freddy Garcia/350	5.00
4	Greg Maddux/750	20.00
5	Tim Hudson/550	8.00
6	Curt Schilling/525	8.00
7	Mark Buehrle/750	5.00
9	Joe Mays/750	5.00
10	Javier Vazquez/500	5.00
11	Mark Mulder/300	6.00
12	Wade Miller/525	5.00
13	Barry Zito/550	8.00
14	Pedro Martinez/550	15.00
15	Al Leiter/525	5.00
16	Chan Ho Park/400	5.00
17	John Burkett/700	5.00
18	C.C. Sabathia/550	5.00
19	Jamie Moyer/700	5.00

Bobblehead

NM/M
Common Bobblehead: 10.00
One per box.

1	Ichiro Suzuki	40.00
2	Cal Ripken Jr.	40.00
3	Derek Jeter	35.00
4	Mark McGwire	35.00
5	Albert Pujols	40.00
6	Ken Griffey Jr.	20.00
7	Nomar Garciaparra	20.00
8	Mike Piazza	20.00
9	Alex Rodriguez	20.00
10	Manny Ramirez	10.00
11	Tsuyoshi Shinjo	10.00
12	Hideo Nomo	10.00
13	Chipper Jones	15.00
14	Sammy Sosa	20.00
15	Roger Clemens	17.50
16	Tony Gwynn	15.00
17	Barry Bonds	35.00
18	Kazuhiro Sasaki	10.00
19	Pedro Martinez	10.00
20	Jeff Bagwell	10.00
21	Ichiro Suzuki ROY	40.00
22	Albert Pujols ROY	40.00

Bobblehead Cards

NM/M
Common Player: 4.00
1-20 2,000 Produced
21-22 1,000 Produced

1	Ichiro Suzuki	15.00
2	Cal Ripken Jr.	12.00
3	Derek Jeter	12.00
4	Mark McGwire	10.00
5	Albert Pujols	10.00
6	Ken Griffey Jr.	8.00
7	Nomar Garciaparra	8.00
8	Mike Piazza	8.00
9	Alex Rodriguez	8.00
10	Manny Ramirez	5.00
11	Tsuyoshi Shinjo	4.00
12	Hideo Nomo	4.00
13	Chipper Jones	6.00
14	Sammy Sosa	8.00
15	Roger Clemens	7.00
16	Tony Gwynn	6.00
17	Barry Bonds	15.00
18	Kazuhiro Sasaki	4.00
19	Pedro Martinez	5.00
20	Jeff Bagwell	5.00
21	Ichiro Suzuki	15.00
22	Albert Pujols	15.00

Crusade

NM/M
Complete Set (25): 125.00
Common Player: 3.00

1	Roger Clemens/275	15.00
02	Luis Gonzalez/275	3.00
3	Troy Glaus/275	6.00
4	Freddy Garcia/300	3.00
5	Sean Casey/285	5.00
6	Bobby Abreu/300	3.00
7	Matt Morris/300	3.00
8	Cal Ripken Jr./275	25.00
9	Miguel Tejada/285	4.00
10	Vladimir Guerrero/275	8.00
11	Mark Buehrle/100	5.00
12	Mike Sweeney/300	3.00
13	Ivan Rodriguez/275	5.00
14	Jeff Bagwell/275	8.00
15	Joe Mays/250	3.00
16	Cliff Floyd/300	3.00
17	Lance Berkman/300	3.00
18	Aramis Ramirez/100	5.00
19	Tony Gwynn/300	10.00
20	Shannon Stewart/100	3.00
21	Todd Helton/275	5.00
22	Chipper Jones/275	12.00
23	Javier Vazquez/100	5.00
24	Shawn Green/275	5.00
25	Barry Bonds/300	25.00

Rookie Crusade

NM/M
Complete Set (25): 110.00
Common Player: 3.00

26	Albert Pujols/250	30.00
27	Wilson Betemit/100	3.00
28	C.C. Sabathia/290	3.00
29	Roy Oswalt/100	4.00
30	Johnny Estrada/100	3.00
31	Nick Johnson/100	4.00
32	Aubrey Huff/100	3.00
33	Corey Patterson/200	4.00
34	Jay Gibbons/100	4.00
35	Marcus Giles/100	3.00
36	Juan Cruz/100	3.00
37	Tsuyoshi Shinjo/300	3.00
38	Ben Sheets/285	3.00
39	Bud Smith/100	3.00
40	Alex Escobar/100	3.00
41	Joe Kennedy/100	3.00
42	Alexis Gomez/100	3.00
43	Jimmy Rollins/300	3.00
44	Josh Towers/100	3.00

1	Ichiro Suzuki	15.00
2	Cal Ripken Jr.	12.00
3	Derek Jeter	12.00
4	Mark McGwire	10.00
5	Albert Pujols	10.00
6	Ken Griffey Jr.	8.00
7	Nomar Garciaparra	8.00
8	Mike Piazza	8.00
9	Alex Rodriguez	8.00
10	Manny Ramirez	5.00
11	Tsuyoshi Shinjo	4.00
12	Hideo Nomo	4.00
13	Chipper Jones	6.00
14	Sammy Sosa	8.00
15	Roger Clemens	7.00
16	Tony Gwynn	6.00
17	Barry Bonds	15.00
18	Kazuhiro Sasaki	4.00
19	Pedro Martinez	5.00
20	Jeff Bagwell	5.00
21	Ichiro Suzuki	15.00
22	Albert Pujols	15.00

Crusade Autographs

NM/M
Common Player: 4.00

11	Mark Buehrle/200	10.00
15	Joe Mays/50	10.00
18	Aramis Ramirez/200	8.00
20	Shannon Stewart/200	8.00
23	Javier Vazquez/100	10.00
26	Albert Pujols/50	750.00
27	Wilson Betemit/200	10.00
29	Roy Oswalt/200	12.00
30	Johnny Estrada/200	8.00
31	Nick Johnson/200	12.00
32	Aubrey Huff/200	8.00
33	Corey Patterson/200	10.00
34	Jay Gibbons/200	20.00
35	Marcus Giles/200	8.00
36	Juan Cruz/200	8.00
39	Bud Smith/200	8.00
40	Alex Escobar/200	8.00
41	Joe Kennedy/200	8.00
42	Alexis Gomez/200	10.00
44	Josh Towers/200	8.00
45	Joe Crede/200	10.00
46	Brandon Duckworth/200	12.00
48	Jose Ortiz/200	8.00
49	Casey Fossum/200	12.00
50	Adam Dunn/100	30.00

Dominators

NM/M
Complete Set (30): 90.00
Common Player: 2.00
Inserted 1:20

1	Manny Ramirez	4.00
2	Lance Berkman	2.00
3	Juan Gonzalez	4.00
4	Albert Pujols	10.00
5	Jason Giambi	3.00
6	Mike Sweeney	2.00
7	Rafael Palmeiro	4.00
8	Luis Gonzalez	2.00
9	Ichiro Suzuki	10.00
10	Cliff Floyd	2.00
11	Roberto Alomar	4.00
12	Paul LoDuca	2.00
13	Shannon Stewart	2.00
14	Barry Bonds	10.00
15	Larry Walker	2.00
16	Shawn Green	3.00
17	Moises Alou	2.00
18	Cal Ripken Jr.	10.00
19	Brian Giles	2.00
20	Magglio Ordonez	3.00
21	Jose Vidro	2.00
22	Edgar Martinez	2.00
23	Aramis Ramirez	2.00
24	Tony Gwynn	5.00
25	Richie Sexson	2.00
26	Todd Helton	4.00
27	Garret Anderson	2.00
28	Chipper Jones	5.00
29	Troy Glaus	4.00
30	Jeff Bagwell	4.00

Diamond Dominators

NM/M
Common Player: 4.00
Varying quantities produced

1	Manny Ramirez/725	8.00
2	Lance Berkman/725	4.00
3	Juan Gonzalez/500	6.00
4	Albert Pujols/125	65.00
5	Jason Giambi/250	8.00
6	Mike Sweeney/325	4.00
7	Rafael Palmeiro/550	8.00
9	Luis Gonzalez/725	4.00
10	Cliff Floyd/725	4.00
11	Roberto Alomar/200	8.00
12	Paul LoDuca/600	4.00
13	Shannon Stewart/725	6.00
14	Barry Bonds/250	30.00
15	Larry Walker/725	6.00
16	Shawn Green/500	6.00
17	Moises Alou/550	4.00
18	Cal Ripken Jr./250	50.00
19	Brian Giles/725	5.00
20	Magglio Ordonez/725	5.00
21	Jose Vidro/725	4.00
22	Edgar Martinez/200	6.00
23	Aramis Ramirez/200	5.00
24	Tony Gwynn/500	10.00
25	Richie Sexson/725	6.00
26	Todd Helton/725	8.00
27	Garret Anderson/725	6.00
28	Chipper Jones/725	12.00
29	Troy Glaus/200	8.00
30	Jeff Bagwell/325	8.00

Rewards

NM/M
Common Player: 5.00
Inserted 1:212

1	Jason Giambi	7.50
2	Ichiro Suzuki	40.00
3	Roger Clemens	20.00
4	Freddy Garcia	5.00
5	Ichiro Suzuki	40.00
6	Albert Pujols	30.00
7	Barry Bonds	30.00
8	Albert Pujols	30.00
9	Randy Johnson	10.00
10	Matt Morris	5.00

Final Rewards

NM/M
Common Player: 5.00
Varying quantities produced

1	Jason Giambi/250	10.00
2	Ichiro Suzuki/50	120.00
3	Roger Clemens/200	8.00

4	Freddy Garcia/250	5.00
5	Ichiro Suzuki/50	120.00
6	Albert Pujols/125	60.00
7	Barry Bonds/200	40.00
8	Albert Pujols/125	60.00
9	Randy Johnson/250	15.00

Rookie Team

	NM/M
Complete Set (15):	65.00
Common Player:	3.00
Inserted 1:83	

1	Jay Gibbons	5.00
2	Alfonso Soriano	6.00
3	Jimmy Rollins	3.00
4	Wilson Betemit	3.00
5	Albert Pujols	20.00
6	Johnny Estrada	3.00
7	Ichiro Suzuki	15.00
8	Tsuyoshi Shinjo	4.00
9	Adam Dunn	5.00
10	C.C. Sabathia	3.00
11	Ben Sheets	3.00
12	Roy Oswalt	4.00
13	Bud Smith	3.00
14	Josh Towers	3.00
15	Juan Cruz	3.00

Rookie Team Materials

	NM/M
Common Player:	5.00
Varying quantities produced	

1	Jay Gibbons/100	8.00
2	Alfonso Soriano/200	15.00
3	Jimmy Rollins/200	5.00
5	Albert Pujols/100	65.00
6	Johnny Estrada/100	5.00
7	Ichiro Suzuki/50	120.00
8	Tsuyoshi Shinjo/200	10.00
9	Adam Dunn/200	8.00
10	C.C. Sabathia/200	5.00
11	Ben Sheets/200	5.00
13	Bud Smith/250	5.00
14	Josh Towers/200	5.00
15	Juan Cruz/200	5.00

Yearbook

	NM/M
Complete Set (25):	85.00
Common Player:	3.00
Inserted 1:24	

1	Barry Bonds	12.00
2	Mark Mulder	3.00
3	Luis Gonzalez	2.00
4	Lance Berkman	2.00

5	Matt Morris	2.00
6	Roy Oswalt	2.50
7	Todd Helton	3.00
8	Tsuyoshi Shinjo	2.00
9	C.C. Sabathia	2.00
10	Curt Schilling	3.00
11	Rickey Henderson	3.00
12	Jamie Moyer	2.00
13	Shawn Green	3.00
14	Randy Johnson	4.00
15	Jim Thome	2.00
16	Larry Walker	2.00
17	Jimmy Rollins	2.00
18	Kazuhiro Sasaki	2.00
19	Hideo Nomo	3.00
20	Roger Clemens	7.50
21	Bud Smith	2.00
22	Ichiro Suzuki	10.00
23	Albert Pujols	15.00
24	Cal Ripken Jr.	15.00
25	Tony Gwynn	5.00

Yearbook Scrapbook

	NM/M
Common Player:	4.00
Varying quantities produced	

1	Barry Bonds/525	30.00
2	Mark Mulder/500	6.00
3	Luis Gonzalez/500	4.00
4	Lance Berkman/525	4.00
6	Roy Oswalt/150	6.00
7	Todd Helton/525	6.00
8	Tsuyoshi Shinjo/75	15.00
9	C.C. Sabathia/500	4.00
10	Curt Schilling/525	6.00
11	Rickey Henderson/200	15.00
12	Jamie Moyer/500	4.00
13	Shawn Green/525	5.00
14	Randy Johnson/500	8.00
15	Jim Thome/400	4.00
16	Larry Walker/500	4.00
18	Kazuhiro Sasaki/500	4.00
19	Hideo Nomo/150	8.00
20	Roger Clemens/475	20.00
21	Bud Smith/525	4.00
22	Ichiro Suzuki/75	80.00
23	Albert Pujols/500	50.00
24	Cal Ripken/525	30.00
25	Tony Gwynn/500	10.00

2001 Donruss Elite

	NM/M
Complete Set (200):	
Common Player:	.25
Common (151-200):	5.00
Production 900	
Common 201-250:	4.00
(#201-250 available by redemption)	
Pack (5):	12.00
Box (18):	180.00

1	Alex Rodriguez	2.00
2	Barry Bonds	2.50
3	Cal Ripken Jr.	2.50
4	Chipper Jones	1.50
5	Derek Jeter	2.50
6	Troy Glaus	.75
7	Frank Thomas	1.00
8	Greg Maddux	1.50
9	Ivan Rodriguez	.75
10	Jeff Bagwell	1.00
11	Jose Canseco	.50
12	Todd Helton	.75
13	Ken Griffey Jr.	1.75
14	Manny Ramirez	1.00
15	Mark McGwire	2.00
16	Mike Piazza	1.75
17	Nomar Garciaparra	1.50
18	Pedro Martinez	1.00
19	Randy Johnson	1.00
20	Rick Ankiel	.25
21	Ricky Henderson	1.00
22	Roger Clemens	1.75
23	Sammy Sosa	1.50
24	Tony Gwynn	1.50
25	Vladimir Guerrero	1.00
26	Eric Davis	.25
27	Roberto Alomar	.35
28	Mark Mulder	.35
29	Pat Burrell	.50
30	Harold Baines	.25
31	Carlos Delgado	.60
32	J.D. Drew	.40
33	Jim Edmonds	.40
34	Darin Erstad	.35
35	Jason Giambi	.40
36	Tom Glavine	.50
37	Juan Gonzalez	.25
38	Mark Grace	.25
39	Shawn Green	.40
40	Tim Hudson	.25
41	Andruw Jones	1.00
42	David Justice	.25
43	Jeff Kent	.25
44	Barry Larkin	.25
45	Pokey Reese	.25
46	Mike Mussina	.40
47	Hideo Nomo	.25
48	Rafael Palmeiro	.65
49	Adam Piatt	.25
50	Scott Rolen	.65
51	Gary Sheffield	.40
52	Bernie Williams	.25
53	Bob Abreu	.25
54	Edgardo Alfonzo	.25
55	Jermaine Clark RC	.25
56	Albert Belle	.25
57	Craig Biggio	.25
58	Andres Galarraga	.25
59	Edgar Martinez	.25
60	Fred McGriff	.25
61	Magglio Ordonez	.25
62	Jim Thome	.65
63	Matt Williams	.25
64	Kerry Wood	.50
65	Moises Alou	.25
66	Brady Anderson	.25
67	Garret Anderson	.25
68	Tony Armas Jr.	.25
69	Tony Batista	.25
70	Jose Cruz Jr.	.25
71	Carlos Beltran	.50
72	Adrian Beltre	.40
73	Kris Benson	.25
74	Lance Berkman	.25
75	Kevin Brown	.25
76	Jay Buhner	.25
77	Jeromy Burnitz	.25
78	Ken Caminiti	.25
79	Sean Casey	.40
80	Luis Castillo	.25
81	Eric Chavez	.40
82	Jeff Cirillo	.25
83	Bartolo Colon	.25
84	David Cone	.25
85	Freddy Garcia	.25
86	Johnny Damon	.50
87	Ray Durham	.25
88	Jermaine Dye	.25
89	Juan Encarnacion	.25
90	Terrence Long	.25
91	Carl Everett	.25
92	Steve Finley	.25
93	Cliff Floyd	.25
94	Brad Fulmer	.25
95	Brian Giles	.25
96	Luis Gonzalez	.25
97	Rusty Greer	.25
98	Jeffrey Hammonds	.25
99	Mike Hampton	.25
100	Orlando Hernandez	.35
101	Richard Hidalgo	.25
102	Geoff Jenkins	.25
103	Jacque Jones	.25
104	Brian Jordan	.25
105	Gabe Kapler	.25
106	Eric Karros	.25
107	Jason Kendall	.25
108	Adam Kennedy	.25
109	Byung-Hyun Kim	.25
110	Ryan Klesko	.25
111	Chuck Knoblauch	.25
112	Paul Konerko	.25
113	Carlos Lee	.25
114	Kenny Lofton	.25
115	Javy Lopez	.25
116	Tino Martinez	.25
117	Ruben Mateo	.25
118	Kevin Millwood	.25
119	Ben Molina	.25
120	Raul Mondesi	.25
121	Trot Nixon	.25
122	John Olerud	.25
123	Paul O'Neill	.25
124	Chan Ho Park	.25
125	Andy Pettitte	.40
126	Jorge Posada	.35
127	Mark Quinn	.25
128	Aramis Ramirez	.25
129	Mariano Rivera	.35
130	Tim Salmon	.25
131	Curt Schilling	.40
132	Richie Sexson	.25
133	John Smoltz	.25
134	J.T. Snow	.25
135	Jay Payton	.25
136	Shannon Stewart	.25
137	B.J. Surhoff	.25
138	Mike Sweeney	.25
139	Fernando Tatis	.25
140	Miguel Tejada	.40
141	Jason Varitek	.25
142	Greg Vaughn	.25
143	Mo Vaughn	.25
144	Robin Ventura	.25
145	Jose Vidro	.25
146	Omar Vizquel	.25
147	Larry Walker	.25
148	David Wells	.25
149	Rondell White	.25
150	Preston Wilson	.25
151	Brent Abernathy	5.00
152	Cory Aldridge RC	5.00
153	Gene Altman RC	5.00
154	Josh Beckett	6.00
155	Wilson Betemit RC	5.00
156	Albert Pujols RC	400.00
157	Joe Crede	5.00
158	Jack Cust	5.00
159	Ben Sheets	5.00
160	Alex Escobar	5.00
161	Adrian Hernandez RC	5.00
162	Pedro Feliz	5.00
163	Nate Frese RC	5.00
164	Carlos Garcia RC	5.00
165	Marcus Giles	5.00
166	Alexis Gomez RC	5.00
167	Jason Hart	5.00
168	Aubrey Huff	5.00
169	Cesar Izturis	5.00
170	Nick Johnson	5.00
171	Jack Wilson RC	10.00
172	Brian Lawrence RC	5.00
173	Christian Parker RC	5.00
174	Nick Maness RC	5.00
175	Jose Mieses RC	5.00
176	Greg Miller RC	5.00
177	Eric Munson	5.00
178	Xavier Nady RC	5.00
179	Blaine Neal RC	5.00
180	Abraham Nunez	5.00
181	Jose Ortiz	5.00
182	Jeremy Owens RC	5.00
183	Jay Gibbons RC	10.00
184	Corey Patterson	5.00
185	Carlos Pena	5.00
186	C.C. Sabathia	5.00
187	Timo Perez	5.00
188	Adam Pettyjohn RC	5.00
189	Donaldo Mendez RC	5.00
190	Jackson Melian RC	5.00
191	Wilken Ruan RC	5.00
192	Duaner Sanchez RC	5.00
193	Alfonso Soriano	5.00
194	Rafael Soriano RC	10.00
195	Ichiro Suzuki RC	150.00
196	Billy Sylvester RC	5.00
197	Juan Uribe RC	5.00
198	Tsuyoshi Shinjo RC	10.00
199	Carlos Valderrama RC	5.00
200	Matt White RC	5.00
201	Adam Dunn	6.00
202	Joe Kennedy	4.00
203	Mike Rivera	4.00
204	Erick Almonte	4.00
205	Brandon Duckworth	4.00
206	Victor Martinez RC	180.00
207	Rick Bauer	4.00
208	Jeff Deardorff	4.00
209	Antonio Perez	4.00
210	Bill Hall	30.00
211	Dennis Tankersley	6.00
212	Jeremy Affeldt	8.00
213	Junior Spivey	8.00
214	Casey Fossum	6.00
215	Brandon Lyon	4.00
216	Angel Santos	4.00
217	Cody Ransom	4.00
218	Jason Lane	35.00
219	David Williams	4.00
220	Alex Herrera	4.00
221	Ryan Drese	4.00
222	Travis Hafner	65.00
223	Bud Smith	4.00
224	Johnny Estrada	25.00
225	Ricardo Rodriguez	4.00
226	Brandon Berger	4.00
227	Claudio Vargas	4.00
228	Luis Garcia	4.00
229	Marlon Byrd	20.00
230	Hee Seop Choi	20.00
231	Corky Miller	4.00
232	Justin Duchscherer	6.00
233	Tim Spooneybarger	4.00
234	Roy Oswalt	4.00
235	Willie Harris	4.00
236	Josh Towers	4.00
237	Juan Pena	4.00
238	Alfredo Amezaga	4.00
239	Geronimo Gil	4.00
240	Juan Cruz	4.00
241	Ed Rogers	4.00
242	Joe Thurston	4.00
243	Orlando Hudson RC	10.00
244	John Buck RC	8.00
245	Martin Vargas	4.00
246	David Brous	4.00
247	Dewon Brazelton	4.00
248	Mark Prior	80.00
249	Angel Berroa	10.00
250	Mark Teixeira	100.00

Aspirations

Cards 1-150 print run	
76-100:	5-10X
1-150 p/r 51-75:	8-15X
1-150 p/r 26-50: 10-25X	
Cards 151-200 print run	
76-100:	1X
151-200 p/r 51-75:	1.5X
151-200 p/r 26-50:	1.5-2X
Varying quantities produced	

Status

Cards 1-150 print run	
76-100:	5-10X
1-150 p/r 51-75:	8-15X
1-150 p/r 26-50:	10-25X
Cards 151-200 print run	
76-100:	1X
151-200 p/r 51-75:	1.5X
151-200 p/r 26-50:	1.5-2X
Varying quantities produced	

Back 2 Back Jacks

	NM/M
Common Player:	15.00
Singles production 100	
Doubles production 50	
SP print runs listed	

1	Ernie Banks/75	20.00
2	Ryne Sandberg/75	40.00
3	Babe Ruth	200.00
4	Lou Gehrig	150.00
5	Eddie Matthews	25.00
6	Troy Glaus	15.00
7	Don Mattingly/50	50.00
8	Todd Helton	15.00
9	Wade Boggs	15.00
10	Tony Gwynn	25.00
11	Robin Yount	25.00
12	Paul Molitor/50	25.00
13	Mike Schmidt/50	40.00
14	Scott Rolen/75	20.00
15	Reggie Jackson	25.00
16	Dave Winfield	15.00
17	Johnny Bench/50	25.00
18	Joe Morgan	15.00
19	Brooks Robinson/50	40.00
20	Cal Ripken Jr.	50.00
21	Ty Cobb	100.00
22	Al Kaline/50	40.00
23	Frank Robinson/50	25.00
24	Frank Thomas	20.00
25	Roberto Clemente	80.00
26	Vladimir Guerrero/50	25.00
27	Harmon Killebrew/50	25.00
28	Kirby Puckett	20.00
29	Yogi Berra/75	35.00
30	Phil Rizzuto/75	30.00
31	Ernie Banks, Ryne Sandberg	80.00
32	Babe Ruth, Lou Gehrig	350.00
33	Troy Glaus, Eddie Matthews	40.00
34	Don Mattingly, Todd Helton	100.00
35	Tony Gwynn, Wade Boggs	75.00
36	Paul Molitor, Robin Yount	50.00
37	Mike Schmidt, Scott Rolen	80.00
38	Dave Winfield, Reggie Jackson	40.00
39	Joe Morgan, Johnny Bench	50.00
40	Brooks Robinson, Cal Ripken/50	100.00
41	Al Kaline, Ty Cobb	175.00
42	Frank Robinson, Frank Thomas	40.00
43	Roberto Clemente, Vladimir Guerrero	100.00
44	Harmon Killebrew, Kirby Puckett	50.00
45	Phil Rizzuto, Yogi Berra/25	100.00

Back 2 Back Jacks Autograph

	NM/M
Common Autograph:	60.00

Print runs listed		
1	Ernie Banks/25	200.00
2	Ryne Sandberg/25	250.00
6	Troy Glaus/50	50.00
7	Don Mattingly/50	200.00
12	Paul Molitor/25	75.00
13	Mike Schmidt/50	150.00
14	Scott Rolen/50	60.00
17	Johnny Bench/50	100.00
19	Brooks Robinson/50	75.00
22	Al Kaline/50	100.00
23	Frank Robinson/50	50.00
26	Vladimir Guerrero/50	100.00
27	Harmon Killebrew/50	100.00
29	Yogi Berra/25	125.00
30	Phil Rizzuto/25	125.00
45	Phil Rizzuto, Yogi Berra/25	200.00

Passing the Torch

	NM/M
Common Player:	3.00
Singles production 1,000	
Doubles production 500	

1	Stan Musial	8.00
2	Tony Gwynn	8.00
3	Willie Mays	10.00
4	Barry Bonds	15.00
5	Mike Schmidt	4.00
6	Scott Rolen	4.00
7	Cal Ripken Jr.	15.00
8	Alex Rodriguez	10.00
9	Hank Aaron	15.00
10	Andruw Jones	4.00
11	Nolan Ryan	15.00
12	Pedro Martinez	5.00
13	Wade Boggs	6.00
14	Nomar Garciaparra	8.00
15	Don Mattingly	10.00
16	Todd Helton	5.00
17	Stan Musial, Tony Gwynn	10.00
18	Barry Bonds, Willie Mays	20.00
19	Mike Schmidt, Scott Rolen	15.00
20	Alex Rodriguez, Cal Ripken Jr.	25.00
21	Andruw Jones, Hank Aaron	15.00
22	Nolan Ryan, Pedro Martinez	25.00
23	Nomar Garciaparra, Wade Boggs	15.00
24	Don Mattingly, Todd Helton	15.00

Passing the Torch Autographs

	NM/M
Common Player:	30.00
Singles production 100	
Doubles production 50	

1	Stan Musial	100.00
2	Tony Gwynn	75.00
3	Willie Mays	200.00
4	Barry Bonds	275.00
5	Mike Schmidt	100.00
6	Scott Rolen	50.00
7	Cal Ripken Jr.	150.00
8	Alex Rodriguez	120.00
9	Hank Aaron	200.00
10	Andruw Jones	30.00
11	Nolan Ryan	125.00
12	Pedro Martinez	75.00
13	Wade Boggs	30.00
14	Nomar Garciaparra	125.00
15	Don Mattingly	40.00
16	Todd Helton	40.00
17	Stan Musial, Tony Gwynn	175.00
18	Barry Bonds, Willie Mays	900.00
19	Mike Schmidt, Scott Rolen	150.00
20	Alex Rodriguez, Cal Ripken Jr.	400.00
21	Andruw Jones, Hank Aaron	250.00
22	Nolan Ryan, Pedro Martinez	300.00
22	Nolan Ryan, Roger Clemens FB redemp.	375.00

| 23 | Wade Boggs FB Redemp. | 25.00 |
| 24 | Don Mattingly, Todd Helton | 200.00 |

Primary Colors

		NM/M
Complete Set (40):		100.00
Common Player:		1.00
Production 975 Sets		
Red Die-Cut:		3-5X
Production 25		
Blues:		1-1.5X
Production 200		
Blue Die-Cut:		1.5-3X
Production 50		
Yellows:		3-5X
Production 25		
Yellow Die-Cut:		1.5-2X
Production 75		
1	Alex Rodriguez	8.00
2	Barry Bonds	10.00
3	Cal Ripken Jr.	10.00
4	Chipper Jones	5.00
5	Derek Jeter	10.00
6	Troy Glaus	4.00
7	Frank Thomas	4.00
8	Greg Maddux	5.00
9	Ivan Rodriguez	2.50
10	Jeff Bagwell	4.00
11	Todd Helton	4.00
12	Ken Griffey Jr.	6.00
13	Manny Ramirez	4.00
14	Mark McGwire	8.00
15	Mike Piazza	6.00
16	Nomar Garciaparra	6.00
17	Pedro Martinez	4.00
18	Randy Johnson	4.00
19	Rick Ankiel	1.25
20	Roger Clemens	5.50
21	Sammy Sosa	6.00
22	Tony Gwynn	5.00
23	Vladimir Guerrero	4.00
24	Carlos Delgado	2.00
25	Jason Giambi	2.50
26	Andruw Jones	4.00
27	Bernie Williams	1.50
28	Roberto Alomar	1.50
29	Shawn Green	1.50
30	Barry Larkin	1.00
31	Scott Rolen	3.00
32	Gary Sheffield	2.00
33	Rafael Palmeiro	3.00
34	Albert Belle	1.00
35	Magglio Ordonez	1.50
36	Jim Thome	1.00
37	Jim Edmonds	1.00
38	Darin Erstad	2.00
39	Kris Benson	1.00
40	Sean Casey	1.50

Prime Numbers

		NM/M
Print runs listed		
1a	Alex Rodriguez/300	8.00
1b	Alex Rodriguez/308	8.00
1c	Alex Rodriguez/350	8.00
2a	Ken Griffey Jr./400	6.00
2b	Ken Griffey Jr./408	6.00
2c	Ken Griffey Jr./430	6.00
3a	Mark McGwire/500	8.00
3b	Mark McGwire/504	8.00
3c	Mark McGwire/550	8.00
4a	Cal Ripken Jr./400	10.00
4b	Cal Ripken Jr./407	10.00
4c	Cal Ripken Jr./410	10.00
5a	Derek Jeter/300	10.00

5b	Derek Jeter/302	10.00
5c	Derek Jeter/320	10.00
6a	Mike Piazza/300	6.00
6b	Mike Piazza/302	6.00
6c	Mike Piazza/360	6.00
7a	Nomar Garciaparra/ 300	6.00
7b	Nomar Garciaparra/ 302	6.00
7c	Nomar Garciaparra/ 370	6.00
8a	Sammy Sosa/300	6.00
8b	Sammy Sosa/306	6.00
8c	Sammy Sosa/380	6.00
9a	Vladimir Guerrero/ 300	4.00
9b	Vladimir Guerrero/ 305	4.00
9c	Vladimir Guerrero/ 340	4.00
10a	Tony Gwynn/300	4.00
10b	Tony Gwynn/304	4.00
10c	Tony Gwynn/390	4.00

Prime Numbers Die-Cut

		NM/M
Print runs listed		
1a	Alex Rodriguez/58	25.00
1b	Alex Rodriguez/50	25.00
2a	Ken Griffey Jr./38	20.00
2b	Ken Griffey Jr./30	20.00
3a	Mark McGwire/54	25.00
3b	Mark McGwire/50	25.00
5a	Derek Jeter/22	75.00
5b	Derek Jeter/20	75.00
6a	Mike Piazza/62	15.00
6b	Mike Piazza/60	15.00
7a	Nomar Garciaparra/ 72	15.00
7b	Nomar Garciaparra/ 70	15.00
8a	Sammy Sosa/86	15.00
8b	Sammy Sosa/80	15.00
9a	Vladimir Guerrero/45	10.00
9b	Vladimir Guerrero/40	10.00
10a	Tony Gwynn/94	10.00
10b	Tony Gwynn/90	10.00

Throwback Threads

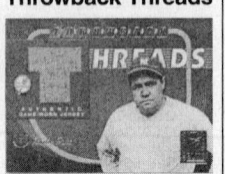

		NM/M
Common Player:		15.00
Singles production 100		
Doubles production 50		
SP production listed		
1	Stan Musial/75	50.00
2	Tony Gwynn/75	25.00
3	Willie McCovey	15.00
4	Barry Bonds	50.00
5	Babe Ruth	250.00
6	Lou Gehrig	200.00
7	Mike Schmidt/75	40.00
8	Scott Rolen	20.00
9	Harmon Killebrew/75	30.00
10	Kirby Puckett	20.00
11	Al Kaline/75	40.00
12	Eddie Matthews	25.00
13	Hank Aaron/75	60.00
14	Andruw Jones/50	20.00
15	Lou Brock	15.00
16	Ozzie Smith	25.00
17	Ernie Banks/75	35.00
18	Ryne Sandberg	50.00
19	Roberto Clemente	100.00
20	Vladimir Guerrero/ 50	30.00
21	Frank Robinson/50	25.00
22	Frank Thomas	15.00
23	Brooks Robinson/25	25.00
24	Cal Ripken Jr.	50.00
25	Roger Clemens	30.00
26	Pedro Martinez	20.00
27	Reggie Jackson	15.00
28	Dave Winfield	15.00
29	Don Mattingly/50	60.00
30	Todd Helton	15.00
31	Stan Musial, Tony Gwynn/25	120.00
32	Barry Bonds, Willie McCovey	85.00
33	Babe Ruth, Lou Gehrig	500.00
34	Mike Schmidt, Scott Rolen/25	150.00
35	Harmon Killebrew, Kirby Puckett	50.00
36	Al Kaline, Eddie Matthews	50.00
37	Andruw Jones, Hank Aaron	85.00
38	Lou Brock, Ozzie Smith	50.00
39	Ernie Banks, Ryne Sandberg/25	125.00

40	Roberto Clemente, Vladimir Guerrero	90.00
41	Frank Robinson, Frank Thomas	40.00
42	Brooks Robinson, Cal Ripken Jr.	85.00
43	Pedro Martinez, Roger Clemens	60.00
44	Dave Winfield, Reggie Jackson	30.00
45	Don Mattingly, Todd Helton	75.00

Throwback Threads Autograph

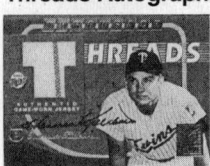

		NM/M
Production listed		
Football Exchange for 21 & 22 will be redeemed for #'s listed for 21 & 22.		
1	Stan Musial/25	150.00
2	Tony Gwynn/25	100.00
7	Mike Schmidt/25	200.00
9	Harmon Killebrew/ 25	125.00
11	Al Kaline/25	120.00
13	Hank Aaron/25	150.00
14	Andruw Jones/50	50.00
17	Ernie Banks/25	150.00
20	Vladimir Guerrero/ 50	75.00
21	Frank Robinson/ 50/FB Redemp	40.00
22	Frank Thomas/ 50 FB redemp	50.00
23	Brooks Robinson/ 50	100.00
29	Don Mattingly/50	150.00
31	Stan Musial, Tony Gwynn/25	225.00
34	Mike Schmidt, Scott Rolen/25	225.00
39	Ernie Banks, Ryne Sandberg/25	250.00

Title Waves

		NM/M
Common Player:		1.00
Numbered to title year.		
Holofoil:		2-3X
Production 100 Sets		
1	Tony Gwynn/1994	5.00
2	Todd Helton/2000	4.00
3	Nomar Garciaparra/ 2000	6.00
4	Frank Thomas/1997	4.00
5	Alex Rodriguez/1996	8.00
6	Jeff Bagwell/1994	4.00
7	Mark McGwire/1998	8.00
8	Sammy Sosa/2000	6.00
9	Ken Griffey Jr./1997	6.00
10	Albert Belle/1995	1.00
11	Barry Bonds/1993	10.00
12	Jose Canseco/1991	2.00
13	Manny Ramirez/1999	4.00
14	Sammy Sosa/1998	6.00
15	Andres Galarraga/ 1996	1.00
16	Todd Helton/2000	4.00
17	Ken Griffey Jr./1997	6.00
18	Jeff Bagwell/1994	4.00
19	Mike Piazza/1995	6.00
20	Alex Rodriguez/1995	8.00
21	Jason Giambi/2000	2.00
22	Ivan Rodriguez/1999	2.50
23	Greg Maddux/1997	5.00
24	Pedro Martinez/1994	4.00
25	Derek Jeter/2000	10.00
26	Bernie Williams/1998	1.50
27	Roger Clemens/1999	4.00
28	Chipper Jones/1995	4.00
29	Mark McGwire/1999	6.00
30	Cal Ripken Jr./1983	10.00

Turn of the Century Autographs

		NM/M
Common Autograph:		8.00
Production 100 Sets		
Redemp. deadline 5/01/03.		
151	Brent Abernathy	8.00
152	Cory Aldridge	8.00
153	Gene Altman	8.00
154	Josh Beckett	50.00

155	Wilson Betemit	25.00
156	Albert Pujols	900.00
157	Joe Crede	40.00
158	Jack Cust	8.00
159	Ben Sheets	30.00
160	Alex Escobar	8.00
161	Adrian Hernandez	8.00
162	Pedro Feliz	8.00
163	Nate Frese	8.00
164	Carlos Garcia	8.00
165	Marcus Giles	20.00
166	Alexis Gomez	10.00
167	Jason Hart	8.00
168	Aubrey Huff	20.00
169	Cesar Izturis	10.00
170	Nick Johnson	20.00
171	Jack Wilson	15.00
172	Brian Lawrence	10.00
173	Christian Parker	8.00
174	Nick Maness	8.00
175	Jose Mieses	10.00
176	Greg Miller	8.00
177	Eric Munson	10.00
178	Xavier Nady	15.00
179	Blaine Neal	8.00
180	Abraham Nunez	8.00
181	Jose Ortiz	10.00
182	Jeremy Owens	8.00
183	Jay Gibbons	25.00
184	Corey Patterson	20.00
185	Carlos Pena	10.00
186	C.C. Sabathia	20.00
187	Timoniel Perez	8.00
188	Adam Pettyjohn	8.00
189	Donaldo Mendez	8.00
190	Jackson Melian	8.00
191	Wilken Ruan	8.00
192	Duaner Sanchez	8.00
193	Alfonso Soriano	60.00
194	Rafael Soriano	10.00
196	Billy Sylvester	8.00
197	Juan Uribe	20.00
199	Carlos Valderrama	10.00
200	Matt White	8.00

2001 Donruss Signature Series

		NM/M
Complete Set (311):		
Common Player:		.50
Common (111-165):		8.00
Auto. print run 330.		
Common (166-311):		4.00
Production 800		
Box:		100.00
1	Alex Rodriguez	3.00
2	Barry Bonds	4.00
3	Cal Ripken Jr.	4.00
4	Chipper Jones	2.00
5	Derek Jeter	4.00
6	Troy Glaus	1.50
7	Frank Thomas	1.50
8	Greg Maddux	2.00
9	Ivan Rodriguez	1.00
10	Jeff Bagwell	1.50
11	John Olerud	.50
12	Todd Helton	1.50
13	Ken Griffey Jr.	2.50
14	Manny Ramirez	1.50
15	Mark McGwire	3.00
16	Mike Piazza	2.50
17	Nomar Garciaparra	2.50
18	Moises Alou	.50
19	Aramis Ramirez	.50
20	Curt Schilling	.75
21	Pat Burrell	.75
22	Doug Mientkiewicz	.50

23	Carlos Delgado	.75
24	J.D. Drew	.50
25	Cliff Floyd	.50
26	Freddy Garcia	.50
27	Roberto Alomar	.75
28	Barry Zito	.75
29	Juan Encarnacion	.50
30	Paul Konerko	.50
31	Mark Mulder	.75
32	Andy Pettitte	.75
33	Jim Edmonds	.50
34	Darin Erstad	1.00
35	Jason Giambi	1.00
36	Tom Glavine	.75
37	Juan Gonzalez	1.50
38	Fred McGriff	.50
39	Shawn Green	.75
40	Tim Hudson	.75
41	Andruw Jones	1.50
42	Jeff Kent	.50
43	Barry Larkin	.50
44	Brad Radke	.50
45	Mike Mussina	.75
46	Hideo Nomo	.75
47	Rafael Palmeiro	1.50
48	Scott Rolen	1.50
49	Gary Sheffield	.75
50	Bernie Williams	.75
51	Bobby Abreu	.50
52	Edgardo Alfonzo	.50
53	Edgar Martinez	.50
54	Magglio Ordonez	.75
55	Kerry Wood	.75
56	Adrian Beltre	.75
57	Lance Berkman	.50
58	Kevin Brown	.65
59	Sean Casey	.65
60	Eric Chavez	.75
61	Bartolo Colon	.50
62	Sammy Sosa	2.50
63	Jermaine Dye	.50
64	Tony Gwynn	2.00
65	Carl Everett	.50
66	Brian Giles	.50
67	Mike Hampton	.50
68	Richard Hidalgo	.50
69	Geoff Jenkins	.50
70	Tony Clark	.50
71	Roger Clemens	2.25
72	Ryan Klesko	.50
73	Chan Ho Park	.50
74	Richie Sexson	.50
75	Mike Sweeney	.50
76	Kazuhiro Sasaki	.50
77	Miguel Tejada	.75
78	Jose Vidro	.50
79	Larry Walker	.50
80	Preston Wilson	.50
81	Craig Biggio	.50
82	Andres Galarraga	.50
83	Jim Thome	.50
84	Vladimir Guerrero	1.50
85	Rafael Furcal	.50
86	Cristian Guzman	.50
87	Terrence Long	.50
88	Bret Boone	.50
89	Wade Miller	.50
90	Eric Milton	.50
91	Gabe Kapler	.50
92	Johnny Damon	.75
93	Carlos Lee	.50
94	Kenny Lofton	.50
95	Raul Mondesi	.50
96	Jorge Posada	.65
97	Mark Grace	.65
98	Robert Fick	.50
99	Joe Mays	.50
100	Aaron Sele	.50
101	Ben Grieve	.50
102	Luis Gonzalez	.65
103	Ray Durham	.50
104	Mark Quinn	.50
105	Jose Canseco	1.00
106	David Justice	.50
107	Pedro Martinez	1.50
108	Randy Johnson	1.50
109	Phil Nevin	.50
110	Ricky Henderson	1.50
111	Alex Escobar/Auto.	8.00
112	Johnny Estrada/ Auto. RC	15.00
113	Pedro Feliz /Auto.	8.00
114	Nate Frese/Auto.	8.00
115	Ricardo Rodriguez/ Auto. RC	8.00
116	Brandon Larson/ Auto. RC	8.00
117	Alexis Gomez/ Auto. RC	8.00
118	Jason Hart/Auto.	8.00
119	C.C. Sabathia/Auto.	15.00
120	Endy Chavez/ Auto. RC	8.00
121	Christian Parker/ Auto. RC	8.00
122	Jackson Melian RC	8.00
123	Joe Kennedy/ Auto. RC	10.00
124	Adrian Hernandez/ Auto. RC	8.00
125	Cesar Izturis/Auto.	10.00
126	Jose Mieses/ Auto. RC	8.00
127	Roy Oswalt/Auto.	30.00
128	Eric Munson/Auto.	8.00
129	Xavier Nady/Auto.	8.00
130	Horacio Ramirez/ Auto. RC	8.00

131	Abraham Nunez/Auto.	8.00
132	Jose Ortiz/Auto.	8.00
133	Jeremy Owens/ Auto. RC	8.00
134	Claudio Vargas/ Auto. RC	8.00
135	Corey Patterson/ Auto.	15.00
136	Carlos Pena	8.00
137	Bud Smith/Auto. RC	8.00
138	Adam Dunn/Auto.	25.00
139	Adam Pettyjohn/Auto.	8.00
140	Elpidio Guzman/ Auto. RC	8.00
141	Jay Gibbons/ Auto. RC	15.00
142	Wilken Ruan/ Auto. RC	8.00
143	Tsuyoshi Shinjo RC	8.00
144	Alfonso Soriano/ Auto.	30.00
145	Marcus Giles/Auto.	10.00
146	Ichiro Suzuki RC	70.00
147	Juan Uribe/Auto.	10.00
148	David Williams/ Auto.	8.00
149	Carlos Valderrama/ Auto. RC	8.00
150	Matt White/Auto. RC	8.00
151	Albert Pujols/ Auto. RC	750.00
152	Donaldo Mendez/ Auto. RC	8.00
153	Cory Aldridge/ Auto. RC	8.00
154	Brandon Duckworth/ Auto. RC	8.00
155	Josh Beckett/Auto.	20.00
156	Wilson Betemit/ Auto. RC	15.00
157	Ben Sheets/Auto.	25.00
158	Andres Torres/ Auto. RC	8.00
159	Aubrey Huff/Auto.	15.00
160	Jack Wilson/ Auto. RC	15.00
161	Rafael Soriano/ Auto. RC	8.00
162	Nick Johnson/Auto.	12.00
163	Carlos Garcia/ Auto. RC	8.00
164	Josh Towers/ Auto. RC	10.00
165	Jason Michaels/ Auto. RC	8.00
166	Ryan Drese RC	4.00
167	Dewon Brazelton RC	4.00
168	Kevin Olsen RC	4.00
169	Benito Baez RC	4.00
170	Mark Prior RC	25.00
171	Wilmy Caceres RC	4.00
172	Mark Teixeira RC	35.00
173	Willie Harris RC	4.00
174	Mike Koplove RC	4.00
175	Brandon Knight RC	4.00
176	John Grabow RC	4.00
177	Jeremy Affeldt RC	4.00
178	Brandon Inge	4.00
179	Casey Fossum RC	6.00
180	Scott Stewart RC	4.00
181	Luke Hudson RC	4.00
182	Ken Vining RC	4.00
183	Toby Hall	4.00
184	Eric Knott RC	4.00
185	Kris Foster RC	4.00
186	David Brous RC	4.00
187	Roy Smith RC	4.00
188	Grant Balfour RC	4.00
189	Jeremy Fikac RC	4.00
190	Morgan Ensberg RC	10.00
191	Ryan Freel RC	4.00
192	Ryan Jensen RC	4.00
193	Lance Davis RC	4.00
194	Delvin James RC	4.00
195	Timo Perez	4.00
196	Michael Cuddyer	4.00
197	Bob File RC	4.00
198	Martin Vargas RC	4.00
199	Kris Keller RC	4.00
200	Tim Spooneybarger RC	4.00
201	Adam Everett	4.00
202	Josh Fogg RC	6.00
203	Kip Wells	4.00
204	Rick Bauer RC	4.00
205	Brent Abernathy	4.00
206	Erick Almonte RC	4.00
207	Pedro Santana RC	4.00
208	Ken Harvey	4.00
209	Jerrod Riggan RC	4.00
210	Nick Punto RC	4.00
211	Steve Green RC	4.00
212	Nick Neugebauer	4.00
213	Chris George	4.00
214	Mike Penny	4.00
215	Bret Prinz RC	4.00
216	Tim Christman RC	4.00
217	Sean Douglass RC	4.00
218	Brett Jodie RC	4.00
219	Juan Diaz RC	4.00
220	Carlos Hernandez RC	4.00
221	Alex Cintron	4.00
222	Juan Cruz RC	4.00
223	Larry Bigbie	4.00
224	Junior Spivey RC	4.00
225	Luis Rivas	4.00
226	Brandon Lyon RC	4.00
227	Tony Cogan RC	4.00

228	Justin Duchscherer RC	6.00
229	Tike Redman	4.00
230	Jimmy Rollins	5.00
231	Scott Podsednik RC	15.00
232	Jose Acevedo RC	4.00
233	Luis Pineda RC	4.00
234	Josh Phelps	4.00
235	Paul Phillips RC	4.00
236	Brian Roberts RC	8.00
237	Orlando Woodwards RC	4.00
238	Bart Miadich RC	4.00
239	Les Walrond RC	4.00
240	Brad Voyles RC	4.00
241	Joe Crede	8.00
242	Juan Moreno RC	4.00
243	Matt Ginter	4.00
244	Brian Rogers RC	4.00
245	Pablo Ozuna	4.00
246	Geronimo Gil RC	4.00
247	Mike Maroth RC	4.00
248	Josue Perez RC	4.00
249	Dee Brown	4.00
250	Victor Zambrano RC	4.00
251	Nick Maness RC	4.00
252	Kyle Lohse RC	6.00
253	Greg Miller RC	4.00
254	Henry Mateo RC	4.00
255	Duaner Sanchez RC	4.00
256	Rob Mackowiak RC	6.00
257	Steve Lomasney	4.00
258	Angel Santos RC	4.00
259	Winston Abreu RC	4.00
260	Brandon Berger RC	4.00
261	Tomas De La Rosa RC	4.00
262	Ramon Vazquez RC	4.00
263	Mickey Callaway RC	4.00
264	Corky Miller RC	4.00
265	Keith Ginter RC	4.00
266	Cody Ransom RC	4.00
267	Doug Nickle RC	4.00
268	Derrick Lewis RC	4.00
269	Eric Hinske RC	6.00
270	Travis Phelps RC	4.00
271	Eric Valent	4.00
272	Michael Rivera RC	4.00
273	Esix Snead RC	4.00
274	Troy Mattes RC	4.00
275	Jermaine Clark	4.00
276	Nate Cornejo	4.00
277	George Perez RC	4.00
278	Juan Rivera	4.00
279	Justin Atchley RC	4.00
280	Adam Johnson	4.00
281	Gene Altman RC	4.00
282	Jason Jennings	4.00
283	Scott MacRae RC	4.00
284	Craig Monroe RC	6.00
285	Bert Snow RC	4.00
286	Stubby Clapp RC	4.00
287	Jack Cust	4.00
288	Will Ohman RC	4.00
289	Wily Mo Pena RC	4.00
290	Joe Beimel RC	4.00
291	Jason Karnuth RC	4.00
292	Bill Ortega	4.00
293	Nate Teut RC	4.00
294	Erik Hiljus RC	4.00
295	Jason Smith RC	4.00
296	Juan Pena	4.00
297	David Espinosa	4.00
298	Tim Redding	4.00
299	Brian Lawrence RC	4.00
300	Brian Reith RC	4.00
301	Chad Durbin	4.00
302	Kurt Ainsworth	4.00
303	Blaine Neal RC	4.00
304	Jorge Julio RC	4.00
305	Adam Bernero	4.00
306	Travis Hafner RC	25.00
307	Dustan Mohr RC	4.00
308	Cesar Crespo RC	4.00
309	Billy Sylvester RC	4.00
310	Zach Day RC	6.00
311	Angel Berroa RC	8.00

Signature Proofs

Stars (1-110): 2-3X
Production 175
Cards (111-311) Production 25

Award Winning Signatures

	NM/M
Common Player:	20.00
Jeff Bagwell/94	65.00
Carlos Beltran/99	40.00
Johnny Bench/68	75.00
Yogi Berra/55	50.00
Craig Biggio/97	25.00
Barry Bonds/93	200.00
Rod Carew/77	50.00
Orlando Cepeda/67	20.00
Andre Dawson/77	20.00
Dennis Eckersley/92	25.00
Dennis Eckersley/92	25.00
Whitey Ford/61	50.00
Jason Giambi/100	20.00
Bob Gibson/68	40.00
Juan Gonzalez/96	35.00
Orel Hershiser/88	25.00
Al Kaline/67	75.00
Fred Lynn/75	15.00
Fred Lynn/75	15.00
Jim Palmer/76	25.00
Cal Ripken/83	150.00
Phil Rizzuto/50	40.00
Brooks Robinson/64	40.00
Scott Rolen/97	30.00
Ryne Sandberg/84	90.00
Warren Spahn/57	50.00
Frank Thomas/94	35.00
Billy Williams/61	20.00
Kerry Wood/98	5.00
Robin Yount/89	60.00

Century Marks

	NM/M
Common Autograph:	5.00
Brent Abernathy/184	5.00
Roberto Alomar/102	40.00
Rick Ankiel/119	8.00
Lance Berkman/121	15.00
Mark Buehrle/224	10.00
Wilmy Caceres/194	5.00
Eric Chavez/170	10.00
Joe Crede/154	5.00
Jack Cust/178	5.00
Brandon Duckworth/ 183	5.00
David Espinosa/199	5.00
Johnny Estrada/198	5.00
Pedro Feliz/180	5.00
Robert Fick/232	5.00
Cliff Floyd/146	8.00
Casey Fossum/100	10.00
Jay Gibbons/175	5.00
Keith Ginter/163	5.00
Troy Glaus/144	20.00
Luis Gonzalez/101	10.00
Vladimir Guerrero/ 187	30.00
Richard Hidalgo/173	5.00
Tim Hudson/145	25.00
Adam Johnson/130	5.00
Gabe Kapler/150	8.00
Joe Kennedy/219	5.00
Ryan Klesko/176	10.00
Carlos Lee/179	8.00
Terrence Long/180	5.00
Edgar Martinez/110	20.00
Joe Mays/209	5.00
Greg Miller/194	5.00
Wade Miller/180	5.00
Mark Mulder/203	20.00
Xavier Nady/180	5.00
Magglio Ordonez/ 104	10.00
Jose Ortiz/187	5.00
Roy Oswalt/192	20.00
Wily Mo Pena/203	10.00
Brad Penny/198	5.00
Aramis Ramirez/241	20.00
Luis Rivas/163	5.00
Alex Rodriguez/110	120.00
Scott Rolen/106	30.00
Mike Sweeney/99	10.00
Eric Valent/163	5.00
Kip Wells/223	5.00
Kerry Wood/109	25.00

Milestone Marks

	NM/M
Common Player:	10.00
Ernie Banks/285	35.00
Yogi Berra/120	50.00
Wade Boggs/98	60.00
Barry Bonds/55	200.00
George Brett/27	150.00
George Brett/23	150.00
Lou Brock/83	25.00
Rod Carew/110	30.00
Steve Carlton/75	35.00
Gary Carter/213	20.00
Bobby Doerr/192	15.00
Bob Feller/202	15.00
Whitey Ford/186	25.00
Steve Garvey/175	10.00
Tony Gwynn/99	50.00
Fergie Jenkins/149	15.00
Al Kaline/149	40.00
Harmon Killebrew/ 127	40.00
Ralph Kiner/105	20.00
Willie McCovey/20	75.00
Paul Molitor/96	40.00
Eddie Murray/46	70.00
Stan Musial/109	75.00
Phil Niekro/300	10.00
Tony Perez/146	15.00
Cal Ripken/25	200.00
Frank Robinson/ 136	20.00
Mike Schmidt/40	125.00
Mike Schmidt/23	150.00
Enos Slaughter/117	20.00
Warren Spahn/300	20.00
Alan Trammell/154	25.00
Hoyt Wilhelm/227	10.00
Dave Winfield/31	50.00
Dave Winfield/15	80.00

Notable Nicknames

	NM/M
Common Player:	30.00
Production 100	
Ernie Banks	75.00
Orlando Cepeda	40.00
Will Clark	80.00
Roger Clemens/50	250.00
Andre Dawson	30.00
Bob Feller	50.00
Carlton Fisk	70.00
Andres Galarraga	40.00
Luis Gonzalez	30.00
Reggie Jackson	75.00
Harmon Killebrew	80.00
Stan Musial	120.00
Brooks Robinson	80.00
Nolan Ryan	250.00
Ryne Sandberg	150.00
Enos Slaughter	50.00
Duke Snider	75.00
Frank Thomas	100.00

Signature Stats

	NM/M
Quantity produced listed	

Roberto Alomar/120	40.00	
Moises Alou/124	6.00	
Luis Aparicio/313	15.00	
Lance Berkman/297	15.00	
Wade Boggs/51	75.00	
Lou Brock/118	15.00	
Gary Carter/32	50.00	
Joe Carter/121	10.00	
Sean Casey/103	10.00	
Darin Erstad/100	15.00	
Bob Feller/26	50.00	
Cliff Floyd/45	15.00	
Whitey Ford/72	40.00	
Andres Galarraga/ 150		8.00
Bob Gibson/112	25.00	
Brian Giles/123	10.00	
Troy Glaus/102	20.00	
Luis Gonzalez/114	10.00	
Vladimir Guerrero/ 131		30.00
Richard Hidalgo/314	6.00	
Bo Jackson/32	85.00	
Al Kaline/128	45.00	
Gabe Kapler/302	6.00	
Ralph Kiner/54	30.00	
Carlos Lee/261	10.00	
Kenny Lofton/210	6.00	
Edgar Martinez/145	20.00	
Joe Mays/115	6.00	
Paul Molitor/41	50.00	
Mark Mulder/88	25.00	
Magglio Ordonez/ 126		10.00
Rafael Palmeiro/47	40.00	
Kirby Puckett/31	100.00	
Manny Ramirez/45	20.00	
Alex Rodriguez/132	85.00	
Ivan Rodriguez/113	30.00	
Shannon Stewart/319	6.00	
Mike Sweeney/144	6.00	
Miguel Tejada/115	35.00	
Joe Torre/230	25.00	
Javier Vazquez/405	6.00	
Jose Vidro/330	6.00	
Hoyt Wilhelm/243	6.00	

Team Trademarks

	NM/M
Rick Ankiel/179	10.00
Ernie Banks/180	50.00
Johnny Bench/20	75.00
Yogi Berra/124	40.00
Wade Boggs/89	75.00
Barry Bonds/77	200.00
Lou Brock/29	35.00
Steve Carlton/174	25.00
Sean Casey/123	15.00
Orlando Cepeda/100	20.00
Roger Clemens/30 (Red Sox)	125.00
Roger Clemens/21 (Yankees)	150.00
Andre Dawson/176	15.00
Bobby Doerr/193	20.00
Whitey Ford/94	40.00
Steve Garvey/182	20.00
Bob Gibson/98	30.00
Juan Gonzalez/40	40.00
Shawn Green/109	20.00
Orel Hershiser/210	25.00
Reggie Jackson/50	50.00
Fergie Jenkins/213	15.00
Chipper Jones/74	50.00
Pedro Martinez/27	85.00
Don Mattingly/72	125.00
Willie Mays/197	125.00
Willie McCovey/26	70.00
Joe Morgan/33	80.00
Eddie Murray/45	75.00
Stan Musial/65	90.00
Mike Mussina/85 (Orioles)	40.00
Mike Mussina/95 (Yankees)	50.00
Phil Niekro/187	10.00
Rafael Palmeiro/99	30.00
Jim Palmer/142	15.00
Tony Perez/73	15.00
Manny Ramirez/57	50.00
Cal Ripken Jr./47	200.00
Phil Rizzuto/98	40.00
Brooks Robinson/ 146	25.00
Frank Robinson/118/ Orioles	25.00
Frank Robinson/116/ Reds	25.00

Alex Rodriguez/100	100.00
Ivan Rodriguez/62	50.00
Scott Rolen/39	40.00
Nolan Ryan/153	100.00
Ryne Sandberg/52	100.00
Curt Schilling/163	40.00
Mike Schmidt/107	75.00
Tom Seaver/25	125.00
Gary Sheffield/194	20.00
Enos Slaughter/215	20.00
Duke Snider/47	50.00
Warren Spahn/140	40.00
Joe Torre/90	40.00
Billy Williams/194	10.00
Kerry Wood/52	40.00

Hawaii

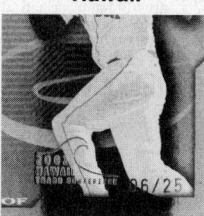

As part of its participation in the 2002 Hawaii Trade Conference, Donruss created special gold-foil enhanced versions of many of the base cards, inserts, parallels and autographs of its Signature Series issues. Cards all carry individual serial numbers from editions as low as 1-of-1 and as high as 25. Because of their scarcity and widely fluctuating demand, values cannot be quoted.

2001 Donruss Studio

Jason Giambi · 1B

	NM/M
Complete Set (200):	
Common Player:	.25
Common SP (151-200):	4.00
Production 700	
Pack (6):	8.00
Box (18) + 5x7 Auto.	140.00
1	Alex Rodriguez	2.00
2	Barry Bonds	2.50
3	Cal Ripken Jr.	2.50
4	Chipper Jones	1.00
5	Derek Jeter	2.50
6	Troy Glaus	.65
7	Frank Thomas	.75
8	Greg Maddux	1.00
9	Ivan Rodriguez	.65
10	Jeff Bagwell	.75
11	Mark Quinn	.25
12	Todd Helton	.65
13	Ken Griffey Jr.	1.50
14	Manny Ramirez	.75
15	Mark McGwire	2.00
16	Mike Piazza	1.50
17	Nomar Garciaparra	1.00
18	Robin Ventura	.25
19	Aramis Ramirez	.25
20	J.T. Snow	.25
21	Pat Burrell	.60
22	Curt Schilling	.50
23	Carlos Delgado	.50
24	J.D. Drew	.40
25	Cliff Floyd	.25
26	Brian Jordan	.25
27	Roberto Alomar	.35
28	Barry Zito	.40
29	Harold Baines	.25
30	Brad Penny	.25
31	Jose Cruz	.25
32	Andy Pettitte	.40
33	Jim Edmonds	.25
34	Darin Erstad	.35
35	Jason Giambi	.60
36	Tom Glavine	.50
37	Juan Gonzalez	.35
38	Mark Grace	.25
39	Shawn Green	.50
40	Tim Hudson	.50

41	Andruw Jones	.75
42	Jeff Kent	.25
43	Barry Larkin	.25
44	Rafael Furcal	.25
45	Mike Mussina	.50
46	Hideo Nomo	.50
47	Rafael Palmeiro	.65
48	Scott Rolen	.60
49	Gary Sheffield	.25
50	Bernie Williams	.25
51	Bobby Abreu	.25
52	Edgardo Alfonzo	.25
53	Edgar Martinez	.25
54	Magglio Ordonez	.25
55	Kerry Wood	.50
56	Matt Morris	.25
57	Lance Berkman	.25
58	Kevin Brown	.25
59	Sean Casey	.40
60	Eric Chavez	.40
61	Bartolo Colon	.25
62	Johnny Damon	.50
63	Jermaine Dye	.25
64	Juan Encarnacion	.25
65	Carl Everett	.25
66	Brian Giles	.25
67	Mike Hampton	.25
68	Richard Hidalgo	.25
69	Geoff Jenkins	.25
70	Jacque Jones	.25
71	Jason Kendall	.25
72	Ryan Klesko	.25
73	Chan Ho Park	.25
74	Richie Sexson	.25
75	Mike Sweeney	.25
76	Fernando Tatis	.25
77	Miguel Tejada	.50
78	Jose Vidro	.25
79	Larry Walker	.25
80	Preston Wilson	.25
81	Craig Biggio	.25
82	Fred McGriff	.25
83	Jim Thome	.65
84	Garret Anderson	.25
85	Mark Mulder	.40
86	Tony Batista	.25
87	Terrence Long	.25
88	Brad Fullmer	.25
89	Rusty Greer	.25
90	Orlando Hernandez	.25
91	Gabe Kapler	.25
92	Paul Konerko	.25
93	Carlos Lee	.25
94	Kenny Lofton	.25
95	Raul Mondesi	.25
96	Jorge Posada	.40
97	Tim Salmon	.25
98	Greg Vaughn	.25
99	Mo Vaughn	.25
100	Omar Vizquel	.25
101	Ben Grieve	.25
102	Luis Gonzalez	.25
103	Ray Durham	.25
104	Ryan Dempster	.25
105	Eric Karros	.25
106	David Justice	.25
107	Pedro Martinez	.75
108	Randy Johnson	.75
109	Rick Ankiel	.25
110	Rickey Henderson	.75
111	Roger Clemens	1.25
112	Sammy Sosa	1.00
113	Tony Gwynn	1.00
114	Vladimir Guerrero	.75
115	Kazuhiro Sasaki	.25
116	Phil Nevin	.25
117	Ruben Mateo	.25
118	Shannon Stewart	.25
119	Matt Williams	.25
120	Tino Martinez	.25
121	Ken Caminiti	.25
122	Edgar Renteria	.25
123	Charles Johnson	.25
124	Aaron Sele	.25
125	Javy Lopez	.25
126	Mariano Rivera	.35
127	Shea Hillenbrand	.25
128	Jeff D'Amico	.25
129	Brady Anderson	.25
130	Kevin Millwood	.25
131	Trot Nixon	.25
132	Mike Lieberthal	.25
133	Juan Pierre	.25
134	Russ Ortiz	.25
135	Jose Macias	.25
136	John Smoltz	.25
137	Jason Varitek	.25
138	Dean Palmer	.25
139	Jeff Cirillo	.25
140	Paul O'Neill	.25
141	Andres Galarraga	.25
142	David Wells	.25
143	Brad Radke	.25
144	Wade Miller	.25
145	John Olerud	.25
146	Moises Alou	.25
147	Carlos Beltran	.50
148	Jeromy Burnitz	.25
149	Steve Finley	.25
150	Joe Mays	.25
151	Alex Escobar	4.00
152	Johnny Estrada RC	8.00
153	Pedro Feliz	4.00
154	Nate Frese RC	4.00
155	Dee Brown	4.00
156	Brandon Larson RC	5.00
157	Alexis Gomez RC	4.00
158	Jason Hart	4.00

159	C.C. Sabathia	4.00
160	Josh Towers RC	6.00
161	Christian Parker RC	4.00
162	Jackson Melian RC	4.00
163	Joe Kennedy RC	4.00
164	Adrian Hernandez RC	4.00
165	Jimmy Rollins	4.00
166	Jose Mieses RC	4.00
167	Roy Oswalt	5.00
168	Eric Munson	4.00
169	Xavier Nady	4.00
170	Horacio Ramirez RC	8.00
171	Abraham Nunez	4.00
172	Jose Ortiz	4.00
173	Jeremy Owens RC	4.00
174	Claudio Vargas RC	4.00
175	Corey Patterson	4.00
176	Carlos Pena	4.00
177	Bud Smith RC	4.00
178	Adam Dunn	4.00
179	Adam Pettyjohn RC	4.00
180	Elpidio Guzman RC	4.00
181	Jay Gibbons RC	10.00
182	Wilkin Ruan RC	4.00
183	Tsuyoshi Shinjo RC	4.00
184	Alfonso Soriano	4.00
185	Marcus Giles	4.00
186	Ichiro Suzuki RC	85.00
187	Juan Uribe RC	6.00
188	David Williams RC	4.00
189	Carlos Valderrama RC	4.00
190	Matt White RC	4.00
191	Albert Pujols RC	240.00
192	Donaldo Mendez RC	4.00
193	Cory Aldridge RC	4.00
194	Endy Chavez RC	4.00
195	Josh Beckett	4.00
196	Wilson Betemit RC	4.00
197	Ben Sheets	4.00
198	Andres Torres RC	4.00
199	Aubrey Huff	4.00
200	Jack Wilson RC	8.00

Proofs

Chipper Jones • 3B
ATLANTA BRAVES

This parallel insert has a metallic holo-foil seal on front and is serially numbered to 25 each.

Values Undetermined
Production 25 Sets

Diamond Collection

		NM/M
	Common Player:	5.00
1	Vladimir Guerrero	10.00
2	Barry Bonds	30.00
3	Cal Ripken Jr.	30.00
4	Nomar Garciaparra	20.00
5	Greg Maddux	15.00
6	Frank Thomas	10.00
7	Roger Clemens	20.00
8	Luis Gonzalez/SP	4.00
9	Tony Gwynn	15.00
10	Carlos Lee/SP	6.00
11	Troy Glaus	5.00
12	Randy Johnson	10.00
13	Manny Ramirez/SP	15.00
14	Pedro Martinez	10.00
15	Todd Helton	10.00
16	Jeff Bagwell	10.00
17	Rickey Henderson	10.00
18	Kazuhiro Sasaki	5.00
19	Albert Pujols SP	50.00
20	Ivan Rodriguez	8.00
21	Darin Erstad	6.00
22	Andruw Jones	6.00
23	Roberto Alomar	6.00
25	Juan Gonzalez	10.00
26	Shawn Green	7.50
27	Lance Berkman	5.00

Abbreviations
SP - Short Print

28	Scott Rolen	9.00
29	Rafael Palmeiro	8.00
30	J.D. Drew	5.00
31	Kerry Wood	8.00
32	Jim Edmonds	5.00
33	Tom Glavine/SP	8.00
34	Hideo Nomo/SP	50.00
36	Tim Hudson	5.00
37	Miguel Tejada	8.00
38	Chipper Jones	15.00
39	Edgar Martinez/SP	8.00
40	Chan Ho Park	5.00
41	Magglio Ordonez	5.00
42	Sean Casey	5.00
43	Larry Walker	5.00
45	Cliff Floyd	5.00
46	Mike Sweeney	5.00
47	Kevin Brown	5.00
48	Richie Sexson	5.00
49	Jermaine Dye	5.00
50	Craig Biggio	5.00

Leather & Lumber

		NM/M
	Common Player:	5.00
	Combos:	No Pricing
	Production 25 Sets	
1	Barry Bonds	25.00
2	Cal Ripken Jr.	25.00
3	Miguel Tejada	5.00
5	Frank Thomas	8.00
6	Greg Maddux	10.00
7	Ivan Rodriguez	8.00
8	Jeff Bagwell/SP	10.00
9	Sean Casey/SP	6.00
10	Todd Helton	8.00
11	Cliff Floyd	5.00
12	Hideo Nomo	40.00
13	Chipper Jones	10.00
14	Rickey Henderson	8.00
15	Richard Hidalgo	5.00
16	Mike Piazza	15.00
17	Larry Walker	5.00
18	Tony Gwynn	10.00
19	Vladimir Guerrero	8.00
20	Rafael Furcal	5.00
21	Roberto Alomar/SP	8.00
23	Albert Pujols	60.00
24	Raul Mondesi	5.00
25	J.D. Drew	5.00
26	Jim Edmonds	5.00
27	Darin Erstad/SP	6.00
28	Craig Biggio	5.00
29	Kenny Lofton	5.00
30	Juan Gonzalez	5.00
31	John Olerud	5.00
32	Shawn Green	5.00
33	Andruw Jones/SP	5.00
34	Moises Alou	5.00
35	Jeff Kent	5.00
36	Ryan Klesko	5.00
37	Luis Gonzalez	5.00
38	Rafael Palmeiro	8.00
40	Scott Rolen	8.00
41	Carlos Lee	5.00
42	Bobby Abreu	5.00
43	Edgardo Alfonzo	5.00
44	Bernie Williams	5.00
45	Brian Giles	5.00
46	Jermaine Dye	5.00
47	Lance Berkman	5.00
48	Edgar Martinez	5.00
49	Richie Sexson	5.00
50	Magglio Ordonez	5.00

Masterstokes

		NM/M
	Common Player:	8.00
	Production 200 Sets	
1	Tony Gwynn	25.00
2	Ivan Rodriguez	10.00
3	J.D. Drew	8.00
4	Cal Ripken Jr.	60.00
5	Hideo Nomo	50.00
6	Darin Erstad	8.00
7	Frank Thomas	12.00

8	Andruw Jones	12.00
9	Roberto Alomar	8.00
10	Larry Walker	8.00
11	Vladimir Guerrero	12.00
12	Barry Bonds	65.00
14	Luis Gonzalez	8.00
16	Juan Gonzalez	12.00
17	Todd Helton	12.00
18	Jeff Bagwell	12.00
19	Albert Pujols	75.00
20	Shawn Green	8.00
21	Magglio Ordonez	8.00
22	Scott Rolen	8.00
23	Rafael Palmeiro	10.00
24	Sean Casey	8.00
25	Jim Edmonds	8.00
26	Chipper Jones	20.00
27	Cliff Floyd	8.00
28	Carlos Lee	8.00
29	Edgar Martinez	8.00
30	Lance Berkman	8.00

Warning Track

		NM/M
	Common Player:	4.00
1	Andruw Jones	8.00
2	Rafael Palmeiro	7.00
3	Gary Sheffield	5.00
4	Larry Walker	4.00
5	Shawn Green	4.00
6	Mike Piazza	12.00
7	Barry Bonds	20.00
8	J.D. Drew	4.00
9	Magglio Ordonez	4.00
10	Todd Helton	8.00
11	Juan Gonzalez	8.00
12	Pat Burrell	5.00
13	Mark McGwire	15.00
14	Frank Robinson	4.00
15	Manny Ramirez	8.00
16	Lance Berkman	4.00
17	Johnny Bench	10.00
18	Chipper Jones	10.00
19	Mike Schmidt	15.00
22	Sammy Sosa	12.00
23	Cal Ripken Jr.	20.00
24	Roberto Alomar	4.00
25	Willie Stargell	4.00
26	Scott Rolen	7.00
28	Roberto Clemente/SP	50.00
29	Tony Gwynn	10.00
30	Ivan Rodriguez	5.00
31	Sean Casey	4.00
32	Frank Thomas	8.00
33	Jeff Bagwell	8.00
34	Jeff Kent	4.00
35	Reggie Jackson	8.00

Private Signings

		NM/M
	Common Player:	8.00
	Inserted 1:Hobby Box	
1	Alex Rodriguez	75.00
2	Miguel Tejada	25.00
3	Ben Sheets	15.00
4	Tony Gwynn/SP/190	60.00
5	Wilson Betemit	8.00
6	Rick Ankiel	8.00
7	Ivan Rodriguez/SP/150	30.00
8	Ryan Klesko	8.00
9	Jason Giambi/SP/250	15.00
10	Brad Penny	8.00
11	Gabe Kapler	8.00
12	Vladimir Guerrero	30.00
13	Alex Escobar	8.00
14	Edgar Martinez	15.00
15	Cal Ripken/SP/50	200.00
16	Brian Giles	8.00
17	Todd Helton/SP/125	25.00
18	Mike Sweeney	8.00
19	Cliff Floyd	8.00
20	Corey Patterson	12.00
21	Alfonso Soriano	40.00
22	Bobby Abreu	8.00
23	Shawn Green/SP/190	20.00
24	C.C. Sabathia	8.00
25	Luis Gonzalez	8.00
26	Barry Bonds/SP/95	200.00
27	Rafael Palmeiro/SP/250	30.00
28	Mike Mussina/SP/144	40.00
29	Roger Clemens/SP/200	100.00
30	Greg Maddux/SP/200	80.00
31	Troy Glaus	20.00
32	Kerry Wood	15.00
33	Roberto Alomar/SP/200	30.00
34	Tom Glavine	30.00
35	Frank Thomas	20.00
36	Carlos Lee	8.00
37	Scott Rolen	20.00
38	Andruw Jones/SP/250	20.00
39	Manny Ramirez/SP/115	40.00
40	Magglio Ordonez	12.00
41	Lance Berkman	8.00
42	Josh Beckett	25.00
43	Adam Dunn	15.00
44	Albert Pujols/SP/50	450.00
45	Darin Erstad	12.00
46	Curt Schilling	30.00
47	Barry Zito	12.00
48	Sean Casey	8.00

Round Trip Tickets

2001 Donruss The Rookies

MARK TEIXEIRA • TEXAS RANGERS • 3B

		NM/M
	Complete Set (105):	80.00
	Complete Factory Set (106):	100.00
	Common Player:	.25
1	Adam Dunn	.50
2	Ryan Drese RC	.40
3	Bud Smith RC	.25
4	Tsuyoshi Shinjo RC	.50
5	Roy Oswalt	.50
6	Wilmy Caceres RC	.25
7	Willie Harris RC	.25
8	Andres Torres RC	.25
9	Brandon Knight RC	.25
10	Horacio Ramirez RC	.75
11	Benito Baez RC	.25
12	Jeremy Affeldt RC	.25
13	Ryan Jensen RC	.25
14	Casey Fossum RC	.50
15	Ramon Vazquez RC	.50
16	Dustan Mohr RC	.25
17	Saul Rivera RC	.25
18	Zach Day RC	.50
19	Erik Hiljus RC	.25
20	Cesar Crespo RC	.25
21	Wilson Guzman RC	.25
22	Travis Hafner RC	6.00
23	Grant Balfour RC	.25
24	Johnny Estrada RC	1.50
25	Morgan Ensberg RC	1.00
26	Jack Wilson RC	1.50
27	Aubrey Huff	.25
28	Endy Chavez RC	.50
29	Delvin James RC	.25
30	Michael Cuddyer	.25
31	Jason Michaels RC	.25
32	Martin Vargas RC	.25
33	Donaldo Mendez RC	.25
34	Jorge Julio RC	.25
35	Tim Spooneybarger RC	.25
36	Kurt Ainsworth RC	.25
37	Josh Fogg RC	.50
38	Brian Reith RC	.25

39	Rick Baurer RC	.25
40	Tim Redding RC	.25
41	Erick Almonte RC	.50
42	Juan Pena	.25
43	Ken Harvey RC	.25
44	David Brous RC	.25
45	Kevin Olsen RC	.25
46	Henry Mateo RC	.25
47	Nick Neugebauer RC	.25
48	Mike Penney RC	.25
49	Jay Gibbons RC	1.00
50	Tim Christman RC	.25
51	Brandon Duckworth RC	.50
52	Brett Jodie RC	.25
53	Christian Parker RC	.25
54	Carlos Hernandez RC	.25
55	Brandon Larson RC	.50
56	Nick Punto RC	.25
57	Elpidio Guzman RC	.25
58	Joe Beimel RC	.25
59	Junior Spivey RC	.50
60	Will Ohman RC	.25
61	Brandon Lyon RC	.25
62	Stubby Clapp RC	.25
63	Justin Duchscherer RC	.50
64	Jimmy Rollins	.40
65	David Williams RC	.40
66	Craig Monroe RC	.25
67	Jose Acevedo RC	.25
68	Jason Jennings	.25
69	Josh Phelps	.25
70	Brian Roberts RC	2.00
71	Claudio Vargas RC	.25
72	Adam Johnson	.25
73	Bart Miadich RC	.25
74	Juan Rivera	.25
75	Brad Voyles RC	.25
76	Nate Cornejo	.25
77	Juan Moreno RC	.25
78	Brian Rogers RC	.25
79	Ricardo Rodriguez RC	.40
80	Geronimo Gil RC	.25
81	Joe Kennedy RC	.40
82	Kevin Joseph RC	.25
83	Josue Perez RC	.25
84	Victor Zambrano RC	.25
85	Josh Towers RC	.40
86	Mike Rivera RC	.25
87	Mark Prior RC	6.00
88	Juan Cruz RC	.40
89	Dewon Brazelton RC	.40
90	Angel Berroa RC	1.00
91	Mark Teixeira RC	15.00
92	Cody Ransom RC	.25
93	Angel Santos RC	.25
94	Corky Miller RC	.40
95	Brandon Berger RC	.40
96	Corey Patterson	.25
97	Albert Pujols RC	60.00
98	Josh Beckett	.50
99	C.C. Sabathia	.25
100	Alfonso Soriano	.75
101	Ben Sheets	.25
102	Rafael Soriano RC	.50
103	Wilson Betemit RC	.50
104	Ichiro Suzuki RC	10.00
105	Jose Ortiz	.25

Rookie Diamond Kings

ICHIRO

		NM/M
	Complete Set (5):	40.00
	Inserted 1:Rookies Set	
106	C.C. Sabathia	5.00
107	Tsuyoshi Shinjo	8.00
108	Albert Pujols	25.00
109	Roy Oswalt	8.00
110	Ichiro Suzuki	12.00

2002 Donruss Samples

Each March 2002, issue of Beckett Baseball Card Monthly included a sample 2002 Donruss card rubber-cemented inside. The cards differ from the issued version only in the appearance on back of a (usually) silver-foil silver-foil "SAMPLE" notation. Some cards were produced with the overprint in gold-foil, in much more limited quantities. The number of different players' cards involved in the promotion is unknown.

	NM/M
Common Player:	.10
Stars:	1.5-2X
Gold:	10X

2002 Donruss

BARRY ZITO • A's

		NM/M
	Complete Set (220):	120.00
	Common Player:	.15
	Common (151-200):	1.00
	Inserted 1:4	
	Common (201-220):	1.00
	Inserted 1:8	
	Pack (5):	2.00
	Box (24):	40.00
1	Alex Rodriguez	1.50
2	Barry Bonds	2.00
3	Derek Jeter	2.00
4	Robert Fick	.15
5	Juan Pierre	.20
6	Torii Hunter	.25
7	Todd Helton	.75
8	Cal Ripken Jr.	2.00
9	Manny Ramirez	.75
10	Johnny Damon	.25
11	Mike Piazza	1.25
12	Nomar Garciaparra	1.25
13	Pedro Martinez	.75
14	Brian Giles	.15
15	Albert Pujols	1.50
16	Roger Clemens	1.00
17	Sammy Sosa	1.25
18	Vladimir Guerrero	.75
19	Tony Gwynn	1.00
20	Pat Burrell	.35
21	Carlos Delgado	.50
22	Tino Martinez	.15
23	Jim Edmonds	.50
24	Jason Giambi	.50
25	Tom Glavine	.30
26	Mark Grace	.25
27	Tony Armas Jr.	.15
28	Andruw Jones	.75
29	Ben Sheets	.15
30	Jeff Kent	.15
31	Barry Larkin	.15
32	Joe Mays	.15
33	Mike Mussina	.40
34	Hideo Nomo	.60
35	Rafael Palmeiro	.65
36	Scott Brosius	.15
37	Scott Rolen	.65
38	Gary Sheffield	.35
39	Bernie Williams	.35
40	Bobby Abreu	.15
41	Edgardo Alfonzo	.15
42	C.C. Sabathia	.15
43	Jeremy Giambi	.15
44	Craig Biggio	.15
45	Andres Galarraga	.15
46	Edgar Martinez	.15
47	Fred McGriff	.25
48	Magglio Ordonez	.25
49	Jim Thome	.25
50	Matt Williams	.15
51	Kerry Wood	.50
52	Moises Alou	.15
53	Brady Anderson	.15
54	Garret Anderson	.15
55	Juan Gonzalez	.75
56	Bret Boone	.15
57	Jose Cruz Jr.	.15
58	Carlos Beltran	.50
59	Adrian Beltre	.15
60	Joe Kennedy	.15
61	Lance Berkman	.25
62	Kevin Brown	.25
63	Tim Hudson	.35
64	Jeromy Burnitz	.15

#	Player	
65	Jarrod Washburn	.15
66	Sean Casey	.20
67	Eric Chavez	.25
68	Bartolo Colon	.15
69	Freddy Garcia	.15
70	Jermaine Dye	.15
71	Terrence Long	.15
72	Cliff Floyd	.15
73	Luis Gonzalez	.25
74	Ichiro Suzuki	1.50
75	Mike Hampton	.15
76	Richard Hidalgo	.15
77	Geoff Jenkins	.15
78	Gabe Kapler	.15
79	Ken Griffey Jr.	1.25
80	Jason Kendall	.15
81	Josh Towers	.15
82	Ryan Klesko	.15
83	Paul Konerko	.15
84	Carlos Lee	.15
85	Kenny Lofton	.15
86	Josh Beckett	.40
87	Raul Mondesi	.15
88	Trot Nixon	.15
89	John Olerud	.15
90	Paul O'Neill	.15
91	Chan Ho Park	.15
92	Andy Pettitte	.35
93	Jorge Posada	.30
94	Mark Quinn	.15
95	Aramis Ramirez	.15
96	Curt Schilling	.40
97	Richie Sexson	.15
98	John Smoltz	.15
99	Wilson Betemit	.15
100	Shannon Stewart	.15
101	Alfonso Soriano	.75
102	Mike Sweeney	.15
103	Miguel Tejada	.40
104	Greg Vaughn	.15
105	Robin Ventura	.15
106	Jose Vidro	.15
107	Larry Walker	.15
108	Preston Wilson	.15
109	Corey Patterson	.20
110	Mark Mulder	.25
111	Tony Clark	.15
112	Roy Oswalt	.25
113	Jimmy Rollins	.40
114	Kazuhiro Sasaki	.15
115	Barry Zito	.40
116	Javier Vazquez	.15
117	Mike Cameron	.15
118	Phil Nevin	.15
119	Bud Smith	.15
120	Cristian Guzman	.15
121	Al Leiter	.15
122	Brad Radke	.15
123	Bobby Higginson	.15
124	Robert Person	.15
125	Adam Dunn	.50
126	Ben Grieve	.15
127	Rafael Furcal	.15
128	Jay Gibbons	.15
129	Paul LoDuca	.15
130	Wade Miller	.15
131	Tsuyoshi Shinjo	.15
132	Eric Milton	.15
133	Rickey Henderson	.75
134	Roberto Alomar	.40
135	Darin Erstad	.50
136	J.D. Drew	.35
137	Shawn Green	.25
138	Randy Johnson	.75
139	Mark McGwire	1.50
139		.15
140	Jose Canseco	.40
141	Jeff Bagwell	.75
142	Greg Maddux	1.00
143	Mark Buehrle	.15
144	Ivan Rodriguez	.65
145	Frank Thomas	.75
146	Rich Aurilia	.15
147	Troy Glaus	.75
148	Ryan Dempster	.15
149	Chipper Jones	1.00
150	Matt Morris	.15
151	Marlon Byrd	2.00
152	Ben Howard RC	4.00
153	Brandon Backe RC	2.00
154	Jorge De La Rosa RC	2.00
155	Corky Miller	1.00
156	Dennis Tankersley	1.00
157	Kyle Kane RC	3.00
158	Justin Duchscherer	1.00
159	Brian Mallette RC	3.00
160	Chris Baker RC	3.00
161	Jason Lane	1.00
162	Hee Seop Choi	1.50
163	Juan Cruz	1.00
164	Rodrigo Rosario RC	1.00
165	Matt Guerrier	1.00
166	Anderson Machado RC	3.00
167	Geronimo Gil	1.00
168	Dewon Brazelton	1.00
169	Mark Prior	5.00
170	Bill Hall	1.00
171	Jorge Padilla RC	4.00
172	Jose Cueto	1.00
173	Allan Simpson RC	3.00
174	Doug DeVore RC	3.00
175	Josh Pearce	1.00
176	Angel Berroa RC	3.00
177	Steve Bechler RC	3.00
178	Antonio Perez	1.00
179	Mark Teixeira	3.00
180	Erick Almonte	1.00
181	Orlando Hudson	1.00
182	Mike Rivera	1.00
183	Raul Chavez RC	2.00
184	Juan Pena	1.00
185	Travis Hughes RC	2.00
186	Ryan Ludwick	1.00
187	Ed Rogers	1.00
188	Andy Pratt RC	2.00
189	Nick Neugebauer	1.00
190	Tom Shearn RC	3.00
191	Eric Cyr RC	3.00
192	Victor Martinez	1.00
193	Brandon Berger	1.00
194	Erik Bedard	1.00
195	Fernando Rodney	1.00
196	Joe Thurston	1.00
197	John Buck	1.00
198	Jeff Deardorff RC	2.00
199	Ryan Jamison RC	1.00
200	Alfredo Amezaga	1.00
201	Luis Gonzalez	1.00
202	Roger Clemens	4.00
203	Barry Zito	1.25
204	Bud Smith	1.00
205	Magglio Ordonez	1.25
206	Kerry Wood	1.50
207	Freddy Garcia	1.00
208	Adam Dunn	1.50
209	Curt Schilling	2.00
210	Lance Berkman	1.50
211	Rafael Palmeiro	2.00
212	Ichiro Suzuki	4.00
213	Bobby Abreu	1.00
214	Mark Mulder	1.00
215	Roy Oswalt	1.50
216	Mike Sweeney	1.00
217	Paul LoDuca	1.00
218	Aramis Ramirez	1.00
219	Randy Johnson	2.00
220	Albert Pujols	5.00

All-Time Diamond Kings

NM/M
Complete Set (10):		80.00
Common Player:		5.00
Production 2,500 Sets		
Studio Series:		2-3X
Production 250 Sets		
1	Ted Williams	15.00
2	Cal Ripken Jr.	15.00
3	Lou Gehrig	10.00
4	Babe Ruth	15.00
5	Roberto Clemente	10.00
6	Don Mattingly	10.00
7	Kirby Puckett	8.00
8	Stan Musial	8.00
9	Yogi Berra	5.00
10	Ernie Banks	5.00

Bat Kings

NM/M
Quantities produced listed		
Studio Series:		1.5-3X
Production 25 or 50		
1	Jason Giambi/250	15.00
2	Alex Rodriguez/250	25.00
3	Mike Piazza/250	20.00
4	Roberto Clemente/125	100.00
5	Babe Ruth/125	220.00

Diamond Kings

NM/M
Complete Set (20):		80.00
Common Player:		2.00
Production 2,500 Sets		
Studio Series:		2-3X
Production 250 Sets		
1	Nomar Garciaparra	6.00
2	Shawn Green	2.00
3	Randy Johnson	4.00
4	Derek Jeter	7.50
5	Carlos Delgado	3.00
6	Roger Clemens	5.00
7	Jeff Bagwell	4.00
8	Vladimir Guerrero	4.00
9	Luis Gonzalez	2.00
10	Mike Piazza	6.00
11	Ichiro Suzuki	6.00
12	Pedro Martinez	4.00
13	Todd Helton	4.00
14	Sammy Sosa	6.00
15	Ivan Rodriguez	3.50
16	Barry Bonds	7.50
17	Albert Pujols	6.00
18	Jim Thome	2.00
19	Alex Rodriguez	6.00
20	Jason Giambi	3.00

Stat Line Career

NM/M
Cards 1-150 print run 251-400:	2-4X
1-150 p/r 151-250:	3-6X
1-150 p/r 101-150:	4-8X
1-150 p/r 61-100:	5-10X
1-150 p/r 31-60:	8-20X
1-150 p/r 15-30:	15-30X
Common 151-200 p/r 251-400:	1.00
Common 151-200 p/r 151-250:	1.00
Common 151-200 p/r 76-150:	2.00
Common 151-200 p/r 30-75:	4.00

Stat Line Season

NM/M
Cards 1-150 print run 151-200:	3-6X
1-150 p/r 101-150:	4-8X
1-150 p/r 76-100:	5-10X
1-150 p/r 51-75:	6-12X
1-150 p/r 31-50:	8-20X
1-150 p/r 15-30:	15-30X
Comm. 151-200 p/r 151-200:	1.00
Comm. 151-200 p/r 101-150:	1.50
Comm. 151-200 p/r 76-100:	2.00
Comm. 151-200 p/r 30-75:	4.00

Autographs

NM/M
Common Autograph:		15.00
Varying quantities produced		
203	Barry Zito/200	25.00
204	Bud Smith/200	15.00
205	Magglio Ordonez/200	20.00
206	Kerry Wood/200	30.00
207	Freddy Garcia/200	15.00
208	Adam Dunn/200	25.00
210	Lance Berkman/175	15.00
211	Rafael Palmeiro/25	20.00
213	Bobby Abreu/200	15.00
214	Mark Mulder/200	15.00
215	Roy Oswalt/200	15.00
216	Mike Sweeney/200	15.00
217	Paul LoDuca/200	15.00
218	Aramis Ramirez/200	15.00
220	Albert Pujols/200	75.00

Elite Series

NM/M
Complete Set (15):		30.00
Common Player:		2.00
Production 2,500 Sets		
Autographs:		No Pricing
Production 25		
1	Barry Bonds	8.00
2	Lance Berkman	3.00
3	Jason Giambi	2.50
4	Nomar Garciaparra	4.00
5	Curt Schilling	2.50
6	Vladimir Guerrero	3.00
7	Shawn Green	2.00
8	Troy Glaus	2.00
9	Jeff Bagwell	3.00
10	Manny Ramirez	3.00
11	Eric Chavez	2.00
12	Carlos Delgado	2.50
13	Mike Sweeney	3.00
14	Todd Helton	3.00
15	Luis Gonzalez	2.00

Elite Series Legends

NM/M
Complete Set (5):		15.00
Common Player:		3.00
Production 2,500		
16	Enos Slaughter	3.00
17	Frank Robinson	4.00
18	Bob Gibson	4.00
19	Warren Spahn	4.00
20	Whitey Ford	4.00

Series Legends Autographs

NM/M
Production 250 Sets		
16	Enos Slaughter	30.00
17	Frank Robinson	30.00
18	Bob Gibson	35.00
19	Warren Spahn	40.00
20	Whitey Ford	40.00

Jersey Kings

NM/M
Quantity produced listed		
Studio Series:		1.5-3X
Production 25 or 50		
1	Alex Rodriguez/250	15.00
2	Jason Giambi/250	10.00
3	Carlos Delgado/250	10.00
4	Barry Bonds	25.00
5	Randy Johnson/250	10.00
6	Jim Thome/250	8.00
7	Shawn Green/250	8.00
8	Pedro Martinez/250	10.00
9	Jeff Bagwell/250	10.00
10	Vladimir Guerrero/250	10.00
11	Ivan Rodriguez/250	10.00
12	Nomar Garciaparra/250	15.00
13	Don Mattingly/125	80.00
14	Ted Williams/125	125.00
15	Lou Gehrig/125	200.00

Longball Leaders

NM/M
Complete Set (20):		40.00
Common Player:		1.00
Production 1,000 Sets		
Seasonal Sum Parallel:		2-4X
Parallel #'d to 2001 HR total.		
1	Barry Bonds	8.00
2	Sammy Sosa	6.00
3	Luis Gonzalez	1.00
4	Alex Rodriguez	6.00
5	Shawn Green	1.50
6	Todd Helton	3.00
7	Jim Thome	3.00
8	Rafael Palmeiro	2.50
9	Richie Sexson	1.00
10	Troy Glaus	3.00
11	Manny Ramirez	3.00
12	Phil Nevin	1.00
13	Jeff Bagwell	3.00
14	Carlos Delgado	2.00
15	Jason Giambi	2.00
16	Chipper Jones	4.00
17	Larry Walker	2.00
18	Albert Pujols	6.00
19	Brian Giles	1.00
20	Bret Boone	1.00

Production Line

NM/M
Common Card:		2.00
Numbered to category stat.		
1	Barry Bonds/515	8.00
2	Jason Giambi/477	2.00
3	Larry Walker/449	2.50
4	Sammy Sosa/437	6.00
5	Todd Helton/432	3.00
6	Lance Berkman/430	2.00
7	Luis Gonzalez/429	2.00
8	Chipper Jones/427	6.00
9	Edgar Martinez/423	2.00
10	Gary Sheffield/417	2.00
11	Jim Thome/416	3.00
12	Roberto Alomar/415	3.00
13	J.D. Drew/414	2.00
14	Jim Edmonds/410	2.00
15	Carlos Delgado/408	3.00
16	Manny Ramirez/405	4.00
17	Brian Giles/404	2.00
18	Albert Pujols/403	8.00
19	John Olerud/401	2.00
20	Alex Rodriguez/399	8.00
21	Barry Bonds/863	5.00
22	Sammy Sosa/737	5.00
23	Luis Gonzalez/688	1.50
24	Todd Helton/685	2.00
25	Larry Walker/662	1.50
26	Jason Giambi/660	2.00
27	Jim Thome/624	2.00
28	Alex Rodriguez/620	5.00
29	Lance Berkman/620	1.50
30	J.D. Drew/613	1.50
31	Albert Pujols/610	5.00
32	Manny Ramirez/609	2.00
33	Chipper Jones/605	2.00
34	Shawn Green/598	1.50
35	Brian Giles/590	1.50
36	Juan Gonzalez/590	2.00
37	Phil Nevin/588	1.50
38	Gary Sheffield/583	1.50
39	Bret Boone/578	1.50
40	Cliff Floyd/578	1.50
41	Barry Bonds/1,378	5.00
42	Sammy Sosa/1,174	4.00
43	Jason Giambi/1,137	1.50
44	Todd Helton/1,117	1.50
45	Luis Gonzalez/1,117	1.50
46	Larry Walker/1,111	1.50
47	Lance Berkman/1,050	1.50
48	Jim Thome/1,040	1.50
49	Chipper Jones/1,032	2.50
50	J.D. Drew/1,027	1.00
51	Alex Rodriguez/1,021	4.00
52	Manny Ramirez/1,014	1.50
53	Albert Pujols/1,013	4.00
54	Gary Sheffield/1,000	1.50
55	Brian Giles/994	1.00
56	Phil Nevin/976	1.50
57	Jim Edmonds/974	1.50
58	Shawn Green/970	1.00
59	Cliff Floyd/968	1.00
60	Edgar Martinez/966	1.00

Recollection Collection

NM/M
Complete Set (47):		
Common Player:		
6	Steve Carlton 83/30	40.00
7	Steve Carlton 87/30	40.00
8	Gary Carter 87/100	25.00
9	Gary Carter 89/100	25.00
11	Joe Carter 87/45	25.00
13	Andre Dawson 81/50	20.00
14	Andre Dawson 83/50	20.00
16	Andre Dawson 87/45	20.00
17	Dennis Eckersley 81/45	20.00
24	Steve Garvey 87/75	20.00
26	Fergie Jenkins 81/40	25.00
46	Tom Seaver 87/60	60.00
47	Don Sutton 87/200	15.00

Rookie Year Materials - Bats

NM/M
Production 250 Sets		
1	Barry Bonds	40.00
2	Cal Ripken Jr.	40.00
3	Kirby Puckett	15.00
4	Johnny Bench	15.00

Rookie Year Materials - Bats Autograph

NM/M
Numbered to debut year.		
1	Barry Bonds/86	125.00
2	Cal Ripken Jr/81	140.00
3	Kirby Puckett/84	120.00
4	Johnny Bench/68	75.00

Rookie Year Materials - Jerseys

NM/M
Quantity produced listed		
Parallel #'d to 25 or 50.		
1	Nomar Garciaparra/250	20.00
2	Randy Johnson/250	10.00
3	Ivan Rodriguez/250	10.00
4	Vladimir Guerrero/250	15.00
5	Stan Musial/50	80.00
6	Yogi Berra/50	50.00

2002 Donruss Classics Samples

Each August, 2002, issue of Beckett Baseball Card Monthly included a sample Donruss Classics card rubber-cemented inside. The cards differ from the issued version only in the appearance on back of a (usually) silver-foil "SAMPLE" notation. Some cards were produced with the overprint in gold-foil, in much more limited quantities. Cards #1-100 from the set can be found in this Sample version.

NM/M
Common Player:	.10
Stars:	1.5-2X
Gold:	10X

2002 Donruss Classics

NM/M
Complete Set (200):		.50
Common Player:		.50
Common (101-150):		3.00
Common (151-200):		2.00
Production 1,500		
Pack (6):		5.00
Box (18):		70.00
1	Alex Rodriguez	3.00
2	Barry Bonds	4.00
3	C.C. Sabathia	.50
4	Chipper Jones	2.00
5	Derek Jeter	4.00
6	Troy Glaus	1.50
7	Frank Thomas	1.50
8	Greg Maddux	2.00
9	Ivan Rodriguez	1.25
10	Jeff Bagwell	1.50
11	Mark Buehrle	.50
12	Todd Helton	1.50
13	Ken Griffey Jr.	2.50
14	Manny Ramirez	1.50
15	Brad Penny	.50
16	Mike Piazza	2.50
17	Nomar Garciaparra	2.50
18	Pedro J. Martinez	1.50
19	Randy Johnson	1.50
20	Bud Smith	.50
21	Rickey Henderson	1.50
22	Roger Clemens	2.25
23	Sammy Sosa	2.50
24	Brandon Duckworth	.50
25	Vladimir Guerrero	1.50
26	Kazuhiro Sasaki	.65
27	Roberto Alomar	.65
28	Barry Zito	.75
29	Rich Aurilia	.50
30	Ben Sheets	.50
31	Carlos Delgado	1.00
32	J.D. Drew	.75
33	Jermaine Dye	.50
34	Darin Erstad	.75
35	Jason Giambi	1.00
36	Tom Glavine	.60
37	Juan Gonzalez	1.50
38	Luis Gonzalez	.35
39	Shawn Green	.75
40	Tim Hudson	.65
41	Andruw Jones	1.50
42	Shannon Stewart	.50
43	Barry Larkin	.50
44	Wade Miller	.50
45	Mike Mussina	.65
46	Hideo Nomo	1.00
47	Rafael Palmeiro	1.25
48	Scott Rolen	1.00
49	Gary Sheffield	.75
50	Bernie Williams	.65
51	Bobby Abreu	.50
52	Javier Vazquez	.50
53	Edgar Martinez	.50
54	Magglio Ordonez	.75
55	Kerry Wood	1.00
56	Adrian Beltre	.65
57	Lance Berkman	.75
58	Kevin Brown	.50
59	Sean Casey	.50
60	Eric Chavez	.75
61	Robert Person	.50
62	Jeremy Giambi	.50
63	Freddy Garcia	.50
64	Alfonso Soriano	1.50
65	Doug Davis	.50
66	Brian Giles	.50
67	Moises Alou	.50
68	Richard Hidalgo	.50
69	Paul LoDuca	.50
70	Aramis Ramirez	.50
71	Andres Galarraga	.50
72	Ryan Klesko	.50
73	Chan Ho Park	.50
74	Richie Sexson	.50
75	Mike Sweeney	.50
76	Aubrey Huff	.50
77	Miguel Tejada	.75
78	Jose Vidro	.50
79	Larry Walker	.50
80	Roy Oswalt	.75
81	Craig Biggio	.50
82	Juan Pierre	.50

83	Jim Thome	.50
84	Josh Towers	.50
85	Alex Escobar	.50
86	Cliff Floyd	.50
87	Terrence Long	.50
88	Curt Schilling	.75
89	Carlos Beltran	1.00
90	Albert Pujols	2.50
91	Gabe Kapler	.50
92	Mark Mulder	.50
93	Carlos Lee	.50
94	Robert Fick	.50
95	Raul Mondesi	.50
96	Ichiro Suzuki	2.50
97	Adam Dunn	.75
98	Corey Patterson	.75
99	Tsuyoshi Shinjo	.50
100	Joe Mays	.50
101	Juan Cruz	3.00
102	Marlon Byrd	5.00
103	Luis Garcia	3.00
104	Jorge Padilla RC	6.00
105	Dennis Tankersley	3.00
106	Josh Pearce	3.00
107	Ramon Vazquez	3.00
108	Chris Baker RC	5.00
109	Eric Cyr RC	3.00
110	Reed Johnson RC	5.00
111	Ryan Jamison RC	3.00
112	Antonio Perez	3.00
113	Satoru Komiyama RC	3.00
114	Austin Kearns	4.00
115	Juan Pena	3.00
116	Orlando Hudson	3.00
117	Kazuhisa Ishii RC	6.00
118	Eric Bedard	3.00
119	Luis Ugueto RC	3.00
120	Ben Howard RC	4.00
121	Morgan Ensberg RC	3.00
122	Doug DeVore RC	4.00
123	Josh Phelps	3.00
124	Angel Berroa	4.00
125	Ed Rogers	3.00
126	Takahito Nomura RC	3.00
127	John Ennis RC	3.00
128	Bill Hall	3.00
129	Dewon Brazelton	3.00
130	Hank Blalock	5.00
131	So Taguchi RC	3.00
132	Jorge De La Rosa RC	3.00
133	Matt Thornton	3.00
134	Brandon Backe RC	3.00
135	Jeff Deardorff RC	3.00
136	Steve Smyth	3.00
137	Anderson Machado RC	5.00
138	John Buck	3.00
139	Mark Prior	15.00
140	Sean Burroughs	3.00
141	Alex Herrera	3.00
142	Francis Beltran RC	3.00
143	Jason Romano	3.00
144	Michael Cuddyer	3.00
145	Steve Bechler RC	3.00
146	Alfredo Amezaga	3.00
147	Ryan Ludwick	3.00
148	Martin Vargas	3.00
149	Allan Simpson RC	3.00
150	Mark Teixeira	4.00
151	Hank Aaron	8.00
152	Ernie Banks	6.00
153	Johnny Bench	6.00
154	George Brett	10.00
155	Lou Brock	3.00
156	Rod Carew	3.00
157	Steve Carlton	4.00
158	Joe Torre	3.00
159	Dennis Eckersley	2.50
160	Reggie Jackson	6.00
161	Al Kaline	6.00
162	Dave Parker	2.00
163	Don Mattingly	10.00
164	Tony Gwynn	6.00
165	Willie McCovey	3.00
166	Joe Morgan	3.00
167	Stan Musial	8.00
168	Jim Palmer	3.00
169	Brooks Robinson	5.00
170	Bo Jackson	5.00
171	Nolan Ryan	15.00
172	Mike Schmidt	8.00
173	Tom Seaver	6.00
174	Cal Ripken Jr.	15.00
175	Robin Yount	6.00
176	Wade Boggs	5.00
177	Gary Carter	3.00
178	Ron Santo	2.00
179	Luis Aparicio	2.00
180	Bobby Doerr	5.00
181	Ryne Sandberg	6.00
182	Yogi Berra	5.00
183	Will Clark	4.00
184	Eddie Murray	4.00
185	Andre Dawson	5.00
186	Duke Snider	5.00
187	Orlando Cepeda	4.00
188	Billy Williams	2.00
189	Juan Marichal	4.00
190	Harmon Killebrew	5.00
191	Kirby Puckett	6.00
192	Carlton Fisk	4.00
193	Dave Winfield	3.00
194	Alan Trammell	3.00
195	Paul Molitor	6.00
196	Tony Perez	6.00
197	Ozzie Smith	6.00
198	Ralph Kiner	2.00
199	Fergie Jenkins	2.00
200	Phil Rizzuto	3.00

Timeless Tributes

Stars (1-100):	2-4X
SP's (101-150):	1-2X
SP's (151-200):	2-3X
Production 100 Sets	

Classic Singles

NM/M
Common Player: 10.00
Some too scarce to price.

1	Cal Ripken Jr./Jsy/50	40.00
2	Eddie Murray/Jsy/100	15.00
3	George Brett/Jsy/100	35.00
4	Bo Jackson/Jsy/100	20.00
5	Ted Williams/Bat/50	200.00
6	Jimmie Foxx/Bat/50	60.00
7	Reggie Jackson/Jsy/100	15.00
8	Steve Carlton/Jsy/50	30.00
9	Mel Ott/Jsy/50	70.00
10	"Catfish" Hunter/Jsy/100	10.00
11	Nolan Ryan/Jsy/100	40.00
12	Rickey Henderson/Jsy/100	25.00
13	Robin Yount/Jsy/100	25.00
14	Orlando Cepeda/Jsy/100	10.00
15	Ty Cobb/Bat/50	150.00
16	Babe Ruth/Bat/50	275.00
17	Dave Parker/Jsy/100	10.00
18	Willie Stargell/Jsy/100	15.00
19	Ernie Banks/Bat/100	25.00
20	Mike Schmidt/Jsy/100	35.00
21	Duke Snider/Jsy/50	25.00
22	Jackie Robinson/Jsy/50	75.00
23	Rickey Henderson/Bat/100	25.00
25	Lou Gehrig/Bat/50	175.00
26	Jimmie Foxx/Bat/50	65.00
28	Tony Gwynn/Bat/100	20.00
29	Bobby Doerr/Jsy/100	15.00
30	Joe Torre/Jsy/100	10.00

Classic Combos

Too scarce to price.

Legendary Hats

NM/M
50 sets produced

1	Don Mattingly/50	150.00
2	George Brett	150.00
3	Wade Boggs	30.00
4	Ryne Sandberg	120.00

Legendary Leather

NM/M
50 sets produced

1	Don Mattingly	125.00
2	Wade Boggs	30.00
4	Kirby Puckett	50.00
5	Mike Schmidt	80.00

Legendary Lumberjacks

NM/M
Varying quantities produced

1	Don Mattingly/500	20.00
2	George Brett/400	20.00
3	Stan Musial/100	35.00
4	Lou Gehrig/50	175.00
5	Mike Piazza/500	10.00
6	Mel Ott/50	75.00
7	Ted Williams/50	150.00
8	Bo Jackson/500	8.00
9	Kirby Puckett/500	15.00
10	Rafael Palmeiro/500	10.00
11	Andre Dawson/500	5.00
12	Ozzie Smith/500	15.00
13	Paul Molitor/500	15.00
14	Babe Ruth/50	220.00
15	Carlton Fisk/500	8.00
16	Rickey Henderson/500	10.00
17	Gary Carter/500	5.00
18	Cal Ripken Jr/100	40.00
19	Eddie Matthews/100	20.00
20	Luis Aparicio/500	5.00
21	Al Kaline/100	25.00
22	Eddie Murray/500	8.00
23	Yogi Berra/100	25.00
24	Alex Rodriguez/500	25.00
25	Tony Gwynn/500	10.00
26	Roberto Clemente/100	80.00
27	Mike Schmidt/400	20.00
28	Reggie Jackson/500	10.00
29	Ryne Sandberg/500	20.00
30	Joe Morgan/400	5.00
31	Joe Torre/500	5.00
32	Gary Sheffield/500	5.00
33	Nomar Garciaparra/500	10.00
34	Jeff Bagwell/500	8.00
35	Manny Ramirez/500	8.00

Legendary Spikes

NM/M
50 sets produced

1	Don Mattingly	125.00
2	Eddie Murray	30.00
3	Paul Molitor	50.00
4	Harmon Killebrew	40.00
5	Mike Schmidt	100.00

New Millennium Classics

NM/M
Common Player: 4.00
Varying quantities produced
All jerseys unless noted.

1	Curt Schilling/500	6.00
2	Vladimir Guerrero/100	15.00
3	Jim Thome/500	8.00
4	Troy Glaus/400	6.00
5	Ivan Rodriguez/200	6.00
6	Todd Helton/400	5.00
7	Sean Casey/500	4.00
8	Scott Rolen/475	8.00
9	Ken Griffey Jr./150/Base	10.00
10	Hideo Nomo/100	25.00
11	Tom Glavine/350	5.00
12	Pedro Martinez/100	15.00
13	Cliff Floyd/500	4.00
14	Shawn Green/125	8.00
15	Rafael Palmeiro/250	8.00
16	Luis Gonzalez/100	5.00
17	Lance Berkman/100	6.00
18	Frank Thomas/500	8.00
19	Randy Johnson/400	8.00
20	Moises Alou/500	4.00
21	Chipper Jones/500	8.00
22	Larry Walker/300	4.00
23	Mike Sweeney/500	4.00
24	Juan Gonzalez/300	5.00
25	Roger Clemens/100	20.00
26	Albert Pujols/300/Base	
27	Magglio Ordonez/500	5.00
28	Alex Rodriguez/400	10.00
29	Jeff Bagwell/125	10.00
30	Kazuhiro Sasaki/500	4.00
31	Barry Larkin/300	6.00
32	Andruw Jones/350	8.00
33	Kerry Wood/200	4.00
34	Rickey Henderson/100	10.00
35	Greg Maddux/100	15.00
36	Brian Giles/400	4.00
37	Craig Biggio/100	5.00
38	Roberto Alomar/400	6.00
39	Mike Piazza/400	10.00
40	Bernie Williams/100	10.00
41	Ichiro Suzuki/150/Ball	30.00
42	Kenny Lofton/450	4.00
43	Mark Mulder/500	4.00
44	Kazuhisa Ishii/500	15.00
45	Darin Erstad/500	4.00
46	Jose Vidro/500	4.00
47	Miguel Tejada/475	6.00
48	Roy Oswalt/500	5.00
51	Barry Zito/500	5.00
51	Manny Ramirez/400	8.00
52	Nomar Garciaparra/400	10.00
53	C.C. Sabathia/500	4.00
54	Carlos Delgado/500	8.00
55	Gary Sheffield/500	8.00
56	J.D. Drew/500	5.00
57	Barry Bonds/150/Ball	25.00
58	Derek Jeter/150/Ball	25.00
59	Edgar Martinez/400	5.00
60	Sammy Sosa/150/Ball	15.00

Significant Signatures

NM/M
Common Prospect Autograph: 5.00
Varying quantities produced.
Many not priced due to scarcity.

101	Juan Cruz/400	6.00
102	Marlon Byrd/500	10.00
103	Luis Garcia/500	6.00
104	Jorge Padilla/500	10.00
105	Dennis Tankersley/250	10.00
106	Josh Pearce/500	8.00
107	Ramon Vazquez/500	10.00
108	Chris Baker/500 RC	6.00
109	Eric Cyr/500	6.00
110	Reed Johnson/500	10.00
111	Ryan Jamison/500	5.00
112	Antonio Perez/500	5.00
113	Satoru Komiyama/50	40.00
114	Austin Kearns/500	15.00
115	Juan Pena/500	5.00
116	Orlando Hudson/400	10.00
117	Kazuhisa Ishii/50	40.00
118	Eric Bedard/500	15.00
119	Luis Ugueto/250	10.00
120	Ben Howard/500	8.00
121	Morgan Ensberg/500	10.00
122	Doug DeVore/500	5.00
123	Josh Phelps/500	8.00
124	Angel Berroa/500	10.00
125	Ed Rogers/500	5.00
127	John Ennis/500	5.00
128	Bill Hall/400	10.00
129	Dewon Brazelton/400	8.00
130	Hank Blalock/100	20.00
131	So Taguchi/150	30.00
132	Jorge De La Rosa/500	5.00
133	Matt Thornton/500	5.00
134	Brandon Backe/500	5.00
135	Jeff Deardorff/500	5.00
136	Steve Smyth/400	5.00
137	Anderson Machado/500	10.00
138	John Buck/500	5.00
139	Mark Prior/250	25.00
140	Sean Burroughs/50	10.00
141	Alex Herrera/500	5.00
142	Francis Beltran/500	5.00
143	Jason Romano/500	5.00
144	Michael Cuddyer/400	8.00
145	Steve Bechler/500	8.00
146	Alfredo Amezaga/500	5.00
147	Ryan Ludwick/500	8.00
148	Martin Vargas/500	5.00
149	Allan Simpson/500	5.00
150	Mark Teixeira/30	30.00
152	Ernie Banks/25	100.00
153	Johnny Bench/25	125.00
154	George Brett/25	260.00
155	Lou Brock/100	30.00
156	Steve Carlton/25	35.00
159	Dennis Eckersley/500	15.00
161	Al Kaline/125	35.00
162	Dave Parker/500	10.00
163	Don Mattingly/25	75.00
167	Jim Palmer/125	25.00
168	Brooks Robinson/125	40.00
177	Gary Carter/150	25.00
178	Ron Santo/500	20.00
179	Luis Aparicio/400	10.00
180	Bobby Doerr/500	15.00
182	Yogi Berra/25	80.00
184	Eddie Murray/25	60.00
185	Andre Dawson/200	20.00
186	Duke Snider/25	70.00
187	Orlando Cepeda/125	25.00
188	Billy Williams/200	15.00
189	Juan Marichal/500	15.00
190	Harmon Killebrew/100	50.00
194	Alan Trammell/200	25.00
195	Paul Molitor/25	60.00
196	Tony Perez/150	15.00
198	Ralph Kiner/125	20.00
199	Fergie Jenkins/200	15.00
200	Phil Rizzuto/125	40.00

Timeless Treasures

NM/M
Some not priced.

5	Ted Williams/Bat/42	140.00
6	Ted Williams/Bat/47	140.00
7	Ted Williams/Bat/46	140.00
8	Ted Williams/Bat/49	140.00
10	Cal Ripken Jr./Jsy/98	50.00
11	Cal Ripken Jr./Jsy/82	50.00
12	Cal Ripken Jr./Jsy/83	50.00
13	Cal Ripken Jr./Jsy/91	50.00

2002 Donruss Diamond Kings Samples

Each May and July 2002 issue of Beckett Baseball Card Monthly included a sample DK card rubber-cemented inside. The cards differ from the issued version only in the appearance on back of a (usually) silver-foil "SAMPLE" notation and, on some cards, the lack of silver-foil graphics on front. Some cards were produced with the back overprint in gold-foil in much more limited quantities. Cards #1-100 were issued in May, and 101-150 in July.

NM/M

Common Player:	.25
Stars:	1.5-2X
Gold:	10X

2002 Donruss Diamond Kings

NM/M

Complete Set (150):	150.00
Common Player:	.40
Common SP (101-150):	2.00
Inserted 1:3	
Pack (4):	4.50
Box (24):	80.00

1	Vladimir Guerrero	1.00
2	Adam Dunn	.75
3	Tsuyoshi Shinjo	.40
4	Adrian Beltre	.60
5	Troy Glaus	1.00
6	Albert Pujols	2.00
7	Trot Nixon	.40
8	Alex Rodriguez	2.50
9	Tom Glavine	1.00
10	Alfonso Soriano	1.00
11	Todd Helton	1.00
12	Joe Torre	.40
13	Tim Hudson	.50
14	Andruw Jones	1.00
15	Shawn Green	.50
16	Aramis Ramirez	.40
17	Shannon Stewart	.40
18	Barry Bonds	3.00
19	Sean Casey	.40
20	Barry Larkin	.40
21	Scott Rolen	.75
22	Barry Zito	.50
23	Sammy Sosa	2.00
24	Bartolo Colon	.40
25	Ryan Klesko	.40
26	Ben Grieve	.40
27	Roy Oswalt	.50
28	Kazuhiro Sasaki	.40
29	Roger Clemens	1.75
30	Bernie Williams	.50
31	Roberto Alomar	.50
32	Bobby Abreu	.40
33	Robert Fick	.40
34	Bret Boone	.40
35	Rickey Henderson	1.00
36	Brian Giles	.40
37	Richie Sexson	.40
38	Bud Smith	.40
39	Richard Hidalgo	.40
40	C.C. Sabathia	.40
41	Rich Aurilia	.40
42	Carlos Beltran	.75
43	Raul Mondesi	.40
44	Carlos Delgado	.50
45	Randy Johnson	1.00
46	Chan Ho Park	.40
47	Rafael Palmeiro	.75
48	Chipper Jones	1.50
49	Phil Nevin	.40
50	Cliff Floyd	.40
51	Pedro Martinez	1.00
52	Craig Biggio	.40
53	Paul LoDuca	.40
54	Cristian Guzman	.40
55	Pat Burrell	.50
56	Curt Schilling	.40
57	Orlando Cabrera	.40
58	Darin Erstad	.65
59	Omar Vizquel	.40
60	Derek Jeter	3.00
61	Nomar Garciaparra	.40
62	Edgar Martinez	.40
63	Moises Alou	.50
64	Eric Chavez	.50
65	Mike Sweeney	.40
66	Frank Thomas	1.00
67	Mike Piazza	2.00
68	Gary Sheffield	.50
69	Mike Mussina	.50
70	Greg Maddux	1.50
71	Juan Gonzalez	1.00
72	Hideo Nomo	.65
73	Miguel Tejada	.40
74	Ichiro Suzuki	2.00
75	Matt Morris	.40
76	Ivan Rodriguez	.75
77	Mark Mulder	.40
78	J.D. Drew	.40
79	Mark Grace	.50
80	Jason Giambi	.50
81	Mark Buehrle	.40
82	Jose Vidro	.40
83	Manny Ramirez	.50
84	Jeff Bagwell	1.00
85	Magglio Ordonez	.50
86	Ken Griffey Jr.	2.00
87	Luis Gonzalez	.40
88	Jim Edmonds	.40
89	Larry Walker	.40
90	Jim Thome	.40
91	Lance Berkman	.50
92	Jorge Posada	.50
93	Kevin Brown	.40
94	Joe Mays	.40
95	Kerry Wood	.75
96	Mark Ellis	.40
97	Austin Kearns	.75
98	Jorge De La Rosa RC	.50
99	Brandon Berger	.40
100	Ryan Ludwick	.40
101	Marlon Byrd	2.00
102	Brandon Backe RC	2.00
103	Juan Cruz	2.00
104	Anderson Machado RC	3.00
105	So Taguchi RC	4.00
106	Dewon Brazelton	3.00
107	Josh Beckett	3.00
108	John Buck	2.00
109	Jorge Padilla RC	3.00
110	Hee Seop Choi	2.00
111	Angel Berroa	2.00
112	Mark Teixeira	3.00
113	Victor Martinez	

114	Kazuhisa Ishii RC	6.00
115	Dennis Tankersley	2.00
116	Wilson Valdez RC	2.00
117	Antonio Perez	2.00
118	Ed Rogers	2.00
119	Wilson Betemit	2.00
120	Mike Rivera	6.00
121	Mark Prior	6.00
122	Roberto Clemente	6.00
123	Roberto Clemente	6.00
124	Roberto Clemente	6.00
125	Roberto Clemente	6.00
126	Roberto Clemente	6.00
127	Babe Ruth	10.00
128	Ted Williams	8.00
129	Andre Dawson	2.00
130	Eddie Murray	3.00
131	Juan Marichal	3.00
132	Kirby Puckett	5.00
133	Alan Trammell	2.00
134	Bobby Doerr	2.00
135	Carlton Fisk	3.00
136	Eddie Mathews	4.00
137	Mike Schmidt	6.00
138	Jim "Catfish" Hunter	2.00
139	Nolan Ryan	10.00
140	George Brett	6.00
141	Gary Carter	2.00
142	Paul Molitor	4.00
143	Lou Gehrig	8.00
144	Ryne Sandberg	5.00
145	Tony Gwynn	5.00
146	Ron Santo	2.00
147	Cal Ripken Jr.	10.00
148	Al Kaline	4.00
149	Bo Jackson	3.00
150	Don Mattingly	8.00

Bronze Foil

Cards 1-100:	1-2X
Cards 101-150:	.5X
Inserted 1:6	
Gold Foil (1-100):	4-8X
Gold Foil (101-150):	2-3X
Production 100 Sets	
Silver Foil (1-100):	3-4X
Silver Foil (101-150):	1-2X
Production 400 Sets	

Diamond Cut

NM/M

Common Signature (1-30):		5.00
1	Vladimir Guerrero/400	30.00
2	Mark Prior/400	50.00
3	Victor Martinez/500	10.00
4	Marlon Byrd/500	15.00
5	Bud Smith/400	10.00
6	Joe Mays/500	10.00
7	Troy Glaus/500	20.00
8	Ron Santo/500	15.00
9	Roy Oswalt/500	20.00
10	Angel Berroa/500	10.00
11	Mark Buehrle/500	15.00
12	John Buck/500	10.00
13	Barry Larkin/250	40.00
14	Gary Carter/300	30.00
15	Mark Teixeira/300	25.00
16	Alan Trammell/500	20.00
17	Kazuhisa Ishii/100	65.00
18	Rafael Palmeiro/125	30.00
19	Austin Kearns/500	25.00
20	Joe Torre/125	40.00
21	J.D. Drew/500	20.00
22	So Taguchi/400	20.00
23	Juan Marichal/500	15.00
24	Bobby Doerr/500	20.00
25	Carlos Beltran/500	10.00
26	Robert Fick/500	10.00
27	Albert Pujols/200	70.00
28	Shannon Stewart/500	10.00
29	Antonio Perez/500	10.00
30	Wilson Betemit/500	10.00

Jerseys (31-80):

31	Alex Rodriguez/500	15.00
32	Curt Schilling/500	8.00
33	George Brett/300	30.00
34	Hideo Nomo/100	40.00
35	Ivan Rodriguez/500	8.00
36	Don Mattingly/200	40.00
37	Joe Mays/500	5.00
38	Lance Berkman/400	5.00
39	Tony Gwynn/500	10.00
40	Darin Erstad/400	5.00
41	Adrian Beltre/500	5.00
42	Frank Thomas/500	8.00
43	Cal Ripken Jr./300	30.00
44	Jose Vidro/500	5.00
45	Randy Johnson/300	8.00
46	Carlos Delgado/500	6.00
47	Roger Clemens/400	20.00
48	Luis Gonzalez/500	5.00
49	Marlon Byrd/500	6.00
50	Carlton Fisk/500	8.00
51	Manny Ramirez/500	8.00

52	Vladimir Guerrero/500	8.00
53	Barry Larkin/500	8.00
54	Aramis Ramirez/500	5.00
55	Todd Helton/300	8.00
56	Carlos Beltran/250	8.00
57	Jeff Bagwell/250	8.00
58	Larry Walker/500	5.00
59	Al Kaline/200	25.00
60	Chipper Jones/500	8.00
61	Bernie Williams/500	6.00
62	Bud Smith/500	5.00
63	Edgar Martinez/500	8.00
64	Pedro Martinez/500	8.00
65	Andre Dawson/200	5.00
66	Mike Piazza/100	40.00
67	Barry Zito/500	6.00
68	Bo Jackson/300	8.00
69	Nolan Ryan/400	50.00
70	Troy Glaus/500	6.00
71	Jorge Posada/500	8.00
72	Ted Williams/100	200.00
73	Nomar Garciaparra/500	15.00
74	"Catfish" Hunter/100	25.00
75	Gary Carter/500	5.00
76	Craig Biggio/500	5.00
77	Andruw Jones/500	8.00
78	Rickey Henderson/250	30.00
79	Greg Maddux/400	15.00
80	Kerry Wood/500	10.00

Bats (81-100):

81	Alex Rodriguez/500	20.00
82	Don Mattingly/425	30.00
83	Craig Biggio/500	5.00
84	Kazuhisa Ishii/375	8.00
85	Eddie Murray/500	8.00
86	Carlton Fisk/500	8.00
87	Tsuyoshi Shinjo/500	5.00
88	Bo Jackson/500	10.00
89	Eddie Mathews/100	30.00
90	Chipper Jones/500	8.00
91	Adam Dunn/375	8.00
92	Tony Gwynn/200	10.00
93	Kirby Puckett/500	15.00
94	Andre Dawson/500	6.00
95	Bernie Williams/500	6.00
96	Roberto Clemente/300	70.00
97	Babe Ruth/100	250.00
98	Roberto Alomar/500	8.00
99	Frank Thomas/500	8.00
100	So Taguchi/500	6.00

DK Originals

NM/M

Complete Set (15):		50.00
Common Player:		2.00
Production 1,000 Sets		
1	Alex Rodriguez	7.00
2	Kazuhisa Ishii	2.00
3	Pedro Martinez	3.00
4	Nomar Garciaparra	6.00
5	Albert Pujols	6.00
6	Chipper Jones	5.00
7	So Taguchi	2.00
8	Jeff Bagwell	3.00
9	Vladimir Guerrero	3.00
10	Derek Jeter	8.00
11	Sammy Sosa	6.00
12	Ichiro Suzuki	6.00
13	Barry Bonds	8.00
14	Jason Giambi	3.00
15	Mike Piazza	6.00

Heritage Collection

NM/M

Complete Set (25):		100.00
Common Player:		2.00
Inserted 1:23		
1	Lou Gehrig	8.00
2	Nolan Ryan	10.00
3	Ryne Sandberg	4.00
4	Ted Williams	8.00
5	Roberto Clemente	8.00
6	Mike Schmidt	5.00
7	Roger Clemens	5.00
8	Kirby Puckett	4.00
9	Andre Dawson	2.00
10	Carlton Fisk	2.00
11	Don Mattingly	8.00
12	Juan Marichal	2.00
13	George Brett	8.00
14	Bo Jackson	2.00
15	Eddie Mathews	3.00
16	Randy Johnson	3.00
17	Alan Trammell	2.00
18	Tony Gwynn	4.00
19	Paul Molitor	3.00
20	Barry Bonds	10.00
21	Eddie Murray	3.00
22	Jim "Catfish" Hunter	2.00
23	Rickey Henderson	2.00
24	Cal Ripken Jr.	10.00
25	Babe Ruth	8.00

Ramly T204

NM/M

Complete Set (25):		120.00
Common Player:		3.00
Production 1,000 Sets		
1	Vladimir Guerrero	4.00
2	Jeff Bagwell	3.00
3	Barry Bonds	15.00
4	Rickey Henderson	4.00
5	Mike Piazza	8.00
6	Derek Jeter	15.00
7	Kazuhisa Ishii	3.00
8	Ichiro Suzuki	10.00
9	Chipper Jones	5.00
10	Sammy Sosa	8.00
11	Don Mattingly	10.00
12	Shawn Green	3.00
13	Nomar Garciaparra	10.00
14	Luis Gonzalez	3.00
15	Albert Pujols	8.00
16	Cal Ripken Jr.	15.00
17	Todd Helton	4.00
18	Hideo Nomo	3.00
19	Alex Rodriguez	10.00
20	So Taguchi	3.00
21	Lance Berkman	3.00
22	Tony Gwynn	5.00
23	Roger Clemens	6.00
24	Jason Giambi	4.00
25	Ken Griffey Jr.	8.00

Recollection Collection

NM/M

Common Player:		
22	Fred Lynn 87 DK/28	15.00
30	Roy Oswalt 01 RDK Black/48	20.00
47	Alan Trammell 88 DK/110	30.00

Timeline

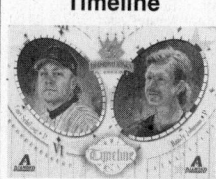

NM/M

Complete Set (10):		60.00
Common Card:		3.00
Inserted 1:60		
1	Lou Gehrig, Don Mattingly	10.00
2	Hideo Nomo, Ichiro Suzuki	10.00
3	Cal Ripken Jr., Alex Rodriguez	10.00
4	Mike Schmidt, Scott Rolen	8.00
5	Ichiro Suzuki, Albert Pujols	8.00
6	Curt Schilling, Randy Johnson	5.00
7	Chipper Jones, Eddie Mathews	5.00
8	Lou Gehrig, Cal Ripken Jr.	10.00
9	Derek Jeter, Roger Clemens	10.00
10	Kazuhiko Ishimine, So Taguchi	3.00

LCS Programs

A perforated sheet of Diamond King cards was inserted into some of the programs sold for the American and National League Championship Series. The 8-1/2" x 11" sheet features eight player cards and a header card advertising the brand. Each 2-1/2" x 3-1/2" card is perforated on all sides and differs from the regularly issued version only in the card number on back. Sheet cards have either an "ALCS-" or "NLCS-" prefix to the number. Other programs could be found with similar sheets of Donruss Originals, Donruss Studio or Playoff Piece of the Game cards.

NM/M

Complete Sheet Set (2):		20.00
Common Player:		.50
ALCS SHEET		10.00
1	Cal Ripken Jr.	3.00
2	Nomar Garciaparra	1.50
3	Roger Clemens	1.25
4	Alex Rodriguez	1.25
5	Troy Glaus	1.00
6	Miguel Tejada	.50
7	Alfonso Soriano	1.00
8	Ted Williams	2.50
--	Header Card	.10
NLCS SHEET		10.00
1	Randy Johnson	1.00
2	Josh Beckett	.75
3	Mike Piazza	1.50
4	Greg Maddux	1.25
5	Lance Berkman	.50
6	Mark Prior	2.00
7	Adam Dunn	1.00
8	Tony Gwynn	1.25
--	Header Card	.10

2002 Donruss Elite Samples

Each June 2002 issue of Beckett Baseball Card Monthly included a sample Elite Series card rubber-cemented inside. The cards differ from the issued version only in the appearance on back of a (usually) silver-foil "SAMPLE" notation. Some cards were produced with the overprint in gold-foil, in much more limited quantities. Cards #1-100 from the set can be found in this Sample version.

NM/M

Common Player:	.25
Stars:	1.5-2X
Gold:	10X

2002 Donruss Elite

NM/M

Complete Set (200):		
Common Player:		.25
Common (101-150):		2.00
Inserted 1:10		
Common (151-200):		3.00
Production 1,500		
Pack (5):		3.00
Box (20):		50.00
1	Vladimir Guerrero	.75
2	Bernie Williams	.35
3	Ichiro Suzuki	1.50
4	Roger Clemens	1.25
5	Greg Maddux	1.00
6	Fred McGriff	.25
7	Jermaine Dye	.25
8	Ken Griffey Jr.	1.50
9	Todd Helton	.75
10	Torii Hunter	.40
11	Pat Burrell	.40
12	Chipper Jones	1.00
13	Ivan Rodriguez	.50
14	Roy Oswalt	.40
15	Shannon Stewart	.25
16	Magglio Ordonez	.40
17	Lance Berkman	.25
18	Mark Mulder	.25
19	Al Leiter	.25
20	Sammy Sosa	1.50
21	Scott Rolen	.75
22	Aramis Ramirez	.25
23	Alfonso Soriano	.75
24	Phil Nevin	.25
25	Barry Bonds	2.50
26	Joe Mays	.25
27	Jeff Kent	.25
28	Mark Quinn	.25
29	Adrian Beltre	.35
30	Freddy Garcia	.25
31	Pedro J. Martinez	.75
32	Darryl Kile	.25
33	Mike Cameron	.25
34	Frank Catalanotto	.25
35	Jose Vidro	.25
36	Jim Thome	.50
37	Javy Lopez	.25
38	Paul Konerko	.25
39	Jeff Bagwell	.75
40	Curt Schilling	.40
41	Miguel Tejada	.40
42	Jim Edmonds	.25
43	Ellis Burks	.25
44	Mark Grace	.25
45	Robb Nen	.25
46	Jeff Conine	.25
47	Derek Jeter	2.50
48	Mike Lowell	.25
49	Javier Vazquez	.25
50	Manny Ramirez	.75
51	Bartolo Colon	.25
52	Carlos Beltran	.50
53	Tim Hudson	.40
54	Rafael Palmeiro	.65
55	Jimmy Rollins	.25
56	Andruw Jones	.75
57	Orlando Cabrera	.25
58	Dean Palmer	.25
59	Bret Boone	.25
60	Carlos Febles	.25
61	Ben Grieve	.25
62	Richie Sexson	.25
63	Alex Rodriguez	2.00
64	Juan Pierre	.25
65	Bobby Higginson	.25
66	Barry Zito	.40
67	Raul Mondesi	.25
68	Albert Pujols	2.00
69	Omar Vizquel	.25
70	Bobby Abreu	.25
71	Corey Koskie	.25
72	Tom Glavine	.40
73	Paul LoDuca	.25
74	Terrence Long	.25
75	Matt Morris	.25
76	Andy Pettitte	.40
77	Rich Aurilia	.25
78	Todd Walker	.25
79	John Olerud	.25
80	Mike Sweeney	.25
81	Ray Durham	.25
82	Fernando Vina	.25
83	Nomar Garciaparra	1.50
84	Mariano Rivera	.35
85	Mike Piazza	1.50
86	Mark Buehrle	.25
87	Adam Dunn	.25
88	Luis Gonzalez	.35
89	Richard Hidalgo	.25
90	Brad Radke	.25
91	Russ Ortiz	.25
92	Brian Giles	.25
93	Billy Wagner	.25
94	Cliff Floyd	.25
95	Eric Milton	.25
96	Bud Smith	.25
97	Wade Miller	.25
98	Jon Lieber	.25
99	Derrek Lee	.25
100	Jose Cruz Jr.	.25
101	Dmitri Young	2.00
102	Mo Vaughn	2.00
103	Tino Martinez	2.00
104	Larry Walker	2.50
105	Chuck Knoblauch	2.00
106	Troy Glaus	3.00
107	Jason Giambi	4.00
108	Travis Fryman	2.00
109	Josh Beckett	4.00
110	Edgar Martinez	2.00
111	Tim Salmon	2.00
112	C.C. Sabathia	2.00
113	Randy Johnson	5.00
114	Juan Gonzalez	4.00
115	Carlos Delgado	4.00
116	Hideo Nomo	4.00
117	Kerry Wood	4.00
118	Brian Jordan	2.00
119	Carlos Pena	2.00
120	Roger Cedeno	2.00
121	Chan Ho Park	2.00
122	Rafael Furcal	2.00
123	Frank Thomas	4.00
124	Mike Mussina	4.00
125	Rickey Henderson	5.00
126	Sean Casey	2.00
127	Barry Larkin	2.00
128	Kazuhiro Sasaki	2.00
129	Moises Alou	2.00
130	Jeff Cirillo	2.00
131	Jason Kendall	2.00
132	Gary Sheffield	3.00
133	Ryan Klesko	2.00
134	Kevin Brown	2.00
135	Darin Erstad	2.00
136	Roberto Alomar	3.00
137	Brad Fullmer	2.00
138	Eric Chavez	2.00
139	Ben Sheets	2.00
140	Trot Nixon	2.00
141	Garret Anderson	2.00
142	Shawn Green	2.50
143	Troy Percival	2.50
144	Craig Biggio	2.50
145	Jorge Posada	2.50
146	J.D. Drew	3.00
147	Johnny Damon	2.00
148	Jeromy Burnitz	2.00
149	Robin Ventura	2.00
150	Aaron Sele	2.00
151	Cam Esslinger RC	3.00
152	Ben Howard RC	4.00
153	Brandon Backe RC	3.00
154	Jorge De La Rosa RC	3.00
155	Austin Kearns	5.00
156	Carlos Zambrano	3.00
157	Kyle Kane RC	3.00
158	So Taguchi RC	5.00
159	Brian Mallette RC	3.00
160	Brett Jodie	3.00
161	Elio Serrano RC	3.00
162	Joe Thurston	3.00
163	Kevin Olsen	3.00
164	Rodrigo Rosario RC	4.00
165	Matt Guerrier	3.00
166	Anderson Machado RC	5.00
167	Bert Snow	3.00
168	Franklyn German RC	3.00
169	Brandon Claussen	3.00
170	Jason Romano	3.00
171	Jorge Padilla RC	5.00
172	Jose Cueto	3.00
173	Allan Simpson RC	3.00
174	Doug DeVore RC	5.00
175	Justin Duchscherer	3.00
176	Josh Pearce	3.00
177	Steve Bechler RC	3.00
178	Josh Phelps	3.00
179	Juan Diaz	3.00
180	Victor Alvarez RC	3.00
181	Ramon Vazquez	3.00
182	Mike Rivera	3.00
183	Kazuhisa Ishii RC	6.00
184	Henry Mateo	3.00
185	Travis Hughes RC	5.00
186	Zach Day	3.00
187	Brad Voyles	3.00
188	Sean Douglass	3.00
189	Nick Neugebauer	3.00
190	Tom Shearn RC	3.00
191	Eric Cyr RC	3.00
192	Adam Johnson	3.00
193	Michael Cuddyer	3.00
194	Erik Bedard	3.00
195	Mark Ellis	3.00
196	Carlos Hernandez	3.00
197	Deivi Santos	3.00
198	Morgan Ensberg	3.00
199	Ryan Jamison RC	3.00
200	Cody Ransom	3.00

Aspirations

1-100 print run 26-50:	15-30X
1-100 p/r 51-80:	8-15X
101-150 p/r 26-50:	1.5-3X
101-150 p/r 51-99:	1-2X

Status

1-100 print run 36-70:	10-20X
1-100 p/r 71-100:	5-10X

101-150 p/r 36-70: 1-2X
101-150 p/r 71-100: 1X

All-Star Salutes

NM/M
Common Player: 1.00
Century: 1-2X
Production 100

1	Ichiro Suzuki	5.00
2	Tony Gwynn	4.00
3	Magglio Ordonez	1.50
4	Cal Ripken Jr.	8.00
5	Tony Gwynn	4.00
6	Kazuhiro Sasaki	1.00
7	Freddy Garcia	1.00
8	Luis Gonzalez	1.00
9	Lance Berkman	1.00
10	Derek Jeter	8.00
11	Chipper Jones	4.00
12	Randy Johnson	3.00
13	Andruw Jones	3.00
14	Pedro J. Martinez	3.00
15	Jim Thome	1.00
16	Rafael Palmeiro	2.50
17	Barry Larkin	1.00
18	Ivan Rodriguez	2.50
19	Omar Vizquel	1.00
20	Edgar Martinez	1.00
21	Larry Walker	1.00
22	Javy Lopez	1.00
23	Mariano Rivera	1.25
24	Frank Thomas	3.00
25	Greg Maddux	4.00

Back to the Future

NM/M
Complete Set (24): 75.00
Common Player: 2.00
Duals 500 produced, singles 1,000

1	Scott Rolen, Marlon Byrd	5.00
2	Joe Crede, Frank Thomas	6.00
3	Lance Berkman, Jeff Bagwell	6.00
4	Marcus Giles, Chipper Jones	10.00
5	Shawn Green, Paul LoDuca	4.00
7	Kerry Wood, Juan Cruz	4.00
8	Vladimir Guerrero, Orlando Cabrera	6.00
9	Scott Rolen	3.00
10	Marlon Byrd	2.00
11	Frank Thomas	4.00
12	Joe Crede	2.00
13	Jeff Bagwell	4.00
14	Lance Berkman	2.00
15	Chipper Jones	6.00
16	Marcus Giles	2.00
17	Shawn Green	2.50
18	Paul LoDuca	2.00
19	Jim Edmonds	2.00
21	Kerry Wood	3.00
22	Juan Cruz	2.00
23	Vladimir Guerrero	4.00
24	Orlando Cabrera	2.00

Back to the Future Threads

NM/M
Common Card: 10.00
Duals 50 produced, singles 100

1	Scott Rolen, Marlon Byrd	30.00
2	Joe Crede, Frank Thomas	40.00
3	Lance Berkman, Jeff Bagwell	40.00
4	Marcus Giles, Chipper Jones	50.00
5	Shawn Green, Paul LoDuca	30.00
7	Kerry Wood, Juan Cruz	35.00
8	Vladimir Guerrero, Orlando Cabrera	40.00
9	Scott Rolen	15.00
10	Marlon Byrd	20.00
11	Frank Thomas	25.00
12	Joe Crede	10.00
13	Jeff Bagwell	25.00
14	Lance Berkman	15.00
15	Chipper Jones	25.00
16	Marcus Giles	10.00
17	Shawn Green	15.00
18	Paul LoDuca	10.00
19	Jim Edmonds	10.00
20	So Taguchi	50.00
21	Kerry Wood	15.00
22	Juan Cruz	10.00
23	Vladimir Guerrero	25.00
24	Orlando Cabrera	10.00

Back 2 Back Jacks

NM/M
Common Card: 10.00
Dual Production 75
Single Production 150

1	Ivan Rodriguez, Alex Rodriguez	40.00
2	Kirby Puckett, Dave Winfield	50.00
3	Ted Williams, Nomar Garciaparra	150.00
4	Jeff Bagwell, Craig Biggio	25.00
5	Eddie Murray, Cal Ripken Jr.	125.00
6	Andruw Jones, Chipper Jones	25.00
7	Roberto Clemente, Willie Stargell	120.00
8	Lou Gehrig, Don Mattingly	180.00
9	Larry Walker, Todd Helton	20.00
10	Manny Ramirez, Trot Nixon	25.00
11	Alex Rodriguez	30.00
12	Ivan Rodriguez	15.00
13	Kirby Puckett	40.00
14	Dave Winfield	15.00
15	Ted Williams	100.00
16	Nomar Garciaparra	40.00
17	Jeff Bagwell	15.00
18	Craig Biggio	10.00
19	Eddie Murray	20.00
20	Cal Ripken Jr.	60.00
21	Andruw Jones	10.00
22	Chipper Jones	20.00
23	Roberto Clemente	80.00
24	Lou Gehrig	160.00
26	Don Mattingly	65.00
27	Larry Walker	10.00
28	Todd Helton	15.00
29	Manny Ramirez	20.00
30	Trot Nixon	10.00

Career Bests

NM/M
Common Player: 2.00

1	Albert Pujols/1,013	8.00
2	Alex Rodriguez/52	20.00
3	Alex Rodriguez/135	15.00
4	Andruw Jones/104	6.00
5	Barry Bonds/73	25.00
6	Barry Bonds/1,379	10.00
7	Barry Bonds/177	20.00
8	C.C. Sabathia/171	4.00
9	Carlos Beltran/876	2.00
10	Chipper Jones/330	6.00
11	Derek Jeter/900	15.00
12	Eric Chavez/114	4.00
13	Frank Catalanotto/330	2.00
14	Ichiro Suzuki/838	15.00
15	Ichiro Suzuki/127	15.00
16	J.D. Drew/27	20.00
17	J.D. Drew/1,027	2.00
18	Jason Giambi/660	5.00
20	Jim Thome/49	25.00
21	Jim Thome/624	4.00
22	Jorge Posada/95	8.00
23	Jose Cruz Jr/856	3.00
24	Kazuhiro Sasaki/45	15.00
25	Kerry Wood/336	3.00
26	Lance Berkman/1,050	3.00
27	Magglio Ordonez/382	3.00
28	Mark Mulder/345	2.00
29	Pat Burrell/27	20.00
30	Pat Burrell/469	3.00
31	Randy Johnson/372	6.00
33	Richie Sexson/547	3.00
34	Roberto Alomar/956	
35	Sammy Sosa/160	12.00
36	Sammy Sosa/1,174	6.00
37	Shawn Green/125	4.00
39	Trot Nixon/150	4.00
40	Troy Glaus/108	5.00

Passing the Torch

NM/M
Common Card: 4.00
Dual 500, single 1,000 produced

1	Fergie Jenkins, Mark Prior	10.00
2	Nolan Ryan, Roy Oswalt	25.00
3	Ozzie Smith, J.D. Drew	8.00
4	George Brett, Carlos Beltran	15.00
5	Kirby Puckett, Michael Cuddyer	10.00
6	Johnny Bench, Adam Dunn	8.00
7	Duke Snider, Paul LoDuca	6.00
8	Tony Gwynn, Xavier Nady	10.00
9	Fergie Jenkins	4.00
10	Mark Prior	8.00
11	Nolan Ryan	15.00
12	Roy Oswalt	5.00
13	Ozzie Smith	6.00
14	J.D. Drew	6.00
15	George Brett	10.00
16	Carlos Beltran	6.00
17	Kirby Puckett	6.00
18	Michael Cuddyer	6.00
19	Johnny Bench	6.00
20	Adam Dunn	6.00
21	Duke Snider	6.00
22	Paul LoDuca	4.00
23	Tony Gwynn	6.00
24	Xavier Nady	4.00

Passing the Torch Autographs

NM/M
Common Autograph: 15.00

1	Ferguson Jenkins, Mark Prior/50	125.00
2	Nolan Ryan, Roy Oswalt/50	180.00
3	Ozzie Smith, J.D. Drew/50	125.00
4	George Brett, Carlos Beltran/25	300.00
5	Kirby Puckett, Michael Cuddyer/50	100.00
6	Johnny Bench, Adam Dunn/50	100.00
7	Duke Snider, Paul LoDuca/50	80.00
8	Tony Gwynn, Xavier Nady/50	120.00
9	Fergie Jenkins/50	40.00
10	Mark Prior/100	80.00
11	Nolan Ryan/100	125.00
12	Roy Oswalt/100	25.00
13	Ozzie Smith/25	160.00
14	J.D. Drew/100	30.00
15	George Brett/25	300.00
16	Carlos Beltran/100	40.00
17	Kirby Puckett/25	120.00
18	Michael Cuddyer/100	15.00
19	Johnny Bench/100	50.00
20	Adam Dunn/50	10.00
21	Duke Snider/100	30.00
22	Paul LoDuca/100	15.00
23	Tony Gwynn/100	50.00
24	Xavier Nady/100	15.00

Recollection Collection

NM/M
Common Player:

2	Alfredo Amezaga 01/50	15.00
13	Orlando Hudson 01/50	20.00
18	Antonio Perez 01/50	15.00
19	Mike Rivera 01/50	15.00
22	Claudio Vargas 01/50	15.00
23	Martin Vargas 01/50	15.00

Throwback Threads

NM/M
Common Card: 15.00
Dual 50, single 100 Produced

1	Manny Ramirez, Ted Williams	125.00
2	Mike Piazza, Carlton Fisk	50.00
3	George Brett, Bo Jackson	125.00
4	Randy Johnson, Curt Schilling	40.00
5	Don Mattingly, Lou Gehrig	250.00
6	Bernie Williams, Dave Winfield	25.00
7	Rickey Henderson, Paul Molitor	75.00
8	Robin Yount	75.00
9	J.D. Drew, Stan Musial	100.00
10	Andre Dawson, Ryne Sandberg	100.00
11	Babe Ruth, Reggie Jackson	325.00
12	Brooks Robinson, Cal Ripken Jr.	120.00
13	Ted Williams, Nomar Garciaparra	125.00
14	Shawn Green, Jackie Robinson	80.00
15	Tony Gwynn, Cal Ripken Jr.	120.00
16	Ted Williams	75.00
17	Manny Ramirez	20.00
18	Carlton Fisk	25.00
19	Mike Piazza	20.00
20	Bo Jackson	20.00
21	George Brett	50.00
22	Curt Schilling	20.00
23	Randy Johnson	20.00
24	Don Mattingly	50.00
25	Lou Gehrig	200.00
26	Bernie Williams	15.00
27	Dave Winfield	15.00
29	Rickey Henderson	40.00
30	Robin Yount	30.00
31	Paul Molitor	25.00
32	Stan Musial	65.00
33	J.D. Drew	15.00
34	Andre Dawson	15.00
35	Ryne Sandberg	50.00
36	Babe Ruth	250.00
37	Reggie Jackson	25.00
38	Brooks Robinson	25.00
39	Cal Ripken Jr.	75.00
40	Nomar Garciaparra	40.00
41	Jackie Robinson	80.00
42	Shawn Green	15.00
43	Pedro J. Martinez	20.00
44	Nolan Ryan	80.00
45	Kazuhiro Sasaki	15.00
46	Tony Gwynn	25.00
47	Carlton Fisk	20.00
48	Cal Ripken Jr.	75.00
49	Rod Carew	20.00
50	Nolan Ryan	80.00
51	Alex Rodriguez	25.00
52	Greg Maddux	25.00
53	Pedro J. Martinez	20.00
54	Rickey Henderson	30.00
55	Rod Carew	20.00
56	Roberto Clemente	100.00
57	Hideo Nomo	40.00
58	Rickey Henderson	40.00
59	Dave Parker	15.00
60	Eddie Mathews	25.00
61	Eddie Murray	20.00
62	Nolan Ryan	80.00
63	Tom Seaver	25.00
64	Roger Clemens	40.00
65	Rickey Henderson	40.00

Throwback Threads Autographs

NM/M
Production 5-25

Turn of the Century

NM/M
Common Player: 8.00

154	Jorge De La Rosa/50	8.00
155	Carlos Zambrano/50	8.00
157	Kyle Kane/50	8.00
158	So Taguchi/25	15.00
159	Brian Mallette/50	8.00
160	Brett Jodie/50	8.00
168	Matt Guerrier/50	8.00
168	Franklyn German/50	8.00
169	Brandon Claussen/50	15.00
171	Jorge Padilla/50	10.00
172	Jose Cueto/50	8.00
176	Josh Pearce/50	8.00
177	Steve Bechler/50	8.00
178	Josh Phelps/50	8.00
180	Victor Alvarez/50	8.00
182	Michael Rivera/50	8.00
183	Kazuhisa Ishii/125	20.00
184	Henry Mateo/50	8.00
186	Zach Day/50	8.00
189	Nick Neugebauer/100	8.00
192	Adam Johnson/125	8.00
193	Michael Cuddyer/50	8.00
195	Mark Ellis/25	10.00
196	Carlos Hernandez/150	8.00
198	Morgan Ensberg/50	8.00
200	Cody Ransom/150	8.00

Turn of the Century Autographs

NM/M
Common Autograph: 10.00

151	Cam Esslinger/150	10.00
152	Ben Howard/150	10.00
153	Brandon Backe/150	15.00
154	Jorge De La Rosa/100	10.00
155	Austin Kearns/150	15.00
156	Carlos Zambrano/100	20.00
157	Kyle Kane/100	10.00
158	So Taguchi/125	20.00
159	Brian Mallette/100	10.00
160	Brett Jodie/100	10.00
161	Elio Serrano/150	10.00
162	Joe Thurston/150	10.00
163	Kevin Olsen/150	10.00
164	Rodrigo Rosario/150	10.00
165	Matt Guerrier/100	10.00
166	Anderson Machado/150	10.00
167	Bert Snow/150	10.00
168	Franklyn German/100	10.00
169	Brandon Claussen/100	15.00
170	Jason Romano/150	10.00
171	Jorge Padilla/100	15.00
172	Jose Cueto/100	10.00
173	Allan Simpson/150	15.00
174	Doug DeVore/150	15.00
175	Justin Duchscherer/150	10.00
176	Josh Pearce/100	10.00
177	Steve Bechler/100	10.00
178	Josh Phelps/150	15.00
179	Juan Diaz/150	10.00
180	Victor Alvarez/100	10.00
181	Ramon Vazquez/150	10.00
182	Michael Rivera/100	10.00
183	Kazuhisa Ishii/150	150.00
184	Henry Mateo/100	10.00
185	Travis Hughes/150	10.00
186	Zach Day/100	10.00
187	Brad Voyles/150	10.00
188	Sean Douglass/150	10.00
189	Nick Neugebauer/50	10.00
190	Tom Shearn/150	10.00
191	Eric Cyr/150	10.00
192	Adam Johnson/25	10.00
193	Michael Cuddyer/100	10.00
194	Erik Bedard/150	20.00
195	Mark Ellis/125	10.00
196	Deivis Santos/150	10.00
198	Morgan Ensberg/150	10.00
199	Ryan Jamison/150	10.00

2002 Donruss Fan Club

NM/M
Complete Set (300):
Common Player: .25
Common (201-260): 3.00
Production 1,350
Common (261-300): 2.00
Production 2,025
Pack (5): 3.50
Box (20): 60.00

1	Alex Rodriguez	2.00
2	Pedro Martinez	.75
3	Vladimir Guerrero	.25
4	Jim Edmonds	.25
5	Derek Jeter	2.50
6	Johnny Damon	.40
7	Rafael Furcal	.25
8	Cal Ripken Jr.	2.50
9	Brad Radke	.25
10	Bret Boone	.25
11	Pat Burrell	.50
12	Roy Oswalt	.50
13	Cliff Floyd	.25
14	Robin Ventura	.25
15	Frank Thomas	.35
16	Mariano Rivera	.35
17	Paul LoDuca	.25
18	Geoff Jenkins	.25
19	Tony Gwynn	1.00
20	Chipper Jones	1.00
21	Eric Chavez	.40
22	Kerry Wood	.60
23	Jorge Posada	.35
24	J.D. Drew	.40
25	Garret Anderson	.25
26	Javier Vazquez	.25
27	Kenny Lofton	.25
28	Paul Konerko	.45
29	Paul Konerko	.45
30	Bernie Williams	.45
31	Eric Milton	.25
32	Craig Wilson	.25
33	Paul O'Neill	.35
34	Dmitri Young	.25
35	Andres Galarraga	.25
36	Gary Sheffield	.40
37	Ben Grieve	.25
38	Scott Rolen	.75
39	Mark Grace	.35
40	Albert Pujols	2.00
41	Barry Zito	.40
42	Edgar Martinez	.25
43	Jarrod Washburn	.25
44	Juan Pierre	.25
45	Mark Buehrle	.25
46	Larry Walker	.25
47	Trot Nixon	.25
48	Wade Miller	.25
49	Robert Fick	.25
50	Sean Casey	.40
51	Joe Mays	.25
52	Brad Fullmer	.25
53	Chan Ho Park	.25
54	Carlos Delgado	.50
55	Phil Nevin	.25
56	Mike Cameron	.25
57	Raul Mondesi	.25
58	Roberto Alomar	.40
59	Ryan Klesko	.25
60	Andruw Jones	.75
61	Gabe Kapler	.25
62	Darin Erstad	.65
63	Cristian Guzman	.25
64	Kazuhiro Sasaki	.25
65	Doug Mientkiewicz	.25
66	Sammy Sosa	1.50
67	Mike Hampton	.25
68	Rickey Henderson	.75
69	Mark Mulder	.35
70	Jeff Conine	.25
71	Freddy Garcia	.25
72	Ivan Rodriguez	.65
73	Terrence Long	.25
74	Adam Dunn	.50
75	Moises Alou	.25
76	Todd Helton	.75
77	Preston Wilson	.25
78	Roger Cedeno	.25
79	Tony Armas Jr.	.25
80	Manny Ramirez	.75
81	Jose Vidro	.25
82	Randy Johnson	.75
83	Richie Sexson	.25
84	Troy Glaus	.75
85	Kevin Brown	.25
86	Woody Williams	.25
87	Adrian Beltre	.40
88	Brian Giles	.25
89	Jermaine Dye	.25
90	Craig Biggio	.25
91	Richard Hidalgo	.25
92	Magglio Ordonez	.40
93	Al Leiter	.25
94	Jeff Kent	.25
95	Curt Schilling	.50
96	Tim Hudson	.25
97	Fred McGriff	.25
98	Barry Larkin	.25
99	Jim Thome	.25
100	Tom Glavine	.40
101	Alfonso Soriano	.75
102	Jamie Moyer	.25
103	Vinny Castilla	.25
104	Rich Aurilia	.25
105	Matt Morris	.25
106	Rafael Palmeiro	.65
107	Joe Crede	.25
108	Barry Bonds	2.50
109	Robert Person	.25
110	Nomar Garciaparra	1.50
111	Brandon Duckworth	.25
112	Russ Ortiz	.25
113	Jeff Weaver	.25
114	Carlos Beltran	.50
115	Ellis Burks	.25
116	Jeremy Giambi	.25
117	Carlos Lee	.25
118	Ken Griffey Jr.	1.50
119	Torii Hunter	.40
120	Andy Pettitte	.40
121	Jose Canseco	.40
122	Charles Johnson	.25
123	Nick Johnson	.25
124	Luis Gonzalez	.35
125	Rondell White	.25
126	Miguel Tejada	.25

127	Jose Cruz Jr.	.25
128	Brent Abernathy	.25
129	Scott Brosius	.25
130	Jon Lieber	.25
131	John Smoltz	.25
132	Mike Sweeney	.25
133	Shannon Stewart	.25
134	Derrek Lee	.25
135	Brian Jordan	.25
136	Rusty Greer	.25
137	Mike Piazza	1.50
138	Billy Wagner	.25
139	Shawn Green	.35
140	Orlando Cabrera	.25
141	Jeff Bagwell	.75
142	Aaron Sele	.25
143	Hideo Nomo	.75
144	Marlon Anderson	.25
145	Todd Walker	.25
146	Bobby Higginson	.25
147	Ichiro Suzuki	2.00
148	Juan Uribe	.25
149	Jason Kendall	.25
150	Mark Quinn	.25
151	Ben Sheets	.25
152	Paul Abbott	.25
153	Aubrey Huff	.25
154	Greg Maddux	1.00
155	Darryl Kile	.25
156	John Burkett	.25
157	Juan Gonzalez	.75
158	Javy Lopez	.25
159	Aramis Ramirez	.25
160	Lance Berkman	.25
161	David Cone	.25
162	Edgar Renteria	.25
163	Roger Clemens	1.25
164	Frank Catalanotto	.25
165	Bartolo Colon	.25
166	Mark McGwire	2.00
167	Jay Gibbons	.25
168	Tony Clark	.25
169	Tsuyoshi Shinjo	.25
170	Brad Penny	.25
171	Marcus Giles	.25
172	Matt Williams	.25
173	Bud Smith	.25
174	Tino Martinez	.25
175	Ryan Dempster	.40
176	Jimmy Rollins	.25
177	Edgardo Alfonzo	.25
178	Jason Giambi	.50
179	Aaron Boone	.25
180	Matt Dunigan	.25
181	Mike Lowell	.25
182	Jose Ortiz	.25
183	Johnny Estrada	.25
184	Shane Reynolds	.25
185	Joe Kennedy	.25
186	Corey Patterson	.25
187	Jeromy Burnitz	.25
188	C.C. Sabathia	.25
189	Doug Davis	.25
190	Omar Vizquel	.25
191	John Olerud	.25
192	Dee Brown	.25
193	Kip Wells	.25
194	A.J. Burnett	.25
195	Josh Towers	.25
196	Jason Varitek	.25
197	Jason Isringhausen	.25
198	Fernando Vina	.25
199	Ramon Ortiz	.25
200	Bobby Abreu	.25
201	Willie Harris	3.00
202	Angel Santos	3.00
203	Corky Miller	3.00
204	Mike Rivera	3.00
205	Justin Duchscherer	3.00
206	Rick Bauer	3.00
207	Angel Berroa	3.00
208	Juan Cruz	3.00
209	Dewon Brazelton	3.00
210	Mark Prior	10.00
211	Mark Teixeira	8.00
212	Geronimo Gil	3.00
213	Casey Fossum	3.00
214	Ken Harvey	3.00
215	Michael Cuddyer	3.00
216	Wilson Betemit	3.00
217	David Brous	3.00
218	Juan Pena	3.00
219	Travis Hafner	4.00
220	Erick Almonte	3.00
221	Morgan Ensberg	3.00
222	Martin Vargas	3.00
223	Brandon Berger	3.00
224	Zach Day	3.00
225	Brad Voyles	3.00
226	Jeremy Affeldt	3.00
227	Nick Neugebauer	3.00
228	Tim Redding	3.00
229	Adam Johnson	3.00
230	Doug DeVore RC	4.00
231	Cody Ransom	3.00
232	Marlon Byrd	3.00
233	Delvin James	3.00
234	Eric Munson	3.00
235	Dennis Tankersley	3.00
236	Josh Beckett	8.00
237	Bill Hall	3.00
238	Kevin Olsen	3.00
239	Francis Beltran RC	3.00
240	Antonio Perez	3.00
241	Orlando Hudson	3.00
242	Anderson Machado RC	6.00
243	Tom Shearn RC	5.00
244	Brian Mallette RC	4.00
245	Raul Chavez RC	4.00
246	Andy Pratt RC	4.00
247	Jorge De La Rosa RC	4.00
248	Jeff Deardorff RC	4.00
249	Ben Howard RC	4.00
250	Brandon Backe RC	4.00
251	Ed Rogers	3.00
252	Travis Hughes RC	4.00
253	Rodrigo Rosario RC	5.00
254	Alfredo Amezaga	3.00
255	Jorge Padilla RC	5.00
256	Victor Martinez	4.00
257	Steve Bechler RC	4.00
258	Chris Baker RC	4.00
259	Ryan Freel	3.00
260	Allan Simpson RC	3.00
261	Alex Rodriguez	6.00
262	Vladimir Guerrero	3.00
263	Bud Smith	2.00
264	Miguel Tejada	2.00
265	Craig Biggio	2.00
266	Luis Gonzalez	2.00
267	Ivan Rodriguez	3.00
268	C.C. Sabathia	2.00
269	Jeff Bagwell	3.00
270	Aramis Ramirez	2.00
271	Bobby Abreu	2.00
272	Rich Aurilia	2.00
273	Jason Giambi	3.00
274	Rickey Henderson	3.00
275	Wade Miller	3.00
276	Andruw Jones	3.00
277	Troy Glaus	3.00
278	Roy Oswalt	3.00
279	Tony Gwynn	3.00
280	Adam Dunn	3.00
281	Larry Walker	2.00
282	Jose Canseco	3.00
283	Todd Helton	3.00
284	Lance Berkman	2.00
285	Cal Ripken Jr.	10.00
286	Albert Pujols	8.00
287	Alfonso Soriano	3.00
288	Mark Mulder	2.00
289	Mike Hampton	2.00
290	Andres Galarraga	2.00
291	Barry Bonds	8.00
292	Ben Sheets	2.00
293	Ichiro Suzuki	6.00
294	J.D. Drew	2.00
295	Jose Ortiz	2.00
296	Kerry Wood	2.00
297	Mark McGwire	8.00
298	Mike Sweeney	2.00
299	Pat Burrell	3.00
300	Tim Hudson	3.00

Autographs

NM/M
Common Player: 5.00
Varying quantities produced

201	Willie Harris/500	5.00
203	Corky Miller/500	5.00
205	Justin Duchscherer/500	8.00
207	Angel Berroa/100	15.00
208	Juan Cruz/175	15.00
209	Dewon Brazelton/52	15.00
210	Mark Prior/425	40.00
211	Mark Teixeira/425	25.00
213	Casey Fossum/100	10.00
215	Michael Cuddyer/52	15.00
216	Wilson Betemit/500	8.00
217	David Brous/500	8.00
218	Juan A. Pena/188	8.00
219	Travis Hafner/375	5.00
221	Morgan Ensberg/52	15.00
222	Martin Vargas/500	5.00
223	Brandon Berger/500	5.00
224	Zach Day/500	5.00
225	Brad Voyles/500	5.00
226	Jeremy Affeldt/250	5.00
227	Nick Neugebauer/225	8.00
228	Tim Redding/500	5.00
229	Adam Johnson/425	5.00
230	Doug DeVore/300	5.00
231	Cody Ransom/500	5.00
232	Marlon Byrd/475	15.00
233	Delvin James/375	5.00
234	Eric Munson/325	8.00
235	Dennis Tankersley/500	5.00
238	Kevin Olsen/325	5.00
240	Antonio Perez/525	5.00
241	Orlando Hudson/525	10.00
248	Jeff Deardorff/475	5.00
251	Ed Rogers/400	5.00
255	Jorge Padilla/450	15.00
260	Allan Simpson/475	5.00
278	Roy Oswalt/75	35.00

Artist

NM/M
Complete Set (14): 60.00
Common Player: 5.00
Production 300 Sets

1	Pedro Martinez	8.00
2	Curt Schilling	6.00
3	Kevin Brown	5.00
4	Tim Hudson	5.00
5	Kerry Wood	7.50
7	Barry Zito	4.00
8	Hideo Nomo	6.00
9	Randy Johnson	6.00
10	Roger Clemens	15.00
11	Kazuhiro Sasaki	3.00
12	Joe Mays	3.00
13	Mark Mulder	3.00
14	Javier Vazquez	3.00

Master Artists

NM/M
Common Player: 5.00
Production 150 Sets

1	Pedro Martinez	15.00
2	Curt Schilling	10.00
3	Kevin Brown	5.00
4	Tim Hudson	6.00
5	Kerry Wood	5.00
6	Barry Zito	8.00
7	Hideo Nomo	15.00
8	Randy Johnson	15.00
9	Greg Maddux	15.00
10	Roger Clemens	20.00
11	Kazuhiro Sasaki	5.00
12	Joe Mays	5.00
13	Mark Mulder	5.00
14	Javier Vazquez	5.00

Artist Autographs

NM/M
Production 15-100

6	Barry Zito/100	35.00

Craftsmen

Complete Set (18): 80.00
Common Player: 3.00
Production 300 Sets

1	Ichiro Suzuki	10.00
2	Todd Helton	5.00
3	Manny Ramirez	5.00
4	Luis Gonzalez	3.00
5	Roberto Alomar	3.50
6	Moises Alou	3.00
7	Darin Erstad	3.00
8	Mike Piazza	10.00
9	Edgar Martinez	3.00
10	Vladimir Guerrero	6.00
11	Juan Gonzalez	3.00
12	Nomar Garciaparra	10.00
13	Tony Gwynn	6.00
14	Jeff Bagwell	5.00
15	Albert Pujols	15.00
16	Larry Walker	3.00
17	Paul LoDuca	3.00
18	Lance Berkman	3.00

Master Craftsmen

NM/M
Common Player: 5.00
Production 150 Sets/H

1	Ichiro Suzuki/Ball/51	75.00
2	Todd Helton	5.00
3	Manny Ramirez	10.00
4	Luis Gonzalez	8.00
5	Roberto Alomar	8.00
6	Moises Alou	8.00
7	Darin Erstad	8.00
8	Mike Piazza	15.00
9	Edgar Martinez	8.00
10	Vladimir Guerrero	15.00
11	Juan Gonzalez	8.00
12	Nomar Garciaparra	20.00
13	Tony Gwynn/175	20.00
14	Jeff Bagwell	8.00
15	Albert Pujols/175	25.00
16	Larry Walker/175	5.00
17	Paul LoDuca/175	5.00
18	Lance Berkman	8.00

Craftsmen Autographs

NM/M
Common Player:

17	Paul LoDuca/100	20.00

Double Features

NM/M
Complete Set (10): 80.00
Common Card: 8.00
Production 125 Sets

1	Larry Walker, Todd Helton	10.00
2	Jose Vidro, Vladimir Guerrero	10.00
3	Jason Giambi, Jeremy Giambi	8.00
4	Nomar Garciaparra, Manny Ramirez	15.00
5	Troy Glaus, Darin Erstad	8.00
6	Shawn Green, Paul LoDuca	8.00
7	Jeff Bagwell, Craig Biggio	10.00
8	Pedro Martinez, Hideo Nomo	12.00
9	Curt Schilling, Randy Johnson	10.00
10	Andruw Jones, Chipper Jones	12.50

Double Features Game-Used

NM/M
Common Card: 10.00
Production 50 Sets

1	Larry Walker, Todd Helton	15.00
2	Jose Vidro, Vladimir Guerrero	20.00
3	Jason Giambi, Jeremy Giambi	15.00
4	Nomar Garciaparra, Manny Ramirez	30.00
5	Troy Glaus, Darin Erstad	15.00
6	Shawn Green, Paul LoDuca	10.00
7	Jeff Bagwell, Craig Biggio	15.00
8	Pedro Martinez, Hideo Nomo	30.00
9	Curt Schilling, Randy Johnson	20.00
10	Andruw Jones, Chipper Jones	20.00

Franchise Features

NM/M
Complete Set (40): 180.00
Common Player: 3.00
Production 300 Sets

1	Cliff Floyd	3.00
2	Mike Piazza	12.00
3	Cal Ripken Jr.	25.00
4	Mike Sweeney	3.00
5	Curt Schilling	3.00
6	Aramis Ramirez	3.00
7	Vladimir Guerrero	8.00
8	Andruw Jones	8.00
9	Tim Hudson	3.00
10	Bernie Williams	8.00
11	Pedro Martinez	8.00
12	Roberto Alomar	3.00
13	Joe Mays	3.00
14	Jason Giambi	8.00
15	Kazuhiro Sasaki	3.00
16	Magglio Ordonez	3.00
17	Nomar Garciaparra	12.00
18	Juan Gonzalez	8.00
19	Carlos Beltran	3.00
20	Javier Vazquez	3.00
21	Miguel Tejada	3.00
22	Luis Gonzalez	3.00
23	Greg Maddux	10.00
24	Rafael Palmeiro	3.00
25	Freddy Garcia	3.00
26	Barry Zito	4.00
27	Paul LoDuca	3.00
28	Robert Fick	3.00
29	Roger Clemens	10.00
30	Eric Chavez	3.00
31	Ivan Rodriguez	8.00
32	Chipper Jones	10.00
33	Kerry Wood	6.00
34	Randy Johnson	8.00
35	Alex Rodriguez	12.00
36	Manny Ramirez	8.00
37	Mark Buehrle	3.00
38	Mark Mulder	3.00
39	Ichiro Suzuki	15.00
40	Troy Glaus	4.00

Franchise Features Autographs

NM/M
Production 15-100

6	Aramis Ramirez/100	20.00
13	Joe Mays/75	10.00
19	Carlos Beltran/100	20.00
25	Freddy Garcia/100	20.00
26	Barry Zito/100	30.00
28	Robert Fick/100	15.00
30	Eric Chavez/50	20.00
37	Mark Buehrle/100	15.00

Franchise Features Game-Used

NM/M
Common Player: 4.00
Production 150 Sets
All Jerseys unless noted

1	Cliff Floyd	4.00
2	Mike Piazza	15.00
3	Cal Ripken Jr.	30.00
4	Mike Sweeney	4.00
5	Curt Schilling	8.00
6	Aramis Ramirez	4.00
7	Vladimir Guerrero	8.00
8	Andruw Jones	8.00
9	Tim Hudson	6.00
10	Bernie Williams	6.00
11	Pedro Martinez	10.00
12	Roberto Alomar	6.00
13	Joe Mays	4.00
14	Jason Giambi	8.00
15	Kazuhiro Sasaki	5.00
16	Magglio Ordonez	6.00
17	Nomar Garciaparra	20.00
18	Juan Gonzalez	8.00
19	Carlos Beltran	8.00
20	Javier Vazquez	4.00
21	Miguel Tejada	8.00
22	Luis Gonzalez	5.00
23	Greg Maddux	15.00
24	Rafael Palmeiro	10.00
25	Freddy Garcia	4.00
26	Barry Zito	8.00
27	Paul LoDuca	4.00
28	Robert Fick	4.00
29	Roger Clemens	20.00
30	Eric Chavez/Bat	4.00
31	Ivan Rodriguez	8.00
32	Chipper Jones	8.00
33	Kerry Wood	10.00
34	Randy Johnson	10.00
35	Alex Rodriguez	15.00
36	Manny Ramirez	8.00
37	Mark Buehrle	4.00
38	Mark Mulder	4.00
39	Ichiro Suzuki/Ball	80.00
40	Troy Glaus	6.00

League Leaders

NM/M
Common Player: 3.00
Production 300 Sets

1	Roger Clemens	12.00
2	Curt Schilling	5.00
3	Matt Morris	3.00
4	Randy Johnson	6.00
5	Mark Mulder	4.00
6	Curt Schilling	5.00
7	Mike Mussina	4.00
8	Joe Mays	3.00
9	Matt Morris	3.00
10	Tim Hudson	3.00
11	Mark Buehrle	4.00
12	Greg Maddux	10.00
13	Freddy Garcia	3.00
14	Randy Johnson	6.00
15	Curt Schilling	5.00
16	Chan Ho Park	3.00
17	Roger Clemens	12.00
18	Mike Mussina	3.00
19	Javier Vazquez	3.00
20	Kerry Wood	8.00
21	Randy Johnson	6.00
22	Barry Zito	4.00
23	Hideo Nomo	8.00
24	Ichiro Suzuki	10.00
25	Todd Helton	5.00
26	Albert Pujols	20.00
27	Alex Rodriguez	12.00
28	Shannon Stewart	3.00
29	Luis Gonzalez	3.00
30	Alex Rodriguez	12.00
31	Barry Bonds	20.00
32	Sammy Sosa	15.00
33	Luis Gonzalez	3.00
34	Todd Helton	5.00
35	Jim Thome	3.00
36	Shawn Green	5.00
37	Jeff Bagwell	7.50
38	Todd Helton	5.00
39	Luis Gonzalez	5.00
40	Lance Berkman	8.00
41	Juan Gonzalez	6.00
42	Larry Walker	3.00
43	Ichiro Suzuki	10.00
44	Lance Berkman	3.00
45	Todd Helton	5.00

League Leaders Autographs

NM/M
Production 15-100

5	Mark Mulder/100	20.00
11	Mark Buehrle/100	15.00
13	Freddy Garcia/100	15.00
19	Javier Vazquez/100	15.00
26	Albert Pujols/100	150.00
28	Shannon Stewart/100	15.00

League Leaders Game-Used

NM/M
Common Player: 4.00
Production 150 or 175

1	Roger Clemens	20.00
2	Curt Schilling	10.00
3	Randy Johnson	8.00
5	Mark Mulder	6.00
6	Curt Schilling	10.00
7	Mike Mussina/Shoe/50	25.00
8	Joe Mays	4.00
10	Tim Hudson	6.00
11	Mark Buehrle	4.00
12	Greg Maddux	15.00
13	Freddy Garcia	4.00
14	Randy Johnson	8.00
15	Curt Schilling	10.00
16	Chan Ho Park	4.00
17	Roger Clemens	20.00
18	Mike Mussina/Shoe/50	25.00
19	Javier Vazquez	4.00
20	Kerry Wood	10.00
21	Randy Johnson	8.00
22	Barry Zito	6.00
23	Hideo Nomo	6.00
24	Ichiro Suzuki/Ball/51	75.00
25	Todd Helton	8.00
27	Albert Pujols	20.00
27	Alex Rodriguez	15.00
29	Shannon Stewart	4.00
29	Luis Gonzalez	5.00
30	Alex Rodriguez	15.00
32	Barry Bonds	25.00
32	Sammy Sosa	15.00
33	Luis Gonzalez	4.00
34	Todd Helton	8.00
35	Jim Thome	10.00
36	Shawn Green	5.00
37	Jeff Bagwell	8.00
38	Todd Helton	8.00
39	Luis Gonzalez	4.00
41	Lance Berkman	4.00
41	Juan Gonzalez	6.00
42	Larry Walker	4.00
43	Ichiro Suzuki/Ball/51	75.00
44	Lance Berkman	4.00
45	Todd Helton	5.00

Pure Power

NM/M
Complete Set (18): 65.00
Common Player: 2.00
Production 300 Sets

1	Sammy Sosa	8.00
2	Lance Berkman	2.00
3	Chipper Jones	6.00
4	Troy Glaus	2.00
5	Barry Bonds	12.00
6	Todd Helton	5.00
7	Manny Ramirez	4.00
8	Jason Giambi	4.00
9	Juan Gonzalez	4.00
10	Albert Pujols	10.00
11	Jim Thome	2.00
12	Mike Piazza	8.00
13	Frank Thomas	4.00
14	Richie Sexson	2.00
15	Jeff Bagwell	4.00
16	Rafael Palmeiro	3.00
17	Luis Gonzalez	2.00
18	Shawn Green	2.50

Pure Power Masters

NM/M
Complete Set (18) 125.00
Common Player: 5.00
Production 150

1	Sammy Sosa	15.00
2	Lance Berkman	5.00
3	Chipper Jones	10.00
4	Troy Glaus	5.00
5	Barry Bonds	25.00
6	Todd Helton	8.00

#	Player	Price
7	Manny Ramirez	8.00
8	Jason Giambi	6.00
9	Juan Gonzalez	8.00
10	Albert Pujols	20.00
11	Jim Thome	5.00
12	Mike Piazza	15.00
13	Frank Thomas	8.00
14	Richie Sexson	5.00
15	Jeff Bagwell	8.00
16	Rafael Palmeiro	6.00
17	Luis Gonzalez	5.00
18	Shawn Green	6.00

Pure Power Autographs

NM/M
Varying quantities produced

#	Player	Price
14	Richie Sexson/100	20.00

Records

NM/M
Complete Set (5): 50.00
Common Player: 8.00
Production 300

#	Player	Price
1	Barry Bonds	15.00
2	Barry Bonds	15.00
3	Barry Bonds	15.00
4	Rickey Henderson	8.00
5	Rickey Henderson	8.00

Records Game-Used

NM/M
Production 150

#	Player	Price
1	Barry Bonds	40.00
2	Barry Bonds	40.00
3	Barry Bonds	40.00
4	Rickey Henderson	20.00
5	Rickey Henderson	20.00

2002 Donruss Originals Samples

Each November 2002, issue of Beckett Baseball Card Monthly included a sample '02 Donruss Originals card rubber-cemented inside. The cards differ from the issued version only in the appearance on back of a (usually) silver-foil silver-foil "SAMPLE" notation. Some cards were produced with the overprint in gold-foil, in much more limited quantities. The number of different players' cards involved in the promotion is unknown.

Common Player:
Stars: 1.5-2X
Gold: 10X

2002 Donruss Originals

NM/M
Complete Set (400): 75.00
Common Player: .10
Common Rated Rookie: .50
Pack (5): 2.00
Hobby Box (24): 40.00

#	Player	Price
1	So Taguchi/RC RC	.75
2	Allan Simpson/RC RC	.50
3	Brian Mallette/RC RC	.50
4	Ben Howard/RC RC	.50
5	Kazuhisa Ishii/RC RC	2.00
6	Francis Beltran/RC RC	.50
7	Jorge Padilla/RC RC	.50
8	Brandon Puffer/RC RC	.50
9	Oliver Perez/RC RC	1.50
10	Kirk Saarloos/RC	.50
11	Travis Driskill/RC RC	.50
12	Jeremy Lambert/RC	.50
13	John Foster/RC RC	.50
14	Steve Kent/RC RC	.50
15	Shawn Sedlacek/RC	.50
16	Alex Rodriguez	1.25
17	Lance Berkman	.10
18	Kevin Brown	.10
19	Garret Anderson	.10
20	Bobby Abreu	.10
21	Richard Hidalgo	.10
22	Matt Morris	.10
23	Manny Ramirez	.60
24	Derek Jeter	1.50
25	Kerry Wood	.25
26	Mark Grace	.15
27	Edgar Martinez	.10
28	Nomar Garciaparra	1.00
29	Roberto Alomar	.25
30	Jason Giambi	.50
31	Juan Gonzalez	.50
32	Albert Pujols	1.00
33	Juan Cruz	.10
34	Troy Glaus	.60
35	Greg Maddux	.75
36	Adam Dunn	.40
37	J.D. Drew	.25
38	Tsuyoshi Shinjo	.10
39	Vladimir Guerrero	.60
40	Barry Bonds	1.50
41	Carlos Delgado	.40
42	Ken Griffey Jr.	1.00
43	Carlos Pena	.10
44	Jeff Kent	.10
45	Roger Clemens	.75
46	Frank Thomas	.60
47	Larry Walker	.10
48	Pedro J. Martinez	.60
49	Moises Alou	.10
50	Andruw Jones	.60
51	Luis Gonzalez	.25
52	Adrian Beltre	.10
53	Bobby Hill	.10
54	Roy Oswalt	.20
55	Tim Hudson	.20
56	Trot Nixon	.10
57	Jeff Bagwell	.60
58	Bernie Williams	.30
59	Magglio Ordonez	.25
60	Bartolo Colon	.10
61	Shawn Green	.20
62	Mark Buehrle	.10
63	Sean Casey	.10
64	Rickey Henderson	.60
65	Aramis Ramirez	.10
66	Ichiro Suzuki	1.00
67	Cliff Floyd	.10
68	Darin Erstad	.40
69	Paul LoDuca	.10
70	Ivan Rodriguez	.50
71	Mo Vaughn	.10
72	Todd Helton	.60
73	Raul Mondesi	.10
74	Sammy Sosa	1.00
75	Cristian Guzman	.10
76	Jimmy Rollins	.25
77	Hideo Nomo	.10
78	C.C. Sabathia	.10
79	Wade Miller	.10
80	Drew Henson	.20
81	Chipper Jones	.75
82	Miguel Tejada	.25
83	Freddy Garcia	.10
84	Richie Sexson	.10
85	Robin Ventura	.10
86	Jose Vidro	.10
87	Rich Aurilia	.10
88	Scott Rolen	.25
89	Carlos Beltran	.40
90	Austin Kearns	.25
91	Kazuhiro Sasaki	.10
92	Carlos Hernandez	.10
93	Randy Johnson	.60
94	Jim Thome	.10
95	Curt Schilling	.10
96	Alfonso Soriano	.50
97	Barry Larkin	.10
98	Rafael Palmeiro	.50
99	Tom Glavine	.25
100	Barry Zito	.10
101	Craig Biggio	.10
102	Mike Piazza	1.00
103	Ben Sheets	.10
104	Mark Mulder	.20
105	Mike Mussina	.25
106	Jim Edmonds	.10
107	Paul Konerko	.10
108	Pat Burrell	.25
109	Chan Ho Park	.10
110	Mike Sweeney	.10
111	Phil Nevin	.10
112	Brian Giles	.10
113	Eric Chavez	.20
114	Corey Patterson	.10
115	Gary Sheffield	.25
116	Kazuhisa Ishii/RC	2.00
117	Kyle Kane/RC RC	.50
118	Eric Junge/RC RC	.50
119	Luis Ugueto/RC RC	.50
120	Cam Esslinger/RC RC	.50
121	Earl Snyder/RC RC	.50
122	Oliver Perez/RC	1.50
123	Victor Alvarez/RC RC	.50
124	Tom Shearn/RC RC	.50
125	Corey Thurman/RC RC	.50
126	Satoru Komiyama/RC	.50
127	Hansel Izquierdo/RC RC	.50
128	Elio Serrano/RC RC	.50
129	Michael Crudale/RC RC	.50
130	Chris Snelling/RC RC	1.50
131	Nomar Garciaparra	1.00
132	Roger Clemens	.75
133	Hank Blalock	.25
134	Eric Chavez	.20
135	Corey Patterson	.20
136	Richie Sexson	.10
137	Freddy Garcia	.10
138	Miguel Tejada	.25
139	Alex Rodriguez/SP	1.50
140	Adrian Beltre	.10
141	Bobby Abreu	.10
142	Bret Boone	.10
143	Tim Hudson	.20
144	Roy Oswalt	.20
145	Derek Jeter	1.50
146	Rich Aurilia	.10
147	Mark Grace	.15
148	Kerry Wood/SP	1.00
149	Geronimo Gil	.10
150	Mark Buehrle	.10
151	Jim Edmonds	.10
152	Ichiro Suzuki	1.00
153	Juan Gonzalez	.60
154	Darin Erstad	.40
155	Barry Bonds/SP	2.50
156	Greg Maddux	.75
157	Adam Dunn	.25
158	Todd Helton	.60
159	Roberto Alomar	.25
160	Sammy Sosa	1.00
161	Sean Burroughs	.10
162	Albert Pujols	1.00
163	Carlos Delgado	.25
164	Frank Thomas	.60
165	Ken Griffey Jr.	1.00
166	Jason Giambi/SP	.50
167	Chipper Jones	.75
168	Ivan Rodriguez	.50
169	Pedro Martinez/SP	1.00
170	Gary Sheffield	.25
171	Andruw Jones	.50
172	Luis Gonzalez	.25
173	Raul Mondesi	.10
174	Jose Vidro	.10
175	Garret Anderson/SP	.50
176	Scott Rolen	.60
177	Kazuhiro Sasaki	.10
178	Jeff Bagwell	.60
179	Manny Ramirez	.60
180	Jim Thome	.10
181	Ben Sheets	.20
182	Randy Johnson	.60
183	Lance Berkman	.10
184	Shawn Green	.10
185	Rickey Henderson	.60
186	Edgar Martinez	.10
187	Barry Larkin	.10
188	Bernie Williams	.30
189	Luis Aparicio	.50
190	Troy Glaus/SP	.50
191	Mike Mussina	.30
192	Pee Wee Reese	.50
193	Craig Biggio	.10
194	Vladimir Guerrero	.60
195	J.D. Drew	.20
196	Jeff Kent	.10
197	Dewon Brazelton	.10
198	Tsuyoshi Shinjo/SP	.40
199	Sean Casey	.10
200	Hideo Nomo	.50
201	C.C. Sabathia	.10
202	Larry Walker	.10
203	Mark Teixeira	.75
204	Mike Sweeney	.10
205	Moises Alou	.10
206	Mark Prior	.75
207	Javier Vazquez	.10
208	Phil Nevin	.10
209	Harmon Killebrew	.50
210	Brian Giles	.10
211	Carlos Beltran	.40
212	Don Drysdale	.40
213	Matt Morris	.10
214	Trot Nixon	.10
215	Magglio Ordonez	.25
216	Curt Schilling/SP	.75
217	Mark Mulder	.50
218	Alfonso Soriano	1.00
219	Rafael Palmeiro/SP	.75
220	Tom Glavine	.25
221	Barry Zito	.25
222	Mike Piazza	1.00
223	Bartolo Colon	.10
224	Cliff Floyd	.10
225	Paul LoDuca	.10
226	Cristian Guzman	.10
227	Mo Vaughn	.10
228	Aramis Ramirez	.10
229	Pat Burrell	.10
230	Chan Ho Park	.10
231	Satoru Komiyama/RC	.50
232	Brandon Backe/RC RC	.50
233	Anderson Machado/RC RC	.50
234	Doug DeVore/RC RC	.50
235	Steve Bechler/RC RC	.50
236	John Ennis/RC RC	.50
237	Rodrigo Rosario/RC RC	.50
238	Jorge Sosa/RC RC	.50
239	Ken Huckaby/RC RC	.50
240	Mike Moriarty/RC RC	.50
241	Kirk Saarloos/RC	1.00
242	Kevin Frederick/RC RC	.50
243	Aaron Guiel/RC	.50
244	Jose Rodriguez/RC	.50
245	So Taguchi/RC	1.00
246	Albert Pujols	1.50
247	Derek Jeter	1.50
248	Brian Giles	.10
249	Mike Cameron	.10
250	Josh Beckett	.25
251	Ken Griffey Jr./SP	1.50
252	Aramis Ramirez	.10
253	Miguel Tejada	.25
254	Carlos Delgado	.25
255	Pedro J. Martinez	.60
256	Raul Mondesi	.10
257	Roger Clemens	.75
258	Gary Sheffield	.25
259	Jose Vidro	.10
260	Alex Rodriguez	1.25
261	Larry Walker	.10
262	Mark Mulder	.20
263	Scott Rolen	.60
264	Tim Hudson	.20
265	Manny Ramirez	.60
266	Rich Aurilia	.10
267	Roy Oswalt	.10
268	Mark Grace	.15
269	Lance Berkman	.10
270	Nomar Garciaparra	1.00
271	Barry Bonds	1.50
272	Ryan Klesko	.10
273	Ichiro Suzuki	1.00
274	Shawn Green	.10
275	Darin Erstad	.40
276	Bernie Williams	.30
277	Greg Maddux/SP	1.00
278	Eric Hinske	.10
279	Randy Johnson	.60
280	Todd Helton	.60
281	Sammy Sosa/SP	1.00
282	Nick Johnson	.10
283	Jose Cruz Jr.	.10
284	Frank Thomas	.60
285	Tsuyoshi Shinjo	.10
286	Troy Glaus	.60
287	Jason Giambi	.10
288	Chipper Jones/SP	1.00
289	Roberto Alomar	.30
290	Bobby Hill	.10
291	Garret Anderson	.10
292	Andruw Jones	.60
293	Luis Gonzalez	.15
294	Mike Mussina	.30
295	Ivan Rodriguez/SP	.75
296	Barry Larkin	.10
297	Kazuhiro Sasaki	.10
298	Alfonso Soriano	.50
299	Jeff Bagwell/SP	.75
300	Bobby Abreu	.10
301	Ben Sheets	.20
302	Curt Schilling	.40
303	Jim Thome	.10
304	Kerry Wood	.50
305	Mark Buehrle	.10
306	Rickey Henderson	.60
307	Rafael Palmeiro	.50
308	Jim Edmonds	.10
309	Mike Piazza	1.00
310	Edgar Martinez	.10
311	Tom Glavine	.25
312	Adrian Beltre	.10
313	Adam Dunn	.40
314	Craig Biggio	.10
315	Vladimir Guerrero/SP	1.00
316	Bret Boone	.10
317	Hideo Nomo/SP	.75
318	Jeff Kent	.10
319	Juan Gonzalez	.60
320	Sean Casey	.10
321	C.C. Sabathia	.10
322	J.D. Drew	.20
323	Torii Hunter/SP	.40
324	Chan Ho Park	.10
325	Mike Sweeney	.10
326	Javier Vazquez	.10
327	Jorge Posada	.25
328	Barry Zito	.25
329	Willie McCovey	.50
330	Kevin Brown	.10
331	Mo Vaughn	.10
332	Carlos Beltran	.40
333	Bobby Doerr	.50
334	Matt Morris	.10
335	Trot Nixon	.10
336	Magglio Ordonez	.25
337	Paul LoDuca	.10
338	Phil Nevin	.10
339	Eric Chavez	.20
340	Corey Patterson	.10
341	Richie Sexson	.10
342	Pat Burrell	.25
343	Freddy Garcia	.10
344	Bartolo Colon	.10
345	Cliff Floyd	.10
346	Deivis Santos/RC	.50
347	Felix Escalona/RC RC	.50
348	Miguel Asencio/RC RC	.50
349	Takahito Nomura/RC RC	.50
350	Jorge Padilla/RC	.50
351	Vladimir Guerrero	.60
352	Ichiro Suzuki	1.00
353	Jay Gibbons	.10
354	Alfonso Soriano	.50
355	Mark Buehrle	.20
356	Shawn Green	.20
357	Barry Larkin	.10
358	Josh Fogg	.10
359	Shannon Stewart	.10
360	Andruw Jones	.60
361	Juan Gonzalez	.60
362	Ken Griffey Jr.	1.00
363	Tim Hudson	.20
364	Roy Oswalt/SP	.50
365	Carlos Delgado	.40
366	Albert Pujols/SP	2.00
367	Willie Stargell	.25
368	Roger Clemens	.75
369	Luis Gonzalez	.25
370	Barry Zito	.25
371	Alex Rodriguez	1.25
372	Troy Glaus	.60
373	Vladimir Guerrero	.60
374	Jeff Bagwell	.60
375	Randy Johnson	.60
376	Manny Ramirez	.60
377	Derek Jeter/SP	2.00
378	C.C. Sabathia	.10
379	Rickey Henderson	.60
380	J.D. Drew	.20
381	Nomar Garciaparra	1.00
382	Darin Erstad	.40
383	Ben Sheets	.20
384	Frank Thomas	.60
385	Barry Bonds	1.50
386	Pedro J. Martinez	.60
387	Mark Mulder	.20
388	Greg Maddux	.75
389	Todd Helton	.60
390	Lance Berkman	.10
391	Sammy Sosa	1.00
392	Mike Piazza	1.00
393	Chipper Jones	.75
394	Adam Dunn	.40
395	Jason Giambi	.50
396	Eric Chavez	.20
397	Bobby Abreu	.10
398	Aramis Ramirez	.10
399	Paul LoDuca	.10
400	Miguel Tejada	.25

Aqueous Glossy

Stars (1-400): 3-5X
Average of 1:Box

All-Stars

NM/M
Complete Set (25): 90.00
Common Player: 2.00
Inserted 1:30

#	Player	Price
1	George Brett	8.00
2	Rickey Henderson	4.00
3	Mike Schmidt	6.00
4	Vladimir Guerrero	3.00
5	Tony Gwynn	3.00
6	Curt Schilling	2.00
7	Don Mattingly	8.00
8	Roberto Alomar	3.00
9	Cal Ripken Jr.	8.00
10	Carlton Fisk	2.00
11	Roger Clemens	5.00
12	Jeff Bagwell	3.00
13	Kirby Puckett	8.00
14	Nolan Ryan	10.00
15	Ryne Sandberg	5.00
16	Ivan Rodriguez	2.00
17	Sammy Sosa	5.00
18	Greg Maddux	5.00
19	Alex Rodriguez	8.00
20	Todd Helton	2.00
21	Randy Johnson	3.00
22	Troy Glaus	2.00
23	Ichiro Suzuki	6.00
24	Barry Bonds	8.00
25	Derek Jeter	10.00

Champions

NM/M
Complete Set (25): 75.00

Common Player: 2.00
Production 800 Sets

#	Player	Price
1	Nolan Ryan	10.00
2	George Brett	6.00
3	Edgar Martinez	2.00
4	Mike Schmidt	6.00
5	Randy Johnson	3.00
6	Tony Gwynn	4.00
7	John Smoltz	2.00
8	Roger Clemens	4.00
9	Mel Ott	2.00
10	Todd Helton	3.00
11	Bernie Williams	2.00
12	Troy Glaus	3.00
13	Steve Carlton	2.00
14	Ryne Sandberg	4.00
15	Ted Williams	8.00
16	Alex Rodriguez	8.00
17	Lou Boudreau	2.00
18	Luis Gonzalez	2.00
19	Rickey Henderson	3.00
20	Jose Canseco	2.00
21	Stan Musial	5.00
22	Randy Johnson	3.00
23	Don Mattingly	6.00
24	Nomar Garciaparra	5.00
25	Wade Boggs	4.00

Champions Materials

NM/M
Common Player: 8.00
Varying quantities produced

#	Player	Price
1	Nolan Ryan/78	65.00
2	George Brett/80	30.00
3	Edgar Martinez/92	10.00
4	Mike Schmidt/80	40.00
5	Randy Johnson/94	15.00
6	Tony Gwynn/84	20.00
7	John Smoltz/96	8.00
8	Roger Clemens/88	20.00
10	Todd Helton/100	10.00
11	Bernie Williams/98	10.00
12	Troy Glaus/100	10.00
13	Steve Carlton/80	15.00
14	Ryne Sandberg/90	40.00
15	Ted Williams/42	200.00
16	Alex Rodriguez/96	20.00
17	Lou Boudreau/44	15.00
18	Luis Gonzalez/99	8.00
19	Rickey Henderson/82	20.00
21	Stan Musial/50	60.00
22	Randy Johnson/88	15.00
23	Don Mattingly/84	60.00
24	Nomar Garciaparra/100	30.00
25	Wade Boggs/88	15.00

Gamers

NM/M
Common Player: 3.00
Varying quantities produced

#	Player	Price
1	Alfonso Soriano/400	8.00
2	Shawn Green/500	5.00
3	Curt Schilling/500	8.00
4	Hideo Nomo/100	20.00
5	Toby Hall/500	4.00
6	Andruw Jones/500	4.00
7	Cliff Floyd/500	3.00
8	Mark Ellis/500	4.00
9	Gabe Kapler/500	3.00
10	Andres Galarraga/500	3.00
11	Freddy Garcia/500	3.00
12	Tsuyoshi Shinjo/200	4.00
13	Robin Ventura/500	3.00
14	Paul LoDuca/500	3.00
15	Manny Ramirez/500	8.00
16	Garret Anderson/250	5.00
17	Joe Kennedy/500	3.00
18	Roger Clemens/500	15.00
19	Gary Sheffield/500	6.00
20	Vernon Wells/500	4.00
22	Hideo Nomo/100	40.00
23	Tim Hudson/500	6.00
24	Larry Bigbie/500	4.00
25	Larry Walker/500	4.00
27	John Olerud/500	3.00
28	Chipper Jones/500	8.00
29	Tony Gwynn/500	10.00
30	Juan Gonzalez/500	8.00
31	Jacque Jones/500	5.00
32	Frank Thomas/500	8.00
33	Luis Gonzalez/500	4.00
34	Geoff Jenkins/500	6.00
35	J.D. Drew/500	5.00
36	Edgardo Alfonzo/500	4.00

ABBREVIATIONS

RC - Rookie Class
SP - Short Print

#	Player	NM/M
37	Todd Helton/500	8.00
38	Brad Penny/500	4.00
39	Robert Fick/500	8.00
40	Will Clark/500	15.00
41	Tony Armas Jr./500	4.00
42	Nick Johnson/400	3.00
43	Ben Grieve/500	3.00
44	Vladimir Guerrero/500	8.00
45	Jason Jennings/500	3.00
46	Carlos Lee/500	3.00
47	Carlos Delgado/500	6.00
48	Chan Ho Park/500	3.00
49	Juan Diaz/500	3.00
50	Alex Rodriguez/400	15.00

Hit List

NM/M
Complete Set (20): 40.00
Common Player: 1.00
Production 1,500 Sets

#	Player	Price
1	Ichiro Suzuki	4.00
2	Shawn Green	1.00
3	Alex Rodriguez	5.00
4	Nomar Garciaparra	4.00
5	Derek Jeter	6.00
6	Barry Bonds	6.00
7	Mike Piazza	4.00
8	Albert Pujols	4.00
9	Chipper Jones	3.00
10	Sammy Sosa	4.00
11	Rickey Henderson	2.00
12	Frank Thomas	2.00
13	Jeff Bagwell	2.00
14	Vladimir Guerrero	2.00
15	Todd Helton	2.00
16	Adam Dunn	1.00
17	Rafael Palmeiro	2.00
18	Manny Ramirez	2.00
19	Lance Berkman	1.00
20	Jason Giambi	1.50

Hit List Total Bases

NM/M
Common Player:
Numbered to career high total bases.

#	Player	Price
1	Ichiro Suzuki/Base/316	15.00
2	Shawn Green/Bat/370	5.00
3	Alex Rodriguez/Bat/393	15.00
4	Nomar Garciaparra/Bat/365	10.00
5	Derek Jeter/346/Base	20.00
6	Barry Bonds/Base/411	20.00
7	Mike Piazza/Bat/355	10.00
8	Albert Pujols/Base/360	10.00
9	Chipper Jones/Bat/359	8.00
10	Sammy Sosa/Base/425	10.00
11	Rickey Henderson/Bat/285	10.00
12	Frank Thomas/Bat/364	8.00
13	Jeff Bagwell/Bat/363	8.00
14	Vladimir Guerrero/Bat/379	8.00
15	Todd Helton/Bat/405	8.00
16	Adam Dunn/Bat/141	8.00
17	Rafael Palmeiro/Bat/356	8.00
18	Manny Ramirez/Bat/346	8.00
19	Lance Berkman/Bat/358	5.00
20	Jason Giambi/Bat/343	6.00

Making History

NM/M
Complete Set (10): 30.00
Common Player: 2.00
Production 800 Sets

#	Player	Price
1	Rafael Palmeiro	2.00
2	Roger Clemens	5.00
3	Greg Maddux	4.00
4	Randy Johnson	3.00
5	Barry Bonds	8.00
6	Mike Piazza	6.00
7	Roberto Alomar	2.00
8	Rickey Henderson	2.00
9	Sammy Sosa	
10	Tom Glavine	2.00

Making History Materials

NM/M
Production 100 Sets

#	Player	Price
1	Rafael Palmeiro	15.00
2	Roger Clemens	20.00
3	Greg Maddux	15.00
4	Randy Johnson	10.00
5	Barry Bonds/Base	20.00
6	Mike Piazza	15.00
7	Roberto Alomar	8.00
8	Rickey Henderson	25.00
9	Sammy Sosa/Base	15.00
10	Tom Glavine	10.00

Mound Marvels

NM/M
Complete Set (15): 30.00
Common Player: 1.00
Inserted 1:40

#	Player	Price
1	Roger Clemens	6.00
2	Matt Morris	1.00
3	Pedro J. Martinez	5.00
4	Randy Johnson	5.00
5	Wade Miller	1.00
6	Tim Hudson	1.50
7	Mike Mussina	3.00
8	C.C. Sabathia	1.00
9	Kazuhiro Sasaki	1.00
10	Curt Schilling	4.00
11	Hideo Nomo	2.50
12	Roger Clemens	6.00
13	Mark Buehrle	1.00
14	Barry Zito	1.50
15	Roy Oswalt	1.50

Mound Marvels High Heat

NM/M
Production 100 Sets

#	Player	Price
1	Roger Clemens	25.00
2	Matt Morris	10.00
3	Pedro J. Martinez	20.00
4	Randy Johnson	15.00
5	Wade Miller	8.00
6	Tim Hudson	10.00
7	Mike Mussina	15.00
8	C.C. Sabathia	10.00
9	Kazuhiro Sasaki	10.00
10	Curt Schilling	15.00
11	Hideo Nomo	40.00
12	Roger Clemens	25.00
13	Mark Buehrle	8.00
14	Barry Zito	15.00
15	Roy Oswalt	8.00

Nifty Fifty Bats

NM/M
Common Player: 5.00
Production 50 Sets

#	Player	Price
1	Alex Rodriguez	20.00
2	Kerry Wood	15.00
3	Ivan Rodriguez	15.00
4	Geronimo Gil	5.00
5	Vladimir Guerrero	15.00
6	Corky Miller	5.00
7	Todd Helton	12.00
8	Rickey Henderson	15.00
9	Andruw Jones	10.00
10	Barry Bonds/Ball	30.00
11	Tom Glavine	10.00
12	Mark Teixeira	10.00
13	Mike Piazza	15.00
14	Austin Kearns	8.00
15	Rickey Henderson	15.00
16	Derek Jeter/Ball	20.00
17	Barry Larkin	8.00
18	Jeff Bagwell	10.00
19	Bernie Williams	10.00
20	Frank Thomas	10.00
21	Lance Berkman	8.00
22	Marlon Byrd	6.00
23	Randy Johnson	15.00
24	Ichiro Suzuki/Ball	40.00
25	Darin Erstad	8.00
26	Jason Lane	5.00
27	Roberto Alomar	8.00
28	Ken Griffey Jr./Ball	20.00
29	Tsuyoshi Shinjo	8.00
30	Pedro Martinez	15.00
31	Rickey Henderson	15.00
32	Albert Pujols/Ball	20.00
33	Nomar Garciaparra	15.00
34	Troy Glaus	10.00
35	Chipper Jones	15.00
36	Adam Dunn	8.00
37	Jason Giambi/Ball	10.00
38	Greg Maddux	20.00
39	Mike Piazza	15.00
40	So Taguchi	8.00
41	Manny Ramirez	15.00
42	Scott Rolen	15.00
43	Sammy Sosa/Ball	15.00
44	Shawn Green	8.00
45	Rickey Henderson	15.00
46	Alex Rodriguez	20.00
47	Hideo Nomo	30.00
48	Kazuhisa Ishii	8.00
49	Luis Gonzalez	8.00
50	Jim Thome	15.00

Nifty Fifty Jersey

NM/M
Common Player: 5.00
Production 50 Sets

#	Player	Price
2	Kerry Wood	15.00
3	Ivan Rodriguez	15.00
4	Geronimo Gil	5.00
5	Vladimir Guerrero	15.00
6	Corky Miller	5.00
7	Todd Helton	12.00
8	Rickey Henderson	15.00
9	Andruw Jones	10.00
10	Tom Glavine	10.00
11	Mark Teixeira	10.00
12	Mike Piazza	15.00
13	Austin Kearns	8.00
14	Rickey Henderson	15.00
15	Derek Jeter/Base	20.00
16	Barry Larkin	8.00
17	Jeff Bagwell	10.00
18	Bernie Williams	10.00
19	Frank Thomas	10.00
20	Lance Berkman	8.00
21	Marlon Byrd	8.00
22	Randy Johnson	15.00
23	Ichiro Suzuki/Base	40.00
24	Darin Erstad	8.00
25	Jason Lane	5.00
26	Roberto Alomar	10.00
27	Ken Griffey Jr./Base	20.00
28	Tsuyoshi Shinjo	8.00
29	Pedro Martinez	15.00
30	Rickey Henderson	15.00
31	Albert Pujols/Base	20.00
32	Nomar Garciaparra	15.00
33	Troy Glaus	15.00
34	Chipper Jones	15.00
35	Adam Dunn	8.00
36	Jason Giambi/Base	15.00
37	Greg Maddux	20.00
38	Mike Piazza	15.00
39	So Taguchi	15.00
40	Manny Ramirez	15.00
41	Scott Rolen	15.00
42	Sammy Sosa/Base	15.00
43	Shawn Green	10.00
44	Rickey Henderson	15.00
45	Alex Rodriguez	20.00
46	Hideo Nomo	30.00
47	Kazuhisa Ishii	8.00
49	Luis Gonzalez	15.00
50	Jim Thome	15.00

Nifty Fifty Combos

NM/M
Production 50 Sets
All bat & jerseys unless noted.

#	Player	Price
1	Alex Rodriguez	30.00
2	Kerry Wood	20.00
3	Ivan Rodriguez	20.00
4	Geronimo Gil	10.00
5	Vladimir Guerrero	20.00
6	Corky Miller	10.00
7	Todd Helton	20.00
8	Rickey Henderson	25.00
9	Andruw Jones	15.00
10	Barry Bonds/Base/Ball	40.00
11	Tom Glavine	20.00
12	Mark Teixeira	20.00
13	Mike Piazza	25.00
14	Austin Kearns	15.00
15	Rickey Henderson	25.00
16	Derek Jeter/Base/Ball	30.00
17	Barry Larkin	15.00
18	Jeff Bagwell	20.00
19	Bernie Williams	20.00
20	Frank Thomas	20.00
21	Lance Berkman	15.00
22	Marlon Byrd	15.00
23	Randy Johnson	20.00
24	Ichiro Suzuki/Base/Ball	60.00
25	Darin Erstad	15.00
26	Jason Lane	10.00
27	Roberto Alomar	15.00
28	Ken Griffey Jr./Ball/Base	25.00
29	Tsuyoshi Shinjo	10.00
30	Pedro Martinez	20.00
31	Rickey Henderson	25.00
32	Albert Pujols/Base/Ball	50.00
33	Nomar Garciaparra	30.00
34	Troy Glaus	15.00
35	Chipper Jones	15.00
36	Adam Dunn	15.00
37	Jason Giambi/Base	20.00
38	Greg Maddux	25.00
39	Mike Piazza	25.00
40	So Taguchi	15.00
41	Manny Ramirez	20.00
42	Scott Rolen	20.00
43	Sammy Sosa/Base/Ball	25.00
44	Shawn Green	10.00
45	Rickey Henderson	25.00
46	Alex Rodriguez	30.00
47	Hideo Nomo	30.00
48	Kazuhisa Ishii	15.00
49	Luis Gonzalez	8.00
50	Jim Thome	20.00

On The Record

NM/M
Complete Set (15): 60.00
Common Player: 3.00
Production 800 Sets

#	Player	Price
1	Ty Cobb	6.00
2	Jimmie Foxx	4.00
3	Lou Gehrig	10.00
4	Dale Murphy	5.00
5	Steve Carlton	3.00
6	Randy Johnson	4.00
7	Greg Maddux	6.00
8	Roger Clemens	8.00
9	Yogi Berra	5.00
10	Don Mattingly	8.00
11	Rickey Henderson	4.00
12	Stan Musial	6.00
13	Jackie Robinson	10.00
14	Roberto Clemente	10.00
15	Mike Schmidt	6.00

On the Record Materials

NM/M
Varying quantities produced

#	Player	Price
3	Lou Gehrig/34	220.00
4	Dale Murphy/83	10.00
5	Steve Carlton/72	10.00
6	Randy Johnson/100	10.00
7	Greg Maddux/93	15.00
8	Roger Clemens/87	20.00
9	Yogi Berra/51	12.00
10	Don Mattingly/85	25.00
11	Rickey Henderson/90	15.00
13	Jackie Robinson/49	50.00
14	Roberto Clemente/66	75.00
15	Mike Schmidt/80	25.00

Power Alley

NM/M
Complete Set (15): 30.00
Common Player: 1.00
Production 1,500 Sets
Die-Cut Parallel: 1.5-2X
Production 100 Sets

#	Player	Price
1	Barry Bonds	6.00
2	Sammy Sosa	3.00
3	Lance Berkman	1.00
4	Luis Gonzalez	1.00
5	Alex Rodriguez	4.00
6	Troy Glaus	2.00
7	Vladimir Guerrero	2.00
8	Jason Giambi	1.50
9	Mike Piazza	3.00
10	Todd Helton	2.00
11	Mike Schmidt	4.00
12	Don Mattingly	4.00
13	Andre Dawson	1.50
14	Reggie Jackson	2.00
15	Dale Murphy	1.50

Signature Marks

NM/M
Common Autograph: 5.00
Varying quantities produced
Many not priced, lack of market info.

What If -'80

NM/M
Complete Set (25): 75.00
Common Player: 1.50
Inserted 1:12

#	Player	Price
2	Eric Hinske/200	8.00
3	Cesar Izturis/200	5.00
4	Roy Oswalt/100	20.00
6	Jack Cust/200	5.00
7	Nick Johnson/200	8.00
8	Jason Hart/200	5.00
8	Mark Prior/100	30.00
9	Luis Garcia/200	5.00
10	Jay Gibbons/200	10.00
11	Corky Miller/200	5.00
12	Antonio Perez/100	8.00
13	Andres Torres/200	5.00
14	Brandon Claussen/200	8.00
16	Ed Rogers/200	5.00
17	Jorge Padilla/200	5.00
18	Francis Beltran/200	5.00
19	Kip Wells/200	6.00
20	Ryan Ludwick/200	8.00
21	Juan Cruz/100	8.00
22	Juan Diaz/200	5.00
22	Marcus Giles/200	10.00
23	Joe Kennedy/200	5.00
24	Wade Miller/100	10.00
25	Corey Patterson/100	10.00
26	Angel Berroa/200	10.00
27	Ricardo Rodriguez/200	5.00
28	Toby Hall/200	8.00
29	Carlos Pena/50	8.00
30	Jason Jennings/200	8.00
31	Rafael Soriano/200	10.00
32	Marlon Byrd/100	10.00
34	Rodrigo Rosario/200	5.00
35	Brent Abernathy/200	5.00
36	Bill Hall/200	5.00
37	Fernando Rodney/200	10.00
38	Josh Pearce/200	8.00
39	Brian Lawrence/200	5.00
42	Tim Redding/200	5.00
43	Jeremy Giambi/200	8.00
43	Victor Martinez/200	25.00
44	Hank Blalock/50	25.00
46	Geronimo Gil/200	5.00
47	So Taguchi/200	25.00
48	Austin Kearns/200	15.00
49	Alfonso Soriano/50	40.00

What If - Rookies

NM/M
Complete Set (23): 75.00
Common Player: 1.50
Inserted 1:12

#	Player	Price
1	Wade Boggs	6.00
2	Ryne Sandberg	6.00
3	Cal Ripken Jr.	12.50
4	Tony Gwynn	6.00
5	Don Mattingly	10.00
6	Wade Boggs	6.00
7	Roger Clemens	7.50
8	Kirby Puckett	6.00
9	Eric Davis	1.50
10	Dwight Gooden	1.50
11	Eric Davis	1.50
12	Roger Clemens	7.50
13	Kirby Puckett	6.00
14	Dwight Gooden	1.50
15	Barry Bonds	12.50
16	Will Clark	1.50
17	Barry Larkin	1.50
18	Greg Maddux	6.00
19	Rafael Palmeiro	4.00
20	Craig Biggio	1.50
21	Gary Sheffield	1.50
22	Randy Johnson	5.00
23	Curt Schilling	1.50

What If -'78

NM/M
Complete Set (27): 75.00
Common Player: 1.50
Inserted 1:12

#	Player	Price
1	Paul Molitor	4.00
2	Alan Trammell	1.50
3	Ozzie Smith	6.00
4	George Brett	10.00
5	Johnny Bench	6.00
6	Rod Carew	2.00
7	Carlton Fisk	1.50
8	Reggie Jackson	5.00
9	Dale Murphy	2.00
10	Joe Morgan	1.50
11	Eddie Murray	4.00
12	Jim Palmer	4.00
13	Tom Seaver	4.00
14	Willie Stargell	2.00
15	Dave Winfield	2.00
16	Dave Parker	1.50
17	Mike Schmidt	8.00
18	Eddie Mathews	4.00
19	Lou Brock	1.50
20	Willie McCovey	1.50
21	Andre Dawson	1.50
22	Dennis Eckersley	4.00
23	Robin Yount	4.00
24	Nolan Ryan	15.00
25	Steve Carlton	1.50
26	Paul Molitor	4.00
27	Ozzie Smith	6.00

#	Player	Price
1	Rickey Henderson	3.00
2	Johnny Bench	6.00
3	George Brett	10.00
4	Steve Carlton	2.50
5	Rod Carew	2.00
6	Gary Carter	1.50
7	Carlton Fisk	1.50
8	Reggie Jackson	5.00
9	Dave Parker	1.50
10	Dale Murphy	3.00
11	Paul Molitor	4.00
12	Mike Schmidt	8.00
13	Alan Trammell	1.50
14	Dave Winfield	4.00
15	Robin Yount	4.00
16	Joe Morgan	1.50
17	Jim Palmer	1.50
18	Nolan Ryan	15.00
19	Tom Seaver	4.00
20	Ozzie Smith	6.00
21	Willie McCovey	1.50
22	Andre Dawson	1.50
23	Eddie Murray	2.00
24	Al Kaline	5.00
25	Duke Snider	4.00

LCS Programs

A perforated sheet of Donruss Originals cards was inserted into some of the programs sold for the American and National League Championship Series. The 8-1/2" x 11" sheet features eight player cards and a header card advertising the brand. Each 2-1/2" x 3-1/2" card is perforated on all sides and differs from the regularly issued version only in the card number on back. Sheet cards have either an "ALCS-" or "NLCS-" prefix to the number. Other programs could be found with similar sheets of Donruss Diamond Kings, Donruss Studio or Playoff Piece of the Game cards.

NM/M
Complete Sheet Set (2): 16.00
Common Player: .50

ALCS SHEET 8.00

#	Player	Price
9	Manny Ramirez (1986 style)	1.00
10	Nolan Ryan (All-Stars)	2.50
11	Roger Clemens (Champions)	1.50
12	Alex Rodriguez (All-Stars)	2.00
13	Paul Konerko (1982 style)	.50
14	Don Mattingly (All-Stars)	1.50
15	Miguel Tejada (1984 style)	.50
16	Rickey Henderson (Making History)	.50
---	Header Card	.10

NLCS SHEET 8.00

#	Player	Price
25	Mike Schmidt (Champions)	2.00
26	Andruw Jones (1986 style)	1.00
27	Lance Berkman (Power Alley)	.50
28	Vladimir Guerrero (All-Stars)	1.00
29	Roberto Clemente (On The Record)	3.00
30	Austin Kearns (1982 style)	.50
31	Curt Schilling (All-Stars)	.50
32	Kazuhisa Ishii (1984 style)	1.00
---	Header Card	.10

2002 Donruss Studio Samples

Each issue of the September 2002, Beckett Baseball Card Monthly included a sample 2002 Donruss Studio card rubber-cemented inside. The cards differ from the issued version only in the appearance on back of a (usually) silver-foil "SAMPLE" notation. Some cards were produced with the overprint in gold-foil, in much more limited quantities. The number of different players' cards involved in the promotion is unknown.

	NM/M
Common Player:	.10
Stars:	1.5-2X
Gold:	10X

2002 Donruss Studio

BRIAN GILES / OF

	NM/M
Complete Set (250):	150.00
Common Player:	.25
Common (201-250):	3.00
Production 1,500	
Pack (5):	3.00
Box (18):	45.00

#	Player	Price
1	Vladimir Guerrero	.75
2	Chipper Jones	1.00
3	Bobby Abreu	.25
4	Barry Zito	.40
5	Larry Walker	.25
6	Miguel Tejada	.40
7	Mike Sweeney	.25
8	Shannon Stewart	.25
9	Sammy Sosa	1.50
10	Bud Smith	.25
11	Wilson Betemit	.25
12	Kevin Brown	.35
13	Ellis Burks	.25
14	Pat Burrell	.40
15	Cliff Floyd	.25
16	Marcus Giles	.25
17	Troy Glaus	.75
18	Barry Larkin	.25
19	Carlos Lee	.25
20	Brian Lawrence	.25
21	Paul LoDuca	.25
22	Ben Grieve	.25
23	Shawn Green	.40
24	Mike Cameron	.40
25	Roger Clemens	1.25
26	Joe Crede	.25
27	Jose Cruz	.25
28	Jeremy Affeldt	.25
29	Adrian Beltre	.25
30	Josh Beckett	.50
31	Roberto Alomar	.40
32	Toby Hall	.25
33	Mike Hampton	.25
34	Eric Milton	.25
35	Eric Munson	.25
36	Trot Nixon	.25
37	Roy Oswalt	.40
38	Chan Ho Park	.25
39	Charles Johnson	.25
40	Nick Johnson	.25
41	Tim Hudson	.40
42	Cristian Guzman	.25
43	Drew Henson	.35
44	Mark Grace	.35
45	Luis Gonzalez	.35
46	Pedro J. Martinez	.75
47	Joe Mays	.25
48	Jorge Posada	.40
49	Aramis Ramirez	.25
50	Kip Wells	.25
51	Moises Alou	.25
52	Omar Vizquel	.25
53	Ichiro Suzuki	1.50
54	Jimmy Rollins	.40
55	Freddy Garcia	.25
56	Steve Green	.25
57	Brian Jordan	.25
58	Paul Konerko	.35
59	Jack Cust	.25
60	Sean Casey	.25
61	Bret Boone	.25
62	Hideo Nomo	.60
63	Magglio Ordonez	.40
64	Frank Thomas	.75
65	Josh Towers	.25
66	Javier Vazquez	.25
67	Robin Ventura	.25
68	Aubrey Huff	.25
69	Richard Hidalgo	.25
70	Brandon Claussen	.25
71	Bartolo Colon	.25
72	John Buck	.25
73	Dee Brown	.25
74	Barry Bonds	2.00
75	Jason Giambi	.50
76	Erick Almonte	.25
77	Ryan Dempster	.25
78	Jim Edmonds	.25
79	Jay Gibbons	.25
80	Shigetoshi Hasegawa	.25
81	Todd Helton	.75
82	Erik Bedard	.25
83	Carlos Beltran	.50
84	Rafael Soriano	.25
85	Gary Sheffield	.40
86	Richie Sexson	.25
87	Mike Rivera	.25
88	Jose Ortiz	.25
89	Abraham Nunez	.25
90	Dave Williams	.25
91	Preston Wilson	.25
92	Jason Jennings	.25
93	Juan Diaz	.25
94	Steve Smyth	.25
95	Phil Nevin	.25
96	John Olerud	.25
97	Brad Penny	.25
98	Andy Pettitte	.40
99	Juan Pierre	.25
100	Manny Ramirez	.75
101	Edgardo Alfonzo	.25
102	Michael Cuddyer	.25
103	Johnny Damon	.40
104	Carlos Zambrano	.35
105	Jose Vidro	.25
106	Tsuyoshi Shinjo	.25
107	Ed Rogers	.25
108	Scott Rolen	.75
109	Mariano Rivera	.35
110	Tim Redding	.25
111	Josh Phelps	.25
112	Gabe Kapler	.25
113	Edgar Martinez	.25
114	Fred McGriff	.25
115	Raul Mondesi	.25
116	Wade Miller	.25
117	Mike Mussina	.40
118	Rafael Palmeiro	.65
119	Adam Johnson	.25
120	Rickey Henderson	.75
121	Bill Hall	.25
122	Ken Griffey Jr.	1.50
123	Geronimo Gil	.25
124	Robert Fick	.25
125	Darin Erstad	.50
126	Brandon Duckworth	.25
127	Garret Anderson	.25
128	Pedro Feliz	.25
129	Jeff Cirillo	.25
130	Brian Giles	.25
131	Craig Biggio	.25
132	Willie Harris	.25
133	Doug Davis	.25
134	Jeff Kent	.25
135	Terrence Long	.25
136	Carlos Delgado	.50
137	Tino Martinez	.25
138	Donaldo Mendez	.25
139	Sean Douglass	.25
140	Eric Chavez	.40
141	Rick Ankiel	.25
142	Jeremy Giambi	.25
143	Juan Pena	.25
144	Bernie Williams	.40
145	Craig Wilson	.25
146	Ricardo Rodriguez	.25
147	Albert Pujols	1.50
148	Antonio Perez	.25
149	Russ Ortiz	.25
150	Corky Miller	.25
151	Rich Aurilia	.25
152	Kerry Wood	.50
153	Joe Thurston	.25
154	Jeff Deardorff RC	.25
155	Jermaine Dye	.25
156	Andruw Jones	.75
157	Victor Martinez	.25
158	Nick Neugebauer	.25
159	Matt Morris	.25
160	Casey Fossum	.25
161	J.D. Drew	.40
162	Matt Childers RC	.50
163	Mark Buehrle	.25
164	Jeff Bagwell	.75
165	Kazuhiro Sasaki	.25
166	Ben Sheets	.40
167	Alex Rodriguez	1.50
168	Adam Pettyjohn	.25
169	Chris Snelling RC	.50
170	Robert Person	.25
171	Juan Uribe	.25
172	Mo Vaughn	.25
173	Alfredo Amezaga	.25
174	Ryan Drese	.25
175	Corey Thurman RC	.25
176	Jim Thome	.25
177	Orlando Cabrera	.25
178	Eric Cyr RC	.25
179	Greg Maddux	1.00
180	Earl Snyder RC	.25
181	C.C. Sabathia	.25
182	Mark Mulder	.40
183	Jose Mieses	.25
184	Joe Kennedy	.25
185	Randy Johnson	.75
186	Tom Glavine	.40
187	Eric Junge RC	.25
188	Mike Piazza	1.50
189	Corey Patterson	.40
190	Carlos Pena	.25
191	Curt Schilling	.40
192	Nomar Garciaparra	1.50
193	Lance Berkman	.25
194	Ryan Klesko	.25
195	Ivan Rodriguez	.65
196	Alfonso Soriano	.75
197	Derek Jeter	2.00
198	David Justice	.25
199	Juan Gonzalez	.75
200	Adam Dunn	.50
201	Victor Alvarez RC	3.00
202	Miguel Asencio RC	3.00
203	Brandon Backe RC	3.00
204	Chris Baker RC	4.00
205	Steve Bechler RC	3.00
206	Francis Beltran RC	4.00
207	Angel Berroa	3.00
208	Hank Blalock	4.00
209	Dewon Brazelton	3.00
210	Sean Burroughs	3.00
211	Marlon Byrd	3.00
212	Raul Chavez RC	4.00
213	Juan Cruz	3.00
214	Jorge De La Rosa RC	3.00
215	Doug DeVore RC	3.00
216	John Ennis RC	3.00
217	Felix Escalona RC	3.00
218	Morgan Ensberg	3.00
219	Cam Esslinger RC	3.00
220	Kevin Frederick RC	3.00
221	Franklyn German RC	3.00
222	Eric Hinske	4.00
223	Ben Howard RC	3.00
224	Orlando Hudson	3.00
225	Travis Hughes RC	5.00
226	Kazuhisa Ishii RC	6.00
227	Ryan Jamison RC	3.00
228	Reed Johnson RC	3.00
229	Kyle Kane RC	3.00
230	Austin Kearns	3.00
231	Satoru Komiyama RC	4.00
232	Jason Lane	3.00
233	Jeremy Lambert RC	3.00
234	Anderson Machado RC	4.00
235	Brian Mallette RC	3.00
236	Takahito Nomura RC	3.00
237	Jorge Padilla RC	4.00
238	Luis Ugueto RC	3.00
239	Mark Prior	10.00
240	Rene Reyes RC	3.00
241	Deivis Santos RC	3.00
242	Elio Serrano RC	3.00
243	Tom Shearn RC	3.00
244	Allan Simpson RC	3.00
245	So Taguchi RC	5.00
246	Dennis Tankersley	3.00
247	Mark Teixeira	6.00
248	Matt Thornton	3.00
249	Bobby Hill	3.00
250	Ramon Vazquez	3.00

Proof

Proofs (1-200):	4-8X
Proofs (201-250):	1-2X
Production 100 Sets	

Private Signings

	NM/M
Common Autograph:	5.00

Varying quantities produced

#	Player	Price
1	Vladimir Guerrero/25	75.00
2	Chipper Jones/15	150.00
3	Bobby Abreu/50	20.00
4	Barry Zito/25	50.00
6	Miguel Tejada/50	30.00
7	Mike Sweeney/50	20.00
8	Shannon Stewart/100	10.00
10	Bud Smith/100	5.00
11	Wilson Betemit/250	8.00
12	Kevin Brown/25	45.00
15	Cliff Floyd/50	15.00
16	Marcus Giles/250	5.00
17	Troy Glaus/50	30.00
19	Carlos Lee/25	20.00
20	Brian Lawrence/250	8.00
21	Paul LoDuca/250	5.00
25	Roger Clemens/15	175.00
26	Joe Crede/250	8.00
28	Jeremy Affeldt/250	8.00
29	Adrian Beltre/25	20.00
30	Josh Beckett/25	40.00
31	Roberto Alomar/25	60.00
32	Toby Hall/250	8.00
37	Roy Oswalt/50	20.00
43	Drew Henson/150	20.00
45	Luis Gonzalez/15	50.00
47	Joe Mays/100	8.00
49	Aramis Ramirez/50	20.00
51	Moises Alou/15	30.00
55	Freddy Garcia/50	15.00
56	Steve Green/250	5.00
59	Jack Cust/250	8.00
60	Sean Casey/50	15.00
63	Magglio Ordonez/15	50.00
66	Javier Vazquez/100	15.00
68	Aubrey Huff/250	5.00
69	Richard Hidalgo/25	20.00
70	Brandon Claussen/250	10.00
72	John Buck/250	5.00
76	Dee Brown/250	8.00
76	Erick Almonte/250	8.00
79	Jay Gibbons/250	15.00
81	Todd Helton/15	85.00
84	Erik Bedard/250	15.00
84	Rafael Soriano/250	10.00
85	Gary Sheffield/25	60.00
86	Richie Sexson/50	15.00
87	Mike Rivera/250	5.00
88	Jose Ortiz/250	8.00
89	Abraham Nunez/250	8.00
90	Dave Williams/250	8.00
92	Jason Jennings/250	8.00
93	Juan Diaz/250	8.00
96	Steve Smyth/250	8.00
97	Brad Penny/80	10.00
99	Juan Pierre/100	10.00
100	Manny Ramirez/15	75.00
102	Michael Cuddyer/250	10.00
104	Carlos Zambrano/250	15.00
105	Jose Vidro/100	15.00
107	Ed Rogers/250	8.00
111	Tim Redding/250	5.00
112	Josh Phelps/250	8.00
113	Gabe Kapler/100	5.00
116	Wade Miller/250	8.00
118	Rafael Palmeiro/25	50.00
121	Bill Hall/250	10.00
123	Geronimo Gil/250	8.00
124	Robert Fick/150	10.00
126	Brandon Duckworth/250	8.00
128	Pedro Feliz/250	8.00
130	Brian Giles/15	50.00
131	Craig Biggio/15	40.00
132	Willie Harris/250	5.00
133	Doug Davis/250	8.00
137	Terrence Long/150	10.00
138	Donaldo Mendez/250	5.00
139	Sean Douglass/250	5.00
140	Eric Chavez/15	50.00
141	Rick Ankiel/250	8.00
142	Jeremy Giambi/100	6.00
143	Juan Pena/250	8.00
144	Bernie Williams/75	75.00
145	Craig Wilson/20	20.00
146	Ricardo Rodriguez/250	10.00
147	Albert Pujols/25	120.00
148	Antonio Perez/250	5.00
150	Corky Miller/250	8.00
151	Rich Aurilia/250	20.00
152	Kerry Wood/25	70.00
153	Joe Thurston/250	8.00
154	Jeff Deardorff/250	8.00
155	Jermaine Dye/15	25.00
157	Victor Martinez/250	15.00
158	Nick Neugebauer/150	5.00
160	Casey Fossum/250	8.00
161	J.D. Drew/25	40.00
162	Matt Childers/250	8.00
163	Mark Buehrle/150	10.00
166	Ben Sheets/100	15.00
167	Alex Rodriguez/15	165.00
168	Adam Pettyjohn/250	5.00
169	Chris Snelling/250	10.00
170	Robert Person/250	5.00
171	Juan Uribe/250	5.00
175	Alfredo Amezaga/250	5.00
175	Corey Thurman/250	8.00
178	Eric Cyr/250	5.00
179	Greg Maddux/15	200.00
180	Earl Snyder/250	5.00
181	C.C. Sabathia/50	20.00
182	Mark Mulder/50	20.00
183	Jose Mieses/250	5.00
184	Joe Kennedy/250	5.00
187	Eric Junge/250	5.00
189	Corey Patterson/205	20.00
190	Carlos Pena/250	10.00
191	Curt Schilling/15	80.00
196	Ivan Rodriguez/15	75.00
196	Alfonso Soriano/250	40.00
201	Victor Alvarez/250	5.00
203	Brandon Backe/250	5.00
204	Chris Baker/250	5.00
205	Steve Bechler/250	5.00
206	Francis Beltran/250	5.00
207	Angel Berroa/250	10.00
208	Hank Blalock/100	25.00
209	Dewon Brazelton/200	5.00
210	Sean Burroughs/50	20.00
211	Marlon Byrd/200	5.00
212	Raul Chavez/250	5.00
213	Juan Cruz/50	15.00
214	Jorge De La Rosa/250	5.00
215	Doug DeVore/250	5.00
216	John Ennis/250	5.00
217	Felix Escalona/250	5.00
218	Morgan Ensberg/250	10.00
219	Cam Esslinger/250	5.00
220	Kevin Frederick/250	5.00
221	Franklyn German/250	5.00
222	Eric Hinske/250	8.00
223	Ben Howard/250	8.00
224	Orlando Hudson/250	10.00
225	Travis Hughes/250	10.00
226	Kazuhisa Ishii/50	50.00
227	Ryan Jamison/250	5.00
228	Reed Johnson/250	10.00
229	Kyle Kane/250	5.00
230	Austin Kearns/250	20.00
231	Satoru Komiyama/50	10.00
232	Jason Lane/200	5.00
233	Jeremy Lambert/250	5.00
234	Anderson Machado/200	10.00
235	Brian Mallette/250	5.00
236	Takahito Nomura/100	20.00
237	Jorge Padilla/200	10.00
238	Luis Ugueto/250	5.00
239	Mark Prior/100	40.00
240	Rene Reyes/250	5.00
241	Deivis Santos/250	5.00
243	Tom Shearn/250	5.00
244	Allan Simpson/250	5.00
245	So Taguchi/100	15.00
246	Dennis Tankersley/100	10.00
247	Mark Teixeira/50	35.00
248	Matt Thornton/250	5.00
249	Bobby Hill/100	5.00
250	Ramon Vazquez/250	5.00

Classic Studio

WILLIE McCOVEY • 1B • SAN FRANCISCO GIANTS

	NM/M
Complete Set (25):	90.00
Common Player:	3.00
Production 1,000 Sets	
First Ballot:	3-4X

Print run based on HOF year.

#	Player	Price
1	Kirby Puckett	5.00
2	George Brett	8.00
3	Nolan Ryan	10.00
4	Mike Schmidt	5.00
5	Steve Carlton	3.00
6	Reggie Jackson	5.00
7	Tom Seaver	3.00
8	Joe Morgan	3.00
9	Jim Palmer	3.00
10	Johnny Bench	5.00
11	Willie McCovey	3.00
12	Brooks Robinson	4.00
13	Al Kaline	5.00
14	Stan Musial	6.00
15	Ozzie Smith	6.00
16	Dave Winfield	3.00
17	Robin Yount	3.00
18	Rod Carew	3.00
19	Willie Stargell	3.00
20	Lou Brock	3.00
21	Ernie Banks	5.00
22	Ted Williams	10.00
23	Jackie Robinson	8.00
24	Roberto Clemente	10.00
25	Lou Gehrig	10.00

Classic Studio Autograph

Production 15-20

Diamond Collection

JASON GIAMBI • 1B

	NM/M
Complete Set (25):	65.00
Common Player:	1.50

Inserted 1:17

#	Player	Price
1	Todd Helton	3.00
2	Chipper Jones	4.00
3	Lance Berkman	1.50
4	Derek Jeter	8.00
5	Hideo Nomo	3.00
6	Kazuhisa Ishii	1.50
7	Barry Bonds	8.00
8	Alex Rodriguez	5.00
9	Ichiro Suzuki	5.00
10	Mike Piazza	5.00
11	Jim Thome	1.50
12	Greg Maddux	4.00
13	Jeff Bagwell	3.00
14	Vladimir Guerrero	3.00
15	Ken Griffey Jr.	3.00
16	Jason Giambi	2.50
17	Nomar Garciaparra	5.00
18	Albert Pujols	6.00
19	Manny Ramirez	3.00
20	Pedro J. Martinez	3.00
21	Roger Clemens	4.50
22	Randy Johnson	3.00
23	Mark Prior	2.00
24	So Taguchi	1.50
25	Sammy Sosa	5.00

Diamond Collection Artist's Proof

	NM/M
Common Jersey card:	4.00

Varying quantities produced

#	Player	Price
1	Todd Helton/200	8.00
2	Chipper Jones/150	10.00
3	Lance Berkman/200	6.00
4	Derek Jeter/200/Base	20.00
5	Hideo Nomo/150	25.00
6	Kazuhisa Ishii/150	8.00
7	Barry Bonds/200/Base	25.00
8	Alex Rodriguez/150	15.00
9	Ichiro Suzuki/200/Base	25.00
10	Mike Piazza/150	15.00
11	Jim Thome/150	10.00
12	Greg Maddux/150	15.00
13	Jeff Bagwell/150	8.00
14	Vladimir Guerrero/200	8.00
15	Ken Griffey Jr./200/Base	10.00
16	Jason Giambi/200/Base	6.00
17	Nomar Garciaparra/150	15.00
18	Albert Pujols/Base/200	10.00
19	Manny Ramirez/150	8.00
20	Pedro Martinez/150	8.00
21	Roger Clemens/150	15.00
22	Randy Johnson/150	8.00
23	So Taguchi/200	5.00
25	Sammy Sosa/200/Base	15.00

Hats Off

	NM/M
Common Player:	8.00
Production 100	
MLB Logo:	No Pricing
Production One Set	

#	Player	Price
10	Carlos Lee	10.00
14	Mark Buehrle	10.00
16	Paul LoDuca	10.00
22	Brandon Duckworth	10.00
23	J.D. Drew	12.00
28	Wade Miller	10.00
30	Brian Giles	10.00
31	Lance Berkman	10.00
32	Shannon Stewart	10.00
33	Kazuhisa Ishii/50	20.00
34	Rafael Palmeiro	20.00
36	Roy Oswalt	15.00
37	Jason Lane	10.00
38	Andruw Jones	15.00
39	Brad Penny	10.00
40	Bud Smith	8.00
41	Carlos Beltran	15.00
42	Magglio Ordonez	20.00
43	Craig Biggio	10.00
45	Jeff Bagwell	25.00
47	Juan Cruz	8.00
48	Kerry Wood	25.00
49	Brandon Berger	8.00
50	Juan Pierre	8.00

Leather & Lumber

	NM/M
Common Player:	5.00
Production 200 unless noted.	
Artist's Proofs:	1.5-2X
Production 50	

#	Player	Price
1	Nomar Garciaparra	15.00
2	Jeff Bagwell/150	15.00
3	Alex Rodriguez	15.00
4	Vladimir Guerrero/100	10.00
5	Luis Gonzalez	10.00
6	Chipper Jones	10.00
7	Shawn Green	8.00
8	Kirby Puckett/100	15.00
9	Juan Gonzalez	8.00
10	Troy Glaus	8.00
11	Don Mattingly/100	30.00
12	Todd Helton	10.00

13	Jim Thome	10.00
14	Rickey Henderson	15.00
15	Mike Schmidt/100	35.00
16	Adam Dunn/100	10.00
17	Ivan Rodriguez	10.00
18	Manny Ramirez/150	10.00
19	Tsuyoshi Shinjo	8.00
20	Andruw Jones/150	10.00
21	Roberto Alomar	8.00
22	Lance Berkman	5.00
23	Derek Jeter/50/Ball	30.00
24	Ichiro Suzuki/50/Ball	60.00
25	Mike Piazza	15.00

Masterstrokes

NM/M
Complete Set (25): 50.00
Common Player: 1.50
Inserted 1:17

1	Vladimir Guerrero	3.00
2	Frank Thomas	3.00
3	Alex Rodriguez	6.00
4	Manny Ramirez	3.00
5	Jeff Bagwell	3.00
6	Jim Thome	1.50
7	Ichiro Suzuki	5.00
8	Andruw Jones	3.00
9	Troy Glaus	3.00
10	Chipper Jones	4.00
11	Juan Gonzalez	3.00
12	Lance Berkman	1.50
13	Mike Piazza	5.00
14	Darin Erstad	2.00
15	Albert Pujols	6.00
16	Kazuhisa Ishii	1.50
17	Shawn Green	1.50
18	Rafael Palmeiro	2.00
19	Todd Helton	3.00
20	Carlos Delgado	1.50
21	Ivan Rodriguez	2.00
22	Luis Gonzalez	1.50
23	Derek Jeter	8.00
24	Nomar Garciaparra	5.00
15	J.D. Drew	1.50

Masterstrokes Artist's Proof

NM/M
All Jersey/Bat unless noted
Varying quantities produced

1	Vladimir Guerrero/ 200	15.00
2	Frank Thomas/200	15.00
3	Alex Rodriguez/100	25.00
4	Manny Ramirez/200	10.00
5	Jeff Bagwell/150	10.00
6	Jim Thome/200	15.00
7	Ichiro Suzuki/100/ Ball/Base	50.00
8	Andruw Jones/200	10.00
9	Troy Glaus/200	10.00
10	Chipper Jones/200	15.00
11	Juan Gonzalez/200	10.00
12	Lance Berkman/200	8.00
13	Mike Piazza/200	25.00
14	Darin Erstad/200	10.00
15	Albert Pujols/100/ Ball/Base	30.00
16	Kazuhisa Ishii/200	15.00
17	Shawn Green/200	10.00
18	Rafael Palmeiro/200	20.00
19	Todd Helton/200	15.00
20	Carlos Delgado/200	10.00
21	Ivan Rodriguez/200	15.00
22	Luis Gonzalez/200	10.00
23	Derek Jeter/100/ Ball/Base	35.00
24	Nomar Garciaparra/ 200	25.00
25	J.D. Drew/150	8.00

Spirit of the Game

NM/M
Complete Set (50): 60.00
Common Player: 1.00
Inserted 1:9

1	Alex Rodriguez	5.00
2	Curt Schilling	1.50
3	Hideo Nomo	2.00
4	Derek Jeter	6.00
5	Mike Sweeney	1.00
6	Mike Piazza	4.00
7	Roger Clemens	3.00
8	Shawn Green	1.50

Spirit of the Game
Designated Hitter
EDGAR MARTINEZ • MARINERS

9	Vladimir Guerrero	2.00
10	Carlos Lee	1.00
11	Edgar Martinez	1.00
12	Albert Pujols	5.00
13	Mark Prior	2.00
14	Mark Buehrle	1.00
15	Chipper Jones	3.00
16	Paul LoDuca	1.00
17	Frank Thomas	3.00
18	Randy Johnson	2.00
19	Cliff Floyd	1.00
20	Todd Helton	3.00
21	Luis Gonzalez	1.00
22	Brandon Duckworth	1.00
23	Jason Giambi	1.50
24	Juan Uribe	1.00
25	Dewon Brazelton	1.00
26	J.D. Drew	1.00
27	Troy Glaus	2.00
28	Wade Miller	1.00
29	Darin Erstad	1.50
30	Brian Giles	1.00
31	Lance Berkman	1.50
32	Shannon Stewart	1.00
33	Kazuhisa Ishii	1.00
34	Corey Patterson	1.50
35	Rafael Palmeiro	1.50
36	Roy Oswalt	1.00
37	Jason Lane	1.00
38	Andruw Jones	2.00
39	Brad Penny	1.00
40	Bud Smith	1.00
41	Carlos Beltran	1.50
42	Magglio Ordonez	1.50
43	Craig Biggio	1.00
44	Hank Blalock	1.50
45	Jeff Bagwell	2.00
46	Josh Beckett	1.50
47	Juan Cruz	1.00
48	Kerry Wood	1.50
49	Brandon Berger	1.00
50	Juan Pierre	1.00

Studio Stars

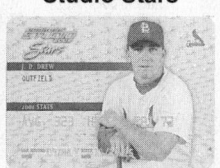

NM/M
Complete Set (50): 60.00
Common Player: 1.00
Production 700 Sets
Golds: 1.5-2X
Production 250 Sets
Platinums: 3-5X
Production 50 Sets

1	Mike Piazza	3.00
2	Ivan Rodriguez	1.50
3	Albert Pujols	4.00
4	Scott Rolen	2.00
5	Alex Rodriguez	4.00
6	Curt Schilling	1.50
7	Vladimir Guerrero	2.00
8	Jim Thome	1.00
9	Derek Jeter	5.00
10	C.C. Sabathia	1.00
11	Sammy Sosa	3.00
12	Adam Dunn	1.50
13	Bernie Williams	1.00
14	Ichiro Suzuki	4.00
15	Barry Bonds	5.00
16	Rickey Henderson	2.00
17	Ken Griffey Jr.	3.00
18	Kazuhisa Ishii	1.00
19	Kerry Wood	1.50
20	Todd Helton	1.50
21	Hideo Nomo	2.00
22	Frank Thomas	3.00
23	Manny Ramirez	2.00
24	Luis Gonzalez	1.00
25	Rafael Palmeiro	1.50
26	Mike Mussina	1.50
27	Roy Oswalt	1.00
28	Darin Erstad	1.50
29	Barry Larkin	1.50
30	Randy Johnson	2.00
31	Tom Glavine	1.00
32	Lance Berkman	1.50
33	Juan Gonzalez	2.00
34	Shawn Green	1.00
35	Nomar Garciaparra	3.00
36	Troy Glaus	2.00
37	Tim Hudson	1.00
38	Carlos Delgado	1.50
39	Jason Giambi	1.50
40	Andruw Jones	2.00
41	Roberto Alomar	1.00
42	Greg Maddux	2.50
43	Pedro J. Martinez	2.00
44	Tony Gwynn	3.00
45	Alfonso Soriano	1.50
46	Chipper Jones	2.50
47	J.D. Drew	1.00
48	Roger Clemens	2.75
49	Barry Zito	1.00
50	Jeff Bagwell	1.50

LCS Programs

A perforated sheet of Donruss Studio cards was inserted into some of the programs sold for the American and National League Championship Series. The 8-1/2" x 11" sheet features eight player cards and a header card advertising the brand. Each 2-1/2" x 3-1/2" card is perforated on all sides and differs from the regularly issued version only in the card number on back. Sheet have either an "ALCS-" or "NLCS-" prefix to the number. Other programs could be found with similar sheets of Donruss Diamond Kings, Donruss Originals or Playoff Piece of the Game cards.

NM/M
Complete Sheet Set (2): 16.00
Common Player: .50

	ALCS SHEET	8.00
25	Eric Hinske	.50
26	Edgar Martinez (Spirit/Game)	.50
27	Pedro Martinez	.75
28	Roger Clemens (Spirit/Game)	1.75
29	Alex Rodriguez (Spirit/Game)	2.50
30	George Brett (Classic)	2.00
31	Dewon Brazelton (Spirit/Game)	.50
32	Barry Zito	.60
---	Header Card	.10
	NLCS SHEET	8.00
17	J.D. Drew (Spirit/Game)	.60
18	Randy Johnson	.75
19	Mike Piazza (Spirit/Game)	2.00
20	Ozzie Smith (Classic)	1.00
21	Jeff Kent	.50
22	Roy Oswalt (Spirit/Game)	.60
23	Pat Burrell	.60
24	Todd Helton (Spirit/Game)	.75
---	Header Card	.10

2002 Donruss The Rookies

NM/M
Complete Set (110): 20.00
Common Player: .15
Common Rookie: .25
Pack (5): 2.00
Box (24): 40.00

1	Kazuhisa Ishii RC	1.00
2	P.J. Bevis RC	.25
3	Jason Simontacchi RC	.50
4	John Lackey	.15
5	Travis Driskill RC	.25
6	Carl Sadler RC	.25
7	Tim Kalita RC	.25
8	Nelson Castro RC	.25
9	Francis Beltran RC	.25
10	So Taguchi RC	.50
11	Ryan Bukvich RC	.25
12	Brian Fitzgerald	.15
13	Kevin Frederick RC	.25
14	Chone Figgins RC	.75
15	Marlon Byrd	.15
16	Ron Calloway RC	.25
17	Jason Lane	.15
18	Satoru Komiyama RC	.25
19	John Ennis RC	.25
20	Juan Brito RC	.25
21	Gustavo Chacin RC	.50
22	Josh Bard RC	.50
23	Brett Myers	.25
24	Mike Smith RC	.25
25	Eric Hinske	.15
26	Jake Peavy	.15
27	Todd Donovan RC	.25
28	Luis Ugueto RC	.25
29	Corey Thurman RC	.25
30	Takahito Nomura RC	.25
31	Andy Shibilo RC	.25
32	Mike Crudale RC	.25
33	Earl Snyder RC	.25
34	Brian Tallet	.50
35	Miguel Asencio RC	.25
36	Felix Escalona RC	.25
37	Drew Henson	.40
38	Steve Kent RC	.25
39	Rene Reyes RC	.25
40	Edwin Almonte RC	.25
41	Chris Snelling RC	.75
42	Franklyn German RC	.25
43	Jeriome Robertson RC	.25
44	Colin Young RC	.25
45	Jeremy Lambert RC	.25
46	Kirk Saarloos RC	.75
47	Matt Childers RC	.25
48	Justin Wayne	.15
49	Jose Valverde RC	.25
50	Wily Mo Pena	.15
51	Victor Alvarez RC	.25
52	Julius Matos RC	.25
53	Aaron Cook RC	.40
54	Jeff Austin RC	.25
55	Adrian Burnside RC	.25
56	Brandon Puffer RC	.25
57	Jeremy Hill RC	.25
58	Jaime Cerda RC	.25
59	Aaron Guiel RC	.25
60	Ron Chiavacci	.15
61	Kevin Cash RC	.25
62	Elio Serrano	.15
63	Julio Mateo RC	.25
64	Cam Esslinger RC	.25
65	Ken Huckaby RC	.25
66	Wiki Nieves RC	.25
67	Luis Martinez RC	.25
68	Scotty Layfield RC	.25
69	Jeremy Guthrie RC	.75
70	Hansel Izquierdo RC	.25
71	Shane Nance RC	.25
72	Jeff Baker RC	.50
73	Clifford Bartosh RC	.25
74	Mitch Wylie RC	.25
75	Oliver Perez RC	.75
76	Matt Thornton	.15
77	John Foster RC	.25
78	Joe Borchard	.15
79	Eric Junge RC	.25
80	Jorge Sosa RC	.25
81	Runelvys Hernandez	.25
82	Kevin Mench	.25
83	Ben Kozlowski RC	.50
84	Trey Hodges RC	.40
85	Reed Johnson RC	.25
86	Eric Eckenstahler RC	.25
87	Franklin Nunez RC	.25
88	Victor Martinez	.50
89	Kevin Gryboski RC	.25
90	Jason Jennings	.15
91	Jim Rushford RC	.25
92	Jeremy Ward RC	.25
93	Adam Walker RC	.25
94	Freddy Sanchez RC	.25
95	Wilson Valdez RC	.25
96	Lee Gardner	.15
97	Eric Good RC	.25
98	Hank Blalock	.25
99	Mark Corey	.15
100	Jason Davis RC	.40
101	Mike Gonzalez RC	.25
102	David Ross RC	.25
103	Tyler Yates RC	.25
104	Cliff Lee RC	.50
105	Mike Moriarty RC	.25
106	Josh Hancock RC	.25
107	Jason Beverlin RC	.25
108	Clay Condrey RC	.25
109	Shawn Sedlacek RC	.25
110	Sean Burroughs	.15

Donruss Originals

401	Runelvys Hernandez RC	.50
402	Wilson Valdez RC	.25
403	Brian Tallet	1.00
404	Chone Figgins RC	.25
405	Jeriome Robertson RC	.50
406	Shane Nance	.25
407	Aaron Cook	.25
408	Trey Hodges RC	.75
409	Matt Childers RC	.40
410	Mitch Wylie RC	.25
411	Rene Reyes RC	.25
412	Mike Smith	.25
413	Jason Simontacchi RC	.75
414	Luis Martinez	.40
415	Kevin Cash	.40
416	Todd Donovan	.25
417	Scotty Layfield	.25
418	Joe Borchard	.25
419	Adrian Burnside	.25
420	Ben Kozlowski	.25
421	Clay Condrey	.25
422	Cliff Lee	1.00
423	Josh Bard	.25
424	Freddy Sanchez	1.00
425	Ron Calloway	.25

Donruss Studio

Common Studio RC: 3.00
Production 1,500

251	Freddy Sanchez RC	3.00
252	Josh Bard RC	3.00
253	Trey Hodges RC	5.00
254	Jorge Sosa RC	3.00
255	Ben Kozlowski RC	3.00
256	Eric Good RC	3.00
257	Brian Tallet RC	5.00
258	P.J. Bevis RC	3.00
259	Rodrigo Rosario RC	3.00
260	Kirk Saarloos RC	5.00
261	Runelvys Hernandez RC	4.00
262	Josh Hancock RC	3.00
263	Tim Kalita RC	3.00
264	Jason Simontacchi RC	5.00
265	Clay Condrey RC	3.00
266	Cliff Lee RC	4.00
267	Aaron Guiel RC	3.00
268	Andy Pratt RC	3.00
269	Wilson Valdez RC	3.00
270	Oliver Perez RC	3.00
271	Joe Borchard RC	3.00
272	Jeriome Robertson RC	4.00
273	Aaron Cook RC	5.00
274	Kevin Cash RC	5.00
275	Chone Figgins RC	3.00

Best of Fan Club

Common Best of Fan Club RC: 3.00
Production 1,350
Best of Fan Club Spotlights: 1.5-3X
Production 100 Sets

201	Kirk Saarloos RC	5.00
202	Oliver Perez RC	5.00
203	So Taguchi RC	6.00
204	Runelvys Hernandez RC	5.00
205	Freddy Sanchez RC	5.00
206	Cliff Lee RC	8.00
207	Kazuhisa Ishii RC	8.00
208	Kevin Cash RC	5.00
209	Trey Hodges RC	6.00
210	Wilson Valdez RC	5.00
211	Satoru Komiyama RC	3.00
212	Luis Ugueto RC	5.00
213	Joe Borchard RC	3.00
214	Brian Tallet RC	4.00
215	Jeriome Robertson RC	5.00
216	Eric Junge RC	5.00
217	Aaron Cook RC	4.00
218	Jason Simontacchi RC	3.00
219	Miguel Asencio RC	3.00
220	Josh Bard RC	3.00
221	Earl Snyder RC	3.00
222	Felix Escalona RC	3.00
223	Rene Reyes RC	3.00
224	Chone Figgins RC	3.00
225	Chris Snelling RC	5.00

Fan Club

Inserted 1:4 Retail

201	Kirk Saarloos	1.50
202	Oliver Perez	1.50
203	So Taguchi RC	2.00
204	Runelvys Hernandez RC	1.50
205	Freddy Sanchez RC	2.00
206	Cliff Lee	1.50
207	Kazuhisa Ishii RC	3.00
208	Kevin Cash	1.00
209	Trey Hodges	1.50
210	Wilson Valdez	1.50
211	Satoru Komiyama RC	1.00
212	Luis Ugueto RC	1.50
213	Joe Borchard	2.00
214	Brian Tallet	1.00
215	Jeriome Robertson RC	1.50
216	Eric Junge	1.50
217	Aaron Cook	1.50
218	Jason Simontacchi	1.50
219	Miguel Asencio	1.50
220	Josh Bard	1.50
221	Earl Snyder	1.00
222	Felix Escalona	1.00
223	Rene Reyes	1.00
224	Chone Figgins	1.00
225	Chris Snelling RC	4.00

Elite

Common Elite RC: 4.00
Production 1,000
Elite Turn of the Century: 1-2.5X
Production 100 Sets

201	Chris Snelling RC	5.00
202	Satoru Komiyama RC	5.00
203	Jason Simontacchi RC	8.00
204	Tim Kalita RC	4.00
205	Runelvys Hernandez RC	5.00
206	Kirk Saarloos RC	4.00
207	Aaron Cook RC	6.00
208	Luis Ugueto RC	5.00
209	Gustavo Chacin RC	5.00
210	Francis Beltran RC	5.00
211	Takahito Nomura RC	5.00
212	Oliver Perez RC	5.00
213	Miguel Asencio RC	4.00
214	Rene Reyes RC	5.00
215	Jeff Baker RC	15.00
216	Jon Adkins RC	5.00
217	Carlos Rivera RC	5.00
218	Corey Thurman RC	5.00
219	Earl Snyder RC	5.00
220	Felix Escalona RC	5.00
221	Jeremy Guthrie RC	15.00
222	Josh Hancock RC	5.00
223	Ben Kozlowski RC	5.00
224	Eric Good RC	5.00
225	Eric Junge RC	5.00
226	Andy Pratt RC	5.00
227	Matt Thornton RC	5.00
228	Jorge Sosa RC	5.00
229	Mike Smith RC	5.00
230	Mitch Wylie RC	5.00
231	John Ennis RC	5.00
232	Reed Johnson RC	5.00
233	Joe Borchard RC	8.00
234	Ron Calloway RC	5.00
235	Brian Tallet RC	5.00
236	Chris Baker RC	5.00
237	Cliff Lee RC	15.00
238	Matt Childers RC	5.00
239	Freddy Sanchez RC	8.00
240	Chone Figgins RC	8.00
241	Kevin Cash RC	5.00
242	Josh Bard RC	5.00
243	Jeriome Robertson RC	5.00
244	Jeremy Hill RC	5.00
245	Shane Nance RC	5.00
246	Wes Obermueller RC	5.00
247	Trey Hodges RC	5.00
248	Eric Eckenstahler RC	5.00
249	Jim Rushford RC	5.00
250	Jose Castillo RC	10.00
251	Garrett Atkins RC	20.00
252	Alexis Rios RC	100.00
253	Ryan Church RC	10.00
254	Jimmy Gobble RC	8.00
255	Corwin Malone	6.00
257	Nic Jackson RC	6.00
258	Tommy Whiteman RC	8.00
259	Mario Ramos	5.00
260	Rob Bowen RC	8.00
261	Josh Wilson RC	5.00
262	Tim Hummel RC	5.00
264	Gerald Laird RC	15.00
265	Vinnie Chulk RC	5.00
266	Jesus Medrano RC	5.00
272	Adam LaRoche RC	20.00
273	Adam Morrissey RC	5.00
274	Henri Stanley RC	5.00
275	Walter Young RC	10.00

Donruss Classics

Common Classics RC: 3.00
Production 1,500
Classics Timeless Tributes: 1.5-3X
Production 100 Sets

201	Oliver Perez RC	3.00
202	Aaron Cook RC	5.00
203	Eric Junge RC	3.00
204	Freddy Sanchez RC	5.00
205	Cliff Lee RC	5.00
206	Runelvys Hernandez RC	5.00
207	Chone Figgins RC	3.00
208	Rodrigo Rosario RC	3.00
209	Kevin Cash RC	3.00
210	Josh Bard RC	3.00
211	Felix Escalona RC	3.00
212	Jeriome Robertson RC	5.00
213	Jason Simontacchi RC	5.00
214	Shane Nance RC	3.00
215	Ben Kozlowski RC	3.00
216	Brian Tallet RC	5.00
217	Earl Snyder RC	3.00
218	Andy Pratt RC	3.00
219	Trey Hodges RC	5.00
220	Kirk Saarloos RC	5.00
221	Rene Reyes RC	3.00
222	Joe Borchard RC	5.00
223	Wilson Valdez RC	3.00
224	Miguel Asencio RC	5.00
225	Chris Snelling RC	5.00

Diamond Kings

Common DK RC: 3.00
Inserted 1:10

151	Chris Snelling RC	4.00
152	Satoru Komiyama RC	3.00
153	Oliver Perez RC	3.00
154	Kirk Saarloos RC	3.00
155	Rene Reyes RC	3.00

156	Runelvys Hernandez RC	3.00
157	Rodrigo Rosario RC	3.00
158	Jason Simontacchi RC	3.00
159	Miguel Asencio RC	3.00
160	Aaron Cook RC	3.00

Autographs

NM/M
Production 15-100 .... 5.00
Print Runs Listed
2	P.J. Bevis/50	20.00
9	Francis Beltran/100	5.00
13	Kevin Frederick/100	5.00
14	Chone Figgins/100	20.00
15	Marlon Byrd/100	10.00
17	Jason Lane/100	8.00
19	John Ennis/100	10.00
22	Josh Bard/100	10.00
25	Eric Hinske/100	5.00
28	Luis Ugueto/100	5.00
29	Corey Thurman/100	5.00
30	Takahito Nomura/100	20.00
33	Earl Snyder/100	10.00
34	Brian Tallet/100	5.00
37	Drew Henson/50	20.00
39	Rene Reyes/50	15.00
40	Edwin Almonte/50	15.00
41	Chris Snelling/50	20.00
42	Franklyn German/100	5.00
45	Jeremy Lambert/100	5.00
46	Kirk Saarloos/100	10.00
47	Matt Childers/100	5.00
50	Wily Mo Pena/100	15.00
51	Victor Alvarez/100	5.00
61	Kevin Cash/100	8.00
62	Elio Serrano/100	5.00
64	Cam Esslinger/100	5.00
69	Jeremy Guthrie/100	15.00
71	Shane Nance/100	8.00
72	Jeff Baker/100	20.00
76	Matt Thornton/100	10.00
78	Joe Borchard/100	10.00
82	Kevin Mench/100	10.00
83	Ben Kozlowski/100	8.00
84	Trey Hodges/100	10.00
85	Reed Johnson/100	15.00
88	Victor Martinez/100	25.00
90	Jason Jennings/100	8.00
95	Wilson Valdez/100	10.00
97	Eric Good/100	10.00
98	Hank Blalock/100	20.00
104	Cliff Lee/100	25.00
110	Sean Burroughs/50	10.00

Donruss Classics Signatures

NM/M
Print Runs Listed
203	Eric Junge/50	10.00
205	Cliff Lee/100	30.00
207	Chone Figgins/100	10.00
208	Rodrigo Rosario/250	10.00
209	Kevin Cash/100	10.00
210	Josh Bard/100	10.00
214	Shane Nance/200	10.00
215	Ben Kozlowski/200	10.00
216	Brian Tallet/100	15.00
217	Earl Snyder/100	10.00
218	Andy Pratt/250	10.00
219	Trey Hodges/250	15.00
220	Kirk Saarloos/100	20.00
221	Rene Reyes/50	10.00
222	Joe Borchard/100	10.00
223	Wilson Valdez/100	10.00
225	Chris Snelling/100	25.00

Donruss Studio Private Signing

NM/M
Print Runs Listed
252	Josh Bard/100	10.00
253	Trey Hodges/250	10.00
255	Ben Kozlowski/200	5.00
257	Brian Tallet/100	15.00
258	P.J. Bevis/50	15.00
259	Rodrigo Rosario/250	5.00
260	Kirk Saarloos/100	10.00
263	Tim Kalita/50	8.00
266	Cliff Lee/100	25.00
268	Andy Pratt/250	10.00
269	Wilson Valdez/200	10.00
271	Joe Borchard/100	15.00
274	Kevin Cash/100	8.00
275	Chone Figgins/100	8.00

Elite Turn of the Century Autograph

NM/M
Common Autograph: ....
Print Runs Listed
201	Chris Snelling/50	30.00
206	Kirk Saarloos/50	20.00
215	Jeff Baker/100	40.00
216	Jon Adkins/100	10.00
217	Carlos Rivera/100	15.00
221	Jeremy Guthrie/100	25.00
223	Ben Kozlowski/100	10.00
224	Eric Good/100	10.00
240	Chone Figgins/100	30.00
241	Kevin Cash/100	10.00
247	Trey Hodges/100	15.00
251	Garrett Atkins/100	15.00
253	Ryan Church/100	35.00
254	Jimmy Gobble/100	10.00
255	Corwin Malone/100	10.00
258	Tom Whiteman/100	15.00
259	Mario Ramos/100	15.00
260	Rob Bowen/100	15.00
261	Josh Wilson/100	15.00
262	Tim Hummel/100	15.00
264	Gerald Laird/100	25.00
266	Jesus Medrano/100	15.00
272	Adam LaRoche/100	60.00
273	Adam Morrissey/100	15.00
274	Henri Stanley/100	15.00

Fan Club Autograph

NM/M
Common Autograph: ....
Print Runs Listed
201	Kirk Saarloos/100	10.00
208	Kevin Cash/50	8.00
209	Trey Hodges/100	10.00
210	Wilson Valdez/50	10.00
212	Luis Ugueto/75	10.00
213	Joe Borchard/50	15.00
214	Brian Tallet/50	15.00
220	Josh Bard/50	8.00
221	Earl Snyder/100	10.00
223	Rene Reyes/50	8.00
224	Chone Figgins/100	8.00

Best of Fan Club Autograph

NM/M
Production 10-100 ....
Print Runs Listed
201	Kirk Saarloos/100	10.00
208	Kevin Cash/50	10.00
209	Trey Hodges/100	10.00
210	Wilson Valdez/50	10.00
212	Luis Ugueto/75	10.00
213	Joe Borchard/50	15.00
214	Brian Tallet/50	15.00
220	Josh Bard/50	8.00
221	Earl Snyder/50	8.00
223	Rene Reyes/50	10.00
224	Chone Figgins/100	8.00
225	Chris Snelling/50	15.00

Phenoms

NM/M
Common Player: 3.00
Production 1,000 Sets
1	Kazuhisa Ishii	5.00
2	Eric Hinske	3.00
3	Jason Lane	3.00
4	Victor Martinez	5.00
5	Mark Prior	6.00

6	Antonio Perez	3.00
7	John Buck	3.00
8	Joe Borchard	3.00
9	Alexis Gomez	3.00
10	Sean Burroughs	3.00
11	Carlos Pena	3.00
12	Bill Hall	3.00
13	Alfredo Amezaga	3.00
14	Ed Rogers	3.00
15	Mark Teixeira	5.00
16	Chris Snelling	4.00
17	Nick Johnson	3.00
18	Angel Berroa	3.00
19	Orlando Hudson	3.00
20	Drew Henson	3.00
21	Austin Kearns	3.00
22	Dewon Brazelton	3.00
23	Dennis Tankersley	3.00
24	Josh Beckett	4.00
25	Marlon Byrd	4.00

Phenoms Autographs

NM/M
Common Autograph: 5.00
Print Runs Listed
2	Eric Hinske/500	10.00
3	Jason Lane/500	5.00
4	Victor Martinez/225	10.00
5	Mark Prior/100	50.00
6	Antonio Perez/500	5.00
7	John Buck/500	5.00
8	Joe Borchard/500	10.00
9	Alexis Gomez/400	5.00
10	Sean Burroughs/150	10.00
11	Carlos Pena/150	8.00
12	Bill Hall/200	8.00
13	Alfredo Amezaga/500	5.00
14	Ed Rogers/500	5.00
15	Mark Teixeira/100	20.00
16	Chris Snelling/100	15.00
17	Nick Johnson/250	8.00
18	Angel Berroa/500	5.00
19	Orlando Hudson/400	15.00
20	Drew Henson/500	25.00
21	Austin Kearns/75	20.00
22	Dewon Brazelton/350	5.00
23	Dennis Tankersley/100	8.00
24	Josh Beckett/125	25.00
25	Marlon Byrd/500	5.00

Rookie Crusade

NM/M
Common Player: 3.00
Production 1,500 Sets
1	Corky Miller	3.00
2	Jack Cust	3.00
3	Erik Bedard	3.00
4	Andres Torres	3.00
5	Geronimo Gil	3.00
6	Rafael Soriano	3.00
7	Johnny Estrada	3.00
8	Steve Bechler	3.00
9	Adam Johnson	3.00
10	So Taguchi	3.00
11	Dee Brown	3.00
12	Kevin Frederick	3.00
13	Allan Simpson	3.00
14	Ricardo Rodriguez	3.00
15	Jason Hart	3.00
16	Matt Childers	3.00
17	Jason Jennings	3.00
18	Anderson Machado	3.00
19	Fernando Rodney	3.00
20	Brandon Larson	3.00
21	Satoru Komiyama	3.00
22	Francis Beltran	3.00
23	Joe Thurston	3.00
24	Josh Pearce	3.00
25	Carlos Hernandez	3.00
26	Ben Howard	3.00
27	Wilson Valdez	3.00
28	Victor Alvarez	3.00
29	Cesar Izturis	3.00
30	Endy Chavez	3.00
31	Michael Cuddyer	4.00
32	Bobby Hill	3.00
33	Willie Harris	3.00
34	Joe Crede	3.00
35	Jorge Padilla	3.00
36	Brandon Backe	3.00
37	Franklyn German	3.00
38	Xavier Nady	3.00
39	Raul Chavez	3.00
40	Shane Nance	3.00

41	Brandon Claussen	4.00
42	Tom Shearn	3.00
43	Freddy Sanchez	3.00
44	Chone Figgins	3.00
45	Cliff Lee	4.00
46	Brian Mallette	3.00
47	Mike Rivera	3.00
48	Elio Serrano	3.00
49	Rodrigo Rosario	3.00
50	Earl Snyder	3.00

Rookie Crusade Autograph

NM/M
Common Autograph: 5.00
Print Runs Listed
1	Corky Miller/500	5.00
2	Jack Cust/500	6.00
3	Erik Bedard/100	10.00
4	Andres Torres/500	5.00
5	Geronimo Gil/500	5.00
6	Rafael Soriano/500	8.00
7	Johnny Estrada/400	5.00
8	Steve Bechler/500	6.00
9	Adam Johnson/500	5.00
11	Dee Brown/500	5.00
12	Kevin Frederick/150	5.00
13	Allan Simpson/150	5.00
14	Ricardo Rodriguez/500	5.00
15	Jason Hart/500	5.00
16	Matt Childers/150	5.00
17	Jason Jennings/500	5.00
18	Anderson Machado/500	8.00
19	Fernando Rodney/500	5.00
20	Brandon Larson/400	5.00
22	Francis Beltran/500	5.00
23	Joe Thurston/500	5.00
24	Josh Pearce/500	5.00
25	Carlos Hernandez/500	5.00
26	Ben Howard/500	6.00
27	Wilson Valdez/500	5.00
28	Victor Alvarez/500	5.00
29	Cesar Izturis/500	8.00
30	Endy Chavez/500	5.00
31	Michael Cuddyer/375	10.00
32	Bobby Hill/250	5.00
33	Willie Harris/300	5.00
34	Joe Crede/100	8.00
35	Jorge Padilla/475	5.00
36	Brandon Backe/350	5.00
37	Franklyn German/500	5.00
38	Xavier Nady/500	8.00
39	Raul Chavez/500	5.00
40	Shane Nance/500	5.00
41	Brandon Claussen/150	10.00
42	Tom Shearn/500	5.00
44	Chone Figgins/500	5.00
45	Cliff Lee/500	10.00
46	Brian Mallette/150	5.00
47	Mike Rivera/400	5.00
48	Elio Serrano/500	5.00
49	Rodrigo Rosario/100	10.00
50	Earl Snyder/100	10.00

2003 Donruss Samples

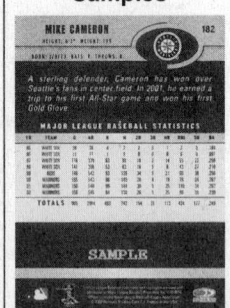

Each issue of the January 2003 Beckett Baseball Card Monthly included a sample 2003 Donruss card rubber-cemented inside. The cards differ from the issued version only in the appearance on back of a (usually) silver-foil "SAMPLE" notation. Some cards were produced with the overprint in gold-foil, in much more limited quantities. The number of different players' cards involved in the promotion is unknown.

NM/M
Common Player: .... .10
Stars: 1.5-2X
Gold: 10X

2003 Donruss

GARRET ANDERSON OF

NM/M
Complete Set (400): 40.00
Common Player: .... .15
Pack (13): 1.50
Box (24): 30.00
1	Vladimir Guerrero	.75
2	Derek Jeter	.50
3	Adam Dunn	.50
4	Greg Maddux	1.00
5	Lance Berkman	.40
6	Ichiro Suzuki	2.00
7	Mike Piazza	1.00
8	Alex Rodriguez	2.00
9	Tom Glavine	.25
10	Randy Johnson	.75
11	Nomar Garciaparra	1.00
12	Jason Giambi	.50
13	Sammy Sosa	1.00
14	Barry Zito	.25
15	Chipper Jones	1.00
16	Magglio Ordonez	.25
17	Larry Walker	.25
18	Alfonso Soriano	.50
19	Curt Schilling	.50
20	Barry Bonds	2.00
21	Joe Borchard	.15
22	Chris Snelling	.15
23	Brian Tallet	.15
24	Cliff Lee	.15
25	Freddy Sanchez	.15
26	Chone Figgins	.15
27	Kevin Cash	.15
28	Josh Bard	.15
29	Jeriome Robertson	.15
30	Jeremy Hill	.15
31	Shane Nance	.15
32	Jake Peavy	.15
33	Trey Hodges	.15
34	Eric Eckenstahler	.15
35	Jim Rushford	.15
36	Oliver Perez	.15
37	Kirk Saarloos	.15
38	Hank Blalock	.50
39	Francisco Rodriguez	.25
40	Runelvys Hernandez	.15
41	Aaron Cook	.15
42	Josh Hancock	.15
43	P.J. Bevis	.15
44	Jon Adkins	.15
45	Tim Kalita	.15
46	Nelson Castro	.15
47	Colin Young	.15
48	Adrian Burnside	.15
49	Luis Martinez	.15
50	Peter Zamora	.15
51	Todd Donovan	.15
52	Jeremy Ward	.15
53	Wilson Valdez	.15
54	Eric Good	.15
55	Jeff Baker	.15
56	Mitch Wylie	.15
57	Ron Calloway	.15
58	Jose Valverde	.15
59	Jason Davis	.15
60	Scotty Layfield	.15
61	Matt Thornton	.15
62	Adam Walker	.15
63	Gustavo Chacin	.15
64	Ron Chiavacci	.15
65	Wiki Nieves	.15
66	Clifford Bartosh	.15
67	Mike Gonzalez	.15
68	Justin Wayne	.15
69	Eric Junge	.15
70	Ben Kozlowski	.15
71	Darin Erstad	.25
72	Garret Anderson	.40
73	Troy Glaus	.40
74	David Eckstein	.15
75	Adam Kennedy	.15
76	Kevin Appier	.15
77	Jarrod Washburn	.15
78	Scott Spiezio	.15
79	Tim Salmon	.25
80	Ramon Ortiz	.15
81	Bengie Molina	.15
82	Brad Fullmer	.15
83	Troy Percival	.15
84	David Segui	.15
85	Jay Gibbons	.15
86	Tony Batista	.15
87	Scott Erickson	.15
88	Jeff Conine	.15
89	Melvin Mora	.15
90	Buddy Groom	.15
91	Rodrigo Lopez	.15
92	Marty Cordova	.15
93	Geronimo Gil	.15
94	Kenny Lofton	.15
95	Shea Hillenbrand	.15
96	Manny Ramirez	.50
97	Pedro Martinez	.75
98	Nomar Garciaparra	1.00
99	Rickey Henderson	.40
100	Johnny Damon	.25
101	Trot Nixon	.15
102	Derek Lowe	.15
103	Hee Seop Choi	.15
104	Mark Teixeira	.40
105	Tim Wakefield	.15
106	Jason Varitek	.25
107	Frank Thomas	.50
108	Joe Crede	.15
109	Magglio Ordonez	.25
110	Ray Durham	.15
111	Mark Buehrle	.15
112	Paul Konerko	.25
113	Jose Valentin	.15
114	Carlos Lee	.15
115	Royce Clayton	.15
116	C.C. Sabathia	.15
117	Ellis Burks	.15
118	Omar Vizquel	.25
119	Jim Thome	.75
120	Matt Lawton	.15
121	Travis Fryman	.15
122	Earl Snyder	.15
123	Ricky Gutierrez	.15
124	Einar Diaz	.15
125	Danys Baez	.15
126	Robert Fick	.15
127	Bobby Higginson	.15
128	Steve Sparks	.15
129	Mike Rivera	.15
130	Wendell Magee	.15
131	Randall Simon	.15
132	Carlos Pena	.15
133	Mark Redman	.15
134	Juan Acevedo	.15
135	Mike Sweeney	.15
136	Aaron Guiel	.15
137	Carlos Beltran	.40
138	Joe Randa	.15
139	Paul Byrd	.15
140	Shawn Sedlacek	.15
141	Raul Ibanez	.15
142	Michael Tucker	.15
143	Torii Hunter	.40
144	Jacque Jones	.15
145	David Ortiz	.40
146	Corey Koskie	.15
147	Brad Radke	.15
148	Doug Mientkiewicz	.15
149	A.J. Pierzynski	.15
150	Dustan Mohr	.15
151	Michael Cuddyer	.15
152	Eddie Guardado	.15
153	Cristian Guzman	.15
154	Derek Jeter	2.00
155	Bernie Williams	.50
156	Roger Clemens	1.50
157	Mike Mussina	.50
158	Jorge Posada	.40
159	Alfonso Soriano	.75
160	Jason Giambi	.50
161	Robin Ventura	.25
162	Andy Pettitte	.25
163	David Wells	.15
164	Nick Johnson	.15
165	Jeff Weaver	.15
166	Raul Mondesi	.15
167	Rondell White	.15
168	Tim Hudson	.25
169	Barry Zito	.40
170	Mark Mulder	.25
171	Miguel Tejada	.40
172	Eric Chavez	.25
173	Billy Koch	.15
174	Jermaine Dye	.15
175	Scott Hatteberg	.15
176	Terrence Long	.15
177	David Justice	.25
178	Ramon Hernandez	.15
179	Ted Lilly	.15
180	Ichiro Suzuki	1.50
181	Edgar Martinez	.25
182	Mike Cameron	.15
183	John Olerud	.25
184	Bret Boone	.15
185	Dan Wilson	.15
186	Freddy Garcia	.15
187	Jamie Moyer	.15
188	Carlos Guillen	.15
189	Ruben Sierra	.15
190	Kazuhiro Sasaki	.15
191	Mark McLemore	.15
192	Chris Snelling	.15
193	Joel Pineiro	.15
194	Jeff Cirillo	.15
195	Rafael Soriano	.15
196	Ben Grieve	.15
197	Aubrey Huff	.15
198	Steve Cox	.15
199	Toby Hall	.15
200	Randy Winn	.15
201	Brent Abernathy	.15
202	Chris Gomez	.15
203	John Flaherty	.15
204	Paul Wilson	.15
205	Chan Ho Park	.15
206	Alex Rodriguez	2.00
207	Juan Gonzalez	.50
208	Rafael Palmeiro	.50
209	Ivan Rodriguez	.50

#	Player	Price		#	Player	Price
210	Rusty Greer	.15		328	Bartolo Colon	.15
211	Kenny Rogers	.15		329	Fernando Tatis	.15
212	Ismael Valdes	.15		330	Brad Wilkerson	.15
213	Frank Catalanotto	.15		331	Masato Yoshii	.15
214	Hank Blalock	.50		332	Mike Piazza	1.00
215	Michael Young	.15		333	Jeromy Burnitz	.15
216	Kevin Mench	.15		334	Roberto Alomar	.50
217	Herbert Perry	.15		335	Mo Vaughn	.15
218	Gabe Kapler	.25		336	Al Leiter	.25
219	Carlos Delgado	.25		337	Pedro Astacio	.15
220	Shannon Stewart	.15		338	Edgardo Alfonzo	.15
221	Eric Hinske	.15		339	Armando Benitez	.15
222	Roy Halladay	.25		340	Timoniel Perez	.15
223	Felipe Lopez	.15		341	Jay Payton	.15
224	Vernon Wells	.15		342	Roger Cedeno	.15
225	Josh Phelps	.15		343	Rey Ordonez	.15
226	Jose Cruz	.15		344	Steve Trachsel	.15
227	Curt Schilling	.50		345	Satoru Komiyama	.15
228	Randy Johnson	.75		346	Scott Rolen	.75
229	Luis Gonzalez	.25		347	Pat Burrell	.40
230	Mark Grace	.40		348	Bobby Abreu	.25
231	Junior Spivey	.15		349	Mike Lieberthal	.15
232	Tony Womack	.15		350	Brandon Duckworth	.15
233	Matt Williams	.25		351	Jimmy Rollins	.25
234	Steve Finley	.15		352	Marlon Anderson	.15
235	Byung-Hyun Kim	.15		353	Travis Lee	.15
236	Craig Counsell	.15		354	Vicente Padilla	.15
237	Greg Maddux	1.00		355	Randy Wolf	.15
238	Tom Glavine	.40		356	Jason Kendall	.15
239	John Smoltz	.25		357	Brian Giles	.25
240	Chipper Jones	1.00		358	Aramis Ramirez	.40
241	Gary Sheffield	.25		359	Pokey Reese	.15
242	Andruw Jones	.40		360	Kip Wells	.15
243	Vinny Castilla	.15		361	Josh Fogg	.15
244	Damian Moss	.15		362	Mike Williams	.15
245	Rafael Furcal	.15		363	Jack Wilson	.15
246	Javy Lopez	.15		364	Craig Wilson	.15
247	Kevin Millwood	.15		365	Kevin Young	.15
248	Kerry Wood	.75		366	Ryan Klesko	.15
249	Fred McGriff	.25		367	Phil Nevin	.15
250	Sammy Sosa	1.00		368	Brian Lawrence	.15
251	Alex Gonzalez	.15		369	Mark Kotsay	.15
252	Corey Patterson	.25		370	Brett Tomko	.15
253	Moises Alou	.15		371	Trevor Hoffman	.15
254	Juan Cruz	.15		372	Deivi Cruz	.15
255	Jon Lieber	.15		373	Bubba Trammell	.15
256	Matt Clement	.15		374	Sean Burroughs	.15
257	Mark Prior	.75		375	Barry Bonds	2.00
258	Ken Griffey Jr.	1.00		376	Jeff Kent	.25
259	Barry Larkin	.25		377	Rich Aurilia	.15
260	Adam Dunn	.50		378	Tsuyoshi Shinjo	.15
261	Sean Casey	.15		379	Benito Santiago	.15
262	Jose Rijo	.15		380	Kirk Rueter	.15
263	Elmer Dessens	.15		381	Livan Hernandez	.15
264	Austin Kearns	.25		382	Russ Ortiz	.15
265	Corky Miller	.15		383	David Bell	.15
266	Todd Walker	.15		384	Jason Schmidt	.40
267	Chris Reitsma	.15		385	Reggie Sanders	.15
268	Ryan Dempster	.15		386	J.T. Snow	.15
269	Aaron Boone	.15		387	Robb Nen	.15
270	Danny Graves	.15		388	Ryan Jensen	.15
271	Brandon Larson	.15		389	Jim Edmonds	.40
272	Larry Walker	.25		390	J.D. Drew	.25
273	Todd Helton	.50		391	Albert Pujols	1.50
274	Juan Uribe	.15		392	Fernando Vina	.15
275	Juan Pierre	.15		393	Tino Martinez	.15
276	Mike Hampton	.15		394	Edgar Renteria	.40
277	Todd Zeile	.15		395	Matt Morris	.15
278	Todd Hollandsworth	.15		396	Woody Williams	.15
279	Jason Jennings	.15		397	Jason Isringhausen	.15
280	Josh Beckett	.40		398	Placido Polanco	.15
281	Mike Lowell	.15		399	Eli Marrero	.15
282	Derrek Lee	.25		400	Jason Simontacchi	.15
283	A.J. Burnett	.15				
284	Luis Castillo	.15				
285	Tim Raines	.15				

Stat Line Career

Cards serial numbered 251-400: 3-6X
Print run 151-250: 4-8X
Print run 101-150: 5-10X
Print run 61-100: 8-15X
Print run 31-60: 10-20X
Numbered to career stat.

Stat Line Season

Cards serial numbered 151-200: 4-8X
Print run 101-150: 5-10X
Print run 61-100: 8-15X
Print run 31-60: 10-20X
Numbered to 2002 stat.

All-Stars

	NM/M
Complete Set (10):	25.00
Common Player:	1.50
Retail only	

(continuing column 1)
286 Preston Wilson .15
287 Juan Encarnacion .15
288 Charles Johnson .15
289 Jeff Bagwell .50
290 Craig Biggio .25
291 Lance Berkman .40
292 Daryle Ward .15
293 Roy Oswalt .40
294 Richard Hidalgo .15
295 Octavio Dotel .15
296 Wade Miller .15
297 Julio Lugo .15
298 Billy Wagner .15
299 Shawn Green .25
300 Adrian Beltre .25
301 Paul Lo Duca .15
302 Eric Karros .15
303 Kevin Brown .15
304 Hideo Nomo .40
305 Odalis Perez .15
306 Eric Gagne .40
307 Brian Jordan .15
308 Cesar Izturis .15
309 Mark Grudzielanek .15
310 Kazuhisa Ishii .15
311 Geoff Jenkins .15
312 Richie Sexson .40
313 Jose Hernandez .15
314 Ben Sheets .25
315 Ruben Quevedo .15
316 Jeffrey Hammonds .15
317 Alex Sanchez .15
318 Eric Young .15
319 Takahito Nomura .15
320 Vladimir Guerrero .75
321 Jose Vidro .15
322 Orlando Cabrera .15
323 Michael Barrett .15
324 Javier Vazquez .15
325 Tony Armas Jr. .15
326 Andres Galarraga .15
327 Tomokazu Ohka .15

#	Player	Price
1	Ichiro Suzuki	5.00
2	Alex Rodriguez	6.00
3	Nomar Garciaparra	5.00
4	Derek Jeter	6.00
5	Manny Ramirez	2.00
6	Barry Bonds	6.00
7	Adam Dunn	1.50
8	Mike Piazza	3.00
9	Sammy Sosa	4.00
10	Todd Helton	1.50

Anniversary 1983

	NM/M
Complete Set (20):	50.00
Common Player:	1.50
Inserted 1:12	

#	Player	Price
1	Dale Murphy	2.00
2	Jim Palmer	2.00
3	Nolan Ryan	6.00
4	Ozzie Smith	4.00
5	Tom Seaver	4.00
6	Mike Schmidt	5.00
7	Steve Carlton	3.00
8	Robin Yount	4.00
9	Ryne Sandberg	4.00
10	Cal Ripken Jr.	8.00
11	Fernando Valenzuela	1.50
12	Andre Dawson	3.00
13	George Brett	6.00
14	Eddie Murray	3.00
15	Dave Winfield	2.00
16	Johnny Bench	5.00
17	Wade Boggs	2.00
18	Tony Gwynn	4.00
19	San Diego Chicken	1.50
20	Ty Cobb	5.00

Bat Kings

	NM/M
Common Player:	10.00
Studio Series:	1.5-3X
Production 25 or 50	

#	Player	Price
1	Scott Rolen/250	20.00
2	Frank Thomas/250	15.00
3	Chipper Jones/250	15.00
4	Ivan Rodriguez/250	15.00
5	Stan Musial/100	40.00
6	Nomar Garciaparra/250	25.00
7	Vladimir Guerrero/250	15.00
8	Adam Dunn/250	15.00
9	Lance Berkman/250	10.00
10	Magglio Ordonez/250	10.00
11	Ernie Banks/50	25.00
12	Manny Ramirez/100	25.00
13	Mike Piazza/100	40.00
14	Alex Rodriguez/100	25.00
15	Todd Helton/100	20.00
16	Andre Dawson/100	15.00
17	Cal Ripken Jr/100	60.00
18	Tony Gwynn/100	25.00
19	Don Mattingly/100	60.00
20	Ryne Sandberg/100	45.00

Diamond Kings

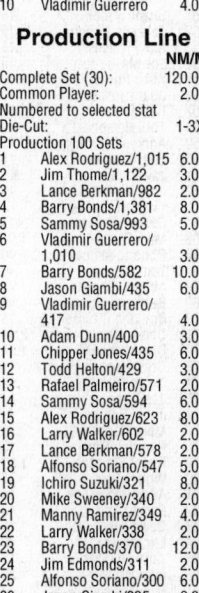

	NM/M
Complete Set (20):	120.00
Common Player:	2.00
Production 2,500 Sets	
Studio Series:	1.5-3X
Production 250 Sets	

#	Player	Price
1	Vladimir Guerrero	5.00
2	Derek Jeter	15.00
3	Adam Dunn	5.00
4	Greg Maddux	8.00
5	Lance Berkman	3.00
6	Ichiro Suzuki	10.00
7	Mike Piazza	10.00
8	Alex Rodriguez	10.00
9	Tom Glavine	3.00
10	Randy Johnson	8.00
11	Nomar Garciaparra	10.00
12	Jason Giambi	5.00
13	Sammy Sosa	8.00
14	Barry Zito	3.00
15	Chipper Jones	8.00
16	Magglio Ordonez	2.00
17	Larry Walker	2.00
18	Alfonso Soriano	8.00
19	Curt Schilling	4.00
20	Barry Bonds	10.00

Elite Series

	NM/M
Complete Set (15):	50.00
Common Player:	2.00
Production 2,500 Sets	
Dominators:	No Pricing
Production 25 Sets	

#	Player	Price
1	Alex Rodriguez	8.00
2	Barry Bonds	10.00
3	Ichiro Suzuki	8.00
4	Vladimir Guerrero	4.00
5	Randy Johnson	4.00
6	Pedro Martinez	4.00
7	Adam Dunn	3.00
8	Sammy Sosa	6.00
9	Jim Edmonds	2.00
10	Greg Maddux	6.00
11	Kazuhisa Ishii	2.00
12	Jason Giambi	4.00
13	Nomar Garciaparra	6.00
14	Tom Glavine	2.00
15	Todd Helton	3.00

Elite Dominators

No Pricing
25 sets produced.

Jersey Kings

	NM/M
Common Player:	10.00
Studio Series:	1.5-3X
Production 25 or 50	

#	Player	Price
1	Juan Gonzalez/250	15.00
2	Greg Maddux/250	20.00
3	Nomar Garciaparra/250	20.00
4	Troy Glaus/250	10.00
5	Reggie Jackson/100	20.00
6	Alex Rodriguez/250	25.00
7	Alfonso Soriano/250	15.00
8	Curt Schilling/250	12.00
9	Vladimir Guerrero/250	15.00
10	Adam Dunn/250	15.00
11	Mark Grace/100	15.00
12	Roger Clemens/100	30.00
13	Jeff Bagwell/100	25.00
14	Tom Glavine/100	25.00
15	Mike Piazza/100	25.00
16	Rod Carew/100	20.00
17	Rickey Henderson/100	20.00
18	Mike Schmidt/100	40.00
19	Cal Ripken Jr./100	60.00
20	Dale Murphy/100	15.00

Longball Leaders

	NM/M
Complete Set (10):	30.00
Common Player:	1.50
Production 1,000 Sets	
Seasonal Sum:	4-6X
Numbered to 2002 HR total	

#	Player	Price
1	Alex Rodriguez	6.00
2	Alfonso Soriano	4.00
3	Rafael Palmeiro	2.00
4	Jim Thome	3.00
5	Jason Giambi	3.00
6	Sammy Sosa	5.00
7	Barry Bonds	8.00
8	Lance Berkman	2.00
9	Shawn Green	1.50
10	Vladimir Guerrero	4.00

Production Line

	NM/M
Complete Set (30):	120.00
Common Player:	2.00
Numbered to selected stat	
Die-Cut:	1-3X
Production 100 Sets	

#	Player	Price
1	Alex Rodriguez/1,015	6.00
2	Jim Thome/1,122	3.00
3	Lance Berkman/982	2.00
4	Barry Bonds/1,381	8.00
5	Sammy Sosa/993	2.00
6	Vladimir Guerrero/1,010	3.00
7	Barry Bonds/582	10.00
8	Jason Giambi/435	6.00
9	Vladimir Guerrero/417	4.00
10	Adam Dunn/400	3.00
11	Chipper Jones/435	6.00
12	Todd Helton/429	3.00
13	Rafael Palmeiro/571	2.00
14	Sammy Sosa/594	6.00
15	Alex Rodriguez/623	8.00
16	Larry Walker/602	2.00
17	Lance Berkman/578	2.00
18	Alfonso Soriano/547	5.00
19	Ichiro Suzuki/321	8.00
20	Mike Sweeney/340	4.00
21	Manny Ramirez/349	4.00
22	Larry Walker/338	2.00
23	Barry Bonds/370	12.00
24	Jim Edmonds/311	2.00
25	Alfonso Soriano/300	5.00
26	Jason Giambi/335	6.00
27	Miguel Tejada/336	4.00
28	Brian Giles/309	3.00
29	Vladimir Guerrero/364	5.00
30	Pat Burrell/319	8.00

Timber and Threads

	NM/M
Common Player:	6.00

#	Player	Price
1	Al Kaline/Bat/125	25.00
2	Alex Rodriguez/Bat/350	20.00
3	Carlos Delgado/Bat/250	8.00
4	Cliff Floyd/Bat/250	8.00
5	Eddie Mathews/Bat/125	25.00
6	Edgar Martinez/Bat/125	10.00
7	Ernie Banks/Bat/50	40.00
8	Ivan Rodriguez/Bat/125	15.00
9	J.D. Drew/Bat/125	8.00
10	Jorge Posada/Bat/300	10.00
11	Lou Brock/Bat/125	20.00
12	Mike Piazza/Bat/125	25.00
13	Mike Schmidt/Bat/125	50.00
14	Reggie Jackson/Bat/125	20.00
15	Rickey Henderson/Bat/125	20.00
16	Robin Yount/Bat/125	35.00
17	Rod Carew/Bat/125	25.00
18	Scott Rolen/Bat/125	20.00
19	Shawn Green/Bat/300	8.00
20	Willie Stargell/Bat/125	15.00
21	Alex Rodriguez/Jsy/175	20.00
22	Andruw Jones/Jsy/275	8.00
23	Brooks Robinson/Jsy/150	25.00
24	Chipper Jones/Jsy/150	20.00
25	Greg Maddux/Jsy/175	20.00
26	Hideo Nomo/Jsy/300	8.00
27	Ivan Rodriguez/Jsy/225	10.00
28	Jack Morris/Jsy/150	8.00
29	J.D. Drew/Jsy/150	8.00
30	Jeff Bagwell/Jsy/500	8.00
31	Jim Thome/Jsy/200	15.00
32	John Smoltz/Jsy/175	8.00
33	John Olerud/Jsy/450	8.00
34	Kerry Wood/Jsy/200	15.00
35	Harmon Killebrew/Jsy/50	60.00
36	Larry Walker/Jsy/500	6.00
37	Magglio Ordonez/Jsy/150	10.00
38	Manny Ramirez/Jsy/500	15.00
39	Mike Piazza/Jsy/300	15.00
40	Mike Sweeney/Jsy/200	8.00
41	Nomar Garciaparra/Jsy/200	25.00
42	Paul Konerko/Jsy/500	10.00
43	Pedro Martinez/Jsy/175	15.00
44	Randy Johnson/Jsy/175	15.00
45	Roger Clemens/Jsy/350	20.00
46	Shawn Green/Jsy/250	8.00
47	Todd Helton/Jsy/175	8.00
48	Tom Glavine/Jsy/225	12.00
49	Tony Gwynn/Jsy/150	25.00
50	Vladimir Guerrero/Jsy/450	15.00

Champions Samples

Each issue of the May., 2003, Beckett Baseball Card Monthly included a sample 2003 Donruss Champions card rubber-cemented inside. The cards differ from the issued version only in the appearance on back of a (usually) silver-foil "SAMPLE" notation. Some cards were produced with the overprint in gold-foil, in much more limited quantities. The number of different players' cards involved in the promotion is unknown.

	NM/M
Common Player:	.10
Stars:	1.5-2X
Gold:	10X

2003 Donruss Champions

	NM/M
Complete Set (300):	40.00
Common Player:	.15
Pack (8):	2.00
Box (24):	40.00

#	Player	Price
1	Adam Kennedy	.15
2	Alfredo Amezaga	.15
3	Chone Figgins	.15
4	Darin Erstad	.25
5	David Eckstein	.15
6	Garret Anderson	.40
7	Jarrod Washburn	.15
8	Nolan Ryan	2.00
9	Tim Salmon	.25
10	Troy Glaus	.40
11	Troy Percival	.15
12	Curt Schilling	.50
13	Junior Spivey	.15
14	Luis Gonzalez	.25
15	Mark Grace	.50
16	Randy Johnson	1.00
17	Steve Finley	.15
18	Andruw Jones	.40

#	Player	Price	#	Player	Price	#	Player	Price
19	Chipper Jones	.75	137	Cesar Izturis	.15	255	Ben Kozlowski	.15
20	Dale Murphy	.50	138	Victor Alvarez	.15	256	Gerald Laird	.15
21	Gary Sheffield	.40	139	Hideo Nomo	.50	257	Hank Blalock	.50
22	Greg Maddux	1.00	140	Joe Thurston	.15	258	Ivan Rodriguez	.50
23	John Smoltz	.25	141	Kazuhisa Ishii	.15	259	Juan Gonzalez	.50
24	Andy Pratt	.15	142	Kevin Brown	.25	260	Kevin Mench	.15
25	Adam LaRoche	.15	143	Odalis Perez	.15	261	Mario Ramos	.15
26	Trey Hodges	.15	144	Paul LoDuca	.15	262	Mark Teixeira	.25
27	Warren Spahn	.75	145	Shawn Green	.25	263	Nolan Ryan	2.00
28	Cal Ripken Jr.	3.00	146	Ben Sheets	.15	264	Rafael Palmeiro	.50
29	Ed Rogers	.15	147	Bill Hall	.15	265	Alexis Rios	.15
30	Brian Roberts	.15	148	Nick Neugebauer	.15	266	Carlos Delgado	.40
31	Geronimo Gil	.15	149	Richie Sexson	.40	267	Eric Hinske	.15
32	Jay Gibbons	.15	150	Robin Yount	1.00	268	Josh Phelps	.15
33	Josh Towers	.15	151	Shane Nance	.15	269	Kevin Cash	.15
34	Casey Fossum	.15	152	Takahito Nomura	.15	270	Orlando Hudson	.15
35	Cliff Floyd	.15	153	A.J. Pierzynski	.15	271	Roy Halladay	.15
36	Derek Lowe	.15	154	Joe Mays	.15	272	Shannon Stewart	.15
37	Fred Lynn	.15	155	Kirby Puckett	1.00	273	Vernon Wells	.15
38	Freddy Sanchez	.15	156	Adam Johnson	.15	274	Vinnie Chulk	.15
39	Manny Ramirez	.50	157	Rob Bowen	.15	275	Jason Anderson	.15
40	Nomar Garciaparra	1.00	158	Torii Hunter	.40	276	Craig Brazell RC	.50
41	Pedro J. Martinez	.50	159	Andres Galarraga	.15	277	Terrmel Sledge RC	.50
42	Rickey Henderson	.50	160	Endy Chavez	.15	278	Ryan Cameron RC	.50
43	Shea Hillenbrand	.15	161	Javier Vazquez	.15	279	Clint Barmes RC	.50
44	Trot Nixon	.15	162	Jose Vidro	.15	280	Jhonny Peralta RC	.50
45	Bobby Hill	.15	163	Vladimir Guerrero	.75	281	Todd Wellemeyer RC	.50
46	Corey Patterson	.15	164	Dwight Gooden	.15	282	Jon Leicester RC	.40
47	Fred McGriff	.25	165	Mike Piazza	1.00	283	Brandon Webb RC	1.00
48	Hee Seop Choi	.15	166	Roberto Alomar	.15	284	Tim Olson RC	.50
49	Juan Cruz	.15	167	Tom Glavine	.40	285	Matt Kata RC	.75
50	Kerry Wood	.75	168	Alfonso Soriano	.75	286	Rob Hammock RC	.50
51	Mark Prior	1.00	169	Bernie Williams	.40	287	Pete LaForest RC	.50
52	Moises Alou	.25	170	Brandon Claussen	.15	288	Nook Logan RC	.50
53	Nic Jackson	.15	171	Derek Jeter	2.00	289	Prentice Redman RC	.40
54	Ryne Sandberg	1.00	172	Don Mattingly	1.50	290	Joe Valentine RC	.40
55	Sammy Sosa	1.50	173	Drew Henson	.15	291	Jose Contreras RC	1.00
56	Carlos Lee	.15	174	Jason Giambi	.50	292	Josh Stewart RC	.40
57	Corwin Malone	.15	175	Joe Torre	.25	293	Mike Nicolas RC	.40
58	Frank Thomas	.50	176	Jorge Posada	.40	294	Marshall McDougall	.15
59	Joe Borchard	.15	177	Mike Mussina	.50	295	Travis Chapman	.15
60	Joe Crede	.15	178	Nick Johnson	.15	296	Jose Morban	.15
61	Magglio Ordonez	.25	179	Roger Clemens	1.50	297	Michael Hessman RC	.40
62	Mark Buehrle	.15	180	Whitey Ford	.75	298	Buddy Hernandez RC	.40
63	Paul Konerko	.25	181	Adam Morrissey	.15	299	Shane Victorino RC	.40
64	Tim Hummel	.15	182	Barry Zito	.40	300	Jason Dubois	.15
65	Jon Adkins	.15	183	David Justice	.15	301	Hideki Matsui RC	3.00
66	Adam Dunn	.50	184	Eric Chavez	.40			
67	Austin Kearns	.15	185	Jermaine Dye	.15			
68	Barry Larkin	.40	186	Mark Mulder	.25			
69	Jose Acevedo	.15	187	Miguel Tejada	.40			
70	Corky Miller	.15	188	Reggie Jackson	.75			
71	Eric Davis	.15	189	Terrence Long	.15			
72	Ken Griffey Jr.	1.00	190	Tim Hudson	.25			
73	Sean Casey	.15	191	Anderson Machado	.15			
74	Wily Mo Pena	.15	192	Bobby Abreu	.40			
75	Bob Feller	.50	193	Brandon Duckworth	.15			
76	Brian Tallet	.15	194	Jim Thome	.40			
77	C.C. Sabathia	.15	195	Eric Junge	.15			
78	Cliff Lee	.15	196	Jeremy Giambi	.15			
79	Earl Snyder	.15	197	Johnny Estrada	.15			
80	Ellis Burks	.15	198	Jorge Padilla	.15			
81	Jeremy Guthrie	.15	199	Marlon Byrd	.15			
82	Travis Hafner	.25	200	Mike Schmidt	1.50			
83	Luis Garcia	.15	201	Pat Burrell	.50			
84	Omar Vizquel	.25	202	Steve Carlton	.25			
85	Ricardo Rodriguez	.15	203	Aramis Ramirez	.25			
86	Ryan Church	.15	204	Brian Giles	.15			
87	Victor Martinez	.15	205	Carlos Rivera	.15			
88	Brandon Phillips	.15	206	Craig Wilson	.15			
89	Jack Cust	.15	207	Dave Williams	.15			
90	Jason Jennings	.15	208	Jack Wilson	.15			
91	Jeff Baker	.15	209	Jose Castillo	.15			
92	Garrett Atkins	.15	210	Kip Wells	.15			
93	Juan Uribe	.15	211	Roberto Clemente	1.50			
94	Larry Walker	.25	212	Walter Young	.15			
95	Rene Reyes	.15	213	Ben Howard	.15			
96	Todd Helton	.50	214	Brian Lawrence	.15			
97	Alan Trammell	.15	215	Clifford Bartosh	.15			
98	Fernando Rodney	.15	216	Dennis Tankersley	.15			
99	Carlos Pena	.15	217	Oliver Perez	.15			
100	Jack Morris	.15	218	Phil Nevin	.15			
101	Bobby Higginson	.15	219	Ryan Klesko	.25			
102	Mike Maroth	.15	220	Sean Burroughs	.15			
103	Robert Fick	.15	221	Tony Gwynn	.75			
104	Jesus Medrano	.15	222	Xavier Nady	.15			
105	Josh Beckett	.40	223	Mike Rivera	.15			
106	Luis Castillo	.15	224	Barry Bonds	2.00			
107	Mike Lowell	.25	225	Benito Santiago	.15			
108	Juan Pierre	.15	226	Jason Schmidt	.40			
109	Josh Wilson	.15	227	Jeff Kent	.25			
110	Tim Redding	.15	228	Kenny Lofton	.15			
111	Carlos Hernandez	.15	229	Rich Aurilia	.15			
112	Craig Biggio	.25	230	Robb Nen	.15			
113	Henri Stanley	.15	231	Tsuyoshi Shinjo	.15			
114	Jason Lane	.15	232	Bret Boone	.15			
115	Jeff Bagwell	.50	233	Chris Snelling	.15			
116	John Buck	.15	234	Edgar Martinez	.25			
117	Kirk Saarloos	.15	235	Freddy Garcia	.15			
118	Lance Berkman	.75	236	Ichiro Suzuki	1.50			
119	Nolan Ryan	2.00	237	John Olerud	.25			
120	Richard Hidalgo	.15	238	Kazuhiro Sasaki	.15			
121	Rodrigo Rosario	.15	239	Mike Cameron	.15			
122	Roy Oswalt	.15	240	Rafael Soriano	.15			
123	Tommy Whiteman RC	.15	241	Albert Pujols	1.50			
124	Wade Miller	.15	242	J.D. Drew	.40			
125	Alexis Gomez	.15	243	Jim Edmonds	.40			
126	Angel Berroa	.15	244	Ozzie Smith	1.00			
127	Brandon Berger	.15	245	Scott Rolen	.75			
128	Carlos Beltran	.40	246	So Taguchi	.15			
129	George Brett	2.00	247	Stan Musial	1.00			
130	Jimmy Gobble	.15	248	Antonio Perez	.15			
131	Dee Brown	.15	249	Aubrey Huff	.15			
132	Mike Sweeney	.15	250	Dewon Brazelton	.15			
133	Raul Ibanez	.15	251	Delvin James	.15			
134	Runelvys Hernandez	.15	252	Joe Kennedy	.15			
135	Adrian Beltre	.40	253	Toby Hall	.15			
136	Brian Jordan	.15	254	Alex Rodriguez	2.00			

Metalized

Stars: 4-8X
RC's: 1-3X
Production 100 Sets
Holofoils: No Pricing
Production 25 Sets

Autographs

NM/M
Common Autograph: 5.00
2 Alfredo Amezaga/325 8.00
3 Chone Figgins/375 10.00
13 Junior Spivey/45 10.00
24 Andy Pratt/475 8.00
25 Adam LaRoche/400 10.00
26 Trey Hodges/305 5.00
29 Ed Rogers/305 5.00
30 Brian Roberts/500 35.00
31 Geronimo Gil/150 8.00
32 Jay Gibbons/475 8.00
33 Josh Towers/500 10.00
34 Casey Fossum/160 10.00
35 Cliff Floyd/70 20.00
37 Fred Lynn/80 20.00
38 Freddy Sanchez/400 15.00
46 Corey Patterson/100 15.00
49 Juan Cruz/250 8.00
51 Mark Prior/50 30.00
53 Nic Jackson/100 10.00

57 Corwin Malone/400 8.00
59 Joe Borchard/215 8.00
64 Tim Hummel/400 5.00
65 Jon Adkins/400 5.00
66 Adam Dunn/100 30.00
67 Austin Kearns/500 20.00
69 Jose Acevedo/315 5.00
70 Corky Miller/295 5.00
71 Eric Davis/45 25.00
74 Wily Mo Pena/450 15.00
77 Brian Tallet/250 8.00
78 Cliff Lee/330 10.00
79 Earl Snyder/225 8.00
81 Jeremy Guthrie/400 8.00
83 Luis Garcia/395 5.00
86 Ryan Church/395 10.00
87 Victor Martinez/250 25.00
88 Brandon Phillips/375 10.00
89 Jack Cust/498 8.00
90 Jason Jennings/375 8.00
91 Jeff Baker/400 8.00
92 Garrett Atkins/400 8.00
95 Rene Reyes/350 8.00
98 Fernando Rodney/500 8.00
100 Jack Morris/50 20.00
102 Mike Maroth/400 8.00
104 Jesus Medrano/500 8.00
109 Josh Wilson/400 8.00
110 Tim Redding/375 8.00
111 Carlos Hernandez/250 8.00
113 Henri Stanley/390 5.00
114 Jason Lane/250 10.00
117 Kirk Saarloos/149 8.00
120 Richard Hidalgo/120 10.00
121 Rodrigo Rosario/500 10.00
122 Roy Oswalt/100 20.00
124 Wade Miller/125 10.00
126 Angel Berroa/400 10.00
127 Brandon Berger/325 8.00
130 Jimmy Gobble/400 8.00
131 Dee Brown/500 8.00
132 Mike Sweeney/45 20.00
134 Runelvys Hernandez/400 5.00
138 Victor Alvarez/308 8.00
144 Paul LoDuca/45 20.00
146 Ben Sheets/500 8.00
147 Bill Hall/450 10.00
148 Nick Neugebauer/375 5.00
151 Shane Nance/150 4.00
152 Takahito Nomura/50 20.00
153 A.J. Pierzynski/250 10.00
156 Adam Johnson/500 8.00
157 Rob Bowen/375 8.00
158 Torii Hunter/45 20.00
160 Endy Chavez/280 8.00
161 Javier Vazquez/50 15.00
162 Jose Vidro/45 15.00
164 Dwight Gooden/45 30.00
170 Brandon Claussen/475 10.00
178 Nick Johnson/500 8.00
181 Adam Morrissey/395 8.00
185 Jermaine Dye/275 15.00
189 Terrence Long/250 10.00
191 Anderson Machado/500 8.00
193 Brandon Duckworth/100 10.00
195 Eric Junge/279 8.00
205 Carlos Rivera/400 8.00
206 Craig Wilson/245 10.00
207 Dave Williams/265 8.00
208 Jack Wilson/500 15.00
212 Walter Young/400 8.00
213 Ben Howard/500 8.00
214 Brian Lawrence/500 8.00
215 Clifford Bartosh/400 8.00
222 Xavier Nady/250 8.00
223 Mike Rivera/90 8.00
233 Chris Snelling/200 8.00
240 Rafael Soriano/500 8.00
248 Antonio Perez/500 8.00
249 Aubrey Huff/475 15.00
250 Dewon Brazelton/50 15.00
251 Delvin James/400 8.00
252 Joe Kennedy/250 8.00
253 Toby Hall/500 8.00
255 Ben Kozlowski/450 8.00
256 Gerald Laird/450 8.00
257 Hank Blalock/50 25.00
260 Kevin Mench/475 10.00
261 Mario Ramos/475 5.00
262 Mark Teixeira/40 40.00
265 Alexis Rios/400 8.00
267 Eric Hinske/390 10.00
269 Kevin Cash/375 8.00
274 Vinnie Chulk/100 8.00
275 Jason Anderson/493 15.00
276 Craig Brazell/500 15.00
277 Terrmel Sledge/500 10.00
278 Ryan Cameron/475 8.00
279 Clint Barmes/500 15.00
280 Jhonny Peralta/500 15.00
281 Todd Wellemeyer/477 10.00
282 Jon Leicester/480 8.00
283 Brandon Webb/500 30.00
284 Tim Olson/500 8.00
285 Matt Kata/487 10.00
286 Rob Hammock/486 8.00
287 Pete LaForest/500 8.00
288 Nook Logan/500 10.00
289 Prentice Redman/488 10.00
290 Joe Valentine/475 8.00
291 Jose Contreras/100 25.00

292 Josh Stewart/485 10.00
293 Mike Nicolas/500 10.00
295 Travis Chapman/100 15.00
296 Jose Morban/475 8.00
297 Michael Hessman/500 8.00
298 Buddy Hernandez/500 8.00
299 Shane Victorino/480 8.00
300 Jason Dubois/480 10.00
302 Ryan Wagner/100 15.00
303 Adam Loewen/100 10.00
304 Chien-Ming Wang/100 200.00
305 Hong-Chih Kuo/100 80.00
307 Dan Haren/100 20.00
309 Ramon Nivar/100 15.00

Call to the Hall

hoyt wilhelm rp

NM/M
Complete Set (10): 30.00
Common Player: 2.00
Metalized: 2-4X
Production 100 Sets
Holofoils: No Pricing
Production 25 Sets
1 Nolan Ryan/2,490 10.00
2 Tom Seaver/2,490 4.00
3 Phil Rizzuto/2,500 4.00
4 Orlando Cepeda/2,500 2.00
5 Al Kaline/2,500 5.00
6 Hoyt Wilhelm/2,500 2.00
7 Luis Aparicio/2,500 2.00
8 Billy Williams/2,500 2.00
9 Jim Palmer/2,500 2.00
10 Mike Schmidt/2,500 6.00

Call to the Hall Autographs

No Pricing
Quantity produced listed

Grand Champions

NM/M
Complete Set (25): 80.00
Common Player: 2.00
Inserted 1:18
Metalized: 2-4X
Production 100 Sets
Holo Foils: No Pricing
Production 25 Sets
1 Stan Musial 6.00
2 Bob Feller 2.00
3 Reggie Jackson 3.00
4 George Brett 8.00
5 Jim Palmer 2.00
6 Harmon Killebrew 4.00
7 Ernie Banks 2.00
8 Frank Robinson 2.00
9 Greg Maddux 4.00
10 Whitey Ford 4.00
11 Bob Gibson 2.00
12 Mike Schmidt 4.00
13 Nolan Ryan 10.00
14 Warren Spahn 4.00
15 Rod Carew 3.00
16 Hoyt Wilhelm 2.00
17 Duke Snider 4.00
18 Tom Seaver 2.00
19 Steve Carlton 3.00
20 Yogi Berra 4.00
21 Cal Ripken Jr. 10.00
22 Tony Gwynn 4.00
23 Wade Boggs 4.00
24 Rickey Henderson 3.00
25 Roger Clemens 8.00

Grand Champions Autographs

No Pricing

Numbers Game

NM/M
Quantity produced listed

1 Vladimir Guerrero/Jsy/200 10.00
2 Nomar Garciaparra/Jsy/200 20.00
3 Magglio Ordonez/Jsy/100 8.00
4 Garret Anderson/Jsy/50 15.00
5 Derek Jeter/Base/200 20.00
6 Jim Thome/Jsy/200 8.00
7 Torii Hunter/Jsy/200 10.00
8 Todd Helton/Jsy/200 10.00
9 Andruw Jones/Jsy/200 6.00
11 Luis Gonzalez/Jsy/200 5.00
12 Manny Ramirez/Jsy/200 12.00
13 Paul Konerko/Jsy/200 6.00
14 Alex Rodriguez/Jsy/200 20.00
15 Carlos Beltran/Jsy/200 4.00
16 Bernie Williams/Jsy/200 8.00
17 Barry Bonds/Base/200 20.00
18 Miguel Tejada/Jsy/200 15.00
19 Jason Giambi/Base/200 8.00
20 Ichiro Suzuki/Base/200 25.00
21 Ivan Rodriguez/Jsy/100 15.00
22 Rafael Palmeiro/Jsy/200 10.00
23 Carlos Delgado/Jsy/200 5.00
24 Vernon Wells/Jsy/200 4.00
25 Sammy Sosa/Jsy/200 20.00
26 Chipper Jones/Jsy/200 12.00
27 Adam Dunn/Jsy/44 25.00
28 Larry Walker/Jsy/200 4.00
29 Shawn Green/Jsy/100 10.00
30 Richie Sexson/Jsy/200 6.00
31 Jose Vidro/Jsy/200 4.00
32 Mike Piazza/Jsy/200 40.00
33 Roberto Alomar/Jsy/100 15.00
34 Bobby Abreu/Jsy/200 5.00
35 Pat Burrell/Jsy/200 8.00
36 Brian Giles/Jsy/200 6.00
37 Albert Pujols/Base/200 15.00
38 Lance Berkman/Jsy/50 15.00
39 Ryan Klesko/Jsy/200 6.00
40 Jeff Kent/Jsy/200 4.00

Statistical Champs

NM/M
Complete Set (30): 40.00
Common Player: 1.00
Inserted 1:10
1 Alex Rodriguez 5.00
2 Alfonso Soriano 2.00
3 Curt Schilling 1.50
4 Eddie Mathews 2.00
5 Fred Lynn 1.00
6 Harmon Killebrew 2.00
7 Hideo Nomo 1.00
8 Jim Thome 1.50
9 Kirby Puckett 3.00
10 Luis Gonzalez 1.00
11 Manny Ramirez 1.50
12 Jason Giambi 1.00
13 Mike Schmidt 4.00
14 Nomar Garciaparra 4.00
15 Lou Brock 1.50
16 Randy Johnson 2.00
17 Reggie Jackson 2.00
18 Rickey Henderson 1.50
19 Roberto Clemente 5.00
20 Barry Zito 1.50
21 Todd Helton 1.50
22 Tom Seaver 3.00
23 Tony Gwynn 2.00
24 Torii Hunter 1.00
25 Troy Glaus 1.00
26 Wade Boggs 1.50
27 Rod Carew 1.50
28 Juan Gonzalez 1.50
29 Sammy Sosa 3.00
30 Warren Spahn 2.00

Statistical Champs Materials

NM/M
Quantity produced listed

1 Alex Rodriguez/ Jsy/250 20.00
3 Curt Schilling/ Jsy/225 8.00
4 Eddie Mathews/ Jsy/250 20.00
6 Harmon Killebrew/ Jsy/250 20.00
7 Hideo Nomo/ Jsy/110 50.00
8 Jim Thome/Jsy/250 8.00
9 Kirby Puckett/ Jsy/250 20.00
10 Luis Gonzalez/ Jsy/250 5.00
11 Manny Ramirez/ Jsy/155 10.00
12 Jason Giambi/ Jsy/250 10.00
13 Mike Schmidt/ Jsy/250 35.00
14 Nomar Garciaparra/ Jsy/99 30.00
15 Lou Brock/Jsy/250 15.00
16 Randy Johnson/ Jsy/100 15.00
17 Reggie Jackson/ Jsy/200 15.00
18 Rickey Henderson/ Jsy/184 15.00
20 Barry Zito/Jsy/100 10.00
21 Todd Helton/Jsy/250 10.00
22 Tom Seaver/Jsy/100 30.00
23 Tony Gwynn/Jsy/200 15.00
24 Torii Hunter/Jsy/200 10.00
25 Troy Glaus/Jsy/125 5.00
26 Wade Boggs/ Jsy/250 15.00
27 Rod Carew/Hat/150 15.00
28 Juan Gonzalez/ Jsy/250 8.00
29 Sammy Sosa/ Jsy/250 20.00
30 Warren Spahn/ Jsy/150 30.00

Team Colors

Complete Set (30): 60.00
Common Player: 1.00
Inserted 1:10
1 Miguel Tejada 1.50
2 Mike Schmidt 5.00
3 George Brett 6.00
4 Magglio Ordonez 1.00
5 Ryne Sandberg 4.00
6 Adam Dunn 1.50
7 Mark Prior 2.00
8 Tony Gwynn 2.00
9 Troy Glaus 1.50
10 Stan Musial 4.00
11 Kirby Puckett 3.00
12 Don Mattingly 1.00
13 Bobby Abreu 1.00
14 Ichiro Suzuki 4.00
15 Cal Ripken Jr. 8.00
16 Chipper Jones 3.00
17 Carlos Beltran 1.50
18 Alfonso Soriano 2.00
19 Albert Pujols 5.00
20 Andruw Jones 1.50
21 Bernie Williams 1.50
22 Todd Helton 1.50
23 Roberto Clemente 6.00
24 Jim Thome 1.50
25 Carlos Delgado 1.00
26 Derek Jeter 6.00
27 Garret Anderson 1.00
28 Nomar Garciaparra 4.00
29 Torii Hunter 1.00
30 Vladimir Guerrero 2.00

Team Colors Materials

NM/M
Quantity produced listed
1 Miguel Tejada/ Jsy/50 15.00
2 Mike Schmidt/ Jsy/200 35.00
3 George Brett/ Jsy/200 35.00
4 Magglio Ordonez/ Jsy/100 8.00
5 Ryne Sandberg/ Jsy/200 30.00

6 Adam Dunn/Jsy/44 20.00
7 Mark Prior/Jsy/200 8.00
8 Tony Gwynn/Jsy/200 15.00
9 Troy Glaus/Jsy/200 8.00
10 Stan Musial/Jsy/200 35.00
11 Kirby Puckett/ Jsy/200 15.00
12 Don Mattingly/ Jsy/200 40.00
13 Bobby Abreu/Jsy/200 5.00
14 Ichiro Suzuki/ Base/200 25.00
15 Cal Ripken Jr./ Jsy/200 40.00
16 Chipper Jones/ Jsy/200 12.00
17 Carlos Beltran/ Jsy/200 8.00
19 Albert Pujols/ Base/200 15.00
20 Andruw Jones/ Jsy/200 6.00
21 Bernie Williams/ Jsy/200 8.00
22 Todd Helton/Jsy/200 10.00
23 Roberto Clemente/ Jsy/200 80.00
24 Jim Thome/Jsy/200 8.00
25 Carlos Delgado/ Jsy/200 5.00
26 Derek Jeter/Base/ 200 20.00
27 Garret Anderson/ Jsy/50 12.00
28 Nomar Garciaparra/ Jsy/200 20.00
29 Torii Hunter/Jsy/200 10.00
30 Vladimir Guerrero/ Jsy/200 10.00

Total Game

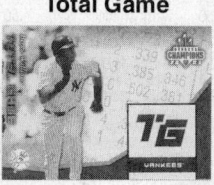

NM/M
Complete Set (40): 60.00
Common Player: 1.00
Inserted 1:9
1 Vladimir Guerrero 2.00
2 Nomar Garciaparra 4.00
3 Magglio Ordonez 1.00
4 Garret Anderson 1.00
5 Derek Jeter 6.00
6 Jim Thome 1.50
7 Torii Hunter 1.50
8 Todd Helton 1.50
9 Andruw Jones 1.50
10 Alfonso Soriano 2.00
11 Luis Gonzalez 1.00
12 Manny Ramirez 1.50
13 Paul Konerko 1.00
14 Alex Rodriguez 5.00
15 Carlos Beltran 1.00
16 Bernie Williams 1.50
17 Barry Bonds 6.00
18 Miguel Tejada 1.50
19 Jason Giambi 1.00
20 Ichiro Suzuki 4.00
21 Ivan Rodriguez 1.50
22 Rafael Palmeiro 1.50
23 Carlos Delgado 1.00
24 Vernon Wells 1.00
25 Sammy Sosa 4.00
26 Chipper Jones 2.00
27 Adam Dunn 1.50
28 Larry Walker 1.00
29 Shawn Green 1.00
30 Richie Sexson 1.00
31 Jose Vidro 1.00
32 Mike Piazza 2.00
33 Roberto Alomar 1.50
34 Bobby Abreu 1.00
35 Pat Burrell 1.00
36 Brian Giles 1.00
37 Albert Pujols 5.00
38 Lance Berkman 1.00
39 Ryan Klesko 1.00
40 Jeff Kent 1.00

World Series Champions

NM/M
Complete Set (15): 20.00
Common Player: 1.50
Production 2,002 Sets
Metalized: 2-3X
Production 100 Sets
Holo Foil: No Pricing

Production 25 Sets
1 Troy Glaus 3.00
2 Jarrod Washburn 1.50
3 Darin Erstad 2.50
4 Troy Percival 1.50
5 David Eckstein 1.50
6 Francisco Rodriguez 2.00
7 Garret Anderson 2.50
8 John Lackey 1.50
9 Tim Salmon 2.00
10 Chone Figgins 1.50
11 Adam Kennedy 1.50
12 Scott Spiezio 1.50
13 Ben Molina 1.50
14 Brad Fullmer 1.50
15 Troy Glaus MVP 3.00

World Series Champions Autograph

No Pricing

2003 Donruss Classics Samples

Each issue of the June 2003 Beckett Baseball Card Monthly included a sample 2003 Donruss Classics card rubber-cemented inside. The cards differ from the issued version only in the appearance on back of a (usually) silver-foil "SAMPLE" notation. Some cards were produced with the overprint in gold-foil, in much more limited quantities. The number of different players' cards involved in the promotion is unknown.

NM/M
Common Player: .10
Stars: 1.5-2X
Gold: 10X

2003 Donruss Classics

RYAN KLESKO

NM/M
Complete Set (200):
Common Player: .40
Common Legends (101-150): 3.00
Production 1,500
Common Prospect (151-200): 3.00
Production 1,500
Pack (7): 4.50
Box (18): 70.00
1 Troy Glaus .50
2 Barry Bonds 3.00
3 Miguel Tejada .50
4 Randy Johnson 1.00
5 Eric Hinske .40
6 Barry Zito .50
7 Jason Jennings .40
8 Derek Jeter 3.00
9 Vladimir Guerrero 1.00
10 Corey Patterson .75
11 Manny Ramirez .75
12 Edgar Martinez .50
13 Roy Oswalt .50
14 Andruw Jones .75
15 Alex Rodriguez 3.00
16 Mark Mulder .50
17 Kazuhisa Ishii .40
18 Gary Sheffield .50
19 Jay Gibbons .40
20 Roberto Alomar .50
21 A.J. Pierzynski .40
22 Eric Chavez .50
23 Roger Clemens 2.00
24 C.C. Sabathia .40
25 Jose Vidro .40
26 Shannon Stewart .40
27 Mark Teixeira .50
28 Joe Thurston .40
29 Josh Beckett .75
30 Jeff Bagwell .75
31 Geronimo Gil .40
32 Curt Schilling .75
33 Frank Thomas .75
34 Lance Berkman .50
35 Adam Dunn .75
36 Christian Parker .40
37 Jim Thome 1.00
38 Shawn Green .50
39 Drew Henson .40
40 Chipper Jones 1.00
41 Kevin Mench .40
42 Hideo Nomo .50
43 Andres Galarraga .40
44 Doug Davis .40
45 Mark Prior 1.00
46 Sean Casey .40
47 Magglio Ordonez .50
48 Tom Glavine .50
49 Marlon Byrd .40
50 Albert Pujols 2.00
51 Mark Buehrle .40
52 Aramis Ramirez .50
53 Pat Burrell .50
54 Craig Biggio .50
55 Alfonso Soriano 1.00
56 Kerry Wood 1.00
57 Wade Miller .40
58 Hank Blalock .75
59 Cliff Floyd .40
60 Jason Giambi .50
61 Carlos Beltran .50
62 Brian Roberts .40
63 Paul LoDuca .40
64 Tim Redding .40
65 Sammy Sosa 2.00
66 Joe Borchard .40
67 Ryan Klesko .40
68 Richie Sexson .50
69 Carlos Lee .40
70 Rickey Henderson .75
71 Brian Tallet .40
72 Luis Gonzalez .50
73 Satoru Komiyama .40
74 Tim Hudson .50
75 Ken Griffey Jr. 1.50
76 Adam Johnson .40
77 Bobby Abreu .60
78 Adrian Beltre .40
79 Rafael Palmeiro .75
80 Ichiro Suzuki 2.00
81 Kenny Lofton .40
82 Brian Giles .50
83 Barry Larkin .50
84 Robert Fick .40
85 Ben Sheets .50
86 Scott Rolen 1.00
87 Nomar Garciaparra 1.50
88 Brandon Phillips .40
89 Ben Kozlowski .40
90 Bernie Williams .75
91 Pedro J. Martinez 1.00
92 Todd Helton .75
93 Jermaine Dye .40
94 Carlos Delgado .50
95 Mike Piazza 1.50
96 Junior Spivey .40
97 Torii Hunter .50
98 Mike Sweeney .40
99 Ivan Rodriguez .75
100 Greg Maddux 1.50
101 Ernie Banks 5.00
102 Steve Garvey 3.00
103 George Brett 8.00
104 Lou Brock 3.00
105 Hoyt Wilhelm 3.00
106 Steve Carlton 4.00
107 Joe Torre 3.00
108 Dennis Eckersley 4.00
109 Reggie Jackson 5.00
110 Al Kaline 8.00
111 Harold Reynolds 3.00
112 Don Mattingly 8.00
113 Tony Gwynn 5.00
114 Willie McCovey 5.00
115 Joe Morgan 3.00
116 Stan Musial 8.00
117 Jim Palmer 3.00
118 Brooks Robinson 8.00
119 Don Sutton 3.00
120 Nolan Ryan 10.00
121 Mike Schmidt 8.00
122 Tom Seaver 5.00
123 Cal Ripken Jr. 8.00
124 Robin Yount 5.00
125 Bob Feller 3.00
126 Joe Carter 3.00
127 Jack Morris 3.00
128 Luis Aparicio 3.00
129 Bobby Doerr 3.00
130 Dave Parker 3.00
131 Yogi Berra 5.00
132 Will Clark 3.00
133 Fred Lynn 3.00
134 Andre Dawson 3.00
135 Duke Snider 4.00
136 Orlando Cepeda 3.00
137 Billy Williams 3.00
138 Dale Murphy 4.00
139 Harmon Killebrew 5.00
140 Carlton Fisk 6.00
141 Eric Davis 3.00
142 Alan Trammell 3.00
143 Paul Molitor 5.00
144 Jose Canseco 3.00
145 Ozzie Smith 5.00
146 Ralph Kiner 3.00
147 Dwight Gooden 3.00
148 Phil Rizzuto 5.00
149 Lenny Dykstra 3.00
150 Adam LaRoche 4.00
151 Tim Hummel 3.00
152 Matt Kata RC 4.00
153 Jeff Baker 3.00
154 Josh Stewart RC 4.00
155 Marshall McDougall 4.00
156 Jhonny Peralta 3.00
157 Mike Nicolas RC 3.00
158 Jeremy Guthrie 3.00
159 Craig Brazell RC 4.00
160 Joe Valentine RC 3.00
161 Buddy Hernandez 4.00
162 Freddy Sanchez 4.00
163 Shane Victorino RC 4.00
164 Corwin Malone 4.00
165 Jason Dubois 3.00
166 Josh Wilson 3.00
167 Tim Olson RC 4.00
168 Clifford Bartosh 3.00
169 Michael Hessman RC 4.00
170 Ryan Church 5.00
171 Garrett Atkins 5.00
172 Jose Morban 3.00
173 Ryan Cameron RC 4.00
174 Todd Wellemeyer RC 4.00
175 Travis Chapman 3.00
176 Jason Anderson 3.00
177 Adam Morrissey 3.00
178 Jose Contreras 5.00
179 Nic Jackson 3.00
180 Rob Hammock RC 3.00
181 Carlos Rivera 3.00
182 Vinnie Chulk 3.00
183 Pete LaForest RC 3.00
184 Jon Leicester RC 4.00
185 Terrmel Sledge RC 4.00
186 Jose Castillo 3.00
187 Gerald Laird 3.00
188 Nook Logan RC 4.00
189 Clint Barmes RC 5.00
190 Jesus Medrano 3.00
191 Henri Stanley 3.00
192 Hideki Matsui RC 10.00
193 Walter Young 3.00
194 Jon Adkins 3.00
195 Tommy Whiteman RC 4.00
196 Rob Bowen 3.00
197 Brandon Webb RC 5.00
198 Prentice Redman RC 4.00
199 Jimmy Gobble 3.00

Dress Code

NM/M
Common Player: 4.00
Quantity produced listed
1 Roger Clemens/ Jsy/500 15.00
2 M. Tejada/Jsy/Hat/ Bat/250 20.00
3 V. Guerrero/Jsy/250 8.00
4 Kazuhisa Ishii/ Jsy/250 10.00
5 Chipper Jones/ Jsy/425 10.00
6 Troy Glaus/Jsy/425 8.00
7 Rafael Palmeiro/ Jsy/500 8.00
8 Rickey Henderson/ Jsy/250 10.00
9 Pedro Martinez/ Jsy/425 8.00
10 Andruw Jones/ Jsy/425 6.00
11 Nomar Garciaparra/ Jsy/500 12.00
12 Carlos Delgado/ Jsy/500 5.00
13 R.Henderson/Jsy/ Hat/250 20.00
14 K. Wood/Jsy/ Hat/250 20.00
15 L. Berkman/Jsy/ Hat/50 20.00
16 Tony Gwynn/ Quad/400 65.00
17 Mark Mulder/Jsy/425 8.00
18 Jim Thome/Jsy/500 8.00
19 Mike Piazza/Jsy/500 15.00
20 Mike Mussina/ Jsy/500 10.00
21 Luis Gonzalez/ Jsy/500 5.00
22 Ryan Klesko/Jsy/500 5.00
23 Richie Sexson/ Jsy/500 6.00
24 Curt Schilling/ Jsy/200 10.00
25 A. Rodriguez/Jsy/ 500 12.00
26 B. Williams/Jsy/425 8.00
27 Cal Ripken Jr./ Jsy/500 35.00
28 C.C. Sabathia/Jsy/ 500 4.00
29 M. Piazza/Bat/Jsy/ 200 30.00
30 Rickey Henderson/ Hat/Jsy/500 15.00
31 Torii Hunter/Jsy/425 8.00
32 Mark Teixeira/Jsy/425 8.00
33 D. Murphy/Jsy/ Bat/300 15.00
34 Todd Helton/Jsy/425 8.00
35 Eric Chavez/Jsy/425 8.00
36 Vernon Wells/Jsy/425 5.00
37 J. Bagwell/Jsy/ Hat/100 25.00
38 Nick Johnson/ Jsy/425 5.00
39 Tim Hudson/ Hat/250 10.00
40 Shawn Green/Jsy/ 425 5.00
41 Mark Buehrle/Jsy/ 500 5.00
42 Garret Anderson/ Jsy/100 5.00
43 Alex Rodriguez/ Jsy/500 12.00
44 Jason Giambi/Jsy/ 500 5.00
45 Carlos Beltran/ Jsy/500 5.00
46 Adam Dunn/Jsy/ Hat/100 30.00
47 Jorge Posada/Jsy/ 425 8.00
48 Roy Oswalt/Jsy/ Hat/100 15.00
49 Rich Aurilia/Jsy/500 5.00
50 Jason Jennings/ Quad/250 15.00
51 Mark Prior/Quad/250 40.00
52 Jim Edmonds/ Jsy/500 8.00
53 Fred McGriff/Jsy/500 6.00
54 A. Soriano/Jsy/ Shoe/100 15.00
55 Jeff Kent/Jsy/425 5.00
56 Hideo Nomo/Jsy/ 200 30.00
57 Manny Ramirez/ Jsy/425 8.00
58 J. Canseco/Jsy/ Bat/350 15.00
59 M. Ordonez/Jsy/500 6.00
60 A. Trammell/Jsy/ Bat/250 10.00
61 Bobby Abreu/Jsy/500 6.00
62 R.Henderson/ Dual/Jsy/200 20.00
63 Josh Beckett/Jsy/500 6.00
64 Barry Larkin/Jsy/500 8.00
65 Randy Johnson/ Jsy/200 10.00
66 Juan Gonzalez/ Jsy/200 8.00
67 Barry Zito/Jsy/ Hat/125 15.00
68 Roger Clemens/ Jsy/500 15.00
69 Rickey Henderson/ Hat/Jsy/100 25.00
70 Hideo Nomo/Jsy/ 100 50.00
71 Paul Konerko/ Jsy/400 6.00
72 Pat Burrell/Jsy/400 8.00
73 F.Thomas/Jsy/ Pants/250 15.00
74 Sammy Sosa/ Jsy/500 15.00
75 G. Maddux/Glv/ Jsy/50 60.00

Legendary Hats

NM/M
Varying quantities produced
1 Roberto Clemente/ 80 100.00
2 Kirby Puckett/50 50.00
3 Mike Schmidt/50 75.00
4 Tony Gwynn/50 50.00
5 Rickey Henderson/ 50 60.00

Legendary Leather

NM/M
Varying quantities produced
1 Nolan Ryan/80 110.00

Legendary Lumberjacks

NM/M
Common Player: 10.00

Legendary Lumberjacks

		NM/M
Complete Set (15):		65.00
Common Player:		3.00
Production 2,500 Sets		
1	Babe Ruth	10.00
2	Steve Carlton	3.00
3	Honus Wagner	6.00
4	Warren Spahn	5.00
5	Eddie Mathews	5.00
6	Nolan Ryan	10.00
7	Rogers Hornsby	5.00
8	Ernie Banks	5.00
9	Harmon Killebrew	5.00
10	Tom Seaver	5.00
11	Jimmie Foxx	6.00
12	Ty Cobb	6.00
13	Frank Robinson	4.00
14	Mel Ott	5.00
15	Lou Gehrig	8.00

Legendary Spikes

Varying quantities produced
1	Babe Ruth/100	180.00
2	Lou Gehrig/80	125.00
3	George Brett/250	25.00
4	Duke Snider/250	20.00
5	Roberto Clemente/25	165.00
6	Ryne Sandberg/400	35.00
7	Robin Yount/300	15.00
8	Harmon Killebrew/250	25.00
9	Al Kaline/250	25.00
10	Eddie Mathews/225	20.00
11	Brooks Robinson/400	25.00
13	Kirby Puckett/375	20.00
14	Jose Canseco/400	15.00
15	Nellie Fox/325	20.00
16	Don Mattingly/400	35.00
17	Joe Torre/250	15.00
18	Cal Ripken Jr/250	40.00
19	Richie Ashburn/250	15.00
20	Mike Schmidt/250	30.00
21	Dale Murphy/250	25.00
22	Thurman Munson/400	15.00
23	Tony Gwynn/400	15.00
24	Orlando Cepeda/225	10.00
25	Ty Cobb/25	225.00
26	Paul Molitor/325	10.00
27	Ralph Kiner/200	15.00
28	Frank Robinson/225	20.00
29	Yogi Berra/50	50.00
30	Reggie Jackson/375	15.00
31	Rod Carew/325	15.00
32	Carlton Fisk/325	15.00
33	Rogers Hornsby/50	60.00
34	Mel Ott/125	30.00
35	Jimmie Foxx/50	60.00

Legendary Spikes

		NM/M
Production 50 Sets		
1	Kirby Puckett	60.00
2	Tony Gwynn	50.00
3	Don Mattingly	125.00
4	Frank Robinson	35.00
5	Gary Carter	30.00

Legends of the Fall

		NM/M
Complete Set (10):		40.00
Common Player:		3.00
Production 2,500 Sets		
1	Reggie Jackson	4.00
2	Duke Snider	4.00
3	Roberto Clemente	8.00
4	Mel Ott	4.00
5	Yogi Berra	6.00
6	Jackie Robinson	5.00
7	Enos Slaughter	3.00
8	Willie Stargell	4.00
9	Bobby Doerr	3.00
10	Thurman Munson	5.00

Legends of the Fall Fabrics

		NM/M
Quantity produced listed		3.00
1	Reggie Jackson/100	20.00
2	Roberto Clemente/50	120.00
6	Jackie Robinson/50	80.00
8	Willie Stargell/100	20.00
9	Bobby Doerr/100	20.00

Membership

Membership VIP Memorabilia

		NM/M
Varying quantities produced		
1	Babe Ruth/Bat/29	325.00
2	Steve Carlton/Jsy/81	25.00
4	Warren Spahn/Jsy/61	50.00
5	Eddie Mathews/Bat/67	60.00
6	Nolan Ryan/Jsy/80	75.00
7	R. Hornsby/Bat/31	75.00
8	Ernie Banks/Jsy/70	35.00
9	H. Killebrew/Jsy/71	60.00
10	Tom Seaver/Jsy/81	30.00
11	Jimmie Foxx/Bat/40	60.00
13	F. Robinson/Jsy/71	25.00
14	Mel Ott/Jsy/45	50.00

Significant Signatures

		NM/M
Common Autograph:		8.00
#'s 201-211 exclusive to Donruss Rookies		
5	Eric Hinske/250	15.00
6	Barry Zito/25	40.00
7	Jason Jennings/250	10.00
10	Corey Patterson/100	15.00
13	Roy Oswalt/100	25.00
16	Mark Mulder/100	25.00
19	Jay Gibbons/250	10.00
21	A.J. Pierzynski/75	20.00
22	Eric Chavez/20	40.00
25	Jose Vidro/75	15.00
27	Mark Teixeira/40	40.00
31	Geronimo Gil/50	15.00
35	Adam Dunn/100	40.00
36	Christian Parker/250	10.00
39	Drew Henson/100	10.00
41	Kevin Mench/250	10.00
45	Mark Prior/50	30.00
56	Kerry Wood/15	60.00
57	Wade Miller/200	10.00
58	Hank Blalock/50	25.00
62	Brian Roberts/50	25.00
63	Paul LoDuca/100	15.00
64	Tim Redding/250	8.00
66	Joe Borchard/100	15.00
68	Richie Sexson/20	40.00
69	Carlos Lee/25	25.00
73	Satoru Komiyama/124	20.00
76	Adam Johnson/200	8.00
84	Robert Fick/50	10.00
88	Brandon Phillips/250	10.00
89	Ben Kozlowski/150	8.00
93	Jermaine Dye/50	15.00
96	Junior Spivey/100	15.00
97	Torii Hunter/50	25.00
102	Steve Garvey/100	25.00
108	Dennis Eckersley/50	30.00
111	Harold Reynolds/50	15.00
119	Don Sutton/100	15.00
120	Nolan Ryan/50	200.00
123	Cal Ripken Jr/50	220.00
126	Joe Carter/100	15.00
127	Jack Morris/100	20.00
128	Luis Aparicio/50	20.00
132	Will Clark/20	125.00
133	Fred Lynn/50	15.00
134	Andre Dawson/50	30.00
136	Orlando Cepeda/100	20.00
137	Billy Williams/100	15.00
142	Eric Davis/50	25.00
143	Alan Trammell/50	35.00

148	Dwight Gooden/50	40.00
149	Phil Rizzuto/20	75.00
150	Lenny Dykstra/50	25.00
151	Adam LaRoche/250	15.00
152	Tim Hummel/500	8.00
153	Matt Kata/500	15.00
154	Jeff Baker/500	10.00
155	Josh Stewart/177	10.00
156	Marshall McDougall/500	10.00
157	Jhonny Peralta/500	8.00
158	Mike Nicolas/500	8.00
159	Jeremy Guthrie/500	10.00
160	Craig Brazell/500	15.00
161	Joe Valentine/172	10.00
162	Buddy Hernandez/500	8.00
163	Freddy Sanchez/500	10.00
164	Shane Victorino/351	8.00
165	Corwin Malone/500	8.00
166	Jason Dubois/500	12.00
167	Josh Wilson/500	8.00
168	Tim Olson/500	8.00
169	Clifford Bartosh/500	8.00
170	Michael Hessman/427	8.00
171	Ryan Church/500	8.00
172	Garrett Atkins/500	8.00
173	Jose Morban/500	8.00
174	Ryan Cameron/500	10.00
175	Todd Wellemeyer/500	10.00
176	Travis Chapman/477	8.00
177	Jason Anderson/500	15.00
178	Adam Morrissey/500	8.00
179	Jose Contreras/100	20.00
180	Nic Jackson/500	8.00
181	Rob Hammock/500	8.00
182	Carlos Rivera/500	8.00
183	Vinnie Chulk/500	8.00
184	Pete LaForest/177	10.00
185	Jon Leicester/500	8.00
186	Terrmel Sledge/500	10.00
187	Jose Castillo/500	10.00
188	Gerald Laird/500	8.00
189	Nook Logan/427	8.00
190	Clint Barmes/500	20.00
191	Jesus Medrano/500	8.00
192	Henri Stanley/500	8.00
193	Walter Young/500	10.00
194	Jon Adkins/500	8.00
196	Tommy Whiteman/500	8.00
197	Rob Bowen/500	8.00
198	Brandon Webb/500	30.00
199	Prentice Redman/127	10.00
200	Jimmy Gobble/500	10.00
201	Jeremy Bonderman/100	50.00
202	Adam Loewen/100	10.00
203	Chien-Ming Wang/50	220.00
205	Ryan Wagner/100	10.00
206	Dan Haren/100	20.00
209	Ramon Nivar/100	15.00

Singles

		NM/M
Common Player:		10.00
Varying quantities produced		
1	Babe Ruth/Jsy/100	275.00
2	Lou Gehrig/Jsy/80	200.00
3	Jackie Robinson/Jsy/80	75.00
5	Bobby Doerr/Jsy/100	15.00
6	Fred Lynn/Jsy/100	12.00
7	Honus Wagner/Seat/100	35.00
8	Roberto Clemente/Jsy/80	100.00
9	Kirby Puckett/Jsy/100	40.00
10	Torii Hunter/Jsy/100	10.00
11	Sammy Sosa/Jsy/100	25.00
12	Ryne Sandberg/Jsy/100	90.00
13	Hideo Nomo/Jsy/100	20.00
14	Kazuhisa Ishii/Jsy/50	15.00
15	Mike Schmidt/Jsy/100	45.00
16	Steve Carlton/Jsy/100	15.00
17	Robin Yount/Jsy/100	30.00
18	Paul Molitor/Jsy/100	25.00
19	Mike Piazza/Jsy/100	35.00
20	Duke Snider/Jsy/50	35.00
21	Al Kaline/Jsy/50	40.00
23	Don Mattingly/Jsy/100	60.00
24	Jason Giambi/Jsy/100	10.00
26	Ozzie Smith/Jsy/100	40.00
27	Roger Clemens/Jsy/100	25.00
28	Pedro Martinez/Jsy/100	20.00
29	Thurman Munson/Jsy/50	50.00
30	Yogi Berra/Jsy/25	70.00

Combos

		NM/M
Varying quantities produced		

CC1	Babe Ruth, Lou Gehrig/50	475.00
CC2	Jackie Robinson, Pee Wee Reese/50	80.00
CC3	Bobby Doerr, Fred Lynn/25	65.00
CC4	Honus Wagner, Roberto Clemente/50	150.00
CC5	Kirby Puckett, Torii Hunter/25	75.00
CC6	Sammy Sosa, Ryne Sandberg/25	100.00
CC7	Hideo Nomo, Kazuhisa Ishii/25	75.00
CC8	Mike Schmidt, Steve Carlton/25	150.00
CC9	Robin Yount, Paul Molitor/25	100.00
CC12	Don Mattingly, Jason Giambi/25	150.00
CC13	Stan Musial, Ozzie Smith/25	100.00

Timeless Treasures

		NM/M
Varying quantities produced		
1	Tony Gwynn, Stan Musial/50	100.00
3	Vladimir Guerrero, Roberto Clemente/50	125.00
5	Jason Giambi, Don Mattingly/50	100.00

2003 Donruss Diamond Kings Samples

Each April 2003 issue of Beckett Baseball Card Monthly included a sample DK card rubber-cemented inside. The cards differ from the issued version only in the appearance on back of a (usually) silver-foil "SAMPLE" notation and, on some cards, the lack of silver-foil graphics on front. Some cards were produced with the back overprint in gold-foil in much more limited quantities.

		NM/M
Common Player:		.25
Stars:		1.5-2X
Gold:		10X

2003 Donruss Diamond Kings

		NM/M
Complete Set (176):		90.00
Common Player:		.40
Common (151-176):		1.00
Pack (5):		4.00
Box (24):		75.00
1	Darin Erstad	.50
2	Garret Anderson	.50
3	Troy Glaus	.50
4	David Eckstein	.40
5	Jarrod Washburn	.40
6	Adam Kennedy	.40
7	Jay Gibbons	.40
8	Tony Batista	.40
9	Melvin Mora	.40
10	Rodrigo Lopez	.40
11	Manny Ramirez	.75
12	Pedro J. Martinez	1.00
13	Nomar Garciaparra	1.50
14	Rickey Henderson	.60
15	Johnny Damon	.50
16	Derek Lowe	.40
17	Cliff Floyd	.40
18	Frank Thomas	.75
19	Magglio Ordonez	.50
20	Paul Konerko	.40
21	Mark Buehrle	.40
22	C.C. Sabathia	.40
23	Omar Vizquel	.40
24	Jim Thome	.75
25	Ellis Burks	.40
26	Robert Fick	.40
27	Bobby Higginson	.40
28	Randall Simon	.40
29	Carlos Pena	.40
30	Carlos Beltran	.75
31	Paul Byrd	.40
32	Raul Ibanez	.40
33	Mike Sweeney	.40
34	Torii Hunter	.50
35	Corey Koskie	.40
36	A.J. Pierzynski	.40
37	Cristian Guzman	.40
38	Jacque Jones	.40
39	Derek Jeter	3.00
40	Bernie Williams	.60
41	Roger Clemens	2.00
42	Mike Mussina	.60
43	Jorge Posada	.50
44	Alfonso Soriano	1.00
45	Jason Giambi	.50
46	Robin Ventura	.40
47	David Wells	.40
48	Tim Hudson	.50
49	Barry Zito	.50
50	Mark Mulder	.50
51	Miguel Tejada	.50
52	Eric Chavez	.50
53	Jermaine Dye	.40
54	Ichiro Suzuki	2.00
55	Edgar Martinez	.50
56	John Olerud	.40
57	Dan Wilson	.40
58	Joel Pineiro	.40
59	Kazuhiro Sasaki	.40
60	Freddy Garcia	.40
61	Aubrey Huff	.40
62	Steve Cox	.40
63	Randy Winn	.40
64	Alex Rodriguez	2.50
65	Juan Gonzalez	.50
66	Rafael Palmeiro	.75
67	Ivan Rodriguez	.75
68	Kenny Rogers	.40
69	Carlos Delgado	.50
70	Eric Hinske	.40
71	Roy Halladay	.40
72	Vernon Wells	.40
73	Shannon Stewart	.40
74	Curt Schilling	.75
75	Randy Johnson	1.00
76	Luis Gonzalez	.40
77	Mark Grace	.50
78	Junior Spivey	.40
79	Greg Maddux	1.50
80	Tom Glavine	.50
81	John Smoltz	.40
82	Chipper Jones	1.00
83	Gary Sheffield	.40
84	Andruw Jones	.50
85	Kerry Wood	1.00
86	Fred McGriff	.50
87	Sammy Sosa	1.50
88	Mark Prior	1.00
89	Ken Griffey Jr.	1.50
90	Barry Larkin	.50
91	Adam Dunn	.50
92	Sean Casey	.40
93	Austin Kearns	.50
94	Aaron Boone	.40
95	Larry Walker	.50
96	Todd Helton	.75
97	Jason Jennings	.40
98	Jay Payton	.40
99	Josh Beckett	.50
100	Mike Lowell	.40
101	A.J. Burnett	.40
102	Jeff Bagwell	.75
103	Craig da Luz	.40
104	Lance Berkman	.50
105	Roy Oswalt	.40
106	Wade Miller	.40
107	Shawn Green	.50
108	Adrian Beltre	.50
109	Hideo Nomo	.50
110	Kazuhisa Ishii	.40
111	Odalis Perez	.40
112	Paul LoDuca	.40
113	Ben Sheets	.40
114	Richie Sexson	.50
115	Jose Hernandez	.40
116	Vladimir Guerrero	.75
117	Jose Vidro	.40
118	Tomokazu Ohka	.40
119	Andres Galarraga	.40
120	Bartolo Colon	.40
121	Mike Piazza	1.50
122	Roberto Alomar	.50
123	Mo Vaughn	.40
124	Al Leiter	.40
125	Edgardo Alfonzo	.40
126	Pat Burrell	.75
127	Bobby Abreu	.50
128	Mike Lieberthal	.40
129	Vicente Padilla	.40
130	Marlon Byrd	.40
131	Jason Kendall	.40
132	Brian Giles	.50
133	Aramis Ramirez	.50
134	Kip Wells	.40
135	Ryan Klesko	.40
136	Phil Nevin	.40
137	Brian Lawrence	.40
138	Sean Burroughs	.40
139	Mark Kotsay	.40
140	Barry Bonds	3.00
141	Jeff Kent	.40
142	Benito Santiago	.40
143	Kirk Reuter	.40
144	Jason Schmidt	.50
145	Jim Edmonds	.50
146	J.D. Drew	.40
147	Albert Pujols	2.00
148	Tino Martinez	.40
149	Matt Morris	.40
150	Scott Rolen	1.00
151	Joe Borchard	2.00
152	Cliff Lee	1.00
153	Brian Tallet	1.00
154	Freddy Sanchez	1.00
155	Chone Figgins	1.00
156	Kevin Cash	1.00
157	Justin Wayne	1.00
158	Ben Kozlowski	1.00
159	Babe Ruth	6.00
160	Jackie Robinson	4.00
161	Ozzie Smith	4.00
162	Lou Gehrig	5.00
163	Stan Musial	4.00
164	Mike Schmidt	5.00
165	Carlton Fisk	2.00
166	George Brett	6.00
167	Dale Murphy	4.00
168	Cal Ripken Jr.	8.00
169	Tony Gwynn	3.00
170	Don Mattingly	6.00
171	Jack Morris	2.00
172	Ty Cobb	6.00
173	Nolan Ryan	6.00
174	Ryne Sandberg	5.00
175	Thurman Munson	4.00
176	Jose Contreras RC	8.00

Framed Portraits Bronze

Cards (1-150):	1-2.5X
Cards (151-176):	.75-1.5X
Silvers (1-150):	3-5X
Silvers (151-176):	2-3X
Production 400 Sets	
Golds (1-150):	5-10X
Golds (151-176):	3-6X
Production 100 Sets	

Diamond Cut

		NM/M
Common Signature (1-25):		10.00
Quantity produced listed		
1	Barry Zito/75	50.00
2	Edgar Martinez/125	50.00
3	Jay Gibbons/150	25.00
4	Joe Borchard/150	20.00
5	Marlon Byrd/150	20.00
6	Adam Dunn/150	40.00
7	Torii Hunter/150	40.00
8	Vladimir Guerrero/25	150.00
9	Wade Miller/150	25.00
10	Alfonso Soriano/100	60.00
11	Brian Lawrence/150	25.00
12	Cliff Floyd/100	25.00
13	Dale Murphy/75	75.00
14	Jack Morris/150	25.00
15	Eric Hinske/150	20.00
16	Jason Jennings/150	20.00
17	Mark Buehrle/150	30.00
18	Mark Prior/150	40.00
19	Mark Mulder/150	25.00
20	Mike Sweeney/150	25.00
21	Nolan Ryan/50	200.00
22	Don Mattingly/75	100.00
23	Andruw Jones/75	40.00
24	Aubrey Huff/75	25.00
	Common Jerseys (26-75):	5.00
26	Nolan Ryan/50	50.00
27	Ozzie Smith/400	15.00
28	Rickey Henderson/300	10.00

#	Player	Price
29	Jack Morris/500	5.00
30	George Brett/350	25.00
31	Cal Ripken Jr./300	40.00
32	Ryne Sandberg/450	20.00
33	Don Mattingly/400	25.00
34	Tony Gwynn/400	15.00
35	Dale Murphy/350	10.00
36	Carlton Fisk/400	10.00
38	Lou Gehrig/50	240.00
39	Garret Anderson/450	8.00
40	Pedro J. Martinez/400	10.00
41	Nomar Garciaparra/350	15.00
42	Magglio Ordonez/450	8.00
43	C.C. Sabathia/500	5.00
44	Omar Vizquel/250	8.00
45	Jim Thome/500	8.00
46	Torii Hunter/500	8.00
47	Roger Clemens/500	15.00
48	Alfonso Soriano/400	10.00
49	Tim Hudson/500	8.00
50	Barry Zito/350	8.00
51	Mark Mulder/500	6.00
52	Miguel Tejada/400	8.00
53	John Olerud/350	5.00
54	Alex Rodriguez/500	15.00
55	Rafael Palmeiro/500	8.00
56	Curt Schilling/500	8.00
57	Randy Johnson/400	10.00
58	Greg Maddux/350	12.00
59	John Smoltz/400	6.00
60	Chipper Jones/450	10.00
61	Andruw Jones/500	8.00
62	Kerry Wood/500	8.00
63	Mark Prior/500	10.00
64	Adam Dunn/350	10.00
65	Larry Walker/500	5.00
66	Todd Helton/500	10.00
67	Jeff Bagwell/500	10.00
68	Roy Oswalt/500	8.00
69	Hideo Nomo/150	15.00
70	Kazuhisa Ishii/250	5.00
71	Vladimir Guerrero/500	10.00
72	Mike Piazza/500	5.00
73	Joe Borchard/500	5.00
74	Ryan Klesko/500	5.00
75	Shawn Green/500	5.00

Common Bat (76-105): 5.00

#	Player	Price
76	George Brett/350	25.00
77	Ozzie Smith/450	15.00
78	Cal Ripken Jr/150	50.00
79	Don Mattingly/400	25.00
80	Babe Ruth/50	200.00
81	Dale Murphy/350	8.00
82	Rickey Henderson/500	10.00
83	Ivan Rodriguez/500	8.00
84	Marlon Byrd/500	5.00
85	Eric Chavez/500	8.00
86	Nomar Garciaparra/500	15.00
87	Alex Rodriguez/500	15.00
88	Vladimir Guerrero/500	10.00
89	Paul LoDuca/500	5.00
90	Richie Sexson/500	6.00
91	Mike Piazza/350	15.00
92	J.D. Drew/500	5.00
93	Juan Gonzalez/500	8.00
94	Pat Burrell/500	5.00
95	Adam Dunn/250	15.00
96	Mike Schmidt/500	20.00
97	Ryne Sandberg/500	20.00
98	Edgardo Alfonzo/500	5.00
99	Andruw Jones/500	8.00
100	Carlos Beltran/500	6.00
101	Jeff Bagwell/500	8.00
102	Lance Berkman/500	8.00
103	Luis Gonzalez/500	5.00
104	Carlos Delgado/500	8.00
105	Jim Edmonds/250	8.00

Combos (106-110):
Some Combos & Autos not priced.

#	Player	Price
106	Alfonso Soriano/75	40.00
107	Greg Maddux/Jsy/Auto./50	140.00
109	Adam Dunn/Bat/Auto./50	60.00
110	Rickey Henderson/Jsy/Bat/50	20.00

DK Evolution

NM/M
Complete Set (25): 85.00
Common Player: 2.00

Inserted 1:18

#	Player	Price
1	Cal Ripken Jr.	10.00
2	Ichiro Suzuki	6.00
3	Randy Johnson	4.00
4	Pedro J. Martinez	4.00
5	Nolan Ryan	10.00
6	Derek Jeter	10.00
7	Kerry Wood	4.00
8	Alex Rodriguez	8.00
9	Magglio Ordonez	2.00
10	Greg Maddux	5.00
11	Todd Helton	4.00
12	Sammy Sosa	5.00
13	Lou Gehrig	8.00
14	Lance Berkman	2.00
15	Barry Zito	2.00
16	Barry Bonds	10.00
17	Tom Glavine	2.00
18	Shawn Green	2.00
19	Roger Clemens	8.00
20	Nomar Garciaparra	6.00
21	Tony Gwynn	4.00
22	Vladimir Guerrero	3.00
23	Albert Pujols	8.00
24	Chipper Jones	4.00
25	Alfonso Soriano	4.00

Hall of Fame Heroes

NM/M
Complete Set (10): 40.00
Common Player: 3.00
Inserted 1:43

#	Player	Price
1	Bob Feller	3.00
2	Al Kaline	6.00
3	Lou Boudreau	4.00
4	Duke Snider	4.00
5	Jackie Robinson	6.00
6	Early Wynn	3.00
7	Yogi Berra	4.00
8	Stan Musial	4.00
9	Ty Cobb	6.00
10	Ted Williams	8.00

HOF Heroes Materials

NM/M
Common Player: 30.00
Production 50 Sets

#	Player	Price
1	Bob Feller/Jsy	70.00
2	Al Kaline/Bat	45.00
3	Lou Boudreau/Jsy	40.00
4	Duke Snider/Bat	30.00
5	Yogi Berra/Bat	40.00
6	Stan Musial/Bat	100.00
7	Ty Cobb/Bat	110.00
10	Ted Williams/Jsy	175.00

Heritage Collection

NM/M
Complete Set (25): 100.00
Common Player: 2.00
Inserted 1:23

#	Player	Price
1	Ozzie Smith	5.00
2	Lou Gehrig	8.00
3	Stan Musial	8.00
4	Mike Schmidt	6.00
5	Carlton Fisk	5.00
6	George Brett	10.00
7	Dale Murphy	4.00
8	Cal Ripken Jr.	10.00
9	Tony Gwynn	4.00
10	Don Mattingly	8.00
11	Jack Morris	2.00
12	Ty Cobb	8.00
13	Nolan Ryan	12.00
14	Ryne Sandberg	6.00
15	Thurman Munson	4.00
16	Ichiro Suzuki	6.00
17	Derek Jeter	10.00
18	Greg Maddux	6.00
19	Sammy Sosa	5.00
20	Pedro J. Martinez	4.00
21	Alex Rodriguez	8.00
22	Roger Clemens	6.00
23	Barry Bonds	10.00
24	Lance Berkman	2.00
25	Vladimir Guerrero	3.00

Recollection

Production 2-15

Recollection Autographs

NM/M
Common Player:

#	Player	Price
1	Adrian Beltre/40	15.00
2	Brandon Berger/99	10.00
9	Mark Buehrle/73	10.00
15	Andre Dawson/24	25.00
16	Andre Dawson/50	20.00
17	Andre Dawson/28	25.00
19	Jorge De La Rosa/148	5.00
24	Rob Fick/150	8.00
37	Tim Hudson/50	15.00
42	Ryan Ludwick/130	5.00
55	Roy Oswalt/65	15.00
56	Roy Oswalt/100	15.00
70	Bud Smith/114	5.00
72	Shannon Stewart/50	8.00

Team Timelines

NM/M
Complete Set (10): 85.00
Common Card: 4.00
Production 1,000 Sets

#	Player	Price
1	Nolan Ryan, Roy Oswalt	15.00
2	Dale Murphy, Chipper Jones	8.00
3	Stan Musial, Jim Edmonds	10.00
4	George Brett, Mike Sweeney	12.00
5	Tony Gwynn, Ryan Klesko	6.00
6	Carlton Fisk, Magglio Ordonez	4.00
7	Mike Schmidt, Pat Burrell	12.00
8	Don Mattingly, Bernie Williams	12.00
9	Ryne Sandberg, Kerry Wood	10.00
10	Lou Gehrig, Alfonso Soriano	10.00

Team Timelines Materials

NM/M
Common Card: 30.00
Production 100 unless noted.

#	Player	Price
1	Nolan Ryan, Roy Oswalt	120.00
2	Dale Murphy, Chipper Jones	40.00
3	Stan Musial, Jim Edmonds	45.00
4	George Brett, Mike Sweeney	65.00
5	Tony Gwynn, Ryan Klesko	40.00
6	Carlton Fisk, Magglio Ordonez	30.00
7	Mike Schmidt, Pat Burrell	90.00
8	Don Mattingly, Bernie Williams	70.00
9	Ryne Sandberg, Kerry Wood	60.00
10	Lou Gehrig, Alfonso Soriano/50	200.00

Inserts Hawaii

At an invitation-only Donruss/ Playoff reception during the SCD Hawaii Trade Conference, attendees were given a a three-card pack with each card embossed with the show logo on front and gold-foil serial numbered on back. The packs had one each of the Diamond Kings inserts Heritage Collection (numbered to 20), Hall of Fame Heroes (50) and Team Timelines (50).

NM/M
Common Player: 4.00

#	Player	Price
1	Ozzie Smith	25.00
2	Lou Gehrig	35.00
3	Stan Musial	25.00
4	Mike Schmidt	35.00
5	Carlton Fisk	20.00
6	George Brett	60.00
7	Dale Murphy	15.00
8	Cal Ripken Jr.	75.00
9	Tony Gwynn	45.00
10	Don Mattingly	45.00
11	Jack Morris	6.00
12	Ty Cobb	35.00
13	Nolan Ryan	75.00
14	Ryne Sandberg	55.00
15	Thurman Munson	15.00
16	Ichiro Suzuki	75.00
17	Derek Jeter	75.00
18	Greg Maddux	25.00
19	Sammy Sosa	45.00
20	Pedro Martinez	9.00
21	Alex Rodriguez	60.00
22	Roger Clemens	25.00
23	Barry Bonds	75.00
24	Lance Berkman	6.00
25	Vladimir Guerrero	9.00
1	Bob Feller	6.00
2	Al Kaline	15.00
3	Lou Boudreau	4.00
4	Duke Snider	10.00
5	Jackie Robinson	15.00
6	Early Wynn	4.00
7	Yogi Berra	10.00
8	Stan Musial	15.00
9	Ty Cobb	9.00
10	Ted Williams	15.00
1	Nolan Ryan, Roy Oswalt	35.00
2	Dale Murphy, Chipper Jones	15.00
3	Stan Musial, Jim Edmonds	10.00
4	George Brett, Mike Sweeney	30.00
5	Tony Gwynn, Ryan Klesko	15.00
6	Carlton Fisk, Magglio Ordonez	10.00
7	Mike Schmidt, Pat Burrell	20.00
8	Don Mattingly, Bernie Williams	25.00
9	Ryne Sandberg, Kerry Wood	25.00
10	Lou Gehrig, Alfonso Soriano	20.00

2003 Donruss Elite

NM/M
Complete Set (200):
Common Player: .25
Common Rookie (181-200): 3.00
Production 1,750
Pack (5): 3.50
Box (20): 60.00

#	Player	Price
1	Darin Erstad	.40
2	David Eckstein	.25
3	Garret Anderson	.40
4	Jarrod Washburn	.25
5	Tim Salmon	.40
6	Troy Glaus	.50
7	Marty Cordova	.25
8	Melvin Mora	.25
9	Rodrigo Lopez	.25
10	Tony Batista	.25
11	Derek Lowe	.25
12	Johnny Damon	.25
13	Manny Ramirez	.50
14	Nomar Garciaparra	1.50
15	Pedro J. Martinez	.75
16	Shea Hillenbrand	.25
17	Carlos Lee	.25
18	Joe Crede	.25
19	Frank Thomas	.50
20	Magglio Ordonez	.40
21	Mark Buehrle	.25
22	Paul Konerko	.25
23	C.C. Sabathia	.25
24	Ellis Burks	.25
25	Omar Vizquel	.40
26	Brian Tallet	.25
27	Bobby Higginson	.25
28	Carlos Pena	.25
29	Mark Redman	.25
30	Steve Sparks	.25
31	Carlos Beltran	.50
32	Joe Randa	.25
33	Mike Sweeney	.25
34	Raul Ibanez	.25
35	Runelvys Hernandez	.25
36	Brad Radke	.25
37	Corey Koskie	.25
38	Cristian Guzman	.25
39	David Ortiz	.50
40	Doug Mientkiewicz	.25
41	Jacque Jones	.25
42	Torii Hunter	.40
43	Alfonso Soriano	.75
44	Andy Pettitte	.40
45	Bernie Williams	.50
46	David Wells	.25
47	Derek Jeter	2.00
48	Jason Giambi	.40
49	Jeff Weaver	.25
50	Jorge Posada	.40
51	Mike Mussina	.50
52	Roger Clemens	1.50
53	Barry Zito	.40
54	Eric Chavez	.40
55	Jermaine Dye	.25
56	Mark Mulder	.40
57	Miguel Tejada	.40
58	Tim Hudson	.40
59	Bret Boone	.25
60	Chris Snelling	.25
61	Edgar Martinez	.40
62	Freddy Garcia	.25
63	Ichiro Suzuki	1.50
64	Jamie Moyer	.25
65	John Olerud	.25
66	Kazuhiro Sasaki	.25
67	Aubrey Huff	.25
68	Joe Kennedy	.25
69	Paul Wilson	.25
70	Alex Rodriguez	1.50
71	Chan Ho Park	.25
72	Hank Blalock	.50
73	Juan Gonzalez	.50
74	Kevin Mench	.25
75	Rafael Palmeiro	.50
76	Carlos Delgado	.40
77	Eric Hinske	.25
78	Josh Phelps	.25
79	Roy Halladay	.25
80	Shannon Stewart	.25
81	Vernon Wells	.25
82	Curt Schilling	.50
83	Junior Spivey	.25
84	Luis Gonzalez	.40
85	Mark Grace	.50
86	Randy Johnson	.50
87	Steve Finley	.25
88	Andruw Jones	.50
89	Chipper Jones	.75
90	Gary Sheffield	.50
91	Greg Maddux	1.00
92	John Smoltz	.40
93	Corey Patterson	.25
94	Kerry Wood	.75
95	Mark Prior	1.00
96	Moises Alou	.40
97	Sammy Sosa	1.50
98	Adam Dunn	.40
99	Austin Kearns	.40
100	Barry Larkin	.40
101	Ken Griffey Jr.	1.00
102	Sean Casey	.25
103	Jason Jennings	.25
104	Jay Payton	.25
105	Larry Walker	.40
106	Todd Helton	.50
107	A.J. Burnett	.50
108	Josh Beckett	.50
109	Juan Encarnacion	.25
110	Mike Lowell	.25
111	Craig Biggio	.40
112	Daryle Ward	.25
113	Jeff Bagwell	.50
114	Lance Berkman	.50
115	Roy Oswalt	.40
116	Jason Lane	.25
117	Adrian Beltre	.50
118	Hideo Nomo	.50
119	Kazuhisa Ishii	.40
120	Kevin Brown	.40
121	Odalis Perez	.25
122	Paul LoDuca	.25
123	Shawn Green	.40
124	Ben Sheets	.40
125	Jeffrey Hammonds	.25
126	Jose Hernandez	.25
127	Richie Sexson	.50
128	Bartolo Colon	.25
129	Brad Wilkerson	.25
130	Javier Vazquez	.25
131	Jose Vidro	.25
132	Michael Barrett	.25
133	Vladimir Guerrero	.75
134	Al Leiter	.25
135	Mike Piazza	1.00
136	Mo Vaughn	.25
137	Pedro Astacio	.25
138	Roberto Alomar	.40
139	Pat Burrell	.40
140	Vicente Padilla	.25
141	Jimmy Rollins	.40
142	Bobby Abreu	.40
143	Marlon Byrd	.40
144	Brian Giles	.40
145	Jason Kendall	.40
146	Aramis Ramirez	.40
147	Josh Fogg	.25
148	Ryan Klesko	.40
149	Phil Nevin	.40
150	Sean Burroughs	.25
151	Mark Kotsay	.25
152	Barry Bonds	2.00
153	Damian Moss	.25
154	Jason Schmidt	.50
155	Benito Santiago	.25
156	Rich Aurilia	.25
157	Scott Rolen	.75
158	J.D. Drew	.40
159	Jim Edmonds	.40
160	Matt Morris	.40
161	Tino Martinez	.25
162	Albert Pujols	1.50
163	Russ Ortiz	.25
164	Rey Ordonez	.25
165	Paul Byrd	.25
166	Kenny Lofton	.25
167	Kenny Rogers	.25
168	Rickey Henderson	.50
169	Fred McGriff	.40
170	Charles Johnson	.25
171	Mike Hampton	.25
172	Jim Thome	.75
173	Travis Hafner	.25
174	Ivan Rodriguez	.50
175	Ray Durham	.25
176	Jeremy Giambi	.25
177	Jeff Kent	.40
178	Cliff Floyd	.25
179	Kevin Millwood	.25
180	Tom Glavine	.50
181	Hideki Matsui RC	10.00
182	Jose Contreras RC	4.00
183	Terrmel Sledge RC	3.00
184	Lew Ford RC	6.00
185	Jhonny Peralta	4.00
186	Alexis Rios	4.00
187	Jeff Baker	3.00
188	Jeremy Guthrie	3.00
189	Jose Castillo	3.00
190	Garrett Atkins	3.00
191	Jeremy Bonderman	8.00
192	Adam LaRoche	3.00
193	Vinnie Chulk	3.00
194	Walter Young	3.00
195	Jimmy Gobble	3.00
196	Prentice Redman RC	4.00
197	Jason Anderson	3.00
198	Nic Jackson	3.00
199	Travis Chapman	3.00
200	Shane Victorino RC	3.00

Aspirations

NM/M
Stars print run 25-50: 10-15X
Rookies (181-200) p/r 25-50: 1-3X
Stars p/r 51-99: 5-10X
Serial numbered to jersey number.
Gold One-of-One's exist.
181 Hideki Matsui/45 125.00

Status

NM/M
Stars print run 25-50: 10-15X
Rookies (181-200) p/r 25-50: 1-3X
Stars p/r 51-99: 5-10X
Gold Status: No Pricing
Production 24 Sets
181 Hideki Matsui/55 120.00

All-Time Career Best

NM/M
Complete Set (45): 120.00
Common Player: 2.00
Inserted 1:9
Gold print run 25-50: 4-8X
Gold print run 51-100: 3-5X
Gold p/r 101-239: 1.5-3X
Numbered to career stat.

#	Player	Price
1	Babe Ruth	6.00
2	Ty Cobb	5.00
3	Jackie Robinson	4.00
4	Lou Gehrig	5.00
5	Thurman Munson	2.00
6	Nolan Ryan	3.00
7	Mike Schmidt	4.00
8	Don Mattingly	5.00
9	Yogi Berra	2.00

10	Rod Carew	2.00
11	Reggie Jackson	3.00
12	Al Kaline	4.00
13	Harmon Killebrew	4.00
14	Eddie Mathews	3.00
15	Stan Musial	4.00
16	Jim Palmer	2.00
17	Phil Rizzuto	2.00
18	Brooks Robinson	3.00
19	Tom Seaver	3.00
20	Robin Yount	4.00
21	Carlton Fisk	3.00
22	Dale Murphy	4.00
23	Cal Ripken Jr.	8.00
24	Tony Gwynn	4.00
25	Andre Dawson	2.00
26	Derek Jeter	6.00
27	Ken Griffey Jr.	4.00
28	Albert Pujols	4.00
29	Sammy Sosa	4.00
30	Jason Giambi	3.00
31	Randy Johnson	3.00
32	Greg Maddux	4.00
33	Rickey Henderson	3.00
34	Pedro Martinez	3.00
35	Jeff Bagwell	3.00
36	Alex Rodriguez	5.00
37	Vladimir Guerrero	3.00
38	Chipper Jones	3.00
39	Shawn Green	2.00
40	Tom Glavine	2.00
41	Curt Schilling	2.00
42	Todd Helton	2.00
43	Roger Clemens	4.00
44	Lance Berkman	2.00
45	Nomar Garciaparra	5.00

All-Time Career Best Materials

NM/M
Common Player: 5.00
Varying quantities produced

1	Babe Ruth/Bat/25	250.00
2	Ty Cobb/Bat/25	150.00
3	Jackie Robinson/Jsy/50	50.00
4	Lou Gehrig/Bat/100	100.00
5	Thurman Munson/Bat/200	15.00
6	Nolan Ryan/Jsy/400	40.00
7	Mike Schmidt/Jsy/400	30.00
8	Don Mattingly/Jsy/250	40.00
9	Yogi Berra/Bat/100	25.00
10	Rod Carew/Bat/400	10.00
11	Reggie Jackson/Bat/400	10.00
12	Al Kaline/Bat/400	20.00
13	Harmon Killebrew/Jsy/400	15.00
14	Eddie Mathews/Bat/200	25.00
15	Stan Musial/Bat/100	40.00
16	Jim Palmer/Jsy/200	10.00
17	Phil Rizzuto/Bat/400	10.00
18	Brooks Robinson/Bat/400	15.00
19	Tom Seaver/Jsy/400	15.00
20	Robin Yount/Bat/400	15.00
21	Carlton Fisk/Bat/400	10.00
22	Dale Murphy/Bat/400	10.00
23	Cal Ripken Jr/Bat/400	35.00
24	Tony Gwynn/Jsy/400	12.00
25	Andre Dawson/Bat/400	5.00
26	Derek Jeter/Base/400	15.00
27	Ken Griffey Jr./Base/400	10.00
28	Albert Pujols/Base/400	15.00
29	Sammy Sosa/Bat/400	12.00
30	Jason Giambi/Bat/400	8.00
31	Randy Johnson/Jsy/400	8.00
32	Greg Maddux/Jsy/400	10.00
33	Rickey Henderson/Bat/400	10.00
34	Pedro Martinez/Jsy/400	10.00
35	Jeff Bagwell/Jsy/400	8.00
36	Alex Rodriguez/Bat/400	12.00
37	Vladimir Guerrero/Bat/400	8.00
38	Chipper Jones/Bat/400	10.00
39	Shawn Green/Bat/400	5.00
40	Tom Glavine/Jsy/400	5.00
41	Curt Schilling/Jsy/400	8.00
42	Todd Helton/Bat/400	8.00
43	Roger Clemens/Jsy/400	20.00
44	Lance Berkman/Bat/400	5.00
45	Nomar Garciaparra/Bat/400	15.00

All-Time Career Best Materials Gold

NM/M
Numbered to career stat.
Some not priced yet.

1	Babe Ruth/60	125.00
4	Lou Gehrig/49	125.00
5	Thurman Munson/105	25.00
7	Mike Schmidt/48	50.00
8	Don Mattingly/53	60.00
9	Yogi Berra/30	50.00
10	Rod Carew/239	10.00
11	Reggie Jackson/39	25.00
12	Al Kaline/29	50.00
13	Harmon Killebrew/140	20.00
14	Eddie Mathews/31	50.00
15	Stan Musial/39	60.00
16	Brooks Robinson/118	20.00
20	Robin Yount/49	40.00
21	Carlton Fisk/107	15.00
22	Dale Murphy/44	40.00
23	Cal Ripken Jr./211	40.00
24	Tony Gwynn/220	10.00
25	Andre Dawson/49	15.00
27	Ken Griffey Jr./56	75.00
28	Albert Pujols/37	30.00
29	Sammy Sosa/66	35.00
30	Jason Giambi/137	10.00
33	Rickey Henderson/130	20.00
35	Jeff Bagwell/47	15.00
36	Alex Rodriguez/393	15.00
37	Vladimir Guerrero/44	25.00
38	Chipper Jones/45	20.00
39	Shawn Green/49	15.00
41	Curt Schilling/35	20.00
42	Todd Helton/59	15.00
44	Lance Berkman/55	15.00
45	Nomar Garciaparra/35	50.00

Back to the Future

NM/M
Complete Set (15): 35.00
Common Card: 2.00
#'s 1-10 production 1,000;
#'s 11-15 production 500

1	Kerry Wood	4.00
2	Mark Prior	4.00
3	Magglio Ordonez	2.50
4	Joe Borchard	2.00
5	Lance Berkman	3.00
6	Jason Lane	2.00
7	Rafael Palmeiro	3.00
8	Mark Teixeira	3.00
9	Carlos Delgado	3.00
10	Josh Phelps	2.00
11	Kerry Wood, Mark Prior	4.00
12	Joe Borchard, Magglio Ordonez	2.50
13	Jason Lane, Lance Berkman	3.00
14	Mark Teixeira, Rafael Palmeiro	3.00
15	Carlos Delgado, Josh Phelps	3.00

Back to the Future Threads

NM/M
Common Card: 4.00
Singles production 250:
Doubles production 125:

1	Kerry Wood	10.00
2	Mark Prior	12.00
3	Magglio Ordonez	5.00
4	Joe Borchard	5.00
5	Lance Berkman	6.00
6	Jason Lane	4.00
7	Rafael Palmeiro	8.00
8	Mark Teixeira	10.00
9	Carlos Delgado	5.00
10	Josh Phelps	6.00
11	Kerry Wood, Mark Prior	20.00
12	Joe Borchard, Magglio Ordonez	8.00
13	Jason Lane, Lance Berkman	8.00
14	Mark Teixeira, Rafael Palmeiro	15.00
15	Carlos Delgado, Josh Phelps	8.00

Back 2 Back Jacks

NM/M
Common Player:

1	Adam Dunn/250	10.00
2	Alex Rodriguez/250	10.00
3	Alfonso Soriano/250	10.00
4	Andruw Jones/250	8.00
5	Chipper Jones/250	10.00
6	Jason Giambi/250	8.00
7	Jeff Bagwell/250	8.00
8	Jim Thome/250	8.00
9	Juan Gonzalez/250	8.00
10	Lance Berkman/250	6.00
11	Magglio Ordonez/250	4.00
12	Manny Ramirez/250	8.00
13	Miguel Tejada/250	6.00
14	Mike Piazza/250	15.00
15	Nomar Garciaparra/250	15.00
16	Rafael Palmeiro/250	8.00
17	Rickey Henderson/250	10.00
18	Sammy Sosa/250	15.00
19	Scott Rolen/250	6.00
20	Shawn Green/250	6.00
21	Todd Helton/250	8.00
22	Vladimir Guerrero/250	8.00
23	Ivan Rodriguez/250	6.00
24	Eric Chavez/250	6.00
25	Larry Walker/250	6.00
26	Troy Glaus/250, Garret Anderson	8.00
27	Adam Dunn, Austin Kearns/125	20.00
28	Alex Rodriguez, Rafael Palmeiro/125	20.00
29	Eric Chavez, Miguel Tejada/125	10.00
30	Frank Thomas, Magglio Ordonez/125	15.00
31	Jeff Bagwell, Lance Berkman/125	15.00
32	Manny Ramirez, Nomar Garciaparra/125	30.00
33	Jose Vidro, Vladimir Guerrero/125	15.00
34	Mike Piazza, Roberto Alomar/125	20.00
35	Larry Walker, Todd Helton/125	15.00
36	Babe Ruth/100	150.00
37	Cal Ripken Jr./100	65.00
38	Don Mattingly/100	15.00
39	Kirby Puckett/100	20.00
40	Roberto Clemente/100	75.00
41	Alfonso Soriano, Phil Rizzuto/75	25.00
42	Andre Dawson, Sammy Sosa/75	40.00
43	Ozzie Smith, Scott Rolen/75	60.00
44	Don Mattingly, Jason Giambi/75	75.00
45	Rickey Henderson, Ty Cobb/75	125.00
46	Joe Morgan, Johnny Bench/50	35.00
47	Brooks Robinson, Cal Ripken Jr./50	100.00
48	Bo Jackson, George Brett/50	100.00
49	Babe Ruth, Lou Gehrig/50	375.00
50	Thurman Munson, Yogi Berra/50	60.00

Career Best

NM/M
Common Player: 3.00
Numbered to statistic

3	Garret Anderson/56	6.00
4	Andruw Jones/83	6.00
6	Magglio Ordonez/38	6.00
7	Magglio Ordonez/135	4.00
8	Adam Dunn/26	15.00
10	Lance Berkman/42	3.00
11	Lance Berkman/128	3.00
12	Shawn Green/385	3.00
13	Alfonso Soriano/39	12.00
14	Alfonso Soriano/300	5.00
15	Jason Giambi/120	5.00
16	Derek Jeter/32	30.00
17	Vladimir Guerrero/40	12.00
18	Vladimir Guerrero/417	5.00
19	Barry Zito/23	8.00
21	Miguel Tejada/34	8.00
22	Barry Bonds/198	15.00
23	Barry Bonds/370	15.00
24	Ichiro Suzuki/388	8.00
24	Alex Rodriguez/57	15.00
25	Alex Rodriguez/142	10.00

Career Best Materials

NM/M
Common Player: 4.00
Production 500 Sets

1	Randy Johnson/Jsy	8.00
2	Curt Schilling/Jsy	8.00
3	Garret Anderson/Bat	4.00
4	Andruw Jones/Bat	4.00
5	Kerry Wood/Shoe	10.00
6	Magglio Ordonez/Bat	4.00
7	Magglio Ordonez/Bat	4.00
8	Adam Dunn/Bat	6.00
9	Roy Oswalt/Jsy	5.00
10	Lance Berkman/Bat	5.00
11	Lance Berkman/Bat	5.00
12	Shawn Green/Bat	4.00
13	Alfonso Soriano/Bat	10.00
14	Alfonso Soriano/Bat	10.00
15	Jason Giambi/Bat	8.00
16	Derek Jeter/Base	15.00
17	Vladimir Guerrero/Bat	8.00
18	Vladimir Guerrero/Bat	8.00
19	Barry Zito/Jsy	6.00
20	Miguel Tejada/Bat	6.00
21	Barry Bonds/Base	15.00
22	Barry Bonds/Base	15.00
23	Ichiro Suzuki/Base	15.00
24	Alex Rodriguez/Jsy	10.00
25	Alex Rodriguez/Jsy	10.00

Career Best Materials Autograph

NM/M
Quantity produced listed

3	Garret Anderson/Bat/75	35.00
9	Adam Dunn/Bat/100	50.00
9	Roy Oswalt/Jsy/250	30.00
17	Vladimir Guerrero/Bat/50	75.00
18	Vladimir Guerrero/Bat/50	75.00
19	Barry Zito/Jsy/75	40.00

Highlights

NM/M
Production 500 Sets

1	Sammy Sosa	10.00
2	Rafael Palmeiro	8.00
3	Hideki Matsui	10.00
4	Jose Contreras	4.00
5	Kevin Millwood	4.00

Highlights Autographs

NM/M
Production 50 Sets

2	Rafael Palmeiro	75.00
4	Jose Contreras	25.00

Passing the Torch

Complete Set (15):		50.00
Common Player:		
1	Stan Musial	6.00
2	Jim Edmonds	2.00
3	Dale Murphy	3.00
4	Andruw Jones	3.00
5	Roger Clemens	3.00
6	Mark Prior	3.00
7	Tom Seaver	3.00
8	Tom Glavine	1.50
9	Mike Schmidt	3.00
10	Pat Burrell	2.00
11	Jim Edmonds, Stan Musial	8.00
12	Andruw Jones, Dale Murphy	5.00
13	Mark Prior, Roger Clemens	8.00
14	Tom Glavine, Tom Seaver	5.00
15	Mike Schmidt, Pat Burrell	10.00

Passing the Torch Autograph

NM/M
Common Auto (1-10): 30.00
#'s 1-10 production 50
#'s 11-15 production 25
No pricing for #'s 11-15.

1	Stan Musial	80.00
2	Jim Edmonds	40.00
3	Dale Murphy	50.00
4	Andruw Jones	40.00
5	Roger Clemens	125.00
6	Mark Prior	40.00
7	Tom Seaver	60.00
8	Tom Glavine	50.00
9	Mike Schmidt	100.00
10	Pat Burrell	30.00

Recollection Autographs

NM/M
Some not priced due to scarcity.

1	Jeremy Affeldt/75	15.00
2	Erick Almonte/75	8.00
4	Adrian Beltre/36	30.00
7	Brandon Berger/83	8.00
8	Angel Berroa/28	25.00
13	Jeff Deardorff/53	8.00
14	Ryan Drese/100	25.00
21	Luis Garcia/28	15.00
22	Geronimo Gil/75	8.00
28	Travis Hafner Black/52	30.00
30	Bill Hall/27	15.00
35	Gerald Laird/46	10.00
36	Jason Lane/27	15.00
44	Victor Martinez/52	100.00
46	Roy Oswalt Black/61	20.00
51	Ricardo Rodriguez/75	8.00
55	Bud Smith/50	10.00
56	Bud Smith/28	15.00
58	Junior Spivey/45	20.00
59	Tim Spooneybarger/100	8.00
61	Shannon Stewart/35	20.00
64	Claudio Vargas/51	8.00

Throwback Threads

NM/M
Common Player: 4.00

1	Randy Johnson/Jsy	8.00
2	Randy Johnson/Hat	10.00
3	Roger Clemens/Jsy	20.00
4	Roger Clemens/Jsy	8.00
5	Manny Ramirez/Jsy	8.00
6	Greg Maddux/Jsy	8.00
7	Jason Giambi/Jsy	6.00
8	Jason Giambi/Jsy	6.00
9	Alex Rodriguez/Jsy	10.00
10	Alex Rodriguez/Jsy	10.00
11	Miguel Tejada/Jsy	8.00
12	Alfonso Soriano/Jsy	8.00
13	Nomar Garciaparra/Jsy	15.00
14	Pedro J. Martinez/Jsy	8.00
15	Pedro J. Martinez/Jsy	8.00
16	Andruw Jones/Jsy	6.00
17	Chipper Jones/Jsy	6.00
18	Barry Zito/Jsy	6.00
19	Mark Mulder/Jsy	4.00
20	Lance Berkman/Jsy	6.00
21	Magglio Ordonez/Jsy	6.00
22	Mike Piazza/Jsy	15.00
23	Mike Piazza/Jsy	15.00
24	Rickey Henderson/Jsy	8.00
25	Rickey Henderson/Jsy	8.00
26	Rickey Henderson/Jsy	8.00
27	Sammy Sosa/Jsy	15.00
28	Shawn Green/Jsy	6.00
29	Troy Glaus/Jsy	8.00
30	Vladimir Guerrero/Jsy	8.00
31	Adam Dunn/Jsy	8.00
32	Jeff Bagwell/Jsy	8.00
33	Curt Schilling/Jsy	8.00
34	Hideo Nomo/Jsy	20.00
35	Hideo Nomo/Jsy	20.00
36	Hideo Nomo/Jsy	20.00
37	Kerry Wood/Jsy	10.00
38	Mark Prior/Jsy	8.00
39	Roberto Alomar/Jsy	6.00
40	Todd Helton/Jsy	8.00
41	Jim Thome/Jsy	8.00
42	Rafael Palmeiro/Jsy	8.00
43	Juan Gonzalez/Jsy	8.00
44	Vernon Wells/Jsy	4.00
45	Torii Hunter/Jsy	6.00
46	Randi Johnson/Jsy	15.00
47	Roger Clemens/Jsy	30.00
48	Jason Giambi/Jsy	10.00
49	Alex Rodriguez/Jsy	25.00
50	Pedro J. Martinez/Jsy	8.00
51	Mike Piazza/Jsy	25.00
52	Rickey Henderson	20.00
53	Rickey Henderson	20.00
54	Rickey Henderson, Hat, Rickey Henderson/Jsy	20.00
55	Hideo Nomo/Jsy	40.00
56	Randy Johnson/Jsy	15.00
57	Curt Schilling, Randy Johnson/Jsy	15.00
58	Alfonso Soriano, Jason Giambi	20.00
59	Barry Zito, Mark Mulder	15.00
60	Andruw Jones, Chipper Jones/Jsy	20.00
61	Greg Maddux, Tom Glavine	40.00
62	Jeff Bagwell, Lance Berkman/Jsy	15.00
63	Mark Prior, Roger Clemens/Jsy	20.00
64	Alex Rodriguez, Rafael Palmeiro/Jsy	20.00
65	Jim Thome, Roberto Alomar/Jsy	20.00
66	Mike Piazza, Roberto Alomar/Jsy	20.00
67	Mark Grace, Sammy Sosa/Jsy	25.00
68	Larry Walker, Todd Helton/Jsy	20.00
69	Adam Dunn, Austin Kearns/Jsy	20.00
70	Alex Rodriguez, Ivan Rodriguez/Jsy	20.00
71	Bobby Abreu, Marlon Byrd/Jsy	15.00
72	Eric Chavez, Miguel Tejada/Jsy	15.00
73	Greg Maddux, John Smoltz/Jsy	30.00
74	Kerry Wood, Mark Prior/Jsy	15.00
75	Barry Zito, Tim Hudson/Jsy	10.00
76	Babe Ruth	250.00
77	Ty Cobb	100.00
78	Jackie Robinson	75.00
79	Lou Gehrig	125.00
80	Thurman Munson	30.00
81	Nolan Ryan	50.00
82	Don Mattingly	50.00
83	Mike Schmidt	35.00
84	Reggie Jackson	20.00
85	George Brett	40.00
86	Cal Ripken Jr.	50.00
87	Tony Gwynn	15.00
88	Yogi Berra	40.00
89	Stan Musial	40.00
90	Jim Palmer	15.00
91	Thurman Munson	50.00
92	Chipper Jones, Dale Murphy	50.00
93	Don Mattingly, Jason Giambi	80.00
94	Andre Dawson, Sammy Sosa	40.00
95	Mark Prior, Nolan Ryan	50.00
96	Babe Ruth, Lou Gehrig	475.00
97	Joe Morgan, Tom Seaver	40.00
98	Harmon Killebrew, Rod Carew	40.00
99	Nolan Ryan	90.00
100	Reggie Jackson	35.00

Throwback Threads Autograph

NM/M
Production 5-75

30	Vladimir Guerrero/50	75.00
31	Adam Dunn/50	75.00
37	Kerry Wood/50	75.00
38	Mark Prior/75	50.00
39	Roberto Alomar/50	75.00

Turn of the Century Autographs

NM/M
Common Autograph: 10.00
Production 50 Sets

182	Jose Contreras	40.00
183	Terrmel Sledge	15.00
184	Lew Ford	20.00
185	Jhonny Peralta	35.00
186	Alexis Rios	40.00
187	Jeff Baker	15.00
188	Jeremy Guthrie	15.00
189	Jose Castillo	15.00
190	Garrett Atkins	15.00
191	Jeremy Bonderman	75.00
192	Adam LaRoche	15.00
193	Vinnie Chulk	15.00
194	Walter Young	15.00
195	Jimmy Gobble	10.00
196	Prentice Redman	15.00
197	Jason Anderson	15.00
198	Nic Jackson	15.00
199	Travis Chapman	15.00
200	Shane Victorino	10.00

Montreal Expos

Over the course of the season in a series of stadium giveaways, fans attending selected

BILL LEE

ADAM LOEWEN

games at Olympic Stadium received a cello-wrapped pack of specially designed Donruss cards featuring many of the team's most popular players since entering the National League in 1969. Cards are the standard 2-1/2" x 3-1/2" format with either black-and-white or color photos on front, bordered in white with red and blue graphics. Backs have a dark blue background with personal data, a line of career stats and highlights.

		NM/M
Complete Set (59):		25.00
Common Player:		.25
Series 1, April 25		4.00
1	Claude Raymond	.75
2	Javier Vasquez	1.50
3	John Boccabella	.75
4	Bill Stoneman	.75
5	Carl Morton	.75
6	Ron Fairly	.75
Series 2, May 9		
7	Bob Bailey	.25
8	Steve Renko	.25
9	Mike Marshall	.25
10	Ron Hunt	.25
11	Ken Singleton	.25
12	Pedro Martinez	3.00
Series 3, May 23		1.50
13	Tim Foli	.25
14	Mike Jorgensen	.25
15	Steve Rogers	.25
16	Willie Davis	.25
17	Larry Parrish	.25
18	Jerry White	.25
Series 4, June 20		8.00
19	Ellis Valentine	.25
20	Woody Fryman	.25
21	Andre Dawson	2.00
22	Warren Cromartie	.25
23	Vladimir Guerrero	2.00
24	Tony Perez	2.00
Series 5, July 11		1.50
25	Chris Speier	.25
26	Dan Schatzeder	.25
27	Ross Grimsley	.25
28	Scott Sanderson	.25
29	Tim Wallach	.25
30	Dave Cash	.25
Series 6, July 25		2.00
31	Bill Gullickson	1.00
32	Tim Raines	1.00
33	Rodney Scott	.25
34	Ron LeFlore	.25
35	Charlie Lea	.25
36	Bill Lee	.25
Series 7, Aug. 1		3.00
37	Jeff Reardon	.25
38	Bryn Smith	.25
39	Al Oliver	.25
40	Hubie Brooks	.25
41	Terry Francona	.25
42	Gary Carter	2.00
Series 8, Aug. 15		4.00
43	Spike Owen	.25
44	Tim Burke	.25
45	Andres Galarraga	.50
46	Marquis Grissom	.25
47	Larry Walker	2.00
48	Moises Alou	.50
49	Dennis Martinez	.25
Series 9, Sept. 12		3.50
50	Denis Boucher	.25
51	Rondell White	.25
52	Mel Rojas	.25
53	Henry Rodriguez	.25
54	David Segui	.25
55	Ugueth Urbina	.25
56	Jose Vidro	1.00
57	Darrin Fletcher	.25
58	Orlando Cabrera	.25
59	John Wetteland	.25

2003 Donruss Rookie & Traded

		NM/M
Complete Set (65):		8.00
Common Player:		.25
Pack (8):		8.00
Box (24):		150.00

1	Jeremy Bonderman	1.00
2	Adam Loewen	.50
3	Dan Haren	.50
4	Jose Contreras RC	.50
5	Hideki Matsui RC	2.00
6	Arnie Munoz	.25
7	Miguel Cabrera	.25
8	Andrew Brown RC	.25
9	Josh Hall RC	.25
10	Josh Stewart RC	.25
11	Clint Barmes RC	.25
12	Luis Ayala RC	.25
13	Brandon Webb RC	.75
14	Greg Aquino	.25
15	Chien-Ming Wang RC	2.00
16	Rickie Weeks RC	1.50
17	Edgar Gonzalez RC	.25
18	Dontrelle Willis	.25
19	Bo Hart RC	.25
20	Rosman Garcia RC	.25
21	Jeremy Griffiths	.25
22	Craig Brazell RC	.50
23	Daniel Cabrera RC	.50
24	Fernando Cabrera RC	.25
25	Termmel Sledge RC	.25
26	Ramon Nivar	.25
27	Rob Hammock RC	.25
28	Francisco Rosario RC	.25
29	Cory Stewart	.25
30	Felix Sanchez	.25
31	Jorge Cordova	.25
32	Rocco Baldelli	.50
33	Beau Kemp RC	.25
34	Micheal Nakamura RC	.25
35	Rett Johnson RC	.25
36	Guillermo Quiroz RC	.25
37	Hong-Chih Kuo RC	1.00
38	Ian Ferguson RC	.25
39	Franklin Perez	.25
40	Tim Olson RC	.25
41	Jerome Williams	.25
42	Rich Fischer	.25
43	Phil Seibel RC	.25
44	Aaron Looper RC	.25
45	Jae Weong Seo	.25
46	Chad Gaudin RC	.25
47	Matt Kata RC	.25
48	Ryan Wagner RC	.25
49	Michel Hernandez RC	.25
50	Diegomar Markwell	.25
51	Doug Waechter	.25
52	Mike Nicolas	.25
53	Prentice Redman RC	.25
54	Shane Bazzell	.25
55	Delmon Young RC	2.00
56	Brian Stokes	.25
57	Matt Bruback	.25
58	Nook Logan RC	.25
59	Oscar Villarreal RC	.25
60	Pete LaForest RC	.25
61	Shea Hillenbrand	.25
62	Aramis Ramirez	.40
63	Aaron Boone	.25
64	Roberto Alomar	.50
65	Rickey Henderson	.50

Team Heroes

Common Player (541-548):		.25
Team Heroes Glossy:		1-2X
541	Rickie Weeks RC	1.00
542	Hideki Matsui RC	1.50
543	Ramon Nivar	.25
544	Adam Loewen RC	.75
545	Brandon Webb RC	.75
546	Dan Haren	.25
547	Delmon Young RC	2.00
548	Ryan Wagner RC	.25

Champions

Common Player (302-309):		.25
Metalized:		4-8X
Production 100		
302	Ryan Wagner RC	.25
303	Adam Loewen RC	.25
304	Chien-Ming Wang RC	2.50
305	Hong-Chih Kuo RC	1.00
306	Delmon Young RC	2.00
307	Dan Haren	.25
308	Rickie Weeks RC	1.50
309	Ramon Nivar	.25

Leaf

Common Player (321-329):		.25
Leaf Red Press Proofs:		4-8X
Production 100		
Leaf Blue Press Proofs:		5-10X
Production 50		
321	Hideki Matsui RC	1.50
322	Ramon Nivar	.25
323	Adam Loewen RC	.25
324	Brandon Webb RC	.75

325	Chien-Ming Wang RC	2.50
326	Delmon Young RC	2.00
327	Ryan Wagner RC	.25
328	Dan Haren	.25
329	Rickie Weeks RC	1.50

Playoff Prestige

Common Player (201-210):		.25
Prestige X-Tra Points:		5-10X
Production 50		
201	Jeremy Bonderman	1.00
202	Brandon Webb RC	.75
203	Adam Loewen RC	.25
204	Chien-Ming Wang RC	2.50
205	Hong-Chih Kuo RC	1.00
206	Delmon Young RC	2.00
207	Ryan Wagner RC	.25
208	Dan Haren	.25
209	Rickie Weeks RC	1.50
210	Ramon Nivar	.25

Classics

Common Player (201-211):		4.00
Production 1,000		
Classics Timeless Tributes:		.75-1.5X
Production 100		
201	Jeremy Bonderman	10.00
202	Adam Loewen	6.00
203	Chien-Ming Wang RC	25.00
204	Hong-Chih Kuo RC	8.00
205	Ryan Wagner RC	4.00
206	Dan Haren	4.00
207	Dontrelle Willis	4.00
208	Rickie Weeks RC	10.00
209	Ramon Nivar	4.00
210	Chad Gaudin RC	4.00
211	Delmon Young RC	15.00

Studio

Common Player (201-211):		3.00
Production 1,500		
Studio Proof:		1-1.5X
Production 100		
201	Adam Loewen RC	3.00
202	Jeremy Bonderman	6.00
203	Brandon Webb RC	3.00
204	Chien-Ming Wang RC	25.00
205	Chad Gaudin RC	3.00
206	Ryan Wagner RC	3.00
207	Hong-Chih Kuo RC	8.00
208	Dan Haren	3.00
209	Rickie Weeks RC	10.00
210	Ramon Nivar	3.00
211	Delmon Young RC	15.00

Diamond Kings

Common Player (177-201):		3.00
Inserted 1:30		
DK Portraits Bronze:		.5-1X
DK Portraits Silver:		1-1.5X
Production 100		
DK Portraits Gold:		1-2X
Production 50		
177	Hideki Matsui RC	10.00
178	Jeremy Bonderman	8.00
179	Brandon Webb RC	8.00
180	Adam Loewen RC	4.00
181	Chien-Ming Wang RC	15.00
182	Hong-Chih Kuo RC	6.00
183	Clint Barmes RC	3.00
184	Guillermo Quiroz RC	4.00
185	Edgar Gonzalez RC	3.00
186	Todd Wellemeyer RC	3.00
187	Dan Haren	3.00
188	Dustin McGowan	3.00
189	Preston Larrison	3.00
191	Kevin Youkilis	8.00
192	Bubba Nelson	3.00
193	Chris Burke	3.00
194	J.D. Durbin	4.00
195	Ryan Howard	30.00
196	Jason Kubel	6.00
197	Brendan Harris	3.00
198	Brian Bruney	3.00
199	Ramon Nivar	3.00
200	Rickie Weeks RC	10.00
201	Delmon Young RC	15.00

Leaf Certified Materials

Mirror Red Signature:		.75-1.5X
Production 100 or 50		
Mirror Blue Signature:		1-1.5X
Mirror Gold Signature:		No Pricing
Mirror Emerald Signature:		No Pricing
Mirror Reds:		.2-.4X
Production 100		
Mirror Blues:		.4-.6X
Production 50		
Mirror Golds:		No Pricing
Production 25		
251	Adam Loewen/ Auto./250 RC	15.00
252	Dan Haren/ Auto./250	15.00
253	Dontrelle Willis/ Auto./150	25.00
254	Ramon Nivar/ Auto./250	10.00
255	Chad Gaudin/ Auto./250 RC	10.00
256	Kevin Correia/ Auto./250 RC	10.00
257	Rickie Weeks/ Auto./100 RC	100.00
258	Ryan Wagner/ Auto./250 RC	15.00
259	Delmon Young/ Auto./100 RC	160.00

Playoff Absolute

Common Player (201-208):		4.00

Production 1,000		
Spectrum:		1-2X
Production 100		
201	Adam Loewen RC	4.00
202	Ramon Nivar	4.00
203	Dan Haren	4.00
204	Dontrelle Willis	4.00
205	Chad Gaudin	4.00
206	Rickie Weeks RC	8.00
207	Ryan Wagner RC	4.00
208	Delmon Young RC	12.00

Elite Extra Edition

Common Player (1-58):		4.00
Production 900		
Elite Status:		1-3X
Numbered to Jersey Number		
Elite Aspirations:		1-2X
Varying quantities produced		
Turn of Century non-Auto:		1-2X
Production 100		
Elite Gold Status:		No Pricing
Production 24		
1	Adam Loewen RC	4.00
2	Brandon Webb RC	10.00
3	Chien-Ming Wang RC	40.00
4	Hong-Chih Kuo RC	20.00
5	Clint Barmes RC	4.00
6	Guillermo Quiroz RC	3.00
7	Edgar Gonzalez RC	3.00
8	Todd Wellemeyer RC	4.00
9	Alfredo Gonzalez RC	3.00
10	Craig Brazell RC	3.00
11	Tim Olson RC	3.00
12	Rich Fischer	3.00
13	Daniel Cabrera RC	5.00
14	Francisco Rosario RC	4.00
15	Francisco Cruceta RC	4.00
16	Alejandro Machado	4.00
17	Andrew Brown RC	4.00
18	Rob Hammock RC	4.00
19	Arnie Munoz	4.00
20	Felix Sanchez	4.00
21	Nook Logan RC	4.00
22	Cory Stewart	4.00
23	Michel Hernandez RC	4.00
24	Rett Johnson RC	4.00
25	Josh Hall RC	4.00
26	Doug Waechter	4.00
27	Matt Kata RC	4.00
28	Dan Haren	4.00
29	Dontrelle Willis	4.00
30	Ramon Nivar	4.00
31	Chad Gaudin RC	4.00
32	Rickie Weeks RC	15.00
33	Ryan Wagner RC	4.00
34	Kevin Correia RC	4.00
35	Bo Hart RC	4.00
36	Oscar Villarreal RC	4.00
37	Josh Willingham RC	5.00
38	Jeff Duncan RC	6.00
39	David DeJesus RC	6.00
40	Dustin McGowan	6.00
41	Preston Larrison	4.00
43	Kevin Youkilis	8.00
44	Bubba Nelson	4.00
45	Chris Burke	6.00
46	J.D. Durbin	4.00
47	Ryan Howard	100.00
48	Jason Kubel RC	8.00
49	Brendan Harris	4.00
50	Brian Bruney	4.00
52	Byron Gettis	4.00
53	Edwin Jackson RC	4.00
55	Daniel Garcia	4.00
57	Chad Cordero RC	4.00
58	Delmon Young RC	25.00

Common Leaf Limited Phenom:

Silver Spotlights:		1X
Production 50		
Gold Spotlights:		No Pricing
Production 10 or 25		
Patch:		No Pricing
Production 25		
Rewards:		No Pricing
Production 10		
201	Delmon Young/ Auto./99 RC	220.00
202	Rickie Weeks/ Auto./99 RC	125.00
203	Edwin Jackson/ Auto./99 RC	20.00
204	Dan Haren/Auto./99	30.00

Signature Series:

151	Delmon Young/ Auto./200 RC	100.00
152	Rickie Weeks/ Auto./200 RC	65.00
153	Edwin Jackson/ Auto./200	15.00

Autographs

Common Player:		4.00
Production 500		
Position:		1-2X
Production 100		
Number:		1-2X
Production 100		
1	Nomar Garciaparra	8.00
2	Alex Rodriguez	8.00
3	Mike Piazza	8.00
4	Greg Maddux	8.00
5	Roger Clemens	10.00
6	Sammy Sosa	8.00
7	Randy Johnson	8.00
8	Albert Pujols	15.00
9	Alfonso Soriano	8.00
10	Chipper Jones	8.00
11	Mark Prior	6.00
12	Hideo Nomo	6.00
13	Adam Dunn	6.00
14	Juan Gonzalez	5.00
15	Vladimir Guerrero	8.00
16	Pedro J. Martinez	8.00
17	Jim Thome	6.00
18	Brandon Webb/200	6.00
19	Mike Mussina	6.00
20	Mark Teixeira	5.00
21	Barry Larkin	5.00
22	Ivan Rodriguez	6.00
23	Hank Blalock	6.00
24	Rafael Palmeiro	6.00
25	Curt Schilling	6.00
26	Troy Glaus	5.00
27	Bernie Williams	6.00
28	Scott Rolen	6.00
29	Torii Hunter	4.00
30	Nick Johnson	4.00
31	Kazuhisa Ishii	4.00
32	Shawn Green	5.00
33	Jeff Bagwell	6.00

34	Lance Berkman	4.00
35	Roy Oswalt	4.00
36	Kerry Wood	4.00
37	Todd Helton	6.00
38	Manny Ramirez	8.00
39	Andruw Jones	5.00
40	Frank Thomas	5.00
41	Gary Sheffield	5.00
42	Magglio Ordonez	5.00
43	Mike Sweeney	4.00
44	Carlos Beltran	6.00
45	Richie Sexson	5.00
46	Jeff Kent	5.00
47	Carlos Delgado	5.00
48	Vernon Wells	4.00
49	Dontrelle Willis	8.00
50	Jae Weong Seo	4.00

Gamers Autograph

		NM/M
Production 5-50		4.00
Many not priced due to scarcity.		
20	Mark Teixeira/50	30.00
23	Hank Blalock/50	30.00
29	Torii Hunter/50	20.00
35	Roy Oswalt/50	20.00
43	Mike Sweeney/50	15.00
48	Vernon Wells/30	20.00
49	Dontrelle Willis/50	25.00

Playoff Prestige Autograph

		NM/M
Quantity produced listed		
201	Jeremy Bonderman/100	50.00
202	Brandon Webb/100	25.00
203	Adam Loewen/100	10.00
204	Chien-Ming Wang/50	300.00
205	Hong-Chih Kuo/100	180.00
207	Ryan Wagner/100	15.00
208	Dan Haren/100	15.00
210	Ramon Nivar/100	15.00

Recollection Autographs

		NM/M
Common Player:		
7	Jack McDowell 88/75	20.00

Stat Line Season/Career

Cards serial #'d from		
101-150:		1-2X
Cards serial #'d from 50-100:		2-3X
Cards serial #'d from 26-49:		3-4X
Cards numbered under 25 not priced.		

R&T Elite Turn of the Century Autograph

		NM/M
Common Player:		10.00
Production 100		
Aspirations:		.75-1.5X
Varying quantities produced		
1	Adam Loewen	15.00
2	Brandon Webb	75.00
3	Chien-Ming Wang	300.00
4	Hong-Chih Kuo	150.00
5	Clint Barmes	25.00
6	Guillermo Quiroz	20.00
7	Edgar Gonzalez	10.00
8	Todd Wellemeyer	10.00
9	Alfredo Gonzalez	10.00
10	Craig Brazell	10.00
11	Tim Olson	10.00
12	Rich Fischer	10.00
13	Daniel Cabrera	30.00
14	Francisco Rosario	10.00
15	Francisco Cruceta	10.00
16	Alejandro Machado	10.00
17	Andrew Brown	10.00
18	Rob Hammock	10.00
19	Arnie Munoz	10.00
20	Felix Sanchez	10.00
21	Nook Logan	10.00
22	Cory Stewart	10.00
23	Michel Hernandez	10.00
24	Rett Johnson	10.00

Gamers

		NM/M
Common Player:		4.00

25	Josh Hall	15.00
26	Doug Waechter	10.00
27	Matt Kata	10.00
28	Dan Haren	40.00
29	Dontrelle Willis/25	60.00
30	Ramon Nivar	10.00
31	Chad Gaudin	10.00
32	Rickie Weeks/25	120.00
33	Ryan Wagner	10.00
35	Bo Hart	10.00
36	Oscar Villarreal	10.00
37	Josh Willingham	30.00
38	Jeff Duncan	10.00
40	Dustin McGowan	15.00
41	Preston Larrison	10.00
43	Kevin Youkilis	40.00
44	Bubba Nelson	15.00
45	Chris Burke	15.00
46	J.D. Durbin	15.00
47	Ryan Howard	1,100
48	Jason Kubel	40.00
49	Brendan Harris	15.00
50	Brian Bruney	10.00
52	Byron Gettis	10.00
53	Edwin Jackson	10.00
55	Daniel Garcia	10.00
58	Delmon Young	225.00

2003 Donruss Signature Series

		NM/M
Complete Set (150):		150.00
Common Player:		.50
Common RK (101-150):		1.00
Inserted 1:Tin		
Tin:		35.00
1	Garret Anderson	.75
2	Tim Salmon	.75
3	Troy Glaus	.75
4	Curt Schilling	1.00
5	Luis Gonzalez	.75
6	Mark Grace	.75
7	Matt Williams	.50
8	Randy Johnson	1.50
9	Andruw Jones	1.00
10	Chipper Jones	1.50
11	Gary Sheffield	.75
12	Greg Maddux	2.00
13	Johnny Damon	.75
14	Manny Ramirez	1.50
15	Nomar Garciaparra	2.50
16	Pedro J. Martinez	1.50
17	Corey Patterson	.50
18	Kerry Wood	1.50
19	Mark Prior	2.00
20	Sammy Sosa	2.50
21	Bartolo Colon	.50
22	Frank Thomas	1.00
23	Magglio Ordonez	.50
24	Paul Konerko	.50
25	Adam Dunn	1.00
26	Austin Kearns	.75
27	Barry Larkin	.75
28	Ken Griffey Jr.	.75
29	C.C. Sabathia	.50
30	Omar Vizquel	.50
31	Larry Walker	.50
32	Todd Helton	1.00
33	Ivan Rodriguez	1.00
34	Josh Beckett	.75
35	Craig Biggio	.75
36	Jeff Bagwell	1.00
37	Jeff Kent	.50
38	Lance Berkman	.75
39	Richard Hidalgo	.50
40	Roy Oswalt	.75
41	Carlos Beltran	1.00
42	Mike Sweeney	.50
43	Runelvys Hernandez	.50
44	Hideo Nomo	.75
45	Kazuhisa Ishii	.50
46	Paul LoDuca	.50
47	Shawn Green	.75
48	Ben Sheets	.75
49	Richie Sexson	.75
50	A.J. Pierzynski	.50
51	Torii Hunter	.75
52	Javier Vazquez	.50
53	Jose Vidro	.50
54	Vladimir Guerrero	1.50
55	Cliff Floyd	.50
56	David Cone	.50
57	Mike Piazza	2.00
58	Roberto Alomar	.75
59	Tom Glavine	.75
60	Alfonso Soriano	1.50
61	Derek Jeter	4.00
62	Drew Henson	.50
63	Jason Giambi	.75
64	Mike Mussina	1.00
65	Nick Johnson	.50
66	Roger Clemens	3.00
67	Barry Zito	.75
68	Eric Chavez	.75
69	Mark Mulder	.75
70	Miguel Tejada	.75
71	Tim Hudson	.75
72	Bobby Abreu	.75
73	Jim Thome	1.00
74	Kevin Millwood	.50
75	Pat Burrell	.50
76	Brian Giles	.50
77	Jason Kendall	.50
78	Kenny Lofton	.50
79	Phil Nevin	.50
80	Ryan Klesko	.50
81	Andres Galarraga	.50

82	Barry Bonds	4.00
83	Rich Aurilia	.50
84	Edgar Martinez	.50
85	Freddy Garcia	.50
86	Ichiro Suzuki	2.50
87	Albert Pujols	3.00
88	Jim Edmonds	.75
89	Scott Rolen	1.50
90	So Taguchi	.50
91	Rocco Baldelli	.50
92	Alex Rodriguez	3.00
93	Hank Blalock	1.00
94	Juan Gonzalez	1.00
95	Mark Teixeira	.75
96	Rafael Palmeiro	1.00
97	Carlos Delgado	.50
98	Eric Hinske	.50
99	Roy Halladay	.75
100	Vernon Wells	.50
101	Hideki Matsui **RC**	10.00
102	Jose Contreras **RC**	3.00
103	Jeremy Bonderman	4.00
104	Bernie Castro **RC**	1.00
105	Alfredo Gonzalez **RC**	1.00
106	Arnie Munoz **RC**	1.00
107	Andrew Brown **RC**	1.50
108	Josh Hall **RC**	1.50
109	Josh Stewart **RC**	1.50
110	Clint Barmes **RC**	1.50
111	Brandon Webb **RC**	2.50
112	Chien-Ming Wang **RC**	15.00
113	Edgar Gonzalez **RC**	1.00
114	Alejandro Machado **RC**	1.00
115	Jeremy Griffiths **RC**	1.00
116	Craig Brazell **RC**	1.50
117	Shane Bazell **RC**	1.50
118	Fernando Cabrera **RC**	1.50
119	Terrmel Sledge **RC**	1.50
120	Rob Hammock **RC**	1.50
121	Francisco Rosario **RC**	1.50
122	Francisco Cruceta **RC**	1.50
123	Rett Johnson **RC**	1.50
124	Guillermo Quiroz **RC**	2.00
125	Hong-Chih Kuo **RC**	2.00
126	Ian Ferguson **RC**	1.50
127	Tim Olson **RC**	1.50
128	Todd Wellemeyer **RC**	1.50
129	Richard Fischer **RC**	1.00
130	Phil Seibel **RC**	1.00
131	Joe Valentine **RC**	1.00
132	Matt Kata **RC**	1.00
133	Michael Hessman **RC**	1.00
134	Michel Hernandez **RC**	1.00
135	Doug Waechter **RC**	1.50
136	Prentice Redman **RC**	1.00
137	Nook Logan **RC**	1.00
138	Oscar Villarreal **RC**	1.00
139	Pete LaForest **RC**	1.00
140	Matt Bruback **RC**	1.00
141	Dontrelle Willis	1.50
142	Greg Aquino **RC**	1.00
143	Lew Ford **RC**	4.00
144	Jeff Duncan **RC**	2.00
145	Dan Haren **RC**	1.50
146	Miguel Ojeda **RC**	1.00
147	Rosman Garcia **RC**	1.00
148	Felix Sanchez **RC**	1.00
149	Jon Leicester **RC**	1.00
150	Roger Deago **RC**	1.00

Century Proofs
Stars (1-100):		2-4X
Century (101-150):		1-2X
Production 100 Sets		

Decade Proofs
Production 10 Sets
No pricing due to scarcity.

Authentic Cuts
Quantity produced listed

Autographs
		NM/M
Common Auto:		8.00
Some not priced due to scarcity.		
1	Garret Anderson	15.00
6	Mark Grace/141	50.00
7	Matt Williams	10.00
8	Randy Johnson/50	60.00
10	Chipper Jones/50	45.00
14	Manny Ramirez/50	40.00
17	Barry Larkin/159	25.00
33	Ivan Rodriguez/50	35.00
38	Lance Berkman/75	15.00
39	Richard Hidalgo	8.00
40	Roy Oswalt/150	15.00
42	Mike Sweeney	8.00
50	A.J. Pierzynski	8.00
51	Torii Hunter	8.00
53	Jose Vidro	6.00
54	Vladimir Guerrero	20.00
55	Cliff Floyd	8.00
56	David Cone/3	10.00
58	Roberto Alomar/50	40.00
65	Nick Johnson	10.00
67	Barry Zito/150	15.00
68	Eric Chavez	10.00
69	Mark Mulder/50	10.00
72	Bobby Abreu	10.00
78	Kenny Lofton/229	10.00
80	Ryan Klesko/150	10.00
81	Andres Galarraga	8.00
83	Rich Aurilia/122	8.00

84	Edgar Martinez	15.00
89	Scott Rolen/200	25.00
90	So Taguchi/220	10.00
95	Mark Teixeira/150	20.00
100	Vernon Wells	10.00
102	Jose Contreras	20.00
141	Dontrelle Willis/150	25.00

Century
		NM/M
Common Auto:		15.00
Production 100 Sets		
Decades:		No Pricing
Production 10 Sets		
1	Garret Anderson	15.00
7	Matt Williams	15.00
27	Barry Larkin	30.00
39	Richard Hidalgo	15.00
42	Mike Sweeney	15.00
50	A.J. Pierzynski	15.00
51	Torii Hunter	20.00
53	Jose Vidro	15.00
54	Vladimir Guerrero	30.00
55	Cliff Floyd	15.00
62	Drew Henson	15.00
65	Nick Johnson	15.00
69	Mark Mulder	25.00
72	Bobby Abreu	20.00
78	Kenny Lofton	15.00
81	Andres Galarraga	15.00
84	Edgar Martinez	25.00
89	Scott Rolen	30.00
90	So Taguchi	15.00
100	Vernon Wells	15.00
102	Jose Contreras	25.00

Century Notations
		NM/M
Production 100 Sets		
Decade Notations:		No Pricing
Production 10 Sets		
1	Garret Anderson	20.00
7	Matt Williams	15.00
50	A.J. Pierzynski	15.00
68	Eric Chavez	15.00
78	Kenny Lofton	15.00
84	Edgar Martinez	25.00

INKredible - Three
		NM/M
Production 50 Sets		
1	Barry Zito, Mark Mulder, Tim Hudson	300.00
2	Andruw Jones, Chipper Jones, Greg Maddux	325.00
3	Ernie Banks, Kerry Wood, Mark Prior	300.00
4	Harmon Killebrew, Kirby Puckett, Torii Hunter	175.00
5	Javier Vazquez, Jose Vidro, Vladimir Guerrero	90.00

INKredible - Four
		NM/M
Production 25 Sets		
Limited pricing due to scarcity.		
4	Brooks Robinson, Cal Ripken Jr., Frank Robinson, Jim Palmer	500.00
6	Bo Jackson, Carlos Beltran, George Brett, Mike Sweeney	225.00
7	Curt Schilling, Junior Spivey, Mark Grace, Randy Johnson	475.00
10	Joe Carter, Roberto Alomar, Ryan Klesko, Tony Gwynn	200.00

INKredible - Six

	NM/M
Production 10 Sets	
Limited pricing due to scarcity.	
3	Andre Dawson, Ernie Banks, Kerry Wood, Mark Grace, Mark Prior, Ryne Sandberg 1,500
5	Alex Rodriguez, Don Mattingly, George Brett, Hideo Nomo, Nolan Ryan, Roger Clemens 3,100

Legends of Summer
		NM/M
Complete Set (40):		125.00
Common Player:		3.00
Production 250 Sets		

Century:		1X
Production 100 Sets		
Decades:		No Pricing
Production 10 Sets		
1	Al Kaline	5.00
2	Alan Trammell	3.00
3	Andre Dawson	3.00
4	Babe Ruth	10.00
5	Billy Williams	3.00
6	Bo Jackson	4.00
7	Bob Feller	3.00
8	Bobby Doerr	3.00
9	Brooks Robinson	5.00
10	Dale Murphy	5.00
11	Dennis Eckersley	3.00
12	Don Mattingly	8.00
13	Duke Snider	3.00
14	Eric Davis	3.00
15	Frank Robinson	3.00
16	Fred Lynn	3.00
17	Gary Carter	3.00
18	Harmon Killebrew	5.00
19	Jack Morris	3.00
20	Jim Palmer	3.00
21	Jim Abbott	3.00
22	Joe Morgan	3.00
23	Joe Torre	3.00
24	Johnny Bench	5.00
25	Jose Canseco	3.00
26	Kirby Puckett	5.00
27	Lenny Dykstra	3.00
28	Lou Brock	3.00
29	Ralph Kiner	3.00
30	Mike Schmidt	6.00
31	Nolan Ryan	9.00
32	Nolan Ryan	10.00
33	Orel Hershiser	3.00
34	Phil Rizzuto	3.00
35	Orlando Cepeda	3.00
36	Ryne Sandberg	3.00
37	Stan Musial	6.00
38	Steve Garvey	3.00
39	Tony Perez	3.00
40	Ty Cobb	6.00

Legends of Summer Autograph
		NM/M
Common Autograph:		8.00
1	Al Kaline	20.00
2	Alan Trammell	10.00
3	Andre Dawson	10.00
5	Billy Williams	8.00
6	Bo Jackson/100	50.00
7	Bob Feller	15.00
8	Bobby Doerr	15.00
9	Brooks Robinson	25.00
10	Dale Murphy/75	40.00
11	Dennis Eckersley	15.00
12	Don Mattingly/50	75.00
13	Duke Snider/225	20.00
14	Eric Davis	8.00
15	Frank Robinson	10.00
16	Fred Lynn	8.00
17	Gary Carter	10.00
18	Harmon Killebrew/171	20.00
19	Jack Morris	10.00
20	Jim Palmer	10.00
21	Jim Abbott	10.00
22	Joe Morgan/125	15.00
23	Joe Torre	10.00
24	Johnny Bench/75	30.00
25	Jose Canseco/75	30.00
26	Kirby Puckett/75	35.00
27	Lenny Dykstra	15.00
28	Lou Brock	15.00
29	Ralph Kiner	15.00
30	Mike Schmidt/75	60.00
31	Nolan Ryan/75	110.00
33	Orel Hershiser	20.00
34	Phil Rizzuto	15.00
35	Orlando Cepeda	15.00
36	Ryne Sandberg/75	60.00
37	Stan Musial/200	30.00
38	Steve Garvey	10.00
39	Tony Perez	10.00

Legends of Summer Century
		NM/M
Production 100 Sets		
Decades:		No Pricing
Production 10 Sets		
1	Al Kaline	25.00
2	Alan Trammell	20.00
3	Andre Dawson	15.00
5	Billy Williams	15.00
6	Bo Jackson	50.00
7	Bob Feller	15.00
8	Bobby Doerr	20.00
9	Brooks Robinson	25.00
11	Dennis Eckersley	15.00
12	Don Mattingly	65.00
14	Eric Davis	15.00
15	Frank Robinson	15.00
16	Fred Lynn	15.00
17	Gary Carter	20.00
19	Jack Morris	15.00
20	Jim Palmer	20.00
21	Jim Abbott	15.00
23	Joe Torre	15.00
27	Lenny Dykstra	15.00
28	Lou Brock	25.00
29	Ralph Kiner	15.00
33	Orel Hershiser	60.00

34	Phil Rizzuto	30.00
35	Orlando Cepeda	20.00
36	Ryne Sandberg	65.00
38	Stan Musial	60.00
39	Steve Garvey	15.00
39	Tony Perez	15.00

Legends of Summer Notations
		NM/M
Common Autograph:		8.00
1	Al Kaline/200	20.00
3	Alan Trammell/250	10.00
3	Andre Dawson/250	10.00
5	Billy Williams/250	8.00
5	Billy Williams/150	8.00
7	Bob Feller/250	15.00
7	Bob Feller/200	15.00
8	Bobby Doerr/250	10.00
9	Brooks Robinson/150	20.00
9	Brooks Robinson/50	40.00
10	Dale Murphy/45	45.00
11	Dennis Eckersley/250	10.00
14	Eric Davis/250	8.00
14	Eric Davis/150	8.00
14	Eric Davis/200	8.00
16	Fred Lynn/240	10.00
16	Fred Lynn/150	10.00
18	Harmon Killebrew/75	40.00
18	Harmon Killebrew/50	40.00
18	Harmon Killebrew/125	30.00
19	Jack Morris/250	10.00
20	Jim Palmer/190	10.00
20	Jim Palmer/140	10.00
20	Jim Palmer/50	20.00
21	Jim Abbott/200	10.00
21	Jim Abbott/100	15.00
21	Jim Abbott/75	15.00
21	Jim Abbott/50	15.00
27	Lenny Dykstra/226	10.00
28	Lou Brock/50	35.00
29	Ralph Kiner/250	15.00
29	Ralph Kiner/100	15.00
29	Ralph Kiner/150	15.00
35	Orlando Cepeda/75	35.00
35	Orlando Cepeda/40	25.00
38	Steve Garvey/150	15.00
38	Steve Garvey/50	20.00
38	Steve Garvey/75	15.00
39	Tony Perez/250	15.00
39	Tony Perez/125	15.00
39	Tony Perez/75	20.00
39	Tony Perez/175	10.00

Notable Nicknames
		NM/M
Complete Set (20):		75.00
Common Player:		3.00
Production 750 Sets		
Century:		1-1.5X
Production 100 Sets		
Decade:		No Pricing
Production 10 Sets		
1	Andre Dawson	3.00
2	Torii Hunter	3.00
3	Brooks Robinson	5.00
4	Carlton Fisk	3.00
5	Mike Mussina	8.00
6	Don Mattingly	8.00
7	Duke Snider	4.00
8	Eric Davis	3.00
9	Frank Thomas	4.00
10	Randy Johnson	5.00
11	Lenny Dykstra	3.00
12	Ivan Rodriguez	3.00
13	Nolan Ryan	10.00
14	Phil Rizzuto	3.00
15	Reggie Jackson	4.00
16	Roger Clemens	8.00
17	Ryne Sandberg	8.00
18	Stan Musial	6.00
19	Luis Gonzalez	3.00
20	Will Clark	4.00

Notable Nicknames Autograph
		NM/M
Quantity produced listed		
Decades:		No Pricing
Production 10 Sets		
1	Andre "The Hawk" Dawson/100	30.00
2	Torii "Spiderman" Hunter/100	30.00
3	Brooks "Hoover" Robinson	60.00
4	Carlton "Pudge" Fisk/100	50.00
5	Mike "Moose" Mussina/100	80.00
6	Don "Donnie Baseball" Mattingly/100	100.00
7	Duke "Duke of Flatbush" Snider/100	60.00
8	Eric "The Red" Davis/40	50.00
9	Frank "The Big Hurt" Thomas/100	60.00

10	Randy "Big Unit" Johnson/100	100.00
11	Lenny "Nails" Dykstra/100	20.00
12	Ivan "Pudge" Rodriguez/75	50.00
14	Phil "Scooter" Rizzuto/100	50.00
15	Reggie "Mr. October" Jackson/100	60.00
16	Roger "The Rocket" Clemens/100	150.00
17	Ryne "Ryno" Sandberg/100	75.00
18	Stan "The Man" Musial/100	85.00
19	Luis "Gonzo" Gonzalez/100	25.00
20	Will "The Thrill" Clark/100	60.00

Notations
		NM/M
Varying quantities produced		
Many not priced due to scarcity.		
1	Garret Anderson/75	20.00
7	Matt Williams/250	10.00
7	Matt Williams/50	20.00
45	Kazuhisa Ishii/35	35.00
50	A.J. Pierzynski/200	15.00
53	Jose Vidro/40	15.00
62	Drew Henson/73	20.00
68	Eric Chavez/50	20.00
78	Kenny Lofton/150	10.00
80	Ryan Klesko/35	20.00
83	Rich Aurilia/61	15.00
84	Edgar Martinez/250	10.00
84	Edgar Martinez/60	20.00
100	Vernon Wells/75	15.00

Players Collection Autograph
		NM/M
Quantity produced listed		
	Roberto Alomar/75	30.00
	Adrian Beltre/104	15.00
	Lance Berkman/50	20.00
	Craig Biggio/26	35.00
	Joe Borchard/53	10.00
	J.D. Drew/52	20.00
	Jim Edmonds/52	25.00
	Todd Helton/50	40.00
	Jason Jennings/49	10.00
	Chipper Jones/51	50.00
	Paul LoDuca/227	8.00
	Magglio Ordonez/102	20.00
	Mark Prior/27	100.00
	Ivan Rodriguez/52	35.00
	Richie Sexson/50	20.00
	Matt Williams/482	8.00

Signature Cuts
		NM/M
Some not priced due to scarcity.		
Decades:		No Pricing
Production 10 Sets		
8	Randy Johnson/40	60.00
33	Ivan Rodriguez/122	30.00
54	Vladimir Guerrero/34	35.00
58	Roberto Alomar/100	30.00
64	Mike Mussina/82	40.00
73	Jim Thome/127	30.00
80	Ryan Klesko/35	20.00
81	Andres Galarraga/51	20.00
89	Scott Rolen/36	40.00

Team Trademarks
		NM/M
Complete Set (40):		150.00
Common Player:		3.00
Production 100 Sets		
Century:		1X
Production 100 Sets		
Decade:		No Pricing
Production 10 Sets		
1	Adam Dunn	3.00
2	Andre Dawson	3.00
3	Babe Ruth	10.00
4	Barry Bonds	10.00
5	Brooks Robinson	4.00
6	Cal Ripken Jr.	10.00
7	Derek Jeter	8.00
8	Don Mattingly	8.00
9	Frank Robinson	3.00
10	Fred Lynn	3.00
11	Gary Carter	3.00
12	George Brett	5.00
13	Greg Maddux	5.00
14	Ichiro Suzuki	6.00
15	Jim Palmer	3.00
16	Jose Contreras	3.00
17	Kerry Wood	4.00
18	Lou Gehrig	8.00
19	Magglio Ordonez	3.00
20	Mark Grace	3.00
21	Mike Schmidt	8.00
22	Nolan Ryan	10.00
23	Nolan Ryan	10.00
24	Reggie Jackson	6.00
25	Rickey Henderson	3.00
26	Roberto Clemente	6.00
27	Roger Clemens	6.00
28	Roger Clemens	6.00
29	Ryne Sandberg	6.00

30	Sammy Sosa	6.00
31	Stan Musial	6.00
32	Steve Carlton	3.00
33	Tim Hudson	3.00
34	Tom Glavine	3.00
35	Tom Seaver	4.00
36	Tony Gwynn	4.00
37	Torii Hunter	3.00
38	Ty Cobb	6.00
39	Vladimir Guerrero	4.00
40	Will Clark	4.00

Team Trademarks Century

NM/M
Production 100 Sets
Decade: No Pricing
Production 10 Sets

2	Andre Dawson	15.00
5	Brooks Robinson	30.00
9	Frank Robinson	15.00
10	Fred Lynn	15.00
11	Gary Carter	20.00
15	Jim Palmer	15.00
16	Jose Contreras	25.00
20	Mark Grace	60.00
29	Ryne Sandberg	65.00
31	Stan Musial	65.00
32	Steve Carlton	25.00
34	Tom Glavine	25.00
37	Steve Hunter	15.00
39	Vladimir Guerrero	25.00

Team Trademarks Autograph

NM/M
Quantity produced listed

1	Adam Dunn/50	35.00
2	Andre Dawson/250	10.00
5	Brooks Robinson/250	20.00
6	Cal Ripken Jr./50	200.00
8	Don Mattingly/75	85.00
10	Fred Lynn/250	8.00
11	Gary Carter/250	10.00
12	George Brett/50	100.00
13	Greg Maddux/50	85.00
16	Jose Contreras/250	15.00
17	Kerry Wood/50	40.00
19	Magglio Ordonez/75	15.00
20	Mark Grace/25	90.00
23	Nolan Ryan/50	110.00
24	Reggie Jackson/75	25.00
25	Rickey Henderson/50	100.00
27	Roger Clemens/50	110.00
28	Roger Clemens/50	110.00
29	Ryne Sandberg/100	60.00
31	Stan Musial/200	50.00
32	Steve Carlton/150	20.00
33	Tim Hudson/100	35.00
34	Tom Glavine/50	35.00
36	Tom Seaver/50	35.00
36	Tony Gwynn/50	60.00
37	Torii Hunter/250	10.00
39	Vladimir Guerrero/250	20.00
40	Will Clark/125	30.00

Team Trademarks Notations

NM/M
Quantity produced listed

2	Andre Dawson/250	10.00
2	Andre Dawson/150	10.00
5	Brooks Robinson/75	35.00
5	Brooks Robinson/125	30.00
10	Fred Lynn/50	20.00
15	Jim Palmer/32	25.00
15	Jim Palmer/128	15.00
15	Jim Palmer/150	15.00
29	Ryne Sandberg/40	80.00
29	Ryne Sandberg/55	20.00
32	Steve Carlton/50	35.00
33	Tim Hudson/50	45.00
40	Will Clark/52	60.00

2003 Donruss Studio Samples

Each August 2003 issue of Beckett Baseball Card Monthly included a sample Donruss Studio card rubber-cemented inside. The cards differ from the issued version only in the appearance on back of a (usually) silver-foil "SAMPLE" notation. Some cards were produced with the back overprint in gold-foil in much more limited quan-

JOE VALENTINE RP

tities. The number of different players' cards involved in the promotion is unknown.

NM/M
Common Player: .10
Stars: 1.5X
Gold: 20X

2003 Donruss Studio

KERRY WOOD P

NM/M
Complete Set (200): 35.00
Common Player: .25
Pack (6): 4.00
Box (20): 60.00

1	Darin Erstad	.40
2	David Eckstein	.25
3	Garret Anderson	.50
4	Jarrod Washburn	.25
5	Tim Salmon	.50
6	Troy Glaus	.50
7	Jay Gibbons	.25
8	Melvin Mora	.25
9	Rodrigo Lopez	.25
10	Tony Batista	.25
11	Freddy Sanchez	.25
12	Derek Lowe	.40
13	Johnny Damon	.40
14	Manny Ramirez	.75
15	Nomar Garciaparra	1.50
16	Pedro J. Martinez	1.00
17	Rickey Henderson	.50
18	Shea Hillenbrand	.25
19	Carlos Lee	.25
20	Frank Thomas	.75
21	Magglio Ordonez	.25
22	Bartolo Colon	.25
23	Paul Konerko	.25
24	Josh Stewart RC	.25
25	C.C. Sabathia	.25
26	Jeremy Guthrie	.25
27	Ellis Burks	.25
28	Omar Vizquel	.40
29	Victor Martinez	.25
30	Cliff Lee	.25
31	Jhonny Peralta	.50
32	Brian Tallet	.25
33	Bobby Higginson	.25
34	Carlos Pena	.25
35	Nook Logan RC	.25
36	Steve Sparks	.25
37	Travis Chapman	.25
38	Carlos Beltran	.75
39	Joe Randa	.25
40	Mike Sweeney	.25
41	Jimmy Gobble	.25
42	Michael Tucker	.25
43	Runelvys Hernandez	.25
44	Brad Radke	.25
45	Corey Koskie	.25
46	Cristian Guzman	.25
47	J.C. Romero	.25
48	Doug Mientkiewicz	.25
49	Lew Ford RC	1.50
50	Jacque Jones	.40
51	Torii Hunter	.50
52	Alfonso Soriano	.75
53	Nick Johnson	.25
54	Bernie Williams	.50
55	Jose Contreras RC	1.50
56	Derek Jeter	3.00
57	Jason Giambi	.50
58	Brandon Claussen	.25
59	Jorge Posada	.50
60	Mike Mussina	.50
61	Roger Clemens	2.00
62	Hideki Matsui RC	5.00
63	Barry Zito	.50
64	Adam Morrissey	.25
65	Eric Chavez	.40
66	Jermaine Dye	.25
67	Mark Mulder	.40
68	Miguel Tejada	.50
69	Joe Valentine RC	.25
70	Tim Hudson	.50
71	Bret Boone	.40
72	Chris Snelling	.25
73	Edgar Martinez	.25
74	Freddy Garcia	.25
75	Ichiro Suzuki	2.00
76	Jamie Moyer	.25
77	John Olerud	.40
78	Kazuhiro Sasaki	.25
79	Aubrey Huff	.25
80	Joe Kennedy	.25
81	Dewon Brazelton	.25
82	Pete LaForest RC	.25
83	Alex Rodriguez	2.50
84	Chan Ho Park	.25
85	Hank Blalock	.75
86	Juan Gonzalez	.75
87	Kevin Mench	.25
88	Rafael Palmeiro	.75
89	Carlos Delgado	.50
90	Eric Hinske	.25
91	Josh Phelps	.25
92	Roy Halladay	.40
93	Shannon Stewart	.25
94	Vernon Wells	.40
95	Vinnie Chulk	.25
96	Curt Schilling	.75
97	Junior Spivey	.25
98	Luis Gonzalez	.50
99	Mark Grace	.50
100	Randy Johnson	1.00
101	Andruw Jones	.75
102	Chipper Jones	1.00
103	Gary Sheffield	.50
104	Greg Maddux	1.50
105	John Smoltz	.50
106	Mike Hampton	.25
107	Adam LaRoche	.25
108	Michael Hessman RC	.50
109	Corey Patterson	.40
110	Kerry Wood	1.00
111	Mark Prior	1.00
112	Moises Alou	.50
113	Sammy Sosa	1.50
114	Adam Dunn	.75
115	Austin Kearns	.40
116	Barry Larkin	.40
117	Ken Griffey Jr.	1.50
118	Sean Casey	.25
119	Jason Jennings	.25
120	Jay Payton	.25
121	Larry Walker	.40
122	Todd Helton	.75
123	Jeff Baker	.25
124	Clint Barmes RC	1.00
125	Ivan Rodriguez	.75
126	Josh Beckett	.50
127	Juan Encarnacion	.25
128	Mike Lowell	.25
129	Craig Biggio	.40
130	Jason Lane	.25
131	Jeff Bagwell	.75
132	Lance Berkman	.50
133	Roy Oswalt	.50
134	Jeff Kent	.40
135	Hideo Nomo	.50
136	Kazuhisa Ishii	.25
137	Kevin Brown	.40
138	Odalis Perez	.25
139	Paul LoDuca	.25
140	Shawn Green	.50
141	Adrian Beltre	.50
142	Ben Sheets	.40
143	Bill Hall	.25
144	Jeffrey Hammonds	.25
145	Richie Sexson	.50
146	Termel Sledge RC	.75
147	Brad Wilkerson	.25
148	Javier Vazquez	.25
149	Jose Vidro	.25
150	Michael Barrett	.25
151	Vladimir Guerrero	.75
152	Al Leiter	.25
153	Mike Piazza	2.00
154	Mo Vaughn	.25
155	Cliff Floyd	.25
156	Roberto Alomar	.50
157	Roger Cedeno	.25
158	Tom Glavine	.50
159	Prentice Redman RC	.25
160	Bobby Abreu	.50
161	Jimmy Rollins	.40
162	Mike Lieberthal	.25
163	Pat Burrell	.50
164	Vicente Padilla	.25
165	Jim Thome	.75
166	Kevin Millwood	.40
167	Aramis Ramirez	.50
168	Brian Giles	.40
169	Jason Kendall	.40
170	Josh Fogg	.25
171	Kip Wells	.25
172	Jose Castillo	.25
173	Mark Kotsay	.25
174	Oliver Perez	.25
175	Phil Nevin	.25
176	Ryan Klesko	.40
177	Sean Burroughs	.25
178	Brian Lawrence	.25
179	Shane Victorino RC	.25
180	Barry Bonds	3.00
181	Benito Santiago	.25
182	Ray Durham	.25
183	Rich Aurilia	.25
184	Damian Moss	.25
185	Albert Pujols	2.00
186	J.D. Drew	.25
187	Jim Edmonds	.50
188	Matt Morris	.40
189	Tino Martinez	.25
190	Scott Rolen	.75
191	Troy Glaus, Tim Salmon	.50
192	Sean Casey, Corky Miller	.25
193	Carlos Lee, Frank Thomas	.50
194	Lance Berkman, Jeff Kent	.25
195	Jose Contreras, Mariano Rivera	1.00
196	Alex Rodriguez, Juan Gonzalez	1.00
197	Andy Pettitte, David Wells	.25
198	Shawn Green, Dave Roberts	.25
199	Mike Lieberthal, Jimmy Rollins	.40
200	Mike Mussina, Hideki Matsui	2.00

Proofs

Stars (1-200): 4-8X
Rookies (1-200): 2-3X
Production 100 Sets

Private Signings

NM/M

7	Jay Gibbons/100	10.00
11	Freddy Sanchez/150	25.00
24	Josh Stewart/200	8.00
26	Jeremy Guthrie/125	8.00
29	Victor Martinez/200	20.00
30	Cliff Lee/150	10.00
31	Jhonny Peralta/200	20.00
35	Nook Logan/100	8.00
37	Travis Chapman/150	8.00
41	Jimmy Gobble/200	8.00
42	J.C. Romero/200	8.00
49	Lew Ford/200	15.00
51	Torii Hunter/50	20.00
53	Nick Johnson/100	10.00
55	Jose Contreras/100	25.00
58	Brandon Claussen/200	10.00
69	Joe Valentine/200	8.00
79	Aubrey Huff/50	10.00
81	Dewon Brazelton/75	10.00
82	Pete LaForest/100	10.00
85	Hank Blalock/50	20.00
87	Kevin Mench/200	8.00
90	Eric Hinske/125	8.00
95	Vinnie Chulk/50	8.00
97	Junior Spivey/50	10.00
107	Adam LaRoche/200	15.00
108	Michael Hessman/200	8.00
111	Mark Prior/50	30.00
119	Jason Jennings/50	8.00
123	Jeff Baker/75	10.00
124	Clint Barmes/200	10.00
130	Jason Lane/100	10.00
139	Paul LoDuca/75	15.00
143	Bill Hall/50	20.00
146	Termel Sledge/125	10.00
149	Jose Vidro/50	15.00
159	Prentice Redman/200	10.00
160	Bobby Abreu/50	20.00
171	Kip Wells/50	10.00
172	Jose Castillo/175	8.00
178	Brian Lawrence/100	10.00
179	Shane Victorino/200	10.00
201	Adam Loewen/100	20.00
202	Jeremy Bonderman/50	40.00
203	Brandon Webb/100	35.00
204	Chien-Ming Wang/50	250.00
206	Ryan Wagner/100	10.00
207	Hong-Chih Kuo/25	175.00
208	Dan Haren/100	15.00
210	Ramon Nivar/100	15.00

Big League Challenge

NM/M
Complete Set (50): 125.00
Common Player: 1.50
Production 400 Sets
Proofs 4-8X
Production 25 Sets

1	Jose Canseco	2.00
2	Magglio Ordonez	1.50
3	Alex Rodriguez	5.00
4	Lance Berkman	1.50
5	Rafael Palmeiro	3.00
6	Nomar Garciaparra	5.00
7	Nomar Garciaparra	5.00
8	Nomar Garciaparra	5.00
9	Troy Glaus	2.00
10	Mark McGwire	6.00
11	Mark McGwire	6.00
12	Mark McGwire	6.00
13	Jim Thome	3.00
14	Chipper Jones	3.00
15	Shawn Green	1.50
16	Alex Rodriguez	5.00
17	Alex Rodriguez	5.00
18	Alex Rodriguez	5.00
21	Jason Giambi	2.00
21	Pat Burrell	1.50
22	Mike Piazza	4.00
23	Mike Piazza	4.00
23	Mike Piazza	4.00
26	Frank Thomas	2.00
27	Rafael Palmeiro	2.00
28	Jose Canseco	2.00
29	Albert Pujols	5.00
31	Troy Glaus	2.00
31	Barry Bonds	6.00
32	Barry Bonds	6.00
33	Barry Bonds	6.00
34	Todd Helton	3.00
35	Rafael Palmeiro	3.00
36	Jim Thome	3.00
37	Ozzie Smith	3.00
38	Troy Glaus	2.00
39	Shawn Green	1.50
40	Barry Bonds	6.00
41	Barry Bonds	6.00
42	Barry Bonds	6.00
43	Magglio Ordonez	1.50
44	Alex Rodriguez	5.00
45	Alex Rodriguez	5.00
46	Alex Rodriguez	5.00
47	Lance Berkman	1.50
48	Rafael Palmeiro	2.00
49	Pat Burrell	1.50
50	Albert Pujols	5.00

Big League Challenge Materials

NM/M
Common Player: 4.00
Inserted 1:20

2	Magglio Ordonez/Jsy	4.00
3	Alex Rodriguez/Jsy	10.00
4	Lance Berkman/Jsy	4.00
15	Shawn Green/Jsy	4.00
29	Albert Pujols/Jsy	15.00
39	Jim Thome/Jsy	6.00
40	Shawn Green/Pants	4.00
41	Barry Bonds/Base	10.00
42	Barry Bonds/Base	10.00
43	Barry Bonds/Base	10.00
43	Magglio Ordonez/Jsy	4.00
45	Alex Rodriguez/Jsy	10.00
46	Alex Rodriguez/Pants	10.00
47	Lance Berkman/Jsy	4.00
48	Rafael Palmeiro/Jsy	6.00
50	Albert Pujols/Pants	10.00

Big League Challenge Prime Material

NM/M
Common Player: 10.00

2	Magglio Ordonez/100	10.00
3	Alex Rodriguez/100	25.00
15	Shawn Green/50	15.00
29	Albert Pujols/100	25.00
39	Jim Thome/50	20.00
45	Alex Rodriguez/100	25.00
48	Rafael Palmeiro/100	15.00

Enshrinement

NM/M
Complete Set (50): 180.00
Common Player: 3.00
Production 750 Sets
Proofs: 5-10X
Production 20 or 21

1	Gary Carter	4.00
2	Ozzie Smith	10.00
3	Kirby Puckett	6.00
4	Carlton Fisk	4.00
5	Tony Perez	3.00
6	Nolan Ryan	15.00
7	George Brett	12.00
8	Robin Yount	10.00
9	Orlando Cepeda	3.00
10	Phil Niekro	3.00
11	Mike Schmidt	10.00
12	Richie Ashburn	6.00
13	Steve Carlton	4.00
14	Phil Rizzuto	4.00
15	Reggie Jackson	6.00
16	Tom Seaver	5.00
17	Rollie Fingers	4.00
18	Rod Carew	5.00
19	Gaylord Perry	3.00
21	Fergie Jenkins	3.00
21	Jim Palmer	3.00
22	Joe Morgan	3.00
23	Johnny Bench	6.00
24	Willie Stargell	3.00
25	Billy Williams	3.00
26	Jim "Catfish" Hunter	3.00
27	Willie McCovey	3.00
28	Bobby Doerr	3.00
29	Lou Brock	4.00
30	Enos Slaughter	3.00
31	Hoyt Wilhelm	3.00
32	Harmon Killebrew	6.00
33	Pee Wee Reese	3.00
34	Luis Aparicio	3.00
35	Brooks Robinson	6.00
36	Juan Marichal	4.00
37	Frank Robinson	5.00
38	Bob Gibson	4.00
39	Al Kaline	6.00
40	Duke Snider	6.00
41	Eddie Mathews	5.00
42	Robin Roberts	3.00
43	Ralph Kiner	3.00
44	Whitey Ford	5.00
45	Roberto Clemente	10.00
46	Warren Spahn	4.00
47	Yogi Berra	5.00
48	Early Wynn	3.00
49	Stan Musial	6.00
50	Bob Feller	4.00

Enshrinement Autographs

NM/M
Varying quantities produced

1	Gary Carter/50	30.00
2	Tony Perez/50	50.00
9	Orlando Cepeda/50	20.00
10	Phil Niekro/50	20.00
13	Steve Carlton/50	40.00
14	Phil Rizzuto/15	50.00
21	Fergie Jenkins/50	20.00
21	Jim Palmer/25	35.00
22	Joe Morgan/10	50.00
28	Bobby Doerr/100	30.00
31	Hoyt Wilhelm/50	25.00
34	Luis Aparicio/100	15.00
35	Brooks Robinson/25	65.00
37	Frank Robinson/25	35.00
43	Ralph Kiner/25	40.00
50	Bob Feller/100	25.00

Leather & Lumber

NM/M
Common Player: 5.00

1	Adam Dunn/400	10.00
2	Alex Rodriguez/250	12.00
3	Alfonso Soriano/250	10.00
4	Andruw Jones/400	8.00
5	Austin Kearns/400	8.00
6	Chipper Jones/400	10.00
7	Derek Jeter/100	35.00
8	Don Mattingly/100	40.00
9	Edgar Martinez	10.00
11	Frank Thomas/400	8.00
11	Fred McGriff/400	8.00
13	Greg Maddux/150	15.00
14	Hideki Matsui/Ball/100	40.00
15	Hideo Nomo/150	15.00
16	Ichiro Suzuki/Ball/100	40.00
17	Ivan Rodriguez/250	8.00
18	Jason Giambi/400	8.00
19	Jeff Bagwell/400	8.00
20	Jim Edmonds/150	8.00
21	Jim Thome/400	10.00
22	Juan Gonzalez/400	8.00
23	Kerry Wood/250	10.00
24	Kirby Puckett/100	25.00
25	Lance Berkman/400	8.00
26	Magglio Ordonez/400	5.00
27	Manny Ramirez/250	10.00
28	Mark Prior/400	8.00
29	Miguel Tejada/200	5.00
30	Mike Piazza/400	10.00
31	Mike Schmidt/200	25.00
32	Nomar Garciaparra/400	15.00
33	Pat Burrell/400	8.00
34	Pedro Martinez/150	10.00
36	Randy Johnson/250	10.00
37	Rickey Henderson/175	10.00
38	Sammy Sosa/300	10.00
39	Shawn Green/400	5.00
40	Vladimir Guerrero/400	8.00

Leather & Lumber Dual

NM/M
Common Player:
Those without bat & ball are noted.

1	Adam Dunn/50	25.00
2	Alex Rodriguez/50	30.00
3	Andruw Jones/50	25.00

5 Austin Kearns/Shoe/50 25.00
6 Chipper Jones/25 45.00
8 Don Mattingly/25 80.00
10 Frank Thomas/50 30.00
13 Greg Maddux/Shoe/50 35.00
17 Ivan Rodriguez/50 25.00
23 Kerry Wood/50 35.00
24 Kirby Puckett/25 35.00
25 Lance Berkman/50 12.00
28 Mark Prior/Shoe/50 50.00
29 Miguel Tejada/25 15.00
33 Pat Burrell/25 20.00
36 Randy Johnson/25 40.00
38 Sammy Sosa/Shoe/25 60.00

Masterstrokes

ALBERT PUJOLS - OUTFIELD

NM/M
Complete Set (25): 50.00
Common Player: 1.00
Production 1,000 Sets
1 Adam Dunn 2.00
2 Albert Pujols 3.00
3 Alex Rodriguez 5.00
4 Alfonso Soriano 3.00
5 Andruw Jones 1.50
6 Chipper Jones 3.00
7 Derek Jeter 6.00
8 Greg Maddux 3.00
9 Hideki Matsui 8.00
10 Hideo Nomo 1.50
11 Ivan Rodriguez 2.00
12 Jason Giambi 1.50
13 Jeff Bagwell 1.50
14 Juan Gonzalez 1.50
15 Ken Griffey Jr. 3.00
16 Lance Berkman 1.00
17 Magglio Ordonez 2.00
18 Manny Ramirez 2.00
19 Mark Prior 2.00
20 Miguel Tejada 1.00
21 Mike Piazza 3.00
22 Nomar Garciaparra 4.00
23 Pat Burrell 1.50
24 Sammy Sosa 4.00
25 Vladimir Guerrero 1.50

Masterstrokes Artist's Proof

NM/M
Common Player: 15.00
Production 50 Sets
1 Adam Dunn 25.00
2 Albert Pujols 50.00
3 Alex Rodriguez 50.00
4 Alfonso Soriano 25.00
5 Andruw Jones 20.00
6 Chipper Jones 30.00
7 Derek Jeter 50.00
8 Greg Maddux 25.00
9 Hideki Matsui 75.00
10 Hideo Nomo 100.00
11 Ivan Rodriguez 20.00
12 Jason Giambi 15.00
13 Jeff Bagwell 25.00
14 Juan Gonzalez 25.00
15 Ken Griffey Jr. 30.00
16 Lance Berkman 15.00
17 Magglio Ordonez 15.00
18 Manny Ramirez 20.00
19 Mark Prior 20.00
20 Miguel Tejada 15.00
21 Mike Piazza 35.00
22 Nomar Garciaparra 40.00
23 Pat Burrell 15.00
24 Sammy Sosa 25.00
25 Vladimir Guerrero 25.00

Players Collection

NM/M
Common Player: 4.00
Production 300 Sets
1 Adam Dunn 8.00
2 Adrian Beltre 6.00
3 Alex Rodriguez 10.00
4 Alfonso Soriano 8.00
5 Andruw Jones 6.00
6 Andy Pettitte 4.00
7 Barry Larkin 6.00
8 Barry Zito 4.00
9 Ben Grieve 4.00
10 Bernie Williams 8.00

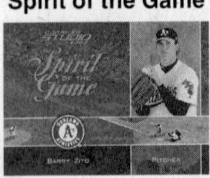

11 Cal Ripken Jr. 30.00
12 Carlos Delgado 5.00
13 C.C. Sabathia 4.00
14 Chipper Jones 10.00
15 Craig Biggio 4.00
16 Curt Schilling 6.00
17 Alex Rodriguez 10.00
18 Frank Thomas 8.00
19 Freddy Garcia 4.00
20 Jay Bell 4.00
21 Roger Clemens 12.00
22 Tony Gwynn 10.00
23 Ivan Rodriguez 6.00
24 Jason Giambi 6.00
25 Jason Jennings 4.00
26 Jay Payton 4.00
27 J.D. Drew 4.00
28 Jeff Bagwell 8.00
29 Jeromy Burnitz 4.00
30 Jim Edmonds 6.00
31 Jim Thome 8.00
32 Joe Borchard 4.00
33 Joe Mays 4.00
34 John Olerud 4.00
35 David Wells 4.00
36 Juan Gonzalez 6.00
37 Kazuhiro Sasaki 4.00
38 Chan Ho Park 4.00
39 Kerry Wood 8.00
40 Kevin Brown 5.00
41 Lance Berkman 4.00
42 Larry Walker 4.00
43 Bret Boone 4.00
44 Magglio Ordonez 4.00
45 Manny Ramirez 6.00
46 Mark Mulder 4.00
47 Mark Prior 8.00
48 Matt Williams 4.00
49 Miguel Tejada 6.00
50 Mike Piazza 8.00
51 Nomar Garciaparra 10.00
52 Doug Davis 4.00
53 Paul Konerko 4.00
54 Paul LoDuca 4.00
55 Pedro J. Martinez 8.00
56 Preston Wilson 4.00
57 Rafael Palmeiro 8.00
58 Marlon Byrd 4.00
59 Reggie Sanders 4.00
60 Richie Sexson 5.00
61 Rickey Henderson 10.00
62 Rickey Henderson 10.00
63 Robert Person 4.00
64 Jeff Bagwell 8.00
65 Roger Clemens 12.00
66 Roy Oswalt 4.00
67 Ryan Klesko 4.00
68 Sammy Sosa 12.00
69 Shawn Green 5.00
70 Steve Finley 4.00
71 Terrence Long 4.00
72 Tim Hudson 4.00
73 Toby Hall 4.00
74 Todd Helton 6.00
75 Travis Lee 4.00
76 Troy Glaus 6.00
77 Tsuyoshi Shinjo 4.00
78 Vernon Wells 4.00
79 Vladimir Guerrero 8.00
80 Wes Helms 4.00
81 Alex Rodriguez 10.00
82 Alfonso Soriano 6.00
83 Barry Larkin 6.00
84 Roberto Alomar 6.00
85 Ivan Rodriguez 6.00
86 Jason Giambi 6.00
87 Jeff Bagwell 8.00
88 Juan Gonzalez 6.00
89 Larry Walker 4.00
90 Luis Gonzalez 4.00
91 Magglio Ordonez 4.00
92 Manny Ramirez 8.00
93 Marlon Byrd 4.00
94 Mike Piazza 10.00
95 Pat Burrell 8.00
96 Todd Helton 6.00
97 Rickey Henderson 10.00
98 Andruw Jones 6.00
99 Craig Biggio 8.00
100 Mark Prior 8.00

Recollection Autographs 5x7

NM/M
3 Sean Casey/125 15.00
5 Troy Glaus/82 20.00

8 Vladimir Guerrero/125 35.00
10 Todd Helton/55 35.00
12 Ryan Klesko/75 15.00
18 Ivan Rodriguez/50 40.00
-19 C.C. Sabathia/50 20.00
20 Curt Schilling/75 30.00
23 Mike Sweeney/42 15.00
24 Miguel Tejada/44 30.00
26 Kerry Wood/200 25.00
27 Barry Zito/200 15.00

Spirit of the Game

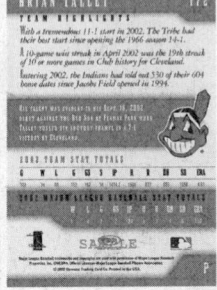

NM/M
Complete Set (35): 60.00
Common Player: 1.00
Production 1,250 Sets
1 Garret Anderson 1.00
2 Nomar Garciaparra 3.00
3 Pedro J. Martinez 2.00
4 Rickey Henderson 1.50
5 Magglio Ordonez 1.00
6 Torii Hunter 1.50
7 Alfonso Soriano 1.50
8 Jose Contreras 1.00
9 Derek Jeter 4.00
10 Jason Giambi 1.50
11 Roger Clemens 4.00
12 Hideki Matsui 6.00
13 Barry Zito 1.50
14 Ichiro Suzuki 3.00
15 Alex Rodriguez 4.00
16 Curt Schilling 1.00
17 Randy Johnson 2.00
18 Andruw Jones 1.50
19 Chipper Jones 2.00
20 Greg Maddux 3.00
21 Sammy Sosa 3.00
22 Adam Dunn 2.00
23 Ken Griffey Jr. 4.00
24 Todd Helton 2.00
25 Ivan Rodriguez 2.00
26 Lance Berkman 1.00
27 Hideo Nomo 1.50
28 Shawn Green 1.00
29 Vladimir Guerrero 2.00
30 Mike Piazza 3.00
31 Roberto Alomar 1.50
32 Jim Thome 2.00
33 Barry Bonds 5.00
34 Albert Pujols 3.00
35 Scott Rolen 2.00

Stars

NM/M
Complete Set (50): 65.00
Common Player: 1.00
Inserted 1:5
Golds: 3-5X
Production 100 Sets
1 Troy Glaus 1.50
2 Manny Ramirez 1.50
3 Nomar Garciaparra 3.00
4 Pedro J. Martinez 2.00
5 Rickey Henderson 1.50
6 Torii Hunter 1.50
7 Frank Thomas 1.50
8 Magglio Ordonez 1.50
9 Alfonso Soriano 2.00
10 Jose Contreras 1.00
11 Derek Jeter 4.00
12 Jason Giambi 1.50
13 Roger Clemens 4.00
14 Mike Mussina 1.50
15 Barry Zito 1.50
16 Miguel Tejada 1.50
17 Ichiro Suzuki 4.00
18 Alex Rodriguez 4.00
19 Juan Gonzalez 1.00
20 Rafael Palmeiro 2.00
21 Hank Blalock 2.00
22 Curt Schilling 2.00
23 Randy Johnson 2.00
24 Junior Spivey 1.00
25 Andruw Jones 2.00
26 Chipper Jones 2.00
27 Greg Maddux 3.00
28 Kerry Wood 2.00
29 Mark Prior 3.00
30 Sammy Sosa 3.00
31 Adam Dunn 2.00
32 Ken Griffey Jr. 3.00
33 Austin Kearns 1.50
34 Larry Walker 1.00
35 Todd Helton 2.00
36 Ivan Rodriguez 2.00

37 Jeff Bagwell 2.00
38 Lance Berkman 1.00
39 Craig Biggio 1.00
40 Hideo Nomo 1.50
41 Shawn Green 1.00
42 Vladimir Guerrero 2.00
43 Mike Piazza 3.00
44 Tom Glavine 1.50
45 Roberto Alomar 1.50
46 Pat Burrell 1.50
47 Jim Thome 2.00
48 Barry Bonds 5.00
49 Albert Pujols 4.00
50 Scott Rolen 2.00

2003 Donruss Team Heroes Samples

Common Player: .10
Stars: 1.5-2X
Gold: 10X

2003 Donruss Team Heroes

Each issue of the February 2003 Beckett Baseball Card Monthly included a sample 2003 Donruss Team Heroes card rubber-cemented inside. The cards differ from the issued version only in the appearance on back of a (usually) silver-foil "SAMPLE" notation. Some cards were produced with the overprint in gold-foil, in much more limited quantities. The number of different players' cards involved in the promotion is unknown.

NM/M
Complete Set (540): 55.00
Common Player: .15
Pack (13): 1.50
Box (24): 25.00
1 Adam Kennedy .15
2 Steve Green .15
3 Rod Carew .40
4 Alfredo Amezaga .15
5 Reggie Jackson .50
6 Jarrod Washburn .15
7 Nolan Ryan 3.00
8 Tim Salmon .25
9 Garret Anderson .25
10 Darin Erstad .25
11 Elpidio Guzman .15
12 David Eckstein .15
13 Troy Percival .15
14 Troy Glaus .75
15 Doug DeVore .15
16 Tony Womack .15
17 Matt Williams .25
18 Junior Spivey .15
19 Mark Grace .50
20 Curt Schilling .75
21 Erubiel Durazo .15
22 Craig Counsell .15
23 Byung-Hyun Kim .15
24 Randy Johnson 1.00
25 Luis Gonzalez .40
26 John Smoltz .15
27 Tim Spooneybarger .15
28 Dale Murphy .50

29 Warren Spahn .50
30 Jason Marquis .15
31 Kevin Millwood .15
32 Javy Lopez .15
33 Vinny Castilla .15
34 Julio Franco .15
35 Trey Hodges .15
36 Chipper Jones 1.50
37 Gary Sheffield .25
38 Billy Sylvester .15
39 Tom Glavine .40
40 Rafael Furcal .15
41 Cory Aldridge .15
42 Greg Maddux 1.50
43 John Ennis .15
44 Wes Helms .15
45 Horacio Ramirez .15
46 Derrick Lewis .15
47 Marcus Giles .15
48 Eddie Mathews .75
49 Wilson Betemit .15
50 Andruw Jones .50
51 Josh Towers .15
52 Ed Rogers .15
53 Kris Foster .15
54 Brooks Robinson .75
55 Cal Ripken Jr. 3.00
56 Brian Roberts .15
57 Luis Rivera .15
58 Rodrigo Lopez .15
59 Geronimo Gil .15
60 Erik Bedard .15
61 Jim Palmer .40
62 Jay Gibbons .15
63 Travis Driskill .15
64 Larry Bigbie .15
65 Eddie Murray .40
66 Hoyt Wilhelm .15
67 Bobby Doerr .15
68 Pedro J. Martinez 1.00
69 Roger Clemens 1.50
70 Nomar Garciaparra 2.00
71 Trot Nixon .15
72 Dennis Eckersley .40
73 John Burkett .15
74 Tim Wakefield .15
75 Wade Boggs .40
76 Cliff Floyd .15
77 Casey Fossum .15
78 Johnny Damon .15
79 Fred Lynn .15
80 Rickey Henderson .40
81 Juan Diaz .15
82 Manny Ramirez .75
83 Carlton Fisk .50
84 Jorge De La Rosa .15
85 Shea Hillenbrand .15
86 Derek Lowe .15
87 Jason Varitek .15
88 Carlos Baerga .15
89 Freddy Sanchez .15
90 Ugueth Urbina .15
91 Rey Sanchez .15
92 Josh Hancock .15
93 Tony Clark .15
94 Dustin Hermanson .15
95 Ryne Sandberg 1.50
96 Fred McGriff .25
97 Alex Gonzalez .15
98 Mark Belhorn .15
99 Fergie Jenkins .25
100 Jon Lieber .15
101 Francis Beltran .15
102 Greg Maddux 1.50
103 Nate Frese .15
104 Andre Dawson .25
105 Carlos Zambrano .15
106 Steve Smyth .15
107 Ernie Banks 1.00
108 Will Ohman .15
109 Kerry Wood .50
110 Bobby Hill .15
111 Moises Alou .15
112 Hee Seop Choi .15
113 Corey Patterson .15
114 Sammy Sosa 1.50
115 Mark Prior .50
116 Juan Cruz .15
117 Ron Santo .15
118 Billy Williams .15
119 Antonio Alfonseca .15
120 Matt Clement .15
121 Carlton Fisk .50
122 Joe Crede .15
123 Magglio Ordonez .40
124 Frank Thomas .75
125 Joe Borchard .15
126 Royce Clayton .15
127 Luis Aparicio .15
128 Willie Harris .15
129 Kyle Kane .15
130 Paul Konerko .25
131 Matt Ginter .15
132 Carlos Lee .15
133 Mark Buehrle .15
134 Adam Dunn .75
135 Eric Davis .15
136 Johnny Bench 1.00
137 Joe Morgan .25
138 Austin Kearns .40
139 Barry Larkin .40
140 Ken Griffey Jr. 2.00
141 Luis Pineda .15
142 Corky Miller .15
143 Brandon Larson .15
144 Wily Mo Pena .15
145 Lance Davis .15
146 Tom Seaver 1.00

147 Luke Hudson .15
148 Sean Casey .15
149 Tony Perez .15
150 Todd Walker .15
151 Aaron Boone .15
152 Jose Rijo .15
153 Ryan Dempster .15
154 Danny Graves .15
155 Matt Lawton .15
156 Cliff Lee .15
157 Ryan Drese .15
158 Danys Baez .15
159 Einar Diaz .15
160 Milton Bradley .15
161 Earl Snyder .15
162 Ellis Burks .15
163 Lou Boudreau .15
164 Bob Feller .15
165 Ricardo Rodriguez .15
166 Victor Martinez .15
167 Alex Herrera .15
168 Omar Vizquel .15
169 David Elder .15
170 C.C. Sabathia .15
171 Alex Escobar .15
172 Brian Tallet .15
173 Jim Thome .75
174 Rene Reyes .15
175 Juan Uribe .15
176 Jason Romano .15
177 Juan Pierre .15
178 Jason Jennings .15
179 Jose Ortiz .15
180 Larry Walker .25
181 Cam Esslinger .15
182 Todd Helton .50
183 Aaron Cook .15
184 Jack Cust .15
185 Jack Morris .15
186 Mike Rivera .15
187 Bobby Higginson .15
188 Fernando Rodney .15
189 Al Kaline 1.00
190 Carlos Pena .15
191 Alan Trammell .15
192 Mike Maroth .15
193 Adam Pettyjohn .15
194 David Espinosa .15
195 Adam Bernero .15
196 Franklyn German .15
197 Robert Fick .15
198 Andres Torres .15
199 Luis Castillo .15
200 Preston Wilson .15
201 Pablo Ozuna .15
202 Brad Penny .15
203 Josh Beckett .15
204 Charles Johnson .15
205 Wilson Valdez .15
206 A.J. Burnett .15
207 Abraham Nunez .15
208 Mike Lowell .15
209 Jose Cueto .15
210 Jeromie Robertson .15
211 Jeff Bagwell .75
212 Kirk Saarloos .15
213 Craig Biggio .25
214 Rodrigo Rosario .15
215 Roy Oswalt .25
216 John Buck .15
217 Tim Redding .15
218 Morgan Ensberg .15
219 Richard Hidalgo .15
220 Wade Miller .15
221 Lance Berkman .50
222 Raul Chavez .15
223 Carlos Hernandez .15
224 Greg Miller .15
225 Tom Shearn .15
226 Jason Lane .15
227 Nolan Ryan 3.00
228 Billy Wagner .15
229 Octavio Dotel .15
230 Shane Reynolds .15
231 Julio Lugo .15
232 Daryle Ward .15
233 Mike Sweeney .15
234 Angel Berroa .15
235 George Brett 1.50
236 Brad Voyles .15
237 Brandon Berger .15
238 Chad Durbin .15
239 Alexis Gomez .15
240 Jeremy Affeldt .15
241 Bo Jackson .75
242 Dee Brown .15
243 Tony Cogan .15
244 Carlos Beltran .15
245 Joe Randa .15
246 Pee Wee Reese .25
247 Andy Ashby .15
248 Cesar Izturis .15
249 Duke Snider .50
250 Mark Grudzielanek .15
251 Chin-Feng Chen .15
252 Brian Jordan .15
253 Steve Garvey .15
254 Odalis Perez .15
255 Hideo Nomo .50
256 Kevin Brown .15
257 Eric Karros .15
258 Joe Thurston .15
259 Carlos Garcia .15
260 Shawn Green .40
261 Paul LoDuca .15
262 Kazuhisa Ishii .15
263 Victor Alvarez .15
264 Eric Gagne .15

#	Player	Price
265	Don Sutton	.15
266	Orel Hershiser	.15
267	Dave Roberts	.15
268	Adrian Beltre	.15
269	Don Drysdale	.50
270	Jackie Robinson	1.50
271	Tyler Houston	.15
272	Omar Daal	.15
273	Marquis Grissom	.15
274	Paul Quantrill	.15
275	Paul Molitor	.15
276	Jose Hernandez	.15
277	Takahito Nomura	.15
278	Nick Neugebauer	.15
279	Jose Mieses	.15
280	Richie Sexson	.40
281	Matt Childers	.15
282	Bill Hall	.15
283	Ben Sheets	.15
284	Brian Mallette	.15
285	Geoff Jenkins	.15
286	Robin Yount	.75
287	Jeff Deardorff	.15
288	Luis Rivas	.15
289	Harmon Killebrew	.50
290	Michael Cuddyer	.15
291	Torii Hunter	.15
292	Kevin Frederick	.15
293	Adam Johnson	.15
294	Jack Morris	.15
295	Rod Carew	.40
296	Kirby Puckett	1.50
297	Joe Mays	.15
298	Jacque Jones	.15
299	Cristian Guzman	.15
300	Kyle Lohse	.15
301	Eric Milton	.15
302	Brad Radke	.15
303	Doug Mientkiewicz	.15
304	Corey Koskie	.15
305	Jose Vidro	.15
306	Claudio Vargas	.15
307	Gary Carter	.25
308	Andre Dawson	.25
309	Henry Mateo	.15
310	Andres Galarraga	.15
311	Zach Day	.15
312	Bartolo Colon	.15
313	Endy Chavez	.15
314	Javier Vazquez	.15
315	Michael Barrett	.15
316	Vladimir Guerrero	1.00
317	Orlando Cabrera	.15
318	Al Leiter	.15
319	Timoniel Perez	.15
320	Rey Ordonez	.15
321	Gary Carter	.15
322	Armando Benitez	.15
323	Dwight Gooden	.15
324	Pedro Astacio	.15
325	Roberto Alomar	.50
326	Edgardo Alfonzo	.15
327	Nolan Ryan	3.00
328	Mo Vaughn	.25
329	Ryan Jamison	.15
330	Satoru Komiyama	.15
331	Mike Piazza	2.50
332	Tom Seaver	1.00
333	Jorge Posada	.40
334	Derek Jeter	2.50
335	Babe Ruth	3.00
336	Lou Gehrig	2.50
337	Andy Pettitte	.40
338	Mariano Rivera	.25
339	Robin Ventura	.15
340	Yogi Berra	1.00
341	Phil Rizzuto	.50
342	Bernie Williams	.50
343	Alfonso Soriano	1.50
344	Drew Henson	.15
345	Erick Almonte	.15
346	Rondell White	.15
347	Christian Parker	.15
348	Joe Torre	.25
349	Nick Johnson	.15
350	Raul Mondesi	.15
351	Brandon Claussen	.15
352	Reggie Jackson	.50
353	Roger Clemens	1.50
354	Don Mattingly	1.50
355	Jason Giambi	1.50
356	Adrian Hernandez	.15
357	Jeff Weaver	.15
358	Mike Mussina	.50
359	Brett Jodie	.15
360	David Wells	.15
361	Enos Slaughter	.50
362	Whitey Ford	.50
363	Eric Chavez	.25
364	Miguel Tejada	.40
365	Barry Zito	.15
366	Bert Snow	.15
367	Rickey Henderson	.50
368	Juan A. Pena	.15
369	Terrence Long	.15
370	Dennis Eckersley	.40
371	Mark Ellis	.15
372	Tim Hudson	.25
373	Jose Canseco	.50
374	Reggie Jackson	.50
375	Mark Mulder	.50
376	David Justice	.25
377	Jermaine Dye	.15
378	Brett Myers	.15
379	Lenny Dykstra	.15
380	Vicente Padilla	.15
381	Bobby Abreu	.15
382	Pat Burrell	.50
383	Jorge Padilla	.15
384	Jeremy Giambi	.15
385	Mike Lieberthal	.15
386	Anderson Machado	.15
387	Marlon Byrd	.15
388	Bud Smith	.15
389	Eric Valent	.15
390	Elio Serrano	.15
391	Jimmy Rollins	.25
392	Brandon Duckworth	.15
393	Robin Roberts	.15
394	Marlon Anderson	.15
395	Robert Person	.15
396	Johnny Estrada	.15
397	Mike Schmidt	1.00
398	Eric Junge	.15
399	Jason Michaels	.15
400	Steve Carlton	.40
401	Placido Polanco	.15
402	John Grabow	.15
403	Tomas De La Rosa	.15
404	Tike Redman	.15
405	Willie Stargell	.40
406	Dave Williams	.15
407	John Candelaria	.15
408	Jack Wilson	.15
409	Matt Guerrier	.15
410	Jason Kendall	.15
411	Josh Fogg	.15
412	Aramis Ramirez	.15
413	Dave Parker	.15
414	Roberto Clemente	2.00
415	Kip Wells	.15
416	Brian Giles	.25
417	Honus Wagner	1.50
418	Ramon Vazquez	.15
419	Oliver Perez	.15
420	Ryan Klesko	.15
421	Brian Lawrence	.15
422	Ben Howard	.15
423	Ozzie Smith	1.00
424	Dennis Tankersley	.15
425	Tony Gwynn	1.00
426	Sean Burroughs	.15
427	Xavier Nady	.15
428	Phil Nevin	.15
429	Trevor Hoffman	.15
430	Jake Peavy	.15
431	Cody Ransom	.15
432	Kenny Lofton	.15
433	Mel Ott	.50
434	Tsuyoshi Shinjo	.15
435	Deivis Santos	.15
436	Rich Aurilia	.15
437	Will Clark	.50
438	Pedro Feliz	.15
439	J.T. Snow	.15
440	Robb Nen	.15
441	Carlos Valderrama	.15
442	Willie McCovey	.15
443	Jeff Kent	.25
444	Orlando Cepeda	.15
445	Barry Bonds	2.50
446	Alex Rodriguez	2.50
447	Allan Simpson	.15
448	Antonio Perez	.15
449	Edgar Martinez	.15
450	Freddy Garcia	.15
451	Chris Snelling	.15
452	Matt Thornton	.15
453	Kazuhiro Sasaki	.15
454	Harold Reynolds	.15
455	Randy Johnson	1.00
456	Bret Boone	.15
457	Rafael Soriano	.15
458	Luis Ugueto	.15
459	Ken Griffey Jr.	2.00
460	Ichiro Suzuki	2.00
461	Jamie Moyer	.15
462	Joel Pineiro	.15
463	Jeff Cirillo	.15
464	John Olerud	.15
465	Mike Cameron	.15
466	Ruben Sierra	.15
467	Mark McLemore	.15
468	Carlos Guillen	.15
469	Dan Wilson	.15
470	Shigetoshi Hasegawa	.15
471	Ben Davis	.15
472	Ozzie Smith	1.00
473	Matt Morris	.15
474	Edgar Renteria	.15
475	Les Walrond	.15
476	Albert Pujols	1.00
477	Stan Musial	1.50
478	J.D. Drew	.15
479	Josh Pearce	.15
480	Enos Slaughter	.15
481	Jason Simontacchi	.15
482	Jeremy Lambert	.15
483	Tino Martinez	.15
484	Rogers Hornsby	.50
485	Rick Ankiel	.15
486	Jim Edmonds	.25
487	Scott Rolen	.50
488	Kevin Joseph	.15
489	Fernando Vina	.15
490	Jason Isringhausen	.15
491	Lou Brock	.40
492	Joe Torre	.15
493	Bob Gibson	.50
494	Chuck Finley	.15
495	So Taguchi	.15
496	Ben Grieve	.15
497	Toby Hall	.15
498	Brent Abernathy	.15
499	Brandon Backe	.15
500	Felix Escalona	.15
501	Matt White	.15
502	Randy Winn	.15
503	Carl Crawford	.15
504	Dewon Brazelton	.15
505	Joe Kennedy	.15
506	Wade Boggs	.50
507	Aubrey Huff	.15
508	Alex Rodriguez	2.50
509	Ivan Rodriguez	.50
510	Will Clark	.75
511	Hank Blalock	.15
512	Travis Hughes	.15
513	Travis Hafner	.15
514	Ryan Ludwick	.15
515	Doug Davis	.15
516	Juan Gonzalez	.50
517	Jason Hart	.15
518	Mark Teixeira	.40
519	Nolan Ryan	3.00
520	Rafael Palmeiro	.50
521	Kevin Mench	.15
522	Chan Ho Park	.15
523	Kenny Rogers	.15
524	Rusty Greer	.15
525	Michael Young	.15
526	Carlos Delgado	.40
527	Vernon Wells	.15
528	Orlando Hudson	.15
529	Shannon Stewart	.15
530	Joe Carter	.15
531	Chris Baker	.15
532	Eric Hinske	.15
533	Corey Thurman	.15
534	Josh Phelps	.15
535	Reed Johnson	.15
536	Brian Bowles	.15
537	Roy Halladay	.15
538	Jose Cruz Jr.	.15
539	Kelvim Escobar	.15
540	Chris Carpenter	.15

Glossy
Stars: 1-2.5X
Inserted 1:1

Stat Line

Cards serial numbered

151-250:	4-8X
Print run 101-150:	5-10X
Print run 51-100:	8-15X
Print run 26-50:	10-20X

Autographs
NM/M
Common Player: 6.00
Some not priced due to scarcity.

#	Player	Price
4	Alfredo Amezaga/250	6.00
11	Elpidio Guzman/100	10.00
15	Doug DeVore/122	6.00
35	Trey Hodges/250	8.00
38	Billy Sylvester/250	6.00
41	Cory Aldridge/250	6.00
45	Horacio Ramirez/200	8.00
46	Derrick Lewis/250	6.00
47	Marcus Giles/200	8.00
49	Wilson Betemit/75	10.00
51	Josh Towers/110	10.00
52	Ed Rogers/250	6.00
53	Kris Foster/250	6.00
56	Brian Roberts/250	35.00
59	Geronimo Gil/60	10.00
60	Erik Bedard/250	8.00
62	Jay Gibbons/181	10.00
64	Larry Bigbie/100	10.00
77	Casey Fossum/250	6.00
79	Fred Lynn/50	20.00
81	Juan Diaz/250	6.00
84	Jorge De La Rosa/250	6.00
99	Fergie Jenkins/50	25.00
101	Francis Beltran/250	8.00
103	Nate Frese/250	6.00
105	Carlos Zambrano/150	20.00
108	Will Ohman/50	10.00
110	Bobby Hill/150	8.00
115	Mark Prior/50	40.00
122	Juan Cruz/50	10.00
122	Joe Crede/250	8.00
122	Joe Borchard/250	10.00
127	Luis Aparicio/50	8.00
128	Willie Harris/129	8.00
129	Kyle Kane/100	10.00
131	Matt Ginter/250	6.00
132	Carlos Lee/250	15.00
133	Mark Buehrle/50	20.00
135	Eric Davis/75	20.00
138	Austin Kearns/71	20.00
142	Corky Miller/75	6.00
143	Brandon Larson/143	10.00
144	Wily Mo Pena/50	15.00
147	Luke Hudson/50	12.00
149	Tony Perez/50	20.00
156	Cliff Lee/250	10.00
159	Earl Snyder/250	8.00
165	Ricardo Rodriguez/250	8.00
166	Victor Martinez/250	25.00
171	Alex Herrera/250	6.00
172	Alex Escobar/125	10.00
176	Brian Tallet/250	10.00
176	Rene Reyes/250	6.00
176	Jason Romano/50	15.00
178	Juan Pierre/66	15.00
178	Jason Jennings/250	10.00
181	Jose Ortiz/250	8.00
181	Cam Esslinger/250	6.00
184	Jack Cust/250	10.00
185	Jack Morris/50	20.00
186	Mike Rivera/250	6.00
186	Fernando Rodney/250	6.00
190	Carlos Pena/96	12.00
192	Mike Maroth/250	6.00
193	Adam Pettyjohn/250	6.00
194	David Espinosa/250	6.00
195	Adam Bernero/250	6.00
197	Franklyn German/250	8.00
197	Robert Fick/50	10.00
201	Andres Torres/250	6.00
205	Pablo Ozuna/250	6.00
207	Wilson Valdez/250	6.00
212	Abraham Nunez/250	8.00
214	Kirk Saarloos/250	8.00
215	Rodrigo Rosario/250	6.00
215	Roy Oswalt/50	20.00
217	Tim Redding/250	6.00
218	Morgan Ensberg/250	6.00
219	Richard Hidalgo/100	10.00
220	Wade Miller/200	10.00
222	Raul Chavez/125	15.00
223	Carlos Hernandez/250	10.00
224	Greg Miller/90	10.00
226	Jason Lane/250	10.00
234	Angel Berroa/200	10.00
236	Brad Voyles/200	10.00
237	Brandon Berger/250	8.00
238	Chad Durbin/250	8.00
239	Alexis Gomez/165	10.00
240	Jeremy Affeldt/71	6.00
242	Dee Brown/50	12.00
243	Tony Cogan/250	6.00
248	Cesar Izturis/200	10.00
253	Steve Garvey/75	30.00
258	Joe Thurston/108	10.00
259	Carlos Garcia/100	8.00
261	Paul LoDuca/50	20.00
263	Victor Alvarez/250	6.00
265	Don Sutton/50	20.00
277	Takahito Nomura/100	20.00
279	Jose Mieses/50	15.00
281	Matt Childers/100	12.00
283	Ben Sheets/100	20.00
284	Brian Mallette/250	10.00
287	Jeff Deardorff/100	6.00
288	Luis Rivas/200	8.00
290	Michael Cuddyer/250	10.00
291	Torii Hunter/100	15.00
294	Jack Morris/50	20.00
305	Jose Vidro/50	15.00
306	Claudio Vargas/150	6.00
309	Henry Mateo/250	6.00
311	Zach Day/250	6.00
313	Endy Chavez/250	6.00
314	Javier Vazquez/250	15.00
323	Dwight Gooden/250	25.00
344	Drew Henson/50	25.00
345	Erick Almonte/250	6.00
347	Christian Parker/200	6.00
351	Brandon Claussen/250	6.00
356	Adrian Hernandez/200	6.00
359	Brett Jodie/250	8.00
366	Bert Snow/250	6.00
371	Juan Pena/250	6.00
371	Mark Ellis/150	6.00
383	Lenny Dykstra/75	25.00
383	Jorge Padilla/250	8.00
386	Jeremy Giambi/100	6.00
386	Anderson Machado/250	6.00
387	Marlon Byrd/200	6.00
388	Bud Smith/125	10.00
389	Eric Valent/100	8.00
390	Elio Serrano/250	6.00
392	Brandon Duckworth/100	10.00
395	Robert Person/100	6.00
396	Johnny Estrada/209	15.00
398	Eric Junge/250	8.00
399	Jason Michaels/221	6.00
402	John Grabow/250	6.00
407	Dave Williams/250	6.00
407	John Candelaria/100	10.00
408	Jack Wilson/50	10.00
409	Matt Guerrier/200	6.00
412	Aramis Ramirez/50	30.00
413	Dave Parker/50	20.00
415	Kip Wells/250	8.00
418	Ramon Vazquez/200	6.00
419	Oliver Perez/150	15.00
421	Brian Lawrence/250	8.00
422	Ben Howard/250	6.00
427	Xavier Nady/50	15.00
431	Cody Ransom/100	10.00
435	Deivis Santos/100	6.00
438	Pedro Feliz/50	15.00
441	Carlos Valderrama/250	6.00
447	Allan Simpson/250	6.00
448	Antonio Perez/250	6.00
451	Chris Snelling/100	10.00
452	Matt Thornton/200	6.00
454	Harold Reynolds/100	15.00
457	Rafael Soriano/250	6.00
458	Luis Ugueto/50	10.00
475	Les Walrond/50	12.00
479	Josh Pearce/200	6.00
497	Toby Hall/200	8.00
498	Brent Abernathy/250	8.00
499	Brandon Backe/250	8.00
500	Felix Escalona/50	10.00
504	Dewon Brazelton/100	10.00
505	Joe Kennedy/200	6.00
512	Aubrey Huff/100	15.00
514	Travis Hughes/200	6.00
515	Ryan Ludwick/250	6.00
516	Doug Davis/250	6.00
517	Jason Hart/123	6.00
518	Mark Teixeira/50	40.00
521	Kevin Mench/250	6.00
528	Orlando Hudson/120	10.00
531	Chris Baker/200	6.00
532	Eric Hinske/250	6.00
533	Corey Thurman/250	8.00
534	Josh Phelps/150	10.00
535	Reed Johnson/250	6.00
536	Brian Bowles/250	6.00
543	Ramon Nivar/100	15.00
544	Adam Loewen/100	15.00
545	Brandon Webb/100	30.00
546	Dan Haren/100	20.00
548	Ryan Wagner/100	15.00

Timeline Threads

NM/M
Common Player:
Quantity produced listed

#	Player	Price
1	Bobby Doerr/39	20.00
2	Phil Rizzuto/47	30.00
3	Yogi Berra/47	35.00
4	Pee Wee Reese/58	15.00
5	Al Kaline/64	40.00
7	Orlando Cepeda/65	15.00
8	Eddie Mathews/66	40.00
9	Lou Brock/66	15.00
10	Juan Marichal/67	15.00
11	Ernie Banks/68	40.00
12	Willie Stargell/68	15.00
13	Jim Palmer/69	15.00
14	Luis Aparicio/69	15.00
15	Tom Seaver/69	15.00
16	Harmon Killebrew/71	50.00
17	Joe Morgan/74	15.00
18	Brooks Robinson/76	30.00
19	Mike Schmidt/81	65.00
20	Willie McCovey/77	15.00
21	Robin Yount/78	40.00
22	Reggie Jackson/79	25.00
23	Rod Carew/85	25.00
24	Nolan Ryan/91	80.00
25	Tony Gwynn/98	25.00
26	Alex Rodriguez/100	25.00
27	Carlos Delgado/101	10.00
28	Lance Berkman/102	10.00
29	Randy Johnson/100	20.00
30	Josh Beckett/101	15.00
31	Eric Davis/89	10.00
32	Todd Helton/101	15.00
33	Jose Canseco/89	25.00
34	Mike Piazza/101	25.00
35	Fred Lynn/75	10.00
36	Mike Sweeney/101	10.00
37	Miguel Tejada/101	15.00
38	Curt Schilling/101	15.00
39	Dale Murphy/87	40.00
40	Jim Thome/101	20.00
41	Adam Dunn/102	15.00
42	Nomar Garciaparra/100	25.00
43	Vladimir Guerrero/100	15.00
44	Alfonso Soriano/102	20.00
45	Wade Boggs/90	15.00
46	Randy Johnson/89	20.00
47	Hal Newhouser/55	15.00
48	Chipper Jones/93	20.00
49	Andruw Jones/96	15.00
50	Frank Thomas/94	15.00

Hawaii

The base set and, it is believed, all inserts including autographs from the Team Heroes issue were produced in a

special edition for attendees at the 2003 SCD Hawaii Trade Conference. Each card is gold-foil stamped with a show logo and "1/1" notation. Because of their unique nature, no catalog values are assigned.

2003 Donruss Timeless Treasures

NM/M
Complete Set (100):
Common Player: 2.00
Production 900 Sets
Tin (4): 100.00

#	Player	Price
1	Adam Dunn	3.00
2	Al Kaline	5.00
3	Alan Trammell	2.00
4	Albert Pujols	8.00
5	Alex Rodriguez	8.00
6	Alfonso Soriano	4.00
7	Andre Dawson	3.00
8	Andruw Jones	3.00
9	Austin Kearns	2.00
10	Babe Ruth	10.00
11	Barry Bonds	10.00
12	Barry Larkin	2.00
13	Barry Zito	3.00
14	Bernie Williams	4.00
15	Bo Jackson	4.00
16	Brooks Robinson	4.00
17	Cal Ripken Jr.	10.00
18	Carlton Fisk	4.00
19	Chipper Jones	4.00
20	Curt Schilling	3.00
21	Dale Murphy	2.00
22	Derek Jeter	10.00
23	Don Mattingly	10.00
24	Duke Snider	3.00
25	Eddie Mathews	3.00
26	Frank Robinson	2.00
27	Frank Thomas	4.00
28	Garret Anderson	2.00
29	Gary Carter	2.00
30	George Brett	8.00
31	Greg Maddux	6.00
32	Harmon Killebrew	4.00
33	Hideki Matsui RC	10.00
34	Hideo Nomo	3.00
35	Ichiro Suzuki	6.00
36	Ivan Rodriguez	4.00
37	Jackie Robinson	6.00
38	Jason Giambi	3.00
39	Jeff Bagwell	4.00
40	Jim Edmonds	4.00
41	Jim Palmer	3.00
42	Jim Thome	4.00
43	Joe Morgan	2.00
44	Jorge Posada	3.00
45	Jose Contreras RC	5.00
46	Juan Gonzalez	2.00
47	Kazuhisa Ishii	2.00
48	Ken Griffey Jr.	5.00
49	Kerry Wood	4.00
50	Kirby Puckett	5.00
51	Lance Berkman	2.00
52	Larry Walker	2.00
53	Lou Brock	3.00
54	Lou Gehrig	8.00
55	Magglio Ordonez	2.00
56	Mark Prior	4.00
57	Miguel Tejada	3.00
58	Mike Mussina	3.00
59	Mike Piazza	6.00
60	Mike Schmidt	8.00
61	Nolan Ryan	10.00

62	Nomar Garciaparra	6.00
63	Ozzie Smith	5.00
64	Pat Burrell	2.00
65	Pedro J. Martinez	4.00
66	Pee Wee Reese	2.00
67	Phil Rizzuto	4.00
68	Rafael Palmeiro	3.00
69	Randy Johnson	5.00
70	Reggie Jackson	4.00
71	Richie Ashburn	2.00
72	Rickey Henderson	3.00
73	Roberto Alomar	3.00
74	Roberto Clemente	8.00
75	Robin Yount	4.00
76	Rod Carew	3.00
77	Roger Clemens	8.00
78	Rogers Hornsby	4.00
79	Roy Oswalt	2.00
80	Ryan Klesko	2.00
81	Ryne Sandberg	6.00
82	Sammy Sosa	6.00
83	Scott Rolen	4.00
84	Shawn Green	3.00
85	Stan Musial	6.00
86	Steve Carlton	3.00
87	Thurman Munson	5.00
88	Todd Helton	4.00
89	Tom Glavine	2.00
90	Tom Seaver	4.00
91	Tony Gwynn	4.00
92	Tony Perez	2.00
93	Torii Hunter	2.00
94	Troy Glaus	3.00
95	Ty Cobb	6.00
96	Vernon Wells	2.00
97	Vladimir Guerrero	4.00
98	Warren Spahn	4.00
99	Willie McCovey	3.00
100	Yogi Berra	5.00

Silver
Stars (1-100): 3-5X
Production 50 Sets
Golds: No Pricing
Production 10 Sets
Platinum 1-of-1's exist.

Award Materials
NM/M
Quantity produced listed

1	Ivan Rodriguez/100	10.00
2	Mike Schmidt/50	60.00
3	Roberto Clemente/50	80.00
4	Roger Clemens/50	25.00
5	Randy Johnson/100	15.00
6	Pedro J. Martinez/100	15.00
7	Ivan Rodriguez/100	15.00
8	Jeff Bagwell/100	15.00
9	Frank Thomas/100	15.00
10	Cal Ripken Jr./75	50.00
11	Tom Seaver/50	25.00

Award Prime Materials
NM/M
Quantity produced listed

6	Pedro J. Martinez/50	30.00
9	Frank Thomas/50	25.00

Award Materials Autograph
Complete Set (1):

Award Winning MLB Logos
Complete Set (2):
Common Player:

Classic Combos
NM/M
Quantity produced listed

1	Jason Giambi/100	15.00
2	Adrian Beltre/100	10.00
3	Alex Rodriguez/100	25.00
4	Alfonso Soriano/100	30.00
5	Andruw Jones/100	15.00
6	Andre Dawson/100	15.00
7	Barry Larkin/100	10.00
8	Barry Zito/100	15.00
9	Cal Ripken Jr./100	60.00
10	Chipper Jones/100	15.00
11	Don Mattingly/10	50.00
12	Eric Chavez/100	10.00
13	Frank Thomas/100	15.00
14	Greg Maddux/100	25.00
15	Ivan Rodriguez/100	15.00
16	Jeff Bagwell/100	15.00
17	Jim Thome/100	15.00
18	Juan Gonzalez/100	15.00
19	Kazuhisa Ishii/100	15.00
20	Kerry Wood/100	15.00
21	Lance Berkman/100	10.00
22	Magglio Ordonez/100	10.00
23	Manny Ramirez/100	15.00
24	Miguel Tejada/100	10.00
25	Mike Piazza/100	20.00
26	Nomar Garciaparra/100	20.00
27	Pedro J. Martinez/100	20.00
28	Randy Johnson/100	15.00
29	Rickey Henderson/100	20.00
30	Ryne Sandberg/100	30.00
32	Shawn Green/100	10.00
33	Todd Helton/100	10.00
34	Tony Gwynn/100	20.00
35	Vladimir Guerrero/100	15.00

Classic Prime Combos
NM/M
Quantity produced listed

6	Andre Dawson/25	40.00
11	Don Mattingly/25	75.00
16	Jeff Bagwell/25	50.00

Classic Combos Autograph
NM/M
Quantity produced listed

8	Barry Zito/25	100.00
22	Magglio Ordonez/25	65.00
34	Tony Gwynn/25	100.00

Game Day Materials
NM/M
Quantity produced listed

1	Tony Gwynn/100	15.00
2	Magglio Ordonez/100	8.00
3	George Brett/100	40.00
4	Rickey Henderson/100	15.00
5	Billy Williams/100	10.00
6	Frank Thomas/100	10.00
7	Tony Gwynn/75	20.00
10	Ryne Sandberg/100	30.00
11	Miguel Tejada/100	10.00

Game Day Materials Autograph
Quantity produced listed

HOF Cuts

NM/M
Production One Set

Ty Cobb (8/03 auction)	6,500

HOF Combos

NM/M
Quantity produced listed

1	Al Kaline/50	50.00
4	Kirby Puckett/75	40.00
6	Mike Schmidt/100	50.00
7	Nolan Ryan/50	100.00
8	Phil Rizzuto/50	30.00
9	Reggie Jackson/25	40.00
11	Rod Carew/50	25.00
14	George Brett/50	85.00
15	Carlton Fisk/100	20.00

Prime Combos

NM/M
Quantity produced listed

HOF Combos Autographs

HOF Induction Year Combos
NM/M
Production 25 Sets

6	Enos Slaughter, Lou Brock/25	60.00
8	Phil Rizzuto, Steve Carlton/25	45.00

10	George Brett, Robin Yount/25	185.00

HOF Letters
Quantity produced listed

HOF Logos
NM/M
Quantity produced listed

29	Eddie Mathews/35	65.00
36	Nolan Ryan/35	100.00
37	Nolan Ryan/35	100.00
38	Nolan Ryan/35	100.00
43	Robin Yount/35	50.00

HOF Materials

NM/M
Quantity produced listed

1	Al Kaline	25.00
2	Babe Ruth/75	140.00
3	Carlton Fisk/100	15.00
4	Eddie Mathews/100	20.00
5	Gary Carter/100	15.00
6	George Brett/100	35.00
7	Harmon Killebrew/100	25.00
8	Joe Morgan/100	10.00
9	Kirby Puckett/100	20.00
10	Lou Gehrig/100	110.00
11	Luis Aparicio/100	15.00
12	Mike Schmidt/100	25.00
13	Ozzie Smith/100	25.00
14	Phil Rizzuto/100	10.00
15	Reggie Jackson/100	15.00
16	Richie Ashburn/100	15.00
17	Roberto Clemente/100	60.00
18	Robin Yount/100	20.00
19	Rod Carew/100	15.00
20	Rogers Hornsby/100	45.00
21	Stan Musial/100	35.00
22	Ty Cobb/100	120.00
23	Willie McCovey/100	10.00
24	Yogi Berra/100	30.00
25	Al Kaline/100	25.00
26	Babe Ruth/50	300.00
27	Bobby Doerr/100	15.00
28	Brooks Robinson/100	15.00
29	Eddie Mathews/100	20.00
30	Harmon Killebrew/100	25.00
31	Ty Cobb/50	150.00
32	Joe Morgan/100	10.00
33	Lou Brock/100	10.00
34	Lou Gehrig/50	225.00
35	Mike Schmidt/100	25.00
36	Nolan Ryan/50	40.00
37	Nolan Ryan/50	40.00
38	Nolan Ryan/50	40.00
39	Phil Rizzuto/100	10.00
40	Reggie Jackson/25	25.00
41	Reggie Jackson/100	15.00
42	Roberto Clemente/50	90.00
43	Robin Yount/100	20.00
44	Rod Carew/100	15.00
45	Stan Musial/100	35.00
46	Tom Seaver/100	20.00
47	Steve Carlton/100	15.00
48	Carlton Fisk/100	15.00
49	Pee Wee Reese/100	15.00
50	Jackie Robinson/50	85.00

HOF Materials Autograph
NM/M
Quantity produced listed

7	Harmon Killebrew/25	80.00
12	Mike Schmidt/15	180.00
24	Yogi Berra/15	150.00
28	Brooks Robinson/25	75.00
30	Harmon Killebrew/50	75.00
39	Phil Rizzuto/25	65.00
43	Robin Yount/25	175.00

HOF Numbers
NM/M
Quantity produced listed

35	Mike Schmidt/50	40.00
36	Nolan Ryan/35	100.00
43	Robin Yount/35	50.00
47	Steve Carlton/40	20.00
48	Carlton Fisk/35	45.00

Home Run Materials
NM/M
Quantity produced listed

1	Harmon Killebrew/100	20.00
2	Harmon Killebrew/100	20.00
3	Jose Canseco/100	15.00
4	Magglio Ordonez/100	8.00
5	Rafael Palmeiro/100	15.00
6	Rafael Palmeiro/100	15.00
7	Rafael Palmeiro/100	15.00
8	Alex Rodriguez/100	15.00
9	Alex Rodriguez/100	15.00
10	Alex Rodriguez/100	15.00
11	Alex Rodriguez/20	75.00
12	Adam Dunn/100	15.00

Home Run Materials Autograph
NM/M
Quantity produced listed

1	Harmon Killebrew/25	80.00
3	Jose Canseco/25	100.00

Material Ink
NM/M
Quantity produced listed

1	Adam Dunn/50	45.00
2	Alan Trammell/100	30.00
3	Alex Rodriguez/25	150.00
4	Andre Dawson/100	30.00
6	Barry Zito/100	45.00
7	Bo Jackson/100	60.00
8	Bob Feller/25	70.00
9	Bobby Doerr/100	45.00
11	Cal Ripken Jr./50	200.00
12	Cal Ripken Jr./50	200.00
13	Cal Ripken Jr./25	225.00
14	Dale Murphy/50	45.00
15	Dave Parker/75	35.00
16	David Cone/100	30.00
17	Don Mattingly/100	85.00
18	Duke Snider/25	75.00
19	Edgar Martinez/50	50.00
20	Gary Carter/100	30.00
21	Harmon Killebrew/75	70.00
22	Jim Edmonds/25	55.00
23	Jim Thome/50	50.00
24	Joe Carter/100	30.00
25	Jose Canseco/50	50.00
26	Jose Vidro/100	40.00
27	Kazuhisa Ishii/100	40.00
28	Kerry Wood/50	60.00
29	Lance Berkman/50	40.00
31	Mark Mulder/25	65.00
32	Mike Schmidt/50	90.00
33	Nick Johnson/25	40.00
34	Nolan Ryan/25	225.00
35	Nolan Ryan/25	225.00
36	Nolan Ryan/25	225.00
37	Paul LoDuca/100	25.00
38	Paul Molitor/50	45.00
39	Reggie Jackson/40	85.00
40	Roberto Alomar/50	50.00
41	Roberto Alomar/100	40.00
43	Robin Yount/50	75.00
47	Ryan Klesko/25	25.00
48	Ryne Sandberg/25	140.00
50	Stan Musial/25	150.00
51	Steve Carlton/100	35.00
52	Steve Carlton/100	35.00
53	Todd Helton/50	60.00
54	Tom Seaver/50	50.00
55	Tony Gwynn/100	100.00
56	Torii Hunter/100	40.00
57	Vladimir Guerrero/100	40.00
58	Will Clark/50	85.00

Material MLB Logo Ink
Complete Set (22)
Common Player

Milestone Materials
NM/M
Quantity produced listed

3	Rickey Henderson/100	15.00

Past and Present
NM/M
Production 100 Sets

1	Alex Rodriguez/100	20.00
2	Hideo Nomo/100	25.00
3	Jason Giambi/100	15.00
4	Juan Gonzalez/100	15.00
5	Mike Piazza/100	20.00
6	Pedro J. Martinez/100	15.00
7	Randy Johnson/100	15.00
8	Rickey Henderson/100	15.00
9	Roberto Alomar/100	15.00
10	Roger Clemens/100	20.00
11	Sammy Sosa/100	35.00

Past & Present Letters
NM/M
Quantity produced listed

1	Alex Rodriguez/75	30.00
3	Hideo Nomo/25	90.00
4	Juan Gonzalez/100	8.00
6	Pedro J. Martinez/75	35.00
7	Randy Johnson/75	40.00

Past and Present Logos
NM/M
Quantity produced listed

2	Hideo Nomo/25	90.00
3	Jason Giambi/75	40.00
5	Mike Piazza/50	40.00

Past & Present Numbers
NM/M
Quantity produced listed

2	Hideo Nomo/25	75.00
3	Jason Giambi/25	40.00
6	Pedro J. Martinez/50	40.00
7	Randy Johnson/50	40.00

Past & Present Patches
Quantity produced listed

Post Season Materials
Quantity produced listed

Post Season Prime Material
NM/M
No Pricing

1	Ozzie Smith/75	50.00

Post Season Materials Autograph
NM/M
Quantity produced listed

1	Ozzie Smith/15	125.00

Prime Materials
NM/M
Quantity produced listed

1	Tony Gwynn/100	15.00
2	Magglio Ordonez/100	8.00
4	Rickey Henderson/100	15.00
6	Frank Thomas/100	10.00
7	Tony Gwynn/75	20.00
10	Ryne Sandberg/100	30.00
11	Miguel Tejada/100	10.00

Prime Material Ink
NM/M
Quantity produced listed

2	Alan Trammell/50	50.00
5	Andre Dawson/50	60.00
7	Bo Jackson/50	100.00
20	Gary Carter/50	50.00
24	Joe Carter/50	50.00
26	Jose Vidro/25	40.00
27	Kazuhisa Ishii/50	45.00
33	Nick Johnson/50	45.00
53	Steve Carlton/50	50.00
58	Torii Hunter/50	50.00
59	Vladimir Guerrero/50	70.00
60	Will Clark/25	180.00

Rookie Year Combos
NM/M
Quantity produced listed

6	Mark Prior/50	40.00
7	Albert Pujols/50	80.00

Rookie Year Materials

NM/M

	Common Player:	8.00
1	Cal Ripken Jr./100	50.00
2	Mike Schmidt/50	40.00
3	Rafael Palmeiro/100	15.00
4	Nomar Garciaparra/100	20.00
5	Stan Musial/42	70.00
6	Yogi Berra/100	30.00
7	Ivan Rodriguez/100	15.00
12	Vladimir Guerrero/100	15.00
14	Ivan Rodriguez/91	10.00
15	Andruw Jones/96	15.00
16	Andruw Jones/100	15.00
17	Fred Lynn/100	8.00
18	Jeff Kent/100	8.00
19	Gary Sheffield/100	10.00
20	Ron Santo/100	15.00
21	Juan Gonzalez/100	15.00
22	Alfonso Soriano/100	25.00
23	Ryan Klesko/92	10.00
24	Adam Dunn/100	12.00
25	Hideo Nomo/100	25.00
26	Mark Prior/100	15.00
27	Pat Burrell/99	15.00
28	Magglio Ordonez/100	8.00
29	Kirby Puckett/84	15.00
30	Albert Pujols/100	30.00
31	Albert Pujols/100	30.00

R.Y. Materials Autograph
NM/M
Quantity produced listed

7	Yogi Berra/15	150.00
26	Mark Prior/25	150.00
28	Magglio Ordonez/25	50.00

Rookie Year Materials Letter
NM/M
Quantity produced listed

4	Nomar Garciaparra/35	40.00
9	Ivan Rodriguez/35	20.00
12	Vladimir Guerrero/35	25.00
15	Andruw Jones/25	35.00
30	Albert Pujols/25	90.00

2003 Donruss Timeless Treasures R.Y. Materials Logos
NM/M
Quantity produced listed

12	Vladimir Guerrero/50	25.00
15	Andruw Jones/50	25.00
17	Fred Lynn/25	25.00
18	Jeff Kent/50	20.00
19	Gary Sheffield/50	25.00
22	Alfonso Soriano/20	60.00
23	Ryan Klesko/50	15.00
30	Albert Pujols/50	75.00

R.Y. Materials Numbers
NM/M
Quantity produced listed

12	Vladimir Guerrero/50	25.00
15	Andruw Jones/15	25.00
17	Fred Lynn/30	25.00
18	Jeff Kent/25	20.00
19	Gary Sheffield/25	30.00
21	Juan Gonzalez/30	30.00
22	Alfonso Soriano/35	50.00
23	Ryan Klesko/35	20.00
26	Mark Prior/35	40.00
30	Albert Pujols/25	90.00

R.Y. Materials Patches
Quantity produced listed

Playoff Babe Ruth Special Edition

Fifteen swatches from the jersey purchased in May 2003 for $265,000 were inserted into a special edition serially numbered card. Card No. 1 was given to Ruth's daughter. Some of the cards were reportedly given to Donruss/Playoff employees as year-end awards.

NM/M

Babe Ruth	2,100

2004 Donruss
NM/M

Complete Set (400):	75.00
Common Player:	.10
Pack (10):	3.50
Box (24):	65.00

Jeff Bagwell

#	Player	Price
1	Derek Jeter	2.00
2	Greg Maddux	1.00
3	Albert Pujols	1.50
4	Ichiro Suzuki	1.00
5	Alex Rodriguez	1.50
6	Roger Clemens	1.50
7	Andruw Jones	.50
8	Barry Bonds	2.00
9	Jeff Bagwell	.50
10	Randy Johnson	.75
11	Scott Rolen	.50
13	Lance Berkman	.40
14	Barry Zito	.25
15	Manny Ramirez	.50
16	Carlos Delgado	.50
17	Alfonso Soriano	.50
18	Todd Helton	.50
19	Mike Mussina	.10
20	Nomar Garciaparra	1.50
21	Chipper Jones	1.00
22	Mark Prior	2.00
23	Jim Thome	.50
24	Vladimir Guerrero	.75
25	Pedro Martinez	.75
26	Sergio Mitre	.10
27	Adam Loewen	.10
28	Alfredo Gonzalez	.10
29	Miguel Ojeda	.10
30	Rosman Garcia	.10
31	Arnie Munoz	.10
32	Andrew Brown	.10
33	Josh Hall	.10
34	Josh Stewart	.10
35	Clint Barmes	.10
36	Brandon Webb	.10
37	Chien-Ming Wang	.40
38	Edgar Gonzalez	.10
39	Alejandro Machado	.10
40	Jeremy Griffiths	.10
41	Craig Brazell	.10
42	Daniel Cabrera	.10
43	Fernando Cabrera	.10
44	Termel Sledge	.10
45	Rob Hammock	.10
46	Francisco Rosario	.10
47	Francisco Cruceta	.10
48	Rett Johnson	.10
49	Guillermo Quiroz	.10
50	Hong-Chih Kuo	.10
51	Ian Ferguson	.10
52	Tim Olson	.10
53	Todd Wellemeyer	.10
54	Rich Fischer	.10
55	Phil Seibel	.10
56	Joe Valentine	.10
57	Matt Kata	.10
58	Michael Hessman	.10
59	Michel Hernandez	.10
60	Doug Waechter	.10
61	Prentice Redman	.10
62	Nook Logan	.10
63	Oscar Villarreal	.10
64	Pete LaForest	.10
65	Matt Bruback	.10
66	Dan Haren	.10
67	Greg Aquino	.10
68	Lew Ford	.10
69	Jeff Duncan	.10
70	Ryan Wagner	.10
71	Bengie Molina	.10
72	Brad Fullmer	.10
73	Darin Erstad	.25
74	David Eckstein	.10
75	Garret Anderson	.10
76	Jarrod Washburn	.10
77	Kevin Appier	.10
78	Scott Spiezio	.10
79	Tim Salmon	.25
80	Troy Glaus	.40
81	Troy Percival	.10
82	Jason Johnson	.10
83	Jay Gibbons	.25
84	Melvin Mora	.10
85	Sidney Ponson	.10
86	Tony Batista	.10
87	Bill Mueller	.10
88	Byung-Hyun Kim	.10
89	David Ortiz	.25
90	Derek Lowe	.25
91	Johnny Damon	.25
92	Casey Fossum	.10
93	Manny Ramirez	.50
94	Nomar Garciaparra	1.50
95	Pedro J. Martinez	.75
96	Todd Walker	.10
97	Trot Nixon	.10
98	Bartolo Colon	.10
99	Carlos Lee	.10

#	Player	Price
100	D'Angelo Jimenez	.10
101	Esteban Loaiza	.10
102	Frank Thomas	.50
103	Joe Crede	.10
104	Jose Valentin	.10
105	Magglio Ordonez	.25
106	Mark Buehrle	.10
107	Paul Konerko	.10
108	Brandon Phillips	.10
109	C.C. Sabathia	.10
110	Ellis Burks	.10
111	Jeremy Guthrie	.10
112	Josh Bard	.10
113	Matt Lawton	.10
114	Milton Bradley	.10
115	Omar Vizquel	.20
116	Travis Hafner	.10
117	Bobby Higginson	.10
118	Carlos Pena	.10
119	Dmitri Young	.20
120	Eric Munson	.10
121	Jeremy Bonderman	.10
122	Nate Cornejo	.10
123	Omar Infante	.10
124	Ramon Santiago	.10
125	Angel Berroa	.10
126	Carlos Beltran	.25
127	Desi Relaford	.10
128	Jeremy Affeldt	.10
129	Joe Randa	.10
130	Ken Harvey	.10
131	Mike MacDougal	.10
132	Michael Tucker	.10
133	Mike Sweeney	.20
134	Raul Ibanez	.20
135	Runelvys Hernandez	.10
136	A.J. Pierzynski	.10
137	Brad Radke	.10
138	Corey Koskie	.10
139	Cristian Guzman	.10
140	Doug Mientkiewicz	.10
141	Dustan Mohr	.10
142	Jacque Jones	.10
143	Kenny Rogers	.10
144	Bobby Kielty	.10
145	Kyle Lohse	.10
146	Luis Rivas	.10
147	Torii Hunter	.25
148	Alfonso Soriano	.75
149	Andy Pettitte	.40
150	Bernie Williams	.40
151	David Wells	.10
152	Derek Jeter	2.00
153	Hideki Matsui	2.00
154	Jason Giambi	.75
155	Jorge Posada	.50
156	Jose Contreras	.40
157	Mike Mussina	.50
158	Nick Johnson	.10
159	Robin Ventura	.10
160	Roger Clemens	1.50
161	Barry Zito	.25
162	Chris Singleton	.10
163	Eric Byrnes	.10
164	Eric Chavez	.25
165	Erubiel Durazo	.10
166	Keith Foulke	.10
167	Mark Ellis	.10
168	Miguel Tejada	.40
169	Mark Mulder	.25
170	Ramon Hernandez	.10
171	Ted Lilly	.10
172	Terrence Long	.10
173	Tim Hudson	.25
174	Bret Boone	.25
175	Carlos Guillen	.10
176	Dan Wilson	.10
177	Edgar Martinez	.10
178	Freddy Garcia	.10
179	Gil Meche	.10
180	Ichiro Suzuki	1.00
181	Jamie Moyer	.10
182	Joel Pineiro	.10
183	John Olerud	.20
184	Mike Cameron	.10
185	Randy Winn	.10
186	Ryan Franklin	.10
187	Kazuhiro Sasaki	.10
188	Aubrey Huff	.10
189	Carl Crawford	.25
190	Joe Kennedy	.10
191	Marlon Anderson	.10
192	Rey Ordonez	.10
193	Rocco Baldelli	.25
194	Toby Hall	.10
195	Travis Lee	.10
196	Alex Rodriguez	1.50
197	Carl Everett	.10
198	Chan Ho Park	.10
199	Einar Diaz	.10
200	Hank Blalock	.25
201	Ismael Valdes	.10
202	Juan Gonzalez	.50
203	Mark Teixeira	.40
204	Mike Young	.10
205	Rafael Palmeiro	.25
206	Carlos Delgado	.50
207	Kelvim Escobar	.10
208	Eric Hinske	.10
209	Frank Catalanotto	.10
210	Josh Phelps	.10
211	Orlando Hudson	.10
212	Roy Halladay	.25
213	Shannon Stewart	.10
214	Vernon Wells	.25
215	Carlos Baerga	.10
216	Curt Schilling	.40
217	Junior Spivey	.10

#	Player	Price
218	Luis Gonzalez	.25
219	Lyle Overbay	.10
220	Mark Grace	.25
221	Matt Williams	.20
222	Randy Johnson	.75
223	Shea Hillenbrand	.10
224	Steve Finley	.10
225	Andruw Jones	.50
226	Chipper Jones	1.00
227	Gary Sheffield	.40
228	Greg Maddux	1.00
229	Javy Lopez	.25
230	John Smoltz	.25
231	Marcus Giles	.10
232	Mike Hampton	.10
233	Rafael Furcal	.25
234	Robert Fick	.10
235	Russ Ortiz	.10
236	Alex Gonzalez	.10
237	Carlos Zambrano	.10
238	Corey Patterson	.10
239	Hee Seop Choi	.10
240	Kerry Wood	.50
241	Mark Belhorn	.10
242	Mark Prior	1.50
243	Moises Alou	.25
244	Sammy Sosa	1.50
245	Aaron Boone	.10
246	Adam Dunn	.40
247	Austin Kearns	.40
248	Barry Larkin	.25
249	Felipe Lopez	.10
250	Jose Guillen	.10
251	Ken Griffey Jr.	1.00
252	Jason LaRue	.10
253	Scott Williamson	.10
254	Sean Casey	.20
255	Shawn Chacon	.10
256	Chris Stynes	.10
257	Jason Jennings	.10
258	Jay Payton	.20
259	Jose Hernandez	.10
260	Larry Walker	.25
261	Preston Wilson	.20
262	Ronnie Belliard	.10
263	Todd Helton	.50
264	A.J. Burnett	.10
265	Alex Gonzalez	.10
266	Brad Penny	.10
267	Derrek Lee	.10
268	Ivan Rodriguez	.40
269	Josh Beckett	.50
270	Juan Encarnacion	.10
271	Juan Pierre	.10
272	Luis Castillo	.10
273	Mike Lowell	.10
274	Todd Hollandsworth	.10
275	Billy Wagner	.25
276	Brad Ausmus	.10
277	Craig Biggio	.25
278	Jeff Bagwell	.50
279	Jeff Kent	.25
280	Lance Berkman	.25
281	Richard Hidalgo	.10
282	Roy Oswalt	.25
283	Wade Miller	.10
284	Adrian Beltre	.10
285	Brian Jordan	.10
286	Cesar Izturis	.10
287	Dave Roberts	.10
288	Eric Gagne	.25
289	Fred McGriff	.25
290	Hideo Nomo	.40
291	Kazuhisa Ishii	.10
292	Kevin Brown	.10
293	Paul LoDuca	.10
294	Shawn Green	.40
295	Ben Sheets	.25
296	Geoff Jenkins	.10
297	Rey Sanchez	.10
298	Richie Sexson	.40
299	Wes Helms	.10
300	Brad Wilkerson	.10
301	Claudio Vargas	.10
302	Endy Chavez	.10
303	Fernando Tatis	.10
304	Javier Vazquez	.25
305	Jose Vidro	.10
306	Michael Barrett	.10
307	Orlando Cabrera	.20
308	Tony Armas Jr.	.10
309	Vladimir Guerrero	.75
310	Zach Day	.10
311	Al Leiter	.10
312	Cliff Floyd	.10
313	Jae Weong Seo	.10
314	Jeromy Burnitz	.10
315	Mike Piazza	1.00
316	Mo Vaughn	.25
317	Roberto Alomar	.40
318	Roger Cedeno	.10
319	Tom Glavine	.25
320	Jose Reyes	.40
321	Bobby Abreu	.20
322	Brett Myers	.10
323	David Bell	.10
324	Jim Thome	.50
325	Jimmy Rollins	.25
326	Kevin Millwood	.10
327	Marlon Byrd	.10
328	Mike Lieberthal	.10
329	Pat Burrell	.40
330	Randy Wolf	.10
331	Aramis Ramirez	.10
332	Brian Giles	.25
333	Jason Kendall	.20
334	Kenny Lofton	.20
335	Kip Wells	.10

#	Player	Price
336	Kris Benson	.10
337	Randall Simon	.10
338	Reggie Sanders	.10
339	Albert Pujols	2.00
340	Edgar Renteria	.10
341	Fernando Vina	.10
342	J.D. Drew	.10
343	Jim Edmonds	.25
344	Matt Morris	.10
345	Mike Matheny	.10
346	Scott Rolen	.50
347	Tino Martinez	.10
348	Woody Williams	.10
349	Brian Lawrence	.10
350	Mark Kotsay	.10
351	Mark Loretta	.10
352	Ramon Vazquez	.10
353	Rondell White	.10
354	Ryan Klesko	.25
355	Sean Burroughs	.10
356	Trevor Hoffman	.10
357	Xavier Nady	.10
358	Andres Galarraga	.10
359	Barry Bonds	2.00
360	Benito Santiago	.10
361	Deivi Cruz	.10
362	Edgardo Alfonzo	.10
363	J.T. Snow	.10
364	Jason Schmidt	.10
365	Kirk Rueter	.10
366	Kurt Ainsworth	.10
367	Marquis Grissom	.10
368	Ray Durham	.10
369	Rich Aurilia	.10
370	Tim Worrell	.10
371	Troy Glaus	.20
372	Melvin Mora	.10
373	Nomar Garciaparra	.75
374	Magglio Ordonez	.20
375	Omar Vizquel	.10
376	Dmitri Young	.10
377	Mike Sweeney	.10
378	Torii Hunter	.25
379	Derek Jeter	1.00
380	Barry Zito	.20
381	Ichiro Suzuki	.50
382	Rocco Baldelli	.20
383	Alex Rodriguez	.75
384	Carlos Delgado	.25
385	Randy Johnson	.40
386	Greg Maddux	.50
387	Sammy Sosa	.75
388	Ken Griffey Jr.	.50
389	Todd Helton	.25
390	Ivan Rodriguez	.25
391	Jeff Bagwell	.25
392	Hideo Nomo	.20
393	Richie Sexson	.20
394	Vladimir Guerrero	.40
395	Mike Piazza	.50
396	Jim Thome	.25
397	Jason Kendall	.10
398	Albert Pujols	1.00
399	Ryan Klesko	.10
400	Barry Bonds	1.00

NATIONAL LEAGUE ALL-STARS

AUSTIN KEARNS

#	Player	Price
1	Alex Rodriguez	5.00
2	Roger Clemens	5.00
3	Ichiro Suzuki	3.00
4	Barry Zito	1.50
5	Garret Anderson	1.50
6	Derek Jeter	5.00
7	Manny Ramirez	2.00
8	Pedro J. Martinez	2.00
9	Alfonso Soriano	2.50
10	Carlos Delgado	1.50
11	Barry Bonds	5.00
12	Andruw Jones	2.00
13	Scott Rolen	2.00
14	Austin Kearns	1.50
15	Mark Prior	4.00
16	Vladimir Guerrero	2.00
17	Jeff Bagwell	2.00
18	Mike Piazza	3.00
19	Albert Pujols	5.00
20	Randy Johnson	2.50

Bat Kings

	NM/M
Common Player:	5.00
Studio Current Player:	1.5X
Production 50	
Studio Retired:	No Pricing
Production 25	

#	Player	Price
1	Alex Rodriguez/250	10.00
2	Albert Pujols/250	15.00
3	Chipper Jones/250	12.00
4	Lance Berkman/250	5.00
5	Cal Ripken Jr./100	50.00
6	George Brett/100	30.00
7	Don Mattingly/100	40.00
8	Roberto Clemente/100	75.00

Craftsmen

CRAFTSMEN

	NM/M
Complete Set (15):	40.00
Common Player:	2.00
Production 2,000 Sets	
Black:	1-2X
Production 275 Sets	
Master Craftsmen:	1-2X
Production 150 Sets	

#	Player	Price
1	Alex Rodriguez	5.00
2	Mark Prior	4.00
3	Ichiro Suzuki	3.00
4	Barry Bonds	5.00
5	Ken Griffey Jr.	4.00
6	Alfonso Soriano	3.00
7	Mike Piazza	3.00
8	Chipper Jones	3.00
9	Derek Jeter	5.00
10	Randy Johnson	2.50
11	Sammy Sosa	4.00
12	Roger Clemens	4.00
13	Nomar Garciaparra	4.00
14	Greg Maddux	4.00
15	Albert Pujols	5.00

Diamond Kings Insert

	NM/M
Complete Set (25):	80.00
Common Player:	2.00
Production 2,500 Sets	
Studio Series:	1-2X
Production 250 Sets	
Black:	1.5-2X
Production 100 Sets	

#	Player	Price
1	Derek Jeter	8.00
2	Greg Maddux	6.00

Black Press Proofs
No pricing due to scarcity.
Production 10 Sets
Hot Pack exclusive.

Career Stat Line

Terrence Long

Cards Serial #'d from 251-500:

251-500:	3-5X
Print run 101-250:	4-6X
Print run 61-100:	4-8X
Print run 26-60:	8-15X

No pricing for P/R 25 or less.
Numbered to career statistic.

Season Stat Line

Print run 101-261:	4-6X
Print run 61-100:	4-8X
Print run 26-60:	8-15X

No pricing for P/R 25 or less.
Numbered to 2003 statistic.

All-Stars

	NM/M
Complete Set (20):	40.00
Common Player:	1.50
Production 1,000 Sets	
Black:	1-2X
Production 250 Sets	

DIAMOND KINGS

#	Player	Price
3	Albert Pujols	8.00
4	Ichiro Suzuki	6.00
5	Alex Rodriguez	6.00
6	Roger Clemens	6.00
7	Andruw Jones	3.00
8	Barry Bonds	3.00
9	Jeff Bagwell	3.00
10	Randy Johnson	3.00
11	Scott Rolen	3.00
12	Lance Berkman	2.00
13	Barry Zito	2.00
14	Manny Ramirez	3.00
15	Carlos Delgado	2.50
16	Alfonso Soriano	4.00
17	Todd Helton	3.00
18	Mike Mussina	2.00
19	Austin Kearns	2.00
20	Nomar Garciaparra	4.00
21	Chipper Jones	4.00
22	Mark Prior	4.00
23	Jim Thome	3.00
24	Vladimir Guerrero	3.00
25	Pedro J. Martinez	3.00

Elite Series

BARRY ZITO — Elite Series

	NM/M
Complete Set (15):	60.00
Common Player:	2.00
Production 1,500 Sets	
Black:	1-2X
Production 150 Sets	
Dominators:	No Pricing
Production 25 Sets	

#	Player	Price
1	Albert Pujols	8.00
2	Barry Zito	3.00
3	Gary Sheffield	3.00
4	Mike Mussina	3.00
5	Lance Berkman	2.00
6	Alfonso Soriano	4.00
7	Randy Johnson	4.00
8	Nomar Garciaparra	8.00
9	Austin Kearns	3.00
10	Manny Ramirez	3.00
11	Mark Prior	6.00
12	Alex Rodriguez	6.00
13	Derek Jeter	8.00
14	Barry Bonds	8.00
15	Roger Clemens	6.00

Inside View

INSIDE VIEW

	NM/M
Complete Set (25):	50.00
Common Player:	1.00
Production 1,250 Sets	
1	Derek Jeter	5.00
2	Greg Maddux	3.00
3	Albert Pujols	5.00

4 Ichiro Suzuki 3.00
5 Alex Rodriguez 4.00
6 Roger Clemens 5.00
7 Andruw Jones 1.50
8 Barry Bonds 5.00
9 Jeff Bagwell 2.00
10 Randy Johnson 2.00
11 Scott Rolen 2.00
12 Lance Berkman 1.00
13 Barry Zito 1.50
14 Manny Ramirez 2.00
15 Carlos Delgado 1.50
16 Alfonso Soriano 2.00
17 Todd Helton 2.00
18 Mike Mussina 1.50
19 Austin Kearns 1.50
20 Nomar Garciaparra 4.00
21 Chipper Jones 3.00
22 Mark Prior 4.00
23 Jim Thome 2.00
24 Vladimir Guerrero 2.00
25 Pedro J. Martinez 2.50

Jersey Kings
NM/M
Quantity produced listed
Studio Current Player: 1.5X
Production 50
Studio Retired: No Pricing
Production 25
1 Alfonso Soriano/250 10.00
2 Sammy Sosa/250 15.00
3 Roger Clemens/250 15.00
4 Nomar Garciaparra/250 12.00
5 Mark Prior/250 10.00
6 Vladimir Guerrero/250 8.00
7 Don Mattingly/100 40.00
8 Roberto Clemente/100 80.00
9 George Brett/100 35.00
10 Nolan Ryan/100 40.00
11 Cal Ripken Jr./100 55.00
12 Mike Schmidt/100 40.00

Longball Leaders

NM/M
Complete Set (10): 20.00
Common Player: 1.50
Production 1,500 Sets
Black: 1-2X
Production 250 Sets
Die-Cut: 1.5-3X
Production 50 Sets
1 Barry Bonds 5.00
2 Alfonso Soriano 3.00
3 Adam Dunn 1.50
4 Alex Rodriguez 5.00
5 Jim Thome 2.00
6 Garret Anderson 1.50
7 Juan Gonzalez 2.00
8 Jeff Bagwell 2.00
9 Gary Sheffield 1.50
10 Sammy Sosa 2.00

Mound Marvels
NM/M
Complete Set (15): 20.00
Common Player: 1.00
Production 750 Sets
Black: 1-2X
Production 175 Sets
1 Mark Prior 4.00
2 Curt Schilling 1.50
3 Mike Mussina 1.50
4 Kevin Brown 1.00
5 Pedro J. Martinez 2.50
6 Mark Mulder 1.00
7 Kerry Wood 1.50
8 Greg Maddux 3.00
9 Kevin Millwood 1.50
10 Barry Zito 1.50
11 Roger Clemens 3.00
12 Randy Johnson 2.50
13 Hideo Nomo 1.50
14 Tim Hudson 1.50
15 Tom Glavine 1.50

Power Alley Red
NM/M
Complete Set (20): 50.00
Common Player: 2.00
Production 2,500 Sets
Red Die-Cuts: 1-2X

Production 250 Sets
Blues: 1X
Production 1,000 Sets
Blue Die-Cuts: 1.5-2X
Production 100 Sets
Purples: 1-2X
Production 250 Sets
Purple Die-Cuts: No Pricing
Production 25 Sets
Yellows: 1.5-2X
Production 100 Sets
Yellow Die-Cut: No Pricing
Production 10 Sets
Greens: No Pricing
Production 25 Sets
Green Die-Cuts: No Pricing
Production 5 Sets
1 Albert Pujols 8.00
2 Mike Piazza 5.00
3 Carlos Delgado 3.00
4 Barry Bonds 8.00
5 Jim Edmonds 3.00
6 Nomar Garciaparra 6.00
7 Alfonso Soriano 4.00
8 Alex Rodriguez 8.00
9 Lance Berkman 2.00
10 Scott Rolen 3.00
11 Manny Ramirez 3.00
12 Rafael Palmeiro 3.00
13 Sammy Sosa 6.00
14 Adam Dunn 2.00
15 Andruw Jones 3.00
16 Jim Thome 3.00
17 Jason Giambi 3.00
18 Jeff Bagwell 3.00
19 Juan Gonzalez 3.00
20 Austin Kearns 2.00

Production Line Average
NM/M
Complete Set (10): 35.00
Common Player: 1-2X
Die-Cut: 1-2X
Production 100 Sets
Black: 2-3X
Production 35 Sets
1 Gary Sheffield/330 3.00
2 Ichiro Suzuki/312 5.00
3 Todd Helton/358 3.00
4 Manny Ramirez/325 3.00
5 Garret Anderson/315 2.00
6 Barry Bonds/341 8.00
7 Albert Pujols/359 8.00
8 Derek Jeter/324 8.00
9 Nomar Garciaparra/301 6.00
10 Hank Blalock/300 3.00

Production Line OBP
NM/M
Complete Set (10): 25.00
Common Player: 2.00
Die-Cut: 1-2X
Production 100 Sets
Black: 2-3X
Production 40 Sets
1 Todd Helton/458 3.00
2 Albert Pujols/439 6.00
3 Larry Walker/422 2.00
4 Barry Bonds/529 6.00
5 Chipper Jones/402 4.00
6 Manny Ramirez/427 3.00
7 Gary Sheffield/419 2.00
8 Lance Berkman/412 2.00
9 Alex Rodriguez/396 6.00
10 Jason Giambi/412 3.00

Production Line OPS
NM/M
Complete Set (10): 25.00
Varying quanties produced
Black: 1-2X
Production 125 Sets
Die-Cut: 1-2X
Production 100 Sets
1 Albert Pujols/1,106 5.00
2 Barry Bonds/1,278 5.00
3 Gary Sheffield/1,023 1.50
4 Todd Helton/1,088 3.00
5 Scott Rolen/910 3.00
6 Manny Ramirez/1,014 3.00
7 Alex Rodriguez/995 5.00
8 Jim Thome/958 3.00
9 Jason Giambi/939 3.00
10 Frank Thomas/952 3.00

Production Line Slugging
NM/M
Complete Set (10): 25.00
Varying quantities produced
Black: 1-2X
Production 75 Sets
Die-Cut: 1-2X
Production 100 Sets
1 Alex Rodriguez/604 6.00
2 Frank Thomas/562 3.00
3 Garret Anderson/541 2.00
4 Albert Pujols/667 5.00
5 Sammy Sosa/553 5.00
6 Gary Sheffield/604 2.00
7 Manny Ramirez/587 3.00
8 Jim Edmonds/617 2.00
9 Barry Bonds/688 6.00
10 Todd Helton/630 3.00

Timber & Threads

NM/M
Common Player: 4.00
Inserted 1:40
Studio Series: 1.5X
Production 50 Sets
1 Adam Dunn 6.00
2 Alex Rodriguez/Blue 10.00
3 Alex Rodriguez/White 10.00
4 Andruw Jones 6.00
5 Austin Kearns 6.00
6 Carlos Beltran 4.00
7 Carlos Lee 4.00
8 Frank Thomas 8.00
9 Greg Maddux 10.00
10 Hideo Nomo 4.00
11 Jeff Bagwell 8.00
12 Lance Berkman 4.00
13 Magglio Ordonez 4.00
14 Mike Sweeney 4.00
15 Randy Johnson 4.00
16 Rocco Baldelli 10.00
17 Roger Clemens 12.00
18 Sammy Sosa 12.00
19 Shawn Green 4.00
20 Tom Glavine 4.00
21 Adam Dunn 6.00
22 Andruw Jones 6.00
23 Bobby Abreu 6.00
24 Hank Blalock 6.00
25 Ivan Rodriguez 6.00
26 Jim Edmonds 6.00
27 Josh Phelps 4.00
28 Juan Gonzalez 4.00
29 Lance Berkman 4.00
30 Larry Walker 4.00
31 Magglio Ordonez 4.00
32 Manny Ramirez 8.00
33 Mike Piazza 10.00
34 Nomar Garciaparra 4.00
35 Paul LoDuca 4.00
36 Roberto Alomar 4.00
37 Rocco Baldelli 10.00
38 Sammy Sosa 12.00
39 Vernon Wells 4.00
40 Vladimir Guerrero 8.00

2004 Donruss Classics

NM/M
Complete Set (213):
Common Player: .40
Common (151-210): 3.00
Production 1,999
Pack (6): 6.00
Box (18): 90.00
1 Albert Pujols 2.50
2 Derek Jeter 3.00
3 Hank Blalock .50
4 Shannon Stewart .40
5 Jason Giambi 1.00
6 Carlos Lee .40
7 Trot Nixon .40
8 Bret Boone .50
9 Mark Mulder .40
10 Mariano Rivera .50
11 Scott Podsednik .75
12 Jim Edmonds .50
13 Mike Lowell .50
14 Robin Ventura .40
15 Brian Giles .50
16 Jose Vidro .40
17 Manny Ramirez .75
18 Alex Rodriguez 2.50
19 Carlos Beltran .50
20 Hideki Matsui 2.50
21 Johan Santana .40
22 Richie Sexson .50
23 Chipper Jones 1.00
24 Steve Finley .40
25 Mark Prior 1.50
26 Alexis Rios .40
27 Rafael Palmeiro .75
28 Jorge Posada .50
29 Barry Zito .50
30 Jamie Moyer .40
31 Preston Wilson .40
32 Miguel Cabrera .75
33 Pedro Martinez 1.00
34 Curt Schilling .75
35 Hee Seop Choi .40
36 Dontrelle Willis .50
37 Rafael Soriano .40
38 Richard Fischer .40
39 Brian Tallet .40
40 Jose Castillo .40
41 Wade Miller .40
42 Jose Contreras .40
43 Runelvys Hernandez .40
44 Joe Borchard .40
45 Kazuhisa Ishii .40
46 Jose Reyes .50
47 Adam Dunn .50
48 Randy Johnson 1.00
49 Brandon Phillips .40
50 Scott Rolen 1.00
51 Ken Griffey Jr. 1.50
52 Tom Glavine .50
53 Cliff Lee .40
54 Chien-Ming Wang .50
55 Roy Oswalt .50
56 Austin Kearns .50
57 Jhonny Peralta .40
58 Greg Maddux 1.50
59 Mark Grace .50
60 Jae Weong Seo .40
61 Nic Jackson .40
62 Roger Clemens 2.50
63 Jimmy Gobble .40
64 Travis Hafner .40
65 Paul Konerko .40
66 Jerome Williams .40
67 Ryan Klesko .50
68 Alexis Gomez .40
69 Omar Vizquel .40
70 Zach Day .40
71 Rickey Henderson .50
72 Morgan Ensberg .40
73 Josh Beckett .75
74 Garrett Atkins .40
75 Sean Casey .40
76 Julio Franco .40
77 Lyle Overbay .40
78 Josh Phelps .40
79 Juan Gonzalez .75
80 Rich Harden .40
81 Bernie Williams .50
82 Torii Hunter .50
83 Angel Berroa .40
84 Jody Gerut .40
85 Roberto Alomar .50
86 Byung-Hyun Kim .40
87 Jay Gibbons .40
88 Chone Figgins .40
89 Fred McGriff .50
90 Rich Aurilia .40
91 Xavier Nady .40
92 Marlon Byrd .40
93 Mike Piazza 1.50
94 Vladimir Guerrero 1.00
95 Shawn Green .50
96 Jeff Kent .50
97 Ivan Rodriguez .75
98 Jay Payton .40
99 Barry Larkin .50
100 Mike Sweeney .40
101 Adrian Beltre .40
102 Robby Hammock .40
103 Orlando Hudson .40
104 Mark Teixeira .50
105 Hong-Chih Kuo .40
106 Eric Chavez .50
107 Nick Johnson .40
108 Jacque Jones .40
109 Ken Harvey .40
110 Aramis Ramirez .40
111 Victor Martinez .40
112 Joe Crede .40
113 Jason Varitek .50
114 Troy Glaus .40
115 Billy Wagner .40
116 Kerry Wood 1.00
117 Hideo Nomo .50
118 Brandon Webb .40
119 Craig Biggio .40
120 Orlando Cabrera .40
121 Sammy Sosa 2.00
122 Bobby Abreu .50
123 Andruw Jones .75
124 Jeff Bagwell .75
125 Jim Thome 1.00
126 Javy Lopez .50
127 Luis Castillo .40
128 Todd Helton .75
129 Roy Halladay .50
130 Mike Mussina .50
131 Eric Byrnes .40
132 Eric Hinske .40
133 Nomar Garciaparra 2.00
134 Edgar Martinez .50
135 Rocco Baldelli .50
136 Miguel Tejada .50
137 Alfonso Soriano 1.00
138 Carlos Delgado .75
139 Rafael Furcal .50
140 Ichiro Suzuki 2.00
141 Aubrey Huff .40
142 Garret Anderson .50
143 Vernon Wells .40
144 Magglio Ordonez .50
145 Brett Myers .40
146 Luis Gonzalez .40
147 Lance Berkman .50
148 Frank Thomas .75
149 Gary Sheffield .50
150 Tim Hudson .50
151 Duke Snider 3.00
152 Carl Yastrzemski 4.00
153 Whitey Ford 3.00
154 Cal Ripken Jr. 8.00
155 Dwight Gooden 2.00
156 Warren Spahn 4.00
157 Bob Gibson 3.00
158 Don Mattingly 6.00
159 Jack Morris 3.00
160 Jim Bunning 2.00
161 Fergie Jenkins 2.00
162 Brooks Robinson 3.00
163 George Kell 2.00
164 Darryl Strawberry 2.00
165 Robin Roberts 2.00
166 Monte Irvin 2.00
167 Ernie Banks 4.00
168 Wade Boggs 3.00
169 Gaylord Perry 2.00
170 Keith Hernandez 2.00
171 Lou Brock 3.00
172 Frank Robinson 3.00
173 Nolan Ryan 8.00
174 Stan Musial 5.00
175 Eddie Murray 3.00
176 Byron Gettis 2.00
177 Merkin Valdez RC 5.00
178 Rickie Weeks 4.00
179 Akinori Otsuka RC 4.00
180 Brian Bruney 3.00
181 Freddy Guzman RC 3.00
182 Brendan Harris 3.00
183 John Gall RC 3.00
184 Jason Kubel 3.00
185 Delmon Young 4.00
186 Ryan Howard 3.00
187 Adam Loewen 3.00
188 J.D. Durbin 3.00
189 Dan Haren 3.00
190 Dustin McGowan 3.00
191 Chad Gaudin 3.00
192 Preston Larrison 3.00
193 Ramon Nivar 3.00
194 Ronald Belisario RC 3.00
195 Mike Gosling 3.00
196 Kevin Youkilis 3.00
197 Ryan Wagner 3.00
198 Bubba Nelson 3.00
199 Edwin Jackson 3.00
200 Chris Burke 3.00
201 Carlos Hines RC 3.00
202 Greg Dobbs RC 3.00
203 Jamie Brown RC 3.00
204 David Crouthers 3.00
205 Ian Snell RC 3.00
206 Gary Carter 3.00
207 Dale Murphy 3.00
208 Ryne Sandberg 3.00
209 Phil Niekro 2.00
210 Don Sutton 2.00
211 Alex Rodriguez/Yankees/SP 5.00
212 Alfonso Soriano/Rangers/SP 1.00
213 Greg Maddux/Cubs/SP 3.00

Timeless Tributes Green
Cards (1-150): 4-6X
Cards (151-210): 1-2X
Production 50 Sets

Timeless Tributes Red

Red (1-150): 2-4X
Red (151-210): 1-1.5X
Production 100 Sets

Timeless Tributes Platinum
No Pricing
Production One Set

Classic Singles Bat
NM/M
Quantity produced listed
1 Babe Ruth/15 250.00
3 Stan Musial/25 30.00
4 Ted Williams/25 100.00
5 Lou Gehrig/50 125.00
6 Eddie Murray/25 15.00
7 Roy Campanella/50 15.00
8 Robin Yount/50 20.00
9 Roberto Clemente/25 70.00
10 Don Mattingly/50 25.00
12 Carl Yastrzemski/50 20.00
13 Mark Grace/50 15.00
15 Rickey Henderson/50 15.00
16 Reggie Jackson/50 15.00
17 Pee Wee Reese/50 15.00
20 Roger Maris/25 40.00
21 Cal Ripken Jr./50 60.00
23 Willie Stargell/50 15.00
24 Paul Molitor/50 20.00
26 Alan Trammell/50 12.00
27 Sammy Sosa/50 20.00
28 Bobby Doerr/50 8.00
29 Rod Carew/50 15.00
30 Yogi Berra/50 20.00
32 George Brett/50 30.00

Classic Singles Jersey
NM/M
Quantity produced listed
Prime: No Pricing
Production One Set
2 Nolan Ryan/50 35.00
3 Stan Musial/15 50.00
6 Eddie Murray/100 10.00
7 Roy Campanella/Pants/50 20.00
8 Robin Yount/100 15.00
9 Roberto Clemente/25 75.00
10 Don Mattingly/100 20.00
11 Bob Gibson/15 25.00
12 Carl Yastrzemski/50 20.00
13 Mark Grace/25 20.00
14 Jack Morris/100 6.00
15 Rickey Henderson/25 20.00
16 Reggie Jackson/50 15.00
17 Pee Wee Reese/50 25.00
18 Marty Marion/100 6.00
19 Tommy John/100 5.00
20 Roger Maris/25 50.00
21 Cal Ripken Jr./25 75.00
22 Red Schoendienst/25 10.00
23 Willie Stargell/100 15.00
24 Paul Molitor/100 10.00
25 Whitey Ford/50 25.00
26 Alan Trammell/100 10.00
27 Sammy Sosa/50 20.00
28 Bobby Doerr/50 8.00
29 Rod Carew/100 10.00
30 Yogi Berra/15 35.00
31 Phil Rizzuto/25 20.00
32 George Brett/25 40.00

Classic Singles Jersey-Bat
NM/M
Quantity produced listed
Prime: No Pricing
Production One Set
2 Nolan Ryan/25 50.00
3 Stan Musial/15 45.00
6 Eddie Murray/25 25.00
7 Roy Campanella/Pants/25 35.00
8 Robin Yount/25 40.00
9 Roberto Clemente/25 125.00
10 Don Mattingly/25 50.00
12 Carl Yastrzemski/25 50.00
13 Mark Grace/25 20.00
15 Rickey Henderson/25 25.00
16 Reggie Jackson/25 25.00
17 Pee Wee Reese/25 25.00
20 Roger Maris/25 75.00
21 Cal Ripken Jr./25 75.00
23 Willie Stargell/25 20.00
24 Paul Molitor/25 25.00
26 Alan Trammell/25 25.00
27 Sammy Sosa/25 25.00
28 Bobby Doerr/25 25.00
29 Rod Carew/25 30.00
30 Yogi Berra/15 40.00
32 George Brett/25 50.00

ABBREVIATIONS
SP - Short Print

Classic Combos Bat

		NM/M
Quantity produced listed		
1	Babe Ruth, Lou Gehrig/25	375.00
2	Roy Campanella, Pee Wee Reese/50	25.00
3	Ted Williams, Carl Yastrzemski/25	125.00
4	Roberto Clemente, Willie Stargell/25	100.00
5	Eddie Murray, Cal Ripken Jr./50	50.00
6	Roger Maris, Yogi Berra/25	65.00
10	Nolan Ryan, Rod Carew/50	35.00
11	Don Mattingly, Rickey Henderson/50	40.00
15	Robin Yount, Paul Molitor/50	40.00
16	Mark Grace, Sammy Sosa/50	30.00
17	Ted Williams, Bobby Doerr/25	80.00
18	Reggie Jackson, Rod Carew/25	25.00

Classic Combos Jersey

		NM/M
Prime:		No Pricing
Production One Set		
1	Babe Ruth/Pants, Lou Gehrig/Pants/15	500.00
2	Roy Campanella/Pants, Pee Wee Reese/25	30.00
3	Ted Williams, Carl Yastrzemski/15	200.00
4	Roberto Clemente, Willie Stargell/25	85.00
5	Eddie Murray, Cal Ripken Jr./25	75.00
6	Roger Maris, Yogi Berra/25	65.00
8	Whitey Ford, Yogi Berra/25	30.00
9	Marty Marion, Stan Musial/25	40.00
10	Nolan Ryan, Rod Carew/25	40.00
11	Don Mattingly, Rickey Henderson/50	40.00
12	Jack Morris, Alan Trammell/50	15.00
13	Whitey Ford, Phil Rizzuto/25	30.00
14	Marty Marion, Red Schoendienst/25	15.00
15	Robin Yount, Paul Molitor/40	40.00
16	Mark Grace, Sammy Sosa/50	30.00
17	Ted Williams, Bobby Doerr/15	150.00
18	Reggie Jackson, Rod Carew/50	25.00

Classic Combos Quad

		NM/M
Quantity produced listed		
Prime:		No Pricing
Production One Set		
2	Roy Campanella/Pants, Pee Wee Reese/25	50.00
3	Ted Williams, Carl Yastrzemski/15	250.00
4	Roberto Clemente, Willie Stargell/25	200.00
5	Eddie Murray, Cal Ripken Jr./25	125.00
6	Roger Maris, Yogi Berra/15	150.00
10	Nolan Ryan, Rod Carew/50	70.00
11	Don Mattingly, Rickey Henderson/25	80.00
15	Robin Yount, Paul Molitor/25	75.00
16	Mark Grace, Sammy Sosa/25	60.00
17	Ted Williams, Bobby Doerr/15	200.00
18	Reggie Jackson, Rod Carew/25	40.00

Dress Code Bat

	NM/M
Common Player:	5.00

Production 50 Sets		
Combo Material:		1-1.5X
Production 50 Sets		
1	Derek Jeter	25.00
2	Kerry Wood	15.00
3	Nomar Garciaparra	15.00
4	Jacque Jones	5.00
5	Mark Teixeira	6.00
6	Troy Glaus	8.00
7	Todd Helton	10.00
8	Miguel Tejada	6.00
9	Mike Piazza	12.00
11	Mike Sweeney	5.00
12	Albert Pujols	20.00
13	Rickey Henderson	10.00
14	Chipper Jones	10.00
15	Don Mattingly	25.00
16	Shawn Green	5.00
17	Mark Grace	10.00
18	Jason Giambi	8.00
19	Barry Zito	10.00
20	Sammy Sosa	15.00
22	Rafael Palmeiro	10.00
23	Frank Thomas	10.00
24	Manny Ramirez	10.00
25	Mike Mussina	10.00
26	Magglio Ordonez	6.00
27	Rocco Baldelli	12.00
28	Andruw Jones	6.00
29	Torii Hunter	6.00
30	Ivan Rodriguez	10.00
31	Jeff Bagwell	10.00
32	Mark Mulder	6.00
33	Trot Nixon	10.00
34	Cal Ripken Jr.	60.00
35	Dontrelle Willis	8.00
36	Hank Blalock	8.00
37	Brandon Webb	8.00
38	Miguel Cabrera	8.00
39	Hideo Nomo	10.00
41	Tim Hudson	8.00
42	Pedro Martinez	12.00
43	Hee Seop Choi	6.00
44	Randy Johnson	10.00
45	Tony Gwynn	15.00
46	Mark Prior	10.00
47	Eric Chavez	6.00
48	Alex Rodriguez	15.00
50	Alfonso Soriano	12.00

Dress Code Jersey

	NM/M
Common Player:	4.00
Production 100 Sets	
Number:	1X
Production 100 Sets	
Prime:	2X
Production 25 Sets	

1	Derek Jeter	25.00
2	Kerry Wood	15.00
3	Nomar Garciaparra	10.00
4	Jacque Jones	5.00
5	Mark Teixeira	5.00
6	Troy Glaus	6.00
7	Todd Helton	6.00
8	Miguel Tejada	5.00
9	Mike Piazza	10.00
11	Mike Sweeney	5.00
12	Albert Pujols	15.00
13	Rickey Henderson	8.00
14	Chipper Jones	8.00
15	Don Mattingly	25.00
16	Shawn Green	5.00
17	Mark Grace	10.00
18	Jason Giambi	8.00
19	Barry Zito	8.00
20	Sammy Sosa	12.00
21	Jay Gibbons	4.00
22	Rafael Palmeiro	8.00
23	Frank Thomas	8.00
24	Manny Ramirez	6.00
25	Mike Mussina	8.00
26	Magglio Ordonez	6.00
27	Rocco Baldelli	6.00
28	Andruw Jones	8.00
29	Torii Hunter	8.00
30	Ivan Rodriguez	8.00
31	Jeff Bagwell	8.00
32	Mark Mulder	6.00
33	Trot Nixon	5.00
34	Cal Ripken Jr./25	80.00
35	Dontrelle Willis	6.00
36	Hank Blalock	5.00
37	Brandon Webb	4.00
38	Miguel Cabrera	12.00
39	Hideo Nomo	8.00
40	Shannon Stewart	4.00
41	Tim Hudson	6.00
42	Pedro Martinez	6.00
43	Hee Seop Choi	4.00
44	Randy Johnson	6.00
45	Tony Gwynn	10.00
46	Mark Prior	6.00
47	Eric Chavez	6.00
48	Alex Rodriguez	10.00
49	Johan Santana	4.00
50	Alfonso Soriano	8.00

Dress Code Combos Signature

		NM/M
Quantity produced listed		
Prime:		No Pricing
Production One Set		
4	Jacque Jones/Jsy/25	15.00
21	Jay Gibbons/Jsy/25	25.00
32	Mark Mulder/Jsy/25	35.00
33	Trot Nixon/Jsy/25	50.00
35	Dontrelle Willis/Jsy/25	40.00
38	Miguel Cabrera/Jsy/25	70.00
40	Shannon Stewart/Jsy/25	20.00
49	Johan Santana/Jsy/25	40.00

Famous Foursomes

		NM/M
Production 99 Sets		
1	Roy Campanella, Pee Wee Reese, Jackie Robinson, Duke Snider	15.00
2	Stan Musial, Bob Gibson, Red Schoendienst, Clete Boyer	15.00

Famous Foursomes Jersey

	NM/M
No Pricing	
Production 10 Sets	
Prime: No Pricing	
Production One Set	

Legendary Hats Material

		NM/M
Quantity produced listed		
2	Mike Schmidt/25	50.00
6	George Brett/25	60.00
14	Cal Ripken Jr./25	100.00
16	Kirby Puckett/25	30.00
20	Reggie Jackson/Yanks/25	25.00
22	Ernie Banks/25	35.00
29	Dave Winfield/25	15.00
40	Wade Boggs/25	25.00
42	Rickey Henderson/A's/25	20.00
49	Reggie Jackson/Angels/25	25.00
51	Rafael Palmeiro/25	20.00
52	Sammy Sosa/25	30.00
55	Steve Carlton/25	20.00
56	Rod Carew/Angels/25	20.00
60	R Henderson/Angels/25	20.00

Legendary Jackets Material

		NM/M
Production 100 Sets		
2	Mike Schmidt	15.00
8	Reggie Jackson/A's	15.00
17	Don Mattingly	20.00
32	Gary Carter	5.00
54	Nolan Ryan	30.00
56	Rod Carew/Angels	10.00

Legendary Jerseys Material

	NM/M
Common Player:	2.00
Production 1,000 Sets	
Spikes:	1-2X
Production 100 Sets	
Hats:	2-3X
Production 50 Sets	
Jackets:	2-3X
Production 50 Sets	
Jerseys:	1X
Production 500 Sets	
Leather:	1-2X
Production 100 Sets	
Pants:	2-3X
Production 50 Sets	

1	Tony Gwynn	3.00
2	Mike Schmidt	5.00
3	Johnny Bench	4.00
4	Roger Maris	5.00
5	Ted Williams	8.00
6	George Brett	6.00
7	Carlton Fisk	2.00
8	Reggie Jackson	3.00
9	Joe Morgan	

10	Bo Jackson	3.00
11	Stan Musial	4.00
12	Andre Dawson	2.00
13	Rickey Henderson	2.00
14	Cal Ripken Jr.	8.00
15	Dale Murphy	2.00
16	Kirby Puckett	4.00
17	Don Mattingly	5.00
18	Brooks Robinson	3.00
19	Orlando Cepeda	2.00
20	Reggie Jackson	3.00
21	Roberto Clemente	3.00
22	Ernie Banks	4.00
23	Frank Robinson	3.00
24	Harmon Killebrew	3.00
25	Willie Stargell	3.00
26	Al Kaline	3.00
27	Carl Yastrzemski	4.00
28	Duke Snider	2.00
29	Dave Winfield	2.00
30	Eddie Murray	3.00
31	Eddie Matthews	3.00
32	Gary Carter	2.00
33	Rod Carew	3.00
34	Jimmie Foxx	4.00
35	Mel Ott	3.00
36	Paul Molitor	3.00
37	Thurman Munson	4.00
38	Rogers Hornsby	3.00
39	Robin Yount	4.00
40	Wade Boggs	3.00
41	Jackie Robinson	5.00
42	Rickey Henderson	2.00
43	Ty Cobb	5.00
44	Yogi Berra	3.00
45	Roy Campanella	3.00
46	Luis Aparicio	2.00
47	Phil Rizzuto	3.00
48	Roger Maris	5.00
49	Reggie Jackson	3.00
50	Lou Gehrig	6.00
51	Rafael Palmeiro	3.00
52	Sammy Sosa	5.00
53	Roger Clemens	6.00
54	Nolan Ryan	5.00
55	Steve Carlton	4.00
56	Rod Carew	3.00
57	Whitey Ford	3.00
58	Fergie Jenkins	2.00
59	Babe Ruth	8.00
60	R Henderson	2.00

Dress Code Combos Signature

	NM/M
Number:	1X
Production 3-50	
No pricing for production 15 or less.	
Prime:	No Pricing
Production One Set	
1	Tony Gwynn/50	20.00
2	Mike Schmidt/25	35.00
3	Johnny Bench/25	15.00
6	George Brett/25	50.00
7	Carlton Fisk/50	15.00
8	Reggie Jackson/25	30.00
9	Joe Morgan/25	15.00
10	Bo Jackson/25	50.00
12	Andre Dawson/50	10.00
13	R Henderson/25	20.00
14	Cal Ripken Jr./25	85.00
15	Dale Murphy/25	20.00
16	Kirby Puckett/50	15.00
18	Brooks Robinson/50	20.00
19	Orlando Cepeda/50	8.00
20	Reggie Jackson/25	25.00
21	Roberto Clemente/25	75.00
23	Frank Robinson/50	10.00
24	Harmon Killebrew/50	15.00
25	Willie Stargell/50	10.00
27	Carl Yastrzemski/50	25.00
29	Dave Winfield/50	10.00
30	Eddie Murray/50	20.00
31	Eddie Mathews/50	25.00
32	Gary Carter/50	8.00
33	Rod Carew/25	20.00
36	Paul Molitor/50	15.00
39	Robin Yount/50	25.00
40	Wade Boggs/50	15.00
42	Rickey Henderson/25	25.00
44	Yogi Berra/15	35.00
46	Luis Aparicio/50	8.00
47	Phil Rizzuto/50	20.00
48	Roger Maris/25	40.00
49	Reggie Jackson/25	15.00
51	Rafael Palmeiro/50	10.00
52	Sammy Sosa/50	20.00
53	Roger Clemens/50	25.00
p4	Nolan Ryan/50	30.00
55	Steve Carlton/50	8.00
56	Rod Carew/50	15.00
57	Whitey Ford/25	35.00

Legendary Leather Material

		NM/M
Quantity produced listed		
16	Kirby Puckett/Fld Glv/25	40.00
32	Gary Carter/Fld Glv/25	35.00
51	Rafael Palmeiro/Fld Glv/25	25.00
52	Sammy Sosa/Btg Glv/25	50.00
55	Steve Carlton/Fld Glv/25	15.00
58	Fergie Jenkins/Fld Glv/25	15.00

Legendary Lumberjacks

	NM/M
Common Player:	2.00
Production 1,000 Sets	
Spikes:	1-2X
Production 100 Sets	
Hats:	2-3X
Production 50 Sets	
Jackets:	2-3X
Production 50 Sets	
Jerseys:	1X
Production 500 Sets	
Leather:	1-2X
Production 100 Sets	
Pants:	2-3X
Production 50 Sets	

Legendary Lumberjacks Material

		NM/M
Quantity produced listed		
1	Tony Gwynn/100	15.00
2	Mike Schmidt/100	15.00
3	Johnny Bench/100	15.00
4	Roger Maris /25	40.00
5	Ted Williams/100	100.00
6	George Brett/100	25.00
7	Carlton Fisk/100	10.00
8	Reggie Jackson /100	12.00
9	Joe Morgan/100	5.00
10	Bo Jackson/100	10.00
11	Stan Musial/25	35.00
12	Andre Dawson/100	5.00
13	R Henderson/100	10.00
14	Cal Ripken Jr./100	40.00
15	Dale Murphy/100	12.00
16	Kirby Puckett/100	15.00
17	Don Mattingly/100	20.00
18	Brooks Robinson/100	15.00
19	Orlando Cepeda/100	5.00
20	Reggie Jackson/100	12.00
21	Roberto Clemente/25	65.00
22	Ernie Banks/100	15.00
23	Frank Robinson/100	15.00
24	Harmon Killebrew/100	20.00
25	Willie Stargell/100	15.00
26	Al Kaline/100	10.00
27	Carl Yastrzemski/100	25.00
29	Dave Winfield/100	5.00
30	Eddie Murray/100	8.00
31	Eddie Mathews/50	20.00
32	Gary Carter/100	8.00
34	Rod Carew/100	5.00
35	Mel Ott/25	35.00
36	Paul Molitor/100	10.00
37	Thurman Munson/50	20.00

Legendary Pants Material

		NM/M
Quantity produced listed		
1	Tony Gwynn/25	25.00
12	Andre Dawson/25	10.00
24	Harmon Killebrew/50	20.00
26	Al Kaline/50	25.00
45	Roy Campanella/25	25.00
46	Luis Aparicio/50	10.00
47	Phil Rizzuto/50	15.00
48	Roger Maris A's/25	30.00
51	Rafael Palmeiro/25	20.00
56	Rod Carew Angels/50	15.00
57	Whitey Ford/25	25.00
58	Fergie Jenkins/25	25.00

Legendary Spikes Material

		NM/M
Quantity produced listed		
13	R Henderson/Yanks./25	30.00
17	Don Mattingly/50	40.00
29	Dave Winfield/50	15.00
42	Rickey Henderson/A's/25	30.00
51	Rafael Palmeiro/25	25.00
52	Sammy Sosa/50	30.00
60	R Henderson/Angels/25	30.00

Legendary Leather Material (col 7)

38	Rogers Hornsby/25	50.00
39	Robin Yount/100	15.00
40	Wade Boggs/50	12.00
42	Rickey Henderson/50	10.00
44	Yogi Berra/25	20.00
46	Roy Campanella/25	30.00
47	Luis Aparicio/100	8.00
48	Roger Maris/25	40.00
49	Reggie Jackson/100	15.00
50	Lou Gehrig/25	125.00
51	Rafael Palmeiro/100	15.00
52	Sammy Sosa/100	15.00
56	Rod Carew/100	8.00
60	R Henderson/100	10.00

Membership

	NM/M
Complete Set (25):	70.00
Common Player:	2.00
Production 2,499 Sets	
1	Stan Musial	4.00
2	Ted Williams	5.00
3	Early Wynn	2.00
4	Roberto Clemente	5.00
5	Al Kaline	4.00
6	Bob Gibson	3.00
7	Lou Brock	2.00
8	Carl Yastrzemski	4.00
9	Gaylord Perry	2.00
10	Fergie Jenkins	2.00
11	Steve Carlton	2.00
12	Reggie Jackson	5.00
13	Rod Carew	3.00
14	Bert Blyleven	2.00
15	Mike Schmidt	4.00
16	Nolan Ryan	6.00
17	Robin Yount	4.00
18	George Brett	6.00
19	Eddie Murray	3.00
20	Tony Gwynn	3.00
21	Cal Ripken Jr.	8.00
22	Randy Johnson	4.00
23	Sammy Sosa	5.00
24	Rafael Palmeiro	3.00
25	Roger Clemens	5.00

Membership VIP Bat

	NM/M
Quantity produced listed	
1	Stan Musial/25	40.00
2	Ted Williams/25	100.00
4	Roberto Clemente/25	65.00
5	Al Kaline/25	20.00
7	Lou Brock/25	20.00
8	Carl Yastrzemski/25	25.00
11	Steve Carlton/25	15.00
12	Reggie Jackson/25	25.00
13	Rod Carew/25	25.00
15	Mike Schmidt/25	30.00
17	Robin Yount/25	25.00
19	Eddie Murray/25	25.00
20	Tony Gwynn/25	25.00
22	Randy Johnson/25	25.00
23	Sammy Sosa/25	30.00
24	Rafael Palmeiro/25	20.00
25	Roger Clemens/25	25.00

Membership VIP Jersey

NM/M

Quantity produced listed
Prime: No Pricing
Production One Set

1	Stan Musial/15	40.00
4	Roberto Clemente/25	75.00
5	Al Kaline/Pants/25	20.00
8	Carl Yastrzemski/25	30.00
9	Gaylord Perry/25	10.00
10	Fergie Jenkins/Pants/25	15.00
11	Steve Carlton/25	15.00
12	Reggie Jackson/25	25.00
13	Rod Carew/25	20.00
14	Bert Blyleven/25	10.00
15	Mike Schmidt/25	30.00
16	Nolan Ryan/25	35.00
17	Robin Yount/25	25.00
18	George Brett/25	40.00
19	Eddie Murray/25	25.00
20	Tony Gwynn/25	25.00
21	Cal Ripken Jr./25	85.00
22	Randy Johnson/25	20.00
23	Sammy Sosa/25	30.00
24	Rafael Palmeiro/25	20.00
25	Roger Clemens/25	25.00

Membership VIP Signatures

NM/M

Quantity produced listed

5	Al Kaline/20	50.00
9	Gaylord Perry/50	15.00
10	Fergie Jenkins/50	20.00
11	Steve Carlton/50	30.00
14	Bert Blyleven/50	10.00

Membership VIP Combos Material

NM/M

Quantity produced listed
Prime: No Pricing
Production One Set

1	Stan Musial/Bat-Jsy/15	40.00
4	Roberto Clemente/Bat-Jsy/25	100.00
5	Al Kaline/Bat-Pants/25	30.00
8	Carl Yastrzemski/Bat-Jsy/25	50.00
10	Fergie Jenkins/Fld Glv-Pants/25	15.00
11	Steve Carlton/Bat-Jsy/25	15.00
12	Reggie Jackson/Bat-Jsy/25	30.00
13	Rod Carew/Bat-Pants/25	25.00
15	Mike Schmidt/Bat-Jsy/25	40.00
16	Nolan Ryan/Bat-Jsy/25	50.00
17	Robin Yount/Bat-Jsy/25	40.00
18	George Brett/Bat-Jsy/25	50.00
19	Eddie Murray/Bat-Jsy/25	30.00
20	Tony Gwynn/Bat-Jsy/25	40.00
21	Cal Ripken Jr./Bat-Jsy/25	80.00
22	Randy Johnson/Bat-Jsy/25	25.00
23	Sammy Sosa/Bat-Jsy/25	35.00
24	Rafael Palmeiro/Bat-Jsy/25	25.00
25	Roger Clemens/Bat-Jsy/25	30.00

Membership VIP Combos Signature

NM/M

Quantity produced listed
Prime: No Pricing
Production One Set

5	Al Kaline/Pants/25	50.00
9	Gaylord Perry/Jsy/50	15.00
10	Fergie Jenkins/Pants/50	20.00
11	Steve Carlton/Jsy/25	40.00
14	Bert Blyleven/Jsy/50	15.00

National Trading Card Day

As part of its participation in NTCD on April 3, Donruss-Playoff issued a foil pack with four baseball player cards and two football, plus a header. Only the baseball players are listed here. Fronts have game-action photos on a ghosted background; backs have recent stats, biographical data and career highlights. The NTCD logo appears on front.

NM/M

Unopened Pack:		3.00
Common Player:		.25
DP-1	Albert Pujols	.50
DP-2	Roger Clemens	.25
DP-3	Mike Piazza	.25
DP-4	Alfonso Soriano	.25

October Heroes

NM/M

Production 2,499 Sets

1	Reggie Jackson	3.00
2	Bob Gibson	3.00
3	Carlton Fisk	2.00
4	Whitey Ford	2.00
5	George Brett	5.00
6	Roberto Clemente	5.00
7	Roy Campanella	3.00
8	Babe Ruth	6.00

October Heroes Bat

NM/M

Quantity produced listed

1	Reggie Jackson/25	25.00
3	Carlton Fisk/25	25.00
4	Roberto Clemente/25	65.00
7	Roy Campanella/25	25.00

October Heroes Fabric

NM/M

Quantity produced listed

2	Bob Gibson/Jsy/15	30.00
3	Carlton Fisk/Jsy/25	20.00
4	Whitey Ford/Jsy/25	20.00
5	George Brett/Jsy/25	40.00
7	Roy Campanella/Pants/25	20.00

October Heroes Signature

NM/M

Quantity produced listed

4	Whitey Ford/50	40.00

October Heroes Combos Material

NM/M

Quantity produced listed

1	Reggie Jackson/Bat-Hat/25	40.00
3	Carlton Fisk/Bat-Jsy/25	30.00
5	George Brett/Bat-Jsy/25	50.00
7	Roy Campanella/Bat-Pants/25	35.00

October Heroes Combos Signature

NM/M

Quantity produced listed

4	Whitey Ford/Jsy/50	45.00

Significant Signatures Green

NM/M

Quantity produced listed

3	Hank Blalock/50	40.00
5	Shannon Stewart/50	10.00
7	Trot Nixon/30	30.00
13	Mike Lowell/25	25.00
14	Robin Ventura/25	15.00
19	Carlos Beltran/25	50.00
21	Johan Santana/50	35.00
24	Steve Finley/25	25.00
26	Alexis Rios/100	25.00
32	Miguel Cabrera/50	45.00
36	Dontrelle Willis/25	25.00
37	Rafael Soriano/100	6.00
38	Richard Fischer/100	6.00
39	Brian Tallet/100	6.00
40	Jose Castillo/100	6.00
41	Wade Miller/25	20.00
43	Runelvys Hernandez/20	10.00
44	Joe Borchard/50	8.00
47	Adam Dunn/50	30.00
49	Brandon Phillips/50	6.00
53	Cliff Lee/50	10.00
54	Chien-Ming Wang/50	150.00
57	Jhonny Peralta/100	6.00
60	Jae Weong Seo/50	15.00
61	Nic Jackson/100	8.00
63	Jimmy Gobble/45	6.00
64	Travis Hafner/100	12.00
66	Jerome Williams/50	6.00
68	Alexis Gomez/50	6.00
70	Zach Day/50	8.00
72	Morgan Ensberg/50	6.00
74	Garrett Atkins/99	6.00
77	Lyle Overbay/100	15.00
78	Josh Phelps/50	10.00
79	Juan Gonzalez/25	45.00
80	Rich Harden/50	15.00
84	Jody Gerut/50	15.00
87	Jay Gibbons/50	15.00
88	Chone Figgins/50	10.00
98	Jay Payton/50	10.00
99	Barry Larkin/50	40.00
102	Robby Hammock/50	6.00
103	Orlando Hudson/50	8.00
105	Hong-Chih Kuo/50	10.00
106	Eric Chavez/50	35.00
108	Jacque Jones/50	10.00
109	Ken Harvey/100	8.00
110	Aramis Ramirez/50	20.00
111	Victor Martinez/50	20.00
112	Joe Crede/50	10.00
113	Jason Varitek/25	40.00
118	Brandon Webb/25	15.00
121	Sammy Sosa/21	150.00
127	Luis Castillo/25	10.00
134	Edgar Martinez/25	40.00
145	Brett Myers/25	8.00
149	Gary Sheffield/25	25.00
151	Duke Snider/25	35.00
153	Whitey Ford/25	40.00
155	Dwight Gooden/50	20.00
158	Don Mattingly/25	100.00
159	Jack Morris/50	10.00
160	Jim Bunning/25	25.00
161	Fergie Jenkins/50	15.00
163	George Kell/50	15.00
164	Darryl Strawberry/50	20.00
165	Robin Roberts/25	30.00
166	Monte Irvin/25	60.00
167	Ernie Banks/25	60.00
168	Wade Boggs/50	40.00
169	Gaylord Perry/50	10.00
170	Keith Hernandez/50	15.00
172	Frank Robinson/25	30.00
173	Nolan Ryan/25	120.00
174	Stan Musial/50	70.00
175	Eddie Murray/50	50.00
176	Byron Gettis/100	6.00
177	Merkin Valdez/100	6.00
178	Rickie Weeks/50	50.00
180	Brian Bruney/100	6.00
181	Freddy Guzman/100	6.00
182	Brendan Harris/100	6.00
183	John Gall/100	8.00
184	Jason Kubel/100	12.00
185	Delmon Young/50	30.00
186	Ryan Howard/100	80.00
187	Adam Loewen/100	15.00
188	J.D. Durbin/100	8.00
189	Dan Haren/100	6.00
190	Dustin McGowan/100	10.00
191	Chad Gaudin/100	6.00
192	Preston Larrison/100	6.00
193	Ramon Nivar/100	6.00
195	Mike Gosling/100	6.00
196	Kevin Youkilis/100	15.00
197	Ryan Wagner/100	10.00
198	Bubba Nelson/100	8.00
199	Edwin Jackson/100	10.00
200	Chris Burke/100	6.00
201	Carlos Hines/100	10.00
202	Greg Dobbs/50	6.00
203	Jamie Brown/100	8.00
204	David Crouthers/100	6.00
205	Ian Snell/100	30.00
206	Gary Carter/50	25.00
207	Dale Murphy/50	40.00
208	Ryne Sandberg/50	75.00
209	Phil Niekro/50	20.00
210	Don Sutton/50	15.00

Significant Signatures Red

NM/M

Quantity produced listed

3	Hank Blalock/50	30.00
4	Shannon Stewart/100	8.00
6	Carlos Lee/25	20.00
7	Trot Nixon/50	20.00
9	Mark Mulder/25	30.00
12	Jim Edmonds/25	30.00
13	Mike Lowell/50	20.00
14	Robin Ventura/50	20.00
16	Jose Vidro/25	20.00
19	Carlos Beltran/50	50.00
21	Johan Santana/100	25.00
24	Steve Finley/100	6.00
26	Alexis Rios/25	25.00
27	Rafael Palmeiro/25	65.00
28	Jorge Posada/25	45.00
32	Miguel Cabrera/100	40.00
36	Dontrelle Willis/25	25.00
37	Rafael Soriano/250	6.00
38	Richard Fischer/250	6.00
39	Brian Tallet/250	6.00
40	Jose Castillo/250	6.00
41	Wade Miller/92	15.00
42	Jose Contreras/25	25.00
43	Runelvys Hernandez/50	8.00
44	Joe Borchard/250	6.00
47	Adam Dunn/25	30.00
49	Brandon Phillips/70	6.00
50	Scott Rolen/25	35.00
53	Cliff Lee/100	8.00
54	Chien-Ming Wang/250	100.00
55	Roy Oswalt/25	30.00
56	Austin Kearns/25	20.00
57	Jhonny Peralta/250	6.00
60	Jae Weong Seo/100	10.00
61	Nic Jackson/250	6.00
63	Jimmy Gobble/200	10.00
64	Travis Hafner/100	12.00
65	Paul Konerko/25	15.00
66	Jerome Williams/250	20.00
68	Alexis Gomez/100	6.00
70	Zach Day/100	6.00
72	Morgan Ensberg/100	8.00
74	Garrett Atkins/245	6.00
76	Julio Franco/25	20.00
77	Lyle Overbay/250	15.00
78	Josh Phelps/50	8.00
79	Juan Gonzalez/25	45.00
80	Rich Harden/150	10.00
82	Torii Hunter/25	30.00
84	Jody Gerut/100	6.00
87	Jay Gibbons/100	15.00
88	Chone Figgins/100	6.00
92	Rich Aurilia/25	15.00
92	Marlon Byrd/25	15.00
98	Jay Payton/100	8.00
99	Barry Larkin/25	40.00
102	Robby Hammock/150	6.00
103	Orlando Hudson/100	6.00
105	Hong-Chih Kuo/100	30.00
106	Eric Chavez/25	35.00
107	Nick Johnson/25	20.00
108	Jacque Jones/100	6.00
109	Ken Harvey/250	6.00
110	Aramis Ramirez/100	20.00
111	Victor Martinez/99	20.00
112	Joe Crede/100	6.00
113	Jason Varitek/25	35.00
114	Troy Glaus/25	30.00
118	Brandon Webb/50	15.00
119	Craig Biggio/25	30.00
120	Orlando Cabrera/100	10.00
121	Sammy Sosa/25	150.00
122	Bobby Abreu/25	15.00
123	Andruw Jones/25	30.00
124	Jeff Bagwell/25	65.00
127	Luis Castillo/50	10.00
131	Eric Byrnes/25	15.00
132	Eric Hinske/25	15.00
134	Edgar Martinez/50	20.00
135	Rocco Baldelli/25	40.00
143	Vernon Wells/25	15.00
144	Magglio Ordonez/25	30.00
145	Brett Myers/100	8.00
149	Gary Sheffield/50	20.00
150	Tim Hudson/50	40.00
151	Duke Snider/50	30.00
153	Whitey Ford/50	40.00
155	Dwight Gooden/100	20.00
156	Warren Spahn/25	45.00
158	Don Mattingly/100	100.00
159	Jack Morris/100	10.00
160	Jim Bunning/100	20.00
161	Fergie Jenkins/100	10.00
163	George Kell/100	15.00
164	Darryl Strawberry/100	20.00
165	Robin Roberts/100	15.00
166	Monte Irvin/100	15.00
167	Ernie Banks/100	50.00
168	Wade Boggs/50	30.00
169	Gaylord Perry/100	10.00
170	Keith Hernandez/100	20.00
171	Lou Brock/25	30.00
172	Frank Robinson/50	25.00
173	Nolan Ryan/50	85.00
174	Stan Musial/50	60.00
175	Eddie Murray/50	50.00
176	Byron Gettis/250	6.00
177	Merkin Valdez/250	15.00
178	Rickie Weeks/250	40.00
180	Brian Bruney/250	6.00
181	Freddy Guzman/250	6.00
182	Brendan Harris/250	6.00
183	John Gall/250	8.00
184	Jason Kubel/250	10.00
185	Delmon Young/100	30.00
186	Ryan Howard/250	70.00
187	Adam Loewen/250	15.00
188	J.D. Durbin/250	8.00
189	Dan Haren/250	10.00
190	Dustin McGowan/250	10.00
191	Chad Gaudin/250	6.00
192	Preston Larrison/250	6.00
193	Ramon Nivar/250	6.00
195	Mike Gosling/250	6.00
196	Kevin Youkilis/250	15.00
197	Ryan Wagner/250	10.00
198	Bubba Nelson/250	8.00
199	Edwin Jackson/250	10.00
200	Chris Burke/250	6.00
201	Carlos Hines/250	10.00
202	Greg Dobbs/100	6.00
203	Jamie Brown/250	8.00
204	David Crouthers/250	6.00
205	Ian Snell/250	25.00
206	Gary Carter/100	20.00
207	Dale Murphy/50	40.00
208	Ryne Sandberg/50	85.00
209	Phil Niekro/50	15.00
210	Don Sutton/100	15.00

Team Colors Bat

NM/M

Quantity produced listed

2	Steve Garvey/50	10.00
3	Eric Davis/50	15.00
4	Al Oliver/50	8.00
6	Bobby Doerr/25	20.00
7	Paul Molitor/50	15.00
9	Dale Murphy/50	20.00
11	Jose Canseco/50	20.00
12	Jim Rice/50	12.00
13	Will Clark/50	25.00
14	Alan Trammell/50	12.00
16	Dwight Evans/50	15.00
18	Dave Parker/Pirates/25	10.00
21	Andre Dawson/Expos/50	10.00
22	Darryl Strawberry/Dgr/50	10.00
23	George Foster/50	10.00
26	Bo Jackson/50	30.00
27	Cal Ripken Jr./50	50.00
28	Deion Sanders/25	15.00
29	Don Mattingly/Jkt/50	25.00
30	Mark Grace/50	15.00
31	Fred Lynn/50	8.00
33	Ernie Banks/25	30.00
34	Gary Carter/50	12.00
35	Roger Maris/25	40.00
36	Ron Santo/50	12.00
38	Tony Gwynn/50	15.00
40	Red Schoendienst/25	15.00
41	Steve Carlton/25	15.00
43	Wade Boggs/25	25.00
44	Luis Aparicio/25	10.00
46	Andre Dawson/Cubs/25	12.00
48	Darryl Strawberry/Mets/50	10.00
49	Dave Parker Reds/50	8.00

Team Colors Jersey

NM/M

Quantity produced listed
Prime: No Pricing
Production One Set

1	Lenny Dykstra/Mets/Fld Glv/25	15.00
2	Steve Garvey/100	6.00
3	Eric Davis/25	15.00
5	Nolan Ryan/25	30.00
6	Bobby Doerr/25	20.00
7	Paul Molitor/100	10.00
8	Dale Murphy/25	8.00
9	Harold Baines/100	8.00
10	Dwight Gooden/50	10.00
11	Jose Canseco/100	15.00
12	Jim Rice/100	8.00
13	Will Clark/25	25.00
14	Alan Trammell/100	8.00
15	Lee Smith/100	5.00
16	Dwight Evans/100	15.00
17	Tony Oliva/100	8.00
18	Dave Parker/Pirates/25	10.00
19	Jack Morris/100	5.00
20	Luis Tiant/100	6.00
21	Andre Dawson/Expos/100	6.00
22	Darryl Strawberry/Dgr/100	8.00
23	George Foster/100	5.00
24	Marty Marion/100	6.00
25	Dennis Eckersley/100	6.00
26	Bo Jackson/50	30.00
27	Cal Ripken Jr./100	35.00
28	Deion Sanders/50	8.00
29	Don Mattingly/Jkt/100	20.00
30	Mark Grace/50	15.00
31	Fred Lynn/50	8.00
33	Ernie Banks/25	30.00
34	Gary Carter/Jkt/100	8.00
37	Keith Hernandez/25	15.00
38	Tony Gwynn/25	15.00
39	Jim Palmer/25	15.00
40	Red Schoendienst/25	15.00
41	Steve Carlton/25	15.00
43	Wade Boggs/25	25.00
44	Tommy John/100	5.00
45	Luis Aparicio/25	5.00
46	Andre Dawson/Cubs/25	15.00
47	Bert Blyleven/100	5.00
48	Darryl Strawberry/Mets/100	8.00
49	Dave Parker/Reds/100	5.00

Team Colors Signatures

NM/M

Quantity produced listed

1	Lenny Dykstra/Mets/15	15.00
2	Steve Garvey/50	25.00
3	Eric Davis/50	20.00
4	Al Oliver/50	15.00
6	Bobby Doerr/50	20.00
9	Harold Baines/50	25.00
10	Dwight Gooden/50	20.00
12	Jim Rice/50	20.00
14	Alan Trammell/50	20.00
15	Lee Smith/50	15.00
16	Dwight Evans/50	20.00
17	Tony Oliva/50	20.00
18	Dave Parker/Pirates/50	15.00
19	Jack Morris/50	10.00
20	Luis Tiant/50	15.00
21	Andre Dawson/Expos/25	25.00
22	Darryl Strawberry/Dgr/50	20.00
23	George Foster/50	15.00
24	Marty Marion/50	15.00
25	Dennis Eckersley/50	15.00
31	Fred Lynn/50	15.00
34	Gary Carter/20	35.00
37	Keith Hernandez/25	35.00
39	Jim Palmer/20	20.00
40	Red Schoendienst/50	15.00
41	Steve Carlton/20	35.00
43	Tommy John/50	15.00
44	Luis Aparicio/50	20.00
45	Bob Feller/50	20.00
46	Andre Dawson/Cubs/25	25.00
47	Bert Blyleven/50	12.00
48	Darryl Strawberry/Mets/50	20.00
49	Dave Parker/Reds/50	15.00
50	Lenny Dykstra/Phils/50	15.00

Team Colors Combos Material

NM/M

Production 25 Sets
Prime: No Pricing
Production One Set

2	Steve Garvey/Bat-Jsy	15.00
3	Eric Davis/Bat-Jsy	20.00
5	Nolan Ryan/Bat-Jsy	25.00
6	Bobby Doerr/Bat-Jsy	25.00
7	Paul Molitor/Bat-Jsy	25.00
9	Dale Murphy/Bat-Jsy	25.00
11	Jose Canseco/Bat-Jsy	30.00
12	Jim Rice/Bat-Jsy	25.00
13	Will Clark/Bat-Jsy	40.00
14	Alan Trammell/Bat-Jsy	30.00
16	Dwight Evans/Bat-Jsy	25.00
18	Dave Parker/Pirates/Bat-Jsy	20.00
21	Andre Dawson/Expos/Bat-Jsy	15.00

22	Darryl Strawberry/Dgr/Bat-Jsy	20.00
23	George Foster/Bat-Jsy	10.00
26	Bo Jackson/Bat-Jsy	40.00
27	Cal Ripken Jr./Bat-Jsy	65.00
28	Deion Sanders/Bat-Jsy	25.00
29	Don Mattingly/Bat-Jsy	45.00
30	Mark Grace/Bat-Jsy	25.00
33	Ernie Banks/Bat-Jsy	45.00
34	Gary Carter/Bat-Jkt	25.00
38	Tony Gwynn/Bat-Jsy	40.00
40	Red Schoendienst/Bat-Jsy	15.00
41	Steve Carlton/Bat-Jsy	20.00
42	Wade Boggs/Bat-Jsy	25.00
44	Luis Aparicio/Bat-Jsy	15.00
46	Andre Dawson/Cubs/Bat-Jsy	15.00
48	Darryl Strawberry/Mets/Bat-Jsy	20.00
49	Dave Parker/Reds/Bat-Jsy	20.00

Team Colors Combos Signature

NM/M
Quantity produced listed
Prime: No Pricing
Production One Set

1	Lenny Dykstra/Mets/Fld Glv/100	15.00
2	Steve Garvey/Jsy/100	15.00
3	Eric Davis/Jsy/100	25.00
4	Al Oliver/Bat/100	20.00
6	Bobby Doerr/Jsy/100	20.00
9	Harold Baines/Jsy/100	20.00
10	Dwight Gooden/Jsy/100	25.00
12	Jim Rice/Jsy/100	25.00
14	Alan Trammell/Jsy/100	25.00
15	Lee Smith/Jsy/100	25.00
16	Dwight Evans/Jsy/100	25.00
17	Tony Oliva/Jsy/100	20.00
18	Dave Parker/Pirates/Jsy/100	15.00
19	Jack Morris/Jsy/100	20.00
20	Luis Tiant/Jsy/100	20.00
21	Andre Dawson/Expos/Jsy/100	25.00
22	Darryl Strawberry/Dgr/Jsy/100	25.00
23	George Foster/Jsy/100	20.00
24	Marty Marion/Jsy/100	20.00
25	Dennis Eckersley/Jsy/100	25.00
31	Fred Lynn/Jsy/100	25.00
33	Ernie Banks/Jsy/25	90.00
34	Gary Carter/Jkt/50	40.00
36	Ron Santo/Bat/25	50.00
37	Keith Hernandez/Jsy/25	45.00
39	Jim Palmer/Jsy/50	35.00
40	Red Schoendienst/Jsy/100	15.00
41	Steve Carlton/Jsy/50	40.00
43	Tommy John/Jsy/100	20.00
44	Luis Aparicio/Jsy/100	15.00
46	Andre Dawson/Cubs/Jsy/50	25.00
47	Bert Blyleven/Jsy/100	25.00
48	Darryl Strawberry/Mets/Jsy/100	25.00
49	Dave Parker/Reds/Jsy/100	15.00
50	Lenny Dykstra/Phils/Btg Glv/30	25.00

Timeless Triples

NM/M
Complete Set (6): 40.00
Common Player:
Production 500 Sets

1. Ted Williams, Carl Yastrzemski, Carlton Fisk — 10.00
2. Lou Gehrig, Roger Maris, Thurman Munson — 8.00
3. Brooks Robinson, Frank Robinson, Cal Ripken Jr. — 10.00
4. Roger Clemens, Andy Pettitte, Roy Oswalt — 6.00
5. Greg Maddux, Mark Prior, Kerry Wood — 8.00
6. Alex Rodriguez, Derek Jeter, Gary Sheffield — 10.00

Timeless Triples Bat

NM/M
Production 25 Sets

1. Ted Williams, Carl Yastrzemski, Carlton Fisk — 185.00
2. Lou Gehrig, Roger Maris, Thurman Munson — 200.00
3. Brooks Robinson, Frank Robinson, Cal Ripken Jr. — 140.00

Timeless Triples Jersey

NM/M
Quantity produced listed
Prime: No Pricing
Production One Set

3. Brooks Robinson, Frank Robinson, Cal Ripken Jr./25 — 140.00

2004 Donruss Diamond Kings

NM/M
Complete Set (175): 75.00
Common Player: .25
Common (151-175): 1.50
Pack (5): 7.50
Box (12): 80.00

1	Alex Rodriguez	2.50
2	Andruw Jones	.75
3	Nomar Garciaparra	2.00
4	Kerry Wood	.75
5	Magglio Ordonez	.50
6	Victor Martinez	.25
7	Jeremy Bonderman	.25
8	Josh Beckett	.75
9	Jeff Kent	.40
10	Carlos Beltran	.50
11	Hideo Nomo	.50
12	Richie Sexson	.50
13	Jose Vidro	.25
14	Jae Weong Seo	.25
15	Alfonso Soriano	1.00
16	Barry Zito	.50
17	Brett Myers	.25
18	Brian Giles	.40
19	Edgar Martinez	.40
20	Jim Edmonds	.50
21	Rocco Baldelli	.75
22	Mark Teixeira	.50
23	Carlos Delgado	.75
24	Julius Matos	.25
25	Jose Reyes	.50
26	Marlon Byrd	.25
27	Albert Pujols	2.50
28	Vernon Wells	.40
29	Garret Anderson	.50
30	Jerome Williams	.25
31	Chipper Jones	1.00
32	Rich Harden	.25
33	Manny Ramirez	.75
34	Derek Jeter	3.00
35	Brandon Webb	.25
36	Mark Prior	1.50
37	Roy Halladay	.50
38	Frank Thomas	.75
39	Rafael Palmeiro	.75
40	Adam Dunn	.50
41	Aubrey Huff	.25
42	Todd Helton	.75
43	Matt Morris	.40
44	Dontrelle Willis	.40
45	Lance Berkman	.50
46	Mike Sweeney	.25
47	Kazuhisa Ishii	.25
48	Torii Hunter	.50
49	Vladimir Guerrero	1.00
50	Mike Piazza	1.50
51	Alexis Rios	.25
52	Shannon Stewart	.25
53	Eric Hinske	.25
54	Jason Jennings	.25
55	Jason Giambi	1.00
56	Brandon Claussen	.25
57	Joe Thurston	.25
58	Ramon Nivar	.25
59	Jay Gibbons	.25
60	Eric Chavez	.50
61	Jimmy Gobble	.25
62	Walter Young	.25
63	Mark Grace	.50
64	Austin Kearns	.50
65	Bobby Abreu	.50
66	Hee Seop Choi	.25
67	Brandon Phillips	.25
68	Rickie Weeks	.50
69	Luis Gonzalez	.50
70	Mariano Rivera	.50
71	Jason Lane	.25
72	Xavier Nady	.25
73	Runelvys Hernandez	.25
74	Aramis Ramirez	.25
75	Ichiro Suzuki	2.00
76	Cliff Lee	.25
77	Chris Snelling	.25
78	Ryan Wagner	.25
79	Miguel Tejada	.50
80	Juan Gonzalez	.75
81	Joe Borchard	.25
82	Gary Sheffield	.50
83	Wade Miller	.25
84	Jeff Bagwell	.75
85	Ryan Church	.25
86	Adrian Beltre	.25
87	Jeff Baker	.25
88	Adam Loewen	.25
89	Bernie Williams	.50
90	Pedro J. Martinez	1.00
91	Carlos Rivera	.25
92	Junior Spivey	.25
93	Tim Hudson	.50
94	Troy Glaus	.50
95	Ken Griffey Jr.	1.50
96	Alexis Gomez	.25
97	Antonio Perez	.25
98	Dan Haren	.25
99	Ivan Rodriguez	.75
100	Randy Johnson	1.00
101	Lyle Overbay	.25
102	Oliver Perez	.25
103	Miguel Cabrera	.75
104	Scott Rolen	1.00
105	Roger Clemens	2.00
106	Brian Tallet	.25
107	Nic Jackson	.25
108	Angel Berroa	.25
109	Hank Blalock	.50
110	Ryan Klesko	.40
111	Jose Castillo	.25
112	Paul Konerko	.25
113	Greg Maddux	1.50
114	Mark Mulder	.50
115	Pat Burrell	.50
116	Garrett Atkins	.25
117	Jeremy Guthrie	.25
118	Orlando Cabrera	.25
119	Nick Johnson	.25
120	Tom Glavine	.50
121	Morgan Ensberg	.25
122	Sean Casey	.25
123	Orlando Hudson	.25
124	Hideki Matsui	2.50
125	Craig Biggio	.25
126	Adam LaRoche	.25
127	Hong-Chih Kuo	.25
128	Paul LoDuca	.25
129	Shawn Green	.50
130	Luis Castillo	.25
131	Joe Crede	.25
132	Ken Harvey	.25
133	Freddy Sanchez	.25
134	Roy Oswalt	.50
135	Curt Schilling	.75
136	Alfredo Amezaga	.25
137	Chien-Ming Wang	.50
138	Barry Larkin	.50
139	Trot Nixon	.25
140	Jim Thome	1.00
141	Bret Boone	.40
142	Jacque Jones	.25
143	Travis Hafner	.25
144	Sammy Sosa	2.00
145	Mike Mussina	.50
146	Vinnie Chulk	.25
147	Chad Gaudin	.25
148	Delmon Young	.50
149	Mike Lowell	.40
150	Rickey Henderson	.50
151	Roger Clemens	4.00
152	Mark Grace	2.00
153	Rickey Henderson	2.00
154	Alex Rodriguez	5.00
155	Rafael Palmeiro	2.00
156	Greg Maddux	3.00
157	Mike Piazza	3.00
158	Mike Mussina	1.50
159	Dale Murphy	1.50
160	Cal Ripken Jr.	6.00
161	Carl Yastrzemski	2.00
162	Marty Marion	1.50
163	Don Mattingly	4.00
164	Robin Yount	2.00
165	Andre Dawson	1.50
166	Jim Palmer	1.50
167	George Brett	5.00
168	Whitey Ford	2.00
169	Roy Campanella	2.00
170	Roger Maris	4.00
171	Duke Snider	2.00
172	Steve Carlton	2.00
173	Stan Musial	3.00
174	Nolan Ryan	6.00
175	Deion Sanders	1.50

Bronze

Bronze (1-150): 4-6X
Bronze (151-175): 2-3X
Production 100 Sets
Bronze Sepia: 2-3X
Production 100

Framed Bronze

Framed Bronze (1-150): 2-3X
Framed Bronze (151-175): 1-2X
Framed Bronze Sepia: 1-2X
Inserted 1:6

Silver

Silver (1-150): 5-10X
Silver (151-175): 2-4X
Production 50 Sets
Silver Sepia: 2-4X
Production 50

Framed Silver

Framed Silver (1-150): 4-8X
Framed Silver (151-175): 2-3X
Production 100 Sets
Framed Silver Sepia: 2-3X
Production 100

Platinum

Platinum: No Pricing
Production One Set
Platinum Sepia: No Pricing
Production One Set

Framed Platinum

Framed Platinum: No Pricing
Production One Set

Diamond Cut Bat

NM/M
Common Player: 6.00
Production 100 unless noted.

1	Alex Rodriguez	15.00
2	Nomar Garciaparra	12.00
3	Hideo Nomo	8.00
4	Alfonso Soriano	10.00
6	Edgar Martinez	8.00
7	Rocco Baldelli	10.00
8	Mark Teixeira	10.00
9	Albert Pujols	20.00
10	Vernon Wells	8.00
11	Garret Anderson	8.00
14	Brandon Webb	6.00
15	Mark Prior	15.00
16	Rafael Palmeiro	10.00
17	Adam Dunn	10.00
18	Dontrelle Willis	8.00
19	Kazuhisa Ishii	6.00
21	Torii Hunter	8.00
21	Vladimir Guerrero	10.00
22	Mike Piazza	15.00
23	Jason Giambi	10.00
27	Bobby Abreu	6.00
28	Hee Seop Choi	6.00
28	Rickie Weeks	12.00
30	Troy Glaus	8.00
31	Ivan Rodriguez	10.00
32	Hank Blalock	10.00
33	Greg Maddux	15.00
34	Nick Johnson	6.00
35	Shawn Green	8.00
36	Sammy Sosa	15.00
37	Dale Murphy/50	15.00
38	Cal Ripken Jr./50	50.00
39	Carl Yastrzemski	15.00
41	Don Mattingly	25.00
43	George Brett/50	40.00
46	Steve Carlton/50	15.00
47	Stan Musial/25	40.00
48	Nolan Ryan/50	35.00
49	Deion Sanders/50	15.00
50	Roberto Clemente/25	120.00

Diamond Cut Jersey

NM/M
Common Player: 6.00
Production 100 unless noted.

1	Alex Rodriguez	15.00
2	Nomar Garciaparra	15.00
3	Hideo Nomo/50	15.00
4	Alfonso Soriano	10.00
5	Brett Myers/50	10.00
6	Edgar Martinez	10.00
7	Rocco Baldelli	12.00
8	Mark Teixeira	10.00
9	Albert Pujols	20.00
10	Vernon Wells	8.00
11	Garret Anderson/50	8.00
12	Jerome Williams	8.00
13	Rich Harden	8.00
14	Brandon Webb	6.00
15	Mark Prior	15.00
16	Rafael Palmeiro	10.00
17	Adam Dunn	10.00
18	Dontrelle Willis	8.00
19	Kazuhisa Ishii	6.00
20	Torii Hunter	10.00
21	Vladimir Guerrero/50	15.00
22	Mike Piazza	15.00
23	Jason Giambi	10.00
25	Ramon Nivar	6.00
26	Bobby Abreu	6.00
27	Hee Seop Choi	8.00
30	Troy Glaus	8.00
31	Ivan Rodriguez	10.00
32	Hank Blalock	10.00
33	Greg Maddux	15.00
34	Nick Johnson	6.00
35	Shawn Green	8.00
36	Sammy Sosa	15.00
37	Dale Murphy/50	20.00
38	Cal Ripken Jr./50	50.00
39	Carl Yastrzemski	20.00
41	Don Mattingly	25.00
43	George Brett/50	35.00
44	Whitey Ford/25	25.00
46	Steve Carlton/50	15.00
48	Nolan Ryan/50	40.00
49	Deion Sanders/50	15.00

Diamond Cut Signature

NM/M
Many not priced due to scarcity.

7	Rocco Baldelli/50	45.00
8	Mark Teixeira/25	30.00
13	Rich Harden/50	25.00
14	Brandon Webb/50	25.00
20	Torii Hunter/25	30.00
24	Ryan Wagner/50	20.00
25	Ramon Nivar/50	10.00
28	Rickie Weeks/50	40.00
29	Adam Loewen/50	20.00
32	Hank Blalock/25	30.00
40	Marty Marion/25	15.00
41	Don Mattingly/23	110.00
42	Jim Palmer/22	45.00
46	Steve Carlton/32	35.00
48	Nolan Ryan/34	125.00

Diamond Cut Combo

NM/M
Common Player: 10.00
Production 50 unless noted.

1	Alex Rodriguez	30.00
2	Nomar Garciaparra	25.00
3	Hideo Nomo/25	30.00
4	Alfonso Soriano	15.00
6	Edgar Martinez	15.00
7	Rocco Baldelli/25	25.00
8	Mark Teixeira/25	20.00
9	Albert Pujols	40.00
10	Vernon Wells/25	15.00
11	Garret Anderson/25	15.00
14	Brandon Webb/25	15.00
16	Rafael Palmeiro/25	20.00
17	Adam Dunn/25	15.00
18	Dontrelle Willis/25	15.00
19	Kazuhisa Ishii/25	15.00
20	Torii Hunter/25	15.00
21	Vladimir Guerrero/25	25.00
22	Mike Piazza	20.00
23	Jason Giambi/25	25.00
26	Bobby Abreu	10.00
27	Hee Seop Choi	10.00
30	Troy Glaus/25	20.00
31	Ivan Rodriguez/25	20.00
32	Hank Blalock/25	20.00
33	Greg Maddux	25.00
34	Nick Johnson/25	12.00
35	Shawn Green/25	15.00
36	Sammy Sosa	25.00
41	Don Mattingly/23	50.00
42	Jim Palmer/25	20.00
46	Steve Carlton/32	50.00
48	Nolan Ryan/34	50.00
49	Deion Sanders/24	25.00
50	Roberto Clemente/21	150.00

Diamond Cut Signature Combo

NM/M
Varying quantities produced

40	Marty Marion/30	30.00
46	Steve Carlton/32	45.00

DK Combos Bronze

NM/M
Varying quantities produced

26	Marlon Byrd/Bat-Jsy/30	20.00
32	Rich Harden/Jsy-Jsy/15	50.00
53	Eric Hinske/Bat-Jsy/30	20.00
57	Joe Thurston/Bat-Jsy/25	15.00
59	Jay Gibbons/Jsy-Jsy/15	35.00
65	Bob Abreu/Bat-Jsy/15	25.00
74	Aramis Ramirez/Bat-Bat/15	25.00
92	Junior Spivey/Bat-Jsy/30	30.00
101	Lyle Overbay/Bat-Jsy/30	15.00
103	Miguel Cabrera/Bat-Jsy/30	35.00
108	Angel Berroa/Bat-Pants/30	15.00
109	Hank Blalock/Bat-Jsy/30	35.00
111	Jose Castillo/Bat-Bat/15	15.00
121	Morgan Ensberg/Bat-Jsy/30	15.00
123	Orlando Hudson/Bat-Jsy/30	15.00
126	Adam LaRoche/Bat-Bat/15	15.00
130	Luis Castillo/Bat-Jsy/30	15.00
143	Travis Hafner/Bat-Jsy/30	12.00
147	Chad Gaudin/Jsy-Jsy/25	12.00

DK Combos Framed Bronze

NM/M
Varying quantities produced

26	Marlon Byrd/Bat-Jsy/25	12.00
35	Brandon Webb/Bat-Jsy/25	25.00
53	Eric Hinske/Bat-Jsy/25	12.00
57	Joe Thurston/Bat-Jsy/25	12.00
59	Jay Gibbons/Jsy-Jsy/15	15.00
62	Walter Young/Bat-Bat/15	12.00
65	Bobby Abreu/Bat-Jsy/15	15.00
71	Jason Lane/Bat-Hat/15	15.00
74	Aramis Ramirez/Bat-Bat/25	20.00
77	Chris Snelling/Bat-Bat/25	12.00
81	Joe Borchard/Bat-Jsy/25	10.00
92	Junior Spivey/Bat-Jsy/25	15.00
97	Antonio Perez/Bat-Pants/25	12.00
98	Dan Haren/Bat-Jsy/25	15.00
101	Lyle Overbay/Bat-Jsy/25	10.00
103	Miguel Cabrera/Bat-Jsy/25	40.00
107	Nic Jackson/Bat-Bat/25	10.00
108	Angel Berroa/Bat-Pants/25	12.00
109	Hank Blalock/Bat-Jsy/25	30.00
110	Ryan Klesko/Bat-Jsy/15	15.00
111	Jose Castillo/Bat-Bat/25	10.00
121	Morgan Ensberg/Bat-Jsy/15	15.00
123	Orlando Hudson/Bat-Jsy/15	15.00
126	Adam LaRoche/Bat-Bat/15	12.00
127	Hong-Chih Kuo/Bat-Bat/25	10.00
130	Luis Castillo/Bat-Jsy/25	12.00
136	Alfredo Amezaga/Bat-Jsy/15	15.00
143	Travis Hafner/Bat-Jsy/15	15.00
147	Chad Gaudin/Jsy-Jsy/25	10.00

DK Combos Silver

NM/M
Varying quantities produced

26	Marlon Byrd/Bat-Jsy/15	15.00
101	Lyle Overbay/Bat-Jsy/15	15.00
102	Miguel Cabrera/Bat-Jsy/15	50.00
108	Angel Berroa/Bat-Pants/15	15.00
109	Hank Blalock/Bat-Jsy/15	50.00
121	Morgan Ensberg/Bat-Jsy/15	20.00
123	Orlando Hudson/Bat-Jsy/15	15.00
126	Adam LaRoche/Bat-Bat/15	20.00

DK Combos Framed Silver

Framed Silver: No Pricing
Production 1-15
Framed Silver Sepia: No Pricing
Production 1-5

DK Combos Gold

Gold Combos: No Pricing
Production 1-5
Gold Combos Sepia: No Pricing
Production One Set

DK Combos Framed Gold

Framed Gold Combos: No Pricing
Production 1-5
Framed Gold Sepia: No Pricing
Production 1-5

DK Combos Platinum

Platinum Combos: No Pricing
Production One Set
Platinum Combos Sepia: No Pricing
Production One Set

DK Combos Framed Platinum

Framed Platinum: No Pricing
Production One Set

DK Materials Bronze

NM/M

Common Player:
No pricing for production 15 or less.

	NM/M
Framed Bronze	1-1.5X
Production 5-100	
Framed Bronze Sepia:	1.5-2X
Production 5-50	
Silver:	1-2X
Production 5-50	
Silver Sepia:	1.5-2X
Production 1-30	
Framed Silver:	1-2X
Production 5-75	
Framed Silver Sepia:	1.5-2X
Production 1-30	
Gold:	1.5-2X
Production 1-50	
Gold Sepia:	No Pricing
Production 1-15	
Framed Gold:	1.5-2X
Production 5-50	
Framed Gold Sepia:	No Pricing
Production 1-15	
Platinums:	No Pricing

All Platinums limited to one set.

1 Alex Rodriguez/ Bat-Jsy/150 20.00
2 Andruw Jones/ Bat-Jsy/150 8.00
3 Nomar Garciaparra/ Bat-Jsy/150 15.00
4 Kerry Wood/ Bat-Jsy/150 15.00
5 Magglio Ordonez/ Bat-Jsy/150 8.00
6 Victor Martinez/ Bat-Bat/100 6.00
7 Jeremy Bonderman/ Jsy-Jsy/30 10.00
8 Josh Beckett/ Bat-Jsy/150 10.00
9 Jeff Kent/Bat-Jsy/150 8.00
10 Carlos Beltran/ Bat-Jsy/150 8.00
11 Hideo Nomo/ Bat-Jsy/150 8.00
12 Richie Sexson/ Bat-Jsy/150 10.00
13 Jose Vidro/Bat-Jsy/50 8.00
14 Jae Weong Seo/ Jsy-Jsy/30 8.00
15 Alfonso Soriano/ Bat-Jsy/150 10.00
16 Barry Zito/ Bat-Jsy/100 10.00
17 Brett Myers/ Jsy-Jsy/30 10.00
18 Brian Giles/ Bat-Bat/100 8.00
19 Edgar Martinez/ Bat-Jsy/150 8.00
20 Jim Edmonds/ Bat-Jsy/150 8.00
21 Rocco Baldelli/ Bat-Jsy/100 12.00
22 Mark Teixeira/ Bat-Jsy/100 8.00
23 Carlos Delgado/ Bat-Jsy/150 8.00
25 Jose Reyes/ Bat-Jsy/100 8.00
26 Marlon Byrd/ Bat-Jsy/100 8.00
27 Albert Pujols/ Bat-Jsy/150 25.00
28 Vernon Wells/ Bat-Jsy/150 8.00
29 Garret Anderson/ Bat-Jsy/15 20.00

30 Jerome Williams/ Jsy-Jsy/150 8.00
31 Chipper Jones/ Bat-Jsy/150 12.00
32 Rich Harden/ Bat-Jsy/150 8.00
33 Manny Ramirez/ Bat-Jsy/150 10.00
34 Derek Jeter/ Base-Base/100 20.00
35 Brandon Webb/ Bat-Jsy/100 8.00
36 Mark Prior/ Bat-Jsy/100 15.00
37 Roy Halladay/ Jsy-Jsy/150 8.00
38 Frank Thomas/ Bat-Jsy/150 12.00
39 Rafael Palmeiro/ Bat-Jsy/150 10.00
40 Adam Dunn/ Bat-Jsy/150 8.00
41 Aubrey Huff/ Bat-Jsy/30 10.00
42 Todd Helton/ Bat-Jsy/150 10.00
43 Matt Morris/ Jsy-Jsy/100 8.00
44 Dontrelle Willis/ Bat-Jsy/100 10.00
45 Lance Berkman/ Bat-Jsy/100 8.00
46 Mike Sweeney/ Bat-Jsy/100 8.00
47 Kazuhisa Ishii/ Bat-Jsy/100 8.00
48 Torii Hunter/ Bat-Jsy/100 8.00
49 Vladimir Guerrero/ Bat-Jsy/150 15.00
50 Mike Piazza/ Bat-Jsy/150 15.00
51 Alexis Rios/ Bat-Jsy/150 12.00
52 Shannon Stewart/ Bat-Bat/100 6.00
53 Eric Hinske/ Bat-Jsy/100 6.00
54 Jason Jennings/ Bat-Jsy/150 6.00
55 Jason Giambi/ Bat-Jsy/150 10.00
57 Joe Thurston/ Bat-Jsy/150 6.00
58 Ramon Nivar/ Bat-Jsy/150 6.00
59 Jay Gibbons/ Jsy-Jsy/150 8.00
60 Eric Chavez/ Bat-Jsy/150 8.00
62 Walter Young/ Bat-Bat/100 6.00
63 Mark Grace/ Bat-Jsy/150 10.00
64 Austin Kearns/ Bat-Jsy/150 8.00
65 Bob Abreu/ Bat-Jsy/150 6.00
66 Hee Seop Choi/ Bat-Jsy/150 6.00
67 Brandon Phillips/ Bat-Jsy/150 6.00
68 Rickie Weeks/ Bat-Bat/100 15.00
69 Luis Gonzalez/ Bat-Jsy/150 6.00
70 Mariano Rivera/ Jsy-Jsy/100 10.00
71 Jason Lane/ Bat-Jsy/100 15.00
73 Runelvys Hernandez/ Jsy-Jsy/30 8.00
75 Ichiro Suzuki/ Ball-Base/15 50.00
77 Chris Snelling/ Bat-Bat/30 8.00
79 Miguel Tejada/ Bat-Jsy/150 8.00
80 Juan Gonzalez/ Bat-Jsy/150 8.00
82 Gary Sheffield/ Bat-Jsy/150 8.00
83 Wade Miller/ Bat-Jsy/50 6.00
84 Jeff Bagwell/ Bat-Jsy/150 15.00
86 Adrian Beltre/ Bat-Jsy/100 6.00
87 Jeff Baker/ Bat-Jsy/100 6.00
89 Bernie Williams/ Bat-Jsy/150 10.00
90 Pedro J. Martinez/ Bat-Jsy/150 15.00
92 Junior Spivey/ Bat-Jsy/150 8.00
93 Tim Hudson/ Bat-Jsy/150 8.00
94 Troy Glaus/ Bat-Jsy/150 8.00
95 Ken Griffey Jr./ Base-Base/100 15.00
96 Alexis Gomez/ Bat-Bat/30 10.00
97 Antonio Perez/ Bat-Pants/100 6.00
98 Dan Haren/ Bat-Jsy/100 6.00

99 Ivan Rodriguez/ Bat-Jsy/150 10.00
100 Randy Johnson/ Bat-Jsy/150 12.00
101 Lyle Overbay/ Bat-Jsy/100 6.00
103 Miguel Cabrera/ Bat-Jsy/150 15.00
104 Scott Rolen/ Bat-Jsy/100 10.00
105 Roger Clemens/ Bat-Jsy/100 20.00
107 Nic Jackson/ Bat-Bat/100 6.00
108 Angel Berroa/ Bat-Pants/30 10.00
109 Hank Blalock/ Bat-Jsy/100 10.00
110 Ryan Klesko/ Bat-Jsy/200 8.00
111 Jose Castillo/ Bat-Jsy/100 6.00
112 Paul Konerko/ Bat-Jsy/100 6.00
113 Greg Maddux/ Bat-Jsy/100 15.00
114 Mark Mulder/ Bat-Jsy/100 8.00
115 Pat Burrell/ Bat-Jsy/100 8.00
116 Garrett Atkins/ Jsy-Jsy/100 6.00
118 Orlando Cabrera/ Bat-Jsy/100 8.00
119 Nick Johnson/ Bat-Jsy/100 6.00
120 Tom Glavine/ Bat-Jsy/100 10.00
121 Morgan Ensberg/ Bat-Jsy/100 6.00
123 Orlando Hudson/ Bat-Jsy/100 6.00
124 Hideki Matsui/ Ball-Base/15 70.00
125 Craig Biggio/ Bat-Jsy/100 8.00
126 Adam LaRoche/ Bat-Bat/100 8.00
127 Hong-Chih Kuo/ Bat-Bat/100 6.00
128 Paul LoDuca/ Bat-Jsy/100 6.00
129 Shawn Green/ Bat-Jsy/100 8.00
130 Luis Castillo/ Bat-Jsy/100 6.00
132 Ken Harvey/ Bat-Bat/100 6.00
133 Freddy Sanchez/ Bat-Jsy/200 6.00
134 Roy Oswalt/ Bat-Jsy/100 8.00
135 Curt Schilling/ Bat-Jsy/100 8.00
136 Alfredo Amezaga/ Bat-Jsy/15 15.00
139 Trot Nixon/ Bat-Jsy/100 10.00
140 Jim Thome/ Bat-Jsy/150 15.00
141 Bret Boone/ Bat-Jsy/100 8.00
142 Jacque Jones/ Bat-Jsy/100 6.00
143 Todd Hafner/ Bat-Jsy/100 8.00
144 Sammy Sosa/ Bat-Jsy/100 20.00
145 Mike Mussina/ Bat-Jsy/100 12.00
147 Chad Gaudin/ Jsy-Jsy/100 6.00
149 Mike Lowell/ Bat-Jsy/100 8.00
151 Rickey Henderson/ Bat-Jsy/100 15.00
151 Roger Clemens/ FB Bat-Jsy/100 20.00
153 Rickey Henderson/ FB Bat-Jsy/30 30.00
154 Alex Rodriguez/ FB Bat-Jsy/100 20.00
155 Rafael Palmeiro/ FB Bat-Jsy/100 10.00
156 Greg Maddux/ FB Bat-Bat/100 15.00
157 Mike Piazza/ FB Bat-Jsy/100 15.00
158 Mike Mussina/ FB Bat-Jsy/100 12.00
159 Dale Murphy LGD/ Bat-Jsy/30 20.00
160 Cal Ripken Jr. LGD/ Bat-Jsy/100 50.00
161 Carl Yastrzemski LGD/ Bat-Jsy/25 25.00
162 Marty Marion LGD/ Jsy-Jsy/30 10.00
163 Don Mattingly LGD/ Bat-Jsy/100 25.00
164 Robin Yount LGD/ Bat-Jsy/100 25.00
165 Andre Dawson LGD/ Bat-Jsy/30 15.00
167 George Brett LGD/ Bat-Jsy/100 50.00
168 Whitey Ford LGD/ Jsy-Pants/30 10.00

172 Steve Carlton LGD/ Bat-Jsy/100 15.00
173 Stan Musial LGD/ Bat-Jsy/30 25.00
174 Nolan Ryan LGD/ Bat-Jsy/30 50.00
175 Deion Sanders LGD/ Bat-Jsy/100 12.00

DK Signatures Bronze

NM/M

No Pricing For Prod. less than 15

	NM/M
Framed Bronze:	1X
Production 1-50	
Bronze Sepia:	No Pricing
Production 1-15	

6 Victor Martinez/200 10.00
13 Jose Vidro/200 10.00
14 Jae Weong Seo/200 15.00
17 Brett Myers/200 10.00
19 Edgar Martinez/25 40.00
26 Marlon Byrd/200 10.00
32 Rich Harden/200 15.00
35 Brandon Webb/25 30.00
41 Aubrey Huff/100 12.00
48 Torii Hunter/100 10.00
51 Alexis Rios/200 20.00
52 Shannon Stewart/200 10.00
53 Eric Hinske/25 20.00
56 Brandon Claussen/200 10.00
57 Joe Thurston/200 8.00
58 Ramon Nivar/200 8.00
59 Jay Gibbons/25 25.00
61 Jimmy Gobble/100 15.00
62 Walter Young/200 8.00
67 Brandon Phillips/100 6.00
68 Rickie Weeks/30 40.00
71 Jason Lane/200 8.00
73 Runelvys Hernandez/50 10.00
74 Aramis Ramirez/100 8.00
76 Cliff Lee/200 10.00
77 Chris Snelling/200 8.00
78 Ryan Wagner/100 15.00
81 Joe Borchard/200 8.00
85 Ryan Church/200 8.00
87 Jeff Baker/100 10.00
88 Adam Loewen/100 20.00
91 Carlos Rivera/100 8.00
92 Junior Spivey/25 20.00
96 Alexis Gomez/200 8.00
97 Antonio Perez/46 10.00
98 Dan Haren/100 12.00
101 Lyle Overbay/200 8.00
102 Oliver Perez/200 8.00
103 Miguel Cabrera/100 35.00
106 Brian Tallet/200 8.00
107 Nic Jackson/200 8.00
108 Angel Berroa/25 8.00
109 Hank Blalock/25 35.00
111 Jose Castillo/200 8.00
114 Mark Mulder/25 30.00
116 Garrett Atkins/100 8.00
117 Jeremy Guthrie/25 8.00
118 Orlando Cabrera/75 12.00
121 Morgan Ensberg/200 10.00
123 Orlando Hudson/100 10.00
126 Adam LaRoche/100 15.00
127 Hong-Chih Kuo/25 75.00
130 Luis Castillo/25 20.00
131 Joe Crede/100 8.00
132 Ken Harvey/200 8.00
133 Freddy Sanchez/50 8.00
136 Alfredo Amezaga/90 8.00
137 Chien-Ming Wang/25 125.00
142 Jacque Jones/25 20.00
143 Travis Hafner/100 10.00
146 Vinnie Chulk/200 8.00
147 Chad Gaudin/100 8.00
149 Mike Lowell/25 20.00

DK Signatures Silver

NM/M

No pricing for prod. less than 15

	NM/M
Framed Silver:	1.5-2X
Production 1-25	
Silver Sepia:	No Pricing
Production 1-10	

6 Victor Martinez/49 15.00
13 Jose Vidro/20 20.00
14 Jae Weong Seo/80 15.00
17 Brett Myers/90 15.00
26 Marlon Byrd/100 10.00
32 Rich Harden/100 15.00
35 Brandon Webb/15 35.00
41 Aubrey Huff/40 12.00
51 Alexis Rios/100 20.00
52 Shannon Stewart/30 15.00
56 Brandon Claussen/100 10.00
57 Joe Thurston/100 8.00
58 Ramon Nivar/30 15.00
61 Jimmy Gobble/100 8.00
62 Walter Young/100 8.00
67 Brandon Phillips/30 8.00
68 Rickie Weeks/20 50.00
71 Jason Lane/100 8.00
73 Runelvys Hernandez/30 10.00
74 Aramis Ramirez/30 25.00
76 Cliff Lee/100 10.00
77 Chris Snelling/100 8.00
78 Ryan Wagner/30 20.00
81 Joe Borchard/100 8.00
85 Ryan Church/100 8.00
87 Jeff Baker/30 15.00
88 Adam Loewen/30 8.00
96 Alexis Gomez/100 8.00
98 Dan Haren/30 15.00
101 Lyle Overbay/100 8.00
102 Oliver Perez/100 8.00
103 Miguel Cabrera/30 40.00
106 Brian Tallet/100 8.00
107 Nic Jackson/100 8.00
109 Hank Blalock/30 35.00
111 Jose Castillo/100 8.00
116 Garrett Atkins/30 10.00
121 Morgan Ensberg/50 15.00
123 Orlando Hudson/30 15.00
126 Adam LaRoche/20 20.00
131 Joe Crede/35 12.00
132 Ken Harvey/30 10.00
136 Alfredo Amezaga/30 10.00
143 Travis Hafner/30 15.00
146 Vinnie Chulk/30 8.00
147 Chad Gaudin/30 10.00

DK Signatures Gold

NM/M

Many not priced due to scarcity.

	NM/M
Framed Gold:	No Pricing
Production 1-5	
Gold Sepia:	No Pricing
Production 1-5	

32 Rich Harden/50 15.00
51 Alexis Rios/50 25.00
56 Brandon Claussen/50 15.00
57 Joe Thurston/50 10.00
62 Walter Young/50 10.00
71 Jason Lane/40 15.00
77 Chris Snelling/50 10.00
81 Joe Borchard/50 10.00
85 Ryan Church/50 10.00
96 Alexis Gomez/50 10.00
101 Lyle Overbay/50 10.00
102 Oliver Perez/50 10.00
106 Brian Tallet/50 10.00
107 Nic Jackson/50 10.00
121 Morgan Ensberg/48 15.00
146 Vinnie Chulk/50 10.00

DK Signatures Platinum

No Pricing
Production One Set
Framed Platinum: No Pricing
Platinum Sepia: No Pricing
Production One Set

Gallery of Stars

NM/M

Complete Set (15): 50.00
Common Player: 2.00
Inserted 1:37

1 Nolan Ryan 8.00
2 Cal Ripken Jr. 8.00
3 George Brett 6.00
4 Don Mattingly 6.00
5 Deion Sanders 2.00
6 Mike Piazza 4.00
7 Hideo Nomo 2.00
8 Rickey Henderson 2.00
9 Roger Clemens 6.00
10 Greg Maddux 4.00
11 Albert Pujols 6.00
12 Alex Rodriguez 6.00
13 Dale Murphy 3.00
14 Mark Prior 4.00
15 Dontrelle Willis 2.00

Heritage Collection

NM/M

Complete Set (25): 75.00
Common Player: 2.00
Inserted 1:22

1 Dale Murphy 3.00
2 Cal Ripken Jr. 8.00
3 Carl Yastrzemski 4.00
4 Don Mattingly 6.00
5 Jim Palmer 2.00
6 Andre Dawson 2.00
7 Roy Campanella 3.00
8 George Brett 6.00
9 Duke Snider 4.00
10 Marty Marion 2.00
11 Deion Sanders 2.00
12 Whitey Ford 3.00
13 Stan Musial 5.00
14 Nolan Ryan 8.00
15 Steve Carlton 2.00
16 Robin Yount 3.00
17 Albert Pujols 6.00
18 Alex Rodriguez 6.00
19 Mike Piazza 4.00
20 Roger Clemens 6.00
21 Hideo Nomo 2.00
22 Mark Prior 4.00
23 Roger Maris 5.00
24 Greg Maddux 4.00
25 Mark Grace 2.00

Heritage Collection Auto.

No Pricing

Heritage Collection Bat

NM/M

Production 50 unless noted.

1 Dale Murphy 20.00
2 Cal Ripken Jr. 40.00
3 Carl Yastrzemski 20.00
4 Don Mattingly 30.00
6 Andre Dawson/25 30.00
7 Roy Campanella/25 30.00
8 George Brett/25 40.00
11 Deion Sanders 10.00
13 Stan Musial/25 35.00
14 Nolan Ryan/25 40.00
15 Steve Carlton/25 20.00
16 Robin Yount 20.00
17 Albert Pujols 25.00
18 Alex Rodriguez 25.00
19 Mike Piazza 25.00
20 Roger Clemens 25.00
21 Hideo Nomo 15.00
22 Mark Prior 15.00
23 Roger Maris/25 50.00
24 Greg Maddux 15.00
25 Mark Grace 10.00

Heritage Collection Jersey

NM/M

Production 50 unless noted.

1 Dale Murphy 15.00
2 Cal Ripken Jr. 40.00
3 Carl Yastrzemski 20.00
4 Don Mattingly 30.00
6 Andre Dawson/25 20.00
7 Roy Campanella/25 40.00
8 George Brett/25 30.00
10 Marty Marion 10.00
11 Deion Sanders 10.00
12 Whitey Ford/25 25.00
14 Nolan Ryan/25 40.00
15 Steve Carlton/25 20.00
16 Robin Yount 20.00
17 Albert Pujols 25.00
18 Alex Rodriguez 25.00
19 Mike Piazza 15.00
20 Roger Clemens 25.00
21 Hideo Nomo 15.00
22 Mark Prior 15.00
23 Roger Maris/25 50.00
24 Greg Maddux 15.00
25 Mark Grace 10.00

HOF Heroes

George Brett

NM/M

Common Player: 2.50

1 George Brett/1,000 6.00
2 George Brett/500 8.00
3 George Brett/250 12.00
4 Mike Schmidt/1,000 5.00
5 Mike Schmidt/250 10.00
6 Nolan Ryan/1,000 8.00
7 Nolan Ryan/500 10.00
8 Nolan Ryan/250 15.00
9 Roberto Clemente/1,000 6.00
10 Roberto Clemente/500 10.00
11 Roberto Clemente/250 15.00
12 Roberto Clemente/100 20.00
13 Carl Yastrzemski/1,000 4.00
14 Robin Yount/1,000 4.00
15 Whitey Ford/1,000 4.00
16 Duke Snider/1,000 4.00
17 Duke Snider/1,000 8.00
18 Carlton Fisk/1,000 3.00
19 Ozzie Smith/1,000 4.00

20	Kirby Puckett/1,000	4.00
21	Bobby Doerr/1,000	2.50
22	Frank Robinson/1,000	3.00
23	Ralph Kiner/1,000	2.50
24	Al Kaline/1,000	4.00
25	Bob Feller/1,000	3.00
26	Yogi Berra/1,000	4.00
27	Stan Musial/1,000	5.00
28	Stan Musial/500	8.00
29	Stan Musial/250	10.00
30	Jim Palmer/1,000	2.50
31	Johnny Bench/1,000	4.00
32	Steve Carlton/1,000	3.00
33	Gary Carter/1,000	3.00
34	Roy Campanella/1,000	3.00
35	Roy Campanella/250	8.00

HOF Heroes Bat

NM/M
Production 25 unless noted.

1	George Brett	35.00
2	George Brett	35.00
3	George Brett	35.00
4	Mike Schmidt	35.00
5	Mike Schmidt	35.00
6	Nolan Ryan	40.00
7	Nolan Ryan	40.00
8	Nolan Ryan	40.00
13	Carl Yastrzemski	30.00
14	Robin Yount	35.00
18	Carlton Fisk	25.00
19	Ozzie Smith	30.00
20	Kirby Puckett	30.00
21	Bobby Doerr	20.00
22	Frank Robinson	15.00
23	Ralph Kiner	15.00
24	Al Kaline	25.00
31	Johnny Bench	25.00
32	Steve Carlton	20.00
33	Gary Carter	20.00
34	Roy Campanella	30.00
35	Roy Campanella	30.00

HOF Heroes Jersey

NM/M
Production 25 unless noted.

1	George Brett	35.00
2	George Brett	35.00
3	George Brett	35.00
4	Mike Schmidt	35.00
5	Mike Schmidt	35.00
6	Nolan Ryan	40.00
7	Nolan Ryan	40.00
8	Nolan Ryan	40.00
13	Carl Yastrzemski	30.00
14	Robin Yount	35.00
15	Whitey Ford	30.00
18	Carlton Fisk	25.00
19	Ozzie Smith	30.00
20	Kirby Puckett	30.00
21	Bobby Doerr	20.00
24	Al Kaline	25.00
32	Steve Carlton	20.00
33	Gary Carter	20.00
34	Roy Campanella	30.00
35	Roy Campanella	30.00

HOF Heroes Combo

Production 25 unless noted.
NM/M

1	George Brett	50.00
2	George Brett	50.00
3	George Brett	50.00
4	Mike Schmidt	40.00
5	Mike Schmidt	40.00
6	Nolan Ryan	50.00
7	Nolan Ryan	50.00
8	Nolan Ryan	50.00
13	Carl Yastrzemski	40.00
14	Robin Yount	40.00
15	Whitey Ford	30.00
18	Carlton Fisk	30.00
19	Ozzie Smith	40.00
20	Kirby Puckett	40.00
21	Bobby Doerr	25.00
23	Ralph Kiner	20.00
24	Al Kaline	35.00
32	Steve Carlton	30.00
33	Gary Carter	25.00
34	Roy Campanella	40.00
35	Roy Campanella	40.00

HOF Heroes Signature

NM/M
Many not priced.

14	Robin Yount/19	70.00
15	Whitey Ford/16	50.00
22	Frank Robinson/20	50.00
25	Bob Feller/19	40.00
30	Jim Palmer/22	40.00
32	Steve Carlton/32	35.00

Recollection Autographs

NM/M
Varying quantities produced

6	Clint Barmes 03 DK Black/82	10.00
7	Clint Barmes 03 DK Blue/72	10.00
8	Carlos Beltran 02 DK/23	20.00
9	Carlos Beltran 03 DK/99	15.00
10	Adrian Beltre 02 DK/40	10.00
19	Chris Burke 03 DK/150	10.00
20	Marlon Byrd 02 DK/23	15.00
21	Marlon Byrd 03 DK/100	10.00
24	Kevin Cash 03 DK/103	10.00
25	Jose Cruz 85 DK/59	10.00
26	J.D. Durbin 03 DK/151	10.00
27	Jim Edmonds 03 DK/24	25.00
32	Julio Franco 87 DK/25	20.00
33	Freddy Garcia 03 DK/50	20.00
34	Jay Gibbons 03 DK/100	12.00
39	Brendan Harris 03 DK/150	8.00
42	Runelvys Hernandez 02 DK/100	8.00
43	Eric Hinske 03 DK/20	20.00
44	Tim Hudson 02 DK/25	30.00
45	Tim Hudson 03 DK/25	30.00
46	Aubrey Huff 03 DK/99	15.00
49	Jason Jennings 03 DK/50	10.00
50	Tommy John 88 DK Black/62	15.00
52	Howard Johnson 90 DK/52	10.00
54	Austin Kearns 02 DK/25	30.00
55	Austin Kearns 03 DK/25	30.00
59	Preston Larrison 03 DK Black/74	10.00
60	Preston Larrison 03 DK Blue/77	10.00
67	Dustin McGowan 03 DK/159	8.00
69	Melvin Mora 03 DK/101	8.00
71	Jack Morris 03 DK/60	10.00
72	Jack Morris 03 DK Her/19	20.00
74	Dale Murphy 03 DK Blue/47	30.00
82	Magglio Ordonez 03 DK/25	30.00
85	Dave Parker 82 DK/20	30.00
86	Dave Parker 90 DK/18	30.00
88	Jorge Posada 02 DK/25	50.00
89	Mark Prior 03 DK/25	100.00
94	Mike Rivera 02 DK/24	15.00
97	Ivan Rodriguez 03 DK/22	40.00
100	Rodrigo Rosario 03 DK/50	8.00
105	Ron Santo 02 DK/29	35.00
106	Richie Sexson 02 DK/25	25.00
107	Richie Sexson 03 DK/25	25.00
109	Chris Snelling 02 DK/46	12.00
119	Shannon Stewart 02 DK/50	15.00
120	Shannon Stewart 03 DK Black/92	12.00
126	Gorman Thomas 82 DK Black/22	20.00
127	Gorman Thomas 82 DK Blue/20	20.00
128	Alan Trammell 02 DK/29	30.00
129	Alan Trammell 02 DK Her/25	30.00
130	Robin Ventura 03 DK/25	20.00
131	Jose Vidro 03 DK/25	20.00
132	Rickie Weeks 03 DK/52	50.00
133	Kevin Youkilis 03 DK/153	15.00

Timeline

NM/M
Common Player: 3.00
Inserted 1:92

1	Roger Clemens	6.00
2	Mark Grace	3.00
3	Mike Mussina	3.00
4	Mike Piazza	4.00
5	Nolan Ryan	8.00
6	Rickey Henderson	3.00

Team Timeline

NM/M
Complete Set (19): 65.00
Common Duo: 2.00
Inserted 1:29

1	Deion Sanders, Andruw Jones	2.00
2	Rickie Weeks, Robin Yount	3.00
3	Don Mattingly, Whitey Ford	8.00
4	Chipper Jones, Dale Murphy	4.00
5	Nomar Garciaparra, Bobby Doerr	5.00
6	Mark Prior, Sammy Sosa	5.00
7	Hideo Nomo, Kazuhisa Ishii	2.00
8	Andre Dawson, Mark Grace	3.00
9	Roger Clemens, Carl Yastrzemski	6.00
10	Mike Mussina, Cal Ripken Jr.	8.00
11	Stan Musial, Albert Pujols	8.00
12	Jim Palmer, Mike Mussina	2.00
13	Marty Marion, Stan Musial	4.00
14	George Brett, Mike Sweeney	6.00
15	Roger Clemens, Roger Maris	6.00
16	Duke Snider, Shawn Green	3.00
17	Jim Thome, Mike Schmidt	4.00
18	Nolan Ryan, Alex Rodriguez	8.00
19	Roy Campanella, Mike Piazza	4.00

Team Timeline Bat

NM/M
Production 25 unless noted.

1	Deion Sanders, Andruw Jones	15.00
2	Rickie Weeks, Robin Yount	40.00
3	Don Mattingly, Whitey Ford	60.00
4	Chipper Jones, Dale Murphy	35.00
5	Nomar Garciaparra, Bobby Doerr	30.00
6	Mark Prior, Sammy Sosa	40.00
7	Hideo Nomo, Kazuhisa Ishii	40.00
8	Andre Dawson, Mark Grace	20.00
9	Roger Clemens, Carl Yastrzemski	50.00
10	Mike Mussina, Cal Ripken Jr.	75.00
11	Stan Musial, Albert Pujols	65.00
12	Jim Palmer, Mike Mussina	25.00
14	George Brett, Mike Sweeney	30.00
15	Roger Clemens, Roger Maris	60.00
17	Jim Thome, Mike Schmidt	40.00
18	Nolan Ryan, Alex Rodriguez	60.00
19	Roy Campanella, Mike Piazza	40.00

Team Timeline Jersey

NM/M
Production 25 Sets
Prime: No Pricing
Production One Set

1	Deion Sanders, Andruw Jones	15.00
2	Rickie Weeks, Robin Yount	40.00
3	Don Mattingly, Whitey Ford	60.00
4	Chipper Jones, Dale Murphy	35.00

5	Nomar Garciaparra, Bobby Doerr	30.00
6	Mark Prior, Sammy Sosa	40.00
7	Hideo Nomo, Kazuhisa Ishii	40.00
8	Andre Dawson, Mark Grace	20.00
9	Roger Clemens, Carl Yastrzemski	50.00
10	Mike Mussina, Cal Ripken Jr.	75.00
14	George Brett, Mike Sweeney	30.00
15	Roger Clemens, Roger Maris	60.00
17	Jim Thome, Mike Schmidt	40.00
18	Nolan Ryan, Alex Rodriguez	60.00
19	Roy Campanella, Mike Piazza	40.00

2004 Donruss Elite

NM/M
Complete Set (205):
Common Player: .25
Common Auto. (151-180): 5.00
Production 250-1,000
Common (181-200): 2.00
Production 1,000
Pack (5): 5.00
Box (24): 100.00

1	Troy Glaus	.40
2	Darin Erstad	.25
3	Garret Anderson	.40
4	Tim Salmon	.40
5	Bartolo Colon	.40
6	Jose Guillen	.25
7	Miguel Tejada	.40
8	Adam Loewen	.25
9	Jay Gibbons	.25
10	Melvin Mora	.25
11	Javy Lopez	.40
12	Pedro J. Martinez	.75
13	Curt Schilling	.50
14	David Ortiz	.50
15	Keith Foulke	.25
16	Nomar Garciaparra	1.00
17	Magglio Ordonez	.40
18	Frank Thomas	.50
19	Carlos Lee	.40
20	Paul Konerko	.40
21	Mark Buehrle	.25
22	Jody Gerut	.25
23	Victor Martinez	.25
24	C.C. Sabathia	.25
25	Ellis Burks	.25
26	Bobby Higginson	.25
27	Jeremy Bonderman	.25
28	Fernando Vina	.25
29	Carlos Pena	.25
30	Dmitri Young	.25
31	Carlos Beltran	.50
32	Benito Santiago	.25
33	Mike Sweeney	.25
34	Angel Berroa	.25
35	Runelvys Hernandez	.25
36	Johan Santana	.40
37	Doug Mientkiewicz	.25
38	Shannon Stewart	.25
39	Torii Hunter	.25
40	Derek Jeter	2.00
41	Jason Giambi	.50
42	Bernie Williams	.50
43	Alfonso Soriano	.50
44	Gary Sheffield	.40
45	Mike Mussina	.50
46	Jorge Posada	.40
47	Hideki Matsui	1.00
48	Kevin Brown	.40
49	Javier Vazquez	.40
50	Mariano Rivera	.40
51	Eric Chavez	.40
52	Tim Hudson	.40
53	Mark Mulder	.40
54	Barry Zito	.40
55	Ichiro Suzuki	1.00
56	Edgar Martinez	.40
57	Bret Boone	.40
58	John Olerud	.40
59	Scott Spiezio	.25
60	Aubrey Huff	.40
61	Rocco Baldelli	.40
62	Jose Cruz Jr.	.25
63	Delmon Young	.40
64	Mark Teixeira	.40
65	Hank Blalock	.50
66	Michael Young	.40
67	Alex Rodriguez	2.00
68	Carlos Delgado	.50
69	Eric Hinske	.40
70	Roy Halladay	.40
71	Vernon Wells	.40
72	Randy Johnson	.75
73	Richie Sexson	.50
74	Brandon Webb	.25
75	Luis Gonzalez	.40
76	Steve Finley	.25
77	Chipper Jones	.75
78	Andruw Jones	.50
79	Marcus Giles	.25
80	Rafael Furcal	.25
81	J.D. Drew	.40
82	Sammy Sosa	1.50
83	Kerry Wood	.75
84	Mark Prior	1.00
85	Derrek Lee	.40
86	Moises Alou	.40
87	Corey Patterson	.40
88	Ken Griffey Jr.	1.00
89	Austin Kearns	.40
90	Adam Dunn	.50
91	Barry Larkin	.40
92	Todd Helton	.50
93	Larry Walker	.40
94	Preston Wilson	.25
95	Charles Johnson	.25
96	Luis Castillo	.25
97	Josh Beckett	.40
98	Mike Lowell	.40
99	Miguel Cabrera	.75
100	Juan Pierre	.25
101	Dontrelle Willis	.40
102	Andy Pettitte	.40
103	Wade Miller	.25
104	Jeff Bagwell	.50
105	Craig Biggio	.40
106	Lance Berkman	.40
107	Jeff Kent	.40
108	Roy Oswalt	.40
109	Hideo Nomo	.40
110	Adrian Beltre	.25
111	Paul LoDuca	.25
112	Shawn Green	.40
113	Fred McGriff	.40
114	Eric Gagne	.40
115	Geoff Jenkins	.40
116	Rickie Weeks	.40
117	Scott Podsednik	.40
118	Nick Johnson	.25
119	Orlando Cabrera	.25
120	Jose Vidro	.25
121	Kazuo Matsui RC	5.00
122	Tom Glavine	.40
123	Al Leiter	.40
124	Mike Piazza	1.00
125	Jose Reyes	.50
126	Mike Cameron	.25
127	Pat Burrell	.40
128	Jim Thome	.75
129	Mike Lieberthal	.25
130	Bobby Abreu	.40
131	Kip Wells	.25
132	Jack Wilson	.25
133	Pokey Reese	.25
134	Brian Giles	.40
135	Sean Burroughs	.25
136	Ryan Klesko	.40
137	Trevor Hoffman	.25
138	Jason Schmidt	.40
139	J.T. Snow	.25
140	A.J. Pierzynski	.25
141	Ray Durham	.25
142	Jim Edmonds	.40
143	Albert Pujols	1.50
144	Edgar Renteria	.40
145	Scott Rolen	.75
146	Matt Morris	.25
147	Ivan Rodriguez	.50
148	Vladimir Guerrero	.75
149	Greg Maddux	1.00
150	Kevin Millwood	.40
151	Hector Gimenez AU/750 RC	5.00
152	Willy Taveras AU/750 RC	15.00
153	Ruddy Yan AU/750 RC	15.00
154	Graham Koonce AU/750	8.00
155	Jose Capellan AU/750 RC	15.00
156	Onil Joseph AU/750 RC	5.00
157	John Gall AU/1000 RC	10.00
158	Carlos Hines AU/750 RC	5.00
159	Jerry Gil AU/750 RC	5.00
160	Mike Gosling AU/750 RC	5.00
161	Jason Frasor AU/750 RC	5.00
162	Justin Knoedler AU/750 RC	5.00
163	Merkin Valdez AU/500 RC	10.00
164	Angel Chavez AU/1000 RC	5.00
165	Ivan Ochoa AU/750 RC	10.00
166	Greg Dobbs AU/750 RC	5.00
167	Ronald Belisario AU/750 RC	5.00
168	Aarom Baldiris AU/750 RC	10.00
170	David Crouthers AU/750	5.00
171	Freddy Guzman AU/750 RC	10.00
172	Akinori Otsuka AU/250 RC	25.00
173	Ian Snell AU/750 RC	30.00
174	Nick Regilio AU/1000 RC	5.00
175	Jamie Brown AU/750 RC	5.00
176	Jerome Gamble AU/750 RC	5.00
177	Roberto Novoa AU/1000 RC	5.00
178	Sean Henn AU/1000	10.00
179	Ramon Ramirez AU/1000 RC	10.00
180	Jason Bartlett AU/1000 RC	10.00
181	Bob Gibson/RET	2.00
182	Cal Ripken Jr./RET	8.00
183	Carl Yastrzemski/RET	4.00
184	Dale Murphy/RET	3.00
185	Don Mattingly/RET	6.00
186	Eddie Murray/RET	2.00
187	George Brett/RET	6.00
188	Jackie Robinson/RET	4.00
189	Jim Palmer/RET	2.00
190	Lou Gehrig/RET	5.00
191	Mike Schmidt/RET	5.00
192	Ozzie Smith/RET	5.00
193	Nolan Ryan/RET	8.00
194	Reggie Jackson/RET	3.00
195	Roberto Clemente/RET	6.00
196	Robin Yount/RET	4.00
197	Stan Musial/RET	5.00
198	Ted Williams/RET	8.00
199	Tony Gwynn/RET	3.00
200	Ty Cobb/RET	5.00
201	James Gandolfini/FG	3.00
202	Freddy Adu/FG	3.00
203	Summer Sanders/FG	1.50
204	Janet Evans/FG	1.50
205	Brandi Chastain/FG	1.50

Aspirations

Cards (1-150) print run

61-99:	4-8X
(1-150) p/r 41-60:	6-10X
(1-150) p/r 21-40:	8-15X
Autos. (151-180):	.75-1.5X
(181-200):	2-3X

Production 19-99

Status

Cards (1-150) print run
61-81: 4-8X
(1-150) p/r 41-60: 6-10X
(1-150) p/r 21-40: 8-15X
Autos (151-180): .75-1X
(181-200): 3-4X
Production 1-81

Status Gold
Gold (1-150): 10-20X
Gold (151-180): No Pricing
Gold (181-200): 3-6X
Production 24 Sets

Back to the Future
NM/M
#1-6
Production 500
#6-9
Production 250
Black: 1-2X
Production 25 or 50
Gold: .75-1.5X
Production 50 or 100
Red: 1X
Production 125 or 250
1 Tim Hudson 2.00
2 Rich Harden 1.50
3 Alex Rodriguez/Rgr 5.00
4 Hank Blalock 3.00
5 Sammy Sosa 5.00
6 Hee Seop Choi 1.50
7 Tim Hudson, Rich Harden 3.00
8 Alex Rodriguez, Hank Blalock 6.00
9 Sammy Sosa, Hee Seop Choi 6.00

Back to the Future Bats
NM/M
#1-6
Production 200
#8-9
Production 100
1 Tim Hudson 4.00
3 Alex Rodriguez 10.00
4 Hank Blalock 6.00
5 Sammy Sosa 10.00
6 Hee Seop Choi 4.00
8 Alex Rodriguez, Hank Blalock 12.00
9 Sammy Sosa, Hee Seop Choi 12.00

Back to the Future Jerseys
NM/M
#1-6
Production 200
#7-9
Production 100
Prime: 1.5-2X
Production 25 or 50
1 Tim Hudson 4.00
2 Rich Harden 4.00
3 Alex Rodriguez/Rgr 10.00
4 Hank Blalock 6.00
5 Sammy Sosa 10.00
6 Hee Seop Choi 4.00
7 Tim Hudson, Rich Harden 8.00
8 Alex Rodriguez, Hank Blalock 12.00
9 Sammy Sosa, Hee Seop Choi 12.00

Back 2 Back Jacks
NM/M
Singles Production 25-125
Duals Production 25-50
1 Albert Pujols/125 15.00
2 Alex Rodriguez/125 10.00
3 Alfonso Soriano/125 8.00
4 Andruw Jones/125 5.00
5 Chipper Jones/125 8.00
6 Derek Jeter/125 20.00
7 Frank Thomas/125 8.00
8 Miguel Cabrera/125 8.00
9 Jason Giambi/125 8.00
10 Jim Thome/125 8.00
11 Mike Piazza/125 10.00
12 Nomar Garciaparra/25 35.00
13 Sammy Sosa/125 8.00
14 Shawn Green/125 4.00
15 Vladimir Guerrero/125 8.00
16 Andruw Jones, Chipper Jones/50 20.00
17 Alfonso Soriano, Derek Jeter/50 30.00
18 Jeff Bagwell, Lance Berkman/50 15.00
19 Alex Rodriguez, Rafael Palmeiro/50 20.00
20 Adam Dunn, Austin Kearns/25 20.00
21 Al Kaline/100 15.00
22 Babe Ruth/50 140.00
23 Cal Ripken Jr./100 20.00
24 Dale Murphy/100 10.00
25 Don Mattingly/100 15.00
26 George Brett/100 20.00
27 Lou Gehrig/100 85.00
28 Mike Schmidt/100 15.00
29 Roberto Clemente/100 50.00
30 Roy Campanella/100 15.00
31 Babe Ruth, Roger Maris/25 200.00
32 Harmon Killebrew, Kirby Puckett/50 35.00
33 Paul Molitor, Robin Yount/50 40.00
34 Reggie Jackson/50 15.00
35 Lou Gehrig, Ty Cobb/50 200.00
36 Don Mattingly, Jason Giambi/50 25.00
37 Ted Williams, Nomar Garciaparra/50 75.00
38 Andre Dawson, Sammy Sosa/50 25.00
39 Dale Murphy, Chipper Jones/50 15.00
40 Stan Musial, Jim Edmonds/50 25.00

Back 2 Back Jacks Combos
NM/M
Singles Production 25-50
Duals Production 10-25
1 Albert Pujols/Bat-Jsy/50 30.00
2 Alex Rodriguez/Bat-Jsy/50 20.00
3 Alfonso Soriano/Bat-Jsy/50 15.00
4 Andruw Jones/Bat-Jsy/50 8.00
5 Chipper Jones/Bat-Jsy/50 12.00
6 Derek Jeter/Bat-Jsy/50 35.00
7 Frank Thomas/Bat-Jsy/50 15.00
8 Miguel Cabrera/Bat-Jsy/50 15.00
9 Jason Giambi/Bat-Jsy/50 15.00
10 Jim Thome/Bat-Jsy/50 15.00
11 Mike Piazza/Bat-Jsy/50 20.00
12 Nomar Garciaparra/Bat-Jsy/50 20.00
13 Sammy Sosa/Bat-Jsy/50 20.00
14 Shawn Green/Bat-Jsy/50 6.00
15 Vladimir Guerrero/Bat-Jsy/50 15.00
16 Andruw Jones, Chipper Jones/25 30.00
17 Alfonso Soriano, Lance Berkman/25 50.00
18 Jeff Bagwell, Lance Berkman/25 20.00
19 Alex Rodriguez, Rafael Palmeiro/25 30.00
20 Adam Dunn, Austin Kearns/25 20.00
21 Al Kaline/Bat-Jsy/25 25.00
22 Babe Ruth/Bat-Jsy/50 350.00
23 Cal Ripken Jr./Bat-Jsy/50 60.00
24 Dale Murphy/Bat-Jsy/50 15.00
25 Don Mattingly/Bat-Jsy/50 25.00
26 George Brett/Bat-Jsy/50 30.00
27 Lou Gehrig/Bat-Jsy/50 150.00
28 Mike Schmidt/Bat-Jsy/50 30.00
29 Roberto Clemente/Bat-Jsy/50 80.00
30 Roy Campanella/Bat-Jsy/50 25.00
31 Babe Ruth, Roger Maris/10 185.00
32 Harmon Killebrew, Kirby Puckett/25 50.00
33 Paul Molitor, Robin Yount/25 50.00
34 Reggie Jackson/25 25.00
35 Lou Gehrig, Ty Cobb/25 350.00
36 Don Mattingly, Jason Giambi/25 35.00
37 Ted Williams, Nomar Garciaparra 140.00
38 Andre Dawson, Sammy Sosa 40.00
39 Dale Murphy, Chipper Jones 20.00
40 Stan Musial, Jim Edmonds 35.00

Career Best
NM/M
Common Player: 1.00
Production 1,000 Sets
Black: 2X
Production 100 Sets
Gold Print Run 200-390: 1.5X
Gold P/R 101-200: 2X
Gold P/R 50-100: 3X
Gold P/R 26-50: 3-5X
Gold P/R 15-25: 5-8X
1 Albert Pujols 3.00
2 Alex Rodriguez 3.00
3 Alfonso Soriano 1.50
4 Andruw Jones 1.00
5 Barry Zito 1.00
6 Cal Ripken Jr. 5.00
7 Chipper Jones 1.50
8 Curt Schilling 1.00
9 Derek Jeter 4.00
10 Don Mattingly 4.00
11 Dontrelle Willis 1.00
12 Doc Gooden 1.00
13 Eddie Murray 1.50
14 Frank Thomas 1.50
15 Gary Sheffield 1.00
16 George Brett 4.00
17 Greg Maddux 2.00
18 Hideo Nomo 1.00
19 Ichiro Suzuki 2.00
20 Ivan Rodriguez 1.50
21 Jason Giambi 1.50
22 Jeff Bagwell 1.50
23 Jim Thome 1.50
24 Kerry Wood 1.50
25 Lance Berkman 1.00
26 Magglio Ordonez 1.00
27 Mark Prior 2.00
28 Mike Piazza 2.00
29 Mike Schmidt 3.00
30 Nomar Garciaparra 2.50
31 Pedro J. Martinez 2.00
32 Randy Johnson 2.00
33 Roger Clemens 3.00
34 Sammy Sosa 2.50
35 Tony Gwynn 1.50

Career Best Bats
NM/M
#1-30
Production 100 or 200
Combo Print Run 50: 1-2X
Combo P/R 25: 2X
Production 25 or 50
1 Albert Pujols/200 15.00
2 Alex Rodriguez/200 10.00
3 Alfonso Soriano/200 8.00
4 Andruw Jones/200 5.00
5 Barry Zito/200 4.00
6 Cal Ripken Jr./200 25.00
7 Chipper Jones/200 8.00
8 Curt Schilling/200 5.00
9 Derek Jeter/200 15.00
10 Don Mattingly/200 15.00
11 Dontrelle Willis/100 6.00
12 Doc Gooden/200 6.00
13 Eddie Murray/200 4.00
14 Frank Thomas/200 8.00
15 Gary Sheffield/200 5.00
16 George Brett/200 15.00
17 Greg Maddux/100 10.00
18 Hideo Nomo/100 4.00
19 Ivan Rodriguez/200 8.00
20 Jason Giambi/200 8.00
21 Jeff Bagwell/200 8.00
22 Jim Thome/200 8.00
23 Kerry Wood/100 8.00
24 Lance Berkman/200 5.00
25 Magglio Ordonez/200 4.00
26 Mark Prior/100 8.00
27 Mike Piazza/200 8.00
28 Mike Schmidt/200 10.00
29 Nomar Garciaparra/200 8.00
30 Pedro J. Martinez/200 8.00
31 Randy Johnson/200 8.00
32 Roger Clemens/200 15.00
33 Sammy Sosa/200 10.00
34 Tony Gwynn/200 8.00

Career Best Jerseys
NM/M
Quantity produced listed
Prime: 1.5-2X
Production 25-50
1 Albert Pujols/200 15.00
2 Alex Rodriguez/200 10.00
3 Alfonso Soriano/200 8.00
4 Andruw Jones/200 5.00
5 Barry Zito/200 4.00
6 Cal Ripken Jr./50 40.00
7 Chipper Jones/200 8.00
8 Curt Schilling/200 5.00
9 Derek Jeter/200 15.00
10 Don Mattingly/50 20.00
11 Dontrelle Willis/200 6.00
12 Doc Gooden/200 6.00
13 Eddie Murray/200 6.00
14 Frank Thomas/200 8.00
15 Gary Sheffield/200 5.00
16 George Brett/50 25.00
17 Greg Maddux/200 10.00
18 Hideo Nomo/200 8.00
20 Ivan Rodriguez/200 8.00
21 Jason Giambi/200 8.00
22 Jeff Bagwell/200 8.00
23 Jim Thome/200 8.00
24 Kerry Wood/200 10.00
25 Lance Berkman/200 4.00
26 Magglio Ordonez/200 4.00
27 Mark Prior/200 8.00
28 Mike Piazza/200 10.00
29 Mike Schmidt/100 10.00
30 Nomar Garciaparra/200 10.00
31 Pedro J. Martinez/200 8.00
32 Randy Johnson/200 8.00
33 Roger Clemens/200 15.00
34 Sammy Sosa/200 8.00
35 Tony Gwynn/50 15.00

Passing the Torch
NM/M
#1-30
Production 1,000
#31-45
Production 500
Black: 1-2X
Production 50 or 100
Blue: 1X
Production 125 or 250
Gold: 1.5-3X
Production 25 or 50
Green: .75-1X
Production 250 or 500
1 Whitey Ford 3.00
2 Andy Pettitte 1.50
3 Willie McCovey 2.00
4 Will Clark 3.00
5 Stan Musial 4.00
6 Albert Pujols 5.00
7 Andre Dawson 2.00
8 Vladimir Guerrero 2.00
9 Dale Murphy 2.00
10 Chipper Jones 2.00
11 Joe Morgan 1.50
12 Barry Larkin 1.50
13 Jim "Catfish" Hunter 1.50
14 Tim Hudson 1.50
15 Jim Rice 1.50
16 Manny Ramirez 2.00
17 Greg Maddux 2.50
18 Mark Prior 2.00
19 Don Mattingly 4.00
20 Jason Giambi 2.00
21 Roy Campanella 2.00
22 Mike Piazza 3.00
23 Ozzie Smith 2.00
24 Scott Rolen 2.00
25 Roger Clemens 2.00
26 Mike Mussina 2.00
27 Babe Ruth 6.00
28 Roger Maris 4.00
29 Nolan Ryan 6.00
30 Roy Oswalt 1.50
31 Whitey Ford, Andy Pettitte 3.00
32 Willie McCovey, Will Clark 3.00
33 Stan Musial, Albert Pujols 6.00
34 Andre Dawson, Vladimir Guerrero 3.00
35 Dale Murphy, Chipper Jones 3.00
36 Joe Morgan, Barry Larkin 3.00
37 Jim "Catfish" Hunter, Tim Hudson 2.00
38 Jim Rice, Manny Ramirez 3.00
39 Greg Maddux, Mark Prior 4.00
40 Don Mattingly, Jason Giambi 8.00
41 Roy Campanella, Mike Piazza 5.00
42 Ozzie Smith, Scott Rolen 5.00
43 Roger Clemens, Mike Mussina 5.00
44 Babe Ruth, Roger Maris 10.00
45 Nolan Ryan, Roy Oswalt 8.00

Passing the Torch Autographs
NM/M
Quantity produced listed
Many not priced due to scarcity.
4 Will Clark/15 100.00
7 Andre Dawson/50 15.00
9 Dale Murphy/50 30.00
11 Joe Morgan/15 25.00
14 Tim Hudson/15 45.00
15 Jim Rice/50 15.00
18 Mark Prior/15 80.00
24 Scott Rolen/15 50.00
30 Roy Oswalt/50 15.00

Passing the Torch Bats
NM/M
Quantity produced listed
2 Andy Pettitte/200 6.00
4 Willie McCovey/100 6.00
5 Will Clark/100 10.00
6 Stan Musial/100 25.00
7 Albert Pujols/200 15.00
8 Andre Dawson/100 8.00
9 Vladimir Guerrero/200 8.00
10 Dale Murphy/100 10.00
11 Chipper Jones/200 8.00
12 Joe Morgan/200 4.00
13 Barry Larkin/200 5.00
14 Tim Hudson/200 5.00
15 Jim Rice/200 5.00
16 Manny Ramirez/200 8.00
17 Greg Maddux/200 10.00
18 Mark Prior/200 8.00
19 Don Mattingly/200 15.00
20 Jason Giambi/200 8.00
21 Roy Campanella/50 30.00
22 Mike Piazza/200 10.00
23 Ozzie Smith/200 15.00
24 Scott Rolen/200 8.00
25 Roger Clemens/200 15.00
26 Mike Mussina/200 8.00
27 Babe Ruth/50 150.00
28 Roger Maris/50 50.00
29 Nolan Ryan/100 25.00
30 Roy Oswalt/200 4.00
32 Willie McCovey, Will Clark/50 20.00
33 Stan Musial, Albert Pujols/50 50.00
34 Andre Dawson, Vladimir Guerrero/50 20.00
35 Dale Murphy, Chipper Jones/50 20.00
36 Joe Morgan, Barry Larkin/50 15.00
37 Jim "Catfish" Hunter, Tim Hudson/50 15.00
38 Jim Rice, Manny Ramirez/50 20.00
40 Don Mattingly, Jason Giambi/50 35.00
41 Roy Campanella, Mike Piazza/25 35.00
42 Ozzie Smith, Scott Rolen/50 30.00
43 Roger Clemens, Mike Mussina/50 30.00
44 Babe Ruth, Roger Maris/25 200.00
45 Nolan Ryan, Roy Oswalt/50 35.00

2004 Donruss Elite Passing the Torch Jerseys
NM/M
Quantity produced listed
1 Whitey Ford/100 15.00
2 Andy Pettitte/200 4.00
3 Willie McCovey/100 6.00
4 Will Clark/100 10.00
5 Stan Musial/100 25.00
6 Albert Pujols/200 15.00
7 Andre Dawson/200 8.00
8 Vladimir Guerrero/200 8.00
9 Dale Murphy/100 10.00
10 Chipper Jones/200 8.00
11 Joe Morgan/100 4.00
12 Barry Larkin/200 5.00
13 Jim "Catfish" Hunter/100 5.00
14 Tim Hudson/200 5.00
15 Jim Rice/200 5.00
16 Manny Ramirez/200 8.00
18 Mark Prior/200 8.00
19 Don Mattingly/100 15.00
20 Jason Giambi/200 8.00
21 Roy Campanella/50 30.00
22 Mike Piazza/200 10.00
23 Ozzie Smith/100 12.00
24 Scott Rolen/200 8.00
25 Roger Clemens/200 15.00
26 Mike Mussina/200 8.00
27 Babe Ruth/25 300.00
28 Roger Maris/50 50.00
29 Nolan Ryan/100 25.00
30 Roy Oswalt/200 4.00
31 Whitey Ford, Andy Pettitte/50 20.00
32 Willie McCovey, Will Clark/50 20.00
33 Stan Musial, Albert Pujols/50 50.00
34 Andre Dawson, Vladimir Guerrero/50 20.00
35 Dale Murphy, Chipper Jones/50 20.00
36 Joe Morgan, Barry Larkin/50 15.00
37 Jim "Catfish" Hunter, Tim Hudson/50 15.00
38 Jim Rice, Manny Ramirez/50 20.00
40 Don Mattingly, Jason Giambi/50 35.00
41 Roy Campanella, Mike Piazza/50 35.00
42 Ozzie Smith, Scott Rolen/50 30.00
43 Roger Clemens, Mike Mussina/50 30.00
45 Nolan Ryan, Roy Oswalt/50 35.00

Recollection Autographs
NM/M
Common Autograph: 8.00
1 Jeremy Affeldt 01/25 8.00
2 Erick Almonte 01/26 10.00
4 Jeff Baker 02/25 30.00
5 Brandon Berger 01/25 8.00
6 Marlon Byrd 01/24 25.00
7 Ryan Drese 02/45 8.00
9 Brandon Duckworth 01/16 15.00
10 Casey Fossum 01/23 15.00
11 Geronimo Gil 01/25 8.00
12 Jeremy Guthrie 02/25 20.00
14 Nic Jackson 02/95

```
21  Ricardo Rodriguez
    01/25                8.00
23  Bud Smith 01/25      8.00
25  Junior Spivey 01/20 20.00
26  Tim Spooneybarger
    01/25               10.00
28  Martin Vargas 01/37  8.00
```

Team

```
                          NM/M
Production 1,500 Sets
Black:                    1X-2X
Production 150 Sets
Gold:                   1-1.5X
Production 250 Sets
1   Cal Ripken Jr.,
    Eddie Murray,
    Jim Palmer            8.00
2   Derek Jeter,
    Roger Clemens,
    Bernie Williams,
    Andy Pettitte         4.00
3   Johnny Bench, Tony Perez,
    George Foster,
    Dave Concepcion       4.00
4   Josh Beckett,
    Dontrelle Willis,
    Ivan Rodriguez        2.00
5   Randy Johnson,
    Curt Schilling,
    Luis Gonzalez,
    Mark Grace            2.00
6   Derek Jeter, Wade Boggs,
    Darryl Strawberry     5.00
7   Chipper Jones,
    Tom Glavine,
    Greg Maddux,
    Ryan Klesko           4.00
8   Dwight Gooden,
    Gary Carter,
    Darryl Strawberry     2.00
9   Jackie Robinson,
    Roy Campanella,
    Duke Snider           3.00
10  Phil Rizzuto, Yogi Berra,
    Whitey Ford           2.00
11  Stan Musial, Curt Schilling,
    Marty Marion,
    Enos Slaughter        4.00
```

Team Bats

```
                          NM/M
Production 100 Sets
2   Derek Jeter,
    Roger Clemens,
    Bernie Williams,
    Andy Pettitte        30.00
3   Johnny Bench, Tony Perez,
    George Foster,
    Dave Concepcion      50.00
4   Josh Beckett,
    Dontrelle Willis,
    Ivan Rodriguez       15.00
5   Randy Johnson,
    Curt Schilling,
    Luis Gonzalez,
    Mark Grace           25.00
6   Derek Jeter, Wade Boggs,
    Darryl Strawberry    30.00
7   Chipper Jones,
    Tom Glavine,
    Greg Maddux,
    Ryan Klesko          25.00
8   Dwight Gooden,
    Gary Carter,
    Darryl Strawberry    20.00
```

Team Jerseys

```
                          NM/M
Production 100 unless noted.
1   Cal Ripken Jr.,
    Eddie Murray,
    Jim Palmer           50.00
2   Derek Jeter,
    Roger Clemens,
    Bernie Williams,
    Andy Pettitte        40.00
4   Josh Beckett,
    Dontrelle Willis,
    Ivan Rodriguez       15.00
5   Randy Johnson,
    Curt Schilling,
    Luis Gonzalez,
    Mark Grace           25.00
6   Derek Jeter, Wade Boggs,
    Darryl Strawberry    30.00
```

```
7   Chipper Jones,
    Tom Glavine,
    Greg Maddux,
    Ryan Klesko          25.00
9   Jackie Robinson,
    Roy Campanella,
    Duke Snider          75.00
10  Phil Rizzuto, Yogi Berra,
    Whitey Ford          35.00
11  Stan Musial, Curt Schilling,
    Marty Marion,
    Enos Slaughter       50.00
```

Throwback Threads

```
                          NM/M
Quantity produced listed
Prime:                  1.5-3X
Prime Singles Production 10-25
Prime Duals Production 5-15
1   Albert Pujols/150    60.00
2   Alex Rodriguez/
    Rgr/150             125.00
3   Alfonso Soriano/
    150                 175.00
4   Chipper Jones/150   120.00
5   Derek Jeter/150      15.00
6   Greg Maddux/150      10.00
7   Hideo Nomo/150        8.00
8   Miguel Cabrera/150    8.00
9   Ivan Rodriguez/150    8.00
10  Jason Giambi/150      8.00
11  Jeff Bagwell/150      8.00
12  Lance Berkman/150     4.00
13  Mark Prior/150        8.00
14  Mike Piazza/150      10.00
15  Nomar Garciaparra/
    150                 10.00
16  Pedro J. Martinez/
    150                  8.00
17  Randy Johnson/150     8.00
18  Sammy Sosa/150        8.00
19  Shawn Green/150       4.00
20  Vladimir Guerrero/
    150                  8.00
21  Adam Dunn,
    Austin Kearns/75     20.00
22  Barry Zito,
    Mark Mulder/75       10.00
23  Curt Schilling/75     10.00
24  Derek Jeter,
    Jason Giambi/75       25.00
25  Dontrelle Willis,
    Josh Beckett/75       15.00
26  Frank Thomas,
    Magglio Ordonez/75    15.00
27  Jim Thome/75          15.00
28  Kerry Wood,
    Mark Prior/75         25.00
29  Hank Blalock,
    Mark Teixeira/75      15.00
30  Albert Pujols,
    Scott Rolen/75        40.00
31  Babe Ruth/50         280.00
32  Cal Ripken Jr./100    40.00
33  Carl Yastrzemski/
    100                  20.00
34  Deion Sanders/100     20.00
35  Don Mattingly/100     20.00
36  George Brett/100      20.00
37  Jim Palmer/100         8.00
38  Kirby Puckett/100     15.00
39  Lou Gehrig/100       125.00
40  Mark Grace/100        10.00
41  Mike Schmidt/100      20.00
42  Nolan Ryan/100        25.00
43  Ozzie Smith/100       20.00
44  Reggie Jackson/100    10.00
45  Rickey Henderson/
    100                  10.00
46  Roberto Clemente/
    100                 75.00
47  Roger Clemens/100     15.00
48  Roger Maris/100       40.00
49  Roy Campanella/
    Pants/100            15.00
50  Tony Gwynn/100        15.00
51  Babe Ruth,
    Lou Gehrig/25        400.00
52  Cal Ripken Jr.,
    Eddie Murray/50       50.00
53  Ted Williams,
    Carl Yastrzemski/50   85.00
54  Andre Dawson,
    Gary Carter/50        20.00
55  Reggie Jackson,
    Rod Carew/50          20.00
56  Derek Jeter,
    Phil Rizzuto/50       40.00
57  Nolan Ryan,
    Roy Oswalt/50         40.00
58  Roger Clemens,
    Mike Mussina/50       25.00
59  Albert Pujols,
    Stan Musial/50        40.00
60  Nomar Garciaparra,
    Stan Musial/50        85.00
```

Throwback Threads Autographs

```
                          NM/M
Production 25 Sets
Prime:              No Pricing
Production 5-10
9   Ivan Rodriguez/25     60.00
13  Mark Prior/25         80.00
18  Sammy Sosa/25        175.00
```

```
35  Don Mattingly/25     120.00
37  Jim Palmer/25         40.00
```

Throwback Threads Prime

```
Quantity produced listed
```

Turn of the Century

BARRY LARKIN

```
Stars (1-150):           2-3X
Production 750
Stars (181-200):          1X
Production 250
```

2004 Donruss Elite Extra Edition

SCOTT ROLEN

```
                          NM/M
Complete Set (288):
Common (1-150):            .25
Common (206-215):         2.00
Production 1,000
Common Auto.(216-355):    6.00
Common No Auto.
(234-254):                3.00
No Auto. Production 1,000
Pack (5):                10.00
Box (12):               100.00
Note: Cards 151-205 do not exist.
1   Troy Glaus            .40
2   John Lackey           .25
3   Garret Anderson       .40
4   Francisco Rodriguez   .25
5   Casey Kotchman        .25
6   Jose Guillen          .25
7   Miguel Tejada         .50
8   Rafael Palmeiro       .50
9   Jay Gibbons           .25
10  Melvin Mora           .25
11  Javy Lopez            .25
12  Pedro Martinez        .75
13  Curt Schilling        .75
14  David Ortiz           .75
15  Manny Ramirez         .75
16  Nomar Garciaparra    1.00
17  Magglio Ordonez       .25
18  Frank Thomas          .75
19  Esteban Loaiza        .25
20  Paul Konerko          .50
21  Mark Buehrle          .25
22  Jody Gerut            .25
23  Victor Martinez       .25
24  C.C. Sabathia         .25
25  Travis Hafner         .25
26  Cliff Lee             .25
27  Jeremy Bonderman      .25
28  Dallas McPherson      .25
29  Jermaine Dye          .25
30  Carlos Guillen        .25
31  Carlos Beltran        .50
32  Ken Harvey            .25
33  Mike Sweeney          .25
34  Angel Berroa          .25
35  Joe Nathan            .25
36  Johan Santana         .40
37  Jacque Jones          .25
38  Shannon Stewart       .25
39  Torii Hunter          .40
```

```
40  Derek Jeter          2.00
41  Jason Giambi          .50
42  Danny Graves          .25
43  Alfonso Soriano       .75
44  Gary Sheffield        .50
45  Mike Mussina          .50
46  Jorge Posada          .50
47  Hideki Matsui        1.00
48  Francisco Cordero     .25
49  Javier Vazquez        .25
50  Mariano Rivera        .40
51  Eric Chavez           .40
52  Tim Hudson            .40
53  Mark Mulder           .40
54  Barry Zito            .40
55  Ichiro Suzuki        1.50
56  Edgar Martinez        .25
57  Bret Boone            .25
58  Lew Ford              .25
59  B.J. Upton            .40
60  Aubrey Huff           .25
61  Rocco Baldelli        .25
62  Carl Crawford         .40
63  Delmon Young          .40
64  Mark Teixeira         .40
65  Hank Blalock          .50
66  Michael Young         .25
67  Alex Rodriguez       1.50
68  Carlos Delgado        .40
69  Milton Bradley        .25
70  Roy Halladay          .40
71  Vernon Wells          .25
72  Randy Johnson         .75
73  Bobby Crosby          .25
74  Lyle Overbay          .25
75  Luis Gonzalez         .25
76  Steve Finley          .25
77  Chipper Jones         .75
78  Andruw Jones          .40
79  Marcus Giles          .25
80  Rafael Furcal         .40
81  J.D. Drew             .40
82  Sammy Sosa           1.00
83  Kerry Wood            .40
84  Mark Prior            .75
85  Derrek Lee            .50
86  Moises Alou           .40
87  Carlos Zambrano       .40
88  Ken Griffey Jr.      1.00
89  Austin Kearns         .40
90  Adam Dunn             .50
91  Barry Larkin          .40
92  Todd Helton           .50
93  Larry Walker          .40
94  Preston Wilson        .25
95  Sean Casey            .25
96  Luis Castillo         .25
97  Josh Beckett          .25
98  Mike Lowell           .25
99  Miguel Cabrera        .75
100 Brad Penny            .25
101 Dontrelle Willis      .25
102 Andy Pettitte         .40
103 Wade Miller           .25
104 Jeff Bagwell          .50
105 Craig Biggio          .40
106 Lance Berkman         .40
107 Jeff Kent             .25
108 Roy Oswalt            .40
109 Hideo Nomo            .40
110 Adrian Beltre         .40
111 Paul LoDuca           .25
112 Shawn Green           .25
113 Roger Clemens        2.00
114 Eric Gagne            .40
115 Danny Kolb            .25
116 Rickie Weeks          .25
117 Scott Podsednik       .25
118 Livan Hernandez       .25
119 Orlando Cabrera       .25
120 Jose Vidro            .25
121 David Wright         1.50
122 Tom Glavine           .40
123 Al Leiter             .25
124 Mike Piazza          1.00
125 Jose Reyes            .50
126 Richard Hidalgo       .25
127 Eric Milton           .25
128 Jim Thome             .75
129 Mike Lieberthal       .25
130 Bobby Abreu           .40
131 Kip Wells             .25
132 Jack Wilson           .25
133 Jason Bay             .40
134 Brian Giles           .25
135 Sean Burroughs        .25
136 Khalil Greene         .25
137 Jake Peavy            .40
138 Jason Schmidt         .40
139 J.T. Snow             .25
140 Craig Wilson          .25
141 Chase Utley           .50
142 Jim Edmonds           .40
143 Albert Pujols        2.00
144 Edgar Renteria        .40
145 Scott Rolen           .75
146 Matt Morris           .25
147 Ivan Rodriguez        .50
148 Vladimir Guerrero     .75
149 Greg Maddux          1.00
150 Ben Sheets            .40
206 Will Clark           2.00
207 Nolan Ryan           8.00
208 Bob Feller           2.00
209 Red Schoendienst     2.00
210 Brooks Robinson      3.00
211 Al Kaline            3.00
212 Ozzie Smith          4.00
```

```
213 Maury Wills          2.00
214 Steve Carlton        2.00
215 Duke Snider          3.00
216 Scott Lewis/
    Auto./465 RC        30.00
217 Josh Johnson/
    Auto./597 RC        10.00
218 Jeff Fiorentino/
    Auto./597 RC        20.00
219 Grant Hansen/
    Auto./599 RC         6.00
220 Yovani Gallardo/
    Auto./803 RC        50.00
221 Eddie Prasch/
    Auto./803 RC        10.00
222 Danny Hill/
    Auto./603 RC         6.00
223 Chuck Lofgren/
    Auto./803 RC        25.00
224 Blake Johnson/
    Auto./811 RC        10.00
225 Cory Dunlap/
    Auto./599 RC        15.00
226 Carlos Vasquez/
    Auto./869 RC         8.00
227 Jesse Crain/
    Auto./1000 RC       10.00
228 Yhency Brazoban/
    Auto./1000 RC        6.00
229 Abe Alvarez/
    Auto./1000 RC        8.00
230 Scott Kazmir/
    Auto./350           60.00
231 J.A. Happ/
    Auto./1195 RC        8.00
232 Mark Jecmen/
    Auto./1047 RC        6.00
234 Kameron Loe/
    Auto./1575 RC        8.00
235 Ervin Santana/
    1000 RC              3.00
239 Josh Karp/1000 RC    3.00
242 Alberto Callaspo/
    1000 RC              3.00
243 Jesse Hoover/
    Auto./1191 RC        8.00
246 Justin Hoyman/
    Auto./1124 RC        8.00
247 Juan Cedeno/
    1000 RC              3.00
250 Jake Dittler/1000    4.00
252 Benjamin Zobrist/
    Auto./1178 RC        8.00
253 Jeff Salazar/1000 RC 3.00
254 Fausto Carmona/
    1000 RC              4.00
256 Jorge Vasquez/
    Auto./1000 RC        6.00
257 Rafael Gonzalez/
    Auto./603 RC         6.00
258 Andrew Dobies/
    Auto./601 RC        10.00
259 Colby Miller/
    Auto./997 RC         6.00
260 K.C. Herren/
    Auto./735 RC         8.00
261 Ryan Meaux/
    Auto./546 RC         6.00
262 Dustin Pedroia/
    Auto./1114 RC       30.00
263 Fernando Nieve/
    Auto./1000 RC       10.00
264 Mariano Gomez/
    Auto./1000 RC        6.00
265 Eric Campbell/
    Auto./260 RC       120.00
266 Billy Killian/
    Auto./703 RC         6.00
267 Mike Rouse/
    Auto./999            6.00
268 Kyle Bono/
    Auto./1203 RC        8.00
269 Mitch Einertson/
    Auto./1047 RC       10.00
270 Scott Proctor/
    Auto./1000 RC        8.00
271 Tim Bittner/
    Auto./1000 RC        6.00
272 Christian Garcia/
    Auto./799 RC        10.00
273 Yadier Molina/
    Auto./1000 RC       20.00
275 Charles Thomas/
    Auto./907 RC         8.00
276 Travis Blackley/
    Auto./1000 RC        6.00
277 Frankie Francisco/
    Auto./1000 RC        6.00
278 Dioner Navarro/
    Auto./1000 RC       10.00
279 Joey Gathright/
    Auto./1000 RC        8.00
280 Kazuhito Tadano/
    Auto./1000 RC       15.00
281 Matt Bush/
    Auto./1100 RC       20.00
282 David Haehnel/
    Auto./865 RC         8.00
283 Tommy Hottovy/
    Auto./825 RC         6.00
284 Chris Carter/
    Auto./973 RC        30.00
285 Mark Rogers/
    Auto./578 RC        20.00
286 Jeremy Sowers/
    Auto./537 RC        30.00
287 Homer Bailey/
    Auto./1571 RC       50.00
```

```
288 Mike Butia/
    Auto./825 RC         8.00
289 Chris Nelson/
    Auto./465 RC        30.00
290 Thomas Diamond/
    Auto./1055 RC       15.00
291 Neil Walker/
    Auto./1343 RC       20.00
292 Sean Gamble/
    Auto./1229 RC        8.00
293 Bill Bray/
    Auto./1073 RC        6.00
294 Reid Brignac/
    Auto./522 RC        60.00
295 Ryan Klosterman/
    Auto./865 RC         6.00
296 David Purcey/
    Auto./1485 RC        8.00
297 Scott Elbert/
    Auto./1617 RC       30.00
298 Josh Fields/
    Auto./961 RC        35.00
299 Chris Lambert/
    Auto./954 RC         8.00
300 Trevor Plouffe/
    Auto./1329 RC       10.00
301 Greg Golson/
    Auto./1334 RC       15.00
302 Josh Baker/
    Auto./525 RC         8.00
303 Phillip Hughes/
    Auto./1073 RC      100.00
304 Matt Macri/
    Auto./979 RC         8.00
305 Kyle Waldrop/
    Auto./823 RC        10.00
306 Richie Robnett/
    Auto./1575 RC       10.00
307 Taylor Tankersley/
    Auto./1073 RC        8.00
308 Blake DeWitt/
    Auto./1562 RC       25.00
309 Daryl Jones/
    Auto./575 RC        15.00
310 Eric Hurley/
    Auto./1021 RC       25.00
311 J.P. Howell/
    Auto./1453 RC       10.00
312 Zach Jackson/
    Auto./1069 RC        8.00
313 Justin Orenduff/
    Auto./473 RC        10.00
314 Tyler Lumsden/
    Auto./473 RC        10.00
315 Matt Fox/
    Auto./473 RC        12.00
316 Danny Putnam/
    Auto./473 RC        10.00
317 Jon Poterson/
    Auto./464 RC        15.00
318 Gio Gonzalez/
    Auto./473 RC        30.00
319 Jay Rainville/
    Auto./823 RC        12.00
320 Huston Street/
    Auto./709 RC        30.00
321 Jeff Marquez/
    Auto./493 RC        10.00
322 Eric Beattie/
    Auto./930 RC         8.00
323 B.J. Szymanski/
    Auto./1327 RC        8.00
324 Seth Smith/
    Auto./1065 RC       10.00
325 Robert Johnson/
    Auto./790 RC         8.00
326 Wes Whisler/
    Auto./473 RC         8.00
327 Billy Buckner/
    Auto./673 RC         8.00
328 Jon Zeringue/
    Auto./473 RC        15.00
329 Curtis Thigpen/
    Auto./673 RC        10.00
330 Donny Lucy/
    Auto./573 RC         6.00
331 Mike Ferris/
    Auto./558 RC        10.00
332 Anthony Swarzak/
    Auto./370 RC        25.00
333 Jason Jaramillo/
    Auto./573 RC         8.00
334 Hunter Pence/
    Auto./672 RC        90.00
335 Mike Rozier/
    Auto./628 RC         8.00
336 Kurt Suzuki/
    Auto./473 RC        20.00
337 Jason Vargas/
    Auto./621 RC        20.00
338 Brian Bixler/
    Auto./665 RC        10.00
340 Dexter Fowler/
    Auto./623 RC        50.00
341 Mark Trumbo/
    Auto./1321 RC       15.00
342 Jeff Frazier/
    Auto./423 RC         8.00
343 Steven Register/
    Auto./673 RC         8.00
344 Michael Schlact/
    Auto./477 RC         8.00
345 Garrett Mock/
    Auto./471 RC        12.00
346 Eric Haberer/
    Auto./473 RC         8.00
347 Matt Tuiasosopo/
    Auto./473 RC        25.00
```

		NM/M
348	Jason Windsor/Auto./473 RC	15.00
349	Grant Johnson/Auto./815 RC	10.00
350	J.C. Holt/Auto./673 RC	10.00
351	Joseph Bauserman/Auto./472 RC	8.00
352	Jamar Walton/Auto./481 RC	15.00
353	Eric Patterson/Auto./1571 RC	15.00
354	Tyler Johnson/Auto./775 RC	15.00
355	Nick Adenhart/Auto./653 RC	85.00

Aspirations
1-150 print run 61-99:	4-8X
1-150 p/r 41-60:	6-12X
1-150 p/r 26-40:	8-15X
1-150 p/r 25 or less:	No pricing
206-355 p/r 51-99:	1-2X no auto.
216-355 p/r 61-99:	.4-1X auto.
216-355 p/r 41-60:	.5-1X auto.
216-355 p/r 26-40:	.75-1X auto.

No Pricing print run 25 or less.

Aspirations Gold
Gold (1-150):	10-20X
Gold (206-215):	3-6X
Gold (216-355):	No Pricing

Production 25 Sets

Status
1-150 print run 61-99:	4-8X
1-150 p/r 41-60:	6-12X
1-150 p/r 26-40:	8-15X
1-150 p/r 25 or less:	No Pricing
206-355 p/r 51-99:	1-2X no auto.
216-355 p/r 61-99:	.4-1X auto.
216-355 p/r 41-60:	.5-1X auto.
216-355 p/r 26-40:	.75-1X auto.

No pricing print run 25 or less.

Status Gold
No Pricing
Production 10 Sets

Turn of the Century
(1-150):	3-5X
Production 250 Sets	
(206-215):	2-3X
(216-355 no auto):	.5-1X
(216-355 auto):	.2-.5X

206-355 production 100

Back to Back Picks Sign.
NM/M
Quantity produced listed
1	Delmon Young, Rickie Weeks/25	50.00
3	Adam Dunn, Austin Kearns/25	50.00
5	Michael Young, Vernon Wells/25	35.00
6	Brian Roberts, Larry Bigbie/50	30.00
7	Ron Cey, Steve Garvey/50	35.00
8	Bill Madlock, Dave Parker/50	40.00
9	Derrek Lee, Torii Hunter, Trot Nixon/50	
11	Chris Nelson, Matt Bush, Reid Brignac/250	65.00
12	B.J. Szymanski, Greg Golson, Jeff Frazier/250	50.00
13	Mark Trumbo, Nick Adenhart, Tyler Johnson/100	50.00
14	Chris Carter, Danny Putnam, Mark Jecmen/100	40.00
15	Billy Killian, Daryl Jones, Matt Bush/100	40.00
16	Blake DeWitt, Justin Orenduff, Scott Elbert/250	40.00
17	Jay Rainville, Kyle Waldrop, Trevor Plouffe/250	50.00
18	Jeff Marquez, Jon Poterson, Phillip Hughes/100	90.00
19	Wes Whisler, Tyler Lumsden, Wes Whisler/100	40.00
20	Curtis Thigpen, David Purcey, Zach Jackson/100	40.00

Career Best All-Stars

Common Player: Production 500 Sets
1	Randy Johnson	3.00
2	David Ortiz	3.00
3	Edgar Renteria	2.00
4	Victor Martinez	2.00
5	Albert Pujols	6.00
6	Hideki Matsui	5.00
7	Mariano Rivera	2.00
8	Carlos Zambrano	2.00
9	Hank Blalock	2.00
10	Michael Young	2.00
11	Mike Piazza	4.00
12	Alfonso Soriano	2.00
13	Carl Crawford	2.00
14	Scott Rolen	3.00
15	Vladimir Guerrero	3.00
16	Lance Berkman	2.00
17	Todd Helton	3.00
18	Curt Schilling	3.00
19	Francisco Cordero	2.00
20	Mark Mulder	2.00
21	Sammy Sosa	4.00
22	Roger Clemens	6.00
23	Miguel Cabrera	3.00
24	Manny Ramirez	3.00
25	Jim Thome	3.00

Career Best A-S Jersey
NM/M
Production 50 Sets
Prime: 1X-2X
Production 5-25
No pricing 15 or less.
1	Randy Johnson	15.00
2	David Ortiz	15.00
3	Edgar Renteria	8.00
4	Victor Martinez	8.00
5	Albert Pujols	25.00
6	Hideki Matsui	40.00
7	Mariano Rivera	10.00
8	Carlos Zambrano	8.00
9	Hank Blalock	10.00
10	Michael Young	8.00
11	Mike Piazza	20.00
12	Alfonso Soriano	15.00
13	Carl Crawford	8.00
14	Scott Rolen	15.00
15	Vladimir Guerrero	15.00
16	Lance Berkman	8.00
17	Todd Helton	10.00
18	Curt Schilling	15.00
19	Francisco Cordero	8.00
20	Mark Mulder	8.00
21	Sammy Sosa	15.00
22	Roger Clemens	20.00
23	Miguel Cabrera	12.00
24	Manny Ramirez	15.00
25	Jim Thome	15.00

Career Best A-S Jersey Prime
NM/M
2	David Ortiz/25	25.00
4	Victor Martinez/25	15.00
5	Albert Pujols/25	40.00
6	Hideki Matsui/25	75.00
8	Carlos Zambrano/25	15.00
9	Hank Blalock/25	20.00
10	Michael Young/25	15.00
11	Mike Piazza/25	30.00
12	Alfonso Soriano/25	25.00
13	Carl Crawford/25	25.00
14	Scott Rolen/25	25.00
15	Vladimir Guerrero/25	25.00
16	Lance Berkman/25	15.00
17	Todd Helton/25	20.00
18	Curt Schilling/25	25.00
20	Mark Mulder/25	15.00
21	Sammy Sosa/25	30.00
22	Roger Clemens/25	40.00
23	Miguel Cabrera/25	25.00
24	Manny Ramirez/25	25.00
25	Jim Thome/25	25.00

Career Best A-S Sig. Black
No Pricing
Production 1-5

Career Best A-S Sign. Gold
No Pricing
Production 1-10

Career Best A-S Sig. Jersey Go
NM/M
Production 1-25
2	David Ortiz/25	75.00
3	Edgar Renteria/25	40.00
4	Victor Martinez/25	40.00
8	Carlos Zambrano/25	40.00
10	Michael Young/25	35.00
13	Carl Crawford/25	30.00
19	Francisco Cordero/25	20.00

Career Best A-S Sig. Jersey Pr
No Pricing
Production 1-10

Draft Class
NM/M
Common Duo: 2.00
Production 500 Sets
1	Johnny Bench, Nolan Ryan	10.00
2	Bert Blyleven, Dwight Evans	2.00
3	Jim Rice, Keith Hernandez	2.00
4	Dennis Eckersley, Gary Carter	3.00
5	Fred Lynn, Robin Yount	5.00
6	Andre Dawson, Lee Smith	2.00
7	Alan Trammell, Jack Morris	2.00
8	Harold Baines, Paul Molitor	3.00
9	Cal Ripken Jr., Kirk Gibson	10.00
10	Don Mattingly, Orel Hershiser	6.00
11	Darryl Strawberry, Eric Davis	2.00
12	Dwight Gooden, Jose Canseco	3.00
13	Rafael Palmeiro, Randy Johnson	4.00
14	Curt Schilling, Gary Sheffield	3.00
15	Mike Piazza, Robin Ventura	4.00
16	Frank Thomas, Jeff Bagwell	3.00
17	Chipper Jones, Mike Mussina	3.00
18	Garret Anderson, Jorge Posada	2.00
19	Scott Rolen, Torii Hunter	3.00
20	Kerry Wood, Todd Helton	3.00
21	Eric Chavez, Roy Oswalt	2.00
22	Johnny Estrada, Vernon Wells	2.00
23	Lance Berkman, Tim Hudson	2.00
24	Mark Buehrle, Mark Mulder	2.00
25	C.C. Sabathia, Sean Burroughs	2.00
26	Albert Pujols, Barry Zito	6.00
27	Rich Harden, Rocco Baldelli	2.00
28	Bobby Crosby, Mark Teixeira	4.00
29	Casey Kotchman, Mark Prior	3.00
30	Dewon Brazelton, Jeremy Bonderman	2.00
31	J.C. Holt, Jon Zeringue	3.00
32	Kyle Bono, Matt Fox	3.00
33	Dexter Fowler, Mike Rozier	3.00
34	Huston Street, J.P. Howell	3.00
35	Grant Johnson, Matt Macri	3.00
36	Eric Beattie, Jeff Frazier	3.00
37	Jason Windsor, Kurt Suzuki	5.00
38	Josh Fields, Matt Tuiasosopo	6.00
39	Joseph Bauserman, K.C. Herren	3.00
40	Chris Lambert, Eric Haberer, Matt Tuiasosopo	

Passing the Torch
NM/M
Common Duo: 3.00
Production 500 Sets
1	Dennis Eckersley, Huston Street	4.00
2	Matt Bush, Tony Gwynn	6.00
3	Homer Bailey, Tom Seaver	4.00
4	Bob Feller, Jeremy Sowers	3.00
5	Josh Fields, Robin Ventura	3.00
6	Nolan Ryan, Thomas Diamond	8.00
7	Eric Patterson, Ryne Sandberg	6.00
8	Richie Robnett, Rickey Henderson	4.00
9	Mike Ferris, Stan Musial	5.00
10	Bobby Doerr, Dustin Pedroia	

Passing the Torch Autograph Black
No Pricing
Production 5-10 Sets

Passing the Torch Autograph Gold
NM/M
Production 5-25
2	Matt Bush, Tony Gwynn/25	90.00
5	Bob Feller, Jeremy Sowers/25	60.00
10	Bobby Doerr, Dustin Pedroia/25	60.00

Round Numbers
NM/M
Common Player: 2.00
Production 500 Sets
1	Ozzie Smith	4.00
2	Derek Jeter	6.00
3	Alex Rodriguez	5.00
4	Paul Molitor	3.00
5	George Brett	3.00
6	Delmon Young	2.00
7	Dontrelle Willis	2.00
8	Gary Carter	2.00
9	Reggie Jackson	2.00
10	Andre Dawson	2.00
11	Neil Walker	2.00
12	Laynce Nix	2.00
13	Matt Bush	6.00
14	Lyle Overbay	2.00
15	Carlos Beltran	3.00
16	Todd Helton	2.00
17	Mark Grace	2.00
18	Fred Lynn	2.00
19	Robin Yount	4.00
20	Mike Schmidt	6.00
21	Roger Clemens	6.00
22	Will Clark	3.00
23	Don Mattingly	5.00
24	Blake DeWitt	2.00
25	Rafael Palmeiro	3.00
26	Wade Boggs	3.00
27	Mark Rogers	5.00
28	Billy Buckner	2.00
29	Jeff Baker	2.00
30	Nolan Ryan	8.00
31	Mike Piazza	4.00
32	Alexis Rios	2.00
33	Eddie Murray	3.00
34	Jose Canseco	3.00
35	Mike Mussina	3.00
36	Eric Beattie	3.00
37	Keith Hernandez	2.00
38	Michael Young	2.00
39	Dwight Evans	2.00
40	Scott Elbert	3.00
41	Adrian Gonzalez	2.00
42	Johnny Bench	3.00
43	Dennis Eckersley	2.00
44	Dale Murphy	3.00
45	Ryne Sandberg	4.00
46	David Wright	3.00
47	Hank Blalock	3.00
48	Orel Hershiser	2.00
49	Sean Casey	2.00
50	Albert Pujols	6.00

Round Numbers Signature
NM/M
Production 5-250
1	Ozzie Smith/25	65.00
4	Paul Molitor/25	35.00
6	Delmon Young/25	20.00
7	Dontrelle Willis/25	20.00
8	Gary Carter/25	20.00
10	Andre Dawson/50	20.00
11	Neil Walker/250	20.00
12	Laynce Nix/50	20.00
13	Matt Bush/100	40.00
14	Lyle Overbay/50	15.00
15	Carlos Beltran/25	50.00
17	Mark Grace/25	35.00
18	Fred Lynn/25	15.00
20	Mike Schmidt/25	85.00
22	Will Clark/20	60.00
23	Don Mattingly/25	65.00
24	Blake DeWitt/25	30.00
27	Mark Rogers/100	40.00
28	Billy Buckner/100	15.00
32	Alexis Rios/50	15.00
34	Jose Canseco/25	50.00
36	Eric Beattie/50	15.00
37	Keith Hernandez/50	20.00
38	Michael Young/50	20.00
39	Dwight Evans/50	25.00
40	Scott Elbert/50	15.00
41	Adrian Gonzalez/50	10.00
43	Dennis Eckersley/50	30.00
44	Dale Murphy/50	20.00
46	David Wright/25	75.00
47	Hank Blalock/50	20.00
49	Sean Casey/50	15.00

Signature
NM/M
Production 1-50
132	Jack Wilson/25	25.00
133	Jason Bay/25	25.00
231	J.A. Happ/50	10.00
233	Mark Jecmen/50	8.00
234	Kameron Loe/50	20.00
235	Ervin Santana/50	40.00
239	Josh Karp/50	15.00
243	Jesse Hoover/50	10.00
246	Justin Hoyman/50	15.00
247	Juan Cedeno/50	15.00
252	Benjamin Zobrist/50	10.00
253	Jeff Salazar/50	30.00
254	Fausto Carmona/50	20.00

Signature Aspirations
NM/M
Production 1-100
Golds: No Pricing
Production 1-25
216	Scott Lewis/50	15.00
217	Josh Johnson/50	15.00
218	Jeff Fiorentino/50	25.00
219	Grant Hansen/50	15.00
220	Yovani Gallardo/50	100.00
221	Eddie Prasch/50	10.00
222	Danny Hill/50	8.00
223	Chuck Lofgren/50	40.00
224	Blake Johnson/50	15.00
225	Cory Dunlap/50	20.00
226	Carlos Vasquez/50	10.00
227	Jesse Crain/50	15.00
228	Yhency Brazoban/50	10.00
229	Abe Alvarez/50	10.00
256	Jorge Vasquez/50	8.00
257	Rafael Gonzalez/50	8.00
258	Andrew Dobies/50	15.00
259	Colby Miller/49	10.00
260	K.C. Herren/50	15.00
261	Ryan Meaux/50	10.00
262	Dustin Pedroia/50	40.00
263	Fernando Nieve/50	8.00
264	Mariano Gomez/50	10.00
266	Billy Killian/50	8.00
267	Mike Rouse/50	10.00
268	Kyle Bono/50	10.00
269	Mitch Einertson/50	25.00
270	Scott Proctor/50	15.00
271	Tim Bittner/50	8.00
272	Christian Garcia/50	10.00
273	Yadier Molina/50	30.00
274	Justin Leone/50	15.00
275	Charles Thomas/50	15.00
276	Travis Blackley/50	10.00
277	Frankie Francisco/50	10.00
278	Dioner Navarro/50	15.00
279	Joey Gathright/50	10.00
280	Kazuhito Tadano/50	20.00
281	Matt Bush/50	30.00
282	David Haehnel/100	10.00
283	Tommy Hottovy/100	10.00
284	Chris Carter/50	35.00
286	Jeremy Sowers/100	40.00
287	Homer Bailey/100	100.00
288	Mike Butia/100	10.00
289	Chris Nelson/100	40.00
290	Thomas Diamond/100	30.00
291	Neil Walker/100	25.00
292	Sean Gamble/100	10.00
293	Bill Bray/100	8.00
294	Reid Brignac/50	80.00
295	Ryan Klosterman/100	8.00
296	David Purcey/100	10.00
297	Scott Elbert/100	50.00
299	Josh Fields/100	40.00
299	Chris Lambert/100	10.00
300	Trevor Plouffe/100	25.00
301	Greg Golson/100	20.00
302	Josh Baker/100	10.00
303	Phillip Hughes/100	150.00
304	Matt Macri/100	12.00
305	Kyle Waldrop/100	25.00
306	Richie Robnett/100	10.00
307	Taylor Tankersley/100	10.00
308	Blake DeWitt/100	50.00
309	Daryl Jones/50	25.00
310	Eric Hurley/100	30.00
311	J.P. Howell/100	20.00
312	Zach Jackson/100	10.00
313	Justin Orenduff/100	20.00
314	Tyler Lumsden/100	20.00
315	Matt Fox/100	15.00
316	Danny Putnam/100	15.00
317	Jon Poterson/100	20.00
318	Gio Gonzalez/100	35.00
319	Jay Rainville/100	20.00
320	Huston Street/100	60.00
321	Jeff Marquez/100	15.00
322	Eric Beattie/100	10.00
323	B.J. Szymanski/100	10.00
324	Seth Smith/100	25.00
325	Robert Johnson/100	10.00
326	Wes Whisler/50	10.00
327	Billy Buckner/50	10.00
328	Jon Zeringue/100	30.00
329	Curtis Thigpen/50	12.00
330	Donny Lucy/50	10.00
331	Mike Ferris/100	12.00
332	Jason Jaramillo/50	15.00
334	Hunter Pence/50	140.00
335	Mike Rozier/50	15.00
336	Kurt Suzuki/100	25.00
337	Jason Vargas/50	50.00
338	Brian Bixler/50	15.00
340	Dexter Fowler/50	70.00
341	Mark Trumbo/50	15.00
342	Jeff Frazier/100	20.00
343	Steven Register/50	10.00
344	Michael Schlact/50	10.00
345	Garrett Mock/50	15.00
346	Eric Haberer/50	10.00
347	Matt Tuiasosopo/100	30.00
348	Jason Windsor/50	15.00
349	Grant Johnson/50	10.00
350	J.C. Holt/50	10.00
351	Joseph Bauserman/50	10.00
352	Jamar Walton/50	10.00
353	Eric Patterson/100	25.00
354	Tyler Johnson/50	15.00
355	Nick Adenhart/100	100.00

Signature Status
NM/M
Production 1-50
Golds: No Pricing
Production 1-10
221	Eddie Prasch/25	15.00
224	Blake Johnson/25	20.00
229	Abe Alvarez/25	15.00
257	Rafael Gonzalez/25	10.00
268	Kyle Bono/25	15.00
272	Christian Garcia/25	15.00
276	Travis Blackley/25	15.00
281	Matt Bush/25	40.00
282	David Haehnel/25	15.00
283	Tommy Hottovy/25	15.00
284	Chris Carter/25	40.00
286	Jeremy Sowers/25	40.00
287	Homer Bailey/25	125.00
288	Mike Butia/25	15.00
289	Chris Nelson/25	40.00
290	Thomas Diamond/50	40.00
291	Neil Walker/25	35.00
292	Sean Gamble/25	15.00
293	Bill Bray/25	10.00
294	Reid Brignac/25	80.00
295	Ryan Klosterman/50	10.00
296	David Purcey/25	15.00
297	Scott Elbert/25	75.00
298	Josh Fields/50	50.00
299	Chris Lambert/25	15.00
300	Greg Golson/25	35.00
301	Greg Golson/25	35.00
302	Josh Baker/25	15.00
303	Phillip Hughes/25	180.00
304	Matt Macri/25	15.00
305	Kyle Waldrop/25	25.00
306	Richie Robnett/25	25.00
307	Taylor Tankersley/50	15.00
308	Blake DeWitt/25	40.00
309	Daryl Jones/25	30.00
310	Eric Hurley/25	40.00
311	J.P. Howell/25	20.00
312	Zach Jackson/25	15.00
313	Justin Orenduff/25	20.00
314	Tyler Lumsden/25	20.00
315	Matt Fox/25	20.00
316	Danny Putnam/25	20.00
317	Jon Poterson/25	20.00
318	Gio Gonzalez/25	40.00
319	Jay Rainville/25	35.00
320	Huston Street/25	60.00
321	Jeff Marquez/25	20.00
322	Eric Beattie/25	15.00
323	B.J. Szymanski/25	15.00
324	Seth Smith/25	30.00
325	Robert Johnson/25	15.00
326	Wes Whisler/25	15.00
327	Billy Buckner/25	15.00
328	Jon Zeringue/25	35.00
329	Curtis Thigpen/25	12.00
330	Donny Lucy/25	15.00
331	Mike Ferris/50	15.00
333	Jason Jaramillo/50	15.00
334	Hunter Pence/25	140.00
335	Mike Rozier/50	15.00
336	Kurt Suzuki/50	25.00
337	Jason Vargas/25	50.00
338	Brian Bixler/50	15.00
340	Dexter Fowler/50	70.00
341	Mark Trumbo/50	25.00
342	Jeff Frazier/50	15.00
343	Steven Register/50	10.00
344	Michael Schlact/50	15.00
346	Eric Haberer/50	10.00
347	Matt Tuiasosopo/50	40.00
348	Jason Windsor/50	20.00
349	Grant Johnson/50	10.00
350	J.C. Holt/50	10.00
351	Joseph Bauserman/50	10.00
352	Jamar Walton/50	25.00
353	Eric Patterson/50	25.00
354	Tyler Johnson/50	15.00
355	Nick Adenhart/50	120.00

Sign. Turn of Century
NM/M
216	Scott Lewis/100	12.00
217	Josh Johnson/100	12.00
218	Jeff Fiorentino/100	10.00
219	Grant Hansen/100	10.00
220	Yovani Gallardo/100	75.00
221	Eddie Prasch/100	10.00
222	Danny Hill/100	8.00
223	Chuck Lofgren/100	35.00
224	Blake Johnson/100	15.00
225	Cory Dunlap/100	20.00
226	Carlos Vasquez/100	10.00
227	Jesse Crain/100	15.00

228 Yhency Brazoban/100 10.00
229 Abe Alvarez/100 10.00
246 Justin Hoyman/250 10.00
252 Benjamin Zobrist/150 10.00
256 Jorge Vasquez/100 8.00
257 Rafael Gonzalez/100 10.00
258 Andrew Dobies/100 15.00
259 Colby Miller/100 10.00
260 K.C. Herren/100 15.00
261 Ryan Meaux/100 10.00
262 Dustin Pedroia/100 35.00
263 Fernando Nieve/100 10.00
264 Mariano Gomez/100 10.00
266 Billy Killian/100 15.00
267 Mike Rouse/100 10.00
268 Kyle Bono/100 10.00
269 Mitch Einertson/100 15.00
270 Scott Proctor/100 10.00
271 Tim Bittner/100 8.00
272 Christian Garcia/100 10.00
273 Yadier Molina/100 30.00
274 Justin Leone/100 10.00
275 Charles Thomas/100 15.00
276 Travis Blackley/100 10.00
277 Frankie Francisco/100 10.00
278 Dioner Navarro/100 15.00
279 Joey Gathright/100 15.00
280 Kazuhito Tadano/100 15.00
281 Matt Bush/250 20.00
282 David Haehnel/250 8.00
283 Tommy Hottovy/250 8.00
284 Chris Carter/250 35.00
285 Mark Rogers/100 30.00
286 Jeremy Sowers/250 35.00
287 Homer Bailey/250 75.00
288 Mike Butia/250 8.00
289 Chris Nelson/250 30.00
290 Thomas Diamond/250 25.00
291 Neil Walker/242 20.00
292 Sean Gamble/250 8.00
293 Bill Bray/250 8.00
294 Reid Brignac/100 60.00
295 Ryan Klosterman/250 8.00
296 David Purcey/250 8.00
297 Scott Elbert/250 50.00
298 Josh Fields/250 40.00
299 Chris Lambert/250 15.00
300 Trevor Plouffe/250 15.00
301 Greg Golson/250 20.00
302 Josh Baker/100 10.00
303 Phillip Hughes/250 125.00
304 Matt Macri/250 15.00
305 Kyle Waldrop/250 15.00
306 Richie Robnett/250 15.00
307 Taylor Tankersley/250 10.00
308 Blake DeWitt/250 25.00
309 Daryl Jones/250 8.00
310 Eric Hurley/250 25.00
311 J.P. Howell/250 10.00
312 Zach Jackson/250 10.00
313 Justin Orenduff/100 15.00
314 Tyler Lumsden/250 10.00
315 Matt Fox/250 12.00
316 Danny Putnam/250 12.00
317 Jon Poterson/238 12.00
318 Gio Gonzalez/250 30.00
319 Jay Rainville/250 20.00
320 Huston Street/250 30.00
321 Jeff Marquez/250 10.00
322 Eric Beattie/250 8.00
323 B.J. Szymanski/250 8.00
324 Seth Smith/250 15.00
325 Robert Johnson/100 10.00
326 Wes Whisler/100 8.00
327 Billy Buckner/100 10.00
328 Jon Zeringue/250 20.00
329 Curtis Thigpen/100 10.00
330 Donny Lucy/100 8.00
331 Mike Ferris/250 10.00
332 Anthony Swarzak/100 25.00
333 Jason Jaramillo/250 8.00
334 Hunter Pence/200 90.00
335 Mike Rozier/250 8.00
336 Kurt Suzuki/250 20.00
337 Jason Vargas/200 20.00
338 Brian Bixler/200 8.00
340 Dexter Fowler/250 40.00
341 Mark Trumbo/250 20.00
342 Jeff Frazier/50 20.00
343 Steven Register/200 8.00
344 Michael Schlact/200 8.00
345 Garrett Mock/200 15.00
346 Eric Haberer/100 8.00
347 Matt Tuiasosopo/250 30.00
348 Jason Windsor/100 15.00
349 Grant Johnson/250 8.00
350 J.C. Holt/100 8.00
351 Joseph Bauserman/100 8.00
352 Jamar Walton/200 12.00
353 Eric Patterson/250 8.00
354 Tyler Johnson/250 15.00
355 Nick Adenhart/100 100.00

Throwback Threads

NM/M
Production 50 Sets
1 Roger Maris 60.00
2 Ted Williams 80.00
3 Cal Ripken Jr. 75.00
4 Duke Snider 20.00
5 George Brett 40.00

Throwback Threads Autograph

No Pricing

2004 Donruss Leather & Lumber

NM/M
Complete Set (175):
Common Player (1-150): .25
Common Auto. (151-173): 6.00
Production 500
Pack (5): 5.00
Box (24): 100.00
1 Bartolo Colon .25
2 Garret Anderson .50
3 Tim Salmon .40
4 Troy Glaus .50
5 Vladimir Guerrero 1.00
6 Brandon Webb .25
7 Luis Gonzalez .40
8 Randy Johnson 1.00
9 Richie Sexson .50
10 Shea Hillenbrand .25
11 Adam LaRoche .25
12 Andruw Jones .50
13 Chipper Jones 1.00
14 Dale Murphy .75
15 J.D. Drew .50
16 Marcus Giles .25
17 Rafael Furcal .25
18 Cal Ripken Jr. 3.00
19 Javy Lopez .50
20 Jay Gibbons .25
21 Luis Matos .25
22 Miguel Tejada .75
23 Rafael Palmeiro .75
24 Curt Schilling .75
25 Jason Varitek .40
26 Manny Ramirez .75
27 Nomar Garciaparra 1.50
28 Pedro J. Martinez 1.00
29 Trot Nixon .25
30 Greg Maddux 1.50
31 Kerry Wood .50
32 Mark Prior 1.00
33 Ryne Sandberg 1.50
34 Sammy Sosa 2.00
35 Carlos Lee .25
36 Frank Thomas .75
37 Magglio Ordonez .40
38 Paul Konerko .25
39 Adam Dunn .75
40 Austin Kearns .25
41 Barry Larkin .50
42 Ken Griffey Jr. 1.50
43 Ryan Wagner .25
44 C.C. Sabathia .25
45 Jody Gerut .25
46 Omar Vizquel .25
47 Larry Walker .40
48 Preston Wilson .25
49 Todd Helton .75
50 Alan Trammell .75
51 Ivan Rodriguez .75
52 Jeremy Bonderman .25
53 Dontrelle Willis .50
54 Josh Beckett .50
55 Luis Castillo .25
56 Miguel Cabrera 1.00
57 Mike Lowell .40
58 Andy Pettitte .40
59 Craig Biggio .40
60 Jeff Bagwell .75
61 Jeff Kent .40
62 Lance Berkman .40
63 Roger Clemens 2.50
64 Roy Oswalt .40
65 Angel Berroa .25
66 Carlos Beltran .75
67 George Brett 2.00
68 Juan Gonzalez .50
69 Mike Sweeney .25
70 Eric Gagne .50
71 Hideo Nomo .25
72 Kazuhisa Ishii .25
73 Paul LoDuca .25
74 Shawn Green .50
75 Geoff Jenkins .25
76 Junior Spivey .25
77 Rickie Weeks .75
78 Robin Yount .75
79 Scott Podsednik .25
80 Jacque Jones .25
81 Johan Santana .50
82 Shannon Stewart .25
83 Torii Hunter .40
84 Andre Dawson .50
85 Chad Cordero .25
86 Jose Vidro .25
87 Nick Johnson .25
88 Orlando Cabrera .40
89 Gary Carter .50
90 Jae Weong Seo .25
91 Jose Reyes .50
92 Mike Piazza 1.50
93 Tom Glavine .50
94 Alex Rodriguez 2.50
95 Bernie Williams .50
96 Derek Jeter 2.50
97 Don Mattingly 2.00
98 Gary Sheffield .50
99 Hideki Matsui 1.50
100 Jason Giambi .50
101 Jorge Posada .50
102 Mike Mussina .50
103 Barry Zito .50
104 Bobby Crosby .25
105 Eric Chavez .40
106 Jermaine Dye .25
107 Mark Mulder .40
108 Rich Harden .25
109 Rickey Henderson .25
110 Tim Hudson .40
111 Bobby Abreu .40
112 Brett Myers .25
113 Jim Thome 1.00
114 Kevin Millwood .25
115 Marlon Byrd .25
116 Mike Schmidt 2.00
117 Pat Burrell .25
118 Dave Parker .25
119 Jason Bay .25
120 Jason Kendall .25
121 Brian Giles .25
122 Jay Payton .25
123 Ryan Klesko .25
124 Tony Gwynn 1.00
125 Edgardo Alfonzo .25
126 Jason Schmidt .50
127 Jerome Williams .25
128 Bret Boone .25
129 Edgar Martinez .25
130 Ichiro Suzuki 2.00
131 Jamie Moyer .25
132 John Olerud .25
133 Albert Pujols 2.00
134 Edgar Renteria .40
135 Jim Edmonds .25
136 Matt Morris .25
137 Scott Rolen 1.00
138 Aubrey Huff .25
139 Carl Crawford .25
140 Delmon Young .25
141 Rocco Baldelli .25
142 Alfonso Soriano 1.00
143 Hank Blalock .75
144 Mark Teixeira .50
145 Michael Young .25
146 Nolan Ryan 2.50
147 Carlos Delgado .50
148 Eric Hinske .25
149 Roy Halladay .25
150 Vernon Wells .25
151 Andres Blanco RC 8.00
152 Kevin Cave RC 6.00
153 Ryan Meaux RC 6.00
154 Tim Bausher RC 6.00
155 Jesse Harper RC 6.00
156 Mike Wuertz RC 8.00
157 Colby Miller RC 6.00
158 Donald Kelly RC 6.00
159 Edwin Moreno RC 6.00
160 Mike Johnston RC 6.00
161 Orlando Rodriguez RC 6.00
162 Phil Stockman RC 8.00
163 Yadier Molina RC 8.00
164 Jorge Vasquez RC 8.00
165 Scott Proctor RC 8.00
166 Jake Woods RC 8.00
167 Aarom Baldiris RC 8.00
168 Jason Bartlett RC 8.00
169 Casey Daigle RC 6.00
170 Dennis Sarfate RC 6.00
171 Edwardo Sierra RC 8.00
172 Merkin Valdez RC 8.00
173 Eddy Rodriguez RC 8.00
174 Kazuo Matsui RC 8.00
175 David Aardsma RC 4.00

Silver

Stars (1-150): 4-8X
SP's (151-175): .5X
Production 100 Sets

Gold

Stars (1-150): 10-15X
SP's (151-175): No Pricing
Production 25 Sets

Platinum

No Pricing
Production One Set

B/W

NM/M
Common Player: 1.50
Production 1,000 Sets
Gold B/W: 4-6X
Production 25 Sets
Silver B/W: 2-3X
Production 100 Sets
Platinum B/W: No Pricing
Production One Set
13 Chipper Jones 2.00
14 Dale Murphy 1.50
18 Cal Ripken Jr. 8.00
27 Nomar Garciaparra 3.00
30 Greg Maddux 2.50
32 Mark Prior 1.50
33 Ryne Sandberg 3.00
34 Sammy Sosa 3.00
63 Roger Clemens 4.00
67 George Brett 4.00
78 Robin Yount 3.00
89 Gary Carter 1.50
92 Mike Piazza 3.00
94 Alex Rodriguez 5.00
96 Derek Jeter 5.00
97 Don Mattingly 4.00
99 Hideki Matsui 3.00
109 Rickey Henderson 1.50
116 Mike Schmidt 3.00
124 Tony Gwynn 2.00
130 Ichiro Suzuki 4.00
133 Albert Pujols 3.00
142 Alfonso Soriano 2.00
146 Nolan Ryan 5.00
174 Kazuo Matsui 6.00

Bat-Spikes

NM/M
Bat/Glove: .75-1.5X
Production 1-50
Bat/Ball: .75-1.5X
Production 5-25
No pricing 15 or less.
Barrel/Jersey: No Pricing
Production 1-5
1 Andruw Jones/25 15.00
6 Angel Berroa/25 10.00
7 Barry Zito/25 15.00
8 Ben Sheets/50 10.00
9 Brad Penny/50 8.00
9 Brian Giles/25 8.00
10 Carlos Lee/50 8.00
11 Corey Patterson/50 15.00
14 Don Mattingly/25 40.00
15 Gary Carter/25 12.00
17 Ivan Rodriguez/50 15.00
19 Jack Cust/50 8.00
19 Jason Jennings/50 8.00
22 Jim Edmonds/50 10.00
22 Joe Borchard/50 8.00
23 Joe Crede/50 8.00
24 Josh Beckett/25 15.00
25 Josh Phelps/50 8.00
27 Juan Pierre/50 8.00
27 Kenny Lofton/50 8.00
29 Lance Berkman/25 10.00
30 Magglio Ordonez/25 10.00
31 Marcus Giles/50 10.00
32 Mark Buehrle/50 8.00
38 Mark Prior/25 20.00
35 Mark Teixeira/25 15.00
35 Marlon Byrd/50 10.00
38 Nick Johnson/25 10.00
39 Orlando Hudson/25 8.00
40 Paul LoDuca/25 10.00
41 Rafael Palmeiro/25 20.00
43 Roy Oswalt/25 15.00
46 Ryan Klesko/50 10.00
46 Sean Casey/50 8.00
47 Travis Hafner/50 15.00
49 Victor Martinez/50 10.00
50 Wade Miller/50 10.00

Cuts

NM/M
Common Player:
1 Adam Dunn/192 20.00
2 Al Kaline/192 35.00
3 Alfonso Soriano/160 40.00
4 Andre Dawson/224 15.00
5 Angel Berroa/224 10.00
6 Harmon Killebrew/192 35.00
7 Bob Gibson/96 30.00
8 Brooks Robinson/192 30.00
9 Cal Ripken Jr./32 200.00
10 Dale Murphy/224 25.00
11 Darryl Strawberry/224 15.00
12 Delmon Young/192 20.00
13 Don Mattingly/96 65.00
14 Duke Snider/96 60.00
15 Dwight Gooden/96 60.00
16 Ozzie Smith/96 60.00
17 Garret Anderson/224 15.00
18 Gary Carter/160 20.00
19 George Kell/224 15.00
20 George Kell/224 15.00
21 Hank Blalock/224 20.00
22 Jim Palmer/192 20.00
23 Kirk Gibson/160 15.00
24 Lou Brock/192 25.00

Cuts Glove

NM/M
Quantity produced listed
1 Adam Dunn/192 20.00
2 Al Kaline/192 35.00
3 Alfonso Soriano/160 40.00
4 Andre Dawson/224 15.00
5 Angel Berroa/224 10.00
6 Harmon Killebrew/192 35.00
7 Bob Gibson/96 30.00
8 Brooks Robinson/192 30.00
9 Cal Ripken Jr./32 200.00
10 Dale Murphy/224 25.00
11 Darryl Strawberry/224 15.00
12 Delmon Young/192 20.00
13 Don Mattingly/96 65.00
14 Duke Snider/96 30.00
15 Dwight Gooden/96 15.00
16 Ozzie Smith/96 60.00
17 Garret Anderson/224 15.00
18 Gary Carter/160 20.00
19 Jason Jennings/50 8.00
20 George Kell/224 15.00
21 Hank Blalock/224 20.00
22 Jim Palmer/192 20.00
23 Kirk Gibson/160 15.00
24 Lou Brock/192 25.00
25 Ryne Sandberg/160 50.00
26 Mark Prior/160 40.00
27 Miguel Cabrera/224 25.00
28 Mike Lowell/160 15.00
29 Nolan Ryan/96 100.00
30 Luis Aparicio/224 15.00
31 Paul Molitor/160 30.00
32 Red Schoendienst/224 25.00
33 Rickie Weeks/224 25.00
34 Ron Santo/224 25.00
35 Roy Oswalt/224 20.00
36 Stan Musial/96 60.00
37 Steve Carlton/192 20.00
38 Tony Gwynn/192 35.00
39 Vernon Wells/160 10.00
40 Will Clark/192 35.00
41 Bob Feller/224 25.00
42 Bobby Doerr/224 20.00
44 Ralph Kiner/224 30.00
45 Torii Hunter/224 15.00
46 Rollie Fingers/224 15.00
48 Steve Garvey/224 15.00
49 Alan Trammell/224 15.00
50 Maury Wills/224 15.00
Gaylord Perry/224 15.00

Hall of Fame

NM/M
Common Player: 2.00
Quantity produced listed
Silver: 1-2X
Production 100 Sets
1 Carl Yastrzemski/1989 4.00
2 Carlton Fisk/2000 2.00
3 George Brett/1999 5.00
4 Johnny Bench/1989 4.00
5 Mike Schmidt/1995 5.00
6 Nolan Ryan/1999 4.00
7 Ozzie Smith/2002 4.00
8 Robin Yount/1999 4.00
9 Rod Carew/1991 3.00
10 Tom Seaver/1992 3.00

Hall of Fame Materials

NM/M
Quantity produced listed
1 Carl Yastrzemski/Jsy/250 15.00
2 Carlton Fisk/Jsy/250 10.00
3 George Brett/Jsy/250 15.00
4 Johnny Bench/Jsy/100 15.00
5 Mike Schmidt/Jkt/250 15.00
6 Nolan Ryan/Pants/100 25.00
7 Ozzie Smith/Jsy/100 20.00
8 Robin Yount/Jsy/250 12.00
9 Rod Carew/Jkt/250 15.00
10 Tom Seaver/Jsy/200 15.00

Leather Cuts Ball

No Pricing
Production 5-10

Leather in Leather

NM/M
Common Player:
Production 2,499 Sets
Silver: 1-2X
Production 100 Sets
1 Garret Anderson BB 1.50
2 Albert Pujols BB 5.00
3 John Smoltz BB 1.50
4 Cal Ripken Jr. BB 8.00
5 Ichiro Suzuki BB 5.00
6 Pedro J. Martinez BB 2.00
7 Shawn Green BB 1.50
8 Juan Gonzalez BB 1.50
9 Mariano Rivera BB 1.50
10 Jason Giambi BB 1.50
11 Dave Parker BG 1.50
12 Dwight Gooden BG 1.50
13 Eric Munson BG 1.50
14 Frank Thomas BG 2.00
15 Joe Carter BG 1.50
16 Jose Canseco BG 1.50
17 Paul O'Neill BG 1.50
18 Tony Gwynn BG 3.00
19 Wade Boggs BG 2.00
20 Xavier Nady BG 1.50
21 Albert Pujols FG 5.00
22 Alex Rodriguez FG 6.00
23 Chipper Jones FG 1.50
24 Derek Jeter FG 6.00
25 Jack Wilson FG 1.50
26 Lenny Dykstra FG 1.50
27 Mark Grace FG 2.00
28 Steve Carlton FG 2.00
29 Tony Perez FG 2.00
30 Vladimir Guerrero FG 3.00
31 Bernie Williams SH 3.00
32 Eddie Murray SH 3.00
33 Frank Robinson SH 3.00
34 Greg Maddux SH 4.00
35 Harmon Killebrew SH 3.00
36 Manny Ramirez SH 2.00
37 Mike Piazza SH 4.00
38 Paul Molitor SH 3.00
39 Sammy Sosa SH 4.00
40 Tim Hudson SH 2.00

Leather Materials

NM/M
Quantity produced listed
1 Garret Anderson/Ball/50 8.00
2 Albert Pujols Ball/50 25.00
3 John Smoltz Ball/50 20.00
4 Cal Ripken Jr./Ball/50 75.00
5 Ichiro Suzuki Ball/50 60.00
6 Pedro J. Martinez/Ball/50 15.00
7 Shawn Green Ball/50 8.00
8 Juan Gonzalez/Ball/50 10.00
9 Mariano Rivera/Ball/50 10.00
10 Jason Giambi Ball/50 10.00
11 Dave Parker/Btg Glv/25 20.00
12 Dwight Gooden/Btg Glv/25 20.00
13 Eric Munson/Btg Glv/50 8.00
14 Frank Thomas/Btg Glv/50 20.00
15 Joe Carter/Btg Glv/50 10.00
16 Jose Canseco/Btg Glv/50 20.00

17	Paul O'Neill/ Btg Glv/50	20.00
18	Tony Gwynn/ Btg Glv/50	30.00
19	Wade Boggs/ Btg Glv/25	10.00
20	Xavier Nady/ Btg Glv/50	8.00
22	Alex Rodriguez/ Fld Glv/25	35.00
23	Chipper Jones/ Fld Glv/50	30.00
24	Derek Jeter/ Fld Glv/25	50.00
25	Jack Wilson/ Fld Glv/50	8.00
26	Lenny Dykstra/ Fld Glv/50	10.00
27	Mark Grace/ Fld Glv/50	15.00
28	Steve Carlton/ Fld Glv/50	12.00
29	Tony Perez/ Fld Glv/25	15.00
31	Bernie Williams/ Spikes/50	10.00
32	Eddie Murray/ Spikes/50	30.00
33	Frank Robinson/ Spikes/50	10.00
34	Greg Maddux/ Spikes/25	30.00
35	Harmon Killebrew/ Spikes/25	35.00

Materials Bat B/W

NM/M
Production 100 unless noted.

13	Chipper Jones	8.00
14	Dale Murphy	4.00
18	Cal Ripken Jr.	30.00
20	Nomar Garciaparra	10.00
30	Greg Maddux	10.00
32	Mark Prior	8.00
33	Ryne Sandberg/50	30.00
34	Sammy Sosa	12.00
63	Roger Clemens	20.00
67	George Brett	15.00
78	Robin Yount	12.00
89	Gary Carter	8.00
92	Mike Piazza	10.00
94	Alex Rodriguez	10.00
96	Derek Jeter	20.00
97	Don Mattingly	20.00
109	Rickey Henderson	10.00
116	Mike Schmidt	15.00
124	Tony Gwynn	10.00
133	Albert Pujols	20.00
142	Alfonso Soriano	8.00
146	Nolan Ryan/25	65.00
174	Kazuo Matsui	

Materials Jersey

NM/M
Common Jersey: 4.00
Quantity produced listed
MLB Logo: No Pricing
Production One Set
Prime: 1-1.25X
Production 1-25
No pricing 15 or less.
Barrel: No Pricing
Production 1-5

2	Garret Anderson/50	8.00
3	Tim Salmon/250	4.00
4	Troy Glaus/200	4.00
6	Brandon Webb/100	4.00
7	Luis Gonzalez/250	4.00
8	Randy Johnson/100	10.00
12	Andruw Jones/250	4.00
13	Chipper Jones/250	8.00
14	Dale Murphy/250	10.00
16	Marcus Giles/250	4.00
17	Rafael Furcal/250	4.00
18	Cal Ripken Jr./100	30.00
19	Javy Lopez/150	4.00
20	Jay Gibbons/250	4.00
21	Luis Matos/250	4.00
22	Miguel Tejada/250	6.00
23	Rafael Palmeiro/250	8.00
25	Jason Varitek/250	8.00
26	Manny Ramirez/250	4.00
28	Pedro J. Martinez/ 250	8.00
29	Trot Nixon/25	10.00
30	Greg Maddux/100	10.00
31	Kerry Wood/250	10.00
32	Mark Prior/250	8.00
33	Ryne Sandberg/50	30.00
34	Sammy Sosa/250	10.00
35	Carlos Lee/250	4.00
36	Frank Thomas/250	8.00
37	Magglio Ordonez/250	4.00
38	Paul Konerko/250	4.00
39	Adam Dunn/250	8.00
40	Austin Kearns/250	4.00
41	Barry Larkin/250	6.00
44	C.C. Sabathia/250	4.00
45	Jody Gerut/250	4.00
46	Omar Vizquel/250	4.00
47	Larry Walker/250	4.00
48	Preston Wilson/250	4.00
49	Todd Helton	8.00
50	Alan Trammell	10.00
51	Ivan Rodriguez/100	10.00
52	Jeremy Bonderman/ 150	4.00
53	Dontrelle Willis/100	4.00
54	Josh Beckett/250	4.00
55	Luis Castillo/250	4.00
56	Miguel Cabrera/50	15.00
57	Mike Lowell/25	10.00
58	Andy Pettitte/250	15.00
59	Craig Biggio/250	4.00
60	Jeff Bagwell/250	8.00
61	Jeff Kent/250	4.00
62	Lance Berkman/250	4.00
64	Roy Oswalt/250	4.00
66	Angel Berroa/50	6.00
67	Carlos Beltran/250	6.00
68	George Brett/250	15.00
69	Mike Sweeney/100	4.00
71	Hideo Nomo/250	6.00
72	Kazuhisa Ishii/250	4.00
73	Paul LoDuca/250	4.00
74	Shawn Green/250	4.00
75	Geoff Jenkins/250	4.00
78	Robin Yount/50	10.00
80	Jacque Jones/250	4.00
81	Johan Santana/250	8.00
82	Shannon Stewart/250	4.00
83	Torii Hunter/250	4.00
84	Andre Dawson/50	10.00
86	Jose Vidro/250	4.00
88	Orlando Cabrera/100	4.00
89	Gary Carter/250	8.00
90	Jae Weong Seo/100	4.00
91	Jose Reyes/250	6.00
92	Mike Piazza/250	10.00
93	Tom Glavine/250	6.00
95	Bernie Williams/250	4.00
96	Derek Jeter/150	20.00
98	Don Mattingly/250	15.00
99	Hideki Matsui/250	20.00
100	Jason Giambi/250	4.00
101	Jorge Posada/250	4.00
102	Mike Mussina/100	8.00
103	Barry Zito/250	4.00
105	Eric Chavez/100	4.00
107	Mark Mulder/250	6.00
108	Rich Harden/250	8.00
109	Rickey Henderson/ 250	10.00
110	Tim Hudson/250	4.00
111	Bobby Abreu/250	4.00
112	Brett Myers/250	4.00
113	Jim Thome/250	8.00
114	Kevin Millwood/250	4.00
115	Marlon Byrd/250	4.00
116	Mike Schmidt/50	25.00
117	Pat Burrell/250	4.00
118	Dave Parker/250	4.00
120	Jason Kendall/50	6.00
123	Ryan Klesko/250	4.00
124	Tony Gwynn/100	12.00
127	Jerome Williams/200	4.00
129	Edgar Martinez/250	6.00
131	Jamie Moyer/250	4.00
132	John Olerud/150	4.00
133	Albert Pujols/250	15.00
134	Edgar Renteria/250	6.00
135	Jim Edmonds/250	4.00
136	Matt Morris/250	4.00
137	Scott Rolen/250	6.00
138	Aubrey Huff/100	4.00
139	Carl Crawford/250	4.00
141	Rocco Baldelli/250	4.00
143	Hank Blalock/250	4.00
146	Nolan Ryan/250	30.00
147	Carlos Delgado/250	4.00
148	Eric Hinske/100	4.00
149	Roy Halladay/100	4.00
150	Vernon Wells/250	4.00

Materials Jersey B/W

NM/M
Common Player: 5.00
Jersey Prime B/W: No Pricing
Production 1-25

13	Chipper Jones/250	8.00
14	Dale Murphy/250	10.00
18	Cal Ripken Jr./100	35.00
30	Greg Maddux/100	10.00
32	Mark Prior/250	8.00
33	Ryne Sandberg/250	30.00
34	Sammy Sosa/250	12.00
67	George Brett/250	10.00
78	Robin Yount/150	10.00
89	Gary Carter/250	5.00
92	Mike Piazza/250	10.00
96	Derek Jeter/100	20.00
97	Don Mattingly/250	15.00
99	Hideki Matsui/250	10.00
109	Rickey Henderson/ 250	8.00
116	Mike Schmidt/50	25.00
124	Tony Gwynn/100	10.00
133	Albert Pujols/250	15.00
146	Nolan Ryan/250	25.00
174	Kazuo Matsui/50	25.00

Naturals

NM/M
Common Player: 1.50
Production 1,499 Sets
Silver: 1-2X
Production 100 Sets

1	Eric Chavez	1.50
2	Garret Anderson	1.50
3	Lance Berkman	1.50
4	Paul Molitor	3.00
5	Rafael Palmeiro	2.00

6	Ralph Kiner	3.00
7	Todd Helton	2.00
8	Tony Gwynn	4.00
9	Wade Boggs	2.00
10	Will Clark	2.00

Naturals Materials Bat

NM/M
Barrel: No Pricing
Production 1-5

1	Eric Chavez/20	12.00
2	Garret Anderson/250	5.00
3	Lance Berkman/250	5.00
4	Paul Molitor/250	8.00
5	Rafael Palmeiro/250	8.00
6	Ralph Kiner/250	10.00
7	Todd Helton/250	8.00
8	Tony Gwynn/250	12.00
9	Wade Boggs/250	8.00
10	Will Clark/250	10.00

Pennants/ Pinstripes

NM/M
Common Player: 1.50
Production 1,499 Sets
Gold: 1-2X
Production 100 Sets

1	Reggie Jackson	2.50
2	Mike Schmidt	5.00
3	Steve Carlton	2.00
4	Dwight Gooden	1.50
5	Darryl Strawberry	1.50
6	Roger Clemens	5.00
7	Curt Schilling	2.00
8	Mark Grace	2.00
9	Ivan Rodriguez	2.00
10	Josh Beckett	1.50

Pennants/ Pinstripes Materials

NM/M
Quantity produced listed

1	Reggie Jackson/ Pants/100	10.00
2	Mike Schmidt/Jsy/25	35.00
3	Steve Carlton/ Jsy/100	8.00
4	Dwight Gooden/ Jsy/250	8.00
5	Darryl Strawberry/ Pants/250	4.00
6	Roger Clemens/ Jsy/250	10.00
7	Curt Schilling/Jsy/250	6.00
8	Mark Grace/Jsy/250	8.00
9	Ivan Rodriguez/ Jsy/250	8.00
10	Josh Beckett/Jsy/100	5.00

Rivals

NM/M
Common Duo: 1.50
Production 1,499 Sets
Silver: 1-2X
Production 100 Sets

1	Derek Jeter, Nomar Garciaparra	6.00
2	Mark Prior, Albert Pujols	4.00
3	Warren Spahn, Stan Musial	4.00
4	Don Sutton, Reggie Jackson	2.00
5	Roger Clemens, Mike Piazza	4.00
6	Dennis Eckersley, M. Williams	1.50
7	Kerry Wood, Frank Thomas	3.00
8	Jim Palmer, Willie Stargell	2.00
9	Tom Seaver, Mike Schmidt	5.00
10	Jack Morris, George Brett	5.00
11	Randy Johnson, Todd Helton	2.00
12	Tommy John, Rod Carew	2.00
13	Pedro J. Martinez, Jason Giambi	2.00
14	Dwight Gooden, Wade Boggs	1.50
15	Bob Gibson, Ernie Banks	3.00
16	Hideo Nomo, Barry Larkin	1.50
17	Roy Halladay, Vladimir Guerrero	2.00
18	Greg Maddux, Jeff Bagwell	3.00
19	Barry Zito, Alex Rodriguez	5.00
20	Steve Carlton, Andre Dawson	1.50
21	Mariano Rivera, Chipper Jones	2.00
22	Tom Glavine, Manny Ramirez	2.00
23	Whitey Ford, Harmon Killebrew	2.00
24	Carl Yastrzemski, Jim "Catfish" Hunter	2.00
25	Nolan Ryan, Robin Ventura	5.00
26	Carlton Fisk, Joe Morgan	1.50
27	Phil Rizzuto, Duke Snider	2.00
28	Fergie Jenkins, Lou Brock	1.50
29	Jose Canseco, Will Clark	1.50
30	Mike Mussina, Josh Beckett	1.50
31	Rickey Henderson, Ivan Rodriguez	2.00
32	Don Mattingly, Eddie Murray	5.00
33	Troy Glaus, Eric Chavez	1.50
34	Ryne Sandberg, Steve Garvey	3.00
35	Bob Gibson, Roger Maris	4.00
36	Roger Clemens, Cal Ripken Jr.	8.00
37	Orel Hershiser, Darryl Strawberry	1.50
38	Curt Schilling, Paul Molitor	2.00
39	Ichiro Suzuki, Hideki Matsui	5.00
40	Sammy Sosa, Jim Thome	2.00

Rivals Materials

NM/M
Quantity produced listed

1	Derek Jeter/Jsy, Nomar Garciaparra/ Bat/250	25.00
2	Mark Prior/Jsy, Albert Pujols/ Jsy/250	20.00
3	Warren Spahn/Pants, Stan Musial/Jsy/100	30.00
5	Roger Clemens/Jsy, Mike Piazza/Jsy/250	20.00
7	Kerry Wood/Jsy, Frank Thomas/ Jsy/100	10.00
8	Jim Palmer/Jsy, Willie Stargell/ Jsy/250	12.00
9	Tom Seaver/Jsy, Mike Schmidt/ Jsy/250	20.00
10	Jack Morris/Jsy, George Brett/Jsy/250	15.00
11	Randy Johnson/Jsy, Todd Helton/Jsy/250	12.00
12	Tommy John/Pants, Rod Carew/Jsy/250	8.00
13	Pedro J. Martinez/Jsy, Jason Giambi/ Jsy/250	12.00
14	Dwight Gooden/Jsy, Wade Boggs/Jsy/250	10.00
15	Bob Gibson/Jsy, Ernie Banks/ Pants/250	20.00
16	Hideo Nomo/Jsy, Barry Larkin/Jsy/250	10.00
17	Roy Halladay/Jsy, Vladimir Guerrero/ Jsy/250	10.00
18	Greg Maddux/Jsy, Jeff Bagwell/Jsy/250	15.00
19	Barry Zito/Jsy, Alex Rodriguez/ Jsy/250	15.00
20	Steve Carlton/Jsy, Andre Dawson/ Jsy/250	10.00
22	Tom Glavine/Jsy, Manny Ramirez/ Jsy/250	10.00
23	Whitey Ford/Pants, Harmon Killebrew/ Jsy/100	35.00
24	Carl Yastrzemski/Jsy, Jim "Catfish" Hunter/ Jsy/250	20.00
25	Nolan Ryan/Pants, Robin Ventura/ Jsy/250	25.00
26	Carlton Fisk/Jsy, Joe Morgan/Jsy/250	10.00
28	Fergie Jenkins/Pants, Lou Brock/Jsy/250	10.00
29	Jose Canseco Bat, Will Clark Bat/250	15.00
30	Mike Mussina/Jsy, Josh Beckett/Jsy/250	10.00
31	Rickey Henderson/Jsy, Ivan Rodriguez/ Jsy/250	10.00
32	Don Mattingly/Pants, Eddie Murray/ Jsy/250	20.00
33	Troy Glaus/Jsy, Eric Chavez/Jsy/250	8.00
34	Ryne Sandberg/Jsy, Steve Garvey/ Jsy/250	20.00
35	Bob Gibson/Jsy, Roger Maris/Jsy/100	40.00
36	Roger Clemens/Jsy, Cal Ripken Jr./ Pants/250	30.00
38	Curt Schilling/Jsy, Paul Molitor/Bat/250	12.00
39	Ichiro Suzuki/Base, Hideki Matsui/ Base/250	40.00
40	Sammy Sosa/Jsy, Jim Thome/Jsy/250	12.00

Signatures Bronze

NM/M
Quantity produced listed

2	Garret Anderson/25	25.00
10	Shea Hillenbrand/ 100	10.00
11	Adam LaRoche/100	10.00
14	Dale Murphy/25	35.00
16	Marcus Giles/50	15.00
17	Rafael Furcal/100	20.00
20	Jay Gibbons/100	10.00
21	Luis Matos/100	10.00
35	Carlos Lee/100	10.00
39	Adam Dunn/25	30.00
44	C.C. Sabathia/100	15.00
48	Preston Wilson/50	15.00
50	Alan Trammell/20	20.00
52	Jeremy Bonderman/ 100	10.00
56	Miguel Cabrera/50	30.00
65	Angel Berroa/100	10.00
66	Carlos Beltran/100	25.00
79	Scott Podsednik/100	10.00
81	Johan Santana/100	40.00
82	Shannon Stewart/ 100	10.00
83	Torii Hunter/100	15.00
85	Andre Dawson/100	15.00
86	Chad Cordero/100	8.00
86	Jose Vidro/100	10.00
88	Orlando Cabrera/100	10.00
106	Bobby Crosby/100	20.00
108	Rich Harden/100	20.00
119	Marlon Byrd/100	15.00
122	Jay Payton/100	10.00
138	Aubrey Huff/50	15.00
145	Carl Crawford/Jkt/250	20.00
151	Andres Blanco/50	10.00
153	Kevin Cave/100	10.00
155	Ryan Meaux/100	8.00
155	Jesse Harper/100	8.00
156	Mike Wuertz/100	10.00
158	Donald Kelly/100	6.00
159	Edwin Moreno/100	6.00
160	Mike Johnston/100	6.00
161	Orlando Rodriguez/ 100	6.00
164	Jorge Vasquez/100	8.00
166	Jake Woods/100	8.00
170	Dennis Sarfate/100	8.00
173	Eddy Rodriguez/100	8.00

Signatures Bronze B/W

No Pricing
Production 1-25

Signatures Silver

NM/M
Quantity produced listed

2	Garret Anderson/50	20.00
10	Shea Hillenbrand/50	15.00
11	Adam LaRoche/50	15.00
14	Dale Murphy/50	25.00
16	Marcus Giles/50	15.00
17	Rafael Furcal/50	15.00
20	Jay Gibbons/50	10.00
21	Luis Matos/25	35.00
32	Mark Prior/50	40.00
35	Carlos Lee/50	15.00
39	Adam Dunn/25	30.00
40	Austin Kearns/25	10.00
43	Ryan Wagner/50	15.00
44	C.C. Sabathia/50	15.00
45	Jody Gerut/50	15.00
48	Preston Wilson/50	15.00
50	Alan Trammell/50	20.00
52	Jeremy Bonderman/ 50	10.00
56	Miguel Cabrera/50	30.00
65	Angel Berroa/50	10.00
66	Carlos Beltran/50	30.00
73	Paul LoDuca/25	20.00
79	Scott Podsednik/50	15.00
80	Jacque Jones/50	15.00
81	Johan Santana/50	40.00
82	Shannon Stewart/50	15.00
83	Torii Hunter/50	15.00
84	Andre Dawson/50	15.00
85	Chad Cordero/50	8.00
86	Jose Vidro/50	10.00
88	Orlando Cabrera/50	12.00
104	Bobby Crosby/50	25.00
106	Jermaine Dye/50	15.00
107	Mark Mulder/25	20.00
108	Rich Harden/50	20.00
115	Marlon Byrd/50	10.00
119	Jason Bay/50	20.00
122	Jay Payton/50	10.00
138	Aubrey Huff/50	15.00
143	Carl Crawford/50	20.00
143	Hank Blalock/50	25.00
145	Michael Young/50	20.00
150	Vernon Wells/50	15.00
151	Andres Blanco/50	10.00
152	Kevin Cave/100	10.00
153	Ryan Meaux/100	8.00
155	Tim Bausher/100	8.00
155	Jesse Harper/100	8.00
158	Mike Wuertz/100	10.00
159	Donald Kelly/100	6.00
160	Edwin Moreno/100	6.00
161	Mike Johnston/100	6.00
164	Orlando Rodriguez/ 100	6.00
166	Jorge Vasquez/100	8.00
170	Jake Woods/50	10.00
167	Aarom Baldiris/100	10.00
170	Dennis Sarfate/100	8.00
173	Eddy Rodriguez/100	8.00

Signatures Silver B/W

No Pricing
Production 1-25

Signatures Gold

NM/M
Quantity produced listed

2	Garret Anderson/25	25.00
10	Shea Hillenbrand/25	20.00
11	Adam LaRoche/25	15.00
14	Dale Murphy/25	35.00
16	Marcus Giles/25	20.00
17	Rafael Furcal/25	20.00
20	Jay Gibbons/25	15.00
21	Luis Matos/25	15.00
35	Carlos Lee/25	15.00
39	Adam Dunn/25	30.00
44	C.C. Sabathia/25	20.00
45	Jody Gerut/25	20.00
48	Preston Wilson/25	20.00
50	Alan Trammell/25	25.00
52	Jeremy Bonderman/ 25	15.00
56	Miguel Cabrera/25	35.00
65	Angel Berroa/25	10.00
66	Carlos Beltran/25	40.00
79	Scott Podsednik/25	20.00
80	Jacque Jones/25	20.00
81	Johan Santana/25	50.00
82	Shannon Stewart/25	20.00
83	Torii Hunter/25	20.00
84	Andre Dawson/25	20.00
85	Chad Cordero/25	10.00
86	Jose Vidro/25	15.00
88	Orlando Cabrera/25	15.00
104	Bobby Crosby/25	30.00
106	Jermaine Dye/25	20.00
115	Marlon Byrd/25	15.00
119	Jason Bay/25	25.00
122	Jay Payton/25	15.00
138	Aubrey Huff/25	20.00
139	Carl Crawford/25	25.00

145	Michael Young/25	30.00
151	Andres Blanco/50	10.00
152	Kevin Cave/50	10.00
153	Ryan Meaux/50	10.00
154	Tim Bausher/50	10.00
155	Jesse Harper/50	10.00
156	Mike Wuertz/50	10.00
158	Donald Kelly/50	10.00
159	Edwin Moreno/50	8.00
160	Mike Johnston/50	8.00
161	Orlando Rodriguez/50	10.00
164	Jorge Vasquez/50	10.00
166	Jake Woods/50	10.00
167	Aarom Baldiris/50	10.00
168	Jason Bartlett/50	12.00
170	Dennis Sarfate/50	8.00
173	Eddy Rodriguez/50	10.00

Signatures Gold B/W

No Pricing
Production 1-25

Signatures Platinum

No Pricing
Production One Set

Signatures Platinum B/W

No Pricing
Production One Set

2004 Donruss Studio

CHIPPER JONES

		NM/M
Complete Set (220):		
Common Player:		.15
Common SP (201-221):		6.00
Production 400-800:		
Pack (6):		4.00
Box (24):		75.00
1	Bartolo Colon	.15
2	Garret Anderson	.40
3	Tim Salmon	.25
4	Troy Glaus	.40
5	Vladimir Guerrero	.75
6	Brandon Webb	.15
7	Brian Bruney	.15
8	Casey Fossum	.15
9	Luis Gonzales	.25
10	Randy Johnson	1.00
11	Richie Sexson	.40
12	Robby Hammock	.15
13	Roberto Alomar	.40
14	Shea Hillenbrand	.15
15	Steve Finley	.15
16	Adam LaRoche	.15
17	Andruw Jones	.50
18	Bubba Nelson	.15
19	Chipper Jones	.75
20	Dale Murphy	.50
21	J.D. Drew	.25
22	Marcus Giles	.15
23	Michael Hessman	.15
24	Rafael Furcal	.25
25	Warren Spahn	.50
26	Adam Loewen	.15
27	Cal Ripken Jr.	3.00
28	Javy Lopez	.40
29	Jay Gibbons	.15
30	Luis Matos	.15
31	Miguel Tejada	.40
32	Rafael Palmeiro	.50
33	Curt Schilling	.50
34	Jason Varitek	.25
35	Kevin Youkilis	.15
36	Manny Ramirez	.50
37	Nomar Garciaparra	.75
38	Pedro Martinez	.75
39	Trot Nixon	.25
40	Aramis Ramirez	.15
41	Brendan Harris	.15
42	Derrek Lee	.25
43	Ernie Banks	1.00
44	Greg Maddux	1.00
45	Kerry Wood	.75
46	Mark Prior	1.00
47	Ryne Sandberg	1.00
48	Sammy Sosa	1.50
49	Todd Wellemeyer	.15
50	Carlos Lee	.15
51	Edwin Almonte	.15
52	Frank Thomas	.50

53	Joe Borchard	.15
54	Joe Crede	.15
55	Magglio Ordonez	.25
56	Adam Dunn	.50
57	Austin Kearns	.25
58	Barry Larkin	.40
59	Brandon Larson	.15
60	Ken Griffey Jr.	1.00
61	Ryan Wagner	.15
62	Sean Casey	.25
63	Brian Tallet	.15
64	C.C. Sabathia	.15
65	Jeremy Guthrie	.15
66	Jody Gerut	.15
67	Travis Hafner	.25
68	Clint Barmes	.15
69	Jeff Baker	.15
70	Joe Kennedy	.15
71	Larry Walker	.25
72	Preston Wilson	.15
73	Todd Helton	.50
74	Dmitri Young	.15
75	Ivan Rodriguez	.50
76	Jeremy Bonderman	.15
77	Preston Larrison	.15
78	Dontrelle Willis	.15
79	Josh Beckett	.50
80	Juan Pierre	.15
81	Luis Castillo	.15
82	Miguel Cabrera	.75
83	Mike Lowell	.25
84	Andy Pettitte	.15
85	Chris Burke	.15
86	Craig Biggio	.25
87	Jeff Bagwell	.25
88	Jeff Kent	.25
89	Lance Berkman	.25
90	Morgan Ensberg	.15
91	Richard Hidalgo	.15
92	Roger Clemens	1.50
93	Roy Oswalt	.25
94	Wade Miller	.15
95	Angel Berroa	.15
96	Byron Gettis	.15
97	Carlos Beltran	.25
98	Juan Gonzalez	.50
99	Mike Sweeney	.15
100	Duke Snider	.50
101	Edwin Jackson	.50
102	Eric Gagne	.50
103	Hideo Nomo	.40
104	Hong-Chih Kuo	.15
105	Kazuhisa Ishii	.15
106	Paul Lo Duca	.15
107	Robin Ventura	.15
108	Shawn Green	.25
109	Junior Spivey	.15
110	Lyle Overbay	.25
111	Rickie Weeks	.25
112	Scott Podsednik	.25
113	J.D. Durbin	.15
114	Jacque Jones	.15
115	Jason Kubel	.15
116	Johan Santana	.25
117	Shannon Stewart	.15
118	Torii Hunter	.25
119	Brad Wilkerson	.15
120	Jose Vidro	.15
121	Nick Johnson	.15
122	Orlando Cabrera	.15
123	Zach Day	.15
124	Gary Carter	.40
125	Jae Weong Seo	.15
126	Kazuo Matsui RC	5.00
127	Mike Piazza	1.00
128	Tom Glavine	.40
129	Alex Rodriguez	2.00
130	Bernie Williams	.40
131	Chien-Ming Wang	.50
132	Derek Jeter	2.00
133	Don Mattingly	2.00
134	Gary Sheffield	.40
135	Hideki Matsui	1.00
136	Jason Giambi	.50
137	Javier Vazquez	.25
138	Jorge Posada	.40
139	Jose Contreras	.15
140	Kevin Brown	.25
141	Mariano Rivera	.40
142	Mike Mussina	.40
143	Whitey Ford	.50
144	Barry Zito	.25
145	Eric Chavez	.25
146	Mark Mulder	.25
147	Rich Harden	.25
148	Tim Hudson	.25
149	Bobby Abreu	.25
150	Jim Thome	.75
151	Kevin Millwood	.25
152	Marlon Byrd	.15
153	Mike Schmidt	1.00
154	Ryan Howard	.75
155	Jack Wilson	.15
156	Jason Kendall	.15
157	Akinori Otsuka RC	1.00
158	Brian Giles	.25
159	David Wells	.15
160	Jay Payton	.15
161	Phil Nevin	.15
162	Ryan Klesko	.15
163	Sean Burroughs	.15
164	A.J. Pierzynski	.15
165	J.T. Snow	.15
166	Jason Schmidt	.25
167	Jerome Williams	.15
168	Merkin Valdez RC	1.00
169	Will Clark	.50
170	Bret Boone	.25

171	Chris Snelling	.15
172	Edgar Martinez	.25
173	Ichiro Suzuki	1.00
174	Jamie Moyer	.15
175	Randy Winn	.15
176	Rich Aurilia	.15
177	Shigetoshi Hasegawa	.15
178	Albert Pujols	1.50
179	Dan Haren	.15
180	Edgar Renteria	.25
181	Jim Edmonds	.25
182	Matt Morris	.15
183	Scott Rolen	.75
184	Stan Musial	1.00
185	Aubrey Huff	.15
186	Chad Gaudin	.15
187	Delmon Young	.15
188	Fred McGriff	.25
189	Rocco Baldelli	.25
190	Alfonso Soriano	.75
191	Hank Blalock	.50
192	Mark Teixeira	.50
193	Nolan Ryan	2.50
194	Alexis Rios	.15
195	Carlos Delgado	.50
196	Dustin McGowan	.15
197	Guillermo Quiroz	.15
198	Josh Phelps	.15
199	Roy Halladay	.25
200	Vernon Wells	.25
201	Mike Gosling AU/400	8.00
202	Ronny Cedeno AU/76 RC	8.00
203	Ronald Belisario AU/400 RC	8.00
204	Justin Hampson AU/800 RC	6.00
205	Carlos Vasquez AU/800 RC	6.00
206	Lincoln Holdzkom AU/800 RC	6.00
207	Casey Daigle AU/550 RC	6.00
208	Jason Bartlett AU/700 RC	6.00
209	Mariano Gomez AU/800 RC	8.00
210	Mike House AU/800 RC	6.00
211	Chris Shelton AU/800 RC	25.00
212	Dennis Sarfate AU/800 RC	8.00
213	Shingo Takatsu AU/800 RC	35.00
214	Justin Leone AU/800 RC	15.00
215	Cory Sullivan AU/800 RC	8.00
216	Mike Wuertz AU/800 RC	8.00
217	Tim Bausher AU/800 RC	8.00
218	Jesse Harper AU/800 RC	8.00
219	Ryan Meaux AU/800 RC	8.00
221	Kevin Cave AU/800 RC	8.00

Proofs Silver

Silver (1-200):	3-6X
Silver (201-225):	.25X
#220, 222-225 exist only in parallel set.	
Production 100 Sets	

Proofs Gold

Gold (1-200):	5-10X
Gold (201-225):	.5X
#220, 222-225 exist only in parallel set.	
Production 50 Sets	

Proofs Platinum

No Pricing
Production 10 Sets

Big League Challenge

		NM/M
Production 999 Sets		6.00
Die-Cut:		1X
Production 500 Sets		
1	Albert Pujols Left	6.00
2	Albert Pujols Right	6.00
3	Alex Rodriguez Rgr Left	5.00
4	Alex Rodriguez Rgr Right	5.00
5	Magglio Ordonez	2.00
6	Rafael Palmeiro	3.00
7	Troy Glaus Follow	2.00
8	Troy Glaus Start	2.00
9	Albert Pujols Bat Up	6.00
10	Alex Rodriguez Rgr Bat Up	5.00

Big League Challenge Material

		NM/M
Production 100 Sets		15.00
Combo:		1-2X
Production 50 Sets		
1	Albert Pujols/Jsy	15.00
2	Albert Pujols/Pants	15.00
3	Alex Rodriguez/ Rgr/Jsy	10.00
4	Alex Rodriguez/ Rgr/Pants	10.00
5	Magglio Ordonez/Jsy	5.00
6	Rafael Palmeiro/Jsy	8.00
7	Troy Glaus/Jsy	6.00
8	Troy Glaus/Pants	6.00
9	Albert Pujols/Hat	20.00
10	Alex Rodriguez/ Rgr Hat	15.00

Diamond Cuts Combo Material

		NM/M
Quantity produced listed		15.00
1	Derek Jeter/ Bat-Jsy/50	40.00
2	Greg Maddux/ Bat-Jsy/50	25.00
4	Miguel Cabrera/ Bat-Jsy/50	20.00
5	Mark Mulder/ Bat-Jsy/50	15.00
6	Rafael Furcal/ Bat-Jsy/50	10.00
7	Mark Prior/ Bat-Jsy/25	20.00
8	Roy Oswalt/ Bat-Jsy/50	10.00
9	Dontrelle Willis/ Bat-Jsy/25	15.00
10	Jay Gibbons/ Bat-Jsy/50	10.00
11	Josh Beckett/ Bat-Jsy/50	15.00
12	Angel Berroa/ Bat-Jsy/50	10.00
13	Adam Dunn/ Bat-Jsy/50	15.00
14	Hank Blalock/ Bat-Jsy/50	15.00
15	Carlos Beltran/ Bat-Jsy/50	15.00
16	Shannon Stewart/ Bat-Jsy/50	10.00
17	Aubrey Huff/ Bat-Jsy/50	10.00
18	Jeff Bagwell/ Bat-Jsy/50	20.00
19	Trot Nixon/ Bat-Jsy/50	15.00
20	Nolan Ryan/ Jkt-Jsy/50	40.00
21	Tony Gwynn/ Bat-Jsy/50	30.00
22	Andre Dawson/ Bat-Jsy/50	15.00
23	Don Mattingly/ Bat-Jkt/50	40.00
24	Dale Murphy/ Bat-Jsy/50	20.00
25	Gary Carter/ Bat-Jsy/50	15.00

Diamond Cuts Combo Material Signature

	NM/M
Production 1-5 Sets	

Diamond Cuts Material Bat

		NM/M
Quantity produced listed		8.00
1	Derek Jeter/100	25.00
2	Greg Maddux/100	10.00
3	Nomar Garciaparra/ 200	10.00
4	Miguel Cabrera/200	8.00
5	Mark Mulder/200	6.00
6	Rafael Furcal/200	4.00

7	Mark Prior/200	8.00
8	Roy Oswalt/200	4.00
9	Dontrelle Willis/100	4.00
10	Jay Gibbons/200	4.00
11	Josh Beckett/200	6.00
12	Angel Berroa/200	4.00
13	Adam Dunn/200	8.00
14	Hank Blalock/200	8.00
15	Carlos Beltran/200	6.00
16	Shannon Stewart/200	4.00
17	Aubrey Huff/200	8.00
18	Jeff Bagwell/200	8.00
19	Trot Nixon/200	6.00
21	Tony Gwynn/200	10.00
22	Andre Dawson/200	4.00
23	Don Mattingly/200	15.00
24	Dale Murphy/200	10.00
25	Gary Carter/200	6.00

Diamond Cuts Material Jersey

		NM/M
Production 250 Sets		8.00
1	Derek Jeter	20.00
2	Greg Maddux	10.00
3	Nomar Garciaparra	10.00
4	Miguel Cabrera	8.00
5	Mark Mulder	6.00
6	Rafael Furcal	4.00
7	Mark Prior	8.00
8	Roy Oswalt	4.00
9	Dontrelle Willis	6.00
10	Jay Gibbons	4.00
11	Josh Beckett	4.00
12	Angel Berroa	4.00
13	Adam Dunn	8.00
14	Hank Blalock	8.00
15	Carlos Beltran	4.00
16	Shannon Stewart	4.00
17	Aubrey Huff	4.00
18	Jeff Bagwell	8.00
19	Trot Nixon	6.00
20	Nolan Ryan/Jkt	25.00
21	Tony Gwynn	10.00
22	Andre Dawson	4.00
23	Don Mattingly/Jkt	15.00
24	Dale Murphy	10.00
25	Gary Carter	6.00

Game Day Souvenirs Number

		NM/M
Quantity produced listed		4.00
Position:		.5-1X
Production 25-300		
1	Garret Anderson/ Jsy/300	4.00
2	Troy Glaus/Jsy/300	6.00
3	Vladimir Guerrero/ Jsy/300	8.00
4	Steve Finley/Jsy/25	4.00
5	Luis Gonzales/Jsy/25	4.00
6	Richie Sexson/ Jsy/300	6.00
7	Andruw Jones/ Jsy/300	8.00
8	Chipper Jones/ Jsy/250	8.00
9	Rafael Furcal/Jsy/250	4.00
13	Curt Schilling/Jsy/300	6.00
14	Pedro Martinez/ Jsy/300	8.00
15	David Ortiz/Jsy/300	8.00
16	Sammy Sosa/ Jsy/300	10.00
17	Corey Patterson/ Jsy/250	6.00
18	Moises Alou/Jsy/300	4.00
19	Magglio Ordonez/ Jsy/250	6.00
20	Paul Konerko/Jsy/300	4.00
21	Frank Thomas/ Jsy/300	8.00
22	Austin Kearns/Jsy/50	8.00
23	Sean Casey/Jsy/250	6.00
24	Adam Dunn/Jsy/200	10.00
26	Omar Vizquel/Jsy/250	4.00
27	C.C. Sabathia/Jsy/250	6.00
28	Jody Gerut/Jsy/250	4.00
29	Todd Helton/Jsy/300	8.00
30	Vinny Castilla/Jsy/300	4.00
30	Jeromy Burnitz/ Jsy/300	
31	Fernando Vina/ Jsy/300	4.00

32	Ivan Rodriguez/ Jsy/300	8.00
33	Jeremy Bonderman/ Jsy/300	4.00
34	Mike Lowell/Jsy/225	4.00
35	Luis Castillo/Jsy/250	4.00
36	Miguel Cabrera/ Jsy/300	8.00
37	Roger Clemens/ Jsy/300	10.00
38	Andy Pettitte/Jsy/300	4.00
39	Jeff Bagwell/Jsy/300	6.00
40	Mike Sweeney/ Jsy/150	4.00
41	Carlos Beltran/Jsy/200	6.00
42	Angel Berroa/Jsy/100	4.00
43	Paul Lo Duca/Jsy/75	4.00
44	Shawn Green/Jsy/150	4.00
45	Adrian Beltre/Jsy/150	4.00
46	Ben Sheets/Jsy/300	4.00
47	Geoff Jenkins/Jsy/250	4.00
48	Junior Spivey/Jsy/300	4.00
49	Doug Mientkiewicz/ Jsy/100	4.00
50	Shannon Stewart/ Jsy/100	4.00
51	Torii Hunter/Jsy/300	6.00
52	Livan Hernandez/ Jsy/300	4.00
53	Jose Vidro/Jsy/200	4.00
54	Orlando Cabrera/ Jsy/300	4.00
55	Mike Piazza/Jsy/250	8.00
56	Mike Cameron/ Jsy/250	4.00
57	Kazuo Matsui/ Jsy/200	30.00
58	Derek Jeter/Jsy/50	30.00
59	Jason Giambi/Jsy/50	10.00
61	Barry Zito/Jsy/200	6.00
62	Eric Chavez/Jsy/150	4.00
63	Eric Byrnes/Jsy/150	4.00
65	Jim Thome/Jsy/300	8.00
66	Jimmy Rollins/ Jsy/250	4.00
67	Jason Kendall/ Jsy/250	4.00
68	Craig Wilson/Jsy/250	4.00
69	Jack Wilson/Jsy/250	4.00
70	Ryan Klesko/Jsy/300	4.00
71	Brian Giles/Jsy/300	4.00
72	Sean Burroughs/ Jsy/300	4.00
73	A.J. Pierzynski/ Jsy/300	4.00
74	J.T. Snow/Jsy/300	4.00
75	Michael Tucker/ Jsy/300	4.00
77	Edgar Martinez/ Jsy/50	10.00
79	Scott Rolen/Jsy/300	8.00
80	Albert Pujols/Jsy/300	15.00
81	Jim Edmonds/Jsy/300	6.00
82	Aubrey Huff/Jsy/100	4.00
83	Tino Martinez/Jsy/100	4.00
84	Rocco Baldelli/Jsy/100	6.00
85	Alfonso Soriano/ Jsy/200	8.00
86	Michael Young/ Jsy/250	6.00
87	Hank Blalock/Jsy/200	6.00
88	Eric Hinske/Jsy/200	4.00
89	Carlos Delgado/ Jsy/300	
90	Vernon Wells/Jsy/250	4.00

Game Day Souvenirs Signature Number

Production 5 Sets

Heritage

	NM/M
Production 999 Sets	4.00
Die-Cut:	2-3X
Production 100 Sets	
1 George Brett	6.00
2 Nolan Ryan	8.00
3 Cal Ripken Jr.	8.00
4 Mike Schmidt	5.00
5 Roberto Clemente	6.00
6 Don Mattingly	5.00
7 Dale Murphy	4.00
8 Ryne Sandberg	5.00
9 Harmon Killebrew	4.00
10 Stan Musial	5.00

Heritage Material Bat

	NM/M
Production 50 Sets	15.00
1 George Brett	30.00
2 Cal Ripken Jr.	40.00
3 Mike Schmidt	20.00
4 Roberto Clemente	60.00
5 Don Mattingly	30.00
6 Dale Murphy	30.00
7 Ryne Sandberg	30.00
8 Harmon Killebrew	30.00
9 Stan Musial	35.00

Heritage Material Jersey

	NM/M
Quantity produced listed	15.00

#	Player	Price
1	George Brett/200	15.00
2	Nolan Ryan/Jkt/200	20.00
3	Cal Ripken Jr./200	30.00
4	Mike Schmidt/Pants/200	15.00
5	Roberto Clemente/50	60.00
6	Don Mattingly/Jkt/200	15.00
7	Dale Murphy/200	8.00
8	Ryne Sandberg/200	20.00
9	Harmon Killebrew/Pants/200	15.00
10	Stan Musial/100	20.00

Heritage Signature Material Jersey

Production 5 Sets

Heroes of the Hall

		NM/M
Production 999 Sets		4.00
Die-Cut:		1X
Production 500 Sets		
1	Fergie Jenkins	3.00
2	Gary Carter	3.00
3	Gaylord Perry	3.00
4	George Brett	6.00
5	Jim Palmer	3.00
6	Nolan Ryan	8.00
7	Paul Molitor	4.00
8	Rod Carew	3.00
9	Steve Carlton	4.00
10	Robin Yount	8.00

Heroes of the Hall Material Bat

		NM/M
Production 100 Sets		
2	Gary Carter	8.00
4	George Brett	20.00
7	Paul Molitor	10.00
8	Rod Carew	8.00
9	Steve Carlton	8.00
10	Robin Yount	15.00

Heroes of the Hall Material Jersey

		NM/M
Production 200 unless noted.		
Prime:		No Pricing
Production 10 Sets		
1	Fergie Jenkins/Pants	8.00
2	Gary Carter	8.00
3	Gaylord Perry/100	8.00
4	George Brett	15.00
5	Jim Palmer	8.00
6	Nolan Ryan	25.00
7	Paul Molitor	10.00
8	Rod Carew	10.00
9	Steve Carlton	8.00
10	Robin Yount	15.00

Heroes of the Hall Material Signature

No Pricing
Production 1-10

Masterstrokes Material Bat

Production 200 Sets		6.00
1	Todd Helton	8.00
2	Jose Vidro	4.00
3	Edgar Renteria	4.00
4	Mike Lowell	4.00
5	Gary Sheffield	6.00
6	Albert Pujols	15.00
7	Javy Lopez	6.00
8	Carlos Delgado	6.00
9	Bret Boone	4.00
10	Alex Rodriguez	10.00
11	Vernon Wells	4.00
12	Manny Ramirez	6.00
13	Jorge Posada	6.00
14	Edgar Martinez	4.00
15	Bernie Williams	6.00
16	Magglio Ordonez	4.00
17	Garret Anderson	4.00
18	Eric Chavez	4.00
19	Alfonso Soriano	8.00
20	Jason Giambi	6.00
21	Jeff Kent	4.00
22	Scott Rolen	8.00
23	Vladimir Guerrero	8.00
24	Sammy Sosa	10.00
25	Mike Piazza	8.00

Masterstrokes Material Jersey

		NM/M
Prime:		No Pricing
Production 5 Sets		
1	Todd Helton/250	8.00
2	Jose Vidro/250	4.00
3	Edgar Renteria/250	6.00
4	Mike Lowell/250	4.00
5	Gary Sheffield/250	6.00
6	Albert Pujols/250	15.00
7	Javy Lopez/250	6.00
8	Carlos Delgado/250	6.00
9	Bret Boone/250	4.00
10	Alex Rodriguez/250	10.00
11	Vernon Wells/250	4.00
12	Manny Ramirez/250	6.00
13	Jorge Posada/250	6.00
14	Edgar Martinez/250	4.00
15	Bernie Williams/250	6.00
16	Magglio Ordonez/250	4.00
17	Garret Anderson/250	4.00
18	Eric Chavez/250	4.00
19	Alfonso Soriano/150	8.00
20	Jason Giambi/250	6.00
21	Jeff Kent/250	4.00
22	Scott Rolen/250	8.00
23	Vladimir Guerrero/250	8.00
24	Sammy Sosa/250	10.00
25	Mike Piazza/250	8.00

Masterstrokes Combo Material

		NM/M
Production 50 Sets		10.00
1	Todd Helton/Bat-Jsy/50	15.00
2	Jose Vidro/Bat-Jsy/50	8.00
3	Edgar Renteria/Bat-Jsy/50	10.00
4	Mike Lowell/Bat-Jsy/50	10.00
5	Gary Sheffield/Bat-Jsy/50	10.00
6	Albert Pujols/Bat-Jsy/50	30.00
7	Javy Lopez/Bat-Jsy/50	10.00
8	Carlos Delgado/Bat-Jsy/50	10.00
9	Bret Boone/Bat-Jsy/50	8.00
10	Alex Rodriguez/Rgr Bat-Jsy/50	20.00
11	Vernon Wells/Bat-Jsy/50	8.00
12	Manny Ramirez/Bat-Jsy/50	10.00
13	Jorge Posada/Bat-Jsy/50	10.00
14	Edgar Martinez/Bat-Jsy/50	10.00
15	Bernie Williams/Bat-Jsy/50	10.00
16	Magglio Ordonez/Bat-Jsy/50	8.00
17	Garret Anderson/Bat-Jsy/50	8.00
18	Eric Chavez/Bat-Jsy/50	8.00
19	Alfonso Soriano/Bat-Jsy/50	15.00
20	Jason Giambi/Bat-Jsy/50	10.00
21	Jeff Kent/Bat-Jsy/50	8.00
22	Scott Rolen/Bat-Jsy/50	20.00
23	Vladimir Guerrero/Bat-Jsy/50	20.00
24	Sammy Sosa/Bat-Jsy/50	25.00
25	Mike Piazza/Bat-Jsy/50	20.00

Masterstrokes Combo Material Signature

No Pricing
Production 1-10

Players Collection Jersey

		NM/M
Common Jersey: Production 150 Sets		
Platinum:		1-2X
Production 50 Sets		
1	Adam Dunn/AS	6.00
2	Adam Dunn/Gray	6.00
3	Adam Dunn/White	6.00
4	Alex Rodriguez	10.00
5	Alex Rodriguez/AS	10.00
6	Alex Rodriguez/Blue	10.00
7	Alex Rodriguez/White	10.00
8	Andruw Jones/Home	6.00
9	Andruw Jones/Road	6.00
10	Austin Kearns	6.00
11	Brandon Webb	4.00
12	C.C. Sabathia	4.00
13	Cal Ripken Jr.	25.00
14	Carlos Beltran	6.00
15	Carlos Delgado	6.00
16	Carlos Lee	4.00
17	Chipper Jones/Home	8.00
18	Chipper Jones/Road	8.00
19	Craig Biggio	6.00
20	Curt Schilling	6.00
21	David Wells	4.00
22	Don Mattingly	20.00
23	Dontrelle Willis	8.00
24	Frank Thomas/Black	8.00
25	Frank Thomas/White	8.00
26	Fred McGriff	6.00
27	Garret Anderson/AS	6.00
28	Gary Sheffield	6.00
29	Gary Sheffield	6.00
30	Greg Maddux/Gray	6.00
31	Hank Blalock/Home	6.00
32	Hank Blalock/Road	6.00
33	Hee Seop Choi	6.00
34	Hideo Nomo	6.00
35	Hideo Nomo/Gray	6.00
36	Hideo Nomo/White	6.00
37	Ivan Rodriguez	6.00
38	Ivan Rodriguez	6.00
39	Jason Giambi/Home	6.00
40	Jim Edmonds	6.00
41	Jim Thorne	6.00
42	John Olerud	4.00
43	John Smoltz	6.00
44	Josh Beckett	6.00
45	Josh Phelps	4.00
46	Juan Gonzalez	6.00
47	Juan Gonzalez	6.00
48	Kazuhisa Ishii	6.00
49	Lance Berkman	6.00
50	Larry Walker/Home	4.00
51	Larry Walker/Road	6.00
52	Luis Gonzalez/AS	6.00
53	Magglio Ordonez/Home	4.00
54	Magglio Ordonez/Road	4.00
55	Manny Ramirez	8.00
56	Manny Ramirez/AS	8.00
57	Mark Prior Home	8.00
58	Mark Prior Road	8.00
59	Mark Teixeira	6.00
60	Mike Mussina	6.00
61	Mike Piazza AS	8.00
62	Mike Piazza Black	8.00
63	Mike Piazza White	8.00
64	Nomar Garciaparra/Gray	8.00
65	Nomar Garciaparra/White	8.00
66	Pat Burrell	6.00
67	Paul Konerko	4.00
68	Paul Lo Duca	4.00
69	Pedro Martinez	8.00
70	Rafael Furcal	4.00
71	Rafael Palmeiro/Blue	6.00
72	Rafael Palmeiro/Gray	6.00
73	Ramon Hernandez	4.00
74	Rickey Henderson	6.00
75	Rickey Henderson/Black	6.00
76	Rickey Henderson/White	6.00
77	Roberto Alomar	6.00
78	Roberto Alomar	6.00
79	Robin Ventura/AS	4.00
80	Roger Clemens/Away	10.00
81	Roger Clemens/Home	10.00
82	Roy Halladay	6.00
83	Sammy Sosa/AS	12.00
84	Sammy Sosa/Gray	12.00
85	Sammy Sosa/White	12.00
86	Scott Rolen	8.00
87	Shannon Stewart	4.00
88	Shawn Green/Blue	4.00
89	Shawn Green/Gray	4.00
90	Shawn Green/White	4.00
91	Terrence Long	4.00
92	Tim Hudson	6.00
93	Todd Helton/Away	8.00
94	Todd Helton/Home	8.00
95	Tom Glavine	6.00
96	Tom Glavine	6.00
97	Torii Hunter	6.00
98	Vernon Wells	4.00
99	Vladimir Guerrero	8.00
100	Vladimir Guerrero/AS	8.00

Private Signings Silver

		NM/M
2	Garret Anderson/25	25.00
6	Brandon Webb/25	15.00
7	Brian Bruney/25	5.00
8	Casey Fossum/63	8.00
14	Shea Hillenbrand/25	20.00
16	Adam LaRoche/26	15.00
18	Bubba Nelson/250	8.00
22	Marcus Giles/25	30.00
24	Rafael Furcal/25	25.00
26	Adam Loewen/25	20.00
29	Jay Gibbons/50	15.00
30	Luis Matos/250	10.00
35	Kevin Youkilis/250	20.00
39	Trot Nixon/25	50.00
40	Aramis Ramirez/25	25.00
41	Brendan Harris/100	8.00
43	Ernie Banks/25	75.00
48	Sammy Sosa/21	150.00
50	Carlos Lee/25	20.00
51	Edwin Almonte/227	5.00
53	Joe Borchard/100	5.00
55	Brandon Larson/100	5.00
61	Ryan Wagner/50	5.00
63	Brian Tallet/250	5.00
65	Jeremy Guthrie/89	8.00
66	Jody Gerut/100	5.00
67	Travis Hafner/26	15.00
68	Clint Barmes/100	8.00
70	Joe Kennedy/50	5.00
72	Preston Wilson/25	25.00
73	Preston Larrison/100	8.00
81	Luis Castillo/25	15.00
82	Miguel Cabrera/25	60.00
85	Chris Burke/50	15.00
90	Morgan Ensberg/50	15.00
95	Byron Gettis/25	10.00
97	Carlos Beltran/50	35.00
100	Duke Snider/50	40.00
101	Edwin Jackson/100	15.00
104	Hong-Chih Kuo/250	30.00
106	Paul Lo Duca/25	25.00
107	Robin Ventura/25	30.00
109	Junior Spivey/50	15.00
112	Scott Podsednik/100	20.00
113	J.D. Durbin/250	5.00
114	Jacque Jones/50	20.00
115	Jason Kubel/100	15.00
116	Johan Santana/25	25.00
117	Shannon Stewart/25	15.00
120	Jose Vidro/15	30.00
124	Gary Carter/50	25.00
131	Chien-Ming Wang/243	100.00
133	Don Mattingly/25	75.00
134	Gary Sheffield/25	25.00
147	Rich Harden/200	15.00
154	Ryan Howard/250	65.00
160	Jay Payton/50	10.00
167	Jerome Williams/57	25.00
168	Merkin Valdez/250	10.00
169	Will Clark/25	75.00
177	Chris Snelling/200	5.00
177	Shigetoshi Hasegawa/25	75.00
179	Dan Haren/250	8.00
184	Stan Musial/25	80.00
185	Aubrey Huff/250	10.00
186	Chad Gaudin/100	5.00
187	Delmon Young/25	40.00
192	Mark Teixeira/23	25.00
193	Nolan Ryan/34	100.00
194	Alexis Rios/250	15.00
196	Dustin McGowan/115	10.00
197	Guillermo Quiroz/120	8.00

Private Signings Gold

		NM/M
2	Garret Anderson/16	35.00
6	Brandon Webb/55	10.00
7	Brian Bruney/10	5.00
14	Shea Hillenbrand/28	25.00
16	Adam LaRoche/25	15.00
22	Marcus Giles/25	30.00
23	Michael Hessman/25	15.00
29	Jay Gibbons/25	20.00
30	Luis Matos/100	10.00
35	Kevin Youkilis/100	25.00
41	Aramis Ramirez/35	35.00
41	Brendan Harris/75	20.00
49	Todd Wellemeyer/50	10.00
50	Carlos Lee/45	15.00
51	Edwin Almonte/56	10.00
53	Joe Borchard/25	10.00
57	Joe Crede/24	15.00
59	Austin Kearns/28	25.00
59	Brandon Larson/16	15.00
61	Ryan Wagner/38	5.00
61	Brian Tallet/50	10.00
65	Jeremy Guthrie/67	8.00
67	Travis Hafner/34	25.00
69	Clint Barmes/36	10.00
69	Jeff Baker/62	10.00
70	Joe Kennedy/37	15.00
73	Todd Helton/17	50.00
77	Preston Larrison/56	10.00
82	Dontrelle Willis/35	40.00
82	Miguel Cabrera/24	60.00
89	Lance Berkman/17	50.00
90	Morgan Ensberg/25	15.00
96	Byron Gettis/100	8.00
97	Carlos Beltran/25	50.00
98	Juan Gonzalez/22	35.00
100	Duke Snider/25	50.00
101	Edwin Jackson/50	20.00
104	Hong-Chih Kuo/100	40.00
105	Kazuhisa Ishii/17	50.00
106	Paul Lo Duca/16	50.00
107	Robin Ventura/25	30.00
108	Shawn Green/15	30.00
109	Junior Spivey/37	15.00
112	Scott Podsednik/20	25.00
113	J.D. Durbin/31	15.00
114	Jacque Jones/25	25.00
116	Johan Santana/57	25.00
117	Shannon Stewart/23	15.00
121	Nick Johnson/21	15.00
121	Orlando Cabrera/18	25.00
124	Gary Carter/25	30.00
124	Jae Weong Seo/25	15.00
131	Chien-Ming Wang/100	125.00
147	Rich Harden/53	20.00
152	Marlon Byrd/29	15.00
154	Ryan Howard/100	75.00
160	Jay Payton/17	20.00
167	Jerome Williams/50	25.00
168	Merkin Valdez/100	15.00
171	Chris Snelling/32	15.00
177	Shigetoshi Hasegawa/17	75.00
179	Dan Haren/100	10.00
184	Stan Musial/25	80.00
185	Aubrey Huff/19	25.00
186	Chad Gaudin/100	5.00
187	Delmon Young/73	20.00
192	Mark Teixeira/25	25.00
194	Alexis Rios/50	20.00
196	Dustin McGowan/50	10.00
198	Josh Phelps/17	15.00

Private Signings Platinum

No Pricing
Production 1-10

Rally Caps

		NM/M
Production 999 Sets		
Die-Cut:		1X
Production 500 Sets		
1	Adam Dunn	2.00
2	Adrian Beltre	1.50
3	Albert Pujols	5.00
4	Alex Rodriguez	5.00
5	Andruw Jones	2.00
6	Angel Berroa	1.50
7	Aubrey Huff	1.50
8	Austin Kearns	1.50
9	Ben Sheets	1.50
10	Brad Penny	1.50
11	Carlos Beltran	1.50
12	Carlos Lee	1.50
13	Casey Fossum	1.50
14	Eric Hinske	1.50
15	Geoff Jenkins	1.50
16	Jack Wilson	1.50
17	Jason Jennings	1.50
18	Joe Kennedy	1.50
19	Lance Berkman	1.50
20	Magglio Ordonez	1.50
21	Kerry Wood	3.00
22	Mark Buehrle	1.50
23	Mark Prior	3.00
24	Mark Teixeira	2.00
25	Michael Cuddyer	1.50
26	Jeff Conine	1.50
27	Mike Mussina	2.50
28	Mike Piazza	4.00
29	Jose Reyes	2.00
30	Paul Lo Duca	1.50
31	Pedro Martinez	2.00
32	Roy Oswalt	2.00
33	Ryan Klesko	2.00
34	Sammy Sosa	4.00
35	Tim Hudson	1.50
36	Todd Helton	2.00
37	Torii Hunter	2.00
38	Vernon Wells	1.50
39	Craig Wilson	1.50
40	Edgar Renteria	1.50

Spirit of the Game

		NM/M
Production 999 Sets		
Die-Cut:		1X
Production 500 Sets		
1	Sammy Sosa	4.00
2	Alex Rodriguez Rgr	4.00
3	Nomar Garciaparra	4.00
4	Derek Jeter	6.00
5	Albert Pujols	5.00
6	Roger Clemens	5.00
7	Mark Prior	3.00
8	Randy Johnson	2.00
9	Pedro Martinez	2.00
10	Vladimir Guerrero	2.00
11	Todd Helton	2.00
12	Jeff Bagwell	2.00
13	Mike Mussina	1.50
14	Josh Beckett	1.50
15	Hideo Nomo	1.50
16	Mike Piazza	2.00
17	Don Mattingly	5.00
18	George Brett	5.00
19	Nolan Ryan	8.00
20	Cal Ripken Jr.	8.00

Spirit of the Game Material Bat

		NM/M
1	Sammy Sosa/100	15.00
2	Alex Rodriguez/Rgr/100	10.00
3	Nomar Garciaparra/100	10.00
4	Derek Jeter/100	20.00
5	Albert Pujols/100	20.00
6	Roger Clemens/50	20.00
7	Mark Prior/100	8.00
8	Randy Johnson/100	15.00

10	Vladimir Guerrero/100	10.00
11	Todd Helton/100	10.00
12	Jeff Bagwell/100	8.00
13	Mike Mussina/50	8.00
14	Josh Beckett/100	8.00
15	Hideo Nomo/100	10.00
16	Mike Piazza/100	10.00
17	Don Mattingly/100	20.00
18	George Brett/100	20.00
20	Cal Ripken Jr./50	50.00

Spirit of the Game Material Jersey

		NM/M
Prime:		No Pricing
Production 1-5		
1	Sammy Sosa/200	10.00
2	Alex Rodriguez/200	10.00
3	Nomar Garciaparra/100	10.00
4	Derek Jeter/200	20.00
5	Albert Pujols/100	20.00
7	Mark Prior/200	8.00
8	Randy Johnson/100	10.00
9	Pedro Martinez/200	10.00
11	Todd Helton/100	10.00
12	Jeff Bagwell/200	8.00
13	Mike Mussina/200	8.00
14	Josh Beckett/200	8.00
15	Hideo Nomo/200	8.00
16	Mike Piazza/200	12.00
17	Don Mattingly/Jkt/200	15.00
18	George Brett/200	15.00
19	Nolan Ryan/100	40.00
20	Cal Ripken Jr./100	40.00

Spirit of the Game Material Signature Jersey

No Pricing
Production 1-5

Stars

		NM/M
Inserted 1:5		
Gold:		1.5-3X
Production 100 Sets		
Platinum:		3-5X
Production 25 Sets		
1	Albert Pujols	3.00
2	Alex Rodriguez	4.00
3	Alfonso Soriano	1.50
4	Andy Pettitte	.50
5	Angel Berroa	.50
6	Aubrey Huff	.50
7	Austin Kearns	.75
8	Barry Zito	.75
9	Brian Giles	.75
10	Carlos Delgado	.75
11	Chipper Jones	1.50
12	Craig Biggio	.75
13	Curt Schilling	1.00
14	Derek Jeter	4.00
15	Edgar Martinez	.50
16	Eric Gagne	1.00
17	Frank Thomas	1.00
18	Hank Blalock	1.00
19	Hideki Matsui	3.00
20	Hideo Nomo	.75
21	Ichiro Suzuki	2.00
22	Ivan Rodriguez	1.00
23	Jason Kendall	.50
24	Jason Schmidt	.50
25	Jeff Bagwell	1.00
26	Jim Edmonds	.50
27	Jim Thome	1.50
28	Josh Beckett	.75
29	Kazuo Matsui	4.00
30	Ken Griffey Jr.	2.50
31	Larry Walker	.50
32	Magglio Ordonez	.50
33	Manny Ramirez	1.00
34	Mark Mulder	.75
35	Mark Prior	2.00
36	Mark Teixeira	1.00
37	Miguel Tejada	1.00
38	Mike Mussina	1.00
39	Mike Piazza	2.50
40	Pedro Martinez	1.50
41	Randy Johnson	1.50
42	Roger Clemens	3.00
43	Roy Halladay	.50

44	Russ Ortiz	.50
45	Sammy Sosa	3.00
46	Scott Podsednik	.50
47	Tim Hudson	.75
48	Todd Helton	1.50
49	Vernon Wells	.50
50	Vladimir Guerrero	2.00

2004 Donruss Team Heroes

		NM/M
Complete Set (465):		75.00
Common Player:		.25
Common SP (441-465):		.50
Pack (8):		2.00
Box (24):		40.00
1	Troy Glaus	.40
2	Garret Anderson	.40
3	John Lackey	.25
4	Jarrod Washburn	.25
5	Bengie Molina	.25
6	Adam Kennedy	.25
7	Francisco Rodriguez	.25
8	Darin Erstad	.25
9	Ramon Ortiz	.25
10	Chone Figgins	.25
11	Rich Fischer	.25
12	David Eckstein	.25
13	Troy Percival	.25
14	Tim Salmon	.40
15	Nolan Ryan Angels	2.00
16	Luis Gonzalez	.25
17	Matt Kata	.25
18	Randy Johnson	.75
19	Oscar Villarreal	.25
20	Tim Olson	.25
21	Rob Hammock	.25
22	Alex Cintron	.25
23	Brian Bruney	.25
24	Brandon Webb	.25
25	Greg Aquino	.25
26	Shea Hillenbrand	.25
27	Steve Finley	.25
28	Rod Barajas	.25
29	Mike Hampton	.25
30	Adam LaRoche	.25
31	Russ Ortiz	.25
32	Chipper Jones	.75
33	John Smoltz	.40
34	Andruw Jones	.50
35	Bubba Nelson	.25
36	Johnny Estrada	.25
37	Marcus Giles	.25
38	Rafael Furcal	.25
39	Horacio Ramirez	.25
40	Dale Murphy	.40
41	Gaylord Perry/Braves	.25
42	Mark DeRosa	.25
43	Adam Loewen	.25
44	Jerry Hairston Jr.	.25
45	Jose Morban	.25
46	Daniel Cabrera	.25
47	Jay Gibbons	.25
48	Larry Bigbie	.25
49	Luis Matos	.25
50	Rodrigo Lopez	.25
51	Melvin Mora	.25
52	Cal Ripken Jr.	2.50
53	Geronimo Gil	.25
54	Tony Batista	.25
55	Jason Johnson	.25
56	Jason Varitek	.25
57	Bill Mueller	.25
58	Todd Walker	.25
59	Trot Nixon	.40
60	Tim Wakefield	.25
61	Kevin Youkilis	.25
62	David Ortiz	.50
63	Johnny Damon	.40
64	Derek Lowe	.25
65	Pedro J. Martinez	.75
66	Carl Yastrzemski	.75
67	Bobby Doerr	.25
68	Matt Clement	.25
69	Sammy Sosa	1.50
70	Randall Simon	.25
71	Nate Frese	.25
72	Carlos Zambrano	.40
73	Moises Alou	.25
74	Mark Prior	1.00
75	Jason Dubois	.25
76	Nic Jackson	.25
77	Corey Patterson	.40
78	John Webb	.25
79	Kerry Wood	.75
80	Aramis Ramirez	.40
81	Brendan Harris	.25

82	Kenny Lofton	.40
83	Alex Gonzalez	.25
84	Gary Matthews Sr.	.25
85	Mark Grace	.25
86	Mark Grudzielanek	.25
87	Joe Borowski	.25
88	Joe Crede	.25
89	Mark Buehrle	.25
90	Paul Konerko	.25
91	Magglio Ordonez	.40
92	Corwin Malone	.25
93	Frank Thomas	.50
94	Jose Valentin	.25
95	Miguel Olivo	.25
96	Esteban Loaiza	.25
97	Carlos Lee	.25
98	Harold Baines	.25
99	Jason LaRue	.25
100	Sean Casey	.40
101	Adam Dunn	.50
102	Josh Hall	.25
103	Danny Graves	.25
104	Barry Larkin	.40
105	Ken Griffey Jr.	1.00
106	Brandon Claussen	.25
107	Austin Kearns	.40
108	D'Angelo Jimenez	.25
109	Ryan Wagner	.25
110	Tim Hummel	.25
111	Johnny Bench	1.00
112	Eric Davis	.25
113	Jose Rijo	.25
114	Travis Hafner	.40
115	Jody Gerut	.25
116	Fernando Cabrera	.25
117	Jhonny Peralta	.25
118	Ryan Church	.25
119	Francisco Cruceta	.25
120	Omar Vizquel	.25
121	Jason Davis	.25
122	Jeremy Guthrie	.25
123	C.C. Sabathia	.25
124	Milton Bradley	.25
125	Cliff Lee	.25
126	Victor Martinez	.25
127	Bob Feller	.50
128	Casey Blake	.25
129	Josh Bard	.25
130	Billy Traber	.25
131	Coco Crisp	.25
132	Larry Walker	.40
133	Jason Jennings	.25
134	Garrett Atkins	.25
135	Rene Reyes	.25
136	Chin-Hui Tsao	.25
137	Preston Wilson	.25
138	Jeff Baker	.25
139	Charles Johnson	.25
140	Shawn Chacon	.25
141	Todd Helton	.50
142	Jay Payton	.25
143	Omar Infante	.25
144	Bobby Higginson	.25
145	Dmitri Young	.25
146	Jorge Cordova	.25
147	Jeremy Bonderman	.25
148	Brandon Inge	.25
149	Franklyn German	.25
150	Nook Logan	.25
151	Alex Sanchez	.25
152	Craig Monroe	.25
153	Preston Larrison	.25
154	Carlos Pena	.25
155	Alan Trammell	.50
156	Jack Morris	.25
157	Eric Munson	.25
158	Mike Maroth	.25
159	Josh Beckett	.40
160	Josh Willingham	.25
161	Mike Lowell	.40
162	Luis Castillo	.25
163	Wilson Valdez	.25
164	Miguel Cabrera	.25
165	Alex Gonzalez	.25
166	Carl Pavano	.25
167	Dontrelle Willis	.40
168	Juan Pierre	.25
169	Juan Encarnacion	.25
170	Brad Penny	.25
171	Ivan Rodriguez/Marlins	.50
172	Josh Wilson	.25
173	Jeff Conine	.25
174	Mark Redman	.25
175	A.J. Burnett	.25
176	Jeff Bagwell	.50
177	Octavio Dotel	.25
178	Craig Biggio	.25
179	John Buck	.25
180	Rodrigo Rosario	.25
181	Tommy Whiteman	.25
182	Kirk Saarloos	.25
183	Jason Lane	.25
184	Wade Miller	.25
185	Lance Berkman	.25
186	Roy Oswalt	.40
187	Tim Redding	.25
188	Jeff Kent	.40
189	Chris Burke	.25
190	Morgan Ensberg	.25
191	Nolan Ryan/Astros	2.00
192	Geoff Blum	.25
193	Jeremy Affeldt	.25
194	Mike Sweeney	.25
195	Angel Berroa	.25
196	Jimmy Gobble	.25
197	Ken Harvey	.25
198	Carlos Beltran	.50
199	Alexis Gomez	.25

200	Byron Gettis	.25
201	Mike MacDougal	.25
202	David DeJesus	.25
203	Runelvys Hernandez	.25
204	George Brett	1.50
205	Amos Otis	.25
206	Joe Randa	.25
207	Aaron Guiel	.25
208	Eric Gagne	.40
209	Shawn Green	.40
210	Kevin Brown	.40
211	Cesar Izturis	.25
212	Kazuhisa Ishii	.25
213	Joe Thurston	.25
214	Odalis Perez	.25
215	Rickey Henderson	.50
216	Hideo Nomo	.40
217	Hong-Chih Kuo	.25
218	Edwin Jackson	.50
219	Paul LoDuca	.25
220	Adrian Beltre	.40
221	Duke Snider	.75
222	Steve Garvey	.50
223	Rickie Weeks	.40
224	Bill Hall	.25
225	Doug Davis	.25
226	Geoff Jenkins	.25
227	Matt Childers	.25
228	Dan Kolb	.25
229	Scott Podsednik	.40
230	Pedro Liriano	.25
231	Ben Sheets	.40
232	Robin Yount	.75
233	Gorman Thomas	.25
234	Ben Oglivie	.25
235	Matt LeCroy	.25
236	Cristian Guzman	.25
237	Lew Ford	.25
238	J.C. Romero	.25
239	Rob Bowen	.25
240	Corey Koskie	.25
241	Jacque Jones	.25
242	Brad Radke	.25
243	Shannon Stewart	.25
244	J.D. Durbin	.25
245	Doug Mientkiewicz	.25
246	Jason Kubel	.25
247	Torii Hunter	.40
248	Johan Santana	.25
249	Kirby Puckett	.75
250	Luis Rivas	.25
251	Orlando Cabrera	.25
252	Tony Armas Jr.	.25
253	Brad Wilkerson	.25
254	Endy Chavez	.25
255	Jose Vidro	.25
256	Zach Day	.25
257	Livan Hernandez	.25
258	Terrmel Sledge	.25
259	Michael Barrett	.25
260	Gary Carter	.50
261	Andre Dawson	.50
262	Craig Brazell	.25
263	Mike Piazza	1.00
264	Jeff Duncan	.25
265	Jason Anderson	.25
266	Tom Glavine	.25
267	Danny Garcia	.25
268	Ty Wigginton	.25
269	Al Leiter	.25
270	Jeremy Griffiths	.25
271	Jose Reyes	.40
272	Prentice Redman	.25
273	Cliff Floyd	.25
274	Jae Weong Seo	.25
275	Nolan Ryan Mets	2.00
276	Keith Hernandez	.25
277	Jason Phillips	.25
278	Kazuo Matsui RC	3.00
279	Jose Contreras	.25
280	Aaron Boone	.25
281	Mike Mussina	.40
282	Jason Giambi	.50
283	Hideki Matsui	1.00
284	Derek Jeter	2.00
285	Mariano Rivera	.40
286	Chien-Ming Wang	.40
287	Bernie Williams	.25
288	Alfonso Soriano/Yanks	.25
289	Jorge Posada	.25
290	Michel Hernandez	.25
291	Erick Almonte	.25
292	Don Mattingly	1.50
293	Roger Clemens/Yanks	1.50
294	Gaylord Perry/Rgr	.25
295	Tommy John	.25
296	Tim Hudson	.25
297	Rich Harden	.25
298	Eric Chavez	.40
299	Adam Morrissey	.25
300	Mark Mulder	.40
301	Eric Byrnes	.25
302	Jermaine Dye	.25
303	Barry Zito	.40
304	Erubiel Durazo	.25
305	Mark Ellis	.25
306	Bobby Crosby	.40
307	Shane Bazzell	.25
308	Mario Ramos	.25
309	Jose Canseco	.50
310	Placido Polanco	.25
311	Jimmy Rollins	.25
312	Jim Thome	.75
313	Brett Myers	.25
314	Jason Michaels	.25
315	Vicente Padilla	.25
316	Bobby Abreu	.40
317	Ryan Howard	.50

318	Chase Utley	.50
319	Pat Burrell	.40
320	Randy Wolf	.25
321	Franklin Perez	.25
322	Marlon Byrd	.25
323	Kevin Millwood	.40
324	Mike Lieberthal	.25
325	Anderson Machado	.25
326	Travis Chapman	.25
327	Steve Carlton	.50
328	Greg Luzinski	.25
329	David Bell	.25
330	Craig Wilson	.25
331	Kris Benson	.25
332	Jose Castillo	.25
333	Josh Fogg	.25
334	Jason Kendall	.25
335	Walter Young	.25
336	Oliver Perez	.25
337	Jason Bay	.25
338	Duaner Sanchez	.25
339	Jack Wilson	.40
340	Carlos Rivera	.25
341	Kip Wells	.25
342	Freddy Sanchez	.25
343	Roberto Clemente	2.00
344	Al Oliver	.25
345	Phil Nevin	.25
346	Trevor Hoffman	.25
347	Ryan Klesko	.40
348	Khalil Greene	.25
349	Freddy Guzman RC	.25
350	Brian Giles	.40
351	Brian Lawrence	.25
352	Sean Burroughs	.25
353	Ben Howard	.25
354	Xavier Nady	.25
355	Mark Loretta	.25
356	Ramon Vazquez	.25
357	Tony Gwynn	.75
358	Adam Eaton	.25
359	Merkin Valdez RC	.75
360	Kevin Correia	.25
361	Edgardo Alfonzo	.25
362	Mike Cameron	.25
363	Ray Durham	.25
364	Jesse Foppert	.25
365	Robb Nen	.25
366	Marquis Grissom	.25
367	Jerome Williams	.25
368	Jason Schmidt	.40
369	Will Clark	.50
370	Bret Boone	.40
371	Freddy Garcia	.25
372	Dan Wilson	.25
373	Rett Johnson	.25
374	Kazuhiro Sasaki	.25
375	Ichiro Suzuki	1.00
376	Edgar Martinez	.40
377	Jamie Moyer	.25
378	Joel Pineiro	.25
379	Carlos Guillen	.25
380	Randy Winn	.25
381	J.J. Putz	.25
382	John Olerud	.40
383	Matt Thornton	.25
384	Rafael Soriano	.25
385	Gil Meche	.25
386	Albert Pujols	1.50
387	Woody Williams	.25
388	Dan Haren	.25
389	Matt Morris	.40
390	Jim Edmonds	.40
391	Edgar Renteria	.40
392	Scott Rolen	.75
393	J.D. Drew	.40
394	Bo Hart	.25
395	Stan Musial	1.00
396	Red Schoendienst	.25
397	Terry Pendleton	.25
398	Mike Matheny	.25
399	Dewon Brazelton	.25
400	Chad Gaudin	.25
401	Aubrey Huff	.25
402	Victor Zambrano	.25
403	Antonio Perez	.25
404	Carl Crawford	.40
405	Joe Kennedy	.25
406	Pete LaForest	.25
407	Delmon Young	.40
408	Rocco Baldelli	.25
409	Doug Waechter	.25
410	Brian Stokes	.25
411	Edwin Almonte	.25
412	Toby Hall	.25
413	Lance Carter	.25
414	Greg Maddux/Braves	1.00
415	Hank Blalock	.50
416	Colby Lewis	.25
417	Mark Teixeira	.25
418	Gerald Laird	.25
419	Ricardo Rodriguez	.25
420	Ben Kozlowski	.25
421	Kevin Mench	.25
422	Michael Young	.25
423	Ramon Nivar	.25
424	Laynce Nix	.25
425	Nolan Ryan/Rgr	2.00
426	Einar Diaz	.25
427	Carlos Delgado	.25
428	Eric Hinske	.25
429	Dustin McGowan	.25
430	Frank Catalanotto	.25
431	Kevin Cash	.25
432	Roy Halladay	.25
433	Orlando Hudson	.25
434	Francisco Rosario	.25
435	Guillermo Quiroz	.25

436	Vernon Wells	.25
437	Josh Phelps	.25
438	Alexis Rios	.25
439	Reed Johnson	.25
440	Chris Woodward	.25
441	Bartolo Colon/SP	.50
442	Richie Sexson/SP	.75
443	Greg Maddux/SP/Cubs	2.00
444	Javy Lopez/SP	.75
445	Gary Sheffield/SP	.75
446	Curt Schilling/SP	1.00
447	Nomar Garciaparra/SP	2.50
448	Manny Ramirez/SP	1.50
449	Derrek Lee/SP	.75
450	Roberto Alomar SP	.75
451	Ivan Rodriguez/SP/Tigers	1.50
452	Junior Spivey/SP	.50
453	Alfonso Soriano/SP/Rgr	1.00
454	Vladimir Guerrero/SP	1.50
455	Nick Johnson/SP	.50
456	Javier Vazquez/SP	.50
457	Andy Pettitte/SP	.75
458	Miguel Tejada/SP	.75
459	Rich Aurilia/SP	.50
460	A.J. Pierzynski/SP	.50
462	Roger Clemens/SP/Astros	3.00
463	Juan Gonzalez/SP	1.00
464	Rafael Palmeiro/SP	1.00
465	Alex Rodriguez/SP/Yanks	4.00

Showdown Bronze

Bronze (1-440):	3-5X
Bronze (441-465):	2-3X
Production 150 Sets	

Showdown Silver

Silver (1-440):	5-10X
Silver (441-465):	3-5X
Production 50 Sets	

Showdown Gold

No Pricing
Production 10 Sets

Autographs

		NM/M
Inserted 1:24		
10	Chone Figgins	10.00
11	Rich Fischer	5.00
17	Matt Kata	5.00
19	Oscar Villarreal	5.00
20	Tim Olson	5.00
21	Rob Hammock/57	10.00
23	Brian Bruney	5.00
25	Greg Aquino	5.00
35	Bubba Nelson	5.00
45	Jose Morban	5.00
46	Daniel Cabrera	5.00
61	Kevin Youkilis/50	15.00
71	Nate Frese	5.00
75	Jason Dubois	5.00
76	Nic Jackson	5.00
78	John Webb	5.00
81	Brendan Harris	10.00

ABBREVIATIONS

SP - Short Print

#	Player	Price
84	Gary Matthews Sr.	10.00
92	Corwin Malone	5.00
102	Josh Hall/25	15.00
106	Brandon Claussen	10.00
110	Tim Hummel	5.00
116	Francisco Cabrera	5.00
117	Jhonny Peralta	5.00
118	Ryan Church	8.00
119	Francisco Cruceta/75	8.00
146	Jorge Cordova	5.00
149	Franklyn German	5.00
150	Nook Logan	5.00
153	Preston Larrison	8.00
160	Josh Willingham	5.00
163	Wilson Valdez	5.00
172	Josh Wilson	5.00
180	Rodrigo Rosario	8.00
181	Tommy Whiteman	5.00
187	Tim Redding/22	10.00
189	Chris Burke	5.00
197	Ken Harvey	15.00
200	Byron Gettis	8.00
205	Amos Otis	10.00
211	Cesar Izturis	5.00
225	Doug Davis	8.00
227	Matt Childers	5.00
230	Pedro Liriano	5.00
233	Gorman Thomas	15.00
234	Ben Oglivie/86	15.00
237	Lew Ford	10.00
238	J.C. Romero	5.00
239	Rob Bowen	5.00
246	Jason Kubel/50	15.00
258	Terrmel Sledge	5.00
262	Craig Brazell	5.00
264	Jeff Duncan	8.00
265	Jason Anderson	5.00
267	Danny Garcia	5.00
270	Jeremy Griffiths	8.00
272	Prentice Redman	8.00
291	Erick Almonte/66	8.00
307	Shane Bazzell	5.00
308	Mario Ramos	5.00
314	Jason Michaels/42	8.00
321	Franklyn Perez	5.00
325	Anderson Machado/50	10.00
326	Travis Chapman	5.00
328	Greg Luzinski	5.00
331	Kris Benson	10.00
335	Walter Young/67	10.00
338	Duaner Sanchez	5.00
353	Ben Howard	5.00
359	Merkin Valdez/50	20.00
360	Kevin Correia	5.00
373	Rett Johnson/76	8.00
381	J.J. Putz	5.00
383	Matt Thornton/50	8.00
384	Rafael Soriano	5.00
406	Pete LaForest	5.00
410	Brian Stokes	5.00
411	Edwin Almonte	5.00
419	Ricardo Rodriguez	5.00
420	Ben Kozlowski	5.00
431	Kevin Cash	5.00
434	Francisco Rosario/48	8.00

2004 Donruss Throwback Threads

NM/M

Complete Set (250):
Common Player: .15
Common (201-225): 1.50
Common (226-250): 3.00
Production 1,000
Hobby Pack (5): 5.00
Hobby Box (24): 90.00

#	Player	Price
1	Bartolo Colon	.15
2	Darin Erstad	.25
3	David Eckstein	.15
4	Garret Anderson	.25
5	Tim Salmon	.25
6	Troy Glaus	.25
7	Vladimir Guerrero	.75
8	Brandon Webb	.15
9	Luis Gonzalez	.25
10	Randy Johnson	.75
11	Richie Sexson	.40
12	Roberto Alomar	.50
13	Shea Hillenbrand	.15
14	Steve Finley	.15
15	Adam LaRoche	.15
16	Andruw Jones	.50
17	Chipper Jones	.75
18	J.D. Drew	.25
19	John Smoltz	.25
20	Rafael Furcal	.25
21	Russ Ortiz	.15
22	Javy Lopez	.25
23	Jay Gibbons	.15
24	Larry Bigbie	.15
25	Luis Matos	.15
26	Melvin Mora	.15
27	Miguel Tejada	.40
28	Rafael Palmeiro	.50
29	Curt Schilling	.50
30	David Ortiz	.75
31	Derek Lowe	.15
32	Jason Varitek	.15
33	Johnny Damon	.25
34	Manny Ramirez	.50
35	Nomar Garciaparra	1.00
36	Pedro J. Martinez	.75
37	Trot Nixon	.15
38	Aramis Ramirez	.40
39	Corey Patterson	.25
40	Derrek Lee	.25
41	Greg Maddux	1.00
42	Kerry Wood	.75
43	Mark Prior	.75
44	Sammy Sosa	1.50
45	Carlos Lee	.15
46	Esteban Loaiza	.15
47	Frank Thomas	.50
48	Joe Borchard	.15
49	Magglio Ordonez	.25
50	Mark Buehrle	.15
51	Paul Konerko	.15
52	Adam Dunn	.50
53	Austin Kearns	.25
54	Barry Larkin	.40
55	Brandon Larson	.15
56	Ken Griffey Jr.	1.00
57	Ryan Wagner	.15
58	Sean Casey	.15
59	C.C. Sabathia	.15
60	Jody Gerut	.15
61	Omar Vizquel	.15
62	Travis Hafner	.25
63	Victor Martinez	.25
64	Charles Johnson	.15
65	Garrett Atkins	.15
66	Jason Jennings	.15
67	Joe Kennedy	.15
68	Larry Walker	.25
69	Preston Wilson	.15
70	Todd Helton	.50
71	Ivan Rodriguez	.50
72	Jeremy Bonderman	.15
73	A.J. Burnett	.15
74	Brad Penny	.15
75	Dontrelle Willis	.50
76	Josh Beckett	.50
77	Juan Pierre	.15
78	Luis Castillo	.15
79	Miguel Cabrera	.75
80	Mike Lowell	.25
81	Andy Pettitte	.25
82	Craig Biggio	.25
83	Jeff Bagwell	.50
84	Jeff Kent	.25
85	Lance Berkman	.25
86	Morgan Ensberg	.15
87	Richard Hidalgo	.15
88	Roger Clemens	1.50
89	Roy Oswalt	.25
90	Wade Miller	.15
91	Angel Berroa	.15
92	Carlos Beltran	.50
93	Juan Gonzalez	.40
94	Ken Harvey	.15
95	Mike Sweeney	.15
96	Runelvys Hernandez	.15
97	Adrian Beltre	.40
98	Edwin Jackson	.15
99	Eric Gagne	.40
100	Hideo Nomo	.25
101	Hong-Chih Kuo	.15
102	Kazuhisa Ishii	.15
103	Paul LoDuca	.15
104	Shawn Green	.25
105	Ben Sheets	.15
106	Geoff Jenkins	.15
107	Junior Spivey	.15
108	Rickie Weeks	.25
109	Scott Podsednik	.25
110	Corey Koskie	.15
111	Doug Mientkiewicz	.15
112	Jacque Jones	.15
113	Joe Mays	.15
114	Johan Santana	.25
115	Shannon Stewart	.15
116	Torii Hunter	.25
117	Brad Wilkerson	.15
118	Carl Everett	.15
119	Chad Cordero	.15
120	Jose Vidro	.15
121	Nick Johnson	.15
122	Orlando Cabrera	.15
123	Al Leiter	.15
124	Cliff Floyd	.15
125	Jae Weong Seo	.15
126	Jose Reyes	.25
127	Mike Cameron	.15
128	Mike Piazza	1.00
129	Tom Glavine	.25
130	Alex Rodriguez	2.00
131	Bernie Williams	.40
132	Chien-Ming Wang	.40
133	Derek Jeter	2.00
134	Gary Sheffield	.50
135	Hideki Matsui	1.00
136	Jason Giambi	.25
137	Javier Vazquez	.15
138	Jorge Posada	.25
139	Jose Contreras	.15
140	Kevin Brown	.15
141	Mariano Rivera	.25
142	Mike Mussina	.40
143	Barry Zito	.15
144	Bobby Crosby	.25
145	Eric Chavez	.25
146	Erubiel Durazo	.15
147	Jermaine Dye	.15
148	Mark Kotsay	.15
149	Mark Mulder	.15
150	Rich Harden	.15
151	Tim Hudson	.25
152	Billy Wagner	.15
153	Bobby Abreu	.25
154	Brett Myers	.15
155	Jim Thome	.75
156	Jimmy Rollins	.25
157	Kevin Millwood	.25
158	Marlon Byrd	.15
159	Pat Burrell	.25
160	Jason Bay	.15
161	Jason Kendall	.15
162	Brian Giles	.15
163	Jay Payton	.15
164	Ryan Klesko	.15
165	Edgardo Alfonzo	.15
166	Jason Schmidt	.40
167	Jerome Williams	.15
168	Todd Linden	.15
169	Bret Boone	.15
170	Edgar Martinez	.25
171	Freddy Garcia	.15
172	Ichiro Suzuki	1.50
173	Jamie Moyer	.15
174	John Olerud	.15
175	Shigetoshi Hasegawa	.15
176	Albert Pujols	1.50
177	Dan Haren	.15
178	Edgar Renteria	.25
179	Jim Edmonds	.25
180	Matt Morris	.25
181	Scott Rolen	.75
182	Aubrey Huff	.15
183	Carl Crawford	.15
184	Chad Gaudin	.15
185	Delmon Young	.25
186	Dewon Brazelton	.15
187	Fred McGriff	.25
188	Rocco Baldelli	.25
189	Alfonso Soriano	.75
190	Hank Blalock	.50
191	Laynce Nix	.15
192	Mark Teixeira	.25
193	Michael Young	.40
194	Carlos Delgado	.40
195	Eric Hinske	.15
196	Frank Catalanotto	.15
197	Josh Phelps	.15
198	Orlando Hudson	.15
199	Roy Halladay	.15
200	Vernon Wells	.15
201	Dale Murphy	2.00
202	Cal Ripken Jr.	10.00
203	Fred Lynn	1.50
204	Wade Boggs	2.00
205	Nolan Ryan	6.00
206	Rod Carew	2.00
207	Andre Dawson	1.50
208	Ernie Banks	3.00
209	Ryne Sandberg	5.00
210	Bo Jackson	3.00
211	Carlton Fisk	3.00
212	Dave Concepcion	1.50
213	Alan Trammell	1.50
214	George Brett	5.00
215	Robin Yount	4.00
216	Gary Carter	1.50
217	Darryl Strawberry	1.50
218	Dwight Gooden	1.50
219	Babe Ruth	6.00
220	Don Mattingly	5.00
221	Reggie Jackson	3.00
222	Mike Schmidt	5.00
223	Tony Gwynn	4.00
224	Keith Hernandez	2.00
225	Hector Gimenez RC	3.00
226	Graham Koonce	3.00
227	John Gall RC	5.00
228	Jerry Gil RC	3.00
229	Jason Frasor RC	3.00
230	Justin Knoedler RC	3.00
231	Ivan Ochoa RC	3.00
232	Greg Dobbs RC	5.00
233	Ronald Belisario RC	3.00
234	Jerome Gamble RC	3.00
235	Roberto Novoa RC	3.00
236	Sean Henn	4.00
237	Willy Taveras RC	8.00
238	Ramon Ramirez RC	3.00
239	Kazuo Matsui RC	8.00
240	Akinori Otsuka RC	5.00
241	Jason Bartlett RC	5.00
242	Fernando Nieve RC	3.00
243	Freddy Guzman RC	3.00
244	Aarom Baldiris RC	5.00
245	Merkin Valdez RC	5.00
246	Mike Gosling	3.00
247	Shingo Takatsu RC	3.00
248	William Bergolla RC	3.00
249	Shawn Hill RC	3.00
250	Justin Germano RC	3.00

Blast From the Past

NM/M

Common Player: 1.50
Production 1,500 Sets
Spectrum: 2-3X
Production 100 Sets

#	Player	Price
1	Albert Pujols	5.00
2	Alex Rodriguez	4.00
3	Babe Ruth	6.00
4	Cal Ripken Jr.	8.00
5	Carlton Fisk	2.00
6	Eddie Mathews	3.00
7	Eddie Murray	2.00
8	Ernie Banks	3.00
9	Frank Robinson	2.00
10	George Foster	1.50
11	Harmon Killebrew	3.00
12	Jim Rice	1.50
13	Jim Thome	2.00
14	Johnny Bench	3.00
15	Jose Canseco	2.00
16	Juan Gonzalez	2.00
17	Ken Griffey Jr.	3.00
18	Mike Piazza	4.00
19	Mike Schmidt	5.00
20	Reggie Jackson	2.00
21	Roger Maris	3.00
22	Sammy Sosa	4.00
23	Stan Musial	4.00
24	Willie McCovey	2.00
25	Willie Stargell	2.00

Blast From the Past Bat

NM/M

Production 250 unless noted.

#	Player	Price
1	Albert Pujols	15.00
2	Alex Rodriguez	10.00
3	Babe Ruth/50	150.00
4	Cal Ripken Jr.	25.00
5	Carlton Fisk	8.00
6	Eddie Mathews	10.00
7	Eddie Murray	8.00
8	Ernie Banks	10.00
9	Frank Robinson	8.00
10	George Foster	6.00
11	Harmon Killebrew	10.00
12	Jim Rice	8.00
13	Jim Thome	8.00
14	Johnny Bench	10.00
15	Jose Canseco/100	10.00
16	Juan Gonzalez	8.00
17	Mike Piazza	15.00
18	Mike Schmidt	15.00
19	Reggie Jackson	8.00
20	Roger Maris	30.00
21	Sammy Sosa	10.00
22	Stan Musial	15.00
23	Willie McCovey	8.00
24	Willie Stargell	8.00

Century Collection Material

NM/M

All Jersey unless noted.

Prime: 1.5-3X
Production 10-25
Combo: .75-2X
Production 5-50
Combo Prime: 2-3X
Production 5-25
No pricing 15 or less.

#	Player	Price
1	Alan Trammell/250	8.00
2	Alex Rodriguez/250	10.00
3	Alfonso Soriano/250	8.00
4	Andre Dawson/250	6.00
5	Andy Pettitte/250	6.00
6	Bert Blyleven/250	6.00
7	Bo Jackson/250	12.00
8	Bobby Doerr/250	8.00
9	Brooks Robinson/25	30.00
10	Carl Yastrzemski/250	15.00
11	Carlos Delgado/250	6.00
12	Carlton Fisk/Jkt/250	8.00
13	Curt Schilling/250	6.00
14	Darryl Strawberry/250	6.00
15	Dave Concepcion/250	6.00
16	Dave Parker/100	8.00
17	Dennis Eckersley/250	8.00
18	Don Sutton/250	6.00
19	Duke Snider/250	10.00
20	Dwight Gooden/250	6.00
21	Eddie Mathews/250	25.00
22	Enos Slaughter/100	8.00
23	Ernie Banks/Pants/250	15.00
24	Frankie Frisch/Jkt/250	12.00
25	Frank Robinson/250	10.00
26	Frank Thomas/250	10.00
27	Garret Anderson/250	6.00
28	Gary Carter/250	6.00
29	Gary Sheffield/250	6.00
30	Harmon Killebrew/50	25.00
31	Harold Baines/250	6.00
32	Hideo Nomo/250	6.00
33	Jack Morris/250	6.00
34	Jason Giambi/250	6.00
35	Jeff Kent/250	4.00
36	Jim "Catfish" Hunter/250	8.00
37	Jim Palmer/50	10.00
38	Jim Rice/250	8.00
39	Jim Thome/250	10.00
40	John Smoltz/250	8.00
41	Johnny Mize/Pants/250	8.00
42	Jose Canseco/250	8.00
43	Juan Gonzalez/250	6.00
44	Juan Marichal/250	6.00
45	Keith Hernandez/250	8.00
46	Kerry Wood/250	10.00
47	Kevin Brown/250	4.00
48	Lance Berkman/250	6.00
49	Larry Walker/250	6.00
50	Lee Smith/250	6.00
51	Lenny Dykstra/Bat/250	6.00
52	Luis Tiant/250	6.00
53	Magglio Ordonez/250	4.00
54	Manny Ramirez/250	8.00
55	Mariano Rivera/100	8.00
56	Mark Grace/250	8.00
57	Mark Mulder/250	6.00
58	Mark Teixeira/150	6.00
59	Marty Marion/25	15.00
60	Mike Mussina/Pants/250	8.00
61	Mike Piazza/250	10.00
62	Nellie Fox/Bat/250	15.00
63	Nolan Ryan/Jkt/250	20.00
64	Ozzie Smith/250	12.00
65	Pedro J. Martinez/250	8.00
66	Pee Wee Reese/Bat/250	8.00
67	Phil Niekro/250	8.00
68	Phil Rizzuto/Pants/250	10.00
70	Rafael Palmeiro/250	6.00
71	Ralph Kiner/Bat/250	8.00
72	Randy Johnson/250	10.00
73	Reggie Jackson/Jkt/250	8.00
74	Rickey Henderson/250	10.00
75	Roberto Alomar/250	6.00
76	Robin Ventura/250	4.00
77	Rod Carew/250	10.00
78	Roger Clemens/250	15.00
79	Ron Santo/Bat/250	10.00
80	Scott Rolen/250	10.00
81	Shawn Green/250	6.00
82	Steve Garvey/250	6.00
83	Tim Hudson/250	4.00
84	Tom Glavine/250	6.00
85	Tom Seaver/25	30.00
86	Adam Dunn/250	6.00
87	Tommy John/250	6.00
88	Tommy Lasorda/250	6.00
89	Tony Oliva/250	6.00
90	Tony Perez/Bat/250	8.00
91	Torii Hunter/250	4.00
92	Troy Glaus/250	4.00
93	Vernon Wells/250	4.00
94	Vladimir Guerrero/250	8.00
95	Wade Boggs/250	6.00
96	Warren Spahn/100	20.00
97	Will Clark/Bat/250	6.00
98	Willie McCovey/250	8.00
99	Willie Stargell/250	8.00
100	George Foster/250	6.00

Century Collection Signature Material

NM/M

All Jersey unless noted.
Prime: No Pricing
Production 5-10
Combo: .75-1.5X
Production 5-25
No pricing 15 or less.
Combo Prime: No Pricing
Production 5-10

#	Player	Price
1	Alan Trammell/50	25.00
2	Alfonso Soriano/50	40.00
4	Andre Dawson/50	25.00
6	Bert Blyleven/50	20.00
8	Bobby Doerr/50	25.00
14	Darryl Strawberry/50	25.00
15	Dave Concepcion/50	25.00
16	Dave Parker/50	20.00
17	Dennis Eckersley/50	40.00
18	Don Sutton/50	25.00
19	Duke Snider/25	40.00
20	Dwight Gooden/50	25.00
22	Garret Anderson/50	25.00
28	Gary Carter/50	25.00
29	Gary Sheffield/25	30.00
31	Harold Baines/50	25.00
33	Jack Morris/50	15.00
37	Jim Palmer/25	25.00
38	Jim Rice/50	20.00
43	Jose Canseco/25	50.00
44	Juan Marichal/50	25.00
47	Keith Hernandez/25	25.00
50	Lee Smith/50	15.00
51	Lenny Dykstra/Bat/50	20.00
52	Luis Tiant/50	15.00
53	Magglio Ordonez/50	25.00
56	Mark Grace/50	40.00
57	Mark Mulder/25	25.00
58	Mark Teixeira/25	40.00
59	Marty Marion/25	40.00
68	Phil Niekro/50	25.00
71	Ralph Kiner/Bat/50	40.00
75	Roberto Alomar/25	50.00
76	Robin Ventura/50	20.00
82	Steve Garvey/50	25.00
87	Tommy John/50	15.00
90	Tony Perez/Bat/25	40.00
91	Torii Hunter/25	30.00
93	Vernon Wells/25	25.00
94	Vladimir Guerrero/50	40.00
100	George Foster/50	20.00

Century Stars

NM/M

Common Player: 1.50
Production 1,500 Sets
Spectrum: 1.5-3X
Production 100 Sets

#	Player	Price
1	Al Kaline	2.00
2	Albert Pujols	5.00
3	Alex Rodriguez	4.00
4	Barry Larkin	3.00
5	Barry Zito	1.50
6	Billy Williams	1.50
7	Bob Feller	1.50
8	Bob Gibson	3.00
9	Cal Ripken Jr.	8.00
10	Chipper Jones	3.00
11	Curt Schilling	2.00
12	Dale Murphy	2.00
13	Dave Parker	1.50
14	Derek Jeter	8.00
15	Don Drysdale	1.50
16	Don Mattingly	3.00
17	Eddie Murray	2.00
18	Fergie Jenkins	1.50
19	Gary Carter	2.00
20	George Brett	5.00
21	Greg Maddux	3.00
22	Ivan Rodriguez	2.00
23	Jeff Bagwell	2.00
24	Joe Morgan	2.00
25	Johnny Bench	3.00
26	Kirby Puckett	3.00
27	Lou Boudreau	1.50
28	Lou Brock	1.50
29	Luis Aparicio	1.50
30	Manny Ramirez	2.00
31	Mark Prior	2.00
32	Miguel Tejada	2.00
33	Mike Mussina	2.00
34	Mike Piazza	4.00
35	Mike Schmidt	5.00

36	Nolan Ryan	6.00
37	Nomar Garciaparra	4.00
38	Ozzie Smith	4.00
39	Paul Molitor	3.00
40	Pedro J. Martinez	3.00
41	Rafael Palmeiro	3.00
42	Randy Johnson	3.00
43	Red Schoendienst	1.50
44	Reggie Jackson	3.00
45	Rickey Henderson	2.00
46	Roberto Alomar	2.00
47	Roberto Clemente	5.00
48	Robin Yount	3.00
49	Rod Carew	4.00
50	Roger Clemens	5.00
51	Ryne Sandberg	4.00
52	Sammy Sosa	4.00
53	Stan Musial	4.00
54	Steve Carlton	2.00
55	Todd Helton	2.00
56	Tom Glavine	2.00
57	Tom Seaver	3.00
58	Tony Gwynn	3.00
59	Wade Boggs	2.00
60	Whitey Ford	3.00

Century Stars Material

NM/M
All Jersey unless noted.
Prime: No Pricing
Production 5 Sets

1	Al Kaline/Pants/25	30.00
2	Albert Pujols/25	25.00
4	Barry Larkin/50	10.00
5	Barry Zito/50	6.00
6	Billy Williams/50	8.00
8	Bob Gibson/25	20.00
9	Cal Ripken Jr./50	60.00
10	Chipper Jones/50	10.00
11	Curt Schilling/50	8.00
12	Dale Murphy/50	12.00
13	Dave Parker/50	8.00
14	Derek Jeter/50	35.00
15	Don Drysdale/50	12.00
16	Don Mattingly/Jkt/50	20.00
17	Eddie Murray/50	15.00
18	Fergie Jenkins/Pants/25	12.00
19	Gary Carter/Pants/50	8.00
20	George Brett/50	25.00
21	Greg Maddux/50	15.00
22	Ivan Rodriguez/50	12.00
23	Jeff Bagwell/50	10.00
24	Joe Morgan/25	10.00
25	Johnny Bench/50	20.00
26	Kirby Puckett/50	15.00
27	Lou Boudreau/50	8.00
28	Lou Brock/25	20.00
29	Luis Aparicio/Pants/50	8.00
30	Manny Ramirez/50	10.00
31	Mark Prior/50	8.00
32	Miguel Tejada/50	8.00
33	Mike Mussina/50	10.00
34	Mike Piazza/50	20.00
35	Mike Schmidt/50	20.00
36	Nolan Ryan/50	35.00
37	Nomar Garciaparra/50	15.00
38	Ozzie Smith/50	25.00
40	Pedro J. Martinez/50	10.00
41	Rafael Palmeiro/25	15.00
42	Randy Johnson/50	12.00
43	Red Schoendienst/50	8.00
44	Reggie Jackson/Pants/50	15.00
45	Rickey Henderson/50	15.00
46	Roberto Alomar/50	12.00
48	Robin Yount/50	20.00
49	Rod Carew/Jkt/50	10.00
50	Roger Clemens/50	15.00
51	Ryne Sandberg/50	20.00
52	Sammy Sosa/50	15.00
54	Steve Carlton/50	15.00
55	Todd Helton/50	12.00
56	Tom Glavine/50	10.00
57	Tom Seaver/50	15.00
58	Tony Gwynn/50	15.00
59	Wade Boggs/50	10.00

Century Stars Signature

NM/M
Signature Material: No Pricing
Production 5 Sets
Sig. Material Prime: No Pricing
Production 5 Sets

1	Al Kaline/25	50.00
6	Billy Williams/25	35.00
7	Bob Feller/25	30.00
8	Bob Gibson/25	35.00
12	Dale Murphy/25	40.00
13	Dave Parker/25	20.00
18	Fergie Jenkins/25	25.00
19	Gary Carter/25	25.00
22	Joe Morgan/25	30.00
28	Lou Brock/25	35.00
29	Luis Aparicio/25	20.00
35	Mike Schmidt/25	60.00
38	Ozzie Smith/25	75.00
53	Stan Musial/25	75.00

Dynasty

NM/M
Common Player: 3.00

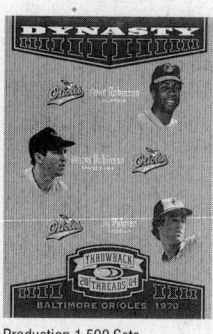

Production 1,500 Sets
Spectrum: 2-3X
Production 100 Sets

1	Phil Rizzuto, Whitey Ford	3.00
2	Pee Wee Reese, Duke Snider, Tom Lasorda	3.00
3	Jim "Catfish" Hunter, Reggie Jackson	3.00
4	Roger Maris, Whitey Ford	5.00
5	Enos Slaughter, Shawn Marion, Stan Musial	5.00
6	Dwight Gooden, Gary Carter, Darryl Strawberry, Keith Hernandez	3.00
7	Johnny Bench, Tony Perez, Joe Morgan, George Foster	3.00
8	Derek Jeter, Jorge Posada, Bernie Williams, Andy Pettitte	6.00
9	Frank Robinson, Brooks Robinson, Jim Palmer	3.00
10	Willie Stargell, Dave Parker, Bill Madlock	3.00
11	Bob Gibson, Lou Brock, Ken Boyer	3.00
12	Rickey Henderson, Paul Molitor, Joe Carter, Roberto Alomar	3.00

Dynasty Material

NM/M
Quantity produced listed
Prime: No Pricing
Production 5 Sets

3	Jim "Catfish" Hunter, Reggie Jackson/25	25.00
6	Dwight Gooden, Gary Carter, Darryl Strawberry, Keith Hernandez/50	35.00
7	Johnny Bench, Tony Perez, Joe Morgan, George Foster/25	80.00
8	Derek Jeter, Jorge Posada, Bernie Williams, Andy Pettitte/25	50.00
10	Willie Stargell, Dave Parker, Bill Madlock/25	30.00
11	Bob Gibson, Lou Brock, Ken Boyer/25	35.00
12	Rickey Henderson, Paul Molitor, Joe Carter, Roberto Alomar/25	60.00

Generations

NM/M
Common Duo: 1.50
Production 1,500 Sets
Spectrum: 2-3X
Production 100 Sets

1	George Brett, Albert Pujols	5.00
2	Wade Boggs, Aubrey Huff	2.00
3	Jim "Catfish" Hunter, Tim Hudson	2.00
4	Steve Garvey, Shawn Green	1.50
5	Tony Gwynn, Garret Anderson	4.00
6	Fergie Jenkins, Mark Prior	2.00
7	Robin Yount, Rickie Weeks	4.00
8	Warren Spahn, Greg Maddux	4.00
9	Brooks Robinson, Cal Ripken Jr., Miguel Tejada	8.00
10	Bobby Doerr, Carl Yastrzemski, Manny Ramirez	5.00
11	Al Kaline, Alan Trammell, Ivan Rodriguez	2.50
12	Tom Seaver, Dwight Gooden, Tom Glavine	4.00
13	Stan Musial, Lou Brock, Jim Edmonds	4.00
14	George Foster, Dave Parker, Austin Kearns	1.50
15	Ed Mathews, Dale Murphy, Chipper Jones	3.00
16	Don Sutton, Nolan Ryan, Roger Clemens	8.00
17	Bernie Williams, Andre Dawson, Sammy Sosa	4.00
18	Whitey Ford, Tommy John, Andy Pettitte	2.00
19	Carlton Fisk, Roger Clemens, Nomar Garciaparra	5.00
20	Shawn Marion, Ozzie Smith, Edgar Renteria	4.00
21	Reggie Jackson, Rickey Henderson, Eric Chavez	2.00
22	Babe Ruth, Don Mattingly, Derek Jeter	8.00
23	Roberto Clemente Jr., Reggie Jackson, Sammy Sosa	6.00
24	Bob Feller, Tom Seaver, Roger Clemens	5.00
25	Ernie Banks, Cal Ripken Jr., Alex Rodriguez	8.00
26	Pee Wee Reese, Ozzie Smith, Derek Jeter	6.00
27	Harmon Killebrew, Mike Schmidt, Alex Rodriguez	5.00
28	Bob Gibson, Dwight Gooden, Josh Beckett	2.00

Generations Material

NM/M
Quantity produced listed
Prime: No Pricing
Production 5 Sets

1	George Brett, Albert Pujols/50	40.00
2	Wade Boggs, Aubrey Huff/50	10.00
3	Jim "Catfish" Hunter, Tim Hudson/25	20.00
5	Tony Gwynn, Garret Anderson/50	20.00
6	Fergie Jenkins, Mark Prior/25	15.00
7	Robin Yount, Rickie Weeks/Bat/50	20.00
8	Warren Spahn, Greg Maddux/25	40.00
11	Al Kaline, Alan Trammell, Ivan Rodriguez/Bat/25	40.00
14	George Foster, Dave Parker, Austin Kearns/25	20.00
16	Don Sutton, Nolan Ryan, Roger Clemens/Bat/50	50.00
17	Billy Williams, Andre Dawson, Sammy Sosa/50	30.00
18	Whitey Ford, Tommy John, Andy Pettitte/25	40.00
19	Carlton Fisk, Roger Clemens, Nomar Garciaparra	40.00
20	Marty Marion, Ozzie Smith, Edgar Renteria/25	40.00
21	Reggie Jackson, Rickey Henderson, Eric Chavez/50	30.00
24	Bob Feller, Tom Seaver, Roger Clemens/25	40.00
25	Ernie Banks, Cal Ripken Jr., Alex Rodriguez	65.00
26	Pee Wee Reese, Ozzie Smith, Derek Jeter/25	50.00
27	Harmon Killebrew, Mike Schmidt, Alex Rodriguez/Bat/25	50.00
28	Bob Gibson, Dwight Gooden, Josh Beckett/25	30.00

Material

NM/M

	Common Player:	4.00
2	Darin Erstad/Jsy/100	6.00
4	Garret Anderson/Jsy/100	6.00
5	Tim Salmon/Jsy/100	6.00
6	Troy Glaus/Jsy/100	6.00
7	Vladimir Guerrero/Bat/100	10.00
8	Brandon Webb/Pants/100	4.00
9	Luis Gonzalez/Jsy/100	4.00
10	Randy Johnson/Jsy/100	10.00
11	Richie Sexson/Bat/50	8.00
12	Roberto Alomar/Bat/100	8.00
14	Steve Finley/Jsy/100	4.00
15	Adam LaRoche/Bat/100	4.00
16	Andruw Jones/Jsy/100	4.00
17	Chipper Jones/Jsy/100	8.00
18	J.D. Drew/Bat/100	4.00
19	John Smoltz/Jsy/100	8.00
20	Rafael Furcal/Jsy/100	4.00
22	Javy Lopez/Bat/100	4.00
23	Jay Gibbons/Jsy/100	4.00
24	Larry Bigbie/Jsy/100	4.00
25	Luis Matos/Jsy/100	4.00
26	Melvin Mora/Jsy/100	4.00
27	Miguel Tejada/Bat/100	6.00
28	Rafael Palmeiro/Jsy/100	8.00
29	Curt Schilling/Bat/100	6.00
30	David Ortiz/Bat/100	10.00
32	Jason Varitek/Jsy/100	8.00
33	Johnny Damon/Bat/100	6.00
34	Manny Ramirez/Jsy/100	8.00
35	Nomar Garciaparra/Jsy/100	8.00
36	Pedro J. Martinez/Jsy/100	8.00
37	Trot Nixon/Bat/100	4.00
38	Aramis Ramirez/Jsy/100	6.00
39	Corey Patterson/Pants/100	4.00
41	Greg Maddux/Bat/100	10.00
42	Kerry Wood/Pants/100	10.00
43	Mark Prior/Jsy/100	6.00
44	Sammy Sosa/Jsy/100	12.00
45	Carlos Lee/Jsy/100	4.00
47	Frank Thomas/Pants/100	8.00
48	Joe Borchard/Jsy/100	4.00
49	Magglio Ordonez/Jsy/100	4.00
50	Mark Buehrle/Jsy/100	4.00
51	Paul Konerko/Jsy/100	4.00
52	Adam Dunn/Jsy/100	8.00
53	Austin Kearns/Jsy/100	6.00
54	Barry Larkin/Jsy/100	6.00
55	Brandon Larson/Fld Glv/100	4.00
58	Sean Casey/Jsy/100	4.00
59	C.C. Sabathia/Jsy/100	4.00
60	Jody Gerut/Jsy/100	4.00
61	Omar Vizquel/Jsy/100	4.00
62	Travis Hafner/Jsy/100	4.00
63	Victor Martinez/Bat/100	6.00
64	Charles Johnson/Bat/100	4.00
65	Garrett Atkins/Jsy/100	4.00
66	Jason Jennings/Jsy/100	4.00
67	Joe Kennedy/Bat/100	4.00
68	Larry Walker/Jsy/100	4.00
69	Preston Wilson/Jsy/100	4.00
70	Todd Helton/Jsy/100	8.00
71	Ivan Rodriguez/Bat/100	8.00
72	Jeremy Bonderman/Jsy/100	4.00
73	A.J. Burnett/Jsy/100	4.00
74	Brad Penny/Jsy/100	4.00
75	Dontrelle Willis/Jsy/100	
76	Josh Beckett/Jsy/100	6.00
77	Juan Pierre/Bat/100	4.00
78	Luis Castillo/Jsy/100	4.00
79	Miguel Cabrera/Jsy/100	8.00
80	Mike Lowell/Jsy/50	8.00
81	Andy Pettitte/Bat/100	4.00
82	Craig Biggio/Jsy/100	6.00
83	Jeff Bagwell/Jsy/100	8.00
84	Jeff Kent/Jsy/100	4.00
85	Lance Berkman/Jsy/100	4.00
86	Morgan Ensberg/Jsy/100	4.00
87	Richard Hidalgo/Pants/100	4.00
88	Roger Clemens/Bat/50	15.00
89	Roy Oswalt/Jsy/100	4.00
90	Wade Miller/Jsy/100	4.00
91	Angel Berroa/Pants/100	4.00
92	Carlos Beltran/Jsy/100	8.00
93	Juan Gonzalez/Bat/100	8.00
94	Ken Harvey/Bat/100	4.00
95	Mike Sweeney/Jsy/100	4.00
96	Runelvys Hernandez/Jsy/100	4.00
97	Adrian Beltre/Jsy/100	4.00
98	Edwin Jackson/Jsy/100	4.00
100	Hideo Nomo/Jsy/100	8.00
101	Hong-Chih Kuo/Jsy/100	4.00
102	Kazuhisa Ishii/Jsy/100	4.00
103	Paul LoDuca/Jsy/100	4.00
104	Shawn Green/Jsy/100	4.00
105	Ben Sheets/Jsy/100	6.00
106	Geoff Jenkins/Jsy/100	4.00
107	Junior Spivey/Bat/50	4.00
108	Rickie Weeks/Bat/50	8.00
111	Doug Mientkiewicz/Bat/100	4.00
112	Jacque Jones/Jsy/100	4.00
113	Joe Mays/Jsy/100	4.00
114	Johan Santana/Jsy/100	8.00
115	Shannon Stewart/Jsy/100	4.00
116	Torii Hunter/Jsy/100	6.00
117	Brad Wilkerson/Bat/100	4.00
118	Carl Everett/Bat/100	4.00
120	Jose Vidro/Jsy/100	4.00
121	Nick Johnson/Bat/100	4.00
122	Orlando Cabrera/Jsy/100	4.00
123	Al Leiter/Jsy/100	4.00
124	Cliff Floyd/Bat/100	4.00
125	Jae Weong Seo/Jsy/100	4.00
126	Jose Reyes/Jsy/100	8.00
127	Mike Piazza/Jsy/100	8.00
129	Tom Glavine/Jsy/100	6.00
130	Alex Rodriguez/Bat/100	10.00
131	Bernie Williams/Jsy/100	6.00
133	Derek Jeter/Jsy/100	20.00
134	Gary Sheffield/Bat/100	6.00
135	Hideki Matsui/Jsy/100	20.00
136	Jason Giambi/Jsy/100	6.00
138	Jorge Posada/Jsy/100	6.00
141	Mariano Rivera/Jsy/50	15.00
142	Mike Mussina/Jsy/100	6.00
143	Barry Zito/Jsy/100	4.00
145	Eric Chavez/Jsy/100	4.00
146	Erubiel Durazo/Bat/100	4.00
147	Jermaine Dye/Bat/100	4.00
149	Mark Mulder/Jsy/100	6.00
150	Rich Harden/Jsy/100	4.00
151	Tim Hudson/Jsy/100	6.00
153	Bobby Abreu/Jsy/100	6.00
154	Brett Myers/Jsy/100	4.00
155	Jim Thome/Jsy/100	8.00
157	Kevin Millwood/Jsy/100	4.00
158	Marlon Byrd/Bat/100	4.00
159	Pat Burrell/Jsy/100	6.00
161	Jason Kendall/Jsy/100	4.00
162	Brian Giles/Bat/100	4.00
164	Ryan Klesko/Jsy/100	4.00
165	Edgardo Alfonzo/Bat/100	4.00
167	Jerome Williams/Jsy/100	4.00
170	Edgar Martinez/Jsy/100	8.00
171	Freddy Garcia/Jsy/100	4.00
173	Jamie Moyer/Jsy/100	4.00
174	John Olerud/Jsy/100	4.00
176	Albert Pujols/Jsy/100	20.00
177	Dan Haren/Jsy/100	4.00
178	Edgar Renteria/Jsy/100	6.00
179	Jim Edmonds/Jsy/100	4.00
180	Matt Morris/Jsy/100	4.00
181	Scott Rolen/Jsy/100	8.00
182	Aubrey Huff/Jsy/100	4.00
183	Carl Crawford/Jsy/100	4.00
184	Chad Gaudin/Jsy/100	4.00
185	Delmon Young/Bat/100	6.00
186	Dewon Brazelton/Jsy/100	4.00
187	Fred McGriff/Jsy/100	6.00
188	Rocco Baldelli/Jsy/100	4.00
189	Alfonso Soriano/Bat/100	6.00
190	Hank Blalock/Jsy/100	6.00
191	Laynce Nix/Bat/100	4.00
192	Mark Teixeira/Jsy/23	15.00
193	Michael Young/Bat/100	6.00
194	Carlos Delgado/Jsy/100	6.00
195	Eric Hinske/Jsy/100	4.00
196	Frank Catalanotto/Jsy/100	4.00
197	Josh Phelps/Jsy/100	4.00
198	Orlando Hudson/Jsy/100	4.00
199	Roy Halladay/Jsy/100	6.00
200	Vernon Wells/Jsy/100	4.00
201	Dale Murphy/Jsy/100	12.00
202	Cal Ripken Jr./Jsy/100	30.00
203	Fred Lynn/Bat/100	8.00
204	Wade Boggs/Jsy/100	8.00
205	Nolan Ryan/Jkt/100	25.00
206	Rod Carew/Jkt/100	10.00
207	Andre Dawson/Pants/100	6.00
208	Ernie Banks/Pants/100	20.00
209	Ryne Sandberg/Jsy/100	25.00
210	Bo Jackson/Jsy/100	12.00
211	Carlton Fisk/Jkt/100	10.00
212	Dave Concepcion/Jsy/100	8.00
213	Alan Trammell/Bat/100	8.00
214	George Brett/Jsy/100	15.00
215	Robin Yount/Jsy/100	15.00
216	Gary Carter/Jsy/100	8.00
217	Darryl Strawberry/Pants/100	8.00
218	Dwight Gooden/Jsy/50	8.00
219	Babe Ruth/Jsy/25	400.00
220	Don Mattingly/Jkt/100	15.00
221	Reggie Jackson/Jkt/100	10.00
222	Mike Schmidt/Jkt/100	15.00
223	Tony Gwynn/Jsy/100	10.00
224	Keith Hernandez/Jsy/100	8.00

Player Threads

NM/M
Common Player: 4.00
Production 250 Sets
Prime: 2-3X
Production 10-25
No pricing 15 or less.

1	Aaron Boone	4.00
2	Alex Rodriguez/M's-Rgr	15.00
3	Andres Galarraga/Braves-Giants-Rgr	10.00
4	Aramis Ramirez	4.00
5	Bartolo Colon	4.00
6	Ben Grieve/A's-D'Rays	4.00
7	Brad Fullmer	4.00
8	Bret Boone/Braves-M's	4.00
9	Brian Giles	4.00
10	Brian Jordan	4.00
11	Byung-Hyun Kim	4.00
12	Casey Fossum	4.00
13	Cesar Izturis	4.00
14	Chan Ho Park	4.00
15	Charles Johnson	4.00
16	Cliff Floyd	4.00
17	Darryl Strawberry/Dgr-Met-Ynk	10.00
18	David Ortiz	10.00

19	David Wells/	
	Jays-Yanks	4.00
20	Derrek Lee	6.00
21	Dmitri Young	4.00
22	Edgardo Alfonzo	4.00
23	Ellis Burks	4.00
24	Gary Sheffield/	
	Braves-Brew-Dgr	8.00
25	Hee Seop Choi	4.00
26	Ivan Rodriguez/	
	Marlins-Rgr	10.00
27	J.D. Drew	6.00
28	Javier Vazquez	4.00
29	Jay Payton	4.00
30	Jeff Kent/	
	Astros-Giants-Jays	4.00
31	Jeromy Burnitz	4.00
32	Jim Thome/	
	Indians-Phils	10.00
33	Joe Kennedy	4.00
34	Joe Torre	8.00
35	Jose Cruz Jr.	4.00
36	Juan Encarnacion	4.00
37	Juan Gonzalez/	
	Indians-Rgr	8.00
38	Juan Pierre	4.00
39	Junior Spivey	4.00
40	Kenny Lofton/	
	Brave-Tribe	8.00
41	Kevin Millwood	6.00
42	Manny Ramirez/	
	Indians-Sox	12.00
43	Mark Grace/	
	Cubs-D'backs	10.00
44	Mike Hampton	4.00
45	Mike Piazza/	
	Dgr-Marlins-Mets	20.00
46	Milton Bradley	4.00
47	Moises Alou	6.00
48	Nick Johnson	4.00
49	Nolan Ryan Ang/	
	Jkt-Ast/Jkt-Rgr	50.00
50	Preston Wilson/	
	Marlins-Rockies	6.00
51	Rafael Palmeiro/	
	O's-Rgr	10.00
52	Ray Durham	4.00
53	Reggie Jackson/	
	A's-Ang-Yank	15.00
54	Reggie Sanders	4.00
55	Rich Aurilia	4.00
56	Richie Sexson	6.00
57	Rickey Henderson	
	A's-M's-Yanks/25	50.00
58	Rickey Henderson/	
	Dgr-Mets-Padres	20.00
59	Robert Fick	4.00
60	Roberto Alomar/	
	Mets-Sox	8.00
61	Roberto Alomar/	
	Indians-O's	8.00
62	Robin Ventura	
	Mets-Sox-Yanks	10.00
63	Rondell White/	
	Cubs-Expos	6.00
64	Ryan Klesko/	
	Braves-Padres	6.00
65	Sean Casey	6.00
66	Shannon Stewart/	
	Jays-Twins	6.00
67	Shawn Green/	
	Jays-Dgr	8.00
68	Shea Hillenbrand	4.00
69	Steve Carlton/	
	Giants-Phils	8.00
70	Terrence Long	4.00
71	Tony Batista	4.00
72	Travis Hafner/	
	Indians-Rgr	6.00
73	Travis Lee	4.00
74	Vladimir Guerrero	8.00
75	Wes Helms	4.00

Player Threads Signature

		NM/M
Quantity produced listed		
4	Aramis Ramirez/25	30.00
17	Darryl Strawberry/	
	Dgr-Met-Ynk/25	40.00
24	Gary Sheffield/	
	Brave-Brw-Dgr/25	40.00
28	Javier Vazquez/25	20.00
29	Jay Payton/25	15.00
37	Juan Gonzalez/	
	Indians-Rgr/25	40.00
39	Junior Spivey/25	15.00
50	Preston Wilson/	
	Marlins-Rockies/25	25.00
55	Rich Aurilia/25	15.00
62	Robin Ventura/	
	Mets-Sox-Yanks/25	40.00
68	Shea Hillenbrand/25	20.00
74	Vladimir Guerrero/25	60.00

Signature Marks

		NM/M
Common Autograph:		8.00
4	Garret Anderson/25	25.00
8	Brandon Webb/50	10.00
13	Shea Hillenbrand/50	15.00
15	Adam LaRoche/50	10.00
20	Rafael Furcal/25	25.00
23	Jay Gibbons/50	10.00
24	Larry Bigbie/50	20.00
25	Luis Matos/50	10.00
26	Melvin Mora/50	10.00
30	David Ortiz/25	40.00
37	Trot Nixon/25	30.00
40	Derrek Lee/25	30.00
43	Mark Prior/25	40.00
45	Carlos Lee/50	10.00
46	Esteban Loaiza/50	12.00
48	Joe Borchard/25	15.00
50	Mark Buehrle/25	25.00
53	Austin Kearns/25	15.00
55	Brandon Larson/25	15.00
60	Jody Gerut/50	20.00
62	Travis Hafner/50	15.00
63	Victor Martinez/50	25.00
69	Preston Wilson/50	15.00
74	Brad Penny/50	15.00
79	Miguel Cabrera/50	40.00
80	Mike Lowell/25	20.00
86	Morgan Ensberg/50	12.00
89	Roy Oswalt/25	25.00
91	Angel Berroa/25	12.00
92	Carlos Beltran/25	35.00
98	Edwin Jackson/50	20.00
101	Hong-Chih Kuo/50	30.00
109	Scott Podsednik/50	15.00
112	Jacque Jones/50	15.00
114	Johan Santana/25	50.00
115	Shannon Stewart/25	20.00
116	Torii Hunter/25	25.00
119	Chad Cordero/50	8.00
120	Jose Vidro/25	15.00
122	Orlando Cabrera/50	15.00
132	Chien-Ming Wang/	
	25	100.00
147	Jermaine Dye/50	12.00
160	Jason Bay/50	20.00
163	Jay Payton/50	15.00
168	Todd Linden/50	15.00
175	Shigetoshi	
	Hasegawa/25	50.00
177	Dan Haren/25	15.00
181	Scott Rolen/25	50.00
182	Aubrey Huff/50	15.00
184	Chad Gaudin/50	10.00
186	Dewon Brazelton/50	10.00
187	Fred McGriff/25	25.00
189	Alfonso Soriano/25	30.00
193	Michael Young/50	20.00
203	Fred Lynn/50	20.00
207	Andre Dawson/50	20.00
216	Gary Carter/25	25.00
217	Darryl Strawberry/50	20.00
218	Dwight Gooden/50	15.00
224	Keith Hernandez/50	20.00
225	Hector Gimenez/100	8.00
226	Graham Koonce/100	8.00
228	Jerry Gil/100	8.00
229	Jason Frasor/100	8.00
230	Justin Knoedler/50	8.00
233	Ronald Belisario/200	8.00
234	Jerome Gamble/200	8.00
235	Roberto Novoa/200	8.00
236	Sean Henn/200	10.00
237	Willy Taveras/100	10.00
238	Ramon Ramirez/200	10.00
241	Jason Bartlett/25	20.00
242	Fernando Nieve/25	12.00
243	Freddy Guzman/25	20.00
248	William Bergolla/100	10.00
249	Shawn Hill/100	8.00
250	Justin Germano/100	8.00

2004 Donruss Timeless Treasures

		NM/M
Complete Set (100):		200.00
Common Player:		1.50
Production 999 Sets		
Tin (4):		125.00
1	Albert Pujols	6.00
2	Garret Anderson	2.00
3	Randy Johnson	3.00
4	Alex Rodriguez/Yanks	8.00
5	Manny Ramirez	3.00
6	Mark Prior	4.00

7	Roberto Alomar	2.00
8	Barry Larkin	2.00
9	Todd Helton	2.50
10	Ivan Rodriguez	3.00
11	Jacque Jones	1.50
12	Jeff Kent	1.50
13	Mike Sweeney	1.50
14	Shawn Green	2.00
15	Richie Sexson	2.00
16	Mike Piazza	5.00
17	Vladimir Guerrero	4.00
18	Mike Mussina	2.00
19	Barry Zito	2.00
20	Don Mattingly	6.00
21	Ichiro Suzuki	5.00
22	Rocco Baldelli	2.00
23	Rafael Palmeiro	3.00
24	Carlos Delgado	2.00
25	Roger Clemens	6.00
26	Luis Gonzalez	2.00
27	Gary Sheffield	2.00
28	Jay Gibbons	1.50
29	Nomar Garciaparra	5.00
30	Aramis Ramirez	2.00
31	Frank Thomas	3.00
32	Ryan Wagner	1.50
33	Preston Wilson	1.50
34	Hideki Matsui	4.00
35	Roy Oswalt	2.00
36	Angel Berroa	1.50
37	Kazuhisa Ishii	1.50
38	Scott Podsednik	1.50
39	Torii Hunter	2.00
40	Tom Glavine	2.00
41	Jason Giambi	3.00
42	Eric Chavez	2.00
43	Jim Thome	3.00
44	Tony Gwynn	3.00
45	Edgar Martinez	2.00
46	Jim Edmonds	2.00
47	Delmon Young	2.00
48	Hank Blalock	2.00
49	Vernon Wells	1.50
50	Curt Schilling	2.50
51	Chipper Jones	3.00
52	Cal Ripken Jr.	8.00
53	Jason Varitek	1.50
54	Kerry Wood	3.00
55	Magglio Ordonez	2.00
56	Adam Dunn	2.00
57	Jay Payton	1.50
58	Josh Beckett	2.00
59	Jeff Bagwell	3.00
60	Carlos Beltran	2.00
61	Hideo Nomo	2.00
62	Rickie Weeks	2.00
63	Alfonso Soriano	2.50
64	Miguel Tejada	2.00
65	Bret Boone	2.00
66	Scott Rolen	3.00
67	Aubrey Huff	1.50
68	Juan Gonzalez	2.50
69	Roy Halladay	2.50
70	Brandon Webb	1.50
71	Andruw Jones	2.50
72	Pedro J. Martinez	3.00
73	Carlos Lee	1.50
74	Lance Berkman	2.00
75	Paul LoDuca	1.50
76	Jorge Posada	2.00
77	Tim Hudson	2.00
78	Stan Musial	4.00
79	Mark Teixeira	2.00
80	Trot Nixon	1.50
81	Fred McGriff	1.50
82	Nick Johnson	1.50
83	Nolan Ryan	8.00
84	Ken Griffey Jr.	4.00
85	Mariano Rivera	2.00
86	Mark Mulder	2.00
87	Bob Gibson	2.50
88	Dale Murphy UER	2.50
89	Bernie Williams	2.00
90	Carl Yastrzemski	3.00
91	Sammy Sosa	5.00
92	Miguel Cabrera	4.00
93	Craig Biggio	2.00
94	George Brett	6.00
95	Rickey Henderson	3.00
96	Derek Jeter	8.00
97	Greg Maddux	4.00
98	Bob Abreu	2.00
99	Troy Glaus	2.00
100	Dontrelle Willis	2.00

Bronze
		NM/M
Bronze:		1-2X
Production 100 Sets		

Silver
Silver:		2-4X
Production 25 Sets		

Gold
Gold:		No Pricing
Production 10 Sets		

Platinum
Platinum:		No Pricing
Production One Set		

Award Materials
		NM/M
Common Player:		10.00
Quantity Produced Listed		
Prime:		1-2X

Production 1-25		
No Pricing 10 or less.		
Number:		.75-1.5X
Production 3-51		
No Pricing 15 or less.		
2	Stan Musial/Jsy/43	25.00
3	Lou Boudreau/	
	Jsy/19	15.00
4	Roger Maris/	
	Pants/61	40.00
	Roger Maris/Bat/61	40.00
6	Roberto Clemente/	
	Bat/66	60.00
7	Bob Gibson 68 CY/	
	Jsy/68	20.00
8	Bob Gibson 68 MVP/	
	Jsy/68	20.00
9	Tom Seaver/Jsy/19	20.00
10	Fred Lynn/Jsy/75	8.00
11	Jim Rice/Jsy/78	10.00
12	Mike Schmidt 80 MVP/	
	Jsy/80	15.00
13	Mike Schmidt 80 MVP/	
	Pants/80	15.00
14	Mike Schmidt/	
	80 MVP Stir/80	15.00
15	Mike Schmidt 81 MVP/	
	Jsy/81	15.00
16	Mike Schmidt 81 MVP/	
	Bat/81	15.00
17	Dale Murphy/Jsy/82	7.00
18	Mike Schmidt/	
	86 MVP Hat/19	35.00
19	Mike Schmidt/	
	86 MVP Shoe/19	35.00
20	Mike Schmidt/	
	86 MVP/Bat/86	15.00
21	Mike Schmidt/	
	86 MVP Stir/19	35.00
22	Jose Canseco/Jsy/88	10.00
23	Frank Thomas/	
	93 MVP/Bat/93	10.00
24	Frank Thomas/	
	93 MVP/Jsy/93	10.00
25	Jeff Bagwell/	
	Pants/94	10.00
26	Frank Thomas	
	94 MVP/Jsy/94	10.00
27	Frank Thomas	
	94 MVP/Pants/94	10.00
28	Jeff Bagwell/Bat/94	10.00
29	Pedro J. Martinez	
	97 CY/Jsy/97	7.00
30	Ivan Rodriguez/	
	Bat/99	10.00
31	Randy Johnson	
	00 CY/Jsy/25	20.00
32	Pedro J. Martinez	
	00 CY/Jsy/25	20.00
33	Roger Clemens/	
	Jsy/50	15.00
34	Randy Johnson	
	02 CY/Jsy/25	20.00
35	Miguel Tejada/	
	Jsy/25	15.00

Award Materials Combos
		NM/M
Prime:		.75-1.5X
Production 19 Sets		
4	Roger Maris/	
	Bat-Pants/61	70.00
12	Mike Schmidt 80M/	
	Jsy-Pants/80	40.00
13	Mike Schmidt	
	80M/Pant-Stir/50	30.00
14	Mike Schmidt 80M/	
	Jsy-Stir/50	30.00
15	Mike Schmidt 81M/	
	Bat-Jsy/50	40.00
16	Mike Schmidt 81M/	
	Bat-Stir/50	30.00
18	Mike Schmidt 86M/	
	Hat-Shoe/50	30.00
19	Mike Schmidt 86M/	
	Hat-Bat/50	30.00
20	Mike Schmidt 86M/	
	Hat-Stir/50	30.00
21	Mike Schmidt 86M/	
	Bat-Shoe/50	30.00
23	Frank Thomas 93M/	
	Bat-Jsy/25	25.00
25	Jeff Bagwell/	
	Bat-Jsy/25	25.00
26	Frank Thomas 94M/	
	Bat-Jsy/25	25.00
35	Miguel Tejada/	
	Bat-Jsy/25	15.00

Award Materials Combo Prime
Production 19 Sets

Award Materials Combo Signature
No Pricing		
Production 5 Sets		
Prime:		No Pricing
Production One Set		

Award Materials Number
Production 3-45

Award Materials Prime
Production 1-25

Award Material Signature Prime

Award Materials Signature
		NM/M
Common Autograph:		
Quantity produced listed		
Number:		1-2X
Production 1-19		
No Pricing 10 or less.		
Prime:		No Pricing
7	Bob Gibson 68 CY/	
	Jsy/19	50.00
8	Bob Gibson 68 MVP/	
	Jsy/19	50.00
10	Fred Lynn/Jsy/75	15.00
11	Jim Rice/Jsy/78	30.00

Game Day Materials
		NM/M
Quantity produced listed		
1	Nellie Fox/Bat/58	40.00
2	Frank Robinson/	
	Bat/61	25.00
3	George Brett/Bat/77	20.00
4	George Brett/Hat/82	30.00
5	Nolan Ryan/Hat/19	80.00
6	Cal Ripken Jr./	
	Hat/85	50.00
7	Rod Carew/Hat/19	25.00
8	Ryne Sandberg/	
	Bat/91	20.00
9	Kirby Puckett/Bat/92	15.00
10	Frank Thomas/Bat/93	10.00
12	Tony Gwynn/	
	Pants/99	15.00
13	Vladimir Guerrero/	
	Bat/99	15.00
14	Tony Gwynn/Hat/99	20.00
15	Magglio Ordonez/	
	Hat/15	15.00
16	Rickey Henderson/	
	Bat/50	10.00

Game Day Material Signature
		NM/M
Many not priced		
due to scarcity.		
2	Frank Robinson/	
	Bat/25	40.00
15	Magglio Ordonez/	
	Hat/25	30.00

HOF Materials Barrel
Production One Set

HOF Materials Bat
		NM/M
1	Al Kaline/25	25.00
2	Babe Ruth/50	200.00
4	Bobby Doerr/25	15.00
5	Brooks Robinson/25	30.00
6	Carl Yastrzemski/25	30.00
7	Carlton Fisk/25	20.00
8	Dave Winfield/25	15.00
10	Eddie Murray/25	25.00
11	Ernie Banks/25	30.00
13	Frank Robinson/25	15.00
18	Joe Morgan/25	15.00
19	Johnny Bench/25	30.00
21	Kirby Puckett/25	30.00
22	Lou Brock/25	20.00
23	Lou Gehrig/25	125.00
24	Luis Aparicio/25	10.00
25	Mel Ott/25	40.00
26	Orlando Cepeda/25	15.00
27	Pee Wee Reese/25	15.00
28	Phil Rizzuto/25	15.00
29	Red Schoendienst/25	10.00
30	Roberto Clemente/25	65.00
31	Roy Campanella/25	25.00
32	Paul Molitor/25	20.00
33	Ty Cobb/25	100.00
35	Willie McCovey/25	15.00
36	Willie Stargell/25	15.00

HOF Materials Bat Signature
		NM/M
1	Al Kaline/50	40.00
4	Bobby Doerr/50	35.00
5	Brooks Robinson/50	40.00
11	Ernie Banks/25	75.00
13	Frank Robinson/25	35.00
18	Joe Morgan/25	40.00
19	Johnny Bench/50	60.00
22	Lou Brock/50	30.00
24	Luis Aparicio/50	20.00
26	Orlando Cepeda/25	25.00
28	Phil Rizzuto/25	35.00

29	Red Schoendienst/	
	50	25.00
32	Paul Molitor/25	50.00

HOF Material Combo Bat-Jsy
		NM/M
Quantity produced listed		
Prime:		No Pricing
Production 1-5		
1	Al Kaline/25	40.00
2	Babe Ruth/25	500.00
5	Bobby Doerr/25	15.00
6	Brooks Robinson/50	30.00
7	Carl Yastrzemski/50	40.00
8	Carlton Fisk/50	20.00
9	Dave Winfield/50	15.00
10	Eddie Murray/50	35.00
13	Frank Robinson/50	20.00
18	Joe Morgan/50	15.00
19	Kirby Puckett/50	30.00
22	Lou Brock/50	15.00
23	Lou Gehrig/25	220.00
24	Luis Aparicio/25	20.00
25	Mel Ott/25	60.00
27	Pee Wee Reese/50	20.00
28	Phil Rizzuto/50	20.00
29	Red Schoendienst/	
	25	15.00
30	Roberto Clemente/	
	50	80.00
32	Paul Molitor/50	20.00
35	Willie McCovey/50	15.00
36	Willie Stargell/50	20.00

HOF Mat. Combo Bat-Jsy Sig
		NM/M
Quantity produced listed		
Prime:		No Pricing
Production 1-5		
4	Bobby Doerr/25	30.00
5	Brooks Robinson/25	80.00
11	Ernie Banks/25	80.00
13	Frank Robinson/25	65.00
18	Joe Morgan/25	40.00
22	Lou Brock/25	40.00
24	Luis Aparicio/25	30.00
29	Red Schoendienst/	
	25	40.00
32	Paul Molitor/25	60.00

HOF Mat. Combo Bat-Pant
		NM/M
Production 25 Sets		
1	Al Kaline/25	35.00
2	Babe Ruth/25	350.00
12	Fergie Jenkins/	
	Fld Glv-Pants/25	15.00
23	Lou Gehrig/25	200.00
24	Luis Aparicio/25	15.00
25	Mel Ott/25	60.00
31	Roy Campanella/25	40.00
33	Ty Cobb/25	100.00

HOF Mat Combo Bat-Pant Signature
		NM/M
1	Al Kaline/25	75.00
12	Fergie Jenkins/	
	Fld Glv-Pants/25	35.00
24	Luis Aparicio/25	25.00

HOF Material Combo Jsy-Pant
		NM/M
2	Babe Ruth/25	500.00
23	Lou Gehrig/25	220.00
24	Luis Aparicio/25	15.00

HOF Mat. Combo Jsy-Pant Signature
		NM/M
Prime:		No Pricing
Production 1-5		
24	Luis Aparicio/25	25.00

HOF Materials Jersey
		NM/M
Quantity produced listed		
Prime:		No Pricing
Production 1-10		
Jersey Number:		.75-1.5X
Production 1-44		
No Pricing 15 or less.		
2	Babe Ruth/25	500.00
3	Bob Feller/10	10.00
4	Bobby Doerr/25	15.00
5	Brooks Robinson/50	15.00
6	Carl Yastrzemski/50	25.00
7	Carlton Fisk/50	10.00
9	Dave Winfield/50	10.00
10	Eddie Murray/50	15.00
13	Frank Robinson/25	20.00
14	Hal Newhouser/25	10.00
16	Hoyt Wilhelm/25	10.00
17	Jim Palmer/50	10.00
18	Joe Morgan/50	10.00
20	Juan Marichal/50	10.00

#	Player	Price
21	Kirby Puckett/50	20.00
22	Lou Brock/25	15.00
23	Lou Gehrig/25	140.00
24	Luis Aparicio/25	10.00
25	Mel Ott/25	40.00
27	Pee Wee Reese/50	15.00
28	Phil Rizzuto/50	15.00
29	Red Schoendienst/25	15.00
30	Roberto Clemente/50	60.00
32	Paul Molitor/50	15.00
34	Warren Spahn/50	20.00
35	Willie McCovey/50	10.00
36	Willie Stargell/50	15.00

HOF Materials Jsy Signature
NM/M
Quantity produced listed
Prime: No Pricing
Production 1-10
Number: 1X
Production 10-25

#	Player	Price
1	Al Kaline/25	50.00
4	Bobby Doerr/50	30.00
5	Brooks Robinson/25	60.00
13	Frank Robinson	35.00
16	Hoyt Wilhelm/25	25.00
17	Jim Palmer/50	30.00
18	Joe Morgan/25	30.00
20	Juan Marichal/50	35.00
22	Lou Brock/25	25.00
24	Luis Aparicio/50	25.00
26	Orlando Cepeda/25	25.00
28	Phil Rizzuto/50	40.00
29	Red Schoendienst/50	20.00
32	Paul Molitor/50	30.00
34	Warren Spahn/25	65.00

HOF Material Jsy Number
NM/M

#	Player	Price
16	Jackie Robinson/42	50.00

HOF Materials Pants
NM/M

#	Player	Price
1	Al Kaline/25	30.00
2	Babe Ruth/50	200.00
12	Fergie Jenkins/25	15.00
23	Lou Gehrig/50	125.00
24	Luis Aparicio/25	15.00
25	Mel Ott/25	40.00
31	Roy Campanella/25	40.00
33	Ty Cobb/25	125.00

HOF Material Pants Signature
NM/M
Production 25 Sets

#	Player	Price
1	Al Kaline	50.00
12	Fergie Jenkins	30.00
24	Luis Aparicio	25.00
28	Phil Rizzuto	40.00

HOF Materials Signature
NM/M
Quantity produced listed
Prime: No Pricing
Production 1-10

#	Player	Price
1	Al Kaline/25	50.00
3	Bob Feller/25	25.00
5	Brooks Robinson	50.00
7	Carlton Fisk/27	50.00
9	Duke Snider/25	40.00
11	Ernie Banks/25	60.00
12	Fergie Jenkins/31	45.00
13	Frank Robinson/20	40.00
15	Hoyt Wilhelm/25	25.00
17	Jim Palmer/22	30.00
20	Juan Marichal/27	30.00
21	Kirby Puckett/34	60.00
22	Lou Brock/20	40.00
26	Orlando Cepeda/30	30.00
28	Phil Rizzuto/25	40.00
29	Red Schoendienst/25	30.00
32	Paul Molitor/25	50.00
34	Warren Spahn/21	50.00
35	Willie McCovey/25	40.00

HOF Material Jsy Signature Prime
NM/M

#	Player	Price
23	Lou Gehrig/1 (7/04 auction)	4,950

Home Away Gamers
NM/M
Quantity produced listed
Prime: No Pricing
Production 3-5

#	Player	Price
1	Babe Ruth/ Jsy-Jsy/25	600.00
3	Wade Boggs/ Jsy-Jsy/50	15.00
4	Tony Gwynn/ Jsy-Jsy/50	30.00
5	Steve Carlton/ Jsy-Jsy/50	15.00
7	Ryne Sandberg/ Jsy-Jsy/50	35.00
8	Rod Carew/ Jsy-Jsy/50	15.00
9	Rickey Henderson/ Jsy-Jsy/50	25.00
11	Ted Williams/ Jsy-Jsy/100	85.00
12	Ozzie Smith/ Jsy-Jsy/50	25.00
13	Mike Schmidt/ Jsy-Jsy/50	30.00
14	Harmon Killebrew/ Jsy-Jsy/50	30.00
15	George Brett/ Jsy-Jsy/100	30.00
16	Don Mattingly/ Jsy-Jsy/25	35.00
17	Dale Murphy/ Jsy-Jsy/50	15.00
18	Cal Ripken Jr./ Jsy-Jsy/100	50.00
19	Lou Gehrig/ Jsy-Jsy/50	200.00
20	Nolan Ryan/ Jsy-Jsy/100	40.00

Home Away Gamers Signature

NM/M

#	Player	Price
5	Steve Carlton/ Jsy-Jsy/25	40.00
13	Mike Schmidt/ Jsy-Jsy/20	100.00
14	Harmon Killebrew/ Jsy-Jsy/25	90.00
16	Don Mattingly/ Jsy-Jsy/25	120.00
17	Dale Murphy/ Jsy-Jsy/25	70.00
19	Lou Gehrig/ Jsy-Jsy/1 (5/04 auction)	7,100

Home Away Gamers Combos
NM/M
Quantity produced listed
Prime: No Pricing
Production 3-10

#	Player	Price
1	Babe Ruth/25	800.00
3	Wade Boggs/50	25.00
4	Tony Gwynn/50	40.00
5	Steve Carlton/50	25.00
6	Stan Musial/50	85.00
7	Ryne Sandberg/50	40.00
8	Rod Carew/50	25.00
9	Rickey Henderson/ 50	25.00
11	Ted Williams/100	150.00
12	Ozzie Smith/50	40.00
13	Mike Schmidt/50	40.00
14	Harmon Killebrew/ 25	40.00
15	George Brett/100	50.00
16	Don Mattingly/50	50.00
17	Dale Murphy/50	25.00
18	Cal Ripken Jr./100	65.00
19	Lou Gehrig/50	400.00
20	Nolan Ryan/100	65.00

Home Away Gamer Combo Signature
No Pricing
Production 1-5
Prime: No Pricing
Production One Set

Home Run Materials
NM/M

#	Player	Price
1	Roger Maris/Bat/61	40.00
3	Harmon Killebrew HR 570/Bat/75	20.00
4	Harmon Killebrew HR 565/Bat/75	20.00
5	Jose Canseco/Bat/96	10.00
6	Alex Rodriguez/ Bat/100	15.00
7	Sammy Sosa/ Jsy/100	15.00
8	Rafael Palmeiro/ Jsy/25	20.00
9	Ivan Rodriguez/ Jsy/25	20.00

Material Ink Bat
NM/M

#	Player	Price
1	Adam Dunn/25	40.00
2	Alan Trammell/25	35.00
4	Andre Dawson/25	35.00
5	Bo Jackson/25	60.00
7	Dale Murphy/25	40.00
12	Don Mattingly/25	65.00
20	Mark Prior/25	80.00
25	Paul O'Neill/25	40.00
29	Ron Santo/25	35.00
30	Ryne Sandberg/25	85.00
32	Tony Gwynn/25	80.00
34	Will Clark/25	45.00

Material Ink Combos
NM/M
Quantity produced listed
Prime: No Pricing
Production 1-10

#	Player	Price
1	Adam Dunn/ Bat-Jsy/25	40.00
2	Alan Trammell/ Bat-Jsy/25	35.00
4	Andre Dawson/ Bat-Jsy/25	35.00
5	Bo Jackson/ Bat-Jsy/25	60.00
7	Dale Murphy/ Bat-Jsy/25	40.00
12	Don Mattingly/ Bat-Jsy/25	100.00
17	Jose Canseco/ Bat-Jsy/25	50.00
30	Ryne Sandberg/ Bat-Jsy/25	85.00
32	Tony Gwynn/ Bat-Jsy/25	80.00
34	Will Clark/ Bat-Jsy/25	40.00

Material Ink Combo Prime
NM/M
Quantity produced listed
No Pricing

Material Ink Jersey
NM/M
Quantity produced listed
Number: .75-1X
Production 1-100
No Pricing 15 or less.
Prime: .75-1.5X
Production 1-25
No Pricing 15 or less.

#	Player	Price
1	Adam Dunn/25	40.00
2	Alan Trammell/100	20.00
4	Andre Dawson/100	25.00
5	Bo Jackson/100	60.00
7	Dale Murphy/50	35.00
8	Darryl Strawberry/ 100	25.00
9	Dave Parker/25	20.00
11	Doc Gooden/100	20.00
12	Don Mattingly/100	65.00
13	Dontrelle Willis/25	40.00
15	Ivan Rodriguez/25	50.00
16	Joe Carter/25	30.00
17	Jose Canseco/25	25.00
20	Mark Prior/50	60.00
21	Mark Teixeira/25	50.00
22	Marty Marion/25	25.00
26	Rocco Baldelli/25	20.00
30	Ryne Sandberg/50	75.00
31	Ernie Banks/50	25.00
33	Vladimir Guerrero/25	60.00
34	Will Clark/50	40.00

Material Ink Jersey Number
NM/M
Quantity produced listed

#	Player	Price
1	Adam Dunn/25	40.00
2	Alan Trammell/100	20.00
4	Andre Dawson/100	20.00
5	Bo Jackson/25	75.00
7	Dale Murphy/50	30.00
8	Darryl Strawberry/ 100	20.00
9	Dave Parker/25	30.00
11	Doc Gooden/100	15.00
12	Don Mattingly/50	50.00
13	Dontrelle Willis/25	40.00
16	Joe Carter/25	40.00
19	Mark Grace/25	40.00
21	Mark Teixeira/25	40.00
22	Marty Marion/25	25.00
26	Rocco Baldelli/25	25.00
31	Ernie Banks/25	65.00
33	Vladimir Guerrero/ 25	50.00
34	Will Clark/50	25.00

Milestone Materials
NM/M
Quantity produced listed
Number: .75-1.5X
Production 9-36
Prime: 1-2X
Production 25 Sets

Milestone Material Signature
NM/M

#	Player	Price
4	Gaylord Perry/ Jsy/82	20.00

Milestone Material Signature Number
NM/M

#	Player	Price
4	Gaylord Perry/ Jsy/82	20.00

Milesone Material Signature Prime
NM/M
Quantity produced listed

#	Player	Price
4	Gaylord Perry/ Jsy/19	30.00

No-Hitters Quad Signature
No Pricing
Production One Set

Rookie Year Materials
NM/M
Quantity produced listed
Prime: No Pricing
Production 5-10
Number: .75-1.5X
Production 3-51
No Pricing 15 or less.

#	Player	Price
1	Stan Musial/Jsy/19	60.00
2	Yogi Berra Stripe/ Jsy/19	40.00
3	Yogi Berra Grey/ Jsy/47	25.00
4	Whitey Ford/Jsy/50	20.00
5	Jim "Catfish" Hunter/ Jsy/65	10.00
6	Johnny Bench/ Bat/68	15.00
7	Mike Schmidt/Bat/72	15.00
8	Gary Carter/Jsy/74	8.00
9	Robin Yount/Jsy/74	20.00
11	Cal Ripken Jr./Bat/81	40.00
12	Kirby Puckett/Bat/84	10.00
13	Roger Clemens/ Jsy/84	20.00
15	Gary Sheffield/Jsy/89	8.00
16	Juan Gonzalez/ Jsy/89	10.00
17	Randy Johnson/ Jsy/89	10.00
18	Ivan Rodriguez/ Jsy/91	10.00
20	Pedro J. Martinez/ Jsy/92	10.00
21	Mike Piazza/Jsy/93	10.00
22	Hideo Nomo/Jsy/95	10.00
23	Hideo Nomo/ Pants/95	10.00
24	Alex Rodriguez/ Jsy/95	15.00
26	Scott Rolen/Jsy/96	10.00
27	Andruw Jones/Jsy/96	8.00
28	Nomar Garciaparra/ Jsy/97	10.00
29	Vladimir Guerrero/ Jsy/97	10.00
31	Alfonso Soriano/ Jsy/100	10.00
32	Albert Pujols White/ Jsy/100	20.00
33	Albert Pujols Grey/ Jsy/100	20.00
34	Albert Pujols/ Bat/100	20.00
36	Mark Prior Blue/ Jsy/100	10.00
37	Mark Prior Grey/ Jsy/100	10.00
38	Dontrelle Willis/ Jsy/35	15.00

Rookie Year Material Signature

NM/M
Quantity produced listed
Prime: 1X
Production 1-35
Number: 1X
No Pricing 15 or less.

#	Player	Price
1	Stan Musial/Jsy/9	125.00
3	Yogi Berra Grey/ Jsy/19	100.00
4	Whitey Ford/Jsy/19	85.00
8	Gary Carter/Jsy/19	35.00
14	Fred Lynn/Jsy/75	15.00
14	Lenny Dykstra/ Fld Glv/85	20.00
16	Juan Gonzalez/ Jsy/19	40.00
25	Garret Anderson/ Jsy/95	20.00
30	Shannon Stewart/ Jsy/97	15.00
36	Mark Prior Blue/ Jsy/22	80.00
37	Mark Prior Grey/ Jsy/22	80.00
38	Dontrelle Willis/ Jsy/35	40.00
39	Rocco Baldelli/ Jsy/19	40.00

Rookie Year Material Combo
NM/M
Quantity produced listed

#	Player	Price
2	Yogi Berra/ Jsy-Jsy/8	60.00
22	Hideo Nomo/ Jsy-Pants/16	30.00
36	Mark Prior/ Jsy-Jsy/22	30.00
38	Dontrelle Willis/ Jsy-Jsy/35	10.00

R.Y. Materials Combos Signature
NM/M

#	Player	Price
36	Mark Prior/ Jsy-Jsy/22	100.00
38	Dontrelle Willis/ Jsy-Jsy/35	40.00

R.Y. Material Combos Prime
NM/M
Quantity produced listed

#	Player	Price
36	Mark Prior/ Jsy-Jsy/22	30.00
38	Dontrelle Willis/ Jsy-Jsy/35	10.00

R.Y. Material Combo Signature Prime
NM/M
Quantity produced listed

#	Player	Price
36	Mark Prior/ Jsy-Jsy/22	100.00
38	Dontrelle Willis/ Jsy-Jsy/35	40.00

Rookie Year Material Dual
NM/M
Production 25 Sets
Prime: No Pricing
Production 10 Sets

#	Player	Price
40	Roger Clemens/Jsy, Nomar Garciaparra/ Jsy	40.00
41	Pedro J. Martinez/ Mike Piazza/Jsy	35.00
42	Mike Piazza/Jsy, Hideo Nomo/Jsy	35.00
43	Pedro J. Martinez/Jsy, Hideo Nomo/Jsy	20.00
44	Yogi Berra/Jsy, Whitey Ford/Jsy	50.00
45	Mike Schmidt/Bat, Scott Rolen/Jsy	40.00
46	Stan Musial/Jsy, Albert Pujols/Jsy	75.00
47	Juan Gonzalez/Jsy, Ivan Rodriguez/Jsy	15.00

Rookie Year Material Dual Signature
No Pricing
Production 5 Sets

Rookie Year Material Dual Prime
No Pricing
Production 10 Sets

Rookie Year Material Number
Quantity produced listed

Rookie Year Material Signature Number
Quantity produced listed

Rookie Year Material Prime
Quantity produced listed

Rookie Year Material Signature Prime
Quantity produced listed

Signature Bronze
NM/M

#	Player	Price
1	Albert Pujols/25	125.00
2	Garret Anderson/16	30.00
4	Alex Rodriguez/25	100.00
5	Manny Ramirez/24	40.00
9	Mark Prior/50	50.00
12	Barry Larkin/25	30.00
14	Todd Helton/17	40.00
14	Shawn Green/15	30.00
17	Vladimir Guerrero	30.00
20	Don Mattingly/50	60.00
23	Rafael Palmeiro/25	45.00
27	Gary Sheffield/50	40.00
37	Kazuhisa Ishii/17	40.00
40	Tom Glavine/25	30.00
42	Eric Chavez/25	25.00
44	Tony Gwynn/50	45.00
46	Jim Edmonds/15	35.00
47	Delmon Young/73	20.00
49	Vernon Wells/25	20.00
50	Curt Schilling/38	40.00
53	Jason Varitek/33	30.00
54	Adam Dunn/25	30.00
58	Josh Beckett/21	30.00
59	Jeff Bagwell/25	50.00
60	Carlos Beltran/15	30.00
68	Juan Gonzalez/25	30.00
71	Andruw Jones/25	30.00
76	Jorge Posada/25	40.00
78	Stan Musial/50	75.00
79	Mark Teixeira/23	35.00
83	Nolan Ryan/50	90.00
87	Bob Gibson/25	40.00
88	Dale Murphy/50	25.00
90	Carl Yastrzemski/25	60.00
91	Sammy Sosa/50	125.00
92	Miguel Cabrera/24	45.00
94	George Brett/25	100.00
95	Rickey Henderson/ 25	25.00
97	Greg Maddux/31	30.00
100	Dontrelle Willis/35	30.00

Signature Silver
NM/M
Quantity produced listed

#	Player	Price
2	Garret Anderson/10	10.00
6	Mark Prior/22	50.00
17	Vladimir Guerrero/27	50.00
20	Don Mattingly/23	90.00
27	Gary Sheffield/25	35.00
44	Tony Gwynn/19	75.00
47	Delmon Young/25	30.00
68	Juan Gonzalez/22	35.00
76	Jorge Posada/20	40.00
78	Stan Musial/25	75.00
83	Nolan Ryan/34	120.00
88	Dale Murphy/40	40.00
91	Sammy Sosa/21	125.00

Signature Gold
No Pricing
Production 1-11

Statistical Champions
NM/M
Number: .75-1.5X
Production 1-51
No Pricing 15 or less.
Prime: No Pricing
Production 5-10

#	Player	Price
2	Stan Musial 43 BA/ Jsy/19	40.00
3	Ralph Kiner/Bat/49	10.00
4	Stan Musial 57 BA/ Jsy/57	30.00
5	Ted Williams/Jsy/25	90.00
6	Warren Spahn/ Jsy/25	30.00
7	Eddie Mathews/ Jsy/19	40.00
8	Roger Maris 61 HR/ Bat/61	40.00
9	Roger Maris 61 HR/ Pants/61	40.00
10	Roger Maris 61 RBI/ Bat/61	40.00
11	Roger Maris 61 RBI/ Pants/61	40.00
12	Roberto Clemente/ Jsy/19	100.00
13	Frank Robinson/ Bat/66	10.00
14	Bob Gibson 68 ERA/ Jsy/68	15.00
15	Bob Gibson 68 K/ Jsy/68	15.00
16	Tom Seaver/Jsy/19	25.00
18	Harmon Killebrew/ Pants/71	15.00
19	Mike Schmidt/ Jsy/74	15.00
20	Reggie Jackson/ Jsy/19	20.00
22	Rod Carew Hat/78	15.00
23	Jim Rice 78 HR/ Jsy/78	10.00
24	Jim Rice 78 RBI/ Jsy/78	10.00
25	Reggie Jackson/ Hat/80	15.00
26	Dale Murphy 82 RBI/ Jsy/82	15.00
27	Steve Carlton/Jsy/83	10.00
28	Dale Murphy 85 HR/ Jsy/85	15.00

29	Wade Boggs 86 BA/Jsy/86	15.00
30	Wade Boggs 87 BA/Jsy/87	15.00
31	Will Clark/Jsy/88	15.00
32	Nolan Ryan 89 K/Jsy/89	20.00
33	Nolan Ryan 90 K/Jsy/90	20.00
34	Nolan Ryan 90 K/Pants/90	20.00
35	Ryne Sandberg/Jsy/90	20.00
36	Roger Clemens 90 K/Jsy/90	20.00
37	George Brett/Jsy/90	20.00
38	Roger Clemens 92 ERA/Jsy/100	20.00
39	Roger Clemens 96 K/Jsy/100	20.00
40	Tony Gwynn/Jsy/25	35.00
41	Pedro Martinez Expos/25	20.00
42	Greg Maddux/Jsy/100	10.00
43	Juan Gonzalez/Pants/25	20.00
44	Manny Ramirez/Bat/25	15.00
45	Nomar Garciaparra 99 BA/Jsy/100	10.00
47	Nomar Garciaparra 00 BA/Jsy/100	10.00
48	Todd Helton 00 BA/Jsy/25	15.00
49	Todd Helton 00 RBI/Jsy/25	15.00
50	Troy Glaus/Jsy/25	10.00
51	Randy Johnson 00 K/Jsy/100	
52	Tom Glavine/Jsy/25	10.00
53	Sammy Sosa 00 HR/Jsy/100	15.00
54	Alex Rodriguez 01 HR/Bat/100	15.00
55	Curt Schilling/Jsy/25	10.00
56	Pedro J. Martinez 99 K/Jsy/25	20.00
57	Alex Rodriguez 01 HR/Jsy/100	15.00
58	Mark Mulder/Jsy/25	10.00
59	Sammy Sosa 01 RBI/Jsy/100	15.00
60	Manny Ramirez/Jsy/25	15.00
61	Lance Berkman/Jsy/25	10.00
62	Randy Johnson 02 W/Jsy/25	15.00
63	Alex Rodriguez 02 HR/Jsy/100	15.00
64	Alex Rodriguez 02 HR/Jsy/100	
65	Alex Rodriguez 02 RBI/Jsy/100	15.00
66	Alex Rodriguez 02 RBI/Bat/100	15.00
67	Pedro J. Martinez 02 K/Jsy/25	20.00
68	Pedro J. Martinez 02 ERA/Jsy/25	20.00
69	Sammy Sosa 02 HR/Jsy/25	15.00
70	Jim Thome/Jsy/25	15.00
71	Alex Rodriguez 03 HR/Bat/100	15.00
72	Albert Pujols/Bat/100	20.00
73	Alex Rodriguez 03 HR/Jsy/100	15.00
74	Albert Pujols/Jsy/100	20.00

Statistical Champion Signature

NM/M

Quantity produced listed
Number: .5-1.5X
Production 1-47
Prime: No Pricing
Production 1-10

		NM/M
3	Ralph Kiner/Bat/49	35.00
6	Warren Spahn/Jsy/25	75.00
13	Frank Robinson/Bat/66	40.00
14	Bob Gibson 68 ERA/Jsy/25	50.00
15	Bob Gibson 68 K/Jsy/25	50.00
17	Harmon Killebrew/Jsy/71	50.00
18	Harmon Killebrew/Pants/71	50.00
19	Mike Schmidt/Jsy/25	75.00
20	Reggie Jackson/Jsy/25	65.00
21	Phil Niekro/Jsy/50	30.00
22	Rod Carew Hat/25	30.00
23	Jim Rice 78 HR/Jsy/78	30.00
24	Jim Rice 78 RBI/Jsy/78	30.00

25	Reggie Jackson/Hat/25	65.00
26	Dale Murphy 82 RBI/Jsy/25	50.00
27	Steve Carlton/Jsy/25	50.00
28	Dale Murphy 85 HR/Jsy/25	50.00
29	Wade Boggs 86 BA/Jsy/25	40.00
30	Wade Boggs 87 BA/Jsy/25	40.00
31	Will Clark/Jsy/88	30.00
32	Nolan Ryan 89 K/Jsy/25	120.00
33	Nolan Ryan 90 K/Jsy/25	120.00
34	Nolan Ryan 90 K/Pants/25	120.00
35	Ryne Sandberg/Jsy/25	80.00
40	Tony Gwynn/Jsy/25	70.00
43	Juan Gonzalez/Pants/19	40.00
50	Troy Glaus/Jsy/25	35.00
52	Tom Glavine/Jsy/20	40.00
53	Sammy Sosa 00 HR/Jsy/25	150.00
55	Curt Schilling/Jsy/25	40.00
58	Mark Mulder/Jsy/25	30.00
59	Sammy Sosa 01 RBI/Jsy/25	150.00
61	Lance Berkman/Jsy/20	40.00
69	Sammy Sosa 02 HR/Jsy/25	150.00

Silver

| Cards (1-50): | 2X |

Production 100 Sets

Gold

| Cards (1-50): | 4-6X |

Production 25 Sets

Gold Autographs

NM/M

Production 25 Sets

3	Adam Dunn	30.00
7	Miguel Cabrera	40.00
9	Carlos Beltran	80.00
15	Garret Anderson	40.00
18	Hank Blalock	30.00
22	Ivan Rodriguez	35.00
26	Juan Gonzalez	60.00
31	Magglio Ordonez	50.00
33	Mark Prior	40.00
44	Scott Rolen	50.00
48	Torii Hunter	45.00
49	Vernon Wells	35.00
50	Vladimir Guerrero	30.00
		70.00

Platinum

No Pricing
Production One Set

Platinum Autographs

NM/M

No Pricing
Production One Set

World Series Materials

NM/M

Quantity produced listed
1	Frank Robinson/Bat/61	15.00
2	Ozzie Smith/Jsy/87	15.00
3	Rickey Henderson/Bat/93	15.00
4	Tom Glavine/Jsy/96	10.00
5	Roger Clemens/Jsy/100	15.00

World Series Material Signature

NM/M

Quantity produced listed
Prime: No Pricing
Production 9-10
| 1 | Frank Robinson/Bat/19 | 50.00 |
| 4 | Tom Glavine/Jsy/19 | 40.00 |

World Series Material Prime

NM/M

Quantity produced listed
2	Ozzie Smith/Jsy/19	25.00
4	Tom Glavine/Jsy/19	20.00
5	Roger Clemens/Jsy/20	30.00

2004 Donruss Timelines

		NM/M
Complete Set (50):	40.00
Common Player:	.75
Pack (5):	40.00
Box (4):	120.00
1	Adam Dunn	.75
2	Albert Pujols	3.00
3	Alex Rodriguez	3.00
4	Alfonso Soriano	1.50
5	Andruw Jones	1.00
6	Austin Kearns	.75
7	Miguel Cabrera	1.00
8	Barry Zito	.75
9	Carlos Beltran	.75
10	Carlos Delgado	1.00
11	Chipper Jones	2.00
12	Curt Schilling	1.00
13	Derek Jeter	4.00
14	Frank Thomas	1.00
15	Garret Anderson	.75
16	Gary Sheffield	.75
17	Greg Maddux	2.00
18	Hank Blalock	.75

19	Hideki Matsui	3.00
20	Hideo Nomo	.75
21	Ichiro Suzuki	2.00
22	Ivan Rodriguez	1.00
23	Jason Giambi	1.50
24	Jeff Bagwell	1.00
25	Jim Thome	1.50
26	Juan Gonzalez	.75
27	Ken Griffey Jr.	2.00
28	Kevin Brown	.75
29	Kerry Wood	1.00
30	Lance Berkman	.75
31	Magglio Ordonez	.75
32	Manny Ramirez	1.00
33	Mark Prior	3.00
34	Mike Mussina	.75
35	Mike Piazza	2.00
36	Nomar Garciaparra	3.00
37	Pedro J. Martinez	1.50
38	Rafael Palmeiro	1.00
39	Randy Johnson	1.50
40	Richie Sexson	.75
41	Roger Clemens	3.00
42	Roy Halladay	.75
43	Sammy Sosa	2.50
44	Scott Rolen	1.50
45	Shawn Green	.75
46	Tim Hudson	.75
47	Todd Helton	1.00
48	Torii Hunter	.75
49	Vernon Wells	.75
50	Vladimir Guerrero	1.50

Boys of Summer Silver Autographs

NM/M

| Common Autograph: | .12.00 |
| Production 100 |
2	Marty Marion	12.00
3	Andre Dawson	15.00
6	Steve Garvey	20.00
8	Darren Daulton	12.00
9	Darryl Strawberry	18.00
10	Dave Parker	12.00
11	Doc Gooden	20.00
12	Don Mattingly	65.00
13	Eric Davis	12.00
15	Fred Lynn	12.00
16	Graig Nettles	15.00
18	Jim Rice	15.00
20	Keith Hernandez	15.00
22	Jack Morris	15.00
24	Vida Blue	15.00

Boys of Summer Gold Autographs

NM/M

| Common Autograph: | 20.00 |
| Production 25 |
1	Alan Trammell	35.00
2	Marty Marion	20.00
3	Andre Dawson	20.00
6	Steve Garvey	20.00
8	Darren Daulton	20.00
9	Darryl Strawberry	20.00
10	Dave Parker	20.00
11	Doc Gooden	20.00
12	Don Mattingly	75.00
13	Eric Davis	20.00
14	Dwight Evans	25.00
15	Fred Lynn	25.00
16	Graig Nettles	25.00
17	Jay Buhner	25.00
18	Jim Rice	25.00
20	Keith Hernandez	20.00
22	Jack Morris	20.00
24	Vida Blue	20.00
25	Will Clark	100.00

Boys of Summer Platinum Autographs

No Pricing
Production One Set

Boys of Summer Materials

		NM/M
Common Player:	5.00
Combos:	1-2X
Production 100 Sets
Prime:	1-2X
Production 100 Sets
3	Andre Dawson	5.00
4	Bo Jackson	10.00
5	Cal Ripken Jr.	20.00
7	Dale Murphy	6.00
9	Darryl Strawberry	5.00
11	Doc Gooden	5.00
12	Don Mattingly	15.00
19	Jose Canseco	6.00
21	Rickey Henderson	8.00
22	Jack Morris	5.00
23	Tony Gwynn	8.00
25	Will Clark	8.00

Boys of Summer Combo Materials

NM/M

Production 100 Sets
3	Andre Dawson	10.00
4	Bo Jackson	15.00
5	Cal Ripken Jr.	30.00
7	Dale Murphy	10.00

12	Don Mattingly	25.00
19	Jose Canseco	10.00
21	Rickey Henderson	15.00
23	Tony Gwynn	10.00
25	Will Clark	10.00

Boys of Summer Material Autograph

NM/M

Varying quantities produced
3	Andre Dawson/50	25.00
9	Darryl Strawberry/150	25.00
11	Doc Gooden/100	25.00
12	Don Mattingly/25	80.00
22	Jack Morris/150	12.00

Boys of Summer Prime Materials

NM/M

| Common Player: | 8.00 |
| Production 100 Sets |
3	Andre Dawson	8.00
4	Bo Jackson	15.00
5	Cal Ripken Jr.	30.00
9	Darryl Strawberry	8.00
12	Doc Gooden	8.00
12	Don Mattingly	25.00
21	Rickey Henderson	15.00
23	Tony Gwynn	12.00
25	Will Clark	12.00

Boys/ Summer Prime Materials Autograph

No Pricing
Production One Set

Call to the Hall

		NM/M
Complete Set (25):	80.00
Common Player:	3.00
Production 250 Sets
Silver:	1X
Production 100 Sets
Gold:	3-4X
Production 25 Sets
Platinum:	No Pricing
Production One Set
1	Babe Ruth	10.00
2	Billy Williams	3.00
3	Bob Feller	3.00
4	Bobby Doerr	3.00
5	Carlton Fisk	3.00
6	Gary Carter	3.00
7	George Brett	8.00
8	Carl Yastrzemski	5.00
9	Harmon Killebrew	5.00
10	Jim Palmer	3.00
11	Joe Morgan	5.00
12	Johnny Bench	5.00
13	Kirby Puckett	5.00
14	Gaylord Perry	3.00
15	Mike Schmidt	6.00
16	Nolan Ryan	10.00
17	Ozzie Smith	5.00
18	Phil Rizzuto	3.00
19	Reggie Jackson	4.00
20	Roberto Clemente	6.00
21	Robin Yount	4.00
22	Rod Carew	3.00
23	Rollie Fingers	3.00
24	Steve Carlton	3.00
25	Tom Seaver	4.00

Call to the Hall Autographs

		NM/M
Common Autograph:	15.00
Silver Autos:	1X
Production 100
3	Bob Feller	15.00
4	Bobby Doerr	15.00
14	Gaylord Perry	15.00
23	Rollie Fingers	15.00

Call to the Hall Gold Autographs

NM/M

Production 25 Sets
| 2 | Billy Williams | 25.00 |

12	Don Mattingly	25.00
19	Jose Canseco	10.00
21	Rickey Henderson	15.00
23	Tony Gwynn	10.00
25	Will Clark	10.00

Boys of Summer Material Autograph

NM/M

Varying quantities produced
3	Andre Dawson/50	25.00
9	Darryl Strawberry/150	25.00
11	Doc Gooden/100	25.00
12	Don Mattingly/25	80.00
22	Jack Morris/150	12.00

Call to the Hall Platinum Autograph

No Pricing
Production One Set

Call to the Hall Materials

		NM/M
Common Player:	6.00
1	Babe Ruth/50	575.00
4	Bobby Doerr	6.00
6	Gary Carter	8.00
7	George Brett	12.00
8	Carl Yastrzemski	12.00
13	Kirby Puckett	10.00
15	Mike Schmidt	12.00
16	Nolan Ryan	20.00
19	Ozzie Smith	8.00
19	Reggie Jackson	8.00
20	Roberto Clemente/100	50.00

Call to the Hall Combo Materials

NM/M

Production 125 Sets
6	Gary Carter	12.00
7	George Brett	25.00
13	Kirby Puckett	20.00
15	Mike Schmidt	25.00
16	Nolan Ryan	35.00
19	Reggie Jackson	20.00

Call to the Hall Material Autograph

NM/M

Varying quantities produced
4	Bobby Doerr/100	25.00
6	Gary Carter/25	45.00
19	Reggie Jackson/25	50.00

Materials

		NM/M
Common Player:	5.00
Combos:	1-2X
Production 125
Primes:	1-2X
Production 125
1	Adam Dunn	5.00
2	Albert Pujols	12.00
3	Alex Rodriguez	10.00
4	Alfonso Soriano	8.00
5	Andruw Jones	5.00
7	Miguel Cabrera/SP	10.00
10	Carlos Delgado	8.00
11	Chipper Jones	8.00
14	Frank Thomas	8.00
17	Greg Maddux	8.00
20	Hideo Nomo	6.00
22	Ivan Rodriguez	6.00
23	Jason Giambi	6.00
24	Jeff Bagwell	6.00
25	Jim Thome	8.00
26	Juan Gonzalez	6.00
30	Lance Berkman	5.00
33	Mark Prior	10.00
35	Mike Piazza	8.00
36	Nomar Garciaparra	10.00
37	Pedro J. Martinez	8.00
39	Randy Johnson	6.00

ABBREVIATIONS

SP - Short Print

12	Don Mattingly	25.00
19	Jose Canseco	10.00
21	Rickey Henderson	15.00
23	Tony Gwynn	10.00
25	Will Clark	10.00

Call to the Hall Platinum Autograph

No Pricing
Production One Set

Call to the Hall Materials

Call to the Hall Materials

3	Bob Feller	40.00
6	Gary Carter	40.00
10	Jim Palmer	30.00
18	Phil Rizzuto	40.00
24	Steve Carlton	40.00

Call to the Hall Platinum Autograph

No Pricing
Production One Set

41 Roger Clemens 10.00
43 Sammy Sosa 10.00
45 Shawn Green 5.00
47 Todd Helton 6.00
49 Vernon Wells 5.00

Materials Autographs
Varying quantities produced
7 Miguel Cabrera/25 85.00
22 Ivan Rodriguez/25 65.00
33 Mark Prior/50 75.00
49 Vernon Wells/25 25.00

Materials Combo

NM/M
Common Player: 8.00
Production 125 Sets
1 Adam Dunn 8.00
2 Albert Pujols 20.00
3 Alex Rodriguez 15.00
4 Alfonso Soriano 10.00
5 Andruw Jones 8.00
7 Miguel Cabrera 20.00
11 Chipper Jones 15.00
14 Frank Thomas 12.00
17 Greg Maddux 15.00
20 Hideo Nomo 10.00
25 Jim Thome 12.00
30 Lance Berkman 8.00
33 Mark Prior 20.00
35 Mike Piazza 15.00
36 Nomar Garciaparra 15.00
37 Pedro J. Martinez 12.00
39 Randy Johnson 10.00
41 Roger Clemens 15.00
43 Sammy Sosa 15.00
45 Shawn Green 10.00
47 Todd Helton 10.00

Materials Prime
NM/M
Common Player: 8.00
Production 125 Sets
1 Adam Dunn 8.00
2 Albert Pujols 20.00
3 Alex Rodriguez 20.00
4 Alfonso Soriano 10.00
5 Andruw Jones 8.00
7 Miguel Cabrera 20.00
10 Carlos Delgado 8.00
11 Chipper Jones 15.00
14 Frank Thomas 12.00
17 Greg Maddux 15.00
20 Hideo Nomo 10.00
25 Jim Thome 12.00
30 Lance Berkman 8.00
33 Mark Prior 20.00
35 Mike Piazza 15.00
36 Nomar Garciaparra 15.00
37 Pedro J. Martinez 12.00
39 Randy Johnson 10.00
41 Roger Clemens 15.00
43 Sammy Sosa 15.00
45 Shawn Green 10.00
47 Todd Helton 10.00
49 Vernon Wells 8.00

Materials Prime Autograph
No Pricing
Production One Set

Recollection Autographs

Complete Set (1576):
Common Player:

2004 Donruss World Series

NM/M
Complete Set (200):
Common Player: .15
Common SP (176-200): 8.00
Pack (6): 6.00
Box (24): 120.00
1 Bartolo Colon .15
2 Darin Erstad .25
3 Garret Anderson .25
4 Tim Salmon .25
5 Troy Glaus .25
6 Vladimir Guerrero .75
7 Brandon Webb .15
8 Luis Gonzalez .15
9 Randy Johnson .75
10 Roberto Alomar .40
11 Shea Hillenbrand .15
12 Steve Finley .15
13 Andruw Jones .40
14 Chipper Jones .75
15 J.D. Drew .25
16 Marcus Giles .25
17 Rafael Furcal .25
18 Javy Lopez .25
19 Jay Gibbons .15
20 Luis Matos .15
21 Melvin Mora .15
22 Miguel Tejada .25
23 Rafael Palmeiro .50
24 Curt Schilling .75
25 Dwight Evans .15
26 Fred Lynn .15
27 Jason Varitek .25
28 Jim Rice .25
29 Johnny Damon .40
30 Luis Tiant .15
31 Manny Ramirez .50
32 Nomar Garciaparra 1.00
33 Pedro Martinez .75
34 Trot Nixon .15
35 Aramis Ramirez .25
36 Corey Patterson .25
37 Derrek Lee .25
38 Greg Maddux 1.00
39 Kerry Wood .75
40 Mark Prior .75
41 Moises Alou .15
42 Sammy Sosa 1.50
43 Carlos Lee .15
44 Frank Thomas .25
45 Luis Aparicio .15
46 Magglio Ordonez .25
47 Mark Buehrle .15
48 Paul Konerko .25
49 Adam Dunn .50
50 Austin Kearns .15
51 Barry Larkin .25
52 Dave Concepcion .15
53 George Foster .15
54 Joe Morgan .15
55 Sean Casey .15
56 Tony Perez .15
57 C.C. Sabathia .15
58 Jody Gerut .15
59 Omar Vizquel .15
60 Victor Martinez .15
61 Charles Johnson .15
62 Jeromy Burnitz .15
63 Larry Walker .25
64 Preston Wilson .15
65 Todd Helton .50
66 Alan Trammell .15
67 Dmitri Young .15
68 Ivan Rodriguez .50
69 Jeremy Bonderman .15
70 A.J. Burnett .15
71 Brad Penny .15
72 Dontrelle Willis .15
73 Josh Beckett .40
74 Juan Pierre .15
75 Luis Castillo .15
76 Miguel Cabrera .25
77 Mike Lowell .25
78 Andy Pettitte .25
79 Craig Biggio .15
80 Jeff Bagwell .50
81 Jeff Kent .25
82 Lance Berkman .25
83 Roger Clemens 2.00
84 Roy Oswalt .25
85 Wade Miller .15
86 Angel Berroa .15

87 Carlos Beltran .50
88 Juan Gonzalez .40
89 Ken Harvey .15
90 Mike Sweeney .15
91 Adrian Beltre .40
92 Hideo Nomo .15
93 Kazuhisa Ishii .15
94 Milton Bradley .15
95 Orel Hershiser .15
96 Paul LoDuca .15
97 Shawn Green .25
98 Ben Sheets .25
99 Geoff Jenkins .15
100 Junior Spivey .15
101 Rickie Weeks .15
102 Scott Podsednik .15
103 Jack Morris .15
104 Jacque Jones .15
105 Johan Santana .50
106 Shannon Stewart .15
107 Torii Hunter .15
108 Jose Vidro .15
109 Orlando Cabrera .25
110 Al Leiter .25
111 Darryl Strawberry .25
112 Dwight Gooden .15
113 Jose Reyes .25
114 Kazuo Matsui RC 2.00
115 Keith Hernandez .15
116 Lenny Dykstra .15
117 Mike Piazza 1.00
118 Tom Glavine .40
119 Alex Rodriguez 2.00
120 Bernie Williams .40
121 Derek Jeter 2.00
122 Gary Sheffield .50
123 Jason Giambi .25
124 Javier Vazquez .25
125 Jorge Posada .25
126 Kenny Lofton .25
127 Kevin Brown .15
128 Mariano Rivera .25
129 Mike Mussina .40
130 Barry Zito .25
131 Eric Chavez .25
132 Jermaine Dye .15
133 Mark Mulder .25
134 Rich Harden .25
135 Tim Hudson .25
136 Brett Myers .15
137 Jim Thome .75
138 Kevin Millwood .15
139 Marlon Byrd .15
140 Mike Lieberthal .15
141 Pat Burrell .15
142 Steve Carlton .25
143 Dave Parker .15
144 Jason Kendall .15
145 Brian Giles .15
146 Jay Payton .15
147 Ryan Klesko .15
148 J.T. Snow .15
149 Jason Schmidt .25
150 Bret Boone .15
151 Edgar Martinez .25
152 Jamie Moyer .15
153 Rich Aurilia .15
154 Shigetoshi Hasegawa .15
155 Albert Pujols 2.00
156 Dan Haren .15
157 Edgar Renteria .15
158 Fernando Vina .15
159 Jim Edmonds .40
160 Matt Morris .15
161 Scott Rolen .75
162 Aubrey Huff .15
163 Carl Crawford .15
164 Dewon Brazelton .15
165 Fred McGriff .25
166 Rocco Baldelli .25
167 Alfonso Soriano .75
168 Hank Blalock .50
169 Kenny Rogers .15
170 Mark Teixeira .25
171 Michael Young .15
172 Carlos Delgado .40
173 Eric Hinske .15
174 Roy Halladay .25
175 Vernon Wells .15
176 Ivan Ochoa/ Auto./487 RC 8.00
177 Jason Bartlett/ Auto./1000 RC 8.00
178 Josh Labandeira/ Auto./703 RC 8.00
179 Phil Stockman/ Auto./1000 RC 8.00
180 Ronny Cedeno/ Auto./715 RC 8.00
181 Shawn Camp/ Auto./1000 RC 8.00
182 Ruddy Yan/ Auto./1000 RC 8.00
183 Roberto Novoa/ Auto./568 RC 10.00
184 Justin Knoedler/ Auto./1000 RC 8.00
185 Jesse Harper/ Auto./1000 RC 8.00
186 Jason Szuminski/ Auto./1000 RC 8.00
187 Jamie Brown/ Auto./800 RC 8.00
188 Eddy Garabito/ Auto./1000 RC 8.00
189 Dennis Sarfate/ Auto./1000 RC 8.00

190 Ryan Meaux/ Auto./1000 RC 8.00
191 Charles Thomas/ Auto./1000 RC 10.00
192 Frank Francisco/ Auto./1000 RC 8.00
193 Orlando Rodriguez/ Auto./500 RC 8.00
194 Joey Gathright/ Auto./1000 RC 10.00
195 Renyel Pinto/ Auto./1000 RC 10.00
196 Justin Leone/ Auto./1000 RC 10.00
197 Tim Bausher/ Auto./834 RC 8.00
198 Travis Blackley/ Auto./1000 RC 10.00
199 Yadier Molina/ Auto./500 RC 15.00
200 Brad Halsey/ Auto./500 RC 10.00

HoloFoil 10
No Pricing
Production 10 Sets

HoloFoil 25
HoloFoil (1-175): 10-20X
HoloFoil (176-200): No Pricing
Production 25 Sets

HoloFoil 50
HoloFoil (1-175): 6-12X
HoloFoil (176-200): .75X
Production 50 Sets

HoloFoil 100
HoloFoil (1-175): 4-8X
HoloFoil (176-200): .5X
Production 100 Sets

Champions
NM/M
Complete Boxed Set (25): 25.00
Common Player: .50
201 Curt Schilling 3.00
202 Pedro Martinez 3.00
203 Derek Lowe .50
204 Tim Wakefield .50
205 Bronson Arroyo .50
206 Mike Timlin .50
207 Curt Leskanic .50
208 Mike Myers .50
209 Alan Embree .50
210 Keith Foulke .50
211 Jason Varitek 2.00
212 Doug Mirabelli .50
213 Doug Mientkiewicz .50
214 Mark Bellhorn .50
215 Pokey Reese .50
216 Orlando Cabrera 1.00
217 Bill Mueller .50
218 Kevin Youkilis .50
219 Manny Ramirez 3.00
220 Johnny Damon 3.00
221 Dave Roberts .50
222 Trot Nixon .50
223 Gabe Kapler .50
224 David Ortiz 3.00

Champions Box Topper
NM/M
Inserted 1:Set
WS1 World Series Champions 2.00

Blue
NM/M
Complete Set (100): 50.00
Common Player: .50
Inserted 1:1
HoloFoil 100: 2-4X
Production 100 Sets
HoloFoil 50: 4-6X
Production 50 Sets
HoloFoil 25: 6-10X
Production 25 Sets
HoloFoil 10: No Pricing
Production 10 Sets
1 Josh Beckett .50
2 Miguel Cabrera 1.00
3 Derek Lee .50
4 Mike Lowell .50
5 Brad Penny .50
6 Ivan Rodriguez 1.00
7 Dontrelle Willis .50
8 Luis Castillo .50
9 Garret Anderson .75
10 Troy Glaus .75
11 John Lackey .50
12 Chone Figgins .50
13 Tim Salmon .50

14 Darin Erstad .50
15 Troy Percival .50
16 Steve Finley .50
17 Mark Grace .75
18 Randy Johnson 1.00
19 Curt Schilling 1.00
20 Luis Gonzalez .50
21 Andy Pettitte .75
22 Bernie Williams .75
23 Jorge Posada .75
24 Mariano Rivera .75
25 Roger Clemens 3.00
26 Jose Canseco 1.00
27 David Justice .75
28 Paul O'Neill .75
29 Darryl Strawberry .50
30 David Wells .50
31 Wade Boggs .75
32 Charles Johnson .50
33 Cliff Floyd .50
34 Moises Alou .50
35 Edgar Renteria .50
36 Chipper Jones 1.50
37 Tom Glavine .75
38 John Smoltz .50
39 Greg Maddux 1.50
40 Ryan Klesko .50
41 Javy Lopez .50
42 Fred McGriff .50
43 Roberto Alomar .50
44 Joe Carter .50
45 Rickey Henderson .50
46 Paul Molitor 1.00
47 Jack Morris .50
48 Jack Morris .50
49 Kirby Puckett 1.50
50 Eric Davis .50
51 Barry Larkin .75
52 Paul O'Neill .75
53 Dennis Eckersley .50
54 Jose Canseco 1.00
55 Rickey Henderson .50
56 Dave Parker .50
57 Orel Hershiser .50
58 Kirk Gibson .50
59 Bert Blyleven .50
60 Dwight Gooden .50
61 Gary Carter .50
62 Lenny Dykstra .50
63 Keith Hernandez .50
64 Darryl Strawberry .50
65 George Brett 3.00
66 Kirk Gibson .50
67 Alan Trammell .50
68 Jim Palmer .75
69 Eddie Murray .75
70 Cal Ripken Jr. 5.00
71 Keith Hernandez .50
72 Ozzie Smith 1.50
73 Steve Garvey .50
74 Steve Carlton 1.00
75 Mike Schmidt 4.00
76 John Candelaria .50
77 Bert Blyleven .50
78 Dave Parker .50
79 Willie Stargell 1.00
80 Reggie Jackson 1.50
81 Johnny Bench 2.00
82 Dave Concepcion .50
83 George Foster .50
84 Joe Morgan .50
85 Tony Perez .50
86 Rollie Fingers .50
87 Jim "Catfish" Hunter .50
88 Reggie Jackson 1.00
89 Al Oliver .50
90 Roberto Clemente 3.00
91 Willie Stargell .75
92 Brooks Robinson 1.00
93 Frank Robinson 1.00
94 Nolan Ryan 3.00
95 Tom Seaver 1.50
96 Al Kaline 1.00
97 Bob Gibson .75
98 Lou Brock .75
99 Orlando Cepeda 1.00
100 Duke Snider 1.00

Blue Material Bat
NM/M
Common Player: 5.00
Production 50 Sets
1 Josh Beckett 8.00
2 Miguel Cabrera 12.00
3 Derek Lee 8.00
4 Mike Lowell 5.00
5 Brad Penny 5.00
6 Ivan Rodriguez 8.00
9 Garret Anderson 5.00
10 Troy Glaus 8.00
13 Tim Salmon 5.00
14 Darin Erstad 5.00
18 Mark Grace 12.00
19 Curt Schilling 12.00
20 Luis Gonzalez 5.00
21 Andy Pettitte 8.00
22 Bernie Williams 8.00
23 Jorge Posada 10.00
25 Roger Clemens 20.00
27 David Justice 5.00
28 Paul O'Neill 10.00
29 Darryl Strawberry 10.00
31 Wade Boggs 15.00
32 Charles Johnson 5.00
33 Cliff Floyd 5.00
34 Moises Alou 8.00

35 Edgar Renteria 8.00
36 Chipper Jones 15.00
37 Tom Glavine 10.00
39 Greg Maddux 20.00
40 Ryan Klesko 5.00
42 Javy Lopez 5.00
44 Joe Carter 8.00
45 Rickey Henderson 15.00
46 Paul Molitor 15.00
49 Kirby Puckett 15.00
50 Eric Davis 5.00
51 Barry Larkin 8.00
53 Paul O'Neill 8.00
55 Rickey Henderson 15.00
56 Dave Parker 8.00
58 Kirk Gibson 10.00
60 Dwight Gooden 8.00
61 Gary Carter 8.00
62 Lenny Dykstra 5.00
63 Keith Hernandez 5.00
64 Darryl Strawberry 5.00
65 George Brett 25.00
66 Kirk Gibson 8.00
67 Alan Trammell 8.00
69 Eddie Murray 8.00
70 Cal Ripken Jr. 70.00
71 Keith Hernandez 8.00
72 Ozzie Smith 20.00
73 Steve Garvey 5.00
74 Steve Carlton 10.00
75 Mike Schmidt 25.00
78 Dave Parker 8.00
79 Willie Stargell 15.00
80 Reggie Jackson 15.00
81 Johnny Bench 20.00
82 Dave Concepcion 5.00
83 George Foster 5.00
84 Joe Morgan 5.00
85 Tony Perez 5.00
88 Reggie Jackson 15.00
89 Al Oliver 5.00
90 Roberto Clemente 60.00
91 Willie Stargell 5.00
92 Brooks Robinson 15.00
93 Frank Robinson 10.00
96 Al Kaline 15.00
98 Lou Brock 15.00
99 Orlando Cepeda 10.00

Blue Material Fabric
NM/M
Common Player: 4.00
Quantity produced listed
1 Josh Beckett/Jsy/103 4.00
2 Miguel Cabrera/ Jsy/103 8.00
3 Derrek Lee/Jsy/103 6.00
4 Mike Lowell/Jsy/103 4.00
5 Brad Penny/Jsy/103 4.00
6 Ivan Rodriguez/ Jsy/103 8.00
7 Dontrelle Willis/ Jsy/103 4.00
9 Garret Anderson/ Jsy/102 4.00
10 Troy Glaus/Jsy/102 4.00
13 Tim Salmon/Jsy/102 4.00
14 Darin Erstad/Jsy/102 4.00
15 Tony Percival/Jsy/102 4.00
16 Steve Finley/Jsy/101 4.00
18 Randy Johnson/ Pants/101 8.00
19 Curt Schilling/ Jsy/101 8.00
20 Luis Gonzalez/ Jsy/101 4.00
21 Andy Pettitte/Jsy/100 6.00
22 Bernie Williams/ Jsy/100 6.00
24 Mariano Rivera/ Jsy/100 6.00
25 Roger Clemens/ Jsy/100 12.00
29 Darryl Strawberry/ Jsy/99 6.00
30 David Wells/Jsy/99 4.00
31 Wade Boggs/Jsy/96 8.00
32 Charles Johnson/ Jsy/97 4.00
33 Cliff Floyd/Jsy/97 4.00
36 Chipper Jones/Jsy/95 8.00
37 Tom Glavine/Jsy/95 6.00
39 Greg Maddux/Jsy/95 10.00
40 Ryan Klesko/Jsy/95 4.00
41 Javy Lopez/Jsy/95 4.00
51 Barry Larkin/Jsy/90 8.00
54 Jose Canseco/ Jsy/89 10.00
55 Rickey Henderson/ Jsy/89 12.00
57 Orel Hershiser/Jsy/88 8.00
59 Bert Blyleven/Jsy/87 6.00
60 Dwight Gooden/ Jsy/86 6.00
61 Gary Carter/Jkt/86 6.00
64 Darryl Strawberry/ Jsy/86 6.00
65 George Brett/Jsy/85 8.00
68 Jim Palmer/Pants/83 8.00
69 Eddie Murray/Jsy/83 15.00
70 Cal Ripken Jr./ Jsy/83 40.00
71 Keith Hernandez/ Jsy/82 6.00
74 Steve Carlton/Jsy/80 6.00

75 Mike Schmidt/Jkt/80 15.00
78 Dave Parker/Jsy/79 6.00
79 Willie Stargell/Jsy/79 8.00
80 Reggie Jackson/ Jsy/78 8.00
81 Johnny Bench/ Jsy/75 12.00
82 Dave Concepcion/ Jsy/75 4.00
83 George Foster/Jsy/75 4.00
86 Rollie Fingers/Jsy/74
87 Jim "Catfish" Hunter/ Jsy/74 8.00
88 Reggie Jackson/ Jkt/73
91 Willie Stargell/Jsy/71 8.00
98 Lou Brock/Jkt/67 8.00
100 Duke Snider/ Pants/55 10.00

Blue Material Fabric AL/NL

NM/M
Common Player: 4.00
Quantity produced listed
1 Josh Beckett/Jsy/100 4.00
2 Miguel Cabrera/ Jsy/100 8.00
3 Derrek Lee/Jsy/100 4.00
4 Mike Lowell/Jsy/100 4.00
5 Brad Penny/Jsy/103 4.00
6 Ivan Rodriguez/ Jsy/100 8.00
7 Dontrelle Willis/ Jsy/100 4.00
9 Garret Anderson/ Jsy/100
10 Troy Glaus/Jsy/100 4.00
13 Tim Salmon/Jsy/100 4.00
14 Darin Erstad/Jsy/100 4.00
15 Tony Percival/
16 Steve Finley/Jsy/100 4.00
18 Randy Johnson/ Pants/100 8.00
19 Curt Schilling/ Jsy/100 8.00
20 Luis Gonzalez/ Jsy/100 4.00
21 Andy Pettitte/Jsy/100 6.00
22 Bernie Williams/ Jsy/100 6.00
24 Mariano Rivera/ Jsy/100 6.00
25 Roger Clemens/ Jsy/100 15.00
29 Darryl Strawberry/ Jsy/100 4.00
30 David Wells/Jsy/10 4.00
31 Wade Boggs/Jsy/100 8.00
32 Charles Johnson/ Jsy/100 4.00
33 Cliff Floyd/Jsy/100 4.00
36 Chipper Jones/ Jsy/100 8.00
37 Tom Glavine/Jsy/100 6.00
39 Greg Maddux/ Jsy/100 10.00
40 Ryan Klesko/Jsy/100 4.00
41 Javy Lopez/Jsy/100 4.00
51 Barry Larkin/Jsy/100 8.00
54 Jose Canseco/ Jsy/100 10.00
55 Rickey Henderson/ Jsy/100 10.00
57 Orel Hershiser/ Jsy/100 8.00
59 Bert Blyleven/Jsy/50 8.00
60 Dwight Gooden/ Jsy/100 6.00
61 Gary Carter/Jkt/100 6.00
64 Darryl Strawberry/ Jsy/100 6.00
65 George Brett/Jsy/25 25.00
68 Jim Palmer/Pants/50 8.00
69 Eddie Murray/Jsy/50 15.00
70 Cal Ripken Jr./ Jsy/50 65.00
71 Keith Hernandez/ Jsy/50 8.00
74 Steve Carlton/Jsy/50 8.00
75 Mike Schmidt/Jkt/50 25.00
78 Dave Parker/Jsy/50 8.00
79 Willie Stargell/Jsy/50 15.00
80 Reggie Jackson/ Jsy/50 15.00
82 Dave Concepcion/ Jsy/50
83 George Foster/Jsy/50 8.00
86 Rollie Fingers/Jsy/50 8.00
87 Jim "Catfish" Hunter/ Jsy/50 15.00
88 Reggie Jackson/ Jkt/50 15.00
91 Willie Stargell/Jsy/50 15.00
98 Lou Brock/Jkt/50 15.00
100 Duke Snider/ Pants/50 15.00

Blue Signature

NM/M
Quantity produced listed
2 Miguel Cabrera/25 40.00
3 Derrek Lee/25 30.00
5 Brad Penny/25 15.00
9 Garret Anderson/25 20.00

11 John Lackey/50 10.00
12 Chone Figgins/25 15.00
16 Steve Finley/25 20.00
29 Darryl Strawberry/25 20.00
42 Fred McGriff/25 40.00
47 Jack Morris/25 20.00
48 Jack Morris/25 20.00
50 Eric Davis/25 25.00
53 Dennis Eckersley/25 40.00
56 Dave Parker/25 20.00
59 Bert Blyleven/25 25.00
60 Dwight Gooden/25 25.00
62 Lenny Dykstra/25 25.00
63 Keith Hernandez/25 25.00
64 Darryl Strawberry/25 25.00
67 Alan Trammell/25 25.00
68 Jim Palmer/25 25.00
71 Keith Hernandez/25 25.00
76 John Candelaria/25 25.00
77 Bert Blyleven/25 25.00
78 Dave Parker/25 20.00
82 Dave Concepcion/25 20.00
83 George Foster/25 20.00
85 Tony Perez/25 35.00
86 Rollie Fingers/25 25.00
89 Al Oliver/25 25.00

Face Off

NM/M
Complete Set (20): 75.00
Common Duo: 2.00
Production 500 Sets
HoloFoil: 2-4X
Production 25 Sets
1 Roger Clemens, Mike Piazza 6.00
2 Mike Mussina, Ivan Rodriguez 3.00
3 Mark Grace, Jorge Posada 4.00
4 Greg Maddux, Jim Thome 5.00
5 Rickey Henderson, Curt Schilling 4.00
6 Kirby Puckett, Tom Glavine 4.00
7 Dennis Eckersley, Will Clark 3.00
8 Bernie Williams, Randy Johnson 4.00
9 Cal Ripken Jr., Steve Carlton 12.00
10 Tom Seaver, Reggie Jackson
11 Mike Schmidt, George Brett 8.00
12 Wade Boggs, Keith Hernandez 3.00
13 Dwight Gooden, Dwight Evans 2.00
14 Johnny Bench, Jim "Catfish" Hunter 4.00
15 Jim Palmer, Dave Parker 4.00
16 Bob Gibson, Al Kaline 4.00
17 Carl Yastrzemski, Lou Brock 6.00
18 Duke Snider, Whitey Ford
19 Carlton Fisk, Tony Perez 4.00
20 Roberto Clemente, Frank Robinson 8.00

Face Off Material

NM/M
Common Duo: 10.00

Quantity produced listed
1 Roger Clemens/Jsy, Mike Piazza/Jsy/100 25.00
2 Mike Mussina/Jsy, Ivan Rodriguez/ Jsy/100 20.00
4 Greg Maddux/Jsy, Jim Thome/Jsy/25 35.00
5 Rickey Henderson/Jsy, Curt Schilling/ Jsy/100 15.00
7 Kirby Puckett/Jsy, Tom Glavine/ Jsy/100 25.00
8 Bernie Williams/Jsy, Randy Johnson/ Pants/100 20.00
9 Cal Ripken Jr./Jsy, Steve Carlton/Jsy/50 75.00
11 Mike Schmidt/Jkt, George Brett/Jsy/50 40.00
13 Dwight Gooden/Jsy, Dwight Evans/ Jsy/50 25.00
15 Jim Palmer/Jsy, Dave Parker/Jsy,
17 Carl Yastrzemski/Jsy, Lou Brock/Jkt/50 40.00
18 Duke Snider/Pants, Whitey Ford/Jsy/50 25.00
19 Carlton Fisk/Jsy, Tony Perez/ Fld Glv/50 20.00

Legends of the Fall

NM/M
Complete Set (20): 75.00
Common Player: 3.00
Production 500 Sets
HoloFoil: 2-4X
Production 25 Sets
1 Bob Gibson 4.00
2 Brooks Robinson 4.00
3 Cal Ripken Jr. 12.00
4 Carl Yastrzemski 6.00
5 Carlton Fisk 4.00
6 Derek Jeter 8.00
7 Duke Snider 4.00
8 Eddie Murray 4.00
9 Frank Robinson 3.00
10 Gary Carter 3.00
11 George Brett 8.00
12 Jim Palmer 3.00
13 Johnny Bench 4.00
14 Marco Rivera 3.00
15 Mike Schmidt 8.00
16 Phil Rizzuto 3.00
17 Red Schoendienst 3.00
18 Reggie Jackson 4.00
19 Rickey Henderson 3.00
20 Whitey Ford 4.00

Legends of the Fall Material

NM/M
Common Player: 5.00
Quantity produced listed
1 Bob Gibson/Jsy/50 12.00
2 Brooks Robinson/ Bat/50 10.00
3 Cal Ripken Jr./ Jkt/100 40.00
4 Carl Yastrzemski/ Bat/50 10.00
5 Carlton Fisk/Bat/50 10.00
7 Duke Snider/ Pants/50 15.00
8 Eddie Murray/Jsy/50 15.00
9 Frank Robinson/ Bat/100 5.00
10 Gary Carter/Jkt/100 5.00
11 George Brett/Bat/50 5.00
12 Jim Palmer/Pants/25 12.00
13 Johnny Bench/ Bat/100 12.00
14 Marco Rivera/ Jsy/100 8.00
15 Mike Schmidt/Jkt/50 25.00
16 Phil Rizzuto/ Pants/50 10.00
17 Red Schoendienst/ Bat/100 5.00
18 Reggie Jackson/ Bat/100 8.00
19 Rickey Henderson/ Bat/100 10.00

Legends of the Fall Signature

NM/M
Common Player:
2 Brooks Robinson/25 30.00
9 Frank Robinson/25 35.00
10 Gary Carter/25 25.00
12 Jim Palmer/25 25.00

16 Phil Rizzuto/25 30.00
17 Red Schoendienst/ 50 20.00

Legends of the Fall Signature Material

NM/M
Quantity produced listed
1 Bob Gibson/Jsy/25 40.00
2 Brooks Robinson/ Bat/50 35.00
8 Duke Snider/ Pants/50 35.00
9 Frank Robinson/ Bat/50 30.00
10 Gary Carter/Jkt/50 25.00
12 Jim Palmer/ Pants/25 25.00
13 Johnny Bench/ Bat/25 70.00
16 Phil Rizzuto/ Pants/50 35.00
17 Red Schoendienst/ Bat/100 20.00

Material Bat

NM/M
Common Player: 4.00
Production 100 Sets
2 Darin Erstad 4.00
3 Garret Anderson 4.00
4 Tim Salmon 4.00
6 Troy Glaus 4.00
8 Vladimir Guerrero 8.00
12 Luis Gonzalez 4.00
13 Andruw Jones 6.00
14 Chipper Jones 8.00
15 J.D. Drew 4.00
16 Marcus Giles 4.00
17 Rafael Furcal 4.00
18 Javy Lopez 4.00
19 Jay Gibbons 4.00
22 Miguel Tejada 6.00
23 Rafael Palmeiro 8.00
25 Dwight Evans 4.00
26 Fred Lynn 4.00
27 Jason Varitek 6.00
28 Jim Rice 8.00
29 Johnny Damon 10.00
31 Manny Ramirez 8.00
32 Nomar Garciaparra 10.00
33 Pedro Martinez 8.00
34 Trot Nixon 4.00
35 Aramis Ramirez 4.00
37 Derrek Lee 6.00
40 Mark Prior 6.00
41 Moises Alou 4.00
42 Sammy Sosa 12.00
43 Carlos Lee 4.00
44 Frank Thomas 8.00
45 Luis Aparicio 4.00
46 Magglio Ordonez 4.00
47 Mark Buehrle 4.00
48 Paul Konerko 4.00
49 Adam Dunn 8.00
50 Austin Kearns 8.00
51 Barry Larkin 8.00
52 Dave Concepcion 4.00
53 George Foster 4.00
54 Joe Morgan 6.00
55 Sean Casey 4.00
56 Tony Perez 4.00
59 Omar Vizquel 4.00
60 Victor Martinez 4.00
61 Charles Johnson 4.00
63 Larry Walker 8.00
64 Preston Wilson 4.00
65 Todd Helton 8.00
66 Alan Trammell 4.00
68 Ivan Rodriguez 8.00
71 Brad Penny 4.00
73 Josh Beckett 6.00
74 Juan Pierre 6.00
75 Luis Castillo 4.00
76 Miguel Cabrera 8.00
77 Mike Lowell 4.00
78 Andy Pettitte 6.00
79 Craig Biggio 6.00
80 Jeff Bagwell 8.00
81 Jeff Kent 4.00
82 Lance Berkman 4.00
83 Roger Clemens 15.00
84 Roy Oswalt 4.00
86 Angel Berroa 4.00
87 Carlos Beltran 6.00
88 Juan Gonzalez 6.00
89 Ken Harvey 4.00
90 Mike Sweeney 4.00
91 Adrian Beltre 6.00
93 Kazuhisa Ishii 4.00
96 Paul LoDuca 4.00
97 Shawn Green 4.00
99 Geoff Jenkins 4.00
104 Jacque Jones 4.00
105 Shannon Stewart 4.00
107 Torii Hunter 6.00
108 Jose Vidro 4.00
109 Orlando Cabrera 4.00
111 Darryl Strawberry 4.00
112 Dwight Gooden 6.00
113 Jose Reyes 6.00
114 Kazuo Matsui 10.00
115 Keith Hernandez 4.00
116 Lenny Dykstra 4.00

118 Tom Glavine 8.00
122 Gary Sheffield 8.00
125 Jorge Posada 8.00
126 Kenny Lofton 4.00
127 Kevin Brown 4.00
129 Mike Mussina 8.00
131 Eric Chavez 4.00
132 Jermaine Dye 4.00
133 Mark Mulder 4.00
135 Tim Hudson 6.00
137 Jim Thome 8.00
139 Marlon Byrd 4.00
141 Pat Burrell 4.00
142 Steve Carlton 6.00
143 Dave Parker 4.00
145 Brian Giles 4.00
147 Ryan Klesko 4.00
151 Edgar Martinez 4.00
153 Rich Aurilia 4.00
155 Albert Pujols 15.00
157 Edgar Renteria 6.00
159 Jim Edmonds 6.00
161 Scott Rolen 8.00
162 Aubrey Huff 4.00
165 Fred McGriff 4.00
166 Rocco Baldelli 4.00
167 Alfonso Soriano 8.00
168 Hank Blalock 8.00
170 Mark Teixeira 6.00
171 Michael Young 4.00
172 Carlos Delgado 4.00
175 Vernon Wells 4.00

Material Fabric AL/NL

NM/M
Common Player: 4.00
Production 250 unless noted.
2 Darin Erstad/Jsy 4.00
3 Garret Anderson/Jsy 4.00
4 Tim Salmon/Jsy 4.00
5 Troy Glaus/Jsy 4.00
6 Vladimir Guerrero/Jsy 8.00
7 Brandon Webb/Pants 4.00
9 Luis Gonzalez/Jsy 4.00
12 Randy Johnson/ Pants/100 10.00
12 Steve Finley/Jsy 4.00
13 Andruw Jones/Jsy 6.00
14 Chipper Jones/Jsy 6.00
16 Marcus Giles/Jsy 4.00
17 Rafael Furcal/Jsy 4.00
19 Jay Gibbons/Jsy 4.00
20 Luis Matos/Jsy 4.00
21 Melvin Mora/Jsy 4.00
22 Miguel Tejada/Jsy 6.00
23 Rafael Palmeiro/ Jsy/100 8.00
25 Dwight Evans/Jsy 4.00
26 Fred Lynn/Jsy 4.00
28 Jim Rice/Jsy 4.00
31 Manny Ramirez/Jsy 8.00
33 Pedro Martinez/Jsy 8.00
35 Aramis Ramirez/Jsy 6.00
38 Greg Maddux/ Jsy/100 12.00
39 Kerry Wood/Pants 8.00
40 Mark Prior/Jsy 4.00
42 Sammy Sosa/Jsy 10.00
43 Carlos Lee/Jsy 4.00
44 Frank Thomas/Jsy 4.00
45 Mark Buehrle/Jsy 4.00
48 Paul Konerko/Jsy 4.00
49 Adam Dunn/Jsy 8.00
50 Austin Kearns/Jsy 4.00
56 Dave Concepcion/Jsy 4.00
57 C.C. Sabathia/Jsy 4.00
58 Jody Gerut/Jsy 4.00
59 Omar Vizquel/Jsy 4.00
62 Victor Martinez/Jsy 4.00
63 Larry Walker/Jsy 8.00
64 Preston Wilson/Jsy 4.00
65 Todd Helton/Jsy 8.00
70 A.J. Burnett/Jsy 4.00
71 Brad Penny/Jsy 4.00
72 Dontrelle Willis/Jsy 6.00
73 Josh Beckett/Jsy 4.00
76 Miguel Cabrera/Jsy 8.00
77 Mike Lowell/Jsy 4.00
79 Craig Biggio/Jsy 6.00
80 Jeff Bagwell/Pants 8.00
81 Jeff Kent/Jsy 4.00
82 Lance Berkman/Jsy 4.00
86 Angel Berroa/Pants 4.00
90 Mike Sweeney/Jsy 4.00

91 Adrian Beltre/Jsy 6.00
92 Hideo Nomo/Jsy 8.00
93 Kazuhisa Ishii/Jsy 4.00
95 Orel Hershiser/ Jsy/100 4.00
96 Paul LoDuca/Jsy 4.00
97 Shawn Green/Jsy 6.00
98 Ben Sheets/Pants 4.00
99 Geoff Jenkins/Jsy 4.00
104 Jacque Jones/Jsy 4.00
105 Johan Santana/Jsy 8.00
106 Shannon Stewart/Jsy 4.00
110 Al Leiter/Jsy 4.00
111 Darryl Strawberry/ Jsy 4.00
117 Mike Piazza/Jsy 10.00
118 Tom Glavine/Jsy 8.00
120 Bernie Williams/Jsy 6.00
123 Jason Giambi/Jsy 4.00
128 Mariano Rivera/Jsy 6.00
129 Mike Mussina/Jsy 8.00
130 Barry Zito/Jsy 4.00
131 Eric Chavez/Jsy 4.00
133 Mark Mulder/Jsy 4.00
135 Tim Hudson/Jsy 4.00
136 Brett Myers/Jsy 4.00
137 Jim Thome/Jsy 8.00
138 Kevin Millwood/Jsy 4.00
139 Marlon Byrd/Jsy 4.00
141 Pat Burrell/Jsy 4.00
142 Steve Carlton/ Jsy/100 6.00
143 Dave Parker/Jsy/100 4.00
147 Ryan Klesko/Jsy 4.00
152 Jamie Moyer/Jsy 4.00
155 Albert Pujols/ Jsy/100 15.00
156 Dan Haren/Jsy 4.00
159 Jim Edmonds/Jsy 6.00
161 Scott Rolen/Jsy 8.00
162 Aubrey Huff/Jsy 4.00
163 Carl Crawford/Jsy 4.00
164 Dewon Brazelton/Jsy 4.00
165 Fred McGriff/Jsy 4.00
166 Rocco Baldelli/Jsy 4.00
168 Hank Blalock/Jsy 8.00
174 Roy Halladay/Jsy 4.00
175 Vernon Wells/Jsy 4.00

Material Fabric Number

NM/M
Common Player:
5 Troy Glaus/Jsy/25 10.00
6 Vladimir Guerrero/ Jsy/27 20.00
7 Brandon Webb/ Pants/55 6.00
8 Luis Gonzalez/Jsy/20 8.00
9 Randy Johnson/ Pants/51 15.00
13 Andruw Jones/ Jsy/25 10.00
16 Marcus Giles/Jsy/22 8.00
19 Jay Gibbons/Jsy/31 8.00
23 Rafael Palmeiro/ Jsy/25 15.00
25 Dwight Evans/Jsy/24 15.00
26 Fred Lynn/Jsy/19 10.00
30 Luis Tiant/Jsy/23 4.00
31 Manny Ramirez/ Jsy/24 20.00
33 Pedro Martinez/ Jsy/45 15.00
38 Greg Maddux/Jsy/31 20.00
39 Kerry Wood/ Pants/34 20.00
40 Mark Prior/Jsy/22 15.00
42 Sammy Sosa/Jsy/45 25.00
44 Carlos Lee/Jsy/45
Jsy/35 15.00
46 Magglio Ordonez/ Jsy/30 8.00
47 Mark Buehrle/Jsy/56 6.00
49 Adam Dunn/Jsy/44 12.00
50 Austin Kearns/ Jsy/28 4.00
57 C.C. Sabathia/Jsy/52 6.00
60 Victor Martinez/ Jsy/41 8.00
63 Larry Walker/Jsy/33 10.00
64 Preston Wilson/ Jsy/44 6.00
65 Todd Helton/Jsy/17 25.00
68 A.J. Burnett/Jsy/34 6.00
71 Brad Penny/Jsy/31 6.00
72 Dontrelle Willis/ Jsy/35 6.00
73 Josh Beckett/Jsy/21 15.00
76 Miguel Cabrera/ Jsy/24 20.00
90 Mike Sweeney/ Jsy/23
91 Adrian Beltre/Jsy/29 15.00
95 Orel Hershiser/ Jsy/55 8.00
105 Johan Santana/ Jsy/23 15.00
106 Shannon Stewart/ Jsy/23
107 Torii Hunter/Jsy/48 10.00
110 Al Leiter/Jsy/22 10.00
117 Mike Piazza/Jsy/31 12.00
118 Tom Glavine/Jsy/47 12.00
120 Bernie Williams/ Jsy/51 12.00

123	Jason Giambi/Jsy/25	10.00
125	Jorge Posada/Jsy/20	15.00
128	Mariano Rivera/Jsy/42	10.00
129	Mike Mussina/Jsy/35	15.00
130	Barry Zito/Jsy/75	8.00
133	Mark Mulder/Jsy/20	15.00
136	Brett Myers/Jsy/39	6.00
137	Jim Thome/Jsy/25	20.00
138	Kevin Millwood/Jsy/34	8.00
139	Marlon Byrd/Jsy/29	8.00
142	Steve Carlton/Jsy/32	12.00
143	Dave Parker/Jsy/39	8.00
147	Ryan Klesko/Jsy/30	10.00
152	Jamie Moyer/Jsy/25	6.00
156	Dan Haren/Jsy/55	6.00
159	Jim Edmonds/Jsy/15	15.00
161	Scott Rolen/Jsy/27	25.00
164	Dewon Brazelton/Jsy/45	6.00
165	Fred McGriff/Jsy/29	15.00
174	Roy Halladay/Jsy/32	8.00

MVP

		NM/M
Complete Set (15):		35.00
Common Player:		2.00
Production 1,000 Sets		
HoloFoil:		2-4X
Production 50 Sets		
1	Whitey Ford	3.00
2	Bob Gibson	3.00
3	Frank Robinson	2.00
4	Brooks Robinson	3.00
5	Roberto Clemente	6.00
6	Reggie Jackson	3.00
7	Rollie Fingers	2.00
8	Johnny Bench	4.00
9	Reggie Jackson	3.00
10	Mike Schmidt	6.00
11	Alan Trammell	2.00
12	Orel Hershiser	2.00
13	Jack Morris	2.00
14	Paul Molitor	4.00
15	Tom Glavine	3.00

MVP Material
NM/M
Quantity produced listed

1	Whitey Ford/Jsy/50	10.00
2	Bob Gibson/Jsy/50	10.00
3	Frank Robinson/Jsy/25	12.00
6	Reggie Jackson/Jkt/100	10.00
7	Rollie Fingers/Jsy/50	5.00
9	Reggie Jackson/Jsy/25	20.00
10	Mike Schmidt/Jsy/50	25.00
12	Orel Hershiser/Jsy/50	5.00
15	Tom Glavine/Jsy/100	8.00

MVP Signature
NM/M
Quantity produced listed

11	Alan Trammell/25	20.00
13	Jack Morris/25	20.00

MVP Signature Material
NM/M
Quantity produced listed

2	Bob Gibson/Jsy/50	35.00
3	Frank Robinson/Shoe/40	40.00
7	Rollie Fingers/Jsy/100	15.00
12	Orel Hershiser/Jsy/25	25.00

October Heroes

		NM/M
Complete Set (20):		40.00
Common Player:		2.00
Production 500 Sets		
HoloFoil:		2-4X
Production 25 Sets		
1	Alan Trammell	2.00
2	Andy Pettitte	3.00
3	Jim "Catfish" Hunter	2.00
4	Chipper Jones	4.00
5	Dave Concepcion	2.00
6	David Wells	2.00
7	Jack Morris	2.00
8	Joe Morgan	3.00
9	Josh Beckett	2.00
10	Kirby Puckett	4.00
11	Kirk Gibson	2.00
12	Marty Marion	4.00
13	Miguel Cabrera	4.00
14	Paul Molitor	3.00
15	Paul O'Neill	2.00
16	Randy Johnson	4.00
17	Roger Clemens	6.00
18	Steve Carlton	3.00
19	Steve Garvey	2.00
20	Wade Boggs	3.00

October Heroes Material

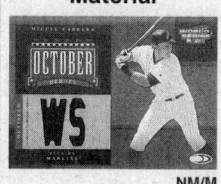

NM/M
Common Player: 4.00

1	Alan Trammell/Jsy/25	10.00
2	Andy Pettitte/Jsy/100	4.00
3	Jim "Catfish" Hunter/Jsy/25	15.00
4	Chipper Jones/Jsy/100	8.00
5	Dave Concepcion/Jsy/100	4.00
6	David Wells/Jsy/25	8.00
9	Josh Beckett/Jsy/100	4.00
10	Kirby Puckett/Jsy/25	25.00
12	Marty Marion/Jsy/25	10.00
13	Miguel Cabrera/Jsy/100	8.00
16	Randy Johnson/Pants/50	12.00
17	Roger Clemens/Jsy/100	12.00
18	Steve Carlton/Jsy/100	6.00
19	Steve Garvey/Jsy/100	6.00
20	Wade Boggs/Jsy/100	8.00

October Heroes Signatures
NM/M
Quantity produced listed

1	Alan Trammell/25	25.00
2	Dave Concepcion/25	20.00
7	Jack Morris/25	20.00
12	Marty Marion/25	20.00
13	Miguel Cabrera/25	40.00
18	Steve Carlton/25	35.00
19	Steve Garvey/25	20.00

October Heroes Signature Material

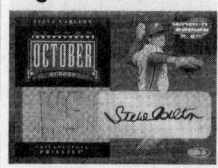

NM/M

1	Alan Trammell/Jsy/100	20.00
5	Dave Concepcion/Jsy/100	15.00
12	Marty Marion/Jsy/100	15.00
13	Miguel Cabrera/Jsy/100	30.00
18	Steve Carlton/Jsy/50	35.00
19	Steve Garvey/Jsy/100	15.00

October Legends

		NM/M
Complete Set (20):		60.00
Common Player:		2.00
Production 500 Sets		
HoloFoil:		2-4X
Production 25 Sets		
1	Bob Gibson	3.00
2	Cal Ripken Jr.	10.00
3	Carl Yastrzemski	6.00
4	Carlton Fisk	3.00
5	Duke Snider	4.00
6	Eddie Murray	4.00
7	Frank Robinson	3.00
8	George Brett	8.00
9	Joe Morgan	2.00
10	Johnny Bench	4.00
11	Lou Brock	3.00
12	Mike Schmidt	8.00
13	Paul Molitor	4.00
14	Phil Rizzuto	3.00
15	Reggie Jackson	4.00
16	Robin Yount	4.00
17	Stan Musial	6.00
18	Steve Carlton	2.00
19	Whitey Ford	3.00
20	Willie McCovey	2.00

October Legends Materials
NM/M
Common Player: 5.00
Quantity produced listed

1	Bob Gibson/Jsy/50	10.00
2	Cal Ripken Jr./Jsy/50	50.00
3	Carl Yastrzemski/Jsy/50	20.00
4	Carlton Fisk/Jsy/100	8.00
5	Duke Snider/Jsy/25	20.00
6	Eddie Murray/Jsy/100	4.00
7	Frank Robinson/Jsy/50	8.00
8	George Brett/Jsy/50	25.00
10	Johnny Bench/Jsy/50	15.00
11	Lou Brock/Jkt/100	8.00
12	Mike Schmidt/Jkt/100	15.00
14	Phil Rizzuto/Pants/25	15.00
15	Reggie Jackson/Jkt/100	8.00
16	Robin Yount/Jsy/100	10.00
18	Steve Carlton/Jsy/100	5.00
19	Whitey Ford/Pants/50	15.00
20	Willie McCovey/Jsy/25	15.00

October Legends Signature
NM/M
Quantity produced listed

11	Lou Brock/25	35.00
14	Phil Rizzuto/25	35.00
18	Steve Carlton/25	30.00

October Legends Signature Material

NM/M

1	Bob Gibson/Jsy/50	40.00
5	Duke Snider/Jsy/50	40.00
7	Frank Robinson/Jsy/50	30.00
11	Lou Brock/Jkt/100	25.00
13	Paul Molitor/Jsy/25	40.00
14	Phil Rizzuto/Pants/50	30.00
16	Robin Yount/Jsy/25	65.00
17	Stan Musial/Jsy/25	90.00
18	Steve Carlton/Jsy/100	25.00
19	Whitey Ford/Pants/25	40.00
20	Willie McCovey/Jsy/25	40.00

Playoff All-Stars

		NM/M
Complete Set (20):		50.00
Common Player:		2.00
Production 500 Sets		
HoloFoil:		2-4X
Production 25 Sets		
1	Mark Prior	3.00
2	Sammy Sosa	6.00
3	Steve Finley	2.00
4	David Ortiz	4.00
5	Mike Piazza	5.00
6	Edgar Martinez	2.00
7	Roy Oswalt	2.00
8	Johan Santana	3.00
9	Jacque Jones	2.00
10	Will Clark	4.00
11	Albert Pujols	8.00
12	Andre Dawson	3.00
13	Nolan Ryan	10.00
14	Fred Lynn	2.00
15	Jim Rice	3.00
16	Dwight Evans	2.00
17	Harmon Killebrew	4.00
18	Maury Wills	2.00
19	Mark Mulder	2.00
20	Frank Thomas	4.00

Playoff All-Stars Material 1
NM/M
Quantity produced listed

1	Mark Prior/Jsy/100	6.00
2	Sammy Sosa/Jsy/100	10.00
3	Steve Finley/Jsy/100	4.00
4	David Ortiz/Jsy/100	10.00
5	Mike Piazza/Jsy/100	10.00
6	Edgar Martinez/Jsy/50	6.00
7	Roy Oswalt/Jsy/100	4.00
8	Johan Santana/Jsy/100	8.00
9	Jacque Jones/Jsy/100	4.00
10	Will Clark/Bat/100	10.00
11	Albert Pujols/Jsy/100	20.00
12	Andre Dawson/Jsy/100	6.00
13	Nolan Ryan/Jsy/100	25.00
14	Fred Lynn/Jsy/50	4.00
15	Jim Rice/Jsy/50	4.00
16	Dwight Evans/Jsy/50	4.00
17	Harmon Killebrew/Jsy/50	20.00
19	Mark Mulder/Jsy/50	4.00
20	Frank Thomas/Jsy/50	8.00

Playoff All-Stars Material 2
NM/M
Common Dual: 6.00

1	Mark Prior/Jsy-Jsy/100	8.00
2	Sammy Sosa/Jsy-Jsy/100	15.00
3	Steve Finley/Jsy-Jsy/100	6.00
4	David Ortiz/Bat-Jsy/100	20.00
5	Mike Piazza/Bat-Jsy/100	15.00
6	Edgar Martinez/Bat-Jsy/100	10.00
7	Roy Oswalt/Bat-Jsy/100	6.00
8	Johan Santana/Jsy-Jsy/100	10.00
9	Jacque Jones/Bat-Jsy/100	6.00
11	Albert Pujols/Jsy-Jsy/100	25.00
12	Andre Dawson/Bat-Jsy/100	8.00
13	Nolan Ryan/Jkt-Jsy/50	40.00
14	Fred Lynn/Bat-Jsy/50	8.00
15	Jim Rice/Bat-Jsy/50	10.00
16	Dwight Evans/Bat-Jsy/50	6.00
17	Harmon Killebrew/Bat-Jsy/25	25.00
19	Mark Mulder/Bat-Jsy/100	6.00
20	Frank Thomas/Bat-Jsy/100	12.00

Playoff All-Stars Material 3
NM/M
Common Triple: 10.00

1	Mark Prior/Bat-Hat-Jsy/100	15.00
2	Sammy Sosa/Bat-Jsy-Jsy/100	20.00
3	Steve Finley/Jsy-Jsy-Jsy/100	10.00
4	David Ortiz/Bat-Jsy-Jsy/100	25.00
5	Mike Piazza/Bat-Jsy-Jsy/100	15.00
6	Edgar Martinez/Bat-Jsy-Jsy/100	10.00
7	Roy Oswalt/Bat-Fld Glv-Jsy/50	10.00
9	Jacque Jones/Bat-Jsy/50	6.00
11	Albert Pujols/Bat-Jsy/100	40.00
13	Nolan Ryan/Bat-Jkt-Jsy/50	65.00
15	Jim Rice/Bat-Jsy/100	10.00
16	Dwight Evans/Bat-Hat-Jsy/100	10.00
17	Harmon Killebrew/Bat-Jsy-Shoe/25	50.00
20	Frank Thomas/Jsy-Jsy-Pants/100	20.00

Playoff All-Stars Signature
NM/M
Quantity produced listed

1	Mark Prior/25	40.00
3	Steve Finley/25	20.00
4	David Ortiz/25	60.00
7	Roy Oswalt/25	20.00
8	Johan Santana/25	20.00
9	Jacque Jones/25	20.00
10	Will Clark/25	50.00
13	Andre Dawson/25	20.00
13	Nolan Ryan/25	125.00
14	Fred Lynn/25	20.00
15	Jim Rice/25	25.00
16	Dwight Evans/25	30.00
18	Maury Wills/25	20.00

Playoff All-Stars Signature Material 1
NM/M
Quantity produced listed
Material 2: .75-1.5X
Production 5-100
Material 3: .75-1.5X
Production 5-100

3	Steve Finley/Jsy/100	15.00
4	David Ortiz/Jsy/100	50.00
6	Edgar Martinez/Jsy/50	30.00
7	Roy Oswalt/Jsy/100	15.00
8	Johan Santana/Jsy/100	35.00
9	Jacque Jones/Jsy/100	15.00
10	Will Clark/Bat/25	65.00
12	Andre Dawson/Jsy/100	20.00
14	Fred Lynn/Jsy/25	20.00
15	Jim Rice/Jsy/25	20.00
16	Dwight Evans/Jsy/50	30.00
19	Mark Mulder/Jsy/50	30.00
20	Frank Thomas/Jsy/25	50.00

Records

		NM/M
Complete Set (5):		10.00
Common Player:		3.00
Production 1,000 Sets		
HoloFoil:		2-4X
Production 50 Sets		
1	Lou Brock	3.00
2	Yogi Berra	4.00
3	Reggie Jackson	3.00
4	Bob Gibson	3.00
5	Whitey Ford	3.00

Records Material
NM/M
Quantity produced listed

1	Lou Brock/Bat/100	10.00
2	Yogi Berra/Bat/50	20.00
3	Reggie Jackson/Bat/100	10.00
7	Whitey Ford/Pants/25	20.00

Records Signature
NM/M
Common Player:

1	Lou Brock/25	30.00

Records Signature Material
NM/M
Quantity produced listed

1	Lou Brock/Bat/100	25.00
3	Reggie Jackson/Bat/20	40.00

Signature
NM/M
Common Autograph: 4.00
201-222 Exclusive to Red Sox Champs Sets

3	Garret Anderson/25	25.00
7	Brandon Webb/25	10.00
11	Shea Hillenbrand/25	10.00
12	Steve Finley/25	15.00
16	Marcus Giles/25	15.00
17	Rafael Furcal/25	15.00
19	Jay Gibbons/25	15.00
20	Luis Matos/25	15.00
21	Melvin Mora/25	20.00
25	Dwight Evans/25	30.00
26	Fred Lynn/25	20.00
28	Jim Rice/25	25.00
30	Luis Tiant/25	20.00
34	Trot Nixon/25	25.00
35	Aramis Ramirez/25	35.00
37	Derrek Lee/25	30.00
40	Mark Prior/25	40.00
43	Carlos Lee/25	10.00
45	Luis Aparicio/25	20.00
46	Magglio Ordonez/25	20.00
48	Mark Buehrle/25	20.00
49	Adam Dunn/25	40.00
51	Austin Kearns/25	20.00
52	Dave Concepcion/25	15.00
53	George Foster/25	15.00
56	Tony Perez/25	35.00
57	C.C. Sabathia/25	20.00
58	Jody Gerut/25	10.00
60	Victor Martinez/25	25.00
64	Preston Wilson/25	15.00
66	Alan Trammell/25	25.00
69	Jeremy Bonderman/25	10.00
71	Brad Penny/25	10.00
76	Miguel Cabrera/25	40.00
84	Roy Oswalt/25	20.00
85	Wade Miller/25	10.00
86	Angel Berroa/25	10.00
87	Carlos Beltran/25	50.00
89	Ken Harvey/25	10.00
94	Milton Bradley/25	20.00
96	Paul LoDuca/25	25.00
101	Rickie Weeks/25	25.00
102	Scott Podsednik/25	20.00
103	Jack Morris/25	20.00
104	Jacque Jones/25	15.00
105	Johan Santana/25	50.00
106	Shannon Stewart/25	15.00
107	Torii Hunter/25	25.00
108	Jose Vidro/25	15.00
109	Orlando Cabrera/25	20.00
111	Darryl Strawberry/25	25.00
112	Dwight Gooden/25	25.00
115	Keith Hernandez/25	25.00
116	Lenny Dykstra/25	20.00
132	Jermaine Dye/25	20.00
133	Mark Mulder/25	20.00
134	Rich Harden/25	25.00
139	Marlon Byrd/25	10.00
142	Steve Carlton/25	35.00
143	Dave Parker/25	25.00
146	Jay Payton/25	10.00
148	J.T. Snow/25	15.00
154	Shigetoshi Hasegawa/25	40.00
156	Dan Haren/25	20.00
162	Aubrey Huff/25	20.00
163	Carl Crawford/25	20.00
164	Dewon Brazelton/25	10.00
168	Hank Blalock/25	25.00
170	Mark Teixeira/25	35.00
171	Michael Young/25	20.00

Signature Trio
NM/M
Quantity produced listed

2	Derek Lee, Brad Penny, Mike Lowell/25	40.00
3	Garret Anderson, John Lackey, Chone Figgins/25	75.00
8	Roberto Alomar, Paul Molitor, Jack Morris/25	125.00
9	Eric Davis, Barry Larkin, Paul O'Neill/25	100.00
10	Dennis Eckersley, Jose Canseco, Dave Parker/25	125.00
11	Keith Hernandez, Dwight Gooden, Gary Carter/25	75.00
12	Lenny Dykstra, George Foster, Darryl Strawberry/25	65.00
13	Alan Trammell, Kirk Gibson, Jack Morris/25	100.00
15	Bert Blyleven, John Candelaria, Dave Parker/25	75.00

Souvenirs Playoff
NM/M
Common Player: 5.00
Production 100 Sets

1	Chipper Jones/Ball	10.00
2	Randy Johnson/Ball	10.00
3	Albert Pujols/Ball	20.00
4	Jason Schmidt/Ball	8.00
5	Gary Sheffield/Ball	8.00
6	Miguel Tejada/Ball	8.00
7	J.D. Drew/Ball	8.00
8	John Smoltz/Ball	10.00
9	Eric Milton/Ball	5.00
10	Mark Grace/Ball	10.00
11	Tim Hudson/Ball	5.00
12	Jeff Bagwell/Ball	10.00
13	Jim Edmonds/Ball	8.00
14	Sammy Sosa/Ball	15.00
15	Albert Pujols/Ball	20.00

Souvenirs World Series
NM/M
Common Player: 5.00
Production 100 Sets

1	Jason Schmidt/Ball	8.00
2	Troy Glaus/Base	5.00
3	Reggie Sanders/Base	5.00
4	Tim Salmon/Base	5.00

5	Garret Anderson/Base	5.00
6	Francisco Rodriguez/Base	5.00
7	Rich Aurilia/Ball	5.00
8	Jeff Kent/Ball	5.00
9	Troy Glaus/Base	5.00
10	Troy Glaus/Base	5.00
11	Jeff Kent/Ball	5.00
12	Scott Spiezio/Base	5.00
13	Tony Percival/Base	5.00
14	Garret Anderson/Base	5.00
15	Darin Erstad/Base	5.00

Triple Threads

		NM/M
	Common Player:	10.00
1	Josh Beckett, Miguel Cabrera, Mike Lowell/100	15.00
2	Luis Castillo, Ivan Rodriguez, Dontrelle Willis/100	20.00
3	Garret Anderson, Troy Glaus, Tim Salmon/100	20.00
4	Curt Schilling, Mark Grace, Randy Johnson/50	25.00
5	Jorge Posada, Bernie Williams, Roger Clemens/50	25.00
6	Andy Pettitte, Wade Boggs, Mariano Rivera/50	20.00
7	Charles Johnson, Cliff Floyd, Moises Alou/100	10.00
8	Chipper Jones, Tom Glavine, Greg Maddux/100	30.00
9	Joe Carter, Rickey Henderson, David Wells/100	25.00
10	Eric Davis, Barry Larkin, Paul O'Neill/100	20.00
11	Dwight Gooden, Gary Carter, Darryl Strawberry/100	20.00
12	Frank White, Willie Wilson, George Brett/100	30.00
13	Jim Palmer, Eddie Murray, Cal Ripken Jr./50	125.00
14	Willie Stargell, Dave Parker, Bill Madlock/100	20.00
15	Johnny Bench, Joe Morgan, Tony Perez/100	35.00
16	Dave Concepcion, George Foster, Johnny Bench/50	40.00
17	Al Oliver, Roberto Clemente, Willie Stargell/50	80.00
18	Jim Palmer, Frank Robinson, Brooks Robinson/50	25.00
19	Bob Gibson, Lou Brock, Orlando Cepeda/50	25.00
20	Stan Musial, Red Schoendienst, Marty Marion/50	40.00

2005 Donruss

	NM/M
Complete Set (400):	120.00
Common Player:	.15

	Common SP (1-70, 371-400):	1.00
	Inserted 1:6	
	Pack (10):	2.50
	Box (24):	50.00
1	Garret Anderson	1.00
2	Vladimir Guerrero	2.00
3	Manny Ramirez	2.00
4	Kerry Wood	2.00
5	Sammy Sosa	3.00
6	Magglio Ordonez	1.00
7	Adam Dunn	1.50
8	Todd Helton	1.50
9	Josh Beckett	1.00
10	Miguel Cabrera	2.00
11	Lance Berkman	1.00
12	Carlos Beltran	1.50
13	Shawn Green	1.00
14	Roger Clemens	4.00
15	Mike Piazza	2.50
16	Alex Rodriguez	3.00
17	Derek Jeter	4.00
18	Mark Mulder	1.00
19	Jim Thome	2.00
20	Albert Pujols	3.00
21	Scott Rolen	2.00
22	Aubrey Huff	1.00
23	Alfonso Soriano	2.00
24	Hank Blalock	1.50
25	Vernon Wells	1.00
26	Kazuo Matsui	1.50
27	B.J. Upton	1.50
28	Charles Thomas	1.00
29	Akinori Otsuka	1.00
30	David Aardsma	1.00
31	Travis Blackley	1.00
32	Brad Halsey	1.00
33	David Wright	5.00
34	Kazuhito Tadano	1.00
35	Casey Kotchman	1.50
36	Khalil Greene	2.00
37	Adrian Gonzalez	1.00
38	Zack Greinke	1.00
39	Chad Cordero	1.00
40	Scott Kazmir	4.00
41	Jeremy Guthrie	1.00
42	Noah Lowry	1.00
43	Chase Utley	1.00
44	Billy Traber	1.00
45	Aarom Baldiris	1.00
46	Abe Alvarez	1.00
47	Angel Chavez	1.00
48	Joe Mauer	1.00
49	Joey Gathright	1.00
50	John Gall	1.00
51	Ronald Belisario	1.00
52	Ryan Wing	1.00
53	Scott Proctor	1.00
54	Yadier Molina	1.00
55	Carlos Hines	1.00
56	Frankie Francisco	1.00
57	Graham Koonce	1.00
58	Jake Woods	1.00
59	Jason Bartlett	1.00
60	Mike Rouse	1.00
61	Phil Stockman	1.00
62	Renyel Pinto	1.00
63	Roberto Novoa	1.00
64	Ryan Meaux	1.00
65	David Crouthers	1.00
66	Justin Knoedler	1.00
67	Justin Leone	1.00
68	Nick Regilio	1.00
69	Mike Gosling	1.00
70	Onil Joseph	1.00
71	Bartolo Colon	.15
72	Brad Fullmer	.15
73	Chone Figgins	.15
74	Darin Erstad	.25
75	Francisco Rodriguez	.15
76	Garret Anderson	.25
77	Jarrod Washburn	.15
78	John Lackey	.15
79	Jose Guillen	.15
80	Robb Quinlan	.15
81	Tim Salmon	.25
82	Troy Glaus	.25
83	Troy Percival	.15
84	Vladimir Guerrero	.50
85	Brandon Webb	.15
86	Casey Fossum	.15
87	Luis Gonzalez	.15
88	Randy Johnson	.50
89	Richie Sexson	.25
90	Robby Hammock	.15
91	Roberto Alomar	.15
92	Adam LaRoche	.15
93	Andruw Jones	.25
94	Bubba Nelson	.15
95	Chipper Jones	.50
96	J.D. Drew	.25
97	John Smoltz	.25
98	Johnny Estrada	.15
99	Marcus Giles	.15
100	Mike Hampton	.15
101	Nick Green	.15
102	Rafael Furcal	.15
103	Russ Ortiz	.15
104	Adam Loewen	.15
105	Brian Roberts	.15
106	Javy Lopez	.25
107	Jay Gibbons	.15
108	Larry Bigbie	.15
109	Luis Matos	.15
110	Melvin Mora	.15
111	Miguel Tejada	.40
112	Rafael Palmeiro	.40
113	Rodrigo Lopez	.15
114	Sidney Ponson	.15
115	Bill Mueller	.15
116	Byung-Hyun Kim	.15
117	Curt Schilling	.40
118	David Ortiz	.40
119	Derek Lowe	.15
120	Doug Mientkiewicz	.15
121	Jason Varitek	.25
122	Johnny Damon	.25
123	Keith Foulke	.15
124	Kevin Youkilis	.15
125	Manny Ramirez	.50
126	Orlando Cabrera	.25
127	Pedro J. Martinez	.50
128	Trot Nixon	.15
129	Aramis Ramirez	.25
130	Carlos Zambrano	.25
131	Corey Patterson	.15
132	Derrek Lee	.25
133	Greg Maddux	.75
134	Kerry Wood	.50
135	Mark Prior	.50
136	Matt Clement	.15
137	Moises Alou	.15
138	Nomar Garciaparra	1.00
139	Sammy Sosa	1.00
140	Todd Walker	.15
141	Angel Guzman	.15
142	Billy Koch	.15
143	Carlos Lee	.15
144	Frank Thomas	.40
145	Magglio Ordonez	.25
146	Mark Buehrle	.15
147	Paul Konerko	.25
148	Wilson Valdez	.15
149	Adam Dunn	.40
150	Austin Kearns	.15
151	Barry Larkin	.25
152	Benito Santiago	.15
153	Jason LaRue	.15
154	Ken Griffey Jr.	.75
155	Ryan Wagner	.15
156	Sean Casey	.15
157	Brandon Phillips	.15
158	Brian Tallet	.15
159	C.C. Sabathia	.15
160	Cliff Lee	.15
161	Jeremy Guthrie	.15
162	Jody Gerut	.15
163	Matt Lawton	.15
164	Omar Vizquel	.15
165	Travis Hafner	.15
166	Victor Martinez	.25
167	Charles Johnson	.15
168	Garrett Atkins	.15
169	Jason Jennings	.15
170	Jay Payton	.15
171	Jeromy Burnitz	.15
172	Joe Kennedy	.15
173	Larry Walker	.25
174	Preston Wilson	.15
175	Todd Helton	.40
176	Vinny Castilla	.15
177	Bobby Higginson	.15
178	Brandon Inge	.15
179	Carlos Guillen	.15
180	Carlos Pena	.15
181	Craig Monroe	.15
182	Dmitri Young	.15
183	Eric Munson	.15
184	Fernando Vina	.15
185	Ivan Rodriguez	.40
186	Jeremy Bonderman	.15
187	Rondell White	.15
188	A.J. Burnett	.15
189	Dontrelle Willis	.25
190	Guillermo Mota	.15
191	Hee Seop Choi	.15
192	Jeff Conine	.15
193	Josh Beckett	.25
194	Juan Encarnacion	.15
195	Juan Pierre	.15
196	Luis Castillo	.15
197	Miguel Cabrera	.50
198	Mike Lowell	.15
199	Paul LoDuca	.15
200	Andy Pettitte	.25
201	Brad Ausmus	.15
202	Carlos Beltran	.40
203	Chris Burke	.15
204	Craig Biggio	.25
205	Jeff Bagwell	.40
206	Jeff Kent	.25
207	Lance Berkman	.25
208	Morgan Ensberg	.15
209	Octavio Dotel	.15
210	Roger Clemens	1.50
211	Roy Oswalt	.25
212	Tim Redding	.15
213	Angel Berroa	.15
214	Juan Gonzalez	.25
215	Ken Harvey	.15
216	Mike Sweeney	.15
217	Adrian Beltre	.25
218	Brad Penny	.15
219	Eric Gagne	.25
220	Hideo Nomo	.15
221	Hong-Chih Kuo	.15
222	Jeff Weaver	.15
223	Kazuhisa Ishii	.15
224	Milton Bradley	.15
225	Shawn Green	.15
226	Steve Finley	.15
227	Danny Kolb	.15
228	Geoff Jenkins	.15
229	Junior Spivey	.15
230	Lyle Overbay	.15
231	Rickie Weeks	.15
232	Scott Podsednik	.15
233	Brad Radke	.15
234	Corey Koskie	.15
235	Cristian Guzman	.15
236	Dustan Mohr	.15
237	Eddie Guardado	.15
238	J.D. Durbin	.15
239	Jacque Jones	.15
240	Joe Nathan	.15
241	Johan Santana	.40
242	Lew Ford	.15
243	Michael Cuddyer	.15
244	Shannon Stewart	.15
245	Torii Hunter	.15
246	Brad Wilkerson	.15
247	Carl Everett	.15
248	Jeff Fassero	.15
249	Jose Vidro	.15
250	Livan Hernandez	.15
251	Michael Barrett	.15
252	Tony Batista	.15
253	Zach Day	.15
254	Al Leiter	.15
255	Cliff Floyd	.15
256	Jae Weong Seo	.15
257	John Olerud	.15
258	Jose Reyes	.40
259	Mike Cameron	.15
260	Mike Piazza	1.00
261	Richard Hidalgo	.15
262	Tom Glavine	.25
263	Vance Wilson	.15
264	Alex Rodriguez	1.50
265	Armando Benitez	.15
266	Bernie Williams	.25
267	Bubba Crosby	.15
268	Chien-Ming Wang	.40
269	Derek Jeter	1.50
270	Esteban Loaiza	.15
271	Gary Sheffield	.25
272	Hideki Matsui	1.00
273	Jason Giambi	.25
274	Javier Vazquez	.15
275	Jorge Posada	.25
276	Jose Contreras	.15
277	Kenny Lofton	.15
278	Kevin Brown	.15
279	Mariano Rivera	.25
280	Mike Mussina	.25
281	Barry Zito	.15
282	Bobby Crosby	.15
283	Eric Byrnes	.15
284	Eric Chavez	.25
285	Erubiel Durazo	.15
286	Jermaine Dye	.15
287	Mark Kotsay	.15
288	Mark Mulder	.25
289	Rich Harden	.15
290	Tim Hudson	.15
291	Billy Wagner	.15
292	Bobby Abreu	.15
293	Brett Myers	.15
294	Eric Milton	.15
295	Jim Thome	.50
296	Jimmy Rollins	.25
297	Kevin Millwood	.15
298	Marlon Byrd	.15
299	Mike Lieberthal	.15
300	Pat Burrell	.15
301	Randy Wolf	.15
302	Craig Wilson	.15
303	Jack Wilson	.15
304	Jacob Cruz	.15
305	Jason Bay	.15
306	Jason Kendall	.15
307	Jose Castillo	.15
308	Kip Wells	.15
309	Brian Giles	.15
310	Brian Lawrence	.15
311	Chris Oxspring	.15
312	David Wells	.15
313	Freddy Guzman	.15
314	Jake Peavy	.15
315	Mark Loretta	.15
316	Ryan Klesko	.15
317	Sean Burroughs	.15
318	Trevor Hoffman	.15
319	Xavier Nady	.15
320	A.J. Pierzynski	.15
321	Edgardo Alfonzo	.15
322	J.T. Snow	.15
323	Jason Schmidt	.15
324	Jerome Williams	.15
325	Kirk Rueter	.15
326	Bret Boone	.15
327	Bucky Jacobsen	.15
328	Edgar Martinez	.15
329	Freddy Garcia	.15
330	Ichiro Suzuki	1.00
331	Jamie Moyer	.15
332	Joel Pineiro	.15
333	Scott Spiezio	.15
334	Shigetoshi Hasegawa	.15
335	Albert Pujols	1.50
336	Edgar Renteria	.25
337	Jason Isringhausen	.15
338	Jim Edmonds	.25
339	Matt Morris	.15
340	Mike Matheny	.15
341	Reggie Sanders	.15
342	Scott Rolen	.50
343	Woody Williams	.15
344	Jeff Suppan	.15
345	Aubrey Huff	.15
346	Carl Crawford	.25
347	Chad Gaudin	.15
348	Delmon Young	.15
349	Dewon Brazelton	.15
350	Jose Cruz Jr.	.15
351	Rocco Baldelli	.25
352	Tino Martinez	.15
353	Toby Hall	.15
354	Alfonso Soriano	.40
355	Brian Jordan	.15
356	Francisco Cordero	.15
357	Hank Blalock	.40
358	Kenny Rogers	.15
359	Kevin Mench	.15
360	Laynce Nix	.15
361	Mark Teixeira	.25
362	Michael Young	.15
363	Alex Gonzalez	.15
364	Alexis Rios	.15
365	Carlos Delgado	.25
366	Eric Hinske	.15
367	Frank Catalanotto	.15
368	Josh Phelps	.15
369	Roy Halladay	.15
370	Vernon Wells	.15
371	Vladimir Guerrero	2.00
372	Randy Johnson	2.00
373	Chipper Jones	2.00
374	Miguel Tejada	1.50
375	Pedro Martinez	2.00
376	Sammy Sosa	3.00
377	Frank Thomas	1.50
378	Ken Griffey Jr.	3.00
379	Victor Martinez	1.50
380	Todd Helton	1.50
381	Ivan Rodriguez	1.50
382	Miguel Cabrera	2.00
383	Roger Clemens	4.00
384	Ken Harvey	1.00
385	Eric Gagne	1.50
386	Lyle Overbay	1.00
387	Shannon Stewart	1.00
388	Brad Wilkerson	1.00
389	Mike Piazza	2.50
390	Alex Rodriguez	3.00
391	Mark Mulder	1.00
392	Jim Thome	2.00
393	Jack Wilson	1.00
394	Khalil Greene	1.50
395	Jason Schmidt	1.00
396	Ichiro Suzuki	3.00
397	Albert Pujols	4.00
398	Rocco Baldelli	1.00
399	Alfonso Soriano	1.50
400	Vernon Wells	1.00

Press Proofs Black
No Pricing
Production 10 Sets

Press Proofs Blue
Blue (71-370): 4-8X
Blue SP's: 2-3X
Production 100 Sets

Press Proofs Gold
Gold (71-370): 10-20X
Gold SP's: 3-6X
Production 25 Sets

Press Proofs Red

Red (71-370): 2-4X
Red SP's: .75-1.5X
Production 200 Sets

Stat Line Career

#71-370 print run 201-400: 2-4X
71-370 p/r 101-200: 3-6X
71-370 p/r 51-100: 4-8X
71-370 p/r 26-50: 6-12X
71-370 p/r 25 or less: No Pricing
SP's print run 200 or more: 1-2X
SP's p/r 101-200: 1.5-2X
SP's p/r 51-100: 2-4X
SP's p/r 26-50: 3-5X
SP's p/r 25 or less: No Pricing
Cards are numbered to career statistic.

Stat Line Season

#71-370 print run 101-200: 3-6X
71-370 p/r 51-100: 4-8X
71-370 p/r 26-50: 6-12X
71-370 p/r 25 or less: No Pricing
SP's p/r 101 or more: 1.5-2X
SP's p/r 51-100: 2-4X
SP's p/r 26-50: 3-5X
SP's p/r 25 or less: No Pricing
Cards are numbered to season statistic.

25th Anniversary
Stars: 10-20X
SP's (1-70, 371-400): 3-6X
Production 25 Sets

All-Stars AL

	NM/M
Common Player:	2.00
Production 1,000 Sets	
Gold:	1-2X
Production 100 Sets	

1	Alex Rodriguez	6.00
2	Alfonso Soriano	3.00
3	Curt Schilling	2.00
4	Derek Jeter	8.00
5	Hank Blalock	2.00
6	Hideki Matsui	6.00
7	Ichiro Suzuki	6.00
8	Ivan Rodriguez	3.00
9	Jason Giambi	2.00
10	Manny Ramirez	3.00
11	Mark Mulder	2.00
12	Michael Young	2.00
13	Tim Hudson	2.00
14	Victor Martinez	2.00
15	Vladimir Guerrero	3.00

All-Stars NL

	NM/M
Common Player:	2.00
Production 1,000 Sets	
Gold:	1-2X
Production 100 Sets	

1	Albert Pujols	8.00
2	Ben Sheets	2.00
3	Edgar Renteria	2.00
4	Eric Gagne	2.00
5	Jack Wilson	2.00
6	Jason Schmidt	2.00
7	Jeff Kent	2.00
8	Jim Thome	3.00
9	Ken Griffey Jr.	4.00
10	Mike Piazza	4.00
11	Roger Clemens	8.00
12	Sammy Sosa	5.00
13	Scott Rolen	3.00
14	Sean Casey	2.00
15	Todd Helton	2.00

Autographs

No Pricing

Bat Kings

		NM/M
Common Player:		5.00
Quantity produced listed		
1	Garret Anderson/250	5.00
2	Vladimir Guerrero/250	8.00
3	Cal Ripken Jr./100	50.00
4	Manny Ramirez/250	8.00
5	Kerry Wood/250	8.00
6	Sammy Sosa/250	12.00
7	Magglio Ordonez/250	5.00
8	Adam Dunn/250	8.00
9	Todd Helton/250	8.00
10	Josh Beckett/250	5.00
11	Miguel Cabrera/250	8.00
12	Lance Berkman/250	5.00
13	Carlos Beltran/250	8.00
14	Shawn Green/250	5.00
15	Roger Clemens/100	15.00
16	Mike Piazza/250	12.00
17	Nolan Ryan/100	50.00
18	Mark Mulder/250	5.00
19	Jim Thome/250	10.00
20	Albert Pujols/250	20.00
21	Scott Rolen/250	10.00
22	Aubrey Huff/250	5.00
23	Alfonso Soriano/250	8.00

Bat Kings Signatures

No Pricing
Production 5 or 10

Craftsmen

		NM/M
Complete Set (30):		40.00
Common Player:		1.00
Production 1,000 Sets		
Black:		1.5-2X
Production 100 Sets		
Master:		1-2X
Production 250 Sets		
Master Black:		No Pricing
Production 10 Sets		
1	Albert Pujols	5.00
2	Alex Rodriguez	4.00
3	Alfonso Soriano	2.00
4	Andruw Jones	1.00
5	Carlos Beltran	1.50
6	Derek Jeter	5.00
7	Greg Maddux	2.50
8	Hank Blalock	1.50
9	Ichiro Suzuki	5.00
10	Jeff Bagwell	1.50
11	Jim Thome	2.00
12	Josh Beckett	1.00
13	Ken Griffey Jr.	2.50
14	Manny Ramirez	2.00
15	Mark Mulder	1.00
16	Mark Prior	2.00
17	Mark Teixeira	1.00
18	Miguel Tejada	1.50
19	Mike Mussina	1.50
20	Mike Piazza	2.00
21	Nomar Garciaparra	3.00
22	Pedro Martinez	2.00
23	Rafael Palmeiro	1.50
24	Randy Johnson	2.00
25	Roger Clemens	5.00
26	Sammy Sosa	3.00
27	Scott Rolen	2.00
28	Tim Hudson	1.00
29	Vernon Wells	1.00
30	Vladimir Guerrero	2.00

Diamond Kings Inserts

	NM/M
Complete Set (25):	40.00
Common Player:	1.50

Studio / Production

Production 2,005 Sets		
Studio:		1.5-2X
Production 250 Sets		
Studio Black:		1.5-3X
Production 100 Sets		
1	Garret Anderson	1.50
2	Vladimir Guerrero	2.00
3	Manny Ramirez	2.00
4	Kerry Wood	1.50
5	Sammy Sosa	4.00
6	Magglio Ordonez	1.50
7	Adam Dunn	1.50
8	Todd Helton	1.50
9	Josh Beckett	1.50
10	Miguel Cabrera	2.00
11	Lance Berkman	1.50
12	Carlos Beltran	2.00
13	Shawn Green	1.50
14	Roger Clemens	6.00
15	Mike Piazza	3.00
16	Alex Rodriguez	5.00
17	Derek Jeter	6.00
18	Mark Mulder	1.50
19	Jim Thome	2.00
20	Albert Pujols	6.00
21	Scott Rolen	2.00
22	Aubrey Huff	1.50
23	Alfonso Soriano	2.00
24	Hank Blalock	1.50
25	Vernon Wells	1.50

Elite Series

		NM/M
Complete Set (25):		50.00
Common Player:		2.00
Production 1,500 Sets		
Black:		1-2X
Production 100 Sets		
Dominator:		1-1.5X
Production 250 Sets		
Dominator Black:		3-5X
Production 25 Sets		
1	Albert Pujols	6.00
2	Alex Rodriguez	5.00
3	Alfonso Soriano	2.00
4	Derek Jeter	5.00
5	Hank Blalock	1.50
6	Ichiro Suzuki	5.00
7	Ivan Rodriguez	2.00
8	Jim Thome	2.00
9	Ken Griffey Jr.	2.00
10	Manny Ramirez	2.00
11	Mark Mulder	1.50
12	Mark Prior	2.00
13	Michael Young	1.50
14	Miguel Cabrera	2.00
15	Miguel Tejada	2.00
16	Mike Piazza	2.00
17	Nomar Garciaparra	4.00
18	Rafael Palmeiro	2.00
19	Randy Johnson	2.00
20	Roger Clemens	6.00
21	Sammy Sosa	4.00
22	Scott Rolen	2.00
23	Tim Hudson	1.50
24	Todd Helton	1.50
25	Vladimir Guerrero	2.00

Fans of the Game

		NM/M
Complete Set (5):		10.00
1	Jesse Ventura	3.00
2	John C. McGinley	2.00
3	Susie Essman	2.00
4	Dean Cain	2.00
5	Meat Loaf	3.00

Fans of the Game Signatures

		NM/M
1	Jesse Ventura	50.00
2	John C. McGinley/SP/300	50.00
3	Susie Essman	60.00
4	Dean Cain/SP/250	90.00
5	Meat Loaf	60.00

Jersey Kings

		NM/M
Common Player:		5.00
1	Garret Anderson/250	5.00
2	Vladimir Guerrero/250	8.00
3	Cal Ripken Jr./100	50.00
4	Manny Ramirez/250	8.00
5	Kerry Wood/250	10.00
6	Sammy Sosa/250	12.00
7	Magglio Ordonez/250	5.00
8	Adam Dunn/250	8.00
9	Todd Helton/250	8.00
10	Josh Beckett/250	5.00
11	Miguel Cabrera/250	8.00
12	Lance Berkman/250	5.00
13	Carlos Beltran/250	5.00
14	Shawn Green/250	5.00
15	Roger Clemens/250	15.00
16	Mike Piazza/250	10.00
17	Nolan Ryan/100	50.00
18	Mark Mulder/250	5.00
19	Jim Thome/250	8.00
20	Albert Pujols/250	20.00
21	Scott Rolen/250	10.00
22	Aubrey Huff/250	5.00
23	Alfonso Soriano/250	8.00
24	Hank Blalock/250	8.00
25	Vernon Wells/250	5.00

Jersey Kings Signatures

No Pricing
Production 5 or 10

Longball Leaders

		NM/M
Complete Set (15):		30.00
Common Player:		2.00
Black:		1-2X
Production 250 Sets		
Die-Cut:		2-3X
Production 50 Sets		
Black Die-Cut:		No Pricing
Production 10 Sets		
1	Adam Dunn	3.00
2	Adrian Beltre	3.00
3	Albert Pujols	6.00
4	Alex Rodriguez	3.00
5	David Ortiz	3.00
6	Hank Blalock	3.00
7	J.D. Drew	2.00
8	Jeromy Burnitz	2.00
9	Jim Edmonds	2.50
10	Jim Thome	3.00
11	Manny Ramirez	3.00
12	Mark Teixeira	2.00
13	Moises Alou	2.00
14	Paul Konerko	2.00
15	Steve Finley	2.00

Mound Marvels

		NM/M
Complete Set (15):		40.00
Common Player:		2.00
Production 1,000 Sets		
Black:		No Pricing
Production 10 Sets		
1	Curt Schilling	4.00
2	Dontrelle Willis	4.00
3	Eric Gagne	4.00
4	Greg Maddux	6.00
5	John Smoltz	3.00
6	Kenny Rogers	2.00
7	Kerry Wood	3.00
8	Mariano Rivera	3.00
9	Mark Mulder	2.00
10	Mark Prior	4.00
11	Mike Mussina	3.00
12	Pedro Martinez	4.00
13	Randy Johnson	4.00
14	Roger Clemens	8.00
15	Tim Hudson	2.00

Power Alley Red

		NM/M
Common Player:		3.00
Black:		1.5-2X
Production 50 Sets		
Die-Cut:		1X
Production 100 Sets		
Black Die-Cut:		2-3X
Production 25 Sets		
1	Albert Pujols/1072	8.00
2	Bobby Abreu/983	4.00
3	Lance Berkman/1017	4.00
4	J.D. Drew/1006	3.00
5	Jorge Posada/977	4.00
6	Ichiro Suzuki/1016	8.00
7	Manny Ramirez/1009	4.00
8	Melvin Mora/1007	3.00
9	Todd Helton/1088	4.00
10	Travis Hafner/993	3.00

	NM/M
Common Player:	1.50
Production 2,500 Sets	
Black:	No Pricing
Production 10 Sets	
Black Die-Cut:	No Pricing
Production 5 Sets	
Blue:	1X
Production 1,000 Sets	
Blue Die-Cut:	2-3X
Production 100 Sets	
Green:	3-5X
Production 25 Sets	
Green Die-Cut:	No Pricing
Production 10 Sets	
Purple:	1-2X
Production 250 Sets	
Purple Die-Cut:	2-3X
Production 50 Sets	
Red Die-Cut:	1-2X
Production 250 Sets	
Yellow:	2-3X
Production 100 Sets	
Yellow Die-Cut:	3-5X

Production 25 Sets

1	Adam Dunn	2.00
2	Adrian Beltre	2.00
3	Albert Pujols	6.00
4	Alex Rodriguez	5.00
5	Alfonso Soriano	3.00
6	Gary Sheffield	2.00
7	Hank Blalock	2.00
8	Hideki Matsui	4.00
9	J.D. Drew	1.50
10	Jeromy Burnitz	1.50
11	Jim Edmonds	2.00
12	Jim Thome	3.00
13	Ken Griffey Jr.	3.00
14	Manny Ramirez	2.00
15	Mark Teixeira	1.50
16	Miguel Cabrera	3.00
17	Miguel Tejada	2.00
18	Mike Lowell	1.50
19	Mike Piazza	3.00
20	Moises Alou	1.50
21	Paul Konerko	1.50
22	Sammy Sosa	4.00
23	Scott Rolen	3.00
24	Todd Helton	2.00
25	Vladimir Guerrero	3.00

Production Line BA

	NM/M
Common Player:	3.00
Black:	2-3X
Production 25 Sets	
Die-Cut:	1X
Production 100 Sets	
Black Die-Cut:	No Pricing
Production 10 Sets	

1	Ichiro Suzuki/372	8.00
2	Ivan Rodriguez/334	5.00
3	Juan Pierre/326	3.00
4	Adrian Beltre/334	5.00
5	Albert Pujols/331	10.00
6	Mark Loretta/335	3.00
7	Melvin Mora/340	3.00
8	Sean Casey/324	3.00
9	Todd Helton/347	4.00
10	Vladimir Guerrero/337	5.00

Production Line OBP

	NM/M
Common Player:	3.00
Black:	2-3X
Production 25 Sets	
Die-Cut:	1X
Production 100 Sets	
Black Die-Cut:	No Pricing
Production 10 Sets	

1	Albert Pujols/415	8.00
2	Bobby Abreu/428	3.00
3	Lance Berkman/450	3.00
4	J.D. Drew/436	3.00
5	Jorge Posada/400	4.00
6	Ichiro Suzuki/414	8.00
7	Manny Ramirez/397	3.00
8	Melvin Mora/419	3.00
9	Todd Helton/469	4.00
10	Travis Hafner/410	3.00

Production Line OPS

	NM/M
Common Player:	3.00
Black:	1.5-2X
Production 50 Sets	
Die-Cut:	1X
Production 100 Sets	
Black Die-Cut:	2-3X
Production 25 Sets	

Production Line Slugging

		NM/M
Common Player:		3.00
Black:		1.5-2X
Production 50 Sets		
Die-Cut:		1X
Production 100 Sets		
Black Die-Cut:		2-3X
Production 25 Sets		
1	Adrian Beltre/629	4.00
2	Albert Pujols/657	8.00
3	Todd Helton/620	4.00
4	J.D. Drew/569	3.00
5	Jim Edmonds/643	3.00
6	Jim Thome/581	4.00
7	Vladimir Guerrero/598	3.00
8	Manny Ramirez/613	4.00
9	Scott Rolen/598	4.00
10	Travis Hafner/583	3.00

Recollection Autographs

No Pricing
Production 1-5

Rookies

	NM/M
Common Player:	2.00
Inserted 1:23	
Black:	No Pricing
Production 10 Sets	
Blue:	1X
Production 100 Sets	
Gold:	2-3X
Production 25 Sets	
Red:	.75-1X
Production 200 Sets	

1	Fernando Nieve	2.00
2	Frankie Francisco	2.00
3	Jorge Vasquez	2.00
4	Travis Blackley	2.00
5	Joey Gathright	4.00
6	Kazuhito Tadano	2.00
7	Edwin Moreno	2.00
8	Lance Cormier	2.00
9	Justin Knoedler	2.00
10	Orlando Rodriguez	2.00
11	Renyel Pinto	2.00
12	Justin Leone	2.00
13	Dennis Sarfate	2.00
14	Sam Narron	2.00
15	Yadier Molina	4.00
16	Carlos Vasquez	2.00
17	Ryan Wing	2.00
18	Brad Halsey	2.00
19	Ryan Meaux	2.00
20	Mike Wuertz	2.00
21	Shawn Camp	2.00
22	Ruddy Yan	2.00
23	Donald Kelly	2.00
24	Jake Woods	2.00
25	Colby Miller	2.00
26	Abe Alvarez	2.00
27	Mike Rouse	2.00
28	Phil Stockman	2.00
29	Kevin Cave	2.00
30	Chris Shelton	4.00
31	Tim Bittner	2.00
32	Mariano Gomez	2.00
33	Angel Chavez	2.00
34	Carlos Hines	2.00
35	Aarom Baldiris	2.00
36	Kazuo Matsui	5.00
37	Nick Regilio	2.00
38	Ivan Ochoa	2.00
39	Graham Koonce	2.00
40	Merkin Valdez	3.00
41	Greg Dobbs	2.00
42	Chris Oxspring	2.00
43	David Crouthers	2.00
44	Freddy Guzman	2.00
45	Akinori Otsuka	2.00
46	Jesse Crain	2.00
47	Casey Daigle	2.00
48	Roberto Novoa	2.00
49	Eddy Rodriguez	2.00
50	Jason Bartlett	2.00

Rookies Stat Line Career

Print run 201-316:	1X
Print run 101-200:	1X

Print run 51-100:	1-1.5X
Print run 26-50:	1-2X
Print run 25 or less:	No Pricing

Cards are numbered to career statistic.

Rookies Stat Line Season

Print run 101-200:	1X
Print run 51-100:	1-1.5X
Print run 26-50:	1-2X
Print run 25 or less:	No Pricing

Cards are numbered to season statistic.

Rookies Autographs

		NM/M
Common Autographs:		5.00
1	Fernando Nieve	5.00
2	Frankie Francisco	5.00
3	Jorge Vasquez	5.00
4	Travis Blackley	5.00
5	Joey Gathright	8.00
6	Edwin Moreno	5.00
8	Lance Cormier	5.00
9	Justin Knoedler	5.00
10	Orlando Rodriguez	5.00
11	Renyel Pinto	5.00
13	Dennis Sarfate	5.00
15	Yadier Molina	10.00
16	Carlos Vasquez	5.00
17	Ryan Wing/SP	10.00
18	Brad Halsey	8.00
19	Ryan Meaux	5.00
20	Mike Wuertz	5.00
22	Ruddy Yan	5.00
23	Donald Kelly	5.00
24	Jake Woods	5.00
25	Colby Miller	5.00
26	Abe Alvarez	8.00
27	Mike Rouse/SP	5.00
28	Phil Stockman	5.00
29	Kevin Cave	5.00
30	Chris Shelton/SP	10.00
31	Tim Bittner	5.00
32	Mariano Gomez	5.00
33	Angel Chavez	5.00
34	Carlos Hines	5.00
35	Aarom Baldiris	5.00
36	Nick Regilio	5.00
37		
38	Ivan Ochoa	5.00
39	Graham Koonce	5.00
42	Chris Oxspring	5.00
43	David Crouthers	5.00
48	Roberto Novoa	5.00
49	Eddy Rodriguez	5.00
50	Jason Bartlett	5.00

Timber and Threads Bat

		NM/M
Common Player:		5.00
1	Albert Pujols	15.00
2	Alfonso Soriano	8.00
3	Andre Dawson	8.00
4	Austin Kearns	5.00
5	Brad Penny	5.00
6	Carlos Beltran	8.00
7	Carlos Lee	5.00
8	Chipper Jones	8.00
9	Dale Murphy	8.00
10	Don Mattingly	20.00
11	Frank Thomas	8.00
12	Garret Anderson	8.00
13	Gary Carter	5.00
14	Hank Blalock	8.00
15	Jacque Jones	5.00
16	Jay Gibbons	5.00
17	Jeff Bagwell	8.00
18	Jermaine Dye	5.00
19	Jim Thome	8.00
20	Jose Vidro	5.00
21	Lance Berkman	5.00
22	Laynce Nix	5.00
23	Magglio Ordonez	5.00
24	Marcus Giles	5.00
25	Mark Prior	10.00
26	Mark Teixeira	5.00
27	Melvin Mora	5.00
28	Michael Young	5.00
29	Miguel Cabrera	8.00
30	Mike Lowell	5.00
31	Roy Oswalt	5.00
32	Sammy Sosa	10.00
33	Scott Rolen	10.00
34	Sean Burroughs	5.00
35	Sean Casey	5.00

ABBREVIATIONS

SP - Short Print

38	Shannon Stewart	5.00
39	Torii Hunter	5.00
40	Travis Hafner	5.00

Timber and Threads Bat Signature

No Pricing
Production 5 or 10

Timber and Threads Combo

		NM/M
1	Albert Pujols/Bat-Jsy	25.00
2	Alfonso Soriano/Bat-Jsy	10.00
3	Andre Dawson/Bat-Jsy	8.00
4	Austin Kearns/Bat-Jsy	8.00
5	Brad Penny/Bat-Jsy	6.00
6	Carlos Beltran/Bat-Jsy	12.00
7	Carlos Lee/Bat-Jsy	6.00
8	Chipper Jones/Bat-Jsy	12.00
9	Dale Murphy/Bat-Jsy	10.00
10	Don Mattingly/Bat-Jsy	25.00
11	Frank Thomas/Bat-Jsy	12.00
12	Garret Anderson/Bat-Jsy	8.00
13	Gary Carter/Bat-Jsy	8.00
14	Hank Blalock/Bat-Jsy	10.00
15	Jacque Jones/Bat-Jsy	6.00
17	Jay Gibbons/Bat-Jsy	6.00
18	Jeff Bagwell/Bat-Jsy	12.00
20	Jermaine Dye/Bat-Jsy	6.00
21	Jim Thome/Bat-Jsy	12.00
22	Jose Vidro/Bat-Jsy	6.00
23	Lance Berkman/Bat-Jsy	6.00
24	Laynce Nix/Bat-Jsy	6.00
25	Magglio Ordonez/Bat-Jsy	8.00
26	Marcus Giles/Bat-Jsy	6.00
27	Mark Prior/Bat-Jsy	15.00
28	Mark Teixeira/Bat-Jsy	8.00
29	Melvin Mora/Bat-Jsy	6.00
30	Michael Young/Bat-Jsy	8.00
31	Miguel Cabrera/Bat-Jsy	12.00
32	Mike Lowell/Bat-Jsy	8.00
33	Roy Oswalt/Bat-Jsy	8.00
34	Sammy Sosa/Bat-Jsy	15.00
35	Scott Rolen/Bat-Jsy	15.00
36	Sean Burroughs/Bat-Jsy	6.00
37	Sean Casey/Bat-Jsy	6.00
38	Shannon Stewart/Bat-Jsy	6.00
39	Torii Hunter/Bat-Jsy	8.00
40	Travis Hafner/Bat-Jsy	8.00

Timber and Threads Combo Signture

No Pricing
Production 5 or 10

Timber and Threads Jersey

		NM/M
Common Player:		5.00
1	Albert Pujols	15.00
2	Alfonso Soriano	8.00
4	Austin Kearns	5.00
5	Brad Penny	8.00
6	Carlos Beltran	8.00
7	Carlos Lee	5.00
9	Dale Murphy	8.00
10	Don Mattingly	25.00
11	Frank Thomas	8.00
12	Garret Anderson	5.00
13	Gary Carter	5.00
14	Hank Blalock	8.00
15	Jacque Jones	5.00
17	Jay Gibbons	5.00
18	Jeff Bagwell	8.00
19	Jeremy Bonderman	5.00
20	Jermaine Dye	5.00
21	Jim Thome	8.00
22	Jose Vidro	5.00
23	Lance Berkman	5.00
24	Laynce Nix	5.00
25	Magglio Ordonez	5.00
26	Marcus Giles	5.00
27	Mark Prior	10.00
28	Mark Teixeira	5.00
29	Melvin Mora	5.00
30	Michael Young	5.00

31	Miguel Cabrera	8.00
32	Mike Lowell	5.00
33	Roy Oswalt	5.00
34	Sammy Sosa	10.00
35	Scott Rolen	10.00
36	Sean Burroughs	5.00
37	Sean Casey	5.00
38	Shannon Stewart	5.00
39	Torii Hunter	5.00
40	Travis Hafner	5.00

Timber and Threads Jersey Signature

No Pricing
Production 5 or 10

'85 Reprints

		NM/M
Complete Set (12):		40.00
Common Player:		2.00
Production 1,985 Sets		
1	Eddie Murray	3.00
2	George Brett	6.00
3	Nolan Ryan	8.00
4	Mike Schmidt	6.00
5	Tony Gwynn	3.00
7	Cal Ripken Jr.	10.00
8	Dwight Gooden	2.00
9	Roger Clemens	8.00
10	Don Mattingly	6.00
11	Kirby Puckett	4.00
12	Orel Hershiser	2.00

'85 Reprints Material

		NM/M
Production 85 Sets		
1	Eddie Murray/Jsy	20.00
2	George Brett/Jsy	35.00
3	Nolan Ryan/Jkt	40.00
4	Mike Schmidt/Jkt	35.00
5	Tony Gwynn/Jsy	20.00
7	Cal Ripken Jr./Jsy	50.00
9	Roger Clemens/Jsy	40.00
10	Don Mattingly/Jsy	35.00
11	Kirby Puckett/Jsy	20.00
12	Orel Hershiser/Jsy	10.00

1965 Minnesota Twins 40th Anniversary

To commemorate the 40th anniversary of the team's 1965 American League championship, this set was produced by Donruss as a stadium giveaway. Fifteen-card cello packs containing cards #1-15 were distributed on August 18. Cards #19-30 were given away the next day. Fronts have black-and-white photos bordered in blue.

		NM/M
Complete Set (30):		15.00
Common Player:		.25
1	Dave Boswell	.25
2	Jim Kaat	.50
3	Jim Merritt	.25
4	Mel Nelson	.25
5	Bill Pleis	.25
6	Dick Stigman	.25
7	Earl Battey	.25
8	Jerry Kindall	.25
9	Frank Quilici	.25
10	Zoilo Versalles	.50
11	Bob Allison	.50
12	Joe Nossek	.25
13	Tony Oliva	3.00
14	Sam Mele	.25
15	John Sain	.25
16	Jim "Mudcat" Grant	.35
17	Johnny Klippstein	.25
18	Camilo Pascual	.40
19	Jim Perry	.35
20	Al Worthington	.25
21	John Sevcik	.25
22	Jerry Zimmerman	.25
23	Harmon Killebrew	5.00
24	Don Mincher	.25
25	Rich Rollins	.25
26	Billy Martin	2.00
27	Jimmie Hall	.25
28	Sandy Valdespino	.25
29	Hal Naragon	.25
30	Jim Lemon	.25

2005 Donruss Classics

		NM/M
Complete Set (250):		
Common Player (1-200):		.25
Common Auto. (201-225):		6.00
Common SP (226-250):		3.00
Production 1,000		
Pack (5):		8.00
Box (18):		120.00
1	Scott Rolen	1.00
2	Derek Jeter	3.00
3	Jose Vidro	.25
4	Johnny Damon	1.00
5	Nomar Garciaparra	2.00
6	Jose Guillen	.25
7	Trot Nixon	.25
8	Mark Loretta	.25
9	Jody Gerut	.25
10	Miguel Tejada	.75
11	Barry Larkin	.50
12	Jeff Kent	.40
13	Carl Crawford	.25
14	Paul Konerko	.40
15	Jim Edmonds	.50
16	Garret Anderson	.40
17	Jay Gibbons	.25
18	Moises Alou	.25
19	Mike Lowell	.25
20	Mark Mulder	.40
21	Josh Beckett	.50
22	Tim Salmon	.25
23	Shannon Stewart	.25
24	Miguel Cabrera	1.00
25	Jim Thome	1.00
26	Kevin Youkilis	.25
27	Justin Morneau	.75
28	Austin Kearns	.25
29	Cliff Lee	.25
30	Ken Griffey Jr.	1.50
31	Mike Piazza	1.50
32	Roy Halladay	.40
33	Larry Walker	.50
34	David Ortiz	1.00
35	Dontrelle Willis	.50
36	Craig Wilson	.25
37	Jeff Suppan	.25
38	Curt Schilling	1.00
39	Larry Bigbie	.25
40	Rich Harden	.40
41	Victor Martinez	.50
42	Jorge Posada	.50
43	Joey Gathright	.25
44	Adam Dunn	.75
45	Pedro Martinez	1.00
46	Dallas McPherson	.50
47	Tom Glavine	.40
48	Torii Hunter	.40
49	Angel Berroa	.25
50	Mark Prior	1.00
51	Ichiro Suzuki	2.00
52	C.C. Sabathia	.25
53	Bobby Abreu	.25
54	Shigetoshi Hasegawa	.25
55	Brandon Webb	.50
56	Mark Buehrle	.50
57	Johan Santana	.75
58	Francisco Rodriguez	.50
59	Roy Oswalt	.50
60	Mike Sweeney	.25
61	Jake Peavy	.50
62	Akinori Otsuka	.25
63	Dioner Navarro	.25
64	Kazuhito Tadano	.25
65	Ryan Wagner	.25
66	Abe Alvarez	.25
67	Mark Teixeira	.75
68	Jermaine Dye	.25
69	Todd Walker	.25
70	Octavio Dotel	.25

71	Frank Thomas	.75
72	Javy Lopez	.50
73	Scott Podsednik	.25
74	B.J. Upton	.50
75	Barry Zito	.40
76	Raul Ibanez	.25
77	Orlando Cabrera	.25
78	Sean Burroughs	.25
79	Esteban Loaiza	.25
80	Jason Schmidt	.50
81	Vinny Castilla	.25
82	Shingo Takatsu	.25
83	Juan Pierre	.25
84	David Dellucci	.25
85	Travis Blackley	.25
86	Brad Penny	.25
87	Nick Johnson	.25
88	Brian Roberts	.50
89	Kazuo Matsui	.25
90	Mike Lieberthal	.25
91	Craig Biggio	.40
92	Sean Casey	.25
93	Andy Pettitte	.50
94	Milton Bradley	.40
95	Rocco Baldelli	.25
96	Adrian Gonzalez	.25
97	Chad Tracy	.25
98	Chad Cordero	.25
99	Albert Pujols	3.00
100	Jason Kubel	.25
101	Rafael Furcal	.25
102	Jack Wilson	.25
103	Eric Chavez	.40
104	Casey Kotchman	.25
105	Jeff Bagwell	.75
106	Melvin Mora	.25
107	Bobby Crosby	.25
108	Preston Wilson	.25
109	Hank Blalock	.25
110	Vernon Wells	.40
111	Francisco Cordero	.25
112	Steve Finley	.25
113	Omar Vizquel	.25
114	Eric Byrnes	.25
115	Tim Hudson	.50
116	Aramis Ramirez	.50
117	Lance Berkman	.40
118	Shea Hillenbrand	.25
119	Aubrey Huff	.25
120	Lew Ford	.25
121	Sammy Sosa	2.00
122	Marcus Giles	.25
123	Rickie Weeks	.25
124	Manny Ramirez	1.00
125	Jason Giambi	.40
126	Adam LaRoche	.25
127	Vladimir Guerrero	1.00
128	Ken Harvey	.25
129	Adrian Beltre	.50
130	Magglio Ordonez	.25
131	Greg Maddux	1.50
132	Russ Ortiz	.25
133	Jason Varitek	.75
134	Kerry Wood	1.00
135	Mike Mussina	.75
136	Joe Nathan	.25
137	Troy Glaus	.50
138	Carlos Zambrano	.50
139	Ben Sheets	.50
140	Jae Weong Seo	.25
141	Derrek Lee	.50
142	Carlos Beltran	.50
143	John Lackey	.25
144	Aaron Rowand	.25
145	Dewon Brazelton	.25
146	Jason Bay	.25
147	Alfonso Soriano	1.00
148	Travis Hafner	.25
149	Ryan Church	.25
150	Bret Boone	.25
151	Bernie Williams	.50
152	Wade Miller	.25
153	Zack Greinke	.25
154	Scott Kazmir	.25
155	Hideki Matsui	2.00
156	Livan Hernandez	.25
157	Jose Capellan	.25
158	David Wright	1.00
159	Chone Figgins	.25
160	Jeremy Reed	.25
161	J.D. Drew	.40
162	Hideo Nomo	.50
163	Merkin Valdez	.25
164	Shawn Green	.40
165	Alexis Rios	.25
166	Johnny Estrada	.25
167	Danny Graves	.25
168	Carlos Lee	.25
169	John Van Benschoten	.25
170	Randy Johnson	1.00
171	Randy Wolf	.25
172	Luis Gonzalez	.40
173	Chipper Jones	1.00
174	Delmon Young	.50
175	Edwin Jackson	.50
176	Carlos Delgado	.50
177	Matt Clement	.25
178	Jacque Jones	.25
179	Gary Sheffield	.50
180	Laynce Nix	.25
181	Tom Gordon	.25
182	Jose Castillo	.25
183	Andruw Jones	.50
184	Brian Giles	.25
185	Paul LoDuca	.25
186	Roger Clemens	3.00
187	Todd Helton	.75
188	Keith Foulke	.25
189	Jeremy Bonderman	.25
190	Troy Percival	.25
191	Michael Young	.25

192	Carlos Guillen	.25
193	Rafael Palmeiro	.75
194	Brett Myers	.25
195	Carl Pavano	.40
196	Alex Rodriguez	2.50
197	Lyle Overbay	.25
198	Ivan Rodriguez	.75
199	Khalil Greene	.40
200	Edgar Renteria	.40
201	Justin Verlander AU/400 **RC**	40.00
202	Miguel Negron AU/1300 **RC**	6.00
204	Paul Reynoso AU/1200 **RC**	8.00
205	Colter Bean AU/1200 **RC**	8.00
206	Raul Tablado AU/1200 **RC**	8.00
207	Mark McLemore AU/1500 **RC**	8.00
208	Russel Rohlicek AU/1200 **RC**	8.00
210	Chris Seddon AU/785 **RC**	8.00
213	Mike Morse AU/1200 **RC**	6.00
215	Randy Messenger AU/1200 **RC**	6.00
217	Carlos Ruiz AU/1200 **RC**	8.00
218	Chris Roberson AU/1200 **RC**	8.00
219	Ryan Speier AU/1200 **RC**	8.00
221	Ambiorix Burgos AU/750 **RC**	8.00
223	David Gassner AU/1200 **RC**	6.00
224	Sean Tracey AU/1200 **RC**	8.00
225	Casey Rogowski AU/1500 **RC**	8.00
226	Billy Williams	3.00
227	Ralph Kiner	3.00
228	Ozzie Smith	5.00
229	Rod Carew	3.00
230	Nolan Ryan	8.00
231	Fergie Jenkins	3.00
232	Paul Molitor	4.00
233	Carlton Fisk	4.00
234	Rollie Fingers	3.00
235	Lou Brock	3.00
236	Gaylord Perry	3.00
237	Don Mattingly	6.00
238	Maury Wills	3.00
239	Luis Aparicio	3.00
240	George Brett	8.00
241	Mike Schmidt	6.00
242	Joe Morgan	3.00
243	Dennis Eckersley	3.00
244	Reggie Jackson	4.00
245	Bobby Doerr	3.00
246	Bob Feller	3.00
247	Cal Ripken Jr.	10.00
248	Harmon Killebrew	4.00
249	Frank Robinson	4.00
250	Stan Musial	5.00

Timeless Tributes Gold

Gold (1-200):	4-8X
Gold (201-225):	.4-.75X
Gold (226-250):	2-4X
Production 50 Sets	

Timeless Tributes Silver

Gold (1-200):	2-4X
Gold (201-225):	.25X
Gold (226-250):	1-2X
Production 100 Sets	

Timeless Tributes Platinum

No Pricing
Production One Set

Classic Combos

		NM/M
Common Combo:		4.00
Production 400 Sets		
Gold:		2-4X
Production 25 Sets		
Platinum:		No Pricing
Production One Set		
33	Babe Ruth, Ted Williams	10.00
34	Roberto Clemente, Vladimir Guerrero	8.00
35	Willie Mays, Willie McCovey	8.00
36	Yogi Berra, Mike Piazza	6.00
37	Sandy Koufax, Nolan Ryan	30.00
38	Harmon Killebrew, Mike Schmidt	8.00
39	Whitey Ford, Randy Johnson	4.00
40	Cal Ripken Jr., George Brett	15.00
41	Hank Aaron, Stan Musial	8.00
42	Carl Yastrzemski, Frank Robinson	6.00
43	Bob Feller, Roger Clemens	6.00
44	Bob Gibson, Tom Seaver	4.00
45	Roger Maris, Jim Thome	4.00
46	Albert Pujols, Don Mattingly	8.00
47	Duke Snider, Sammy Sosa	4.00
48	Rickey Henderson, Bo Jackson	4.00
49	Ernie Banks, Reggie Jackson	4.00
50	Burleigh Grimes, Greg Maddux	6.00

Classic Combos Bat

No Pricing
Production 5 Sets

Classic Combos Jersey

		NM/M
Production 5-50		
Prime:		No Pricing
Production 1-5		
38	Harmon Killebrew, Mike Schmidt/50	30.00
39	Whitey Ford, Randy Johnson/25	25.00
40	Cal Ripken Jr., George Brett/50	50.00
45	Roger Maris, Jim Thome/25	50.00
46	Albert Pujols, Don Mattingly/50	40.00
47	Duke Snider, Sammy Sosa/25	30.00
48	Rickey Henderson, Bo Jackson/50	25.00

Classic Combos Materials

		NM/M
Production 1-25		
Prime:		No Pricing
Production 5 Sets		
46	Albert Pujols, Don Mattingly/25	50.00
48	Rickey Henderson, Bo Jackson/25	30.00

Classic Combos Materials HR

		NM/M
Production 1-25		
46	Albert Pujols, Don Mattingly/25	50.00
48	Rickey Henderson, Bo Jackson/25	30.00

Classic Combos Signature
No Pricing
Production One Set

Classic Combos Signature Bat
No Pricing
Production One Set

Classic Combos Signature Jersey
No Pricing
Production 1-5

Classic Combos Signature Material
No Pricing
Production One Set

Classic Combos Signature Materials HR
No Pricing
Production One Set

Classic Singles
NM/M
Complete Set (32): 120.00
Common Player: 3.00
Production 400 Sets
Gold: 2-4X
Production 25 Sets
Platinum: No Pricing
Production One Set

1 Hank Aaron 8.00
2 Tom Seaver 4.00
3 Harmon Killebrew 4.00
4 Paul Molitor 4.00
5 Brooks Robinson 4.00
6 Stan Musial 5.00
7 Bobby Doerr 3.00
8 Cal Ripken Jr. 12.00
9 Phil Niekro 3.00
10 Eddie Murray 4.00
11 Randy Johnson 4.00
12 Steve Carlton 3.00
13 Rickey Henderson 3.00
14 Ernie Banks 4.00
15 Curt Schilling 4.00
16 Whitey Ford 4.00
17 Al Kaline 4.00
18 Gary Carter 3.00
19 Robin Yount 4.00
20 Johnny Bench 4.00
21 Bob Feller 3.00
22 Jim Palmer 3.00
23 Don Mattingly 6.00
24 Willie Mays 6.00
25 Dave Righetti 3.00
26 Roger Clemens 6.00
27 Juan Marichal 3.00
28 Tony Gwynn 4.00
29 Nolan Ryan 8.00
30 Carlton Fisk 3.00
31 Greg Maddux 5.00
32 Sandy Koufax 25.00

Classic Singles Bat
NM/M
Production 25-50

1 Hank Aaron/25 50.00
2 Tom Seaver/50 15.00
4 Paul Molitor/50 15.00
5 Brooks Robinson/50 15.00
6 Stan Musial/50 30.00
7 Bobby Doerr/25 10.00
8 Cal Ripken Jr./25 70.00
9 Phil Niekro/50 8.00
10 Eddie Murray/50 15.00
11 Randy Johnson/50 20.00
12 Steve Carlton/25 10.00
13 Rickey Henderson/50 15.00
14 Ernie Banks/50 20.00
17 Al Kaline/25 25.00
18 Gary Carter/50 8.00
19 Robin Yount/50 15.00
20 Johnny Bench/25 20.00
23 Don Mattingly/25 30.00
24 Willie Mays/25 50.00
28 Tony Gwynn/50 15.00
29 Nolan Ryan/25 40.00
30 Carlton Fisk/50 15.00

Classic Singles Jersey
NM/M
Production 10-100
Prime: No Pricing
Production 1-5

2 Tom Seaver/25 20.00
3 Harmon Killebrew/25 20.00
4 Paul Molitor/50 15.00
5 Brooks Robinson/50 15.00
6 Bobby Doerr/Pants/100 10.00
8 Cal Ripken Jr./25 70.00
9 Phil Niekro/50 8.00
10 Eddie Murray/50 15.00
11 Randy Johnson/100 12.00
12 Steve Carlton/25 12.00
13 Rickey Henderson/100 —
14 Ernie Banks/25 25.00
15 Curt Schilling/100 15.00
16 Whitey Ford/75 20.00
18 Gary Carter/100 8.00
19 Robin Yount/50 15.00
20 Johnny Bench/50 15.00
21 Bob Feller/Pants/25 20.00
22 Jim Palmer/100 8.00
23 Don Mattingly/100 25.00
24 Willie Mays/25 50.00
25 Dave Righetti/50 8.00
26 Roger Clemens/25 25.00
27 Juan Marichal/25 15.00
28 Tony Gwynn/100 15.00
29 Nolan Ryan/50 30.00
31 Carlton Fisk/25 15.00
31 Greg Maddux/25 15.00
32 Sandy Koufax/25 375.00

Classic Singles Materials
NM/M
Production 10-25
Prime: No Pricing
Production 10-25

2 Tom Seaver/Bat-Jsy/25 20.00
3 Harmon Killebrew/Bat-Jys/25 25.00
4 Paul Molitor/Bat-Jsy/25 20.00
5 Brooks Robinson/Bat-Jsy/25 —
7 Bobby Doerr/Bat-Pants/25 10.00
11 Randy Johnson/Bat-Jsy/25 20.00
12 Steve Carlton/Bat-Jsy/25 15.00
13 Rickey Henderson/Bat-Jsy/25 30.00
18 Gary Carter/Bat-Jsy/25 15.00
19 Robin Yount/Bat-Jsy/25 25.00
20 Johnny Bench/Bat-Jsy/25 25.00
23 Don Mattingly/Bat-Jsy/25 35.00
28 Tony Gwynn/Bat-Jsy/25 25.00
29 Nolan Ryan/Bat-Jsy/25 40.00
30 Carlton Fisk/Bat-Jsy/25 15.00

Classic Singles Materials HR
NM/M
Production 10-25

2 Tom Seaver/Bat-Jsy/25 20.00
3 Harmon Killebrew/Bat-Jsy/25 25.00
4 Paul Molitor/Bat-Jsy/25 20.00
5 Brooks Robinson/Bat-Jsy/25 20.00
7 Bobby Doerr/Bat-Pants/25 10.00
11 Randy Johnson/Bat-Jsy/25 20.00
12 Steve Carlton/Bat-Pants/25 15.00
13 Rickey Henderson/Bat-Jsy/25 30.00
18 Gary Carter/Bat-Jsy/25 15.00
19 Robin Yount/Bat-Jsy/25 25.00
20 Johnny Bench/Bat-Jsy/25 25.00
23 Don Mattingly/Bat-Jsy/25 35.00
28 Tony Gwynn/Bat-Jsy/25 25.00

Classic Singles Signature
No Pricing
Production 1-5

Classic Singles Signature Bat
No Pricing
Production 1-10

Classic Singles Signature Jersey
No Pricing
Production 1-5

Classic Singles Signature Materials
No Pricing
Production 1-10

Classic Singles Signature Materials HR
No Pricing
Production 1-10

Dress Code Bat
NM/M
Production 50-100

1 Albert Pujols/100 25.00
2 Bernie Williams/50 10.00
4 Carlos Beltran/100 10.00
5 Chipper Jones/100 10.00
7 David Ortiz/100 12.00
8 Hank Blalock/100 15.00
9 Hideki Matsui/100 30.00
10 Jim Edmonds/100 8.00
11 Jim Thome/100 15.00
14 Mark Prior/50 8.00
15 Mark Teixeira/100 6.00
16 Miguel Cabrera/100 8.00
17 Miguel Tejada/100 6.00
18 Mike Piazza/100 12.00
22 Sammy Sosa/100 12.00
23 Scott Rolen/100 10.00
26 Torii Hunter/100 6.00
30 Vladimir Guerrero/100 10.00

Dress Code Jersey Number
NM/M
Production 5-57

2 Bernie Williams/51 10.00
4 Carlos Beltran/15 8.00
6 Curt Schilling/38 15.00
7 David Ortiz/34 20.00
9 Hideki Matsui/55 —
11 Jim Thome/25 15.00
12 Johan Santana/57 12.00
13 Mark Mulder/20 15.00
14 Mark Prior/22 15.00
15 Mark Teixeira/23 10.00
16 Miguel Cabrera/24 15.00
18 Mike Piazza/31 15.00
19 Pedro J. Martinez/45 10.00
20 Randy Johnson/Pants/51 12.00
21 Roger Clemens/23 25.00
22 Sammy Sosa/21 15.00
23 Scott Rolen/27 15.00
26 Torii Hunter/48 6.00
27 Travis Hafner/48 6.00
29 Victor Martinez/51 8.00
30 Vladimir Guerrero/27 20.00

Dress Code Jersey Prime
NM/M
Production 25 Sets

1 Albert Pujols 75.00
2 Bernie Williams 20.00
3 Carl Crawford 12.00
4 Carlos Beltran 25.00
5 Chipper Jones 30.00
6 Curt Schilling 30.00
7 David Ortiz 30.00
8 Hank Blalock 20.00
10 Jim Edmonds 20.00
11 Jim Thome 25.00
12 Johan Santana 30.00
13 Mark Mulder 20.00
14 Mark Prior 20.00
15 Mark Teixeira 15.00
16 Miguel Cabrera 25.00
17 Miguel Tejada 25.00
18 Mike Piazza 25.00
19 Pedro J. Martinez 25.00
20 Randy Johnson 30.00
21 Roger Clemens 50.00
22 Sammy Sosa 30.00
23 Scott Rolen 30.00
24 Tim Hudson 20.00
25 Todd Helton 20.00
26 Torii Hunter 15.00
27 Travis Hafner 10.00
28 Vernon Wells 10.00
29 Victor Martinez 15.00
30 Vladimir Guerrero 30.00

Dress Code Materials
NM/M
Production 5-100
Prime: No Pricing
Production 5 Sets

1 Albert Pujols/Bat-Jsy/100 25.00
2 Bernie Williams/Bat-Jsy/50 10.00
4 Carlos Beltran/Bat-Jsy-Jsy/100 10.00
5 Chipper Jones/Bat-Jsy/100 12.00
6 Curt Schilling/Bat-Jsy/50 15.00
7 David Ortiz/Bat-Hat/100 15.00
8 Hank Blalock/Bat-Jsy/100 8.00
9 Hideki Matsui/Bat-Jsy/100 30.00
10 Jim Edmonds 10.00
11 Jim Thome/Jsy-Jsy/100 12.00
15 Mark Teixeira/Bat-Jsy/100 8.00
16 Miguel Cabrera/Jsy/100 10.00
17 Miguel Tejada/Bat-Jsy/100 8.00
18 Mike Piazza/Bat-Jsy/100 12.00
19 Pedro J. Martinez/Bat-Jsy/100 12.00
22 Sammy Sosa/Bat-Jsy/100 12.00
23 Scott Rolen/Jsy-Jsy/50 12.00
25 Todd Helton/Jsy-Jsy/50 12.00
26 Torii Hunter/Bat-Jsy/100 8.00
27 Travis Hafner/Jsy-Shoes/100 8.00
28 Vernon Wells/Jsy-Jsy/100 8.00
29 Victor Martinez/Jsy-Jsy/50 8.00
30 Vladimir Guerrero/Bat-Jsy/100 12.00

Dress Code Signature Bat
NM/M
Production 1-25

7 David Ortiz/25 50.00
8 Hank Blalock/25 30.00
16 Miguel Cabrera/25 50.00
26 Torii Hunter/25 30.00
27 Travis Hafner/25 25.00
28 Vernon Wells/25 25.00

Dress Code Signature Jersey
NM/M
Production 5-25

7 David Ortiz/25 50.00
8 Hank Blalock/25 30.00
12 Johan Santana/25 50.00
16 Miguel Cabrera/25 50.00
26 Torii Hunter/25 30.00
27 Travis Hafner/25 25.00
28 Vernon Wells/25 25.00
29 Victor Martinez/25 25.00

Dress Code Signature Jersey Number
NM/M
Production 1-25
Prime: No Pricing
Production 1-5

7 David Ortiz/25 50.00
8 Hank Blalock/25 30.00
12 Johan Santana/25 50.00
26 Torii Hunter/25 30.00
27 Travis Hafner/25 25.00
29 Victor Martinez/25 25.00

Dress Code Signature Materials
No Pricing
Production 1-5

Home Run Heroes

NM/M
Complete Set (50): 90.00
Common Player: 1.50
Production 1,000 Sets
Gold: 2-4X
Production 50 Sets
Platinum: No Pricing
Production One Set

1 Mike Schmidt 4.00
2 Ken Griffey Jr. 4.00
3 Babe Ruth 6.00
4 Duke Snider 3.00
5 Johnny Bench 3.00
6 Stan Musial 3.00
7 Willie McCovey 2.00
8 Willie Stargell 2.00
9 Ted Williams 5.00
10 Frank Thomas 3.00
11 Gary Sheffield 2.00
12 Jim Thome 2.00
13 Harmon Killebrew 2.00
14 Ernie Banks 3.00
15 George Foster 1.50
16 Albert Pujols 5.00
17 Tony Perez 1.50
18 Richie Sexson 1.50
19 Juan Gonzalez 1.50
20 Frank Robinson 2.00
21 Sammy Sosa 3.00
22 Jeff Bagwell 1.50
23 Mark Teixeira 1.50
24 Willie Mays 5.00
25 Rafael Palmeiro 2.00
26 Billy Williams 1.50
27 Vladimir Guerrero 2.00
28 Gary Carter 2.00
29 Fred McGriff 1.50
30 Orlando Cepeda 1.50
31 Dave Winfield 2.00
32 Shawn Green 1.50
33 Jose Canseco 1.50
34 Hideki Matsui 4.00
35 Roger Maris 4.00
36 Andre Dawson 2.00
37 Paul Konerko 1.50
38 Darryl Strawberry 1.50
39 Dave Parker 1.50
40 Adam Dunn 2.00
41 Ralph Kiner 2.00
42 Miguel Tejada 2.00
43 Dale Murphy 2.00
44 Hank Aaron 6.00
45 Mike Piazza 3.00
46 Reggie Jackson 2.00
47 Adrian Beltre 2.00
48 Cal Ripken Jr. 8.00
49 Manny Ramirez 3.00
49 Alex Rodriguez 5.00

Home Run Heroes Jersey HR
NM/M
Production 1-66
Prime: No Pricing
Production One Set

1 Mike Schmidt/48 25.00
3 Babe Ruth/25 165.00
5 Johnny Bench/45 15.00
7 Willie McCovey/23 15.00
8 Willie Stargell/48 15.00
9 Ted Williams/43 60.00
10 Frank Thomas/43 12.00
11 Gary Sheffield/36 8.00
12 Jim Thome/47 15.00
13 Harmon Killebrew/49 20.00
14 Ernie Banks/Pants/ 20.00
15 Gene Foster/25 10.00
16 Albert Pujols/45 35.00
18 Richie Sexson/45 8.00
19 Juan Gonzalez/47 8.00
21 Sammy Sosa/66 12.00
22 Jeff Bagwell/47 10.00
23 Mark Teixeira/38 8.00
24 Willie Mays/51 50.00
25 Rafael Palmeiro/ 10.00
26 Billy Williams/26 12.00
27 Vladimir Guerrero/44 12.00
28 Gary Carter/31 8.00
29 Fred McGriff/32 12.00
30 Orlando Cepeda/Pants/46 8.00
31 Dave Winfield/34 10.00
32 Shawn Green/49 8.00
33 Jose Canseco/44 10.00
34 Hideki Matsui/Pants/31 40.00
35 Roger Maris/Pants/19 50.00
36 Andre Dawson/49 8.00
38 Darryl Strawberry/24 10.00
39 Dave Parker/34 8.00
40 Adam Dunn/ —
42 Miguel Tejada/34 10.00
43 Dale Murphy/44 10.00
44 Hank Aaron/47 50.00
45 Mike Piazza/39 15.00
46 Reggie Jackson/39 —
47 Adrian Beltre/48 8.00
48 Cal Ripken Jr./34 —
49 Manny Ramirez/43 12.00

Home Run Heroes Materials
NM/M
Production 1-66
Prime: No Pricing
Production One Set

1 Mike Schmidt/Bat-Jsy/48 30.00
3 Babe Ruth/Bat-Jsy/25 300.00
5 Johnny Bench/Bat-Jsy/45 20.00
7 Willie McCovey/Bat-Jsy/23 20.00
8 Willie Stargell/Bat-Jsy/48 20.00
9 Ted Williams/Bat-Jsy/43 85.00
10 Frank Thomas/Jsy-Jsy/43 15.00
11 Gary Sheffield/Bat-Jsy/36 10.00
12 Jim Thome/Bat-Jsy/47 15.00
13 Harmon Killebrew/Bat-Jsy/49 25.00
14 Ernie Banks/Bat-Pants/47 25.00
15 George Foster/Bat-Jsy/52 10.00
16 Albert Pujols/Jsy-Jsy/46 40.00
17 Tony Perez/Bat-Fld Glv/24 15.00
18 Richie Sexson/Bat-Jsy/45 10.00
19 Juan Gonzalez/Bat-Jsy/47 10.00
21 Sammy Sosa/Bat-Jsy/66 15.00
22 Jeff Bagwell/Bat-Jsy/47 12.00
23 Mark Teixeira/Bat-Jsy/38 10.00
24 Willie Mays/Bat-Jsy/51 50.00
25 Rafael Palmeiro/Bat-Jsy/47 12.00
26 Billy Williams/Bat-Jsy/26 10.00
27 Vladimir Guerrero/Bat-Jsy/44 15.00
28 Gary Carter/Bat-Jsy/31 12.00
29 Fred McGriff/Bat-Jsy/32 15.00
30 Orlando Cepeda/Bat-Pants/34 12.00
31 Dave Winfield/Bat-Jsy/34 15.00
32 Shawn Green/Bat-Jsy/49 10.00
33 Jose Canseco/Hat-Jsy/44 12.00
34 Hideki Matsui/Bat-Pants/31 60.00
35 Roger Maris/Bat-Pants/19 50.00
36 Andre Dawson/Bat-Jsy/49 10.00
38 Darryl Strawberry/Jsy-Jsy/24 12.00
39 Dave Parker/Bat-Jsy/34 12.00
40 Adam Dunn/Bat-Jsy/46 15.00
42 Miguel Tejada/Bat-Jsy/34 15.00
43 Dale Murphy/Jsy-Jsy/44 15.00
44 Hank Aaron/Bat-Jsy/47 50.00
45 Mike Piazza/Jsy-Jsy/40 15.00
46 Reggie Jackson/Bat-Jsy/39 15.00
47 Adrian Beltre/Bat-Jsy/48 12.00
48 Cal Ripken Jr./Bat-Jsy/34 60.00
49 Manny Ramirez/Jsy-Jsy/43 15.00

Home Run Heroes Signature
No Pricing
Production 1-10

Home Run Heroes Signature Materials
No Pricing
Production 1-10

Legendary Lumberjacks
NM/M
Common Player: 2.00
Production 400 Sets
Gold: 2-4X
Production 50 Sets
Platinum: No Pricing
Production One Set

1 Al Kaline 4.00
2 Babe Ruth 8.00
3 Billy Williams 2.00
4 Bob Feller 3.00
5 Bob Gibson 3.00
6 Brooks Robinson 3.00
7 Cal Ripken Jr. 10.00
8 Carlton Fisk 3.00
9 Dennis Eckersley 2.00
10 Don Mattingly 6.00
11 Duke Snider 3.00
12 Eddie Murray 3.00
13 Ernie Banks 3.00
14 Fergie Jenkins 2.00
15 Frank Robinson 3.00
16 Gaylord Perry 2.00
17 George Brett 6.00
18 George Kell 2.00
19 Harmon Killebrew 4.00
20 Jim Palmer 2.00
21 Joe Morgan 2.00
22 Johnny Bench 3.00
23 Juan Marichal 2.00
24 Lou Brock 3.00
25 Maury Wills 2.00
26 Mike Schmidt 6.00
27 Nolan Ryan 4.00
28 Ozzie Smith 4.00
29 Paul Molitor 3.00
30 Pee Wee Reese 2.00
31 Phil Niekro 3.00
32 Phil Rizzuto 3.00
33 Ralph Kiner 2.00

34	Reggie Jackson	3.00
35	Rickey Henderson	3.00
36	Roberto Clemente	8.00
37	Robin Yount	4.00
38	Rod Carew	2.00
39	Roger Maris	5.00
40	Stan Musial	5.00
41	Steve Carlton	8.00
42	Ted Williams	2.00
43	Tom Seaver	3.00
44	Tony Gwynn	3.00
45	Tony Perez	2.00
46	Wade Boggs	3.00
47	Warren Spahn	4.00
48	Whitey Ford	4.00
49	Willie McCovey	3.00
50	Yogi Berra	4.00

Legendary Lumberjacks Bat
NM/M
Production 1-50

2	Babe Ruth/25	200.00
6	Brooks Robinson/50	15.00
7	Cal Ripken Jr./50	50.00
8	Carlton Fisk/50	10.00
10	Don Mattingly/50	25.00
12	Eddie Murray/50	15.00
13	Ernie Banks/50	15.00
15	Frank Robinson/50	15.00
17	George Brett/50	15.00
19	Harmon Killebrew/50	15.00
21	Joe Morgan/50	10.00
22	Johnny Bench/50	15.00
24	Lou Brock/50	10.00
26	Mike Schmidt/50	15.00
28	Ozzie Smith/50	15.00
29	Paul Molitor/50	12.00
30	Pee Wee Reese/50	15.00
34	Reggie Jackson/50	12.00
35	Rickey Henderson/50	12.00
36	Roberto Clemente/50	50.00
37	Robin Yount/50	15.00
38	Rod Carew/50	10.00
39	Roger Maris/50	40.00
40	Stan Musial/25	25.00
42	Ted Williams/25	60.00
44	Tony Gwynn/25	15.00
46	Wade Boggs/50	12.00
49	Willie McCovey/50	15.00
50	Yogi Berra/25	25.00

Legendary Lumberjacks Jersey
NM/M
Production 1-50

3	Billy Williams/25	12.00
6	Brooks Robinson/50	25.00
7	Cal Ripken Jr./50	50.00
8	Carlton Fisk/25	15.00
10	Don Mattingly/50	25.00
12	Eddie Murray/50	15.00
13	Ernie Banks/50	20.00
19	Harmon Killebrew/25	20.00
22	Johnny Bench/25	10.00
24	Lou Brock/25	12.00
25	Maury Wills/25	12.00
26	Mike Schmidt/25	20.00
28	Ozzie Smith/25	20.00
29	Paul Molitor/25	12.00
34	Reggie Jackson/25	15.00
35	Rickey Henderson/50	12.00
37	Robin Yount/50	15.00
38	Rod Carew/50	10.00

Legendary Lumberjacks Jersey HR
NM/M
Production 1-25

6	Brooks Robinson/25	20.00
7	Cal Ripken Jr./25	60.00
10	Don Mattingly/25	30.00
12	Eddie Murray/25	20.00
29	Paul Molitor/25	20.00
35	Rickey Henderson/25	20.00
37	Robin Yount/25	20.00
38	Rod Carew/25	15.00
44	Tony Gwynn/25	20.00
45	Tony Perez/25	15.00
46	Wade Boggs/25	15.00
49	Willie McCovey/25	15.00

Legendary Lumberjacks Materials
NM/M
Production 1-50

2	Babe Ruth/Bat-Jsy/25	300.00
6	Brooks Robinson/Bat-Jsy/50	20.00
7	Cal Ripken Jr./Bat-Jsy/25	60.00
8	Carlton Fisk/Bat-Jsy/25	15.00
10	Don Mattingly/Bat-Jsy/50	30.00
12	Eddie Murray/Bat-Jsy/50	20.00
13	Ernie Banks/Bat-Jsy/25	25.00
19	Harmon Killebrew/Bat-Jsy/50	20.00
22	Johnny Bench/Bat-Jsy/50	20.00
24	Lou Brock/Bat-Jsy/50	12.00
26	Mike Schmidt/Bat-Jsy/50	25.00
29	Paul Molitor/Bat-Jsy/50	15.00
34	Reggie Jackson/Bat-Jsy/50	20.00
35	Rickey Henderson/Bat-Jsy/50	15.00
37	Robin Yount/Bat-Jsy/50	20.00
38	Rod Carew/Bat-Jsy/50	15.00
44	Tony Gwynn/Bat-Jsy/50	20.00
46	Wade Boggs/Bat-Jsy/50	15.00
49	Willie McCovey/Bat-Jsy/44	15.00

Legendary Players
NM/M
Common Player: 1.50
Production 800 Sets
Gold: 2-3X
Production 75 Sets
Platinum: No Pricing
Production One Set

1	Al Kaline	3.00
2	Babe Ruth	6.00
3	Billy Williams	1.50
4	Bob Feller	2.00
5	Bob Gibson	2.00
6	Brooks Robinson	3.00
7	Cal Ripken Jr.	8.00
8	Carlton Fisk	2.00
9	Dennis Eckersley	2.00
10	Don Mattingly	5.00
11	Duke Snider	2.00
12	Eddie Murray	2.00
13	Ernie Banks	3.00
14	Fergie Jenkins	1.50
15	Frank Robinson	3.00
16	Gaylord Perry	1.50
17	George Brett	5.00
18	George Kell	1.50
19	Harmon Killebrew	3.00
20	Jim Palmer	1.50
21	Joe Morgan	1.50
22	Johnny Bench	4.00
23	Juan Marichal	1.50
24	Lou Brock	2.00
25	Maury Wills	1.50
26	Mike Schmidt	5.00
27	Nolan Ryan	8.00
28	Ozzie Smith	3.00
29	Paul Molitor	2.00
30	Pee Wee Reese	1.50
31	Phil Niekro	1.50
32	Phil Rizzuto	2.00
33	Ralph Kiner	1.50
34	Reggie Jackson	2.00
35	Rickey Henderson	2.00
36	Roberto Clemente	6.00
37	Robin Yount	3.00
38	Rod Carew	2.00
39	Roger Maris	4.00
40	Stan Musial	4.00
41	Steve Carlton	1.50
42	Ted Williams	6.00
43	Tom Seaver	2.00
44	Tony Gwynn	2.00
45	Tony Perez	1.50
46	Wade Boggs	2.00
47	Warren Spahn	3.00
48	Whitey Ford	3.00
49	Willie McCovey	2.00
50	Yogi Berra	3.00

Legendary Players Hat
NM/M
Production 1-25

10	Don Mattingly/25	30.00
13	Ernie Banks/25	20.00
17	George Brett/25	30.00
20	Jim Palmer/25	10.00
26	Mike Schmidt/25	30.00
28	Ozzie Smith/25	25.00
37	Robin Yount/25	25.00
44	Tony Gwynn/25	20.00

Legendary Players Jacket
NM/M
Production 25 Sets

7	Cal Ripken Jr.	60.00
8	Carlton Fisk	12.00
10	Don Mattingly	40.00
24	Lou Brock	15.00
26	Mike Schmidt	35.00
27	Nolan Ryan	50.00
34	Reggie Jackson	15.00
35	Rickey Henderson	20.00
38	Rod Carew	20.00
42	Ted Williams	85.00

Legendary Players Jersey Number
NM/M
Production 1-44
Prime: No Pricing
Production One Set

3	Billy Williams/26	10.00
8	Carlton Fisk/72	10.00
9	Dennis Eckersley/43	10.00
10	Don Mattingly/23	30.00
12	Eddie Murray/33	15.00
16	Gaylord Perry/36	8.00
20	Jim Palmer/22	15.00
23	Juan Marichal/27	10.00
24	Lou Brock/20	15.00
25	Maury Wills/30	8.00
26	Mike Schmidt/20	15.00
27	Nolan Ryan/34	40.00
31	Phil Niekro/35	8.00
35	Rickey Henderson/24	15.00
37	Robin Yount/19	25.00
38	Rod Carew/29	15.00
41	Steve Carlton/32	15.00
44	Tony Gwynn/19	20.00
45	Tony Perez/24	15.00
46	Wade Boggs/26	15.00
47	Warren Spahn/24	20.00
49	Willie McCovey/44	12.00

Legendary Players Leather
NM/M
Production 10-25

10	Don Mattingly/Btg Glv/25	40.00
14	Fergie Jenkins/Fld Glv/25	15.00
26	Mike Schmidt/Fld Glv/25	40.00
35	Rickey Henderson/Btg Glv/25	25.00
41	Steve Carlton/Fld Glv/25	15.00
44	Tony Gwynn/Btg Glv/25	30.00
45	Tony Perez/Fld Glv/25	15.00

Legendary Players Pants
NM/M
Production 1-25

4	Bob Feller/19	20.00
7	Cal Ripken Jr./25	60.00
11	Duke Snider/25	20.00
12	Eddie Murray/25	20.00
14	Fergie Jenkins/25	10.00
20	Jim Palmer/25	10.00
23	Juan Marichal/25	10.00
28	Ozzie Smith/25	25.00
29	Paul Molitor/25	15.00
35	Rickey Henderson/25	20.00
38	Rod Carew/25	15.00
39	Roger Maris/25	50.00
43	Tom Seaver/25	15.00
44	Tony Gwynn/25	20.00
47	Warren Spahn/24	20.00
49	Willie McCovey/25	15.00

Legendary Players Signature
No Pricing
Production 1-10

Legendary Players Spikes
NM/M
Production 1-25

| 15 | Frank Robinson/25 | 20.00 |
| 44 | Tony Gwynn/25 | 30.00 |

Membership
NM/M
Common Player: 1.50
Production 1,000 Sets
Gold: 2-4X
Production 50 Sets
Platinum: No Pricing
Production One Set

1	Bobby Doerr	1.50
2	Tom Seaver	2.00
3	Cal Ripken Jr.	8.00
4	Paul Molitor	2.00
5	Brooks Robinson	2.00
6	Al Kaline	4.00
7	Steve Carlton	2.00
8	Carl Yastrzemski	4.00
9	Bob Feller	2.00
10	Fred Lynn	1.50
11	Luis Aparicio	1.50
12	Hank Aaron	6.00
13	Willie Mays	6.00
14	Bob Gibson	3.00
15	Joe Morgan	2.00
16	Whitey Ford	3.00
17	Don Sutton	1.50
18	Harmon Killebrew	3.00
19	Tony Gwynn	3.00
20	Lou Brock	1.50
21	Dennis Eckersley	1.50
22	Jim Palmer	1.50
23	Don Mattingly	5.00
24	Carlton Fisk	2.00
25	Gaylord Perry	1.50
26	Mike Schmidt	5.00
27	Nolan Ryan	6.00
28	Sandy Koufax	10.00
29	Rod Carew	2.00
30	Maury Wills	1.50

Membership VIP Bat
NM/M
Production 25 Sets

1	Bobby Doerr	10.00
2	Tom Seaver	20.00
3	Cal Ripken Jr.	60.00
4	Paul Molitor	15.00
5	Brooks Robinson	15.00
6	Al Kaline	20.00
7	Steve Carlton	10.00
8	Carl Yastrzemski	20.00
10	Fred Lynn	8.00
11	Luis Aparicio	8.00
12	Hank Aaron	40.00
13	Willie Mays	50.00
15	Joe Morgan	10.00
18	Harmon Killebrew	20.00
19	Tony Gwynn	20.00
20	Lou Brock	15.00
23	Don Mattingly	30.00
24	Carlton Fisk	15.00
29	Rod Carew	12.00

Membership VIP Jersey
NM/M
Production 5-50
Prime: No Pricing
Production One Set

7	Steve Carlton/25	10.00
10	Fred Lynn/25	10.00
11	Luis Aparicio/25	10.00
15	Joe Morgan/25	10.00
17	Don Sutton/50	8.00
19	Tony Gwynn/50	15.00
20	Lou Brock/25	15.00
21	Dennis Eckersley/50	8.00
22	Jim Palmer/25	15.00
23	Don Mattingly/25	30.00
24	Carlton Fisk/25	15.00
25	Gaylord Perry/50	8.00
26	Mike Schmidt/50	20.00
27	Nolan Ryan/25	40.00
29	Rod Carew/50	10.00

Membership VIP Materials
NM/M
Production 5-25
Prime: No Pricing
Production One Set

1	Bobby Doerr/Bat-Pants/25	10.00
2	Tom Seaver/Bat-Jsy/25	20.00
3	Cal Ripken Jr./Bat-Jsy/25	75.00
4	Paul Molitor/Bat-Jsy/25	20.00
5	Brooks Robinson/Bat-Jsy/25	25.00
7	Steve Carlton/Bat-Jsy/25	15.00
10	Fred Lynn/Bat-Jsy/25	10.00
11	Luis Aparicio/Bat-Jsy/25	10.00
15	Joe Morgan/Bat-Jsy/25	12.00
18	Harmon Killebrew/Bat-Jsy/25	25.00
19	Tony Gwynn/Bat-Jsy/25	25.00
20	Lou Brock/Bat-Jsy/25	25.00
23	Don Mattingly/Bat-Jsy/25	35.00
27	Nolan Ryan/Bat-Jsy/25	50.00
29	Rod Carew/Bat-Jsy/25	20.00

Membership VIP Materials Awards
No Pricing
Production 5-10

Membership VIP Materials HOF
No Pricing
Production 10 Sets

Membership VIP Materials HR
NM/M
Production 6-49

1	Bobby Doerr/Jsy-Pants/27	15.00
3	Cal Ripken Jr./Jsy-Pants/34	60.00
4	Paul Molitor/Bat-Jsy/22	15.00
8	Carl Yastrzemski/Bat-Jsy/44	25.00
10	Fred Lynn/Bat-Jsy/39	8.00
12	Hank Aaron/Bat-Jsy/47	50.00
15	Joe Morgan/Bat-Jsy/27	12.00
18	Harmon Killebrew/Bat-Jsy/49	20.00
20	Lou Brock/Bat-Jsy/21	15.00
23	Don Mattingly/Bat-Jsy/40	40.00
24	Carlton Fisk/Bat-Jsy/37	15.00
26	Mike Schmidt/Bat-Jsy/48	25.00

Membership VIP Materials Stats
No Pricing
Production 10 Sets

Membership VIP Signature
No Pricing
Production 1-5

Membership VIP Signature Bat
No Pricing
Production 1-10

Membership VIP Signature Jersey
No Pricing
Production 1-10

Membership VIP Signature Material
NM/M
Production 1-25
Prime: No Pricing
Production One Set

1	Bobby Doerr/Bat-Pants/25	35.00
10	Fred Lynn/Bat-Jsy/25	30.00
11	Luis Aparicio/Bat-Jsy/25	30.00
20	Lou Brock/Bat-Jsy/25	50.00

Membership VIP Sign. Mat. Awards
No Pricing
Production 1-10

Membership VIP Signature Materials HOF
No Pricing
Production 1-10

Membership VIP Signature Materials HR
No Pricing
Production 1-10

Membership VIP Signture Material Stats
No Pricing
Production 5-10

Significant Signatures Silver
NM/M
Production 1-200
Gold: .75-1.5X
Production 1-100
No pricing 20 or less.
Platinum: No Pricing
Production One Set

17	Jay Gibbons/25	15.00
26	Tim Salmon/100	15.00
26	Kevin Youkilis/25	12.00
29	Cliff Lee/200	8.00
37	Jeff Suppan/200	10.00
39	Larry Bigbie/100	15.00
40	Rich Harden/100	15.00
43	Victor Martinez/25	20.00
43	Joey Gathright/100	8.00
61	Jake Peavy/25	40.00
63	Dioner Navarro/100	15.00
64	Kazuhito Tadano/100	15.00
65	Ryan Wagner/50	10.00
66	Abe Alvarez/100	15.00
69	Jermaine Dye/25	15.00
73	Todd Walker/25	15.00
76	Octavio Dotel/25	15.00
73	Scott Podsednik/25	20.00
76	Raul Ibanez/50	15.00
79	Orlando Cabrera/25	20.00
84	Esteban Loaiza/50	15.00
85	David Dellucci/25	20.00
86	Travis Blackley/200	8.00
88	Brad Penny/25	35.00
90	Brian Roberts/100	35.00
94	Mike Lieberthal/25	15.00
96	Milton Bradley/100	15.00
96	Adrian Gonzalez/200	12.00
98	Chad Tracy/100	15.00
102	Chad Cordero/100	8.00
102	Jason Kubel/200	12.00
104	Jack Wilson/100	10.00
104	Casey Kotchman/100	12.00
106	Melvin Mora/100	15.00
107	Bobby Crosby/100	15.00
111	Francisco Cordero/50	15.00
114	Eric Byrnes/50	10.00
118	Shea Hillenbrand/25	15.00
119	Aubrey Huff/25	20.00
120	Lew Ford/25	20.00
126	Adam LaRoche/25	15.00
128	Ken Harvey/50	10.00
132	Russ Ortiz/25	15.00
133	Jason Varitek/25	15.00
136	Joe Nathan/100	20.00
138	Carlos Zambrano/25	35.00
143	John Lackey/100	15.00
145	Dewon Brazelton/200	10.00
146	Jason Bay/25	25.00
148	Travis Hafner/100	12.00
152	Wade Miller/50	12.00
154	Scott Kazmir/25	15.00
156	Livan Hernandez/25	15.00
158	David Wright/25	85.00
159	Chone Figgins/100	12.00
163	Merkin Valdez/200	10.00
165	Alexis Rios/50	15.00
166	Johnny Estrada/200	10.00
167	Danny Graves/50	15.00
168	Carlos Lee/25	25.00
171	Randy Wolf/25	15.00
175	Edwin Jackson/25	12.00
178	Jacque Jones/25	15.00
180	Laynce Nix/200	10.00
181	Tom Gordon/25	15.00
182	Jose Castillo/100	12.00
188	Keith Foulke/25	60.00
189	Jeremy Bonderman/50	20.00
190	Troy Percival/25	15.00
194	Brett Myers/15	15.00
197	Lyle Overbay/25	20.00
202	Miguel Negron/100	8.00
204	Paulino Reynoso/100	10.00
205	Colter Bean/100	10.00
206	Raul Tablado/100	8.00
207	Mark McLemore/100	8.00
208	Russel Rohlicek/100	8.00
210	Chris Seddon/100	8.00
213	Mike Morse/100	20.00
217	Carlos Ruiz/100	15.00
218	Chris Roberson/100	8.00
219	Ryan Speier/100	8.00
221	Ambiorix Burgos/100	8.00
223	David Gassner/100	8.00
224	Sean Tracey/100	8.00
225	Casey Rogowski/100	8.00
236	Gaylord Perry LGD/25	25.00
245	Bobby Doerr LGD/25	25.00
246	Bob Feller LGD/25	30.00

Stars of Summer

NM/M
Common Player: 1.50
Production 1,000 Sets
Gold: 2-4X
Production 50 Sets
Platinum: No Pricing
Production One Set

1	Andre Dawson	2.00
2	Bert Blyleven	2.00
3	Bill Madlock	1.50
4	Dale Murphy	3.00
5	Darryl Strawberry	2.00
6	Dave Parker	2.00

7	Dave Righetti	2.00
8	Dwight Evans	2.00
9	Dwight Gooden	2.00
10	Fred Lynn	1.50
11	George Foster	2.00
12	Harold Baines	2.00
13	Jack Morris	1.50
14	Jim Rice	3.00
15	Keith Hernandez	2.00
16	Kirk Gibson	2.00
17	Luis Aparicio	2.00
18	Mark Grace	2.00
19	Marty Marion	1.50
20	Orel Hershiser	2.00
21	Ron Guidry	3.00
22	Ron Santo	2.00
23	Steve Garvey	2.00
24	Tony Oliva	2.00
25	Will Clark	3.00

Stars of Summer Material

NM/M

Production 100-250

1	Andre Dawson/Jsy/250	8.00
2	Bert Blyleven/Jsy/150	8.00
3	Bill Madlock/Bat/250	5.00
4	Dale Murphy/Jsy/100	12.00
5	Darryl Strawberry/Jsy/250	8.00
6	Dave Parker/Jsy/100	10.00
7	Dave Righetti/Jsy/100	8.00
8	Dwight Evans/Bat/250	8.00
9	Dwight Gooden/Bat/150	8.00
10	Fred Lynn/Jsy/100	5.00
11	George Foster/Bat/250	5.00
12	Harold Baines/Jsy/250	5.00
13	Jack Morris/Jsy/100	5.00
14	Jim Rice/Pants/250	8.00
15	Keith Hernandez/Bat/100	5.00
16	Kirk Gibson/Jsy/250	8.00
17	Luis Aparicio/Bat/250	8.00
18	Mark Grace/Bat/250	10.00
22	Ron Santo/Bat/150	10.00
23	Steve Garvey/Jsy/250	8.00
24	Tony Oliva/Jsy/250	8.00
25	Will Clark/Bat/250	10.00

Stars of Summer Signature Material

NM/M

Production 25-100

1	Andre Dawson/Jsy/100	20.00
2	Bert Blyleven/Jsy/50	20.00
3	Bill Madlock/Bat/100	20.00
4	Dale Murphy/Jsy/25	40.00
6	Dave Parker/Jsy/50	20.00
7	Dave Righetti/Jsy/50	20.00
8	Dwight Evans/Jsy/50	30.00
9	Dwight Gooden/Bat/25	25.00
10	Fred Lynn/Jsy/100	15.00
11	George Foster/Bat/50	20.00
12	Harold Baines/Jsy/100	25.00
13	Jack Morris/Jsy/100	15.00
14	Jim Rice/Pants/50	25.00
15	Keith Hernandez/Jsy/50	
16	Kirk Gibson/Jsy/25	40.00
17	Luis Aparicio/Bat/50	20.00
18	Mark Grace/Bat/50	40.00
22	Ron Santo/Bat/50	35.00
23	Steve Garvey/Jsy/50	20.00
24	Tony Oliva/Jsy/50	20.00
25	Will Clark/Bat/25	40.00

Team Colors

NM/M

Common Player: 1.50

Production 800 Sets

Gold: 2-4X

Production 50 Sets

Platinum: No Pricing

Production One Set

1	Adam Dunn	2.00
2	Albert Pujols	6.00
3	Andruw Jones	2.00
4	Aramis Ramirez	2.00
5	Aubrey Huff	1.50
6	Bobby Abreu	2.00
7	Cal Ripken Jr.	8.00
8	Carlos Lee	1.50
9	Craig Biggio	2.00
10	Derrek Lee	2.00
11	Garret Anderson	2.00
12	Gary Carter	2.00
13	Geoff Jenkins	1.50
14	Greg Maddux	4.00
15	Hank Blalock	2.00
16	Hideki Matsui	5.00
17	Jake Peavy	2.00
18	Jim Edmonds	2.00
19	Jim Palmer	2.00
20	Jose Guillen	1.50
21	Jose Vidro	1.50
22	Juan Pierre	1.50
23	Lew Ford	1.50
24	Lyle Overbay	1.50
25	Manny Ramirez	3.00
26	Mark Loretta	1.50
27	Mark Teixeira	3.00
28	Melvin Mora	1.50
29	Michael Young	2.00
30	Miguel Cabrera	4.00
31	Mike Lowell	1.50
32	Mike Mussina	2.00
33	Milton Bradley	2.00
34	Randy Johnson	4.00
35	Roger Clemens	6.00
36	Sean Casey	2.00
37	Shawn Green	2.00
38	Steve Carlton	2.00
39	Todd Helton	2.00
40	Travis Hafner	1.50

Team Colors Bat

NM/M

Production 100 Sets

1	Adam Dunn	8.00
2	Albert Pujols	20.00
3	Andruw Jones	5.00
4	Aramis Ramirez	8.00
7	Cal Ripken Jr.	30.00
9	Craig Biggio	8.00
10	Derrek Lee	8.00
11	Garret Anderson	5.00
12	Gary Carter	5.00
15	Hank Blalock	8.00
16	Hideki Matsui	30.00
18	Jim Edmonds	10.00
21	Jose Vidro	5.00
22	Juan Pierre	5.00
23	Lew Ford	5.00
27	Mark Teixeira	5.00
28	Melvin Mora	5.00
29	Michael Young	5.00
30	Miguel Cabrera	10.00
31	Mike Lowell	5.00
36	Sean Casey	5.00
37	Shawn Green	5.00

Team Colors Materials

NM/M

Production 25-100

Prime: No Pricing

Production 5 Sets

1	Adam Dunn/Bat-Jsy/100	10.00
2	Albert Pujols/Bat-Jsy/100	25.00
3	Andruw Jones/Bat-Jsy/100	8.00
4	Aramis Ramirez/Bat-Jsy/100	10.00
6	Bobby Abreu/Jsy-Jsy/100	10.00
7	Cal Ripken Jr./Bat-Jsy/100	40.00
8	Carlos Lee/Jsy-Jsy/100	8.00
9	Craig Biggio/Bat-Jsy/100	8.00
11	Garret Anderson/Bat-Jsy/50	8.00
12	Gary Carter/Bat-Jsy/50	8.00
13	Geoff Jenkins/Jsy-Pants/100	8.00
15	Hank Blalock/Bat-Jsy/100	10.00
16	Hideki Matsui/Bat-Jsy/50	45.00
18	Jim Edmonds/Bat-Jkt/25	12.00
19	Jim Palmer/Jsy-Pants/25	12.00
21	Jose Vidro/Bat-Jsy/50	8.00
23	Lew Ford/Bat-Jsy/100	8.00
25	Manny Ramirez/Jsy-Jsy/100	15.00
27	Mark Teixeira/Bat-Jsy/100	10.00
29	Melvin Mora/Bat-Jsy/100	8.00
30	Michael Young/Bat-Jsy/100	8.00
30	Miguel Cabrera/Bat-Jsy/100	15.00
31	Mike Lowell/Bat-Jsy/100	8.00
36	Sean Casey/Bat-Jsy/100	8.00
37	Shawn Green/Bat-Jsy/100	8.00
39	Todd Helton/Jsy-Jsy/50	10.00

Team Colors Signature

NM/M

Production 1-25

4	Aramis Ramirez/25	40.00
5	Aubrey Huff/25	20.00
8	Carlos Lee/25	25.00
17	Jake Peavy/25	40.00
20	Jose Guillen/25	25.00
21	Jose Vidro/25	20.00
23	Lew Ford/25	20.00
24	Lyle Overbay/25	25.00
26	Mark Loretta/25	25.00
28	Melvin Mora/25	25.00
33	Milton Bradley/25	25.00
40	Travis Hafner/25	20.00

Team Colors Signature Bat

NM/M

Production 5-25

1	Adam Dunn/25	40.00
4	Aramis Ramirez/25	40.00
5	Aubrey Huff/25	20.00
10	Derrek Lee/25	35.00
11	Garret Anderson/25	25.00
15	Hank Blalock/25	30.00
21	Jose Vidro/25	20.00
23	Lew Ford/25	20.00
29	Michael Young/25	20.00

Team Colors Signature Jersey

NM/M

Production 1-25

Prime: No Pricing

Production One Set

1	Adam Dunn/25	40.00
4	Aramis Ramirez/25	40.00
5	Aubrey Huff/25	20.00
8	Carlos Lee/25	25.00
11	Garret Anderson/25	25.00
12	Gary Carter/25	30.00
15	Hank Blalock/25	30.00
21	Jose Vidro/25	20.00
23	Lew Ford/25	20.00
24	Lyle Overbay/25	25.00
28	Melvin Mora/25	25.00
29	Michael Young/25	20.00
40	Travis Hafner/25	20.00

Team Colors Signature Materials

NM/M

Production 5-25

Prime: No Pricing

Production One Set

4	Aramis Ramirez/Bat-Jsy/25	50.00
5	Aubrey Huff/Jsy-Jsy/25	25.00
8	Carlos Lee/Jsy-Jsy/25	30.00
11	Garret Anderson/Bat-Jsy/25	30.00
15	Hank Blalock/Bat-Jsy/25	40.00
21	Jose Vidro/BatBat-Jsy/25	25.00
23	Lew Ford/Bat-Jsy/25	25.00
28	Melvin Mora/Bat-Jsy/25	30.00
29	Michael Young/Bat-Jsy/25	30.00
40	Travis Hafner/Jsy-Jsy/25	25.00

Texas Rangers Hall of Fame

This cello-wrapped set was a stadium giveaway.

NM/M

Complete Set (9): 7.00

Common Player: .25

(1)	Buddy Bell	.50
(2)	Mark Holtz (Broadcaster)	.25
(3)	Charlie Hough	.50
(4)	Ferguson Jenkins	.75
(5)	Johnny Oates	.25
(6)	Nolan Ryan	5.00
(7)	Jim Sundberg	.50
(8)	Tom Vandergriff (Broadcaster)	.25
(9)	John Wetteland	.50

2005 Donruss Diamond Kings

NM/M

Complete Set (300): 85.00

Complete Update Set (150): 40.00

Common Player: .25

Pack (5): 8.00

Box (12): 75.00

Update Pack (5): 5.00

Update Box (16): 75.00

1	Garret Anderson	.40
2	Vladimir Guerrero	.75
3	Jose Guillen	.40
4	Troy Glaus	.40
5	Tim Salmon	.25
6	Casey Kotchman	.25
7	Chone Figgins	.25
8	Robb Quinlan	.25
9	Francisco Rodriguez	.25
10	Troy Percival	.25
11	Randy Johnson	.75
12	Brandon Webb	.25
13	Richie Sexson	.40
14	Shea Hillenbrand	.25
15	Chad Tracy	.25
16	Alex Cintron	.25
17	Luis Gonzalez	.25
18	Rafael Furcal	.25
19	Andruw Jones	.50
20	Marcus Giles	.25
21	John Smoltz	.50
22	Adam LaRoche	.25
23	Russ Ortiz	.25
24	J.D. Drew	.25
25	Chipper Jones	.75
26	Nick Green	.25
27	Rafael Palmeiro	.50
28	Miguel Tejada	.50
29	Javy Lopez	.25
30	Luis Matos	.25
31	Larry Bigbie	.25
32	Rodrigo Lopez	.25
33	Brian Roberts	.25
34	Melvin Mora	.25
35	Adam Loewen	.25
36	Manny Ramirez	.50
37	Jason Varitek	.50
38	Trot Nixon	.25
39	Curt Schilling	.75
40	Keith Foulke	.25
41	Pedro Martinez	.75
42	Johnny Damon	.75
43	Kevin Youkilis	.25
44	Orlando Cabrera	.25
45	Abe Alvarez	.25
46	David Ortiz	.75
47	Kerry Wood	.75
48	Mark Prior	.75
49	Aramis Ramirez	.25
50	Greg Maddux	1.00
51	Carlos Zambrano	.40
52	Derrek Lee	.50
53	Corey Patterson	.40
54	Moises Alou	.40
55	Matt Clement	.25
56	Sammy Sosa	1.50
57	Nomar Garciaparra	1.00
58	Todd Walker	.25
59	Angel Guzman	.25
60	Magglio Ordonez	.40
61	Carlos Lee	.25
62	Joe Crede	.25
63	Paul Konerko	.25
64	Shingo Takatsu	.25
65	Frank Thomas	.50
66	Freddy Garcia	.25
67	Aaron Rowand	.25
68	Jose Contreras	.25
69	Adam Dunn	.50
70	Austin Kearns	.25
71	Barry Larkin	.40
72	Ken Griffey Jr.	1.00
73	Ryan Wagner	.25
74	Sean Casey	.25
75	Danny Graves	.25
76	C.C. Sabathia	.40
77	Jody Gerut	.25
78	Omar Vizquel	.40
79	Victor Martinez	.40
80	Matt Lawton	.25
81	Jake Westbrook	.25
82	Kazuhito Tadano	.25
83	Travis Hafner	.25
84	Todd Helton	.50
85	Preston Wilson	.25
86	Matt Holliday	.25
87	Jeromy Burnitz	.25
88	Vinny Castilla	.25
89	Jeremy Bonderman	.25
90	Ivan Rodriguez	.50
91	Carlos Guillen	.25
92	Brandon Inge	.25
93	Rondell White	.25
94	Dontrelle Willis	.25
95	Miguel Cabrera	.75
96	Josh Beckett	.40
97	Mike Lowell	.25
98	Luis Castillo	.25
99	Juan Pierre	.25
100	Paul LoDuca	.25
101	Guillermo Mota	.25
102	Craig Biggio	.25
103	Lance Berkman	.25
104	Roy Oswalt	.25
105	Roger Clemens	2.00
106	Jeff Kent	.25
107	Morgan Ensberg	.25
108	Jeff Bagwell	.25
109	Carlos Beltran	.50
110	Angel Berroa	.25
111	Mike Sweeney	.25
112	Jeremy Affeldt	.25
113	Zack Greinke	.25
114	Juan Gonzalez	.25
115	Andres Blanco	.25
116	Shawn Green	.25
117	Milton Bradley	.25
118	Adrian Beltre	.50
119	Hideo Nomo	.50
120	Steve Finley	.25
121	Eric Gagne	.25
122	Brad Penny	.25
123	Scott Podsednik	.25
124	Ben Sheets	.40
125	Lyle Overbay	.25
126	Junior Spivey	.25
127	Bill Hall	.25
128	Rickie Weeks	.25
129	Jacque Jones	.25
130	Torii Hunter	.40
131	Johan Santana	.25
132	Lew Ford	.25
133	Joe Mauer	.75
134	Justin Morneau	.25
135	Jason Kubel	.25
136	Jose Vidro	.25
137	Chad Cordero	.25
138	Brad Wilkerson	.25
139	Nick Johnson	.25
140	Livan Hernandez	.25
141	Tom Glavine	.40
142	Jae Weong Seo	.25
143	Jose Reyes	.50
144	Al Leiter	.25
145	Mike Piazza	1.00
146	Kazuo Matsui	.25
147	Richard Hidalgo	.25
148	David Wright	.75
149	Mariano Rivera	.50
150	Mike Mussina	.25
151	Alex Rodriguez	1.50
152	Derek Jeter	1.50
153	Jorge Posada	.50
154	Jason Giambi	.25
155	Gary Sheffield	.50
156	Bubba Crosby	.25
157	Javier Vazquez	.25
158	Kevin Brown	.25
159	Tom Gordon	.25
160	Esteban Loaiza	.25
161	Hideki Matsui	1.50
162	Eric Chavez	.40
163	Mark Mulder	.40
164	Barry Zito	.40
165	Tim Hudson	.40
166	Jermaine Dye	.25
167	Octavio Dotel	.25
168	Bobby Crosby	.25
169	Mark Kotsay	.25
170	Scott Hatteberg	.25
171	Jim Thome	.75
172	Bobby Abreu	.40
173	Kevin Millwood	.25
174	Mike Lieberthal	.25
175	Jimmy Rollins	.50
176	Chase Utley	.50
177	Randy Wolf	.25
178	Craig Wilson	.25
179	Jason Kendall	.25
180	Jack Wilson	.25
181	Jose Castillo	.25
182	Robert Mackowiak	.25
183	Oliver Perez	.25
184	Oliver Perez	.25
185	Sean Burroughs	.25
186	Jay Payton	.25
187	Brian Giles	.25
188	Akinori Otsuka	.25
189	Jake Peavy	.25
190	Phil Nevin	.25
191	Mark Loretta	.25
192	Khalil Greene	.40
193	Trevor Hoffman	.25
194	Freddy Guzman	.25
195	Jerome Williams	.25
196	Jason Schmidt	.40
197	Todd Linden	.25
198	Merkin Valdez	.25
199	J.T. Snow	.25
200	A.J. Pierzynski	.40
201	Edgar Martinez	.40
202	Ichiro Suzuki	1.50
203	Raul Ibanez	.25
204	Bret Boone	.25
205	Shigetoshi Hasegawa	.25
206	Miguel Olivo	.25
207	Bucky Jacobsen	.25
208	Jamie Moyer	.25
209	Jim Edmonds	.50
210	Scott Rolen	.75
211	Edgar Renteria	.50
212	Dan Haren	.25
213	Matt Morris	.25
214	Albert Pujols	2.00
215	Larry Walker	.40
216	Jason Isringhausen	.25
217	Chris Carpenter	.25
218	Jason Marquis	.25
219	Jeff Suppan	.25
220	Aubrey Huff	.25
221	Carl Crawford	.25
222	Rocco Baldelli	.25
223	Fred McGriff	.25
224	Dewon Brazelton	.25
225	B.J. Upton	.40
226	Joey Gathright	.25
227	Scott Kazmir	.40
228	Hank Blalock	.50
229	Mark Teixeira	.50
230	Michael Young	.25
231	Adrian Gonzalez	.25
232	Laynce Nix	.25
233	Alfonso Soriano	.75
234	Rafael Palmeiro	.50
235	Kevin Mench	.25
236	David Dellucci	.25
237	Francisco Cordero	.25
238	Kenny Rogers	.25
239	Roy Halladay	.25
240	Carlos Delgado	.40
241	Alexis Rios	.25
242	Vernon Wells	.25
243	Yadier Molina	.25
244	Rene Rivera	.25
245	Logan Kensing	.25
246	Gavin Floyd	.25
247	Russ Adams	.25
248	Dioner Navarro	.25
249	Ryan Howard	1.00
250	Ryan Church	.25
251	Jeff Francis	.25
252	John Van Benschoten	.25
253	Yhency Brazoban	.25
254	David Krynzel	.25
255	Victor Diaz	.25
256	Jairo Garcia	.25
257	Scott Proctor	.25
258	Shawn Hill	.25
259	Jeff Baker	.25
260	Matt Peterson	.25
261	Josh Kroeger	.25
262	Grady Sizemore	.50
263	Clint Nageotte	.25
264	Andy Green	.25
265	Justin Verlander RC	2.00
266	Jim Thome	.75
267	Larry Walker	.40
268	Ivan Rodriguez	.50
269	Brad Penny	.25
270	Carlos Beltran	.50
271	Paul LoDuca	.25
272	Orlando Cabrera	.25
273	Nomar Garciaparra	1.00
274	Esteban Loaiza	.25
275	Richard Hidalgo	.25
276	John Olerud	.25
277	Greg Maddux	1.00
278	Roger Clemens	2.00
279	Alfonso Soriano	.75

280	Dale Murphy	.50
281	Cal Ripken Jr.	4.00
282	Dwight Evans	.25
283	Ron Santo	.25
284	Andre Dawson	.50
285	Harold Baines	.25
286	Jack Morris	.25
287	Kirk Gibson	.25
288	Bo Jackson	.75
289	Orel Hershiser	.25
290	Maury Wills	.25
291	Tony Oliva	.25
292	Darryl Strawberry	.25
293	Roger Maris	1.00
294	Don Mattingly	2.00
295	Rickey Henderson	.50
296	Dave Stewart	.25
297	Dave Parker	.25
298	Steve Garvey	.25
299	Matt Williams	.25
300	Keith Hernandez	.25
301	John Lackey	.25
302	Vladimir Guerrero	.75
303	Garret Anderson	.25
304	Dallas McPherson	.25
305	Orlando Cabrera	.25
306	Steve Finley	.25
307	Luis Gonzalez	.25
308	Randy Johnson	.75
309	Scott Hairston	.25
310	Shawn Green	.25
311	Troy Glaus	.40
312	Javier Vazquez	.25
313	Russ Ortiz	.25
314	Chipper Jones	.75
315	Johnny Estrada	.25
316	Andruw Jones	.50
317	Tim Hudson	.25
318	Danny Kolb	.25
319	Jay Gibbons	.25
320	Melvin Mora	.25
321	Rafael Palmeiro	.25
322	Val Majewski	.25
323	David Ortiz	.75
324	Manny Ramirez	.75
325	Edgar Renteria	.25
326	Matt Clement	.25
327	Curt Schilling	.75
328	Sammy Sosa	1.00
329	Mark Prior	.75
330	Greg Maddux	1.00
331	Nomar Garciaparra	1.00
332	Frank Thomas	.50
333	Mark Buehrle	.25
334	Jermaine Dye	.25
335	Scott Podsednik	.25
336	Sean Casey	.25
337	Adam Dunn	.50
338	Ken Griffey Jr.	1.00
339	Travis Hafner	.25
340	Victor Martinez	.25
341	Cliff Lee	.25
342	Todd Helton	.50
343	Preston Wilson	.25
344	Ivan Rodriguez	.50
345	Dmitri Young	.25
346	Nate Robertson	.25
347	Miguel Cabrera	.75
348	Jeff Bagwell	.40
349	Andy Pettitte	.40
350	Roger Clemens	2.00
351	Ken Harvey	.25
352	Danny Bautista	.25
353	Hideo Nomo	.50
354	Kazuhisa Ishii	.25
355	Edwin Jackson	.25
356	J.D. Drew	.25
357	Jeff Kent	.25
358	Geoff Jenkins	.25
359	Carlos Lee	.25
360	Shannon Stewart	.25
361	Joe Nathan	.25
362	Johan Santana	.50
363	Mike Piazza	1.00
364	Hideki Matsui	.25
365	Carlos Beltran	.50
366	Pedro Martinez	.75
367	Ambiorix Concepcion RC	.40
368	Hideki Matsui	1.50
369	Bernie Williams	.40
370	Gary Sheffield	.50
371	Randy Johnson	.75
372	Jaret Wright	.25
373	Carl Pavano	.25
374	Derek Jeter	2.00
375	Alex Rodriguez	1.50
376	Eric Byrnes	.25
377	Rich Harden	.25
378	Mark Mulder	.40
379	Nick Swisher	.25
380	Eric Chavez	.25
381	Jason Kendall	.25
382	Marlon Byrd	.25
383	Pat Burrell	.25
384	Brett Myers	.25
385	Jim Thome	.50
386	Jason Bay	.25
387	Jake Peavy	.25
388	Moises Alou	.25
389	Omar Vizquel	.25
390	Travis Blackley	.25
391	Jose Lopez	.25
392	Jeremy Reed	.25
393	Adrian Beltre	.25
394	Richie Sexson	.25
395	Wladimir Balentien RC	1.50
396	Ichiro Suzuki	1.50
397	Albert Pujols	2.00
398	Scott Rolen	.75
399	Mark Mulder	.40
400	David Eckstein	.25
401	Delmon Young	.25
402	Aubrey Huff	.25
403	Alfonso Soriano	.50
404	Hank Blalock	.25
405	Richard Hidalgo	.25
406	Vernon Wells	.25
407	Orlando Hudson	.25
408	Alexis Rios	.25
409	Shea Hillenbrand	.25
410	Jose Guillen	.25
411	Vinny Castilla	.25
412	Jose Vidro	.25
413	Nick Johnson	.25
414	Livan Hernandez	.25
415	Miguel Tejada	.50
416	Gary Sheffield	.50
417	Curt Schilling	.75
418	Rafael Palmeiro	.50
419	Scott Rolen	.75
420	Aramis Ramirez	.40
421	Vladimir Guerrero	.75
422	Steve Finley	.25
423	Roger Clemens	2.00
424	Mike Piazza	1.00
425	Ivan Rodriguez	.50
426	David Justice	.25
427	Mark Grace	.40
428	Alan Trammell	.25
429	Bert Blyleven	.25
430	Dwight Gooden	.25
431	Deion Sanders	.25
432	Joe Torre	.25
433	Jose Canseco	.40
434	Tony Gwynn	.75
435	Will Clark	.40
436	Marty Marion	.25
437	Nolan Ryan	3.00
438	Billy Martin	.25
439	Carlos Delgado	.25
440	Magglio Ordonez	.25
441	Sammy Sosa	1.00
442	Keiichi Yabu RC	.50
443	Yuniesky Betancourt RC	1.00
444	Jeff Niemann RC	1.50
445	Brandon McCarthy RC	1.50
446	Philip Humber RC	1.50
447	Tadahito Iguchi RC	2.00
448	Cal Ripken Jr.	4.00
449	Ryne Sandberg	2.00
450	Willie Mays	2.00

Non-Canvas
No Pricing
Production 20 Sets

Bronze

Stars: 3-5X
Production 100 Sets
Update Bronze (301-450): 3-5X
Production 50

Silver
Silvers: 4-8X
Production 50 Sets
Update (301-450): No Pricing
Production 25 Sets

Silver B/W
Silvers: 4-8X
Production 50 Sets

Gold
Golds: 5-10X
Production 25 Sets
Gold Update (301-450): No Pricing
Production 10 Sets

Platinum
No Pricing
Production One Set
Framed Platinums: No Pricing
Production One Set

Framed Black
Stars: 5-10X
Production 25 Sets

Framed Blue

Stars: 5-10X
Production 25 Sets

Framed Green
Stars: 4-8X
Production 50 Sets

Framed Red
Stars: 1-3X
Inserted 1:3

Diamond Cuts Bat
NM/M
Common Player: 4.00

1	Adam Dunn/200	8.00
2	Adrian Beltre/200	6.00
3	Alfonso Soriano/50	8.00
4	Andruw Jones/200	4.00
5	Andy Pettitte/50	6.00
6	Aramis Ramirez/100	6.00
8	Brian Giles/200	4.00
10	Carlos Beltran/200	6.00
12	Craig Wilson/200	4.00
13	Curt Schilling/50	10.00
14	Darin Erstad/200	6.00
16	Derrek Lee/200	6.00
17	Fred McGriff/100	6.00
19	Ivan Rodriguez/200	6.00
21	Jason Bay/200	4.00
22	Jason Giambi/100	4.00
23	Jeff Kent/200	4.00
25	Juan Gonzalez/200	6.00
27	Kazuhisa Ishii/50	6.00
28	Kevin Brown/100	6.00
29	Larry Walker/200	6.00
31	Mark Teixeira/200	6.00
32	Melvin Mora/50	4.00
33	Michael Young/200	4.00
34	Miguel Tejada/100	8.00
35	Mike Mussina/50	8.00
36	Paul LoDuca/200	6.00
37	Preston Wilson/200	4.00
38	Randy Johnson/200	10.00
39	Richie Sexson/200	6.00
40	Roger Clemens/200	15.00
41	Scott Rolen/100	8.00
42	Sean Burroughs/200	4.00
43	Sean Casey/200	4.00
44	Shannon Stewart/200	4.00
45	Shawn Green/200	4.00
47	Tim Salmon/200	4.00
48	Tom Glavine/200	6.00
49	Torii Hunter/200	6.00

Diamond Cuts Jersey
NM/M
Common Player: 4.00
Prime: No Pricing
Production One Set

1	Adam Dunn/50	10.00
2	Adrian Beltre/200	6.00
3	Alfonso Soriano/200	8.00
4	Andruw Jones/200	4.00
5	Andy Pettitte/100	6.00
6	Aramis Ramirez/200	6.00
7	Brian Giles/200	4.00
8	C.C. Sabathia/200	4.00
9	Carl Crawford/200	4.00
10	Carlos Beltran/200	8.00
11	Carlos Lee/200	4.00
12	Craig Wilson/200	4.00
13	Curt Schilling/50	10.00
14	Darin Erstad/200	4.00
16	Fred McGriff/200	4.00
18	Greg Maddux/50	12.00
19	Ivan Rodriguez/200	8.00
20	Jason Bay/200	4.00
21	Jason Giambi/200	4.00
22	Jay Gibbons/100	4.00
23	Jeff Kent/200	4.00
24	John Olerud/200	4.00
25	Juan Gonzalez/Pants/200	4.00
26	Junior Spivey/200	4.00
27	Kazuhisa Ishii/200	6.00
28	Kevin Brown/100	4.00
29	Larry Walker/Rockies/200	6.00
30	Lyle Overbay/200	4.00
31	Mark Teixeira/100	6.00
32	Melvin Mora/200	4.00
33	Michael Young/200	4.00
34	Miguel Tejada/200	8.00
35	Mike Mussina/200	8.00
36	Paul LoDuca/50	6.00
37	Preston Wilson/200	4.00
38	Randy Johnson/200	8.00
39	Richie Sexson/200	6.00
40	Roger Clemens/50	15.00
41	Scott Rolen/50	10.00
42	Sean Burroughs/200	4.00
43	Sean Casey/200	4.00
44	Shannon Stewart/100	4.00
45	Shawn Green/200	4.00
46	Steve Finley/200	4.00
48	Tom Glavine/200	6.00
50	Travis Hafner/100	4.00

Diamond Cuts Combos
NM/M
Common Player: 6.00
Prime: No Pricing
Production One Set

1	Adam Dunn/ Bat-Jsy/100	10.00
2	Adrian Beltre/ Bat-Jsy/100	8.00
3	Alfonso Soriano/ Bat-Jsy/100	10.00
4	Andruw Jones/ Bat-Jsy/100	8.00
5	Andy Pettitte/ Jsy/100	10.00
6	Aramis Ramirez/ Bat-Jsy/100	8.00
7	Brian Giles/ Bat-Jsy/100	8.00
10	Carlos Beltran/ Bat-Jsy/50	15.00
11	Carlos Lee/ Jsy/100	6.00
12	Craig Wilson/ Bat-Jsy/100	6.00
13	Curt Schilling/ Bat-Jsy/100	12.00
14	Darin Erstad/ Bat-Jsy/100	6.00
17	Fred McGriff/ Bat-Jsy/100	6.00
19	Ivan Rodriguez/ Bat-Jsy/100	10.00
21	Jason Giambi/ Bat-Jsy/50	8.00
22	Jay Gibbons/ Bat-Jsy/50	8.00
23	Jeff Kent/ Bat-Jsy/100	6.00
24	John Olerud/ Bat-Jsy/200	6.00
25	Juan Gonzalez/ Bat-Pants/100	8.00
27	Kazuhisa Ishii/ Bat-Jsy/100	6.00
28	Kevin Brown/ Bat-Jsy/100	6.00
29	Larry Walker/ Bat-Jsy/100	8.00
31	Mark Teixeira/ Bat-Jsy/100	10.00
34	Miguel Tejada/ Jsy-Jsy/100	10.00
35	Mike Mussina/ Bat-Pants/50	12.00
36	Paul LoDuca/ Bat-Jsy/50	6.00
37	Preston Wilson/ Bat-Jsy/100	6.00
38	Randy Johnson/ Bat-Jsy/50	15.00
40	Roger Clemens/ Bat-Jsy/50	20.00
44	Shannon Stewart/ Bat-Jsy/100	6.00
45	Shawn Green/ Bat-Jsy/100	6.00
48	Tom Glavine/ Bat-Jsy/100	8.00
49	Torii Hunter/ Bat-Jsy/25	8.00

Diamond Cuts Signature

NM/M
Production 1-100
#26-35 inserted 1:76
#26-35 as DK Update exclusive

8	C.C. Sabathia/25	20.00
9	Carl Crawford/50	20.00
11	Carlos Lee/100	15.00
12	Craig Wilson/100	15.00
20	Jason Bay/100	15.00
22	Jay Gibbons/100	15.00
30	Lyle Overbay/100	15.00
32	Melvin Mora/50	15.00
44	Shannon Stewart/25	20.00
47	Tim Salmon/100	20.00
50	Travis Hafner/100	15.00

Diamond Cuts Signature Bat
NM/M
Production 5-100

1	Adam Dunn/25	40.00
2	Adrian Beltre/50	35.00
6	Aramis Ramirez/100	30.00
10	Carlos Beltran/50	40.00
12	Craig Wilson/50	15.00
16	Derrek Lee/100	20.00
17	Fred McGriff/25	50.00
22	Jay Gibbons/100	10.00
31	Mark Teixeira/25	40.00
33	Michael Young/100	20.00
36	Paul LoDuca/25	25.00
43	Sean Casey/25	25.00
44	Shannon Stewart/25	20.00
49	Torii Hunter/25	25.00

Diamond Cuts Signature Jersey
NM/M
Prime: No Pricing
Production 5-100

2	Adrian Beltre/100	25.00
6	Aramis Ramirez/100	30.00
8	C.C. Sabathia/100	15.00
9	Carl Crawford/50	20.00
11	Carlos Lee/100	15.00
12	Craig Wilson/100	15.00
30	Lyle Overbay/100	15.00
31	Mark Teixeira/25	40.00
32	Melvin Mora/50	15.00
33	Michael Young/100	20.00
36	Paul LoDuca/25	25.00
42	Sean Burroughs/50	10.00
43	Sean Casey/25	25.00
45	Shannon Stewart/25	20.00
46	Steve Finley/25	25.00
50	Travis Hafner/25	20.00
57	Mark Mulder/25	25.00
60	Victor Martinez/25	20.00

Diamond Cuts Signature Combos
NM/M
Production 1-100
Prime: No Pricing
Production One Set

1	Adam Dunn/ Bat-Jsy/25	40.00
2	Adrian Beltre/ Bat-Bat/25	40.00
6	Aramis Ramirez/ Bat-Jsy/100	30.00
8	C.C. Sabathia/ Jsy/100	25.00
11	Carlos Lee/ Jsy-Jsy/100	20.00
12	Craig Wilson/ Bat-Bat/100	15.00
17	Fred McGriff/ Bat-Jsy/25	50.00
22	Jay Gibbons/ Bat-Bat/50	10.00
25	Juan Gonzalez/ Bat-Jsy/100	25.00
27	Kazuhisa Ishii/ Bat-Jsy/50	50.00
31	Mark Teixeira/ Bat-Bat/25	40.00
33	Michael Young/ Bat-Jsy/50	25.00
36	Paul LoDuca/ Bat-Bat/25	25.00
43	Sean Casey/ Bat-Jsy/25	25.00
49	Torii Hunter/ Bat-Jsy/25	25.00
51	Aramis Ramirez/ Jsy/24	25.00
60	Victor Martinez/25	20.00

Heritage Collection

NM/M
Common Player: 1.50
Inserted 1:21

1	Andre Dawson	1.50
2	Bob Gibson	2.50
3	Cal Ripken Jr.	8.00
4	Dale Murphy	2.00
5	Darryl Strawberry	1.50
6	Dennis Eckersley	1.50
7	Don Mattingly	6.00
8	Duke Snider	3.00
9	Dwight Gooden	1.50
10	Eddie Murray	3.00
11	Frank Robinson	3.00
12	Gary Carter	2.00
13	George Brett	6.00
14	Harmon Killebrew	3.00
15	Jack Morris	1.50
16	Jim Palmer	1.50
17	Lou Brock	2.00
18	Mike Schmidt	6.00
19	Nolan Ryan	8.00
20	Ozzie Smith	4.00
21	Phil Niekro	1.50
22	Rod Carew	2.00
23	Rollie Fingers	1.50
24	Steve Carlton	1.50
25	Tony Gwynn	3.00
26	Curt Schilling	1.50
27	Bobby Doerr	1.50
28	Edgar Martinez	1.50
29	Jim Thorpe	4.00
30	Mark Grace	1.50
31	Matt Williams	1.50
32	Paul Molitor	2.50
33	Robin Yount	4.00
34	Ryne Sandberg	5.00
35	Will Clark	2.00

Heritage Collection Bat
NM/M
Production 50-100

1	Andre Dawson/50	5.00
3	Cal Ripken Jr./100	40.00
4	Dale Murphy/100	10.00
5	Darryl Strawberry/50	8.00
7	Don Mattingly/100	20.00
9	Dwight Gooden/100	5.00
10	Eddie Murray/100	15.00
11	Frank Robinson/50	8.00
12	Gary Carter/100	5.00
13	George Brett/100	15.00
14	Harmon Killebrew/100	10.00
17	Lou Brock/100	8.00
18	Mike Schmidt/100	20.00
19	Nolan Ryan/50	30.00
20	Ozzie Smith/100	15.00
21	Phil Niekro/50	8.00
22	Rod Carew/100	8.00
24	Steve Carlton/100	5.00
25	Tony Gwynn/100	10.00

Heritage Collection Jersey
NM/M
Production 25-100
Prime: No Pricing
Production One Set

1	Andre Dawson/100	8.00
2	Bob Gibson/50	10.00
3	Cal Ripken Jr./100	40.00
4	Dale Murphy/100	10.00
5	Darryl Strawberry/25	10.00
6	Dennis Eckersley/100	5.00
7	Don Mattingly/100	20.00
8	Duke Snider/50	15.00
9	Dwight Gooden/100	5.00
10	Eddie Murray/100	15.00
12	Gary Carter/100	5.00
13	George Brett/50	20.00
14	Harmon Killebrew/100	10.00
15	Jack Morris/100	5.00
16	Jim Palmer/100	5.00
17	Lou Brock/100	8.00
18	Mike Schmidt/Jkt/100	20.00
19	Nolan Ryan/100	25.00
20	Ozzie Smith/Pants/100	15.00
21	Phil Niekro/100	8.00
22	Rod Carew/100	8.00
23	Rollie Fingers/100	8.00
24	Steve Carlton/100	5.00
25	Tony Gwynn/100	10.00

Heritage Collection Combos
NM/M
Production 25-100
Prime: No Pricing
Production One Set

1	Andre Dawson/ Bat-Jsy/50	8.00
3	Cal Ripken Jr./ Bat-Jsy/50	60.00
4	Dale Murphy/ Bat-Jsy/25	20.00
7	Don Mattingly/ Bat-Jkt/100	25.00
8	Duke Snider/ Jsy-Pants/25	20.00
9	Dwight Gooden/ Bat-Jsy/50	10.00
10	Eddie Murray/ Bat-Jsy/100	20.00
14	Harmon Killebrew/ Bat-Jsy/100	15.00
16	Jim Palmer/ Jsy-Pants/100	10.00
17	Lou Brock/ Bat-Jkt/50	10.00
18	Mike Schmidt/ Bat-Jsy/100	25.00

19	Nolan Ryan/ Jsy-Pants/50	40.00
20	Ozzie Smith/ Bat-Pants/100	20.00
21	Phil Niekro/ Bat-Jsy/50	10.00
22	Rod Carew/ Bat-Jsy/100	10.00
24	Steve Carlton/ Bat-Jsy/100	8.00
25	Tony Gwynn/ Bat-Jsy/50	15.00

Heritage Collection Signature
NM/M

Production 1-50
1	Andre Dawson/50	25.00
5	Darryl Strawberry/50	25.00
9	Dwight Gooden/25	25.00
15	Jack Morris/50	20.00
23	Rollie Fingers/25	40.00

Heritage Collection Signature Bat
NM/M

Production 5-100
#26-35 are DK Update exclusive
1	Andre Dawson/50	25.00
4	Dale Murphy/25	40.00
7	Don Mattingly/25	75.00
9	Dwight Gooden/100	25.00
11	Frank Robinson/25	40.00
14	Harmon Killebrew/50	50.00
17	Lou Brock/50	35.00
20	Ozzie Smith/25	65.00
21	Phil Niekro/20	30.00
22	Rod Carew/25	40.00
24	Steve Carlton/25	40.00
25	Tony Gwynn/25	50.00
28	Edgar Martinez/25	40.00
31	Matt Williams/25	35.00
35	Will Clark/25	40.00

Heritage Collection Signature Jersey
NM/M

Production 5-100
#26-35 are DK Update exclusive
Prime: No Pricing
Production One Set
1	Andre Dawson/100	25.00
2	Bob Gibson/25	40.00
4	Dale Murphy/50	40.00
5	Darryl Strawberry/ Pants/100	20.00
6	Dennis Eckersley/50	25.00
7	Don Mattingly/25	85.00
8	Duke Snider/50	35.00
9	Dwight Gooden/100	20.00
11	Frank Robinson/25	40.00
12	Gary Carter/50	25.00
14	Harmon Killebrew/ 50	50.00
15	Jack Morris/100	15.00
16	Jim Palmer/25	35.00
17	Lou Brock/50	35.00
20	Ozzie Smith/25	60.00
21	Phil Niekro/25	30.00
22	Rod Carew/25	40.00
23	Rollie Fingers/25	30.00
24	Steve Carlton/25	40.00
27	Bobby Doerr/25	
28	Edgar Martinez/25	35.00
31	Matt Williams/25	35.00
35	Will Clark/25	40.00

Heritage Collection Signature Combos
NM/M

Production 5-100
#26-35 are DK Update exclusive
Prime: No Pricing
Production One Set
1	Andre Dawson/ Bat/25	25.00
4	Dale Murphy/ Bat/25	40.00
6	Dennis Eckersley/ Jsy-Jsy/25	25.00
7	Don Mattingly/ Bat-Jkt/25	80.00
9	Dwight Gooden/ Bat-Jsy/100	25.00
12	Gary Carter/ Jkt/25	25.00
14	Harmon Killebrew/ Bat-Bat/25	50.00
15	Jack Morris/ Jsy/25	30.00
16	Jim Palmer/ Jsy-Pants/25	30.00
17	Lou Brock/ Bat-Jsy/50	40.00
21	Phil Niekro/ Bat-Jsy/50	25.00
22	Rod Carew/ Bat-Jkt/25	40.00
24	Steve Carlton/ Bat-Jsy/25	40.00
25	Tony Gwynn/ Jsy/50	50.00
27	Bobby Doerr/ Jsy/Pants/25	25.00

HOF Heroes

NM/M

#51-100 are DK Update exclusive
Common Player: 1.50
Non Canvas:	No Pricing	
Production 20 Sets		
Bronze:	1-2X	
Production 100 Sets		
Gold:	3-5X	
Production 25 Sets		
Platinum:	No Pricing	
Production One Set		
Silver:	2-4X	
Production 50 Sets		
Frame Black:	3-5X	
Production 25 Sets		
Frame Blue:	1-2X	
Production 100 Sets		
Frame Green:	2-4X	
Production 50 Sets		
Frame Red:	1X	
Inserted 1:18		
1	Phil Niekro	1.50
2	Brooks Robinson	2.00
3	Jim Palmer	2.00
4	Carl Yastrzemski	3.00
5	Ted Williams	5.00
6	Duke Snider	3.00
7	Burleigh Grimes	1.50
8	Don Sutton	1.50
9	Nolan Ryan	6.00
10	Fergie Jenkins	1.50
11	Carlton Fisk	2.00
12	Tom Seaver	2.00
13	Bob Feller	2.00
14	Nolan Ryan	6.00
15	George Brett	5.00
16	Warren Spahn	3.00
17	Paul Molitor	3.00
18	Rod Carew	3.00
19	Harmon Killebrew	3.00
20	Monte Irvin	2.00
21	Gary Carter	2.00
22	Phil Rizzuto	2.00
23	Babe Ruth	6.00
24	Reggie Jackson	5.00
25	Mike Schmidt	5.00
26	Roberto Clemente	5.00
27	Juan Marichal	1.50
28	Willie McCovey	2.00
29	Stan Musial	4.00
30	Ozzie Smith	3.00
31	Dennis Eckersley	1.50
32	Phil Niekro	1.50
33	Jim Palmer	2.00
34	Carl Yastrzemski	3.00
35	Duke Snider	3.00
36	Don Sutton	1.50
37	Nolan Ryan	6.00
38	Carlton Fisk	2.00
39	Tom Seaver	2.00
40	Bob Feller	2.00
41	Nolan Ryan	6.00
42	George Brett	5.00
43	Harmon Killebrew	3.00
44	Gary Carter	1.50
45	Mike Schmidt	5.00
46	Stan Musial	4.00
47	Ozzie Smith	3.00
48	Dennis Eckersley	1.50
49	Fergie Jenkins	1.50
50	Brooks Robinson	2.00
51	Eddie Murray	2.00
52	Frank Robinson	2.00
53	Carlton Fisk	1.50
54	Ted Williams	5.00
55	Rod Carew	2.00
56	Ernie Banks	3.00
57	Luis Aparicio	1.50
58	Johnny Bench	3.00
59	Al Kaline	2.00
60	George Kell	1.50
61	Robin Yount	3.00
62	Nolan Ryan	6.00
63	Whitey Ford	1.50
64	Reggie Jackson	2.00
65	Babe Ruth	6.00
66	Rollie Fingers	1.50
67	Steve Carlton	1.50
68	Robin Roberts	1.50
69	Ralph Kiner	1.50
70	Willie Stargell	2.00
71	Roberto Clemente	5.00
72	Gaylord Perry	1.50
73	Bob Gibson	2.00
74	Lou Brock	1.50
75	Frankie Frisch	1.50
76	Eddie Murray	2.00
77	Frank Robinson	2.00
78	Carlton Fisk	1.50
79	Ted Williams	5.00
80	Rod Carew	2.00
81	Ernie Banks	3.00
82	Luis Aparicio	1.50
83	Johnny Bench	3.00
84	Al Kaline	2.00
85	Willie Mays	5.00
86	Robin Yount	3.00
87	Nolan Ryan	5.00
88	Whitey Ford	2.00
89	Reggie Jackson	5.00
90	Babe Ruth	6.00
91	Rollie Fingers	1.50
92	Steve Carlton	1.50
93	Wade Boggs	2.00
94	Wade Boggs	2.00
95	Willie Stargell	2.00
96	Roberto Clemente	5.00
97	Gaylord Perry	1.50
98	Bob Gibson	2.00
99	Lou Brock	1.50
100	Frankie Frisch	1.50

HOF Heroes Materials Bronze
NM/M

Production 1-100
No pricing 20 or less.
Gold:	.75-1.5X	
Production 1-25		
Silver:	.75-1.5X	
Production 10-50		
Framed Black:	No Pricing	
Production 1-10		
Framed Blue:	.75-1.5X	
Production 1-25		
Framed Red:	.75-1.5X	
Production 10-50		
1	Phil Niekro/ Bat-Jsy/100	8.00
2	Brooks Robinson/ Bat-Jsy/100	12.00
3	Jim Palmer/ Jsy-Pants/100	8.00
4	Carl Yastrzemski/ Bat-Pants/50	20.00
6	Duke Snider/ Jsy-Pants/50	15.00
7	Burleigh Grimes/ Pants-Pants/25	75.00
8	Don Sutton/ Jsy-Jsy/100	8.00
9	Nolan Ryan/ Bat-Jsy/50	40.00
10	Fergie Jenkins/ Pants-Pants/100	8.00
11	Carlton Fisk/ Bat-Jkt/100	12.00
12	Tom Seaver/ Jsy-Pants/50	15.00
13	Bob Feller/ Pants-Pants/25	20.00
14	Nolan Ryan/ Bat-Jsy/50	40.00
15	George Brett/ Bat-Bat/25	40.00
16	Warren Spahn/ Jsy-Jsy/25	30.00
17	Paul Molitor/ Bat-Jsy/100	15.00
18	Rod Carew/ Bat-Jsy/50	15.00
19	Harmon Killebrew/ Bat-Jsy/50	20.00
21	Gary Carter/ Bat-Jsy/100	8.00
23	Babe Ruth/ Pants-Pants/25	300.00
24	Reggie Jackson/ Bat-Jkt/100	15.00
25	Mike Schmidt/ Bat-Jsy/50	30.00
26	Roberto Clemente/ Bat-Bat/50	60.00
27	Juan Marichal/ Pants-Pants/25	12.00
28	Willie McCovey/ Pants/100	10.00
29	Stan Musial/ Bat-Bat/25	30.00
30	Ozzie Smith/ Pants-Pants/100	20.00
31	Dennis Eckersley/ Jsy-Jsy/100	8.00
32	Phil Niekro/ Bat-Jsy/100	8.00
33	Jim Palmer/ Jsy-Jsy/25	12.00
34	Carl Yastrzemski/ Pants-Pants/25	30.00
35	Duke Snider/ Jsy-Pants	20.00
36	Don Sutton/ Jsy-Jsy/100	8.00
37	Nolan Ryan/ Bat-Jkt/25	50.00

38	Carlton Fisk/ Bat-Jkt/100	12.00
39	Tom Seaver/ Bat-Jsy/25	20.00
40	Bob Feller/ Pants-Pants/25	20.00
41	Nolan Ryan/ Bat-Jkt/25	50.00
42	George Brett/ Bat-Bat/25	40.00
43	Harmon Killebrew/ Bat-Jsy/25	25.00
44	Gary Carter/ Bat-Jsy/100	8.00
45	Mike Schmidt/ Bat-Jsy/25	40.00
46	Stan Musial/ Bat-Bat/30	30.00
47	Ozzie Smith/ Bat-Jsy/100	20.00
48	Dennis Eckersley/ Jsy-Jsy/100	8.00
49	Fergie Jenkins/ Pants-Pants/25	12.00
50	Brooks Robinson/ Bat-Jsy/20	20.00
51	Eddie Murray/ Bat-Jsy/25	12.00
52	Frank Robinson/ Bat/Bat/50	12.00
53	Carlton Fisk/ Bat/Jsy/100	10.00
55	Rod Carew/ Jsy/Jsy/25	12.00
56	Ernie Banks/ Bat/Pants/50	15.00
57	Luis Aparicio/ Bat/Bat/50	8.00
58	Johnny Bench/ Jsy/Jsy/15	15.00
59	Al Kaline/Bat/Bat/25	20.00
61	Robin Yount/ Bat/Jsy/25	15.00
62	Nolan Ryan/ Bat/Jsy/25	50.00
63	Whitey Ford/ Jsy/Jsy/25	25.00
64	Reggie Jackson/ Bat/Jsy/25	15.00
66	Rollie Fingers/ Jsy/Jsy/25	8.00
67	Steve Carlton/ Bat/Jsy/25	10.00
70	Willie Stargell/ Bat/Jsy/25	15.00
72	Gaylord Perry/ Jsy/Jsy/25	8.00
73	Bob Gibson/ Jsy/Jsy/25	15.00
74	Lou Brock/Bat/Bat/Jsy/50	12.00
76	Eddie Murray/ Bat/Bat/25	12.00
77	Frank Robinson/ Bat/Bat/50	12.00
78	Carlton Fisk/ Bat/Jsy/50	12.00
80	Rod Carew/ Bat/Jkt/50	12.00
81	Ernie Banks/ Jsy/Jsy/15	15.00
82	Luis Aparicio/ Bat/Bat/50	8.00
83	Johnny Bench/ Jsy/Jsy/25	15.00
86	Robin Yount/ Bat/Jsy/25	15.00
87	Nolan Ryan/ Bat/Jsy/40	40.00
88	Whitey Ford/ Jsy/Jsy/25	25.00
89	Reggie Jackson/ Bat/Jsy/25	15.00
91	Rollie Fingers/ Jsy/Jsy/25	8.00
92	Steve Carlton/ Bat/Jsy/25	10.00
95	Willie Stargell/ Bat/Jsy/25	15.00
97	Gaylord Perry/ Jsy/Jsy/25	8.00
99	Lou Brock/ Bat/Jsy/50	10.00

HOF Heroes Signatures Bronze
NM/M

Production 1-25
No pricing 20 or less.
Gold:	No Pricing	
Production 1-10		
Platinum:	No Pricing	
Production One Set		
Silver:	1X	
Production 1-25		
Framed Blue:	No Pricing	
Production One Set		
Framed Black:	No Pricing	
Production One Set		
Framed Green:	No Pricing	
Production 1-10		
Framed Red:	No Pricing	
Production 1-25		
Cards #52-99 are seeded in DK Update.		
13	Bob Feller/25	35.00
40	Bob Feller/25	35.00
52	Frank Robinson/25	35.00

57	Luis Aparicio/25	15.00
59	Al Kaline/25	40.00
60	George Kell/25	20.00
66	Rollie Fingers/25	15.00
67	Steve Carlton/25	20.00
68	Robin Roberts/25	15.00
69	Ralph Kiner/25	35.00
72	Gaylord Perry/15	20.00
74	Lou Brock/25	35.00
82	Luis Aparicio/25	15.00
84	Al Kaline/25	40.00
91	Rollie Fingers/25	15.00
92	Steve Carlton/25	20.00
93	Wade Boggs/ Yanks/25	30.00
94	Wade Boggs/Sox/25	30.00
97	Gaylord Perry/25	15.00
99	Lou Brock/25	35.00

HOF Heroes Signature Materials Bronze
NM/M

Production 5-50
No pricing 20 or less.
Gold:	.75-1.5X	
Production 5-25		
Platinum:	No Pricing	
Production One Set		
Silver:	.75-1X	
Production 5-50		
Framed Black:	No Pricing	
Production 5-10		
Framed Blue:	.75-1.5X	
Production 5-25		
Framed Green:	No Pricing	
Production 1-10		
Framed Red:	.75-1.5X	
Production 1-25		
#53-99 are found in DK Update		
2	Brooks Robinson/ Bat-Jsy/	50.00
3	Jim Palmer/ Jsy-Pants/25	40.00
6	Duke Snider/ Jsy-Pants/25	40.00
8	Don Sutton/ Jsy-Jsy/25	30.00
10	Fergie Jenkins/ Pants-Pants/25	30.00
13	Bob Feller/ Pants-Pants/25	35.00
18	Rod Carew/ Bat-Jsy/50	40.00
19	Harmon Killebrew/ Bat-Jsy/50	50.00
21	Gary Carter/ Bat-Jsy/25	25.00
27	Juan Marichal/ Pants-Pants/25	40.00
28	Willie McCovey/ Jsy-Pants/25	50.00
29	Stan Musial/ Bat-Bat/25	85.00
30	Ozzie Smith/ Bat-Pants/25	75.00
31	Dennis Eckersley/ Jsy-Jsy/25	35.00
32	Phil Niekro/ Bat-Jsy/25	30.00
33	Jim Palmer/ Bat-Jsy/25	40.00
35	Duke Snider/ Jsy-Jsy/25	40.00
36	Don Sutton/ Bat-Jsy/25	30.00
40	Bob Feller/ Pants-Pants/25	35.00
43	Harmon Killebrew/ Bat-Jsy/50	40.00
44	Gary Carter/ Bat-Jsy/50	25.00
47	Ozzie Smith/ Bat-Pants/25	75.00
48	Dennis Eckersley/ Jsy-Jsy/25	25.00
49	Fergie Jenkins/ Pants-Pants/50	30.00
50	Brooks Robinson/ Bat-Jsy/50	50.00
61	Robin Yount/ Bat-Jsy/50	50.00
66	Rollie Fingers/ Jsy-Jsy/50	15.00
72	Gaylord Perry/ Jsy-Jsy/50	15.00
74	Lou Brock/ Bat-Jsy/30	30.00
80	Rod Carew/ Bat-Jsy/25	25.00
99	Lou Brock/ Bat-Jsy/50	40.00

Materials Bronze
NM/M

Production 10-200
No pricing 20 or less.
Gold:	.75-1.5X	
Production 25-50		
Silver:	.75-1.5X	
Production 25-100		
Platinum:	No Pricing	
Production One Set		
Framed Black:	No Pricing	
Production 10 Sets		
Framed Blue:	.75-1.5X	

Production 50 Sets		
Framed Green:		
Production 25 Sets		
Framed Red:	.75-1.5X	
Production 25-100		
#302-450 are found in DK Update		
1	Garret Anderson/ Bat-Jsy/200	5.00
2	Vladimir Guerrero/ Bat-Jsy/200	10.00
4	Troy Glaus/ Bat-Jsy/200	5.00
5	Tim Salmon/ Bat-Jsy/200	5.00
7	Chone Figgins/ Jsy-Jsy/200	5.00
10	Tony Percival/ Jsy-Jsy/200	5.00
12	Brandon Webb/ Bat-Pants/200	5.00
13	Richie Sexson/ Bat-Bat/200	5.00
17	Luis Gonzalez/ Jsy-Jsy/200	5.00
18	Rafael Furcal/ Bat-Jsy/200	5.00
19	Andruw Jones/ Bat-Jsy/200	8.00
21	John Smoltz/ Jsy-Jsy/200	8.00
24	J.D. Drew/ Bat-Bat/200	5.00
25	Chipper Jones/ Bat-Jsy/200	10.00
27	Rafael Palmeiro/ Bat-Jsy/200	8.00
28	Miguel Tejada/ Bat-Jsy/200	10.00
29	Javy Lopez/ Bat-Jsy/25	10.00
30	Luis Matos/ Jsy-Jsy/100	5.00
31	Larry Bigbie/ Jsy-Jsy/200	5.00
32	Rodrigo Lopez/ Jsy-Jsy/200	5.00
34	Melvin Mora/ Bat-Jsy/200	5.00
36	Manny Ramirez/ Bat-Jsy/200	10.00
38	Trot Nixon/ Bat-Bat/200	10.00
39	Curt Schilling/ Bat-Jsy/200	10.00
41	Pedro Martinez/ Bat-Jsy/200	10.00
42	Johnny Damon/ Bat-Bat/200	15.00
43	Kevin Youkilis/ Bat-Bat/200	5.00
46	David Ortiz/ Bat-Jsy/200	10.00
47	Kerry Wood/ Jsy-Pants/200	10.00
48	Mark Prior/ Bat-Jsy/200	8.00
49	Aramis Ramirez/ Bat-Jsy/200	8.00
50	Greg Maddux/ Bat-Jsy/100	15.00
51	Carlos Zambrano/ Jsy-Jsy/200	8.00
52	Derrek Lee/ Bat-Bat/200	8.00
54	Moises Alou/ Bat-Bat/200	8.00
56	Sammy Sosa/ Bat-Jsy/200	10.00
57	Nomar Garciaparra/ Bat-Bat/200	10.00
60	Magglio Ordonez/ Bat-Jsy/200	5.00
61	Carlos Lee/ Bat-Jsy/200	5.00
62	Joe Crede/ Bat-Bat/200	5.00
65	Frank Thomas/ Bat-Jsy/200	8.00
69	Adam Dunn/ Bat-Jsy/200	5.00
70	Austin Kearns/ Bat-Bat/200	5.00
74	Sean Casey/ Jsy-Pants/200	5.00
76	C.C. Sabathia/ Bat-Jsy/200	5.00
77	Jody Gerut/ Bat-Jsy/200	5.00
78	Omar Vizquel/ Bat-Jsy/200	5.00
79	Victor Martinez/ Bat-Jsy/200	5.00
80	Matt Lawton/ Bat-Bat/200	5.00
84	Todd Helton/ Bat-Jsy/200	5.00
85	Preston Wilson/ Bat-Jsy/200	5.00
90	Ivan Rodriguez/ Bat-Jsy/200	8.00
92	Brandon Inge/ Bat-Jsy/200	5.00
94	Dontrelle Willis/ Bat-Jsy/200	5.00
95	Miguel Cabrera/ Bat-Jsy/200	10.00
96	Josh Beckett/ Bat-Bat/100	5.00

#	Description	Price
97	Mike Lowell/ Bat-Jsy/100	5.00
98	Luis Castillo/ Bat-Bat/200	5.00
99	Juan Pierre/ Bat-Jsy/200	5.00
100	Paul LoDuca/ Bat-Bat/200	5.00
102	Craig Biggio/ Bat-Pants/200	5.00
103	Lance Berkman/ Bat-Jsy/200	5.00
104	Roy Oswalt/ Jsy-Jsy/200	5.00
105	Roger Clemens/ Bat-Jsy/200	15.00
106	Jeff Kent/ Bat-Jsy/100	5.00
108	Jeff Bagwell/ Bat-Jsy/200	8.00
109	Carlos Beltran/ Bat-Jsy/200	8.00
110	Angel Berroa/ Bat-Bat/200	5.00
111	Mike Sweeney/ Bat-Jsy/200	5.00
112	Jeremy Affeldt/ Pants-Pants/200	5.00
114	Juan Gonzalez/ Bat-Jsy/200	8.00
116	Shawn Green/ Bat-Jsy/200	5.00
118	Adrian Beltre/ Bat-Jsy/200	8.00
119	Hideo Nomo/ Bat-Jsy/200	8.00
123	Scott Podsednik/ Bat-Jsy/200	5.00
124	Ben Sheets/ Bat-Pants/200	8.00
125	Lyle Overbay/ Jsy-Jsy/200	5.00
126	Junior Spivey/ Jsy-Jsy/200	5.00
127	Bill Hall/ Bat-Jsy/200	5.00
129	Jacque Jones/ Bat-Jsy/200	5.00
130	Torii Hunter/ Bat-Jsy/200	5.00
131	Johan Santana/ Bat-Jsy/200	10.00
132	Lew Ford/ Bat-Jsy/200	5.00
136	Jose Vidro/ Bat-Jsy/200	5.00
138	Brad Wilkerson/ Bat-Bat/100	5.00
139	Nick Johnson/ Bat-Bat/100	5.00
140	Livan Hernandez/ Jsy-Jsy/25	5.00
141	Tom Glavine/ Bat-Bat/200	8.00
143	Jose Reyes/ Bat-Jsy/200	6.00
144	Al Leiter/Jsy-Jsy/200	5.00
145	Mike Piazza/ Jsy-Jsy/100	15.00
146	Kazuo Matsui/ Bat-Jsy/200	8.00
147	Richard Hidalgo/ Bat-Jsy/200	5.00
149	Mariano Rivera/ Bat-Jsy/200	8.00
150	Mike Mussina/ Bat-Jsy/200	8.00
153	Jorge Posada/ Bat-Jsy/200	8.00
154	Jason Giambi/ Bat-Jsy/200	5.00
155	Gary Sheffield/ Bat-Jsy/200	8.00
158	Kevin Brown/ Bat-Jsy/100	5.00
160	Esteban Loaiza/ Bat-Bat/100	5.00
161	Hideki Matsui/ Jsy-Pants/200	20.00
162	Eric Chavez/ Bat-Jsy/200	5.00
163	Mark Mulder/ Bat-Jsy/25	10.00
164	Barry Zito/ Bat-Jsy/200	5.00
165	Tim Hudson/ Bat-Jsy/200	8.00
166	Jermaine Dye/ Bat-Jsy/200	5.00
168	Bobby Crosby/ Bat-Jsy/200	8.00
171	Jim Thome/ Bat-Jsy/200	8.00
172	Bobby Abreu/ Jsy-Jsy/200	5.00
173	Kevin Millwood/ Jsy-Jsy/200	5.00
178	Craig Wilson/ Bat-Jsy/200	5.00
180	Jack Wilson/ Bat-Bat/200	5.00
181	Jose Castillo/ Bat-Jsy/200	5.00
184	Jason Bay/ Bat-Jsy/200	5.00
185	Sean Burroughs/ Bat-Jsy/200	8.00
187	Brian Giles/ Bat-Bat/100	5.00
193	Trevor Hoffman/ Jsy-Jsy/200	5.00
199	J.T. Snow/Jsy-Jsy/25	5.00
200	A.J. Pierzynski/ Jsy-Jsy/100	5.00
201	Edgar Martinez/ Bat-Bat/200	5.00
204	Bret Boone/ Jsy-Jsy/200	5.00
208	Jamie Moyer/ Bat-Jsy/200	5.00
209	Jim Edmonds/ Bat-Jsy/200	8.00
210	Scott Rolen/ Bat-Jsy/200	10.00
211	Edgar Renteria/ Bat-Jsy/200	8.00
212	Dan Haren/ Bat-Jsy/100	5.00
213	Matt Morris/ Bat-Jsy/200	5.00
214	Albert Pujols/ Jsy-Jsy/200	20.00
215	Larry Walker/ Bat-Jsy/200	5.00
220	Aubrey Huff/ Bat-Bat/100	5.00
221	Carl Crawford/ Bat-Jsy/200	5.00
222	Rocco Baldelli/ Bat-Jsy/200	5.00
223	Fred McGriff/ Bat-Jsy/200	5.00
224	Dewon Brazelton/ Bat-Jsy/200	5.00
225	B.J. Upton/ Bat-Bat/200	8.00
226	Joey Gathright/ Bat-Jsy/200	5.00
228	Hank Blalock/ Bat-Jsy/100	8.00
229	Mark Teixeira/ Bat-Jsy/200	8.00
230	Michael Young/ Bat-Jsy/200	5.00
232	Laynce Nix/ Bat-Jsy/200	5.00
233	Alfonso Soriano/ Bat-Jsy/200	8.00
234	Rafael Palmeiro/ Bat-Jsy/200	8.00
235	Kevin Mench/ Bat-Jsy/200	5.00
236	David Dellucci/ Jsy-Jsy/200	8.00
237	Francisco Cordero/ Jsy-Jsy/200	5.00
239	Roy Halladay/ Jsy-Jsy/200	5.00
240	Carlos Delgado/ Jsy-Jsy/200	5.00
242	Vernon Wells/ Bat-Jsy/200	5.00
267	Larry Walker/ Jsy-Jsy/200	8.00
268	Ivan Rodriguez/ Jsy-Jsy/200	8.00
269	Brad Penny/ Bat-Jsy/200	5.00
270	Carlos Beltran/ Bat-Jsy/200	8.00
271	Paul LoDuca/ Bat-Jsy/200	5.00
273	Nomar Garciaparra/ Bat-Bat/100	10.00
274	Esteban Loaiza/ Bat-Bat/100	5.00
275	Richard Hidalgo/ Jkt-Pants/200	5.00
276	John Olerud/ Bat-Bat/200	5.00
277	Greg Maddux/ Bat-Jsy/200	12.00
278	Roger Clemens/ Bat-Jsy/200	15.00
279	Alfonso Soriano/ Bat-Jsy/200	8.00
280	Dale Murphy/ Jsy-Jsy/200	8.00
281	Cal Ripken Jr./ Bat-Jsy/200	30.00
282	Dwight Evans/ Bat-Jsy/200	8.00
283	Ron Santo/ Bat-Bat/200	10.00
284	Andre Dawson/ Bat-Jsy/200	8.00
285	Harold Baines/ Bat-Jsy/200	8.00
286	Jack Morris/ Jsy-Jsy/100	8.00
287	Kirk Gibson/ Bat-Jsy/200	8.00
288	Bo Jackson/ Bat-Jsy/200	10.00
289	Orel Hershiser/ Jsy-Jsy/50	8.00
291	Tony Oliva/ Bat-Jsy/200	10.00
292	Darryl Strawberry/ Bat-Jsy/200	8.00
293	Roger Maris/ Bat-Jsy/200	50.00
294	Don Mattingly/ Bat-Jsy/100	25.00
295	Rickey Henderson/ Bat-Jsy/100	10.00
297	Dave Parker/ Bat-Jsy/200	8.00
298	Steve Garvey/ Bat-Jsy/200	8.00
299	Matt Williams/ Jsy-Jsy/200	8.00
300	Keith Hernandez/ Bat-Jsy/200	8.00
302	Vladimir Guerrero/ Bat-Jsy/200	10.00
303	Garret Anderson/ Bat-Jsy/200	5.00
307	Luis Gonzalez/ Bat-Jsy/200	5.00
310	Shawn Green/ Bat-Jsy/200	5.00
311	Troy Glaus/ Bat-Jsy/200	5.00
314	Chipper Jones/ Jsy-Jsy/100	10.00
315	Johnny Estrada/ Jsy-Jsy/200	5.00
316	Andruw Jones/ Bat-Jsy/200	8.00
319	Jay Gibbons/ Bat-Bat/200	5.00
320	Melvin Mora/ Bat-Jsy/200	5.00
321	Rafael Palmeiro/ Bat-Jsy/200	8.00
323	David Ortiz/ Bat-Jsy/200	8.00
324	Manny Ramirez/ Bat-Jsy/200	10.00
327	Curt Schilling/ Bat-Jsy/200	10.00
328	Sammy Sosa/ Bat-Jsy/200	10.00
329	Mark Prior/ Bat-Jsy/200	8.00
330	Greg Maddux/ Jsy-Jsy/25	15.00
332	Frank Thomas/ Bat-Pants/200	10.00
333	Mark Buehrle/ Bat-Jsy/200	5.00
336	Sean Casey/ Bat-Jsy/200	5.00
337	Adam Dunn/ Bat-Jsy/200	8.00
339	Travis Hafner/ Jsy-Jsy/200	5.00
340	Victor Martinez/ Bat-Jsy/200	5.00
341	Cliff Lee/Jsy-Jsy/200	5.00
342	Todd Helton/ Bat-Jsy/25	8.00
343	Preston Wilson/ Jsy-Jsy/200	5.00
344	Ivan Rodriguez/ Bat-Jsy/200	8.00
347	Miguel Cabrera/ Bat-Jsy/200	10.00
348	Jeff Bagwell/ Bat-Jsy/200	8.00
349	Andy Pettitte/ Bat-Jsy/200	8.00
350	Roger Clemens/ Bat-Jsy/200	15.00
351	Ken Harvey/ Bat-Jsy/200	5.00
353	Hideo Nomo/ Bat-Jsy/200	8.00
354	Kazuhisa Ishii/ Jsy-Jsy/200	5.00
355	Edwin Jackson/ Jsy-Jsy/200	5.00
356	J.D. Drew/ Bat-Bat/200	5.00
357	Jeff Kent/ Bat-Bat/25	5.00
358	Geoff Jenkins/ Jsy-Pants/200	5.00
359	Carlos Lee/ Bat-Bat/200	5.00
360	Shannon Stewart/ Jsy-Jsy/200	5.00
362	Johan Santana/ Jsy-Jsy/100	10.00
363	Mike Piazza/ Jsy-Jsy/100	12.00
364	Kazuo Matsui/ Jsy-Jsy/100	5.00
366	Pedro Martinez/ Bat-Jsy/100	10.00
368	Hideki Matsui/ Bat-Jsy/100	20.00
369	Bernie Williams/ Bat-Jsy/200	8.00
370	Gary Sheffield/ Bat-Jsy/200	8.00
371	Randy Johnson/ Bat-Bat/25	10.00
378	Mark Mulder/ Bat-Bat/50	8.00
380	Eric Chavez/ Jsy-Jsy/100	5.00
382	Marlon Byrd/ Jsy-Jsy/200	5.00
383	Pat Burrell/ Bat-Jsy/200	5.00
385	Jim Thome/ Bat-Bat/200	8.00
388	Moises Alou/ Bat-Bat/200	5.00
393	Adrian Beltre/ Bat-Bat/50	5.00
394	Richie Sexson/ Bat-Bat/200	5.00
397	Albert Pujols/ Bat-Jsy/200	20.00
398	Scott Rolen/ Bat-Jsy/200	5.00
401	Delmon Young/ Bat-Bat/200	5.00
402	Aubrey Huff/ Bat-Jsy/50	5.00
403	Alfonso Soriano/ Bat-Jsy/200	8.00
404	Hank Blalock/ Bat-Jsy/200	5.00
405	Richard Hidalgo/ Bat-Jsy/200	5.00
406	Vernon Wells/ Jsy-Jsy/200	5.00
407	Orlando Hudson/ Bat-Bat/200	5.00
412	Jose Vidro/ Bat-Jsy/5	5.00
415	Miguel Tejada/ Bat-Jsy/200	8.00
416	Gary Sheffield/ Bat-Bat/200	8.00
417	Curt Schilling/ Bat-Jsy/200	10.00
418	Rafael Palmeiro/ Bat-Jsy/50	8.00
419	Scott Rolen/ Bat-Jsy/200	10.00
420	Aramis Ramirez/ Jsy-Jsy/200	8.00
421	Vladimir Guerrero/ Bat-Bat/200	10.00
422	Steve Finley/ Jsy-Jsy/200	5.00
423	Roger Clemens/ Bat-Jsy/200	15.00
424	Mike Piazza/ Jsy-Jsy/200	12.00
425	Ivan Rodriguez/ Bat-Jsy/200	8.00
426	David Justice/ Jsy-Jsy/200	5.00
427	Mark Grace/ Bat-Jsy/200	8.00
428	Alan Trammell/ Bat-Jsy/100	5.00
430	Dwight Gooden/ Bat-Jsy/200	5.00
431	Deion Sanders/ Bat-Jsy/200	5.00
432	Joe Torre/ Bat-Bat/100	5.00
433	Jose Canseco/ Jsy-Jsy/100	8.00
434	Tony Gwynn/ Bat-Pants/200	8.00
435	Will Clark/ Bat-Jsy/200	8.00
437	Nolan Ryan/ Bat-Jsy/50	15.00
438	Billy Martin/ Jsy-Pants/200	10.00
439	Carlos Delgado/ Bat-Bat/200	5.00
440	Magglio Ordonez/ Bat-Bat/200	5.00
441	Sammy Sosa/ Bat-Jsy/25	10.00
449	Ryne Sandberg/ Bat-Jsy/100	10.00

Recollection Autographs Gold

No Pricing
Production One Set
Silver: No Pricing
Production One Set
Platinum: No Pricing
Production One Set

Signature Bronze

NM/M

Production 1-100
No pricing 20 or less.
Black: No Pricing
Production One Set
Gold: .75-1.5X
Production 1-50
Silver: .75-1.5X
Production 1-100
Platinum: No Pricing
Production One Set
Framed Blue: .75-1.5X
Production 1-50
Framed Green: .75-1.5X
Production 1-25
Framed Red: .75-1.5X
#303-450 found in DK Update

#	Player	Price
3	Jose Guillen/100	15.00
5	Tim Salmon/100	20.00
6	Casey Kotchman/100	15.00
7	Chone Figgins/100	15.00
8	Robb Quinlan/100	8.00
9	Francisco Rodriguez/ 50	40.00
10	Troy Percival/50	15.00
14	Shea Hillenbrand/100	10.00
15	Chad Tracy/100	10.00
16	Alex Cintron/100	8.00
22	Adam LaRoche/50	10.00
23	Russ Ortiz/50	12.00
26	Nick Green/50	8.00
30	Luis Matos/100	10.00
31	Larry Bigbie/100	10.00
32	Rodrigo Lopez/100	15.00
33	Brian Roberts/100	25.00
34	Melvin Mora/100	15.00
40	Keith Foulke/50	40.00
43	Kevin Youkilis/100	15.00
44	Orlando Cabrera/50	20.00
45	Abe Alvarez/100	8.00
51	Carlos Zambrano/50	30.00
58	Todd Walker/50	15.00
59	Angel Guzman/50	15.00
61	Carlos Lee/100	15.00
73	Ryan Wagner/100	10.00
75	Danny Graves/100	12.00
76	C.C. Sabathia/50	20.00
77	Jody Gerut/100	8.00
79	Victor Martinez/50	20.00
82	Kazuhito Tadano/100	20.00
83	Travis Hafner/100	15.00
89	Jeremy Bonderman/ 100	15.00
92	Brandon Inge/100	10.00
101	Guillermo Mota/50	10.00
107	Morgan Ensberg/100	10.00
112	Jeremy Affeldt/100	10.00
117	Milton Bradley/100	15.00
122	Brad Penny/100	10.00
123	Scott Podsednik/50	15.00
125	Lyle Overbay/100	12.00
127	Bill Hall/100	8.00
132	Lew Ford/100	15.00
135	Jason Kubel/100	15.00
137	Chad Cordero/100	10.00
140	Livan Hernandez/25	15.00
156	Bubba Crosby/100	10.00
159	Tom Gordon/25	20.00
160	Esteban Loaiza/100	10.00
166	Jermaine Dye/50	15.00
168	Octavio Dotel/50	15.00
169	Bobby Crosby/100	20.00
174	Mike Lieberthal/100	12.00
177	Randy Wolf/100	10.00
178	Craig Wilson/100	10.00
180	Jack Wilson/100	12.00
181	Jose Castillo/100	10.00
184	Jason Bay/100	15.00
186	Jay Payton/50	10.00
189	Jake Peavy/50	30.00
194	Freddy Guzman/100	10.00
197	Todd Linden/50	10.00
198	Merkin Valdez/100	10.00
203	Raul Ibanez/100	10.00
206	Miguel Olivo/50	10.00
207	Bucky Jacobsen/100	12.00
208	Jamie Moyer/50	15.00
212	Dan Haren/100	12.00
219	Jeff Suppan/100	10.00
220	Aubrey Huff/50	15.00
221	Carl Crawford/25	20.00
224	Dewon Brazelton/100	8.00
226	Joey Gathright/100	10.00
227	Scott Kazmir/25	25.00
230	Michael Young/100	20.00
231	Adrian Gonzalez/100	10.00
232	Laynce Nix/100	10.00
236	David Dellucci/100	20.00
237	Francisco Cordero/ 100	15.00
241	Alexis Rios/100	15.00
248	Dioner Navarro/100	15.00
253	Yhency Brazoban/ 100	10.00
257	Scott Proctor/100	8.00
260	Matt Peterson/100	8.00
269	Brad Penny/50	10.00
272	Orlando Cabrera/50	10.00
274	Esteban Loaiza/100	10.00
284	Andre Dawson/50	20.00
285	Harold Baines/50	15.00
286	Jack Morris/100	10.00
290	Maury Wills/100	15.00
292	Darryl Strawberry/ 100	15.00
297	Dave Parker/100	20.00
299	Matt Williams/25	25.00
303	Garret Anderson/50	15.00
304	Dallas McPherson/ 100	15.00
305	Orlando Cabrera/25	10.00
306	Steve Finley/50	10.00
313	Russ Ortiz/50	10.00
315	Johnny Estrada/100	8.00
318	Danny Kolb/50	8.00
319	Jay Gibbons/50	8.00
320	Melvin Mora/50	10.00
325	Edgar Renteria/50	15.00
333	Mark Buehrle/50	20.00
336	Sean Casey/25	15.00
339	Travis Hafner/50	15.00
340	Victor Martinez/50	10.00
341	Cliff Lee/100	15.00
351	Preston Wilson/50	15.00
351	Ken Harvey/100	8.00
355	Edwin Jackson/50	10.00
355	Carlos Lee/100	10.00
360	Shannon Stewart/25	15.00
361	Joe Nathan/100	15.00
376	Eric Byrnes/100	8.00
377	Rich Harden/100	15.00
378	Mark Mulder/25	20.00
380	Eric Chavez/25	15.00
382	Marlon Byrd/100	8.00
384	Brett Myers/100	15.00
386	Jason Bay/50	15.00
387	Jake Peavy/50	25.00
402	Aubrey Huff/50	15.00
407	Orlando Hudson/25	10.00
410	Jose Guillen/25	15.00
429	Bert Blyleven/50	10.00
430	Dwight Gooden/25	15.00
436	Marty Marion/50	15.00

Signature Materials Bronze

NM/M

Production 1-200
No pricing 20 or less.
Platinum: No Pricing
Production One Set
Framed Black: No Pricing
Production 1-10
Framed Blue: No Pricing
Production 1-50
Framed Green: 1-2X
Production 1-25
Framed Red: .75-1.5X
Production 1-100

#	Description	Price
1	Garret Anderson/	25.00
7	Chone Figgins/ Bat-Jsy/200	15.00
18	Rafael Furcal/ Bat-Jsy/50	20.00
19	Andruw Jones/ Bat-Jsy/25	35.00
31	Larry Bigbie/ Jsy-Jsy/200	15.00
32	Rodrigo Lopez/ Jsy-Jsy/200	15.00
38	Trot Nixon/ Bat-Jsy/100	30.00
46	David Ortiz/ Bat-Jsy/100	50.00
48	Mark Prior/ Bat-Jsy/25	40.00
49	Aramis Ramirez/ Bat-Jsy/100	25.00
51	Carlos Zambrano/ Jsy-Jsy/200	25.00
52	Derrek Lee/ Bat-Jsy/100	20.00
61	Carlos Lee/ Bat-Jsy/100	10.00
76	C.C. Sabathia/ Jsy-Jsy/100	20.00
78	Omar Vizquel/ Jsy-Jsy/100	40.00
95	Miguel Cabrera/ Bat-Jsy/200	50.00
109	Carlos Beltran/ Bat-Jsy/100	40.00
112	Jeremy Affeldt/ Pants-Pants/100	10.00
127	Bill Hall/Bat-Bat/100	10.00
129	Jacque Jones/ Bat-Jsy/200	20.00
131	Johan Santana/ Jsy-Jsy/50	40.00
132	Lew Ford/ Bat-Jsy/200	15.00
139	Nick Johnson/ Bat-Bat/50	12.00
153	Jorge Posada/ Bat-Jsy/200	40.00
162	Eric Chavez/ Bat-Jsy/25	25.00
178	Craig Wilson/ Jsy-Jsy/200	15.00
185	Sean Burroughs/ Bat-Jsy/100	10.00
201	Edgar Martinez/ Bat-Jsy/200	40.00
211	Edgar Renteria/ Bat-Jsy/25	30.00
221	Carl Crawford/ Jsy-Jsy/200	15.00
229	Mark Teixeira/ Bat-Jsy/25	40.00
230	Michael Young/ Bat-Jsy/200	20.00
232	Laynce Nix/ Bat-Bat/25	12.00
233	Alfonso Soriano/ Bat-Jsy/25	50.00
239	Roy Halladay/ Jsy-Jsy/50	50.00
269	Brad Penny/ Jsy-Jsy/200	10.00
280	Dale Murphy/ Jsy-Jsy/50	35.00
282	Dwight Evans/ Bat-Jsy/25	25.00
283	Ron Santo/ Bat-Jsy/50	35.00
284	Andre Dawson/ Jsy-Jsy/100	25.00
286	Jack Morris/ Jsy-Jsy/200	20.00
287	Kirk Gibson/ Bat-Jsy/25	25.00
289	Orel Hershiser/ Jsy-Jsy/25	35.00
291	Tony Oliva/ Bat-Jsy/25	25.00
294	Don Mattingly/ Jsy-Jsy/25	90.00
297	Dave Parker/ Bat-Jsy/50	25.00
298	Steve Garvey/ Bat-Jsy/50	25.00

300	Keith Hernandez/Bat-Jsy/100	20.00
303	Garret Anderson/Bat-Jsy/100	20.00
315	Johnny Estrada/Jsy-Jsy/100	12.00
319	Jay Gibbons/Bat-Bat/50	12.00
320	Melvin Mora/Jsy-Jsy/50	15.00
323	David Ortiz/Jsy-Jsy/25	50.00
333	Mark Buehrle/Jsy-Jsy/25	25.00
339	Travis Hafner/Jsy-Jsy/25	25.00
340	Victor Martinez/Jsy-Jsy/25	20.00
341	Cliff Lee/Jsy-Jsy/25	15.00
343	Preston Wilson/Bat-Jsy/25	20.00
351	Ken Harvey/Jsy-Jsy/25	12.00
382	Marlon Byrd/Bat-Jsy/25	12.00
401	Delmon Young/Bat-Bat/25	25.00
407	Orlando Hudson/Bat-Bat/25	12.00
419	Scott Rolen/Jsy-Jsy/25	30.00
428	Alan Trammell/Jsy-Jsy/25	25.00
430	Dwight Gooden/Bat-Jsy/25	25.00
434	Tony Gwynn/Bat-Jsy/25	40.00

Signature Materials Silver

NM/M

Production 1-100

7	Chone Figgins/Bat-Jsy/100	15.00
18	Rafael Furcal/Bat-Jsy/100	30.00
31	Larry Bigbie/Jsy-Jsy/100	15.00
32	Rodrigo Lopez/Jsy-Jsy/100	15.00
46	David Ortiz/Bat-Jsy/50	60.00
49	Aramis Ramirez/Bat-Jsy/50	35.00
51	Carlos Zambrano/Jsy-Jsy/100	30.00
61	Carlos Lee/Bat-Jsy/100	10.00
76	C.C. Sabathia/Jsy-Jsy/100	20.00
104	Roy Oswalt/Jsy-Jsy/100	30.00
112	Jeremy Affeldt/Pants-Pants/100	10.00
127	Bill Hall/Bat-Bat/100	10.00
129	Jacque Jones/Bat-Jsy/50	20.00
132	Lew Ford/Bat-Jsy/100	15.00
178	Craig Wilson/Jsy-Jsy/100	15.00
221	Carl Crawford/Jsy-Jsy/100	15.00
230	Michael Young/Bat-Jsy/50	25.00
232	Laynce Nix/Bat-Jsy/100	15.00
269	Brad Penny/Jsy-Jsy/50	15.00
280	Dale Murphy/Jsy-Jsy/25	50.00
282	Dwight Evans/Bat-Jsy/50	30.00
283	Ron Santo/Bat-Bat/50	45.00
284	Andre Dawson/Bat-Jsy/50	30.00
285	Harold Baines/Bat-Jsy/25	25.00
286	Jack Morris/Jsy-Jsy/25	25.00
291	Tony Oliva/Bat-Jsy/50	30.00
297	Dave Parker/Bat-Jsy/50	30.00
298	Steve Garvey/Bat-Jsy/50	30.00
299	Matt Williams/Jsy-Jsy/50	35.00
300	Keith Hernandez/Bat-Jsy/50	25.00

Signature Materials Gold

NM/M

Production 1-50

7	Chone Figgins/Bat-Jsy/20	20.00
18	Rafael Furcal/Bat-Jsy/30	30.00
31	Larry Bigbie/Jsy-Jsy/20	20.00
32	Rodrigo Lopez/Jsy-Jsy/50	20.00

46	David Ortiz/Bat-Jsy/50	60.00
49	Aramis Ramirez/Bat-Jsy/50	35.00
51	Carlos Zambrano/Jsy-Jsy/50	35.00
76	C.C. Sabathia/Jsy-Jsy/50	25.00
104	Roy Oswalt/Jsy-Jsy/50	30.00
112	Jeremy Affeldt/Pants-Pants/50	15.00
127	Bill Hall/Bat-Bat/50	15.00
129	Jacque Jones/Bat-Jsy/50	20.00
132	Lew Ford/Bat-Jsy/50	20.00
178	Craig Wilson/Bat-Jsy/50	20.00
221	Carl Crawford/Jsy-Jsy/50	20.00
230	Michael Young/Bat-Jsy/50	25.00
269	Brad Penny/Bat-Jsy/50	15.00
280	Dale Murphy/Jsy-Jsy/25	50.00
282	Dwight Evans/Bat-Jsy/50	30.00
283	Ron Santo/Bat-Bat/50	45.00
284	Andre Dawson/Bat-Jsy/50	30.00
285	Harold Baines/Bat-Jsy/50	25.00
286	Jack Morris/Jsy-Jsy/50	25.00
291	Tony Oliva/Bat-Jsy/50	30.00
297	Dave Parker/Bat-Jsy/50	30.00
299	Matt Williams/Jsy-Jsy/50	35.00

Teams Timeline Materials Jersey

NM/M

Common Duo: 8.00

Production 100 Sets

Prime: No Pricing

Production One Set

#26-30 found in DK Update

1	Albert Pujols, Scott Rolen	40.00
2	Roger Clemens, Andy Pettitte	25.00
3	Tim Hudson, Mark Mulder	8.00
4	Hank Blalock, Mark Teixeira	10.00
7	Miguel Tejada, Cal Ripken Jr.	40.00
8	Vladimir Guerrero, Reggie Jackson	15.00
9	Mike Schmidt/Jkt., Jim Thome	30.00
10	Chipper Jones, Greg Maddux	20.00
13	Don Mattingly/Jkt., Hideki Matsui	50.00
14	Carlos Delgado, Vernon Wells	8.00
15	Todd Helton, Larry Walker	10.00
16	Duke Snider, Adrian Beltre	10.00
18	Rafael Palmeiro, Eddie Murray	15.00
19	Manny Ramirez, Carl Yastrzemski	25.00
21	Johnny Bench, Adam Dunn	15.00
22	Robin Yount, Lyle Overbay	15.00
24	Gary Carter, Mike Piazza	15.00
25	Carlton Fisk, Frank Thomas	15.00
26	Nolan Ryan, Mike Piazza	30.00
27	Roger Clemens, Jeff Bagwell	20.00
30	Albert Pujols, Stan Musial	40.00

Timeline

NM/M

Complete Set (25): 50.00

Common Player: 1.50

Inserted 1:21

#26-30 found in DK Update

1	Roger Clemens	6.00
2	Nolan Ryan	8.00
3	Carlos Beltran	3.00
4	Ivan Rodriguez	3.00
5	Jim Thome	3.00
6	Mike Piazza	4.00
7	Miguel Tejada	3.00
8	Rafael Palmeiro	2.00
9	Greg Maddux	4.00
10	Tom Glavine	1.50
11	Vladimir Guerrero	2.00
12	Curt Schilling	1.50
13	Mike Mussina	2.00
14	Rickey Henderson	2.00
15	Scott Rolen	3.00
16	Alfonso Soriano	3.00
17	Gary Sheffield	2.00
18	Carlton Fisk	3.00
19	Aramis Ramirez	1.50
20	Mark Grace	1.50
21	Jason Giambi	1.50
22	Juan Gonzalez	1.50
23	Brad Penny	1.50
24	Nomar Garciaparra	4.00
25	Larry Walker	2.00
26	Curt Schilling	2.00
27	Reggie Jackson	2.00
28	Gary Carter	1.50
29	Roger Clemens	6.00
30	Nolan Ryan	8.00

Team Timeline Materials Bat

NM/M

Production 25-100

2	Roger Clemens, Andy Pettitte/50	25.00
5	Miguel Cabrera, Mike Lowell/100	15.00
8	Vladimir Guerrero, Reggie Jackson/75	20.00
9	Mike Schmidt, Jim Thome/50	30.00
13	Don Mattingly, Hideki Matsui/50	50.00
15	Todd Helton, Larry Walker/100	10.00
17	Al Kaline, Ivan Rodriguez/25	30.00
18	Rafael Palmeiro, Eddie Murray/100	15.00
21	Johnny Bench, Adam Dunn/100	15.00
22	Robin Yount, Lyle Overbay/100	20.00
23	Nolan Ryan, Randy Johnson/25	40.00

Teams Timeline Materials Jersey

NM/M

Production 50-200

Prime: No Pricing

Production One Set

#26-30 found in DK Update

1	Roger Clemens	15.00
2	Nolan Ryan	25.00
3	Carlos Beltran	10.00
4	Ivan Rodriguez	8.00
7	Mike Piazza	15.00
7	Miguel Tejada	10.00
8	Rafael Palmeiro	10.00
9	Greg Maddux	15.00
11	Vladimir Guerrero	15.00
12	Curt Schilling	10.00
13	Mike Mussina	10.00
14	Rickey Henderson	10.00
15	Scott Rolen	15.00
16	Alfonso Soriano	10.00
18	Carlton Fisk	10.00
19	Aramis Ramirez	10.00
21	Jason Giambi	8.00
22	Juan Gonzalez	8.00
26	Curt Schilling	10.00
27	Reggie Jackson	8.00
28	Gary Carter	8.00
29	Roger Clemens	15.00
30	Nolan Ryan	25.00

Update B/W

B/W: 1X

Inserted 1:2

Update Gallery of Stars

NM/M

Complete Set (25): 30.00

Common Player: 1.50

Inserted 1:8

1	Andre Dawson	1.50
2	Bob Feller	2.00
3	Bobby Doerr	1.50
4	C.C. Sabathia	1.50
5	Carl Crawford	1.50
6	Dale Murphy	2.00
7	Danny Kolb	1.50
8	Darryl Strawberry	1.50
9	Dave Parker	1.50
10	David Ortiz	1.50
11	Dwight Gooden	1.50
12	Garret Anderson	1.50
13	Jack Morris	1.50
14	Jacque Jones	1.50
15	Jim Palmer	2.00
16	Johan Santana	3.00
17	Ken Harvey	1.50
18	Lyle Overbay	1.50
19	Marty Marion	1.50
20	Melvin Mora	1.50
21	Michael Young	1.50
22	Miguel Cabrera	3.00
23	Preston Wilson	1.50
24	Sean Casey	1.50
25	Victor Martinez	1.50

Update Gallery of Stars Autograph

NM/M

Production 5-100

1	Andre Dawson/100	15.00
2	Bob Feller/100	25.00
3	Bobby Doerr/100	15.00
4	C.C. Sabathia/25	15.00
5	Carl Crawford/100	12.00
6	Dale Murphy/100	20.00
7	Danny Kolb/100	10.00
8	Darryl Strawberry/100	15.00
9	Dave Parker/100	15.00
11	Dwight Gooden/100	15.00
13	Jack Morris/100	12.00
14	Jacque Jones/50	10.00

Timeline Materials Bat

NM/M

Production 25-100

1	Roger Clemens	30.00
2	Nolan Ryan	50.00
3	Carlos Beltran	10.00
4	Ivan Rodriguez	10.00
5	Jim Thome	20.00
8	Rafael Palmeiro	10.00
9	Greg Maddux	30.00
10	Tom Glavine	10.00
11	Vladimir Guerrero	15.00
12	Curt Schilling	20.00
13	Mike Mussina	10.00
14	Rickey Henderson	10.00
15	Scott Rolen	20.00
17	Gary Sheffield	10.00
18	Carlton Fisk	10.00
19	Aramis Ramirez	10.00
20	Mark Grace	10.00
22	Juan Gonzalez	10.00
25	Larry Walker	10.00

Timeline Materials Jersey

NM/M

Production 50-200

Prime: No Pricing

Production One Set

#26-30 found in DK Update

1	Roger Clemens	15.00
2	Nolan Ryan	25.00
3	Carlos Beltran	10.00
4	Ivan Rodriguez	8.00
7	Miguel Tejada	10.00
8	Rafael Palmeiro	10.00
9	Greg Maddux	15.00
11	Vladimir Guerrero	15.00
12	Curt Schilling	10.00
13	Mike Mussina	10.00
14	Rickey Henderson	10.00
15	Scott Rolen	15.00
16	Alfonso Soriano	10.00
18	Carlton Fisk	10.00
19	Aramis Ramirez	10.00
21	Jason Giambi	8.00
22	Juan Gonzalez	8.00
26	Curt Schilling	10.00
27	Reggie Jackson	8.00
28	Gary Carter	8.00
29	Roger Clemens	15.00
30	Nolan Ryan	25.00

Update Gallery of Stars Jersey Autograph

NM/M

Production 25-100

Prime: No Pricing

Production One Set

1	Andre Dawson/25	25.00
2	Bob Feller/30	30.00
3	Bobby Doerr/100	15.00
4	C.C. Sabathia/100	15.00
5	Carl Crawford/50	15.00
6	Dale Murphy/50	25.00
9	Dave Parker/100	15.00
10	David Ortiz/50	40.00
11	Dwight Gooden/100	20.00
12	Garret Anderson/50	20.00
13	Jack Morris/50	15.00
14	Jacque Jones/25	15.00
15	Jim Palmer/25	25.00
17	Ken Harvey/50	15.00
18	Lyle Overbay/100	10.00
19	Marty Marion/25	20.00
20	Melvin Mora/50	15.00
24	Sean Casey/25	20.00
25	Victor Martinez/100	20.00

Update Gallery of Star Combo

NM/M

Production 50-200

Prime: No Pricing

Production One Set

1	Andre Dawson/100	10.00
3	Bobby Doerr/100	8.00
6	Dale Murphy/100	10.00
9	Dave Parker/200	8.00
10	David Ortiz/200	12.00
11	Dwight Gooden/100	5.00
12	Garret Anderson/100	5.00
14	Jacque Jones/50	5.00
15	Jim Palmer/50	5.00

17	Ken Harvey/100	8.00
18	Lyle Overbay/50	10.00
19	Marty Marion/25	20.00
20	Melvin Mora/100	12.00
25	Victor Martinez/100	12.00

Update Gallery of Stars Bat

NM/M

Production 50-200

1	Andre Dawson/50	8.00
3	Bobby Doerr/100	4.00
6	Dale Murphy/100	4.00
8	Darryl Strawberry/100	4.00
9	Dave Parker/100	4.00
10	David Ortiz/200	10.00
11	Dwight Gooden/100	4.00
12	Garret Anderson/100	4.00
18	Lyle Overbay/100	4.00
21	Michael Young/200	4.00
22	Miguel Cabrera/100	8.00
23	Preston Wilson/200	4.00
24	Sean Casey/200	4.00

Update Gallery of Stars Bat Autograph

NM/M

Production 5-200

1	Andre Dawson/25	25.00
3	Bobby Doerr/200	15.00
9	Dave Parker/200	15.00
11	Dwight Gooden/100	20.00
12	Garret Anderson/100	15.00
14	Jacque Jones/100	15.00
17	Ken Harvey/25	12.00
21	Michael Young/100	15.00
22	Miguel Cabrera/35	35.00
24	Sean Casey/50	20.00

Update Gallery of Stars Jersey

NM/M

Production 25-100

Prime: No Pricing

Production One Set

1	Andre Dawson/100	6.00
2	Bob Feller/100	8.00
3	Bobby Doerr/100	4.00
4	C.C. Sabathia/100	4.00
5	Carl Crawford/100	4.00
6	Dale Murphy/100	8.00
7	Darryl Strawberry/25	6.00
9	Dave Parker/100	4.00
10	David Ortiz/100	8.00
11	Dwight Gooden/25	5.00
12	Garret Anderson/50	4.00
13	Jack Morris/100	4.00
14	Jacque Jones/100	4.00
15	Jim Palmer/100	6.00
17	Ken Harvey/100	4.00
18	Lyle Overbay/100	4.00
20	Melvin Mora/100	4.00
21	Michael Young/100	4.00
22	Miguel Cabrera/100	8.00
23	Preston Wilson/100	4.00
24	Sean Casey/100	4.00
25	Victor Martinez/25	6.00

Update Gallery of Stars Jersey Autograph

NM/M

Production 25-100

Prime: No Pricing

Production One Set

1	Andre Dawson/25	25.00
2	Bob Feller/50	30.00
3	Bobby Doerr/100	15.00
4	C.C. Sabathia/100	15.00
5	Carl Crawford/50	15.00
6	Dale Murphy/50	25.00
9	Dave Parker/100	15.00
10	David Ortiz/50	40.00
11	Dwight Gooden/100	20.00
12	Garret Anderson/50	20.00
13	Jack Morris/50	15.00
14	Jacque Jones/25	15.00
15	Jim Palmer/25	25.00
17	Ken Harvey/50	15.00
18	Lyle Overbay/100	10.00
19	Marty Marion/25	20.00
20	Melvin Mora/50	15.00
24	Sean Casey/25	20.00
25	Victor Martinez/100	20.00

18	Lyle Overbay/50	5.00
21	Michael Young/200	5.00
22	Miguel Cabrera/200	10.00
23	Preston Wilson/200	5.00
24	Sean Casey/200	5.00

Update Gallery of Stars Combo Autograph

NM/M

Production 25-200

Prime: No Pricing

Production One Set

1	Andre Dawson/50	25.00
3	Bobby Doerr/200	20.00
6	Dale Murphy/50	30.00
9	Dave Parker/100	15.00
10	David Ortiz/50	40.00
11	Dwight Gooden/100	20.00
12	Garret Anderson/50	20.00
14	Jacque Jones/50	25.00
15	Jim Palmer/50	25.00
17	Ken Harvey/25	15.00
21	Michael Young/50	20.00
22	Miguel Cabrera/50	35.00
24	Sean Casey/50	20.00
25	Victor Martinez/100	20.00

Update HOF Sluggers

NM/M

Common Player: 2.00

1	Duke Snider	2.00
2	Eddie Murray	2.00
3	Frank Robinson	2.00
4	George Brett	5.00
5	Harmon Killebrew	3.00
6	Mike Schmidt	5.00
7	Reggie Jackson	3.00
8	Roberto Clemente	6.00
9	Stan Musial	4.00
10	Willie Mays	5.00

Update HOF Sluggers Jersey

NM/M

Production 5-50

1	Duke Snider/Pants/25	10.00
2	Eddie Murray/50	10.00
5	Harmon Killebrew/25	15.00
6	Mike Schmidt/50	15.00
7	Reggie Jackson/Pants/50	8.00
9	Stan Musial/Pants/25	20.00
10	Willie Mays/Pants/50	25.00

Update Masters of the Game

NM/M

Common Player: 2.00

1	Albert Pujols	4.00
2	Cal Ripken Jr.	6.00
3	Don Mattingly	4.00
4	Greg Maddux	4.00
5	Jim Thorpe	4.00
6	Nolan Ryan	5.00
7	Randy Johnson	4.00
8	Roberto Clemente	6.00
9	Roger Clemens	5.00
10	Willie Mays	4.00

Update Masters of the Game Jersey

NM/M

Production 25-50

1	Albert Pujols/50	20.00
2	Cal Ripken Jr./50	30.00
3	Don Mattingly/25	20.00
4	Greg Maddux/50	10.00
5	Jim Thorpe/25	250.00
6	Nolan Ryan/25	10.00
7	Randy Johnson/25	10.00
9	Roger Clemens/25	10.00
10	Willie Mays/Pants/25	30.00

Inner Column (between col 1 and 2) — Team Timeline

Team Timeline

NM/M

Complete Set (25): 65.00

Common Duo: 1.50

Inserted 1:21

#26-30 found in DK Update

1	Albert Pujols, Scott Rolen	6.00
2	Roger Clemens, Andy Pettitte	6.00
3	Tim Hudson, Mark Mulder	1.50
4	Hank Blalock, Mark Teixeira	2.00
5	Miguel Cabrera, Mike Lowell	2.00
6	Greg Maddux, Sammy Sosa	4.00
7	Miguel Tejada, Cal Ripken Jr.	8.00
8	Vladimir Guerrero, Reggie Jackson	3.00
9	Mike Schmidt, Jim Thome	4.00
10	Chipper Jones, Greg Maddux	4.00
11	George Brett, Ken Harvey	5.00
12	Don Mattingly, Hideki Matsui	5.00
13	Torii Hunter, Johan Santana	2.00
14	Carlos Delgado, Vernon Wells	1.50
15	Todd Helton, Larry Walker	2.00
16	Duke Snider, Adrian Beltre	2.00
17	Al Kaline, Ivan Rodriguez	3.00
18	Rafael Palmeiro, Eddie Murray	2.00
19	Manny Ramirez, Carl Yastrzemski	3.00
20	Ralph Kiner, Jason Bay	1.50
21	Johnny Bench, Adam Dunn	3.00
22	Robin Yount, Lyle Overbay	4.00
23	Nolan Ryan, Randy Johnson	8.00
24	Gary Carter, Mike Piazza	4.00
25	Carlton Fisk, Frank Thomas	3.00
26	Nolan Ryan, Mike Piazza	8.00
27	Roger Clemens, Jeff Bagwell	8.00
28	Cal Ripken Jr., Sammy Sosa	8.00
29	Willie Mays, Jim Thorpe	8.00
30	Albert Pujols, Stan Musial	8.00

2005 Donruss Elite

		NM/M
Complete Set (200):		
Common Player (1-150):		.25
Common SP (151-170):		3.00
Production 1,250		
Common Auto. (171-200):		8.00
Production 500 to 1,500		
Pack (5):		5.00
Box (20):		90.00
1	Bartolo Colon	.25
2	Casey Kotchman	.25
3	Chone Figgins	.25
4	Darin Erstad	.25
5	Garret Anderson	.40
6	Jose Guillen	.25
7	Vladimir Guerrero	.75
8	Luis Gonzalez	.25
9	Randy Johnson	.75
10	Troy Glaus	.40
11	Andruw Jones	.40
12	Chipper Jones	.75
13	J.D. Drew	.25
14	John Smoltz	.40
15	Johnny Estrada	.25
16	Marcus Giles	.25
17	Rafael Furcal	.25
18	Javy Lopez	.40
19	Jay Gibbons	.25
20	Melvin Mora	.25
21	Miguel Tejada	.50
22	Rafael Palmeiro	.50
23	Sidney Ponson	.25
24	Curt Schilling	.75
25	David Ortiz	.75
26	Derek Lowe	.25
27	Jason Varitek	.40
28	Johnny Damon	.75
29	Manny Ramirez	.75
30	Pedro Martinez	.75
31	Aramis Ramirez	.40
32	Carlos Zambrano	.40
33	Corey Patterson	.25
34	Derrek Lee	.50
35	Greg Maddux	1.00
36	Kerry Wood	.50
37	Mark Prior	.75
38	Moises Alou	.40
39	Nomar Garciaparra	1.00
40	Sammy Sosa	1.00
41	Carlos Lee	.25
42	Frank Thomas	.50
43	Jermaine Dye	.25
44	Magglio Ordonez	.25
45	Mark Buehrle	.25
46	Paul Konerko	.25
47	Adam Dunn	.50
48	Austin Kearns	.25
49	Barry Larkin	.40
50	Ken Griffey Jr.	1.00
51	Sean Casey	.25
52	C.C. Sabathia	.25
53	Cliff Lee	.25
54	Travis Hafner	.25
55	Victor Martinez	.25
56	Jeromy Burnitz	.25
57	Preston Wilson	.25
58	Todd Helton	.40
59	Brandon Inge	.25
60	Ivan Rodriguez	.50
61	Jeremy Bonderman	.25
62	Troy Percival	.25
63	Dontrelle Willis	.40
64	Josh Beckett	.40
65	Juan Pierre	.25
66	Miguel Cabrera	.75
67	Mike Lowell	.25
68	Paul LoDuca	.25
69	Andy Pettitte	.40
70	Brad Ausmus	.25
71	Carlos Beltran	.50
72	Craig Biggio	.40
73	Jeff Bagwell	.50
74	Lance Berkman	.40
75	Roger Clemens	2.00
76	Roy Oswalt	.25
77	Juan Gonzalez	.40
78	Mike Sweeney	.25
79	Zack Greinke	.25
80	Adrian Beltre	.25
81	Hideo Nomo	.25
82	Jeff Kent	.25
83	Milton Bradley	.25
84	Shawn Green	.25
85	Steve Finley	.25
86	Ben Sheets	.25
87	Lyle Overbay	.25
88	Scott Podsednik	.25
89	Lew Ford	.25
90	Shannon Stewart	.25
91	Torii Hunter	.25
92	David Wright	.75
93	Jose Reyes	.50
94	Kazuo Matsui	.25
95	Mike Piazza	1.00
96	Tom Glavine	.40
97	Alex Rodriguez	1.50
98	Bernie Williams	.40
99	Derek Jeter	2.00
100	Gary Sheffield	.50
101	Hideki Matsui	1.50
102	Jason Giambi	.25
103	Kevin Brown	.25
104	Mike Mussina	.40
105	Barry Zito	.25
106	Bobby Crosby	.40
107	Eric Chavez	.40
108	Jason Kendall	.25
109	Mark Mulder	.40
110	Bobby Abreu	.40
111	Jim Thome	.75
112	Kevin Millwood	.25
113	Pat Burrell	.25
114	Craig Wilson	.25
115	Jack Wilson	.25
116	Jason Bay	.40
117	Brian Giles	.25
118	Khalil Greene	.40
119	Mark Loretta	.25
120	Ryan Klesko	.25
121	Sean Burroughs	.25
122	Edgardo Alfonzo	.25
123	J.T. Snow	.25
124	Jason Schmidt	.25
125	Omar Vizquel	.25
126	Ichiro Suzuki	1.50
127	Jamie Moyer	.25
128	Bret Boone	.25
129	Richie Sexson	.40
130	Albert Pujols	2.00
131	Edgar Renteria	.40
132	Jeff Suppan	.25
133	Jim Edmonds	.40
134	Larry Walker	.40
135	Scott Rolen	.75
136	Aubrey Huff	.25
137	B.J. Upton	.25
138	Carl Crawford	.25
139	Rocco Baldelli	.25
140	Alfonso Soriano	.75
141	Hank Blalock	.40
142	Kenny Rogers	.25
143	Laynce Nix	.25
144	Mark Teixeira	.50
145	Michael Young	.25
146	Carlos Delgado	.40
147	Eric Hinske	.25
148	Roy Halladay	.25
149	Vernon Wells	.25
150	Jose Vidro	.25
151	Bob Gibson	3.00
152	Brooks Robinson	3.00
153	Cal Ripken Jr.	10.00
154	Carl Yastrzemski	4.00
155	Don Mattingly	5.00
156	Eddie Murray	3.00
157	Ernie Banks	4.00
158	Frank Robinson	3.00
159	George Brett	5.00
160	Harmon Killebrew	4.00
161	Johnny Bench	4.00
162	Mike Schmidt	5.00
163	Nolan Ryan	4.00
164	Paul Molitor	4.00
165	Stan Musial	5.00
166	Steve Carlton	3.00
167	Tony Gwynn	4.00
168	Warren Spahn	4.00
169	Willie Mays	6.00
170	Willie McCovey	3.00
171	Miguel Negron AU/1500 RC	8.00
172	Mike Morse AU/1000 RC	15.00
173	Wladimir Balentien AU/1500 RC	10.00
174	Alberto Concepcion AU/651 RC	10.00
175	Ubaldo Jimenez AU/500 RC	10.00
176	Justin Verlander AU/500 RC	50.00
177	Ryan Speier AU/1000 RC	8.00
178	Geovany Soto AU/500 RC	8.00
179	Mark McLemore AU/1200 RC	8.00
180	Ambiorix Burgos AU/599 RC	8.00
181	Chris Roberson AU/1000 RC	10.00
182	Colter Bean AU/625 RC	10.00
183	Erick Threets AU/500 RC	8.00
184	Carlos Ruiz AU/1000 RC	15.00
186	Jared Gothreaux AU/1500 RC	10.00
187	Luis Hernandez AU/1000 RC	8.00
188	Agustin Montero/ 1000 RC	2.00
189	Paulino Reynoso/ 1000 RC	2.00
190	Garrett Jones AU/500 RC	8.00
191	Sean Thompson AU/500 RC	8.00
192	Matt Lindstrom AU/1500 RC	8.00
193	Nate McLouth AU/500 RC	10.00
194	Luke Scott AU/671 RC	25.00
195	Keith Hattig AU/500	10.00
196	Jason Hammel AU/1500 RC	10.00
197	Danny Rueckel AU/671 RC	8.00
198	Justin Wechsler AU/500 RC	8.00
199	Chris Resop AU/500 RC	15.00
200	Jeff Miller AU/500 RC	10.00

Aspirations

Cards (1-150) print run	
61-99:	4-8X
(1-150) p/r 41-60:	6-10X
(1-150) p/r 21-40:	8-15X
(151-170) p/r 36-80:	1.5-3X
Autos. (171-200) p/r	
40-99:	.5-1.5X
No pricing production 20 or less.	
Production 15-99	

Status

Cards (1-150) print run	
61-81:	4-8X
(1-150) p/r 41-60:	6-10X
(1-150) p/r 21-40:	8-15X
(151-170) p/r 36-81:	1.5-3X
Autos. (171-200) p/r	
40-81:	.5-1.5X
No pricing production 20 or less.	
Production 1-81	

Status Gold

Gold (1-150):	10-20X
Gold (151-170):	3-5X
Gold (171-200):	No Pricing
Production 24 Sets	

Turn of the Century

Stars (1-150):	2-3X
Production 750	
(151-170):	1X
Production 250	
Rookies (171-200):	.25-1X
Production 500	

Back 2 Back Jacks

		NM/M
Production 25-200		
1	Adam Dunn/200	8.00
2	Albert Pujols/100	15.00
4	Babe Ruth/50	160.00
5	Cal Ripken Jr./100	30.00
6	David Ortiz/200	10.00
7	Eddie Murray/150	8.00
8	Ernie Banks/50	15.00
9	Frank Robinson/50	8.00
10	Gary Sheffield/200	5.00
11	George Foster/125	5.00
12	Don Mattingly/10	15.00
13	Hideki Matsui/25	30.00
16	Jason Giambi/50	5.00
17	Jim Rice/125	8.00
18	Jim Thome/200	8.00
19	Johnny Bench/125	10.00
20	Lance Berkman/200	5.00
21	Manny Ramirez/200	8.00
22	Mike Piazza/200	10.00
23	Mike Schmidt/125	15.00
24	Rafael Palmeiro/125	8.00
25	Reggie Jackson/125	10.00
26	Sammy Sosa/100	10.00
27	Scott Rolen/200	8.00
28	Stan Musial/125	10.00
29	Willie Mays/50	40.00
30	Kirk Gibson/125	5.00
31	Will Clark/125	5.00
32	Willie Mays, Sammy Sosa/50	50.00
	Eddie Murray, Mike Piazza/50	20.00
33	Mike Schmidt, Jim Thome/50	30.00
34	Rafael Palmeiro, Kirk Gibson/50	10.00
35	Jim Rice, Manny Ramirez/50	15.00
36	Adrian Beltre, Will Clark/50	15.00
37	Reggie Jackson, David Ortiz/50	15.00
38	Johnny Bench, Adam Dunn/50	20.00

Back 2 Back Jacks Combos

		NM/M
1	Adam Dunn/ Bat-Jsy/100	10.00
2	Adrian Beltre/ Bat-Jsy/100	8.00

5	Cal Ripken Jr./ Bat-Jsy/50	40.00
6	David Ortiz/ Bat-Jsy/50	12.00
7	Eddie Murray/ Bat-Jsy/50	10.00
8	Ernie Banks/ Bat-Jsy/10	20.00
10	Gary Sheffield/ Bat-Jsy/100	8.00
11	George Foster/ Bat-Jsy/50	8.00
12	Don Mattingly/ Bat-Jsy/20	20.00
13	Hideki Matsui/ Bat-Jsy/25	40.00
14	Jason Giambi/ Bat-Jsy/50	8.00
15	Jim Edmonds/ Bat-Jsy/100	10.00
17	Jim Thome/ Bat-Jsy/100	8.00
18	Johnny Bench/ Bat-Jsy/15	15.00
19	Lance Berkman/ Bat-Jsy/100	8.00
20	Manny Ramirez/ Bat-Jsy/100	12.00
21	Mike Piazza/ Bat-Jsy/100	15.00
22	Mike Schmidt/ Bat-Jsy/50	20.00
23	Rafael Palmeiro/ Bat-Jsy/50	10.00
24	Reggie Jackson/ Bat-Jsy/50	15.00
25	Sammy Sosa/ Bat-Jsy/100	15.00
26	Scott Rolen/ Bat-Jsy/100	12.00
27	Stan Musial/ Bat-Pants/50	25.00
28	Willie Mays/ Bat-Jsy/50	60.00
29	Kirk Gibson/ Bat-Jsy/50	10.00
30	Will Clark/ Bat-Jsy/50	12.00
32	Eddie Murray, Mike Piazza/25	30.00
33	Mike Schmidt, Jim Thome/25	50.00
34	Rafael Palmeiro, Kirk Gibson/25	20.00
35	Jim Rice, Manny Ramirez/50	25.00
36	Adrian Beltre, Will Clark/50	15.00
37	Reggie Jackson, David Ortiz/25	30.00
38	Johnny Bench, Adam Dunn/25	30.00
40	Cal Ripken Jr., Albert Pujols/25	100.00

Career Best

		NM/M
Common Player:		1.00
Production 1,500 Sets		
Black:		1-2X
Production 150 Sets		
Blue:		1-2X
Production 250 Sets		
Gold:		1-1.5X
Production 500 Sets		
1	Adam Dunn	1.50
2	Adrian Beltre	1.00
3	Albert Pujols	4.00
4	Andruw Jones	1.50
5	Ben Sheets	1.00
6	Bo Jackson	2.00
7	Brooks Robinson	2.00
8	Cal Ripken Jr.	6.00
9	Dale Murphy	1.50
10	Don Mattingly	3.00
11	Eddie Murray	1.50
12	George Brett	3.00
13	Hank Blalock	1.50
14	Ichiro Suzuki	3.00
15	Jim Thome	1.50
16	Kerry Wood	1.50
17	Lance Berkman	1.00
18	Mark Prior	2.00
19	Mark Teixeira	1.50
20	Mike Schmidt	3.00
21	Pedro Martinez	2.00
22	Randy Johnson	2.00
23	Rickey Henderson	1.50
24	Sammy Sosa	3.00
25	Tony Gwynn	

Career Best Bats

		NM/M
Production 50-250		
1	Adam Dunn/250	8.00
2	Adrian Beltre/250	5.00

3	Albert Pujols/250	15.00
4	Andruw Jones/250	5.00
5	Ben Sheets/250	5.00
6	Bo Jackson/250	8.00
7	Brooks Robinson/250	8.00
8	Cal Ripken Jr./250	25.00
9	Dale Murphy/150	10.00
10	Don Mattingly/250	12.00
11	Eddie Murray/250	8.00
12	George Brett/250	15.00
13	Hank Blalock/250	8.00
14	Jim Thome/100	8.00
16	Kerry Wood/250	8.00
17	Lance Berkman/250	5.00
18	Mark Prior/150	6.00
19	Mark Teixeira/250	8.00
20	Mike Schmidt/250	12.00
21	Pedro Martinez/100	8.00
22	Randy Johnson/100	10.00
23	Rickey Henderson/ 250	8.00
24	Sammy Sosa/100	8.00
25	Tony Gwynn/100	10.00

Career Best Jerseys

		NM/M
Production 100-250		
1	Adam Dunn/250	8.00
2	Adrian Beltre/250	5.00
3	Albert Pujols/250	15.00
4	Andruw Jones/250	5.00
5	Ben Sheets/250	5.00
6	Bo Jackson/250	10.00
7	Brooks Robinson/50	10.00
8	Cal Ripken Jr./150	25.00
9	Dale Murphy/100	10.00
10	Don Mattingly/150	12.00
11	Eddie Murray/100	8.00
12	George Brett/100	15.00
13	Hank Blalock/250	8.00
14	Jim Thome/250	8.00
16	Kerry Wood/250	8.00
17	Lance Berkman/250	8.00
18	Mark Prior/250	6.00
19	Mark Teixeira/250	8.00
20	Mike Schmidt/100	12.00
21	Pedro Martinez/250	8.00
22	Randy Johnson/100	10.00
23	Rickey Henderson/50	8.00
24	Sammy Sosa/100	8.00
25	Tony Gwynn/250	10.00

Career Best Combos

		NM/M
Production 25-150		
1	Adam Dunn/ Bat-Jsy/150	10.00
2	Adrian Beltre/ Bat-Jsy/150	8.00
3	Albert Pujols/ Bat-Jsy/150	20.00
4	Andruw Jones/ Bat-Jsy/150	8.00
5	Ben Sheets/ Bat-Jsy/150	8.00
6	Bo Jackson/ Bat-Jsy/25	20.00
7	Brooks Robinson/ Bat-Jsy/25	25.00
8	Cal Ripken Jr./ Bat-Jsy/25	40.00
9	Dale Murphy/ Bat-Jsy/25	10.00
10	Don Mattingly/ Bat-Jsy/25	20.00
11	Eddie Murray/ Bat-Jsy/25	12.00
12	George Brett/ Bat-Jsy/25	25.00
13	Hank Blalock/ Bat-Jsy/150	10.00
15	Jim Thome/ Bat-Jsy/150	10.00
16	Kerry Wood/ Bat-Pants/150	10.00
17	Lance Berkman/ Bat-Jsy/150	8.00
18	Mark Prior/ Bat-Jsy/150	8.00
19	Mark Teixeira/ Bat-Jsy/150	12.00
21	Pedro Martinez/ Bat-Jsy/125	10.00
23	Rickey Henderson/ Bat-Jsy/25	15.00
24	Sammy Sosa/ Bat-Jsy/150	12.00
25	Tony Gwynn/ Bat-Jsy/25	15.00

Face 2 Face

		NM/M
Complete Set (20):		35.00
Common Duo:		
Production 1,500 Sets		
Black:		1-1.5X
Production 500 Sets		
Gold:		1-2X
Production 250 Sets		
Red:		1X
Production 750 Sets		
1	Roger Clemens, Scott Rolen	3.00
2	Greg Maddux, Jeff Bagwell	3.00
3	Mark Prior, Mike Piazza	3.00
4	Mike Mussina, Ivan Rodriguez	2.00
5	Josh Beckett, Sammy Sosa	2.00
6	Roy Oswalt, Miguel Cabrera	2.00
7	Roger Clemens, Albert Pujols	4.00
8	Pedro Martinez, Vladimir Guerrero	2.00
9	Randy Johnson, Jim Edmonds	2.00
10	Curt Schilling, Derek Jeter	4.00
11	Kerry Wood, Lance Berkman	1.50
12	Tim Hudson, Garret Anderson	1.00
13	Pedro Martinez, Gary Sheffield	2.00
14	Barry Zito, Magglio Ordonez	1.00
15	Kerry Wood, Shawn Green	1.50
16	Mike Mussina, Miguel Tejada	2.00
17	Randy Johnson, Albert Pujols	4.00
18	Nolan Ryan, George Brett	4.00
19	Tom Seaver, Mike Schmidt	3.00
20	Jim Palmer, Harmon Killebrew	2.00

Face 2 Face Bats

		NM/M
Production 25-150		
3	Mark Prior, Mike Piazza/10	8.00
4	Mike Mussina, Ivan Rodriguez/100	8.00
5	Josh Beckett, Sammy Sosa/50	10.00
6	Roy Oswalt, Miguel Cabrera/100	10.00
8	Pedro Martinez, Vladimir Guerrero/50	10.00
9	Randy Johnson, Jim Edmonds/50	10.00
11	Kerry Wood, Lance Berkman/150	8.00
12	Tim Hudson, Garret Anderson/150	8.00
13	Pedro Martinez, Gary Sheffield/150	8.00
14	Barry Zito, Magglio Ordonez/50	8.00
15	Kerry Wood, Shawn Green/150	8.00
18	Nolan Ryan, George Brett/100	25.00
19	Tom Seaver, Mike Schmidt/150	15.00

Face 2 Face Jerseys

		NM/M
Production 25-200		
1	Roger Clemens, Scott Rolen/200	15.00
2	Greg Maddux, Jeff Bagwell/75	10.00
3	Mark Prior, Mike Piazza/200	8.00
4	Mike Mussina, Ivan Rodriguez/200	8.00
5	Josh Beckett, Sammy Sosa/200	12.00
6	Roy Oswalt, Miguel Cabrera/200	8.00
7	Roger Clemens, Albert Pujols/200	20.00
8	Pedro Martinez, Vladimir Guerrero/75	10.00
11	Kerry Wood, Lance Berkman/200	8.00
12	Tim Hudson, Garret Anderson/75	8.00
13	Pedro Martinez, Gary Sheffield/75	10.00

14 Barry Zito, Magglio Ordonez/200 8.00
15 Kerry Wood, Shawn Green/200 8.00
16 Mike Mussina, Miguel Tejada/200 10.00
17 Randy Johnson, Albert Pujols/75 20.00
19 Tom Seaver, Mike Schmidt/50 20.00

Face 2 Face Combos
NM/M
Production 25-250
1 Roger Clemens/Jsy, Scott Rolen/Bat/100 15.00
2 Greg Maddux/Jsy, Jeff Bagwell/Bat/100 10.00
3 Mark Prior/Jsy, Mike Piazza/Bat/250 8.00
4 Mike Mussina/Jsy, Ivan Rodriguez/Bat/250 8.00
5 Josh Beckett/Jsy, Sammy Sosa/Bat/250 10.00
6 Roy Oswalt/Jsy, Miguel Cabrera/Bat/250 8.00
8 Pedro Martinez/Jsy, Vladimir Guerrero/Bat/75 10.00
11 Kerry Wood/Bat, Lance Berkman/Jsy/250 8.00
12 Tim Hudson/Jsy, Garret Anderson/Bat/100 8.00
13 Pedro Martinez/Bat, Gary Sheffield/Jsy/75 12.00
14 Barry Zito/Jsy, Magglio Ordonez/Bat/250 8.00
15 Kerry Wood/Bat, Shawn Green/Bat/250 8.00
16 Mike Mussina/Jsy, Miguel Tejada/Bat/250 10.00
19 Tom Seaver/Jsy, Mike Schmidt/Bat/50 20.00

Passing the Torch

NM/M
Common Player: 1.50
1-30 Production 1,000
31-45 Production 500
Black:
1-30 Production 50 — 2-3X
31-45 Production 25
Gold:
1-30 Production 100 — 1-2X
31-45 Production 50
Green:
1-30 Production 250 — 1-1.5X
31-45 Production 125
Red:
1-30 Production 500 — 1X
31-45 Production 250
1 Adrian Beltre 1.50
2 Albert Pujols 5.00
3 Alex Rodriguez 4.00
4 Andruw Jones 1.50
5 Babe Ruth 6.00
6 Ben Sheets 1.50
7 Brooks Robinson 2.00
8 Cal Ripken Jr. 8.00
9 Carl Yastrzemski 3.00
10 Dale Murphy 2.00
11 David Ortiz 2.00
12 Derek Jeter 5.00
13 Don Mattingly 4.00
14 George Brett 4.00
15 Greg Maddux 3.00
16 Hank Blalock 1.50
17 Jeff Bagwell 1.50
18 Johnny Bench 3.00
19 Magglio Ordonez 1.50
20 Mark Prior 2.00
21 Mark Teixeira 2.00
22 Miguel Cabrera 2.00
23 Mike Schmidt 3.00
24 Nolan Ryan 6.00
25 Pedro Martinez 2.00
26 Sammy Sosa 3.00
27 Scott Rolen 2.00
28 Tom Seaver 2.00
29 Vladimir Guerrero 2.00
30 Willie Mays 4.00
31 Carlton Fisk, Magglio Ordonez 3.00
32 Nolan Ryan, Ben Sheets 8.00
33 Babe Ruth, Alex Rodriguez 8.00
34 Cal Ripken Jr., B.J. Upton 10.00
35 Willie Mays, Andruw Jones 5.00
36 George Brett, Hank Blalock 5.00
37 Greg Maddux, Whitey Ford 4.00
38 Harmon Killebrew, Mark Prior 3.00
39 Tom Seaver, Mark Prior 3.00
40 Don Mattingly, Mark Teixeira 5.00
41 Stan Musial, Carlos Beltran 3.00
43 Willie McCovey, Jeff Bagwell 3.00
44 Andre Dawson, Miguel Cabrera 3.00
45 Brooks Robinson, Scott Rolen 4.00

Passing the Torch Autographs
NM/M
Production 5-100
1 Adrian Beltre/75 15.00
6 Ben Sheets/75 15.00
7 Brooks Robinson/100 25.00
10 Dale Murphy/100 20.00
13 Don Mattingly/50 50.00
18 Johnny Bench/25 50.00
19 Magglio Ordonez/75 10.00
20 Mark Prior/25 40.00
21 Mark Teixeira/75 25.00
22 Miguel Cabrera/75 25.00
23 Mike Schmidt/25 50.00
27 Scott Rolen/25 40.00
28 Tom Seaver/25 50.00
31 Carlton Fisk, Magglio Ordonez/25 50.00
44 Andre Dawson, Miguel Cabrera/25 50.00
45 Brooks Robinson, Scott Rolen/25 75.00

Passing the Torch Bats
Production 25-250
1 Adrian Beltre/250 4.00
2 Albert Pujols/250 15.00
4 Andruw Jones/250 4.00
6 Ben Sheets/250 4.00
7 Brooks Robinson/150 10.00
8 Cal Ripken Jr./150 25.00
9 Carl Yastrzemski/150 10.00
10 Dale Murphy/150 6.00
11 David Ortiz/250 8.00
13 Don Mattingly/150 10.00
16 George Brett/150 10.00
17 Hank Blalock/250 4.00
18 Jeff Bagwell/250 6.00
19 Johnny Bench/150 10.00
20 Magglio Ordonez/250 4.00
21 Mark Prior/50 10.00
22 Mark Teixeira/250 6.00
23 Miguel Cabrera/250 8.00
24 Mike Schmidt/150 10.00
25 Nolan Ryan/50 20.00
26 Pedro Martinez/150 8.00
27 Sammy Sosa/250 8.00
28 Scott Rolen/250 8.00
29 Vladimir Guerrero/250 8.00
30 Willie Mays/50 30.00
31 Carlton Fisk, Magglio Ordonez/250 6.00
32 Nolan Ryan, Ben Sheets/50 35.00
34 Cal Ripken Jr., B.J. Upton/50 50.00
35 Willie Mays, Andruw Jones/50 35.00
36 George Brett, Hank Blalock/50 15.00
39 Tom Seaver, Mark Prior/25 20.00
40 Don Mattingly, Mark Teixeira/150 15.00
42 Dale Murphy, Lance Berkman/50 12.00
43 Willie McCovey, Jeff Bagwell/25 20.00
44 Andre Dawson, Miguel Cabrera/150 10.00
45 Brooks Robinson, Scott Rolen/150 15.00

Passing the Torch Jerseys
NM/M
Production 25-250
1 Adrian Beltre/250 4.00
2 Albert Pujols/250 15.00
4 Andruw Jones/250 4.00
6 Ben Sheets/250 4.00
8 Cal Ripken Jr./250 20.00
9 Carl Yastrzemski/Pants/50 10.00
10 Dale Murphy/250 6.00
11 David Ortiz/250 8.00
13 Don Mattingly/150 10.00
14 George Brett/50 12.00
15 Greg Maddux/250 10.00
16 Hank Blalock/250 4.00
17 Jeff Bagwell/250 6.00
18 Johnny Bench/Pants/150 10.00
19 Magglio Ordonez/250 4.00
20 Mark Prior/250 8.00
21 Mark Teixeira/250 6.00
22 Miguel Cabrera/250 8.00
23 Mike Schmidt/150 8.00
24 Nolan Ryan/50 20.00
25 Pedro Martinez/250 8.00
26 Sammy Sosa/250 8.00
27 Scott Rolen/250 8.00
28 Tom Seaver/50 8.00
29 Vladimir Guerrero/250 8.00
31 Carlton Fisk, Magglio Ordonez/50 8.00
32 Nolan Ryan, Ben Sheets/50 35.00
34 Cal Ripken Jr., B.J. Upton/50 50.00
35 Willie Mays, Andruw Jones/50 35.00
36 George Brett, Hank Blalock/50 15.00
39 Tom Seaver, Mark Prior/25 20.00
40 Don Mattingly, Mark Teixeira/100 15.00
42 Dale Murphy, Lance Berkman/150 10.00
43 Willie McCovey, Jeff Bagwell/50 15.00
44 Andre Dawson, Miguel Cabrera/150 10.00

Recollection Autographs
Production 10-25

Teams

NM/M
Common Card:
Production 1,500 Sets
Black: 1X-2X
Production 250 Sets
Blue: 1X
Production 1,000 Sets
Gold: 2X-3X
Production 100 Sets
Green: 1X-1.5X
Production 750 Sets
Red: 1X-1.5X
Production 500 Sets
1 Manny Ramirez, Pedro Martinez, David Ortiz 4.00
2 Albert Pujols, Scott Rolen, Jim Edmonds 4.00
3 Roger Clemens, Jeff Bagwell, Lance Berkman, Craig Biggio 4.00
4 Miguel Cabrera, Josh Beckett, Mike Lowell 2.00
5 Kerry Wood, Mark Prior, Sammy Sosa, Greg Maddux 4.00
6 Adrian Beltre, Shawn Green, Hideo Nomo, Kazuhisa Ishii 2.00
7 Cal Ripken Jr., Eddie Murray, Jim Palmer 8.00
8 George Brett, Bo Jackson, Frank White 4.00
9 Roger Clemens, Mike Mussina, Alfonso Soriano, Bernie Williams 4.00
10 Tom Glavine, Greg Maddux, Ryan Klesko, David Justice 4.00

Teams Bats
NM/M
Production 50-100
1 Manny Ramirez, Pedro Martinez, David Ortiz/150 20.00
2 Albert Pujols, Scott Rolen, Jim Edmonds/100 40.00
3 Roger Clemens, Jeff Bagwell, Lance Berkman, Craig Biggio/50 35.00
4 Miguel Cabrera, Josh Beckett, Mike Lowell/100 10.00
6 Adrian Beltre, Shawn Green, Hideo Nomo, Kazuhisa Ishii/50 20.00
8 George Brett, Bo Jackson, Frank White/50 25.00

Teams Jerseys
NM/M
Production 50-150
1 Manny Ramirez, Pedro Martinez, David Ortiz/150 20.00
2 Albert Pujols, Scott Rolen, Jim Edmonds/150 30.00
3 Roger Clemens, Jeff Bagwell, Lance Berkman, Craig Biggio/150 25.00
4 Miguel Cabrera, Josh Beckett, Mike Lowell/150 15.00
5 Kerry Wood, Mark Prior, Sammy Sosa, Greg Maddux/150 25.00
6 Adrian Beltre, Shawn Green, Hideo Nomo, Kazuhisa Ishii/50 20.00
7 Cal Ripken Jr., Eddie Murray, Jim Palmer/100 35.00
9 Roger Clemens, Mike Mussina, Alfonso Soriano, Bernie Williams/100 25.00
10 Tom Glavine, Greg Maddux, Ryan Klesko, David Justice/100 30.00

Throwback Threads
NM/M
Production 10-200
1 Albert Pujols/200 15.00
3 Bert Blyleven/200 4.00
4 Bobby Doerr/Pants/200 6.00
6 Cal Ripken Jr./150 25.00
7 Carl Yastrzemski/Pants/150 12.00
9 Dale Murphy/150 8.00
10 Dennis Eckersley/50 8.00
11 Don Mattingly/200 10.00
12 Don Sutton/100 4.00
13 Early Wynn/50 6.00
14 Eddie Murray/100 8.00
16 Greg Maddux/150 8.00
17 Harmon Killebrew/100 8.00
18 Hoyt Wilhelm/150 6.00
19 Jim Edmonds/200 8.00
21 Lou Boudreau/100 8.00
22 Lou Brock/50 8.00
23 Miguel Cabrera/200 8.00
24 Mike Mussina/150 8.00
25 Mike Piazza/150 8.00
26 Mike Schmidt/150 15.00
27 Nolan Ryan/50 20.00
28 Phil Niekro/100 6.00
29 Randy Johnson/150 8.00
30 Rickey Henderson/150 8.00
31 Sammy Sosa/150 8.00
32 Scott Rolen/200 8.00
34 Steve Carlton/100 8.00
36 Tommy John/150 6.00
37 Vladimir Guerrero/200 8.00
38 Whitey Ford/25 15.00
39 Willie Mays/50 40.00
40 Willie McCovey/150 8.00
46 Lou Brock, Rickey Henderson/100 15.00
49 Bo Jackson, Deion Sanders/150 15.00
50 Nolan Ryan, Curt Schilling/100 25.00
51 Don Sutton, Greg Maddux/100 15.00
52 Harmon Killebrew, Rafael Palmeiro/150 15.00
53 Dale Murphy, Dwight Evans/150 12.00
55 Carl Yastrzemski, Vladimir Guerrero/50 15.00
56 Eddie Murray, Mike Piazza/100 12.00
57 Johnny Bench, Ivan Rodriguez/50 12.00
58 Jim Palmer, Tim Hudson/50 10.00
59 Cal Ripken Jr., Hank Blalock/50 35.00
60 Jim Rice, Manny Ramirez/100 12.00

Throwback Threads Autographs
NM/M
Prime: No Pricing
Production 1-10
3 Bert Blyleven/100 15.00
4 Bobby Doerr/Pants/100 20.00
5 Brooks Robinson/50 30.00
8 Dale Murphy/100 25.00
9 Dennis Eckersley/75 20.00
11 Don Sutton/50 20.00
17 Harmon Killebrew/75 30.00
20 Jim Palmer/75 15.00
22 Lou Brock/Jkt/75 30.00
23 Miguel Cabrera/75 30.00

Throwback Threads Prime
Production 1-25

2005 Donruss Greats
NM/M
Complete Set (150): 50.00
Common Player: .50
Pack (5): 9.00
Box (15): 120.00
1 Al Kaline .75
2 Alan Trammell .50
3 Andre Dawson .50
4 Barry Larkin .75
5 Bert Blyleven .50
6 Billy Williams .50
7 Bo Jackson 1.00
8 Bob Feller .75
9 Bobby Doerr .50
10 Brooks Robinson 1.00
11 Cal Ripken Jr. 4.00
12 Dale Murphy .50
13 Darryl Strawberry .50
14 Dave Parker .50
15 Dave Stewart .50
16 David Cone .50
17 Dennis Eckersley .50
18 Don Larsen .50
19 Don Mattingly 2.00
20 Don Sutton .50
21 Duke Snider 1.00
22 Dwight Evans .50
23 Dwight Gooden .50
24 Earl Weaver .50
25 Fergie Jenkins .50
26 Frank Robinson .50
27 Fred Lynn .50
28 Gary Carter .50
29 Gaylord Perry .50
30 George Brett 2.50
31 George Foster .50
32 George Kell .50
33 Harmon Killebrew 1.50
34 Harold Baines .50
35 Harold Reynolds .50
36 Jack Morris .50
37 Jim Abbott .50
38 Jim Bunning .50
39 Jim Palmer .50
40 Jim Rice .50
41 Jim Leyritz .50
42 Joe Morgan .50
43 John Kruk .50
44 Johnny Bench 2.00
45 Johnny Podres .50
46 Jose Canseco 1.00
47 Juan Marichal .50
48 Keith Hernandez .50
49 Kent Hrbek .50
50 Kirby Puckett 2.00
51 Lee Smith .50
52 Lenny Dykstra .50
53 Luis Aparicio .50
54 Luis Tiant .50
55 Mark Grace .50
56 Marty Marion .50
57 Matt Williams .50
58 Maury Wills .50
59 Mike Schmidt 2.00
60 Minnie Minoso .50
61 Nolan Ryan 3.00
62 Ozzie Smith 1.00
63 Paul Molitor .75
64 Phil Rizzuto .75
65 Ralph Kiner .50
66 Randy Jones .50
67 Red Schoendienst .50
68 Rich "Goose" Gossage .50
69 Rob Dibble .50
70 Robin Roberts .50
71 Rod Carew .50
72 Rollie Fingers .50
73 Ron Guidry .50
74 Ron Santo .50
75 Ryne Sandberg 2.00
76 Stan Musial 2.00
77 Steve Carlton .50
78 Steve Garvey .50
79 Steve Stone .50
80 Terry Pendleton .50
81 Terry Steinbach .50
82 Tom Seaver 1.00
83 Tommy John .50
84 Tony Gwynn 1.00
85 Tony Oliva .50
86 Whitey Ford 1.00
87 Will Clark .75
88 Willie Mays 3.00
89 Willie McCovey 1.00
90 Roberto Clemente 2.50
91 Roger Maris 2.00
92 Bob Gibson .75
93 Carl Yastrzemski 1.50
94 Jim "Catfish" Hunter .50
95 Warren Spahn 1.00
96 Reggie Jackson 1.00
97 Lou Brock .75
98 Joe Morgan .50
99 Carlton Fisk .50
100 Eddie Murray .50
101 Roger Clemens 3.00
102 Greg Maddux 2.00
103 Derek Jeter 3.00
104 Albert Pujols 3.00
105 Ken Griffey Jr. 2.00
106 Alex Rodriguez 3.00
107 Mike Piazza 1.50
108 Manny Ramirez 1.00
109 Sammy Sosa 1.00
110 Rafael Palmeiro .75
111 Randy Johnson 1.00
112 Vladimir Guerrero 1.00
113 Ichiro Suzuki 2.00
114 David Ortiz 1.00
115 Miguel Cabrera 1.00
116 Frank Thomas 1.00
117 Pedro Martinez 1.00
118 Chipper Jones 1.00
119 Todd Helton .75
120 Alfonso Soriano 1.00
121 Ivan Rodriguez .75
122 Carlos Delgado .50
123 Carlos Beltran .75
124 Jeff Kent .50
125 Curt Schilling .75
126 Derrek Lee .75
127 Jason Bay .50
128 Mark Teixeira .75
129 Craig Biggio .50
130 Miguel Tejada .50
131 Johan Santana .75
132 Jim Thome .50
133 Tim Hudson .50
134 Barry Zito .50
135 Mark Mulder .50
136 Hideki Matsui 2.00
137 John Smoltz .50
138 Mark Prior .75
139 Andruw Jones .75
140 Adam Dunn .75
141 Prince Fielder .50
142 Tadahito Iguchi RC 2.00
143 Randy Johnson 1.00
144 Pedro Martinez 1.00
145 Alex Rodriguez 3.00
146 Roger Clemens 3.00
147 Vladimir Guerrero 1.00
148 Greg Maddux 2.00
149 Ken Griffey Jr. 2.00
150 Roger Clemens 3.00

Gold Holofoil
Gold Holofoil: 3-4X
Production 100 Sets

Platinum Holofoil
Platinum Holofoil: 3-5X
Production 50 Sets

Silver Holofoil
Silver Holofoil: 1-2X
Inserted 1:3

Dodger Blues Brooklyn Material
NM/M
Common Player: 5.00
Prime: No Pricing
Production 10
1 Sandy Koufax/43 140.00
2 Duke Snider/27 40.00
3 Burleigh Grimes 40.00
4 Tommy Lasorda 10.00

Dodger Blues Brooklyn Signature Material
NM/M
1 Sandy Koufax/37 300.00

Dodger Blues LA Material
NM/M
Common Player: 10.00
Prime: No Pricing
Production 1-10
1 Sandy Koufax/43 140.00
2 Duke Snider/55 35.00
4 Tommy Lasorda 10.00
5 Orel Hershiser 10.00
6 Don Sutton 10.00

Dodger Blues LA Signature Material
NM/M
Production 10-37
Prime: No Pricing
Production 1-5
1 Sandy Koufax/37 300.00

Hall of Fame Souvenirs

		NM/M
Common Player:		2.00
1	Willie Mays/Giants	4.00
2	Hank Aaron/Mil.	4.00
3	Hank Aaron/Atl.	4.00
4	Willie Mays/Mets	4.00
5	Nolan Ryan	6.00
6	Roberto Clemente/	
	Kneeling	4.00
7	Nellie Fox	2.00
8	Pee Wee Reese	3.00
9	Babe Ruth	6.00
10	Bobby Doerr	3.00
11	Brooks Robinson	3.00
12	Carlton Fisk	3.00
13	Eddie Murray	3.00
14	Ernie Banks	4.00
15	Frank Robinson	3.00
16	Gary Carter	2.00
17	Hack Wilson	2.00
18	Harmon Killebrew	4.00
19	Joe Morgan	2.00
20	Kirby Puckett	4.00
21	Lou Brock	3.00
22	Orlando Cepeda	2.00
23	Red Schoendienst	2.00
24	Richie Ashburn	2.00
25	Stan Musial	5.00
26	Roberto Clemente/	
	Standing	6.00
27	Wade Boggs/Sox	3.00
28	Wade Boggs/Yanks	4.00

Hall of Fame Souvenirs Material Bat

		NM/M
Common Player:		10.00
1	Willie Mays	25.00
2	Hank Aaron	25.00
3	Hank Aaron	25.00
4	Willie Mays	25.00
5	Nolan Ryan/30	25.00
6	Roberto Clemente	40.00
7	Nellie Fox	10.00
8	Pee Wee Reese	10.00
9	Babe Ruth	140.00
11	Brooks Robinson	10.00
12	Carlton Fisk	10.00
13	Eddie Murray	10.00
14	Ernie Banks	15.00
15	Frank Robinson	8.00
16	Gary Carter	8.00
17	Hack Wilson	30.00
18	Harmon Killebrew	10.00
19	Joe Morgan	8.00
20	Kirby Puckett	10.00
21	Lou Brock	8.00
22	Orlando Cepeda	8.00
23	Red Schoendienst	8.00
24	Richie Ashburn	8.00
25	Stan Musial	20.00
26	Roberto Clemente	40.00
27	Wade Boggs	8.00
28	Wade Boggs	10.00

HOF Souvenirs Material Combo

		NM/M
Common Combo:		10.00
1	Willie Mays/Giants	50.00
2	Hank Aaron/Mil.	50.00
3	Hank Aaron/Atl.	50.00
4	Willie Mays/25	50.00
5	Nolan Ryan/25	40.00
8	Pee Wee Reese/38	25.00
9	Babe Ruth/50	300.00
10	Bobby Doerr	10.00
11	Brooks Robinson/29	20.00
12	Carlton Fisk	10.00
13	Eddie Murray	10.00
14	Ernie Banks	10.00
16	Gary Carter	10.00
18	Harmon Killebrew	15.00
23	Red Schoendienst	10.00
26	Roberto Clemente	75.00
27	Wade Boggs	10.00
28	Wade Boggs	25.00

HOF Souvenirs Material Jersey

		NM/M
Common Player:		10.00
1	Willie Mays/25	40.00
2	Hank Aaron/25	40.00
3	Hank Aaron/25	40.00
4	Willie Mays/25	40.00
5	Nolan Ryan/25	25.00
9	Babe Ruth/25	225.00
10	Bobby Doerr	10.00
12	Carlton Fisk	10.00
24	Richie Ashburn	10.00
25	Stan Musial	25.00
27	Wade Boggs	12.00

Hall of Fame Souvenirs Signature

No Pricing

HOF Souvenirs Signature Material Bat

		NM/M

No pricing production 22 or less.

10	Bobby Doerr	20.00
11	Brooks Robinson	30.00
12	Carlton Fisk	30.00
15	Frank Robinson	30.00
16	Gary Carter	20.00
18	Harmon Killebrew	30.00
19	Joe Morgan	20.00
20	Kirby Puckett/52	90.00
21	Lou Brock	25.00
22	Orlando Cepeda	25.00
23	Red Schoendienst	25.00
25	Stan Musial/50	60.00

HOF Souvenirs Signature Material Combo

		NM/M
Common Signature:		20.00
10	Bobby Doerr	20.00
11	Brooks Robinson	40.00
12	Carlton Fisk/50	40.00
15	Frank Robinson/39	30.00
16	Gary Carter	20.00
18	Harmon Killebrew	30.00
19	Joe Morgan/23	25.00
20	Kirby Puckett/45	125.00
22	Orlando Cepeda	25.00
25	Stan Musial	80.00
27	Wade Boggs/50	40.00
28	Wade Boggs/31	40.00

HOF Souvenirs Signature Material Jersey

		NM/M
Common Signature:		20.00
10	Bobby Doerr	20.00
11	Brooks Robinson	40.00
12	Carlton Fisk	30.00
15	Frank Robinson	30.00
16	Gary Carter/63	20.00
18	Harmon Killebrew	30.00
22	Orlando Cepeda/68	25.00
23	Red Schoendienst	25.00
25	Stan Musial	65.00
27	Wade Boggs/50	40.00
28	Wade Boggs/3	40.00

Redbirds Material

		NM/M
Common Player:		8.00
Prime:		No Pricing
Production 1-25		
1	Stan Musial/w/Glv/	
	Jsy T2	35.00
2	Ozzie Smith/Jkt T4	20.00
3	Enos Slaughter/	
	Jsy T4	15.00
4	Frankie Frisch/Jkt T3	20.00
5	Lou Brock/Jsy T2	15.00
6	Bob Gibson/Jsy T2	20.00
7	Ken Boyer/Jsy T3	25.00
8	Lee Smith/Jsy T4	8.00
9	Albert Pujols/Jsy T2	35.00
10	Stan Musial	
	w/Bant/Pants T2	35.00

Redbirds Signature Material

		NM/M
Prime:		No Pricing
Production 1-5		
8	Lee Smith/50	20.00

Signature Gold HoloFoil

	NM/M
Tier 1 Production 1-50	
Tier 2 Production 51-100	
Tier 3 Production 101-250	
Tier 4 Production 251-800	
Tier 5 Production 801-1200	
Tier 6 Production 1201-2000	
Cards are not serial numbered.	
1	Al Kaline T2	30.00
2	Alan Trammell T3	15.00
3	Andre Dawson T5	10.00
4	Barry Larkin T2/55	30.00
5	Bert Blyleven T4	15.00
6	Billy Williams T2/55	15.00
7	Bo Jackson T1/35	50.00
8	Bob Feller T6	15.00
9	Bobby Doerr T5	20.00
10	Brooks Robinson T2	30.00
11	Cal Ripken Jr. T3	120.00
12	Dale Murphy T3	15.00
13	Darryl Strawberry T6	15.00
14	Dave Parker T3	10.00
15	Dave Stewart T3	10.00
16	David Cone T2	15.00
17	Dennis Eckersley T3	10.00
18	Don Larsen T4	20.00
19	Don Mattingly T1/45	75.00
20	Don Sutton T3	15.00

(continued)

21	Duke Snider T2/55	25.00
22	Dwight Evans T3	15.00
23	Dwight Gooden T3	15.00
24	Earl Weaver T4	15.00
25	Fergie Jenkins T3	15.00
26	Frank Robinson T2	25.00
27	Fred Lynn T4	10.00
28	Gary Carter T2/55	15.00
29	Gaylord Perry T3	15.00
30	George Brett T1/35	75.00
31	George Foster T5	10.00
32	George Kell T6	15.00
33	Harmon Killebrew	
	T2/55	30.00
34	Harold Baines T4	10.00
35	Harold Reynolds T4	10.00
36	Jack Morris T5	10.00
37	Jim Abbott T4	15.00
38	Jim Bunning T2	25.00
39	Jim Palmer T3	15.00
40	Jim Rice T2	20.00
41	Jim Leyritz T3	10.00
42	Joe Morgan T1/35	20.00
43	John Kruk T2	10.00
44	Johnny Bench T1/35	50.00
45	Johnny Podres T6	10.00
46	Jose Canseco T1/45	35.00
47	Juan Marichal T2	20.00
48	Keith Hernandez T5	15.00
49	Kent Hrbek T5	10.00
50	Kirby Puckett T1/35	85.00
51	Lee Smith T5	10.00
52	Lenny Dykstra T4	10.00
53	Luis Aparicio T3	15.00
54	Luis Tiant T3	15.00
55	Mark Grace T1/45	25.00
56	Marty Marion T4	15.00
57	Matt Williams T3	15.00
58	Maury Wills T4	15.00
59	Mike Schmidt T1/35	50.00
60	Minnie Minoso T5	10.00
61	Nolan Ryan T2/75	80.00
62	Ozzie Smith T2/55	40.00
63	Paul Molitor T2/55	30.00
64	Phil Rizzuto T2/55	30.00
65	Ralph Kiner T5	25.00
66	Randy Jones T4	10.00
67	Red Schoendienst T3	10.00
68	Rich "Goose"	
	Gossage T3	10.00
69	Rob Dibble T4	10.00
70	Robin Roberts T2	30.00
71	Rod Carew T2/55	25.00
72	Rollie Fingers T3	15.00
73	Ron Guidry T3	15.00
74	Ron Santo T3	20.00
75	Ryne Sandberg	
	T1/35	60.00
76	Stan Musial	20.00
77	Steve Carlton T2	15.00
78	Steve Garvey T3	15.00
79	Steve Stone T3	10.00
81	Terry Steinbach T3	10.00
82	Tom Seaver T1/35	40.00
83	Tommy John T6	10.00
84	Tony Gwynn T1/45	40.00
85	Tony Oliva T5	15.00
86	Whitey Ford T1/35	40.00
87	Will Clark T2/55	25.00
88	Willie Mays T2	150.00
89	Willie McCovey	
	T1/45	35.00

Signature Platinum HoloFoil

		NM/M
Production 1-50		
Cards are not serial #'d.		
2	Andre Dawson	15.00
5	Bert Blyleven	15.00
8	Bob Feller	25.00
9	Bobby Doerr	20.00
13	Darryl Strawberry	15.00
14	Dave Parker	15.00
18	Don Larsen	30.00
23	Dwight Gooden	20.00
25	Fergie Jenkins	25.00
27	Fred Lynn	15.00
31	George Foster	15.00
32	George Kell	25.00
34	Harold Baines	20.00
35	Harold Reynolds	15.00
36	Jack Morris	15.00
39	Jim Palmer	20.00
45	Johnny Podres	20.00
48	Keith Hernandez	20.00
49	Kent Hrbek	20.00
51	Lee Smith	20.00
52	Lenny Dykstra	20.00
54	Luis Tiant	20.00
56	Marty Marion	25.00
57	Matt Williams	20.00
58	Maury Wills	25.00
60	Minnie Minoso	25.00
65	Ralph Kiner	40.00
66	Randy Jones	15.00
67	Red Schoendienst	25.00
69	Rob Dibble	15.00
74	Ron Santo	30.00
79	Steve Stone	20.00
81	Terry Steinbach	15.00
83	Tommy John	15.00
85	Tony Oliva	20.00

Souvenirs

		NM/M
Common Player:		2.00

1	Jim Thorpe	4.00
2	Joe Carter	2.00
3	Will Clark	3.00
4	Cal Ripken Jr.	6.00
5	Dwight Evans	2.00
6	George Foster	2.00
7	Steve Garvey	2.00
8	Don Mattingly	4.00
9	Deion Sanders	3.00
10	Ron Santo	3.00
11	Alan Trammell	2.00
12	Robin Ventura	2.00
13	Matt Williams	3.00

Souvenirs Material Bat

		NM/M
Common Player:		5.00
2	Joe Carter	5.00
3	Will Clark	8.00
5	Dwight Evans	5.00
6	George Foster	5.00
7	Steve Garvey	5.00
8	Don Mattingly	15.00
9	Deion Sanders	8.00
10	Ron Santo	8.00
11	Alan Trammell	8.00
12	Robin Ventura	5.00
13	Matt Williams	5.00

Souvenirs Material Combo

		NM/M
Common Combo:		5.00
2	Joe Carter/50	10.00
3	Will Clark	12.00
9	Deion Sanders	12.00
11	Alan Trammell	10.00
13	Matt Williams	10.00

Souvenirs Material Jersey

		NM/M
Common Player:		5.00
1	Jim Thorpe	120.00
3	Will Clark	10.00
4	Cal Ripken Jr.	25.00
9	Deion Sanders	10.00
11	Alan Trammell/68	10.00
12	Robin Ventura/48	5.00
13	Matt Williams	8.00

Souvenirs Signature

		NM/M
Common Auto.:		15.00
3	Will Clark	25.00
5	Dwight Evans/25	20.00
7	Steve Garvey	15.00
10	Ron Santo	25.00
11	Alan Trammell	20.00

Souvenirs Signature Material Bat

		NM/M
Common Player:		15.00
3	Will Clark	25.00
5	Dwight Evans	20.00
7	Steve Garvey	15.00
10	Ron Santo	25.00
11	Alan Trammell	20.00
12	Robin Ventura	15.00

Souvenirs Signature Material Combo

		NM/M
Common Player:		20.00
3	Will Clark	30.00
7	Steve Garvey	20.00
11	Alan Trammell	20.00

Souvenirs Signature Material Jersey

		NM/M
Common Player:		15.00
3	Will Clark	25.00
5	Dwight Evans	25.00
7	Steve Garvey	15.00
11	Alan Trammell	20.00

Sox Nation Material

		NM/M
Common Player:		10.00
Prime:		No Pricing
Production 1-10		
1	Ted Williams	75.00
2	Bobby Doerr	20.00
3	Roger Clemens/55	40.00
4	Carl Yastrzemski	25.00
5	Carl Yastrzemski	25.00
6	Jim Rice	15.00
7	Jim Rice	15.00
8	Joe Cronin	15.00
9	Joe Cronin	15.00
10	Carlton Fisk	20.00
11	Fred Lynn	10.00

12	Wade Boggs	25.00
13	Wade Boggs/55	25.00

Sox Nation Signature Material

		NM/M
Prime:		No Pricing
Production 1-5		
6	Bobby Doerr/50	25.00
7	Jim Rice/50	25.00
7	Jim Rice/50	25.00
8	Fred Lynn/50	15.00

Yankee Clippings Material

		NM/M
Common Player:		8.00
Prime:		No Pricing
Production 1-33		
2	Babe Ruth	300.00
3	Billy Martin	40.00
4	Billy Martin	40.00
5	Bobby Murcer	15.00
6	Bucky Dent	15.00
7	Jim "Catfish" Hunter	15.00
8	Jim "Catfish" Hunter	15.00
9	Darryl Strawberry	8.00
10	Dave Righetti	8.00
11	Dave Winfield	10.00
12	Deion Sanders	15.00
13	Deion Sanders	15.00
14	Don Mattingly	35.00
15	Elston Howard	15.00
16	Graig Nettles	15.00
17	Roger Clemens/43	50.00
18	Luis Tiant	8.00
19	Mickey Rivers	15.00
20	Phil Rizzuto	15.00
21	Reggie Jackson	20.00
22	Rickey Henderson	15.00
23	Roger Maris	50.00
24	Roger Maris	50.00
25	Ron Guidry	15.00
26	Sparky Lyle	8.00
27	Phil Niekro	20.00
28	Tommy John	15.00
29	Whitey Ford	40.00
30	Yogi Berra	60.00

Yankee Clippings Signature Material

		NM/M
Prime:		No Pricing
Production 1-5		
9	Darryl Strawberry/25	30.00
18	Luis Tiant/50	30.00
20	Phil Rizzuto/25	60.00
25	Ron Guidry/25	50.00
28	Tommy John/25	30.00

2005 Donruss Leather & Lumber

		NM/M
Complete Set (177):		
Common Player (1-150):		.25
Common Auto. (151-175):		8.00
Production 256		
Card #176 doesn't exist.		
Pack (5):		7.00
Box (18):		100.00
1	Adam Dunn	.50
2	Adrian Beltre	.40
3	Akinori Otsuka	.25
4	Al Leiter	.25
5	Albert Pujols	2.00
6	Alex Rodriguez	1.50
7	Alfonso Soriano	.75
8	Andy Pettitte	.40
9	Aramis Ramirez	.25
10	Aubrey Huff	.25
11	Austin Kearns	.25
12	Barry Larkin	.40
13	Barry Zito	.40
14	Bartolo Colon	.25
15	Bernie Williams	.40
16	Bobby Abreu	.40
17	Bobby Crosby	.40
18	Brad Penny	.25
19	Brian Giles	.25
20	C.C. Sabathia	.25
21	Carl Crawford	.40
22	Carl Pavano	.25
23	Carlos Beltran	.50
24	Carlos Delgado	.40

25	Carlos Lee	.40
26	Carlos Zambrano	.40
27	Casey Kotchman	.40
28	Chipper Jones	.75
29	Chone Figgins	.25
30	Craig Biggio	.25
31	Craig Monroe	.25
32	Cristian Guzman	.25
33	Curt Schilling	.75
34	Danny Haren	.25
35	Darin Erstad	.25
36	David Dellucci	.25
37	David Ortiz	.75
38	David Wells	.25
39	Derek Jeter	2.00
40	Dontrelle Willis	.40
41	Edgar Renteria	.40
42	Eric Gagne	.40
43	Frank Thomas	.50
44	Garret Anderson	.50
45	Gary Sheffield	.50
46	Geoff Jenkins	.25
47	Greg Maddux	1.50
48	Hideo Nomo	.25
49	Ichiro Suzuki	1.50
50	Ivan Rodriguez	.50
51	J.D. Drew	.40
52	Jake Peavy	.40
53	Jamie Moyer	.25
54	Jason Giambi	.25
55	Jason Kendall	.25
56	Jason Schmidt	.25
57	Jason Varitek	.40
58	Javy Lopez	.25
59	Jay Gibbons	.25
60	Jeff Bagwell	.50
61	Jeff Bagwell	.50
62	Jeremy Bonderman	.25
63	Jermaine Dye	.25
64	Jim Edmonds	.40
65	Jim Thome	.50
66	Joe Nathan	.25
67	Johan Santana	.50
68	John Olerud	.25
69	John Smoltz	.40
70	Johnny Damon	.25
71	Johnny Estrada	.25
72	Jose Reyes	.50
73	Jose Vidro	.25
74	Josh Beckett	.40
75	Juan Pierre	.25
76	Junior Spivey	.25
77	Justin Morneau	.25
78	Kazuhisa Ishii	.25
79	Kazuo Matsui	.25
80	Ken Griffey Jr.	1.50
81	Kerry Wood	.40
82	Kevin Brown	.25
83	Kevin Millwood	.25
84	Khalil Greene	.25
85	Lance Berkman	.25
86	Larry Walker	.25
87	Laynce Nix	.25
88	Lyle Overbay	.25
89	Magglio Ordonez	.25
90	Manny Ramirez	.50
91	Marcus Giles	.25
92	Mark Loretta	.25
93	Mark Mulder	.40
94	Mark Prior	.50
95	Mark Teixeira	.40
96	Melvin Mora	.25
97	Michael Young	.25
98	Miguel Tejada	.50
99	Mike Lieberthal	.25
100	Mike Lowell	.40
101	Mike Mussina	.40
102	Mike Piazza	1.00
103	Milton Bradley	.25
104	Moises Alou	.40
105	Morgan Ensberg	.25
106	Nomar Garciaparra	1.00
107	Omar Vizquel	.25
108	Paul Konerko	.40
109	Paul LoDuca	.25
110	Pedro Martinez	.75
111	Rafael Furcal	.25
112	Rafael Palmeiro	.40
113	Randy Johnson	.75
114	Richie Sexson	.25
115	Rocco Baldelli	.25
116	Roger Clemens	2.00
117	Roy Halladay	.40
118	Sammy Sosa	.75
119	Scott Podsednik	.25
120	Scott Rolen	.75
121	Sean Burroughs	.25
122	Sean Casey	.25
123	Shannon Stewart	.25
124	Shawn Green	.40
125	Steve Finley	.25
126	Tim Hudson	.40
127	Tim Salmon	.40
128	Todd Helton	.50
129	Tom Glavine	.40
130	Torii Hunter	.40
131	Travis Hafner	.40
132	Troy Glaus	.40
133	Troy Percival	.25
134	Vernon Wells	.40
135	Victor Martinez	.25
136	Vladimir Guerrero	.75
137	Andre Dawson	.40
138	Brooks Robinson	.50
139	Cal Ripken Jr.	3.00
140	Dale Murphy	.50
141	Darryl Strawberry	.40
142	George Brett	2.00

143	Harmon Killebrew	1.00
144	Jim Palmer	.50
145	Lou Brock	.75
146	Mike Schmidt	1.00
147	Nolan Ryan	2.00
148	Steve Carlton	.50
149	Tony Gwynn	1.00
150	Willie Mays	1.00
151	Agustin Montero **RC**	10.00
152	Carlos Ruiz **RC**	15.00
153	Casey Rogowski **RC**	8.00
154	Chris Resop **RC**	15.00
155	Chris Roberson **RC**	15.00
156	Colter Bean **RC**	15.00
157	Danny Rueckel **RC**	8.00
158	David Gassner **RC**	8.00
159	Geovany Soto **RC**	12.00
160	John Hattig Jr. **RC**	8.00
161	Justin Wechsler **RC**	10.00
162	Luke Scott **RC**	25.00
163	Mark McLemore **RC**	10.00
164	Miguel Negron **RC**	8.00
165	Mike Morse **RC**	20.00
166	Nate McLouth **RC**	8.00
167	Philip Humber **RC**	8.00
168	Randy Messenger **RC**	8.00
169	Raul Tablado **RC**	8.00
170	Russel Rohlicek **RC**	8.00
171	Ryan Speier **RC**	8.00
172	Scott Munter **RC**	10.00
173	Sean Thompson **RC**	10.00
174	Sean Tracey **RC**	10.00
175	Wladimir Balentien **RC**	25.00
177	Norihiro Nakamura/128 **RC**	75.00

Silver
Silver (1-150): 3-5X
Production 100 Sets

Gold
Gold (1-150): 4-8X
Production 50 Sets

Platinum
Platinum: No Pricing
Production One Set

Big Bang
NM/M
Common Player: 1.50
Production 2,000 Sets
Gold: 1-2X
Production 100 Sets
Silver: 1-2X
Production 200 Sets
Platinum: No Pricing
Production One Set

1	Adam Dunn	2.00
2	Adrian Beltre	1.50
3	Albert Pujols	6.00
4	Alex Rodriguez	5.00
5	Chipper Jones	2.00
6	Dale Murphy	2.00
7	Darryl Strawberry	2.00
8	Dave Parker	1.50
9	David Ortiz	2.00
10	Duke Snider	2.00
11	Frank Robinson	2.00
12	Gary Sheffield	1.50
13	George Foster	1.50
14	Harmon Killebrew	3.00
15	Jim Edmonds	1.50
16	Jim Rice	1.50
17	Jim Thome	2.00
18	Ken Griffey Jr.	4.00
19	Manny Ramirez	2.00
20	Matt Williams	1.50
21	Mike Piazza	3.00
22	Mike Schmidt	5.00
23	Rafael Palmeiro	2.00
24	Sammy Sosa	3.00
25	Ted Williams	5.00

Big Bang Bat
NM/M
Production 50-250

3	Albert Pujols/250	15.00
8	Dave Parker/250	4.00
9	David Ortiz/250	8.00
11	Frank Robinson/100	8.00
12	George Foster/250	4.00
16	Jim Rice/50	6.00
19	Manny Ramirez/250	8.00
22	Mike Schmidt/250	15.00
23	Rafael Palmeiro/250	6.00
24	Sammy Sosa/250	8.00
25	Ted Williams/100	60.00

Big Bang Jersey
NM/M
Production 25-250
Prime: No Pricing
Production 5 Sets

1	Adam Dunn/250	6.00
3	Albert Pujols/250	15.00
5	Chipper Jones/250	8.00
6	Dale Murphy/250	8.00
7	Darryl Strawberry/Pants/250	6.00
8	Dave Parker/250	4.00
9	David Ortiz/250	8.00
10	Duke Snider/25	12.00
12	Gary Sheffield/250	6.00
14	Harmon Killebrew/100	10.00
15	Jim Edmonds/250	6.00
16	Jim Rice/Pants/250	6.00
17	Jim Thome/250	8.00
19	Manny Ramirez/100	8.00
20	Matt Williams/250	8.00
21	Mike Piazza/250	8.00
22	Mike Schmidt/100	15.00
23	Rafael Palmeiro/Pants/250	6.00
24	Sammy Sosa/250	8.00
25	Ted Williams/Jkt/250	40.00

Big Bang Combos
NM/M
Production 25-100
Prime: No Pricing
Production 5 Sets

1	Adam Dunn/Bat-Jsy/25	12.00
2	Adrian Beltre/Bat-Jsy/25	8.00
3	Albert Pujols/Bat-Jsy/10	25.00
7	Darryl Strawberry/Jsy-Pants/100	8.00
8	Dave Parker/Bat-Jsy/100	8.00
9	David Ortiz/Bat-Jsy/100	15.00
15	Jim Edmonds/Jsy-Jsy/100	10.00
16	Jim Rice/Jsy-Jsy/100	10.00
19	Manny Ramirez/Bat-Jsy/100	12.00
20	Matt Williams/Bat-Jsy/100	8.00
21	Mike Piazza/Bat-Jsy/50	15.00
22	Mike Schmidt/Bat-Jsy/100	20.00
23	Rafael Palmeiro/Bat-Jsy/100	10.00
24	Sammy Sosa/Bat-Jsy/100	12.00

Big Bang Signatures
No Pricing
Production 1-10

Game Ball Signatures
NM/M
Production 1-50

1	Ben Grieve/50	10.00
3	Eli Marrero/24	12.00
4	Jeff Fassero/24	25.00
5	Jose Guillen/47	25.00
7	Mark Grudzielanek/23	30.00
9	Paul Konerko/45	25.00

Great Gloves
NM/M
Common Player: 1.50
Production 2,000 Sets
Gold: 2-3X
Production 50 Sets
Silver: 1-2X
Production 100 Sets
Platinum: No Pricing
Production One Set

1	Austin Kearns	1.50
2	Gary Carter	2.00
3	Ivan Rodriguez	2.00
4	Mark Grace	2.00
5	Mark Teixeira	2.00
6	Mike Schmidt	5.00
7	Omar Vizquel	1.50
8	Scott Rolen	1.50
9	Tony Gwynn	3.00
10	Willie Mays	5.00

Great Gloves Fielding Glove
NM/M
Production 25 Sets

1	Austin Kearns/25	10.00
2	Gary Carter/25	20.00
3	Ivan Rodriguez/25	15.00
4	Mark Grace/25	20.00
5	Mark Teixeira/25	15.00
6	Mike Schmidt/25	40.00
9	Tony Gwynn/25	20.00

Great Gloves Jersey
NM/M
Production 25-50
Prime: No Pricing
Production 5 Sets

1	Austin Kearns/50	8.00
2	Gary Carter/50	8.00
3	Ivan Rodriguez/50	8.00
4	Mark Grace/50	10.00
5	Mark Teixeira/50	8.00
6	Mike Schmidt/50	20.00
7	Omar Vizquel/50	8.00
8	Scott Rolen/50	10.00
9	Tony Gwynn/50	12.00
10	Willie Mays/25	40.00

Hitters Inc.
NM/M
Common Player: 1.50
Production 2,000 Sets
Gold: 2-3X
Production 50 Sets
Silver: 1-2X
Production 100 Sets
Platinum: No Pricing
Production One Set

1	Albert Pujols	6.00
2	Alfonso Soriano	2.00
3	Cal Ripken Jr.	8.00
4	Don Mattingly	5.00
5	Dwight Evans	1.50
6	George Brett	5.00
7	Hank Blalock	1.50
8	Ichiro Suzuki	5.00
9	Ivan Rodriguez	2.00
10	Jack Wilson	1.50
11	Keith Hernandez	1.50
12	Larry Walker	2.00
13	Lou Brock	2.00
14	Lyle Overbay	1.50
15	Michael Young	1.50
16	Paul Molitor	2.00
17	Rod Carew	2.00
18	Sean Casey	1.50
19	Steve Garvey	1.50
20	Todd Helton	2.00
21	Tony Gwynn	3.00
22	Travis Hafner	1.50
23	Ted Williams	2.00
24	Wade Boggs	2.00
25	Willie Mays	5.00

Hitters Inc. Bat
NM/M
Production 25-100

1	Albert Pujols/100	15.00
2	Alfonso Soriano/50	6.00
3	Cal Ripken Jr./100	25.00
4	Don Mattingly/100	6.00
5	Dwight Evans/100	6.00
6	George Brett/50	6.00
7	Hank Blalock/100	6.00
9	Ivan Rodriguez/100	6.00
10	Jack Wilson/100	4.00
12	Larry Walker/100	6.00
13	Lou Brock/100	6.00
15	Michael Young/100	4.00
16	Paul Molitor/100	8.00
17	Rod Carew/100	8.00
18	Sean Casey/100	4.00
19	Steve Garvey/100	6.00
21	Tony Gwynn/100	8.00
23	Ted Williams/50	60.00
24	Wade Boggs/100	6.00
25	Willie Mays/40	40.00

Hitters Inc. Signature Bat
NM/M
Production 5-25

5	Dwight Evans/25	20.00
7	Hank Blalock/25	25.00
10	Jack Wilson/25	15.00
13	Lou Brock/25	30.00
15	Michael Young/25	15.00
18	Sean Casey/25	15.00
19	Steve Garvey/25	30.00

Hitters Inc. Jersey
NM/M
Production 25-100

1	Albert Pujols/100	15.00
2	Alfonso Soriano/100	6.00
3	Cal Ripken Jr./100	25.00
4	Don Mattingly/100	15.00
5	Dwight Evans/100	6.00
7	Hank Blalock/100	4.00
9	Ivan Rodriguez/100	6.00
10	Jack Wilson/100	4.00
12	Larry Walker/100	6.00
13	Lou Brock/50	8.00
14	Lyle Overbay/100	4.00
16	Paul Molitor/100	8.00
17	Rod Carew/100	8.00
18	Sean Casey/100	6.00
19	Steve Garvey/100	6.00
20	Todd Helton/100	6.00
21	Tony Gwynn/100	10.00
22	Travis Hafner/100	4.00
23	Ted Williams/Jkt/100	40.00
24	Wade Boggs/100	8.00
25	Willie Mays/50	40.00

Hitters Inc. Signature Jersey
NM/M
Production 5-25

5	Dwight Evans/25	20.00
7	Hank Blalock/25	25.00
10	Jack Wilson/25	15.00
13	Lou Brock/25	30.00
15	Lyle Overbay/25	15.00
18	Sean Casey/25	15.00
19	Steve Garvey/25	30.00
22	Travis Hafner/25	20.00

Hitters Inc. Signatures
No Pricing
Production 5-10

Leather Cuts
NM/M
Production 1-128

2	Andre Dawson/128	15.00
3	Bert Blyleven/128	15.00
4	Lee Smith/32	15.00
5	Billy Williams/64	15.00
6	Bob Feller/128	25.00
7	Joe Pepitone/128	20.00
8	Bobby Doerr/128	15.00
9	Juan Marichal/112	20.00
12	Dale Murphy/96	25.00
13	Darryl Strawberry/128	15.00
14	Johnny Podres/128	20.00
18	Duke Snider/128	25.00
20	Dwight Gooden/128	15.00
21	Fergie Jenkins/96	15.00
23	Fred Lynn/128	15.00
24	Justin Morneau/128	20.00
27	Gaylord Perry/128	15.00
28	George Foster/128	10.00
29	Harmon Killebrew/64	30.00
30	Jack Morris/128	15.00
31	Jim Palmer/128	15.00
32	Jim Rice/128	15.00
33	John Kruk/128	20.00
34	Randy Jones/128	15.00
35	Keith Hernandez/128	15.00
36	Lenny Dykstra/128	15.00
37	Lou Brock/64	35.00
38	Luis Aparicio/128	15.00
39	Lyle Overbay/128	10.00
40	Maury Wills/128	15.00
41	Earl Weaver/128	15.00
42	Miguel Cabrera/64	40.00
44	Monte Irvin/96	20.00
46	Kent Hrbek/128	15.00
47	Red Schoendienst/128	20.00
48	Rich "Goose" Gossage/128	20.00
50	Minnie Minoso/128	20.00
54	Sean Casey/64	15.00
57	Steve Stone/128	15.00
57	Tommy John/128	15.00
57	Victor Martinez/128	15.00
61	Lee Smith/128	15.00

Lumber Cuts Bat
NM/M
Production 6-128

1	Al Kaline	40.00
10	Cal Ripken Jr./60	125.00
13	Darryl Strawberry/96	20.00
19	Dwight Evans/128	25.00
20	Dwight Gooden/128	15.00
22	Frank Robinson/40	25.00
23	Fred Lynn/96	15.00
27	George Foster/128	15.00
31	Jim Rice/32	25.00
36	Lenny Dykstra/128	15.00
37	Lou Brock/128	30.00
38	Luis Aparicio/128	15.00
39	Lyle Overbay/128	10.00
55	Sean Casey/32	15.00
57	Tommy John/128	15.00
57	Victor Martinez/128	15.00

Leather Cuts Bat
NM/M
Production 6-128

1	Al Kaline/58	40.00
10	Cal Ripken Jr./60	125.00
13	Darryl Strawberry/96	20.00
19	Dwight Evans/128	25.00
20	Dwight Gooden/128	15.00
22	Frank Robinson/40	25.00
23	Fred Lynn/96	15.00
27	George Foster/128	15.00
31	Jim Rice/32	25.00
36	Lenny Dykstra/128	15.00
37	Lou Brock/128	30.00
38	Luis Aparicio/128	15.00
39	Lyle Overbay/128	10.00
51	Sean Casey/32	15.00
55	Tommy John/128	15.00
57	Victor Martinez/128	15.00

Leather Cuts Jersey
NM/M
Production 1-128

2	Andre Dawson/128	20.00
3	Bert Blyleven/128	15.00
4	Lee Smith/96	15.00
8	Bobby Doerr/Pants/128	20.00
9	Juan Marichal/112	20.00
10	Cal Ripken Jr./60	125.00
12	Dale Murphy/96	25.00
13	Darryl Strawberry/96	20.00
16	Dave Righetti/48	20.00
19	David Cone/120	8.00
19	Dwight Evans/44	30.00
20	Dwight Gooden/128	15.00
21	Fergie Jenkins/Pants/128	20.00
23	Fred Lynn/96	15.00
27	Gaylord Perry/128	15.00
28	Harmon Killebrew/32	40.00
29	Jack Morris/64	15.00
31	Jim Rice/Pants/128	20.00
33	John Kruk/128	20.00
35	Keith Hernandez/32	20.00
36	Lenny Dykstra/128	15.00
38	Luis Aparicio/128	15.00
39	Lyle Overbay/128	15.00
42	Miguel Cabrera/64	40.00
51	Sean Casey/32	15.00
55	Tommy John/128	15.00
57	Victor Martinez/128	15.00

Lumber Cuts
NM/M
Production 1-128

2	Andre Dawson/128	15.00
3	Bert Blyleven/128	15.00
4	Lee Smith/32	20.00
5	Billy Williams/64	15.00
6	Bob Feller/128	25.00
7	Joe Pepitone/128	20.00
8	Bobby Doerr/128	15.00
9	Juan Marichal/112	20.00
12	Dale Murphy/96	25.00
13	Darryl Strawberry/128	15.00
14	Johnny Podres/128	15.00
18	Duke Snider/128	15.00
21	Fergie Jenkins/96	15.00
23	Fred Lynn/128	15.00
24	Justin Morneau/128	20.00
27	Gaylord Perry/128	15.00
29	Harmon Killebrew/64	30.00
30	Jack Morris/128	15.00
31	Jim Palmer/128	15.00
32	Jim Rice/128	15.00
33	John Kruk/128	20.00
35	Keith Hernandez/128	15.00
37	Lenny Dykstra/128	15.00
39	Lou Brock/64	35.00
40	Luis Aparicio/128	15.00
41	Earl Weaver/128	15.00
42	Miguel Cabrera/64	40.00
46	Kent Hrbek/128	15.00
47	Red Schoendienst/128	20.00
48	Rich "Goose" Gossage/128	20.00
50	Minnie Minoso/128	20.00
54	Sean Casey/64	15.00
57	Steve Stone/128	15.00
57	Tommy John/128	15.00
57	Victor Martinez/128	15.00
61	Lee Smith/128	15.00

Lumber Cuts Jersey

NM/M
Production 7-128

2	Andre Dawson/128	20.00
3	Bert Blyleven/128	15.00
8	Bobby Doerr/Pants/128	20.00
9	Juan Marichal/112	20.00
10	Cal Ripken Jr./60	125.00
12	Dale Murphy/96	25.00
13	Darryl Strawberry/96	20.00
16	Dave Righetti/48	20.00
19	David Cone/120	8.00
19	Dwight Evans/44	30.00
20	Dwight Gooden/128	15.00
21	Fergie Jenkins/Pants/128	20.00
23	Fred Lynn/96	15.00
27	Gaylord Perry/128	15.00
28	Harmon Killebrew/32	40.00
29	Jack Morris/64	15.00
31	Jim Rice/Pants/128	20.00
33	John Kruk/128	20.00
35	Keith Hernandez/32	20.00
36	Lenny Dykstra/128	15.00
38	Luis Aparicio/128	15.00
39	Lyle Overbay/128	15.00
42	Miguel Cabrera/64	40.00
51	Sean Casey/32	15.00
55	Tommy John/128	15.00
57	Victor Martinez/128	15.00

Lumber/Leather
NM/M
Common Player: 1.50
Production 2,000 Sets
Gold: 2-3X
Production 50 Sets
Silver: 1-2X
Production 100 Sets
Platinum: No Pricing
Production One Set

1	Albert Pujols	6.00
2	Alex Rodriguez	5.00
3	Alfonso Soriano	
4	Cal Ripken Jr.	8.00
5	Carlos Lee	2.00
6	Derek Jeter	6.00
7	Don Mattingly	5.00
8	Ichiro Suzuki	4.00
9	Ivan Rodriguez	2.00
10	Jack Wilson	1.50
11	Josh Beckett	1.50
12	Ken Griffey Jr.	4.00
13	Lance Berkman	2.00
14	Magglio Ordonez	1.50
15	Mark Grace	2.00
16	Mark Prior	2.00
17	Mark Teixeira	2.00
18	Mike Schmidt	4.00
19	Nolan Ryan	6.00
20	Nomar Garciaparra	2.00
21	Paul LoDuca	1.50
22	Rafael Palmeiro	2.00
23	Randy Johnson	2.00
24	Richie Sexson	2.00
25	Rickey Henderson	2.00
26	Roger Clemens	6.00
27	Ryan Klesko	1.50
28	Stan Musial	3.00
29	Steve Carlton	2.00
30	Tim Hudson	2.00
31	Tony Gwynn	2.00
32	Travis Hafner	1.50
33	Victor Martinez	1.50
34	Wade Boggs	2.00
35	Willie Mays	5.00

Lumber/Leather Barrel
No Pricing
Production One Set

L/L Barrel-Jersey
No Pricing
Production One Set

L/L Bat-Btg Glove
NM/M
Production 1-25

3	Alfonso Soriano/25	15.00
5	Carlos Lee/25	12.00
7	Don Mattingly/25	40.00
9	Ivan Rodriguez/25	15.00
13	Lance Berkman/25	15.00
14	Magglio Ordonez/25	10.00
18	Mike Schmidt/25	40.00
21	Paul LoDuca/25	10.00
22	Rafael Palmeiro/25	15.00
24	Richie Sexson/25	15.00
25	Rickey Henderson/25	20.00
27	Ryan Klesko/25	10.00
31	Tony Gwynn/25	20.00

L/L Bat-Fld Glove
NM/M
Production 5-25

5	Carlos Lee/25	12.00
9	Ivan Rodriguez/25	15.00
10	Jack Wilson/25	10.00
13	Lance Berkman/25	15.00
15	Mark Grace/25	15.00
16	Mark Prior/25	20.00
18	Mike Schmidt/25	40.00
21	Paul LoDuca/25	10.00
22	Rafael Palmeiro/25	15.00
24	Richie Sexson/25	10.00
29	Ryan Klesko/25	10.00
30	Steve Carlton/25	15.00
31	Tim Hudson/25	15.00
31	Tony Gwynn/25	20.00

Lumber/Leather Bat-Spikes
NM/M
Production 1-25

1	Albert Pujols/25	40.00
5	Carlos Lee/25	12.00
9	Ivan Rodriguez/25	12.00
11	Josh Beckett/25	12.00
13	Lance Berkman/25	15.00
14	Magglio Ordonez/25	10.00
16	Mark Prior/25	20.00
21	Paul LoDuca/25	10.00
22	Rafael Palmeiro/25	15.00
24	Richie Sexson/25	15.00
25	Rickey Henderson/25	20.00
27	Ryan Klesko/25	15.00
30	Tim Hudson/25	15.00
31	Tony Gwynn/25	20.00

Materials Barrel
No Pricing
Production 1-4

Materials Bat
NM/M
Production 25-250

1	Adam Dunn/250	6.00
5	Adrian Beltre/100	4.00
6	Albert Pujols/250	15.00
7	Alfonso Soriano/100	6.00
8	Andy Pettitte/100	6.00
9	Aramis Ramirez/100	6.00
10	Aubrey Huff/75	6.00
11	Austin Kearns/100	4.00
12	Barry Larkin/200	6.00
13	Barry Zito/25	8.00
15	Bernie Williams/250	6.00

18	Brad Penny/75	4.00
19	Brian Giles/50	4.00
23	Carlos Beltran/100	8.00
24	Carlos Delgado/250	4.00
25	Carlos Lee/150	4.00
27	Casey Kotchman/250	4.00
29	Chone Figgins/250	4.00
30	Craig Biggio/250	6.00
31	Craig Monroe/250	4.00
33	Curt Schilling/100	8.00
35	Darin Erstad/250	4.00
37	David Ortiz/250	8.00
40	Dontrelle Willis/250	6.00
43	Frank Thomas/50	4.00
44	Garret Anderson/250	4.00
46	Geoff Jenkins/50	4.00
47	Greg Maddux/250	10.00
51	J.D. Drew/250	4.00
57	Jason Varitek/100	4.00
58	Javy Lopez/250	4.00
59	Jay Gibbons/250	4.00
60	Jeff Bagwell/250	6.00
61	Jeff Kent/250	4.00
68	John Olerud/250	4.00
72	Jose Reyes/250	6.00
73	Jose Vidro/250	4.00
75	Juan Pierre/250	4.00
81	Kerry Wood/100	4.00
82	Kevin Brown/100	4.00
85	Lance Berkman/250	4.00
87	Laynce Nix/250	4.00
89	Magglio Ordonez/250	4.00
90	Manny Ramirez/100	8.00
94	Mark Prior/250	6.00
97	Michael Young/250	4.00
104	Moises Alou/250	4.00
106	Nomar Garciaparra/100	8.00
109	Paul LoDuca/250	4.00
111	Rafael Furcal/250	4.00
112	Rafael Palmeiro/250	6.00
114	Richie Sexson/250	4.00
115	Rocco Baldelli/250	8.00
118	Sammy Sosa/100	4.00
122	Sean Casey/100	4.00
123	Shannon Stewart/50	4.00
124	Shawn Green/250	4.00
126	Tim Hudson/50	6.00
127	Tim Salmon/250	4.00
129	Tom Glavine/250	4.00
130	Torii Hunter/250	4.00
132	Troy Glaus/250	4.00
138	Brooks Robinson/100	8.00
139	Cal Ripken Jr./50	30.00
145	Lou Brock/100	4.00
146	Mike Schmidt/50	15.00
147	Nolan Ryan/50	25.00
149	Tony Gwynn/100	10.00
150	Willie Mays/25	40.00

Materials Jersey
NM/M

Production 20-250

1	Adam Dunn/150	6.00
5	Albert Pujols/250	15.00
7	Alfonso Soriano/150	6.00
9	Andy Pettitte/150	6.00
9	Aramis Ramirez/250	4.00
10	Aubrey Huff/250	6.00
12	Barry Larkin/250	6.00
13	Barry Zito/150	6.00
15	Bernie Williams/150	6.00
16	Bobby Abreu/250	4.00
17	Bobby Crosby/150	4.00
20	C.C. Sabathia/250	4.00
21	Carl Crawford/200	6.00
26	Carlos Zambrano/250	4.00
27	Casey Kotchman/140	4.00
28	Chipper Jones/250	8.00
29	Chone Figgins/200	6.00
30	Craig Biggio/200	6.00
33	Curt Schilling/250	8.00
35	Darin Erstad/150	4.00
36	David Dellucci/250	4.00
37	David Ortiz/250	8.00
40	Dontrelle Willis/250	4.00
43	Frank Thomas/Pants/150	8.00
44	Garret Anderson/250	4.00
45	Gary Sheffield/250	6.00
46	Geoff Jenkins/250	4.00
47	Greg Maddux/25	15.00
48	Hideo Nomo/250	6.00
50	Ivan Rodriguez/150	6.00
53	Jamie Moyer/50	4.00
54	Jason Giambi/250	4.00
57	Jason Varitek/100	10.00
58	Javy Lopez/250	4.00
59	Jay Gibbons/75	4.00
60	Jeff Bagwell/250	6.00
62	Jeremy Bonderman/150	4.00
64	Jim Edmonds/250	6.00
65	Jim Thome/150	6.00
67	Johan Santana/250	8.00
69	John Smoltz/250	6.00
70	Johnny Damon/250	8.00
71	Johnny Estrada/250	4.00
72	Jose Reyes/150	6.00
73	Jose Vidro/150	4.00
74	Josh Beckett/50	4.00
76	Junior Spivey/50	4.00
77	Justin Morneau/250	4.00
78	Kazuhisa Ishii/250	4.00
79	Kazuo Matsui/250	4.00
81	Kerry Wood/Pants/150	6.00

85	Lance Berkman/250	4.00
86	Larry Walker/250	4.00
87	Laynce Nix/250	4.00
88	Lyle Overbay/200	4.00
90	Manny Ramirez/250	8.00
91	Marcus Giles/150	4.00
94	Mark Prior/250	6.00
95	Mark Teixeira/250	6.00
96	Melvin Mora/250	4.00
97	Michael Young/25	6.00
98	Miguel Tejada/250	6.00
100	Mike Lowell/250	4.00
101	Mike Mussina/250	6.00
102	Mike Piazza/250	8.00
105	Morgan Ensberg/150	4.00
108	Paul Konerko/150	6.00
111	Rafael Furcal/150	4.00
112	Rafael Palmeiro/250	6.00
115	Rocco Baldelli/250	6.00
116	Roger Clemens/150	10.00
117	Roy Halladay/150	4.00
119	Scott Podsednik/250	4.00
120	Scott Rolen/250	6.00
121	Sean Burroughs/150	4.00
122	Sean Casey/250	4.00
123	Shannon Stewart/150	4.00
128	Todd Helton/250	6.00
130	Torii Hunter/250	4.00
131	Travis Hafner/250	6.00
134	Vernon Wells/250	4.00
135	Victor Martinez/150	4.00
136	Vladimir Guerrero/250	8.00
137	Andre Dawson/50	4.00
139	Cal Ripken Jr./250	20.00
140	Dale Murphy/250	6.00
141	Darryl Strawberry/Pants/150	4.00
143	Harmon Killebrew/100	8.00
145	Lou Brock/Jkt/250	4.00
146	Mike Schmidt/50	15.00
147	Nolan Ryan/50	15.00
148	Steve Carlton/100	10.00
149	Tony Gwynn/250	8.00
150	Willie Mays/Pants/25	40.00

Naturals
NM/M

Common Player:
Production 2,000 Sets
Gold: 2-3X
Production 50 Sets
Silver: 1-2X
Production 100 Sets
Platinum: No Pricing
Production One Set

1	Andruw Jones	2.00
2	Bernie Williams	1.50
3	Brooks Robinson	2.00
4	Cal Ripken Jr.	8.00
5	Casey Kotchman	1.50
6	Craig Biggio	2.00
7	Craig Wilson	1.50
8	David Ortiz	3.00
9	Eddie Murray	2.00
10	Javy Lopez	1.50
11	Jeff Bagwell	2.00
12	Lance Berkman	1.50
13	Magglio Ordonez	1.50
14	Michael Young	1.50
15	Rafael Palmeiro	2.00
16	Reggie Jackson	2.00
17	Rickey Henderson	2.00
18	Rocco Baldelli	1.50
19	Sammy Sosa	4.00
20	Shawn Green	1.50
21	Ted Williams	6.00
22	Tony Gwynn	3.00
23	Wade Boggs	2.00
24	Will Clark	2.00
25	Willie Mays	5.00

Naturals Barrel
No Pricing
Production 1-3

Naturals Bat
NM/M

Production 25-100

1	Andruw Jones/100	6.00
2	Bernie Williams/100	4.00
3	Brooks Robinson/100	8.00
4	Cal Ripken Jr./100	25.00
5	Casey Kotchman/100	4.00
6	Craig Biggio/100	6.00
7	Craig Wilson/100	4.00
8	David Ortiz/100	10.00
9	Eddie Murray/100	8.00
10	Javy Lopez/100	6.00
11	Jeff Bagwell/100	6.00
12	Lance Berkman/100	4.00
13	Magglio Ordonez/100	4.00
14	Michael Young/100	4.00
15	Rafael Palmeiro/100	6.00
16	Reggie Jackson/100	8.00
17	Rickey Henderson/100	8.00
18	Rocco Baldelli/100	4.00
19	Sammy Sosa/100	8.00
20	Shawn Green/100	4.00
21	Ted Williams/50	50.00
22	Tony Gwynn/100	10.00
23	Wade Boggs/100	8.00
24	Will Clark/100	4.00
25	Willie Mays/25	40.00

Naturals Jersey
NM/M

Production 25-100
Prime: No Pricing
Production 5 Sets

1	Andruw Jones/100	6.00
2	Bernie Williams/100	6.00
4	Cal Ripken Jr./100	25.00
5	Casey Kotchman/100	4.00
6	Craig Biggio/100	6.00
7	Craig Wilson/100	4.00
9	David Ortiz/100	10.00
9	Eddie Murray/100	8.00
10	Javy Lopez/100	4.00
11	Jeff Bagwell/100	6.00
12	Lance Berkman/100	4.00
13	Magglio Ordonez/50	4.00
14	Michael Young/50	4.00
15	Rafael Palmeiro/100	6.00
16	Reggie Jackson/100	8.00
17	Rickey Henderson/Jkt/100	
18	Rocco Baldelli/100	4.00
19	Sammy Sosa/100	8.00
20	Shawn Green/100	4.00
21	Ted Williams/Jkt/100	40.00
22	Tony Gwynn/100	8.00
23	Wade Boggs/100	8.00
24	Will Clark/50	4.00
25	Willie Mays/25	40.00

Naturals Combos
NM/M

Production 25-100
Prime: No Pricing
Production 5 Sets

1	Andruw Jones/Bat-Jsy/100	8.00
2	Bernie Williams/Bat-Jsy/100	8.00
3	Brooks Robinson/Bat-Jsy/100	15.00
4	Cal Ripken Jr./Bat-Jsy/100	30.00
5	Casey Kotchman/Bat-Jsy/100	6.00
6	Craig Biggio/Bat-Jsy/100	8.00
7	Craig Wilson/Bat-Jsy/100	6.00
8	David Ortiz/Bat-Jsy/100	12.00
9	Eddie Murray/Bat-Jsy/100	10.00
10	Javy Lopez/Bat-Jsy/100	6.00
11	Jeff Bagwell/Bat-Jsy/100	8.00
12	Lance Berkman/Bat-Jsy/100	6.00
13	Magglio Ordonez/Bat-Jsy/25	8.00
14	Michael Young/Bat-Jsy/100	6.00
15	Rafael Palmeiro/Bat-Jsy/100	8.00
16	Reggie Jackson/Bat-Jsy/100	12.00
17	Rickey Henderson/Bat-Jkt/100	10.00
18	Rocco Baldelli/Bat-Jsy/100	6.00
19	Sammy Sosa/Bat-Jsy/100	10.00
20	Shawn Green/Bat-Jsy/100	6.00
21	Ted Williams/Bat-Jkt/50	60.00
22	Tony Gwynn/Bat-Jsy/100	12.00
23	Wade Boggs/Bat-Jsy/100	10.00
24	Will Clark/Bat-Jsy/100	10.00
25	Willie Mays/Bat-Jsy/25	50.00

Rivals
NM/M

Common Duo: 1.50
Production 2,000 Sets
Gold: 2-3X
Production 50 Sets
Silver: 1-2X
Production 100 Sets
Platinum: No Pricing
Production One Set

1	Ichiro Suzuki, Hideki Matsui	5.00
2	Mark Mulder, Vladimir Guerrero	2.00
3	Tim Hudson, Mark Teixeira	2.00
4	Roger Clemens, Albert Pujols	6.00
5	Greg Maddux, Jeff Bagwell	4.00
6	Randy Johnson, Adrian Beltre	3.00
7	Kerry Wood, Larry Walker	2.00
8	Mike Mussina, Manny Ramirez	2.00
9	C.C. Sabathia, Torii Hunter	1.50
10	Josh Beckett, Chipper Jones	2.00
11	Derek Jeter, Miguel Tejada	6.00
12	Alex Rodriguez, Hank Blalock	5.00
13	Carlos Beltran, Sammy Sosa	3.00
14	Mark Prior, Jim Thome	2.00
15	Miguel Cabrera, Andruw Jones	2.00
16	Johan Santana, Magglio Ordonez	2.00
17	Josh Beckett, Craig Biggio	2.00
18	Adam Dunn, Shawn Green	2.00
19	J. Morris, Rod Carew	2.00
20	Jim Palmer, Paul Molitor	2.00
21	Mike Schmidt, George Brett	5.00
22	Cal Ripken Jr., Don Mattingly	8.00
23	Bob Gibson, Ernie Banks	4.00
24	Eddie Murray, Bert Blyleven	3.00
25	Warren Spahn, Willie Mays	6.00

Rivals Bat
NM/M

Production 50-100

3	Tim Hudson, Mark Teixeira/50	10.00
4	Roger Clemens, Albert Pujols/100	25.00
5	Greg Maddux, Jeff Bagwell/100	15.00
7	Kerry Wood, Larry Walker/100	15.00
10	Josh Beckett, Chipper Jones/50	15.00
13	Carlos Beltran, Sammy Sosa/100	15.00
14	Mark Prior, Jim Thome/50	15.00
18	Adam Dunn, Shawn Green/100	10.00
21	Mike Schmidt, George Brett/100	20.00
22	Cal Ripken Jr., Don Mattingly/100	30.00

Rivals Jersey
NM/M

Production 50-250
Prime: No Pricing
Production 5 Sets

2	Mark Mulder, Vladimir Guerrero/100	10.00
3	Tim Hudson, Mark Teixeira/100	10.00
4	Roger Clemens, Albert Pujols/100	20.00
5	Greg Maddux, Jeff Bagwell/250	10.00
7	Kerry Wood, Larry Walker/250	8.00
9	C.C. Sabathia, Torii Hunter/150	10.00
10	Josh Beckett/Pants, Chipper Jones/150	10.00
13	Carlos Beltran, Sammy Sosa/250	10.00
14	Mark Prior, Jim Thome/250	10.00
15	Miguel Cabrera, Andruw Jones/250	10.00
16	Johan Santana, Magglio Ordonez/100	10.00
18	Adam Dunn, Shawn Green/100	10.00
19	J. Morris, Rod Carew/250	10.00
21	Mike Schmidt, George Brett/100	15.00
22	Cal Ripken Jr., Don Mattingly/100	40.00
23	Bob Gibson, Ernie Banks/50	15.00
24	Eddie Murray, Bert Blyleven	10.00
25	Warren Spahn/Pant, Willie Mays/Pant/50	60.00

Signatures Gold
NM/M

Production 5-100
Platinum: No Pricing
Production One Set

1	Adam Dunn/25	35.00
2	Adrian Beltre/25	25.00
3	Akinori Otsuka/50	30.00
5	Aubrey Huff/50	15.00
11	Austin Kearns/25	15.00
17	Bobby Crosby/15	15.00
18	Brad Penny/100	15.00
25	Carlos Lee/100	15.00
26	Carlos Zambrano/100	25.00
27	Casey Kotchman/100	10.00
29	Chone Figgins/100	15.00
31	Craig Monroe/100	10.00
34	Danny Haren/100	10.00
36	David Dellucci/100	15.00
52	Jake Peavy/100	25.00
53	Jamie Moyer/100	15.00
59	Jay Gibbons/100	10.00
62	Jeremy Bonderman/100	10.00
63	Jermaine Dye/100	12.00
66	Joe Nathan/100	10.00
71	Johnny Estrada/50	10.00
87	Laynce Nix/100	10.00
88	Lyle Overbay/100	10.00
92	Mark Loretta/100	15.00
99	Mike Lieberthal/100	10.00
104	Milton Bradley/100	12.00
105	Morgan Ensberg/100	12.00
108	Paul Konerko/25	20.00
111	Rafael Furcal/25	15.00
117	Roy Halladay/25	25.00
119	Scott Podsednik/50	15.00
121	Sean Burroughs/100	8.00
122	Sean Casey/25	15.00
123	Shannon Stewart/100	8.00
126	Steve Finley/50	15.00
127	Tim Hudson/25	30.00
129	Tim Salmon/100	15.00
130	Torii Hunter/25	20.00
131	Travis Hafner/100	12.00
133	Troy Percival/50	15.00
134	Vernon Wells/25	15.00
135	Victor Martinez/100	15.00
137	Andre Dawson/25	15.00
138	Brooks Robinson/25	30.00
140	Dale Murphy/50	25.00
141	Darryl Strawberry/100	15.00
143	Harmon Killebrew/30	30.00
145	Jim Palmer/25	20.00
146	Lou Brock/25	30.00
148	Mike Schmidt/25	60.00
149	Steve Carlton/50	25.00
149	Tony Gwynn/25	50.00

Signatures Lumber Cuts
NM/M

Production 256 Sets

151	Agustin Montero	8.00
152	Carlos Ruiz	8.00
153	Casey Rogowski	10.00
154	Chris Resop	15.00
155	Chris Roberson	10.00
156	Colter Bean	10.00
157	Danny Rueckel	8.00
158	David Gassner	8.00
159	Geovany Soto	8.00
160	John Hattig Jr.	8.00
161	Justin Wechsler	8.00
162	Luke Scott	15.00
163	Mark McLemore	8.00
164	Miguel Negron	8.00
165	Mike Morse	40.00
166	Nate McLouth/254	10.00
167	Philip Humber	20.00
168	Randy Messenger	8.00
169	Raul Tablado	8.00
170	Russel Rohlicek	8.00
171	Ryan Speier	8.00
172	Scott Munter	12.00
173	Sean Thompson	10.00
174	Sean Tracey	10.00
175	Wladimir Balentien	20.00
177	Norihiro Nakamura/128	75.00

2005 Donruss Cal Ripken 10th Anniversary

This card marking the 10th anniversary of Ripken's 2,131st consecutive game was issued in the September 4 issue of the Baltimore Sun newspaper.

NM/M
Cal Ripken Jr. 4.00

2005 Donruss Studio
NM/M

Complete Set (300):
Common Player: .25

	Pack (6):	4.00
	Box (24):	90.00
1	Casey Kotchman	.25
2	Chone Figgins	.25
3	Dallas McPherson	.25
4	Darin Erstad	.25
5	Ervin Santana	.25
6	Garret Anderson	.40
7	Norihiro Nakamura RC	2.00
8	John Lackey	.25
9	Orlando Cabrera	.25
10	Robb Quinlan	.25
11	Steve Finley	.25
12	Tim Salmon	.25
13	Vladimir Guerrero	.75
14	Brandon Webb	.25
15	Craig Counsell	.25
16	Javier Vazquez	.25
17	Luis Gonzalez	.25
18	Tony Pena RC	.40
19	Russ Ortiz	.25
20	Scott Hairston	.25
21	Shawn Green	.25
22	Jose Cruz Jr.	.25
23	Troy Glaus	.40
24	Adam LaRoche	.25
25	Andruw Jones	.50
26	Chipper Jones	.75
27	Danny Kolb	.25
28	John Smoltz	.40
29	Johnny Estrada	.25
30	Marcus Giles	.25
31	Nick Green	.25
32	Rafael Furcal	.25
33	Tim Hudson	.40
34	Brian Roberts	.25
35	Javy Lopez	.25
36	Jay Gibbons	.25
37	Melvin Mora	.25
38	Miguel Tejada	.50
39	Rafael Palmeiro	.50
40	Rodrigo Lopez	.25
41	Sidney Ponson	.25
42	Abe Alvarez	.25
43	Bill Mueller	.25
44	Curt Schilling	.75
45	David Ortiz	.75
46	David Wells	.25
47	Edgar Renteria	.25
48	Jason Varitek	.50
49	Jay Payton	.25
50	Johnny Damon	.75
51	Juan Cedeno	.25
52	Manny Ramirez	.75
53	Matt Clement	.25
54	Trot Nixon	.25
55	Wade Miller	.25
56	Aramis Ramirez	.40
57	Carlos Zambrano	.40
58	Corey Patterson	.25
59	Derrek Lee	.50
60	Greg Maddux	1.50
61	Kerry Wood	.40
62	Mark Prior	.75
63	Nomar Garciaparra	.75
64	Sammy Sosa	1.00
65	Todd Walker	.25
66	A.J. Pierzynski	.25
67	Aaron Rowand	.25
68	Frank Thomas	.50
69	Freddy Garcia	.25
70	Jermaine Dye	.25
71	Mark Buehrle	.40
72	Paul Konerko	.25
73	Tadahito Iguchi RC	3.00
74	Pedro Lopez RC	.40
75	Scott Podsednik	.25
76	Shingo Takatsu	.25
77	Adam Dunn	.50
78	Austin Kearns	.25
79	Barry Larkin	.50
80	Bubba Nelson	.25
81	Danny Graves	.25
82	Eric Milton	.25
83	Ken Griffey Jr.	1.50
84	Ryan Wagner	.25
85	Sean Casey	.25
86	C.C. Sabathia	.25
87	Cliff Lee	.25
88	Fausto Carmona	.25
89	Grady Sizemore	.40
90	Jake Westbrook	.25
91	Jody Gerut	.25
92	Juan Gonzalez	.40
93	Kazuhito Tadano	.25
94	Travis Hafner	.25
95	Victor Martinez	.25
96	Charles Johnson	.25
97	Clint Barmes	.25
98	Cory Sullivan	.25
99	Jeff Baker	.25
100	Jeff Francis	.25
101	Jeff Salazar	.25
102	Jeromy Burnitz	.25
103	Joe Kennedy	.25
104	Matt Holliday	.25
105	Preston Wilson	.25
106	Todd Helton	.50
107	Ubaldo Jimenez RC	.40
108	Brandon Inge	.25
109	Carlos Guillen	.25
110	Carlos Pena	.25
111	Craig Monroe	.25
112	Ivan Rodriguez	.50
113	Jeremy Bonderman	.25
114	Justin Verlander RC	2.00
115	Magglio Ordonez	.25
116	Troy Percival	.25

117	Vance Wilson	.25
118	A.J. Burnett	.25
119	Al Leiter	.25
120	Dontrelle Willis	.25
121	Josh Beckett	.40
122	Juan Pierre	.25
123	Miguel Cabrera	.75
124	Mike Lowell	.25
125	Paul LoDuca	.25
126	Randy Messenger RC	.40
127	Yorman Bazardo RC	.25
128	Andy Pettitte	.40
129	Brad Lidge	.25
130	Chris Burke	.25
131	Craig Biggio	.40
132	Fernando Nieve	.25
133	Jason Lane	.25
134	Jeff Bagwell	.50
135	Lance Berkman	.40
136	Morgan Ensberg	.25
137	Roger Clemens	2.00
138	Roy Oswalt	.25
139	Ambiorix Burgos RC	.40
140	David DeJesus	.25
141	Jeremy Affeldt	.25
142	Jose Lima	.25
143	Ken Harvey	.25
144	Mike MacDougal	.25
145	Mike Sweeney	.25
146	Terrence Long	.25
147	Zack Greinke	.25
148	Brad Penny	.25
149	Derek Lowe	.25
150	Dioner Navarro	.25
151	Edwin Jackson	.25
152	Eric Gagne	.25
153	Hee Seop Choi	.25
154	Hideo Nomo	.50
155	J.D. Drew	.25
156	Jeff Kent	.25
157	Jeff Weaver	.25
158	Milton Bradley	.25
159	Yhency Brazoban	.25
160	Ben Sheets	.40
161	Bill Hall	.25
162	Carlos Lee	.25
163	Gustavo Chacin	.25
164	Geoff Jenkins	.25
165	Jose Capellan	.25
166	Lyle Overbay	.25
167	Rickie Weeks	.40
168	Jacque Jones	.40
169	Joe Mauer	.50
170	Joe Nathan	.25
171	Johan Santana	.50
172	Justin Morneau	.40
173	Lew Ford	.25
174	Michael Cuddyer	.25
175	Shannon Stewart	.25
176	Torii Hunter	.25
177	Brad Radke	.25
178	Ambiorix Concepcion RC	.40
179	Carlos Beltran	.50
180	David Wright	.75
181	Jose Reyes	.50
182	Kazuo Matsui	.25
183	Kris Benson	.25
184	Mike Piazza	1.00
185	Pedro Martinez	.75
186	Philip Humber RC	1.00
187	Tom Glavine	.40
188	Alex Rodriguez	1.50
189	Carl Pavano	.25
190	Derek Jeter	2.00
191	Yuniesky Betancourt RC	1.00
192	Hideki Matsui	1.50
193	Jorge Posada	.40
194	Kevin Brown	.25
195	Mariano Rivera	.50
196	Mike Mussina	.40
197	Randy Johnson	.75
198	Scott Proctor	.25
199	Tom Gordon	.25
200	Barry Zito	.40
201	Bobby Crosby	.40
202	Danny Haren	.25
203	Eric Chavez	.40
204	Keiichi Yabu RC	.25
205	Jason Kendall	.25
206	Joe Blanton	.25
207	Mark Kotsay	.25
208	Nick Swisher	.25
209	Octavio Dotel	.25
210	Rich Harden	.40
211	Billy Wagner	.40
212	Bobby Abreu	.40
213	Chase Utley	.50
214	Gavin Floyd	.25
215	Jim Thome	.50
216	Jimmy Rollins	.50
217	Jon Lieber	.25
218	Kenny Lofton	.25
219	Mike Lieberthal	.25
220	Pat Burrell	.25
221	Randy Wolf	.25
222	Craig Wilson	.25
223	Jack Wilson	.25
224	Jason Bay	.25
225	John Van Benschoten	.25
226	Jose Castillo	.25
227	Kip Wells	.25
228	Matt Lawton	.25
229	Akinori Otsuka	.25
230	Brian Giles	.25
231	Freddy Guzman	.25
232	Jake Peavy	.40

233	Khalil Greene	.40
234	Mark Loretta	.25
235	Sean Burroughs	.25
236	Trevor Hoffman	.25
237	Woody Williams	.25
238	Armando Benitez	.25
239	Edgardo Alfonzo	.25
240	Erick Threets RC	.40
241	Jason Schmidt	.40
242	Marquis Grissom	.25
243	Merkin Valdez	.25
244	Michael Tucker	.25
245	Moises Alou	.40
246	Omar Vizquel	.40
247	Adrian Beltre	.40
248	Bret Boone	.25
249	Bucky Jacobsen	.25
250	Clint Nageotte	.25
251	Ichiro Suzuki	1.50
252	J.J. Putz	.25
253	Jeremy Reed	.25
254	Miguel Olivo	.25
255	Mike Morse RC	2.00
256	Richie Sexson	.40
257	Wladimir Balentien RC	1.00
258	Albert Pujols	2.00
259	Jason Isringhausen	.25
260	Jeff Suppan	.25
261	Jim Edmonds	.40
262	Larry Walker	.40
263	Mark Mulder	.40
264	Rick Ankiel	.50
265	Scott Rolen	.75
266	Yadier Molina	.25
267	Aubrey Huff	.25
268	B.J. Upton	.25
269	Carl Crawford	.25
270	Chris Seddon RC	.40
271	Delmon Young	.25
272	Dewon Brazelton	.25
273	Jeff Niemann RC	1.00
274	Rocco Baldelli	.25
275	Scott Kazmir	.25
276	Adrian Gonzalez	.25
277	Alfonso Soriano	.75
278	Francisco Cordero	.25
279	Hank Blalock	.40
280	Kameron Loe	.25
281	Kenny Rogers	.25
282	Laynce Nix	.25
283	Mark Teixeira	.40
284	Michael Young	.25
285	Corey Koskie	.25
286	David Bush	.25
287	Frank Catalanotto	.25
288	Gabe Gross	.25
289	Raul Tablado RC	.40
290	Roy Halladay	.40
291	Shea Hillenbrand	.25
292	Vernon Wells	.25
293	Chad Cordero	.25
294	Cristian Guzman	.25
295	Jose Guillen	.25
296	Jose Vidro	.25
297	Josh Karp	.25
298	Livan Hernandez	.25
299	Nick Johnson	.25
300	Vinny Castilla	.25

Proofs Silver

Stars:	3-5X
Production 100 Sets	

Proofs Gold

Stars:	8-12X
Production 25 Sets	

Proofs Platinum

No Pricing
Production 10 Sets

Autographs

No Pricing

Diamond Cuts

		NM/M
Common Player:		1.00
Production 1,250 Sets		
Die-Cut:		1-1.5X
Production 250 Sets		
Die-Cut Gold:		1.5-3X
Production 75 Sets		
1	Roger Clemens	4.00
2	Manny Ramirez	1.50
3	Francisco Rodriguez	1.00
4	Brian Roberts	1.00

5	Javy Lopez	1.00
6	Vernon Wells	1.00
7	Johan Santana	1.50
8	Torii Hunter	1.00
9	Mike Mussina	1.50
10	Sammy Sosa	2.50
11	Ryan Wagner	1.00
12	Jack Wilson	1.00
13	Ichiro Suzuki	3.00
14	Greg Maddux	3.00
15	Albert Pujols	4.00
16	Jeremy Bonderman	1.00
17	Johnny Estrada	1.00
18	Mark Buehrle	1.00
19	Jorge Posada	1.00
20	Carl Crawford	1.00
21	Paul Konerko	1.00
22	Victor Martinez	1.00
23	Jose Vidro	1.00
24	Jim Thome	1.50
25	Andruw Jones	1.50

Diamond Cuts Bat

		NM/M
Production 5-300		
1	Roger Clemens/50	15.00
2	Manny Ramirez/200	8.00
5	Javy Lopez/300	4.00
8	Torii Hunter/300	4.00
10	Sammy Sosa/25	15.00
12	Jack Wilson/300	4.00
14	Greg Maddux/225	10.00
15	Albert Pujols/300	15.00
21	Paul Konerko/50	6.00
22	Victor Martinez/300	4.00
23	Jose Vidro/300	4.00
25	Andruw Jones/300	6.00

Diamond Cuts Jersey

		NM/M
Production 15-250		
Prime:		No Pricing
Production 5-10		
1	Roger Clemens/125	10.00
2	Manny Ramirez/250	8.00
3	Francisco Rodriguez/250	4.00
4	Brian Roberts/250	6.00
5	Javy Lopez/250	4.00
6	Vernon Wells/250	4.00
7	Johan Santana/175	8.00
8	Torii Hunter/250	4.00
9	Mike Mussina/250	6.00
10	Sammy Sosa/250	8.00
11	Ryan Wagner/250	4.00
14	Greg Maddux/250	8.00
15	Albert Pujols/250	20.00
16	Jeremy Bonderman/250	4.00
17	Johnny Estrada/250	4.00
18	Mark Buehrle/250	4.00
19	Jorge Posada/250	4.00
20	Carl Crawford/250	4.00
21	Paul Konerko/250	4.00
22	Victor Martinez/250	4.00
23	Jose Vidro/175	4.00
24	Jim Thome/250	6.00
25	Andruw Jones/250	6.00

Diamond Cuts Combo

		NM/M
Production 5-50		
Prime:		No Pricing
Production 10 Sets		
1	Roger Clemens/Bat-Jsy/50	20.00
2	Manny Ramirez/Bat-Jsy/50	12.00
3	Freddy Rodriguez/Jsy-Jsy/50	10.00
5	Javy Lopez/Bat-Jsy/50	8.00
6	Vernon Wells/Jsy-Jsy/50	8.00
8	Torii Hunter/Bat-Jsy/50	8.00
10	Sammy Sosa/Jsy-Jsy/50	12.00
11	Ryan Wagner/Jsy-Jsy/50	8.00
12	Jack Wilson/Bat-Jsy/50	8.00
14	Greg Maddux/Bat-Jsy/50	15.00
15	Albert Pujols/Bat-Jsy/50	30.00
17	Johnny Estrada/Fld Glve-Jsy/50	10.00
21	Paul Konerko/Jsy-Jsy/50	10.00
22	Victor Martinez/Bat-Jsy/50	10.00
23	Jose Vidro/Bat-Jsy/50	8.00
24	Jim Thome/Jsy-Jsy/45	12.00
25	Andruw Jones/Bat-Jsy/50	10.00

Diamond Cuts Signature Combo

		NM/M
Production 25-50		

Prime:		No Pricing
Production 10 Sets		
3	Freddy Rodriguez/Jsy-Jsy/25	40.00
6	Vernon Wells/Jsy-Jsy/25	25.00
8	Torii Hunter/Bat-Jsy/50	20.00
11	Ryan Wagner/Jsy-Jsy/50	15.00
12	Jack Wilson/Bat-Jsy/50	20.00
16	Jeremy Bonderman/Jsy-Jsy/50	20.00
17	Johnny Estrada/Fld Glv-Jsy/50	15.00
21	Paul Konerko/Jsy-Jsy/25	25.00

Heritage

		NM/M
Common Player:		1.00
Production 1,000 Sets		
Die-Cut:		1-1.5X
Production 200 Sets		
Die-Cut Gold:		2-3X
Production 50 Sets		
1	Rickey Henderson	1.50
2	Jeff Bagwell	1.50
3	Steve Garvey	1.00
4	Albert Pujols	5.00
5	Don Mattingly	4.00
6	Frank Thomas	1.50
7	Tony Gwynn	2.00
8	Gary Sheffield	1.50
9	Dale Murphy	1.50
10	Kerry Wood	1.50
11	Cal Ripken Jr.	6.00
12	Miguel Cabrera	2.00
13	Dwight Gooden	1.00
14	Barry Zito	1.00
15	Darryl Strawberry	1.00

Heritage Bat

		NM/M
Production 150 Sets		
1	Rickey Henderson	8.00
2	Jeff Bagwell	6.00
3	Steve Garvey	4.00
4	Albert Pujols	15.00
5	Don Mattingly	10.00
6	Frank Thomas	6.00
7	Tony Gwynn	8.00
8	Gary Sheffield	6.00
9	Dale Murphy	6.00
11	Cal Ripken Jr.	20.00
12	Miguel Cabrera	6.00
13	Dwight Gooden	4.00
15	Darryl Strawberry	4.00

Heritage Jersey

		NM/M
Production 50-250		
Prime:		No Pricing
Production 10 Sets		
1	Rickey Henderson/250	8.00
2	Jeff Bagwell/250	6.00
3	Steve Garvey/250	6.00
4	Albert Pujols/250	8.00
5	Don Mattingly/250	12.00
6	Frank Thomas/250	6.00
7	Tony Gwynn/250	8.00
9	Dale Murphy/250	6.00
10	Kerry Wood/250	4.00
11	Cal Ripken Jr./250	20.00
12	Miguel Cabrera/50	8.00
13	Dwight Gooden/250	4.00
14	Barry Zito/250	4.00
15	Darryl Strawberry/250	4.00

Heritage Combo

		NM/M
Production 10-50		
Prime:		No Pricing
Production 10 Sets		
1	Rickey Henderson/Bat-Jsy/50	15.00
2	Jeff Bagwell/Bat-Jsy/50	10.00
3	Steve Garvey/Bat-Jsy/50	10.00
4	Albert Pujols/Bat-Jsy/50	25.00
5	Don Mattingly/Bat-Jsy/50	20.00
6	Frank Thomas/Bat-Jsy/50	10.00
7	Tony Gwynn/Bat-Jsy/50	15.00
8	Gary Sheffield/Bat-Jsy/50	10.00
9	Dale Murphy/Bat-Jsy/50	12.00
10	Kerry Wood/Jsy-Pants/25	10.00
11	Cal Ripken Jr./Bat-Jsy/50	4.00
12	Miguel Cabrera/Bat-Jsy/50	12.00
13	Dwight Gooden/Bat-Jsy/50	10.00
15	Darryl Strawberry/Bat-Jsy/50	10.00

Heritage Signature Combo

		NM/M
Production 10-50		
Prime:		No Pricing
Production 5-10		
3	Steve Garvey/Bat-Jsy/50	25.00
5	Don Mattingly/Bat-Jsy/50	75.00
9	Dale Murphy/Bat-Jsy/50	40.00
11	Cal Ripken Jr./Bat-Jsy/50	160.00
12	Miguel Cabrera/Bat-Jsy/25	50.00
13	Dwight Gooden/Bat-Jsy/25	25.00
15	Darryl Strawberry/Bat-Jsy/25	25.00

Heroes of the Hall

		NM/M
Common Player:		2.00
Production 350 Sets		
Die-Cut:		1-1.5X
Die-Cut Gold:		2-3X
Production 25 Sets		
1	Luis Aparicio	2.00
2	Dennis Eckersley	2.00
3	Brooks Robinson	4.00
4	Carlton Fisk	2.00
5	Tom Seaver	4.00
6	Paul Molitor	2.00
7	Rod Carew	3.00
8	George Brett	6.00
9	Nolan Ryan	8.00
10	Mike Schmidt	6.00
11	Willie Mays	8.00
12	Gary Carter	2.00
13	Lou Brock	2.00
14	Steve Carlton	2.00
15	Harmon Killebrew	4.00

Heroes of the Hall Bat

		NM/M
Production 100-150		
1	Luis Aparicio/150	4.00
3	Brooks Robinson/150	8.00
4	Carlton Fisk/150	6.00
6	Paul Molitor/150	8.00
8	George Brett/150	12.00
10	Mike Schmidt/125	15.00
11	Willie Mays/100	35.00
12	Gary Carter/125	6.00
13	Lou Brock/150	6.00
15	Harmon Killebrew/150	8.00

Heroes of the Hall Jersey

		NM/M
Production 50-150		
Prime:		No Pricing
Production 5-10		
1	Luis Aparicio/150	4.00
2	Dennis Eckersley/150	6.00
3	Brooks Robinson/50	10.00
4	Carlton Fisk/150	4.00
5	Tom Seaver/150	8.00
6	Paul Molitor/150	8.00
7	Rod Carew/150	4.00
8	George Brett/150	12.00
9	Nolan Ryan/100	20.00
10	Mike Schmidt/100	15.00
11	Willie Mays/50	40.00
12	Gary Carter/150	6.00
14	Steve Carlton/150	4.00
15	Harmon Killebrew/150	8.00

Heroes of the Hall Combo

		NM/M
Production 25-50		
Prime:		No Pricing
Production 5-10		
1	Luis Aparicio/Bat-Jsy/50	10.00
2	Dennis Eckersley/Jsy-Pants/50	10.00
3	Brooks Robinson/Bat-Jsy/50	15.00
4	Carlton Fisk/Bat-Jsy/50	10.00
5	Tom Seaver/Jsy-Pants/50	15.00
6	Paul Molitor/Bat-Jsy/50	12.00
8	George Brett/Bat-Jsy/50	20.00
9	Nolan Ryan/Bat-Jsy/50	25.00
10	Mike Schmidt/Bat-Jsy/50	20.00
11	Willie Mays/Bat-Jsy/50	60.00
12	Gary Carter/Bat-Jsy/50	10.00
13	Lou Brock/Bat-Jkt/50	15.00

15	Harmon Killebrew/Bat-Jsy/50	15.00

Heroes of the Hall Signature Combo

		NM/M
Production 5-50		
Prime:		No Pricing
Production 5-10		
1	Luis Aparicio/Bat-Jsy/50	20.00
2	Dennis Eckersley/Jsy-Pants/25	30.00
4	Carlton Fisk/Bat-Jsy/25	40.00
6	Paul Molitor/Bat-Jsy/25	35.00
14	Steve Carlton/Bat-Jsy/25	35.00
15	Harmon Killebrew/Bat-Jsy/25	40.00

Masterstrokes

		NM/M
Common Player:		1.50
Production 750 Sets		
Die-Cut:		1-1.5X
Production 150 Sets		
Die-Cut Gold:		1.5-2X
Production 50 Sets		
1	Hideki Matsui	6.00
2	David Ortiz	3.00
3	Aramis Ramirez	2.00
4	Lance Berkman	1.50
5	Ichiro Suzuki	6.00
6	Mike Piazza	4.00
7	Ivan Rodriguez	2.00
8	Hideo Nomo	2.00
9	Jeff Bagwell	2.00
10	Travis Hafner	1.50
11	Casey Kotchman	1.50
12	Jim Edmonds	2.00
13	Michael Young	1.50
14	Lyle Overbay	1.50
15	Eric Chavez	2.00
16	Jason Bay	1.50
17	Hank Blalock	2.00
18	Frank Thomas	2.00
19	Craig Biggio	2.00
20	Miguel Cabrera	3.00
21	Vladimir Guerrero	3.00
22	Sammy Sosa	3.00
23	Chipper Jones	3.00
24	Rafael Palmeiro	2.00
25	Adam Dunn	2.00

Masterstrokes Bat

		NM/M
Production 25-250		
1	Hideki Matsui/25	30.00
2	David Ortiz/30	8.00
3	Aramis Ramirez/35	8.00
4	Lance Berkman/250	4.00
6	Mike Piazza/100	10.00
7	Ivan Rodriguez/250	6.00
9	Jeff Bagwell/250	6.00
10	Travis Hafner/250	4.00
11	Casey Kotchman/250	4.00
13	Michael Young/250	4.00
14	Lyle Overbay/250	4.00
16	Jason Bay/250	4.00
17	Hank Blalock/50	6.00
18	Frank Thomas/250	6.00
19	Craig Biggio/250	6.00
20	Miguel Cabrera/250	8.00
21	Vladimir Guerrero/250	8.00
22	Sammy Sosa/250	8.00
23	Chipper Jones/250	6.00
25	Adam Dunn/250	6.00

Masterstrokes Jersey

		NM/M
Production 40-250		
Prime:		No Pricing
Production 10 Sets		
1	Hideki Matsui/250	20.00
2	David Ortiz/250	8.00
3	Aramis Ramirez/250	4.00
4	Lance Berkman/250	4.00
6	Mike Piazza/250	8.00
7	Ivan Rodriguez/250	6.00
8	Hideo Nomo/250	6.00
9	Jeff Bagwell/250	6.00
10	Travis Hafner/200	4.00

11	Casey Kotchman/250	4.00
12	Jim Edmonds/250	6.00
13	Michael Young/150	4.00
14	Lyle Overbay/250	4.00
15	Eric Chavez/250	4.00
16	Jason Bay/250	4.00
17	Hank Blalock/250	4.00
18	Frank Thomas/250	6.00
19	Craig Biggio/250	6.00
20	Miguel Cabrera/250	6.00
21	Vladimir Guerrero/50	10.00
22	Sammy Sosa/250	8.00
23	Chipper Jones/250	6.00
24	Rafael Palmeiro/40	8.00
25	Adam Dunn/250	6.00

Masterstrokes Combo
NM/M
Production 15-50
Prime: No Pricing
Production 10 Sets

2	David Ortiz/ Bat-Jsy/	15.00
3	Aramis Ramirez/ Jsy-Jsy/50	10.00
4	Lance Berkman/ Bat-Jsy/50	8.00
6	Mike Piazza/ Jsy-Jsy/50	15.00
7	Ivan Rodriguez/ Bat-Jsy/50	10.00
8	Hideo Nomo/ Jsy-Jsy/50	12.00
9	Jeff Bagwell/ Bat-Jsy/50	10.00
10	Travis Hafner/ Bat-Jsy/	8.00
11	Casey Kotchman/ Jsy-Jsy/50	10.00
12	Jim Edmonds/ Jsy-Jsy/50	10.00
13	Michael Young/ Bat-Jsy/50	10.00
14	Lyle Overbay/ Bat-Jsy/50	8.00
15	Eric Chavez/ Bat-Jsy/50	10.00
16	Jason Bay/ Bat-Jsy/50	8.00
17	Hank Blalock/ Jsy-Jsy/50	10.00
18	Frank Thomas/ Bat-Jsy/50	12.00
19	Craig Biggio/ Bat-Jsy/50	10.00
20	Miguel Cabrera/ Bat-Jsy/50	15.00
21	Vladimir Guerrero/ Bat-Jsy/50	15.00
22	Sammy Sosa/ Bat-Jsy/50	15.00
23	Chipper Jones/ Bat-Jsy/50	12.00
24	Rafael Palmeiro/ Bat-Pants/50	12.00
25	Adam Dunn/ Bat-Jsy/50	10.00

Masterstrokes Signature Combo
NM/M
Production 5-50
Prime: No Pricing
Production 5-10

10	Travis Hafner/ Bat-Jsy/50	25.00
11	Casey Kotchman/ Bat-Jsy/50	20.00
14	Lyle Overbay/ Bat-Jsy/50	12.00
15	Eric Chavez/ Bat-Jsy/25	25.00
16	Jason Bay/ Bat-Jsy/50	25.00
17	Hank Blalock/ Jsy-Jsy/25	30.00
20	Miguel Cabrera/ Bat-Jsy/25	50.00

Portraits Zenith White
NM/M
Common Player: 2.00
Production 70 Sets
Parallel #'d 40-60: .75-1X
Parallel #'d 20-35: .75-1.5X
No pricing 15 or less.

1	Ozzie Smith	6.00
2	Derek Jeter	8.00
3	Eric Chavez	2.00
4	Duke Snider	4.00
5	Albert Pujols	8.00
6	Stan Musial	6.00
7	Ivan Rodriguez	3.00
8	Cal Ripken Jr.	15.00
9	Hank Blalock	2.00
10	Chipper Jones	3.00
11	Gary Sheffield	2.00
12	Alfonso Soriano	3.00
13	Carl Crawford	2.00
14	Lou Brock	4.00
15	Jim Edmonds	3.00
16	Bo Jackson	4.00
17	Todd Helton	3.00
18	Javy Lopez	2.00
19	Tony Gwynn	5.00
20	Mark Mulder	4.00
21	Sammy Sosa	4.00
22	Roger Clemens	6.00
23	Don Mattingly	8.00
24	Willie Mays	8.00
25	Andruw Jones	3.00
26	Steve Garvey	4.00
27	Scott Rolen	3.00
28	George Brett	4.00
29	Rod Carew	4.00
30	Ken Griffey Jr.	6.00
31	Mike Piazza	5.00
32	Steve Carlton	3.00
33	Larry Walker	2.00
34	Kerry Wood	2.00
35	Frank Thomas	3.00
36	Lance Berkman	2.00
37	Nomar Garciaparra	4.00
38	Curt Schilling	3.00
39	Carl Yastrzemski	6.00
40	Mark Grace	3.00
41	Tom Seaver	4.00
42	Mariano Rivera	3.00
43	Carlos Beltran	3.00
44	Reggie Jackson	4.00
45	Pedro Martinez	3.00
46	Richie Sexson	2.00
47	Tom Glavine	3.00
48	Torii Hunter	2.00
49	Ron Guidry	2.00
50	Michael Young	3.00
51	Ichiro Suzuki	6.00
52	C.C. Sabathia	2.00
53	Johnny Bench	4.00
54	Mark Teixeira	3.00
55	Hideki Matsui	6.00
56	Mike Mussina	3.00
57	Johan Santana	3.00
58	Fergie Jenkins	2.00
59	Hideo Nomo	3.00
60	Nolan Ryan	10.00
61	Whitey Ford	3.00
62	Jim Thome	3.00
63	Gary Carter	3.00
64	Randy Johnson	3.00
65	Vladimir Guerrero	3.00
66	Harmon Killebrew	4.00
67	Tim Hudson	3.00
68	Josh Beckett	2.00
69	Eddie Murray	4.00
70	Greg Maddux	5.00
71	J.D. Drew	2.00
72	Bob Feller	4.00
73	Adrian Beltre	2.00
74	Wade Boggs	4.00
75	Barry Zito	2.00
76	David Ortiz	3.00
77	Mike Schmidt	8.00
78	Miguel Cabrera	4.00
79	Carlos Delgado	2.00
80	Andre Dawson	2.00
81	Garret Anderson	2.00
82	Rickey Henderson	3.00
83	Shawn Green	2.00
84	Dale Murphy	3.00
85	Alex Rodriguez	6.00
86	Mark Prior	3.00
87	Paul Molitor	4.00
88	Jeff Bagwell	3.00
89	Eric Gagne	2.00
90	Troy Glaus	2.00
91	Robin Yount	4.00
92	Miguel Tejada	3.00
93	Kirk Gibson	2.00
94	Manny Ramirez	3.00
95	Rafael Palmeiro	3.00
96	Maury Wills	2.00
97	Craig Biggio	2.00
98	Jim Palmer	3.00
99	Adam Dunn	2.00
100	Carlton Fisk	3.00

Private Signings Silver
NM/M
Common Autograph: 8.00
Production 100 Sets

1	Casey Kotchman	15.00
2	Chone Figgins	8.00
5	Ervin Santana	8.00
9	Orlando Cabrera	12.00
12	Tim Salmon	12.00
18	Tony Pena	8.00
19	Russ Ortiz	8.00
24	Adam LaRoche	10.00
27	Danny Kolb	8.00
31	Nick Green	8.00
34	Brian Roberts	15.00
36	Jay Gibbons	8.00
49	Jay Payton	12.00
51	Juan Cedeno	8.00
55	Wade Miller	8.00
57	Carlos Zambrano	20.00
65	Todd Walker	10.00
70	Jermaine Dye	12.00
81	Bubba Nelson	8.00
83	Danny Graves	8.00
84	Ryan Wagner	8.00
87	Cliff Lee	8.00
91	Fausto Carmona	8.00
94	Jody Gerut	8.00
96	Travis Hafner	12.00
98	Cory Sullivan	8.00
101	Jeff Salazar	8.00
103	Joe Kennedy	8.00
108	Brandon Inge	8.00
111	Craig Monroe	8.00
113	Jeremy Bonderman	12.00
117	Vance Wilson	8.00
127	Yorman Bazardo	8.00
127	Yorman Bazardo	8.00
133	Jason Lane	8.00
136	Morgan Ensberg	12.00
141	Jeremy Affeldt	8.00
143	Ken Harvey	8.00
150	Dioner Navarro	12.00
151	Edwin Jackson	8.00
158	Milton Bradley	10.00
159	Yhency Brazoban	8.00
161	Bill Hall	8.00
162	Carlos Lee	12.00
166	Lyle Overbay	8.00
173	Lew Ford	8.00
191	Yuniesky Betancourt	25.00
198	Scott Proctor	8.00
201	Bobby Crosby	10.00
209	Danny Haren	8.00
209	Octavio Dotel	8.00
210	Rich Harden	12.00
219	Mike Lieberthal	8.00
221	Randy Wolf	8.00
222	Craig Wilson	8.00
223	Jack Wilson	8.00
224	Jason Bay	10.00
226	Jose Castillo	8.00
231	Freddy Guzman	8.00
232	Jake Peavy	25.00
234	Mark Loretta	10.00
250	Clint Nageotte	8.00
252	J.J. Putz	8.00
260	Jeff Suppan	8.00
276	Adrian Gonzalez	8.00
278	Francisco Cordero	8.00
280	Kameron Loe	8.00
282	Laynce Nix	8.00
291	Shea Hillenbrand	8.00
293	Chad Cordero	10.00
295	Jose Guillen	8.00
297	Josh Karp	8.00
298	Livan Hernandez	12.00

Private Signings Gold
NM/M
Common Autograph: 8.00
Production 50 Sets

1	Casey Kotchman	20.00
2	Chone Figgins	10.00
5	Ervin Santana	10.00
9	Garret Anderson	15.00
9	Orlando Cabrera	15.00
10	Robb Quinlan	8.00
11	Steve Finley	15.00
12	Tim Salmon	15.00
14	Brandon Webb	10.00
18	Tony Pena	8.00
19	Russ Ortiz	10.00
24	Adam LaRoche	10.00
27	Danny Kolb	10.00
31	Johnny Estrada	10.00
31	Nick Green	8.00
32	Rafael Furcal	15.00
34	Brian Roberts	20.00
36	Jay Gibbons	10.00
40	Rodrigo Lopez	10.00
47	Edgar Renteria	25.00
49	Jay Payton	10.00
51	Juan Cedeno	8.00
53	Matt Clement	30.00
54	Trot Nixon	20.00
56	Wade Miller	10.00
57	Carlos Zambrano	25.00
59	Derek Lee	40.00
65	Todd Walker	12.00
70	Jermaine Dye	15.00
71	Mark Buehrle	25.00
72	Paul Konerko	15.00
76	Shingo Takatsu	20.00
78	Austin Kearns	10.00
80	Bubba Nelson	8.00
81	Danny Graves	8.00
83	Ryan Wagner	10.00
87	Cliff Lee	10.00
88	Fausto Carmona	8.00
93	Jody Gerut	10.00
94	Kazuhito Tadano	15.00
94	Travis Hafner	15.00
98	Cory Sullivan	8.00
101	Jeff Salazar	8.00
108	Joe Kennedy	8.00
108	Brandon Inge	10.00
111	Craig Monroe	10.00
113	Jeremy Bonderman	15.00
116	Troy Percival	15.00
117	Vance Wilson	8.00
123	Miguel Cabrera	35.00
127	Yorman Bazardo	10.00
133	Jason Lane	8.00
136	Morgan Ensberg	15.00
141	Jeremy Affeldt	8.00
143	Ken Harvey	8.00
148	Brad Penny	10.00
150	Dioner Navarro	15.00
158	Edwin Jackson	10.00
158	Milton Bradley	12.00
159	Yhency Brazoban	8.00
161	Bill Hall	10.00
162	Carlos Lee	15.00
166	Lyle Overbay	8.00
168	Jacque Jones	8.00
170	Joe Nathan	12.00
173	Lew Ford	10.00
175	Shannon Stewart	10.00
191	Yuniesky Betancourt	30.00
198	Scott Proctor	10.00
199	Tom Gordon	12.00
201	Bobby Crosby	20.00
209	Danny Haren	10.00
209	Octavio Dotel	10.00
210	Rich Harden	15.00
219	Mike Lieberthal	15.00
221	Randy Wolf	8.00
222	Craig Wilson	10.00
223	Jack Wilson	10.00
224	Jason Bay	15.00
226	Jose Castillo	10.00
229	Akinori Otsuka	20.00
231	Freddy Guzman	10.00
232	Jake Peavy	30.00
234	Mark Loretta	12.00
235	Sean Burroughs	8.00
243	Merkin Valdez	10.00
249	Omar Vizquel	8.00
249	Bucky Jacobsen	10.00
250	Clint Nageotte	15.00
252	J.J. Putz	15.00
254	Miguel Olivo	8.00
260	Jeff Suppan	12.00
266	Yadier Molina	12.00
267	Aubrey Huff	12.00
268	B.J. Upton	20.00
269	Carl Crawford	20.00
271	Delmon Young	25.00
272	Dewon Brazelton	10.00
276	Adrian Gonzalez	10.00
278	Francisco Cordero	10.00
280	Kameron Loe	10.00
282	Laynce Nix	10.00
284	Michael Young	15.00
291	Shea Hillenbrand	12.00
293	Chad Cordero	12.00
295	Jose Guillen	12.00
297	Josh Karp	8.00
298	Livan Hernandez	15.00
299	Nick Johnson	15.00

Spirit of the Game
NM/M
Common Player: 1.50
Production 600 Sets
Die-Cut: 1-1.5X
Production 125 Sets
Die-Cut Gold: 2-4X
Production 25 Sets

1	Mark Prior	3.00
2	Sean Casey	1.50
3	Ichiro Suzuki	6.00
4	Andruw Jones	2.00
5	Francisco Cordero	1.50
6	Ben Sheets	2.00
7	Rocco Baldelli	1.50
8	Rafael Furcal	1.50
9	Angel Berroa	1.50
10	Roy Oswalt	1.50
11	Jose Reyes	1.50
12	Shannon Stewart	1.50
13	Greg Maddux	5.00
14	Alfonso Soriano	3.00
15	Curt Schilling	3.00
16	Jody Gerut	1.50
17	Brandon Webb	1.50
18	Josh Beckett	1.50
19	Laynce Nix	1.50
20	Scott Rolen	3.00

Spirit of the Game Bat
NM/M
Production 75-300

1	Mark Prior/300	6.00
4	Andruw Jones/300	6.00
6	Ben Sheets/300	4.00
7	Rocco Baldelli/300	4.00
8	Rafael Furcal/300	4.00
11	Jose Reyes/300	4.00
12	Shannon Stewart/75	4.00
13	Greg Maddux/300	4.00
14	Alfonso Soriano/225	6.00
16	Jody Gerut/300	4.00
17	Brandon Webb/300	4.00
19	Laynce Nix/300	4.00

Spirit of the Game Jersey
NM/M
Production 125-250
Prime: No Pricing
Production 10 Sets

1	Mark Prior/250	6.00
2	Sean Casey/250	4.00
4	Andruw Jones/250	6.00
5	Francisco Cordero/ 250	4.00
6	Ben Sheets/250	4.00
7	Rocco Baldelli/250	4.00
8	Rafael Furcal/250	4.00
10	Roy Oswalt/250	4.00
11	Jose Reyes/250	4.00
12	Shannon Stewart/250	4.00
13	Greg Maddux/250	4.00
14	Alfonso Soriano/250	6.00
15	Curt Schilling/250	6.00
16	Jody Gerut/125	6.00
18	Josh Beckett/250	4.00
19	Laynce Nix/250	4.00
20	Scott Rolen/250	6.00

Spirit of the Game Combo
NM/M
Production 50 Sets
Prime: No Pricing
Production 10 Sets

1	Mark Prior/Bat-Jsy	12.00
4	Sean Casey/Jsy-Jsy	6.00
4	Andruw Jones/ Bat-Jsy	8.00
6	Ben Sheets/Bat-Jsy	8.00
7	Rocco Baldelli/ Bat-Jsy	6.00
8	Rafael Furcal/Bat-Jsy	6.00
10	Roy Oswalt/Bat-Jsy	6.00
11	Jose Reyes/Bat-Jsy	8.00
12	Shannon Stewart/ Jsy-Jsy	6.00
13	Greg Maddux/ Bat-Jsy	15.00
14	Alfonso Soriano/ Jsy-Jsy	12.00
15	Curt Schilling/ Bat-Jsy	12.00
16	Jody Gerut/Bat-Jsy	6.00
19	Laynce Nix/Bat-Jsy	6.00
22	Scott Rolen/Jsy-Jsy	12.00

Spirit of the Game Signature Combo
NM/M
Production 10-25
Prime: No Pricing
Production 5-10

2	Sean Casey/ Jsy-Jsy/	20.00
8	Rafael Furcal/ Bat-Jsy/	25.00
12	Shannon Stewart/ Jsy-Jsy/	20.00
16	Jody Gerut/ Bat-Jsy/25	15.00
19	Laynce Nix/ Bat-Jsy/25	15.00

Stars
NM/M
Common Player: 1.00
Inserted 1:6
Gold: 1-2X
Production 500 Sets
Platinum: 2-4X
Production 50 Sets

1	Carlos Beltran	1.50
2	Sean Casey	1.00
3	Ichiro Suzuki	3.00
4	Vladimir Guerrero	1.50
5	Tim Hudson	1.50
6	Alex Rodriguez	4.00
7	Miguel Tejada	1.50
8	Curt Schilling	1.50
9	Roger Clemens	4.00
10	Ben Sheets	1.50
11	Todd Helton	1.50
12	Mark Mulder	1.00
13	Scott Podsednik	1.00
14	Victor Martinez	1.00
15	Mark Prior	1.50
16	Ivan Rodriguez	1.50
17	Dontrelle Willis	1.00
18	Andy Pettitte	1.00
19	Khalil Greene	1.50
20	Jeff Kent	1.00
21	Paul Konerko	1.50
22	Joe Mauer	1.50
23	Bobby Crosby	1.00
24	Pedro Martinez	2.00
25	John Smoltz	1.00
26	Derek Jeter	4.00
27	Moises Alou	1.00
28	Rich Harden	1.00
29	Jim Thome	1.50
30	Jason Bay	2.00
31	Aramis Ramirez	3.00
32	Carlos Lee	1.00
33	B.J. Upton	1.00
34	Nomar Garciaparra	1.00
35	Ken Griffey Jr.	1.00
36	Darin Erstad	1.00
37	Larry Walker	1.00
38	Jose Vidro	1.00
39	Zack Greinke	1.00
40	Michael Young	1.00
41	David Wright	2.00
42	Albert Pujols	4.00
43	Vernon Wells	1.00
44	Mark Teixeira	1.50
45	Jacque Jones	1.00
46	Brian Giles	1.00
47	Austin Kearns	1.00
48	Omar Vizquel	1.00
49	Randy Johnson	1.50
50	Jason Varitek	1.50

2005 Donruss Team Heroes
NM/M
Complete Set (440): 80.00
Common Player: .15
Pack (8): 1.75
Box (24): 35.00

1	Adam Kennedy	.15
2	Bartolo Colon	.15
3	Bengie Molina	.15
4	Casey Kotchman	.15
5	Chone Figgins	.15
6	Dallas McPherson	.25
7	Darin Erstad	.15
8	David Eckstein	.15
9	Francisco Rodriguez	.25
10	Garret Anderson	.15
11	Jarrod Washburn	.15
12	John Lackey	.15
13	Jose Guillen	.25
14	Robb Quinlan	.15
15	Tim Bittner	.15
16	Tim Salmon	.15
17	Vladimir Guerrero	.40
18	Alex Cintron	.15
19	Craig Counsell	.15
20	Brandon Webb	.15
21	Chad Tracy	.15
22	Doug DeVore	.15
23	Luis Gonzalez	.25
24	Mark Grace	.25
25	Randy Johnson	.75
26	Scott Hairston	.15
27	Shea Hillenbrand	.15
28	Tim Olson	.15
29	Adam LaRoche	.15
30	Andruw Jones	.40
31	Charles Thomas	.15
32	Chipper Jones	.75
33	Dale Murphy	.50
34	John Smoltz	.25
35	Johnny Estrada	.15
36	Jose Capellan	.15
37	Marcus Giles	.15
38	Nick Green	.15
39	Phil Niekro	.25
40	Rafael Furcal	.25
41	Brian Roberts	.50
42	Cal Ripken Jr.	4.00
43	Javy Lopez	.25
44	Jay Gibbons	.15
45	Larry Bigbie	.15
46	Luis Matos	.15
47	Melvin Mora	.15
48	Miguel Tejada	.50
49	Rafael Palmeiro	.50
50	Rodrigo Lopez	.15
51	Sidney Ponson	.15
52	Abe Alvarez	.15
53	Bill Mueller	.15
54	Curt Schilling	.75
55	David Ortiz	.75
56	Doug Mientkiewicz	.15
57	Dwight Evans	.15
58	Fred Lynn	.15
59	Jim Rice	.40
60	Johnny Damon	.75
61	Keith Foulke	.15
62	Kevin Youkilis	.15
63	Manny Ramirez	.75
64	Tim Wakefield	.15
65	Trot Nixon	.15
66	Angel Guzman	.15
67	Aramis Ramirez	.40
68	Carlos Zambrano	.40
69	Corey Patterson	.40
70	Derrek Lee	.40
71	Greg Maddux	1.00
72	Kerry Wood	.75
73	Lee Smith	.15
74	Mark Prior	.75
75	Sammy Sosa	1.50
76	Aaron Rowand	.15
77	Carlos Lee	.15
78	Frank Thomas	.50
79	Freddy Garcia	.15
80	Harold Baines	.15
81	Jose Contreras	.15
82	Juan Uribe	.15
83	Mark Buehrle	.15
84	Paul Konerko	.15
85	Shingo Takatsu	.15
86	Adam Dunn	.50
87	Austin Kearns	.15
88	Danny Graves	.15
89	Eric Davis	.15
90	Jacob Cruz	.15
91	Jason LaRue	.15
92	Ken Griffey Jr.	1.50
93	Ryan Wagner	.15
94	Sean Casey	.25
95	Casey Blake	.15
96	C.C. Sabathia	.15
97	Cliff Lee	.15
98	Grady Sizemore	.25
99	Jake Westbrook	.15
100	Jody Gerut	.15
101	Kazuhito Tadano	.15
102	Matt Lawton	.15
103	Travis Hafner	.15
104	Victor Martinez	.15
105	Charles Johnson	.15
106	Clint Barmes	.25
107	Garrett Atkins	.15
108	Jason Jennings	.15
109	Jeff Francis	.15
110	Joe Kennedy	.15
111	Matt Holliday	.15
112	Preston Wilson	.15
113	Todd Helton	.50
114	Alan Trammell	.40
115	Bobby Higginson	.15
116	Brandon Inge	.15
117	Carlos Guillen	.15
118	Carlos Pena	.15
119	Craig Monroe	.15
120	Dmitri Young	.15
121	Eric Munson	.15

#	Player	
122	Ivan Rodriguez	.50
123	Jeremy Bonderman	.15
124	Roberto Novoa	.15
125	A.J. Burnett	.15
126	Alex Gonzalez	.15
127	Dontrelle Willis	.40
128	Guillermo Mota	.15
129	Josh Beckett	.40
130	Juan Pierre	.15
131	Luis Castillo	.15
132	Miguel Cabrera	.75
133	Paul LoDuca	.15
134	Adam Everett	.15
135	Andy Pettitte	.25
136	Brad Ausmus	.15
137	Chris Burke	.15
138	Craig Biggio	.25
139	Jeff Bagwell	.50
140	Lance Berkman	.15
141	Morgan Ensberg	.15
142	Nolan Ryan	3.00
143	Roger Clemens	2.00
144	Roy Oswalt	.25
145	Tim Redding	.15
146	Wade Miller	.15
147	Andres Blanco	.15
148	Angel Berroa	.15
149	Benito Santiago	.15
150	Byron Gettis	.15
151	George Brett	2.00
152	Jeremy Affeldt	.15
153	Ken Harvey	.15
154	Mike MacDougal	.15
155	Mike Sweeney	.15
156	Shawn Camp	.15
157	Zack Greinke	.15
158	Brad Penny	.15
159	Cesar Izturis	.15
160	Edwin Jackson	.15
161	Eric Gagne	.40
162	Jerry Hairston	.15
163	Jeff Weaver	.15
164	Kazuhisa Ishii	.15
165	Milton Bradley	.15
166	Orel Hershiser	.25
167	Shawn Green	.25
168	Steve Garvey	.15
169	Tommy John	.15
170	Yhency Brazoban	.15
171	Ben Sheets	.25
172	Bill Hall	.15
173	Danny Kolb	.15
174	Lyle Overbay	.15
175	Paul Molitor	.50
176	Robin Yount	1.00
177	Rollie Fingers	.15
178	Rickie Weeks	.15
179	Scott Podsednik	.15
180	Jack Morris	.15
181	Jacque Jones	.15
182	Jason Kubel	.15
183	Joe Mauer	.50
184	Joe Nathan	.15
185	Johan Santana	.50
186	Justin Morneau	.15
187	Lew Ford	.15
188	Matthew LeCroy	.15
189	Rod Carew	.50
190	Shannon Stewart	.15
191	Torii Hunter	.25
192	Aarom Baldiris	.15
193	Cliff Floyd	.15
194	Darryl Strawberry	.15
195	Dwight Gooden	.15
196	David Wright	.75
197	Victor Zambrano	.15
198	Jose Reyes	.25
199	Kazuo Matsui	.15
200	Keith Hernandez	.15
201	Mike Piazza	1.00
202	Tom Glavine	.15
203	Vance Wilson	.15
204	Tom Seaver	.75
205	Alex Rodriguez	1.50
206	Bernie Williams	.15
207	Chien-Ming Wang	.40
208	Derek Jeter	2.00
209	Dioner Navarro	.15
210	Don Mattingly	1.50
211	Gary Sheffield	.50
212	Hideki Matsui	1.50
213	Jason Giambi	.25
214	Javier Vazquez	.15
215	Jim Leyritz	.15
216	Jorge Posada	.40
217	Kevin Brown	.15
218	Mariano Rivera	.40
219	Mike Mussina	.40
220	Scott Proctor	.15
221	Tom Gordon	.15
222	Barry Zito	.25
223	Bobby Crosby	.25
224	Dave Stewart	.15
225	Dennis Eckersley	.50
226	Eric Byrnes	.15
227	Eric Chavez	.25
228	Erubiel Durazo	.15
229	Mark Kotsay	.15
230	Mark Mulder	.40
231	Octavio Dotel	.15
232	Rich Harden	.15
233	Tim Hudson	.40
234	Billy Wagner	.15
235	Bobby Abreu	.40
236	Brett Myers	.15
237	Chase Utley	.25
238	Jim Thome	.75
239	Jimmy Rollins	.25
240	Lenny Dykstra	.15
241	Marlon Byrd	.15
242	Mike Lieberthal	.15
243	Mike Schmidt	1.50
244	Pat Burrell	.25
245	Randy Wolf	.15
246	Ryan Howard	.75
247	Steve Carlton	.15
248	Bert Blyleven	.15
249	Bill Madlock	.15
250	Dave Parker	.40
251	Craig Wilson	.15
252	Jack Wilson	.15
253	Jason Bay	.25
254	Jason Kendall	.15
255	Jose Castillo	.15
256	Kip Wells	.15
257	Akinori Otsuka	.15
258	Brian Giles	.25
259	Brian Lawrence	.15
260	Freddy Guzman	.15
261	Gaylord Perry	.15
262	Jake Peavy	.25
263	Jay Payton	.15
264	Khalil Greene	.15
265	Mark Loretta	.15
266	Phil Nevin	.15
267	Ryan Klesko	.15
268	Sean Burroughs	.15
269	Tony Gwynn	.75
270	Trevor Hoffman	.15
271	A.J. Pierzynski	.15
272	Dustan Mohr	.15
273	Edgardo Alfonzo	.15
274	Jason Schmidt	.40
275	Jerome Williams	.15
276	Matt Williams	.15
277	Merkin Valdez	.15
278	Todd Linden	.15
279	Will Clark	.50
280	Bret Boone	.15
281	Bucky Jacobsen	.15
282	Clint Nageotte	.15
283	Ichiro Suzuki	1.50
284	J.J. Putz	.15
285	Jamie Moyer	.15
286	Bobby Madritsch	.15
287	Mike Morse RC	.25
288	Joel Pineiro	.15
289	Shigetoshi Hasegawa	.15
290	Travis Blackley	.15
291	Albert Pujols	2.00
292	Dan Haren	.15
293	Jason Isringhausen	.15
294	Jason Marquis	.15
295	Jeff Suppan	.15
296	Jim Edmonds	.40
297	Larry Walker	.40
298	Reggie Sanders	.15
299	Scott Rolen	.75
300	Yadier Molina	.15
301	Aubrey Huff	.15
302	B.J. Upton	.15
303	Carl Crawford	.15
304	Chad Gaudin	.15
305	Delmon Young	.40
306	Dewon Brazelton	.15
307	Joey Gathright	.15
308	Jose Cruz Jr.	.15
309	Rocco Baldelli	.15
310	Wade Boggs	.50
311	Adrian Gonzalez	.15
312	Alfonso Soriano	.75
313	Francisco Cordero	.15
314	Frankie Francisco	.15
315	Hank Blalock	.50
316	Kenny Rogers	.15
317	Laynce Nix	.15
318	Mark Teixeira	.50
319	Michael Young	.15
320	Alexis Rios	.15
321	David Bush	.15
322	Eric Hinske	.15
323	Frank Catalanotto	.15
324	Gabe Gross	.15
325	Guillermo Quiroz	.15
326	Rickey Henderson	.50
327	Orlando Hudson	.15
328	Roy Halladay	.40
329	Ted Lilly	.15
330	Vernon Wells	.15
331	Alberto Callaspo	.15
332	Jeff Mathis	.15
333	Ervin Santana	.15
334	Troy Percival	.15
335	Troy Glaus	.40
336	Greg Aquino	.15
337	Tony Pena RC	.25
338	Luis Terrero	.15
339	J.D. Drew	.15
340	Jon Lieber	.15
341	Russ Ortiz	.15
342	Daniel Cabrera	.15
343	Val Majewski	.15
344	Orlando Cabrera	.15
345	Hanley Ramirez	.15
346	Pedro Martinez	.75
347	Jason Varitek	.50
348	Pedro Martinez	.75
349	Derek Lowe	.15
350	Juan Cedeno	.15
351	Todd Walker	.15
352	Matt Clement	.25
353	Moises Alou	.15
354	Nomar Garciaparra	1.00
355	Michael Barrett	.15
356	Todd Hollandsworth	.15
357	Jose Valentin	.15
358	Magglio Ordonez	.15
359	Pedro Lopez RC	.25
360	Barry Larkin	.25
361	Jaret Wright	.15
362	Elizardo Ramirez	.15
363	Omar Vizquel	.15
364	Fausto Carmona	.15
365	Jake Dittler	.15
366	Jeff Salazar	.15
367	Jeromy Burnitz	.15
368	Jayson Nix	.15
369	Ubaldo Jimenez RC	.25
370	Vinny Castilla	.15
371	Justin Verlander RC	.75
372	Armando Benitez	.15
373	Carl Pavano	.25
374	Chris Aguila	.15
375	Logan Kensing	.15
376	Mike Lowell	.15
377	Yorman Bazardo RC	.25
378	Willy Taveras	.15
379	Jeff Kent	.25
380	Carlos Beltran	.50
381	Kevin Millwood	.15
382	Juan Gonzalez	.15
383	Steve Finley	.15
384	Hideo Nomo	.40
385	Adrian Beltre	.15
386	David Krynzel	.15
387	Richie Sexson	.15
388	Jesse Crain	.15
389	Brad Radke	.15
390	Jason Lane	.15
391	Corey Koskie	.15
392	Cristian Guzman	.15
393	Brad Wilkerson	.15
394	Brendan Harris	.15
395	Chad Cordero	.15
396	Endy Chavez	.15
397	Jose Vidro	.15
398	Josh Karp	.15
399	Livan Hernandez	.15
400	Nick Johnson	.15
401	Ryan Church	.15
402	Terrmel Sledge	.15
403	Philip Humber RC	1.50
404	Ambiorix Concepcion RC	.25
405	Al Leiter	.15
406	Richard Hidalgo	.15
407	Kris Benson	.15
408	Mike Cameron	.15
409	Victor Diaz	.15
410	Tony Womack	.15
411	Ferdin Tejeda	.15
412	Nick Swisher	.15
413	Jairo Garcia	.15
414	Jermaine Dye	.15
415	Joe Blanton	.15
416	Eric Milton	.15
417	Gavin Floyd	.15
418	John Van Benschoten	.15
419	Matt Peterson	.15
420	David Wells	.15
421	J.T. Snow	.15
422	Willie Mays	2.00
423	Jeremy Reed	.15
424	Jose Lopez	.15
425	Raul Ibanez	.15
426	Wladimir Balentien RC	1.50
427	Matt Morris	.15
428	Mike Matheny	.15
429	Edgar Renteria	.25
430	Woody Williams	.15
431	Jeff Niemann RC	4.00
432	Scott Kazmir	.15
433	Tino Martinez	.15
434	Chris Young RC	.50
435	David Dellucci	.15
436	Kameron Loe	.15
437	Nolan Ryan	3.00
438	John-Ford Griffin	.15
439	Carlos Delgado	.40
440	Russ Adams	.15

Autographs

#	Player	NM/M
4	Casey Kotchman/SP	20.00
14	Robb Quinlan	8.00
15	Tim Bittner	5.00
18	Alex Cintron/SP	5.00
22	Doug DeVore	5.00
28	Tim Olson	5.00
38	Nick Green	5.00
44	Jay Gibbons/SP	12.00
50	Rodrigo Lopez/SP	5.00
66	Angel Guzman	12.00
90	Jacob Cruz	5.00
97	Cliff Lee SP	10.00
101	Kazuhito Tadano	5.00
104	Victor Martinez/SP	20.00
110	Joe Kennedy	5.00
116	Brandon Inge	10.00
119	Craig Monroe	8.00
124	Roberto Novoa	8.00
150	Byron Gettis/SP	8.00
156	Shawn Camp	5.00
170	Yhency Brazoban	8.00
172	Bill Hall/SP	8.00
182	Jason Kubel/SP	12.00
192	Aarom Baldiris/SP	10.00
203	Vance Wilson	5.00
220	Scott Proctor	8.00
277	Merkin Valdez	5.00
278	Todd Linden/SP	25.00
281	Bucky Jacobsen	5.00
282	Clint Nageotte	5.00
290	Travis Blackley	5.00
292	Dan Haren/SP	12.00
295	Jeff Suppan	10.00
306	Dewon Brazelton	8.00
307	Joey Gathright/SP	10.00
311	Adrian Gonzalez	10.00
313	Francisco Cordero/ SP	10.00
314	Frankie Francisco	5.00
317	Laynce Nix	5.00
333	Ervin Santana	10.00
337	Tony Pena	8.00
346	Hanley Ramirez	15.00
350	Juan Cedeno	8.00
359	Pedro Lopez	15.00
364	Fausto Carmona	5.00
365	Jake Dittler	10.00
366	Jeff Salazar	10.00
368	Jayson Nix	5.00
377	Yorman Bazardo	8.00
378	Willy Taveras/SP	15.00
398	Josh Karp	5.00
411	Ferdin Tejeda	5.00
419	Matt Peterson	5.00
435	David Dellucci/SP	20.00
436	Kameron Loe	5.00

ABBREVIATIONS

SP - Short Print

Movie Gallery

		NM/M
1	Cal Ripken Jr.	1.00

Showdown Blue

Blue: 3-5X

Showdown Bronze

Bronze: 4-6X
Production 100 Sets

Showdown Gold

Gold: No Pricing
Production 10 Sets

Showdown Red

Red: 1.5-3X

Showdown Silver

Silver: 6-8X
Production 50 Sets

National Convention

These cello-wrapped team sets were available at the National Sports Collectors Convention to persons who redeemed a free coupon available at Wal-Mart. Cards share the basic design of Donruss Team Heroes but have a National Convention logo on front and are numbered "X of 6" on back.

		NM/M
Complete Set (12):		
Common Player:		.25
	Chicago Cubs Team Heroes (6)	3.00
1	Kerry Wood	.50
2	Aramis Ramirez	.25
3	Mark Prior	.50
4	Nomar Garciaparra	.50
5	Greg Maddux	.50
6	Derek Lee	1.00
	Chicago White Sox Team Heroes (6)	2.00
1	Frank Thomas	1.00
2	Shingo Takatsu	.25
3	Aaron Rowand	.25
4	Paul Konerko	.25
5	Jermaine Dye	.25
6	Mark Buehrle	.25

2005 Donruss Throwback Threads

	NM/M
Complete Set (300):	

GARY SHEFFIELD

	NM/M
Common Player:	.20
Pack (5):	3.00
Box (24):	65.00

#	Player	
1	Luis Castillo	.20
2	Derek Jeter	1.50
3	Eric Chavez	.20
4	Angel Berroa	.20
5	Jeff Bagwell	.40
6	J.T. Snow	.20
7	Craig Biggio	.30
8	Michael Barrett	.20
9	Hank Blalock	.40
10	Chipper Jones	.50
11	Jacque Jones	.20
12	Mark Teixeira	.50
13	Omar Vizquel	.20
14	Paul LoDuca	.20
15	Jim Edmonds	.30
16	Aramis Ramirez	.20
17	Lance Berkman	.30
18	Javy Lopez	.30
19	Adam LaRoche	.20
20	Jorge Posada	.40
21	Sean Casey	.20
22	Mark Prior	.40
23	Phil Nevin	.20
24	Manny Ramirez	.50
25	Andruw Jones	.40
26	Matt Lawton	.20
27	Vladimir Guerrero	.50
28	Austin Kearns	.20
29	John Smoltz	.20
30	Ken Griffey Jr.	1.00
31	Mike Piazza	.75
32	Jason Jennings	.20
33	Jason Varitek	.40
34	David Ortiz	.50
35	Mike Mussina	.40
36	Joe Nathan	.20
37	Kenny Rogers	.20
38	Carlos Zambrano	.30
39	Eric Byrnes	.20
40	Clint Barmes	.20
41	Danny Kolb	.20
42	Mariano Rivera	.40
43	Joey Gathright	.20
44	Adam Dunn	.40
45	Carlos Lee	.20
46	Yhency Brazoban	.20
47	Roy Oswalt	.20
48	Torii Hunter	.20
49	Scott Podsednik	.20
50	Jason Hammel RC	.20
51	Ichiro Suzuki	1.00
52	C.C. Sabathia	.20
53	Bobby Abreu	.40
54	Jon Garland	.20
55	Brandon Webb	.20
56	Mark Buehrle	.20
57	Johan Santana	.40
58	Mike Sweeney	.20
59	Tadahito Iguchi RC	1.50
60	Edgar Renteria	.20
61	Aaron Rowand	.20
62	Craig Wilson	.20
63	J.D. Drew	.30
64	Bobby Crosby	.20
65	Justin Morneau	.40
66	Scott Rolen	.50
67	Jose Vidro	.20
68	Carlos Beltran	.40
69	Jeff Weaver	.20
70	Jason Schmidt	.20
71	Brad Wilkerson	.20
72	Yuniesky Betancourt RC	1.50
73	Octavio Dotel	.20
74	Mike Cameron	.20
75	Barry Zito	.40
76	Woody Williams	.20
77	Russel Rohlicek RC	.20
78	Mark Kotsay	.20
79	Jeff Suppan	.20
80	Eric Gagne	.40
81	Tim Salmon	.20
82	Troy Glaus	.20
83	Kevin Mench	.20
84	Ivan Rodriguez	.40
85	Sean Burroughs	.20
86	Dallas McPherson	.20
87	Jamie Moyer	.20
88	Orlando Cabrera	.20
89	Wladimir Balentien RC	1.00
90	Philip Humber RC	.20
91	Francisco Cordero	.20
92	Danny Graves	.20
93	Bucky Jacobsen	.20
94	Cliff Lee	.20
95	Oliver Perez	.20
96	Jake Peavy	.30
97	Doug Mientkiewicz	.20
98	Brad Radke	.20
99	Jeremy Reed	.20
100	Garret Anderson	.30
101	Rafael Furcal	.20
102	Jack Wilson	.20
103	Bernie Williams	.20
104	Josh Beckett	.20
105	Albert Pujols	1.50
106	Ubaldo Jimenez RC	.40
107	Richard Hidalgo	.20
108	Luke Scott RC	1.00
109	Hideo Nomo	.40
110	Vernon Wells	.30
111	Richie Sexson	.40
112	Chad Cordero	.20
113	Alex Rodriguez	1.50
114	Paul Konerko	.30
115	Carlos Guillen	.20
116	Francisco Rodriguez	.20
117	Johnny Damon	.50
118	David Wright	1.00
119	Lyle Overbay	.20
120	Brian Roberts	.20
121	Sammy Sosa	1.00
122	Roger Clemens	1.50
123	Rickie Weeks	.20
124	Larry Bigbie	.20
125	Rafael Palmeiro	.40
126	Jason Giambi	.20
127	Hideki Matsui	1.00
128	Brad Lidge	.20
129	Jeremy Affeldt	.20
130	Mike MacDougal	.20
131	Troy Percival	.20
132	Matt Morris	.20
133	David Gassner RC	.40
134	Kerry Wood	.40
135	Dontrelle Willis	.40
136	Michael Young	.30
137	Andy Pettitte	.40
138	Kris Benson	.20
139	Miguel Negron RC	.20
140	Rich Harden	.20
141	Bret Boone	.20
142	Danny Rueckel RC	.20
143	Jeff Niemann RC	1.00
144	Randy Messenger RC	.20
145	Pedro Martinez	.50
146	Kazuhisa Ishii	.20
147	Carlos Delgado	.30
148	Tom Glavine	.30
149	Russ Ortiz	.20
150	Gavin Floyd	.20
151	Randy Johnson	.50
152	Prince Fielder	8.00
153	Nomar Garciaparra	.75
154	Pat Burrell	.30
155	Melvin Mora	.20
156	Jose Reyes	.50
157	Trot Nixon	.20
158	B.J. Upton	.20
159	Jody Gerut	.20
160	Juan Pierre	.20
161	Miguel Tejada	.40
162	Barry Larkin	.40
163	Carl Crawford	.20
164	Ben Sheets	.30
165	Tim Hudson	.40
166	Darin Erstad	.20
167	Todd Helton	.40
168	Luis Gonzalez	.30
169	Mark Mulder	.30
170	David Dellucci	.20
171	Marcus Giles	.20
172	Shannon Stewart	.20
173	Zack Greinke	.40
174	Miguel Cabrera	.50
175	Nick Johnson	.20
176	Derek Lee	.50
177	Jim Thome	.50
178	Ken Harvey	.20
179	Ambiorix Concepcion RC	.40
180	Roy Halladay	.50
181	Larry Walker	.30
182	Greg Maddux	1.00
183	Frank Thomas	.50
184	Travis Hafner	.30
185	Matt Holliday	.20
186	Victor Martinez	.20
187	Jason Isringhausen	.20
188	Bill Mueller	.20
189	Dewon Brazelton	.20
190	Adrian Beltre	.40
191	Tim Wakefield	.20
192	Alexis Rios	.20
193	Alfonso Soriano	.50
194	Fernando Vina	.20
195	Armando Benitez	.20
196	Bartolo Colon	.30
197	A.J. Burnett	.20
198	Milton Bradley	.20
199	Brad Penny	.20
200	Rocco Baldelli	.20
201	Curt Schilling	.50
202	Ryan Wagner	.20
203	Preston Wilson	.20
204	Akinori Otsuka	.20
205	Bill McCarthy RC	.60
206	Edgardo Alfonzo	.20
207	Mike Lieberthal	.20
208	Shea Hillenbrand	.20
209	Tom Gordon	.20
210	Kip Wells	.20
211	Frank Catalanotto	.20

212	Casey Kotchman	.20
213	Justin Verlander **RC**	1.50
214	Brandon Inge	.20
215	Terrmel Sledge	.20
216	Gary Sheffield	.40
217	Steve Finley	.20
218	Kenny Lofton	.20
219	Chris Carpenter	.30
220	Danny Haren	.20
221	Brett Myers	.20
222	Joe Mauer	.50
223	David Wells	.20
224	Brian Giles	.20
225	Moises Alou	.30
226	Casey Rogowski **RC**	.40
227	Chase Utley	.50
228	Corey Koskie	.20
229	Derek Lowe	.20
230	Erick Threets **RC**	.40
231	Grady Sizemore	.40
232	Jason Lane	.20
233	Jeremy Bonderman	.20
234	Livan Hernandez	.20
235	Ryan Klesko	.20
236	Sidney Ponson	.20
237	Jimmy Rollins	.20
238	Eric Milton	.20
239	Shingo Takatsu	.20
240	Scott Kazmir	.20
241	Shawn Green	.30
242	Nick Swisher	.20
243	Shawn Chacon	.20
244	Javier Vazquez	.20
245	Mark Loretta	.20
246	Dmitri Young	.20
247	Charles Johnson	.20
248	Magglio Ordonez	.20
249	Sean Thompson **RC**	.20
250	Jared Gothreaux **RC**	.40
251	Kevin Millwood	.20
252	Mike Lowell	.20
253	Cristian Guzman	.20
254	Nate McLouth **RC**	.40
255	Delmon Young	.40
256	Jeromy Burnitz	.20
257	Garrett Atkins	.20
258	Junior Spivey	.20
259	Morgan Ensberg	.20
260	Chone Figgins	.20
261	Hayden Penn **RC**	.50
262	Jason Bay	.40
263	Jose Cruz Jr.	.20
264	Khalil Greene	.40
265	Ray Durham	.20
266	Juan Gonzalez	.40
267	Jeff Kent	.20
268	Dioner Navarro	.20
269	Rodrigo Lopez	.20
270	Geoff Jenkins	.20
271	Jermaine Dye	.20
272	Orlando Hudson	.20
273	Jose Lima	.20
274	Jeff Francis	.20
275	Luis Matos	.20
276	Jason Kendall	.20
277	Mike Hampton	.20
278	Al Kaline	.75
279	Bert Blyleven	.20
280	Bill Madlock	.20
281	Cal Ripken Jr.	3.00
282	Dale Murphy	.50
283	Gary Carter	.50
284	George Brett	2.00
285	Harmon Killebrew	1.00
286	Harold Baines	.40
287	John Kruk	.50
288	Keith Hernandez	.40
289	Willie Mays	3.00
290	Matt Williams	.20
291	Nolan Ryan	2.50
292	Paul Molitor	.50
293	Reggie Jackson	.75
294	Rickey Henderson	.50
295	Ron Cey	.20
296	Ryne Sandberg	1.00
297	Ted Williams	2.50
298	Tom Seaver	.75
299	Tony Gwynn	.75
300	Babe Ruth/SP	20.00

Century Proof Blue
Blue (1-299): 3-6X
Production 150 Sets

Century Proof Green
Green (1-299): 3-6X

Century Proof Gold
Gold (1-299): 3-6X
Production 100 Sets

Century Stars

		NM/M
Common Player:		1.00
Spectrum:		1.5-3X
Production 100 Sets		
1	Bobby Doerr	1.00
2	Derek Jeter	4.00
3	Harmon Killebrew	1.50
4	Paul Molitor	1.50
5	Brooks Robinson	1.00
6	Steve Garvey	1.00
7	Ivan Rodriguez	1.00
8	Carl Yastrzemski	2.50
9	Nomar Garciaparra	2.00

10	Miguel Tejada	1.00
11	Edgar Martinez	1.00
12	Kevin Brown	1.00
13	Alex Rodriguez	3.00
14	Carlton Fisk	1.00
15	Craig Biggio	1.00
16	Dwight Gooden	1.00
17	Jim Palmer	1.00
18	Ken Griffey Jr.	2.00
19	Bob Feller	1.50
20	Don Sutton	1.00
21	Al Kaline	1.50
22	Roger Clemens	4.00
23	Kirk Gibson	1.00
24	Willie Mays	3.00
25	Frank Robinson	1.00
26	Randy Johnson	1.50
27	Jim "Catfish" Hunter	1.00
28	Austin Kearns	1.00
29	John Smoltz	1.00
30	Nolan Ryan	4.00
31	Duke Snider	1.50
32	Bernie Williams	1.00
33	David Wells	1.00
34	Bo Jackson	1.50
35	Mike Mussina	1.00
36	Gaylord Perry	1.00
37	Andre Dawson	1.00
38	Curt Schilling	1.50
39	Darryl Strawberry	1.00
40	Willie McCovey	1.00
41	Tom Seaver	1.50
42	Mariano Rivera	1.00
43	Dennis Eckersley	1.00
44	David Cone	1.00
45	Bret Boone	1.00
46	Will Clark	1.00
47	Jack Morris	1.00
48	Ichiro Suzuki	3.00
49	Alan Trammell	1.00
50	Cal Ripken Jr.	4.00

Century Stars Material

		NM/M
Common Player:		4.00
Production 20-50		
Prime:		No Pricing
Production 5 Sets		
1	Bobby Doerr/Pants/50	8.00
3	Harmon Killebrew/Jsy/50	15.00
4	Paul Molitor/Jsy/50	10.00
5	Brooks Robinson/Bat/50	10.00
6	Steve Garvey/Jsy/50	4.00
7	Ivan Rodriguez/Jsy/50	8.00
8	Carl Yastrzemski/Jsy/50	15.00
10	Miguel Tejada/Jsy/50	6.00
11	Edgar Martinez/Jsy/50	6.00
12	Kevin Brown/Jsy/50	4.00
14	Carlton Fisk/Jsy/50	8.00
15	Craig Biggio/Jsy/50	8.00
16	Dwight Gooden/Jsy/50	4.00
17	Jim Palmer/Jsy/50	6.00
20	Don Sutton/Jsy/50	4.00
21	Al Kaline/Bat/50	15.00
22	Roger Clemens/Jsy/50	15.00
23	Kirk Gibson/Jsy/50	4.00
25	Frank Robinson/Bat/50	6.00
26	Randy Johnson/Jsy/50	8.00
28	Austin Kearns/Jsy/50	4.00
29	John Smoltz/Jsy/50	8.00
30	Nolan Ryan/Jkt/50	25.00
32	Bernie Williams/Jsy/50	6.00
33	David Wells/Jsy/50	4.00
34	Bo Jackson/Jsy/50	10.00
35	Mike Mussina/Jsy/50	8.00
36	Gaylord Perry/Jsy/50	6.00
37	Andre Dawson/Jsy/50	6.00
38	Curt Schilling/Jsy/50	8.00
39	Darryl Strawberry/Jsy/50	6.00
40	Willie McCovey/Jsy/50	8.00
42	Mariano Rivera/Jsy/50	10.00
43	Dennis Eckersley/Jsy/50	6.00
44	David Cone/Jsy/50	4.00
45	Bret Boone/Jsy/50	4.00
47	Jack Morris/Jsy/50	4.00
49	Alan Trammell/Jsy/50	6.00
50	Cal Ripken Jr./Jsy/50	30.00

Century Stars Signature Material

No Pricing
Production 10 Sets
Prime: No Pricing
Production 5 Sets

Dynasty

	NM/M
Common Trio:	2.00

Spectrum:		1.25X
Production 100 Sets		
1	Reggie Jackson, Jim "Catfish" Hunter, Sparky Lyle	2.00
2	Cal Ripken Jr., Jim Palmer, Eddie Murray	8.00
3	Dwight Gooden, Gary Carter, Darryl Strawberry	2.00
4	Rickey Henderson, Dennis Eckersley, Jose Canseco	2.00
5	Chipper Jones, Greg Maddux, David Justice	3.00
6	Roger Clemens, Alfonso Soriano, Bernie Williams	6.00
8	Randy Johnson, Curt Schilling, Matt Williams	3.00
9	Troy Glaus, Garret Anderson, Francisco Rodriguez	2.00
	Josh Beckett, Miguel Cabrera, Mike Lowell	2.00
10	Curt Schilling, Manny Ramirez, Jason Varitek	8.00

Dynasty Material

		NM/M
Production 20-50		
Prime:		No Pricing
Production 5 Sets		
1	Reggie Jackson/Pants, Jim "Catfish" Hunter/Pants, Sparky Lyle/Pants/50	20.00
2	Cal Ripken Jr./Jsy, Jim Palmer/Jsy, Eddie Murray/Jsy/50	40.00
3	Dwight Gooden/Jsy, Gary Carter/Jsy, Darryl Strawberry/Pants/20	15.00
4	Rickey Henderson/Jsy, Dennis Eckersley/Pants, Jose Canseco/Jsy/50	35.00
5	Chipper Jones/Jsy, Greg Maddux/Jsy, David Justice/Jsy/50	25.00
6	Roger Clemens/Jsy, Alfonso Soriano/Jsy, Bernie Williams/Jsy/50	30.00
7	Randy Johnson/Jsy, Curt Schilling/Jsy, Matt Willaims/Jsy/50	20.00
8	Troy Glaus/Jsy, Garret Anderson/Jsy, Francisco Rodriguez/Jsy/50	15.00
10	Curt Schilling/Jsy, Manny Ramirez/Jsy, Jason Varitek/Jsy/50	40.00

Generations

		NM/M
Common Player:		2.00
Spectrum:		1-2.5X
Production 100 Sets		
1	Duke Snider, Reggie Jackson, Sammy Sosa	2.00
2	Rod Carew, John Kruk, Eric Chavez	2.00
3	Bo Jackson, Deion Sanders, Brian Jordan	3.00
4	Brett George, Tony Gwynn, Todd Helton	4.00
5	Babe Ruth, Ted Williams, Willie Mays	5.00
6	Rickey Henderson, Lenny Dykstra, Ichiro Suzuki	3.00
7	Keith Hernandez, Don Mattingly, Casey Kotchman	3.00
8	Wade Boggs, Mark Grace, Hank Blalock	2.00
9	Gary Carter, Ivan Rodriguez, Victor Martinez	2.00
10	Gaylord Perry, Morris, Greg Maddux	2.00
11	Joe Morgan, Ryne Sandberg, Alfonso Soriano	3.00
12	Juan Marichal, Luis Tiant, Pedro Martinez	2.00
13	Stan Musial, Carl Yastrzemski, Lance Berkman	3.00
14	Johnny Bench, Carlton Fisk, Mike Piazza	3.00
15	Harmon Killebrew, Cal Ripken Jr., Albert Pujols	5.00
16	Frank Robinson, Andre Dawson, Gary Sheffield	2.00

17	Bob Feller, Roger Clemens, Kerry Wood	4.00
18	Steve Carlton, Tom Glavine, Barry Zito	2.00
19	Murray, Rafael Palmeiro, Mark Teixeira	2.00
20	Brooks Robinson, Mike Schmidt, Scott Rolen	3.00
21	Luis Aparicio, Omar Vizquel, Rafael Furcal	2.00
22	Don Sutton, David Cone, Roy Oswalt	2.00
23	Fred Lynn, Dale Murphy, Jim Edmonds	2.00
24	Ozzie, Barry Larkin, B.J. Upton	3.00
25	Gibson, Nolan Ryan, Mark Prior	4.00

Generations Material

		NM/M
Production 20-50		
Prime:		No Pricing
Production 10 Sets		
2	Rod Carew/Jsy, John Kruk/Jsy, Eric Chavez/Jsy/50	15.00
3	Bo Jackson/Jsy, Deion Sanders/Jsy, Brian Jordan/Jsy/50	25.00
4	Brett George/Jsy, Tony Gwynn/Jsy, Todd Helton/Jsy/50	25.00
7	Keith Hernandez/Jsy, Don Mattingly/Pants, Casey Kotchman/Jsy/20	30.00
8	Wade Boggs/Jsy, Mark Grace/Jsy, Hank Blalock/Jsy/50	15.00
9	Gary Carter/Jsy, Ivan Rodriguez/Jsy, Victor Martinez/Jsy/50	15.00
10	Gaylord Perry/Jsy, Morris/Jsy, Greg Maddux/Jsy/50	25.00
11	Joe Morgan/Jsy, Ryne Sandberg/Jsy, Alfonso Soriano/Jsy/50	35.00
12	Juan Marichal/Pants, Luis Tiant/Pants, Pedro Martinez/Jsy/50	20.00
14	Johnny Bench/Pants, Carlton Fisk/Jsy, Mike Piazza/Jsy/50	20.00
15	Harmon Killebrew/Jsy, Cal Ripken Jr./Jsy, Albert Pujols/Jsy/50	50.00
16	Frank Robinson/Bat, Andre Dawson/Jsy, Gary Sheffield/Jsy/20	15.00
17	Bob Feller/Pants, Roger Clemens/Jsy, Kerry Wood/Jsy/20	50.00
18	Steve Carlton/Jsy, Tom Glavine/Jsy, Barry Zito/Jsy/50	20.00
19	Murray/Jsy, Rafael Palmeiro/Jsy, Mark Teixeira/Jsy/50	20.00

Material Bat

		NM/M
Common Player:		4.00
Production 5-250		
1	Luis Castillo/250	4.00
4	Angel Berroa/250	4.00
6	Jeff Bagwell/250	6.00
7	Craig Biggio/250	6.00
14	Paul LoDuca/250	4.00
17	Lance Berkman/250	4.00
18	Javy Lopez/250	4.00
21	Sean Casey/250	6.00
25	Andruw Jones/250	4.00
28	Matt Lawton/250	4.00
32	Jason Jennings/250	4.00
33	Jason Varitek/50	12.00
34	David Ortiz/250	8.00
43	Joey Gathright/250	4.00
48	Torii Hunter/250	4.00
55	Brandon Webb/250	4.00
58	Mike Sweeney/250	4.00
62	Craig Wilson/250	4.00
63	J.D. Drew/250	4.00
67	Jose Vidro/250	4.00
68	Carlos Beltran/250	4.00
81	Tim Salmon/250	4.00
82	Troy Glaus/250	4.00
83	Kevin Mench/250	4.00
101	Rafael Furcal/150	6.00
102	Jack Wilson/250	4.00
103	Bernie Williams/250	4.00
107	Richard Hidalgo/250	4.00
111	Richie Sexson/100	6.00
121	Sammy Sosa/250	6.00
125	Rafael Palmeiro/250	6.00
135	Dontrelle Willis/50	6.00

136	Michael Young/250	4.00
141	Bret Boone/50	4.00
147	Carlos Delgado/250	4.00
148	Tom Glavine/250	4.00
153	Nomar Garciaparra/150	8.00
154	Pat Burrell/150	4.00
156	Jose Reyes/50	6.00
158	B.J. Upton/250	6.00
159	Jody Gerut/250	4.00
160	Juan Pierre/250	4.00
162	Barry Larkin/100	6.00
164	Ben Sheets/250	4.00
165	Tim Hudson/50	6.00
168	Darin Erstad/50	4.00
174	Miguel Cabrera/250	4.00
175	Nick Johnson/250	4.00
192	Alex Rios/50	4.00
197	A.J. Burnett/250	4.00
200	Rocco Baldelli/250	4.00
203	Preston Wilson/150	4.00
206	Edgardo Alfonzo/250	4.00
212	Casey Kotchman/250	4.00
215	Terrmel Sledge/250	4.00
218	Kenny Lofton/150	4.00
224	Brian Giles/35	4.00
225	Moises Alou/50	6.00
232	Jason Lane/250	4.00
235	Ryan Klesko/250	4.00
241	Shawn Green/250	4.00
247	Charles Johnson/250	4.00
248	Magglio Ordonez/250	4.00
252	Mike Lowell/50	6.00
255	Delmon Young/250	4.00
259	Morgan Ensberg/25	6.00
260	Chone Figgins/250	4.00
262	Jason Bay/175	6.00
265	Ray Durham/200	4.00
266	Juan Gonzalez/250	6.00
267	Jeff Kent/250	4.00
272	Orlando Hudson/250	4.00
280	Bill Madlock/100	4.00
281	Cal Ripken Jr./150	25.00
283	Gary Carter/250	8.00
284	George Brett/25	25.00
286	Harold Baines/50	6.00
288	Keith Hernandez/25	8.00
289	Willie Mays/25	35.00
291	Nolan Ryan/25	25.00
292	Paul Molitor/150	6.00
293	Reggie Jackson/250	10.00
294	Rickey Henderson/250	8.00
296	Ryne Sandberg/50	15.00
297	Ted Williams/50	50.00
299	Tony Gwynn/50	10.00
300	Babe Ruth/25	180.00

Material Jersey

		NM/M
Common Player:		4.00
Production 5-250		
Prime:		1-2X
Production 10-100		
No pricing 20 or less.		
1	Luis Castillo/45	4.00
3	Eric Chavez/250	4.00
6	Jeff Bagwell/250	6.00
7	J.T. Snow/250	4.00
9	Craig Biggio/250	6.00
9	Hank Blalock/25	6.00
10	Chipper Jones/250	8.00
11	Jacque Jones/250	4.00
12	Mark Teixeira/150	6.00
13	Jim Edmonds/250	6.00
16	Aramis Ramirez/250	4.00
17	Lance Berkman/250	4.00
18	Javy Lopez/250	4.00
20	Jorge Posada/250	4.00
22	Sean Casey/250	4.00
22	Mark Prior/250	8.00
24	Phil Nevin/50	4.00
24	Manny Ramirez/250	8.00
25	Andruw Jones/250	6.00
27	Vladimir Guerrero/250	8.00
28	Austin Kearns/250	4.00
31	John Smoltz/250	8.00
31	Mike Piazza/250	8.00
32	Jason Jennings/250	4.00
34	David Ortiz/250	10.00
38	Carlos Zambrano/250	6.00
42	Mariano Rivera/50	8.00
43	Joey Gathright/100	4.00

44	Adam Dunn/250	6.00
47	Roy Oswalt/250	4.00
48	Torii Hunter/100	4.00
52	C.C. Sabathia/250	4.00
53	Bobby Abreu/250	4.00
56	Mark Buehrle/250	4.00
57	Johan Santana/75	4.00
60	Mike Sweeney/75	4.00
62	Craig Wilson/250	4.00
64	Bobby Crosby/100	4.00
66	Scott Rolen/250	6.00
67	Jose Vidro/75	4.00
74	Mike Cameron/250	4.00
75	Barry Zito/250	4.00
83	Kevin Mench/250	4.00
87	Ivan Rodriguez/250	6.00
91	Jamie Moyer/50	4.00
91	Francisco Cordero/250	4.00
94	Cliff Lee/250	4.00
98	Brad Radke/250	4.00
100	Garret Anderson/50	4.00
101	Rafael Furcal/100	4.00
103	Bernie Williams/250	6.00
104	Josh Beckett/25	4.00
108	Albert Pujols/250	15.00
109	Hideo Nomo/250	8.00
110	Vernon Wells/250	4.00
114	Paul Konerko/250	4.00
116	Francisco Rodriguez/250	4.00
117	Johnny Damon/250	8.00
118	David Wright/250	10.00
119	Lyle Overbay/250	4.00
120	Brian Roberts/100	4.00
122	Roger Clemens/100	12.00
124	Larry Bigbie/200	4.00
125	Rafael Palmeiro/250	6.00
126	Jason Giambi/250	4.00
127	Hideki Matsui/250	15.00
134	Kerry Wood/250	6.00
135	Dontrelle Willis/250	6.00
136	Michael Young/250	6.00
137	Andy Pettitte/250	6.00
145	Bret Boone/250	4.00
146	Kazuhisa Ishii/250	4.00
147	Carlos Delgado/250	4.00
148	Tom Glavine/250	4.00
154	Pat Burrell/250	4.00
155	Melvin Mora/250	4.00
156	Jose Reyes/200	4.00
157	Trot Nixon/250	4.00
158	B.J. Upton/250	4.00
159	Jody Gerut/100	4.00
161	Miguel Tejada/35	8.00
162	Barry Larkin/40	8.00
163	Carl Crawford/40	6.00
164	Ben Sheets/250	4.00
167	Darin Erstad/25	6.00
167	Todd Helton/150	4.00
169	Luis Gonzalez/250	4.00
170	David Dellucci/150	4.00
172	Shannon Stewart/250	4.00
174	Miguel Cabrera/100	8.00
176	Derrek Lee/250	8.00
179	Jim Thome/250	6.00
180	Ken Harvey/150	4.00
180	Roy Halladay/250	8.00
182	Greg Maddux/250	8.00
186	Victor Martinez/250	4.00
189	Dewon Brazelton/250	4.00
190	Adrian Beltre/250	4.00
193	Alfonso Soriano/250	8.00
197	A.J. Burnett/250	4.00
201	Rocco Baldelli/250	4.00
202	Curt Schilling/250	6.00
202	Ryan Wagner/250	4.00
203	Preston Wilson/250	4.00
211	Frank Catalanotto/250	4.00
212	Casey Kotchman/250	4.00
214	Brandon Inge/250	4.00
221	Brett Myers/50	4.00
232	Jason Lane/95	4.00
233	Jeremy Bonderman/250	4.00
234	Livan Hernandez/250	4.00
235	Ryan Klesko/250	4.00
237	Jimmy Rollins/35	6.00
252	Mike Lowell/250	4.00
257	Garrett Atkins/250	4.00
258	Junior Spivey/250	4.00
259	Morgan Ensberg/150	4.00
260	Chone Figgins/250	4.00
262	Jason Bay/250	6.00
269	Rodrigo Lopez/250	4.00
270	Geoff Jenkins/250	4.00
275	Luis Matos/250	4.00
279	Bert Blyleven/50	6.00
281	Cal Ripken Jr./250	30.00
282	Dale Murphy/250	10.00
283	Gary Carter/50	8.00
284	George Brett/50	15.00
285	Harmon Killebrew/25	15.00
286	Harold Baines/50	8.00
287	John Kruk/50	6.00
289	Willie Mays/Pants/25	40.00
290	Matt Williams/50	8.00
291	Nolan Ryan/50	25.00
292	Paul Molitor/50	10.00
293	Reggie Jackson/25	10.00
294	Rickey Henderson/50	10.00
295	Ron Cey/50	4.00
296	Ryne Sandberg/50	15.00
297	Ted Williams/25	60.00
298	Tom Seaver/25	15.00
299	Tony Gwynn/50	12.00
300	Babe Ruth/25	200.00

Material Combo

		NM/M
Common Player:		6.00
Production 10-100		
Prime:		1-2X
Production 5-40		
No pricing 20 or less.		
1	Luis Castillo/	
	Bat-Jsy/90	6.00
3	Eric Chavez/	
	Bat-Jsy/25	8.00
5	Jeff Bagwell/	
	Bat-Jsy/100	8.00
7	Craig Biggio/	
	Bat-Jsy/25	10.00
12	Mark Teixeira/	
	Bat-Jsy/25	10.00
17	Lance Berkman/	
	Bat-Jsy/100	6.00
21	Sean Casey/	
	Bat-Jsy/100	6.00
22	Mark Prior/	
	Bat-Jsy/25	6.00
25	Andruw Jones/	
	Bat-Jsy/100	8.00
32	Jason Jennings/	
	Bat-Jsy/100	6.00
34	David Ortiz/	
	Bat-Jsy/25	20.00
43	Joey Gathright/	
	Bat-Jsy/65	6.00
55	Brandon Webb/	
	Bat-Pants/100	6.00
58	Mike Sweeney/	
	Bat-Jsy/65	6.00
62	Craig Wilson/	
	Bat-Jsy/100	6.00
67	Jose Vidro/	
	Bat-Jsy/100	6.00
83	Kevin Mench/	
	Bat-Jsy/100	6.00
101	Rafael Furcal/	
	Bat-Jsy/25	6.00
103	Bernie Williams/	
	Bat-Jsy/25	8.00
104	Josh Beckett/	
	Bat-Jsy/25	8.00
110	Vernon Wells/	
	Hat-Jsy/100	6.00
124	Larry Bigbie/	
	Jsy-Jsy/100	6.00
126	Jason Giambi/	
	Jsy-Jsy/100	8.00
136	Michael Young/	
	Bat-Jsy/100	8.00
146	Kazuhisa Ishii/	
	Hat-Jsy/25	10.00
154	Pat Burrell/Bat-Jsy/50	8.00
156	Jose Reyes/	
	Jsy/25	8.00
157	Trot Nixon/	
	Bat-Jsy/25	10.00
160	Juan Pierre/	
	Bat-Fld Glv/95	6.00
164	Ben Sheets/	
	Jsy-Jsy/100	6.00
168	Luis Gonzalez/	
	Jsy-Jsy/100	6.00
171	Marcus Giles/	
	Hat-Jsy/50	6.00
172	Shannon Stewart/	
	Jsy-Jsy/30	6.00
174	Miguel Cabrera/	
	Bat-Jsy/25	12.00
180	Roy Halladay/	
	Jsy-Jsy/85	8.00
183	Frank Thomas/	
	Hat-Jsy/25	15.00
186	Victor Martinez/	
	Fld Glv-Jsy/40	8.00
197	A.J. Burnett/	
	Bat-Jsy/100	6.00
200	Rocco Baldelli/	
	Bat-Jsy/100	6.00
201	Curt Schilling/	
	Bat-Jsy/25	12.00
202	Ryan Wagner/	
	Jsy-Jsy/100	6.00
203	Preston Wilson/	
	Bat-Jsy/85	6.00
212	Casey Kotchman/	
	Bat-Jsy/50	6.00
218	Kenny Lofton/	
	Bat-Fld Glv/100	6.00
232	Jason Lane/	
	Bat-Hat/50	6.00
235	Ryan Klesko/	
	Hat-Jsy/100	6.00
252	Mike Lowell/	
	Jsy-Jsy/100	6.00
257	Garrett Atkins/	
	Jsy-Jsy/100	6.00
259	Morgan Ensberg/	
	Bat-Jsy/100	8.00
260	Chone Figgins/	
	Bat-Jsy/50	6.00
262	Jason Bay/	
	Bat-Jsy/50	8.00
272	Orlando Hudson/	
	Bat-Jsy/40	6.00
275	Luis Matos/	
	Jsy-Jsy/50	6.00
281	Cal Ripken Jr./	
	Bat-Jsy/50	40.00
283	Gary Carter/	
	Jsy-Pants/25	15.00

284	George Brett/	
	Bat-Jsy/25	30.00
286	Harold Baines/	
	Bat-Jsy/50	10.00
288	Keith Hernandez/	
	Bat-Jsy/50	10.00
289	Willie Mays/	
	Bat-Pants/25	50.00
291	Nolan Ryan/	
	Bat-Jsy/50	25.00
292	Paul Molitor/	
	Bat-Jsy/50	15.00
293	Reggie Jackson/	
	Bat-Jsy/50	15.00
294	Rickey Henderson/	
	Bat-Jsy/50	15.00
296	Ryne Sandberg/	
	Bat-Jsy/50	25.00
297	Ted Williams/	
	Bat-Jsy/25	75.00
298	Tom Seaver/	
	Jsy-Pants/25	15.00
299	Tony Gwynn/	
	Jsy-Pants/50	15.00
300	Babe Ruth/	
	Bat-Jsy/25	375.00

Player Timelines

		NM/M
Common Player:		1.00
Spectrum:		1-2.5X
Production 100 Sets		
1	Dale Murphy	2.00
2	Greg Maddux	3.00
3	Tom Glavine	2.00
4	David Ortiz	3.00
5	Bo Jackson	2.00
6	Lyle Overbay	1.00
7	Tommy John	1.00
8	Shawn Green	1.00
9	Aramis Ramirez	1.50
10	Javy Lopez	1.00
11	Vladimir Guerrero	3.00
12	Travis Hafner	1.00
13	Junior Spivey	1.00
14	Alfonso Soriano	1.00
15	Andre Dawson	1.00
16	Sammy Sosa	3.00
17	Andy Pettitte	1.50
18	Jim Edmonds	1.50
19	Willie McCovey	2.00
20	Scott Rolen	1.00
21	Jermaine Dye	1.00
22	Pedro Martinez	2.50
23	Don Sutton	1.00
24	Randy Johnson	2.00
25	Nolan Ryan	3.00
26	Dennis Eckersley	1.00
27	Reggie Jackson	2.00
28	Deion Sanders	1.00
29	Curt Schilling	1.00
30	Rickey Henderson	1.00
31	Mike Piazza	2.00
32	Gary Carter	1.00
33	Roberto Alomar	1.00
34	Hideo Nomo	1.00
35	Andres Galarraga	1.00
36	Juan Gonzalez	1.00
37	Roger Clemens	4.00
38	Jeff Kent	1.00
39	Steve Carlton	1.00
40	Wade Boggs	1.50

Player Timeline Material

		NM/M
Production 25-250		
1	Dale Murphy/50	10.00
2	Greg Maddux/100	10.00
3	Tom Glavine/50	8.00
4	David Ortiz/250	10.00
5	Bo Jackson/100	12.00
6	Lyle Overbay/250	4.00
7	Tommy John/	
	Pants/250	
8	Shawn Green/100	4.00
9	Aramis Ramirez/250	6.00
10	Javy Lopez/100	4.00
11	Vladimir Guerrero/25	15.00
12	Travis Hafner/250	8.00
13	Junior Spivey/250	4.00
14	Alfonso Soriano/100	8.00
16	Sammy Sosa/250	8.00
17	Andy Pettitte/100	8.00
18	Jim Edmonds/100	8.00
19	Willie McCovey/	
	Pants/50	12.00
20	Scott Rolen/50	10.00
21	Jermaine Dye/100	4.00
22	Pedro Martinez/100	12.00
23	Don Sutton/50	6.00
24	Randy Johnson/50	15.00
25	Nolan Ryan/Jkt/50	40.00
27	Reggie Jackson/	
	Pants/50	15.00
28	Deion Sanders/25	15.00
29	Curt Schilling/50	10.00
30	Rickey Henderson/	
	Pants/100	15.00
31	Mike Piazza/50	15.00
32	Gary Carter/Pants/50	15.00
33	Roberto Alomar/250	8.00
34	Hideo Nomo/50	15.00
36	Andres Galarraga/250	6.00
37	Roger Clemens/25	30.00

38	Jeff Kent/50	6.00

Player Timelines Signature Material

		NM/M
Production 5-50		
Prime:		No Pricing
Production 5-10		
1	Dale Murphy/50	30.00
6	Lyle Overbay/50	12.00
7	Tommy John/	
	Pants/10	15.00
12	Travis Hafner/25	20.00
13	Junior Spivey/50	12.00
15	Andre Dawson/25	25.00
21	Jermaine Dye/50	15.00
23	Don Sutton/25	20.00
32	Gary Carter/Pants/50	20.00
36	Juan Gonzalez/25	40.00

Polo Grounds 85 HIT Long Fly

		NM/M
Common Player:		1.50
Production 85 sets		
Parallel #'d 40-75:		.75-1.5X
Parallel #'d 20-35:		1-2X
No pricing 15 or less.		
1	Ken Griffey Jr.	4.00
2	Roger Clemens	6.00
3	Barry Zito	2.00
4	Alex Rodriguez	5.00
5	Melvin Mora	1.50
6	Kevin Brown	1.50
7	Chipper Jones	3.00
8	Scott Kazmir	2.00
9	Kip Wells	1.50
10	Khalil Greene	2.00
11	Kevin Millwood	1.50
12	Kerry Wood	1.50
13	Mark Kotsay	1.50
14	Jeff Bagwell	2.00
15	Hank Blalock	2.00
16	Scott Rolen	2.00
17	Lance Berkman	2.00
18	Mike Mussina	2.00
19	Jim Edmonds	2.00
20	Jorge Posada	2.00
21	Curt Schilling	3.00
22	Vernon Wells	1.50
23	Pedro Martinez	3.00
24	Jeremy Reed	1.50
25	Hideki Matsui	4.00
26	Steve Finley	1.50
27	Gavin Floyd	1.50
28	Darin Erstad	1.50
29	Bernie Williams	2.00
30	Mark Mulder	2.00
31	Rafael Palmeiro	2.00
32	Andruw Jones	2.00
33	Roy Halladay	2.00
34	Dontrelle Willis	2.00
35	Bret Boone	2.00
36	Andy Pettitte	2.00
37	Vladimir Guerrero	3.00
38	Randy Johnson	2.00
39	Michael Young	2.00
40	Frank Thomas	2.00
41	Todd Helton	2.00
42	Johan Santana	3.00
43	Mark Teixeira	2.00
44	Justin Morneau	1.50
45	Brad Radke	1.50
46	Dallas McPherson	1.50
47	Tim Hudson	2.00
48	Carl Crawford	1.50
49	Eric Gagne	2.00
50	Mark Prior	3.00
51	Tom Glavine	2.00
52	Craig Biggio	2.00
53	John Smoltz	2.00
54	Manny Ramirez	2.00
55	Ivan Rodriguez	2.00
56	Gary Sheffield	2.00
57	Josh Beckett	2.00
58	Miguel Tejada	2.00
59	Bobby Abreu	1.50
60	Ichiro Suzuki	4.00
61	Sammy Sosa	2.50
62	Garret Anderson	2.00
63	Sean Casey	1.50
64	Troy Glaus	2.00
65	Larry Walker	2.00
66	Alfonso Soriano	2.00
67	Luis Gonzalez	2.00
68	Eric Chavez	2.00

69	Adrian Beltre	2.00
70	Miguel Cabrera	3.00
71	Carlos Beltran	2.00
72	Jim Thome	2.00
73	David Ortiz	3.00
74	Adam Dunn	2.00
75	Jacque Jones	1.50
76	Shawn Green	1.50
77	Victor Martinez	1.50
78	Torii Hunter	1.50
79	Carlos Lee	1.50
80	C.C. Sabathia	1.50
81	Joe Mauer	2.00
82	Kris Benson	1.50
83	Zack Greinke	1.50
84	Greg Maddux	4.00
85	David Wright	4.00
86	Mike Piazza	4.00
87	Johnny Damon	3.00
88	Derek Jeter	6.00
89	B.J. Upton	1.50
90	Albert Pujols	6.00
91	Cal Ripken Jr.	6.00
92	Nolan Ryan	5.00
93	George Brett	5.00
94	Don Mattingly	4.00
95	Ryne Sandberg	4.00
96	Rickey Henderson	3.00
97	Robin Yount	3.00
98	Mike Schmidt	4.00
99	Tony Gwynn	3.00
100	Willie Mays	5.00

Signature Marks

		NM/M
Production 5-1,000		
4	Angel Berroa/25	12.00
19	Adam LaRoche/50	20.00
36	Joe Nathan/25	20.00
38	Carlos Zambrano/25	30.00
39	Eric Byrnes/50	10.00
41	Danny Kolb/25	10.00
45	Carlos Lee/25	10.00
49	Scott Podsednik/20	20.00
52	C.C. Sabathia/25	15.00
54	Mark Buehrle/25	30.00
62	Craig Wilson/50	15.00
64	Bobby Crosby/100	15.00
67	Jose Vidro/25	15.00
73	Octavio Dotel/25	12.00
77	Russel Rohlicek/250	15.00
81	Tim Salmon/25	20.00
85	Sean Burroughs/25	10.00
87	Jamie Moyer/25	15.00
88	Orlando Cabrera/25	20.00
91	Philip Humber/50	15.00
91	Francisco Cordero/50	15.00
92	Danny Graves/25	15.00
93	Bucky Jacobsen/64	8.00
94	Cliff Lee/50	10.00
96	Jake Peavy/25	35.00
101	Rafael Furcal/25	20.00
102	Jack Wilson/100	10.00
108	Luke Scott/250	15.00
110	Vernon Wells/25	15.00
112	Chad Cordero/25	15.00
114	Paul Konerko/25	20.00
116	Francisco Rodriguez/	
	25	20.00
118	David Wright/25	85.00
119	Lyle Overbay/25	10.00
120	Brian Roberts/100	15.00
124	Larry Bigbie/75	8.00
129	Jeremy Affeldt/25	10.00
131	Troy Percival/25	15.00
133	David Gassner/1000	5.00
136	Michael Young/25	20.00
139	Miguel Negron/250	5.00
140	Rich Harden/25	25.00
142	Danny Rueckel/250	5.00
144	Randy Messenger/	
	500	5.00
149	Russ Ortiz/25	15.00
157	Trot Nixon/25	25.00
158	B.J. Upton/25	15.00
159	Jody Gerut/25	10.00
170	David Dellucci/50	15.00
172	Shannon Stewart/25	15.00
175	Nick Johnson/25	15.00
176	Derrek Lee/25	40.00
178	Ken Harvey/50	8.00
179	Ambiorix Concepcion/	
	500	5.00
184	Travis Hafner/50	15.00
189	Dewon Brazelton/66	8.00
192	Alexis Rios/25	15.00
198	Milton Bradley/100	12.00
199	Brad Penny/25	10.00
202	Ryan Wagner/25	10.00
204	Akinori Otsuka/25	20.00
207	Mike Lieberthal/25	15.00
209	Shea Hillenbrand/25	20.00
211	Tom Gordon/25	20.00
212	Casey Kotchman/100	10.00
213	Justin Verlander/25	40.00
220	Danny Haren/25	15.00
226	Casey Rogowski/25	10.00
230	Erick Threets/500	5.00
232	Jason Lane/25	10.00
232	Jeremy Bonderman/	
	50	15.00
234	Livan Hernandez/25	15.00
239	Shingo Takatsu/25	15.00
245	Mark Loretta/25	20.00
250	Jared Gothreaux/1000	5.00
254	Nate McLouth/1000	8.00
258	Junior Spivey/25	10.00

259	Morgan Ensberg/25	20.00
260	Chone Figgins/50	10.00
262	Jason Bay/186	15.00
268	Dioner Navarro/75	8.00
271	Jermaine Dye/25	15.00
275	Orlando Hudson/100	8.00
275	Luis Matos/50	10.00
279	Bert Blyleven/25	15.00
280	Bill Madlock/50	15.00
281	Cal Ripken Jr./25	150.00
282	Dale Murphy/25	30.00
286	Harold Baines/25	15.00
288	Keith Hernandez/25	15.00
290	Matt Williams/25	30.00

Throwback Collection

		NM/M
Common Player:		1.00
Spectrum:		1-2.5X
Production 100 Sets		
1	Billy Martin	2.00
2	Tony Gwynn	2.00
3	Babe Ruth	4.00
4	Angel Berroa	1.00
5	Jeff Bagwell	1.50
6	Tony Oliva	1.00
7	Ivan Rodriguez	1.50
8	Gary Carter	1.50
9	Ted Williams	4.00
10	Chipper Jones	2.00
11	Al Oliver	1.00
12	Roberto Alomar	1.00
13	Omar Vizquel	1.00
14	Ernie Banks	2.00
15	Carlos Beltran	1.50
16	Garret Anderson	1.00
17	Mark Grace	1.00
18	Jason Giambi	1.00
19	Dave Righetti	1.00
20	Mike Schmidt	3.00
21	Roger Clemens	4.00
22	Juan Gonzalez	1.50
23	Carlos Delgado	1.00
24	Manny Ramirez	2.00
25	Jim Thome	1.50
26	Wade Boggs	2.00
27	Luis Tiant	1.00
28	Kerry Wood	1.50
29	Rod Carew	1.50
30	Dwight Evans	1.00
31	Mike Piazza	2.00
32	Billy Williams	1.00
33	Larry Walker	1.00
34	Nolan Ryan	4.00
35	Edgar Renteria	1.00
36	Greg Maddux	2.50
37	Gaylord Perry	1.00
38	Curt Schilling	1.00
39	Dave Parker	1.00
40	Andruw Jones	1.50
41	Orlando Cepeda	1.50
42	Fergie Jenkins	1.00
43	Kirby Puckett	2.00
44	Reggie Jackson	2.00
45	Bob Gibson	2.00
46	Rickey Henderson	2.00
47	Lee Smith	1.00
48	Lou Brock	1.50
49	Fred Lynn	1.00
50	Lance Berkman	1.00
51	Shawn Green	1.00
52	Hoyt Wilhelm	1.00
53	Sammy Sosa	2.50
54	Tim Hudson	1.50
55	Matt Williams	1.00
56	Marty Marion	1.00
57	Eric Chavez	1.00
58	Rafael Palmeiro	1.50
59	Randy Johnson	2.00
60	David Ortiz	2.00
61	Hank Blalock	1.00
62	Jim Rice	1.00
63	Mark Mulder	1.50
64	Kazuo Matsui	1.00
65	Pedro Martinez	2.00
66	Sean Casey	1.00
67	Carlos Lee	1.00
68	Stan Musial	3.00
69	Fred McGriff	1.00
70	Darryl Strawberry	1.00
71	Tommy John	1.00
72	Hideo Nomo	1.00
73	Johnny Bench	2.00
74	Cal Ripken Jr.	5.00
75	Harold Baines	1.00

Throwback Collection Material

		NM/M
Production 5-500		
Prime:		1-2X
Production 5-25		
No pricing 20 or less.		
1	Billy Martin/Pants/250	8.00
2	Tony Gwynn/Jsy/250	8.00
4	Angel Berroa/	
	Pants/100	4.00
5	Jeff Bagwell/Jsy/500	4.00
6	Tony Oliva/Jsy/250	4.00
7	Ivan Rodriguez/	
	Chest Prot-Jsy/100	6.00
8	Gary Carter/	
	Jsy-Pants/100	4.00
10	Chipper Jones/	
	Bat-Jsy/100	6.00
11	Al Oliver/	
	Bat-Jsy/100	6.00
12	Roberto Alomar/	
	Bat-Jsy/100	8.00
13	Omar Vizquel/	
	Bat-Jsy/100	8.00
15	Carlos Beltran/	
	Bat-Jsy/50	8.00
17	Mark Grace/	
	Bat-Jsy/50	10.00

12	Roberto Alomar/	
	Jsy/500	6.00
13	Omar Vizquel/Jsy/500	4.00
15	Carlos Beltran/	
	Jsy/100	6.00
16	Garret Anderson/	
	Jsy/50	4.00
17	Mark Grace/Jsy/250	6.00
18	Jason Giambi/Jsy/500	4.00
19	Dave Righetti/Jsy/250	4.00
21	Roger Clemens/	
	Jsy/250	10.00
22	Juan Gonzalez/	
	Jsy/150	4.00
23	Carlos Delgado/	
	Jsy/150	4.00
24	Manny Ramirez/	
	Jsy/50	10.00
25	Jim Thome/Jsy/500	4.00
26	Wade Boggs/Jsy/500	4.00
27	Luis Tiant/Pants/500	4.00
28	Kerry Wood/Jsy/500	4.00
29	Rod Carew/Jkt/250	6.00
30	Dwight Evans/Jsy/50	6.00
31	Mike Piazza/Jsy/50	8.00
32	Billy Williams/Jsy/100	4.00
33	Larry Walker/Jsy/500	4.00
34	Nolan Ryan/	
	Pants/100	15.00
35	Edgar Renteria/	
	Jsy/500	4.00
36	Greg Maddux/Jsy/375	8.00
37	Gaylord Perry/	
	Jsyu/250	4.00
38	Curt Schilling/Jsy/500	4.00
39	Dave Parker/Jsy/50	4.00
40	Andruw Jones/	
	Jsy/500	4.00
41	Orlando Cepeda/	
	Pants/250	4.00
42	Fergie Jenkins/	
	Jsy/250	4.00
43	Kirby Puckett/Jsy/400	6.00
44	Reggie Jackson/	
	Jsy/250	6.00
45	Bob Gibson/Jsy/100	8.00
46	Rickey Henderson/	
	Jsy/500	6.00
47	Lee Smith/Jsy/250	4.00
49	Fred Lynn/Jsy/250	4.00
50	Lance Berkman/	
	Jsy/500	4.00
51	Shawn Green/Jsy/500	4.00
52	Hoyt Wilhelm/Jsy/250	4.00
53	Sammy Sosa/Jsy/500	8.00
54	Tim Hudson/Jsy/500	4.00
55	Matt Williams/Jsy/250	4.00
57	Eric Chavez/Jsy/500	4.00
58	Rafael Palmeiro/	
	Jsy/500	6.00
59	Randy Johnson/	
	Jsy/250	6.00
60	David Ortiz/Jsy/500	8.00
61	Hank Blalock/Jsy/50	4.00
62	Jim Rice/Pants/250	4.00
63	Mark Mulder/Jsy/100	4.00
64	Kazuo Matsui/Jsy/500	4.00
65	Pedro Martinez/	
	Jsy/250	6.00
66	Sean Casey/Jsy/500	4.00
67	Carlos Lee/Jsy/500	4.00
68	Stan Musial/	
	Pants/100	20.00
69	Fred McGriff/Jsy/250	4.00
70	Darryl Strawberry/	
	Jsy/250	4.00
71	Tommy John/Jsy/250	4.00
72	Hideo Nomo/Jsy/500	6.00
73	Johnny Bench/	
	Pants/100	8.00
74	Cal Ripken Jr./	
	Jsy/250	20.00
75	Harold Baines/	
	Jsy/250	4.00

Throwback Colletion Material Combo

		NM/M
Production 5-100		
1	Billy Martin/	
	Jsy-Pants/100	10.00
2	Tony Gwynn/	
	Jsy-Pants/100	12.00
4	Angel Berroa/	
	Bat-Pants/100	4.00
5	Jeff Bagwell/	
	Jsy-Pants/100	8.00
6	Tony Oliva/	
	Bat-Jsy/100	8.00
7	Ivan Rodriguez/	
	Chest Prot-Jsy/100	6.00
8	Gary Carter/	
	Jsy-Pants/100	4.00
10	Chipper Jones/	
	Bat-Jsy/100	6.00
11	Al Oliver/	
	Bat-Jsy/100	6.00
12	Roberto Alomar/	
	Bat-Jsy/100	8.00
13	Omar Vizquel/	
	Bat-Jsy/100	8.00
15	Carlos Beltran/	
	Bat-Jsy/50	8.00
17	Mark Grace/	
	Bat-Jsy/50	10.00

18 Jason Giambi/Jsy-Jsy/100 6.00
19 Dave Righetti/Jsy-Jsy/100 6.00
21 Roger Clemens/Jsy-Jsy/100 15.00
22 Juan Gonzalez/Bat-Jsy/100 6.00
23 Carlos Delgado/Bat-Jsy/100 4.00
26 Wade Boggs/Bat-Jsy/100 10.00
29 Rod Carew/Jkt-Jsy/100 10.00
33 Larry Walker/Jsy-Jsy/100 6.00
34 Nolan Ryan/Bat-Pants/100 20.00
36 Greg Maddux/Jsy-Jsy/100 12.00
38 Curt Schilling/Bat-Jsy/100 6.00
40 Andruw Jones/Bat-Jsy/100 8.00
41 Orlando Cepeda/Bat-Pants/100 8.00
43 Kirby Puckett/Bat-Jsy/100 12.00
44 Reggie Jackson/Bat-Jsy/100 10.00
46 Rickey Henderson/Bat-Jsy/100 10.00
47 Lee Smith/Jsy-Jsy/100 6.00
49 Fred Lynn/Bat-Jsy/100 4.00
50 Lance Berkman/Bat-Jsy/100 4.00
51 Shawn Green/Bat-Jsy/100 4.00
52 Hoyt Wilhelm/Jsy-Jsy/100 4.00
53 Sammy Sosa/Hat-Jsy/100 8.00
54 Tim Hudson/Jsy-Jsy/100 4.00
57 Eric Chavez/Jsy-Jsy/100 6.00
58 Rafael Palmeiro/Bat-Jsy/100 8.00
59 Randy Johnson/Jsy-Pants/100 10.00
60 David Ortiz/Jsy-Jsy/100 10.00
61 Hank Blalock/Jsy-Jsy/100 6.00
62 Jim Rice/Jsy-Pants/100 6.00
64 Kazuo Matsui/Bat-Jsy/100 4.00
65 Pedro Martinez/Jsy-Jsy/100 8.00
66 Sean Casey/Jsy-Pants/100 4.00
67 Carlos Lee/Hat-Jsy/100 4.00
69 Fred McGriff/Bat-Jsy/100 8.00
70 Darryl Strawberry/Jsy-Jsy/100 6.00
71 Tommy John/Bat-Jsy/100 4.00
72 Hideo Nomo/Jsy-Jsy/100 10.00
73 Johnny Bench/Bat-Pants/100 12.00
74 Cal Ripken Jr./Bat-Jsy/100 30.00
75 Harold Baines/Bat-Jsy/100 4.00

Throwback Collection Signature Material
NM/M
Production 5-50
2 Tony Gwynn/Jsy/50 40.00
4 Angel Berroa/Pants/50 10.00
6 Tony Oliva/Jsy/50 20.00
8 Gary Carter/Pants/50 20.00
12 Roberto Alomar/Jsy/50 30.00
13 Omar Vizquel/Jsy/50 30.00
15 Carlos Beltran/Jsy/50 30.00
17 Mark Grace/Jsy/50 30.00
19 Dave Righetti/Jsy/50 20.00
26 Wade Boggs/Jsy/50 35.00
27 Luis Tiant/Pants/50 20.00
29 Rod Carew/Jkt/50 30.00
30 Dwight Evans/Jsy/50 25.00
32 Billy Williams/Jsy/50 20.00
35 Edgar Renteria/Jsy/50 20.00
37 Gaylord Perry/Jsy/50 15.00
39 Dave Parker/Jsy/50 20.00
41 Orlando Cepeda/Pants/25 25.00
42 Fergie Jenkins/Jsy/50 20.00
44 Reggie Jackson/Jsy/50 50.00
45 Bob Gibson/Jsy/25 40.00
49 Fred Lynn/Jsy/50 20.00

54 Tim Hudson/Jsy/25 25.00
55 Matt Williams/Jsy/50 30.00
57 Eric Chavez/Jsy/50 20.00
62 Jim Rice/Pants/50 25.00
63 Mark Mulder/Jsy/50 20.00
66 Sean Casey/Jsy/50 20.00
67 Carlos Lee/Jsy/50 20.00
68 Stan Musial/Pants/25 75.00
70 Darryl Strawberry/Jsy/50 20.00
71 Tommy John/Jsy/50 15.00
75 Harold Baines/Jsy/50 15.00

Throwback Collection Signature Material Combo
NM/M
Production 5-25
2 Tony Gwynn/Jsy-Pants/25 50.00
4 Angel Berroa/Bat-Pants/25 15.00
6 Tony Oliva/Bat-Jsy/25 25.00
8 Gary Carter/Jsy-Pants/25 25.00
12 Roberto Alomar/Bat-Jsy/25 40.00
15 Carlos Beltran/Bat-Jsy/25 35.00
17 Mark Grace/Bat-Jsy/25 35.00
19 Dave Righetti/Bat-Jsy/25 25.00
26 Wade Boggs/Bat-Jsy/25 40.00
29 Rod Carew/Jkt-Jsy/25 40.00
44 Reggie Jackson/Bat-Jsy/25 50.00
49 Fred Lynn/Bat-Jsy/25 25.00
62 Jim Rice/Jsy-Pants/25 30.00
67 Carlos Lee/Hat-Jsy/25 25.00
68 Stan Musial/Bat-Pants/25 75.00
70 Darryl Strawberry/Jsy/25 20.00
75 Harold Baines/Jsy/25 20.00

2005 Donruss Timeless Treasures

Complete Set (100):
Common Player: 1.50
Production 799 Sets
Tin (4): 100.00
1 David Ortiz 3.00
2 Derek Jeter 8.00
3 Edgar Renteria 2.00
4 Paul Molitor 3.00
5 Jeff Bagwell 2.00
6 Melvin Mora 1.50
7 Bobby Crosby 1.50
8 Cal Ripken Jr. 10.00
9 Hank Blalock 2.00
10 Hideo Nomo 2.00
11 Gary Sheffield 2.00
12 Alfonso Soriano 3.00
13 Carl Crawford 2.00
14 Paul Konerko 1.50
15 Jim Edmonds 2.00
16 Garret Anderson 1.50
17 Lance Berkman 1.50
18 Javy Lopez 1.50
19 Tony Gwynn 3.00
20 Mark Mulder 1.50
21 Sammy Sosa 5.00
22 Roger Clemens 8.00
23 Mark Teixeira 3.00
24 Miguel Cabrera 3.00
25 Jim Thome 3.00
26 Mike Piazza 4.00
27 Vladimir Guerrero 3.00
28 Austin Kearns 1.50
29 Rod Carew 5.00
30 Ken Griffey Jr. 5.00
31 Mike Piazza 4.00

32 David Wright 3.00
33 Jason Varitek 2.00
34 Kerry Wood 3.00
35 Frank Thomas 4.00
36 Mark Prior 3.00
37 Mike Mussina 3.00
38 Curt Schilling 3.00
39 Greg Maddux 4.00
40 Miguel Tejada 3.00
41 Tom Seaver 3.00
42 Mariano Rivera 4.00
43 Jason Giambi 1.50
44 Roy Oswalt 1.50
45 Pedro Martinez 2.00
46 Jeff Niemann RC 5.00
47 Tom Glavine 1.50
48 Torii Hunter 1.50
49 Scott Rolen 3.00
50 Curt Schilling 2.00
51 Randy Johnson 3.00
52 C.C. Sabathia 1.50
53 Rafael Palmeiro 2.00
54 Jake Peavy 2.00
55 Hideki Matsui 6.00
56 Ichiro Suzuki 6.00
57 Johan Santana 3.00
58 Todd Helton 2.00
59 Justin Verlander RC 8.00
60 Kazuo Matsui 1.50
61 Rafael Palmeiro 2.00
62 Sean Casey 1.50
63 Nolan Ryan 8.00
64 Magglio Ordonez 1.50
65 Craig Biggio 2.00
66 Vernon Wells 1.50
67 Manny Ramirez 3.00
68 Aramis Ramirez 2.00
69 Omar Vizquel 1.50
70 Eric Gagne 1.50
71 Troy Glaus 2.00
72 Carlton Fisk 2.00
73 Victor Martinez 1.50
74 Adrian Beltre 2.00
75 Barry Zito 1.50
76 Josh Beckett 2.00
77 Michael Young 1.50
78 Eric Chavez 1.50
79 Hideo Nomo 2.00
80 Andruw Jones 2.00
81 Ivan Rodriguez 2.00
82 Don Mattingly 6.00
83 Larry Walker 2.00
84 Philip Humber RC 5.00
85 Juan Gonzalez 1.50
86 Tim Hudson 2.00
87 Alex Rodriguez 6.00
88 Greg Maddux 4.00
89 J.D. Drew 2.00
90 Shawn Green 1.50
91 Roger Clemens 8.00
92 Nomar Garciaparra 4.00
93 Andy Pettitte 2.00
94 Khalil Greene 1.50
95 Mike Schmidt 5.00
96 Carlos Beltran 2.00
97 Mike Mussina 2.00
98 Ben Sheets 1.50
99 Chipper Jones 3.00
100 Albert Pujols 8.00

Bronze
Bronze: 1-2X
Production 100 Sets

Silver
Gold: 2-3X
Production 50 Sets

Gold
Gold: 3-5X
Production 25 Sets

Platinum
No Pricing
Production One Set

Award Materials Number
NM/M
Production 1-29
Prime: No Pricing
Production 1-5
9 Jim Palmer/Pants/22 12.00
10 Rod Carew/Jsy/29 15.00
12 Mike Schmidt/Jsy/20 25.00
13 Robin Yount/Jsy/19 25.00
15 Roger Clemens/Jsy/21 25.00

Award Material Signature Number
No Pricing
Production 1-5

Award Materials Year
NM/M
Production 1-99
1 Lou Boudreau/Jsy/48 20.00
2 Roger Maris/Pants/61 40.00

6 Johnny Bench/Jsy/72 15.00
9 Jim Palmer/Pants/76 20.00
10 Rod Carew/Jsy/77 10.00
12 Mike Schmidt/Jsy/81 20.00
13 Robin Yount/Jsy/89 15.00
14 Dale Murphy/Jsy/83 10.00
15 Roger Clemens/Jsy/86 20.00
16 Cal Ripken Jr./Jsy/91 40.00
17 Tom Glavine/Jsy/91 8.00
18 Frank Thomas/Jsy/94 10.00
19 Jeff Bagwell/Pants/94 8.00
20 Randy Johnson/Jsy/95 10.00
21 Pedro Martinez/Jsy/97 10.00
22 Ivan Rodriguez/Jsy/99 10.00

Award Material Signature Year
NM/M
Production 1-25
Prime: No Pricing
Production 1-5
6 Johnny Bench/Jsy/25 60.00
9 Jim Palmer/Pants/25 35.00
10 Rod Carew/Jsy/25 50.00
12 Mike Schmidt/Jsy/25 75.00
14 Dale Murphy/Jsy/25 50.00

Game Day Materials
NM/M
Production 5-100
1 Rod Carew/Hat/25 20.00
2 Kirby Puckett/Bat/100 15.00
5 Nellie Fox/Bat/25 60.00
6 Vladimir Guerrero/Fld Glv/25 15.00
7 Tony Gwynn/Jsy/100 15.00
8 Rickey Henderson/Bat/100 10.00
9 David Ortiz/Hat/100 15.00
10 Carlos Beltran/Jsy/50 10.00

Game Day Material Signature
NM/M
Production 3-25
7 Tony Gwynn/Jsy/25 50.00

Gamers NY
NM/M
Production 25 Sets
1 Jim Thorpe/Jsy-Jsy/25 450.00
2 Willie Mays/Jsy-Pants/25 75.00
3 Nolan Ryan/Bat-Jsy/25 65.00

Gamers NY Signatures
NM/M
Production 25 Sets
2 Willie Mays/Jsy-Pants/25 250.00
3 Nolan Ryan/Bat-Jsy/25 125.00

HOF Cuts
No Pricing
Production 1-10

HOF Cuts Materials
No Pricing
Production 1-10

HOF Materials Barrel
Production One Set

HOF Materials Bat
NM/M
Production 5-50
1 Pee Wee Reese/25 20.00
2 Harmon Killebrew/25 20.00
4 Hack Wilson/50 65.00
5 Brooks Robinson/50 20.00
6 Stan Musial/50 40.00
8 Carl Yastrzemski/50 20.00
9 Ted Williams/50 50.00
11 Luis Aparicio/25 15.00
12 Bobby Doerr/25 15.00
14 Ernie Banks/50 15.00
15 Ralph Kiner/25 15.00
17 Mike Schmidt/50 40.00
21 Roberto Clemente/50 75.00
24 Willie Mays/50 40.00
25 Willie Stargell/25 25.00
26 Frank Robinson/50 10.00
28 Reggie Jackson/50 15.00
30 Orlando Cepeda/50 10.00
34 Nolan Ryan/50 30.00

35 George Brett/50 25.00
39 Nellie Fox/50 40.00
43 Johnny Bench/50 20.00
47 Hank Aaron/50 40.00
50 Al Kaline/50 20.00

HOF Material Signature Bat
NM/M
Production 1-25
3 Harmon Killebrew/25 50.00
5 Brooks Robinson/25 50.00
6 Stan Musial/25 85.00
11 Luis Aparicio/25 25.00
12 Bobby Doerr/25 50.00
15 Ralph Kiner/25 50.00
17 Mike Schmidt/25 75.00
24 Willie Mays/25 240.00
26 Frank Robinson/25 40.00
30 Orlando Cepeda/25 25.00
34 Nolan Ryan/25 120.00
43 Johnny Bench/25 60.00
50 Al Kaline/25 50.00

HOF Materials Hat
No Pricing

HOF Materials Signature Hat
Production 5-10

HOF Materials Jersey
NM/M
Production 1-100
Prime: No Pricing
Production 1-5
3 Harmon Killebrew/100 15.00
5 Brooks Robinson/100 15.00
6 Stan Musial/100 25.00
8 Carl Yastrzemski/100 15.00
9 Ted Williams/100 60.00
14 Ernie Banks/100 15.00
15 Whitey Ford/100 15.00
17 Duke Snider/25 20.00
19 Willie McCovey/25 20.00
20 Mike Schmidt/50 25.00
22 Jim Palmer/25 12.00
23 Enos Slaughter/50 15.00
24 Willie Mays/100 40.00
25 Willie Stargell/50 20.00
28 Reggie Jackson/25 25.00
29 Warren Spahn/25 25.00
31 Hoyt Wilhelm/50 10.00
32 Sandy Koufax/25 250.00
33 Hal Newhouser/50 10.00
34 Nolan Ryan/50 30.00
35 George Brett/25 25.00
37 Jim "Catfish" Hunter/25 15.00
38 Frankie Frisch/Jkt/50 15.00
40 Lou Boudreau/25 15.00
43 Johnny Bench/25 15.00
44 Hank Aaron/100 40.00
45 Joe Cronin/25 20.00
49 Early Wynn/50 15.00

HOF Material Signature Jersey
NM/M
Production 1-25
Prime: No Pricing
Production 1-5
3 Harmon Killebrew/25 50.00
5 Brooks Robinson/25 50.00
6 Stan Musial/25 85.00
17 Duke Snider/25 40.00
19 Willie McCovey/25 50.00
20 Mike Schmidt/25 75.00
22 Jim Palmer/25 25.00
24 Willie Mays/25 240.00
34 Nolan Ryan/25 120.00
43 Johnny Bench/25 60.00

HOF Material Jersey Number
NM/M
Production 1-44
18 Willie McCovey/44 15.00
20 Mike Schmidt/20 30.00
22 Jim Palmer/22 12.00
24 Willie Mays/24 65.00
28 Reggie Jackson/44 15.00
29 Warren Spahn/21 20.00
31 Hoyt Wilhelm/31 10.00
32 Sandy Koufax/32 250.00
34 Nolan Ryan/34 30.00
37 Jim "Catfish" Hunter/29 15.00
44 Hank Aaron/44 50.00
49 Early Wynn/15 15.00

HOF Materials Signature Jersey Number
NM/M
Production 1-44
18 Willie McCovey/44 50.00
20 Mike Schmidt/20 75.00
22 Jim Palmer/22 40.00

24 Willie Mays/24 240.0X
34 Nolan Ryan/34 120.00

HOF Materials Combos
NM/M
Production 1-25
Prime: No Pricing
Production 1-5
3 Harmon Killebrew/Bat-Jsy/25 25.00
5 Brooks Robinson/Bat-Jsy/25 30.00
6 Stan Musial/Bat-Jsy/25 40.00
8 Carl Yastrzemski/Bat-Jsy/25 30.00
9 Ted Williams/Bat-Jsy/25 85.00
12 Bobby Doerr/Bat-Pants/25 15.00
14 Ernie Banks/Bat-Jsy/25 25.00
18 Willie McCovey/Jsy-Pants/25 25.00
20 Mike Schmidt/Bat-Jsy/25 30.00
24 Willie Mays/Bat-Jsy/25 75.00
25 Willie Stargell/Bat-Jsy/25 30.00
28 Reggie Jackson/Bat-Jsy/25 30.00
29 Warren Spahn/Jsy-Pants/25 30.00
34 Nolan Ryan/Jsy-Pants/25 50.00
35 George Brett/Bat-Jsy/25 30.00
43 Johnny Bench/Bat-Jsy/25 25.00
44 Hank Aaron/Bat-Jsy/25 60.00

HOF Material Signature Combos
NM/M
Production 1-25
Prime: No Pricing
Production 1-5
3 Harmon Killebrew/Bat-Jsy/25 65.00
5 Brooks Robinson/Bat-Jsy/25 65.00
6 Stan Musial/Bat-Jsy/25 100.00
12 Bobby Doerr/Bat-Pants/25 30.00
18 Willie McCovey/Jsy-Pants/25 60.00
20 Mike Schmidt/Bat-Jsy/25 85.00
24 Willie Mays/Bat-Jsy/25 250.00
30 Orlando Cepeda/Bat-Pants/25 30.00
34 Nolan Ryan/Jsy-Pants/25 120.00
43 Johnny Bench/Bat-Jsy/25 60.00

HOF Materials Pants
NM/M
Production 1-50
6 Stan Musial/50 30.00
8 Carl Yastrzemski/50 20.00
12 Bobby Doerr/50 10.00
17 Duke Snider/50 20.00
18 Willie McCovey/50 15.00
19 Bob Feller/50 20.00
22 Jim Palmer/50 10.00
24 Willie Mays/50 40.00
29 Warren Spahn/25 25.00
30 Orlando Cepeda/50 10.00
34 Nolan Ryan/50 25.00
42 Burleigh Grimes/50 75.00
43 Johnny Bench/50 15.00
45 Joe Cronin/50 20.00
46 Fergie Jenkins/50 10.00

HOF Material Signature Pants
NM/M
Production 1-50
6 Stan Musial/25 85.00
12 Bobby Doerr/50 25.00
17 Duke Snider/50 40.00
18 Willie McCovey/50 50.00
22 Jim Palmer/25 40.00
24 Willie Mays/50 240.00
30 Orlando Cepeda/25 25.00
34 Nolan Ryan/25 120.00
43 Johnny Bench/25 60.00
46 Fergie Jenkins/25 30.00

HOF Silver
NM/M
Common Player: 4.00
Production 500 Sets
Gold: 2-4X
Production 25 Sets
Platinum: No Pricing

Production One Set

#	Player	Price
1	Pee Wee Reese	4.00
2	Red Schoendienst	4.00
3	Harmon Killebrew	5.00
4	Hack Wilson	4.00
5	Brooks Robinson	5.00
6	Stan Musial	6.00
7	Al Simmons	4.00
8	Carl Yastrzemski	5.00
9	Ted Williams	8.00
10	Phil Rizzuto	4.00
11	Luis Aparicio	4.00
12	Bobby Doerr	4.00
13	Bob Lemon	4.00
14	Ernie Banks	5.00
15	Ralph Kiner	4.00
16	Whitey Ford	4.00
17	Duke Snider	4.00
18	Willie McCovey	4.00
19	Bob Feller	4.00
20	Mike Schmidt	6.00
21	Roberto Clemente	8.00
22	Jim Palmer	4.00
23	Enos Slaughter	4.00
24	Willie Mays	8.00
25	Willie Stargell	4.00
26	Frank Robinson	4.00
27	Carl Hubbell	4.00
28	Reggie Jackson	4.00
29	Warren Spahn	5.00
30	Orlando Cepeda	4.00
31	Hoyt Wilhelm	4.00
32	Sandy Koufax	15.00
33	Hal Newhouser	4.00
34	Nolan Ryan	8.00
35	George Brett	6.00
36	Bill Dickey	4.00
37	Jim "Catfish" Hunter	4.00
38	Frankie Frisch	4.00
39	Nellie Fox	4.00
40	Lou Boudreau	4.00
41	Hank Greenberg	5.00
42	Burleigh Grimes	4.00
43	Johnny Bench	5.00
44	Hank Aaron	8.00
45	Joe Cronin	4.00
46	Fergie Jenkins	4.00
47	Luke Appling	4.00
48	Yogi Berra	5.00
49	Early Wynn	4.00
50	Al Kaline	5.00

Home Road Gamers Duos
NM/M
Production 1-100
Prime: No Pricing
Production 1-10

#	Player	Price
3	Babe Ruth/ Jsy-Jsy/25	450.00
4	Paul Molitor/ Jsy-Pants/100	15.00
7	Ivan Rodriguez/ Jsy-Jsy/100	10.00
9	Ted Williams/ Jsy-Jsy/25	85.00
10	Andre Dawson/ Jsy-Jsy/15	15.00
11	Darryl Strawberry/ Jsy-Jsy/25	12.00
14	Ernie Banks/ Jsy-Jsy/25	30.00
15	Jim Edmonds/ Jsy-Jsy/25	15.00
16	Bo Jackson/ Jsy-Jsy/25	20.00
17	Mark Grace/ Jsy-Jsy/100	15.00
18	Albert Pujols/ Jsy-Jsy/100	25.00
19	Tony Gwynn/ Jsy-Jsy/100	15.00
20	Cal Ripken Jr./ Jsy-Jsy/100	40.00
21	Chipper Jones/ Jsy-Jsy/50	15.00
23	Don Mattingly/ Jsy-Jsy/100	25.00
24	Willie Mays/ Jsy-Jsy/25	80.00
25	Tony Oliva/ Jsy-Jsy/50	10.00
28	Reggie Jackson/ Jsy-Jsy/50	15.00
29	Rod Carew/ Jsy-Jsy/100	15.00
30	Harmon Killebrew/ Jsy-Pants/25	25.00
32	Nolan Ryan/ Jsy-Jsy/100	30.00
33	Eddie Murray/ Jsy-Pants/100	15.00
35	Rickey Henderson/ Jsy-Jsy/50	12.00
36	Jim Rice/Jsy-Jsy/50	12.00
37	Hoyt Wilhelm/ Jsy-Jsy/50	10.00
38	Curt Schilling/ Jsy-Jsy/100	15.00
42	Greg Maddux/ Jsy-Jsy/100	15.00
43	Dennis Eckersley/ Jsy-Jsy/50	10.00
44	Willie McCovey/ Jsy-Pants/100	15.00
45	Willie Stargell/ Jsy-Jsy/50	20.00
46	Mike Mussina/ Jsy-Pants/50	15.00
47	Gary Carter/ Jsy-Jsy/50	15.00
48	Dale Murphy/ Jsy-Jsy/50	15.00
49	Mike Piazza/ Jsy-Jsy/50	20.00
50	Jim Palmer/ Jsy-Pants/100	10.00

Home Road Gamers Signature Duos
NM/M
Production 1-25

#	Player	Price
4	Paul Molitor/ Jsy-Pants/25	60.00
11	Darryl Strawberry/ Jsy-Jsy/25	30.00
17	Mark Grace/ Jsy-Jsy/25	50.00
19	Tony Gwynn/ Jsy-Jsy/25	50.00
23	Don Mattingly/ Jsy-Jsy/25	80.00
25	Tony Oliva/ Jsy-Jsy/25	30.00
29	Rod Carew/ Jsy-Jsy/25	50.00
30	Harmon Killebrew/ Jsy-Jsy/25	50.00
36	Jim Rice/Jsy-Jsy/25	35.00
43	Dennis Eckersley/ Jsy-Jsy/25	30.00
44	Willie McCovey/ Jsy-Jsy/25	50.00
47	Gary Carter/ Jsy-Jsy/25	30.00
48	Dale Murphy/ Jsy-Jsy/25	50.00
50	Jim Palmer/ Jsy-Pants/25	40.00

Home Road Gamer Signature Trios
NM/M
Production 1-25
Prime: No Pricing
Production 1-5

#	Player	Price
4	Paul Molitor/ Bat-Jsy-Pants/25	75.00
11	Darryl Strawberry Fld Glv- Jsy-Jsy/25	40.00
17	Mark Grace/ Bat-Jsy-Jsy/25	60.00
19	Tony Gwynn/ Bat-Jsy-Jsy/25	70.00
23	Don Mattingly/ Bat-Jsy-Jsy/25	90.00
25	Tony Oliva/ Bat-Jsy-Jsy/25	35.00
29	Rod Carew/ Bat-Jsy-Jsy/25	60.00
30	Harmon Killebrew/ Bat-Jsy-Jsy/25	70.00
36	Jim Rice/ Bat-Jsy-Jsy/25	40.00

Home Road Gamers Trios
NM/M
Production 1-100
Prime: No Pricing
Production 1-10

#	Player	Price
4	Paul Molitor/ Bat-Jsy-Pants/100	25.00
7	Ivan Rodriguez/ Jsy-Jsy-Jsy/100	15.00
9	Ted Williams/ Jsy-Jsy-Jsy/100	120.00
11	Darryl Strawberry/ Fld Glv-Jsy-Jsy/25	20.00
14	Ernie Banks/ Bat-Jsy-Jsy/25	40.00
15	Jim Edmonds/ Bat-Jsy-Jsy/25	25.00
17	Mark Grace/ Bat-Jsy-Jsy/100	25.00
18	Albert Pujols/ Bat-Jsy-Jsy/100	40.00
19	Tony Gwynn/ Jsy-Jsy-Jsy/100	25.00
20	Cal Ripken Jr./ Jsy-Jsy-Jsy/100	60.00
21	Chipper Jones/ Bat-Jsy-Jsy/50	20.00
23	Don Mattingly/ Bat-Jsy-Jsy/100	30.00
24	Willie Mays/ Bat-Jsy-Jsy/25	75.00
25	Tony Oliva/ Bat-Jsy-Jsy/50	20.00
28	Reggie Jackson/ Bat-Jsy-Jsy/100	20.00
29	Rod Carew/ Bat-Jsy-Jsy/100	20.00
30	Harmon Killebrew/ Bat-Jsy-Jsy/25	35.00
32	Nolan Ryan/ Jkt-Jsy-Jsy/100	35.00
33	Eddie Murray/ Bat-Jsy-Pants/100	20.00
35	Rickey Henderson/ Bat-Jsy-Jsy/100	20.00
36	Jim Rice/ Bat-Jsy-Jsy/25	20.00
38	Curt Schilling/ Bat-Jsy-Jsy/50	15.00
44	Willie McCovey/ Bat-Jsy-Jsy/100	20.00
45	Willie Stargell/ Bat-Jsy-Jsy/50	20.00
46	Mike Mussina/ Bat-Jsy-Pants/25	35.00
47	Gary Carter/ Bat-Jsy-Jsy/50	25.00
48	Dale Murphy/ Bat-Jsy-Jsy/50	30.00
49	Mike Piazza/ Jsy-Jsy-Jsy/25	35.00

Home Run Materials
NM/M
Production 1-100

#	Player	Price
1	Ernie Banks/Bat/60	15.00
2	Roger Maris/Bat/61	50.00
4	Johnny Bench/ Pants/71	10.00
5	Harmon Killebrew/ Bat/75	10.00
6	Jose Canseco/Bat/25	15.00
8	Sammy Sosa/ Jsy/100	10.00
9	Jim Thome/Jsy/50	10.00
10	Rafael Palmeiro/ Jsy/50	8.00

Home Run Materials Signature
NM/M
Production 3-25

#	Player	Price
1	Ernie Banks/Bat/25	60.00
4	Johnny Bench/ Pants/25	60.00
5	Harmon Killebrew/ Bat/25	50.00

Material Ink Bat
No Pricing
Production 1-10

Material Ink Jersey
NM/M
Production 1-50

#	Player	Price
2	Fred Lynn/50	15.00
3	Dale Murphy/50	30.00
4	Paul Molitor/50	15.00
5	Alan Trammell/50	15.00
8	Gary Carter/50	20.00
10	Andre Dawson/50	15.00
11	Luis Aparicio/50	15.00
14	Darryl Strawberry/50	15.00
18	Kirk Gibson/50	20.00
20	Don Sutton/50	20.00
23	Don Mattingly/Jkt/50	75.00
24	Tony Perez/50	50.00
27	Carlton Fisk/25	40.00
29	Fred McGriff/25	40.00
30	John Kruk/25	50.00
32	Dwight Evans/50	25.00
33	Gaylord Perry/50	25.00
34	Bo Jackson/25	65.00
36	Gaylord Perry/50	20.00
39	Dave Parker/25	20.00
42	Harmon Killebrew/50	50.00
43	Dennis Eckersley/25	25.00
44	Willie McCovey/25	50.00
46	Luis Tiant/50	20.00
48	Mark Grace/50	40.00

Material Ink Jersey Number
NM/M
Production 1-44

#	Player	Price
2	Fred Lynn/19	30.00
14	Darryl Strawberry/44	20.00
20	Don Sutton/20	25.00
22	Mark Prior/22	50.00
23	Don Mattingly/Jkt/23	80.00
24	Tony Perez/34	30.00
27	Carlton Fisk/27	40.00
29	Fred McGriff/29	40.00
30	John Kruk/29	50.00
32	Dwight Evans/24	35.00
36	Gaylord Perry/36	20.00
40	Mark Teixeira/23	40.00
43	Dennis Eckersley/43	20.00
44	Willie McCovey/44	40.00
46	Luis Tiant/27	25.00

Material Ink Combos
NM/M
Production 1-25
Prime: No Pricing
Production 1-5

#	Player	Price
2	Fred Lynn/ Bat-Jsy/25	35.00
8	Gary Carter/ Bat-Jsy/25	30.00
10	Andre Dawson/ Bat-Jsy/25	30.00
11	Luis Aparicio/ Bat-Jsy/25	30.00
14	Darryl Strawberry/ Bat-Jsy/25	30.00
27	Carlton Fisk/ Bat-Jsy/25	40.00
37	Miguel Cabrera/ Bat-Jsy/25	50.00
39	Dave Parker/ Bat-Jsy/25	25.00
48	Mark Grace/ Bat-Jsy/50	25.00

Milestone Material Number
NM/M
Production 1-31

#	Player	Price
2	Nolan Ryan/Jsy/30	35.00
10	Greg Maddux/Jsy/31	20.00

Milestone Materials Signature Number
NM/M
No Pricing
Production 1-10

Milestone Material Year
NM/M
Production 10-25
Prime: No Pricing
Production 1-10

#	Player	Price
1	Roger Maris/ Pants/25	40.00
2	Nolan Ryan/Jsy/25	30.00
5	Steve Garvey/Jsy/25	10.00
6	Wade Boggs/Jsy/25	20.00
7	Tony Gwynn/Jsy/25	20.00
8	Sammy Sosa/Jsy/25	20.00
9	Randy Johnson/ Jsy/25	15.00
10	Greg Maddux/Jsy/25	20.00

Milestone Materials Signature Year
NM/M
Production 1-25
Prime: No Pricing
Production 1-10

#	Player	Price
2	Nolan Ryan/Jsy/25	120.00
5	Steve Garvey/Jsy/25	25.00
7	Tony Gwynn/Jsy/25	40.00

No-Hitters
NM/M
Production 3-25

#	Player	Price
7	Dennis Eckersley, Bert Blyleven/25	35.00
8	Juan Marichal, Gaylord Perry/25	35.00
9	Jim Palmer, Bob Gibson/25	40.00

Rookie Year Materials Number
NM/M
Production 1-44

#	Player	Price
1	Rod Carew/Jsy/29	20.00
6	Juan Marichal/Jsy/27	12.00
8	Jim Palmer/Hat/22	15.00
16	Kirk Gibson/Hat/23	15.00
18	Roger Clemens/ Jsy/21	25.00
20	David Cone/Jsy/44	8.00
23	Deion Sanders/ Jsy/21	20.00
24	Dwight Gooden/ Jsy/16	15.00
28	Mike Piazza/Jsy/31	20.00
33	Andruw Jones/ Jsy/10	10.00
34	Vladimir Guerrero/ Jsy/27	15.00
37	Kerry Wood/Jsy/34	15.00
38	Magglio Ordonez/ Jsy/30	8.00
40	Mark Mulder/Jsy/20	10.00
41	Lance Berkman/ Jsy/17	10.00
42	Alfonso Soriano/ Jsy/33	10.00
46	Mark Prior/Jsy/22	10.00
47	Mark Teixeira/Jsy/23	10.00
48	Miguel Cabrera/ Jsy/20	15.00
50	Victor Martinez/ Jsy/41	8.00

Rookie Year Material Signature Number
NM/M
Production 1-30

#	Player	Price
1	Rod Carew/Jsy/29	35.00
4	Duke Snider/Jsy/25	40.00
6	Juan Marichal/ Jsy/25	25.00
11	Gary Carter/Jsy/25	30.00
12	Robin Yount/Jsy/19	65.00
13	Keith Hernandez/ Jsy/18	35.00
15	Ozzie Smith/Jsy/25	50.00
20	David Cone/Jsy/25	25.00
21	Gary Sheffield/ Jsy/25	40.00
24	Dwight Gooden/ Jsy/25	25.00
38	Magglio Ordonez/ Jsy/30	20.00
46	Mark Prior/Jsy/22	40.00
47	Mark Teixeira/Jsy/23	40.00
48	Miguel Cabrera/ Jsy/20	50.00
50	Victor Martinez/ Jsy/25	20.00

Rookie Year Materials Year
NM/M
Production 1-100
Prime: No Pricing
Production 5 Sets

#	Player	Price
1	Rod Carew/Jsy/100	12.00
4	Duke Snider/Jsy/100	12.00
6	Juan Marichal/ Jsy/100	10.00
11	Gary Carter/Jsy/100	8.00
12	Robin Yount/Jsy/100	15.00
13	Keith Hernandez/ Jsy/100	10.00
15	Ozzie Smith/Jsy/25	10.00
17	Dave Righetti/Jsy/25	20.00
18	Roger Clemens/ Jsy/25	15.00
19	Greg Maddux/Jsy/25	25.00
20	David Cone/Jsy/100	8.00
21	Gary Sheffield/ Jsy/100	10.00
22	Randy Johnson/ Jsy/100	10.00
23	Deion Sanders/ Jsy/100	10.00
24	Dwight Gooden/ Jsy/25	8.00
25	Ivan Rodriguez/ Jsy/100	8.00
26	Jeff Bagwell/ Pants/25	8.00
27	Pedro Martinez/ Jsy/100	10.00
28	Mike Piazza/Jsy/100	12.00
29	Chipper Jones/ Jsy/100	10.00
30	Hideo Nomo/Jsy/100	12.00
32	Scott Rolen/Jsy/100	10.00
33	Andruw Jones/ Jsy/100	8.00
34	Vladimir Guerrero/ Jsy/100	10.00
35	Sean Casey/Jsy/25	10.00
36	Paul LoDuca/Jsy/25	8.00
37	Kerry Wood/Jsy/100	12.00
38	Magglio Ordonez/ Jsy/25	8.00
39	Vernon Wells/Jsy/25	8.00
40	Mark Mulder/Jsy/25	8.00
41	Lance Berkman/ Jsy/100	8.00
42	Alfonso Soriano/ Jsy/100	8.00
43	Albert Pujols/ Jsy/100	20.00
44	Ben Sheets/Jsy/25	10.00
45	Roy Oswalt/Jsy/100	10.00
46	Mark Prior/Jsy/100	8.00
47	Mark Teixeira/Jsy/100	8.00
48	Miguel Cabrera/ Jsy/100	10.00
49	Travis Hafner/Jsy/100	10.00
50	Victor Martinez/ Jsy/100	10.00

Rookie Year Materials Signature Year
NM/M
Production 1-25
Prime: No Pricing
Production 1-5

#	Player	Price
1	Rod Carew/Jsy/25	35.00
4	Duke Snider/Jsy/25	40.00
6	Juan Marichal/ Jsy/25	25.00
11	Gary Carter/Jsy/25	30.00
12	Robin Yount/Jsy/25	65.00
13	Keith Hernandez/ Jsy/25	30.00
15	Ozzie Smith/Jsy/25	50.00
17	Dave Righetti/Jsy/25	50.00
20	David Cone/Jsy/25	25.00
21	Gary Sheffield/ Jsy/25	40.00
24	Dwight Gooden/ Jsy/25	25.00
32	Scott Rolen/Jsy/25	50.00
35	Sean Casey/Jsy/25	50.00
36	Paul LoDuca/Jsy/25	20.00
38	Magglio Ordonez/ Jsy/25	20.00
39	Vernon Wells/Jsy/25	20.00
40	Mark Mulder/Jsy/25	20.00
42	Alfonso Soriano/ Jsy/25	35.00
44	Ben Sheets/Jsy/25	25.00
46	Mark Prior/Jsy/25	40.00
47	Mark Teixeira/Jsy/25	40.00
48	Miguel Cabrera/ Jsy/25	50.00
49	Travis Hafner/Jsy/25	20.00
50	Victor Martinez/ Jsy/25	20.00

Salutations Signature
NM/M
Production 1-24

#	Player	Price
4	Al Kaline/24	70.00
5	Dale Murphy/24	50.00
7	Duke Snider/24	50.00
17	Johnny Bench/24	60.00
19	Steve Carlton/24	40.00

Signature Bronze
NM/M
Production 10-100
Platinum: No Pricing
Production One Set

#	Player	Price
3	Edgar Renteria/50	30.00
4	Paul Molitor/100	25.00
7	Bobby Crosby/25	25.00
8	Cal Ripken Jr./25	200.00
9	Hank Blalock/50	20.00
11	Gary Sheffield/50	35.00
12	Alfonso Soriano/50	25.00
14	Paul Konerko/50	25.00
15	Jim Edmonds/50	30.00
19	Tony Gwynn/100	40.00
20	Mark Mulder/100	25.00
23	Mark Teixeira/50	30.00
24	Miguel Cabrera/50	30.00
28	Austin Kearns/50	15.00
29	Rod Carew/100	25.00
34	David Wright/25	75.00
34	Kerry Wood/50	35.00
36	Mark Prior/100	40.00
41	Tom Seaver/100	25.00
44	Roy Oswalt/25	40.00
46	Jeff Niemann/100	35.00
48	Torii Hunter/50	20.00
49	Scott Rolen/50	40.00
52	C.C. Sabathia/25	25.00
53	Rafael Palmeiro/25	50.00
57	Johan Santana/50	40.00
59	Justin Verlander/100	30.00
61	Rafael Palmeiro/25	50.00
62	Sean Casey/25	20.00
63	Nolan Ryan/85	85.00
64	Magglio Ordonez/50	15.00
65	Craig Biggio/50	30.00
66	Vernon Wells/25	20.00
67	Manny Ramirez/25	50.00
69	Omar Vizquel/50	40.00
72	Carlton Fisk/100	25.00
73	Victor Martinez/50	15.00
74	Adrian Beltre/50	25.00
75	Barry Zito/50	20.00
76	Josh Beckett/25	35.00
77	Michael Young/50	20.00
82	Eric Chavez/50	15.00
82	Don Mattingly/100	60.00
85	Philip Humber/100	25.00
85	Juan Gonzalez/50	25.00
90	Tim Hudson/50	30.00
90	Shawn Green/50	30.00
95	Mike Schmidt/100	50.00
99	Ben Sheets/25	25.00
99	Chipper Jones/25	60.00

Signature Silver
NM/M
Production 5-50

#	Player	Price
3	Edgar Renteria/25	40.00
4	Paul Molitor/25	30.00
9	Hank Blalock/25	25.00
11	Gary Sheffield/25	40.00
12	Alfonso Soriano/25	35.00
14	Paul Konerko/25	35.00
15	Jim Edmonds/25	35.00
16	Garret Anderson/25	25.00
19	Tony Gwynn/50	60.00
20	Mark Mulder/50	25.00
23	Mark Teixeira/25	25.00
24	Miguel Cabrera/25	40.00
28	Austin Kearns/25	20.00
29	Rod Carew/50	30.00
34	Kerry Wood/25	40.00
36	Mark Prior/50	40.00
41	Tom Seaver/50	50.00
46	Jeff Niemann/50	40.00
48	Torii Hunter/25	25.00
49	Scott Rolen/50	50.00
57	Johan Santana/50	50.00
59	Justin Verlander/25	35.00
63	Nolan Ryan/50	100.00
64	Magglio Ordonez/25	20.00
65	Craig Biggio/25	35.00
69	Omar Vizquel/25	40.00
72	Carlton Fisk/50	25.00
73	Victor Martinez/25	20.00
74	Adrian Beltre/25	25.00
75	Barry Zito/25	20.00
77	Michael Young/25	20.00
78	Eric Chavez/25	20.00
82	Don Mattingly/50	60.00
84	Philip Humber/50	30.00
86	Juan Gonzalez/25	40.00
86	Tim Hudson/25	30.00
95	Mike Schmidt/50	65.00

Signature Gold
NM/M
Production 3-25

4	Paul Molitor/25	35.00
19	Tony Gwynn/25	50.00
20	Mark Mulder/25	30.00
29	Rod Carew/25	35.00
36	Mark Prior/25	50.00
41	Tom Seaver/25	60.00
63	Nolan Ryan/25	120.00
72	Carlton Fisk/25	35.00
82	Don Mattingly/25	80.00
95	Mike Schmidt/25	85.00

Statistical Champions Material Number

NM/M

Production 1-47

1	Nolan Ryan/Jsy/34	30.00
2	Lee Smith/Jsy/47	8.00
4	Kerry Wood/Jsy/34	12.00
6	Curt Schilling/Jsy/38	10.00
20	Mark Mulder/Jsy/20	10.00
21	Roger Clemens/ Jsy/21	25.00
22	Will Clark/Jsy/22	20.00
23	Don Mattingly/ Jsy/23	25.00
24	Manny Ramirez/ Jsy/24	12.00
25	Billy Williams/Jsy/26	10.00
26	Wade Boggs/Jsy/26	15.00
27	Kevin Brown/Jsy/27	8.00
29	Adrian Beltre/Jsy/29	8.00
32	Sandy Koufax/ Jsy/32	250.00
33	Jose Canseco/ Jsy/33	12.00
34	Kirby Puckett/Jsy/34	15.00
35	Rickey Henderson/ Jsy/35	15.00
38	Curt Schilling/Jsy/38	10.00
41	Nolan Ryan/Jsy/34	30.00
44	Roy Oswalt/Jsy/44	8.00

Stat. Champion Materials Signature Number

NM/M

Production 1-34

1	Nolan Ryan/Jsy/34	120.00
19	Tony Gwynn/Jsy/19	75.00
20	Mark Mulder/Jsy/20	25.00
22	Will Clark/Jsy/22	40.00
23	Don Mattingly/ Jsy/23	75.00
26	Wade Boggs/Jsy/26	40.00
29	Adrian Beltre/Jsy/29	35.00
39	Don Sutton/Jsy/20	30.00
41	Nolan Ryan/Jsy/34	120.00

Statistical Champions Materials Year

NM/M

Production 1-100
Prime: No Pricing
Production 1-5

1	Nolan Ryan/Jsy/100	25.00
2	Lee Smith/Jsy/25	10.00
3	Harmon Killebrew/ Jsy/100	12.00
4	Kerry Wood/Jsy/100	12.00
5	Albert Pujols/ Jsy/100	20.00
6	Curt Schilling/Jsy/100	8.00
7	Joe Cronin/ Pants/100	12.00
8	Cal Ripken Jr./ Jsy/100	30.00
9	Barry Zito/Jsy/100	8.00
10	Miguel Tejada/ Jsy/100	10.00
11	Edgar Martinez/ Jsy/25	8.00
14	Andre Dawson/ Jsy/25	10.00
17	Todd Helton/Jsy/100	8.00
19	Tony Gwynn/Jsy/100	12.00
20	Mark Mulder/Jsy/100	5.00
21	Roger Clemens/ Jsy/100	15.00
22	Will Clark/Jsy/25	20.00
23	Don Mattingly/ Jsy/100	20.00
24	Manny Ramirez/ Jsy/100	10.00
25	Billy Williams/ Jsy/100	8.00
26	Wade Boggs/ Jsy/100	10.00
27	Kevin Brown/Jsy/25	8.00
28	George Brett/ Jsy/100	20.00
29	Adrian Beltre/Jsy/25	10.00
30	Lance Berkman/ Jsy/100	5.00
31	Sammy Sosa/ Jsy/100	10.00
32	Sandy Koufax/ Jsy/25	250.00
33	Jose Canseco/ Jsy/25	15.00
34	Kirby Puckett/ Jsy/100	10.00

35	Rickey Henderson/ Jsy/100	12.00
36	Juan Gonzalez/ Jsy/100	8.00
38	Curt Schilling/Jsy/100	8.00
39	Don Sutton/Jsy/100	8.00
40	Johan Santana/ Jsy/100	10.00
41	Nolan Ryan/Jsy/100	25.00
43	Lou Brock/Jsy/100	8.00
44	Roy Oswalt/Jsy/25	8.00
45	Dale Murphy/ Jsy/100	10.00

Statistical Champions Materials Signature Year

NM/M

Production 1-50
Prime: No Pricing
Production 1-5

1	Nolan Ryan/Jsy/50	100.00
3	Harmon Killebrew/ Jsy/50	40.00
4	Kerry Wood/Jsy/50	40.00
8	Cal Ripken Jr./ Jsy/25	175.00
9	Barry Zito/Jsy/25	25.00
11	Edgar Martinez/ Jsy/25	40.00
19	Tony Gwynn/Jsy/50	60.00
20	Mark Mulder/Jsy/25	40.00
22	Will Clark/Jsy/25	40.00
23	Don Mattingly/ Jsy/50	60.00
26	Wade Boggs/Jsy/25	40.00
29	Adrian Beltre/Jsy/25	35.00
39	Don Sutton/Jsy/25	30.00
40	Johan Santana/ Jsy/25	60.00
41	Nolan Ryan/Jsy/50	100.00
43	Lou Brock/Jsy/50	40.00
45	Dale Murphy/Jsy/50	30.00

World Series Materials

NM/M

Production 1-100

1	Frank Robinson/ Bat/100	10.00
3	Carl Yastrzemski/ Bat/100	25.00
4	Jack Morris/Jsy/50	8.00
7	Wade Boggs/Bat/100	12.00
8	Andruw Jones/ Jsy/100	8.00
10	Darryl Strawberry/ Jsy/100	10.00

World Series Materials Signatures

NM/M

Production 1-25
Prime: No Pricing
Production 1-10

4	Jack Morris/Jsy/25	25.00
7	Wade Boggs/Bat/25	40.00
10	Darryl Strawberry/ Jsy/25	25.00

2005 Donruss Zenith Promos

This 7-1/2" x 10" Dufex foil-technology card was distributed as a wrapper redemption at the National Sports Collectors Convention in Chicago. The back has a promo overprint.

NM/M

32	Sandy Koufax	12.00

2005 Donruss Zenith

NM/M

Complete Set (250):		50.00
Common Player:		.25
Hobby Pack (5):		5.00

Hobby Box (18):		80.00
1	Curt Schilling	.50
2	Jim Edmonds	.40
3	Ichiro Suzuki	1.50
4	Jody Gerut	.25
5	Carlos Beltran	.50
6	Miguel Tejada	.50
7	Ted Lilly	.25
8	Bobby Abreu	.40
9	Mark Teixeira	.50
10	Manny Ramirez	.75
11	Eric Gagne	.40
12	Adrian Beltre	.40
13	Dmitri Young	.25
14	Alfonso Soriano	.50
15	Vladimir Guerrero	.75
16	Carl Crawford	.25
17	David Ortiz	.75
18	Jose Guillen	.25
19	Miguel Cabrera	.75
20	Alex Rodriguez	2.00
21	Brad Lidge	.25
22	Francisco Rodriguez	.25
23	Carlos Lee	.25
24	Ben Sheets	.40
25	Jason Schmidt	.25
26	Cesar Izturis	.25
27	Corey Patterson	.25
28	Marcus Giles	.25
29	Melvin Mora	.25
30	Yadier Molina	.25
31	Juan Pierre	.25
32	Aubrey Huff	.25
33	Rafael Furcal	.25
34	David Dellucci	.25
35	Jake Peavy	.40
36	Aramis Ramirez	.40
37	Javy Lopez	.25
38	Aaron Rowand	.25
39	Raul Ibanez	.25
40	Jason Bay	.40
41	Michael Young	.25
42	Ivan Rodriguez	.50
43	Derrek Lee	.50
44	Adam Dunn	.50
45	Eric Chavez	.40
46	Pedro Martinez	.75
47	Roy Oswalt	.40
48	Kevin Millwood	.25
49	Carlos Delgado	.40
50	Derek Jeter	2.00
51	Johnny Damon	.50
52	Richie Sexson	.40
53	Nomar Garciaparra	.75
54	Edgar Renteria	.25
55	Carl Pavano	.25
56	Tim Wakefield	.25
57	Michael Barrett	.25
58	Johnny Estrada	.25
59	Jeff Kent	.25
60	Mark Loretta	.25
61	Greg Maddux	1.00
62	Hank Blalock	.40
63	Moises Alou	.40
64	Brad Radke	.25
65	Brad Wilkerson	.25
66	Sean Casey	.25
67	Oliver Perez	.40
68	Scott Hatteberg	.25
69	Mike Lowell	.25
70	Kazuo Matsui	.25
71	Mark Prior	.50
72	Hideki Matsui	1.50
73	Geoff Jenkins	.25
74	Gary Sheffield	.50
75	A.J. Burnett	.25
76	Vernon Wells	.25
77	Kenny Rogers	.25
78	Jose Reyes	.50
79	Victor Martinez	.25
80	Jorge Posada	.40
81	Rich Harden	.25
82	Travis Hafner	.25
83	Bret Boone	.25
84	Chipper Jones	.75
85	Bartolo Colon	.25
86	Scott Podsednik	.25
87	Coco Crisp	.25
88	Luis Castillo	.25
89	John Smoltz	.40
90	Andruw Jones	.50
91	Milton Bradley	.25
92	Torii Hunter	.25
93	Shawn Green	.40
94	Paul Konerko	.40
95	David Wells	.25
96	Scott Rolen	.50
97	Rodrigo Lopez	.25

98	Garret Anderson	.40
99	Tim Hudson	.40
100	Sammy Sosa	.75
101	Jason Varitek	.50
102	Lance Berkman	.40
103	Troy Glaus	.40
104	Carlos Guillen	.25
105	Jeff Bagwell	.50
106	Phil Nevin	.25
107	Freddy Garcia	.25
108	Jake Westbrook	.25
109	Marquis Grissom	.25
110	Johan Santana	.75
111	Kerry Wood	.40
112	Jose Vidro	.25
113	Mike Mussina	.40
114	Josh Beckett	.40
115	Matt Lawton	.25
116	Craig Biggio	.40
117	Reggie Sanders	.25
118	Jason Kendall	.25
119	Larry Walker	.25
120	Roger Clemens	2.00
121	C.C. Sabathia	.25
122	Javier Vazquez	.25
123	Barry Zito	.40
124	Jon Lieber	.25
125	Kris Benson	.25
126	Jacque Jones	.25
127	Ray Durham	.25
128	Mark Kotsay	.25
129	Jack Wilson	.25
130	Bobby Crosby	.25
131	Todd Helton	.50
132	Lyle Overbay	.25
133	Jon Garland	.25
134	Roy Halladay	.40
135	Orlando Cabrera	.25
136	Danny Kolb	.25
137	Austin Kearns	.25
138	Paul LoDuca	.25
139	Magglio Ordonez	.40
140	Rafael Palmeiro	.50
141	Omar Vizquel	.25
142	Mike Piazza	1.00
143	Mark Mulder	.40
144	Dontrelle Willis	.40
145	Tom Glavine	.40
146	Khalil Greene	.25
147	Ken Griffey Jr.	1.50
148	Mike Sweeney	.25
149	Trot Nixon	.25
150	Randy Johnson	.75
151	Doug Mientkiewicz	.25
152	Jeromy Burnitz	.25
153	Brandon Webb	.25
154	Kevin Brown	.25
155	Carlos Zambrano	.40
156	Shingo Takatsu	.25
157	Erubiel Durazo	.25
158	Jason Isringhausen	.25
159	Corey Koskie	.25
160	Aaron Boone	.25
161	Joe Nathan	.25
162	Nick Johnson	.25
163	Michael Tucker	.25
164	Chris Carpenter	.25
165	Preston Wilson	.25
166	J.T. Snow	.25
167	Hideo Nomo	.40
168	Miguel Olivo	.25
169	Jarrod Washburn	.25
170	Derek Lowe	.25
171	Eric Milton	.25
172	Andy Pettitte	.40
173	Jason Giambi	.40
174	Richard Hidalgo	.25
175	Jayson Werth	.25
176	Juan Gonzalez	.25
177	Rocco Baldelli	.25
178	Steve Finley	.25
179	Frank Thomas	.40
180	Kenny Lofton	.25
181	Randy Winn	.25
182	Brandon McCarthy RC	1.50
183	Lew Ford	.25
184	Mike Cameron	.25
185	Carlos Pena	.25
186	Brian Roberts	.25
187	Jeremy Bonderman	.25
188	Luis Gonzalez	.25
189	J.D. Drew	.25
190	Frank Catalanotto	.25
191	John Buck	.25
192	Pat Burrell	.25
193	Ryan Klesko	.25
194	Jermaine Dye	.25
195	Mariano Rivera	.40
196	Angel Berroa	.25
197	Carlos Zambrano	.25
198	Joel Pineiro	.25
199	Jay Gibbons	.25
200	Albert Pujols	2.00
201	Billy Wagner	.25
202	Darin Erstad	.25
203	Jim Thome	.50
204	Adam LaRoche	.25
205	Cliff Floyd	.25
206	Grady Sizemore	.50
207	Garrett Atkins	.25
208	Philip Humber RC	.25
209	Zack Greinke	.25
210	Wladimir Balentien RC	1.00
211	Ubaldo Jimenez RC	.50
212	Dallas McPherson	.25
213	Justin Verlander RC	3.00
214	Justin Morneau	.50
215	Chase Utley	.50

216	Casey Kotchman	.25
217	Tadahito Iguchi RC	3.00
218	Hanley Ramirez	.25
219	Scott Kazmir	.25
220	J.J. Hardy	.25
221	Ambiorix Concepcion RC	.50
222	Jeff Niemann RC	1.00
223	David Wright	1.00
224	Joe Mauer	.50
225	Rickie Weeks	.25
226	Yuniesky Betancourt RC	1.00
227	Brady Clark	.25
228	Keiichi Yabu RC	.50
229	Delmon Young	.50
230	Nick Swisher	.25
231	George Brett	1.00
232	Ryne Sandberg	1.00
233	Mike Schmidt	1.00
234	Tony Gwynn	.75
235	Rickey Henderson	.50
236	Ozzie Smith	.50
237	Reggie Jackson	.75
238	Steve Carlton	.40
239	Robin Yount	.40
240	Tom Seaver	.40
241	Ted Williams	1.50
242	Don Mattingly	.50
243	Mark Grace	.40
244	Rod Carew	.40
245	Willie Mays	1.50
246	Gary Carter	.40
247	Wade Boggs	.50
248	Dale Murphy	.40
249	Nolan Ryan	2.00
250	Cal Ripken Jr.	3.00

Artist's Proofs Silver

Silver AP (1-250): 3-5X
Inserted 1:16

Artist's Proofs Gold

Gold AP (1-250): 5-10X
Production 50 Sets

Museum Collection

Museum (1-250): 2-3X
Inserted 1:3

Epix Orange Play

NM/M

Common Player:	1.50
Production 750 Sets	
Black Game:	1-2X
Production 75 Sets	
Black Moment:	2-3X
Production 25 Sets	
Black Play:	1X
Production 100 Sets	
Black Season:	1-2X
Production 50 Sets	
Blue Game:	1X
Production 350	
Blue Moment:	1X
Production 150 Sets	
Blue Play:	1X
Production 500 Sets	
Blue Season:	1X
Production 250 Sets	
Emerald Game:	1X
Production 100 Sets	
Emerald Moment:	1-2X
Production 50 Sets	
Emerald Play:	1X
Production 150 Sets	
Emerald Season:	1X
Production 75 Sets	
Orange Game:	1X
Production 500 Sets	
Orange Moment:	1X
Production 250 Sets	
Orange Season:	1X
Production 350 Sets	
Purple Game:	1X
Production 250 Sets	
Purple Moment:	1X
Production 100 Sets	
Purple Play:	1X
Production 350 Sets	
Purple Season:	1X
Production 150 Sets	
Red Game:	1X
Production 150 Sets	
Red Moment:	1-2X
Production 50 Sets	
Red Play:	1X
Production 250 Sets	
Red Season:	1X
Production 100 Sets	

1	Vladimir Guerrero	3.00
2	Alex Rodriguez	6.00
3	Johan Santana	3.00
4	Todd Helton	2.00
5	Mark Teixeira	2.00
6	Manny Ramirez	3.00
7	Scott Rolen	2.00
8	Gary Sheffield	2.00
9	Miguel Cabrera	3.00
10	Jim Thome	2.00
11	Eric Chavez	1.50
12	Roger Clemens	6.00

13	Pedro Martinez	3.00
14	Roy Oswalt	1.50
15	Carlos Delgado	1.50
16	Nomar Garciaparra	2.00
17	Hideki Matsui	5.00
18	Shawn Green	1.50
19	Greg Maddux	4.00
20	Ted Williams	6.00
21	Don Mattingly	5.00
22	Cal Ripken Jr.	10.00
23	George Brett	6.00
24	Nolan Ryan	8.00
25	Willie Mays	6.00

Mozaics

NM/M

Common Trio: 1.00
Inserted 1:8

1	Pedro Martinez, Carlos Beltran, Tom Glavine	2.00
2	Albert Pujols, Jim Edmonds, Mark Mulder	5.00
3	Sammy Sosa, Miguel Tejada, Rafael Palmeiro	2.00
4	Mark Teixeira, Hank Blalock, Michael Young	2.00
5	Andruw Jones, Rafael Furcal, Johnny Estrada	1.50
6	Bobby Crosby, Eric Chavez, Barry Zito	1.00
7	Shawn Green, Troy Glaus, Luis Gonzalez	1.00
8	Austin Kearns, Adam Dunn, Sean Casey	1.00
9	Jim Thome, Bobby Abreu, Pat Burrell	1.50
10	Lance Berkman, Jeff Bagwell, Craig Biggio	1.50
11	Orlando Cabrera, Steve Finley, Darin Erstad	1.00
12	J.D. Drew, Jeff Kent, Milton Bradley	1.00
13	Dontrelle Willis, Mike Lowell, A.J. Burnett	1.00
14	Adrian Beltre, Jeremy Reed, Richie Sexson	1.00
15	Joe Mauer, Justin Morneau, Jacque Jones	1.00
16	Gary Sheffield, Hideki Matsui, Mike Mussina	4.00

Mozaics Materials Single

NM/M

Common Player:		4.00
1	Pedro Martinez/Jsy	4.00
2	Albert Pujols/Bat	15.00
3	Miguel Tejada/Jsy	6.00
4	Mark Teixeira/Bat	6.00
5	Andruw Jones/Bat	6.00
6	Luis Gonzalez/Bat	6.00
8	Adam Dunn/Bat	6.00
9	Bobby Abreu/Jsy	4.00
10	Craig Biggio/Bat	4.00
11	Darin Erstad/Bat	4.00
12	J.D. Drew/Bat	4.00
13	A.J. Burnett/Bat	4.00
14	Richie Sexson/Bat	4.00
15	Jacque Jones/Bat	4.00
16	Gary Sheffield/Fld Glv	6.00

Mozaics Materials Triple Jerseys

NM/M

Production 5-100
Prime: No Pricing
Production 5-10

5	Mark Teixeira, Hank Blalock, Michael Young/100	10.00
6	Bobby Crosby, Eric Chavez, Barry Zito/25	10.00
8	Austin Kearns, Adam Dunn, Sean Casey/100	10.00

9 Jim Thome, Bobby Abreu, Pat Burrell/100 10.00
10 Lance Berkman, Jeff Bagwell, Craig Biggio/100 10.00
16 Gary Sheffield, Hideki Matsui, Mike Mussina/50 25.00

Positions

Common Card: Inserted 1:21
Gold: 1X-2X
Production 100 Sets
1 Randy Johnson, Mark Prior, Roger Clemens 4.00
2 Ivan Rodriguez, Mike Piazza, Victor Martinez 2.00
3 Albert Pujols, Todd Helton, David Ortiz 5.00
4 Marcus Giles, Mark Loretta, Bret Boone 1.00
5 Scott Rolen, Aramis Ramirez, Chipper Jones 2.00
6 Kazuo Matsui, Miguel Tejada, Michael Young 1.50
7 Brian Giles, Manny Ramirez, Shannon Stewart 2.00
8 Rocco Baldelli, Andruw Jones, Vernon Wells 1.50
9 Miguel Cabrera, Lance Berkman, Vladimir Guerrero 2.00

Positions Materials Single
NM/M
Common Player: 4.00
1 Mark Prior/Bat 4.00
2 Ivan Rodriguez/Bat 6.00
3 Albert Pujols 15.00
4 Bret Boone/Jsy 4.00
5 Chipper Jones/Bat 6.00
6 Kazuo Matsui/Jsy 4.00
7 Manny Ramirez/Bat 6.00
8 Andruw Jones/Bat 4.00
9 Lance Berkman/Bat 4.00

Positions Materials Triple Jersey
NM/M
Production 5-100
2 Ivan Rodriguez, Mike Piazza, Victor Martinez/50 15.00
3 Albert Pujols, Todd Helton, David Ortiz/50 25.00
5 Scott Rolen, Aramis Ramirez, Chipper Jones/100 15.00
6 Kazuo Matsui, Miguel Tejada, Michael Young/75 10.00
8 Rocco Baldelli, Andruw Jones, Vernon Wells/100 10.00
9 Miguel Cabrera, Lance Berkman, Vladimir Guerrero/100 15.00

Positions Material Triple Jersey Prime
NM/M
Production 5-25
2 Ivan Rodriguez, Mike Piazza, Victor Martinez/25 35.00
5 Scott Rolen, Aramis Ramirez, Chipper Jones/25 35.00
6 Kazuo Matsui, Miguel Tejada, Michael Young/25 25.00
7 Brian Giles, Manny Ramirez, Shannon Stewart/25 20.00
8 Rocco Baldelli, Andruw Jones, Vernon Wells/25 25.00
9 Miguel Cabrera, Lance Berkman, Vladimir Guerrero/25 35.00

Red Hot
NM/M
Common Player: Inserted 1:16
1 Scott Rolen 1.50
2 Johan Santana 1.50
3 Josh Beckett 1.00
4 Aubrey Huff 1.00
5 Alfonso Soriano 1.50
6 Jeff Bagwell 1.50
7 Ted Williams 5.00
8 Mark Prior 1.50
9 Todd Helton 1.50
10 Vladimir Guerrero 2.00

Red Hot Bats
NM/M
Production 50-150
1 Scott Rolen/150 6.00
4 Aubrey Huff/150 4.00
5 Alfonso Soriano/150 6.00
6 Jeff Bagwell/150 6.00
7 Ted Williams/50 40.00
8 Mark Prior/150 6.00
9 Todd Helton/150 6.00
10 Vladimir Guerrero/150 8.00

Red Hot Jerseys
NM/M
Production 25-300
1 Scott Rolen/150 6.00
2 Johan Santana/150 4.00
3 Josh Beckett/300 4.00
4 Aubrey Huff/25 6.00
5 Alfonso Soriano/150 6.00
6 Jeff Bagwell/300 6.00
7 Ted Williams/25 60.00
8 Mark Prior/250 6.00
9 Todd Helton/165 6.00
10 Vladimir Guerrero/150 8.00

Red Hot Jerseys Prime
NM/M
Production 1-25
1 Scott Rolen/25 20.00
2 Johan Santana/25 20.00
3 Josh Beckett/25 15.00
4 Aubrey Huff/25 20.00
5 Alfonso Soriano/25 15.00
6 Jeff Bagwell/25 20.00
8 Mark Prior/25 20.00
9 Todd Helton/25 20.00
10 Vladimir Guerrero/25 25.00

White Hot
NM/M
Common Player: Inserted 1:65
1 Scott Rolen 2.00
2 Johan Santana 2.00
3 Josh Beckett 1.50
4 Aubrey Huff 1.50
5 Alfonso Soriano 2.00
6 Jeff Bagwell 2.00
7 Ted Williams 6.00
8 Mark Prior 2.00
9 Todd Helton 2.00
10 Vladimir Guerrero 2.00

White Hot Bats
NM/M
Production 50 Sets
1 Scott Rolen/50 8.00
4 Aubrey Huff/50 4.00
5 Alfonso Soriano/50 6.00
6 Jeff Bagwell/50 6.00
7 Ted Williams/50 40.00
8 Mark Prior/50 8.00
9 Todd Helton/50 8.00
10 Vladimir Guerrero/50 8.00

White Hot Jerseys
NM/M
Production 1-200
Prime: No Pricing
Production 1-10
1 Scott Rolen/50 8.00
2 Johan Santana/50 8.00
3 Josh Beckett/185 4.00
5 Alfonso Soriano/50 6.00
6 Jeff Bagwell/200 6.00
8 Mark Prior/200 6.00
9 Todd Helton/151 6.00
10 Vladimir Guerrero/50 8.00

Roll Call Autographs
NM/M
Inserted 1:24
1 Hanley Ramirez 20.00
2 Sean Tracey 8.00
3 Justin Wechsler 8.00
4 Matt Lindstrom 6.00
5 Garrett Jones 8.00
6 Ambiorix Concepcion 8.00
7 Casey Rogowski 6.00
8 Kelly Shoppach 6.00
9 Sean Thompson 8.00
10 Jeff Miller 6.00
11 Chris Resop 10.00
12 Justin Verlander 25.00
13 Geovany Soto 8.00
14 Paulino Reynoso 6.00
15 Chris Roberson 8.00
16 Justin Leone 6.00
17 Jeff Niemann 15.00
18 Mark Woodyard 6.00
19 Raul Tablado 8.00
20 Norihiro Nakamura 40.00
21 Tony Pena 8.00
22 Wladimir Balentien 10.00
23 Miguel Negron 6.00
24 Eude Brito 8.00
25 Ubaldo Jimenez 6.00
26 Mike Morse 10.00
27 Devon Lowery 6.00
28 Philip Humber 12.00
29 Nate McLouth 10.00
30 Jason Hammel 8.00

Spellbound
NM/M
Common Maddux (1-4) 3.00
Common Clemens (5-9) 4.00
Common A-Rod (10-13) 4.00
Common Pujols (14-19) 4.00
Inserted 1:11
1 Greg Maddux/G 3.00
2 Greg Maddux/R 3.00
3 Greg Maddux/E 3.00
4 Greg Maddux/G 3.00
5 Roger Clemens/R 4.00
6 Roger Clemens/O 4.00
7 Roger Clemens/G 4.00
8 Roger Clemens/E 4.00
9 Roger Clemens/R 4.00
10 Alex Rodriguez/A 4.00
11 Alex Rodriguez/L 4.00
12 Alex Rodriguez/E 4.00
13 Alex Rodriguez/X 4.00
14 Albert Pujols/ A 4.00
15 Albert Pujols/L 4.00
16 Albert Pujols/B 4.00
17 Albert Pujols/R 4.00
18 Albert Pujols/R 4.00
19 Albert Pujols/T 4.00

Spellbound Jerseys
NM/M
Production 150-250
1 Greg Maddux G/150 12.00
2 Greg Maddux R/150 12.00
3 Greg Maddux E/150 12.00
4 Greg Maddux G/150 12.00
5 Roger Clemens R/150 15.00
6 Roger Clemens O/150 15.00
7 Roger Clemens G/150 15.00
8 Roger Clemens E/150 15.00
9 Roger Clemens R/150 15.00
14 Albert Pujols A/250 15.00
15 Albert Pujols L/250 15.00
16 Albert Pujols B/250 15.00
17 Albert Pujols E/250 15.00
18 Albert Pujols R/250 15.00
19 Albert Pujols T/250 15.00

Spellbound Jerseys Prime
NM/M
Production 10-25
5 Roger Clemens R/25 40.00
6 Roger Clemens O/25 40.00
7 Roger Clemens G/25 40.00
8 Roger Clemens E/25 40.00
9 Roger Clemens R/25 40.00

Team Zenith
NM/M
Common Player: Inserted 1:31
Gold: 1-2X
Production 100 Sets
1 Ichiro Suzuki 5.00
2 Jim Edmonds 2.00
3 Hideki Matsui 5.00
4 Alex Rodriguez 5.00
5 Derek Jeter 6.00
6 Alfonso Soriano 2.00
7 Jim Thome 2.00
8 Jorge Posada 1.50
9 Barry Zito 1.50
10 Curt Schilling 2.00
11 Willie Mays 4.00

Team Zenith Bats
NM/M
Production 15-25
3 Hideki Matsui/50 25.00
7 Jim Thome/150 6.00
8 Jorge Posada/25 8.00
11 Willie Mays/25 70.00

Team Zenith Jerseys
NM/M
Production 15-300
3 Hideki Matsui/165 20.00
7 Jim Thome/175 6.00
8 Jorge Posada/300 6.00
9 Barry Zito/150 4.00
10 Curt Schilling/150 6.00
11 Willie Mays/175 30.00

Team Zenith Jerseys Prime
NM/M
Production 25 Sets
3 Jim Edmonds/25 15.00
6 Alfonso Soriano/25 15.00
7 Jim Thome/25 20.00
8 Jorge Posada/25 15.00
9 Barry Zito/25 15.00
10 Curt Schilling/25 20.00

Z-Graphs

NICK JOHNSON

NM/M
Production 1-250
1 Danny Haren/250 10.00
2 Dallas McPherson/250 12.00
5 Jeremy Bonderman/200 15.00
7 Craig Wilson/250 8.00
8 Adam LaRoche/250 12.00
9 Nick Johnson/250 10.00
11 Dontrelle Willis/25 83.00
17 Morgan Ensberg/250 10.00
19 B.J. Upton/50 20.00
21 Brian Roberts/250 15.00
22 Omar Vizquel/100 20.00
   Shannon Stewart/100 10.00
24 Angel Berroa/250 10.00
26 Brandon Webb/100 10.00
29 Magglio Ordonez/100 12.00
30 Cal Ripken Jr./100 90.00
31 Johnny Estrada/50 10.00
32 Austin Kearns/100 10.00
33 Nolan Ryan/34 80.00
34 Orlando Cabrera/100 10.00
35 Roy Oswalt/100 15.00
36 Roy Halladay/50 20.00
38 Bobby Crosby/100 20.00
39 Jack Wilson/100 10.00
40 Jacque Jones/250 12.00
41 Eric Byrnes/250 8.00
52 Tony Gwynn/25 40.00
   Paul Molitor/25 30.00
55 Ryne Sandberg/25 50.00
57 Casey Kotchman/100 12.00
60 Paul Konerko/100 10.00
62 David Wright/100 60.00
63 Milton Bradley/100 10.00
68 Rich Harden/250 15.00
69 Travis Hafner/250 10.00
   Victor Martinez/25 20.00
70 Vernon Wells/25 20.00
72 Francisco Rodriguez/100 10.00
73 Mark Prior/25 40.00
75 Sean Casey/25 15.00
77 Carlos Zambrano/50 20.00
80 Livan Hernandez/100 12.00
84 Mark Buehrle/100 15.00
85 Keith Foulke/100 10.00
86 Edgar Renteria/50 15.00
88 Derek Lee/100 25.00
89 Joe Nathan/100 10.00
90 Michael Young/50 15.00
91 Dale Murphy/100 20.00
93 Francisco Cordero/100 8.00
94 Jake Peavy/100 20.00
95 Aubrey Huff/100 15.00
96 Ben Sheets/50 20.00
97 Carlos Lee/25 15.00
98 Miguel Cabrera/25 40.00
99 Mark Teixeira/25 40.00

Z-Bats
NM/M
Common Player: 4.00
3 Rickey Henderson 8.00
4 Andy Pettitte 8.00
7 Craig Wilson 4.00
9 Nick Johnson 4.00
10 Bernie Williams 6.00
11 Dontrelle Willis 6.00
12 Kenny Lofton 6.00
13 Tom Glavine 4.00
14 Kazuo Matsui/SP 6.00
15 Morgan Ensberg/SP 6.00
16 Mike Piazza 8.00
17 Trot Nixon/SP 8.00
18 Ryan Klesko/SP 6.00
19 B.J. Upton 4.00
22 Omar Vizquel 4.00
23 Shannon Stewart 4.00
24 Preston Wilson 4.00
26 Angel Berroa 4.00
27 Brandon Webb 4.00
28 Rafael Palmeiro 6.00
29 Mike Sweeney 4.00
30 Magglio Ordonez 4.00
30 Cal Ripken Jr. 25.00
31 Johnny Estrada 4.00
32 Austin Kearns 4.00
34 Nolan Ryan 20.00
34 Orlando Cabrera 4.00
35 Roy Oswalt 4.00
36 Roy Halladay 6.00
37 Lyle Overbay 4.00
39 Jack Wilson 4.00
40 Jacque Jones 4.00
44 Tony Gwynn 8.00
45 Mike Cameron 4.00
46 Geoff Jenkins 4.00
47 Bo Jackson 8.00
48 Luis Gonzalez 4.00
50 Craig Biggio 6.00
51 Josh Beckett 4.00
52 Paul Molitor 6.00
55 Ryne Sandberg 10.00
56 Jeff Bagwell 6.00
57 Casey Kotchman 4.00
58 Chipper Jones 6.00
60 Paul Konerko 6.00
61 Kevin Mench 4.00
62 David Wright 10.00
64 Andruw Jones 6.00
65 Garret Anderson 4.00
66 Jorge Posada 4.00
68 Travis Hafner 4.00
69 Victor Martinez 4.00
70 Vernon Wells 4.00
71 A.J. Burnett 4.00
72 Mark Prior 4.00
73 Mike Lowell 4.00
76 Brad Wilkerson 4.00
79 Moises Alou 4.00
81 Hank Blalock 4.00
82 J.D. Drew 4.00
83 Reggie Jackson/SP 8.00
84 Mark Buehrle/SP 6.00
87 Adam Dunn 6.00
88 Derek Lee 6.00
90 Michael Young 4.00
91 Dale Murphy 6.00
92 Aramis Ramirez 4.00
95 Aubrey Huff 4.00
96 Ben Sheets 4.00
97 Carlos Lee 4.00
98 Miguel Cabrera 8.00
99 Mark Teixeira 8.00
100 Albert Pujols 15.00

Z-Batgraphs
NM/M
Production 1-100
7 Craig Wilson/100 12.00
9 Nick Johnson/100 15.00
11 Dontrelle Willis/25 40.00
24 Angel Berroa/100 8.00
29 Magglio Ordonez/100 10.00
39 Jack Wilson/100 15.00
44 Tony Gwynn/25 50.00
52 Paul Molitor/25 30.00
55 Ryne Sandberg/25 65.00
57 Casey Kotchman/100 20.00
59 Chone Figgins/50 15.00
69 Victor Martinez/25 25.00
73 Mark Prior/25 40.00
90 Michael Young/100 15.00
91 Dale Murphy/100 20.00
97 Carlos Lee/50 20.00
99 Mark Teixeira/25 40.00

Z-Jerseys
NM/M
Common Player: 4.00
1 Danny Haren 6.00
2 Rickey Henderson 8.00
4 Andy Pettitte 4.00
5 Jeremy Bonderman 4.00
6 Pat Burrell 4.00
7 Craig Wilson 4.00
10 Bernie Williams 4.00
11 Dontrelle Willis 6.00
13 Tom Glavine 6.00
14 Kazuo Matsui 4.00
16 Mike Piazza 8.00
17 Trot Nixon 4.00
18 Ryan Klesko 4.00
19 B.J. Upton 4.00
21 Brian Roberts 4.00
22 Omar Vizquel 4.00
23 Shannon Stewart 4.00
25 Preston Wilson 4.00
25 Garrett Atkins 4.00
27 Rafael Palmeiro 6.00
28 Mike Sweeney 4.00
29 Magglio Ordonez 4.00
30 Cal Ripken Jr. 25.00
32 Austin Kearns 4.00
33 Nolan Ryan 20.00
34 Orlando Cabrera 4.00
35 Roy Oswalt 4.00
36 Roy Halladay 6.00
37 Lyle Overbay 4.00
39 Jack Wilson 4.00
40 Jacque Jones 4.00
41 Eric Byrnes 4.00
42 Barry Zito 4.00
43 C.C. Sabathia 8.00
44 Tony Gwynn 8.00
45 Mike Cameron 4.00
47 Geoff Jenkins 4.00
48 Bo Jackson 8.00
48 Luis Gonzalez 4.00
49 Johnny Damon 6.00
50 Craig Biggio 6.00
51 Josh Beckett 4.00
52 Paul Molitor 8.00
53 Kerry Wood 4.00
54 Lew Ford 4.00
55 Ryne Sandberg 10.00
56 Jeff Bagwell 6.00
57 Casey Kotchman 4.00
58 Chipper Jones 4.00
59 Chone Figgins 4.00
60 Paul Konerko 4.00
61 Kevin Mench 4.00
62 David Wright 10.00
64 Andruw Jones 6.00
65 Garret Anderson 4.00
66 Jorge Posada 4.00
68 Travis Hafner 4.00
69 Victor Martinez 4.00
70 Vernon Wells 4.00
71 A.J. Burnett 4.00
72 Francisco Rodriguez 4.00
73 Mark Prior 6.00
74 Mike Lowell 4.00
75 Sean Casey 4.00
77 Carlos Zambrano 4.00
78 Brad Radke 4.00
79 Moises Alou 4.00
80 Livan Hernandez 4.00
81 Hank Blalock 4.00
82 J.D. Drew 4.00
83 Reggie Jackson 8.00
84 Mark Buehrle 6.00
86 Edgar Renteria 4.00
87 Adam Dunn 6.00
88 Derek Lee 6.00
90 Michael Young 4.00
91 Dale Murphy 6.00
92 Aramis Ramirez 4.00
95 Aubrey Huff 4.00
96 Ben Sheets 4.00
97 Carlos Lee 4.00
98 Miguel Cabrera 8.00
99 Mark Teixeira 8.00
100 Albert Pujols 15.00

Z-Jerseygraphs
NM/M
Production 1-100
5 Jeremy Bonderman/100 20.00
7 Craig Wilson/100 10.00
11 Dontrelle Willis/25 35.00
15 Morgan Ensberg/25 20.00
17 Trot Nixon/25 25.00
19 B.J. Upton/50 25.00
21 Brian Roberts/100 25.00
22 Shannon Stewart/100 15.00
31 Johnny Estrada/100 10.00
35 Roy Oswalt/20 25.00
36 Roy Halladay/25 25.00
37 Lyle Overbay/25 15.00
38 Bobby Crosby/25 25.00
40 Jacque Jones/100 15.00
44 Tony Gwynn/25 50.00
52 Paul Molitor/25 35.00
55 Ryne Sandberg/25 65.00
57 Casey Kotchman/100 20.00
59 Chone Figgins/50 20.00
60 Paul Konerko/25 35.00
68 Travis Hafner/25 20.00
69 Victor Martinez/25 25.00
70 Vernon Wells/25 20.00
72 Francisco Rodriguez/100 25.00
73 Mark Prior/25 50.00
75 Sean Casey/25 20.00
80 Livan Hernandez/25 15.00
84 Mark Buehrle/100 25.00
88 Derek Lee/100 30.00
90 Michael Young/100 25.00
91 Dale Murphy/100 25.00
93 Francisco Cordero/100 12.00
96 Ben Sheets/25 20.00
99 Mark Teixeira/25 50.00

Z-Jerseys Prime
NM/M
Production 1-150
3 Rickey Henderson/150 15.00
4 Andy Pettitte/100 15.00
5 Jeremy Bonderman/150 8.00
6 Pat Burrell/150 8.00
7 Craig Wilson/150 8.00
10 Bernie Williams/50 10.00
11 Dontrelle Willis/150 10.00
14 Kazuo Matsui/150 8.00
17 Trot Nixon/25 12.00
18 Ryan Klesko/150 8.00

ABBREVIATIONS
SP - Short Print

19	B.J. Upton/50	10.00
20	Brian Roberts/50	10.00
22	Shannon Stewart/150	8.00
23	Preston Wilson/150	8.00
25	Garrett Atkins/150	8.00
27	Rafael Palmeiro/150	10.00
28	Mike Sweeney/150	8.00
30	Cal Ripken Jr./25	50.00
31	Johnny Estrada/150	8.00
32	Austin Kearns/150	8.00
33	Nolan Ryan/100	30.00
35	Roy Oswalt/100	10.00
36	Roy Halladay/100	10.00
37	Lyle Overbay/100	8.00
40	Jacque Jones/100	8.00
41	Eric Byrnes/50	8.00
42	Barry Zito/150	10.00
43	C.C. Sabathia/150	8.00
44	Tony Gwynn/150	15.00
45	Mike Cameron/100	8.00
46	Geoff Jenkins/50	8.00
47	Bo Jackson/100	20.00
48	Luis Gonzalez/150	8.00
49	Johnny Damon/25	20.00
51	Josh Beckett/50	8.00
52	Paul Molitor/70	15.00
54	Lew Ford/150	8.00
55	Ryne Sandberg/50	25.00
56	Jeff Bagwell/150	12.00
57	Casey Kotchman/50	10.00
58	Chipper Jones/150	10.00
60	Paul Konerko/50	10.00
61	Kevin Mench/150	10.00
64	Andruw Jones/150	12.00
65	Garret Anderson/25	15.00
66	Jorge Posada/50	12.00
68	Travis Hafner/100	8.00
69	Victor Martinez/25	12.00
70	Vernon Wells/150	10.00
71	A.J. Burnett/150	10.00
72	Francisco Rodriguez/100	8.00
73	Mark Prior/50	15.00
74	Mike Lowell/150	8.00
75	Sean Casey/150	8.00
77	Carlos Zambrano/100	10.00
78	Brad Radke/150	8.00
80	Livan Hernandez/50	10.00
81	Hank Blalock/100	10.00
83	Reggie Jackson/150	15.00
84	Mark Buehrle/50	12.00
87	Adam Dunn/150	10.00
88	Derrek Lee/25	15.00
90	Michael Young/50	10.00
91	Dale Murphy/50	20.00
92	Aramis Ramirez/100	10.00
93	Francisco Cordero/50	10.00
95	Aubrey Huff/150	8.00
96	Ben Sheets/150	10.00
98	Miguel Cabrera/150	15.00
99	Mark Teixeira/100	10.00

Z-Jerseygraphs Prime

NM/M
Production 1-25

5	Jeremy Bonderman/25	35.00
7	Craig Wilson/25	35.00
11	Dontrelle Willis/25	50.00
17	Trot Nixon/25	40.00
19	B.J. Upton/25	50.00
20	Brian Roberts/25	40.00
22	Shannon Stewart/25	25.00
24	Angel Berroa/25	20.00
31	Johnny Estrada/25	20.00
32	Austin Kearns/25	20.00
35	Roy Oswalt/25	35.00
36	Roy Halladay/25	45.00
40	Jacque Jones/25	25.00
41	Eric Byrnes/25	20.00
44	Tony Gwynn/25	65.00
52	Paul Molitor/25	50.00
55	Ryne Sandberg/25	80.00
57	Casey Kotchman/25	30.00
60	Paul Konerko/25	30.00
68	Travis Hafner/25	35.00
69	Victor Martinez/25	30.00
70	Vernon Wells/25	30.00
72	Francisco Rodriguez/25	40.00
73	Mark Prior/25	60.00
75	Sean Casey/25	30.00
77	Carlos Zambrano/25	30.00
80	Livan Hernandez/25	25.00
84	Mark Buehrle/25	30.00
88	Derrek Lee/25	50.00
90	Michael Young/25	30.00
91	Dale Murphy/25	40.00
93	Francisco Cordero/25	20.00
95	Aubrey Huff/25	25.00
96	Ben Sheets/25	35.00
98	Miguel Cabrera/25	40.00
99	Mark Teixeira/25	60.00

Z-Combos

NM/M
Production 1-150
Cards are bat/jsy unless noted.

3	Rickey Henderson/100	12.00
7	Craig Wilson/150	6.00
10	Bernie Williams/150	8.00
11	Dontrelle Willis/25	8.00
14	Kazuo Matsui/50	8.00

19	B.J. Upton/25	10.00
24	Angel Berroa/Bat-Pants/100	6.00
26	Brandon Webb/Bat-Pants/100	6.00
30	Cal Ripken Jr./100	30.00
33	Nolan Ryan/50	40.00
44	Tony Gwynn/100	12.00
47	Bo Jackson/100	10.00
50	Craig Biggio/50	10.00
52	Paul Molitor/100	12.00
53	Kerry Wood/25	8.00
54	Lew Ford/25	8.00
55	Ryne Sandberg/100	20.00
56	Jeff Bagwell/50	10.00
57	Casey Kotchman/50	8.00
58	Chipper Jones/100	10.00
59	Chone Figgins/100	6.00
61	Kevin Mench/100	6.00
64	Andruw Jones/100	10.00
69	Victor Martinez/100	8.00
71	A.J. Burnett/100	6.00
73	Mark Prior/100	10.00
81	Hank Blalock/100	8.00
87	Adam Dunn/25	10.00
88	Derrek Lee/25	12.00
90	Michael Young/100	6.00
91	Dale Murphy/100	10.00
99	Mark Teixeira/Bat-Hat/100	12.00

Z-Combos Prime

NM/M
Production 1-25
All are bat/patch.

3	Rickey Henderson/25	25.00
7	Craig Wilson/25	10.00
10	Bernie Williams/25	15.00
11	Dontrelle Willis/25	15.00
14	Kazuo Matsui/25	10.00
19	B.J. Upton/25	15.00
27	Rafael Palmeiro/25	15.00
30	Cal Ripken Jr./25	65.00
33	Nolan Ryan/25	50.00
44	Tony Gwynn/25	25.00
47	Bo Jackson/25	25.00
55	Ryne Sandberg/25	35.00
56	Jeff Bagwell/25	15.00
57	Casey Kotchman/25	15.00
58	Chipper Jones/25	15.00
61	Kevin Mench/25	10.00
64	Andruw Jones/25	10.00
65	Garret Anderson/25	15.00
69	Victor Martinez/25	10.00
71	A.J. Burnett/25	10.00
73	Mark Prior/25	15.00
74	Mike Lowell/25	15.00
81	Hank Blalock/25	15.00
87	Adam Dunn/25	15.00
88	Derrek Lee/25	20.00
90	Michael Young/25	20.00
91	Dale Murphy/25	20.00
96	Ben Sheets/25	15.00
99	Mark Teixeira/25	25.00

Z-Team

NM/M
Common Player:
Inserted 1:11
Gold: 1-2X
Production 100 Sets

1	Albert Pujols	5.00
2	Carlos Beltran	1.50
3	Randy Johnson	2.00
4	Miguel Tejada	1.50
5	Ichiro Suzuki	4.00
6	Eric Gagne	1.00
7	Adrian Beltre	1.00
8	Alfonso Soriano	1.50
9	Jim Edmonds	1.50
10	David Ortiz	2.00
11	Curt Schilling	2.00
12	Mariano Rivera	1.50
13	Derek Jeter	5.00
14	Ivan Rodriguez	1.50
15	Johnny Damon	1.50
16	Mark Prior	1.50
17	Vernon Wells	1.00
18	Chipper Jones	2.00
19	Torii Hunter	1.00
20	Tim Hudson	1.50
21	Lance Berkman	1.00
22	Troy Glaus	2.50
23	Mike Piazza	2.50
24	Mark Mulder	1.00
25	Ken Griffey Jr.	3.00

1986 Dorman's Cheese

Found in specially-marked packages of Dorman's American Cheese Singles, this set consists of 10 two-card panels of baseball superstars. Labeled

"Super Star Limited Edition," the panels measure 2" x 1-1/2" and have a perforation line in the center. Fronts have a color photo along with the Dorman's logo and the player's name, team and position. Due to a lack of MLB licensing, all team insignias have been airbrushed from the players' caps. Backs contain brief player statistics. The unnumbered panels and cards are listed here alphabetically by the player on the left.

		NM/M
Complete Panel Set (10):		5.00
Complete Singles Set (20):		4.00
Common Panel:		.50
Common Player:		.20
	Panel 1	1.00
(1)	George Brett	.75
(2)	Jack Morris	.20
	Panel 2	1.50
(3)	Gary Carter	.40
(4)	Cal Ripken Jr.	1.00
	Panel 3	.65
(5)	Dwight Gooden	.20
(6)	Kent Hrbek	.20
	Panel 4	1.00
(7)	Rickey Henderson	.40
(8)	Mike Schmidt	.75
	Panel 5	.75
(9)	Keith Hernandez	.20
(10)	Dale Murphy	.25
	Panel 6	1.00
(11)	Reggie Jackson	.60
(12)	Eddie Murray	.40
	Panel 7	1.25
(13)	Don Mattingly	.75
(14)	Ryne Sandberg	.60
	Panel 8	1.00
(15)	Willie McGee	.20
(16)	Robin Yount	.40
	Panel 9	1.00
(17)	Rick Sutcliffe (Sutcliffe)	.20
(18)	Wade Boggs	.60
	Panel 10	1.00
(19)	Dave Winfield	.40
(20)	Jim Rice	.25

1981 Drake's

Producing its first baseball card set since 1950, Drake Bakeries, in conjunction with Topps, issued a 33-card set entitled "Big Hitters." The cards, in standard 2-1/2" x 3-1/2" size, feature 19 American League and 14 National League sluggers. Full-color action photos, containing a facsimile autograph, are positioned in red frames for A.L. players and blue frames for N.L. hitters. The player's name, team, position, and Drake's logo are also on front. Backs, which are similar to the regular 1981 Topps issue, contain the card number, statistical and biographical information, and the Drake's logo.

		NM/M
Complete Set (33):		6.00
Common Player:		.25
1	Carl Yastrzemski	1.50
2	Rod Carew	1.00
3	Pete Rose	3.00
4	Dave Parker	.25
5	George Brett	2.00
6	Eddie Murray	1.00
7	Mike Schmidt	2.00
8	Jim Rice	.50
9	Fred Lynn	.25
10	Reggie Jackson	1.50
11	Steve Garvey	.50
12	Ken Singleton	.25
13	Bill Buckner	.25
14	Dave Winfield	1.00
15	Jack Clark	.25
16	Cecil Cooper	.25
17	Bob Horner	.25
18	George Foster	.25
19	Dave Kingman	.25
20	Cesar Cedeno	.25
21	Joe Charboneau	.75
22	George Hendrick	.25
23	Gary Carter	1.00
24	Al Oliver	.25
25	Bruce Bochte	.25
26	Jerry Mumphrey	.25
27	Steve Kemp	.25
28	Bob Watson	.25
29	John Castino	.25
30	Tony Armas	.25
31	John Mayberry	.25
32	Carlton Fisk	1.00
33	Lee Mazzilli	.25

1982 Drake's

Drake Bakeries produced, in conjunction with Topps, a "2nd Annual Collectors' Edition" in 1982. Thirty-three standard-size cards (2-1/2" x 3-1/2") make up the set. Like the previous year, the set is entitled "Big Hitters" and is comprised of 19 American League players and 14 from the National League. Fronts have a mounted photo appearance and contain a facsimile autograph. The player's name, team, position, and the Drake's logo also are on front. Backs, other than being numbered 1-33 and containing a Drake's copyright line, are identical to the regular 1982 Topps.

		NM/M
Complete Set (33):		5.00
Common Player:		.25
1	Tony Armas	.25
2	Buddy Bell	.25
3	Johnny Bench	.50
4	George Brett	1.00
5	Bill Buckner	.25
6	Rod Carew	.50
7	Gary Carter	.50
8	Jack Clark	.25
9	Cecil Cooper	.25
10	Jose Cruz	.25
11	Dwight Evans	.25
12	Carlton Fisk	.50
13	George Foster	.25
14	Steve Garvey	.40
15	Kirk Gibson	.25
16	Mike Hargrove	.25
17	George Hendrick	.25
18	Bob Horner	.25
19	Reggie Jackson	.75
20	Terry Kennedy	.25
21	Dave Kingman	.25
22	Greg Luzinski	.25
23	Bill Madlock	.25
24	John Mayberry	.25
25	Eddie Murray	.50
26	Graig Nettles	.25
27	Jim Rice	.40
28	Pete Rose	2.00
29	Mike Schmidt	1.00
30	Ken Singleton	.25
31	Dave Winfield	.50
32	Butch Wynegar	.25
33	Richie Zisk	.25

1983 Drake's

Seventeen American League and 16 National League "Big Hitters" make up the 33-card "3rd Annual Collectors' Edition" set issued by Drake Bakeries in 1983. The Topps-

produced cards measure 2-1/2" x 3-1/2". Fronts are somewhat similar in design to the previous year's set. Backs are identical to the 1983 Topps regular issue except for being numbered 1-33 and containing a Drake's logo and copyright line.

		NM/M
Complete Set (33)		5.00
Common Player:		.25
1	Don Baylor	.25
2	Bill Buckner	.25
3	Rod Carew	.60
4	Gary Carter	.60
5	Jack Clark	.25
6	Cecil Cooper	.25
7	Dwight Evans	.25
8	George Foster	.25
9	Pedro Guerrero	.25
10	George Hendrick	.25
11	Bob Horner	.25
12	Reggie Jackson	.75
13	Steve Kemp	.25
14	Dave Kingman	.25
15	Bill Madlock	.25
16	Gary Matthews	.25
17	Hal McRae	.25
18	Dale Murphy	.60
19	Eddie Murray	.60
20	Ben Oglivie	.25
21	Al Oliver	.25
22	Jim Rice	.40
23	Cal Ripken, Jr.	3.00
24	Pete Rose	2.00
25	Mike Schmidt	1.50
26	Ken Singleton	.25
27	Gorman Thomas	.25
28	Jason Thompson	.25
29	Mookie Wilson	.25
30	Willie Wilson	.25
31	Dave Winfield	.60
32	Carl Yastrzemski	.75
33	Robin Yount	.60

1984 Drake's

For the fourth year in a row, Drake Bakeries issued a 33-card "Big Hitters" set. The 1984 edition, produced again by Topps, includes 17 National League players and 16 from the American League. As in all previous years, card fronts feature the player in a batting pose. Backs are identical to the 1984 Topps regular issue except for being numbered 1-33 and carrying the Drake's logo and copyright line. The cards are the standard 2-1/2" x 3-1/2".

		NM/M
Complete Set (33):		4.00
Common Player:		.25
1	Don Baylor	.25
2	Wade Boggs	.75
3	George Brett	1.00
4	Bill Buckner	.25
5	Rod Carew	.50
6	Gary Carter	.50
7	Ron Cey	.25

1985 Drake's

The "5th Annual Collectors' Edition" set produced by Topps for Drake Bakeries consists of 33 "Big Hitters" and 11 "Super Pitchers." The new "Super Pitchers" feature increased the set's size from the usual 33 cards to 44. The 2-1/2" x 3-1/2" cards show the player in a game-action photo. Backs differ from the regular 1985 Topps issue only in that they are numbered 1-44 and carry the Drake's logo.

		NM/M
Complete Set (44):		3.00
Common Player:		.15
1	Tony Armas	.15
2	Harold Baines	.15
3	Don Baylor	.15
4	George Brett	.75
5	Gary Carter	.40
6	Ron Cey	.15
7	Jose Cruz	.15
8	Alvin Davis	.15
9	Chili Davis	.15
10	Dwight Evans	.15
11	Steve Garvey	.25
12	Kirk Gibson	.15
13	Pedro Guerrero	.15
14	Tony Gwynn	.50
15	Keith Hernandez	.15
16	Kent Hrbek	.15
17	Reggie Jackson	.50
18	Gary Matthews	.15
19	Don Mattingly	.75
20	Dale Murphy	.40
21	Eddie Murray	.40
22	Dave Parker	.15
23	Lance Parrish	.15
24	Tim Raines	.15
25	Jim Rice	.25
26	Cal Ripken, Jr.	1.50
27	Juan Samuel	.15
28	Ryne Sandberg	.50
29	Mike Schmidt	.50
30	Darryl Strawberry	.15
31	Alan Trammell	.15
32	Dave Winfield	.40
33	Robin Yount	.40
34	Mike Boddicker	.15
35	Steve Carlton	.15
36	Dwight Gooden	.15
37	Willie Hernandez	.15
38	Mark Langston	.15
39	Dan Quisenberry	.15
40	Dave Righetti	.15
41	Tom Seaver	.40
42	Bob Stanley	.15
43	Rick Sutcliffe	.15
44	Bruce Sutter	.30

1986 Drake's

For the sixth consecutive year, Drake Bakeries issued a baseball card set. The 1986 set

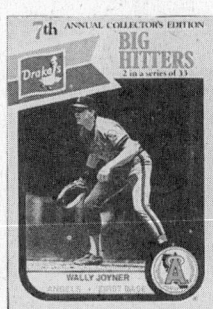

was the first in that sequence not produced by Topps. Cards were available only by buying the snack products on whose boxes the cards were printed. Cards, measuring 2-1/2" x 3-1/2", were issued in either two-, three-, or four-card panels. Fourteen panels, consisting of 37 different players, comprise the set. The players who make up the set are tabbed as either "Big Hitters" or "Super Pitchers." Logos of various Drake's products can be found on the panel backs. The value of the set is higher when collected in either panel or complete box form.

	NM/M
Complete Panel Set (14):	20.00
Complete Singles Set (37):	12.00
Common Panel:	.25
Common Player:	.25
Panel (1)	.75
1 Gary Carter	.40
2 Dwight Evans	.25
Panel (2)	1.00
3 Reggie Jackson	.50
4 Dave Parker	.25
Panel (3)	1.50
5 Rickey Henderson	.40
6 Pedro Guerrero	.25
Panel (4)	3.00
7 Don Mattingly	.75
8 Mike Marshall	.25
9 Keith Moreland	.25
Panel (5)	4.00
10 Keith Hernandez	.25
11 Cal Ripken Jr.	2.50
Panel (6)	2.50
12 Dale Murphy	.35
13 Jim Rice	.35
Panel (7)	3.00
14 George Brett	.75
15 Tim Raines	.25
Panel (8)	1.50
16 Darryl Strawberry	.25
17 Bill Buckner	.25
Panel (9)	3.00
18 Dave Winfield	.40
19 Ryne Sandberg	.25
20 Steve Balboni	.25
21 Tommy Herr	.25
Panel (10)	3.00
22 Pete Rose	1.50
23 Willie McGee	.25
24 Harold Baines	.25
25 Eddie Murray	.40
Panel (11)	3.00
26 Mike Schmidt	.75
27 Wade Boggs	.50
28 Kirk Gibson	.25
Panel (12)	1.50
29 Bret Saberhagen	.25
30 John Tudor	.25
31 Orel Hershiser	.25
Panel (13)	4.00
32 Ron Guidry	.25
33 Nolan Ryan	2.50
34 Dave Steib	.25
Panel (14)	1.50
35 Dwight Gooden	.25
36 Fernando Valenzuela	.25
37 Tom Browning	.25

1987 Drake's

For the seventh consecutive season, Drake Bakeries produced a baseball card set. The 2-1/2" x 3-1/2" cards were printed in either two-, three-, or four-card panels on boxes of various snack products distributed in the eastern U.S. The set is comprised of 33 cards, with 25 players branded as "Big Hitters" and eight as "Super Pitchers." Fronts carry a game-action photo and the Drake's logo sur-

rounded by a brown and yellow border. Backs have the player's complete major league record.

	NM/M
Complete Panel Set (12):	20.00
Complete Singles Set (33):	12.00
Common Panel:	1.50
Common Single Player:	.25
Panel (1)	1.00
1 Darryl Strawberry	.25
2 Wally Joyner	.25
Panel (2)	1.00
3 Von Hayes	.25
4 Jose Canseco	.40
Panel (3)	5.00
5 Dave Winfield	.60
6 Cal Ripken Jr.	2.50
7 Keith Moreland	.25
Panel (4)	2.50
8 Don Mattingly	1.00
9 Willie McGee	.25
Panel (5)	2.00
10 Keith Hernandez	.25
11 Tony Gwynn	.75
Panel (6)	3.00
12 Rickey Henderson	.60
13 Dale Murphy	.35
14 George Brett	.35
15 Jim Rice	.35
Panel (7)	5.00
16 Wade Boggs	.75
17 Kevin Bass	.25
18 Dave Parker	.25
19 Kirby Puckett	.75
Panel (8)	2.00
20 Gary Carter	.60
21 Ryne Sandberg	.75
22 Harold Baines	.25
Panel (9)	3.00
23 Mike Schmidt	1.00
24 Eddie Murray	.60
25 Steve Sax	.25
Panel (10)	1.00
26 Dwight Gooden	.25
27 Jack Morris	.25
28 Ron Darling	.25
29 Fernando Valenzuela	.25
30 John Tudor	.25
Panel (12)	7.50
31 Roger Clemens	1.00
32 Nolan Ryan	2.50
33 Mike Scott	.25

1988 Drake's

The 8th annual edition of this set includes 33 glossy full-color cards printed on cut-out panels of two, three of four cards on Drake's dessert snack boxes. Card fronts have white borders with a large red and blue "Super Pitchers" (six cards) or "Big Hitters" (27 cards) caption upper-left, beside the "8th Annual Collector's Edition" label. Backs are printed in black and include the card number, personal data, batting/pitching record and sponsor logos.

	NM/M
Complete Panel Set (12):	20.00
Complete Singles Set (33):	10.00
Common Panel:	1.50
Common Player:	.25
Panel (1)	2.00
1 Don Mattingly	1.00
2 Tim Raines	.25
Panel (2)	1.00

---

3 Darryl Strawberry	.25
4 Wade Boggs	.75
Panel (3)	6.00
5 Keith Hernandez	.25
6 Mark McGwire	1.50
Panel (4)	3.00
7 Rickey Henderson	.60
8 Mike Schmidt	1.00
9 Dwight Evans	.25
Panel (5)	2.00
10 Gary Carter	.60
11 Paul Molitor	.60
Panel (6)	3.50
12 Dave Winfield	.60
13 Alan Trammell	.25
14 Tony Gwynn	.75
Panel (7)	2.50
15 Dale Murphy	.35
16 Andre Dawson	.35
17 Von Hayes	.25
18 Willie Randolph	.25
Panel (8)	3.50
19 Kirby Puckett	.75
20 Juan Samuel	.25
21 Eddie Murray	.60
Panel (9)	1.00
22 George Bell	.25
23 Larry Sheets	.25
24 Eric Davis	.25
Panel (10)	5.00
25 Cal Ripken Jr.	2.00
26 Pedro Guerrero	.25
27 Will Clark	.25
Panel (11)	1.00
28 Dwight Gooden	.25
29 Frank Viola	.25
Panel (12)	3.00
30 Roger Clemens	1.00
31 Rick Sutcliffe	.25
32 Jack Morris	.25
33 John Tudor	.25

1989 Dubuque Braves

Given away at Sunday home games to correspond with player appearances at a stadium autograph booth, these 2-3/8" x 3-1/2" cards were sponsored by the Braves hot dog concessionaire, Dubuque Meats. Cards have player photos centered within a dark blue border. A Braves cap is at upper-left, the hot dog company's logo at lower-left. The player's name, team and position are in white. Backs, printed in black on white, have the Braves logo, a few personal facts and figures and previous year/career stats. Because only 15,000 of each card were distributed over the course of the season, compilation of complete sets is extremely challenging. The checklist here is arranged in alphabetical order.

	NM/M
Complete Set (33):	40.00
Common Player:	.50
(1) Paul Assenmacher	.50
(2) Jim Acker	.50
(3) Jose Alvarez	.50
(4) Bruce Benedict	.50
(5) Geronimo Berroa/SP	8.00
(6) Jeff Blauser	.50
(7) Joe Boever	.50
(8) Marty Clary	.50
(9) Bruce dal Canton	.50
(10) Jody Davis	.50
(11) Mark Eichhorn	.50
(12) Ron Gant	1.50
(13) Tom Glavine	5.00
(14) Tommy Gregg	.50

---

(15) Dion James/SP	4.00
(16) Clarence Jones	.50
(17) Derek Lilliquist	.50
(18) Roy Majtyka	.50
(19) Oddibe McDowell	.50
(20) Dale Murphy	6.00
(21) Russ Nixon	.50
(22) Gerald Perry	.50
(23) John Russell	.50
(24) Lonnie Smith	.50
(25) Pete Smith	.50
(26) Zane Smith	.50
(27) John Smoltz	4.00
(28) Brian Snitker	.50
(29) Andres Thomas	.50
(30) Jeff Treadway	.50
(31) Jeff Wetherby	.50
(32) Ed Whited	.50
(33) Bobby Wine	.50

1990 Dubuque Braves

For a second season, the Braves' hot dog vendor, Dubuque Meats, sponsored this season-long promotion. Up to four different player cards were given out at Sunday home games, corresponding with player appearances at an autograph booth. Some player cards were distributed more than once, while others, such as Dale Murphy, who was traded, were only given out one day. Players were added to the set right up through the final Sunday home game of the season. Complete sets are extremely difficult to assemble. The player photo on these 2-3/8" x 3-1/2" cards have a white border. A red banner beneath the photo has the player's name, uniform number and position printed in black. Backs are printed in dark blue and feature full minor and major league stats. The checklist here is arranged alphabetically.

	NM/M
Complete Set (35):	25.00
Common Player:	.50
(1) Steve Avery	.50
(2) Jeff Blauser	.50
(3) Joe Boever	.50
(4) Francisco Cabrera	.50
(5) Pat Corrales	.50
(6) Bobby Cox	.50
(7) Nick Esasky	.50
(8) Ron Gant	1.50
(9) Tom Glavine	4.00
(10) Mark Grant	.50
(11) Tommy Gregg	.50
(12) Dwayne Henry	.50
(13) Alexis Infante	.50
(14) Clarence Jones	.50
(15) Dave Justice	4.50
(16) Jimmy Kremers	.50
(17) Charlie Leibrandt	.50
(18) Mark Lemke	.50
(19) Roy Majtyka	.50
(20) Leo Mazzone	.50
(21) Oddibe McDowell	.50
(22) Dale Murphy	5.00
(23) Phil Niekro	3.00
(24) Greg Olson	.50
(25) Jim Presley	.50
(26) Lonnie Smith	.50
(27) Pete Smith	.50
(28) John Smoltz	1.50
(29) Brian Snitker	.50
(30) Andres Thomas	.50
(31) Jeff Treadway	.50
(32) Ernie Whitt	.50
(33) Jimy Williams	.50
(34) Homer the Brave/ Mascot	.50
(35) Rally/Mascot	.50

ABBREVIATIONS

SP - Short Print

Team Photo Set

This three-panel team set was given away at an early-season game, commemorating the Braves 25th season in Atlanta. The sheet measures 11" x 28-1/2". The top panel is a team photo. The two lower panels contain 30 individual cards, 2-1/2" x 3-1/4", perforated to allow them to be separated. Backs are printed in red and blue. The perforated team set is much more common than the Dubuque cards given out a few at a time during Sunday home games. The checklist below is arranged according to uniform numbers which appear on the front of each card.

	NM/M
Complete Panel:	9.00
Common Player:	.25
1 Oddibe McDowell	.25
2 Russ Nixon	.25
3 Dale Murphy	3.00
4 Jeff Blauser	.25
8 Ron Gant	.50
10 Greg Olson	.25
12 Ernie Whitt	.25
14 Andres Thomas	.25
15 Jeff Treadway	.25
17 Tommy Gregg	.25
17 Nick Esasky	.25
18 Jim Presley	.25
19 Francisco Cabrera	.25
20 Mark Lemke	.25
23 Dave Justice	2.00
24 Derek Lilliquist	.25
25 Pete Smith	.25
27 Lonnie Smith	.25
30 John Smoltz	1.00
30 Mike Stanton	.25
36 Tony Castillo	.25
37 Joe Boever	.25
40 Charlie Kerfeld	.25
45 Charlie Leibrandt	.25
46 Dwayne Henry	.25
47 Tom Glavine	1.50
48 Marty Clary	.25
49 Rick Luecken	.25
58a Joe Hesketh	.25
58b Alexis Infante	.25

1991 Dubuque Braves

At each Sunday home game the Braves distributed some 15,000 of each of three to six player cards to kids under 14. The cards corresponded to appearances by those players at an autograph session. That method of distribution makes accumulation of complete sets very difficult. Sponsor of the set for

---

the third straight year was the stadium's hot dog concession-aire, Dubuque Meats. Their logo appears in the upper-left corner of the player photo. At lower-right on the 2-1/4" x 3-1/2" cards is a baseball diamond figure with the team and player name and the year of issue. There is a white outer border on the card, with the photo framed in white-pin-striped dark blue. Backs are printed in dark blue, with logos, complete stats, biographical information and the player's uniform number. Cards are checklisted here in alphabetical order.

	NM/M
Complete Set (41):	25.00
Common Player:	.50
(1) Steve Avery	.50
(2) Jim Beauchamp	.50
(3) Mike Bell	.50
(4) Rafael Belliard	.50
(5) Juan Berenguer	.50
(6) Jeff Blauser	.50
(7) Sid Bream	.50
(8) Francisco Cabrera	.50
(9) Jim Clancy	.50
(10) Pat Corrales	.50
(11) Bobby Cox	.50
(12) Nick Esasky	.50
(13) Marvin Freeman	.50
(14) Ron Gant	1.00
(15) Tom Glavine	3.00
(16) Mark Grant	.50
(17) Tommy Gregg	.50
(18) Mike Heath	.50
(19) Brian Hunter	.50
(20) Clarence Jones	.50
(21) David Justice	2.00
(22) Charlie Leibrandt	.50
(23) Mark Lemke	.50
(24) Leo Mazzone	.50
(25) Kent Mercker	.50
(26) Keith Mitchell	.50
(27) Otis Nixon	.50
(28) Greg Olson	.50
(29) Jeff Parrett	.50
(30) Terry Pendleton	.50
(31) Armando Reynoso	.50
(32) Deion Sanders	3.00
(33) Lonnie Smith	.50
(34) Pete Smith	.50
(35) John Smoltz	1.50
(36) Mike Stanton	.50
(37) Jeff Treadway	.50
(38) Jimy Williams	.50
(39) Ned Yost	.50
(40) Homer the Brave/ Mascot	.50
(41) Rally/Mascot	.50

Team Photo Set

This team photo/player card triptych was an early season give-away. Each of the three fold-out panels measures about 9-1/2" x 10-1/2". The 30 individual player cards have perforated edges for easy removal from the sheet. The 2-1/8" x 3-1/8" cards have a player portrait photo at center, with blue diamond designs at the corners. A red box below the photo has the player's name and uniform number. Blue Braves and Dubuque logos appear at the lower corners of the white border. Backs are printed in red and blue and include full stats and a facsimile autograph, plus a few biographical details. The team sheet cards are considered much more common than the other Braves baseball card promotional giveaways, especially in complete sets. Cards are checklisted here alphabetically.

	NM/M
Complete Panel:	15.00
Common Player:	.50
(1) Steve Avery	.50
(2) Rafael Belliard	.50
(3) Juan Berenguer	.50
(4) Jeff Blauser	.50
(5) Sid Bream	.50
(6) Francisco Cabrera	.50
(7) Bobby Cox	.50
(8) Nick Esasky	.50
(9) Marvin Freeman	.50
(10) Ron Gant	.75
(11) Tom Glavine	3.00
(12) Mark Grant	.50
(13) Tommy Gregg	.50
(14) Mike Heath	.50
(15) Danny Heep	.50
(16) David Justice	2.00
(17) Charlie Leibrandt	.50
(18) Mark Lemke	.50
(19) Kent Mercker	.50
(20) Otis Nixon	.50
(21) Greg Olson	.50
(22) Jeff Parrett	.50
(23) Terry Pendleton	.50
(24) Deion Sanders	2.00
(25) Doug Sisk	.50
(26) Lonnie Smith	.50
(27) Pete Smith	.50
(28) John Smoltz	1.50
(29) Mike Stanton	.50
(30) Jeff Treadway	.50

1992 Dunkin' Donuts Red Sox

The 1992 Boston Red Sox were the subject of a set of 30 cards, including the manager and coaches. Co-sponsored by Dunkin Donuts and WVIT-TV and released in May in Connecticut, the set was sold as an uncut, perforated sheet of 30 cards, measuring about 9-1/2" x 10-3/4". Individual perforated cards could be removed from the sheet; they measure 2-1/8" x 3-1/8". Fronts have a player photo framed in black on a white background. In the border beneath the photo are the player's name, position, uniform number and sponsors' logos. Backs have complete major and minor league stats. The cards are checklisted here by uniform number, which appears on the card front.

	NM/M
Complete Panel:	7.50
Common Player:	.25
2 Luis Rivera	.25
3 Jody Reed	.25
6 Tony Pena	.25
7 Rick Burleson	.25
11 Tim Naehring	.25
12 Ellis Burks	.25
16 Frank Viola	.25
17 Butch Hobson	.25
18 Carlos Quintana	.25
20 John Marzano	.25
21 Roger Clemens	6.00
23 Tom Brunansky	.25
25 Jack Clark	.25
26 Wade Boggs	3.00
27 Greg Harris	.25
29 Phil Plantier	.25
30 Matt Young	.25
32 Gary Allenson	.25
34 Don Zimmer	.25
35 Rich Gale	.25
37 Al Bumbry	.25
39 Mike Greenwell	.25
41 Jeff Reardon	.25
42 Mo Vaughn	.35
43 Kevin Morton	.25
44 Danny Darwin	.25
47 Mike Gardiner	.25
48 Tony Fossas	.25

50 Tom Bolton	.25
55 Joe Hesketh	.25

1993 Duracell Power Players

The Duracell battery company issued a 48-card set in 1993 that was presented in two 24-card series. The cards were available through the mail with proofs of purchase from selected Duracell products. Cards feature a Duracell logo at top, with a black and orange border surrounding a color photo of the player. The player's name is printed in yellow with team and position in white on top of a green background. Because the set was not licensed to use major league uniform logos, they were airbrushed off the photos. Backs have a player portrait photo, a facsimile autograph, recent stats and a few biographical and career details printed over a ballpark scene. Series I cards are number "X of 24;" Series II cards are so indicated beneath the card number.

	NM/M
Complete Set (48):	4.00
Common Player:	.10
Series 1	2.00
1 Roger Clemens	.60
2 Frank Thomas	.40
3 Andre Dawson	.25
4 Orel Hershiser	.10
5 Kirby Puckett	.50
6 Edgar Martinez	.25
7 Craig Biggio	.10
8 Terry Pendleton	.10
9 Mark McGwire	.75
10 Dave Stewart	.10
11 Ozzie Smith	.50
12 Doug Drabek	.10
13 Dwight Gooden	.25
14 Tony Gwynn	.50
15 Carlos Baerga	.10
16 Robin Yount	.40
17 Barry Bonds	1.00
18 Bip Roberts	.10
19 Don Mattingly	.60
20 Nolan Ryan	1.00
21 Tom Glavine	.25
22 Will Clark	.10
23 Cecil Fielder	.10
24 Dave Winfield	.40
Series 2	2.00
1 Cal Ripken, Jr.	1.00
2 Melido Perez	.10
3 John Kruk	.10
4 Charlie Hayes	.10
5 George Brett	.60
6 Ruben Sierra	.10
7 Deion Sanders	.15
8 Andy Van Slyke	.10
9 Fred McGriff	.10
10 Benito Santiago	.10
11 Charles Nagy	.10
12 Greg Maddux	.50
13 Ryne Sandberg	.50
14 Dennis Martinez	.10
15 Ken Griffey Jr.	.75
16 Jim Abbott	.10
17 Barry Larkin	.10
18 Gary Sheffield	.30
19 Jose Canseco	.25
20 Jack McDowell	.10
21 Darryl Strawberry	.10
22 Delino DeShields	.10
23 Dennis Eckersley	.40
24 Paul Molitor	.40

E

2003 Easton Gloves

A set of standard-format cards featuring members of

the Easton Advisory Staff was issued as a premium for the purchase of youth model baseball gloves. The cards were distributed in four-card cello packs. Fronts have black borders, game-action photos, a facsimile autograph, player identification and Easton logos. Backs have a smaller photo, personal data and recent stats.

	NM/M
Complete Set (12):	20.00
Common Player:	2.00
1 Bobby Abreu	2.00
2 Luis Castillo	2.00
3 Eric Chavez	2.00
4 Eric Gagne	2.00
5 Luis Gonzalez	2.00
6 Eddie Guardado	2.00
7 Jeff Kent	2.00
8 Javy Lopez	2.00
9 John Olerud	2.00
10 Vicente Padilla	2.00
11 Sammy Sosa	7.50
12 Mike Williams	2.00

2005 Easton Gloves

A set of standard-format cards featuring members of the Easton Advisory Staff was issued as a premium for the purchase of youth model baseball gloves. Card fronts have game-action photos, a facsimile autograph and player identification. Backs have a smaller photo, personal data and recent stats.

	NM/M
Complete Set (12):	8.00
Common Player:	1.00
1 Sammy Sosa	2.50
2 Orlando Cabrera	1.00
3 Eric Chavez	1.00
4 Luis Gonzalez	1.00
5 Jeff Kent	1.00
6 Javy Lopez	1.00
7 Aramis Ramirez	1.00
8 Edgar Renteria	1.00
9 Luis Castillo	1.00
10 Eric Gagne	1.00
11 Michael Barrett	1.00
12 Bobby Abreu	1.00

1990 Eclipse Stars of the Negro Leagues

OSCAR CHARLESTON

Better known in the field of comic books than baseball cards, Eclipse of California produced this set of cards honoring stars of the defunct Negro Leagues. The 2-1/2" x 3-1/2" cards have water color paintings (by Mark Chiarello) of the players on front. Well-written (by Jack Morelli) career summaries on back give

a real flavor for this brand of pro ball and its era. Copyright lines for all parties are at bottom back. The issue was sold only as a boxed set.

	NM/M
Complete Set (36):	16.00
Common Player:	.50
1 Header Card	.25
2a Josh Gibson (Wrong picture, "H" on cap.)	4.00
2b Josh Gibson (Correct picture, "G" on cap.)	4.00
3 Cannonball Redding	.50
4 Biz Mackey	2.00
5 Pop Lloyd	1.00
6 Bingo DeMoss	1.00
7 Willard Brown	2.00
8 John Donaldson	.50
9 Monte Irvin	1.50
10 Ben Taylor	2.00
11 Willie Wells	1.25
12 Dave Brown	.50
13 Leon Day	1.00
14 Ray Dandridge	1.00
15 Turkey Stearnes	1.00
16 Rube Foster	1.00
17 Oliver Marcelle	.50
18 Judy Johnson	1.00
19 Christobel Torrienti	2.00
20 Satchel Paige	4.00
21 Mule Suttles	.50
22 John Beckwith	.50
23 Martin Dihigo	1.00
24 Willie Foster	.50
25 Dick Lundy	.50
26 Buck Leonard	1.00
27 Smokey Joe Williams	1.00
28 Cool Papa Bell	1.00
29 Bullet Rogan	1.00
30 Newt Allen	.75
31 Bruce Petway	.50
32 Jose Mendez	2.00
33 Louis Santop	2.00
34 Jud Wilson	2.00
35 Sammy Hughes	.50
36a Oscar Charleston (Wrong picture, "G" on cap.)	1.00
36b Oscar Charleston (Correct picture, "H" on cap.)	1.00

1992 Eclipse Negro League BPA - Paul Lee

RAY DANDRIDGE Third Base

Four Negro League baseball cards were handed out to the first 50,000 fans attending Negro League Baseball Players Association night at Shea Stadium on June 2. Cards feature the artwork of Paul Lee on front. Backs have a career summary and biographical details, along with the Mets and Eclipse logos.

	NM/M
Complete Set (4):	4.00
Common Player:	1.50
1 Monte Irvin	1.50
2 "Buck" Leonard	1.00
3 Josh Gibson	3.00
4 Ray Dandridge	1.00

Negro League BPA - John Clapp

Sponsored by Kraft, and produced by Eclipse, 15,000 sets of these cards were made for distribution at The Negro League Baseball Players Association night, August 9 at Lackawanna County Stadium, home of the Scranton Wilkes-Barre Red Barons. The 2-1/2" x 3-1/2" cards have watercolor player pictures on front, by artist John Clapp. Backs have

MARTINEZ JACKSON Second Base

career summaries, sponsor and issuer logos and copyright information.

	NM/M
Complete Set (18):	6.00
Common Player:	.50
1 Leon Day	1.50
2 Clinton (Casey) Jones	.50
3 Lester Lockett	.50
4 Monte Irvin	2.00
5 Armando Vazquez	.50
6 Jimmie Crutchfield	.50
7 Ted Radcliffe	.50
8 Albert Haywood	.50
9 Artie Wilson	1.50
10 Sam Jethroe	1.25
11 Edsall Walker	.50
12 Bill Wright	.50
13 Jim Cohen	.50
14 Andy Porter	.50
15 Tommy Sampson	.50
16 Buck Leonard	1.50
17 Josh Gibson	2.00
18 Martinez Jackson	1.50

1990 Elite Senior League

EARL WEAVER

This 126-card set features the players of the first Senior League season. Cards are printed on high quality stock with full-color photos. The card backs feature statistics. Earl Weaver and Mike Easler cards were distributed as promo cards. Original retail price was about $12 per boxed set, the only manner of distribution.

	NM/M
Complete Set (126):	4.00
Common Player:	.05
1 Curt Flood	.15
2 Bob Tolan	.05
3 Dick Bosman	.05
4 Ivan DeJesus	.05
5 Dock Ellis	.05
6 Roy Howell	.05
7 Lamar Johnson	.05
8 Steve Kemp	.05
9 Ken Landreaux	.05
10 Randy Lerch	.05
11 Jon Matlack	.05
12 Gary Rajsich	.05
13 Lenny Randle	.05
14 Elias Sosa	.05
15 Ozzie Virgil	.05
16 Milt Wilcox	.05
17 Steve Henderson	.05
18 Ray Burris	.05
19 Mike Easler	.05
20 Juan Eichelberger	.05
21 Rollie Fingers	.50
22 Toby Harrah	.05
23 Randy Johnson	.05
24 Dave Kingman	.15
25 Lee Lacy	.05
26 Tito Landrum	.05
27 Paul Mirabella	.05
28 Mickey Rivers	.10
29 Rodney Scott	.05
30 Tim Stoddard	.05
31 Ron Washington	.05

32 Jerry White	.05
33 Dick Williams	.05
34 Clete Boyer	.10
35 Steve Dillard	.05
36 Garth Iorg	.05
37 Bruce Kison	.05
38 Wayne Krenchicki	.05
39 Ron LeFlore	.10
40 Tippy Martinez	.05
41 Omar Moreno	.05
42 Jim Morrison	.05
43 Graig Nettles	.15
44 Jim Nettles	.05
45 Wayne Nordhagen	.05
46 Al Oliver	.15
47 Jerry Royster	.05
48 Sammy Stewart	.05
49 Randy Bass	.05
50 Vida Blue	.10
51 Bruce Bochy	.05
52 Doug Corbett	.05
53 Jose Cruz	.05
54 Jamie Easterly	.05
55 Pete Falcone	.05
56 Bob Galasso	.05
57 Johnny Grubb	.05
58 Bake McBride	.05
59 Dyar Miller	.05
60 Tom Paciorek	.05
61 Ken Reitz	.05
62 U.L. Washington	.05
63 Alan Ashby	.05
64 Pat Dobson	.05
65 Doug Bird	.05
66 Marty Castillo	.05
67 Dan Driessen	.05
68 Wayne Garland	.05
69 Tim Ireland	.05
70 Ron Jackson	.05
71 Bobby Jones	.05
72 Dennis Leonard	.05
73 Rick Manning	.05
74 Amos Otis	.05
75 Pat Putnam	.05
76 Eric Rasmussen	.05
77 Paul Blair	.05
78 Bert Campaneris	.05
79 Cesar Cedeno	.10
80 Ed Figueroa	.05
81 Ross Grimsley	.05
82 George Hendrick	.05
83 Cliff Johnson	.05
84 Mike Kekich	.05
85 Rafael Landestoy	.05
86 Larry Milbourne	.05
87 Bobby Molinaro	.05
88 Sid Monge	.05
89 Rennie Stennett	.05
90 Derrell Thomas	.05
91 Earl Weaver	.30
92 Gary Allenson	.05
93 Pedro Borbon	.05
94 Al Bumbry	.05
95 Bill Campbell	.05
96 Bernie Carbo	.05
97 Ferguson Jenkins	.50
98 Pete LaCock	.05
99 Bill Lee	.05
100 Tommy McMillan	.05
101 Joe Pittman	.05
102 Gene Richards	.05
103 Leon Roberts	.05
104 Tony Scott	.05
105 Doug Simunic	.05
106 Rick Wise	.05
107 Willie Aikens	.05
108 Juan Beniquez	.05
109 Bobby Bonds	.10
110 Sergio Ferrer	.05
111 Chuck Ficks	.05
112 George Foster	.10
113 Dave Hilton	.05
114 Al Holland	.05
115 Clint Hurdle	.05
116 Bill Madlock	.10
117 Steve Ontiveros	.05
118 Roy Thomas	.05
119 Luis Tiant	.10
120 Walt Williams	.05
121 Vida Blue	.10
122 Bobby Bonds	.05
123 Rollie Fingers	.50
124 George Foster	.10
125 Fergie Jenkins	.50
126 Dave Kingman	.10

2003 El Nueva Dia Montreal Expos

En la Isla Sosa con los Cachorros

To commemorate the series played by the Expos in Puerto Rico, a local newspaper sponsored this set given away to fans at Hiram Bithorn Stadium on September 11 at the final San Juan "home" game. The cello-wrapped set has nine colorful 4-3/4" x 5-5/8" blank-back cards arranged like a newspaper page. At top is the sponsor's logo and the logo created for the historic series of games throughout the 2003 season. At bottom are one or two color photos with captions. In between are a headline and story summary about one of the series. All text is in Spanish. Each player named or prominently pictured on the card is listed.

	NM/M
Complete Set (9):	12.50
Common Card:	.60
1 Montreal pisa el 'home' (Jose Vidro, Wilfredo Cordero, Mark Grudzielanek)	1.25
2 Ovacion a Robero Alomar (Roberto Alomar)	2.50
3 Abuso casero de los Expos (Javier Vazquez, Javier Lopez, Marcus Giles)	1.25
4 Javy Lopez carga a los Bravos (Henry Mateo, Rocky Biddle, Javy Lopez, Andruw Jones)	1.25
5 Reaccion por todo lo alto (Javier Vazquez, Brian Schneider)	.25
6 Recibe el Bithorn a los campeones (Bengie Molina, Jose Molina)	.60
7 Puerto Rico (Juan Gonzalez)	2.50
8 Card' (Dontrelle Willis, Ivan Rodriguez, Braden Looper)	1.25
9 En la Isla Sosa con los Cachorros (Sammy Sosa)	5.00

1983 English's Chicken Baltimore Orioles Lids

The World Champion O's were featured on this set of fried chicken bucket lids. Printed on thick cardboard discs with the blank backs heavily waxed, the lids come in two sizes, 8-3/8" diameter and 7-1/4". The design is the same on each, with a black, white and orange player portrait at center, flanked by some personal data and '83 stats. His name is in orange below, with his position and team in black beneath that. In the wide orange border is "English's Salutes/1983 Champions." The player's union logo is at right of the portrait, but cap logos are missing because the issue was not licensed through MLB. The lids are not numbered.

	NM/M
Complete Set (13):	45.00
Common Player:	2.00
(1) Mike Boddicker	2.00
(2) Rich Dauer	2.00
(3) Storm Davis	2.00
(4) Mike Flanagan	2.00
(5) John Lowenstein	2.00
(6) Tippy Martinez	2.00
(7) Gary Roenicke	2.00
(8) Ken Singleton	2.00
(9) Rick Dempsey	2.00
(10) Scott McGregor	2.00
(11) Eddie Murray	6.00

(12) Jim Palmer	6.00
(13) Cal Ripken, Jr.	30.00

1991 Enor Kevin Maas Story

This 20-card set was produced by one of the hobby's leading manufacturers of plastic supplies. Not surprisingly, the set was housed in a 6" by 8-1/4" plastic album with eight four-card plastic sheets inside. Besides the cards and album, the set came with a biographical brochure on the 1990 A.L. Rookie of the Year runner-up. Each of the 2-1/2" x 3-1/2" cards features one or more color photos of the player on front. A series of red stripes at the top of the card features the player's name in the uppermost stripe. Backs have the same stripe motif at top and include career information or stats at center. The logos of MLB, the Yankees and Enor appear at the bottom.

	NM/M
Complete Set w/Album (20):	4.00
Single Card:	.10

F

1981 Family Fun Centers Padres

Six Padres players or staff are featured on these 13" x 10" coupon sheets. At the right end of each glossy paper sheet is a group of coupons and advertising for the recreation centers, printed in black, yellow and green. At left are six photos. Each of the 3" x 4" photos has a color player pose. At either top or bottom, depending on placement on the sheet, is the player name in black, "FAMILY FUN CENTER" in green and a red building logo. Backs are blank and the sheets are not perforated.

	NM/M
Complete Set (4):	110.00
Common Player:	10.00
(1) Randy Bass, Frank Howard, Gary Lucas, Gene Richards, Ozzie Smith, Jerry Turner	60.00
(2) Kurt Bevacqua, Dave Cash, Paul Dade, Rollie Fingers, Don Williams, Dave Winfield	25.00
(3) Dan Boone, Chuck Estrada, Joe Lefebvre, Tim Lollar, Ed Stevens, Steve Swisher	10.00

(4) John Curtis, Barry Evans, Tim Flannery, Terry Kennedy, Steve Mura, Bob Tolan	10.00
(5) Von Joshua, Fred Kendall, Dennis Kinney, Jerry Mumphrey, Steve Mura, Dick Phillips	10.00

1994 FanFest Roberto Clemente Commemorative

In an unprecedented show of co-operation, the five Major League Baseball trading card licensees created this set of Roberto Clemente commemorative cards for distribution at the All-Star Fan Fest. Cards were available at participating manufacturers' booths, making complete sets somewhat difficult to assemble. Topps and Fleer based their commemorative cards on their companies' respective 1955 and 1963 Clemente cards. Donruss had artist Dick Perez create a Diamond King card of Clemente, while Upper Deck and Score Select created new designs. It is believed fewer than 10,000 of each card exist.

	NM/M
Complete Set (5):	30.00
Common Card:	6.00
1 Roberto Clemente (Donruss Diamond King)	6.00
2 Roberto Clemente (Fleer 1963 reprint.)	6.00
3 Roberto Clemente (Score Select)	6.00
4 Roberto Clemente (Topps 1955 reprint.)	10.00
5 Roberto Clemente (Upper Deck)	6.00

1995 FanFest Nolan Ryan Commemorative

At the July 7-11, 1995, FanFest, held in Dallas, Tex., site of the All-Star Game, five of Major League Baseball's principal licensees combined on a wrapper redemption program which offered Nolan Ryan Tribute cards. With 3,000 of the cards pegged as each day's maximum giveaway, only 15,000 total sets were available. Most of the companies opted for gold-leaf and/or foil-print extravaganzas, while Topps chose to re-create a single-player 1968-style Nolan Ryan rookie card with full career stats on back.

	NM/M
Complete Set (5):	16.00
Common Card:	4.00
1 Nolan Ryan (Upper Deck)	4.00
2 Nolan Ryan (Topps)	4.50

3 Nolan Ryan (Pinnacle)	4.00
4 Nolan Ryan (Fleer Ultra)	4.00
5 Nolan Ryan (Donruss)	4.00

1996 FanFest Steve Carlton Commemorative

Philadelphia's most famous Lefty (before Rocky Balboa) was chosen as the subject of the '96 All-Star FanFest multi-company card tribute. Each of the five largest baseball card licensees produced a Carlton card for use in a wrapper redemption promotion at the annual show. Each of the cards featured the Liberty Bell All-Star Game logo along with such bells and whistles as embossing, metallic-foil highlights, etc.

	NM/M
Complete Set (5):	12.50
Common Card:	3.00
1 Steve Carlton (Donruss)	3.00
2 Steve Carlton (Fleer Ultra)	3.00
3 Steve Carlton (Pinnacle)	3.00
4 Steve Carlton (Topps)	4.00
5 Steve Carlton (Upper Deck)	3.00

1997 FanFest Jackie Robinson Commemorative

In conjunction with FanFest in Cleveland, July 4-8, preceding the All-Star Game, five of the major card companies combined to create a card set honoring Jackie Robinson. Each company made its card available at the show in a wrapper redemption exchange. In most cases the tribute cards showcased the respective companies' technical expertise. Production of each card was limited to 15,000.

	NM/M
Complete Set (5):	12.00
Common Card:	2.50
1 Jackie Robinson (Pinnacle Dufex)	2.50
2 Jackie Robinson (Topps Finest '52 reprint.)	3.00
3 Jackie Robinson (Upper Deck)	2.50
4 Jackie Robinson (Donruss - 1948 Leaf reprint.)	2.50
5 Jackie Robinson (Fleer)	2.50

1998 FanFest Lou Brock Commemorative

In the years before the Rockies joined the National League, Denver's "home team" was the St. Louis Cardinals. One of that team's greatest players of the 1960s and 1970s, Hall of Famer Lou Brock, was selected to be honored in the annual All-Star FanFest commemorative series used by the card companies as a wrapper redemption premium (five wrappers for each card). Card fronts include the All-Star Game logo, backs have the Cooperstown Collection logo. Topps' card is a chromium version reproduction of Brock's 1962 rookie card, which depicts him as a Cub.

	NM/M
Complete Set (5):	3.00
Common Card:	.50
1 Lou Brock (Topps)	2.00
2 Lou Brock (Pinnacle)	1.00
3 Lou Brock (Fleer)	.50
4 Lou Brock (Donruss DK)	1.00
5 Lou Brock (Upper Deck)	.50

1999 FanFest Carl Yastrzemski Commemorative

One of the modern Red Sox most popular players of the of the 1960s-1980s, Hall of Famer Carl Yastrzemski, was selected to be honored in the 1999 Boston All-Star FanFest commemorative series used by the card companies as a wrapper redemption premium (five wrappers for each card). Card fronts include the All-Star Game logo.

	NM/M
Complete Set (4):	7.50
Common Card:	2.00
1 Carl Yastrzemski (Topps)	2.75
2 Carl Yastrzemski (Ultra)	2.00
3 Carl Yastrzemski (Upper Deck)	2.00
4 Carl Yastrzemski (Pacific)	2.00

2000 FanFest Hank Aaron Commemorative

As in past years, each of Major League Baseball's major card licensees pro-

duced a special card in conjunction with FanFest in Atlanta prior to the All-Star Game. Visitors to the Collector's Showcase area of FanFest could obtain one card from each company's booth via a wrapper redemption.

	NM/M
Complete Set (4):	7.50
Common Card:	2.50
1 Hank Aaron (Topps)	2.50
2 Hank Aaron (Fleer)	2.50
3 Hank Aaron (Upper Deck)	2.50
4 Hank Aaron (Pacific)	2.50

2000 FanFest Hank Aaron Rookie Reprint

It has been reported that Topps originally intended to use this rookie reprint as its redemption card at FanFest, but later switched to a version of the Aaron card which appeared in 2000 Topps. It is said the rookie version was only distributed to a few of the vendors. Like the other cards in the redemption program, the '54 Topps reprint has the event logo on front. It is numbered "1 of 4" on back.

	NM/M
1 Hank Aaron (1954 Topps reprint)	4.00

2001 FanFest Seattle Mariners

A multi-manufacturer wrapper-redemption promotion at the July 6-10 All-Star FanFest in Seattle allowed collectors to acquire a special set of nine cards featuring current and former M's stars. Cards were generally available by visiting the booth of each manufacturer and opening five packs of that company's 2001 baseball cards. Original artwork, and metallic-foil highlights were featured on some cards. Production was 10,000 of each card.

	NM/M
Complete Set (9):	20.00
Common Player:	2.00
1 Ken Griffey Jr. (Upper Deck)	4.00
2 Alex Rodriguez (Donruss Diamond Kings)	5.00
3 Ichiro Suzuki (Fleer)	7.50
4 Edgar Martinez (Topps Gallery)	2.00
5 John Olerud (Topps Gallery)	2.00
6 Jay Buhner (Fleer)	2.00
7 Randy Johnson (Donruss Diamond Kings)	3.50
8 Lou Piniella (Upper Deck)	2.00
9 Alvin Davis, Harold Reynolds (Tuff Stuff)	2.00

2002 FanFest

BARRY BONDS / OF

All of the major baseball card licensees participated in a wrapper redemption program at the 2002 FanFest in Milwaukee. Each company produced one card of a Brewers star and one from another team. Five wrappers from selected products could be traded in for one of the cards. Wrappers from super-premium brands could be exchanged for cards featuring game-used base swatches. All cards carry special All-Star Game logos.

	NM/M
Complete Set (8):	10.00
Common Player:	2.00
1 Derek Jeter (Fleer)	3.00
2 Ichiro (Upper Deck)	4.00
3a Sammy Sosa (Topps Finest)	2.50
3b Sammy Sosa (Topps Finest Refractor)	12.00
4 Barry Bonds (Donruss Studio)	3.00
5 Robin Yount (Donruss Studio)	2.00
6 Geoff Jenkins (Topps Finest)	2.00
7 Ben Sheets (Upper Deck)	2.00
8 Richie Sexson (Fleer)	2.00

Game-Used Base Cards

All of the major baseball card licensees participated in a wrapper redemption program at the 2002 FanFest in Milwaukee. Each company produced one card of a Brewers star and one from another team. Five wrappers from selected products could be redeemed for base brand-type cards while opening high-priced packs would net a game-used base card. Ten thousand of each of the regular redemption and Ryan-Clemens cards were produced; the game-used cards were in an edition of 1,000 each. Cards feature the All-Star Game and FanFest logos and are numbered within the edition of 12.

	NM/M
Complete Set GU Base Cards (4):	35.00
Common Player:	5.00
GU1a Derek Jeter (Fleer, First Base)	6.00
GU1b Derek Jeter (Fleer, Second Base)	6.00
GU2 Ichiro (Upper Deck)	20.00
GU3 Sammy Sosa (Topps)	5.00
GU4 Barry Bonds (Donruss Studio)	7.50

2003 FanFest

By opening packs of specified brands at various card companies' FanFest booths, collectors could receive one of eight redemption cards. Low-priced card wrappers could be redeemed for base brand-type cards while opening high-priced packs would net a game-used base card. Cards feature the All-Star Game logo and are numbered within the edition of eight.

	NM/M
Complete Set (8):	35.00
Common Player:	2.00
1 Hideki Matsui (Upper Deck, g-u base)	7.50
2 Barry Bonds (Topps, g-u base)	10.00
3 Derek Jeter (Fleer, g-u base)	10.00
4 Sammy Sosa (Donruss, g-u base)	7.50
5 Frank Thomas (Upper Deck)	3.00
6 Bartolo Colon (Topps)	2.00
7 Paul Konerko (Fleer)	2.00
8 Magglio Ordonez (Donruss)	2.00

2004 FanFest

By opening packs of specified brands at various card companies' FanFest booths at the All-Star related event in Houston, collectors could receive one of 12 redemption cards featuring current and former (Ryan) Astros players. Low-priced card wrappers could be redeemed for base brand-type cards while opening high-priced packs would net a game-used base card. Ten thousand of each of the regular redemption and Ryan-Clemens cards were produced; the game-used cards were in an edition of 1,000 each. Cards feature the All-Star Game and FanFest logos and are numbered within the edition of 12.

	NM/M
Complete Set (12):	45.00
Common Player:	2.00
1 Roger Clemens (Fleer GU)	10.00
2 Andy Pettitte (Upper Deck GU)	5.00
3 Jeff Bagwell (Donruss GU)	7.50
4 Lance Berkman (Topps GU)	5.00
5 Roy Oswalt (Topps)	2.00

6 Craig Biggio (Donruss)	2.00
7 Jeff Kent (Upper Deck)	.75
8 Adam Everett (Fleer)	2.00
9 Roger Clemens, Nolan Ryan (Fleer)	5.00
10 Roger Clemens, Nolan Ryan (Upper Deck)	5.00
11 Roger Clemens, Nolan Ryan (Donruss)	5.00
12 Roger Clemens, Nolan Ryan (Topps)	5.00

2005 FanFest

By opening packs of specified brands at various card companies' FanFest booths at the All-Star related event in Detroit, collectors could receive one of nine redemption cards. Low-priced card wrappers could be redeemed for base brand-type cards while opening high-priced packs would net a game-used jersey card. Ten thousand of each of the regular redemption and dual-player cards were produced; the game-used cards were in an edition of 1,000 each. Cards feature the All-Star Game and FanFest logos.

	NM/M
Complete Set (9):	25.00
Common Player:	1.00
1 Ivan Rodriguez (Topps jersey)	12.50
2 Jeremy Bonderman (UD jersey)	6.00
3 Dmitri Young (Donruss jersey)	6.00
4 Derek Jeter (UD)	3.00
5 Alex Rodriguez (Topps)	3.00
6 Albert Pujols (Donruss)	3.00
7 Al Kaline, Ivan Rodriguez/UD	1.00
8 Al Kaline, Ivan Rodriguez (Donruss)	1.00
9 Al Kaline, Ivan Rodriguez (Topps)	1.00

1988 Fantastic Sam's

This set of color player discs (2-1/2" diameter) was distributed during a Superstar Sweepstakes sponsored by Fantastic Sam's Family Haircutters' 1,800 stores nationwide. Each card consists of two connected discs (bright orange fronts, white backs) perforated for easy separation. One disc features the baseball player photo, the other carries the sweepstakes logo and a list of prizes. Player discs carry a Fantastic Sam's Baseball Superstars header curved above the photo, with player name, team and position printed in black. Backs are black-and-white and include personal info, card number and 1987 stats. Sweepstakes discs list contest prizes (Grand Prize was 4 tickets to a 1988 Championship game) on the front and an entry form on the flipside. Below the prize list is a silver scratch-off rectangle which may reveal an instant prize.

	NM/M
Complete Set (20):	4.00

Uncut Sheet:	10.00
Common Player:	.10
1 Kirby Puckett	.50
2 George Brett	.50
3 Mark McGwire	1.00
4 Wally Joyner	.10
5 Paul Molitor	.45
6 Alan Trammell	.10
7 George Bell	.10
8 Wade Boggs	.50
9 Don Mattingly	.75
10 Julio Franco	.10
11 Ozzie Smith	.50
12 Will Clark	.10
13 Dale Murphy	.15
14 Eric Davis	.10
15 Andre Dawson	.25
16 Tim Raines	.10
17 Darryl Strawberry	.10
18 Tony Gwynn	.50
19 Mike Schmidt	.75
20 Pedro Guerrero	.10

1984 Farmer Jack Detroit Tigers

Though there is no indication on the pictures themselves, this issue was a promotion by the Farmer Jack grocery store chain. Printed on semi-gloss paper, the color photos are bordered in white and measure 6" x 9". A facsimile autograph is printed on front. The unnumbered pictures are blank-backed and are checklisted here in alphabetical order.

	NM/M
Complete Set (16):	15.00
Common Player:	.50
(1) Dave Bergman	.50
(2) Darrell Evans	1.25
(3) Barbaro Garbey	.50
(4) Kirk Gibson	1.00
(5) John Grubb	.50
(6) Willie Hernandez	.50
(7) Larry Herndon	.50
(8) Howard Johnson	.90
(9) Chet Lemon	.75
(10) Jack Morris	.90
(11) Lance Parrish	1.00
(12) Dan Petry	.50
(13) Dave Rozema	.50
(14) Alan Trammell	4.00
(15) Lou Whitaker	2.50
(16) Milt Wilcox	.50

1987 Farmland Dairies Mets

#8 Catcher

The New York Mets and Farmland Dairies produced a nine-card panel of baseball cards for members of the Junior Mets Club. Members of the club, kids 14 years of age and younger, received the perforated panel as part of a package featuring gifts and special privileges. The cards are the standard 2-1/2" x 3-1/2" with fronts containing a full-color photo encompassed by a blue border. The backs are designed on a vertical format and have player statistics and career highlights. The Farmland Dairies and Junior Mets Club logos are also carried on the card backs.

	NM/M
Complete Panel Set:	4.50
Complete Singles Set (9):	3.00
Common Single Player:	.25
1 Mookie Wilson	.35
3 Lenny Dykstra	.35
8 Gary Carter	1.50
12 Ron Darling	.25
16 Darryl Strawberry	.35
19 Bob Ojeda	.25
22 Kevin McReynolds	.25
42 Roger McDowell	.25
--- Team card	.25

1988 Farmland Dairies Mets

Part of the Junior Mets Fan Club membership package, this set of nine standard size cards was printed on a single panel. Card fronts feature full-color action shots framed in orange and blue. A white player name runs across the top border, with a large team logo, uniform number and position printed below the photo. Card backs are blue on brown and include personal data, stats and 1987 season highlights. The set was offered to fans 14 years and younger for a $6 fan club membership fee, with a $1 discount for those who sent in two proofs of purchase from Farmland Dairies milk cartons.

	NM/M
Complete Panel Set:	4.50
Complete Singles Set (9):	2.50
Common Single Player:	.25
8 Gary Carter	1.50
16 Dwight Gooden	.25
17 Keith Hernandez	.40
18 Darryl Strawberry	.25
20 Howard Johnson	.25
21 Kevin Elster	.25
42 Roger McDowell	.25
48 Randy Myers	.25
50 Sid Fernandez	.25

1989 Farmland Dairies Mets

For the third consecutive year in 1989, Farmland Dairies sponsored the Junior Mets fan club. One of the club's membership benefits was a nine-card set issued on a 7-1/2" x 10-1/2" perforated sheet. Individual cards measure the standard 2-1/2" x 3-1/2" with team-

color borders of blue and gold. Backs have the Junior Mets and Farmland logos along with 1988 highlights and stats, career stats and some biographical data. The checklist is by uniform number as shown on the cards' front.

	NM/M
Complete Set, Sheet	3.50
Complete Set, Singles (9):	3.00
Common Player:	.50
8 Gary Carter	1.50
9 Gregg Jefferies	.50
16 Dwight Gooden	.25
18 Darryl Strawberry	.25
19 Kevin McReynolds	.25
25 Keith Miller	.25
42 Roger McDowell	.25
44 David Cone	.50
--- 1988 Eastern Division Champs (Team photo.)	.25

1993 Fax Pax

Roger Clemens

Titled "Fax Pax World of Sports," this 40-card set was issued in Great Britain and features top athletes from many sports around the world. The 2-1/2" x 3-1/2" cards have borderless color action photos on front. A white strip near the bottom carries the player's name and the flag of his nation. Black, white and red backs have biographical data, stats and a career summary. Only the baseball players are listed here.

	NM/M
Common Player:	1.00
1 Roger Clemens	1.50
2 Ken Griffey Jr.	2.00
3 John Olerud	1.00
4 Nolan Ryan	3.00

1982 FBI Foods Discs

This set was issued in the form of a pair of 2-7/8" diameter discs printed on the bottoms of six-pack cartons of Canadian soft drinks. The discs have black-and-white player portrait photos at center, with cap logos airbrushed off. At top is a green and orange FBI logo. Player identification flanks the photo. The copyright and logo of the players' association appear at right. The initials of the set's producer, Mike Schechter Associates, appear at lower-left. The unnumbered discs are checklisted here in alphabetical order. Because of their appearance on the bottom of a cardboard box, many cards suffer scuffing on the front, or show indentations from the soda cans. A premium of 25-50 percent attaches to intact boxes or panels.

	NM/M
Complete Set, Singles (30):	650.00
Common Player:	10.00
(1) Vida Blue	10.00

(2)	George Brett	100.00
(3)	Rod Carew	25.00
(4)	Steve Carlton	30.00
(5)	Gary Carter	30.00
(6)	Warren Cromartie	10.00
(7)	Andre Dawson	15.00
(8)	Rollie Fingers	20.00
(9)	Carlton Fisk	30.00
(10)	Steve Garvey	15.00
(11)	Goose Gossage	10.00
(12)	Bill Gullickson	10.00
(13)	Steve Henderson	10.00
(14)	Keith Hernandez	10.00
(15)	John Mayberry	10.00
(16)	Al Oliver	10.00
(17)	Dave Parker	10.00
(18)	Tim Raines	10.00
(19)	Jim Rice	15.00
(20)	Steve Rogers	10.00
(21)	Pete Rose	150.00
(22)	Nolan Ryan	150.00
(23)	Mike Schmidt	100.00
(24)	Tom Seaver	30.00
(25)	Ken Singleton	10.00
(26)	Dave Steib	10.00
(27)	Bruce Sutter	20.00
(28)	Ellis Valentine	10.00
(29)	Fernando Valenzuela	10.00
(30)	Dave Winfield	30.00

1993 Finest Promos

Debuting at the 1993 National Convention in Chicago, this three-card set introduced the hobby to the Topps Finest baseball issue. While the promos are identical in high-tech format to the regular Finest cards issued later, including the same card numbers, there are differences in the promos; some subtle, some glaring. For instance, the Ryan and Alomar cards were issued in promo form in the "gray" style of the basic set. In the regularly issued set, those cards were in the green All-Star format. Each of the promos is overprinted in red on the back, "Promotional Sample 1 of 5000." Of considerably greater rarity are refractor versions of these promo cards, with production numbers unknown.

		NM/M
Complete Set (3):		25.00
Complete Set, Refractors (3):		1,500
88	Roberto Alomar	3.50
88r	Roberto Alomar (Refractor)	300.00
98	Don Mattingly	10.00
98r	Don Mattingly (Refractor)	500.00
107	Nolan Ryan	15.00
107r	Nolan Ryan (Refractor)	750.00

1993 Finest

This 199-card set uses a process of multi-color metallization; this chromium technology adds depth and dimension to the card. The set has a 33-card subset of All-Stars; a parallel version of these cards (Refractors) were also created with refracting foil using the metallization enhancement process. There is one refracting foil card in every nine packs. Packs have five cards. Each 18-count box contains a 5" x 7" version of one of the 33 All-Star players in the set.

		NM/M
Complete Set (199):		75.00
Common Player:		.50
Refractors:		40-50X
Pack (6):		15.00
Wax Box (18):		300.00
1	Dave Justice	.50
2	Lou Whitaker	.50
3	Bryan Harvey	.50
4	Carlos Garcia	.50
5	Sid Fernandez	.50
6	Brett Butler	.50
7	Scott Cooper	.50
8	B.J. Surhoff	.50
9	Steve Finley	.50
10	Curt Schilling	2.00
11	Jeff Bagwell	4.00
12	Alex Cole	.50
13	John Olerud	.50
14	John Smiley	.50
15	Bip Roberts	.50
16	Albert Belle	.50
17	Duane Ward	.50
18	Alan Trammell	.50
19	Andy Benes	.50
20	Reggie Sanders	.50
21	Todd Zeile	.50
22	Rick Aguilera	.50
23	Dave Hollins	.50
24	Jose Rijo	.50
25	Matt Williams	.50
26	Sandy Alomar	.50
27	Alex Fernandez	.50
28	Ozzie Smith	6.00
29	Ramon Martinez	.50
30	Bernie Williams	.50
31	Gary Sheffield	1.00
32	Eric Karros	.50
33	Frank Viola	.50
34	Kevin Young	.50
35	Ken Hill	.50
36	Tony Fernandez	.50
37	Tim Wakefield	.50
38	John Kruk	.50
39	Chris Sabo	.50
40	Marquis Grissom	.50
41	Glenn Davis	.50
42	Jeff Montgomery	.50
43	Kenny Lofton	.50
44	John Burkett	.50
45	Darryl Hamilton	.50
46	Jim Abbott	.50
47	Ivan Rodriguez	3.00
48	Eric Young	.50
49	Mitch Williams	.50
50	Harold Reynolds	.50
51	Brian Harper	.50
52	Rafael Palmeiro	3.00
53	Bret Saberhagen	.50
54	Jeff Conine	.50
55	Ivan Calderon	.50
56	Juan Guzman	.50
57	Carlos Baerga	.50
58	Charles Nagy	.50
59	Wally Joyner	.50
60	Charlie Hayes	.50
61	Shane Mack	.50
62	Pete Harnisch	.50
63	George Brett	8.00
64	Lance Johnson	.50
65	Ben McDonald	.50
66	Bobby Bonilla	.50
67	Terry Steinbach	.50
68	Ron Gant	.50
69	Doug Jones	.50
70	Paul Molitor	4.00
71	Brady Anderson	.50
72	Chuck Finley	.50
73	Mark Grace	.75
74	Mike Devereaux	.50
75	Tony Phillips	.50
76	Chuck Knoblauch	.50
77	Tony Gwynn	6.00
78	Kevin Appier	.50
79	Sammy Sosa	6.00
80	Mickey Tettleton	.50
81	Felix Jose	.50
82	Mark Langston	.50
83	Gregg Jefferies	.50
84	Andre Dawson/AS	1.00

85	Greg Maddux/AS	6.00
86	Rickey Henderson/AS	4.00
87	Tom Glavine/AS	2.50
88	Roberto Alomar/AS	.50
89	Darryl Strawberry/AS	.50
90	Wade Boggs/AS	6.00
91	Bo Jackson/AS	1.00
92	Mark McGwire/AS	6.00
93	Robin Ventura/AS	.50
94	Joe Carter/AS	.50
95	Lee Smith/AS	.50
96	Cal Ripken, Jr./AS	10.00
97	Larry Walker/AS	.50
98	Don Mattingly/AS	8.00
99	Jose Canseco/AS	2.50
100	Dennis Eckersley/AS	3.00
101	Terry Pendleton/AS	.50
102	Frank Thomas/AS	10.00
103	Barry Bonds /AS	8.00
104	Roger Clemens/AS	8.00
105	Ryne Sandberg/AS	6.00
106	Fred McGriff/AS	.50
107	Nolan Ryan/AS	10.00
108	Will Clark/AS	.50
109	Pat Listach/AS	.50
110	Ken Griffey Jr./AS	6.00
111	Cecil Fielder/AS	.50
112	Kirby Puckett/AS	6.00
113	Dwight Gooden/AS	.50
114	Barry Larkin/AS	.50
115	David Cone/AS	.50
116	Juan Gonzalez/AS	2.50
117	Kent Hrbek	.50
118	Tim Wallach	.50
119	Craig Biggio	.50
120	Bobby Kelly	.50
121	Greg Olson	.50
122	Eddie Murray	4.00
123	Wil Cordero	.50
124	Jay Buhner	.50
125	Carlton Fisk	4.00
126	Eric Davis	.50
127	Doug Drabek	.50
128	Ozzie Guillen	.50
129	John Wetteland	.50
130	Andres Galarraga	.50
131	Ken Caminiti	.50
132	Tom Candiotti	.50
133	Pat Borders	.50
134	Kevin Brown	.50
135	Travis Fryman	.50
136	Kevin Mitchell	.50
137	Greg Swindell	.50
138	Benny Santiago	.50
139	Reggie Jefferson	.50
140	Chris Bosio	.50
141	Deion Sanders	.60
142	Scott Erickson	.50
143	Howard Johnson	.50
144	Orestes Destrade	.50
145	Jose Guzman	.50
146	Chad Curtis	.50
147	Cal Eldred	.50
148	Willie Greene	.50
149	Tommy Greene	.50
150	Erik Hanson	.50
151	Bob Welch	.50
152	John Jaha	.50
153	Harold Baines	.50
154	Randy Johnson	4.00
155	Al Martin	.50
156	J.T. Snow RC	1.50
157	Mike Mussina	2.50
158	Ruben Sierra	.50
159	Dean Palmer	.50
160	Steve Avery	.50
161	Julio Franco	.50
162	Dave Winfield	4.00
163	Tim Salmon	.50
164	Tom Henke	.50
165	Mo Vaughn	.50
166	John Smoltz	.50
167	Danny Tartabull	.50
168	Delino DeShields	.50
169	Charlie Hough	.50
170	Paul O'Neill	.50
171	Darren Daulton	.50
172	Jack McDowell	.50
173	Junior Felix	.50
174	Jimmy Key	.50
175	George Bell	.50
176	Mike Stanton	.50
177	Len Dykstra	.50
178	Norm Charlton	.50
179	Eric Anthony	.50
180	Bob Dibble	.50
181	Otis Nixon	.50
182	Randy Myers	.50
183	Tim Raines	.50
184	Orel Hershiser	.50
185	Andy Van Slyke	.50
186	Mike Lansing RC	1.00
187	Ray Lankford	.50
188	Mike Morgan	.50
189	Moises Alou	.50
190	Edgar Martinez	.50
191	John Franco	.50
192	Robin Yount	5.00
193	Bob Tewksbury	.50
194	Jay Bell	.50
195	Luis Gonzalez	.50
196	Dave Fleming	.50
197	Mike Greenwell	.50
198	David Nied	.50
199	Mike Piazza	10.00

Refractors

This parallel insert set comprises each of the 199 cards from the regular Topps Finest set recreated with refracting foil using the metallization enhancement process. One refractor card was inserted in every nine packs, on average. Estimated production was about 250 of each card, though short-prints are known. In the mid 2000s large quantities of the refractors began appearing in the market, fueling speculation that some form of unissued remainder inventory had been released from the printer.

		NM/M
Common Player:		15.00
1	Dave Justice	15.00
2	Lou Whitaker	15.00
3	Bryan Harvey/SP	45.00
4	Carlos Garcia	15.00
5	Sid Fernandez	15.00
6	Brett Butler	15.00
7	Scott Cooper	15.00
8	B.J. Surhoff	15.00
9	Steve Finley	15.00
10	Curt Schilling	50.00
11	Jeff Bagwell	100.00
12	Alex Cole	15.00
13	John Olerud	15.00
14	John Smiley	15.00
15	Bip Roberts	15.00
16	Albert Belle	15.00
17	Duane Ward	15.00
18	Alan Trammell	15.00
19	Andy Benes	15.00
20	Reggie Sanders	15.00
21	Todd Zeile	15.00
22	Rick Aguilera	15.00
23	Dave Hollins	15.00
24	Jose Rijo	15.00
25	Matt Williams	15.00
26	Sandy Alomar	15.00
27	Alex Fernandez	15.00
28	Ozzie Smith	100.00
29	Ramon Martinez	15.00
30	Bernie Williams	15.00
31	Gary Sheffield	40.00
32	Eric Karros	15.00
33	Frank Viola	15.00
34	Kevin Young	15.00
35	Ken Hill	15.00
36	Tony Fernandez	15.00
37	Tim Wakefield	15.00
38	John Kruk	15.00
39	Chris Sabo/SP	75.00
40	Marquis Grissom	15.00
41	Glenn Davis/SP	50.00
42	Jeff Montgomery	15.00
43	Kenny Lofton	15.00
44	John Burkett	15.00
45	Darryl Hamilton	15.00
46	Jim Abbott	15.00
47	Ivan Rodriguez	150.00
48	Eric Young	15.00
49	Mitch Williams	15.00
50	Harold Reynolds	15.00
51	Brian Harper	15.00
52	Rafael Palmeiro	75.00
53	Bret Saberhagen	15.00
54	Jeff Conine	15.00
55	Ivan Calderon	15.00
56	Juan Guzman	15.00
57	Carlos Baerga	15.00
58	Charles Nagy	15.00
59	Wally Joyner	15.00
60	Charlie Hayes	15.00
61	Shane Mack	15.00
62	Pete Harnisch	15.00
63	George Brett	125.00
64	Lance Johnson	15.00
65	Ben McDonald	15.00
66	Bobby Bonilla	15.00
67	Terry Steinbach	15.00
68	Ron Gant	15.00
69	Doug Jones	15.00
70	Paul Molitor	100.00
71	Brady Anderson	15.00
72	Chuck Finley	15.00
73	Mark Grace	15.00
74	Mike Devereaux	15.00

75	Tony Phillips	15.00
76	Chuck Knoblauch	15.00
77	Tony Gwynn	100.00
78	Kevin Appier	15.00
79	Sammy Sosa	150.00
80	Mickey Tettleton	15.00
81	Felix Jose	15.00
82	Mark Langston	15.00
83	Gregg Jefferies	15.00
84	Andre Dawson/AS	35.00
85	Greg Maddux/AS	15.00
86	Rickey Henderson/AS	125.00
87	Tom Glavine/AS	50.00
88	Roberto Alomar/AS	45.00
89	Darryl Strawberry/AS	15.00
90	Wade Boggs/AS	100.00
91	Bo Jackson/AS	60.00
92	Mark McGwire/AS	200.00
93	Robin Ventura/AS	15.00
94	Joe Carter/AS/SP	50.00
95	Lee Smith/AS	15.00
96	Cal Ripken, Jr./AS	500.00
97	Larry Walker/AS/SP	100.00
98	Don Mattingly/AS	100.00
99	Jose Canseco/AS	50.00
100	Dennis Eckersley/AS	75.00
101	Terry Pendleton/AS	15.00
102	Frank Thomas/AS/SP	200.00
103	Barry Bonds/AS	300.00
104	Roger Clemens/AS	200.00
105	Ryne Sandberg/AS	125.00
106	Fred McGriff/AS	15.00
107	Nolan Ryan/AS	500.00
108	Will Clark/AS/SP	75.00
109	Pat Listach/AS	15.00
110	Ken Griffey Jr./AS	450.00
111	Cecil Fielder/AS	15.00
112	Kirby Puckett/AS	100.00
113	Dwight Gooden/AS	15.00
114	Barry Larkin/AS	15.00
115	David Cone/AS	15.00
116	Juan Gonzalez/AS/SP	150.00
117	Kent Hrbek	15.00
118	Tim Wallach	15.00
119	Craig Biggio	15.00
120	Bobby Kelly	15.00
121	Greg Olson	15.00
122	Eddie Murray	100.00
123	Wil Cordero	15.00
124	Jay Buhner	15.00
125	Carlton Fisk	75.00
126	Eric Davis	15.00
127	Doug Drabek	15.00
128	Ozzie Guillen	15.00
129	John Wetteland	15.00
130	Andres Galarraga	15.00
131	Ken Caminiti	15.00
132	Tom Candiotti	15.00
133	Pat Borders	15.00
134	Kevin Brown	15.00
135	Travis Fryman	15.00
136	Kevin Mitchell	15.00
137	Greg Swindell	15.00
138	Benny Santiago	15.00
139	Reggie Jefferson	15.00
140	Chris Bosio	15.00
141	Deion Sanders	15.00
142	Scott Erickson	15.00
143	Howard Johnson	15.00
144	Orestes Destrade	15.00
145	Jose Guzman	15.00
146	Chad Curtis	15.00
147	Cal Eldred	15.00
148	Willie Greene/SP	75.00
149	Tommy Greene	15.00
150	Erik Hanson	15.00
151	Bob Welch	15.00
152	John Jaha	15.00
153	Harold Baines	15.00
154	Randy Johnson	100.00
155	Al Martin	15.00
156	J.T. Snow	15.00
157	Mike Mussina	45.00
158	Ruben Sierra	15.00
159	Dean Palmer	15.00
160	Steve Avery	15.00
161	Julio Franco	15.00
162	Dave Winfield	15.00
163	Tim Salmon/SP	50.00
164	Tom Henke	15.00
165	Mo Vaughn	15.00
166	John Smoltz	15.00
167	Danny Tartabull	15.00
168	Delino DeShields	15.00
169	Charlie Hough	15.00
170	Paul O'Neill	15.00
171	Darren Daulton	15.00
172	Jack McDowell	15.00
173	Junior Felix	15.00
174	Jimmy Key	15.00
175	George Bell	15.00
176	Mike Stanton	15.00
177	Len Dykstra	15.00
178	Norm Charlton	15.00
179	Eric Anthony	15.00
180	Bob Dibble	15.00
181	Otis Nixon	15.00
182	Randy Myers	15.00
183	Tim Raines	15.00
184	Orel Hershiser	15.00
185	Andy Van Slyke	15.00
186	Mike Lansing	15.00
187	Ray Lankford	15.00
188	Mike Morgan	15.00

189	Moises Alou	15.00
190	Edgar Martinez	15.00
191	John Franco	15.00
192	Robin Yount	90.00
193	Bob Tewksbury	15.00
194	Jay Bell	15.00
195	Luis Gonzalez	15.00
196	Dave Fleming	15.00
197	Mike Greenwell	15.00
198	David Nied	15.00
199	Mike Piazza	250.00

Jumbo All-Stars

These 4-1/2" x 6" cards were produced using the chromium metallization process. Each 18-pack Finest box contains one of the All-Star jumbo cards. Based on '93 Finest production, it is estimated fewer than 1,500 of each were issued.

		NM/M
Complete Set (33):		185.00
Common Player:		2.00
84	Andre Dawson	2.50
85	Greg Maddux	10.00
86	Rickey Henderson	7.50
87	Tom Glavine	3.00
88	Roberto Alomar	3.00
89	Darryl Strawberry	2.00
90	Wade Boggs	10.00
91	Bo Jackson	2.00
92	Mark McGwire	20.00
93	Robin Ventura	2.00
94	Joe Carter	2.00
95	Lee Smith	2.00
96	Cal Ripken, Jr.	30.00
97	Larry Walker	2.00
98	Don Mattingly	12.00
99	Jose Canseco	3.50
100	Dennis Eckersley	6.00
101	Terry Pendleton	2.00
102	Frank Thomas	7.50
103	Barry Bonds	30.00
104	Roger Clemens	12.00
105	Ryne Sandberg	10.00
106	Fred McGriff	2.00
107	Nolan Ryan	30.00
108	Will Clark	2.50
109	Pat Listach	2.00
110	Ken Griffey Jr.	15.00
111	Cecil Fielder	2.00
112	Kirby Puckett	10.00
113	Dwight Gooden	2.00
114	Barry Larkin	2.00
115	David Cone	2.00
116	Juan Gonzalez	7.50

1994 Finest Pre-Production

Forty cards premiering the upcoming 1994 Topps Finest set were a random insert in packs of Topps Series 2 regular-issue cards. The promos are in the same format as the regular-issue Finest cards and share the same card numbers. On back there is a red "Pre-Production" notice printed diagonally over the statistics.

1994 Finest Pre-Production

		NM/M
Complete Set (40):		35.00
Common Player:		1.00
22	Deion Sanders	1.00
23	Jose Offerman	1.00
26	Alex Fernandez	1.00
31	Steve Finley	1.00
35	Andres Galarraga	1.00
43	Reggie Sanders	1.00
47	Dave Hollins	1.00
52	David Cone	1.00
59	Dante Bichette	1.00
61	Orlando Merced	1.00
62	Brian McRae	1.00
66	Mike Mussina	2.50
76	Mike Stanley	1.00
78	Mark McGwire	6.00
79	Pat Listach	1.00
82	Dwight Gooden	1.00
84	Phil Plantier	1.00
90	Jeff Russell	1.00
92	Gregg Jefferies	1.00
93	Jose Guzman	1.00
100	John Smoltz	1.00
102	Jim Thome	3.00
121	Moises Alou	1.00
125	Devon White	1.00
126	Ivan Rodriguez	3.00
130	Dave Magadan	1.00
136	Ozzie Smith	4.00
141	Chris Hoiles	1.00
149	Jim Abbott	1.00
151	Bill Swift	1.00
154	Edgar Martinez	1.00
157	J.T. Snow	1.00
159	Alan Trammell	1.00
163	Roberto Kelly	1.00
166	Scott Erickson	1.00
168	Scott Cooper	1.00
169	Rod Beck	1.00
177	Dean Palmer	1.00
182	Todd Van Poppel	1.00
185	Paul Sorrento	1.00

1994 Finest

The 1994 Finest set comprises two series of 220 cards each; subsets of 20 superstars and 20 top rookies are featured in each series. Each card has a metallic look to it, using Topps Finest technology. Backs picture the player on the top half and statistics on the bottom. Baseball's Finest was limited to 4,000 cases and available to dealers through an allocation process, based on their sales the previous year. Along with the regular-issue set, there was a parallel set, called Refractors, of 440 cards and a 4 x 6-inch version of the 80 subset cards.

		NM/M
Complete Set (440):		40.00
Common Player:		.15
Refractors:		3X
Series 1 or 2 Pack (7):		1.50
Series 1 or 2 Box (24):		25.00
1	Mike Piazza	3.00
2	Kevin Stocker	.15
3	Greg McMichael	.15
4	Jeff Conine	.15
5	Rene Arocha	.15
6	Aaron Sele	.15
7	Brent Gates	.15
8	Chuck Carr	.15
9	Kirk Rueter	.15
10	Mike Lansing	.15
11	Al Martin	.15
12	Jason Bere	.15
13	Troy Neel	.15
14	Armando Reynoso	.15
15	Jeromy Burnitz	.15
16	Rich Amaral	.15
17	David McCarty	.15
18	Tim Salmon	.15
19	Steve Cooke	.15
20	Wil Cordero	.15
21	Kevin Tapani	.15
22	Deion Sanders	.15
23	Jose Offerman	.15
24	Mark Langston	.15
25	Ken Hill	.15
26	Alex Fernandez	.15
27	Jeff Blauser	.15
28	Royce Clayton	.15
29	Brad Ausmus	.15
30	Ryan Bowen	.15
31	Steve Finley	.15
32	Charlie Hayes	.15
33	Jeff Kent	.15
34	Mike Henneman	.15
35	Andres Galarraga	.15
36	Wayne Kirby	.15
37	Joe Oliver	.15
38	Terry Steinbach	.15
39	Ryan Thompson	.15
40	Luis Alicea	.15
41	Randy Velarde	.15
42	Bob Tewksbury	.15
43	Reggie Sanders	.15
44	Brian Williams	.15
45	Joe Orsulak	.15
46	Jose Lind	.15
47	Dave Hollins	.15
48	Graeme Lloyd	.15
49	Jim Gott	.15
50	Andre Dawson	.40
51	Steve Buechele	.15
52	David Cone	.15
53	Ricky Gutierrez	.15
54	Lance Johnson	.15
55	Tino Martinez	.15
56	Phil Hiatt	.15
57	Carlos Garcia	.15
58	Danny Darwin	.15
59	Dante Bichette	.15
60	Scott Kamieniecki	.15
61	Orlando Merced	.15
62	Brian McRae	.15
63	Pat Kelly	.15
64	Tom Henke	.15
65	Jeff King	.15
66	Mike Mussina	.75
67	Tim Pugh	.15
68	Robby Thompson	.15
69	Paul O'Neill	.15
70	Hal Morris	.15
71	Ron Karkovice	.15
72	Joe Girardi	.15
73	Eduardo Perez	.15
74	Raul Mondesi	.15
75	Mike Gallego	.15
76	Mike Stanley	.15
77	Kevin Roberson	.15
78	Mark McGwire	4.00
79	Pat Listach	.15
80	Eric Davis	.15
81	Mike Bordick	.15
82	Dwight Gooden	.15
83	Mike Moore	.15
84	Phil Plantier	.15
85	Darren Lewis	.15
86	Rick Wilkins	.15
87	Darryl Strawberry	.30
88	Rob Dibble	.15
89	Greg Vaughn	.15
90	Jeff Russell	.15
91	Mark Lewis	.15
92	Gregg Jefferies	.15
93	Jose Guzman	.15
94	Kenny Rogers	.15
95	Mark Lemke	.15
96	Mike Morgan	.15
97	Andujar Cedeno	.15
98	Orel Hershiser	.15
99	Greg Swindell	.15
100	John Smoltz	.15
101	Pedro Martinez	.15
102	Jim Thome	1.00
103	David Segui	.15
104	Charles Nagy	.15
105	Shane Mack	.15
106	John Jaha	.15
107	Tom Candiotti	.15
108	David Wells	.15
109	Bobby Jones	.15
110	Bob Hamelin	.15
111	Bernard Gilkey	.15
112	Chili Davis	.15
113	Todd Stottlemyre	.15
114	Derek Bell	.15
115	Mark McLemore	.15
116	Mark Whiten	.15
117	Mike Devereaux	.15
118	Terry Pendleton	.15
119	Pat Meares	.15
120	Pete Harnisch	.15
121	Moises Alou	.15
122	Jay Buhner	.15
123	Wes Chamberlain	.15
124	Mike Perez	.15
125	Devon White	.15
126	Ivan Rodriguez	1.25
127	Don Slaught	.15
128	John Valentin	.15
129	Jaime Navarro	.15
130	Dave Magadan	.15
131	Brady Anderson	.15
132	Juan Guzman	.15
133	John Wetteland	.15
134	Dave Stewart	.15
135	Scott Servais	.15
136	Ozzie Smith	2.50
137	Darrin Fletcher	.15
138	Jose Mesa	.15
139	Wilson Alvarez	.15
140	Pete Incaviglia	.15
141	Chris Hoiles	.15
142	Darryl Hamilton	.15
143	Chuck Finley	.15
144	Archi Cianfrocco	.15
145	Bill Wegman	.15
146	Joey Cora	.15
147	Darrell Whitmore	.15
148	David Hulse	.15
149	Jim Abbott	.15
150	Curt Schilling	.40
151	Bill Swift	.15
152	Tommy Greene	.15
153	Roberto Mejia	.15
154	Edgar Martinez	.15
155	Roger Pavlik	.15
156	Randy Tomlin	.15
157	J.T. Snow	.15
158	Bob Welch	.15
159	Alan Trammell	.15
160	Ed Sprague	.15
161	Ben McDonald	.15
162	Derrick May	.15
163	Roberto Kelly	.15
164	Bryan Harvey	.15
165	Ron Gant	.15
166	Scott Erickson	.15
167	Anthony Young	.15
168	Scott Cooper	.15
169	Rod Beck	.15
170	John Franco	.15
171	Gary DiSarcina	.15
172	Dave Fleming	.15
173	Wade Boggs	2.50
174	Kevin Appier	.15
175	Jose Bautista	.15
176	Wally Joyner	.15
177	Dean Palmer	.15
178	Tony Phillips	.15
179	John Smiley	.15
180	Charlie Hough	.15
181	Scott Fletcher	.15
182	Todd Van Poppel	.15
183	Mike Blowers	.15
184	Willie McGee	.15
185	Paul Sorrento	.15
186	Eric Young	.15
187	Bret Barberie	.15
188	Manuel Lee	.15
189	Jeff Branson	.15
190	Jim Deshaies	.15
191	Ken Caminiti	.15
192	Tim Raines	.15
193	Joe Grahe	.15
194	Hipolito Pichardo	.15
195	Denny Neagle	.15
196	Jeff Gardner	.15
197	Mike Benjamin	.15
198	Milt Thompson	.15
199	Bruce Ruffin	.15
200	Chris Hammond	.15
201	Tony Gwynn	2.50
202	Robin Ventura	.15
203	Frank Thomas	1.50
204	Kirby Puckett	2.50
205	Roberto Alomar	.30
206	Dennis Eckersley	1.25
207	Joe Carter	.15
208	Albert Belle	.15
209	Greg Maddux	2.50
210	Ryne Sandberg	2.50
211	Juan Gonzalez	.75
212	Jeff Bagwell	1.50
213	Randy Johnson	1.50
214	Matt Williams	.15
215	Dave Winfield	1.50
216	Larry Walker	.15
217	Roger Clemens	2.75
218	Kenny Lofton	.15
219	Cecil Fielder	.15
220	Darren Daulton	.15
221	John Olerud	.15
222	Jose Canseco	.75
223	Rickey Henderson	1.50
224	Fred McGriff	.15
225	Gary Sheffield	.50
226	Jack McDowell	.15
227	Rafael Palmeiro	1.25
228	Travis Fryman	.15
229	Marquis Grissom	.15
230	Barry Bonds	5.00
231	Carlos Baerga	.15
232	Ken Griffey Jr.	3.00
233	Dave Justice	.15
234	Bobby Bonilla	.15
235	Cal Ripken	5.00
236	Sammy Sosa	2.50
237	Len Dykstra	.15
238	Will Clark	.15
239	Paul Molitor	1.50
240	Barry Larkin	.15
241	Bo Jackson	.35
242	Mitch Williams	.15
243	Ron Darling	.15
244	Darryl Kile	.15
245	Geronimo Berroa	.15
246	Gregg Olson	.15
247	Brian Harper	.15
248	Rheal Cormier	.15
249	Rey Sanchez	.15
250	Jeff Fassero	.15
251	Sandy Alomar	.15
252	Chris Bosio	.15
253	Andy Stankiewicz	.15
254	Harold Baines	.15
255	Andy Ashby	.15
256	Tyler Green	.15
257	Kevin Brown	.15
258	Mo Vaughn	.15
259	Mike Harkey	.15
260	Dave Henderson	.15
261	Kent Hrbek	.15
262	Darrin Jackson	.15
263	Bob Wickman	.15
264	Spike Owen	.15
265	Todd Jones	.15
266	Pat Borders	.15
267	Tom Glavine	.45
268	Dave Nilsson	.15
269	Rich Batchelor	.15
270	Delino DeShields	.15
271	Felix Fermin	.15
272	Orestes Destrade	.15
273	Mickey Morandini	.15
274	Otis Nixon	.15
275	Ellis Burks	.15
276	Greg Gagne	.15
277	John Doherty	.15
278	Julio Franco	.15
279	Bernie Williams	.15
280	Rick Aguilera	.15
281	Mickey Tettleton	.15
282	David Nied	.15
283	Johnny Ruffin	.15
284	Dan Wilson	.15
285	Omar Vizquel	.15
286	Willie Banks	.15
287	Erik Pappas	.15
288	Cal Eldred	.15
289	Bobby Witt	.15
290	Luis Gonzalez	.15
291	Greg Pirkl	.15
292	Alex Cole	.15
293	Ricky Bones	.15
294	Denis Boucher	.15
295	John Burkett	.15
296	Steve Trachsel	.15
297	Ricky Jordan	.15
298	Mark Dewey	.15
299	Jimmy Key	.15
300	Mike MacFarlane	.15
301	Tim Belcher	.15
302	Carlos Reyes	.15
303	Greg Harris	.15
304	Brian Anderson **RC**	.15
305	Terry Mulholland	.15
306	Felix Jose	.15
307	Darren Holmes	.15
308	Jose Rijo	.15
309	Paul Wagner	.15
310	Bob Scanlan	.15
311	Mike Jackson	.15
312	Jose Vizcaino	.15
313	Rob Butler	.15
314	Kevin Seitzer	.15
315	Geronimo Pena	.15
316	Hector Carrasco	.15
317	Eddie Murray	1.50
318	Roger Salkeld	.15
319	Todd Hundley	.15
320	Danny Jackson	.15
321	Kevin Young	.15
322	Mike Greenwell	.15
323	Kevin Mitchell	.15
324	Chuck Knoblauch	.15
325	Danny Tartabull	.15
326	Vince Coleman	.15
327	Marvin Freeman	.15
328	Andy Benes	.15
329	Mike Kelly	.15
330	Karl Rhodes	.15
331	Allen Watson	.15
332	Damion Easley	.15
333	Reggie Jefferson	.15
334	Kevin McReynolds	.15
335	Arthur Rhodes	.15
336	Brian Hunter	.15
337	Tom Browning	.15
338	Pedro Munoz	.15
339	Billy Ripken	.15
340	Gene Harris	.15
341	Fernando Vina	.15
342	Sean Berry	.15
343	Pedro Astacio	.15
344	B.J. Surhoff	.15
345	Doug Drabek	.15
346	Jody Reed	.15
347	Ray Lankford	.15
348	Steve Farr	.15
349	Eric Anthony	.15
350	Pete Smith	.15
351	Lee Smith	.15
352	Mariano Duncan	.15
353	Doug Strange	.15
354	Tim Bogar	.15
355	Dave Weathers	.15
356	Eric Karros	.15
357	Randy Myers	.15
358	Chad Curtis	.15
359	Steve Avery	.15
360	Brian Jordan	.15
361	Tim Wallach	.15
362	Pedro Martinez	1.50
363	Bip Roberts	.15
364	Lou Whitaker	.15
365	Luis Polonia	.15
366	Benny Santiago	.15
367	Brett Butler	.15
368	Shawon Dunston	.15
369	Kelly Stinnett	.15
370	Chris Turner	.15
371	Ruben Sierra	.15
372	Greg Harris	.15
373	Xavier Hernandez	.15
374	Howard Johnson	.15
375	Duane Ward	.15
376	Roberto Hernandez	.15
377	Scott Leius	.15
378	Dave Valle	.15
379	Sid Fernandez	.15
380	Doug Jones	.15
381	Zane Smith	.15
382	Craig Biggio	.15
383	Rick White	.15
384	Tom Pagnozzi	.15
385	Chris James	.15
386	Bret Boone	.15
387	Jeff Montgomery	.15
388	Chad Kreuter	.15
389	Greg Hibbard	.15
390	Mark Grace	.15
391	Phil Leftwich	.15
392	Don Mattingly	2.75
393	Ozzie Guillen	.15
394	Gary Gaetti	.15
395	Erik Hanson	.15
396	Scott Brosius	.15
397	Tom Gordon	.15
398	Bill Gullickson	.15
399	Matt Mieske	.15
400	Pat Hentgen	.15
401	Walt Weiss	.15
402	Greg Blosser	.15
403	Stan Javier	.15
404	Doug Henry	.15
405	Ramon Martinez	.15
406	Frank Viola	.15
407	Mike Hampton	.15
408	Andy Van Slyke	.15
409	Bobby Ayala	.15
410	Todd Zeile	.15
411	Jay Bell	.15
412	Denny Martinez	.15
413	Mark Portugal	.15
414	Bobby Munoz	.15
415	Kirt Manwaring	.15
416	John Kruk	.15
417	Trevor Hoffman	.15
418	Chris Sabo	.15
419	Bret Saberhagen	.15
420	Chris Nabholz	.15
421	James Mouton	.15
422	Tony Tarasco	.15
423	Carlos Delgado	.75
424	Rondell White	.15
425	Javier Lopez	.15
426	Chan Ho Park **RC**	1.00
427	Cliff Floyd	.15
428	Dave Staton	.15
429	J.R. Phillips	.15
430	Manny Ramirez	1.50
431	Kurt Abbott	.15
432	Melvin Nieves	.15
433	Alex Gonzalez	.15
434	Rick Helling	.15
435	Danny Bautista	.15
436	Matt Walbeck	.15
437	Ryan Klesko	.15
438	Steve Karsay	.15
439	Salomon Torres	.15
440	Scott Ruffcorn	.15

Refractors

It takes an experienced eye and good light to detect a Refractor parallel card from a regular-issue Topps Finest. The Refractor utilizes a variation of the Finest metallic printing process to produce rainbow-effect highlights on the card front. The Refractors share the checklist with the regular-issue Finest and were inserted at a rate of about one per 10 packs.

		NM/M
Complete Set (440):		300.00
Common Player:		1.00
Stars/Rookies:		3X

Superstar Jumbos

Identical in format to the Superstars subset in the Finest issue, these cards measure about 4" x 5-1/2" and were distributed one per box in Finest foil packs. Backs carry a card number under the banner with the player's name and po-

sition. There were 20 rookies and 20 superstars from both Series 1 and Series 2.

		NM/M
Complete Set (80):		140.00
Common Player:		1.00
1	Mike Piazza	12.50
2	Kevin Stocker	1.00
3	Greg McMichael	1.00
4	Jeff Conine	1.00
5	Rene Arocha	1.00
6	Aaron Sele	1.00
7	Brent Gates	1.00
8	Chuck Carr	1.00
9	Kirk Rueter	1.00
10	Mike Lansing	1.00
11	Al Martin	1.00
12	Jason Bere	1.00
13	Troy Neel	1.00
14	Armando Reynoso	1.00
15	Jeromy Burnitz	1.00
16	Rich Amaral	1.00
17	David McCarty	1.00
18	Tim Salmon	1.00
19	Steve Cooke	1.00
20	Wil Cordero	1.00
201	Tony Gwynn	7.50
202	Robin Ventura	1.00
203	Frank Thomas	6.00
204	Kirby Puckett	7.50
205	Roberto Alomar	2.00
206	Dennis Eckersley	5.00
207	Joe Carter	1.00
208	Albert Belle	1.00
209	Greg Maddux	7.50
210	Ryne Sandberg	7.50
211	Juan Gonzalez	3.00
212	Jeff Bagwell	6.00
213	Randy Johnson	6.00
214	Matt Williams	1.00
215	Dave Winfield	7.50
216	Larry Walker	1.00
217	Roger Clemens	10.00
218	Kenny Lofton	1.00
219	Cecil Fielder	1.00
220	Darren Daulton	1.00
221	John Olerud	1.00
222	Jose Canseco	4.00
223	Rickey Henderson	6.00
224	Fred McGriff	1.00
225	Gary Sheffield	2.00
226	Jack McDowell	1.00
227	Rafael Palmeiro	5.00
228	Travis Fryman	1.00
229	Marquis Grissom	1.00
230	Barry Bonds	20.00
231	Carlos Baerga	1.00
232	Ken Griffey Jr.	12.50
233	Dave Justice	1.00
234	Bobby Bonilla	1.00
235	Cal Ripken	20.00
236	Sammy Sosa	7.50
237	Len Dykstra	1.00
238	Will Clark	1.00
239	Paul Molitor	6.00
240	Barry Larkin	1.00
421	James Mouton	1.00
422	Tony Tarasco	1.00
423	Carlos Delgado	3.00
424	Rondell White	1.00
425	Javier Lopez	1.00
426	Chan Ho Park	1.00
427	Cliff Floyd	1.00
428	Dave Staton	1.00
429	J.R. Phillips	1.00
430	Manny Ramirez	6.00
431	Kurt Abbott	1.00
432	Melvin Nieves	1.00
433	Alex Gonzalez	1.00
434	Rick Helling	1.00
435	Danny Bautista	1.00
436	Matt Walbeck	1.00
437	Ryan Klesko	1.00
438	Steve Karsay	1.00
439	Salomon Torres	1.00
440	Scott Ruffcorn	1.00

Superstar Sampler

This special version of 45 of the biggest-name stars from the 1994 Topps Finest set was issued in a three-card cello pack with the same player's '94 Bowman and Stadium Club cards. The packs were

67	145	20	5	20	73
292	616	115	11	74	306

st Mon

first player from a new e...

...ter, then slugged 2-run ho

PS COMPANY INC. LICENSED BY MLB...
TENT #4,933,218 #5,082,703 #5,106,126

available only in 1994 Topps retail factory sets. Cards are identical to the regular-issue Finest cards except for a round, red "Topps Superstar Sampler" logo printed at bottom center on back.

		NM/M
Complete Set (45):		400.00
Common Player:		4.00
1	Mike Piazza	35.00
18	Tim Salmon	4.00
35	Andres Galarraga	4.00
74	Raul Mondesi	4.00
92	Gregg Jefferies	4.00
201	Tony Gwynn	20.00
203	Frank Thomas	15.00
204	Kirby Puckett	20.00
205	Roberto Alomar	6.00
207	Joe Carter	4.00
208	Albert Belle	4.00
209	Greg Maddux	20.00
210	Ryne Sandberg	20.00
211	Juan Gonzalez	7.50
212	Jeff Bagwell	15.00
213	Randy Johnson	15.00
214	Matt Williams	4.00
216	Larry Walker	4.00
217	Roger Clemens	30.00
219	Cecil Fielder	4.00
220	Darren Daulton	4.00
221	John Olerud	4.00
222	Jose Canseco	7.50
224	Fred McGriff	4.00
225	Gary Sheffield	6.00
226	Jack McDowell	4.00
227	Rafael Palmeiro	12.00
229	Marquis Grissom	4.00
230	Barry Bonds	65.00
231	Carlos Baerga	4.00
232	Ken Griffey Jr.	35.00
233	Dave Justice	4.00
234	Bobby Bonilla	4.00
235	Cal Ripken Jr.	65.00
237	Len Dykstra	4.00
238	Will Clark	4.00
239	Paul Molitor	15.00
240	Barry Larkin	4.00
258	Mo Vaughn	4.00
267	Tom Glavine	7.50
390	Mark Grace	4.00
392	Don Mattingly	30.00
408	Andy Van Slyke	4.00
427	Cliff Floyd	4.00
430	Manny Ramirez	15.00

Bronze

This three-card set was included as part of the purchase of a 1994 Topps Stadium Club Members Only set, but was also made available on a limited basis via newspaper ads. The cards feature a version of Topps' Finest technology with the multi-colored front design laminated to a bronze base by a heavy lucite overlay. Backs are engraved in black on bronze and contain complete major and minor league stats and a few personal data. The Finest bronze cards are slightly larger than current standard suze, measuring 2-3/4" x 3-3/4".

	NM/M
Complete Set (3):	40.00
Common Player:	10.00

1	Barry Bonds	20.00
2	Ken Griffey Jr.	15.00
3	Frank Thomas	10.00

1995 Finest

In its third year Finest baseball was reduced to a 220-card base set. All cards feature the chrome-printing technology associated with the Finest logo and include a peel-off plastic protector on the card front. Backgrounds are green with gold pinstripes. Behind the action photo at center is a large diamond with each corner intersected by a silver semi-circle. On the Finest Rookies subset which makes up the first 30 cards of the issue, the diamond has a graduated pink to orange center, with flecks of red throughout. Veterans cards have a graduated blue to purple center of the diamond. On the rookies cards there is a teal brand name at top, while the vets show a gold "FINEST." Backs repeat the front background motif in shades of green. There is a player photo at right, with biographical data, 1994 and career stats, and a "Finest Moment" career highlight at left. Finest was sold in seven-card packs with a suggested retail price of $4.99.

	NM/M
Complete Set (220):	75.00
Common Player:	.25
Refractors:	5X
Series 1 or 2 Pack (7):	2.00
Series 1 or 2 Wax Box (24):	30.00

1	Raul Mondesi (Rookie Theme)	.25
2	Kurt Abbott (Rookie Theme)	.25
3	Chris Gomez (Rookie Theme)	.25
4	Manny Ramirez (Rookie Theme)	1.50
5	Rondell White (Rookie Theme)	.25
6	William Van Landingham (Rookie Theme)	.25
7	Jon Lieber (Rookie Theme)	.25
8	Ryan Klesko (Rookie Theme)	.25
9	John Hudek (Rookie Theme)	.25
10	Joey Hamilton (Rookie Theme)	.25
11	Bob Hamelin (Rookie Theme)	.25
12	Brian Anderson (Rookie Theme)	.25
13	Mike Lieberthal (Rookie Theme)	.25
14	Rico Brogna (Rookie Theme)	.25
15	Rusty Greer (Rookie Theme)	.25
16	Carlos Delgado (Rookie Theme)	1.00
17	Jim Edmonds (Rookie Theme)	.65
18	Steve Trachsel (Rookie Theme)	.25
19	Matt Walbeck (Rookie Theme)	.25
20	Armando Benitez (Rookie Theme)	.25
21	Steve Karsay (Rookie Theme)	.25
22	Jose Oliva (Rookie Theme)	.25
23	Cliff Floyd (Rookie Theme)	.25
24	Kevin Foster (Rookie Theme)	.25
25	Javier Lopez (Rookie Theme)	.25
26	Jose Valentin (Rookie Theme)	.25
27	James Mouton (Rookie Theme)	.25
28	Hector Carrasco (Rookie Theme)	.25
29	Orlando Miller (Rookie Theme)	.25
30	Garret Anderson (Rookie Theme)	.25
31	Marvin Freeman	.25
32	Brett Butler	.25
33	Roberto Kelly	.25
34	Rod Beck	.25
35	Jose Rijo	.25
36	Edgar Martinez	.25
37	Jim Thome	.65
38	Rick Wilkins	.25
39	Wally Joyner	.25
40	Wil Cordero	.25
41	Tommy Greene	.25
42	Travis Fryman	.25
43	Don Slaught	.25
44	Brady Anderson	.25
45	Matt Williams	.25
46	Rene Arocha	.25
47	Rickey Henderson	1.50
48	Mike Mussina	.75
49	Greg McMichael	.25
50	Jody Reed	.25
51	Tino Martinez	.25
52	Dave Clark	.25
53	John Valentin	.25
54	Bret Boone	.25
55	Walt Weiss	.25
56	Kenny Lofton	.25
57	Scott Leius	.25
58	Eric Karros	.25
59	John Olerud	.25
60	Chris Hoiles	.25
61	Sandy Alomar	.25
62	Tim Wallach	.25
63	Cal Eldred	.25
64	Tom Glavine	.50
65	Mark Grace	.25
66	Rey Sanchez	.25
67	Bobby Ayala	.25
68	Dante Bichette	.25
69	Andres Galarraga	.25
70	Chuck Carr	.25
71	Bobby Witt	.25
72	Steve Avery	.25
73	Bobby Jones	.25
74	Delino DeShields	.25
75	Kevin Tapani	.25
76	Randy Johnson	1.50
77	David Nied	.25
78	Pat Hentgen	.25
79	Tim Salmon	.25
80	Todd Zeile	.25
81	John Wetteland	.25
82	Albert Belle	.25
83	Ben McDonald	.25
84	Bobby Munoz	.25
85	Bip Roberts	.25
86	Mo Vaughn	.25
87	Chuck Finley	.25
88	Chuck Knoblauch	.25
89	Frank Thomas	1.50
90	Danny Tartabull	.25
91	Dean Palmer	.25
92	Len Dykstra	.25
93	J.R. Phillips	.25
94	Tom Candiotti	.25
95	Marquis Grissom	.25
96	Barry Larkin	.25
97	Bryan Harvey	.25
98	Dave Justice	.25
99	David Cone	.25
100	Wade Boggs	2.50
101	Jason Bere	.25
102	Hal Morris	.25
103	Fred McGriff	.25
104	Bobby Bonilla	.25
105	Jay Buhner	.25
106	Allen Watson	.25
107	Mickey Tettleton	.25
108	Kevin Appier	.25
109	Ivan Rodriguez	1.00
110	Carlos Garcia	.25
111	Andy Benes	.25
112	Eddie Murray	1.50
113	Mike Piazza	3.50
114	Greg Vaughn	.25
115	Paul Molitor	1.50
116	Terry Steinbach	.25
117	Jeff Bagwell	1.50
118	Ken Griffey Jr.	3.50
119	Gary Sheffield	.75
120	Cal Ripken Jr.	5.00
121	Jeff Kent	.25
122	Jay Bell	.25
123	Will Clark	.25
124	Cecil Fielder	.25
125	Alex Fernandez	.25
126	Don Mattingly	3.00
127	Reggie Sanders	.25
128	Moises Alou	.25
129	Craig Biggio	.25
130	Eddie Williams	.25
131	John Franco	.25
132	John Kruk	.25
133	Jeff King	.25
134	Royce Clayton	.25
135	Doug Drabek	.25
136	Ray Lankford	.25
137	Roberto Alomar	.50
138	Todd Hundley	.25
139	Alex Cole	.25
140	Shawon Dunston	.25
141	John Roper	.25
142	Mark Langston	.25
143	Tom Pagnozzi	.25
144	Wilson Alvarez	.25
145	Scott Cooper	.25
146	Kevin Mitchell	.25
147	Mark Whiten	.25
148	Jeff Conine	.25
149	Chili Davis	.25
150	Luis Gonzalez	.25
151	Juan Guzman	.25
152	Mike Greenwell	.25
153	Mike Henneman	.25
154	Rick Aguilera	.25
155	Dennis Eckersley	1.00
156	Darrin Fletcher	.25
157	Darren Lewis	.25
158	Juan Gonzalez	.75
159	Dave Hollins	.25
160	Jimmy Key	.25
161	Roberto Hernandez	.25
162	Randy Myers	.25
163	Joe Carter	.25
164	Darren Daulton	.25
165	Mike MacFarlane	.25
166	Bret Saberhagen	.25
167	Kirby Puckett	2.50
168	Lance Johnson	.25
169	Mark McGwire	4.00
170	Jose Canseco	.75
171	Mike Stanley	.25
172	Lee Smith	.25
173	Robin Ventura	.25
174	Greg Gagne	.25
175	Brian McRae	.25
176	Mike Bordick	.25
177	Rafael Palmeiro	1.00
178	Kenny Rogers	.25
179	Chad Curtis	.25
180	Devon White	.25
181	Paul O'Neill	.25
182	Ken Caminiti	.25
183	Dave Nilsson	.25
184	Tim Naehring	.25
185	Roger Clemens	3.00
186	Otis Nixon	.25
187	Tim Raines	.25
188	Dennis Martinez	.25
189	Pedro Martinez	1.50
190	Jim Abbott	.25
191	Ryan Thompson	.25
192	Barry Bonds	5.00
193	Joe Girardi	.25
194	Steve Finley	.25
195	John Jaha	.25
196	Tony Gwynn	2.50
197	Sammy Sosa	2.50
198	John Burkett	.25
199	Carlos Baerga	.25
200	Ramon Martinez	.25
201	Aaron Sele	.25
202	Eduardo Perez	.25
203	Alan Trammell	.25
204	Orlando Merced	.25
205	Deion Sanders	.35
206	Robb Nen	.25
207	Jack McDowell	.25
208	Ruben Sierra	.25
209	Bernie Williams	.25
210	Kevin Seitzer	.25
211	Charles Nagy	.25
212	Tony Phillips	.25
213	Greg Maddux	2.50
214	Jeff Montgomery	.25
215	Larry Walker	.25
216	Andy Van Slyke	.25
217	Ozzie Smith	2.50
218	Geronimo Pena	.25
219	Gregg Jefferies	.25
220	Lou Whitaker	.25

Refractors

A parallel set with a counterpart to each of the 220 cards in the regular Finest emission, the Refractors are printed in a version of the Finest chrome technology that produces a rainbow effect when viewed at the proper an-gle. The relatively open spaces of the 1995 Finest design make the Refractors easier to spot than the previous years' versions, but just to assist the identification process, Topps placed a small black "RE-FRACTOR" in the dark green background on the cards' backs, as well. Advertised rate of insertion for the Refractors was about one per 12 packs.

	NM/M
Complete Set (220):	400.00
Common Player:	1.00
Stars:	5X

Flame Throwers

The scarcest of the Finest inserts is the nine-card set of baseball hardest throwing pitchers. Flame Throwers cards are found at an average rate of one per 48 packs. Fronts have a central photo of a pitcher bringing his best heat. Behind the photo is the Flame Throwers typographic logo in tones of red, yellow and orange. Backs have another photo and a bar graph rating the pitcher's skill levels.

		NM/M
Complete Set (9):		20.00
Common Player:		1.50
1	Jason Bere	1.50
2	Roger Clemens	8.00
3	Juan Guzman	1.50
4	John Hudek	1.50
5	Randy Johnson	5.00
6	Pedro Martinez	4.00
7	Jose Rijo	1.50
8	Bret Saberhagen	1.50
9	John Wetteland	1.50

Power Kings

The emphasis is on youth in this chase set of baseball's top distance threats. Found at a rate of one per 24 packs, on average, the Power Kings inserts have a central photo of the player in batting action. The background, in shades of blue, features lightning strokes. Backs feature another pair of player photos and a bar graph charting the hitter's power skills.

		NM/M
Complete Set (18):		35.00
Common Player:		.75
1	Bob Hamelin	.75
2	Raul Mondesi	.75
3	Ryan Klesko	.75
4	Carlos Delgado	1.50
5	Manny Ramirez	3.00
6	Mike Piazza	5.00
7	Jeff Bagwell	3.00
8	Mo Vaughn	.75
9	Frank Thomas	3.00
10	Ken Griffey Jr.	5.00
11	Albert Belle	.75
12	Sammy Sosa	4.00
13	Dante Bichette	.75
14	Gary Sheffield	.75
15	Matt Williams	.75
16	Fred McGriff	.75
17	Barry Bonds	7.50
18	Cecil Fielder	.75

Update

Players who changed teams through trades or free agent signings and more of the season's rookie player crop are included in the Finest Update series of 110 cards. The cards are numbered contiguously with the base Finest set and share the same design. Once again, Refractor cards were found on an average of once per 12 packs. Finest Update was sold in seven-card packs with a suggested retail price of $4.99.

	NM/M
Complete Set (110):	20.00
Common Player:	.25
Refractors:	5X
Wax Pack (7):	1.25
Wax Box (24):	20.00

221	Chipper Jones	2.50
222	Benji Gil	.25
223	Tony Phillips	.25
224	Trevor Wilson	.25
225	Tony Tarasco	.25
226	Roberto Petagine	.25
227	Mike MacFarlane	.25
228	Hideo Nomo RC	3.00
229	Mark McLemore	.25
230	Ron Gant	.25
231	Andujar Cedeno	.25
232	Mike Mimbs RC	.25
233	Jim Abbott	.25
234	Ricky Bones	.25
235	Marty Cordova	.25
236	Mark Johnson	.25
237	Marquis Grissom	.25
238	Tom Henke	.25
239	Terry Pendleton	.25
240	John Wetteland	.25
241	Lee Smith	.25
242	Jaime Navarro	.25
243	Luis Alicea	.25
244	Scott Cooper	.25
245	Gary Gaetti	.25
246	Edgardo Alfonzo	.25
247	Brad Clontz	.25
248	Dave Mlicki	.25
249	Dave Winfield	1.50
250	Mark Grudzielanek RC	.50
251	Alex Gonzalez	.25
252	Kevin Brown	.25
253	Esteban Loaiza	.25
254	Vaughn Eshelman	.25
255	Bill Swift	.25
256	Brian McRae	.25
257	Bobby Higginson RC	.50
258	Jack McDowell	.25
259	Scott Stahoviak	.25
260	Jon Nunnally	.25
261	Charlie Hayes	.25
262	Jacob Brumfield	.25
263	Chad Curtis	.25
264	Heathcliff Slocumb	.25
265	Mark Whiten	.25
266	Mickey Tettleton	.25
267	Jose Mesa	.25
268	Doug Jones	.25
269	Trevor Hoffman	.25
270	Paul Sorrento	.25
271	Shane Andrews	.25
272	Brett Butler	.25
273	Curtis Goodwin	.25
274	Larry Walker	.25
275	Phil Plantier	.25
276	Ken Hill	.25
277	Vinny Castilla	.25
278	Billy Ashley	.25
279	Derek Jeter	6.00
280	Bob Tewksbury	.25
281	Jose Offerman	.25

282	Glenallen Hill	.25
283	Tony Fernandez	.25
284	Mike Devereaux	.25
285	John Burkett	.25
286	Geronimo Berroa	.25
287	Quilvio Veras	.25
288	Jason Bates	.25
289	Lee Tinsley	.25
290	Derek Bell	.25
291	Jeff Fassero	.25
292	Ray Durham	.25
293	Chad Ogea	.25
294	Bill Pulsipher	.25
295	Phil Nevin	.25
296	Carlos Perez RC	.25
297	Roberto Kelly	.25
298	Tim Wakefield	.25
299	Jeff Manto	.25
300	Brian Hunter	.25
301	C.J. Nitkowski	.25
302	Dustin Hermanson	.25
303	John Mabry	.25
304	Orel Hershiser	.25
305	Ron Villone	.25
306	Sean Bergman	.25
307	Tom Goodwin	.25
308	Al Reyes	.25
309	Todd Stottlemyre	.25
310	Rich Becker	.25
311	Joey Cora	.25
312	Ed Sprague	.25
313	John Smoltz	.25
314	Frank Castillo	.25
315	Chris Hammond	.25
316	Ismael Valdes	.25
317	Pete Harnisch	.25
318	Bernard Gilkey	.25
319	John Kruk	.25
320	Marc Newfield	.25
321	Brian Johnson	.25
322	Mark Portugal	.25
323	David Hulse	.25
324	Luis Ortiz	.25
325	Mike Benjamin	.25
326	Brian Jordan	.25
327	Shawn Green	.75
328	Joe Oliver	.25
329	Felipe Lira	.25
330	Andre Dawson	.25

Update Refractors

The special version of Topps' chromium printing process which creates a rainbow effect was applied to a limited number of each card in the Finest Update set to create a parallel Refractor edition. To assist in identification, a small black "REFRACTOR" is printed on the cards' backs, as well. Refractors are found on average once every 12 packs of Finest Update.

	NM/M
Complete Set (110):	100.00
Common Player:	1.00
Stars:	5X

Bronze League Leaders

Available only by mail directly from Topps, this set features N.L. and A.L. leaders in various batting categories for the 1994 season. Fronts employ Topps' Finest technology with a stained-glass effect in the background, overlaid with a heavy layer of resin. Backs are bronze and feature 1994 stats and highlights embossed in blue. The cards are oversized, measuring 2-3/4" x 3-3/4".

	NM/M
Complete Set (6):	20.00
Common Player:	2.50
1 Matt Williams	2.50
2 Tony Gwynn	6.50
3 Jeff Bagwell	5.00
4 Ken Griffey Jr.	9.00

5	Paul O'Neill	2.50
6	Frank Thomas	5.00

1996 Finest

Utilizing three levels of base-card scarcity, the 359-card Finest set comprises 220 Commons (Bronze), 91 Uncommons (Silver) and 49 Rares (Gold). Cards were somewhat randomly assigned a status. Uncommon cards are found one in four packs; Rare cards are seeded one per 24 packs. The set has eight themes. Series 1 themes are Phenoms, Intimidators, Gamers and Sterling, the latter of which consists of star players already included within the first three themes. Series 2 themes are Franchise, Additions, Prodigies and Sterling. Regular-issue cards are not only numbered from 1-359 in the set as a whole, but also numbered within each subset. Finest Refractor parallel cards were also made. Rare Refractor cards are found one every 288 packs (fewer than 150 of each produced), while Uncommon Refractors are found one per 48 packs. Common Refractors are seeded 1:12.

	NM/M
Complete Set (359):	300.00
Bronze Set (220):	60.00
Common Bronze:	.15
Silver Set (91):	90.00
Typical Silver:	.50
Gold Set (47):	200.00
Typical Gold:	2.00
Series 1 Pack (6):	1.50
Series 1 Wax Box (24):	30.00
Series 2 Pack (6):	1.50
Series 2 Wax Box (24):	30.00
1 Greg Maddux/S (Intimidators)	3.00
2 Bernie Williams/S (Gamers)	.50
3 Ivan Rodriguez/S (Intimidators)	1.50
4 Marty Cordova/G (Phenoms)	2.00
5 Roberto Hernandez (Intimidators)	.15
6 Tony Gwynn/G (Gamers)	7.50
7 Barry Larkin/S (Sterling)	.50
8 Terry Pendleton (Gamers)	.15
9 Albert Belle/G (Gamers)	2.00
10 Ray Lankford/S (Gamers)	.50
11 Mike Piazza/S (Sterling)	4.00
12 Ken Caminiti (Gamers)	.15
13 Larry Walker/S (Intimidators)	.50
14 Matt Williams/S (Intimidators)	.50
15 Dan Miceli (Phenoms)	.15
16 Chipper Jones (Sterling)	2.00
17 John Wetteland (Intimidators)	.15
18 Kirby Puckett/G (Sterling)	7.50
19 Tim Naehring (Gamers)	.15
20 Karim Garcia/G (Phenoms)	2.00
21 Eddie Murray (Gamers)	1.25
22 Tim Salmon/S (Intimidators)	.50
23 Kevin Appier (Intimidators)	.15

24	Ken Griffey Jr. (Sterling)	3.00
25	Cal Ripken Jr./G (Gamers)	15.00
26	Brian McRae (Gamers)	.15
27	Pedro Martinez (Intimidators)	1.25
28	Brian Jordan (Gamers)	.15
29	Mike Fetters (Intimidators)	.15
30	Carlos Delgado (Phenoms)	.65
31	Shane Reynolds (Intimidators)	.15
32	Terry Steinbach (Gamers)	.15
33	Hideo Nomo/G (Sterling)	2.50
34	Mark Leiter (Gamers)	.15
35	Edgar Martinez/S (Intimidators)	.50
36	David Segui (Gamers)	.15
37	Gregg Jefferies (Gamers)	.15
38	Bill Pulsipher/S (Phenoms)	.50
39	Ryne Sandberg/S (Gamers)	7.50
40	Fred McGriff (Intimidators)	.15
41	Shawn Green/S (Phenoms)	.75
42	Jeff Bagwell/G (Sterling)	5.00
43	Jim Abbott/S (Gamers)	.50
44	Glenallen Hill (Intimidators)	.15
45	Brady Anderson (Gamers)	.15
46	Roger Clemens/S (Intimidators)	3.50
47	Jim Thome (Gamers)	.60
48	Frank Thomas (Sterling)	1.25
49	Chuck Knoblauch (Gamers)	.15
50	Lenny Dykstra (Gamers)	.15
51	Jason Isringhausen/G (Phenoms)	2.00
52	Rondell White/S (Phenoms)	.50
53	Tom Pagnozzi (Gamers)	.15
54	Dennis Eckersley S (Intimidators)	1.50
55	Ricky Bones (Gamers)	.15
56	David Justice (Intimidators)	.15
57	Steve Avery (Gamers)	.15
58	Robby Thompson (Gamers)	.15
59	Hideo Nomo/S (Phenoms)	1.00
60	Gary Sheffield/S (Intimidators)	.75
61	Tony Gwynn (Sterling)	2.00
62	Will Clark/S (Gamers)	.50
63	Denny Neagle (Gamers)	.15
64	Mo Vaughn/G (Intimidators)	2.00
65	Bret Boone/S (Gamers)	.50
66	Dante Bichette/G (Sterling)	2.00
67	Robin Ventura (Gamers)	.15
68	Rafael Palmeiro/S (Intimidators)	1.50
69	Carlos Baerga/S (Gamers)	.50
70	Kevin Seitzer (Gamers)	.15
71	Ramon Martinez (Intimidators)	.15
72	Tom Glavine/S (Gamers)	1.00
73	Garret Anderson/S (Phenoms)	.50
74	Mark McGwire/S (Intimidators)	12.00
75	Brian Hunter (Phenoms)	.15
76	Alan Benes (Phenoms)	.15
77	Randy Johnson/S (Intimidators)	2.00
78	Jeff King/S (Gamers)	.50
79	Kirby Puckett/G (Intimidators)	3.00
80	Ozzie Guillen (Gamers)	.15
81	Kenny Lofton/S (Intimidators)	2.00
82	Benji Gil (Phenoms)	.15
83	Jim Edmonds/G (Gamers)	2.00
84	Cecil Fielder/S (Intimidators)	.50
85	Todd Hundley (Gamers)	.15
86	Reggie Sanders/S (Intimidators)	.50
87	Pat Hentgen (Gamers)	.15
88	Ryan Klesko/S (Intimidators)	.50
89	Chuck Finley (Gamers)	.15
90	Mike Mussina/S (Intimidators)	2.50
91	John Valentin/S (Intimidators)	.50

92	Derek Jeter (Phenoms)	4.00
93	Paul O'Neill (Intimidators)	.15
94	Darrin Fletcher (Gamers)	.15
95	Manny Ramirez/S (Phenoms)	2.00
96	Delino DeShields (Gamers)	.15
97	Tim Salmon (Sterling)	.15
98	John Olerud (Gamers)	.15
99	Vinny Castilla/S (Intimidators)	.50
100	Jeff Conine/S (Gamers)	2.00
101	Tim Wakefield (Gamers)	.15
102	Johnny Damon/G (Phenoms)	3.50
103	Dave Stevens (Gamers)	.15
104	Orlando Merced (Gamers)	.15
105	Barry Bonds/G (Sterling)	15.00
106	Jay Bell (Gamers)	.15
107	John Burkett (Gamers)	.15
108	Chris Hoiles (Gamers)	.15
109	Carlos Perez/S (Phenoms)	.50
110	Dave Nilsson (Gamers)	.15
111	Rod Beck (Intimidators)	.15
112	Craig Biggio/S (Gamers)	.50
113	Mike Piazza (Intimidators)	3.00
114	Mark Langston (Gamers)	.15
115	Juan Gonzalez/S (Intimidators)	1.00
116	Rico Brogna (Gamers)	.15
117	Jose Canseco/G (Intimidators)	3.00
118	Tom Goodwin (Gamers)	.15
119	Bryan Rekar (Phenoms)	.15
120	David Cone (Intimidators)	.15
121	Ray Durham/S (Phenoms)	.50
122	Andy Pettitte (Phenoms)	.40
123	Chili Davis (Intimidators)	.15
124	John Smoltz (Gamers)	.15
125	Heathcliff Slocumb (Intimidators)	.15
126	Dante Bichette (Intimidators)	.15
127	C.J. Nitkowski/S (Phenoms)	.50
128	Alex Gonzalez (Phenoms)	.15
129	Jeff Montgomery (Intimidators)	.15
130	Raul Mondesi/S (Intimidators)	.50
131	Denny Martinez (Gamers)	.15
132	Mel Rojas (Intimidators)	.15
133	Derek Bell (Gamers)	.15
134	Trevor Hoffman (Intimidators)	.15
135	Ken Griffey Jr./S (Intimidators)	9.00
136	Darren Daulton (Gamers)	.15
137	Pete Schourek (Gamers)	.15
138	Phil Nevin (Phenoms)	.15
139	Andres Galarraga (Intimidators)	.15
140	Chad Fonville (Phenoms)	.15
141	Chipper Jones/G (Phenoms)	7.50
142	Lee Smith/S (Intimidators)	.50
143	Joe Carter/S (Gamers)	.50
144	J.T. Snow (Gamers)	.15
145	Greg Maddux/S (Sterling)	7.50
146	Barry Bonds (Intimidators)	4.00
147	Orel Hershiser (Gamers)	.15
148	Quilvio Veras (Phenoms)	.15
149	Will Clark (Sterling)	.15
150	Jose Rijo (Gamers)	.15
151	Mo Vaughn/S (Sterling)	.50
152	Travis Fryman (Gamers)	.15
153	Frank Rodriguez/S (Phenoms)	.50
154	Alex Fernandez (Gamers)	.15
155	Wade Boggs (Gamers)	2.00
156	Troy Percival (Phenoms)	.15
157	Moises Alou (Gamers)	.15
158	Javy Lopez (Gamers)	.15
159	Jason Giambi (Phenoms)	.50
160	Steve Finley/S (Gamers)	.50

161	Jeff Bagwell/S (Intimidators)	2.00
162	Mark McGwire (Sterling)	3.50
163	Eric Karros (Gamers)	.15
164	Jay Buhner/S (Intimidators)	2.00
165	Cal Ripken Jr./S (Sterling)	6.00
166	Mickey Tettleton (Intimidators)	.15
167	Barry Larkin (Intimidators)	.15
168	Lyle Mouton/S (Phenoms)	.50
169	Ruben Sierra (Intimidators)	.15
170	Bill Swift (Gamers)	.15
171	Sammy Sosa/S (Intimidators)	3.00
172	Chad Curtis (Gamers)	.15
173	Dean Palmer (Gamers)	.15
174	John Franco/S (Gamers)	.50
175	Bobby Bonilla (Intimidators)	.15
176	Greg Colbrunn (Gamers)	.15
177	Jose Mesa (Intimidators)	.15
178	Mike Greenwell (Gamers)	.15
179	Greg Vaughn/S (Intimidators)	.50
180	Mark Wohlers/S (Intimidators)	.50
181	Doug Drabek (Gamers)	.15
182	Paul O'Neill S (Sterling)	.50
183	Wilson Alvarez (Gamers)	.15
184	Marty Cordova (Sterling)	.15
185	Hal Morris (Gamers)	.15
186	Frank Thomas/G (Intimidators)	6.00
187	Carlos Garcia (Gamers)	.15
188	Albert Belle/S (Intimidators)	.50
189	Mark Grace/S (Gamers)	.50
190	Marquis Grissom (Gamers)	.15
191	Checklist	.15
192	Chipper Jones/G (Sterling)	7.50
193	Will Clark	.15
194	Paul Molitor	1.25
195	Kenny Rogers	.15
196	Reggie Sanders	.15
197	Roberto Alomar/G (Gamers)	2.50
198	Dennis Eckersley/G	4.00
199	Raul Mondesi	.15
200	Lance Johnson	.15
201	Alvin Mormon	.15
202	George Arias/G (Gamers)	2.00
203	Jack McDowell	.15
204	Randy Myers	.15
205	Harold Baines	.15
206	Marty Cordova	.15
207	Rich Hunter RC	.15
208	Al Leiter	.15
209	Greg Gagne	.15
210	Ben McDonald	.15
211	Ernie Young/S	.50
212	Terry Adams	.15
213	Paul Sorrento	.15
214	Albert Belle	.15
215	Mike Blowers	.15
216	Jim Edmonds	.15
217	Felipe Crespo	.15
218	Fred McGriff/S	.50
219	Shawon Dunston	.15
220	Jimmy Haynes	.15
221	Jose Canseco	.50
222	Eric Davis	.15
223	Kimera Bartee/S	.50
224	Tim Raines	.15
225	Tony Phillips	.15
226	Charlie Hayes	.15
227	Eric Owens	.15
228	Roberto Alomar	.30
229	Rickey Henderson/S	.50
230	Sterling Hitchcock/S	.50
231	Bernard Gilkey/S	.50
232	Hideo Nomo/G	2.50
233	Kenny Lofton	.15
234	Ryne Sandberg/S	3.00
235	Greg Maddux/S	3.00
236	Mark McGwire	3.50
237	Jay Buhner	.15
238	Craig Biggio	.15
239	Todd Stottlemyre/S	.50
240	Barry Bonds	4.00
241	Jason Kendall	.15
242	Paul O'Neill/S	.50
243	Chris Snopek/G	.15
244	Ron Gant	.15
245	Paul Wilson	.15
246	Todd Hollandsworth	.15
247	Todd Zeile	.15
248	David Justice	.15
249	Tim Salmon/S	2.00
250	Moises Alou	.15
251	Bob Wolcott	.15
252	David Wells	.15
253	Juan Gonzalez	.65
254	Andres Galarraga	.15
255	Dave Hollins	.15
256	Devon White/S	.50
257	Sammy Sosa	2.00

258	Ivan Rodriguez	.75
259	Bip Roberts	.15
260	Tino Martinez	.15
261	Chuck Knoblauch/S	.15
262	Mike Stanley	.15
263	Wally Joyner/S	.15
264	Butch Huskey	.15
265	Jeff Conine	.15
266	Matt Williams/G	2.00
267	Mark Grace	.15
268	Jason Schmidt	.15
269	Otis Nixon	.15
270	Randy Johnson/G	5.00
271	Kirby Puckett	2.00
272	Andy Fox/S RC	.50
273	Andy Benes	.15
274	Sean Berry/S	.50
275	Mike Piazza	3.00
276	Rey Ordonez	.15
277	Benito Santiago/S	.50
278	Gary Gaetti	.15
279	Paul Molitor/S	5.00
280	Robin Ventura	.15
281	Cal Ripken Jr.	4.00
282	Carlos Baerga	.15
283	Roger Cedeno	.15
284	Chad Mottola/S	.50
285	Terrell Wade	.15
286	Kevin Brown	.15
287	Rafael Palmeiro	1.00
288	Mo Vaughn	.15
289	Dante Bichette/S	.50
290	Cecil Fielder/G	2.00
291	Doc Gooden/S	.50
292	Bob Tewksbury	.15
293	Kevin Mitchell/S	.50
294	Livan Hernandez RC	2.00
295	Russ Davis/S	.50
296	Chan Ho Park/S	.50
297	T.J. Mathews	.15
298	Manny Ramirez	1.25
299	Jeff Bagwell	1.25
300	Marty Janzen/G RC	.50
301	Wade Boggs	2.00
302	Larry Walker/S	.50
303	Steve Gibralter	.15
304	B.J. Surhoff	.15
305	Ken Griffey Jr./S	4.00
306	Royce Clayton	.15
307	Sal Fasano	.15
308	Ron Gant/G	2.00
309	Gary Sheffield	.40
310	Ken Hill	.15
311	Joe Girardi	.15
312	Matt Lawton RC	.15
313	Billy Wagner/S	.50
314	Julio Franco	.15
315	Joe Carter	.50
316	Brooks Kieschnick	.15
317	Mike Grace/S RC	.50
318	Heathcliff Slocumb	.15
319	Barry Larkin	.15
320	Tony Gwynn	2.00
321	Ryan Klesko/G	2.00
322	Frank Thomas	1.25
323	Edgar Martinez	.15
324	Jermaine Dye/G	2.00
325	Henry Rodriguez	.15
326	Marvin Benard RC	.15
327	Kenny Lofton/S	.50
328	Derek Bell/S	.50
329	Ugueth Urbina	.15
330	Jason Giambi/G	3.00
331	Roger Salkeld	.15
332	Edgar Renteria	.15
333	Ryan Klesko	.15
334	Ray Lankford	.15
335	Edgar Martinez/S	.15
336	Justin Thompson	.15
337	Gary Sheffield/S	.75
338	Rey Ordonez/S	2.00
339	Mark Clark	.15
340	Ruben Rivera	.15
341	Mark Grace/S	.50
342	Matt Williams	.15
343	Francisco Cordova RC	.25
344	Cecil Fielder	.15
345	Andres Galarraga/S	.15
346	Brady Anderson/S	.15
347	Sammy Sosa/S	7.50
348	Mark Grudzielanek	.15
349	Ron Coomer	.15
350	Derek Jeter/S	6.00
351	Rich Aurilia	.15
352	Jose Herrera	.15
353	Jay Buhner/S	.15
354	Juan Gonzalez/G	2.50
355	Craig Biggio/G	2.00
356	Tony Clark	.15
357	Tino Martinez/S	.50
358	Dan Naulty RC	.15
359	Checklist	.15

Refractors

Finest Refractor cards were created as a parallel set to Topps' 1996 Finest set. Rare Refractor cards are found about one per 288 packs (less than 150 of these sets were produced), while Uncommon Refractors are found one every 48 packs. Common Refractors are seeded one every 12 packs.

	NM/M
Complete Set (359):	900.00

found every four packs and golds every 24 packs. Each card has a parallel Refractor version: bronze (1:12), silver (1:48) and gold (1:288). In addition, silver and gold cards have an additional parallel set. Silvers are found in an embossed version (1:16) and embossed Refractor version (1:192), while golds are found in a die-cut embossed version (1:96) and a die-cut embossed Refractor (1:1152).

	NM/M
Complete Set (350):	200.00
Bronze Set (200):	15.00
Common Bronze:	.15
Silver Set (100):	75.00
Typical Silver:	.50
Embossed Silvers:	2X
Gold Set (50):	150.00
Typical Gold:	1.50
Embossed Die-Cut Golds:	1.5X
Series 1 or 2 Pack (6):	1.50
Series 1 or 2 Wax Box (24):	25.00

1	Barry Bonds/B	2.00
2	Ryne Sandberg/B	.75
3	Brian Jordan/B	.15
4	Rocky Coppinger/B	.15
5	Dante Bichette/B	.15
6	Al Martin/B	.15
7	Charles Nagy/B	.15
8	Otis Nixon/B	.15
9	Mark Johnson/B	.15
10	Jeff Bagwell/B	.60
11	Ken Hill/B	.15
12	Willie Adams/B	.15
13	Raul Mondesi/B	.15
14	Reggie Sanders/B	.15
15	Derek Jeter/B	2.00
16	Jermaine Dye/B	.15
17	Edgar Renteria/B	.15
18	Travis Fryman/B	.15
19	Roberto Hernandez/B	.15
20	Sammy Sosa/B	.75
21	Garret Anderson/B	.15
22	Rey Ordonez/B	.15
23	Glenallen Hill/B	.15
24	Dave Nilsson/B	.15
25	Kevin Brown/B	.15
26	Brian McRae/B	.15
27	Joey Hamilton/B	.15
28	Jamey Wright/B	.15
29	Frank Thomas/B	.60
30	Mark McGwire/B	1.50
31	Ramon Martinez/B	.15
32	Jaime Bluma/B	.15
33	Frank Rodriguez/B	.15
34	Andy Benes/B	.15
35	Jay Buhner/B	.15
36	Justin Thompson/B	.15
37	Darin Erstad/B	.30
38	Gregg Jefferies/B	.15
39	Jeff D'Amico/B	.15
40	Pedro Martinez/B	.60
41	Nomar Garciaparra/B	.75
42	Jose Valentin/B	.15
43	Pat Hentgen/B	.15
44	Will Clark/B	.15
45	Bernie Williams/B	.15
46	Luis Castillo/B	.15
47	B.J. Surhoff/B	.15
48	Greg Gagne/B	.15
49	Pete Schourek/B	.15
50	Mike Piazza/B	1.00
51	Dwight Gooden/B	.15
52	Javy Lopez/B	.15
53	Chuck Finley/B	.15
54	James Baldwin/B	.15
55	Jack McDowell/B	.15
56	Royce Clayton/B	.15
57	Carlos Delgado/B	.35
58	Neifi Perez/B	.15
59	Eddie Taubensee/B	.15
60	Rafael Palmeiro/B	.50
61	Marty Cordova/B	.15
62	Wade Boggs/B	.75
63	Rickey Henderson/B	.60
64	Mike Hampton/B	.15
65	Troy Percival/B	.15
66	Barry Larkin/B	.15
67	Jermaine Allensworth/B	.15
68	Mark Clark/B	.15
69	Mike Lansing/B	.15
70	Mark Grudzielanek/B	.15
71	Todd Stottlemyre/B	.15
72	Juan Guzman/B	.15
73	John Burkett/B	.15
74	Wilson Alvarez/B	.15
75	Ellis Burks/B	.15
76	Bobby Higginson/B	.15
77	Ricky Bottalico/B	.15
78	Omar Vizquel/B	.15
79	Paul Sorrento/B	.15
80	Denny Neagle/B	.15
81	Roger Pavlik/B	.15
82	Mike Lieberthal/B	.15
83	Devon White/B	.15
84	John Olerud/B	.15
85	Kevin Appier/B	.15
86	Joe Girardi/B	.15
87	Paul O'Neill/B	.15
88	Mike Sweeney/B	.15
89	John Smiley/B	.15
90	Ivan Rodriguez/B	.50
91	Randy Myers/B	.15
92	Bip Roberts/B	.15
93	Jose Mesa/B	.15
94	Paul Wilson/B	.15
95	Mike Mussina/B	.30
96	Ben McDonald/B	.15
97	John Mabry/B	.15
98	Tom Goodwin/B	.15
99	Edgar Martinez/B	.15
100	Andruw Jones/B	.60
101	Jose Canseco/S	.75
102	Billy Wagner/S	.50
103	Dante Bichette/S	.50
104	Curt Schilling/S	1.00
105	Dean Palmer/S	.50
106	Larry Walker/S	.50
107	Bernie Williams/S	.50
108	Chipper Jones/S	2.00
109	Gary Sheffield/S	1.00
110	Randy Johnson/S	1.50
111	Roberto Alomar/S	.75
112	Todd Walker/S	.50
113	Sandy Alomar/S	.50
114	John Jaha/S	.50
115	Ken Caminiti/S	.50
116	Ryan Klesko/S	.50
117	Mariano Rivera/S	.75
118	Jason Giambi/S	1.00
119	Lance Johnson/S	.50
120	Robin Ventura/S	.50
121	Todd Hollandsworth/S	.50
122	Johnny Damon/S	.75
123	William Van Landingham/S	.50
124	Jason Kendall/S	.50
125	Vinny Castilla/S	.50
126	Harold Baines/S	.50
127	Joe Carter/S	.50
128	Craig Biggio/S	.50
129	Tony Clark/S	.50
130	Ron Gant/S	.50
131	David Segui/S	.50
132	Steve Trachsel/S	.50
133	Scott Rolen/S	1.25
134	Mike Stanley/S	.50
135	Cal Ripken Jr./S	5.00
136	John Smoltz/S	.50
137	Bobby Jones/S	.50
138	Manny Ramirez/S	1.50
139	Ken Griffey Jr./S	3.00
140	Chuck Knoblauch/S	.50
141	Mark Grace/S	.50
142	Chris Snopek/S	.50
143	Hideo Nomo/S	.75
144	Tim Salmon/S	.50
145	David Cone/S	.50
146	Eric Young/S	.50
147	Jeff Brantley/S	.50
148	Jim Thome/S	1.00
149	Trevor Hoffman/S	.50
150	Juan Gonzalez/S	.75
151	Mike Piazza/G	10.00
152	Ivan Rodriguez/G	4.50
153	Mo Vaughn/G	2.00
154	Brady Anderson/G	2.00
155	Mark McGwire/G	11.00
156	Rafael Palmeiro/G	4.50
157	Barry Larkin/G	2.00
158	Greg Maddux/G	7.50
159	Jeff Bagwell/G	6.00
160	Frank Thomas/G	6.00
161	Ken Caminiti/G	2.00
162	Andruw Jones/G	6.00
163	Dennis Eckersley/G	4.50
164	Jeff Conine/G	2.00
165	Jim Edmonds/G	2.00
166	Derek Jeter/G	12.50
167	Vladimir Guerrero/G	6.00
168	Sammy Sosa/G	7.50
169	Tony Gwynn/G	7.50
170	Andres Galarraga/G	2.00
171	Todd Hundley/G	2.00
172	Jay Buhner/G	2.00
173	Paul Molitor/G	2.00
174	Kenny Lofton/G	2.00
175	Barry Bonds/G	12.50
176	Gary Sheffield/B	.35
177	Dmitri Young/B	.15
178	Jay Bell/B	.15
179	David Wells/B	.15
180	Walt Weiss/B	.15
181	Paul Molitor/B	.60
182	Jose Guillen/B	.15
183	Al Leiter/B	.15
184	Mike Fetters/B	.15
185	Mark Langston/B	.15
186	Fred McGriff/B	.50
187	Darrin Fletcher/B	.15
188	Brant Brown/B	.15
189	Geronimo Berroa/B	.15
190	Jim Thome/B	.50
191	Jose Vizcaino/B	.15
192	Andy Ashby/B	.15
193	Rusty Greer/B	.15
194	Brian Hunter/B	.15
195	Chris Hoiles/B	.15
196	Orlando Merced/B	.15
197	Brett Butler/B	.15
198	Derek Bell/B	.15
199	Bobby Bonilla/B	.15
200	Alex Ochoa/B	.15
201	Wally Joyner/B	.15
202	Mo Vaughn/B	.15
203	Doug Drabek/B	.15
204	Tino Martinez/B	.15
205	Roberto Alomar/B	.30
206	Brian Giles/B **RC**	.75
207	Todd Worrell/B	.15
208	Alan Benes/B	.15
209	Jim Leyritz/B	.15
210	Darryl Hamilton/B	.15
211	Jimmy Key/B	.15
212	Juan Gonzalez/B	.35
213	Vinny Castilla/B	.15
214	Chuck Knoblauch/B	.15
215	Tony Phillips/B	.15
216	Jeff Cirillo/B	.15
217	Carlos Garcia/B	.15
218	Brooks Kieschnick/B	.15
219	Marquis Grissom/B	.15
220	Dan Wilson/B	.15
222	Greg Vaughn/B	.15
223	John Wetteland/B	.15
224	Andres Galarraga/B	.15
225	Ozzie Guillen/B	.15
226	Kevin Elster/B	.15
227	Bernard Gilkey/B	.15
228	Mike MacFarlane/B	.15
229	Heathcliff Slocumb/B	.15
230	Wendell Magee Jr./B	.15
231	Carlos Baerga/B	.15
232	Kevin Seitzer/B	.15
233	Henry Rodriguez/B	.15
234	Roger Clemens/B	.85
235	Mark Wohlers/B	.15
236	Eddie Murray/B	.60
237	Todd Zeile/B	.15
238	J.T. Snow/B	.15
239	Ken Griffey Jr./B	1.00
240	Sterling Hitchcock/B	.15
241	Albert Belle/B	.15
242	Terry Steinbach/B	.15
243	Robb Nen/B	.15
244	Mark McLemore/B	.15
245	Jeff King/B	.15
246	Tony Clark/B	.15
247	Tim Salmon/B	.15
248	Benito Santiago/B	.15
249	Robin Ventura/B	.15
250	Bubba Trammell/B **RC**	.15
251	Chili Davis/B	.15
252	John Valentin/B	.15
253	Cal Ripken Jr./B	2.00
254	Matt Williams/B	.15
255	Jeff Kent/B	.15
256	Eric Karros/B	.15
257	Ray Lankford/B	.15
258	Ed Sprague/B	.15
259	Shane Reynolds/B	.15
260	Jaime Navarro/B	.15
261	Eric Davis/B	.15
262	Orel Hershiser/B	.15
263	Mark Grace/B	.15
264	Rod Beck/B	.15
265	Ismael Valdes/B	.15
266	Manny Ramirez/B	.60
267	Ken Caminiti/B	.15
268	Tim Naehring/B	.15
269	Jose Rosado/B	.15
270	Greg Colbrunn/B	.15
271	Dean Palmer/B	.15
272	David Justice/B	.15
273	Scott Spiezio/B	.15
274	Chipper Jones/S	.75
275	Mel Rojas/B	.15
276	Bartolo Colon/B	.15
277	Darin Erstad/S	1.00
278	Sammy Sosa/S	2.00
279	Rafael Palmeiro/S	1.25
280	Frank Thomas/S	1.50
281	Ruben Rivera/S	.50
282	Hal Morris/S	.50
283	Jay Buhner/S	.50
284	Kenny Lofton/S	.50
285	Jose Canseco/S	.75
286	Alex Fernandez/S	.50
287	Todd Helton/S	1.25
288	Andy Pettitte/S	1.00
289	John Franco/S	.50
290	Ivan Rodriguez/S	1.25
291	Ellis Burks/S	.50
292	Julio Franco/S	.50
293	Mike Piazza/S	3.00
294	Brian Jordan/S	.50
295	Greg Maddux/S	2.00
296	Bob Abreu/S	.50
297	Rondell White/S	.50
298	Moises Alou/S	.50
299	Tony Gwynn/S	2.00
300	Deion Sanders/S	.50
301	Jeff Montgomery/S	.50
302	Ray Durham/S	.50
303	John Wasdin/S	.50
304	Ryne Sandberg/S	2.00
305	Delino DeShields/S	.50
306	Mark McGwire/S	4.00
307	Andruw Jones/S	1.50
308	Kevin Orie/S	.50
309	Matt Williams/S	.50
310	Karim Garcia/S	.50
311	Derek Jeter/S	5.00
312	Mo Vaughn/S	.50
313	Brady Anderson/S	.50
314	Barry Bonds/S	5.00
315	Steve Finley/S	.50
316	Vladimir Guerrero/S	1.50
317	Matt Morris/S	.50
318	Tom Glavine/S	1.00
319	Jeff Bagwell/S	1.50
320	Albert Belle/S	.50
321	Hideki Irabu/S **RC**	1.00
322	Andres Galarraga/S	.50
323	Cecil Fielder/S	.50
324	Barry Larkin/S	.50
325	Todd Hundley/S	.50
326	Fred McGriff/S	.50
327	Gary Sheffield/G	3.00
328	Craig Biggio/G	2.00
329	Raul Mondesi/G	2.00
330	Edgar Martinez/G	2.00
331	Chipper Jones/G	7.50
332	Bernie Williams/G	3.00
333	Juan Gonzalez/G	3.00
334	Ron Gant/G	2.00
335	Cal Ripken Jr./G	12.50
336	Larry Walker/G	2.00
337	Matt Williams/G	2.00
338	Jose Cruz Jr./G	2.00
339	Joe Carter/G	2.00
340	Wilton Guerrero/G	2.00
341	Cecil Fielder/G	2.00
342	Todd Walker/G	2.00
343	Ken Griffey Jr./G	10.00
344	Ryan Klesko/G	2.00
345	Roger Clemens/G	9.00
346	Hideo Nomo/G	3.00
347	Dante Bichette/G	2.00
348	Albert Belle/G	2.00
349	Randy Johnson/G	6.00
350	Manny Ramirez/G	6.00
	John Smoltz/G	2.00

1997 Finest Samples

Many of the subsets included in the 1997 Finest issue were previewed with a cello-wrapped pack of five cards distributed to hobby dealers. Cards are virtually identical to the issued versions and are designated a Refractor on back. Overprinted on back is a red notice, "PROMOTIONAL SAMPLE / NOT FOR RESALE."

	NM/M
Complete Set (5):	15.00
Common Player:	2.00

1	Barry Bonds	3.50
15	Derek Jeter	3.50
30	Mark McGwire	3.00
143	Hideo Nomo	2.50
159	Jeff Bagwell	2.50

1997 Finest

Finest returned for 1997 in its three-tiered format from 1996, but added several new twists. Issued in two series of 175 cards each, cards numbered 1-100 and 176-275 are bronze; 101-150 and 276-325 are silver and 151-175 and 326-350 are gold. All cards are designated among one of five different subsets per series. In Series 1 they are: Warriors, Blue Chips, Power, Hurlers and Masters. Series 2 subsets are: Power, Masters, Blue Chips, Competitors and Acquisitions. The bronze cards are the "common" card, while silvers are

Embossed

Each Uncommon (silver) and Rare (gold) card in both Series 1 and 2 Finest was also issued in a parallel Embossed version. The Embossed Silver were a 1:16 find, while the die-cut Embossed Gold were found on average of just one per 96 packs.

	NM/M
Common Embossed Silver:	1.00
Embossed Silver Stars:	2X
Common Embossed Gold:	3.00
Embossed/Die-Cut Gold Stars:	1.5X

Refractors

Every card in '97 Finest - both regular and embossed parallel - has a Refractor version. The Uncommon parallel set of Refractors features a mosaic pattern in the background while the Rare embossed die-cut parallel set of Refractors are produced with a hyper-plaid foil design. The number of cards and the insertion ratios for each level of Refractors is as follows: Common (200 cards, 1:12 packs), Uncommon (100, 1:48), Rare (50, 1:288), Embossed Uncommon (100, 1:192), Embossed Die-cut Rare (50, 1:1152).

	NM/M
Common Bronze:	2.00
Bronze Stars:	6X
Typical Silver:	8.00
Silver Stars:	3X
Typical Gold:	8.00
Gold Stars:	2X
Typical Embossed Silver:	7.50
Embossed Silver Stars:	7X

(Left margin box, below img_1:)

Bronze Set (220):	300.00
Common Bronze:	1.00
Bronze Stars:	4X
Silver Set (91):	250.00
Typical Silver:	2.00
Silver Stars:	2.5X
Gold Set (48):	600.00
Typical Gold:	6.00
Gold Stars:	2X

1998 Finest Pre-Production

Five-card cello packs of '98 Finest were distributed in the hobby market to preview the always-popular issue. The cards are virtually identical to the issued versions except for the card number, which bears a "PP" prefix.

	NM/M
Complete Set (5):	8.00
Common Player:	1.00

1	Nomar Garciaparra	2.25
2	Mark McGwire	3.00
3	Ivan Rodriguez	2.00
4	Ken Griffey Jr.	2.50
5	Roger Clemens	2.25

1998 Finest

Finest dropped its three-tiered format in 1998 and produced a 275-card set on a thicker 26-point stock, with 150 cards in Series 1 and 125 in Series 2. The catch in 1998 was that each card arrived in Protector, No-Protector, Protector Refractor and No-Protector Refractor versions. Six-card packs sold for a suggested retail price of $5. Finest also included insert sets for the first time since 1995. Included in Series 1 packs were Centurions, Mystery Finest and Power Zone inserts. Series 2 had Mystery Finest, Stadium Stars and The Man. Throughout both series, Finest Protector cards are considered base cards, while No-Protector cards are inserted one per two packs (HTA odds 1:1), No-Protector Refractors are seeded 1:24 packs (HTA odds 1:10) and Finest Refractors are seeded 1:12 packs (HTA odds 1:5).

	NM/M
Complete Set (275):	30.00
Common Player:	.15
No-Protector:	2.5X
Refractors:	4X
No-Protector Refractor:	8X
Pack (6):	1.50
Wax Box (24):	25.00
Jumbo Pack (13):	2.50
Jumbo Box (12):	25.00

1	Larry Walker	.15
2	Andruw Jones	.75
3	Ramon Martinez	.15
4	Geronimo Berroa	.15
5	David Justice	.15
6	Rusty Greer	.15
7	Chad Ogea	.15
8	Tom Goodwin	.15
9	Tino Martinez	.15
10	Jose Guillen	.15
11	Jeffrey Hammonds	.15
12	Brian McRae	.15
13	Jeremi Gonzalez	.15
14	Craig Counsell	.15
15	Mike Piazza	1.50
16	Greg Maddux	1.00
17	Todd Greene	.15
18	Rondell White	.15
19	Kirk Rueter	.15
20	Tony Clark	.15
21	Brad Radke	.15
22	Jaret Wright	.35
23	Carlos Delgado	.50
24	Dustin Hermanson	.15
25	Gary Sheffield	.40
26	Jose Canseco	.35
27	Kevin Young	.15
28	David Wells	.15

29	Mariano Rivera	.25
30	Reggie Sanders	.15
31	Mike Cameron	.15
32	Bobby Witt	.15
33	Kevin Orie	.15
34	Royce Clayton	.15
35	Edgar Martinez	.15
36	Neifi Perez	.15
37	Kevin Appier	.15
38	Darryl Hamilton	.15
39	Michael Tucker	.15
40	Roger Clemens	1.25
41	Carl Everett	.15
42	Mike Sweeney	.15
43	Pat Meares	.15
44	Brian Giles	.15
45	Matt Morris	.15
46	Jason Dickson	.15
47	Rich Loiselle	.15
48	Joe Girardi	.15
49	Steve Trachsel	.15
50	Ben Grieve	.15
51	Jose Vizcaino	.15
52	Hideki Irabu	.15
53	J.T. Snow	.15
54	Mike Hampton	.15
55	Dave Nilsson	.15
56	Alex Fernandez	.15
57	Brett Tomko	.15
58	Wally Joyner	.15
59	Kelvim Escobar	.15
60	Roberto Alomar	.30
61	Todd Jones	.15
62	Paul O'Neill	.15
63	Jamie Moyer	.15
64	Mark Wohlers	.15
65	Jose Cruz Jr.	.15
66	Troy Percival	.15
67	Rick Reed	.15
68	Will Clark	.15
69	Jamey Wright	.15
70	Mike Mussina	.35
71	David Cone	.15
72	Ryan Klesko	.15
73	Scott Hatteberg	.15
74	James Baldwin	.15
75	Tony Womack	.15
76	Carlos Perez	.15
77	Charles Nagy	.15
78	Jeromy Burnitz	.15
79	Shane Reynolds	.15
80	Cliff Floyd	.15
81	Jason Kendall	.15
82	Chad Curtis	.15
83	Matt Karchner	.15
84	Ricky Bottalico	.15
85	Sammy Sosa	1.00
86	Javy Lopez	.15
87	Jeff Kent	.15
88	Shawn Green	.25
89	Devon White	.15
90	Tony Gwynn	1.00
91	Bob Tewksbury	.15
92	Derek Jeter	2.50
93	Eric Davis	.15
94	Jeff Fassero	.15
95	Denny Neagle	.15
96	Ismael Valdes	.15
97	Tim Salmon	.15
98	Mark Grudzielanek	.15
99	Curt Schilling	.35
100	Ken Griffey Jr.	1.50
101	Edgardo Alfonzo	.15
102	Vinny Castilla	.15
103	Jose Rosado	.15
104	Scott Erickson	.15
105	Alan Benes	.15
106	Shannon Stewart	.15
107	Delino DeShields	.15
108	Mark Loretta	.15
109	Todd Hundley	.15
110	Chuck Knoblauch	.15
111	Quinton McCracken	.15
112	F.P. Santangelo	.15
113	Gerald Williams	.15
114	Omar Vizquel	.15
115	John Valentin	.15
116	Damion Easley	.15
117	Matt Lawton	.15
118	Jim Thome	.60
119	Sandy Alomar	.15
120	Albert Belle	.15
121	Chris Stynes	.15
122	Butch Huskey	.15
123	Shawn Estes	.15
124	Terry Adams	.15
125	Ivan Rodriguez	.60
126	Ron Gant	.15
127	John Mabry	.15
128	Jeff Shaw	.15
129	Jeff Montgomery	.15
130	Justin Thompson	.15
131	Livan Hernandez	.15
132	Ugueth Urbina	.15
133	Doug Glanville	.15
134	Troy O'Leary	.15
135	Cal Ripken Jr.	2.50
136	Quilvio Veras	.15
137	Pedro Astacio	.15
138	Willie Greene	.15
139	Lance Johnson	.15
140	Nomar Garciaparra	1.00
141	Jose Offerman	.15
142	Scott Rolen	.60
143	Derek Bell	.15
144	Johnny Damon	.35
145	Mark McGwire	2.00
146	Chan Ho Park	.15

147	Edgar Renteria	.15
148	Eric Young	.15
149	Craig Biggio	.15
150	Checklist 1-150	.15
151	Frank Thomas	.75
152	John Wetteland	.15
153	Mike Lansing	.15
154	Pedro Martinez	.75
155	Rico Brogna	.15
156	Kevin Brown	.15
157	Alex Rodriguez	2.00
158	Wade Boggs	1.00
159	Richard Hidalgo	.15
160	Mark Grace	.15
161	Jose Mesa	.15
162	John Olerud	.15
163	Tim Belcher	.15
164	Chuck Finley	.15
165	Brian Hunter	.15
166	Joe Carter	.15
167	Stan Javier	.15
168	Jay Bell	.15
169	Ray Lankford	.15
170	John Smoltz	.15
171	Ed Sprague	.15
172	Jason Giambi	.50
173	Todd Walker	.15
174	Paul Konerko	.15
175	Rey Ordonez	.15
176	Dante Bichette	.15
177	Bernie Williams	.15
178	Jon Nunnally	.15
179	Rafael Palmeiro	.60
180	Jay Buhner	.15
181	Devon White	.15
182	Jeff D'Amico	.15
183	Walt Weiss	.15
184	Scott Spiezio	.15
185	Moises Alou	.15
186	Carlos Baerga	.15
187	Todd Zeile	.15
188	Gregg Jefferies	.15
189	Mo Vaughn	.15
190	Terry Steinbach	.15
191	Ray Durham	.15
192	Robin Ventura	.15
193	Jeff Reed	.15
194	Ken Caminiti	.15
195	Eric Karros	.15
196	Wilson Alvarez	.15
197	Gary Gaetti	.15
198	Andres Galarraga	.15
199	Alex Gonzalez	.15
200	Garret Anderson	.15
201	Andy Benes	.15
202	Harold Baines	.15
203	Ron Coomer	.15
204	Dean Palmer	.15
205	Reggie Jefferson	.15
206	John Burkett	.15
207	Jermaine Allensworth	.15
208	Bernard Gilkey	.15
209	Jeff Bagwell	.75
210	Kenny Lofton	.15
211	Bobby Jones	.15
212	Bartolo Colon	.15
213	Jim Edmonds	.15
214	Pat Hentgen	.15
215	Matt Williams	.15
216	Bob Abreu	.15
217	Jorge Posada	.15
218	Marty Cordova	.15
219	Ken Hill	.15
220	Steve Finley	.15
221	Jeff King	.15
222	Quinton McCracken	.15
223	Matt Stairs	.15
224	Darin Erstad	.35
225	Fred McGriff	.15
226	Marquis Grissom	.15
227	Doug Glanville	.15
228	Tom Glavine	.35
229	John Franco	.15
230	Darren Bragg	.15
231	Barry Larkin	.15
232	Trevor Hoffman	.15
233	Brady Anderson	.15
234	Al Martin	.15
235	B.J. Surhoff	.15
236	Ellis Burks	.15
237	Randy Johnson	.75
238	Mark Clark	.15
239	Tony Saunders	.15
240	Hideo Nomo	.40
241	Brad Fullmer	.15
242	Chipper Jones	1.00
243	Jose Valentin	.15
244	Manny Ramirez	.75
245	Derrek Lee	.50
246	Jimmy Key	.15
247	Tim Naehring	.15
248	Bobby Higginson	.15
249	Charles Johnson	.15
250	Chili Davis	.15
251	Tom Gordon	.15
252	Mike Lieberthal	.15
253	Billy Wagner	.15
254	Juan Guzman	.15
255	Todd Stottlemyre	.15
256	Brian Jordan	.15
257	Barry Bonds	2.50
258	Dan Wilson	.15
259	Paul Molitor	.75
260	Juan Gonzalez	.40
261	Francisco Cordova	.15
262	Cecil Fielder	.15
263	Travis Lee	.15
264	Kevin Tapani	.15

265	Raul Mondesi	.15
266	Travis Fryman	.15
267	Armando Benitez	.15
268	Pokey Reese	.15
269	Rick Aguilera	.15
270	Andy Pettitte	.35
271	Jose Vizcaino	.15
272	Kerry Wood	.40
273	Vladimir Guerrero	.75
274	John Smiley	.15
275	Checklist 151-275	.15

	NM/M
Complete Set (275):	400.00
Common Player:	2.00
Stars/Rookies:	8X

Refractors

All 275 cards from Finest Series 1 and 2 are available in a Refractor version. seeded one per 12 packs. Besides the refractive quality of the printing of front, Refractors are designated with an "R" suffix to the card number on back.

	NM/M
Complete Set (275):	200.00
Common Player:	1.00
Stars/Rookies:	4X

No-Protector

This parallel to the 275-card base set foregoes the peel-off front protector and adds Finest technology to the back of the card. Stated insertion rates were one per two packs or one per pack in Home Team Advantage (HTA) boxes.

	NM/M
Complete Set (275):	150.00
Common Player:	.50
Stars/Rookies:	2.5X

No-Protector Refractor

A Refractor parallel to the 275 No-Protector parallel cards was a 1:24 pack insert. In Series 1, only the refractive quality of the front and back printing reveals this insert. Series 2 No-Protector Refractors have an "R" suffix to the card number on back.

Centurions

Centurions is a 20-card insert found only Series 1 hobby (1:153) and Home Team Advantage packs (1:71). The theme of the insert to top players who will lead the game into the next century. Each card is sequentially numbered on the back to 500, while Refractor versions are numbered to 75.

		NM/M
Complete Set (20):		75.00
Common Player:		1.50
Production 500 Sets		
Refractors (75 Sets):		4X
C1	Andruw Jones	4.50
C2	Vladimir Guerrero	4.50
C3	Nomar Garciaparra	6.00
C4	Scott Rolen	3.50
C5	Ken Griffey Jr.	8.00
C6	Jose Cruz Jr.	1.50
C7	Barry Bonds	12.00
C8	Mark McGwire	10.00
C9	Juan Gonzalez	2.50
C10	Jeff Bagwell	4.50
C11	Frank Thomas	4.50
C12	Paul Konerko	2.00
C13	Alex Rodriguez	10.00
C14	Mike Piazza	8.00
C15	Travis Lee	1.50
C16	Chipper Jones	6.00
C17	Larry Walker	1.50
C18	Mo Vaughn	1.50
C19	Livan Hernandez	1.50
C20	Jaret Wright	1.50

Mystery Finest

This 50-card insert was seeded one per 36 Series 1 packs and one per 15 HTA packs. The set includes 20 top players, each matched on a double-sided card with three other players and once with himself. Each side of the card is printed on a chromium finish and arrives with a black opaque protector. Mystery Finest inserts are numbered with an "M" prefix. Refractor versions were seeded one per 64 packs (HTA odds 1:15).

		NM/M
Complete Set (50):		125.00
Common Player:		1.50
Refractors:		4X
M1	Frank Thomas, Ken Griffey Jr.	3.00
M2	Frank Thomas, Mike Piazza	3.00
M3	Frank Thomas, Mark McGwire	4.00
M4	Frank Thomas, Frank Thomas	2.00
M5	Ken Griffey Jr., Mike Piazza	3.00

M6	Ken Griffey Jr., Mark McGwire	4.00
M7	Ken Griffey Jr., Ken Griffey Jr.	4.00
M8	Mike Piazza, Mark McGwire	4.00
M9	Mike Piazza, Mike Piazza	4.00
M10	Mark McGwire, Mark McGwire	6.00
M11	Nomar Garciaparra, Jose Cruz Jr.	2.50
M12	Nomar Garciaparra, Derek Jeter	5.00
M13	Nomar Garciaparra, Andruw Jones	2.50
M14	Nomar Garciaparra, Nomar Garciaparra	3.00
M15	Jose Cruz Jr., Derek Jeter	5.00
M16	Jose Cruz Jr., Andruw Jones	1.50
M17	Jose Cruz Jr., Jose Cruz Jr.	1.50
M18	Derek Jeter, Andruw Jones	5.00
M19	Derek Jeter, Derek Jeter	7.50
M20	Andruw Jones, Andruw Jones	2.00
M21	Cal Ripken Jr., Tony Gwynn	5.00
M22	Cal Ripken Jr., Barry Bonds	5.00
M23	Cal Ripken Jr., Greg Maddux	5.00
M24	Cal Ripken Jr., Cal Ripken Jr.	7.50
M25	Tony Gwynn, Barry Bonds	5.00
M26	Tony Gwynn, Greg Maddux	2.50
M27	Tony Gwynn, Tony Gwynn	3.00
M28	Barry Bonds, Greg Maddux	5.00
M29	Barry Bonds, Barry Bonds	7.50
M30	Greg Maddux, Greg Maddux	3.00
M31	Juan Gonzalez, Larry Walker	1.50
M32	Juan Gonzalez, Andres Galarraga	1.50
M33	Juan Gonzalez, Chipper Jones	2.50
M34	Juan Gonzalez, Juan Gonzalez	1.50
M35	Larry Walker, Andres Galarraga	1.50
M36	Larry Walker, Chipper Jones	2.50
M37	Larry Walker, Larry Walker	1.50
M38	Andres Galarraga, Chipper Jones	2.50
M39	Andres Galarraga, Andres Galarraga	1.50
M40	Chipper Jones, Chipper Jones	3.00
M41	Gary Sheffield, Sammy Sosa	3.00
M42	Gary Sheffield, Jeff Bagwell	1.50
M43	Gary Sheffield, Tino Martinez	1.50
M44	Gary Sheffield, Gary Sheffield	2.00
M45	Sammy Sosa, Jeff Bagwell	3.00
M46	Sammy Sosa, Tino Martinez	3.00
M47	Sammy Sosa, Sammy Sosa	3.00
M48	Jeff Bagwell, Tino Martinez	1.50
M49	Jeff Bagwell, Jeff Bagwell	2.00
M50	Tino Martinez, Tino Martinez	1.50

Mystery Finest 2

Forty more Mystery Finest inserts were seeded in Series 2 packs at a rate of one per 36 packs (HTA odds 1:15), with Refrators every 1:144

packs (HTA odds 1:64). As with Series 1, 20 players are in the checklist; some players are found with another player on the back or by himself on each side. Each side is printed in Finest technology with an opaque black protector.

		NM/M
Complete Set (40):		100.00
Common Player:		2.00
Refractors:		4X
M1	Nomar Garciaparra, Frank Thomas	3.50
M2	Nomar Garciaparra, Albert Belle	3.50
M3	Nomar Garciaparra, Scott Rolen	3.50
M4	Frank Thomas, Albert Belle	2.50
M5	Frank Thomas, Scott Rolen	2.50
M6	Albert Belle, Scott Rolen	1.50
M7	Ken Griffey Jr., Jose Cruz	4.00
M8	Ken Griffey Jr., Alex Rodriguez	6.00
M9	Ken Griffey Jr., Roger Clemens	4.50
M10	Jose Cruz, Alex Rodriguez	6.00
M11	Jose Cruz, Roger Clemens	3.00
M12	Alex Rodriguez, Roger Clemens	6.00
M13	Mike Piazza, Barry Bonds	6.00
M14	Mike Piazza, Derek Jeter	6.00
M15	Mike Piazza, Bernie Williams	5.00
M16	Barry Bonds, Derek Jeter	6.50
M17	Barry Bonds, Bernie Williams	4.00
M18	Derek Jeter, Bernie Williams	6.00
M19	Mark McGwire, Jeff Bagwell	4.50
M20	Mark McGwire, Mo Vaughn	5.00
M21	Mark McGwire, Jim Thome	5.00
M22	Jeff Bagwell, Mo Vaughn	2.00
M23	Jeff Bagwell, Jim Thome	1.50
M24	Mo Vaughn, Jim Thome	1.50
M25	Juan Gonzalez, Travis Lee	1.50
M26	Juan Gonzalez, Ben Grieve	1.50
M27	Juan Gonzalez, Fred McGriff	1.50
M28	Travis Lee, Ben Grieve	1.50
M29	Travis Lee, Fred McGriff	1.50
M30	Ben Grieve, Fred McGriff	1.50
M31	Albert Belle, Albert Belle	1.50
M32	Scott Rolen, Scott Rolen	2.00
M33	Alex Rodriguez, Alex Rodriguez	6.00
M34	Roger Clemens, Roger Clemens	4.00
M35	Bernie Williams, Bernie Williams	1.50
M36	Mo Vaughn, Mo Vaughn	1.50
M37	Jim Thome, Jim Thome	2.00
M38	Travis Lee, Travis Lee	1.50
M39	Fred McGriff, Fred McGriff	1.50
M40	Ben Grieve, Ben Grieve	1.50

Mystery Finest Jumbo

Series 2 Home Team Advantage (HTA) boxes were the exclusive venue for these large-format (3" x 5") versions of Mystery Finest. Regular cards were found one per six boxes of HTA, while Refractor versions were a 1:12 seed.

		NM/M
Complete Set (3):		12.50
Common Card:		4.00
Refractor:		1.5X
1	Ken Griffey Jr., Alex Rodriguez	4.00
2	Derek Jeter, Bernie Williams	5.00
3	Mark McGwire, Jeff Bagwell	4.00

Power Zone

This Series 1 insert features Topps' new "Flop Inks" technology which changes the color of the card depending at what angle it is viewed. They are inserted one per 72 hobby packs (HTA odds 1:32). Cards are numbered with a "P" prefix.

		NM/M
Complete Set (20):		25.00
Common Player:		.50
1	Ken Griffey Jr.	3.00
2	Jeff Bagwell	2.00
3	Jose Cruz Jr.	.50
4	Barry Bonds	5.00
5	Mark McGwire	4.00
6	Jim Thome	1.50
7	Mo Vaughn	.50
8	Gary Sheffield	1.00
9	Andres Galarraga	.50
10	Nomar Garciaparra	2.50
11	Rafael Palmeiro	.50
12	Sammy Sosa	2.50
13	Jay Buhner	.50
14	Tony Clark	.50
15	Mike Piazza	3.00
16	Larry Walker	.50
17	Albert Belle	.50
18	Tino Martinez	.50
19	Juan Gonzalez	1.25
20	Frank Thomas	2.00

Stadium Stars

Stadium Stars is a 24-card insert that features Topps' new lenticular holographic chromium technology. These are exclusive to Series 2 packs and carried an insertion rate of one per 72 packs (HTA odds 1:32).

		NM/M
Complete Set (24):		95.00
Common Player:		1.00
SS1	Ken Griffey Jr.	8.00
SS2	Alex Rodriguez	10.00
SS3	Mo Vaughn	1.00
SS4	Nomar Garciaparra	6.00
SS5	Frank Thomas	4.50
SS6	Albert Belle	1.00
SS7	Derek Jeter	12.00
SS8	Chipper Jones	6.00
SS9	Cal Ripken Jr.	12.00
SS10	Jim Thome	3.00
SS11	Mike Piazza	8.00
SS12	Juan Gonzalez	2.50
SS13	Jeff Bagwell	4.50
SS14	Sammy Sosa	6.00
SS15	Jose Cruz Jr.	1.00
SS16	Gary Sheffield	2.00
SS17	Larry Walker	1.00
SS18	Tony Gwynn	6.00
SS19	Mark McGwire	10.00
SS20	Barry Bonds	12.00
SS21	Tino Martinez	1.00
SS22	Manny Ramirez	4.50
SS23	Ken Caminiti	1.00
SS24	Andres Galarraga	1.00

The Man

This 20-card insert features the top players in baseball and was exlusively found in Series 2 packs. Regular versions

are sequentially numbered to 500 and inserted one per 119 packs, while Refractor versions are numbered to 75 and inserted one per 793 packs.

		NM/M
Complete Set (20):		125.00
Common Player:		1.50
Refractors:		3X
TM1	Ken Griffey Jr.	10.00
TM2	Barry Bonds	15.00
TM3	Frank Thomas	6.00
TM4	Chipper Jones	7.50
TM5	Cal Ripken Jr.	15.00
TM6	Nomar Garciaparra	7.50
TM7	Mark McGwire	12.50
TM8	Mike Piazza	.50
TM9	Derek Jeter	15.00
TM10	Alex Rodriguez	12.50
TM11	Jose Cruz Jr.	1.50
TM12	Larry Walker	1.50
TM13	Jeff Bagwell	6.00
TM14	Tony Gwynn	7.50
TM15	Travis Lee	2.00
TM16	Juan Gonzalez	6.00
TM17	Scott Rolen	4.50
TM18	Randy Johnson	6.00
TM19	Roger Clemens	9.00
TM20	Greg Maddux	7.50

Jumbo

Eight oversized cards were inserted into both Series 1 and Series 2 boxes as box toppers. The cards measure 3" x 5" and are inserted one per three boxes, with Refractor versions every six boxes. The oversized cards are similar to the regular-issue cards except for the numbering which designates each "X of 8."

		NM/M
Complete Set (16):		30.00
Common Player:		1.00
Refractors:		1.5X
1	Mark McGwire	4.00
2	Cal Ripken Jr.	6.00
3	Nomar Garciaparra	2.00
4	Mike Piazza	3.00
5	Greg Maddux	2.00
6	Jose Cruz Jr.	1.00
7	Roger Clemens	2.50
8	Ken Griffey Jr.	3.00
1	Frank Thomas	1.50
2	Bernie Williams	1.50
3	Randy Johnson	1.50
4	Chipper Jones	2.00
5	Manny Ramirez	1.50
6	Barry Bonds	5.00
7	Juan Gonzalez	1.25
8	Jeff Bagwell	1.50

1999 Finest

Released in two series, with each consisting of 100 regular and 50 subset cards divided into three categories: Gems, Sensations and Rookies in Series 1, and Sterling, Gamers and Rookies in the second

series. The subset cards are short-printed, seeded one per pack. Cards are printed on 27 pt. stock utilizing chromium technology. There are two parallels: Refractors and die-cut Gold Refractors. Refractors are seeded 1:12 packs, while Gold Refractors are numbered to 100 sets. Six-cards packs carried an SRP of $4.99.

		NM/M
Complete Set (300):		80.00
Complete Series 1 (150):		30.00
Complete Series 2 (150):		50.00
Common Player:		.15
Common SP		
(101-150, 251-300):		.50
Star Refractors:		6X
SP Refractors:		3X
Star Gold Refractors:		15X
SP Gold Refractors:		10X
Pack (6):		1.50
Wax Box (24):		30.00
1	Darin Erstad	.35
2	Javy Lopez	.15
3	Vinny Castilla	.15
4	Jim Thome	.60
5	Tino Martinez	.15
6	Mark Grace	.15
7	Shawn Green	.40
8	Dustin Hermanson	.15
9	Kevin Young	.15
10	Tony Clark	.15
11	Scott Brosius	.15
12	Craig Biggio	.15
13	Brian McRae	.15
14	Chan Ho Park	.15
15	Manny Ramirez	1.00
16	Chipper Jones	1.50
17	Rico Brogna	.15
18	Quinton McCracken	.15
19	J.T. Snow Jr.	.15
20	Tony Gwynn	1.50
21	Juan Guzman	.15
22	John Valentin	.15
23	Rick Helling	.15
24	Sandy Alomar	.15
25	Frank Thomas	1.00
26	Jorge Posada	.15
27	Dmitri Young	.15
28	Rick Reed	.15
29	Kevin Tapani	.15
30	Troy Glaus	.75
31	Kenny Rogers	.15
32	Jeromy Burnitz	.15
33	Mark Grudzielanek	.15
34	Mike Mussina	.50
35	Scott Rolen	.75
36	Neifi Perez	.15
37	Brad Radke	.15
38	Darryl Strawberry	.15
39	Robb Nen	.15
40	Moises Alou	.15
41	Eric Young	.15
42	Livan Hernandez	.15
43	John Wetteland	.15
44	Matt Lawton	.15
45	Ben Grieve	.15
46	Fernando Tatis	.15
47	Travis Fryman	.15
48	David Segui	.15
49	Bob Abreu	.15
50	Nomar Garciaparra	1.50
51	Paul O'Neill	.15
52	Jeff King	.15
53	Francisco Cordova	.15
54	John Olerud	.15
55	Vladimir Guerrero	1.00
56	Fernando Vina	.15
57	Shane Reynolds	.15
58	Chuck Finley	.15
59	Rondell White	.15
60	Greg Vaughn	.15
61	Ryan Minor	.15
62	Tom Gordon	.15
63	Damion Easley	.15
64	Ray Durham	.15
65	Orlando Hernandez	.15
66	Bartolo Colon	.15
67	Jaret Wright	.15
68	Royce Clayton	.15
69	Tim Salmon	.15
70	Mark McGwire	2.50
71	Alex Gonzalez	.15
72	Tom Glavine	.40
73	David Justice	.15
74	Omar Vizquel	.15
75	Juan Gonzalez	.50
76	Bobby Higginson	.15
77	Todd Walker	.15
78	Dante Bichette	.15
79	Kevin Millwood	.15
80	Roger Clemens	1.75
81	Kerry Wood	.50
82	Cal Ripken Jr.	3.00
83	Jay Bell	.15
84	Barry Bonds	3.00
85	Alex Rodriguez	2.50
86	Doug Glanville	.15
87	Jason Kendall	.15
88	Sean Casey	.25
89	Aaron Sele	.15
90	Derek Jeter	3.00
91	Andy Ashby	.15
92	Rusty Greer	.15
93	Rod Beck	.15
94	Matt Williams	.15
95	Mike Piazza	2.00
96	Wally Joyner	.15
97	Barry Larkin	.15
98	Eric Milton	.15
99	Gary Sheffield	.50
100	Greg Maddux	1.50
101	Ken Griffey Jr. (Gem)	4.00
102	Frank Thomas (Gem)	2.00
103	Nomar Garciaparra (Gem)	3.00
104	Mark McGwire (Gem)	5.00
105	Alex Rodriguez (Gem)	5.00
106	Tony Gwynn (Gem)	3.00
107	Juan Gonzalez (Gem)	.75
108	Jeff Bagwell (Gem)	2.00
109	Sammy Sosa (Gem)	3.00
110	Vladimir Guerrero (Gem)	2.00
111	Roger Clemens (Gem)	3.50
112	Barry Bonds (Gem)	6.00
113	Darin Erstad (Gem)	.50
114	Mike Piazza (Gem)	4.00
115	Derek Jeter (Gem)	6.00
116	Chipper Jones (Gem)	3.00
117	Larry Walker (Gem)	.50
118	Scott Rolen (Gem)	1.50
119	Cal Ripken Jr. (Gem)	6.00
120	Greg Maddux (Gem)	3.00
121	Troy Glaus (Sensations)	1.50
122	Ben Grieve (Sensations)	.50
123	Ryan Minor (Sensations)	.50
124	Kerry Wood (Sensations)	.50
125	Travis Lee (Sensations)	.50
126	Adrian Beltre (Sensations)	.50
127	Brad Fullmer (Sensations)	.50
128	Aramis Ramirez (Sensations)	.50
129	Eric Chavez (Sensations)	.50
130	Todd Helton (Sensations)	1.50
131	Pat Burrell RC (Finest Rookies)	4.00
132	Ryan Mills RC (Finest Rookies)	.50
133	Austin Kearns RC (Finest Rookies)	3.00
134	Josh McKinley RC (Finest Rookies)	.50
135	Adam Everett RC (Finest Rookies)	.75
136	Marlon Anderson	.50
137	Bruce Chen	.50
138	Matt Clement	.50
139	Alex Gonzalez	.50
140	Roy Halladay	.50
141	Calvin Pickering	.50
142	Randy Wolf	.50
143	Ryan Anderson	.50
144	Ruben Mateo	.50
145	Alex Escobar RC	.50
146	Jeremy Giambi	.50
147	Lance Berkman	.50
148	Michael Barrett	.50
149	Preston Wilson	.50
150	Gabe Kapler	.50
151	Roger Clemens	1.75
152	Jay Buhner	.15
153	Brad Fullmer	.15
154	Ray Lankford	.15
155	Jim Edmonds	.15
156	Jason Giambi	.60
157	Bret Boone	.15
158	Jeff Cirillo	.15
159	Rickey Henderson	1.00
160	Edgar Martinez	.15
161	Ron Gant	.15
162	Mark Kotsay	.15
163	Trevor Hoffman	.15
164	Jason Schmidt	.15
165	Brett Tomko	.15
166	David Ortiz	.50
167	Dean Palmer	.15
168	Hideki Irabu	.15
169	Mike Cameron	.15
170	Pedro Martinez	1.00
171	Tom Goodwin	.15
172	Brian Hunter	.15
173	Al Leiter	.15
174	Charles Johnson	.15
175	Curt Schilling	.50
176	Robin Ventura	.15
177	Travis Lee	.15
178	Jeff Shaw	.15
179	Ugueth Urbina	.15
180	Roberto Alomar	.30
181	Cliff Floyd	.15
182	Adrian Beltre	.25
183	Tony Womack	.15
184	Brian Jordan	.15
185	Randy Johnson	1.00
186	Mickey Morandini	.15
187	Todd Hundley	.15
188	Jose Valentin	.15
189	Eric Davis	.15
190	Ken Caminiti	.15
191	David Wells	.15
192	Ryan Klesko	.15
193	Garret Anderson	.15
194	Eric Karros	.15
195	Ivan Rodriguez	.75
196	Aramis Ramirez	.15
197	Mike Lieberthal	.15
198	Will Clark	.15
199	Rey Ordonez	.15
200	Ken Griffey Jr.	2.00
201	Jose Guillen	.15
202	Scott Erickson	.15
203	Paul Konerko	.15
204	Johnny Damon	.40
205	Larry Walker	.15
206	Denny Neagle	.15
207	Jose Offerman	.15
208	Andy Pettitte	.30
209	Bobby Jones	.15
210	Kevin Brown	.15
211	John Smoltz	.15
212	Henry Rodriguez	.15
213	Tim Belcher	.15
214	Carlos Delgado	.50
215	Andruw Jones	1.00
216	Andy Benes	.15
217	Fred McGriff	.15
218	Edgar Renteria	.15
219	Miguel Tejada	.25
220	Bernie Williams	.15
221	Justin Thompson	.15
222	Marty Cordova	.15
223	Delino DeShields	.15
224	Ellis Burks	.15
225	Kenny Lofton	.15
226	Steve Finley	.15
227	Eric Chavez	.25
228	Jose Cruz Jr.	.15
229	Marquis Grissom	.15
230	Jeff Bagwell	1.00
231	Jose Canseco	.50
232	Edgardo Alfonzo	.15
233	Richie Sexson	.15
234	Jeff Kent	.15
235	Rafael Palmeiro	.75
236	David Cone	.15
237	Gregg Jefferies	.15
238	Mike Lansing	.15
239	Mariano Rivera	.25
240	Albert Belle	.15
241	Chuck Knoblauch	.15
242	Derek Bell	.15
243	Pat Hentgen	.15
244	Andres Galarraga	.15
245	Mo Vaughn	.15
246	Wade Boggs	1.50
247	Devon White	.15
248	Todd Helton	.75
249	Raul Mondesi	.15
250	Sammy Sosa	1.50
251	Nomar Garciaparra (Sterling)	3.00
252	Mark McGwire (Sterling)	5.00
253	Alex Rodriguez (Sterling)	5.00
254	Juan Gonzalez (Sterling)	.75
255	Vladimir Guerrero (Sterling)	2.00
256	Ken Griffey Jr. (Sterling)	4.00
257	Mike Piazza (Sterling)	4.00
258	Derek Jeter (Sterling)	6.00
259	Albert Belle (Sterling)	.50
260	Greg Vaughn (Sterling)	.50
261	Sammy Sosa (Sterling)	3.00
262	Greg Maddux (Sterling)	3.00
263	Frank Thomas (Sterling)	2.00
264	Mark Grace (Sterling)	.50
265	Ivan Rodriguez (Sterling)	1.25
266	Roger Clemens (Gamers)	3.50
267	Mo Vaughn (Gamers)	.50
268	Jim Thome (Gamers)	.75
269	Darin Erstad (Gamers)	.65
270	Chipper Jones (Gamers)	2.50
271	Larry Walker (Gamers)	.50
272	Cal Ripken Jr. (Gamers)	6.00
273	Scott Rolen (Gamers)	1.25
274	Randy Johnson (Gamers)	2.00
275	Tony Gwynn (Gamers)	2.50
276	Barry Bonds (Gamers)	6.00
277	Sean Burroughs RC	1.50
278	J.M. Gold RC	.50
279	Carlos Lee	.50
280	George Lombard	.50
281	Carlos Beltran	1.50
282	Fernando Seguignol	.50
283	Eric Chavez	.65
284	Carlos Pena RC	.75
285	Corey Patterson RC	2.00
286	Alfonso Soriano RC	12.00
287	Nick Johnson RC	2.00
288	Jorge Toca RC	.50
289	A.J. Burnett RC	1.00
290	Andy Brown RC	.50
291	Doug Mientkiewicz RC	1.00
292	Bobby Seay RC	.50
293	Chip Ambres RC	.50
294	C.C. Sabathia RC	2.50
295	Choo Freeman RC	1.00
296	Eric Valent RC	.50
297	Matt Belisle RC	.50
298	Jason Tyner RC	.50
299	Masao Kida RC	.50
300	Hank Aaron, Mark McGwire (Homerun Kings)	3.00

Refractors

Inserted at the rate of one card per 12 packs, Refractors use special technology to impart a more colorful sheen to the card fronts. To eliminate doubt, the backs have the word "REFRACTOR" printed to the right of the card number at top.

	NM/M
Complete Set (300):	750.00
Common Player:	1.00
Stars:	6X
SP's:	3X

Gold Refractors

At the top of Finest's chase-card line-up for 1999 are the Gold Refractors. Fronts have an overall gold tone in the background. Backs are individually serial numbered in gold foil with an edition of 100 each, and have the words "GOLD REFRACTOR" printed at top, to the right of the card number. The Gold Refractors are die-cut along the edges to create a deckled effect. Stated pack insertion rates were between 1:26 and 1:82 depending on series and type.

	NM/M
Common Player:	3.00
Stars:	15X
SP's:	10X

Complements

This Series 2 insert set pairs two players on a "split-screen" card front. There are three different versions for each card, Non-Refractor/Refractor (1:56), Refractor/Non-Refractor (1:56) and Refractor/Refractor (1:168). Each card is numbered with a "C" prefix. Values shown are for cards with either the left- or right-side player as Refractor; dual-refractor cards valued at 2X.

		NM/M
Complete Set (7):		25.00
Common Player:		2.50
Inserted 1:56		
Dual-Refractors		2X
Inserted 1:168		
1	Mike Piazza, Ivan Rodriguez	4.00
2	Tony Gwynn, Wade Boggs	3.00
3	Kerry Wood, Roger Clemens	3.50
4	Juan Gonzalez, Sammy Sosa	3.00
5	Derek Jeter, Nomar Garciaparra	6.00
6	Mark McGwire, Frank Thomas	5.00
7	Vladimir Guerrero, Andruw Jones	2.50

Double Feature

Similar to Finest Complements, this Series 2 set utilizes split-screen fronts to accomodate two players on a horizontal format. Each card has three versions: Non-Refractor/Refractor (1:56), Refractor/Non-Refractor (1:56) and Refractor/Refractor (1:168). Card numbers have a "DF" prefix. Values shown are for cards with either left- or right-side Refractor; Dual-Refractor cards are valued at 2X.

		NM/M
Complete Set (7):		30.00
Common Player:		2.00
Dual-Refractors:		2X
1	Ken Griffey Jr., Alex Rodriguez	10.00
2	Chipper Jones, Andruw Jones	6.00
3	Darin Erstad, Mo Vaughn	2.00
4	Craig Biggio, Jeff Bagwell	4.00
5	Ben Grieve, Eric Chavez	2.00
6	Albert Belle, Cal Ripken Jr.	10.00
7	Scott Rolen, Pat Burrell	3.00

Franchise Records

This Series 2 insert set focuses on players who led their teams in various statistical categories. They are randomly seeded in 1:129 packs, while a parallel Refractor version is inserted 1:378. Card numbers have a "FR" prefix.

		NM/M
Complete Set (10):		35.00
Common Player:		2.00
Refractors:		3X
1	Frank Thomas	2.50
2	Ken Griffey Jr.	5.00
3	Mark McGwire	6.00
4	Juan Gonzalez	2.00
5	Nomar Garciaparra	3.00
6	Mike Piazza	5.00
7	Cal Ripken Jr.	7.50
8	Sammy Sosa	3.00
9	Barry Bonds	7.50
10	Tony Gwynn	3.00

Future's Finest

This Series 2 insert focuses on up-and-coming players who are primed to emerge as superstars. These are seeded 1:171 packs and limited to 500 numbered sets. Card numbers have a "FF" prefix.

		NM/M
Complete Set (10):		35.00
Common Player:		2.00
1	Pat Burrell	10.00
2	Troy Glaus	12.50
3	Eric Chavez	3.00
4	Ryan Anderson	2.00
5	Ruben Mateo	2.00
6	Gabe Kapler	2.00
7	Alex Gonzalez	2.00
8	Michael Barrett	2.00
9	Lance Berkman	2.00
10	Fernando Seguignol	2.00

Hank Aaron Award Contenders

This insert set focuses on nine players who had the best chance to win baseball's newest award. Production varies from card to card, with nine times as many of card #9 as of card #1, and so on. Insertion odds thus vary greatly, from 1:12 to 1:216. Refractor versions are found at odds which vary from 1:96 to 1:1728. Card numbers have an "HA" prefix.

		NM/M
Complete Set (9):		20.00
Common Player:		2.00
Refractors:		3X
1	Juan Gonzalez	2.00
2	Vladimir Guerrero	2.50
3	Nomar Garciaparra	3.00
4	Albert Belle	2.00
5	Frank Thomas	2.50
6	Sammy Sosa	3.00
7	Alex Rodriguez	5.00
8	Ken Griffey Jr.	4.00
9	Mark McGwire	

Leading Indicators

Utilizing a heat-sensitive, thermal ink technology, these cards highlight the 1998 home run totals of 10 players. Touching the left, right or center field portion of the card behind each player's image reveals his 1998 season home run total in that specific direction. These are seeded in Series 1 packs.

		NM/M
Complete Set (10):		20.00
Common Player:		.50
Inserted 1:24		
L1	Mark McGwire	5.00
L2	Sammy Sosa	3.00
L3	Ken Griffey Jr.	4.00
L4	Greg Vaughn	.50
L5	Albert Belle	.50
L6	Juan Gonzalez	.75
L7	Andres Galarraga	.50
L8	Alex Rodriguez	5.00
L9	Barry Bonds	6.00
L10	Jeff Bagwell	1.50

Milestones

This Series 2 insert set is fractured into four subsets, each focusing on a statistical category: Hits, Home Runs, RBIs and Doubles. The Hits category is limited to 3,000 numbered sets. Home Runs are limited to 500 numbered sets. RBIs are limited to 1,400 numbered sets and Doubles is limited to 500 numbered sets. Each card number carries an "M" prefix.

		NM/M
Complete Set (40):		125.00
Common Hits (1-10):		.50
Common Homeruns (11-20):		2.00
Common RBI (21-30):		1.00
Common Doubles (31-40):		2.00
1	Tony Gwynn (Hits)	1.50
2	Cal Ripken Jr. (Hits)	3.00
3	Wade Boggs (Hits)	1.50
4	Ken Griffey Jr. (Hits)	2.00
5	Frank Thomas (Hits)	1.00
6	Barry Bonds (Hits)	3.00
7	Travis Lee (Hits)	.50
8	Alex Rodriguez (Hits)	2.50
9	Derek Jeter (Hits)	3.00
10	Vladimir Guerrero (Hits)	1.00
11	Mark McGwire (Home Runs)	8.00
12	Ken Griffey Jr. (Home Runs)	7.00
13	Vladimir Guerrero (Home Runs)	4.00
14	Alex Rodriguez (Home Runs)	8.00
15	Barry Bonds (Home Runs)	10.00
16	Sammy Sosa (Home Runs)	5.00
17	Albert Belle (Home Runs)	5.00
18	Frank Thomas (Home Runs)	4.00
19	Jose Canseco (Home Runs)	3.00
20	Mike Piazza (Home Runs)	7.00
21	Jeff Bagwell (RBI)	2.00
22	Barry Bonds (RBI)	6.00
23	Ken Griffey Jr. (RBI)	4.00
24	Albert Belle (RBI)	1.00
25	Juan Gonzalez (RBI)	1.50
26	Vinny Castilla (RBI)	1.00
27	Mark McGwire (RBI)	5.00
28	Alex Rodriguez (RBI)	5.00
29	Nomar Garciaparra (RBI)	3.00
30	Frank Thomas (RBI)	2.50
31	Barry Bonds (Doubles)	10.00
32	Albert Belle (Doubles)	2.00
33	Ben Grieve (Doubles)	2.00
34	Craig Biggio (Doubles)	2.00
35	Vladimir Guerrero (Doubles)	4.00
36	Nomar Garciaparra (Doubles)	5.00
37	Alex Rodriguez (Doubles)	7.00
38	Derek Jeter (Doubles)	10.00
39	Ken Griffey Jr. (Doubles)	7.00
40	Brad Fullmer (Doubles)	2.00

Peel & Reveal

This Series 1 insert offers 20 players produced in varying levels of scarcity designated by background design: Sparkle is common, Hyperplaid is uncommon and Stadium Stars is rare. Each card has a peel-off opaque protective coating on both front and back. Stated insertion odds are: Sparkle 1:30; Hyperplaid 1:60, and Stadium Stars 1:120. Home Team Advantage (HTA) boxes have odds which are twice as good.

		NM/M
Complete Set (20):		40.00
Common Player:		1.00
Hyperplaid:		1.5X
Stadium Stars:		2.5X
1	Kerry Wood	1.50
2	Mark McGwire	5.00
3	Sammy Sosa	3.00
4	Ken Griffey Jr.	4.00
5	Nomar Garciaparra	3.00
6	Greg Maddux	3.00
7	Derek Jeter	6.00
8	Andres Galarraga	1.00
9	Alex Rodriguez	5.00
10	Frank Thomas	2.00
11	Roger Clemens	3.50
12	Juan Gonzalez	1.50
13	Ben Grieve	1.00
14	Jeff Bagwell	2.00
15	Todd Helton	2.00
16	Chipper Jones	3.00
17	Barry Bonds	6.00
18	Travis Lee	1.00
19	Vladimir Guerrero	2.00
20	Pat Burrell	1.50

Prominent Figures

Fifty cards on Refractor technology highlight superstars chasing the all-time records in five different statistical categories: Home Runs, Slugging Percentage, Batting Average, RBIs and Total Bases. Ten players are featured in each category, each sequentially numbered to the all-time single season record statistic for that category. Home Run category is numbered to 70, Slugging Percentage to 847, Batting Average to 424, RBIs to 190 and Total Bases to 457.

		NM/M
Complete Set (50):		250.00
Common Home Runs (1-10):		
#'d to 70:		3.00
Common Slugging % (11-20):		
#'d to 847:		1.00
Common Batting Ave. (21-30):		
#'d to 424:		1.75
Common RBIs (31-40):		
#'d to 190:		2.00
Common Total Bases (41-50):		
#'d to 457:		1.75
1	Mark McGwire (HR)	25.00
2	Sammy Sosa (HR)	10.00
3	Ken Griffey Jr. (HR)	15.00
4	Mike Piazza (HR)	15.00
5	Juan Gonzalez (HR)	5.00
6	Greg Vaughn (HR)	3.00
7	Alex Rodriguez (HR)	25.00
8	Manny Ramirez (HR)	7.50
9	Jeff Bagwell (HR)	7.50
10	Andres Galarraga (HR)	3.00
11	Mark McGwire (S%)	6.00
12	Sammy Sosa (S%)	5.00
13	Juan Gonzalez (S%)	2.50
14	Ken Griffey Jr. (S%)	5.00
15	Barry Bonds (S%)	7.50
16	Greg Vaughn (S%)	1.00
17	Larry Walker (S%)	1.00
18	Andres Galarraga (S%)	1.00
19	Jeff Bagwell (S%)	2.50
20	Albert Belle (S%)	1.00
21	Tony Gwynn (BA)	5.00
22	Mike Piazza (BA)	6.00
23	Larry Walker (BA)	1.75
24	Alex Rodriguez (BA)	7.50
25	John Olerud (BA)	1.75
26	Frank Thomas (BA)	3.50
27	Bernie Williams (BA)	1.75
28	Chipper Jones (BA)	3.50
29	Jim Thome (BA)	2.50
30	Barry Bonds (BA)	9.00
31	Juan Gonzalez (RBI)	3.00
32	Sammy Sosa (RBI)	9.00
33	Mark McGwire (RBI)	20.00
34	Albert Belle (RBI)	2.00
35	Ken Griffey Jr. (RBI)	15.00
36	Jeff Bagwell (RBI)	6.00
37	Chipper Jones (RBI)	9.00
38	Vinny Castilla (RBI)	2.00
39	Alex Rodriguez (RBI)	20.00
40	Andres Galarraga (RBI)	2.00
41	Sammy Sosa (TB)	6.00
42	Mark McGwire (TB)	7.50
43	Albert Belle (TB)	1.75
44	Ken Griffey Jr. (TB)	6.00
45	Jeff Bagwell (TB)	3.50
46	Juan Gonzalez (TB)	3.50
47	Barry Bonds (TB)	9.00
48	Vladimir Guerrero (TB)	3.50
49	Larry Walker (TB)	1.75
50	Alex Rodriguez (TB)	7.50

Split Screen

Players who share a common bond are highlighted in this Series 1 insert set which includes 14 paired players. Each card is available in three variations: Non-Refractor/Refractor (1:28), Refractor/Non-Refractor (1:28) and Refractor/Refractor (1:84). Values shown are for a card with either left- or right-side Refractor; dual-Refractor cards are worth 2X.

		NM/M
Complete Set (14):		30.00
Common Card:		1.00
Dual-Refractor:		2X
1	Mark McGwire, Sammy Sosa	4.00
2	Ken Griffey Jr., Alex Rodriguez	4.00

Team Finest

The first 10 cards are showcased in Series 1 while the last 10 cards showcased in Series 2. Team Finest are available in three colors: Blue, Red and Gold (Red and Gold are only available in Home Team Advantage packs). All Team Finest are serially numbered as follows: Blue, numbered to 1,500; Blue Refractors to 150; Red to 500; Red Refractors to 50; Gold to 250 and Gold Refractors to 25. Cards have a TF prefix to the card number.

		NM/M
Complete Set (20):		25.00
Common Blue:		1.00
Production 1,500 Sets		
Blue Refractors:		3X
Production 150 Sets		
Reds:		1.5X
Production 500 Sets		
Red Refractors:		7X
Production 50 Sets		
Golds:		2X
Production 250 Sets		
Gold Refractors:		10X
Production 25 Sets		
1	Greg Maddux	2.50
2	Mark McGwire	4.50
3	Sammy Sosa	2.50
4	Juan Gonzalez	1.25
5	Alex Rodriguez	4.50
6	Travis Lee	1.00
7	Roger Clemens	2.75
8	Darin Erstad	1.25
9	Todd Helton	1.75
10	Mike Piazza	3.50
11	Kerry Wood	1.25
12	Ken Griffey Jr.	3.50
13	Frank Thomas	2.00
14	Jeff Bagwell	2.00
15	Nomar Garciaparra	2.50
16	Derek Jeter	6.00
17	Chipper Jones	2.50
18	Barry Bonds	6.00
19	Tony Gwynn	2.50
20	Ben Grieve	1.00

2000 Finest

3	Nomar Garciaparra, Derek Jeter	5.00
4	Barry Bonds, Albert Belle	4.00
5	Cal Ripken Jr., Tony Gwynn	4.00
6	Manny Ramirez, Juan Gonzalez	1.50
7	Frank Thomas, Andres Galarraga	1.50
8	Scott Rolen, Chipper Jones	2.00
9	Ivan Rodriguez, Mike Piazza	3.00
10	Kerry Wood, Roger Clemens	2.50
11	Greg Maddux, Tom Glavine	2.00
12	Troy Glaus, Eric Chavez	1.50
13	Ben Grieve, Todd Helton	1.00
14	Travis Lee, Pat Burrell	2.50

The 286-card base set has the traditional chromium finish with the Topps Finest logo in the upper left portion on the front. Also in the upper left portion is a partial image of a baseball with seams in the background of the player photo. Card backs have a small photo with '99 stats and career totals. The rookies from Series 1 are serial numbered to 2,000 and in Series 2 to 3,000.

	NM/M
Complete Set (286):	250.00
Complete Series 1 (147):	175.00
Complete Series 2 (140):	125.00
Common Player:	.25
Common Rookie (101-120):	4.00
Production 2,000	
Common Rookie (247-266):	4.00
Production 3,000	
Common Counterpart	
(267-276):	.75
Inserted 1:8	
Common Gem (136-145):	1.50
Inserted 1:24	
Pack (6):	2.00
Series 1 & 2 Box (24):	40.00

1	Nomar Garciaparra	2.00
2	Chipper Jones	1.50
3	Erubiel Durazo	.25
4	Robin Ventura	.25
5	Garret Anderson	.25
6	Dean Palmer	.25
7	Mariano Rivera	.35
8	Rusty Greer	.25
9	Jim Thome	.25
10	Jeff Bagwell	1.00
11	Jason Giambi	.75
12	Jeromy Burnitz	.25
13	Mark Grace	.35
14	Russ Ortiz	.25
15	Kevin Brown	.25
16	Kevin Millwood	.25
17	Scott Williamson	.25
18	Orlando Hernandez	.25
19	Todd Walker	.25
20	Carlos Beltran	.50
21	Ruben Rivera	.25
22	Curt Schilling	.40
23	Brian Giles	.25
24	Eric Karros	.25
25	Preston Wilson	.25
26	Al Leiter	.25
27	Juan Encarnacion	.25
28	Tim Salmon	.40
29	B.J. Surhoff	.25
30	Bernie Williams	.45
31	Lee Stevens	.25
32	Pokey Reese	.25
33	Mike Sweeney	.25
34	Corey Koskie	.25
35	Roberto Alomar	.40
36	Tim Hudson	.40
37	Tom Glavine	.40
38	Jeff Kent	.25
39	Mike Lieberthal	.25
40	Barry Larkin	.25
41	Paul O'Neill	.25
42	Rico Brogna	.25
43	Brian Daubach	.25
44	Rich Aurilia	.25
45	Vladimir Guerrero	1.00
46	Luis Castillo	.25
47	Bartolo Colon	.25
48	Kevin Appier	.25
49	Mo Vaughn	.25
50	Alex Rodriguez	2.50
51	Randy Johnson	1.00
52	Kris Benson	.25
53	Tony Clark	.25
54	Chad Allen	.25
55	Larry Walker	.25
56	Freddy Garcia	.25
57	Paul Konerko	.35
58	Edgardo Alfonzo	.25
59	Brady Anderson	.25
60	Derek Jeter	3.00
61	Mike Hampton	.25
62	Jeff Cirillo	.25
63	Shannon Stewart	.25
64	Greg Maddux	1.50
65	Mark McGwire	2.50
66	Gary Sheffield	.50
67	Kevin Young	.25
68	Tony Gwynn	1.50
69	Rey Ordonez	.25
70	Cal Ripken Jr.	3.00
71	Todd Helton	1.00
72	Brian Jordan	.25
73	Jose Canseco	.50
74	Luis Gonzalez	.40
75	Barry Bonds	3.00
76	Jermaine Dye	.25
77	Jose Offerman	.25
78	Magglio Ordonez	.40
79	Fred McGriff	.25
80	Ivan Rodriguez	.60
81	Josh Hamilton (Prospects)	.50
82	Vernon Wells (Prospects)	.25
83	Mark Mulder (Prospects)	.35

84	John Patterson (Prospects)	.25
85	Nick Johnson (Prospects)	.50
86	Pablo Ozuna (Prospects)	.25
87	A.J. Burnett (Prospects)	.25
88	Jack Cust (Prospects)	.25
89	Adam Piatt (Prospects)	.25
90	Rob Ryan (Prospects)	.25
91	Sean Burroughs (Prospects)	.35
92	D'Angelo Jimenez (Prospects)	.25
93	Chad Hermansen (Prospects)	.25
94	Rob Fick (Prospects)	.25
95	Ruben Mateo (Prospects)	.25
96	Alex Escobar (Prospects)	.25
97	Willi Mo Pena (Prospects)	.25
98	Corey Patterson (Prospects)	.50
99	Eric Munson (Prospects)	.25
100	Pat Burrell (Prospects)	.75
101	Michael Tejera RC	4.00
102	Bobby Bradley RC	4.00
103	Larry Bigbie RC	6.00
104	B.J. Garbe RC	.25
105	Josh Kalinowski RC	4.00
106	Brett Myers RC	15.00
107	Chris Mears RC	4.00
108	Aaron Rowand RC	10.00
109	Corey Myers RC	4.00
110	John Sneed RC	4.00
111	Ryan Christensen RC	4.00
112	Kyle Snyder RC	4.00
113	Mike Paradis RC	4.00
114	Chance Caple RC	4.00
115	Ben Christiansen RC	4.00
116	Brad Baker RC	4.00
117	Rob Purvis RC	4.00
118	Rick Asadoorian RC	4.00
119	Ruben Salazar RC	4.00
120	Julio Zuleta RC	4.00
121	Ken Griffey Jr., Alex Rodriguez (Features)	4.00
122	Nomar Garciaparra, Derek Jeter (Features)	5.00
123	Mark McGwire, Sammy Sosa (Features)	4.00
124	Randy Johnson, Pedro Martinez (Features)	2.00
125	Mike Piazza, Ivan Rodriguez (Features)	3.00
126	Manny Ramirez, Roberto Alomar (Features)	2.00
127	Chipper Jones, Andruw Jones (Features)	3.00
128	Cal Ripken Jr., Tony Gwynn (Features)	5.00
129	Jeff Bagwell, Craig Biggio (Features)	1.50
130	Vladimir Guerrero, Barry Bonds (Features)	5.00
131	Alfonso Soriano, Nick Johnson (Features)	2.00
132	Josh Hamilton, Pat Burrell (Features)	1.50
133	Corey Patterson, Ruben Mateo (Features)	.75
134	Larry Walker, Todd Helton (Features)	1.50
135	Edgardo Alfonzo, Rey Ordonez (Features)	.75
136	Derek Jeter (Gems)	10.00
137	Alex Rodriguez (Gems)	8.00
138	Chipper Jones (Gems)	5.00
139	Mike Piazza (Gems)	6.00
140	Mark McGwire (Gems)	8.00
141	Ivan Rodriguez (Gems)	2.00
142	Cal Ripken Jr. (Gems)	10.00
143	Vladimir Guerrero (Gems)	3.00
144	Randy Johnson (Gems)	3.00
145	Jeff Bagwell (Gems)	3.00
146	Ken Griffey Jr. field	1.50
146a	Ken Griffey Jr. press	1.50
147	Andruw Jones	1.50
148	Kerry Wood	.50
149	Jim Edmonds	.25
150	Pedro Martinez	1.00
151	Warren Morris	.25
152	Trevor Hoffman	.25
153	Eric Young	.25
154	Andy Pettitte	.40
155	Frank Thomas	1.00
156	Damion Easley	.25
157	Cliff Floyd	.25
158	Ben Davis	.25
159	John Valentin	.25

160	Rafael Palmeiro	.65
161	Andy Ashby	.25
162	J.D. Drew	.40
163	Jay Bell	.25
164	Adam Kennedy	.25
165	Manny Ramirez	1.00
166	John Halama	.25
167	Octavio Dotel	.25
168	Darin Erstad	.40
169	Jose Lima	.25
170	Andres Galarraga	.25
171	Scott Rolen	.75
172	Delino DeShields	.25
173	J.T. Snow Jr.	.25
174	Tony Womack	.25
175	John Olerud	.25
176	Jason Kendall	.25
177	Carlos Lee	.25
178	Eric Milton	.25
179	Jeff Cirillo	.25
180	Gabe Kapler	.25
181	Greg Vaughn	.25
182	Denny Neagle	.25
183	Tino Martinez	.25
184	Doug Mientkiewicz	.25
185	Juan Gonzalez	1.00
186	Ellis Burks	.25
187	Mike Hampton	.25
188	Royce Clayton	.25
189	Mike Mussina	.50
190	Carlos Delgado	.50
191	Ben Grieve	.25
192	Fernando Tatis	.25
193	Matt Williams	.25
194	Rondell White	.25
195	Shawn Green	.50
196	Justin Thompson	.25
197	Troy Glaus	1.00
198	Roger Cedeno	.25
199	Ray Lankford	.25
200	Sammy Sosa	2.00
201	Kenny Lofton	.25
202	Edgar Martinez	.25
203	Mark Kotsay	.25
204	David Wells	.25
205	Craig Biggio	.25
206	Ray Durham	.25
207	Troy O'Leary	.25
208	Rickey Henderson	.75
209	Bob Abreu	.25
210	Neifi Perez	.25
211	Carlos Febles	.25
212	Chuck Knoblauch	.25
213	Moises Alou	.25
214	Omar Vizquel	.25
215	Vinny Castilla	.25
216	Javy Lopez	.25
217	Johnny Damon	.40
218	Roger Clemens	1.75
219	Miguel Tejada	.40
220	Deion Sanders	.35
221	Matt Lawton	.25
222	Albert Belle	.25
223	Adrian Beltre	.50
224	Dante Bichette	.25
225	Raul Mondesi	.25
226	Mike Piazza	2.00
227	Brad Penny (Prospects)	.25
228	Kip Wells (Prospects)	.25
229	Adam Everett (Prospects)	.25
230	Eddie Yarnall (Prospects)	.25
231	Matt LeCroy (Prospects)	.25
232	Ryan Anderson (Prospects)	.25
233	Rick Ankiel (Prospects)	.25
234	Daryle Ward (Prospects)	.25
235	Rafael Furcal (Prospects)	.25
236	Dee Brown (Prospects)	.25
237	Travis Dawkins (Prospects)	.25
238	Eric Valent (Prospects)	.25
239	Peter Bergeron (Prospects)	.25
240	Alfonso Soriano (Prospects)	1.50
241	John Patterson (Prospects)	.25
242	Jorge Toca (Prospects)	.25
243	Ryan Anderson (Prospects)	.25
244	Jason Dallaero (Prospects)	.25
245	Jason Grilli (Prospects)	.25
246	Chad Hermansen (Prospects)	.25
247	Scott Downs RC	4.00
248	Keith Reed RC	4.00
249	Edgar Cruz RC	4.00
250	Wes Anderson RC	4.00
251	Lyle Overbay RC	10.00
252	Mike Lamb RC	4.00
253	Vince Faison RC	4.00
254	Chad Alexander RC	4.00
255	Chris Wakeland RC	4.00
256	Aaron McNeal RC	4.00
257	Tomokazu Ohka RC	4.00
258	Ty Howington RC	6.00
259	Javier Colina RC	4.00
260	Jason Jennings RC	4.00
261	Ramon Santiago RC	4.00
262	Johan Santana RC	75.00
263	Quincey Foster RC	4.00
264	Junior Brignac RC	4.00

265	Rico Washington RC	4.00
266	Scott Sobkowiak RC	4.00
267	Pedro Martinez, Rick Ankiel (Counterparts)	2.00
268	Manny Ramirez, Vladimir Guerrero (Counterparts)	2.00
269	A.J. Burnett, Mark Mulder (Counterparts)	.75
270	Mike Piazza, Eric Munson (Counterparts)	2.50
271	Josh Hamilton, Corey Patterson (Counterparts)	1.00
272	Ken Griffey Jr., Sammy Sosa (Counterparts)	3.00
273	Derek Jeter, Alfonso Soriano (Counterparts)	5.00
274	Mark McGwire, Pat Burrell (Counterparts)	4.00
275	Chipper Jones, Cal Ripken Jr. (Counterparts)	5.00
276	Nomar Garciaparra, Alex Rodriguez (Counterparts)	4.00
277	Pedro Martinez (Gems)	3.00
278	Tony Gwynn (Gems)	5.00
279	Barry Bonds (Gems)	10.00
280	Juan Gonzalez (Gems)	3.00
281	Larry Walker (Gems)	1.50
282	Nomar Garciaparra (Gems)	8.00
283	Ken Griffey Jr. (Gems)	6.00
284	Manny Ramirez (Gems)	3.00
285	Shawn Green (Gems)	2.00
286	Sammy Sosa (Gems)	6.00

Refractor

AL LEITER

These are a parallel to the base set and have a mirror like sheen. Card backs have "refractor" written underneath the card number.

	NM/M
Stars (1-100):	5-10X
Inserted 1:24	
Rookies (101-120,247-266):	.5-1X
Production 500 Sets	
Features (121-135):	2-3X
Inserted 1:96	
Counterparts (267-276):	2-3X
Inserted 1:96	
Gems (136-145,277-286):	2-3X
Inserted 1:288	

Gold Refractor

A parallel to the base set, these have the usual mirror like appearance with a deckle edged border. Regular cards are seeded 1:240 packs, Rookies are limited to 100 serial numbered sets, Features and Counterparts subsets (1:960) and Gems (1:2,880).

Stars (1-100):	20-40X
Inserted 1:240	
Rookies (101-120, 247-266):1-2X	
Production 100 Sets	
Features:	4-8X
Inserted 1:960	
Counterparts:	4-8X
Inserted 1:960	
Gems:	5-10X
Inserted 1:2,880	

Ballpark Bounties

Seeded across both Series 1 and 2 these inserts use Serigraph Fresnal technology and have a metallic looking image of a baseball in the background of the player photo. Card backs are numbered with a "BB" prefix.

	NM/M
Complete Set (30):	85.00
Complete Series 1 (15):	45.00

Scott Rolen

Complete Series 2 (15):	45.00
Common Player:	1.50
Inserted 1:24	
1	Chipper Jones	5.00
2	Mike Piazza	6.00
3	Vladimir Guerrero	3.00
4	Sammy Sosa	6.00
5	Nomar Garciaparra	6.00
6	Manny Ramirez	3.00
7	Jeff Bagwell	3.00
8	Scott Rolen	2.00
9	Carlos Beltran	2.50
10	Pedro Martinez	3.00
11	Greg Maddux	5.00
12	Josh Hamilton	2.00
13	Adam Piatt	1.50
14	Pat Burrell	2.00
15	Alfonso Soriano	3.00
16	Alex Rodriguez	8.00
17	Derek Jeter	10.00
18	Cal Ripken Jr.	10.00
19	Larry Walker	1.50
20	Barry Bonds	10.00
21	Ken Griffey Jr.	6.00
22	Mark McGwire	8.00
23	Ivan Rodriguez	2.00
24	Andruw Jones	2.50
25	Todd Helton	2.50
26	Randy Johnson	3.00
27	Ruben Mateo	1.50
28	Corey Patterson	1.50
29	Sean Burroughs	1.50
30	Eric Munson	1.50

Dream Cast

DREAM CAST

These inserts are found exclusively in Series 2 packs and utilize Duflex technology. The card fronts try to portray a "dream sequence" with sky and clouds in the background. They are numbered with a "DC" prefix on the card back.

	NM/M
Complete Set (10):	40.00
Common Player:	2.00
Inserted 1:36	
1	Mark McGwire	8.00
2	Roberto Alomar	2.00
3	Chipper Jones	5.00
4	Derek Jeter	10.00
5	Barry Bonds	10.00
6	Ken Griffey Jr.	6.00
7	Sammy Sosa	6.00
8	Mike Piazza	6.00
9	Pedro Martinez	3.00
10	Randy Johnson	3.00

Finest Moments

Finest Moments

This four-card set pays tribute to milestone achievements accomplished during the 1999 season. They are numbered with a "FM" prefix. A Refractor parallel version is seeded 1:20 packs.

	NM/M
Complete Set (4):	6.00
Common Player:	1.00
Inserted 1:9	
Refractor:	1-2X
Inserted 1:20	
1	Chipper Jones	3.00
2	Ivan Rodriguez	1.50
3	Tony Gwynn	3.00
4	Wade Boggs	3.00

Moments Autographs

Finest Moments

1999 NL MVP

An autographed version of the four-card set, these were seeded 1:425 packs.

	NM/M
Common Autograph:	25.00
Inserted 1:425	
1	Chipper Jones	50.00
2	Ivan Rodriguez	25.00
3	Tony Gwynn	50.00
4	Wade Boggs	25.00

For The Record

FOR THE RECORD

CHIPPER JONES

Printed on Finest Clear Card technology, each of the 10 players featured has three cards. Each card sequentially numbered to the distance of the outfield wall in their home ballpark (left, center and right). Combining all three cards forms a panoramic view of the stadium.

	NM/M
Complete Set (30):	300.00
Common Player:	8.00
1A	Derek Jeter/318	20.00
1B	Derek Jeter/408	20.00
1C	Derek Jeter/314	20.00
2A	Mark McGwire/330	15.00
2B	Mark McGwire/402	15.00
2C	Mark McGwire/330	15.00
3A	Ken Griffey Jr./331	10.00
3B	Ken Griffey Jr./405	10.00
3C	Ken Griffey Jr./327	10.00
4A	Alex Rodriguez/331	15.00
4B	Alex Rodriguez/405	15.00
4C	Alex Rodriguez/327	15.00
5A	Nomar Garciaparra/310	10.00
5B	Nomar Garciaparra/390	10.00
5C	Nomar Garciaparra/302	10.00
6A	Cal Ripken Jr./333	20.00
6B	Cal Ripken Jr./410	20.00
6C	Cal Ripken Jr./318	20.00
7A	Sammy Sosa/355	10.00
7B	Sammy Sosa/400	10.00
7C	Sammy Sosa/353	10.00
8A	Manny Ramirez/325	8.00
8B	Manny Ramirez/410	8.00
8C	Manny Ramirez/325	8.00
9A	Mike Piazza/338	10.00

9B Mike Piazza/410 10.00
9C Mike Piazza/338 10.00
10A Chipper Jones/335 9.00
10B Chipper Jones/401 9.00
10C Chipper Jones/330 9.00

Gems Oversized

Each of the 10 Gems subset cards in series 1 and 2 were also done on an oversized format. The oversized cards were added as a box topper to each box. Home Team Advantage stores received Refractor versions of the Gems Oversized cards as a box topper.

		NM/M
Complete Set (20):		50.00
Common Player:		1.00
Inserted 1:Box		
1	Derek Jeter	6.00
2	Alex Rodriguez	5.00
3	Chipper Jones	3.00
4	Mike Piazza	4.00
5	Mark McGwire	5.00
6	Ivan Rodriguez	1.25
7	Cal Ripken Jr.	6.00
8	Vladimir Guerrero	2.00
9	Randy Johnson	2.00
10	Jeff Bagwell	4.00
11	Nomar Garciaparra	4.00
12	Ken Griffey Jr.	4.00
13	Manny Ramirez	2.00
14	Shawn Green	1.50
15	Sammy Sosa	4.00
16	Pedro Martinez	2.00
17	Tony Gwynn	2.00
18	Barry Bonds	6.00
19	Juan Gonzalez	1.50
20	Larry Walker	1.00

Going the Distance

This 12-card set highlights the top hitters in baseball, utilizing Photopolymer hologram technology. Card backs are numbered with a "GTD" prefix.

		NM/M
Complete Set (12):		45.00
Common Player:		3.00
Inserted 1:24		
1	Tony Gwynn	3.50
2	Alex Rodriguez	6.00
3	Derek Jeter	8.00
4	Chipper Jones	3.50
5	Nomar Garciaparra	4.00
6	Sammy Sosa	4.00
7	Ken Griffey Jr.	4.00
8	Vladimir Guerrero	3.00
9	Mark McGwire	6.00
10	Mike Piazza	4.00
11	Manny Ramirez	3.00
12	Cal Ripken Jr.	8.00

2001 Finest

	NM/M
Complete Set (140):	250.00
Common Player:	.25
Common Standout Veteran (10):	5.00
Production 1999	
Common Rookie (111-140):	4.00
Production 999	

Pack (6):		6.00
Box (20):		100.00
1	Mike Piazza/SV	10.00
2	Andruw Jones	1.00
3	Jason Giambi	.75
4	Fred McGriff	.25
5	Vladimir Guerrero/SV	6.00
6	Adrian Gonzalez	.25
7	Pedro Martinez	1.00
8	Mike Lieberthal	.25
9	Warren Morris	.25
10	Juan Gonzalez	1.00
11	Jose Canseco	.50
12	Jose Valentin	.25
13	Jeff Cirillo	.25
14	Pokey Reese	.25
15	Scott Rolen	.75
16	Greg Maddux	1.50
17	Carlos Delgado	.50
18	Rick Ankiel	.25
19	Steve Finley	.25
20	Shawn Green	.40
21	Orlando Cabrera	.25
22	Roberto Alomar	.45
23	John Olerud	.25
24	Albert Belle	.35
25	Edgardo Alfonzo	.25
26	Rafael Palmeiro	.75
27	Mike Sweeney	.25
28	Bernie Williams	.35
29	Larry Walker	.25
30	Barry Bonds/SV	15.00
31	Orlando Hernandez	.25
32	Randy Johnson	1.00
33	Shannon Stewart	.25
34	Mark Grace	.35
35	Alex Rodriguez/SV	12.00
36	Tino Martinez	.25
37	Carlos Febles	.25
38	Al Leiter	.25
39	Omar Vizquel	.25
40	Chuck Knoblauch	.25
41	Tim Salmon	.40
42	Brian Jordan	.25
43	Edgar Renteria	.25
44	Preston Wilson	.25
45	Mariano Rivera	.40
46	Gabe Kapler	.25
47	Jason Kendall	.25
48	Rickey Henderson	.75
49	Luis Gonzalez	.40
50	Tom Glavine	.40
51	Jeromy Burnitz	.25
52	Garret Anderson	.25
53	Craig Biggio	.25
54	Vinny Castilla	.25
55	Jeff Kent	.25
56	Gary Sheffield	.50
57	Jorge Posada	.40
58	Sean Casey	.40
59	Johnny Damon	.40
60	Dean Palmer	.25
61	Todd Helton	1.00
62	Barry Larkin	.25
63	Robin Ventura	.25
64	Kenny Lofton	.25
65	Sammy Sosa/SV	10.00
66	Rafael Furcal	.25
67	Jay Bell	.25
68	J.T. Snow Jr.	.25
69	Jose Vidro	.25
70	Ivan Rodriguez	.75
71	Jermaine Dye	.25
72	Chipper Jones/SV	8.00
73	Fernando Vina	.25
74	Ben Grieve	.25
75	Mark McGwire/SV	12.00
76	Matt Williams	.25
77	Mark Grudzielanek	.25
78	Mike Hampton	.25
79	Brian Giles	.25
80	Tony Gwynn	1.50
81	Carlos Beltran	.50
82	Ray Durham	.25
83	Brad Radke	.25
84	David Justice	.25
85	Frank Thomas	1.00
86	Todd Zeile	.25
87	Pat Burrell	.75
88	Jim Thome	.25
89	Greg Vaughn	.25
90	Ken Griffey Jr./SV	10.00
91	Mike Mussina	.40
92	Magglio Ordonez	.25
93	Bobby Abreu	.25
94	Alex Gonzalez	.25
95	Kevin Brown	.25
96	Jay Buhner	.25
97	Roger Clemens	2.00
98	Nomar Garciaparra/SV	10.00
99	Derek Lee	.25
100	Derek Jeter/SV	15.00
101	Adrian Beltre	.45
102	Geoff Jenkins	.25
103	Javy Lopez	.25
104	Raul Mondesi	.25
105	Troy Glaus	1.00
106	Jeff Bagwell	1.00
107	Eric Karros	.25
108	Mo Vaughn	.25
109	Cal Ripken Jr.	3.00
110	Manny Ramirez	1.00
111	Scott Heard	4.00
112	Luis Montanez RC	5.00
113	Ben Diggins	4.00
114	Shaun Boyd RC	4.00
115	Sean Burnett	4.00
116	Carmen Cali RC	4.00
117	Derek Thompson	4.00
118	David Parrish RC	4.00
119	Dominic Rich RC	4.00
120	Chad Petty RC	4.00
121	Steve Smyth RC	4.00
122	John Lackey	4.00
123	Matt Galante RC	4.00
124	Danny Borrell RC	4.00
125	Bob Keppel RC	4.00
126	Justin Wayne RC	8.00
127	J.R. House	4.00
128	Brian Sellier RC	4.00
129	Dan Moylan RC	4.00
130	Scott Pratt RC	4.00
131	Victor Hall RC	4.00
132	Joel Pineiro	8.00
133	Josh Axelson RC	4.00
134	Jose Reyes RC	200.00
135	Greg Runser RC	4.00
136	Bryan Hebson RC	4.00
137	Sammy Serrano RC	4.00
138	Kevin Joseph RC	4.00
139	Juan Richardson RC	8.00
140	Mark Fischer RC	4.00

Refractors

Stars (1-110)	4-8X
Production 499	
SP's:	.5-1.5X
Production 399	
Cards (111-140):	1-2X
Production 241	

All-Stars

		NM/M
Complete Set (10):		30.00
Common Player:		2.00
Inserted 1:10		
Refractors:		1.5-2X
Inserted 1:40		
1	Mark McGwire	5.00
2	Derek Jeter	6.00
3	Alex Rodriguez	5.00
4	Chipper Jones	3.00
5	Nomar Garciaparra	4.00
6	Sammy Sosa	4.00
7	Mike Piazza	4.00
8	Barry Bonds	6.00
9	Vladimir Guerrero	2.00
10	Ken Griffey Jr.	4.00

Autographed

		NM/M
Common Player:		5.00
Inserted 1:22		
MB	Milton Bradley	10.00
GB	Sean Burnett	5.00
BKC	Brian Cole	5.00
JC	Joe Crede	6.00
BC	Brad Creese	5.00
BD	Ben Diggins	5.00
CD	Chad Durham	5.00
TF	Troy Farnsworth	5.00
RF	Rafael Furcal	8.00
KG	Keith Ginter	5.00
AG	Adrian Gonzalez	15.00
JHH	Josh Hamilton	40.00
JH	Jason Hart	5.00
JRH	J.R. House	5.00
AH	Adam Hyzdu	5.00
DKC	David Kelton	5.00
AK	Adam Kennedy	5.00
DK	David Krynzel	8.00
ML	Mike Lamb	5.00
TL	Terrence Long	5.00
KM	Kevin Mench	5.00
BM	Ben Molina	5.00
JM	Justin Morneau	100.00
CM	Chad Mottola	5.00
JO	Jose Ortiz	5.00
DP	David Parrish	5.00
DCP	Corey Patterson	15.00
JP	Jay Payton	6.00
CP	Carlos Pena	5.00
AP	Albert Pujols	320.00
MQ	Mark Quinn	5.00
MR	Mark Redman	5.00
BS	Ben Sheets	15.00
JS	Juan Silvestre	5.00
JNS	Jamal Strong	5.00
BZ	Barry Zito	20.00

Moments

		NM/M
Complete Set (25):		45.00
Common Player:		1.00
Inserted 1:12		
Refractors:		1.5-2X
Inserted 1:40		
1	Pat Burrell	2.00
2	Adam Kennedy	1.00
3	Mike Lamb	1.00
4	Rafael Furcal	1.00
5	Terrence Long	1.00
6	Jay Payton	1.00
7	Mark Quinn	1.00
8	Ben Molina	1.00
9	Kazuhiro Sasaki	1.00
10	Mark Redman	1.00
11	Barry Bonds	8.00
12	Alex Rodriguez	6.00
13	Roger Clemens	5.00
14	Jim Edmonds	1.00
15	Jason Giambi	2.00
16	Todd Helton	2.50
17	Troy Glaus	2.50
18	Carlos Delgado	2.00
19	Darin Erstad	2.00
20	Cal Ripken Jr.	8.00
21	Paul Molitor	3.00
22	Robin Yount	2.50
23	George Brett	5.00
24	Dave Winfield	2.50
25	Wade Boggs	3.00

Moments Autographs

		NM/M
Inserted 1:250		
BB	Barry Bonds	180.00
GB	George Brett	75.00
JG	Jason Giambi	25.00
TH	Todd Helton	30.00
PM	Paul Molitor	30.00
EM	Eddie Murray	20.00
CR	Cal Ripken Jr.	125.00
DW	Dave Winfield	20.00
RY	Robin Yount	50.00

Origins

		NM/M
Complete Set (15):		18.00
Common Player:		1.00
Inserted 1:7		
Refractors:		1.5-2X
Inserted 1:40		
1	Derek Jeter	5.00
2	Jason Kendall	1.00
3	Jose Vidro	1.00
4	Preston Wilson	1.00
5	Jim Edmonds	1.00
6	Vladimir Guerrero	2.00
7	Andruw Jones	1.50
8	Scott Rolen	1.50
9	Edgardo Alfonzo	1.00
10	Mike Sweeney	1.00
11	Alex Rodriguez	4.00
12	Jermaine Dye	1.00
13	Charles Johnson	1.00
14	Darren Dreifort	1.00
15	Neifi Perez	1.00

2002 Finest

		NM/M
Complete Set (110):		125.00
Common Player:		.25
Common SP Auto. (101-110):		8.00
Pack (5):		4.00
Box (18):		60.00
1	Mike Mussina	.50
2	Steve Sparks	.25
3	Randy Johnson	1.00
4	Orlando Cabrera	.25
5	Jeff Kent	.25
6	Carlos Delgado	.75
7	Ivan Rodriguez	.75
8	Jose Cruz	.25
9	Jason Giambi	.75
10	Brad Penny	.25
11	Moises Alou	.25
12	Mike Piazza	2.00
13	Ben Grieve	.25
14	Derek Jeter	3.00
15	Roy Oswalt	.40
16	Pat Burrell	.65
17	Preston Wilson	.25
18	Kevin Brown	.25
19	Barry Bonds	3.00
20	Phil Nevin	.25
21	Juan Gonzalez	1.00
22	Carlos Beltran	.60
23	Chipper Jones	1.50
24	Curt Schilling	.50
25	Jorge Posada	.40
26	Alfonso Soriano	1.00
27	Cliff Floyd	.25
28	Rafael Palmeiro	.75
29	Terrence Long	.25
30	Ken Griffey Jr.	2.00
31	Jason Kendall	.25
32	Jose Vidro	.25
33	Jermaine Dye	.25
34	Bobby Higginson	.25
35	Albert Pujols	2.50
36	Miguel Tejada	.40
37	Jim Edmonds	.40
38	Barry Zito	.40
39	Jimmy Rollins	.50
40	Rafael Furcal	.25
41	Omar Vizquel	.25
42	Kazuhiro Sasaki	.25
43	Brian Giles	.25
44	Darin Erstad	.50
45	Mariano Rivera	.40
46	Troy Percival	.25
47	Mike Sweeney	.25
48	Vladimir Guerrero	1.00
49	Troy Glaus	1.00
50	Hideo Nomo	.65
51	Edgardo Alfonzo	.25
52	Roger Clemens	1.75
53	Eric Chavez	.40
54	Alex Rodriguez	2.50
55	Cristian Guzman	.25
56	Jeff Bagwell	1.00
57	Bernie Williams	.40
58	Kerry Wood	.60
59	Ryan Klesko	.25
60	Ichiro Suzuki	2.00
61	Larry Walker	.25
62	Nomar Garciaparra	2.00
63	Craig Biggio	.25
64	J.D. Drew	.40
65	Juan Pierre	.25
66	Roberto Alomar	.50
67	Luis Gonzalez	.40
68	Bud Smith	.25
69	Magglio Ordonez	.50
70	Scott Rolen	1.00
71	Tsuyoshi Shinjo	.25
72	Reggie Sanders	.25
73	Garret Anderson	.25
74	Tim Hudson	.40
75	Adam Dunn	.75
76	Gary Sheffield	.50
77	Johnny Damon	.25
78	Todd Helton	1.00
79	Geoff Jenkins	.25
80	Shawn Green	.40
81	C.C. Sabathia	.25
82	Kazuhisa Ishii RC	3.00
83	Rich Aurilia	.25
84	Mike Hampton	.25
85	Ben Sheets	.25
86	Andruw Jones	1.00
87	Richie Sexson	.25
88	Jim Thome	.25
89	Sammy Sosa	2.00
90	Greg Maddux	1.50
91	Pedro Martinez	1.00
92	Jeromy Burnitz	.25
93	Raul Mondesi	.25
94	Bret Boone	.25
95	Jerry Hairston Jr.	.25
96	Carlos Pena	.25
97	Juan Cruz	.25
98	Morgan Ensberg	.25
99	Nathan Haynes	.25
100	Xavier Nady	.25
101	Nic Jackson/ Auto.	10.00
102	Mauricio Lara/ Auto. RC	8.00
103	Freddy Sanchez/ Auto. RC	20.00
104	Clint Nageotte/ Auto. RC	15.00
105	Beltran Perez/ Auto. RC	8.00
106	Garrett Gentry/ Auto. RC	8.00
107	Chad Qualls/Auto. RC	8.00
108	Jason Bay/Auto. RC	65.00
109	Michael Hill/Auto. RC	8.00
110	Brian Tallet/Auto.	10.00

Refractors

Star Refractors	2-5X
Numbered to 499	
X-Fractors	3-6X
Numbered to 299	
X-Fractor Protector:	5-10X
X-Fract. Protector (101-110):	1-2X
Numbered to 99.	

Moments Autographs

		NM/M
Common Autograph:		10.00
Inserted 1:18		
LA	Luis Aparicio	15.00
YB	Yogi Berra	30.00
JB	Jim Bunning	10.00
BG	Bob Gibson	25.00
GG	Rich "Goose" Gossage	10.00
FJ	Fergie Jenkins	15.00
DL	Don Larsen	15.00
DM	Don Mattingly	75.00
GP	Gaylord Perry	10.00
BR	Bobby Richardson	35.00
BRO	Brooks Robinson	35.00
JS	Johnny Sain	10.00
MS	Mike Schmidt	50.00
RS	Red Schoendienst	10.00
BT	Bobby Thomson	15.00

Bat Relics

	NM/M
Common Player:	5.00

Inserted 1:72

BB	Barry Bonds	25.00
BBO	Bret Boone	5.00
NG	Nomar Garciaparra	15.00
LG	Luis Gonzalez	5.00
TG	Tony Gwynn	10.00
TH	Todd Helton	8.00
AJ	Andruw Jones	5.00
CJ	Chipper Jones	10.00
MP	Mike Piazza	10.00
AP	Albert Pujols	20.00
AR	Alex Rodriguez	10.00
IR	Ivan Rodriguez	8.00
TS	Tsuyoshi Shinjo	5.00
AS	Alfonso Soriano	8.00
BW	Bernie Williams	8.00

Team Topps Legends

Common Autograph

Uniform Relics

		NM/M
Common Player:		5.00
Inserted 1:24		
RA	Roberto Alomar	8.00
JB	Jeff Bagwell	8.00
BB	Barry Bonds	20.00
BBO	Bret Boone	5.00
CD	Carlos Delgado	8.00
LG	Luis Gonzalez	5.00
MG	Mark Grace	8.00
SG	Shawn Green	5.00
TG	Tony Gwynn	10.00
TH	Todd Helton	8.00
RH	Rickey Henderson	15.00
AJ	Andruw Jones	8.00
CJ	Chipper Jones	10.00
GM	Greg Maddux	10.00
PM	Pedro Martinez	10.00
HN	Hideo Nomo	20.00
RP	Rafael Palmeiro	10.00
MP	Mike Piazza	10.00
AR	Alex Rodriguez	10.00
IR	Ivan Rodriguez	8.00
CS	Curt Schilling	10.00
TS	Tsuyoshi Shinjo	5.00
FT	Frank Thomas	8.00
LW	Larry Walker	5.00

2003 Finest

	NM/M
Complete Set (110):	
Common Player:	.25
Common Auto. (101-110):	10.00
Pack (5):	5.00
Box (18):	75.00

1	Sammy Sosa	2.00
2	Paul Konerko	.25
3	Todd Helton	.75
4	Mike Lowell	.25
5	Lance Berkman	.25
6	Kazuhisa Ishii	.25
7	A.J. Pierzynski	.25
8	Jose Vidro	.25
9	Roberto Alomar	.40
10	Derek Jeter	3.00
11	Barry Zito	.50
12	Jimmy Rollins	.50
13	Brian Giles	.25
14	Ryan Klesko	.25
15	Rich Aurilia	.25
16	Jim Edmonds	.25
17	Aubrey Huff	.25
18	Ivan Rodriguez	.65
19	Eric Hinske	.25
20	Barry Bonds	3.00
21	Darin Erstad	.60
22	Curt Schilling	.50
23	Andruw Jones	.75
24	Jay Gibbons	.25
25	Nomar Garciaparra	1.50
26	Kerry Wood	.60
27	Magglio Ordonez	.50
28	Austin Kearns	.50
29	Jason Jennings	.25
30	Jason Giambi	.50
31	Tim Hudson	.40
32	Edgar Martinez	.25
33	Carl Crawford	.75
34	Hee Seop Choi	35.00
35	Vladimir Guerrero	.75
36	Jeff Kent	.25
37	John Smoltz	.25
38	Frank Thomas	.75
39	Cliff Floyd	.25
40	Mike Piazza	1.50
41	Mark Prior	.75
42	Tim Salmon	.40
43	Shawn Green	.50
44	Bernie Williams	.40
45	Jim Thome	.40
46	John Olerud	.25
47	Orlando Hudson	.25
48	Mark Teixeira	.75
49	Gary Sheffield	.50
50	Ichiro Suzuki	2.00
51	Tom Glavine	.40
52	Torii Hunter	.25
53	Craig Biggio	.25
54	Carlos Beltran	.75
55	Bartolo Colon	.25
56	Jorge Posada	.35
57	Pat Burrell	.65
58	Edgar Renteria	.25
59	Rafael Palmeiro	.65
60	Alfonso Soriano	.75
61	Brandon Phillips	.25
62	Luis Gonzalez	.40
63	Manny Ramirez	.75
64	Garret Anderson	.25
65	Ken Griffey Jr.	1.50
66	A.J. Burnett	.25
67	Mike Sweeney	.25
68	Doug Mientkiewicz	.25
69	Eric Chavez	.50
70	Adam Dunn	.75
71	Shea Hillenbrand	.25
72	Troy Glaus	.75
73	Rodrigo Lopez	.25
74	Moises Alou	.25
75	Chipper Jones	1.00
76	Bobby Abreu	.50
77	Mark Mulder	.40
78	Kevin Brown	.25
79	Josh Beckett	.50
80	Larry Walker	.25
81	Randy Johnson	.75
82	Greg Maddux	1.00
83	Johnny Damon	.25
84	Omar Vizquel	.25
85	Jeff Bagwell	.75
86	Carlos Pena	.25
87	Roy Oswalt	.40
88	Richie Sexson	.25
89	Roger Clemens	1.25
90	Miguel Tejada	.40
91	Vicente Padilla	.25
92	Phil Nevin	.25
93	Edgardo Alfonzo	.25
94	Bret Boone	.25
95	Albert Pujols	2.00
96	Carlos Delgado	.50
97	Marlon Byrd	.25
98	Scott Rolen	.75
99	Pedro J. Martinez	.75
100	Alex Rodriguez	2.00
101	Adam LaRoche RC	60.00
102	Andy Marte RC	60.00
103	Daryl Clark RC	10.00
104	J.D. Durbin RC	10.00
105	Craig Brazell RC	15.00
106	Brian Burgamy RC	10.00
107	Tyler Johnson RC	10.00
108	Joey Gomes	10.00
109	Bryan Bullington RC	25.00
110	Byron Gettis RC	10.00

Refractors

Stars (1-100):		2-4X
Rookie Autos. (101-110):		.75-1.5X
Inserted 1:6		

X-Fractors

Stars (1-100):	5-10X
Rookie Autos. (101-110):	1-2.5X
Production 99 Sets	
X-Fractor Golds (1-100):	3-6X
Golds Rk Autos. (101-110):	1-2X
Production 199 Sets	

Bat Relics

		NM/M
Common Player:		8.00
Inserted 1:6		
JB	Jeff Bagwell	8.00
LB	Lance Berkman	8.00
WB	Wade Boggs	8.00
BB	Barry Bonds	20.00
RC	Rod Carew	10.00
RCL	Roger Clemens	15.00
AD	Adam Dunn	8.00
NG	Nomar Garciaparra	20.00
TH	Todd Helton	10.00
RH	Rickey Henderson	8.00
CJ	Chipper Jones	8.00
AK	Austin Kearns	8.00
GM	Greg Maddux	15.00
PM	Paul Molitor	15.00
DM	Dale Murphy	15.00
RP	Rafael Palmeiro	8.00
MP	Mike Piazza	15.00
KP	Kirby Puckett	15.00
AP	Albert Pujols	15.00
MR	Manny Ramirez	8.00
CR	Cal Ripken Jr.	35.00
AR	Alex Rodriguez	12.00
IR	Ivan Rodriguez	8.00
MS	Mike Schmidt	20.00
AS	Alfonso Soriano	8.00
MT	Miguel Tejada	8.00
JT	Jim Thome	10.00

Moments Autographs

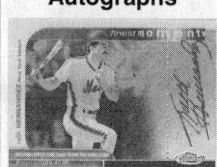

		NM/M
Common Player:		10.00
EB	Ernie Banks	60.00
PB	Paul Blair	10.00
LB	Lou Brock	25.00
GC	Gary Carter	15.00
OC	Orlando Cepeda	15.00
GF	George Foster	15.00
GG	Rich "Goose" Gossage	15.00
KH	Keith Hernandez	15.00
DL	Don Larsen	15.00
WMA	Willie Mays	150.00
JP	Jim Palmer	15.00
GP	Gaylord Perry	15.00
JS	Johnny Sain	10.00

Team Topps Legends Autograph

		NM/M
Common Autograph:		10.00
	Luis Aparicio	15.00
	Paul Blair	10.00
	Lou Brock	25.00
	Rich "Goose" Gossage	15.00
	Al Kaline	35.00
	Don Larsen	20.00
	Vern Law	12.00
	Stan Musial	75.00

Uniform Relics

		NM/M
Common Player:		5.00
BB	Barry Bonds	20.00
EC	Eric Chavez	5.00
AD	Adam Dunn	10.00
LG	Luis Gonzalez	5.00
TH	Todd Helton	8.00
RJ	Randy Johnson	8.00
AJ	Andruw Jones	8.00

CJ	Chipper Jones	10.00
GM	Greg Maddux	12.00
WM	Willie Mays	30.00
MM	Mark Mulder	6.00
RO	Roy Oswalt	5.00
RP	Rafael Palmeiro	8.00
MP	Mike Piazza	12.00
AP	Albert Pujols	15.00
MR	Manny Ramirez	8.00
AR	Alex Rodriguez	15.00
CS	Curt Schilling	8.00
AS	Alfonso Soriano	8.00
SS	Sammy Sosa	15.00
MSW	Mike Sweeney	5.00
LW	Larry Walker	5.00

2004 Finest

TRAVIS BLACKLEY

	NM/M
Complete Set (122):	
Common Player:	.40
Common Star Relic (101-110):	8.00
Inserted 1:42	
Common FYP Autograph (111-122):	10.00
Inserted 1:18	
Pack (5):	6.00
Box (18):	85.00
Mini-Box (6):	30.00

1	Juan Pierre	.40
2	Derek Jeter	3.00
3	Garret Anderson	.50
4	Javy Lopez	.50
5	Corey Patterson	.50
6	Todd Helton	.75
7	Roy Oswalt	.50
8	Shawn Green	.50
9	Vladimir Guerrero	1.00
10	Jorge Posada	.50
11	Jason Kendall	.40
12	Scott Rolen	1.00
13	Randy Johnson	1.00
14	Bill Mueller	.40
15	Magglio Ordonez	.50
16	Larry Walker	.50
17	Lance Berkman	.50
18	Richie Sexson	.75
19	Orlando Cabrera	.40
20	Alfonso Soriano	1.00
21	Kevin Millwood	.50
22	Edgar Martinez	.50
23	Aubrey Huff	.40
24	Carlos Delgado	.75
25	Vernon Wells	.50
26	Mark Teixeira	.40
27	Troy Glaus	.50
28	Jeff Kent	.50
29	Hideo Nomo	.50
30	Torii Hunter	.50
31	Hank Blalock	.50
32	Brandon Webb	.40
33	Tony Batista	.40
34	Bret Boone	.40
35	Ryan Klesko	.50
36	Barry Zito	.50
37	Aaron Boone	.40
38	Geoff Jenkins	.40
39	Jeff Bagwell	.75
40	Dontrelle Willis	.50
41	Adam Dunn	.75
42	Mark Buehrle	.40
43	Esteban Loaiza	.40
44	Angel Berroa	.40
45	Ivan Rodriguez	.75
46	Jose Vidro	.40
47	Mark Mulder	.50
48	Marlon Byrd	.40
49	Jim Edmonds	.50
50	Eric Gagne	.50
51	Marcus Giles	.40
52	Curt Schilling	.75
53	Ken Griffey Jr.	1.50
54	Jason Schmidt	.50
55	Miguel Tejada	.50
56	Dmitri Young	.40
57	Mike Lowell	.50
58	Mike Sweeney	.40
59	Scott Podsednik	.75
60	Miguel Cabrera	1.00
61	Johan Santana	.40
62	Bernie Williams	.50
63	Eric Chavez	.50
64	Bobby Abreu	.50
65	Brian Giles	.50
66	Michael Young	.40
67	Paul LoDuca	.40
68	Austin Kearns	.40

69	Jody Gerut	.40
70	Kerry Wood	1.00
71	Luis Matos	.40
72	Greg Maddux	1.50
73	Alex Rodriguez	4.00
74	Mike Lieberthal	.40
75	Jim Thome	1.00
76	Javier Vazquez	.40
77	Bartolo Colon	.50
78	Manny Ramirez	.75
79	Jacque Jones	.40
80	Johnny Damon	.40
81	Carlos Beltran	.75
82	C.C. Sabathia	.40
83	Preston Wilson	.40
84	Luis Castillo	.40
85	Kevin Brown	.50
86	Shannon Stewart	.40
87	Cliff Floyd	.40
88	Mike Mussina	.50
89	Rafael Furcal	.40
90	Roy Halladay	.50
91	Frank Thomas	.75
92	Melvin Mora	.40
93	Andruw Jones	.75
94	Luis Gonzalez	.50
95	David Ortiz	.75
96	Gary Sheffield	.50
97	Tim Hudson	.50
98	Phil Nevin	.40
99	Ichiro Suzuki	2.00
100	Albert Pujols	2.50
101	Nomar Garciaparra	15.00
102	Sammy Sosa	15.00
103	Josh Beckett	8.00
104	Jason Giambi	8.00
105	Rocco Baldelli	8.00
106	Jose Reyes	8.00
107	Chipper Jones	10.00
108	Pedro J. Martinez	10.00
109	Mike Piazza	8.00
110	Mark Prior	8.00
111	Craig Ansman RC	10.00
112	Jeff Allison	8.00
113	David Murphy	15.00
114	Jason Hirsh	20.00
115	Matt Moses	8.00
116	Estee Harris RC	10.00
117	Logan Kensing RC	8.00
118	Lastings Milledge	60.00
119	Merkin Valdez RC	15.00
120	Travis Blackley RC	15.00
121	Vito Chiaravalloti RC	10.00
122	Dioner Navarro RC	25.00

Refractor

Refractor (1-100):	2-4X
Inserted 1:6	
Refractor (101-110):	1-2X
Inserted 1:156	
Refractor (111-122):	1-2X
Inserted 1:132	

Gold Refractor

Gold Refractor (1-100):	6-12X
Gold Refr. (101-110):	1.5-2X
Gold Refr. (111-122):	2-4X
Production 50 Sets	

Uncirculated X-Fractor

CURT SCHILLING

Stars (1-100):	4-8X
Relics (101-110):	1-2X
Autographs (111-122):	1-2X
Inserted as a box topper.	
Production 139 Sets	

Moments Autographs

		NM/M
Common Autograph:		10.00
JA	Jim Abbott	15.00
VB	Vida Blue	12.00
OC	Orlando Cepeda	12.00
LD	Lenny Dykstra	10.00
GS	George Foster	10.00
EK	Ed Kranepool	10.00
WM	Willie Mays	100.00
JP	Johnny Podres	10.00
DS	Duke Snider	40.00
RY	Robin Yount	75.00

Relics

MARLON BYRD

		NM/M
Common Player:		4.00
JB	Jeff Bagwell	8.00
RB1	Rocco Baldelli/Jsy	6.00
RB3	Rocco Baldelli/Jsy	6.00
JPB1	Josh Beckett	8.00
LB1	Lance Berkman/Bat	5.00
LB2	Lance Berkman/Jsy	5.00
AB	Angel Berroa	4.00
HB1	Hank Blalock/Bat	8.00
HB2	Hank Blalock/Jsy	8.00
PB	Pat Burrell	10.00
SB	Sean Burroughs	5.00
MB	Marlon Byrd	4.00
MC	Miguel Cabrera	10.00
EC	Eric Chavez	6.00
AD	Adam Dunn	8.00
DE	Darin Erstad	4.00
NG	Nomar Garciaparra	12.00
TG	Troy Glaus	6.00
AG	Adrian Gonzalez	4.00
LG	Luis Gonzalez	4.00
SG	Shawn Green	6.00
VG	Vladimir Guerrero	8.00
CG	Cristian Guzman	4.00
RH	Rich Harden	5.00
TH1	Todd Helton/Bat	8.00
TH2	Todd Helton/Jsy	8.00
TH	Tim Hudson	5.00
TKH1	Torii Hunter/Bat	6.00
TKH2	Torii Hunter/Jsy	6.00
KI	Kazuhisa Ishii	4.00
RJ	Randy Johnson	8.00
AJ	Andruw Jones	6.00
JL	Javy Lopez	6.00
DL	Derek Lowe	4.00
ML1	Mike Lowell/Jsy	5.00
ML2	Mike Lowell/Jsy	5.00
GM	Greg Maddux	10.00
KM	Kevin Millwood	6.00
MM	Mark Mulder	4.00
BM1	Brett Myers/Jsy	4.00
BM2	Brett Myers/Jsy	4.00
MO1	Magglio Ordonez/Jsy	6.00
MO2	Magglio Ordonez/Bat	6.00
RP1	Rafael Palmeiro/Bat	8.00
RP2	Rafael Palmeiro/Jsy	8.00
RP3	Rafael Palmeiro/Jsy	8.00
AP	Andy Pettitte	6.00
JP	Juan Pierre	4.00
MP	Mark Prior	10.00
AP1	Albert Pujols/Jsy	15.00
AP2	Albert Pujols/Bat	15.00
JR1	Jose Reyes/Jsy	8.00
JR2	Jose Reyes/Bat	8.00
JR3	Jose Reyes/Jsy	8.00
MR	Mariano Rivera	10.00
AR1	Alex Rodriguez/Rangers	10.00
AR2	Alex Rodriguez/Yanks.	20.00
IR1	Ivan Rodriguez/Jsy	4.00
IR2	Ivan Rodriguez/Jsy	8.00
IR3	Ivan Rodriguez/Bat	8.00
SR	Scott Rolen	8.00
CCS	C.C. Sabathia	6.00
KS	Kazuhiro Sasaki	4.00
CS	Curt Schilling	6.00
GS	Gary Sheffield	8.00
JS	John Smoltz	8.00
AS	Alfonso Soriano	8.00
SS	Sammy Sosa	12.00
MT1	Miguel Tejada/Bat	6.00
MT2	Miguel Tejada/Jsy	6.00
FT	Frank Thomas	8.00
JT	Jim Thome	10.00
LW	Larry Walker	4.00
VW	Vernon Wells	5.00
BW	Bernie Williams	6.00
DW	Dontrelle Willis	6.00
PW	Preston Wilson	4.00
KW1	Kerry Wood/Jsy	10.00
KW2	Kerry Wood/Bat	10.00

DY	Delmon Young	8.00
BZ	Barry Zito	8.00

2005 Finest

NM/M

Complete Set (166):
Common Player: .40
Common Auto. (141-156): 10.00
Production 970, unless noted.
Pack (5): 10.00
Box (18): 150.00

1	Alexis Rios	.40
2	Hank Blalock	.50
3	Bobby Abreu	.50
4	Curt Schilling	1.00
5	Albert Pujols	3.00
6	Aaron Rowand	.40
7	B.J. Upton	.50
8	Andruw Jones	.75
9	Jeff Francis	.40
10	Sammy Sosa	1.50
11	Aramis Ramirez	.75
12	Carl Pavano	.40
13	Bartolo Colon	.40
14	Greg Maddux	2.00
15	Scott Kazmir	.50
16	Melvin Mora	.40
17	Brandon Backe	.40
18	Bobby Crosby	.40
19	Carlos Lee	.50
20	Carl Crawford	.50
21	Brian Giles	.40
22	Jeff Bagwell	.75
23	J.D. Drew	.50
24	C.C. Sabathia	.50
25	Alfonso Soriano	1.00
26	Chipper Jones	1.00
27	Austin Kearns	.40
28	Carlos Delgado	.75
29	Jack Wilson	.40
30	Dmitri Young	.40
31	Carlos Guillen	.40
32	Jim Thome	1.00
33	Eric Chavez	.50
34	Jason Schmidt	.50
35	Brad Radke	.40
36	Frank Thomas	.75
37	Darin Erstad	.40
38	Javier Vazquez	.40
39	Garret Anderson	.50
40	David Ortiz	1.00
41	Javy Lopez	.40
42	Geoff Jenkins	.40
43	Jose Vidro	.40
44	Aubrey Huff	.40
45	Bernie Williams	.50
46	Dontrelle Willis	.50
47	Jim Edmonds	.50
48	Ivan Rodriguez	.75
49	Gary Sheffield	.50
50	Alex Rodriguez	2.50
51	John Buck	.40
52	Andy Pettitte	.50
53	Ichiro Suzuki	2.50
54	Johnny Estrada	.40
55	Jake Peavy	.50
56	Carlos Zambrano	.50
57	Jose Reyes	.75
58	Bret Boone	.40
59	Jason Bay	.50
60	David Wright	1.50
61	Jeromy Burnitz	.40
62	Corey Patterson	.50
63	Juan Pierre	.40
64	Zack Greinke	.40
65	Mike Lowell	.40
66	Ken Griffey Jr.	2.00
67	Marcus Giles	.40
68	Edgar Renteria	.50
69	Ken Harvey	.40
70	Pedro Martinez	1.00
71	Johnny Damon	1.00
72	Lyle Overbay	.50
73	Mike Maroth	.40
74	Jorge Posada	.50
75	Carlos Beltran	.75
76	Mark Buehrle	.50
77	Khalil Greene	.40
78	Josh Beckett	.50
79	Mark Loretta	.40
80	Rafael Palmeiro	.75
81	Justin Morneau	.50
82	Rocco Baldelli	.50
83	Ben Sheets	.50
84	Kerry Wood	.50
85	Miguel Tejada	.75
86	Magglio Ordonez	.50
87	Livan Hernandez	.40
88	Kazuo Matsui	.40
89	Manny Ramirez	1.00
90	Hideki Matsui	2.00
91	Jeff Kent	.50
92	Matt Lawton	.40
93	Richie Sexson	.50
94	Mike Mussina	.75
95	Adam Dunn	.75
96	Johan Santana	.75
97	Nomar Garciaparra	1.50
98	Michael Young	.40
99	Victor Martinez	.50
100	Barry Bonds	3.00
101	Oliver Perez	.40
102	Randy Johnson	1.00
103	Mark Mulder	.50
104	Pat Burrell	.40
105	Mike Sweeney	.40
106	Mark Teixeira	.75
107	Paul LoDuca	.40
108	Jon Lieber	.40
109	Mike Piazza	1.50
110	Roger Clemens	3.00
111	Rafael Furcal	.50
112	Troy Glaus	.50
113	Miguel Cabrera	1.00
114	Randy Wolf	.40
115	Lance Berkman	.75
116	Mark Prior	.75
117	Rich Harden	.40
118	Preston Wilson	.40
119	Roy Oswalt	.50
120	Luis Gonzalez	.40
121	Ronnie Belliard	.40
122	Sean Casey	.40
123	Barry Zito	.50
124	Larry Walker	.50
125	Derek Jeter	3.00
126	Tim Hudson	.50
127	Tom Glavine	.50
128	Scott Rolen	1.00
129	Torii Hunter	.50
130	Paul Konerko	.75
131	Shawn Green	.40
132	Travis Hafner	.50
133	Vernon Wells	.40
134	Sidney Ponson	.40
135	Vladimir Guerrero	1.00
136	Mark Kotsay	.40
137	Todd Helton	.75
138	Adrian Beltre	.50
139	Wily Mo Pena	.40
140	Joe Mauer	.75
141	Brian Stavisky **RC**	12.00
142	Nate McLouth **RC**	15.00
143	Glen Perkins **RC**	15.00
144	Chip Cannon **RC**	15.00
145	Shane Costa **RC**	10.00
146	Wes Swackhamer **RC**	12.00
147	Kevin Melillo **RC**	15.00
148	Billy Butler **RC**	50.00
149	Landon Powell **RC**	15.00
150	Scott Mathieson **RC**	10.00
151	Chris Roberson **RC**	10.00
152	Chad Orvella/375 **RC**	15.00
153	Eric Nielsen **RC**	10.00
154	Matt Campbell **RC**	10.00
155	Mike Rogers **RC**	10.00
156	Melky Cabrera **RC**	40.00
157	Nolan Ryan	4.00
158	Bo Jackson	1.00
159	Wade Boggs	1.00
160	Andre Dawson	.75
161	Dave Winfield	1.00
162	Reggie Jackson	1.00
163	David Justice	.50
164	Dale Murphy	1.00
165	Paul O'Neill	.75
166	Tom Seaver	1.50

2005 Finest Refractors

Refrac. (1-140, 157-166): 2-4X
Autograph (141-156): .5-1X
Production 399 Sets

Black

Refrac. (1-140, 157-166): 4-8X
Autograph (141-156): 1-2X
Production 99 Sets

Blue

Refrac. (1-140, 157-166): 2-4X
Autograph (141-156): .5-1X
Production 299 Sets

Gold

Refrac. (1-140, 157-166): 5-10X
Autograph (141-156): 2-4X
Production 49 Sets

Green

Refrac. (1-140, 157-166): 2-4X
Autograph (141-156): .5-1.5X
Production 199 Sets

White Framed

No Pricing
Production One Set

Super Fractor

No Pricing
Production One Set

2005 Finest X-Fractor

Refrac. (1-140, 157-166): 2-4X
Autograph (141-156): .5-1X
Production 250 Sets

Black

Refrac. (1-140, 157-166): 8-15X
Autograph (141-156): No Pricing
Production 25 Sets

Blue

Refrac. (1-140, 157-166): 3-5X
Autograph (141-156): .5-1.5X
Production 150 Sets

Gold

No Pricing
Production 10 Sets

Green

Refrac. (1-140, 157-166): 5-10X
Autograph (141-156): 1.5-3X
Production 50 Sets

White Framed

No Pricing
Production One Set

Autographs

NM/M

X-Fractor: 1.5-2X
Production 25 Sets

JB	Jason Bay	25.00
CB	Carlos Beltran	30.00
BB	Barry Bonds	280.00
MB	Milton Bradley	15.00
EC	Eric Chavez	20.00
JE	Johnny Estrada	15.00
EG	Eric Gagne	30.00
KM	Kevin Millar	15.00
DO	David Ortiz	50.00
MR	Mariano Rivera	60.00
JS	Johan Santana	40.00
GS	Gary Sheffield	30.00
AS	Alfonso Soriano	30.00
JST	Jacob Stevens	10.00
DW	David Wright	80.00

Finest Moment Autographs

No Pricing
Production 50

Printing Plates

No Pricing
Production one set for each color.

Alex Rodriguez Finest Moments

NM/M

A-Rod 1-49: 10.00
Production 190 Sets
FAM1-49 Alex Rodriguez 10.00

Alex Rodriguez Finest Moments Autograph

NM/M

Production 13 Sets
A-Rod Auto. 1-49: 150.00
FAM1-49 Alex Rodriguez 150.00

2 of a Kind Autographs

No Pricing
Production 13

2006 Finest

NM/M

Complete Set (155):
Common Player: .40
Common Auto. (141-155):
Pack (5): 9.00
Box (18): 150.00

1	Vladimir Guerrero	1.00
2	Troy Glaus	.50
3	Andruw Jones	1.00
4	Miguel Tejada	.75
5	Manny Ramirez	1.00
6	Curt Schilling	1.00
7	Mark Prior	.75
8	Kerry Wood	.50
9	Tadahito Iguchi	.40
10	Freddy Garcia	.40
11	Ryan Howard	1.50
12	Mark Buehrle	.40
13	Wily Mo Pena	.40
14	C.C. Sabathia	.40
15	Garret Anderson	.40
16	Shawn Green	.40
17	Rafael Furcal	.40
18	Jeff Francoeur	.40
19	Ken Griffey Jr.	2.00
20	Derek Lee	.75
21	Paul Konerko	.75
22	Rickie Weeks	.40
23	Magglio Ordonez	.40
24	Juan Pierre	.40
25	Felix Hernandez	1.00
26	Roger Clemens	3.00
27	Zack Greinke	.40
28	Johan Santana	1.00
29	Jose Reyes	.75
30	Bobby Crosby	.40
31	Jason Schmidt	.40
32	Khalil Greene	.40
33	Richie Sexson	.50
34	Mark Mulder	.40
35	Mark Teixeira	.75
36	Nick Johnson	.40
37	Vernon Wells	.50
38	Scott Kazmir	.50
39	Jim Edmonds	.50
40	Adrian Beltre	.40
41	Dan Johnson	.40
42	Carlos Lee	.50
43	Lance Berkman	.75
44	Josh Beckett	.50
45	Morgan Ensberg	.40
46	Garrett Atkins	.40
47	Chase Utley	.50
48	Joe Mauer	.75
49	Travis Hafner	.75
50	Alex Rodriguez	3.00
51	Austin Kearns	.40
52	Scott Podsednik	.40
53	Jose Contreras	.40
54	Greg Maddux	2.00
55	Hideki Matsui	2.00
56	Matt Clement	.40
57	Javy Lopez	.40
58	Tim Hudson	.50
59	Luis Gonzalez	.50
60	Bartolo Colon	.50
61	Marcus Giles	.40
62	Justin Morneau	.75
63	Nomar Garciaparra	.75
64	Robinson Cano	1.00
65	Ervin Santana	.40
66	Brady Clark	.40
67	Edgar Renteria	.40
68	Jon Garland	.40
69	Felipe Lopez	.40
70	Ivan Rodriguez	.75
71	Dontrelle Willis	.50
72	Carlos Guillen	.40
73	J.D. Drew	.40
74	Rich Harden	.40
75	Albert Pujols	3.00
76	Livan Hernandez	.40
77	Roy Halladay	.50
78	Hank Blalock	.50
79	David Wright	1.50
80	Jimmy Rollins	.50
81	John Smoltz	.50
82	Miguel Cabrera	1.00
83	David DeJesus	.40
84	Torii Hunter	.50
85	Adam Dunn	.75
86	Randy Johnson	1.00
87	Roy Oswalt	.50
88	Bobby Abreu	.50
89	Rocco Baldelli	.40
90	Ichiro Suzuki	2.00
91	Jorge Cantu	.40
92	Jack Wilson	.40
93	Jose Vidro	.40
94	Kevin Millwood	.50
95	David Ortiz	1.00
96	Victor Martinez	.50
97	Jeremy Bonderman	.40
98	Todd Helton	.75
99	Carlos Beltran	.75
100	Barry Bonds	3.00
101	Jeff Kent	.50
102	Mike Sweeney	.40
103	Ben Sheets	.40
104	Melvin Mora	.40
105	Gary Sheffield	.75
106	Craig Wilson	.40
107	Chris Carpenter	.75
108	Michael Young	.50
109	Gustavo Chacin	.40
110	Chipper Jones	1.00
111	Mark Loretta	.40
112	Andy Pettitte	.50
113	Carlos Delgado	.50
114	Pat Burrell	.50
115	Jason Bay	.50
116	Brian Roberts	.50
117	Joe Crede	.40
118	Jake Peavy	.50
119	Aubrey Huff	.40
120	Pedro Martinez	1.00
121	Jorge Posada	.50
122	Barry Zito	.50
123	Scott Rolen	.75
124	Brett Myers	.40
125	Derek Jeter	3.00
126	Eric Chavez	.50
127	Carl Crawford	.50
128	Jim Thome	1.00
129	Johnny Damon	1.00
130	Alfonso Soriano	1.00
131	Clint Barmes	.40
132	Dustin Nippert **(RC)**	1.00
133	Hanley Ramirez **(RC)**	2.00
134	Matt Capps **(RC)**	1.00
135	Miguel Perez **(RC)**	1.00
136	Tom Gorzelanny **(RC)**	1.00
137	Charlton Jimerson **(RC)**	1.00
138	Bryan Bullington **(RC)**	1.00
139	Kenji Johjima **RC**	4.00
140	Craig Hansen **RC**	3.00
141	Craig Breslow **RC**	15.00
142	Adam Wainwright **(RC)**	30.00
143	Joey Devine **RC**	20.00
144	Hong-Chih Kuo **(RC)**	40.00
145	Jason Botts **(RC)**	20.00
146	Josh Johnson **(RC)**	20.00
147	Jason Bergmann **RC**	20.00
148	Scott Olsen **(RC)**	15.00
149	Darrell Rasner **(RC)**	15.00
150	Daniel Ortmeier **(RC)**	15.00
151	Chuck James **(RC)**	20.00
152	Ryan Garko **(RC)**	20.00
153	Nelson Cruz **(RC)**	20.00
154	Anthony Lerew **(RC)**	12.00
155	Francisco Liriano **(RC)**	35.00

SuperFractor

No Pricing
Production One Set

Gold Refractor

Stars (1-140): 6-12X
Autos. (141-155): 2-3X
Production One Set

Black Refractor

Stars (1-140): 4-8X
Autos. (141-155): 1-2X
Production 99 Sets

Green Refractor

Stars (1-140): 2-5X
Autos. (141-155): .75-1.5X
Production 199 Sets

Blue Refractor

Stars (1-140): 2-5X
Autos. (141-155): .75-1X
Production 299 Sets

Refractor

Stars (1-140): 2-4X
Autos. (141-155): .5-1X
Production 399 Sets

White Framed Refractor

No Pricing
Production One Set

Gold X-Fractor

No Pricing
Production 10 Sets

Black X-Fractor

Stars (1-140): 8-15X
Autos. (141-155): No Pricing
Production 25 Sets

Green X-Fractor

Stars (1-140): 6-12X
Autos. (141-155): 2-3X
Production 50 Sets

Blue X-Fractor

Stars (1-140): 3-5X
Autos. (141-155): 1-1.5X
Production 150 Sets

X-Fractor

Stars (1-140): 2-5X
Autos. (141-155): .75-1X
Production 250 Sets

Mickey Mantle Finest Moments

NM/M

Common Mantle: 10.00
Production 850 Sets
Refractor: 1X
Production 399 Sets
Blue Refractor: 1-1.5X
Production 299 Sets
Green Refractor: 1-2X
Production 199 Sets
Black Refractor: 1.5-3X
Production 99 Sets
Gold Refractor: 3-4X
Production 49 Sets
X-Fractor: 1-1.5X
Production 250 Sets
Blue X-Fractor: 1-2X
Production 150 Sets
Green X-Fractor: 3-4X
Production 50 Sets
Black X-Fractor: 4-6X
Production 25 Sets
Gold X-Fractor: No Pricing
Production 10 Sets
1-20 Mickey Mantle 10.00

Autographs

NM/M

JB	Jason Bay	25.00
MC	Miguel Cabrera	40.00
RC	Robinson Cano	50.00
EC	Eric Chavez	20.00
MG	Marcus Giles	15.00
VG	Vladimir Guerrero	50.00
JG	Jose Guillen	12.00
RH	Rich Harden	20.00
KJ	Kenji Johjima	80.00

AJ	Andruw Jones	50.00
CJ	Chipper Jones	60.00
DL	Derrek Lee	30.00
RO	Roy Oswalt	25.00
AR	Alex Rodriguez	160.00
GS	Gary Sheffield	30.00
DWI	Dontrelle Willis	25.00
CW	Craig Wilson	10.00
DW	David Wright	70.00

Barry Bonds Finest Moments Autographs

No Pricing

Barry Bonds Finest Moments

	NM/M
Common Bonds:	10.00
Production 425 Sets	
Gold Refractor:	1-2X
Production 199 Sets	
1-25 Barry Bonds	10.00

Mickey Mantle Finest Moments Cut Signature

No Pricing
Production One Set

2007 Finest

		NM/M
Complete Set (165):		
Common player (1-135):		.25
Common RC (136-150):		1.00
Common RC Auto. (151-165):		10.00
Pack (5):		8.00
Box (18):		125.00
1	David Wright	2.00
2	Jered Weaver	.50
3	Chipper Jones	1.00
4	Magglio Ordonez	.25
5	Ben Sheets	.50
6	Nick Johnson	.25
7	Melvin Mora	.25
8	Chien-Ming Wang	1.00
9	Andre Ethier	.50
10	Carlos Beltran	1.00
11	Ryan Zimmerman	1.00
12	Troy Glaus	.50
13	Hanley Ramirez	.50
14	Mark Buehrle	.50
15	Dan Uggla	.50
16	Richie Sexson	.75
17	Scott Kazmir	.50
18	Garrett Atkins	.25
19	Matt Cain	.50
20	Jorge Posada	.50
21	Brett Myers	.50
22	Jeff Francoeur	.50
23	Scott Rolen	1.00
24	Derrek Lee	.75
25	Manny Ramirez	1.00
26	Johnny Damon	1.00
27	Mark Teixeira	1.00
28	Mark Prior	.50
29	Victor Martinez	.50
30	Greg Maddux	2.00
31	Prince Fielder	.75
32	Jeremy Bonderman	.50
33	Paul LoDuca	.50
34	Brandon Webb	.50
35	Robinson Cano	.50
36	Josh Beckett	.50
37	David DeJesus	.25
38	Kenny Rogers	.25
39	Jim Thome	.50
40	Brian McCann	.50
41	Lance Berkman	.50
42	Adam Dunn	.75
43	Rocco Baldelli	.50
44	Brian Roberts	.50
45	Vladimir Guerrero	.50
46	Dontrelle Willis	.50
47	Eric Chavez	.50
48	Carlos Zambrano	.50
49	Ivan Rodriguez	1.00
50	Alex Rodriguez	3.00
51	Curt Schilling	.50
52	Carlos Delgado	.75
53	Matt Holliday	.25
54	Mark Teahen	.25
55	Frank Thomas	1.00
56	Grady Sizemore	.75
57	Aramis Ramirez	.50
58	Rafael Furcal	.50
59	David Ortiz	1.00
60	Paul Konerko	.50
61	Barry Zito	.50
62	Travis Hafner	.50
63	Nick Swisher	.50
64	Johan Santana	1.00
65	Miguel Tejada	.75
66	Carl Crawford	.50
67	Kenji Johjima	.50
68	Derek Jeter	3.00
69	Francisco Liriano	.50
70	Ken Griffey Jr.	.50
71	Pat Burrell	.50
72	Adrian Gonzalez	.25
73	Miguel Cabrera	1.00
74	Albert Pujols	3.00
75	Justin Verlander	.75
76	Carlos Lee	.50
77	John Smoltz	.50
78	Orlando Hudson	.25
79	Joe Mauer	.50
80	Freddy Sanchez	.50
81	Bobby Abreu	.50
82	Pedro Martinez	1.00
83	Vernon Wells	.50
84	Justin Morneau	.75
85	Bill Hall	.50
86	Jason Schmidt	.25
87	Michael Young	.50
88	Tadahito Iguchi	.25
89	Kevin Millwood	.25
90	Randy Johnson	1.00
91	Roy Halladay	.50
92	Mike Lowell	.25
93	Jake Peavy	.50
94	Jason Varitek	.75
95	Todd Helton	.75
96	Mark Loretta	.25
97	Gary Matthews	.25
98	Ryan Howard	2.00
99	Jose Reyes	1.00
100	Chris Carpenter	.50
101	Hideki Matsui	2.00
102	Brian Giles	.25
103	Torii Hunter	.25
104	Rich Harden	.25
105	Ichiro Suzuki	2.00
106	Chase Utley	1.00
107	Nicholas Markakis	.50
108	Marcus Giles	.25
109	Gary Sheffield	.75
110	Jim Edmonds	.50
111	Brandon Phillips	.25
112	Roy Oswalt	.50
113	Jeff Kent	.50
114	Jason Bay	.50
115	Raul Ibanez	.50
116	Stephen Drew	.50
117	Hank Blalock	.50
118	Tom Glavine	.50
119	Andruw Jones	.75
120	Alfonso Soriano	1.00
121	Mariano Rivera	.50
122	Garret Anderson	.50
123	Erik Bedard	.50
124	Huston Street	.50
125	Austin Kearns	.50
126	Jermaine Dye	.25
127	C.C. Sabathia	.25
128	Joe Nathan	.25
129	Craig Monroe	.25
130	Aubrey Huff	.25
131	Billy Wagner	.25
132	Jorge Cantu	.25
133	Trevor Hoffman	.25
134	Ronnie Belliard	.25
135	B.J. Ryan	.25
136	Adam Lind (RC)	1.00
137	Hector Gimenez (RC)	1.00
138	Shawn Riggans (RC)	1.00
139	Joaquin Arias (RC)	1.00
140	Drew Anderson (RC)	1.00
141	Mike Rabelo RC	1.00
142	Chris Narveson (RC)	1.00
143	Ryan Feierabend (RC)	1.00
144	Vinny Rottino (RC)	2.00
145	Jon Knott (RC)	1.00
146	Oswaldo Navarro RC	1.00
147	Brian Stokes (RC)	1.00
148	Glen Perkins (RC)	1.00
149	Mitch Maier (RC)	1.00
150	Delmon Young (RC)	2.00
151	Andrew Miller RC	50.00
152	Troy Tulowitzki (RC)	20.00
153	Philip Humber (RC)	20.00
154	Kevin Kouzmanoff (RC)	20.00
155	Michael Bourn (RC)	15.00
156	Miguel Montero (RC)	15.00
157	David Murphy (RC)	15.00
158	Ryan Sweeney (RC)	15.00
159	Jeff Baker (RC)	10.00
160	Jeff Salazar (RC)	10.00
161	Jose Garcia (RC)	10.00
162	Josh Fields (RC)	15.00
163	Delwyn Young (RC)	15.00
164	Fred Lewis (RC)	10.00
165	Scott Moore (RC)	15.00

Printing Plates

Production one set per color.

Gold Refractor

Gold Refractor (1-150):	5-10X
Production 50	
RC Autos.:	2X
Production 49	

Black Refractor

Black Refractor (1-150):	4-8X
RC Autos.:	1.5X
Production 99 Sets	

Green Refractor

Green Refractor (1-150):	2-5X
RC Autos.:	1-1.5X
Production 199 Sets	

Blue Refractor

Blue Refractor (1-150):	2-5X
Production 399 Sets	
RC Autos.:	.75-1X
Production 299	

Refractor

Refractor (1-150):	2-4X
RC Autographs:	.5-1X
Production 399 only autos serial #'d	

SuperFractor

Production One Set

X-Fractor

X-Fractor (1-135):	10-20X
RC Autos.:	No Pricing
Production 25 Sets	

Dual Rookies Finest Moments Autograph

		NM/M
Refractors:		No Pricing
Production 25 Sets		
VR	Justin Verlander, Hanley Ramirez	60.00
RP	Mariano Rivera, Jorge Posada	80.00
OP	Roy Oswalt, Mark Prior	40.00
UW	Chase Utley, David Wright	100.00
CY	Robinson Cano, Michael Young	50.00
WW	Chien-Ming Wang, Brandon Webb	175.00
JH	Chuck James, Cole Hamels	40.00
PO	Yusmeiro Petit, Scott Olsen	20.00
PP	Jonathan Papelbon, Dustin Pedroia	75.00
CC	Eric Chavez, Miguel Cabrera	40.00
CK	Nelson Cruz, Matthew Kemp	25.00
HJ	Rich Hill, Josh Johnson	30.00
HM	Cole Hamels, Brett Myers	60.00
MC	Lastings Milledge, Melky Cabrera	35.00
CR	Matt Cain, Anthony Reyes	25.00
BM	Jason Bay, Justin Morneau	35.00
MG	Russell Martin, Ryan Garko	25.00
MN	Kendry Morales, Michael Napoli	25.00
MK	Lastings Milledge, Matthew Kemp	30.00
RU	Hanley Ramirez, Dan Uggla	40.00

Rookies Finest Moments Autograph

		NM/M
Common Autograph:		10.00
Refractors:		No Pricing
Production 25 Sets		
DO	David Ortiz	50.00
DW	David Wright	75.00
JN	Joe Nathan	10.00
AR	Alex Rodriguez	125.00
TH	Travis Hafner	20.00
RH	Ryan Howard	100.00
AS	Anibal Sanchez	20.00
BP	Brandon Phillips	10.00
CH	Cole Hamels	40.00
DWW	Dontrelle Willis	20.00
LM	Lastings Milledge	25.00
RC	Robinson Cano	50.00
MN	Michael Napoli	20.00
DU	Dan Uggla	15.00
BW	Brad Wilkerson	15.00
MC	Melky Cabrera	35.00
AW	Adam Wainwright	30.00
CQ	Carlos Quentin	15.00
RJH	Rich Hill	30.00
YP	Yusmeiro Petit	15.00
FC	Fausto Carmona	15.00
CJ	Chuck James	20.00
JM	Justin Morneau	25.00
RZ	Ryan Zimmerman	35.00
RM	Russell Martin	15.00
JP	Jonathan Papelbon	50.00
HR	Hanley Ramirez	20.00
MTC	Matt Cain	25.00
DY	Delmon Young	30.00

Ryan Howard HR History

	NM/M
Common Howard (1-58):	4.00
Inserted 2:Box	
Production 459 Sets	
Refractor:	1.5-2X
Production 149 Sets	
X-Fractor:	2-4X
Production 50 Sets	
Gold Refractor:	No Pricing
Production One Set	

Mantle Cut Signature

Production One

Rookies Finest Moments

		NM/M
Common Player:		.50
Refractor:		2-3X
Blue Refractor:		2-4X
Production 299 Sets		
Green Refractor:		2-4X
Production 199 Sets		
Black Refractor:		4-6X
Production 99 Sets		
Gold Refractor:		4-8X
Production 50 Sets		
X-Fractor:		10-15X
Production 25 Sets		
AD	Adam Dunn	1.00
AJ	Andruw Jones	1.50
AP	Albert Pujols	4.00
AR	Alex Rodriguez	4.00
CB	Carlos Beltran	1.50
CC	Carl Crawford	.50
CJ	Chipper Jones	1.50
DJ	Derek Jeter	4.00
DL	Derrek Lee	1.50
DO	David Ortiz	1.50
DW	David Wright	2.50
DWW	Dontrelle Willis	1.00
HM	Hideki Matsui	2.50
IS	Ichiro Suzuki	2.50
JB	Jason Bay	1.00
JM	Joe Mauer	1.00
JR	Jose Reyes	2.00
KG	Ken Griffey Jr.	3.00
MC	Miguel Cabrera	1.50
MP	Mike Piazza	2.00
MR	Manny Ramirez	1.50
MT	Miguel Tejada	1.50
NG	Nomar Garciaparra	1.50
RH	Ryan Howard	3.00
VG	Vladimir Guerrero	1.50
AS	Anibal Sanchez	.50
JP	Jonathan Papelbon	1.50
DU	Dan Uggla	.50
HR	Hanley Ramirez	1.00
JV	Justin Verlander	1.00
FL	Francisco Liriano	1.00
SD	Stephen Drew	1.00
JW	Jered Weaver	1.00
JS	Jeremy Sowers	1.00
KJ	Kenji Johjima	1.00
MCA	Melky Cabrera	1.00
NM	Nicholas Markakis	1.00
PF	Prince Fielder	1.50
RM	Russell Martin	.50
AE	Andre Ethier	1.00
MK	Matthew Kemp	1.00
JH	Jason Hirsh	.50
CH	Cole Hamels	2.00
JBA	Josh Barfield	.50
IK	Ian Kinsler	.50
AW	Adam Wainwright	1.00
JST	Brian Stokes	.50
MN	Michael Napoli	.50
CQ	Carlos Quentin	1.00
NC	Nelson Cruz	.50

A-Rod Road to 500

	NM/M
Common A-Rod (26-50):	2.00
Inserted 2:Box	

1993 Flair Promos

Among the scarcest modern baseball promo cards are those produced to introduce Fleer's new premium product for 1993, Flair. Basically similar to the issued versions, the promo cards have "000" in place of the card number on back. The promos are checklisted here in alphabetical order.

		NM/M
Complete Set (8):		200.00
Common Player:		10.00
(1)	Will Clark	10.00
(2)	Darren Daulton	10.00
(3)	Andres Galarraga	10.00
(4)	Bryan Harvey	10.00
(5)	David Justice	10.00
(6)	Jody Reed	10.00
(7)	Nolan Ryan	100.00
(8)	Sammy Sosa	60.00

1993 Flair

Designed as Fleer's super-premium card brand, this 300-card set contains extra-thick cards which feature gold-foil highlights and UV coating front and back. Portrait and action photos are combined in a high-tech front picture and there is a muted photo on the back, as well.

		NM/M
Complete Set (300):		15.00
Common Player:		.10
Pack (10):		1.50
Wax Box (24):		20.00
1	Steve Avery	.10
2	Jeff Blauser	.10
3	Ron Gant	.10
4	Tom Glavine	.25
5	Dave Justice	.10
6	Mark Lemke	.10
7	Greg Maddux	1.00
8	Fred McGriff	.10
9	Terry Pendleton	.10
10	Deion Sanders	.15
11	John Smoltz	.10
12	Mike Stanton	.10
13	Steve Buechele	.10
14	Mark Grace	.10
15	Greg Hibbard	.10
16	Derrick May	.10
17	Chuck McElroy	.10
18	Mike Morgan	.10
19	Randy Myers	.10
20	Ryne Sandberg	1.00
21	Dwight Smith	.10
22	Sammy Sosa	1.00
23	Jose Vizcaino	.10
24	Tim Belcher	.10
25	Rob Dibble	.10
26	Roberto Kelly	.10
27	Barry Larkin	.25
28	Kevin Mitchell	.10
29	Hal Morris	.10
30	Joe Oliver	.10
31	Jose Rijo	.10
32	Bip Roberts	.10
33	Chris Sabo	.10
34	Reggie Sanders	.10
35	Dante Bichette	.10
36	Willie Blair	.10
37	Jerald Clark	.10
38	Alex Cole	.10
39	Andres Galarraga	.10
40	Joe Girardi	.10
41	Charlie Hayes	.10
42	Chris Jones	.10
43	David Nied	.10
44	Eric Young	.10
45	Alex Arias	.10
46	Jack Armstrong	.10
47	Bret Barberie	.10
48	Chuck Carr	.10
49	Jeff Conine	.10
50	Orestes Destrade	.10
51	Chris Hammond	.10
52	Bryan Harvey	.10
53	Benito Santiago	.10
54	Gary Sheffield	.35
55	Walt Weiss	.10
56	Eric Anthony	.10
57	Jeff Bagwell	.75
58	Craig Biggio	.10
59	Ken Caminiti	.10
60	Andujar Cedeno	.10
61	Doug Drabek	.10
62	Steve Finley	.10
63	Luis Gonzalez	.10
64	Pete Harnisch	.10
65	Doug Jones	.10
66	Darryl Kile	.10
67	Greg Swindell	.10
68	Brett Butler	.10
69	Jim Gott	.10
70	Orel Hershiser	.10
71	Eric Karros	.10
72	Pedro Martinez	.75
73	Ramon Martinez	.10
74	Roger McDowell	.10
75	Mike Piazza	1.50
76	Jody Reed	.10
77	Tim Wallach	.10
78	Moises Alou	.10
79	Greg Colbrunn	.10
80	Wil Cordero	.10
81	Delino DeShields	.10
82	Jeff Fassero	.10
83	Marquis Grissom	.10
84	Ken Hill	.10
85	Mike Lansing RC	.25
86	Dennis Martinez	.10
87	Larry Walker	.10
88	John Wetteland	.10
89	Bobby Bonilla	.10
90	Vince Coleman	.10
91	Dwight Gooden	.10
92	Todd Hundley	.10
93	Howard Johnson	.10
94	Eddie Murray	.75
95	Joe Orsulak	.10
96	Bret Saberhagen	.10
97	Darren Daulton	.10
98	Mariano Duncan	.10
99	Len Dykstra	.10
100	Jim Eisenreich	.10
101	Tommy Greene	.10
102	Dave Hollins	.10
103	Pete Incaviglia	.10
104	Danny Jackson	.10
105	John Kruk	.10
106	Terry Mulholland	.10
107	Curt Schilling	.25
108	Mitch Williams	.10
109	Stan Belinda	.10
110	Jay Bell	.10
111	Steve Cooke	.10
112	Carlos Garcia	.10
113	Jeff King	.10
114	Al Martin	.10
115	Orlando Merced	.10
116	Don Slaught	.10
117	Andy Van Slyke	.10
118	Tim Wakefield	.10
119	Rene Arocha RC	.10
120	Bernard Gilkey	.10
121	Gregg Jefferies	.10
122	Ray Lankford	.10
123	Donovan Osborne	.10
124	Tom Pagnozzi	.10
125	Erik Pappas	.10
126	Geronimo Pena	.10
127	Lee Smith	.10
128	Ozzie Smith	1.00
129	Bob Tewksbury	.10
130	Mark Whiten	.10
131	Derek Bell	.10
132	Andy Benes	.10
133	Tony Gwynn	1.00
134	Gene Harris	.10
135	Trevor Hoffman	.10
136	Phil Plantier	.10
137	Rod Beck	.10
138	Barry Bonds	2.50
139	John Burkett	.10
140	Will Clark	.10
141	Royce Clayton	.10
142	Mike Jackson	.10
143	Darren Lewis	.10
144	Kirt Manwaring	.10
145	Willie McGee	.10
146	Bill Swift	.10
147	Robby Thompson	.10
148	Matt Williams	.10
149	Brady Anderson	.10
150	Mike Devereaux	.10
151	Chris Hoiles	.10
152	Ben McDonald	.10
153	Mark McLemore	.10
154	Mike Mussina	.40
155	Gregg Olson	.10
156	Harold Reynolds	.10
157	Cal Ripken, Jr.	2.50
158	Rick Sutcliffe	.10
159	Fernando Valenzuela	.10
160	Roger Clemens	1.25
161	Scott Cooper	.10
162	Andre Dawson	.30
163	Scott Fletcher	.10
164	Mike Greenwell	.10
165	Greg Harris	.10
166	Billy Hatcher	.10
167	Jeff Russell	.10
168	Mo Vaughn	.10
169	Frank Viola	.10
170	Chad Curtis	.10
171	Chili Davis	.10
172	Gary DiSarcina	.10
173	Damion Easley	.10

174	Chuck Finley	.10
175	Mark Langston	.10
176	Luis Polonia	.10
177	Tim Salmon	.10
178	Scott Sanderson	.10
179	J.T. Snow RC	.50
180	Wilson Alvarez	.10
181	Ellis Burks	.10
182	Joey Cora	.10
183	Alex Fernandez	.10
184	Ozzie Guillen	.10
185	Roberto Hernandez	.10
186	Bo Jackson	.20
187	Lance Johnson	.10
188	Jack McDowell	.10
189	Frank Thomas	.75
190	Robin Ventura	.10
191	Carlos Baerga	.10
192	Albert Belle	.10
193	Wayne Kirby	.10
194	Derek Lilliquist	.10
195	Kenny Lofton	.10
196	Carlos Martinez	.10
197	Jose Mesa	.10
198	Eric Plunk	.10
199	Paul Sorrento	.10
200	John Doherty	.10
201	Cecil Fielder	.10
202	Travis Fryman	.10
203	Kirk Gibson	.10
204	Mike Henneman	.10
205	Chad Kreuter	.10
206	Scott Livingstone	.10
207	Tony Phillips	.10
208	Mickey Tettleton	.10
209	Alan Trammell	.10
210	David Wells	.10
211	Lou Whitaker	.10
212	Kevin Appier	.10
213	George Brett	1.25
214	David Cone	.10
215	Tom Gordon	.10
216	Phil Hiatt	.10
217	Felix Jose	.10
218	Wally Joyner	.10
219	Jose Lind	.10
220	Mike Macfarlane	.10
221	Brian McRae	.10
222	Jeff Montgomery	.10
223	Cal Eldred	.10
224	Darryl Hamilton	.10
225	John Jaha	.10
226	Pat Listach	.10
227	Graeme Lloyd RC	.10
228	Kevin Reimer	.10
229	Bill Spiers	.10
230	B.J. Surhoff	.10
231	Greg Vaughn	.10
232	Robin Yount	.75
233	Rick Aguilera	.10
234	Jim Deshaies	.10
235	Brian Harper	.10
236	Kent Hrbek	.10
237	Chuck Knoblauch	.10
238	Shane Mack	.10
239	David McCarty	.10
240	Pedro Munoz	.10
241	Mike Pagliarulo	.10
242	Kirby Puckett	1.00
243	Dave Winfield	.75
244	Jim Abbott	.10
245	Wade Boggs	1.00
246	Pat Kelly	.10
247	Jimmy Key	.10
248	Jim Leyritz	.10
249	Don Mattingly	1.25
250	Matt Nokes	.10
251	Paul O'Neill	.10
252	Mike Stanley	.10
253	Danny Tartabull	.10
254	Bob Wickman	.10
255	Bernie Williams	.10
256	Mike Bordick	.10
257	Dennis Eckersley	.60
258	Brent Gates	.10
259	Goose Gossage	.10
260	Rickey Henderson	.75
261	Mark McGwire	2.00
262	Ruben Sierra	.10
263	Terry Steinbach	.10
264	Bob Welch	.10
265	Bobby Witt	.10
266	Rich Amaral	.10
267	Chris Bosio	.10
268	Jay Buhner	.10
269	Norm Charlton	.10
270	Ken Griffey Jr.	1.50
271	Erik Hanson	.10
272	Randy Johnson	.75
273	Edgar Martinez	.10
274	Tino Martinez	.10
275	Dave Valle	.10
276	Omar Vizquel	.10
277	Kevin Brown	.10
278	Jose Canseco	.45
279	Julio Franco	.10
280	Juan Gonzalez	.40
281	Tom Henke	.10
282	David Hulse	.10
283	Rafael Palmeiro	.65
284	Dean Palmer	.10
285	Ivan Rodriguez	.65
286	Nolan Ryan	2.50
287	Roberto Alomar	.25
288	Pat Borders	.10
289	Joe Carter	.10
290	Juan Guzman	.10
291	Pat Hentgen	.10
292	Paul Molitor	.75
293	John Olerud	.10
294	Ed Sprague	.10
295	Dave Stewart	.10
296	Duane Ward	.10
297	Devon White	.10
298	Checklist	.05
299	Checklist	.05
300	Checklist	.05

Wave of the Future

The game's top prospects are featured in this insert issue randomly packaged in Flair packs. Cards #19-20, Darrell Whitmore and Nigel Wilson, were printed with each other's back; no corrected version was made.

		NM/M
Complete Set (20):		6.00
Common Player:		.15
1	Jason Bere	.15
2	Jeremy Burnitz	.15
3	Russ Davis	.15
4	Jim Edmonds	.25
5	Cliff Floyd	.15
6	Jeffrey Hammonds	.15
7	Trevor Hoffman	.15
8	Domingo Jean	.15
9	David McCarty	.15
10	Bobby Munoz	.15
11	Brad Pennington	.15
12	Mike Piazza	3.00
13	Manny Ramirez	2.00
14	John Roper	.15
15	Tim Salmon	.25
16	Aaron Sele	.15
17	Allen Watson	.15
18	Rondell White	.15
19	Darell Whitmore	.15
20	Nigel Wilson	.15

1994 Flair

One of the success stories of 1993 returned with the release of Fleer Flair for 1994. At $4 per pack this was pricey stuff, but collectors apparently liked the look that includes an extremely thick card stock, full-bleed photos and gold-foil graphics on both sides with a protective polyester laminate described as "far beyond mere UV coating." In addition to the 250 regular-issue cards, there are three 10-card, insert sets; Wave of the Future, Outfield Power and Hot Numbers in Series 1, the last with players' images printed on 100 percent etched foil. Series 2 has 200 base cards and Hot Glove, In-field Power and 10 more Wave of the Future insert cards.

	NM/M
Complete Set (450):	60.00
Common Player:	.10
Series 1 Pack (10):	1.50
Series 1 Box (24):	20.00
Series 2 Pack (10):	3.00
Series 2 Box (24):	50.00

1	Harold Baines	.10
2	Jeffrey Hammonds	.10
3	Chris Hoiles	.10
4	Ben McDonald	.10
5	Mark McLemore	.10
6	Jamie Moyer	.10
7	Jim Poole	.10
8	Cal Ripken, Jr.	3.00
9	Chris Sabo	.10
10	Scott Bankhead	.10
11	Scott Cooper	.10
12	Danny Darwin	.10
13	Andre Dawson	.30
14	Billy Hatcher	.10
15	Aaron Sele	.10
15a	Aaron Sele/OPS	2.00
16	John Valentin	.10
17	Dave Valle	.10
18	Mo Vaughn	.10
19	Brian Anderson RC	.50
20	Gary DiSarcina	.10
21	Jim Edmonds	.10
22	Chuck Finley	.10
23	Bo Jackson	.20
24	Mark Leiter	.10
25	Greg Myers	.10
26	Eduardo Perez	.10
27	Tim Salmon	.10
28	Wilson Alvarez	.10
29	Jason Bere	.10
30	Alex Fernandez	.10
31	Ozzie Guillen	.10
32	Joe Hall	.10
33	Darrin Jackson	.10
34	Kirk McCaskill	.10
35	Tim Raines	.10
36	Frank Thomas	1.00
37	Carlos Baerga	.10
38	Albert Belle	.10
39	Mark Clark	.10
40	Wayne Kirby	.10
41	Dennis Martinez	.10
42	Charles Nagy	.10
43	Manny Ramirez	1.00
44	Paul Sorrento	.10
45	Jim Thome	.65
46	Eric Davis	.10
47	John Doherty	.10
48	Junior Felix	.10
49	Cecil Fielder	.10
50	Kirk Gibson	.10
51	Mike Moore	.10
52	Tony Phillips	.10
53	Alan Trammell	.10
54	Kevin Appier	.10
55	Stan Belinda	.10
56	Vince Coleman	.10
57	Greg Gagne	.10
58	Bob Hamelin	.10
59	Dave Henderson	.10
60	Wally Joyner	.10
61	Mike Macfarlane	.10
62	Jeff Montgomery	.10
63	Ricky Bones	.10
64	Jeff Bronkey	.10
65	Alex Diaz	.10
66	Cal Eldred	.10
67	Darryl Hamilton	.10
68	John Jaha	.10
69	Mark Kiefer	.10
70	Kevin Seitzer	.10
71	Turner Ward	.10
72	Rich Becker	.10
73	Scott Erickson	.10
74	Keith Garagozzo	.10
75	Kent Hrbek	.10
76	Scott Leius	.10
77	Kirby Puckett	1.50
78	Matt Walkbeck	.10
79	Dave Winfield	1.00
80	Mike Gallego	.10
81	Xavier Hernandez	.10
82	Jimmy Key	.10
83	Jim Leyritz	.10
84	Don Mattingly	1.75
85	Matt Nokes	.10
86	Paul O'Neill	.10
87	Melido Perez	.10
88	Danny Tartabull	.10
89	Mike Bordick	.10
90	Ron Darling	.10
91	Dennis Eckersley	.75
92	Stan Javier	.10
93	Steve Karsay	.10
94	Mark McGwire	2.50
95	Troy Neel	.10
96	Terry Steinbach	.10
97	Bill Taylor	.10
98	Eric Anthony	.10
99	Chris Bosio	.10
100	Tim Davis	.10
101	Felix Fermin	.10
102	Dave Fleming	.10
103	Ken Griffey Jr.	2.00
104	Greg Hibbard	.10
105	Reggie Jefferson	.10
106	Tino Martinez	.10
107	Jack Armstrong	.10
108	Will Clark	.10
109	Juan Gonzalez	.50
110	Rick Helling	.10
111	Tom Henke	.10
112	David Hulse	.10
113	Manuel Lee	.10
114	Doug Strange	.10
115	Roberto Alomar	.25
116	Joe Carter	.10
117	Carlos Delgado	.50
118	Pat Hentgen	.10
119	Paul Molitor	1.00
120	John Olerud	.10
121	Dave Stewart	.10
122	Todd Stottlemyre	.10
123	Mike Timlin	.10
124	Jeff Blauser	.10
125	Tom Glavine	.30
126	Dave Justice	.10
127	Mike Kelly	.10
128	Ryan Klesko	.10
129	Javier Lopez	.10
130	Greg Maddux	1.50
131	Fred McGriff	.10
132	Kent Mercker	.10
133	Mark Wohlers	.10
134	Willie Banks	.10
135	Steve Buechele	.10
136	Shawon Dunston	.10
137	Jose Guzman	.10
138	Glenallen Hill	.10
139	Randy Myers	.10
140	Karl Rhodes	.10
141	Ryne Sandberg	1.50
142	Steve Trachsel	.10
143	Bret Boone	.10
144	Tom Browning	.10
145	Hector Carrasco	.10
146	Barry Larkin	.10
147	Hal Morris	.10
148	Jose Rijo	.10
149	Reggie Sanders	.10
150	John Smiley	.10
151	Dante Bichette	.10
152	Ellis Burks	.10
153	Joe Girardi	.10
154	Mike Harkey	.10
155	Roberto Mejia	.10
156	Marcus Moore	.10
157	Armando Reynoso	.10
158	Bruce Ruffin	.10
159	Eric Young	.10
160	Kurt Abbott RC	.10
161	Jeff Conine	.10
162	Orestes Destrade	.10
163	Chris Hammond	.10
164	Bryan Harvey	.10
165	Dave Magadan	.10
166	Gary Sheffield	.40
167	David Weathers	.10
168	Andujar Cedeno	.10
169	Tom Edens	.10
170	Luis Gonzalez	.10
171	Pete Harnisch	.10
172	Todd Jones	.10
173	Darryl Kile	.10
174	James Mouton	.10
175	Scott Servais	.10
176	Mitch Williams	.10
177	Pedro Astacio	.10
178	Orel Hershiser	.10
179	Raul Mondesi	.10
180	Jose Offerman	.10
181	Chan Ho Park RC	1.00
182	Mike Piazza	2.00
183	Cory Snyder	.10
184	Tim Wallach	.10
185	Todd Worrell	.10
186	Sean Berry	.10
187	Wil Cordero	.10
188	Darrin Fletcher	.10
189	Cliff Floyd	.10
190	Marquis Grissom	.10
191	Rod Henderson	.10
192	Ken Hill	.10
193	Pedro Martinez	1.00
194	Kirk Rueter	.10
195	Jeromy Burnitz	.10
196	John Franco	.10
197	Dwight Gooden	.10
198	Todd Hundley	.10
199	Bobby Jones	.10
200	Jeff Kent	.10
201	Mike Maddux	.10
202	Ryan Thompson	.10
203	Jose Vizcaino	.10
204	Darren Daulton	.10
205	Len Dykstra	.10
206	Jim Eisenreich	.10
207	Dave Hollins	.10
208	Danny Jackson	.10
209	Doug Jones	.10
210	Jeff Juden	.10
211	Ben Rivera	.10
212	Kevin Stocker	.10
213	Milt Thompson	.10
214	Jay Bell	.10
215	Steve Cooke	.10
216	Mark Dewey	.10
217	Al Martin	.10
218	Orlando Merced	.10
219	Don Slaught	.10
220	Zane Smith	.10
221	Rick White	.10
222	Kevin Young	.10
223	Rene Arocha	.10
224	Rheal Cormier	.10
225	Brian Jordan	.10
226	Ray Lankford	.10
227	Mike Perez	.10
228	Ozzie Smith	1.50
229	Mark Whiten	.10
230	Todd Zeile	.10
231	Derek Bell	.10
232	Archi Cianfrocco	.10
233	Ricky Gutierrez	.10
234	Trevor Hoffman	.10
235	Phil Plantier	.10
236	Dave Staton	.10
237	Wally Whitehurst	.10
238	Todd Benzinger	.10
239	Barry Bonds	3.00
240	John Burkett	.10
241	Royce Clayton	.10
242	Bryan Hickerson	.10
243	Mike Jackson	.10
244	Darren Lewis	.10
245	Kirt Manwaring	.10
246	Mark Portugal	.10
247	Salomon Torres	.10
248	Checklist	.10
249	Checklist	.10
250	Checklist	.10
251	Brady Anderson	.10
252	Mike Devereaux	.10
253	Sid Fernandez	.10
254	Leo Gomez	.10
255	Mike Mussina	.40
256	Mike Oquist	.10
257	Rafael Palmeiro	.75
258	Lee Smith	.10
259	Damon Berryhill	.10
260	Wes Chamberlain	.10
261	Roger Clemens	1.75
262	Gar Finnvold	.10
263	Mike Greenwell	.10
264	Tim Naehring	.10
265	Otis Nixon	.10
266	Ken Ryan	.10
267	Chad Curtis	.10
268	Chili Davis	.10
269	Damion Easley	.10
270	Jorge Fabregas	.10
271	Mark Langston	.10
272	Phil Leftwich	.10
273	Harold Reynolds	.10
274	J.T. Snow	.10
275	Joey Cora	.10
276	Julio Franco	.10
277	Roberto Hernandez	.10
278	Lance Johnson	.10
279	Ron Karkovice	.10
280	Jack McDowell	.10
281	Robin Ventura	.10
282	Sandy Alomar Jr.	.10
283	Kenny Lofton	.10
284	Jose Mesa	.10
285	Jack Morris	.10
286	Eddie Murray	1.00
287	Chad Ogea	.10
288	Eric Plunk	.10
289	Paul Shuey	.10
290	Omar Vizquel	.10
291	Danny Bautista	.10
292	Travis Fryman	.10
293	Greg Gohr	.10
294	Chris Gomez	.10
295	Mickey Tettleton	.10
296	Lou Whitaker	.10
297	David Cone	.10
298	Gary Gaetti	.10
299	Tom Gordon	.10
300	Felix Jose	.10
301	Jose Lind	.10
302	Brian McRae	.10
303	Mike Fetters	.10
304	Brian Harper	.10
305	Pat Listach	.10
306	Matt Mieske	.10
307	Dave Nilsson	.10
308	Jody Reed	.10
309	Greg Vaughn	.10
310	Bill Wegman	.10
311	Rick Aguilera	.10
312	Alex Cole	.10
313	Denny Hocking	.10
314	Chuck Knoblauch	.10
315	Shane Mack	.10
316	Pat Meares	.10
317	Kevin Tapani	.10
318	Jim Abbott	.10
319	Wade Boggs	1.00
320	Sterling Hitchcock	.10
321	Pat Kelly	.10
322	Terry Mulholland	.10
323	Luis Polonia	.10
324	Mike Stanley	.10
325	Bob Wickman	.10
326	Bernie Williams	.10
327	Mark Acre	.10
328	Geronimo Berroa	.10
329	Scott Brosius	.10
330	Brent Gates	.10
331	Rickey Henderson	1.00
332	Carlos Reyes	.10
333	Ruben Sierra	.10
334	Bobby Witt	.10
335	Bobby Ayala	.10
336	Jay Buhner	.10
337	Randy Johnson	1.00
338	Edgar Martinez	.10
339	Bill Risley	.10
340	Alex Rodriguez RC	40.00
341	Roger Salkeld	.10
342	Dan Wilson	.10
343	Kevin Brown	.10
344	Jose Canseco	.45
345	Dean Palmer	.10
346	Ivan Rodriguez	.75
347	Kenny Rogers	.10
348	Pat Borders	.10
349	Juan Guzman	.10
350	Ed Sprague	.10
351	Devon White	.10
352	Steve Avery	.10
353	Roberto Kelly	.10
354	Mark Lemke	.10
355	Greg McMichael	.10
356	Terry Pendleton	.10
357	John Smoltz	.10
358	Mike Stanton	.10
359	Tony Tarasco	.10
360	Mark Grace	.10
361	Derrick May	.10
362	Rey Sanchez	.10
363	Sammy Sosa	1.50
364	Rick Wilkins	.10
365	Jeff Brantley	.10
366	Tony Fernandez	.10
367	Chuck McElroy	.10
368	Kevin Mitchell	.10
369	John Roper	.10
370	Johnny Ruffin	.10
371	Deion Sanders	.15
372	Marvin Freeman	.10
373	Andres Galarraga	.10
374	Charlie Hayes	.10
375	Nelson Liriano	.10
376	David Nied	.10
377	Walt Weiss	.10
378	Bret Barberie	.10
379	Jerry Browne	.10
380	Chuck Carr	.10
381	Greg Colbrunn	.10
382	Charlie Hough	.10
383	Kurt Miller	.10
384	Benito Santiago	.10
385	Jeff Bagwell	1.00
386	Craig Biggio	.10
387	Ken Caminiti	.10
388	Doug Drabek	.10
389	Steve Finley	.10
390	John Hudek	.10
391	Orlando Miller	.10
392	Shane Reynolds	.10
393	Brett Butler	.10
394	Tom Candiotti	.10
395	Delino DeShields	.10
396	Kevin Gross	.10
397	Eric Karros	.10
398	Ramon Martinez	.10
399	Henry Rodriguez	.10
400	Moises Alou	.10
401	Jeff Fassero	.10
402	Mike Lansing	.10
403	Mel Rojas	.10
404	Larry Walker	.10
405	John Wetteland	.10
406	Gabe White	.10
407	Bobby Bonilla	.10
408	Josias Manzanillo	.10
409	Bret Saberhagen	.10
410	David Segui	.10
411	Mariano Duncan	.10
412	Tommy Greene	.10
413	Billy Hatcher	.10
414	Ricky Jordan	.10
415	John Kruk	.10
416	Bobby Munoz	.10
417	Curt Schilling	.30
418	Fernando Valenzuela	.10
419	David West	.10
420	Carlos Garcia	.10
421	Brian Hunter	.10
422	Jeff King	.10
423	Jon Lieber	.10
424	Ravelo Manzanillo	.10
425	Denny Neagle	.10
426	Andy Van Slyke	.10
427	Bryan Eversgerd	.10
428	Bernard Gilkey	.10
429	Gregg Jefferies	.10
430	Tom Pagnozzi	.10
431	Bob Tewksbury	.10
432	Allen Watson	.10
433	Andy Ashby	.10
434	Andy Benes	.10
435	Donnie Elliott	.10
436	Tony Gwynn	1.50
437	Joey Hamilton	.10
438	Tim Hyers	.10
439	Luis Lopez	.10
440	Bip Roberts	.10
441	Scott Sanders	.10
442	Rod Beck	.10
443	Dave Burba	.10
444	Darryl Strawberry	.10
445	Bill Swift	.10
446	Robby Thompson	.10
447	William Van Landingham RC	.10
448	Matt Williams	.10
449	Checklist	.10
450	Checklist	.10

Hot Gloves

Hot Glove

Hot Glove is a 10-card Series 2 insert set. It focuses on players with outstanding defensive ability. Cards feature a die-cut design, with the player photo in front of a baseball glove. Player identification and a "Hot Glove" logo are in gold foil in the lower-left corner.

		NM/M
Complete Set (10):		40.00
Common Player:		2.00
1	Barry Bonds	10.00
2	Will Clark	2.00
3	Ken Griffey Jr.	7.50
4	Kenny Lofton	2.00
5	Greg Maddux	5.00
6	Don Mattingly	6.50
7	Kirby Puckett	5.00
8	Cal Ripken, Jr.	10.00
9	Tim Salmon	2.00
10	Matt Williams	2.00

Hot Numbers

Hot Numbers is an insert set found in Series 1 packs at an average rate of 1:24. Each card is printed on 100 percent etched foil and displays the player in the forefront with a background made up of floating numbers. The player's name is in gold foil across the bottom-right side and a large foil "Hot Numbers" and that player's uniform number are in a square at bottom-left.

		NM/M
Complete Set (10):		15.00
Common Player:		.50
1	Roberto Alomar	1.00
2	Carlos Baerga	.50
3	Will Clark	.50
4	Fred McGriff	.50
5	Paul Molitor	3.00
6	John Olerud	.50
7	Mike Piazza	4.50
8	Cal Ripken, Jr.	6.00
9	Ryne Sandberg	4.00
10	Frank Thomas	3.00

Infield Power

Infield Power is a horizontally formatted insert set. Cards show the player batting on one half and in the field on the other half of the card, divided by a black, diagonal strip that reads "Infield Power" and the player's name. The set spotlights infielders that often hit the longball. Infield Power was inserted into Series 2 packs at an average rate of 1:5.

		NM/M
Complete Set (10):		5.00
Common Player:		.25
1	Jeff Bagwell	.75
2	Will Clark	.25
3	Darren Daulton	.25
4	Don Mattingly	1.25
5	Fred McGriff	.25
6	Rafael Palmeiro	.65
7	Mike Piazza	1.50
8	Cal Ripken, Jr.	2.50
9	Frank Thomas	.75
10	Matt Williams	.25

Outfield Power

Flair's Outfield Power was randomly inserted in Series 1 packs at a 1:5 rate. This vertically formatted card shows the player in the field on top, while the bottom half shows the player at the plate. The photos divided by a black strip with "Outfield Power" and the player's name on it.

		NM/M
Complete Set (10):		5.00
Common Player:		.30
1	Albert Belle	.30
2	Barry Bonds	2.00
3	Joe Carter	.30
4	Len Dykstra	.30
5	Juan Gonzalez	.45
6	Ken Griffey Jr.	1.50
7	Dave Justice	.30
8	Kirby Puckett	.50
9	Tim Salmon	.30
10	Dave Winfield	.75

Wave of the Future 1

Series 1 Wave of the Future is horizontally formatted and depicts 10 outstanding 1994 rookies who have the potential to become superstars. Each player is featured on a colorful wavelike background. A Wave of the Future gold-foil stamp is placed in the bottom-right corner with the player name in gold foil starting in the opposite bottom corner and running across the bottom. Advertised insertion rate was 1:5.

		NM/M
Complete Set (10):		6.00
Common Player:		.25
1	Kurt Abbott	.25
2	Carlos Delgado	5.00
3	Steve Karsay	.25
4	Ryan Klesko	.25
5	Javier Lopez	.25
6	Raul Mondesi	.25
7	James Mouton	.25
8	Chan Ho Park	.25
9	Dave Staton	.25
10	Rick White	.25

Wave of the Future 2

Series 2 Flair also has a Wave of the Future insert set. Unlike the earlier series, this 10-card set is vertically formated. The Wave of the Future logo appears in the bottom-left with the player's name stretching across the rest of the bottom. The background has a swirling water effect, on which the player is superimposed. Insertion rate is one per five packs.

		NM/M
Complete Set (10):		22.50
Common Player:		.50
1	Mark Acre	.50
2	Chris Gomez	.50
3	Joey Hamilton	.50
4	John Hudek	.50
5	Jon Lieber	.50
6	Matt Mieske	.50
7	Orlando Miller	.50
8	Alex Rodriguez	20.00
9	Tony Tarasco	.50
10	Bill Van Landingham	.50

1995 Flair

There's no mistaking that 1995 Flair is Fleer's super-premium brand. Cards are printed on double-thick cardboard with a background of etched metallic foil: Gold for National Leaguers, silver for American. A portrait and an action photo are featured on the horizontal front design. Backs are vertically formatted with a borderless action photo, several years worth of stats and foil trim. The basic set was issued in two series of 216 basic cards each, along with several insert sets exclusive to each series. Cards were sold in a hard pack of nine with a suggested retail price of $5.

		NM/M
Complete Set (432):		30.00
Common Player:		.10
Series 1 or 2 Pack (9):		1.00
Series 1 or 2 Wax Box (24):		15.00
1	Brady Anderson	.10
2	Harold Baines	.10
3	Leo Gomez	.10
4	Alan Mills	.10
5	Jamie Moyer	.10
6	Mike Mussina	.40
7	Mike Oquist	.10
8	Arthur Rhodes	.10
9	Cal Ripken Jr.	3.00
10	Roger Clemens	1.75
11	Scott Cooper	.10
12	Mike Greenwell	.10
13	Aaron Sele	.10
14	John Valentin	.10
15	Mo Vaughn	.10
16	Chad Curtis	.10
17	Gary DiSarcina	.10
18	Chuck Finley	.10
19	Andrew Lorraine	.10
20	Spike Owen	.10
21	Tim Salmon	.10
22	J.T. Snow	.10
23	Wilson Alvarez	.10
24	Jason Bere	.10
25	Ozzie Guillen	.10
26	Mike LaValliere	.10
27	Frank Thomas	1.00
28	Robin Ventura	.10
29	Carlos Baerga	.10
30	Albert Belle	.10
31	Jason Grimsley	.10
32	Dennis Martinez	.10
33	Eddie Murray	1.00
34	Charles Nagy	.10
35	Manny Ramirez	1.00
36	Paul Sorrento	.10
37	John Doherty	.10
38	Cecil Fielder	.10
39	Travis Fryman	.10
40	Chris Gomez	.10
41	Tony Phillips	.10
42	Lou Whitaker	.10
43	David Cone	.10
44	Gary Gaetti	.10
45	Mark Gubicza	.10
46	Bob Hamelin	.10
47	Wally Joyner	.10
48	Rusty Meacham	.10
49	Jeff Montgomery	.10
50	Ricky Bones	.10
51	Cal Eldred	.10
52	Pat Listach	.10
53	Matt Mieske	.10
54	Dave Nilsson	.10
55	Greg Vaughn	.10
56	Bill Wegman	.10
57	Chuck Knoblauch	.10
58	Scott Leius	.10
59	Pat Mahomes	.10
60	Pat Meares	.10
61	Pedro Munoz	.10
62	Kirby Puckett	1.50
63	Wade Boggs	1.00
64	Jimmy Key	.10
65	Jim Leyritz	.10
66	Don Mattingly	1.75
67	Paul O'Neill	.10
68	Melido Perez	.10
69	Danny Tartabull	.10
70	John Briscoe	.10
71	Scott Brosius	.10
72	Ron Darling	.10
73	Brent Gates	.10
74	Rickey Henderson	1.00
75	Stan Javier	.10
76	Mark McGwire	2.50
77	Todd Van Poppel	.10
78	Bobby Ayala	.10
79	Mike Blowers	.10
80	Jay Buhner	.10
81	Ken Griffey Jr.	2.00
82	Randy Johnson	1.00
83	Tino Martinez	.10
84	Jeff Nelson	.10
85	Alex Rodriguez	2.50
86	Will Clark	.10
87	Jeff Frye	.10
88	Juan Gonzalez	.50
89	Rusty Greer	.10
90	Darren Oliver	.10
91	Dean Palmer	.10
92	Ivan Rodriguez	.75
93	Matt Whiteside	.10
94	Roberto Alomar	.25
95	Joe Carter	.10
96	Tony Castillo	.10
97	Juan Guzman	.10
98	Pat Hentgen	.10
99	Mike Huff	.10
100	John Olerud	.10
101	Woody Williams	.10
102	Roberto Kelly	.10
103	Ryan Klesko	.10
104	Javier Lopez	.10
105	Greg Maddux	1.50
106	Fred McGriff	.10
107	Jose Oliva	.10
108	John Smoltz	.10
109	Tony Tarasco	.10
110	Mark Wohlers	.10
111	Jim Bullinger	.10
112	Shawon Dunston	.10
113	Derrick May	.10
114	Randy Myers	.10
115	Karl Rhodes	.10
116	Rey Sanchez	.10
117	Steve Trachsel	.10
118	Eddie Zambrano	.10
119	Bret Boone	.10
120	Brian Dorsett	.10
121	Hal Morris	.10
122	Jose Rijo	.10
123	John Roper	.10
124	Reggie Sanders	.10
125	Pete Schourek	.10
126	John Smiley	.10
127	Ellis Burks	.10
128	Vinny Castilla	.10
129	Marvin Freeman	.10
130	Andres Galarraga	.10
131	Mike Munoz	.10
132	David Nied	.10
133	Bruce Ruffin	.10
134	Walt Weiss	.10
135	Eric Young	.10
136	Greg Colbrunn	.10
137	Jeff Conine	.10
138	Jeremy Hernandez	.10
139	Charles Johnson	.10
140	Robb Nen	.10
141	Gary Sheffield	.40
142	Dave Weathers	.10
143	Jeff Bagwell	1.00
144	Craig Biggio	.10
145	Tony Eusebio	.10
146	Luis Gonzalez	.10
147	John Hudek	.10
148	Darryl Kile	.10
149	Dave Veres	.10
150	Billy Ashley	.10
151	Pedro Astacio	.10
152	Rafael Bournigal	.10
153	Delino DeShields	.10
154	Raul Mondesi	.10
155	Mike Piazza	2.00
156	Rudy Seanez	.10
157	Ismael Valdes	.10
158	Tim Wallach	.10
159	Todd Worrell	.10
160	Moises Alou	.10
161	Cliff Floyd	.10
162	Gil Heredia	.10
163	Mike Lansing	.10
164	Pedro Martinez	1.00
165	Kirk Rueter	.10
166	Tim Scott	.10
167	Jeff Shaw	.10
168	Rondell White	.10
169	Bobby Bonilla	.10
170	Rico Brogna	.10
171	Todd Hundley	.10
172	Jeff Kent	.10
173	Jim Lindeman	.10
174	Joe Orsulak	.10
175	Bret Saberhagen	.10
176	Toby Borland	.10
177	Darren Daulton	.10
178	Lenny Dykstra	.10
179	Jim Eisenreich	.10
180	Tommy Greene	.10
181	Tony Longmire	.10
182	Bobby Munoz	.10
183	Kevin Stocker	.10
184	Jay Bell	.10
185	Steve Cooke	.10
186	Ravelo Manzanillo	.10
187	Al Martin	.10
188	Denny Neagle	.10
189	Don Slaught	.10
190	Paul Wagner	.10
191	Rene Arocha	.10
192	Bernard Gilkey	.10
193	Jose Oquendo	.10
194	Tom Pagnozzi	.10
195	Ozzie Smith	1.50
196	Allen Watson	.10
197	Mark Whiten	.10
198	Andy Ashby	.10
199	Donnie Elliott	.10
200	Bryce Florie	.10
201	Tony Gwynn	1.50
202	Trevor Hoffman	.10
203	Brian Johnson	.10
204	Tim Mauser	.10
205	Bip Roberts	.10
206	Rod Beck	.10
207	Barry Bonds	3.00
208	Royce Clayton	.10
209	Darren Lewis	.10
210	Mark Portugal	.10
211	Kevin Rogers	.10
212	William Van Landingham	.10
213	Matt Williams	.10
214	Checklist	.10
215	Checklist	.10
216	Checklist	.10
217	Bret Barberie	.10
218	Armando Benitez	.10
219	Kevin Brown	.10
220	Sid Fernandez	.10
221	Chris Hoiles	.10
222	Doug Jones	.10
223	Ben McDonald	.10
224	Rafael Palmeiro	.75
225	Andy Van Slyke	.10
226	Jose Canseco	.40
227	Vaughn Eshelman	.10
228	Mike Macfarlane	.10
229	Tim Naehring	.10
230	Frank Rodriguez	.10
231	Lee Tinsley	.10
232	Mark Whiten	.10
233	Garret Anderson	.10
234	Chili Davis	.10
235	Jim Edmonds	.10
236	Mark Langston	.10
237	Troy Percival	.10
238	Tony Phillips	.10
239	Lee Smith	.10
240	Jim Abbott	.10
241	James Baldwin	.10
242	Mike Devereaux	.10
243	Ray Durham	.10
244	Alex Fernandez	.10
245	Roberto Hernandez	.10
246	Lance Johnson	.10
247	Ron Karkovice	.10
248	Tim Raines	.10
249	Sandy Alomar Jr.	.10
250	Orel Hershiser	.10
251	Julian Tavarez	.10
252	Jim Thome	.65
253	Omar Vizquel	.10
254	Dave Winfield	1.00
255	Chad Curtis	.10
256	Kirk Gibson	.10
257	Mike Henneman	.10
258	Bob Higginson RC	.25
259	Felipe Lira	.10
260	Rudy Pemberton	.10
261	Alan Trammell	.10
262	Kevin Appier	.10
263	Pat Borders	.10
264	Tom Gordon	.10
265	Jose Lind	.10
266	Jon Nunnally	.10
267	Dilson Torres	.10
268	Michael Tucker	.10
269	Jeff Cirillo	.10
270	Darryl Hamilton	.10
271	David Hulse	.10
272	Mark Kiefer	.10
273	Graeme Lloyd	.10
274	Joe Oliver	.10
275	Al Reyes	.10
276	Kevin Seitzer	.10
277	Rick Aguilera	.10
278	Marty Cordova	.10
279	Scott Erickson	.10
280	LaTroy Hawkins	.10
281	Brad Radke	.10
282	Kevin Tapani	.10
283	Tony Fernandez	.10
284	Sterling Hitchcock	.10
285	Pat Kelly	.10
286	Jack McDowell	.10
287	Andy Pettitte	.30
288	Mike Stanley	.10
289	John Wetteland	.10
290	Bernie Williams	.10
291	Mark Acre	.10
292	Geronimo Berroa	.10
293	Dennis Eckersley	.75
294	Steve Ontiveros	.10
295	Ruben Sierra	.10
296	Terry Steinbach	.10
297	Dave Stewart	.10
298	Todd Stottlemyre	.10
299	Darren Bragg	.10
300	Joey Cora	.10
301	Edgar Martinez	.10
302	Bill Risley	.10
303	Ron Villone	.10
304	Dan Wilson	.10
305	Benji Gil	.10
306	Wilson Heredia	.10
307	Mark McLemore	.10
308	Otis Nixon	.10
309	Kenny Rogers	.10
310	Jeff Russell	.10
311	Mickey Tettleton	.10
312	Bob Tewksbury	.10
313	David Cone	.10
314	Carlos Delgado	.50
315	Alex Gonzalez	.10
316	Shawn Green	.40
317	Paul Molitor	1.00
318	Ed Sprague	.10
319	Devon White	.10
320	Steve Avery	.10
321	Jeff Blauser	.10
322	Brad Clontz	.10
323	Tom Glavine	.30
324	Marquis Grissom	.10
325	Chipper Jones	1.50
326	Dave Justice	.10
327	Mark Lemke	.10
328	Kent Merckner	.10
329	Jason Schmidt	.10
330	Steve Buechele	.10
331	Kevin Foster	.10
332	Mark Grace	.10
333	Brian McRae	.10
334	Sammy Sosa	1.50
335	Ozzie Timmons	.10
336	Rick Wilkins	.10
337	Hector Carrasco	.10
338	Ron Gant	.10
339	Barry Larkin	.10
340	Deion Sanders	.15
341	Benito Santiago	.10
342	Roger Bailey	.10
343	Jason Bates	.10
344	Dante Bichette	.10
345	Joe Girardi	.10
346	Bill Swift	.10
347	Mark Thompson	.10
348	Larry Walker	.10
349	Kurt Abbott	.10
350	John Burkett	.10
351	Chuck Carr	.10
352	Andre Dawson	.30
353	Chris Hammond	.10
354	Charles Johnson	.10
355	Terry Pendleton	.10
356	Quivio Veras	.10
357	Derek Bell	.10
358	Jim Dougherty	.10
359	Doug Drabek	.10
360	Todd Jones	.10
361	Orlando Miller	.10
362	James Mouton	.10
363	Phil Plantier	.10
364	Shane Reynolds	.10
365	Todd Hollandsworth	.10
366	Eric Karros	.10
367	Ramon Martinez	.10
368	Hideo Nomo RC	3.00
369	Jose Offerman	.10
370	Antonio Osuna	.10
371	Todd Williams	.10
372	Shane Andrews	.10
373	Wil Cordero	.10
374	Jeff Fassero	.10
375	Darrin Fletcher	.10
376	Mark Grudzielanek RC	.50
377	Carlos Perez RC	.25
378	Mel Rojas	.10
379	Tony Tarasco	.10
380	Edgardo Alfonzo	.10
381	Brett Butler	.10
382	Carl Everett	.10
383	John Franco	.10
384	Pete Harnisch	.10
385	Bobby Jones	.10
386	Dave Mlicki	.10
387	Jose Vizcaino	.10
388	Ricky Bottalico	.10
389	Tyler Green	.10
390	Charlie Hayes	.10
391	Dave Hollins	.10
392	Gregg Jefferies	.10
393	Michael Mimbs RC	.10
394	Mickey Morandini	.10
395	Curt Schilling	.10
396	Heathcliff Slocumb	.10
397	Jason Christiansen	.10
398	Midre Cummings	.10
399	Carlos Garcia	.10
400	Mark Johnson	.10
401	Jeff King	.10
402	Jon Lieber	.10
403	Esteban Loaiza	.10

404	Orlando Merced	.10
405	Gary Wilson RC	.10
406	Scott Cooper	.10
407	Tom Henke	.10
408	Ken Hill	.10
409	Danny Jackson	.10
410	Brian Jordan	.10
411	Ray Lankford	.10
412	John Mabry	.10
413	Todd Zeile	.10
414	Andy Benes	.10
415	Andres Berumen	.10
416	Ken Caminiti	.10
417	Andujar Cedeno	.10
418	Steve Finley	.10
419	Joey Hamilton	.10
420	Dustin Hermanson	.10
421	Melvin Nieves	.10
422	Roberto Petagine	.10
423	Eddie Williams	.10
424	Glenallen Hill	.10
425	Kirt Manwaring	.10
426	Terry Mulholland	.10
427	J.R. Phillips	.10
428	Joe Rosselli	.10
429	Robby Thompson	.10
430	Checklist	.10
431	Checklist	.10
432	Checklist	.10

Cal Ripken, Jr. Enduring Flair

The career of Cal Ripken, Jr., is traced in this insert set found in Series 2 Flair at the average rate of once per dozen packs. Each card has a vintage photo on front, with a large silver-foil "ENDURING" logo toward bottom. Backs have another color photo, a quote and other information about the milestone. The series was extended by a special mail-in offer for five additional cards which chronicled Ripken's record-breaking 1995 season.

		NM/M
Complete Set (15):		40.00
Common Card:		4.00
1	Rookie Of The Year	4.00
2	1st MVP Season	4.00
3	World Series Highlight	4.00
4	Family Tradition	4.00
5	8,243 Consecutive Innings	4.00
6	95 Consecutive Errorless Games	4.00
7	All-Star MVP	4.00
8	1,000th RBI	4.00
9	287th Home Run	4.00
10	2,000th Consecutive Game	4.00
11	Record-tying Game	6.00
12	Record-breaking Game	6.00
13	Defensive Prowess	6.00
14	Literacy Work	6.00
15	2,153 and Counting	6.00

Hot Gloves

The cream of the crop among Series 2 Flair inserts is this set featuring fine fielders. Cards have a background of an embossed gold-foil glove, with a color player photo centered in front. Silver foil comprises the card title and player name at bottom and the Flair logo at top. Backs have a white background, a photo of a glove with a career summary overprinted and a player portrait photo in a lower corner. These inserts are found at the average rate of once per 25 packs.

		NM/M
Complete Set (12):		35.00
Common Player:		1.25
1	Roberto Alomar	2.00
2	Barry Bonds	10.00
3	Ken Griffey Jr.	7.50
4	Marquis Grissom	1.25
5	Barry Larkin	1.25
6	Darren Lewis	1.25
7	Kenny Lofton	1.25
8	Don Mattingly	6.00
9	Cal Ripken Jr.	10.00
10	Ivan Rodriguez	2.50
11	Devon White	1.25
12	Matt Williams	1.25

Hot Numbers

These Series 1 inserts are a 1:9 find. Gold metallic-foil background with 1994 seasonal stat numbers are the background for a color action photo on front. Horizontal backs have a ghosted portrait photo at right and career highlights at left.

		NM/M
Complete Set (10):		10.00
Common Player:		.50
1	Jeff Bagwell	1.00
2	Albert Belle	.50
3	Barry Bonds	2.25
4	Ken Griffey Jr.	2.00
5	Kenny Lofton	.50
6	Greg Maddux	1.25
7	Mike Piazza	2.00
8	Cal Ripken Jr.	2.25
9	Frank Thomas	1.00
10	Matt Williams	.50

Infield Power

Power rays and waves emanating from the player's bat in an action photo are the front design of this Series 2 chase set. The card title, name and team are at bottom, and the Flair logo at top are in silver foil. Backs repeat the wave theme with a player photo on one end and a career summary at the other. These inserts are seeded at the average rate of one per five packs.

		NM/M
Complete Set (10):		4.00
Common Player:		.25
1	Jeff Bagwell	.75
2	Darren Daulton	.25
3	Cecil Fielder	.25
4	Andres Galarraga	.25
5	Fred McGriff	.25
6	Rafael Palmeiro	.65
7	Mike Piazza	1.50
8	Frank Thomas	1.00
9	Mo Vaughn	.25
10	Matt Williams	.25

Outfield Power

Laser-like colored rays are the background to the action photo on front and portrait on back of this series. The card title, player identification and Flair logo on front are in silver foil. Backs are horizontal, silver-foil enhanced and include a career summary. This chase set is seeded at the average rate of one card per six packs of Series 1 Flair.

		NM/M
Complete Set (10):		7.50
Common Player:		.35
1	Jason Bates	.25
2	Armando Benitez	.25
3	Marty Cordova	.25
4	Ray Durham	.25
5	Vaughn Eshelman	.25
6	Carl Everett	.25
7	Shawn Green	1.50
8	Dustin Hermanson	.25
9	Chipper Jones	4.00
10	Hideo Nomo	1.50

Today's Spotlight

The premier insert set in Flair Series I, found once every 30 packs or so, this die-cut issue has the player action photo spotlighted in a 2-3/8" bright spot, with the rest of the photo muted in gray and dark gray. The card title, Flair logo, player name and team are in silver foil. The horizontal backs have a portrait photo in the spotlight and career summary on the side.

		NM/M
Complete Set (12):		15.00
Common Player:		1.00
1	Jeff Bagwell	3.00
2	Jason Bere	1.00
3	Cliff Floyd	1.00
4	Chuck Knoblauch	1.00
5	Kenny Lofton	1.00
6	Javier Lopez	1.00
7	Raul Mondesi	1.00
8	Mike Mussina	1.50
9	Mike Piazza	5.00
10	Manny Ramirez	3.00
11	Tim Salmon	1.00
12	Frank Thomas	3.00

Wave Of The Future

The cream of baseball's rookie crop is featured in this Series 2 insert set, found once per eight packs on average. Fronts have a graduated color background with a baseball/wave morph, which is repeated at the bottom in silver foil, along with the player name. A color action photo is at center. The player's name, team and "Wave of the Future" are repeated in horizontal rows behind the photo. Horizontal backs repeat the wave logo, have another player photo and a career summary.

1996 Flair Promotional Sheet

Three samples of Flair's 1996 issue and an information card are included on this 5" x 7" promotional sheet. Sheets are found with either a gold or silver finish.

	NM/M
Complete Sheet:	5.00

1996 Flair

Fleer's 1996 Flair baseball set has 400 cards, a parallel set and four insert types. Regular card fronts have two photos of the featured player; backs have a photo and career statistics. All cards have a silver-foil version and a gold-foil version, with each version appearing in equal numbers. Seven-card packs carried an issue price of $4.99.

		NM/M
Complete Set (400):		50.00
Common Player:		.15
Pack (9):		3.00
Wax Box (18):		40.00
1	Roberto Alomar	.30
2	Brady Anderson	.15
3	Bobby Bonilla	.15
4	Scott Erickson	.15
5	Jeffrey Hammonds	.15
6	Jimmy Haynes	.15
7	Chris Hoiles	.15
8	Kent Mercker	.15
9	Mike Mussina	.50
10	Randy Myers	.15
11	Rafael Palmeiro	.75
12	Cal Ripken Jr.	3.00
(12p)	Cal Ripken Jr./OPS (No card #)	3.00
13	B.J. Surhoff	.15
14	David Wells	.15
15	Jose Canseco	.50
16	Roger Clemens	1.75
17	Wil Cordero	.15
18	Tom Gordon	.15
19	Mike Greenwell	.15
20	Dwayne Hosey	.15
21	Jose Malave	.15
22	Tim Naehring	.15
23	Troy O'Leary	.15
24	Aaron Sele	.15
25	Heathcliff Slocumb	.15
26	Mike Stanley	.15
27	Jeff Suppan	.15
28	John Valentin	.15
29	Mo Vaughn	.15
30	Tim Wakefield	.15
31	Jim Abbott	.15
32	Garret Anderson	.15
33	George Arias	.15
34	Chili Davis	.15
35	Gary DiSarcina	.15
36	Jim Edmonds	.15
37	Chuck Finley	.15
38	Todd Greene	.15
39	Mark Langston	.15
40	Troy Percival	.15
41	Tim Salmon	.15
42	Lee Smith	.15
43	J.T. Snow	.15
44	Randy Velarde	.15
45	Tim Wallach	.15
46	Wilson Alvarez	.15
47	Harold Baines	.15
48	Jason Bere	.15
49	Ray Durham	.15
50	Alex Fernandez	.15
51	Ozzie Guillen	.15
52	Roberto Hernandez	.15
53	Ron Karkovice	.15
54	Darren Lewis	.15
55	Lyle Mouton	.15
56	Tony Phillips	.15
57	Chris Snopek	.15
58	Kevin Tapani	.15
59	Danny Tartabull	.15
60	Frank Thomas	1.00
61	Robin Ventura	.15
62	Sandy Alomar	.15
63	Carlos Baerga	.15
64	Albert Belle	.15
65	Julio Franco	.15
66	Orel Hershiser	.15
67	Kenny Lofton	.15
68	Dennis Martinez	.15
69	Jack McDowell	.15
70	Jose Mesa	.15
71	Eddie Murray	1.00
72	Charles Nagy	.15
73	Tony Pena	.15
74	Manny Ramirez	1.00
75	Julian Tavarez	.15
76	Jim Thome	.65
77	Omar Vizquel	.15
78	Chad Curtis	.15
79	Cecil Fielder	.15
80	Travis Fryman	.15
81	Chris Gomez	.15
82	Bob Higginson	.15
83	Mark Lewis	.15
84	Felipe Lira	.15
85	Alan Trammell	.15
86	Kevin Appier	.15
87	Johnny Damon	.50
88	Tom Goodwin	.15
89	Mark Gubicza	.15
90	Bob Hamelin	.15
91	Keith Lockhart	.15
92	Jeff Montgomery	.15
93	Jon Nunnally	.15
94	Bip Roberts	.15
95	Michael Tucker	.15
96	Joe Vitiello	.15
97	Ricky Bones	.15
98	Chuck Carr	.15
99	Jeff Cirillo	.15
100	Mike Fetters	.15
101	John Jaha	.15
102	Mike Matheny	.15
103	Ben McDonald	.15
104	Matt Mieske	.15
105	Dave Nilsson	.15
106	Kevin Seitzer	.15
107	Steve Sparks	.15
108	Jose Valentin	.15
109	Greg Vaughn	.15
110	Rick Aguilera	.15
111	Rich Becker	.15
112	Marty Cordova	.15
113	LaTroy Hawkins	.15
114	Dave Hollins	.15
115	Roberto Kelly	.15
116	Chuck Knoblauch	.15
117	Matt Lawton RC	.50
118	Pat Meares	.15
119	Paul Molitor	1.00
120	Kirby Puckett	1.50
121	Brad Radke	.15
122	Frank Rodriguez	.15
123	Scott Stahoviak	.15
124	Matt Walbeck	.15
125	Wade Boggs	1.00
126	David Cone	.15
127	Joe Girardi	.15
128	Dwight Gooden	.15
129	Derek Jeter	3.00
130	Jimmy Key	.15
131	Jim Leyritz	.15
132	Tino Martinez	.15
133	Paul O'Neill	.15
134	Andy Pettitte	.40
135	Tim Raines	.15
136	Ruben Rivera	.15
137	Kenny Rogers	.15
138	Ruben Sierra	.15
139	John Wetteland	.15
140	Bernie Williams	.15
141	Tony Batista RC	.50
142	Allen Battle	.15
143	Geronimo Berroa	.15
144	Mike Bordick	.15
145	Scott Brosius	.15
146	Steve Cox	.15
147	Brent Gates	.15
148	Jason Giambi	.65
149	Doug Johns	.15
150	Mark McGwire	2.50
151	Pedro Munoz	.15
152	Ariel Prieto	.15
153	Terry Steinbach	.15
154	Todd Van Poppel	.15
155	Bobby Ayala	.15
156	Chris Bosio	.15
157	Jay Buhner	.15
158	Joey Cora	.15
159	Russ Davis	.15
160	Ken Griffey Jr.	2.00
161	Sterling Hitchcock	.15
162	Randy Johnson	1.00
163	Edgar Martinez	.15
164	Alex Rodriguez	2.50
165	Paul Sorrento	.15
166	Dan Wilson	.15
167	Will Clark	.15
168	Benji Gil	.15
169	Juan Gonzalez	.50
170	Rusty Greer	.15
171	Kevin Gross	.15
172	Darryl Hamilton	.15
173	Mike Henneman	.15
174	Ken Hill	.15
175	Mark McLemore	.15
176	Dean Palmer	.15
177	Roger Pavlik	.15
178	Ivan Rodriguez	.75
179	Mickey Tettleton	.15
180	Bobby Witt	.15
181	Joe Carter	.15
182	Felipe Crespo	.15
183	Alex Gonzalez	.15
184	Shawn Green	.40
185	Juan Guzman	.15
186	Erik Hanson	.15
187	Pat Hentgen	.15
188	Sandy Martinez RC	.15
189	Otis Nixon	.15
190	John Olerud	.15
191	Paul Quantrill	.15
192	Bill Risley	.15
193	Ed Sprague	.15
194	Steve Avery	.15
195	Jeff Blauser	.15
196	Brad Clontz	.15
197	Jermaine Dye	.15
198	Tom Glavine	.40
199	Marquis Grissom	.15
200	Chipper Jones	1.50
201	David Justice	.15
202	Ryan Klesko	.15
203	Mark Lemke	.15
204	Javier Lopez	.15
205	Greg Maddux	1.50
206	Fred McGriff	.15
207	Greg McMichael	.15
208	Wonderful Monds	.15
209	Jason Schmidt	.15
210	John Smoltz	.15
211	Mark Wohlers	.15
212	Jim Bullinger	.15
213	Frank Castillo	.15
214	Kevin Foster	.15
215	Luis Gonzalez	.15
216	Mark Grace	.15
217	Robin Jennings RC	.15
218	Doug Jones	.15
219	Dave Magadan	.15
220	Brian McRae	.15
221	Jaime Navarro	.15

222	Rey Sanchez	.15
223	Ryne Sandberg	1.50
224	Scott Servais	.15
225	Sammy Sosa	1.50
226	Ozzie Timmons	.15
227	Bret Boone	.15
228	Jeff Branson	.15
229	Jeff Brantley	.15
230	Dave Burba	.15
231	Vince Coleman	.15
232	Steve Gibralter	.15
233	Mike Kelly	.15
234	Barry Larkin	.15
235	Hal Morris	.15
236	Mark Portugal	.15
237	Jose Rijo	.15
238	Reggie Sanders	.15
239	Pete Schourek	.15
240	John Smiley	.15
241	Eddie Taubensee	.15
242	Jason Bates	.15
243	Dante Bichette	.15
244	Ellis Burks	.15
245	Vinny Castilla	.15
246	Andres Galarraga	.15
247	Darren Holmes	.15
248	Curt Leskanic	.15
249	Steve Reed	.15
250	Kevin Ritz	.15
251	Bret Saberhagen	.15
252	Bill Swift	.15
253	Larry Walker	.15
254	Walt Weiss	.15
255	Eric Young	.15
256	Kurt Abbott	.15
257	Kevin Brown	.15
258	John Burkett	.15
259	Greg Colbrunn	.15
260	Jeff Conine	.15
261	Andre Dawson	.40
262	Chris Hammond	.15
263	Charles Johnson	.15
264	Al Leiter	.15
265	Robb Nen	.15
266	Terry Pendleton	.15
267	Pat Rapp	.15
268	Gary Sheffield	.50
269	Quilvio Veras	.15
270	Devon White	.15
271	Bob Abreu	.15
272	Jeff Bagwell	1.00
273	Derek Bell	.15
274	Sean Berry	.15
275	Craig Biggio	.15
276	Doug Drabek	.15
277	Tony Eusebio	.15
278	Richard Hidalgo	.15
279	Brian Hunter	.15
280	Todd Jones	.15
281	Derrick May	.15
282	Orlando Miller	.15
283	James Mouton	.15
284	Shane Reynolds	.15
285	Greg Swindell	.15
286	Mike Blowers	.15
287	Brett Butler	.15
288	Tom Candiotti	.15
289	Roger Cedeno	.15
290	Delino DeShields	.15
291	Greg Gagne	.15
292	Karim Garcia	.15
293	Todd Hollandsworth	.15
294	Eric Karros	.15
295	Ramon Martinez	.15
296	Raul Mondesi	.15
297	Hideo Nomo	.50
298	Mike Piazza	2.00
299	Ismael Valdes	.15
300	Todd Worrell	.15
301	Moises Alou	.15
302	Shane Andrews	.15
303	Yamil Benitez	.15
304	Jeff Fassero	.15
305	Darrin Fletcher	.15
306	Cliff Floyd	.15
307	Mark Grudzielanek	.15
308	Mike Lansing	.15
309	Pedro Martinez	1.00
310	Ryan McGuire	.15
311	Carlos Perez	.15
312	Mel Rojas	.15
313	David Segui	.15
314	Rondell White	.15
315	Edgardo Alfonzo	.15
316	Rico Brogna	.15
317	Carl Everett	.15
318	John Franco	.15
319	Bernard Gilkey	.15
320	Todd Hundley	.15
321	Jason Isringhausen	.15
322	Lance Johnson	.15
323	Bobby Jones	.15
324	Jeff Kent	.15
325	Rey Ordonez	.15
326	Bill Pulsipher	.15
327	Jose Vizcaino	.15
328	Paul Wilson	.15
329	Ricky Bottalico	.15
330	Darren Daulton	.15
331	David Doster **RC**	.15
332	Lenny Dykstra	.15
333	Jim Eisenreich	.15
334	Sid Fernandez	.15
335	Gregg Jefferies	.15
336	Mickey Morandini	.15
337	Benito Santiago	.15
338	Curt Schilling	.40
339	Kevin Stocker	.15

340	David West	.15
341	Mark Whiten	.15
342	Todd Zeile	.15
343	Jay Bell	.15
344	John Ericks	.15
345	Carlos Garcia	.15
346	Charlie Hayes	.15
347	Jason Kendall	.15
348	Jeff King	.15
349	Mike Kingery	.15
350	Al Martin	.15
351	Orlando Merced	.15
352	Dan Miceli	.15
353	Denny Neagle	.15
354	Alan Benes	.15
355	Andy Benes	.15
356	Royce Clayton	.15
357	Dennis Eckersley	.75
358	Gary Gaetti	.15
359	Ron Gant	.15
360	Brian Jordan	.15
361	Ray Lankford	.15
362	John Mabry	.15
363	T.J. Mathews	.15
364	Mike Morgan	.15
365	Donovan Osborne	.15
366	Tom Pagnozzi	.15
367	Ozzie Smith	1.50
368	Todd Stottlemyre	.15
369	Andy Ashby	.15
370	Brad Ausmus	.15
371	Ken Caminiti	.15
372	Andujar Cedeno	.15
373	Steve Finley	.15
374	Tony Gwynn	1.50
375	Joey Hamilton	.15
376	Rickey Henderson	1.00
377	Trevor Hoffman	.15
378	Wally Joyner	.15
379	Marc Newfield	.15
380	Jody Reed	.15
381	Bob Tewksbury	.15
382	Fernando Valenzuela	.15
383	Rod Beck	.15
384	Barry Bonds	3.00
385	Mark Carreon	.15
386	Shawon Dunston	.15
387	Osvaldo Fernandez **RC**	.40
388	Glenallen Hill	.15
389	Stan Javier	.15
390	Mark Leiter	.15
391	Kirt Manwaring	.15
392	Robby Thompson	.15
393	William Van Landingham	.15
394	Allen Watson	.15
395	Matt Williams	.15
396	Checklist	.15
397	Checklist	.15
398	Checklist	.15
399	Checklist	.15
400	Checklist	.15

Hot Gloves can only be found in hobby packs, at a rate of one per every 90 packs.

		NM/M
Complete Set (10):		60.00
Common Player:		3.00
1	Roberto Alomar	4.00
2	Barry Bonds	15.00
3	Will Clark	3.00
4	Ken Griffey Jr.	10.00
5	Kenny Lofton	3.00
6	Greg Maddux	7.50
7	Mike Piazza	10.00
8	Cal Ripken Jr.	15.00
9	Ivan Rodriguez	6.00
10	Matt Williams	3.00

Powerline

Ten of baseball's top sluggers are featured on these Flair inserts. They are the easiest of the Flair inserts to obtain; seeded one per six packs. Fronts combine yellow-green artwork with the player photo. Backs have a vertical color photo and career information.

		NM/M
Complete Set (10):		6.00
Common Player:		.25
1	Albert Belle	.75
2	Barry Bonds	2.00
3	Juan Gonzalez	.35
4	Ken Griffey Jr.	.75
5	Mark McGwire	1.00
6	Mike Piazza	.75
7	Manny Ramirez	.50
8	Sammy Sosa	.65
9	Frank Thomas	.75
10	Matt Williams	.25

Wave of the Future

These inserts feature up-and-coming young talent in baseball. Twenty 1996 rookies and prospects are printed on lenticular cards. They are seeded one per every 72 packs.

		NM/M
Complete Set (20):		30.00
Common Player:		2.00
1	Bob Abreu	3.00

2	George Arias	2.00
3	Tony Batista	2.00
4	Alan Benes	2.00
5	Yamil Benitez	2.00
6	Steve Cox	2.00
7	David Doster	2.00
8	Jermaine Dye	2.00
9	Osvaldo Fernandez	2.00
10	Karim Garcia	3.00
11	Steve Gibralter	2.00
12	Todd Greene	2.00
13	Richard Hidalgo	2.00
14	Robin Jennings	2.00
15	Jason Kendall	2.00
16	Jose Malave	2.00
17	Wonderful Monds	2.00
18	Rey Ordonez	2.00
19	Ruben Rivera	2.00
20	Paul Wilson	2.00

1997 Flair Showcase Promo Strip

The concept of Flair Showcase's Style-Grace-Showcase set composition is debuted on this 7-1/2" x 3-1/2" strip featuring three cards of Alex Rodriguez. The cards are overprinted in gold on front and black on back with "PRO-MOTIONAL SAMPLE."

	NM/M
Complete Strip (3):	5.00

1997 Flair Showcase Row 2 (Style)

The 1997 Flair issue is actually three different versions of a 180-player set printed on a super-glossy thick stock. The most common version, Style, is designated Row 2 on back. Fronts have a color action photo with a black-and-white portrait image in the background, all printed on silver foil. Cards #1-60 are designated "Showtime" on back; #61-120 are "Show-piece" and #121-180 are labeled "Showstopper" and were inserted in varying ratios: Showtime - 1.5:1; Showpiece 1:1.5 and Showstopper 1:1. Cards were sold exclusively at hobby shops in five-card packs for $4.99.

	NM/M
Complete Set (180):	15.00
Common Showtime (1-60):	.15
Common Showpiece (61-120):	.25
Common Showstopper (121-180):	.20
A-Rod Glove Exchange:	125.00
Pack (5):	2.00
Wax Box (24):	35.00

1	Andruw Jones	1.25
2	Derek Jeter	3.00
3	Alex Rodriguez	2.25
4	Paul Molitor	1.25
5	Jeff Bagwell	1.25
6	Scott Rolen	1.25
7	Kenny Lofton	.50
8	Cal Ripken Jr.	3.00
9	Brady Anderson	.15
10	Chipper Jones	1.50
11	Todd Greene	.20
12	Todd Walker	.15
13	Billy Wagner	.15
14	Craig Biggio	.15
15	Kevin Orie	.15

16	Hideo Nomo	.65
17	Kevin Appier	.15
18	Bubba Trammell **RC**	.15
19	Juan Gonzalez	.65
20	Randy Johnson	1.25
21	Roger Clemens	1.75
22	Johnny Damon	.35
23	Ryne Sandberg	1.50
24	Ken Griffey Jr.	2.00
25	Barry Bonds	3.00
26	Nomar Garciaparra	1.50
27	Vladimir Guerrero	1.25
28	Ron Gant	.15
29	Joe Carter	.15
30	Tim Salmon	.15
31	Mike Piazza	2.00
32	Barry Larkin	.15
33	Manny Ramirez	1.25
34	Sammy Sosa	1.50
35	Frank Thomas	1.25
36	Melvin Nieves	.15
37	Tony Gwynn	1.50
38	Gary Sheffield	.35
39	Darin Erstad	.50
40	Ken Caminiti	.15
41	Jermaine Dye	.15
42	Mo Vaughn	.15
43	Raul Mondesi	.15
44	Greg Maddux	1.50
45	Chuck Knoblauch	.15
46	Andy Pettitte	.50
47	Deion Sanders	.15
48	Albert Belle	.25
49	Jamey Wright	.15
50	Rey Ordonez	.15
51	Bernie Williams	.25
52	Mark McGwire	2.25
53	Mike Mussina	.50
54	Bob Abreu	.20
55	Reggie Sanders	.15
56	Brian Jordan	.15
57	Ivan Rodriguez	1.00
58	Roberto Alomar	.30
59	Tim Naehring	.15
60	Edgar Renteria	.15
61	Dean Palmer	.25
62	Benito Santiago	.25
63	David Cone	.25
64	Carlos Delgado	.75
65	Brian Giles **RC**	.75
66	Alex Ochoa	.25
67	Rondell White	.25
68	Robin Ventura	.25
69	Eric Karros	.25
70	Jose Valentin	.25
71	Rafael Palmeiro	1.00
72	Chris Snopek	.25
73	David Justice	.25
74	Tom Glavine	.45
75	Rudy Pemberton	.25
76	Larry Walker	.25
77	Jim Thome	.75
78	Charles Johnson	.25
79	Dante Powell	.25
80	Derrek Lee	.75
81	Jason Kendall	.25
82	Todd Hollandsworth	.25
83	Bernard Gilkey	.25
84	Mel Rojas	.25
85	Dmitri Young	.25
86	Bret Boone	.25
87	Pat Hentgen	.25
88	Bobby Bonilla	.25
89	John Wetteland	.25
90	Todd Hundley	.25
91	Wilton Guerrero	.25
92	Geronimo Berroa	.25
93	Al Martin	.25
94	Danny Tartabull	.25
95	Brian McRae	.25
96	Steve Finley	.25
97	Todd Stottlemyre	.25
98	John Smoltz	.50
99	Matt Williams	.50
100	Eddie Murray	1.25
101	Henry Rodriguez	.25
102	Marty Cordova	.25
103	Juan Guzman	.25
104	Chili Davis	.25
105	Eric Young	.25
106	Jeff Abbott	.25
107	Shannon Stewart	.25
108	Rocky Coppinger	.25
109	Jose Canseco	.65
110	Dante Bichette	.25
111	Dwight Gooden	.25
112	Scott Brosius	.25
113	Steve Avery	.25
114	Andres Galarraga	.25
115	Sandy Alomar Jr.	.25
116	Ray Lankford	.25
117	Jorge Posada	.25
118	Ryan Klesko	.25
119	Jay Buhner	.25
120	Jose Guillen	.25
121	Paul O'Neill	.20
122	Jimmy Key	.20
123	Hal Morris	.20
124	Travis Fryman	.20
125	Jim Edmonds	.20
126	Jeff Cirillo	.20
127	Fred McGriff	.20
128	Alan Benes	.20
129	Derek Bell	.20
130	Tony Graffanino	.20
131	Shawn Green	.40
132	Denny Neagle	.20
133	Alex Fernandez	.20

134	Mickey Morandini	.20
135	Royce Clayton	.20
136	Jose Mesa	.20
137	Edgar Martinez	.20
138	Curt Schilling	.40
139	Lance Johnson	.20
140	Andy Benes	.20
141	Charles Nagy	.20
142	Mariano Rivera	.40
143	Mark Wohlers	.20
144	Ken Hill	.20
145	Jay Bell	.20
146	Bob Higginson	.20
147	Mark Grudzielanek	.20
148	Ray Durham	.20
149	John Olerud	.20
150	Joey Hamilton	.20
151	Trevor Hoffman	.20
152	Dan Wilson	.20
153	J.T. Snow	.20
154	Marquis Grissom	.20
155	Yamil Benitez	.20
156	Rusty Greer	.20
157	Darryl Kile	.20
158	Ismael Valdes	.20
159	Jeff Conine	.20
160	Darren Daulton	.20
161	Chan Ho Park	.20
162	Troy Percival	.20
163	Wade Boggs	1.50
164	Dave Nilsson	.20
165	Vinny Castilla	.20
166	Kevin Brown	.20
167	Dennis Eckersley	1.00
168	Wendell Magee Jr.	.20
169	John Jaha	.20
170	Garret Anderson	.20
171	Jason Giambi	.75
172	Mark Grace	.20
173	Tony Clark	.20
174	Moises Alou	.20
175	Brett Butler	.20
176	Cecil Fielder	.20
177	Chris Widger	.20
178	Doug Drabek	.20
179	Ellis Burks	.20
180	Shigetosi Hasegawa	.20

Showcase Row 1 (Grace)

The second level of '97 Flair scarcity is represented by the Row 1/Grace cards (so designated on back). These are visually differentiated on front by the use of a full background to the action photo, and the addition of a color portrait. Row 1/Grace cards are further broken down by their designation on back as: "Showstopper" (#1-60; seeded 1:2.5 packs), "Showtime" (#61-120; 1:2) and "Showpiece" (#121-180; 1:3) with varying insertion rates as shown.

	NM/M
Complete Set (180):	50.00
Common Showstopper (1-60):	.35
Stars:	1.5X
Common Showtime (61-120):	.25
Stars:	1X
Common Showpiece (121-180):	.60
Stars:	1.5X

Showcase Row 0 (Showcase)

The scarcest level of '97 Flair is the Row 0/Showcase cards (so designated on front and back). These are identifiable on front by the use of a color portrait in the foreground, with a large action photo behind, printed on a gold-flecked metallic background. Row 0/Showcase cards are further broken down by their designation on back as: "Showpiece" (#1-60; seeded

Diamond Cuts

Ten of the game's top stars are showcased on these 1996 Flair inserts. They are seeded one per 20 packs. Fronts have a textured background rainbow metallic foil and silver glitter.

		NM/M
Complete Set (12):		25.00
Common Player:		1.00
1	Jeff Bagwell	2.50
2	Albert Belle	1.00
3	Barry Bonds	6.00
4	Juan Gonzalez	1.25
5	Ken Griffey Jr.	4.00
6	Greg Maddux	3.00
7	Eddie Murray	2.50
8	Mike Piazza	4.00
9	Cal Ripken Jr.	6.00
10	Frank Thomas	2.50
11	Mo Vaughn	1.00
12	Matt Williams	1.00

Hot Gloves

Ten top defensive players are highlighted on these die-cut insert cards, a design first made popular in 1994.

1:24 packs), "Showstopper" (#61-120; 1:12) and "Show-time" (#121-180; 1:5) with varying insertion rates as shown.

	NM/M
Complete Set (180):	200.00
Common Showpiece (1-60):	1.50
Stars:	2X
Common Showstopper (61-120):	.75
Stars:	4X
Common Showtime (121-180):	.35
Stars:	3X

Showcase Legacy Collection

This 540-card parallel set is printed on matte-finish stock rather than the high-gloss of the regular cards. Front graphic highlights are in blue foil, as is the serial number on back from within each card's edition of just 100. Stated odds of insertion are one per 30 packs. Because all Legacies are printed in identical numbers, there is no premium for cards of different rows.

	NM/M
Common Player:	10.00
Stars:	25X

Showcase Legacy Masterpiece

The insert card chase reached its inevitable zenith with the creation of this series of one-of-a-kind inserts. Each of the 180 players' three cards (Row 2/Style, Row 1/Grace, Row 0/Showcase) in the '97 Flair Legacy Collection was also produced in an edition of one card and inserted at a rate of about one per 3,000 packs. Instead of the blue metallic foil highlights on front and back of the regular Legacy cards, the one-of-a-kind Masterpieces are highlighted in purple and carry a notation on back, "The Only 1 of 1 Masterpiece". Because of the unique nature of each card, value depends solely on demand, thus presentation of meaningful "catalog" values is not possible.

	NM/M
Common Player:	100.00

Showcase Diamond Cuts

This 20-card insert, found 1:20 packs, features a die-cut design with an action

photo of the player appearing above a baseball diamond in the lower background.

		NM/M
Complete Set (20):		55.00
Common Player:		1.50
1	Jeff Bagwell	3.00
2	Albert Belle	1.50
3	Ken Caminiti	1.50
4	Juan Gonzalez	2.00
5	Ken Griffey Jr.	4.50
6	Tony Gwynn	4.00
7	Todd Hundley	1.50
8	Andruw Jones	3.00
9	Chipper Jones	4.00
10	Greg Maddux	4.00
11	Mark McGwire	5.00
12	Mike Piazza	4.50
13	Derek Jeter	6.00
14	Manny Ramirez	3.00
15	Cal Ripken Jr.	6.00
16	Alex Rodriguez	5.00
17	Frank Thomas	3.00
18	Mo Vaughn	1.50
19	Bernie Williams	1.50
20	Matt Williams	1.50

Showcase Hot Gloves

Inserted 1:90 packs, Hot Gloves features 15 cards with a die-cut "flaming glove" design printed in thermally active inks and saluting some of baseball's best defensive players.

		NM/M
Complete Set (15):		125.00
Common Player:		2.50
1	Roberto Alomar	3.00
2	Barry Bonds	20.00
3	Juan Gonzalez	6.00
4	Ken Griffey Jr.	15.00
5	Marquis Grissom	2.50
6	Derek Jeter	20.00
7	Chipper Jones	12.00
8	Barry Larkin	2.50
9	Kenny Lofton	2.50
10	Greg Maddux	12.00
11	Mike Piazza	15.00
12	Cal Ripken Jr.	20.00
13	Alex Rodriguez	17.50
14	Ivan Rodriguez	7.50
15	Frank Thomas	10.00

Showcase Wave of the Future

This insert focuses on some of the up-and-coming young stars in the game. Cards were seeded 1:4 packs. A large ocean wave makes up the background of each card front.

		NM/M
Complete Set (27):		10.00
Common Player:		.25
1	Todd Greene	.25
2	Andruw Jones	1.50
3	Randall Simon	.25
4	Wady Almonte	.25
5	Pat Cline	.25
6	Jeff Abbott	.25
7	Justin Towle	.25
8	Richie Sexson	.25
9	Bubba Trammell	.35
10	Bob Abreu	.35
11	David Arias (Last name actually Ortiz.)	9.00
12	Todd Walker	.25
13	Orlando Cabrera	.25
14	Vladimir Guerrero	1.50
15	Ricky Ledee	.25
16	Jorge Posada	.25
17	Ruben Rivera	.25
18	Scott Spiezio	.25
19	Scott Rolen	1.00
20	Emil Brown	.25
21	Jose Guillen	.25
22	T.J. Staton	.25
23	Elieser Marrero	.25
24	Fernando Tatis	.25
25	Ryan Jones	.25
WF1	Hideki Irabu	.25
WF2	Jose Cruz Jr.	.25

1998 Flair Showcase Promo Strip

Each of the Row 0, 1, 2 and 3 variations of Cal Ripken's cards are featured on this 10" x 3-1/2" promo strip. The front of each card has "PROMOTIONAL SAMPLE" printed diagonally in gold; on the back the notice is printed in black-and-white.

	NM/M
Complete Promo Strip:	5.00

1998 Flair Showcase Row 3

Row 3, or Flair, cards are considered the base cards of '98 Showcase. They feature a close-up black-and-white portrait photo in the background and an action shot in front, overprinted on a silver-foil background. Flair/Showtime (#1-30) cards are inserted 1:9 packs, Flair/Showstopper (#31-60) are found 1:1.1 packs, Flair/Showdown (#61-90) cards are inserted 1:1.5 packs and Flair/Showdown (#91-120) cards are inserted 1:2 packs.

		NM/M
Complete Set (120):		20.00
Common Player (1-30):		.25
Common Player (31-60):		.25
Common Player (61-90):		.35
Common Player (91-120):		.45
Pack (5):		2.50
Wax Box (24):		45.00
1	Ken Griffey Jr.	2.00
2	Travis Lee	.25
3	Frank Thomas	1.25
4	Ben Grieve	.25
5	Nomar Garciaparra	1.50
6	Jose Cruz Jr.	.25

7	Alex Rodriguez	2.50
8	Cal Ripken Jr.	3.00
9	Mark McGwire	2.50
10	Chipper Jones	1.50
11	Paul Konerko	.40
12	Todd Helton	1.00
13	Greg Maddux	1.50
14	Derek Jeter	3.00
15	Jaret Wright	.25
16	Livan Hernandez	.25
17	Mike Piazza	2.00
18	Juan Encarnacion	.25
19	Tony Gwynn	1.50
20	Scott Rolen	1.00
21	Roger Clemens	1.75
22	Tony Clark	.25
23	Albert Belle	.25
24	Mo Vaughn	.25
25	Andruw Jones	1.25
26	Jason Dickson	.25
27	Fernando Tatis	.25
28	Ivan Rodriguez	.75
29	Ricky Ledee	.25
30	Darin Erstad	.50
31	Brian Rose	.25
32	Magglio Ordonez RC	2.00
33	Larry Walker	.25
34	Bobby Higginson	.25
35	Chili Davis	.25
36	Barry Bonds	3.00
37	Vladimir Guerrero	1.25
38	Jeff Bagwell	1.25
39	Kenny Lofton	.25
40	Ryan Klesko	.25
41	Mike Cameron	.25
42	Charles Johnson	.25
43	Andy Pettitte	.40
44	Juan Gonzalez	.25
45	Tim Salmon	.25
46	Hideki Irabu	.25
47	Paul Molitor	1.25
48	Edgar Renteria	.25
49	Manny Ramirez	1.25
50	Jim Edmonds	.25
51	Bernie Williams	.25
52	Roberto Alomar	.40
53	David Justice	.25
54	Rey Ordonez	.25
55	Ken Caminiti	.25
56	Jose Guillen	.25
57	Randy Johnson	1.25
58	Brady Anderson	.25
59	Hideo Nomo	.50
60	Tino Martinez	.25
61	John Smoltz	.35
62	Joe Carter	.35
63	Matt Williams	.35
64	Robin Ventura	.35
65	Barry Larkin	.35
66	Dante Bichette	.35
67	Travis Fryman	.35
68	Gary Sheffield	.60
69	Eric Karros	.35
70	Matt Stairs	.35
71	Al Martin	.35
72	Jay Buhner	.35
73	Ray Lankford	.35
74	Carlos Delgado	.65
75	Edgardo Alfonzo	.35
76	Rondell White	.35
77	Chuck Knoblauch	.35
78	Raul Mondesi	.35
79	Johnny Damon	.60
80	Matt Morris	.35
81	Tom Glavine	.60
82	Kevin Brown	.35
83	Garret Anderson	.35
84	Mike Mussina	.40
85	Pedro Martinez	1.25
86	Craig Biggio	.35
87	Darryl Kile	.35
88	Rafael Palmeiro	.75
89	Jim Thome	.60
90	Andres Galarraga	.35
91	Sammy Sosa	1.50
92	Willie Greene	.45
93	Vinny Castilla	.45
94	Justin Thompson	.45
95	Jeff King	.45
96	Jeff Cirillo	.45
97	Mark Grudzielanek	.45
98	Brad Radke	.45
99	John Olerud	.45
100	Curt Schilling	.65
101	Steve Finley	.45
102	J.T. Snow	.45
103	Edgar Martinez	.45
104	Wilson Alvarez	.45
105	Rusty Greer	.45
106	Pat Hentgen	.45
107	David Cone	.45
108	Fred McGriff	.45
109	Jason Giambi	.75
110	Tony Womack	.45
111	Bernard Gilkey	.45
112	Alan Benes	.45
113	Mark Grace	.45
114	Reggie Sanders	.45
115	Moises Alou	.45
116	John Jaha	.45
117	Henry Rodriguez	.45
118	Dean Palmer	.45
119	Mike Lieberthal	.45
120	Shawn Estes	.45

Showcase Row 2

Row 2, or Style (as they are designated on front) cards in Flair Showcase are the second easiest type of card to pull from packs. Fronts are similar to Row 3 base cards, but include the entire background of the action photo and have a color portrait photo. Cards #1-30 are inserted one per three packs, #31-60 are found 1:2.5 packs, #61-90 cards are 1:4 and #91-120 are inserted one per three packs.

	NM/M
Complete Set (120):	40.00
Common Player:	.50
Stars:	1.5-2X

Showcase Row 1

Row 1, also referred to as Grace, was the second most difficult type of card to pull from Flair Showcase. The front design has an action photo overprinted on a large portrait which is printed on a rainbow metallic-foil background. Cards #1-30 are seeded one per 16 packs, #31-60 are 1:24, #61-90 are 1:6 and #91-120 are 1:10.

	NM/M
Complete Set (1-120):	100.00
Commons (1-30):	1.00
Stars:	2X
Commons (31-60):	1.25
Stars:	3X
Commons (61-90):	.35
Stars:	1X
Commons (91-120):	.75
Stars:	1.5X

Showcase Row 0

Row 0 is the most difficult of the four tiers to obtain from packs. Two action photos are combined on a horizontal format with one in a prismatic foil background. The first 30 cards are serially numbered to 250, cards #30-60 are numbered to 500, #61-90 are numbered to 1,000 and #91-120 are numbered within an edition of 2,000.

	NM/M
Complete Set (120):	350.00

Common Player (1-30):	5.00
Stars:	10X
Common Player (31-60):	3.00
Stars:	8X
Common Player (61-90):	2.00
Stars:	6X
Common Player (91-120):	1.00
Stars:	4X

Showcase Legacy Collection

Legacy Collection parallels all 480 cards in the Flair Showcase set. Each Legacy Collection card displays the player's name in black plate laminated on the back, with the card's sequential numbering to 100 in gold foil.

	NM/M
Common Player:	7.50
Stars:	25X

Showcase Legacy Masterpiece

Each of the 120 players' four cards (Rows 3, 2, 1 and 0) in the '98 Flair Legacy Collection was also produced in an edition of one card and inserted at a rate of about one per 3,000 packs. The one-of-a-kind cards carry a notation on back: "The Only 1 of 1 Masterpiece." With supply a fixed quantity, value depends on demand at any particular time, thus it is not possible to present meaningful "catalog" values.

	NM/M
Common Player:	50.00

Showcase Perfect 10

Perfect 10 features the game's most popular players on a silk-screen technology design. The cards were serial numbered to 10 on the back and were inserted into packs of Flair Showcase.

	NM/M
Complete Set (10):	1,600
Common Player:	100.00
1 Ken Griffey Jr.	200.00
2 Cal Ripken Jr.	300.00
3 Frank Thomas	125.00
4 Mike Piazza	200.00
5 Greg Maddux	150.00
6 Nomar Garciaparra	150.00
7 Mark McGwire	250.00
8 Scott Rolen	100.00
9 Alex Rodriguez	250.00
10 Roger Clemens	175.00

Showcase Wave of the Future

Twelve up-and-coming players with hot minor league stats and Major League potential are displayed in Wave of the Future. The cards contain a clear acetate card inside a plastic covering that is filled with vegetable oil and glitter. These were inserted one per 20 packs and are numbered with a "WF" prefix.

	NM/M
Complete Set (12):	10.00
Common Player:	.50
WF1 Travis Lee	.50
WF2 Todd Helton	5.00
WF3 Ben Grieve	.50
WF4 Juan Encarnacion	.50
WF5 Brad Fullmer	.50
WF6 Ruben Rivera	.50
WF7 Paul Konerko	.75
WF8 Derrek Lee	1.50
WF9 Mike Lowell	.50
WF10 Magglio Ordonez	2.00
WF11 Rich Butler	.50
WF12 Eli Marrero	.50

1999 Flair Showcase Row 3 (Power)

Power is one of three tiers in 1999 Showcase. The front on this base-level version is rainbow holofoil including the large portrait photo in the background. In the foreground is a color action photo. Matte textured silver spot embossing is printed over the player's name and team at lower-right. All three Rows of Showcase can be found with three different back designs. Showtime presents traditional annual and career stats. Horizontally formatted Showpiece cards have a black-and-white player photo as a "Classic Matchup" of the player's stats to those of a past star. Showdown backs have a color action photo on a brightly-colored wave-pattern background. A stat box at center offers career numbers in four unique categories like day-night, grass-turf, etc. Each of these three back-design levels of scarcity has a different advertised insertion rate. Within Row 3/Power, these vary only between one card in .9 packs, and one card in 1.2 packs, thus there is no practical value differential. Five-card packs of Flair Showcase had a $4.99 SRP.

	NM/M
Complete Set (144):	25.00
Common Player:	.25
Pack (5):	3.00
Wax Box (24):	45.00
1 Mark McGwire	2.50
2 Sammy Sosa	1.50
3 Ken Griffey Jr.	2.00
4 Chipper Jones	1.50
5 Ben Grieve	.25
6 J.D. Drew	.75
7 Jeff Bagwell	1.00
8 Cal Ripken Jr.	3.00
9 Tony Gwynn	1.50
10 Nomar Garciaparra	1.50
11 Travis Lee	.35
12 Troy Glaus	.75
13 Mike Piazza	2.00
14 Alex Rodriguez	2.50
15 Kevin Brown	.25
16 Darin Erstad	.50
17 Scott Rolen	.50
18 Micah Bowie RC	.25
19 Juan Gonzalez	.50
20 Kerry Wood	.50
21 Roger Clemens	1.75
22 Derek Jeter	3.00
23 Pat Burrell RC	3.00
24 Tim Salmon	.25
25 Barry Bonds	3.00
26 Roosevelt Brown RC	.25
27 Vladimir Guerrero	1.00
28 Randy Johnson	1.00
29 Mo Vaughn	.25
30 Fernando Seguignol	.25
31 Greg Maddux	1.50
32 Tony Clark	.25
33 Eric Chavez	.40
34 Kris Benson	.25
35 Frank Thomas	1.00
36 Mario Encarnacion	.25
37 Gabe Kapler	.25
38 Jeremy Giambi	.25
39 Peter Tucci RC	.25
40 Manny Ramirez	1.00
41 Albert Belle	.25
42 Warren Morris	.25
43 Michael Barrett	.25
44 Andruw Jones	1.00
45 Carlos Delgado	.60
46 Jaret Wright	.25
47 Juan Encarnacion	.25
48 Scott Hunter	.25
49 Tino Martinez	.25
50 Craig Biggio	.25
51 Jim Thome	.60
52 Vinny Castilla	.25
53 Tom Glavine	.40
54 Bob Higginson	.25
55 Moises Alou	.25
56 Robin Ventura	.25
57 Bernie Williams	.25
58 Pedro J. Martinez	1.00
59 Greg Vaughn	.25
60 Ray Lankford	.25
61 Jose Canseco	.40
62 Ivan Rodriguez	.75
63 Shawn Green	.40
64 Rafael Palmeiro	.75
65 Ellis Burks	.25
66 Jason Kendall	.25
67 David Wells	.25
68 Rondell White	.25
69 Gary Sheffield	.40
70 Ken Caminiti	.25
71 Cliff Floyd	.25
72 Larry Walker	.25
73 Bartolo Colon	.25
74 Barry Larkin	.25
75 Calvin Pickering	.25
76 Jim Edmonds	.25
77 Henry Rodriguez	.25
78 Roberto Alomar	.40
79 Andres Galarraga	.25
80 Richie Sexson	.75
81 Todd Helton	.75
82 Damion Easley	.25
83 Livan Hernandez	.25
84 Carlos Beltran	.60
85 Todd Hundley	.25
86 Todd Walker	.25
87 Scott Brosius	.25
88 Bob Abreu	.25
89 Corey Koskie	.25
90 Ruben Rivera	.25
91 Edgar Renteria	.25
92 Quinton McCracken	.25
93 Bernard Gilkey	.25
94 Shannon Stewart	.25
95 Dustin Hermanson	.25
96 Mike Caruso	.25
97 Alex Gonzalez	.25
98 Raul Mondesi	.25
99 David Cone	.25
100 Curt Schilling	.40
101 Brian Giles	.25
102 Edgar Martinez	.25
103 Rolando Arrojo	.25
104 Derek Bell	.25
105 Denny Neagle	.25
106 Marquis Grissom	.25
107 Bret Boone	.25
108 Mike Mussina	.50
109 John Smoltz	.25
110 Brett Tomko	.25
111 David Justice	.25
112 Andy Pettitte	.40
113 Eric Karros	.25
114 Dante Bichette	.25
115 Jeromy Burnitz	.25
116 Paul Konerko	.40
117 Steve Finley	.25
118 Ricky Ledee	.25
119 Edgardo Alfonzo	.25
120 Dean Palmer	.25
121 Rusty Greer	.25
122 Luis Gonzalez	.25
123 Randy Winn	.25
124 Jeff Kent	.25
125 Doug Glanville	.25
126 Justin Thompson	.25
127 Bret Saberhagen	.25
128 Wade Boggs	1.50
129 Al Leiter	.25
130 Paul O'Neill	.25
131 Chan Ho Park	.25
132 Johnny Damon	.60
133 Darryl Kile	.25
134 Reggie Sanders	.25
135 Kevin Millwood	.25
136 Charles Johnson	.25
137 Ray Durham	.25
138 Rico Brogna	.25
139 Matt Williams	.25
140 Sandy Alomar	.25
141 Jeff Cirillo	.25
142 Devon White	.25
143 Andy Benes	.25
144 Mike Stanley	.25
Checklist card	.05

Showcase Row 2 (Passion)

Juan Gonzalez
Texas Rangers

The metallic-foil background in the second level of Flair Showcase - Row 2/Passion - has an action photo printed in front of large textured numerals representing the player's uniform number. In the foreground is another action shot. Backs have the same three designs as Row 3, but only vary in insertion rate from one card per 1.3 packs to one card per three packs.

	NM/M
Complete Set (144):	65.00
Common Player:	.25
Showdown (1-48):	2X
Showpiece (49-96):	1X
Showtime (97-144):	1X

Showcase Row 1 (Showcase)

Tony Gwynn

Showcase level - Row 1 - presents two portraits and an action photo and the player's uniform number on a plastic laminate in a horizontal format. A gold-foil serial number is stamped into the upper-left corner in one of three levels of scarcity: Showpiece (#1-48) is limited to 1,500 numbered sets, Showtime (#49-96) is limited to 3,000 sets and Showdown (#97-144) is numbered to 6,000 sets.

	NM/M
Complete Set (144):	300.00
Common Showpiece (1-48):	2.00
Showpiece Stars:	5X
Common Showtime (49-96):	1.00
Showtime Stars:	3X
Common Showdown (97-144):	.50
Showdown Stars:	2X

Showcase Legacy /Masterpiece

Each of the 432 total cards in Flair Showcase was also produced in a pair of extremely limited parallels. The blue-foil enhanced Legacy Collection cards are serially numbered within an edition of just 99. The presence of purple foil on front signifies a Legacy Masterpiece card, which is identified on front by the notation, "The Only 1 of 1 Masterpiece." Because of their unique nature, determination of a "book value" for Masterpiece cards is not possible.

	NM/M
Common Legacy:	6.00
Legacy Stars:	20X
Common Masterpiece:	50.00

Showcase Measure of Greatness

Chipper Jones

This 15-card set captures baseball's top superstars who were closing in on milestones during the 1999 season. Each card is sequentially numbered to 500.

	NM/M
Complete Set (15):	100.00
Common Player:	3.00
Production 500 Sets	
1 Roger Clemens	7.50
2 Nomar Garciaparra	6.50
3 Juan Gonzalez	3.00
4 Ken Griffey Jr.	9.00
5 Vladimir Guerrero	5.00
6 Tony Gwynn	6.50
7 Derek Jeter	15.00
8 Chipper Jones	6.50
9 Mark McGwire	12.50
10 Mike Piazza	9.00
11 Manny Ramirez	5.00
12 Cal Ripken Jr.	15.00
13 Alex Rodriguez	12.50
14 Sammy Sosa	6.50
15 Frank Thomas	5.00

Showcase Wave of the Future

This insert set spotlights young stars on the rise and is limited to 1,000 serial numbered sets.

	NM/M
Complete Set (15):	40.00

Wave of the Future
J.D. Drew

	NM/M
Common Player:	1.50
Production 1,000 Sets	
1 Kerry Wood	4.00
2 Ben Grieve	1.50
3 J.D. Drew	4.00
4 Juan Encarnacion	1.50
5 Travis Lee	2.00
6 Todd Helton	7.50
7 Troy Glaus	7.50
8 Ricky Ledee	1.50
9 Eric Chavez	2.00
10 Ben Davis	1.50
11 George Lombard	1.50
12 Jeremy Giambi	1.50
13 Roosevelt Brown	1.50
14 Pat Burrell	6.00
15 Preston Wilson	1.50

2003 Flair

	NM/M
Complete Set (125):	
Common Player:	.25
Common SP (91-125):	4.00
Production 500	
Pack (5):	3.50
Box (20):	50.00
1 Hideo Nomo	.60
2 Derek Jeter	3.00
3 Junior Spivey	.25
4 Rich Aurilia	.25
5 Luis Gonzalez	.35
6 Sean Burroughs	.25
7 Pedro J. Martinez	1.00
8 Randy Winn	.25
9 Carlos Delgado	.50
10 Pat Burrell	.50
11 Barry Larkin	.25
12 Roberto Alomar	.40
13 Tony Batista	.25
14 Barry Bonds	3.00
15 Craig Biggio	.25
16 Ivan Rodriguez	.65
17 Javier Vazquez	.25
18 Joe Borchard	.25
19 Josh Phelps	.25
20 Omar Vizquel	.25
21 Tom Glavine	.40
22 Darin Erstad	.50
23 Hee Seop Choi	.25
24 Roger Clemens	1.75
25 Michael Cuddyer	.25
26 Mike Sweeney	.25
27 Phil Nevin	.25
28 Torii Hunter	.25
29 Vladimir Guerrero	1.00
30 Ellis Burks	.25
31 Jimmy Rollins	.50
32 Ken Griffey Jr.	2.00
33 Magglio Ordonez	.40
34 Mark Prior	1.00
35 Mike Lieberthal	.25
36 Jorge Posada	.30
37 Rodrigo Lopez	.25
38 Todd Helton	1.00
39 Adam Kennedy	.25
40 Curt Schilling	.40
41 Jim Thome	.50
42 Josh Beckett	.25
43 Carlos Pena	.25
44 Jason Kendall	.25
45 Sammy Sosa	2.00
46 Scott Rolen	.75
47 Alex Rodriguez	2.50
48 Aubrey Huff	.25
49 Bobby Abreu	.25
50 Jeff Kent	.25
51 Joe Randa	.25
52 Lance Berkman	.25
53 Orlando Cabrera	.25
54 Richie Sexson	.25
55 Albert Pujols	2.00
56 Alfonso Soriano	.50
57 Greg Maddux	1.50
58 Jason Giambi	.75
59 Jeff Bagwell	1.00
60 Kerry Wood	.50
61 Manny Ramirez	1.00
62 Eric Chavez	.40
63 Preston Wilson	.25
64 Shawn Green	.50
65 Shea Hillenbrand	.25
66 Austin Kearns	.75
67 Cliff Floyd	.25
68 Edgardo Alfonzo	.25
69 J.D. Drew	.40
70 Larry Walker	.25
71 Mike Piazza	2.00
72 Andruw Jones	.75
73 Ben Grieve	.25
74 Eric Hinske	.25
75 Geoff Jenkins	.25
76 Kazuhiro Sasaki	.25
77 Matt Morris	.25
78 Miguel Tejada	.40
79 Aramis Ramirez	.25
80 Troy Glaus	1.00
81 Ichiro Suzuki	2.00
82 Mark Teixeira	.50
83 Nomar Garciaparra	2.00
84 Chipper Jones	1.50
85 Frank Thomas	1.00
86 Paul LoDuca	.25
87 Bernie Williams	.35
88 Adam Dunn	.75
89 Randy Johnson	1.00
90 Barry Zito	.40
91 Lew Ford RC	8.00
92 Joe Valentine RC	3.00
93 Jhonny Peralta RC	3.00
94 Hideki Matsui RC	20.00
95 Francisco Rosario RC	3.00
96 Adam LaRoche RC	4.00
97 Josh Hall RC	6.00
98 Chien-Ming Wang RC	25.00
99 Josh Willingham RC	6.00
100 Guillermo Quiroz RC	6.00
101 Terrmel Sledge RC	3.00
102 Prentice Redman RC	3.00
103 Matt Bruback RC	6.00
104 Alejandro Machado RC	3.00
105 Shane Victorino RC	6.00
106 Chris Waters RC	3.00
107 Jose Contreras RC	8.00
108 Pete LaForest RC	3.00
109 Nook Logan RC	3.00
110 Hector Luna RC	6.00
111 Daniel Cabrera RC	6.00
112 Matt Kata RC	6.00
113 Rontrez Johnson RC	6.00
114 Josh Stewart RC	8.00
115 Michael Hessman RC	3.00
116 Felix Sanchez RC	6.00
117 Michel Hernandez RC	3.00
118 Arnaldo Munoz RC	3.00
119 Ian Ferguson RC	6.00
120 Clint Barmes RC	6.00
121 Brian Stokes RC	3.00
122 Craig Brazell RC	6.00
123 John Webb RC	3.00
124 Tim Olson RC	6.00
125 Jeremy Bonderman RC	10.00

Row 1

Stars (1-90):	5-10X
Rookies (91-125):	.75-1.5X
Production 150 Sets	
Row 2:	No Pricing
Production 25 Sets	

Diamond Cuts

DIAMOND CUTS
SCOTT ROLEN

	NM/M
Common Player:	4.00
Inserted 1:10	
Golds:	1-2X
Production 100 Sets	
1DC Alex Rodriguez	12.00
2DC Roberto Alomar	4.00
3DC Scott Rolen	5.00
4DC Alfonso Soriano	6.00
5DC Chipper Jones	7.50
6DC Pat Burrell	5.00
7DC Derek Jeter	15.00
8DC Mike Piazza	10.00
9DC J.D. Drew	4.00
10DC Vladimir Guerrero	6.00
11DC Greg Maddux	7.50
12DC Barry Zito	4.00
13DC Troy Glaus	5.00
14DC Roy Oswalt	4.00
15DC Roger Clemens	9.00

Hot Numbers

	NM/M
Common Player:	15.00

Production 100 Sets

1HN	Alex Rodriguez	35.00
2HN	Roberto Alomar	20.00
3HN	Scott Rolen	30.00
4HN	Alfonso Soriano	30.00
5HN	Chipper Jones	25.00
6HN	Pat Burrell	15.00
7HN	Derek Jeter	40.00
8HN	Mike Piazza	30.00
9HN	J.D. Drew	15.00
10HN	Vladimir Guerrero	20.00
11HN	Greg Maddux	30.00
12HN	Barry Zito	15.00
13HN	Troy Glaus	15.00
14HN	Roy Oswalt	15.00

Hot Numbers Dual
Production 25 Sets: No Pricing

Power Tools
NM/M
Common Player: 5.00
Production 500 Sets
Golds: 1-1.5X
Production 100 Sets

1PT	Nomar Garciaparra	15.00
2PT	Derek Jeter	25.00
3PT	Sammy Sosa	12.00
4PT	Miguel Tejada	5.00
5PT	Austin Kearns	10.00
6PT	Jason Giambi	8.00
7PT	Adam Dunn	8.00
8PT	Jim Thome	8.00
9PT	Lance Berkman	6.00
10PT	Alfonso Soriano	15.00
12PT	Alex Rodriguez	15.00
13PT	Mike Piazza	10.00
14PT	Bernie Williams	8.00
15PT	Jeff Bagwell	8.00
16PT	Andruw Jones	10.00
17PT	Scott Rolen	12.00
19PT	Juan Gonzalez	6.00

Power Tools - Dual

NM/M
Common Duo: 5.00
Production 200 Sets

1PTD	Nomar Garciaparra, Derek Jeter	40.00
3PTD	Adam Dunn, Austin Kearns	25.00
4PTD	Jim Thome, Sammy Sosa	15.00
5PTD	Alex Rodriguez, Nomar Garciaparra	20.00
6PTD	Jason Giambi, Bernie Williams	15.00
7PTD	Derek Jeter, Alfonso Soriano	25.00
8PTD	Lance Berkman, Jeff Bagwell	10.00
9PTD	Miguel Tejada, Alex Rodriguez	20.00
10PTD	Jason Giambi, Mike Piazza	20.00

Sweet Swatch
NM/M
Common Player: 5.00
Production 250 Sets

Derek Jeter	20.00
Sammy Sosa	15.00
Hideo Nomo	20.00
Vladimir Guerrero	6.00
Jason Giambi	8.00
Nomar Garciaparra	15.00
Randy Johnson	12.00
Miguel Tejada	5.00
Pedro J. Martinez	10.00
Adam Dunn	8.00
Roger Clemens	15.00
Mark Prior	8.00
Chipper Jones	10.00
Alex Rodriguez	15.00
Bernie Williams	6.00
Lance Berkman	6.00
Kazuhiro Sasaki	6.00
Alfonso Soriano	12.00

Sweet Swatch Oversized
NM/M
Common Player: 6.00
1:Hobby Box

Masterpiece One-of-One's exist.

Derek Jeter/150	20.00
Sammy Sosa/279	15.00
Hideo Nomo/970	12.00
Jason Giambi/350	15.00
Nomar Garciaparra/727	15.00
Randy Johnson/274	15.00
Miguel Tejada/518	6.00
Pedro Martinez/1,480	10.00
Adam Dunn/1,090	8.00
Roger Clemens/97	25.00
Mark Prior/1,195	10.00
Chipper Jones/80	15.00
Alex Rodriguez/150	15.00
Bernie Williams/1,420	8.00
Lance Berkman/1,465	6.00
Kazuhiro Sasaki/505	10.00

Sweet Swatch Autograph Oversized
NM/M
Common Player:
Golds: 1.5-2X
Production 25, Jeter 50
Masterpiece One-of-Ones exist.

Derek Jeter/312	90.00
Randy Johnson/218	60.00
Adam Dunn/218	30.00
Jeff Bagwell/218	40.00

Sweet Swatch Patch
NM/M
Common Player: 15.00
Production 50 Sets

Sammy Sosa	50.00
Hideo Nomo	50.00
Jason Giambi	20.00
Nomar Garciaparra	45.00
Randy Johnson	40.00
Miguel Tejada	15.00
Pedro J. Martinez	40.00
Adam Dunn	35.00
Roger Clemens	50.00
Mark Prior	25.00
Alex Rodriguez	45.00
Bernie Williams	40.00
Kazuhiro Sasaki	30.00
Alfonso Soriano	35.00

Sweet Swatch Patch Oversized
NM/M
Common Player: 15.00

Derek Jeter/35	75.00
Sammy Sosa/190	40.00
Hideo Nomo/114	50.00
Vladimir Guerrero/290	35.00
Nomar Garciaparra/124	40.00
Miguel Tejada/183	15.00
Pedro Martinez/185	40.00
Adam Dunn/130	30.00
Mark Prior/290	25.00
Chipper Jones/284	25.00
Alex Rodriguez/298	40.00
Bernie Williams/123	25.00
Lance Berkman/287	25.00
Kazuhiro Sasaki/90	40.00

Sweet Swatch Dual Oversized
Production 25 Sets: No Pricing

Wave of the Future
NM/M
Common Player: 3.00
Production 500 Sets
Golds: 1-2X
Production 100 Sets

1WOF	Francisco Rodriguez	3.00
2WOF	Carl Crawford	4.00
3WOF	Austin Kearns	10.00
4WOF	Hank Blalock	8.00
5WOF	Marlon Byrd	3.00
6WOF	Michael Restovich	3.00
7WOF	Joe Borchard	3.00
8WOF	Sean Burroughs	4.00
9WOF	Aubrey Huff	3.00
10WOF	Josh Phelps	5.00

2003 Flair Greats of the Game

NM/M

Complete Set (95):	35.00
Common Player:	.40
Pack (5):	6.00
Box (20):	100.00

1	Ozzie Smith	1.00
2	Red Schoendienst	.40
3	Harmon Killebrew	1.50
4	Ralph Kiner	.40
5	Johnny Bench	2.00
6	Al Kaline	1.00
7	Bobby Doerr	.40
8	Cal Ripken Jr.	4.00
9	Enos Slaughter	.40
10	Phil Rizzuto	1.00
11	Luis Aparicio	.40
12	Pee Wee Reese	.40
13	Richie Ashburn	.40
14	Ernie Banks	2.00
15	Earl Weaver	.40
16	Whitey Ford	1.50
17	Brooks Robinson	1.00
18	Lou Boudreau	.40
19	Robin Yount	1.00
20	Mike Schmidt	2.50
21	Bob Lemon	.40
22	Stan Musial	2.50
23	Joe Morgan	.60
24	Early Wynn	.40
25	Willie Stargell	.75
26	Yogi Berra	2.00
27	Juan Marichal	.40
28	Rick Ferrell	.40
29	Rod Carew	.75
30	Jim Bunning	.40
31	Ferguson Jenkins	.40
32	Steve Carlton	.75
33	Larry Doby	.40
34	Nolan Ryan	4.00
35	Phil Niekro	.40
36	Billy Williams	.40
37	Hal Newhouser	.40
38	Bob Feller	.75
39	Lou Brock	.75
40	Monte Irvin	.75
41	Eddie Mathews	1.00
42	Rollie Fingers	.40
43	Gaylord Perry	.40
44	Reggie Jackson	1.50
45	Bob Gibson	1.00
46	Robin Roberts	.40
47	Tom Seaver	1.00
48	Willie McCovey	.40
49	Hoyt Wilhelm	.40
50	George Kell	.40
51	Warren Spahn	1.00
52	Jim "Catfish" Hunter	.40
53	Dom DiMaggio	.40
54	Joe Medwick	.40
55	Johnny Pesky	.40
56	Steve Garvey	.40
57	Harry Heilmann	.40
58	Dave Winfield	.75
59	Andre Dawson	.40
60	Jimmie Foxx	1.00
61	Buddy Bell	.40
62	Gabby Hartnett	.40
63	Babe Ruth	4.00
64	Dizzy Dean	1.50
65	Hank Greenberg	.40
66	Don Drysdale	.75
67	Gary Carter	.40
68	Wade Boggs	.75
69	Tony Perez	.40
70	Mickey Cochrane	.75
71	Bill Dickey	.40
72	George Brett	3.00
73	Honus Wagner	3.00
74	George Sisler	1.00
75	Walter Johnson	2.00
76	Ron Santo	.40
77	Roy Campanella	1.00
78	Roger Maris	2.50
79	Kirby Puckett	2.50
80	Alan Trammell	.40
81	Don Mattingly	4.00
82	Ty Cobb	3.00
83	Lou Gehrig	3.00
84	Jackie Robinson	3.00
85	Billy Martin	.75
86	Paul Molitor	.75
87	Duke Snider	1.00
88	Thurman Munson	1.50
89	Luke Appling	.40
90	Ernie Lombardi	.40
91	Rube Waddell	.40
92	Travis Jackson	.40
93	Joe Sewell	.40
94	King Kelly	.40
95	Heinie Manush	.40

Common Home Team (96-133): 2.00

96HT	Bobby Doerr	2.00
97HT	Johnny Pesky	2.00
98HT	Wade Boggs	3.00
99HT	Tony Conigliaro	2.00
100HT	Carlton Fisk	3.00
101HT	Rico Petrocelli	2.00
102HT	Jim Rice	2.00
103HT	Al Lopez	2.00
104HT	Pee Wee Reese	2.00
105HT	Tommy Lasorda	2.00
106HT	Gil Hodges	3.00
107HT	Jackie Robinson	6.00
108HT	Duke Snider	4.00
109HT	Don Drysdale	4.00
110HT	Steve Garvey	2.00
111HT	Hoyt Wilhelm	2.00
112HT	Juan Marichal	3.00
113HT	Monte Irvin	3.00
114HT	Willie McCovey	3.00
115HT	Travis Jackson	3.00
116HT	Bobby Bonds	3.00
117HT	Orlando Cepeda	3.00
118HT	Whitey Ford	4.00
119HT	Phil Rizzuto	4.00
120HT	Reggie Jackson	4.00
121HT	Yogi Berra	5.00
122HT	Roger Maris	6.00
123HT	Don Mattingly	10.00
124HT	Babe Ruth	10.00
125HT	Dave Winfield	4.00
126HT	Bob Gibson	3.00
127HT	Enos Slaughter	2.00
128HT	Joe Medwick	2.00
129HT	Lou Brock	3.00
130HT	Ozzie Smith	5.00
131HT	Stan Musial	6.00
132HT	Steve Carlton	3.00
133HT	Dizzy Dean	4.00

Ballpark Heroes

NM/M

Complete Set (9):	25.00
Common Player:	2.00
Inserted 1:10	
1BH	Nolan Ryan	5.00
2BH	Babe Ruth	5.00
3BH	Honus Wagner	3.00
4BH	Ty Cobb	4.00
5BH	Ernie Banks	3.00
6BH	Mike Schmidt	3.00
7BH	Duke Snider	2.00
8BH	Cal Ripken Jr.	5.00
9BH	Stan Musial	3.00

Bat Rack Triple
NM/M
Common Card: 15.00
Production 300

Eddie Murray, Cal Ripken Jr., Brooks Robinson	75.00
Ryne Sandberg, Ron Santo, Billy Williams	45.00
Johnny Bench, Joe Morgan, Tony Perez	35.00
Eddie Mathews, Paul Molitor, Robin Yount	40.00
Tommie Agee, Jerry Grote, Bud Harrelson	
Reggie Jackson, Don Mattingly, Dave Winfield	45.00
Dave Parker, Willie Stargell	20.00

Bat Rack Quad

Common Card: 50.00
Numbered to 150

Don Mattingly, Joe Morgan, Cal Ripken Jr., Brooks Robinson	90.00
Ryne Sandberg, Ron Santo, Billy Williams, Andre Dawson	60.00
Dave Winfield, Cal Ripken Jr., Paul Molitor, Robin Yount	80.00
Eddie Murray, Eddie Mathews, Reggie Jackson, Willie McCovey	50.00

Classic Numbers

NM/M

Complete Set (13):	50.00
Common Player:	3.00
Inserted 1:20	
1CN	Jackie Robinson	6.00
2CN	Willie McCovey	3.00
3CN	Brooks Robinson	5.00
4CN	Reggie Jackson	6.00
5CN	Ozzie Smith	5.00
6CN	Johnny Bench	6.00
7CN	Yogi Berra	6.00
8CN	Cal Ripken Jr.	10.00
9CN	George Brett	8.00
10CN	Thurman Munson	5.00
11CN	Joe Morgan	3.00
12CN	Nolan Ryan	10.00
13CN	Steve Carlton	3.00

Classic Numbers Game-Used
NM/M
Common Player: 10.00
Inserted 1:24

Willie McCovey	12.00
George Brett	20.00
Joe Morgan	10.00
Yogi Berra	20.00
Cal Ripken Jr.	25.00
Nolan Ryan	35.00
Ozzie Smith	15.00
Johnny Bench	15.00
Ryne Sandberg	25.00
Thurman Munson	20.00
Steve Carlton	10.00

Classic Numbers Dual-Side
NM/M
Common Card: 25.00
Production 250 Sets

Yogi Berra, Thurman Munson	45.00
Nolan Ryan, Steve Carlton	65.00
Johnny Bench, Thurman Munson	35.00
Cal Ripken Jr., Ozzie Smith	60.00
Joe Morgan, Ryne Sandberg	35.00
Willie McCovey, Johnny Bench	25.00
Yogi Berra, Cal Ripken Jr.	50.00
George Brett, Nolan Ryan	75.00

Cut of History

NM/M
Common Player: 5.00
Inserted 1:10

Paul O'Neill	5.00
Dennis Eckersley	8.00
Jim Palmer	6.00
Graig Nettles	8.00
Frank Baker	30.00
Wade Boggs	8.00
Roger Maris	60.00
Jim "Catfish" Hunter	8.00
Alan Trammell	12.00
Eddie Murray	20.00
Steve Carlton	10.00
Tom Seaver	8.00

Gary Carter	8.00
Phil Niekro	6.00
Luis Aparicio	8.00
Reggie Jackson	12.00
Fergie Jenkins	8.00
Kirby Puckett	15.00
Billy Martin	15.00
Joe Medwick	25.00
Buddy Bell	5.00
Early Wynn	10.00
Cal Ripken Jr.	25.00
Hoyt Wilhelm	8.00
Willie McCovey	10.00

Cut of History Autograph
NM/M
Common Player:

Alan Trammell/211	25.00
Steve Carlton/506	30.00
Cal Ripken Jr/155	150.00
Johnny Bench/161	50.00

Greats of the Grain
NM/M
Production 50 Sets

1GOG	Ty Cobb	100.00
2GOG	Mike Schmidt	50.00
3GOG	Babe Ruth	140.00
4GOG	Lou Gehrig	80.00
5GOG	George Brett	160.00
6GOG	Stan Musial	75.00
7GOG	Don Mattingly	110.00
8GOG	Cal Ripken Jr.	100.00
9GOG	Eddie Mathews	75.00

HOF Postmark
NM/M
Production 2,002

Ozzie Smith	20.00
Ozzie Smith/Auto./202	100.00

Home Team Cut
NM/M
Common Player: 8.00
Patch: 2-5X
Production 25 Sets

Wade Boggs	15.00
Carlton Fisk	20.00
Jim Rice	15.00
Pee Wee Reese	15.00
Duke Snider	20.00
Steve Garvey	10.00
Tommy Lasorda	15.00
Juan Marichal	10.00
Bobby Bonds	8.00
Willie McCovey	10.00
Billy Martin	15.00
Roger Maris	65.00
Reggie Jackson	15.00
Dave Winfield	12.00
Red Schoendienst	8.00
Ozzie Smith	35.00
Joe Medwick	25.00

Sweet Swatch Bat

NM/M
Common Player: 15.00

Cal Ripken Jr./305	40.00
George Brett/320	30.00
Johnny Bench/175	20.00
Reggie Jackson/155	20.00
Don Mattingly/340	40.00
Willie McCovey/155	15.00
Jose Canseco/175	25.00
Kirby Puckett/251	40.00
Orlando Cepeda/165	15.00
Eddie Mathews/185	40.00
Pee Wee Reese/165	30.00
Andre Dawson/310	15.00

Sweet Swatch Jersey

NM/M
Common Player: 15.00

Jerry Coleman/528	20.00
Ryne Sandberg/374	25.00
Johnny Bench/410	20.00
Paul Molitor/592	15.00
Cal Ripken Jr/557	45.00
Gil Hodges/545	20.00
Carlton Fisk/1,200	8.00

Nolan Ryan/590	40.00
Tom Seaver/385	20.00
Don Mattingly/880	35.00
Jose Canseco/1,329	15.00
George Brett/384	30.00
Jim Palmer/335	15.00
Kirby Puckett/445	20.00
Juan Marichal/385	15.00
Robin Yount/340	25.00
Andre Dawson/335	15.00

Sweet Swatch Jersey Autograph

NM/M

Common Autograph:	
Cal Ripken Jr/40	240.00
Johnny Bench/40	130.00
Alan Trammell/40	75.00

Poland Springs Yankees Greats

The "Official Bottled Water of the N.Y. Yankees" sponsored this stadium give-away card set. The first 18,000 youngsters through the gates at the May 14 game received five-card cello packs which included four player cards and a sponsor's card. The player cards are virtually identical to the regular-issue versions except for the addition on a Poland Springs logo on front and, in the case of Berra, a card number change on back.

NM/M

Complete Set (5):		6.00
Common Player:		1.50
8	Yogi Berra	2.00
10	Phil Rizzuto	1.50
16	Whitey Ford	2.00
44	Reggie Jackson	2.00
---	Sponsor's Card	.10

2006 Flair Showcase

Jason Bay

NM/M

Complete Set (200):		
Common Player (1-100):		.50
Common Player (101-150):		1.50
Inserted 1:4 Hobby		
Common Player (151-200):		2.00
Inserted 1:8 Hobby		
Pack (5):		5.00
Box (18):		80.00
1	Jeremy Hermida (RC)	.50
2	Albert Pujols	3.00
3	Ryan Shealy (RC)	.50
4	Mark Prior	.75
5	Chuck James (RC)	1.00
6	Shawn Green	.50
7	Rickie Weeks	.50
8	Roy Halladay	.50
9	Luis Gonzalez	.50
10	David Ortiz	1.50
11	Josh Beckett	.75
12	Gary Sheffield	.75
13	Jose Reyes	.75
14	Brandon Watson (RC)	.50
15	Tadahito Iguchi	.50
16	Rich Harden	.50
17	Skip Schumaker (RC)	.50
18	Vladimir Guerrero	1.00
19	Chris Carpenter	.75
20	Brian Roberts	.50
21	Roy Oswalt	.50
22	Ben Johnson (RC)	.50
23	Todd Helton	.75
24	Wilbert Nieves (RC)	.50
25	Michael Young	.50
26	A.J. Burnett	.50
27	J.D. Drew	.50
28	Adrian Beltre	.50
29	Tim Hudson	.50
30	Jake Peavy	.50
31	Magglio Ordonez	.50
32	Brad Wilkerson	.50
33	Ryan Freel	.50
34	Javier Vazquez	.50
35	Tom Glavine	.50
36	Jason Bergmann RC	1.00
37	Marcus Giles	.50
38	Jim Thome	1.00
39	Ichiro Suzuki	2.00
40	Jeff Harris RC	.75
41	Miguel Cabrera	1.00
42	Nomar Garciaparra	1.00
43	Brian Giles	.50
44	Jeremy Accardo RC	1.00
45	Taylor Buchholz (RC)	.50
46	Mike Jacobs	.50
47	Chris Denorfia (RC)	.50
48	Ivan Rodriguez	.75
49	Mike Piazza	1.50
50	Curt Schilling	1.00
51	Kelly Stoppach (RC)	.50
52	Jason Kubel (RC)	.50
53	Craig Biggio	.50
54	Livan Hernandez	.50
55	Joe Mauer	.75
56	Scott Feldman RC	1.00
57	Garret Anderson	.50
58	Steve Stemle RC	1.00
59	Boof Bonser RC	.50
60	Jose Guillen	.50
61	Rafael Furcal	.50
62	John Van Benschoten (RC)	.50
63	Dontrelle Willis	.75
64	Jose Vidro	.50
65	David Wright	2.00
66	Alfonso Soriano	1.00
67	Scott Podsednik	.50
68	Felix Hernandez	.75
69	Richie Sexson	.75
70	Jeff Francoeur	.50
71	Conor Jackson	.50
72	Javy Lopez	.50
73	Jonathan Papelbon (RC)	6.00
74	Frank Thomas	.75
75	Greg Maddux	2.00
76	Josh Rupe (RC)	.50
77	Eric Chavez	.50
78	Ben Sheets	.50
79	Chase Utley	.75
80	Derek Lee	.75
81	Manny Ramirez	1.00
82	Pedro Martinez	1.00
83	Hideki Matsui	.75
84	Jeremy Bonderman	.50
85	Ronny Cedeno	.50
86	Trevor Hoffman	.50
87	Mark Buehrle	.50
88	Jason Bay	.75
89	Reggie Sanders	.50
90	Brian Anderson (RC)	.50
91	Travis Hafner	.50
92	Carlos Beltran	.75
93	Cody Ross (RC)	.50
94	Melvin Mora	.50
95	Chris Duffy	.50
96	Vernon Wells	.50
97	Bartolo Colon	.50
98	Aubrey Huff	.50
99	Paul Konerko	.50
100	Cesar Izturis	.50
101	Josh Willingham (RC)	1.50
102	Matt Cain (RC)	2.00
103	Macay McBride (RC)	.50
104	Jeff Mathis	1.50
105	Alex Rodriguez	8.00
106	Justin Morneau	2.00
107	Felipe Lopez	1.50
108	Justin Verlander (RC)	8.00
109	Ryan Howard	5.00
110	Mike Sweeney	1.50
111	Scott Rolen	3.00
112	Hank Blalock	1.50
113	Kerry Wood	1.50
114	B.J. Ryan	1.50
115	Garrett Atkins	1.50
116	Carlos Delgado	2.50
117	Zack Greinke	1.50
118	Chad Cordero	1.50
119	Julio Lugo	1.50
120	Bobby Crosby	1.50
121	Barry Zito	2.00
122	Jhonny Peralta	1.50
123	Miguel Tejada	2.50
124	Grady Sizemore	2.00
125	Derek Jeter	10.00
126	Cliff Lee	1.50
127	Khalil Greene	1.50
128	Lance Berkman	2.00
129	Huston Street	1.50
130	Jermaine Dye	2.00
131	Chone Figgins	1.50
132	Torii Hunter	2.00
133	Jorge Cantu	1.50
134	Jason Giambi	3.00
135	Johan Santana	3.00
136	Chad Tracy	1.50
137	Troy Glaus	2.00
138	Moises Alou	2.00
139	Jason Schmidt	2.00
140	Ken Griffey Jr.	8.00
141	Jason Varitek	3.00
142	John Smoltz	2.50
143	Andy Pettitte	2.00
144	Jeff Kent	2.00
145	Coco Crisp	2.00
146	Jonny Gomes	1.50
147	Aaron Rowand	1.50
148	Mike Mussina	2.50
149	Johnny Damon	4.00
150	Edgar Renteria	1.50
151	Scott Kazmir	2.00
152	Lyle Overbay	2.00
153	Placido Polanco	2.00
154	Mariano Rivera	3.00
155	Hanley Ramirez (RC)	3.00
156	Morgan Ensberg	2.00
157	Kenny Rogers	2.00
158	Brad Lidge	2.00
159	A.J. Pierzynski	2.00
160	Aramis Ramirez	3.00
161	Mark Teixeira	3.00
162	Carl Crawford	3.00
163	Ryan Zimmerman (RC)	10.00
164	Adam Dunn	3.00
165	Joe Nathan	2.00
166	Juan Pierre	2.00
167	Pat Burrell	2.00
168	Carlos Lee	3.00
169	Billy Wagner	2.00
170	Prince Fielder (RC)	8.00
171	Randy Johnson	4.00
172	Andruw Jones	4.00
173	Francisco Rodriguez	2.00
174	Robinson Cano	3.00
175	Matt Holliday	2.00
176	Jim Edmonds	2.00
177	Josh Barfield (RC)	2.00
178	Chipper Jones	4.00
179	Bobby Jenks	2.00
180	Carlos Zambrano	3.00
181	Bobby Abreu	3.00
182	Brandon Webb	2.00
183	Kevin Millwood	2.00
184	Zachary Duke	2.00
185	Randy Winn	2.00
186	Eric Gagne	2.00
187	Kenji Johjima RC	10.00
188	John Patterson	2.00
189	Mark Loretta	2.00
190	Anderson Hernandez (RC)	2.00
191	Chris Resop (RC)	2.00
192	Ian Kinsler (RC)	8.00
193	Francisco Liriano (RC)	8.00
194	Noah Lowry	2.00
195	Brett Myers	2.00
196	Rocco Baldelli	2.00
197	Cliff Floyd	2.00
198	Sean Casey	2.00
199	Geoff Jenkins	2.00
200	Clint Barmes	2.00

Printing Plates

No Pricing
Production one set per color.

Legacy Blue

Joe Nathan 025/150

Blue (1-100):	2-4X
Blue (101-150):	1-1.5X
Blue (151-200):	1X
Production 150 Sets	

Legacy Emerald

Jeremy Bonderman

Emerald (1-100):	2-4X
Emerald (101-150):	1-1.5X
Emerald (151-200):	1X
Production 150 Sets	

Autographics

NM/M

Common Autograph:		8.00
BA	Bronson Arroyo	20.00
JB	Jason Bay	20.00
HB	Hank Blalock	10.00
BO	Jeremy Bonderman	20.00
SC	Sean Casey/SP	15.00
GC	Gustavo Chacin	10.00
BC	Brandon Claussen	10.00
CH	Chad Cordero	8.00
CO	Craig Counsell	8.00
CA	Carl Crawford	15.00
CC	Coco Crisp	25.00
KG	Ken Griffey Jr./SP	75.00
JG	Jose Guillen	8.00
TH	Travis Hafner/SP	15.00
AH	Aaron Harang	15.00
LH	Livan Hernandez	8.00
CI	Cesar Izturis	8.00
MK	Mark Kotsay	8.00
CL	Cliff Lee	8.00
JM	Justin Morneau	20.00
XN	Xavier Nady	10.00
RO	Roy Oswalt/SP	15.00
WP	Wily Mo Pena	15.00
JH	Jhonny Peralta	10.00
JP	Joel Pineiro	8.00
RA	Aramis Ramirez	15.00
AR	Aaron Rowand	15.00
CU	Chase Utley/SP/100	25.00
JV	Javier Vazquez/SP	8.00
OV	Omar Vizquel	30.00
RZ	Ryan Zimmerman	50.00

Fresh Ink

NM/M

Common Auto.:		10.00
GA	Garrett Atkins	10.00
CB	Clint Barmes/SP	15.00
JB	Joe Blanton	15.00
MC	Miguel Cabrera/SP	25.00
MA	Matt Cain SP	25.00
BC	Bobby Crosby	10.00
DD	David DeJesus	15.00
GF	Gavin Floyd	10.00
JG	Jonny Gomes	15.00
KG	Khalil Greene/SP	25.00
ZG	Zack Greinke	10.00
HA	Rich Harden	15.00
DH	Danny Haren	15.00
RH	Rich Hill	30.00
TI	Tadahito Iguchi	40.00
SK	Scott Kazmir	15.00
CK	Casey Kotchman	10.00
NL	Noah Lowry	10.00
VM	Victor Martinez	15.00
BM	Brandon McCarthy	10.00
OP	Odalis Perez	10.00
RE	Jeremy Reed	10.00
BR	Brian Roberts	15.00
ES	Ervin Santana	10.00
JS	Johan Santana/SP	50.00
CS	Chris Shelton	15.00
HS	Huston Street	15.00
MT	Mark Teahen	10.00
DW	Dontrelle Willis	15.00
WR	David Wright/SP/100	60.00
KY	Kevin Youkilis	15.00
MY	Michael Young/SP/100	20.00

Hot Gloves

NM/M

Common Player:		10.00
Inserted 1:108 Hobby		
1	Derrek Lee	15.00
2	Andruw Jones	15.00
3	Bobby Abreu	10.00
4	Luis Castillo	10.00
5	Mike Matheny	10.00
6	Cesar Izturis	10.00
7	Craig Biggio	15.00
8	Darin Erstad	10.00
9	Derek Jeter	40.00
10	Eric Chavez	10.00
11	Greg Maddux	40.00
12	Ichiro Suzuki	35.00
13	Ivan Rodriguez	15.00
14	J.T. Snow	10.00
15	Jim Edmonds	15.00
16	Steve Finley	10.00
17	Kenny Rogers	10.00
18	Jason Varitek	20.00

Abbreviations

SP - Short Print

19	Ken Griffey Jr.	40.00
20	Mark Teixeira	15.00
21	Orlando Hudson	10.00
22	Mike Hampton	10.00
23	Mike Mussina	15.00
24	Vernon Wells	15.00
25	Omar Vizquel	10.00
26	Alex Rodriguez	40.00
27	Mike Cameron	15.00
28	Scott Rolen	25.00
29	Todd Helton	15.00
30	Torii Hunter	15.00

Hot Numbers

Albert Pujols Cardinals 1B

NM/M

Common Player:		1.50
Inserted 1:6 Hobby		
1	Albert Pujols	8.00
2	Alex Rodriguez	8.00
3	Andruw Jones	3.00
4	Bobby Abreu	1.50
5	Chipper Jones	3.00
6	Curt Schilling	3.00
7	David Ortiz	3.00
8	David Wright	5.00
9	Derek Jeter	8.00
10	Derrek Lee	3.00
11	Eric Gagne	1.50
12	Greg Maddux	5.00
13	Hideki Matsui	5.00
14	Ichiro Suzuki	5.00
15	Ivan Rodriguez	2.00
16	Johan Santana	2.00
17	Johnny Damon	3.00
18	Ken Griffey Jr.	5.00
19	Manny Ramirez	3.00
20	Mark Prior	2.00
21	Mark Teixeira	3.00
22	Miguel Cabrera	3.00
23	Miguel Tejada	2.00
24	Pedro Martinez	3.00
25	Randy Johnson	3.00
26	Rickie Weeks	1.50
27	Roger Clemens	6.00
28	Todd Helton	3.00
29	Torii Hunter	1.50
30	Vladimir Guerrero	5.00

Lettermen

No Pricing
Production 3-9

Showcase Signatures

NM/M

Production 35 Sets		
JE	Jeremy Bonderman	30.00
SC	Sean Casey	20.00
CD	Chad Cordero	10.00
JG	Jose Guillen	10.00
AH	Aaron Harang	20.00
HA	Rich Harden	30.00
CI	Cesar Izturis	10.00
XN	Xavier Nady	20.00
RO	Roy Oswalt	20.00
WM	Wily Mo Pena	20.00
PE	Jhonny Peralta	15.00
BR	Brian Roberts	20.00
CS	Chris Shelton	20.00
KY	Kevin Youkilis	20.00
RZ	Ryan Zimmerman	65.00

Stitches

NM/M

Common Player:		4.00
Inserted 1:9		
BA	Bobby Abreu	4.00
MA	Moises Alou	5.00
RB	Rocco Baldelli	6.00
JO	Josh Beckett	6.00
CB	Carlos Beltran	8.00
LB	Lance Berkman	4.00
HB	Hank Blalock	6.00
BO	Jeremy Bonderman	6.00
MB	Mark Buehrle	4.00
MC	Miguel Cabrera	10.00
RC	Robinson Cano	12.00
JC	Jorge Cantu	6.00
EC	Eric Chavez	6.00
CO	Michael Collins	4.00
CA	Carl Crawford	6.00
BC	Bobby Crosby	6.00
JD	Johnny Damon	10.00
CD	Carlos Delgado	6.00
DR	J.D. Drew	6.00
AD	Adam Dunn	6.00
JE	Jim Edmonds	6.00
RF	Rafael Furcal	6.00
EG	Eric Gagne	6.00
FG	Freddy Garcia	4.00
JG	Jason Giambi	8.00
BG	Brian Giles	4.00
TG	Tom Glavine	8.00
LG	Luis Gonzalez	4.00
GR	Khalil Greene	4.00
KG	Ken Griffey Jr.	10.00
VG	Vladimir Guerrero	8.00
TR	Travis Hafner	8.00
RH	Roy Halladay	6.00
RI	Rich Harden	6.00
HA	J.J. Hardy	4.00
TH	Todd Helton	8.00
HO	Trevor Hoffman	4.00
MH	Matt Holliday	4.00
HU	Tim Hudson	6.00
TO	Torii Hunter	6.00
DJ	Derek Jeter	20.00
RJ	Randy Johnson	8.00
AJ	Andruw Jones	8.00
CJ	Chipper Jones	8.00
JJ	Jacque Jones	4.00
SK	Scott Kazmir	6.00
JK	Jeff Kent	6.00
CL	Carlos Lee	4.00
DL	Derrek Lee	8.00
PL	Paul LoDuca	4.00
JL	Javy Lopez	4.00
GM	Greg Maddux	10.00
PM	Pedro Martinez	10.00
KM	Kazuo Matsui	6.00
DM	Daisuke Matsuzaka	125.00
JM	Joe Mauer	8.00
KE	Kevin Millwood	4.00
MM	Mike Mussina	8.00
TN	Trot Nixon	8.00
DO	David Ortiz	10.00
JP	Jake Peavy	6.00
AN	Andy Pettitte	6.00
MI	Mike Piazza	10.00
MP	Mark Prior	6.00
AP	Albert Pujols	20.00
AR	Aramis Ramirez	6.00
MR	Manny Ramirez	8.00
RE	Jeremy Reed	4.00
JR	Jose Reyes	10.00
BR	Brian Roberts	4.00
FR	Francisco Rodriguez	4.00
IR	Ivan Rodriguez	8.00
SR	Scott Rolen	8.00
CC	C.C. Sabathia	4.00
JS	Johan Santana	8.00
JA	Jason Schmidt	6.00
RS	Richie Sexson	4.00
BS	Ben Sheets	4.00
GS	Gary Sheffield	8.00
SM	John Smoltz	8.00
AS	Alfonso Soriano	8.00
SW	Mike Sweeney	4.00
MT	Mark Teixeira	8.00
TE	Miguel Tejada	8.00
FT	Frank Thomas	10.00
JT	Jim Thome	8.00
JU	Juan Uribe	4.00
JV	Jason Varitek	10.00
OV	Omar Vizquel	6.00
RW	Rickie Weeks	6.00
VW	Vernon Wells	6.00
DW	Dontrelle Willis	6.00
PW	Preston Wilson	4.00
KW	Kerry Wood	4.00
WR	David Wright	15.00
MY	Michael Young	6.00
BZ	Barry Zito	4.00

Wave of the Future

Rickie Weeks 2B

NM/M

Common Player:		1.00
Inserted 1:2		
WF-1	Jeremy Hermida	1.00
WF-2	Kelly Stoppach	1.00
WF-3	Adam Wainwright	1.00
WF-4	Ryan Zimmerman	4.00
WF-5	Josh Willingham	1.00
WF-6	Brandon McCarthy	1.00
WF-7	Conor Jackson	1.00
WF-8	Grady Sizemore	1.50
WF-9	Curtis Granderson	1.00
WF-10	Jose Capellan	1.00
WF-11	Mike Jacobs	1.00
WF-12	Gavin Floyd	1.00

WF-13	Hanley Ramirez	1.50
WF-14	Jason Kubel	1.00
WF-15	Nate McLouth	1.00
WF-16	Felix Hernandez	1.50
WF-17	Jeff Francoeur	1.00
WF-18	Wilbert Nieves	1.00
WF-19	Cody Ross	1.00
WF-20	Justin Verlander	5.00
WF-21	Ben Johnson	1.00
WF-22	Guillermo Quiroz	1.00
WF-23	Jonathan Papelbon	4.00
WF-24	Prince Fielder	1.50
WF-25	Rickie Weeks	1.50
WF-26	Robinson Cano	2.00
WF-27	Kenji Johjima	4.00
WF-28	Anderson Hernandez	1.00
WF-29	Yuniesky Betancourt	1.00
WF-30	Zachary Duke	1.00

WBC Classic Moments

		NM/M
	Common Player:	1.50
	Inserted 1:8	
CM-1	Adam Stern	1.50
CM-2	Jason Bay	2.00
CM-3	Wei Wang	1.50
CM-4	Yung-Chi Chen	3.00
CM-5	Pedro Luis Lazo	2.00
CM-6	Yoandy Garlobo	1.50
CM-7	Ormari Romero	1.50
CM-8	Frederich Cepeda	1.50
CM-9	Yulieski Gourriel	1.50
CM-10	Yadel Marti	1.50
CM-11	David Ortiz	2.50
CM-12	Albert Pujols	5.00
CM-13	Adrian Beltre	1.50
CM-14	Alberto Castillo	1.50
CM-15	Odalis Perez	1.50
CM-16	Jason Grilli	1.50
CM-17	Daisuke Matsuzaka	5.00
CM-18	Sadaharu Oh	10.00
CM-19	Nobuhiko Matsunaka	3.00
CM-20	Ichiro Suzuki	5.00
CM-21	Akinori Otsuka	3.00
CM-22	Koji Uehara	3.00
CM-23	Kosuke Fukudome	5.00
CM-24	Daisuke Matsuzaka	5.00
CM-25	Ichiro Suzuki	5.00
CM-26	Seung-Yeop Lee	2.00
CM-27	Seung-Yeop Lee	2.00
CM-28	Jong Beom Lee	1.50
CM-29	Jae Weong Seo	1.50
CM-30	Chan Ho Park	1.50
CM-31	Hee Seop Choi	1.50
CM-32	Jorge Cantu	1.50
CM-33	Oliver Perez	1.50
CM-34	Vinny Castilla	1.50
CM-35	Esteban Loaiza	1.50
CM-36	Shairon Martis	1.50
CM-37	Bernie Williams	2.00
CM-38	Javier Vazquez	1.50
CM-39	Carlos Beltran	2.00
CM-40	Bernie Williams	2.00
CM-41	Roger Clemens	5.00
CM-42	Ken Griffey Jr.	5.00
CM-43	Alex Rodriguez	5.00
CM-44	Derrek Lee	2.00
CM-45	Derek Jeter	5.00
CM-46	Chipper Jones	2.00
CM-47	Miguel Cabrera	2.00
CM-48	Francisco Rodriguez	1.50
CM-49	Victor Martinez	1.50
CM-50	Freddy Garcia	1.50

1981 Fleer

STEVE CARLTON PITCHER OF THE YEAR

For the first time in 18 years, Fleer issued a baseball card set featuring current players. The 660-card effort included numerous errors in the first print run which were subsequently corrected. The 2-1/2" x 3-1/2" cards are numbered by team in order of the previous season's finish. Card fronts feature a full-color photo inside a border which is color-coded by team. Backs are printed in black, grey and yellow on white stock and carry full player statistical information. The player's batting average or earned run average is located in a circle in the upper-right corner of the back. The complete set price in the checklist that follows does not include the higher priced variations.

		NM/M
	Complete Set (660):	30.00
	Common Player:	.05
	Wax Pack (17):	1.75
	Wax Box (38):	50.00
	Vending Box (500):	20.00
1	Pete Rose	3.00
2	Larry Bowa	.05
3	Manny Trillo	.05
4	Bob Boone	.05
5a	Mike Schmidt/Portrait	2.50
5b	Mike Schmidt/Btg	2.00
6a	Steve Carlton ("Lefty" on front.)	1.00
6b	Steve Carlton (Pitcher of the Year on front, date 1066 on back.)	2.00
6c	Steve Carlton (Pitcher of the Year on front, date 1966 on back.)	2.50
7a	Tug McGraw (Game Saver on front.)	.50
7b	Tug McGraw (Pitcher on front.)	.05
8	Larry Christenson	.05
9	Bake McBride	.05
10	Greg Luzinski	.05
11	Ron Reed	.05
12	Dickie Noles	.05
13	Keith Moreland RC	.15
14	Bob Walk	.05
15	Lonnie Smith	.05
16	Dick Ruthven	.05
17	Sparky Lyle	.05
18	Greg Gross	.05
19	Garry Maddox	.05
20	Nino Espinosa	.05
21	George Vukovich	.05
22	John Vukovich	.05
23	Ramon Aviles	.05
24a	Kevin Saucier (Ken Saucier on back)	.10
24b	Kevin Saucier (Kevin Saucier on back)	.50
25	Randy Lerch	.05
26	Del Unser	.05
27	Tim McCarver	.15
28a	George Brett/Btg	2.00
28b	George Brett/Portrait	2.00
29a	Willie Wilson/Portrait	.50
29b	Willie Wilson/Btg	.15
30	Paul Splittorff	.05
31	Dan Quisenberry	.05
32a	Amos Otis/Btg	.50
32b	Amos Otis/Portrait	.10
33	Steve Busby	.05
34	U.L. Washington	.05
35	Dave Chalk	.05
36	Darrell Porter	.05
37	Marty Pattin	.05
38	Larry Gura	.05
39	Renie Martin	.05
40	Rich Gale	.05
41a	Hal McRae (Dark blue "Royals" on front.)	.40
41b	Hal McRae (Light blue "Royals" on front.)	.10
42	Dennis Leonard	.05
43	Willie Aikens	.05
44	Frank White	.05
45	Clint Hurdle	.05
46	John Wathan	.05
47	Pete LaCock	.05
48	Rance Mulliniks	.05
49	Jeff Twitty	.05
50	Jamie Quirk	.05
51	Art Howe	.05
52	Ken Forsch	.05
53	Vern Ruhle	.05
54	Joe Niekro	.05
55	Frank LaCorte	.05
56	J.R. Richard	.05
57	Nolan Ryan	4.00
58	Enos Cabell	.05
59	Cesar Cedeno	.05
60	Jose Cruz	.05
61	Bill Virdon	.05
62	Terry Puhl	.05
63	Joaquin Andujar	.05

64	Alan Ashby	.05
65	Joe Sambito	.05
66	Denny Walling	.05
67	Jeff Leonard	.05
68	Luis Pujols	.05
69	Bruce Bochy	.05
70	Rafael Landestoy	.05
71	Dave Smith RC	.05
72	Danny Heep RC	.05
73	Julio Gonzalez	.05
74	Craig Reynolds	.05
75	Gary Woods	.05
76	Dave Bergman	.05
77	Randy Niemann	.05
78	Joe Morgan	1.00
79a	Reggie Jackson/Portrait	2.50
79b	Reggie Jackson/Btg	2.00
80	Bucky Dent	.10
81	Tommy John	.10
82	Luis Tiant	.05
83	Rick Cerone	.05
84	Dick Howser	.05
85	Lou Piniella	.10
86	Ron Davis	.05
87a	Graig Nettles (Craig on back.)	4.50
87b	Graig Nettles (Graig on back.)	.15
88	Ron Guidry	.10
89	Rich Gossage	.10
90	Rudy May	.05
91	Gaylord Perry	.75
92	Eric Soderholm	.05
93	Bob Watson	.05
94	Bobby Murcer	.10
95	Bobby Brown	.05
96	Jim Spencer	.05
97	Tom Underwood	.05
98	Oscar Gamble	.05
99	Johnny Oates	.05
100	Fred Stanley	.05
101	Ruppert Jones	.05
102	Dennis Werth	.05
103	Joe Lefebvre	.05
104	Brian Doyle	.05
105	Aurelio Rodriguez	.05
106	Doug Bird	.05
107	Mike Griffin	.05
108	Tim Lollar	.05
109	Willie Randolph	.05
110	Steve Garvey	.30
111	Reggie Smith	.05
112	Don Sutton	.75
113	Burt Hooton	.05
114a	Davy Lopes (Davey) (No finger on back.)	.05
114b	Davy Lopes (Davey) (Small finger on back.)	.50
115	Dusty Baker	.05
116	Tom Lasorda	.10
117	Bill Russell	.05
118	Jerry Reuss	.05
119	Terry Forster	.05
120a	Bob Welch (Bob on back.)	.10
120b	Bob Welch (Robert)	.50
121	Don Stanhouse	.05
122	Rick Monday	.05
123	Derrel Thomas	.05
124	Joe Ferguson	.05
125	Rick Sutcliffe	.10
126a	Ron Cey (No finger on back.)	.05
126b	Ron Cey (Small finger on back.)	.50
127	Dave Goltz	.05
128	Jay Johnstone	.05
129	Steve Yeager	.05
130	Gary Weiss	.05
131	Mike Scioscia RC	.50
132	Vic Davalillo	.05
133	Doug Rau	.05
134	Pepe Frias	.05
135	Mickey Hatcher	.05
136	Steve Howe RC	.10
137	Robert Castillo	.05
138	Gary Thomasson	.05
139	Rudy Law	.05
140	Fernando Valenzuela RC	1.50
141	Manny Mota	.05
142	Gary Carter	1.00
143	Steve Rogers	.05
144	Warren Cromartie	.05
145	Andre Dawson	.40
146	Larry Parrish	.05
147	Rowland Office	.05
148	Ellis Valentine	.05
149	Dick Williams	.05
150	Bill Gullickson RC	.15
151	Elias Sosa	.05
152	John Tamargo	.05
153	Chris Speier	.05
154	Ron LeFlore	.05
155	Rodney Scott	.05
156	Stan Bahnsen	.05
157	Bill Lee	.05
158	Fred Norman	.05
159	Woodie Fryman	.05
160	Dave Palmer	.05
161	Jerry White	.05
162	Roberto Ramos	.05
163	John D'Acquisto	.05
164	Tommy Hutton	.05
165	Charlie Lea	.15
166	Scott Sanderson	.05
167	Ken Macha	.05

168	Tony Bernazard	.05
169	Jim Palmer	1.00
170	Steve Stone	.10
171	Mike Flanagan	.05
172	Al Bumbry	.05
173	Doug DeCinces	.05
174	Scott McGregor	.05
175	Mark Belanger	.05
176	Tim Stoddard	.05
177a	Rick Dempsey (No finger on front.)	.05
177b	Rick Dempsey (Small finger on front.)	.50
178	Earl Weaver	.25
179	Tippy Martinez	.05
180	Dennis Martinez	.05
181	Sammy Stewart	.05
182	Rich Dauer	.05
183	Lee May	.05
184	Eddie Murray	1.00
185	Benny Ayala	.05
186	John Lowenstein	.05
187	Gary Roenicke	.05
188	Ken Singleton	.05
189	Dan Graham	.05
190	Terry Crowley	.05
191	Kiko Garcia	.05
192	Dave Ford	.05
193	Mark Corey	.05
194	Lenn Sakata	.05
195	Doug DeCinces	.05
196	Johnny Bench	1.00
197	Dave Concepcion	.05
198	Ray Knight	.05
199	Ken Griffey	.10
200	Tom Seaver	1.00
201	Dave Collins	.05
202	George Foster	.05
203	Junior Kennedy	.05
204	Frank Pastore	.05
205	Dan Driessen	.05
206	Hector Cruz	.05
207	Paul Moskau	.05
208	Charlie Leibrandt RC	.25
209	Harry Spilman	.05
210	Joe Price RC	.05
211	Tom Hume	.05
212	Joe Nolan	.05
213	Doug Bair	.05
214	Mario Soto	.05
215a	Bill Bonham (No finger on back.)	.05
215b	Bill Bonham (Small finger on back.)	.50
216a	George Foster (Slugger on front.)	.25
216b	George Foster (Outfield on front.)	.15
217	Paul Householder	.05
218	Ron Oester	.05
219	Sam Mejias	.05
220	Sheldon Burnside	.05
221	Carl Yastrzemski	1.00
222	Jim Rice	.40
223	Fred Lynn	.05
224	Carlton Fisk	1.00
225	Rick Burleson	.05
226	Dennis Eckersley	.75
227	Butch Hobson	.05
228	Tom Burgmeier	.05
229	Garry Hancock	.05
230	Don Zimmer	.05
231	Steve Renko	.05
232	Dwight Evans	.05
233	Mike Torrez	.05
234	Bob Stanley	.05
235	Jim Dwyer	.05
236	Dave Stapleton	.05
237	Glenn Hoffman	.05
238	Jerry Remy	.05
239	Dick Drago	.05
240	Bill Campbell	.05
241	Tony Perez	.75
242	Phil Niekro	.75
243	Dale Murphy	.30
244	Bob Horner	.05
245	Jeff Burroughs	.05
246	Rick Camp	.05
247	Bob Cox	.05
248	Bruce Benedict	.05
249	Gene Garber	.05
250	Jerry Royster	.05
251a	Gary Matthews (No finger on back.)	.05
251b	Gary Matthews (Small finger on back.)	.50
252	Chris Chambliss	.05
253	Luis Gomez	.05
254	Bill Nahorodny	.05
255	Doyle Alexander	.05
256	Brian Asselstine	.05
257	Biff Pocoroba	.05
258	Mike Lum	.05
259	Charlie Spikes	.05
260	Glenn Hubbard	.05
261	Tommy Boggs	.05
262	Al Hrabosky	.05
263	Rick Matula	.05
264	Preston Hanna	.05
265	Larry Bradford	.05
266	Rafael Ramirez RC	.05
267	Larry McWilliams	.05
268	Rod Carew	1.00
269	Bobby Grich	.05
270	Carney Lansford	.05
271	Don Baylor	.05
272	Joe Rudi	.05
273	Dan Ford	.05

274	Jim Fregosi	.05
275	Dave Frost	.05
276	Frank Tanana	.05
277	Dickie Thon	.05
278	Jason Thompson	.05
279	Rick Miller	.05
280	Bert Campaneris	.05
281	Tom Donohue	.05
282	Brian Downing	.05
283	Fred Patek	.05
284	Bruce Kison	.05
285	Dave LaRoche	.05
286	Don Aase	.05
287	Jim Barr	.05
288	Alfredo Martinez	.05
289	Larry Harlow	.05
290	Andy Hassler	.05
291	Dave Kingman	.05
292	Bill Buckner	.05
293	Rick Reuschel	.05
294	Bruce Sutter	.75
295	Jerry Martin	.05
296	Scot Thompson	.05
297	Ivan DeJesus	.05
298	Steve Dillard	.05
299	Dick Tidrow	.05
300	Randy Martz	.05
301	Lenny Randle	.05
302	Lynn McGlothen	.05
303	Cliff Johnson	.05
304	Tim Blackwell	.05
305	Dennis Lamp	.05
306	Bill Caudill	.05
307	Carlos Lezcano	.05
308	Jim Tracy	.05
309	Doug Capilla	.05
310	Willie Hernandez	.05
311	Mike Vail	.05
312	Mike Krukow	.05
313	Barry Foote	.05
314	Larry Biittner	.05
315	Mike Tyson	.05
316	Lee Mazzilli	.05
317	John Stearns	.05
318	Alex Trevino	.05
319	Craig Swan	.05
320	Frank Taveras	.05
321	Steve Henderson	.05
322	Neil Allen	.05
323	Mark Bomback	.05
324	Mike Jorgensen	.05
325	Joe Torre	.25
326	Elliott Maddox	.05
327	Pete Falcone	.05
328	Ray Burris	.05
329	Claudell Washington	.05
330	Doug Flynn	.05
331	Joel Youngblood	.05
332	Bill Almon	.05
333	Tom Hausman	.05
334	Pat Zachry	.05
335	Jeff Reardon RC	2.00
336	Wally Backman RC	.15
337	Dan Norman	.05
338	Jerry Morales	.05
339	Ed Farmer	.05
340	Bob Molinaro	.05
341	Todd Cruz	.05
342a	Britt Burns RC (No finger on front.)	.10
342b	Britt Burns RC (Small finger on front.)	.50
343	Kevin Bell	.05
344	Tony LaRussa	.25
345	Steve Trout	.05
346	Harold Baines RC	3.00
347	Richard Wortham	.05
348	Wayne Nordhagen	.05
349	Mike Squires	.05
350	Lamar Johnson	.05
351	Rickey Henderson	2.50
352	Francisco Barrios	.05
353	Thad Bosley	.05
354	Chet Lemon	.05
355	Bruce Kimm	.05
356	Richard Dotson RC	.05
357	Jim Morrison	.05
358	Mike Proly	.05
359	Greg Pryor	.05
360	Dave Parker	.05
361	Omar Moreno	.05
362a	Kent Tekulve (1071 Waterbury on back)	.15
362b	Kent Tekulve (1971 Waterbury on back)	.50
363	Willie Stargell	1.00
364	Phil Garner	.05
365	Ed Ott	.05
366	Don Robinson	.05
367	Chuck Tanner	.05
368	Jim Rooker	.05
369	Dale Berra	.05
370	Jim Bibby	.05
371	Steve Nicosia	.05
372	Mike Easler	.05
373	Bill Robinson	.05
374	Lee Lacy	.05
375	John Candelaria	.05
376	Manny Sanguillen	.05
377	Rick Rhoden	.05
378	Grant Jackson	.05
379	Tim Foli	.05
380	Rod Scurry RC	.05
381	Bill Madlock	.05
382a	Kurt Bevacqua (Photo reversed, backwards "P" on cap.)	.15

382b	Kurt Bevacqua (correct photo)	.50
383	Bert Blyleven	.10
384	Eddie Solomon	.05
385	Enrique Romo	.05
386	John Milner	.05
387	Mike Hargrove	.05
388	Jorge Orta	.05
389	Toby Harrah	.05
390	Tom Veryzer	.05
391	Miguel Dilone	.05
392	Dan Spillner	.05
393	Jack Brohamer	.05
394	Wayne Garland	.05
395	Sid Monge	.05
396	Rick Waits	.05
397	Joe Charboneau RC	.50
398	Gary Alexander	.05
399	Jerry Dybzinski	.05
400	Mike Stanton	.05
401	Mike Paxton	.05
402	Gary Gray	.05
403	Rick Manning	.05
404	Bo Diaz	.05
405	Ron Hassey	.05
406	Ross Grimsley	.05
407	Victor Cruz	.05
408	Len Barker	.05
409	Bob Bailor	.05
410	Otto Velez	.05
411	Ernie Whitt	.05
412	Jim Clancy	.05
413	Barry Bonnell	.05
414	Dave Stieb	.05
415	Damaso Garcia RC	.10
416	John Mayberry	.05
417	Roy Howell	.05
418	Dan Ainge RC	3.00
419a	Jesse Jefferson (Pirates on back.)	.10
419b	Jesse Jefferson (Blue Jays on back.)	.50
420	Joey McLaughlin	.05
421	Lloyd Moseby RC	.10
422	Al Woods	.05
423	Garth Iorg	.05
424	Doug Ault	.05
425	Ken Schrom RC	.05
426	Mike Willis	.05
427	Steve Braun	.05
428	Bob Davis	.05
429	Jerry Garvin	.05
430	Alfredo Griffin	.05
431	Bob Mattick	.05
432	Vida Blue	.05
433	Jack Clark	.05
434	Willie McCovey	1.00
435	Mike Ivie	.05
436a	Darrel Evans (Darrel on front.)	.15
436b	Darrell Evans (Darrell on front.)	.50
437	Terry Whitfield	.05
438	Rennie Stennett	.05
439	John Montefusco	.05
440	Jim Wohlford	.05
441	Bill North	.05
442	Milt May	.05
443	Max Venable	.05
444	Ed Whitson	.05
445	Al Holland RC	.05
446	Randy Moffitt	.05
447	Bob Knepper	.05
448	Gary Lavelle	.05
449	Greg Minton	.05
450	Johnnie LeMaster	.05
451	Larry Herndon	.05
452	Rich Murray	.05
453	Joe Pettini	.05
454	Allen Ripley	.05
455	Dennis Littlejohn	.05
456	Tom Griffin	.05
457	Alan Hargesheimer	.05
458	Joe Strain	.05
459	Steve Kemp	.05
460	Sparky Anderson	.25
461	Alan Trammell	.25
462	Mark Fidrych	.25
463	Lou Whitaker	.05
464	Dave Rozema	.05
465	Milt Wilcox	.05
466	Champ Summers	.05
467	Lance Parrish	.05
468	Dan Petry	.05
469	Pat Underwood	.05
470	Rick Peters	.05
471	Al Cowens	.05
472	John Wockenfuss	.05
473	Tom Brookens	.05
474	Richie Hebner	.05
475	Jack Morris	.05
476	Jim Lentine	.05
477	Bruce Robbins	.05
478	Mark Wagner	.05
479	Tim Corcoran	.05
480a	Stan Papi (Pitcher on front.)	.15
480b	Stan Papi (Shortstop on front.)	.50
481	Kirk Gibson RC	3.00
482	Dan Schatzeder	.05
483	Amos Otis	.05
484	Dave Winfield	1.00
485	Rollie Fingers	.75
486	Gene Richards	.05
487	Randy Jones	.05
488	Ozzie Smith	2.00
489	Gene Tenace	.05

490 Bill Fahey .05
491 John Curtis .05
492 Dave Cash .05
493a Tim Flannery (Photo reversed, batting righty.) .15
493b Tim Flannery (Photo correct, batting lefty.) .50
494 Jerry Mumphrey .05
495 Bob Shirley .05
496 Steve Mura .05
497 Eric Rasmussen .05
498 Broderick Perkins .05
499 Barry Evans .05
500 Chuck Baker .05
501 Luis Salazar **RC** .05
502 Gary Lucas .05
503 Mike Armstrong .05
504 Jerry Turner .05
505 Dennis Kinney .05
506 Willy Montanez (Willie) .05
507 Gorman Thomas .05
508 Ben Oglivie .05
509 Larry Hisle .05
510 Sal Bando .05
511 Robin Yount 1.00
512 Mike Caldwell .05
513 Sixto Lezcano .05
514a Jerry Augustine (Billy Travers photo.) .15
514b Billy Travers (Correct name with photo.) .50
515 Paul Molitor 1.00
516 Moose Haas .05
517 Bill Castro .05
518 Jim Slaton .05
519 Lary Sorensen .05
520 Bob McClure .05
521 Charlie Moore .05
522 Jim Gantner .05
523 Reggie Cleveland .05
524 Don Money .05
525 Billy Travers .05
526 Buck Martinez .05
527 Dick Davis .05
528 Ted Simmons .05
529 Garry Templeton .05
530 Ken Reitz .05
531 Tony Scott .05
532 Ken Oberkfell .05
533 Bob Sykes .05
534 Keith Smith .05
535 John Littlefield .05
536 Jim Kaat .05
537 Bob Forsch .05
538 Mike Phillips .05
539 Terry Landrum **RC** .05
540 Leon Durham **RC** .10
541 Terry Kennedy .05
542 George Hendrick .05
543 Dane Iorg .05
544 Mark Littell (Photo actually Jeff Little.) .05
545 Keith Hernandez .15
546 Silvio Martinez .05
547a Pete Vuckovich (Photo actually Don Hood.) .15
547b Don Hood (Correct name with photo.) .50
548 Bobby Bonds .10
549 Mike Ramsey .05
550 Tom Herr .05
551 Roy Smalley .05
552 Jerry Koosman .05
553 Ken Landreaux .05
554 John Castino .05
555 Doug Corbett .05
556 Bombo Rivera .05
557 Ron Jackson .05
558 Butch Wynegar .05
559 Hosken Powell .05
560 Pete Redfern .05
561 Roger Erickson .05
562 Glenn Adams .05
563 Rick Sofield .05
564 Geoff Zahn .05
565 Pete Mackanin .05
566 Mike Cubbage .05
567 Darrell Jackson .05
568 Dave Edwards .05
569 Rob Wilfong .05
570 Sal Butera .05
571 Jose Morales .05
572 Rick Langford .05
573 Mike Norris .05
574 Rickey Henderson 2.50
575 Tony Armas .05
576 Dave Revering .05
577 Jeff Newman .05
578 Bob Lacey .05
579 Brian Kingman (Photo actually Alan Wirth.) .05
580 Mitchell Page .05
581 Billy Martin .25
582 Rob Picciolo .05
583 Mike Heath .05
584 Mickey Klutts .05
585 Orlando Gonzalez .05
586 Mike Davis **RC** .05
587 Wayne Gross .05
588 Matt Keough .05
589 Steve McCatty .05
590 Dwayne Murphy .05
591 Mario Guerrero .05
592 Dave McKay .05
593 Jim Essian .05
594 Dave Heaverlo .05
595 Maury Wills .10

596 Juan Beniquez .05
597 Rodney Craig .05
598 Jim Anderson .05
599 Floyd Bannister .05
600 Bruce Bochte .05
601 Julio Cruz .05
602 Ted Cox .05
603 Dan Meyer .05
604 Larry Cox .05
605 Bill Stein .05
606 Steve Garvey .30
607 Dave Roberts .05
608 Leon Roberts .05
609 Reggie Walton .05
610 Dave Edler .05
611 Larry Milbourne .05
612 Kim Allen .05
613 Mario Mendoza .05
614 Tom Paciorek .05
615 Glenn Abbott .05
616 Joe Simpson .05
617 Mickey Rivers .05
618 Jim Kern .05
619 Jim Sundberg .05
620 Richie Zisk .05
621 Jon Matlack .05
622 Fergie Jenkins .75
623 Pat Corrales .05
624 Ed Figueroa .05
625 Buddy Bell .05
626 Al Oliver .05
627 Doc Medich .05
628 Bump Wills .05
629 Rusty Staub .05
630 Pat Putnam .05
631 John Grubb .05
632 Danny Darwin .05
633 Ken Clay .05
634 Jim Norris .05
635 John Butcher .05
636 Dave Roberts .05
637 Billy Sample .05
638 Carl Yastrzemski 1.00
639 Cecil Cooper .05
640 Mike Schmidt 2.00
641a Checklist 1-50 (41 Hal McRae) .10
641b Checklist 1-50 (41 Hal McRae Double Threat) .10
642 Checklist 51-109 .05
643 Checklist 110-168 .05
644a Checklist 169-220 (202 George Foster) .10
644b Checklist 169-220 (202 George Foster "Slugger") .10
(645a) Triple Threat Larry Bowa, Pete Rose, Mike Schmidt (No number on back.) 2.00
645b Triple Threat Pete Rose, Larry Bowa, Mike Schmidt (Number on back.) 2.00
646 Checklist 221-267 .05
647 Checklist 268-315 .05
648 Checklist 316-359 .05
649 Checklist 360-408 .05
650 Reggie Jackson 2.00
651 Checklist 409-458 .05
652a Checklist 459-509 (483 Aurelio Lopez) .10
652b Checklist 459-506 (no 483) .10
653 Willie Wilson .05
654a Checklist 507-550 (514 Jerry Augustine) .10
654b Checklist 507-550 (514 Billy Travers) .10
655 George Brett 3.00
656 Checklist 551-593 .05
657 Tug McGraw .05
658 Checklist 594-637 .05
659a Checklist 640-660 (Last number on front is 551.) .10
659b Checklist 640-660 (Last number on front is 483.) .15
660a Steve Carlton (Date 1066 on back.) 1.00
660b Steve Carlton (Date 1966 on back.) 2.00

All Star Game/Team Logo Stickers

Highlights of previous All-Star Games are presented in Robert Laughlin cartoons on the cardboard backings of these stickers which feature team logos, caps or patches. Though none of the players are named on the cards, many are identifiable by the pictures, uniform numbers and/or game-action descriptions on the cards. Where a specific player is clearly depicted, his name is listed.

	NM/M
Complete Set (47):	15.00
Common Card:	.50

1933 AL wins newsman's first "Dream Game" (Babe Ruth) 1.00
1934 out (Carl Hubbell, Babe Ruth, Lou Gehrig, Jimmie Foxx, Al Simmons, Joe Cronin) .50
1935 in row (Mel Harder, Lefty Gomez) .60
1936 first time (Dizzy Dean) .75
1937 lineup (Lou Gehrig) .75
1938 gets strong pitching (Johnny VanderMeer) .60
1939 in World's Fair city (Joe DiMaggio) .75
1940 shutout (Paul Derringer) .50
1941 Two-out homer in 9th wins for AL (Ted Williams) .65
1942 victory (Lou Boudreau, Rudy York) .50
1943 anyway .50
1944 easiest win .50
1946 most lopsided win .50
1947 AL pinch hits break up pitchers' battle .50
1948 AL wins despite stars on injury list .50
1949 gains 12-4 series lead (George Kell, Johnny Mize) .50
1950 park .50
1951 NL bombs rivals with four homers (Ralph Kiner) .60
1952 Two NL homers win rain-shortened game (Jackie Robinson, Hank Sauer) .65
1953 first eight innings (Red Schoendienst, Minnie Minoso) .50
1954 slugfest (Al Rosen) .50
1955 in 12th (Stan Musial) .65
1956 NL scores in five straight innings (Ted Williams) .75
1957 in ninth (Mickey Mantle) 1.00
1958 of no extra-base hits (Nellie Fox) .65
1959 two games (Frank Robinson, Al Kaline) .60
1960 NL wins both games in AL parks .50
1961 for only tie (Stu Miller) .50
1962 year of two games is split .50
1963 NL is outhit 11-6 but wins anyway .50
1964 All-Star series .50
1965 All-Star series (Willie Mays) .75
1966 NL takes pitchers' battle in 10th (Juan Marichal, Denny McLain) .60
1967 30 batters fan in 15-inning marathon .50
1968 AL scoreless streak reaches 18 innings .50
1969 runaway (Willie McCovey) .60
1970 12th (Bud Harrelson) .50
1971 triumph from 1963 to 1980 (Reggie Jackson, Harmon Killebrew, Frank Robinson) .65
1972 games (Hank Aaron) .75
1973 they win again .50
1974 Dodgers are heroes in easy NL victory .50
1975 9th .50
1976 NL breezes .50
1977 win again .50
1978 with four in 8th .50
1979 row to win seesaw 50th game .50
1980 series lead of 32-18 (1 tie) .50

Star Stickers

The 128-card 1981 Fleer Star Sticker set was designed to allow the card fronts to be peeled away from the cardboard backs. Fronts feature color photos with blue and yellow trim. Backs are identical in design to the regular 1981 Fleer set except for color and numbering. The set contains three unnumbered checklist cards whose fronts depict Reggie Jackson, George Brett and Mike Schmidt. The sticker-cards, which are the standard 2-1/2" x 3-1/2", were issued in gum wax packs.

	NM/M
Complete Set (128):	15.00
Common Player:	.15
Wax Pack (5):	1.25
Wax Box (36):	15.00

1 Steve Garvey .40
2 Ron LeFlore .15
3 Ron Cey .15
4 Dave Revering .15
5 Tony Armas .15
6 Mike Norris .15
7 Steve Kemp .15
8 Bruce Bochte .15
9 Mike Schmidt 2.00
10 Scott McGregor .15
11 Buddy Bell .15
12 Carney Lansford .15
13 Carl Yastrzemski 1.00
14 Ben Oglivie .15
15 Willie Stargell 1.00
16 Cecil Cooper .15
17 Gene Richards .15
18 Jim Kern .15
19 Jerry Koosman .15
20 Larry Bowa .15
21 Kent Tekulve .15
22 Dan Driessen .15
23 Phil Niekro .75
24 Dan Quisenberry .15
25 Dave Winfield 1.00
26 Dave Parker .15
27 Rick Langford .15
28 Amos Otis .15
29 Bill Buckner .15
30 Al Bumbry .15
31 Bake McBride .15
32 Mickey Rivers .15
33 Rick Burleson .15
34 Dennis Eckersley .75
35 Cesar Cedeno .15
36 Enos Cabell .15
37 Johnny Bench 1.00
38 Robin Yount 1.00
39 Mark Belanger .15
40 Rod Carew 1.00
41 George Foster .15
42 Lee Mazzilli .15
43 Triple Threat (Larry Bowa, Pete Rose, Mike Schmidt) 2.00
44 J.R. Richard .15
45 Lou Piniella .15
46 Ken Landreaux .15
47 Rollie Fingers .75
48 Joaquin Andujar .15
49 Tom Seaver 1.00
50 Bobby Grich .15
51 Jon Matlack .15
52 Jack Clark .15
53 Jim Rice .15
54 Rickey Henderson 3.00
55 Roy Smalley .15
56 Mike Flanagan .15
57 Steve Rogers .15
58 Carlton Fisk 1.00
59 Don Sutton .75
60 Ken Griffey .15
61 Burt Hooton .15
62 Dusty Baker .15
63 Vida Blue .15
64 Al Oliver .15
65 Jim Bibby .15
66 Tony Perez .15
67 Davy Lopes (Davey) .15
68 Bill Russell .15
69 Larry Parrish .15
70 Garry Maddox .15
71 Phil Garner .15
72 Graig Nettles .20
73 Gary Carter 1.00
74 Pete Rose 3.00
75 Greg Luzinski .15
76 Ron Guidry .15
77 Gorman Thomas .15
78 Jose Cruz .15
79 Bob Boone .15
80 Bruce Sutter .15
81 Chris Chambliss .15
82 Paul Molitor .15
83 Tug McGraw .15
84 Ferguson Jenkins .75
85 Steve Carlton 1.00
86 Miguel Dilone .15
87 Reggie Smith .15
88 Rick Cerone .15
89 Alan Trammell .15
90 Doug DeCinces .15
91 Sparky Lyle .15
92 Warren Cromartie .15
93 Rick Reuschel .15
94 Larry Hisle .15
95 Paul Splittorff .15
96 Manny Trillo .15
97 Frank White .15
98 Fred Lynn .15
99 Bob Horner .15
100 Omar Moreno .15
101 Dave Concepcion .15
102 Larry Gura .15
103 Ken Singleton .15
104 Steve Stone .15
105 Richie Zisk .15
106 Willie Wilson .15
107 Willie Randolph .15
108 Nolan Ryan 3.00
109 Joe Morgan 1.00
110 Bucky Dent .20
111 Dave Kingman .15
112 John Castino .15
113 Joe Rudi .15
114 Ed Farmer .15
115 Reggie Jackson 2.50
116 George Brett 2.00
117 Eddie Murray 1.00
118 Rich Gossage .20
119 Dale Murphy .40
120 Ted Simmons .15
121 Tommy John .20
122 Don Baylor .15
123 Andre Dawson .60
124 Jim Palmer 1.00
125 Garry Templeton .15
----- Checklist 1-42 (Reggie Jackson) .50
----- Checklist 43-83 (George Brett) .50
----- Checklist 84-125 (Mike Schmidt) .50

Superstar Stickers

While these small (about 1-1/2" x 2") stickers carry the Fleer name and were, indeed, produced by Fleer, they are more akin to collectors' issues than a legitimate product. Wrappers of 1981 Fleer Star Stickers offered the opportunity to put one's own photo, or the photo of someone else, on 24 stickers for a couple of dollars and proofs of purchase. Some enterprising hobbyists sent in several different pictures of Mickey Mantle and pictures of then-current stars and had them made into stickers. Because they are unauthorized by Mantle, or the other players seen (Boggs, Mattingly, Yaz, etc.), there is no collector value.

1982 Fleer

Fleer's 1982 set did not match the quality of the previous year's effort. Many of the card photos are blurred and have muddied backgrounds. The 2-1/2" x 3-1/2" cards feature color photos bordered by a frame which is color-coded by team. Backs are blue, white, and yellow and contain the player's team logo plus the logos of Major League Baseball and the Major League Baseball Players Association. Due to a lawsuit by Topps, Fleer was forced to issue the set with team logo stickers rather than gum. The complete set price does not include the higher priced variations.

	NM/M
Complete Set (660):	45.00
Common Player:	.05
Wax Pack (15):	3.00
Wax Box (36):	85.00
Cello Pack (28):	4.00
Cello Box (24):	85.00
Vending Box (500):	40.00

1 Dusty Baker .05
2 Robert Castillo .05
3 Ron Cey .05
4 Terry Forster .05
5 Steve Garvey .30
6 Dave Goltz .05
7 Pedro Guerrero .05
8 Burt Hooton .05
9 Steve Howe .05
10 Jay Johnstone .05
11 Ken Landreaux .05
12 Davey Lopes .05
13 Mike Marshall **RC** .15
14 Bobby Mitchell .05
15 Rick Monday .05
16 Tom Niedenfuer **RC** .05
17 Ted Power **RC** .05
18 Jerry Reuss .05
19 Ron Roenicke .05
20 Bill Russell .05
21 Steve Sax **RC** .45
22 Mike Scioscia .05
23 Reggie Smith .05
24 Dave Stewart **RC** 1.50
25 Rick Sutcliffe .05
26 Derrel Thomas .05
27 Fernando Valenzuela .10
28 Bob Welch .05
29 Steve Yeager .05
30 Bobby Brown .05
31 Rick Cerone .05
32 Ron Davis .05
33 Bucky Dent .10
34 Barry Foote .05
35 George Frazier .05
36 Oscar Gamble .05
37 Rich Gossage .10
38 Ron Guidry .05
39 Reggie Jackson 1.50
40 Tommy John .10
41 Rudy May .05
42 Larry Milbourne .05
43 Jerry Mumphrey .05
44 Bobby Murcer .10
45 Gene Nelson **RC** .05
46 Graig Nettles .10
47 Johnny Oates .05
48 Lou Piniella .05
49 Willie Randolph .05
50 Rick Reuschel .05
51 Dave Revering .05
52 Dave Righetti **RC** .45
53 Aurelio Rodriguez .05
54 Bob Watson .05
55 Dennis Werth .05
56 Dave Winfield 1.00
57 Johnny Bench 1.00
58 Bruce Berenyi .05
59 Larry Biittner .05
60 Scott Brown .05
61 Dave Collins .05
62 Geoff Combe .05
63 Dave Concepcion .05
64 Dan Driessen .05
65 Joe Edelen .05
66 George Foster .05
67 Ken Griffey .05
68 Paul Householder .05
69 Tom Hume .05
70 Junior Kennedy .05
71 Ray Knight .05
72 Mike LaCoss .05
73 Rafael Landestoy .05
74 Charlie Leibrandt .05
75 Sam Mejias .05
76 Paul Moskau .05
77 Joe Nolan .05
78 Mike O'Berry .05
79 Ron Oester .05
80 Frank Pastore .05
81 Joe Price .05
82 Tom Seaver 1.00
83 Mario Soto .05
84 Mike Vail .05
85 Tony Armas .05
86 Shooty Babitt .05
87 Dave Beard .05
88 Rick Bosetti .05
89 Keith Drumright .05
90 Wayne Gross .05
91 Mike Heath .05
92 Rickey Henderson 1.00
93 Cliff Johnson .05
94 Jeff Jones .05
95 Matt Keough .05

No.	Player	Price
96	Brian Kingman	.05
97	Mickey Klutts	.05
98	Rick Langford	.05
99	Steve McCatty	.05
100	Dave McKay	.05
101	Dwayne Murphy	.05
102	Jeff Newman	.05
103	Mike Norris	.05
104	Bob Owchinko	.05
105	Mitchell Page	.05
106	Rob Picciolo	.05
107	Jim Spencer	.05
108	Fred Stanley	.05
109	Tom Underwood	.05
110	Joaquin Andujar	.05
111	Steve Braun	.05
112	Bob Forsch	.05
113	George Hendrick	.05
114	Keith Hernandez	.05
115	Tom Herr	.05
116	Dane Iorg	.05
117	Jim Kaat	.10
118	Tito Landrum	.05
119	Sixto Lezcano	.05
120	Mark Littell	.05
121	John Martin	.05
122	Silvio Martinez	.05
123	Ken Oberkfell	.05
124	Darrell Porter	.05
125	Mike Ramsey	.05
126	Orlando Sanchez	.05
127	Bob Shirley	.05
128	Lary Sorensen	.05
129	Bruce Sutter	.75
130	Bob Sykes	.05
131	Garry Templeton	.05
132	Gene Tenace	.05
133	Jerry Augustine	.05
134	Sal Bando	.05
135	Mark Brouhard	.05
136	Mike Caldwell	.05
137	Reggie Cleveland	.05
138	Cecil Cooper	.05
139	Jamie Easterly	.05
140	Marshall Edwards	.05
141	Rollie Fingers	.75
142	Jim Gantner	.05
143	Moose Haas	.05
144	Larry Hisle	.05
145	Roy Howell	.05
146	Rickey Keeton	.05
147	Randy Lerch	.05
148	Paul Molitor	1.00
149	Don Money	.05
150	Charlie Moore	.05
151	Ben Oglivie	.05
152	Ted Simmons	.05
153	Jim Slaton	.05
154	Gorman Thomas	.05
155	Robin Yount	1.00
156	Pete Vukovich	.05
157	Benny Ayala	.05
158	Mark Belanger	.05
159	Al Bumbry	.05
160	Terry Crowley	.05
161	Rich Dauer	.05
162	Doug DeCinces	.05
163	Rick Dempsey	.05
164	Jim Dwyer	.05
165	Mike Flanagan	.05
166	Dave Ford	.05
167	Dan Graham	.05
168	Wayne Krenchicki	.05
169	John Lowenstein	.05
170	Dennis Martinez	.05
171	Tippy Martinez	.05
172	Scott McGregor	.05
173	Jose Morales	.05
174	Eddie Murray	1.00
175	Jim Palmer	.75
176	Cal Ripken, Jr. RC	35.00
177	Gary Roenicke	.05
178	Lenn Sakata	.05
179	Ken Singleton	.05
180	Sammy Stewart	.05
181	Tim Stoddard	.05
182	Steve Stone	.05
183	Stan Bahnsen	.05
184	Ray Burris	.05
185	Gary Carter	1.00
186	Warren Cromartie	.50
187	Andre Dawson	.50
188	Terry Francona RC	.05
189	Woodie Fryman	.05
190	Bill Gullickson	.05
191	Grant Jackson	.05
192	Wallace Johnson	.09
193	Charlie Lea	.05
194	Bill Lee	.05
195	Jerry Manuel	.05
196	Brad Mills	.05
197	John Milner	.05
198	Rowland Office	.05
199	David Palmer	.05
200	Larry Parrish	.05
201	Mike Phillips	.05
202	Tim Raines	.25
203	Bobby Ramos	.05
204	Jeff Reardon	.50
205	Steve Rogers	.05
206	Scott Sanderson	.05
207	Rodney Scott (Photo actually Tim Raines.)	.10
208	Elias Sosa	.05
209	Chris Speier	.05
210	Tim Wallach RC	1.00
211	Jerry White	.05
212	Alan Ashby	.05
213	Cesar Cedeno	.05
214	Jose Cruz	.05
215	Kiko Garcia	.05
216	Phil Garner	.05
217	Danny Heep	.05
218	Art Howe	.05
219	Bob Knepper	.05
220	Frank LaCorte	.05
221	Joe Niekro	.05
222	Joe Pittman	.05
223	Terry Puhl	.05
224	Luis Pujols	.05
225	Craig Reynolds	.05
226	J.R. Richard	.05
227	Dave Roberts	.05
228	Vern Ruhle	.05
229	Nolan Ryan	3.00
230	Joe Sambito	.05
231	Tony Scott	.05
232	Dave Smith	.05
233	Harry Spilman	.05
234	Don Sutton	.75
235	Dickie Thon	.05
236	Denny Walling	.05
237	Gary Woods	.05
238	Luis Aguayo RC	.05
239	Ramon Aviles	.05
240	Bob Boone	.05
241	Larry Bowa	.05
242	Warren Brusstar	.05
243	Steve Carlton	1.00
244	Larry Christenson	.05
245	Dick Davis	.05
246	Greg Gross	.05
247	Sparky Lyle	.05
248	Garry Maddox	.05
249	Gary Matthews	.05
250	Bake McBride	.05
251	Tug McGraw	.05
252	Keith Moreland	.05
253	Dickie Noles	.05
254	Mike Proly	.05
255	Ron Reed	.05
256	Pete Rose	2.50
257	Dick Ruthven	.05
258	Mike Schmidt	2.00
259	Lonnie Smith	.05
260	Manny Trillo	.05
261	Del Unser	.05
262	George Vukovich	.05
263	Tom Brookens	.05
264	George Cappuzzello	.05
265	Marty Castillo	.05
266	Al Cowens	.05
267	Kirk Gibson	.05
268	Richie Hebner	.05
269	Ron Jackson	.05
270	Lynn Jones	.05
271	Steve Kemp	.05
272	Rick Leach RC	.25
273	Aurelio Lopez	.05
274	Jack Morris	.05
275	Kevin Saucier	.05
276	Lance Parrish	.05
277	Rick Peters	.05
278	Dan Petry	.05
279	David Rozema	.05
280	Stan Papi	.05
281	Dan Schatzeder	.05
282	Champ Summers	.05
283	Alan Trammell	.05
284	Lou Whitaker	.05
285	Milt Wilcox	.05
286	John Wockenfuss	.05
287	Gary Allenson	.05
288	Tom Burgmeier	.05
289	Bill Campbell	.05
290	Mark Clear	.05
291	Steve Crawford	.05
292	Dennis Eckersley	.75
293	Dwight Evans	.05
294	Rich Gedman RC	.10
295	Garry Hancock	.05
296	Glenn Hoffman	.05
297	Bruce Hurst	.05
298	Carney Lansford	.05
299	Rick Miller	.05
300	Reid Nichols	.05
301	Bob Ojeda RC	.25
302	Tony Perez	.75
303	Chuck Rainey	.05
304	Jerry Remy	.05
305	Jim Rice	.50
306	Joe Rudi	.05
307	Bob Stanley	.05
308	Dave Stapleton	.05
309	Frank Tanana	.05
310	Mike Torrez	.05
311	John Tudor	.05
312	Carl Yastrzemski	1.00
313	Buddy Bell	.05
314	Steve Comer	.05
315	Danny Darwin	.05
316	John Ellis	.05
317	John Grubb	.05
318	Rick Honeycutt	.05
319	Charlie Hough	.05
320	Fergie Jenkins	.75
321	John Henry Johnson	.05
322	Jim Kern	.05
323	Jon Matlack	.05
324	Doc Medich	.05
325	Mario Mendoza	.05
326	Al Oliver	.05
327	Pat Putnam	.05
328	Mickey Rivers	.05
329	Leon Roberts	.05
330	Billy Sample	.05
331	Bill Stein	.05
332	Jim Sundberg	.05
333	Mark Wagner	.05
334	Bump Wills	.05
335	Bill Almon	.05
336	Harold Baines	.05
337	Ross Baumgarten	.05
338	Tony Bernazard	.05
339	Britt Burns	.05
340	Richard Dotson	.05
341	Jim Essian	.05
342	Ed Farmer	.05
343	Carlton Fisk	1.00
344	Kevin Hickey	.05
345	Lamarr Hoyt (LaMarr)	.05
346	Lamar Johnson	.05
347	Jerry Koosman	.05
348	Rusty Kuntz	.05
349	Dennis Lamp	.05
350	Ron LeFlore	.05
351	Chet Lemon	.05
352	Greg Luzinski	.05
353	Bob Molinaro	.05
354	Jim Morrison	.05
355	Wayne Nordhagen	.05
356	Greg Pryor	.05
357	Mike Squires	.05
358	Steve Trout	.05
359	Alan Bannister	.05
360	Len Barker	.05
361	Bert Blyleven	.10
362	Joe Charboneau	.10
363	John Denny	.05
364	Bo Diaz	.05
365	Miguel Dilone	.05
366	Jerry Dybzinski	.05
367	Wayne Garland	.05
368	Mike Hargrove	.05
369	Toby Harrah	.05
370	Ron Hassey	.05
371	Von Hayes RC	.25
372	Pat Kelly	.05
373	Duane Kuiper	.05
374	Rick Manning	.05
375	Sid Monge	.05
376	Jorge Orta	.05
377	Dave Rosello	.05
378	Dan Spillner	.05
379	Mike Stanton	.05
380	Andre Thornton	.05
381	Tom Veryzer	.05
382	Rick Waits	.05
383	Doyle Alexander	.05
384	Vida Blue	.05
385	Fred Breining	.05
386	Enos Cabell	.05
387	Jack Clark	.05
388	Darrell Evans	.05
389	Tom Griffin	.05
390	Larry Herndon	.05
391	Al Holland	.05
392	Gary Lavelle	.05
393	Johnnie LeMaster	.05
394	Jerry Martin	.05
395	Milt May	.05
396	Greg Minton	.05
397	Joe Morgan	1.00
398	Joe Pettini	.05
399	Alan Ripley	.05
400	Billy Smith	.05
401	Rennie Stennett	.05
402	Ed Whitson	.05
403	Jim Wohlford	.05
404	Willie Aikens	.05
405	George Brett	2.00
406	Ken Brett	.05
407	Dave Chalk	.05
408	Rich Gale	.05
409	Cesar Geronimo	.05
410	Larry Gura	.05
411	Clint Hurdle	.05
412	Mike Jones	.05
413	Dennis Leonard	.05
414	Renie Martin	.05
415	Lee May	.05
416	Hal McRae	.05
417	Darryl Motley	.05
418	Rance Mulliniks	.05
419	Amos Otis	.05
420	Ken Phelps RC	.05
421	Jamie Quirk	.05
422	Dan Quisenberry	.05
423	Paul Splittorff	.05
424	U.L. Washington	.05
425	John Wathan	.05
426	Frank White	.05
427	Willie Wilson	.05
428	Brian Asselstine	.05
429	Bruce Benedict	.05
430	Tom Boggs	.05
431	Larry Bradford	.05
432	Rick Camp	.05
433	Chris Chambliss	.05
434	Gene Garber	.05
435	Preston Hanna	.05
436	Bob Horner	.05
437	Glenn Hubbard	.05
438a	Al Hrabosky (All Hrabosky, 5'1" on back.)	4.50
438b	Al Hrabosky (Al Hrabosky, 5'1" on back.)	1.00
438c	Al Hrabosky (Al Hrabosky, 5'10" on back.)	.25
439	Rufino Linares	.05
440	Rick Mahler RC	.05
441	Ed Miller	.05
442	John Montefusco	.10
443	Dale Murphy	.50
444	Phil Niekro	.75
445	Gaylord Perry	.75
446	Biff Pocoroba	.05
447	Rafael Ramirez	.05
448	Jerry Royster	.05
449	Claudell Washington	.05
450	Don Aase	.05
451	Don Baylor	.05
452	Juan Beniquez	.05
453	Rick Burleson	.05
454	Bert Campaneris	.05
455	Rod Carew	1.00
456	Bob Clark	.05
457	Brian Downing	.05
458	Dan Ford	.05
459	Ken Forsch	.05
460	Dave Frost	.05
461	Bobby Grich	.05
462	Larry Harlow	.05
463	John Harris	.05
464	Andy Hassler	.05
465	Butch Hobson	.05
466	Jesse Jefferson	.05
467	Bruce Kison	.05
468	Fred Lynn	.05
469	Angel Moreno	.05
470	Ed Ott	.05
471	Fred Patek	.05
472	Steve Renko	.05
473	Mike Witt RC	.10
474	Geoff Zahn	.05
475	Gary Alexander	.05
476	Dale Berra	.05
477	Kurt Bevacqua	.05
478	Jim Bibby	.05
479	John Candelaria	.05
480	Victor Cruz	.05
481	Mike Easler	.05
482	Tim Foli	.05
483	Lee Lacy	.05
484	Vance Law	.05
485	Bill Madlock	.05
486	Willie Montanez	.05
487	Omar Moreno	.05
488	Steve Nicosia	.05
489	Dave Parker	.05
490	Tony Pena	.05
491	Pascual Perez	.05
492	Johnny Ray RC	.05
493	Rick Rhoden	.05
494	Bill Robinson	.05
495	Don Robinson	.05
496	Enrique Romo	.05
497	Rod Scurry	.05
498	Eddie Solomon	.05
499	Willie Stargell	1.00
500	Kent Tekulve	.05
501	Jason Thompson	.05
502	Glenn Abbott	.05
503	Jim Anderson	.05
504	Floyd Bannister	.05
505	Bruce Bochte	.05
506	Jeff Burroughs	.05
507	Bryan Clark	.05
508	Ken Clay	.05
509	Julio Cruz	.05
510	Dick Drago	.05
511	Gary Gray	.05
512	Dan Meyer	.05
513	Jerry Narron	.05
514	Tom Paciorek	.05
515	Casey Parsons	.05
516	Lenny Randle	.05
517	Shane Rawley	.05
518	Joe Simpson	.05
519	Richie Zisk	.05
520	Neil Allen	.05
521	Bob Bailor	.05
522	Hubie Brooks	.05
523	Mike Cubbage	.05
524	Pete Falcone	.05
525	Doug Flynn	.05
526	Tom Hausman	.05
527	Ron Hodges	.05
528	Randy Jones	.05
529	Mike Jorgensen	.05
530	Dave Kingman	.05
531	Ed Lynch	.05
532	Mike Marshall	.05
533	Lee Mazzilli	.05
534	Dyar Miller	.05
535	Mike Scott	.05
536	Rusty Staub	.05
537	John Stearns	.05
538	Craig Swan	.05
539	Frank Taveras	.05
540	Alex Trevino	.05
541	Ellis Valentine	.05
542	Mookie Wilson	.05
543	Joel Youngblood	.05
544	Pat Zachry	.05
545	Glenn Adams	.05
546	Fernando Arroyo	.05
547	John Verhoeven	.05
548	Sal Butera	.05
549	John Castino	.05
550	Don Cooper	.05
551	Doug Corbett	.05
552	Dave Engle	.05
553	Roger Erickson	.05
554	Danny Goodwin	.05
555a	Darrell Jackson (Black cap.)	.65
555b	Darrell Jackson (Red cap w/speck of white.)	3.00
555c	Darrell Jackson (Red cap w/white T.)	.10
556	Pete Mackanin	.05
557	Jack O'Connor	.05
558	Hosken Powell	.05
559	Pete Redfern	.05
560	Roy Smalley	.05
561	Chuck Baker	.05
562	Gary Ward	.05
563	Rob Wilfong	.05
564	Al Williams	.05
565	Butch Wynegar	.05
566	Randy Bass	.05
567	Juan Bonilla	.05
568	Danny Boone	.05
569	John Curtis	.05
570	Juan Eichelberger	.05
571	Barry Evans	.05
572	Tim Flannery	.05
573	Ruppert Jones	.05
574	Terry Kennedy	.05
575	Joe Lefebvre	.05
576a	John Littlefield (Pitching lefty.)	80.00
576b	John Littlefield (Pitching righty.)	.05
577	Gary Lucas	.05
578	Steve Mura	.05
579	Broderick Perkins	.05
580	Gene Richards	.05
581	Luis Salazar	.05
582	Ozzie Smith	1.50
583	John Urrea	.05
584	Chris Welsh	.05
585	Rick Wise	.05
586	Doug Bird	.05
587	Tim Blackwell	.05
588	Bobby Bonds	.10
589	Bill Buckner	.05
590	Bill Caudill	.05
591	Hector Cruz	.05
592	Jody Davis RC	.10
593	Ivan DeJesus	.05
594	Steve Dillard	.05
595	Leon Durham	.05
596	Rawly Eastwick	.05
597	Steve Henderson	.05
598	Mike Krukow	.05
599	Mike Lum	.05
600	Randy Martz	.05
601	Jerry Morales	.05
602	Ken Reitz	.05
603a	Lee Smith RC (Cubs logo reversed on back.)	2.50
603b	Lee Smith RC (corrected)	2.50
604	Dick Tidrow	.05
605	Jim Tracy	.05
606	Mike Tyson	.05
607	Ty Waller	.05
608	Danny Ainge	.50
609	Jorge Bell RC	1.00
610	Mark Bomback	.05
611	Barry Bonnell	.05
612	Jim Clancy	.05
613	Damaso Garcia	.05
614	Jerry Garvin	.05
615	Alfredo Griffin	.05
616	Garth Iorg	.05
617	Luis Leal	.05
618	Ken Macha	.05
619	John Mayberry	.05
620	Joey McLaughlin	.05
621	Lloyd Moseby	.05
622	Dave Stieb	.05
623	Jackson Todd	.05
624	Willie Upshaw RC	.05
625	Otto Velez	.05
626	Ernie Whitt	.05
627	Al Woods	.05
628	1981 All-Star Game	.05
629	All-Star Infielders (Bucky Dent, Frank White)	.05
630	Big Red Machine (Dave Concepcion, Dan Driessen, George Foster)	.10
631	Top N.L. Relief Pitcher (Bruce Sutter)	.30
632	Steve & Carlton (Steve Carlton, Carlton Fisk)	.25
633	3000th Game, May 25, 1981 (Carl Yastrzemski)	.35
634	Dynamic Duo (Johnny Bench, Tom Seaver)	.30
635	West Meets East (Gary Carter, Fernando Valenzuela)	.20
636a	N.L. Strikeout King Fernando Valenzuela ("...led the National League...")	.50
636b	N.L. Strikeout King Fernando Valenzuela ("... led the National League...")	.25
637	Home Run King (Mike Schmidt)	.50
638	N.L. All-Stars (Gary Carter, Dave Parker)	.25
639	Perfect Game! (Len Barker, Bo Diaz)	.05
640	Pete Rose, Pete Rose, Jr. (Re-Pete)	2.00
641	Phillies' Finest (Steve Carlton, Mike Schmidt, Lonnie Smith)	.50
642	Red Sox Reunion (Dwight Evans, Fred Lynn)	.10
643	Most Hits and Runs (Rickey Henderson)	1.00
644	Most Saves 1981 A.L. (Rollie Fingers)	.15
645	Most 1981 Wins (Tom Seaver)	.25
646a	Yankee Powerhouse Reggie Jackson, Dave Winfield (Comma after "outfielder" on back.)	1.50
646b	Yankee Powerhouse Reggie Jackson, Dave Winfield (No comma.)	2.00
647	Checklist 1-56	.05
648	Checklist 57-109	.05
649	Checklist 110-156	.05
650	Checklist 157-211	.05
651	Checklist 212-262	.05
652	Checklist 263-312	.05
653	Checklist 313-358	.05
654	Checklist 359-403	.05
655	Checklist 404-449	.05
656	Checklist 450-501	.05
657	Checklist 502-544	.05
658	Checklist 545-585	.05
659	Checklist 586-627	.05
660	Checklist 628-646	.05

Proofs

Ken Griffey
REDS • OUTFIELD

More than two dozen proof cards which differ significantly from the issued versions in 1982 Fleer are known, though the quantities in which they have made their way into the hobby market are not known. Blank-backed and hand-cut from press sheets, the proofs include a number of Hall of Famers and high-demand stars. The manner in which the proof card differs from the issued version is listed parenthetically.

No.	Description	NM/M
---	Dave Patterson (No issued version.)	75.00
4	Terry Forster (Green photo border.)	50.00
31	Rick Cerone (Game-action, catching.)	75.00
37	Rich Gossage (Pose to knees.)	75.00
48	Lou Piniella (Game-action, trotting.)	75.00
49	Willie Randolph/Btg (Game-action.)	75.00
61	Dave Collins/Btg (Game-action.)	50.00
67	Ken Griffey (Home uniform.)	60.00
82	Tom Seaver/Pitching (Game-action.)	600.00
312	Carl Yastrzemski (Misspelled "Yastrzemski.")	350.00
395	Milt May (Ed Whitson photo.)	60.00
402	Ed Whitson (Milt May photo.)	60.00
416	Hal McRae (Position: OF.)	25.00
427	Willie Wilson (Pose, no microphone.)	50.00
449	Claudell Washington/Btg (Game-action.)	50.00
503	Jim Anderson (Incorrect name: Mike.)	25.00
555	Darrell Jackson (Pictures unidentifed pitcher.)	45.00
629	All-Star Infielders (Captioned: "Dent & White.")	25.00
632	Steve & Carlton (Captioned: "Carlton & Steve / FISK & CARLTON.")	40.00
635	West Meets East (Captioned: "East Meets West.")	25.00
638	N.L. All Stars (Captioned: "Parker & Carter.")	25.00

644	Most Saves 1981 (Captioned: "A.L. Most Saves in 1981.")	25.00
646	Yankee Powerhouse (Captioned: "Winfield & Jackson.")	45.00
652	Checklist (Lists #275 as Stan Papi.)	15.00
655	Checklist (McRae's position: OF)	15.00
660	Checklist (White border, incorrect captions as above.)	15.00

Test Cards

To test a proposed cardboard stock from International Paper Co., a run of 100 sheets of test cards was printed and delivered to Fleer officials. The cards on the sheet include various combinations of correct picture/name combinations, incorrect picture/name combinations and cards with no player identification. All cards have the words "TEST CARD" overprinted in black in the player identification area at bottom center, along with the letters "o," "n" or both vertically at the left end of the oblong. Backs are blank. At least half of the 132-card test sheets have made their way into the hobby where they are offered both as complete sheets and as hand-cut single cards or panels. A number of the photos seen on the test sheets did not appear in Fleer's 1982 card set. The checklist here is arranged by row and card number on the sheets. Player names are as printed, if the photo is not that player it is identified in parentheses. Each of the 66 cards is double-printed on the sheet.

		NM/M
	Complete Sheet (132):	1,500
	Complete Set (66):	900.00
	Common Card:	10.00
1-1	Jon Matlack (Steve Christmas)	10.00
1-2	Wayne Gross (Jose Brito)	10.00
1-3	Mario Mendoza (John Lickert)	10.00
1-4	Mike Heath (Daryl Sconiers)	10.00
1-5	Bump Wills (Lee Mazzilli)	10.00
1-6	Steve McCatty (Jose Rodriguez)	10.00
1-7	Steve Stone	25.00
1-8	No identification (Brian Harper)	10.00
1-9	Dennis Martinez (Cubs player)	15.00
1-10	No identification (Julio Valdez)	10.00
1-11	Jim Palmer (Del Unser)	25.00
2-1	Billy Sample (Bill Doran)	10.00
2-2	Tony Armas (Tony Armas)	10.00
2-3	Rick Honeycutt (Rick Honeycutt)	10.00
2-4	Cliff Jackson (Tim Ireland)	10.00
2-5	John Ellis (Floyd Rayford)	10.00
2-6	Dave McKay (Jim Wright)	10.00
2-7	Ken Singleton (Larry Milbourne)	10.00
2-8	No identification (Steve Balboni)	10.00
2-9	John Lowenstein (Mickey Mahler)	10.00
2-10	No identification (Ty Waller)	10.00
2-11	Doug DeCinces (Mike Patterson)	10.00
3-1	Mickey Rivers (Pat Putnam)	10.00
3-2	Rickey Henderson (Mike Norris)	25.00
3-3	Jim Sundberg (Jim Kern)	10.00
3-4	Bob Owchinko (Fred Stanley)	10.00
3-5	Buddy Bell (Danny Darwin)	10.00
3-6	Shooty Babbitt (Rick Langford)	10.00
3-7	Sammy Stewart (Tippy Martinez)	10.00
3-8	No identification (Juan Eichelberger)	10.00
3-9	Lenn Sakata (Eddie Murray)	25.00
3-10	No identification (Juan Bonilla)	10.00
3-11	Benny Ayala (Terry Crowley)	10.00
4-1	Al Oliver (Bill Stein)	10.00
4-2	Dwayne Murphy (Matt Keough)	10.00
4-3	Leon Roberts (John Grubb)	10.00
4-4	Rob Picciolo (Brian Kingman)	10.00
4-5	Mark Wagner (Steve Comer)	10.00
4-6	Jeff Jones (Jeff Neumann)	10.00
4-7	Tim Stoddard (Mike Flanagan)	10.00
4-8	No identification (John Urrea)	10.00
4-9	Rick Dempsey (Mark Belanger)	10.00
4-10	No identification (Luis Salazar)	10.00
4-11	Dave Ford (Cal Ripken Jr.)	250.00
5-1	Pat Putnam	15.00
5-2	Mike Norris	15.00
5-3	Jim Kern	15.00
5-4	Fred Stanley	15.00
5-5	Danny Darwin	15.00
5-6	Rick Langford	15.00
5-7	Tippy Martinez	15.00
5-8	No identification (Juan Eichelberger)	10.00
5-9	Eddie Murray	30.00
5-10	No identification (Juan Bonilla)	10.00
5-11	Terry Crowley	15.00
6-1	Bill Stein	15.00
6-2	Matt Keough	15.00
6-3	John Grubb	15.00
6-4	Brian Kingman	15.00
6-5	Steve Comer	15.00
6-6	Jeff Neumann	15.00
6-7	Mike Flanagan	15.00
6-8	No identification (John Urrea)	10.00
6-9	Mark Belanger	15.00
6-10	No identification (Luis Salazar)	10.00
6-11	Cal Ripken, Jr.	400.00

Stamps

Issued by Fleer in 1982, this set consists of 242 player stamps, each measuring 1-13/16" x 2-1/2". Originally issued in perforated strips of 10, the full-color stamps are numbered in the lower-left corner and were designed to be placed in an album. Six stamps feature two players each.

		NM/M
	Complete Set (242):	10.00
	Common Player:	.05
	Stamp Album:	1.50
	Wax Pack (10):	.35
	Wax Box (60):	12.50
1	Fernando Valenzuela	.05
2	Rick Monday	.05
3	Ron Cey	.05
4	Dusty Baker	.05
5	Burt Hooton	.05
6	Pedro Guerrero	.05
7	Jerry Reuss	.05
8	Bill Russell	.05
9	Steve Garvey	.15
10	Davey Lopes	.05
11	Tom Seaver	.25
12	George Foster	.05
13	Frank Pastore	.05
14	Dave Collins	.05
15	Dave Concepcion	.05
16	Ken Griffey	.05
17	Johnny Bench	.25
18	Ray Knight	.05
19	Mario Soto	.05
20	Ron Oester	.05
21	Ken Oberkfell	.05
22	Bob Forsch	.05
23	Keith Hernandez	.05
24	Dane Iorg	.05
25	George Hendrick	.05
26	Gene Tenace	.05
27	Garry Templeton	.05
28	Bruce Sutter	.20
29	Darrell Porter	.05
30	Tom Herr	.05
31	Tim Raines	.05
32	Chris Speier	.05
33	Warren Cromartie	.05
34	Larry Parrish	.05
35	Andre Dawson	.25
36	Steve Rogers	.05
37	Jeff Reardon	.05
38	Rodney Scott	.05
39	Gary Carter	.25
40	Scott Sanderson	.05
41	Cesar Cedeno	.05
42	Nolan Ryan	1.00
43	Don Sutton	.20
44	Terry Puhl	.05
45	Joe Niekro	.05
46	Tony Scott	.05
47	Joe Sambito	.05
48	Art Howe	.05
49	Bob Knepper	.05
50	Jose Cruz	.05
51	Pete Rose	.50
52	Dick Ruthven	.05
53	Mike Schmidt	.35
54	Steve Carlton	.25
55	Tug McGraw	.05
56	Larry Bowa	.05
57	Garry Maddox	.05
58	Gary Matthews	.05
59	Manny Trillo	.05
60	Lonnie Smith	.05
61	Vida Blue	.05
62	Milt May	.05
63	Joe Morgan	.25
64	Enos Cabell	.05
65	Jack Clark	.05
66	Claudell Washington	.05
67	Gaylord Perry	.20
68	Phil Niekro	.20
69	Bob Horner	.05
70	Chris Chambliss	.05
71	Dave Parker	.05
72	Tony Pena	.05
73	Kent Tekulve	.05
74	Mike Easler	.05
75	Tim Foli	.05
76	Willie Stargell	.25
77	Bill Madlock	.05
78	Jim Bibby	.05
79	Omar Moreno	.05
80	Lee Lacy	.05
81	Hubie Brooks	.05
82	Rusty Staub	.05
83	Ellis Valentine	.05
84	Neil Allen	.05
85	Dave Kingman	.05
86	Mookie Wilson	.05
87	Doug Flynn	.05
88	Pat Zachry	.05
89	John Stearns	.05
90	Lee Mazzilli	.05
91	Ken Reitz	.05
92	Mike Krukow	.05
93	Jerry Morales	.05
94	Leon Durham	.05
95	Ivan DeJesus	.05
96	Bill Buckner	.05
97	Jim Tracy	.05
98	Steve Henderson	.05
99	Dick Tidrow	.05
100	Mike Tyson	.05
101	Ozzie Smith	.35
102	Ruppert Jones	.05
103	Broderick Perkins	.05
104	Gene Richrds	.05
105	Terry Kennedy	.05
106	Jim Bibby, Willie Stargell	.10
107	Larry Bowa, Pete Rose	.25
108	Warren Spahn, Fernando Valenzuela	.10
109	Dave Concepcion, Pete Rose	.25
110	Reggie Jackson, Dave Winfield	.20
111	Tom Lasorda, Fernando Valenzuela	.20
112	Reggie Jackson	.35
113	Dave Winfield	.25
114	Lou Piniella	.10
115	Tommy John	.10
116	Rich Gossage	.10
117	Ron Davis	.05
118	Rick Cerone	.05
119	Graig Nettles	.05
120	Ron Guidry	.05
121	Willie Randolph	.05
122	Dwayne Murphy	.05
123	Rickey Henderson	.25
124	Wayne Gross	.05
125	Mike Norris	.05
126	Rick Langford	.05
127	Jim Spencer	.05
128	Tony Armas	.05
129	Matt Keough	.05
130	Jeff Jones	.05
131	Steve McCatty	.05
132	Rollie Fingers	.20
133	Jim Gantner	.05
134	Gorman Thomas	.05
135	Robin Yount	.05
136	Paul Molitor	.25
137	Ted Simmons	.05
138	Ben Oglivie	.05
139	Moose Haas	.05
140	Cecil Cooper	.05
141	Pete Vuckovich	.05
142	Doug DeCinces	.05
143	Jim Palmer	.25
144	Steve Stone	.05
145	Mike Flanagan	.05
146	Rick Dempsey	.05
147	Al Bumbry	.05
148	Mark Belanger	.05
149	Scott McGregor	.05
150	Ken Singleton	.05
151	Eddie Murray	.25
152	Lance Parrish	.05
153	David Rozema	.05
154	Champ Summers	.05
155	Alan Trammell	.05
156	Lou Whitaker	.05
157	Milt Wilcox	.05
158	Kevin Saucier	.05
159	Jack Morris	.05
160	Steve Kemp	.05
161	Kirk Gibson	.05
162	Carl Yastrzemski	.25
163	Jim Rice	.05
164	Carney Lansford	.05
165	Dennis Eckersley	.20
166	Mike Torrez	.05
167	Dwight Evans	.05
168	Glenn Hoffman	.05
169	Bob Stanley	.05
170	Tony Perez	.05
171	Jerry Remy	.05
172	Buddy Bell	.05
173	Ferguson Jenkins	.05
174	Mickey Rivers	.05
175	Bump Wills	.05
176	Jon Matlack	.05
177	Steve Comer	.05
178	Al Oliver	.05
179	Bill Stein	.05
180	Pat Putnam	.05
181	Jim Sundberg	.05
182	Ron LeFlore	.05
183	Carlton Fisk	.25
184	Harold Baines	.05
185	Bill Almon	.05
186	Richard Dotson	.05
187	Greg Luzinski	.05
188	Mike Squires	.05
189	Britt Burns	.05
190	Lamarr Hoyt	.05
191	Chet Lemon	.05
192	Joe Charboneau	.10
193	Toby Harrah	.05
194	John Denny	.05
195	Rick Manning	.05
196	Miguel Dilone	.05
197	Bo Diaz	.05
198	Mike Hargrove	.05
199	Bert Blyleven	.05
200	Len Barker	.05
201	Andre Thornton	.05
202	George Brett	.35
203	U.L. Washington	.05
204	Dan Quisenberry	.05
205	Larry Gura	.05
206	Willie Aikens	.05
207	Willie Wilson	.05
208	Dennis Leonard	.05
209	Frank White	.05
210	Hal McRae	.05
211	Amos Otis	.05
212	Don Aase	.05
213	Butch Hobson	.05
214	Fred Lynn	.05
215	Brian Downing	.05
216	Dan Ford	.05
217	Rod Carew	.25
218	Bobby Grich	.05
219	Rick Burleson	.05
220	Don Baylor	.05
221	Ken Forsch	.05
222	Bruce Bochte	.05
223	Richie Zisk	.05
224	Tom Paciorek	.05
225	Julio Cruz	.05
226	Jeff Burroughs	.05
227	Doug Corbett	.05
228	Roy Smalley	.05
229	Gary Ward	.05
230	John Castino	.05
231	Rob Wilfong	.05
232	Dave Stieb	.05
233	Otto Velez	.05
234	Damaso Garcia	.05
235	John Mayberry	.05
236	Alfredo Griffin	.05
237	Ted Williams, Carl Yastrzemski	.50
238	Rick Cerone, Graig Nettles	.05
239	Buddy Bell, George Brett	.15
240	Steve Carlton, Jim Kaat	.10
241	Steve Carlton, Dave Parker	.10
242	Ron Davis, Nolan Ryan	.40

1983 Fleer Promo Sheet

YOU GET MORE WITH FLEER BASEBALL

The consumer, rather than dealer, was the target audience for this sheet premiering '83 Fleer. Six player cards, identical to the issued versions, appear on the 9-5/8" x 7-1/2" sheet, along with advertising messages on front and back. Versions of the sheet can be found with the name of hobby publications which inserted the sample into their issues.

	NM/M
Uncut Sheet:	5.00

1983 Fleer

Reggie Smith — FIRST BASE

The 1983 Fleer set features color photos set inside a light brown border. The cards are standard 2-1/2" x 3-1/2". A team logo is located at the card bottom and the word "Fleer" is found at the top. The card backs are designed on a vertical format and include a small black and white photo of the player along with biographical and statistical information. The reverses are done in two shades of brown on white stock. The set was issued with team logo stickers.

		NM/M
	Complete Set (660):	40.00
	Common Player:	.05
	Wax Pack (15):	3.00
	Wax Box (38):	100.00
	Cello Pack (28):	4.00
	Cello Box (24):	80.00
	Vending Box (500):	35.00
1	Joaquin Andujar	.05
2	Doug Bair	.05
3	Steve Braun	.05
4	Glenn Brummer	.05
5	Bob Forsch	.05
6	David Green	.05
7	George Hendrick	.05
8	Keith Hernandez	.05
9	Tom Herr	.05
10	Dane Iorg	.05
11	Jim Kaat	.10
12	Jeff Lahti	.05
13	Tito Landrum	.05
14	Dave LaPoint RC	.05
15	Willie McGee RC	1.50
16	Steve Mura	.05
17	Ken Oberkfell	.05
18	Darrell Porter	.05
19	Mike Ramsey	.05
20	Gene Roof	.05
21	Lonnie Smith	.05
22	Ozzie Smith	1.50
23	John Stuper	.05
24	Bruce Sutter	.65
25	Gene Tenace	.05
26	Jerry Augustine	.05
27	Dwight Bernard	.05
28	Mark Brouhard	.05
29	Mike Caldwell	.05
30	Cecil Cooper	.05
31	Jamie Easterly	.05
32	Marshall Edwards	.05
33	Rollie Fingers	.65
34	Jim Gantner	.05
35	Moose Haas	.05
36	Roy Howell	.05
37	Peter Ladd	.05
38	Bob McClure	.05
39	Doc Medich	.05
40	Paul Molitor	.75
41	Don Money	.05
42	Charlie Moore	.05
43	Ben Oglivie	.05
44	Ed Romero	.05
45	Ted Simmons	.05
46	Jim Slaton	.05
47	Don Sutton	.65
48	Gorman Thomas	.05
49	Pete Vuckovich	.05
50	Ned Yost	.05
51	Robin Yount	.75
52	Benny Ayala	.05
53	Bob Bonner	.05
54	Al Bumbry	.05
55	Terry Crowley	.05
56	Storm Davis RC	.10
57	Rich Dauer	.05
58	Rick Dempsey	.05
59	Jim Dwyer	.05
60	Mike Flanagan	.05
61	Dan Ford	.05
62	Glenn Gulliver	.05
63	John Lowenstein	.05
64	Dennis Martinez	.05
65	Tippy Martinez	.05
66	Scott McGregor	.05
67	Eddie Murray	.75
68	Joe Nolan	.05
69	Jim Palmer	.75
70	Cal Ripken, Jr.	6.00
71	Gary Roenicke	.05
72	Lenn Sakata	.05
73	Ken Singleton	.05
74	Sammy Stewart	.05
75	Tim Stoddard	.05
76	Don Aase	.05
77	Don Baylor	.05
78	Juan Beniquez	.05
79	Bob Boone	.05
80	Rick Burleson	.05
81	Rod Carew	.75
82	Bobby Clark	.05
83	Doug Corbett	.05
84	John Curtis	.05
85	Doug DeCinces	.05
86	Brian Downing	.05
87	Joe Ferguson	.05
88	Tim Foli	.05
89	Ken Forsch	.05
90	Dave Goltz	.05
91	Bobby Grich	.05
92	Andy Hassler	.05
93	Reggie Jackson	1.50
94	Ron Jackson	.05
95	Tommy John	.10
96	Bruce Kison	.05
97	Fred Lynn	.05
98	Ed Ott	.05
99	Steve Renko	.05
100	Luis Sanchez	.05
101	Rob Wilfong	.05
102	Mike Witt	.05
103	Geoff Zahn	.05
104	Willie Aikens	.05
105	Mike Armstrong	.05
106	Vida Blue	.05
107	Bud Black RC	.50
108	George Brett	2.00
109	Bill Castro	.05
110	Onix Concepcion	.05
111	Dave Frost	.05
112	Cesar Geronimo	.05
113	Larry Gura	.05
114	Steve Hammond	.05
115	Don Hood	.05
116	Dennis Leonard	.05
117	Jerry Martin	.05
118	Lee May	.05
119	Hal McRae	.05
120	Amos Otis	.05
121	Greg Pryor	.05
122	Dan Quisenberry	.05
123	Don Slaught RC	.20
124	Paul Splittorff	.05
125	U.L. Washington	.05
126	John Wathan	.05
127	Frank White	.05
128	Willie Wilson	.05
129	Steve Bedrosian	.05
130	Bruce Benedict	.05
131	Tommy Boggs	.05
132	Brett Butler	.05
133	Rick Camp	.05
134	Chris Chambliss	.05
135	Ken Dayley	.05
136	Gene Garber	.05
137	Terry Harper	.05
138	Bob Horner	.05
139	Glenn Hubbard	.05
140	Rufino Linares	.05
141	Rick Mahler	.05
142	Dale Murphy	.50
143	Phil Niekro	.65
144	Pascual Perez	.05
145	Biff Pocoroba	.05

No.	Player	Price
146	Rafael Ramirez	.05
147	Jerry Royster	.05
148	Ken Smith	.05
149	Bob Walk	.05
150	Claudell Washington	.05
151	Bob Watson	.05
152	Larry Whisenton	.05
153	Porfirio Altamirano	.05
154	Marty Bystrom	.05
155	Steve Carlton	.75
156	Larry Christenson	.05
157	Ivan DeJesus	.05
158	John Denny	.05
159	Bob Dernier	.05
160	Bo Diaz	.05
161	Ed Farmer	.05
162	Greg Gross	.05
163	Mike Krukow	.05
164	Garry Maddox	.05
165	Gary Matthews	.05
166	Tug McGraw	.05
167	Bob Molinaro	.05
168	Sid Monge	.05
169	Ron Reed	.05
170	Bill Robinson	.05
171	Pete Rose	3.00
172	Dick Ruthven	.05
173	Mike Schmidt	2.00
174	Manny Trillo	.05
175	Ozzie Virgil	.05
176	George Vukovich	.05
177	Gary Allenson	.05
178	Luis Aponte	.05
179	Wade Boggs RC	10.00
180	Tom Burgmeier	.05
181	Mark Clear	.05
182	Dennis Eckersley	.65
183	Dwight Evans	.05
184	Rich Gedman	.05
185	Glenn Hoffman	.05
186	Bruce Hurst	.05
187	Carney Lansford	.05
188	Rick Miller	.05
189	Reid Nichols	.05
190	Bob Ojeda	.05
191	Tony Perez	.65
192	Chuck Rainey	.05
193	Jerry Remy	.05
194	Jim Rice	.35
195	Bob Stanley	.05
196	Dave Stapleton	.05
197	Mike Torrez	.05
198	John Tudor	.05
199	Julio Valdez	.05
200	Carl Yastrzemski	.75
201	Dusty Baker	.05
202	Joe Beckwith	.05
203	Greg Brock RC	.05
204	Ron Cey	.05
205	Terry Forster	.05
206	Steve Garvey	.30
207	Pedro Guerrero	.05
208	Burt Hooton	.05
209	Steve Howe	.05
210	Ken Landreaux	.05
211	Mike Marshall	.05
212	Candy Maldonado RC	.05
213	Rick Monday	.05
214	Tom Niedenfuer	.05
215	Jorge Orta	.05
216	Jerry Reuss	.05
217	Ron Roenicke	.05
218	Vicente Romo	.05
219	Bill Russell	.05
220	Steve Sax	.05
221	Mike Scioscia	.05
222	Dave Stewart	.05
223	Derrel Thomas	.05
224	Fernando Valenzuela	.05
225	Bob Welch	.05
226	Ricky Wright	.05
227	Steve Yeager	.05
228	Bill Almon	.05
229	Harold Baines	.05
230	Salome Barojas	.05
231	Tony Bernazard	.05
232	Britt Burns	.05
233	Richard Dotson	.05
234	Ernesto Escarrega	.05
235	Carlton Fisk	.75
236	Jerry Hairston Sr.	.05
237	Kevin Hickey	.05
238	LaMarr Hoyt	.05
239	Steve Kemp	.05
240	Jim Kern	.05
241	Ron Kittle RC	.25
242	Jerry Koosman	.05
243	Dennis Lamp	.05
244	Rudy Law	.05
245	Vance Law	.05
246	Ron LeFlore	.05
247	Greg Luzinski	.05
248	Tom Paciorek	.05
249	Aurelio Rodriguez	.05
250	Mike Squires	.05
251	Steve Trout	.05
252	Jim Barr	.05
253	Dave Bergman	.05
254	Fred Breining	.05
255	Bob Brenly	.05
256	Jack Clark	.05
257	Chili Davis	.05
258	Darrell Evans	.05
259	Alan Fowlkes	.05
260	Rich Gale	.05
261	Atlee Hammaker	.05
262	Al Holland	.05
263	Duane Kuiper	.05
264	Bill Laskey	.05
265	Gary Lavelle	.05
266	Johnnie LeMaster	.05
267	Renie Martin	.05
268	Milt May	.05
269	Greg Minton	.05
270	Joe Morgan	.75
271	Tom O'Malley	.05
272	Reggie Smith	.05
273	Guy Sularz	.05
274	Champ Summers	.05
275	Max Venable	.05
276	Jim Wohlford	.05
277	Ray Burris	.05
278	Gary Carter	.75
279	Warren Cromartie	.05
280	Andre Dawson	.40
281	Terry Francona	.05
282	Doug Flynn	.05
283	Woody Fryman	.05
284	Bill Gullickson	.05
285	Wallace Johnson	.05
286	Charlie Lea	.05
287	Randy Lerch	.05
288	Brad Mills	.05
289	Dan Norman	.05
290	Al Oliver	.05
291	David Palmer	.05
292	Tim Raines	.05
293	Jeff Reardon	.05
294	Steve Rogers	.05
295	Scott Sanderson	.05
296	Dan Schatzeder	.05
297	Bryn Smith	.05
298	Chris Speier	.05
299	Tim Wallach	.05
300	Jerry White	.05
301	Joel Youngblood	.05
302	Ross Baumgarten	.05
303	Dale Berra	.05
304	John Candelaria	.05
305	Dick Davis	.05
306	Mike Easler	.05
307	Richie Hebner	.05
308	Lee Lacy	.05
309	Bill Madlock	.05
310	Larry McWilliams	.05
311	John Milner	.05
312	Omar Moreno	.05
313	Jim Morrison	.05
314	Steve Nicosia	.05
315	Dave Parker	.05
316	Tony Pena	.05
317	Johnny Ray	.05
318	Rick Rhoden	.05
319	Don Robinson	.05
320	Enrique Romo	.05
321	Manny Sarmiento	.05
322	Rod Scurry	.05
323	Jim Smith	.05
324	Willie Stargell	.75
325	Jason Thompson	.05
326	Kent Tekulve	.05
327a	Tom Brookens (Narrow (1/4") brown box at bottom on back.)	.45
327b	Tom Brookens (Wide (1-1/4") brown box at bottom on back.)	.05
328	Enos Cabell	.05
329	Kirk Gibson	.05
330	Larry Herndon	.05
331	Mike Ivie	.05
332	Howard Johnson RC	1.00
333	Lynn Jones	.05
334	Rick Leach	.05
335	Chet Lemon	.05
336	Jack Morris	.05
337	Lance Parrish	.05
338	Larry Pashnick	.05
339	Dan Petry	.05
340	Dave Rozema	.05
341	Dave Rucker	.05
342	Elias Sosa	.05
343	Dave Tobik	.05
344	Alan Trammell	.05
345	Jerry Turner	.05
346	Jerry Ujdur	.05
347	Pat Underwood	.05
348	Lou Whitaker	.05
349	Milt Wilcox	.05
350	Glenn Wilson RC	.05
351	John Wockenfuss	.05
352	Kurt Bevacqua	.05
353	Juan Bonilla	.05
354	Floyd Chiffer	.05
355	Luis DeLeon	.05
356	Dave Dravecky RC	.30
357	Dave Edwards	.05
358	Juan Eichelberger	.05
359	Tim Flannery	.05
360	Tony Gwynn RC	15.00
361	Ruppert Jones	.05
362	Terry Kennedy	.05
363	Joe Lefebvre	.05
364	Sixto Lezcano	.05
365	Tim Lollar	.05
366	Gary Lucas	.05
367	John Montefusco	.05
368	Broderick Perkins	.05
369	Joe Pittman	.05
370	Gene Richards	.05
371	Luis Salazar	.05
372	Eric Show RC	.05
373	Garry Templeton	.05
374	Chris Welsh	.05
375	Alan Wiggins	.05
376	Rick Cerone	.05
377	Dave Collins	.05
378	Roger Erickson	.05
379	George Frazier	.05
380	Oscar Gamble	.05
381	Goose Gossage	.10
382	Ken Griffey	.05
383	Ron Guidry	.10
384	Dave LaRoche	.05
385	Rudy May	.05
386	John Mayberry	.05
387	Lee Mazzilli	.05
388	Mike Morgan	.05
389	Jerry Mumphrey	.05
390	Bobby Murcer	.05
391	Graig Nettles	.10
392	Lou Piniella	.10
393	Willie Randolph	.05
394	Shane Rawley	.05
395	Dave Righetti	.05
396	Andre Robertson	.05
397	Roy Smalley	.05
398	Dave Winfield	.75
399	Butch Wynegar	.05
400	Chris Bando	.05
401	Alan Bannister	.05
402	Len Barker	.05
403	Tom Brennan	.05
404	Carmelo Castillo RC	.05
405	Miguel Dilone	.05
406	Jerry Dybzinski	.05
407	Mike Fischlin	.05
408	Ed Glynn (Photo actually Bud Anderson.)	.05
409	Mike Hargrove	.05
410	Toby Harrah	.05
411	Ron Hassey	.05
412	Von Hayes	.05
413	Rick Manning	.05
414	Bake McBride	.05
415	Larry Milbourne	.05
416	Bill Nahorodny	.05
417	Jack Perconte	.05
418	Larry Sorensen	.05
419	Dan Spillner	.05
420	Rick Sutcliffe	.05
421	Andre Thornton	.05
422	Rick Waits	.05
423	Eddie Whitson	.05
424	Jesse Barfield	.05
425	Barry Bonnell	.05
426	Jim Clancy	.05
427	Damaso Garcia	.05
428	Jerry Garvin	.05
429	Alfredo Griffin	.05
430	Garth Iorg	.05
431	Roy Lee Jackson	.05
432	Luis Leal	.05
433	Buck Martinez	.05
434	Joey McLaughlin	.05
435	Lloyd Moseby	.05
436	Rance Mulliniks	.05
437	Dale Murray	.05
438	Wayne Nordhagen	.05
439	Gene Petralli RC	.05
440	Hosken Powell	.05
441	Dave Stieb	.05
442	Willie Upshaw	.05
443	Ernie Whitt	.05
444	Al Woods	.05
445	Alan Ashby	.05
446	Jose Cruz	.05
447	Kiko Garcia	.05
448	Phil Garner	.05
449	Danny Heep	.05
450	Art Howe	.05
451	Bob Knepper	.05
452	Alan Knicely	.05
453	Ray Knight	.05
454	Frank LaCorte	.05
455	Mike LaCoss	.05
456	Randy Moffitt	.05
457	Joe Niekro	.05
458	Terry Puhl	.05
459	Luis Pujols	.05
460	Craig Reynolds	.05
461	Bert Roberge	.05
462	Vern Ruhle	.05
463	Nolan Ryan	4.00
464	Joe Sambito	.05
465	Tony Scott	.05
466	Dave Smith	.05
467	Harry Spilman	.05
468	Dickie Thon	.05
469	Denny Walling	.05
470	Larry Andersen	.05
471	Floyd Bannister	.05
472	Jim Beattie	.05
473	Bruce Bochte	.05
474	Manny Castillo	.05
475	Bill Caudill	.05
476	Bryan Clark	.05
477	Al Cowens	.05
478	Julio Cruz	.05
479	Todd Cruz	.05
480	Gary Gray	.05
481	Dave Henderson	.05
482	Mike Moore RC	.05
483	Gaylord Perry	.65
484	Dave Revering	.05
485	Joe Simpson	.05
486	Mike Stanton	.05
487	Rick Sweet	.05
488	Ed Vande Berg RC	.05
489	Richie Zisk	.05
490	Doug Bird	.05
491	Larry Bowa	.05
492	Bill Buckner	.05
493	Bill Campbell	.05
494	Jody Davis	.05
495	Leon Durham	.05
496	Steve Henderson	.05
497	Willie Hernandez	.05
498	Fergie Jenkins	.65
499	Jay Johnstone	.05
500	Junior Kennedy	.05
501	Randy Martz	.05
502	Jerry Morales	.05
503	Keith Moreland	.05
504	Dickie Noles	.05
505	Mike Proly	.05
506	Allen Ripley	.05
507	Ryne Sandberg RC	10.00
508	Lee Smith	1.00
509	Pat Tabler	.05
510	Dick Tidrow	.05
511	Bump Wills	.05
512	Gary Woods	.05
513	Tony Armas	.05
514	Dave Beard	.05
515	Jeff Burroughs	.05
516	John D'Acquisto	.05
517	Wayne Gross	.05
518	Mike Heath	.05
519	Rickey Henderson	.75
520	Cliff Johnson	.05
521	Matt Keough	.05
522	Brian Kingman	.05
523	Rick Langford	.05
524	Davey Lopes	.05
525	Steve McCatty	.05
526	Dave McKay	.05
527	Dan Meyer	.05
528	Dwayne Murphy	.05
529	Jeff Newman	.05
530	Mike Norris	.05
531	Bob Owchinko	.05
532	Joe Rudi	.05
533	Jimmy Sexton	.05
534	Fred Stanley	.05
535	Tom Underwood	.05
536	Neil Allen	.05
537	Wally Backman	.05
538	Bob Bailor	.05
539	Hubie Brooks	.05
540	Carlos Diaz	.05
541	Pete Falcone	.05
542	George Foster	.05
543	Ron Gardenhire	.05
544	Brian Giles	.05
545	Ron Hodges	.05
546	Randy Jones	.05
547	Mike Jorgensen	.05
548	Dave Kingman	.05
549	Ed Lynch	.05
550	Jesse Orosco	.05
551	Rick Ownbey	.05
552	Charlie Puleo RC	.05
553	Gary Rajsich	.05
554	Mike Scott	.05
555	Rusty Staub	.05
556	John Stearns	.05
557	Craig Swan	.05
558	Ellis Valentine	.05
559	Tom Veryzer	.05
560	Mookie Wilson	.05
561	Pat Zachry	.05
562	Buddy Bell	.05
563	John Butcher	.05
564	Steve Comer	.05
565	Danny Darwin	.05
566	Bucky Dent	.05
567	John Grubb	.05
568	Rick Honeycutt	.05
569	Dave Hostetler	.05
570	Charlie Hough	.05
571	Lamar Johnson	.05
572	Jon Matlack	.05
573	Paul Mirabella	.05
574	Larry Parrish	.05
575	Mike Richardt	.05
576	Mickey Rivers	.05
577	Billy Sample	.05
578	Dave Schmidt RC	.05
579	Bill Stein	.05
580	Jim Sundberg	.05
581	Frank Tanana	.05
582	Mark Wagner	.05
583	George Wright	.05
584	Johnny Bench	.75
585	Bruce Berenyi	.05
586	Larry Biittner	.05
587	Cesar Cedeno	.05
588	Dave Concepcion	.05
589	Dan Driessen	.05
590	Greg Harris	.05
591	Ben Hayes	.05
592	Paul Householder	.05
593	Tom Hume	.05
594	Wayne Krenchicki	.05
595	Rafael Landestoy	.05
596	Charlie Leibrandt	.05
597	Eddie Milner RC	.05
598	Ron Oester	.05
599	Frank Pastore	.05
600	Joe Price	.05
601	Tom Seaver	.75
602	Bob Shirley	.05
603	Mario Soto	.05
604	Alex Trevino	.05
605	Mike Vail	.05
606	Duane Walker	.05
607	Tom Brunansky	.05
608	Bobby Castillo	.05
609	John Castino	.05
610	Ron Davis	.05
611	Lenny Faedo	.05
612	Terry Felton	.05
613	Gary Gaetti RC	.35
614	Mickey Hatcher	.05
615	Brad Havens	.05
616	Kent Hrbek	.05
617	Randy S. Johnson	.05
618	Tim Laudner	.05
619	Jeff Little	.05
620	Bob Mitchell	.05
621	Jack O'Connor	.05
622	John Pacella	.05
623	Pete Redfern	.05
624	Jesus Vega	.05
625	Frank Viola RC	1.00
626	Ron Washington	.05
627	Gary Ward	.05
628	Al Williams	.05
629	Red Sox All-Stars (Mark Clear, Dennis Eckersley, Carl Yastrzemski)	.25
630	300 Career Wins (Terry Bulling, Gaylord Perry)	.10
631	Pride of Venezuela (Dave Concepcion, Manny Trillo)	.10
632	All-Star Infielders (Buddy Bell, Robin Yount)	.20
633	Mr. Vet & Mr. Rookie (Kent Hrbek, Dave Winfield)	.25
634	Fountain of Youth (Pete Rose, Willie Stargell)	.40
635	Big Chiefs (Toby Harrah, Andre Thornton)	.05
636	"Smith Bros." (Lonnie Smith, Ozzie Smith)	.15
637	Base Stealers' Threat (Gary Carter, Bo Diaz)	.10
638	All-Star Catchers (Gary Carter, Carlton Fisk)	.15
639	Rickey Henderson (In Action)	.50
640	Home Run Threats (Reggie Jackson, Ben Oglivie)	.25
641	Two Teams - Same Day (Joel Youngblood)	.05
642	Last Perfect Game (Len Barker, Ron Hassey)	.05
643	Blue (Vida Blue)	.05
644	Black & (Bud Black)	.05
645	Power (Reggie Jackson)	.30
646	Speed & (Rickey Henderson)	.30
647	Checklist 1-51	.05
648	Checklist 52-103	.05
649	Checklist 104-152	.05
650	Checklist 153-200	.05
651	Checklist 201-251	.05
652	Checklist 252-301	.05
653	Checklist 302-351	.05
654	Checklist 352-399	.05
655	Checklist 400-444	.05
656	Checklist 445-489	.05
657	Checklist 490-535	.05
658	Checklist 536-583	.05
659	Checklist 584-628	.05
660	Checklist 629-646	.05

(checklisted below) and in "Vend-A-Stamp" dispensers of 18 stamps each. Sixteen different dispenser strips were needed to complete the set (strips 1-4 comprise Sheet 1; strips 5-8 comprise Sheet 2; strips 9-12 comprise Sheet 3; and strips 13-16 comprise Sheet 4.) Stamps measure 1-1/4" x 1-13/16".

	NM/M
Complete Sheet Set (4):	5.00
Complete Vend-A-Stamp Set (288):	5.00
Common Sheet:	2.50
Common Stamp Dispenser:	.35
Common Single Stamp:	.01

1	Sheet 1 (A's Logo, Angels Logo, Willie Upshaw, Fernando Valenzuela, U.L. Washington, Bump Wills, Dave Winfield, Robin Yount, Pat Zachry, Astros Logo, Cardinals Logo, Cubs Logo, Dodgers Logo, Expos Logo, Giants Logo, Indians Logo, Mets Logo, Orioles Logo, Phillies Logo, Pirates Logo, Red Sox Logo, Twins Logo, White Sox Logo, Neil Allen, Harold Baines, Buddy Bell, Dale Berra, Wade Boggs, George Brett, Bill Buckner, Jack Clark, Dave Concepcion, Warren Cromar)	2.50
2	Sheet 2 (Angels Logo, Astros Logo, Gorman Thomas, Jason Thompson, Tom Underwood, Mookie Wilson, Willie Wilson, John Wockenfuss, Carl Yastrzemski, Braves Logo, Cardinals Logo, Dodgers Logo, Expos Logo, Indians Logo, Mariners Logo, Mets Logo, Phillies Logo, Pirates Logo, Rangers Logo, Reds Logo, Royals Logo, Tigers Logo, Yankees Logo, Willie Aikens, Bob Bailor, Dusty Baker, Floyd Bannister, Len Barker, Hubie Brooks, Tom Brunansky, Chris Chambliss, Mark Clea)	2.50
3	Sheet 3 (A's Logo, Angels Logo, Blue Jays Logo, Braves Logo, Brewers Logo, Andre Thornton, Manny Trillo, Frank White, Milt Wilcox, John Tudor, Ed Vande Berg, Bob Watson, Dodgers Logo, Giants Logo, Indians Logo, Mariners Logo, Orioles Logo, Padres Logo, Reds Logo, Royals Logo, Tigers Logo, Twins Logo, White Sox Logo, Alan Ashby, Dave Beard, Jim Beattie, Johnny Bench, Larry Biittner, Bob Boone, Rod Carew, Gary Carter, Bobby Castillo, Bill Caudill, Cecil Coo)	2.50
4	Sheet 4 (Blue Jays Logo, Braves logo, Ellis Valentine, Pete Vuckovich, Gary Ward, Claudell Washington, Lou Whitaker, Al Williams, Richie Zisk, Brewers Logo, Cubs Logo, Expos Logo, Giants Logo, Padres Logo, Phillies Logo, Pirates Logo, Rangers Logo, Red Sox Logo, Reds Logo, Royals Logo, Twins Logo, White Sox Logo, Yankees Logo, Joaquin Andujar, Don Baylor, Vida Blue, Bruce Bochte, Larry Bowa, Al Bumbry, Jeff Burroughs, Enos Cabell, Steve Carlton, Cesar Ced)	2.50

Star Stamps

WHAT ATL. BRAVE STARTED AS CATCHER AND IS NOW A NL ALL-STAR OUTFIELDER?

DALE MURPHY OF

The 1983 Fleer Stamp set consists of 288 stamps, including 224 player stamps and 64 team logo stamps. They were originally issued on four different sheets of 72 stamps each

Star Stamps Poster

Available via a wrapper redemption offer, this huge (31-3/4" x 21-3/4") poster is printed in red and blue on glossy white paper stock. Besides blue-tone photos of each stamp, the poster has trivia questions and the logos of each team, league, MLB and the Players Association. Sheets were folded to 9-1/2" x 12-1/2" for mailing.

FLEER'S 1983 BASEBALL STAR STAMPS

NM/M
Star Stamp Poster 10.00

Stickers

ROD CAREW 1B

This 270-sticker set consists of both player stickers and team logo stickers, all measuring 1-13/16" x 2-1/2". The player stickers are numbered on the back. The front features a full-color photo surrounded by a blue border with two stars at the top. The stickers were issued in strips of ten player stickers plus two team logo stickers. The 26 logo stickers have been assigned numbers 271 through 296.

NM/M

Complete Set (296):		10.00
Common Player:		.05
Wax Pack (12):		.30
Wax Box (48):		10.00
1	Bruce Sutter	.20
2	Willie McGee	.05
3	Darrell Porter	.05
4	Lonnie Smith	.05
5	Dane Iorg	.05
6	Keith Hernandez	.05
7	Joaquin Andujar	.05
8	Ken Oberkfell	.05
9	John Stuper	.05
10	Ozzie Smith	.40
11	Bob Forsch	.05
12	Jim Gantner	.05
13	Rollie Fingers	.20
14	Pete Vuckovich	.05
15	Ben Oglivie	.05
16	Don Sutton	.20
17	Bob McClure	.05
18	Robin Yount	.25
19	Paul Molitor	.25
20	Gorman Thomas	.05
21	Mike Caldwell	.05
22	Ted Simmons	.05
23	Cecil Cooper	.05
24	Steve Renko	.05
25	Tommy John	.10
26	Rod Carew	.25
27	Bruce Kison	.05
28	Ken Forsch	.05
29	Geoff Zahn	.05
30	Doug DiCinces	.05
31	Fred Lynn	.05
32	Reggie Jackson	.40
33	Don Baylor	.05
34	Bob Boone	.05
35	Brian Downing	.05
36	Goose Gossage	.05
37	Roy Smalley	.05
38	Graig Nettles	.05
39	Dave Winfield	.25
40	Lee Mazzilli	.05
41	Jerry Mumphrey	.05
42	Dave Collins	.05
43	Rick Cerone	.05
44	Willie Randolph	.05
45	Lou Piniella	.10
46	Ken Griffey	.05
47	Ron Guidry	.05
48	Jack Clark	.05
49	Reggie Smith	.05
50	Atlee Hammaker	.05
51	Fred Breining	.05
52	Gary Lavelle	.05
53	Chili Davis	.05
54	Greg Minton	.05
55	Joe Morgan	.25
56	Al Holland	.05
57	Bill Laskey	.05
58	Duane Kuiper	.05
59	Tom Burgmeier	.05
60	Carl Yastrzemski	.50
61	Mark Clear	.05
62	Mike Torrez	.05
63	Dennis Eckersley	.20
64	Wade Boggs	.50
65	Bob Stanley	.05
66	Jim Rice	.15
67	Carney Lansford	.05
68	Jerry Remy	.05
69	Dwight Evans	.05
70	John Candelaria	.05
71	Bill Madlock	.05
72	Dave Parker	.05
73	Kent Tekulve	.05
74	Tony Pena	.05
75	Manny Sarmiento	.05
76	Johnny Ray	.05
77	Dale Berra	.05
78	Lee Lacy	.05
79	Jason Thompson	.05
80	Mike Easler	.05
81	Willie Stargell	.25
82	Rick Camp	.05
83	Bob Watson	.05
84	Bob Horner	.05
85	Rafael Ramirez	.05
86	Chris Chambliss	.05
87	Gene Garber	.05
88	Claudell Washington	.05
89	Steve Bedrosian	.05
90	Dale Murphy	.15
91	Phil Niekro	.05
92	Jerry Royster	.05
93	Bob Walk	.05
94	Frank White	.05
95	Dennis Leonard	.05
96	Vida Blue	.05
97	U.L. Washington	.05
98	George Brett	.45
99	Amos Otis	.05
100	Dan Quisenberry	.05
101	Willie Aikens	.05
102	Hal McRae	.05
103	Larry Gura	.05
104	Willie Wilson	.05
105	Damaso Garcia	.05
106	Hosken Powell	.05
107	Joey McLaughlin	.05
108	Jim Clancy	.05
109	Barry Bonnell	.05
110	Garth Iorg	.05
111	Dave Stieb	.05
112	Fernando Valenzuela	.05
113	Steve Garvey	.10
114	Rick Monday	.05
115	Burt Hooton	.05
116	Bill Russell	.05
117	Pedro Guerrero	.05
118	Steve Sax	.05
119	Steve Howe	.05
120	Ken Landreaux	.05
121	Dusty Baker	.05
122	Ron Cey	.05
123	Jerry Reuss	.05
124	Bump Wills	.05
125	Keith Moreland	.05
126	Dick Tidrow	.05
127	Bill Campbell	.05
128	Larry Bowa	.05
129	Randy Martz	.05
130	Ferguson Jenkins	.20
131	Leon Durham	.05
132	Bill Buckner	.05
133	Ron Davis	.05
134	Jack O'Connor	.05
135	Kent Hrbek	.05
136	Gary Ward	.05
137	Al Williams	.05
138	Tom Brunansky	.05
139	Bobby Castillo	.05
140	Dusty Baker, Dale Murphy	.10
141	Nolan Ryan	.65
142	Lee Lacy (Lacy), Omar Moreno	.05
143	Al Oliver, Pete Rose	.25
144	Rickey Henderson	.05
145	Ray Knight, Pete Rose, Mike Schmidt	.30
146	Hal McRae, Ben Oglivie	.05
147	Tom Hume, Ray Knight	.05
148	Buddy Bell, Carlton Fisk	.05
149	Steve Kemp	.05
150	Rudy Law	.05
151	Ron LeFlore	.05
152	Jerry Koosman	.05
153	Carlton Fisk	.25
154	Salome Barojas	.05
155	Harold Baines	.05
156	Britt Burns	.05
157	Tom Paciorek	.05
158	Greg Luzinski	.05
159	LaMarr Hoyt	.05
160	George Wright	.05
161	Danny Darwin	.05
162	Lamar Johnson	.05
163	Charlie Hough	.05
164	Buddy Bell	.05
165	John Matlack (Jon)	.05
166	Billy Sample	.05
167	John Grubb	.05
168	Larry Parrish	.05
169	Ivan DeJesus	.05
170	Mike Schmidt	.45
171	Tug McGraw	.05
172	Ron Reed	.05
173	Garry Maddox	.05
174	Pete Rose	.50
175	Manny Trillo	.05
176	Steve Carlton	.25
177	Bo Diaz	.05
178	Gary Matthews	.05
179	Bill Caudill	.05
180	Ed Vande Berg	.05
181	Gaylord Perry	.20
182	Floyd Bannister	.05
183	Richie Zisk	.05
184	Al Cowens	.05
185	Bruce Bochte	.05
186	Jeff Burroughs	.05
187	Dave Beard	.05
188	Davey Lopes	.05
189	Dwayne Murphy	.05
190	Rick Langford	.05
191	Tom Underwood	.05
192	Rickey Henderson	.25
193	Mike Flanagan	.05
194	Scott McGregor	.05
195	Ken Singleton	.05
196	Rich Dauer	.05
197	John Lowenstein	.05
198	Cal Ripken, Jr.	1.00
199	Dennis Martinez	.05
200	Jim Palmer	.25
201	Tippy Martinez	.05
202	Eddie Murray	.25
203	Al Bumbry	.05
204	Dickie Thon	.05
205	Phil Garner	.05
206	Jose Cruz	.05
207	Nolan Ryan	.65
208	Ray Knight	.05
209	Terry Puhl	.05
210	Joe Niekro	.05
211	Art Howe	.05
212	Alan Ashby	.05
213	Tom Hume	.05
214	Johnny Bench	.25
215	Larry Biittner	.05
216	Mario Soto	.05
217	Dan Driessen	.05
218	Tom Seaver	.25
219	Dave Concepcion	.05
220	Wayne Krenchicki	.05
221	Cesar Cedeno	.05
222	Ruppert Jones	.05
223	Terry Kennedy	.05
224	Luis DeLeon	.05
225	Eric Show	.05
226	Tim Flannery	.05
227	Garry Templeton	.05
228	Tim Lollar	.05
229	Sixto Lezcano	.05
230	Bob Bailor	.05
231	Craig Swan	.05
232	Dave Kingman	.05
233	Mookie Wilson	.05
234	John Stearns	.05
235	Ellis Valentine	.05
236	Neil Allen	.05
237	Pat Zachry	.05
238	Rusty Staub	.05
239	George Foster	.05
240	Rick Sutcliffe	.05
241	Andre Thornton	.05
242	Mike Hargrove	.05
243	Dan Spillner	.05
244	Lary Sorensen	.05
245	Len Barker	.05
246	Rick Manning	.05
247	Toby Harrah	.05
248	Milt Wilcox	.05
249	Lou Whitaker	.05
250	Tom Brookens	.05
251	Chet Lemon	.05
252	Jack Morris	.05
253	Alan Trammell	.05
254	John Wockenfuss	.05
255	Lance Parrish	.05
256	Larry Herndon	.05
257	Chris Speier	.05
258	Woody Fryman	.05
259	Scott Sanderson	.05
260	Steve Rogers	.05
261	Warren Cromartie	.05
262	Gary Carter	.25
263	Bill Gullickson	.05
264	Andre Dawson	.15
265	Tim Raines	.05
266	Charlie Lea	.05
267	Jeff Reardon	.05
268	Al Oliver	.05
269	George Hendrick	.05
270	John Montefusco	.05
(271)	A's Logo	.05
(272)	Angels Logo	.05
(273)	Astros Logo	.05
(274)	Blue Jays Logo	.05
(275)	Braves Logo	.05
(276)	Brewers Logo	.05
(277)	Cardinals Logo	.05
(278)	Cubs Logo	.05
(279)	Dodgers Logo	.05
(280)	Expos Logo	.05
(281)	Giants Logo	.05
(282)	Indians Logo	.05
(283)	Mariners Logo	.05
(284)	Mets Logo	.05
(285)	Orioles Logo	.05
(286)	Padres Logo	.05
(287)	Phillies Logo	.05
(288)	Pirates Logo	.05
(289)	Rangers Logo	.05
(290)	Red Sox Logo	.05
(291)	Reds Logo	.05
(292)	Royals Logo	.05
(293)	Tigers Logo	.05
(294)	Twins Logo	.05
(295)	Yankees Logo	.05
(296)	White Sox Logo	.05

1984 Fleer Sample Sheet

Reportedly available only as an insert in a trade magazine for the grocery industry, this full-color 7-7/8" x 10-7/8" sheet is printed on glossy paper rather than cardboard. The full-color front reproduces nine cards from the forthcoming '84 Fleer issue. The black and red back has details of the cards and ordering informartion.

NM/M

Sample Sheet:
George Foster,
Keith Hernandez,
Ron Oester, Charlie Puleo,
Steve Rogers,
Dan Schatzeder,
Bill Scherrer, Bryn Smith,
Darryl Strawberry 10.00

1984 Fleer

Kent Hrbek FIRST BASE

The 1984 Fleer set contained 660 cards for the fourth consecutive year. The 2-1/2" x 3-1/2" cards feature a color photo surrounded by white borders and horizontal dark blue stripes. The top stripe contains the word "Fleer" with the lower carrying the player's name. Backs have a small black-and-white player photo and are done in blue ink on white stock. The set was issued with team logo stickers.

NM/M

Complete Set (660):		40.00
Common Player:		.05
Wax Pack (15):		2.50
Wax Box (36):		75.00
Cello Pack (28):		4.50
Cello Box (24):		85.00
Vending Box (500):		40.00
1	Mike Boddicker RC	.05
2	Al Bumbry	.05
3	Todd Cruz	.05
4	Rich Dauer	.05
5	Storm Davis	.05
6	Rick Dempsey	.05
7	Jim Dwyer	.05
8	Mike Flanagan	.05
9	Dan Ford	.05
10	John Lowenstein	.05
11	Dennis Martinez	.05
12	Tippy Martinez	.05
13	Scott McGregor	.05
14	Eddie Murray	1.00
15	Joe Nolan	.05
16	Jim Palmer	1.00
17	Cal Ripken, Jr.	4.00
18	Gary Roenicke	.05
19	Lenn Sakata	.05
20	John Shelby RC	.05
21	Ken Singleton	.05
22	Sammy Stewart	.05
23	Tim Stoddard	.05
24	Marty Bystrom	.05
25	Steve Carlton	1.00
26	Ivan DeJesus	.05
27	John Denny	.05
28	Bob Dernier	.05
29	Bo Diaz	.05
30	Kiko Garcia	.05
31	Greg Gross	.05
32	Kevin Gross RC	.05
33	Von Hayes	.05
34	Willie Hernandez	.05
35	Al Holland	.05
36	Charles Hudson RC	.05
37	Joe Lefebvre	.05
38	Sixto Lezcano	.05
39	Garry Maddox	.05
40	Gary Matthews	.05
41	Len Matuszek	.05
42	Tug McGraw	.05
43	Joe Morgan	1.00
44	Tony Perez	.75
45	Ron Reed	.05
46	Pete Rose	3.00
47	Juan Samuel RC	.25
48	Mike Schmidt	2.50
49	Ozzie Virgil	.05
50	Juan Agosto RC	.05
51	Harold Baines	.05
52	Floyd Bannister	.05
53	Salome Barojas	.05
54	Britt Burns	.05
55	Julio Cruz	.05
56	Richard Dotson	.05
57	Jerry Dybzinski	.05
58	Carlton Fisk	1.00
59	Scott Fletcher RC	.05
60	Jerry Hairston Sr.	.05
61	Kevin Hickey	.05
62	Marc Hill	.05
63	LaMarr Hoyt	.05
64	Ron Kittle	.05
65	Jerry Koosman	.05
66	Dennis Lamp	.05
67	Rudy Law	.05
68	Vance Law	.05
69	Greg Luzinski	.05
70	Tom Paciorek	.05
71	Mike Squires	.05
72	Dick Tidrow	.05
73	Greg Walker RC	.05
74	Glenn Abbott	.05
75	Howard Bailey	.05
76	Doug Bair	.05
77	Juan Berenguer	.05
78	Tom Brookens	.05
79	Enos Cabell	.05
80	Kirk Gibson	.05
81	John Grubb	.05
82	Larry Herndon	.05
83	Wayne Krenchicki	.05
84	Rick Leach	.05
85	Chet Lemon	.05
86	Aurelio Lopez	.05
87	Jack Morris	.05
88	Lance Parrish	.05
89	Dan Petry	.05
90	Dave Rozema	.05
91	Alan Trammell	.05
92	Lou Whitaker	.05
93	Milt Wilcox	.05
94	Glenn Wilson	.05
95	John Wockenfuss	.05
96	Dusty Baker	.05
97	Joe Beckwith	.05
98	Greg Brock	.05
99	Jack Fimple	.05
100	Pedro Guerrero	.05
101	Rick Honeycutt	.05
102	Burt Hooton	.05
103	Steve Howe	.05
104	Ken Landreaux	.05
105	Mike Marshall	.05
106	Rick Monday	.05
107	Jose Morales	.05
108	Tom Niedenfuer	.05
109	Alejandro Pena RC	.05
110	Jerry Reuss	.05
111	Bill Russell	.05
112	Steve Sax	.05
113	Mike Scioscia	.05
114	Derrel Thomas	.05
115	Fernando Valenzuela	.05
116	Bob Welch	.05
117	Steve Yeager	.05
118	Pat Zachry	.05
119	Don Baylor	.05
120	Bert Campaneris	.05
121	Rick Cerone	.05
122	Ray Fontenot RC	.05
123	George Frazier	.05
124	Oscar Gamble	.05
125	Goose Gossage	.10
126	Ken Griffey	.05
127	Ron Guidry	.10
128	Jay Howell RC	.05
129	Steve Kemp	.05
130	Matt Keough	.05
131	Don Mattingly RC	20.00
132	John Montefusco	.05
133	Omar Moreno	.05
134	Dale Murray	.05
135	Graig Nettles	.05
136	Lou Piniella	.10
137	Willie Randolph	.05
138	Shane Rawley	.05
139	Dave Righetti	.05
140	Andre Robertson	.05
141	Bob Shirley	.05
142	Roy Smalley	.05
143	Dave Winfield	1.00
144	Butch Wynegar	.05
145	Jim Acker RC	.05
146	Doyle Alexander	.05
147	Jesse Barfield	.05
148	George Bell	.05
149	Barry Bonnell	.05
150	Jim Clancy	.05
151	Dave Collins	.05
152	Tony Fernandez RC	.50
153	Damaso Garcia	.05
154	Dave Geisel	.05
155	Jim Gott RC	.05
156	Alfredo Griffin	.05
157	Garth Iorg	.05
158	Roy Lee Jackson	.05
159	Cliff Johnson	.05
160	Luis Leal	.05
161	Buck Martinez	.05
162	Joey McLaughlin	.05
163	Randy Moffitt	.05
164	Lloyd Moseby	.05
165	Rance Mulliniks	.05
166	Jorge Orta	.05
167	Dave Stieb	.05
168	Willie Upshaw	.05
169	Ernie Whitt	.05
170	Len Barker	.05
171	Steve Bedrosian	.05
172	Bruce Benedict	.05
173	Brett Butler	.05
174	Rick Camp	.05
175	Chris Chambliss	.05
176	Ken Dayley	.05
177	Pete Falcone	.05
178	Terry Forster	.05
179	Gene Garber	.05
180	Terry Harper	.05
181	Bob Horner	.05
182	Glenn Hubbard	.05
183	Randy Johnson	.05
184	Craig McMurtry RC	.05
185	Donnie Moore RC	.05
186	Dale Murphy	.60
187	Phil Niekro	.75
188	Pascual Perez	.05
189	Biff Pocoroba	.05
190	Rafael Ramirez	.05
191	Jerry Royster	.05
192	Claudell Washington	.05
193	Bob Watson	.05
194	Jerry Augustine	.05
195	Mark Brouhard	.05
196	Mike Caldwell	.05
197	Tom Candiotti RC	.25
198	Cecil Cooper	.05
199	Rollie Fingers	.75
200	Jim Gantner	.05
201	Bob L. Gibson	.05
202	Moose Haas	.05
203	Roy Howell	.05
204	Pete Ladd	.05
205	Rick Manning	.05
206	Bob McClure	.05
207	Paul Molitor	1.00
208	Don Money	.05
209	Charlie Moore	.05
210	Ben Oglivie	.05
211	Chuck Porter	.05
212	Ed Romero	.05
213	Ted Simmons	.05
214	Jim Slaton	.05
215	Don Sutton	.75
216	Tom Tellmann	.05
217	Pete Vuckovich	.05
218	Ned Yost	.05
219	Robin Yount	1.00
220	Alan Ashby	.05
221	Kevin Bass RC	.05
222	Jose Cruz	.05
223	Bill Dawley RC	.05
224	Frank DiPino	.05
225	Bill Doran RC	.05
226	Phil Garner	.05
227	Art Howe	.05
228	Bob Knepper	.05
229	Ray Knight	.05
230	Frank LaCorte	.05
231	Mike LaCoss	.05
232	Mike Madden	.05
233	Jerry Mumphrey	.05
234	Joe Niekro	.05
235	Terry Puhl	.05
236	Luis Pujols	.05
237	Craig Reynolds	.05
238	Vern Ruhle	.05
239	Nolan Ryan	4.00
240	Mike Scott	.05
241	Tony Scott	.05
242	Dave Smith	.05
243	Dickie Thon	.05
244	Denny Walling	.05
245	Dale Berra	.05
246	Jim Bibby	.05
247	John Candelaria	.05
248	Jose DeLeon RC	.05
249	Mike Easler	.05

No.	Player	Price
250	Cecilio Guante RC	.05
251	Richie Hebner	.05
252	Lee Lacy	.05
253	Bill Madlock	.05
254	Milt May	.05
255	Lee Mazzilli	.05
256	Larry McWilliams	.05
257	Jim Morrison	.05
258	Dave Parker	.05
259	Tony Pena	.05
260	Johnny Ray	.05
261	Rick Rhoden	.05
262	Don Robinson	.05
263	Manny Sarmiento	.05
264	Rod Scurry	.05
265	Kent Tekulve	.05
266	Gene Tenace	.05
267	Jason Thompson	.05
268	Lee Tunnell RC	.05
269	Marvell Wynne RC	.05
270	Ray Burris	.05
271	Gary Carter	1.00
272	Warren Cromartie	.05
273	Andre Dawson	.25
274	Doug Flynn	.05
275	Terry Francona	.05
276	Bill Gullickson	.05
277	Bob James	.05
278	Charlie Lea	.05
279	Bryan Little	.05
280	Al Oliver	.05
281	Tim Raines	.05
282	Bobby Ramos	.05
283	Jeff Reardon	.05
284	Steve Rogers	.05
285	Scott Sanderson	.05
286	Dan Schatzeder	.05
287	Bryn Smith	.05
288	Chris Speier	.05
289	Manny Trillo	.05
290	Mike Vail	.05
291	Tim Wallach	.05
292	Chris Welsh	.05
293	Jim Wohlford	.05
294	Kurt Bevacqua	.05
295	Juan Bonilla	.05
296	Bobby Brown	.05
297	Luis DeLeon	.05
298	Dave Dravecky	.05
299	Tim Flannery	.05
300	Steve Garvey	.25
301	Tony Gwynn	2.00
302	Andy Hawkins RC	.10
303	Ruppert Jones	.05
304	Terry Kennedy	.05
305	Tim Lollar	.05
306	Gary Lucas	.05
307	Kevin McReynolds RC	.25
308	Sid Monge	.05
309	Mario Ramirez	.05
310	Gene Richards	.05
311	Luis Salazar	.05
312	Eric Show	.05
313	Elias Sosa	.05
314	Garry Templeton	.05
315	Mark Thurmond RC	.05
316	Ed Whitson	.05
317	Alan Wiggins	.05
318	Neil Allen	.05
319	Joaquin Andujar	.05
320	Steve Braun	.05
321	Glenn Brummer	.05
322	Bob Forsch	.05
323	David Green	.05
324	George Hendrick	.05
325	Tom Herr	.05
326	Dane Iorg	.05
327	Jeff Lahti	.05
328	Dave LaPoint	.05
329	Willie McGee	.05
330	Ken Oberkfell	.05
331	Darrell Porter	.05
332	Jamie Quirk	.05
333	Mike Ramsey	.05
334	Floyd Rayford	.05
335	Lonnie Smith	.05
336	Ozzie Smith	2.00
337	John Stuper	.05
338	Bruce Sutter	.75
339	Andy Van Slyke RC	1.00
340	Dave Von Ohlen	.05
341	Willie Aikens	.05
342	Mike Armstrong	.05
343	Bud Black	.05
344	George Brett	2.50
345	Onix Concepcion	.05
346	Keith Creel	.05
347	Larry Gura	.05
348	Don Hood	.05
349	Dennis Leonard	.05
350	Hal McRae	.05
351	Amos Otis	.05
352	Gaylord Perry	.75
353	Greg Pryor	.05
354	Dan Quisenberry	.05
355	Steve Renko	.05
356	Leon Roberts	.05
357	Pat Sheridan RC	.05
358	Joe Simpson	.05
359	Don Slaught	.05
360	Paul Splittorff	.05
361	U.L. Washington	.05
362	John Wathan	.05
363	Frank White	.05
364	Willie Wilson	.05
365	Jim Barr	.05
366	Dave Bergman	.05
367	Fred Breining	.05
368	Bob Brenly	.05
369	Jack Clark	.05
370	Chili Davis	.05
371	Mark Davis RC	.05
372	Darrell Evans	.05
373	Atlee Hammaker	.05
374	Mike Krukow	.05
375	Duane Kuiper	.05
376	Bill Laskey	.05
377	Gary Lavelle	.05
378	Johnnie LeMaster	.05
379	Jeff Leonard	.05
380	Randy Lerch	.05
381	Renie Martin	.05
382	Andy McGaffigan	.05
383	Greg Minton	.05
384	Tom O'Malley	.05
385	Max Venable	.05
386	Brad Wellman	.05
387	Joel Youngblood	.05
388	Gary Allenson	.05
389	Luis Aponte	.05
390	Tony Armas	.05
391	Doug Bird	.05
392	Wade Boggs	2.00
393	Dennis Boyd RC	.05
394	Mike Brown	.05
395	Mark Clear	.05
396	Dennis Eckersley	.75
397	Dwight Evans	.05
398	Rich Gedman	.05
399	Glenn Hoffman	.05
400	Bruce Hurst	.05
401	John Henry Johnson	.05
402	Ed Jurak	.05
403	Rick Miller	.05
404	Jeff Newman	.05
405	Reid Nichols	.05
406	Bob Ojeda	.05
407	Jerry Remy	.05
408	Jim Rice	.05
409	Bob Stanley	.05
410	Dave Stapleton	.05
411	John Tudor	.05
412	Carl Yastrzemski	1.50
413	Buddy Bell	.05
414	Larry Biittner	.05
415	John Butcher	.05
416	Danny Darwin	.05
417	Bucky Dent	.05
418	Dave Hostetler	.05
419	Charlie Hough	.05
420	Bobby Johnson	.05
421	Odell Jones	.05
422	Jon Matlack	.05
423	Pete O'Brien RC	.05
424	Larry Parrish	.05
425	Mickey Rivers	.05
426	Billy Sample	.05
427	Dave Schmidt	.05
428	Mike Smithson RC	.05
429	Bill Stein	.05
430	Dave Stewart	.05
431	Jim Sundberg	.05
432	Frank Tanana	.05
433	Dave Tobik	.05
434	Wayne Tolleson RC	.05
435	George Wright	.05
436	Bill Almon	.05
437	Keith Atherton RC	.05
438	Dave Beard	.05
439	Tom Burgmeier	.05
440	Jeff Burroughs	.05
441	Chris Codiroli RC	.05
442	Tim Conroy RC	.05
443	Mike Davis	.05
444	Wayne Gross	.05
445	Garry Hancock	.05
446	Mike Heath	.05
447	Rickey Henderson	1.00
448	Don Hill RC	.05
449	Bob Kearney	.05
450	Bill Krueger	.05
451	Rick Langford	.05
452	Carney Lansford	.05
453	Davey Lopes	.05
454	Steve McCatty	.05
455	Dan Meyer	.05
456	Dwayne Murphy	.05
457	Mike Norris	.05
458	Ricky Peters	.05
459	Tony Phillips	.05
460	Tom Underwood	.05
461	Mike Warren	.05
462	Johnny Bench	1.50
463	Bruce Berenyi	.05
464	Dann Bilardello	.05
465	Cesar Cedeno	.05
466	Dave Concepcion	.05
467	Dan Driessen	.05
468	Nick Esasky RC	.05
469	Rich Gale	.05
470	Ben Hayes	.05
471	Paul Householder	.05
472	Tom Hume	.05
473	Alan Knicely	.05
474	Eddie Milner	.05
475	Ron Oester	.05
476	Kelly Paris	.05
477	Frank Pastore	.05
478	Ted Power	.05
479	Joe Price	.05
480	Charlie Puleo	.05
481	Gary Redus RC	.05
482	Bill Scherrer	.05
483	Mario Soto	.05
484	Alex Trevino	.05
485	Duane Walker	.05
486	Larry Bowa	.05
487	Warren Brusstar	.05
488	Bill Buckner	.05
489	Bill Campbell	.05
490	Ron Cey	.05
491	Jody Davis	.05
492	Leon Durham	.05
493	Mel Hall RC	.05
494	Fergie Jenkins	.75
495	Jay Johnstone	.05
496	Craig Lefferts RC	.10
497	Carmelo Martinez RC	.05
498	Jerry Morales	.05
499	Keith Moreland	.05
500	Dickie Noles	.05
501	Mike Proly	.05
502	Chuck Rainey	.05
503	Dick Ruthven	.05
504	Ryne Sandberg	2.00
505	Lee Smith	.05
506	Steve Trout	.05
507	Gary Woods	.05
508	Juan Beniquez	.05
509	Bob Boone	.05
510	Rick Burleson	.05
511	Rod Carew	1.00
512	Bobby Clark	.05
513	John Curtis	.05
514	Doug DeCinces	.10
515	Brian Downing	.05
516	Tim Foli	.05
517	Ken Forsch	.05
518	Bobby Grich	.05
519	Andy Hassler	.05
520	Reggie Jackson	1.50
521	Ron Jackson	.05
522	Tommy John	.10
523	Bruce Kison	.05
524	Steve Lubratich	.05
525	Fred Lynn	.05
526	Gary Pettis RC	.05
527	Luis Sanchez	.05
528	Daryl Sconiers	.05
529	Ellis Valentine	.05
530	Rob Wilfong	.05
531	Mike Witt	.05
532	Geoff Zahn	.05
533	Bud Anderson	.05
534	Chris Bando	.05
535	Alan Bannister	.05
536	Bert Blyleven	.10
537	Tom Brennan	.05
538	Jamie Easterly	.05
539	Juan Eichelberger	.05
540	Jim Essian	.05
541	Mike Fischlin	.05
542	Julio Franco	.05
543	Mike Hargrove	.05
544	Toby Harrah	.05
545	Ron Hassey	.05
546	Neal Heaton RC	.05
547	Bake McBride	.05
548	Broderick Perkins	.05
549	Lary Sorensen	.05
550	Dan Spillner	.05
551	Rick Sutcliffe	.05
552	Pat Tabler	.05
553	Gorman Thomas	.05
554	Andre Thornton	.05
555	George Vukovich	.05
556	Darrell Brown	.05
557	Tom Brunansky	.05
558	Randy Bush RC	.05
559	Bobby Castillo	.05
560	John Castino	.05
561	Ron Davis	.05
562	Dave Engle	.05
563	Lenny Faedo	.05
564	Pete Filson	.05
565	Gary Gaetti	.05
566	Mickey Hatcher	.05
567	Kent Hrbek	.05
568	Rusty Kuntz	.05
569	Tim Laudner	.05
570	Rick Lysander	.05
571	Bobby Mitchell	.05
572	Ken Schrom	.05
573	Ray Smith	.05
574	Tim Teufel RC	.05
575	Frank Viola	.05
576	Gary Ward	.05
577	Ron Washington	.05
578	Len Whitehouse	.05
579	Al Williams	.05
580	Bob Bailor	.05
581	Mark Bradley	.05
582	Hubie Brooks	.05
583	Carlos Diaz	.05
584	George Foster	.05
585	Brian Giles	.05
586	Danny Heep	.05
587	Keith Hernandez	.05
588	Ron Hodges	.05
589	Scott Holman	.05
590	Dave Kingman	.05
591	Ed Lynch	.05
592	Jose Oquendo RC	.05
593	Jesse Orosco	.05
594	Junior Ortiz RC	.05
595	Tom Seaver	1.00
596	Doug Sisk RC	.05
597	Rusty Staub	.05
598	John Stearns	.05
599	Darryl Strawberry	.25
600	Craig Swan	.05
601	Walt Terrell RC	.05
602	Mike Torrez	.05
603	Mookie Wilson	.05

Brett Butler — OUTFIELD — CLEVELAND INDIANS

No.	Player	Price
604	Jamie Allen	.05
605	Jim Beattie	.05
606	Tony Bernazard	.05
607	Manny Castillo	.05
608	Bill Caudill	.05
609	Bryan Clark	.05
610	Al Cowens	.05
611	Dave Henderson	.05
612	Steve Henderson	.05
613	Orlando Mercado	.05
614	Mike Moore	.05
615	Ricky Nelson	.05
616	Spike Owen RC	.10
617	Pat Putnam	.05
618	Ron Roenicke	.05
619	Mike Stanton	.05
620	Bob Stoddard	.05
621	Rick Sweet	.05
622	Roy Thomas	.05
623	Ed Vande Berg	.05
624	Matt Young RC	.05
625	Richie Zisk	.05
626	'83 All-Star Game Record Breaker (Fred Lynn)	.05
627	'83 All-Star Game Record Breaker (Manny Trillo)	.05
628	N.L. Iron Man (Steve Garvey)	.10
629	A.L. Batting Runner-Up (Rod Carew)	.15
630	A.L. Batting Champion (Wade Boggs)	.50
631	Letting Go Of The Raines (Tim Raines)	.10
632	Double Trouble (Al Oliver)	.05
633	All-Star Second Base (Steve Sax)	.05
634	All-Star Shortstop (Dickie Thon)	.05
635	Ace Firemen (Tippy Martinez, Dan Quisenberry)	.05
636	Reds Reunited (Joe Morgan, Tony Perez, Pete Rose)	.75
637	Backstop Stars (Bob Boone, Lance Parrish)	.05
638	The Pine Tar Incident, 7/24/83 (George Brett, Gaylord Perry)	.25
639	1983 No-Hitters (Bob Forsch, Dave Righetti, Mike Warren)	.05
640	Retiring Superstars (Johnny Bench, Carl Yastrzemski)	.50
641	Going Out In Style (Gaylord Perry)	.05
642	300 Club & Strikeout Record (Steve Carlton)	.10
643	The Managers (Joe Altobelli, Paul Owens)	.05
644	The MVP (Rick Dempsey)	.05
645	The Rookie Winner (Mike Boddicker)	.05
646	The Clincher (Scott McGregor)	.05
647	Checklist: Orioles/Royals (Joe Altobelli)	.05
648	Checklist: Phillies/Giants (Paul Owens)	.05
649	Checklist: White Sox/Red Sox (Tony LaRussa)	.05
650	Checklist: Tigers/Rangers (Sparky Anderson)	.10
651	Checklist: Dodgers/A's (Tommy Lasorda)	.10
652	Checklist: Yankees/Reds (Billy Martin)	.05
653	Checklist: Blue Jays/Cubs (Bobby Cox)	.10
654	Checklist: Braves/Angels (Joe Torre)	.10
655	Checklist: Brewers/Indians (Rene Lacheman)	.05
656	Checklist: Astros/Twins (Bob Lillis)	.05
657	Checklist: Pirates/Mets (Chuck Tanner)	.05
658	Checklist: Expos/Mariners (Bill Virdon)	.05
659	Checklist: Padres/Specials (Dick Williams)	.05
660	Checklist: Cardinals/Specials (Whitey Herzog)	.05

Update

Following the lead of Topps, Fleer issued near the end of the baseball season a 132-card set to update player trades and include rookies not depicted in the regular issue. The cards are identical in design to the regular issue but are numbered U-1 through U-132. Available only as a boxed set through hobby dealers, the set was printed in limited quantities. Sets were not factory sealed.

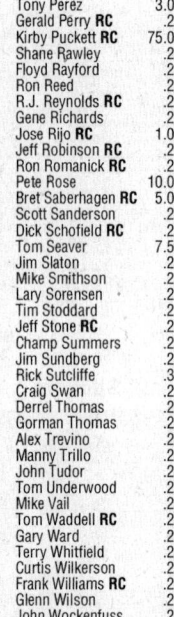

No.	Player	NM/M
Complete Set (132):		300.00
Common Player:		.25
1	Willie Aikens	.25
2	Luis Aponte	.25
3	Mark Bailey RC	.25
4	Bob Bailor	.25
5	Dusty Baker	.25
6	Steve Balboni RC	.25
7	Alan Bannister	.25
8	Marty Barrett RC	.25
9	Dave Beard	.25
10	Joe Beckwith	.25
11	Dave Bergman	.25
12	Tony Bernazard	.25
13	Bruce Bochte	.25
14	Barry Bonnell	.25
15	Phil Bradley RC	.25
16	Fred Breining	.25
17	Mike Brown	.25
18	Bill Buckner	.25
19	Ray Burris	.25
20	John Butcher	.25
21	Brett Butler	.25
22	Enos Cabell	.25
23	Bill Campbell	.25
24	Bill Caudill	.25
25	Bobby Clark	.25
26	Bryan Clark	.25
27	Roger Clemens RC	250.00
28	Jaime Cocanower	.25
29	Ron Darling RC	1.00
30	Alvin Davis RC	.25
31	Bob Dernier	.25
32	Carlos Diaz	.25
33	Mike Easler	.25
34	Dennis Eckersley	4.00
35	Jim Essian	.25
36	Darrell Evans	.25
37	Mike Fitzgerald RC	.25
38	Tim Foli	.25
39	John Franco RC	3.00
40	George Frazier	.25
41	Rich Gale	.25
42	Barbaro Garbey	.25
43	Dwight Gooden RC	7.50
44	Goose Gossage	.40
45	Wayne Gross	.25
46	Mark Gubicza RC	1.00
47	Jackie Gutierrez	.25
48	Toby Harrah	.25
49	Ron Hassey	.25
50	Richie Hebner	.25
51	Willie Hernandez	.25
52	Ed Hodge	.25
53	Ricky Horton RC	.25
54	Art Howe	.25
55	Dane Iorg	.25
56	Brook Jacoby RC	.25
57	Dion James RC	.25
58	Mike Jeffcoat RC	.25
59	Ruppert Jones	.25
60	Bob Kearney	.25
61	Jimmy Key RC	1.00
62	Dave Kingman	.25
63	Brad Komminsk RC	.25
64	Jerry Koosman	.25
65	Wayne Krenchicki	.25
66	Rusty Kuntz	.25
67	Frank LaCorte	.25
68	Dennis Lamp	.25
69	Tito Landrum	.25
70	Mark Langston RC	4.00
71	Rick Leach	.25
72	Craig Lefferts RC	.25
73	Gary Lucas	.25
74	Jerry Martin	.25
75	Carmelo Martinez	.25
76	Mike Mason RC	.25
77	Gary Matthews	.25
78	Andy McGaffigan	.25
79	Joey McLaughlin	.25
80	Joe Morgan	5.00
81	Darryl Motley	.25
82	Graig Nettles	.40
83	Phil Niekro	3.00
84	Ken Oberkfell	.25
85	Al Oliver	.25
86	Jorge Orta	.25
87	Amos Otis	.25
88	Bob Owchinko	.25
89	Dave Parker	.25
90	Jack Perconte	.25
91	Tony Perez	3.00
92	Gerald Perry RC	.25
93	Kirby Puckett RC	75.00
94	Shane Rawley	.25
95	Floyd Rayford	.25
96	Ron Reed	.25
97	R.J. Reynolds RC	.25
98	Gene Richards	.25
99	Jose Rijo RC	1.00
100	Jeff Robinson RC	.25
101	Ron Romanick RC	.25
102	Pete Rose	10.00
103	Bret Saberhagen RC	5.00
104	Scott Sanderson	.25
105	Dick Schofield RC	.25
106	Tom Seaver	7.50
107	Jim Slaton	.25
108	Mike Smithson	.25
109	Lary Sorensen	.25
110	Tim Stoddard	.25
111	Jeff Stone RC	.25
112	Champ Summers	.25
113	Jim Sundberg	.25
114	Rick Sutcliffe	.35
115	Craig Swan	.25
116	Derrel Thomas	.25
117	Gorman Thomas	.25
118	Alex Trevino	.25
119	Manny Trillo	.25
120	John Tudor	.25
121	Tom Underwood	.25
122	Mike Vail	.25
123	Tom Waddell RC	.25
124	Gary Ward	.25
125	Terry Whitfield	.25
126	Curtis Wilkerson	.25
127	Frank Williams RC	.25
128	Glenn Wilson	.25
129	John Wockenfuss	.25
130	Ned Yost	.25
131	Mike Young RC	.25
132	Checklist 1-132	.10

Stickers

This set was designed to be housed in a special collector's album that was organized according to various league leader categories, resulting in some players being pictured on more than one sticker. Each full-color sticker measures 1-15/16" x 2-1/2" and is framed with a beige border. The stickers, which were sold in packs of six, are numbered on the back.

No.	Player	NM/M
Complete Set (126):		9.00
Common Player:		.05
Sticker Album:		1.00
Wax Box (100):		12.00
1	Dickie Thon	.05
2	Ken Landreaux	.05
3	Darrell Evans	.05
4	Harold Baines	.25
5	Dave Winfield	.25
6	Bill Madlock	.05
7	Lonnie Smith	.05
8	Jose Cruz	.05
9	George Hendrick	.05
10	Ray Knight	.05
11	Wade Boggs	.30
12	Rod Carew	.25
13	Lou Whitaker	.05
14	Alan Trammell	.05
15	Cal Ripken, Jr.	.50
16	Mike Schmidt	.40
17	Dale Murphy	.40
18	Andre Dawson	.15
19	Pedro Guerrero	.05
20	Jim Rice	.15
21	Tony Armas	.05
22	Ron Kittle	.05
23	Eddie Murray	.25
24	Jose Cruz	.05
25	Andre Dawson	.15
26	Rafael Ramirez	.05
27	Al Oliver	.05
28	Wade Boggs	.30
29	Cal Ripken, Jr.	.50
30	Lou Whitaker	.05
31	Cecil Cooper	.05
32	Dale Murphy	.20
33	Andre Dawson	.15
34	Pedro Guerrero	.05

#	Player	Price
35	Mike Schmidt	.40
36	George Brett	.40
37	Jim Rice	.15
38	Eddie Murray	.25
39	Carlton Fisk	.25
40	Rusty Staub	.05
41	Duane Walker	.05
42	Steve Braun	.05
43	Kurt Bevacqua	.05
44	Hal McRae	.05
45	Don Baylor	.05
46	Ken Singleton	.05
47	Greg Luzinski	.05
48	Mike Schmidt	.40
49	Keith Hernandez	.05
50	Dale Murphy	.20
51	Tim Raines	.05
52	Wade Boggs	.30
53	Rickey Henderson	.25
54	Rod Carew	.25
55	Ken Singleton	.05
56	John Denny	.05
57	John Candelaria	.05
58	Larry McWilliams	.05
59	Pascual Perez	.05
60	Jesse Orosco	.05
61	Moose Haas	.05
62	Richard Dotson	.05
63	Mike Flanagan	.05
64	Scott McGregor	.05
65	Atlee Hammaker	.05
66	Rick Honeycutt	.05
67	Lee Smith	.05
68	Al Holland	.05
69	Greg Minton	.05
70	Bruce Sutter	.20
71	Jeff Reardon	.05
72	Frank DiPino	.05
73	Dan Quisenberry	.05
74	Bob Stanley	.05
75	Ron Davis	.05
76	Bill Caudill	.05
77	Peter Ladd	.05
78	Steve Carlton	.25
79	Mario Soto	.05
80	Larry McWilliams	.05
81	Fernando Valenzuela	.05
82	Nolan Ryan	.75
83	Jack Morris	.05
84	Floyd Bannister	.05
85	Dave Stieb	.05
86	Dave Righetti	.05
87	Rick Sutcliffe	.05
88	Tim Raines	.05
89	Alan Wiggins	.05
90	Steve Sax	.05
91	Mookie Wilson	.05
92	Rickey Henderson	.25
93	Rudy Law	.05
94	Willie Wilson	.05
95	Julio Cruz	.05
96	Johnny Bench	.30
97	Carl Yastrzemski	.25
98	Gaylord Perry	.15
99	Pete Rose	.45
100	Joe Morgan	.25
101	Steve Carlton	.25
102	Jim Palmer	.25
103	Rod Carew	.25
104	Darryl Strawberry	.20
105	Craig McMurtry	.05
106	Mel Hall	.05
107	Lee Tunnell	.05
108	Bill Dawley	.05
109	Ron Kittle	.05
110	Mike Boddicker	.05
111	Julio Franco	.05
112	Daryl Sconiers	.05
113	Neal Heaton	.05
114	John Shelby	.05
115	Rick Dempsey	.05
116	John Lowenstein	.05
117	Jim Dwyer	.05
118	Bo Diaz	.05
119	Pete Rose	.45
120	Joe Morgan	.25
121	Gary Matthews	.05
122	Garry Maddox	.05
123	Paul Owens	.05
124	Tom Lasorda	.05
125	Joe Altobelli	.05
126	Tony LaRussa	.05

1985 Fleer

The 1985 Fleer set consists of 660 cards, each measuring 2-1/2" x 3-1/2". Card fronts feature a color photo plus the player's team logo and the word "Fleer." The photos have a color-coded frame which corresponds to the player's team. A grey border surrounds the frame. Backs are similar in design to previous years, but have two shades of red and black ink on white stock. For the fourth consecutive year, Fleer included special cards and team checklists in the set. Also incorporated in a set for the first time were ten "Major League Prospect" cards, each featuring two rookie hopefuls. The set was issued with team logo stickers.

	NM/M
Unopened Factory Set (660):	50.00
Complete Set (660):	40.00
Common Player:	.05
Wax Pack (15):	4.50
Wax Box (36):	150.00
Cello Pack (28):	6.00
Cello Box (24):	150.00
Rack Pack (45):	8.00
Vending Box (500):	35.00

#	Player	Price
1	Doug Bair	.05
2	Juan Berenguer	.05
3	Dave Bergman	.05
4	Tom Brookens	.05
5	Marty Castillo	.05
6	Darrell Evans	.05
7	Barbaro Garbey	.05
8	Kirk Gibson	.05
9	John Grubb	.05
10	Willie Hernandez	.05
11	Larry Herndon	.05
12	Howard Johnson	.05
13	Ruppert Jones	.05
14	Rusty Kuntz	.05
15	Chet Lemon	.05
16	Aurelio Lopez	.05
17	Sid Monge	.05
18	Jack Morris	.05
19	Lance Parrish	.05
20	Dan Petry	.05
21	Dave Rozema	.05
22	Bill Scherrer	.05
23	Alan Trammell	.05
24	Lou Whitaker	.05
25	Milt Wilcox	.05
26	Kurt Bevacqua	.05
27	Greg Booker RC	.05
28	Bobby Brown	.05
29	Luis DeLeon	.05
30	Dave Dravecky	.05
31	Tim Flannery	.05
32	Steve Garvey	.40
33	Goose Gossage	.10
34	Tony Gwynn	2.00
35	Greg Harris	.05
36	Andy Hawkins	.05
37	Terry Kennedy	.05
38	Craig Lefferts	.05
39	Tim Lollar	.05
40	Carmelo Martinez	.05
41	Kevin McReynolds	.05
42	Graig Nettles	.05
43	Luis Salazar	.05
44	Eric Show	.05
45	Garry Templeton	.05
46	Mark Thurmond	.05
47	Ed Whitson	.05
48	Alan Wiggins	.05
49	Rich Bordi	.05
50	Larry Bowa	.05
51	Warren Brusstar	.05
52	Ron Cey	.05
53	Henry Cotto RC	.05
54	Jody Davis	.05
55	Bob Dernier	.05
56	Leon Durham	.05
57	Dennis Eckersley	.75
58	George Frazier	.05
59	Richie Hebner	.05
60	Dave Lopes	.05
61	Gary Matthews	.05
62	Keith Moreland	.05
63	Rick Reuschel	.05
64	Dick Ruthven	.05
65	Ryne Sandberg	2.00
66	Scott Sanderson	.05
67	Lee Smith	.05
68	Tim Stoddard	.05
69	Rick Sutcliffe	.05
70	Steve Trout	.05
71	Gary Woods	.05
72	Wally Backman	.05
73	Bruce Berenyi	.05
74	Hubie Brooks	.05
75	Kelvin Chapman	.05
76	Ron Darling	.05
77	Sid Fernandez RC	.05
78	Mike Fitzgerald	.05
79	George Foster	.05
80	Brent Gaff	.05
81	Ron Gardenhire	.05
82	Dwight Gooden	.50
83	Tom Gorman	.05
84	Danny Heep	.05
85	Keith Hernandez	.05
86	Ray Knight	.05
87	Ed Lynch	.05
88	Jose Oquendo	.05
89	Jesse Orosco	.05
90	Rafael Santana RC	.05
91	Doug Sisk	.05
92	Rusty Staub	.05
93	Darryl Strawberry	.10
94	Walt Terrell	.05
95	Mookie Wilson	.05
96	Jim Acker	.05
97	Willie Aikens	.05
98	Doyle Alexander	.05
99	Jesse Barfield	.05
100	George Bell	.05
101	Jim Clancy	.05
102	Dave Collins	.05
103	Tony Fernandez	.05
104	Damaso Garcia	.05
105	Jim Gott	.05
106	Alfredo Griffin	.05
107	Garth Iorg	.05
108	Roy Lee Jackson	.05
109	Cliff Johnson	.05
110	Jimmy Key	.05
111	Dennis Lamp	.05
112	Rick Leach	.05
113	Luis Leal	.05
114	Buck Martinez	.05
115	Lloyd Moseby	.05
116	Rance Mulliniks	.05
117	Dave Stieb	.05
118	Willie Upshaw	.05
119	Ernie Whitt	.05
120	Mike Armstrong	.05
121	Don Baylor	.05
122	Marty Bystrom	.05
123	Rick Cerone	.05
124	Joe Cowley RC	.05
125	Brian Dayett RC	.05
126	Tim Foli	.05
127	Ray Fontenot	.05
128	Ken Griffey	.05
129	Ron Guidry	.10
130	Toby Harrah	.05
131	Jay Howell	.05
132	Steve Kemp	.05
133	Don Mattingly	2.50
134	Bobby Meacham	.05
135	John Montefusco	.05
136	Omar Moreno	.05
137	Dale Murray	.05
138	Phil Niekro	.75
139	Mike Pagliarulo RC	.20
140	Willie Randolph	.05
141	Dennis Rasmussen RC	.05
142	Dave Righetti	.05
143	Jose Rijo	.05
144	Andre Robertson	.05
145	Bob Shirley	.05
146	Dave Winfield	1.00
147	Butch Wynegar	.05
148	Gary Allenson	.05
149	Tony Armas	.05
150	Marty Barrett	.05
151	Wade Boggs	2.00
152	Dennis Boyd	.05
153	Bill Buckner	.05
154	Mark Clear	.05
155	Roger Clemens	40.00
156	Steve Crawford	.05
157	Mike Easler	.05
158	Dwight Evans	.05
159	Rich Gedman	.05
160	Jackie Gutierrez	.05
161	Bruce Hurst	.05
162	John Henry Johnson	.05
163	Rick Miller	.05
164	Reid Nichols	.05
165	Al Nipper RC	.05
166	Bob Ojeda	.05
167	Jerry Remy	.05
168	Jim Rice	.25
169	Bob Stanley	.05
170	Mike Boddicker	.05
171	Al Bumbry	.05
172	Todd Cruz	.05
173	Rich Dauer	.05
174	Storm Davis	.05
175	Rick Dempsey	.05
176	Jim Dwyer	.05
177	Mike Flanagan	.05
178	Dan Ford	.05
179	Wayne Gross	.05
180	John Lowenstein	.05
181	Dennis Martinez	.05
182	Tippy Martinez	.05
183	Scott McGregor	.05
184	Eddie Murray	1.00
185	Joe Nolan	.05
186	Floyd Rayford	.05
187	Cal Ripken, Jr.	4.00
188	Gary Roenicke	.05
189	Lenn Sakata	.05
190	John Shelby	.05
191	Ken Singleton	.05
192	Sammy Stewart	.05
193	Bill Swaggerty	.05
194	Tom Underwood	.05
195	Mike Young	.05
196	Steve Balboni	.05
197	Joe Beckwith	.05
198	Bud Black	.05
199	George Brett	2.50
200	Onix Concepcion	.05
201	Mark Gubicza RC	.50
202	Larry Gura	.05
203	Mark Huismann RC	.05
204	Dane Iorg	.05
205	Danny Jackson RC	.05
206	Charlie Leibrandt	.05
207	Hal McRae	.05
208	Darryl Motley RC	.05
209	Jorge Orta	.05
210	Greg Pryor	.05
211	Dan Quisenberry	.05
212	Bret Saberhagen	.25
213	Pat Sheridan	.05
214	Don Slaught	.05
215	U.L. Washington	.05
216	John Wathan	.05
217	Frank White	.05
218	Willie Wilson	.05
219	Neil Allen	.05
220	Joaquin Andujar	.05
221	Steve Braun	.05
222	Danny Cox RC	.05
223	Bob Forsch	.05
224	David Green	.05
225	George Hendrick	.05
226	Tom Herr	.05
227	Ricky Horton RC	.05
228	Art Howe	.05
229	Mike Jorgensen	.05
230	Kurt Kepshire	.05
231	Jeff Lahti	.05
232	Tito Landrum	.05
233	Dave LaPoint	.05
234	Willie McGee	.05
235	Tom Nieto RC	.05
236	Terry Pendleton RC	1.00
237	Darrell Porter	.05
238	Dave Rucker	.05
239	Lonnie Smith	.05
240	Ozzie Smith	2.00
241	Bruce Sutter	.75
242	Andy Van Slyke	.05
243	Dave Von Ohlen	.05
244	Larry Andersen	.05
245	Bill Campbell	.05
246	Steve Carlton	1.00
247	Tim Corcoran	.05
248	Ivan DeJesus	.05
249	John Denny	.05
250	Bo Diaz	.05
251	Greg Gross	.05
252	Kevin Gross	.05
253	Von Hayes	.05
254	Al Holland	.05
255	Charles Hudson	.05
256	Jerry Koosman	.05
257	Joe Lefebvre	.05
258	Sixto Lezcano	.05
259	Garry Maddox	.05
260	Len Matuszek	.05
261	Tug McGraw	.05
262	Al Oliver	.05
263	Shane Rawley	.05
264	Juan Samuel	.05
265	Mike Schmidt	2.50
266	Jeff Stone RC	.05
267	Ozzie Virgil	.05
268	Glenn Wilson	.05
269	John Wockenfuss	.05
270	Darrell Brown	.05
271	Tom Brunansky	.05
272	Randy Bush	.05
273	John Butcher	.05
274	Bobby Castillo	.05
275	Ron Davis	.05
276	Dave Engle	.05
277	Pete Filson	.05
278	Gary Gaetti	.05
279	Mickey Hatcher	.05
280	Ed Hodge	.05
281	Kent Hrbek	.05
282	Houston Jimenez	.05
283	Tim Laudner	.05
284	Rick Lysander	.05
285	Dave Meier	.05
286	Kirby Puckett	8.00
287	Pat Putnam	.05
288	Ken Schrom	.05
289	Mike Smithson	.05
290	Tim Teufel	.05
291	Frank Viola	.05
292	Ron Washington	.05
293	Don Aase	.05
294	Juan Beniquez	.05
295	Bob Boone	.05
296	Mike Brown	.05
297	Rod Carew	1.00
298	Doug Corbett	.05
299	Doug DeCinces	.05
300	Brian Downing	.05
301	Ken Forsch	.05
302	Bobby Grich	.05
303	Reggie Jackson	2.00
304	Tommy John	.10
305	Curt Kaufman	.05
306	Bruce Kison	.05
307	Fred Lynn	.05
308	Gary Pettis	.05
309	Ron Romanick RC	.05
310	Luis Sanchez	.05
311	Dick Schofield	.05
312	Daryl Sconiers	.05
313	Jim Slaton	.05
314	Derrel Thomas	.05
315	Rob Wilfong	.05
316	Mike Witt	.05
317	Geoff Zahn	.05
318	Len Barker	.05
319	Steve Bedrosian	.05
320	Bruce Benedict	.05
321	Rick Camp	.05
322	Chris Chambliss	.05
323	Jeff Dedmon RC	.05
324	Terry Forster	.05
325	Gene Garber	.05
326	Albert Hall RC	.05
327	Terry Harper	.05
328	Bob Horner	.05
329	Glenn Hubbard	.05
330	Randy Johnson	.05
331	Brad Komminsk	.05
332	Rick Mahler	.05
333	Craig McMurtry	.05
334	Donnie Moore	.05
335	Dale Murphy	.40
336	Ken Oberkfell	.05
337	Pascual Perez	.05
338	Gerald Perry	.05
339	Rafael Ramirez	.05
340	Jerry Royster	.05
341	Alex Trevino	.05
342	Claudell Washington	.05
343	Alan Ashby	.05
344	Mark Bailey RC	.05
345	Kevin Bass	.05
346	Enos Cabell	.05
347	Jose Cruz	.05
348	Bill Dawley	.05
349	Frank DiPino	.05
350	Bill Doran	.05
351	Phil Garner	.05
352	Bob Knepper	.05
353	Mike LaCoss	.05
354	Jerry Mumphrey	.05
355	Joe Niekro	.05
356	Terry Puhl	.05
357	Craig Reynolds	.05
358	Vern Ruhle	.05
359	Nolan Ryan	4.00
360	Joe Sambito	.05
361	Mike Scott	.05
362	Dave Smith	.05
363	Julio Solano RC	.05
364	Dickie Thon	.05
365	Denny Walling	.05
366	Dave Anderson	.05
367	Bob Bailor	.05
368	Greg Brock	.05
369	Carlos Diaz	.05
370	Pedro Guerrero	.05
371	Orel Hershiser RC	3.00
372	Rick Honeycutt	.05
373	Burt Hooton	.05
374	Ken Howell RC	.05
375	Ken Landreaux	.05
376	Candy Maldonado	.05
377	Mike Marshall	.05
378	Tom Niedenfuer	.05
379	Alejandro Pena	.05
380	Jerry Reuss	.05
381	R.J. Reynolds RC	.05
382	German Rivera	.05
383	Bill Russell	.05
384	Steve Sax	.05
385	Mike Scioscia	.05
386	Franklin Stubbs RC	.05
387	Fernando Valenzuela	.05
388	Bob Welch	.05
389	Terry Whitfield	.05
390	Steve Yeager	.05
391	Pat Zachry	.05
392	Fred Breining	.05
393	Gary Carter	1.00
394	Andre Dawson	.25
395	Miguel Dilone	.05
396	Dan Driessen	.05
397	Doug Flynn	.05
398	Terry Francona	.05
399	Bill Gullickson	.05
400	Bob James	.05
401	Charlie Lea	.05
402	Bryan Little	.05
403	Gary Lucas	.05
404	David Palmer	.05
405	Tim Raines	.05
406	Mike Ramsey	.05
407	Jeff Reardon	.05
408	Steve Rogers	.05
409	Dan Schatzeder	.05
410	Bryn Smith	.05
411	Mike Stenhouse	.05
412	Tim Wallach	.05
413	Jim Wohlford	.05
414	Bill Almon	.05
415	Keith Atherton	.05
416	Bruce Bochte	.05
417	Tom Burgmeier	.05
418	Ray Burris	.05
419	Bill Caudill	.05
420	Chris Codiroli	.05
421	Tim Conroy	.05
422	Mike Davis	.05
423	Jim Essian	.05
424	Mike Heath	.05
425	Rickey Henderson	1.00
426	Donnie Hill	.05
427	Dave Kingman	.05
428	Bill Krueger	.05
429	Carney Lansford	.05
430	Steve McCatty	.05
431	Joe Morgan	1.00
432	Dwayne Murphy	.05
433	Tony Phillips	.05
434	Lary Sorensen	.05
435	Mike Warren	.05
436	Curt Young RC	.05
437	Luis Aponte	.05
438	Chris Bando	.05
439	Tony Bernazard	.05
440	Bert Blyleven	.10
441	Brett Butler	.05
442	Ernie Camacho	.05
443	Joe Carter	.25
444	Carmelo Castillo	.05
445	Jamie Easterly	.05
446	Steve Farr RC	.05
447	Mike Fischlin	.05
448	Julio Franco	.05
449	Mel Hall	.05
450	Mike Hargrove	.05
451	Neal Heaton	.05
452	Brook Jacoby	.05
453	Mike Jeffcoat RC	.05
454	Don Schulze RC	.05
455	Roy Smith	.05
456	Pat Tabler	.05
457	Andre Thornton	.05
458	George Vukovich	.05
459	Tom Waddell	.05
460	Jerry Willard	.05
461	Dale Berra	.05
462	John Candelaria	.05
463	Jose DeLeon	.05
464	Doug Frobel	.05
465	Cecilio Guante	.05
466	Brian Harper	.05
467	Lee Lacy	.05
468	Bill Madlock	.05
469	Lee Mazzilli	.05
470	Larry McWilliams	.05
471	Jim Morrison	.05
472	Tony Pena	.05
473	Johnny Ray	.05
474	Rick Rhoden	.05
475	Don Robinson	.05
476	Rod Scurry	.05
477	Kent Tekulve	.05
478	Jason Thompson	.05
479	John Tudor	.05
480	Lee Tunnell	.05
481	Marvell Wynne	.05
482	Salome Barojas	.05
483	Dave Beard	.05
484	Jim Beattie	.05
485	Barry Bonnell	.05
486	Phil Bradley RC	.05
487	Al Cowens	.05
488	Alvin Davis	.05
489	Dave Henderson	.05
490	Steve Henderson	.05
491	Bob Kearney	.05
492	Mark Langston	.15
493	Larry Milbourne	.05
494	Paul Mirabella	.05
495	Mike Moore	.05
496	Edwin Nunez RC	.05
497	Spike Owen	.05
498	Jack Perconte	.05
499	Ken Phelps	.05
500	Jim Presley RC	.05
501	Mike Stanton	.05
502	Bob Stoddard	.05
503	Gorman Thomas	.05
504	Ed Vande Berg	.05
505	Matt Young	.05
506	Juan Agosto	.05
507	Harold Baines	.05
508	Floyd Bannister	.05
509	Britt Burns	.05
510	Julio Cruz	.05
511	Richard Dotson	.05
512	Jerry Dybzinski	.05
513	Carlton Fisk	1.00
514	Scott Fletcher	.05
515	Jerry Hairston Sr.	.05
516	Marc Hill	.05
517	LaMarr Hoyt	.05
518	Ron Kittle	.05
519	Rudy Law	.05
520	Vance Law	.05
521	Greg Luzinski	.05
522	Gene Nelson	.05
523	Tom Paciorek	.05
524	Ron Reed	.05
525	Bert Roberge	.05
526	Tom Seaver	1.00
527	Roy Smalley	.05
528	Dan Spillner	.05
529	Mike Squires	.05
530	Greg Walker	.05
531	Cesar Cedeno	.05
532	Dave Concepcion	.05
533	Eric Davis RC	2.00
534	Nick Esasky	.05
535	Tom Foley	.05
536	John Franco	.05
537	Brad Gulden	.05
538	Tom Hume	.05
539	Wayne Krenchicki	.05
540	Andy McGaffigan	.05
541	Eddie Milner	.05
542	Ron Oester	.05
543	Bob Owchinko	.05
544	Dave Parker	.05
545	Frank Pastore	.05
546	Tony Perez	.75
547	Ted Power	.05
548	Joe Price	.05
549	Gary Redus	.05
550	Pete Rose	3.00
551	Jeff Russell RC	.05
552	Mario Soto	.05
553	Jay Tibbs RC	.05
554	Duane Walker	.05
555	Alan Bannister	.05
556	Buddy Bell	.05

557	Danny Darwin	.05
558	Charlie Hough	.05
559	Bobby Jones	.05
560	Odell Jones	.05
561	Jeff Kunkel RC	.05
562	Mike Mason RC	.05
563	Pete O'Brien	.05
564	Larry Parrish	.05
565	Mickey Rivers	.05
566	Billy Sample	.05
567	Dave Schmidt	.05
568	Donnie Scott	.05
569	Dave Stewart	.05
570	Frank Tanana	.05
571	Wayne Tolleson	.05
572	Gary Ward	.05
573	Curtis Wilkerson	.05
574	George Wright	.05
575	Ned Yost	.05
576	Mark Brouhard	.05
577	Mike Caldwell	.05
578	Bobby Clark	.05
579	Jaime Cocanower	.05
580	Cecil Cooper	.05
581	Rollie Fingers	.75
582	Jim Gantner	.05
583	Moose Haas	.05
584	Dion James	.05
585	Pete Ladd	.05
586	Rick Manning	.05
587	Bob McClure	.05
588	Paul Molitor	1.00
589	Charlie Moore	.05
590	Ben Oglivie	.05
591	Chuck Porter	.05
592	Randy Ready RC	.05
593	Ed Romero	.05
594	Bill Schroeder RC	.05
595	Ray Searage	.05
596	Ted Simmons	.05
597	Jim Sundberg	.05
598	Don Sutton	.75
599	Tom Tellmann	.05
600	Rick Waits	.05
601	Robin Yount	1.00
602	Dusty Baker	.05
603	Bob Brenly	.05
604	Jack Clark	.05
605	Chili Davis	.05
606	Mark Davis	.05
607	Dan Gladden RC	.25
608	Atlee Hammaker	.05
609	Mike Krukow	.05
610	Duane Kuiper	.05
611	Bob Lacey	.05
612	Bill Laskey	.05
613	Gary Lavelle	.05
614	Johnnie LeMaster	.05
615	Jeff Leonard	.05
616	Randy Lerch	.05
617	Greg Minton	.05
618	Steve Nicosia	.05
619	Gene Richards	.05
620	Jeff Robinson RC	.05
621	Scot Thompson	.05
622	Manny Trillo	.05
623	Brad Wellman	.05
624	Frank Williams RC	.05
625	Joel Youngblood	.05
626	Cal Ripken, Jr. (In Action)	1.00
627	Mike Schmidt (In Action)	.50
628	Giving the Signs (Sparky Anderson)	.05
629	A.L. Pitcher's Nightmare (Rickey Henderson, Dave Winfield)	.50
630	N.L. Pitcher's Nightmare (Ryne Sandberg, Mike Schmidt)	1.00
631	N.L. All-Stars (Gary Carter, Steve Garvey, Ozzie Smith, Darryl Strawberry)	.25
632	All-Star Game Winning Battery (Gary Carter, Charlie Lea)	.10
633	N.L. Pennant Clinchers (Steve Garvey, Goose Gossage)	.10
634	N.L. Rookie Phenoms (Dwight Gooden, Juan Samuel)	.05
635	Toronto's Big Guns (Willie Upshaw)	.05
636	Toronto's Big Guns (Lloyd Moseby)	.05
637	Holland (Al Holland)	.05
638	Tunnell (Lee Tunnell)	.05
639	Reggie Jackson (In Action)	.50
640	Pete Rose (In Action)	.75
641	Father & Son (Cal Ripken, Jr., Cal Ripken, Sr.)	1.00
642	Cubs team	.10
643	1984's Two Perfect Games & One No-Hitter (Jack Morris, David Palmer, Mike Witt)	.05
644	Major League Prospect (Willie Lozado, Vic Mata)	.05
645	Major League Prospect (Kelly Gruber RC, Randy O'Neal RC)	.15

646	Major League Prospect (Jose Roman RC, Joel Skinner RC)	.05
647	Major League Prospect (Steve Kiefer RC, Danny Tartabull RC)	.50
648	Major League Prospect (Rob Deer RC, Alejandro Sanchez RC)	.25
649	Major League Prospect (Shawon Dunston RC, Bill Hatcher RC)	1.00
650	Major League Prospect (Mike Bielecki RC, Ron Robinson RC)	.10
651	Major League Prospect (Zane Smith RC, Paul Zuvella RC)	.10
652	Major League Prospect (Glenn Davis RC, Joe Hesketh RC)	.20
653	Major League Prospect (Steve Jeltz RC, John Russell RC)	.10
654	Checklist 1-95	.05
655	Checklist 96-195	.05
656	Checklist 196-292	.05
657	Checklist 293-391	.05
658	Checklist 392-481	.05
659	Checklist 482-575	.05
660	Checklist 576-660	.05

Update

For the second straight year, Fleer issued a 132-card update set. Cards portray traded players on their new teams and also include rookies not depicted in the regular issue. The cards are identical in design to the 1985 Fleer set but are numbered U-1 through U-132. The set was issued with team logo stickers in a specially designed box and was available only through hobby dealers.

		NM/M
	Complete Set (132):	5.00
	Common Player:	.10
1	Don Aase	.10
2	Bill Almon	.10
3	Dusty Baker	.10
4	Dale Berra	.10
5	Karl Best RC	.10
6	Tim Birtsas RC	.10
7	Vida Blue	.10
8	Rich Bordi	.10
9	Daryl Boston RC	.10
10	Hubie Brooks	.10
11	Chris Brown RC	.10
12	Tom Browning RC	.10
13	Al Bumbry	.10
14	Tim Burke RC	.10
15	Ray Burris	.10
16	Jeff Burroughs	.10
17	Ivan Calderon RC	.10
18	Jeff Calhoun	.10
19	Bill Campbell	.10
20	Don Carman RC	.10
21	Gary Carter	.50
22	Bobby Castillo	.10
23	Bill Caudill	.10
24	Rick Cerone	.10
25	Jack Clark	.10
26	Pat Clements RC	.10
27	Stewart Cliburn RC	.10
28	Vince Coleman RC	.10
29	Dave Collins	.10
30	Fritz Connally	.10
31	Henry Cotto RC	.10
32	Danny Darwin	.10
33	Darren Daulton RC	1.00
34	Jerry Davis	.10
35	Brian Dayett	.10
36	Ken Dixon RC	.10
37	Tommy Dunbar	.10
38	Mariano Duncan RC	.10
39	Bob Fallon	.10
40	Brian Fisher RC	.10
41	Mike Fitzgerald	.10
42	Ray Fontenot	.10
43	Greg Gagne RC	.10
44	Oscar Gamble	.10
45	Jim Gott	.10
46	David Green	.10

47	Alfredo Griffin	.10
48	Ozzie Guillen RC	2.00
49	Toby Harrah	.10
50	Ron Hassey	.10
51	Rickey Henderson	3.00
52	Steve Henderson	.10
53	George Hendrick	.10
54	Teddy Higuera RC	.10
55	Al Holland	.10
56	Burt Hooton	.10
57	Jay Howell	.10
58	LaMarr Hoyt	.10
59	Tim Hulett RC	.10
60	Bob James	.10
61	Cliff Johnson	.10
62	Howard Johnson	.10
63	Ruppert Jones	.10
64	Steve Kemp	.10
65	Bruce Kison	.10
66	Mike LaCoss	.10
67	Lee Lacy	.10
68	Dave LaPoint	.10
69	Gary Lavelle	.10
70	Vance Law	.10
71	Manny Lee RC	.10
72	Sixto Lezcano	.10
73	Tim Lollar	.10
74	Urbano Lugo RC	.10
75	Fred Lynn	.10
76	Steve Lyons RC	.10
77	Mickey Mahler	.10
78	Ron Mathis RC	.10
79	Len Matuszek	.10
80	Oddibe McDowell RC	.10
81	Roger McDowell RC	.10
82	Donnie Moore	.10
83	Ron Musselman	.10
84	Al Oliver	.10
85	Joe Orsulak RC	.10
86	Dan Pasqua RC	.10
87	Chris Pittaro RC	.10
88	Rick Reuschel	.10
89	Earnie Riles RC	.10
90	Jerry Royster	.10
91	Dave Rozema	.10
92	Dave Rucker	.10
93	Vern Ruhle	.10
94	Mark Salas RC	.10
95	Luis Salazar	.10
96	Joe Sambito	.10
97	Billy Sample	.10
98	Alex Sanchez	.10
99	Calvin Schiraldi RC	.10
100	Rick Schu RC	.10
101	Larry Sheets RC	.10
102	Ron Shepherd	.10
103	Nelson Simmons RC	.10
104	Don Slaught	.10
105	Roy Smalley	.10
106	Lonnie Smith	.10
107	Nate Snell RC	.10
108	Lary Sorensen	.10
109	Chris Speier	.10
110	Mike Stenhouse	.10
111	Tim Stoddard	.10
112	John Stuper	.10
113	Jim Sundberg	.10
114	Bruce Sutter	.40
115	Don Sutton	.50
116	Bruce Tanner RC	.10
117	Kent Tekulve	.10
118	Walt Terrell	.10
119	Mickey Tettleton RC	1.00
120	Rich Thompson	.10
121	Louis Thornton RC	.10
122	Alex Trevino	.10
123	John Tudor	.10
124	Jose Uribe RC	.10
125	Dave Valle RC	.10
126	Dave Von Ohlen	.10
127	Curt Wardle	.10
128	U.L. Washington	.10
129	Ed Whitson	.10
130	Herm Winningham RC	.10
131	Rich Yett RC	.10
132	Checklist	.10

Limited Edition

Dale Murphy

The 1985 Fleer Limited Edition boxed set was distributed through several chains of retail stores. The cards, which are the standard 2-1/2" x 3-1/2", have full-color photos inside a red and yellow frame. The backs are set in

black type against two different shades of yellow and contain the player's personal and statistical information. The set was issued in a specially designed box which carried the complete checklist for the set on the back. Six team logo stickers were also included with the set.

		NM/M
	Complete Set (44):	4.00
	Common Player:	.10
1	Buddy Bell	.10
2	Bert Blyleven	.15
3	Wade Boggs	.60
4	George Brett	.75
5	Rod Carew	.50
6	Steve Carlton	.50
7	Alvin Davis	.10
8	Andre Dawson	.25
9	Steve Garvey	.15
10	Goose Gossage	.15
11	Tony Gwynn	.60
12	Keith Hernandez	.10
13	Kent Hrbek	.10
14	Reggie Jackson	.60
15	Dave Kingman	.10
16	Ron Kittle	.10
17	Mark Langston	.10
18	Jeff Leonard	.10
19	Bill Madlock	.10
20	Don Mattingly	.75
21	Jack Morris	.10
22	Dale Murphy	.15
23	Eddie Murray	.50
24	Tony Pena	.10
25	Dan Quisenberry	.10
26	Tim Raines	.10
27	Jim Rice	.25
28	Cal Ripken, Jr.	1.00
29	Pete Rose	.85
30	Nolan Ryan	1.00
31	Ryne Sandberg	.60
32	Steve Sax	.10
33	Mike Schmidt	.75
34	Tom Seaver	.50
35	Ozzie Smith	.60
36	Mario Soto	.10
37	Dave Stieb	.10
38	Darryl Strawberry	.10
39	Rick Sutcliffe	.10
40	Alan Trammell	.10
41	Willie Upshaw	.10
42	Fernando Valenzuela	.10
43	Dave Winfield	.50
44	Robin Yount	.50

Star Stickers

The 1985 Fleer sticker set consists of 126 player stickers, each measuring 1-15/16" x 2-1/2". Numbered on the back, the stickers were designed to be put in a special album. Distributed in packs of six, the 1985 stickers are the scarcest of all Fleer baseball sticker issues.

		NM/M
	Complete Set (126):	12.50
	Common Player:	
	Sticker Album:	1.25
	Wax Pack (6):	.25
	Wax Box (100):	16.00
1	Pete Rose	1.00
2	Pete Rose	1.00
3	Pete Rose	1.00
4	Don Mattingly	1.50
5	Dave Winfield	.40
6	Wade Boggs	.50
7	Buddy Bell	.05
8	Tony Gwynn	.40
9	Lee Lacy	.05
10	Chili Davis	.05
11	Ryne Sandberg	.50
12	Tony Armas	.05
13	Jim Rice	.15
14	Dave Kingman	.05
15	Alvin Davis	.05
16	Gary Carter	.25
17	Mike Schmidt	1.00
18	Dale Murphy	.20
19	Ron Cey	.05

20	Eddie Murray	.40
21	Harold Baines	.05
22	Kirk Gibson	.05
23	Jim Rice	.15
24	Gary Matthews	.05
25	Keith Hernandez	.05
26	Gary Carter	.25
27	George Hendrick	.05
28	Tony Armas	.05
29	Dave Kingman	.05
30	Dwayne Murphy	.05
31	Lance Parrish	.05
32	Andre Thornton	.05
33	Dale Murphy	.20
34	Mike Schmidt	1.00
35	Gary Carter	.25
36	Darryl Strawberry	.05
37	Don Mattingly	1.50
38	Larry Parrish	.05
39	George Bell	.05
40	Dwight Evans	.05
41	Cal Ripken, Jr.	2.00
42	Tim Raines	.05
43	Johnny Ray	.05
44	Juan Samuel	.05
45	Ryne Sandberg	.50
46	Mike Easler	.05
47	Andre Thornton	.05
48	Dave Kingman	.05
49	Don Baylor	.05
50	Rusty Staub	.05
51	Steve Braun	.05
52	Kevin Bass	.05
53	Greg Gross	.05
54	Rickey Henderson	.40
55	Dave Collins	.05
56	Brett Butler	.05
57	Gary Pettis	.05
58	Tim Raines	.05
59	Juan Samuel	.05
60	Alan Wiggins	.05
61	Lonnie Smith	.05
62	Eddie Murray	.05
63	Eddie Murray	.05
64	Eddie Murray	.05
65	Eddie Murray	.05
66	Eddie Murray	.05
67	Eddie Murray	.05
68	Tom Seaver	.05
69	Tom Seaver	.05
70	Tom Seaver	.05
71	Tom Seaver	.05
72	Tom Seaver	.05
73	Tom Seaver	.05
74	Mike Schmidt	.25
75	Mike Schmidt	.25
76	Mike Schmidt	.25
77	Mike Schmidt	.25
78	Mike Schmidt	.25
79	Mike Schmidt	.25
80	Mike Boddicker	.05
81	Bert Blyleven	.05
82	Jack Morris	.05
83	Dan Petry	.05
84	Frank Viola	.05
85	Joaquin Andujar	.05
86	Mario Soto	.05
87	Dwight Gooden	.05
88	Joe Niekro	.05
89	Rick Sutcliffe	.05
90	Mike Boddicker	.05
91	Dave Stieb	.05
92	Bert Blyleven	.05
93	Phil Niekro	.25
94	Alejandro Pena	.05
95	Dwight Gooden	.05
96	Orel Hershiser	.15
97	Rick Rhoden	.05
98	John Candelaria	.05
99	Dan Quisenberry	.05
100	Bill Caudill	.05
101	Willie Hernandez	.05
102	Dave Righetti	.05
103	Ron Davis	.05
104	Bruce Sutter	.20
105	Lee Smith	.05
106	Jesse Orosco	.05
107	Al Holland	.05
108	Goose Gossage	.05
109	Mark Langston	.05
110	Dave Stieb	.05
111	Mike Witt	.05
112	Bert Blyleven	.05
113	Dwight Gooden	.05
114	Fernando Valenzuela	.05
115	Nolan Ryan	2.00
116	Mario Soto	.05
117	Ron Darling	.05
118	Dan Gladden	.05
119	Jeff Stone	.05
120	John Franco	.05
121	Barbaro Garbey	.05
122	Kirby Puckett	1.50
123	Roger Clemens	7.50
124	Bret Saberhagen	.05
125	Sparky Anderson	.05
126	Dick Williams	.05

1986 Fleer

The 1986 Fleer set contains 660 color cards measuring 2-1/2" x 3-1/2". The card fronts feature a player photo enclosed by a dark blue border. The card backs are minus the black-and-white photo

that was included in past Fleer efforts. Player biographical and statistical information appear in black and yellow on white stock. As in 1985, Fleer devoted ten cards, entitled "Major League Prospects," to twenty promising rookie players. The 1986 set, as in the previous four years was issued with team logo stickers.

		NM/M
	Unopened Fact. Set (660):	30.00
	Complete Set (660):	25.00
	Common Player:	.05
	Wax Pack (15):	1.50
	Wax Box (36):	45.00
	Cello Pack (28):	2.00
	Cello Box (24):	40.00
	Rack Pack (45):	4.00
	Rack Box (24):	65.00
1	Steve Balboni	.05
2	Joe Beckwith	.05
3	Buddy Biancalana	.05
4	Bud Black	.05
5	George Brett	2.00
6	Onix Concepcion	.05
7	Steve Farr	.05
8	Mark Gubicza	.05
9	Dane Iorg	.05
10	Danny Jackson	.05
11	Lynn Jones	.05
12	Mike Jones	.05
13	Charlie Leibrandt	.05
14	Hal McRae	.05
15	Omar Moreno	.05
16	Darryl Motley	.05
17	Jorge Orta	.05
18	Dan Quisenberry	.05
19	Bret Saberhagen	.05
20	Pat Sheridan	.05
21	Lonnie Smith	.05
22	Jim Sundberg	.05
23	John Wathan	.05
24	Frank White	.05
25	Willie Wilson	.05
26	Joaquin Andujar	.05
27	Steve Braun	.05
28	Bill Campbell	.05
29	Cesar Cedeno	.05
30	Jack Clark	.05
31	Vince Coleman	.05
32	Danny Cox	.05
33	Ken Dayley	.05
34	Ivan DeJesus	.05
35	Bob Forsch	.05
36	Brian Harper	.05
37	Tom Herr	.05
38	Ricky Horton	.05
39	Kurt Kepshire	.05
40	Jeff Lahti	.05
41	Tito Landrum	.05
42	Willie McGee	.05
43	Tom Nieto	.05
44	Terry Pendleton	.05
45	Darrell Porter	.05
46	Ozzie Smith	1.50
47	John Tudor	.05
48	Andy Van Slyke	.05
49	Todd Worrell RC	.25
50	Jim Acker	.05
51	Doyle Alexander	.05
52	Jesse Barfield	.05
53	George Bell	.05
54	Jeff Burroughs	.05
55	Bill Caudill	.05
56	Jim Clancy	.05
57	Tony Fernandez	.05
58	Tom Filer	.05
59	Damaso Garcia	.05
60	Tom Henke	.05
61	Garth Iorg	.05
62	Cliff Johnson	.05
63	Jimmy Key	.05
64	Dennis Lamp	.05
65	Gary Lavelle	.05
66	Buck Martinez	.05
67	Lloyd Moseby	.05
68	Rance Mulliniks	.05
69	Al Oliver	.05
70	Dave Stieb	.05
71	Louis Thornton	.05
72	Willie Upshaw	.05
73	Ernie Whitt	.05
74	Rick Aguilera RC	.75

#	Player	Price
75	Wally Backman	.05
76	Gary Carter	1.00
77	Ron Darling	.05
78	Len Dykstra RC	2.00
79	Sid Fernandez	.05
80	George Foster	.05
81	Dwight Gooden	.05
82	Tom Gorman	.05
83	Danny Heep	.05
84	Keith Hernandez	.05
85	Howard Johnson	.05
86	Ray Knight	.05
87	Terry Leach	.05
88	Ed Lynch	.05
89	Roger McDowell	.05
90	Jesse Orosco	.05
91	Tom Paciorek	.05
92	Ronn Reynolds	.05
93	Rafael Santana	.05
94	Doug Sisk	.05
95	Rusty Staub	.05
96	Darryl Strawberry	.05
97	Mookie Wilson	.05
98	Neil Allen	.05
99	Don Baylor	.05
100	Dale Berra	.05
101	Rich Bordi	.05
102	Marty Bystrom	.05
103	Joe Cowley	.05
104	Brian Fisher RC	.05
105	Ken Griffey	.05
106	Ron Guidry	.10
107	Ron Hassey	.05
108	Rickey Henderson	1.00
109	Don Mattingly	2.00
110	Bobby Meacham	.05
111	John Montefusco	.05
112	Phil Niekro	.75
113	Mike Pagliarulo	.05
114	Dan Pasqua	.05
115	Willie Randolph	.05
116	Dave Righetti	.05
117	Andre Robertson	.05
118	Billy Sample	.05
119	Bob Shirley	.05
120	Ed Whitson	.05
121	Dave Winfield	1.00
122	Butch Wynegar	.05
123	Dave Anderson	.05
124	Bob Bailor	.05
125	Greg Brock	.05
126	Enos Cabell	.05
127	Bobby Castillo	.05
128	Carlos Diaz	.05
129	Mariano Duncan	.05
130	Pedro Guerrero	.05
131	Orel Hershiser	.05
132	Rick Honeycutt	.05
133	Ken Howell	.05
134	Ken Landreaux	.05
135	Bill Madlock	.05
136	Candy Maldonado	.05
137	Mike Marshall	.05
138	Len Matuszek	.05
139	Tom Niedenfuer	.05
140	Alejandro Pena	.05
141	Jerry Reuss	.05
142	Bill Russell	.05
143	Steve Sax	.05
144	Mike Scioscia	.05
145	Fernando Valenzuela	.05
146	Bob Welch	.05
147	Terry Whitfield	.05
148	Juan Beniquez	.05
149	Bob Boone	.05
150	John Candelaria	.05
151	Rod Carew	1.00
152	Stewart Cliburn RC	.05
153	Doug DeCinces	.05
154	Brian Downing	.05
155	Ken Forsch	.05
156	Craig Gerber	.05
157	Bobby Grich	.05
158	George Hendrick	.05
159	Al Holland	.10
160	Reggie Jackson	1.50
161	Ruppert Jones	.05
162	Urbano Lugo RC	.05
163	Kirk McCaskill RC	.25
164	Donnie Moore	.05
165	Gary Pettis	.05
166	Ron Romanick	.05
167	Dick Schofield	.05
168	Daryl Sconiers	.05
169	Jim Slaton	.05
170	Don Sutton	.75
171	Mike Witt	.05
172	Buddy Bell	.05
173	Tom Browning	.05
174	Dave Concepcion	.05
175	Eric Davis	.05
176	Bo Diaz	.05
177	Nick Esasky	.05
178	John Franco	.05
179	Tom Hume	.05
180	Wayne Krenchicki	.05
181	Andy McGaffigan	.05
182	Eddie Milner	.05
183	Ron Oester	.05
184	Dave Parker	.05
185	Frank Pastore	.05
186	Tony Perez	.75
187	Ted Power	.05
188	Joe Price	.05
189	Gary Redus	.05
190	Ron Robinson	.05
191	Pete Rose	2.50
192	Mario Soto	.05
193	John Stuper	.05
194	Jay Tibbs	.05
195	Dave Van Gorder	.05
196	Max Venable	.05
197	Juan Agosto	.05
198	Harold Baines	.05
199	Floyd Bannister	.05
200	Britt Burns	.05
201	Julio Cruz	.05
202	Joel Davis RC	.05
203	Richard Dotson	.05
204	Carlton Fisk	1.00
205	Scott Fletcher	.05
206	Ozzie Guillen	.05
207	Jerry Hairston Sr.	.05
208	Tim Hulett	.05
209	Bob James	.05
210	Ron Kittle	.05
211	Rudy Law	.05
212	Bryan Little	.05
213	Gene Nelson	.05
214	Reid Nichols	.05
215	Luis Salazar	.05
216	Tom Seaver	1.00
217	Dan Spillner	.05
218	Bruce Tanner	.05
219	Greg Walker	.05
220	Dave Wehrmeister	.05
221	Juan Berenguer	.05
222	Dave Bergman	.05
223	Tom Brookens	.05
224	Darrell Evans	.05
225	Barbaro Garbey	.05
226	Kirk Gibson	.05
227	John Grubb	.05
228	Willie Hernandez	.05
229	Larry Herndon	.05
230	Chet Lemon	.05
231	Aurelio Lopez	.05
232	Jack Morris	.05
233	Randy O'Neal	.05
234	Lance Parrish	.05
235	Dan Petry	.05
236	Alex Sanchez	.05
237	Bill Scherrer	.05
238	Nelson Simmons	.05
239	Frank Tanana	.05
240	Walt Terrell	.05
241	Alan Trammell	.05
242	Lou Whitaker	.05
243	Milt Wilcox	.05
244	Hubie Brooks	.05
245	Tim Burke RC	.05
246	Andre Dawson	.35
247	Mike Fitzgerald	.05
248	Terry Francona	.05
249	Bill Gullickson	.05
250	Joe Hesketh	.05
251	Bill Laskey	.05
252	Vance Law	.05
253	Charlie Lea	.05
254	Gary Lucas	.05
255	David Palmer	.05
256	Tim Raines	.05
257	Jeff Reardon	.05
258	Bert Roberge	.05
259	Dan Schatzeder	.05
260	Bryn Smith	.05
261	Randy St. Claire RC	.05
262	Scot Thompson	.05
263	Tim Wallach	.05
264	U.L. Washington	.05
265	Mitch Webster RC	.05
266	Herm Winningham RC	.05
267	Floyd Youmans RC	.05
268	Don Aase	.05
269	Mike Boddicker	.05
270	Rich Dauer	.05
271	Storm Davis	.05
272	Rick Dempsey	.05
273	Ken Dixon	.05
274	Jim Dwyer	.05
275	Mike Flanagan	.05
276	Wayne Gross	.05
277	Lee Lacy	.05
278	Fred Lynn	.05
279	Tippy Martinez	.05
280	Dennis Martinez	.05
281	Scott McGregor	.05
282	Eddie Murray	1.00
283	Floyd Rayford	.05
284	Cal Ripken, Jr.	3.00
285	Gary Roenicke	.05
286	Larry Sheets	.05
287	John Shelby	.05
288	Nate Snell	.05
289	Sammy Stewart	.05
290	Alan Wiggins	.05
291	Mike Young	.05
292	Alan Ashby	.05
293	Mark Bailey	.05
294	Kevin Bass	.05
295	Jeff Calhoun	.05
296	Jose Cruz	.05
297	Glenn Davis	.05
298	Bill Dawley	.05
299	Frank DiPino	.05
300	Bill Doran	.05
301	Phil Garner	.05
302	Jeff Heathcock RC	.05
303	Charlie Kerfeld RC	.05
304	Bob Knepper	.05
305	Ron Mathis	.05
306	Jerry Mumphrey	.05
307	Jim Pankovits	.05
308	Terry Puhl	.05
309	Craig Reynolds	.05
310	Nolan Ryan	3.00
311	Mike Scott	.05
312	Dave Smith	.05
313	Dickie Thon	.05
314	Denny Walling	.05
315	Kurt Bevacqua	.05
316	Al Bumbry	.05
317	Jerry Davis	.05
318	Luis DeLeon	.05
319	Dave Dravecky	.05
320	Tim Flannery	.05
321	Steve Garvey	.30
322	Goose Gossage	.05
323	Tony Gwynn	1.50
324	Andy Hawkins	.05
325	LaMarr Hoyt	.05
326	Roy Lee Jackson	.05
327	Terry Kennedy	.05
328	Craig Lefferts	.05
329	Carmelo Martinez	.05
330	Lance McCullers RC	.05
331	Kevin McReynolds	.05
332	Graig Nettles	.05
333	Jerry Royster	.05
334	Eric Show	.05
335	Tim Stoddard	.05
336	Garry Templeton	.05
337	Mark Thurmond	.05
338	Ed Wojna	.05
339	Tony Armas	.05
340	Marty Barrett	.05
341	Wade Boggs	1.50
342	Dennis Boyd	.05
343	Bill Buckner	.05
344	Mark Clear	.05
345	Roger Clemens	2.00
346	Steve Crawford	.05
347	Mike Easler	.05
348	Dwight Evans	.05
349	Rich Gedman	.05
350	Jackie Gutierrez	.05
351	Glenn Hoffman	.05
352	Bruce Hurst	.05
353	Bruce Kison	.05
354	Tim Lollar	.05
355	Steve Lyons	.05
356	Al Nipper	.05
357	Bob Ojeda	.05
358	Jim Rice	.30
359	Bob Stanley	.05
360	Mike Trujillo	.05
361	Thad Bosley	.05
362	Warren Brusstar	.05
363	Ron Cey	.05
364	Jody Davis	.05
365	Bob Dernier	.05
366	Shawon Dunston	.05
367	Leon Durham	.05
368	Dennis Eckersley	.75
369	Ray Fontenot	.05
370	George Frazier	.05
371	Bill Hatcher	.05
372	Dave Lopes	.05
373	Gary Matthews	.05
374	Ron Meredith	.05
375	Keith Moreland	.05
376	Reggie Patterson	.05
377	Dick Ruthven	.05
378	Ryne Sandberg	1.50
379	Scott Sanderson	.05
380	Lee Smith	.05
381	Lary Sorensen	.05
382	Chris Speier	.05
383	Rick Sutcliffe	.05
384	Steve Trout	.05
385	Gary Woods	.05
386	Bert Blyleven	.10
387	Tom Brunansky	.05
388	Randy Bush	.05
389	John Butcher	.05
390	Ron Davis	.05
391	Dave Engle	.05
392	Frank Eufemia	.05
393	Pete Filson	.05
394	Gary Gaetti	.05
395	Greg Gagne	.05
396	Mickey Hatcher	.05
397	Kent Hrbek	.05
398	Tim Laudner	.05
399	Rick Lysander	.05
400	Dave Meier	.05
401	Kirby Puckett	1.50
402	Mark Salas	.05
403	Ken Schrom	.05
404	Roy Smalley	.05
405	Mike Smithson	.05
406	Mike Stenhouse	.05
407	Tim Teufel	.05
408	Frank Viola	.05
409	Ron Washington	.05
410	Keith Atherton	.05
411	Dusty Baker	.05
412	Tim Birtsas RC	.05
413	Bruce Bochte	.05
414	Chris Codiroli	.05
415	Dave Collins	.05
416	Mike Davis	.05
417	Alfredo Griffin	.05
418	Mike Heath	.05
419	Steve Henderson	.05
420	Donnie Hill	.05
421	Jay Howell	.05
422	Tommy John	.10
423	Dave Kingman	.05
424	Bill Krueger	.05
425	Rick Langford	.05
426	Carney Lansford	.05
427	Steve McCatty	.05
428	Dwayne Murphy	.05
429	Steve Ontiveros RC	.05
430	Tony Phillips	.05
431	Jose Rijo	.05
432	Mickey Tettleton RC	.05
433	Luis Aguayo	.05
434	Larry Andersen	.05
435	Steve Carlton	1.00
436	Don Carman RC	.05
437	Tim Corcoran	.05
438	Darren Daulton	.05
439	John Denny	.05
440	Tom Foley	.05
441	Greg Gross	.05
442	Kevin Gross	.05
443	Von Hayes	.05
444	Charles Hudson	.05
445	Garry Maddox	.05
446	Shane Rawley	.05
447	Dave Rucker	.05
448	John Russell	.05
449	Juan Samuel	.05
450	Mike Schmidt	2.00
451	Rick Schu	.05
452	Dave Shipanoff	.05
453	Dave Stewart	.05
454	Jeff Stone	.05
455	Kent Tekulve	.05
456	Ozzie Virgil	.05
457	Glenn Wilson	.05
458	Jim Beattie	.05
459	Karl Best	.05
460	Barry Bonnell	.05
461	Phil Bradley	.05
462	Ivan Calderon RC	.05
463	Al Cowens	.05
464	Alvin Davis	.05
465	Dave Henderson	.05
466	Bob Kearney	.05
467	Mark Langston	.05
468	Bob Long	.05
469	Mike Moore	.05
470	Edwin Nunez	.05
471	Spike Owen	.05
472	Jack Perconte	.05
473	Jim Presley	.05
474	Donnie Scott	.05
475	Bill Swift RC	.05
476	Danny Tartabull	.05
477	Gorman Thomas	.05
478	Roy Thomas	.05
479	Ed Vande Berg	.05
480	Frank Wills	.05
481	Matt Young	.05
482	Ray Burris	.05
483	Jaime Cocanower	.05
484	Cecil Cooper	.05
485	Danny Darwin	.05
486	Rollie Fingers	.75
487	Jim Gantner	.05
488	Bob Gibson	.05
489	Moose Haas	.05
490	Teddy Higuera RC	.05
491	Paul Householder	.05
492	Pete Ladd	.05
493	Rick Manning	.05
494	Bob McClure	.05
495	Paul Molitor	1.00
496	Charlie Moore	.05
497	Ben Oglivie	.05
498	Randy Ready	.05
499	Earnie Riles RC	.05
500	Ed Romero	.05
501	Bill Schroeder	.05
502	Ray Searage	.05
503	Ted Simmons	.05
504	Pete Vuckovich	.05
505	Rick Waits	.05
506	Robin Yount	1.00
507	Len Barker	.05
508	Steve Bedrosian	.05
509	Bruce Benedict	.05
510	Rick Camp	.05
511	Rick Cerone	.05
512	Chris Chambliss	.05
513	Jeff Dedmon	.05
514	Terry Forster	.05
515	Gene Garber	.05
516	Terry Harper	.05
517	Bob Horner	.05
518	Glenn Hubbard	.05
519	Joe Johnson RC	.05
520	Brad Komminsk	.05
521	Rick Mahler	.05
522	Dale Murphy	.30
523	Ken Oberkfell	.05
524	Pascual Perez	.05
525	Gerald Perry	.05
526	Rafael Ramirez	.05
527	Steve Shields RC	.05
528	Zane Smith	.05
529	Bruce Sutter	.75
530	Milt Thompson RC	.05
531	Claudell Washington	.05
532	Paul Zuvella	.05
533	Vida Blue	.05
534	Bob Brenly	.05
535	Chris Brown	.05
536	Chili Davis	.05
537	Mark Davis	.05
538	Rob Deer	.05
539	Dan Driessen	.05
540	Scott Garrelts	.05
541	Dan Gladden	.05
542	Jim Gott	.05
543	David Green	.05
544	Atlee Hammaker	.05
545	Mike Jeffcoat	.05
546	Mike Krukow	.05
547	Dave LaPoint	.05
548	Jeff Leonard	.05
549	Greg Minton	.05
550	Alex Trevino	.05
551	Manny Trillo	.05
552	Jose Uribe RC	.05
553	Brad Wellman	.05
554	Frank Williams	.05
555	Joel Youngblood	.05
556	Alan Bannister	.05
557	Glenn Brummer	.05
558	Steve Buechele RC	.05
559	Jose Guzman RC	.05
560	Toby Harrah	.05
561	Greg Harris	.05
562	Dwayne Henry RC	.05
563	Burt Hooton	.05
564	Charlie Hough	.05
565	Mike Mason	.05
566	Oddibe McDowell RC	.05
567	Pete O'Brien	.05
568	Larry Parrish	.05
569	Dave Rozema	.05
570	Dave Schmidt	.05
571	Don Slaught	.05
572	Wayne Tolleson	.05
573	Duane Walker	.05
574	Gary Ward	.05
575	Chris Welsh	.05
576	Curtis Wilkerson	.05
577	George Wright	.05
578	Chris Bando	.05
579	Tony Bernazard	.05
580	Brett Butler	.05
581	Ernie Camacho	.05
582	Joe Carter	.05
583	Carmello Castillo (Carmelo)	.05
585	Jamie Easterly	.05
586	Julio Franco	.05
587	Mel Hall	.05
588	Mike Hargrove	.05
589	Neal Heaton	.05
590	Brook Jacoby	.05
591	Otis Nixon RC	.25
592	Jerry Reed	.05
593	Vern Ruhle	.05
594	Pat Tabler	.05
595	Rich Thompson	.05
596	Andre Thornton	.05
597	Dave Von Ohlen	.05
598	George Vukovich	.05
599	Tom Waddell	.05
600	Curt Wardle	.05
601	Jerry Willard	.05
602	Bill Almon	.05
603	Mike Bielecki	.05
604	Sid Bream	.05
605	Mike Brown	.05
606	Pat Clements RC	.05
607	Jose DeLeon	.05
608	Denny Gonzalez	.05
609	Cecilio Guante	.05
610	Steve Kemp	.05
611	Sam Khalifa	.05
612	Lee Mazzilli	.05
613	Larry McWilliams	.05
614	Jim Morrison	.05
615	Joe Orsulak RC	.25
616	Tony Pena	.05
617	Johnny Ray	.05
618	Rick Reuschel	.05
619	R.J. Reynolds	.05
620	Rick Rhoden	.05
621	Don Robinson	.05
622	Jason Thompson	.05
623	Lee Tunnell	.05
624	Jim Winn	.05
625	Marvell Wynne	.05
626	Dwight Gooden (In Action)	.05
627	Don Mattingly (In Action)	.50
628	Pete Rose (4,192 Hits)	.50
629	Rod Carew (3,000 Hits)	.25
630	Phil Niekro, Tom Seaver (300 Wins)	.25
631	Ouch! (Don Baylor)	.05
632	Instant Offense (Tim Raines, Darryl Strawberry)	.05
633	Shortstops Supreme (Cal Ripken, Jr., Alan Trammell)	1.00
634	Boggs & "Hero" (Wade Boggs, George Brett)	1.00
635	Braves Dynamic Duo (Bob Horner, Dale Murphy)	.25
636	Cardinal Ignitors (Vince Coleman, Willie McGee)	.25
637	Terror on the Basepaths (Vince Coleman)	.05
638	Charlie Hustle & Dr. K (Dwight Gooden, Pete Rose)	.50
639	1984 and 1985 A.L. Batting Champs (Wade Boggs, Don Mattingly)	1.00
640	N.L. West Sluggers (Steve Garvey, Dale Murphy, Dave Parker)	.25
641	Staff Aces (Dwight Gooden, Fernando Valenzuela)	.10
642	Blue Jay Stoppers (Jimmy Key, Dave Stieb)	.05
643	A.L. All-Star Backstops (Carlton Fisk, Rich Gedman)	.10
644	Major League Prospect (Benito Santiago RC, Gene Walter RC)	1.00
645	Major League Prospect (Colin Ward RC, Mike Woodard RC)	.10
646	Major League Prospect (Kal Daniels RC, Paul O'Neill RC)	2.00
647	Major League Prospect (Andres Galarraga RC, Fred Toliver RC)	3.00
648	Major League Prospect (Curt Ford RC, Bob Kipper RC)	.10
649	Major League Prospect (Jose Canseco RC, Eric Plunk RC)	5.00
650	Major League Prospect (Mark McLemore RC, Gus Polidor RC)	.75
651	Major League Prospect (Mickey Brantley RC, Rob Woodward RC)	.10
652	Major League Prospect (Mark Funderburk RC, Billy Joe Robidoux RC)	.10
653	Major League Prospect (Cecil Fielder RC, Cory Snyder RC)	1.50
654	Checklist 1-97	
655	Checklist 98-196	.05
656	Checklist 197-291	.05
657	Checklist 292-385	.05
658	Checklist 386-482	.05
659	Checklist 483-578	.05
660	Checklist 579-660	.05

All Stars

Gary Carter — METS • CATCHER

Fleer's choices for a major league All-Star team make up this 12-card set. The cards were randomly inserted in 35¢ wax packs and 59¢ cello packs. The card fronts have a color photo set against a bright red background for A.L. players or a bright blue background for N.L. players. Backs feature the player's career highlights on a red and blue background.

		NM/M
Complete Set (12):		7.50
Common Player:		.10
1	Don Mattingly	2.00
2	Tom Herr	.10
3	George Brett	2.00
4	Gary Carter	.75
5	Cal Ripken, Jr.	4.00
6	Dave Parker	.10
7	Rickey Henderson	.75
8	Pedro Guerrero	.10
9	Dan Quisenberry	.10
10	Dwight Gooden	.10
11	Gorman Thomas	.10
12	John Tudor	.10

Future Hall Of Famers

PETE ROSE — REDS • MANAGER-1B

The 1986 Future Hall of Famers set is comprised of six players Fleer felt would gain eventual entrance into the Baseball Hall of Fame. The cards are the standard 2-1/2" x 3-1/2" and were randomly inserted in three-pack rack packs. Card fronts feature a player photo set against a blue background with horizontal light blue stripes. Backs are printed in black on blue and feature career highlights in narrative form.

		NM/M
Complete Set (6):		5.00
Common Player:		.75
1	Pete Rose	2.00
2	Steve Carlton	.75
3	Tom Seaver	.75
4	Rod Carew	.75
5	Nolan Ryan	3.00
6	Reggie Jackson	1.00

Box Panels

Picking up on a Donruss idea, Fleer issued eight cards in panels of four on the bottoms of the wax and cello pack boxes. The cards are numbered C-1 through C-8 and are 2-1/2" x 3-1/2", with a complete panel measuring 5"x 7-1/8". Included in the eight cards are six players and two team logo/checklist cards.

		NM/M
Complete Panel Set (2):		4.00
Complete Singles Set (8):		4.00
Common Single Player:		.20
Panel		2.50
1	Royals logo/Checklist	.05
2	George Brett	2.00
3	Ozzie Guillen	.20
4	Dale Murphy	.40
Panel		1.50
5	Cardinals Logo/ Checklist	.05
6	Tom Browning	.20
7	Gary Carter	1.00
8	Carlton Fisk	1.00

Update

Issued near the end of the baseball season, the 1986 Fleer Update set consists of cards numbered U-1 through U-132. The 2-1/2" x 3-1/2" cards are identical in design to the regular 1986 Fleer set. The purpose of the set is to update player trades and include rookies not depicted in the regular issue. The set was issued with team logo stickers in a specially designed box and was available only through hobby dealers.

	NM/M
Unopened Fact. Set (132):	40.00

Complete Set (132):		30.00
Common Player:		.05
1	Mike Aldrete RC	.05
2	Andy Allanson RC	.05
3	Neil Allen	.05
4	Joaquin Andujar	.05
5	Paul Assenmacher RC	.05
6	Scott Bailes RC	.05
7	Jay Baller RC	.05
8	Scott Bankhead RC	.05
9	Bill Bathe RC	.05
10	Don Baylor	.05
11	Billy Beane RC	.05
12	Steve Bedrosian	.05
13	Juan Beniquez	.05
14	Barry Bonds RC	25.00
15	Bobby Bonilla RC	1.00
16	Rich Bordi	.05
17	Bill Campbell	.05
18	Tom Candiotti	.05
19	John Cangelosi RC	.05
20	Jose Canseco	4.00
21	Chuck Cary RC	.05
22	Juan Castillo RC	.05
23	Rick Cerone	.05
24	John Cerutti RC	.05
25	Will Clark RC	1.00
26	Mark Clear	.05
27	Darnell Coles RC	.05
28	Dave Collins	.05
29	Tim Conroy	.05
30	Ed Correa RC	.05
31	Joe Cowley	.05
32	Bill Dawley	.05
33	Rob Deer	.05
34	John Denny	.05
35	Jim DeShaies RC	.05
36	Doug Drabek RC	1.00
37	Mike Easler	.05
38	Mark Eichhorn RC	.05
39	Dave Engle	.05
40	Mike Fischlin	.05
41	Scott Fletcher	.05
42	Terry Forster	.05
43	Terry Francona	.05
44	Andres Galarraga	.50
45	Lee Guetterman RC	.05
46	Bill Gullickson	.05
47	Jackie Gutierrez	.05
48	Moose Haas	.05
49	Billy Hatcher	.05
50	Mike Heath	.05
51	Guy Hoffman RC	.05
52	Tom Hume	.05
53	Pete Incaviglia RC	.50
54	Dane Iorg	.05
55	Chris James RC	.05
56	Stan Javier RC	.05
57	Tommy John	.15
58	Tracy Jones RC	.05
59	Wally Joyner RC	1.00
60	Wayne Krenchicki	.05
61	John Kruk RC	1.00
62	Mike LaCoss	.05
63	Pete Ladd	.05
64	Dave LaPoint	.05
65	Mike LaValliere RC	.05
66	Rudy Law	.05
67	Dennis Leonard	.05
68	Steve Lombardozzi RC	.05
69	Aurelio Lopez	.05
70	Mickey Mahler	.05
71	Candy Maldonado	.05
72	Roger Mason RC	.05
73	Greg Mathews RC	.05
74	Andy McGaffigan	.05
75	Joel McKeon RC	.05
76	Kevin Mitchell RC	.50
77	Bill Mooneyham RC	.05
78	Omar Moreno	.05
79	Jerry Mumphrey	.05
80	Al Newman RC	.05
81	Phil Niekro	.50
82	Randy Niemann	.05
83	Juan Nieves RC	.05
84	Bob Ojeda	.05
85	Rick Ownbey	.05
86	Tom Paciorek	.05
87	David Palmer	.05
88	Jeff Parrett RC	.05
89	Pat Perry RC	.05
90	Dan Plesac RC	.05
91	Darrell Porter	.05
92	Luis Quinones RC	.05
93	Rey Quinonez RC	.05
94	Gary Redus	.05
95	Jeff Reed RC	.05
96	Bip Roberts RC	.05
97	Billy Joe Robidoux RC	.05
98	Gary Roenicke	.05
99	Ron Roenicke	.05
100	Angel Salazar	.05
101	Joe Sambito	.05
102	Billy Sample	.05
103	Dave Schmidt	.05
104	Ken Schrom	.05
105	Ruben Sierra RC	.75
106	Ted Simmons	.05
107	Sammy Stewart	.05
108	Kurt Stillwell RC	.05
109	Dale Sveum RC	.05
110	Tim Teufel	.05
111	Bob Tewksbury RC	.05
112	Andres Thomas RC	.05
113	Jason Thompson	.05
114	Milt Thompson	.05
115	Rob Thompson RC	.05
116	Jay Tibbs	.05
117	Fred Toliver	.05
118	Wayne Tolleson	.05
119	Alex Trevino	.05
120	Manny Trillo	.05
121	Ed Vande Berg	.05
122	Ozzie Virgil	.05
123	Tony Walker RC	.05
124	Gene Walter	.05
125	Duane Ward RC	.05
126	Jerry Willard	.05
127	Mitch Williams RC	.05
128	Reggie Williams RC	.05
129	Bobby Witt RC	.05
130	Marvell Wynne	.05
131	Steve Yeager	.05
132	Checklist	.05

Baseball's Best

The 1986 Fleer Baseball's Best set was produced for the McCrory's retail chain and its affiliated stores. Subtitled "Sluggers vs. Pitchers," the set contains 22 each of the game's best hitters and pitchers. The 2-1/2" x 3-1/2" cards have color action photos on front. Backs are done in blue and red and carry players' personal and statistical data. The sets were issued in a specially designed box with six team logo stickers.

		NM/M
Complete Set (44):		4.00
Common Player:		.10
1	Bert Blyleven	.25
2	Wade Boggs	.75
3	George Brett	1.00
4	Tom Browning	.10
5	Jose Canseco	.60
6	Will Clark	.15
7	Roger Clemens	1.00
8	Alvin Davis	.10
9	Julio Franco	.10
10	Kirk Gibson	.10
11	Dwight Gooden	.10
12	Goose Gossage	.10
13	Pedro Guerrero	.10
14	Ron Guidry	.10
15	Tony Gwynn	.75
16	Orel Hershiser	.10
17	Kent Hrbek	.10
18	Reggie Jackson	.75
19	Wally Joyner	.15
20	Charlie Leibrandt	.10
21	Don Mattingly	1.00
22	Willie McGee	.10
23	Jack Morris	.10
24	Dale Murphy	.25
25	Eddie Murray	.50
26	Jeff Reardon	.10
27	Rick Reuschel	.10
28	Cal Ripken, Jr.	2.00
29	Pete Rose	1.50
30	Nolan Ryan	2.00
31	Bret Saberhagen	.10
32	Ryne Sandberg	.75
33	Mike Schmidt	1.00
34	Tom Seaver	.50
35	Bryn Smith	.05
36	Mario Soto	.05
37	Dave Stieb	.05
38	Darryl Strawberry	.10
39	Rick Sutcliffe	.05
40	John Tudor	.10
41	Fernando Valenzuela	.05
42	Bobby Witt	.10
43	Mike Witt	.10
44	Robin Yount	.50

League Leaders

Fleer's 1986 "League Leaders" set features 44 of the game's top players and was issued through the Walgreen's drug store chain. Fronts contain a color photo and feature player name, team and position in a blue band near the bottom of the card. The words "League Leaders" appear in a red band at the top of the card.

		NM/M
Complete Set (44):		4.00

Ozzie Smith
CARDINALS—SHORTSTOP

The background for the card fronts is alternating blue and white stripes. The card backs are printed in blue, red and white and carry statistical information and team logo. Cards are the standard 2-1/2" x 3-1/2". The set was issued in a special cardboard box, along with six team logo stickers.

		NM/M
Complete Set (44):		4.00
Common Player:		.10
1	Wade Boggs	.60
2	George Brett	.75
3	Jose Canseco	.60
4	Rod Carew	.40
5	Gary Carter	.40
6	Jack Clark	.10
7	Vince Coleman	.10
8	Jose Cruz	.10
9	Alvin Davis	.10
10	Mariano Duncan	.10
11	Leon Durham	.10
12	Carlton Fisk	.40
13	Julio Franco	.10
14	Scott Garrelts	.10
15	Steve Garvey	.25
16	Dwight Gooden	.10
17	Ozzie Guillen	.10
18	Willie Hernandez	.10
19	Bob Horner	.10
20	Kent Hrbek	.10
21	Charlie Leibrandt	.10
22	Don Mattingly	.75
23	Oddibe McDowell	.10
24	Willie McGee	.10
25	Keith Moreland	.10
26	Lloyd Moseby	.10
27	Dale Murphy	.25
28	Phil Niekro	.35
29	Joe Orsulak	.10
30	Dave Parker	.10
31	Lance Parrish	.10
32	Kirby Puckett	.60
33	Tim Raines	.10
34	Earnie Riles	.10
35	Cal Ripken, Jr.	1.50
36	Pete Rose	1.00
37	Bret Saberhagen	.10
38	Juan Samuel	.10
39	Ryne Sandberg	.60
40	Tom Seaver	.40
41	Lee Smith	.10
42	Ozzie Smith	.60
43	Dave Stieb	.10
44	Robin Yount	.40

Limited Edition

VINCE COLEMAN
CARDINALS—OUTFIELD

Produced for the McCrory's store chain and its affiliates for the second year in a row, the Limited Edition set contains 44 cards. In standard 2-1/2" x 3-1/2" size, cards have color photos enclosed by green, red and yellow trim. Backs carry black print on two shades of red. The set was issued in a special cardboard box, along with six team logo stickers.

		NM/M
Complete Set (44):		4.00

Common Player:			.10
1	Doyle Alexander		.10
2	Joaquin Andujar		.10
3	Harold Baines		.10
4	Wade Boggs		.60
5	Phil Bradley		.10
6	George Brett		.75
7	Hubie Brooks		.10
8	Chris Brown		.10
9	Tom Brunansky		.10
10	Gary Carter		.50
11	Vince Coleman		.10
12	Cecil Cooper		.10
13	Jose Cruz		.10
14	Mike Davis		.10
15	Carlton Fisk		.50
16	Julio Franco		.10
17	Damaso Garcia		.10
18	Rich Gedman		.10
19	Kirk Gibson		.10
20	Dwight Gooden		.10
21	Pedro Guerrero		.10
22	Tony Gwynn		.60
23	Rickey Henderson		.50
24	Orel Hershiser		.10
25	LaMarr Hoyt		.10
26	Reggie Jackson		.60
27	Don Mattingly		.75
28	Oddibe McDowell		.10
29	Willie McGee		.10
30	Paul Molitor		.50
31	Dale Murphy		.20
32	Eddie Murray		.50
33	Dave Parker		.10
34	Tony Pena		.10
35	Jeff Reardon		.10
36	Cal Ripken, Jr.		1.50
37	Pete Rose		1.00
38	Bret Saberhagen		.10
39	Juan Samuel		.10
40	Ryne Sandberg		.60
41	Mike Schmidt		.75
42	Lee Smith		.10
43	Don Sutton		.40
44	Lou Whitaker		.10

Mini

DAVE WINFIELD
OUTFIELD

Fleer's 1986 "Classic Miniatures" set contains 120 cards that measure 1-13/16" x 2-9/16". The design of the high-gloss cards is identical to the regular 1986 Fleer set but the player photos are entirely different. The set, which was issued in a specially designed box along with 18 team logo stickers, was available only through hobby dealers.

		NM/M
Complete Set (120):		3.50
Common Player:		.05
1	George Brett	.65
2	Dan Quisenberry	.05
3	Bret Saberhagen	.05
4	Lonnie Smith	.05
5	Willie Wilson	.05
6	Jack Clark	.05
7	Vince Coleman	.05
8	Tom Herr	.05
9	Willie McGee	.05
10	Ozzie Smith	.50
11	John Tudor	.05
12	Jesse Barfield	.05
13	George Bell	.05
14	Tony Fernandez	.05
15	Damaso Garcia	.05
16	Dave Stieb	.05
17	Gary Carter	.40
18	Ron Darling	.05
19	Dwight Gooden	.05
20	Keith Hernandez	.05
21	Darryl Strawberry	.05
22	Ron Guidry	.05
23	Rickey Henderson	.40
24	Don Mattingly	.65
25	Dave Righetti	.05
26	Dave Winfield	.40
27	Mariano Duncan	.05
28	Pedro Guerrero	.05
29	Bill Madlock	.05
30	Mike Marshall	.05
31	Fernando Valenzuela	.05
32	Reggie Jackson	.50
33	Gary Pettis	.05

34	Ron Romanick	.05
35	Don Sutton	.30
36	Mike Witt	.05
37	Buddy Bell	.05
38	Tom Browning	.05
39	Dave Parker	.05
40	Pete Rose	.75
41	Mario Soto	.05
42	Harold Baines	.05
43	Carlton Fisk	.40
44	Ozzie Guillen	.05
45	Ron Kittle	.05
46	Tom Seaver	.40
47	Kirk Gibson	.05
48	Jack Morris	.05
49	Lance Parrish	.05
50	Alan Trammell	.05
51	Lou Whitaker	.05
52	Hubie Brooks	.05
53	Andre Dawson	.25
54	Tim Raines	.05
55	Bryn Smith	.05
56	Tim Wallach	.05
57	Mike Boddicker	.05
58	Eddie Murray	.40
59	Cal Ripken, Jr.	1.25
60	John Shelby	.05
61	Mike Young	.05
62	Jose Cruz	.05
63	Glenn Davis	.05
64	Phil Garner	.05
65	Nolan Ryan	1.25
66	Mike Scott	.05
67	Steve Garvey	.15
68	Goose Gossage	.05
69	Tony Gwynn	.50
70	Andy Hawkins	.05
71	Garry Templeton	.05
72	Wade Boggs	.50
73	Roger Clemens	.65
74	Dwight Evans	.05
75	Rich Gedman	.05
76	Jim Rice	.25
77	Shawon Dunston	.05
78	Leon Durham	.05
79	Keith Moreland	.05
80	Ryne Sandberg	.50
81	Rick Sutcliffe	.05
82	Bert Blyleven	.05
83	Tom Brunansky	.05
84	Kent Hrbek	.05
85	Kirby Puckett	.50
86	Bruce Bochte	.05
87	Jose Canseco	.40
88	Mike Davis	.05
89	Jay Howell	.05
90	Dwayne Murphy	.05
91	Steve Carlton	.40
92	Von Hayes	.05
93	Juan Samuel	.05
94	Mike Schmidt	.65
95	Glenn Wilson	.05
96	Phil Bradley	.05
97	Alvin Davis	.05
98	Jim Presley	.05
99	Danny Tartabull	.05
100	Cecil Cooper	.05
101	Paul Molitor	.40
102	Earnie Riles	.05
103	Robin Yount	.40
104	Bob Horner	.05
105	Dale Murphy	.40
106	Bruce Sutter	.30
107	Claudell Washington	.05
108	Chris Brown	.05
109	Chili Davis	.05
110	Scott Garrelts	.05
111	Oddibe McDowell	.05
112	Pete O'Brien	.05
113	Gary Ward	.05
114	Brett Butler	.05
115	Julio Franco	.05
116	Brook Jacoby	.05
117	Mike Brown	.05
118	Joe Orsulak	.05
119	Tony Pena	.05
120	R.J. Reynolds	.05

Star Stickers

STEVE GARVEY
PADRES · FIRST BASE

Fleer's 1986 sticker-card set again measures 2-1/2" x 3-1/2" and features color photos inside dark maroon borders. Backs are identical to the 1986 baseball card issue except for the 1-132 numbering system and blue ink instead of yellow. Card #132 is a multi-player card featuring Dwight Gooden and Dale Murphy on the front and a complete checklist for the set on the reverse. The cards were sold in wax packs with team logo stickers.

		NM/M
Complete Set (132):		7.00
Common Player:		.05
Wax Pack (5):		1.00
Wax Box (36):		12.00
1	Harold Baines	.05
2	Jesse Barfield	.05
3	Don Baylor	.05
4	Juan Beniquez	.05
5	Tim Birtsas	.05
6	Bert Blyleven	.10
7	Bruce Bochte	.05
8	Wade Boggs	.50
9	Dennis Boyd	.05
10	Phil Bradley	.05
11	George Brett	.65
12	Hubie Brooks	.05
13	Chris Brown	.05
14	Tom Browning	.05
15	Tom Brunansky	.05
16	Bill Buckner	.05
17	Britt Burns	.05
18	Brett Butler	.05
19	Jose Canseco	.40
20	Rod Carew	.40
21	Steve Carlton	.40
22	Don Carman	.05
23	Gary Carter	.40
24	Jack Clark	.05
25	Vince Coleman	.05
26	Cecil Cooper	.05
27	Jose Cruz	.05
28	Ron Darling	.05
29	Alvin Davis	.05
30	Jody Davis	.05
31	Mike Davis	.05
32	Andre Dawson	.25
33	Mariano Duncan	.05
34	Shawon Dunston	.05
35	Leon Durham	.05
36	Darrell Evans	.05
37	Tony Fernandez	.05
38	Carlton Fisk	.40
39	John Franco	.05
40	Julio Franco	.05
41	Damaso Garcia	.05
42	Scott Garrelts	.05
43	Steve Garvey	.15
44	Rich Gedman	.05
45	Kirk Gibson	.05
46	Dwight Gooden	.05
47	Pedro Guerrero	.05
48	Ron Guidry	.05
49	Ozzie Guillen	.05
50	Tony Gwynn	.50
51	Andy Hawkins	.05
52	Von Hayes	.05
53	Rickey Henderson	.40
54	Tom Henke	.05
55	Keith Hernandez	.05
56	Willie Hernandez	.05
57	Tom Herr	.05
58	Orel Hershiser	.05
59	Teddy Higuera	.05
60	Bob Horner	.05
61	Charlie Hough	.05
62	Jay Howell	.05
63	LaMarr Hoyt	.05
64	Kent Hrbek	.05
65	Reggie Jackson	.50
66	Bob James	.05
67	Dave Kingman	.05
68	Ron Kittle	.05
69	Charlie Leibrandt	.05
70	Fred Lynn	.05
71	Mike Marshall	.05
72	Don Mattingly	.65
73	Oddibe McDowell	.05
74	Willie McGee	.05
75	Scott McGregor	.05
76	Paul Molitor	.40
77	Donnie Moore	.05
78	Keith Moreland	.05
79	Jack Morris	.05
80	Dale Murphy	.15
81	Eddie Murray	.40
82	Phil Niekro	.35
83	Joe Orsulak	.05
84	Dave Parker	.05
85	Lance Parrish	.05
86	Larry Parrish	.05
87	Tony Pena	.05
88	Gary Pettis	.05
89	Jim Presley	.05
90	Kirby Puckett	.50
91	Dan Quisenberry	.05
92	Tim Raines	.05
93	Johnny Ray	.05
94	Jeff Reardon	.05
95	Rick Reuschel	.05
96	Jim Rice	.25
97	Dave Righetti	.05
98	Earnie Riles	.05
99	Cal Ripken, Jr.	1.25
100	Ron Romanick	.05
101	Pete Rose	.85

102	Nolan Ryan	1.25
103	Bret Saberhagen	.05
104	Mark Salas	.05
105	Juan Samuel	.05
106	Ryne Sandberg	.50
107	Mike Schmidt	.65
108	Mike Scott	.05
109	Tom Seaver	.40
110	Bryn Smith	.05
111	Dave Smith	.05
112	Lee Smith	.05
113	Ozzie Smith	.50
114	Mario Soto	.05
115	Dave Stieb	.05
116	Darryl Strawberry	.05
117	Bruce Sutter	.35
118	Garry Templeton	.05
119	Gorman Thomas	.05
120	Andre Thornton	.05
121	Alan Trammell	.05
122	John Tudor	.05
123	Fernando Valenzuela	.05
124	Frank Viola	.05
125	Gary Ward	.05
126	Lou Whitaker	.05
127	Frank White	.05
128	Glenn Wilson	.05
129	Willie Wilson	.05
130	Dave Winfield	.40
131	Robin Yount	.40
132	Dwight Gooden, Dale Murphy	.10

Star Stickers Box Panels

Four cards, numbered S-1 through S-4, were placed on the bottoms of 1986 Fleer Star Stickers wax pack boxes. The cards are nearly identical in format to the regular issue sticker cards. Individual cards measure 2-1/2" x 3-1/2" in size, while a complete panel of four measures 5" x 7-1/8".

		NM/M
Complete Panel Set:		2.00
Complete Singles Set (4):		2.00
Common Single Player:		.30
1	Dodgers logo	.05
2	Wade Boggs	1.25
3	Steve Garvey	.30
4	Dave Winfield	1.00

1987 Fleer

The 1987 Fleer set consists of 660 cards. Fronts feature a graduated blue-to-white border design. The player's name and position appear in the upper-left corner of the card; his team logo is located in the lower-right. Backs are done in blue, red and white and contain an innovative "Pro Scouts Report" feature which rates the player's batting or pitching skills. For the third year in a row, Fleer included its "Major League Prospects" subset. Fleer produced a glossy-finish Collectors Edition set which came housed in a specially-de-

signed tin box. After experiencing a dramatic hike in price during 1987, the glossy set now sells for only a few dollars more than the regular issue.

		NM/M
Unopened Fact. Set (672):		65.00
Complete Set (660):		50.00
Common Player:		.05
Wax Pack (15/17):		3.00
Wax Box (36):		100.00
Cello Pack (28):		5.00
Cello Box (24):		100.00
Rack Pack (51):		8.00
Rack Box (24):		160.00
1	Rick Aguilera	.05
2	Richard Anderson	.05
3	Wally Backman	.05
4	Gary Carter	.75
5	Ron Darling	.05
6	Len Dykstra	.05
7	Kevin Elster RC	.15
8	Sid Fernandez	.05
9	Dwight Gooden	.05
10	Ed Hearn RC	.05
11	Danny Heep	.05
12	Keith Hernandez	.05
13	Howard Johnson	.05
14	Ray Knight	.05
15	Lee Mazzilli	.05
16	Roger McDowell	.05
17	Kevin Mitchell	.05
18	Randy Niemann	.05
19	Bob Ojeda	.05
20	Jesse Orosco	.05
21	Rafael Santana	.05
22	Doug Sisk	.05
23	Darryl Strawberry	.05
24	Tim Teufel	.05
25	Mookie Wilson	.05
26	Tony Armas	.05
27	Marty Barrett	.05
28	Don Baylor	.05
29	Wade Boggs	1.00
30	Oil Can Boyd	.05
31	Bill Buckner	.05
32	Roger Clemens	2.00
33	Steve Crawford	.05
34	Dwight Evans	.05
35	Rich Gedman	.05
36	Dave Henderson	.05
37	Bruce Hurst	.05
38	Tim Lollar	.05
39	Al Nipper	.05
40	Spike Owen	.05
41	Jim Rice	.30
42	Ed Romero	.05
43	Joe Sambito	.05
44	Calvin Schiraldi	.05
45	Tom Seaver	.75
46	Jeff Sellers RC	.05
47	Bob Stanley	.05
48	Sammy Stewart	.05
49	Larry Andersen	.05
50	Alan Ashby	.05
51	Kevin Bass	.05
52	Jeff Calhoun	.05
53	Jose Cruz	.05
54	Danny Darwin	.05
55	Glenn Davis	.05
56	Jim Deshaies RC	.10
57	Bill Doran	.05
58	Phil Garner	.05
59	Billy Hatcher	.05
60	Charlie Kerfeld	.05
61	Bob Knepper	.05
62	Dave Lopes	.05
63	Aurelio Lopez	.05
64	Jim Pankovits	.05
65	Terry Puhl	.05
66	Craig Reynolds	.05
67	Nolan Ryan	3.00
68	Mike Scott	.05
69	Dave Smith	.05
70	Dickie Thon	.05
71	Tony Walker	.05
72	Denny Walling	.05
73	Bob Boone	.05
74	Rick Burleson	.05
75	John Candelaria	.05
76	Doug Corbett	.05
77	Doug DeCinces	.05
78	Brian Downing	.05
79	Chuck Finley RC	1.00
80	Terry Forster	.05
81	Bobby Grich	.05
82	George Hendrick	.05
83	Jack Howell RC	.05
84	Reggie Jackson	1.00
85	Ruppert Jones	.05
86	Wally Joyner	.05
87	Gary Lucas	.05
88	Kirk McCaskill	.05
89	Donnie Moore	.05
90	Gary Pettis	.05
91	Vern Ruhle	.05
92	Dick Schofield	.05
93	Don Sutton	.65
94	Rob Wilfong	.05
95	Mike Witt	.05
96	Doug Drabek RC	.05
97	Mike Easler	.05
98	Mike Fischlin	.05
99	Brian Fisher	.05
100	Ron Guidry	.10
101	Rickey Henderson	.75

102	Tommy John	.10
103	Ron Kittle	.05
104	Don Mattingly	2.00
105	Bobby Meacham	.05
106	Joe Niekro	.05
107	Mike Pagliarulo	.05
108	Dan Pasqua	.05
109	Willie Randolph	.05
110	Dennis Rasmussen	.05
111	Dave Righetti	.05
112	Gary Roenicke	.05
113	Rod Scurry	.05
114	Bob Shirley	.05
115	Joel Skinner	.05
116	Tim Stoddard	.05
117	Bob Tewksbury RC	.35
118	Wayne Tolleson	.05
119	Claudell Washington	.05
120	Dave Winfield	.75
121	Steve Buechele	.05
122	Ed Correa RC	.05
123	Scott Fletcher	.05
124	Jose Guzman	.05
125	Toby Harrah	.05
126	Greg Harris	.05
127	Charlie Hough	.05
128	Pete Incaviglia	.05
129	Mike Mason	.05
130	Oddibe McDowell	.05
131	Dale Mohorcic RC	.05
132	Pete O'Brien	.05
133	Tom Paciorek	.05
134	Larry Parrish	.05
135	Geno Petralli	.05
136	Darrell Porter	.05
137	Jeff Russell	.05
138	Ruben Sierra	.05
139	Don Slaught	.05
140	Gary Ward	.05
141	Curtis Wilkerson	.05
142	Mitch Williams RC	.10
143	Bobby Witt RC	.10
144	Dave Bergman	.05
145	Tom Brookens	.05
146	Bill Campbell	.05
147	Chuck Cary RC	.05
148	Darnell Coles	.05
149	Dave Collins	.05
150	Darrell Evans	.05
151	Kirk Gibson	.05
152	John Grubb	.05
153	Willie Hernandez	.05
154	Larry Herndon	.05
155	Eric King RC	.05
156	Chet Lemon	.05
157	Dwight Lowry	.05
158	Jack Morris	.05
159	Randy O'Neal	.05
160	Lance Parrish	.05
161	Dan Petry	.05
162	Pat Sheridan	.05
163	Jim Slaton	.05
164	Frank Tanana	.05
165	Walt Terrell	.05
166	Mark Thurmond	.05
167	Alan Trammell	.05
168	Lou Whitaker	.05
169	Luis Aguayo	.05
170	Steve Bedrosian	.05
171	Don Carman	.05
172	Darren Daulton	.05
173	Greg Gross	.05
174	Kevin Gross	.05
175	Von Hayes	.05
176	Charles Hudson	.05
177	Tom Hume	.05
178	Steve Jeltz	.05
179	Mike Maddux RC	.05
180	Shane Rawley	.05
181	Gary Redus	.05
182	Ron Roenicke	.05
183	Bruce Ruffin RC	.10
184	John Russell	.05
185	Juan Samuel	.05
186	Dan Schatzeder	.05
187	Mike Schmidt	2.00
188	Rick Schu	.05
189	Jeff Stone	.05
190	Kent Tekulve	.05
191	Milt Thompson	.05
192	Glenn Wilson	.05
193	Buddy Bell	.05
194	Tom Browning	.05
195	Sal Butera	.05
196	Dave Concepcion	.05
197	Kal Daniels	.05
198	Eric Davis	.05
199	John Denny	.05
200	Bo Diaz	.05
201	Nick Esasky	.05
202	John Franco	.05
203	Bill Gullickson	.05
204	Barry Larkin RC	2.00
205	Eddie Milner	.05
206	Rob Murphy RC	.05
207	Ron Oester	.05
208	Dave Parker	.05
209	Tony Perez	.65
210	Ted Power	.05
211	Joe Price	.05
212	Ron Robinson	.05
213	Pete Rose	2.50
214	Mario Soto	.05
215	Kurt Stillwell RC	.05
216	Max Venable	.05
217	Chris Welsh	.05
218	Carl Willis RC	.05
219	Jesse Barfield	.05

220	George Bell	.05
221	Bill Caudill	.05
222	John Cerutti RC	.05
223	Jim Clancy	.05
224	Mark Eichhorn RC	.10
225	Tony Fernandez	.05
226	Damaso Garcia	.05
227	Kelly Gruber	.05
228	Tom Henke	.05
229	Garth Iorg	.05
230	Cliff Johnson	.05
231	Joe Johnson	.05
232	Jimmy Key	.05
233	Dennis Lamp	.05
234	Rick Leach	.05
235	Buck Martinez	.05
236	Lloyd Moseby	.05
237	Rance Mulliniks	.05
238	Dave Stieb	.05
239	Willie Upshaw	.05
240	Ernie Whitt	.05
241	Andy Allanson RC	.05
242	Scott Bailes RC	.05
243	Chris Bando	.05
244	Tony Bernazard	.05
245	John Butcher	.05
246	Brett Butler	.05
247	Ernie Camacho	.05
248	Tom Candiotti	.05
249	Joe Carter	.05
250	Carmen Castillo	.05
251	Julio Franco	.05
252	Mel Hall	.05
253	Brook Jacoby	.05
254	Phil Niekro	.65
255	Otis Nixon	.05
256	Dickie Noles	.05
257	Bryan Oelkers	.05
258	Ken Schrom	.05
259	Don Schulze	.05
260	Cory Snyder	.05
261	Pat Tabler	.05
262	Andre Thornton	.05
263	Rich Yett RC	.05
264	Mike Aldrete RC	.05
265	Juan Berenguer	.05
266	Vida Blue	.05
267	Bob Brenly	.05
268	Chris Brown	.05
269	Will Clark	.05
270	Chili Davis	.05
271	Mark Davis	.05
272	Kelly Downs RC	.05
273	Scott Garrelts	.05
274	Dan Gladden	.05
275	Mike Krukow	.05
276	Randy Kutcher RC	.05
277	Mike LaCoss	.05
278	Jeff Leonard	.05
279	Candy Maldonado	.05
280	Roger Mason	.05
281	Bob Melvin RC	.05
282	Greg Minton	.05
283	Jeff Robinson	.05
284	Harry Spilman	.05
285	Rob Thompson RC	.05
286	Jose Uribe	.05
287	Frank Williams	.05
288	Joel Youngblood	.05
289	Jack Clark	.05
290	Vince Coleman	.05
291	Tim Conroy	.05
292	Danny Cox	.05
293	Ken Dayley	.05
294	Curt Ford	.05
295	Bob Forsch	.05
296	Tom Herr	.05
297	Ricky Horton	.05
298	Clint Hurdle	.05
299	Jeff Lahti	.05
300	Steve Lake	.05
301	Tito Landrum	.05
302	Mike LaValliere RC	.05
303	Greg Mathews RC	.05
304	Willie McGee	.05
305	Jose Oquendo	.05
306	Terry Pendleton	.05
307	Pat Perry	.05
308	Ozzie Smith	1.50
309	Ray Soff	.05
310	John Tudor	.05
311	Andy Van Slyke	.05
312	Todd Worrell	.05
313	Dann Bilardello	.05
314	Hubie Brooks	.05
315	Tim Burke	.05
316	Andre Dawson	.35
317	Mike Fitzgerald	.05
318	Tom Foley	.05
319	Andres Galarraga	.05
320	Joe Hesketh	.05
321	Wallace Johnson	.05
322	Wayne Krenchicki	.05
323	Vance Law	.05
324	Dennis Martinez	.05
325	Bob McClure	.05
326	Andy McGaffigan	.05
327	Al Newman RC	.05
328	Tim Raines	.05
329	Jeff Reardon	.05
330	Luis Rivera RC	.05
331	Bob Sebra RC	.05
332	Bryn Smith	.05
333	Jay Tibbs	.05
334	Tim Wallach	.05
335	Mitch Webster	.05
336	Jim Wohlford	.05
337	Floyd Youmans	.05

338	Chris Bosio RC	.25
339	Glenn Braggs RC	.05
340	Rick Cerone	.05
341	Mark Clear	.05
342	Bryan Clutterbuck RC	.05
343	Cecil Cooper	.05
344	Rob Deer	.05
345	Jim Gantner	.05
346	Ted Higuera	.05
347	John Henry Johnson	.05
348	Tim Leary RC	.05
349	Rick Manning	.05
350	Paul Molitor	.75
351	Charlie Moore	.05
352	Juan Nieves	.05
353	Ben Oglivie	.05
354	Dan Plesac RC	.10
355	Ernest Riles	.05
356	Billy Joe Robidoux	.05
357	Bill Schroeder	.05
358	Dale Sveum RC	.05
359	Gorman Thomas	.05
360	Bill Wegman RC	.05
361	Robin Yount	.75
362	Steve Balboni	.05
363	Scott Bankhead RC	.05
364	Buddy Biancalana	.05
365	Bud Black	.05
366	George Brett	2.00
367	Steve Farr	.05
368	Mark Gubicza	.05
369	Bo Jackson	.75
370	Danny Jackson	.05
371	Mike Kingery RC	.05
372	Rudy Law	.05
373	Charlie Leibrandt	.05
374	Dennis Leonard	.05
375	Hal McRae	.05
376	Jorge Orta	.05
377	Jamie Quirk	.05
378	Dan Quisenberry	.05
379	Bret Saberhagen	.05
380	Angel Salazar	.05
381	Lonnie Smith	.05
382	Jim Sundberg	.05
383	Frank White	.05
384	Willie Wilson	.05
385	Joaquin Andujar	.05
386	Doug Bair	.05
387	Dusty Baker	.05
388	Bruce Bochte	.05
389	Jose Canseco	.65
390	Chris Codiroli	.05
391	Mike Davis	.05
392	Alfredo Griffin	.05
393	Moose Haas	.05
394	Donnie Hill	.05
395	Jay Howell	.05
396	Dave Kingman	.05
397	Carney Lansford	.05
398	David Leiper RC	.05
399	Bill Mooneyham RC	.05
400	Dwayne Murphy	.05
401	Steve Ontiveros	.05
402	Tony Phillips	.05
403	Eric Plunk	.05
404	Jose Rijo	.05
405	Terry Steinbach RC	.50
406	Dave Stewart	.05
407	Mickey Tettleton	.05
408	Dave Von Ohlen	.05
409	Jerry Willard	.05
410	Curt Young	.05
411	Bruce Bochy	.05
412	Dave Dravecky	.05
413	Tim Flannery	.05
414	Steve Garvey	.25
415	Goose Gossage	.10
416	Tony Gwynn	1.50
417	Andy Hawkins	.05
418	LaMarr Hoyt	.05
419	Terry Kennedy	.05
420	John Kruk	.05
421	Dave LaPoint	.05
422	Craig Lefferts	.05
423	Carmelo Martinez	.05
424	Lance McCullers	.05
425	Kevin McReynolds	.05
426	Graig Nettles	.05
427	Bip Roberts	.05
428	Jerry Royster	.05
429	Benito Santiago	.05
430	Eric Show	.05
431	Bob Stoddard	.05
432	Garry Templeton	.05
433	Gene Walter	.05
434	Ed Whitson	.05
435	Marvell Wynne	.05
436	Dave Anderson	.05
437	Greg Brock	.05
438	Enos Cabell	.05
439	Mariano Duncan	.05
440	Pedro Guerrero	.05
441	Orel Hershiser	.05
442	Rick Honeycutt	.05
443	Ken Howell	.05
444	Ken Landreaux	.05
445	Bill Madlock	.05
446	Mike Marshall	.05
447	Len Matuszek	.05
448	Tom Niedenfuer	.05
449	Alejandro Pena	.05
450	Dennis Powell RC	.05
451	Jerry Reuss	.05
452	Bill Russell	.05
453	Steve Sax	.05
454	Mike Scioscia	.05
455	Franklin Stubbs	.05

456	Alex Trevino	.05
457	Fernando Valenzuela	.05
458	Ed Vande Berg	.05
459	Bob Welch	.05
460	Reggie Williams RC	.05
461	Don Aase	.05
462	Juan Beniquez	.05
463	Mike Boddicker	.05
464	Juan Bonilla	.05
465	Rich Bordi	.05
466	Storm Davis	.05
467	Rick Dempsey	.05
468	Ken Dixon	.05
469	Jim Dwyer	.05
470	Mike Flanagan	.05
471	Jackie Gutierrez	.05
472	Brad Havens	.05
473	Lee Lacy	.05
474	Fred Lynn	.05
475	Scott McGregor	.05
476	Eddie Murray	.75
477	Tom O'Malley	.05
478	Cal Ripken, Jr.	3.00
479	Larry Sheets	.05
480	John Shelby	.05
481	Nate Snell	.05
482	Jim Traber RC	.05
483	Mike Young	.05
484	Neil Allen	.05
485	Harold Baines	.05
486	Floyd Bannister	.05
487	Daryl Boston	.05
488	Ivan Calderon	.05
489	John Cangelosi RC	.05
490	Steve Carlton	.75
491	Joe Cowley	.05
492	Julio Cruz	.05
493	Bill Dawley	.05
494	Jose DeLeon	.05
495	Richard Dotson	.05
496	Carlton Fisk	.75
497	Ozzie Guillen	.05
498	Jerry Hairston Sr.	.05
499	Ron Hassey	.05
500	Tim Hulett	.05
501	Bob James	.05
502	Steve Lyons	.05
503	Joel McKeon RC	.05
504	Gene Nelson	.05
505	Dave Schmidt	.05
506	Ray Searage	.05
507	Bobby Thigpen RC	.15
508	Greg Walker	.05
509	Jim Acker	.05
510	Doyle Alexander	.05
511	Paul Assenmacher RC	.05
512	Bruce Benedict	.05
513	Chris Chambliss	.05
514	Jeff Dedmon	.05
515	Gene Garber	.05
516	Ken Griffey	.05
517	Terry Harper	.05
518	Bob Horner	.05
519	Glenn Hubbard	.05
520	Rick Mahler	.05
521	Omar Moreno	.05
522	Dale Murphy	.35
523	Ken Oberkfell	.05
524	Ed Olwine	.05
525	David Palmer	.05
526	Rafael Ramirez	.05
527	Billy Sample	.05
528	Ted Simmons	.05
529	Zane Smith	.05
530	Bruce Sutter	.65
531	Andres Thomas RC	.05
532	Ozzie Virgil	.05
533	Allan Anderson RC	.05
534	Keith Atherton	.05
535	Billy Beane	.05
536	Bert Blyleven	.10
537	Tom Brunansky	.05
538	Randy Bush	.05
539	George Frazier	.05
540	Gary Gaetti	.05
541	Greg Gagne	.05
542	Mickey Hatcher	.05
543	Neal Heaton	.05
544	Kent Hrbek	.05
545	Roy Lee Jackson	.05
546	Tim Laudner	.05
547	Steve Lombardozzi	.05
548	Mark Portugal RC	.10
549	Kirby Puckett	1.50
550	Jeff Reed	.05
551	Mark Salas	.05
552	Roy Smalley	.05
553	Mike Smithson	.05
554	Frank Viola	.05
555	Thad Bosley	.05
556	Ron Cey	.05
557	Jody Davis	.05
558	Ron Davis	.05
559	Bob Dernier	.05
560	Frank DiPino	.05
561	Shawon Dunston	.05
562	Leon Durham	.05
563	Dennis Eckersley	.65
564	Terry Francona	.05
565	Dave Gumpert	.05
566	Guy Hoffman	.05
567	Ed Lynch	.05
568	Gary Matthews	.05
569	Keith Moreland	.05
570	Jamie Moyer RC	.05
571	Jerry Mumphrey	.05
572	Ryne Sandberg	1.00
573	Scott Sanderson	.05

574	Lee Smith	.05
575	Chris Speier	.05
576	Rick Sutcliffe	.05
577	Manny Trillo	.05
578	Steve Trout	.05
579	Karl Best	.05
580	Scott Bradley RC	.05
581	Phil Bradley	.05
582	Mickey Brantley	.05
583	Mike Brown	.05
584	Alvin Davis	.05
585	Lee Guetterman RC	.05
586	Mark Huismann	.05
587	Bob Kearney	.05
588	Pete Ladd	.05
589	Mark Langston	.05
590	Mike Moore	.05
591	Mike Morgan	.05
592	John Moses	.05
593	Ken Phelps	.05
594	Jim Presley	.05
595	Rey Quinonez (Quinones) RC	.05
596	Harold Reynolds	.05
597	Billy Swift	.05
598	Danny Tartabull	.05
599	Steve Yeager	.05
600	Matt Young	.05
601	Bill Almon	.05
602	Rafael Belliard RC	.05
603	Mike Bielecki	.05
604	Barry Bonds	40.00
605	Bobby Bonilla	.05
606	Sid Bream	.05
607	Mike Brown	.05
608	Pat Clements	.05
609	Mike Diaz RC	.05
610	Cecilio Guante	.05
611	Barry Jones RC	.05
612	Bob Kipper	.05
613	Larry McWilliams	.05
614	Jim Morrison	.05
615	Joe Orsulak	.05
616	Junior Ortiz	.05
617	Tony Pena	.05
618	Johnny Ray	.05
619	Rick Reuschel	.05
620	R.J. Reynolds	.05
621	Rick Rhoden	.05
622	Don Robinson	.05
623	Bob Walk	.05
624	Jim Winn	.05
625	Youthful Power (Jose Canseco, Pete Incaviglia)	.15
626	300 Game Winners (Phil Niekro, Don Sutton)	.25
627	A.L. Firemen (Don Aase, Dave Righetti)	.05
628	Rookie All-Stars (Jose Canseco, Wally Joyner)	.25
629	Magic Mets (Gary Carter, Dwight Gooden, Keith Hernandez, Darryl Strawberry)	.15
630	N.L. Best Righties (Mike Krukow, Mike Scott)	.05
631	Sensational Southpaws (John Franco, Fernando Valenzuela)	.05
632	Count 'Em (Bob Horner)	.05
633	A.L. Pitcher's Nightmare (Jose Canseco, Kirby Puckett, Jim Rice)	.25
634	All Star Battery (Gary Carter, Roger Clemens)	.50
635	4,000 Strikeouts (Steve Carlton)	.15
636	Big Bats At First Sack (Glenn Davis, Eddie Murray)	.15
637	On Base (Wade Boggs, Keith Hernandez)	.25
638	Sluggers From Left Side (Don Mattingly, Darryl Strawberry)	.50
639	Former MVP's (Dave Parker, Ryne Sandberg)	.25
640	Dr. K. & Super K (Roger Clemens, Dwight Gooden)	.50
641	A.L. West Stoppers (Charlie Hough, Mike Witt)	.05
642	Doubles & Triples (Tim Raines, Juan Samuel)	.05
643	Outfielders With Punch (Harold Baines, Jesse Barfield)	.05
644	Major League Prospects (Dave Clark RC, Greg Swindell RC)	.35
645	Major League Prospects (Ron Karkovice RC, Russ Morman RC)	.05
646	Major League Prospects (Willie Fraser RC, Devon White RC)	1.00
647	Major League Prospects (Jerry Browne RC, Mike Stanley RC)	.25

648	Major League Prospects (Phil Lombardi RC, Dave Magadan RC)	.20
649	Major League Prospects (Ralph Bryant RC, Jose Gonzalez RC)	.10
650	Major League Prospects (Randy Asadoor RC, Jimmy Jones RC)	.10
651	Major League Prospects (Marvin Freeman RC, Tracy Jones RC)	.10
652	Major League Prospects (Kevin Seitzer RC, John Stefero RC)	.25
653	Major League Prospects (Steve Fireovid RC, Rob Nelson RC)	.10
654	Checklist 1-95	.05
655	Checklist 96-192	.05
656	Checklist 193-288	.05
657	Checklist 289-384	.05
658	Checklist 385-483	.05
659	Checklist 484-578	.05
660	Checklist 579-660	.05

All Stars

As in 1986, Fleer All Star Team cards were randomly inserted in wax and cello packs. Twelve cards, measuring the standard 2-1/2" x 3-1/2", comprise the set. Fronts feature a full-color player photo set against a gray background for American League players and a black background for National Leaguers. Backs are printed in black, red and white and feature a lengthy player biography. Fleer's choices for a major league All-Star team is once again the theme for the set.

		NM/M
Complete Set (12):		8.00
Common Player:		.25
1	Don Mattingly	2.00
2	Gary Carter	1.00
3	Tony Fernandez	.25
4	Steve Sax	.25
5	Kirby Puckett	1.50
6	Mike Schmidt	2.00
7	Mike Easler	.25
8	Todd Worrell	.25
9	George Bell	.25
10	Fernando Valenzuela	.25
11	Roger Clemens	2.00
12	Tim Raines	.25

Headliners

A continuation of the 1986 Future Hall of Famers idea, Fleer encountered legal problems with using the Hall of Fame name and abated them by entitling the set "Headliners." The cards were randomly inserted in three-pack rack packs. Fronts feature a player photo set against a beige background with bright red stripes. Backs are printed in black, red

and gray and offer a brief biography with an emphasis on the player's performance during the 1986 season.

		NM/M
Complete Set (6):		4.00
Common Player:		.50
1	Wade Boggs	1.50
2	Jose Canseco	1.00
3	Dwight Gooden	.50
4	Rickey Henderson	1.00
5	Keith Hernandez	.50
6	Jim Rice	.75

'86 World Series

WORLD SERIES 1986 • DARLING PICKS UP THE SLACK

Fleer issued a set of 12 cards highlighting the 1986 World Series between the Boston Red Sox and New York Mets. The sets were available only with Fleer factory sets, both regular and glossy. The cards, 2-1/2" x 3-1/2", have either horizontal or vertical formats. The fronts are bordered in red, white and blue stars and stripes with a thin gold frame around the photo. Backs are printed in red and blue on white stock and include information regarding the photo on the card fronts.

		NM/M
Complete Set, Regular (12):		6.00
Complete Set, Glossy (12):		6.00
Common Card:		.25
1	Left-Hand Finesse Beats Mets (Bruce Hurst)	.25
2	Wade Boggs, Keith Hernandez	1.25
3	Roger Clemens	4.00
4	Gary Carter	1.00
5	Ron Darling	.25
6	.433 Series Batting Average (Marty Barrett)	.25
7	Dwight Gooden	.50
8	Strategy At Work	.25
9	Dewey! (Dwight Evans)	.25
10	One Strike From Boston Victory (Dave Henderson, Spike Owen)	.25
11	Ray Knight, Darryl Strawberry	.25
12	Series M.V.P. (Ray Knight)	.25

Box Panels

For the second straight year, Fleer produced a special set of cards designed to stimulate sales of their wax and cello pack boxes. In 1987, Fleer issued 16 cards in panels of four on the bottoms of retail boxes. The cards are numbered C-1 through C-16 and are 2-1/2" x 3-1/2" in size. The cards have the same de-

sign as the regular issue set with the player photos and card numbers being different.

		NM/M
Complete Panel Set (4):		6.00
Complete Singles Set (16):		6.00
Common Panel:		1.50
Common Single Player:		.15
Panel		1.50
1	Mets Logo	.05
6	Keith Hernandez	.25
8	Dale Murphy	.45
14	Ryne Sandberg	1.00
Panel		2.50
2	Jesse Barfield	.15
3	George Brett	1.50
5	Red Sox Logo	.05
11	Kirby Puckett	1.00
Panel		1.50
4	Dwight Gooden	.15
9	Astros Logo	.05
10	Dave Parker	.15
15	Mike Schmidt	1.50
Panel		1.00
7	Wally Joyner	.25
12	Dave Righetti	.15
13	Angels Logo	.05
16	Robin Yount	.75

Glossy Tin

The three-year run of limited edition, glossy collectors' issues by Fleer from 1987-89 has become known to the hobby as "tins" for the colorful lithographed metal boxes in which complete sets were sold. In their debut year a reported 100,000 sets were made, each serial numbered on a sticker attached to the shrink-wrapped tin box. While the glossy version of the 1987 Fleer set once enjoyed a significant premium over regular cards, today that premium has evaporated and, indeed, it can be harder to find a buyer for the glossy version.

	NM/M
Unopened Set (672):	75.00
Complete Set (672):	50.00
Common Player:	.10

Update

Steve Carlton PITCHER

The 1987 update edition brings the regular Fleer set up to date by including traded players and hot rookies. The cards measure 2-1/2" x 3-1/2" and are housed in a specially designed box with 25 team logo stickers. A glossy-coated Fleer Collectors Edition set was also produced.

		NM/M
Complete Set (132):		9.00
Common Player:		.05
1	Scott Bankhead	.05
2	Eric Bell RC	.05
3	Juan Beniquez	.05
4	Juan Berenguer	.05
5	Mike Birkbeck RC	.05
6	Randy Bockus RC	.05
7	Rod Booker RC	.05
8	Thad Bosley	.05
9	Greg Brock	.05
10	Bob Brower RC	.05
11	Chris Brown	.05
12	Jerry Browne	.05
13	Ralph Bryant	.05
14	DeWayne Buice RC	.05

15	Ellis Burks RC	.05
16	Casey Candaele RC	.05
17	Steve Carlton	.50
18	Juan Castillo	.05
19	Chuck Crim RC	.05
20	Mark Davidson RC	.05
21	Mark Davis	.05
22	Storm Davis	.05
23	Bill Dawley	.05
24	Andre Dawson	.30
25	Brian Dayett	.05
26	Rick Dempsey	.05
27	Ken Dowell RC	.05
28	Dave Dravecky	.05
29	Mike Dunne RC	.05
30	Dennis Eckersley	.40
31	Cecil Fielder	.05
32	Brian Fisher	.05
33	Willie Fraser	.05
34	Ken Gerhart RC	.05
35	Jim Gott	.05
36	Dan Gladden	.05
37	Mike Greenwell RC	.05
38	Cecilio Guante	.05
39	Albert Hall	.05
40	Atlee Hammaker	.05
41	Mickey Hatcher	.05
42	Mike Heath	.05
43	Neal Heaton	.05
44	Mike Henneman RC	.05
45	Guy Hoffman	.05
46	Charles Hudson	.05
47	Chuck Jackson RC	.05
48	Mike Jackson RC	.05
49	Reggie Jackson	.75
50	Chris James	.05
51	Dion James	.05
52	Stan Javier	.05
53	Stan Jefferson RC	.05
54	Jimmy Jones	.05
55	Tracy Jones	.05
56	Terry Kennedy	.05
57	Mike Kingery	.05
58	Ray Knight	.05
59	Gene Larkin RC	.05
60	Mike LaValliere	.05
61	Jack Lazorko RC	.05
62	Terry Leach	.05
63	Rick Leach	.05
64	Craig Lefferts	.05
65	Jim Lindeman RC	.05
66	Bill Long RC	.05
67	Mike Loynd RC	.05
68	Greg Maddux RC	6.00
69	Bill Madlock	.05
70	Dave Magadan	.05
71	Joe Magrane RC	.05
72	Fred Manrique RC	.05
73	Mike Mason	.05
74	Lloyd McClendon RC	.05
75	Fred McGriff RC	.05
76	Mark McGwire	3.00
77	Mark McLemore	.05
78	Kevin McReynolds	.05
79	Dave Meads RC	.05
80	Greg Minton	.05
81	John Mitchell RC	.05
82	Kevin Mitchell	.05
83	John Morris	.05
84	Jeff Musselman RC	.05
85	Randy Myers RC	.05
86	Gene Nelson	.05
87	Joe Niekro	.05
88	Tom Nieto	.05
89	Reid Nichols	.05
90	Matt Nokes RC	.05
91	Dickie Noles	.05
92	Edwin Nunez	.05
93	Jose Nunez RC	.05
94	Paul O'Neill	.05
95	Jim Paciorek RC	.05
96	Lance Parrish	.05
97	Bill Pecota RC	.05
98	Tony Pena	.05
99	Luis Polonia RC	.05
100	Randy Ready	.05
101	Jeff Reardon	.05
102	Gary Redus	.05
103	Rick Rhoden	.05
104	Wally Ritchie RC	.05
105	Jeff Robinson RC	.05
106	Mark Salas	.05
107	Dave Schmidt	.05
108	Kevin Seitzer	.05
109	John Shelby	.05
110	John Smiley RC	.05
111	Lary Sorensen	.05
112	Chris Speier	.05
113	Randy St. Claire	.05
114	Jim Sundberg	.05
115	B.J. Surhoff RC	.05
116	Greg Swindell	.05
117	Danny Tartabull	.05
118	Dorn Taylor RC	.05
119	Lee Tunnell	.05
120	Ed Vande Berg	.05
121	Andy Van Slyke	.05
122	Gary Ward	.05
123	Devon White	.05
124	Alan Wiggins	.05
125	Bill Wilkinson RC	.05
126	Jim Winn	.05
127	Frank Williams	.05
128	Ken Williams RC	.05
129	Matt Williams RC	1.00
130	Herm Winningham	.05
131	Matt Young	.05
132	Checklist 1-132	.05

Update Glossy Tin

The 1987 Fleer glossy tin update set is identical to the regular-issue updates, except for the high-gloss coating on the cards' fronts and the lithographed metal box in which the sets were sold. Production was estimated at 100,000. Because of perceived overproduction, the glossy tin update set and singles currently carry little, if any, premium over the regular-issue updates.

	NM/M
Unopened Set (132):	12.00
Complete Set (132):	7.50
Common Player:	.10

Award Winners

Cardinal Comeback Player of the Year

The 1987 Fleer Award Winners boxed set was prepared for distribution by 7-Eleven stores. The 2-1/2" x 3-1/2" cards feature players who have won various major league awards during their careers. Fronts contain full-color photos surrounded by a yellow border. The name of the award the player won is printed at the bottom of the card in an oval-shaped band designed to resemble a metal nameplate on a trophy. Backs are printed in black, yellow and white, and include lifetime major and minor league statistics along with typical personal information. Each boxed set contained six team logo stickers.

		NM/M
Complete Set (44):		5.00
Common Player:		.10
1	Marty Barrett	.10
2	George Bell	.10
3	Bert Blyleven	.20
4	Bob Boone	.10
5	John Candelaria	.10
6	Jose Canseco	.45
7	Gary Carter	.50
8	Joe Carter	.10
9	Roger Clemens	1.00
10	Cecil Cooper	.10
11	Eric Davis	.10
12	Tony Fernandez	.10
13	Scott Fletcher	.10
14	Bob Forsch	.10
15	Dwight Gooden	.10
16	Ron Guidry	.10
17	Ozzie Guillen	.10
18	Bill Gullickson	.10
19	Tony Gwynn	.75
20	Bob Knepper	.10
21	Ray Knight	.10
22	Mark Langston	.10
23	Candy Maldonado	.10
24	Don Mattingly	.85
25	Roger McDowell	.10
26	Dale Murphy	.20
27	Dave Parker	.10
28	Lance Parrish	.10
29	Gary Pettis	.10
30	Kirby Puckett	.75
31	Johnny Ray	.10
32	Dave Righetti	.10
33	Cal Ripken, Jr.	1.50
34	Bret Saberhagen	.10
35	Ryne Sandberg	.75
36	Mike Schmidt	1.00
37	Mike Scott	.10
38	Ozzie Smith	.75
39	Robbie Thompson	.10
40	Fernando Valenzuela	.10
41	Mitch Webster	.10
42	Frank White	.10
43	Mike Witt	.10
44	Todd Worrell	.10

Baseball All Stars

JOSE CANSECO, OUTFIELD • A'S

Produced by Fleer for exclusive distribution through Ben Franklin stores, the "Baseball All Stars" set is comprised of 44 cards in the standard 2-1/2" x 3-1/2" format. Cards have full-color photos surrounded by a bright red border with white pinstripes at the top and bottom. Backs are printed in blue, white and dark red and include complete major and minor league statistics. The set was issued in a special cardboard box with a handful of team logo stickers.

		NM/M
Complete Set (44):		5.00
Common Player:		.10
1	Harold Baines	.10
2	Jesse Barfield	.10
3	Wade Boggs	.65
4	Dennis "Oil Can" Boyd	.10
5	Scott Bradley	.10
6	Jose Canseco	.40
7	Gary Carter	.50
8	Joe Carter	.10
9	Mark Clear	.10
10	Roger Clemens	.85
11	Jose Cruz	.10
12	Chili Davis	.10
13	Jody Davis	.10
14	Rob Deer	.10
15	Brian Downing	.10
16	Sid Fernandez	.10
17	John Franco	.10
18	Andres Galarraga	.10
19	Dwight Gooden	.10
20	Tony Gwynn	.65
21	Charlie Hough	.10
22	Bruce Hurst	.10
23	Wally Joyner	.10
24	Carney Lansford	.10
25	Fred Lynn	.10
26	Don Mattingly	.85
27	Willie McGee	.10
28	Jack Morris	.10
29	Dale Murphy	.20
30	Bob Ojeda	.10
31	Tony Pena	.10
32	Kirby Puckett	.65
33	Dan Quisenberry	.10
34	Tim Raines	.10
35	Willie Randolph	.10
36	Cal Ripken, Jr.	1.50
37	Pete Rose	1.00
38	Nolan Ryan	1.50
39	Juan Samuel	.10
40	Mike Schmidt	.85
41	Ozzie Smith	.65
42	Andres Thomas	.10
43	Fernando Valenzuela	.10
44	Mike Witt	.10

Baseball's Best
Box Bottom

These special cards were printed on the bottom of retail boxes of Fleer's "Baseball's Best" boxed sets. The box-bottom cards are in the same format as the boxed cards, with red, white and blue borders and a yellow title strip at top. Backs are also similar in design to the regular-issue cards, carrying player data and stats. Cards are numbered with a "M" prefix.

		NM/M
Complete Panel:		3.00
Complete Set (6):		3.00
Common Player:		.50
1	Steve Bedrosian	.50
2	Will Clark	1.00
3	Vince Coleman	.50
4	Bo Jackson	2.00
5	Cory Snyder	.50
---	K.C. Royals logo	.10

Baseball's Best

BRET SABERHAGEN 3.41 ERA

For a second straight baseball card season, Fleer produced for McCrory's stores and their affiliates a 44-card "Baseball's Best" set. Subtitled "Sluggers vs. Pitchers," 28 everyday players and 16 pitchers are featured. The card design is nearly identical to the previous year's effort. The cards were sold in a specially designed box along with six team logo stickers.

		NM/M
Complete Set (44):		4.00
Common Player:		.10
1	Kevin Bass	.10
2	Jesse Barfield	.10
3	George Bell	.10
4	Wade Boggs	.65
5	Sid Bream	.10
6	George Brett	.85
7	Ivan Calderon	.10
8	Jose Canseco	.50
9	Jack Clark	.10
10	Roger Clemens	.85
11	Eric Davis	.10
12	Andre Dawson	.25
13	Sid Fernandez	.10
14	John Franco	.10
15	Dwight Gooden	.10
16	Pedro Guerrero	.10
17	Tony Gwynn	.65
18	Rickey Henderson	.60
19	Tom Henke	.10
20	Ted Higuera	.10
21	Pete Incaviglia	.10
22	Wally Joyner	.10
23	Jeff Leonard	.10
24	Joe Magrane	.10
25	Don Mattingly	.85
26	Mark McGwire	1.00
27	Jack Morris	.10
28	Dale Murphy	.20
29	Dave Parker	.10
30	Ken Phelps	.10
31	Kirby Puckett	.65
32	Tim Raines	.10
33	Jeff Reardon	.10
34	Dave Righetti	.10
35	Cal Ripken, Jr.	1.50
36	Bret Saberhagen	.10
37	Mike Schmidt	.85
38	Mike Scott	.10
39	Kevin Seitzer	.10
40	Darryl Strawberry	.10
41	Rick Sutcliffe	.10
42	Pat Tabler	.10
43	Fernando Valenzuela	.10
44	Mike Witt	.10

Exciting Stars

CORY SNYDER, INDIANS • OF

Another entry into the Fleer lineup of individual boxed sets, the "Baseball's Exciting Stars" set was produced for Cumberland Farms stores. The card fronts feature a red, white and blue border with the words "Exciting Stars" printed in yellow at the top. The backs are printed in red and blue and carry complete major and minor league statistics. Included with the boxed set of 44 cards were six team logo stickers.

		NM/M
Complete Set (44):		4.00
Common Player:		.10
1	Don Aase	.10
2	Rick Aguilera	.10
3	Jesse Barfield	.10
4	Wade Boggs	.65
5	Dennis "Oil Can" Boyd	.10
6	Sid Bream	.10
7	Jose Canseco	.45
8	Steve Carlton	.50
9	Gary Carter	.50
10	Will Clark	.10
11	Roger Clemens	.85
12	Danny Cox	.10
13	Alvin Davis	.10
14	Eric Davis	.10
15	Rob Deer	.10
16	Brian Downing	.10
17	Gene Garber	.10
18	Steve Garvey	.20
19	Dwight Gooden	.10
20	Mark Gubicza	.10
21	Mel Hall	.10
22	Terry Harper	.10
23	Von Hayes	.10
24	Rickey Henderson	.50
25	Tom Henke	.10
26	Willie Hernandez	.10
27	Ted Higuera	.10
28	Rick Honeycutt	.10
29	Kent Hrbek	.08
30	Wally Joyner	.10
31	Charlie Kerfeld	.10
32	Fred Lynn	.10
33	Don Mattingly	.85
34	Tim Raines	.10
35	Dennis Rasmussen	.10
36	Johnny Ray	.10
37	Jim Rice	.25
38	Pete Rose	1.00
39	Lee Smith	.10
40	Cory Snyder	.10
41	Darryl Strawberry	.10
42	Kent Tekulve	.10
43	Willie Wilson	.10
44	Bobby Witt	.10

Game Winners

KEVIN McREYNOLDS, 14 GAME WINNING RUNS BATTED IN

The 1987 Fleer "Baseball's Game Winners" boxed set was produced for distribution through Bi-Mart Discount Drug, Pay'n-Save, Mott's 5 & 10, M.E. Moses, and Winn's stores. Cards have a light blue border with the player's name and game winning RBI or games-won statistics in a yellow oval band at the top. Backs are similar to the regular-issue 1987 Fleer, with full professional stats. Included with the boxed set were six team logo stickers.

		NM/M
Complete Set (44):		4.00
Common Player:		.10
1	Harold Baines	.10
2	Don Baylor	.10
3	George Bell	.10

Hottest Stars

MARK EICHHORN, BLUE JAYS • PITCHER

The "Baseball's Hottest Stars" set was produced by Fleer for the Revco Drug Store chain. Measuring the standard 2-1/2" x 3-1/2", the cards feature full-color photos surrounded by a red, white and blue border. Card backs are printed in red, white and black and contain the player's lifetime professional statistics. The set was sold in a special cardboard box with six team logo stickers.

		NM/M
Unopened Set (44):		45.00
Complete Set (44):		25.00
Common Player:		.10
1	Joaquin Andujar	.10
2	Harold Baines	.10
3	Kevin Bass	.10
4	Don Baylor	.10
5	Barry Bonds	20.00
6	George Brett	1.00
7	Tom Brunansky	.10
8	Brett Butler	.10
9	Jose Canseco	.60
10	Roger Clemens	1.00
11	Ron Darling	.10
12	Eric Davis	.10
13	Andre Dawson	.25
14	Doug DeCinces	.10
15	Leon Durham	.10
16	Mark Eichhorn	.10
17	Scott Garrelts	.10
18	Dwight Gooden	.10
19	Dave Henderson	.10
20	Rickey Henderson	.60
21	Keith Hernandez	.10
22	Ted Higuera	.10
23	Bob Horner	.10
24	Pete Incaviglia	.10
25	Wally Joyner	.10
26	Mark Langston	.10
27	Don Mattingly	1.00
28	Dale Murphy	.20
29	Kirk McCaskill	.10
30	Willie McGee	.10
31	Dave Righetti	.10
32	Pete Rose	1.50
33	Bruce Ruffin	.10

4	Tony Bernazard	.10
5	Wade Boggs	.75
6	George Brett	.85
7	Hubie Brooks	.10
8	Jose Canseco	.50
9	Gary Carter	.60
10	Roger Clemens	.85
11	Eric Davis	.10
12	Glenn Davis	.10
13	Shawon Dunston	.10
14	Mark Eichhorn	.10
15	Gary Gaetti	.10
16	Steve Garvey	.15
17	Kirk Gibson	.10
18	Dwight Gooden	.10
19	Von Hayes	.10
20	Willie Hernandez	.10
21	Ted Higuera	.10
22	Wally Joyner	.10
23	Bob Knepper	.10
24	Mike Krukow	.10
25	Jeff Leonard	.10
26	Don Mattingly	.85
27	Kirk McCaskill	.10
28	Kevin McReynolds	.10
29	Jim Morrison	.10
30	Dale Murphy	.15
31	Pete O'Brien	.10
32	Bob Ojeda	.10
33	Larry Parrish	.10
34	Ken Phelps	.10
35	Dennis Rasmussen	.10
36	Ernest Riles	.10
37	Cal Ripken, Jr.	1.00
38	Ron Robinson	.10
39	Steve Sax	.10
40	Mike Schmidt	.85
41	John Tudor	.10
42	Fernando Valenzuela	.10
43	Mike Witt	.10
44	Curt Young	.10

34	Steve Sax	.10
35	Mike Schmidt	1.00
36	Larry Sheets	.10
37	Eric Show	.10
38	Dave Smith	.10
39	Cory Snyder	.10
40	Frank Tanana	.10
41	Alan Trammell	.10
42	Reggie Williams	.10
43	Mookie Wilson	.10
44	Todd Worrell	.10

League Leaders

TODD WORRELL, ST. LOUIS CARDINALS

For a second year, Fleer produced a 44- card "League Leaders" set for Walgreens. The card fronts feature a border style which is identical to that used in 1986. However, a trapezoidal shaped full-color player photo is placed diagonally on the front. "1987 Fleer League Leaders" appears in the upper left corner of the front although nowhere on the card does it state in which pitching, hitting or fielding department was the player a league leader. Backs are printed in red and blue on white stock. The cards in the boxed set are the standard 2-1/2" x 3-1/2" size.

		NM/M
Complete Set (44):		4.00
Common Player:		.10
1	Jesse Barfield	.10
2	Mike Boddicker	.10
3	Wade Boggs	.65
4	Phil Bradley	.10
5	George Brett	.85
6	Hubie Brooks	.10
7	Chris Brown	.10
8	Jose Canseco	.50
9	Joe Carter	.10
10	Roger Clemens	.85
11	Vince Coleman	.10
12	Joe Cowley	.10
13	Kal Daniels	.10
14	Glenn Davis	.10
15	Jody Davis	.10
16	Darrell Evans	.10
17	Dwight Evans	.10
18	John Franco	.10
19	Julio Franco	.10
20	Dwight Gooden	.10
21	Goose Gossage	.10
22	Tom Herr	.10
23	Ted Higuera	.10
24	Bob Horner	.10
25	Pete Incaviglia	.10
26	Wally Joyner	.10
27	Dave Kingman	.10
28	Don Mattingly	.85
29	Willie McGee	.10
30	Donnie Moore	.10
31	Keith Moreland	.10
32	Eddie Murray	.60
33	Mike Pagliarulo	.10
34	Larry Parrish	.10
35	Tony Pena	.10
36	Kirby Puckett	.65
37	Pete Rose	1.00
38	Juan Samuel	.10
39	Ryne Sandberg	.65
40	Mike Schmidt	.85
41	Darryl Strawberry	.10
42	Greg Walker	.10
43	Bob Welch	.10
44	Todd Worrell	.10

Limited Edition

For the third straight year, Fleer produced a Limited Edition set for the McCrory's store chain and its affiliates. The cards are the standard 2-1/2" x 3-1/2" and feature light blue borders at the top and bottom and a diagonal red and white border running along both sides. The set was issued in a specially prepared cardboard box, along with six team logo stickers.

		NM/M
Complete Set (44):		4.00
Common Player:		.10
1	Floyd Bannister	.10
2	Marty Barrett	.10
3	Steve Bedrosian	.10
4	George Bell	.10
5	George Brett	.85
6	Jose Canseco	.40
7	Joe Carter	.10
8	Will Clark	.10
9	Roger Clemens	.85
10	Vince Coleman	.10
11	Glenn Davis	.10
12	Mike Davis	.10
13	Len Dykstra	.10
14	John Franco	.10
15	Julio Franco	.10
16	Steve Garvey	.25
17	Kirk Gibson	.10
18	Dwight Gooden	.10
19	Tony Gwynn	.65
20	Keith Hernandez	.10
21	Teddy Higuera	.10
22	Kent Hrbek	.10
23	Wally Joyner	.10
24	Mike Krukow	.10
25	Mike Marshall	.10
26	Don Mattingly	.85
27	Oddibe McDowell	.10
28	Jack Morris	.10
29	Lloyd Moseby	.10
30	Dale Murphy	.20
31	Eddie Murray	.50
32	Tony Pena	.10
33	Jim Presley	.10
34	Jeff Reardon	.10
35	Jim Rice	.25
36	Pete Rose	1.00
37	Mike Schmidt	.85
38	Mike Scott	.10
39	Lee Smith	.10
40	Lonnie Smith	.10
41	Gary Ward	.10
42	Dave Winfield	.50
43	Todd Worrell	.10
44	Robin Yount	.50

Limited Edition Box Bottom

These special cards were printed on the bottom of retail boxes of Fleer's "Limited Edition" boxed sets. The box-bottom cards are in the same format as the boxed cards, with red, white and blue borders. Backs are also similar in design to the regular-issue cards, carrying player data and stats.

		NM/M
Complete Panel:		2.00
Complete Set (6):		2.00
Common Player:		.50
C1	Ron Darling	.50
C2	Bill Buckner	.50
C3	John Candelaria	.50
C4	Jack Clark	.50
C5	Bret Saberhagen	.50
C6	Houston Astros logo	.25

Mini

Continuing with an idea originated the previous year, the Fleer "Classic Miniatures" set consists of 120 cards that measure 1-13/16" x 2-9/16". The cards are identical in design to the regular-issue set, but use completely different photos. The set was issued in a specially prepared collectors box along with 18 team logo stickers. The mini set was available only through hobby dealers.

		NM/M
Complete Set (120):		4.00
Common Player:		.05
1	Don Aase	.05
2	Joaquin Andujar	.05
3	Harold Baines	.05
4	Jesse Barfield	.05
5	Kevin Bass	.05
6	Don Baylor	.05
7	George Bell	.05
8	Tony Bernazard	.05
9	Bert Blyleven	.05
10	Wade Boggs	.65
11	Phil Bradley	.05
12	Sid Bream	.05
13	George Brett	.85
14	Hubie Brooks	.05
15	Chris Brown	.05
16	Tom Candiotti	.05
17	Jose Canseco	.40
18	Gary Carter	.50
19	Joe Carter	.05
20	Roger Clemens	.85
21	Vince Coleman	.05
22	Cecil Cooper	.05
23	Ron Darling	.05
24	Alvin Davis	.05
25	Chili Davis	.05
26	Eric Davis	.05
27	Glenn Davis	.05
28	Mike Davis	.05
29	Doug DeCinces	.05
30	Rob Deer	.05
31	Jim Deshaies	.05
32	Bo Diaz	.05
33	Richard Dotson	.05
34	Brian Downing	.05
35	Shawon Dunston	.05
36	Mark Eichhorn	.05
37	Dwight Evans	.05
38	Tony Fernandez	.05
39	Julio Franco	.05
40	Gary Gaetti	.05
41	Andres Galarraga	.05
42	Scott Garrelts	.05
43	Steve Garvey	.15
44	Kirk Gibson	.05
45	Dwight Gooden	.05
46	Ken Griffey	.05
47	Mark Gubicza	.05
48	Ozzie Guillen	.05
49	Bill Gullickson	.05
50	Tony Gwynn	.65
51	Von Hayes	.05
52	Rickey Henderson	.50
53	Keith Hernandez	.05
54	Willie Hernandez	.05
55	Ted Higuera	.05
56	Charlie Hough	.05
57	Kent Hrbek	.05
58	Pete Incaviglia	.05
59	Wally Joyner	.05
60	Bob Knepper	.05
61	Mike Krukow	.05
62	Mark Langston	.05
63	Carney Lansford	.05
64	Jim Lindeman	.05
65	Bill Madlock	.05
66	Don Mattingly	.85
67	Kirk McCaskill	.05
68	Lance McCullers	.05
69	Keith Moreland	.05
70	Jack Morris	.05
71	Jim Morrison	.05
72	Lloyd Moseby	.05
73	Jerry Mumphrey	.05
74	Dale Murphy	.15
75	Eddie Murray	.50
76	Pete O'Brien	.05
77	Bob Ojeda	.05
78	Jesse Orosco	.05
79	Dan Pasqua	.05
80	Dave Parker	.05
81	Larry Parrish	.05
82	Jim Presley	.05
83	Kirby Puckett	.65
84	Dan Quisenberry	.05
85	Tim Raines	.05
86	Dennis Rasmussen	.05
87	Johnny Ray	.05
88	Jeff Reardon	.05
89	Jim Rice	.25
90	Dave Righetti	.05
91	Earnest Riles	.05
92	Cal Ripken, Jr.	1.50
93	Ron Robinson	.05
94	Juan Samuel	.05
95	Ryne Sandberg	.65
96	Steve Sax	.05
97	Mike Schmidt	.85
98	Ken Schrom	.05

99	Mike Scott	.05
100	Ruben Sierra	.05
101	Lee Smith	.05
102	Ozzie Smith	.65
103	Cory Snyder	.05
104	Kent Tekulve	.05
105	Andres Thomas	.05
106	Rob Thompson	.05
107	Alan Trammell	.05
108	John Tudor	.05
109	Fernando Valenzuela	.05
110	Greg Walker	.05
111	Mitch Webster	.05
112	Lou Whitaker	.05
113	Frank White	.05
114	Reggie Williams	.05
115	Glenn Wilson	.05
116	Willie Wilson	.05
117	Dave Winfield	.50
118	Mike Witt	.05
119	Todd Worrell	.05
120	Floyd Youmans	.05

Record Setters

Produced by Fleer for the Eckerd Drug chain, the Record Setters set contains 44 cards in standard 2-1/2" x 3-1/2" size. Although the set is titled "Record Setters," the actual records the players have set is not specified anywhere on the cards. Given that several players included in the set were young prospects, a better title for those cards might have been "Possible Record Setters." The set came housed in a special cardboard box with six team logo stickers.

		NM/M
Complete Set (44):		4.00
Common Player:		.10
1	George Brett	.85
2	Chris Brown	.10
3	Jose Canseco	.40
4	Roger Clemens	.85
5	Alvin Davis	.10
6	Shawon Dunston	.10
7	Tony Fernandez	.10
8	Carlton Fisk	.45
9	Gary Gaetti	.10
10	Gene Garber	.10
11	Rich Gedman	.10
12	Dwight Gooden	.10
13	Ozzie Guillen	.10
14	Bill Gullickson	.10
15	Billy Hatcher	.10
16	Orel Hershiser	.10
17	Wally Joyner	.10
18	Ray Knight	.10
19	Craig Lefferts	.10
20	Don Mattingly	.85
21	Kevin Mitchell	.10
22	Lloyd Moseby	.10
23	Dale Murphy	.15
24	Eddie Murray	.45
25	Phil Niekro	.30
26	Ben Oglivie	.10
27	Jesse Orosco	.10
28	Joe Orsulak	.10
29	Larry Parrish	.10
30	Tim Raines	.10
31	Shane Rawley	.10
32	Dave Righetti	.10
33	Pete Rose	1.00
34	Steve Sax	.10
35	Mike Schmidt	.85
36	Mike Scott	.10
37	Don Sutton	.30
38	Alan Trammell	.10
39	John Tudor	.10
40	Gary Ward	.10
41	Lou Whitaker	.10
42	Willie Wilson	.10
43	Todd Worrell	.10
44	Floyd Youmans	.10

Star Stickers

The 1987 Fleer Star Stickers set contains 132 cards which become stickers if the

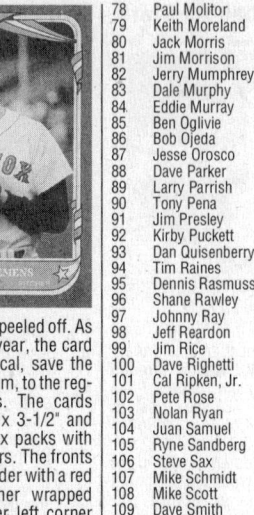

back is bent and peeled off. As in the previous year, the card backs are identical, save the numbering system, to the regular-issue cards. The cards measure 2-1/2" x 3-1/2" and were sold in wax packs with team logo stickers. The fronts have a green border with a red and white banner wrapped across the upper left corner and the sides. The backs are printed in green and yellow.

		NM/M
Complete Set (132):		6.00
Common Player:		.05
Wax Pack (5):		.50
Wax Box (36):		12.00
1	Don Aase	.05
2	Harold Baines	.05
3	Floyd Bannister	.05
4	Jesse Barfield	.05
5	Marty Barrett	.05
6	Kevin Bass	.05
7	Don Baylor	.05
8	Steve Bedrosian	.05
9	George Bell	.05
10	Bert Blyleven	.05
11	Mike Boddicker	.05
12	Wade Boggs	.65
13	Phil Bradley	.05
14	Sid Bream	.05
15	George Brett	.85
16	Hubie Brooks	.05
17	Tom Brunansky	.05
18	Tom Candiotti	.05
19	Jose Canseco	.40
20	Gary Carter	.50
21	Joe Carter	.05
22	Will Clark	.05
23	Mark Clear	.05
24	Roger Clemens	.85
25	Vince Coleman	.05
26	Jose Cruz	.05
27	Ron Darling	.05
28	Alvin Davis	.05
29	Chili Davis	.05
30	Eric Davis	.05
31	Glenn Davis	.05
32	Mike Davis	.05
33	Andre Dawson	.25
34	Doug DeCinces	.05
35	Brian Downing	.05
36	Shawon Dunston	.05
37	Mark Eichhorn	.05
38	Dwight Evans	.05
39	Tony Fernandez	.05
40	Bob Forsch	.05
41	John Franco	.05
42	Julio Franco	.05
43	Gary Gaetti	.05
44	Gene Garber	.05
45	Scott Garrelts	.05
46	Steve Garvey	.20
47	Kirk Gibson	.05
48	Dwight Gooden	.05
49	Ken Griffey	.05
50	Ozzie Guillen	.05
51	Bill Gullickson	.05
52	Tony Gwynn	.65
53	Mel Hall	.05
54	Greg Harris	.05
55	Von Hayes	.05
56	Rickey Henderson	.50
57	Tom Henke	.05
58	Keith Hernandez	.05
59	Willie Hernandez	.05
60	Ted Higuera	.05
61	Bob Horner	.05
62	Charlie Hough	.05
63	Jay Howell	.05
64	Kent Hrbek	.05
65	Bruce Hurst	.05
66	Pete Incaviglia	.05
67	Bob James	.05
68	Wally Joyner	.05
69	Mike Krukow	.05
70	Mark Langston	.05
71	Carney Lansford	.05
72	Fred Lynn	.05
73	Bill Madlock	.05
74	Don Mattingly	.85
75	Kirk McCaskill	.05
76	Lance McCullers	.05
77	Oddibe McDowell	.05

78	Paul Molitor	.50
79	Keith Moreland	.05
80	Jack Morris	.05
81	Jim Morrison	.05
82	Jerry Mumphrey	.05
83	Dale Murphy	.20
84	Eddie Murray	.05
85	Ben Oglivie	.05
86	Bob Ojeda	.05
87	Jesse Orosco	.05
88	Dave Parker	.05
89	Larry Parrish	.05
90	Tony Pena	.05
91	Jim Presley	.05
92	Kirby Puckett	.65
93	Dan Quisenberry	.05
94	Tim Raines	.05
95	Dennis Rasmussen	.05
96	Shane Rawley	.05
97	Johnny Ray	.05
98	Jeff Reardon	.05
99	Jim Rice	.25
100	Dave Righetti	.05
101	Cal Ripken, Jr.	2.00
102	Pete Rose	1.00
103	Nolan Ryan	2.00
104	Juan Samuel	.05
105	Ryne Sandberg	.65
106	Steve Sax	.05
107	Mike Schmidt	.85
108	Mike Scott	.05
109	Dave Smith	.05
110	Lee Smith	.05
111	Lonnie Smith	.05
112	Ozzie Smith	.65
113	Cory Snyder	.05
114	Darryl Strawberry	.05
115	Don Sutton	.45
116	Kent Tekulve	.05
117	Gorman Thomas	.05
118	Alan Trammell	.05
119	John Tudor	.05
120	Fernando Valenzuela	.05
121	Bob Welch	.05
122	Lou Whitaker	.05
123	Frank White	.05
124	Reggie Williams	.05
125	Willie Wilson	.05
126	Dave Winfield	.50
127	Mike Witt	.05
128	Todd Worrell	.05
129	Curt Young	.05
130	Robin Yount	.50
131	Checklist (Jose Canseco, Don Mattingly)	.25
132	Checklist (Bo Jackson, Eric Davis)	.05

Star Stickers Box Panels

Fleer issued on the bottoms of its Fleer Star Stickers wax pack boxes six player cards plus two team logo/checklist cards. The cards, which measure 2-1/2" x 3-1/2", are numbered S-1 through S-8, and are identical in design to the Star Stickers.

		NM/M
Complete Panel Set (2):		2.50
Complete Singles Set (8):		2.50
Common Single Player:		.10
Panel		2.00
2	Wade Boggs	.75
3	Bert Blyleven	.10
6	Phillies Logo	.05
8	Don Mattingly	1.50
Panel		1.00
1	Tigers Logo	.05
4	Jose Cruz	.10
5	Glenn Davis	.10
7	Bob Horner	.10

1988 Fleer

A clean, uncluttered look was featured in the 1988 Fleer set. Cards in the standard 2-1/2" x 3-1/2" format feature blue and red diagonal lines on a white background. Player identification and team logo appears at top. Backs include personal in-

formation and career statistics, plus a new feature called "At Their Best." This feature graphically shows a player's pitching or hitting statistics for home and road games and how he fared during day games as opposed to night contests. The set includes 19 special cards (#622-640) and 12 "Major League Prospects" cards.

		NM/M
Retail Factory Set (672):		12.00
Hobby Factory Set (672):		10.00
Complete Set (660):		8.00
Common Player:		.05
Wax Pack (15):		.75
Wax Box (36):		12.00
Cello Pack (28):		1.25
Cello Box (24):		16.00
1	Keith Atherton	.05
2	Don Baylor	.05
3	Juan Berenguer	.05
4	Bert Blyleven	.10
5	Tom Brunansky	.05
6	Randy Bush	.05
7	Steve Carlton	.50
8	Mark Davidson RC	.05
9	George Frazier	.05
10	Gary Gaetti	.05
11	Greg Gagne	.05
12	Dan Gladden	.05
13	Kent Hrbek	.05
14	Gene Larkin RC	.05
15	Tim Laudner	.05
16	Steve Lombardozzi	.05
17	Al Newman	.05
18	Joe Niekro	.05
19	Kirby Puckett	.65
20	Jeff Reardon	.05
21a	Dan Schatzader (Incorrect spelling.)	.10
21b	Dan Schatzeder (Correct spelling.)	.05
22	Roy Smalley	.05
23	Mike Smithson	.05
24	Les Straker RC	.05
25	Frank Viola	.05
26	Jack Clark	.05
27	Vince Coleman	.05
28	Danny Cox	.05
29	Bill Dawley	.05
30	Ken Dayley	.05
31	Doug DeCinces	.05
32	Curt Ford	.05
33	Bob Forsch	.05
34	David Green	.05
35	Tom Herr	.05
36	Ricky Horton	.05
37	Lance Johnson RC	.25
38	Steve Lake	.05
39	Jim Lindeman	.05
40	Joe Magrane RC	.10
41	Greg Mathews	.05
42	Willie McGee	.05
43	John Morris	.05
44	Jose Oquendo	.05
45	Tony Pena	.05
46	Terry Pendleton	.05
47	Ozzie Smith	.65
48	John Tudor	.05
49	Lee Tunnell	.05
50	Todd Worrell	.05
51	Doyle Alexander	.05
52	Dave Bergman	.05
53	Tom Brookens	.05
54	Darrell Evans	.05
55	Kirk Gibson	.05
56	Mike Heath	.05
57	Mike Henneman	.05
58	Willie Hernandez	.05
59	Larry Herndon	.05
60	Eric King	.05
61	Chet Lemon	.05
62	Scott Lusader RC	.05
63	Bill Madlock	.05
64	Jack Morris	.05
65	Jim Morrison	.05
66	Matt Nokes	.05
67	Dan Petry	.05
68a	Jeff Robinson RC (Born 12-13-60 on back.)	.25
68b	Jeff Robinson RC (Born 12/14/61 on back.)	.10
69	Pat Sheridan	

No.	Player	Price
70	Nate Snell	.05
71	Frank Tanana	.05
72	Walt Terrell	.05
73	Mark Thurmond	.05
74	Alan Trammell	.05
75	Lou Whitaker	.05
76	Mike Aldrete	.05
77	Bob Brenly	.05
78	Will Clark	.05
79	Chili Davis	.05
80	Kelly Downs	.05
81	Dave Dravecky	.05
82	Scott Garrelts	.05
83	Atlee Hammaker	.05
84	Dave Henderson	.05
85	Mike Krukow	.05
86	Mike LaCoss	.05
87	Craig Lefferts	.05
88	Jeff Leonard	.05
89	Candy Maldonado	.05
90	Ed Milner	.05
91	Bob Melvin	.05
92	Kevin Mitchell	.05
93	Jon Perlman RC	.05
94	Rick Reuschel	.05
95	Don Robinson	.05
96	Chris Speier	.05
97	Harry Spilman	.05
98	Robbie Thompson	.05
99	Jose Uribe	.05
100	Mark Wasinger RC	.05
101	Matt Williams	.05
102	Jesse Barfield	.05
103	George Bell	.05
104	Juan Beniquez	.05
105	John Cerutti	.05
106	Jim Clancy	.05
107	Rob Ducey RC	.05
108	Mark Eichhorn	.05
109	Tony Fernandez	.05
110	Cecil Fielder	.05
111	Kelly Gruber	.05
112	Tom Henke	.05
113	Garth Iorg (Iorg)	.05
114	Jimmy Key	.05
115	Rick Leach	.05
116	Manny Lee	.05
117	Nelson Liriano RC	.05
118	Fred McGriff	.05
119	Lloyd Moseby	.05
120	Rance Mulliniks	.05
121	Jeff Musselman	.05
122	Jose Nunez RC	.05
123	Dave Stieb	.05
124	Willie Upshaw	.05
125	Duane Ward RC	.05
126	Ernie Whitt	.05
127	Rick Aguilera	.05
128	Wally Backman	.05
129	Mark Carreon RC	.10
130	Gary Carter	.50
131	David Cone RC	.05
132	Ron Darling	.05
133	Len Dykstra	.05
134	Sid Fernandez	.05
135	Dwight Gooden	.05
136	Keith Hernandez	.05
137	Gregg Jefferies RC	.50
138	Howard Johnson	.05
139	Terry Leach	.05
140	Barry Lyons RC	.05
141	Dave Magadan	.05
142	Roger McDowell	.05
143	Kevin McReynolds	.05
144	Keith Miller RC	.05
145	John Mitchell RC	.05
146	Randy Myers	.05
147	Bob Ojeda	.05
148	Jesse Orosco	.05
149	Rafael Santana	.05
150	Doug Sisk	.05
151	Darryl Strawberry	.05
152	Tim Teufel	.05
153	Gene Walter	.05
154	Mookie Wilson	.05
155	Jay Aldrich RC	.05
156	Chris Bosio	.05
157	Glenn Braggs	.05
158	Greg Brock	.05
159	Juan Castillo	.05
160	Mark Clear	.05
161	Cecil Cooper	.05
162	Chuck Crim RC	.05
163	Rob Deer	.05
164	Mike Felder	.05
165	Jim Gantner	.05
166	Ted Higuera	.05
167	Steve Kiefer	.05
168	Rick Manning	.05
169	Paul Molitor	.50
170	Juan Nieves	.05
171	Dan Plesac	.05
172	Earnest Riles	.05
173	Bill Schroeder	.05
174	Steve Stanicek RC	.05
175	B.J. Surhoff	.05
176	Dale Sveum	.05
177	Bill Wegman	.05
178	Robin Yount	.50
179	Hubie Brooks	.05
180	Tim Burke	.05
181	Casey Candaele	.05
182	Mike Fitzgerald	.05
183	Tom Foley	.05
184	Andres Galarraga	.05
185	Neal Heaton	.05
186	Wallace Johnson	.05
187	Vance Law	.05
188	Dennis Martinez	.05
189	Bob McClure	.05
190	Andy McGaffigan	.05
191	Reid Nichols	.05
192	Pascual Perez	.05
193	Tim Raines	.05
194	Jeff Reed	.05
195	Bob Sebra	.05
196	Bryn Smith	.05
197	Randy St. Claire	.05
198	Tim Wallach	.05
199	Mitch Webster	.05
200	Herm Winningham	.05
201	Floyd Youmans	.05
202	Brad Arnsberg RC	.05
203	Rick Cerone	.05
204	Pat Clements	.05
205	Henry Cotto	.05
206	Mike Easler	.05
207	Ron Guidry	.10
208	Bill Gullickson	.05
209	Rickey Henderson	.50
210	Charles Hudson	.05
211	Tommy John	.10
212	Roberto Kelly	.25
213	Ron Kittle	.05
214	Don Mattingly	.75
215	Bobby Meacham	.05
216	Mike Pagliarulo	.05
217	Dan Pasqua	.05
218	Willie Randolph	.05
219	Rick Rhoden	.05
220	Dave Righetti	.05
221	Jerry Royster	.05
222	Tim Stoddard	.05
223	Wayne Tolleson	.05
224	Gary Ward	.05
225	Claudell Washington	.05
226	Dave Winfield	.50
227	Buddy Bell	.05
228	Tom Browning	.05
229	Dave Concepcion	.05
230	Kal Daniels	.05
231	Eric Davis	.05
232	Bo Diaz	.05
233	Nick Esasky	.05
234	John Franco	.05
235	Guy Hoffman	.05
236	Tom Hume	.05
237	Tracy Jones	.05
238	Bill Landrum RC	.05
239	Barry Larkin	.05
240	Terry McGriff RC	.05
241	Rob Murphy	.05
242	Ron Oester	.05
243	Dave Parker	.05
244	Pat Perry	.05
245	Ted Power	.05
246	Dennis Rasmussen	.05
247	Ron Robinson	.05
248	Kurt Stillwell	.05
249	Jeff Treadway RC	.05
250	Frank Williams	.05
251	Steve Balboni	.05
252	Bud Black	.05
253	Thad Bosley	.05
254	George Brett	.75
255	John Davis RC	.05
256	Steve Farr	.05
257	Gene Garber	.05
258	Jerry Gleaton	.05
259	Mark Gubicza	.05
260	Bo Jackson	.10
261	Danny Jackson	.05
262	Ross Jones RC	.05
263	Charlie Leibrandt	.05
264	Bill Pecota RC	.05
265	Melido Perez RC	.05
266	Jamie Quirk	.05
267	Dan Quisenberry	.05
268	Bret Saberhagen	.05
269	Angel Salazar	.05
270	Kevin Seitzer	.05
271	Danny Tartabull	.05
272	Gary Thurman RC	.05
273	Frank White	.05
274	Willie Wilson	.05
275	Tony Bernazard	.05
276	Jose Canseco	.30
277	Mike Davis	.05
278	Storm Davis	.05
279	Dennis Eckersley	.40
280	Alfredo Griffin	.05
281	Rick Honeycutt	.05
282	Jay Howell	.05
283	Reggie Jackson	.65
284	Dennis Lamp	.05
285	Carney Lansford	.05
286	Mark McGwire	.85
287	Dwayne Murphy	.05
288	Gene Nelson	.05
289	Steve Ontiveros	.05
290	Tony Phillips	.05
291	Eric Plunk	.05
292	Luis Polonia RC	.15
293	Rick Rodriguez RC	.05
294	Terry Steinbach	.05
295	Dave Stewart	.05
296	Curt Young	.05
297	Luis Aguayo	.05
298	Steve Bedrosian	.05
299	Jeff Calhoun	.05
300	Don Carman	.05
301	Todd Frohwirth RC	.05
302	Greg Gross	.05
303	Kevin Gross	.05
304	Von Hayes	.05
305	Keith Hughes RC	.05
306	Mike Jackson RC	.05
307	Chris James	.05
308	Steve Jeltz	.05
309	Mike Maddux	.05
310	Lance Parrish	.05
311	Shane Rawley	.05
312	Wally Ritchie RC	.05
313	Bruce Ruffin	.05
314	Juan Samuel	.05
315	Mike Schmidt	.75
316	Rick Schu	.05
317	Jeff Stone	.05
318	Kent Tekulve	.05
319	Milt Thompson	.05
320	Glenn Wilson	.05
321	Rafael Belliard	.05
322	Barry Bonds	1.00
323	Bobby Bonilla	.05
324	Sid Bream	.05
325	John Cangelosi	.05
326	Mike Diaz	.05
327	Doug Drabek	.05
328	Mike Dunne RC	.05
329	Brian Fisher	.05
330	Brett Gideon RC	.05
331	Terry Harper	.05
332	Bob Kipper	.05
333	Mike LaValliere	.05
334	Jose Lind RC	.15
335	Junior Ortiz	.05
336	Vicente Palacios RC	.05
337	Bob Patterson RC	.05
338	Al Pedrique RC	.05
339	R.J. Reynolds	.05
340	John Smiley	.05
341	Andy Van Slyke	.05
342	Bob Walk	.05
343	Marty Barrett	.05
344	Todd Benzinger RC	.05
345	Wade Boggs	.65
346	Tom Bolton RC	.05
347	Oil Can Boyd	.05
348	Ellis Burks	.05
349	Roger Clemens	.75
350	Steve Crawford	.05
351	Dwight Evans	.05
352	Wes Gardner RC	.05
353	Rich Gedman	.05
354	Mike Greenwell	.05
355	Sam Horn RC	.05
356	Bruce Hurst	.05
357	John Marzano RC	.05
358	Al Nipper	.05
359	Spike Owen	.05
360	Jody Reed RC	.15
361	Jim Rice	.20
362	Ed Romero	.05
363	Kevin Romine RC	.05
364	Joe Sambito	.05
365	Calvin Schiraldi	.05
366	Jeff Sellers	.05
367	Bob Stanley	.05
368	Scott Bankhead	.05
369	Phil Bradley	.05
370	Scott Bradley	.05
371	Mickey Brantley	.05
372	Mike Campbell RC	.05
373	Alvin Davis	.05
374	Lee Guetterman	.05
375	Dave Hengel RC	.05
376	Mike Kingery	.05
377	Mark Langston	.05
378	Edgar Martinez RC	1.00
379	Mike Moore	.05
380	Mike Morgan	.05
381	John Moses	.05
382	Donnell Nixon RC	.05
383	Edwin Nunez	.05
384	Ken Phelps	.05
385	Jim Presley	.05
386	Rey Quinones	.05
387	Jerry Reed	.05
388	Harold Reynolds	.05
389	Dave Valle	.05
390	Bill Wilkinson RC	.05
391	Harold Baines	.05
392	Floyd Bannister	.05
393	Daryl Boston	.05
394	Ivan Calderon	.05
395	Jose DeLeon	.05
396	Richard Dotson	.05
397	Carlton Fisk	.50
398	Ozzie Guillen	.05
399	Ron Hassey	.05
400	Donnie Hill	.05
401	Bob James	.05
402	Dave LaPoint	.05
403	Bill Lindsey RC	.05
404	Bill Long RC	.05
405	Steve Lyons	.05
406	Fred Manrique RC	.05
407	Jack McDowell RC	.25
408	Gary Redus	.05
409	Ray Searage	.05
410	Bobby Thigpen	.05
411	Greg Walker	.05
412	Kenny Williams RC	.05
413	Jim Winn	.05
414	Jody Davis	.05
415	Andre Dawson	.25
416	Brian Dayett	.05
417	Bob Dernier	.05
418	Frank DiPino	.05
419	Shawon Dunston	.05
420	Leon Durham	.05
421	Les Lancaster RC	.10
422	Ed Lynch	.05
423	Greg Maddux	.75
424	Dave Martinez RC	.05
425a	Keith Moreland (Bunting, photo actually Jody Davis.)	2.00
425b	Keith Moreland (Standing upright, correct photo.)	.05
426	Jamie Moyer	.05
427	Jerry Mumphrey	.05
428	Paul Noce RC	.05
429	Rafael Palmeiro	.40
430	Wade Rowdon RC	.05
431	Ryne Sandberg	.65
432	Scott Sanderson	.05
433	Lee Smith	.05
434	Jim Sundberg	.05
435	Rick Sutcliffe	.05
436	Manny Trillo	.05
437	Juan Agosto	.05
438	Larry Andersen	.05
439	Alan Ashby	.05
440	Kevin Bass	.05
441	Ken Caminiti	.25
442	Rocky Childress RC	.05
443	Jose Cruz	.05
444	Danny Darwin	.05
445	Glenn Davis	.05
446	Jim Deshaies	.05
447	Bill Doran	.05
448	Ty Gainey	.05
449	Billy Hatcher	.05
450	Jeff Heathcock	.05
451	Bob Knepper	.05
452	Rob Mallicoat RC	.05
453	Dave Meads RC	.05
454	Craig Reynolds	.05
455	Nolan Ryan	1.00
456	Mike Scott	.05
457	Dave Smith	.05
458	Denny Walling	.05
459	Robbie Wine RC	.05
460	Gerald Young RC	.05
461	Bob Brower	.05
462a	Jerry Browne (White player, photo actually Bob Brower.)	2.00
462b	Jerry Browne (Black player, correct photo.)	.05
463	Steve Buechele	.05
464	Edwin Correa	.05
465	Cecil Espy RC	.05
466	Scott Fletcher	.05
467	Jose Guzman	.05
468	Greg Harris	.05
469	Charlie Hough	.05
470	Pete Incaviglia	.05
471	Paul Kilgus RC	.05
472	Mike Loynd	.05
473	Oddibe McDowell	.05
474	Dale Mohorcic	.05
475	Pete O'Brien	.05
476	Larry Parrish	.05
477	Geno Petralli	.05
478	Jeff Russell	.05
479	Ruben Sierra	.05
480	Mike Stanley	.05
481	Curtis Wilkerson	.05
482	Mitch Williams	.05
483	Bobby Witt	.05
484	Tony Armas	.05
485	Bob Boone	.05
486	Bill Buckner	.05
487	DeWayne Buice RC	.05
488	Brian Downing	.05
489	Chuck Finley	.05
490	Willie Fraser	.05
491	Jack Howell	.05
492	Ruppert Jones	.05
493	Wally Joyner	.05
494	Jack Lazorko	.05
495	Gary Lucas	.05
496	Kirk McCaskill	.05
497	Mark McLemore	.05
498	Darrell Miller	.05
499	Greg Minton	.05
500	Donnie Moore	.05
501	Gus Polidor	.05
502	Johnny Ray	.05
503	Mark Ryal RC	.05
504	Dick Schofield	.05
505	Don Sutton	.40
506	Devon White	.05
507	Mike Witt	.05
508	Dave Anderson	.05
509	Tim Belcher RC	.05
510	Ralph Bryant	.05
511	Tim Crews RC	.15
512	Mike Devereaux RC	.10
513	Mariano Duncan	.05
514	Pedro Guerrero	.05
515	Jeff Hamilton RC	.05
516	Mickey Hatcher	.05
517	Brad Havens	.05
518	Orel Hershiser	.05
519	Shawn Hillegas RC	.05
520	Ken Howell	.05
521	Tim Leary	.05
522	Mike Marshall	.05
523	Steve Sax	.05
524	Mike Scioscia	.05
525	Mike Sharperson RC	.05
526	John Shelby	.05
527	Franklin Stubbs	.05
528	Fernando Valenzuela	.05
529	Bob Welch	.05
530	Matt Young	.05
531	Jim Acker	.05
532	Paul Assenmacher	.05
533	Jeff Blauser RC	.10
534	Joe Boever RC	.05
535	Martin Clary RC	.05
536	Kevin Coffman RC	.05
537	Jeff Dedmon	.05
538	Ron Gant RC	.50
539	Tom Glavine RC	2.00
540	Ken Griffey	.05
541	Al Hall	.05
542	Glenn Hubbard	.05
543	Dion James	.05
544	Dale Murphy	.20
545	Ken Oberkfell	.05
546	David Palmer	.05
547	Gerald Perry	.05
548	Charlie Puleo	.05
549	Ted Simmons	.05
550	Zane Smith	.05
551	Andres Thomas	.05
552	Ozzie Virgil	.05
553	Don Aase	.05
554	Jeff Ballard RC	.05
555	Eric Bell	.05
556	Mike Boddicker	.05
557	Ken Dixon	.05
558	Jim Dwyer	.05
559	Ken Gerhart	.05
560	Rene Gonzales RC	.05
561	Mike Griffin	.05
562	John Hayban (Habyan)	.05
563	Terry Kennedy	.05
564	Ray Knight	.05
565	Lee Lacy	.05
566	Fred Lynn	.05
567	Eddie Murray	.50
568	Tom Niedenfuer	.05
569	Bill Ripken RC	.05
570	Cal Ripken, Jr.	1.00
571	Dave Schmidt	.05
572	Larry Sheets	.05
573	Pete Stanicek RC	.05
574	Mark Williamson RC	.05
575	Mike Young	.05
576	Shawn Abner RC	.05
577	Greg Booker	.05
578	Chris Brown	.05
579	Keith Comstock RC	.05
580	Joey Cora RC	.05
581	Mark Davis	.05
582	Tim Flannery	.05
583	Goose Gossage	.05
584	Mark Grant	.05
585	Tony Gwynn	.65
586	Andy Hawkins	.05
587	Stan Jefferson	.05
588	Jimmy Jones	.05
589	John Kruk	.05
590	Shane Mack RC	.10
591	Carmelo Martinez	.05
592	Lance McCullers	.05
593	Eric Nolte RC	.05
594	Randy Ready	.05
595	Luis Salazar	.05
596	Benito Santiago	.05
597	Eric Show	.05
598	Garry Templeton	.05
599	Ed Whitson	.05
600	Scott Bailes	.05
601	Chris Bando	.05
602	Jay Bell RC	.50
603	Brett Butler	.05
604	Tom Candiotti	.05
605	Joe Carter	.05
606	Carmen Castillo	.05
607	Brian Dorsett RC	.05
608	John Farrell RC	.05
609	Julio Franco	.05
610	Mel Hall	.05
611	Tommy Hinzo RC	.05
612	Brook Jacoby	.05
613	Doug Jones RC	.10
614	Ken Schrom	.05
615	Cory Snyder	.05
616	Sammy Stewart	.05
617	Greg Swindell	.05
618	Pat Tabler	.05
619	Ed Vande Berg	.05
620	Eddie Williams RC	.05
621	Rich Yett	.05
622	Slugging Sophomores (Wally Joyner, Cory Snyder)	.10
623	Dominican Dynamite (George Bell, Pedro Guerrero)	.05
624	Oakland's Power Team (Jose Canseco, Mark McGwire)	.50
625	Classic Relief (Dan Plesac, Dave Righetti)	.05
626	All Star Righties (Jack Morris, Bret Saberhagen, Mike Witt)	.05
627	Game Closers (Steve Bedrosian, John Franco)	.05
628	Masters of the Double Play (Ryne Sandberg, Ozzie Smith)	.50
629	Rookie Record Setter (Mark McGwire)	.10
630	Changing the Guard in Boston (Todd Benzinger, Ellis Burks, Mike Greenwell)	.10
631	N.L. Batting Champs (Tony Gwynn, Tim Raines)	.20
632	Pitching Magic (Orel Hershiser, Mike Scott)	.05
633	Big Bats At First (Mark McGwire, Pat Tabler)	.50
634	Hitting King and the Thief (Tony Gwynn, Vince Coleman)	.15
635	A.L. Slugging Shortstops (Tony Fernandez, Cal Ripken, Jr., Alan Trammell)	.40
636	Tried and True Sluggers (Gary Carter, Mike Schmidt)	.40
637	Crunch Time (Eric Davis)	.05
638	A.L. All Stars (Matt Nokes, Kirby Puckett)	.25
639	N.L. All Stars (Keith Hernandez, Dale Murphy)	.10
640	The "O's" Brothers (Bill Ripken, Cal Ripken, Jr.)	.50
641	Major League Prospects (Mark Grace RC, Darrin Jackson RC)	1.00
642	Major League Prospects (Damon Berryhill RC, Jeff Montgomery RC)	.20
643	Major League Prospects (Felix Fermin RC, Jessie Reid RC)	.05
644	Major League Prospects (Greg Myers RC, Greg Tabor RC)	.05
645	Major League Prospects (Jim Eppard RC, Joey Meyer RC)	.05
646	Major League Prospects (Adam Peterson RC, Randy Velarde RC)	.10
647	Major League Prospects (Chris Gwynn RC, Peter Smith RC)	.15
648	Major League Prospects (Greg Jelks RC, Tom Newell RC)	.05
649	Major League Prospects (Mario Diaz RC, Clay Parker RC)	.05
650	Major League Prospects (Jack Savage RC, Todd Simmons RC)	.05
651	Major League Prospects (John Burkett RC, Kirt Manwaring RC)	.30
652	Major League Prospects (Dave Otto RC, Walt Weiss RC)	.25
653	Major League Prospects (Randell Byers (Randall) RC, Jeff King RC)	.05
654a	Checklist 1-101 (21 is Schatzeder)	.10
654b	Checklist 1-101 (21 is Schatzeder)	.05
655	Checklist 102-201	.05
656	Checklist 202-296	.05
657	Checklist 297-390	.05
658	Checklist 391-483	.05
659	Checklist 484-575	.05
660	Checklist 576-660	.05

All-Stars

For the third consecutive year, Fleer randomly inserted All Star Team cards in its wax and cello packs. Twelve cards make up the set, with players chosen for the set being Fleer's idea of a major league All-Star team.

		NM/M
	Complete Set (12):	3.00
	Common Player:	.10
1	Matt Nokes	.10
2	Tom Henke	.10
3	Ted Higuera	.10
4	Roger Clemens	1.50
5	George Bell	.10
6	Andre Dawson	.25
7	Eric Davis	.10

		NM/M
8	Wade Boggs	.85
9	Alan Trammell	.10
10	Juan Samuel	.10
11	Jack Clark	.10
12	Paul Molitor	.75

Headliners

This six-card set was inserted in Fleer three-packs, sold by retail outlets and hobby dealers nationwide. The card fronts feature crisp full-color player cut-outs printed on a gray and white facsimile sports page. "Fleer Headliners 1988" is printed in black and red on a white banner across the top of the card, both front and back. A similar white banner across the card bottom bears the black and white National or American League logo and a red player/team name. Card backs are black on grey with red accents and include the card number and a narrative career summary.

		NM/M
Complete Set (6):		3.00
Common Player:		.25
1	Don Mattingly	1.50
2	Mark McGwire	2.00
3	Jack Morris	.15
4	Darryl Strawberry	.15
5	Dwight Gooden	.15
6	Tim Raines	.15

'87 World Series

Highlights of the 1987 Series are captured in this full-color insert set found only in Fleer's regular 660-card factory sets. This second World Series edition by Fleer features cards framed in red, with a blue and white starred bunting draped over the upper edges of the photo and a brief photo caption printed on a yellow band across the lower border. Numbered card backs are red, white and blue and include a description of the action pictured on the front, with stats for the Series.

		NM/M
Complete Set (12):		2.50
Common Player:		.25
1	"Grand" Hero In Game 1 (Dan Gladden)	.25
2	The Cardinals "Bush" Whacked (Randy Bush, Tony Pena)	.25
3	Masterful Performance Turns Momentum (John Tudor)	.25
4	Ozzie Smith	1.00
5	Throw Smoke! (Tony Pena, Todd Worrell)	.25
6	Cardinal Attack - Disruptive Speed (Vince Coleman)	.25
7	Herr's Wallop (Dan Driessen, Tom Herr)	.25
8	Kirby Puckett	1.00
9	Kent Hrbek	.25
10	Rich Hacker/Coach, Tom Herr, Lee Weyer/Umpire	.25
11	Game 7's Play At The Plate Don Baylor, Dave Phillips/Umpire	.25
12	Frank Viola	.25

Box Panels

Fleer's third annual box-bottom issue once again included 16 full-color trading cards printed on the bottoms of four different wax and cello pack retail display boxes. Each box contains three player cards and one team logo card. Player cards follow the same design as the basic 1988 Fleer issue. Standard size, the cards are numbered C-1 through C-16.

		NM/M
Complete Panel Set (4):		4.00
Complete Singles Set (16):		4.00
Common Panel:		1.00
Common Single Player:		.10
Panel		1.50
1	Cardinals Logo	1.00
11	Mike Schmidt	1.00
14	Dave Stewart	.10
15	Tim Wallach	.10
Panel		1.00
2	Dwight Evans	.10
8	Shane Rawley	.10
10	Ryne Sandberg	.75
13	Tigers Logo	.05
Panel		1.25
3	Andres Galarraga	.10
6	Dale Murphy	.45
9	Giants Logo	.05
12	Kevin Seitzer	.10
Panel		1.00
4	Wally Joyner	.10
5	Twins Logo	.05
7	Kirby Puckett	1.00
16	Todd Worrell	.10

Glossy Tin

In its second year of production, Fleer radically reduced production numbers on its glossy version of the 1988 baseball card set. With production estimates in the 60,000 set range, values of the '88 tin glossies are about double those of the regular issue cards. Once again the issue was sold only as complete sets in colorful lithographed metal boxes.

	NM/M
Complete Set (672):	20.00
Common Player:	.15

Update

This update set (numbered U-1 through U-132 are 2-1/2" x 3-1/2") features traded veterans and rookies in a mixture of full-color action shots and close-ups, framed by white borders with red and blue stripes. The backs are red, white and blue-gray and include personal info, along with yearly and "At Their Best" (day, night, home, road) stats charts. The set was packaged in white cardboard boxes with red and blue stripes. A glossy-coated edition of the update set was issued in its own box and is valued at two times the regular issue.

		NM/M
Complete Set (132):		5.00
Common Player:		.05
1	Jose Bautista	.05
2	Joe Orsulak	.05
3	Doug Sisk	.05
4	Craig Worthington RC	.05
5	Mike Boddicker	.05
6	Rick Cerone	.05
7	Larry Parrish	.05
8	Lee Smith	.10
9	Mike Smithson	.05
10	John Trautwein RC	.05
11	Sherman Corbett RC	.05
12	Chili Davis	.05
13	Jim Eppard	.05
14	Bryan Harvey RC	.05
15	John Davis	.05
16	Dave Gallagher RC	.05
17	Ricky Horton	.05
18	Dan Pasqua	.05
19	Melido Perez	.05
20	Jose Segura RC	.05
21	Andy Allanson	.05
22	Jon Perlman	.05
23	Domingo Ramos	.05
24	Rick Rodriguez	.05
25	Willie Upshaw	.05
26	Paul Gibson RC	.05
27	Don Heinkel RC	.05
28	Ray Knight	.05
29	Gary Pettis	.05
30	Luis Salazar	.05
31	Mike MacFarlane RC	.05
32	Jeff Montgomery RC	.05
33	Ted Power	.05
34	Israel Sanchez RC	.05
35	Kurt Stillwell	.05
36	Pat Tabler	.05
37	Don August RC	.05
38	Darryl Hamilton RC	.05
39	Jeff Leonard	.05
40	Joey Meyer	.05
41	Allan Anderson	.05
42	Brian Harper	.05
43	Tom Herr	.05
44	Charlie Lea	.05
45	John Moses	.05
46	John Candelaria	.05
47	Jack Clark	.05
48	Richard Dotson	.05
49	Al Leiter RC	.05
50	Rafael Santana	.05
51	Don Slaught	.05
52	Todd Burns RC	.05
53	Dave Henderson	.05
54	Doug Jennings RC	.05
55	Dave Parker	.05
56	Walt Weiss	.05
57	Bob Welch	.05
58	Henry Cotto	.05
59	Marion Diaz (Mario)	.05
60	Mike Jackson	.05
61	Bill Swift	.05
62	Jose Cecena RC	.05
63	Ray Hayward RC	.05
64	Jim Steels RC	.05
65	Pat Borders RC	.05
66	Sil Campusano RC	.05
67	Mike Flanagan	.05
68	Todd Stottlemyre RC	.05
69	David Wells RC	.05
70	Jose Alvarez RC	.05
71	Paul Runge	.05
72	Cesar Jimenez RC (German)	.05
73	Pete Smith	.05
74	John Smoltz RC	1.50
75	Damon Berryhill RC	.05
76	Goose Gossage	.05
77	Mark Grace	.10
78	Darrin Jackson	.05
79	Vance Law	.05
80	Jeff Pico RC	.05
81	Gary Varsho RC	.05
82	Tim Birtsas	.05
83	Rob Dibble RC	.05
84	Danny Jackson	.05
85	Paul O'Neill	.05
86	Jose Rijo	.05
87	Chris Sabo RC	.25
88	John Fishel RC	.05
89	Craig Biggio RC	2.00
90	Terry Puhl	.05
91	Rafael Ramirez	.05
92	Louie Meadows RC	.05
93	Kirk Gibson	.05
94	Alfredo Griffin	.05
95	Jay Howell	.05
96	Jesse Orosco	.05
97	Alejandro Pena	.05
98	Tracy Woodson RC	.05
99	John Dopson RC	.05
100	Brian Holman RC	.05
101	Rex Hudler RC	.05
102	Jeff Parrett RC	.05
103	Nelson Santovenia RC	.05
104	Kevin Elster	.05
105	Jeff Innis RC	.05
106	Mackey Sasser RC	.05
107	Phil Bradley	.05
108	Danny Clay RC	.05
109	Greg Harris	.05
110	Ricky Jordan RC	.05
111	David Palmer	.05
112	Jim Gott	.05
113	Tommy Gregg RC (Photo actually Randy Milligan.)	.05
114	Barry Jones	.05
115	Randy Milligan RC	.05
116	Luis Alicea RC	.05
117	Tom Brunansky	.05
118	John Costello RC	.05
119	Jose DeLeon	.05
120	Bob Horner	.05
121	Scott Terry RC	.05
122	Roberto Alomar RC	1.50
123	Dave Leiper	.05
124	Keith Moreland	.05
125	Mark Parent RC	.05
126	Dennis Rasmussen	.05
127	Randy Bockus	.05
128	Brett Butler	.05
129	Donell Nixon	.05
130	Earnest Riles	.05
131	Roger Samuels RC	.05
132	Checklist	.05

Update Glossy Tin

The glossy version of the 1988 Fleer Update set differs from the regular-issue Update set only in the high-gloss finish applied to the cards' fronts and the lithographed metal box in which sets were sold.

	NM/M
Complete Set (132):	9.00
Common Player:	.05

Award Winners

This limited edition boxed set of 1987 award-winning player cards also includes six team logo sticker cards. Red, white, blue and yellow bands border the sharp, full-color player photos printed below a "Fleer Award Winners 1988" banner. The player's name and award are printed beneath the photo. Flip sides are red, white and blue and list personal information, career data, team logo and card number. This set was sold exclusively at 7-11 stores nationwide.

		NM/M
Complete Set (44):		3.50
Common Player:		.05
1	Steve Bedrosian	.05
2	George Bell	.05
3	Wade Boggs	.65
4	Jose Canseco	.30
5	Will Clark	.05
6	Roger Clemens	.75
7	Kal Daniels	.05
8	Eric Davis	.05
9	Andre Dawson	.25
10	Mike Dunne	.05
11	Dwight Evans	.05
12	Carlton Fisk	.50
13	Julio Franco	.05
14	Dwight Gooden	.05
15	Pedro Guerrero	.05
16	Tony Gwynn	.65
17	Orel Hershiser	.05
18	Tom Henke	.05
19	Ted Higuera	.05
20	Charlie Hough	.05
21	Wally Joyner	.05
22	Jimmy Key	.05
23	Don Mattingly	.75
24	Mark McGwire	1.50
25	Paul Molitor	.50
26	Jack Morris	.05
27	Dale Murphy	.20
28	Terry Pendleton	.05
29	Kirby Puckett	.65
30	Tim Raines	.05
31	Jeff Reardon	.05
32	Harold Reynolds	.05
33	Dave Righetti	.05
34	Benito Santiago	.05
35	Mike Schmidt	.75
36	Mike Scott	.05
37	Kevin Seitzer	.05
38	Larry Sheets	.05
39	Ozzie Smith	.65
40	Darryl Strawberry	.05
41	Rick Sutcliffe	.05
42	Danny Tartabull	.05
43	Alan Trammell	.05
44	Tim Wallach	.05

Baseball All-Stars

This limited edition boxed set features major league All-Stars. The standard-size cards feature a sporty bright blue and yellow striped background. Card backs feature a blue and white striped design with a yellow highlighted section at the top that contains the player name, card number, team, position and personal data, followed by lifetime career stats. Fleer All Stars are cello-wrapped in blue and yellow striped boxes with checklist backs. The set includes six team logo sticker cards that feature black-and-white aerial shots of major league ballparks. The set was marketed exclusively by Ben Franklin stores.

		NM/M
Complete Set (44):		4.00
Common Player:		.05
1	George Bell	.05
2	Wade Boggs	.65
3	Bobby Bonilla	.05
4	George Brett	.85
5	Jose Canseco	.35
6	Jack Clark	.05
7	Will Clark	.05
8	Roger Clemens	.85
9	Eric Davis	.05
10	Andre Dawson	.25
11	Julio Franco	.05
12	Dwight Gooden	.05
13	Tony Gwynn	.65
14	Orel Hershiser	.05
15	Teddy Higuera	.05
16	Charlie Hough	.05
17	Kent Hrbek	.05
18	Bruce Hurst	.05
19	Wally Joyner	.05
20	Mark Langston	.05
21	Dave LaPoint	.05
22	Candy Maldonado	.05
23	Don Mattingly	.85
24	Roger McDowell	.05
25	Mark McGwire	1.00
26	Jack Morris	.05
27	Dale Murphy	.20
28	Eddie Murray	.05
29	Matt Nokes	.05
30	Kirby Puckett	.05
31	Tim Raines	.05
32	Willie Randolph	.05
33	Jeff Reardon	.05
34	Nolan Ryan	1.00
35	Juan Samuel	.05
36	Mike Schmidt	.85
37	Mike Scott	.05
38	Kevin Seitzer	.05
39	Ozzie Smith	.65
40	Darryl Strawberry	.05
41	Rick Sutcliffe	.05
42	Alan Trammell	.05
43	Tim Wallach	.05
44	Dave Winfield	.50

Baseball's Best

This boxed set of 44 standard-size cards (2-1/2" x 3-1/2") and six team logo stickers is the third annual issue from Fleer highlighting the best major league sluggers and pitchers. Five additional player cards were printed on retail display box bottoms, along with a checklist logo card (numbered C-1 through C-6). Full-color player photos are framed by a green border that fades to yellow. A red (slugger) or blue (pitcher) player name is printed beneath the photo. Backs are printed in green on a white background with yellow highlights. Card number, player name and personal info appear in a green vertical box on the left-hand side of the card back with a yellow cartoon-style team logo overprinted across a stats chart on the right. This set was produced by Fleer for exclusive distribution by McCrory's stores (McCrory, McClellan, J.J. Newberry, H.L. Green, TG&Y).

		NM/M
Complete Set (44):		4.00
Common Player:		.05
1	George Bell	.05
2	Wade Boggs	.65
3	Bobby Bonilla	.05
4	Tom Brunansky	.05
5	Ellis Burks	.05
6	Jose Canseco	.40
7	Joe Carter	.05
8	Will Clark	.05
9	Roger Clemens	.85
10	Eric Davis	.05
11	Glenn Davis	.05
12	Andre Dawson	.25
13	Dennis Eckersley	.45
14	Andres Galarraga	.05
15	Dwight Gooden	.05
16	Pedro Guerrero	.05
17	Tony Gwynn	.65
18	Orel Hershiser	.05
19	Ted Higuera	.05
20	Pete Incaviglia	.05
21	Danny Jackson	.05
22	Doug Jennings	.05
23	Mark Langston	.05
24	Dave LaPoint	.05
25	Mike LaValliere	.05
26	Don Mattingly	.85
27	Mark McGwire	1.00
28	Dale Murphy	.20
29	Ken Phelps	.05
30	Kirby Puckett	.65
31	Johnny Ray	.05
32	Jeff Reardon	.05
33	Dave Righetti	.05
34	Cal Ripkin, Jr. (Ripken)	1.50
35	Chris Sabo	.05
36	Mike Schmidt	.85
37	Mike Scott	.05
38	Kevin Seitzer	.05
39	Ozzie Smith	.65
40	Darryl Strawberry	.05
41	Greg Swindell	.05
42	Frank Tanana	.05
43	Dave Winfield	.50
44	Todd Worrell	.05

Baseball's Best Box Panel

Six cards were placed on the bottoms of retail boxes of the Fleer Baseball's Best boxed sets in 1988. The cards, 2-1/2" x 3-1/2", are identical in design to cards found in the 44-card set. The cards are numbered C-1 through C-6 and were produced for distribution by McCrory stores and its affiliates.

		NM/M
Complete Panel Set:		1.50
Complete Singles Set (6):		1.50
Common Single Player:		.10
1	Ron Darling	.10
2	Rickey Henderson	.75
3	Carney Lansford	.10
4	Rafael Palmeiro	.60
5	Frank Viola	.10
6	Minnesota Twins logo	.05

Exciting Stars

This boxed set showcases star major leaguers. Player photos are slanted upwards to the right, framed by a blue border with a red and white stripe across the middle. Card backs are numbered and printed in red, white and blue. The set was packaged in a checklist box, with six team logo sticker cards featuring black-and-white stadium photos on the flip sides. Exciting Stars was distributed via Cumberland Farm stores throughout the northeastern U.S. and Florida.

		NM/M
Complete Set (44):		3.00
Common Player:		.05
1	Harold Baines	.05
2	Kevin Bass	.05
3	George Bell	.05
4	Wade Boggs	.65
5	Mickey Brantley	.05
6	Sid Bream	.05
7	Jose Canseco	.30
8	Jack Clark	.05
9	Will Clark	.05
10	Roger Clemens	.85
11	Vince Coleman	.05
12	Eric Davis	.05
13	Andre Dawson	.25
14	Julio Franco	.05
15	Dwight Gooden	.05
16	Mike Greenwell	.05
17	Tony Gwynn	.05
18	Von Hayes	.02
19	Tom Henke	.05
20	Orel Hershiser	.05
21	Teddy Higuera	.05
22	Brook Jacoby	.05
23	Wally Joyner	.05
24	Jimmy Key	.05
25	Don Mattingly	.85
26	Mark McGwire	1.00
27	Jack Morris	.05
28	Dale Murphy	.20
29	Matt Nokes	.05
30	Kirby Puckett	.65
31	Tim Raines	.05
32	Ryne Sandberg	.65
33	Benito Santiago	.05
34	Mike Schmidt	.85
35	Mike Scott	.05
36	Kevin Seitzer	.05
37	Larry Sheets	.05
38	Ruben Sierra	.05
39	Darryl Strawberry	.05
40	Rick Sutcliffe	.05
41	Danny Tartabull	.05
42	Alan Trammell	.05
43	Fernando Valenzuela	.05
44	Devon White	.05

Hottest Stars

This boxed set of standard-size player cards and six team logo stickers was produced by Fleer for exclusive distribution at Revco drug stores nationwide. Card fronts feature full-color photos of players representing every major league team. Photos are framed in red, orange and yellow, with a blue-and-white player name printed at bottom. A flaming baseball logo bearing the words "Hottest Stars" appears in the lower-left corner of the photo. Card backs are red, white and blue. The player's name, position, card number and team logo are printed at top, followed by a stats box and personal data. The set also includes six team logo sticker cards with flipside stadium photos in black-and-white.

		NM/M
Complete Set (44):		3.50
Common Player:		.05
1	George Bell	.05
2	Wade Boggs	.65
3	Bobby Bonilla	.05
4	George Brett	.85
5	Jose Canseco	.30
6	Will Clark	.05
7	Roger Clemens	.85
8	Eric Davis	.05
9	Andre Dawson	.25
10	Tony Fernandez	.05
11	Julio Franco	.05
12	Gary Gaetti	.05
13	Dwight Gooden	.05
14	Mike Greenwell	.05
15	Tony Gwynn	.05
16	Rickey Henderson	.50
17	Keith Hernandez	.05
18	Tom Herr	.05
19	Orel Hershiser	.05
20	Ted Higuera	.05
21	Wally Joyner	.05
22	Jimmy Key	.05
23	Mark Langston	.05
24	Don Mattingly	.85
25	Jack McDowell	.05
26	Mark McGwire	1.00
27	Kevin Mitchell	.05
28	Jack Morris	.05
29	Dale Murphy	.20
30	Kirby Puckett	.65
31	Tim Raines	.05
32	Shane Rawley	.05
33	Benito Santiago	.05
34	Mike Schmidt	.85
35	Mike Scott	.05
36	Kevin Seitzer	.05
37	Larry Sheets	.05
38	Ruben Sierra	.05
39	Dave Smith	.05
40	Ozzie Smith	.65
41	Darryl Strawberry	.05
42	Rick Sutcliffe	.05
43	Pat Tabler	.05
44	Alan Trammell	.05

League Leaders

This third annual issue of miniatures (1-7/8" x 2-5/8") includes 120 high-gloss cards featuring new photos, not copies from the regular issue, although the card designs are identical. Card backs are red, white and blue and include personal data, yearly career stats and a stats breakdown of batting average, slugging percentage and on-base average, listed for day, night, home and road games. Card backs are numbered in alphabetical order by teams which are also listed al-

phabetically. The set includes 18 team logo stickers with black-and-white aerial stadium photos on the flip sides.

		NM/M
Complete Set (120):		3.50
Common Player:		.05
1	Eddie Murray	.05
2	Dave Schmidt	.05
3	Larry Sheets	.05
4	Wade Boggs	.65
5	Roger Clemens	.85
6	Dwight Evans	.05
7	Mike Greenwell	.05
8	Sam Horn	.05
9	Lee Smith	.05
10	Brian Downing	.05
11	Wally Joyner	.05
12	Devon White	.05
13	Mike Witt	.05
14	Ivan Calderon	.05
15	Ozzie Guillen	.05
16	Jack McDowell	.05
17	Kenny Williams	.05
18	Joe Carter	.05
19	Julio Franco	.05
20	Pat Tabler	.05
21	Doyle Alexander	.05
22	Jack Morris	.05
23	Matt Nokes	.05
24	Walt Terrell	.05
25	Alan Trammell	.05
26	Bret Saberhagen	.05
27	Kevin Seitzer	.05
28	Danny Tartabull	.05
29	Gary Thurman	.05
30	Ted Higuera	.05
31	Paul Molitor	.50
32	Dan Plesac	.05
33	Robin Yount	.50
34	Gary Gaetti	.05
35	Kent Hrbek	.05
36	Kirby Puckett	.65
37	Jeff Reardon	.05
38	Frank Viola	.05
39	Jack Clark	.05
40	Rickey Henderson	.50
41	Don Mattingly	.85
42	Willie Randolph	.05
43	Dave Righetti	.05
44	Dave Winfield	.50
45	Jose Canseco	.30
46	Mark McGwire	1.00
47	Dave Parker	.05
48	Dave Stewart	.05
49	Walt Weiss	.05
50	Bob Welch	.05
51	Mickey Brantley	.05
52	Mark Langston	.05
53	Harold Reynolds	.05
54	Scott Fletcher	.05
55	Charlie Hough	.05
56	Pete Incaviglia	.05
57	Larry Parrish	.05
58	Ruben Sierra	.05
59	George Bell	.05
60	Mark Eichhorn	.05
61	Tony Fernandez	.05
62	Tom Henke	.05
63	Jimmy Key	.05
64	Dion James	.05
65	Dale Murphy	.20
66	Zane Smith	.05
67	Andre Dawson	.25
68	Mark Grace	.25
69	Jerry Mumphrey	.05
70	Ryne Sandberg	.65
71	Rick Sutcliffe	.05
72	Kal Daniels	.05
73	Eric Davis	.05
74	John Franco	.05
75	Ron Robinson	.05
76	Jeff Treadway	.05
77	Kevin Bass	.05
78	Glenn Davis	.05
79	Nolan Ryan	1.00
80	Mike Scott	.05
81	Dave Smith	.05
82	Kirk Gibson	.05
83	Pedro Guerrero	.05
84	Orel Hershiser	.05
85	Steve Sax	.05
86	Fernando Valenzuela	.05
87	Tim Burke	.05
88	Andres Galarraga	.05
89	Neal Heaton	.05
90	Tim Raines	.05
91	Tim Wallach	.05
92	Dwight Gooden	.05
93	Keith Hernandez	.05
94	Gregg Jefferies	.10
95	Howard Johnson	.05
96	Roger McDowell	.05
97	Darryl Strawberry	.05
98	Steve Bedrosian	.05
99	Von Hayes	.05
100	Shane Rawley	.05
101	Juan Samuel	.05
102	Mike Schmidt	.85
103	Bobby Bonilla	.05
104	Mike Dunne	.05
105	Andy Van Slyke	.05
106	Vince Coleman	.05
107	Bob Horner	.05
108	Willie McGee	.05
109	Ozzie Smith	.65
110	John Tudor	.05
111	Todd Worrell	.05
112	Tony Gwynn	.65
113	John Kruk	.05
114	Lance McCullers	.05
115	Benito Santiago	.05
116	Will Clark	.05
117	Jeff Leonard	.05
118	Candy Maldonado	.05
119	Kirt Manwaring	.05
120	Don Robinson	.05

Mini

This third annual issue of miniatures (1-7/8" x 2-5/8") includes 120 high-gloss cards featuring new photos, not copies from the regular issue, although the card designs are identical. Card backs are red, white and blue and include personal data, yearly career stats and a stats breakdown of batting average, slugging percentage and on-base average, listed for day, night, home and road games. Card backs are numbered in alphabetical order by teams which are also listed al-

MVP

This boxed set of 44 standard-size cards and six team logo stickers was produced by Fleer for exclusive distribution at Toys "R" Us stores. This premiere edition features full-color player photos framed by a yellow and blue border. Card backs are yellow and blue on a white background. The player's team, position and personal data are followed by stats, logo and a blue banner bearing the player's name, team logo and card number. The six sticker cards feature black-and-white stadium photos on the backs.

		NM/M
Complete Set (44):		3.50
Common Player:		.05
1	George Bell	.05
2	Wade Boggs	.65
3	Jose Canseco	.30
4	Ivan Calderon	.05
5	Will Clark	.05
6	Roger Clemens	.85
7	Vince Coleman	.05
8	Eric Davis	.05
9	Andre Dawson	.25
10	Dave Dravecky	.05
11	Mike Dunne	.05
12	Dwight Evans	.05
13	Sid Fernandez	.05
14	Tony Fernandez	.05
15	Julio Franco	.05
16	Dwight Gooden	.05
17	Tony Gwynn	.65
18	Ted Higuera	.05
19	Charlie Hough	.05
20	Wally Joyner	.05
21	Mark Langston	.05
22	Don Mattingly	.85
23	Mark McGwire	1.00
24	Jack Morris	.05
25	Dale Murphy	.20
26	Kirby Puckett	.65
27	Tim Raines	.05
28	Willie Randolph	.05
29	Ryne Sandberg	.65
30	Benito Santiago	.05
31	Mike Schmidt	.05
32	Mike Scott	.05
33	Kevin Seitzer	.05
34	Larry Sheets	.05
35	Ozzie Smith	.65
36	Dave Stewart	.05
37	Darryl Strawberry	.05
38	Rick Sutcliffe	.05
39	Alan Trammell	.05
40	Fernando Valenzuela	.05
41	Frank Viola	.05
42	Tim Wallach	.05
43	Dave Winfield	.50
44	Robin Yount	.50

Record Setters

For the second consecutive year, Fleer issued this set for exclusive distribution by Eckerd Drug stores. Cards are standard size with red and blue borders framing the full-color player photos. Card backs list personal information and career stats in red and blue on a white background. Each 44-card set comes cello-

wrapped in a checklist box that contains six additional cards with peel-off team logo stickers. The sticker cards feature black-and-white aerial photos of major league ballparks, along with stadium statistics such as field size, seating capacity and date of the first game played.

		NM/M
Complete Set (44):		3.50
Common Player:		.05
1	Jesse Barfield	.05
2	George Bell	.05
3	Wade Boggs	.65
4	Jose Canseco	.35
5	Jack Clark	.05
6	Will Clark	.05
7	Roger Clemens	.85
8	Alvin Davis	.05
9	Eric Davis	.05
10	Andre Dawson	.25
11	Mike Dunne	.05
12	John Franco	.05
13	Julio Franco	.05
14	Dwight Gooden	.05
15	Mark Gubicza	.05
16	Ozzie Guillen	.05
17	Tony Gwynn	.65
18	Orel Hershiser	.05
19	Teddy Higuera	.05
20	Howard Johnson	.05
21	Wally Joyner	.05
22	Jimmy Key	.05
23	Jeff Leonard	.05
24	Don Mattingly	.85
25	Mark McGwire	1.00
26	Jack Morris	.05
27	Dale Murphy	.20
28	Larry Parrish	.05
29	Kirby Puckett	.65
30	Tim Raines	.05
31	Harold Reynolds	.05
32	Dave Righetti	.05
33	Cal Ripken, Jr.	1.00
34	Benito Santiago	.05
35	Mike Schmidt	.85
36	Mike Scott	.05
37	Kevin Seitzer	.05
38	Ozzie Smith	.65
39	Darryl Strawberry	.05
40	Rick Sutcliffe	.05
41	Alan Trammell	.05
42	Frank Viola	.05
43	Mitch Williams	.05
44	Todd Worrell	.05

Star Stickers

This set of 132 standard-size sticker cards (including a checklist card) features exclusive player photos, different from those in the Fleer regular issue. Card fronts have light gray backgrounds sprinkled with multi-colored stars. Card backs are printed in red, gray and black on white and include personal data and a breakdown of pitching and batting stats into day, night, home and road categories.

Cards were marketed in two different display boxes that feature six players and two team logos on the bottoms.

		NM/M
Complete Set (132):		7.50
Common Player:		.05
Wax Pack (5):		.50
Wax Box (36):		10.00
1	Mike Boddicker	.05
2	Eddie Murray	.50
3	Cal Ripken, Jr.	1.50
4	Larry Sheets	.05
5	Wade Boggs	.65
6	Ellis Burks	.05
7	Roger Clemens	.85
8	Dwight Evans	.05
9	Mike Greenwell	.05
10	Bruce Hurst	.05
11	Brian Downing	.05
12	Wally Joyner	.05
13	Mike Witt	.05
14	Ivan Calderon	.05
15	Jose DeLeon	.05
16	Ozzie Guillen	.05
17	Bobby Thigpen	.05
18	Joe Carter	.05
19	Julio Franco	.05
20	Brook Jacoby	.05
21	Cory Snyder	.05
22	Pat Tabler	.05
23	Doyle Alexander	.05
24	Kirk Gibson	.15
25	Mike Henneman	.05
26	Jack Morris	.05
27	Matt Nokes	.05
28	Walt Terrell	.05
29	Alan Trammell	.05
30	George Brett	.85
31	Charlie Leibrandt	.05
32	Bret Saberhagen	.05
33	Kevin Seitzer	.05
34	Danny Tartabull	.05
35	Frank White	.05
36	Rob Deer	.05
37	Ted Higuera	.05
38	Paul Molitor	.50
39	Dan Plesac	.05
40	Robin Yount	.50
41	Bert Blyleven	.05
42	Tom Brunansky	.05
43	Gary Gaetti	.05
44	Kent Hrbek	.05
45	Kirby Puckett	.65
46	Jeff Reardon	.05
47	Frank Viola	.05
48	Don Mattingly	.85
49	Mike Pagliarulo	.05
50	Willie Randolph	.05
51	Rick Rhoden	.05
52	Dave Righetti	.05
53	Dave Winfield	.50
54	Jose Canseco	.30
55	Carney Lansford	.05
56	Mark McGwire	1.00
57	Dave Stewart	.05
58	Curt Young	.05
59	Alvin Davis	.05
60	Mark Langston	.05
61	Ken Phelps	.05
62	Harold Reynolds	.05
63	Scott Fletcher	.05
64	Charlie Hough	.05
65	Pete Incaviglia	.05
66	Oddibe McDowell	.05
67	Pete O'Brien	.05
68	Larry Parrish	.05
69	Ruben Sierra	.05
70	Jesse Barfield	.05
71	George Bell	.05
72	Tony Fernandez	.05
73	Tom Henke	.05
74	Jimmy Key	.05
75	Lloyd Moseby	.05
76	Dion James	.05
77	Dale Murphy	.20
78	Zane Smith	.05
79	Andre Dawson	.25
80	Ryne Sandberg	.65
81	Rick Sutcliffe	.05
82	Kal Daniels	.05
83	Eric Davis	.05
84	John Franco	.05
85	Kevin Bass	.05
86	Glenn Davis	.05
87	Bill Doran	.05
88	Nolan Ryan	1.50
89	Mike Scott	.05
90	Dave Smith	.05
91	Pedro Guerrero	.05
92	Orel Hershiser	.05
93	Steve Sax	.05
94	Fernando Valenzuela	.05
95	Tim Burke	.05
96	Andres Galarraga	.05
97	Tim Raines	.05
98	Tim Wallach	.05
99	Mitch Webster	.05
100	Ron Darling	.05
101	Sid Fernandez	.05
102	Dwight Gooden	.05
103	Keith Hernandez	.05
104	Howard Johnson	.05
105	Roger McDowell	.05
106	Darryl Strawberry	.05
107	Steve Bedrosian	.05
108	Von Hayes	.05
109	Shane Rawley	.05
110	Juan Samuel	.05
111	Mike Schmidt	.85
112	Milt Thompson	.05
113	Sid Bream	.05
114	Bobby Bonilla	.05
115	Mike Dunne	.05
116	Andy Van Slyke	.05
117	Vince Coleman	.05
118	Willie McGee	.05
119	Terry Pendleton	.05
120	Ozzie Smith	.65
121	John Tudor	.05
122	Todd Worrell	.05
123	Tony Gwynn	.65
124	John Kruk	.05
125	Benito Santiago	.05
126	Will Clark	.05
127	Dave Dravecky	.05
128	Jeff Leonard	.05
129	Candy Maldonado	.05
130	Rick Rueschel	.05
131	Don Robinson	.05
132	Checklist	.05

Star Stickers Box Panels

RON GUIDRY

This set of eight box-bottom cards was printed on two different retail display boxes. Six players and two team logo sticker cards are included in the set, three player photos and one team photo per box. The full-color player photos are exclusive to the Fleer Star Sticker set. The cards, which measure 2-1/2" x 3-1/2", have a light gray border sprinkled with multicolor stars. The backs are printed in navy blue and red.

		NM/M
Complete Panel Set (2):		1.50
Complete Singles Set (8):		1.50
Common Singles Player:		.15
Panel		1.00
1	Eric Davis	.10
3	Kevin Mitchell	.10
5	Rickey Henderson	.75
7	Tigers Logo	.05
Panel		1.00
2	Gary Carter	.75
4	Ron Guidry	.10
6	Don Baylor	.10
8	Giants Logo	.05

Superstars

OREL HERSHISER

This is the fourth edition of Fleer boxed sets produced for distribution by McCrory's (1985-87 issues were titled "Fleer Limited Edition"). The Superstars standard-size card set features full-color player photos framed by red, white and blue striped top and bottom borders. Card fronts have a semi-glossy slightly textured finish. Card backs are red and blue on white and include card numbers, personal data and statistics. Six team logo sticker cards are also included in this set which was marketed in red, white and blue boxes with checklist backs. Boxed sets were sold exclusively at McCrory's stores and its affiliates.

		NM/M
Complete Set (44):		5.00
Common Player:		.10
1	Steve Bedrosian	.10
2	George Bell	.10
3	Wade Boggs	.65
4	Barry Bonds	1.50
5	Jose Canseco	.45
6	Joe Carter	.10
7	Jack Clark	.10
8	Will Clark	.10
9	Roger Clemens	.85
10	Alvin Davis	.10
11	Eric Davis	.10
12	Glenn Davis	.10
13	Andre Dawson	.25
14	Dwight Gooden	.10
15	Orel Hershiser	.10
16	Teddy Higuera	.10
17	Kent Hrbek	.10
18	Wally Joyner	.10
19	Jimmy Key	.10
20	John Kruk	.10
21	Jeff Leonard	.10
22	Don Mattingly	.85
23	Mark McGwire	1.00
24	Kevin McReynolds	.10
25	Dale Murphy	.15
26	Matt Nokes	.10
27	Terry Pendleton	.10
28	Kirby Puckett	.65
29	Tim Raines	.10
30	Rick Rhoden	.10
31	Cal Ripken, Jr.	1.50
32	Benito Santiago	.10
33	Mike Schmidt	.85
34	Mike Scott	.10
35	Kevin Seitzer	.10
36	Ruben Sierra	.10
37	Cory Snyder	.10
38	Darryl Strawberry	.10
39	Rick Sutcliffe	.10
40	Danny Tartabull	.10
41	Alan Trammell	.10
42	Ken Williams	.10
43	Mike Witt	.10
44	Robin Yount	.50

Superstars Box Panel

SHANE RAWLEY Phillies • Pitcher

Six cards were placed on the bottoms of retail boxes of the Fleer Superstars boxed sets. in 1988. The cards, 2-1/2" x 3-1/2", are identical in design to cards found in the 44-card set. The cards are numbered C-1 through C-6 and were produced for distribution by McCrory stores and its affiliates.

		NM/M
Complete Panel:		2.50
Complete Set (6):		2.50
Common Player:		.25
C1	Pete Incaviglia	.15
C2	Rickey Henderson	1.00
C3	Tony Fernandez	.15
C4	Shane Rawley	.15
C5	Ryne Sandberg	1.50
C6	St. Louis Cardinals logo/checklist	.10

1989 Fleer

This set includes 660 standard-size cards and was issued with 45 team logo stickers. Individual card fronts feature a gray and white striped background with full-color player photos framed by a bright line of color that slants upward to the right. The set also includes two subsets: 15 Major League

KEVIN ROMINE OUTFIELD

Prospects and 12 SuperStar Specials. A special bonus set of 12 All-Star Team cards was randomly inserted in individual wax packs of 15 cards. The last seven cards in the set are checklists, with players listed alphabetically by teams.

		NM/M
Retail Factory Set (660):		17.50
Hobby Factory Set (672):		20.00
Complete Set (660):		15.00
Common Player:		.05
Wax Pack (15):		1.00
Wax Box (36):		25.00
Cello Pack (36):		1.50
Cello Box (24):		20.00
Rack Pack (42+1):		1.50
Rack Box (24):		25.00
1	Don Baylor	.05
2	Lance Blankenship RC	.05
3	Todd Burns RC	.05
4	Greg Cadaret RC	.05
5	Jose Canseco	.35
6	Storm Davis	.05
7	Dennis Eckersley	.35
8	Mike Gallego RC	.05
9	Ron Hassey	.05
10	Dave Henderson	.05
11	Rick Honeycutt	.05
12	Glenn Hubbard	.05
13	Stan Javier	.05
14	Doug Jennings RC	.05
15	Felix Jose RC	.05
16	Carney Lansford	.05
17	Mark McGwire	.65
18	Gene Nelson	.05
19	Dave Parker	.05
20	Eric Plunk	.05
21	Luis Polonia	.05
22	Terry Steinbach	.05
23	Dave Stewart	.05
24	Walt Weiss	.05
25	Bob Welch	.05
26	Curt Young	.05
27	Rick Aguilera	.05
28	Wally Backman	.05
29	Mark Carreon	.05
30	Gary Carter	.40
31	David Cone	.05
32	Ron Darling	.05
33	Len Dykstra	.05
34	Kevin Elster	.05
35	Sid Fernandez	.05
36	Dwight Gooden	.05
37	Keith Hernandez	.05
38	Gregg Jefferies	.05
39	Howard Johnson	.05
40	Terry Leach	.05
41	Dave Magadan	.05
42	Bob McClure	.05
43	Roger McDowell	.05
44	Kevin McReynolds	.05
45	Keith Miller	.05
46	Randy Myers	.05
47	Bob Ojeda	.05
48	Mackey Sasser	.05
49	Darryl Strawberry	.05
50	Tim Teufel	.05
51	Dave West RC	.05
52	Mookie Wilson	.05
53	Dave Anderson	.05
54	Tim Belcher	.05
55	Mike Davis	.05
56	Mike Devereaux	.05
57	Kirk Gibson	.05
58	Alfredo Griffin	.05
59	Chris Gwynn	.05
60	Jeff Hamilton	.05
61a	Danny Heep (Home: San Antonio, TX)	.25
61b	Danny Heep (Home: Lake Hills, TX)	.05
62	Orel Hershiser	.05
63	Brian Holton RC	.05
64	Jay Howell	.05
65	Tim Leary	.05
66	Mike Marshall	.05
67	Ramon Martinez RC	.25
68	Jesse Orosco	.05
69	Alejandro Pena	.05
70	Steve Sax	.05
71	Mike Scioscia	.05
72	Mike Sharperson	.05
73	John Shelby	.05
74	Franklin Stubbs	.05
75	John Tudor	.05
76	Fernando Valenzuela	.05
77	Tracy Woodson	.05
78	Marty Barrett	.05
79	Todd Benzinger	.05
80	Mike Boddicker	.05
81	Wade Boggs	.50
82	"Oil Can" Boyd	.05
83	Ellis Burks	.05
84	Rick Cerone	.05
85	Roger Clemens	.60
86	Steve Curry RC	.05
87	Dwight Evans	.05
88	Wes Gardner	.05
89	Rich Gedman	.05
90	Mike Greenwell	.05
91	Bruce Hurst	.05
92	Dennis Lamp	.05
93	Spike Owen	.05
94	Larry Parrish	.05
95	Carlos Quintana RC	.05
96	Jody Reed	.05
97	Jim Rice	.05
98a	Kevin Romine (Batting follow-thru, photo actually Randy Kutcher.)	.25
98b	Kevin Romine (Arms crossed on chest, correct photo.)	.25
99	Lee Smith	.05
100	Mike Smithson	.05
101	Bob Stanley	.05
102	Allan Anderson	.05
103	Keith Atherton	.05
104	Juan Berenguer	.05
105	Bert Blyleven	.10
106	Eric Bullock RC	.05
107	Randy Bush	.05
108	John Christensen RC	.05
109	Mark Davidson	.05
110	Gary Gaetti	.05
111	Greg Gagne	.05
112	Dan Gladden	.05
113	German Gonzalez RC	.05
114	Brian Harper	.05
115	Tom Herr	.05
116	Kent Hrbek	.05
117	Gene Larkin	.05
118	Tim Laudner	.05
119	Charlie Lea	.05
120	Steve Lombardozzi	.05
121a	John Moses (Home: Phoenix, AZ)	.25
121b	John Moses (Home: Tempe, AZ)	.05
122	Al Newman	.05
123	Mark Portugal	.05
124	Kirby Puckett	.50
125	Jeff Reardon	.05
126	Fred Toliver	.05
127	Frank Viola	.05
128	Doyle Alexander	.05
129	Dave Bergman	.05
130a	Tom Brookens (Mike Heath stats on back.)	.50
130b	Tom Brookens (Correct stats on back.)	.05
131	Paul Gibson RC	.05
132a	Mike Heath (Tom Brookens stats on back.)	.50
132b	Mike Heath (Correct stats on back.)	.05
133	Don Heinkel RC	.05
134	Mike Henneman	.05
135	Guillermo Hernandez	.05
136	Eric King	.05
137	Chet Lemon	.05
138	Fred Lynn	.05
139	Jack Morris	.05
140	Matt Nokes	.05
141	Gary Pettis	.05
142	Ted Power	.05
143	Jeff Robinson	.05
144	Luis Salazar	.05
145	Steve Searcy RC	.05
146	Pat Sheridan	.05
147	Frank Tanana	.05
148	Alan Trammell	.05
149	Walt Terrell	.05
150	Jim Walewander RC	.05
151	Lou Whitaker	.05
152	Tim Birtsas	.05
153	Tom Browning	.05
154	Keith Brown RC	.05
155	Norm Charlton RC	.15
156	Dave Concepcion	.05
157	Kal Daniels	.05
158	Eric Davis	.05
159	Bo Diaz	.05
160	Rob Dibble	.05
161	Nick Esasky	.05
162	John Franco	.05
163	Danny Jackson	.05
164	Barry Larkin	.05
165	Rob Murphy	.05
166	Paul O'Neill	.05
167	Jeff Reed	.05
168	Jose Rijo	.05
169	Ron Robinson	.05
170	Chris Sabo	.05
171	Candy Sierra RC	.05
172	Van Snider RC	.05
173a	Jeff Treadway (Blue "target" above head.)	75.00
173b	Jeff Treadway (No "target.")	.05
174	Frank Williams	.05
175	Herm Winningham	.05
176	Jim Adduci RC	.05
177	Don August	.05
178	Mike Birkbeck	.05
179	Chris Bosio	.05
180	Glenn Braggs	.05
181	Greg Brock	.05
182	Mark Clear	.05
183	Chuck Crim	.05
184	Rob Deer	.05
185	Tom Filer	.05
186	Jim Gantner	.05
187	Darryl Hamilton	.05
188	Ted Higuera	.05
189	Odell Jones	.05
190	Jeffrey Leonard	.05
191	Joey Meyer	.05
192	Paul Mirabella	.05
193	Paul Molitor	.40
194	Charlie O'Brien RC	.05
195	Dan Plesac	.05
196	Gary Sheffield RC	1.00
197	B.J. Surhoff	.05
198	Dale Sveum	.05
199	Bill Wegman	.05
200	Robin Yount	.40
201	Rafael Belliard	.05
202	Barry Bonds	.75
203	Bobby Bonilla	.05
204	Sid Bream	.05
205	Benny Distefano RC	.05
206	Doug Drabek	.05
207	Mike Dunne	.05
208	Felix Fermin	.05
209	Brian Fisher	.05
210	Jim Gott	.05
211	Bob Kipper	.05
212	Dave LaPoint	.05
213	Mike LaValliere	.05
214	Jose Lind	.05
215	Junior Ortiz	.05
216	Vicente Palacios	.05
217	Tom Prince RC	.05
218	Gary Redus	.05
219	R.J. Reynolds	.05
220	Jeff Robinson	.05
221	John Smiley	.05
222	Andy Van Slyke	.05
223	Bob Walk	.05
224	Glenn Wilson	.05
225	Jesse Barfield	.05
226	George Bell	.05
227	Pat Borders	.05
228	John Cerutti	.05
229	Jim Clancy	.05
230	Mark Eichhorn	.05
231	Tony Fernandez	.05
232	Cecil Fielder	.05
233	Mike Flanagan	.05
234	Kelly Gruber	.05
235	Tom Henke	.05
236	Jimmy Key	.05
237	Rick Leach	.05
238	Manny Lee	.05
239	Nelson Liriano	.05
240	Fred McGriff	.05
241	Lloyd Moseby	.05
242	Rance Mulliniks	.05
243	Jeff Musselman	.05
244	Dave Stieb	.05
245	Todd Stottlemyre RC	.05
246	Duane Ward	.05
247	David Wells	.05
248	Ernie Whitt	.05
249	Luis Aguayo	.05
250a	Neil Allen (Home: Sarasota, FL)	.25
250b	Neil Allen (Home: Syosset, NY)	.05
251	John Candelaria	.05
252	Jack Clark	.05
253	Richard Dotson	.05
254	Rickey Henderson	.40
255	Tommy John	.10
256	Roberto Kelly	.05
257	Al Leiter	.05
258	Don Mattingly	.60
259	Dale Mohorcic	.05
260	Hal Morris	.25
261	Scott Nielsen RC	.05
262	Mike Pagliarulo	.05
263	Hipolito Pena RC	.05
264	Ken Phelps	.05
265	Willie Randolph	.05
266	Rick Rhoden	.05
267	Dave Righetti	.05
268	Rafael Santana	.05
269	Steve Shields RC	.05
270	Joel Skinner	.05
271	Don Slaught	.05
272	Claudell Washington	.05
273	Gary Ward	.05
274	Dave Winfield	.40
275	Luis Aquino RC	.05
276	Floyd Bannister	.05
277	George Brett	.60
278	Bill Buckner	.05
279	Nick Capra RC	.05
280	Jose DeJesus RC	.05
281	Steve Farr	.05
282	Jerry Gleaton	.05
283	Mark Gubicza	.05
284	Tom Gordon RC	.05
285	Bo Jackson	.10
286	Charlie Leibrandt	.05
287	Mike Macfarlane RC	.10
288	Jeff Montgomery	.05
289	Bill Pecota	.05
290	Jamie Quirk	.05

#	Player	Price
291	Bret Saberhagen	.05
292	Kevin Seitzer	.05
293	Kurt Stillwell	.05
294	Pat Tabler	.05
295	Danny Tartabull	.05
296	Gary Thurman	.05
297	Frank White	.05
298	Willie Wilson	.05
299	Roberto Alomar	.20
300	Sandy Alomar, Jr. RC	.25
301	Chris Brown	.05
302	Mike Brumley RC	.05
303	Mark Davis	.05
304	Mark Grant	.05
305	Tony Gwynn	.50
306	Greg Harris RC	.05
307	Andy Hawkins	.05
308	Jimmy Jones	.05
309	John Kruk	.05
310	Dave Leiper	.05
311	Carmelo Martinez	.05
312	Lance McCullers	.05
313	Keith Moreland	.05
314	Dennis Rasmussen	.05
315	Randy Ready	.05
316	Benito Santiago	.05
317	Eric Show	.05
318	Todd Simmons	.05
319	Garry Templeton	.05
320	Dickie Thon	.05
321	Ed Whitson	.05
322	Marvell Wynne	.05
323	Mike Aldrete	.05
324	Brett Butler	.05
325	Will Clark	.05
326	Kelly Downs	.05
327	Dave Dravecky	.05
328	Scott Garrelts	.05
329	Atlee Hammaker	.05
330	Charlie Hayes RC	.10
331	Mike Krukow	.05
332	Craig Lefferts	.05
333	Candy Maldonado	.05
334	Kirt Manwaring	.05
335	Bob Melvin	.05
336	Kevin Mitchell	.05
337	Donell Nixon	.05
338	Tony Perezchica RC	.05
339	Joe Price	.05
340	Rick Reuschel	.05
341	Earnest Riles	.05
342	Don Robinson	.05
343	Chris Speier	.05
344	Robby Thompson	.05
345	Jose Uribe	.05
346	Matt Williams	.05
347	Trevor Wilson RC	.15
348	Juan Agosto	.05
349	Larry Andersen	.05
350a	Alan Ashby ("Throws Right")	.25
350b	Alan Ashby ("Throws Right")	.05
351	Kevin Bass	.05
352	Buddy Bell	.05
353	Craig Biggio	.05
354	Danny Darwin	.05
355	Glenn Davis	.05
356	Jim Deshaies	.05
357	Bill Doran	.05
358	John Fishel RC	.05
359	Billy Hatcher	.05
360	Bob Knepper	.05
361	Louie Meadows RC	.05
362	Dave Meads	.05
363	Jim Pankovits	.05
364	Terry Puhl	.05
365	Rafael Ramirez	.05
366	Craig Reynolds	.05
367	Mike Scott	.05
368	Nolan Ryan	.75
369	Dave Smith	.05
370	Gerald Young	.05
371	Hubie Brooks	.05
372	Tim Burke	.05
373	John Dopson RC	.05
374	Mike Fitzgerald	.05
375	Tom Foley	.05
376	Andres Galarraga	.05
377	Neal Heaton	.05
378	Joe Hesketh	.05
379	Brian Holman RC	.05
380	Rex Hudler	.05
381a	Randy Johnson RC (Marlboro ad on scoreboard.)	40.00
381b	Randy Johnson (Ad partially obscured.)	10.00
381c	Randy Johnson RC (Ad completely blacked out.)	3.00
382	Wallace Johnson	.05
383	Tracy Jones	.05
384	Dave Martinez	.05
385	Dennis Martinez	.05
386	Andy McGaffigan	.05
387	Otis Nixon	.05
388	Johnny Paredes RC	.05
389	Jeff Parrett	.05
390	Pascual Perez	.05
391	Tim Raines	.05
392	Luis Rivera	.05
393	Nelson Santovenia RC	.05
394	Bryn Smith	.05
395	Tim Wallach	.05
396	Andy Allanson	.05
397	Rod Allen RC	.05
398	Scott Bailes	.05

#	Player	Price
399	Tom Candiotti	.05
400	Joe Carter	.05
401	Carmen Castillo	.05
402	Dave Clark	.05
403	John Farrell	.05
404	Julio Franco	.05
405	Don Gordon	.05
406	Mel Hall	.05
407	Brad Havens	.05
408	Brook Jacoby	.05
409	Doug Jones	.05
410	Jeff Kaiser RC	.05
411	Luis Medina RC	.05
412	Cory Snyder	.05
413	Greg Swindell	.05
414	Ron Tingley RC	.05
415	Willie Upshaw	.05
416	Ron Washington	.05
417	Rich Yett	.05
418	Damon Berryhill	.05
419	Mike Bielecki	.05
420	Doug Dascenzo RC	.05
421	Jody Davis	.05
422	Andre Dawson	.25
423	Frank DiPino	.05
424	Shawon Dunston	.05
425	"Goose" Gossage	.10
426	Mark Grace	.25
427	Mike Harkey RC	.05
428	Darrin Jackson	.05
429	Les Lancaster	.05
430	Vance Law	.05
431	Greg Maddux	.50
432	Jamie Moyer	.05
433	Al Nipper	.05
434	Rafael Palmeiro	.35
435	Pat Perry	.05
436	Jeff Pico RC	.05
437	Ryne Sandberg	.50
438	Calvin Schiraldi	.05
439	Rick Sutcliffe	.05
440a	Manny Trillo ("Throws Rig")	.35
440b	Manny Trillo ("Throws Right")	.05
441	Gary Varsho RC	.05
442	Mitch Webster	.05
443	Luis Alicea	.05
444	Tom Brunansky	.05
445	Vince Coleman	.05
446	John Costello RC	.05
447	Danny Cox	.05
448	Ken Dayley	.05
449	Jose DeLeon	.05
450	Curt Ford	.05
451	Pedro Guerrero	.05
452	Bob Horner	.05
453	Tim Jones RC	.05
454	Steve Lake	.05
455	Joe Magrane	.05
456	Greg Mathews	.05
457	Willie McGee	.05
458	Larry McWilliams	.05
459	Jose Oquendo	.05
460	Tony Pena	.05
461	Terry Pendleton	.05
462	Steve Peters RC	.05
463	Ozzie Smith	.50
464	Scott Terry	.05
465	Denny Walling	.05
466	Todd Worrell	.05
467	Tony Armas	.05
468	Dante Bichette RC	.25
469	Bob Boone	.05
470	Terry Clark RC	.05
471	Stew Cliburn RC	.05
472	Mike Cook RC	.05
473	Sherman Corbett RC	.05
474	Chili Davis	.05
475	Brian Downing	.05
476	Jim Eppard RC	.05
477	Chuck Finley	.05
478	Willie Fraser	.05
479	Bryan Harvey	.05
480	Jack Howell	.05
481	Wally Joyner	.05
482	Jack Lazorko	.05
483	Kirk McCaskill	.05
484	Mark McLemore	.05
485	Greg Minton	.05
486	Dan Petry	.05
487	Johnny Ray	.05
488	Dick Schofield	.05
489	Devon White	.05
490	Mike Witt	.05
491	Harold Baines	.05
492	Daryl Boston	.05
493	Ivan Calderon	.05
494	Mike Diaz	.05
495	Carlton Fisk	.40
496	Dave Gallagher RC	.05
497	Ozzie Guillen	.05
498	Shawn Hillegas	.05
499	Lance Johnson	.05
500	Barry Jones	.05
501	Bill Long	.05
502	Steve Lyons	.05
503	Fred Manrique	.05
504	Jack McDowell	.05
505	Donn Pall RC	.05
506	Kelly Paris	.05
507	Dan Pasqua	.05
508	Ken Patterson RC	.05
509	Melido Perez	.05
510	Jerry Reuss	.05
511	Mark Salas	.05
512	Bobby Thigpen	.05
513	Mike Woodard	.05

#	Player	Price
514	Bob Brower	.05
515	Steve Buechele	.05
516	Jose Cecena RC	.05
517	Cecil Espy	.05
518	Scott Fletcher	.05
519	Cecilio Guante	.05
520	Jose Guzman	.05
521	Ray Hayward	.05
522	Charlie Hough	.05
523	Pete Incaviglia	.05
524	Mike Jeffcoat	.05
525	Paul Kilgus	.05
526	Chad Kreuter RC	.15
527	Jeff Kunkel	.05
528	Oddibe McDowell	.05
529	Pete O'Brien	.05
530	Geno Petralli	.05
531	Jeff Russell	.05
532	Ruben Sierra	.05
533	Mike Stanley	.05
534	Ed Vande Berg	.05
535	Curtis Wilkerson	.05
536	Mitch Williams	.05
537	Bobby Witt	.05
538	Steve Balboni	.05
539	Scott Bankhead	.05
540	Scott Bradley	.05
541	Mickey Brantley	.05
542	Jay Buhner	.05
543	Mike Campbell	.05
544	Darnell Coles	.05
545	Henry Cotto	.05
546	Alvin Davis	.05
547	Mario Diaz	.05
548	Ken Griffey Jr. RC	6.00
549	Erik Hanson RC	.05
550	Mike Jackson	.05
551	Mark Langston	.05
552	Edgar Martinez	.05
553	Bill McGuire RC	.05
554	Mike Moore	.05
555	Jim Presley	.05
556	Rey Quinones	.05
557	Jerry Reed	.05
558	Harold Reynolds	.05
559	Mike Schooler RC	.05
560	Bill Swift	.05
561	Dave Valle	.05
562	Steve Bedrosian	.05
563	Phil Bradley	.05
564	Don Carman	.05
565	Bob Dernier	.05
566	Marvin Freeman	.05
567	Todd Frohwirth	.05
568	Greg Gross	.05
569	Kevin Gross	.05
570	Greg Harris	.05
571	Von Hayes	.05
572	Chris James	.05
573	Steve Jeltz	.05
574	Ron Jones RC	.05
575	Ricky Jordan RC	.05
576	Mike Maddux	.05
577	David Palmer	.05
578	Lance Parrish	.05
579	Shane Rawley	.05
580	Bruce Ruffin	.05
581	Juan Samuel	.05
582	Mike Schmidt	.60
583	Kent Tekulve	.05
584	Milt Thompson	.05
585	Jose Alvarez RC	.05
586	Paul Assenmacher	.05
587	Bruce Benedict	.05
588	Jeff Blauser	.05
589	Terry Blocker RC	.05
590	Ron Gant	.05
591	Tom Glavine	.30
592	Tommy Gregg	.05
593	Albert Hall	.05
594	Dion James	.05
595	Rick Mahler	.05
596	Dale Murphy	.25
597	Gerald Perry	.05
598	Charlie Puleo	.05
599	Ted Simmons	.05
600	Pete Smith	.05
601	Zane Smith	.05
602	John Smoltz	.50
603	Bruce Sutter	.35
604	Andres Thomas	.05
605	Ozzie Virgil	.05
606	Brady Anderson	.05
607	Jeff Ballard	.05
608	Jose Bautista RC	.05
609	Ken Gerhart	.05
610	Terry Kennedy	.05
611	Eddie Murray	.40
612	Carl Nichols RC	.05
613	Tom Niedenfuer	.05
614	Joe Orsulak	.05
615	Oswaldo Peraza RC (Oswald)	.05
616a	Bill Ripken (Vulgarity on bat knob.)	8.00
616b	Bill Ripken (Scribble over vulgarity.)	6.00
616c	Bill Ripken (Black box over vulgarity.)	.10
616d	Bill Ripken (Vulgarity whited out.) (Many fake "white out" cards exist, created by erasures.)	250.00
616e	Billy Ripken (Strip cut out of bottom of card.)	
617	Cal Ripken, Jr.	.75
618	Dave Schmidt	.05

#	Player	Price
619	Rick Schu	.05
620	Larry Sheets	.05
621	Doug Sisk	.05
622	Pete Stanicek	.05
623	Mickey Tettleton	.05
624	Jay Tibbs	.05
625	Jim Traber	.05
626	Mark Williamson	.05
627	Craig Worthington RC	.05
628	Speed and Power (Jose Canseco)	.20
629	Pitcher Perfect (Tom Browning)	.05
630	Like Father Like Sons (Roberto Alomar, Sandy Alomar, Jr.)	.20
631	N.L. All-Stars (Will Clark, Rafael Palmeiro)	.10
632	Homeruns Coast to Coast (Will Clark, Darryl Strawberry)	.05
633	Hot Corner's Hot Hitters (Wade Boggs, Carney Lansford)	.25
634	Triple A's (Jose Canseco, Mark McGwire, Terry Steinbach)	.40
635	Dual Heat (Mark Davis, Dwight Gooden)	.05
636	N.L. Pitching Power (David Cone, Danny Jackson)	.05
637	Cannon Arms (Bobby Bonilla, Chris Sabo)	.05
638	Double Trouble (Andres Galarraga, Gerald Perry)	.05
639	Power Center (Eric Davis)	.05
640	Major League Prospects (Cameron Drew RC, Steve Wilson RC)	.05
641	Major League Prospects (Kevin Brown, Kevin Reimer RC)	.30
642	Major League Prospects (Jerald Clark RC, Brad Pounders RC)	.05
643	Major League Prospects (Mike Capel RC, Drew Hall RC)	.05
644	Major League Prospects (Joe Girardi RC, Rolando Roomes RC)	.20
645	Major League Prospects (Marty Brown RC, Lenny Harris RC)	.15
646	Major League Prospects (Luis de los Santos RC, Jim Campbell RC)	.05
647	Major League Prospects (Miguel Garcia RC, Randy Kramer RC)	.05
648	Major League Prospects (Torey Lovullo RC, Robert Palacios RC)	.05
649	Major League Prospects (Jim Corsi RC, Bob Milacki RC)	.05
650	Major League Prospects (Grady Hall RC, Mike Rochford RC)	.05
651	Major League Prospects (Vance Lovelace RC, Terry Taylor RC)	.05
652	Major League Prospects (Dennis Cook RC, Ken Hill RC)	.20
653	Major League Prospects (Scott Service RC, Shane Turner RC)	.05
654	Checklist 1-101	.05
655	Checklist 102-200	.05
656	Checklist 201-298	.05
657	Checklist 299-395	.05
658	Checklist 396-490	.05
659	Checklist 491-584	.05
660	Checklist 585-660	.05

and cello packs. The cards feature two player photos set against a green background with the "89 Fleer All Star Team" logo bannered across the top, and the player's name, position and team in the lower left corner. The backs contain a narrative player profile.

	NM/M
Complete Set (12):	2.50
Common Player:	.25
1 Bobby Bonilla	.25
2 Jose Canseco	.75
3 Will Clark	.40
4 Dennis Eckersley	.50
5 Julio Franco	.25
6 Mike Greenwell	.25
7 Orel Hershiser	.25
8 Paul Molitor	1.00
9 Mike Scioscia	.25
10 Darryl Strawberry	.25
11 Alan Trammell	.25
12 Frank Viola	.25

For The Record

Fleer's "For the Record" set features six players and their achievements from 1988. Fronts of the standard 2-1/2" x 3-1/2" cards feature a photo of the player set against a red scoreboard background. Card backs are grey and describe individual accomplishments. The cards were distributed randomly in rack packs.

	NM/M
Complete Set (6):	2.50
Common Player:	.25
1 Wade Boggs	.75
2 Roger Clemens	1.00
3 Andres Galarraga	.25
4 Kirk Gibson	.25
5 Greg Maddux	.75
6 Don Mattingly	1.00

World Series

This 12-card set, which depicts highlights of the 1988 World Series, was included as a special sub-set with the regular and glossy factory-collated Fleer set. It was not available as individual cards in wax packs, cello packs or any other form.

	NM/M
Complete Set, Regular (12):	2.00
Common Card:	.10
1 Dodgers Secret Weapon (Mickey Hatcher)	.10
2 Rookie Starts Series (Tim Belcher)	.10
3 Jose Canseco	.25
4 Dramatic Comeback (Mike Scioscia)	.10
5 Kirk Gibson	.10
6 Orel Hershiser	.10
7 One Swings, Three RBIs (Mike Marshall)	.10
8 Mark McGwire	1.00

All-Star Team

FRANK VIOLA LEFT HAND PITCHER-TWINS

This special 12-card set represents Fleer's choices for its 1989 Major League All-Star Team. For the fourth consecutive year, Fleer inserted the special cards randomly in wax

9 Sax's Speed Wins Game 4 (Steve Sax)	.10
10 Series Caps Award Winning Year (Walt Weiss)	.10
11 Orel Hershiser	.15
12 Dodger Blue, World Champs	.25

Box Panels

For the fourth consecutive year, Fleer issued a series of cards on the bottom panels of its regular 1989 wax pack boxes. The 28-card set includes 20 players and eight team logo cards, all designed in the identical style of the regular 1989 Fleer set. The box-bottom cards were randomly printed, four cards (three player cards and one team logo) on each bottom panel. Cards are numbered C-1 to C-28.

	NM/M
Complete Panel Set (7):	6.00
Complete Singles Set (28):	3.00
Common Single Player:	.15
1 Mets Logo	.05
2 Wade Boggs	.75
3 George Brett	1.25
4 Jose Canseco	.50
5 A's Logo	.05
6 Will Clark	.10
7 David Cone	.10
8 Andres Galarraga	.10
9 Dodgers Logo	.10
10 Kirk Gibson	.10
11 Mike Greenwell	.10
12 Tony Gwynn	.75
13 Tigers Logo	.10
14 Orel Hershiser	.10
15 Danny Jackson	.10
16 Wally Joyner	.10
17 Red Sox Logo	.05
18 Yankees Logo	.10
19 Fred McGriff	.10
20 Kirby Puckett	.75
21 Chris Sabo	.10
22 Kevin Seitzer	.10
23 Pirates logo	.05
24 Astros logo	.05
25 Darryl Strawberry	.10
26 Alan Trammell	.10
27 Andy Van Slyke	.10
28 Frank Viola	.10

Glossy Tin

The last of the limited-edition, collector-version glossy tin sets is estimated to have been produced in an edition of 30,000-60,000, creating a significant premium over their counterparts in the regular Fleer set. The issue was sold only in complete-set form in a lithographed metal box. The 1989 glossies differ from the regular cards on back in the use of blue, rather than yellow ink, and the appearance at center of a large baseball logo with 1989

/ Collector's Edition / Fleer at center. No glossy version of the '89 Update set was made. Fleer glossy sets were originally wholesaled at $40 each.

	NM/M
Unopened Set (672):	75.00
Complete Set (672):	50.00
Common Player:	.25

Update

ROBIN VENTURA
THIRD BASE

Fleer produced its sixth consecutive "Update" set in 1989 to supplement the company's regular set. As in the past, the set consisted of 132 cards (numbered U-1 through U-132) that were sold by hobby dealers in special collector's boxes.

		NM/M
Complete Set (132):		6.00
Common Player:		.05
1	Phil Bradley	.05
2	Mike Devereaux	.05
3	Steve Finley RC	.05
4	Kevin Hickey	.05
5	Brian Holton	.05
6	Bob Milacki	.05
7	Randy Milligan	.05
8	John Dopson	.05
9	Nick Esasky	.05
10	Rob Murphy	.05
11	Jim Abbott RC	.05
12	Bert Blyleven	.10
13	Jeff Manto RC	.05
14	Bob McClure	.05
15	Lance Parrish	.05
16	Lee Stevens RC	.05
17	Claudell Washington	.05
18	Mark Davis	.05
19	Eric King	.05
20	Ron Kittle	.05
21	Matt Merullo RC	.05
22	Steve Rosenberg RC	.05
23	Robin Ventura RC	.25
24	Keith Atherton	.05
25	Joey (Albert) Belle RC	1.00
26	Jerry Browne	.05
27	Felix Fermin	.05
28	Brad Komminsk	.05
29	Pete O'Brien	.05
30	Mike Brumley	.05
31	Tracy Jones	.05
32	Mike Schwabe RC	.05
33	Gary Ward	.05
34	Frank Williams	.05
35	Kevin Appier RC	.05
36	Bob Boone	.05
37	Luis de los Santos	.05
38	Jim Eisenreich RC	.05
39	Jaime Navarro RC	.05
40	Bill Spiers RC	.05
41	Greg Vaughn RC	.25
42	Randy Veres RC	.05
43	Wally Backman	.05
44	Shane Rawley	.05
45	Steve Balboni	.05
46	Jesse Barfield	.05
47	Alvaro Espinoza RC	.05
48	Bob Geren RC	.05
49	Mel Hall	.05
50	Andy Hawkins	.05
51	Hensley Meulens RC	.05
52	Steve Sax	.05
53	Deion Sanders RC	.05
54	Rickey Henderson	.40
55	Mike Moore	.05
56	Tony Phillips	.05
57	Greg Briley	.05
58	Gene Harris	.05
59	Randy Johnson	2.00
60	Jeffrey Leonard	.05
61	Dennis Powell	.05
62	Omar Vizquel	.05
63	Kevin Brown	.05
64	Julio Franco	.05
65	Jamie Moyer	.05
66	Rafael Palmeiro	.35
67	Nolan Ryan	1.00
68	Francisco Cabrera RC	.05
69	Junior Felix RC	.05
70	Al Leiter	.05
71	Alex Sanchez RC	.05
72	Geronimo Berroa RC	.05

73	Derek Lilliquist RC	.05
74	Lonnie Smith	.05
75	Jeff Treadway	.05
76	Paul Kilgus	.05
77	Lloyd McClendon	.05
78	Scott Sanderson	.05
79	Dwight Smith RC	.05
80	Jerome Walton RC	.05
81	Mitch Williams	.05
82	Steve Wilson	.05
83	Todd Benzinger	.05
84	Ken Griffey	.05
85	Rick Mahler	.05
86	Rolando Roomes	.05
87	Scott Scudder RC	.05
88	Jim Clancy	.05
89	Rick Rhoden	.05
90	Dan Schatzeder	.05
91	Mike Morgan	.05
92	Eddie Murray	.40
93	Willie Randolph	.05
94	Ray Searage	.05
95	Mike Aldrete	.05
96	Kevin Gross	.05
97	Mark Langston	.05
98	Spike Owen	.05
99	Zane Smith	.05
100	Don Aase	.05
101	Barry Lyons	.05
102	Juan Samuel	.05
103	Wally Whitehurst RC	.05
104	Dennis Cook	.05
105	Len Dykstra	.05
106	Charlie Hayes RC	.05
107	Tommy Herr	.05
108	Ken Howell	.05
109	John Kruk	.05
110	Roger McDowell	.05
111	Terry Mulholland RC	.05
112	Jeff Parrett	.05
113	Neal Heaton	.05
114	Jeff King	.05
115	Randy Kramer	.05
116	Bill Landrum	.05
117	Cris Carpenter RC	.05
118	Frank DiPino	.05
119	Ken Hill	.05
120	Dan Quisenberry	.05
121	Milt Thompson	.05
122	Todd Zeile RC	.25
123	Jack Clark	.05
124	Bruce Hurst	.05
125	Mark Parent	.05
126	Bip Roberts	.05
127	Jeff Brantley RC	.05
128	Terry Kennedy	.05
129	Mike LaCoss	.05
130	Greg Litton RC	.05
131	Mike Schmidt	.65
132	Checklist	.05

Bill Ripken FF 'Test'

BILL RIPKEN
SECOND BASE

At the height of the furor over the vulgarity shown on the initial print run of Bill Ripken's card, when genuine examples were selling for as high as $125, this fantasy card surfaced to prey on collectors. In standard size, the card is printed in black-and-white on front and back, reproducing a genuine card. On the back, typography was also added to make the piece look like a test card. This fraudulent product has no collectible value.

Baseball All Stars

FLEER BASEBALL ALL STARS

DON MATTINGLY YANKEES FIRST BASE

This specially-boxed set was produced by Fleer for the Ben Franklin store chain. The full-color player photos are surrounded by a border of pink and yellow vertical bands. "Fleer Baseball All-Stars" appears along the top in red, white and blue. The set was sold in a box with a checklist on the back.

		NM/M
Complete Set (44):		4.00
Common Player:		.10
1	Doyle Alexander	.10
2	George Bell	.10
3	Wade Boggs	.65
4	Bobby Bonilla	.10
5	Jose Canseco	.40
6	Will Clark	.10
7	Roger Clemens	.75
8	Vince Coleman	.10
9	David Cone	.10
10	Mark Davis	.10
11	Andre Dawson	.25
12	Dennis Eckersley	.45
13	Andres Galarraga	.10
14	Kirk Gibson	.10
15	Dwight Gooden	.10
16	Mike Greenwell	.10
17	Mark Gubicza	.10
18	Ozzie Guillen	.10
19	Tony Gwynn	.65
20	Rickey Henderson	.10
21	Orel Hershiser	.10
22	Danny Jackson	.10
23	Doug Jones	.10
24	Ricky Jordan	.10
25	Bob Knepper	.10
26	Barry Larkin	.10
27	Vance Law	.10
28	Don Mattingly	.75
29	Mark McGwire	1.00
30	Paul Molitor	.50
31	Gerald Perry	.10
32	Kirby Puckett	.65
33	Johnny Ray	.10
34	Harold Reynolds	.10
35	Cal Ripken, Jr.	1.50
36	Don Robinson	.10
37	Ruben Sierra	.10
38	Dave Smith	.10
39	Darryl Strawberry	.10
40	Dave Steib	.10
41	Alan Trammell	.10
42	Andy Van Slyke	.10
43	Frank Viola	.10
44	Dave Winfield	.50

Exciting Stars

BASEBALL EXCITING STARS

WILL CLARK
FIRST BASE
FLEER '89

Sold exclusively in Cumberland Farm stores, this boxed set pictures the game's top stars. The card fronts feature a color player photo surrounded by a blue border with "Baseball's Exciting Stars" along the top. The cards were numbered alphabetically and packed in a special box with a complete checklist on the back.

		NM/M
Complete Set (44):		4.00
Common Player:		.10
1	Harold Baines	.10
2	Wade Boggs	.65
3	Jose Canseco	.50
4	Joe Carter	.10
5	Will Clark	.10
6	Roger Clemens	.75
7	Vince Coleman	.10
8	David Cone	.10
9	Eric Davis	.10
10	Glenn Davis	.10
11	Andre Dawson	.25
12	Dwight Evans	.10
13	Andres Galarraga	.10
14	Kirk Gibson	.10
15	Dwight Gooden	.10
16	Jim Gott	.10
17	Mark Grace	.10
18	Mike Greenwell	.10
19	Mark Gubicza	.10
20	Tony Gwynn	.65
21	Rickey Henderson	.60
22	Tom Henke	.10
23	Mike Henneman	.10
24	Orel Hershiser	.10
25	Danny Jackson	.10
26	Gregg Jefferies	.10
27	Ricky Jordan	.10
28	Wally Joyner	.10
29	Mark Langston	.10
30	Tim Leary	.10
31	Don Mattingly	.75
32	Mark McGwire	1.50
33	Dale Murphy	.15
34	Kirby Puckett	.65
35	Chris Sabo	.10
36	Kevin Seitzer	.10
37	Ruben Sierra	.10
38	Ozzie Smith	.65
39	Dave Stewart	.10
40	Darryl Strawberry	.10
41	Alan Trammell	.10
42	Frank Viola	.10
43	Dave Winfield	.60
44	Robin Yount	.60

Heroes of Baseball

'89 HEROES of BASEBALL
Orel Hershiser
DODGERS PITCHER

This boxed set was produced by Fleer for the Woolworth store chain. The fronts of the cards are designed in a red and blue color scheme and feature full-color photos that fade into a soft focus on all edges. The set was numbered alphabetically and was packaged in a special box with a checklist on the back.

		NM/M
Complete Set (44):		4.00
Common Player:		.10
1	George Bell	.10
2	Wade Boggs	.75
3	Barry Bonds	1.50
4	Tom Brunansky	.10
5	Jose Canseco	.40
6	Joe Carter	.10
7	Will Clark	.10
8	Roger Clemens	.85
9	David Cone	.10
10	Eric Davis	.10
11	Glenn Davis	.10
12	Andre Dawson	.25
13	Dennis Eckersley	.50
14	John Franco	.10
15	Gary Gaetti	.10
16	Andres Galarraga	.10
17	Kirk Gibson	.10
18	Dwight Gooden	.10
19	Mike Greenwell	.10
20	Tony Gwynn	.75
21	Bryan Harvey	.10
22	Orel Hershiser	.10
23	Ted Higuera	.10
24	Danny Jackson	.10
25	Ricky Jordan	.10
26	Don Mattingly	.85
27	Fred McGriff	.10
28	Mark McGwire	1.00
29	Kevin McReynolds	.10
30	Gerald Perry	.10
31	Kirby Puckett	.75
32	Johnny Ray	.10
33	Harold Reynolds	.10
34	Cal Ripken, Jr.	1.50
35	Ryne Sandberg	.75
36	Kevin Seitzer	.10
37	Ruben Sierra	.10
38	Darryl Strawberry	.10
39	Bobby Thigpen	.10
40	Alan Trammell	.10
41	Andy Van Slyke	.10
42	Frank Viola	.10
43	Dave Winfield	.65
44	Robin Yount	.65

League Leaders

Another of the various small, boxed sets issued by Fleer, "League Leaders" was produced for Walgreen stores. The standard-size cards feature color photos on the front

FLEER League Leaders

Robin Yount
BREWERS OUTFIELD

surrounded by a red border with "Fleer League Leaders" across the top. The backs include player stats and data and the team logo. The cards are numbered alphabetically and packaged in a special box that includes the full checklist on the back.

		NM/M
Complete Set (44):		3.00
Common Player:		.10
1	Allan Anderson	.10
2	Wade Boggs	.75
3	Jose Canseco	.50
4	Will Clark	.10
5	Roger Clemens	.85
6	Vince Coleman	.10
7	David Cone	.10
8	Kal Daniels	.10
9	Chili Davis	.10
10	Eric Davis	.10
11	Glenn Davis	.10
12	Andre Dawson	.25
13	John Franco	.10
14	Andres Galarraga	.10
15	Kirk Gibson	.10
16	Dwight Gooden	.10
17	Mark Grace	.10
18	Mike Greenwell	.10
19	Tony Gwynn	.75
20	Orel Hershiser	.10
21	Pete Incaviglia	.10
22	Danny Jackson	.10
23	Gregg Jefferies	.10
24	Joe Magrane	.10
25	Don Mattingly	.85
26	Fred McGriff	.10
27	Mark McGwire	1.00
28	Dale Murphy	.15
29	Dan Plesac	.10
30	Kirby Puckett	.75
31	Harold Reynolds	.10
32	Cal Ripken, Jr.	1.50
33	Jeff Robinson	.10
34	Mike Scott	.10
35	Ozzie Smith	.75
36	Dave Stewart	.10
37	Darryl Strawberry	.10
38	Greg Swindell	.10
39	Bobby Thigpen	.10
40	Alan Trammell	.10
41	Andy Van Slyke	.10
42	Frank Viola	.10
43	Dave Winfield	.65
44	Robin Yount	.65

MVP

MIKE GREENWELL
RED SOX OUTFIELD
FLEER Baseball MVP

Filled with superstars, this boxed set was produced by Fleer in 1989 for the Toys "R" Us chain. The fronts of the cards are designed in a yellow and green color scheme and include a "Fleer Baseball MVP" logo above the color player photo. The backs are printed in shades of green and yellow and include biographical notes and stats. The set was issued in a special box with a checklist on the back.

	NM/M
Complete Set (44):	5.00

Superstars

FLEER

WADE BOGGS
THIRD BASE

This boxed set was produced by Fleer for the McCrory store chain. The cards are standard 2-1/2" x 3-1/2" and the full-color player photos are outlined in red with a tan-and-white striped border. The backs carry yellow and white stripes and include the Fleer "SuperStars" logo, player stats and biographical information. The cards are numbered alphabetically and packaged in a special box that includes a checklist on the back.

		NM/M
Complete Set (44):		4.00
Common Player:		.10
1	Roberto Alomar	.35
2	Harold Baines	.10
3	Tim Belcher	.10
4	Wade Boggs	.65
5	George Brett	.85
6	Jose Canseco	.50
7	Gary Carter	.60
8	Will Clark	.10
9	Roger Clemens	.85
10	Kal Daniels	.10
11	Eric Davis	.10
12	Andre Dawson	.25
13	Tony Fernandez	.10
14	Scott Fletcher	.10
15	Andres Galarraga	.10
16	Kirk Gibson	.10
17	Dwight Gooden	.10
18	Jim Gott	.10
19	Mark Grace	.10
20	Mike Greenwell	.10
21	Tony Gwynn	.75
22	Rickey Henderson	.60
23	Orel Hershiser	.10
24	Ted Higuera	.10
25	Gregg Jefferies	.10
26	Wally Joyner	.10
27	Mark Langston	.10
28	Greg Maddux	.75
29	Don Mattingly	.85

	Common Player:	.10
1	Steve Bedrosian	.10
2	George Bell	.10
3	Wade Boggs	.75
4	George Brett	.85
5	Hubie Brooks	.10
6	Jose Canseco	.50
7	Will Clark	.10
8	Roger Clemens	.85
9	Eric Davis	.10
10	Glenn Davis	.10
11	Andre Dawson	.25
12	Andres Galarraga	.10
13	Kirk Gibson	.10
14	Dwight Gooden	.10
15	Mark Grace	.10
16	Mike Greenwell	.10
17	Tony Gwynn	.75
18	Bryan Harvey	.10
19	Orel Hershiser	.10
20	Ted Higuera	.10
21	Danny Jackson	.10
22	Mike Jackson	.10
23	Doug Jones	.10
24	Greg Maddux	.75
25	Mike Marshall	.10
26	Don Mattingly	.85
27	Fred McGriff	.10
28	Mark McGwire	1.50
29	Kevin McReynolds	.10
30	Jack Morris	.10
31	Gerald Perry	.10
32	Kirby Puckett	.75
33	Chris Sabo	.10
34	Mike Scott	.10
35	Ruben Sierra	.10
36	Darryl Strawberry	.10
37	Danny Tartabull	.10
38	Bobby Thigpen	.10
39	Alan Trammell	.10
40	Andy Van Slyke	.10
41	Frank Viola	.10
42	Walt Weiss	.10
43	Dave Winfield	.65
44	Todd Worrell	.10

The cards are numbered alphabetically and packaged in a special box that includes the full checklist on the back.

30	Fred McGriff	.10
31	Mark McGwire	1.50
32	Dan Plesac	.10
33	Kirby Puckett	.75
34	Jeff Reardon	.10
35	Chris Sabo	.10
36	Mike Schmidt	.85
37	Mike Scott	.10
38	Cory Snyder	.10
39	Darryl Strawberry	.10
40	Alan Trammell	.10
41	Frank Viola	.10
42	Walt Weiss	.10
43	Dave Winfield	.60
44	Todd Worrell	.10

1990 Fleer

George Brett — FIRST BASE

Fleer's 1990 set, its 10th annual baseball card offering, again consisted of 660 cards numbered by team. The front of the cards feature mostly action photos surrounded by one of several different color bands and a white border. The set includes various special cards, including a series of "Major League Prospects," Players of the Decade, team checklist cards and a series of multi-player cards. The backs include complete career stats, player data, and a special "Vital Signs" section showing on-base percentage, slugging percentage, etc. for batters; and strikeout and walk ratios, opposing batting averages, etc. for pitchers.

	NM/M
Factory Hobby Set (672):	12.50
Retail Hobby Set (660):	12.00
Complete Set (660):	10.00
Common Player:	.05
Wax Pack (15):	.50
Wax Box (36):	10.00
Cello Pack (33):	1.00
Cello Box (24):	12.00

1	Lance Blankenship	.05
2	Todd Burns	.05
3	Jose Canseco	.30
4	Jim Corsi	.05
5	Storm Davis	.05
6	Dennis Eckersley	.35
7	Mike Gallego	.05
8	Ron Hassey	.05
9	Dave Henderson	.05
10	Rickey Henderson	.40
11	Rick Honeycutt	.05
12	Stan Javier	.05
13	Felix Jose	.05
14	Carney Lansford	.05
15	Mark McGwire	.65
16	Mike Moore	.05
17	Gene Nelson	.05
18	Dave Parker	.05
19	Tony Phillips	.05
20	Terry Steinbach	.05
21	Dave Stewart	.05
22	Walt Weiss	.05
23	Bob Welch	.05
24	Curt Young	.05
25	Paul Assenmacher	.05
26	Damon Berryhill	.05
27	Mike Bielecki	.05
28	Kevin Blankenship	.05
29	Andre Dawson	.25
30	Shawon Dunston	.05
31	Joe Girardi	.05
32	Mark Grace	.05
33	Mike Harkey	.05
34	Paul Kilgus	.05
35	Les Lancaster	.05
36	Vance Law	.05
37	Greg Maddux	.50
38	Lloyd McClendon	.05
39	Jeff Pico	.05
40	Ryne Sandberg	.50
41	Scott Sanderson	.05
42	Dwight Smith	.05
43	Rick Sutcliffe	.05
44	Jerome Walton RC	.05
45	Mitch Webster	.05

46	Curt Wilkerson	.05
47	Dean Wilkins RC	.05
48	Mitch Williams	.05
49	Steve Wilson	.05
50	Steve Bedrosian	.05
51	Mike Benjamin RC	.05
52	Jeff Brantley RC	.10
53	Brett Butler	.05
54	Will Clark	.50
55	Kelly Downs	.05
56	Scott Garrelts	.05
57	Atlee Hammaker	.05
58	Terry Kennedy	.05
59	Mike LaCoss	.05
60	Craig Lefferts	.05
61	Greg Litton RC	.05
62	Candy Maldonado	.05
63	Kirt Manwaring	.05
64	Randy McCament RC	.05
65	Kevin Mitchell	.05
66	Donell Nixon	.05
67	Ken Oberkfell	.05
68	Rick Reuschel	.05
69	Ernest Riles	.05
70	Don Robinson	.05
71	Pat Sheridan	.05
72	Chris Speier	.05
73	Robby Thompson	.05
74	Jose Uribe	.05
75	Matt Williams	.05
76	George Bell	.05
77	Pat Borders	.05
78	John Cerutti	.05
79	Junior Felix RC	.05
80	Tony Fernandez	.05
81	Mike Flanagan	.05
82	Mauro Gozzo RC	.05
83	Kelly Gruber	.05
84	Tom Henke	.05
85	Jimmy Key	.05
86	Manny Lee	.05
87	Nelson Liriano	.05
88	Lee Mazzilli	.05
89	Fred McGriff	.05
90	Lloyd Moseby	.05
91	Rance Mulliniks	.05
92	Alex Sanchez	.05
93	Dave Steib	.05
94	Todd Stottlemyre	.05
95	Duane Ward	.05
96	David Wells	.05
97	Ernie Whitt	.05
98	Frank Wills	.05
99	Mookie Wilson	.05
100	Kevin Appier	.05
101	Luis Aquino	.05
102	Bob Boone	.05
103	George Brett	.60
104	Jose DeJesus	.05
105	Luis de los Santos	.05
106	Jim Eisenreich	.05
107	Steve Farr	.05
108	Tom Gordon	.05
109	Mark Gubicza	.05
110	Bo Jackson	.10
111	Terry Leach	.05
112	Charlie Leibrandt	.05
113	Rick Luecken RC	.05
114	Mike Macfarlane	.05
115	Jeff Montgomery	.05
116	Bret Saberhagen	.05
117	Kevin Seitzer	.05
118	Kurt Stillwell	.05
119	Pat Tabler	.05
120	Danny Tartabull	.05
121	Gary Thurman	.05
122	Frank White	.05
123	Willie Wilson	.05
124	Matt Winters RC	.05
125	Jim Abbott	.05
126	Tony Armas	.05
127	Dante Bichette	.05
128	Bert Blyleven	.10
129	Chili Davis	.05
130	Brian Downing	.05
131	Mike Fetters RC	.05
132	Chuck Finley	.05
133	Willie Fraser	.05
134	Bryan Harvey	.05
135	Jack Howell	.05
136	Wally Joyner	.05
137	Jeff Manto RC	.05
138	Kirk McCaskill	.05
139	Bob McClure	.05
140	Greg Minton	.05
141	Lance Parrish	.05
142	Dan Petry	.05
143	Johnny Ray	.05
144	Dick Schofield	.05
145	Lee Stevens RC	.05
146	Claudell Washington	.05
147	Devon White	.05
148	Mike Witt	.05
149	Roberto Alomar	.20
150	Sandy Alomar, Jr.	.05
151	Andy Benes	.05
152	Jack Clark	.05
153	Pat Clements	.05
154	Joey Cora	.05
155	Mark Davis	.05
156	Mark Grant	.05
157	Tony Gwynn	.50
158	Greg Harris	.05
159	Bruce Hurst	.05
160	Darrin Jackson	.05
161	Chris James	.05
162	Carmelo Martinez	.05
163	Mike Pagliarulo	.05

164	Mark Parent	.05
165	Dennis Rasmussen	.05
166	Bip Roberts	.05
167	Benito Santiago	.05
168	Calvin Schiraldi	.05
169	Eric Show	.05
170	Garry Templeton	.05
171	Ed Whitson	.05
172	Brady Anderson	.05
173	Jeff Ballard	.05
174	Phil Bradley	.05
175	Mike Devereaux	.05
176	Steve Finley	.05
177	Pete Harnisch RC	.05
178	Kevin Hickey	.05
179	Brian Holton	.05
180	Ben McDonald RC	.15
181	Bob Melvin	.05
182	Bob Milacki	.05
183	Randy Milligan	.05
184	Gregg Olson RC	.05
185	Joe Orsulak	.05
186	Bill Ripken	.05
187	Cal Ripken, Jr.	.75
188	Dave Schmidt	.05
189	Larry Sheets	.05
190	Mickey Tettleton	.05
191	Mark Thurmond	.05
192	Jay Tibbs	.05
193	Jim Traber	.05
194	Mark Williamson	.05
195	Craig Worthington	.05
196	Don Aase	.05
197	Blaine Beatty RC	.05
198	Mark Carreon	.05
199	Gary Carter	.40
200	David Cone	.05
201	Ron Darling	.05
202	Kevin Elster	.05
203	Sid Fernandez	.05
204	Dwight Gooden	.05
205	Keith Hernandez	.05
206	Jeff Innis RC	.05
207	Gregg Jefferies	.05
208	Howard Johnson	.05
209	Barry Lyons	.05
210	Dave Magadan	.05
211	Kevin McReynolds	.05
212	Jeff Musselman	.05
213	Randy Myers	.05
214	Bob Ojeda	.05
215	Juan Samuel	.05
216	Mackey Sasser	.05
217	Darryl Strawberry	.05
218	Tim Teufel	.05
219	Frank Viola	.05
220	Juan Agosto	.05
221	Larry Anderson	.05
222	Eric Anthony RC	.10
223	Kevin Bass	.05
224	Craig Biggio	.05
225	Ken Caminiti	.05
226	Jim Clancy	.05
227	Danny Darwin	.05
228	Glenn Davis	.05
229	Jim Deshaies	.05
230	Bill Doran	.05
231	Bob Forsch	.05
232	Brian Meyer	.05
233	Terry Puhl	.05
234	Rafael Ramirez	.05
235	Rick Rhoden	.05
236	Dan Schatzeder	.05
237	Mike Scott	.05
238	Dave Smith	.05
239	Alex Trevino	.05
240	Glenn Wilson	.05
241	Gerald Young	.05
242	Tom Brunansky	.05
243	Cris Carpenter	.05
244	Alex Cole RC	.05
245	Vince Coleman	.05
246	John Costello	.05
247	Ken Dayley	.05
248	Jose DeLeon	.05
249	Frank DiPino	.05
250	Pedro Guerrero	.05
251	Ken Hill	.05
252	Joe Magrane	.05
253	Willie McGee	.05
254	John Morris	.05
255	Jose Oquendo	.05
256	Tony Pena	.05
257	Terry Pendleton	.05
258	Ted Power	.05
259	Dan Quisenberry	.05
260	Ozzie Smith	.50
261	Scott Terry	.05
262	Milt Thompson	.05
263	Denny Walling	.05
264	Todd Worrell	.05
265	Todd Zeile	.05
266	Marty Barrett	.05
267	Mike Boddicker	.05
268	Wade Boggs	.50
269	Ellis Burks	.05
270	Rick Cerone	.05
271	Roger Clemens	.60
272	John Dopson	.05
273	Nick Esasky	.05
274	Dwight Evans	.05
275	Wes Gardner	.05
276	Rich Gedman	.05
277	Mike Greenwell	.05
278	Danny Heep	.05
279	Eric Hetzel	.05
280	Dennis Lamp	.05
281	Rob Murphy	.05

282	Joe Price	.05
283	Carlos Quintana	.05
284	Jody Reed	.05
285	Luis Rivera	.05
286	Kevin Romine	.05
287	Lee Smith	.05
288	Mike Smithson	.05
289	Bob Stanley	.05
290	Harold Baines	.05
291	Kevin Brown	.05
292	Steve Buechele	.05
293	Scott Coolbaugh RC	.05
294	Jack Daugherty RC	.05
295	Cecil Espy	.05
296	Julio Franco	.05
297	Juan Gonzalez RC	2.00
298	Cecilio Guante	.05
299	Drew Hall	.05
300	Charlie Hough	.05
301	Pete Incaviglia	.05
302	Mike Jeffcoat	.05
303	Chad Kreuter	.05
304	Jeff Kunkel	.05
305	Rick Leach	.05
306	Fred Manrique	.05
307	Jamie Moyer	.05
308	Rafael Palmeiro	.35
309	Geno Petralli	.05
310	Kevin Reimer	.05
311	Kenny Rogers RC	.10
312	Jeff Russell	.05
313	Nolan Ryan	.75
314	Ruben Sierra	.05
315	Bobby Witt	.05
316	Chris Bosio	.05
317	Glenn Braggs	.05
318	Greg Brock	.05
319	Chuck Crim	.05
320	Rob Deer	.05
321	Mike Felder	.05
322	Tom Filer	.05
323	Tony Fossas RC	.05
324	Jim Gantner	.05
325	Darryl Hamilton	.05
326	Ted Higuera	.05
327	Mark Knudson RC	.05
328	Bill Krueger	.05
329	Tim McIntosh RC	.05
330	Paul Molitor	.40
331	Jaime Navarro	.05
332	Charlie O'Brien	.05
333	Jeff Peterek RC	.05
334	Dan Plesac	.05
335	Jerry Reuss	.05
336	Gary Sheffield	.35
337	Bill Spiers RC	.05
338	B.J. Surhoff	.05
339	Greg Vaughn	.05
340	Robin Yount	.40
341	Hubie Brooks	.05
342	Tim Burke	.05
343	Mike Fitzgerald	.05
344	Tom Foley	.05
345	Andres Galarraga	.05
346	Damaso Garcia	.05
347	Marquis Grissom RC	.50
348	Kevin Gross	.05
349	Joe Hesketh	.05
350	Jeff Huson RC	.05
351	Wallace Johnson	.05
352	Mark Langston	.05
353a	Dave Martinez (Yellow 90.)	6.00
353b	Dave Martinez (Red 90.)	.05
354	Dennis Martinez	.05
355	Andy McGaffigan	.05
356	Otis Nixon	.05
357	Spike Owen	.05
358	Pascual Perez	.05
359	Tim Raines	.05
360	Nelson Santovenia	.05
361	Bryn Smith	.05
362	Zane Smith	.05
363	Larry Walker	.75
364	Tim Wallach	.05
365	Rick Aguilera	.05
366	Allan Anderson	.05
367	Wally Backman	.05
368	Doug Baker RC	.05
369	Juan Berenguer	.05
370	Randy Bush	.05
371	Carmen Castillo	.05
372	Mike Dyer RC	.05
373	Gary Gaetti	.05
374	Greg Gagne	.05
375	Dan Gladden	.05
376	German Gonzalez	.05
377	Brian Harper	.05
378	Kent Hrbek	.05
379	Gene Larkin	.05
380	Tim Laudner	.05
381	John Moses	.05
382	Al Newman	.05
383	Kirby Puckett	.50
384	Shane Rawley	.05
385	Jeff Reardon	.05
386	Roy Smith	.05
387	Gary Wayne RC	.05
388	Dave West	.05
389	Tim Belcher	.05
390	Tim Crews	.05
391	Mike Davis	.05
392	Rick Dempsey	.05
393	Kirk Gibson	.05
394	Jose Gonzalez	.05
395	Alfredo Griffin	.05
396	Jeff Hamilton	.05

397	Lenny Harris	.05
398	Mickey Hatcher	.05
399	Orel Hershiser	.05
400	Jay Howell	.05
401	Mike Marshall	.05
402	Ramon Martinez	.05
403	Mike Morgan	.05
404	Eddie Murray	.40
405	Alejandro Pena	.05
406	Willie Randolph	.05
407	Mike Scioscia	.05
408	Ray Searage	.05
409	Fernando Valenzuela	.05
410	Jose Vizcaino RC	.10
411	John Wetteland RC	.20
412	Jack Armstrong	.05
413	Todd Benzinger	.05
414	Tim Birtsas	.05
415	Tom Browning	.05
416	Norm Charlton	.05
417	Eric Davis	.05
418	Rob Dibble	.05
419	John Franco	.05
420	Ken Griffey Sr.	.05
421	Chris Hammond RC	.15
422	Danny Jackson	.05
423	Barry Larkin	.05
424	Tim Leary	.05
425	Rick Mahler	.05
426	Joe Oliver	.05
427	Paul O'Neill	.05
428	Luis Quinones	.05
429	Jeff Reed	.05
430	Jose Rijo	.05
431	Ron Robinson	.05
432	Rolando Roomes	.05
433	Chris Sabo	.05
434	Scott Scudder RC	.05
435	Herm Winningham	.05
436	Steve Balboni	.05
437	Jesse Barfield	.05
438	Mike Blowers RC	.05
439	Tom Brookens	.05
440	Greg Cadaret	.05
441	Alvaro Espinoza	.05
442	Bob Geren RC	.05
443	Lee Guetterman	.05
444	Mel Hall	.05
445	Andy Hawkins	.05
446	Roberto Kelly	.05
447	Don Mattingly	.60
448	Lance McCullers	.05
449	Hensley Meulens	.05
450	Dale Mohorcic	.05
451	Clay Parker	.05
452	Eric Plunk	.05
453	Dave Righetti	.05
454	Deion Sanders	.10
455	Steve Sax	.05
456	Don Slaught	.05
457	Walt Terrell	.05
458	Dave Winfield	.40
459	Jay Bell	.05
460	Rafael Belliard	.05
461	Barry Bonds	.75
462	Bobby Bonilla	.05
463	Sid Bream	.05
464	Benny Distefano	.05
465	Doug Drabek	.05
466	Jim Gott	.05
467	Billy Hatcher	.05
468	Neal Heaton	.05
469	Jeff King	.05
470	Bob Kipper	.05
471	Randy Kramer	.05
472	Bill Landrum	.05
473	Mike LaValliere	.05
474	Jose Lind	.05
475	Junior Ortiz	.05
476	Gary Redus	.05
477	Rick Reed RC	.05
478	R.J. Reynolds	.05
479	Jeff Robinson	.05
480	John Smiley	.05
481	Andy Van Slyke	.05
482	Bob Walk	.05
483	Andy Allanson	.05
484	Scott Bailes	.05
485	Albert Belle	.05
486	Bud Black	.05
487	Jerry Browne	.05
488	Tom Candiotti	.05
489	Joe Carter	.05
490	David Clark	.05
491	John Farrell	.05
492	Felix Fermin	.05
493	Brook Jacoby	.05
494	Dion James	.05
495	Doug Jones	.05
496	Brad Komminsk	.05
497	Rod Nichols	.05
498	Pete O'Brien	.05
499	Steve Olin RC	.05
500	Jesse Orosco	.05
501	Joel Skinner	.05
502	Cory Snyder	.05
503	Greg Swindell	.05
504	Rich Yett	.05
505	Scott Bankhead	.05
506	Scott Bradley	.05
507	Greg Briley	.05
508	Jay Buhner	.05
509	Darnell Coles	.05
510	Keith Comstock	.05
511	Henry Cotto	.05
512	Alvin Davis	.05
513	Ken Griffey Jr.	.65
514	Erik Hanson	.05

515	Gene Harris	.05
516	Brian Holman	.05
517	Mike Jackson	.05
518	Randy Johnson	.40
519	Jeffrey Leonard	.05
520	Edgar Martinez	.05
521	Dennis Powell	.05
522	Jim Presley	.05
523	Jerry Reed	.05
524	Harold Reynolds	.05
525	Mike Schooler	.05
526	Bill Swift	.05
527	David Valle	.05
528	Omar Vizquel	.05
529	Ivan Calderon	.05
530	Carlton Fisk	.40
531	Scott Fletcher	.05
532	Dave Gallagher	.05
533	Ozzie Guillen	.05
534	Greg Hibbard RC	.05
535	Shawn Hillegas	.05
536	Lance Johnson	.05
537	Eric King	.05
538	Ron Kittle	.05
539	Steve Lyons	.05
540	Carlos Martinez	.05
541	Tom McCarthy RC	.05
542	Matt Merullo RC	.05
543	Donn Pall	.05
544	Dan Pasqua	.05
545	Ken Patterson	.05
546	Melido Perez	.05
547	Steve Rosenberg	.05
548	Sammy Sosa RC	5.00
549	Bobby Thigpen	.05
550	Robin Ventura	.05
551	Greg Walker	.05
552	Don Carman	.05
553	Pat Combs RC	.05
554	Dennis Cook	.05
555	Darren Daulton	.05
556	Len Dykstra	.05
557	Curt Ford	.05
558	Charlie Hayes	.05
559	Von Hayes	.05
560	Tom Herr	.05
561	Ken Howell	.05
562	Steve Jeltz	.05
563	Ron Jones	.05
564	Ricky Jordan	.05
565	John Kruk	.05
566	Steve Lake	.05
567	Roger McDowell	.05
568	Terry Mulholland	.05
569	Dwayne Murphy	.05
570	Jeff Parrett	.05
571	Randy Ready	.05
572	Bruce Ruffin	.05
573	Dickie Thon	.05
574	Jose Alvarez	.05
575	Geronimo Berroa	.05
576	Jeff Blauser	.05
577	Joe Boever	.05
578	Marty Clary	.05
579	Jody Davis	.05
580	Mark Eichhorn	.05
581	Darrell Evans	.05
582	Ron Gant	.05
583	Tom Glavine	.25
584	Tommy Greene RC	.05
585	Tommy Gregg	.05
586	Dave Justice RC	.40
587	Mark Lemke RC	.05
588	Derek Lilliquist	.05
589	Oddibe McDowell	.05
590	Kent Mercker RC	.05
591	Dale Murphy	.20
592	Gerald Perry	.05
593	Lonnie Smith	.05
594	Pete Smith	.05
595	John Smoltz	.05
596	Mike Stanton RC	.05
597	Andres Thomas	.05
598	Jeff Treadway	.05
599	Doyle Alexander	.05
600	Dave Bergman	.05
601	Brian Dubois RC	.05
602	Paul Gibson	.05
603	Mike Heath	.05
604	Mike Henneman	.05
605	Guillermo Hernandez	.05
606	Shawn Holman RC	.05
607	Tracy Jones	.05
608	Chet Lemon	.05
609	Fred Lynn	.05
610	Jack Morris	.05
611	Matt Nokes	.05
612	Gary Pettis	.05
613	Kevin Ritz RC	.05
614	Jeff Robinson	.05
615	Steve Searcy	.05
616	Frank Tanana	.05
617	Alan Trammell	.05
618	Gary Ward	.05
619	Lou Whitaker	.05
620	Frank Williams	.05
621a	Players of the Decade - 1980 George Brett (... 10 .390 hitting ...)	1.00
621b	Players of the Decade - 1980 (George Brett)	.25
622	Players of the Decade - 1981 (Fernando Valenzuela)	.05
623	Players of the Decade - 1982 (Dale Murphy)	.05

		NM/M
624a	Players of the Decade - 1983 Cal Ripkin, Jr. (Ripken)	1.50
624b	Player of the Decade - 1983 (Cal Ripken, Jr.)	.30
625	Players of the Decade - 1984 (Ryne Sandberg)	.25
626	Players of the Decade - 1985 (Don Mattingly)	.30
627	Players of the Decade - 1986 (Roger Clemens)	.30
628	Players of the Decade - 1987 (George Bell)	.05
629	Players of the Decade - 1988 (Jose Canseco)	.10
630a	Players of the Decade - 1989 Will Clark (Total bases 32.)	.35
630b	Players of the Decade - 1989 Will Clark (Total bases 321.)	.05
631	Game Savers (Mark Davis, Mitch Williams)	.05
632	Boston Igniters (Wade Boggs, Mike Greenwell)	.15
633	Starter & Stopper (Mark Gubicza, Jeff Russell)	.05
634	League's Best Shortstops (Tony Fernandez, Cal Ripken Jr.)	.30
635	Human Dynamos (Kirby Puckett, Bo Jackson)	.20
636	300 Strikeout Club (Mike Scott, Nolan Ryan)	.30
637	The Dynamic Duo (Will Clark, Kevin Mitchell)	.05
638	A.L. All-Stars (Don Mattingly, Mark McGwire)	.65
639	N.L. East Rivals (Howard Johnson, Ryne Sandberg)	.20
640	Major League Prospects (Rudy Seanez RC, Colin Charland RC)	.05
641	Major League Prospects (George Canale RC, Kevin Maas RC)	.10
642	Major League Prospects (Kelly Mann RC, Dave Hansen RC)	.05
643	Major League Prospects (Greg Smith RC, Stu Tate RC)	.05
644	Major League Prospects (Tom Drees RC, Dan Howitt RC)	.05
645	Major League Prospects (Mike Roesler RC, Derrick May RC)	.05
646	Major League Prospects (Scott Hemond RC, Mark Gardner RC)	.10
647	Major League Prospects (John Orton RC, Scott Leius RC)	.10
648	Major League Prospects (Rich Monteleone RC, Dana Williams RC)	.05
649	Major League Prospects (Mike Huff RC, Steve Frey RC)	.05
650	Major League Prospects (Chuck McElroy RC, Moises Alou RC)	.50
651	Major League Prospects (Bobby Rose RC, Mike Hartley RC)	.10
652	Major League Prospects (Matt Kinzer RC, Wayne Edwards RC)	.05
653	Major League Prospects (Delino DeShields RC, Jason Grimsley RC)	.15
654	Athletics, Cubs, Giants & Blue Jays (Checklist)	.05
655	Royals, Angels, Padres & Orioles (Checklist)	.05
656	Mets, Astros, Cardinals & Red Sox (Checklist)	.05
657	Rangers, Brewers, Expos & Twins (Checklist)	.05
658	Dodgers, Reds, Yankees & Pirates (Checklist)	.05
659	Indians, Mariners, White Sox & Phillies (Checklist)	.05
660	Braves, Tigers & Special Cards (Checklist)	.05

All-Stars

The top players at each position, as selected by Fleer, are featured in this 12-card set inserted in cello packs and some wax packs. The cards measure 2-1/2" x 3-1/2" and feature a unique two-photo format on the card fronts.

NM/M
Complete Set (12): 4.00

	Common Player:	.20
1	Harold Baines	.20
2	Will Clark	.20
3	Mark Davis	.20
4	Howard Johnson	.20
5	Joe Magrane	.20
6	Kevin Mitchell	.20
7	Kirby Puckett	1.00
8	Cal Ripken	2.00
9	Ryne Sandberg	1.00
10	Mike Scott	.20
11	Ruben Sierra	.20
12	Mickey Tettleton	.20

League Standouts

Fleer's "League Standouts" are six of baseball's top players distributed randomly in Fleer rack packs. Fronts feature full color photos with a six-dimensional effect. A black and gold frame borders the photo. Backs are yellow and describe the player's accomplishments. The cards measure 2-1/2" x 3-1/2".

NM/M
Complete Set (6): 3.00
Common Player: .50

1	Barry Larkin	.50
2	Don Mattingly	1.50
3	Darryl Strawberry	.50
4	Jose Canseco	.75
5	Wade Boggs	.50
6	Mark Grace	.50

Soaring Stars

Cards from this 12-card set could be found in 1990 Fleer jumbo cello packs. The cards are styled with a cartoon flavor, featuring astronomical graphics surrounding the player. Backs feature information about the promising young player.

NM/M
Complete Set (12): 5.00
Common Player: .10

1	Todd Zeile	.25
2	Mike Stanton	.25
3	Larry Walker	.50
4	Robin Ventura	.50
5	Scott Coolbaugh	.25
6	Ken Griffey Jr.	4.00
7	Tom Gordon	.25
8	Jerome Walton	.25
9	Junior Felix	.25
10	Jim Abbott	.25
11	Ricky Jordan	.25
12	Dwight Smith	.25

World Series

This 12-card set depicts highlights of the 1989 World Series and was included in the factory-collated Fleer set. Single World Series cards were discovered in cello and rack packs, but this was not intended to happen. Fronts of the 2-1/2" x 3-1/2" cards feature action photos set against a white background with a red and blue "'89 World Series" banner. Backs are pink and white and describe the events of the 1989 Fall Classic.

NM/M
Complete Set (12): 1.50
Common Player: .10

1	The Final Piece To The Puzzle (Mike Moore)	.10
2	Kevin Mitchell	.15
3	Game Two's Crushing Blow	.20
4	Will Clark	.15
5	Jose Canseco	.75
6	Great Leather in the Field	.10
7	Game One And A's Break Out On Top	.10
8	Dave Stewart	.10
9	Parker's Bat Produces Power (Dave Parker)	.25
10	World Series Record Book Game 3	.10
11	Rickey Henderson	.75
12	Oakland A's - Baseball's Best In '89	.25

Box Panels

For the fifth consecutive year, Fleer issued a series of cards on the bottom panels of its wax pack boxes. This 28-card set features both players and team logos. The cards were numbered C-1 to C-28.

NM/M
Complete Set, Panels (7): 7.00
Complete Set, Singles (28): 7.00
Common Player: .05

1	Giants Logo	.05
2	Tim Belcher	.05
3	Roger Clemens	1.00
4	Eric Davis	.05
5	Glenn Davis	.05
6	Cubs Logo	.05
7	John Franco	.05
8	Mike Greenwell	.05
9	Athletics logo	.05
10	Ken Griffey Jr.	2.00
11	Pedro Guerrero	.05
12	Tony Gwynn	.75
13	Blue Jays Logo	.05
14	Orel Hershiser	.05
15	Bo Jackson	.10
16	Howard Johnson	.05
17	Mets Logo	.05
18	Cardinals Logo	.05
19	Don Mattingly	1.00
20	Mark McGwire	2.00
21	Kevin Mitchell	.05
22	Kirby Puckett	.75
23	Royals Logo	.05
24	Orioles Logo	.05
25	Ruben Sierra	.05
26	Dave Stewart	.05
27	Jerome Walton	.05
28	Robin Yount	.60

Printed in Canada

Whether these cards were printed for distribution in Canada or simply the work of a Canadian printer engaged by Fleer to meet U.S. demand is unknown. Each of the 660 cards in the 1990 Fleer issue can be found with a "1990 FLEER LTD./LTEE PTD. IN CANADA" copyright notice on back in the bottom border. Except for various superstar cards, little demand attaches to this variation.

NM/M
Complete Set (660): 25.00
Common Player: .25
Wax Pack (10): 1.50
Wax Box (48): 50.00

Update

Fleer produced its seventh consecutive "Update" set in 1990. As in the past, the set consists of 132 cards (numbered U-1 through U-132) that were sold by hobby dealers in special collectors boxes. The cards are designed in the same style as the regular issue. A special Nolan Ryan commemorative card is included in the set.

NM/M
Complete Set (132): 3.00
Common Player: .05

1	Steve Avery RC	.05
2	Francisco Cabrera RC	.05
3	Nick Esasky	.05
4	Jim Kremers RC	.05
5	Greg Olson RC	.05
6	Jim Presley	.05
7	Shawn Boskie RC	.05
8	Joe Kraemer RC	.05
9	Luis Salazar	.05
10	Hector Villanueva RC	.05
11	Glenn Braggs	.05
12	Mariano Duncan	.05
13	Billy Hatcher	.05
14	Tim Layana RC	.05
15	Hal Morris	.05
16	Javier Ortiz RC	.05
17	Dave Rohde RC	.05
18	Eric Yelding RC	.05
19	Hubie Brooks	.05
20	Kal Daniels	.05
21	Dave Hansen	.05
22	Mike Hartley	.05
23	Stan Javier	.05
24	Jose Offerman RC	.05
25	Juan Samuel	.05
26	Dennis Boyd	.05
27	Delino DeShields	.05
28	Steve Frey	.05
29	Mark Gardner	.05
30	Chris Nabholz RC	.05
31	Bill Sampen RC	.05
32	Dave Schmidt	.05
33	Daryl Boston	.05
34	Chuck Carr RC	.05
35	John Franco	.05
36	Todd Hundley RC	.05
37	Julio Machado RC	.05
38	Alejandro Pena	.05
39	Darren Reed RC	.05
40	Kelvin Torve RC	.05
41	Darrel Akerfelds RC	.05
42	Jose DeJesus	.05
43	Dave Hollins RC	.05
44	Carmelo Martinez	.05
45	Brad Moore RC	.05
46	Dale Murphy	.15
47	Wally Backman	.05
48	Stan Belinda RC	.05
49	Bob Patterson	.05
50	Ted Power	.05
51	Don Slaught	.05
52	Geronimo Pena RC	.05
53	Lee Smith	.05
54	John Tudor	.05
55	Joe Carter	.05
56	Tom Howard RC	.05
57	Craig Lefferts	.05
58	Rafael Valdez RC	.05
59	Dave Anderson	.05
60	Kevin Bass	.05
61	John Burkett	.05
62	Gary Carter	.40
63	Rick Parker RC	.05
64	Trevor Wilson	.05
65	Chris Hoiles RC	.05
66	Tim Hulett	.05
67	Dave Johnson RC	.05
68	Curt Schilling RC	.35
69	David Segui RC	.05
70	Tom Brunansky	.05
71	Greg Harris	.05
72	Dana Kiecker RC	.05
73	Tim Naehring RC	.05
74	Tony Pena	.05
75	Jeff Reardon	.05
76	Jerry Reed	.05
77	Mark Eichhorn	.05
78	Mark Langston	.05
79	John Orton	.05
80	Luis Polonia	.05
81	Dave Winfield	.40
82	Cliff Young RC	.05
83	Wayne Edwards	.05
84	Alex Fernandez RC	.05
85	Craig Grebeck RC	.05
86	Scott Radinsky RC	.05
87	Frank Thomas RC	2.00
88	Beau Allred RC	.05
89	Sandy Alomar, Jr.	.05
90	Carlos Baerga RC	.10
91	Kevin Bearse RC	.05
92	Chris James	.05
93	Candy Maldonado	.05
94	Jeff Manto	.05
95	Cecil Fielder	.05
96	Travis Fryman RC	.25
97	Lloyd Moseby	.05
98	Edwin Nunez	.05
99	Tony Phillips	.05
100	Larry Sheets	.05
101	Mark Davis	.05
102	Storm Davis	.05
103	Gerald Perry	.05
104	Terry Shumpert	.05
105	Edgar Diaz RC	.05
106	Dave Parker	.05
107	Tim Drummond RC	.05
108	Junior Ortiz	.05
109	Park Pittman RC	.05
110	Kevin Tapani RC	.05
111	Oscar Azocar RC	.05
112	Jim Leyritz RC	.05
113	Kevin Maas	.05
114	Alan Mills RC	.05
115	Matt Nokes	.05
116	Pascual Perez	.05
117	Ozzie Canseco RC	.05
118	Scott Sanderson	.05
119	Tino Martinez RC	.05
120	Jeff Schaefer RC	.05
121	Matt Young	.05
122	Brian Bohanon RC	.05
123	Jeff Huson	.05
124	Ramon Manon RC	.05
125	Gary Mielke RC	.05
126	Willie Blair RC	.05
127	Glenallen Hill RC	.05
128	John Olerud RC	.35
129	Luis Sojo RC	.05
130	Mark Whiten RC	.05
131	Three Decades of No Hitters (Nolan Ryan)	1.00
132	Checklist	.05

Award Winners

Hill's department stores and 7-Eleven outlets exclusively sold the 1990 Fleer "Award Winners." This 44-card boxed set includes baseball's statistical leaders of 1989. Card fronts feature a full-color player photo framed by a winner's cup design and blue border. Backs showcase player statistics in

blue on a yellow and white background. The cards measure 2-1/2" x 3-1/2". The checklist provided on the back of each box lists Bob Boone's team as the Angels and card #10 as Ron Darling. Darryl Strawberry (#38) is not checklisted and all cards #10-38 are off by a number. This is one of the scarcer Fleer box sets of the era.

NM/M
Complete Set (44): 6.00
Common Player: .05

1	Jeff Ballard	.05
2	Tim Belcher	.05
3	Bert Blyleven	.05
4	Wade Boggs	.75
5	Bob Boone	.05
6	Jose Canseco	.50
7	Will Clark	.05
8	Jack Clark	.05
9	Vince Coleman	.05
10	Eric Davis	.05
11	Jose DeLeon	.05
12	Tony Fernandez	.05
13	Carlton Fisk	.60
14	Scott Garrelts	.05
15	Tom Gordon	.05
16	Ken Griffey Jr.	1.50
17	Von Hayes	.05
18	Rickey Henderson	.60
19	Bo Jackson	.10
20	Howard Johnson	.05
21	Don Mattingly	1.00
22	Fred McGriff	.05
23	Kevin Mitchell	.05
24	Gregg Olson	.05
25	Gary Pettis	.05
26	Kirby Puckett	.75
27	Harold Reynolds	.05
28	Jeff Russell	.05
29	Nolan Ryan	2.00
30	Bret Saberhagen	.05
31	Ryne Sandberg	.05
32	Benito Santiago	.05
33	Mike Scott	.05
34	Ruben Sierra	.05
35	Lonnie Smith	.05
36	Ozzie Smith	.75
37	Dave Stewart	.05
38	Darryl Strawberry	.05
39	Greg Swindell	.05
40	Andy Van Slyke	.05
41	Tim Wallach	.05
42	Jerome Walton	.05
43	Mitch Williams	.05
44	Robin Yount	.60

Baseball All-Stars

Sold exclusively in Ben Franklin stores, this boxed set showcases the game's top players. Fronts feature a player photo surrounded by a pin-striped tan border. Backs have statistics and data printed in shades of red and dark blue. The cards measure 2-1/2" x 3-1/2" and are packed in a special box with a complete checklist on the back. Like other Fleer boxed sets, the cards are numbered alphabetically. All cards carry a "Printed in Canada" note on back.

		NM/M
Complete Set (44):		6.00
Common Player:		.05
1	Wade Boggs	.75
2	Bobby Bonilla	.05
3	Tim Burke	.05
4	Jose Canseco	.50
5	Will Clark	.05
6	Eric Davis	.05
7	Glenn Davis	.05
8	Julio Franco	.05
9	Tony Fernandez	.05
10	Gary Gaetti	.05
11	Scott Garrelts	.05
12	Mark Grace	.05
13	Mike Greenwell	.05
14	Ken Griffey Jr.	1.00
15	Mark Gubicza	.05
16	Pedro Guerrero	.05
17	Von Hayes	.05
18	Orel Hershiser	.05
19	Bruce Hurst	.05
20	Bo Jackson	.10
21	Howard Johnson	.05
22	Doug Jones	.05
23	Barry Larkin	.05
24	Don Mattingly	.85
25	Mark McGwire	1.00
26	Kevin McReynolds	.05
27	Kevin Mitchell	.05
28	Dan Plesac	.05
29	Kirby Puckett	.75
30	Cal Ripken, Jr.	1.50
31	Bret Saberhagen	.05
32	Ryne Sandberg	.75
33	Steve Sax	.05
34	Ruben Sierra	.05
35	Ozzie Smith	.75
36	John Smoltz	.05
37	Darryl Strawberry	.05
38	Terry Steinbach	.05
39	Dave Stewart	.05
40	Bobby Thigpen	.05
41	Alan Trammell	.05
42	Devon White	.05
43	Mitch Williams	.05
44	Robin Yount	.60

League Leaders

For the fifth consecutive year Fleer released a "League Leaders" boxed set of 44 top Major League players. Card number 42 (Jerome Walton) pictures a player other than Walton. The 2-1/2" x 3-1/2" cards display a full-color photo bordered by a blue frame. Backs feature complete statistics. The cards are numbered alphabetically and a complete checklist is displayed on the back of the box. The set was available at Walgreen drug stores. Cards carry a "Printed in Canada" notice on back.

		NM/M
Complete Set (44):		6.00
Common Player:		.10
1	Roberto Alomar	.25
2	Tim Belcher	.10
3	George Bell	.10
4	Wade Boggs	.75
5	Jose Canseco	.50
6	Will Clark	.10
7	David Cone	.10
8	Eric Davis	.10
9	Glenn Davis	.10
10	Nick Esasky	.10
11	Dennis Eckersley	.55
12	Mark Grace	.10
13	Mike Greenwell	.10
14	Ken Griffey Jr.	1.25
15	Mark Gubicza	.10
16	Pedro Guerrero	.10
17	Tony Gwynn	.75
18	Rickey Henderson	.60
19	Bo Jackson	.15
20	Doug Jones	.10
21	Ricky Jordan	.10

22	Barry Larkin	.10
23	Don Mattingly	.85
24	Fred McGriff	.10
25	Mark McGwire	1.25
26	Kevin Mitchell	.10
27	Jack Morris	.10
28	Gregg Olson	.10
29	Dan Plesac	.10
30	Kirby Puckett	.75
31	Nolan Ryan	1.50
32	Bret Saberhagen	.10
33	Ryne Sandberg	.75
34	Steve Sax	.10
35	Mike Scott	.10
36	Ruben Sierra	.10
37	Lonnie Smith	.10
38	Darryl Strawberry	.10
39	Bobby Thigpen	.10
40	Andy Van Slyke	.10
41	Tim Wallach	.10
42	Jerome Walton	.10
43	Devon White	.10
44	Robin Yount	.60

MVP

This 44-card boxed set was produced by Fleer for the Toys R Us chain. Fronts are designed with graduating black-to-white borders, surrounding a color player photo. Backs contain individual data and career statistics. The back of each box carries a checklist of all the players in the set. Six peel-off team logo stickers featuring a baseball trivia quiz on the back are also included with each set. The cards are 2-1/2" x 3-1/2" and numbered alphabetically. All cards carry a "Printed in Canada" notation on the back at bottom.

		NM/M
Complete Set (44):		6.00
Common Player:		.10
1	George Bell	.10
2	Bert Blyleven	.10
3	Wade Boggs	.65
4	Bobby Bonilla	.10
5	George Brett	.85
6	Jose Canseco	.45
7	Will Clark	.10
8	Roger Clemens	.85
9	Eric Davis	.10
10	Glenn Davis	.10
11	Tony Fernandez	.10
12	Dwight Gooden	.10
13	Mike Greenwell	.10
14	Ken Griffey Jr.	1.25
15	Pedro Guerrero	.10
16	Tony Gwynn	.65
17	Rickey Henderson	.50
18	Tom Herr	.10
19	Orel Hershiser	.10
20	Kent Hrbek	.10
21	Bo Jackson	.15
22	Howard Johnson	.10
23	Don Mattingly	.85
24	Fred McGriff	.10
25	Mark McGwire	1.25
26	Kevin Mitchell	.10
27	Paul Molitor	.50
28	Dale Murphy	.25
29	Kirby Puckett	.65
30	Tim Raines	.10
31	Cal Ripken, Jr.	1.50
32	Bret Saberhagen	.10
33	Ryne Sandberg	.65
34	Ruben Sierra	.10
35	Dwight Smith	.10
36	Ozzie Smith	.65
37	Darryl Strawberry	.10
38	Dave Stewart	.10
39	Greg Swindell	.10
40	Bobby Thigpen	.10
41	Alan Trammell	.10
42	Jerome Walton	.10
43	Mitch Williams	.10
44	Robin Yount	.50

1991 Fleer Promo Strip

This three-card strip was issued to introduce Fleer's 1991 baseball card set. The cards on the 7-1/2" x 3-1/2" strip are identical to the players' regular issue cards.

	NM/M
Three-card Strip:	4.00

1991 Fleer

Fleer expanded its 1991 set to include 720 cards. The cards feature yellow-green surrounding full-color action photos. Backs feature a circular portrait photo, biographical information, complete statistics, and career highlights. Once again the cards are numbered alphabetically within team. Because Fleer used more than one printer, many minor variations in photo cropping and typography can be found. The most notable are included in the checklist here.

		NM/M
Unopened Factory Set (732):		12.00
Complete Set (720):		10.00
Common Player:		.05
Wax Pack (15):		.50
Wax Box (36):		12.50
Jumbo Wax Pack (53):		1.25
Jumbo Wax Box (24):		20.00
Cello Pack (30):		1.00
Cello Box (24):		16.00
1	Troy Afenir RC	.05
2	Harold Baines	.05
3	Lance Blankenship	.05
4	Todd Burns	.05
5	Jose Canseco	.30
6	Dennis Eckersley	.35
7	Mike Gallego	.05
8	Ron Hassey	.05
9	Dave Henderson	.05
10	Rickey Henderson	.40
11	Rick Honeycutt	.05
12	Doug Jennings	.05
13	Joe Klink RC	.05
14	Carney Lansford	.05
15	Darren Lewis RC	.05
16	Willie McGee	.05
17a	Mark McGwire (Six-line career summary.)	.65
17b	Mark McGwire (Seven-line career summary.)	.65
18	Mike Moore	.05
19	Gene Nelson	.05
20	Dave Otto	.05
21	Jamie Quirk	.05
22	Willie Randolph	.05
23	Scott Sanderson	.05
24	Terry Steinbach	.05
25	Dave Stewart	.05
26	Walt Weiss	.05
27	Bob Welch	.05
28	Curt Young	.05
29	Wally Backman	.05
30	Stan Belinda RC	.05
31	Jay Bell	.05
32	Rafael Belliard	.05
33	Barry Bonds	.75
34	Bobby Bonilla	.05
35	Sid Bream	.05
36	Doug Drabek	.05
37	Carlos Garcia RC	.10
38	Neal Heaton	.05
39	Jeff King	.05
40	Bob Kipper	.05
41	Bill Landrum	.05
42	Mike LaValliere	.05

43	Jose Lind	.05
44	Carmelo Martinez	.05
45	Bob Patterson	.05
46	Ted Power	.05
47	Gary Redus	.05
48	R.J. Reynolds	.05
49	Don Slaught	.05
50	John Smiley	.05
51	Zane Smith	.05
52	Randy Tomlin RC	.10
53	Andy Van Slyke	.05
54	Bob Walk	.05
55	Jack Armstrong	.05
56	Todd Benzinger	.05
57	Glenn Braggs	.05
58	Keith Brown	.05
59	Tom Browning	.05
60	Norm Charlton	.05
61	Eric Davis	.05
62	Rob Dibble	.05
63	Bill Doran	.05
64	Mariano Duncan	.05
65	Chris Hammond	.05
66	Billy Hatcher	.05
67	Danny Jackson	.05
68	Barry Larkin	.05
69	Tim Layana RC	.05
70	Terry Lee RC	.05
71	Rick Mahler	.05
72	Hal Morris	.05
73	Randy Myers	.05
74	Ron Oester	.05
75	Joe Oliver	.05
76	Paul O'Neill	.05
77	Luis Quinones	.05
78	Jeff Reed	.05
79	Jose Rijo	.05
80	Chris Sabo	.05
81	Scott Scudder	.05
82	Herm Winningham	.05
83	Larry Andersen	.05
84	Marty Barrett	.05
85	Mike Boddicker	.05
86	Wade Boggs	.50
87	Tom Bolton	.05
88	Tom Brunansky	.05
89	Ellis Burks	.05
90	Roger Clemens	.55
91	Scott Cooper RC	.05
92	John Dopson	.05
93	Dwight Evans	.05
94	Wes Gardner	.05
95	Jeff Gray RC	.05
96	Mike Greenwell	.05
97	Greg Harris	.05
98	Daryl Irvine RC	.05
99	Dana Kiecker RC	.05
100	Randy Kutcher	.05
101	Dennis Lamp	.05
102	Mike Marshall	.05
103	John Marzano	.05
104	Rob Murphy	.05
105a	Tim Naehring RC (Seven-line career summary.)	.05
105b	Tim Naehring RC (Nine-line career summary.)	.05
106	Tony Pena	.05
107	Phil Plantier RC	.05
108	Carlos Quintana	.05
109	Jeff Reardon	.05
110	Jerry Reed	.05
111	Jody Reed	.05
112	Luis Rivera	.05
113a	Kevin Romine (One-line career summary.)	.05
113b	Kevin Romine (Two-line career summary.)	.05
114	Phil Bradley	.05
115	Ivan Calderon	.05
116	Wayne Edwards	.05
117	Alex Fernandez	.05
118	Carlton Fisk	.40
119	Scott Fletcher	.05
120	Craig Grebeck RC	.05
121	Ozzie Guillen	.05
122	Greg Hibbard	.05
123	Lance Johnson	.05
124	Barry Jones	.05
125a	Ron Karkovice (Two-line career summary.)	.05
125b	Ron Karkovice (One-line career summary.)	.05
126	Eric King	.05
127	Steve Lyons	.05
128	Carlos Martinez	.05
129	Jack McDowell	.05
130	Donn Pall	.05
131	Dan Pasqua	.05
132	Ken Patterson	.05
133	Melido Perez	.05
134	Adam Peterson	.05
135	Scott Radinsky RC	.05
136	Sammy Sosa	.50
137	Bobby Thigpen	.05
138	Frank Thomas	.40
139	Robin Ventura	.05
140	Daryl Boston	.05
141	Chuck Carr RC	.05
142	Mark Carreon	.05
143	David Cone	.05
144	Ron Darling	.05
145	Kevin Elster	.05
146	Sid Fernandez	.05
147	John Franco	.05
148	Dwight Gooden	.05
149	Tom Herr	.05
150	Todd Hundley	.05
151	Gregg Jefferies	.05

152	Howard Johnson	.05
153	Dave Magadan	.05
154	Kevin McReynolds	.05
155	Keith Miller	.05
156	Bob Ojeda	.05
157	Tom O'Malley	.05
158	Alejandro Pena	.05
159	Darren Reed RC	.05
160	Mackey Sasser	.05
161	Darryl Strawberry	.05
162	Tim Teufel	.05
163	Kelvin Torve	.05
164	Julio Valera	.05
165	Frank Viola	.05
166	Wally Whitehurst	.05
167	Jim Acker	.05
168	Derek Bell RC	.10
169	George Bell	.05
170	Willie Blair RC	.05
171	Pat Borders	.05
172	John Cerutti	.05
173	Junior Felix	.05
174	Tony Fernandez	.05
175	Kelly Gruber	.05
176	Tom Henke	.05
177	Glenallen Hill	.05
178	Jimmy Key	.05
179	Manny Lee	.05
180	Fred McGriff	.05
181	Rance Mulliniks	.05
182	Greg Myers	.05
183	John Olerud	.05
184	Luis Sojo	.05
185	Dave Steib	.05
186	Todd Stottlemyre	.05
187	Duane Ward	.05
188	David Wells	.05
189	Mark Whiten RC	.05
190	Ken Williams	.05
191	Frank Wills	.05
192	Mookie Wilson	.05
193	Don Aase	.05
194	Tim Belcher	.05
195	Hubie Brooks	.05
196	Dennis Cook	.05
197	Tim Crews	.05
198	Kal Daniels	.05
199	Kirk Gibson	.05
200	Jim Gott	.05
201	Alfredo Griffin	.05
202	Chris Gwynn	.05
203	Dave Hansen	.05
204	Lenny Harris	.05
205	Mike Hartley	.05
206	Mickey Hatcher	.05
207	Carlos Hernandez RC	.05
208	Orel Hershiser	.05
209	Jay Howell	.05
210	Mike Huff	.05
211	Stan Javier	.05
212	Ramon Martinez	.05
213	Mike Morgan	.05
214	Eddie Murray	.40
215	Jim Neidlinger RC	.05
216	Jose Offerman	.05
217	Jim Poole RC	.05
218	Juan Samuel	.05
219	Mike Scioscia	.05
220	Ray Searage	.05
221	Mike Sharperson	.05
222	Fernando Valenzuela	.05
223	Jose Vizcaino	.05
224	Mike Aldrete	.05
225	Scott Anderson RC	.05
226	Dennis Boyd	.05
227	Tim Burke	.05
228	Delino DeShields	.05
229	Mike Fitzgerald	.05
230	Tom Foley	.05
231	Steve Frey	.05
232	Andres Galarraga	.05
233	Mark Gardner	.05
234	Marquis Grissom	.05
235	Kevin Gross	.05
236	Drew Hall	.05
237	Dave Martinez	.05
238	Dennis Martinez	.05
239	Dale Mohorcic	.05
240	Chris Nabholz RC	.05
241	Otis Nixon	.05
242	Junior Noboa RC	.05
243	Spike Owen	.05
244	Tim Raines	.05
245	Mel Rojas RC	.10
246	Scott Ruskin RC	.05
247	Bill Sampen RC	.05
248	Nelson Santovenia	.05
249	Dave Schmidt	.05
250	Larry Walker	.05
251	Tim Wallach	.05
252	Dave Anderson	.05
253	Kevin Bass	.05
254	Steve Bedrosian	.05
255	Jeff Brantley	.05
256	John Burkett	.05
257	Brett Butler	.05
258	Gary Carter	.40
259	Will Clark	.05
260	Steve Decker RC	.05
261	Kelly Downs	.05
262	Scott Garrelts	.05
263	Terry Kennedy	.05
264	Mike LaCoss (Photo on back actually Ken Oberkfell.)	.05
265	Mark Leonard RC	.05
266	Greg Litton	.05
267	Kevin Mitchell	.05

268	Randy O'Neal RC	.05
269	Rick Parker RC	.05
270	Rick Reuschel	.05
271	Ernest Riles	.05
272	Don Robinson	.05
273	Robby Thompson	.05
274	Mark Thurmond	.05
275	Jose Uribe	.05
276	Matt Williams	.05
277	Trevor Wilson	.05
278	Gerald Alexander RC	.05
279	Brad Arnsberg	.05
280	Kevin Belcher RC	.05
281	Joe Bitker RC	.05
282	Kevin Brown	.05
283	Steve Buechele	.05
284	Jack Daugherty	.05
285	Julio Franco	.05
286	Juan Gonzalez	.20
287	Bill Haselman RC	.05
288	Charlie Hough	.05
289	Jeff Huson	.05
290	Pete Incaviglia	.05
291	Mike Jeffcoat	.05
292	Jeff Kunkel	.05
293	Gary Mielke	.05
294	Jamie Moyer	.05
295	Rafael Palmeiro	.35
296	Geno Petralli	.05
297	Gary Pettis	.05
298	Kevin Reimer	.05
299	Kenny Rogers	.05
300	Jeff Russell	.05
301	John Russell	.05
302a	Nolan Ryan (First horizontal line between 1979/1980.)	.75
302b	Nolan Ryan (First horizontal line between 1980/1981.)	.75
303	Ruben Sierra	.05
304	Bobby Witt	.05
305	Jim Abbott	.05
306	Kent Anderson RC	.05
307	Dante Bichette	.05
308	Bert Blyleven	.05
309	Chili Davis	.05
310	Brian Downing	.05
311	Mark Eichhorn	.05
312	Mike Fetters	.05
313	Chuck Finley	.05
314	Willie Fraser	.05
315	Bryan Harvey	.05
316	Donnie Hill	.05
317	Wally Joyner	.05
318	Mark Langston	.05
319	Kirk McCaskill	.05
320	John Orton	.05
321	Lance Parrish	.05
322	Luis Polonia	.05
323	Johnny Ray	.05
324	Bobby Rose	.05
325	Dick Schofield	.05
326	Rick Schu	.05
327a	Lee Stevens (Six-line career summary.)	.05
327b	Lee Stevens (Seven-line career summary.)	.05
328	Devon White	.05
329	Dave Winfield	.40
330	Cliff Young RC	.05
331	Dave Bergman	.05
332	Phil Clark RC	.05
333	Darnell Coles	.05
334	Milt Cuyler RC	.05
335	Cecil Fielder	.05
336	Travis Fryman	.05
337	Paul Gibson	.05
338	Jerry Don Gleaton	.05
339	Mike Heath	.05
340	Mike Henneman	.05
341	Chet Lemon	.05
342	Lance McCullers	.05
343	Jack Morris	.05
344	Lloyd Moseby	.05
345	Edwin Nunez	.05
346	Clay Parker	.05
347	Dan Petry	.05
348	Tony Phillips	.05
349	Jeff Robinson	.05
350	Mark Salas	.05
351	Mike Schwabe RC	.05
352	Larry Sheets	.05
353	John Shelby	.05
354	Frank Tanana	.05
355	Alan Trammell	.05
356	Gary Ward	.05
357	Lou Whitaker	.05
358	Beau Allred	.05
359	Sandy Alomar, Jr.	.05
360	Carlos Baerga	.05
361	Kevin Bearse RC	.05
362	Tom Brookens	.05
363	Jerry Browne	.05
364	Tom Candiotti	.05
365	Alex Cole	.05
366	John Farrell	.05
367	Felix Fermin	.05
368	Keith Hernandez	.05
369	Brook Jacoby	.05
370	Chris James	.05
371	Dion James	.05
372	Doug Jones	.05
373	Candy Maldonado	.05
374	Steve Olin	.05
375	Jesse Orosco	.05
376	Rudy Seanez	.05
377	Joel Skinner	.05

#	Player	Price
378	Cory Snyder	.05
379	Greg Swindell	.05
380	Sergio Valdez RC	.05
381	Mike Walker RC	.05
382	Colby Ward RC	.05
383	Turner Ward RC	.05
384	Mitch Webster	.05
385	Kevin Wickander RC	.05
386	Darrel Akerfelds	.05
387	Joe Boever	.05
388a	Rod Booker (No 1981 stats.)	.05
388b	Rod Booker (1981 stats included)	.05
389	Sil Campusano	.05
390	Don Carman	.05
391	Wes Chamberlain RC	.05
392	Pat Combs	.05
393	Darren Daulton	.05
394	Jose DeJesus	.05
395	Len Dykstra	.05
396	Jason Grimsley	.05
397	Charlie Hayes	.05
398	Von Hayes	.05
399	Dave Hollins RC	.05
400	Ken Howell	.05
401	Ricky Jordan	.05
402	John Kruk	.05
403	Steve Lake	.05
404	Chuck Malone RC	.05
405	Roger McDowell	.05
406	Chuck McElroy	.05
407	Mickey Morandini RC	.05
408	Terry Mulholland	.05
409	Dale Murphy	.15
410	Randy Ready	.05
411	Bruce Ruffin	.05
412	Dickie Thon	.05
413	Paul Assenmacher	.05
414	Damon Berryhill	.05
415	Mike Bielecki	.05
416	Shawn Boskie RC	.05
417	Dave Clark	.05
418	Doug Dascenzo	.05
419a	Andre Dawson (No 1976 stats.)	.25
419b	Andre Dawson (1976 stats included)	.25
420	Shawon Dunston	.05
421	Joe Girardi	.05
422	Mark Grace	.05
423	Mike Harkey	.05
424	Les Lancaster	.05
425	Bill Long	.05
426	Greg Maddux	.50
427	Derrick May	.05
428	Jeff Pico	.05
429	Domingo Ramos	.05
430	Luis Salazar	.05
431	Ryne Sandberg	.50
432	Dwight Smith	.05
433	Greg Smith	.05
434	Rick Sutcliffe	.05
435	Gary Varsho	.05
436	Hector Villanueva RC	.05
437	Jerome Walton	.05
438	Curtis Wilkerson	.05
439	Mitch Williams	.05
440	Steve Wilson	.05
441	Marvell Wynne	.05
442	Scott Bankhead	.05
443	Scott Bradley	.05
444	Greg Briley	.05
445	Mike Brumley	.05
446	Jay Buhner	.05
447	Dave Burba RC	.05
448	Henry Cotto	.05
449	Alvin Davis	.05
450	Ken Griffey Jr.	.60
451	Erik Hanson	.05
452	Gene Harris	.05
453	Brian Holman	.05
454	Mike Jackson	.05
455	Randy Johnson	.40
456	Jeffrey Leonard	.05
457	Edgar Martinez	.05
458	Tino Martinez	.05
459	Pete O'Brien	.05
460	Harold Reynolds	.05
461	Mike Schooler	.05
462	Bill Swift	.05
463	David Valle	.05
464	Omar Vizquel	.05
465	Matt Young	.05
466	Brady Anderson	.05
467	Jeff Ballard	.05
468	Juan Bell RC	.05
469a	Mike Devereaux ("Six" last word in career summary top line.)	.05
469b	Mike Devereaux ("Runs" last word in career summary top line.)	.05
470	Steve Finley	.05
471	Dave Gallagher	.05
472	Leo Gomez RC	.05
473	Rene Gonzales	.05
474	Pete Harnisch	.05
475	Kevin Hickey	.05
476	Chris Hoiles RC	.10
477	Sam Horn	.05
478	Tim Hulett	.05
479	Dave Johnson	.05
480	Ron Kittle	.05
481	Ben McDonald	.05
482	Bob Melvin	.05
483	Bob Milacki	.05
484	Randy Milligan	.05
485	John Mitchell RC	.05
486	Gregg Olson	.05
487	Joe Orsulak	.05
488	Joe Price	.05
489	Bill Ripken	.05
490	Cal Ripken, Jr.	.75
491	Curt Schilling	.25
492	David Segui RC	.10
493	Anthony Telford RC	.05
494	Mickey Tettleton	.05
495	Mark Williamson	.05
496	Craig Worthington	.05
497	Juan Agosto	.05
498	Eric Anthony	.05
499	Craig Biggio	.05
500	Ken Caminiti	.05
501	Casey Candaele	.05
502	Andujar Cedeno RC	.05
503	Danny Darwin	.05
504	Mark Davidson	.05
505	Glenn Davis	.05
506	Jim Deshaies	.05
507	Luis Gonzalez RC	1.00
508	Bill Gullickson	.05
509	Xavier Hernandez RC	.05
510	Brian Meyer	.05
511	Ken Oberkfell	.05
512	Mark Portugal	.05
513	Rafael Ramirez	.05
514	Karl Rhodes RC	.10
515	Mike Scott	.05
516	Mike Simms RC	.05
517	Dave Smith	.05
518	Franklin Stubbs	.05
519	Glenn Wilson	.05
520	Eric Yelding	.05
521	Gerald Young	.05
522	Shawn Abner	.05
523	Roberto Alomar	.20
524	Andy Benes	.05
525	Joe Carter	.05
526	Jack Clark	.05
527	Joey Cora	.05
528	Paul Faries RC	.05
529	Tony Gwynn	.50
530	Atlee Hammaker	.05
531	Greg Harris	.05
532	Thomas Howard RC	.05
533	Bruce Hurst	.05
534	Craig Lefferts	.05
535	Derek Lilliquist	.05
536	Fred Lynn	.05
537	Mike Pagliarulo	.05
538	Mark Parent	.05
539	Dennis Rasmussen	.05
540	Bip Roberts	.05
541	Richard Rodriguez RC	.05
542	Benito Santiago	.05
543	Calvin Schiraldi	.05
544	Eric Show	.05
545	Phil Stephenson	.05
546	Garry Templeton	.05
547	Ed Whitson	.05
548	Eddie Williams	.05
549	Kevin Appier	.05
550	Luis Aquino	.05
551	Bob Boone	.05
552	George Brett	.55
553	Jeff Conine RC	.30
554	Steve Crawford	.05
555	Mark Davis	.05
556	Storm Davis	.05
557	Jim Eisenreich	.05
558	Steve Farr	.05
559	Tom Gordon	.05
560	Mark Gubicza	.05
561	Bo Jackson	.10
562	Mike Macfarlane	.05
563	Brian McRae RC	.10
564	Jeff Montgomery	.05
565	Bill Pecota	.05
566	Gerald Perry	.05
567	Bret Saberhagen	.05
568	Jeff Schulz RC	.05
569	Kevin Seitzer	.05
570	Terry Shumpert RC	.05
571	Kurt Stillwell	.05
572	Danny Tartabull	.05
573	Gary Thurman	.05
574	Frank White	.05
575	Willie Wilson	.05
576	Chris Bosio	.05
577	Greg Brock	.05
578	George Canale	.05
579	Chuck Crim	.05
580	Rob Deer	.05
581	Edgar Diaz RC	.05
582	Tom Edens RC	.05
583	Mike Felder	.05
584	Jim Gantner	.05
585	Darryl Hamilton	.05
586	Ted Higuera	.05
587	Mark Knudson	.05
588	Bill Krueger	.05
589	Tim McIntosh	.05
590	Paul Mirabella	.05
591	Paul Molitor	.40
592	Jaime Navarro	.05
593	Dave Parker	.05
594	Dan Plesac	.05
595	Ron Robinson	.05
596	Gary Sheffield	.30
597	Bill Spiers	.05
598	B.J. Surhoff	.05
599	Greg Vaughn	.05
600	Randy Veres	.05
601	Robin Yount	.40
602a	Rick Aguilera (Five-line career summary.)	.05
602b	Rick Aguilera (Four-line career summary.)	.05
603	Allan Anderson	.05
604	Juan Berenguer	.05
605	Randy Bush	.05
606	Carmen Castillo	.05
607	Tim Drummond	.05
608	Scott Erickson RC	.10
609	Gary Gaetti	.05
610a	Greg Gagne (Horizontal lines under 82 Ft. Lauderdale, 84 Toledo and 87 Twins.)	.05
610b	Greg Gagne (Horizontal lines under 82 Orlando, 84 Twins and 88 Twins.)	.05
611	Dan Gladden	.05
612	Mark Guthrie	.05
613	Brian Harper	.05
614	Kent Hrbek	.05
615	Gene Larkin	.05
616	Terry Leach	.05
617	Nelson Liriano	.05
618	Shane Mack	.05
619	John Moses	.05
620	Pedro Munoz RC	.05
621	Al Newman	.05
622	Junior Ortiz	.05
623	Kirby Puckett	.50
624	Roy Smith	.05
625	Kevin Tapani	.05
626	Gary Wayne	.05
627	David West	.05
628	Cris Carpenter	.05
629	Vince Coleman	.05
630	Ken Dayley	.05
631	Jose DeLeon	.05
632	Frank DiPino	.05
633	Bernard Gilkey RC	.25
634	Pedro Guerrero	.05
635	Ken Hill	.05
636	Felix Jose	.05
637	Ray Lankford RC	.25
638	Joe Magrane	.05
639	Tom Niedenfuer	.05
640	Jose Oquendo	.05
641	Tom Pagnozzi	.05
642	Terry Pendleton	.05
643	Mike Perez RC	.05
644	Bryn Smith	.05
645	Lee Smith	.05
646	Ozzie Smith	.50
647	Scott Terry	.05
648	Bob Tewksbury	.05
649	Milt Thompson	.05
650	John Tudor	.05
651	Denny Walling	.05
652	Craig Wilson RC	.05
653	Todd Worrell	.05
654	Todd Zeile	.05
655	Oscar Azocar RC	.05
656	Steve Balboni	.05
657	Jesse Barfield	.05
658	Greg Cadaret	.05
659	Chuck Cary	.05
660	Rick Cerone	.05
661	Dave Eiland RC	.05
662a	Alvaro Espinoza (No 1979-80 stats.)	.05
662b	Alvaro Espinoza (1979-80 stats included)	.05
663	Bob Geren	.05
664	Lee Guetterman	.05
665	Mel Hall	.05
666a	Andy Hawkins (No 1978 stats.)	.05
666b	Andy Hawkins (1978 stats included)	.05
667	Jimmy Jones	.05
668	Roberto Kelly	.05
669	Dave LaPoint	.05
670	Tim Leary	.05
671	Jim Leyritz RC	.10
672	Kevin Maas	.05
673	Don Mattingly	.60
674	Matt Nokes	.05
675	Pascual Perez	.05
676	Eric Plunk	.05
677	Dave Righetti	.05
678	Jeff Robinson	.05
679	Steve Sax	.05
680	Mike Witt	.05
681	Steve Avery	.05
682	Mike Bell	.05
683	Jeff Blauser	.05
684	Francisco Cabrera	.05
685	Tony Castillo RC	.05
686	Marty Clary	.05
687	Nick Esasky	.05
688	Ron Gant	.05
689	Tom Glavine	.25
690	Mark Grant	.05
691	Tommy Gregg	.05
692	Dwayne Henry	.05
693	Dave Justice	.40
694	Jimmy Kremers RC	.05
695	Charlie Leibrandt	.05
696	Mark Lemke	.05
697	Oddibe McDowell	.05
698	Greg Olson RC	.05
699	Jeff Parrett	.05
700	Jim Presley	.05
701	Victor Rosario RC	.05
702	Lonnie Smith	.05
703	Pete Smith	.05
704	John Smoltz	.05
705	Mike Stanton	.05
706	Andres Thomas	.05
707	Jeff Treadway	.05
708	Jim Vatcher RC	.05
709	Home Run Kings (Ryne Sandberg, Cecil Fielder)	.10
710	Second Generation Superstars (Barry Bonds, Ken Griffey Jr.)	.65
711	NLCS Team Leaders (Bobby Bonilla, Barry Larkin)	.05
712	Top Game Savers (Bobby Thigpen, John Franco)	.05
713	Chicago's 100 Club (Andre Dawson, Ryne Sandberg)	.10
714	Checklists (Athletics, Pirates, Reds, Red Sox)	.05
715	Checklists (Dodgers)	.05
716	Checklists (Expos, Giants, Rangers, Angels)	.05
717	Checklists (Tigers, Indians, Phillies, Cubs)	.05
718	Checklists (Mariners, Orioles, Astros, Padres)	.05
719	Checklists (Royals, Brewers, Twins, Cardinals)	.05
720	Checklists (Yankees, Braves, Super Stars)	.05

All-Stars

Three player photos are featured on each card in this special insert set. An action shot and portrait close-up are featured on the front, while a full-figure pose is showcased on the back. The cards were inserted into 1991 Fleer cello packs.

		NM/M
Complete Set (10):		5.00
Common Player:		.25
1	Ryne Sandberg	.75
2	Barry Larkin	.25
3	Matt Williams	.25
4	Cecil Fielder	.25
5	Barry Bonds	2.00
6	Rickey Henderson	.50
7	Ken Griffey Jr.	1.50
8	Jose Canseco	.25
9	Benito Santiago	.25
10	Roger Clemens	1.00

World Series

Once again Fleer released a set in honor of the World Series from the previous season. The 1991 issue features only eight cards compared to twelve in 1990. The cards feature white borders surrounding full-color action shots from the 1990 Fall Classic. The card backs feature an overview of the World Series action.

		NM/M
Complete Set (8):		1.50
Common Player:		.25
1	Eric Davis	.25
2	Billy Hatcher	.25
3	Jose Canseco	.35
4	Rickey Henderson	.45
5	Chris Sabo, Carney Lansford	.25
6	Dave Stewart	.25
7	Jose Rijo	.25
8	Reds Celebrate	.25

Box Panels

Unlike past box panel sets, the 1991 Fleer box panels feature a theme; 1990 no-hitters are celebrated on the three different boxes. The cards feature blank backs and are numbered in order of no-hitter on the front. A team logo was included on each box. The card fronts are styled after the 1991 Fleer cards. A special no-hitter logo appears in the lower left corner.

		NM/M
Complete Set, Singles (10):		3.00
Complete Set, Panels (3):		3.00
Common Player:		.10
1	Mark Langston, Mike Witt	.10
2	Randy Johnson	1.00
3	Nolan Ryan	2.00
4	Dave Stewart	.10
5	Fernando Valenzuela	.10
6	Andy Hawkins	.10
7	Melido Perez	.10
8	Terry Mulholland	.10
9	Dave Steib	.10
----	Team Logos	.05

Update

Fleer produced its eighth consecutive "Update" set in 1991 to supplement the company's regular set. As in the past, the set consists of 132 cards that were sold by hobby dealers in special collectors boxes. The cards are designed in the same style as the regular Fleer issue.

		NM/M
Complete Set (132):		3.00
Common Player:		.05
1	Glenn Davis	.05
2	Dwight Evans	.05
3	Jose Mesa RC	.05
4	Jack Clark	.05
5	Danny Darwin	.05
6	Steve Lyons	.05
7	Mo Vaughn RC	.05
8	Floyd Bannister	.05
9	Gary Gaetti	.05
10	Dave Parker	.05
11	Joey Cora	.05
12	Charlie Hough	.05
13	Matt Merullo	.05
14	Warren Newson RC	.05
15	Tim Raines	.05
16	Albert Belle	.05
17	Glenallen Hill	.05
18	Shawn Hillegas	.05
19	Mark Lewis RC	.05
20	Charles Nagy RC	.05
21	Mark Whiten	.05
22	John Cerutti	.05
23	Rob Deer	.05
24	Mickey Tettleton	.05
25	Warren Cromartie	.05
26	Kirk Gibson	.05
27	David Howard RC	.05
28	Brent Mayne RC	.05
29	Dante Bichette	.05
30	Mark Lee RC	.05
31	Julio Machado	.05
32	Edwin Nunez	.05
33	Willie Randolph	.05
34	Franklin Stubbs	.05
35	Bill Wegman	.05
36	Chili Davis	.05
37	Chuck Knoblauch RC	.05
38	Scott Leius	.05
39	Jack Morris	.05
40	Mike Pagliarulo	.05
41	Lenny Webster RC	.05
42	John Habyan RC	.05
43	Steve Howe	.05
44	Jeff Johnson RC	.05
45	Scott Kamieniecki RC	.05
46	Pat Kelly RC	.05
47	Hensley Meulens	.05
48	Wade Taylor RC	.05
49	Bernie Williams RC	.20
50	Kirk Dressendorfer RC	.05
51	Ernest Riles	.05
52	Rich DeLucia RC	.05
53	Tracy Jones	.05
54	Bill Krueger	.05
55	Alonzo Powell RC	.05
56	Jeff Schaefer	.05
57	Russ Swan RC	.05
58	John Barfield RC	.05
59	Rich Gossage	.10
60	Jose Guzman	.05
61	Dean Palmer RC	.05
62	Ivan Rodriguez RC	1.50
63	Roberto Alomar	.20
64	Tom Candiotti	.05
65	Joe Carter	.05
66	Ed Sprague RC	.05
67	Pat Tabler	.05
68	Mike Timlin RC	.05
69	Devon White	.05
70	Rafael Belliard	.05
71	Juan Berenguer	.05
72	Sid Bream	.05
73	Marvin Freeman	.05
74	Kent Mercker	.05
75	Otis Nixon	.05
76	Terry Pendleton	.05
77	George Bell	.05
78	Danny Jackson	.05
79	Chuck McElroy	.05
80	Gary Scott RC	.05
81	Heathcliff Slocumb RC	.05
82	Dave Smith	.05
83	Rick Wilkins RC	.05
84	Freddie Benavides RC	.05
85	Ted Power	.05
86	Mo Sanford RC	.05
87	Jeff Bagwell RC	2.00
88	Steve Finley	.05
89	Pete Harnisch	.05
90	Darryl Kile RC	.05
91	Brett Butler	.05
92	John Candelaria	.05
93	Gary Carter	.40
94	Kevin Gross	.05
95	Bob Ojeda	.05
96	Darryl Strawberry	.05
97	Ivan Calderon	.05
98	Ron Hassey	.05
99	Gilberto Reyes	.05
100	Hubie Brooks	.05
101	Rick Cerone	.05
102	Vince Coleman	.05
103	Jeff Innis	.05
104	Pete Schourek RC	.05
105	Andy Ashby RC	.05
106	Wally Backman	.05
107	Darrin Fletcher RC	.05
108	Tommy Greene	.05
109	John Morris	.05
110	Mitch Williams	.05
111	Lloyd McClendon	.05
112	Orlando Merced RC	.05
113	Vicente Palacios	.05
114	Gary Varsho	.05
115	John Wehner RC	.05
116	Rex Hudler	.05
117	Tim Jones	.05
118	Geronimo Pena RC	.05
119	Gerald Perry	.05
120	Larry Andersen	.05
121	Jerald Clark	.05
122	Scott Coolbaugh	.05
123	Tony Fernandez	.05
124	Darrin Jackson	.05
125	Fred McGriff	.05
126	Jose Mota RC	.05
127	Tim Teufel	.05
128	Bud Black	.05
129	Mike Felder	.05
130	Willie McGee	.05
131	Dave Righetti	.05
132	Checklist	.05

ProVisions

The illustrations of artist Terry Smith are showcased in this special set. Twelve fantasy portraits were produced for cards inserted into rack packs. Four other ProVision cards were inserted into factory sets. The rack pack cards fea-

RICKEY HENDERSON

ture black borders, while the factory set cards have white borders. Information on the card backs explains the manner in which Smith painted each player. Factory insert ProVisions are indicated by an "F" suffix in the checklist here.

	NM/M
Complete Set (12):	5.00
Common Player:	.15
Complete Factory Set (4):	5.00
Common Player:	.25

1	Kirby Puckett	.75
2	Will Clark	.15
3	Ruben Sierra	.15
4	Mark McGwire	1.50
5	Bo Jackson	.25
6	Jose Canseco	.50
7	Dwight Gooden	.15
8	Mike Greenwell	.15
9	Roger Clemens	1.00
10	Eric Davis	.15
11	Don Mattingly	1.00
12	Darryl Strawberry	.15
1F	Barry Bonds	3.50
2F	Rickey Henderson	.50
3F	Ryne Sandberg	1.00
4F	Dave Stewart	.25

1992 Fleer Promo

It has been reported that only 100 of this sample card were made for distribution at the 1991 FanFest event. The card differs from the issued Kirby Puckett card in the '92 Fleer set in the card number, the absence of 1991 stats and the overprinting of a sample card notice, all on the back.

		NM/M
123	Kirby Puckett	400.00

1992 Fleer

CAL RIPKEN

For the second consecutive year, Fleer produced a 720-card set. The standard card fronts feature full-color action photos bordered in green with the player's name, position and team logo on the right border. The backs feature another full-color action photo, biographical information and statistics. A special 12-card Roger Clemens subset is also included in the 1992 Fleer set. Three more Clemens cards were available through a mail-in offer, and 2,000 Roger Clemens autographed cards were inserted in 1992 packs. Once again the cards are numbered according to team. Subsets in the issue included Major League Propects (#652-680), Record Setters

(#681-687), League Leaders (#688-697), Superstar Specials (#698-707) and ProVisions (#708-713), which for the first time were part of the regular numbered set rather than limited edition insert cards.

	NM/M
Unopened Factory Set (732):	17.50
Complete Set (720):	8.00
Common Player:	.05
Wax Pack (15):	.45
Wax Box (36):	10.00
Cello Pack (35):	1.00
Cello Box (24):	16.00

1	Brady Anderson	.05
2	Jose Bautista	.05
3	Juan Bell	.05
4	Glenn Davis	.05
5	Mike Devereaux	.05
6	Dwight Evans	.05
7	Mike Flanagan	.05
8	Leo Gomez	.05
9	Chris Hoiles	.05
10	Sam Horn	.05
11	Tim Hulett	.05
12	Dave Johnson	.05
13	Chito Martinez RC	.05
14	Ben McDonald	.05
15	Bob Melvin	.05
16	Luis Mercedes RC	.10
17	Jose Mesa	.05
18	Bob Milacki	.05
19	Randy Milligan	.05
20	Mike Mussina	.30
21	Gregg Olson	.05
22	Joe Orsulak	.05
23	Jim Poole	.05
24	Arthur Rhodes RC	.10
25	Billy Ripken	.05
26	Cal Ripken, Jr.	1.00
27	David Segui	.05
28	Roy Smith	.05
29	Anthony Telford	.05
30	Mark Williamson	.05
31	Craig Worthington	.05
32	Wade Boggs	.55
33	Tom Bolton	.05
34	Tom Brunansky	.05
35	Ellis Burks	.05
36	Jack Clark	.05
37	Roger Clemens	.60
38	Danny Darwin	.05
39	Mike Greenwell	.05
40	Joe Hesketh	.05
41	Daryl Irvine	.05
42	Dennis Lamp	.05
43	Tony Pena	.05
44	Phil Plantier	.05
45	Carlos Quintana	.05
46	Jeff Reardon	.05
47	Jody Reed	.05
48	Luis Rivera	.05
49	Mo Vaughn	.05
50	Jim Abbott	.05
51	Kyle Abbott	.05
52	Ruben Amaro Jr. RC	.05
53	Scott Bailes	.05
54	Chris Beasley RC	.05
55	Mark Eichhorn	.05
56	Mike Fetters	.05
57	Chuck Finley	.05
58	Gary Gaetti	.05
59	Dave Gallagher	.05
60	Donnie Hill	.05
61	Bryan Harvey	.05
62	Wally Joyner	.05
63	Mark Langston	.05
64	Kirk McCaskill	.05
65	John Orton	.05
66	Lance Parrish	.05
67	Luis Polonia	.05
68	Bobby Rose	.05
69	Dick Schofield	.05
70	Luis Sojo	.05
71	Lee Stevens	.05
72	Dave Winfield	.50
73	Cliff Young	.05
74	Wilson Alvarez	.05
75	Esteban Beltre RC	.05
76	Joey Cora	.05
77	Brian Drahman RC	.05
78	Alex Fernandez	.05
79	Carlton Fisk	.50
80	Scott Fletcher	.05
81	Craig Grebeck	.05
82	Ozzie Guillen	.05
83	Greg Hibbard	.05
84	Charlie Hough	.05
85	Mike Huff	.05
86	Bo Jackson	.10
87	Lance Johnson	.05
88	Ron Karkovice	.05
89	Jack McDowell	.05
90	Matt Merullo	.05
91	Warren Newson RC	.05
92	Donn Pall	.05
93	Dan Pasqua	.05
94	Ken Patterson	.05
95	Melido Perez	.05
96	Scott Radinsky	.05
97	Tim Raines	.05
98	Sammy Sosa	.55
99	Bobby Thigpen	.05
100	Frank Thomas	.50

101	Robin Ventura	.05
102	Mike Aldrete	.05
103	Sandy Alomar, Jr.	.05
104	Carlos Baerga	.05
105	Albert Belle	.05
106	Willie Blair	.05
107	Jerry Browne	.05
108	Alex Cole	.05
109	Felix Fermin	.05
110	Glenallen Hill	.05
111	Shawn Hillegas	.05
112	Chris James	.05
113	Reggie Jefferson RC	.05
114	Doug Jones	.05
115	Eric King	.05
116	Mark Lewis	.05
117	Carlos Martinez	.05
118	Charles Nagy	.05
119	Rod Nichols	.05
120	Steve Olin	.05
121	Jesse Orosco	.05
122	Rudy Seanez	.05
123	Joel Skinner	.05
124	Greg Swindell	.05
125	Jim Thome RC	.50
126	Mark Whiten	.05
127	Scott Aldred	.05
128	Andy Allanson	.05
129	John Cerutti	.05
130	Milt Cuyler	.05
131	Mike Dalton RC	.05
132	Rob Deer	.05
133	Cecil Fielder	.05
134	Travis Fryman	.05
135	Dan Gakeler RC	.05
136	Paul Gibson	.05
137	Bill Gullickson	.05
138	Mike Henneman	.05
139	Pete Incaviglia	.05
140	Mark Leiter RC	.05
141	Scott Livingstone RC	.10
142	Lloyd Moseby	.05
143	Tony Phillips	.05
144	Mark Salas	.05
145	Frank Tanana	.05
146	Walt Terrell	.05
147	Mickey Tettleton	.05
148	Alan Trammell	.05
149	Lou Whitaker	.05
150	Kevin Appier	.05
151	Luis Aquino	.05
152	Todd Benzinger	.05
153	Mike Boddicker	.05
154	George Brett	.60
155	Storm Davis	.05
156	Jim Eisenreich	.05
157	Kirk Gibson	.05
158	Tom Gordon	.05
159	Mark Gubicza	.05
160	David Howard RC	.05
161	Mike Macfarlane	.05
162	Brent Mayne	.05
163	Brian McRae	.05
164	Jeff Montgomery	.05
165	Bill Pecota	.05
166	Harvey Pulliam RC	.05
167	Bret Saberhagen	.05
168	Kevin Seitzer	.05
169	Terry Shumpert	.05
170	Kurt Stillwell	.05
171	Danny Tartabull	.05
172	Gary Thurman	.05
173	Dante Bichette	.05
174	Kevin Brown	.05
175	Chuck Crim	.05
176	Jim Gantner	.05
177	Darryl Hamilton	.05
178	Ted Higuera	.05
179	Darren Holmes	.05
180	Mark Lee	.05
181	Julio Machado	.05
182	Paul Molitor	.50
183	Jaime Navarro	.05
184	Edwin Nunez	.05
185	Dan Plesac	.05
186	Willie Randolph	.05
187	Ron Robinson	.05
188	Gary Sheffield	.30
189	Bill Spiers	.05
190	B.J. Surhoff	.05
191	Dale Sveum	.05
192	Greg Vaughn	.05
193	Bill Wegman	.05
194	Robin Yount	.50
195	Rick Aguilera	.05
196	Allan Anderson	.05
197	Steve Bedrosian	.05
198	Randy Bush	.05
199	Larry Casian RC	.05
200	Chili Davis	.05
201	Scott Erickson	.05
202	Greg Gagne	.05
203	Dan Gladden	.05
204	Brian Harper	.05
205	Kent Hrbek	.05
206	Chuck Knoblauch	.05
207	Gene Larkin	.05
208	Terry Leach	.05
209	Scott Leius	.05
210	Shane Mack	.05
211	Jack Morris	.05
212	Pedro Munoz RC	.05
213	Denny Neagle RC	.10
214	Al Newman	.05
215	Junior Ortiz	.05
216	Mike Pagliarulo	.05
217	Kirby Puckett	.55
218	Paul Sorrento	.05

219	Kevin Tapani	.05
220	Lenny Webster	.05
221	Jesse Barfield	.05
222	Greg Cadaret	.05
223	Dave Eiland	.05
224	Alvaro Espinoza	.05
225	Steve Farr	.05
226	Bob Geren	.05
227	Lee Guetterman	.05
228	John Habyan	.05
229	Mel Hall	.05
230	Steve Howe	.05
231	Mike Humphreys RC	.05
232	Scott Kamieniecki RC	.10
233	Pat Kelly	.05
234	Roberto Kelly	.05
235	Tim Leary	.05
236	Kevin Maas	.05
237	Don Mattingly	.60
238	Hensley Meulens	.05
239	Matt Nokes	.05
240	Pascual Perez	.05
241	Eric Plunk	.05
242	John Ramos RC	.05
243	Scott Sanderson	.05
244	Steve Sax	.05
245	Wade Taylor RC	.05
246	Randy Velarde	.05
247	Bernie Williams	.05
248	Troy Afenir	.05
249	Harold Baines	.05
250	Lance Blankenship	.05
251	Mike Bordick	.10
252	Jose Canseco	.30
253	Steve Chitren	.05
254	Ron Darling	.05
255	Dennis Eckersley	.45
256	Mike Gallego	.05
257	Dave Henderson	.05
258	Rickey Henderson	.50
259	Rick Honeycutt	.05
260	Brook Jacoby	.05
261	Carney Lansford	.05
262	Mark McGwire	.75
263	Mike Moore	.05
264	Gene Nelson	.05
265	Jamie Quirk	.05
266	Joe Slusarski RC	.10
267	Terry Steinbach	.05
268	Dave Stewart	.05
269	Todd Van Poppel RC	.05
270	Walt Weiss	.05
271	Bob Welch	.05
272	Curt Young	.05
273	Scott Bradley	.05
274	Greg Briley	.05
275	Jay Buhner	.05
276	Henry Cotto	.05
277	Alvin Davis	.05
278	Rich DeLucia	.05
279	Ken Griffey Jr.	.65
280	Erik Hanson	.05
281	Brian Holman	.05
282	Mike Jackson	.05
283	Randy Johnson	.50
284	Tracy Jones	.05
285	Bill Krueger	.05
286	Edgar Martinez	.05
287	Tino Martinez	.05
288	Rob Murphy	.05
289	Pete O'Brien	.05
290	Alonzo Powell	.05
291	Harold Reynolds	.05
292	Mike Schooler	.05
293	Russ Swan	.05
294	Bill Swift	.05
295	Dave Valle	.05
296	Omar Vizquel	.05
297	Gerald Alexander	.05
298	Brad Arnsberg	.05
299	Kevin Brown	.05
300	Jack Daugherty	.05
301	Mario Diaz	.05
302	Brian Downing	.05
303	Julio Franco	.05
304	Juan Gonzalez	.25
305	Rich Gossage	.10
306	Jose Guzman	.05
307	Jose Hernandez RC	.05
308	Jeff Huson	.05
309	Mike Jeffcoat	.05
310	Terry Mathews RC	.05
311	Rafael Palmeiro	.45
312	Dean Palmer	.05
313	Geno Petralli	.05
314	Gary Pettis	.05
315	Kevin Reimer	.05
316	Ivan Rodriguez	.45
317	Kenny Rogers	.05
318	Wayne Rosenthal RC	.05
319	Jeff Russell	.05
320	Nolan Ryan	1.00
321	Ruben Sierra	.05
322	Jim Acker	.05
323	Roberto Alomar	.20
324	Derek Bell	.05
325	Pat Borders	.05
326	Tom Candiotti	.05
327	Joe Carter	.05
328	Rob Ducey	.05
329	Kelly Gruber	.05
330	Juan Guzman RC	.25
331	Tom Henke	.05
332	Jimmy Key	.05
333	Manny Lee	.05
334	Al Leiter	.05
335	Bob MacDonald RC	.05
336	Candy Maldonado	.05

337	Rance Mulliniks	.05
338	Greg Myers	.05
339	John Olerud	.05
340	Ed Sprague RC	.10
341	Dave Stieb	.05
342	Todd Stottlemyre	.05
343	Mike Timlin RC	.10
344	Duane Ward	.05
345	David Wells	.05
346	Devon White	.05
347	Mookie Wilson	.05
348	Eddie Zosky	.05
349	Steve Avery	.05
350	Mike Bell	.05
351	Rafael Belliard	.05
352	Juan Berenguer	.05
353	Jeff Blauser	.05
354	Sid Bream	.05
355	Francisco Cabrera	.05
356	Marvin Freeman	.05
357	Ron Gant	.05
358	Tom Glavine	.30
359	Brian Hunter RC	.05
360	Dave Justice	.05
361	Charlie Leibrandt	.05
362	Mark Lemke	.05
363	Kent Mercker	.05
364	Keith Mitchell RC	.05
365	Greg Olson	.05
366	Terry Pendleton	.05
367	Armando Reynoso RC	.05
368	Deion Sanders	.10
369	Lonnie Smith	.05
370	Pete Smith	.05
371	John Smoltz	.05
372	Mike Stanton	.05
373	Jeff Treadway	.05
374	Mark Wohlers RC	.05
375	Paul Assenmacher	.05
376	George Bell	.05
377	Shawn Boskie	.05
378	Frank Castillo RC	.05
379	Andre Dawson	.25
380	Shawon Dunston	.05
381	Mark Grace	.05
382	Mike Harkey	.05
383	Danny Jackson	.05
384	Les Lancaster	.05
385	Cedric Landrum RC	.05
386	Greg Maddux	.55
387	Derrick May	.05
388	Chuck McElroy	.05
389	Ryne Sandberg	.55
390	Heathcliff Slocumb RC	.10
391	Dave Smith	.05
392	Dwight Smith	.05
393	Rick Sutcliffe	.05
394	Hector Villanueva	.05
395	Chico Walker RC	.05
396	Jerome Walton	.05
397	Rick Wilkins RC	.15
398	Jack Armstrong	.05
399	Freddie Benavides RC	.05
400	Glenn Braggs	.05
401	Tom Browning	.05
402	Norm Charlton	.05
403	Eric Davis	.05
404	Rob Dibble	.05
405	Bill Doran	.05
406	Mariano Duncan	.05
407	Kip Gross RC	.05
408	Chris Hammond	.05
409	Billy Hatcher	.05
410	Chris Jones RC	.05
411	Barry Larkin	.05
412	Hal Morris	.05
413	Randy Myers	.05
414	Joe Oliver	.05
415	Paul O'Neill	.05
416	Ted Power	.05
417	Luis Quinones	.05
418	Jeff Reed	.05
419	Jose Rijo	.05
420	Chris Sabo	.05
421	Reggie Sanders RC	.05
422	Scott Scudder	.05
423	Glenn Sutko	.05
424	Eric Anthony	.05
425	Jeff Bagwell	.50
426	Craig Biggio	.05
427	Ken Caminiti	.05
428	Casey Candaele	.05
429	Mike Capel	.05
430	Andujar Cedeno	.05
431	Jim Corsi	.05
432	Mark Davidson	.05
433	Steve Finley	.05
434	Luis Gonzalez	.05
435	Pete Harnisch	.05
436	Dwayne Henry	.05
437	Xavier Hernandez	.05
438	Jimmy Jones	.05
439	Darryl Kile RC	.05
440	Rob Mallicoat RC	.05
441	Andy Mota RC	.05
442	Al Osuna	.05
443	Mark Portugal	.05
444	Scott Servais RC	.10
445	Mike Simms	.05
446	Gerald Young	.05
447	Tim Belcher	.05
448	Brett Butler	.05
449	John Candelaria	.05
450	Gary Carter	.50
451	Dennis Cook	.05
452	Tim Crews	.05
453	Kal Daniels	.05
454	Jim Gott	.05

455	Alfredo Griffin	.05
456	Kevin Gross	.05
457	Chris Gwynn	.05
458	Lenny Harris	.05
459	Orel Hershiser	.05
460	Jay Howell	.05
461	Stan Javier	.05
462	Eric Karros	.05
463	Ramon Martinez	.05
464	Roger McDowell	.05
465	Mike Morgan	.05
466	Eddie Murray	.50
467	Jose Offerman	.05
468	Bob Ojeda	.05
469	Juan Samuel	.05
470	Mike Scioscia	.05
471	Darryl Strawberry	.05
472	Bret Barberie RC	.10
473	Brian Barnes	.05
474	Eric Bullock	.05
475	Ivan Calderon	.05
476	Delino DeShields	.05
477	Jeff Fassero RC	.10
478	Mike Fitzgerald	.05
479	Steve Frey	.05
480	Andres Galarraga	.05
481	Mark Gardner	.05
482	Marquis Grissom	.05
483	Chris Haney RC	.05
484	Barry Jones	.05
485	Dave Martinez	.05
486	Dennis Martinez	.05
487	Chris Nabholz	.05
488	Spike Owen	.05
489	Gilberto Reyes	.05
490	Mel Rojas	.05
491	Scott Ruskin	.05
492	Bill Sampen	.05
493	Larry Walker	.05
494	Tim Wallach	.05
495	Daryl Boston	.05
496	Hubie Brooks	.05
497	Tim Burke	.05
498	Mark Carreon	.05
499	Tony Castillo	.05
500	Vince Coleman	.05
501	David Cone	.05
502	Kevin Elster	.05
503	Sid Fernandez	.05
504	John Franco	.05
505	Dwight Gooden	.05
506	Todd Hundley	.05
507	Jeff Innis	.05
508	Gregg Jefferies	.05
509	Howard Johnson	.05
510	Dave Magadan	.05
511	Terry McDaniel RC	.05
512	Kevin McReynolds	.05
513	Keith Miller	.05
514	Charlie O'Brien	.05
515	Mackey Sasser	.05
516	Pete Schourek RC	.05
517	Julio Valera	.05
518	Frank Viola	.05
519	Wally Whitehurst	.05
520	Anthony Young RC	.05
521	Andy Ashby RC	.10
522	Kim Batiste RC	.05
523	Joe Boever	.05
524	Wes Chamberlain	.05
525	Pat Combs	.05
526	Danny Cox	.05
527	Darren Daulton	.05
528	Jose DeJesus	.05
529	Len Dykstra	.05
530	Darrin Fletcher	.05
531	Tommy Greene	.05
532	Jason Grimsley	.05
533	Charlie Hayes	.05
534	Von Hayes	.05
535	Dave Hollins	.05
536	Ricky Jordan	.05
537	John Kruk	.05
538	Jim Lindeman	.05
539	Mickey Morandini	.05
540	Terry Mulholland	.05
541	Dale Murphy	.20
542	Randy Ready	.05
543	Wally Ritchie	.05
544	Bruce Ruffin	.05
545	Steve Searcy	.05
546	Dickie Thon	.05
547	Mitch Williams	.05
548	Stan Belinda	.05
549	Jay Bell	.05
550	Barry Bonds	1.00
551	Bobby Bonilla	.05
552	Steve Buechele	.05
553	Doug Drabek	.05
554	Neal Heaton	.05
555	Jeff King	.05
556	Bob Kipper	.05
557	Bill Landrum	.05
558	Mike LaValliere	.05
559	Jose Lind	.05
560	Lloyd McClendon	.05
561	Orlando Merced	.05
562	Bob Patterson	.05
563	Joe Redfield RC	.05
564	Gary Redus	.05
565	Rosario Rodriguez	.05
566	Don Slaught	.05
567	John Smiley	.05
568	Zane Smith	.05
569	Randy Tomlin	.05
570	Andy Van Slyke	.05
571	Gary Varsho	.05
572	Bob Walk	.05

573	John Wehner RC	.05
574	Juan Agosto	.05
575	Cris Carpenter	.05
576	Jose DeLeon	.05
577	Rich Gedman	.05
578	Bernard Gilkey	.05
579	Pedro Guerrero	.05
580	Ken Hill	.05
581	Rex Hudler	.05
582	Felix Jose	.05
583	Ray Lankford	.05
584	Omar Olivares	.05
585	Jose Oquendo	.05
586	Tom Pagnozzi	.05
587	Geronimo Pena	.05
588	Mike Perez	.05
589	Gerald Perry	.05
590	Bryn Smith	.05
591	Lee Smith	.05
592	Ozzie Smith	.55
593	Scott Terry	.05
594	Bob Tewksbury	.05
595	Milt Thompson	.05
596	Todd Zeile	.05
597	Larry Andersen	.05
598	Oscar Azocar	.05
599	Andy Benes	.05
600	Ricky Bones RC	.05
601	Jerald Clark	.05
602	Pat Clements	.05
603	Paul Faries	.05
604	Tony Fernandez	.05
605	Tony Gwynn	.55
606	Greg Harris	.05
607	Thomas Howard	.05
608	Bruce Hurst	.05
609	Darrin Jackson	.05
610	Tom Lampkin	.05
611	Craig Lefferts	.05
612	Jim Lewis RC	.05
613	Mike Maddux	.05
614	Fred McGriff	.05
615	Jose Melendez RC	.05
616	Jose Mota RC	.05
617	Dennis Rasmussen	.05
618	Bip Roberts	.05
619	Rich Rodriguez	.05
620	Benito Santiago	.05
621	Craig Shipley RC	.05
622	Tim Teufel	.05
623	Kevin Ward RC	.05
624	Ed Whitson	.05
625	Dave Anderson	.05
626	Kevin Bass	.05
627	Rod Beck RC	.10
628	Bud Black	.05
629	Jeff Brantley	.05
630	John Burkett	.05
631	Will Clark	.05
632	Royce Clayton RC	.05
633	Steve Decker	.05
634	Kelly Downs	.05
635	Mike Felder	.05
636	Scott Garrelts	.05
637	Eric Gunderson	.05
638	Bryan Hickerson RC	.05
639	Darren Lewis	.05
640	Greg Litton	.05
641	Kirt Manwaring	.05
642	Paul McClellan RC	.05
643	Willie McGee	.05
644	Kevin Mitchell	.05
645	Francisco Olivares	.05
646	Mike Remlinger RC	.10
647	Dave Righetti	.05
648	Robby Thompson	.05
649	Jose Uribe	.05
650	Matt Williams	.05
651	Trevor Wilson	.05
652	Tom Goodwin RC (Prospects)	.05
653	Terry Bross RC (Prospects)	.05
654	Mike Christopher RC (Prospects)	.05
655	Kenny Lofton (Prospects)	.05
656	Chris Cron RC (Prospects)	.05
657	Willie Banks RC (Prospects)	.05
658	Pat Rice RC (Prospects)	.05
659a	Rob Mauer RC (Prospects)(Last name misspelled.)	.75
659b	Rob Maurer RC (Prospects)(corrected)	.05
660	Don Harris RC (Prospects)	.05
661	Henry Rodriguez RC (Prospects)	.05
662	Cliff Brantley RC (Prospects)	.05
663	Mike Linskey RC (Prospects)	.05
664	Gary Disarcina RC (Prospects)	.05
665	Gil Heredia RC (Prospects)	.10
666	Vinny Castilla RC (Prospects)	.50
667	Paul Abbott RC (Prospects)	.05
668	Monty Fariss RC (Prospects)	.05
669	Jarvis Brown RC (Prospects)	.05

670	Wayne Kirby RC (Prospects)	.05
671	Scott Brosius RC (Prospects)	.05
672	Bob Hamelin RC (Prospects)	.05
673	Joel Johnston RC (Prospects)	.05
674	Tim Spehr RC (Prospects)	.05
675	Jeff Gardner RC (Prospects)	.05
676	Rico Rossy RC (Prospects)	.05
677	Roberto Hernandez RC (Prospects)	.20
678	Ted Wood RC (Prospects)	.05
679	Cal Eldred (Prospects)	.05
680	Sean Berry RC (Prospects)	.05
681	Rickey Henderson (Stolen Base Record)	.20
682	Nolan Ryan (Record 7th No-hitter)	.25
683	Dennis Martinez (Perfect Game)	.05
684	Wilson Alvarez (Rookie No-hitter)	.05
685	Joe Carter (3 100 RBI Seasons)	.05
686	Dave Winfield (400 Home Runs)	.20
687	David Cone (Ties NL Record Strikeouts)	.05
688	Jose Canseco (League Leaders)	.15
689	Howard Johnson (League Leaders)	.05
690	Julio Franco (League Leaders)	.05
691	Terry Pendleton (League Leaders)	.05
692	Cecil Fielder (League Leaders)	.05
693	Scott Erickson (League Leaders)	.05
694	Tom Glavine (League Leaders)	.05
695	Dennis Martinez (League Leaders)	.05
696	Bryan Harvey (League Leaders)	.05
697	Lee Smith (League Leaders)	.05
698	Super Siblings (Roberto & Sandy Alomar, Roberto & Sandy Alomar)	.10
699	The Indispensables (Bobby Bonilla, Will Clark)	.05
700	Teamwork (Mark Wohlers, Kent Mercker, Alejandro Pena)	.05
701	Tiger Tandems (Chris Jones, Bo Jackson, Gregg Olson, Frank Thomas)	.05
702	The Ignitors (Brett Butler, Paul Molitor)	.10
703	The Indispensables II (Cal Ripken Jr., Joe Carter)	.05
704	Power Packs (Barry Larkin, Kirby Puckett)	.15
705	Today and Tomorrow (Mo Vaughn, Cecil Fielder)	.05
706	Teenage Sensations (Ramon Martinez, Ozzie Guillen)	.05
707	Designated Hitters (Harold Baines, Wade Boggs)	.20
708	Robin Yount (ProVision)	.35
709	Ken Griffey Jr. (ProVision)	.60
710	Nolan Ryan (ProVision)	.75
711	Cal Ripken, Jr. (ProVision)	.75
712	Frank Thomas (ProVision)	.50
713	Dave Justice (ProVision)	.35
714	Checklist 1-101	.05
715	Checklist 102-194	.05
716	Checklist 195-296	.05
717	Checklist 297-397	.05
718	Checklist 398-494	.05
719	Checklist 495-596	.05
720a	Checklist 597-720 (659 Rob Mauer)	.05
720b	Checklist 597-720 (659 Rob Maurer)	.05

All-Stars

Black borders with gold highlights are featured on these special wax pack insert cards. The fronts feature glossy action photos with a portrait photo inset. Backs feature career highlights.

	NM/M
Complete Set (24):	8.00

Common Player:		.10
1	Felix Jose	.10
2	Tony Gwynn	1.25
3	Barry Bonds	3.00
4	Bobby Bonilla	.10
5	Mike LaValliere	.10
6	Tom Glavine	.40
7	Ramon Martinez	.10
8	Lee Smith	.10
9	Mickey Tettleton	.10
10	Scott Erickson	.10
11	Frank Thomas	.75
12	Danny Tartabull	.10
13	Will Clark	.10
14	Ryne Sandberg	1.25
15	Terry Pendleton	.10
16	Barry Larkin	.10
17	Rafael Palmeiro	.65
18	Julio Franco	.10
19	Robin Ventura	.10
20	Cal Ripken, Jr.	3.00
21	Joe Carter	.10
22	Kirby Puckett	1.25
23	Ken Griffey Jr.	2.25
24	Jose Canseco	.50

Roger Clemens

This set chronicles the career highlights of Roger Clemens. The initial 12 cards from the set were inserted in 1992 Fleer wax packs. A limited number of autographed cards were inserted as well. The additional three cards from the set were available through a mail-in offer. The card fronts feature black borders with metallic gold type. The flip side is yellow with black borders.

	NM/M
Complete Set (15):	6.00
Common Card:	.50
Autographed Card:	40.00

1	Quiet Storm	.50
2	Courted by the Mets and Twins	.50
3	The Show	.50
4	A Rocket Launched	.50
5	Time of Trial	.50
6	Break Through	.50
7	Play it Again Roger	.50
8	Business as Usual	.50
9	Heee's Back	.50
10	Blood, Sweat and Tears	.50
11	Prime of Life	.50
12	Man for Every Season	.50
13	Cooperstown Bound	1.50
14	The Heat of the Moment	1.50
15	Final Words	1.50

Lumber Co.

Baseball's top power hitters at each position are featured in this nine-card set. Fronts feature full-color action photos bordered in black. Backs feature posed player photos and career highlights. The set was included only in factory sets released to the hobby trade.

	NM/M
Complete Set (9):	5.00

Common Player:		.25
1	Cecil Fielder	.25
2	Mickey Tettleton	.25
3	Darryl Strawberry	.25
4	Ryne Sandberg	1.00
5	Jose Canseco	.40
6	Matt Williams	.25
7	Cal Ripken, Jr.	2.00
8	Barry Bonds	2.00
9	Ron Gant	.25

Rookie Sensations

This 20-card set features the top rookies of 1991 and rookie prospects from 1992. The card fronts feature blue borders with "Rookie Sensations" in gold along the top border. The flip sides feature background information on the player. The cards were randomly inserted in 1992 Fleer cello packs. This issue saw very high prices when initially released then suffered long-term declines as the hobby became inundated with more and more insert sets.

	NM/M
Complete Set (20):	13.50

Common Player:		.35
1	Frank Thomas	6.00
2	Todd Van Poppel	.35
3	Orlando Merced	.35
4	Jeff Bagwell	6.00
5	Jeff Fassero	.35
6	Darren Lewis	.35
7	Milt Cuyler	.35
8	Mike Timlin	.35
9	Brian McRae	.35
10	Chuck Knoblauch	.35
11	Rich DeLucia	.35
12	Ivan Rodriguez	4.50
13	Juan Guzman	.35
14	Steve Chitren	.35
15	Mark Wohlers	.35
16	Wes Chamberlain	.35
17	Ray Lankford	.35
18	Chito Martinez	.35
19	Phil Plantier	.35
20	Scott Leius	.35

Smoke 'N Heat

	NM/M
Complete Set (136):	60.00

This 12-card set of top pitchers was included in factory sets designated for sale within the general retail trade. Card numbers have an "S" prefix.

	NM/M
Complete Set (12):	7.50

Common Player:		.25
1	Lee Smith	.25
2	Jack McDowell	.25
3	David Cone	.25
4	Roger Clemens	2.00
5	Nolan Ryan	3.00
6	Scott Erickson	.25
7	Tom Glavine	.50
8	Dwight Gooden	.25
9	Andy Benes	.25
10	Steve Avery	.25
11	Randy Johnson	1.00
12	Jim Abbott	.25

Team Leaders

White and green borders highlight this insert set from Fleer. The card fronts also feature a special gold-foil "team leaders" logo beneath the full-color player photo. The card backs feature player information. The cards were randomly inserted in 1992 Fleer rack packs.

	NM/M
Complete Set (20):	10.00

Common Player:		.50
1	Don Mattingly	2.00
2	Howard Johnson	.50
3	Chris Sabo	.50
4	Carlton Fisk	1.25
5	Kirby Puckett	1.50
6	Cecil Fielder	.50
7	Tony Gwynn	1.50
8	Will Clark	.50
9	Bobby Bonilla	.50
10	Len Dykstra	.50
11	Tom Glavine	.75
12	Rafael Palmeiro	1.00
13	Wade Boggs	1.50
14	Joe Carter	.50
15	Ken Griffey Jr.	2.50
16	Darryl Strawberry	.50
17	Cal Ripken, Jr.	3.00
18	Danny Tartabull	.50
19	Jose Canseco	.75
20	Andre Dawson	.50

Update

This 132-card set was released in boxed set form and features traded players, free agents and top rookies from 1992. The cards are styled after the regular 1992 Fleer and are numbered alphabetically according to team. This set marks the ninth year that Fleer has released an update set. The set includes four black-bordered "Headliner" cards.

Common Player:	.05
H1	1992 All-Star Game MVP (Ken Griffey Jr.)	1.50
H2	3000 Career Hits (Robin Yount)	.50
H3	Major League Career Saves Record (Jeff Reardon)	.10
H4	Record RBI Performance (Cecil Fielder)	.05

1	Todd Frohwirth	.05
2	Alan Mills	.05
3	Rick Sutcliffe	.05
4	John Valentin RC	.25
5	Frank Viola	.05
6	Bob Zupcic RC	.05
7	Mike Butcher RC	.05
8	Chad Curtis RC	.50
9	Damion Easley RC	.25
10	Tim Salmon RC	.50
11	Julio Valera	.05
12	George Bell	.05
13	Roberto Hernandez RC	.05
14	Shawn Jeter RC	.05
15	Thomas Howard	.05
16	Jesse Levis RC	.05
17	Kenny Lofton	.05
18	Paul Sorrento	.05
19	Rico Brogna RC	.05
20	John Doherty RC	.05
21	Dan Gladden	.05
22	Buddy Groom RC	.05
23	Shawn Hare RC	.05
24	John Kiely RC	.05
25	Kurt Knudsen RC	.05
26	Gregg Jefferies	.05
27	Wally Joyner	.05
28	Kevin Koslofski RC	.05
29	Kevin McReynolds	.05
30	Rusty Meacham	.05
31	Keith Miller	.05
32	Hipolito Pichardo RC	.05
33	James Austin RC	.05
34	Scott Fletcher	.05
35	John Jaha RC	.05
36	Pat Listach RC	.05
37	Dave Nilsson RC	.05
38	Kevin Seitzer	.05
39	Tom Edens	.05
40	Pat Mahomes RC	.05
41	John Smiley	.05
42	Charlie Hayes	.05
43	Sam Militello RC	.05
44	Andy Stankiewicz RC	.05
45	Danny Tartabull	.05
46	Bob Wickman RC	.05
47	Jerry Browne	.05
48	Kevin Campbell RC	.05
49	Vince Horsman RC	.05
50	Troy Neel RC	.05
51	Ruben Sierra	.05
52	Bruce Walton RC	.05
53	Willie Wilson	.05
54	Bret Boone RC	.50
55	Dave Fleming RC	.50
56	Kevin Mitchell	.05
57	Jeff Nelson RC	.05
58	Shane Turner RC	.05
59	Jose Canseco	.65
60	Jeff Frye RC	.05
61	Damilo Leon RC	.05
62	Roger Pavlik RC	.05
63	David Cone	.05
64	Pat Hentgen RC	.05
65	Randy Knorr RC	.05
66	Jack Morris	.05
67	Dave Winfield	1.00
68	David Nied RC	.05
69	Otis Nixon	.05
70	Alejandro Pena	.05
71	Jeff Reardon	.05
72	Alex Arias RC	.05
73	Jim Bullinger RC	.05
74	Mike Morgan	.05
75	Rey Sanchez RC	.05
76	Bob Scanlan	.05
77	Sammy Sosa	3.00
78	Scott Bankhead	.05
79	Tim Belcher	.05
80	Steve Foster RC	.05
81	Willie Greene RC	.05
82	Bip Roberts	.05
83	Scott Ruskin	.05
84	Greg Swindell	.05
85	Juan Guerrero RC	.05
86	Butch Henry RC	.05
87	Doug Jones	.05
88	Brian Williams RC	.05
89	Tom Candiotti	.05
90	Eric Davis	.05
91	Carlos Hernandez RC	.05
92	Mike Piazza RC	45.00
93	Mike Sharperson	.05
94	Eric Young RC	.05
95	Moises Alou	.05
96	Greg Colbrunn	.05
97	Wil Cordero RC	.05
98	Ken Hill	.05
99	John Vander Wal RC	.05
100	John Wetteland	.05
101	Bobby Bonilla	.05
102	Eric Hilman RC	.05
103	Pat Howell RC	.05
104	Jeff Kent RC	15.00
105	Dick Schofield	.05
106	Ryan Thompson RC	.05
107	Chico Walker	.05
108	Juan Bell	.05
109	Mariano Duncan	.05

110	Jeff Grotewold RC	.05
111	Ben Rivera RC	.05
112	Curt Schilling	.65
113	Victor Cole RC	.05
114	Al Martin RC	.05
115	Roger Mason RC	.05
116	Blas Minor RC	.05
117	Tim Wakefield RC	4.00
118	Mark Clark RC	.05
119	Rheal Cormier RC	.05
120	Donovan Osborne RC	.05
121	Todd Worrell	.05
122	Jeremy Hernandez RC	.05
123	Randy Myers	.05
124	Frank Seminara RC	.05
125	Gary Sheffield	.75
126	Dan Walters RC	.05
127	Steve Hosey RC	.05
128	Mike Jackson	.05
129	Jim Pena RC	.05
130	Cory Snyder	.05
131	Bill Swift	.05
132	Checklist	.05

7-Eleven

The 1992 Performer Collection was a combined effort from Fleer and 7-11. Customers at 7-11 stores received a packet of five cards with gasoline purchases to build the 24-card set of major stars. The cards are standard size, with virtually the identical design to the regular issue Fleer set of 1992, with only the addition of "The Performer" logo on the front of the card and a pair of sponsors' logos on back.

		NM/M
	Complete Set (24):	9.00
	Common Player:	.20
1	Nolan Ryan	1.50
2	Frank Thomas	.65
3	Ryne Sandberg	.75
4	Ken Griffey Jr.	1.00
5	Cal Ripken, Jr.	1.50
6	Roger Clemens	.85
7	Cecil Fielder	.20
8	Dave Justice	.20
9	Wade Boggs	.75
10	Tony Gwynn	.75
11	Kirby Puckett	.75
12	Darryl Strawberry	.20
13	Jose Canseco	.50
14	Barry Larkin	.20
15	Terry Pendleton	.20
16	Don Mattingly	.85
17	Rickey Henderson	.65
18	Ruben Sierra	.20
19	Jeff Bagwell	.65
20	Tom Glavine	.45
21	Ramon Martinez	.20
22	Will Clark	.50
23	Barry Bonds	1.50
24	Roberto Alomar	.40

1993 Fleer

The card fronts feature silver borders with the player's name, team and position in a banner along the left side of the card. The backs feature an action photo of the player with his name in bold behind him. A box featuring biographical information, statistics and player information is located to the right of the action photo. The cards are numbered alphabetically by team. The basic Fleer issue for 1993 was issued in two series of 360 cards each. The 720-card set included a number of subsets and could be found in many different types of packaging with an unprecedented number of inserts sets to spice up each offering.

		NM/M
	Complete Set (720):	10.00
	Common Player:	.05
	Series 1 or 2 Pack (15):	.50
	Series 1 or 2 Box (36):	12.50
1	Steve Avery	.05
2	Sid Bream	.05
3	Ron Gant	.05
4	Tom Glavine	.25
5	Brian Hunter	.05
6	Ryan Klesko	.05
7	Charlie Leibrandt	.05
8	Kent Mercker	.05
9	David Nied	.05
10	Otis Nixon	.05
11	Greg Olson	.05
12	Terry Pendleton	.05
13	Deion Sanders	.10
14	John Smoltz	.05
15	Mike Stanton	.05
16	Mark Wohlers	.05
17	Paul Assenmacher	.05
18	Steve Buechele	.05
19	Shawon Dunston	.05
20	Mark Grace	.05
21	Derrick May	.05
22	Chuck McElroy	.05
23	Mike Morgan	.05
24	Rey Sanchez	.05
25	Ryne Sandberg	.60
26	Bob Scanlan	.05
27	Sammy Sosa	.05
28	Rick Wilkins	.05
29	Bobby Ayala RC	.05
30	Tim Belcher	.05
31	Jeff Branson RC	.05
32	Norm Charlton	.05
33	Steve Foster RC	.05
34	Willie Greene RC	.05
35	Chris Hammond	.05
36	Milt Hill RC	.05
37	Hal Morris	.05
38	Joe Oliver	.05
39	Paul O'Neill	.05
40	Tim Pugh RC	.05
41	Jose Rijo	.05
42	Bip Roberts	.05
43	Chris Sabo	.05
44	Reggie Sanders	.05
45	Eric Anthony	.05
46	Jeff Bagwell	.50
47	Craig Biggio	.05
48	Joe Boever	.05
49	Casey Candaele	.05
50	Steve Finley	.05
51	Luis Gonzalez	.05
52	Pete Harnisch	.05
53	Xavier Hernandez	.05
54	Doug Jones	.05
55	Eddie Taubensee	.05
56	Brian Williams	.05
57	Pedro Astacio RC	.10
58	Todd Benzinger	.05
59	Brett Butler	.05
60	Tom Candiotti	.05
61	Lenny Harris	.05
62	Carlos Hernandez	.05
63	Orel Hershiser	.05
64	Eric Karros	.05
65	Ramon Martinez	.05
66	Jose Offerman	.05
67	Mike Scioscia	.05
68	Mike Sharperson	.05
69	Eric Young RC	.10
70	Moises Alou	.05
71	Ivan Calderon	.05
72	Archi Cianfrocco RC	.05
73	Wil Cordero	.05
74	Delino DeShields	.05
75	Mark Gardner	.05
76	Ken Hill	.05
77	Tim Laker RC	.05
78	Chris Nabholz	.05
79	Mel Rojas	.05
80	John Vander Wal RC	.10
81	Larry Walker	.05
82	Tim Wallach	.05
83	John Wetteland	.05
84	Bobby Bonilla	.05
85	Daryl Boston	.05
86	Sid Fernandez	.05
87	Eric Hillman RC	.05
88	Todd Hundley	.05
89	Howard Johnson	.05
90	Jeff Kent	.05
91	Eddie Murray	.50
92	Bill Pecota	.05
93	Bret Saberhagen	.05
94	Dick Schofield	.05
95	Pete Schourek	.05
96	Anthony Young	.05
97	Ruben Amaro Jr.	.05
98	Juan Bell	.05
99	Wes Chamberlain	.05
100	Darren Daulton	.05
101	Mariano Duncan	.05
102	Mike Hartley	.05
103	Ricky Jordan	.05
104	John Kruk	.05
105	Mickey Morandini	.05
106	Terry Mulholland	.05
107	Ben Rivera RC	.05
108	Curt Schilling	.25
109	Keith Shepherd RC	.05
110	Stan Belinda	.05
111	Jay Bell	.05
112	Barry Bonds	1.00
113	Jeff King	.05
114	Mike LaValliere	.05
115	Jose Lind	.05
116	Roger Mason	.05
117	Orlando Merced	.05
118	Bob Patterson	.05
119	Don Slaught	.05
120	Zane Smith	.05
121	Randy Tomlin	.05
122	Andy Van Slyke	.05
123	Tim Wakefield RC	.10
124	Rheal Cormier	.05
125	Bernard Gilkey	.05
126	Felix Jose	.05
127	Ray Lankford	.05
128	Bob McClure	.05
129	Donovan Osborne	.05
130	Tom Pagnozzi	.05
131	Geronimo Pena	.05
132	Mike Perez	.05
133	Lee Smith	.05
134	Bob Tewksbury	.05
135	Todd Worrell	.05
136	Todd Zeile	.05
137	Jerald Clark	.05
138	Tony Gwynn	.60
139	Greg Harris	.05
140	Jeremy Hernandez	.05
141	Darrin Jackson	.05
142	Mike Maddux	.05
143	Fred McGriff	.05
144	Jose Melendez	.05
145	Rich Rodriguez	.05
146	Frank Seminara	.05
147	Gary Sheffield	.35
148	Kurt Stillwell	.05
149	Dan Walters RC	.05
150	Rod Beck	.05
151	Bud Black	.05
152	Jeff Brantley	.05
153	John Burkett	.05
154	Will Clark	.05
155	Royce Clayton	.05
156	Mike Jackson	.05
157	Darren Lewis	.05
158	Kirt Manwaring	.05
159	Willie McGee	.05
160	Cory Snyder	.05
161	Bill Swift	.05
162	Trevor Wilson	.05
163	Brady Anderson	.05
164	Glenn Davis	.05
165	Mike Devereaux	.05
166	Todd Frohwirth	.05
167	Leo Gomez	.05
168	Chris Hoiles	.05
169	Ben McDonald	.05
170	Randy Milligan	.05
171	Alan Mills	.05
172	Mike Mussina	.30
173	Gregg Olson	.05
174	Arthur Rhodes	.05
175	David Segui	.05
176	Ellis Burks	.05
177	Roger Clemens	.65
178	Scott Cooper	.05
179	Danny Darwin	.05
180	Tony Fossas	.05
181	Paul Quantrill RC	.10
182	Jody Reed	.05
183	John Valentin RC	.10
184	Mo Vaughn	.05
185	Frank Viola	.05
186	Bob Zupcic	.05
187	Jim Abbott	.05
188	Gary DiSarcina	.05
189	Damion Easley RC	.10
190	Junior Felix	.05
191	Chuck Finley	.05
192	Joe Grahe	.05
193	Bryan Harvey	.05
194	Mark Langston	.05
195	John Orton	.05
196	Luis Polonia	.05
197	Tim Salmon	.05
198	Luis Sojo	.05
199	Wilson Alvarez	.05
200	George Bell	.05
201	Alex Fernandez	.05
202	Craig Grebeck	.05
203	Ozzie Guillen	.05
204	Lance Johnson	.05
205	Ron Karkovice	.05
206	Kirk McCaskill	.05
207	Jack McDowell	.05
208	Scott Radinsky	.05
209	Tim Raines	.05
210	Frank Thomas	.50
211	Robin Ventura	.05
212	Sandy Alomar Jr.	.05
213	Carlos Baerga	.05
214	Dennis Cook	.05
215	Thomas Howard	.05
216	Mark Lewis	.05
217	Derek Lilliquist	.05
218	Kenny Lofton	.05
219	Charles Nagy	.05
220	Steve Olin	.05
221	Paul Sorrento	.05
222	Jim Thome	.40
223	Mark Whiten	.05
224	Milt Cuyler	.05
225	Rob Deer	.05
226	John Doherty RC	.05
227	Cecil Fielder	.05
228	Travis Fryman	.05
229	Mike Henneman	.05
230	John Kiely RC	.05
231	Kurt Knudsen RC	.05
232	Scott Livingstone	.05
233	Tony Phillips	.05
234	Mickey Tettleton	.05
235	Kevin Appier	.05
236	George Brett	.65
237	Tom Gordon	.05
238	Gregg Jefferies	.05
239	Wally Joyner	.05
240	Kevin Koslofski RC	.05
241	Mike Macfarlane	.05
242	Brian McRae	.05
243	Rusty Meacham	.05
244	Keith Miller	.05
245	Jeff Montgomery	.05
246	Hipolito Pichardo RC	.05
247	Ricky Bones	.05
248	Cal Eldred	.05
249	Mike Fetters	.05
250	Darryl Hamilton	.05
251	Doug Henry	.05
252	John Jaha	.05
253	Pat Listach	.05
254	Paul Molitor	.50
255	Jaime Navarro	.05
256	Kevin Seitzer	.05
257	B.J. Surhoff	.05
258	Greg Vaughn	.05
259	Bill Wegman	.05
260	Robin Yount	.50
261	Rick Aguilera	.05
262	Chili Davis	.05
263	Scott Erickson	.05
264	Greg Gagne	.05
265	Mark Guthrie	.05
266	Brian Harper	.05
267	Kent Hrbek	.05
268	Terry Jorgensen	.05
269	Gene Larkin	.05
270	Scott Leius	.05
271	Pat Mahomes	.05
272	Pedro Munoz	.05
273	Kirby Puckett	.60
274	Kevin Tapani	.05
275	Carl Willis	.05
276	Steve Farr	.05
277	John Habyan	.05
278	Mel Hall	.05
279	Charlie Hayes	.05
280	Pat Kelly	.05
281	Don Mattingly	.65
282	Sam Militello	.05
283	Matt Nokes	.05
284	Melido Perez	.05
285	Andy Stankiewicz	.05
286	Danny Tartabull	.05
287	Randy Velarde	.05
288	Bob Wickman	.05
289	Bernie Williams	.05
290	Lance Blankenship	.05
291	Mike Bordick	.05
292	Jerry Browne	.05
293	Dennis Eckersley	.40
294	Rickey Henderson	.50
295	Vince Horsman RC	.05
296	Mark McGwire	.85
297	Jeff Parrett	.05
298	Ruben Sierra	.05
299	Terry Steinbach	.05
300	Walt Weiss	.05
301	Bob Welch	.05
302	Willie Wilson	.05
303	Bobby Witt	.05
304	Bret Boone	.05
305	Jay Buhner	.05
306	Dave Fleming	.05
307	Ken Griffey Jr.	.75
308	Erik Hanson	.05
309	Edgar Martinez	.05
310	Tino Martinez	.05
311	Jeff Nelson	.05
312	Dennis Powell	.05
313	Mike Schooler	.05
314	Russ Swan	.05
315	Dave Valle	.05
316	Omar Vizquel	.05
317	Kevin Brown	.05
318	Todd Burns	.05
319	Jose Canseco	.35
320	Julio Franco	.05
321	Jeff Frye	.05
322	Juan Gonzalez	.30
323	Jose Guzman	.05
324	Jeff Huson	.05
325	Dean Palmer	.05
326	Kevin Reimer	.05
327	Ivan Rodriguez	.40
328	Kenny Rogers	.05
329	Dan Smith RC	.05
330	Roberto Alomar	.20
331	Derek Bell	.05
332	Pat Borders	.05
333	Joe Carter	.05
334	Kelly Gruber	.05
335	Tom Henke	.05
336	Jimmy Key	.05
337	Manuel Lee	.05
338	Candy Maldonado	.05
339	John Olerud	.05
340	Todd Stottlemyre	.05
341	Duane Ward	.05
342	Devon White	.05
343	Dave Winfield	.50
344	Edgar Martinez (League Leaders)	.05
345	Cecil Fielder (League Leaders)	.35
346	Kenny Lofton (League Leaders)	.05
347	Jack Morris (League Leaders)	.05
348	Roger Clemens (League Leaders)	.35
349	Fred McGriff (Round Trippers)	.05
350	Barry Bonds (Round Trippers)	.60
351	Gary Sheffield (Round Trippers)	.05
352	Darren Daulton (Round Trippers)	.05
353	Dave Hollins (Round Trippers)	.05
354	Brothers In Blue (Pedro Martinez, Ramon Martinez)	.25
355	Power Packs (Ivan Rodriguez, Kirby Puckett)	.25
356	Triple Threats (Ryne Sandberg, Gary Sheffield)	.20
357	Infield Trifecta (Roberto Alomar, Chuck Knoblauch, Carlos Baerga)	.05
358	Checklist	.05
359	Checklist	.05
360	Checklist	.05
361	Rafael Belliard	.05
362	Damon Berryhill	.05
363	Mike Bielecki	.05
364	Jeff Blauser	.05
365	Francisco Cabrera	.05
366	Marvin Freeman	.05
367	Dave Justice	.05
368	Mark Lemke	.05
369	Alejandro Pena	.05
370	Jeff Reardon	.05
371	Lonnie Smith	.05
372	Pete Smith	.05
373	Shawn Boskie	.05
374	Jim Bullinger	.05
375	Frank Castillo	.05
376	Doug Dascenzo	.05
377	Andre Dawson	.25
378	Mike Harkey	.05
379	Greg Hibbard	.05
380	Greg Maddux	.60
381	Ken Patterson	.05
382	Jeff Robinson	.05
383	Luis Salazar	.05
384	Dwight Smith	.05
385	Jose Vizcaino	.05
386	Scott Bankhead	.05
387	Tom Browning	.05
388	Darnell Coles	.05
389	Rob Dibble	.05
390	Bill Doran	.05
391	Dwayne Henry	.05
392	Cesar Hernandez	.05
393	Roberto Kelly	.05
394	Barry Larkin	.05
395	Dave Martinez	.05
396	Kevin Mitchell	.05
397	Jeff Reed	.05
398	Scott Ruskin	.05
399	Greg Swindell	.05
400	Dan Wilson	.05
401	Andy Ashby	.05
402	Freddie Benavides	.05
403	Dante Bichette	.05
404	Willie Blair	.05
405	Denis Boucher	.05
406	Vinny Castilla	.05
407	Braulio Castillo	.05
408	Alex Cole	.05
409	Andres Galarraga	.05
410	Joe Girardi	.05
411	Butch Henry	.05
412	Darren Holmes	.05
413	Calvin Jones	.05
414	Steve Reed RC	.05
415	Kevin Ritz	.05
416	Jim Tatum RC	.05
417	Jack Armstrong	.05
418	Bret Barberie	.05
419	Ryan Bowen	.05
420	Cris Carpenter	.05
421	Chuck Carr	.05
422	Scott Chiamparino	.05
423	Jeff Conine	.05
424	Jim Corsi	.05
425	Steve Decker	.05
426	Chris Donnels	.05
427	Monty Fariss	.05
428	Bob Natal	.05
429	Pat Rapp RC	.05
430	Dave Weathers	.05
431	Nigel Wilson RC	.05
432	Ken Caminiti	.05
433	Andujar Cedeno	.05
434	Tom Edens	.05
435	Juan Guerrero	.05
436	Pete Incaviglia	.05
437	Jimmy Jones	.05
438	Darryl Kile	.05
439	Rob Murphy	.05
440	Al Osuna	.05
441	Mark Portugal	.05
442	Scott Servais	.05
443	John Candelaria	.05
444	Tim Crews	.05
445	Eric Davis	.05
446	Tom Goodwin	.05
447	Jim Gott	.05
448	Kevin Gross	.05
449	Dave Hansen	.05
450	Jay Howell	.05
451	Roger McDowell	.05
452	Bob Ojeda	.05
453	Henry Rodriguez	.05
454	Darryl Strawberry	.05
455	Mitch Webster	.05
456	Steve Wilson	.05
457	Brian Barnes	.05
458	Sean Berry	.05
459	Jeff Fassero	.05
460	Darrin Fletcher	.05
461	Marquis Grissom	.05
462	Dennis Martinez	.05
463	Spike Owen	.05
464	Matt Stairs	.05
465	Sergio Valdez	.05
466	Kevin Bass	.05
467	Vince Coleman	.05
468	Mark Dewey	.05
469	Kevin Elster	.05
470	Tony Fernandez	.05
471	John Franco	.05
472	Dave Gallagher	.05
473	Paul Gibson	.05
474	Dwight Gooden	.05
475	Lee Guetterman	.05
476	Jeff Innis	.05
477	Dave Magadan	.05
478	Charlie O'Brien	.05
479	Willie Randolph	.05
480	Mackey Sasser	.05
481	Ryan Thompson	.05
482	Chico Walker	.05
483	Kyle Abbott	.05
484	Bob Ayrault	.05
485	Kim Batiste	.05
486	Cliff Brantley	.05
487	Jose DeLeon	.05
488	Len Dykstra	.05
489	Tommy Greene	.05
490	Jeff Grotewold	.05
491	Dave Hollins	.05
492	Danny Jackson	.05
493	Stan Javier	.05
494	Tom Marsh	.05
495	Greg Matthews	.05
496	Dale Murphy	.15
497	Todd Pratt RC	.05
498	Mitch Williams	.05
499	Danny Cox	.05
500	Doug Drabek	.05
501	Carlos Garcia	.05
502	Lloyd McClendon	.05
503	Denny Neagle	.05
504	Gary Redus	.05
505	Bob Walk	.05
506	John Wehner	.05
507	Luis Alicea	.05
508	Mark Clark	.05
509	Pedro Guerrero	.05
510	Rex Hudler	.05
511	Brian Jordan	.05
512	Omar Olivares	.05
513	Jose Oquendo	.05
514	Gerald Perry	.05
515	Bryn Smith	.05
516	Craig Wilson	.05
517	Tracy Woodson	.05
518	Larry Anderson	.05
519	Andy Benes	.05
520	Jim Deshaies	.05
521	Bruce Hurst	.05
522	Randy Myers	.05
523	Benito Santiago	.05
524	Tim Scott	.05
525	Tim Teufel	.05
526	Mike Benjamin	.05
527	Dave Burba	.05
528	Craig Colbert	.05
529	Mike Felder	.05
530	Bryan Hickerson	.05
531	Chris James	.05
532	Mark Leonard	.05
533	Greg Litton	.05
534	Francisco Oliveras	.05
535	John Patterson	.05
536	Jim Pena	.05
537	Dave Righetti	.05
538	Robby Thompson	.05
539	Jose Uribe	.05
540	Matt Williams	.05
541	Storm Davis	.05
542	Sam Horn	.05
543	Tim Hulett	.05
544	Craig Lefferts	.05
545	Chito Martinez	.05
546	Mark McLemore	.05

547	Luis Mercedes	.05
548	Bob Milacki	.05
549	Joe Orsulak	.05
550	Billy Ripken	.05
551	Cal Ripken, Jr.	1.00
552	Rick Sutcliffe	.05
553	Jeff Tackett	.05
554	Wade Boggs	.60
555	Tom Brunansky	.05
556	Jack Clark	.05
557	John Dopson	.05
558	Mike Gardiner	.05
559	Mike Greenwell	.05
560	Greg Harris	.05
561	Billy Hatcher	.05
562	Joe Hesketh	.05
563	Tony Pena	.05
564	Phil Plantier	.05
565	Luis Rivera	.05
566	Herm Winningham	.05
567	Matt Young	.05
568	Bert Blyleven	.05
569	Mike Butcher	.05
570	Chuck Crim	.05
571	Chad Curtis RC	.15
572	Tim Fortugno	.05
573	Steve Frey	.05
574	Gary Gaetti	.05
575	Scott Lewis	.05
576	Lee Stevens	.05
577	Ron Tingley	.05
578	Julio Valera	.05
579	Shawn Abner	.05
580	Joey Cora	.05
581	Chris Cron	.05
582	Carlton Fisk	.50
583	Roberto Hernandez	.05
584	Charlie Hough	.05
585	Terry Leach	.05
586	Donn Pall	.05
587	Dan Pasqua	.05
588	Steve Sax	.05
589	Bobby Thigpen	.05
590	Albert Belle	.05
591	Felix Fermin	.05
592	Glenallen Hill	.05
593	Brook Jacoby	.05
594	Reggie Jefferson	.05
595	Carlos Martinez	.05
596	Jose Mesa	.05
597	Rod Nichols	.05
598	Junior Ortiz	.05
599	Eric Plunk	.05
600	Ted Power	.05
601	Scott Scudder	.05
602	Kevin Wickander	.05
603	Skeeter Barnes	.05
604	Mark Carreon	.05
605	Dan Gladden	.05
606	Bill Gullickson	.05
607	Chad Kreuter	.05
608	Mark Leiter	.05
609	Mike Munoz	.05
610	Rich Rowland	.05
611	Frank Tanana	.05
612	Walt Terrell	.05
613	Alan Trammell	.05
614	Lou Whitaker	.05
615	Luis Aquino	.05
616	Mike Boddicker	.05
617	Jim Eisenreich	.05
618	Mark Gubicza	.05
619	David Howard	.05
620	Mike Magnante	.05
621	Brent Mayne	.05
622	Kevin McReynolds	.05
623	Eddie Pierce RC	.05
624	Bill Sampen	.05
625	Steve Shifflett	.05
626	Gary Thurman	.05
627	Curtis Wikerson	.05
628	Chris Bosio	.05
629	Scott Fletcher	.05
630	Jim Gantner	.05
631	Dave Nilsson	.05
632	Jesse Orosco	.05
633	Dan Plesac	.05
634	Ron Robinson	.05
635	Bill Spiers	.05
636	Franklin Stubbs	.05
637	Willie Banks	.05
638	Randy Bush	.05
639	Chuck Knoblauch	.05
640	Shane Mack	.05
641	Mike Pagliarulo	.05
642	Jeff Reboulet	.05
643	John Smiley	.05
644	Mike Trombley RC	.05
645	Gary Wayne	.05
646	Lenny Webster	.05
647	Tim Burke	.05
648	Mike Gallego	.05
649	Dion James	.05
650	Jeff Johnson	.05
651	Scott Kamieniecki	.05
652	Kevin Maas	.05
653	Rich Monteleone	.05
654	Jerry Nielsen	.05
655	Scott Sanderson	.05
656	Mike Stanley	.05
657	Gerald Williams	.05
658	Curt Young	.05
659	Harold Baines	.05
660	Kevin Campbell	.05
661	Ron Darling	.05
662	Kelly Downs	.05
663	Eric Fox	.05
664	Dave Henderson	.05
665	Rick Honeycutt	.05
666	Mike Moore	.05
667	Jamie Quirk	.05
668	Jeff Russell	.05
669	Dave Stewart	.05
670	Greg Briley	.05
671	Dave Cochrane	.05
672	Henry Cotto	.05
673	Rich DeLucia	.05
674	Brian Fisher	.05
675	Mark Grant	.05
676	Randy Johnson	.50
677	Tim Leary	.05
678	Pete O'Brien	.05
679	Lance Parrish	.05
680	Harold Reynolds	.05
681	Shane Turner	.05
682	Jack Daugherty	.05
683	David Hulse RC	.05
684	Terry Mathews	.05
685	Al Newman	.05
686	Edwin Nunez	.05
687	Rafael Palmeiro	.40
688	Roger Pavlik	.05
689	Geno Petralli	.05
690	Nolan Ryan	1.00
691	David Cone	.05
692	Alfredo Griffin	.05
693	Juan Guzman	.05
694	Pat Hentgen	.05
695	Randy Knorr	.05
696	Bob MacDonald	.05
697	Jack Morris	.05
698	Ed Sprague	.05
699	Dave Stieb	.05
700	Pat Tabler	.05
701	Mike Timlin	.05
702	David Wells	.05
703	Eddie Zosky	.05
704	Gary Sheffield (League Leaders)	.05
705	Darren Daulton (League Leaders)	.05
706	Marquis Grissom (League Leaders)	.05
707	Greg Maddux (League Leaders)	.10
708	Bill Swift (League Leaders)	.05
709	Juan Gonzalez (Round Trippers)	.15
710	Mark McGwire (Round Trippers)	.50
711	Cecil Fielder (Round Trippers)	.05
712	Albert Belle (Round Trippers)	.05
713	Joe Carter (Round Trippers)	.05
714	Power Brokers (Frank Thomas, Cecil Fielder)	.10
715	Unsung Heroes (Larry Walker, Darren Daulton)	.05
716	Hot Corner Hammers (Edgar Martinez, Robin Ventura)	.05
717	Start to Finish (Roger Clemens, Dennis Eckersley)	.25
718	Checklist	.05
719	Checklist	.05
720	Checklist	.05

All-Stars

Horizontal-format All-Star cards comprised one of the many 1993 Fleer insert issues. Twelve cards of National League All-Stars were included in Series I wax packs, while a dozen American League All-Stars were found in Series II packs. They are among the more popular and valuable of the '93 Fleer inserts.

		NM/M
Complete Set A.L. (12):		6.00
Complete Set N.L. (12):		3.75
Common Player:		.15
	AMERICAN LEAGUE	
1	Frank Thomas	.85
2	Roberto Alomar	.40
3	Edgar Martinez	.15
4	Pat Listach	.15
5	Cecil Fielder	.15
6	Juan Gonzalez	.40
7	Ken Griffey Jr.	2.00
8	Joe Carter	.15
9	Kirby Puckett	1.00
10	Brian Harper	.15
11	Dave Fleming	.15
12	Jack McDowell	.15
	NATIONAL LEAGUE	
1	Fred McGriff	.15
2	Delino DeShields	.15
3	Gary Sheffield	.40
4	Barry Larkin	.15
5	Felix Jose	.15
6	Larry Walker	.15
7	Barry Bonds	2.50
8	Andy Van Slyke	.15
9	Darren Daulton	.15
10	Greg Maddux	.75
11	Tom Glavine	.25
12	Lee Smith	.15

Tom Glavine Career Highlights

This 15-card insert set spotlighted career highlights of Fleer's 1993 spokesman, Tom Glavine. Twelve cards were available in Series 1 and Series 2 packs; cards #13-15 could be obtained only via a special mail offer. A limited number of certified autograph cards were also inserted into packs. Cards #1-4 and 7-10 can each be found with two variations of the writeups on the back. The versions found in Series 2 packaging are the "correct" backs. Neither version carries a premium value.

	NM/M
Complete Set (15):	5.00
Common Card:	.50
Autographed Card:	30.00
1-15 Tom Glavine	.50

Golden Moments

Three cards of this insert set were available in both series of wax packs. Fronts feature black borders with gold-foil baseballs in the corners. The player's name appears in a "Golden Moments" banner at the bottom of the photo. Backs have a portrait photo of the player at top-center and a information on the highlight. The cards are unnumbered and are checklisted here alphabetically within series.

		NM/M
Complete Set (6):		4.00
Common Player:		.25
	SERIES 1	2.00
(1)	George Brett	1.50
(2)	Mickey Morandini	.25
(3)	Dave Winfield	.50
	SERIES 2	2.00
(1)	Dennis Eckersley	.40
(2)	Bip Roberts	.25
(3)	Frank Thomas, Juan Gonzalez	1.50

Major League Prospects

Yet another way to package currently hot rookies and future prospects to increase sales of

the base product, there were 18 insert cards found in each series' wax packs. Fronts are bordered in black and have gold-foil highlights. Most of the depicted players were a few seasons away from everyday play in the major leagues.

		NM/M
Complete Set (36):		7.50
Common Player:		.15
	SERIES 1	5.00
1	Melvin Nieves	.15
2	Sterling Hitchcock	.15
3	Tim Costo	.15
4	Manny Alexander	.15
5	Alan Embree	.15
6	Kevin Young	.15
7	J.T. Snow	.15
8	Russ Springer	.15
9	Billy Ashley	.15
10	Kevin Rogers	.15
11	Steve Hosey	.15
12	Eric Wedge	.15
13	Mike Piazza	3.50
14	Jesse Levis	.15
15	Rico Brogna	.15
16	Alex Arias	.15
17	Rod Brewer	.15
18	Troy Neel	.15
	SERIES 2	2.50
1	Scooter Tucker	.15
2	Kerry Woodson	.15
3	Greg Colbrunn	.15
4	Pedro Martinez	1.50
5	Dave Silvestri	.15
6	Kent Bottenfield	.15
7	Rafael Bournigal	.15
8	J.T. Bruett	.15
9	Dave Mlicki	.15
10	Paul Wagner	.15
11	Mike Williams	.15
12	Henry Mercedes	.15
13	Scott Taylor	.15
14	Dennis Moeller	.15
15	Javier Lopez	.15
16	Steve Cooke	.15
17	Pete Young	.15
18	Ken Ryan	.15

ProVisions

This three-card insert set in Series I wax packs features the baseball art of Wayne Still. Black-bordered fronts feature a player-fantasy painting at center, with the player's name gold-foil stamped beneath. Backs are also bordered in black and have a white box with a career summary.

		NM/M
Complete Set (6):		3.00
Common Player:		.40
	SERIES 1	2.00
1	Roberto Alomar	.65
2	Dennis Eckersley	1.00
3	Gary Sheffield	.75
	SERIES 2	
1	Andy Van Slyke	.40
2	Tom Glavine	.75
3	Cecil Fielder	.40

Rookie Sensations

Ten rookie sensations - some of whom had not been true rookies for several seasons - were featured in this insert issue packaged exclusively in Series 1 and Series 2 cello packs. Card fronts have a player photo set against a silver background and surrounded by a blue border. The player's name and other front printing are in gold foil. Backs are also printed in silver with a blue border. There is a player portrait photo and career summary.

		NM/M
Complete Set (20):		6.25
Common Player:		.25
	SERIES 1	3.00
1	Kenny Lofton	.50
2	Cal Eldred	.25
3	Pat Listach	.25
4	Roberto Hernandez	.25
5	Dave Fleming	.25
6	Eric Karros	.25
7	Reggie Sanders	.25
8	Derrick May	.25
9	Mike Perez	.25
10	Donovan Osborne	.25
	SERIES 2	2.00
1	Moises Alou	.50
2	Pedro Astacio	.25
3	Jim Austin	.25
4	Chad Curtis	.25
5	Gary DiSarcina	.25
6	Scott Livingstone	.25
7	Sam Militello	.25
8	Arthur Rhodes	.25
9	Tim Wakefield	.35
10	Bob Zupcic	.25

Team Leaders

This 20-card insert issue was exclusive to Series 1 and 2 rack packs. Fronts have a portrait photo, with a small action photo superimposed. At the side is a colored bar with the player's name and "Team Leaders" printed vertically. On back is a career summary. Card borders are a light metallic green and both sides of the card are UV coated.

		NM/M
Complete Set (20):		12.50
Common Player:		.40
	SERIES 1	10.00
1	Kirby Puckett	1.25
2	Mark McGwire	3.00
3	Pat Listach	.40
4	Roger Clemens	1.50
5	Frank Thomas	1.00
6	Carlos Baerga	.40
7	Brady Anderson	.40
8	Juan Gonzalez	.50
9	Roberto Alomar	.40
10	Ken Griffey Jr.	2.00
	SERIES 2	4.00
1	Will Clark	.40
2	Terry Pendleton	.40
3	Ray Lankford	.40
4	Eric Karros	.40
5	Gary Sheffield	.75
6	Ryne Sandberg	1.25
7	Marquis Grissom	.40
8	John Kruk	.40
9	Jeff Bagwell	1.00
10	Andy Van Slyke	.40

Final Edition

This 310-card set was sold as a complete set in its own box. Card numbers have the prefix "F." The set also includes 10 Diamond Tribute cards, which are numbered DT1-DT10.

		NM/M
Complete Set (310):		7.50
Common Player:		.05
1	Steve Bedrosian	.05
2	Jay Howell	.05
3	Greg Maddux	.65
4	Greg McMichael RC	.05
5	Tony Tarasco RC	.05
6	Jose Bautista	.05
7	Jose Guzman	.05
8	Greg Hibbard	.05
9	Candy Maldonado	.05
10	Randy Myers	.05
11	Matt Walbeck RC	.05
12	Turk Wendell	.05
13	Willie Nelson	.05
14	Greg Cadaret	.05
15	Roberto Kelly	.05
16	Randy Milligan	.05
17	Kevin Mitchell	.05
18	Jeff Reardon	.05
19	John Roper	.05
20	John Smiley	.05
21	Andy Ashby	.05
22	Dante Bichette	.05
23	Willie Blair	.05
24	Pedro Castellano	.05
25	Vinny Castilla	.05
26	Jerald Clark	.05
27	Alex Cole	.05
28	Scott Fredrickson RC	.05
29	Jay Gainer RC	.05
30	Andres Galarraga	.05
31	Joe Girardi	.05
32	Ryan Hawblitzel	.05
33	Charlie Hayes	.05
34	Darren Holmes	.05
35	Chris Jones	.05
36	David Nied	.05
37	J. Owens RC	.05
38	Lance Painter RC	.05
39	Jeff Parrett	.05
40	Steve Reed RC	.05
41	Armando Reynoso	.05
42	Bruce Ruffin	.05
43	Danny Sheaffer RC	.05
44	Keith Shepherd	.05
45	Jim Tatum	.05
46	Gary Wayne	.05
47	Eric Young	.05
48	Luis Aquino	.05
49	Alex Arias	.05
50	Jack Armstrong	.05
51	Bret Barberie	.05
52	Geronimo Berroa	.05
53	Ryan Bowen	.05
54	Greg Briley	.05
55	Chris Carpenter	.05
56	Chuck Carr	.05
57	Jeff Conine	.05
58	Jim Corsi	.05
59	Orestes Destrade	.05
60	Junior Felix	.05
61	Chris Hammond	.05
62	Bryan Harvey	.05
63	Charlie Hough	.05
64	Joe Klink	.05
65	Richie Lewis RC	.05
66	Mitch Lyden RC	.05
67	Bob Natal	.05
68	Scott Pose RC	.05
69	Rich Renteria	.05
70	Benito Santiago	.05
71	Gary Sheffield	.15
72	Matt Turner RC	.05
73	Walt Weiss	.05
74	Darrell Whitmore RC	.05
75	Nigel Wilson	.05
76	Kevin Bass	.05

77	Doug Drabek	.05
78	Tom Edens	.05
79	Chris James	.05
80	Greg Swindell	.05
81	Omar Daal RC	.05
82	Raul Mondesi	.05
83	Jody Reed	.05
84	Cory Snyder	.05
85	Rick Trlicek	.05
86	Tim Wallach	.05
87	Todd Worrell	.05
88	Tavo Alvarez	.05
89	Frank Bolick	.05
90	Kent Bottenfield	.05
91	Greg Colbrunn	.05
92	Cliff Floyd	.05
93	Lou Frazier RC	.05
94	Mike Gardiner	.05
95	Mike Lansing RC	.25
96	Bill Risley	.05
97	Jeff Shaw	.05
98	Kevin Baez	.05
99	Tim Bogar RC	.05
100	Jeromy Burnitz	.05
101	Mike Draper	.05
102	Darrin Jackson	.05
103	Mike Maddux	.05
104	Joe Orsulak	.05
105	Doug Saunders	.05
106	Frank Tanana	.05
107	Dave Telgheder	.05
108	Larry Anderson	.05
109	Jim Eisenreich	.05
110	Pete Incaviglia	.05
111	Danny Jackson	.05
112	David West	.05
113	Al Martin	.05
114	Blas Minor	.05
115	Dennis Moeller	.05
116	Will Pennyfeather	.05
117	Rich Robertson	.05
118	Ben Shelton	.05
119	Lonnie Smith	.05
120	Freddie Toliver	.05
121	Paul Wagner	.05
122	Kevin Young	.05
123	Rene Arocha RC	.05
124	Gregg Jefferies	.05
125	Paul Kilgus	.05
126	Les Lancaster	.05
127	Joe Magrane	.05
128	Rob Murphy	.05
129	Erik Pappas	.05
130	Stan Royer	.05
131	Ozzie Smith	.65
132	Tom Urbani	.05
133	Mark Whiten	.05
134	Derek Bell	.05
135	Doug Brocail	.05
136	Phil Clark	.05
137	Mark Ettles RC	.05
138	Jeff Gardner	.05
139	Pat Gomez RC	.05
140	Ricky Gutierrez	.05
141	Gene Harris	.05
142	Kevin Higgins RC	.05
143	Trevor Hoffman	.05
144	Phil Plantier	.05
145	Kerry Taylor RC	.05
146	Guillermo Velasquez	.05
147	Wally Whitehurst	.05
148	Tim Worrell RC	.05
149	Todd Benzinger	.05
150	Barry Bonds	2.00
151	Greg Brummett	.05
152	Mark Carreon	.05
153	Dave Martinez	.05
154	Jeff Reed	.05
155	Kevin Rogers	.05
156	Harold Baines	.05
157	Damon Buford	.05
158	Paul Carey RC	.05
159	Jeffrey Hammonds	.05
160	Jamie Moyer	.05
161	Sherman Obando RC	.05
162	John O'Donoghue RC	.05
163	Brad Pennington	.05
164	Jim Poole	.05
165	Harold Reynolds	.05
166	Fernando Valenzuela	.05
167	Jack Voight RC	.05
168	Mark Williamson	.05
169	Scott Bankhead	.05
170	Greg Blosser	.05
171	Jim Byrd RC	.05
172	Ivan Calderon	.05
173	Andre Dawson	.25
174	Scott Fletcher	.05
175	Jose Melendez	.05
176	Carlos Quintana	.05
177	Jeff Russell	.05
178	Aaron Sele	.05
179	Rod Correia RC	.05
180	Chili Davis	.05
181	Jim Edmonds RC	3.00
182	Rene Gonzales	.05
183	Hilly Hathaway RC	.05
184	Torey Lovullo	.05
185	Greg Myers	.05
186	Gene Nelson	.05
187	Troy Percival RC	.05
188	Scott Sanderson	.05
189	Darryl Scott RC	.05
190	J.T. Snow RC	.50
191	Russ Springer	.05
192	Jason Bere	.05
193	Rodney Bolton	.05
194	Ellis Burks	.05
195	Bo Jackson	.15
196	Mike LaValliere	.05
197	Scott Ruffcorn	.05
198	Jeff Schwartz RC	.05
199	Jerry DiPoto	.05
200	Alvaro Espinoza	.05
201	Wayne Kirby	.05
202	Tom Kramer RC	.05
203	Jesse Levis	.05
204	Manny Ramirez	.50
205	Jeff Treadway	.05
206	Bill Wertz RC	.05
207	Cliff Young	.05
208	Matt Young	.05
209	Kirk Gibson	.05
210	Greg Gohr	.05
211	Bill Krueger	.05
212	Bob MacDonald	.05
213	Mike Moore	.05
214	David Wells	.05
215	Billy Brewer RC	.05
216	David Cone	.05
217	Greg Gagne	.05
218	Mark Gardner	.05
219	Chis Haney	.05
220	Phil Hiatt	.05
221	Jose Lind	.05
222	Juan Bell	.05
223	Tom Brunansky	.05
224	Mike Ignasiak	.05
225	Joe Kmak	.05
226	Tom Lampkin	.05
227	Graeme Lloyd RC	.05
228	Carlos Maldonado	.05
229	Matt Mieske	.05
230	Angel Miranda	.05
231	Troy O'Leary RC	.10
232	Kevin Reimer	.05
233	Larry Casian	.05
234	Jim Deshaies	.05
235	Eddie Guardado RC	.10
236	Chip Hale	.05
237	Mike Maksudian RC	.05
238	David McCarty	.05
239	Pat Meares RC	.05
240	George Tsamis RC	.05
241	Dave Winfield	.50
242	Jim Abbott	.05
243	Wade Boggs	.65
244	Andy Cook RC	.05
245	Russ Davis RC	.10
246	Mike Humphreys	.05
247	Jimmy Key	.05
248	Jim Leyritz	.05
249	Bobby Munoz	.05
250	Paul O'Neill	.05
251	Spike Owen	.05
252	Dave Silvestri	.05
253	Marcos Armas RC	.05
254	Brent Gates	.05
255	Goose Gossage	.25
256	Scott Lydy RC	.05
257	Henry Mercedes	.05
258	Mike Mohler RC	.05
259	Troy Neel	.05
260	Edwin Nunez	.05
261	Craig Paquette	.05
262	Kevin Seitzer	.05
263	Rich Amaral	.05
264	Mike Blowers	.05
265	Chris Bosio	.05
266	Norm Charlton	.05
267	Jim Converse RC	.05
268	John Cummings RC	.05
269	Mike Felder	.05
270	Mike Hampton	.05
271	Bill Haselman	.05
272	Dwayne Henry	.05
273	Greg Litton	.05
274	Mackey Sasser	.05
275	Lee Tinsley	.05
276	David Wainhouse	.05
277	Jeff Bronkey RC	.05
278	Benji Gil	.05
279	Tom Henke	.05
280	Charlie Leibrandt	.05
281	Robb Nen	.05
282	Bill Ripken	.05
283	Jon Shave RC	.05
284	Doug Strange	.05
285	Matt Whiteside RC	.05
286	Scott Brow RC	.05
287	Willie Canate RC	.05
288	Tony Castillo	.05
289	Domingo Cedeno RC	.05
290	Darnell Coles	.05
291	Danny Cox	.05
292	Mark Eichhorn	.05
293	Tony Fernandez	.05
294	Al Leiter	.05
295	Paul Molitor	.50
296	Dave Stewart	.05
297	Woody Williams RC	.05
298	Checklist	.05
299	Checklist	.05
300	Checklist	.05
1DT	Wade Boggs	.65
2DT	George Brett	.75
3DT	Andre Dawson	.25
4DT	Carlton Fisk	.50
5DT	Paul Molitor	.50
6DT	Nolan Ryan	2.00
7DT	Lee Smith	.05
8DT	Ozzie Smith	.65
9DT	Dave Winfield	.50
10DT	Robin Yount	.50

Atlantic

The Atlantic Collectors Edition set of 1993 features 24 of the top players in the game (plus one checklist) portrayed in a style matching the regular-issue Fleer set, with the addition of the Atlantic logo and a gold border. The cards were given away five at a time with gasoline purchases at gas stations in New York and Pennsylvania during the summer.

		NM/M
Complete Set (25):		3.50
Common Player:		.12
1	Roberto Alomar	.20
2	Barry Bonds	1.00
3	Bobby Bonilla	.10
4	Will Clark	.10
5	Roger Clemens	.60
6	Darren Daulton	.10
7	Dennis Eckersley	.30
8	Cecil Fielder	.10
9	Tom Glavine	.25
10	Juan Gonzalez	.25
11	Ken Griffey Jr.	.75
12	John Kruk	.10
13	Greg Maddux	.60
14	Don Mattingly	.60
15	Fred McGriff	.10
16	Mark McGwire	.85
17	Terry Pendleton	.10
18	Kirby Puckett	.50
19	Cal Ripken Jr.	1.00
20	Nolan Ryan	1.00
21	Ryne Sandberg	.50
22	Gary Sheffield	.25
23	Frank Thomas	.40
24	Andy Van Slyke	.10
25	Checklist	.05

Fruit of the Loom

Fruit of the Loom and Fleer combined to create a 66-card baseball set in 1993 that featured many of the top players in the game. The cards, with the same design as the regular-issue Fleer cards, also display the Fruit of the Loom logo in the upper-left corner. Three cards were inserted in specially marked packages of the company's products.

		NM/M
Complete Set (66):		30.00
Common Player:		.25
1	Roberto Alomar	.45
2	Brady Anderson	.25
3	Jeff Bagwell	1.00
4	Albert Belle	.25
5	Craig Biggio	.25
6	Barry Bonds	3.00
7	George Brett	1.75
8	Brett Butler	.25
9	Jose Canseco	.65
10	Joe Carter	.25
11	Will Clark	.25
12	Roger Clemens	1.75
13	Darren Daulton	.25
14	Andre Dawson	.40
15	Delino DeShields	.25
16	Rob Dibble	.25
17	Doug Drabek	.25
18	Dennis Eckersley	.85
19	Cecil Fielder	.25
20	Travis Fryman	.25
21	Tom Glavine	.45
22	Juan Gonzalez	.50
23	Dwight Gooden	.25
24	Mark Grace	.25
25	Ken Griffey Jr.	2.00
26	Marquis Grissom	.25
27	Juan Guzman	.25
28	Tony Gwynn	1.50
29	Rickey Henderson	1.00
30	David Justice	.25
31	Eric Karros	.25
32	Chuck Knoblauch	.25
33	John Kruk	.25
34	Ray Lankford	.25
35	Barry Larkin	.25
36	Pat Listach	.25
37	Kenny Lofton	.25
38	Shane Mack	.25
39	Greg Maddux	1.50
40	Dennis Martinez	.25
41	Edgar Martinez	.25
42	Ramon Martinez	.25
43	Don Mattingly	1.75
44	Jack McDowell	.25
45	Fred McGriff	.25
46	Mark McGwire	2.50
47	Jeff Montgomery	.25
48	Eddie Murray	1.00
49	Charles Nagy	.25
50	Tom Pagnozzi	.25
51	Terry Pendleton	.25
52	Kirby Puckett	1.50
53	Jose Rijo	.25
54	Cal Ripken, Jr.	3.00
55	Nolan Ryan	3.00
56	Ryne Sandberg	1.50
57	Gary Sheffield	.65
58	Bill Swift	.25
59	Danny Tartabull	.25
60	Mickey Tettleton	.25
61	Frank Thomas	1.00
62	Andy Van Slyke	.25
63	Robin Ventura	.25
64	Larry Walker	.25
65	Robin Yount	1.00
66	Checklist	.05

1994 Fleer "Highlights" Promo Sheet

To introduce its special insert card series honoring 1993 A.L. Rookie of the Year Tim Salmon and Phillies stars John Kruk and Darren Daulton, Fleer issued this 5" x 7" promo sheet. The three player cards on the sheet are similar to the issued versions except they have black overprinting on front and back which reads, "PROMOTIONAL SAMPLE." The non-player segment of the sheet has details about the inserts and special mail-in offers for additional cards.

	NM/M
Sheet:	6.00

1994 Fleer

Fleer's 720-card 1994 set, released in one series, includes another 204 insert cards to be pursued by collectors. Every pack includes one of the cards, randomly inserted from among the 12 insert sets. Regular cards have action photos on front, with a team logo in one of the lower corners. The player's name and position is stamped in gold foil around the logo. On back, another color player photo is overprinted with color boxes, data and stats, leaving a clear image of the player's face, 1-1/2" x 1-3/4" in size. Cards are UV coated on both sides.

		NM/M
Complete Set (720):		12.50
Common Player:		.05
Pack (15):		.50
Wax Box (36):		12.50
1	Brady Anderson	.05
2	Harold Baines	.05
3	Mike Devereaux	.05
4	Todd Frohwirth	.05
5	Jeffrey Hammonds	.05
6	Chris Hoiles	.05
7	Tim Hulett	.05
8	Ben McDonald	.05
9	Mark McLemore	.05
10	Alan Mills	.05
11	Jamie Moyer	.05
12	Mike Mussina	.40
13	Gregg Olson	.05
14	Mike Pagliarulo	.05
15	Brad Pennington	.05
16	Jim Poole	.05
17	Harold Reynolds	.05
18	Arthur Rhodes	.05
19	Cal Ripken, Jr.	2.00
20	David Segui	.05
21	Rick Sutcliffe	.05
22	Fernando Valenzuela	.05
23	Jack Voigt	.05
24	Mark Williamson	.05
25	Scott Bankhead	.05
26	Roger Clemens	1.00
27	Scott Cooper	.05
28	Danny Darwin	.05
29	Andre Dawson	.25
30	Rob Deer	.05
31	John Dopson	.05
32	Scott Fletcher	.05
33	Mike Greenwell	.05
34	Greg Harris	.05
35	Billy Hatcher	.05
36	Bob Melvin	.05
37	Tony Pena	.05
38	Paul Quantrill	.05
39	Carlos Quintana	.05
40	Ernest Riles	.05
41	Jeff Russell	.05
42	Ken Ryan	.05
43	Aaron Sele	.05
44	John Valentin	.05
45	Mo Vaughn	.05
46	Frank Viola	.05
47	Bob Zupcic	.05
48	Mike Butcher	.05
49	Rod Correia	.05
50	Chad Curtis	.05
51	Chili Davis	.05
52	Gary DiSarcina	.05
53	Damion Easley	.05
54	Jim Edmonds	.05
55	Chuck Finley	.05
56	Steve Frey	.05
57	Rene Gonzales	.05
58	Joe Grahe	.05
59	Hilly Hathaway	.05
60	Stan Javier	.05
61	Mark Langston	.05
62	Phil Leftwich	.05
63	Torey Lovullo	.05
64	Joe Magrane	.05
65	Greg Myers	.05
66	Ken Patterson	.05
67	Eduardo Perez	.05
68	Luis Polonia	.05
69	Tim Salmon	.20
69a	Tim Salmon/OPS	2.00
70	J.T. Snow	.05
71	Ron Tingley	.05
72	Julio Valera	.05
73	Wilson Alvarez	.05
74	Tim Belcher	.05
75	George Bell	.05
76	Jason Bere	.05
77	Rod Bolton	.05
78	Ellis Burks	.05
79	Joey Cora	.05
80	Alex Fernandez	.05
81	Craig Grebeck	.05
82	Ozzie Guillen	.05
83	Roberto Hernandez	.05
84	Bo Jackson	.10
85	Lance Johnson	.05
86	Ron Karkovice	.05
87	Mike LaValliere	.05
88	Kirk McCaskill	.05
89	Jack McDowell	.05
90	Warren Newson	.05
91	Dan Pasqua	.05
92	Scott Radinsky	.05
93	Tim Raines	.05
94	Steve Sax	.05
95	Jeff Schwarz	.05
96	Frank Thomas	.75
97	Robin Ventura	.05
98	Sandy Alomar, Jr.	.05
99	Carlos Baerga	.05
100	Albert Belle	.05
101	Mark Clark	.05
102	Jerry DiPoto	.05
103	Alvaro Espinoza	.05
104	Felix Fermin	.05
105	Jeremy Hernandez	.05
106	Reggie Jefferson	.05
107	Wayne Kirby	.05
108	Tom Kramer	.05
109	Mark Lewis	.05
110	Derek Lilliquist	.05
111	Kenny Lofton	.05
112	Candy Maldonado	.05
113	Jose Mesa	.05
114	Jeff Mutis	.05
115	Charles Nagy	.05
116	Bob Ojeda	.05
117	Junior Ortiz	.05
118	Eric Plunk	.05
119	Manny Ramirez	.75
120	Paul Sorrento	.05
121	Jim Thome	.60
122	Jeff Treadway	.05
123	Bill Wertz	.05
124	Skeeter Barnes	.05
125	Milt Cuyler	.05
126	Eric Davis	.05
127	John Doherty	.05
128	Cecil Fielder	.05
129	Travis Fryman	.05
130	Kirk Gibson	.05
131	Dan Gladden	.05
132	Greg Gohr	.05
133	Chris Gomez	.05
134	Bill Gullickson	.05
135	Mike Henneman	.05
136	Kurt Knudsen	.05
137	Chad Kreuter	.05
138	Bill Krueger	.05
139	Scott Livingstone	.05
140	Bob MacDonald	.05
141	Mike Moore	.05
142	Tony Phillips	.05
143	Mickey Tettleton	.05
144	Alan Trammell	.05
145	David Wells	.05
146	Lou Whitaker	.05
147	Kevin Appier	.05
148	Stan Belinda	.05
149	George Brett	1.00
150	Billy Brewer	.05
151	Hubie Brooks	.05
152	David Cone	.05
153	Gary Gaetti	.05
154	Greg Gagne	.05
155	Tom Gordon	.05
156	Mark Gubicza	.05
157	Chris Gwynn	.05
158	John Habyan	.05
159	Chris Haney	.05
160	Phil Hiatt	.05
161	Felix Jose	.05
162	Wally Joyner	.05
163	Jose Lind	.05
164	Mike Macfarlane	.05
165	Mike Magnante	.05
166	Brent Mayne	.05
167	Brian McRae	.05
168	Kevin McReynolds	.05
169	Keith Miller	.05
170	Jeff Montgomery	.05
171	Hipolito Pichardo	.05
172	Rico Rossy	.05
173	Juan Bell	.05
174	Ricky Bones	.05
175	Cal Eldred	.05
176	Mike Fetters	.05
177	Darryl Hamilton	.05
178	Doug Henry	.05
179	Mike Ignasiak	.05
180	John Jaha	.05
181	Pat Listach	.05
182	Graeme Lloyd	.05
183	Matt Mieske	.05
184	Angel Miranda	.05
185	Jaime Navarro	.05
186	Dave Nilsson	.05
187	Troy O'Leary	.05
188	Jesse Orosco	.05
189	Kevin Reimer	.05
190	Kevin Seitzer	.05
191	Bill Spiers	.05
192	B.J. Surhoff	.05
193	Dickie Thon	.05
194	Jose Valentin	.05
195	Greg Vaughn	.05
196	Bill Wegman	.05
197	Robin Yount	.75
198	Rick Aguilera	.05
199	Willie Banks	.05
200	Bernardo Brito	.05
201	Larry Casian	.05
202	Scott Erickson	.05
203	Eddie Guardado	.05
204	Mark Guthrie	.05

No	Player	Price
205	Chip Hale	.05
206	Brian Harper	.05
207	Mike Hartley	.05
208	Kent Hrbek	.05
209	Terry Jorgensen	.05
210	Chuck Knoblauch	.05
211	Gene Larkin	.05
212	Shane Mack	.05
213	David McCarty	.05
214	Pat Meares	.05
215	Pedro Munoz	.05
216	Derek Parks	.05
217	Kirby Puckett	.85
218	Jeff Reboulet	.05
219	Kevin Tapani	.05
220	Mike Trombley	.05
221	George Tsamis	.05
222	Carl Willis	.05
223	Dave Winfield	.75
224	Jim Abbott	.05
225	Paul Assenmacher	.05
226	Wade Boggs	.85
227	Russ Davis	.05
228	Steve Farr	.05
229	Mike Gallego	.05
230	Paul Gibson	.05
231	Steve Howe	.05
232	Dion James	.05
233	Domingo Jean	.05
234	Scott Kamieniecki	.05
235	Pat Kelly	.05
236	Jimmy Key	.05
237	Jim Leyritz	.05
238	Kevin Maas	.05
239	Don Mattingly	1.00
240	Rich Monteleone	.05
241	Bobby Munoz	.05
242	Matt Nokes	.05
243	Paul O'Neill	.05
244	Spike Owen	.05
245	Melido Perez	.05
246	Lee Smith	.05
247	Mike Stanley	.05
248	Danny Tartabull	.05
249	Randy Velarde	.05
250	Bob Wickman	.05
251	Bernie Williams	.20
252	Mike Aldrete	.05
253	Marcos Armas	.05
254	Lance Blankenship	.05
255	Mike Bordick	.05
256	Scott Brosius	.05
257	Jerry Browne	.05
258	Ron Darling	.05
259	Kelly Downs	.05
260	Dennis Eckersley	.60
261	Brent Gates	.05
262	Goose Gossage	.05
263	Scott Hemond	.05
264	Dave Henderson	.05
265	Rick Honeycutt	.05
266	Vince Horsman	.05
267	Scott Lydy	.05
268	Mark McGwire	1.50
269	Mike Mohler	.05
270	Troy Neel	.05
271	Edwin Nunez	.05
272	Craig Paquette	.05
273	Ruben Sierra	.05
274	Terry Steinbach	.05
275	Todd Van Poppel	.05
276	Bob Welch	.05
277	Bobby Witt	.05
278	Rich Amaral	.05
279	Mike Blowers	.05
280	Bret Boone	.05
281	Chris Bosio	.05
282	Jay Buhner	.05
283	Norm Charlton	.05
284	Mike Felder	.05
285	Dave Fleming	.05
286	Ken Griffey Jr.	1.25
287	Erik Hanson	.05
288	Bill Haselman	.05
289	Brad Holman RC	.05
290	Randy Johnson	.75
291	Tim Leary	.05
292	Greg Litton	.05
293	Dave Magadan	.05
294	Edgar Martinez	.05
295	Tino Martinez	.05
296	Jeff Nelson	.05
297	Erik Plantenberg RC	.05
298	Mackey Sasser	.05
299	Brian Turang RC	.05
300	Dave Valle	.05
301	Omar Vizquel	.05
302	Brian Bohanon	.05
303	Kevin Brown	.05
304	Jose Canseco	.40
305	Mario Diaz	.05
306	Julio Franco	.05
307	Juan Gonzalez	.75
308	Tom Henke	.05
309	David Hulse	.05
310	Manuel Lee	.05
311	Craig Lefferts	.05
312	Charlie Leibrandt	.05
313	Rafael Palmeiro	.75
314	Dean Palmer	.05
315	Roger Pavlik	.05
316	Dan Peltier	.05
317	Geno Petralli	.05
318	Gary Redus	.05
319	Ivan Rodriguez	.65
320	Kenny Rogers	.05
321	Nolan Ryan	2.00
322	Doug Strange	.05
323	Matt Whiteside	.05
324	Roberto Alomar	.30
325	Pat Borders	.05
326	Joe Carter	.05
327	Tony Castillo	.05
328	Darnell Coles	.05
329	Danny Cox	.05
330	Mark Eichhorn	.05
331	Tony Fernandez	.05
332	Alfredo Griffin	.05
333	Juan Guzman	.05
334	Rickey Henderson	.75
335	Pat Hentgen	.05
336	Randy Knorr	.05
337	Al Leiter	.05
338	Paul Molitor	.75
339	Jack Morris	.05
340	John Olerud	.05
341	Dick Schofield	.05
342	Ed Sprague	.05
343	Dave Stewart	.05
344	Todd Stottlemyre	.05
345	Mike Timlin	.05
346	Duane Ward	.05
347	Turner Ward	.05
348	Devon White	.05
349	Woody Williams	.05
350	Steve Avery	.05
351	Steve Bedrosian	.05
352	Rafael Belliard	.05
353	Damon Berryhill	.05
354	Jeff Blauser	.05
355	Sid Bream	.05
356	Francisco Cabrera	.05
357	Marvin Freeman	.05
358	Ron Gant	.05
359	Tom Glavine	.25
360	Jay Howell	.05
361	Dave Justice	.05
362	Ryan Klesko	.05
363	Mark Lemke	.05
364	Javier Lopez	.05
365	Greg Maddux	.85
366	Fred McGriff	.05
367	Greg McMichael	.05
368	Kent Mercker	.05
369	Otis Nixon	.05
370	Greg Olson	.05
371	Bill Pecota	.05
372	Terry Pendleton	.05
373	Deion Sanders	.05
374	Pete Smith	.05
375	John Smoltz	.05
376	Mike Stanton	.05
377	Tony Tarasco	.05
378	Mark Wohlers	.05
379	Jose Bautista	.05
380	Shawn Boskie	.05
381	Steve Buechele	.05
382	Frank Castillo	.05
383	Mark Grace	.10
384	Jose Guzman	.05
385	Mike Harkey	.05
386	Greg Hibbard	.05
387	Glenallen Hill	.05
388	Steve Lake	.05
389	Derrick May	.05
390	Chuck McElroy	.05
391	Mike Morgan	.05
392	Randy Myers	.05
393	Dan Plesac	.05
394	Kevin Roberson	.05
395	Rey Sanchez	.05
396	Ryne Sandberg	.85
397	Bob Scanlan	.05
398	Dwight Smith	.05
399	Sammy Sosa	1.25
400	Jose Vizcaino	.05
401	Rick Wilkins	.05
402	Willie Wilson	.05
403	Eric Yelding	.05
404	Bobby Ayala	.05
405	Jeff Branson	.05
406	Tom Browning	.05
407	Jacob Brumfield	.05
408	Tim Costo	.05
409	Rob Dibble	.05
410	Willie Greene	.05
411	Thomas Howard	.05
412	Roberto Kelly	.05
413	Bill Landrum	.05
414	Barry Larkin	.05
415	Larry Luebbers RC	.05
416	Kevin Mitchell	.05
417	Hal Morris	.05
418	Joe Oliver	.05
419	Tim Pugh	.05
420	Jeff Reardon	.05
421	Jose Rijo	.05
422	Bip Roberts	.05
423	John Roper	.05
424	Johnny Ruffin	.05
425	Chris Sabo	.05
426	Juan Samuel	.05
427	Reggie Sanders	.05
428	Scott Service	.05
429	John Smiley	.05
430	Jerry Spradlin RC	.05
431	Kevin Wickander	.05
432	Freddie Benavides	.05
433	Dante Bichette	.05
434	Willie Blair	.05
435	Daryl Boston	.05
436	Kent Bottenfield	.05
437	Vinny Castilla	.05
438	Jerald Clark	.05
439	Alex Cole	.05
440	Andres Galarraga	.05
441	Joe Girardi	.05
442	Greg Harris	.05
443	Charlie Hayes	.05
444	Darren Holmes	.05
445	Chris Jones	.05
446	Roberto Mejia	.05
447	David Nied	.05
448	J. Owens	.05
449	Jeff Parrett	.05
450	Steve Reed	.05
451	Armando Reynoso	.05
452	Bruce Ruffin	.05
453	Mo Sanford	.05
454	Danny Sheaffer	.05
455	Jim Tatum	.05
456	Gary Wayne	.05
457	Eric Young	.05
458	Luis Aquino	.05
459	Alex Arias	.05
460	Jack Armstrong	.05
461	Bret Barberie	.05
462	Ryan Bowen	.05
463	Chuck Carr	.05
464	Jeff Conine	.05
465	Henry Cotto	.05
466	Orestes Destrade	.05
467	Chris Hammond	.05
468	Bryan Harvey	.05
469	Charlie Hough	.05
470	Joe Klink	.05
471	Richie Lewis	.05
472	Bob Natal RC	.05
473	Pat Rapp RC	.05
474	Rich Renteria RC	.10
475	Rich Rodriguez	.05
476	Benito Santiago	.05
477	Gary Sheffield	.35
478	Matt Turner	.05
479	David Weathers	.05
480	Walt Weiss	.05
481	Darrell Whitmore	.05
482	Eric Anthony	.05
483	Jeff Bagwell	.75
484	Kevin Bass	.05
485	Craig Biggio	.05
486	Ken Caminiti	.05
487	Andujar Cedeno	.05
488	Chris Donnels	.05
489	Doug Drabek	.05
490	Steve Finley	.05
491	Luis Gonzalez	.25
492	Pete Harnisch	.05
493	Xavier Hernandez	.05
494	Doug Jones	.05
495	Todd Jones	.05
496	Darryl Kile	.05
497	Al Osuna	.05
498	Mark Portugal	.05
499	Scott Servais	.05
500	Greg Swindell	.05
501	Eddie Taubensee	.05
502	Jose Uribe	.05
503	Brian Williams	.05
504	Billy Ashley	.05
505	Pedro Astacio	.05
506	Brett Butler	.05
507	Tom Candiotti	.05
508	Omar Daal	.05
509	Jim Gott	.05
510	Kevin Gross	.05
511	Dave Hansen	.05
512	Carlos Hernandez	.05
513	Orel Hershiser	.05
514	Eric Karros	.05
515	Pedro Martinez	.75
516	Ramon Martinez	.05
517	Roger McDowell	.05
518	Raul Mondesi	.05
519	Jose Offerman	.05
520	Mike Piazza	1.25
521	Jody Reed	.05
522	Henry Rodriguez	.05
523	Mike Sharperson	.05
524	Cory Snyder	.05
525	Darryl Strawberry	.05
526	Rick Trlicek	.05
527	Tim Wallach	.05
528	Mitch Webster	.05
529	Steve Wilson	.05
530	Todd Worrell	.05
531	Moises Alou	.05
532	Brian Barnes	.05
533	Sean Berry	.05
534	Greg Colbrunn	.05
535	Delino DeShields	.05
536	Jeff Fassero	.05
537	Darrin Fletcher	.05
538	Cliff Floyd	.05
539	Lou Frazier	.05
540	Marquis Grissom	.05
541	Butch Henry	.05
542	Ken Hill	.05
543	Mike Lansing	.05
544	Brian Looney RC	.05
545	Dennis Martinez	.05
546	Chris Nabholz	.05
547	Randy Ready	.05
548	Mel Rojas	.05
549	Kirk Rueter	.05
550	Tim Scott	.05
551	Jeff Shaw	.05
552	Tim Spehr	.05
553	John VanderWal	.05
554	Larry Walker	.05
555	John Wetteland	.05
556	Rondell White	.05
557	Tim Bogar	.05
558	Bobby Bonilla	.05
559	Jeromy Burnitz	.05
560	Sid Fernandez	.05
561	John Franco	.05
562	Dave Gallagher	.05
563	Dwight Gooden	.05
564	Eric Hillman	.05
565	Todd Hundley	.05
566	Jeff Innis	.05
567	Darrin Jackson	.05
568	Howard Johnson	.05
569	Bobby Jones	.05
570	Jeff Kent	.05
571	Mike Maddux	.05
572	Jeff McKnight	.05
573	Eddie Murray	.75
574	Charlie O'Brien	.05
575	Joe Orsulak	.05
576	Bret Saberhagen	.05
577	Pete Schourek	.05
578	Dave Telgheder	.05
579	Ryan Thompson	.05
580	Anthony Young	.05
581	Ruben Amaro	.05
582	Larry Andersen	.05
583	Kim Batiste	.05
584	Wes Chamberlain	.05
585	Darren Daulton	.05
586	Mariano Duncan	.05
587	Len Dykstra	.05
588	Jim Eisenreich	.05
589	Tommy Greene	.05
590	Dave Hollins	.05
591	Pete Incaviglia	.05
592	Danny Jackson	.05
593	Ricky Jordan	.05
594	John Kruk	.05
595	Roger Mason	.05
596	Mickey Morandini	.05
597	Terry Mulholland	.05
598	Todd Pratt	.05
599	Ben Rivera	.05
600	Curt Schilling	.25
601	Kevin Stocker	.05
602	Milt Thompson	.05
603	David West	.05
604	Mitch Williams	.05
605	Jay Bell	.05
606	Dave Clark	.05
607	Steve Cooke	.05
608	Tom Foley	.05
609	Carlos Garcia	.05
610	Joel Johnston	.05
611	Jeff King	.05
612	Al Martin	.05
613	Lloyd McClendon	.05
614	Orlando Merced	.05
615	Blas Minor	.05
616	Denny Neagle	.05
617	Mark Petkovsek RC	.05
618	Tom Prince	.05
619	Don Slaught	.05
620	Zane Smith	.05
621	Randy Tomlin	.05
622	Andy Van Slyke	.05
623	Paul Wagner	.05
624	Tim Wakefield	.05
625	Bob Walk	.05
626	Kevin Young	.05
627	Luis Alicea	.05
628	Rene Arocha	.05
629	Rod Brewer	.05
630	Rheal Cormier	.05
631	Bernard Gilkey	.05
632	Lee Guetterman	.05
633	Gregg Jefferies	.05
634	Brian Jordan	.05
635	Les Lancaster	.05
636	Ray Lankford	.05
637	Rob Murphy	.05
638	Omar Olivares	.05
639	Jose Oquendo	.05
640	Donovan Osborne	.05
641	Tom Pagnozzi	.05
642	Erik Pappas	.05
643	Geronimo Pena	.05
644	Mike Perez	.05
645	Gerald Perry	.05
646	Ozzie Smith	.85
647	Bob Tewksbury	.05
648	Allen Watson	.05
649	Mark Whiten	.05
650	Tracy Woodson	.05
651	Todd Zeile	.05
652	Andy Ashby	.05
653	Brad Ausmus	.05
654	Billy Bean	.05
655	Derek Bell	.05
656	Andy Benes	.05
657	Doug Brocail	.05
658	Jarvis Brown	.05
659	Archi Cianfrocco	.05
660	Phil Clark	.05
661	Mark Davis	.05
662	Jeff Gardner	.05
663	Pat Gomez	.05
664	Ricky Gutierrez	.05
665	Tony Gwynn	.85
666	Gene Harris	.05
667	Kevin Higgins	.05
668	Trevor Hoffman	.05
669	Pedro A. Martinez RC	.05
670	Tim Mauser	.05
671	Melvin Nieves	.05
672	Phil Plantier	.05
673	Frank Seminara	.05
674	Craig Shipley	.05
675	Kerry Taylor	.05
676	Tim Teufel	.05
677	Guillermo Velasquez	.05
678	Wally Whitehurst	.05
679	Tim Worrell	.05
680	Rod Beck	.05
681	Mike Benjamin	.05
682	Todd Benzinger	.05
683	Bud Black	.05
684	Barry Bonds	2.00
685	Jeff Brantley	.05
686	Dave Burba	.05
687	John Burkett	.05
688	Mark Carreon	.05
689	Will Clark	.10
690	Royce Clayton	.05
691	Bryan Hickerson	.05
692	Mike Jackson	.05
693	Darren Lewis	.05
694	Kirt Manwaring	.05
695	Dave Martinez	.05
696	Willie McGee	.05
697	John Patterson	.05
698	Jeff Reed	.05
699	Kevin Rogers	.05
700	Scott Sanderson	.05
701	Steve Scarsone	.05
702	Billy Swift	.05
703	Robby Thompson	.05
704	Matt Williams	.05
705	Trevor Wilson	.05
706	"Brave New World" (Fred McGriff, Ron Gant, Dave Justice)	.10
707	"1-2 Punch" (Paul Molitor, John Olerud)	.10
708	"American Heat" (Mike Mussina, Jack McDowell)	.10
709	"Together Again" (Lou Whitaker, Alan Trammell)	.10
710	"Lone Star Lumber" (Rafael Palmeiro, Juan Gonzalez)	.25
711	"Batmen" (Brett Butler, Tony Gwynn)	.10
712	"Twin Peaks" (Kirby Puckett, Chuck Knoblauch)	.20
713	"Back to Back" (Mike Piazza, Eric Karros)	.25
714	Checklist	.05
715	Checklist	.05
716	Checklist	.05
717	Checklist	.05
718	Checklist	.05
719	Checklist	.05
720	Checklist	.05
14	Mark Langston	.10
15	Jack McDowell	.10
16	Paul Molitor	.60
17	Jeff Montgomery	.10
18	Mike Mussina	.40
19	John Olerud	.10
20	Kirby Puckett	.75
21	Cal Ripken, Jr.	2.00
22	Ivan Rodriguez	.50
23	Frank Thomas	.65
24	Greg Vaughn	.10
25	Duane Ward	.10
26	Steve Avery	.10
27	Rod Beck	.10
28	Jay Bell	.10
29	Andy Benes	.10
30	Jeff Blauser	.10
31	Barry Bonds	2.00
32	Bobby Bonilla	.10
33	John Burkett	.10
34	Darren Daulton	.10
35	Andres Galarraga	.10
36	Tom Glavine	.30
37	Mark Grace	.25
38	Marquis Grissom	.10
39	Tony Gwynn	.75
40	Bryan Harvey	.10
41	Dave Hollins	.10
42	Dave Justice	.10
43	Darryl Kile	.10
44	John Kruk	.10
45	Barry Larkin	.10
46	Terry Mulholland	.10
47	Mike Piazza	1.50
48	Ryne Sandberg	.75
49	Gary Sheffield	.30
50	John Smoltz	.10

Award Winners

The 1993 MVP, Cy Young and Rookie of the Year award winners from each league are featured in this insert set. Cards are UV coated on both sides. Three different croppings of the same player action photo are featured on the front, with the player's name and other printing in gold foil. Backs have a player portrait and short summary of his previous season's performance. According to the company, odds of finding one of these horizontal-format inserts were one in 37 packs.

	NM/M
Complete Set (6):	4.50
Common Player:	.25
1 Frank Thomas	.75
2 Barry Bonds	2.00
3 Jack McDowell	.25
4 Greg Maddux	1.00
5 Tim Salmon	1.00
6 Mike Piazza	1.50

All-Stars

Each league's 25 representatives for the 1993 All-Star Game are featured in this insert set. Fronts have a player action photo with a rippling American flag in the top half of the background. The '93 All-Star logo is featured at the bottom, along with a gold-foil impression of the player's name. The flag motif is repeated at top of the card back, along with a player portrait photo set against a red (American League) or blue (National League) background. Odds of finding one of the 50 All-Star inserts are one in every two 15-card foil packs.

	NM/M
Complete Set (50):	10.00
Common Player:	.10
1 Roberto Alomar	.10
2 Carlos Baerga	.10
3 Albert Belle	.10
4 Wade Boggs	.75
5 Joe Carter	.10
6 Scott Cooper	.10
7 Cecil Fielder	.10
8 Travis Fryman	.10
9 Juan Gonzalez	.60
10 Ken Griffey Jr.	1.50
11 Pat Hentgen	.10
12 Randy Johnson	.60
13 Jimmy Key	.10

Golden Moments

Ten highlights from the 1993 Major League baseball season are commemorated in this insert set. Each of the cards has a title which summarizes the historical moment. These inserts were available exclusively in Fleer cards packaged for large retail outlets.

	NM/M
Complete Set (10):	5.00
Common Player:	.10
1 "Four in One" (Mark Whiten)	.10

2	"Left and Right" (Carlos Baerga)	.10
3	"3,000 Hit Club" (Dave Winfield)	.50
4	"Eight Straight" (Ken Griffey Jr.)	1.50
5	"Triumphant Return" (Bo Jackson)	.25
6	"Farewell to Baseball" (George Brett)	1.00
7	"Farewell to Baseball" (Nolan Ryan)	2.00
8	"Thirty Times Six" (Fred McGriff)	.10
9	"Enters 5th Dimension" (Frank Thomas)	.75
10	"The No-Hit Parade" (Chris Bosio, Jim Abbott, Darryl Kile)	.10

Golden Moments Super

Super-size (3-1/2" x 5") versions of the Golden Moments insert set were included in hobby cases at the rate of one set, in a specially-printed folder, per 20-box case. Each card carries a serial number designating its position in an edition of 10,000.

		NM/M
Complete Set (10):		7.50
Common Player:		.50
1	"Four in One" (Mark Whiten)	.50
2	"Left and Right" (Carlos Baerga)	.50
3	"3,000 Hit Club" (Dave Winfield)	.75
4	"Eight Straight" (Ken Griffey Jr.)	2.00
5	"Triumphant Return" (Bo Jackson)	.75
6	"Farewell to Baseball" (George Brett)	1.50
7	"Farewell to Baseball" (Nolan Ryan)	2.50
8	"Thirty Times Six" (Fred McGriff)	.50
9	"Enters 5th Dimension" (Frank Thomas)	1.00
10	"The No-Hit Parade" (Chris Bosio, Jim Abbott, Darryl Kile)	.50

League Leaders

Twelve players who led the major leagues in various statistical categories in 1993 are featured in this insert set. Cards are UV coated and have gold-foil stamping on both sides. Within a light metallic green border, card fronts feature a color action photo superimposed over a similar photo in black-and-white. The category in which the player led his league is printed down the right border. Other printing is gold-foil. On back is a color photo and details of the league-leading performance. Stated odds of finding a League Leaders card were one per 17 packs.

		NM/M
Complete Set (12):		3.00
Common Player:		.10
1	John Olerud	.10
2	Albert Belle	.10
3	Rafael Palmeiro	.75
4	Kenny Lofton	.10
5	Jack McDowell	.10
6	Kevin Appier	.10
7	Andres Galarraga	.10
8	Barry Bonds	2.00
9	Len Dykstra	.10
10	Chuck Carr	.10
11	Tom Glavine	.30
12	Greg Maddux	1.00

Lumber Co.

This insert set features the major leagues' top home run hitters. Inserted only in 21-card jumbo packs, odds of finding one were given as one per five packs. Card fronts feature player action photos against a background resembling the label area of a baseball bat. On back is a background photo of a row of bats on the dirt. A player write-up and close-up photo complete the design.

		NM/M
Complete Set (10):		7.50
Common Player:		.40
1	Albert Belle	.40
2	Barry Bonds	2.50
3	Ron Gant	.40
4	Juan Gonzalez	1.00
5	Ken Griffey Jr.	2.00
6	Dave Justice	.40
7	Fred McGriff	.40
8	Rafael Palmeiro	.75
9	Frank Thomas	1.25
10	Matt Williams	.40

Major League Prospects

Thirty-five of the game's promising young stars are featured in this insert set. A light green metallic border frames a player photo, with his team logo lightly printed over the background. Most of the printing is gold-foil stamped. Backs have a player photo against a pin-striped background. A light blue box contains career details. Given odds of finding a "Major League Prospects" card are one in six packs.

		NM/M
Complete Set (35):		4.00
Common Player:		.10
1	Kurt Abbott	.10
2	Brian Anderson	.10
3	Rich Aude	.10
4	Cory Bailey	.10
5	Danny Bautista	.10
6	Marty Cordova	.10
7	Tripp Cromer	.10
8	Midre Cummings	.10
9	Carlos Delgado	1.50
10	Steve Dreyer	.10
11	Steve Dunn	.10
12	Jeff Granger	.10
13	Tyrone Hill	.10
14	Denny Hocking	.10
15	John Hope	.10
16	Butch Huskey	.10
17	Miguel Jimenez	.10
18	Chipper Jones	2.50
19	Steve Karsay	.10
20	Mike Kelly	.10
21	Mike Lieberthal	.20
22	Albie Lopez	.10
23	Jeff McNeely	.10
24	Dan Miceli	.10
25	Nate Minchey	.10
26	Marc Newfield	.10
27	Darren Oliver	.10
28	Luis Ortiz	.10
29	Curtis Pride	.10
30	Roger Salkeld	.10
31	Scott Sanders	.10
32	Dave Staton	.10
33	Salomon Torres	.10
34	Steve Trachsel	.10
35	Chris Turner	.10

ProVisions

Nine players are featured in this insert set. Cards feature the fantasy artwork of Wayne Still in a format that produces one large image when all nine cards are properly arranged. Besides the art, card fronts feature the player's name in gold-foil. Backs have a background in several shades of red, with the player's name and team at the top in white. A short career summary is printed in black. Odds of finding this particular insert in a pack are one in 12.

		NM/M
Complete Set (9):		4.00
Common Player:		.25
1	Darren Daulton	.25
2	John Olerud	.25
3	Matt Williams	.25
4	Carlos Baerga	.25
5	Ozzie Smith	1.00
6	Juan Gonzalez	.75
7	Jack McDowell	.25
8	Mike Piazza	2.00
9	Tony Gwynn	1.00

Rookie Sensations

This insert set features the top rookies from 1993. These inserts were available only in 21-card jumbo packs, with stated odds of one in four packs. Full-bleed fronts have a pair of player photos - one highlighted by a neon outline - superimposed on a graduated background approximating the team colors. Team uniform logo details appear vertically at the right or left side. The player's name is gold-foil stamped in a banner at bottom. The Rookie Sensations and Fleer logos are also gold-imprinted. On back, the team uniform logo is repeated on a white background, along with another player photo and a short write-up.

		NM/M
Complete Set (20):		6.00
Common Player:		.25
1	Rene Arocha	.25
2	Jason Bere	.25
3	Jeromy Burnitz	.25
4	Chuck Carr	.25
5	Jeff Conine	.25
6	Steve Cooke	.25
7	Cliff Floyd	.25
8	Jeffrey Hammonds	.25
9	Wayne Kirby	.25
10	Mike Lansing	.25
11	Al Martin	.25
12	Greg McMichael	.25
13	Troy Neel	.25
14	Mike Piazza	4.00
15	Armando Reynoso	.25
16	Kirk Rueter	.25
17	Tim Salmon	1.00
18	Aaron Sele	.25
19	J.T. Snow	.25
20	Kevin Stocker	.25

Tim Salmon A.L. Rookie of the Year

The popular Angels Rookie of the Year is featured in a 15-card set produced in what Fleer terms "metallized" format. The first 12 cards in the set were inserted into foil packs at the rate of about one card per box. Three additional cards could be obtained by sending $1.50 and 10 '94 Fleer wrappers to a mail-in offer. On both front and back, the cards have a color player photo set against a metallic-image background.

		NM/M
Complete Set (15):		12.50
Common Player:		1.00
Autograph/2,000:		15.00
1	Tim Salmon	1.00
2	Tim Salmon	1.00
3	Tim Salmon	1.00
4	Tim Salmon	1.00
5	Tim Salmon	1.00
6	Tim Salmon	1.00
7	Tim Salmon	1.00
8	Tim Salmon	1.00
9	Tim Salmon	1.00
10	Tim Salmon	1.00
11	Tim Salmon	1.00
12	Tim Salmon	1.00
13	Tim Salmon	1.50
14	Tim Salmon	1.50
15	Tim Salmon	1.50

Smoke N' Heat

Among the scarcest of the '94 Fleer inserts, available at a stated rate of one per 30 packs, these feature 10 of the top strikeout pitchers in the major leagues. "Metallized" card fronts have a player photo set against an infernal background with large letters, "Smoke 'N Heat." The player's name is in gold foil at bottom.

Backs have a similar chaotic hot-red background, a player photo and career summary.

		NM/M
Complete Set (12):		10.00
Common Player:		.20
1	Roger Clemens	3.50
2	David Cone	.20
3	Juan Guzman	.20
4	Pete Harnisch	.20
5	Randy Johnson	2.00
6	Mark Langston	.20
7	Greg Maddux	2.50
8	Mike Mussina	.75
9	Jose Rijo	.20
10	Nolan Ryan	4.50
11	Curt Schilling	.75
12	John Smoltz	.25

Team Leaders

A player from each major league team has been chosen for this 28-card insert set. Fronts feature a team logo against a background of graduated team colors. Player portrait and action photos are superimposed. At bottom is the player name, team and position, all in gold foil. Backs have a team logo and player photo set against a white background, with a short write-up justifying the player's selection as a "Team Leader." Odds of finding one of these inserts were given as one in eight packs.

		NM/M
Complete Set (28):		7.50
Common Player:		.10
1	Cal Ripken, Jr.	2.00
2	Mo Vaughn	.10
3	Tim Salmon	.15
4	Frank Thomas	.50
5	Carlos Baerga	.10
6	Cecil Fielder	.10
7	Brian McRae	.10
8	Greg Vaughn	.10
9	Kirby Puckett	.65
10	Don Mattingly	.75
11	Mark McGwire	1.50
12	Ken Griffey Jr.	1.00
13	Juan Gonzalez	.50
14	Paul Molitor	.50
15	Dave Justice	.50
16	Ryne Sandberg	.65
17	Barry Larkin	.10
18	Andres Galarraga	.10
19	Gary Sheffield	.25
20	Jeff Bagwell	.50
21	Mike Piazza	1.00
22	Marquis Grissom	.10
23	Bobby Bonilla	.10
24	Len Dykstra	.10
25	Jay Bell	.10
26	Gregg Jefferies	.10
27	Tony Gwynn	.65
28	Will Clark	.15

All-Rookie Team

Sharing the format of the basic 1994 Fleer issue, this nine-card set of rookies was available only by redemption of a trade card randomly inserted into foil packs. The exchange card expired Sept. 30, 1994. The cards are numbered with an "M" prefix.

		NM/M
Complete Set (9):		3.00
Common Player:		.25
Exchange Card:		.25
1	Kurt Abbott	.25
2	Rich Becker	.25
3	Carlos Delgado	2.00
4	Jorge Fabregas	.25
5	Bob Hamelin	.25
6	John Hudek	.25
7	Tim Hyers	.25
8	Luis Lopez	.25
9	James Mouton	.25

Update

Rookies, traded players and free agents who changed teams were included in the annual update issue. In the same format as the regular-issue '94 Fleer set, cards are numbered alphabetically within team. Ten special Diamond Tribute cards included in the Update set feature baseball's proven superstars.

		NM/M
Complete Set (210):		50.00
Common Player:		.05
1	Mark Eichhorn	.05
2	Sid Fernandez	.05
3	Leo Gomez	.05
4	Mike Oquist	.05
5	Rafael Palmeiro	.60
6	Chris Sabo	.05
7	Dwight Smith	.05
8	Lee Smith	.05
9	Damon Berryhill	.05
10	Wes Chamberlain	.05
11	Gar Finnvold	.05
12	Chris Howard	.05
13	Tim Naehring	.05
14	Otis Nixon	.05
15	Brian Anderson	.05
16	Jorge Fabregas	.05
17	Rex Hudler	.05
18	Bo Jackson	.15
19	Mark Leiter	.05
20	Spike Owen	.05
21	Harold Reynolds	.05
22	Chris Turner	.05
23	Dennis Cook	.05
24	Jose DeLeon	.05
25	Julio Franco	.05
26	Joe Hall	.05
27	Darrin Jackson	.05
28	Dane Johnson	.05
29	Norberto Martin	.05
30	Scott Sanderson	.05
31	Jason Grimsley	.05
32	Dennis Martinez	.05
33	Jack Morris	.05
34	Eddie Murray	.75
35	Chad Ogea	.05
36	Tony Pena	.05
37	Paul Shuey	.05
38	Omar Vizquel	.05
39	Danny Bautista	.05

No.	Player	Price
40	Tim Belcher	.05
41	Joe Boever	.05
42	Storm Davis	.05
43	Junior Felix	.05
44	Mike Gardiner	.05
45	Buddy Groom	.05
46	Juan Samuel	.05
47	Vince Coleman	.05
48	Bob Hamelin	.05
49	Dave Henderson	.05
50	Rusty Meacham	.05
51	Terry Shumpert	.05
52	Jeff Bronkey	.05
53	Alex Diaz	.05
54	Brian Harper	.05
55	Jose Mercedes	.05
56	Jody Reed	.05
57	Bob Scanlan	.05
58	Turner Ward	.05
59	Rich Becker	.05
60	Alex Cole	.05
61	Denny Hocking	.05
62	Scott Leius	.05
63	Pat Mahomes	.05
64	Carlos Pulido	.05
65	Dave Stevens	.05
66	Matt Walbeck	.05
67	Xavier Hernandez	.05
68	Sterling Hitchcock	.05
69	Terry Mulholland	.05
70	Luis Polonia	.05
71	Gerald Williams	.05
72	Mark Acre	.05
73	Geronimo Berroa	.05
74	Rickey Henderson	.75
75	Stan Javier	.05
76	Steve Karsay	.05
77	Carlos Reyes	.05
78	Bill Taylor	.05
79	Eric Anthony	.05
80	Bobby Ayala	.05
81	Tim Davis	.05
82	Felix Fermin	.05
83	Reggie Jefferson	.05
84	Keith Mitchell	.05
85	Bill Risley	.05
86	Alex Rodriguez RC	40.00
87	Roger Salkeld	.05
88	Dan Wilson	.05
89	Cris Carpenter	.05
90	Will Clark	.10
91	Jeff Frye	.05
92	Rick Helling	.05
93	Chris James	.05
94	Oddibe McDowell	.05
95	Billy Ripken	.05
96	Carlos Delgado	.60
97	Alex Gonzalez	.05
98	Shawn Green	.50
99	Darren Hall	.05
100	Mike Huff	.05
101	Mike Kelly	.05
102	Roberto Kelly	.05
103	Charlie O'Brien	.05
104	Jose Oliva	.05
105	Gregg Olson	.05
106	Willie Banks	.05
107	Jim Bullinger	.05
108	Chuck Crim	.05
109	Shawon Dunston	.05
110	Karl Rhodes	.05
111	Steve Trachsel	.05
112	Anthony Young	.05
113	Eddie Zambrano	.05
114	Bret Boone	.05
115	Jeff Brantley	.05
116	Hector Carrasco	.05
117	Tony Fernandez	.05
118	Tim Fortugno	.05
119	Erik Hanson	.05
120	Chuck McElroy	.05
121	Deion Sanders	.05
122	Ellis Burks	.05
123	Marvin Freeman	.05
124	Mike Harkey	.05
125	Howard Johnson	.05
126	Mike Kingery	.05
127	Nelson Liriano	.05
128	Marcus Moore	.05
129	Mike Munoz	.05
130	Kevin Ritz	.05
131	Walt Weiss	.05
132	Kurt Abbott	.05
133	Jerry Browne	.05
134	Greg Colbrunn	.05
135	Jeremy Hernandez	.05
136	Dave Magadan	.05
137	Kurt Miller	.05
138	Robb Nen	.05
139	Jesus Tavarez	.05
140	Sid Bream	.05
141	Tom Edens	.05
142	Tony Eusebio	.05
143	John Hudek	.05
144	Brian Hunter	.05
145	Orlando Miller	.05
146	James Mouton	.05
147	Shane Reynolds	.05
148	Rafael Bournigal	.05
149	Delino DeShields	.05
150	Garey Ingram	.05
151	Chan Ho Park	.05
152	Wil Cordero	.05
153	Pedro Martinez	.75
154	Randy Milligan	.05
155	Lenny Webster	.05
156	Rico Brogna	.05
157	Josias Manzanillo	.05
158	Kevin McReynolds	.05
159	Mike Remlinger	.05
160	David Segui	.05
161	Pete Smith	.05
162	Kelly Stinnett	.05
163	Jose Vizcaino	.05
164	Billy Hatcher	.05
165	Doug Jones	.05
166	Mike Lieberthal	.05
167	Tony Longmire	.05
168	Bobby Munoz	.05
169	Paul Quantrill	.05
170	Heathcliff Slocumb	.05
171	Fernando Valenzuela	.05
172	Mark Dewey	.05
173	Brian Hunter	.05
174	Jon Lieber	.05
175	Ravelo Manzanillo	.05
176	Dan Miceli	.05
177	Rick White	.05
178	Bryan Eversgerd	.05
179	John Habyan	.05
180	Terry McGriff	.05
181	Vicente Palacios	.05
182	Rich Rodriguez	.05
183	Rick Sutcliffe	.05
184	Donnie Elliott	.05
185	Joey Hamilton	.05
186	Tim Hyers	.05
187	Luis Lopez	.05
188	Ray McDavid	.05
189	Bip Roberts	.05
190	Scott Sanders	.05
191	Eddie Williams	.05
192	Steve Frey	.05
193	Pat Gomez	.05
194	Rich Monteleone	.05
195	Mark Portugal	.05
196	Darryl Strawberry	.05
197	Salomon Torres	.05
198	W. Van Landingham	.05
199	Checklist	.05
200	Checklist	.05

DIAMOND TRIBUTE

No.	Player	Price
DT1	Barry Bonds	2.00
DT2	Joe Carter	.75
DT3	Will Clark	.10
DT4	Roger Clemens	1.50
DT5	Tony Gwynn	1.00
DT6	Don Mattingly	1.50
DT7	Fred McGriff	.05
DT8	Eddie Murray	.75
DT9	Kirby Puckett	1.00
DT10	Cal Ripken Jr.	2.00

Atlantic

Five-card packs of this special Fleer set were given away with an eight-gallon premium gasoline purchase at Atlantic/Sunoco stations in the Eastern U.S. between June 1 and July 31. Many of the cards suffered damaged borders from the packaging process. Cards are in the basic 1994 Fleer format, though the name and position around the team logo at top are in white on these cards, rather than gold-foil. Different front and back photos are used in this set. Backs include the gas station logos at bottom.

		NM/M
Complete Set (25):		3.00
Common Player:		.10
1	Roberto Alomar	.20
2	Carlos Baerga	.10
3	Jeff Bagwell	.40
4	Jay Bell	.10
5	Barry Bonds	1.00
6	Joe Carter	.10
7	Roger Clemens	.60
8	Darren Daulton	.10
9	Lenny Dykstra	.10
10	Cecil Fielder	.10
11	Tom Glavine	.35
12	Juan Gonzalez	.40
13	Ken Griffey Jr.	.75
14	Dave Justice	.10
15	John Kruk	.10
16	Greg Maddux	.50
17	Don Mattingly	.60
18	Jack McDowell	.10
19	John Olerud	.10
20	Mike Piazza	.75
21	Kirby Puckett	.50
22	Tim Salmon	.25
23	Frank Thomas	.40
24	Andy Van Slyke	.10
25	Checklist	.05

Extra Bases

Extra Bases was a 400-card, oversized set, plus 80 insert cards in four different subsets. The cards, 4-11/16" by 2-1/2", have a full-bleed photo on the front and back, as well as UV coating and color coding by team. As was the case in other Fleer products, Extra Bases contained an insert card in every pack. All 80 insert cards feature gold or silver foil stamping.

		NM/M
Complete Set (400):		15.00
Common Player:		.10
Wax Pack:		.45
Wax Box (36):		10.00
1	Brady Anderson	.10
2	Harold Baines	.10
3	Mike Devereaux	.10
4	Sid Fernandez	.10
5	Jeffrey Hammonds	.10
6	Chris Hoiles	.10
7	Ben McDonald	.10
8	Mark McLemore	.10
9	Mike Mussina	.40
10	Mike Oquist	.10
11	Rafael Palmeiro	.75
12	Cal Ripken, Jr.	2.50
13	Chris Sabo	.10
14	Lee Smith	.10
15	Wes Chamberlain	.10
16	Roger Clemens	1.25
17	Scott Cooper	.10
18	Danny Darwin	.10
19	Andre Dawson	.25
20	Mike Greenwell	.10
21	Tim Naehring	.10
22	Otis Nixon	.10
23	Jeff Russell	.10
24	Ken Ryan	.10
25	Aaron Sele	.10
26	John Valentin	.10
27	Mo Vaughn	.10
28	Frank Viola	.10
29	Brian Anderson RC	.15
30	Chad Curtis	.10
31	Chili Davis	.10
32	Gary DiSarcina	.10
33	Damion Easley	.10
34	Jim Edmonds	.10
35	Chuck Finley	.10
36	Bo Jackson	.15
37	Mark Langston	.10
38	Harold Reynolds	.10
39	Tim Salmon	.20
40	Wilson Alvarez	.10
41	James Baldwin	.10
42	Jason Bere	.10
43	Joey Cora	.10
44	Ray Durham RC	.50
45	Alex Fernandez	.10
46	Julio Franco	.10
47	Ozzie Guillen	.10
48	Darrin Jackson	.10
49	Lance Johnson	.10
50	Ron Karkovice	.10
51	Jack McDowell	.10
52	Tim Raines	.10
53	Frank Thomas	.75
54	Robin Ventura	.10
55	Sandy Alomar Jr.	.10
56	Carlos Baerga	.10
57	Albert Belle	.10
58	Mark Clark	.10
59	Wayne Kirby	.10
60	Kenny Lofton	.10
61	Dennis Martinez	.10
62	Jose Mesa	.10
63	Jack Morris	.10
64	Eddie Murray	.75
65	Charles Nagy	.10
66	Manny Ramirez	.75
67	Paul Shuey	.10
68	Paul Sorrento	.10
69	Jim Thome	.50
70	Omar Vizquel	.10
71	Eric Davis	.10
72	John Doherty	.10
73	Cecil Fielder	.10
74	Travis Fryman	.10
75	Kirk Gibson	.10
76	Gene Harris	.10
77	Mike Henneman	.10
78	Mike Moore	.10
79	Tony Phillips	.10
80	Mickey Tettleton	.10
81	Alan Trammell	.10
82	Lou Whitaker	.10
83	Kevin Appier	.10
84	Vince Coleman	.10
85	David Cone	.10
86	Gary Gaetti	.10
87	Greg Gagne	.10
88	Tom Gordon	.10
89	Jeff Granger	.10
90	Bob Hamelin	.10
91	Dave Henderson	.10
92	Felix Jose	.10
93	Wally Joyner	.10
94	Jose Lind	.10
95	Mike Macfarlane	.10
96	Brian McRae	.10
97	Jeff Montgomery	.10
98	Ricky Bones	.10
99	Jeff Bronkey	.10
100	Alex Diaz	.10
101	Cal Eldred	.10
102	Darryl Hamilton	.10
103	Brian Harper	.10
104	John Jaha	.10
105	Pat Listach	.10
106	Dave Nilsson	.10
107	Jody Reed	.10
108	Kevin Seitzer	.10
109	Greg Vaughn	.10
110	Turner Ward	.10
111	Wes Weger	.10
112	Bill Wegman	.10
113	Rick Aguilera	.10
114	Rich Becker	.10
115	Alex Cole	.10
116	Scott Erickson	.10
117	Kent Hrbek	.10
118	Chuck Knoblauch	.10
119	Scott Leius	.10
120	Shane Mack	.10
121	Pat Mahomes	.10
122	Pat Meares	.10
123	Kirby Puckett	1.00
124	Kevin Tapani	.10
125	Matt Walbeck	.10
126	Dave Winfield	.75
127	Jim Abbott	.10
128	Wade Boggs	1.00
129	Mike Gallego	.10
130	Xavier Hernandez	.10
131	Pat Kelly	.10
132	Jimmy Key	.10
133	Don Mattingly	1.25
134	Terry Mulholland	.10
135	Matt Nokes	.10
136	Paul O'Neill	.10
137	Melido Perez	.10
138	Luis Polonia	.10
139	Mike Stanley	.10
140	Danny Tartabull	.10
141	Randy Velarde	.10
142	Bernie Williams	.20
143	Mark Acre	.10
144	Geronimo Berroa	.10
145	Mike Bordick	.10
146	Scott Brosius	.10
147	Ron Darling	.10
148	Dennis Eckersley	.65
149	Brent Gates	.10
150	Rickey Henderson	.75
151	Stan Javier	.10
152	Steve Karsay	.10
153	Mark McGwire	2.00
154	Troy Neel	.10
155	Ruben Sierra	.10
156	Terry Steinbach	.10
157	Bill Taylor	.10
158	Rich Amaral	.10
159	Eric Anthony	.10
160	Bobby Ayala	.10
161	Chris Bosio	.10
162	Jay Buhner	.10
163	Tim Davis	.10
164	Felix Fermin	.10
165	Dave Fleming	.10
166	Ken Griffey Jr.	1.50
167	Reggie Jefferson	.10
168	Randy Johnson	.75
169	Edgar Martinez	.10
170	Tino Martinez	.10
171	Bill Risley	.10
172	Roger Salkeld	.10
173	Mac Suzuki RC	.20
174	Dan Wilson	.10
175	Kevin Brown	.10
176	Jose Canseco	.40
177	Will Clark	.15
178	Juan Gonzalez	.75
179	Rick Helling	.10
180	Tom Henke	.10
181	Chris James	.10
182	Manuel Lee	.10
183	Dean Palmer	.10
184	Ivan Rodriguez	.65
185	Kenny Rogers	.10
186	Roberto Alomar	.20
187	Pat Borders	.10
188	Joe Carter	.10
189	Carlos Delgado	.50
190	Juan Guzman	.10
191	Pat Hentgen	.10
192	Paul Molitor	.75
192a	Paul Molitor (Promotional sample.)	2.00
193	John Olerud	.10
194	Ed Sprague	.10
195	Dave Stewart	.10
196	Todd Stottlemyre	.10
197	Duane Ward	.10
198	Devon White	.10
199	Steve Avery	.10
200	Jeff Blauser	.10
201	Tom Glavine	.30
202	Dave Justice	.10
203	Mike Kelly	.10
204	Roberto Kelly	.10
205	Ryan Klesko	.10
206	Mark Lemke	.10
207	Javier Lopez	.10
208	Greg Maddux	1.00
209	Fred McGriff	.10
210	Greg McMichael	.10
211	Kent Mercker	.10
212	Terry Pendleton	.10
213	John Smoltz	.10
214	Tony Tarasco	.10
215	Willie Banks	.10
216	Steve Buechele	.10
217	Shawon Dunston	.10
218	Mark Grace	.15
219	Brooks Kieschnick RC	.10
220	Derrick May	.10
221	Randy Myers	.10
222	Karl Rhodes	.10
223	Rey Sanchez	.10
224	Sammy Sosa	1.50
225	Steve Traschel	.10
226	Rick Wilkins	.10
227	Bret Boone	.15
228	Jeff Brantley	.10
229	Tom Browning	.10
230	Hector Carrasco	.10
231	Rob Dibble	.10
232	Erik Hanson	.10
233	Barry Larkin	.10
234	Kevin Mitchell	.10
235	Hal Morris	.10
236	Joe Oliver	.10
237	Jose Rijo	.10
238	Johnny Ruffin	.10
239	Deion Sanders	.15
240	Reggie Sanders	.10
241	John Smiley	.10
242	Dante Bichette	.10
243	Ellis Burks	.10
244	Andres Galarraga	.10
245	Joe Girardi	.10
246	Greg Harris	.10
247	Charlie Hayes	.10
248	Howard Johnson	.10
249	Roberto Mejia	.10
250	Marcus Moore	.10
251	David Nied	.10
252	Armando Reynoso	.10
253	Bruce Ruffin	.10
254	Mark Thompson	.10
255	Walt Weiss	.10
256	Kurt Abbott RC	.20
257	Bret Barberie	.10
258	Chuck Carr	.10
259	Jeff Conine	.10
260	Chris Hammond	.10
261	Bryan Harvey	.10
262	Jeremy Hernandez	.10
263	Charlie Hough	.10
264	Dave Magadan	.10
265	Benito Santiago	.10
266	Gary Sheffield	.25
267	David Weathers	.10
268	Jeff Bagwell	.75
269	Craig Biggio	.10
270	Ken Caminiti	.10
271	Andujar Cedeno	.10
272	Doug Drabek	.10
273	Steve Finley	.10
274	Luis Gonzalez	.20
275	Pete Harnisch	.10
276	John Hudek	.10
277	Darryl Kile	.10
278	Orlando Miller	.10
279	James Mouton	.10
280	Shane Reynolds	.10
281	Scott Servais	.10
282	Greg Swindell	.10
283	Pedro Astacio	.10
284	Brett Butler	.10
285	Tom Candiotti	.10
286	Delino DeShields	.10
287	Kevin Gross	.10
288	Orel Hershiser	.10
289	Eric Karros	.10
290	Ramon Martinez	.10
291	Raul Mondesi	.10
292	Jose Offerman	.10
293	Chan Ho Park RC	.75
294	Mike Piazza	1.50
295	Henry Rodriguez	.10
296	Cory Snyder	.10
297	Tim Wallach	.10
298	Todd Worrell	.10
299	Moises Alou	.10
300	Sean Berry	.10
301	Wil Cordero	.10
302	Joey Eischen	.10
303	Jeff Fassero	.10
304	Darrin Fletcher	.10
305	Cliff Floyd	.10
306	Marquis Grissom	.10
307	Ken Hill	.10
308	Mike Lansing	.10
309	Pedro Martinez	.75
310	Mel Rojas	.10
311	Kirk Rueter	.10
312	Larry Walker	.10
313	John Wetteland	.10
314	Rondell White	.10
315	Bobby Bonilla	.10
316	John Franco	.10
317	Dwight Gooden	.10
318	Todd Hundley	.10
319	Bobby Jones	.10
320	Jeff Kent	.10
321	Kevin McReynolds	.10
322	Bill Pulsipher	.10
323	Bret Saberhagen	.10
324	David Segui	.10
325	Pete Smith	.10
326	Kelly Stinnett	.10
327	Ryan Thompson	.10
328	Jose Vizcaino	.10
329	Ricky Bottalico	.10
330	Darren Daulton	.10
331	Mariano Duncan	.10
332	Len Dykstra	.10
333	Tommy Greene	.10
334	Billy Hatcher	.10
335	Dave Hollins	.10
336	Pete Incaviglia	.10
337	Danny Jackson	.10
338	Doug Jones	.10
339	Ricky Jordan	.10
340	John Kruk	.10
341	Curt Schilling	.30
342	Kevin Stocker	.10
343	Jay Bell	.10
344	Steve Cooke	.10
345	Carlos Garcia	.10
346	Brian Hunter	.10
347	Jeff King	.10
348	Al Martin	.10
349	Orlando Merced	.10
350	Denny Neagle	.10
351	Don Slaught	.10
352	Andy Van Slyke	.10
353	Paul Wagner	.10
354	Rick White	.10
355	Luis Alicea	.10
356	Rene Arocha	.10
357	Rheal Cormier	.10
358	Bernard Gilkey	.10
359	Gregg Jefferies	.10
360	Ray Lankford	.10
361	Tom Pagnozzi	.10
362	Mike Perez	.10
363	Ozzie Smith	1.00
364	Bob Tewksbury	.10
365	Mark Whiten	.10
366	Todd Zeile	.10
367	Andy Ashby	.10
368	Brad Ausmus	.10
369	Derek Bell	.10
370	Andy Benes	.10
371	Archi Cianfrocco	.10
372	Tony Gwynn	1.00
373	Trevor Hoffman	.10
374	Tim Hyers	.10
375	Pedro Martinez	.10
376	Phil Plantier	.10
377	Bip Roberts	.10
378	Scott Sanders	.10
379	Dave Staton	.10
380	Wally Whitehurst	.10
381	Rod Beck	.10
382	Todd Benzinger	.10
383	Barry Bonds	2.50
384	John Burkett	.10
385	Royce Clayton	.10
386	Bryan Hickerson	.10
387	Mike Jackson	.10
388	Darren Lewis	.10
389	Kirt Manwaring	.10
390	Willie McGee	.10
391	Mark Portugal	.10
392	Bill Swift	.10
393	Robby Thompson	.10
394	Salomon Torres	.10
395	Matt Williams	.10
396	Checklist	.10
397	Checklist	.10
398	Checklist	.10
399	Checklist	.10
400	Checklist	.10

Extra Bases Game Breakers

Game Breakers featured 30 big-name stars from both leagues who have exhibited offensive firepower. This insert set was done in a horizontal format picturing the player in two different shots, one close-up and one slightly further away. The words "Game Breakers" is written across the bottom, with the player name and team in much smaller letters, printed under it.

		NM/M
	Complete Set (30):	15.00
	Common Player:	.25
1	Jeff Bagwell	.75
2	Rod Beck	.25
3	Albert Belle	.25
4	Barry Bonds	3.00
5	Jose Canseco	.65
6	Joe Carter	.25
7	Roger Clemens	1.50
8	Darren Daulton	.25
9	Len Dykstra	.25
10	Cecil Fielder	.25
11	Tom Glavine	.50
12	Juan Gonzalez	.75
13	Mark Grace	.35
14	Ken Griffey Jr.	2.00
15	Dave Justice	.25
16	Greg Maddux	1.25
17	Don Mattingly	1.50
18	Ben McDonald	.25
19	Fred McGriff	.25
20	Paul Molitor	.75
21	John Olerud	.25
22	Mike Piazza	2.00
23	Kirby Puckett	1.25
24	Cal Ripken, Jr.	3.00
25	Tim Salmon	.35
26	Gary Sheffield	.50
27	Frank Thomas	1.00
28	Mo Vaughn	.25
29	Matt Williams	.25
30	Dave Winfield	.75

Extra Bases Major League Hopefuls

MAJOR LEAGUE HOPEFUL
RAY DURHAM

Minor league standouts with impressive credentials were showcased in Major League Hopefuls. Each card in this insert set shows the player over a computer enhanced background, with three smaller photos running down the top half, on the left side of the card. The insert set title runs across the bottom and the player's name is just under it on a black strip.

		NM/M
	Complete Set (10):	2.00
	Common Player:	.25
1	James Baldwin	.25
2	Ricky Bottalico	.25
3	Ray Durham	.25
4	Joey Eischen	.25
5	Brooks Kieschnick	.25
6	Orlando Miller	.25
7	Bill Pulsipher	.25
8	Mac Suzuki	.25
9	Mark Thompson	.25
10	Wes Weger	.25

Extra Bases Rookie Standouts

Rookie Standouts highlights 20 of the best and brightest first-year players of the 1994 season. Cards picture the player on a baseball

CLIFF FLOYD

background, with a black, jagged-edged "aura" around the player. Names and teams were placed in the bottom-left corner, running up the side. The Rookie Standouts logo, which is a gold glove with a baseball in it and "Rookie Standouts" printed under it, was placed in the bottom-right corner and the Extra Bases logo appears in the upper-left.

		NM/M
	Complete Set (20):	7.50
	Common Player:	.25
1	Kurt Abbott	.25
2	Brian Anderson	.25
3	Hector Carrasco	.25
4	Tim Davis	.25
5	Carlos Delgado	2.50
6	Cliff Floyd	.25
7	Bob Hamelin	.25
8	Jeffrey Hammonds	.25
9	Rick Helling	.25
10	Steve Karsay	.25
11	Ryan Klesko	.25
12	Javier Lopez	.25
13	Raul Mondesi	.25
14	James Mouton	.25
15	Chan Ho Park	.25
16	Manny Ramirez	3.00
17	Tony Tarasco	.25
18	Steve Trachsel	.25
19	Rick White	.25
20	Rondell White	.25

Extra Bases Second Year Stars

Second-Year Stars contains 1993 rookies who were expected to have an even bigger impact in the 1994 season. Each card features five photos of the player. Four are in a filmstrip down the left side; the remaining two-thirds of the card contain a larger photo. "Second-Year Stars" is printed across the bottom, along with the player name and team. Backs repeat the film-strip motif.

		NM/M
	Complete Set (20):	5.00
	Common Player:	.25
1	Bobby Ayala	.25
2	Jason Bere	.25
3	Chuck Carr	.25
4	Jeff Conine	.25
5	Steve Cooke	.25
6	Wil Cordero	.25
7	Carlos Garcia	.25
8	Brent Gates	.25
9	Trevor Hoffman	.25
10	Wayne Kirby	.25
11	Al Martin	.25
12	Pedro Martinez	1.50
13	Greg McMichael	.25
14	Troy Neel	.25
15	David Nied	.25
16	Mike Piazza	3.00
17	Kirk Rueter	.25
18	Tim Salmon	.50
19	Aaron Sele	.25
20	Kevin Stocker	.25

Extra Bases Pitcher's Duel

Pitcher's Duel was available to collectors who mailed in 10 Extra Bases wrappers. The set features 20 of the top pitchers in baseball. Contained in the set were five American League and five National League cards, with two pitchers from the same league on each card. The front background pictures a wide-angle photo of a major league stadium, viewed from above the diamond, behind home plate. Backs have two more action photos set against a sepia-toned background photo of an Old West street to enhance the shootout theme of the set. Cards are numbered with an "M" prefix.

		NM/M
	Complete Set (10):	7.50
	Common Player:	.50
1	Roger Clemens, Jack McDowell	2.50
2	Ben McDonald, Randy Johnson	1.50
3	Jimmy Key, David Cone	.50
4	Mike Mussina, Aaron Sele	1.00
5	Chuck Finley, Wilson Alvarez	.50
6	Steve Avery, Curt Schilling	.75
7	Greg Maddux, Jose Rijo	2.00
8	Bret Saberhagen, Bob Tewksbury	.50
9	Tom Glavine, Bill Swift	.75
10	Doug Drabek, Orel Hershiser	.50

1995 Fleer Promos

This eight-player (plus a header card), cello-wrapped promo set was included in a special "Fleer" national newsstand magazine in early 1995. At first glance the cards seem identical to the regularly issued cards of the same players, but there are subtle differences on the back of each card.

		NM/M
	Complete Set (9):	4.00
	Common Player:	.50
26	Roger Clemens (1988 291 SO and 1992 2.41 ERA boxed)	2.00
78	Paul O'Neill (1991 boxed)	.50
155	David Cone (1990 233 SO boxed, white shadow on team names)	.50
235	Tim Salmon (No box on 1992 101 R.)	.50
285	Juan Gonzalez (Black stats, 1993 boxed.)	1.00
351	Marquis Grissom (No box on 1988 291 AB.)	.50
509	Ozzie Smith (Black stats, no box on 1986 Cardinals:)	1.50
514	Dante Bichette (Black stats.)	.50
--	Header Card "Different by Design"	.05

1995 Fleer

Fleer baseball in 1995 offered six different designs, one for each division. The basic set contains 600 cards and was sold in 12- and 18-card packs. National League West cards feature many smaller pictures in the background that are identical to the picture in the forefront, while AL West cards contain an action photo over top of a close-up on the right side and a water colored look on the left side. AL Central cards exhibit numbers pertinant to each player throughout the front design, with the player in the middle. NL East players appear in action on the left half of the card with a colorful, encripted look on the rest. National League Central and American League East feature more standard designs with the player in the forefront, with vital numbers and a color background.

		NM/M
	Complete Set (600):	15.00
	Common Player:	.05
	Pack (12):	.75
	Wax Box (36):	17.50
1	Brady Anderson	.05
2	Harold Baines	.05
3	Damon Buford	.05
4	Mike Devereaux	.05
5	Mark Eichhorn	.05
6	Sid Fernandez	.05
7	Leo Gomez	.05
8	Jeffrey Hammonds	.05
9	Chris Hoiles	.05
10	Rick Krivda	.05
11	Ben McDonald	.05
12	Mark McLemore	.05
13	Alan Mills	.05
14	Jamie Moyer	.05
15	Mike Mussina	.40
16	Mike Oquist	.05
17	Rafael Palmeiro	.65
18	Arthur Rhodes	.05
19	Cal Ripken, Jr.	2.50
20	Chris Sabo	.05
21	Lee Smith	.05
22	Jack Voight	.05
23	Damon Berryhill	.05
24	Tom Brunansky	.05
25	Wes Chamberlain	.05
26	Roger Clemens	1.25
27	Scott Cooper	.05
28	Andre Dawson	.25
29	Gar Finnvold	.05
30	Tony Fossas	.05
31	Mike Greenwell	.05
32	Joe Hesketh	.05
33	Chris Howard	.05
34	Chris Nabholz	.05
35	Tim Naehring	.05
36	Otis Nixon	.05
37	Carlos Rodriguez	.05
38	Rich Rowland	.05
39	Ken Ryan	.05
40	Aaron Sele	.05
41	John Valentin	.05
42	Mo Vaughn	.25
43	Frank Viola	.05
44	Danny Bautista	.05
45	Joe Boeven	.05
46	Milt Cuyler	.05
47	Storm Davis	.05
48	John Doherty	.05
49	Junior Felix	.05
50	Cecil Fielder	.05
51	Travis Fryman	.05
52	Mike Gardiner	.05
53	Kirk Gibson	.05
54	Chris Gomez	.05
55	Buddy Groom	.05
56	Mike Henneman	.05
57	Chad Kreuter	.05
58	Mike Moore	.05
59	Tony Phillips	.05
60	Juan Samuel	.05
61	Mickey Tettleton	.05
62	Alan Trammell	.05
63	David Wells	.05
64	Lou Whitaker	.05
65	Jim Abbott	.05
66	Joe Ausanio	.05
67	Wade Boggs	1.00
68	Mike Gallego	.05
69	Xavier Hernandez	.05
70	Sterling Hitchcock	.05
71	Steve Howe	.05
72	Scott Kamieniecki	.05
73	Pat Kelly	.05
74	Jimmy Key	.05
75	Jim Leyritz	.05
76	Don Mattingly	1.25
77	Terry Mulholland	.05
78	Paul O'Neill	.05
79	Melido Perez	.05
80	Luis Polonia	.05
81	Mike Stanley	.05
82	Danny Tartabull	.05
83	Randy Velarde	.05
84	Bob Wickman	.05
85	Bernie Williams	.10
86	Gerald Williams	.05
87	Roberto Alomar	.05
88	Pat Borders	.05
89	Joe Carter	.05
90	Tony Castillo	.05
91	Brad Cornett	.05
92	Carlos Delgado	.50
93	Alex Gonzalez	.05
94	Shawn Green	.40
95	Juan Guzman	.05
96	Darren Hall	.05
97	Pat Hentgen	.05
98	Mike Huff	.05
99	Randy Knorr	.05
100	Al Leiter	.05
101	Paul Molitor	.75
102	John Olerud	.05
103	Dick Schofield	.05
104	Ed Sprague	.05
105	Dave Stewart	.05
106	Todd Stottlemyre	.05
107	Devon White	.05
108	Woody Williams	.05
109	Wilson Alvarez	.05
110	Paul Assenmacher	.05
111	Jason Bere	.05
112	Dennis Cook	.05
113	Joey Cora	.05
114	Jose DeLeon	.05
115	Alex Fernandez	.05
116	Julio Franco	.05
117	Craig Graboeck	.05
118	Ozzie Guillen	.05
119	Roberto Hernandez	.05
120	Darrin Jackson	.05
121	Lance Johnson	.05
122	Ron Karkovice	.05
123	Mike LaValliere	.05
124	Norberto Martin	.05
125	Kirk McCaskill	.05
126	Jack McDowell	.05
127	Tim Raines	.05
128	Frank Thomas	.75
129	Robin Ventura	.05
130	Sandy Alomar Jr.	.05
131	Carlos Baerga	.05
132	Albert Belle	.05
133	Mark Clark	.05
134	Alvaro Espinoza	.05
135	Jason Grimsley	.05
136	Wayne Kirby	.05
137	Kenny Lofton	.05
138	Albie Lopez	.05
139	Dennis Martinez	.05
140	Jose Mesa	.05
141	Eddie Murray	.75
142	Charles Nagy	.05
143	Tony Pena	.05
144	Eric Plunk	.05
145	Manny Ramirez	.05
146	Jeff Russell	.05
147	Paul Shuey	.05
148	Paul Sorrento	.05
149	Jim Thome	.65
150	Omar Vizquel	.05
151	Dave Winfield	.75
152	Kevin Appier	.05
153	Billy Brewer	.05
154	Vince Coleman	.05
155	David Cone	.05
156	Gary Gaetti	.05
157	Greg Gagne	.05
158	Tom Gordon	.05
159	Mark Gubicza	.05
160	Bob Hamelin	.05
161	Dave Henderson	.05
162	Felix Jose	.05
163	Wally Joyner	.05
164	Jose Lind	.05
165	Mike Macfarlane	.05
166	Mike Magnante	.05
167	Brent Mayne	.05
168	Brian McRae	.05
169	Rusty Meacham	.05
170	Jeff Montgomery	.05
171	Hipolito Pichardo	.05
172	Terry Shumpert	.05
173	Michael Tucker	.05
174	Ricky Bones	.05
175	Jeff Cirillo **RC**	.30
176	Alex Diaz	.05
177	Cal Eldred	.05
178	Mike Fetters	.05
179	Darryl Hamilton	.05
180	Brian Harper	.05
181	John Jaha	.05
182	Pat Listach	.05
183	Graeme Lloyd	.05
184	Jose Mercedes	.05
185	Matt Mieske	.05
186	Dave Nilsson	.05
187	Jody Reed	.05
188	Bob Scanlan	.05
189	Kevin Seitzer	.05
190	Bill Spiers	.05
191	B.J. Surhoff	.05
192	Jose Valentin	.05
193	Greg Vaughn	.05
194	Turner Ward	.05
195	Bill Wegman	.05
196	Rick Aguilera	.05
197	Rich Becker	.05
198	Alex Cole	.05
199	Marty Cordova	.05
200	Steve Dunn	.05
201	Scott Erickson	.05
202	Mark Guthrie	.05
203	Chip Hale	.05
204	LaTroy Hawkins	.05
205	Denny Hocking	.05
206	Chuck Knoblauch	.05
207	Scott Leius	.05
208	Shane Mack	.05
209	Pat Mahomes	.05
210	Pat Meares	.05
211	Pedro Munoz	.05
212	Kirby Puckett	1.00
213	Jeff Reboulet	.05
214	Dave Stevens	.05
215	Kevin Tapani	.05
216	Matt Walbeck	.05
217	Carl Willis	.05
218	Brian Anderson	.05
219	Chad Curtis	.05
220	Chili Davis	.05
221	Gary DiSarcina	.05
222	Damion Easley	.05
223	Jim Edmonds	.05
224	Chuck Finley	.05
225	Joe Grahe	.05
226	Rex Hudler	.05
227	Bo Jackson	.10
228	Mark Langston	.05
229	Phil Leftwich	.05
230	Mark Leiter	.05
231	Spike Owen	.05
232	Bob Patterson	.05
233	Troy Percival	.05
234	Eduardo Perez	.05
235	Tim Salmon	.10
236	J.T. Snow	.05
237	Chris Turner	.05
238	Mark Acre	.05
239	Geronimo Berroa	.05
240	Mike Bordick	.05
241	John Briscoe	.05
242	Scott Brosius	.05
243	Ron Darling	.05
244	Dennis Eckersley	.65
245	Brent Gates	.05
246	Rickey Henderson	.75
247	Stan Javier	.05
248	Steve Karsay	.05
249	Mark McGwire	2.00
250	Troy Neel	.05
251	Steve Ontiveros	.05
252	Carlos Reyes	.05
253	Ruben Sierra	.05
254	Terry Steinbach	.05
255	Bill Taylor	.05
256	Todd Van Poppel	.05
257	Bobby Witt	.05
258	Rich Amaral	.05
259	Eric Anthony	.05
260	Bobby Ayala	.05
261	Mike Blowers	.05
262	Chris Bosio	.05
263	Jay Buhner	.05
264	John Cummings	.05
265	Tim Davis	.05
266	Felix Fermin	.05
267	Dave Fleming	.05
268	Goose Gossage	.05
269	Ken Griffey Jr.	1.50
270	Reggie Jefferson	.05
271	Randy Johnson	.75
272	Edgar Martinez	.05
273	Tino Martinez	.05
274	Greg Pirkl	.05
275	Bill Risley	.05
276	Roger Salkeld	.05
277	Luis Sojo	.05
278	Mac Suzuki	.05
279	Dan Wilson	.05

No.	Player	Price
280	Kevin Brown	.05
281	Jose Canseco	.40
282	Cris Carpenter	.05
283	Will Clark	.10
284	Jeff Frye	.05
285	Juan Gonzalez	.65
286	Rick Helling	.05
287	Tom Henke	.05
288	David Hulse	.05
289	Chris James	.05
290	Manuel Lee	.05
291	Oddibe McDowell	.05
292	Dean Palmer	.05
293	Roger Pavlik	.05
294	Bill Ripken	.05
295	Ivan Rodriguez	.65
296	Kenny Rogers	.05
297	Doug Strange	.05
298	Matt Whiteside	.05
299	Steve Avery	.05
300	Steve Bedrosian	.05
301	Rafael Belliard	.05
302	Jeff Blauser	.05
303	Dave Gallagher	.05
304	Tom Glavine	.30
305	Dave Justice	.05
306	Mike Kelly	.05
307	Roberto Kelly	.05
308	Ryan Klesko	.05
309	Mark Lemke	.05
310	Javier Lopez	.05
311	Greg Maddux	1.00
312	Fred McGriff	.05
313	Greg McMichael	.05
314	Kent Mercker	.05
315	Charlie O'Brien	.05
316	Jose Oliva	.05
317	Terry Pendleton	.05
318	John Smoltz	.05
319	Mike Stanton	.05
320	Tony Tarasco	.05
321	Terrell Wade	.05
322	Mark Wohlers	.05
323	Kurt Abbott	.05
324	Luis Aquino	.05
325	Bret Barberie	.05
326	Ryan Bowen	.05
327	Jerry Browne	.05
328	Chuck Carr	.05
329	Matias Carrillo	.05
330	Greg Colbrunn	.05
331	Jeff Conine	.05
332	Mark Gardner	.05
333	Chris Hammond	.05
334	Bryan Harvey	.05
335	Richie Lewis	.05
336	Dave Magadan	.05
337	Terry Mathews	.05
338	Robb Nen	.05
339	Yorkis Perez	.05
340	Pat Rapp	.05
341	Benito Santiago	.05
342	Gary Sheffield	.40
343	Dave Weathers	.05
344	Moises Alou	.05
345	Sean Berry	.05
346	Wil Cordero	.05
347	Joe Eischen	.05
348	Jeff Fassero	.05
349	Darrin Fletcher	.05
350	Cliff Floyd	.05
351	Marquis Grissom	.05
352	Butch Henry	.05
353	Gil Heredia	.05
354	Ken Hill	.05
355	Mike Lansing	.05
356	Pedro Martinez	.75
357	Mel Rojas	.05
358	Kirk Rueter	.05
359	Tim Scott	.05
360	Jeff Shaw	.05
361	Larry Walker	.05
362	Lenny Webster	.05
363	John Wetteland	.05
364	Rondell White	.05
365	Bobby Bonilla	.05
366	Rico Brogna	.05
367	Jeromy Burnitz	.05
368	John Franco	.05
369	Dwight Gooden	.05
370	Todd Hundley	.05
371	Jason Jacome	.05
372	Bobby Jones	.05
373	Jeff Kent	.05
374	Jim Lindeman	.05
375	Josias Manzanillo	.05
376	Roger Mason	.05
377	Kevin McReynolds	.05
378	Joe Orsulak	.05
379	Bill Pulsipher	.05
380	Bret Saberhagen	.05
381	David Segui	.05
382	Pete Smith	.05
383	Kelly Stinnett	.05
384	Ryan Thompson	.05
385	Jose Vizcaino	.05
386	Toby Borland	.05
387	Ricky Bottalico	.05
388	Darren Daulton	.05
389	Mariano Duncan	.05
390	Len Dykstra	.05
391	Jim Eisenreich	.05
392	Tommy Greene	.05
393	Dave Hollins	.05
394	Pete Incaviglia	.05
395	Danny Jackson	.05
396	Doug Jones	.05
397	Ricky Jordan	.05

No.	Player	Price
398	John Kruk	.05
399	Mike Lieberthal	.05
400	Tony Longmire	.05
401	Mickey Morandini	.05
402	Bobby Munoz	.05
403	Curt Schilling	.25
404	Heathcliff Slocumb	.05
405	Kevin Stocker	.05
406	Fernando Valenzuela	.05
407	David West	.05
408	Willie Banks	.05
409	Jose Bautista	.05
410	Steve Buechele	.05
411	Jim Bullinger	.05
412	Chuck Crim	.05
413	Shawon Dunston	.05
414	Kevin Foster	.05
415	Mark Grace	.10
416	Jose Hernandez	.05
417	Glenallen Hill	.05
418	Brooks Kieschnick	.05
419	Derrick May	.05
420	Randy Myers	.05
421	Dan Plesac	.05
422	Karl Rhodes	.05
423	Rey Sanchez	.05
424	Sammy Sosa	1.50
425	Steve Trachsel	.05
426	Rick Wilkins	.05
427	Anthony Young	.05
428	Eddie Zambrano	.05
429	Bret Boone	.05
430	Jeff Branson	.05
431	Jeff Brantley	.05
432	Hector Carrasco	.05
433	Brian Dorsett	.05
434	Tony Fernandez	.05
435	Tim Fortugno	.05
436	Erik Hanson	.05
437	Thomas Howard	.05
438	Kevin Jarvis	.05
439	Barry Larkin	.05
440	Chuck McElroy	.05
441	Kevin Mitchell	.05
442	Hal Morris	.05
443	Jose Rijo	.05
444	John Roper	.05
445	Johnny Ruffin	.05
446	Deion Sanders	.05
447	Reggie Sanders	.05
448	Pete Schourek	.05
449	John Smiley	.05
450	Eddie Taubensee	.05
451	Jeff Bagwell	.75
452	Kevin Bass	.05
453	Craig Biggio	.05
454	Ken Caminiti	.05
455	Andujar Cedeno	.05
456	Doug Drabek	.05
457	Tony Eusebio	.05
458	Mike Felder	.05
459	Steve Finley	.05
460	Luis Gonzalez	.10
461	Mike Hampton	.05
462	Pete Harnisch	.05
463	John Hudek	.05
464	Todd Jones	.05
465	Darryl Kile	.05
466	James Mouton	.05
467	Shane Reynolds	.05
468	Scott Servais	.05
469	Greg Swindell	.05
470	Dave Veres	.05
471	Brian Williams	.05
472	Jay Bell	.05
473	Jacob Brumfield	.05
474	Dave Clark	.05
475	Steve Cooke	.05
476	Midre Cummings	.05
477	Mark Dewey	.05
478	Tom Foley	.05
479	Carlos Garcia	.05
480	Jeff King	.05
481	Jon Lieber	.05
482	Ravelo Manzanillo	.05
483	Al Martin	.05
484	Orlando Merced	.05
485	Danny Miceli	.05
486	Denny Neagle	.05
487	Lance Parrish	.05
488	Don Slaught	.05
489	Zane Smith	.05
490	Andy Van Slyke	.05
491	Paul Wagner	.05
492	Rick White	.05
493	Luis Alicea	.05
494	Rene Arocha	.05
495	Rheal Cormier	.05
496	Bryan Eversgerd	.05
497	Bernard Gilkey	.05
498	John Habyan	.05
499	Gregg Jefferies	.05
500	Brian Jordan	.05
501	Ray Lankford	.05
502	John Mabry	.05
503	Terry McGriff	.05
504	Tom Pagnozzi	.05
505	Vicente Palacios	.05
506	Geronimo Pena	.05
507	Gerald Perry	.05
508	Rich Rodriguez	.05
509	Ozzie Smith	1.00
510	Bob Tewksbury	.05
511	Allen Watson	.05
512	Mark Whiten	.05
513	Todd Zeile	.05
514	Dante Bichette	.05
515	Willie Blair	.05

No.	Player	Price
516	Ellis Burks	.05
517	Marvin Freeman	.05
518	Andres Galarraga	.05
519	Joe Girardi	.05
520	Greg Harris	.05
521	Charlie Hayes	.05
522	Mike Kingery	.05
523	Nelson Liriano	.05
524	Mike Munoz	.05
525	David Nied	.05
526	Steve Reed	.05
527	Kevin Ritz	.05
528	Bruce Ruffin	.05
529	John Vander Wal	.05
530	Walt Weiss	.05
531	Eric Young	.05
532	Billy Ashley	.05
533	Pedro Astacio	.05
534	Rafael Bournigal	.05
535	Brett Butler	.05
536	Tom Candiotti	.05
537	Omar Daal	.05
538	Delino DeShields	.05
539	Darren Dreifort	.05
540	Kevin Gross	.05
541	Orel Hershiser	.05
542	Garey Ingram	.05
543	Eric Karros	.05
544	Ramon Martinez	.05
545	Raul Mondesi	.05
546	Chan Ho Park	.05
547	Mike Piazza	1.50
548	Henry Rodriguez	.05
549	Rudy Seanez	.05
550	Ismael Valdes	.05
551	Tim Wallach	.05
552	Todd Worrell	.05
553	Andy Ashby	.05
554	Brad Ausmus	.05
555	Derek Bell	.05
556	Andy Benes	.05
557	Phil Clark	.05
558	Donnie Elliott	.05
559	Ricky Gutierrez	.05
560	Tony Gwynn	1.00
561	Joey Hamilton	.05
562	Trevor Hoffman	.05
563	Luis Lopez	.05
564	Pedro Martinez	.05
565	Tim Mauser	.05
566	Phil Plantier	.05
567	Bip Roberts	.05
568	Scott Sanders	.05
569	Craig Shipley	.05
570	Jeff Tabaka	.05
571	Eddie Williams	.05
572	Rod Beck	.05
573	Mike Benjamin	.05
574	Barry Bonds	2.50
575	Dave Burba	.05
576	John Burkett	.05
577	Mark Carreon	.05
578	Royce Clayton	.05
579	Steve Frey	.05
580	Bryan Hickerson	.05
581	Mike Jackson	.05
582	Darren Lewis	.05
583	Kirt Manwaring	.05
584	Rich Monteleone	.05
585	John Patterson	.05
586	J.R. Phillips	.05
587	Mark Portugal	.05
588	Joe Rosselli	.05
589	Darryl Strawberry	.05
590	Bill Swift	.05
591	Robby Thompson	.05
592	William Van Landingham	.05
593	Matt Williams	.05
594	Checklist	.05
595	Checklist	.05
596	Checklist	.05
597	Checklist	.05
598	Checklist	.05
599	Checklist	.05
600	Checklist	.05

All-Stars

All-Stars are a horizontal, two-sided insert set consisting of 25 cards. A National League All-Star is on one side, while an American League All-Star is on the other, by position. All-Stars are the most common insert in Fleer 1995 baseball, with an insertion ratio of one per three packs.

		NM/M
Complete Set (25):		8.00
Common Card:		.20
1	Ivan Rodriguez, Mike Piazza	.75
2	Frank Thomas, Gregg Jefferies	.50
3	Roberto Alomar, Mariano Duncan	.40
4	Wade Boggs, Matt Williams	.65
5	Cal Ripken, Jr., Ozzie Smith	1.50
6	Joe Carter, Barry Bonds	1.50
7	Ken Griffey Jr., Tony Gwynn	.75
8	Kirby Puckett, Dave Justice	.65
9	Jimmy Key, Greg Maddux	.65
10	Chuck Knoblauch, Wil Cordero	.20
11	Scott Cooper, Ken Caminiti	.20
12	Will Clark, Carlos Garcia	.50
13	Paul Molitor, Jeff Bagwell	.50
14	Travis Fryman, Craig Biggio	.20
15	Mickey Tettleton, Fred McGriff	.20
16	Kenny Lofton, Moises Alou	.20
17	Albert Belle, Marquis Grissom	.20
18	Paul O'Neill, Dante Bichette	.20
19	David Cone, Ken Hill	.20
20	Mike Mussina, Doug Drabek	.50
21	Randy Johnson, John Hudek	.50
22	Pat Hentgen, Danny Jackson	.20
23	Wilson Alvarez, Rod Beck	.20
24	Lee Smith, Randy Myers	.20
25	Jason Bere, Doug Jones	.20

Award Winners

Fleer Award Winners contain Fleer's choices of baseball's most outstanding players. This six-card set was only inserted at a rate of one per 24 packs. Each card has an embossed gold foil design, with the gold strip running up the left side and containing the words "Fleer Award Winner" and the player name.

		NM/M
Complete Set (6):		4.00
Common Player:		.25
1	Frank Thomas	1.50
2	Jeff Bagwell	1.50
3	David Cone	.25
4	Greg Maddux	2.00
5	Bob Hamelin	.25
6	Raul Mondesi	.25

League Leaders

League Leaders feature players on a horizontal format from 10 statistical categories from both leagues. "League Leader" is placed in a blue strip down the left-side of the card, with their respective league and their name in it. These were inserted at a rate of one per 12 packs.

		NM/M
Complete Set (10):		4.00
Common Player:		.25
1	Paul O'Neill	.25
2	Ken Griffey Jr.	1.50
3	Kirby Puckett	.75
4	Jimmy Key	.25
5	Randy Johnson	.65
6	Tony Gwynn	.75
7	Matt Williams	.25
8	Jeff Bagwell	.50
9	Greg Maddux, Ken Hill	.75
10	Andy Benes	.25

Lumber Co.

Ten of the top longball hitters were featured in Lumber Co., which were inserted into every 24 12-card retail packs. They show the power hitter in action, with a wood-grain Lumber Co. logo across the bottom, contain the player's name and team.

		NM/M
Complete Set (10):		12.00
Common Player:		.40
1	Jeff Bagwell	1.50
2	Albert Belle	.40
3	Barry Bonds	3.50
4	Jose Canseco	.75
5	Joe Carter	.40
6	Ken Griffey Jr.	2.50
7	Fred McGriff	.40
8	Kevin Mitchell	.40
9	Frank Thomas	1.75
10	Matt Williams	.40

Major League Prospects

Major League Prospects showcases 10 of 1995's most promising young players. The set title is repeatedly printed across the background, with the player's name and team in a grey strip across the bottom. These cards were inserted into one every six packs.

		NM/M
Complete Set (10):		6.00
Common Player:		.25
1	Garret Anderson	.50
2	James Baldwin	.25
3	Alan Benes	.25
4	Armando Benitez	.25
5	Ray Durham	.25
6	Brian Hunter	.25
7a	Derek Jeter (No licensor logos on back.)	4.00
7b	Derek Jeter (Licensor logos on back.)	4.00
8	Charles Johnson	.25
9	Orlando Miller	.25
10	Alex Rodriguez	3.00

Pro-Visions

Pro-Visions contain six interlocking cards that form one giant picture. These original art cards exhibit the player in a fantasy art background and are inserted into every nine packs.

	NM/M
Complete Set (6):	2.00
Common Player:	.25
1 Mike Mussina	.40
2 Raul Mondesi	.25
3 Jeff Bagwell	.75
4 Greg Maddux	1.00
5 Tim Salmon	.25
6 Manny Ramirez	.75

Rookie Sensations

A perennial favorite within Fleer products, Rookie Sensations cards were inserted in 18-card packs only, at a rate of one per 16 packs. This 20-card set featured the top rookies from the 1994 season. The player's name and team run up the right side of the card, while the words "Rookie Sensations" appear in the bottom-left corner, separated by a colorful, zig-zagged image of a player.

	NM/M
Complete Set (20):	5.00
Common Player:	.25
1 Kurt Abbott	.25
2 Rico Brogna	.25
3 Hector Carrasco	.25
4 Kevin Foster	.25
5 Chris Gomez	.25
6 Darren Hall	.25
7 Bob Hamelin	.25
8 Joey Hamilton	.25
9 John Hudek	.25
10 Ryan Klesko	.25
11 Javier Lopez	.25
12 Matt Mieske	.25
13 Raul Mondesi	.25
14 Manny Ramirez	4.00
15 Shane Reynolds	.25
16 Bill Risley	.25
17 Johnny Ruffin	.25
18 Steve Trachsel	.25
19 William Van Landingham	.25
20 Rondell White	.25

Team Leaders

Team Leaders are two-player cards featuring the leading hitter and pitcher from each major league team, one on each side. Inserted at a rate of one per 24 packs, these are only found in 12-card hobby packs. Team Leaders consisted of 28 cards and included a Team Leader logo in the bottom-left corner.

		NM/M
Complete Set (28):		50.00
Common Card:		.50
1	Cal Ripken, Jr.,	
	Mike Mussina	7.50
2	Mo Vaughn,	
	Roger Clemens	4.50
3	Tim Salmon,	
	Chuck Finley	.75
4	Frank Thomas,	
	Jack McDowell	2.50
5	Albert Belle,	
	Dennis Martinez	.50
6	Cecil Fielder,	
	Mike Moore	.50
7	Bob Hamelin,	
	David Cone	.50
8	Greg Vaughn,	
	Ricky Bones	.50
9	Kirby Puckett,	
	Rick Aguilera	3.00
10	Don Mattingly,	
	Jimmy Key	4.50
11	Ruben Sierra,	
	Dennis Eckersley	1.50
12	Ken Griffey Jr.,	
	Randy Johnson	6.00
13	Jose Canseco,	
	Kenny Rogers	1.00
14	Joe Carter,	
	Pat Hentgen	.50
15	Dave Justice,	
	Greg Maddux	3.00
16	Sammy Sosa,	
	Steve Trachsel	5.00
17	Kevin Mitchell,	
	Jose Rijo	.50
18	Dante Bichette,	
	Bruce Ruffin	.50
19	Jeff Conine, Robb Nen	.50
20	Jeff Bagwell,	
	Doug Drabek	2.50
21	Mike Piazza,	
	Ramon Martinez	5.00
22	Moises Alou, Ken Hill	.50
23	Bobby Bonilla,	
	Bret Saberhagen	.50
24	Darren Daulton,	
	Danny Jackson	.50
25	Jay Bell, Zane Smith	.50
26	Gregg Jefferies,	
	Bob Tewksbury	.50
27	Tony Gwynn,	
	Andy Benes	3.00
28	Matt Williams,	
	Rod Beck	.50

All-Fleer 9

Available only by mailing in 10 Fleer wrappers and $3, this set presents an all-star lineup in a unique design. Colored scribbles down one side of the card front offer a background for gold-foil printing of the card title, player name, position and team. Backs repeat the colored scribbles across virtually the entire surface, making it extremely difficult to read the career summary printed in white over it.

		NM/M
Complete Set (9):		4.00
Common Player:		.25
1	Mike Piazza	1.00
2	Frank Thomas	.50
3	Roberto Alomar	.40
4	Cal Ripken Jr.	2.50
5	Matt Williams	.25
6	Barry Bonds	2.50
7	Ken Griffey Jr.	1.00
8	Tony Gwynn	.65
9	Greg Maddux	.65

All-Rookies

This mail-in set was available by redeeming a randomly inserted trade card found in

packs. The cards feature action player photos on a muted background, with the player ID in gold-foil beneath a huge rookie banner. Horizontal backs have a player photo at left and professional highlights at right. Cards have an "M" prefix to the card number.

		NM/M
Complete Set (9):		1.50
Common Player:		.25
Trade Card: 2X		.12
1	Edgardo Alfonzo	.25
2	Jason Bates	.25
3	Brian Boehringer	.25
4	Darren Bragg	.25
5	Brad Clontz	.25
6	Jim Dougherty	.25
7	Todd Hollandsworth	.25
8	Rudy Pemberton	.25
9	Frank Rodriguez	.25

Update

Fleer carried its "different by design" concept of six formats (one for each division in each league) from the regular set into its 1995 Update issue. The issue consists of 200 cards of 1995's traded, rookie and free agent players, plus five different insert sets. One insert card was found in each regular (12-card, $1.49) and jumbo (18-card, $2.29) pack. Cards are numbered with a "U" prefix.

		NM/M
Complete Set (200):		7.00
Common Player:		.05
Pack (12):		.50
Wax Box (36):		7.50
1	Manny Alexander	.05
2	Bret Barberie	.05
3	Armando Benitez	.05
4	Kevin Brown	.05
5	Doug Jones	.05
6	Sherman Obando	.05
7	Andy Van Slyke	.05
8	Stan Belinda	.05
9	Jose Canseco	.30
10	Vaughn Eshelman	.05
11	Mike Macfarlane	.05
12	Troy O'Leary	.05
13	Steve Rodriguez	.05
14	Lee Tinsley	.05
15	Tim Vanegmond	.05
16	Mark Whiten	.05
17	Sean Bergman	.05
18	Chad Curtis	.05
19	John Flaherty	.05
20	Bob Higginson RC	.15
21	Felipe Lira	.05
22	Shannon Penn	.05
23	Todd Steverson	.05
24	Sean Whiteside	.05
25	Tony Fernandez	.05
26	Jack McDowell	.05
27	Andy Pettite	.15
28	John Wetteland	.05
29	David Cone	.05
30	Mike Timlin	.05

31	Duane Ward	.05
32	Jim Abbott	.05
33	James Baldwin	.05
34	Mike Devereaux	.05
35	Ray Durham	.05
36	Tim Fortugno	.05
37	Scott Ruffcorn	.05
38	Chris Sabo	.05
39	Paul Assenmacher	.05
40	Bud Black	.05
41	Orel Hershiser	.05
42	Julian Tavarez	.05
43	Dave Winfield	.60
44	Pat Borders	.05
45	Melvin Bunch RC	.05
46	Tom Goodwin	.05
47	Jon Nunnally	.05
48	Joe Randa	.05
49	Dilson Torres RC	.05
50	Joe Vitiello	.05
51	David Hulse	.05
52	Scott Karl	.05
53	Mark Kiefer	.05
54	Derrick May	.05
55	Joe Oliver	.05
56	Al Reyes	.05
57	Steve Sparks RC	.05
58	Jerald Clark	.05
59	Eddie Guardado	.05
60	Kevin Maas	.05
61	David McCarty	.05
62	Brad Radke RC	.50
63	Scott Stahoviak	.05
64	Garret Anderson	.05
65	Shawn Boskie	.05
66	Mike James	.05
67	Tony Phillips	.05
68	Lee Smith	.05
69	Mitch Williams	.05
70	Jim Corsi	.05
71	Mark Harkey	.05
72	Dave Stewart	.05
73	Todd Stottlemyre	.05
74	Joey Cora	.05
75	Chad Kreuter	.05
76	Jeff Nelson	.05
77	Alex Rodriguez	2.00
78	Ron Villone	.05
79	Bob Wells RC	.05
80	Jose Alberro RC	.05
81	Terry Burrows	.05
82	Kevin Gross	.05
83	Wilson Heredia	.05
84	Mark McLemore	.05
85	Otis Nixon	.05
86	Jeff Russell	.05
87	Mickey Tettleton	.05
88	Bob Tewksbury	.05
89	Pedro Borbon	.05
90	Marquis Grissom	.05
91	Chipper Jones	.75
92	Mike Mordecai	.05
93	Jason Schmidt	.15
94	John Burkett	.05
95	Andre Dawson	.25
96	Matt Dunbar RC	.05
97	Charles Johnson	.05
98	Terry Pendleton	.05
99	Rich Scheid	.05
100	Quilvio Veras	.05
101	Bobby Witt	.05
102	Eddie Zosky	.05
103	Shane Andrews	.05
104	Reid Cornelius	.05
105	Chad Fonville RC	.05
106	Mark Grudzielanek RC	.25
107	Roberto Kelly	.05
108	Carlos Perez RC	.05
109	Tony Tarasco	.05
110	Brett Butler	.05
111	Carl Everett	.05
112	Pete Harnisch	.05
113	Doug Henry	.05
114	Kevin Lomon	.05
115	Blas Minor	.05
116	Dave Mlicki	.05
117	Ricky Otero RC	.05
118	Norm Charlton	.05
119	Tyler Green	.05
120	Gene Harris	.05
121	Charlie Hayes	.05
122	Gregg Jefferies	.05
123	Michael Mimbs RC	.05
124	Paul Quantrill	.05
125	Frank Castillo	.05
126	Brian McRae	.05
127	Jaime Navarro	.05
128	Mike Perez	.05
129	Tanyon Sturtze	.05
130	Ozzie Timmons	.05
131	John Courtright	.05
132	Ron Gant	.05
133	Xavier Hernandez	.05
134	Brian Hunter	.05
135	Benito Santiago	.05
136	Pete Smith	.05
137	Scott Sullivan	.05
138	Derek Bell	.05
139	Doug Brocail	.05
140	Ricky Gutierrez	.05
141	Pedro Martinez	.05
142	Orlando Miller	.05
143	Phil Plantier	.05
144	Craig Shipley	.05
145	Rich Aude	.05
146	Jason Christiansen RC	.05
147	Freddy Garcia RC	.25
148	Jim Gott	.05

149	Mark Johnson RC	.05
150	Esteban Loaiza	.05
151	Dan Plesac	.05
152	Gary Wilson RC	.05
153	Allen Battle	.05
154	Terry Bradshaw	.05
155	Scott Cooper	.05
156	Tripp Cromer	.05
157	John Frascatore	.05
158	John Habyan	.05
159	Tom Henke	.05
160	Ken Hill	.05
161	Danny Jackson	.05
162	Donovan Osborne	.05
163	Tom Urbani	.05
164	Roger Bailey	.05
165	Jorge Brito RC	.05
166	Vinny Castilla	.05
167	Darren Holmes	.05
168	Roberto Mejia	.05
169	Bill Swift	.05
170	Mark Thompson	.05
171	Larry Walker	.05
172	Greg Hansell	.05
173	Dave Hansen	.05
174	Carlos Hernandez	.05
175	Hideo Nomo RC	2.00
176	Jose Offerman	.05
177	Antonio Osuna	.05
178	Reggie Williams	.05
179	Todd Williams	.05
180	Andres Berumen	.05
181	Ken Caminiti	.05
182	Andujar Cedeno	.05
183	Steve Finley	.05
184	Bryce Florie	.05
185	Dustin Hermanson	.05
186	Ray Holbert	.05
187	Melvin Nieves	.05
188	Roberto Petagine	.05
189	Jody Reed	.05
190	Fernando Valenzuela	.05
191	Brian Williams	.05
192	Mark Dewey	.05
193	Glenallen Hill	.05
194	Chris Hook RC	.05
195	Terry Mulholland	.05
196	Steve Scarsone	.05
197	Trevor Wilson	.05
198	Checklist	.05
199	Checklist	.05
200	Checklist	.05

Update Diamond Tribute

Borderless action photos and gold-foil graphics are front features of this chase set honoring perhaps the 10 top names among baseball's veteran players. Backs have another photo and a few sentences describing what makes the player worthy of inclusion in such a set. The Diamond Tribute cards are found on the average of one per five packs.

		NM/M
Complete Set (10):		6.00
Common Player:		.25
1	Jeff Bagwell	.75
2	Albert Belle	.25
3	Barry Bonds	3.00
4	David Cone	.25
5	Dennis Eckersley	.25
6	Ken Griffey Jr.	1.50
7	Rickey Henderson	.60
8	Greg Maddux	1.00
9	Frank Thomas	.75
10	Matt Williams	.25

Update Headliners

The most common of the Fleer Update inserts are the Headliners cards found on average of one per three packs. Fronts have an action photo set against a collage of newspaper clippings. The graphics are gold-foil. Backs have another color photo and a "Fleer Times"

newspaper background with career summary and/or quotes about the featured player.

		NM/M
Complete Set (20):		8.00
Common Player:		.10
1	Jeff Bagwell	.50
2	Albert Belle	.15
3	Barry Bonds	3.00
4	Jose Canseco	.40
5	Joe Carter	.15
6	Will Clark	.25
7	Roger Clemens	2.00
8	Lenny Dykstra	.15
9	Cecil Fielder	.15
10	Juan Gonzalez	.40
11	Ken Griffey Jr.	2.00
12	Kenny Lofton	.15
13	Greg Maddux	.75
14	Fred McGriff	.15
15	Mike Piazza	1.50
16	Kirby Puckett	.75
17	Tim Salmon	.15
18	Frank Thomas	.50
19	Mo Vaughn	.15
20	Matt Williams	.15

Update Rookie Update

Ten of 1995's top rookies are featured in this horizontally formatted insert set. Fronts have an action photo with a large gold-foil "ROOKIE UPDATE" headline at top. Backs have another photo and career summary. Rookie Update chase cards are found on the average of one per four packs.

		NM/M
Complete Set (10):		4.00
Common Player:		.10
1	Shane Andrews	.10
2	Ray Durham	.10
3	Shawn Green	.40
4	Charles Johnson	.10
5	Chipper Jones	1.50
6	Esteban Loaiza	.10
7	Hideo Nomo	1.00
8	Jon Nunnally	.10
9	Alex Rodriguez	2.00
10	Julian Tavarez	.10

Update Smooth Leather

These inserts featuring top fielders were found only in pre-priced (magazine) foil packs, at an average rate of one card per 12 packs. Fronts are highlighted with gold-foil

graphics. Backs have a glove in the background and explain the player's defensive abilities.

		NM/M
Complete Set (10):		7.50
Common Player:		.25
1	Roberto Alomar	.50
2	Barry Bonds	2.50
3	Ken Griffey Jr.	1.50
4	Marquis Grissom	.25
5	Darren Lewis	.25
6	Kenny Lofton	.25
7	Don Mattingly	1.00
8	Cal Ripken Jr.	2.50
9	Ivan Rodriguez	.75
10	Matt Williams	.25

Update Soaring Stars

A metallic foil-etched background behind the color player action photo identifies this chase set as the toughest among those in the 1995 Fleer Update issue. The Soaring Star cards are found at the average rate of one per box. Backs are conventionally printed and featured a colorful posterized version of the front background, along with another color photo and a career summary.

		NM/M
Complete Set (9):		3.50
Common Player:		.15
1	Moises Alou	.35
2	Jason Bere	.25
3	Jeff Conine	.25
4	Cliff Floyd	.25
5	Pat Hentgen	.25
6	Kenny Lofton	.25
7	Raul Mondesi	.25
8	Mike Piazza	3.00
9	Tim Salmon	.35

Panini Stickers

Following Fleer's purchase of the well-known Italian sticker company, Panini, it was no surprise to see the companies produce a 1995 baseball issue. Titled "Major League Baseball All-Stars," the set consists of 156 player and team logo stickers. A 36-page color album to house the stickers was sold for $1.19. Sold in six-sticker packs for about .50, the individual stickers measure 1-15/16" x 3". Borders are team color-coded and have the player name and team logo at bottom, with the position abbreviation in a diamond at top-right. Backs are printed in black-and-white and include a sticker number, copyright notice and large logos of the licensors and Fleer/Panini. Each sticker can be found with backs that do, or do not, include a promotional message beginning, "Collect all 156 . . ."

	NM/M
Complete Set (156):	3.00
Common Player:	.05
Album:	1.00
Wax Pack (6):	.25
Wax Box (100):	15.00

1	Tom Glavine	.15
2	Doug Drabek	.05
3	Rod Beck	.05
4	Pedro J. Martinez	.25
5	Danny Jackson	.05
6	Greg Maddux	.30
7	Bret Saberhagen	.05
8	Ken Hill	.05
9	Marvin Freeman	.05
10	Andy Benes	.05
11	Wilson Alvarez	.05
12	Jimmy Key	.05
13	Mike Mussina	.15
14	Roger Clemens	.35
15	Pat Hentgen	.05
16	Randy Johnson	.25
17	Lee Smith	.05
18	David Cone	.05
19	Jason Bere	.05
20	Dennis Martinez	.05
21	Darren Daulton	.05
22	Darrin Fletcher	.05
23	Tom Pagnozzi	.05
24	Mike Piazza	.40
25	Benito Santiago	.05
26	Sandy Alomar Jr.	.05
27	Chris Hoiles	.05
28	Ivan Rodriguez	.20
29	Mike Stanley	.05
30	Dave Nilsson	.05
31	Jeff Bagwell	.25
32	Mark Grace	.10
33	Gregg Jefferies	.05
34	Andres Galarraga	.05
35	Fred McGriff	.05
36	Will Clark	.10
37	Mo Vaughn	.05
38	Don Mattingly	.35
39	Frank Thomas	.25
40	Cecil Fielder	.05
41	Robby Thompson	.05
42	Delino DeShields	.05
43	Carlos Garcia	.05
44	Bret Boone	.05
45	Craig Biggio	.05
46	Roberto Alomar	.10
47	Chuck Knoblauch	.05
48	Jose Lind	.05
49	Carlos Baerga	.05
50	Lou Whitaker	.05
51	Bobby Bonilla	.05
52	Tim Wallach	.05
53	Todd Zeile	.05
54	Matt Williams	.05
55	Ken Caminiti	.05
56	Robin Ventura	.05
57	Wade Boggs	.30
58	Scott Cooper	.05
59	Travis Fryman	.05
60	Dean Palmer	.05
61	Jay Bell	.05
62	Barry Larkin	.05
63	Ozzie Smith	.30
64	Wil Cordero	.05
65	Royce Clayton	.05
66	Chris Gomez	.05
67	Ozzie Guillen	.05
68	Cal Ripken Jr.	.50
69	Omar Vizquel	.05
70	Gary DiSarcina	.05
71	Dante Bichette	.05
72	Lenny Dykstra	.05
73	Barry Bonds	.50
74	Gary Sheffield	.20
75	Larry Walker	.05
76	Raul Mondesi	.05
77	Dave Justice	.05
78	Moises Alou	.05
79	Tony Gwynn	.30
80	Deion Sanders	.05
81	Kenny Lofton	.05
82	Kirby Puckett	.30
83	Juan Gonzalez	.20
84	Jay Buhner	.05
85	Joe Carter	.05
86	Ken Griffey Jr.	.40
87	Ruben Sierra	.05
88	Tim Salmon	.05
89	Paul O'Neill	.05
90	Albert Belle	.05
91	Danny Tartabull	.05
92	Jose Canseco	.20
93	Harold Baines	.05
94	Kirk Gibson	.05
95	Chili Davis	.05
96	Eddie Murray	.05
97	Bob Hamelin	.05
98	Paul Molitor	.05
99	Raul Mondesi	.05
100	Ryan Klesko	.05
101	Cliff Floyd	.05
102	William Van Landingham	.05

103	Joey Hamilton	.05
104	John Hudek	.05
105	Manny Ramirez	.25
106	Bob Hamelin	.05
107	Rusty Greer	.05
108	Chris Gomez	.05
109	Greg Maddux	.20
110	Jeff Bagwell	.15
111	Raul Mondesi	.05
112	David Cone	.05
113	Frank Thomas	.25
114	Bob Hamelin	.05
115	Tony Gwynn	.20
116	Matt Williams	.05
117	Jeff Bagwell	.15
118	Craig Biggio	.05
119	Andy Benes	.05
120	Greg Maddux	.20
121	John Franco	.05
122	Paul O'Neill	.05
123	Ken Griffey Jr.	.35
124	Kirby Puckett	.20
125	Kenny Lofton	.05
126	Randy Johnson	.05
127	Jimmy Key	.05
128	Lee Smith	.05
129	San Francisco Giants logo	.05
130	Montreal Expos logo	.05
131	Cincinnati Reds logo	.05
132	Los Angeles Dodgers logo	.05
133	New York Mets logo	.05
134	San Diego Padres logo	.05
135	Colorado Rockies logo	.05
136	Pittsburgh Pirates logo	.05
137	Florida Marlins logo	.05
138	Philadelphia Phillies logo	.05
139	Atlanta Braves logo	.05
140	Houston Astros logo	.05
141	St. Louis Cardinals logo	.05
142	Chicago Cubs logo	.05
143	Cleveland Indians logo	.05
144	New York Yankees logo	.05
145	Kansas City Royals logo	.05
146	Chicago White Sox logo	.05
147	Baltimore Orioles logo	.05
148	Seattle Mariners logo	.05
149	Boston Red Sox logo	.05
150	California Angels logo	.05
151	Toronto Blue Jays logo	.05
152	Detroit Tigers logo	.05
153	Texas Rangers logo	.05
154	Oakland A's logo	.05
155	Milwaukee Brewers logo	.05
156	Minnesota Twins logo	.05

Revco Cleveland Indians

In the midst of their pennant winning season in 1995, the Cleveland Indians were the subject of a special "Update" set produced by Fleer and sold exclusively by Revco stores and the team itself. Seventeen of the 20 cards in the set are virtually identical to the regular-issue 1995 Fleer cards, except for a change in card number on the back, designating each card as "X of 20," and the use of silver foil on front, as opposed to the gold foil found on regular cards. The Dave Winfield card in the Update issue pictures him in an Indians uniform, instead of the Twins uniform in which he appears in the regular set. Logo and checklist cards were added to the team set. Cards were sold in 10-card foil packs.

	NM/M
Complete Set (20):	6.00
Common Player:	.10

1	Sandy Alomar Jr.	.10
2	Carlos Baerga	.10
3	Albert Belle	.10
4	Mark Clark	.10
5	Alvaro Espinoza	.10
6	Wayne Kirby	.10
7	Kenny Lofton	.10
8	Dennis Martinez	.10
9	Jose Mesa	.10
10	Eddie Murray	2.00
11	Charles Nagy	.10
12	Tony Pena	.10
13	Eric Plunk	.10
14	Manny Ramirez	2.00
15	Paul Sorrento	.10
16	Jim Thome	1.00
17	Omar Vizquel	.10
18	Dave Winfield	2.00
19	Indians/Fleer logo card	.05
20	Checklist/Indians logo	.05

1996 Fleer

In a radical departure from the UV-coated standard for even base-brand baseball cards, Fleer's 1996 issue is printed on a matte surface. Fronts feature borderless game-action photos with minimal (player ID, Fleer logo) graphic enhancement in gold foil. Backs have a white background, a portrait photo, full pro stats and a few career highlights. The single-series set was sold in basic 11-card packs with one of nearly a dozen insert-set cards in each $1.49 pack. The set is arranged alphabetically by player within team and league. A glossy-surface Tiffany Collection parallel was included in each pack.

	NM/M
Complete Set (600):	20.00
Common Player:	.05
Complete Tiffany Set (600):	100.00
Tiffanies:	2X
Pack (11):	.75
Wax Box (36):	16.00

1	Manny Alexander	.05
2	Brady Anderson	.05
3	Harold Baines	.05
4	Armando Benitez	.05
5	Bobby Bonilla	.05
6	Kevin Brown	.05
7	Scott Erickson	.05
8	Curtis Goodwin	.05
9	Jeffrey Hammonds	.05
10	Jimmy Haynes	.05
11	Chris Hoiles	.05
12	Doug Jones	.05
13	Rick Krivda	.05
14	Jeff Manto	.05
15	Ben McDonald	.05
16	Jamie Moyer	.05
17	Mike Mussina	.50
18	Jesse Orosco	.05
19	Rafael Palmeiro	.65
20	Cal Ripken Jr.	2.50
20(p)	Cal Ripken Jr./OPS	2.50
21	Rick Aguilera	.05
22	Luis Alicea	.05
23	Stan Belinda	.05
24	Jose Canseco	.50
25	Roger Clemens	1.25
26	Vaughn Eshelman	.05
27	Mike Greenwell	.05
28	Erik Hanson	.05
29	Dwayne Hosey	.05
30	Mike Macfarlane	.05
31	Tim Naehring	.05
32	Troy O'Leary	.05
33	Aaron Sele	.05
34	Zane Smith	.05

35	Jeff Suppan	.05
36	Lee Tinsley	.05
37	John Valentin	.05
38	Mo Vaughn	.25
39	Tim Wakefield	.05
40	Jim Abbott	.05
41	Brian Anderson	.05
42	Garret Anderson	.05
43	Chili Davis	.05
44	Gary DiSarcina	.05
45	Damion Easley	.05
46	Jim Edmonds	.05
47	Chuck Finley	.05
48	Todd Greene	.05
49	Mike Harkey	.05
50	Mike James	.05
51	Mark Langston	.05
52	Greg Myers	.05
53	Orlando Palmeiro	.05
54	Bob Patterson	.05
55	Troy Percival	.05
56	Tony Phillips	.05
57	Tim Salmon	.10
58	Lee Smith	.05
59	J.T. Snow	.05
60	Randy Velarde	.05
61	Wilson Alvarez	.05
62	Luis Andujar RC	.05
63	Jason Bere	.05
64	Ray Durham	.05
65	Alex Fernandez	.05
66	Ozzie Guillen	.05
67	Roberto Hernandez	.05
68	Lance Johnson	.05
69	Matt Karchner	.05
70	Ron Karkovice	.05
71	Norberto Martin	.05
72	Dave Martinez	.05
73	Kirk McCaskill	.05
74	Lyle Mouton	.05
75	Tim Raines	.05
76	Mike Sirotka RC	.05
77	Frank Thomas	.75
78	Larry Thomas	.05
79	Robin Ventura	.05
80	Sandy Alomar Jr.	.05
81	Paul Assenmacher	.05
82	Carlos Baerga	.05
83	Albert Belle	.05
84	Mark Clark	.05
85	Alan Embree	.05
86	Alvaro Espinoza	.05
87	Orel Hershiser	.05
88	Ken Hill	.05
89	Kenny Lofton	.05
90	Dennis Martinez	.05
91	Jose Mesa	.05
92	Eddie Murray	.75
93	Charles Nagy	.05
94	Chad Ogea	.05
95	Tony Pena	.05
96	Herb Perry	.05
97	Eric Plunk	.05
98	Jim Poole	.05
99	Manny Ramirez	.75
100	Paul Sorrento	.05
101	Julian Travarez	.05
102	Jim Thome	.60
103	Omar Vizquel	.05
104	Dave Winfield	.75
105	Danny Bautista	.05
106	Joe Boever	.05
107	Chad Curtis	.05
108	John Doherty	.05
109	Cecil Fielder	.05
110	John Flaherty	.05
111	Travis Fryman	.05
112	Chris Gomez	.05
113	Bob Higginson	.05
114	Mark Lewis	.05
115	Jose Lima	.05
116	Felipe Lira	.05
117	Brian Maxcy	.05
118	C.J. Nitkowski	.05
119	Phil Plantier	.05
120	Clint Sodowsky	.05
121	Alan Trammell	.05
122	Lou Whitaker	.05
123	Kevin Appier	.05
124	Johnny Damon	.35
125	Gary Gaetti	.05
126	Tom Goodwin	.05
127	Tom Gordon	.05
128	Mark Gubicza	.05
129	Bob Hamelin	.05
130	David Howard	.05
131	Jason Jacome	.05
132	Wally Joyner	.05
133	Keith Lockhart	.05
134	Brent Mayne	.05
135	Jeff Montgomery	.05
136	Jon Nunnally	.05
137	Juan Samuel	.05
138	Mike Sweeney RC	.50
139	Michael Tucker	.05
140	Joe Vitiello	.05
141	Ricky Bones	.05
142	Chuck Carr	.05
143	Jeff Cirillo	.05
144	Mike Fetters	.05
145	Darryl Hamilton	.05
146	David Hulse	.05
147	John Jaha	.05
148	Scott Karl	.05
149	Mark Kiefer	.05
150	Pat Listach	.05
151	Mark Loretta	.05
152	Mike Matheny	.05

153	Matt Mieske	.05
154	Dave Nilsson	.05
155	Joe Oliver	.05
156	Al Reyes	.05
157	Kevin Seitzer	.05
158	Steve Sparks	.05
159	B.J. Surhoff	.05
160	Jose Valentin	.05
161	Greg Vaughn	.05
162	Fernando Vina	.05
163	Rich Becker	.05
164	Ron Coomer	.05
165	Marty Cordova	.05
166	Chuck Knoblauch	.05
167	Matt Lawton RC	.30
168	Pat Meares	.05
169	Paul Molitor	.75
170	Pedro Munoz	.05
171	Jose Parra	.05
172	Kirby Puckett	1.00
173	Brad Radke	.05
174	Jeff Reboulet	.05
175	Rich Robertson	.05
176	Frank Rodriguez	.05
177	Scott Stahoviak	.05
178	Dave Stevens	.05
179	Matt Walbeck	.05
180	Wade Boggs	1.00
181	David Cone	.05
182	Tony Fernandez	.05
183	Joe Girardi	.05
184	Derek Jeter	2.50
185	Scott Kamieniecki	.05
186	Pat Kelly	.05
187	Jim Leyritz	.05
188	Tino Martinez	.05
189	Don Mattingly	1.25
190	Jack McDowell	.05
191	Jeff Nelson	.05
192	Paul O'Neill	.05
193	Melido Perez	.05
194	Andy Pettitte	.30
195	Mariano Rivera	.15
196	Ruben Sierra	.05
197	Mike Stanley	.05
198	Darryl Strawberry	.05
199	John Wetteland	.05
200	Bob Wickman	.05
201	Bernie Williams	.10
202	Mark Acre	.05
203	Geronimo Berroa	.05
204	Mike Bordick	.05
205	Scott Brosius	.05
206	Dennis Eckersley	.65
207	Brent Gates	.05
208	Jason Giambi	.60
209	Rickey Henderson	.75
210	Jose Herrera	.05
211	Stan Javier	.05
212	Doug Johns	.05
213	Mark McGwire	2.00
214	Steve Ontiveros	.05
215	Craig Paquette	.05
216	Ariel Prieto	.05
217	Carlos Reyes	.05
218	Terry Steinbach	.05
219	Todd Stottlemyre	.05
220	Danny Tartabull	.05
221	Todd Van Poppel	.05
222	John Wasdin	.05
223	George Williams	.05
224	Steve Wojciechowski	.05
225	Rich Amaral	.05
226	Bobby Ayala	.05
227	Tim Belcher	.05
228	Andy Benes	.05
229	Chris Bosio	.05
230	Darren Bragg	.05
231	Jay Buhner	.05
232	Norm Charlton	.05
233	Vince Coleman	.05
234	Joey Cora	.05
235	Russ Davis	.05
236	Alex Diaz	.05
237	Felix Fermin	.05
238	Ken Griffey Jr.	1.75
239	Sterling Hitchcock	.05
240	Randy Johnson	.75
241	Edgar Martinez	.25
242	Bill Risley	.05
243	Alex Rodriguez	2.00
244	Luis Sojo	.05
245	Dan Wilson	.05
246	Bob Wolcott	.05
247	Will Clark	.10
248	Jeff Frye	.05
249	Benji Gil	.05
250	Juan Gonzalez	.65
251	Rusty Greer	.05
252	Kevin Gross	.05
253	Roger McDowell	.05
254	Mark McLemore	.05
255	Otis Nixon	.05
256	Luis Ortiz	.05
257	Mike Pagliarulo	.05
258	Dean Palmer	.05
259	Roger Pavlik	.05
260	Ivan Rodriguez	.65
261	Kenny Rogers	.05
262	Jeff Russell	.05
263	Mickey Tettleton	.05
264	Bob Tewksbury	.05
265	Dave Valle	.05
266	Matt Whiteside	.05
267	Roberto Alomar	.10
268	Joe Carter	.05
269	Tony Castillo	.05
270	Domingo Cedeno	.05

271	Timothy Crabtree	.05
272	Carlos Delgado	.60
273	Alex Gonzalez	.05
274	Shawn Green	.20
275	Juan Guzman	.05
276	Pat Hentgen	.05
277	Al Leiter	.05
278	Sandy Martinez RC	.05
279	Paul Menhart	.05
280	John Olerud	.05
281	Paul Quantrill	.05
282	Ken Robinson	.05
283	Ed Sprague	.05
284	Mike Timlin	.05
285	Steve Avery	.05
286	Rafael Belliard	.05
287	Jeff Blauser	.05
288	Pedro Borbon	.05
289	Brad Clontz	.05
290	Mike Devereaux	.05
291	Tom Glavine	.25
292	Marquis Grissom	.05
293	Chipper Jones	1.00
294	David Justice	.05
295	Mike Kelly	.05
296	Ryan Klesko	.05
297	Mark Lemke	.05
298	Javier Lopez	.05
299	Greg Maddux	1.00
300	Fred McGriff	.05
301	Greg McMichael	.05
302	Kent Mercker	.05
303	Mike Mordecai	.05
304	Charlie O'Brien	.05
305	Eduardo Perez	.05
306	Luis Polonia	.05
307	Jason Schmidt	.05
308	John Smoltz	.05
309	Terrell Wade	.05
310	Mark Wohlers	.05
311	Scott Bullett	.05
312	Jim Bullinger	.05
313	Larry Casian	.05
314	Frank Castillo	.05
315	Shawon Dunston	.05
316	Kevin Foster	.05
317	Matt Franco	.05
318	Luis Gonzalez	.10
319	Mark Grace	.10
320	Jose Hernandez	.05
321	Mike Hubbard	.05
322	Brian McRae	.05
323	Randy Myers	.05
324	Jaime Navarro	.05
325	Mark Parent	.05
326	Mike Perez	.05
327	Rey Sanchez	.05
328	Ryne Sandberg	1.00
329	Scott Servais	.05
330	Sammy Sosa	1.50
331	Ozzie Timmons	.05
332	Steve Trachsel	.05
333	Todd Zeile	.05
334	Bret Boone	.10
335	Jeff Branson	.05
336	Jeff Brantley	.05
337	Dave Burba	.05
338	Hector Carrasco	.05
339	Mariano Duncan	.05
340	Ron Gant	.05
341	Lenny Harris	.05
342	Xavier Hernandez	.05
343	Thomas Howard	.05
344	Mike Jackson	.05
345	Barry Larkin	.05
346	Darren Lewis	.05
347	Hal Morris	.05
348	Eric Owens	.05
349	Mark Portugal	.05
350	Jose Rijo	.05
351	Reggie Sanders	.05
352	Benito Santiago	.05
353	Pete Schourek	.05
354	John Smiley	.05
355	Eddie Taubensee	.05
356	Jerome Walton	.05
357	David Wells	.05
358	Roger Bailey	.05
359	Jason Bates	.05
360	Dante Bichette	.05
361	Ellis Burks	.05
362	Vinny Castilla	.05
363	Andres Galarraga	.05
364	Darren Holmes	.05
365	Mike Kingery	.05
366	Curt Leskanic	.05
367	Quinton McCracken	.05
368	Mike Munoz	.05
369	David Nied	.05
370	Steve Reed	.05
371	Bryan Rekar	.05
372	Kevin Ritz	.05
373	Bruce Ruffin	.05
374	Bret Saberhagen	.05
375	Bill Swift	.05
376	John Vander Wal	.05
377	Larry Walker	.05
378	Walt Weiss	.05
379	Eric Young	.05
380	Kurt Abbott	.05
381	Alex Arias	.05
382	Jerry Browne	.05
383	John Burkett	.05
384	Greg Colbrunn	.05
385	Jeff Conine	.05
386	Andre Dawson	.35
387	Chris Hammond	.05
388	Charles Johnson	.05

389	Terry Mathews	.05
390	Robb Nen	.05
391	Joe Orsulak	.05
392	Terry Pendleton	.05
393	Pat Rapp	.05
394	Gary Sheffield	.45
395	Jesus Tavarez	.05
396	Marc Valdes	.05
397	Quilvio Veras	.05
398	Randy Veres	.05
399	Devon White	.05
400	Jeff Bagwell	.75
401	Derek Bell	.05
402	Craig Biggio	.05
403	John Cangelosi	.05
404	Jim Dougherty	.05
405	Doug Drabek	.05
406	Tony Eusebio	.05
407	Ricky Gutierrez	.05
408	Mike Hampton	.05
409	Dean Hartgraves	.05
410	John Hudek	.05
411	Brian Hunter	.05
412	Todd Jones	.05
413	Darryl Kile	.05
414	Dave Magadan	.05
415	Derrick May	.05
416	Orlando Miller	.05
417	James Mouton	.05
418	Shane Reynolds	.05
419	Greg Swindell	.05
420	Jeff Tabaka	.05
421	Dave Veres	.05
422	Billy Wagner	.05
423	Donne Wall RC	.05
424	Rick Wilkins	.05
425	Billy Ashley	.05
426	Mike Blowers	.05
427	Brett Butler	.05
428	Tom Candiotti	.05
429	Juan Castro	.05
430	John Cummings	.05
431	Delino DeShields	.05
432	Joey Eischen	.05
433	Chad Fonville	.05
434	Greg Gagne	.05
435	Dave Hansen	.05
436	Carlos Hernandez	.05
437	Todd Hollandsworth	.05
438	Eric Karros	.05
439	Roberto Kelly	.05
440	Ramon Martinez	.05
441	Raul Mondesi	.05
442	Hideo Nomo	.65
443	Antonio Osuna	.05
444	Chan Ho Park	.05
445	Mike Piazza	1.75
446	Felix Rodriguez	.05
447	Kevin Tapani	.05
448	Ismael Valdes	.05
449	Todd Worrell	.05
450	Moises Alou	.05
451	Shane Andrews	.05
452	Yamil Benitez	.05
453	Sean Berry	.05
454	Wil Cordero	.05
455	Jeff Fassero	.05
456	Darrin Fletcher	.05
457	Cliff Floyd	.05
458	Mark Grudzielanek	.05
459	Gil Heredia	.05
460	Tim Laker	.05
461	Mike Lansing	.05
462	Pedro Martinez	.75
463	Carlos Perez	.05
464	Curtis Pride	.05
465	Mel Rojas	.05
466	Kirk Rueter	.05
467	F.P. Santangelo RC	.05
468	Tim Scott	.05
469	David Segui	.05
470	Tony Tarasco	.05
471	Rondell White	.05
472	Edgardo Alfonzo	.05
473	Tim Bogar	.05
474	Rico Brogna	.05
475	Damon Buford	.05
476	Paul Byrd	.05
477	Carl Everett	.10
478	John Franco	.05
479	Todd Hundley	.05
480	Butch Huskey	.05
481	Jason Isringhausen	.05
482	Bobby Jones	.05
483	Chris Jones	.05
484	Jeff Kent	.10
485	Dave Mlicki	.05
486	Robert Person	.05
487	Bill Pulsipher	.05
488	Kelly Stinnett	.05
489	Ryan Thompson	.05
490	Jose Vizcaino	.05
491	Howard Battle	.05
492	Toby Borland	.05
493	Ricky Bottalico	.05
494	Darren Daulton	.05
495	Lenny Dykstra	.05
496	Jim Eisenreich	.05
497	Sid Fernandez	.05
498	Tyler Green	.05
499	Charlie Hayes	.05
500	Gregg Jefferies	.05
501	Kevin Jordan	.05
502	Tony Longmire	.05
503	Tom Marsh	.05
504	Michael Mimbs	.05
505	Mickey Morandini	.05
506	Gene Schall	.05

507	Curt Schilling	.25
508	Heathcliff Slocumb	.05
509	Kevin Stocker	.05
510	Andy Van Slyke	.05
511	Lenny Webster	.05
512	Mark Whiten	.05
513	Mike Williams	.05
514	Jay Bell	.05
515	Jacob Brumfield	.05
516	Jason Christiansen	.05
517	Dave Clark	.05
518	Midre Cummings	.05
519	Angelo Encarnacion	.05
520	John Ericks	.05
521	Carlos Garcia	.05
522	Mark Johnson	.05
523	Jeff King	.05
524	Nelson Liriano	.05
525	Esteban Loaiza	.05
526	Al Martin	.05
527	Orlando Merced	.05
528	Dan Miceli	.05
529	Ramon Morel	.05
530	Denny Neagle	.05
531	Steve Parris	.05
532	Dan Plesac	.05
533	Don Slaught	.05
534	Paul Wagner	.05
535	John Wehner	.05
536	Kevin Young	.05
537	Allen Battle	.05
538	David Bell	.05
539	Alan Benes	.05
540	Scott Cooper	.05
541	Tripp Cromer	.05
542	Tony Fossas	.05
543	Bernard Gilkey	.05
544	Tom Henke	.05
545	Brian Jordan	.05
546	Ray Lankford	.05
547	John Mabry	.05
548	T.J. Mathews	.05
549	Mike Morgan	.05
550	Jose Oliva	.05
551	Jose Oquendo	.05
552	Donovan Osborne	.05
553	Tom Pagnozzi	.05
554	Mark Petkovsek	.05
555	Danny Sheaffer	.05
556	Ozzie Smith	1.00
557	Mark Sweeney	.05
558	Allen Watson	.05
559	Andy Ashby	.05
560	Brad Ausmus	.05
561	Willie Blair	.05
562	Ken Caminiti	.05
563	Andujar Cedeno	.05
564	Glenn Dishman	.05
565	Steve Finley	.05
566	Bryce Florie	.05
567	Tony Gwynn	1.00
568	Joey Hamilton	.05
569	Dustin Hermanson	.05
570	Trevor Hoffman	.05
571	Brian Johnson	.05
572	Marc Kroon	.05
573	Scott Livingstone	.05
574	Marc Newfield	.05
575	Melvin Nieves	.05
576	Jody Reed	.05
577	Bip Roberts	.05
578	Scott Sanders	.05
579	Fernando Valenzuela	.05
580	Eddie Williams	.05
581	Rod Beck	.05
582	Marvin Benard RC	.10
583	Barry Bonds	2.50
584	Jamie Brewington	.05
585	Mark Carreon	.05
586	Royce Clayton	.05
587	Shawn Estes	.05
588	Glenallen Hill	.05
589	Mark Leiter	.05
590	Kirt Manwaring	.05
591	David McCarty	.05
592	Terry Mulholland	.05
593	John Patterson	.05
594	J.R. Phillips	.05
595	Deion Sanders	.05
596	Steve Scarsone	.05
597	Robby Thompson	.05
598	Sergio Valdez	.05
599	William Van Landingham	.05
600	Matt Williams	.05

While Fleer's basic card set for 1996 feature matte-surface cards, a glossy version of each regular card was also issued as a parallel insert set. Other than the UV coating on front and back and the use of silver- rather than gold-foil typography on front, the cards are identical to the regular '96 Fleer player cards. One glossy version card is found in each pack.

	NM/M
Complete Set (600):	100.00
Common Player:	.15
Stars:	2X

Checklists

Checklist cards are treated as an insert set in 1996 Fleer, appearing on average once every six packs. Like all other Fleer hobby inserts in the baseball set, the checklists are UV-coated front and back, in contrast to the matte-finish regular issue cards. Checklists have borderless game-action photos on front, with gold-foil typography. Backs have a large Fleer logo and checklist data on a white background.

		NM/M
Complete Set (10):		5.00
Common Player:		.25
1	Barry Bonds	2.00
2	Ken Griffey Jr.	1.00
3	Chipper Jones	.75
4	Greg Maddux	.75
5	Mike Piazza	1.00
6	Manny Ramirez	.60
7	Cal Ripken Jr.	2.00
8	Frank Thomas	.60
9	Mo Vaughn	.25
10	Matt Williams	.25

Golden Memories

Some of the 1995 season's greatest moments are captured in this insert set, a one per 10 pack pick. Fronts have two photos of the player, one in full color in the foreground and one in monochrome as a backdrop. Typography is in prismatic foil vertically down one side. Backs have another color player photo, along with details of the milestone. Two of the cards feature multiple players.

		NM/M
Complete Set (10):		6.00
Common Player:		.10
1	Albert Belle	.10
2	Barry Bonds, Sammy Sosa	1.50
3	Greg Maddux	1.00
4	Edgar Martinez	.10
5	Ramon Martinez	.10
6	Mark McGwire	1.50
7	Eddie Murray	.75
8	Cal Ripken Jr.	2.00
9	Frank Thomas	.75
10	Alan Trammell, Lou Whitaker	.15

Tiffany

Lumber Company

Once again for 1996, a Fleer "Lumber Company" chase set honors the game's top sluggers. The '96 version has a horizontal format with a rather small player action photo on a background resembling the trademark area of a bat. The "trademark" is actually the player and team name along with the "Lumber Company" ID, printed in textured glossy black ink. Backs repeat the trademark motif and also include a close-up player photo and a few words about his power-hitting numbers. Lumber Company cards are a one per nine pack pick, on average, found only in retail packs.

		NM/M
Complete Set (12):		12.50
Common Player:		.50
1	Albert Belle	.50
2	Dante Bichette	.50
3	Barry Bonds	3.00
4	Ken Griffey Jr.	1.50
5	Mark McGwire	2.00
6	Mike Piazza	1.50
7	Manny Ramirez	.50
8	Tim Salmon	.60
9	Sammy Sosa	1.25
10	Frank Thomas	1.00
11	Mo Vaughn	.50
12	Matt Williams	.50

Post-Season Glory

Highlights of the 1995 postseason are featured in this small chase card set. Against a stadium background are multiple photos of the featured player, arranged horizontally. The vertical backs have another player photo down one side, and a description of his play-off performance on the other. Stated odds of picking one of these cards are one per five packs.

		NM/M
Complete Set (5):		1.50
Common Player:		.15
1	Tom Glavine	.25
2	Ken Griffey Jr.	1.00
3	Orel Hershiser	.15
4	Randy Johnson	1.00
5	Jim Thome	.50

Prospects

Minor leaguers who are expected to make it big in the big time are featured in this insert issue. Fronts feature large portrait photos against pastel backgrounds with player and set ID in prismatic foil. Backs have an action photo and repeat the front background color in a box which details the player's potential and career to date. Average odds of finding a Prospects card are one per six packs.

		NM/M
Complete Set (10):		1.00
Common Player:		.15
1	Yamil Benitez	.15
2	Roger Cedeno	.15
3	Tony Clark	.15
4	Micah Franklin	.15
5	Karim Garcia	.30
6	Todd Greene	.15
7	Alex Ochoa	.15
8	Ruben Rivera	.15
9	Chris Snopek	.15
10	Shannon Stewart	.15

Road Warriors

A black-and-white country highway photo is the background for the color player action photo on this insert set. Front typography is in silver foil. The players featured are those whose performance on the road is considered outstanding. Backs have a white background, portrait photo and stats bearing out the away-game superiority. These inserts are found at an average pace of one per 13 packs.

		NM/M
Complete Set (10):		9.00
Common Player:		.35
1	Derek Bell	.40
2	Tony Gwynn	1.25
3	Greg Maddux	1.25
4	Mark McGwire	2.50
5	Mike Piazza	2.00
6	Manny Ramirez	1.00
7	Tim Salmon	.50
8	Frank Thomas	1.00
9	Mo Vaughn	.40
10	Matt Williams	.40

Rookie Sensations

Top rookies of the 1995 season are featured on this chase card set. Horizontally formatted, the cards have an action photo on one side and a large prismatic-foil end strip which displays the player name, team logo and card company identifiers. Backs have a portrait photo on a white background with a few sentences about the player's rookie season. Stated odds of finding one of these inserts is one per 11 packs, on average.

		NM/M
Complete Set (15):		5.00
Common Player:		.25
1	Garret Anderson	.40
2	Marty Cordova	.25
3	Johnny Damon	1.00
4	Ray Durham	.25
5	Carl Everett	.25
6	Shawn Green	.50
7	Brian Hunter	.25
8	Jason Isringhausen	.25
9	Charles Johnson	.25
10	Chipper Jones	2.00
11	John Mabry	.25
12	Hideo Nomo	.50
13	Troy Percival	.25
14	Andy Pettitte	.50
15	Quilvio Veras	.25

Smoke 'N Heat

Once more using the "Smoke 'N Heat" identifier for a chase set of the game's hardest throwers, Fleer presents these select pitchers in action photos against a black-and-flame background. Front typography is in gold foil. Backs have a large portrait photo, repeat the flame motif as background and have a description of the pitcher's prowess in a black box. The cards are found, on average, once per nine packs.

		NM/M
Complete Set (10):		4.00
Common Player:		.15
1	Kevin Appier	.15
2	Roger Clemens	1.50
3	David Cone	.15
4	Chuck Finley	.15
5	Randy Johnson	.75
6	Greg Maddux	1.00
7	Pedro Martinez	.75
8	Hideo Nomo	.50
9	John Smoltz	.30
10	Todd Stottlemyre	.15

Team Leaders

One player from each club has been selected for inclusion in the "Team Leaders" chase set. Fronts have action player photos on a background of metallic foil littered with multiple representations of the team logo. Gold-foil lettering identifies the player, team and chase set. Backs have a white background, portrait photo and description of the player's leadership role. Stated rate of insertion for this set is one card per nine packs, on average, found only in hobby packs.

		NM/M
Complete Set (28):		30.00
Common Player:		.50
1	Cal Ripken Jr.	6.00
2	Mo Vaughn	.50
3	Jim Edmonds	1.00
4	Frank Thomas	2.00
5	Kenny Lofton	.50

#	Player	Price
6	Travis Fryman	.50
7	Gary Gaetti	.50
8	B.J. Surhoff	.50
9	Kirby Puckett	2.50
10	Don Mattingly	3.00
11	Mark McGwire	4.00
12	Ken Griffey Jr.	3.00
13	Juan Gonzalez	1.00
14	Joe Carter	.50
15	Greg Maddux	2.50
16	Sammy Sosa	3.00
17	Barry Larkin	.50
18	Dante Bichette	.50
19	Jeff Conine	.50
20	Jeff Bagwell	2.00
21	Mike Piazza	3.00
22	Rondell White	.50
23	Rico Brogna	.50
24	Darren Daulton	.50
25	Jeff King	.50
26	Ray Lankford	.50
27	Tony Gwynn	2.50
28	Barry Bonds	6.00

Tomorrow's Legends

In this insert set the projected stars of tomorrow are featured in action poses on a busy multi-colored, quartered background of baseball symbols and the globe. Typography is in silver foil. Backs have a portrait photo and large team logo along with an early-career summary. Odds of finding a "Tomorrow's Legends" card are posted at one per 13 packs, on average.

		NM/M
Complete Set (10):		3.50
Common Player:		.25
1	Garret Anderson	.25
2	Jim Edmonds	.50
3	Brian Hunter	.25
4	Jason Isringhausen	.25
5	Charles Johnson	.25
6	Chipper Jones	2.00
7	Ryan Klesko	.25
8	Hideo Nomo	1.00
9	Manny Ramirez	1.50
10	Rondell White	.25

Zone

The toughest pull (one in 90 packs, average) among the '96 Fleer chase cards is this set evoking the "zone" that the game's great players seek in which their performance is at its peak. The cards have action photos with a background of prismatic foil. Backs are conventionally printed but simulate the foil background and include a player portrait photo plus quotes about the player.

	NM/M
Complete Set (12):	20.00
Common Player:	.75

#	Player	Price
1	Albert Belle	.75
2	Barry Bonds	6.00
3	Ken Griffey Jr.	4.00
4	Tony Gwynn	3.00
5	Randy Johnson	2.00
6	Kenny Lofton	.75
7	Greg Maddux	3.00
8	Edgar Martinez	.75
9	Mike Piazza	4.00
10	Frank Thomas	2.00
11	Mo Vaughn	.75
12	Matt Williams	.75

Update

Fleer Update Baseball has 250 cards, including more than 55 rookies, plus traded players and free agents in their new uniforms, 35 Encore sub-set cards and five checklists. Each card in the regular-issue set also has a parallel "Tiffany Collection" version, which has UV coating and holographic foil stamping in contrast to the matte finish and gold foil of the regular cards. Insert cards include Diamond Tribute, New Horizons, Smooth Leather and Soaring Stars. Each pack also contains a Fleer "Thanks a Million" scratch-off game card, redeemable for prizes. Cards are numbered with a "U" prefix.

	NM/M
Complete Set (250):	12.00
Common Player:	.05
Complete Tiffany Set (250):	40.00
Tiffany Stars:	2X
Pack (11):	1.00
Wax Box (24):	15.00

#	Player	Price
1	Roberto Alomar	.10
2	Mike Devereaux	.05
3	Scott McClain RC	.05
4	Roger McDowell	.05
5	Kent Mercker	.05
6	Jimmy Myers	.05
7	Randy Myers	.05
8	B.J. Surhoff	.05
9	Tony Tarasco	.05
10	David Wells	.05
11	Wil Cordero	.05
12	Tom Gordon	.05
13	Reggie Jefferson	.05
14	Jose Malave	.05
15	Kevin Mitchell	.05
16	Jamie Moyer	.05
17	Heathcliff Slocumb	.05
18	Mike Stanley	.05
19	George Arias	.05
20	Jorge Fabregas	.05
21	Don Slaught	.05
22	Randy Velarde	.05
23	Harold Baines	.05
24	Mike Cameron RC	.75
25	Darren Lewis	.05
26	Tony Phillips	.05
27	Bill Simas	.05
28	Chris Snopek	.05
29	Kevin Tapani	.05
30	Danny Tartabull	.05
31	Julio Franco	.05
32	Jack McDowell	.05
33	Kimera Bartee	.05
34	Mark Lewis	.05
35	Melvin Nieves	.05
36	Mark Parent	.05
37	Eddie Williams	.05
38	Tim Belcher	.05
39	Sal Fasano	.05
40	Chris Haney	.05
41	Mike Macfarlane	.05
42	Jose Offerman	.05
43	Joe Randa	.05
44	Bip Roberts	.05
45	Chuck Carr	.05
46	Bobby Hughes	.05
47	Graeme Lloyd	.05
48	Ben McDowell	.05
49	Kevin Wickander	.05
50	Rick Aguilera	.05
51	Mike Durant	.05
52	Chip Hale	.05
53	LaTroy Hawkins	.05
54	Dave Hollins	.05
55	Roberto Kelly	.05
56	Paul Molitor	.75
57	Dan Naulty RC	.05
58	Mariano Duncan	.05
59	Andy Fox RC	.05
60	Joe Girardi	.05
61	Dwight Gooden	.05
62	Jimmy Key	.05
63	Matt Luke RC	.05
64	Tino Martinez	.05
65	Jeff Nelson	.05
66	Tim Raines	.05
67	Ruben Rivera	.05
68	Kenny Rogers	.05
69	Gerald Williams	.05
70	Tony Batista RC	.50
71	Allen Battle	.05
72	Jim Corsi	.05
73	Steve Cox	.05
74	Pedro Munoz	.05
75	Phil Plantier	.05
76	Scott Spiezio	.05
77	Ernie Young	.05
78	Russ Davis	.05
79	Sterling Hitchcock	.05
80	Edwin Hurtado	.05
81	Raul Ibanez RC	.05
82	Mike Jackson	.05
83	Ricky Jordan	.05
84	Paul Sorrento	.05
85	Doug Strange	.05
86	Mark Brandenburg	.05
87	Damon Buford	.05
88	Kevin Elster	.05
89	Darryl Hamilton	.05
90	Ken Hill	.05
91	Ed Vosberg	.05
92	Craig Worthington	.05
93	Tilson Brito	.05
94	Giovanni Carrara	.05
95	Felipe Crespo	.05
96	Erik Hanson	.05
97	Marty Janzen RC	.05
98	Otis Nixon	.05
99	Charlie O'Brien	.05
100	Robert Perez	.05
101	Paul Quantrill	.05
102	Bill Risley	.05
103	Juan Samuel	.05
104	Jermaine Dye	.05
105	Wonderful Monds	.05
106	Dwight Smith	.05
107	Jerome Walton	.05
108	Terry Adams	.05
109	Leo Gomez	.05
110	Robin Jennings RC	.05
111	Doug Jones	.05
112	Brooks Kieschnick	.05
113	Dave Magadan	.05
114	Jason Maxwell RC	.05
115	Rodney Myers	.05
116	Eric Anthony	.05
117	Vince Coleman	.05
118	Eric Davis	.05
119	Steve Gibralter	.05
120	Curtis Goodwin	.05
121	Willie Greene	.05
122	Mike Kelly	.05
123	Marcus Moore	.05
124	Chad Mottola	.05
125	Chris Sabo	.05
126	Roger Salkeld	.05
127	Pedro Castellano	.05
128	Trenidad Hubbard	.05
129	Jayhawk Owens	.05
130	Jeff Reed	.05
131	Kevin Brown	.05
132	Al Leiter	.05
133	Matt Mantei RC	.05
134	Dave Weathers	.05
135	Devon White	.05
136	Bob Abreu	.05
137	Sean Berry	.05
138	Doug Brocail	.05
139	Richard Hidalgo	.05
140	Alvin Morman	.05
141	Mike Blowers	.05
142	Roger Cedeno	.05
143	Greg Gagne	.05
144	Karim Garcia	.10
145	Wilton Guerrero RC	.05
146	Israel Alcantara RC	.05
147	Omar Daal	.05
148	Ryan McGuire	.05
149	Sherman Obando	.05
150	Jose Paniagua	.05
151	Henry Rodriguez	.05
152	Andy Stankiewicz	.05
153	Dave Veres	.05
154	Juan Acevedo	.05
155	Mark Clark	.05
156	Bernard Gilkey	.05
157	Pete Harnisch	.05
158	Lance Johnson	.05
159	Brent Mayne	.05
160	Rey Ordonez	.05
161	Kevin Roberson	.05
162	Paul Wilson	.05
163	David Doster RC	.05
164	Mike Grace RC	.05
165	Rich Hunter RC	.05
166	Pete Incaviglia	.05
167	Mike Lieberthal	.05
168	Terry Mulholland	.05
169	Ken Ryan	.05
170	Benito Santiago	.05
171	Kevin Sefcik RC	.05
172	Lee Tinsley	.05
173	Todd Zeile	.05
174	Francisco Cordova RC	.05
175	Danny Darwin	.05
176	Charlie Hayes	.05
177	Jason Kendall	.05
178	Mike Kingery	.05
179	Jon Lieber	.05
180	Zane Smith	.05
181	Luis Alicea	.05
182	Cory Bailey	.05
183	Andy Benes	.05
184	Pat Borders	.05
185	Mike Busby RC	.05
186	Royce Clayton	.05
187	Dennis Eckersley	.65
188	Gary Gaetti	.05
189	Ron Gant	.05
190	Aaron Holbert	.05
191	Willie McGee	.05
192	Miguel Mejia RC	.05
193	Jeff Parrett	.05
194	Todd Stottlemyre	.05
195	Sean Bergman	.05
196	Archi Cianfrocco	.05
197	Rickey Henderson	.75
198	Wally Joyner	.05
199	Craig Shipley	.05
200	Bob Tewksbury	.05
201	Tim Worrell	.05
202	Rich Aurilia RC	.05
203	Doug Creek	.05
204	Shawon Dunston	.05
205	Osvaldo Fernandez RC	.05
206	Mark Gardner	.05
207	Stan Javier	.05
208	Marcus Jensen	.05
209	Chris Singleton RC	.05
210	Allen Watson	.05
211	Jeff Bagwell (Encore)	.75
212	Derek Bell (Encore)	.05
213	Albert Belle (Encore)	.05
214	Wade Boggs (Encore)	1.00
215	Barry Bonds (Encore)	2.00
216	Jose Canseco (Encore)	.50
217	Marty Cordova (Encore)	.05
218	Jim Edmonds (Encore)	.05
219	Cecil Fielder (Encore)	.05
220	Andres Galarraga (Encore)	.05
221	Juan Gonzalez (Encore)	.65
222	Mark Grace (Encore)	.10
223	Ken Griffey Jr. (Encore)	1.50
224	Tony Gwynn (Encore)	1.00
225	Jason Isringhausen (Encore)	.05
226	Derek Jeter (Encore)	2.00
227	Randy Johnson (Encore)	.75
228	Chipper Jones (Encore)	1.00
229	Ryan Klesko (Encore)	.05
230	Barry Larkin (Encore)	.05
231	Kenny Lofton (Encore)	.05
232	Greg Maddux (Encore)	1.00
233	Raul Mondesi (Encore)	.05
234	Hideo Nomo (Encore)	.65
235	Mike Piazza (Encore)	1.50
236	Manny Ramirez (Encore)	.75
237	Cal Ripken Jr. (Encore)	2.00
238	Tim Salmon (Encore)	.10
239	Ryne Sandberg (Encore)	1.00
240	Reggie Sanders (Encore)	.05
241	Gary Sheffield (Encore)	.30
242	Sammy Sosa (Encore)	1.25
243	Frank Thomas (Encore)	.75
244	Mo Vaughn (Encore)	.05
245	Matt Williams (Encore)	.05
246	Checklist	.05
247	Checklist	.05
248	Checklist	.05
249	Checklist	.05
250	Checklist	.05

Update Tiffany

	NM/M
Complete Set (250):	45.00
Common Player:	.15
Glossy Stars:	2X

Update Diamond Tribute

These insert cards are the most difficult to pull from 1996 Fleer Update packs; they are seeded one per every 100 packs. The 10-card set features cards of future Hall of Famers on stock utilizing two different holographic foils and a diamond design, similar to the "Zone" insert cards in Fleer Baseball.

		NM/M
Complete Set (10):		50.00
Common Player:		4.00
1	Wade Boggs	6.00
2	Barry Bonds	10.00
3	Ken Griffey Jr.	7.50
4	Tony Gwynn	6.00
5	Rickey Henderson	4.00
6	Greg Maddux	6.00
7	Eddie Murray	4.00
8	Cal Ripken Jr.	10.00
9	Ozzie Smith	6.00
10	Frank Thomas	5.00

Update Headliners

These 20 cards feature newsmakers from 1996. The cards were random inserts in 1996 Fleer Update packs, one per every five retail packs.

		NM/M
Complete Set (20):		20.00
Common Player:		.25
1	Roberto Alomar	.50
2	Jeff Bagwell	1.00
3	Albert Belle	.25
4	Barry Bonds	3.50
5	Cecil Fielder	.25
6	Juan Gonzalez	.75
7	Ken Griffey Jr.	2.25
8	Tony Gwynn	1.50
9	Randy Johnson	1.00
10	Chipper Jones	1.50
11	Ryan Klesko	.25
12	Kenny Lofton	.25
13	Greg Maddux	1.50
14	Hideo Nomo	.75
15	Mike Piazza	2.25
16	Manny Ramirez	1.00
17	Cal Ripken Jr.	3.50
18	Tim Salmon	.40
19	Frank Thomas	1.50
20	Matt Williams	.25

Update New Horizons

These 1996 Fleer Update inserts feature 20 promising youngsters with bright futures in the majors. The cards were seeded one per every five hobby packs.

		NM/M
Complete Set (20):		2.00
Common Player:		.25
1	Bob Abreu	.45
2	George Arias	.25
3	Tony Batista	.25
4	Steve Cox	.25
5	David Doster	.25
6	Jermaine Dye	.25
7	Andy Fox	.25
8	Mike Grace	.25
9	Todd Greene	.25
10	Wilton Guerrero	.25
11	Richard Hidalgo	.25
12	Raul Ibanez	.25
13	Robin Jennings	.25
14	Marcus Jensen	.25
15	Jason Kendall	.35
16	Brooks Kieschnick	.25
17	Ryan McGuire	.25
18	Miguel Mejia	.25
19	Rey Ordonez	.25
20	Paul Wilson	.25

Update Smooth Leather

Ten of the game's top fielders are showcased on these 1996 Fleer Update insert cards. The cards were seeded one per every five packs.

		NM/M
Complete Set (10):		7.00
Common Player:		.40
1	Roberto Alomar	.50
1p	Roberto Alomar /Promo	2.00
2	Barry Bonds	2.50
3	Will Clark	.45
4	Ken Griffey Jr.	1.75
5	Kenny Lofton	.40
6	Greg Maddux	1.00
7	Raul Mondesi	.40
8	Rey Ordonez	.40
9	Cal Ripken Jr.	2.50
9p	Cal Ripken Jr./Promo	6.00
10	Matt Williams	.40

Update Soaring Stars

Ten of the game's top players are spotlighted on these 1996 Fleer Update inserts. The cards were seeded one per every 11 packs.

		NM/M
Complete Set (10):		6.00
Common Player:		.25
1	Jeff Bagwell	.75
2	Barry Bonds	2.00
3	Juan Gonzalez	.75
4	Ken Griffey Jr.	1.50
5	Chipper Jones	1.00
6	Greg Maddux	1.00
7	Mike Piazza	1.50
8	Manny Ramirez	.75
9	Frank Thomas	.75
10	Matt Williams	.25

Baseball '96

For a second consecutive year Fleer issued a special version of its Cleveland Indians cards for sale at Revco stores and Jacobs Field. Sold in 10-card packs with a suggested retail price of $1.49, the Revco version Indians team set differs from the regular Fleer cards in the application of UV coating on front and back, the use of silver- rather than gold-foil highlights and the numbering "X of 20." Following up on the Indians team-set issue, Fleer also issued 20-card sets for several other teams, distributed regionally. They were also sold in 10-card packs ($1.99 SRP) and feature UV coating, silver-foil graphics and special numbering. Some cards were updated and feature new photos reflecting trades, free agent signings, etc.

	NM/M
Complete Set (180):	27.00
Common Player:	.09

Atlanta Braves
Team Set: 4.00
1 Steve Avery .10
2 Jeff Blauser .10
3 Brad Clontz .10
4 Tom Glavine .35
5 Marquis Grissom .10
6 Chipper Jones 1.25
7 David Justice .10
8 Ryan Klesko .10
9 Mark Lemke .10
10 Javier Lopez .10
11 Greg Maddux 1.25
12 Fred McGriff .10
13 Greg McMichael .10
14 Eddie Perez .10
15 Jason Schmidt .10
16 John Smoltz .10
17 Terrell Wade .10
18 Mark Wohlers .10
19 Logo card .10
20 Checklist .10

Baltimore Orioles
Team Set: 5.00
1 Roberto Alomar .20
2 Brady Anderson .10
3 Armando Benitez .10
4 Bobby Bonilla .10
5 Scott Erickson .10
6 Jeffrey Hammonds .10
7 Jimmy Haynes .10
8 Chris Hoiles .10
9 Rick Krivda .10
10 Kent Mercker .10
11 Mike Mussina .45
12 Randy Myers .10
13 Jesse Orosco .10
14 Rafael Palmeiro .75
15 Cal Ripken Jr. 2.50
16 B.J. Surhoff .10
17 Tony Tarasco .10
18 David Wells .10
19 Logo card .10
20 Checklist .10

Boston Red Sox
Team Set: 3.00
1 Stan Belinda .10
2 Jose Canseco .50
3 Roger Clemens 2.00
4 Wil Cordero .10
5 Vaughn Eshelman .10
6 Tom Gordon .10
7 Mike Greenwell .10
8 Dwayne Hosey .10
9 Kevin Mitchell .10
10 Tim Naehring .10
11 Troy O'Leary .10
12 Aaron Sele .10
13 Heathcliff Slocumb .10
14 Mike Stanley .10
15 Jeff Suppan .10
16 John Valentin .10
17 Mo Vaughn .10
18 Tim Wakefield .10
19 Logo card .10
20 Checklist .10

Chicago Cubs
Team Set: 4.00
1 Terry Adams .10
2 Jim Bullinger .10
3 Frank Castillo .10
4 Kevin Foster .10
5 Leo Gomez .10
6 Luis Gonzalez .20
7 Mark Grace .15
8 Jose Hernandez .10
9 Robin Jennings **RC** .10
10 Doug Jones .10
11 Brooks Kieschnick .10
12 Brian McRae .10
13 Jaime Navarro .10
14 Rey Sanchez .10
15 Ryne Sandberg 1.25
16 Scott Servais .10
17 Sammy Sosa 1.50
18 Steve Trachsel .10
19 Logo card .10
20 Checklist .10

Chicago White Sox
Team Set: 4.00
1 Wilson Alvarez .10
2 Harold Baines .10
3 Jason Bere .10
4 Ray Durham .10
5 Alex Fernandez .10
6 Ozzie Guillen .10
7 Roberto Hernandez .10
8 Matt Karchner .10
9 Ron Karkovice .10
10 Darren Lewis .10
11 Dave Martinez .10
12 Lyle Mouton .10
13 Tony Phillips .10
14 Chris Snopek .10
15 Kevin Tapani .10
16 Danny Tartabull .10
17 Frank Thomas 1.00
18 Robin Ventura .10
19 Logo card .10
20 Checklist .10

Cleveland Indians
Team Set: 4.00
1 Sandy Alomar Jr. .10
2 Paul Assenmacher .10
3 Carlos Baerga .10
4 Albert Belle .09
5 Orel Hershiser .10
6 Kenny Lofton .10
7 Dennis Martinez .10
8 Jose Mesa .10
9 Eddie Murray 1.00
10 Charles Nagy .10
11 Tony Pena .10
12 Herb Perry .10
13 Eric Plunk .10
14 Jim Poole .10
15 Manny Ramirez 1.00
16 Julian Tavarez .10
17 Jim Thome .75
18 Omar Vizquel .10
19 Logo card .10
20 Checklist .10

Colorado Rockies
Team Set: 2.75
1 Jason Bates .10
2 Dante Bichette .10
3 Ellis Burks .10
4 Vinny Castilla .10
5 Andres Galarraga .10
6 Darren Holmes .10
7 Curt Leskanic .10
8 Quinton McCracken .10
9 Mike Munoz .10
10 Jayhawk Owens .10
11 Steve Reed .10
12 Kevin Ritz .10
13 Bret Saberhagen .10
14 Bill Swift .10
15 John Vander Wal .10
16 Larry Walker .10
17 Walt Weiss .10
18 Eric Young .10
19 Logo card .10
20 Checklist .10

L.A. Dodgers
Team Set: 4.00
1 Mike Blowers .10
2 Brett Butler .10
3 Tom Candiotti .10
4 Roger Cedeno .10
5 Delino DeShields .10
6 Chad Fonville .10
7 Greg Gagne .10
8 Karim Garcia .15
9 Todd Hollandsworth .10
10 Eric Karros .10
11 Ramon Martinez .10
12 Raul Mondesi .10
13 Hideo Nomo .75
14 Antonio Osuna .10
15 Chan Ho Park .10
16 Mike Piazza 2.00
17 Ismael Valdes .10
18 Todd Worrell .10
19 Logo card .10
20 Checklist .10

Texas Rangers
Team Set: 2.75
1 Mark Brandenburg .10
2 Damon Buford .10
3 Will Clark .15
4 Kevin Elster .10
5 Benji Gil .10
6 Juan Gonzalez .75
7 Rusty Greer .10
8 Kevin Gross .10
9 Darryl Hamilton .10
10 Ken Hill .10
11 Mark McLemore .10
12 Dean Palmer .10
13 Roger Pavlik .10
14 Ivan Rodriguez .75
15 Mickey Tettleton .10
16 Dave Valle .10
17 Ed Vosberg .10
18 Matt Whiteside .10
19 Logo card .10
20 Checklist .10

Panini Stickers

For the second year of distribution by Fleer/SkyBox, the annual baseball sticker set once again used Panini as the dominant brand identification. Printed in Italy, the stickers were sold in packs of six for 49 cents in the U.S., 69 cents in Canada. At 2-1/8"

x 3", the basic player stickers have a green border around the color action photo; a second, ghosted, version of the photo appear in the background. Team logo and player ID are in a bat at bottom. Backs are printed in blue with the sticker number, Panini and licensor logos, along with copyright information. Team logo and special rookie stickers were printed on silver foil. A 60-page album was issued to house the set.

	NM/M
Complete Set (246):	4.00
Common Player:	.05
Album:	.75

1 David Justice .05
2 Tom Glavine .20
3 Javier Lopez .05
4 Greg Maddux .45
5 Marquis Grissom .05
6 Braves logo .05
7 Ryan Klesko .05
8 Chipper Jones .45
9 Quilvio Veras .05
10 Chris Hammond .05
11 Charles Johnson .05
12 John Burkett .05
13 Marlins logo .05
14 Jeff Conine .05
15 Gary Sheffield .25
16 Greg Colbrunn .05
17 Moises Alou .05
18 Pedro J. Martinez .35
19 Rondell White .05
20 Tony Tarasco .05
21 Expos logo .05
22 Carlos Perez .05
23 David Segui .05
24 Wil Cordero .05
25 Jason Isringhausen .05
26 Rico Brogna .05
27 Edgardo Alfonzo .05
28 Todd Hundley .05
29 Mets logo .05
30 Bill Pulsipher .05
31 Carl Everett .05
32 Jose Vizcaino .05
33 Lenny Dykstra .05
34 Charlie Hayes .05
35 Heathcliff Slocumb .05
36 Darren Daulton .05
37 Phillies logo .05
38 Mickey Morandini .05
39 Gregg Jefferies .05
40 Jim Eisenreich .05
41 Brian McRae .05
42 Luis Gonzalez .10
43 Randy Myers .05
44 Shawon Dunston .05
45 Cubs logo .05
46 Jaime Navarro .05
47 Mark Grace .10
48 Sammy Sosa .50
49 Barry Larkin .50
50 Pete Schourek .05
51 John Smiley .05
52 Reggie Sanders .05
53 Reds logo .05
54 Hal Morris .05
55 Ron Gant .05
56 Bret Boone .05
57 Craig Biggio .05
58 Brian L. Hunter .05
59 Jeff Bagwell .35
60 Shane Reynolds .05
61 Astros logo .05
62 Derek Bell .05
63 Doug Drabek .05
64 Orlando Miller .05
65 Jay Bell .05
66 Dan Miceli .05
67 Orlando Merced .05
68 Jeff King .05
69 Carlos Garcia .05
70 Pirates logo .05
71 Al Martin .05
72 Denny Neagle .05
73 Ray Lankford .05
74 Ozzie Smith .45
75 Bernard Gilkey .05
76 John Mabry .05
77 Cardinals logo .05
78 Brian Jordan .05
79 Scott Cooper .05
80 Allen Watson .05
81 Dante Bichette .05
82 Bret Saberhagen .05
83 Walt Weiss .05
84 Andres Galarraga .05
85 Rockies logo .05
86 Larry Walker .05
87 Bill Swift .05
88 Vinny Castilla .05
89 Raul Mondesi .05
90 Roger Cedeno .05
91 Chad Fonville .05
92 Hideo Nomo .30
93 Dodgers logo .05
94 Ramon Martinez .05
95 Mike Piazza .60
96 Eric Karros .05
97 Tony Gwynn .45
98 Brad Ausmus .05
99 Trevor Hoffman .05
100 Ken Caminiti .05
101 Padres logo .05
102 Andy Ashby .05
103 Steve Finley .05
104 Joey Hamilton .05
105 Matt Williams .05
106 Rod Beck .05
107 Barry Bonds .75
108 William Van Landingham .05
109 Giants logo .05
110 Deion Sanders .05
111 Royce Clayton .05
112 Glenallen Hill .05
113 Tony Gwynn (League Leader - BA) .20
114 Dante Bichette (League Leader - HR) .05
115 Dante Bichette (League Leader - RBI) .05
116 Quilvio Veras (League Leader - SB) .05
117 Hideo Nomo (League Leader - K) .15
118 Greg Maddux (League Leader - W) .20
119 Randy Myers(League Leader - Saves) .05
120 Edgar Martinez (League Leader - BA) .05
121 Albert Belle (League Leader - HR) .05
122 Mo Vaughn (League Leader - RBI) .05
123 Kenny Lofton (League Leader - SB) .05
124 Randy Johnson (League Leader - K) .15
125 Mike Mussina (League Leader - W) .10
126 Jose Mesa (League Leader - Saves) .05
127 Mike Mussina .20
128 Cal Ripken Jr. .75
129 Rafael Palmeiro .30
130 Ben McDonald .05
131 Orioles logo .05
132 Chris Hoiles .05
133 Bobby Bonilla .05
134 Brady Anderson .05
135 Jose Canseco .20
136 Roger Clemens .05
137 Mo Vaughn .05
138 Mike Greenwell .05
139 Red Sox logo .05
140 Tim Wakefield .05
141 John Valentin .05
142 Tim Naehring .05
143 Travis Fryman .05
144 Chad Curtis .05
145 Felipe Lira .05
146 Cecil Fielder .05
147 Tigers logo .05
148 John Flaherty .05
149 Chris Gomez .05
150 Sean Bergman .05
151 Don Mattingly .50
152 Andy Pettitte .05
153 Wade Boggs .45
154 Paul O'Neill .05
155 Yankees logo .05
156 Bernie Williams .10
157 Jack McDowell .05
158 David Cone .05
159 Roberto Alomar .10
160 Paul Molitor .35
161 Shawn Green .05
162 Joe Carter .05
163 Blue Jays logo .05
164 Alex Gonzalez .05
165 Al Leiter .05
166 John Olerud .05
167 Alex Fernandez .05
168 Ray Durham .05
169 Lance Johnson .05
170 Ozzie Guillen .05
171 White Sox logo .05
172 Robin Ventura .05
173 Frank Thomas .35
174 Tim Raines .05
175 Albert Belle .05
176 Manny Ramirez .35
177 Eddie Murray .35
178 Orel Hershiser .05
179 Indians logo .05
180 Kenny Lofton .05
181 Carlos Baerga .05
182 Jose Mesa .05
183 Gary Gaetti .05
184 Tom Goodwin .05
185 Kevin Appier .05
186 Jon Nunnally .05
187 Royals logo .05
188 Wally Joyner .05
189 Jeff Montgomery .05
190 Johnny Damon .25
191 B.J. Surhoff .05
192 Ricky Bones .05
193 John Jaha .05
194 Dave Nilsson .05
195 Brewers logo .05
196 Greg Vaughn .05
197 Kevin Seitzer .05
198 Joe Oliver .05
199 Chuck Knoblauch .05
200 Kirby Puckett .45
201 Marty Cordova .05
202 Pat Meares .05
203 Twins logo .05
204 Scott Stahoviak .05
205 Matt Walbeck .05
206 Pedro Munoz .05
207 Garret Anderson .05
208 Chili Davis .05
209 Tim Salmon .10
210 J.T. Snow .05
211 Angels logo .05
212 Jim Edmonds .05
213 Chuck Finley .05
214 Mark Langston .05
215 Dennis Eckersley .30
216 Todd Stottlemyre .05
217 Geronimo Berroa .05
218 Mark McGwire .65
219 A's logo .05
220 Brent Gates .05
221 Terry Steinbach .05
222 Rickey Henderson .35
223 Ken Griffey Jr. .60
224 Alex Rodriguez .65
225 Tino Martinez .05
226 Randy Johnson .35
227 Mariners logo .05
228 Jay Buhner .05
229 Vince Coleman .05
230 Edgar Martinez .05
231 Will Clark .10
232 Juan Gonzalez .35
233 Kenny Rogers .05
234 Ivan Rodriguez .30
235 Rangers logo .05
236 Mickey Tettleton .05
237 Dean Palmer .05
238 Otis Nixon .05
239 Hideo Nomo (Rookie) .20
240 Quilvio Veras (Rookie) .05
241 Jason Isringhausen (Rookie) .05
242 Andy Pettitte (Rookie) .05
243 Chipper Jones (Rookie) .25
244 Garret Anderson (Rookie) .05
245 Charles Johnson (Rookie) .05
246 Marty Cordova (Rookie) .05

1997 Fleer

Fleer maintained its matte-finish coating for 1997 after it debuted in the 1996 product. The regular-issue Series 1 has 500 cards equipped with icons designating All-Stars, League Leaders and World Series cards. There were also 10 checklist cards in the regular-issue set, featuring stars on the front. Fleer arrived in 10-card packs and had a Tiffany Collection parallel set and six different insert sets, including Rookie Sensations, Golden Memories, Team Leaders, Night and Day, Zone and Lumber Company. Series 2 comprises 261 cards plus inserts Decade of Excellence, Bleacher Bashers, Diamond Tributes, Goudey Greats, Headliners, New Horizons and Soaring Stars.

	NM/M
Complete Set (761):	100.00
Complete Series One Set (500):	30.00
Complete Series 2 Set (261):	70.00
Common Player:	.05
Complete Tiffany Set (1-761):	500.00
Tiffany Stars/RC's:	8X
A. Jones Circa AU/200:	35.00
Series 2 Pack (10):	3.00
Series 2 Wax Box (36):	90.00

1 Roberto Alomar .10
2 Brady Anderson .05
3 Bobby Bonilla .05
4 Rocky Coppinger .05
5 Cesar Devarez .05
6 Scott Erickson .05
7 Jeffrey Hammonds .05
8 Chris Hoiles .05
9 Eddie Murray 1.00
10 Mike Mussina .40
11 Randy Myers .05
12 Rafael Palmeiro .75
13 Cal Ripken Jr. 2.50
14 B.J. Surhoff .05
15 David Wells .05
16 Todd Zeile .05
17 Darren Bragg .05
18 Jose Canseco .40
19 Roger Clemens 1.75
20 Wil Cordero .05
21 Jeff Frye .05
22 Nomar Garciaparra 1.75
23 Tom Gordon .05
24 Mike Greenwell .05
25 Reggie Jefferson .05
26 Jose Malave .05
27 Tim Naehring .05
28 Troy O'Leary .05
29 Heathcliff Slocumb .05
30 Mike Stanley .05
31 John Valentin .05
32 Mo Vaughn .05
33 Tim Wakefield .05
34 Garret Anderson .05
35 George Arias .05
36 Shawn Boskie .05
37 Chili Davis .05
38 Jason Dickson .05
39 Gary DiSarcina .05
40 Jim Edmonds .05
41 Darin Erstad .10
42 Jorge Fabregas .05
43 Chuck Finley .05
44 Todd Greene .05
45 Mike Holtz **RC** .05
46 Rex Hudler .05
47 Mike James .05
48 Mark Langston .05
49 Troy Percival .05
50 Tim Salmon .15
51 Jeff Schmidt .05
52 J.T. Snow .05
53 Randy Velarde .05
54 Wilson Alvarez .05
55 Harold Baines .05
56 James Baldwin .05
57 Jason Bere .05
58 Mike Cameron .05
59 Ray Durham .05
60 Alex Fernandez .05
61 Ozzie Guillen .05
62 Roberto Hernandez .05
63 Ron Karkovice .05
64 Darren Lewis .05
65 Dave Martinez .05
66 Lyle Mouton .05
67 Greg Norton .05
68 Tony Phillips .05
69 Chris Snopek .05
70 Kevin Tapani .05
71 Danny Tartabull .05
72 Frank Thomas 1.00
73 Robin Ventura .05
74 Sandy Alomar Jr. .05
75 Albert Belle .05
76 Mark Carreon .05
77 Julio Franco .05
78 Brian Giles **RC** 1.00
79 Orel Hershiser .05
80 Kenny Lofton .05
81 Dennis Martinez .05
82 Jack McDowell .05
83 Jose Mesa .05
84 Charles Nagy .05
85 Chad Ogea .05
86 Eric Plunk .05
87 Manny Ramirez 1.00
88 Kevin Seitzer .05
89 Julian Tavarez .05
90 Jim Thome .65
91 Jose Vizcaino .05
92 Omar Vizquel .05
93 Brad Ausmus .05
94 Kimera Bartee .05
95 Raul Casanova .05
96 Tony Clark .05
97 John Cummings .05
98 Travis Fryman .05
99 Bob Higginson .05
100 Mark Lewis .05

No.	Player	Value
101	Felipe Lira	.05
102	Phil Nevin	.05
103	Melvin Nieves	.05
104	Curtis Pride	.05
105	A.J. Sager	.05
106	Ruben Sierra	.05
107	Justin Thompson	.05
108	Alan Trammell	.05
109	Kevin Appier	.05
110	Tim Belcher	.05
111	Jaime Bluma	.05
112	Johnny Damon	.35
113	Tom Goodwin	.05
114	Chris Haney	.05
115	Keith Lockhart	.05
116	Mike Macfarlane	.05
117	Jeff Montgomery	.05
118	Jose Offerman	.05
119	Craig Paquette	.05
120	Joe Randa	.05
121	Bip Roberts	.05
122	Jose Rosado	.05
123	Mike Sweeney	.05
124	Michael Tucker	.05
125	Jeromy Burnitz	.05
126	Jeff Cirillo	.05
127	Jeff D'Amico	.05
128	Mike Fetters	.05
129	John Jaha	.05
130	Scott Karl	.05
131	Jesse Levis	.05
132	Mark Loretta	.05
133	Mike Matheny	.05
134	Ben McDonald	.05
135	Matt Mieske	.05
136	Marc Newfield	.05
137	Dave Nilsson	.05
138	Jose Valentin	.05
139	Fernando Vina	.05
140	Bob Wickman	.05
141	Gerald Williams	.05
142	Rick Aguilera	.05
143	Rich Becker	.05
144	Ron Coomer	.05
145	Marty Cordova	.05
146	Roberto Kelly	.05
147	Chuck Knoblauch	.05
148	Matt Lawton	.05
149	Pat Meares	.05
150	Travis Miller	.05
151	Paul Molitor	1.00
152	Greg Myers	.05
153	Dan Naulty	.05
154	Kirby Puckett	1.50
155	Brad Radke	.05
156	Frank Rodriguez	.05
157	Scott Stahoviak	.05
158	Dave Stevens	.05
159	Matt Walbeck	.05
160	Todd Walker	.05
161	Wade Boggs	1.50
162	David Cone	.05
163	Mariano Duncan	.05
164	Cecil Fielder	.05
165	Joe Girardi	.05
166	Dwight Gooden	.05
167	Charlie Hayes	.05
168	Derek Jeter	2.50
169	Jimmy Key	.05
170	Jim Leyritz	.05
171	Tino Martinez	.05
172	Ramiro Mendoza RC	.10
173	Jeff Nelson	.05
174	Paul O'Neill	.05
175	Andy Pettitte	.35
176	Mariano Rivera	.15
177	Ruben Rivera	.05
178	Kenny Rogers	.05
179	Darryl Strawberry	.05
180	John Wetteland	.05
181	Bernie Williams	.10
182	Willie Adams	.05
183	Tony Batista	.05
184	Geronimo Berroa	.05
185	Mike Bordick	.05
186	Scott Brosius	.05
187	Bobby Chouinard	.05
188	Jim Corsi	.05
189	Brent Gates	.05
190	Jason Giambi	.50
191	Jose Herrera	.05
192	Damon Mashore RC	.05
193	Mark McGwire	2.25
194	Mike Mohler	.05
195	Scott Spiezio	.05
196	Terry Steinbach	.05
197	Bill Taylor	.05
198	John Wasdin	.05
199	Steve Wojciechowski	.05
200	Ernie Young	.05
201	Rich Amaral	.05
202	Jay Buhner	.05
203	Norm Charlton	.05
204	Joey Cora	.05
205	Russ Davis	.05
206	Ken Griffey Jr.	2.00
207	Sterling Hitchcock	.05
208	Brian Hunter	.05
209	Raul Ibanez	.05
210	Randy Johnson	1.00
211	Edgar Martinez	.05
212	Jamie Moyer	.05
213	Alex Rodriguez	2.25
214	Paul Sorrento	.05
215	Matt Wagner	.05
216	Bob Wells	.05
217	Dan Wilson	.05
218	Damon Buford	.05
219	Will Clark	.10
220	Kevin Elster	.05
221	Juan Gonzalez	.75
222	Rusty Greer	.05
223	Kevin Gross	.05
224	Darryl Hamilton	.05
225	Mike Henneman	.05
226	Ken Hill	.05
227	Mark McLemore	.05
228	Darren Oliver	.05
229	Dean Palmer	.05
230	Roger Pavlik	.05
231	Ivan Rodriguez	.75
232	Mickey Tettleton	.05
233	Bobby Witt	.05
234	Jacob Brumfield	.05
235	Joe Carter	.05
236	Tim Crabtree	.05
237	Carlos Delgado	.50
238	Huck Flener	.05
239	Alex Gonzalez	.05
240	Shawn Green	.20
241	Juan Guzman	.05
242	Pat Hentgen	.05
243	Marty Janzen	.05
244	Sandy Martinez	.05
245	Otis Nixon	.05
246	Charlie O'Brien	.05
247	John Olerud	.05
248	Robert Perez	.05
249	Ed Sprague	.05
250	Mike Timlin	.05
251	Steve Avery	.05
252	Jeff Blauser	.05
253	Brad Clontz	.05
254	Jermaine Dye	.05
255	Tom Glavine	.30
256	Marquis Grissom	.05
257	Andruw Jones	1.00
258	Chipper Jones	1.50
259	David Justice	.05
260	Ryan Klesko	.05
261	Mark Lemke	.05
262	Javier Lopez	.05
263	Greg Maddux	1.50
264	Fred McGriff	.05
265	Greg McMichael	.05
266	Denny Neagle	.05
267	Terry Pendleton	.05
268	Eddie Perez	.05
269	John Smoltz	.05
270	Terrell Wade	.05
271	Mark Wohlers	.05
272	Terry Adams	.05
273	Brant Brown	.05
274	Leo Gomez	.05
275	Luis Gonzalez	.10
276	Mark Grace	.10
277	Tyler Houston	.05
278	Robin Jennings	.05
279	Brooks Kieschnick	.05
280	Brian McRae	.05
281	Jaime Navarro	.05
282	Ryne Sandberg	1.50
283	Scott Servais	.05
284	Sammy Sosa	1.75
285	Dave Swartzbaugh RC	.05
286	Amaury Telemaco	.05
287	Steve Trachsel	.05
288	Pedro Valdes RC	.05
289	Turk Wendell	.05
290	Bret Boone	.05
291	Jeff Branson	.05
292	Jeff Brantley	.05
293	Eric Davis	.05
294	Willie Greene	.05
295	Thomas Howard	.05
296	Barry Larkin	.05
297	Kevin Mitchell	.05
298	Hal Morris	.05
299	Chad Mottola	.05
300	Joe Oliver	.05
301	Mark Portugal	.05
302	Roger Salkeld	.05
303	Reggie Sanders	.05
304	Pete Schourek	.05
305	John Smiley	.05
306	Eddie Taubensee	.05
307	Dante Bichette	.05
308	Ellis Burks	.05
309	Vinny Castilla	.05
310	Andres Galarraga	.05
311	Curt Leskanic	.05
312	Quinton McCracken	.05
313	Neifi Perez	.05
314	Jeff Reed	.05
315	Steve Reed	.05
316	Armando Reynoso	.05
317	Kevin Ritz	.05
318	Bruce Ruffin	.05
319	Larry Walker	.05
320	Walt Weiss	.05
321	Jamey Wright	.05
322	Eric Young	.05
323	Kurt Abbott	.05
324	Alex Arias	.05
325	Kevin Brown	.05
326	Luis Castillo	.05
327	Greg Colbrunn	.05
328	Jeff Conine	.05
329	Andre Dawson	.25
330	Charles Johnson	.05
331	Al Leiter	.05
332	Ralph Milliard	.05
333	Robb Nen	.05
334	Pat Rapp	.05
335	Edgar Renteria	.05
336	Gary Sheffield	.35
337	Devon White	.05
338	Bob Abreu	.05
339	Jeff Bagwell	1.00
340	Derek Bell	.05
341	Sean Berry	.05
342	Craig Biggio	.05
343	Doug Drabek	.05
344	Tony Eusebio	.05
345	Ricky Gutierrez	.05
346	Mike Hampton	.05
347	Brian Hunter	.05
348	Todd Jones	.05
349	Darryl Kile	.05
350	Derrick May	.05
351	Orlando Miller	.05
352	James Mouton	.05
353	Shane Reynolds	.05
354	Billy Wagner	.05
355	Donne Wall	.05
356	Mike Blowers	.05
357	Brett Butler	.05
358	Roger Cedeno	.05
359	Chad Curtis	.05
360	Delino DeShields	.05
361	Greg Gagne	.05
362	Karim Garcia	.10
363	Wilton Guerrero	.05
364	Todd Hollandsworth	.05
365	Eric Karros	.05
366	Ramon Martinez	.05
367	Raul Mondesi	.05
368	Hideo Nomo	.75
369	Antonio Osuna	.05
370	Chan Ho Park	.05
371	Mike Piazza	2.00
372	Ismael Valdes	.05
373	Todd Worrell	.05
374	Moises Alou	.05
375	Shane Andrews	.05
376	Yamil Benitez	.05
377	Jeff Fassero	.05
378	Darrin Fletcher	.05
379	Cliff Floyd	.05
380	Mark Grudzielanek	.05
381	Mike Lansing	.05
382	Barry Manuel	.05
383	Pedro Martinez	1.00
384	Henry Rodriguez	.05
385	Mel Rojas	.05
386	F.P. Santangelo	.05
387	David Segui	.05
388	Ugueth Urbina	.05
389	Rondell White	.05
390	Edgardo Alfonzo	.05
391	Carlos Baerga	.05
392	Mark Clark	.05
393	Alvaro Espinoza	.05
394	John Franco	.05
395	Bernard Gilkey	.05
396	Pete Harnisch	.05
397	Todd Hundley	.05
398	Butch Huskey	.05
399	Jason Isringhausen	.05
400	Lance Johnson	.05
401	Bobby Jones	.05
402	Alex Ochoa	.05
403	Rey Ordonez	.05
404	Robert Person	.05
405	Paul Wilson	.05
406	Matt Beech	.05
407	Ron Blazier	.05
408	Ricky Bottalico	.05
409	Lenny Dykstra	.05
410	Jim Eisenreich	.05
411	Bobby Estalella	.05
412	Mike Grace	.05
413	Gregg Jefferies	.05
414	Mike Lieberthal	.05
415	Wendell Magee Jr.	.05
416	Mickey Morandini	.05
417	Ricky Otero	.05
418	Scott Rolen	.75
419	Ken Ryan	.05
420	Benito Santiago	.05
421	Curt Schilling	.25
422	Kevin Sefcik	.05
423	Jermaine Allensworth	.05
424	Trey Beamon	.05
425	Jay Bell	.05
426	Francisco Cordova	.05
427	Carlos Garcia	.05
428	Mark Johnson	.05
429	Jason Kendall	.05
430	Jeff King	.05
431	Jon Lieber	.05
432	Al Martin	.05
433	Orlando Merced	.05
434	Ramon Morel	.05
435	Matt Ruebel	.05
436	Jason Schmidt	.05
437	Marc Wilkins RC	.05
438	Alan Benes	.05
439	Andy Benes	.05
440	Royce Clayton	.05
441	Dennis Eckersley	.65
442	Gary Gaetti	.05
443	Ron Gant	.05
444	Aaron Holbert	.05
445	Brian Jordan	.05
446	Ray Lankford	.05
447	John Mabry	.05
448	T.J. Mathews	.05
449	Willie McGee	.05
450	Donovan Osborne	.05
451	Tom Pagnozzi	.05
452	Ozzie Smith	1.50
453	Todd Stottlemyre	.05
454	Mark Sweeney	.05
455	Dmitri Young	.05
456	Andy Ashby	.05
457	Ken Caminiti	.05
458	Archi Cianfrocco	.05
459	Steve Finley	.05
460	John Flaherty	.05
461	Chris Gomez	.05
462	Tony Gwynn	1.50
463	Joey Hamilton	.05
464	Rickey Henderson	1.00
465	Trevor Hoffman	.05
466	Brian Johnson	.05
467	Wally Joyner	.05
468	Jody Reed	.05
469	Scott Sanders	.05
470	Bob Tewksbury	.05
471	Fernando Valenzuela	.05
472	Greg Vaughn	.05
473	Tim Worrell	.05
474	Rich Aurilia	.05
475	Rod Beck	.05
476	Marvin Benard	.05
477	Barry Bonds	2.50
478	Jay Canizaro	.05
479	Shawon Dunston	.05
480	Shawn Estes	.05
481	Mark Gardner	.05
482	Glenallen Hill	.05
483	Stan Javier	.05
484	Marcus Jensen	.05
485	Bill Mueller RC	1.50
486	William Van Landingham	.05
487	Allen Watson	.05
488	Rick Wilkins	.05
489	Matt Williams	.05
489p	Matt Williams/OPS	1.50
490	Desi Wilson	.05
491	Checklist (Albert Belle)	.05
492	Checklist (Ken Griffey Jr.)	.85
493	Checklist (Andruw Jones)	.40
494	Checklist (Chipper Jones)	.60
495	Checklist (Mark McGwire)	1.00
496	Checklist (Paul Molitor)	.45
497	Checklist (Mike Piazza)	.85
498	Checklist (Cal Ripken Jr.)	1.25
499	Checklist (Alex Rodriguez)	1.00
500	Checklist (Frank Thomas)	.45
501	Kenny Lofton	.05
502	Carlos Perez	.05
503	Tim Raines	.05
504	Danny Patterson RC	.05
505	Derrick May	.05
506	Dave Hollins	.05
507	Felipe Crespo	.05
508	Brian Banks	.05
509	Jeff Kent	.05
510	Bubba Trammell RC	.25
511	Robert Person	.05
512	David Arias RC (Ortiz)	60.00
513	Ryan Jones	.05
514	David Justice	.05
515	Will Cunnane	.05
516	Russ Johnson	.05
517	John Burkett	.05
518	Robinson Checo RC	.05
519	Ricardo Rincon RC	.05
520	Woody Williams	.05
521	Rick Helling	.05
522	Jorge Posada	.05
523	Kevin Orie	.05
524	Fernando Tatis RC	.15
525	Jermaine Dye	.05
526	Brian Hunter	.05
527	Greg McMichael	.05
528	Matt Wagner	.05
529	Richie Sexson	.05
530	Scott Ruffcorn	.05
531	Luis Gonzalez	.10
532	Mike Johnson	.05
533	Mark Petkovsek	.05
534	Doug Drabek	.05
535	Jose Canseco	.40
536	Bobby Bonilla	.05
537	J.T. Snow	.05
538	Shawon Dunston	.05
539	John Ericks	.05
540	Terry Steinbach	.05
541	Jay Bell	.05
542	Joe Borowski	.05
543	David Wells	.05
544	Justin Towle RC	.10
545	Mike Blowers	.05
546	Shannon Stewart	.05
547	Rudy Pemberton	.05
548	Bill Swift	.05
549	Osvaldo Fernandez	.05
550	Eddie Murray	1.00
551	Don Wengert	.05
552	Brad Ausmus	.05
553	Carlos Garcia	.05
554	Jose Guillen	.05
555	Rheal Cormier	.05
556	Doug Brocail	.05
557	Rex Hudler	.05
558	Armando Benitez	.05
559	Elieser Marrero	.05
560	Ricky Ledee RC	.25
561	Bartolo Colon	.05
562	Quilvio Veras	.05
563	Alex Fernandez	.05
564	Darren Dreifort	.05
565	Benji Gil	.05
566	Kent Mercker	.05
567	Glendon Rusch	.05
568	Ramon Tatis RC	.05
569	Roger Clemens	1.75
570	Mark Lewis	.05
571	Emil Brown RC	.05
572	Jaime Navarro	.05
573	Sherman Obando	.05
574	John Wasdin	.05
575	Calvin Maduro	.05
576	Todd Jones	.05
577	Orlando Merced	.05
578	Cal Eldred	.05
579	Mark Gubicza	.05
580	Michael Tucker	.05
581	Tony Saunders RC	.05
582	Garvin Alston	.05
583	Joe Roa	.05
584	Brady Raggio RC	.05
585	Jimmy Key	.05
586	Marc Sagmoen RC	.05
587	Jim Bullinger	.05
588	Yorkis Perez	.05
589	Jose Cruz Jr. RC	.75
590	Mike Stanton	.05
591	Deivi Cruz RC	.25
592	Steve Karsay	.05
593	Mike Trombley	.05
594	Doug Glanville	.05
595	Scott Sanders	.05
596	Thomas Howard	.05
597	T.J. Staton	.05
598	Garrett Stephenson	.05
599	Rico Brogna	.05
600	Albert Belle	.05
601	Jose Vizcaino	.05
602	Chili Davis	.05
603	Shane Mack	.05
604	Jim Eisenreich	.05
605	Todd Zeile	.05
606	Brian Boehringer	.05
607	Paul Shuey	.05
608	Kevin Tapani	.05
609	John Wetteland	.05
610	Jim Leyritz	.05
611	Ray Montgomery	.05
612	Doug Bochtler	.05
613	Wady Almonte	.05
614	Danny Tartabull	.05
615	Orlando Miller	.05
616	Bobby Ayala	.05
617	Tony Graffanino	.05
618	Marc Valdes	.05
619	Ron Villone	.05
620	Derrek Lee	.05
621	Greg Colbrunn	.05
622	Felix Heredia RC	.10
623	Carl Everett	.05
624	Mark Thompson	.05
625	Jeff Granger	.05
626	Damian Jackson	.05
627	Mark Leiter	.05
628	Chris Holt	.05
629	Dario Veras RC	.05
630	Dave Burba	.05
631	Darryl Hamilton	.05
632	Mark Acre	.05
633	Fernando Hernandez	.05
634	Terry Mulholland	.05
635	Dustin Hermanson	.05
636	Delino DeShields	.05
637	Steve Avery	.05
638	Tony Womack RC	.10
639	Mark Whiten	.05
640	Marquis Grissom	.05
641	Xavier Hernandez	.05
642	Eric Davis	.05
643	Bob Tewksbury	.05
644	Dante Powell	.05
645	Carlos Castillo	.05
646	Chris Widger	.05
647	Moises Alou	.05
648	Pat Listach	.05
649	Edgar Ramos	.05
650	Deion Sanders	.05
651	John Olerud	.05
652	Todd Dunwoody	.05
653	Randall Simon RC	.10
654	Dan Carlson	.05
655	Matt Williams	.05
656	Jeff King	.05
657	Luis Alicea	.05
658	Brian Moehler	.05
659	Ariel Prieto	.05
660	Kevin Elster	.05
661	Mark Hutton	.05
662	Aaron Sele	.05
663	Graeme Lloyd	.05
664	John Burke	.05
665	Mel Rojas	.05
666	Sid Fernandez	.05
667	Pedro Astacio	.05
668	Jeff Abbott	.05
669	Darren Daulton	.05
670	Mike Bordick	.05
671	Sterling Hitchcock	.05
672	Damion Easley	.05
673	Armando Reynoso	.05
674	Pat Cline	.05
675	Orlando Cabrera RC	.50
676	Alan Embree	.05
677	Brian Bevil	.05
678	David Weathers	.05
679	Cliff Floyd	.05
680	Joe Randa	.05
681	Bill Haselman	.05
682	Jeff Fassero	.05
683	Matt Morris	.05
684	Mark Portugal	.05
685	Lee Smith	.05
686	Pokey Reese	.05
687	Benito Santiago	.05
688	Brian Johnson	.05
689	Brent Brede RC	.05
690	Shigetosi Hasegawa	.05
691	Julio Santana	.05
692	Steve Kline	.05
693	Julian Tavarez	.05
694	John Hudek	.05
695	Manny Alexander	.05
696	Roberto Alomar (Encore)	.10
697	Jeff Bagwell (Encore)	.45
698	Barry Bonds (Encore)	1.25
699	Ken Caminiti (Encore)	.05
700	Juan Gonzalez (Encore)	.35
701	Ken Griffey Jr. (Encore)	.85
702	Tony Gwynn (Encore)	.60
703	Derek Jeter (Encore)	1.25
704	Andruw Jones (Encore)	.45
705	Chipper Jones (Encore)	.60
706	Barry Larkin (Encore)	.05
707	Greg Maddux (Encore)	.60
708	Mark McGwire (Encore)	1.00
709	Paul Molitor (Encore)	.45
710	Hideo Nomo (Encore)	.35
711	Andy Pettitte (Encore)	.30
712	Mike Piazza (Encore)	.85
713	Manny Ramirez (Encore)	.45
714	Cal Ripken Jr. (Encore)	1.25
715	Alex Rodriguez (Encore)	1.00
716	Ryne Sandberg (Encore)	.60
717	John Smoltz (Encore)	.05
718	Frank Thomas (Encore)	.05
719	Mo Vaughn (Encore)	.05
720	Bernie Williams (Encore)	.10
721	Checklist (Tim Salmon)	.05
722	Checklist (Greg Maddux)	.60
723	Checklist (Cal Ripken Jr.)	1.25
724	Checklist (Mo Vaughn)	.05
725	Checklist (Ryne Sandberg)	.45
726	Checklist (Frank Thomas)	.50
727	Checklist (Barry Larkin)	.05
728	Checklist (Manny Ramirez)	.45
729	Checklist (Andres Galarraga)	.05
730	Checklist (Tony Clark)	.05
731	Checklist (Gary Sheffield)	.20
732	Checklist (Jeff Bagwell)	.40
733	Checklist (Kevin Appier)	.05
734	Checklist (Mike Piazza)	.85
735	Checklist (Jeff Cirillo)	.05
736	Checklist (Paul Molitor)	.40
737	Checklist (Henry Rodriguez)	.05
738	Checklist (Todd Hundley)	.05
739	Checklist (Derek Jeter)	1.25
740	Checklist (Mark McGwire)	1.00
741	Checklist (Curt Schilling)	.15
742	Checklist (Jason Kendall)	.05
743	Checklist (Tony Gwynn)	.60
744	Checklist (Barry Bonds)	1.25
745	Checklist (Ken Griffey Jr.)	.85
746	Checklist (Brian Jordan)	.05
747	Checklist (Juan Gonzalez)	.40
748	Checklist (Joe Carter)	.05
749	Arizona Diamondbacks	.05
750	Tampa Bay Devil Rays	.05
751	Hideki Irabu RC	.15
752	Jeremi Gonzalez RC	.15
753	Mario Valdez RC	.05
754	Aaron Boone	.05
755	Brett Tomko	.05
756	Jaret Wright RC	1.00
757	Ryan McGuire	.05
758	Jason McDonald	.05
759	Adrian Brown RC	.05
760	Keith Foulke RC	.25
761	Checklist	

ABBREVIATIONS

OPS - Overprinted "Promotional Sample"

Tiffany

Insertion odds were considerably lengthened for the UV-coated Tiffany Collection parallels in 1997 Fleer - to one card per 20 packs.

	NM/M
Complete Set (761):	500.00
Common Player:	1.00
Stars/RC's:	8X
512 David Arias (Ortiz)	140.00

Bleacher Blasters

This 10-card insert features some of the game's top power hitters and was found in retail packs only. Cards featured a die-cut "burst" pattern on an etched foil background. Backs have a portrait photo and career highlights. Cards were inserted 1:36 packs.

		NM/M
Complete Set (10):		40.00
Common Player:		1.50
1	Albert Belle	1.50
2	Barry Bonds	10.00
3	Juan Gonzalez	2.00
4	Ken Griffey Jr.	6.00
5	Mark McGwire	8.00
6	Mike Piazza	6.00
7	Alex Rodriguez	8.00
8	Frank Thomas	4.00
9	Mo Vaughn	1.50
10	Matt Williams	1.50

Decade of Excellence

A 12-card insert found 1:36 in hobby shop packs, cards are in a format similar to the 1987 Fleer set and feature vintage photos of players who started their careers no later than the '87 season. Ten percent of the press run (1:360 packs) received a special foil treatment and designation as "Rare Traditions."

		NM/M
Complete Set (12):		35.00
Common Player:		1.50
Rare Tradition:		12X
1	Wade Boggs	4.50
2	Barry Bonds	9.00
3	Roger Clemens	6.00
4	Tony Gwynn	4.50
5	Rickey Henderson	3.00
6	Greg Maddux	4.50
7	Mark McGwire	6.00
8	Paul Molitor	3.00
9	Eddie Murray	3.00
10	Cal Ripken Jr.	9.00
11	Ryne Sandberg	4.50
12	Matt Williams	1.50

Diamond Tribute

Twelve of the game's top stars are highlighted in this set. Fronts feature an em-

bossed rainbow prismatic foil background and gold lettering. Backs have an action photo and a few sentences about the player. They were inserted 1:288 packs.

		NM/M
Complete Set (12):		120.00
Common Player:		3.00
1	Albert Belle	3.00
2	Barry Bonds	20.00
3	Juan Gonzalez	5.00
4	Ken Griffey Jr.	12.50
5	Tony Gwynn	10.00
6	Greg Maddux	10.00
7	Mark McGwire	15.00
8	Eddie Murray	8.00
9	Mike Piazza	12.50
10	Cal Ripken Jr.	20.00
11	Alex Rodriguez	15.00
12	Frank Thomas	8.00

Golden Memories

Golden Memories captures 10 different highlights from the 1996 season, and is inserted one per 16 packs. Moments like Dwight Gooden's no hitter, Paul Molitor's 3000th hit and Eddie Murray's 500th home run are highlighted on a horizontal format.

		NM/M
Complete Set (10):		6.00
Common Player:		.25
1	Barry Bonds	2.00
2	Dwight Gooden	.25
3	Todd Hundley	.25
4	Mark McGwire	1.50
5	Paul Molitor	.75
6	Eddie Murray	.75
7	Hideo Nomo	.50
8	Mike Piazza	1.25
9	Cal Ripken Jr.	2.00
10	Ozzie Smith	1.00

Goudey Greats

Using a 2-3/8" x 2-7/8" format reminiscent of 1933 Goudey cards, this 15-card insert offers today's top players in classic old-time design. Cards were inserted 1:8 packs. A limited number (1% of press run) of cards received a special gold-foil treatment and were found only in hobby packs.

		NM/M
Complete Set (15):		20.00
Common Player:		.50
Foils:		15X
1	Barry Bonds	4.00
2	Ken Griffey Jr.	3.00

3	Tony Gwynn	2.00
4	Derek Jeter	4.00
5	Chipper Jones	2.00
6	Kenny Lofton	.50
7	Greg Maddux	2.00
8	Mark McGwire	3.50
9	Eddie Murray	1.50
10	Mike Piazza	3.00
11	Cal Ripken Jr.	4.00
12	Alex Rodriguez	3.50
13	Ryne Sandberg	2.00
14	Frank Thomas	1.50
15	Mo Vaughn	.50

Headliners

This 20-card insert highlights the personal achievements of each of the players depicted. Cards were inserted 1:2 packs and feature multicolor foil stamping on the fronts and a newspaper-style account of the player's achievement on the back.

		NM/M
Complete Set (20):		5.00
Common Player:		.10
1	Jeff Bagwell	.25
2	Albert Belle	.10
3	Barry Bonds	1.00
4	Ken Caminiti	.10
5	Juan Gonzalez	.20
6	Ken Griffey Jr.	.60
7	Tony Gwynn	.40
8	Derek Jeter	1.00
9	Andruw Jones	.25
10	Chipper Jones	.40
11	Greg Maddux	.40
12	Mark McGwire	.75
13	Paul Molitor	.25
14	Eddie Murray	.25
15	Mike Piazza	.60
16	Cal Ripken Jr.	1.00
17	Alex Rodriguez	.75
18	Ryne Sandberg	.40
19	John Smoltz	.20
20	Frank Thomas	.25

Lumber Co.

Lumber Co. inserts were found every 48 retail packs. The cards were printed on a die-cut, spherical wood-like pattern, with the player imposed on the left side. Eighteen of the top power hitters in baseball are highlighted.

		NM/M
Complete Set (18):		45.00
Common Player:		1.00
1	Brady Anderson	1.00
2	Jeff Bagwell	3.00
3	Albert Belle	1.00
4	Barry Bonds	8.00
5	Jay Buhner	1.00
6	Ellis Burks	1.00
7	Andres Galarraga	1.00
8	Juan Gonzalez	2.00
9	Ken Griffey Jr.	5.00
10	Todd Hundley	1.00
11	Ryan Klesko	1.00
12	Mark McGwire	6.00
13	Mike Piazza	5.00
14	Alex Rodriguez	6.00
15	Gary Sheffield	2.00
16	Sammy Sosa	4.00
17	Frank Thomas	3.00
18	Mo Vaughn	1.00

New Horizons

Rookies and prospects expected to make an impact during the 1996 season were fea-

1997-98 Fleer Million Dollar Moments

By assembling a complete set of 50 baseball "Million Dollar Moments" cards prior to July 31, 1998, a collector could win $50,000 a year through 2018. The catch, of course, is that cards #46-50 were printed in very limited quantities, with only one card #50. (Stated odds of winning the million were one in nearly 46,000,000.) The Moments cards have player action photos on front vignetted into a black border. The Fleer Million Dollar Moments logo is at top, with the player name and the date and details of his highlight at bottom in orange and white. Backs have the contest rules in fine print. Instant Win versions of some cards were also issued.

		NM/M
Complete Set (45):		2.00
Common Player:		.05
1	Checklist	.05
2	Derek Jeter	.45
3	Babe Ruth	.25
4	Barry Bonds	.25
5	Brooks Robinson	.05
6	Todd Hundley	.05
7	Johnny Vander Meer	.05
8	Cal Ripken Jr.	.45
9	Bill Mazeroski	.05
10	Chipper Jones	.25
11	Frank Robinson	.05
12	Roger Clemens	.35
13	Bob Feller	.30
14	Mike Piazza	.30
15	Joe Nuxhall	.05
16	Hideo Nomo	.15
17	Jackie Robinson	.05
18	Orel Hershiser	.05
19	Bobby Richardson	.05
20	Joe Carter	.05
21	Al Kaline	.05
22	Bernie Williams	.05
23	Don Larsen	.05
24	Rickey Henderson	.15
25	Maury Wills	.05
26	Andruw Jones	.15
27	Bobby Richardson	.05
28	Alex Rodriguez	.35
29	Jim Bunning	.05
30	Ken Caminiti	.05
31	Bob Gibson	.05
32	Frank Thomas	.20
33	Mickey Lolich	.05
34	John Smoltz	.05
35	Ron Swoboda	.05
36	Albert Belle	.05
37	Chris Chambliss	.05
38	Juan Gonzalez	.10
39	Ron Blomberg	.05
40	John Wetteland	.05
41	Carlton Fisk	.05
42	Mo Vaughn	.05
43	Bucky Dent	.05
44	Greg Maddux	.25
45	Willie Stargell	.05

tured in this 15-card insert set. Card fronts feature a rainbow foil background with the words "New Horizon" featured prominently on the bottom under the player's name. Cards were inserted 1:4 packs.

		NM/M
Complete Set (15):		2.00
Common Player:		.05
1	Bob Abreu	.10
2	Jose Cruz Jr.	.05
3	Darin Erstad	.10
4	Nomar Garciaparra	.75
5	Vladimir Guerrero	.60
6	Wilton Guerrero	.05
7	Jose Guillen	.05
8	Hideki Irabu	.05
9	Andruw Jones	.60
10	Kevin Orie	.05
11	Scott Rolen	.50
12	Scott Spiezio	.05
13	Bubba Trammell	.05
14	Todd Walker	.05
15	Dmitri Young	.05

Night & Day

Night and Day spotlighted 10 stars with unusual prowess during night or day games. These lenticular cards carried the toughest insert ratios in Fleer Baseball at one per 288 packs.

		NM/M
Complete Set (10):		45.00
Common Player:		1.00
1	Barry Bonds	12.00
2	Ellis Burks	1.00
3	Juan Gonzalez	2.00
4	Ken Griffey Jr.	6.00
5	Mark McGwire	7.50
6	Mike Piazza	6.00
7	Manny Ramirez	4.00
8	Alex Rodriguez	8.00
9	John Smoltz	2.00
10	Frank Thomas	4.00

Rookie Sensations

Rookies Sensations showcased 20 of the top up-and-coming stars in baseball. Appearing every six packs, these inserts have the feaured player in the foreground, with the background look of painted brush strokes.

		NM/M
Complete Set (20):		6.00
Common Player:		.25
1	Jermaine Allensworth	.25
2	James Baldwin	.25
3	Alan Benes	.25
4	Jermaine Dye	.25
5	Darin Erstad	.50
6	Todd Hollandsworth	.25
7	Derek Jeter	2.50
8	Jason Kendall	.25
9	Alex Ochoa	.25
10	Rey Ordonez	.25
11	Edgar Renteria	.25
12	Bob Abreu	.50
13	Nomar Garciaparra	1.50

14	Wilton Guerrero	.25
15	Andruw Jones	1.00
16	Wendell Magee	.25
17	Neifi Perez	.25
18	Scott Rolen	.75
19	Scott Spiezio	.25
20	Todd Walker	.25

Soaring Stars

A 12-card insert found 1:12 packs designed to profile players with outstanding statistical performances early in their careers. Fronts have player action photos set against a background of rainbow holographic stars which appear, disappear and twinkle as the viewing angle is changed. Conventionally printed backs have another player photo and a few sentences about his career. A parallel version on which the background stars glow was issued at a greatly reduced rate.

		NM/M
Complete Set (12):		10.00
Common Player:		.25
Glowing:		6X
1	Albert Belle	.25
2	Barry Bonds	2.00
3	Juan Gonzalez	.50
4	Ken Griffey Jr.	1.25
5	Derek Jeter	2.00
6	Andruw Jones	.60
7	Chipper Jones	1.00
8	Greg Maddux	1.00
9	Mark McGwire	1.50
10	Mike Piazza	1.25
11	Alex Rodriguez	1.50
12	Frank Thomas	.75

Team Leaders

Team Leaders captured the statistical and/or inspirational leaders from all 28 teams. Inserted every 20 packs, these inserts were printed on a horizontal format, with the player's face die-cut in the perimeter of the card.

		NM/M
Complete Set (28):		25.00
Common Player:		.25
1	Cal Ripken Jr.	5.00
2	Mo Vaughn	.25
3	Jim Edmonds	.40
4	Frank Thomas	1.50
5	Albert Belle	.25
6	Bob Higginson	.25
7	Kevin Appier	.25
8	John Jaha	.25
9	Paul Molitor	1.50
10	Andy Pettitte	.65
11	Mark McGwire	4.00
12	Ken Griffey Jr.	3.00
13	Juan Gonzalez	.75
14	Pat Hentgen	.25
15	Chipper Jones	2.00
16	Mark Grace	.35
17	Barry Larkin	.25
18	Ellis Burks	.25
19	Gary Sheffield	.60
20	Jeff Bagwell	1.50
21	Mike Piazza	2.00
22	Henry Rodriguez	.25
23	Todd Hundley	.25
24	Curt Schilling	.60
25	Jeff King	.25
26	Brian Jordan	.25
27	Tony Gwynn	1.50
28	Barry Bonds	5.00

Zone

Twenty of the top hitters in baseball are featured on these holographic cards with the words Zone printed across the front. Zone inserts were found only in hobby packs at a rate of one per 80.

		NM/M
	Complete Set (20):	80.00
	Common Player:	1.50
1	Jeff Bagwell	5.00
2	Albert Belle	1.50
3	Barry Bonds	15.00
4	Ken Caminiti	1.50
5	Andres Galarraga	1.50
6	Juan Gonzalez	2.50
7	Ken Griffey Jr.	8.00
8	Tony Gwynn	6.00
9	Chipper Jones	6.00
10	Greg Maddux	6.00
11	Mark McGwire	10.00
12	Dean Palmer	1.50
13	Andy Petitte	3.00
14	Mike Piazza	8.00
15	Alex Rodriguez	12.00
16	Gary Sheffield	2.50
17	John Smoltz	2.50
18	Frank Thomas	5.00
19	Jim Thome	4.00
20	Matt Williams	1.50

1998 Fleer

Fleer was issued in two series in 1998, with 350 cards in Series 1 and 250 in Series 2. Each card features a borderless color action shot, with backs containing player information. Subsets in Series 1 included Smoke 'N Heat (301-310), Golden Memories (311-320) and Tale of the Tape (321-340). Golden Memories (1:6 packs) and Tale of the Tape (1:4) were shortprinted. Series 2 subsets included 25 short-printed (1:4) Unforgetable Moments (571-595). Inserts in Series 1 were Vintage '63, Vintage '63 Classic, Decade of Excellence, Decade of Excellence Rare Traditions, Diamond Ink, Diamond Standouts, Lumber Company, Power Game, Rookie Sensations and Zone. Series 2 inserts include: Vintage '63, Vintage '63 Classic, Promising Forecast, In the Clutch, Mickey Mantle: Monumental Moments, Mickey Mantle: Monumental Moments Gold Edition, Diamond Tribute and Diamond Ink.

		NM/M
	Complete Set (600):	65.00
	Complete Series 1 (350):	37.50
	Complete Series 2 (250):	27.50
	Common Player:	.05
	Series 1 or 2 Pack (10):	1.00
	Series 1 or 2 Wax Box (36):	20.00

ABBREVIATIONS

OPS - Overprinted
"Promotional Sample"

#	Player	Price
1	Ken Griffey Jr.	1.50
2	Derek Jeter	2.50
3	Gerald Williams	.05
4	Carlos Delgado	.50
5	Nomar Garciaparra	1.50
6	Gary Sheffield	.30
7	Jeff King	.05
8	Cal Ripken Jr.	2.50
9	Matt Williams	.05
10	Chipper Jones	1.00
11	Chuck Knoblauch	.05
12	Mark Grudzielanek	.05
13	Edgardo Alfonzo	.05
14	Andres Galarraga	.05
15	Tim Salmon	.15
16	Reggie Sanders	.05
17	Tony Clark	.05
18	Jason Kendall	.05
19	Juan Gonzalez	.65
20	Ben Grieve	.10
21	Roger Clemens	1.25
22	Raul Mondesi	.05
23	Robin Ventura	.05
24	Derek Lee	.05
25	Mark McGwire	2.00
26	Luis Gonzalez	.10
27	Kevin Brown	.05
28	Kirk Rueter	.05
29	Bobby Estalella	.05
30	Shawn Green	.35
31	Greg Maddux	1.00
32	Jorge Velandia	.05
33	Larry Walker	.05
34	Joey Cora	.05
35	Frank Thomas	.85
36	Curtis Goodwin	.05
37	Aaron Boone	.05
38	Curt Schilling	.25
39	Bruce Aven	.05
40	Ben McDonald	.05
41	Andy Ashby	.05
42	Jason McDonald	.05
43	Eric Davis	.05
44	Mark Grace	.10
45	Pedro Martinez	.75
46	Lou Collier	.05
47	Chan Ho Park	.05
48	Shane Halter	.05
49	Brian Hunter	.05
50	Jeff Bagwell	.75
51	Bernie Williams	.10
52	J.T. Snow	.05
53	Todd Greene	.05
54	Shannon Stewart	.05
55	Darren Bragg	.05
56	Fernando Tatis	.05
57	Darryl Kile	.05
58	Chris Stynes	.05
59	Javier Valentin	.05
60	Brian McRae	.05
61	Tom Evans	.05
62	Randall Simon	.05
63	Darrin Fletcher	.05
64	Jaret Wright	.05
65	Luis Ordaz	.05
66	Jose Canseco	.40
67	Edgar Renteria	.05
68	Jay Buhner	.05
69	Paul Konerko	.10
70	Adrian Brown	.05
71	Chris Carpenter	.05
72	Mike Lieberthal	.05
73	Dean Palmer	.05
74	Jorge Fabregas	.05
75	Stan Javier	.05
76	Damion Easley	.05
77	David Cone	.05
78	Aaron Sele	.05
79	Antonio Alfonseca	.05
80	Bobby Jones	.05
81	David Justice	.05
82	Jeffrey Hammonds	.05
83	Doug Glanville	.05
84	Jason Dickson	.05
85	Brad Radke	.05
86	David Segui	.05
87	Greg Vaughn	.05
88	Mike Cather RC	.05
89	Alex Fernandez	.05
90	Billy Taylor	.05
91	Jason Schmidt	.05
92	Mike DeJean RC	.05
93	Domingo Cedeno	.05
94	Jeff Cirillo	.05
95	Manny Aybar RC	.10
96	Jaime Navarro	.05
97	Dennis Reyes	.05
98	Barry Larkin	.05
99	Troy O'Leary	.05
100	Alex Rodriguez	2.00
100p	Alex Rodriguez/OPS	2.00
101	Pat Hentgen	.05
102	Bubba Trammell	.05
103	Glendon Rusch	.05
104	Kenny Lofton	.05
105	Craig Biggio	.05
106	Kelvim Escobar	.05
107	Mark Kotsay	.05
108	Rondell White	.05
109	Darren Oliver	.05
110	Jim Thome	.65
111	Rich Becker	.05
112	Chad Curtis	.05
113	Dave Hollins	.05
114	Bill Mueller	.05
115	Antone Williamson	.05
116	Tony Womack	.05
117	Randy Myers	.05
118	Rico Brogna	.05
119	Pat Watkins	.05
120	Eli Marrero	.05
121	Jay Bell	.05
122	Kevin Tapani	.05
123	Todd Erdos RC	.10
124	Neifi Perez	.05
125	Todd Hundley	.05
126	Jeff Abbott	.05
127	Todd Zeile	.05
128	Travis Fryman	.05
129	Sandy Alomar	.05
130	Fred McGriff	.05
131	Richard Hidalgo	.05
132	Scott Spiezio	.05
133	John Valentin	.05
134	Quivlio Veras	.05
135	Mike Lansing	.05
136	Paul Molitor	.75
137	Randy Johnson	.75
138	Harold Baines	.05
139	Doug Jones	.05
140	Abraham Nunez	.05
141	Alan Benes	.05
142	Matt Perisho	.05
143	Chris Clemons	.05
144	Andy Pettitte	.30
145	Jason Giambi	.40
146	Moises Alou	.05
147	Chad Fox RC	.05
148	Felix Martinez	.05
149	Carlos Mendoza RC	.05
150	Scott Rolen	.65
151	Jose Cabrera RC	.05
152	Justin Thompson	.05
153	Ellis Burks	.05
154	Pokey Reese	.05
155	Bartolo Colon	.05
156	Ray Durham	.05
157	Ugueth Urbina	.05
158	Tom Goodwin	.05
159	David Dellucci RC	.25
160	Rod Beck	.05
161	Ramon Martinez	.05
162	Joe Carter	.05
163	Kevin Orie	.05
164	Trevor Hoffman	.05
165	Emil Brown	.05
166	Robb Nen	.05
167	Paul O'Neill	.05
168	Ryan Long	.05
169	Ray Lankford	.05
170	Ivan Rodriguez	.65
171	Rick Aguilera	.05
172	Deivi Cruz	.05
173	Ricky Bottalico	.05
174	Garret Anderson	.05
175	Jose Vizcaino	.05
176	Omar Vizquel	.05
177	Jeff Blauser	.05
178	Orlando Cabrera	.05
179	Russ Johnson	.05
180	Matt Stairs	.05
181	Will Cunnane	.05
182	Adam Riggs	.05
183	Matt Morris	.05
184	Mario Valdez	.05
185	Larry Sutton	.05
186	Marc Pisciotta RC	.05
187	Dan Wilson	.05
188	John Franco	.05
189	Darren Daulton	.05
190	Todd Helton	.75
191	Brady Anderson	.05
192	Ricardo Rincon	.05
193	Kevin Stocker	.05
194	Jose Valentin	.05
195	Ed Sprague	.05
196	Ryan McGuire	.05
197	Scott Eyre RC	.05
198	Steve Finley	.05
199	T.J. Mathews	.05
200	Mike Piazza	1.50
201	Mark Wohlers	.05
202	Brian Giles	.05
203	Eduardo Perez	.05
204	Shigetosi Hasegawa	.05
205	Mariano Rivera	.15
206	Jose Rosado	.05
207	Michael Coleman	.05
208	James Baldwin	.05
209	Russ Davis	.05
210	Billy Wagner	.05
211	Sammy Sosa	1.50
212	Frank Catalanotto RC	.15
213	Delino DeShields	.05
214	John Olerud	.05
215	Heath Murray	.05
216	Jose Vidro	.05
217	Jim Edmonds	.05
218	Shawon Dunston	.05
219	Homer Bush	.05
220	Midre Cummings	.05
221	Tony Saunders	.05
222	Jeromy Burnitz	.05
223	Enrique Wilson	.05
224	Chili Davis	.05
225	Jerry DiPoto	.05
226	Dante Powell	.05
227	Javier Lopez	.05
228	Kevin Polcovich RC	.10
229	Deion Sanders	.05
230	Jimmy Key	.05
231	Rusty Greer	.05
232	Reggie Jefferson	.05
233	Ron Coomer	.05
234	Bobby Higginson	.05
235	Magglio Ordonez RC	2.00
236	Miguel Tejada	.25
237	Rick Gorecki	.05
238	Charles Johnson	.05
239	Lance Johnson	.05
240	Derek Bell	.05
241	Will Clark	.10
242	Brady Raggio	.05
243	Orel Hershiser	.05
244	Vladimir Guerrero	.75
245	John LeRoy	.05
246	Shawn Estes	.05
247	Brett Tomko	.05
248	Dave Nilsson	.05
249	Edgar Martinez	.05
250	Tony Gwynn	1.00
251	Mark Bellhorn	.05
252	Jed Hansen	.05
253	Butch Huskey	.05
254	Eric Young	.05
255	Vinny Castilla	.05
256	Hideki Irabu	.05
257	Mike Cameron	.05
258	Juan Encarnacion	.05
259	Brian Rose	.05
260	Brad Ausmus	.05
261	Dan Serafini	.05
262	Willie Greene	.05
263	Troy Percival	.05
264	Jeff Wallace RC	.05
265	Richie Sexson	.05
266	Rafael Palmeiro	.65
267	Brad Fullmer	.05
268	Jeremi Gonzalez	.05
269	Rob Stanifer RC	.05
270	Mickey Morandini	.05
271	Andruw Jones	.75
272	Royce Clayton	.05
273	Takashi Kashiwada	.05
274	Steve Woodard RC	.10
275	Jose Cruz Jr.	.05
276	Keith Foulke	.05
277	Brad Rigby	.05
278	Tino Martinez	.05
279	Todd Jones	.05
280	John Wetteland	.05
281	Alex Gonzalez	.05
282	Ken Cloude	.05
283	Jose Guillen	.05
284	Danny Clyburn	.05
285	David Ortiz	.05
286	John Thomson	.05
287	Kevin Appier	.05
288	Ismael Valdes	.05
289	Gary DiSarcina	.05
290	Todd Dunwoody	.05
291	Wally Joyner	.05
292	Charles Nagy	.05
293	Jeff Shaw	.05
294	Kevin Millwood RC	1.00
295	Rigo Beltran RC	.05
296	Jeff Frye	.05
297	Oscar Henriquez	.05
298	Mike Thurman	.05
299	Garrett Stephenson	.05
300	Barry Bonds	2.50
301	Roger Clemens (Smoke 'N Heat)	.75
302	David Cone (Smoke 'N Heat)	.05
303	Hideki Irabu (Smoke 'N Heat)	.05
304	Randy Johnson (Smoke 'N Heat)	.40
305	Greg Maddux (Smoke 'N Heat)	.50
306	Pedro Martinez (Smoke 'N Heat)	.35
307	Mike Mussina (Smoke 'N Heat)	.25
308	Andy Pettitte (Smoke 'N Heat)	.15
309	Curt Schilling (Smoke 'N Heat)	.10
310	John Smoltz (Smoke 'N Heat)	.05
311	Roger Clemens (Golden Memories)	1.00
312	Jose Cruz Jr. (Golden Memories)	.05
313	Nomar Garciaparra (Golden Memories)	1.00
314	Ken Griffey Jr. (Golden Memories)	1.00
315	Tony Gwynn (Golden Memories)	.75
316	Hideki Irabu (Golden Memories)	.25
317	Randy Johnson (Golden Memories)	.60
318	Mark McGwire (Golden Memories)	1.50
319	Curt Schilling (Golden Memories)	.35
320	Larry Walker (Golden Memories)	.15
321	Jeff Bagwell (Tale of the Tape)	.60
322	Albert Belle (Tale of the Tape)	.15
323	Barry Bonds (Tale of the Tape)	1.50
324	Jay Buhner (Tale of the Tape)	.15
325	Tony Clark (Tale of the Tape)	.15
326	Jose Cruz Jr. (Tale of the Tape)	.15
327	Andres Galarraga (Tale of the Tape)	.15
328	Juan Gonzalez (Tale of the Tape)	.30
329	Ken Griffey Jr. (Tale of the Tape)	.85
330	Andruw Jones (Tale of the Tape)	.60
331	Tino Martinez (Tale of the Tape)	.15
332	Mark McGwire (Tale of the Tape)	1.00
333	Rafael Palmeiro (Tale of the Tape)	.50
334	Mike Piazza (Tale of the Tape)	.85
335	Manny Ramirez (Tale of the Tape)	.65
336	Alex Rodriguez (Tale of the Tape)	1.00
337	Frank Thomas (Tale of the Tape)	.65
338	Jim Thome (Tale of the Tape)	.65
339	Mo Vaughn (Tale of the Tape)	.15
340	Larry Walker (Tale of the Tape)	.05
341	Checklist (Jose Cruz Jr.)	.15
342	Checklist (Ken Griffey Jr.)	.65
343	Checklist (Derek Jeter)	1.00
344	Checklist (Andruw Jones)	.40
345	Checklist (Chipper Jones)	.50
346	Checklist (Greg Maddux)	.50
347	Checklist (Mike Piazza)	.65
348	Checklist (Cal Ripken Jr.)	1.00
349	Checklist (Alex Rodriguez)	.75
350	Checklist (Frank Thomas)	.45
351	Mo Vaughn	.05
352	Andres Galarraga	.05
353	Roberto Alomar	.10
354	Darin Erstad	.10
355	Albert Belle	.05
356	Matt Williams	.05
357	Darryl Kile	.05
358	Kenny Lofton	.05
359	Orel Hershiser	.05
360	Bob Abreu	.05
361	Chris Widger	.05
362	Glenallen Hill	.05
363	Chili Davis	.05
364	Kevin Brown	.05
365	Marquis Grissom	.05
366	Livan Hernandez	.05
367	Moises Alou	.05
368	Matt Lawton	.05
369	Rey Ordonez	.05
370	Kenny Rogers	.05
371	Lee Stevens	.05
372	Wade Boggs	1.00
373	Luis Gonzalez	.05
374	Jeff Conine	.05
375	Esteban Loaiza	.05
376	Jose Canseco	.40
377	Henry Rodriguez	.05
378	Dave Burba	.05
379	Todd Hollandsworth	.05
380	Ron Gant	.05
381	Pedro Martinez	.75
382	Ryan Klesko	.05
383	Derrek Lee	.05
384	Doug Glanville	.05
385	David Wells	.05
386	Ken Caminiti	.05
387	Damon Hollins	.05
388	Manny Ramirez	.75
389	Mike Mussina	.45
390	Jay Bell	.05
391	Mike Piazza	1.50
392	Mike Lansing	.05
393	Mike Hampton	.05
394	Geoff Jenkins	.05
395	Jimmy Haynes	.05
396	Scott Servais	.05
397	Kent Mercker	.05
398	Jeff Kent	.05
399	Kevin Elster	.05
400	Masato Yoshii RC	.50
401	Jose Vizcaino	.05
402	Javier Martinez	.05
403	David Segui	.05
404	Tony Saunders	.05
405	Karim Garcia	.05
406	Armando Benitez	.05
407	Joe Randa	.05
408	Vic Darensbourg	.05
409	Sean Casey	.20
410	Eric Milton	.05
411	Trey Moore	.05
412	Mike Stanley	.05
413	Tom Gordon	.05
414	Hal Morris	.05
415	Braden Looper	.05
416	Mike Kelly	.05
417	John Smoltz	.05
418	Roger Cedeno	.05
419	Al Leiter	.05
420	Chuck Knoblauch	.05
421	Felix Rodriguez	.05
422	Bip Roberts	.05
423	Ken Hill	.05
424	Jermaine Allensworth	.05
425	Esteban Yan	.05
426	Scott Karl	.05
427	Sean Berry	.05
428	Rafael Medina	.05
429	Javier Vazquez	.05
430	Rickey Henderson	.75
431	Adam Butler RC	.05
432	Todd Stottlemyre	.05
433	Yamil Benitez	.05
434	Sterling Hitchcock	.05
435	Paul Sorrento	.05
436	Bobby Ayala	.05
437	Tim Raines	.05
438	Chris Hoiles	.05
439	Rod Beck	.05
440	Donnie Sadler	.05
441	Charles Johnson	.05
442	Russ Ortiz	.05
443	Pedro Astacio	.05
444	Wilson Alvarez	.05
445	Mike Blowers	.05
446	Todd Zeile	.05
447	Mel Rojas	.05
448	F.P. Santangelo	.05
449	Dmitri Young	.05
450	Brian Anderson	.05
451	Cecil Fielder	.05
452	Roberto Hernandez	.05
453	Todd Walker	.05
454	Tyler Green	.05
455	Jorge Posada	.05
456	Geronimo Berroa	.05
457	Jose Silva	.05
458	Bobby Bonilla	.05
459	Walt Weiss	.05
460	Darren Dreifort	.05
461	B.J. Surhoff	.05
462	Quinton McCracken	.05
463	Derek Lowe	.05
464	Jorge Fabregas	.05
465	Joey Hamilton	.05
466	Brian Jordan	.05
467	Allen Watson	.05
468	John Jaha	.05
469	Heathcliff Slocumb	.05
470	Gregg Jefferies	.05
471	Scott Brosius	.05
472	Chad Ogea	.05
473	A.J. Hinch	.05
474	Bobby Smith	.05
475	Brian Moehler	.05
476	DaRond Stovall	.05
477	Kevin Young	.05
478	Jeff Suppan	.05
479	Marty Cordova	.05
480	John Halama RC	.25
481	Bubba Trammell	.05
482	Mike Caruso	.05
483	Eric Karros	.05
484	Jamey Wright	.05
485	Mike Sweeney	.05
486	Aaron Sele	.05
487	Cliff Floyd	.05
488	Jeff Brantley	.05
489	Jim Leyritz	.05
490	Denny Neagle	.05
491	Travis Fryman	.05
492	Carlos Baerga	.05
493	Eddie Taubensee	.05
494	Darryl Strawberry	.05
495	Brian Johnson	.05
496	Randy Myers	.05
497	Jeff Blauser	.05
498	Jason Wood	.05
499	Rolando Arrojo RC	.25
500	Johnny Damon	.05
501	Jose Mercedes	.05
502	Tony Batista	.05
503	Mike Piazza	1.50
504	Hideo Nomo	.65
505	Chris Gomez	.05
506	Jesus Sanchez RC	.05
507	Al Martin	.05
508	Brian Edmondson	.05
509	Joe Girardi	.05
510	Shayne Bennett	.05
511	Joe Carter	.05
512	Dave Mlicki	.05
513	Rich Butler RC	.10
514	Dennis Eckersley	.65
515	Travis Lee	.10
516	John Mabry	.05
517	Jose Mesa	.05
518	Phil Nevin	.05
519	Raul Casanova	.05
520	Mike Fetters	.05
521	Gary Sheffield	.30
522	Terry Steinbach	.05
523	Steve Trachsel	.05
524	Josh Booty	.05
525	Darryl Hamilton	.05
526	Mark McLemore	.05
527	Kevin Stocker	.05
528	Bret Boone	.05
529	Shane Andrews	.05
530	Robb Nen	.05
531	Carl Everett	.05

532	LaTroy Hawkins	.05
533	Fernando Vina	.05
534	Michael Tucker	.05
535	Mark Langston	.05
536	Mickey Mantle	2.00
537	Bernard Gilkey	.05
538	Francisco Cordova	.05
539	Mike Bordick	.05
540	Fred McGriff	.05
541	Cliff Politte	.05
542	Jason Varitek	.05
543	Shawon Dunston	.05
544	Brian Meadows	.05
545	Pat Meares	.05
546	Carlos Perez	.05
547	Desi Relaford	.05
548	Antonio Osuna	.05
549	Devon White	.05
550	Sean Runyan	.05
551	Mickey Morandini	.05
552	Dave Martinez	.05
553	Jeff Fassero	.05
554	Ryan Jackson **RC**	.05
555	Stan Javier	.05
556	Jaime Navarro	.05
557	Jose Offerman	.05
558	Mike Lowell **RC**	.50
559	Darrin Fletcher	.05
560	Mark Lewis	.05
561	Dante Bichette	.05
562	Chuck Finley	.05
563	Kerry Wood	.35
564	Andy Benes	.05
565	Freddy Garcia	.05
566	Tom Glavine	.25
567	Jon Nunnally	.05
568	Miguel Cairo	.05
569	Shane Reynolds	.05
570	Roberto Kelly	.05
571	Checklist (Jose Cruz Jr.)	.25
572	Checklist (Ken Griffey Jr.)	.65
573	Checklist (Mark McGwire)	.75
574	Checklist (Cal Ripken Jr.)	1.00
575	Checklist (Frank Thomas)	.45
576	Jeff Bagwell (Unforgettable Moments)	1.00
577	Barry Bonds (Unforgettable Moments)	3.00
578	Tony Clark (Unforgettable Moments)	.25
579	Roger Clemens (Unforgettable Moments)	.25
580	Jose Cruz Jr. (Unforgettable Moments)	.25
581	Nomar Garciaparra (Unforgettable Moments)	1.50
582	Juan Gonzalez (Unforgettable Moments)	1.00
583	Ben Grieve (Unforgettable Moments)	.25
584	Ken Griffey Jr. (Unforgettable Moments)	2.00
585	Tony Gwynn (Unforgettable Moments)	1.50
586	Derek Jeter (Unforgettable Moments)	3.00
587	Randy Johnson (Unforgettable Moments)	1.00
588	Chipper Jones (Unforgettable Moments)	1.50
589	Greg Maddux (Unforgettable Moments)	1.50
590	Mark McGwire (Unforgettable Moments)	2.50
591	Andy Pettitte (Unforgettable Moments)	.45
592	Paul Molitor (Unforgettable Moments)	1.00
593	Cal Ripken Jr. (Unforgettable Moments)	3.00
594	Alex Rodriguez (Unforgettable Moments)	2.50
595	Scott Rolen (Unforgettable Moments)	.50
596	Curt Schilling (Unforgettable Moments)	.50
597	Frank Thomas (Unforgettable Moments)	1.25
598	Jim Thome (Unforgettable Moments)	.75
599	Larry Walker (Unforgettable Moments)	.25
600	Bernie Williams (Unforgettable Moments)	.30

Decade of Excellence

Decade of Excellence inserts were found in one per 72 Series 1 hobby packs of Fleer Tradition. The 12-card set features 1988 season photos in Fleer's 1988 card design. The set includes only those current players who have been in baseball for 10 years or more. The use of blue and red metallic foil stripes in the background differentiates a scarcer (1:720 hobby packs) "Rare Traditions" parallel to the insert.

		NM/M
Complete Set (12):		35.00
Common Player:		1.00
Inserted 1:72		
Rare Traditions:		3X
Inserted 1:720		
1	Roberto Alomar	1.50
2	Barry Bonds	8.00
3	Roger Clemens	5.00
4	David Cone	1.00
5	Andres Galarraga	1.00
6	Mark Grace	1.00
7	Tony Gwynn	4.00
8	Randy Johnson	3.00
9	Greg Maddux	4.00
10	Mark McGwire	6.00
11	Paul O'Neill	1.00
12	Cal Ripken Jr.	8.00

Diamond Ink

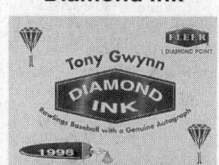

These one-per-pack inserts offer collectors a chance to acquire genuine autographed baseballs. Issued in denominations of 1, 5 and 10 points, the cards had to be accumulated to a total of 500 points of the same player to be redeemed for an autographed ball of that player. Cards are the standard 3-1/2" x 2-1/2" and are printed in black and purple on front and black and yellow on back. The point value of each card is embossed at center to prevent counterfeiting. The rules of the exchange program are printed on back. The deadline for redemption was Dec. 31, 1998. Values shown are for 1-pt. cards. The unnumbered players in the series are listed alphabetically.

		NM/M
Complete Set, 1 pt. (11):		1.00
Common Player, 1 pt.:		.05
5-pt. Cards:		5X
10-pt. Cards:		10X
(1)	Jay Buhner	.05
(2)	Roger Clemens	.20
(3)	Jose Cruz Jr.	.05
(4)	Nomar Garciaparra	.20
(5)	Tony Gwynn	.15
(6)	Roberto Hernandez	.05
(7)	Greg Maddux	.15
(8)	Cal Ripken Jr.	.30
(9)	Alex Rodriguez	.25
(10)	Scott Rolen	.10
(11)	Tony Womack	.05

Diamond Standouts

Diamond Standouts were inserted into Series I packs at a rate of one per 12. The 20-card insert set features players over a diamond design silver foil background.

		NM/M
Complete Set (20):		25.00
Common Player:		.50
1	Jeff Bagwell	1.00
2	Barry Bonds	4.00
3	Roger Clemens	2.00
4	Jose Cruz Jr.	.50
5	Andres Galarraga	.50
6	Nomar Garciaparra	2.00
7	Juan Gonzalez	.75
8	Ken Griffey Jr.	2.00
9	Derek Jeter	4.00
10	Randy Johnson	1.00
11	Chipper Jones	1.50
12	Kenny Lofton	.50
13	Greg Maddux	1.50
14	Pedro Martinez	1.00
15	Mark McGwire	3.00
16	Mike Piazza	2.00
17	Alex Rodriguez	3.00
18	Curt Schilling	.75
19	Frank Thomas	1.00
20	Larry Walker	.50

Diamond Tribute

This 10-card insert was exclusive to Series 2 packs and seeded one per 300 packs. Cards were printed on a leather-like laminated stock and had silver holofoil stamping.

		NM/M
Complete Set (10):		90.00
Common Player:		5.00
DT1	Jeff Bagwell	7.50
DT2	Roger Clemens	10.00
DT3	Nomar Garciaparra	10.00
DT4	Juan Gonzalez	5.00
DT5	Ken Griffey Jr.	12.00
DT6	Mark McGwire	15.00
DT7	Mike Piazza	12.00
DT8	Cal Ripken Jr.	20.00
DT9	Alex Rodriguez	15.00
DT10	Frank Thomas	7.50

For Kids Commemorative Card

More than two dozen nominees for Players Choice Awards are featured in action photos on both sides of this 11" x 8-1/2" card.

	NM/M
Commemorative Card:	3.00

In the Clutch

This Series 2 insert features stars who can stand up to pressure of big league ball.

Fronts have embossed action photos on a prismatic metallic foil background. Backs have a portrait photo and a few words about the player. Stated insertion rate for the inserts was one per 20 packs on average.

		NM/M
Complete Set (15):		25.00
Common Player:		.40
IC1	Jeff Bagwell	1.00
IC2	Barry Bonds	5.00
IC3	Roger Clemens	2.00
IC4	Jose Cruz Jr.	.40
IC5	Nomar Garciaparra	2.00
IC6	Juan Gonzalez	.75
IC7	Ken Griffey Jr.	2.50
IC8	Tony Gwynn	1.50
IC9	Derek Jeter	5.00
IC10	Chipper Jones	1.50
IC11	Greg Maddux	1.50
IC12	Mark McGwire	4.00
IC13	Mike Piazza	2.50
IC14	Frank Thomas	1.50
IC15	Larry Walker	.40

Lumber Company

This 15-card set was exclusive to Series I retail packs and inserted one per 36 packs. It included power hitters and featured the insert name in large letters across the top.

		NM/M
Complete Set (15):		50.00
Common Player:		.70
Inserted 1:36 R		
1	Jeff Bagwell	2.50
2	Barry Bonds	8.00
3	Jose Cruz Jr.	.75
4	Nomar Garciaparra	4.00
5	Juan Gonzalez	1.50
6	Ken Griffey Jr.	5.00
7	Tony Gwynn	3.00
8	Chipper Jones	3.00
9	Tino Martinez	.75
10	Mark McGwire	6.00
11	Mike Piazza	5.00
12	Cal Ripken Jr.	8.00
13	Alex Rodriguez	6.00
14	Frank Thomas	2.50
15	Larry Walker	.75

Mickey Mantle Monumental Moments

This 10-card insert honors Hall of Famer Mickey Mantle's legendary career and was seeded one per 68 packs of Series 2. Fleer/Sky-Box worked closely with Mantle's family with each photo in the set personally selected by them. A gold-enhanced version was issued with each card serially numbered to 51.

		NM/M
Complete Set (10):		40.00
Common Card:		5.00
Inserted 1:68		
Gold (51 sets):		3X
1	Armed and Dangerous	5.00
2	Getting Ready in Spring Training	5.00
3	Mantle and Rizzuto Celebrate	5.00
4	Posed for Action	5.00
5	Signed, Sealed and Ready to Deliver	5.00
6	Triple Crown 1956 Season	5.00
7	Number 7 . . .	5.00
8	Mantle's Powerful Swing . . .	5.00
9	Old-Timers Day Introduction	5.00
10	Portrait of Determination	5.00

Promising Forecast

Potential future stars are showcased in this Series 2 insert. Both front and back have a background of a colorful weather map. Fronts have a glossy player action photo on a matte-finish background. Backs are all-glossy and have a second photo and a few words about the player's potential. Average odds of pulling a Promising Forecast card were stated as one per 12 packs.

		NM/M
Complete Set (20):		7.00
Common Player:		.25
Inserted 1:12		
PF1	Rolando Arrojo	.25
PF2	Sean Casey	.40
PF3	Brad Fullmer	.25
PF4	Karim Garcia	.35
PF5	Ben Grieve	.25
PF6	Todd Helton	3.00
PF7	Richard Hidalgo	.25
PF8	A.J. Hinch	.25
PF9	Paul Konerko	.35
PF10	Mark Kotsay	.25
PF11	Derek Lee	1.00
PF12	Travis Lee	.35
PF13	Eric Milton	.25
PF14	Magglio Ordonez	.50
PF15	David Ortiz	.50
PF16	Brian Rose	.25
PF17	Miguel Tejada	.40
PF18	Jason Varitek	.35
PF19	Enrique Wilson	.25
PF20	Kerry Wood	1.00

Rookie Sensations

Rookie Sensations included 20 gray-bordered cards of the 1997 most promising players who were eligible for the Rookie of the Year award. Each card contained a multi-colored background and was inserted one per 18 packs.

		NM/M
Complete Set (20):		12.00
Common Player:		.50
Inserted 1:18		
1	Mike Cameron	.50
2	Jose Cruz Jr.	.50
3	Jason Dickson	.50
4	Kelvim Escobar	.50
5	Nomar Garciaparra	3.00
6	Ben Grieve	.50
7	Vladimir Guerrero	3.00
8	Wilton Guerrero	.50
9	Jose Guillen	.50
10	Todd Helton	2.00
11	Livan Hernandez	.50
12	Hideki Irabu	.50
13	Andruw Jones	3.00
14	Matt Morris	.50
15	Magglio Ordonez	1.00
16	Neifi Perez	.50
17	Scott Rolen	2.00
18	Fernando Tatis	.50
19	Brett Tomko	.50
20	Jaret Wright	.50

The Power Game

Pitchers and hitters are pictured over a purple metallic background with UV coating in this 20-card insert. Power Game inserts were exclusive to Series I and seeded one per 36 packs.

		NM/M
Complete Set (20):		30.00
Common Player:		.50
Inserted 1:36		
1	Jeff Bagwell	2.00
2	Albert Belle	.50
3	Barry Bonds	6.00
4	Tony Clark	.50
5	Roger Clemens	3.50
6	Jose Cruz Jr.	.50
7	Andres Galarraga	.50
8	Nomar Garciaparra	3.50
9	Juan Gonzalez	1.00
10	Ken Griffey Jr.	4.00
11	Randy Johnson	2.00
12	Greg Maddux	3.00
13	Pedro Martinez	2.00
14	Tino Martinez	.50
15	Mark McGwire	5.00
16	Mike Piazza	4.00
17	Curt Schilling	.75
18	Frank Thomas	2.00
19	Jim Thome	2.00
20	Larry Walker	.50

Vintage '63

Vintage featured 126 different players, with 63 in Series I and 63 in Series II, on the design of 1963 Fleer cards. The insert commemorated the 35th anniversary of Fleer and was seeded one per hobby pack. In addition, Series II featured Mickey Mantle on card No. 67, which completed the original 1963 Fleer set that ended at card No. 66 and wasn't able to include Mantle for licensing reasons. The Mantle card was printed in vintage looking stock and was purposely made to look and feel like the originals. Fleer also printed a Classic parallel version to this insert that contained gold foil on the front and was sequentially numbered to 63 with a "C" prefix on the back.

		NM/M
Complete Set (126):		20.00
Complete Series 1 (63):		10.00
Complete Series 2 (63):		10.00
Common Player:		.10
Classics (63 sets): 20X		
1	Jason Dickson	.10
2	Tim Salmon	.25
3	Andruw Jones	.75
4	Chipper Jones	1.00
5	Kenny Lofton	.10
6	Greg Maddux	1.00
7	Rafael Palmeiro	.65
8	Cal Ripken Jr.	2.50
9	Nomar Garciaparra	1.25
10	Mark Grace	.10
11	Sammy Sosa	1.25
12	Frank Thomas	.75
13	Deion Sanders	.10
14	Sandy Alomar	.10
15	David Justice	.10
16	Jim Thome	.75
17	Matt Williams	.10
18	Jaret Wright	.10
19	Vinny Castilla	.10
20	Andres Galarraga	.10
21	Todd Helton	.75
22	Larry Walker	.10
23	Tony Clark	.10
24	Moises Alou	.10
25	Kevin Brown	.10
26	Charles Johnson	.10
27	Edgar Renteria	.10
28	Gary Sheffield	.50
29	Jeff Bagwell	.75
30	Craig Biggio	.10
31	Raul Mondesi	.10
32	Mike Piazza	1.50
33	Chuck Knoblauch	.10
34	Paul Molitor	.75
35	Vladimir Guerrero	.75
36	Pedro Martinez	.75
37	Todd Hundley	.10
38	Derek Jeter	2.50
39	Tino Martinez	.10
40	Paul O'Neill	.10
41	Andy Pettitte	.35
42	Mariano Rivera	.20
43	Bernie Williams	.20
44	Ben Grieve	.10
45	Scott Rolen	.65
46	Curt Schilling	.45
47	Jason Kendall	.10
48	Tony Womack	.10
49	Ray Lankford	.10
50	Mark McGwire	2.00
51	Matt Morris	.10
52	Tony Gwynn	1.00
53	Barry Bonds	2.50
54	Jay Buhner	.10
55	Ken Griffey Jr.	1.50
56	Randy Johnson	.75
57	Edgar Martinez	.10
58	Alex Rodriguez	2.00
59	Juan Gonzalez	.65
60	Rusty Greer	.10
61	Ivan Rodriguez	.65
62	Roger Clemens	1.25
63	Jose Cruz Jr.	.10
	Checklist #1-63	.10
64	Darin Erstad	.20
65	Jay Bell	.10
66	Andy Benes	.10
67	Mickey Mantle	2.00
68	Karim Garcia	.10
69	Travis Lee	.10
70	Matt Williams	.10
71	Andres Galarraga	.10
72	Tom Glavine	.35
73	Ryan Klesko	.10
74	Denny Neagle	.10
75	John Smoltz	.10
76	Roberto Alomar	.20
77	Joe Carter	.10
78	Mike Mussina	.50
79	B.J. Surhoff	.10
80	Dennis Eckersley	.65
81	Pedro Martinez	.75
82	Mo Vaughn	.10
83	Jeff Blauser	.10
84	Henry Rodriguez	.10
85	Albert Belle	.10
86	Sean Casey	.25
87	Travis Fryman	.10
88	Kenny Lofton	.10
89	Darryl Kile	.10
90	Mike Lansing	.10
91	Bobby Bonilla	.10
92	Cliff Floyd	.10
93	Livan Hernandez	.10
94	Derrek Lee	.10
95	Moises Alou	.10
96	Shane Reynolds	.10
97	Jeff Conine	.10
98	Johnny Damon	.35
99	Eric Karros	.10
100	Hideo Nomo	.65
101	Marquis Grissom	.10
102	Matt Lawton	.10
103	Todd Walker	.10
104	Gary Sheffield	.50
105	Bernard Gilkey	.10
106	Rey Ordonez	.10
107	Chili Davis	.10
108	Chuck Knoblauch	.10
109	Charles Johnson	.10
110	Rickey Henderson	.75
111	Bob Abreu	.10
112	Doug Glanville	.10
113	Gregg Jefferies	.10
114	Al Martin	.10
115	Kevin Young	.10
116	Ron Gant	.10
117	Kevin Brown	.10
118	Ken Caminiti	.10
119	Joey Hamilton	.10
120	Jeff Kent	.10
121	Wade Boggs	1.00
122	Quinton McCracken	.10
123	Fred McGriff	.10
124	Paul Sorrento	.10
125	Jose Canseco	.50
126	Randy Myers	.10
	Checklist #64-126	.10

Vintage '63 Classic

Vintage '63 Classic paralleled all 126 Vintage '63 inserts throughout Series 1 and 2, plus the checklists. These cards feature gold-foil stamping on front, specifically around the diamond in the lower-left corner, and are sequentially numbered to 63 sets. Cards have a "C" suffix to the card number.

	NM/M
Complete Set (128):	650.00
Common Player:	4.00
Stars/RC's :	20X

Zone

Inserted in one per 288 packs of Series I Fleer Tradition, Zone featured 15 top players printed on rainbow foil and etching.

		NM/M
Complete Set (15):		130.00
Common Player:		4.00
Inserted 1:288		
1	Jeff Bagwell	7.50
2	Barry Bonds	25.00
3	Roger Clemens	10.00
4	Jose Cruz Jr.	4.00
5	Nomar Garciaparra	10.00
6	Juan Gonzalez	6.00
7	Ken Griffey Jr.	12.00
8	Tony Gwynn	9.00
9	Chipper Jones	9.00
10	Greg Maddux	9.00
11	Mark McGwire	15.00
12	Mike Piazza	12.00
13	Alex Rodriguez	20.00
14	Frank Thomas	7.50
15	Larry Walker	4.00

Update

Fleer's first Update set since 1994 is this 100-card boxed set. It arrived soon after the conclusion of the 1998 World Series and focused on rookies who made their major league debut in September and had not yet had a rookie card. The set had 70 rookies, including 15 making their major league debut, 20 traded players and free agents. There was one subset called Season's Highlights that focused on feats like Mark McGwire's 70th home run, Sammy Sosa's single-month home run record and Kerry Wood's 20 strikeout performance.

		NM/M
Complete Set (100):		12.50
Common Player:		.05
U1	Mark McGwire (Season Highlights)	.75
U2	Sammy Sosa (Season Highlights)	.45
U3	Roger Clemens (Season Highlights)	.45
U4	Barry Bonds (Season Highlights)	1.00
U5	Kerry Wood (Season Highlights)	.20
U6	Paul Molitor (Season Highlights)	.25
U7	Ken Griffey Jr. (Season Highlights)	.50
U8	Cal Ripken Jr. (Season Highlights)	1.00
U9	David Wells (Season Highlights)	.05
U10	Alex Rodriguez (Season Highlights)	.75
U11	Angel Pena RC	.25
U12	Bruce Chen	.05
U13	Craig Wilson	.05
U14	Orlando Hernandez RC	1.50
U15	Aramis Ramirez	.10
U16	Aaron Boone	.05
U17	Bob Henley	.05
U18	Juan Guzman	.05
U19	Darryl Hamilton	.05
U20	Jay Payton	.05
U21	Jeremy Powell RC	.05
U22	Ben Davis	.05
U23	Preston Wilson	.10
U24	Jim Parque RC	.15
U25	Odalis Perez	.25
U26	Ron Belliard	.05
U27	Royce Clayton	.05
U28	George Lombard	.05
U29	Tony Phillips	.05
U30	Fernando Seguignol RC	.15
U31	Armando Rios RC	.05
U32	Jerry Hairston Jr. RC	.25
U33	Justin Baughman RC	.05
U34	Seth Greisinger	.05
U35	Alex Gonzalez	.05
U36	Michael Barrett	.05
U37	Carlos Beltran	.35
U38	Ellis Burks	.05
U39	Jose Jimenez	.05
U40	Carlos Guillen	.05
U41	Marlon Anderson	.05
U42	Scott Elarton	.05
U43	Glenallen Hill	.05
U44	Shane Monahan	.05
U45	Dennis Martinez	.05
U46	Carlos Febles RC	.05
U47	Carlos Perez	.05
U48	Wilton Guerrero	.05
U49	Randy Johnson	.45
U50	Brian Simmons RC	.05
U51	Carlton Loewer	.05
U52	Mark DeRosa RC	.50
U53	Tim Young RC	.05
U54	Gary Gaetti	.05
U55	Eric Chavez	.25
U56	Carl Pavano	.15
U57	Mike Stanley	.05
U58	Todd Stottlemyre	.05
U59	Gabe Kapler RC	.50
U60	Mike Jerzembeck RC	.05
U61	Mitch Meluskey RC	.15
U62	Bill Pulsipher	.05
U63	Derrick Gibson	.05
U64	John Rocker RC	.75
U65	Calvin Pickering	.05
U66	Blake Stein	.05
U67	Fernando Tatis	.05
U68	Gabe Alvarez	.05
U69	Jeffrey Hammonds	.05
U70	Adrian Beltre	.25
U71	Ryan Bradley RC	.10
U72	Edgar Clemente RC	.05
U73	Rick Croushore RC	.05
U74	Matt Clement	.15
U75	Dermal Brown	.05
U76	Paul Bako	.05
U77	Placido Polanco RC	1.00
U78	Jay Tessmer	.05
U79	Jarrod Washburn	.05
U80	Kevin Witt	.05
U81	Mike Metcalfe	.05
U82	Daryle Ward	.05
U83	Benj Sampson RC	.05
U84	Mike Kinkade RC	.20
U85	Randy Winn	.05
U86	Jeff Shaw	.05
U87	Troy Glaus RC	4.00
U88	Hideo Nomo	.35
U89	Mark Grudzielanek	.05
U90	Mike Frank RC	.05
U91	Bobby Howry RC	.10
U92	Ryan Minor RC	.15
U93	Corey Koskie RC	1.00
U94	Matt Anderson RC	.20
U95	Joe Carter	.05
U96	Paul Konerko	.15
U97	Sidney Ponson	.05
U98	Jeremy Giambi RC	.25
U99	Jeff Kubenka RC	.05
U100	J.D. Drew RC	5.00

Diamond Skills Commemorative Sheet

In conjunction with its sponsorship of the Diamond Skills program, Fleer and its 2,500 direct dealers distributed this eight-player sheet to 7-14 year olds participating in the event. Participants could get a sheet by redeeming Fleer wrappers at a local card store. The 10" x 9" sheet features full size Fleer Tradition card reproductions. At top is a list of 1997 Diamond Skills winners.

	NM/M
Complete Sheet:	2.00

Mantle & Sons

As part of its participation in SportsFest in May 1998, Fleer issued a promotional card featuring a vintage color photo of Mickey Mantle and his sons, David and Danny. The back of the card announced Fleer's first-ever inclusion of Mickey Mantle cards in some of its forthcoming releases.

	NM/M
Mickey Mantle, Danny Mantle, David Mantle	3.00

Mickey Mantle Promo Postcard

This 4-1/4" x 5-1/2" color postcard was sent to Fleer dealers to announce a Mickey Mantle commemorative series in its Series 2 product. The address side has the Fleer Tradition logo in black, blue and red. The picture side has a color photo of one of the Mantle cards to be issued in the format of the 1963 Fleer issue. Cards are individually serial numbered within an edition of 3,500.

	NM/M
Mickey Mantle	4.00

Mark McGwire 62nd HR 23K Gold Commemorative

Marketed as a retail-exclusive "Official 62nd HR 23 Kt. Gold Commemorative Card," this 2-1/2" x 3-1/2" card was sold in a colorful blister pack. Embossed in 23-karat gold foil is an image of McGwire in action. Also on front are a 62-HR logo and a facsimile autograph, along with the legend "Smashing the Record." On back is a small picture of McGwire with the large 9-8-98 date and the details of the record blast. There are appropriate licensing logos and a serial number from within an edition of 200,000.

	NM/M
Mark McGwire	5.00

National Convention Commemorative Set

In conjunction with its participation at the 19th National Sports Collectors Convention in Chicago in August, 1998, Fleer distributed this commemorative set to persons purchasing VIP admission packages. The set includes a specially numbered (NC1) Fleer Tradition Mickey Mantle card, a card picturing Mick with his sons, one of seven large-format (3-1/2" x 5") cards reproducing Mantle Monumental Moments inserts, and an unnumbered header card. The Monumental Moments reproductions are printed on a pinstriped-sky background.

		NM/M
Complete Set (8):		15.00
Common Card:		2.25
NC1	Mickey Mantle (Fleer Tradition)	2.25
NC2	Mickey Mantle (with sons)	2.25
NC3	Mickey Mantle (Monumental Moments - accepting trophy)	2.25
NC4	Mickey Mantle (Monumental Moments - making a throw)	2.25
NC5	Mickey Mantle (Monumental Moments - in sliding pit)	2.25
NC6	Mickey Mantle (Monumental Moments - batting)	2.25
NC7	Mickey Mantle (Monumental Moments - number retired)	2.25
	Header Card	.25

1999 Fleer

Released as a single series in 10-card packs with a suggested retail price of $1.59, the base set consists of 600 cards, including 10 checklists and a 15-card Franchise Futures subset. Cards are UV coated, with borderless photos and gold-foil graphics. Backs have personal bio-information along with year-by-year career stats and a small photo. There are two parallels, Starting Nine, which are hobby-exclusive, numbered to nine sets with blue foil stamping and Warning Track. Found exclusively in retail packs, Warning Tracks can be identified by red foil stamping and a Warning Track logo.

		NM/M
Complete Set (600):		25.00
Common Player:		.05
Warning Track:		2X
Inserted 1:1 R		
Pack (10):		1.00
Wax Box (36):		25.00
1	Mark McGwire	2.00
2	Sammy Sosa	1.25
3	Ken Griffey Jr.	1.50
4	Kerry Wood	.30
5	Derek Jeter	2.50
6	Stan Musial	2.00
7	J.D. Drew	.65
7p	J.D. Drew/OPS	1.50
8	Cal Ripken Jr.	2.50
9	Alex Rodriguez	2.00
10	Travis Lee	.15

No.	Player	Price
11	Andres Galarraga	.05
12	Nomar Garciaparra	1.25
13	Albert Belle	.05
14	Barry Larkin	.05
15	Dante Bichette	.05
16	Tony Clark	.05
17	Moises Alou	.05
18	Rafael Palmeiro	.65
19	Raul Mondesi	.05
20	Vladimir Guerrero	.75
21	John Olerud	.05
22	Bernie Williams	.10
23	Ben Grieve	.05
24	Scott Rolen	.65
25	Jeromy Burnitz	.05
26	Ken Caminiti	.05
27	Barry Bonds	2.50
28	Todd Helton	.75
29	Juan Gonzalez	.65
30	Roger Clemens	1.25
31	Andruw Jones	.75
32	Mo Vaughn	.05
33	Larry Walker	.05
34	Frank Thomas	.75
35	Manny Ramirez	.75
36	Randy Johnson	.75
37	Vinny Castilla	.05
38	Juan Encarnacion	.05
39	Jeff Bagwell	.75
40	Gary Sheffield	.50
41	Mike Piazza	1.50
42	Richie Sexson	.05
43	Tony Gwynn	1.00
44	Chipper Jones	1.00
45	Jim Thome	.65
46	Craig Biggio	.05
47	Carlos Delgado	.40
48	Greg Vaughn	.05
49	Greg Maddux	1.00
50	Troy Glaus	.65
51	Roberto Alomar	.10
52	Dennis Eckersley	.60
53	Mike Caruso	.05
54	Bruce Chen	.05
55	Aaron Boone	.05
56	Bartolo Colon	.05
57	Derrick Gibson	.05
58	Brian Anderson	.05
59	Gabe Alvarez	.05
60	Todd Dunwoody	.05
61	Rod Beck	.05
62	Derek Bell	.05
63	Francisco Cordova	.05
64	Johnny Damon	.25
65	Adrian Beltre	.15
66	Garret Anderson	.05
67	Armando Benitez	.05
68	Edgardo Alfonzo	.05
69	Ryan Bradley	.05
70	Eric Chavez	.30
71	Bobby Abreu	.05
72	Andy Ashby	.05
73	Ellis Burks	.05
74	Jeff Cirillo	.05
75	Jay Buhner	.05
76	Ron Gant	.05
77	Rolando Arrojo	.05
78	Will Clark	.10
79	Chris Carpenter	.05
80	Jim Edmonds	.05
81	Tony Batista	.05
82	Shane Andrews	.05
83	Mark DeRosa	.05
84	Brady Anderson	.05
85	Tony Gordon	.05
86	Brant Brown	.05
87	Ray Durham	.05
88	Ron Coomer	.05
89	Bret Boone	.05
90	Travis Fryman	.05
91	Darryl Kile	.05
92	Paul Bako	.05
93	Cliff Floyd	.05
94	Scott Elarton	.05
95	Jeremy Giambi	.05
96	Darren Dreifort	.05
97	Marquis Grissom	.05
98	Marty Cordova	.05
99	Fernando Seguignol	.05
100	Orlando Hernandez	.05
101	Jose Cruz Jr.	.05
102	Jason Giambi	.60
103	Damion Easley	.05
104	Freddy Garcia	.05
105	Marlon Anderson	.05
106	Kevin Brown	.05
107	Joe Carter	.05
108	Russ Davis	.05
109	Brian Jordan	.05
110	Wade Boggs	1.00
111	Tom Goodwin	.05
112	Scott Brosius	.05
113	Darin Erstad	.10
114	Jay Bell	.05
115	Tom Glavine	.25
116	Pedro Martinez	.75
117	Mark Grace	.10
118	Russ Ortiz	.05
119	Magglio Ordonez	.10
120	Sean Casey	.15
121	Rafael Roque RC	.05
122	Brian Giles	.05
123	Mike Lansing	.05
124	David Cone	.05
125	Alex Gonzalez	.05
126	Carl Everett	.05
127	Jeff King	.05
128	Charles Johnson	.05
129	Geoff Jenkins	.05
130	Corey Koskie	.05
131	Brad Fullmer	.05
132	Al Leiter	.05
133	Rickey Henderson	.75
134	Rico Brogna	.05
135	Jose Guillen	.05
136	Matt Clement	.05
137	Carlos Guillen	.05
138	Orel Hershiser	.05
139	Ray Lankford	.05
140	Miguel Cairo	.05
141	Chuck Finley	.05
142	Rusty Greer	.05
143	Kelvim Escobar	.05
144	Ryan Klesko	.05
145	Andy Benes	.05
146	Eric Davis	.05
147	David Wells	.05
148	Trot Nixon	.05
149	Jose Hernandez	.05
150	Mark Johnson	.05
151	Mike Frank	.05
152	Joey Hamilton	.05
153	David Justice	.05
154	Mike Mussina	.40
155	Neifi Perez	.05
156	Luis Gonzalez	.10
157	Livan Hernandez	.05
158	Dermal Brown	.05
159	Jose Lima	.05
160	Eric Karros	.05
161	Ronnie Belliard	.05
162	Matt Lawton	.05
163	Dustin Hermanson	.05
164	Brian McRae	.05
165	Mike Kinkade	.05
166	A.J. Hinch	.05
167	Doug Glanville	.05
168	Hideo Nomo	.65
169	Jason Kendall	.05
170	Steve Finley	.05
171	Jeff Kent	.05
172	Ben Davis	.05
173	Edgar Martinez	.05
174	Eli Marrero	.05
175	Quinton McCracken	.05
176	Rick Helling	.05
177	Tom Evans	.05
178	Carl Pavano	.10
179	Todd Greene	.05
180	Omar Daal	.05
181	George Lombard	.05
182	Ryan Minor	.05
183	Troy O'Leary	.05
184	Robb Nen	.05
185	Mickey Morandini	.05
186	Robin Ventura	.05
187	Pete Harnisch	.05
188	Kenny Lofton	.05
189	Eric Milton	.05
190	Bobby Higginson	.05
191	Jamie Moyer	.05
192	Mark Kotsay	.05
193	Shane Reynolds	.05
194	Carlos Febles	.05
195	Jeff Kubenka	.05
196	Chuck Knoblauch	.05
197	Kenny Rogers	.05
198	Bill Mueller	.05
199	Shane Monahan	.05
200	Matt Morris	.05
201	Fred McGriff	.05
202	Ivan Rodriguez	.65
203	Kevin Witt	.05
204	Troy Percival	.05
205	David Dellucci	.05
206	Kevin Millwood	.05
207	Jerry Hairston Jr.	.05
208	Mike Stanley	.05
209	Henry Rodriguez	.05
210	Trevor Hoffman	.05
211	Craig Wilson	.05
212	Reggie Sanders	.05
213	Carlton Loewer	.05
214	Omar Vizquel	.05
215	Gabe Kapler	.05
216	Derrek Lee	.05
217	Billy Wagner	.05
218	Dean Palmer	.05
219	Chan Ho Park	.05
220	Fernando Vina	.05
221	Roy Halladay	.05
222	Paul Molitor	.75
223	Ugueth Urbina	.05
224	Rey Ordonez	.05
225	Ricky Ledee	.05
226	Scott Spiezio	.05
227	Wendell Magee Jr.	.05
228	Aramis Ramirez	.05
229	Brian Simmons	.05
230	Fernando Tatis	.05
231	Bobby Smith	.05
232	Aaron Sele	.05
233	Shawn Green	.20
234	Mariano Rivera	.15
235	Tim Salmon	.10
236	Andy Fox	.05
237	Denny Neagle	.05
238	John Valentin	.05
239	Kevin Tapani	.05
240	Paul Konerko	.10
241	Robert Fick	.05
242	Edgar Renteria	.05
243	Brett Tomko	.05
244	Daryle Ward	.05
245	Carlos Beltran	.30
246	Angel Pena	.05
247	Steve Woodard	.05
248	David Ortiz	.05
249	Justin Thompson	.05
250	Rondell White	.05
251	Jaret Wright	.05
252	Ed Sprague	.05
253	Jay Payton	.05
254	Mike Lowell	.05
255	Orlando Cabrera	.05
256	Jason Schmidt	.05
257	David Segui	.05
258	Paul Sorrento	.05
259	John Wetteland	.05
260	Devon White	.05
261	Odalis Perez	.05
262	Calvin Pickering	.05
263	Alex Ramirez	.05
264	Preston Wilson	.05
265	Brad Radke	.05
266	Walt Weiss	.05
267	Tim Young	.05
268	Tino Martinez	.05
269	Matt Stairs	.05
270	Curt Schilling	.25
271	Tony Womack	.05
272	Ismael Valdes	.05
273	Wally Joyner	.05
274	Armando Rios	.05
275	Andy Pettitte	.25
276	Bubba Trammell	.05
277	Todd Zeile	.05
278	Shannon Stewart	.05
279	Matt Williams	.05
280	John Rocker	.05
281	B.J. Surhoff	.05
282	Eric Young	.05
283	Dmitri Young	.05
284	John Smoltz	.05
285	Todd Walker	.05
286	Paul O'Neill	.05
287	Blake Stein	.05
288	Kevin Young	.05
289	Quilvio Veras	.05
290	Kirk Rueter	.05
291	Randy Winn	.05
292	Miguel Tejada	.05
293	J.T. Snow	.05
294	Michael Tucker	.05
295	Jay Tessmer	.05
296	Scott Erickson	.05
297	Tim Wakefield	.05
298	Jeff Abbott	.05
299	Eddie Taubensee	.05
300	Darryl Hamilton	.05
301	Kevin Orie	.05
302	Jose Offerman	.05
303	Scott Karl	.05
304	Chris Widger	.05
305	Todd Hundley	.05
306	Desi Relaford	.05
307	Sterling Hitchcock	.05
308	Delino DeShields	.05
309	Alex Gonzalez	.05
310	Justin Baughman	.05
311	Jamey Wright	.05
312	Wes Helms	.05
313	Dante Powell	.05
314	Jim Abbott	.05
315	Manny Alexander	.05
316	Harold Baines	.05
317	Danny Graves	.05
318	Sandy Alomar	.05
319	Pedro Astacio	.05
320	Jermaine Allensworth	.05
321	Matt Anderson	.05
322	Chad Curtis	.05
323	Antonio Osuna	.05
324	Brad Ausmus	.05
325	Steve Trachsel	.05
326	Mike Blowers	.05
327	Brian Bohanon	.05
328	Chris Gomez	.05
329	Valerio de los Santos	.05
330	Rich Aurilia	.05
331	Michael Barrett	.05
332	Rick Aguilera	.05
333	Adrian Brown	.05
334	Bill Spiers	.05
335	Matt Beech	.05
336	David Bell	.05
337	Juan Acevedo	.05
338	Jose Canseco	.50
339	Wilson Alvarez	.05
340	Luis Alicea	.05
341	Jason Dickson	.05
342	Mike Bordick	.05
343	Ben Ford	.05
344	Keith Lockhart	.05
345	Jason Christiansen	.05
346	Darren Bragg	.05
347	Doug Brocail	.05
348	Jeff Blauser	.05
349	James Baldwin	.05
350	Jeffrey Hammonds	.05
351	Ricky Bottalico	.05
352	Russ Branyon	.05
353	Mark Brownson	.05
354	Dave Berg	.05
355	Sean Bergman	.05
356	Jeff Conine	.05
357	Shayne Bennett	.05
358	Bobby Bonilla	.05
359	Bob Wickman	.05
360	Carlos Baerga	.05
361	Chris Fussell	.05
362	Chili Davis	.05
363	Jerry Spradlin	.05
364	Carlos Hernandez	.05
365	Roberto Hernandez	.05
366	Marvin Benard	.05
367	Ken Cloude	.05
368	Tony Fernandez	.05
369	John Burkett	.05
370	Gary DiSarcina	.05
371	Alan Benes	.05
372	Karim Garcia	.05
373	Carlos Perez	.05
374	Damon Buford	.05
375	Mark Clark	.05
376	Edgard Clemente RC	.05
377	Chad Bradford	.05
378	Frank Catalanotto	.05
379	Vic Darensbourg	.05
380	Sean Berry	.05
381	Dave Burba	.05
382	Sal Fasano	.05
383	Steve Parris	.05
384	Roger Cedeno	.05
385	Chad Fox	.05
386	Wilton Guerrero	.05
387	Dennis Cook	.05
388	Joe Girardi	.05
389	LaTroy Hawkins	.05
390	Ryan Christenson	.05
391	Paul Byrd	.05
392	Lou Collier	.05
393	Jeff Fassero	.05
394	Jim Leyritz	.05
395	Shawn Estes	.05
396	Mike Kelly	.05
397	Rich Croushore	.05
398	Royce Clayton	.05
399	Rudy Seanez	.05
400	Darrin Fletcher	.05
401	Shigetosi Hasegawa	.05
402	Bernard Gilkey	.05
403	Juan Guzman	.05
404	Jeff Frye	.05
405	Marino Santana	.05
406	Alex Fernandez	.05
407	Gary Gaetti	.05
408	Dan Miceli	.05
409	Mike Cameron	.05
410	Mike Remlinger	.05
411	Joey Cora	.05
412	Mark Gardner	.05
413	Aaron Ledesma	.05
414	Jerry Dipoto	.05
415	Ricky Gutierrez	.05
416	John Franco	.05
417	Mendy Lopez	.05
418	Hideki Irabu	.05
419	Mark Grudzielanek	.05
420	Bobby Hughes	.05
421	Pat Meares	.05
422	Jimmy Haynes	.05
423	Bob Henley	.05
424	Bobby Estalella	.05
425	Jon Lieber	.05
426	Giomar Guevara RC	.05
427	Jose Jimenez	.05
428	Deivi Cruz	.05
429	Jonathan Johnson	.05
430	Ken Hill	.05
431	Craig Grebeck	.05
432	Jose Rosado	.05
433	Danny Klassen	.05
434	Bobby Howry	.05
435	Gerald Williams	.05
436	Omar Olivares	.05
437	Chris Hoiles	.05
438	Seth Greisinger	.05
439	Scott Hatteberg	.05
440	Jeremi Gonzalez	.05
441	Wil Cordero	.05
442	Jeff Montgomery	.05
443	Chris Stynes	.05
444	Tony Saunders	.05
445	Einar Diaz	.05
446	Laril Gonzalez	.05
447	Ryan Jackson	.05
448	Mike Hampton	.05
449	Todd Hollandsworth	.05
450	Gabe White	.05
451	John Jaha	.05
452	Bret Saberhagen	.05
453	Otis Nixon	.05
454	Steve Kline	.05
455	Butch Huskey	.05
456	Mike Jerzembeck	.05
457	Wayne Gomes	.05
458	Mike Macfarlane	.05
459	Jesus Sanchez	.05
460	Al Martin	.05
461	Dwight Gooden	.05
462	Ruben Rivera	.05
463	Pat Hentgen	.05
464	Jose Valentin	.05
465	Vladimir Nunez	.05
466	Charlie Hayes	.05
467	Jay Powell	.05
468	Raul Ibanez	.05
469	Kent Mercker	.05
470	John Mabry	.05
471	Woody Williams	.05
472	Roberto Kelly	.05
473	Jim Mecir	.05
474	Dave Hollins	.05
475	Rafael Medina	.05
476	Darren Lewis	.05
477	Felix Heredia	.05
478	Brian Hunter	.05
479	Matt Mantei	.05
480	Richard Hidalgo	.05
481	Bobby Jones	.05
482	Hal Morris	.05
483	Ramiro Mendoza	.05
484	Matt Luke	.05
485	Esteban Loaiza	.05
486	Mark Loretta	.05
487	A.J. Pierzynski	.05
488	Charles Nagy	.05
489	Kevin Sefcik	.05
490	Jason McDonald	.05
491	Jeremy Powell	.05
492	Scott Servais	.05
493	Abraham Nunez	.05
494	Stan Spencer	.05
495	Stan Javier	.05
496	Jose Paniagua	.05
497	Gregg Jefferies	.05
498	Gregg Olson	.05
499	Derek Lowe	.05
500	Willis Otanez	.05
501	Brian Moehler	.05
502	Glenallen Hill	.05
503	Bobby Jones	.05
504	Greg Norton	.05
505	Mike Jackson	.05
506	Kirt Manwaring	.05
507	Eric Weaver	.05
508	Mitch Meluskey	.05
509	Todd Jones	.05
510	Mike Matheny	.05
511	Benj Sampson	.05
512	Tony Phillips	.05
513	Mike Thurman	.05
514	Jorge Posada	.05
515	Bill Taylor	.05
516	Mike Sweeney	.05
517	Jose Silva	.05
518	Mark Lewis	.05
519	Chris Peters	.05
520	Brian Johnson	.05
521	Mike Timlin	.05
522	Mark McLemore	.05
523	Dan Plesac	.05
524	Kelly Stinnett	.05
525	Sidney Ponson	.05
526	Jim Parque	.05
527	Tyler Houston	.05
528	John Thomson	.05
529	Mike Metcalfe	.05
530	Robert Person	.05
531	Marc Newfield	.05
532	Javier Vazquez	.05
533	Terry Steinbach	.05
534	Turk Wendell	.05
535	Tim Raines	.05
536	Brian Meadows	.05
537	Mike Lieberthal	.05
538	Ricardo Rincon	.05
539	Dan Wilson	.05
540	John Johnstone	.05
541	Todd Stottlemyre	.05
542	Kevin Stocker	.05
543	Ramon Martinez	.05
544	Mike Simms	.05
545	Paul Quantrill	.05
546	Matt Walbeck	.05
547	Turner Ward	.05
548	Bill Pulsipher	.05
549	Donnie Sadler	.05
550	Lance Johnson	.05
551	Bill Simas	.05
552	Jeff Reed	.05
553	Jeff Shaw	.05
554	Joe Randa	.05
555	Paul Shuey	.05
556	Mike Redmond	.05
557	Sean Runyan	.05
558	Enrique Wilson	.05
559	Scott Radinsky	.05
560	Larry Sutton	.05
561	Masato Yoshii	.05
562	David Nilsson	.05
563	Mike Trombley	.05
564	Darryl Strawberry	.05
565	Dave Mlicki	.05
566	Placido Polanco	.05
567	Yorkis Perez	.05
568	Esteban Yan	.05
569	Lee Stevens	.05
570	Steve Sinclair	.05
571	Jarrod Washburn	.05
572	Lenny Webster	.05
573	Mike Sirotka	.05
574	Jason Varitek	.05
575	Terry Mulholland	.05
576	Adrian Beltre (Franchise Futures)	.10
577	Eric Chavez (Franchise Futures)	.20
578	J.D. Drew (Franchise Futures)	.35
579	Juan Encarnacion (Franchise Futures)	.05
580	Nomar Garciaparra (Franchise Futures)	.65
581	Troy Glaus (Franchise Futures)	.35
582	Ben Grieve (Franchise Futures)	.05
583	Vladimir Guerrero (Franchise Futures)	.40
584	Todd Helton (Franchise Futures)	.35
585	Derek Jeter (Franchise Futures)	1.25
586	Travis Lee (Franchise Futures)	.10
587	Alex Rodriguez (Franchise Futures)	1.00
588	Scott Rolen (Franchise Futures)	.30
589	Richie Sexson (Franchise Futures)	.05
590	Kerry Wood (Franchise Futures)	.20
591	Ken Griffey Jr. (Checklist)	.75
592	Chipper Jones (Checklist)	.50
593	Alex Rodriguez (Checklist)	1.00
594	Sammy Sosa (Checklist)	.65
595	Mark McGwire (Checklist)	1.00
596	Cal Ripken Jr. (Checklist)	1.25
597	Nomar Garciaparra (Checklist)	.65
598	Derek Jeter (Checklist)	1.25
599	Kerry Wood (Checklist)	.20
600	J.D. Drew (Checklist)	.40

Starting Nine

This ultra-scarce, hobby-only parallel insert, found at the rate of about two cards per case, includes just nine cards of each player. Sharing the basic design of the Fleer Traditional set, the cards have blue metallic foil printing on front, including a "STARTING 9 NINE" logo at lower-right. At bottom right, the card's individual serial number from within the edition of nine is printed. Backs have an "S" suffix to the card number.

	NM/M
Common Player:	20.00

Warning Track Collection

Each of the cards in '99 Fleer Tradition was paralleled in this retail-only issue found one per pack. Warning Track cards are distinguished by the use of red metallic foil on front for the player's name, team, position that are in gold-foil on the regular version. There is also a special "Warning Track Collection" logo in red foil at bottom-right. On back, WTC cards have a "W" suffix to the card number.

	NM/M
Complete Set (600):	160.00
Common Player:	.50
Stars:	2X

Date With Destiny

This 10-card set takes a look at what Hall of Fame plaques might look like for some of today's great players. These are serially numbered to 100 sets.

		NM/M
Complete Set (10):		300.00
Common Player:		20.00
Production 100 Sets		
1	Barry Bonds	60.00
2	Roger Clemens	35.00
3	Ken Griffey Jr.	40.00
4	Tony Gwynn	30.00
5	Greg Maddux	30.00
6	Mark McGwire	50.00
7	Mike Piazza	40.00
8	Cal Ripken Jr.	60.00
9	Alex Rodriguez	50.00
10	Frank Thomas	20.00

Diamond Magic

A multi-layer card, where collectors turn a "wheel" for a kaleidoscope effect behind the player image. These are seeded 1:96 packs.

		NM/M
Complete Set (15):		50.00
Common Player:		1.00
Inserted 1:96		
1	Barry Bonds	9.00
2	Roger Clemens	4.50
3	Nomar Garciaparra	4.50
4	Ken Griffey Jr.	5.00
5	Tony Gwynn	3.75
6	Orlando Hernandez	1.00
7	Derek Jeter	9.00
8	Randy Johnson	3.00
9	Chipper Jones	3.75
10	Greg Maddux	3.75
11	Mark McGwire	6.00
12	Alex Rodriguez	7.50
13	Sammy Sosa	4.50
14	Bernie Williams	1.50
15	Kerry Wood	2.00

Going Yard

This 15-card set features the top home run hitters from the '98 season. These 1:18 pack inserts unfold to be twice as wide as regular cards and takes an unorthodox look at how far the longest home runs went.

	NM/M
Complete Set (15):	4.00

Common Player:		.10
Inserted 1:18		
1	Moises Alou	.10
2	Albert Belle	.10
3	José Canseco	.30
4	Vinny Castilla	.10
5	Andres Galarraga	.10
6	Juan Gonzalez	.20
7	Ken Griffey Jr.	.75
8	Chipper Jones	.50
9	Mark McGwire	1.00
10	Rafael Palmeiro	.35
11	Mike Piazza	.75
12	Alex Rodriguez	1.00
13	Sammy Sosa	.65
14	Greg Vaughn	.10
15	Mo Vaughn	.10

Golden Memories

This 15-card set pays tribute to the great moments from the 1998 season including David Wells perfect game and McGwire's record breaking season. These are seeded 1:54 packs on an embossed frame design.

		NM/M
Complete Set (15):		45.00
Common Player:		.75
Inserted 1:54		
1	Albert Belle	.75
2	Barry Bonds	7.50
3	Roger Clemens	4.50
4	Nomar Garciaparra	4.50
5	Juan Gonzalez	1.50
6	Ken Griffey Jr.	3.75
7	Randy Johnson	2.75
8	Greg Maddux	3.25
9	Mark McGwire	5.00
10	Mike Piazza	3.75
11	Cal Ripken Jr.	7.50
12	Alex Rodriguez	6.00
13	Sammy Sosa	4.50
14	David Wells	.75
15	Kerry Wood	2.00

Home Run Heroes

These cards were part of an unannounced multi-manufacturer (Fleer, Upper Deck, Topps, Pacific) insert program which was exclusive to Wal-Mart. Each company produced cards of Mark McGwire and Sammy Sosa, along with two other premier sluggers. Each company's cards share a "Power Elite" logo at top and "Home Run Heroes" logo vertically at right.

		NM/M
Complete Set (4):		7.50
Common Player:		1.50
1	Mark McGwire	
	(Tradition)	3.00
2	Sammy Sosa	
	(Sports Illustrated)	2.00
3	Mike Piazza	
	(SkyBox Thunder)	2.00
4	Nomar Garciaparra	
	(SkyBox Thunder)	2.00

Stan Musial Monumental Moments

Great moments and insight from and about the St. Louis Cardinals great. This 10-card tribute set chronicles Musial's legendary career. These are seeded 1:36 packs with 500 autographed cards randomly seeded.

		NM/M
Complete Set (10):		15.00
Common Musial:		2.00
Autographed Card:		60.00
1	Life in Donora	2.00
2	Values	2.00
3	In the Beginning	2.00
4	In the Navy	2.00
5	The 1948 Season	
	(w/Red Schoendienst)	2.00
6	Success Stories	
	(w/Pres. Kennedy)	2.00
7	Mr. Cardinal	2.00
8	Most Valuable Player	2.00
9	... baseball's perfect knight	2.00
10	Hall of Fame	2.00

Rookie Flashback

This 15-card set features the impact rookies from the 1998 season. These are seeded 1:6 packs and feature sculpture embossing.

		NM/M
Complete Set (15):		5.00
Common Player:		.25
Inserted 1:6		
1	Matt Anderson	.25
2	Rolando Arrojo	.25
3	Adrian Beltre	.50
4	Mike Caruso	.25
5	Eric Chavez	.40
6	J.D. Drew	.75
7	Juan Encarnacion	.25
8	Brad Fullmer	.25
9	Troy Glaus	1.50
10	Ben Grieve	.25
11	Todd Helton	1.50
12	Orlando Hernandez	.25
13	Travis Lee	.40
14	Richie Sexson	.25
15	Kerry Wood	.65

Vintage '61

This 50-card set takes the first 50 cards from the base set and showcases them in the 1961 Fleer "Baseball Greats" card design. These are seeded one per hobby pack.

		NM/M
Complete Set (50):		7.50
Common Player:		.05
Inserted 1:1		
1	Mark McGwire	.75
2	Sammy Sosa	.50
3	Ken Griffey Jr.	.60
4	Kerry Wood	.25
5	Derek Jeter	1.00
6	Stan Musial	.75
7	J.D. Drew	.30
8	Cal Ripken Jr.	1.00
9	Alex Rodriguez	.75
10	Travis Lee	.10
11	Andres Galarraga	.05
12	Nomar Garciaparra	.50
13	Albert Belle	.05
14	Barry Larkin	.05
15	Dante Bichette	.05
16	Tony Clark	.05
17	Moises Alou	.05
18	Rafael Palmeiro	.30
19	Raul Mondesi	.05
20	Vladimir Guerrero	.35
21	John Olerud	.05
22	Bernie Williams	.10
23	Ben Grieve	.30
24	Scott Rolen	.30
25	Jeromy Burnitz	.05
26	Ken Caminiti	.05
27	Barry Bonds	1.00
28	Todd Helton	.35
29	Juan Gonzalez	.25
30	Roger Clemens	.50
31	Andruw Jones	.35
32	Mo Vaughn	.05
33	Larry Walker	.05
34	Frank Thomas	.35
35	Manny Ramirez	.35
36	Randy Johnson	.35
37	Vinny Castilla	.05
38	Juan Encarnacion	.05
39	Jeff Bagwell	.35
40	Gary Sheffield	.25
41	Mike Piazza	.60
42	Richie Sexson	.05
43	Tony Gwynn	.45
44	Chipper Jones	.45
45	Jim Thome	.30
46	Craig Biggio	.05
47	Carlos Delgado	.25
48	Greg Vaughn	.05
49	Greg Maddux	.45
50	Troy Glaus	.25

Update

Distributed as a 150-card boxed set, the main focus for this release is the inclusion of rookie cards of players called up late in the '99 season, including Rick Ankiel. Besides rookies, the set also features 10 traded players/ free agents and a 10-card Season Highlights subset.

		NM/M
Complete Set (150):		22.50
Common Player:		.10
1	Rick Ankiel RC	.25
2	Peter Bergeron RC	.25
3	Pat Burrell RC	1.50
4	Eric Munson RC	.35
5	Alfonso Soriano RC	3.00
6	Tim Hudson RC	1.50
7	Erubiel Durazo RC	.25
8	Chad Hermansen RC	.10
9	Jeff Zimmerman RC	.10
10	Jesus Pena RC	.10
11	Ramon Hernandez RC	.10
12	Trent Durrington RC	.25
13	Tony Armas Jr. RC	.10
14	Mike Fyhrie RC	.10
15	Danny Kolb RC	.10
16	Mike Porzio RC	.10
17	Will Brunson RC	.10
18	Mike Duvall RC	.10
19	Doug Mientkiewicz RC	.75
20	Gabe Molina RC	.15
21	Luis Vizcaino RC	.20
22	Robinson Cancel RC	.10
23	Brett Laxton RC	.10
24	Joe McEwing RC	.25
25	Justin Speier RC	.20
26	Kip Wells RC	.25
27	Armando Almanza RC	.10
28	Joe Davenport RC	.10
29	Yamid Haad RC	.10
30	John Halama	.10
31	Adam Kennedy	.25
32	Vicente Padilla RC	.25
33	Travis Dawkins RC	.25
34	Ryan Rupe RC	.25
35	B.J. Ryan RC	.10
36	Chance Sanford RC	.10
37	Anthony Shumaker RC	.10
38	Ryan Glynn RC	.10
39	Matt Herges RC	.20
40	Ben Molina	.10
41	Scott Williamson	.10
42	Eric Gagne RC	3.00
43	John McDonald RC	.10
44	Scott Sauerbeck RC	.10
45	Mike Venafro RC	.10
46	Edwards Guzman RC	.10
47	Richard Barker RC	.10
48	Braden Looper	.10
49	Chad Meyers RC	.10
50	Scott Strickland RC	.10
51	Billy Koch	.10
52	Dave Newhan RC	.10
53	David Riske RC	.10
54	Jose Santiago	.10
55	Miguel Del Toro RC	.10
56	Orber Moreno RC	.10
57	Dave Roberts	.10
58	Tim Byrdak RC	.10
59	David Lee RC	.10
60	Guillermo Mota RC	.15
61	Wilton Veras RC	.15
62	Joe Mays RC	.35
63	Jose Fernandez RC	.10
64	Ray King RC	.10
65	Chris Petersen RC	.10
66	Vernon Wells	.15
67	Ruben Mateo	.10
68	Ben Petrick	.10
69	Chris Tremie RC	.10
70	Lance Berkman	.10
71	Dan Smith	.10
72	Carlos Hernandez RC	.10
73	Chad Harville RC	.25
74	Damaso Marte RC	.10
75	Aaron Myette RC	.15
76	Willis Roberts RC	.10
77	Erik Sabel RC	.10
78	Hector Almonte RC	.10
79	Kris Benson	.10
80	Pat Daneker RC	.10
81	Freddy Garcia RC	.50
82	Byung-Hyun Kim RC	.25
83	Wily Pena RC	1.00
84	Dan Wheeler RC	.15
85	Tim Harikkala RC	.10
86	Derrin Ebert RC	.10
87	Horacio Estrada RC	.10
88	Liu Rodriguez RC	.10
89	Jordan Zimmerman RC	.10
90	A.J. Burnett RC	.40
91	Doug Davis RC	.10
92	Robert Ramsey RC	.10
93	Ryan Franklin RC	.10
94	Charlie Greene RC	.10
95	Bo Porter RC	.10
96	Jorge Toca RC	.10
97	Casey Blake RC	.20
98	Amaury Garcia RC	.10
99	Jose Molina RC	.10
100	Melvin Mora RC	1.00
101	Joe Nathan RC	.10
102	Juan Pena RC	.25
103	Dave Borkowski RC	.10
104	Eddie Gaillard RC	.10
105	Rob Radlosky RC	.10
106	Brett Hinchliffe RC	.10
107	Carlos Lee	.10
108	Rob Ryan RC	.10
109	Jeff Weaver RC	.50
110	Ed Yarnall	.10
111	Nelson Cruz RC	.10
112	Cleatus Davidson RC	.10
113	Tim Kubinski RC	.10
114	Sean Spencer RC	.10
115	Joe Winkelsas RC	.10
116	Chris Clapinski RC	.10
117	Tom Davey RC	.10
118	Warren Morris	.10
119	Dan Murray RC	.10
120	Jose Nieves RC	.10
121	Mark Quinn RC	.10
122	Josh Beckett RC	6.00
123	Chad Allen RC	.10
124	Mike Figga	.10
125	Beiker Graterol RC	.10
126	Aaron Scheffer RC	.10
127	Wiki Gonzalez RC	.10
128	Ramon E. Martinez	.10
129	Matt Riley RC	.25
130	Chris Woodward RC	.10
131	Albert Belle	.10
132	Roger Cedeno	.10
133	Roger Clemens	.75
134	Brian Giles	.10
135	Rickey Henderson	.60
136	Randy Johnson	.60
137	Brian Jordan	.10
138	Paul Konerko	.15
139	Hideo Nomo	.50
140	Kenny Rogers	.10
141	Wade Boggs	.65
142	Jose Canseco	.45
143	Roger Clemens	.75
144	David Cone	.10
145	Tony Gwynn	.65
146	Mark McGwire	1.00
147	Cal Ripken Jr.	1.50
148	Alex Rodriguez	1.00
149	Fernando Tatis	.10
150	Robin Ventura	.10

Millennium

This special edition of '99 Fleer Tradition was issued only in factory sets, for sale on Shop at Home. Besides the 600 cards in the regular Tradition issue, these sets include 20 renumbered rookie and highlight cards from the Fleer Update set. Each set is sealed with gold-foil on which is a serial number from with an edition of 5,000 sets. Each card in the edition has a special gold-foil "2000" logo on front.

		NM/M
Complete Factory Set (620):		30.00
Common Player:		.50
Stars:		5X
601	Rick Ankiel	.75
602	Peter Bergeron	.50
603	Pat Burrell	2.00
604	Eric Munson	.50
605	Alfonso Soriano	2.00
606	Tim Hudson	1.25
607	Erubiel Durazo	.50
608	Chad Hermansen	.50
609	Jeff Zimmerman	.50
610	Jesus Pena	.50
611	Wade Boggs	
	(Highlights)	.75
612	Jose Canseco	
	(Highlights)	.50
613	Roger Clemens	
	(Highlights)	1.00
614	David Cone	
	(Highlights)	.50
615	Tony Gwynn	
	(Highlights)	.75
616	Mark McGwire	
	(Highlights)	1.50
617	Cal Ripken Jr.	
	(Highlights)	2.00
618	Alex Rodriguez	
	(Highlights)	1.50
619	Fernando Tatis	
	(Highlights)	.50
620	Robin Ventura	
	(Highlights)	.50

Brilliants Sample

To preview of the introduction of its Brilliants brand of premium quality cards into baseball, Fleer issued a promo card of J.D. Drew. Like the issued cards, the sample is printed on plastic with a mirrored silver

background on front. Both front and back are overprinted, "PROMOTIONAL SAMPLE."

	NM/M
J.D. Drew	3.00

Brilliants

This 175-card set features an action photo on a complete silver-foiled background swirl pattern. The featured player's name, team and postion are stamped in gold foil. Card backs have a small photo, vital information, 1998 statistics and a brief overview of the player's '98 season. Cards numbered 126-175 are part of a short-printed Rookies subset and are seeded 1:2 packs.

	NM/M
Complete Set (175):	60.00
Common Player:	.25
Common SP (126-175):	.50
Blues (1:3):	1.5X
SP Blues (1:6):	1X
Golds:	8X
SP Golds:	3X
Production 99 Sets	
24 Karat Golds:	40X
SP's:	15X
Production 24 Sets	
Pack (5):	2.00
Wax Box (24):	32.50
1	Mark McGwire	2.50
2	Derek Jeter	3.00
3	Nomar Garciaparra	1.75
4	Travis Lee	.25
5	Jeff Bagwell	.75
6	Andres Galarraga	.25
7	Pedro Martinez	.75
8	Cal Ripken Jr.	3.00
9	Vladimir Guerrero	.75
10	Chipper Jones	1.50
11	Rusty Greer	.25
12	Omar Vizquel	.25
13	Quinton McCracken	.25
14	Jaret Wright	.25
15	Mike Mussina	.50
16	Jason Giambi	.60
17	Tony Clark	.25
18	Troy O'Leary	.25
19	Troy Percival	.25
20	Kerry Wood	.50
21	Vinny Castilla	.25
22	Chris Carpenter	.25
23	Richie Sexson	.25
24	Ken Griffey Jr.	2.00
25	Barry Bonds	3.00
26	Carlos Delgado	.60
27	Frank Thomas	.75
28	Manny Ramirez	.75
29	Shawn Green	.50
30	Mike Piazza	2.00
31	Tino Martinez	.25
32	Dante Bichette	.25
33	Scott Rolen	.65
34	Gabe Alvarez	.25
35	Raul Mondesi	.25
36	Damion Easley	.25
37	Jeff Kent	.25
38	Al Leiter	.25
39	Alex Rodriguez	2.50
40	Jeff King	.25
41	Mark Grace	.25
42	Larry Walker	.25
43	Moises Alou	.25
44	Juan Gonzalez	.65
45	Rolando Arrojo	.25
46	Tom Glavine	.45
47	Johnny Damon	.45
48	Livan Hernandez	.25
49	Craig Biggio	.25
50	Dmitri Young	.25
51	Chan Ho Park	.25
52	Todd Walker	.25
53	Derrek Lee	.25
54	Todd Helton	.75
55	Ray Lankford	.25
56	Jim Thome	.65
57	Matt Lawton	.25
58	Matt Anderson	.25

59	Jose Offerman	.25
60	Eric Karros	.25
61	Orlando Hernandez	.25
62	Ben Grieve	.25
63	Bobby Abreu	.25
64	Kevin Young	.25
65	John Olerud	.25
66	Sammy Sosa	1.75
67	Andy Ashby	.25
68	Juan Encarnacion	.25
69	Shane Reynolds	.25
70	Bernie Williams	.35
71	Mike Cameron	.25
72	Troy Glaus	.75
73	Gary Sheffield	.60
74	Jeromy Burnitz	.25
75	Mike Caruso	.25
76	Chuck Knoblauch	.25
77	Kenny Rogers	.25
78	David Cone	.25
79	Tony Gwynn	1.50
80	Aramis Ramirez	.25
81	Paul O'Neill	.25
82	Charles Nagy	.25
83	Javy Lopez	.25
84	Scott Erickson	.25
85	Trevor Hoffman	.25
86	Andruw Jones	.75
87	Ray Durham	.25
88	Jorge Posada	.25
89	Edgar Martinez	.25
90	Tim Salmon	.35
91	Bobby Higginson	.25
92	Adrian Beltre	.45
93	Jason Kendall	.25
94	Henry Rodriguez	.25
95	Greg Maddux	1.50
96	David Justice	.25
97	Ivan Rodriguez	.65
98	Curt Schilling	.45
99	Matt Williams	.25
100	Darin Erstad	.50
101	Rafael Palmeiro	.65
102	David Wells	.25
103	Barry Larkin	.25
104	Robin Ventura	.25
105	Edgar Renteria	.25
106	Andy Pettitte	.25
107	Albert Belle	.25
108	Steve Finley	.25
109	Fernando Vina	.25
110	Rondell White	.25
111	Kevin Brown	.25
112	Jose Canseco	.50
113	Roger Clemens	1.75
114	Todd Hundley	.25
115	Will Clark	.35
116	Jim Edmonds	.25
117	Randy Johnson	.75
118	Denny Neagle	.25
119	Brian Jordan	.25
120	Dean Palmer	.25
121	Roberto Alomar	.45
122	Ken Caminiti	.25
123	Brian Giles	.25
124	Todd Stottlemyre	.25
125	Mo Vaughn	.25
126	J.D. Drew	1.00
127	Ryan Minor	.50
128	Gabe Kapler	.50
129	Jeremy Giambi	.50
130	Eric Chavez	1.00
131	Ben Davis	.50
132	Rob Fick	.50
133	George Lombard	.50
134	Calvin Pickering	.50
135	Preston Wilson	.50
136	Corey Koskie	.75
137	Russell Branyan	.50
138	Bruce Chen	.50
139	Matt Clement	.75
140	Pat Burrell **RC**	2.50
141	Freddy Garcia **RC**	1.00
142	Brian Simmons	.50
143	Carlos Febles	.50
144	Carlos Guillen	.50
145	Fernando Seguignol	.50
146	Carlos Beltran	1.00
147	Edgard Clemente	.50
148	Mitch Meluskey	.50
149	Ryan Bradley	.50
150	Marlon Anderson	.50
151	A.J. Burnett **RC**	1.00
152	Scott Hunter **RC**	.50
153	Mark Johnson	.50
154	Angel Pena	.50
155	Roy Halladay	.75
156	Chad Allen **RC**	.50
157	Trot Nixon	.75
158	Ricky Ledee	.50
159	Gary Bennett **RC**	.50
160	Micah Bowie **RC**	.50
161	Doug Mientkiewicz	.60
162	Danny Klassen	.50
163	Willis Otanez	.50
164	Jin Ho Cho	.50
165	Mike Lowell	.60
166	Armando Rios	.50
167	Tom Evans	.50
168	Michael Barrett	.50
169	Alex Gonzalez	.50
170	Masao Kida **RC**	.60
171	Peter Tucci **RC**	.50
172	Luis Saturria **RC**	.50
173	Kris Benson	.50
174	Mario Encarnacion **RC**	.50
175	Roosevelt Brown **RC**	.50

Brilliants Blue/Golds

The 175 Fleer Brilliants base cards are paralleled in three insert sets of differing degrees of scarcity. Brilliant Blue parallels have a mirrored blue foil background on front and a "B" suffix to the card number on back. They are seeded one per three packs (125 veterans) and one per six packs (50 rookies). Gold parallels are printed with gold foil background and a "G" suffix. Each card is serially numbered on back within an edition of 99. The 24-karat Gold parallels have gold rainbow holographic foil backgrounds, a 24-karat gold logo and are serially numbered to just 24 of each card; numbers have a TG sugffix.

	NM/M
Brilliants Blue Common:	.50
Brilliants Blue Stars:	1.5X
Brilliants Blue Rookies:	1X
Brilliants Gold Common:	3.00
Brilliants Gold Stars:	8X
Brilliants Gold Rookies:	3X
Brilliants 24K Gold Common:	10.00
Brilliants 24K Gold Stars:	40X
Brilliants 24K Gold Rookies:	15X

Brilliants Illuminators

This 15-card set highlights baseball's top young prospects on a team color-coded fully foiled front. Card backs are numbered with an "I" suffix and are inserted 1:10 packs.

	NM/M
Complete Set (15):	10.00
Common Player:	.75
Inserted 1:10	
1	Kerry Wood	2.00
2	Ben Grieve	.75
3	J.D. Drew	1.50
4	Juan Encarnacion	.75
5	Travis Lee	.75
6	Todd Helton	3.00
7	Troy Glaus	2.00
8	Ricky Ledee	.75
9	Eric Chavez	1.50
10	Ben Davis	.75
11	George Lombard	.75
12	Jeremy Giambi	.75
13	Richie Sexson	.75
14	Corey Koskie	.75
15	Russell Branyan	.75

Brilliants Shining Stars

Shining Stars is a 15-card set printed on styrene with two-sided mirrored foil.

Alex Rodriguez•SS

Card backs are numbered with a "S" suffix and are seeded.1:20 packs. Pulsars are a parallel set that are printed on two-sided rainbow holographic foil and styrene with an embossed star pattern in the background. Pulsars are seeded 1:400 packs.

	NM/M
Complete Set (15):	30.00
Common Player:	1.50
Inserted 1:20	
Pulsars:	4X
Inserted 1:400	
1	Ken Griffey Jr.	2.50
2	Mark McGwire	3.00
3	Sammy Sosa	2.25
4	Derek Jeter	4.00
5	Nomar Garciaparra	2.25
6	Alex Rodriguez	3.00
7	Mike Piazza	2.50
8	Juan Gonzalez	1.50
9	Chipper Jones	2.00
10	Cal Ripken Jr.	4.00
11	Frank Thomas	1.50
12	Greg Maddux	2.00
13	Roger Clemens	2.25
14	Vladimir Guerrero	1.50
15	Manny Ramirez	1.50

Mystique

The "Mystique" of this issue lay partly in the fact that each four-card $4.99 pack included a card which was covered with a peel-off coating, either a short-printed star card from the #1-100 base set, one of the short-printed Rookie (#101-150) or Stars (#151-160) cards or one of the inserts. The Rookie cards are serial numbered to 2,999 apiece, while the red-foil highlighted Stars cards are in an edition of 2,500 each. Fronts have metallic foil backgrounds, backs have a player portrait photo, biographical and career notes and stats.

	NM/M
Complete Set (160):	125.00
Common Player:	.20
Common SP (1-100):	.75
Common (101-150):	1.00
Production 2,999 Sets	
Common (151-160):	2.00
Production 2,500 Sets	
Pack (4):	3.00
Wax Box (24):	60.00
1	Ken Griffey Jr. /SP	2.50
2	Livan Hernandez	.20
3	Jeff Kent	.20
4	Brian Jordan	.20
5	Kevin Young	.20

6	Vinny Castilla	.20
7	Orlando Hernandez/SP	.75
8	Bobby Abreu	.20
9	Vladimir Guerrero/SP	1.50
10	Chuck Knoblauch	.20
11	Nomar Garciaparra/SP	2.25
12	Jeff Bagwell	1.00
13	Todd Walker	.20
14	Johnny Damon	.45
15	Mike Caruso	.20
16	Cliff Floyd	.20
17	Andy Pettitte	.35
18	Cal Ripken Jr./SP	4.00
19	Brian Giles	.20
20	Robin Ventura	.20
21	Alex Gonzalez	.20
22	Randy Johnson	.75
23	Raul Mondesi	.20
24	Ken Caminiti	.20
25	Tom Glavine	.40
26	Derek Jeter/SP	4.00
27	Carlos Delgado	.50
28	Adrian Beltre	.35
29	Tino Martinez	.20
30	Todd Helton	.20
31	Juan Gonzalez/SP	1.25
32	Henry Rodriguez	.20
33	Jim Thome	.65
34	Paul O'Neill	.20
35	Scott Rolen/SP	1.25
36	Rafael Palmeiro	.20
37	Will Clark	.25
38	Todd Hundley	.20
39	Andruw Jones/SP	1.50
40	Luis Rolando Arrojo	.20
41	Barry Larkin	.20
42	Tim Salmon	.25
43	Rondell White	.20
44	Curt Schilling	.40
45	Chipper Jones/SP	2.00
46	Jeromy Burnitz	.20
47	Mo Vaughn	.20
48	Tony Clark	.20
49	Fernando Tatis	.20
50	Dmitri Young	.20
51	Wade Boggs	1.50
52	Rickey Henderson	.75
53	Manny Ramirez/SP	1.50
54	Edgar Martinez	.20
55	Jason Giambi	.65
56	Jason Kendall	.20
57	Eric Karros	.20
58	Jose Canseco/SP	.75
59	Shawn Green	.40
60	Ellis Burks	.20
61	Derek Bell	.20
62	Shannon Stewart	.20
63	Roger Clemens/SP	2.25
64	Sean Casey/SP	.75
65	Jose Offerman	.20
66	Sammy Sosa/SP	2.25
67	Frank Thomas/SP	1.50
68	Tony Gwynn/SP	2.00
69	Roberto Alomar	.35
70	Mark McGwire/SP	3.00
71	Troy Glaus	1.00
72	Ray Durham	.20
73	Jeff Cirillo	.20
74	Alex Rodriguez/SP	3.00
75	Jose Cruz Jr.	.20
76	Juan Encarnacion	.20
77	Mark Grace	.20
78	Barry Bonds/SP	4.00
79	Ivan Rodriguez/SP	1.25
80	Greg Vaughn	.20
81	Greg Maddux/SP	2.00
82	Albert Belle	.20
83	John Olerud	.20
84	Kenny Lofton	.20
85	Bernie Williams	.30
86	Matt Williams	.20
87	Ray Lankford	.20
88	Darin Erstad	.40
89	Ben Grieve	.20
90	Craig Biggio	.20
91	Dean Palmer	.20
92	Reggie Sanders	.20
93	Dante Bichette	.20
94	Pedro Martinez/SP	1.50
95	Larry Walker	.20
96	David Wells	.20
97	Travis Lee/SP	.75
98	Mike Piazza/SP	2.50
99	Mike Mussina	.45
100	Kevin Brown	.20
101	Ruben Mateo (Rookie)	1.00
102	Roberto Ramirez (Rookie)	1.00
103	Glen Barker **RC** (Rookie)	1.00
104	Clay Bellinger **RC** (Rookie)	1.00
105	Carlos Guillen (Rookie)	1.00
106	Scott Schoeneweis (Rookie)	1.00
107	Creighton Gubanich (Rookie)	1.00
108	Scott Williamson (Rookie)	1.00
109	Edwards Guzman **RC** (Rookie)	1.00
110	A.J. Burnett **RC** (Rookie)	4.00
111	Jeremy Giambi (Rookie)	1.00
112	Trot Nixon (Rookie)	1.50

113	J.D. Drew (Rookie)	3.00
114	Roy Halladay (Rookie)	1.50
115	Jose Macias **RC** (Rookie)	2.00
116	Corey Koskie (Rookie)	2.00
117	Ryan Rupe **RC** (Rookie)	1.50
118	Scott Hunter (Rookie)	1.00
119	Rob Fick (Rookie)	1.00
120	McKay Christensen (Rookie)	1.50
121	Carlos Febles (Rookie)	2.00
122	Gabe Kapler (Rookie)	1.50
123	Jeff Liefer (Rookie)	1.00
124	Warren Morris (Rookie)	1.00
125	Chris Pritchett (Rookie)	1.00
126	Torii Hunter (Rookie)	3.00
127	Armando Rios (Rookie)	1.00
128	Ricky Ledee (Rookie)	1.00
129	Kelly Dransfeldt **RC** (Rookie)	1.00
130	Jeff Zimmerman (Rookie)	1.50
131	Eric Chavez (Rookie)	2.00
132	Freddy Garcia (Rookie)	3.00
133	Jose Jimenez (Rookie)	1.00
134	Pat Burrell **RC** (Rookie)	20.00
135	Joe McEwing (Rookie)	1.50
136	Kris Benson (Rookie)	1.50
137	Joe Mays **RC** (Rookie)	2.00
138	Rafael Roque (Rookie)	1.00
139	Cristian Guzman (Rookie)	1.50
140	Michael Barrett (Rookie)	1.50
141	Doug Mientkiewicz (Rookie)	1.50
142	Jeff Weaver **RC** (Rookie)	4.00
143	Mike Lowell (Rookie)	1.50
144	Jason Phillips **RC** (Rookie)	2.00
145	Marlon Anderson (Rookie)	1.50
146	Brett Hinchliffe **RC** (Rookie)	1.00
147	Matt Clement (Rookie)	1.50
148	Terrence Long (Rookie)	1.00
149	Carlos Beltran (Rookie)	2.50
150	Preston Wilson (Rookie)	1.50
151	Ken Griffey Jr. (Stars)	2.00
152	Mark McGwire (Stars)	3.00
153	Sammy Sosa (Stars)	1.50
154	Mike Piazza (Stars)	1.50
155	Alex Rodriguez (Stars)	3.00
156	Nomar Garciaparra (Stars)	1.50
157	Cal Ripken Jr. (Stars)	4.00
158	Greg Maddux (Stars)	1.50
159	Derek Jeter (Stars)	4.00
160	Juan Gonzalez (Stars)	1.00
	Checklist card	.10

1999 Fleer Mystique Gold

The first 100 cards of the base set are paralleled in this insert which features gold-foil highlights on front. Gold versions are found in one of eight packs, on average.

	NM/M
Common Player:	1.00
Stars (1-100):	1.5X
Inserted 1:8	

Mystique Masterpiece

Each of the cards in Fleer Mystique was also produced in a unique Masterpiece version. The super-rarities are labeled on front "The Only 1 of 1 / Masterpiece."

NM/M
Common Player: 50.00

Mystique Destiny

A silver holofoil background on front and a serial number within an edition of 999 each marks this insert set. Backs have another photo along with career highlights.

	NM/M
Complete Set (10):	35.00
Common Player:	2.00
Production 999 Sets	
1 Tony Gwynn	5.00
2 Juan Gonzalez	3.00
3 Scott Rolen	4.00
4 Nomar Garciaparra	6.00
5 Orlando Hernandez	2.00
6 Andruw Jones	4.00
7 Vladimir Guerrero	4.00
8 Darin Erstad	2.00
9 Manny Ramirez	4.00
10 Roger Clemens	6.00

Mystique Established

A plastic stock, red holofoil background and silver foil highlights complement the action photo of a top star in this insert set. Backs have another photo, some career highlights and a serial number from within an edition of 100 each.

	NM/M
Complete Set (10):	300.00
Common Player:	15.00
Production 100 Sets	
1 Ken Griffey Jr.	30.00
2 Derek Jeter	60.00
3 Chipper Jones	20.00
4 Greg Maddux	20.00
5 Mark McGwire	45.00
6 Mike Piazza	30.00
7 Cal Ripken Jr.	60.00
8 Alex Rodriguez	45.00
9 Sammy Sosa	25.00
10 Frank Thomas	15.00

Mystique Feel the Game

Swatches of various game-used equipment are featured in this insert series. Each card is hand-numbered from editions which range between 345 and 450.

	NM/M
Common Player:	10.00

Adrian Beltre/ Shoe/430	15.00
J.D. Drew/Jsy/450	15.00
Juan Gonzalez/ Bat Glv/415)	10.00
Tony Gwynn/Jsy/435	15.00
Kevin Millwood/ Jsy/435	10.00
Alex Rodriguez/ Bat/345	30.00
Frank Thomas/ Jsy/450	15.00

Mystique Fresh Ink

These inserts, found about one per 48 packs, have a white oval at bottom front containing an autograph of the player pictured. At bottom is a white panel with a hand-printed serial number from within each card's edition, which ranged from 140 to 1,000. Backs have a Fleer seal and statement of authenticity pertinent to the autograph. The unnumbered cards are listed here in alphabetical order.

	NM/M
Complete Set (26):	300.00
Common Player:	4.00
Inserted 1:48	
Roberto Alomar/500	10.00
Michael Barrett/1,000	6.00
Kris Benson/500	8.00
Micah Bowie/1,000	4.00
A.J. Burnett/500	10.00
Pat Burrell/500	15.00
Ken Caminiti/250	10.00
Jose Canseco/250	25.00
Sean Casey/1,000	8.00
Edgard Clemente/ 1,000	4.00
Bartolo Colon/500	8.00
J.D. Drew/400	15.00
Juan Encarnacion/ 1,000	4.00
Troy Glaus/400	15.00
Juan Gonzalez/250	15.00
Shawn Green/250	15.00
Tony Gwynn/250	30.00
Chipper Jones/500	30.00
Gabe Kapler/750	6.00
Barry Larkin/250	25.00
Doug Mientkiewicz/ 500	6.00
Alex Rodriguez/200	30.00
Scott Rolen/140	30.00
Fernando Tatis/750	4.00
Robin Ventura/500	6.00
Todd Walker/1,000	6.00

Mystique Prophetic

Blue holofoil with silver highlights is the graphic treatment found on this insert set of young stars. Each card is numbered on front from within an edition of 1,999. Backs have a portrait photo and a few words about the player.

	NM/M
Complete Set (10):	15.00
Common Player:	1.00
Production 1,999 Sets	
1 Eric Chavez	1.50
2 J.D. Drew	2.00
3 A.J. Burnett	1.00
4 Ben Grieve	1.00
5 Gabe Kapler	1.00
6 Todd Helton	2.50
7 Troy Glaus	4.00
8 Travis Lee	1.00
9 Pat Burrell	5.00
10 Kerry Wood	1.50

Diamond Skills Commemorative Sheet

In conjunction with its sponsorship of the Diamond Skills program, Fleer distributed this eight-player sheet to 7-14 year olds participating in the event. Participants could get a sheet by redeeming Fleer wrappers at a local card store. The 10" x 9" sheet features full size Fleer Tradition cards. At top is a list of 1997 Diamond Skills winners.

	NM/M
Complete Sheet:	3.00

National Convention Commemorative Set

In conjunction with its participation at the 20th National Sports Collectors Convention in Atlanta in July, 1999, Fleer distributed this cello-wrapped commemorative set to persons purchasing VIP admission packages. The set includes a specially numbered (NC1) version of the Stan Musial card from '99 Fleer Tradition, three large-format (3-1/2" x 5") cards reproducing Musial Monumental Moments inserts, and an unnumbered header card. The Monumental Moments reproductions are printed on a red background with the famed St. Louis arch.

	NM/M
Complete Set (5):	10.00
Common Card:	2.00
NC1 Stan Musial (Fleer Tradition)	2.00
NC2 Stan Musial (Life in Donora - Monumental Moment)	2.00
NC3 Stan Musial (The 1948 Season - Monumental Moment)	2.00
NC4 Stan Musial (Hall of Fame - Monumental Season) Header Card	.25

2000 Fleer Focus

The 250-card base set has two versions for the Prospects subset card numbers

226-250. The portrait versions are serial numbered from 1-999, while the remaining serial numbered from 1,000 to 3,999 capture an action shot. The base set design has a white border with gold foil stamping. Card backs have complete year-by-year statistics along with a career note and small photo.

	NM/M
Complete Set (250):	100.00
Common Player:	.15
Common Prospect (226-250):	4.00
Production 2,999 Sets	
Common Portrait (226-250):	8.00
Portraits:	2X
Production 999 Sets	
Pack:	.15
Wax Box (24):	35.00
1 Nomar Garciaparra	1.25
2 Adrian Beltre	.35
3 Miguel Tejada	.35
4 Joe Randa	.15
5 Larry Walker	.15
6 Jeff Weaver	.15
7 Jay Bell	.15
8 Ivan Rodriguez	.50
9 Edgar Martinez	.15
10 Desi Relaford	.15
11 Derek Jeter	2.50
12 Delino DeShields	.15
13 Craig Biggio	.15
14 Chuck Knoblauch	.15
15 Chuck Finley	.15
16 Brett Tomko	.15
17 Bobby Higginson	.15
18 Pedro Martinez	.75
19 Troy O'Leary	.15
20 Rickey Henderson	.75
21 Robb Nen	.15
22 Rolando Arrojo	.15
23 Rondell White	.15
24 Royce Clayton	.15
25 Rusty Greer	.15
26 Stan Spencer	.15
27 Steve Finley	.15
28 Tom Goodwin	.15
29 Troy Percival	.15
30 Wilton Guerrero	.15
31 Roberto Alomar	.30
32 Mike Hampton	.15
33 Michael Barrett	.15
34 Curt Schilling	.40
35 Bill Mueller	.15
36 Bernie Williams	.30
37 John Smoltz	.15
38 B.J. Surhoff	.15
39 Pete Harnisch	.15
40 Juan Encarnacion	.15
41 Derrek Lee	.15
42 Jeff Shaw	.15
43 David Cone	.15
44 Jason Christiansen	.15
45 Jeff Kent	.15
46 Randy Johnson	.75
47 Todd Walker	.15
48 Jose Lima	.15
49 Jason Giambi	.50
50 Ken Griffey Jr.	1.50
51 Bartolo Colon	.15
52 Mike Lieberthal	.15
53 Shane Reynolds	.15
54 Travis Lee	.15
55 Travis Fryman	.15
56 John Valentin	.15
57 Joey Hamilton	.15
58 Jay Buhner	.15
59 Brad Radke	.15
60 A.J. Burnett	.15
61 Roy Halladay	.25
62 Raul Mondesi	.15
63 Matt Mantei	.15
64 Mark Grace	.15
65 David Justice	.15
66 Billy Wagner	.15
67 Eric Milton	.15
68 Eric Chavez	.25
69 Doug Glanville	.15
70 Ray Durham	.15
71 Mike Sirotka	.15
72 Greg Vaughn	.15
73 Brian Jordan	.15
74 Alex Gonzalez	.15
75 Alex Rodriguez	2.00
76 David Nilsson	.15
77 Robin Ventura	.15
78 Kevin Young	.15
79 Wilson Alvarez	.15
80 Matt Williams	.15
81 Ismael Valdes	.15
82 Kenny Lofton	.15
83 Carlos Beltran	.45
84 Doug Mientkiewicz	.15
85 Wally Joyner	.15
86 J.D. Drew	.35
87 Carlos Delgado	.50
88 Tony Womack	.15
89 Eric Young	.15
90 Manny Ramirez	.75
91 Johnny Damon	.15
92 Torii Hunter	.25
93 Kenny Rogers	.15
94 Trevor Hoffman	.15
95 John Wetteland	.15
96 Ray Lankford	.15
97 Tom Glavine	.30
98 Carlos Lee	.15
99 Richie Sexson	.15
100 Carlos Febles	.15
101 Chad Allen	.15
102 Sterling Hitchcock	.15
103 Joe McEwing	.15
104 Justin Thompson	.15
105 Jim Edmonds	.15
106 Kerry Wood	.40
107 Jim Thome	.65
108 Jeremy Giambi	.15
109 Mike Piazza	1.50
110 Darryl Kile	.15
111 Darin Erstad	.30
112 Kyle Farnsworth	.15
113 Omar Vizquel	.15
114 Orber Moreno	.15
115 Al Leiter	.15
116 John Olerud	.15
117 Aaron Sele	.15
118 Chipper Jones	1.00
119 Paul Konerko	.25
120 Chris Singleton	.15
121 Fernando Vina	.15
122 Andy Ashby	.15
123 Eli Marrero	.15
124 Edgar Renteria	.15
125 Roberto Hernandez	.15
126 Andruw Jones	.75
127 Magglio Ordonez	.25
128 Bob Wickman	.15
129 Tony Gwynn	1.00
130 Mark McGwire	2.00
131 Albert Belle	.15
132 Pokey Reese	.15
133 Tony Clark	.15
134 Jeff Bagwell	.75
135 Mark Grudzielanek	.15
136 Dustin Hermanson	.15
137 Reggie Sanders	.15
138 Ryan Rupe	.15
139 Kevin Millwood	.15
140 Bret Saberhagen	.15
141 Juan Guzman	.15
142 Alex Gonzalez	.15
143 Gary Sheffield	.30
144 Roger Clemens	1.25
145 Ben Grieve	.15
146 Bobby Abreu	.15
147 Brian Giles	.15
148 Quinton McCracken	.15
149 Freddy Garcia	.15
150 Erubiel Durazo	.15
151 Sidney Ponson	.15
152 Scott Williamson	.15
153 Ken Caminiti	.15
154 Vladimir Guerrero	.75
155 Andy Pettitte	.25
156 Edwards Guzman	.15
157 Shannon Stewart	.15
158 Greg Maddux	1.00
159 Mike Stanley	.15
160 Sean Casey	.25
161 Cliff Floyd	.15
162 Devon White	.15
163 Scott Brosius	.15
164 Marlon Anderson	.15
165 Jason Kendall	.15
166 Ryan Klesko	.15
167 Sammy Sosa	1.25
168 Frank Thomas	.75
169 Geoff Jenkins	.15
170 Jason Schmidt	.15
171 Dan Wilson	.15
172 Jose Canseco	.40
173 Troy Glaus	.75
174 Mariano Rivera	.20
175 Scott Rolen	.65
176 J.T. Snow	.15
177 Rafael Palmeiro	.65
178 A.J. Hinch	.15
179 Jose Offerman	.15
180 Jeff Cirillo	.15
181 Dean Palmer	.15
182 Jose Rosado	.15
183 Armando Benitez	.15
184 Brady Anderson	.15
185 Cal Ripken Jr.	2.50
186 Barry Larkin	.15
187 Damion Easley	.15
188 Moises Alou	.15
189 Todd Hundley	.15
190 Tim Hudson	.25
191 Livan Hernandez	.15
192 Fred McGriff	.15
193 Orlando Hernandez	.25
194 Tim Salmon	.20
195 Mike Mussina	.40
196 Todd Helton	.75
197 Juan Gonzalez	.50
198 Kevin Brown	.15
199 Ugueth Urbina	.15
200 Matt Stairs	.15
201 Shawn Estes	.15
202 Gabe Kapler	.15
203 Javy Lopez	.15
204 Henry Rodriguez	.15
205 Dante Bichette	.15
206 Jeromy Burnitz	.15
207 Todd Zeile	.15
208 Rico Brogna	.15
209 Warren Morris	.15
210 David Segui	.15
211 Vinny Castilla	.15
212 Mo Vaughn	.15
213 Charles Johnson	.15
214 Neifi Perez	.15
215 Shawn Green	.40
216 Carl Pavano	.15
217 Tino Martinez	.15
218 Barry Bonds	2.50
219 David Wells	.15
220 Paul O'Neill	.15
221 Masato Yoshii	.15
222 Kris Benson	.15
223 Fernando Tatis	.15
224 Lee Stevens	.15
225 Jose Cruz Jr.	.15
226 Rick Ankiel (Prospect)	4.00
227 Matt Riley (Prospect)	4.00
228 Norm Hutchins (Prospect)	4.00
229 Ruben Mateo (Prospect)	4.00
230 Ben Petrick (Prospect)	4.00
231 Mario Encarnacion (Prospect)	4.00
232 Nick Johnson (Prospect)	6.00
233 Adam Piatt (Prospect)	6.00
234 Mike Darr (Prospect)	4.00
235 Chad Hermansen (Prospect)	4.00
236 Wily Pena (Prospect)	6.00
237 Octavio Dotel (Prospect)	4.00
238 Vernon Wells (Prospect)	6.00
239 Daryle Ward (Prospect)	4.00
240 Adam Kennedy (Prospect)	4.00
241 Angel Pena (Prospect)	4.00
242 Lance Berkman (Prospect)	6.00
243 Gabe Molina (Prospect)	4.00
244 Steve Lomasney (Prospect)	4.00
245 Jacob Cruz (Prospect)	4.00
246 Mark Quinn (Prospect)	4.00
247 Eric Munson (Prospect)	4.00
248 Alfonso Soriano (Prospect)	6.00
249 Kip Wells (Prospect)	4.00
250 Josh Beckett (Prospect)	6.00
Checklist #171	.05
Checklist #172-25, inserts	.05
Checklist inserts	.05

Green

Green, rather than gold, ink is used on front for the player name, team and position to distinguish this parallel insert set. On back, each card is numbered from within an edition of 300 each.

	NM/M
Common Player:	3.00
Stars:	5-10X
Young Stars & RC's (226-250):	1-2X
Production 300 Sets	

Masterpiece

Each of the cards in Fleer Focus was issued in a parallel edition of just one piece each. Fronts of Masterpiece 1/1s have purple metallic ink, instead of gold, for the player identification. On back, there is a notation "The Only 1 of 1 Masterpiece" along with an "M" suffix to the card number. An error version has all the attributes of the true Masterpiece, but lacks the "Only 1 . . ." notation on back (see 2000 Fleer Focus Masterpiece Errors).

	NM/M
Common Player:	100.00

Masterpiece Errors

DAVID SEGUI
Blue Jays • First Base

Thousands of collectors' hopes were crushed when it was determined that an unknown number of uncompleted Masterpiece 1-of-1 cards were erroneously inserted in Focus foil packs. Like the true Masterpiece cards, the fronts of the error cards have the player name, team and position at bottom front in purple, rather than gold foil. On back, the cards even have the "M" suffix to the card number at lower-right. Unfortunately, these do not have the foil-stamped "The Only 1 of 1 Masterpiece" notation on back; greatly reducing the value.

	NM/M
Complete Set (25):	250.00
Common Player:	4.00
50M Ken Griffey Jr.	100.00
202M Gabe Kapler	8.00
203M Javy Lopez	6.00
204M Henry Rodriguez	4.00
205M Dante Bichette	5.00
206M Jeromy Burnitz	5.00
207M Todd Zeile	4.00
208M Rico Brogna	4.00
209M Warren Morris	4.00
210M David Segui	4.00
211M Vinny Castilla	4.00
212M Mo Vaughn	6.00
213M Charles Johnson	5.00
214M Neifi Perez	5.00
215M Shawn Green	20.00
216M Carl Pavano	4.00
217M Tino Martinez	5.00
218M Barry Bonds	30.00
219M David Wells	8.00
220M Paul O'Neill	6.00
221M Masato Yoshii	5.00
222M Kris Benson	8.00
223M Fernando Tatis	6.00
224M Lee Stevens	4.00
225M Jose Cruz Jr.	6.00

Club 3000

These inserts are die-cut around the numbers 3,000 and features three players who either have 3,000 hits or strikeouts, this set spotlights Stan Musial, Steve Carlton and Paul Molitor. These are seeded 1:36 packs.

	NM/M
Complete Set (3):	4.00
Common Player:	1.50
(1) Steve Carlton	1.50
(2) Paul Molitor	1.50
(3) Stan Musial	1.50

Club 3000 Memorabilia

Five tiers featuring memorabilia from game-used bats, caps etc... make up this hand numbered set. Besides a bat and cap insert others include jersey, bat and jersey combo and a bat, jersey and cap combo.

	NM/M
Steve Carlton/ Bat/325	25.00
Steve Carlton/Hat/65	75.00
Steve Carlton/ Jsy/750	20.00
Steve Carlton/ Bat, Hat,/Jsy/25	200.00
Paul Molitor/ Bat/355	30.00
Paul Molitor/Hat/65	85.00
Paul Molitor/Jsy/975	20.00
Paul Molitor/ Bat,/Jsy/100	60.00
Stan Musial/ Bat/325	50.00
Stan Musial/Hat/65	125.00
Stan Musial/Jsy/975	35.00
Stan Musial/ Bat/Jsy/100	80.00

Feel the Game

This 10-card set offers pieces of player-worn jersey from some of baseball's biggest stars embedded into the card front. These were seeded 1:288 packs.

	NM/M
Common Player:	5.00
Inserted 1:288	
Adrian Beltre	7.50
Tom Glavine	10.00
Vladimir Guerrero	15.00
Randy Johnson	15.00
Javy Lopez	5.00
Alex Rodriguez	30.00
Scott Rolen	10.00
Cal Ripken Jr.	40.00
Tim Salmon	6.00
Miguel Tejada	10.00

Focal Points

This 15-card set has silver foil etching around the border and silver foil stamp-ing. These were seeded 1:6 packs and are numbered with an "F" suffix on the card back.

	NM/M
Complete Set (15):	15.00
Common Player:	.75
Inserted 1:6	
1 Mark McGwire	2.50
2 Tony Gwynn	1.00
3 Nomar Garciaparra	2.00
4 Juan Gonzalez	.75
5 Jeff Bagwell	.75
6 Chipper Jones	1.00
7 Cal Ripken Jr.	3.00
8 Alex Rodriguez	2.50
9 Scott Rolen	.75
10 Vladimir Guerrero	.75
11 Mike Piazza	1.50
12 Frank Thomas	.75
13 Ken Griffey Jr.	1.50
14 Sammy Sosa	1.50
15 Derek Jeter	3.00

Focus Pocus

This 10-card set has a silver prismatic, holofoil background with silver foil stamping. These were seeded 1:14 packs and are numbered with an "FP" suffix.

	NM/M
Complete Set (10):	12.00
Common Player:	1.00
Inserted 1:14	
1 Cal Ripken Jr.	3.00
2 Tony Gwynn	1.50
3 Nomar Garciaparra	2.00
4 Juan Gonzalez	1.00
5 Mike Piazza	2.00
6 Mark McGwire	2.50
7 Chipper Jones	1.50
8 Ken Griffey Jr.	2.00
9 Derek Jeter	3.00
10 Alex Rodriguez	2.50

Fresh Ink

These autographed inserts are seeded 1:96 packs.

	NM/M
Common Player:	5.00
Inserted 1:96	
Chad Allen	5.00
Michael Barrett	5.00
Josh Beckett	20.00
Rob Bell	5.00
Adrian Beltre	15.00
Milton Bradley	8.00
Rico Brogna	5.00
Mike Cameron	8.00
Eric Chavez	15.00
Bruce Chen	5.00
Johnny Damon	20.00
Ben Davis	5.00
J.D. Drew	15.00
Erubiel Durazo	10.00
Jeremy Giambi	6.00
Jason Giambi	25.00
Doug Glanville	6.00
Troy Glaus	25.00
Shawn Green	20.00
Mike Hampton	10.00
Tim Hudson	15.00
John Jaha	5.00
Derek Jeter	150.00
D'Angelo Jimenez	5.00
Nick Johnson	8.00
Andruw Jones	20.00
Jason Kendall	10.00
Adam Kennedy	6.00
Mike Lieberthal	8.00
Edgar Martinez	15.00
Aaron McNeal	5.00
Kevin Millwood	10.00
Mike Mussina	30.00
Magglio Ordonez	15.00
Eric Owens	5.00
Rafael Palmeiro	20.00
Wily Pena	15.00
Adam Piatt	8.00
Cal Ripken Jr.	100.00
Alex Rodriguez	65.00
Scott Rolen	20.00
Tim Salmon	15.00
Chris Singleton	5.00
Mike Sweeney	10.00
Jose Vidro	8.00
Rondell White	8.00
Jaret Wright	5.00

Future Vision

This 15-card set highlights the top prospects over a holo-foiled background with red foil etching and stamping. These were seeded 1:9 packs and are numbered with an "FV" suffix.

	NM/M
Complete Set (15):	8.00
Common Player:	.40
Inserted 1:9	
1 Rick Ankiel	.40
2 Matt Riley	.40
3 Ruben Mateo	.40
4 Ben Petrick	.40
5 Mario Encarnacion	.40
6 Octavio Dotel	.40
7 Vernon Wells	.65
8 Adam Kennedy	.40
9 Lance Berkman	.40
10 Chad Hermansen	.40
11 Mark Quinn	.40
12 Eric Munson	.40
13 Alfonso Soriano	2.00
14 Kip Wells	.40
15 Josh Beckett	.75

2000 Fleer Gamers

DEREK JETER
NEW YORK YANKEES • SHORTSTOP

The 120-card base set has silver foil etching down the left portion of the card with vertical stripes running down the right portion of the card front. The card back has career statistical totals as well as a small photo. Two short-printed subsets also make up the 120-card set. Next Gamers (91-110) are seeded 1:3 packs and Fame Game (111-120) are seeded 1:8 packs.

	NM/M
Complete Set (120):	50.00
Common Player (1-90):	.15
Common (91-110):	1.00
Inserted 1:3	
Common (111-120):	1.50
Inserted 1:8	
Pack:	2.00
Wax Box:	35.00
1 Cal Ripken Jr.	2.00
2 Derek Jeter	2.00
3 Alex Rodriguez	1.50
4 Alex Gonzalez	.15
5 Nomar Garciaparra	1.25
6 Brian Giles	.15
7 Chris Singleton	.15
8 Kevin Brown	.15
9 J.D. Drew	.25
10 Raul Mondesi	.15
11 Sammy Sosa	1.25
12 Carlos Beltran	.50
13 Eric Chavez	.15
14 Gabe Kapler	.15
15 Tim Salmon	.25
16 Manny Ramirez	.75
17 Orlando Hernandez	.15
18 Jeff Kent	.15
19 Juan Gonzalez	.75
20 Moises Alou	.15
21 Jason Giambi	.50
22 Ivan Rodriguez	.60
23 Geoff Jenkins	.15
24 Ken Griffey Jr.	1.25
25 Mark McGwire	1.50
26 Jose Canseco	.40
27 Roberto Alomar	.40
28 Craig Biggio	.15
29 Scott Rolen	.65
30 Vinny Castilla	.15
31 Greg Maddux	1.00
32 Pedro J. Martinez	.75
33 Mike Piazza	1.25
34 Albert Belle	.15
35 Frank Thomas	.75
36 Bobby Abreu	.15
37 Edgar Martinez	.15
38 Pokey Reese	.15
39 Preston Wilson	.15
40 Mike Lieberthal	.15
41 Andruw Jones	.75
42 Damion Easley	.15
43 Mike Cameron	.15
44 Todd Walker	.15
45 Jason Kendall	.15
46 Sean Casey	.15
47 Corey Koskie	.15
48 Warren Morris	.15
49 Andres Galarraga	.15
50 Dean Palmer	.15
51 Jose Vidro	.15
52 Brian Jordan	.15
53 Tony Clark	.15
54 Vladimir Guerrero	.75
55 Mo Vaughn	.15
56 Richie Sexson	.15
57 Tino Martinez	.15
58 Eric Owens	.15
59 Matt Williams	.15
60 Omar Vizquel	.15
61 Rickey Henderson	.75
62 J.T. Snow	.15
63 Mark Grace	.25
64 Carlos Febles	.15
65 Paul O'Neill	.15
66 Randy Johnson	.75
67 Kenny Lofton	.15
68 Roger Cedeno	.15
69 Shawn Green	.35
70 Chipper Jones	1.00
71 Jeff Cirillo	.15
72 Robin Ventura	.15
73 Paul Konerko	.15
74 Jeromy Burnitz	.15
75 Ben Grieve	.15
76 Troy Glaus	.75
77 Jim Thome	.25
78 Bernie Williams	.25
79 Barry Bonds	2.00
80 Ray Durham	.15
81 Adrian Beltre	.15
82 Ray Lankford	.15
83 Carlos Delgado	.50
84 Erubiel Durazo	.15
85 Larry Walker	.15
86 Edgardo Alfonzo	.15
87 Rafael Palmeiro	.65
88 Magglio Ordonez	.25
89 Jeff Bagwell	.75
90 Tony Gwynn	1.00
91 Norm Hutchins (Next Gamers)	1.00
92 Derrick Turnbow RC (Next Gamers)	1.50
93 Matt Riley (Next Gamers)	1.00
94 David Eckstein (Next Gamers)	1.00
95 Dernell Stenson (Next Gamers)	1.00
96 Joe Crede (Next Gamers)	1.00
97 Ben Petrick (Next Gamers)	1.00
98 Eric Munson (Next Gamers)	1.00
99 Pablo Ozuna (Next Gamers)	1.00
100 Josh Beckett (Next Gamers)	3.00
101 Aaron McNeal RC (Next Gamers)	1.50
102 Milton Bradley (Next Gamers)	1.50
103 Alex Escobar (Next Gamers)	1.50
104 Alfonso Soriano (Next Gamers)	4.00
105 Wily Pena (Next Gamers)	1.50
106 Nick Johnson (Next Gamers)	1.50
107 Adam Piatt (Next Gamers)	1.00
108 Pat Burrell (Next Gamers)	2.00
109 Rick Ankiel (Next Gamers)	1.00
110 Vernon Wells (Next Gamers)	2.00
111 Alex Rodriguez (Fame Game)	3.00
112 Cal Ripken Jr. (Fame Game)	4.00
113 Mark McGwire (Fame Game)	3.00
114 Ken Griffey Jr. (Fame Game)	2.00
115 Mike Piazza (Fame Game)	2.00
116 Nomar Garciaparra (Fame Game)	3.00
117 Derek Jeter (Fame Game)	4.00
118 Chipper Jones (Fame Game)	1.50
119 Sammy Sosa (Fame Game)	2.00
120 Tony Gwynn (Fame Game)	1.50

Extra

RAY LANKFORD

A parallel to the 120-card base set, the gold foiled card front and "Extra" written down the right portion of the card can be used to differentiate these from regular cards. "Extra" is also written underneath the card number on the back as well. Extras 1-90 are seeded 1:24 packs and numbers 91-120 are seeded 1:36 packs.

Stars (1-90):	5-10X
Inserted 1:24	
Next Gamers (91-110):	1-2X
Inserted 1:36	
Fame Game (110-120):	1-2X
Inserted 1:36	

Cal to Greatness

This 15-card tribute insert set to baseball's "Iron Man" is broken into three tiers. Cards 1-5 are seeded 1:9 packs, cards 6-10 are found 1:25 packs and cards 11-15 are inserted 1:144 packs. Card backs are numbered with a "C" suffix.

	NM/M
Complete Set (15):	100.00
Common Ripken (1-5):	3.00
Inserted 1:9	
Common Ripken (6-10):	6.00
Inserted 1:25	
Common Ripken (11-15):	20.00
Inserted 1:144	

1	Cal Ripken Jr.	3.00
2	Cal Ripken Jr.	3.00
3	Cal Ripken Jr.	3.00
4	Cal Ripken Jr.	3.00
5	Cal Ripken Jr.	3.00
6	Cal Ripken Jr.	6.00
7	Cal Ripken Jr.	6.00
8	Cal Ripken Jr.	6.00
9	Cal Ripken Jr.	6.00
10	Cal Ripken Jr.	6.00
11	Cal Ripken Jr.	20.00
12	Cal Ripken Jr.	20.00
13	Cal Ripken Jr.	20.00
14	Cal Ripken Jr.	20.00
15	Cal Ripken Jr.	20.00

Change the Game

This 15-card set has a holofoiled front with Change the Game printed behind the player image. Seeded 1:24 packs, card backs are numbered with a "CG" suffix.

		NM/M
Complete Set (15):		50.00
Common Player:		1.50
Inserted 1:24		
1	Alex Rodriguez	6.00
2	Cal Ripken Jr.	7.50
3	Chipper Jones	3.00
4	Derek Jeter	7.50
5	Ken Griffey Jr.	4.00
6	Mark McGwire	6.00
7	Mike Piazza	4.00
8	Nomar Garciaparra	4.00
9	Sammy Sosa	4.00
10	Tony Gwynn	3.00
11	Ivan Rodriguez	1.50
12	Pedro Martinez	2.00
13	Juan Gonzalez	2.00
14	Vladimir Guerrero	2.00
15	Manny Ramirez	2.00

Determined

This 15-card set has a holo-foiled front with two player images on the card front. The second player photo is smaller than the primary image and is a close-up shot. Card backs are numbered with a "D" suffix and are seeded 1:12 packs.

		NM/M
Complete Set (15):		25.00
Common Player:		.50
Inserted 1:12		
1	Nomar Garciaparra	2.50
2	Chipper Jones	2.00
3	Derek Jeter	4.00
4	Mike Piazza	2.50
5	Jeff Bagwell	1.00
6	Mark McGwire	3.00
7	Greg Maddux	2.50
8	Sammy Sosa	2.50
9	Ken Griffey Jr.	2.50
10	Alex Rodriguez	3.00
11	Tony Gwynn	2.00
12	Barry Larkin	4.00
13	Barry Bonds	4.00
14	Juan Gonzalez	1.00
15	Sean Casey	.50

Lumber

Seeded 1:36 packs, these inserts have a piece of game-used bat embedded into the card front and are numbered with an "GL" suffix.

		NM/M
Common Player:		5.00
Inserted 1:36		
1	Alex Rodriguez	30.00
2	Carlos Delgado	10.00
3	Jose Vidro	5.00
4	Carlos Febles	5.00
5	J.D. Drew	7.50
6	Mike Cameron	5.00
7	Derek Jeter	40.00
8	Eric Chavez	6.00
9	Cal Ripken Jr.	40.00
10	Gabe Kapler	5.00
11	Damion Easley	5.00
12	Frank Thomas	15.00
13	Chris Singleton	5.00
14	Norm Hutchins	5.00
15	Pokey Reese	5.00
16	Rafael Palmeiro	12.00
17	Ray Durham	5.00
18	Ray Lankford	5.00
19	Roger Cedeno	5.00
20	Shawn Green	6.00
21	Wade Boggs	20.00
22	Roberto Alomar	7.50
23	Moises Alou	5.00
24	Adrian Beltre	6.00
25	Barry Bonds	40.00
26	Jason Giambi	10.00
27	Jason Kendall	5.00
28	Paul Konerko	5.00
29	Mike Lieberthal	5.00
30	Edgar Martinez	5.00
31	Raul Mondesi	5.00
32	Scott Rolen	12.00
33	Alfonso Soriano	10.00
34	Ivan Rodriguez	10.00
35	Magglio Ordonez	7.50
36	Chipper Jones	20.00
37	Sean Casey	6.00
38	Edgardo Alfonzo	5.00
39	Robin Ventura	5.00
40	Bernie Williams	6.00
41	Vladimir Guerrero	15.00
42	Tony Clark	5.00
43	Carlos Beltran	10.00
44	Warren Morris	5.00
45	Jim Thome	5.00
46	Jeromy Burnitz	5.00
47	Matt Williams	5.00
48	Erubiel Durazo	5.00

Lumber Autograph

Twelve players also signed a limited number of their Lumber inserts. The number signed by each player is listed after the player name. These were seeded 1:287 packs.

		NM/M
Common Player:		15.00
Inserted 1:287		
1	Derek Jeter	150.00
2	Eric Chavez	20.00
3	Rafael Palmeiro	40.00
4	Shawn Green	35.00
5	Roberto Alomar	45.00
6	Paul Konerko	15.00
7	Sean Casey	15.00
8	Alex Rodriguez	80.00
9	Robin Ventura	20.00
10	Erubiel Durazo	15.00
11	Tony Clark	15.00
12	Alfonso Soriano	60.00

2000 Fleer Greats of the Game

The base set consists of 107-cards of retired stars. Card fronts have a brown border with "Fleer Greats of the Game" stamped in silver foil. Backs

have a small photo along with complete career statistics and a brief career highlight.

		NM/M
Complete Set (108):		50.00
Common Player:		.50
Pack (6):		10.00
Wax Box (24):		200.00
1	Mickey Mantle	8.00
2	Gil Hodges	1.00
3	Monte Irvin	1.00
4	Satchel Paige	2.50
5	Roy Campanella	2.00
6	Richie Ashburn	1.00
7	Roger Maris	3.00
8	Ozzie Smith	2.00
9	Reggie Jackson	2.50
10	Eddie Mathews	2.00
11	Dave Righetti	.50
12	Dave Winfield	1.00
13	Lou Whitaker	.50
14	Phil Garner	.50
15	Ron Cey	.50
16	Brooks Robinson	2.50
17	Bruce Sutter	.50
18	Dave Parker	.50
19	Johnny Bench	2.50
20	Fernando Valenzuela	.50
21	George Brett	4.00
22	Paul Molitor	.50
23	Hoyt Wilhelm	.50
24	Luis Aparicio	.50
25	Frank White	.50
26	Herb Score	.50
27	Kirk Gibson	.50
28	Mike Schmidt	3.00
29	Don Baylor	.50
30	Joe Pepitone	.50
31	Hal McRae	.50
32	Lee Smith	.50
33	Nolan Ryan	7.00
33	Nolan Ryan/OPS	5.00
34	Bill Mazeroski	.75
35	Bobby Doerr	.50
36	Duke Snider	1.00
37	Dick Groat	.50
38	Larry Doby	.50
39	Kirby Puckett	2.00
40	Steve Carlton	1.00
41	Dennis Eckersley	.50
42	Jim Bunning	.50
43	Ron Guidry	.50
44	Alan Trammell	1.00
45	Bob Feller	1.50
46	Dave Concepcion	.50
47	Dwight Evans	.50
48	Enos Slaughter	.50
49	Tom Seaver	2.50
50	Tony Oliva	1.00
51	Mel Stottlemyre	.50
52	Tommy John	.50
53	Willie McCovey	1.00
54	Red Schoendienst	.50
55	Gorman Thomas	.50
56	Ralph Kiner	1.00
57	Robin Yount	2.00
58	Andre Dawson	1.00
59	Al Kaline	2.50
60	Dom DiMaggio	.50
61	Juan Marichal	1.00
62	Jack Morris	.50
63	Warren Spahn	1.50
64	Preacher Roe	.50
65	Darrell Evans	.50
66	Jim Bouton	.50
67	Rocky Colavito	.75
68	Bob Gibson	1.50
69	Whitey Ford	1.50
70	Moose Skowron	.50
71	Boog Powell	1.00
72	Al Lopez	.50
73	Lou Brock	1.00
74	Mickey Lolich	.50
75	Rod Carew	2.00
76	Bob Lemon	.50
77	Frank Howard	.50
78	Phil Rizzuto	1.50
79	Carl Yastrzemski	2.00

ABBREVIATIONS

OPS - Overprinted "Promotional Sample"
SP - Short Print

80	Rico Carty	.50
81	Jim Kaat	.50
82	Bert Blyleven	.50
83	George Kell	.50
84	Jim Palmer	1.00
85	Maury Wills	1.00
86	Jim Rice	.50
87	Joe Carter	.50
88	Clete Boyer	.50
89	Yogi Berra	2.00
90	Cecil Cooper	.50
91	Davey Johnson	.50
92	Lou Boudreau	.50
93	Orlando Cepeda	1.00
94	Tommy Henrich	.50
95	Hank Bauer	.50
96	Don Larsen	1.50
97	Vida Blue	1.00
98	Ben Oglivie	.50
99	Don Mattingly	5.00
100	Dale Murphy	1.00
101	Ferguson Jenkins	1.00
102	Bobby Bonds	.75
103	Dick Allen	.50
104	Stan Musial	3.00
105	Gaylord Perry	.50
106	Willie Randolph	.50
107	Willie Stargell	1.50
108	Checklist	.50

Autographs

George Brett

Seeded in every six packs, Autographs feature the signature on the bottom half of the card front in black Sharpie. The autographed set features 89 retired players. Some cards were issued in considerably lower quantities than others, as noted in the checklist.

		NM/M
Common Player:		10.00
Inserted 1:6		
	Luis Aparicio	20.00
	Hank Bauer	10.00
	Don Baylor	20.00
	Johnny Bench	180.00
	Yogi Berra	150.00
	Vida Blue	20.00
	Bert Blyleven	10.00
	Bobby Bonds	10.00
	Lou Boudreau	75.00
	Jim Bouton	20.00
	Clete Boyer	15.00
	George Brett	
	(275 or less)	180.00
	Lou Brock	20.00
	Jim Bunning	30.00
	Rod Carew	40.00
	Steve Carlton	20.00
	Joe Carter/SP	75.00
	Orlando Cepeda	15.00
	Ron Cey	15.00
	Rocky Colavito	30.00
	Dave Concepcion	
	(Black autograph.)	15.00
	Dave Concepcion	
	(Red autograph.)	15.00
	Cecil Cooper	10.00
	Andre Dawson	15.00
	Dom DiMaggio	75.00
	Bobby Doerr	15.00
	Darrell Evans	15.00
	Bob Feller	
	(300 or less)	100.00
	Whitey Ford	
	Phil Garner	10.00
	Bob Gibson	25.00
	Kirk Gibson	20.00
	Dick Groat	10.00
	Ron Guidry	20.00
	Tommy Henrich	
	(300 or less)	100.00
	Frank Howard	10.00
	Reggie Jackson	
	(250 or less)	120.00
	Ferguson Jenkins	15.00
	Tommy John	10.00
	Davey Johnson	10.00
	Jim Kaat	15.00
	Al Kaline	35.00
	George Kell	15.00
	Ralph Kiner	20.00
	Don Larsen	25.00
	Mickey Lolich	10.00

	Juan Marichal	40.00
	Eddie Mathews	80.00
	Don Mattingly	
	(300 or less)	250.00
	Bill Mazeroski	20.00
	Willie McCovey	80.00
	Hal McRae	10.00
	Paul Molitor	40.00
	Jack Morris	10.00
	Dale Murphy	35.00
	Stan Musial	100.00
	Ben Oglivie	10.00
	Tony Oliva	15.00
	Jim Palmer/SP	80.00
	Dave Parker	15.00
	Joe Pepitone	15.00
	Gaylord Perry	15.00
	Boog Powell	15.00
	Kirby Puckett	
	(200 or less)	120.00
	Willie Randolph	15.00
	Jim Rice	15.00
	Dave Righetti	10.00
	Phil Rizzuto	
	(200 or less)	140.00
	Brooks Robinson	30.00
	Preacher Roe	15.00
	Nolan Ryan	150.00
	Mike Schmidt	
	(175 or less)	250.00
	Red Schoendienst	15.00
	Herb Score	25.00
	Tom Seaver	75.00
	Moose Skowron	15.00
	Enos Slaughter	20.00
	Lee Smith	10.00
	Ozzie Smith/SP	150.00
	Duke Snider/SP	140.00
	Warren Spahn/SP	100.00
	Bruce Sutter	12.50
	Gorman Thomas	10.00
	Alan Trammell	20.00
	Frank White	10.00
	Hoyt Wilhelm	15.00
	Maury Wills	15.00
	Dave Winfield	150.00
	Carl Yastrzemski	60.00
	Robin Yount/SP	125.00

Memorable Moments Autograph

		NM/M
Common Player:		60.00
1	Ron Guidry/78	75.00
2	Nolan Ryan/99	300.00
3	Herb Score/55	40.00
4	Tom Seaver/69	180.00

Retrospection

The 15-card Retrospection insert set highlights some of the all-time greats with a design borrowed from 1960 Fleer. Former greats including Stan Musial and Al Kaline are featured. They were seeded 1:6 packs.

		NM/M
Complete Set (15):		75.00
Common Player:		4.00
Inserted 1:6		
1	Rod Carew	4.00
2	Stan Musial	8.00
3	Nolan Ryan	15.00
4	Tom Seaver	6.00
5	Brooks Robinson	5.00
6	Al Kaline	6.00
7	Mike Schmidt	10.00
8	Thurman Munson	8.00
9	Steve Carlton	4.00
10	Roger Maris	5.00
11	Duke Snider	5.00
12	Yogi Berra	6.00
13	Carl Yastrzemski	5.00
14	Reggie Jackson	6.00
15	Johnny Bench	8.00

Yankees Clippings

This 15-card memorabilia insert features an actual piece of New York Yankee

uniform worn by former stars. The jersey swatch is formed in the shape of the interlocking "NY" logo and are seeded 1:48 packs.

		NM/M
Common Player:		20.00
Inserted 1:48		
1	Mickey Mantle	200.00
2	Ron Guidry	40.00
3	Don Larsen	40.00
4	Elston Howard	40.00
5	Mel Stottlemyre	25.00
6	Don Mattingly	100.00
7	Reggie Jackson	50.00
8	Tommy John	20.00
9	Dave Winfield	25.00
10	Willie Randolph	20.00
11	Tommy Henrich	20.00
12	Billy Martin	50.00
13	Dave Righetti	20.00
14	Joe Pepitone	20.00
15	Thurman Munson	80.00

2000 Fleer Impact

The base set consists of 200 cards with 25 of those being Prospect subset cards. The featured player's team logo appears beside the player name on the bottom portion with the Impact logo on the top left portion. Card backs have a maximum of 10 years of statistics along with a small photo and vital information. Impact was sold in 10-card packs with an SRP of $.99 per pack.

		NM/M
Complete Set (200):		15.00
Common Player:		.10
Pack (10):		1.00
Box (36):		20.00
1	Cal Ripken Jr.	1.50
2	Jose Canseco	.25
3	Manny Ramirez	.60
4	Bernie Williams	.30
5	Troy Glaus	.60
6	Jeff Bagwell	.60
7	Corey Koskie	.10
8	Barry Larkin	.10
9	Mark Quinn	.10
10	Russ Ortiz	.10
11	Tim Salmon	.15
12	Preston Wilson	.10
13	Mo Vaughn	.10
14	Ray Lankford	.10
15	Sterling Hitchcock	.10
16	Al Leiter	.10
17	Jim Morris	.10
18	Freddy Garcia	.10
19	Adrian Beltre	.20
20	Eric Chavez	.20
21	Robinson Cancel	.10
22	Edgar Renteria	.10
23	John Jaha	.10
24	Chuck Finley	.10
25	Andres Galarraga	.10
26	Paul Byrd	.10
27	John Halama	.10
28	Eric Karros	.10
29	Mike Piazza	1.00
30	Ryan Rupe	.10
31	Frank Thomas	.60
32	Randy Velarde	.10
33	Bobby Abreu	.10
34	Randy Johnson	.60
35	Matt Williams	.10
36	Tony Gwynn	.75
37	Dean Palmer	.10
38	Aaron Sele	.10
39	Rondell White	.10
40	Erubiel Durazo	.10
41	Curt Schilling	.10

42	Kip Wells	.10
43	Craig Biggio	.10
44	Tom Glavine	.25
45	Trevor Hoffman	.10
46	Greg Vaughn	.10
47	Edgar Martinez	.10
48	Magglio Ordonez	.20
49	Mark Mulder	.10
50	John Rocker	.10
51	Kenny Rogers	.10
52	Gary Sheffield	.25
53	Brian Simmons	.10
54	Tony Womack	.10
55	Ken Caminiti	.10
56	Jeff Cirillo	.10
57	Ray Durham	.10
58	Mike Lieberthal	.10
59	Ruben Mateo	.10
60	Mike Cameron	.10
61	Rusty Greer	.10
62	Alex Rodriguez	1.25
63	Robin Ventura	.10
64	Pokey Reese	.10
65	Jose Lima	.10
66	Neifi Perez	.10
67	Rafael Palmeiro	.50
68	Scott Rolen	.50
69	Mike Hampton	.10
70	Sammy Sosa	1.00
71	Mike Stanley	.10
72	Dan Wilson	.10
73	Kerry Wood	.50
74	Mike Mussina	.30
75	Masato Yoshii	.10
76	Peter Bergeron	.10
77	Carlos Delgado	.50
78	Juan Encarnacion	.10
79	Nomar Garciaparra	1.00
80	Jason Kendall	.10
81	Pedro Martinez	.60
82	Darin Erstad	.40
83	Larry Walker	.10
84	Rick Ankiel	.10
85	Scott Erickson	.10
86	Roger Clemens	.85
87	Matt Lawton	.10
88	Jon Lieber	.10
89	Shane Reynolds	.10
90	Ivan Rodriguez	.50
91	Pat Burrell	.50
92	Kent Bottenfield	.10
93	David Cone	.10
94	Mark Grace	.15
95	Paul Konerko	.10
96	Eric Milton	.10
97	Lee Stevens	.10
98	B.J. Surhoff	.10
99	Billy Wagner	.10
100	Ken Griffey Jr.	1.00
101	Randy Wolf	.10
102	Henry Rodriguez	.10
103	Carlos Beltran	.40
104	Rich Aurilia	.10
105	Chipper Jones	.75
106	Homer Bush	.10
107	Johnny Damon	.10
108	J.D. Drew	.40
109	Orlando Hernandez	.10
110	Brad Radke	.10
111	Wilton Veras	.10
112	Dmitri Young	.10
113	Jermaine Dye	.10
114	Kris Benson	.10
115	Derek Jeter	1.50
116	Cole Liniak	.10
117	Jim Thome	.10
118	Pedro Astacio	.10
119	Carlos Febles	.10
120	Darryl Kile	.10
121	Alfonso Soriano	.50
122	Michael Barrett	.10
123	Ellis Burks	.10
124	Chad Hermansen	.10
125	Trot Nixon	.10
126	Bobby Higginson	.10
127	Rick Helling	.10
128	Chris Carpenter	.10
129	Vinny Castilla	.10
130	Brian Giles	.10
131	Todd Helton	.60
132	Jason Varitek	.10
133	Rob Ducey	.10
134	Octavio Dotel	.10
135	Adam Kennedy	.10
136	Jeff Kent	.10
137	Aaron Boone	.10
138	Todd Walker	.10
139	Jeromy Burnitz	.10
140	Roberto Hernandez	.10
141	Matt LeCroy	.10
142	Ugueth Urbina	.10
143	David Wells	.25
144	Luis Gonzalez	.25
145	Andruw Jones	.50
146	Juan Gonzalez	.60
147	Moises Alou	.10
148	Michael Tejera	.10
149	Brian Jordan	.10
150	Mark McGwire	1.25
151	Shawn Green	.25
152	Jay Bell	.10
153	Fred McGriff	.10
154	Rey Ordonez	.10
155	Matt Stairs	.10
156	A.J. Burnett	.10
157	Omar Vizquel	.10
158	Damion Easley	.10
159	Dante Bichette	.10
160	Javy Lopez	.10
161	Fernando Seguignol	.10
162	Richie Sexson	.10
163	Vladimir Guerrero	.60
164	Kevin Young	.10
165	Josh Beckett	.10
166	Albert Belle	.10
167	Cliff Floyd	.10
168	Gabe Kapler	.10
169	Nick Johnson	.15
170	Raul Mondesi	.10
171	Warren Morris	.10
172	Kenny Lofton	.10
173	Reggie Sanders	.10
174	Mike Sweeney	.10
175	Robert Fick	.10
176	Barry Bonds	1.50
177	Luis Castillo	.10
178	Roger Cedeno	.10
179	Jim Edmonds	.10
180	Geoff Jenkins	.10
181	Adam Piatt	.10
182	Phil Nevin	.10
183	Roberto Alomar	.30
184	Kevin Brown	.10
185	D.T. Cromer	.10
186	Jason Giambi	.50
187	Fernando Tatis	.10
188	Brady Anderson	.10
189	Tony Clark	.10
190	Alex Fernandez	.10
191	Matt Blank	.10
192	Greg Maddux	.75
193	Kevin Millwood	.10
194	Jason Schmidt	.10
195	Shannon Stewart	.10
196	Rolando Arrojo	.10
197	Darren Dreifort	.10
198	Ben Grieve	.10
199	Bartolo Colon	.10
200	Sean Casey	.10

Autographics

This autographed set has the player signature on the bottom portion of the card. These were seeded 1:216 packs.

NM/M
Common Player: 5.00
Inserted 1:216
Silvers: 1-2X
Production 250 Sets
Golds: 1-2X
Production 50 Sets

1	Bobby Abreu	15.00
2	Marlon Anderson	5.00
3	Rick Ankiel	8.00
4	Rob Bell	5.00
5	Carlos Beltran	25.00
6	Wade Boggs	30.00
7	Barry Bonds	200.00
8	Milton Bradley	8.00
9	Pat Burrell	25.00
10	Orlando Cabrera	10.00
11	Chris Carpenter	5.00
12	Sean Casey	8.00
13	Carlos Delgado	20.00
14	J.D. Drew	15.00
15	Ray Durham	8.00
16	Kelvim Escobar	6.00
17	Vladimir Guerrero	30.00
18	Tony Gwynn	35.00
19	Jerry Hairston Jr.	5.00
20	Todd Helton	25.00
21	Nick Johnson	8.00
22	Jason Kendall	8.00
23	Mark Kotsay	8.00
24	Cole Liniak	5.00
25	Jose Macias	5.00
26	Greg Maddux	60.00
27	Ruben Mateo	8.00
28	Ober Moreno	5.00
29	Eric Munson	8.00
30	Joe Nathan	5.00
31	Angel Pena	5.00
32	Adam Piatt	6.00
33	Matt Riley	5.00
34	Cal Ripken Jr.	100.00
35	Alex Rodriguez	75.00
36	Scott Rolen	25.00
37	Jimmy Rollins	15.00
38	B.J. Ryan	5.00
39	Alfonso Soriano	40.00
40	Frank Thomas	25.00
41	Wilton Veras	5.00
42	Billy Wagner	10.00
43	Jeff Weaver	8.00
44	Scott Williamson	6.00

Genuine Coverage

This memorabilia insert set has pieces of game-used batting gloves embedded into

the card front. They were seeded 1:720 packs.

NM/M
Common Player: 5.00
Inserted 1:720

1	Alex Rodriguez	65.00
2	Cole Liniak	5.00
3	Barry Bonds	75.00
4	Ben Davis	5.00
5	Bobby Abreu	7.50
6	Mike Sweeney	7.50
7	Rafael Palmeiro	35.00
8	Carlos Lee	5.00
9	Glen Barker	5.00
10	Jason Giambi	30.00
11	Jacque Jones	7.50
12	Joe Nathan	5.00
13	Jason LaRue	5.00
14	Magglio Ordonez	7.50
15	Shannon Stewart	5.00
16	Matt Lawton	5.00
18	Trevor Hoffman	5.00

Mighty Fine in '99

This 40-card set honors the 1999 World Series Champion New York Yankees as well as other various award winners from the '99 season. These were seeded one per pack.

NM/M
Complete Set (40): 8.00
Common Player: .15
Inserted 1:1

1	Clay Bellinger	.15
2	Scott Brosius	.15
3	Roger Clemens	.75
4	David Cone	.15
5	Chad Curtis	.15
6	Chili Davis	.15
7	Joe Girardi	.15
8	Jason Grimsley	.15
9	Orlando Hernandez	.15
10	Hideki Irabu	.15
11	Derek Jeter	2.00
12	Chuck Knoblauch	.15
13	Ricky Ledee	.15
14	Jim Leyritz	.15
15	Tino Martinez	.15
16	Ramiro Mendoza	.15
17	Jeff Nelson	.15
18	Paul O'Neill	.15
19	Andy Pettitte	.25
20	Jorge Posada	.25
21	Mariano Rivera	.25
22	Luis Sojo	.15
23	Mike Stanton	.15
24	Allen Watson	.15
25	Bernie Williams	.30
26	Chipper Jones	.60
27	Ivan Rodriguez	.45
28	Randy Johnson	.50
29	Pedro Martinez	.50
30	Scott Williamson	.15
31	Carlos Beltran	.40
32	Mark McGwire	1.50
33	Ken Griffey Jr.	1.00
34	Robin Ventura	.15
35	Tony Gwynn	.60
36	Wade Boggs	.60
37	Cal Ripken Jr.	2.00
38	Jose Canseco	.40
39	Alex Rodriguez	1.50
40	Fernando Tatis	.15

Point of Impact

Point of Impact honors some of the game's top sluggers on a die-cut design. Card fronts have silver foil stamping and cross hairs where the featured player finds his sweet

spot. These were seeded 1:30 packs and are numbered with an "PI" suffix on the card back.

NM/M
Complete Set (10): 20.00
Common Player: 1.00
Inserted 1:30

1	Ken Griffey Jr.	2.00
2	Mark McGwire	3.00
3	Sammy Sosa	2.00
4	Jeff Bagwell	1.00
5	Derek Jeter	4.00
6	Chipper Jones	1.50
7	Nomar Garciaparra	2.00
8	Cal Ripken Jr.	4.00
9	Barry Bonds	4.00
10	Alex Rodriguez	3.00

2000 Fleer Mystique

The base set consists of 175-cards including a 50-card Prospects subset that each card is serially numbered to 2,000 and covered. The card fronts have a full bleed design with gold foil stamping. Card backs have complete year-by-year statistics and a small photo.

NM/M
Complete Set (175): 350.00
Common Player: .20
Common 126-175: 6.00
Production 2,000 sets
Pack (5): 3.00
Box (20): 50.00

1	Derek Jeter	3.00
2	David Justice	.20
3	Kevin Brown	.20
4	Jason Giambi	.75
5	Jose Canseco	.50
6	Mark Grace	.30
7	Hideo Nomo	.65
8	Edgardo Alfonzo	.20
9	Barry Bonds	3.00
10	Pedro Martinez	1.00
11	Juan Gonzalez	1.00
12	Vladimir Guerrero	1.00
13	Chuck Finley	.20
14	Brian Jordan	.20
15	Richie Sexson	.20
16	Chan Ho Park	.20
17	Tim Hudson	.40
18	Fred McGriff	.20
19	Darin Erstad	.60
20	Chris Singleton	.20
21	Jeff Bagwell	1.00
22	David Cone	.20
23	Edgar Martinez	.20
24	Greg Maddux	1.50
25	Jim Thome	.20
26	Eric Karros	.20
27	Bobby Abreu	.20
28	Greg Vaughn	.20
29	Kevin Millwood	.20
30	Omar Vizquel	.20
31	Marquis Grissom	.20
32	Mike Lieberthal	.20
33	Gabe Kapler	.20
34	Brady Anderson	.20
35	Jeff Cirillo	.20
36	Geoff Jenkins	.20
37	Scott Rolen	.75
38	Rafael Palmeiro	.65
39	Randy Johnson	1.00
40	Barry Larkin	.20
41	Johnny Damon	.40
42	Andy Pettitte	.40
43	Mark McGwire	2.50
44	Albert Belle	.20
45	Derrick Gibson	.20
46	Corey Koskie	.20
47	Curt Schilling	.50
48	Ivan Rodriguez	.65
49	Mike Mussina	.50
50	Todd Helton	1.00
51	Matt Lawton	.20
52	Jason Kendall	.20
53	Kenny Rogers	.20
54	Cal Ripken Jr.	3.00
55	Larry Walker	.20
56	Eric Milton	.20
57	Warren Morris	.20
58	Carlos Delgado	.50
59	Kerry Wood	.65
60	Cliff Floyd	.20
61	Mike Piazza	2.00
62	Jeff Kent	.20
63	Sammy Sosa	2.00
64	Alex Fernandez	.20
65	Mike Hampton	.20
66	Livan Hernandez	.20
67	Matt Williams	.20
68	Roberto Alomar	.45
69	Jermaine Dye	.20
70	Bernie Williams	.35
71	Edgar Renteria	.20
72	Tom Glavine	.40
73	Bartolo Colon	.20
74	Jason Varitek	.20
75	Eric Chavez	.40
76	Fernando Tatis	.20
77	Adrian Beltre	.40
78	Paul Konerko	.20
79	Mike Lowell	.20
80	Robin Ventura	.20
81	Russ Ortiz	.20
82	Troy Glaus	1.00
83	Frank Thomas	1.00
84	Craig Biggio	.20
85	Orlando Hernandez	.20
86	John Olerud	.20
87	Chipper Jones	1.50
88	Manny Ramirez	1.00
89	Shawn Green	.40
90	Ben Grieve	.20
91	Vinny Castilla	.20
92	Tim Salmon	.35
93	Dante Bichette	.20
94	Ken Caminiti	.20
95	Andruw Jones	.75
96	Alex Rodriguez	2.50
97	Erubiel Durazo	.20
98	Sean Casey	.30
99	Carlos Beltran	.50
100	Paul O'Neill	.20
101	Ray Lankford	.20
102	Troy O'Leary	.20
103	Bobby Higginson	.20
104	Rondell White	.20
105	Tony Gwynn	1.50
106	Jim Edmonds	.20
107	Magglio Ordonez	.40
108	Preston Wilson	.20
109	Roger Clemens	1.75
110	Ken Griffey Jr.	2.00
111	Nomar Garciaparra	2.00
112	Juan Encarnacion	.20
113	Michael Barrett	.20
114	Matt Clement	.20
115	David Wells	.20
116	Mo Vaughn	.20
117	Mike Cameron	.20
118	Jose Lima	.20
119	Tino Martinez	.20
120	J.D. Drew	.40
121	Carl Everett	.20
122	Tony Clark	.20
123	Brad Radke	.20
124	Kevin Young	.20
125	Raul Mondesi	.20
126	Cole Liniak (Prospects)	6.00
127	Alfonso Soriano (Prospects)	8.00
128	Lance Berkman (Prospects)	8.00
129	Danny Young (Prospects)	6.00
130	Francisco Cordero (Prospects)	6.00
131	Rob Fick (Prospects)	6.00
132	Matt LeCroy (Prospects)	6.00
133	Adam Piatt (Prospects)	6.00
134	Derrick Turnbow RC (Prospects)	6.00
135	Mark Quinn (Prospects)	6.00
136	Kip Wells (Prospects)	6.00
137	Rob Bell (Prospects)	6.00
138	Brad Penny (Prospects)	6.00
139	Pat Burrell (Prospects)	10.00
140	Danys Baez RC (Prospects)	6.00
141	Chad Hermansen (Prospects)	6.00
142	Steve Lomasney (Prospects)	6.00
143	Peter Bergeron (Prospects)	6.00
144	Jimmy Anderson (Prospects)	6.00
145	Mike Darr (Prospects)	6.00
146	Jacob Cruz (Prospects)	6.00
147	Kazuhiro Sasaki RC (Prospects)	10.00
148	Ben Petrick (Prospects)	6.00
149	Rick Ankiel (Prospects)	6.00
150	Aaron McNeal RC (Prospects)	6.00
152	Octavio Dotel (Prospects)	6.00
152	Juan Pena (Prospects)	6.00
153	Nick Johnson (Prospects)	8.00
154	Wilton Veras (Prospects)	6.00
155	Wily Pena (Prospects)	6.00
156	Mark Mulder (Prospects)	6.00
157	Daryle Ward (Prospects)	6.00
158	Chad Durbin RC (Prospects)	6.00
159	Angel Pena (Prospects)	6.00
160	Dewayne Wise (Prospects)	6.00
161	Tarrik Brock (Prospects)	6.00
162	Marcus Jensen (Prospects)	6.00
163	Kevin Barker (Prospects)	6.00
164	B.J. Ryan (Prospects)	6.00
165	Cesar King (Prospects)	6.00
166	Geoff Blum (Prospects)	6.00
167	Ruben Mateo (Prospects)	6.00
168	Ramon Ortiz (Prospects)	6.00
169	Eric Munson (Prospects)	6.00
170	Josh Beckett (Prospects)	8.00
171	Rafael Furcal (Prospects)	6.00
172	Matt Riley (Prospects)	6.00
173	Johan Santana RC (Prospects)	45.00
174	Mark Johnson (Prospects)	6.00
175	Adam Kennedy (Prospects)	6.00

Gold

These parallel inserts to the 175-card base set are identical to the base cards besides gold highlights throughout the background of the player photo. The word "Gold" also appears underneath the card number on the back. These were seeded 1:20 packs.

Stars (1-125): 4-8X
SP's (126-175): 1X
Inserted 1:20

Club 3000

This three-card set is die-cut around the 3,000 numerals with a date on the left side when the featured player reached the 3,000 milestone. The player name is stamped in silver holo-foil. Card backs are not numbered and have a brief career note. These were seeded 1:20 packs.

NM/M
Complete Set (3): 6.00
Common Player: 1.50
Inserted 1:20

1	Cal Ripken Jr.	5.00
2	Bob Gibson	1.50
3	Dave Winfield	1.50

Club 3000 Memorabilia

Five different memorabilia versions of each player exist, using pieces of game-used bat, jersey and cap which are embedded into each card. The amount of each card produced is listed after the player name.

	NM/M
Cal Ripken Jr./Jsy/825	40.00
Cal Ripken Jr./Bat/265	75.00
Cal Ripken Jr./Hat/55	120.00
Cal Ripken Jr./Jsy/100	100.00
Bob Gibson/Jsy/825	20.00
Bob Gibson/Bat/265	30.00
Bob Gibson/Bat/Jsy/100	50.00
Bob Gibson/Hat/Jsy/100	50.00
Bob Gibson/Hat/55	75.00
Dave Winfield/Jsy/825	15.00
Dave Winfield/Bat/270	25.00
Dave Winfield/Bat/Jsy/100	50.00
Dave Winfield/Hat/55	60.00

Diamond Dominators

This 10-card set spotlights baseball's most dominating performers. Card fronts have a holofoil appearance. These were seeded 1:5 packs and are numbered with an "DD" suffix.

		NM/M
Complete Set (10):		15.00
Common Player:		.75
Inserted 1:5		
1	Manny Ramirez	1.00
2	Pedro Martinez	1.00
3	Sean Casey	.75
4	Vladimir Guerrero	1.00
5	Sammy Sosa	1.50
6	Nomar Garciaparra	1.50
7	Mark McGwire	2.50
8	Ken Griffey Jr.	1.50
9	Derek Jeter	3.00
10	Alex Rodriguez	2.50

Feel the Game

This game-used memorabilia set features either game-used jerseys or bats from today's top stars. These were seeded 1:120 packs.

		NM/M
Common Player:		5.00
Inserted 1:120		
1	Tony Gwynn/Jsy	20.00
2	Alex Rodriguez/Jsy	25.00
3	Chipper Jones/Jsy	20.00
4	Cal Ripken Jr./Jsy	40.00
5	Derek Jeter/Pants	40.00
6	Alex Rodriguez/Bat	30.00
7	Frank Thomas/Bat	15.00
8	Barry Bonds/Bat	40.00

9	Carlos Beltran/Bat	5.00
10	Shawn Green/Bat	8.00
11	Michael Barrett/Bat	5.00
12	Rafael Palmeiro/Bat	10.00
13	Vladimir Guerrero/Bat	15.00
14	Pat Burrell/Bat	12.00

Fresh Ink

This autographed set features signatures from many of the game's top players and are seeded 1:40 packs.

		NM/M
Common Player:		5.00
Inserted 1:40		
1	Chad Allen	5.00
2	Glen Barker	5.00
3	Michael Barrett	5.00
4	Josh Beckett	20.00
5	Rob Bell	5.00
6	Lance Berkman	25.00
7	Kent Bottenfield	5.00
8	Milton Bradley	8.00
9	Orlando Cabrera	10.00
10	Sean Casey	10.00
11	Roger Cedeno	6.00
12	Will Clark	25.00
13	Russ Davis	5.00
14	Carlos Delgado	15.00
15	Einar Diaz	5.00
16	J.D. Drew	10.00
17	Erubiel Durazo	10.00
18	Damion Easley	5.00
19	Carlos Febles	5.00
20	Doug Glanville	6.00
21	Alex Gonzalez	5.00
22	Tony Gwynn	40.00
23	Mike Hampton	8.00
24	Bobby Howry	5.00
25	John Jaha	5.00
26	Nick Johnson	10.00
27	Andruw Jones	20.00
28	Adam Kennedy	8.00
29	Mike Lieberthal	5.00
30	Jose Macias	5.00
31	Ruben Mateo	8.00
32	Raul Mondesi	8.00
33	Heath Murray	5.00
34	Mike Mussina	30.00
35	Hideo Nomo	250.00
36	Magglio Ordonez	15.00
37	Eric Owens	5.00
38	Adam Piatt	5.00
39	Cal Ripken Jr.	100.00
40	Tim Salmon	15.00
41	Chris Singleton	5.00
42	J.T. Snow	8.00
43	Mike Sweeney	10.00
44	Wilton Veras	5.00
45	Jose Vidro	8.00
46	Rondell White	10.00
47	Jaret Wright	5.00

High Praise

This 10-card set has a holo-foiled card front with a "sky" background. These were inserted 1:20 packs and are numbered on the card back with an "HP" suffix.

	NM/M
Complete Set (10):	18.00
Common Player:	.75

1	Mark McGwire	3.00
2	Ken Griffey Jr.	2.00
3	Alex Rodriguez	3.00
4	Derek Jeter	4.00
5	Sammy Sosa	2.00
6	Mike Piazza	2.00
7	Nomar Garciaparra	2.00
8	Cal Ripken Jr.	4.00
9	Tony Gwynn	1.50
10	Shawn Green	.75

Rookie I.P.O.

This 10-card set highlights the top young rookies on a holofoil design. Card backs are numbered with an "RI" suffix and are seeded 1:10 packs.

	NM/M
Complete Set (10):	8.00
Common Player:	.50
Inserted 1:10	

1	Josh Beckett	1.00
2	Eric Munson	.50
3	Pat Burrell	2.00
4	Alfonso Soriano	1.50
5	Rick Ankiel	.50
6	Ruben Mateo	.50
7	Mark Quinn	.50
8	Kip Wells	.50
9	Ben Petrick	.50
10	Nick Johnson	.75

Seismic Activity

This 10-card set spotlights the top power hitters in the game. The player image is in the foreground of a warp like setting with golden highlights. Card backs are numbered with an "SA" suffix and are seeded 1:40 packs. A serial numbered parallel called Richter 100 is randomly seeded and is limited to 100 serial numbered sets.

		NM/M
Complete Set (10):		45.00
Common Player:		3.00
Inserted 1:40		
Richter Parallel:		3-5X
Production 100 Sets		
1	Ken Griffey Jr.	5.00
2	Sammy Sosa	5.00
3	Derek Jeter	10.00
4	Mark McGwire	8.00
5	Manny Ramirez	3.00
6	Mike Piazza	5.00
7	Vladimir Guerrero	3.00
8	Chipper Jones	4.00
9	Alex Rodriguez	8.00
10	Jeff Bagwell	3.00

Supernaturals

This 10-card set has a warp like image of the player on the front with silver holo-foil highlights around the player image and gold foil stamping. Card backs are numbered with an "S" suffix. These were seeded 1:10 packs.

	NM/M
Complete Set (10):	18.00
Common Player:	.75

		NM/M
Complete Set (10):		15.00
Common Player:		1.00
Inserted 1:10		
1	Alex Rodriguez	3.00
2	Chipper Jones	1.75
3	Derek Jeter	4.00
4	Ivan Rodriguez	1.00
5	Ken Griffey Jr.	2.00
6	Mark McGwire	3.00
7	Mike Piazza	2.00
8	Nomar Garciaparra	2.00
9	Sammy Sosa	2.00
10	Vladimir Guerrero	1.50

Dave Winfield Autograph Memorabilia

This two-card set consists of 40 game-used helmet Winfield cards and 20 game-used ball cards.

		NM/M
Complete Set (2):		
1	Dave Winfield/Bat/20	140.00
2	Dave Winfield/Helmet/40	125.00

2000 Fleer Showcase

The base set consists of 140 cards, including 40 Prospect Showcase subset cards. Cards 101-115 are serially numbered to 1,000 and cards 116-140 are serially numbered to 2,000. The card fronts are holo-foiled, with the player name and team stamped in gold foil. Card backs have year-by-year statistics and a small close-up photo. Five-card packs carried an SRP of $4.99.

	NM/M
Complete Set (140):	200.00
Common Player (1-100):	.25
Common (101-115):	6.00
Production 1,000 Sets	
Common (116-140):	4.00
Production 2,000 Sets	
Pack (5):	2.50
Box (24):	50.00

1	Alex Rodriguez	2.50
2	Derek Jeter	3.00
3	Jeromy Burnitz	.25
4	John Olerud	.25
5	Paul Konerko	.25
6	Johnny Damon	.40
7	Curt Schilling	.50
8	Barry Larkin	.40
9	Adrian Beltre	.40
10	Scott Rolen	.75
11	Carlos Delgado	.50
12	Pedro J. Martinez	1.00
13	Todd Helton	1.00
14	Jacque Jones	.25
15	Jeff Kent	.25
16	Darin Erstad	.65
17	Juan Encarnacion	.25
18	Roger Clemens	1.75
19	Tony Gwynn	1.50

20	Nomar Garciaparra	2.00
21	Roberto Alomar	.40
22	Matt Lawton	.25
23	Rich Aurilia	.25
24	Charles Johnson	.25
25	Jim Thome	.25
26	Eric Milton	.25
27	Barry Bonds	3.00
28	Albert Belle	.25
29	Travis Fryman	.25
30	Ken Griffey Jr.	2.00
31	Phil Nevin	.25
32	Chipper Jones	1.50
33	Craig Biggio	.25
34	Mike Hampton	.25
35	Fred McGriff	.25
36	Cal Ripken Jr.	3.00
37	Manny Ramirez	1.00
38	Jose Vidro	.25
39	Trevor Hoffman	.25
40	Tom Glavine	.50
41	Frank Thomas	1.00
42	Chris Widger	.25
43	J.D. Drew	.50
44	Andres Galarraga	.25
45	Pokey Reese	.25
46	Mike Piazza	2.00
47	Kevin Young	.25
48	Sean Casey	.25
49	Carlos Beltran	.60
50	Jason Kendall	.25
51	Vladimir Guerrero	1.00
52	Jermaine Dye	.25
53	Brian Giles	.25
54	Andruw Jones	1.00
55	Richard Hidalgo	.25
56	Robin Ventura	.25
57	Ivan Rodriguez	.65
58	Greg Maddux	1.50
59	Billy Wagner	.25
60	Ruben Mateo	.25
61	Troy Glaus	1.00
62	Dean Palmer	.25
63	Eric Chavez	.40
64	Edgar Martinez	.25
65	Randy Johnson	1.00
66	Preston Wilson	.25
67	Orlando Hernandez	.25
68	Jim Edmonds	.25
69	Carl Everett	.25
70	Larry Walker	.25
71	Ron Belliard	.25
72	Sammy Sosa	2.00
73	Matt Williams	.25
74	Cliff Floyd	.25
75	Bernie Williams	.40
76	Fernando Tatis	.25
77	Steve Finley	.25
78	Jeff Bagwell	1.00
79	Edgardo Alfonzo	.25
80	Jose Canseco	.40
81	Magglio Ordonez	.40
82	Shawn Green	.40
83	Bobby Abreu	.25
84	Tony Batista	.25
85	Mo Vaughn	.25
86	Juan Gonzalez	1.00
87	Paul O'Neill	.25
88	Mark McGwire	2.50
89	Mark Grace	.35
90	Kevin Brown	.25
91	Ben Grieve	.25
92	Shannon Stewart	.25
93	Erubiel Durazo	.25
94	Antonio Alfonseca	.25
95	Jeff Cirillo	.25
96	Greg Vaughn	.25
97	Kerry Wood	.60
98	Geoff Jenkins	.25
99	Jason Giambi	.75
100	Rafael Palmeiro	.65
101	Rafael Furcal	6.00
102	Pablo Ozuna	6.00
103	Brad Penny	6.00
104	Mark Mulder	6.00
105	Adam Piatt	6.00
106	Mike Lamb RC	6.00
107	Kazuhiro Sasaki RC	15.00
108	Aaron McNeal RC	6.00
109	Pat Burrell	8.00
110	Rick Ankiel	6.00
111	Eric Munson	6.00
112	Josh Beckett	8.00
113	Adam Kennedy	6.00
114	Alex Escobar	6.00
115	Chad Hermansen	6.00
116	Kip Wells	4.00
117	Matt LeCroy	4.00
118	Julio Ramirez	4.00
119	Ben Petrick	4.00
120	Nick Johnson	6.00
121	Gookie Dawkins	4.00
122	Julio Zuleta RC	4.00
123	Alfonso Soriano	8.00
124	Keith McDonald RC	4.00
125	Kory DeHaan	4.00
126	Vernon Wells	4.00
127	Dernell Stenson	4.00
128	David Eckstein	4.00
129	Robert Fick	4.00
130	Cole Liniak	4.00
131	Mark Quinn	4.00
132	Eric Gagne	5.00
133	Wily Pena	4.00
134	Andy Thompson RC	4.00
135	Steve Sisco RC	4.00
136	Paul Rigdon RC	6.00
137	Rob Bell	4.00

138	Carlos Guillen	5.00
139	Jimmy Rollins	5.00
140	Jason Conti	4.00

Legacy

A parallel to the 140-card base set these feature a matte and holo-foil design and are serially numbered to 20.

Stars (1-100):	30-50X
Prospects (101-140):	3-6X
Production 20 Sets	

Masterpiece

Each card in 2000 Showcase was issued in a unique Masterpiece edition. The front is enhanced with gold ink while on back is printed the notice "The Only 1 Of 1 / Masterpiece."

Prospect Showcase First

A parallel of the 40-card Prospects subset. These differ from the base cards in that they have a horizontal format and are serially numbered to 500.

Prospects (101-140):	1-2X
Production 500 Sets	

Club 3000

This two-card set pays tribute to Lou Brock and Nolan Ryan. Each card is die-cut around the numerals 3,000 with a date displaying the day Brock or Ryan reached their 3,000 milestone. The player name is stamped in silver holo-foil. These were inserted 1:24 packs.

		NM/M
Common Player:		3.00
Inserted 1:24		
1	Lou Brock	2.00
2	Nolan Ryan	8.00

Club 3000 Memorabilia

These inserts feature actual game-used pieces of memorabilia from Nolan Ryan and Lou Brock and are serial numbered. The number produced is listed after the player name.

	NM/M
Lou Brock/Jsy/680	15.00

	NM/M
Lou Brock/Bat/270	25.00
Lou Brock/Hat, Bat, Jsy/25	100.00
Nolan Ryan/Jsy/780	40.00
Nolan Ryan/Hat/65	120.00
Nolan Ryan/Bat/265	60.00
Nolan Ryan/Bat, Jsy/100	120.00

Consummate Prose

Consummate Prose — Sammy Sosa

This 15-card set has an image of a worn scroll of paper with consummate prose written on it in the background of the player image. The Showcase logo, player name and Consummate Prose are stamped in gold foil. Card backs are numbered with an "CP" suffix and are inserted 1:6 packs.

	NM/M
Complete Set (15):	20.00
Common Player:	.50
Inserted 1:6	
1 Jeff Bagwell	1.50
2 Alex Rodriguez	3.00
3 Chipper Jones	2.00
4 Derek Jeter	4.00
5 Manny Ramirez	1.50
6 Tony Gwynn	2.00
7 Sammy Sosa	2.50
8 Ivan Rodriguez	1.00
9 Greg Maddux	2.00
10 Ken Griffey Jr.	2.50
11 Rick Ankiel	.50
12 Cal Ripken Jr.	4.00
13 Pedro Martinez	1.50
14 Mike Piazza	2.50
15 Mark McGwire	3.00

Feel the Game

This set has swatches of game worn jersey embedded into the card front.

	NM/M
Common Player:	5.00
Inserted 1:72	
1 Barry Bonds	30.00
2 Gookie Dawkins	5.00
3 Darin Erstad	8.00
4 Troy Glaus	10.00
5 Scott Rolen	10.00
6 Alex Rodriguez	25.00
7 Andruw Jones	10.00
8 Robin Ventura	5.00
9 Sean Casey	5.00
10 Cal Ripken Jr.	40.00

Final Answer

These foiled inserts have a green border with the player inside a frame with question marks in the background. The card backs have trivia questions about the featured player. Card backs are numbered with a "FA" suffix. These were seeded 1:10 packs.

	NM/M
Complete Set (10):	20.00
Common Player:	1.00
Inserted 1:10	
1 Alex Rodriguez	3.00
2 Vladimir Guerrero	1.00
3 Cal Ripken Jr.	4.00
4 Sammy Sosa	2.00
5 Barry Bonds	4.00
6 Derek Jeter	4.00
7 Ken Griffey Jr.	2.00
8 Randy Johnson	2.00
9 Sammy Sosa	4.00
10 Alex Rodriguez	5.00

Fresh Ink

Jose Cruz, Jr. • Blue Jays — FreshINK

These autographed inserts are inserted 1:24 packs.

	NM/M
Common Player:	5.00
Inserted 1:24	
1 Rick Ankiel	8.00
2 Josh Beckett	20.00
3 Barry Bonds	200.00
4 A.J. Burnett	10.00
5 Pat Burrell	15.00
6 Ken Caminiti	8.00
7 Sean Casey	10.00
8 Jose Cruz Jr.	10.00
9 Gookie Dawkins	5.00
10 Erubiel Durazo	8.00
11 Juan Encarnacion	8.00
12 Darin Erstad	15.00
13 Rafael Furcal	15.00
14 Nomar Garciaparra	100.00
15 Jason Giambi	20.00
16 Jeremy Giambi	6.00
17 Brian Giles	15.00
18 Troy Glaus	20.00
19 Vladimir Guerrero	30.00
20 Chad Hermansen	5.00
23 Trevor Hoffman	8.00
24 Randy Johnson	60.00
25 Andruw Jones	15.00
26 Jason Kendall	8.00
27 Paul Konerko	10.00
28 Mike Lowell	10.00
29 Aaron McNeal	5.00
30 Warren Morris	5.00
31 Paul O'Neill	20.00
32 Magglio Ordonez	10.00
33 Pablo Ozuna	5.00
34 Brad Penny	8.00
35 Ben Petrick	5.00
36 Pokey Reese	5.00
37 Cal Ripken Jr.	125.00
38 Alex Rodriguez	75.00
39 Scott Rolen	30.00
40 Jose Vidro	8.00
41 Kip Wells	5.00

License to Skill

License to Skill have a rounded, die-cut top with a concentric-circles background. Silver and gold foil etching and foil stamping are used as well. Card backs are numbered with an "LS" suffix.

	NM/M
Complete Set (10):	25.00
Common Player:	1.50
Inserted 1:10	
1 Vladimir Guerrero	2.00
2 Pedro J. Martinez	1.50
3 Nomar Garciaparra	4.00
4 Ivan Rodriguez	1.50
5 Mark McGwire	5.00
6 Derek Jeter	6.00
7 Ken Griffey Jr.	4.00
8 Randy Johnson	2.00
9 Sammy Sosa	4.00
10 Alex Rodriguez	5.00

Long Gone

VLADIMIR GUERRERO — OLYMPIC STADIUM

These inserts are die-cut around the card top to mimic the outfield dimensions of the featured players' stadium. Gold foil stamping is also used. Card backs are numbered with an "LG" suffix and have an insertion ratio of 1:20 packs.

	NM/M
Complete Set (10):	25.00
Common Player:	2.00
Inserted 1:20	
1 Sammy Sosa	4.00
2 Derek Jeter	6.00
3 Nomar Garciaparra	4.00
4 Juan Gonzalez	2.00
5 Vladimir Guerrero	2.00
6 Barry Bonds	6.00
7 Jeff Bagwell	2.00
8 Alex Rodriguez	5.00
9 Ken Griffey Jr.	4.00
10 Mark McGwire	5.00

Noise of Summer

NOISE of SUMMER — MARK McGWIRE — ST. LOUIS CARDINALS

This 10-card set has a kaleidoscope background with the insert name stamped in red foil and the logo, player name and team name stamped in gold foil. Card backs are numbered with an "NS" suffix. These were seeded 1:10 packs.

	NM/M
Complete Set (10):	15.00
Common Player:	1.00
Inserted 1:10	
1 Chipper Jones	1.50
2 Jeff Bagwell	1.00
3 Manny Ramirez	1.00
4 Mark McGwire	3.00
5 Ken Griffey Jr.	2.00
6 Mike Piazza	2.00
7 Pedro J. Martinez	1.00
8 Alex Rodriguez	3.00
9 Derek Jeter	4.00
10 Randy Johnson	1.00

Sweet Sigs

These autographed inserts have the featured players' autograph on an actual "sweet spot" from an authen-

tic Major League baseball. These have an insertion ratio of 1:250 packs.

	NM/M
Common Player:	10.00
Inserted 1:250	
1 Nomar Garciaparra/53	150.00
2 Alex Rodriguez/67	200.00
3 Tony Gwynn	40.00
4 Roger Clemens/79	140.00
5 Scott Rolen	50.00
6 Greg Maddux	80.00
7 Jose Cruz Jr.	15.00
8 Tony Womack	10.00
9 Jay Buhner	10.00
10 Nolan Ryan	125.00

2000 Fleer Tradition

MOISES ALOU — HOUSTON ASTROS — outfield

The Fleer Tradition base set consists of 450 cards including a 30-card rookies/prospects subset, 30 team cards, 10 league leaders, 6 award winners, 10 postseason recaps and 6 checklists. The card fronts have a close-up photo of the featured player as well as a small action photo surrounded by a white border. Like the fronts the card backs have a "throwback" look, which includes complete year-by-year statistics, a brief career note and vital information. 10-card packs had a SRP of $1.49.

	NM/M
Complete Set (450):	50.00
Common Player:	.10
Complete Glossy Factory Set (500):	450.00
Complete Glossy Factory Set (455):	90.00
Glossy (1-450):	1-2X
Common Glossy (451-500):	8.00
Five Glossy (451-500) per factory set 1,000 produced (451-500)	
Pack (10):	1.50
Wax Box:	35.00
1 AL HRs	.50
2 NL HRs	.50
3 AL RBIs	.50
4 NL RBIs	.50
5 AL Avg.	.50
6 NL Avg.	.15
7 AL Wins	.20
8 NL Wins	.40
9 AL ERA	.20
10 NL ERA	.25
11 Matt Mantei	.10
12 John Rocker	.10
13 Kyle Farnsworth	.10
14 Juan Guzman	.10
15 Manny Ramirez	.75
16 Matt Riley-P, Calvin Pickering-1B	.10
17 Tony Clark	.10
18 Brian Meadows	.10
19 Orber Moreno	.10
20 Eric Karros	.10
21 Steve Woodard	.10
22 Scott Brosius	.10
23 Gary Bennett	.10
24 Jason Wood-3B, Dave Borkowski-P	.10
25 Joe McEwing	.10
26 Juan Gonzalez	.75
27 Roy Halladay	.25
28 Trevor Hoffman	.10
29 Arizona Diamondbacks	.10
30 Domingo Guzman-P RC, Wiki Gonzalez-C	.25
31 Bret Boone	.10
32 Nomar Garciaparra	2.00
33 Bo Porter	.10
34 Eddie Taubensee	.10
35 Pedro Astacio	.10
36 Derek Bell	.10
37 Jacque Jones	.10
38 Ricky Ledee	.10
39 Jeff Kent	.10
40 Matt Williams	.10
41 Alfonso Soriano-SS, D'Angelo Jimenez-3B	.75
42 B.J. Surhoff	.10
43 Denny Neagle	.10
44 Omar Vizquel	.10
45 Jeff Bagwell	.75
46 Mark Grudzielanek	.10
47 LaTroy Hawkins	.10
48 Orlando Hernandez	.10
49 Ken Griffey Jr.	2.00
50 Fernando Tatis	.10
51 Quilvio Veras	.10
52 Wayne Gomes	.10
53 Rick Helling	.10
54 Shannon Stewart	.10
55 Dermal Brown-OF, Mark Quinn-OF	.20
56 Randy Johnson	1.00
57 Greg Maddux	1.50
58 Mike Cameron	.10
59 Matt Anderson	.10
60 Milwaukee Brewers	.10
61 Derrek Lee	.10
62 Mike Sweeney	.10
63 Fernando Vina	.10
64 Orlando Cabrera	.20
65 Doug Glanville	.10
66 Stan Spencer	.10
67 Ray Lankford	.10
68 Kelly Dransfeldt	.10
69 Alex Gonzalez	.10
70 Russell Branyan-3B, Danny Peoples-OF	.10
71 Jim Edmonds	.10
72 Brady Anderson	.10
73 Mike Stanley	.10
74 Travis Fryman	.10
75 Carlos Febles	.10
76 Bobby Higginson	.10
77 Carlos Perez	.10
78 Steve Cox-1B, Alex Sanchez-OF	.10
79 Dustin Hermanson	.10
80 Kenny Rogers	.10
81 Miguel Tejada	.25
82 Ben Davis	.10
83 Reggie Sanders	.10
84 Eric Davis	.10
85 J.D. Drew	.45
86 Ryan Rupe	.10
87 Bobby Smith	.10
88 Jose Cruz Jr.	.10
89 Carlos Delgado	.50
90 Toronto Blue Jays	.10
91 Denny Stark-P RC, Gil Meche-P	.25
92 Randy Velarde	.10
93 Aaron Boone	.10
94 Javy Lopez	.10
95 Johnny Damon	.25
96 Jon Lieber	.10
97 Montreal Expos	.10
98 Mark Kotsay	.10
99 Luis Gonzalez	.25
100 Larry Walker	.10
101 Adrian Beltre	.25
102 Alex Ochoa	.10
103 Michael Barrett	.10
104 Tampa Bay Devil Rays	.10
105 Rey Ordonez	.10
106 Derek Jeter	3.00
107 Mike Lieberthal	.10
108 Ellis Burks	.10
109 Steve Finley	.10
110 Ryan Klesko	.10
111 Steve Avery	.10
112 Dave Veres	.10
113 Cliff Floyd	.10
114 Shane Reynolds	.10
115 Kevin Brown	.10
116 David Nilsson	.10
117 Mike Trombley	.10
118 Todd Walker	.10
119 John Olerud	.10
120 Chuck Knoblauch	.10
121 Nomar Garciaparra	2.00
122 Trot Nixon	.10
123 Erubiel Durazo	.10
124 Edwards Guzman	.10
125 Curt Schilling	.50
126 Brian Jordan	.10
127 Cleveland Indians	.10
128 Benito Santiago	.10
129 Frank Thomas	.75
130 Neifi Perez	.10
131 Alex Fernandez	.10
132 Jose Lima	.10
133 Jorge Toca-1B, Melvin Mora-OF	.10
134 Scott Karl	.10
135 Brad Radke	.10
136 Paul O'Neill	.10
137 Kris Benson	.10
138 Colorado Rockies	.10
139 Jason Phillips	.10
140 Robb Nen	.10
141 Ken Hill	.10
142 Charles Johnson	.10
143 Paul Konerko	.10
144 Dmitri Young	.10
145 Justin Thompson	.10
146 Mark Loretta	.10
147 Edgardo Alfonzo	.10
148 Armando Benitez	.10
149 Octavio Dotel	.10
150 Wade Boggs	1.50
151 Ramon Hernandez	.10
152 Freddy Garcia	.10
153 Edgar Martinez	.10
154 Ivan Rodriguez	.65
155 Kansas City Royals	.10
156 Cleatus Davidson-2B, Cristian Guzman-SS	.10
157 Andy Benes	.10
158 Todd Dunwoody	.10
159 Pedro Martinez	1.00
160 Mike Caruso	.10
161 Mike Sirotka	.10
162 Houston Astros	.10
163 Darryl Kile	.10
164 Chipper Jones	1.50
165 Carl Everett	.10
166 Geoff Jenkins	.10
167 Dan Perkins	.10
168 Andy Pettitte	.25
169 Francisco Cordova	.10
170 Jay Buhner	.10
171 Jay Bell	.10
172 Andruw Jones	.75
173 Bobby Howry	.10
174 Chris Singleton	.10
175 Todd Helton	.75
176 A.J. Burnett	.10
177 Marquis Grissom	.10
178 Eric Milton	.10
179 Los Angeles Dodgers	.10
180 Kevin Appier	.10
181 Brian Giles	.10
182 Tom Davey	.10
183 Mo Vaughn	.10
184 Jose Hernandez	.10
185 Jim Parque	.10
186 Derrick Gibson	.10
187 Bruce Aven	.10
188 Jeff Cirillo	.10
189 Doug Mientkiewicz	.10
190 Eric Chavez	.25
191 Al Martin	.10
192 Tom Glavine	.25
193 Butch Huskey	.10
194 Ray Durham	.10
195 Greg Vaughn	.10
196 Vinny Castilla	.10
197 Ken Caminiti	.10
198 Joe Mays	.10
199 Chicago White Sox	.10
200 Mariano Rivera	.20
201 Mark McGwire	2.50
202 Pat Meares	.10
203 Andres Galarraga	.10
204 Tom Gordon	.10
205 Henry Rodriguez	.10
206 Brett Tomko	.10
207 Dante Bichette	.10
208 Craig Biggio	.10
209 Matt Lawton	.10
210 Tino Martinez	.10
211 Aaron Myette-P, Josh Paul-C	.10
212 Warren Morris	.10
213 San Diego Padres	.10
214 Ramon E. Martinez	.10
215 Troy Percival	.10
216 Jason Johnson	.10
217 Carlos Lee	.10
218 Scott Williamson	.10
219 Jeff Weaver	.10
220 Ronnie Belliard	.10
221 Jason Giambi	.65
222 Ken Griffey Jr.	2.00
223 John Halama	.10
224 Brett Hinchliffe	.10
225 Wilson Alvarez	.10
226 Rolando Arrojo	.10
227 Ruben Mateo	.10
228 Rafael Palmeiro	.65
229 David Wells	.10
230 Eric Gagne-P, Jeff Williams-P	.10
231 Tim Salmon	.30
232 Mike Mussina	.50
233 Magglio Ordonez	.25
234 Ron Villone	.10
235 Antonio Alfonseca	.10
236 Jeromy Burnitz	.10
237 Ben Grieve	.10
238 Giomar Guevara	.10
239 Garret Anderson	.10
240 John Smoltz	.10
241 Mark Grace	.15
242 Cole Liniak-3B, Jose Molina-C	.10
243 Damion Easley	.10
244 Jeff Montgomery	.10
245 Kenny Lofton	.10
246 Masato Yoshii	.10
247 Philadelphia Phillies	.10
248 Raul Mondesi	.10
249 Marlon Anderson	.10
250 Shawn Green	.40
251 Sterling Hitchcock	.10
252 Randy Wolf-P, Anthony Shumaker-P	.10
253 Jeff Fassero	.10
254 Eli Marrero	.10
255 Cincinnati Reds	.10

#	Player	Price
256	Rick Ankiel-P, Adam Kennedy-2B	.50
257	Darin Erstad	.60
258	Albert Belle	.20
259	Bartolo Colon	.10
260	Bret Saberhagen	.10
261	Carlos Beltran	.50
262	Glenallen Hill	.10
263	Gregg Jefferies	.10
264	Matt Clement	.10
265	Miguel Del Toro	.10
266	Robinson Cancel-C, Kevin Barker-1B	.10
267	San Francisco Giants	.10
268	Kent Bottenfield	.10
269	Fred McGriff	.10
270	Chris Carpenter	.10
271	Atlanta Braves	.10
272	Wilton Veras-3B, Tomokazu Ohka-P RC	.50
273	Will Clark	.20
274	Troy O'Leary	.10
275	Sammy Sosa	2.00
276	Travis Lee	.15
277	Sean Casey	.25
278	Ron Gant	.10
279	Roger Clemens	1.75
280	Phil Nevin	.10
281	Mike Piazza	2.00
282	Mike Lowell	.10
283	Kevin Millwood	.10
284	Joe Randa	.10
285	Jeff Shaw	.10
286	Jason Varitek	.10
287	Harold Baines	.10
288	Gabe Kapler	.10
289	Chuck Finley	.10
290	Carl Pavano	.10
291	Brad Ausmus	.10
292	Brad Fullmer	.10
293	Boston Red Sox	.10
294	Bob Wickman	.10
295	Billy Wagner	.10
296	Shawn Estes	.10
297	Gary Sheffield	.40
298	Fernando Seguignol	.10
299	Omar Olivares	.10
300	Baltimore Orioles	.10
301	Matt Stairs	.10
302	Andy Ashby	.10
303	Todd Greene	.10
304	Jesse Garcia	.10
305	Kerry Wood	.50
306	Roberto Alomar	.40
307	New York Mets	.10
308	Dean Palmer	.10
309	Mike Hampton	.10
310	Devon White	.10
311	Chad Hermansen-OF, Mike Garcia-P	.10
312	Tim Hudson	.40
313	John Franco	.10
314	Jason Schmidt	.10
315	J.T. Snow	.10
316	Ed Sprague	.10
317	Chris Widger	.10
318	Ben Petrick-C, Luther Hackman-P RC	.25
319	Jose Mesa	.10
320	Jose Canseco	.50
321	John Wetteland	.10
322	Minnesota Twins	.10
323	Jeff DaVanon-OF RC, Brian Cooper-P	.25
324	Tony Womack	.10
325	Rod Beck	.10
326	Mickey Morandini	.10
327	Pokey Reese	.10
328	Jaret Wright	.10
329	Glen Barker	.10
330	Darren Dreifort	.10
331	Torii Hunter	.15
332	Tony Armas Jr.-P, Peter Bergeron-OF	.10
333	Hideki Irabu	.10
334	Desi Relaford	.10
335	Barry Bonds	3.00
336	Gary DiSarcina	.10
337	Gerald Williams	.10
338	John Valentin	.10
339	David Justice	.10
340	Juan Encarnacion	.10
341	Jeremy Giambi	.10
342	Chan Ho Park	.10
343	Vladimir Guerrero	1.00
344	Robin Ventura	.10
345	Bobby Abreu	.10
346	Tony Gwynn	1.50
347	Jose Jimenez	.10
348	Royce Clayton	.10
349	Kelvim Escobar	.10
350	Chicago Cubs	.10
351	Travis Dawkins-SS, Jason LaRue-C	.10
352	Barry Larkin	.10
353	Cal Ripken Jr.	3.00
353s	Cal Ripken Jr./OPS	4.00
354	Alex Rodriguez	2.50
355	Todd Stottlemyre	.10
356	Terry Adams	.10
357	Pittsburgh Pirates	.10
358	Jim Thome	.10
359	Corey Lee-P, Doug Davis-P	.10
360	Moises Alou	.10
361	Todd Hollandsworth	.10
362	Marty Cordova	.10
363	David Cone	.10
364	Joe Nathan-P, Wilson Delgado-SS	.10
365	Paul Byrd	.10
366	Edgar Renteria	.10
367	Rusty Greer	.10
368	David Segui	.10
369	New York Yankees	.50
370	Daryle Ward-OF/1B, Carlos Hernandez-2B	.10
371	Troy Glaus	.75
372	Delino DeShields	.10
373	Jose Offerman	.10
374	Sammy Sosa	2.00
375	Sandy Alomar Jr.	.10
376	Masao Kida	.10
377	Richard Hidalgo	.10
378	Ismael Valdes	.10
379	Ugueth Urbina	.10
380	Darryl Hamilton	.10
381	John Jaha	.10
382	St. Louis Cardinals	.10
383	Scott Sauerbeck	.10
384	Russ Ortiz	.10
385	Jamie Moyer	.10
386	Dave Martinez	.10
387	Todd Zeile	.10
388	Anaheim Angels	.10
389	Rob Ryan-OF	.10
390	Nick Bierbrodt-P, Rickey Henderson	.75
391	Alex Rodriguez	2.50
392	Texas Rangers	.10
393	Roberto Hernandez	.10
394	Tony Batista	.10
395	Oakland Athletics	.10
396	Randall Simon-1B, David Cortes-P RC	.20
397	Gregg Olson	.10
398	Sidney Ponson	.10
399	Micah Bowie	.10
400	Mark McGwire	2.50
401	Florida Marlins	.10
402	Chad Allen	.10
403	Casey Blake-3B, Vernon Wells-OF	.10
404	Pete Harnisch	.10
405	Preston Wilson	.10
406	Richie Sexson	.10
407	Rico Brogna	.10
408	Todd Hundley	.10
409	Wally Joyner	.10
410	Tom Goodwin	.10
411	Joey Hamilton	.10
412	Detroit Tigers	.10
413	Michael Tejera-P RC, Ramon Castro-C	.25
414	Alex Gonzalez	.10
415	Jermaine Dye	.10
416	Jose Rosado	.10
417	Wilton Guerrero	.10
418	Rondell White	.10
419	Al Leiter	.10
420	Bernie Williams	.25
421	A.J. Hinch	.10
422	Pat Burrell	.50
423	Scott Rolen	.65
424	Jason Kendall	.10
425	Kevin Young	.10
426	Eric Owens	.10
427	Derek Jeter	1.00
428	Livan Hernandez	.10
429	Russ Davis	.10
430	Dan Wilson	.10
431	Quinton McCracken	.10
432	Homer Bush	.10
433	Seattle Mariners	.10
434	Chad Harville-P, Luis Vizcaino-P	.10
435	Carlos Beltran	.45
436	Scott Williamson	.10
437	Pedro Martinez	.75
438	Randy Johnson	.75
439	Ivan Rodriguez	.75
440	Chipper Jones	.75
441	AL Division (Bernie Williams)	.15
442	AL Division (Pedro Martinez)	.50
443	AL Champ (Derek Jeter)	1.00
444	NL Division (Brian Jordan)	.10
445	NL Division (Todd Pratt)	.10
446	NL Champ (Kevin Millwood)	.10
447	World Series (Orlando Hernandez)	.10
448	World Series (Derek Jeter)	1.00
449	World Series (Chad Curtis)	.10
450	World Series (Roger Clemens)	.75
451	Carlos Casimiro RC	8.00
452	Adam Melhuse RC	8.00
453	Adam Bernero RC	8.00
454	Dusty Allen RC	8.00
455	Chan Perry RC	8.00
456	Damian Rolls RC	8.00
457	Josh Phelps RC	10.00
458	Barry Zito RC	25.00
459	Hector Ortiz RC	8.00
460	Juan Pierre RC	10.00
461	Jose Ortiz RC	15.00
462	Chad Zerbe RC	8.00
463	Julio Zuleta RC	8.00
464	Eric Byrnes RC	10.00
465	Wilfredo Rodriguez RC	10.00
466	Wascar Serrano RC	8.00
467	Aaron McNeal RC	8.00
468	Paul Rigdon RC	8.00
469	John Snyder RC	8.00
470	J.C. Romero RC	8.00
471	Talmadge Nunnari RC	8.00
472	Mike Lamb RC	8.00
473	Ryan Kohlmeier RC	8.00
474	Rodney Lindsey RC	8.00
475	Elvis Pena RC	8.00
476	Alex Cabrera RC	10.00
477	Chris Richard RC	8.00
478	Pedro Feliz RC	10.00
479	Ross Gload RC	8.00
480	Timoniel Perez RC	8.00
481	Jason Woolf RC	8.00
482	Kenny Kelly RC	8.00
483	Sang-Hoon Lee RC	8.00
484	John Riedling RC	8.00
485	Chris Wakeland RC	8.00
486	Britt Reames RC	8.00
487	Greg LaRocca RC	8.00
488	Randy Keisler RC	8.00
489	Xavier Nady RC	20.00
490	Keith Ginter RC	10.00
491	Joey Nation RC	8.00
492	Kazuhiro Sasaki RC	25.00
493	Lesli Brea RC	8.00
494	Jace Brewer RC	8.00
495	Yohanny Valera RC	8.00
496	Adam Piatt	10.00
497	Nate Rolison	8.00
498	Aubrey Huff	10.00
499	Jason Tyner	8.00
500	Corey Patterson	12.00

format. Card fronts have silver foil stamping, a red border and are seeded 1:6 packs. They are numbered on the back with a "D" suffix.

	NM/M
Complete Set (15):	15.00
Common Player:	.50
Inserted 1:6	
1 Alex Rodriguez	2.50
2 Ben Grieve	.50
3 Cal Ripken Jr.	3.00
4 Chipper Jones	1.50
5 Derek Jeter	3.00
6 Frank Thomas	
7 Jeff Bagwell	1.00
8 Sammy Sosa	2.00
9 Tony Gwynn	1.50
10 Scott Rolen	.75
11 Nomar Garciaparra	
12 Mike Piazza	2.00
13 Mark McGwire	2.50
14 Ken Griffey Jr.	2.00
15 Juan Gonzalez	1.00

Club 3000

The Club 3000 inserts are die-cut around the number 3,000, commemmorating their reaching the 3,000 hit achievement. These are seeded 1:36 packs and features George Brett, Rod Carew and Robin Yount.

	NM/M
Complete Set (3):	5.00
Common Player:	3.00
Inserted 1:36	
(1) George Brett	4.00
(2) Rod Carew	2.00
(3) Robin Yount	2.00

Club 3000 Memorabilia

These are a parallel to the base version and has five different memorabilia based tiers. Level 2 (cap), Level 3 (bat), Level 4 (jersey), Level 5 (bat and jersey) and Level 6 (bat, jersey and cap). Each card is hand-numbered.

	NM/M
George Brett/Bat/250	60.00
George Brett/Hat/100	75.00
George Brett/Jsy/445	30.00
George Brett/Bat, Jsy/100	90.00
Rod Carew/Bat/225	30.00
Rod Carew/Hat/100	50.00
Rod Carew/Jsy/440	20.00
Rod Carew/Bat, Jsy/100	65.00
Robin Yount/Bat/250	40.00
Robin Yount/Hat/100	60.00
Robin Yount/Jsy/440	40.00
Robin Yount/Bat, Jsy/100	75.00

Dividends

This insert set consists of 15 cards and spotlights the top players on a horizontal

Fresh Ink

This autographed insert set consists of 38 cards on a vertical format with the autograph on the bottom third of the card below the player image. These were inserted 1:144 packs.

	NM/M
Common Player:	5.00
Inserted 1:144	
Rick Ankiel	8.00
Carlos Beltran	25.00
Pat Burrell	15.00
Miguel Cairo	5.00
Sean Casey	8.00
Will Clark	30.00
Mike Darr	5.00
J.D. Drew	10.00
Erubiel Durazo	10.00
Carlos Febles	6.00
Freddy Garcia	8.00
Greg Maddux	80.00
Jason Grilli	5.00
Vladimir Guerrero	35.00
Tony Gwynn	40.00
Jerry Hairston Jr.	8.00
Tim Hudson	15.00
John Jaha	5.00
D'Angelo Jimenez	5.00
Andruw Jones	20.00
Gabe Kapler	6.00
Cesar King	6.00
Jason LaRue	6.00
Mike Lieberthal	8.00
Pedro Martinez	50.00
Gary Matthews Jr.	5.00
Orber Moreno	5.00
Eric Munson	5.00
Rafael Palmeiro	35.00
Jim Parque	6.00
Willi Mo Pena	15.00
Cal Ripken Jr.	100.00
Alex Rodriguez	80.00
Tim Salmon	15.00
Chris Singleton	5.00
Alfonso Soriano	50.00
Ed Yarnall	5.00

Grasskickers

This 15-card set has a close-up photo of the featured player with holographic silver foil stamping. These are seeded 1:30 packs and are numbered on the back with a "GK" suffix.

Hall's Well

This 15-card set spotlights superstars destined for Cooperstown, featured on a transparent plastic stock with overlays of silver foil stamping. These were seeded 1:30 packs and are numbered with a "HW" suffix.

	NM/M
Complete Set (15):	50.00
Common Player:	1.50
Inserted 1:30	
1 Mark McGwire	6.00
2 Alex Rodriguez	8.00
3 Cal Ripken Jr.	8.00
4 Chipper Jones	3.00
5 Derek Jeter	8.00
6 Frank Thomas	2.00
7 Greg Maddux	3.00
8 Juan Gonzalez	2.00
9 Ken Griffey Jr.	4.00
10 Mike Piazza	4.00
11 Nomar Garciaparra	4.00
12 Sammy Sosa	4.00
13 Roger Clemens	3.50
14 Ivan Rodriguez	1.50
15 Tony Gwynn	3.00

Opening Day 2K

As part of a multi-manufacturer promotion, Fleer issued eight cards of an "Opening Day 2K" set. Packages containing some of the 32 cards in the issue were distributed by MLB teams early in the season. The cards were also available exclusively as inserts in packs sold at KMart stores early in the season. The Fleer Tradition OD2K cards have gold-foil graphic

highlights on front. Backs are in the basic format of the rest of the Tradition issue, and are numbered "XX of 32/OD."

	NM/M
Complete Set (8):	6.00
Common Player:	.50
9 Cal Ripken Jr.	2.00
10 Alex Rodriguez	2.00
11 Mike Piazza	1.00
12 Jeff Bagwell	.75
13 Randy Johnson	.75
14 Jason Kendall	.50
15 Magglio Ordonez	.50
16 Carlos Delgado	.50

Ripken Collection

This 10-card set is devoted to Cal Ripken Jr. and features 10 different Fleer retro designs. These were seeded 1:30 packs.

	NM/M
Complete Set (10):	50.00
Common Card:	6.00
Inserted 1:30	

Ten-4

This 10-card insert set focuses on baseball's home run kings on a die-cut design enhanced with silver foil stamping. These were seeded 1:18 packs and are numbered on the card back with a "TF" suffix.

	NM/M
Complete Set (10):	20.00
Common Player:	2.00
Inserted 1:18	
1 Sammy Sosa	2.00
2 Nomar Garciaparra	2.00
3 Mike Piazza	2.00
4 Mark McGwire	3.00
5 Ken Griffey Jr.	2.00
6 Juan Gonzalez	1.00
7 Derek Jeter	4.00
8 Chipper Jones	1.50
9 Cal Ripken Jr.	4.00
10 Alex Rodriguez	3.00

Who To Watch

Top prospects for the 2000 season are highlighted in this 15-card set, including Rick Ankiel. They have a die-cut design with gold foil stamping. These were inserted 1:3 packs and numbered on the back with a "WW" suffix.

	NM/M
Complete Set (15):	5.00

Common Player: .25
Inserted 1:3

1	Rick Ankiel	.40
2	Matt Riley	.25
3	Wilton Veras	.25
4	Ben Petrick	.25
5	Chad Hermansen	.25
6	Peter Bergeron	.25
7	Mark Quinn	.25
8	Russell Branyan	.25
9	Alfonso Soriano	1.50
10	Randy Wolf	.50
11	Ben Davis	.25
12	Jeff DaVanon	.25
13	D'Angelo Jimenez	.25
14	Vernon Wells	1.00
15	Adam Kennedy	.40

Glossy Lumberjacks

Common Player: 8.00
One per factory set.
Production listed

1	Edgardo Alfonzo/145	10.00
2	Roberto Alomar/627	10.00
3	Moises Alou/529	8.00
4	Carlos Beltran/489	8.00
5	Adrian Beltre/127	10.00
7	Barry Bonds/305	40.00
9	Pat Burrell/45	25.00
10	Sean Casey/50	15.00
11	Eric Chavez/259	10.00
12	Tony Clark/70	10.00
13	Carlos Delgado/70	20.00
14	J.D. Drew/135	10.00
15	Erubiel Durazo/70	10.00
17	Carlos Febles/120	10.00
18	Jason Giambi/220	15.00
19	Shawn Green/429	10.00
20	Vladimir Guerrero/809	15.00
21	Derek Jeter/180	50.00
22	Chipper Jones/725	15.00
23	Gabe Kapler/160	8.00
27	Paul Konerko/70	10.00
27	Mike Lieberthal/45	10.00
28	Edgar Martinez/211	10.00
29	Raul Mondesi/458	8.00
30	Warren Morris/35	10.00
31	Magglio Ordonez/190	10.00
32	Rafael Palmeiro/49	15.00
33	Pokey Reese/110	8.00
34	Cal Ripken/235	50.00
35	Alex Rodriguez/292	25.00
36	Ivan Rodriguez/602	10.00
37	Scott Rolen/502	10.00
38	Chris Singleton/68	8.00
39	Alfonso Soriano/285	15.00
40	Frank Thomas/489	10.00
41	Jim Thome/479	10.00
42	Robin Ventura/114	10.00
43	Jose Vidro/60	10.00
44	Bernie Williams/215	10.00
45	Matt Williams/152	8.00

Update

CHAD DURBIN
KANSAS CITY ROYALS-PITCHER

Card #50 was supposed to be Indians prospect C.C. Sabathia but it was never issued because he was not called up during the 2000 season.

NM/M
Complete Set (149): 15.00
Common Player: .15

1	Ken Griffey Jr. (Season Highlights)	.50
2	Cal Ripken Jr. (Season Highlights)	1.00
3	Randy Velarde (Season Highlights)	.15
4	Fred McGriff (Season Highlights)	.15
5	Derek Jeter (Season Highlights)	1.00
6	Tom Glavine (Season Highlights)	.25
7	Brent Mayne (Season Highlights)	.15
8	Alex Ochoa (Season Highlights)	.15
9	Scott Sheldon (Season Highlights)	.15
10	Randy Johnson (Season Highlights)	.35
11	Daniel Garibay RC	.15
12	Brad Fullmer	.15
13	Kazuhiro Sasaki RC	.50
14	Andy Tracy	.15
15	Bret Boone	.15
16	Chad Durbin RC	.25
17	Mark Buehrle RC	1.50
18	Julio Zuleta RC	.15
19	Jeremy Giambi	.15
20	Gene Stechschulte RC	.15
21	Lou Pote	.15
22	Darrell Einertson	.15
23	Ken Griffey Jr.	.75
24	Jeff Sparks RC	.25
25	Aaron Fultz RC	.15
26	Derek Bell	.15
27	Rob Bell	.15
28	Rob Fick	.15
29	Darryl Kile	.15
30	Clayton Andrews	.15
31	Dave Veres	.15
32	Hector Mercado RC	.15
33	Willie Morales	.15
34	Kelly Wunsch	.15
35	Hideki Irabu	.15
36	Sean DePaula	.15
37	Dewayne Wise	.15
38	Curt Schilling	.25
39	Mark Johnson	.15
40	Mike Cameron	.15
41	Scott Sheldon	.15
42	Brett Tomko	.15
43	Johan Santana RC	8.00
44	Andy Benes	.15
45	Matt LeCroy	.15
46	Ryan Klesko	.15
47	Andy Ashby	.15
49	Octavio Dotel	.15
49	Eric Byrnes RC	1.00
51	Kenny Rogers	.15
52	Ben Weber	.15
53	Matt Blank	.15
54	Tom Goodwin	.15
55	Jim Edmonds	.15
56	Derrick Turnbow RC	.25
57	Mark Mulder	.15
58	Tarrik Brock	.15
59	Danny Young	.15
60	Fernando Vina	.15
61	Justin Brunette RC	.15
62	Jimmy Anderson	.15
63	Reggie Sanders	.15
64	Adam Kennedy	.15
65	Jesse Garcia	.15
66	Al Martin	.15
67	Kevin Walker	.15
68	Brad Penny	.15
69	B.J. Surhoff	.15
70	Geoff Blum	.15
71	Jose Jimenez	.15
72	Chuck Finley	.15
73	Valerio De Los Santos	.15
74	Terry Adams	.15
75	Rafael Furcal	.15
76	Mike Darr	.15
77	Quilvio Veras	.15
78	Armando Almanza	.15
79	Greg Vaughn	.15
80	Keith McDonald RC	.15
81	Eric Cammack	.15
82	Horacio Estrada	.15
83	Kory DeHaan	.15
84	Kevin Hodges	.15
85	Mike Lamb RC	.25
86	Shawn Green	.40
87	Dan Reichert	.15
88	Adam Piatt	.15
89	Mike Garcia	.15
90	Rodrigo Lopez RC	1.00
91	John Olerud	.15
92	Barry Zito	1.00
93	Jimmy Rollins	.15
94	Denny Neagle	.15
95	Rickey Henderson	.50
96	Adam Eaton	.15
97	Brian O'Connor	.15
98	Andy Thompson	.15
99	Jason Boyd	.15
100	Carlos Guillen	.15
101	Raul Gonzalez	.15
102	Brandon Kolb RC	.25
103	Jason Maxwell	.15
104	Luis Matos RC	.50
105	Morgan Burkhart RC	.25
106	Ismael Villegas	.15
107	David Justice	.15
108	Pablo Ozuna	.15
109	Jose Canseco	.40
110	Alex Cora	.15
111	Will Clark	.25
112	Keith Luuloa	.15
113	Bruce Chen	.15
114	Adam Hyzdu	.15
115	Scott Forster	.15
116	Allen McDill	.15
117	Kevin Nicholson	.15
118	Israel Alcantara	.15
119	Juan Alvarez	.15
120	Julio Lugo	.15
121	B.J. Waszgis	.15
122	Jeff D'Amico	.15
123	Ricky Ledee	.15
124	Mark DeRosa	.15
125	Alex Cabrera RC	.50
126	Gary Matthews	.15
127	Richie Sexson	.15
128	Santiago Perez	.15
129	Rondell White	.15
130	Craig House RC	.15
131	Kevin Beirne	.15
132	Wayne Franklin	.15
133	Henry Rodriguez	.15
134	Jay Payton	.15
135	Ron Gant	.15
136	Paxton Crawford RC	.25
137	Kent Bottenfield	.15
138	Rocky Biddle RC	.15
139	Travis Lee	.15
140	Ryan Vogelsong	.15
141	Jason Conti	.15
142	Tim Drew	.15
143	John Parrish RC	.15
144	Javier Cardona RC	.15
145	Tike Redman RC	.15
146	Brian Schneider	.15
147	Pasqual Coco RC	.15
148	Lorenzo Barcelo RC	.15
149	Jace Brewer RC	.25
150	Milton Bradley	.15

Update Mantle Pieces

Inserted 1:80 sets
1 Mickey Mantle 150.00

Diamond Skills Commemorative Sheet

Utilizing the same format and card reproductions as the souvenir sheet issued in conjunction with the season-opener Cubs-Mets series in Japan, Fleer issued this commemorative sheet for distribution to participants in the 2000 Diamond Skills competition. The 10" x 9" sheets depict star players from Fleer's 2000 Tradition set.

NM/M
Derek Jeter, Chipper Jones, Pedro Martinez, Mike Piazza, Cal Ripken Jr., Ivan Rodriguez, Sammy Sosa, Mo Vaughn 10.00

Japan Commemorative Sheet

To commemorate the opening of the 2000 Major League Baseball season with a Cubs-Mets series in Japan, Fleer created this commemorative sheet for distribution at the opening game on March 29 (20,000) and at the Xebio Sporting Goods stores and Pro Pacific Hobby stores in Japan (5,000 each). The 10" x 9" sheets depict on front cards from Fleer's 2000 Tradition set.

NM/M
Derek Jeter, Chipper Jones, Pedro Martinez, Mike Piazza, Cal Ripken Jr., Ivan Rodriguez, Sammy Sosa, Mo Vaughn 20.00

Oreo

In a nationwide promotional contest in which children stacked Oreo cookies at grocery stores, a pair of hot star cards were given away as consolation prizes. Each 2-1/2" x 3-1/2" card has blue borders with a color photo at center. Jeter's card shows him stacking cookies, while Junior's card (in his new Reds uniform) shows him holding a bag of cookies. Backs have personal information, stats, an action photo and logos of MLB, Fleer and Oreo.

NM/M
Complete Set (2): 6.00
(1) Ken Griffey Jr. 3.00
(2) Derek Jeter 3.00

SportsCards Greats of the Game

The Fleer SportsCards exclusive card set

The first-ever fully-licensed baseball card set to be issued in the form of a magazine insert, this set comprises the game's top players in the design of Fleer's very popular Greats of the Game issue (which depicted only former stars). The cards were issued six per month in uncut sheet form (8-1/4" x 11-1/8") in SportsCards magazine issues dated February through July, 2001. The cards were only inserted in newsstand and card-shop copies. Persons who subscribed to the magazine in a special offer received the complete set in unbound format. If cut from the sheet, individual cards measure the standard 2-1/2" x 3-1/2". On front are action photos on a white background with maroon borders. Backs have player identification, licensor logos and 2000 season stats.

NM/M
Complete Set, Sheets (6): 35.00
Complete Set, Singles (36): 25.00
Common Player: .50

	Sheet 1, February	6.00
1	Rick Ankiel	.75
2	Jeff Bagwell	1.00
3	Barry Bonds	3.00
4	Pat Burrell	.65
5	Roger Clemens	1.50
6	Carlos Delgado	.65
	Sheet 2, March	4.00
7	J.D. Drew	.65
8	Jim Edmonds	.50
9	Darin Erstad	.65
10	Andres Galarraga	.50
11	Nomar Garciaparra	2.00
12	Jason Giambi	.65
	Sheet 3, April	6.00
13	Troy Glaus	1.00
14	Roberto Alomar	.50
15	Ken Griffey Jr.	2.00
16	Vladimir Guerrero	1.00
17	Tony Gwynn	1.25
18	Todd Helton	1.00
	Sheet 4, May	7.50
19	Derek Jeter	7.00
20	Randy Johnson	1.25
21	Chipper Jones	1.25
22	Andruw Jones	1.00
23	Greg Maddux	1.25
24	Pedro Martinez	1.00
	Sheet 5, June	10.00
25	Mark McGwire	2.50
26	Magglio Ordonez	.50
27	Mike Piazza	1.00
28	Manny Ramirez	1.00
29	Cal Ripken Jr.	3.00
30	Alex Rodriguez	2.50
	Sheet 6, July	4.00
31	Ivan Rodriguez	.65
32	Jeff Kent	.50
33	Gary Sheffield	.50
34	Sammy Sosa	2.00
35	Frank Thomas	1.00
36	Bernie Williams	.50

Twizzlers

CAL RIPKEN, JR.
BALTIMORE ORIOLES-THIRD BASE

A dozen of baseball's biggest stars were reproduced in a format only slightly different from 2000 Fleer Tradition for inclusion in packages of Twizzlers candy. The candy version features UV coating on both front and back, has a small Twizzlers logo at lower-right on back and is numbered "X of 12." Cards were included in large (26.5 oz.) packages of candy or a complete set could be obtained for $1.50 and 15 proofs of purchase from smaller packages.

NM/M
Complete Set (12): 7.50
Common Player: .25

1	Mark McGwire	1.50
2	Cal Ripken Jr.	2.00
3	Chipper Jones	.75
4	Bernie Williams	.35
5	Alex Rodriguez	1.50
6	Curt Schilling	.35
7	Ken Griffey Jr.	1.00
8	Sammy Sosa	1.00
9	Mike Piazza	1.00
10	Pedro Martinez	.50
11	Kenny Lofton	.25
12	Larry Walker	.25

2001 Fleer Authority

ICHIRO

NM/M
Complete Set (150): 265.00
Common Player: .25
Common (101-150): 3.00
Production 2,001
Pack (5): 6.00
Box (22 + 2 Graded Packs): 120.00

1	Mark Grace	.35
2	Paul Konerko	.25
3	Sean Casey	.35
4	Jim Thome	.25
5	Todd Helton	.75
6	Tony Clark	.25
7	Jeff Bagwell	.75
8	Mike Sweeney	.25
9	Eric Karros	.25
10	Richie Sexson	.25
11	Doug Mientkiewicz	.25
12	Ryan Klesko	.25
13	John Olerud	.25
14	Mark McGwire	2.00
15	Fred McGriff	.65
16	Rafael Palmeiro	.65
17	Carlos Delgado	.50
18	Roberto Alomar	.40
19	Craig Biggio	.25
20	Jose Vidro	.25
21	Edgardo Alfonzo	.25
22	Jeff Kent	.25
23	Bret Boone	.25
24	Rafael Furcal	.25
25	Nomar Garciaparra	1.50
26	Barry Larkin	.25
27	Cristian Guzman	.25
28	Derek Jeter	2.50
29	Miguel Tejada	.40
30	Jimmy Rollins	.40
31	Rich Aurilia	.25
32	Alex Rodriguez	2.50
33	Cal Ripken Jr.	2.50
34	Troy Glaus	.75
35	Matt Williams	.25
36	Chipper Jones	1.00
37	Jeff Cirillo	.25
38	Robin Ventura	.25
39	Eric Chavez	.35
40	Scott Rolen	.65
41	Phil Nevin	.25
42	Mike Piazza	1.50
43	Jorge Posada	.35
44	Jason Kendall	.25
45	Ivan Rodriguez	.65
46	Frank Thomas	.75
47	Edgar Martinez	.25
48	Darin Erstad	.25
49	Tim Salmon	.35
50	Luis Gonzalez	.25
51	Andruw Jones	.75
52	Carl Everett	.25
53	Manny Ramirez	.75
54	Sammy Sosa	1.50
55	Rondell White	.25
56	Magglio Ordonez	.40
57	Ken Griffey Jr.	1.50
58	Juan Gonzalez	.75
59	Larry Walker	.25
60	Bobby Higginson	.25
61	Cliff Floyd	.25
62	Preston Wilson	.25
63	Moises Alou	.25
64	Lance Berkman	.25
65	Richard Hidalgo	.25
66	Jermaine Dye	.25
67	Mark Quinn	.25
68	Shawn Green	.50
69	Gary Sheffield	.40
70	Jeromy Burnitz	.25
71	Geoff Jenkins	.25
72	Vladimir Guerrero	.75
73	Bernie Williams	.35
74	Johnny Damon	.40
75	Jason Giambi	.60
76	Bobby Abreu	.25
77	Pat Burrell	.50
78	Brian Giles	.25
79	Tony Gwynn	1.00
80	Barry Bonds	2.50
81	J.D. Drew	.40
82	Jim Edmonds	.25
83	Greg Vaughn	.25
84	Raul Mondesi	.25
85	Shannon Stewart	.25
86	Randy Johnson	.75
87	Curt Schilling	.50
88	Tom Glavine	.40
89	Greg Maddux	1.00
90	Pedro Martinez	.75
91	Kerry Wood	.25
92	David Wells	.25
93	Bartolo Colon	.25
94	Mike Hampton	.25
95	Kevin Brown	.25
96	Al Leiter	.25
97	Roger Clemens	1.75
98	Mike Mussina	.25
99	Tim Hudson	.35
100	Kazuhiro Sasaki	.25
101	Ichiro Suzuki RC	35.00
102	Albert Pujols RC	100.00
103	Drew Henson RC	6.00
104	Adam Pettyjohn RC	3.00
105	Adrian Hernandez RC	3.00
106	Andy Morales RC	3.00
107	Tsuyoshi Shinjo RC	3.00
108	Juan Uribe RC	3.00
109	Jack Wilson RC	5.00
110	Jason Smith RC	3.00
111	Junior Spivey RC	4.00
112	Wilson Betemit RC	4.00
113	Elpidio Guzman RC	3.00
114	Esix Snead RC	3.00
115	Winston Abreu RC	3.00
116	Jeremy Owens RC	3.00
117	Jay Gibbons RC	8.00
118	Luis Lopez RC	3.00
119	Ryan Freel RC	4.00
120	Rafael Soriano RC	4.00
121	Johnny Estrada RC	6.00

122	Bud Smith RC	3.00
123	Jackson Melian RC	3.00
124	Matt White RC	3.00
125	Travis Hafner RC	12.00
126	Morgan Ensberg RC	5.00
127	Endy Chavez RC	3.00
128	Bret Prinz RC	3.00
129	Juan Diaz RC	4.00
130	Erick Almonte RC	4.00
131	Rob Mackowiak RC	3.00
132	Carlos Valderrama RC	3.00
133	Wilkin Ruan RC	3.00
134	Angel Berroa RC	5.00
135	Henry Mateo RC	3.00
136	Bill Ortega	3.00
137	Billy Sylvester RC	3.00
138	Andres Torres RC	3.00
139	Nate Frese	3.00
140	Casey Fossum RC	4.00
141	Ricardo Rodriguez RC	3.00
142	Brian Roberts RC	6.00
143	Carlos Garcia RC	3.00
144	Brian Lawrence RC	4.00
145	Cory Aldridge RC	3.00
146	Mark Teixeira RC	25.00
147	Juan Cruz RC	3.00
148	Brandon Duckworth RC	
		3.00
149	Dewon Brazelton RC	3.00
150	Mark Prior RC	20.00

Graded

Mint:	1-1.5X
NrMt+:	.8-1X
NrMt:	.4-.6X

No Multipliers for Gem Mint.

Prominence

Stars (1-100):	5-10X
Production 125	
SP's (101-150):	3-5X
Production 75	

Authority Figures

	NM/M
Complete Set (20):	75.00
Common Card:	2.00
1AF	Mark McGwire, Albert Pujols	8.00
2AF	Kazuhiro Sasaki, Ichiro Suzuki	8.00
3AF	Derek Jeter, Drew Henson	10.00

4AF	Ken Griffey Jr., Jackson Melian	6.00
5AF	Wilson Betemit, Chipper Jones	4.50
6AF	Jeff Bagwell, Morgan Ensberg	4.00
7AF	Cal Ripken Jr., Jay Gibbons	10.00
8AF	Mike Piazza, Tsuyoshi Shinjo	6.00
9AF	Luis Gonzalez, Junior Spivey	2.00
10AF	Barry Bonds, Carlos Valderrama	10.00
11AF	Todd Helton, Juan Uribe	4.00
12AF	Roger Clemens, Adrian Hernandez	5.00
13AF	Alex Rodriguez, Travis Hafner	8.00
14AF	Scott Rolen, Johnny Estrada	3.00
15AF	Brian Giles, Rob Mackowiak	2.00
16AF	Randy Johnson, Bret Prinz	4.00
17AF	Carlos Delgado, Luis Lopez	3.00
18AF	Manny Ramirez, Juan Diaz	4.00
19AF	Mike Sweeney, Endy Chavez	2.00
20AF	Sammy Sosa, Jaisen Randolph	6.00

Diamond Cuts

	NM/M
Common Player:	4.00
Inserted 1:10	
Rick Ankiel/Shoe	4.00
Jeff Bagwell/Jsy	8.00
Adrian Beltre/Hat	4.00
Craig Biggio/Bat	4.00
Barry Bonds/Hat	35.00
Barry Bonds/Jsy	20.00
Barry Bonds/Pants	20.00
Barry Bonds/Shoe	30.00
Barry Bonds/ Wristband/100	50.00
Kevin Brown/Hat	6.00
Kevin Brown/Pants	4.00
Eric Byrnes/Bat	4.00
Sean Casey/Jsy	4.00
Eric Chavez/Hat	6.00
Chipper Jones/Jsy	10.00
Chipper Jones/Bat	10.00
Bartolo Colon/Hat	6.00
Erubiel Durazo/Bat	4.00
Ray Durham/Hat	4.00
Jim Edmonds/Hat	6.00
Jim Edmonds/Shoe	10.00
Darin Erstad/Hat	6.00
Carlos Febles/Bat	4.00
Carlos Febles/Shoe	4.00
Rafael Furcal/Hat	6.00
Juan Gonzalez/ Bat Glv	10.00
Juan Gonzalez/Hat	8.00
Luis Gonzalez	6.00
Shawn Green/ Bat Glv	10.00
Shawn Green/Bat	6.00
Vladimir Guerrero/Bat	8.00
Tony Gwynn/Bat	8.00
Mike Hampton/Hat	5.00
Mike Hampton/Shoe	5.00
Jerry Hairston Jr./Hat	4.00
Jason Hart/Bat	4.00
Todd Helton/Jsy	8.00
Todd Helton/Pants	8.00
Orlando Hernandez/ Bat	4.00
Richard Hidalgo/Bat	4.00
Richard Hidalgo/ Bat Glv	15.00
Derek Jeter/Bat	30.00
Derek Jeter/ Bat Glv	60.00
Derek Jeter/Jsy	30.00
Derek Jeter/Pants	30.00
Derek Jeter/Shoe	40.00
Randy Johnson/Hat	30.00
Andruw Jones/Bat	6.00
Andruw Jones/Hat	8.00
Jason Kendall/Hat	4.00
Barry Larkin/Jsy	5.00
Matt Lawton/Hat	6.00
Mike Lieberthal/ Bat	6.00
Kenny Lofton/Bat	4.00
Edgar Martinez/ Bat Glv	8.00
Pedro Martinez/Shoe	10.00
Raul Mondesi/Bat	4.00
Raul Mondesi/ Bat Glv	6.00
Hideo Nomo/Bat	15.00

	Hideo Nomo/Hat	40.00
	Magglio Ordonez/ Bat Glv	8.00
	Magglio Ordonez/Hat	6.00
	David Ortiz/Bat	4.00
	Rafael Palmeiro/Bat	8.00
	Rafael Palmeiro/Hat	10.00
	Chan Ho Park/Hat	5.00
	Mike Piazza/Bat	15.00
	Mike Piazza/Jsy	15.00
	Mike Piazza/Shoe	25.00
	Albert Pujols/Pants	30.00
	Manny Ramirez/Bat	8.00
	Manny Ramirez/ Bat Glv	15.00
	Manny Ramirez/Hat	15.00
	Cal Ripken Jr./ Bat Glv	65.00
	Cal Ripken Jr./Pants	25.00
	Ivan Rodriguez/ Bat Glv	10.00
	Ivan Rodriguez/Hat	10.00
	Ivan Rodriguez/Pants	8.00
	Ivan Rodriguez/Shoe	10.00
	Scott Rolen/Hat	6.00
	Jared Sandberg/Bat	4.00
	Deion Sanders/Bat	4.00
	Tsuyoshi Shinjo/ Wristband	6.00
	Tsuyoshi Shinjo/Bat	6.00
	J.T. Snow	4.00
	Alfonso Soriano/Hat	20.00
	Ichiro Suzuki/Bat	50.00
	Ichiro Suzuki/Hat	65.00
	Mike Sweeney/Hat	6.00
	Miguel Tejada/Hat	6.00
	Frank Thomas/Bat	8.00
	Frank Thomas/Hat	10.00
	Jim Thome/Bat	6.00
	Larry Walker/Bat	4.00
	Larry Walker/Jsy	4.00
	Bernie Williams/Bat	6.00
	Brian Giles/Pants	5.00

Derek Jeter Monumental Moments

	NM/M
MM4 Derek Jeter/2000	5.00
MM4AU Derek Jeter/ Auto./100	100.00

Derek Jeter Reprint Autographs

	NM/M
1DJRA Derek Jeter/500	90.00

Seal of Approval

	NM/M
Complete Set (15):	45.00
Common Player:	1.50
1SA	Derek Jeter	6.00
2SA	Alex Rodriguez	6.00
3SA	Nomar Garciaparra	4.00
4SA	Cal Ripken Jr.	6.00
5SA	Mike Piazza	4.00
6SA	Mark McGwire	5.00
7SA	Tony Gwynn	3.00
8SA	Barry Bonds	6.00
9SA	Greg Maddux	3.00
10SA	Chipper Jones	3.00
11SA	Roger Clemens	3.50
12SA	Ken Griffey Jr.	4.00
13SA	Vladimir Guerrero	2.00
14SA	Sammy Sosa	4.00
15SA	Todd Helton	1.50

2001 Fleer Boston Red Sox 100th Anniversary

		NM/M
Complete Set (100):		40.00
Common Player:		.25
Pack (5):		6.00
Box (24):		125.00
1	Carl Yastrzemski	2.50
2	Mel Parnell	.25
3	Birdie Tebbetts	.25
4	Tex Hughson	.25
5	Nomar Garciaparra	4.00
6	Fred Lynn	.50
7	John Valentin	.25
8	Rico Petrocelli	.25
9	Ted Williams	5.00
10	Roger Clemens	3.00
11	Luis Aparicio	.40
12	Cy Young	1.50
13	Carlton Fisk	1.00
14	Pedro Martinez	2.00
15	Joe Dobson	.25
16	Babe Ruth	5.00
17	Doc Cramer	.25
18	Pete Runnels	.25
19	Tony Conigliaro	.25
20	Bill Monbouquette	.25
21	Boo Ferriss	.25
22	Harry Hooper	.25
23	Tony Armas	.25
24	Joe Cronin	1.00
25	Rick Ferrell	.25
26	Wade Boggs	2.25
27	Don Baylor	.25
28	Jeff Reardon	.25
29	Smokey Joe Wood	.25
30	Mo Vaughn	.40
31	Walt Dropo	.25
32	Vern Stephens	.25
33	Bernie Carbo	.25
34	George Scott	.25
35	Lefty Grove	1.00
36	Dom DiMaggio	1.00
37	Dennis Eckersley	.75
38	Johnny Pesky	.25
39	Jim Lonborg	.25
40	Jimmy Piersall	.25
41	Tris Speaker	1.50
42	Frank Malzone	.25
43	Bobby Doerr	.75
44	Jimmie Foxx	2.00
45	Tony Pena	.25
46	Billy Goodman	.25
47	Jim Rice	.25
48	Reggie Smith	.25
49	Bill Buckner	.25
50	Earl Wilson	.25
51	Rick Burleson	.25
52	George Kell	.25
53	Dick Radatz	.25
54	Dwight Evans	.25
55	Luis Tiant	.25
56	Elijah "Pumpsie" Green	.25
57	Gene Conley	.25
58	Jackie Jensen	.25
59	Mike Fornieles	.25
60	Dutch Leonard	.25
61	Jake Stahl	.25
62	Don Schwall	.25
63	Jimmy Collins	.25
64	Herb Pennock	.25
65		
66	Carney Lansford	.25
67	Dick Stuart	.25
68	Dave Morehead	.25
69	Harry Agganis	.25
70	Lou Boudreau	.25
71	Joe Morgan	.75
72	Don Zimmer	.75
73	Tom Yawkey	.25
74	Jean Yawkey	.25
75	Origin of the Red Sox	.25
76	First Season	.25
77	World Series History	.25
78	Carl Yastrzemski (Beantown's Best)	1.00
79	Carlton Fisk (Beantown's Best)	.50
80	Dom DiMaggio (Beantown's Best)	.50

81	Wade Boggs (Beantown's Best)	.75
82	Nomar Garciaparra (Beantown's Best)	2.00
83	Pedro Martinez (Beantown's Best)	1.00
84	Ted Williams (Beantown's Best)	2.50
85	Jim Rice (Beantown's Best)	.25
86	Fred Lynn (Beantown's Best)	.25
87	Mo Vaughn (Beantown's Best)	.25
88	Bobby Doerr (Beantown's Best)	.40
89	Bernie Carbo (Beantown's Best)	.25
90	Dennis Eckersley (Beantown's Best)	.35
91	Jimmy Piersall (Beantown's Best)	.25
92	Luis Tiant (Beantown's Best)	.25
93	Jimmy Fund signage (Fenway Through the Years)	.25
94	Green Monster w/Ads (Fenway Through the Years)	.25
95	Green Monster w/All-Star logo (Fenway Through the Years)	.25
96	Ladder shot on Green Monster (Fenway Through the Years)	.25
97	Manual Scoreboard (Fenway Through the Years)	.25
98	Panoramic of Fenway (Fenway Through the Years)	.25
99	Lansdowne St. (Fenway Through the Years)	.25
100	1999 All-Star Game (Fenway Through the Years)	.25

Autograph Caps

Each box of Red Sox 100th Anniversary product includes one fitted, authentically autographed genuine MLB Red Sox cap. A certificate of authentication was included with each cap and each had a Fleer hologram attached.

		NM/M
Complete Set (18):		825.00
Common Player:		15.00
(1)	Wade Boggs	75.00
(2)	Bill Buckner	20.00
(3)	Bernie Carbo	15.00
(4)	Roger Clemens	200.00
(5)	Dom DiMaggio	30.00
(6)	Bobby Doerr	25.00
(7)	Dennis Eckersley	50.00
(8)	Dwight Evans	40.00
(9)	Carlton Fisk	125.00
(10)	Nomar Garciaparra	125.00
(11)	Jim Lonborg	20.00
(12)	Johnny Pesky	15.00
(13)	Rico Petrocelli	20.00
(14)	Jimmy Piersall	30.00
(15)	Jim Rice	40.00
(16)	Luis Tiant	30.00
(17)	Carl Yastrzemski	200.00
(18)	Don Zimmer	30.00

BoSox Sigs

	NM/M
Complete Set (16):	1,000
Common Autograph:	15.00
Inserted 1:96	
Wade Boggs	80.00
Bill Buckner	20.00
Bernie Carbo	15.00
Roger Clemens/100	200.00
Dom DiMaggio	75.00
Bobby Doerr	40.00
Dwight Evans	35.00
Carlton Fisk	80.00
Nomar Garciaparra	100.00
Jim Lonborg	15.00
Fred Lynn	40.00
Rico Petrocelli	15.00
Jim Rice	40.00
Luis Tiant	30.00

Carl Yastrzemski/ 200	180.00

Field the Game

A total of 7,150 exchange cards for Field the Game memorabilia cards was inserted randomly in packs. Collectors exchanging the cards received one of four types of card.

		NM/M
Complete Set (4):		75.00
(1)	Piece of Green Monster outfield wall	20.00
(2)	Piece of base from 100th anniver. game	20.00
(3)	Piece of baseball from 100th anniv. game	20.00
(4)	anniv. game	20.00

Splendid Splinters

	NM/M
Complete Set (15):	20.00
Common Player:	1.00
Inserted 1:10	
SS1	Babe Ruth	6.00
SS2	Dom DiMaggio	1.50
SS3	Carlton Fisk	2.00
SS4	Carl Yastrzemski	3.00
SS5	Nomar Garciaparra	5.00
SS6	Wade Boggs	2.50
SS7	Ted Williams	5.00
SS8	Jim Rice	1.00
SS9	Mo Vaughn	1.00
SS10	Tris Speaker	2.00
SS11	Dwight Evans	1.00
SS12	Jimmie Foxx	2.50
SS13	Bobby Doerr	1.50
SS14	Fred Lynn	1.00
SS15	Johnny Pesky	1.00

Splendid Splinters Game Bat

	NM/M
Complete Set (8):	800.00
Common Player:	15.00
Inserted 1:96	
Babe Ruth/SP/100	400.00
Carl Yastrzemski	75.00
Nomar Garciaparra	30.00
Wade Boggs	25.00
Ted Williams/ SP/100	200.00
Jim Rice	15.00
Dwight Evans	15.00
Jimmie Foxx/ SP/100	200.00

Threads

ABBREVIATIONS
SP - Short Print

Complete Set (9): 400.00
Common Player: 15.00
Inserted 1:96
Wade Boggs 25.00
Roger Clemens 50.00
Dwight Evans 15.00
Carlton Fisk/100 40.00
Pedro Martinez/100 40.00
Jim Rice 20.00
Ted Williams/100 180.00
Carl Yastrzemski 40.00
Don Zimmer 15.00

Yawkey's Heroes

Complete Set (20): 15.00
Common Player: .50
Inserted 1:4
1YH Bobby Doerr .75
2YH Dom DiMaggio 1.00
3YH Jim Rice .50
4YH Wade Boggs 1.50
5YH Carlton Fisk 1.00
6YH Nomar Garciaparra 3.00
7YH Dennis Eckersley 1.00
8YH Carl Yastrzemski 2.00
9YH Ted Williams 4.00
10YH Tony Conigliaro .75
11YH Tony Armas .50
12YH Joe Cronin 1.00
13YH Mo Vaughn .50
14YH Johnny Pesky .50
15YH Jim Lonborg .50
16YH Luis Tiant .50
17YH Tony Pena .50
18YH Dwight Evans .50
19YH Fred Lynn .75
20YH Jimmy Piersall .50

Cal Ripken Jr. Commemoratives

The two "commemorative cards" were produced for sale on a television home shopping program. One card is a reprint of Ripken's 1982 Fleer rookie card, with the addition of a Ripken logo at lower-right. The other is a specially designed and authentically autographed card, horizontal in format, with a game photo of Ripken at right, thre signature at left and the special logo. On back is a statement of authenticity from Fleer, along with a ghost-image portrait photo.

Cal Ripken Jr. (1982 reprint) 10.00
Cal Ripken Jr. (autograph card) 125.00

2001 E-X

Complete Set (130): 150.00
Common Player: .25
Common SP (101-130): 4.00
Production listed
Pack (5): 4.00
Box (24): 80.00
1 Jason Kendall .25
2 Derek Jeter 3.00
3 Greg Vaughn .25
4 Eric Chavez .40
5 Nomar Garciaparra 2.00
6 Roberto Alomar .50
7 Barry Larkin .25
8 Matt Lawton .25
9 Larry Walker .25

10 Chipper Jones 1.50
11 Scott Rolen .75
12 Carlos Lee .25
13 Adrian Beltre .40
14 Ben Grieve .25
15 Mike Sweeney .25
16 John Olerud .25
17 Gabe Kapler .25
18 Brian Giles .25
19 Luis Gonzalez .40
20 Sammy Sosa 2.00
21 Roger Clemens 1.75
22 Vladimir Guerrero 1.00
23 Ken Griffey Jr. 2.00
24 Mark McGwire 2.50
25 Orlando Hernandez .25
26 Shannon Stewart .25
27 Fred McGriff .25
28 Lance Berkman .25
29 Carlos Delgado .75
30 Mike Piazza 2.00
31 Juan Encarnacion .25
32 David Justice .25
33 Greg Maddux 1.50
34 Frank Thomas 1.00
35 Jason Giambi .75
36 Ruben Mateo .25
37 Todd Helton 1.00
38 Jim Edmonds .25
39 Steve Finley .25
40 Tom Glavine .40
41 Mo Vaughn .25
42 Phil Nevin .25
43 Richie Sexson .25
44 Craig Biggio .50
45 Kerry Wood .50
46 Pat Burrell .60
47 Edgar Martinez .25
48 Jim Thome .25
49 Jeff Bagwell 1.00
50 Bernie Williams .45
51 Andruw Jones 1.00
52 Gary Sheffield .40
53 Johnny Damon .40
54 Rondell White .25
55 J.D. Drew .50
56 Tony Batista .25
57 Paul Konerko .25
58 Rafael Palmeiro .75
59 Cal Ripken Jr. 3.00
60 Darin Erstad .60
61 Ivan Rodriguez .75
62 Barry Bonds 3.00
63 Edgardo Alfonzo .25
64 Ellis Burks .25
65 Mike Lieberthal .25
66 Robin Ventura .25
67 Richard Hidalgo .25
68 Magglio Ordonez .40
69 Kazuhiro Sasaki .25
70 Miguel Tejada .50
71 David Wells .25
72 Troy Glaus .50
73 Jose Vidro .25
74 Shawn Green .50
75 Barry Zito .50
76 Jermaine Dye .25
77 Geoff Jenkins .25
78 Jeff Kent .25
79 Al Leiter .25
80 Deivi Cruz .25
81 Eric Karros .25
82 Albert Belle .25
83 Pedro Martinez 1.00
84 Raul Mondesi .25
85 Preston Wilson .25
86 Rafael Furcal .25
87 Rick Ankiel .25
88 Randy Johnson 1.00
89 Kevin Brown .25
90 Sean Casey .35
91 Mike Mussina .50
92 Alex Rodriguez 2.50
93 Andres Galarraga .25
94 Juan Gonzalez 1.00
95 Manny Ramirez 1.00
96 Mark Grace .35
97 Carl Everett .25
98 Tony Gwynn 1.50
99 Mike Hampton .25
100 Ken Caminiti .25
101 Jason Hart/1749 4.00
102 Corey Patterson/1199 5.00
103 Timo Perez/1999 4.00
104 Marcus Giles/1999 4.00

Behind the Numbers Autograph

105 Ichiro Suzuki/1999 RC 50.00
106 Aubrey Huff/1499 8.00

107 Joe Crede/1999 5.00
108 Larry Barnes/1499 4.00
109 Esix Snead/1499 RC 4.00
110 Kenny Kelly/2249 4.00
111 Justin Miller/2249 4.00
112 Jack Cust/1999 4.00
113 Xavier Nady/999 4.00
114 Eric Munson/1499 4.00
115 Elpidio Guzman/1749 RC 4.00
116 Juan Pierre/2189 4.00
117 Winston Abreu/1749 RC 4.00
118 Keith Ginter/1999 4.00
119 Jace Brewer/2699 4.00
120 Paxton Crawford/2249 4.00
121 Jason Tyner/2249 4.00
122 Tike Redman/1999 4.00
123 John Riedling/2499 4.00
124 Jose Ortiz/1499 4.00
125 Oswaldo Mairena/2499 4.00
126 Eric Byrnes/2249 4.00
127 Brian Cole/999 4.00
128 Adam Piatt/2249 4.00
129 Nate Rolison/2499 4.00
130 Keith McDonald/2249 4.00

Base Inks

Random Inserts
Derek Jeter AU/500 110.00

Behind the Numbers

Common Player: 5.00
Inserted 1:33
1BN Johnny Bench 10.00
2BN Wade Boggs 15.00
3BN George Brett 20.00
4BN Lou Brock 5.00
5BN Rollie Fingers 5.00
6BN Carlton Fisk 10.00
7BN Reggie Jackson 10.00
8BN Al Kaline 10.00
10BN Willie McCovey 5.00
11BN Paul Molitor 10.00
12BN Eddie Murray 10.00
13BN Jim Palmer 5.00
14BN Ozzie Smith 15.00
15BN Nolan Ryan 30.00
16BN Mike Schmidt 20.00
17BN Tom Seaver 10.00
18BN Dave Winfield 5.00
19BN Ted Williams 75.00
20BN Robin Yount 10.00
21BN Brady Anderson 5.00
22BN Rick Ankiel 5.00
23BN Albert Belle 5.00
24BN Adrian Beltre 7.50
25BN Barry Bonds 30.00
26BN Eric Chavez 5.00
27BN J.D. Drew 6.00
28BN Darin Erstad 5.00
29BN Troy Glaus 6.00
30BN Mark Grace 6.00
31BN Ben Grieve 5.00
32BN Tony Gwynn 15.00
33BN Todd Helton 10.00
34BN Derek Jeter 30.00
35BN Jeff Kent 5.00
36BN Jason Kendall 5.00
37BN Greg Maddux 15.00
38BN John Olerud 5.00
39BN Cal Ripken Jr. 30.00
40BN Chipper Jones 15.00
41BN John Smoltz 5.00
42BN Frank Thomas 10.00
43BN Robin Ventura 5.00
44BN Bernie Williams 6.00

Quantity produced listed
2BN Wade Boggs/26 150.00
4BN Lou Brock/20 50.00
5BN Rollie Fingers/34 50.00
6BN Carlton Fisk/27 125.00
7BN Reggie Jackson/44 80.00
10BN Willie McCovey/44 80.00
12BN Eddie Murray/33 100.00
13BN Jim Palmer/22 100.00
15BN Nolan Ryan/34 350.00
16BN Mike Schmidt/20 200.00
17BN Tom Seaver/41 80.00
18BN Dave Winfield/31 60.00
20BN Robin Yount/19 180.00
22BN Rick Ankiel/66 20.00
23BN Albert Belle/88 20.00
24BN Adrian Beltre/29 25.00
25BN Barry Bonds/25 250.00
28BN Darin Erstad/17 30.00
29BN Troy Glaus/25 80.00
30BN Mark Grace/17 80.00
32BN Tony Gwynn/19 150.00
33BN Todd Helton/17 125.00
35BN Jeff Kent/21 50.00
36BN Jason Kendall/18 40.00
37BN Greg Maddux/31 250.00
41BN John Smoltz/29 40.00
42BN Frank Thomas/35 75.00
44BN Bernie Williams/51 75.00

Derek Jeter Monumental Moments

2DJMM Derek Jeter (Edition of 1,996.) 5.00
2DJMM Derek Jeter (Autographed edition of 96.) 80.00

Essential Credentials

Stars (1-100): 3-6X
Production 299
Common (101-130): 10.00
Minor Stars (101-130): 15.00
Production 29

E-Xtra Innings

Complete Set (10): 30.00
Common Player: 2.00
Inserted 1:20 R
1XI Mark McGwire 5.00
2XI Sammy Sosa 4.00
3XI Chipper Jones 4.00
4XI Mike Piazza 4.00
5XI Cal Ripken Jr. 6.00
6XI Ken Griffey Jr. 6.00
7XI Alex Rodriguez 5.00
8XI Vladimir Guerrero 4.00
9XI Nomar Garciaparra 4.00
10XI Derek Jeter 6.00

Prospects Autograph

Common Autograph: 8.00
Prod. #'s listed
101 Jason Hart/250 8.00
102 Corey Patterson/800 15.00
103 Timoniel Perez/1000 8.00
104 Marcus Giles/500 10.00
106 Aubrey Huff/500 15.00
107 Joe Crede/500 10.00
108 Larry Barnes/500 8.00
109 Esix Snead/500 8.00
110 Kenny Kelly/250 8.00
111 Justin Miller/250 8.00
112 Jack Cust/1000 8.00
113 Xavier Nady/1000 10.00
114 Eric Munson/1500 8.00
115 Elpidio Guzman/250 8.00
116 Juan Pierre/810 10.00
117 Winston Abreu/250 8.00
118 Keith Ginter/500 8.00
119 Jace Brewer/300 8.00
120 Paxton Crawford/250 8.00
121 Jason Tyner/250 8.00
122 Tike Redman/500 8.00
123 John Riedling/500 8.00
124 Jose Ortiz/500 8.00
125 Oswaldo Mairena/500 8.00
126 Eric Byrnes/250 8.00
127 Brian Cole/2000 8.00
128 Adam Piatt/250 8.00
129 Nate Rolison/250 8.00
130 Keith McDonald/250 8.00

Wall of Fame

Common Player: 4.00
Inserted 1:24
1WF Robin Yount 8.00
2WF Paul Molitor 8.00
3WF Geoff Jenkins 4.00
4WF Mark McGwire 15.00
5WF Sammy Sosa 12.00
6WF Greg Maddux 10.00
7WF Mike Piazza 12.00
8WF Cal Ripken Jr. 20.00
9WF Todd Helton 8.00
10WF Ken Griffey Jr. 12.00
11WF Alex Rodriguez 15.00
12WF Vladimir Guerrero 8.00
13WF Jeff Bagwell 8.00
14WF Ivan Rodriguez 6.00
15WF Juan Gonzalez 8.00
16WF Barry Bonds 20.00
17WF Derek Jeter 20.00
18WF Chipper Jones 10.00
19WF Frank Thomas 8.00
20WF Tony Gwynn 10.00
21WF Nomar Garciaparra 12.00
22WF Manny Ramirez 8.00
23WF Andruw Jones 8.00
24WF Scott Rolen 6.00
25WF Jason Kendall 4.00
26WF Roger Clemens 15.00
27WF Troy Glaus 6.00
28WF Pedro Martinez 8.00
29WF Jason Giambi 5.00
30WF Pat Burrell 5.00

2001 Fleer Focus

Complete Set (240): 140.00
Common Player: .15
Common Prospect (201-224): 3.00
Common Prospect (225-250): 3.00
Pack (10): 2.50
Box (10): 50.00
1 Derek Jeter 2.00
2 Manny Ramirez .75
3 Ken Griffey Jr. 1.25
4 Ken Caminiti .15

5 Joe Randa .15
6 Jason Kendall .15
7 Ron Coomer .15
8 Rondell White .15
9 Tino Martinez .15
10 Nomar Garciaparra 1.25
11 Tony Batista .15
12 Todd Stottlemyre .15
13 Ryan Klesko .15
14 Darin Erstad .50
15 Todd Walker .15
16 Al Leiter .15
17 Carl Everett .15
18 Bobby Abreu .15
19 Raul Mondesi .15
20 Vladimir Guerrero .75
21 Mike Bordick .15
22 Aaron Sele .15
23 Ray Lankford .15
24 Roger Clemens 1.00
25 Kevin Young .15
26 Brad Radke .15
27 Todd Hundley .15
28 Ellis Burks .15
29 Lee Stevens .15
30 Eric Karros .15
31 Darren Dreifort .15
32 Ivan Rodriguez .60
33 Pedro Martinez .75
34 Travis Fryman .15
35 Garret Anderson .15
36 Rafael Palmeiro .60
37 Jason Giambi .50
38 Jeromy Burnitz .15
39 Robin Ventura .15
40 Derek Bell .15
41 Carlos Guillen .15
42 Albert Belle .15
43 Henry Rodriguez .15
44 Brian Jordan .15
45 Mike Sweeney .15
46 Ruben Rivera .15
47 Greg Maddux 1.00
48 Corey Koskie .15
49 Sandy Alomar Jr. .15
50 Mike Mussina .40
51 Tom Glavine .25
52 Aaron Boone .15
53 Frank Thomas .75
54 Kenny Lofton .15
55 Danny Graves .15
56 Jose Valentin .15
57 Travis Lee .15
58 Jim Edmonds .15
59 Jim Thome .15
60 Steve Finley .15
61 Shawn Green .45
62 Lance Berkman .15
63 Mark Quinn .15
64 Randy Johnson .75
65 Dmitri Young .15
66 Andy Pettitte .25
67 Paul O'Neill .15
68 Gil Heredia .15
69 Russell Branyan .15
70 Alex Rodriguez 1.50
71 Geoff Jenkins .15
72 Eric Chavez .25
73 Cal Ripken Jr. 2.00
74 Mark Kotsay .15
75 Jeff D'Amico .15
76 Tony Womack .15
77 Eric Milton .15
78 Joe Girardi .15
79 Peter Bergeron .15
80 Miguel Tejada .25
81 Luis Gonzalez .25
82 Doug Glanville .15
83 Gerald Williams .15
84 Troy O'Leary .15
85 Brian Giles .15
86 Miguel Cairo .15
87 Magglio Ordonez .25
88 Rick Helling .15
89 Bruce Chen .15
90 Jason Varitek .15
91 Mike Lieberthal .15
92 Shawn Estes .15
93 Rick Ankiel .25
94 Tim Salmon .25
95 Jacque Jones .15
96 Johnny Damon .25
97 Larry Walker .15
98 Ruben Mateo .15
99 Brad Fullmer .15
100 Edgardo Alfonzo .15
101 Mark Mulder .15
102 Tony Gwynn 1.00

103 Mike Cameron .15
104 Richie Sexson .15
105 Barry Larkin .15
106 Mike Piazza 1.25
107 Eric Young .15
108 Edgar Renteria .15
109 Todd Zeile .15
110 Luis Castillo .15
111 Sammy Sosa 1.25
112 David Justice .15
113 Delino DeShields .15
114 Mariano Rivera .25
115 Edgar Martinez .15
116 Ray Durham .15
117 Brady Anderson .15
118 Eric Owens .15
119 Alex Gonzalez .15
120 Jay Buhner .15
121 Greg Vaughn .15
122 Mike Lowell .15
123 Marquis Grissom .15
124 Matt Williams .15
125 Dean Palmer .15
126 Troy Glaus .75
127 Bret Boone .15
128 David Ortiz .25
129 Glenallen Hill .15
130 Chipper Jones 1.00
131 Tony Clark .15
132 Terrence Long .15
133 Chuck Finley .15
134 Jeff Bagwell .75
135 J.T. Snow .15
136 Andruw Jones .75
137 Carlos Delgado .50
138 Mo Vaughn .15
139 Derek Lee .15
140 Bobby Estalella .15
141 Kerry Wood .60
142 Jose Vidro .15
143 Ben Grieve .15
144 Barry Bonds 2.00
145 Javy Lopez .15
146 Adam Kennedy .15
147 Jeff Cirillo .15
148 Cliff Floyd .15
149 Carl Pavano .25
150 Bobby Higginson .15
151 Kevin Brown .15
152 Fernando Tatis .15
153 Matt Lawton .15
154 Damion Easley .15
155 Curt Schilling .25
156 Mark McGwire 1.50
157 Mark Grace .25
158 Adrian Beltre .30
159 Jorge Posada .25
160 Richard Hidalgo .15
161 Vinny Castilla .15
162 Bernie Williams .30
163 John Olerud .15
164 Todd Helton .75
165 Craig Biggio .15
166 David Wells .15
167 Phil Nevin .15
168 Andres Galarraga .15
169 Moises Alou .15
170 Denny Neagle .15
171 Jeffrey Hammonds .15
172 Sean Casey .30
173 Gary Sheffield .40
174 Carlos Lee .15
175 Juan Encarnacion .15
176 Roberto Alomar .40
177 Kenny Rogers .15
178 Charles Johnson .15
179 Shannon Stewart .15
180 B.J. Surhoff .15
181 Paul Konerko .15
182 Jermaine Dye .15
183 Scott Rolen .60
184 Fred McGriff .15
185 Juan Gonzalez .75
186 Carlos Beltran .40
187 Jay Payton .15
188 Chad Hermansen .15
189 Pat Burrell .50
190 Omar Vizquel .15
191 Trot Nixon .15
192 Mike Hampton .15
193 Kris Benson .15
194 Gabe Kapler .15
195 Rickey Henderson .75
196 J.D. Drew .45
197 Pokey Reese .15
198 Jeff Kent .15
199 Jose Cruz Jr. .15
200 Preston Wilson .15
201 Eric Munson 2,499 (Prospects) 3.00
202 Alex Cabrera 2,499 (Prospects) 3.00
203 Nate Rolison 2,499 (Prospects) 3.00
204 Julio Zuleta 2,499 (Prospects) 3.00
205 Chris Richard 2,499 (Prospects) 3.00
206 Dernell Stenson 2,499 (Prospects) 3.00
207 Aaron McNeal 2,499 (Prospects) 3.00
208 Aubrey Huff 2,999 (Prospects) 5.00
209 Mike Lamb 2,999 (Prospects) 3.00
210 Xavier Nady 2,999 (Prospects) 4.00

211 Joe Crede 2,999 (Prospects) 4.00
212 Ben Petrick 3,499 (Prospects) 3.00
213 Morgan Burkhart 3,499 (Prospects) 3.00
214 Jason Tyner 1,999 (Prospects) 3.00
215 Juan Pierre 1,999 (Prospects) 5.00
216 Adam Dunn 1,999 (Prospects) 5.00
117 Adam Piatt 1,999 (Prospects) 3.00
218 Eric Byrnes 1,999 (Prospects) 4.00
219 Corey Patterson 1,999 (Prospects) 4.00
220 Kenny Kelly 1,999 (Prospects) 3.00
221 Tike Redman 1,999 (Prospects) 3.00
222 Luis Matos 1,999 (Prospects) 4.00
223 Timoniel Perez 1,999 (Prospects) 3.00
224 Vernon Wells 1,999 (Prospects) 3.00
225 Barry Zito 4,999 (Prospects) 5.00
226 Adam Bernero 4,999 (Prospects) 3.00
227 Kazuhiro Sasaki 4,999 (Prospects) 6.00
228 Oswaldo Mairena 4,999 (Prospects) 3.00
229 Mark Buehrle 4,999 (Prospects) 4.00
230 Ryan Dempster 4,999 (Prospects) 3.00
231 Tim Hudson 4,999 (Prospects) 5.00
232 Scott Downs 4,999 (Prospects) 3.00
233 A.J. Burnett 4,999 (Prospects) 4.00
234 Adam Eaton 4,999 (Prospects) 3.00
235 Paxton Crawford 4,999 (Prospects) 3.00
236 Jace Brewer 3,999 (Prospects) 3.00
237 Jose Ortiz 3,999 (Prospects) 3.00
238 Rafael Furcal 3,999 (Prospects) 4.00
239 Julio Lugo 3,999 (Prospects) 3.00
240 Tomas de la Rosa 3,999 (Prospects) 3.00

Green

NM/M
Common Player: 1.00
Random inserts in packs.
Stated print runs listed below.
1 Derek Jeter/339 10.00
2 Manny Ramirez/351 4.00
3 Ken Griffey Jr./271 8.00
4 Ken Caminiti/303 1.00
5 Joe Randa/304 1.00
6 Jason Kendall/270 1.50
7 Ron Coomer/270 1.00
8 Rondell White/258 1.50
9 Tino Martinez/258 2.00
10 Nomar Garciaparra/372 10.00
11 Tony Batista/263 1.00
12 Todd Stottlemyre/491 1.00
13 Ryan Klesko/283 1.50
14 Darin Erstad/355 1.50
15 Todd Walker/290 1.00
16 Al Leiter/320 1.00
17 Carl Everett/300 1.00
18 Bobby Abreu/316 1.50
19 Raul Mondesi/271 1.00
20 Vladimir Guerrero/345 5.00
21 Mike Bordick/285 1.00
22 Aaron Sele/451 1.00
23 Ray Lankford/253 1.00
24 Roger Clemens/370 10.00
25 Kevin Young/258 1.00
26 Brad Radke/445 1.00
27 Todd Hundley/284 1.00
28 Ellis Burks/344 1.00
29 Lee Stevens/265 1.00
30 Eric Karros/250 1.00

31 Darren Dreifort/416 1.00
32 Ivan Rodriguez/347 4.00
33 Pedro Martinez/174 5.00
34 Travis Fryman/321 1.50
35 Garret Anderson/286 2.00
36 Rafael Palmeiro/285 2.00
37 Jason Giambi/333 5.00
38 Jeromy Burnitz/232 1.00
39 Robin Ventura/232 1.50
40 Derek Bell/266 1.00
41 Carlos Guillen/257 1.00
42 Albert Belle/281 1.00
43 Henry Rodriguez/256 1.00
44 Brian Jordan/264 1.00
45 Mike Sweeney/333 1.00
46 Ruben Rivera/208 1.00
47 Greg Maddux/300 8.00
48 Corey Koskie/300 1.00
49 Sandy Alomar Jr./289 1.00
50 Mike Mussina/379 3.00
51 Tom Glavine/340 2.00
52 Aaron Boone/285 1.00
53 Frank Thomas/328 4.00
54 Kenny Lofton/278 2.00
55 Danny Graves/256 1.00
56 Jose Valentin/273 1.00
57 Travis Lee/235 1.00
58 Jim Edmonds/295 2.00
59 Jim Thome/269 4.00
60 Steve Finley/280 1.00
61 Shawn Green/269 2.00
62 Lance Berkman/297 2.00
63 Mark Quinn/294 1.00
64 Randy Johnson/264 5.00
65 Dmitri Young/303 1.00
66 Andy Pettitte/435 2.00
67 Paul O'Neill/283 2.00
68 Gil Heredia/412 1.00
69 Russell Branyan/238 1.00
70 Alex Rodriguez/316 10.00
71 Geoff Jenkins/303 1.50
72 Eric Chavez/277 2.00
73 Cal Ripken Jr./256 15.00
74 Mark Kotsay/298 1.00
75 Jeff D'Amico/266 1.00
76 Tony Womack/271 1.00
77 Eric Milton/486 1.00
78 Joe Girardi/278 1.00
79 Peter Bergeron/245 1.00
80 Miguel Tejada/275 2.00
81 Luis Gonzalez/311 2.00
82 Doug Glanville/275 1.00
83 Gerald Williams/274 1.00
84 Troy O'Leary/261 1.00
85 Brian Giles/315 2.00
86 Miguel Cairo/261 1.00
87 Magglio Ordonez/315 2.00
88 Rick Helling/448 1.00
89 Bruce Chen/329 1.00
90 Jason Varitek/248 1.00
91 Mike Lieberthal/278 1.00
92 Shawn Estes/426 1.00
93 Rick Ankiel/350 1.00
94 Tim Salmon/290 2.00
95 Jacque Jones/285 1.00
96 Johnny Damon/327 1.50
97 Larry Walker/309 2.00
98 Ruben Mateo/291 1.00
99 Brad Fullmer/295 1.00
100 Edgardo Alfonzo/324 1.00
101 Mark Mulder/544 2.00
102 Tony Gwynn/323 5.00
103 Mike Cameron/267 1.00
104 Richie Sexson/272 1.00
105 Barry Larkin/313 2.00
106 Mike Piazza/324 8.00
107 Eric Young/297 1.00
108 Edgar Renteria/278 1.00
109 Todd Zeile/268 1.00
110 Luis Castillo/334 1.00
111 Sammy Sosa/320 10.00
112 David Justice/286 1.50
113 Delino DeShields/296 1.00
114 Mariano Rivera/285 1.00
115 Edgar Martinez/324 2.00
116 Ray Durham/280 1.00
117 Brady Anderson/257 1.00
118 Eric Owens/293 1.00
119 Alex Gonzalez/252 1.00
120 Jay Buhner/253 1.00
121 Greg Vaughn/254 1.00
122 Mike Lowell/270 1.00
123 Marquis Grissom/244 1.00
124 Matt Williams/257 1.50
125 Dean Palmer/256 1.00
126 Troy Glaus/284 3.00
127 Bret Boone/251 1.50
128 David Ortiz/282 1.00
129 Glenallen Hill/293 1.00
130 Chipper Jones/311 8.00
131 Tony Clark/274 1.00
132 Terrence Long/288 1.00
133 Chuck Finley/417 1.00
134 Jeff Bagwell/310 4.00
135 J.T. Snow/284 1.00
136 Andruw Jones/303 3.00
137 Carlos Delgado/344 2.00
138 Mo Vaughn/272 1.50
139 Derek Lee/281 1.00
140 Bobby Estalella/234 1.00
141 Kerry Wood/480 3.00
142 Jose Vidro/330 1.00
143 Ben Grieve/279 1.00
144 Barry Bonds/306 12.00
145 Javy Lopez/287 2.00
146 Adam Kennedy/266 1.00
147 Jeff Cirillo/326 1.00
148 Cliff Floyd/300 1.00

149 Carl Pavano/306 1.00
150 Bobby Higginson/300 1.00
151 Kevin Brown/258 2.00
152 Fernando Tatis/253 1.00
153 Matt Lawton/305 1.00
154 Damion Easley/259 1.00
155 Curt Schilling/381 3.00
156 Mark McGwire/305 10.00
157 Mark Grace/280 2.50
158 Adrian Beltre/290 1.00
159 Jorge Posada/287 2.00
160 Richard Hidalgo/314 1.00
161 Vinny Castilla/221 1.00
162 Bernie Williams/307 3.00
163 John Olerud/285 1.50
164 Todd Helton/372 4.00
165 Craig Biggio/268 1.50
166 David Wells/411 1.00
167 Phil Nevin/303 1.00
168 Andres Galarraga/302 1.00
169 Moises Alou/355 1.00
170 Denny Neagle/452 1.00
171 Jeffrey Hammonds/335 1.00
172 Sean Casey/315 1.00
173 Gary Sheffield/325 2.00
174 Carlos Lee/301 1.00
175 Juan Encarnacion/289 1.00
176 Roberto Alomar/310 3.00
177 Kenny Rogers/455 1.00
178 Charles Johnson/304 1.00
179 Shannon Stewart/319 1.00
180 B.J. Surhoff/291 1.00
181 Paul Konerko/298 1.00
182 Jermaine Dye/321 1.00
183 Scott Rolen/298 4.00
184 Fred McGriff/277 2.00
185 Juan Gonzalez/289 4.00
186 Carlos Beltran/247 1.50
187 Jay Payton/291 1.50
188 Chad Hermansen/185 1.00
189 Pat Burrell/260 3.00
190 Omar Vizquel/287 1.00
191 Trot Nixon/276 1.00
192 Mike Hampton/314 1.00
193 Kris Benson/385 1.00
194 Gabe Kapler/302 1.00
195 Rickey Henderson/233 3.00
196 J.D. Drew/295 2.00
197 Pokey Reese/255 1.00
198 Jeff Kent/334 1.50
199 Jose Cruz Jr./242 1.00
200 Preston Wilson/264 1.00
201 Eric Munson/252 1.00
202 Alex Cabrera/263 1.00
203 Nate Rolison/77 1.00
204 Julio Zuleta/294 1.00
205 Chris Richard/265 1.00
206 Dernell Stenson/268 1.00
207 Aaron McNeal/310 1.00
208 Aubrey Huff/287 1.00
209 Mike Lamb/278 1.00
210 Joe Crede/357 2.00
211 Ben Petrick/322 2.00
212 Morgan Burkhart/288 1.00
213 Jason Tyner/226 1.00
214 Juan Pierre/310 3.00
215 Adam Dunn/281 4.00
216 Adam Piatt/299 1.00
217 Eric Byrnes/300 1.00
218 Corey Patterson/167 2.00
219 Kenny Kelly/252 1.00
220 Tike Redman/333 1.00
221 Luis Matos/225 1.00
222 Timo Perez/286 1.00
223 Vernon Wells/243 2.00
224 Barry Zito/272 3.00
225 Adam Bernero/419 1.00
226 Kazuhiro Sasaki/316 1.00
227 Oswaldo Mairena/18 5.00
228 Mark Buehrle/421 1.50
229 Ryan Dempster/366 1.00
230 Tim Hudson/414 2.00
231 Scott Downs/529 1.00
232 A.J. Burnett/479 1.00
233 Adam Eaton/413 1.00
234 Paxton Crawford/341 1.00
235 Jose Ortiz/182 1.00
236 Rafael Furcal/295 1.00
237 Julio Lugo/283 1.00
238 Tomas De La Rosa/288 1.00

2001 Fleer Focus Autographics

NM/M
Common Player: 5.00
Inserted 1:72
Silvers: 1-1.5X
Production 250 Sets
Golds: 1-1.5X
Production 50 Sets
Roberto Alomar 30.00
Rick Ankiel 5.00
Albert Belle 5.00
Adrian Beltre 15.00

Lance Berkman 8.00
Barry Bonds 200.00
Jeromy Burnitz 5.00
Pat Burrell 10.00
Sean Casey 8.00
Eric Chavez 10.00
Carlos Delgado 10.00
J.D. Drew 10.00
Jermaine Dye 5.00
Jim Edmonds 10.00
Troy Glaus 15.00
Ben Grieve 5.00
Tony Gwynn 30.00
Randy Johnson 40.00
Chipper Jones 40.00
Mike Lamb 5.00
Mike Lieberthal 5.00
Terrence Long 5.00
Greg Maddux 50.00
Edgar Martinez 15.00
Kevin Millwood 5.00
Mike Mussina 25.00
Corey Patterson 10.00
Jay Payton 8.00
Juan Pierre 5.00
Brad Radke 5.00
Scott Rolen 20.00
Gary Sheffield 15.00
Fernando Tatis 5.00
Robin Ventura 5.00
Kerry Wood 20.00

Bat Company

NM/M
Complete Set (10): 25.00
Common Player: 1.00
Inserted 1:24
1 Barry Bonds 5.00
2 Mark McGwire 4.00
3 Sammy Sosa 3.00
4 Ken Griffey Jr. 3.00
5 Mike Piazza 3.00
6 Derek Jeter 5.00
7 Gary Sheffield 1.50
8 Frank Thomas 1.50
9 Chipper Jones 2.00
10 Alex Rodriguez 4.00

Big Innings

NM/M
Complete Set (25): 15.00
Common Player: .50
Inserted 1:6
VIP: 5-10X
Production 50 Sets
1 Rick Ankiel .50
2 Andruw Jones .50
3 Brian Giles .50
4 Derek Jeter 4.00
5 Rafael Furcal .50
6 Richie Sexson .50
7 Jay Payton .50
8 Carlos Delgado .75
9 Jermaine Dye .50
10 Darin Erstad .75
11 Pat Burrell .75
12 Richard Hidalgo .50
13 Adrian Beltre .60
14 Todd Helton .75
15 Vladimir Guerrero 1.00
16 Nomar Garciaparra 2.00
17 Gabe Kapler .50
18 Carlos Lee .50
19 J.D. Drew .60
20 Troy Glaus 1.00
21 Scott Rolen 1.00
22 Alex Rodriguez 3.00
23 Magglio Ordonez .60
24 Miguel Tejada .60
25 Ruben Mateo .50

Diamond Vision

NM/M
Complete Set (15): 25.00
Common Player: 1.00

Inserted 1:12
1 Derek Jeter 4.00
2 Nomar Garciaparra 2.50
3 Cal Ripken Jr. 4.00
4 Jeff Bagwell 1.50
5 Mark McGwire 3.00
6 Ken Griffey Jr. 2.50
7 Pedro Martinez 1.50
8 Carlos Delgado 1.00
9 Chipper Jones 2.00
10 Barry Bonds 4.00
11 Mike Piazza 2.50
12 Sammy Sosa 2.50
13 Alex Rodriguez 3.00
14 Frank Thomas 1.50
15 Randy Johnson 1.50

Feel the Game

NM/M
Common Player: 5.00
Inserted 1:72
Moises Alou 6.00
Brady Anderson 5.00
Dante Bichette 5.00
Jermaine Dye 5.00
Brian Giles 5.00
Juan Gonzalez 10.00
Rickey Henderson 15.00
Javy Lopez 6.00
Tino Martinez 6.00
Phil Nevin 5.00
Matt Stairs 5.00
Shannon Stewart 5.00
Jose Vidro 5.00

ROY Collection

NM/M
Complete Set (25): 75.00
Common Player: 2.00
Inserted 1:24
1 Luis Aparicio 2.00
2 Johnny Bench 3.00
3 Joe Black 2.00
4 Rod Carew 2.00
5 Orlando Cepeda 2.00
6 Carlton Fisk 2.00
7 Ben Grieve 2.00
8 Frank Howard 2.00
9 Derek Jeter 10.00
10 Fred Lynn 2.00
11 Willie Mays 8.00
12 Willie McCovey 2.00
13 Mark McGwire 8.00
14 Raul Mondesi 2.00
15 Thurman Munson 4.00
16 Eddie Murray 2.00
17 Mike Piazza 6.00
18 Cal Ripken Jr. 10.00
19 Frank Robinson 2.00
20 Jackie Robinson 8.00
21 Scott Rolen 2.00
22 Tom Seaver 2.00
23 Fernando Valenzuela 2.00
24 David Justice 2.00
25 Billy Williams 2.00

ROY Collection Memorabilia

NM/M
Common Player: 8.00
Inserted 1:288
1 Luis Aparicio/Bat 8.00
2 Johnny Bench/Jsy 15.00
3 Orlando Cepeda/Bat 8.00
4 Carlton Fisk/Jsy 10.00
5 Ben Grieve/Bat 8.00
6 Frank Howard/Bat 8.00
7 Derek Jeter/Jsy 50.00
8 Fred Lynn/Bat 8.00
9 Willie Mays/Jsy 60.00
10 Willie McCovey/Bat 8.00
11 Mark McGwire/Ball 50.00
12 Raul Mondesi/Bat 8.00

13	Thurman Munson/Bat	25.00
14	Eddie Murray/Jsy	10.00
15	Mike Piazza/Base	.75
16	Cal Ripken/Jsy	50.00
17	Frank Robinson/Base	10.00
18	Jackie Robinson/Jsy	75.00
19	Scott Rolen/Bat	15.00
20	Tom Seaver/Jsy	15.00
22	David Justice/Jsy	8.00

ROY Collection Signed Memorabilia

NM/M

Common Player:		25.00
1	Luis Aparicio/Jsy/56	40.00
2	Johnny Bench/68	85.00
3	Orlando Cepeda/58	25.00
4	Carlton Fisk/72	50.00
5	Ben Grieve/98	15.00
6	Frank Howard/60	25.00
7	Derek Jeter/96	200.00
8	Fred Lynn/75	25.00
9	Willie Mays/Jsy/51	200.00
10	Willie McCovey/Bat/59	40.00
11	Raul Mondesi/94	25.00
12	Eddie Murray/77	50.00
13	Cal Ripken/82	275.00
14	Frank Robinson/Bat/225	50.00
15	Scott Rolen/97	50.00
16	Tom Seaver/67	90.00
18	David Justice/90	25.00

2001 Fleer Futures

NM/M

Complete Set (220):		20.00
Common Player:		.15
Pack (8):		1.50
Box (28):		30.00
1	Darin Erstad	.60
2	Manny Ramirez	.75
3	Darryl Kile	.15
4	Troy O'Leary	.15
5	Mark Quinn	.15
6	Brian Giles	.15
7	Randy Johnson	.75
8	Todd Walker	.15
9	Mike Piazza	1.50
10	Fred McGriff	.15
11	Sammy Sosa	1.50
12	Chan Ho Park	.15
13	John Rocker	.15
14	Luis Castillo	.15
15	Eric Chavez	.25
16	Carlos Delgado	.50
17	Sean Casey	.25
18	Corey Koskie	.15
19	John Olerud	.15
20	Nomar Garciaparra	1.50
21	Craig Biggio	.15
22	Pat Burrell	.40
23	Bengie Molina	.15
24	Jim Thome	.15
25	Rey Ordonez	.15
26	Fernando Tatis	.15
27	Eric Young	.15
28	Eric Karros	.15
29	Adam Eaton	.15
30	Brian Jordan	.15
31	Jorge Posada	.25
32	Gabe Kapler	.15
33	Keith Foulke	.15
34	Ron Coomer	.15
35	Chipper Jones	1.00
36	Miguel Tejada	.25
37	David Wells	.15
38	Carlos Lee	.15
39	Barry Bonds	2.50
40	Derrek Lee	.15
41	Tim Hudson	.25
42	Billy Koch	.15
43	Dmitri Young	.15
44	Vladimir Guerrero	.75
45	Rickey Henderson	.75

46	Jeff Bagwell	.75
47	Robert Person	.15
48	Brady Anderson	.15
49	Lance Berkman	.15
50	Mike Lieberthal	.15
51	Adam Kennedy	.15
52	Russ Branyan	.15
53	Robin Ventura	.15
54	Mark McGwire	2.00
55	Tony Gwynn	1.00
56	Matt Williams	.15
57	Jeff Cirillo	.15
58	Roger Clemens	1.25
59	Ivan Rodriguez	.65
60	Brad Radke	.15
61	Kazuhiro Sasaki	.15
62	Cal Ripken Jr.	2.50
63	Ken Caminiti	.15
64	Bobby Abreu	.15
65	Troy Glaus	.75
66	Sandy Alomar Jr.	.15
67	Jose Vidro	.15
68	Pedro Martinez	.75
69	Kevin Young	.15
70	Jay Bell	.15
71	Larry Walker	.15
72	Derek Jeter	2.50
73	Miguel Cairo	.15
74	Magglio Ordonez	.15
75	Jeromy Burnitz	.15
76	J.T. Snow	.15
77	Andres Galarraga	.15
78	Ryan Dempster	.15
79	Ken Griffey Jr.	1.50
80	Aaron Sele	.15
81	Tom Glavine	.25
82	Hideo Nomo	.65
83	Orlando Hernandez	.15
84	Tony Batista	.15
85	Aaron Boone	.15
86	Jacque Jones	.15
87	Delino DeShields	.15
88	Garret Anderson	.15
89	Fernando Seguignol	.15
90	Jim Edmonds	.15
91	Frank Thomas	.75
92	Adrian Beltre	.30
93	Ellis Burks	.15
94	Andruw Jones	.75
95	Tony Clark	.15
96	Danny Graves	.15
97	Alex Rodriguez	2.00
98	Mike Mussina	.40
99	Scott Elarton	.15
100	Jason Giambi	.50
101	Jay Payton	.15
102	Gerald Williams	.15
103	Kerry Wood	.50
104	Shawn Green	.35
105	Greg Maddux	1.00
106	Juan Encarnacion	.15
107	Bernie Williams	.30
108	Mike Lamb	.15
109	Charles Johnson	.15
110	Richie Sexson	.15
111	Jeff Kent	.15
112	Albert Belle	.15
113	Cliff Floyd	.15
114	Ben Grieve	.15
115	Tim Salmon	.25
116	Carl Pavano	.15
117	Rick Ankiel	.15
118	Dante Bichette	.15
119	Johnny Damon	.30
120	Brian Anderson	.15
121	Roberto Alomar	.40
122	Mike Hampton	.15
123	Greg Vaughn	.15
124	Carl Everett	.15
125	Moises Alou	.15
126	Jason Kendall	.15
127	Omar Vizquel	.15
128	Mark Grace	.25
129	Kevin Brown	.15
130	Phil Nevin	.15
131	Kevin Millwood	.15
132	Bobby Higginson	.15
133	Ruben Mateo	.15
134	Luis Gonzalez	.25
135	Dean Palmer	.15
136	Mariano Rivera	.25
137	Rick Helling	.15
138	Paul Konerko	.15
139	Marquis Grissom	.15
140	Robb Nen	.15
141	Javy Lopez	.15
142	Preston Wilson	.15
143	Terrence Long	.15
144	Shannon Stewart	.15
145	Barry Larkin	.15
146	Cristian Guzman	.15
147	Jay Buhner	.15
148	Jermaine Dye	.15
149	Kris Benson	.15
150	Curt Schilling	.40
151	Todd Helton	.75
152	Paul O'Neill	.15
153	Rafael Palmeiro	.65
154	Ray Durham	.15
155	Geoff Jenkins	.15
156	Livan Hernandez	.15
157	Rafael Furcal	.15
158	Juan Gonzalez	.15
159	Tino Martinez	.15
160	Raul Mondesi	.15
161	Matt Lawton	.15
162	Edgar Martinez	.15
163	Richard Hidalgo	.15

164	Scott Rolen	.65
165	Chuck Finley	.15
166	Edgardo Alfonzo	.15
167	J.D. Drew	.35
168	Trot Nixon	.15
169	Carlos Beltran	.50
170	Ryan Klesko	.15
171	Mo Vaughn	.15
172	Kenny Lofton	.15
173	Al Leiter	.15
174	Rondell White	.15
175	Mike Sweeney	.15
176	Trevor Hoffman	.15
177	Steve Finley	.15
178	Jeffrey Hammonds	.15
179	David Justice	.15
180	Gary Sheffield	.40
181	Eric Munson (Bright Futures)	.15
182	Luis Matos (Bright Futures)	.15
183	Alex Cabrera (Bright Futures)	.15
184	Randy Keisler (Bright Futures)	.15
185	Nate Rolison (Bright Futures)	.15
186	Jason Hart (Bright Futures)	.15
187	Timo Perez (Bright Futures)	.15
188	Adam Bernero (Bright Futures)	.15
189	Barry Zito (Bright Futures)	.50
190	Ryan Kohlmeier (Bright Futures)	.15
191	Joey Nation (Bright Futures)	.15
192	Oswaldo Mairena (Bright Futures)	.15
193	Aubrey Huff (Bright Futures)	.15
194	Mark Buehrle (Bright Futures)	.15
195	Jace Brewer (Bright Futures)	.15
196	Julio Zuleta (Bright Futures)	.15
197	Xavier Nady (Bright Futures)	.15
198	Vernon Wells (Bright Futures)	.25
199	Joe Crede (Bright Futures)	.15
200	Scott Downs (Bright Futures)	.15
201	Ben Petrick (Bright Futures)	.15
202	A.J. Burnett (Bright Futures)	.15
203	Esix Snead **RC** (Bright Futures)	.15
204	Dernell Stenson (Bright Futures)	.15
205	Jose Ortiz (Bright Futures)	.15
206	Paxton Crawford (Bright Futures)	.15
207	Jason Tyner (Bright Futures)	.15
208	Jimmy Rollins (Bright Futures)	.25
209	Juan Pierre (Bright Futures)	.25
210	Keith Ginter (Bright Futures)	.15
211	Adam Dunn (Bright Futures)	.40
212	Larry Barnes (Bright Futures)	.15
213	Adam Piatt (Bright Futures)	.15
214	Rodney Lindsey (Bright Futures)	.15
215	Eric Byrnes (Bright Futures)	.15
216	Julio Lugo (Bright Futures)	.15
217	Corey Patterson (Bright Futures)	.25
218	Reggie Taylor (Bright Futures)	.15
219	Kenny Kelly (Bright Futures)	.15
220	Tike Redman (Bright Futures)	.15

Black Gold

Production 499 Sets:	3-6X

Bases Loaded

NM/M

Common Player:		4.00
Inserted 1:134		
BL1	Ken Griffey Jr.	10.00
BL2	Mark McGwire	12.00
BL3	Carlos Delgado	4.00
BL4	Chipper Jones	7.50
BL5	Nomar Garciaparra	10.00
BL6	Cal Ripken Jr.	15.00
BL7	Sammy Sosa	10.00
BL8	Jeff Bagwell	6.00
BL9	Vladimir Guerrero	6.00
BL10	Tony Gwynn	7.50
BL11	Frank Thomas	6.00
BL12	Mike Piazza	10.00
BL13	Jason Giambi	5.00
BL14	Troy Glaus	6.00
BL15	Pat Burrell	4.00

Bats to the Future

NM/M

Complete Set (25):		60.00
Common Player:		1.00
Inserted 1:28		
1BF	Mike Schmidt	6.00
2BF	Carlton Fisk	3.00
3BF	Paul Molitor	3.00
4BF	Vladimir Guerrero	3.00
5BF	Dave Parker	1.00
6BF	Chipper Jones	5.00
7BF	Carlos Delgado	3.00
8BF	Tony Gwynn	5.00
9BF	Reggie Jackson	5.00
10BF	Eddie Murray	1.50
11BF	Robin Yount	3.00
12BF	Alan Trammell	1.00
13BF	Frank Thomas	3.00
14BF	Cal Ripken Jr.	8.00
15BF	Don Mattingly	6.00
16BF	Jim Rice	1.00
17BF	Barry Bonds	3.00
18BF	Todd Helton	3.00
19BF	George Brett	6.00
20BF	Barry Bonds	8.00
21BF	Kirk Gibson	1.00
22BF	Matt Williams	1.00
23BF	Dave Winfield	1.50
24BF	Ryne Sandberg	5.00
25BF	Ivan Rodriguez	2.00

Bats to the Future Game Bat

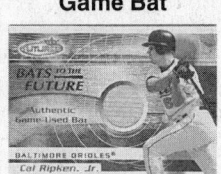

NM/M

Common Player:		5.00
Inserted 1:114		
1BF	Mike Schmidt	25.00
2BF	Carlton Fisk	10.00
3BF	Paul Molitor	15.00
4BF	Vladimir Guerrero	8.00
5BF	Dave Parker	5.00
6BF	Chipper Jones	10.00
7BF	Chris Delgado	8.00
8BF	Tony Gwynn	10.00
9BF	Reggie Jackson	10.00
10BF	Eddie Murray	8.00
11BF	Robin Yount	15.00
12BF	Alan Trammell	8.00
13BF	Frank Thomas	8.00
14BF	Cal Ripken Jr.	30.00
15BF	Don Mattingly	30.00
16BF	Jim Rice	5.00
17BF	Juan Gonzalez	8.00
18BF	Todd Helton	8.00
19BF	George Brett	25.00
20BF	Barry Bonds	25.00
21BF	Kirk Gibson	5.00
22BF	Matt Williams	8.00
23BF	Dave Winfield	8.00
24BF	Ryne Sandberg	15.00
25BF	Ivan Rodriguez	8.00

Bats to the Future Game Bat Autograph

NM/M

Common Autograph:		40.00
Production 50 Sets		
1BF	Mike Schmidt	150.00
2BF	Carlton Fisk	50.00
3BF	Paul Molitor	50.00
4BF	Vladimir Guerrero	80.00
5BF	Dave Parker	40.00
6BF	Chipper Jones	75.00
7BF	Carlos Delgado	50.00
8BF	Tony Gwynn	75.00
9BF	Reggie Jackson	
10BF	Eddie Murray	70.00
11BF	Robin Yount	80.00
12BF	Alan Trammell	40.00
13BF	Frank Thomas	60.00
14BF	Cal Ripken Jr.	200.00
15BF	Don Mattingly	150.00
16BF	Jim Rice	40.00
17BF	Juan Gonzalez	50.00
18BF	Todd Helton	50.00
19BF	George Brett	150.00
20BF	Barry Bonds	200.00
21BF	Kirk Gibson	40.00
22BF	Matt Williams	40.00
23BF	Dave Winfield	60.00
24BF	Ryne Sandberg	125.00
25BF	Ivan Rodriguez	60.00

Characteristics

NM/M

Complete Set (15):		20.00
Common Player:		.75
Inserted 1:9		
1C	Derek Jeter	4.00
2C	Mark McGwire	3.00
3C	Nomar Garciaparra	2.50
4C	Sammy Sosa	2.50
5C	Pedro Martinez	1.50
6C	Chipper Jones	2.00
7C	Cal Ripken Jr.	4.00
8C	Todd Helton	1.50
9C	Jim Edmonds	.75
10C	Ken Griffey Jr.	2.50
11C	Alex Rodriguez	3.00
12C	Mike Piazza	2.50
13C	Vladimir Guerrero	1.50
14C	Frank Thomas	1.50
15C	Carlos Delgado	1.00

Hot Commodities

NM/M

Complete Set (10):		20.00
Common Player:		1.00
Inserted 1:14		
1HC	Mark McGwire	3.00
2HC	Ken Griffey Jr.	2.50
3HC	Derek Jeter	4.00
4HC	Cal Ripken Jr.	4.00
5HC	Chipper Jones	2.00
6HC	Barry Bonds	4.00
7HC	Mike Piazza	2.50
8HC	Sammy Sosa	2.50
9HC	Alex Rodriguez	3.00
10HC	Frank Thomas	1.00

September Call-Ups Memorabilia

NM/M

Common Card:		4.00
Production 200 Sets		
184	Randy Keisler/Cap/Cleat	4.00
185	Nate Rolison/Bat	4.00
187	Timoniel Perez/Bat	4.00
191	Joey Nation/Glv	4.00
192	Oswaldo Mairena/Glv	4.00
195	Jace Brewer/Bat	4.00
197	Xavier Nady/Glv	6.00
199	Joe Crede/Bat	6.00
205	Jose Ortiz/Bat	4.00
208	Jimmy Rollins/Glv	6.00
210	Keith Ginter/Bat	4.00
214	Rodney Lindsey/Bat	4.00
217	Corey Patterson/Bat	8.00
218	Reggie Taylor/Bat	4.00
219	Kenny Kelly/Bat	4.00

2001 Fleer Game Time

NM/M

Complete Set (121):		
Common Player:		.15
Common (91-121):		3.00
Production 2,000		
Pack (5):		4.00
Box (24):		80.00
1	Derek Jeter	2.00
2	Nomar Garciaparra	1.25
3	Alex Rodriguez	1.50
4	Jason Kendall	.15
5	Barry Bonds	2.00
6	David Wells	.15
7	Craig Biggio	.15
8	Adrian Beltre	.30
9	Pat Burrell	.15
10	Rafael Palmeiro	.60
11	Jim Thome	.15
12	Mike Lowell	.15
13	Trevor Hoffman	.15
14	Pokey Reese	.15
15	Juan Encarnacion	.15
16	Shawn Green	.40
17	Kerry Wood	.50
18	Richard Hidalgo	.15
19	Scott Rolen	.60
20	Jeff Kent	.15
21	Alex Gonzalez	.15
22	Matt Williams	.15
23	Mike Sweeney	.15
24	Edgar Martinez	.15
25	Sammy Sosa	1.25
26	Bobby Higginson	.15
27	Kevin Brown	.15
28	Mike Lieberthal	.15
29	Pedro J. Martinez	.75
30	Jeff Weaver	.15
31	Greg Maddux	1.00
32	Mike Hampton	.15
33	Vladimir Guerrero	.75
34	Greg Vaughn	.15
35	Manny Ramirez	.75
36	Carlos Beltran	.40
37	Eric Chavez	.25
38	Troy Glaus	.75
39	Todd Helton	.75
40	Gary Sheffield	.40
41	Brady Anderson	.15
42	Juan Gonzalez	.75
43	Tim Hudson	.30
44	Kenny Lofton	.15
45	Al Leiter	.15
46	Eric Owens	.15
47	Roberto Alomar	.40
48	Preston Wilson	.15
49	Tony Gwynn	1.00
50	Cal Ripken Jr.	2.00

51	Ben Petrick	.15
52	Jason Giambi	.50
53	Ben Grieve	.15
54	Albert Belle	.15
55	Jose Vidro	.15
56	Barry Zito	.30
57	Ivan Rodriguez	.60
58	Jeff Bagwell	.75
59	Geoff Jenkins	.15
60	Roger Clemens	1.00
61	John Olerud	.15
62	Randy Johnson	.75
63	Matt Lawton	.15
64	Mark McGwire	1.50
65	Brad Radke	.15
66	Frank Thomas	.75
67	Edgardo Alfonzo	.15
68	Brian Giles	.15
69	J.T. Snow	.15
70	Carlos Delgado	.50
71	Chipper Jones	1.00
72	Mark Quinn	.15
73	Mike Mussina	.40
74	Rick Ankiel	.15
75	Rafael Furcal	.15
76	Jim Edmonds	.15
77	Vinny Castilla	.15
78	Sean Casey	.25
79	Derrek Lee	.15
80	Mike Piazza	1.25
81	Warren Morris	.15
82	Tim Salmon	.15
83	Jeromy Burnitz	.15
84	Freddy Garcia	.15
85	Ken Griffey Jr.	1.25
86	Andruw Jones	.75
87	Darryl Kile	.15
88	Magglio Ordonez	.15
89	Bernie Williams	.30
90	Timo Perez	.15
91	Ichiro Suzuki RC	
	(Next Game)	35.00
92	Larry Barnes, Darin Erstad	
	(Next Game)	3.00
93	Jaisen Randolph RC	
	(Next Game)	3.00
94	Paul Phillips RC	
	(Next Game)	3.00
95	Esix Snead RC	
	(Next Game)	3.00
96	Matt White RC	
	(Next Game)	3.00
97	Ryan Freel RC	
	(Next Game)	3.00
98	Winston Abreu RC	
	(Next Game)	3.00
99	Junior Spivey RC	
	(Next Game)	5.00
100	Randy Keisler,	
	Roger Clemens	
	(Next Game)	5.00
101	Brian Cole, Mike Piazza	
	(Next Game)	4.00
102	Aubrey Huff, Chipper Jones	
	(Next Game)	3.00
103	Corey Patterson,	
	Sammy Sosa	
	(Next Game)	5.00
104	Sun-Woo Kim,	
	Pedro Martinez	
	(Next Game)	4.00
105	Drew Henson RC	
	(Next Game)	5.00
106	Claudio Vargas RC	
	(Next Game)	3.00
107	Cesar Izturis, Rafael Furcal	
	(Next Game)	3.00
108	Paxton Crawford,	
	Pedro Martinez	
	(Next Game)	3.00
109	Adrian Hernandez RC	
	(Next Game)	3.00
110	Jace Brewer, Derek Jeter	
	(Next Game)	8.00
111	Andy Morales RC	
	(Next Game)	3.00
112	Wilson Betemit RC	
	(Next Game)	3.00
113	Juan Diaz RC	
	(Next Game)	3.00
114	Erick Almonte RC	
	(Next Game)	4.00
115	Nick Punto RC	
	(Next Game)	3.00
116	Tsuyoshi Shinjo RC	
	(Next Game)	4.00
117	Jay Gibbons RC	
	(Next Game)	5.00
118	Andres Torres RC	
	(Next Game)	3.00
119	Alexis Gomez RC	
	(Next Game)	4.00
120	Wilken Ruan RC	
	(Next Game)	3.00
121	Albert Pujols RC	
	(Next Game)	80.00

Next Game Extra

Cards (91-121) 2-3X
Production 200 Sets

Famers Lumber

		NM/M
Common Player:		8.00
Production 100 Sets		
1FL	Luis Aparicio	8.00
2FL	Hank Bauer	8.00

3FL	Paul Blair	8.00
4FL	Bobby Bonds	8.00
5FL	Orlando Cepeda	8.00
6FL	Roberto Clemente	100.00
7FL	Rocky Colavito	10.00
8FL	Bucky Dent	8.00
9FL	Bill Dickey	10.00
10FL	Larry Doby	10.00
11FL	Carlton Fisk	10.00
12FL	Hank Greenberg	25.00
13FL	Elston Howard	8.00
14FL	Frank Howard	8.00
15FL	Reggie Jackson	15.00
16FL	Harmon Killebrew	20.00
17FL	Tony Lazzeri	8.00
18FL	Roger Maris	60.00
19FL	Johnny Mize	10.00
20FL	Thurman Munson	40.00
21FL	Tony Perez	10.00
22FL	Jim Rice	8.00
23FL	Phil Rizzuto	10.00
24FL	Bill Skowron	8.00
25FL	Enos Slaughter	10.00
26FL	Duke Snider	15.00
27FL	Willie Stargell	15.00
28FL	Bill Terry	8.00
29FL	Ted Williams	100.00

Famers Lumber Autograph

		NM/M
Common Player:		40.00
Production 25 Sets		
1FLS	Hank Bauer	40.00
2FLS	Bobby Bonds	50.00
3FLS	Orlando Cepeda	50.00
4FLS	Rocky Colavito	50.00
5FLS	Bucky Dent	40.00
6FLS	Larry Doby	50.00
7FLS	Carlton Fisk	65.00
8FLS	Frank Howard	40.00
9FLS	Reggie Jackson	100.00
10FLS	Harmon Killebrew	120.00
11FLS	Tony Perez	40.00
12FLS	Jim Rice	40.00
13FLS	Phil Rizzuto	60.00
14FLS	Bill Skowron	40.00
15FLS	Enos Slaughter	40.00
16FLS	Duke Snider	75.00

Derek Jeter's Monumental Moments

		NM/M
Complete Set (1):		
1JM	Derek Jeter/1996	8.00
1JMS	Derek Jeter/Auto./96	80.00

Let's Play Two!

		NM/M
Complete Set (15):		30.00
Common Card:		1.50
Inserted 1:24		
1LT	Derek Jeter,	
	Nomar Garciaparra	4.00
2LT	Mark McGwire,	
	Sammy Sosa	3.00
3LT	Pedro J. Martinez,	
	Randy Johnson	1.50
4LT	Vladimir Guerrero,	
	Carlos Delgado	1.50
5LT	Mike Piazza,	
	Roger Clemens	2.50
6LT	Alex Rodriguez,	
	Miguel Tejada	3.00
7LT	Troy Glaus,	
	Chipper Jones	2.00
8LT	Derek Jeter,	
	Alex Rodriguez	4.00
9LT	Cal Ripken Jr.,	
	Derek Jeter	4.00
10LT	Jason Giambi,	
	Mark McGwire	3.00
11LT	Jeff Bagwell,	
	Craig Biggio	1.50
12LT	Tom Glavine,	
	Greg Maddux	2.00
13LT	Ken Griffey Jr.,	
	Barry Bonds	4.00
14LT	Manny Ramirez,	
	Pedro J. Martinez	1.50
15LT	Alex Rodriguez,	
	Ivan Rodriguez	3.00

Lumber

JUAN GONZALEZ Cleveland Indians

		NM/M
Common Player:		4.00
Inserted 1:40		
1GL	Roberto Alomar	6.00
2GL	Rick Ankiel	4.00
3GL	Adrian Beltre	6.00
4GL	Barry Bonds	25.00
5GL	Kevin Brown	4.00
7GL	Ken Caminiti	4.00
8GL	Eric Chavez	5.00
9GL	Carlos Delgado	5.00
10GL	J.D. Drew	5.00
11GL	Erubiel Durazo	4.00
12GL	Carl Everett	4.00
13GL	Rafael Furcal	4.00
14GL	Brian Giles	5.00
15GL	Juan Gonzalez	6.00
16GL	Todd Helton	8.00
18GL	Randy Johnson	10.00
19GL	Chipper Jones	8.00
20GL	Pedro J. Martinez	10.00
21GL	Tino Martinez	5.00
23GL	Cal Ripken SP/275	40.00
24GL	Ivan Rodriguez	8.00
25GL	Frank Thomas	8.00
26GL	Jim Thome	8.00
27GL	Bernie Williams	6.00
28GL	Nomar Garciaparra	15.00

New Order

		NM/M
Complete Set (20):		30.00
Common Player:		1.50
Inserted 1:12		
1NO	Derek Jeter	6.00
2NO	Nomar Garciaparra	4.00
3NO	Alex Rodriguez	5.00
4NO	Mark McGwire	5.00
5NO	Sammy Sosa	4.00
6NO	Carlos Delgado	1.50
7NO	Troy Glaus	1.50
8NO	Jason Giambi	1.50
9NO	Mike Piazza	4.00
10NO	Todd Helton	1.50
11NO	Vladimir Guerrero	2.00
12NO	Manny Ramirez	1.50
13NO	Frank Thomas	1.50
14NO	Ken Griffey Jr.	4.00
15NO	Chipper Jones	3.00

Sticktoitness

		NM/M
Complete Set (20):		15.00
Common Player:		.50
Inserted 1:8		
1S	Derek Jeter	4.00
2S	Nomar Garciaparra	3.00
3S	Alex Rodriguez	3.00
4S	Jeff Bagwell	1.00
5S	Bernie Williams	.50
6S	Eric Chavez	.50
7S	Richard Hidalgo	.50
8S	Ichiro Suzuki	4.00
9S	Troy Glaus	.75
10S	Magglio Ordonez	.50
11S	Corey Patterson	.50
12S	Todd Helton	1.00
13S	Jim Edmonds	.50
14S	Rafael Furcal	.50
15S	Mo Vaughn	.50
16S	Pat Burrell	.65
17S	Alex Rodriguez	.60
18S	Andruw Jones	1.00
19S	Manny Ramirez	1.00
20S	Sean Casey	.65

Uniformity

ANDRES GALARRAGA Texas Rangers

		NM/M
Common Player:		4.00
Inserted 1:25		
1GU	Andres Galarraga	4.00
2GU	Barry Bonds	25.00
3GU	Ben Petrick	4.00
4GU	Brad Radke	4.00
5GU	Brian Jordan	4.00
6GU	Carlos Guillen	4.00
7GU	Fernando Seguignol	4.00
8GU	Fred McGriff	4.00
9GU	Gary Sheffield	5.00
10GU	Greg Maddux	15.00
11GU	Ivan Rodriguez	8.00
12GU	Jay Buhner	4.00
13GU	Jeromy Burnitz	4.00
14GU	John Olerud	4.00
15GU	Kevin Brown	4.00
16GU	Larry Walker	4.00
17GU	Magglio Ordonez	4.00
18GU	Matt Williams	4.00
19GU	Robin Ventura	4.00
20GU	Rondell White	4.00
21GU	Tony Gwynn	15.00
22GU	Troy Glaus	8.00
23GU	Vladimir Guerrero	8.00

2001 Fleer Genuine

		NM/M
Complete Set (130):		150.00
Common Player:		.25
Common (101-130):		3.00
Production 1,500		
Pack (5):		4.00
Box (24):		80.00
1	Derek Jeter	6.00
2	Nomar Garciaparra	2.00
3	Alex Rodriguez	2.50
4	Frank Thomas	1.00
5	Travis Fryman	.25
6	Gary Sheffield	.40
7	Jason Giambi	.75
8	Trevor Hoffman	.25
9	Todd Helton	1.00
10	Ivan Rodriguez	.75
11	Roberto Alomar	.40
12	Barry Zito	.40
13	Kevin Brown	.25
14	Shawn Green	.40
15	Kenny Lofton	.25
16	Jeff Weaver	.25
17	Geoff Jenkins	.25
18	Carlos Delgado	.65
19	Mark Grace	.35
20	Ken Griffey Jr.	2.00
21	David Justice	.25
22	Brian Giles	.25
23	Scott Williamson	.25
24	Richie Sexson	.25
25	John Olerud	.25
26	Sammy Sosa	2.00
27	Bobby Higginson	.25
28	Matt Lawton	.25
29	Vinny Castilla	.25
30	Alex S. Gonzalez	.25
31	Manny Ramirez	1.00
32	Brad Radke	.25
33	Cal Ripken Jr.	3.00
34	Richard Hidalgo	.25
35	Al Leiter	.25
36	Freddy Garcia	.25
37	Juan Encarnacion	.25
38	Corey Koskie	.25
39	Greg Vaughn	.25
40	Rafael Palmeiro	.35
41	Vladimir Guerrero	1.00
42	Troy Glaus	.75
43	Mike Hampton	.25
44	Jose Vidro	.25
45	Ryan Rupe	.25
46	Troy O'Leary	.25
47	Ben Petrick	.25
48	Mike Lieberthal	.25
49	Mike Sweeney	.25
50	Scott Rolen	.75

51	Albert Belle	.25
52	Mark Quinn	.25
53	Mike Piazza	2.00
54	Mark McGwire	2.50
55	Brady Anderson	.25
56	Carlos Beltran	.45
57	Michael Barrett	.25
58	Jason Kendall	.25
59	Jim Edmonds	.25
60	Matt Williams	.25
61	Pokey Reese	.25
62	Bernie Williams	.25
63	Barry Bonds	3.00
64	David Wells	.25
65	Chipper Jones	1.50
66	Jim Parque	.25
67	Derrek Lee	.25
68	Darin Erstad	.60
69	Edgar Martinez	.25
70	Kerry Wood	.60
71	Omar Vizquel	.25
72	Jeromy Burnitz	.25
73	Warren Morris	.25
74	Rick Ankiel	.25
75	Andruw Jones	1.00
76	Paul Konerko	.25
77	Mike Lowell	.25
78	Roger Clemens	1.75
79	Tim Hudson	.35
80	Rafael Furcal	.25
81	Craig Biggio	.25
82	Edgardo Alfonzo	.25
83	Pat Burrell	.50
84	Adrian Beltre	.35
85	Tony Gwynn	1.50
86	J.T. Snow	.25
87	Randy Johnson	1.00
88	Sean Casey	.35
89	Preston Wilson	.25
90	Mike Mussina	.50
91	Eric Chavez	.35
92	Tim Salmon	.25
93	Pedro Martinez	1.00
94	Darryl Kile	.25
95	Greg Maddux	1.50
96	Magglio Ordonez	.25
97	Jeff Bagwell	1.00
98	Timo Perez	.25
99	Jeff Kent	.25
100	Eric Owens	.25
101	Ichiro Suzuki RC	
	(Genuine Upside)	35.00
102	Elpidio Guzman RC	
	(Genuine Upside)	3.00
103	Tsuyoshi Shinjo RC	
	(Genuine Upside)	6.00
104	Travis Hafner RC	
	(Genuine Upside)	10.00
105	Larry Barnes	
	(Genuine Upside)	3.00
106	Jaisen Randolph RC	
	(Genuine Upside)	3.00
107	Paul Phillips RC	
	(Genuine Upside)	3.00
108	Erick Almonte RC	
	(Genuine Upside)	3.00
109	Nick Punto RC	
	(Genuine Upside)	3.00
110	Jack Wilson RC	
	(Genuine Upside)	3.00
111	Jeremy Owens RC	
	(Genuine Upside)	3.00
112	Esix Snead RC	
	(Genuine Upside)	3.00
113	Jay Gibbons RC	
	(Genuine Upside)	8.00
114	Adrian Hernandez RC	
	(Genuine Upside)	4.00
115	Matt White RC	
	(Genuine Upside)	3.00
116	Ryan Freel RC	
	(Genuine Upside)	3.00
117	Martin Vargas RC	
	(Genuine Upside)	3.00
118	Winston Abreu RC	
	(Genuine Upside)	3.00
119	Junior Spivey RC	
	(Genuine Upside)	5.00
120	Paxton Crawford	
	(Genuine Upside)	3.00
121	Randy Keisler	
	(Genuine Upside)	3.00
122	Juan Diaz RC	
	(Genuine Upside)	3.00
123	Aaron Rowand	
	(Genuine Upside)	3.00
124	Toby Hall	
	(Genuine Upside)	3.00
125	Brian Cole	
	(Genuine Upside)	3.00
126	Aubrey Huff	
	(Genuine Upside)	4.00
127	Corey Patterson	
	(Genuine Upside)	4.00
128	Sun-Woo Kim	
	(Genuine Upside)	3.00
129	Jace Brewer	
	(Genuine Upside)	3.00
130	Cesar Izturis	
	(Genuine Upside)	3.00

@ LG (At Large)

		NM/M
Complete Set (15):		50.00
Common Player:		1.50
Inserted 1:23		
1AL	Derek Jeter	7.50
2AL	Nomar Garciaparra	4.00
3AL	Mark McGwire	6.00

4AL	Pedro Martinez	3.00
5AL	Tony Gwynn	3.50
6AL	Roger Clemens	3.50
7AL	Ivan Rodriguez	2.00
8AL	Sammy Sosa	4.00
9AL	Magglio Ordonez	1.50
10AL	Jason Giambi	2.00
11AL	Carlos Delgado	2.00
12AL	Chipper Jones	3.50
13AL	Mike Piazza	4.00
14AL	Cal Ripken Jr.	7.50
15AL	Ken Griffey Jr.	4.00

Final Cut

Final Cut cards of Ron Guidry, Don Larsen and Reggie Jackson were prepared, but not intended for release. At least a few of each have made their way into hobby channels. Because of limited numbers extant, their values cannot be determined. Some, perhaps all, of Edgar Martinez' Final Cut cards have jersey patches rather than the described glove piece.

		NM/M
Common Player:		4.00
Inserted 1:30		
	Miguel Tejada SP/170	6.00
	Barry Bonds/SP/330	40.00
	Robin Ventura	8.00
	Greg Maddux	15.00
	Andruw Jones/SP/135	10.00
	J.D. Drew SP/75	10.00
	Chipper Jones	10.00
	Tim Salmon	4.00
	Edgar Martinez/SP/130	8.00
	Troy Glaus	8.00
	Frank Thomas	8.00
	Pokey Reese	4.00
	Larry Walker	4.00
	Ivan Rodriguez/SP/120	10.00
	Scott Rolen	8.00
	Cal Ripken Jr.	30.00
	Tony Gwynn	10.00
	Wade Boggs	10.00
	George Brett	30.00
	Sean Casey	4.00
	Bob Gibson	6.00
	Matt Williams	6.00
	Robin Yount	8.00
	Ron Guidry (Not officially released.)	150.00
	Reggie Jackson (Not officially released.)	250.00
	Don Larsen (Not officially released.)	140.00

Genuine Coverage PLUS

Common Player

	NM/M
Common Player:	6.00

Production 150 Sets

Troy Glaus	8.00
Randy Johnson	10.00
Andruw Jones	8.00
Frank Thomas	8.00
Darin Erstad	6.00
Chipper Jones	15.00
Derek Jeter	35.00
Tony Gwynn	15.00
Barry Bonds	35.00
Cal Ripken Jr.	35.00

High Interest

	NM/M
Complete Set (15):	40.00
Common Player:	1.50

Inserted 1:23

1HI	Derek Jeter	6.00
2HI	Nomar Garciaparra	4.00
3HI	Greg Maddux	3.00
4HI	Todd Helton	2.00
5HI	Sammy Sosa	4.00
6HI	Jeff Bagwell	2.00
7HI	Jason Giambi	1.50
8HI	Frank Thomas	2.00
9HI	Andruw Jones	2.00
10HI	Jim Edmonds	1.50
11HI	Bernie Williams	1.50
12HI	Randy Johnson	2.00
13HI	Ken Griffey Jr.	4.00
14HI	Pedro Martinez	2.00
15HI	Mark McGwire	5.00

Material Issue

	NM/M
Common Player:	5.00

Inserted 1:30

Randy Johnson	10.00
Scott Rolen	8.00
Robin Ventura	5.00
Tony Gwynn	15.00
Troy Glaus	10.00
Kevin Millwood	5.00
Chipper Jones	15.00
Tom Glavine	5.00
Pedro Martinez/SP/60	40.00
Greg Maddux	15.00
Frank Thomas	15.00
Curt Schilling/SP/120	10.00
Edgar Martinez	5.00
Darin Erstad	5.00
J.D. Drew	5.00
Cal Ripken Jr.	30.00
Nolan Ryan	40.00
Steve Carlton	5.00

Names of the Game - Autographs

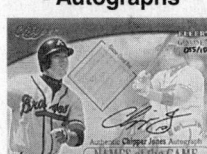

	NM/M
Common Player:	25.00
Yogi Berra	60.00
Orlando Cepeda	20.00
Rocky Colavito	60.00
Andre Dawson	20.00
Bucky Dent	20.00
Rollie Fingers	20.00
Carlton Fisk	40.00
Whitey Ford	40.00
Reggie Jackson	50.00
Randy Johnson	60.00
Chipper Jones	50.00
Harmon Killebrew	60.00
Don Mattingly	90.00
Willie McCovey	25.00
Cal Ripken Jr.	150.00
Ivan Rodriguez	50.00
Preacher Roe	35.00
Nolan Ryan	100.00
Tom Seaver	50.00
Bill Skowron	25.00
Enos Slaughter	30.00
Duke Snider	40.00

Names of the Game - Game Used

	NM/M
Common Player:	10.00

Production 50 Sets

Yogi Berra/Bat	25.00
Orlando Cepeda/Bat	10.00
Rocky Colavito/Bat	20.00
Andre Dawson/Jsy	10.00
Bucky Dent/Bat	10.00
Rollie Fingers/Jsy	10.00
Carlton Fisk/Bat	15.00
Whitey Ford/Jsy	25.00
Jimmie Foxx/Bat	80.00
Hank Greenberg/Bat	50.00
"Catfish" Hunter/Jsy	25.00
Reggie Jackson/Jsy	30.00
Randy Johnson/Jsy	30.00
Chipper Jones/Bat	30.00
Harmon Killebrew/Bat	25.00
Tony Lazzeri/Bat	10.00
Don Mattingly/Bat	65.00
Willie McCovey/Bat	20.00
Johnny Mize/Bat	15.00
Pee Wee Reese/Jsy	15.00
Cal Ripken Jr./Bat	75.00
Phil Rizzuto/Bat	25.00
Ivan Rodriguez/Bat	25.00
Preacher Roe/Jsy	15.00
Babe Ruth/Bat	300.00
Nolan Ryan/Bat	90.00
Tom Seaver/Jsy	25.00
Bill Skowron/Bat	10.00
Enos Slaughter/Bat	10.00
Duke Snider/Bat	25.00
Willie Stargell/Bat	15.00
Bill Terry/Bat	10.00
Ted Williams/Bat	200.00
Hack Wilson/Bat	75.00

Pennant Aggression

	NM/M
Complete Set (10):	30.00

Inserted 1:23

1PA	Derek Jeter	6.00
2PA	Alex Rodriguez	5.00
3PA	Nomar Garciaparra	4.00
4PA	Mark McGwire	5.00
5PA	Ken Griffey Jr.	4.00
6PA	Mike Piazza	4.00
7PA	Sammy Sosa	4.00
8PA	Barry Bonds	6.00
9PA	Chipper Jones	3.00
10PA	Pedro Martinez	2.00

Tip of the Cap

	NM/M
Common Player:	8.00

Production 150 Sets

Barry Bonds	40.00
Eric Chavez	8.00
Shawn Green	8.00
Vladimir Guerrero	15.00
Randy Johnson	20.00
Andruw Jones	10.00
Javy Lopez	8.00
Rafael Palmeiro	10.00
Ivan Rodriguez	10.00
Miguel Tejada	8.00
Roberto Alomar	10.00
Pedro Martinez	15.00

2001 Fleer Greats of the Game

	NM/M
Complete Set (137):	50.00
Common Player:	.25
Hobby Pack (5):	15.00
Hobby Box (24):	200.00

1	Roberto Clemente	2.50
2	George "Sparky" Anderson	.25
3	Babe Ruth	4.00
4	Paul Molitor	1.00
5	Don Larsen	.25
6	Cy Young	1.00
7	Billy Martin	.50
8	Lou Brock	1.00
9	Fred Lynn	.25
10	Johnny Vander Meer	.25
11	Harmon Killebrew	1.00
12	Dave Winfield	1.00
13	Orlando Cepeda	.25
14	Johnny Mize	.75
15	Walter Johnson	1.00
16	Roy Campanella	1.00
17	Monte Irvin	.50
18	Mookie Wilson	.25
19	Elston Howard	.25
20	Walter Alston	.25
21	Rollie Fingers	.25
22	Brooks Robinson	1.00
23	Hank Greenberg	1.00
24	Maury Wills	.25
25	Rich Gossage	.25
26	Leon Day	.25
27	Jimmie Foxx	2.00
28	Alan Trammell	.50
29	Dennis Martinez	.25
30	Don Drysdale	.75
31	Bob Feller	1.00
32	Jackie Robinson	3.00
33	Whitey Ford	1.00
34	Enos Slaughter	.75
35	Rod Carew	.75
36	Eddie Mathews	1.00
37	Ron Cey	.25
38	Thurman Munson	1.00
39	Henry Kimbro	.25
40	Ty Cobb	3.00
41	Rocky Colavito	.50
42	Satchel Paige	1.50
43	Andre Dawson	.50
44	Phil Rizzuto	1.00
45	Roger Maris	2.50
46	Bobby Bonds	.25
47	Joe Carter	.25
48	Christy Mathewson	.75
49	Tony Lazzeri	.25
50	Gil Hodges	.25
51	Ray Dandridge	.25
52	Gaylord Perry	.25
53	Ernie Banks	2.00
54	Lou Gehrig	3.00
55	George Kell	.25
56	Wes Parker	.25
57	Sam Jethroe	.25
58	Joe Morgan	.75
59	Steve Garvey	.50
60	Joe Torre	.75
61	Roger Craig	.25
62	Warren Spahn	1.00
63	Willie McCovey	.25
64	Cool Papa Bell	1.00
65	Frank Robinson	1.00
66	Richie Allen	.25
67	Bucky Dent	.25
68	George Foster	.25
69	Hoyt Wilhelm	.25
70	Phil Niekro	.25
71	Buck Leonard	.25
72	Preacher Roe	.25
73	Yogi Berra	1.50
74	Joe Black	.25
75	Nolan Ryan	4.00
76	Pop Lloyd	.25
77	Lester Lockett	.25
78	Paul Blair	.25
79	Ryne Sandberg	.25
80	Bill Perkins	.25
81	Frank Howard	.25
82	Hack Wilson	1.00
83	Robin Yount	.25
84	Harry Heilmann	.25
85	Mike Schmidt	3.00
86	Vida Blue	.25
87	George Brett	3.00
88	Juan Marichal	.50
89	Tom Seaver	1.50
90	Bill Skowron	.25
91	Don Mattingly	2.00
92	Jim Bunning	.25
93	Eddie Murray	1.00
94	Tommy Lasorda	.25
95	Pee Wee Reese	.50
96	Bill Dickey	.50
97	Ozzie Smith	1.50
98	Dale Murphy	.25
99	Artie Wilson	.25
100	Bill Terry	.25
101	Jim "Catfish" Hunter	.25
102	Don Sutton	.25
103	Luis Aparicio	.25
104	Reggie Jackson	1.50
105	Ted Radcliffe	.25
106	Carl Erskine	.25
107	Johnny Bench	2.00
108	Carl Furillo	.25
109	Stan Musial	2.00
110	Carlton Fisk	.75
111	Rube Foster	.25
112	Tony Oliva	.25
113	Hank Bauer	.25
114	Jim Rice	.25
115	Willie Mays	3.00
116	Ralph Kiner	.50
117	Al Kaline	1.00
118	Billy Williams	.25
119	Buck O'Neil	.25
120	Tony Perez	.25
121	Dave Parker	.25
122	Kirk Gibson	.25
123	Lou Piniella	.25
124	Ted Williams	4.00
125	Steve Carlton	.75
126	Dizzy Dean	.25
127	Willie Stargell	.50
128	Joe Niekro	.25
129	Lloyd Waner	.25
130	Wade Boggs	2.00
131	Wilmer Fields	.25
132	Bill Mazeroski	.50
133	Duke Snider	1.00
134	Smoky Joe Williams	.25
135	Bob Gibson	1.50
136	Jim Palmer	.75
137	Oscar Charleston	.25

Autographs

	NM/M
Common Player:	10.00

Inserted 1:8

1	Richie Allen	10.00
2	George "Sparky" Anderson	10.00
3	Luis Aparicio	10.00
4	Ernie Banks/SP/250	80.00
5	Hank Bauer	10.00
6	Johnny Bench/SP/400	80.00
7	Yogi Berra SP/500	50.00
8	Joe Black	10.00
9	Paul Blair	10.00
9a	Paul Blair/Double Signed	10.00
10	Vida Blue	10.00
11	Wade Boggs	40.00
12	Bobby Bonds	15.00
13	George Brett/SP/247	150.00
14	Lou Brock/SP/500	40.00
15	Jim Bunning	25.00
16	Rod Carew	20.00
17	Steve Carlton	25.00
18	Joe Carter	10.00
19	Orlando Cepeda	15.00
20	Ron Cey	10.00
21	Rocky Colavito	25.00
22	Roger Craig	10.00
23	Andre Dawson	15.00
24	Bucky Dent	10.00
25	Larry Doby	35.00
26	Carl Erskine	15.00
27	Bob Feller	15.00
28	Wilmer Fields	10.00
29	Rollie Fingers	15.00
30	Carlton Fisk	40.00
31	Whitey Ford	30.00
32	George Foster	10.00
33	Steve Garvey/SP/400	40.00
34	Bob Gibson	20.00
35	Kirk Gibson	20.00
36	Rich Gossage	10.00
37	Frank Howard	10.00
38	Monte Irvin	20.00
39	Reggie Jackson/SP/400	60.00
40	Sam Jethroe	10.00
41	Al Kaline	30.00
42	George Kell	10.00
43	Harmon Killebrew	30.00
44	Ralph Kiner	20.00
45	Don Larsen	15.00
46	Tommy Lasorda/SP/400	40.00
47	Lester Lockett	10.00
48	Fred Lynn	10.00
49	Juan Marichal	20.00
50	Dennis Martinez	10.00
51	Don Mattingly	75.00
52	Willie Mays/SP/100	450.00
53	Bill Mazeroski	20.00
54	Willie McCovey	20.00
55	Paul Molitor	25.00
56	Joe Morgan	20.00
57	Dale Murphy	30.00
58	Eddie Murray/SP/140	200.00
59	Stan Musial/SP/525	75.00
60	Joe Niekro	10.00
61	Phil Niekro	10.00
62	Tony Oliva	10.00
63	Buck O'Neil	20.00
64	Jim Palmer/SP/600	20.00
65	Dave Parker	10.00
66	Tony Perez	20.00
67	Gaylord Perry	10.00
68	Lou Piniella	10.00
69	Ted Radcliffe	10.00
70	Jim Rice	10.00
71	Phil Rizzuto/SP/425	80.00
72	Brooks Robinson	25.00
73	Frank Robinson	20.00
74	Preacher Roe	10.00
75	Nolan Ryan/SP/650	100.00
76	Ryne Sandberg	50.00
77	Mike Schmidt/SP/213	175.00
78	Tom Seaver	50.00
79	Bill Skowron	10.00
80	Enos Slaughter	15.00
81	Ozzie Smith	50.00
82	Duke Snider/SP/600	50.00
83	Warren Spahn	40.00
84	Willie Stargell (Redemption card only, none signed.)	10.00
85	Don Sutton	10.00
86	Joe Torre SP/500	40.00
87	Alan Trammell	15.00
88	Hoyt Wilhelm	10.00
89	Billy Williams	10.00
90	Maury Wills	10.00
91	Artie Wilson	10.00
92	Mookie Wilson	10.00
93	Dave Winfield/SP/370	60.00
94	Robin Yount/SP/400	80.00

Dodger Blues

	NM/M
Common Player:	10.00

Inserted 1:36

(1)	Walter Alston/Jsy	10.00
(2)	Walt Alston/Uni.	10.00
(3)	Roy Campanella/SP/Uni.	75.00
(4)	Roger Craig/Jsy	10.00
(5)	Don Drysdale/Jsy	20.00
(6)	Carl Furillo/Jsy	10.00
(7)	Steve Garvey/Jsy	10.00
(8)	Gil Hodges/Uni.	20.00
(9)	Wes Parker/Bat	10.00
(10)	Wes Parker/Jsy	10.00
(11)	Pee Wee Reese/Jsy	15.00
(12)	Jackie Robinson/SP/Uni.	150.00
(13)	Preacher Roe/Jsy	10.00
(14)	Duke Snider/SP/Bat	75.00
(15)	Don Sutton/Jsy	10.00

Feel the Game Classics

	NM/M
Common Player:	5.00

Inserted 1:72

1	Luis Aparicio/Bat	5.00
2	George Brett/Jsy	30.00
3	Lou Brock/Jsy	15.00
4	Orlando Cepeda/Bat	15.00
5	Whitey Ford/Jsy	15.00
6	Hank Greenberg/Bat	40.00
7	Elston Howard/Bat	5.00
8	"Catfish" Hunter/Jsy	8.00
9	Harmon Killebrew/Bat	25.00
10	Roger Maris/Bat	50.00
11	Eddie Mathews/Bat	15.00
12	W. McCovey/Bat/SP/200	15.00
13	Johnny Mize/Bat	5.00
14	Paul Molitor/Jsy	5.00
15	Jim Palmer/Jsy	10.00
16	Tony Perez/Bat	5.00
17	Brooks Robinson/Bat/144	25.00
18	Babe Ruth/Bat/250	200.00
19	Mike Schmidt/Jsy	25.00
20	Tom Seaver/Jsy	10.00
21	Enos Slaughter	10.00
22	Willie Stargell	10.00
23	Hack Wilson	10.00
24	Harry Heilmann	5.00

Retrospection Collection

MIKE SCHMIDT
Philadelphia Phillies

	NM/M
Complete Set (10):	20.00
Common Player:	1.00

Inserted 1:6

1	Babe Ruth	5.00
2	Stan Musial	3.00
3	Jimmie Foxx	3.00
4	Roberto Clemente	4.00
5	Ted Williams	4.00
6	Mike Schmidt	4.00
7	Cy Young	1.50
8	Satchel Paige	2.00
9	Hank Greenberg	1.50
10	Jim Bunning	1.00

2001 Fleer Legacy

	NM/M
Complete Set (105):	
Common Player:	.50
Common (91-105):	8.00
Production 799 Sets	
Pack (5):	8.00
Box (15 + Cap):	140.00

1	Pedro J. Martinez	1.50
2	Andruw Jones	1.50
3	Mike Hampton	.50
4	Gary Sheffield	.65
5	Barry Zito	.65
6	J.D. Drew	.75
7	Charles Johnson	.50
8	David Wells	.50
9	Kazuhiro Sasaki	.50
10	Vladimir Guerrero	1.50
11	Pat Burrell	.75
12	Ruben Mateo	.50
13	Greg Maddux	2.00
14	Sean Casey	.65
15	Craig Biggio	.65
16	Bernie Williams	.65
17	Jeff Kent	.50
18	Nomar Garciaparra	2.50
19	Cal Ripken Jr.	.50
20	Larry Walker	.50
21	Adrian Beltre	.65
22	Johnny Damon	.75
23	Rick Ankiel	.50
24	Matt Williams	.50
25	Magglio Ordonez	.50
26	Richard Hidalgo	.50
27	Robin Ventura	.50
28	Jason Kendall	.50
29	Tony Batista	.50
30	Chipper Jones	2.00

ABBREVIATIONS

SP - Short Print

31	Jim Thome	.50
32	Kevin Brown	.50
33	Mike Mussina	.65
34	Mark McGwire	3.00
35	Darin Erstad	.75
36	Manny Ramirez	1.50
37	Bobby Higginson	.50
38	Richie Sexson	.50
39	Jason Giambi	1.00
40	Alex Rodriguez	3.00
41	Mark Grace	.65
42	Ken Griffey Jr.	2.50
43	Moises Alou	.50
44	Edgardo Alfonzo	.50
45	Phil Nevin	.50
46	Rafael Palmeiro	1.25
47	Javy Lopez	.50
48	Juan Gonzalez	1.50
49	Jermaine Dye	.50
50	Roger Clemens	2.25
51	Barry Bonds	4.00
52	Carl Everett	.50
53	Ben Sheets	.50
54	Juan Encarnacion	.50
55	Jeromy Burnitz	.50
56	Miguel Tejada	.65
57	Ben Grieve	.50
58	Randy Johnson	1.50
59	Frank Thomas	1.50
60	Preston Wilson	.50
61	Mike Piazza	2.50
62	Brian Giles	.50
63	Carlos Delgado	1.00
64	Tom Glavine	.75
65	Roberto Alomar	.65
66	Mike Sweeney	.50
67	Orlando Hernandez	.50
68	Edgar Martinez	.50
69	Tim Salmon	.75
70	Kerry Wood	1.00
71	Jack Wilson RC	3.00
72	Matt Lawton	.50
73	Scott Rolen	1.25
74	Ivan Rodriguez	1.25
75	Steve Finley	.50
76	Barry Larkin	.50
77	Jeff Bagwell	1.50
78	Derek Jeter	4.00
79	Tony Gwynn	2.00
80	Raul Mondesi	.50
81	Rafael Furcal	.50
82	Todd Helton	1.50
83	Shawn Green	.75
84	Tim Hudson	.65
85	Jim Edmonds	.50
86	Troy Glaus	1.50
87	Sammy Sosa	2.50
88	Cliff Floyd	.50
89	Jose Vidro	.50
90	Bobby Abreu	.50
91	Drew Henson/ Auto. RC	40.00
92	Andy Morales/ Auto. RC	8.00
93	Wilson Betemit/ Auto. RC	10.00
94	Elpidio Guzman RC	8.00
95	Esix Snead RC	8.00
96	Winston Abreu RC	8.00
97	Jeremy Owens RC	8.00
99	Junior Spivey RC	15.00
100	Jaisen Randolph RC	8.00
101	Ichiro Suzuki RC	60.00
102	Albert Pujols/ 499 RC	160.00
102	Albert Pujols/ Auto./300 RC	750.00
103	Tsuyoshi Shinjo RC	10.00
104	Jay Gibbons RC	10.00
105	Juan Uribe RC	10.00

Ultimate Legacy

Stars (1-90):	3-5X
Rookies (91-100):	.3-.75X
Rookies (101-105):	.75-1X
Production 250 Sets	

Autographed MLB Fitted Cap

	NM/M
Common Player:	25.00
Inserted 1:15	
Edgardo Alfonzo	25.00
Roberto Alomar	50.00
Ernie Banks/100	100.00

Adrian Beltre	40.00
Johnny Bench/100	125.00
Lance Berkman	30.00
Yogi Berra/200	120.00
Craig Biggio	30.00
Barry Bonds	280.00
Jeromy Burnitz	25.00
Pat Burrell	30.00
Steve Carlton	40.00
Sean Casey	30.00
Orlando Cepeda	30.00
Eric Chavez	25.00
Tony Clark	25.00
Roger Clemens/100	200.00
Johnny Damon	40.00
Dom DiMaggio/200	45.00
J.D. Drew	40.00
Jermaine Dye	25.00
Darin Erstad	40.00
Carlton Fisk/150	80.00
Rafael Furcal	25.00
Nomar Garciaparra/ 150	150.00
Jason Giambi	50.00
Troy Glaus	35.00
Tom Glavine	50.00
Juan Gonzalez	50.00
Luis Gonzalez	30.00
Tony Gwynn	85.00
Drew Henson	30.00
Derek Jeter	250.00
Andruw Jones	40.00
David Justice	30.00
Paul Konerko	25.00
Don Mattingly	150.00
Willie McCovey	30.00
Paul Molitor	60.00
Stan Musial/200	125.00
Mike Mussina	50.00
Jim Palmer	25.00
Corey Patterson	30.00
Kirby Puckett/200	75.00
Cal Ripken/200	200.00
Brooks Robinson	60.00
Ivan Rodriguez	50.00
Scott Rolen	50.00
Nolan Ryan/150	200.00
Mike Schmidt/150	125.00
Tom Seaver/100	125.00
Ben Sheets	40.00
Ozzie Smith	85.00
Duke Snider	40.00
Miguel Tejada	50.00
Jim Thome	60.00
Matt Williams	25.00
Dave Winfield/150	75.00
Carl Yastrzemski/ 150	100.00
Robin Yount	100.00
Barry Zito	40.00

Hit Kings

	NM/M
Common Player:	5.00
Inserted 1:13	
Stan Musial	15.00
Barry Bonds	25.00
Corey Patterson	6.00
Shawn Green	6.00
Ralph Kiner	5.00
Troy O'Leary	5.00
Ivan Rodriguez	6.00
Jose Vidro	5.00
Carlos Beltran	8.00
Jose Canseco	5.00
Juan Encarnacion	5.00
Reggie Jackson	10.00
Ruben Mateo	5.00
Juan Pierre	5.00
Tim Salmon	5.00
Adrian Beltre	6.00
Roger Cedeno	5.00
Troy Glaus	8.00
Jason Kendall	5.00
Rick Ankiel	5.00
Andruw Jones	8.00
Jim Thome	5.00
Tony Batista	5.00
George Brett	20.00
Vladimir Guerrero	10.00
Billy Martin	5.00
Magglio Ordonez	5.00
Johnny Damon	6.00

Hit Kings Short Prints

	NM/M
Common Player:	25.00
Inserted 1:15	
Edgardo Alfonzo	25.00
Roberto Alomar	50.00
Ernie Banks/100	100.00

	NM/M
Common Player:	15.00
Production 100 Sets	
Robin Yount	20.00
Scott Rolen	15.00
Johnny Bench	25.00
Steve Garvey	15.00
Joe Morgan	15.00
Frank Thomas	20.00
Eddie Mathews	20.00
Tony Gwynn	25.00
Roger Clemens	40.00
Wade Boggs	25.00

Hot Gloves

		NM/M
Common Player:		15.00
Inserted 1:180		
1HG	Andruw Jones	15.00
2HG	Mike Mussina	15.00
3HG	Roberto Alomar	15.00
4HG	Tony Gwynn	30.00
5HG	Bernie Williams	15.00
6HG	Ivan Rodriguez	15.00
7HG	Ken Griffey Jr.	40.00
8HG	Robin Ventura	15.00
9HG	Cal Ripken Jr.	60.00
10HG	Jeff Bagwell	20.00
11HG	Mark McGwire	50.00
12HG	Rafael Palmeiro	15.00
13HG	Scott Rolen	15.00
14HG	Barry Bonds	60.00
15HG	Greg Maddux	30.00

MLB Game Issue - Base

		NM/M
Common Player:		4.00
Inserted 1:52		
1GI	Mark McGwire	15.00
2GI	Ken Griffey Jr.	10.00
3GI	Sammy Sosa	10.00
4GI	Mike Piazza	10.00
5GI	Alex Rodriguez	15.00
6GI	Derek Jeter	20.00
7GI	Cal Ripken Jr.	20.00
8GI	Todd Helton	6.00
9GI	Tony Gwynn	8.00
10GI	Chipper Jones	8.00
11GI	Frank Thomas	6.00
12GI	Barry Bonds	20.00
13GI	Troy Glaus	4.00
14GI	Pat Burrell	4.00
15GI	Scott Rolen	5.00

MLB Game Issue - Base/Ball

	NM/M
Common Player:	10.00
Production 100 Sets	
Mark McGwire	50.00
Ken Griffey Jr.	40.00
Sammy Sosa	40.00
Mike Piazza	40.00
Alex Rodriguez	50.00
Derek Jeter	60.00
Cal Ripken Jr.	60.00
Todd Helton	15.00
Tony Gwynn	25.00
Chipper Jones	25.00
Frank Thomas	15.00
Barry Bonds	60.00
Troy Glaus	10.00
Pat Burrell	10.00
Scott Rolen	12.50

MLB Game Issue - Base/Ball/Jersey

	NM/M
Common Card:	25.00
Production 50 Sets	
Derek Jeter	100.00
Cal Ripken Jr.	100.00
Todd Helton	30.00
Tony Gwynn	50.00
Chipper Jones	50.00
Frank Thomas	30.00
Barry Bonds	100.00
Troy Glaus	25.00
Pat Burrell	25.00
Scott Rolen	30.00

Tailor Made

		NM/M
Common Player:		4.00
Inserted 1:15		
2TM	Cal Ripken Jr.	40.00
3TM	Orlando Cepeda	6.00
4TM	Willie McCovey	6.00
5TM	Dave Winfield	6.00
6TM	Don Mattingly	35.00
7TM	Nolan Ryan	40.00
8TM	Manny Ramirez	8.00
9TM	Edgardo Alfonzo	4.00
10TM	Rondell White	4.00
11TM	Lou Piniella	4.00
12TM	Ivan Rodriguez	8.00
13TM	J.D. Drew	4.00
14TM	Barry Bonds	40.00
15TM	Greg Maddux	8.00
16TM	Rick Ankiel	4.00
17TM	Carlos Delgado	8.00
18TM	Kevin Brown	4.00
20TM	Reggie Jackson	10.00
21TM	Shawn Green	6.00
22TM	Jason Kendall	4.00
23TM	Rafael Palmeiro	8.00
24TM	Todd Helton	8.00
25	Curt Schilling	6.00

2001 Fleer Platinum

JEFF BAGWELL FIRST BASE

	NM/M
Complete Set (301):	140.00
Common Player:	.15
Common SP (251-300):	1.00
Inserted 1:6	
Card #301 production 1,500	
Pack (10):	5.00
Box (24):	100.00

1	Bobby Abreu	.15
2	Brad Radke	.15
3	Bill Mueller	.15
4	Adam Eaton	.15
5	Antonio Alfonseca	.15
6	Manny Ramirez	.75
7	Adam Kennedy	.15
8	Jose Valentin	.15
9	Jaret Wright	.15
10	Aramis Ramirez	.15
11	Jeff Kent	.15
12	Juan Encarnacion	.15
13	Sandy Alomar Jr.	.15
14	Joe Randa	.15
15	Darryl Kile	.15
16	Darren Dreifort	.15
17	Matt Kinney	.15
18	Pokey Reese	.15
19	Ryan Klesko	.15
20	Shawn Estes	.15
21	Moises Alou	.15
22	Edgar Renteria	.15
23	Chuck Knoblauch	.15
24	Carl Everett	.15
25	Garret Anderson	.15
26	Shane Reynolds	.15
27	Billy Koch	.15
28	Carlos Febles	.15
29	Brian Anderson	.15
30	Armando Rios	.15
31	Ryan Kohlmeier	.15
32	Steve Finley	.15

33	Brady Anderson	.15
34	Cal Ripken Jr.	2.50
35	Paul Konerko	.15
36	Chuck Finley	.15
37	Rick Ankiel	.15
38	Mariano Rivera	.25
39	Corey Koskie	.15
40	Cliff Floyd	.15
41	Kevin Appier	.15
42	Henry Rodriguez	.15
43	Mark Kotsay	.15
44	Brook Fordyce	.15
45	Brad Ausmus	.15
46	Alfonso Soriano	.50
47	Ray Lankford	.15
48	Keith Foulke	.15
49	Rich Aurilia	.15
50	Alex Rodriguez	2.00
51	Eric Byrnes	.15
52	Travis Fryman	.15
53	Jeff Bagwell	.75
54	Scott Rolen	.65
55	Matt Lawton	.15
56	Brad Fullmer	.15
57	Tony Batista	.15
58	Nate Rolison	.15
59	Carlos Lee	.15
60	Rafael Furcal	.15
61	Jay Bell	.15
62	Jimmy Rollins	.25
63	Derek Lee	.15
64	Andres Galarraga	.15
65	Derek Bell	.15
66	Tim Salmon	.25
67	Travis Lee	.15
68	Kevin Millwood	.15
69	Albert Belle	.15
70	Kazuhiro Sasaki	.15
71	Al Leiter	.15
72	Britt Reames	.15
73	Carlos Beltran	.45
74	Curt Schilling	.50
75	Curtis Leskanic	.15
76	Jeremy Giambi	.15
77	Adrian Beltre	.35
78	David Segui	.15
79	Mike Lieberthal	.15
80	Brian Giles	.15
81	Marvin Benard	.15
82	Aaron Sele	.15
83	Kenny Lofton	.15
84	Doug Glanville	.15
85	Kris Benson	.15
86	Richie Sexson	.15
87	Javy Lopez	.15
88	Doug Mientkiewicz	.15
89	Peter Bergeron	.15
90	Gary Sheffield	.40
91	Derek Lowe	.15
92	Tom Glavine	.40
93	Lance Berkman	.15
94	Chris Singleton	.15
95	Mike Lowell	.25
96	Luis Gonzalez	.30
97	Dante Bichette	.15
98	Mike Sirotka	.15
99	Julio Lugo	.15
100	Juan Gonzalez	.75
101	Craig Biggio	.15
102	Armando Benitez	.15
103	Greg Maddux	1.00
104	Mark Grace	.25
105	John Smoltz	.15
106	J.T. Snow	.15
107	Al Martin	.15
108	Danny Graves	.15
109	Barry Bonds	2.50
110	Lee Stevens	.15
111	Pedro Martinez	.75
112	Shawn Green	.40
113	Bret Boone	.15
114	Matt Stairs	.15
115	Tino Martinez	.15
116	Rusty Greer	.15
117	Mike Bordick	.15
118	Garrett Stephenson	.15
119	Edgar Martinez	.15
120	Ben Grieve	.15
121	Milton Bradley	.15
122	Aaron Boone	.15
123	Ruben Mateo	.15
124	Ken Griffey Jr.	1.50
125	Russell Branyan	.15
126	Shannon Stewart	.15
127	Fred McGriff	.15
128	Ben Petrick	.15
129	Kevin Brown	.15
130	B.J. Surhoff	.15
131	Mark McGwire	2.00
132	Carlos Guillen	.15
133	Adrian Brown	.15
134	Mike Sweeney	.15
135	Eric Milton	.15
136	Cristian Guzman	.15
137	Ellis Burks	.15
138	Fernando Tatis	.15
139	Ben Molina	.15
140	Tony Gwynn	1.00
141	Jeromy Burnitz	.15
142	Miguel Tejada	.25
143	Raul Mondesi	.15
144	Jeffrey Hammonds	.15
145	Pat Burrell	.40
146	Frank Thomas	.75
147	Eric Munson	.15
148	Mike Hampton	.15
149	Mike Cameron	.15
150	Jim Thome	.15

151	Mike Mussina	.50
152	Rick Helling	.15
153	Ken Caminiti	.15
154	John Vander Wal	.15
155	Denny Neagle	.15
156	Robb Nen	.15
157	Jose Canseco	.50
158	Mo Vaughn	.15
159	Phil Nevin	.15
160	Pat Hentgen	.15
161	Sean Casey	.25
162	Greg Vaughn	.15
163	Trot Nixon	.15
164	Roberto Hernandez	.15
165	Vinny Castilla	.15
166	Robin Ventura	.15
167	Alex Ochoa	.15
168	Orlando Hernandez	.15
169	Luis Castillo	.15
170	Quivio Veras	.15
171	Troy O'Leary	.15
172	Livan Hernandez	.15
173	Roger Cedeno	.15
174	Jose Vidro	.15
175	John Olerud	.15
176	Richard Hidalgo	.15
177	Eric Chavez	.25
178	Fernando Vina	.15
179	Chris Stynes	.15
180	Bobby Higginson	.15
181	Bruce Chen	.15
182	Omar Vizquel	.15
183	Rey Ordonez	.15
184	Trevor Hoffman	.15
185	Jeff Cirillo	.15
186	Billy Wagner	.15
187	David Ortiz	.15
188	Tim Hudson	.40
189	Tony Clark	.15
190	Larry Walker	.15
191	Eric Owens	.15
192	Aubrey Huff	.15
193	Royce Clayton	.15
194	Todd Walker	.15
195	Rafael Palmeiro	.65
196	Todd Hundley	.15
197	Roger Clemens	1.25
198	Jeff Weaver	.15
199	Dean Palmer	.15
200	Geoff Jenkins	.15
201	Matt Clement	.15
202	David Wells	.15
203	Chan Ho Park	.15
204	Hideo Nomo	.65
205	Bartolo Colon	.15
206	John Wetteland	.15
207	Corey Patterson	.15
208	Freddy Garcia	.15
209	David Cone	.15
210	Rondell White	.15
211	Carl Pavano	.15
212	Charles Johnson	.15
213	Ron Coomer	.15
214	Matt Williams	.15
215	Jay Payton	.15
216	Nick Johnson	.15
217	Deivi Cruz	.15
218	Scott Elarton	.15
219	Neifi Perez	.15
220	Jason Isringhausen	.15
221	Jose Cruz	.15
222	Gerald Williams	.15
223	Timo Perez	.15
224	Damion Easley	.15
225	Jeff D'Amico (Photo actually Jamey Wright.)	.15
226	Preston Wilson	.15
227	Robert Person	.15
228	Jacque Jones	.15
229	Johnny Damon	.25
230	Tony Womack	.15
231	Adam Piatt	.15
232	Brian Jordan	.15
233	Ben Davis	.15
234	Kerry Wood	.50
235	Mike Piazza	1.50
236	David Justice	.15
237	Dave Veres	.15
238	Eric Young	.15
239	Juan Pierre	.15
240	Gabe Kapler	.15
241	Ryan Dempster	.15
242	Dmitri Young	.15
243	Jorge Posada	.35
244	Eric Karros	.15
245	J.D. Drew	.25
246	Todd Zeile	.15
247	Mark Quinn	.15
248	Kenny Kelly	.15
249	Jermaine Dye	.15
250	Barry Zito	.30
251	Jason Hart, Larry Barnes	1.00
252	Ichiro Suzuki RC, Elpidio Guzman RC	20.00
253	Tsuyoshi Shinjo RC, Brian Cole	3.00
254	John Barnes, Adrian Hernandez RC	1.00
255	Jason Tyner, Jace Brewer	1.00
256	Brian Buchanan, Luis Rivas	1.00
257	Brent Abernathy, Jose Ortiz	1.00
258	Marcus Giles, Keith Ginter	1.00

259 Tike Redman,
   Jaisen Randolph **RC** 1.00
260 Dane Sardinha,
   David Espinosa 1.00
261 Josh Beckett,
   Craig House 1.00
262 Jack Cust,
   Hiram Bocachica 1.00
263 Alex Escobar,
   Esix Snead **RC** 1.00
264 Chris Richard,
   Vernon Wells 1.00
265 Pedro Feliz,
   Xavier Nady 1.00
266 Brandon Inge,
   Joe Crede 1.00
267 Ben Sheets,
   Roy Oswalt 1.00
268 Drew Henson **RC**,
   Andy Morales **RC** 4.00
269 C.C. Sabathia,
   Justin Miller 1.00
270 David Eckstein,
   Jason Gabrowski 1.00
271 Dee Brown,
   Chris Wakeland 1.00
272 Junior Spivey **RC**,
   Alex Cintron 3.00
273 Elvis Pena,
   Juan Uribe **RC** 2.00
274 Carlos Pena,
   Jason Romano 1.00
275 Winston Abreu **RC**,
   Wilson Betemit **RC** 1.50
276 Jose Mieses **RC**,
   Nick Neugebauer 1.00
277 Shea Hillenbrand,
   Dernell Stenson 1.00
278 Jared Sandberg,
   Toby Hall 1.00
279 Jay Gibbons **RC**,
   Ivanon Coffie 3.00
280 Pablo Ozuna,
   Santiago Perez 1.00
281 Nomar Garciaparra/AS 6.00
282 Derek Jeter/AS 6.00
283 Jason Giambi/AS 2.50
284 Magglio Ordonez/AS 1.00
285 Ivan Rodriguez/AS 2.00
286 Troy Glaus/AS 2.00
287 Carlos Delgado/AS 2.00
288 Darin Erstad/AS 1.00
289 Bernie Williams/AS 2.00
290 Roberto Alomar/AS 1.50
291 Barry Larkin /AS 1.50
292 Chipper Jones/AS 4.00
293 Vladimir Guerrero/AS 3.00
294 Sammy Sosa/AS 5.00
295 Todd Helton/AS 3.00
296 Randy Johnson/AS 3.00
297 Jason Kendall/AS 1.00
298 Jim Edmonds/AS 1.50
299 Andruw Jones/AS 2.00
300 Edgardo Alfonzo/AS 1.00
301 Albert Pujols,
   Donaldo Mendez **RC** 80.00

Platinum Edition

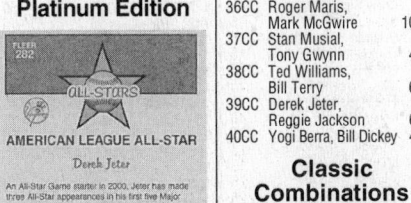

AMERICAN LEAGUE ALL-STAR
Derek Jeter

An All-Star Game starter in 2000, Jeter has made three All-Star appearances in his first five Major League seasons. He was an impressive 3-for-3 with a run scored, knocking in two runs in the pivotal fourth inning that put the AL ahead for good in a 6-9 victory. The later used in the game went directly to Cooperstown for display in the Hall of Fame. Why? He's the first New York Yankee to earn an MVP Award in the Midsummer Classic.

21 / 21

Cards (1-250): 4-8X
Production 201 Sets
SP's (251-280): 8-20X
SP's (281-300): 5-10X
SP Production 21 Sets

Classic Combinations

NM/M
Common Card: 4.00
#1-10 numbered to 250
11-20 numbered to 500
21-30 numbered to 1,000
31-40 numbered to 2,000
1CC Derek Jeter,
   Alex Rodriguez 20.00

2CC Willie Mays,
   Willie McCovey 15.00
3CC Lou Gehrig,
   Babe Ruth 20.00
4CC Mark McGwire,
   Ken Griffey Jr. 15.00
5CC Johnny Bench,
   Roy Campanella 10.00
6CC Ted Williams,
   Nomar Garciaparra 20.00
7CC Yogi Berra,
   Mike Piazza 15.00
8CC Ernie Banks,
   Sammy Sosa 12.00
9CC Nolan Ryan,
   Randy Johnson 25.00
10CC Roberto Clemente,
   Vladimir Guerrero 15.00
11CC Lou Gehrig,
   Stan Musial 15.00
12CC Bill Mazeroski,
   Roberto Clemente 10.00
13CC Ernie Banks,
   Alex Rodriguez 10.00
14CC Phil Rizzuto,
   Derek Jeter 10.00
15CC Mike Piazza,
   Johnny Bench 8.00
16CC Mark McGwire,
   Sammy Sosa 10.00
17CC Ted Williams,
   Tony Gwynn 12.00
18CC Eddie Mathews,
   Mike Schmidt 10.00
19CC Barry Bonds,
   Willie Mays 10.00
20CC Nolan Ryan,
   Pedro Martinez 15.00
21CC Barry Bonds,
   Ken Griffey Jr. 10.00
22CC Willie McCovey,
   Reggie Jackson 5.00
23CC Roberto Clemente,
   Sammy Sosa 8.00
24CC Willie Mays,
   Ernie Banks 8.00
25CC Eddie Mathews,
   Chipper Jones 5.00
26CC Mike Schmidt,
   Brooks Robinson 6.00
27CC Stan Musial,
   Mark McGwire 8.00
28CC Ted Williams,
   Roger Maris 8.00
29CC Yogi Berra,
   Roy Campanella 5.00
30CC Johnny Bench,
   Tony Perez 5.00
31CC Bill Mazeroski,
   Joe Carter 3.00
32CC Mike Piazza,
   Roy Campanella 5.00
33CC Ernie Banks,
   Craig Biggio 4.00
34CC Frank Robinson,
   Brooks Robinson 4.00
35CC Mike Schmidt,
   Scott Rolen 5.00
36CC Roger Maris,
   Mark McGwire 10.00
37CC Stan Musial,
   Tony Gwynn 4.00
38CC Ted Williams,
   Bill Terry 6.00
39CC Derek Jeter,
   Reggie Jackson 6.00
40CC Yogi Berra, Bill Dickey 4.00

Classic Combinations Memorabilia

Classic Combinations

NM/M
Production 25 Sets
1 Yogi Berra,
   Bill Dickey 75.00
2 Yogi Berra,
   Roy Campanella 100.00
3 Roberto Clemente,
   Vladimir Guerrero 200.00
4 Eddie Mathews,
   Chipper Jones 80.00
5 Willie McCovey,
   Reggie Jackson 75.00
6 Phil Rizzuto,
   Derek Jeter 180.00
7 Brooks Robinson,
   Frank Robinson 85.00
8 Brooks Robinson,
   Mike Schmidt 180.00
9 Mike Schmidt,
   Scott Rolen 160.00
10 Ted Williams,
   Bill Terry 300.00
11 Ted Williams,
   Tony Gwynn 375.00

Grandstand Greats

Grandstand Greats

NM/M
Complete Set (20): 25.00
Common Player: 1.00
Inserted 1:12
1GG Chipper Jones 2.00
2GG Alex Rodriguez 3.00
3GG Jeff Bagwell 1.50
4GG Troy Glaus 1.50
5GG Manny Ramirez 1.50
6GG Derek Jeter 4.00
7GG Tony Gwynn 2.00
8GG Greg Maddux 2.00
9GG Nomar Garciaparra 2.50
10GG Sammy Sosa 2.50
11GG Mike Piazza 2.50
12GG Barry Bonds 4.00
13GG Mark McGwire 3.00
14GG Vladimir Guerrero 1.50
15GG Ivan Rodriguez 1.00
16GG Ken Griffey Jr. 2.50
17GG Todd Helton 1.50
18GG Cal Ripken Jr. 4.00
19GG Pedro Martinez 1.50
20GG Frank Thomas 1.50

Nameplates

NM/M
Common Player: 15.00
Inserted 1:12
Cal Ripken/19 200.00
Cal Ripke /21 200.00
Cal Ripken/23 200.00
Cal Ripken/110 100.00
Randy Johnson/99 40.00
Nolan Ryan/49 200.00
Javy Lopez/49 20.00
Frank Thomas/35 40.00
Frank Thomas/75 30.00
Frank Thomas/80 30.00
Jeffrey Hammonds/135 15.00
Larry Walker/79 15.00
Larry Walker/85 15.00
Dave Winfield/80 20.00
Vladimir Guerrero/80 25.00
Vladimir Guerrero/90 25.00
Kevin Millwood/130 15.00
Mike Mussina/91 15.00
Edgar Martinez/87 25.00
Edgar Martinez/120 20.00
Scott Rolen/65 30.00
Ivan Rodriguez/177 25.00
Manny Ramirez/75 25.00
Manny Ramirez/105 25.00
J.D. Drew/170 15.00
Greg Maddux/180 50.00
Chipper Jones/95 40.00
Carlos Beltran/90 15.00
Adrian Beltre 15.00
Matt Williams/175 15.00
Curt Schilling 20.00
Pedro Martinez/120 30.00
Robin Ventura/99 15.00
Tom Glavine/125 15.00
Tony Gwynn/35 75.00
Tony Gwynn/65 40.00
Tony Gwynn/70 40.00
Troy Glaus/85 20.00
Sean Casey/21 35.00
Darin Erstad/39 30.00
Stan Musial/30 150.00

National Patch Time

NM/M
Common Player: 4.00
Inserted 1:24 H
Tony Gwynn 8.00
Manny Ramirez 6.00
Freddy Garcia 4.00
Rondell White 4.00
Ivan Rodriguez 5.00

Brady Anderson 4.00
Adam Piatt 4.00
Carl Everett 4.00
Magglio Ordonez 4.00
Edgardo Alfonzo 4.00
Jason Kendall 4.00
Greg Maddux 8.00
Cal Ripken Jr. 30.00
Fred McGriff 4.00
Pedro Martinez 6.00
Roger Clemens 10.00
Wade Boggs 8.00
George Brett 15.00
Ozzie Smith 8.00
Dave Winfield 6.00
Tom Seaver 6.00
Rollie Fingers 4.00
Mike Schmidt 15.00
Eddie Murray 6.00
Nolan Ryan 30.00
Jeff Cirillo 4.00
Mike Mussina 5.00

Rack Pack Autographs

NM/M
Common Player: 5.00
Hank Aaron
1997/90 100.00
Roger Clemens
1998/125 100.00
Jose Cruz Jr. 1997 5.00
Bob Gibson
1998/300 25.00
Ben Grieve 100 6.00
Tony Gwynn
1998/125 50.00
Wes Helms 1997 5.00
Harmon Killebrew
1998/300 30.00
Paul Konerko 135 5.00
Willie Mays
1997/115 120.00
Willie Mays
1998/120 120.00
Kirby Puckett
1997/105 50.00
Brooks Robinson
1998/40 75.00
Frank Robinson
1998/115 20.00
Scott Rolen
1998/150 25.00
Alex Rodriguez
1997/94 100.00
Alex Rodriguez
1998/150 70.00

Tickets

Complete Set (44):
Common Player:

Tickets Autographs

Complete Set (9):
Common Player:

20th Anniversary Reprints

KIRBY PUCKETT Outfield

NM/M
Complete Set (18): 25.00
Common Player: .50
Inserted 1:8
1AR Cal Ripken Jr. 4.00
2AR Wade Boggs 1.50
3AR Ryne Sandberg 1.50

4AR Tony Gwynn 1.50
5AR Don Mattingly 3.00
6AR Roger Clemens 2.00
7AR Kirby Puckett 1.50
8AR Jose Canseco .75
9AR Barry Bonds 4.00
10AR Ken Griffey Jr. 2.50
11AR Sammy Sosa 2.50
12AR Ivan Rodriguez .75
13AR Jeff Bagwell 1.00
14AR J.D. Drew .75
15AR Troy Glaus 1.00
16AR Rick Ankiel .50
17AR Xavier Nady .50
18AR Jose Ortiz .50

2001 Fleer Platinum RC

ALEX RODRIGUEZ RANGERS — TEAM LEADERS

NM/M
Complete Set (300): 150.00
Common Player: .15
Common (502-601): 1.00
Inserted 1:3 Hobby
Pack (10): 7.00
Box (24): 140.00
302 Shawn Wooten .15
303 Todd Walker .15
304 Brian Buchanan .15
305 Jim Edmonds .25
306 Jarrod Washburn .15
307 Jose Rijo .15
308 Tim Raines .15
309 Matt Morris .15
310 Troy Glaus .50
311 Barry Larkin .40
312 Javier Vazquez .15
313 Placido Polanco .15
314 Darin Erstad .25
315 Marty Cordova .15
316 Vladimir Guerrero .75
317 Kerry Robinson .15
318 Byung-Hyun Kim .15
319 C.C. Sabathia .15
320 Edgardo Alfonzo .15
321 Jason Tyner .15
322 Reggie Sanders .15
323 Roberto Alomar .60
324 Matt Lawton .15
325 Brett Abernathy .15
326 Randy Johnson .75
327 Todd Helton .75
328 Andy Pettitte .40
329 Josh Beckett .40
330 Mark DeRosa .15
331 Jose Ortiz .15
332 Derek Jeter 2.00
333 Toby Hall .15
334 Wes Helms .15
335 Jose Macias .15
336 Bernie Williams .60
337 Ivan Rodriguez .75
338 Chipper Jones 1.25
339 Brandon Inge .15
340 Jason Giambi .75
341 Frank Catalanotto .15
342 Andruw Jones .50
343 Carlos Hernandez **RC** .40
344 Jermaine Dye .15
345 Mike Lamb .15
346 Ken Caminiti .15
347 A.J. Burnett .15
348 Terrence Long .15
349 Ruben Sierra .15
350 Marcus Giles .15
351 Wade Miller .15
352 Mark Mulder .15
353 Carlos Delgado .50
354 Chris Richard .15
355 Daryle Ward .15
356 Brad Penny .15
357 Vernon Wells .25
358 Jason Johnson .15
359 Tim Redding .15
360 Marlon Anderson .15
361 Carlos Pena .15
362 Nomar Garciaparra 2.00
363 Roy Oswalt .40
364 Todd Ritchie .15
365 Jose Mesa .15
366 Shea Hillenbrand .15
367 Dee Brown .15
368 Jason Kendall .25
369 Vinny Castilla .15
370 Fred McGriff .25
371 Neifi Perez .15
372 Xavier Nady .15
373 Abraham Nunez .15

374 Jon Lieber .15
375 Paul LoDuca .15
376 Bubba Trammell .15
377 Brady Clark .15
378 Joel Pineiro .15
379 Mark Grudzielanek .15
380 D'Angelo Jimenez .15
381 Junior Herndon .15
382 Magglio Ordonez .40
383 Ben Sheets .25
384 John Vander Wal .15
385 Pedro Astacio .15
386 Jose Canseco .40
387 Jose Hernandez .15
388 Eric Davis .15
389 Sammy Sosa 1.25
390 Mark Buehrle .15
391 Mark Loretta .15
392 Andres Galarraga .25
393 Scott Spiezio .15
394 Joe Crede .15
395 Luis Rivas .15
396 David Bell .15
397 Einar Diaz .15
398 Adam Dunn .75
399 A.J. Pierzynski .15
400 Jamie Moyer .15
401 Nick Johnson .15
402 Freddy Garcia 4.00
403 Hideo Nomo .50
404 Mark Mulder .25
405 Steve Sparks .15
406 Mariano Rivera .25
407 Mark Buehrle,
   Mike Mussina .25
408 Randy Johnson .50
409 Randy Johnson .50
410 Curt Schilling .15
   Matt Morris .25
411 Greg Maddux .60
412 Robb Nen .15
413 Randy Johnson .50
414 Barry Bonds 1.00
415 Jason Giambi .40
416 Ichiro Suzuki 2.50
417 Ichiro Suzuki 2.50
418 Alex Rodriguez 1.00
419 Bret Boone .25
420 Ichiro Suzuki 2.50
421 Alex Rodriguez 1.00
422 Jason Giambi .40
423 Alex Rodriguez 1.00
424 Larry Walker .25
425 Rich Aurilia .15
426 Barry Bonds 1.00
427 Sammy Sosa .75
428 Jimmy Rollins .15
   Juan Pierre .25
429 Sammy Sosa .75
430 Lance Berkman .25
431 Sammy Sosa .75
432 Carlos Delgado .25
433 Alex Rodriguez 1.00
434 Greg Vaughn .15
435 Albert Pujols 10.00
436 Ichiro Suzuki 2.50
437 Barry Bonds 1.00
438 Phil Nevin .25
439 Brian Giles .25
440 Bobby Abreu .25
441 Jason Giambi .40
442 Derek Jeter 1.00
443 Mike Piazza .75
444 Vladimir Guerrero .50
445 Corey Koskie .25
446 Richie Sexson .25
447 Shawn Green .25
448 Mike Sweeney .15
449 Jeff Bagwell .40
450 Cliff Floyd .15
451 Roger Cedeno .15
452 Todd Helton .40
453 Juan Gonzalez .30
454 Sean Casey .15
455 Magglio Ordonez .25
456 Sammy Sosa .75
457 Manny Ramirez .40
458 Jeff Conine .15
459 Chipper Jones .60
460 Luis Gonzalez .15
461 Troy Glaus .25
462 Ivan Rodriguez .40
463 Luis Gonzalez,
   Jack Cust .25
464 Jim Thome,
   C.C. Sabathia .25
465 Jason Hart,
   Jason Giambi .25
466 Jeff Bagwell,
   Roy Oswalt .30
467 Sammy Sosa,
   Corey Patterson .50
468 Mike Piazza,
   Alex Escobar .75
469 Ken Griffey Jr.,
   Adam Dunn .75
470 Roger Clemens,
   Nick Johnson .75
471 Cliff Floyd,
   Josh Beckett .15
472 Cal Ripken Jr.,
   Jerry Hairston Jr. .75
473 Phil Nevin, Xavier Nady .15
474 Scott Rolen,
   Jimmy Rollins .40
475 Barry Larkin,
   David Espinosa .25

#	Player	Price
476	Larry Walker, Jose Ortiz	.15
477	Chipper Jones, Marcus Giles	.40
478	Craig Biggio, Keith Ginter	.15
479	Magglio Ordonez, Aaron Rowand	.25
480	Alex Rodriguez, Carlos Pena	.75
481	Derek Jeter, Alfonso Soriano	.75
482	Curt Schilling (Post Season Glory)	.20
483	(Post Season Glory)	.25
484	(Post Season Glory)	.25
485	(Post Season Glory)	.25
486	(Post Season Glory)	.25
487	(Post Season Glory)	.25
488	(Post Season Glory)	.25
489	Rudolph Giuliani (Post Season Glory)	.50
490	George Bush (Post Season Glory)	.50
491	(Post Season Glory)	.25
492	(Post Season Glory)	.25
493	(Post Season Glory)	.25
494	Derek Jeter (Post Season Glory)	.75
495	(Post Season Glory)	.25
496	(Post Season Glory)	.25
497	(Post Season Glory)	.25
498	(Post Season Glory)	.25
499	(Post Season Glory)	.25
500	(Post Season Glory)	.25
501	(Post Season Glory)	.25
502	Josh Fogg RC	1.00
503	Elpidio Guzman	1.00
504	Corky Miller RC	1.00
505	Cesar Crespo RC	1.00
506	Carlos Garcia RC	1.00
507	Carlos Valderrama RC	1.00
508	Joe Kennedy RC	1.00
509	Henry Mateo RC	1.00
510	Brandon Duckworth RC	1.00
511	Ichiro Suzuki	15.00
512	Zach Day RC	2.00
513	Ryan Freel RC	1.00
514	Brian Lawrence RC	2.00
515	Alexis Gomez RC	1.00
516	Will Ohman RC	1.00
517	Juan Diaz RC	1.00
518	Juan Moreno RC	1.00
519	Rob Mackowiak RC	1.00
520	Horacio Ramirez RC	1.50
521	Albert Pujols	75.00
522	Tsuyoshi Shinjo	2.50
523	Ryan Drese RC	1.00
524	Angel Berroa RC	3.00
525	Josh Towers RC	2.50
526	Junior Spivey	1.50
527	Greg Miller RC	1.00
528	Esix Snead RC	1.00
529	Mark Prior RC	15.00
530	Drew Henson	3.00
531	Brian Reith RC	1.00
532	Andres Torres RC	1.00
533	Casey Fossum RC	2.00
534	Wilmy Caceres RC	1.00
535	Matt White RC	1.00
536	Wilkin Ruan RC	1.00
537	Rick Bauer RC	1.00
538	Morgan Ensberg RC	2.00
539	Geronimo Gil RC	1.00
540	Dewon Brazelton RC	1.00
541	Johnny Estrada RC	1.50
542	Claudio Vargas RC	1.00
543	Donaldo Mendez RC	1.00
544	Kyle Lohse RC	2.00
545	Nate Frese RC	1.00
546	Christian Parker RC	1.00
547	Blaine Neal RC	1.00
548	Travis Hafner RC	4.00
549	Billy Sylvester RC	1.00
550	Adam Pettyjohn	1.00
551	Bill Ortega RC	1.00
552	Jose Acevedo RC	1.00
553	Steve Green RC	1.00
554	Jay Gibbons RC	2.50
555	Bert Snow RC	1.00
556	Erick Almonte RC	1.50
557	Jeremy Owens RC	1.00
558	Sean Douglass RC	1.00
559	Jason Smith RC	1.00
560	Ricardo Rodriguez RC	1.00
561	Mark Teixeira RC	15.00
562	Tyler Walker RC	1.00
563	Juan Uribe RC	1.50
564	Bud Smith RC	1.00
565	Angel Santos RC	1.00
566	Brandon Lyon RC	1.00
567	Eric Hinske RC	2.50
568	Nick Punto RC	1.00
569	Winston Abreu RC	1.00
570	Jason Phillips RC	4.00
571	Rafael Soriano RC	1.50
572	Wilson Betemit RC	1.00
573	Endy Chavez RC	1.00
574	Juan Cruz RC	1.00
575	Cory Aldridge RC	1.00
576	Adrian Hernandez RC	1.00
577	Brandon Larson RC	1.50
578	Bret Prinz RC	1.00
579	Jackson Melian RC	1.00
580	Dave Maurer RC	1.00
581	Jason Michaels RC	1.00
582	Travis Phelps RC	1.00
583	Cody Ransom RC	1.00
584	Benito Baez RC	1.00
585	Brian Roberts RC	1.00
586	Nate Teut RC	1.00
587	Jack Wilson RC	1.00
588	Willie Harris RC	1.00
589	Martin Vargas RC	1.00
590	Steve Torrealba RC	1.00
591	Stubby Clapp RC	1.00
592	Danny Wright RC	1.00
593	Mike Rivera RC	1.00
594	Luis Pineda RC	1.00
595	Lance Davis RC	1.00
596	Ramon Vazquez RC	1.00
597	Dustan Mohr RC	1.00
598	Troy Mattes RC	1.00
599	Grant Balfour RC	1.00
600	Jared Fernandez RC	1.00
601	Jorge Julio	2.00

E-X

#	Player	Price
131	Albert Pujols/499 RC	300.00
132	Bud Smith/499 RC	8.00
133	Tsuyoshi Shinjo/499 RC	10.00
134	Wilson Betemit/499 RC	8.00
135	Adrian Hernandez/499 RC	8.00
136	Jackson Melian/499	8.00
137	Jay Gibbons/499 RC	10.00
138	Johnny Estrada/499 RC	15.00
139	Morgan Ensberg/499 RC	10.00
140	Drew Henson/499 RC	20.00

Focus

#	Player	Price
241	Tsuyoshi Shinjo/999 RC	5.00
242	Wilson Betemit/999 RC	5.00
243	Jeremy Owens/999 RC	5.00
244	Drew Henson/999 RC	8.00
245	Albert Pujols/999 RC	100.00
246	Travis Hafner/999 RC	12.00
247	Ichiro Suzuki/999 RC	40.00
248	Elpidio Guzman/999 RC	6.00
249	Matt White/999 RC	6.00
250	Junior Spivey/999 RC	8.00

Futures

#	Player	Price
221	Drew Henson/2499 RC	5.00
222	Johnny Estrada/2499 RC	5.00
223	Elpidio Guzman/2499 RC	3.00
224	Albert Pujols/2499 RC	60.00
225	Wilson Betemit/2499 RC	4.00
226	Mark Teixeira/2499 RC	15.00
227	Tsuyoshi Shinjo/2499 RC	5.00
228	Matt White/2499 RC	3.00
229	Adrian Hernandez/2499 RC	3.00
230	Ichiro Suzuki/2499 RC	30.00

Triple Crown

#	Player	Price
301	Elpidio Guzman/2999 RC	4.00
302	Drew Henson/2999 RC	5.00
303	Bud Smith/2999 RC	2.00
304	Carlos Valderrama/2999 RC	2.00
305	Tsuyoshi Shinjo/2999 RC	4.00
306	Ichiro Suzuki/2999 RC	30.00
307	Jackson Melian/2999	2.00
308	Morgan Ensberg/2999 RC	4.00
309	Albert Pujols/2999 RC	90.00
310	Johnny Estrada/2999 RC	5.00

Ultra

#	Player	Price
276	Junior Spivey RC, Juan Uribe RC	5.00
277	Albert Pujols RC, Bud Smith RC	80.00
278	Ichiro Suzuki RC, Tsuyoshi Shinjo RC	25.00
279	Drew Henson RC, Jackson Melian	5.00
280	Matt White RC, Adrian Hernandez RC	2.00

Platinum

Cards (302-501): 4-8X
Production 201
SP's (502-601):
Production 21 not priced.

Lumberjacks

	NM/M
Common Player:	4.00
Inserted 1:1 Rack Pack	
Barry Bonds	20.00
Derek Jeter	20.00
Luis Gonzalez	4.00
Mike Sweeney	4.00
Albert Pujols	15.00
Tony Gwynn	10.00
Adam Dunn	5.00
J.D. Drew	4.00
Brian Giles	4.00
Adrian Beltre	5.00
Bret Boone	4.00
Chipper Jones	10.00
Cliff Floyd	4.00
Darin Erstad	5.00
Gary Sheffield	8.00
Manny Ramirez	8.00
Mike Piazza	12.00
Todd Helton	8.00
Ivan Rodriguez	6.00
Lance Berkman	4.00
Vladimir Guerrero	8.00
Drew Henson	6.00
Cristian Guzman	4.00
Roberto Alomar	5.00
Moises Alou	4.00
Larry Walker	4.00

Lumberjacks Autographs

	NM/M
Production 100 Sets	
Barry Bonds	200.00
J.D. Drew	40.00
Adam Dunn	60.00
Luis Gonzalez	20.00
Derek Jeter	150.00
Albert Pujols	500.00
Cal Ripken Jr.	150.00
Mike Sweeney	20.00

National Patch Time

	NM/M
Common Player:	4.00
Inserted 1:24 H	
Edgardo Alfonzo	4.00
Brady Anderson	4.00
Adrian Beltre	4.00
Barry Bonds	20.00
Jeromy Burnitz	4.00
Eric Chavez	4.00
Roger Clemens	15.00
J.D. Drew	5.00
Darin Erstad	5.00
Carl Everett	4.00
Freddy Garcia	4.00
Jason Giambi	8.00
Juan Gonzalez	6.00
Mark Grace	6.00
Shawn Green	4.00
Ben Grieve	4.00
Vladimir Guerrero	8.00
Tony Gwynn	10.00
Randy Johnson	8.00
Chipper Jones	10.00
David Justice	4.00
Jeff Kent	4.00
Greg Maddux	10.00
Fred McGriff	4.00
John Olerud	4.00
Magglio Ordonez	4.00
Jorge Posada	5.00
Cal Ripken Jr.	20.00
Mariano Rivera	6.00
Ivan Rodriguez	6.00
Scott Rolen	6.00
Kazuhiro Sasaki	4.00
Aaron Sele	4.00
Gary Sheffield	4.00
John Smoltz	4.00
Frank Thomas	8.00
Mo Vaughn	4.00
Robin Ventura	4.00
Bernie Williams	5.00
Carlos Delgado	6.00
Chan Ho Park	4.00
Todd Helton	8.00
Craig Biggio	8.00
Jeff Bagwell	8.00
Paul LoDuca	4.00

2001 Fleer Platinum RC Prime Numbers

		NM/M
Common Player:		8.00
Inserted 1:12 Jumbo Pack		
1PN	Jeff Bagwell	15.00
2PN	Cal Ripken Jr.	50.00
3PN	Barry Bonds	50.00
4PN	Todd Helton	15.00
5PN	Derek Jeter	50.00
6PN	Tony Gwynn	20.00
7PN	Kazuhiro Sasaki	8.00
8PN	Chan Ho Park	8.00
9PN	Sean Casey	10.00
10PN	Chipper Jones	20.00
11PN	Pedro Martinez	15.00
12PN	Mike Piazza	30.00
13PN	Carlos Delgado	8.00
15PN	Roger Clemens	25.00

Winning Combinations

		NM/M
Common Card:		3.00
Varying quantities produced		
1WC	Derek Jeter, Ozzie Smith/2000	8.00
2WC	Barry Bonds, Mark McGwire/500	10.00
3WC	Ichiro Suzuki, Albert Pujols/250	30.00
4WC	Ted Williams, Manny Ramirez/1000	10.00
5WC	Tony Gwynn, Cal Ripken/250	15.00
6WC	Mike Piazza, Derek Jeter/500	10.00
7WC	Dave Winfield, Tony Gwynn/2000	5.00
8WC	Hideo Nomo, Ichiro Suzuki/2000	10.00
9WC	Cal Ripken, Ozzie Smith/1000	10.00
10WC	Mark McGwire, Albert Pujols/2000	10.00
11WC	Jeff Bagwell, Craig Biggio/1000	3.00
12WC	Bobby Bonds, Barry Bonds/250	10.00
13WC	Ted Williams, Stan Musial/250	10.00
14WC	Babe Ruth, Reggie Jackson/500	15.00
15WC	Kazuhiro Sasaki, Ichiro Suzuki/500	10.00
16WC	Nolan Ryan, Roger Clemens/500	15.00
17WC	Roger Clemens, Derek Jeter/250	15.00
18WC	Ivan Rodriguez, Mike Piazza/1000	6.00
19WC	Vladimir Guerrero, Sammy Sosa/2000	6.00
20WC	Barry Bonds, Sammy Sosa/250	10.00
21WC	Roger Clemens, Greg Maddux/1000	8.00
22WC	Juan Gonzalez, Manny Ramirez/2000	3.00
23WC	Todd Helton, Jason Giambi/2000	3.00
24WC	Jeff Bagwell, Lance Berkman/2000	3.00
25WC	Mike Sweeney, George Brett/1000	6.00
26WC	Luis Gonzalez, Babe Ruth/2000	10.00
27WC	Bill Skowron, Don Mattingly/250	10.00
28WC	Yogi Berra, Cal Ripken/2000	10.00
29WC	Pedro Martinez, Nomar Garciaparra/500	8.00
30WC	Ted Kluszewski, Frank Robinson/1000	3.00
31WC	Curt Schilling, Randy Johnson/1000	5.00
32WC	Ken Griffey Jr., Cal Ripken/1000	10.00
33WC	Mike Piazza, Johnny Bench/1000	6.00
34WC	Stan Musial, Albert Pujols/500	10.00
35WC	Jackie Robinson, Nellie Fox/500	8.00
36WC	Lefty Grove, Steve Carlton/250	5.00
37WC	Ty Cobb, Tony Gwynn/250	10.00
38WC	Albert Pujols, Frank Robinson/1000	10.00
39WC	Ryne Sandberg, Sammy Sosa/500	10.00
40WC	Cal Ripken Jr., Lou Gehrig/250	20.00

2001 Fleer Premium

		NM/M
Complete Set (235):		
Common Player:		.15
Common SP (201-230):		4.00
Production 1,999		
Cards 231-235 are redemptions.		
Hobby Pack (8):		5.00
Hobby Box (24):		100.00
1	Cal Ripken Jr.	2.00
2	Derek Jeter	2.00
3	Edgardo Alfonzo	.15
4	Luis Castillo	.15
5	Mike Lieberthal	.15
6	Kazuhiro Sasaki	.15
7	Jeff Kent	.15
8	Eric Karros	.15
9	Tom Glavine	.40
10	Jeromy Burnitz	.15
11	Travis Fryman	.15
12	Ron Coomer	.15
13	Jeff D'Amico	.15
14	Carlos Febles	.15
15	Kevin Brown	.15
16	Deivi Cruz	.15
17	Tino Martinez	.15
18	Bobby Abreu	.15
19	Roger Clemens	1.00
20	Jeffrey Hammonds	.15
21	Peter Bergeron	.15
22	Ray Lankford	.15
23	Scott Rolen	.60
24	Jermaine Dye	.15
25	Rusty Greer	.15
26	Frank Thomas	.75
27	Jeff Bagwell	.75
28	Cliff Floyd	.15
29	Chris Singleton	.15
30	Steve Finley	.15
31	Orlando Hernandez	.15
32	Tom Goodwin	.15
33	Larry Walker	.15
34	Mike Sweeney	.15
35	Tim Hudson	.30
36	Kerry Wood	.40
37	Mike Lowell	.15
38	Andruw Jones	.75
39	Alex S. Gonzalez	.15
40	Juan Gonzalez	.75
41	J.D. Drew	.25
42	Mark McLemore	.15
43	Royce Clayton	.15
44	Paul O'Neill	.15
45	Carlos Beltran	.45
46	Phil Nevin	.15
47	Rondell White	.15
48	Gerald Williams	.15
49	Geoff Jenkins	.15
50	Marvin Benard	.15
51	Alex Rodriguez	1.50
52	Moises Alou	.15
53	Mike Lansing	.15
54	Omar Vizquel	.15
55	Eric Chavez	.30
56	Mark Quinn	.15
57	Mike Lamb	.15
58	Rick Ankiel	.15
59	Lance Berkman	.15
60	Jeff Conine	.15
61	B.J. Surhoff	.15
62	Todd Helton	.75
63	J.T. Snow	.15
64	John Vander Wal	.15
65	Johnny Damon	.25
66	Bobby Higginson	.15
67	Carlos Delgado	.40
68	Shawn Green	.35
69	Mike Redmond	.15
70	Mike Piazza	1.25
71	Adrian Beltre	.35
72	Juan Encarnacion	.15
73	Chipper Jones	1.00
74	Garret Anderson	.15
75	Paul Konerko	.15
76	Barry Larkin	.15
77	Tony Gwynn	1.00
78	Rafael Palmeiro	.60
79	Randy Johnson	.75
80	Mark Grace	.25
81	Javy Lopez	.15
82	Gabe Kapler	.15
83	Henry Rodriguez	.15
84	Raul Mondesi	.15
85	Adam Piatt	.15
86	Marquis Grissom	.15
87	Charles Johnson	.15
88	Sean Casey	.25
89	Manny Ramirez	.75
90	Curt Schilling	.40
91	Fernando Tatis	.15
92	Derek Bell	.15
93	Tony Clark	.15
94	Homer Bush	.15
95	Nomar Garciaparra	1.25
96	Vinny Castilla	.15
97	Ben Davis	.15
98	Carl Everett	.15
99	Damion Easley	.15
100	Craig Biggio	.15
101	Todd Hollandsworth	.15
102	Jay Payton	.15
103	Gary Sheffield	.35
104	Sandy Alomar Jr.	.15
105	Doug Glanville	.15
106	Barry Bonds	2.00
107	Tim Salmon	.25
108	Terrence Long	.15
109	Jorge Posada	.30
110	Jose Offerman	.15
111	Edgar Martinez	.15
112	Jeremy Giambi	.15
113	Dean Palmer	.15
114	Roberto Alomar	.35
115	Aaron Boone	.15
116	Adam Kennedy	.15
117	Joe Randa	.15
118	Jose Vidro	.15
119	Tony Batista	.15
120	Kevin Young	.15
121	Preston Wilson	.15
122	Jason Kendall	.15
123	Mark Kotsay	.15
124	Timoniel Perez	.15
125	Eric Young	.15
126	Greg Maddux	1.00
127	Richard Hidalgo	.15
128	Brian Giles	.15
129	Fred McGriff	.15
130	Troy Glaus	.75
131	Todd Walker	.15
132	Brady Anderson	.15
133	Jim Edmonds	.15
134	Ben Grieve	.15
135	Greg Vaughn	.15
136	Robin Ventura	.15
137	Sammy Sosa	1.25
138	Rich Aurilia	.15
139	Jose Valentin	.15
140	Trot Nixon	.15
141	Troy Percival	.15
142	Bernie Williams	.35
143	Warren Morris	.15
144	Jacque Jones	.15
145	Danny Bautista	.15
146	A.J. Pierzynski	.15
147	Mark McGwire	1.50
148	Rafael Furcal	.15
149	Ray Durham	.15
150	Mike Mussina	.40
151	Jay Bell	.15
152	David Wells	.15
153	Ken Caminiti	.15
154	Jim Thome	.15
155	Ivan Rodriguez	.60
156	Milton Bradley	.15
157	Ken Griffey Jr.	1.25
158	Al Leiter	.15
159	Corey Koskie	.15
160	Shannon Stewart	.15
161	Mo Vaughn	.15
162	Pedro Martinez	.75
163	Todd Hundley	.15
164	Darin Erstad	.60
165	Ruben Rivera	.15
166	Richie Sexson	.15
167	Andres Galarraga	.15
168	Darryl Kile	.15
169	Jose Cruz Jr.	.15
170	David Justice	.15
171	Vladimir Guerrero	.75
172	Jeff Cirillo	.15
173	John Olerud	.15
174	Devon White	.15
175	Ron Belliard	.15
176	Pokey Reese	.15
177	Mike Hampton	.15
178	David Ortiz	.15
179	Magglio Ordonez	.15
180	Ruben Mateo	.15
181	Carlos Lee	.15
182	Matt Williams	.15
183	Miguel Tejada	.25
184	Scott Elarton	.15
185	Bret Boone	.15
186	Pat Burrell	.15
187	Brad Radke	.15
188	Brian Jordan	.15
189	Matt Lawton	.15
190	Al Martin	.15
191	Albert Belle	.15
192	Tony Womack	.15
193	Roger Cedeno	.15
194	Travis Lee	.15
195	Dmitri Young	.15

196	Jay Buhner	.15
197	Jason Giambi	.50
198	Jason Tyner	.15
199	Ben Petrick	.15
200	Jose Canseco	.40
201	Nick Johnson	4.00
202	Jace Brewer	4.00
203	Ryan Freel RC	4.00
204	Jaisen Randolph RC	4.00
205	Marcus Giles	4.00
206	Claudio Vargas RC	4.00
207	Brian Cole	4.00
208	Scott Hodges	4.00
209	Winston Abreu RC	4.00
210	Shea Hillenbrand	4.00
211	Larry Barnes	4.00
212	Paul Phillips RC	4.00
213	Pedro Santana RC	4.00
214	Ivanon Coffie	4.00
215	Junior Spivey RC	8.00
216	Donzell McDonald	4.00
217	Vernon Wells	5.00
218	Corey Patterson	5.00
219	Sang-Hoon Lee	4.00
220	Jack Cust	4.00
221	Jason Romano	4.00
222	Jack Wilson RC	8.00
223	Adam Everett	4.00
224	Esix Snead RC	4.00
225	Jason Hart	4.00
226	Joe Lawrence	4.00
227	Brandon Inge	4.00
228	Alex Escobar	4.00
229	Abraham Nunez	4.00
230	Jared Sandberg	4.00
231	Ichiro Suzuki RC	50.00
232	Tsuyoshi Shinjo RC	6.00
233	Albert Pujols RC	100.00
234	Wilson Betemit RC	5.00
235	Drew Henson RC	6.00

Star Ruby

Stars (1-200): 5-10X
SPs (201-230): .4-.8X
Production 125 Sets

A Time for Heroes

NM/M
Complete Set (20): 30.00
Common Player: 1.00
Inserted 1:20

Darin Erstad	1.00
Alex Rodriguez	4.00
Shawn Green	1.00
Jeff Bagwell	1.50
Sammy Sosa	1.00
Derek Jeter	5.00
Nomar Garciaparra	3.00
Carlos Delgado	1.00
Pat Burrell	1.00
Tony Gwynn	2.50
Chipper Jones	2.50
Jason Giambi	1.00
Magglio Ordonez	1.00
Troy Glaus	1.00
Ivan Rodriguez	1.00
Andruw Jones	1.50
Vladimir Guerrero	2.00
Ken Griffey Jr.	3.00
J.D. Drew	1.00
Todd Helton	1.50

A Time for Heroes Memorabilia

NM/M
Common Player: 4.00
Inserted 1:82

Shawn Green	5.00
Derek Jeter	25.00
Pat Burrell	5.00
Chipper Jones	10.00
Jason Giambi	8.00
Troy Glaus	5.00
Ivan Rodriguez	6.00
Andruw Jones	8.00

J.D. Drew	4.00
Todd Helton	8.00

Brother Wood

NM/M
Common Player: 5.00
Inserted 1:108

1BW	Vladimir Guerrero	10.00
2BW	Andruw Jones	6.00
3BW	Corey Patterson	5.00
4BW	Magglio Ordonez	5.00
5BW	Jason Giambi	8.00
6BW	Rafael Palmeiro	8.00
7BW	Eric Chavez	5.00
8BW	Pat Burrell	6.00
9BW	Adrian Beltre	5.00

Decades of Excellence

NM/M
Complete Set (50): 140.00
Common Player: 1.00
Inserted 1:12
Card #17 does not exist.

Babe Ruth, Lou Gehrig	10.00
Lloyd Waner	1.00
Jimmie Foxx	3.00
Hank Greenberg	2.00
Ted Williams	8.00
Johnny Mize	2.00
Enos Slaughter	1.00
Jackie Robinson	6.00
Stan Musial	3.00
Duke Snider	3.00
Eddie Mathews	3.00
Roy Campanella	2.50
Yogi Berra	4.00
Pee Wee Reese	2.00
Phil Rizzuto	2.00
Al Kaline	4.00
Frank Howard	1.00
Roberto Clemente	8.00
Bob Gibson	3.00
Roger Maris	4.00
Don Drysdale	2.50
Maury Wills	1.00
Tom Seaver	3.00
Reggie Jackson	3.00
Johnny Bench	4.00
Carlton Fisk	2.50
Rod Carew	2.00
Steve Carlton	2.00
Mike Schmidt	6.00
Nolan Ryan	10.00
Rickey Henderson	3.00
Roger Clemens	5.00
Don Mattingly	4.00
George Brett	6.00
Greg Maddux	5.00
Cal Ripken Jr.	10.00
Chipper Jones	5.00
Barry Bonds	10.00
Ivan Rodriguez	2.50
Sammy Sosa, Mark McGwire	8.00
Ken Griffey Jr.	6.00
Tony Gwynn	4.00
Vladimir Guerrero	3.00
Shawn Green	1.00
Alex Rodriguez, Derek Jeter, Nomar Garciaparra	8.00
Pat Burrell	2.00
Rick Ankiel	2.00
Eric Chavez, Troy Glaus	2.00

Decades of Excellence Autograph

NM/M
Common Autograph: 20.00

Production #'s listed.

1	Rick Ankiel/99	10.00
2	Johnny Bench/67	65.00
3	Barry Bonds/86	200.00
4	George Brett/73	100.00
5	Rod Carew/67	30.00
6	Steve Carlton/65	30.00
7	Eric Chavez/98	20.00
8	Carlton Fisk/69	50.00
9	Bob Gibson/59	40.00
10	Tony Gwynn/82	50.00
11	Reggie Jackson/67	60.00
12	Chipper Jones/93	60.00
13	Al Kaline/53	80.00
14	Don Mattingly/82	100.00
15	Cal Ripken Jr./82	150.00
16	Nolan Ryan/66	125.00
17	Mike Schmidt/72	80.00
18	Tom Seaver/67	50.00
19	Enos Slaughter/38	40.00
20	Maury Wills/59	20.00

Decades of Excellence Memorabilia

NM/M
Common Player: 8.00
Inserted 1:217 H

1	Rick Ankiel/Jsy	8.00
2	Barry Bonds/Jsy	15.00
3	Pat Burrell/Jsy	10.00
4	Roy Campanella/Bat/50	50.00
5	Eric Chavez/Bat	8.00
6	Roberto Clemente/Bat/50	125.00
7	Carlton Fisk/Uni.	8.00
8	Jimmie Foxx/Bat/50	80.00
9	Shawn Green/Bat	8.00
10	Tony Gwynn/Jsy	15.00
11	Reggie Jackson/Jsy	15.00
12	Greg Maddux/Jsy	20.00
13	Roger Maris/Uni.	35.00
14	Pee Wee Reese/Jsy	8.00
15	Cal Ripken/Jsy/50	35.00
16	Ivan Rodriguez/Bat	8.00
17	Nolan Ryan/Jsy	50.00
18	Mike Schmidt/Jsy	20.00
19	Tom Seaver/Jsy	8.00
20	Duke Snider/Bat	15.00
21	Ted Williams/Jsy/50	250.00

Diamond Dominators

NM/M
Common Player: 4.00
Inserted 1:51

1DD	Troy Glaus	6.00
2DD	Darin Erstad	5.00
3DD	J.D. Drew	4.00
4DD	Barry Bonds	25.00
5DD	Roger Clemens	20.00
6DD	Vladimir Guerrero	8.00
7DD	Tony Gwynn	10.00
8DD	Greg Maddux	10.00
9DD	Cal Ripken Jr.	10.00
10DD	Ivan Rodriguez	6.00
11DD	Frank Thomas	8.00
12DD	Bernie Williams	4.00
13DD	Jeromy Burnitz	4.00
14DD	Juan Gonzalez	6.00

Diamond Dominators Patches

NM/M
Common Player: 15.00
Production 100 Sets

1DD	Troy Glaus	25.00
2DD	Darin Erstad	15.00
3DD	J.D. Drew	15.00
4DD	Barry Bonds	75.00
5DD	Roger Clemens	60.00
6DD	Vladimir Guerrero	25.00
7DD	Tony Gwynn	50.00
8DD	Greg Maddux	50.00
9DD	Cal Ripken Jr.	75.00
10DD	Ivan Rodriguez	20.00
11DD	Frank Thomas	25.00
12DD	Bernie Williams	20.00
13DD	Jeromy Burnitz	15.00
14DD	Juan Gonzalez	25.00

Grip It and Rip It

NM/M
Complete Set (15): 10.00
Common Player: .50
Inserted 1:6

1GRP	Roger Clemens, Derek Jeter	2.00

2GRP	Scott Rolen, Pat Burrell	.50
3GRP	Greg Maddux, Andruw Jones	1.00
4GRP	Shannon Stewart, Carlos Delgado	.50
5GRP	Shawn Estes, Barry Bonds	2.00
6GRP	Cal Eldred, Frank Thomas	.50
7GRP	Mark McGwire, Jim Edmonds	2.00
8GRP	Jose Vidro, Vladimir Guerrero	.75
9GRP	Pedro Martinez, Nomar Garciaparra	1.50
10GRP	Tom Glavine, Chipper Jones	1.00
11GRP	Ken Griffey Jr., Sean Casey	1.00
12GRP	Jeff Bagwell, Moises Alou	1.00
13GRP	Troy Glaus, Darin Erstad	.50
14GRP	Mike Piazza, Robin Ventura	1.00
15GRP	Eric Chavez, Jason Giambi	.50

Grip It and Rip It Plus

NM/M
Common Card: 8.00
200 Base/Bat Produced
100 Ball/Bat Produced

Roger Clemens, Derek Jeter/100	50.00
Scott Rolen, Pat Burrell/200	8.00
Greg Maddux, Andruw Jones/100	40.00
Shannon Stewart, Carlos Delgado/200	8.00
Shawn Estes, Barry Bonds/100	50.00
Cal Eldred, Frank Thomas/200	15.00
Mark McGwire, Jim Edmonds/100	60.00
Jose Vidro, Vladimir Guerrero/200	15.00
Pedro Martinez, Nomar Garciaparra/100	50.00
Tom Glavine, Chipper Jones/200	15.00
Ken Griffey Jr., Sean Casey/200	20.00
Jeff Bagwell, Moises Alou/200	10.00
Troy Glaus, Darin Erstad/200	10.00
Mike Piazza, Robin Ventura/100	40.00
Eric Chavez, Jason Giambi/200	10.00

Home Field Advantage

NM/M
Complete Set (15): 60.00
Common Player: 2.00
Inserted 1:72

Mike Piazza	6.00
Derek Jeter	10.00
Ken Griffey Jr.	6.00
Carlos Delgado	2.00
Chipper Jones	5.00
Alex Rodriguez	8.00
Sammy Sosa	4.00
Scott Rolen	3.00
Nomar Garciaparra	6.00
Todd Helton	3.00
Vladimir Guerrero	3.00

Jeff Bagwell	3.00
Barry Bonds	10.00
Cal Ripken Jr.	10.00
Mark McGwire	8.00

Home Field Advantage Game Wall

NM/M
Common Player: 6.00
Production 100 Sets

Mike Piazza	15.00
Derek Jeter	25.00
Ken Griffey Jr.	15.00
Carlos Delgado	6.00
Chipper Jones	10.00
Alex Rodriguez	20.00
Sammy Sosa	15.00
Scott Rolen	8.00
Nomar Garciaparra	15.00
Todd Helton	8.00
Vladimir Guerrero	8.00
Jeff Bagwell	8.00
Barry Bonds	25.00
Cal Ripken Jr.	25.00
Mark McGwire	20.00

Derek Jeter Monumental Moments

NM/M
Numbered to 1,995.
Autograph numbered to 95.

DJMM	Derek Jeter	8.00
DJMM	Derek Jeter/ Auto./95	80.00

Solid Performers

NM/M
Complete Set (15): 30.00
Common Player: 1.50
Inserted 1:20

1SP	Mark McGwire	4.00
2SP	Alex Rodriguez	4.00
3SP	Nomar Garciaparra	2.50
4SP	Derek Jeter	5.00
5SP	Vladimir Guerrero	1.50
6SP	Todd Helton	1.50
7SP	Chipper Jones	2.00
8SP	Mike Piazza	2.50
9SP	Ivan Rodriguez	1.50
10SP	Tony Gwynn	2.00
11SP	Cal Ripken Jr.	5.00
12SP	Barry Bonds	5.00
13SP	Jeff Bagwell	1.50
14SP	Ken Griffey Jr.	2.50
15SP	Sammy Sosa	2.50

Solid Performers Game Base

NM/M
Common Player: 5.00
Production 150 Sets

1SP	Mark McGwire	15.00
2SP	Alex Rodriguez	15.00
3SP	Nomar Garciaparra	12.00
4SP	Derek Jeter	20.00
5SP	Vladimir Guerrero	8.00
6SP	Todd Helton	8.00
7SP	Chipper Jones	10.00
8SP	Mike Piazza	12.00
9SP	Ivan Rodriguez	8.00

10SP	Tony Gwynn	10.00
11SP	Cal Ripken Jr.	20.00
12SP	Barry Bonds	20.00
13SP	Jeff Bagwell	12.00
14SP	Ken Griffey Jr.	12.00
15SP	Sammy Sosa	12.00

2001 Fleer Showcase

NM/M
Complete Set (160):
Common Player: .25
Common SP (116-125): 10.00
Production 500
Common SP (126-145): 4.00
Production 1,500
Common SP (146-160): 4.00
Production 2,000
Pack (5): 10.00
Box (24): 200.00

1	Tony Gwynn	1.50
2	Barry Larkin	.25
3	Chan Ho Park	.25
4	Darin Erstad	.65
5	Rafael Furcal	.25
6	Roger Cedeno	.25
7	Timo Perez	.25
8	Rick Ankiel	.25
9	Pokey Reese	.25
10	Jeromy Burnitz	.25
11	Phil Nevin	.25
12	Matt Williams	.25
13	Mike Hampton	.25
14	Fernando Tatis	.25
15	Kazuhiro Sasaki	.25
16	Jim Thome	.25
17	Geoff Jenkins	.25
18	Jeff Kent	.25
19	Tom Glavine	.40
20	Dean Palmer	.25
21	Todd Zeile	.25
22	Edgar Renteria	.25
23	Andruw Jones	1.00
24	Juan Encarnacion	.25
25	Robin Ventura	.25
26	J.D. Drew	.25
27	Ray Durham	.25
28	Richard Hidalgo	.25
29	Eric Chavez	.35
30	Rafael Palmeiro	.75
31	Steve Finley	.25
32	Jeff Weaver	.25
33	Al Leiter	.25
34	Jim Edmonds	.25
35	Garret Anderson	.25
36	Larry Walker	.25
37	Jose Vidro	.25
38	Mike Cameron	.25
39	Brady Anderson	.25
40	Mike Lowell	.25
41	Bernie Williams	.35
42	Gary Sheffield	.40
43	John Smoltz	.25
44	Mike Mussina	.25
45	Greg Vaughn	.25
46	Juan Gonzalez	.75
47	Matt Lawton	.25
48	Robb Nen	.25
49	Brad Radke	.25
50	Edgar Martinez	.25
51	Mike Bordick	.25
52	Shawn Green	.40
53	Carl Everett	.25
54	Adrian Beltre	.40
55	Kerry Wood	.50
56	Kevin Brown	.25
57	Brian Giles	.25
58	Greg Maddux	1.50
59	Preston Wilson	.25
60	Orlando Hernandez	.25
61	Ben Grieve	.25
62	Jermaine Dye	.25
63	Travis Lee	.25
64	Jose Cruz Jr.	.25
65	Rondell White	.25
66	Carlos Beltran	.45
67	Scott Rolen	.75
68	Brad Fullmer	.25
69	David Wells	.25
70	Mike Sweeney	.25
71	Barry Zito	.40
72	Tony Batista	.25
73	Curt Schilling	.40
74	Jeff Cirillo	.25
75	Edgardo Alfonzo	.25
76	John Olerud	.25
77	Carlos Lee	.25

78	Moises Alou	.25
79	Tim Hudson	.35
80	Andres Galarraga	.25
81	Roberto Alomar	.45
82	Richie Sexson	.25
83	Trevor Hoffman	.25
84	Omar Vizquel	.25
85	Jacque Jones	.25
86	J.T. Snow	.25
87	Sean Casey	.25
88	Craig Biggio	.40
89	Mariano Rivera	.35
90	Rusty Greer	.25
91	Barry Bonds	3.00
92	Pedro Martinez	1.00
93	Cal Ripken Jr.	3.00
94	Pat Burrell	.50
95	Chipper Jones	1.50
96	Magglio Ordonez	.25
97	Jeff Bagwell	1.00
98	Randy Johnson	1.00
99	Frank Thomas	1.00
100	Jason Kendall	.25
101	Nomar Garciaparra (Avant Card)	6.00
102	Mark McGwire (Avant Card)	8.00
103	Troy Glaus (Avant Card)	3.00
104	Ivan Rodriguez (Avant Card)	2.50
105	Manny Ramirez (Avant Card)	3.00
106	Derek Jeter (Avant Card)	10.00
107	Alex Rodriguez (Avant Card)	8.00
108	Ken Griffey Jr. (Avant Card)	6.00
109	Todd Helton (Avant Card)	3.00
110	Sammy Sosa (Avant Card)	6.00
111	Vladimir Guerrero (Avant Card)	3.00
112	Mike Piazza (Avant Card)	6.00
113	Roger Clemens (Avant Card)	5.00
114	Jason Giambi (Avant Card)	2.50
115	Carlos Delgado (Avant Card)	2.00
116	Ichiro Suzuki RC (Rookie Avant)	100.00
117	Morgan Ensberg RC (Rookie Avant)	20.00
118	Carlos Valderrama RC (Rookie Avant)	10.00
119	Erick Almonte RC (Rookie Avant)	10.00
120	Tsuyoshi Shinjo RC (Rookie Avant)	10.00
121	Albert Pujols RC (Rookie Avant)	240.00
122	Wilson Betemit RC (Rookie Avant)	10.00
123	Adrian Hernandez RC (Rookie Avant)	10.00
124	Jackson Melian RC (Rookie Avant)	10.00
125	Drew Henson RC (Rookie Avant)	12.00
126	Paul Phillips RC	4.00
127	Esix Snead RC	4.00
128	Ryan Freel RC	4.00
129	Junior Spivey RC	4.00
130	Elpidio Guzman RC	6.00
131	Juan Diaz RC	4.00
132	Andres Torres RC	4.00
133	Jay Gibbons RC	10.00
134	Bill Ortega RC	4.00
135	Alexis Gomez RC	4.00
136	Wilken Ruan RC	4.00
137	Henry Mateo RC	4.00
138	Juan Uribe RC	8.00
139	Johnny Estrada RC	4.00
140	Jaisen Randolph RC	4.00
141	Eric Hinske RC	8.00
142	Jack Wilson RC	10.00
143	Cody Ransom RC	4.00
144	Nate Frese RC	4.00
145	John Grabow RC	4.00
146	Christian Parker RC	4.00
147	Brian Lawrence RC	6.00
148	Brandon Duckworth RC	4.00
149	Winston Abreu RC	4.00
150	Horacio Ramirez RC	8.00
151	Nick Maness RC	4.00
152	Blaine Neal RC	4.00
153	Billy Sylvester RC	4.00
154	David Elder RC	4.00
155	Bert Snow RC	4.00
156	Claudio Vargas RC	4.00
157	Martin Vargas RC	4.00
158	Grant Balfour RC	4.00
159	Randy Keisler RC	4.00
160	Zach Day RC	4.00

Legacy

Stars (1-100): 10-15X
Avant (101-115): 2-4X
RC's (116-125): .75-1.5X
RC's (126-160): 1-2X
Production 50 Sets

Autographics

PAUL KONERKO Chicago White Sox™

NM/M

Common Player: 5.00
Silvers: 1X
Production 250 Sets
Golds: 1-2X
Production 50 Sets

Roberto Alomar	30.00
Rick Ankiel	5.00
Albert Belle	8.00
Carlos Beltran	25.00
Adrian Beltre	10.00
Milton Bradley	5.00
Dee Brown	5.00
Jeromy Burnitz	5.00
Pat Burrell	10.00
Sean Casey	5.00
Joseph Crede	5.00
Jose Cruz Jr.	5.00
Ryan Dempster	5.00
J.D. Drew	10.00
Adam Dunn	15.00
Erubiel Durazo	5.00
Jermaine Dye	5.00
David Eckstein	5.00
Alex Escobar	5.00
Seth Etherton	5.00
Adam Everett	5.00
Carlos Febles	5.00
Troy Glaus	15.00
Ben Grieve	5.00
Toby Hall	5.00
Todd Helton	20.00
Shea Hillenbrand	6.00
Aubrey Huff	6.00
D'Angelo Jimenez	5.00
Paul Konerko	8.00
Mike Lamb	5.00
Matt Lawton	5.00
Derrek Lee	5.00
Mike Lieberthal	5.00
Mike Lowell	8.00
Julio Lugo	5.00
Jason Marquis	5.00
Edgar Martinez	15.00
Kevin Millwood	10.00
Eric Milton	5.00
Bengie Molina	5.00
Mike Mussina	25.00
Russ Ortiz	5.00
Corey Patterson	10.00
Jay Payton	5.00
Adam Piatt	5.00
Juan Pierre	5.00
Brad Radke	5.00
John Rocker	5.00
Alex Rodriguez	60.00
Scott Rolen	20.00
Richie Sexson	10.00
Gary Sheffield	15.00
Shannon Stewart	5.00
Miguel Tejada	25.00
Robin Ventura	5.00
Jose Vidro	5.00
Billy Wagner	8.00
Kip Wells	5.00
Rondell White	5.00
Preston Wilson	5.00
Kerry Wood	20.00
Julio Zuleta	5.00

Awards Showcase

Rafael Furcal Braves™ Shortstop

NM/M

Complete Set (20): 30.00
Common Player: 1.00
Inserted 1:20 Retail

Derek Jeter	5.00
Derek Jeter	5.00
Jason Giambi	1.50
Jeff Kent	1.00
Pedro Martinez	2.00
Randy Johnson	1.00
Kazuhiro Sasaki	1.00
Rafael Furcal	1.00
Carlos Delgado	1.50
Todd Helton	2.00
Ivan Rodriguez	1.50
Darin Erstad	1.50
Bernie Williams	1.00
Greg Maddux	3.00
Jim Edmonds	2.00
Andruw Jones	2.00
Nomar Garciaparra	4.00
Todd Helton	2.00
Troy Glaus	2.00
Sammy Sosa	4.00

Awards Showcase Autographs

Tom Seaver Mets™ Pitcher

NM/M

Production 25 Sets

Johnny Bench	100.00
Yogi Berra	90.00
George Brett	200.00
Steve Carlton	60.00
Roger Clemens	180.00
Andre Dawson	40.00
Whitey Ford	80.00
Tom Glavine	50.00
Juan Gonzalez	50.00
Reggie Jackson	80.00
Randy Johnson	90.00
Chipper Jones	80.00
Harmon Killebrew	75.00
Fred Lynn	25.00
Greg Maddux	150.00
Don Mattingly	175.00
Willie McCovey	40.00
Jim Palmer	40.00
Jim Rice	25.00
Brooks Robinson	75.00
Frank Robinson	50.00
Ivan Rodriguez	50.00
Mike Schmidt	125.00
Tom Seaver	100.00

Awards Showcase Memorabilia

Mike Schmidt Phillies™ Third Base

NM/M

Common Player: 10.00
Production 100 Sets

Johnny Bench	20.00
Yogi Berra	15.00
George Brett	40.00
Lou Brock	10.00
Roy Campanella	25.00
Steve Carlton	10.00
Roger Clemens	40.00
Andre Dawson	10.00
Whitey Ford	15.00
Jimmie Foxx	45.00
Kirk Gibson	10.00
Tom Glavine	10.00
Juan Gonzalez	10.00
Elston Howard	10.00
Jim "Catfish" Hunter	10.00
Reggie Jackson	20.00
Randy Johnson	15.00
Chipper Jones	15.00
Harmon Killebrew	20.00
Greg Maddux	25.00
Don Mattingly	75.00
Willie McCovey	10.00
Jim Palmer	10.00
Jim Rice	10.00
Brooks Robinson	20.00
Frank Robinson	15.00
Jackie Robinson	75.00
Ivan Rodriguez	15.00
Mike Schmidt	40.00
Tom Seaver	15.00
Willie Stargell	10.00
Ted Williams	150.00
Robin Yount	25.00

Derek Jeter's Monumental Moments

Derek Jeter 2000 World Series MVP Monumental Moments

NM/M

Production 2,000:

MM5	Derek Jeter	8.00
	Derek Jeter/ Auto./100	90.00

Showcase Sticks

NM/M

Common Player: 4.00
Inserted 1:24

Roberto Alomar	6.00
Adrian Beltre	5.00
Pat Burrell	6.00
J.D. Drew	4.00
Juan Gonzalez	6.00
Andruw Jones	8.00
Chipper Jones	10.00
Magglio Ordonez	4.00
Ivan Rodriguez	8.00
Scott Rolen	8.00
Frank Thomas	8.00
Roger Cedeno	4.00
Shawn Green	5.00
Richard Hidalgo	4.00
Tony Clark	4.00
Preston Wilson	4.00
Barry Bonds	30.00
Rafael Furcal	4.00
Randy Johnson	8.00
Vladimir Guerrero	8.00
Al Kaline	10.00
George Kell	4.00
Jason Kendall	4.00
Carlos Delgado	5.00
Adam Piatt	4.00
Alex Gonzalez	4.00
Jorge Posada	6.00
Jose Vidro	4.00
Roger Clemens	20.00
Steve Finley	4.00
Reggie Jackson	8.00
Shannon Stewart	4.00
Rick Ankiel	4.00
Jim Thome	8.00
Tsuyoshi Shinjo	6.00
Ichiro Suzuki	25.00

Sweet Sigs

NM/M

Common Player: 10.00
Inserted 1:24
Prices for Lumber
Wall: 1X
Leather: 1-1.5X

Bobby Abreu	15.00
Wilson Betemit	10.00
Russell Branyan	10.00
Pat Burrell	20.00
Eric Chavez	20.00
Rafael Furcal	15.00
Nomar Garciaparra	100.00
Juan Gonzalez	35.00
Elpidio Guzman	10.00
Drew Henson	15.00
Brandon Inge	10.00
Derek Jeter	130.00
Andruw Jones	30.00
Willie Mays	180.00
Jackson Melian	10.00
Xavier Nady	10.00
Jose Ortiz	10.00
Ben Sheets	15.00
Mike Sweeney	10.00
Miguel Tejada	35.00
Albert Pujols	450.00

2001 Fleer Tradition

ROGER CLEMENS New York Yankees™ Pitcher

NM/M

Complete Set (450): 35.00
Common Player: .15
Comp. Factory Set (485): 100.00
Pack (10): 2.00
Box (36): 55.00

1	Andres Galarraga	.15
2	Armando Rios	.15
3	Julio Lugo	.15
4	Darryl Hamilton	.15
5	Dave Veres	.15
6	Edgardo Alfonzo	.15
7	Brook Fordyce	.15
8	Eric Karros	.15
9	Neifi Perez	.15
10	Jim Edmonds	.15
11	Barry Larkin	.15
12	Trot Nixon	.15
13	Andy Pettitte	.35
14	Jose Guillen	.15
15	David Wells	.15
16	Magglio Ordonez	.15
17	David Segui	.15
18	Juan Encarnacion	.15
19	Robert Person	.15
20	Quilvio Veras	.15
21	Mo Vaughn	.15
22	B.J. Surhoff	.15
23	Ken Caminiti	.15
24	Frank Catalanotto	.15
25	Luis Gonzalez	.25
26	Pete Harnisch	.15
27	Alex Gonzalez	.15
28	Mark Quinn	.15
29	Luis Castillo	.15
30	Rick Helling	.15
31	Barry Bonds	2.00
32	Warren Morris	.15
33	Aaron Boone	.15
34	Ricky Gutierrez	.15
35	Preston Wilson	.15
36	Erubiel Durazo	.15
37	Jermaine Dye	.15
38	John Rocker	.15
39	Mark Grudzielanek	.15
40	Pedro Martinez	.75
41	Phil Nevin	.15
42	Luis Matos	.15
43	Orlando Hernandez	.15
44	Steve Cox	.15
45	James Baldwin	.15
46	Rafael Furcal	.15
47	Todd Zeile	.15
48	Elmer Dessens	.15
49	Russell Branyan	.15
50	Juan Gonzalez	.75
51	Mac Suzuki	.15
52	Adam Kennedy	.15
53	Randy Velarde	.15
54	David Bell	.15
55	Royce Clayton	.15
56	Greg Colbrunn	.15
57	Rey Ordonez	.15
58	Kevin Millwood	.15
59	Fernando Vina	.15
60	Eddie Taubensee	.15
61	Enrique Wilson	.15
62	Jay Bell	.15
63	Brian Moehler	.15
64	Brad Fullmer	.15
65	Ben Petrick	.15
66	Orlando Cabrera	.25
67	Shane Reynolds	.15
68	Mitch Meluskey	.15
69	Jeff Shaw	.15
70	Chipper Jones	1.00
71	Tomo Ohka	.15
72	Ruben Rivera	.15
73	Mike Sirotka	.15
74	Scott Rolen	.60
75	Glendon Rusch	.15
76	Miguel Tejada	.35
77	Brady Anderson	.15
78	Bartolo Colon	.15
79	Ron Coomer	.15
80	Gary DiSarcina	.15
81	Geoff Jenkins	.15
82	Billy Koch	.15
83	Mike Lamb	.15
84	Alex Rodriguez	1.50
85	Denny Neagle	.15
86	Michael Tucker	.15
87	Edgar Renteria	.15
88	Brian Anderson	.15
89	Glenallen Hill	.15
90	Aramis Ramirez	.15
91	Rondell White	.15
92	Tony Womack	.15
93	Jeffrey Hammonds	.15
94	Freddy Garcia	.15
95	Bill Mueller	.15
96	Mike Lieberthal	.15
97	Michael Barrett	.15
98	Derek Lee	.15
99	Bill Spiers	.15
100	Derek Lowe	.15
101	Javy Lopez	.15
102	Adrian Beltre	.30
103	Jim Parque	.15
104	Marquis Grissom	.15
105	Eric Chavez	.25
106	Todd Jones	.15
107	Eric Owens	.15
108	Roger Clemens	1.00
109	Denny Hocking	.15
110	Roberto Hernandez	.15
111	Albert Belle	.15
112	Troy Glaus	.75
113	Ivan Rodriguez	.60
114	Carlos Guillen	.15
115	Chuck Finley	.15
116	Dmitri Young	.15
117	Paul Konerko	.15
118	Damon Buford	.15
119	Fernando Tatis	.15
120	Larry Walker	.35
121	Jason Kendall	.15
122	Matt Williams	.15
123	Henry Rodriguez	.15
124	Placido Polanco	.15
125	Bobby Estalella	.15
126	Pat Burrell	.50
127	Mark Loretta	.15
128	Moises Alou	.15
129	Tino Martinez	.15
130	Milton Bradley	.15
131	Todd Hundley	.15
132	Keith Foulke	.15
133	Robert Fick	.15
134	Cristian Guzman	.15
135	Rusty Greer	.15
136	John Olerud	.15
137	Mariano Rivera	.25
138	Jeromy Burnitz	.15
139	Dave Burba	.15
140	Ken Griffey Jr.	1.25
141	Tony Gwynn	1.00
142	Carlos Delgado	.50
143	Edgar Martinez	.15
144	Ramon Hernandez	.15
145	Pedro Astacio	.15
146	Ray Lankford	.15
147	Mike Mussina	.40
148	Ray Durham	.15
149	Lee Stevens	.15
150	Jay Canizaro	.15
151	Adrian Brown	.15
152	Mike Piazza	1.25
153	Cliff Floyd	.15
154	Jose Vidro	.15
155	Jason Giambi	.50
156	Andruw Jones	.75
157	Robin Ventura	.15
158	Gary Sheffield	.40
159	Jeff D'Amico	.15
160	Chuck Knoblauch	.15
161	Roger Cedeno	.15
162	Jim Thome	.15
163	Peter Bergeron	.15
164	Kerry Wood	.50
165	Gabe Kapler	.15
166	Corey Koskie	.15
167	Doug Glanville	.15
168	Brent Mayne	.15
169	Scott Spiezio	.15
170	Steve Karsay	.15
171	Al Martin	.15
172	Fred McGriff	.15
173	Gabe White	.15
174	Alex Gonzalez	.15
175	Mike Darr	.15
176	Bengie Molina	.15
177	Ben Grieve	.15
178	Marlon Anderson	.15
179	Brian Giles	.15
180	Jose Valentin	.15
181	Brian Jordan	.15
182	Randy Johnson	.75
183	Ricky Ledee	.15
184	Russ Ortiz	.15
185	Mike Lowell	.15
186	Curtis Leskanic	.15
187	Bobby Abreu	.15
188	Derek Jeter	2.00
189	Lance Berkman	.15
190	Roberto Alomar	.40
191	Darin Erstad	.60
192	Richie Sexson	.15
193	Alex Ochoa	.15
194	Carlos Febles	.15
195	David Ortiz	.15
196	Shawn Green	.35
197	Mike Sweeney	.15
198	Vladimir Guerrero	.75
199	Jose Jimenez	.15
200	Travis Lee	.15
201	Rickey Henderson	.75
202	Bob Wickman	.15
203	Miguel Cairo	.15
204	Steve Finley	.15
205	Tony Batista	.15
206	Jamey Wright	.15
207	Terrence Long	.15
208	Trevor Hoffman	.15
209	John Vander Wal	.15
210	Greg Maddux	1.00
211	Tim Salmon	.25
212	Herbert Perry	.15
213	Marvin Benard	.15
214	Jose Offerman	.15
215	Jay Payton	.15
216	Jon Lieber	.15
217	Mark Kotsay	.15
218	Scott Brosius	.15
219	Scott Williamson	.15
220	Omar Vizquel	.15
221	Mike Hampton	.15
222	Richard Hidalgo	.15
223	Rey Sanchez	.15
224	Matt Lawton	.15
225	Bruce Chen	.15
226	Ryan Klesko	.15
227	Garret Anderson	.15
228	Kevin Brown	.15
229	Mike Cameron	.15
230	Tony Clark	.15
231	Curt Schilling	.40
232	Vinny Castilla	.15
233	Carl Pavano	.15
234	Eric Davis	.15
235	Darrin Fletcher	.15
236	Matt Stairs	.15
237	Octavio Dotel	.15
238	Mark Grace	.25
239	John Smoltz	.15
240	Matt Clement	.15

241	Ellis Burks	.15
242	Charles Johnson	.15
243	Jeff Bagwell	.75
244	Derek Bell	.15
245	Nomar Garciaparra	1.25
246	Jorge Posada	.35
247	Ryan Dempster	.15
248	J.T. Snow	.15
249	Eric Young	.15
250	Daryle Ward	.15
251	Joe Randa	.15
252	Travis Fryman	.15
253	Mike Williams	.15
254	Jacque Jones	.15
255	Scott Elarton	.15
256	Mark McGwire	1.50
257	Jay Buhner	.15
258	Randy Wolf	.15
259	Sammy Sosa	1.25
260	Chan Ho Park	.15
261	Damion Easley	.15
262	Rick Ankiel	.15
263	Frank Thomas	.75
264	Kris Benson	.15
265	Luis Alicea	.15
266	Jeremy Giambi	.15
267	Geoff Blum	.15
268	Joe Girardi	.15
269	Livan Hernandez	.15
270	Jeff Conine	.15
271	Danny Graves	.15
272	Craig Biggio	.15
273	Jose Canseco	.35
274	Tom Glavine	.30
275	Ruben Mateo	.15
276	Jeff Kent	.15
277	Kevin Young	.15
278	A.J. Burnett	.15
279	Dante Bichette	.15
280	Sandy Alomar Jr.	.15
281	John Wetteland	.15
282	Torii Hunter	.15
283	Jarrod Washburn	.15
284	Rich Aurilia	.15
285	Jeff Cirillo	.15
286	Fernando Seguignol	.15
287	Darren Dreifort	.15
288	Deivi Cruz	.15
289	Pokey Reese	.15
290	Garrett Stephenson	.15
291	Pat Boone	.15
292	Tim Hudson	.35
293	John Flaherty	.15
294	Shannon Stewart	.15
295	Shawn Estes	.15
296	Wilton Guerrero	.15
297	Delino DeShields	.15
298	David Justice	.15
299	Harold Baines	.15
300	Al Leiter	.15
301	Wil Cordero	.15
302	Antonio Alfonseca	.15
303	Sean Casey	.25
304	Carlos Beltran	.40
305	Brad Radke	.15
306	Jason Varitek	.15
307	Shigetosi Hasegawa	.15
308	Todd Stottlemyre	.15
309	Raul Mondesi	.15
310	Mike Bordick	.15
311	Darryl Kile	.15
312	Dean Palmer	.15
313	Johnny Damon	.30
314	Todd Helton	.75
315	Chad Hermansen	.15
316	Kevin Appier	.15
317	Greg Vaughn	.15
318	Robb Nen	.15
319	Jose Cruz Jr.	.15
320	Ron Belliard	.15
321	Bernie Williams	.35
322	Melvin Mora	.15
323	Kenny Lofton	.15
324	Armando Benitez	.15
325	Carlos Lee	.15
326	Damian Jackson	.15
327	Eric Milton	.15
328	J.D. Drew	.30
329	Byung-Hyun Kim	.15
330	Chris Stynes	.15
331	Kazuhiro Sasaki	.15
332	Troy O'Leary	.15
333	Pat Hentgen	.15
334	Brad Ausmus	.15
335	Todd Walker	.15
336	Jason Isringhausen	.15
337	Gerald Williams	.15
338	Aaron Sele	.15
339	Paul O'Neill	.15
340	Cal Ripken Jr.	2.00
341	Manny Ramirez	.75
342	Will Clark	.35
343	Mark Redman	.15
344	Bubba Trammell	.15
345	Troy Percival	.15
346	Chris Singleton	.15
347	Rafael Palmeiro	.60
348	Carl Everett	.15
349	Andy Benes	.15
350	Bobby Higginson	.15
351	Alex Cabrera (Prospects)	.15
352	Barry Zito (Prospects)	.40
353	Jace Brewer (Prospects)	.15
354	Paxton Crawford (Prospects)	.15

355	Oswaldo Mairena (Prospects)	.15
356	Joe Crede (Prospects)	.15
357	A.J. Pierzynski (Prospects)	.15
358	Daniel Garibay (Prospects)	.15
359	Jason Tyner (Prospects)	.15
360	Nate Rolison (Prospects)	.15
361	Scott Downs (Prospects)	.15
362	Keith Ginter (Prospects)	.15
363	Juan Pierre (Prospects)	.15
364	Adam Bernero (Prospects)	.15
365	Chris Richard (Prospects)	.15
366	Joey Nation (Prospects)	.15
367	Aubrey Huff (Prospects)	.15
368	Adam Eaton (Prospects)	.15
369	Jose Ortiz (Prospects)	.15
370	Eric Munson (Prospects)	.15
371	Matt Kinney (Prospects)	.15
372	Eric Byrnes (Prospects)	.15
373	Keith McDonald (Prospects)	.15
374	Matt Wise (Prospects)	.15
375	Timo Perez (Prospects)	.15
376	Julio Zuleta (Prospects)	.15
377	Jimmy Rollins (Prospects)	.25
378	Xavier Nady (Prospects)	.15
379	Ryan Kohlmeier (Prospects)	.15
380	Corey Patterson (Prospects)	.15
381	Todd Helton (League Leaders)	.40
382	Moises Alou (League Leaders)	.15
383	Vladimir Guerrero (League Leaders)	.40
384	Luis Castillo (League Leaders)	.15
385	Jeffrey Hammonds (League Leaders)	.15
386	Nomar Garciaparra (League Leaders)	.75
387	Carlos Delgado (League Leaders)	.25
388	Darin Erstad (League Leaders)	.15
389	Manny Ramirez (League Leaders)	.40
390	Mike Sweeney (League Leaders)	.15
391	Sammy Sosa (League Leaders)	.75
392	Barry Bonds (League Leaders)	1.00
393	Jeff Bagwell (League Leaders)	.40
394	Richard Hidalgo (League Leaders)	.15
395	Vladimir Guerrero (League Leaders)	.40
396	Troy Glaus (League Leaders)	.30
397	Frank Thomas (League Leaders)	.40
398	Carlos Delgado (League Leaders)	.25
399	David Justice (League Leaders)	.15
400	Jason Giambi (League Leaders)	.25
401	Randy Johnson (League Leaders)	.40
402	Kevin Brown (League Leaders)	.15
403	Greg Maddux (League Leaders)	.50
404	Al Leiter (League Leaders)	.15
405	Mike Hampton (League Leaders)	.15
406	Pedro Martinez (League Leaders)	.40
407	Roger Clemens (League Leaders)	.65
408	Mike Sirotka (League Leaders)	.15
409	Mike Mussina (League Leaders)	.25
410	Bartolo Colon (League Leaders)	.15
411	World Series Update	.15
412	World Series Update	.15
413	World Series Update	.15
414	World Series Update	.15
415	World Series Update	.15
416	World Series Update	.15
417	World Series Update	.15
418	World Series Update	.15
419	World Series Update	.15
420	World Series Update	.15
421	Atlanta Braves (Team Checklists)	.15

422	New York Mets (Team Checklists)	.15
423	Florida Marlins (Team Checklists)	.15
424	Philadelphia Phillies (Team Checklists)	.15
425	Montreal Expos (Team Checklists)	.15
426	St. Louis Cardinals (Team Checklists)	.15
427	Cincinnati Reds (Team Checklists)	.15
428	Chicago Cubs (Team Checklists)	.15
429	Milwaukee Brewers (Team Checklists)	.15
430	Houston Astros (Team Checklists)	.15
431	Pittsburgh Pirates (Team Checklists)	.15
432	San Francisco Giants (Team Checklists)	.15
433	Arizona Diamondbacks (Team Checklists)	.15
434	Los Angeles Dodgers (Team Checklists)	.15
435	Colorado Rockies (Team Checklists)	.15
436	San Diego Padres (Team Checklists)	.15
437	New York Yankees (Team Checklists)	.15
438	Boston Red Sox (Team Checklists)	.15
439	Baltimore Orioles (Team Checklists)	.15
440	Toronto Blue Jays (Team Checklists)	.15
441	Tampa Bay Devil Rays (Team Checklists)	.15
442	Chicago White Sox (Team Checklists)	.15
443	Cleveland Indians (Team Checklists)	.15
444	Detroit Tigers (Team Checklists)	.15
445	Kansas City Royals (Team Checklists)	.15
446	Minnesota Twins (Team Checklists)	.15
447	Seattle Mariners (Team Checklists)	.15
448	Oakland Athletics (Team Checklists)	.15
449	Anaheim Angels (Team Checklists)	.15
450	Texas Rangers (Team Checklists)	.15
451	Albert Pujols RC	70.00
452	Ichiro Suzuki RC	15.00
453	Tsuyoshi Shinjo RC	.75
454	Johnny Estrada RC	.75
455	Elpidio Guzman RC	.40
456	Adrian Hernandez RC	.30
457	Rafael Soriano RC	.30
458	Drew Henson RC	1.00
459	Juan Uribe RC	.75
460	Matt White RC	.40
461	Endy Chavez RC	.30
462	Bud Smith RC	.25
463	Morgan Ensberg RC	.75
464	Jay Gibbons RC	2.00
465	Jackson Melian RC	.30
466	Junior Spivey RC	.75
467	Juan Cruz RC	.50
468	Wilson Betemit RC	.40
469	Alexis Gomez RC	.30
470	Mark Teixeira RC	15.00
471	Erick Almonte RC	.30
472	Travis Hafner RC	5.00
473	Carlos Valderrama RC	.30
474	Brandon Duckworth RC	.75
475	Ryan Freel RC	.30
476	Wilkin Ruan RC	.30
477	Andres Torres RC	.30
478	Josh Towers RC	.50
479	Kyle Lohse RC	.75
480	Jason Michaels RC	.30
481	Alfonso Soriano RC	.50
482	C.C. Sabathia RC	.75
483	Roy Oswalt RC	.15
484	Ben Sheets	.15
485	Adam Dunn	.50

Diamond Tributes

Complete Set (30):		35.00
Common Player:		.50
Inserted 1:7		
1	Jackie Robinson	2.00
2	Mike Piazza	2.00
3	Alex Rodriguez	3.00
4	Barry Bonds	4.00
5	Nomar Garciaparra	2.00
6	Roger Clemens	1.75
7	Ivan Rodriguez	.75
8	Cal Ripken Jr.	4.00

9	Manny Ramirez	1.00
10	Chipper Jones	1.50
11	Barry Larkin	.50
12	Carlos Delgado	.75
13	J.D. Drew	.60
14	Carl Everett	.50
15	Todd Helton	1.00
16	Greg Maddux	1.50
17	Scott Rolen	.75
18	Troy Glaus	1.00
19	Brian Giles	.50
20	Jeff Bagwell	1.00
21	Sammy Sosa	2.00
22	Randy Johnson	1.00
23	Andruw Jones	1.00
24	Ken Griffey Jr.	2.00
25	Mark McGwire	3.00
26	Derek Jeter	4.00
27	Vladimir Guerrero	1.00
28	Frank Thomas	1.00
29	Pedro Martinez	1.00
30	Bernie Williams	.50

Grass Roots

		NM/M
Complete Set (15):		25.00
Common Player:		1.00
Inserted 1:18		
1	Derek Jeter	4.00
2	Greg Maddux	2.00
3	Sammy Sosa	2.50
4	Alex Rodriguez	3.00
5	Vladimir Guerrero	1.50
6	Scott Rolen	1.00
7	Frank Thomas	1.50
8	Nomar Garciaparra	2.50
9	Cal Ripken Jr.	4.00
10	Mike Piazza	2.50
11	Ivan Rodriguez	1.00
12	Chipper Jones	2.00
13	Tony Gwynn	2.00
14	Ken Griffey Jr.	2.50
15	Mark McGwire	3.00

Lumber Company

		NM/M
Complete Set (20):		25.00
Common Player:		.50
Inserted 1:12		
1	Vladimir Guerrero	1.50
2	Mo Vaughn	.50
3	Ken Griffey Jr.	2.50
4	Juan Gonzalez	1.50
5	Tony Gwynn	2.00
6	Jim Edmonds	.50
7	Jason Giambi	1.00
8	Alex Rodriguez	3.00
9	Derek Jeter	4.00
10	Darin Erstad	1.00
11	Andruw Jones	1.50
12	Cal Ripken Jr.	4.00
13	Magglio Ordonez	.50
14	Nomar Garciaparra	2.50
15	Chipper Jones	2.00
16	Sean Casey	.60
17	Shawn Green	.60
18	Mike Piazza	2.50
19	Sammy Sosa	2.50
20	Barry Bonds	4.00

Season Pass

Complete Set (6):		
Common Player:		
Values Undetermined		

Stitches in Time

		NM/M
Complete Set (25):		40.00
Common Player:		1.50
Inserted 1:18		
1	Henry Kimbro	1.50
2	Ernie Banks	3.00
3	James "Cool Papa" Bell	2.00
4	Joe Black	1.50

5	Roy Campanella	2.00
6	Ray Dandridge	1.50
7	Leon Day	1.50
8	Larry Doby	2.00
9	Josh Gibson	2.00
10	Elston Howard	2.00
11	Monte Irvin	2.00
12	Buck Leonard	2.00
13	Max Manning	1.50
14	Willie Mays	6.00
15	Buck O'Neil	2.00
16	Satchel Paige	3.00
17	Ted Radcliffe	2.00
18	Jackie Robinson	4.00
19	Bill Perkins	1.50
20	Andrew "Rube" Foster	2.00
21	William "Judy" Johnson	1.50
22	Oscar Charleston	1.50
23	John Henry "Pop" Lloyd	1.50
24	Artie Wilson	1.50
25	Sam Jethroe	1.50

Stitches in Time Autographs

		NM/M
Common Autograph:		20.00
2	Ernie Banks	50.00
3	Joe Black	25.00
11	Monte Irvin	30.00
14	Willie Mays	150.00
15	Buck O'Neil	30.00
17	Ted Radcliffe	25.00
24	Artie Wilson	25.00

Stitches in Time Game-Used

		NM/M
Common Card:		25.00
5	Roy Campanella	60.00
8	Larry Doby/Bat	25.00
10	Elston Howard/Bat	25.00
14	Willie Mays/Jsy	125.00
18	Jackie Robinson/ Jsy	100.00

Turn Back the Clock

		NM/M
Common Card:		8.00
Inserted 1:352		
1	Tom Glavine	10.00
2	Greg Maddux	20.00
3	Sean Casey	8.00
4	Pokey Reese	8.00

5	Jason Giambi	15.00
6	Tim Hudson	8.00
7	Larry Walker	8.00
8	Jeffrey Hammonds	8.00
9	Scott Rolen	15.00
10	Pat Burrell	10.00
11	Chipper Jones	20.00
13	Troy Glaus	15.00
14	Tony Gwynn	20.00
15	Cal Ripken Jr.	50.00
16	Tom Glavine, Greg Maddux	75.00
17	Sean Casey, Pokey Reese	30.00
18	Chipper Jones, Greg Maddux	100.00
19	Larry Walker, Jeffrey Hammonds	30.00
20	Scott Rolen, Pat Burrell	40.00
21	Jason Giambi, Tim Hudson	40.00

Warning Track

		NM/M
Complete Set (23):		120.00
Common Player:		2.00
Inserted 1:72		
1	Josh Gibson	5.00
2	Willie Mays	10.00
3	Mark McGwire	12.00
4	Barry Bonds	15.00
5	Jose Canseco	4.00
6	Ken Griffey Jr.	10.00
7	Cal Ripken Jr.	15.00
8	Rafael Palmeiro	5.00
9	Sammy Sosa	10.00
10	Juan Gonzalez	6.00
11	Frank Thomas	6.00
12	Jeff Bagwell	6.00
13	Gary Sheffield	2.50
14	Larry Walker	2.00
15	Mike Piazza	10.00
16	Larry Doby	4.00
17	Roy Campanella	5.00
18	Manny Ramirez	6.00
19	Chipper Jones	8.00
20	Alex Rodriguez	12.00
21	Ivan Rodriguez	6.00
22	Vladimir Guerrero	5.00
23	Nomar Garciaparra	10.00
24	Andres Galarraga	2.00
25	Jim Thome	2.00

Milwaukee Brewers

This 10-1/2" x 7-1/2" sheet was distributed to the first 10,000 fans attending the Brewers' September 2 game at Miller Park. Eight of the team's Fleer Tradition cards are reproduced on the sheet, with a team logo at center.

		NM/M
Sheet:		12.00

2001 Fleer Triple Crown

		NM/M
Complete Set (300):		25.00
Common Player:		.15
Pack (10):		2.00
Box (24):		40.00

#	Player	Price
1	Derek Jeter	2.00
2	Vladimir Guerrero	.75
3	Henry Rodriguez	.15
4	Jason Giambi	.50
5	Nomar Garciaparra	1.25
6	Jeff Kent	.15
7	Garret Anderson	.15
8	Todd Helton	.75
9	Barry Bonds	2.00
10	Preston Wilson	.15
11	Troy Glaus	.75
12	Geoff Jenkins	.15
13	Jim Edmonds	.15
14	Bobby Higginson	.15
15	Mark Quinn	.15
16	Barry Larkin	.15
17	Richie Sexson	.15
18	Fernando Tatis	.15
19	John Vander Wal	.15
20	Darin Erstad	.60
21	Shawn Green	.40
22	Scott Rolen	.60
23	Tony Batista	.15
24	Phil Nevin	.15
25	Tim Salmon	.25
26	Gary Sheffield	.35
27	Ben Grieve	.15
28	Jermaine Dye	.15
29	Andres Galarraga	.15
30	Adrian Beltre	.35
31	Rafael Palmeiro	.60
32	J.T. Snow	.15
33	Edgardo Alfonzo	.15
34	Paul Konerko	.15
35	Jim Thome	.15
36	Andruw Jones	.75
37	Mike Sweeney	.15
38	Jose Cruz Jr.	.15
39	David Ortiz	.15
40	Pat Burrell	.40
41	Chipper Jones	1.00
42	Jeff Bagwell	.75
43	Raul Mondesi	.15
44	Rondell White	.15
45	Edgar Martinez	.15
46	Cal Ripken Jr.	2.00
47	Moises Alou	.15
48	Shannon Stewart	.15
49	Tino Martinez	.15
50	Jason Kendall	.15
51	Richard Hidalgo	.15
52	Albert Belle	.15
53	Jay Payton	.15
54	Cliff Floyd	.15
55	Rusty Greer	.15
56	Matt Williams	.15
57	Sammy Sosa	1.25
58	Carl Everett	.15
59	Carlos Delgado	.50
60	Jeremy Giambi	.15
61	Jose Canseco	.40
62	David Segui	.15
63	Jose Vidro	.15
64	Matt Stairs	.15
65	Travis Fryman	.15
66	Ken Griffey Jr.	1.25
67	Mike Piazza	1.25
68	Mark McGwire	1.50
69	Craig Biggio	.15
70	Eric Chavez	.25
71	Mo Vaughn	.15
72	Matt Lawton	.15
73	Miguel Tejada	.25
74	Brian Giles	.15
75	Sean Casey	.25
76	Robin Ventura	.15
77	Ivan Rodriguez	.60
78	Dean Palmer	.15
79	Frank Thomas	.75
80	Bernie Williams	.30
81	Juan Encarnacion	.15
82	John Olerud	.15
83	Rich Aurilia	.15
84	Juan Gonzalez	.75
85	Ray Durham	.15
86	Steve Finley	.15
87	Ken Caminiti	.15
88	Roberto Alomar	.40
89	Jeremy Burnitz	.15
90	J.D. Drew	.15
91	Lance Berkman	.15
92	Gabe Kapler	.15
93	Larry Walker	.15
94	Alex Rodriguez	1.50
95	Jeffrey Hammonds	.15
96	Magglio Ordonez	.15
97	David Justice	.15
98	Eric Karros	.15
99	Manny Ramirez	.75
100	Paul O'Neill	.15
101	Ron Gant	.15
102	Erubiel Durazo	.15
103	Jason Varitek	.15
104	Chan Ho Park	.15
105	Corey Koskie	.15
106	Jeff Conine	.15
107	Kevin Tapani	.15
108	Mike Lowell	.15
109	Tim Hudson	.25
110	Bobby Abreu	.15
111	Bret Boone	.15
112	David Wells	.15
113	Brian Jordan	.15
114	Mitch Meluskey	.15
115	Terrence Long	.15
116	Matt Clement	.15
117	Fernando Vina	.15
118	Luis Alicea	.15
119	Jay Bell	.15
120	Mark Grace	.25
121	Carlos Febles	.15
122	Mark Redman	.15
123	Kevin Jordan	.15
124	Pat Meares	.15
125	Mark McLemore	.15
126	Chris Singleton	.15
127	Trot Nixon	.15
128	Carlos Beltran	.40
129	Lee Stevens	.15
130	Kris Benson	.15
131	Jay Buhner	.15
132	Greg Vaughn	.15
133	Eric Young	.15
134	Tony Womack	.15
135	Roger Cedeno	.15
136	Travis Lee	.15
137	Marvin Benard	.15
138	Aaron Sele	.15
139	Rick Ankiel	.15
140	Ruben Mateo	.15
141	Randy Johnson	.75
142	Jason Tyner	.15
143	Mike Redmond	.15
144	Ron Coomer	.15
145	Scott Elarton	.15
146	Javy Lopez	.15
147	Carlos Lee	.15
148	Tony Clark	.15
149	Roger Clemens	1.00
150	Mike Lieberthal	.15
151	Shawn Estes	.15
152	Vinny Castilla	.15
153	Alex Gonzalez	.15
154	Troy Percival	.15
155	Pokey Reese	.15
156	Todd Hollandsworth	.15
157	Marquis Grissom	.15
158	Greg Maddux	1.00
159	Dante Bichette	.15
160	Hideo Nomo	.75
161	Jacque Jones	.15
162	Kevin Young	.15
163	B.J. Surhoff	.15
164	Eddie Taubensee	.15
165	Neifi Perez	.15
166	Orlando Hernandez	.15
167	Francisco Cordova	.15
168	Miguel Cairo	.15
169	Rafael Furcal	.15
170	Sandy Alomar Jr.	.15
171	Jeff Cirillo	.15
172	A.J. Pierzynski	.15
173	Fred McGriff	.15
174	Mike Mussina	.40
175	Aaron Boone	.15
176	Nick Johnson	.15
177	Kent Bottenfield	.15
178	Felipe Crespo	.15
179	Ryan Minor	.15
180	Charles Johnson	.15
181	Damion Easley	.15
182	Michael Barrett	.15
183	Doug Glanville	.15
184	Ben Davis	.15
185	Rickey Henderson	.75
186	Edgard Clemente	.15
187	Dmitri Young	.15
188	Tom Goodwin	.15
189	Mike Hampton	.15
190	Gerald Williams	.15
191	Omar Vizquel	.15
192	Ben Petrick	.15
193	Brad Radke	.15
194	Russ Davis	.15
195	Milton Bradley	.40
196	John Parrish	.15
197	Todd Hundley	.15
198	Carl Pavano	.15
199	Bruce Chen	.15
200	Royce Clayton	.15
201	Homer Bush	.15
202	Mark Grudzielanek	.15
203	Mike Lansing	.15
204	Daryle Ward	.15
205	Jeff D'Amico	.15
206	Ray Lankford	.15
207	Curt Schilling	.40
208	Pedro Martinez	.75
209	Johnny Damon	.30
210	Al Leiter	.15
211	Ruben Rivera	.15
212	Kazuhiro Sasaki	.15
213	Will Clark	.25
214	Rick Helling	.15
215	Adam Piatt	.15
216	Joe Girardi	.15
217	A.J. Burnett	.15
218	Mike Bordick	.15
219	Mike Cameron	.15
220	Tony Gwynn	1.00
221	Deivi Cruz	.15
222	Bubba Trammell	.15
223	Scott Erickson	.15
224	Kerry Wood	.50
225	Derrek Lee	.15
226	Peter Bergeron	.15
227	Chris Gomez	.15
228	Al Martin	.15
229	Brady Anderson	.15
230	Ramon Martinez	.15
231	Darryl Kile	.15
232	Devon White	.15
233	Charlie Hayes	.15
234	Aramis Ramirez	.15
235	Mike Lamb	.15
236	Tom Glavine	.30
237	Troy O'Leary	.15
238	Joe Randa	.15
239	Dustin Hermanson	.15
240	Adam Kennedy	.15
241	Jose Valentin	.15
242	Derek Bell	.15
243	Mark Kotsay	.15
244	Ron Belliard	.15
245	Warren Morris	.15
246	Ozzie Guillen	.15
247	Andy Ashby	.15
248	Jose Offerman	.15
249	Kevin Brown	.15
250	Jorge Posada	.35
251	Alex Cabrera (Prospects)	.15
252	Chan Perry (Prospects)	.15
253	Augie Ojeda (Prospects)	.15
254	Santiago Perez (Prospects)	.15
255	Grant Roberts (Prospects)	.15
256	Dusty Allen (Prospects)	.15
257	Elvis Pena (Prospects)	.15
258	Matt Kinney (Prospects)	.15
259	Timoniel Perez (Prospects)	.15
260	Adam Eaton (Prospects)	.15
261	Geraldo Guzman (Prospects)	.15
262	Damian Rolls (Prospects)	.15
263	Alfonso Soriano (Prospects)	.50
264	Corey Patterson (Prospects)	.15
265	Juan Alvarez (Prospects)	.15
266	Shawn Gilbert (Prospects)	.15
267	Adam Bernero (Prospects)	.15
268	Ben Weber (Prospects)	.15
269	Tike Redman (Prospects)	.15
270	Willie Morales (Prospects)	.15
271	Tomas De La Rosa (Prospects)	.15
272	Rodney Lindsey (Prospects)	.15
273	Carlos Casimiro (Prospects)	.15
274	Jim Mann (Prospects)	.15
275	Pasqual Coco (Prospects)	.15
276	Julio Zuleta (Prospects)	.15
277	Damon Minor (Prospects)	.15
278	Jose Ortiz (Prospects)	.15
279	Eric Munson (Prospects)	.15
280	Andy Thompson (Prospects)	.15
281	Aubrey Huff (Prospects)	.15
282	Chris Richard (Prospects)	.15
283	Ross Gload (Prospects)	.15
284	Travis Dawkins (Prospects)	.15
285	Tim Drew (Prospects)	.15
286	Barry Zito (Prospects)	.40
287	Andy Tracy (Prospects)	.15
288	Julio Lugo (Prospects)	.15
289	Matt DeWitt (Prospects)	.15
290	Keith McDonald (Prospects)	.15
291	J.C. Romero (Prospects)	.15
292	Adam Melhuse (Prospects)	.15
293	Ryan Kohlmeier (Prospects)	.15
294	John Bale (Prospects)	.15
295	Eric Cammack (Prospects)	.15
296	Morgan Burkhart (Prospects)	.15
297	Kory DeHaan (Prospects)	.15
298	Raul Gonzalez (Prospects)	.15
299	Hector Ortiz (Prospects)	.15
300	Talmadge Nunnari (Prospects)	.15

Blue

NM/M
Common Player: 3.00
Produced to # of 2000 HR's.

#	Player	Price
1	Derek Jeter/15	150.00
2	Vladimir Guerrero/44	25.00
3	Henry Rodriguez/20	3.00
4	Jason Giambi/43	15.00
5	Nomar Garciaparra/21	25.00
6	Jeff Kent/33	8.00
7	Garret Anderson/35	4.00
8	Todd Helton/42	15.00
9	Barry Bonds/49	40.00
10	Preston Wilson/31	3.00
11	Troy Glaus/47	10.00
12	Geoff Jenkins/34	8.00
13	Jim Edmonds/42	10.00
14	Bobby Higginson/30	3.00
15	Mark Quinn/20	5.00
16	Barry Larkin/11	15.00
17	Richie Sexson/30	10.00
18	Fernando Tatis/18	3.00
19	John Vander Wal/24	3.00
20	Darin Erstad/25	10.00
21	Shawn Green/24	10.00
22	Scott Rolen/26	15.00
23	Tony Batista/41	3.00
24	Phil Nevin/31	3.00
25	Tim Salmon/34	5.00
26	Gary Sheffield/43	8.00
27	Ben Grieve/27	5.00
28	Jermaine Dye/33	3.00
29	Andres Galarraga/28	5.00
30	Adrian Beltre/20	8.00
31	Rafael Palmeiro/39	10.00
32	J.T. Snow/19	5.00
33	Edgardo Alfonzo/25	5.00
34	Paul Konerko/21	5.00
35	Jim Thome/37	8.00
36	Andruw Jones/36	10.00
37	Mike Sweeney/29	3.00
38	Jose Cruz Jr./31	3.00
39	David Ortiz/10	8.00
40	Pat Burrell/18	15.00
41	Chipper Jones/36	15.00
42	Jeff Bagwell/47	10.00
43	Raul Mondesi/24	5.00
44	Rondell White/13	10.00
45	Edgar Martinez/37	5.00
46	Cal Ripken Jr./15	150.00
47	Moises Alou/30	5.00
48	Shannon Stewart/21	3.00
49	Tino Martinez/16	5.00
50	Jason Kendall/14	5.00
51	Richard Hidalgo/44	3.00
52	Albert Belle/23	5.00
53	Jay Payton/17	3.00
54	Cliff Floyd/22	5.00
55	Rusty Greer/8	8.00
56	Matt Williams/12	5.00
57	Sammy Sosa/50	25.00
58	Carl Everett/34	3.00
59	Carlos Delgado/41	5.00
60	Jeremy Giambi/10	5.00
61	Jose Canseco/15	10.00
62	David Segui/19	3.00
63	Jose Vidro/24	3.00
64	Matt Stairs/21	3.00
65	Travis Fryman/22	5.00
66	Ken Griffey Jr./40	15.00
67	Mike Piazza/38	15.00
68	Mark McGwire/32	20.00
69	Craig Biggio/8	10.00
70	Eric Chavez/26	10.00
71	Mo Vaughn/36	5.00
72	Matt Lawton/13	5.00
73	Miguel Tejada/30	10.00
74	Brian Giles/35	5.00
75	Sean Casey/20	5.00
76	Robin Ventura/24	5.00
77	Ivan Rodriguez/27	8.00
78	Dean Palmer/29	5.00
79	Frank Thomas/43	10.00
80	Bernie Williams/30	5.00
81	Juan Encarnacion/14	5.00
82	John Olerud/14	5.00
83	Rich Aurilia/20	3.00
84	Juan Gonzalez/22	8.00
85	Ray Durham/17	5.00
86	Steve Finley/35	3.00
87	Ken Caminiti/15	5.00
88	Roberto Alomar/19	15.00
89	Jeromy Burnitz/31	3.00
90	J.D. Drew/18	8.00
91	Lance Berkman/21	8.00
92	Gabe Kapler/14	5.00
93	Larry Walker/9	10.00
94	Alex Rodriguez/41	20.00
95	Jeffrey Hammonds/20	5.00
96	Magglio Ordonez/32	5.00
97	David Justice/41	5.00
98	Eric Karros/31	5.00
99	Manny Ramirez/38	10.00
100	Paul O'Neill/18	8.00

Green

NM/M
Common Player: 1.00
Produced to # of 2000 RBI's.

#	Player	Price
1	Derek Jeter/73	20.00
2	Vladimir Guerrero/123	5.00
3	Henry Rodriguez/61	1.00
4	Jason Giambi/137	5.00
5	Nomar Garciaparra/96	10.00
6	Jeff Kent/125	3.00
7	Garret Anderson/117	3.00
8	Todd Helton/147	5.00
9	Barry Bonds/106	20.00
10	Preston Wilson/121	1.00
11	Troy Glaus/102	4.00
12	Geoff Jenkins/94	3.00
13	Jim Edmonds/108	4.00
14	Bobby Higginson/102	1.00
15	Mark Quinn/78	1.00
16	Barry Larkin/41	4.00
17	Richie Sexson/91	4.00
18	Fernando Tatis/64	1.00
19	John Vander Wal/94	1.00
20	Darin Erstad/100	3.00
21	Shawn Green/99	3.00
22	Scott Rolen/89	4.00
23	Tony Batista/114	1.00
24	Phil Nevin/107	3.00
25	Tim Salmon/97	3.00
26	Gary Sheffield/109	3.00
27	Ben Grieve/104	1.00
28	Jermaine Dye/118	1.00
29	Andres Galarraga/100	1.50
30	Adrian Beltre/85	1.00
31	Rafael Palmeiro/120	3.00
32	J.T. Snow/96	1.00
33	Edgardo Alfonzo/94	1.00
34	Paul Konerko/97	1.50
35	Jim Thome/106	4.00
36	Andruw Jones/104	3.00
37	Mike Sweeney/144	3.00
38	Jose Cruz Jr./76	1.00
39	David Ortiz/63	1.00
40	Pat Burrell/79	4.00
41	Chipper Jones/111	8.00
42	Jeff Bagwell/132	5.00
43	Raul Mondesi/67	2.00
44	Rondell White/61	1.50
45	Edgar Martinez/145	2.00
46	Cal Ripken Jr./25	25.00
47	Moises Alou/114	1.00
48	Shannon Stewart/69	1.00
49	Tino Martinez/91	2.00
50	Jason Kendall/58	1.00
51	Richard Hidalgo/122	1.00
52	Albert Belle/103	1.00
53	Jay Payton/62	1.00
54	Cliff Floyd/91	1.00
55	Rusty Greer/65	1.00
56	Matt Williams/47	2.00
57	Sammy Sosa/138	10.00
58	Carl Everett/108	1.00
59	Carlos Delgad/137	3.00
60	Jeremy Giambi/50	1.00
61	Jose Canseco/49	5.00
62	David Segui/103	1.00
63	Jose Vidro/97	1.00
64	Matt Stairs/81	1.00
65	Travis Fryman/106	2.00
66	Ken Griffey Jr./118	10.00
67	Mike Piazza/113	10.00
68	Mark McGwire/73	15.00
69	Craig Biggio/35	4.00
70	Eric Chavez/86	4.00
71	Mo Vaughn/117	3.00
72	Matt Lawton/88	1.00
73	Miguel Tejada/115	4.00
74	Brian Giles/123	4.00
75	Sean Casey/85	2.00
76	Robin Ventura/84	2.00
77	Ivan Rodriguez/83	5.00
78	Dean Palmer/102	1.00
79	Frank Thomas/143	5.00
80	Bernie Williams/121	4.00
81	Juan Encarnacion/72	1.00
82	John Olerud/103	3.00
83	Rich Aurilia/79	1.00
84	Juan Gonzalez/67	3.00
85	Ray Durham/96	1.00
86	Steve Finley/96	1.00
87	Ken Caminiti/45	2.00
88	Roberto Alomar/89	5.00
89	Jeromy Burnitz/98	1.50
90	J.D. Drew/57	3.00
91	Lance Berkman/57	2.00
92	Gabe Kapler/66	2.00
93	Larry Walker/51	3.00
94	Alex Rodriguez/132	15.00
95	Jeffrey Hammonds/106	1.00
96	Magglio Ordonez/126	3.00
97	David Justice/118	3.00
98	Eric Karros/106	1.00
99	Manny Ramirez/122	5.00
100	Paul O'Neill/100	2.00

Red

NM/M
Common Player (1-100): 4-8X
Stars:
Produced to 2000 Bat Avg.

Autographics

NM/M
Common Autograph: 5.00
Inserted 1:72
Silvers: 1X
Production 250 Sets
Golds: 1-2X
Production 50 Sets

#	Player	Price
1	Roberto Alomar	30.00
2	Jimmy Anderson	5.00
3	Ryan Anderson	5.00
4	Rick Ankiel	5.00
5	Adrian Beltre	10.00
6	Peter Bergeron	5.00
7	Lance Berkman	8.00
8	Barry Bonds	200.00
9	Milton Bradley	5.00
10	Dee Brown	5.00
11	Roosevelt Brown	5.00
12	Pat Burrell	10.00
13	Sean Casey	8.00
14	Eric Chavez	10.00
15	Giuseppe Chiaramonte	5.00
16	Joe Crede	5.00
17	Jose Cruz Jr.	5.00
18	Carlos Delgado	10.00
19	Ryan Dempster	5.00
20	Adam Dunn	15.00
21	David Eckstein	5.00
22	Jim Edmonds	10.00
23	Troy Glaus	15.00
24	Chad Green	5.00
25	Tony Gwynn	30.00
26	Todd Helton	20.00
27	Chad Hermansen	5.00
28	Shea Hillenbrand	6.00
29	Aubrey Huff	6.00
30	Randy Johnson	40.00
31	Chipper Jones	40.00
32	Mike Lamb	5.00
33	Corey Lee	5.00
34	Steve Lomasney	5.00
35	Terrence Long	5.00
36	Julio Lugo	5.00
37	Jason Marquis	5.00
38	Bengie Molina	5.00
39	Mike Mussina	25.00
40	Pablo Ozuna	5.00
41	Corey Patterson	10.00
42	Jay Payton	6.00
43	Wily Pena	15.00
44	Josh Phelps	8.00
45	Adam Piatt	5.00
46	Matt Riley	5.00
47	Alex Rodriguez	75.00
48	Alex Sanchez	5.00
49	Gary Sheffield	5.00
50	Alfonso Soriano	40.00
51	Shannon Stewart	6.00
52	Fernando Tatis	5.00
53	Jose Vidro	5.00
54	Preston Wilson	8.00
55	Kerry Wood	25.00
56	Julio Zuleta	5.00

Crowning Achievements

NM/M
Complete Set (15): 15.00
Common Player: .50
Inserted 1:9

#	Player	Price
1	Troy Glaus	1.00
2	Mark McGwire	2.50
3	Barry Larkin, Craig Biggio	.50
4	Ken Griffey Jr.	2.00
5	Rafael Palmeiro	.75
6	Alex Rodriguez	2.50
7	Roger Clemens	1.75
8	Mike Piazza	2.00
9	Cal Ripken Jr.	3.00
10	Randy Johnson	1.00
11	Jeff Bagwell	1.00
12	Sammy Sosa	2.00
13	Greg Maddux	1.50
14	Barry Bonds	3.00
15	Fred McGriff	.50

Crowns of Gold

	NM/M
Common Player:	4.00

Random inserts in Hobby packs.

	NM/M
Rick Ankiel/Jsy	4.00
Steve Carlton/Jsy	10.00
Roger Clemens/Jsy	40.00
Carlos Delgado/Bat	8.00
Darin Erstad/Bat	6.00
Jimmie Foxx/Bat	100.00
Todd Helton/Bat	10.00
Randy Johnson/Jsy	10.00
Frank Robinson/Bat	10.00
Gary Sheffield/Jsy	8.00
Frank Thomas/Bat	10.00
Ted Williams/Bat	200.00

Crowns of Gold Autograph

	NM/M

Random inserts in Hobby packs.

Steve Carlton/Jsy/72	80.00
Roger Clemens/ Jsy/98	200.00
Frank Robinson/ Bat/66	80.00

Feel the Game

	NM/M
Common Player:	4.00
Inserted 1:72	
Golds:	1.5-2X
Production 50 Sets	
Adrian Beltre	6.00
Dante Bichette	4.00
Roger Cedeno	4.00
Ben Davis	4.00
Carlos Delgado	6.00
J.D. Drew	6.00
Jason Giambi	6.00
Brian Giles	4.00
Juan Gonzalez	8.00
Richard Hidalgo	4.00
Chipper Jones	10.00
Eric Karros	4.00
Javy Lopez	4.00
Tino Martinez	4.00
Raul Mondesi	4.00
Phil Nevin	4.00
Chan Ho Park	4.00
Ivan Rodriguez	6.00
Shannon Stewart	4.00
Frank Thomas	8.00
Jose Vidro	4.00
Matt Williams	4.00
Preston Wilson	4.00

Future Threats

	NM/M
Complete Set (15):	15.00
Common Player:	.50
Inserted 1:7	
1 Derek Jeter	3.00
2 Alex Rodriguez	2.50
3 Magglio Ordonez, Shawn Green	.50
4 Larry Walker	.50
5 Vladimir Guerrero	1.00
6 Nomar Garciaparra	2.00
7 Ken Griffey Jr.	2.00
8 Barry Bonds	3.00
9 Chipper Jones	1.50
10 Todd Helton	1.00
11 Ivan Rodriguez	.75
12 Jeff Bagwell	1.00
13 Frank Thomas	1.00
14 Carlos Delgado	.65
15 Mike Piazza	2.00

Glamour Boys

	NM/M
Complete Set (15):	40.00

Common Player:	1.50
Inserted 1:24	
1 Derek Jeter	6.00
2 Vladimir Guerrero	2.00
3 Scott Rolen, Jeff Bagwell	1.50
4 Sammy Sosa	4.00
5 Ken Griffey Jr.	4.00
6 Mark McGwire	5.00
7 Ivan Rodriguez	1.50
8 Mike Piazza	4.00
9 Nomar Garciaparra	4.00
10 Cal Ripken Jr.	6.00
11 Tony Gwynn	3.00
12 Barry Bonds	6.00
13 Randy Johnson	2.00
14 Alex Rodriguez	5.00
15 Pedro Martinez	2.00

Ritz-Oreo

In conjunction with its sponsorship of the 2001 All-Star Game in Seattle, Ritz-Oreo issued a pair of Jeter cards distributed in product packages. In standard 2-1/2" x 3-1/2" format, one card is bordered in red and pictures him batting; a blue bordered card has a picture of him throwing. Backs have biographical data with height measured in Oreos, and weight measured in Ritz, recent stats, a quote and logos of all parties involved. The cards were also available packaged with a pair of Upper Deck Griffey cards in a mail-in offer.

	NM/M
Complete Set (2):	3.00
Common Card:	2.00
Derek Jeter/Btg	2.00
Derek Jeter/Throwing	2.00

2002 Fleer

	NM/M
Complete Set (540):	75.00
Common Player:	.15
Pack (10):	2.00
Box (24):	40.00
31 Miguel Tejada	.25
32 Todd Hollandsworth	.15
33 Marlon Anderson	.15
34 Kerry Robinson	.15
35 Chris Richard	.15
36 Jamey Wright	.15
37 Ray Lankford	.15
38 Mike Bordick	.15
39 Danny Graves	.15
40 A.J. Pierzynski	.15
41 Shannon Stewart	.15
42 Tony Armas Jr.	.15
43 Brad Ausmus	.15
44 Alfonso Soriano	.50
45 Junior Spivey	.15
46 Brent Mayne	.15
47 Jim Thome	.15
48 Dan Wilson	.15
49 Geoff Jenkins	.15
50 Kris Benson	.15
51 Rafael Furcal	.15
52 Wiki Gonzalez	.15
53 Jeff Kent	.15
54 Curt Schilling	.40
55 Ken Harvey	.15
56 Roosevelt Brown	.15
57 David Segui	.15
58 Mario Valdez	.15
59 Adam Dunn	.50
60 Bob Howry	.15
61 Michael Barrett	.15
62 Garret Anderson	.15
63 Kelvim Escobar	.15
64 Ben Grieve	.15
65 Randy Johnson	.75
66 Jose Offerman	.15
67 Jason Kendall	.15
68 Joel Pineiro	.15
69 Alex Escobar	.15
70 Chris George	.15
71 Bobby Higginson	.15
72 Nomar Garciaparra	1.50
73 Pat Burrell	.40
74 Lee Stevens	.15
75 Felipe Lopez	.15
76 Al Leiter	.15
77 Jim Edmonds	.15
78 Al Levine	.15
79 Raul Mondesi	.15
80 Jose Valentin	.15
81 Matt Clement	.15
82 Richard Hidalgo	.15
83 Jamie Moyer	.15
84 Brian Schneider	.15
85 John Franco	.15
86 Brian Buchanan	.15
87 Roy Oswalt	.25
88 Johnny Estrada	.15
89 Marcus Giles	.15
90 Carlos Valderrama	.15
91 Mark Mulder	.15
92 Mark Grace	.25
93 Andy Ashby	.15
94 Woody Williams	.15
95 Ben Petrick	.15
96 Roy Halladay	.30
97 Fred McGriff	.15
98 Shawn Green	.40
99 Todd Hundley	.15
100 Carlos Febles	.15
101 Jason Marquis	.15
102 Mike Redmond	.15
103 Shane Halter	.15
104 Trot Nixon	.15
105 Jeremy Giambi	.15
106 Carlos Delgado	.50
107 Richie Sexson	.15
108 Russ Ortiz	.15
109 David Ortiz	.25
110 Curtis Leskanic	.15
111 Jay Payton	.15
112 Travis Phelps	.15
113 J.T. Snow	.15
114 Edgar Renteria	.15
115 Freddy Garcia	.15
116 Cliff Floyd	.15
117 Charles Nagy	.15
118 Tony Batista	.15
119 Rafael Palmeiro	.65
120 Darren Dreifort	.15
121 Warren Morris	.15
122 Augie Ojeda	.15
123 Rusty Greer	.15
124 Esteban Yan	.15
125 Corey Patterson	.15
126 Matt Ginter	.15
127 Matt Lawton	.15
128 Miguel Batista	.15
129 Randy Winn	.15
130 Eric Milton	.15
131 Jack Wilson	.15
132 Sean Casey	.25
133 Mike Sweeney	.15
134 Jason Tyner	.15
135 Carlos Hernandez	.15
136 Shea Hillenbrand	.15
137 Shawn Wooten	.15
138 Peter Bergeron	.15
139 Travis Lee	.15
140 Craig Wilson	.15
141 Carlos Guillen	.15
142 Chipper Jones	1.00
143 Gabe Kapler	.15
144 Raul Ibanez	.15
145 Eric Chavez	.25
146 D'Angelo Jimenez	.15
147 Chad Hermansen	.15
148 Joe Kennedy	.15
149 Mariano Rivera	.15
150 Jeff Bagwell	.75
151 Joe McEwing	.15
152 Ronnie Belliard	.15
153 Desi Relaford	.15
154 Vinny Castilla	.15
155 Tim Hudson	.25
156 Wilton Guerrero	.15
157 Raul Casanova	.15
158 Edgardo Alfonzo	.15
159 Derrek Lee	.15
160 Phil Nevin	.15
161 Roger Clemens	1.25
162 Jason LaRue	.15
163 Brian Lawrence	.15
164 Adrian Beltre	.30
165 Troy Glaus	.75
166 Jeff Weaver	.15
167 B.J. Surhoff	.15
168 Eric Byrnes	.15
169 Mike Sirotka	.15
170 Bill Haselman	.15
171 Javier Vazquez	.15
172 Sidney Ponson	.15
173 Adam Everett	.15
174 Bubba Trammell	.15
175 Robb Nen	.15
176 Barry Larkin	.15
177 Tony Graffanino	.15
178 Rich Garces	.15
179 Juan Uribe	.15
180 Tom Glavine	.25
181 Eric Karros	.15
182 Michael Cuddyer	.15
183 Wade Miller	.15
184 Matt Williams	.15
185 Matt Morris	.15
186 Rickey Henderson	.75
187 Trevor Hoffman	.15
188 Wilson Betemit	.15
189 Steve Karsay	.15
190 Frank Catalanotto	.15
191 Jason Schmidt	.15
192 Roger Cedeno	.15
193 Magglio Ordonez	.15
194 Pat Hentgen	.15
195 Mike Lieberthal	.15
196 Andy Pettitte	.30
197 Jay Gibbons	.15
198 Rolando Arrojo	.15
199 Joe Mays	.15
200 Aubrey Huff	.15
201 Nelson Figueroa	.15
202 Paul Konerko	.25
203 Ken Griffey Jr.	1.50
204 Brandon Duckworth	.15
205 Sammy Sosa	1.50
206 Carl Everett	.15
207 Scott Rolen	.65
208 Orlando Hernandez	.15
209 Todd Helton	.75
210 Preston Wilson	.15
211 Gil Meche	.15
212 Bill Mueller	.15
213 Craig Biggio	.15
214 Dean Palmer	.15
215 Randy Wolf	.15
216 Jeff Suppan	.15
217 Jimmy Rollins	.25
218 Alexis Gomez	.15
219 Ellis Burks	.15
220 Ramon E. Martinez	.15
221 Ramiro Mendoza	.15
222 Einar Diaz	.15
223 Brent Abernathy	.15
224 Darin Erstad	.25
225 Reggie Taylor	.15
226 Jason Jennings	.15
227 Ray Durham	.15
228 John Parrish	.15
229 Kevin Young	.15
230 Xavier Nady	.15
231 Juan Cruz	.15
232 Greg Norton	.15
233 Barry Bonds	2.00
234 Kip Wells	.15
235 Paul LoDuca	.15
236 Javy Lopez	.25
237 Luis Castillo	.15
238 Tom Gordon	.15
239 Mike Mordecai	.15
240 Damian Rolls	.15
241 Julio Lugo	.15
242 Ichiro Suzuki	1.00
243 Tony Womack	.15
244 Matt Anderson	.15
245 Carlos Lee	.15
246 Alex Rodriguez	1.75
247 Bernie Williams	.30
248 Scott Sullivan	.15
249 Mike Hampton	.15
250 Orlando Cabrera	.15
251 Benito Santiago	.15
252 Steve Finley	.15
253 Dave Williams	.15
254 Adam Kennedy	.15
255 Omar Vizquel	.15
256 Garrett Stephenson	.15
257 Fernando Tatis	.15
258 Mike Piazza	1.50
259 Scott Spiezio	.15
260 Jacque Jones	.15
261 Russell Branyan	.15
262 Mark McLemore	.15
263 Mitch Meluskey	.15
264 Marlon Byrd	.15
265 Kyle Farnsworth	.15
266 Billy Sylvester	.15
267 C.C. Sabathia	.15
268 Mark Buehrle	.15
269 Geoff Blum	.15
270 Bret Prinz	.15
271 Placido Polanco	.15
272 John Olerud	.15
273 Pedro J. Martinez	.75
274 Doug Mientkiewicz	.15
275 Jason Bere	.15
276 Bud Smith	.15
277 Terrence Long	.15
278 Troy Percival	.15
279 Derek Jeter	2.00
280 Eric Owens	.15
281 Jay Bell	.15
282 Mike Cameron	.15
283 Joe Randa	.15
284 Brian Roberts	.15
285 Ryan Klesko	.15
286 Ryan Dempster	.15
287 Cristian Guzman	.15
288 Tim Salmon	.25
289 Mark Johnson	.15
290 Brian Giles	.15
291 Jon Lieber	.15
292 Fernando Vina	.15
293 Mike Mussina	.40
294 Juan Pierre	.15
295 Carlos Beltran	.40
296 Vladimir Guerrero	.75
297 Orlando Merced	.15
298 Jose Hernandez	.15
299 Mike Lamb	.15
300 David Eckstein	.15
301 Mark Loretta	.15
302 Greg Vaughn	.15
303 Jose Vidro	.15
304 Jose Ortiz	.15
305 Mark Grudzielanek	.15
306 Rob Bell	.15
307 Elmer Dessens	.15
308 Tomas Perez	.15
309 Jerry Hairston Jr.	.15
310 Mike Stanton	.15
311 Todd Walker	.15
312 Jason Varitek	.15
313 Masato Yoshii	.15
314 Ben Sheets	.15
315 Roberto Hernandez	.15
316 Eli Marrero	.15
317 Josh Beckett	.50
318 Robert Fick	.15
319 Aramis Ramirez	.15
320 Bartolo Colon	.15
321 Kenny Kelly	.15
322 Luis Gonzalez	.25
323 John Smoltz	.15
324 Homer Bush	.15
325 Kevin Millwood	.15
326 Manny Ramirez	.75
327 Armando Benitez	.15
328 Luis Alicea	.15
329 Mark Kotsay	.15
330 Felix Rodriguez	.15
331 Eddie Taubensee	.15
332 John Burkett	.15
333 Ramon Ortiz	.15
334 Daryle Ward	.15
335 Jarrod Washburn	.15
336 Benji Gil	.15
337 Mike Lowell	.15
338 Larry Walker	.15
339 Andruw Jones	.75
340 Scott Elarton	.15
341 Tony McKnight	.15
342 Frank Thomas	.50
343 Kevin Brown	.15
344 Jermaine Dye	.15
345 Luis Rivas	.15
346 Jeff Conine	.15
347 Bobby Kielty	.15
348 Jeffrey Hammonds	.15
349 Keith Foulke	.15
350 Dave Martinez	.15
351 Adam Eaton	.15
352 Brandon Inge	.15
353 Tyler Houston	.15
354 Bobby Abreu	.15
355 Ivan Rodriguez	.65
356 Doug Glanville	.15
357 Jorge Julio	.15
358 Kerry Wood	.50
359 Eric Munson	.15
360 Joe Crede	.15
361 Denny Neagle	.15
362 Vance Wilson	.15
363 Neifi Perez	.15
364 Darryl Kile	.15
365 Jose Macias	.15
366 Michael Coleman	.15
367 Erubiel Durazo	.15
368 Darrin Fletcher	.15
369 Matt White	.15
370 Marvin Benard	.15
371 Brad Penny	.15
372 Chuck Finley	.15
373 Delino DeShields	.15
374 Adrian Brown	.15
375 Corey Koskie	.15
376 Kazuhiro Sasaki	.15
377 Brent Butler	.15
378 Paul Wilson	.15
379 Scott Williamson	.15
380 Mike Young	.15
381 Toby Hall	.15
382 Shane Reynolds	.15
383 Tom Goodwin	.15
384 Seth Etherton	.15
385 Billy Wagner	.15
386 Josh Phelps	.15
387 Kyle Lohse	.15
388 Jeremy Fikac	.15
389 Jorge Posada	.30
390 Bret Boone	.15
391 Angel Berroa	.15
392 Matt Mantei	.15
393 Alex Gonzalez	.15
394 Scott Strickland	.15
395 Charles Johnson	.15
396 Ramon Hernandez	.15
397 Damian Jackson	.15
398 Albert Pujols	1.50
399 Gary Bennett	.15
400 Edgar Martinez	.15
401 Carl Pavano	.15
402 Chris Gomez	.15
403 Jaret Wright	.15
404 Lance Berkman	.15
405 Robert Person	.15
406 Brook Fordyce	.15
407 Adam Pettyjohn	.15
408 Chris Carpenter	.15
409 Rey Ordonez	.15
410 Eric Gagne	.25
411 Damion Easley	.15
412 A.J. Burnett	.15
413 Aaron Boone	.15
414 J.D. Drew	.25
415 Kelly Stinnett	.15
416 Mark Quinn	.15
417 Brad Radke	.15
418 Jose Cruz Jr.	.15
419 Greg Maddux	1.00
420 Steve Cox	.15
421 Torii Hunter	.15
422 Sandy Alomar	.15
423 Barry Zito	.40
424 Bill Hall	.15
425 Marquis Grissom	.15
426 Rich Aurilia	.15
427 Royce Clayton	.15
428 Travis Fryman	.15
429 Pablo Ozuna	.15
430 David Dellucci	.15
431 Vernon Wells	.15
432 Gregg Zaun	.15
433 Alex Gonzalez	.15
434 Hideo Nomo	.40
435 Jeromy Burnitz	.15
436 Gary Sheffield	.25
437 Tino Martinez	.15
438 Tsuyoshi Shinjo	.15
439 Chan Ho Park	.15
440 Tony Clark	.15
441 Brad Fullmer	.15
442 Jason Giambi	.50
443 Billy Koch	.15
444 Mo Vaughn	.15
445 Alex Ochoa	.15
446 Darren Lewis	.15
447 John Rocker	.15
448 Scott Hatteberg	.15
449 Brady Anderson	.15
450 Chuck Knoblauch	.15
451 Pokey Reese	.15
452 Brian Jordan	.15
453 Albie Lopez	.15
454 David Bell	.15
455 Juan Gonzalez	.75
456 Terry Adams	.15
457 Kenny Lofton	.15
458 Shawn Estes	.15
459 Josh Fogg	.15
460 Dmitri Young	.15
461 Johnny Damon	.25
462 Chris Singleton	.15
463 Ricky Ledee	.15
464 Dustin Hermanson	.15
465 Aaron Sele	.15
466 Chris Stynes	.15
467 Matt Stairs	.15
468 Kevin Appier	.15
469 Omar Daal	.15
470 Moises Alou	.15
471 Juan Encarnacion	.15
472 Robin Ventura	.15
473 Eric Hinske	.15
474 Rondell White	.15
475 Carlos Pena	.15
476 Craig Paquette	.15
477 Marty Cordova	.15
478 Brett Tomko	.15
479 Reggie Sanders	.15
480 Roberto Alomar	.15
481 Jeff Cirillo	.15
482 Todd Zeile	.15
483 John Vander Wal	.15
484 Rick Helling	.15
485 Jeff D'Amico	.15
486 David Justice	.15
487 Jason Isringhausen	.15
488 Shigetoshi Hasegawa	.15
489 Eric Young	.15
490 David Wells	.15
491 Boehm Sierra	.15
492 Aaron Cook RC	.50
493 Takahito Nomura RC	.50
494 Austin Kearns	.15
495 Kazuhisa Ishii RC	2.00
496 Mark Teixeira	.50
497 Rene Reyes RC	.50
498 Timo Shosveberger	.15
499 Ben Broussard	.15
500 Eric Cyr RC	.25
501 Anastacio Martinez RC	.50
502 Morgan Ensberg	.25
503 Steve Kent RC	.25
504 Franklin Nunez RC	.25
505 Adam Walker RC	.25

506	Anderson Machado RC	.50
507	Ryan Drese	.15
508	Luis Ugueto RC	.25
509	Jorge Nunez RC	.25
510	Colby Lewis	.15
511	Ron Calloway RC	.25
512	Hansel Izquierdo RC	.50
513	Jason Lane	.15
514	Rafael Soriano	.15
515	Jackson Melian	.15
516	Edwin Almonte RC	.15
517	Satoru Komiyama RC	.15
518	Corey Thurman RC	.15
519	Jorge De La Rosa RC	.50
520	Victor Martinez	.15
521	Dewan Brazleton	.15
522	Marlon Byrd	.50
523	Jae Weong Seo	.15
524	Orlando Hudson	.15
525	Sean Burroughs	.15
526	Ryan Langerhans	.15
527	David Kelton	.15
528	So Taguchi RC	.50
529	Tyler Walker	.15
530	Hank Blalock	.50
531	Mark Prior	.75
532	Yankee Stadium	.50
533	Fenway Park	.50
534	Wrigley Field	.15
535	Dodger Stadium	.15
536	Camden Yards	.15
537	PacBell Park	.15
538	Jacobs Field	.15
539	SAFECO Field	.15
540	Miller Field	.15

Mini
Mini (1-540): 8-15X
Production 50 Sets
Retail exclusive

Tiffany
Stars (1-540): 4-8X
Production 200 Sets

Barry Bonds Career Highlights

		NM/M
Complete Set (10):		40.00
Common Bonds 1-3:		3.00
Common 4-6 inserted		
1:125 H		4.00
7-9 1:250 H		6.00
#10 1:383		6.00
1CH	Barry Bonds	3.00
2CH	Barry Bonds	3.00
3CH	Barry Bonds	3.00
4CH	Barry Bonds	4.00
5CH	Barry Bonds	4.00
6CH	Barry Bonds	4.00
7CH	Barry Bonds	6.00
8CH	Barry Bonds	6.00
9CH	Barry Bonds	6.00
10CH	Barry Bonds	6.00

Barry Bonds Career Highlights Autographs
No Pricing
25 Sets Produced

Barry Bonds Chasing History

This special edition of 600 was sold exclusively via a home shopping tv program. The 3-1/2" x 2-1/2" card features on front a piece of game-used Bonds bat in the form of the two 0s in "600." At right are an authentic autograph and portrait and action photos. On back is a statement of authenticity and a serial number.

NM/M
Barry Bonds 125.00

Barry Bonds 4X MVP Super

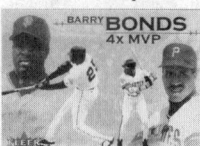

Bonds/ status as the only four-time MVP winner was marked with the issue of this home shopping channel exclusive. The 5-1/2" x 3-1/2" card is serially numbered on back from within an edition of 5,000.

NM/M
Barry Bonds 15.00

Barry Bonds 600 HR Supers

To commemorate his career 600th home run, Fleer produced a pair of jumbo-format (3-1/2" x 5") cards for sale on a TV home shopping show. One version of the card bears a facsimile autograph. A premium version, limited to 600 numbered cards, has a game-used bat chip and an authentic Bonds signature.

	NM/M
Barry Bonds (Facsimile signature.)	55.00
Barry Bonds (Autograph w/Bat chip.)	250.00

Classic Cuts Autographs

		NM/M
Inserted 1:432		
LA-A	Luis Aparicio	15.00
RC-A	Ron Cey	8.00
HK-A	Harmon Killebrew	35.00
JM-A	Juan Marichal	15.00
GP-A	Gaylord Perry/ SP/225	15.00
PR-A	Phil Rizzuto/SP/125	50.00
BR-A	Brooks Robinson/ SP/200	40.00

Classic Cuts Game-Used

		NM/M
Common Player:		5.00
Inserted 1:24		
SA-P	Sparky Anderson/ Pants	5.00
HB-B	Hank Bauer/Bat	5.00
JB-J	Johnny Bench/Jsy	15.00
PB-B	Paul Blair/Bat	5.00
WB-B	Wade Boggs/Bat/99	20.00
WB-J	Wade Boggs/Jsy	10.00
BB-B	Bobby Bonds/Bat	5.00
BB-J	Bobby Bonds/Jsy	5.00
GB-B	George Brett/Bat/250	30.00
GB-J	George Brett/ Jsy/250	30.00
SC-P	Steve Carlton/Pants	6.00
OC-P	Orlando Cepeda/ Pants	5.00
AD-J	Andre Dawson/Jsy	8.00
BD-B	Bill Dickey/Bat/200	15.00
LD-B	Larry Doby/Bat/250	10.00
DE-B	Dwight Evans/ Bat/250	10.00
DE-J	Dwight Evans/Jsy	5.00
RF-J	Rollie Fingers/Jsy	10.00
CF-B	Carlton Fisk/Bat	10.00
CF-J	Carlton Fisk/Jsy/150	20.00
NF-B	Nellie Fox/Bat/200	20.00
SG-B	Steve Garvey/Bat	5.00
KG-B	Kirk Gibson/Bat	5.00
GH-B	Gil Hodges/Bat/200	15.00
CH-J	Jim Hunter/Jsy	10.00
BJ-J	Bo Jackson/Jsy	15.00
RJ-P	Reggie Jackson/ Pants	10.00
GK-B	George Kell/Bat/150	15.00
TK-B	Ted Kluszewski/ Bat/200	15.00
TK-P	Ted Kluszewski/ Pants	10.00
RM-P	Roger Maris/ Pants/200	60.00
EM-B	Eddie Mathews/ Bat/200	20.00
DM-B	Don Mattingly/ Bat/200	50.00
DM-J	Don Mattingly/Jsy	40.00
WM-J	Willie McCovey/ Jsy/300	10.00
PM-B	Paul Molitor/Bat/250	25.00
JM-B	Joe Morgan/Bat/250	8.00
EM-B	Eddie Murray/Bat	10.00
EM-J	Eddie Murray/Jsy	10.00
JP-J	Jim Palmer/Jsy/273	8.00
DP-B	Dave Parker/Bat	5.00
TP-B	Tony Perez/Bat/250	10.00
TP-J	Tony Perez/Jsy	8.00
LP-P	Lou Piniella/Pants	5.00
KP-J	Kirby Puckett/Jsy	15.00
JR-B	Jim Rice/Bat/225	8.00
CR-BG	Cal Ripken Jr./ Btg Glv/100	75.00
CR-FG	Cal Ripken Jr./ Fld Glv/50	125.00
CR-J	Cal Ripken Jr./Jsy	35.00
CR-P	Cal Ripken Jr./ Pants/200	40.00
BR-B	Brooks Robinson/ Bat/250	15.00
NR-J	Nolan Ryan/Jsy	50.00
NR-P	Nolan Ryan/ Pants/200	60.00
RS-B	Ryne Sandberg/Bat	25.00
OS-J	Ozzie Smith/Jsy/250	15.00
WS-B	Willie Stargell/ Bat	15.00
JT-J	Joe Torre/Jsy/125	15.00
AT-B	Alan Trammell/Bat	5.00
EW-J	Earl Weaver/Jsy	5.00
HW-P	Hoyt Wilhelm/ Pants/150	15.00
TW-B	Ted Williams/Bat	85.00
TW-P	Ted Williams/Pants	120.00
DW-B	Dave Winfield/Bat	8.00
DW-J	Dave Winfield/ Jsy/231	10.00
DW-P	Dave Winfield/Pants	8.00
RY-B	Robin Yount/Bat	15.00

Classic Cuts Game-Used Autographs

		NM/M
Varying quantities produced		
LA-B	Luis Aparicio/Bat/45	25.00
BR-B	Brooks Robinson/ Bat/45	80.00

Diamond Standouts

		NM/M
Complete Set (10):		40.00
Common Player:		2.00
Production 1,200 Sets		
1DS	Mike Piazza	4.00
2DS	Derek Jeter	8.00
3DS	Ken Griffey Jr.	4.00
4DS	Barry Bonds	8.00
5DS	Sammy Sosa	4.00
6DS	Alex Rodriguez	4.00
7DS	Ichiro Suzuki	4.00
8DS	Greg Maddux	3.00
9DS	Jason Giambi	2.00
10DS	Nomar Garciaparra	4.00

Golden Memories

Eest meets West as Ichiro makes his Mariners' debut

		NM/M
Complete Set (15):		20.00
Common Player:		1.00
Inserted 1:24		
1GM	Frank Thomas	1.50
2GM	Derek Jeter	4.00
3GM	Albert Pujols	3.00
4GM	Barry Bonds	4.00
5GM	Alex Rodriguez	3.00
6GM	Randy Johnson	1.50
7GM	Jeff Bagwell	1.50
8GM	Greg Maddux	2.00
9GM	Ivan Rodriguez	1.00
10GM	Ichiro Suzuki	2.50
11GM	Mike Piazza	2.50
12GM	Pat Burrell	1.00
13GM	Rickey Henderson	1.50
14GM	Vladimir Guerrero	1.50
15GM	Sammy Sosa	2.50

Headliners

LUIS GONZALEZ • ARIZONA DIAMONDBACKS

		NM/M
Complete Set (20):		10.00
Common Player:		.25
Inserted 1:8		
1HL	Randy Johnson	.75
2HL	Alex Rodriguez	1.50
3HL	Todd Helton	.75
4HL	Pedro J. Martinez	1.00
5HL	Ichiro Suzuki	1.50
6HL	Vladimir Guerrero	.75
7HL	Derek Jeter	2.00
8HL	Adam Dunn	.40
9HL	Luis Gonzalez	.25
10HL	Kazuhiro Sasaki	.25
11HL	Sammy Sosa	1.25
12HL	Jason Giambi	.60
13HL	Ken Griffey Jr.	1.25
14HL	Roger Clemens	1.00
15HL	Brandon Duckworth	.25
16HL	Nomar Garciaparra	1.25
17HL	Bud Smith	.25
18HL	Juan Gonzalez	.75
19HL	Chipper Jones	1.00
20HL	Barry Bonds	2.00

Rookie Flashback

		NM/M
Complete Set (20):		6.00
Common Player:		.25
Inserted 1:3 Retail		
1RF	Bret Prinz	.25
2RF	Albert Pujols	2.00
3RF	C.C. Sabathia	.25
4RF	Ichiro Suzuki	1.50
5RF	Juan Cruz	.25
6RF	Jay Gibbons	.50
7RF	Bud Smith	.25
8RF	Johnny Estrada	.25
9RF	Roy Oswalt	.50
10RF	Tsuyoshi Shinjo	.25
11RF	Brandon Duckworth	.25
12RF	Jackson Melian	.25
13RF	Josh Beckett	1.00
14RF	Morgan Ensberg	.25
15RF	Brian Lawrence	.25
16RF	Eric Hinske	.25
17RF	Juan Uribe	.25
18RF	Matt White	.25
19RF	Junior Spivey	.25
20RF	Wilson Betemit	.25

Rookie Sensations

ICHIRO / Seattle Mariners

		NM/M
Complete Set (20):		40.00
Common Player:		2.00
Production 1,500 Sets		
1RS	Bret Prinz	2.00
2RS	Albert Pujols	10.00
3RS	C.C. Sabathia	2.00
4RS	Ichiro Suzuki	8.00
5RS	Juan Cruz	2.00
6RS	Jay Gibbons	3.00
7RS	Bud Smith	2.00
8RS	Johnny Estrada	2.00
9RS	Roy Oswalt	4.00
10RS	Tsuyoshi Shinjo	2.00
11RS	Brandon Duckworth	2.00
12RS	Jackson Melian	2.00
13RS	Josh Beckett	4.00
14RS	Morgan Ensberg	2.00
15RS	Brian Lawrence	2.00
16RS	Eric Hinske	2.00
17RS	Juan Uribe	2.00
18RS	Matt White	2.00
19RS	Junior Spivey	2.00
20RS	Wilson Betemit	2.00

Then and Now

		NM/M
Common Card:		5.00
Production 275 Sets		
1TN	Eddie Mathews, Chipper Jones	5.00
2TN	Willie McCovey, Barry Bonds	15.00
3TN	Johnny Bench, Mike Piazza	5.00
4TN	Ernie Banks, Alex Rodriguez	8.00
5TN	Rickey Henderson, Ichiro Suzuki	10.00
6TN	Tom Seaver, Roger Clemens	10.00
7TN	Juan Marichal, Pedro J. Martinez	5.00
8TN	Reggie Jackson, Derek Jeter	15.00
9TN	Nolan Ryan, Kerry Wood	20.00
10TN	Joe Morgan, Ken Griffey Jr.	10.00

2002 Fleer Authentix

MANNY RAMIREZ

		NM/M
Complete Set (170):		85.00
Common Player:		.25
Common SP (151-170):		3.00
Production 1,850		
Pack (5):		3.00
Box (24):		60.00
1	Derek Jeter	2.00
2	Tim Hudson	.35
3	Robert Fick	.25
4	Javy Lopez	.25
5	Alfonso Soriano	.50
6	Ken Griffey Jr.	1.25
7	Rafael Palmeiro	.65
8	Bernie Williams	.35
9	Adam Dunn	.50
10	Ivan Rodriguez	.65
11	Vladimir Guerrero	.75
12	Pedro J. Martinez	.75
13	Bret Boone	.25
14	Paul LoDuca	.25
15	Tony Batista	.25
16	Barry Bonds	2.00
17	Craig Biggio	.25
18	Garret Anderson	.25
19	Mark Mulder	.25
20	Frank Thomas	.75
21	Alex Rodriguez	1.50
22	Cristian Guzman	.25
23	Sammy Sosa	1.25
24	Ichiro Suzuki	1.25
25	Carlos Beltran	.50
26	Edgardo Alfonzo	.25
27	Josh Beckett	.50
28	Eric Chavez	.40
29	Roberto Alomar	.40
30	Raul Mondesi	.25
31	Mike Piazza	1.25
32	Barry Larkin	.25
33	Ruben Sierra	.25
34	Tsuyoshi Shinjo	.25
35	Magglio Ordonez	.25
36	Ben Grieve	.25
37	Richie Sexson	.25
38	Manny Ramirez	.75
39	Jeff Kent	.25
40	Shawn Green	.40
41	Andruw Jones	.75
42	Aramis Ramirez	.25
43	Cliff Floyd	.25
44	Juan Pierre	.25
45	Jose Vidro	.25
46	Paul Konerko	.25
47	Greg Vaughn	.25
48	Geoff Jenkins	.25
49	Greg Maddux	1.00
50	Ryan Klesko	.25
51	Corey Koskie	.25
52	Nomar Garciaparra	1.25
53	Edgar Martinez	.25
54	Gary Sheffield	.40
55	Randy Johnson	.75
56	Bobby Abreu	.25
57	Mike Sweeney	.25
58	Chipper Jones	1.00
59	Brian Giles	.25
60	Charles Johnson	.25
61	Ben Sheets	.25
62	Jason Giambi	.60
63	Todd Helton	.75
64	David Eckstein	.25
65	Troy Glaus	.75
66	Sean Casey	.35
67	Gabe Kapler	.25
68	Doug Mientkiewicz	.25
69	Curt Schilling	.40
70	Pat Burrell	.40
71	Albert Pujols	1.25
72	Jermaine Dye	.25
73	Miguel Tejada	.40
74	Jim Thome	.40
75	Carlos Delgado	.40
76	Fred McGriff	.25
77	Mike Cameron	.25
78	Jeromy Burnitz	.25
79	Jay Gibbons	.25
80	Rich Aurilia	.25
81	Lance Berkman	.25
82	Brian Jordan	.25
83	Phil Nevin	.25
84	Moises Alou	.25
85	Reggie Sanders	.25
86	Scott Rolen	.65
87	Larry Walker	.25
88	Matt Williams	.25
89	Roger Clemens	1.00
90	Juan Gonzalez	.75
91	Jose Cruz Jr.	.25
92	Tino Martinez	.25
93	Kerry Wood	.65
94	Freddy Garcia	.25
95	Jeff Bagwell	.75
96	Luis Gonzalez	.35
97	Jimmy Rollins	.50
98	Bobby Higginson	.25
99	Rondell White	.25
100	Jorge Posada	.35
101	Trot Nixon	.25
102	Jason Kendall	.25
103	Preston Wilson	.25
104	Corey Patterson	.25
105	Jose Valentin	.25
106	Carlos Lee	.25
107	Chris Richard	.25
108	Todd Walker	.25
109	Ellis Burks	.25
110	Brady Anderson	.25
111	Kazuhiro Sasaki	.25
112	Roy Oswalt	.35
113	Kevin Brown	.25
114	Jeff Weaver	.25
115	Todd Hollandsworth	.25
116	Joe Crede	.25
117	Tom Glavine	.40
118	Mike Lieberthal	.25
119	Tim Salmon	.35
120	Johnny Damon	.40
121	Brad Fullmer	.25
122	Mo Vaughn	.25
123	Torii Hunter	.25
124	Jamie Moyer	.25
125	Terrence Long	.25
126	Travis Lee	.25
127	Jacque Jones	.25
128	Lee Stevens	.25
129	Russ Ortiz	.25
130	Jeremy Giambi	.25
131	Mike Mussina	.45
132	Orlando Cabrera	.25
133	Barry Zito	.40
134	Robert Person	.25
135	Andy Pettitte	.40
136	Drew Henson	.40
137	Mark Teixeira	.50
138	David Espinosa	.25
139	Orlando Hudson	.25
140	Colby Lewis	.25
141	Bill Hall	.25
142	Michael Restovich	.25
143	Angel Berroa	.40
144	Dewon Brazleton	.25
145	Joe Thurston	.25
146	Mark Prior	.50
147	Dane Sardinha	.25
148	Marlon Byrd	.25
149	Jeff Deardorff RC	.25
150	Austin Kearns	.40
151	Anderson Machado RC	5.00
152	Kazuhisa Ishii	8.00
153	Eric Junge RC	3.00
154	Mark Corey RC	3.00
155	So Taguchi RC	5.00
156	Jorge Padilla RC	5.00
157	Steve Kent RC	3.00
158	Jaime Cerda RC	3.00
159	Hansel Izquierdo RC	3.00
160	Rene Reyes RC	3.00
161	Jorge Nunez RC	3.00
162	Corey Thurman RC	4.00
163	Jorge Sosa RC	3.00
164	Franklin Nunez RC	3.00
165	Adam Walker RC	3.00
166	Ryan Baerlocher RC	3.00
167	Ron Calloway RC	3.00
168	Miguel Asencio RC	3.00
169	Luis Ugueto RC	3.00
170	Felix Escalona RC	3.00

Front Row
Front Row: 4-8X

(Front Row, continued)

Front Row SP: 1-2X
Production 150 Sets

Second Row
Second Row: 3-5X
Second Row SP: .75-1.5X
Production 250 Sets

Autographed AuthenTIX
NM/M
Common Autograph: 10.00
Inserted 1:780
Unripped no pricing.
Numbered to 25
- Derek Jeter 200.00
- Mark Teixeira/25 35.00
- Brooks Robinson/145 40.00
- Ben Sheets/25 30.00
- Mark Prior 40.00
- Kazuhisa Ishii 25.00
- So Taguchi 15.00
- Dane Sardinha 10.00
- David Espinosa 10.00

Autographed Jersey AuthenTIX
NM/M
Inserted 1:1,387
- Derek Jeter 200.00
- Jeff Bagwell 80.00

Ballpark Classics

NM/M
Complete Set (15): 50.00
Common Player: 1.50
Inserted 1:22
- 1BC Reggie Jackson 3.00
- 2BC Don Mattingly 6.00
- 3BC Duke Snider 2.00
- 4BC Carlton Fisk 2.00
- 5BC Cal Ripken Jr. 6.00
- 6BC Willie McCovey 1.50
- 7BC Robin Yount 3.00
- 8BC Paul Molitor 3.00
- 9BC George Brett 6.00
- 10BC Ryne Sandberg 3.00
- 11BC Nolan Ryan 8.00
- 12BC Thurman Munson 3.00
- 13BC Joe Morgan 1.50
- 14BC Jim Rice 1.50
- 15BC Babe Ruth 8.00

Ballpark Classics Memorabilia

NM/M
Common Player: 5.00
Inserted 1:83
Golds: 2X
Production 100
- RJ Reggie Jackson 15.00
- DM Don Mattingly 30.00
- DS Duke Snider 15.00
- CF Carlton Fisk 10.00
- CR Cal Ripken Jr. 40.00
- WC Willie McCovey 15.00
- RY Robin Yount 25.00
- PM Paul Molitor 15.00
- GB George Brett 30.00
- RS Ryne Sandberg/SP 75.00
- NR Nolan Ryan 30.00
- TM Thurman Munson/Cap/SP 50.00
- JM Joe Morgan 5.00
- JR Jim Rice 5.00
- BR Babe Ruth/Seat 150.00

Bat AuthenTIX
NM/M
Common Player: 5.00
Inserted 1:68
Unripped: 2-3X
Production 50
- Pat Burrell 8.00
- Ray Durham/SP/52 5.00

ABBREVIATIONS
SP - Short Print

(Autographed AuthenTIX, continued)

- Juan Gonzalez 8.00
- Drew Henson 5.00
- Orlando Hernandez 5.00
- Hideo Nomo/SP/41 30.00
- Jimmy Rollins 5.00
- Manny Ramirez 8.00
- Bernie Williams/SP/44 10.00
- Derek Jeter/197 40.00
- Andruw Jones 8.00
- Chipper Jones/SP/37 20.00
- Barry Bonds 20.00
- Nomar Garciaparra 25.00

Jersey AuthenTIX
NM/M
Common Player: 5.00
Inserted 1:12
Unripped: 2-3X
Production 50
- Barry Bonds 20.00
- Chipper Jones 8.00
- Scott Rolen/SP 12.00
- Greg Maddux 10.00
- Curt Schilling/SP 10.00
- Mike Piazza 10.00
- Nomar Garciaparra/SP 15.00
- Derek Jeter 20.00
- Luis Gonzalez/SP 8.00
- Jeff Bagwell 8.00
- Frank Thomas 8.00
- Manny Ramirez/SP 10.00
- Shawn Green 5.00
- Todd Helton 8.00
- Jim Edmonds/SP 5.00
- Paul LoDuca 5.00
- Alex Rodriguez 10.00
- Roberto Alomar 6.00
- Andruw Jones/SP 10.00
- Barry Zito 8.00
- J.D. Drew 5.00
- Magglio Ordonez 5.00
- Eric Chavez 5.00
- Darin Erstad/SP 8.00
- Freddy Garcia 5.00
- Jim Thome/SP 12.00
- Pedro J. Martinez 10.00
- Ivan Rodriguez 8.00
- Bernie Williams/SP 10.00
- Randy Johnson 8.00

Derek Jeter 1996 Autographics
NM/M
Production 100
- Derek Jeter 150.00

Power Alley
NM/M
Complete Set (15): 20.00
Common Player: .50
Inserted 1:11
- 1PA Sammy Sosa 2.00
- 2PA Ken Griffey Jr. .50
- 3PA Luis Gonzalez .50
- 4PA Alex Rodriguez 3.00
- 5PA Shawn Green .75
- 6PA Barry Bonds 4.00
- 7PA Todd Helton 1.00
- 8PA Jim Thome .50
- 9PA Troy Glaus .75
- 10PA Manny Ramirez 1.00
- 11PA Jeff Bagwell 1.00
- 12PA Jason Giambi .75
- 13PA Chipper Jones 1.50
- 14PA Mike Piazza 2.00
- 15PA Albert Pujols 3.00

2002 Fleer Box Score
NM/M
Complete Set (310):
Common Player: .25
Common (126-150): 3.00
Production 2,499
Complete Rising Star Set (40): 30.00
Common (151-190): 1.00
Complete Intl. Set (40): 18.00
Common (191-230): 1.00
Complete All-Star Set (40): 20.00

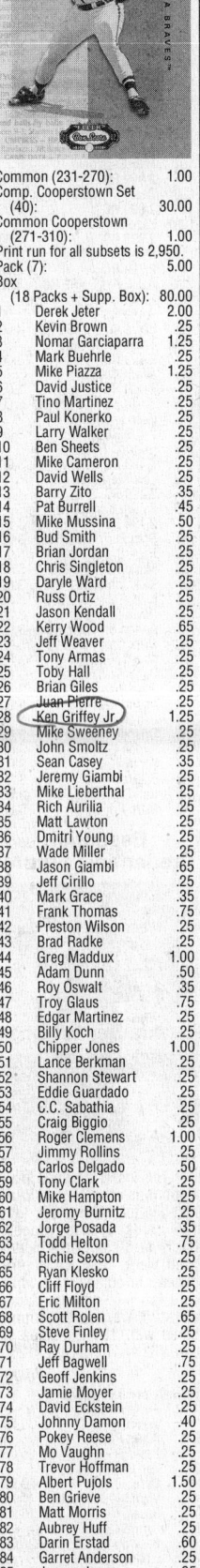

Common (231-270): 1.00
Comp. Cooperstown Set (40): 30.00
Common Cooperstown (271-310): 1.00
Print run for all subsets is 2,950.
Pack (7): 5.00
Box (18 Packs + Supp. Box): 80.00

- 1 Derek Jeter 2.00
- 2 Kevin Brown .25
- 3 Nomar Garciaparra 1.25
- 4 Mark Buehrle .25
- 5 Mike Piazza 1.25
- 6 David Justice .25
- 7 Tino Martinez .25
- 8 Paul Konerko .25
- 9 Larry Walker .25
- 10 Ben Sheets .25
- 11 Mike Cameron .25
- 12 David Wells .25
- 13 Barry Zito .35
- 14 Pat Burrell .45
- 15 Mike Mussina .50
- 16 Bud Smith .25
- 17 Brian Jordan .25
- 18 Chris Singleton .25
- 19 Daryle Ward .25
- 20 Russ Ortiz .25
- 21 Jason Kendall .25
- 22 Kerry Wood .65
- 23 Jeff Weaver .25
- 24 Tony Armas .25
- 25 Toby Hall .25
- 26 Brian Giles .25
- 27 Juan Pierre .25
- 28 Ken Griffey Jr 1.25
- 29 Mike Sweeney .25
- 30 John Smoltz .35
- 31 Sean Casey .25
- 32 Jeremy Giambi .25
- 33 Mike Lieberthal .25
- 34 Rich Aurilia .25
- 35 Matt Lawton .25
- 36 Dmitri Young .25
- 37 Wade Miller .25
- 38 Jason Giambi .65
- 39 Jeff Cirillo .25
- 40 Mark Grace .35
- 41 Frank Thomas .75
- 42 Preston Wilson .25
- 43 Brad Radke .25
- 44 Greg Maddux 1.00
- 45 Adam Dunn .50
- 46 Roy Oswalt .35
- 47 Troy Glaus .75
- 48 Edgar Martinez .25
- 49 Billy Koch .25
- 50 Chipper Jones 1.00
- 51 Lance Berkman .25
- 52 Shannon Stewart .25
- 53 Eddie Guardado .25
- 54 C.C. Sabathia .25
- 55 Craig Biggio .25
- 56 Roger Clemens 1.00
- 57 Jimmy Rollins .25
- 58 Carlos Delgado .50
- 59 Tony Clark .25
- 60 Mike Hampton .25
- 61 Jeromy Burnitz .25
- 62 Jorge Posada .35
- 63 Todd Helton .25
- 64 Richie Sexson .25
- 65 Ryan Klesko .25
- 66 Cliff Floyd .25
- 67 Eric Milton .25
- 68 Scott Rolen .65
- 69 Steve Finley .25
- 70 Ray Durham .25
- 71 Jeff Bagwell .75
- 72 Geoff Jenkins .25
- 73 Jamie Moyer .25
- 74 David Eckstein .25
- 75 Johnny Damon .40
- 76 Pokey Reese .25
- 77 Mo Vaughn .25
- 78 Trevor Hoffman .25
- 79 Albert Pujols 1.50
- 80 Ben Grieve .25
- 81 Matt Morris .25
- 82 Aubrey Huff .25
- 83 Darin Erstad .60
- 84 Garret Anderson .25
- 85 Jacque Jones .25
- 86 Matt Anderson .25
- 87 Jose Vidro .25
- 88 Carlos Lee .25
- 89 Jeff Suppan .25

- 90 Al Leiter .25
- 91 Jeff Kent .25
- 92 Randy Johnson .75
- 93 Moises Alou .25
- 94 Bobby Higginson .25
- 95 Phil Nevin .25
- 96 Alex Rodriguez 1.50
- 97 Luis Gonzalez .40
- 98 A.J. Burnett .25
- 99 Torii Hunter .25
- 100 Ivan Rodriguez .60
- 101 Pedro J. Martinez .75
- 102 Brady Anderson .25
- 103 Paul LoDuca .25
- 104 Eric Chavez .35
- 105 Tim Salmon .35
- 106 Javier Vazquez .25
- 107 Bret Boone .25
- 108 Greg Vaughn .25
- 109 J.D. Drew .40
- 110 Jay Gibbons .25
- 111 Jim Thome .75
- 112 Shawn Green .40
- 113 Tim Hudson .35
- 114 John Olerud .25
- 115 Raul Mondesi .25
- 116 Curt Schilling .50
- 117 Corey Patterson .25
- 118 Robert Fick .25
- 119 Corey Koskie .25
- 120 Juan Gonzalez .75
- 121 Jerry Hairston Jr. .25
- 122 Gary Sheffield .40
- 123 Mark Mulder .25
- 124 Barry Bonds 2.00
- 125 Jim Edmonds .25
- 126 Franklyn German RC 3.00
- 127 Rodrigo Rosario RC 3.00
- 128 Ryan Ludwick RC 3.00
- 129 Jorge de la Rosa RC 4.00
- 130 Jason Lane 3.00
- 131 Brian Mallette RC 3.00
- 132 Chris Baker RC 3.00
- 133 Kyle Kane RC 3.00
- 134 Doug DeVore RC 3.00
- 135 Raul Chavez RC 3.00
- 136 Miguel Asencio RC 3.00
- 137 Luis Garcia RC 3.00
- 138 Nick Johnson 3.00
- 139 Michael Crudale RC 3.00
- 140 P.J. Bevis RC 3.00
- 141 Josh Hancock RC 3.00
- 142 Jeremy Lambert RC 3.00
- 143 Ben Broussard 3.00
- 144 John Ennis RC 3.00
- 145 Wilson Valdez RC 3.00
- 146 Eric Good RC 3.00
- 147 Elio Serrano RC 3.00
- 148 Jaime Cerda RC 3.00
- 149 Hank Blalock 5.00
- 150 Brandon Duckworth 3.00
- 151 Drew Henson 1.50
- 152 Kazuhisa Ishii RC 3.00
- 153 Earl Snyder RC 1.00
- 154 J.M. Gold 1.00
- 155 Satoru Komiyama RC 1.00
- 156 Marlon Byrd 1.00
- 157 So Taguchi RC 2.00
- 158 Eric Hinske 1.00
- 159 Mark Prior 3.00
- 160 Jorge Padilla RC 1.50
- 161 Rene Reyes RC 1.00
- 162 Jorge Nunez RC 1.00
- 163 Nelson Castro RC 1.00
- 164 Anderson Machado RC 2.00
- 165 Mark Teixeira 2.00
- 166 Orlando Hudson RC 1.00
- 167 Edwin Almonte RC 1.00
- 168 Luis Ugueto RC 1.00
- 169 Felix Escalona RC 1.00
- 170 Ron Calloway RC 1.00
- 171 Kevin Mench 1.00
- 172 Takahito Nomura RC 1.00
- 173 Sean Burroughs 1.00
- 174 Steve Kent RC 1.00
- 175 Jorge Sosa RC 1.00
- 176 Mike Moriarty RC 1.00
- 177 Carlos Pena 1.00
- 178 Anastacio Martinez RC 1.00
- 179 Reed Johnson RC 1.00
- 180 Juan Brito RC 1.00
- 181 Wilson Betemit 1.00
- 182 Mike Rivera 1.00
- 183 David Espinosa 1.00
- 184 Todd Donovan RC 1.00
- 185 Morgan Ensberg 1.00
- 186 Dewon Brazelton 1.00
- 187 Ben Howard RC 1.00
- 188 Austin Kearns 2.00
- 189 Josh Beckett 2.00
- 190 Brandon Backe RC 1.50
- 191 Ichiro Suzuki 4.00
- 192 Tsuyoshi Shinjo 1.00
- 193 Hideo Nomo 2.00
- 194 Kazuhiro Sasaki 1.00
- 195 Edgardo Alfonzo 1.00
- 196 Chan Ho Park 1.00
- 197 Carlos Hernandez 1.00
- 198 Byung Kim 1.00
- 199 Omar Vizquel 1.00
- 200 Freddy Garcia 1.00
- 201 Richard Hidalgo 1.00
- 202 Magglio Ordonez 1.00
- 203 Bobby Abreu 1.00
- 204 Roger Cedeno 1.00
- 205 Andruw Jones 1.00
- 206 Mariano Rivera 1.50
- 207 Jose Macias 1.00

- 208 Orlando Hernandez 1.00
- 209 Rafael Palmeiro 2.00
- 210 Danys Baez 1.00
- 211 Bernie Williams 1.25
- 212 Carlos Beltran 3.00
- 213 Roberto Alomar 1.50
- 214 Jose Cruz Jr. 1.00
- 215 Ryan Dempster 1.00
- 216 Erubiel Durazo 1.00
- 217 Carlos Pena 1.00
- 218 Sammy Sosa 4.00
- 219 Adrian Beltre 1.50
- 220 Aramis Ramirez 1.00
- 221 Alfonso Soriano 2.00
- 222 Vladimir Guerrero 2.00
- 223 Juan Uribe 1.00
- 224 Cristian Guzman 1.00
- 225 Manny Ramirez 2.00
- 226 Juan Cruz 1.00
- 227 Ramon Ortiz 1.00
- 228 Juan Encarnacion 1.00
- 229 Bartolo Colon 1.00
- 230 Miguel Tejada 1.25
- 231 Cal Ripken Jr. 6.00
- 232 Derek Jeter 6.00
- 233 Pedro J. Martinez 2.00
- 234 Roberto Alomar 1.50
- 235 Sandy Alomar 1.00
- 236 Mike Piazza 4.00
- 237 Jeff Conine 1.00
- 238 Fred McGriff 1.00
- 239 Kirby Puckett 3.00
- 240 Ken Griffey Jr. 4.00
- 241 Roger Clemens 3.50
- 242 Joe Morgan 1.00
- 243 Willie McCovey 1.00
- 244 Brooks Robinson 1.00
- 245 Juan Marichal 1.00
- 246 Todd Helton 2.00
- 247 Alex Rodriguez 5.00
- 248 Barry Bonds 6.00
- 249 Nomar Garciaparra 4.00
- 250 Jeff Bagwell 2.00
- 251 Kenny Lofton 1.00
- 252 Barry Larkin 1.00
- 253 Tom Glavine 1.50
- 254 Magglio Ordonez 1.00
- 255 Randy Johnson 2.00
- 256 Chipper Jones 3.00
- 257 Kevin Brown 1.00
- 258 Rickey Henderson 2.00
- 259 Greg Maddux 3.00
- 260 Jim Thome 1.00
- 261 Rafael Palmeiro 1.50
- 262 Frank Thomas 2.00
- 263 Manny Ramirez 2.00
- 264 Travis Fryman 1.00
- 265 Gary Sheffield 1.25
- 266 Bernie Williams 1.25
- 267 Matt Williams 1.00
- 268 Ivan Rodriguez 1.50
- 269 Mike Mussina 1.25
- 270 Larry Walker 1.00
- 271 Jim Palmer 1.00
- 272 Cal Ripken Jr. 6.00
- 273 Brooks Robinson 1.00
- 274 Bobby Doerr 1.00
- 275 Ernie Banks 2.00
- 276 Fergie Jenkins 1.00
- 277 Luis Aparicio 1.00
- 278 Hoyt Wilhelm 1.00
- 279 Tom Seaver 1.50
- 280 Joe Morgan 1.00
- 281 Lou Boudreau 1.00
- 282 Larry Doby 1.00
- 283 Jim Bunning 1.00
- 284 George Kell 1.00
- 285 Pee Wee Reese 1.50
- 286 Eddie Mathews 1.00
- 287 Robin Yount 2.00
- 288 Rod Carew 1.00
- 289 Monte Irvin 1.00
- 290 Yogi Berra 2.00
- 291 Whitey Ford 1.00
- 292 Reggie Jackson 2.00
- 293 Rollie Fingers 1.00
- 294 Jim "Catfish" Hunter 1.00
- 295 Richie Ashburn 1.00
- 296 Willie Stargell 1.00
- 297 Ralph Kiner 1.00
- 298 Orlando Cepeda 1.00
- 299 Juan Marichal 1.00
- 300 Gaylord Perry 1.00
- 301 Willie McCovey 1.00
- 302 Red Schoendienst 1.00
- 303 Nolan Ryan 8.00
- 304 Bob Gibson 1.00
- 305 Al Kaline 1.00
- 306 Harmon Killebrew 1.00
- 307 Stan Musial 3.00
- 308 Phil Rizzuto 1.00
- 309 Mike Schmidt 4.00
- 310 Enos Slaughter 1.00

Classic Miniatures
NM/M
Complete Set (40): 25.00
Stars: 1.5-3X base card
Production 2,950 Sets
One set per classic mini box.
First Editions: 4-8X
Production 100 Sets

Classic Miniatures Game-Used
NM/M
Common Player: 6.00

One per Classic Mini box.
- Derek Jeter/Bat 20.00
- Mike Piazza/Jsy 10.00
- Adam Dunn/Jsy 6.00
- Chipper Jones/Bat 10.00
- Roger Clemens/Jsy 15.00
- Alex Rodriguez/Jsy 10.00
- Pedro Martinez/Jsy 10.00
- Jim Thome/Bat 10.00
- Curt Schilling/Jsy 8.00
- Barry Bonds/Bat 20.00

First Edition
Cards (1-125): 4-8X
Cards (126-150): .5-1X
Cards (151-310): 1-2X
Production 100 Sets

All-Star Lineup
NM/M
Common Card: 15.00
1:All-Stars Box
- Derek Jeter, Nomar Garciaparra, Alex Rodriguez 50.00
- Joe Morgan, Willie McCovey, Brooks Robinson 15.00
- Alex Rodriguez, Ivan Rodriguez, Rafael Palmeiro 20.00
- Derek Jeter, Mike Mussina, Bernie Williams 35.00
- Barry Bonds, Cal Ripken Jr., Frank Thomas 60.00
- Cal Ripken Jr., Derek Jeter, Roberto Alomar, Pedro J. Martinez 60.00
- Mike Piazza, Barry Bonds, Ken Griffey Jr., Jeff Bagwell 40.00
- Roger Clemens, Greg Maddux, Randy Johnson, Pedro J. Martinez 35.00
- Todd Helton, Roberto Alomar, Alex Rodriguez, Chipper Jones 25.00
- Ken Griffey Jr., Barry Bonds, Larry Walker, Manny Ramirez 35.00

Amazing Greats
NM/M
Complete Set (20): 20.00
Common Player: .50
Inserted 1:5
- 1AG Derek Jeter 4.00
- 2AG Barry Bonds 4.00
- 3AG Mike Piazza 2.50
- 4AG Ivan Rodriguez .75
- 5AG Todd Helton 1.00
- 6AG Nomar Garciaparra 2.50
- 7AG Jim Thome .50
- 8AG Bernie Williams .50
- 9AG Kazuhisa Sasaki .50
- 10AG Torii Hunter .50
- 11AG Bret Boone .50
- 12AG Tim Hudson .50
- 13AG Randy Johnson 1.00
- 14AG Rafael Palmeiro .75
- 15AG Scott Rolen .75
- 16AG Carlos Delgado .75
- 17AG Chipper Jones 2.00
- 18AG Lance Berkman .50
- 19AG Frank Thomas 2.00
- 20AG Greg Maddux 2.00

Amazing Greats Single Swatch
NM/M
Common Player: 5.00
Inserted 1:13
Dual Swatches: 1-2X
Inserted 1:90
- Derek Jeter 20.00
- Barry Bonds 20.00
- Mike Piazza 10.00
- Ivan Rodriguez 8.00
- Nomar Garciaparra 15.00
- Jim Thome/Bat 10.00
- Bernie Williams 8.00
- Kazuhiro Sasaki 5.00
- Torii Hunter 6.00
- Bret Boone 5.00
- Rafael Palmeiro 8.00
- Scott Rolen 8.00
- Carlos Delgado 8.00
- Lance Berkman 5.00
- Frank Thomas 8.00
- Greg Maddux 10.00

Amazing Greats Patch

NM/M
Common Player: 15.00
Production 150 Sets
Derek Jeter 50.00
Barry Bonds 50.00
Mike Piazza 25.00
Ivan Rodriguez 25.00
Nomar Garciaparra 40.00
Bernie Williams 25.00
Kazuhiro Sasaki 15.00
Torii Hunter 25.00
Bret Boone 15.00
Rafael Palmeiro 25.00
Scott Rolen 25.00
Carlos Delgado 20.00
Lance Berkman 15.00
Frank Thomas 25.00
Greg Maddux 30.00

Bat Rack

NM/M
Common Card: 20.00
Production 300 Sets
1BR Derek Jeter, Alfonso Soriano, Bernie Williams 60.00
2BR Mike Piazza, Roberto Alomar, Mo Vaughn 30.00
3BR Jeff Bagwell, Lance Berkman, Craig Biggio 30.00
4BR Eric Chavez, Miguel Tejada, Carlos Pena 15.00
5BR Alex Rodriguez, Ivan Rodriguez, Rafael Palmeiro 30.00
6BR Chipper Jones, Gary Sheffield, Andruw Jones 20.00
7BR Carlos Delgado, Jim Thome, Frank Thomas 20.00
8BR Derek Jeter, Nomar Garciaparra, Alex Rodriguez 60.00
9BR Barry Bonds, Adam Dunn, Chipper Jones 35.00
10BR Magglio Ordonez, Juan Gonzalez, Manny Ramirez 20.00

Bat Rack Quad

NM/M
Common Card 25.00
Production 150 Sets
Torii Hunter, Cristian Guzman, Frank Thomas, Magglio Ordonez 25.00
Alex Rodriguez, Ivan Rodriguez, Eric Chavez, Miguel Tejada 40.00
Mike Piazza, Roberto Alomar, Alfonso Soriano, Derek Jeter 80.00
Barry Bonds, Lance Berkman, Alex Rodriguez, Nomar Garciaparra 75.00
Barry Bonds, Chipper Jones, Mike Piazza, Ivan Rodriguez 75.00
Derek Jeter, Miguel Tejada, Nomar Garciaparra, Alex Rodriguez 75.00
Roberto Alomar, Mo Vaughn, Jeff Bagwell, Craig Biggio 25.00
Jim Palmer, Carlos Delgado, Jim Thome, Frank Thomas 25.00
Magglio Ordonez, Bernie Williams, Juan Gonzalez, Manny Ramirez 25.00
Chipper Jones, Adam Dunn, Jeff Bagwell, Mo Vaughn 25.00
Alex Rodriguez, Jim Palmer, Bernie Williams, Alfonso Soriano 40.00
Carlos Pena, Eric Chavez, Carlos Delgado, Juan Gonzalez 20.00
Adam Dunn, Lance Berkman, Jim Thome, Manny Ramirez 25.00

Box Score Debuts

NM/M
Complete Set (15): 40.00
Common Player: 2.50
Production 2,002 Sets
1 Hank Blalock 6.00
2 Eric Hinske 3.00
3 Kazuhisa Ishii 5.00
4 Sean Burroughs 3.00
5 Andres Torres 2.50
6 Satoru Komiyama 2.50
7 Mark Prior 10.00
8 Kevin Mench 2.50
9 Austin Kearns 3.00
10 Earl Snyder 2.50
11 Jon Rauch 2.50
12 Jason Lane 2.50
13 Ben Howard 2.50
14 Bobby Hill 2.50
15 Dennis Tankersley 2.50

Hall of Fame Material

NM/M
Common Player: 8.00
1:Cooperstown Box
Jim Palmer/Jsy 8.00
Cal Ripken Jr./Jsy 25.00
Brooks Robinson/Bat 10.00
Joe Morgan/Bat 8.00
Eddie Mathews/Bat 10.00
Robin Yount/Jsy 15.00
Reggie Jackson/Jsy 8.00
"Catfish" Hunter/Jsy 8.00
Willie McCovey/Jsy 8.00
Nolan Ryan/Jsy 30.00

Press Clippings

NM/M
Complete Set (20): 90.00
Common Player: 4.00
Inserted 1:90
1PC Mark Mulder 4.00
2PC Curt Schilling 6.00
3PC Alfonso Soriano 7.50
4PC Jeff Bagwell 7.50
5PC J.D. Drew 5.00
6PC Pedro J. Martinez 7.50
7PC Bobby Abreu 4.00
8PC Alex Rodriguez 12.00
9PC Mike Sweeney 4.00
10PC Carlos Pena 4.00
11PC Josh Beckett 6.00
12PC Roger Clemens 9.00
13PC Manny Ramirez 7.50
14PC Adam Dunn 6.00
15PC Kazuhisa Ishii 7.50
16PC Ken Griffey Jr. 10.00
17PC Sammy Sosa 9.00
18PC Ichiro Suzuki 9.00
19PC Albert Pujols 10.00
20PC Troy Glaus 7.50

Press Clippings Game-Used

NM/M
Common Player: 5.00
Inserted 1:13
Mark Mulder/Jsy 5.00
Curt Schilling/Jsy 5.00
Alfonso Soriano/Bat 10.00
Jeff Bagwell/Jsy 8.00
J.D. Drew/Jsy 5.00
Pedro Martinez/Jsy 10.00
Bobby Abreu/Jsy 5.00
Alex Rodriguez/Jsy 10.00
Mike Sweeney/Jsy 5.00
Carlos Pena/Jsy 5.00
Josh Beckett/Jsy 5.00
Manny Ramirez/Jsy 10.00
Adam Dunn/Jsy 6.00
Kazuhisa Ishii/Jsy 8.00
Ken Griffey Jr./Base 10.00
Sammy Sosa/Base 15.00
Ichiro Suzuki/Base 15.00
Albert Pujols/Base 10.00
Troy Glaus/Base 5.00

Wave of the Future

NM/M
Common Player: 4.00
1: Rising Stars Box
1WF Drew Henson/Bat 5.00
2WF Kazuhisa Ishii/Bat 4.00
3WF Marlon Byrd/Jsy 4.00
4WF So Taguchi/Bat 4.00
5WF Jorge Padilla/Pants/75 10.00
6WF Rene Reyes/Jsy 4.00
7WF Mark Teixeira/100 10.00
8WF Carlos Pena/Bat 4.00
9WF Austin Kearns/Pants 6.00
10WF Josh Beckett/Jsy/50 15.00

World Piece

NM/M
Common Player: 4.00
1:International Box
1WP Ichiro Suzuki/Base 20.00
2WP Tsuyoshi Shinjo/Bat 4.00
3WP Hideo Nomo/Jsy 20.00
4WP Kazuhisa Sasaki/Jsy 4.00
5WP Chan Ho Park/Jsy 4.00
6WP Magglio Ordonez/Jsy 6.00
7WP Andruw Jones/Jsy 4.00
8WP Rafael Palmeiro/Jsy 10.00
9WP Bernie Williams/Jsy 6.00
10WP Roberto Alomar/Bat 6.00

2002 Fleer E-X

NM/M
Complete Set (140):

Common Player: .25
Common SP (101-125): 3.00
Common (126-140): 5.00
Inserted 1:24
Pack (4): 2.50
Box (24): 40.00
1 Alex Rodriguez 1.50
2 Albert Pujols 1.50
3 Ken Griffey Jr. 1.25
4 Vladimir Guerrero .75
5 Sammy Sosa 1.25
6 Ichiro Suzuki 1.25
7 Jorge Posada .35
8 Matt Williams .25
9 Adrian Beltre .40
10 Pat Burrell .40
11 Roger Cedeno .25
12 Tony Clark .25
13 Steve Finley .25
14 Rafael Furcal .25
15 Rickey Henderson .75
16 Richard Hidalgo .25
17 Jason Kendall .25
18 Tino Martinez .25
19 Scott Rolen .65
20 Shannon Stewart .25
21 Jose Vidro .25
22 Preston Wilson .25
23 Raul Mondesi .25
24 Lance Berkman .25
25 Rick Ankiel .25
26 Kevin Brown .25
27 Jeromy Burnitz .25
28 Jeff Cirillo .25
29 Carl Everett .25
30 Eric Chavez .35
31 Freddy Garcia .25
32 Mark Grace .35
33 David Justice .25
34 Fred McGriff .25
35 Mike Mussina .50
36 John Olerud .25
37 Magglio Ordonez .25
38 Curt Schilling .50
39 Aaron Sele .25
40 Robin Ventura .25
41 Adam Dunn .50
42 Jeff Bagwell .75
43 Barry Bonds 2.00
44 Roger Clemens 1.00
45 Cliff Floyd .25
46 Jason Giambi .50
47 Juan Gonzalez .75
48 Luis Gonzalez .35
49 Cristian Guzman .25
50 Todd Helton .75
51 Derek Jeter 2.00
52 Rafael Palmeiro .65
53 Mike Sweeney .25
54 Ben Grieve .25
55 Phil Nevin .25
56 Mike Piazza 1.25
57 Moises Alou .25
58 Ivan Rodriguez .65
59 Manny Ramirez .75
60 Brian Giles .25
61 Jim Thome .25
62 Larry Walker .25
63 Bobby Abreu .25
64 Troy Glaus .75
65 Garret Anderson .40
66 Roberto Alomar .40
67 Bret Boone .25
68 Marty Cordova .25
69 Craig Biggio .25
70 Omar Vizquel .25
71 Jermaine Dye .25
72 Darin Erstad .60
73 Carlos Delgado .50
74 Nomar Garciaparra 1.25
75 Greg Maddux 1.00
76 Tom Glavine .40
77 Frank Thomas .75
78 Shawn Green .40
79 Bobby Higginson .25
80 Jeff Kent .25
81 Chuck Knoblauch .25
82 Paul Konerko .25
83 Carlos Lee .25
84 Jon Lieber .25
85 Paul LoDuca .25
86 Mike Lowell .25
87 Edgar Martinez .25
88 Doug Mientkiewicz .25
89 Pedro J. Martinez .75
90 Randy Johnson .75
91 Aramis Ramirez .25
92 J.D. Drew .40
93 Chris Richard .25
94 Jimmy Rollins .50
95 Ryan Klesko .25
96 Gary Sheffield .40
97 Chipper Jones 1.00
98 Greg Vaughn .25
99 Mo Vaughn .25
100 Bernie Williams .35
101 John Foster/2,999 RC 3.00
102 Jorge De La Rosa/2,999 RC 4.00
103 Edwin Almonte/2,999 RC 3.00
104 Chris Booker/2,999 RC 3.00
105 Victor Alvarez/2,999 RC 3.00
106 Clifford Bartosh/2,999 RC 3.00
107 Felix Escalona/2,999 RC 3.00
108 Corey Thurman/2,999 RC 3.00
109 Kazuhisa Ishii/2,999 RC 6.00
110 Miguel Ascencio/2,999 RC 3.00
111 P.J. Bevis/2,499 RC 3.00
112 Gustavo Chacin/2,499 RC 3.00
113 Steve Kent/2,499 RC 3.00
114 Takahito Nomura/2,499 RC 3.00
115 Adam Walker/2,499 RC 3.00
116 So Taguchi/2,499 RC 5.00
117 Reed Johnson/2,499 RC 5.00
118 Rodrigo Rosario/2,499 RC 3.00
119 Luis Martinez/2,499 RC 4.00
120 Satoru Komiyama/2,499 RC 3.00
121 Sean Burroughs/1,999 3.00
122 Hank Blalock/1,999 5.00
123 Marlon Byrd/1,999 3.00
124 Nick Johnson/1,999 3.00
125 Mark Teixeira/1,999 5.00
126 David Espinosa 3.00
127 Adrian Burnside RC 3.00
128 Mark Corey RC 3.00
129 Matt Thornton 3.00
130 Dane Sardinha 3.00
131 Juan Rivera 3.00
132 Austin Kearns 5.00
133 Ben Broussard 3.00
134 Orlando Hudson 3.00
135 Carlos Pena 3.00
136 Kenny Kelly 3.00
137 Bill Hall 3.00
138 Ron Chiavacci 3.00
139 Mark Prior 6.00

Essential Credentials Future

This insert is issued in an edition inverse to the card number, paralleling the first 125 cards in two groups. Cards #1-60 include a game-used piece; card #1 is produced in an edition of 60, while card #60 is unique, etc. Cards #61-125 are inversely numbered with 125 examples of card #61 and 61 of card #125.

NM/M
Quantity produced listed
1 Alex Rodriguez/Jsy/60 30.00
2 Albert Pujols/Base/59 25.00
3 Ken Griffey Jr./Base/58 20.00
4 Vladimir Guerrero/Base/57 15.00
5 Sammy Sosa/Base/56 25.00
6 Ichiro Suzuki/Base/55 40.00
7 Jorge Posada/Bat/54 12.00
8 Matt Williams/Bat/53 8.00
9 Adrian Beltre/Bat/52 8.00
10 Pat Burrell/Bat/51 10.00
11 Roger Cedeno/Bat/50 8.00
12 Tony Clark/Bat/49 8.00
13 Steve Finley/Bat/48 8.00
14 Rafael Furcal/Bat/47 12.00
15 Rickey Henderson/Bat/46 20.00
16 Richard Hidalgo/Bat/45 10.00
17 Jason Kendall/Bat/44 10.00
18 Tino Martinez/Bat/43 15.00
19 Scott Stewart/Bat/42 20.00
20 Shannon Stewart/Bat/41 10.00
21 Jose Vidro/Bat/40 10.00
22 Preston Wilson/Bat/39 10.00
23 Raul Mondesi/Bat/38 10.00
24 Lance Berkman/Bat/37 10.00
25 Rick Ankiel/Jsy/36 8.00
26 Kevin Brown/Jsy/35 8.00
27 Jeromy Burnitz/Bat/34 8.00
28 Jeff Cirillo/Jsy/33 8.00
29 Carl Everett/Jsy/32 8.00
30 Eric Chavez/Bat/31 10.00
31 Freddy Garcia/Jsy/30 10.00
32 Mark Grace/Jsy/29 20.00
33 David Justice/Jsy/28 15.00
34 Fred McGriff/Jsy/27 15.00
37 Magglio Ordonez/Jsy/24 15.00
38 Curt Schilling/Jsy/23 30.00
61 Jim Thome/125
62 Larry Walker/124 4.00
63 Bobby Abreu/123 4.00
64 Troy Glaus/122 6.00
65 Garret Anderson/121 6.00
66 Roberto Alomar/120 6.00
67 Bret Boone/119 6.00
68 Marty Cordova/118 4.00
69 Craig Biggio/117 4.00
70 Omar Vizquel/116 4.00
71 Jermaine Dye/115 4.00
72 Darin Erstad/114 4.00
73 Carlos Delgado/113 6.00
74 Nomar Garciaparra/112 10.00
75 Greg Maddux/111 10.00
76 Tom Glavine/110 6.00
77 Frank Thomas/109 6.00
78 Shawn Green/108 5.00
79 Bobby Higginson/107 3.00
80 Jeff Kent/106 4.00
81 Chuck Knoblauch/105 3.00
82 Paul Konerko/104 3.00
83 Carlos Lee/103 3.00
84 Jon Lieber/102 3.00
85 Paul LoDuca/101 3.00
86 Mike Lowell/100 4.00
87 Edgar Martinez/99 4.00
88 Doug Mientkiewicz/98 3.00
89 Pedro J. Martinez/97 8.00
90 Randy Johnson/96 8.00
91 Aramis Ramirez/95 4.00
92 J.D. Drew/94 4.00
93 Chris Richard/93 3.00
94 Jimmy Rollins/92 4.00
95 Ryan Klesko/91 3.00
96 Gary Sheffield/90 4.00
97 Chipper Jones/89 8.00
98 Greg Vaughn/88 3.00
99 Mo Vaughn/87 3.00
100 Bernie Williams/86 5.00
101 John Foster NT/85 3.00
102 Jorge De La Rosa NT/84 3.00
103 Edwin Almonte NT/83 3.00
104 Chris Booker NT/82 3.00
105 Victor Alvarez NT/81 3.00
106 Clifford Bartosh NT/80 3.00
107 Felix Escalona NT/79 3.00
108 Corey Thurman NT/78 3.00
109 Kazuhisa Ishii NT/77 12.00
110 Miguel Asencio NT/76 3.00
111 P.J. Bevis NT/75 3.00
112 Gustavo Chacin NT/74 3.00
113 Steve Kent NT/73 3.00
114 Takahito Nomura NT/72
115 Adam Walker NT/71 3.00
116 So Taguchi NT/70 6.00
117 Reed Johnson NT/69 6.00
118 Rodrigo Rosario NT/68
119 Luis Martinez NT/67 5.00
120 Satoru Komiyama NT/66 4.00
121 Sean Burroughs NT/65 5.00
122 Hank Blalock NT/64 6.00
123 Marlon Byrd NT/63 6.00
124 Nick Johnson NT/62 4.00
125 Mark Teixeira NT/61 6.00

Essential Credentials Now

This insert parallels the first 125 cards in E-X. Each card is in an edition equal to its card number. Cards of the first 60 players include a game-used piece.

NM/M
Quantity produced listed
19 Scott Rolen/Bat/19 45.00

22 Preston Wilson/Bat/22 15.00
24 Lance Berkman/Bat/24 20.00
25 Rick Ankiel/Jsy/25 20.00
26 Kevin Brown/Jsy/26 20.00
27 Jeromy Burnitz/Bat/27 20.00
28 Jeff Cirillo/Jsy/28 15.00
29 Carl Everett/Jsy/29 15.00
30 Eric Chavez/Bat/30 20.00
31 Freddy Garcia/Jsy/31 15.00
32 Mark Grace/Jsy/32
33 David Justice/Jsy/33 15.00
34 Fred McGriff/Jsy/34 15.00
35 Mike Mussina/Jsy/35 25.00
36 John Olerud/Jsy/36 10.00
37 Magglio Ordonez/Jsy/37 15.00
38 Curt Schilling/Jsy/38 20.00
39 Aaron Sele/Jsy/39
40 Robin Ventura/Jsy/40 10.00
41 Adam Dunn/Bat/41 15.00
42 Jeff Bagwell/Jsy/42 15.00
43 Barry Bonds/Pants/43 75.00
44 Roger Clemens/Bat/44 50.00
45 Cliff Floyd/Bat/45 10.00
46 Jason Giambi/Base/46 15.00
47 Juan Gonzalez/Jsy/47 15.00
48 Luis Gonzalez/Base/48 15.00
49 Cristian Guzman/Bat/49 15.00
50 Todd Helton Base/50 15.00
51 Derek Jeter/Bat/51 60.00
52 Rafael Palmeiro/Bat/52 20.00
53 Mike Sweeney/Bat/53 10.00
54 Ben Grieve/Jsy/54 5.00
55 Phil Nevin/Bat/55 8.00
56 Mike Piazza Base/56 20.00
57 Moises Alou/Bat/57 10.00
58 Ivan Rodriguez/Jsy/58 15.00
59 Manny Ramirez/Base/59 10.00
60 Brian Giles/Bat/60 10.00
61 Jim Thome/61 15.00
62 Larry Walker/62 5.00
63 Bobby Abreu/63 5.00
64 Troy Glaus/64 8.00
65 Garret Anderson/65 8.00
66 Roberto Alomar/66 8.00
67 Bret Boone/67 5.00
68 Marty Cordova/68 4.00
69 Craig Biggio/69 5.00
70 Omar Vizquel/70 4.00
71 Jermaine Dye/71 4.00
72 Darin Erstad/72 5.00
73 Carlos Delgado/73 6.00
74 Nomar Garciaparra/74 15.00
75 Greg Maddux/75 15.00
76 Tom Glavine/76 5.00
77 Frank Thomas/77 8.00
78 Shawn Green/78 5.00
79 Bobby Higginson/79 4.00
80 Jeff Kent/80 5.00
81 Chuck Knoblauch/81 4.00
82 Paul Konerko/82 5.00
83 Carlos Lee/83 5.00
84 Jon Lieber/84 5.00
85 Paul LoDuca/85 5.00
86 Mike Lowell/86 6.00
87 Edgar Martinez/87 5.00
88 Doug Mientkiewicz/88 5.00
89 Pedro J. Martinez/89 10.00
90 Randy Johnson/90 10.00
91 Aramis Ramirez/91 6.00
92 J.D. Drew/92 6.00
93 Chris Richard/93 4.00
94 Jimmy Rollins/94 10.00
95 Ryan Klesko/95 6.00
96 Gary Sheffield/96 6.00
97 Chipper Jones/97 10.00
98 Greg Vaughn/98 4.00
99 Mo Vaughn/99 6.00
100 Bernie Williams/100 6.00
101 John Foster NT/101 4.00
102 Jorge De La Rosa NT/102 4.00

103	Edwin Almonte NT/103	4.00
104	Chris Booker NT/104	4.00
105	Victor Alvarez NT/105	4.00
106	Clifford Bartosh NT/106	4.00
107	Felix Escalona NT/107	4.00
108	Corey Thurman NT/108	4.00
109	Kazuhisa Ishii NT/109	10.00
110	Miguel Asencio NT/110	4.00
111	P.J. Bevis NT/111	4.00
112	Gustavo Chacin NT/112	4.00
113	Steve Kent NT/113	4.00
114	Takahito Nomura NT/114	4.00
115	Adam Walker NT/115	4.00
116	So Taguchi NT/116	4.00
117	Reed Johnson NT/117	6.00
118	Rodrigo Rosario NT/118	4.00
119	Luis Martinez NT/119	4.00
120	Satoru Komiyama NT/120	4.00
121	Sean Burroughs NT/121	5.00
122	Hank Blalock NT/122	6.00
123	Marlon Byrd NT/123	4.00
124	Nick Johnson NT/124	4.00
125	Mark Teixeira NT/125	6.00

Behind the Numbers

NM/M
Complete Set (35): 75.00
Common Player: 1.00
Inserted 1:8

1BTN	Ichiro Suzuki	5.00
2BTN	Jason Giambi	2.50
3BTN	Mike Piazza	5.00
4BTN	Brian Giles	1.00
5BTN	Barry Bonds	8.00
6BTN	Pedro J. Martinez	3.00
7BTN	Nomar Garciaparra	5.00
8BTN	Randy Johnson	3.00
9BTN	Craig Biggio	1.00
10BTN	Manny Ramirez	3.00
11BTN	Mike Mussina	1.50
12BTN	Kerry Wood	2.50
13BTN	Jim Edmonds	1.00
14BTN	Ivan Rodriguez	2.50
15BTN	Jeff Bagwell	3.00
16BTN	Roger Clemens	4.50
17BTN	Chipper Jones	4.00
18BTN	Shawn Green	1.25
19BTN	Albert Pujols	6.00
20BTN	Andruw Jones	3.00
21BTN	Luis Gonzalez	1.00
22BTN	Todd Helton	3.00
23BTN	Jorge Posada	1.25
24BTN	Scott Rolen	2.50
25BTN	Ben Sheets	1.00
26BTN	Alfonso Soriano	2.50
27BTN	Greg Maddux	4.00
28BTN	Gary Sheffield	1.25
29BTN	Barry Zito	1.25
30BTN	Alex Rodriguez	6.00
31BTN	Larry Walker	1.00
32BTN	Derek Jeter	8.00
33BTN	Ken Griffey Jr.	5.00
34BTN	Vladimir Guerrero	3.00
35BTN	Sammy Sosa	5.00

Behind the Numbers Game Jersey

NM/M
Common Player: 5.00
Inserted 1:24

1	Jeff Bagwell	10.00
2	Craig Biggio/Pants	5.00
4	Roger Clemens	20.00
5	Jim Edmonds	5.00
6	Brian Giles	5.00
7	Luis Gonzalez	5.00
8	Shawn Green	5.00
9	Todd Helton	5.00
10	Derek Jeter/SP	30.00
11	Randy Johnson/SP	10.00
12	Andruw Jones	5.00
13	Chipper Jones	10.00
14	Greg Maddux	10.00
15	Pedro J. Martinez	10.00
16	Mike Mussina	10.00
17	Mike Piazza/Pants	10.00

ABBREVIATIONS

SP - Short Print

18	Jorge Posada	8.00
19	Manny Ramirez	8.00
20	Alex Rodriguez	10.00
21	Ivan Rodriguez	8.00
22	Scott Rolen	8.00
23	Alfonso Soriano/SP	10.00
24	Barry Zito	6.00

Behind the Numbers Game Jersey Dual

No Pricing
Production 25 Sets

Barry Bonds 4X MVP

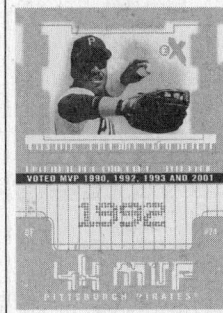

NM/M
Complete Set (4): 20.00
Common Bonds: 6.00

1BB4X	Barry Bonds/1,990	6.00
2BB4X	Barry Bonds/1,992	6.00
3BB4X	Barry Bonds/1,993	6.00
4BB4X	Barry Bonds/2,001	6.00

Game Essentials

NM/M
Common Player: 5.00

Carlos Beltran	5.00
Kevin Brown	5.00
Jeromy Burnitz	5.00
Carlos Delgado	8.00
Jason Hart/SP	8.00
Rickey Henderson	20.00
Drew Henson/Shoe	5.00
Drew Henson/Glv	8.00
Derek Jeter/Shoe	40.00
Jason Kendall	5.00
Jeff Kent	10.00
Barry Larkin/Glv	20.00
Javy Lopez	8.00
Raul Mondesi/Btg Glv	8.00
Rafael Palmeiro	10.00
Adam Piatt	5.00
Brad Radke	5.00
Cal Ripken Jr.	30.00
Mariano Rivera	10.00
Alex Rodriguez/Btg Glv	15.00
Ivan Rodriguez/Shoe	10.00
Kazuhiro Sasaki	5.00
J.T. Snow	5.00
Mo Vaughn	5.00
Robin Ventura	5.00
Jose Vidro	5.00
Matt Williams	5.00

HardWear

NM/M
Complete Set (10): 60.00
Common Player: 4.00
Inserted 1:72 Hobby

1HW	Ivan Rodriguez	4.00
2HW	Mike Piazza	8.00
3HW	Derek Jeter	15.00
4HW	Barry Bonds	15.00
5HW	Todd Helton	4.00
6HW	Roberto Alomar	4.00
7HW	Albert Pujols	10.00
8HW	Ichiro Suzuki	8.00
9HW	Ken Griffey Jr.	8.00
10HW	Jason Giambi	5.00

Hit and Run

NM/M
Complete Set (30): 50.00
Common Player: 1.00
Inserted 1:12

1	Adam Dunn	1.00
2	Derek Jeter	6.00
3	Frank Thomas	2.00
4	Albert Pujols	4.00
5	J.D. Drew	1.00
6	Richard Hidalgo	1.00
7	John Olerud	1.00
8	Roberto Alomar	1.00
9	Pat Burrell	1.50
10	Darin Erstad	1.50
11	Mark Grace	1.00
12	Chipper Jones	3.00
13	Jose Vidro	1.00
14	Cliff Floyd	1.00
15	Mo Vaughn	1.00
16	Nomar Garciaparra	4.00
17	Ivan Rodriguez	1.50
18	Luis Gonzalez	1.00
19	Jason Giambi	1.50
20	Bernie Williams	1.00
21	Mike Piazza	4.00
22	Barry Bonds	6.00
23	Jose Ortiz	1.00
24	Magglio Ordonez	1.00
25	Troy Glaus	2.00
26	Alex Rodriguez	5.00
27	Ichiro Suzuki	4.00
28	Sammy Sosa	4.00
29	Ken Griffey Jr.	4.00
30	Vladimir Guerrero	2.00

Hit and Run Game Base

NM/M
Inserted 1:120

1	J.D. Drew	4.00
2	Adam Dunn	6.00
3	Jason Giambi	4.00
4	Troy Glaus	4.00
5	Ken Griffey Jr.	10.00
6	Vladimir Guerrero	8.00
7	Albert Pujols	15.00
8	Sammy Sosa	10.00
9	Ichiro Suzuki	15.00
10	Bernie Williams	6.00

Hit and Run Game Bat

NM/M
Common Player: 4.00
Inserted 1:24

1	Roberto Alomar	6.00
2	J.D. Drew	4.00
3	Darin Erstad	4.00
4	Cliff Floyd	4.00
5	Nomar Garciaparra	15.00
6	Luis Gonzalez	6.00
7	Richard Hidalgo	4.00
8	Derek Jeter	25.00
9	Chipper Jones	8.00
10	John Olerud	4.00
11	Magglio Ordonez	6.00
12	Jose Ortiz	4.00
13	Mike Piazza	10.00
14	Alex Rodriguez	15.00
15	Ivan Rodriguez	8.00
16	Frank Thomas	8.00
17	Mo Vaughn	4.00
18	Jose Vidro	4.00
19	Bernie Williams	8.00

Hit and Run Game Bat and Base

NM/M
Common Player: 10.00
Inserted 1:240

1	Roberto Alomar	15.00
2	Barry Bonds SP	50.00
3	Nomar Garciaparra	15.00
4	Derek Jeter	40.00
5	Chipper Jones	15.00
6	Mike Piazza	20.00
7	Alex Rodriguez	25.00
8	Mo Vaughn	10.00

Derek Jeter 4X Champ

NM/M
Complete Set (4): 20.00
Common Jeter: 6.00

1DJFX	Derek Jeter/1,996	6.00
2DJFX	Derek Jeter/1,998	6.00
3DJFX	Derek Jeter/1,999	6.00
4DJFX	Derek Jeter/2,000	6.00

2002 Fleer Fall Classic

NM/M
Complete Set (100): 30.00
Common Player: .25
Common SP: 3.00
Inserted 1:18 Hobby
Pack (5): 5.00
Box (24): 100.00

1	Rabbit Maranville	.25
2	Tris Speaker	.75
3	Harmon Killebrew	1.00
4	Lou Gehrig	2.00
5	Lou Boudreau	.25
6	Al Kaline	1.00
7	Paul Molitor	1.00
7	Paul Molitor/Brewers	4.00
8	Cal Ripken Jr.	3.00
9	Yogi Berra	1.00
10	Phil Rizzuto	.75
11	Luis Aparicio	.25
11	Luis Aparicio/Orioles	4.00
12	Stan Musial	2.00
13	Mel Ott	.75
14	Larry Doby	.25
15	Ozzie Smith	1.00
16	Babe Ruth	4.00
16	Babe Ruth/Red Sox	10.00
17	Red Schoendienst	.25
17	Red Schoendienst/Cards	3.00
18	Rollie Fingers	.25
19	Thurman Munson	1.50
20	Lou Brock	.25
21	Paul O'Neill	.25
21	Paul O'Neill/Reds	3.00
22	Jim Palmer	.50
23	Kirby Puckett	1.00
24	Tony Perez	.25
24	Tony Perez/Phila.	3.00
25	Don Larsen	.25
26	Steve Garvey	.25
26	Steve Garvey/Padres	3.00
27	Jim "Catfish" Hunter	.25
27	"Catfish" Hunter/Yanks	4.00
28	Juan Marichal	.50
29	Pee Wee Reese	.25
30	Orlando Cepeda	.25
31	Rich "Goose" Gossage	.25
32	Ray Knight	.25
33	Eddie Murray	.75
34	Nolan Ryan	3.00
35	Alan Trammell	.50
36	Grover Alexander	.75
37	Joe Carter	.25
38	Rogers Hornsby	1.00
39	Jimmie Foxx	1.00
40	Mike Schmidt	1.50
41	Eddie Mathews	1.00
42	Jackie Robinson	1.50
43	Eddie Collins	.25
43	Eddie Collins/White Sox	3.00
44	Willie McCovey	.25
45	Bob Gibson	1.00
46	Keith Hernandez	.50
46	Keith Hernandez/Cards	4.00
47	Brooks Robinson	.25
48	Mordecai Brown	.25
49	Gary Carter	.50
50	Kirk Gibson	.25
50	Kirk Gibson/Tigers	3.00
51	Johnny Mize	.25
52	Johnny Podres	.25
53	Darrell Porter	.25
54	Willie Stargell	.75
55	Lenny Dykstra	.25
55	Lenny Dykstra/Phila.	3.00
56	Christy Mathewson	.75
57	Walter Johnson	1.00
58	Whitey Ford	.75
59	Lefty Grove	.50
60	Duke Snider	.75
61	Cy Young	1.00
62	Dave Winfield	.75
63	Dave Winfield/Yanks	5.00
63	Robin Yount	1.00
64	Fred Lynn	.25
65	Ty Cobb	2.00
66	Joe Morgan	.25
67	Bill Mazeroski	.25
68	Frank Baker	.25
69	Chief Bender	.25
70	Carlton Fisk	.50
71	Jerry Coleman	.25
72	Frankie Frisch	.25
73	Wade Boggs	1.00
73	Wade Boggs/Yanks	4.00
74	Johnny Bench	1.00
75	Roger Maris	2.00
75	Roger Maris/Cards	8.00
76	Dom DiMaggio	.25
77	George Brett	3.00
78	Dave Parker	.25
78	Dave Parker/A's	3.00
79	Hank Greenberg	.25
80	Pepper Martin	.25
81	Graig Nettles	.25
81	Graig Nettles/Padres	3.00
82	Dennis Eckersley	.50
83	Don Clendenon	.25
84	Tom Seaver	1.00
85	Honus Wagner	1.50
86	Reggie Jackson	.75
86	Reggie Jackson/A's	5.00
87	Goose Goslin	.25
87	Goose Goslin/Tigers	3.00
88	Tony Kubek	.25
89	Roy Campanella	1.00
90	Steve Carlton/Cards	4.00
91	Lou Gehrig, Mel Ott	2.00
92	Eddie Collins, Joe Morgan	.25
93	George Brett, Mike Schmidt	2.00
94	Cal Ripken Jr., Ozzie Smith	3.00
95	Thurman Munson, Johnny Bench	1.50
96	Willie Stargell, Stan Musial, Pepper Martin	1.00
97	Babe Ruth, Kirby Puckett, Reggie Jackson	3.00
98	Cy Young, Bob Gibson	1.00
99	Whitey Ford, Steve Carlton	1.00
100	Paul Molitor, Lou Brock	.50

Championship Gold

Golds:	5-10X
Gold SP's:	1-2X
Production 50 Sets	

HOF Plaque

Young's all-time record of 511 career wins will never be broken, and it's only fitting that he won two games in the inaugural 1903 World Series. He led ...

NM/M
Complete Set (30): 90.00
Common Player: 3.00
#'d to HOF induction year

1HOF	Babe Ruth	8.00
2HOF	Christy Mathewson	3.00
3HOF	Honus Wagner	4.00
4HOF	Ty Cobb	5.00
5HOF	Walter Johnson	4.00
6HOF	Cy Young	4.00
7HOF	Tris Speaker	3.00
8HOF	Eddie Collins	3.00
9HOF	Lou Gehrig	6.00
10HOF	Jimmie Foxx	4.00
11HOF	Jackie Robinson	6.00
12HOF	Stan Musial	5.00
13HOF	Yogi Berra	4.00
14HOF	Duke Snider	5.00
15HOF	Juan Marichal	3.00
16HOF	Luis Aparicio	3.00
17HOF	Pee Wee Reese	3.00
18HOF	Willie McCovey	3.00
19HOF	Willie Stargell	3.00
20HOF	Johnny Bench	5.00
21HOF	Joe Morgan	3.00
22HOF	Jim Palmer	3.00
23HOF	Tom Seaver	3.00
24HOF	Reggie Jackson	4.00
25HOF	Steve Carlton	4.00
26HOF	George Brett	6.00
27HOF	Nolan Ryan	8.00
28HOF	Robin Yount	4.00
29HOF	Kirby Puckett	5.00
30HOF	Ozzie Smith	4.00

MVP Collection Game-Used

NM/M
Common Player: 5.00
Inserted 1:100
Golds: .75-2X
Production 100 Sets

JB	Johnny Bench/200	20.00
DC	Donn Clendenon	5.00
RF	Rollie Fingers/200	5.00
RJOK	Reggie Jackson/50	20.00
RJNY	Reggie Jackson	10.00
RK	Ray Knight	5.00
PM	Paul Molitor/250	15.00
DP	Darrell Porter/250	5.00
BR	Brooks Robinson/250	20.00
WS	Willie Stargell/200	10.00
AT	Alan Trammell	10.00

MVP Collection Patch

NM/M
Numbered to MVP Year

JB	Johnny Bench/76	45.00
RF	Rollie Fingers/74	20.00
RJNY	Reggie Jackson/77	40.00
BR	Brooks Robinson/70	40.00
AT	Alan Trammell/84	30.00

October Legends

NM/M
Common Player: 5.00
Inserted 1:48
Golds: .75-1.5X
Production 100 Sets

Joe Morgan	5.00
Wade Boggs/60	20.00
Keith Hernandez/100	15.00
Robin Yount	10.00
Eddie Murray	10.00
Lenny Dykstra/200	8.00
Paul O'Neill	8.00
Red Schoendienst/210	8.00
Pepper Martin/50	15.00
Keith Hernandez/150	20.00
Willie Stargell/225	12.00
George Brett	20.00
Dave Parker/50	10.00
Tony Perez	5.00
Rollie Fingers	5.00
Gary Carter/200	10.00
Dennis Eckersley	5.00
Juan Marichal	8.00
Pee Wee Reese/200	15.00
Roger Maris	60.00
Duke Snider/200	15.00
Darrell Porter/150	5.00
Willie McCovey/150	10.00
Paul Molitor/150	15.00

October Legends Dual

NM/M
Common Card: 10.00
SP's noted

Rollie Fingers, Dennis Eckersley	12.00
Keith Hernandez, Red Schoendienst	12.00
Joe Morgan, Tony Perez	10.00
Wade Boggs, Keith Hernandez	20.00
Lenny Dykstra, Gary Carter	12.00
Robin Yount, Paul Molitor/150	35.00
Roger Maris, Paul O'Neill/200	50.00
Duke Snider, Pee Wee Reese/200	25.00
Juan Marichal, Willie McCovey	15.00
George Brett, Darrell Porter/150	35.00
Willie Stargell, Dave Parker	15.00
Gary Carter, Keith Hernandez	10.00
Cal Ripken Jr., Eddie Murray/200	40.00
Cal Ripken Jr., Eddie Murray/100	50.00
Pepper Martin, Frankie Frisch	15.00

Pennant Chase

NM/M
Common Player: 10.00
Inserted 1:48 Hobby

Yogi Berra/Pants/150	20.00
Carlton Fisk/Bat	10.00
Reggie Jackson/Jsy	10.00
Fred Lynn/Bat	10.00
Thurman Munson/Bat	30.00

Wade Boggs/Jsy 10.00
Dave Winfield/Bat 10.00

Pennant Chase Dual

NM/M
Production 50 Sets
CFRJ Carlton Fisk/Bat, Reggie Jackson/Jsy 30.00
FLTM Fred Lynn/Bat, Thurman Munson/Bat 50.00
WBDW Wade Boggs/Jsy, Dave Winfield/Bat 30.00

Rival Factions

NM/M
Common Card: 2.00
1-24 #'d to 1,000
25-36 #'d to 500
37-43 #'d to 50 not priced
1RF Carlton Fisk, Thurman Munson 3.00
2RF Frank Baker, Babe Ruth 8.00
3RF Jimmie Foxx, Lou Gehrig 6.00
4RF Steve Carlton, Nolan Ryan 8.00
5RF Mordecai Brown, Honus Wagner 3.00
6RF Frankie Frisch, Duke Snider 3.00
7RF Ozzie Smith, Alan Trammell 3.00
8RF Larry Doby, Jackie Robinson 5.00
9RF Steve Garvey, Tony Perez 2.00
10RF Johnny Bench, Willie Stargell 4.00
11RF Ty Cobb, Eddie Collins 5.00
12RF Reggie Jackson, Brooks Robinson 4.00
13RF Yogi Berra, Roy Campanella 4.00
14RF Orlando Cepeda, Willie McCovey 2.00
15RF Al Kaline, Jim Palmer 4.00
16RF George Brett, Kirby Puckett 6.00
17RF Bob Gibson, Tom Seaver 4.00
18RF Cal Ripken Jr., Robin Yount 8.00
19RF Johnny Mize, Mel Ott 3.00
20RF Stan Musial, Pee Wee Reese 4.00
21RF Phil Rizzuto, Ted Williams 8.00
22RF Hank Greenberg, Lefty Grove 2.00
23RF Dave Parker, Mike Schmidt 4.00
24RF Bill Mazeroski, Joe Morgan 2.00
25RF Johnny Bench, Carlton Fisk 5.00
26RF George Brett, Mike Schmidt 6.00
27RF Pee Wee Reese, Phil Rizzuto 4.00
28RF Stan Musial, Ted Williams 10.00
29RF Cal Ripken Jr., Alan Trammell 10.00
30RF Jim "Catfish" Hunter, Tom Seaver 4.00
31RF Ty Cobb, Honus Wagner 5.00
32RF Steve Carlton, Lefty Grove 2.00
33RF Ozzie Smith, Robin Yount 4.00
34RF Frankie Frisch, Joe Morgan 2.00
35RF Hank Greenberg, Jackie Robinson 6.00
36RF Jimmie Foxx, Pepper Martin 4.00

Rival Factions Game-Used Single

NM/M
Common Card: 8.00

Inserted 1:32
Carlton Fisk, Thurman Munson 25.00
Frank Baker, Babe Ruth 25.00
Jimmie Foxx, Lou Gehrig 35.00
Steve Carlton, Nolan Ryan 25.00
Frankie Frisch, Duke Snider 20.00
Ozzie Smith, Alan Trammell 15.00
Larry Doby, Jackie Robinson 15.00
Steve Garvey, Tony Perez 10.00
Johnny Bench, Willie Stargell 10.00
Reggie Jackson, Brooks Robinson 12.00
Orlando Cepeda, Willie McCovey 10.00
Al Kaline, Jim Palmer 10.00
George Brett, Kirby Puckett 25.00
Bob Gibson, Tom Seaver 20.00
Cal Ripken Jr., Robin Yount 30.00
Stan Musial, Pee Wee Reese 25.00
Hank Greenberg, Lefty Grove 20.00
Bill Mazeroski, Joe Morgan 8.00
Johnny Bench, Carlton Fisk 10.00
George Brett, Mike Schmidt 25.00
Pee Wee Reese, Phil Rizzuto 15.00
Cal Ripken Jr., Alan Trammell 35.00
Steve Carlton, Lefty Grove 15.00
Ozzie Smith, Robin Yount 15.00
Frankie Frisch, Joe Morgan 25.00
Hank Greenberg, Jackie Robinson 20.00
Jimmie Foxx, Pepper Martin 30.00
Lou Gehrig, Cal Ripken Jr. 40.00
Reggie Jackson, Dave Winfield 10.00
Babe Ruth, Roger Maris 60.00
Nolan Ryan, Tom Seaver 35.00

Rival Factions Game-Used Dual

NM/M
Common Card: 12.00
Carlton Fisk, Thurman Munson 30.00
Steve Carlton, Nolan Ryan 40.00
Frankie Frisch, Duke Snider 15.00
Ozzie Smith, Alan Trammell 25.00
Larry Doby, Jackie Robinson/75 60.00
Steve Garvey, Tony Perez 10.00
Johnny Bench, Willie Stargell 20.00
Reggie Jackson, Brooks Robinson 20.00
Orlando Cepeda, Willie McCovey/200 15.00
George Brett, Kirby Puckett 40.00
Cal Ripken Jr., Robin Yount 30.00
Johnny Bench, Carlton Fisk 20.00
Cal Ripken Jr., Alan Trammell 30.00
Jim "Catfish" Hunter, Tom Seaver 15.00
Ozzie Smith, Robin Yount 25.00
Frankie Frisch, Joe Morgan 15.00
Hank Greenberg, Jackie Robinson/50 100.00
Jimmie Foxx, Pepper Martin/200 40.00
Reggie Jackson, Dave Winfield/150 20.00
Yogi Berra, Thurman Munson 40.00
Nolan Ryan, Tom Seaver 45.00
Joe Morgan, Jackie Robinson/50 50.00

Rival Factions Dual Patch

NM/M
Production 50 Sets 12.00
Carlton Fisk, Thurman Munson 60.00
Steve Carlton, Nolan Ryan 100.00
Ozzie Smith, Alan Trammell 50.00
Steve Garvey, Tony Perez 30.00
Johnny Bench, Willie Stargell 50.00
Cal Ripken Jr., Robin Yount 125.00
Johnny Bench, Carlton Fisk 50.00
Cal Ripken Jr., Alan Trammell 100.00
Ozzie Smith, Robin Yount 60.00
Reggie Jackson, Dave Winfield 40.00

Series of Champions

NM/M
Complete Set (20): 25.00
Common Player: 1.00
Inserted 1:6
1 Yogi Berra 2.00
2 Wade Boggs 2.00
3 Dave Parker 1.00
4 Joe Carter 1.00
5 Kirk Gibson 1.00
6 Reggie Jackson 2.00
7 Tony Kubek 1.00
8 Don Larsen 1.00
9 Bill Mazeroski 1.00
10 Eddie Murray 1.50
11 Graig Nettles 1.00
12 Tony Perez 1.00
13 Phil Rizzuto 1.50
14 Mike Schmidt 2.50
15 Red Schoendienst 1.00
16 Duke Snider 2.00
17 Ty Cobb 2.50
18 Lou Gehrig 3.00
19 Babe Ruth 4.00

Series of Champions Game-Used

NM/M
Common Player: 5.00
Inserted 1:36
Golds: .75-1.5X
Production 100 Sets
Bat Knob numbered to 10 not priced.
Yogi Berra/Bat 10.00
Wade Boggs/Jsy 10.00
Dave Parker/Bat 5.00
Joe Carter/Bat 5.00
Kirk Gibson/Bat 5.00
Reggie Jackson/Bat 10.00
Tony Kubek/Bat 10.00
Eddie Murray/Bat 10.00
Graig Nettles/Bat 5.00
Tony Perez/Bat 5.00
Red Schoendienst/Jsy 5.00
Duke Snider/Bat 10.00
Babe Ruth/Bat/25 180.00

2002 Fleer Flair

NM/M
Complete Set (138):
Common Player: .25
Common (101-138): 3.00
Production 1,750
Pack (5): 4.00

Hobby Box (20): 70.00
1 Scott Rolen .75
2 Derek Jeter 3.00
3 Sean Casey .40
4 Hideo Nomo .75
5 Craig Biggio .25
6 Randy Johnson 1.00
7 J.D. Drew .50
8 Greg Maddux 1.50
9 Paul LoDuca .25
10 John Olerud .25
11 Barry Larkin .25
12 Mark Grace .35
13 Jimmy Rollins .50
14 Todd Helton 1.00
15 Jim Edmonds .25
16 Roy Oswalt .35
17 Phil Nevin .25
18 Tim Salmon .35
19 Magglio Ordonez .25
20 Roger Clemens 1.75
21 Raul Mondesi .25
22 Edgar Martinez .25
23 Pedro J. Martinez 1.00
24 Edgardo Alfonzo .25
25 Bernie Williams .35
26 Gary Sheffield .40
27 D'Angelo Jimenez .25
28 Toby Hall .25
29 Joe Mays .25
30 Alfonso Soriano .75
31 Mike Piazza 2.00
32 Lance Berkman .25
33 Jim Thome .25
34 Ben Sheets .25
35 Brandon Inge .25
36 Luis Gonzalez .35
37 Jeff Kent .25
38 Ben Grieve .25
39 Carlos Delgado .50
40 Pat Burrell .50
41 Mark Buehrle .25
42 Cristian Guzman .25
43 Shawn Green .40
44 Nomar Garciaparra 2.00
45 Carlos Beltran .60
46 Troy Glaus .75
47 Paul Konerko .25
48 Moises Alou .25
49 Kerry Wood .75
50 Jose Vidro .25
51 Juan Encarnacion .25
52 Bobby Abreu .25
53 C.C. Sabathia .25
54 Alex Rodriguez 2.50
55 Albert Pujols 2.50
56 Bret Boone .25
57 Orlando Hernandez .25
58 Jason Kendall .25
59 Tim Hudson .40
60 Darin Erstad .60
61 Mike Mussina .40
62 Ken Griffey Jr. 2.00
63 Adrian Beltre .35
64 Jeff Bagwell 1.00
65 Vladimir Guerrero 1.00
66 Mike Sweeney .25
67 Sammy Sosa 2.00
68 Andruw Jones .75
69 Richie Sexson .25
70 Matt Morris .25
71 Ivan Rodriguez .75
72 Shannon Stewart .25
73 Barry Bonds 3.00
74 Matt Williams .25
75 Jason Giambi .60
76 Brian Giles .25
77 Cliff Floyd .25
78 Tino Martinez .25
79 Juan Gonzalez 1.00
80 Frank Thomas 1.00
81 Ichiro Suzuki 2.00
82 Barry Zito .35
83 Chipper Jones 1.50
84 Adam Dunn .75
85 Kazuhiro Sasaki .25
86 Mark Quinn .25
87 Rafael Palmeiro .60
88 Jeromy Burnitz .25
89 Curt Schilling .50
90 Chris Richards .25
91 Jon Leiber .25
92 Doug Mientkiewicz .25
93 Roberto Alomar .40
94 Rich Aurilia .25
95 Eric Chavez .35
96 Larry Walker .25
97 Manny Ramirez 1.00

---

98 Tony Clark .25
99 Tsuyoshi Shinjo .25
100 Josh Beckett .50
101 Dewon Brazelton 3.00
102 Jeremy Lambert RC 3.00
103 Andres Torres 3.00
104 Matt Childers RC 4.00
105 Wilson Betemit 3.00
106 Willie Harris 3.00
107 Drew Henson 4.00
108 Rafael Soriano 3.00
109 Carlos Valderrama 3.00
110 Victor Martinez 6.00
111 Juan Rivera 3.00
112 Felipe Lopez 3.00
113 Brandon Duckworth 3.00
114 Jeremy Owens 3.00
115 Aaron Cook RC 3.00
116 Derrick Lewis 3.00
117 Mark Teixeira 6.00
118 Ken Harvey 5.00
119 Tim Spooneybarger 3.00
120 Bill Hall 3.00
121 Adam Pettyjohn 3.00
122 Ramon Castro 3.00
123 Marlon Byrd 4.00
124 Matt White 3.00
125 Eric Cyr RC 3.00
126 Morgan Ensberg 3.00
127 Horacio Ramirez 4.00
128 Ron Calloway RC 3.00
129 Nick Punto 3.00
130 Joe Kennedy 3.00
131 So Taguchi RC 5.00
132 Austin Kearns 4.00
133 Mark Prior 6.00
134 Kazuhisa Ishii RC 8.00
135 Steve Torrealba 3.00
136 Adam Walker RC 3.00
137 Travis Hafner 4.00
138 Zach Day 3.00

Collection

Collection (1-100): 4-6X
Production 175
Collection (101-138): 1-2X
Production 50

Hot Numbers

NM/M
Common Player: 15.00
Production 100 Sets
Manny Ramirez 30.00
Randy Johnson 30.00
Curt Schilling 25.00
Pedro J. Martinez 30.00
Nomar Garciaparra 50.00
Barry Larkin 15.00
Todd Helton 30.00
Larry Walker 15.00
Sean Casey 20.00
Jeff Bagwell 30.00
Craig Biggio 15.00
Shawn Green 15.00
Edgardo Alfonzo 15.00
Mike Piazza 50.00
Derek Jeter 75.00
Chipper Jones 40.00
Jim Edmonds 15.00
J.D. Drew 20.00
Ivan Rodriguez 25.00
Rafael Palmeiro 25.00
Alex Rodriguez 60.00
Greg Maddux 40.00
Carlos Delgado 20.00

Jersey Heights

NM/M
Common Player: 4.00
Inserted 1:18 Hobby
1JH Edgardo Alfonzo 4.00
2JH Jeff Bagwell 8.00
3JH Craig Biggio 8.00
4JH Barry Bonds 20.00
5JH Sean Casey 4.00
6JH Roger Clemens 15.00
7JH Carlos Delgado 6.00
8JH J.D. Drew 6.00
9JH Jim Edmonds 6.00
10JH Nomar Garciaparra 15.00
11JH Shawn Green 5.00
12JH Todd Helton 8.00
13JH Derek Jeter 20.00
14JH Randy Johnson 8.00
15JH Chipper Jones 8.00
16JH Barry Larkin 6.00
17JH Greg Maddux 10.00

18JH Pedro J. Martinez 8.00
19JH Rafael Palmeiro 8.00
20JH Mike Piazza 10.00
21JH Manny Ramirez 8.00
22JH Alex Rodriguez 15.00
23JH Ivan Rodriguez 6.00
24JH Curt Schilling 6.00
25JH Larry Walker 4.00

Jersey Heights (Dual)

NM/M
Common Card: 15.00
Production 100 Sets
Randy Johnson, Curt Schilling 30.00
Pedro J. Martinez, Nomar Garciaparra 50.00
Edgardo Alfonzo, Mike Piazza 30.00
Derek Jeter, Roger Clemens 75.00
Greg Maddux, Chipper Jones 40.00
Jim Edmonds, Jeff Bagwell 20.00
Craig Biggio, Rafael Palmeiro 25.00
Ivan Rodriguez, Carlos Delgado, Shawn Green 15.00
Todd Helton, Larry Walker 20.00
Sean Casey, Barry Larkin 25.00
Alex Rodriguez, Manny Ramirez 40.00

Power Tools

NM/M
Common Player: 4.00
Inserted 1:19
Golds: 1-2.5X
Production 100
1PT Roberto Alomar 6.00
2PT Jeff Bagwell/150 8.00
3PT Craig Biggio 4.00
4PT Barry Bonds 15.00
5PT Bret Boone 4.00
6PT Pat Burrell/225 6.00
8PT Eric Chavez 5.00
9PT J.D. Drew/150 8.00
10PT Jim Edmonds 6.00
11PT Juan Gonzalez 6.00
12PT Luis Gonzalez 4.00
13PT Shawn Green 5.00
15PT Derek Jeter 25.00
16PT Doug Mientkiewicz 4.00
17PT Magglio Ordonez 5.00
18PT Rafael Palmeiro/100 8.00
19PT Mike Piazza 10.00
20PT Alex Rodriguez 15.00
21PT Ivan Rodriguez 8.00
22PT Scott Rolen/42 15.00
23PT Reggie Sanders/120 4.00
24PT Gary Sheffield 6.00
25PT Tsuyoshi Shinjo 5.00
26PT Miguel Tejada 6.00
27PT Frank Thomas 8.00
28PT Jim Thome/225 15.00
29PT Larry Walker 4.00
30PT Bernie Williams 6.00

Power Tools Dual

NM/M
Common Card: 10.00
Inserted 1:40
Golds: 1-2.5X
Production 50 Sets
1 Eric Chavez, Miguel Tejada 10.00
2 Barry Bonds, Tsuyoshi Shinjo 25.00
3 Jim Edmonds, J.D. Drew 15.00
4 Jeff Bagwell, Craig Biggio 15.00
5 Bernie Williams, Derek Jeter 35.00
6 Roberto Alomar, Mike Piazza 20.00
7 Sean Casey, Jim Thome/40 30.00
8 Pat Burrell, Scott Rolen 15.00

9	Gary Sheffield, Shawn Green	10.00
10	Ivan Rodriguez, Alex Rodriguez	15.00
11	Juan Gonzalez, Rafael Palmeiro	15.00
12	Magglio Ordonez, Frank Thomas	15.00
13	Larry Walker, Todd Helton/225	10.00
14	Luis Gonzalez, Reggie Sanders	10.00
15	Doug Mientkiewicz, Bret Boone	10.00

Sweet Swatch Autographs
NM/M
Common Player: 15.00
Quantity produced listed
Golds: No Pricing
Production 15 Sets

Derek Jeter/375	100.00
Barry Bonds/35	200.00
Drew Henson/785	40.00
Mark Teixeira/185	40.00
Dewon Brazelton/185	15.00
Mark Prior/285	40.00
Marlon Byrd/185	15.00
Ozzie Smith/185	65.00
Ron Cey/285	20.00
Paul Molitor/85	50.00
Maury Wills/285	40.00
Dale Murphy/285	60.00
David Espinosa/485	15.00
Dane Sardinha/485	15.00
Ben Sheets/85	50.00
Tony Perez/115	20.00
Brooks Robinson/185	50.00
So Taguchi/335	30.00
Al Kaline/285	30.00
Kazuhisa Ishii/335	30.00
Albert Pujols/50	125.00
Don Mattingly/85	150.00

Sweet Swatch Game-Used
NM/M
Common Player: 8.00
1:Hobby Box

Jeff Bagwell/490	10.00
Josh Beckett/500	10.00
Darin Erstad/525	8.00
Freddy Garcia/620	8.00
Brian Giles/445	10.00
Juan Gonzalez/505	10.00
Mark Grace/795	15.00
Derek Jeter/525	40.00
Jason Kendall/990	10.00
Paul LoDuca/440	10.00
Greg Maddux/475	15.00
Magglio Ordonez/495	10.00
Rafael Palmeiro/535	10.00
Mike Piazza/1,000	15.00
Alex Rodriguez/550	25.00
Ivan Rodriguez/475	10.00
Tim Salmon/465	10.00
Kazuhiro Sasaki/770	8.00
Alfonso Soriano/775	10.00
Larry Walker/430	15.00
Ted Williams/250	125.00

Sweet Swatch Patch
NM/M
Common Player: 25.00
Random Box Topper

Jeff Bagwell/45	75.00
Josh Beckett/60	55.00
Darin Erstad/50	40.00
Freddy Garcia/50	40.00
Juan Gonzalez/55	75.00
Mark Grace/75	60.00
Jason Kendall/120	25.00
Paul LoDuca/50	35.00
Greg Maddux/90	90.00
Magglio Ordonez/55	40.00
Rafael Palmeiro/60	40.00
Mike Piazza/95	100.00
Alex Rodriguez/50	90.00
Ivan Rodriguez/50	40.00
Tim Salmon/40	40.00
Kazuhiro Sasaki/80	50.00
Alfonso Soriano/75	65.00
Larry Walker/60	40.00

2002 Fleer Focus Jersey Edition
NM/M
Complete Set (260): 60.00
Common Player: .15
Common (226-260): 1.00
Inserted 1:4
Pack (10): 2.00
Box (24): 40.00

1	Mike Piazza	1.50
2	Jason Giambi	.50
3	Jim Thome	.15
4	John Olerud	.15
5	J.D. Drew	.30
6	Richard Hidalgo	.15
7	Rusty Greer	.15
8	Tony Batista	.15
9	Omar Vizquel	.15
10	Randy Johnson	.75
11	Cristian Guzman	.15
12	Mark Grace	.25
13	Jeff Cirillo	.15
14	Mike Cameron	.15
15	Jeromy Burnitz	.15
16	Pokey Reese	.15
17	Richie Sexson	.15
18	Joe Randa	.15
19	Aramis Ramirez	.15
20	Pedro J. Martinez	.75
21	Todd Hollandsworth	.15
22	Rondell White	.15
23	Tsuyoshi Shinjo	.15
24	Melvin Mora	.15
25	Tim Hudson	.30
26	Darrin Fletcher	.15
27	Bill Mueller	.15
28	Jeff Weaver	.15
29	Tony Clark	.15
30	Tom Glavine	.40
31	Jarrod Washburn	.15
32	Greg Vaughn	.15
33	Lee Stevens	.15
34	Charles Johnson	.15
35	Lance Berkman	.15
36	Bud Smith	.15
37	Keith Foulke	.15
38	Ben Davis	.15
39	Daryle Ward	.15
40	Bernie Williams	.30
41	Dean Palmer	.15
42	Mark Mulder	.15
43	Jason LaRue	.15
44	Jay Gibbons	.15
45	Brandon Duckworth	.15
46	Carlos Delgado	.40
47	Barry Zito	.25
48	Matt Morris	.15
49	J.T. Snow	.15
50	Albert Pujols	1.50
51	Brad Fullmer	.15
52	Damion Easley	.15
53	Pat Burrell	.40
54	Kevin Brown	.15
55	Todd Walker	.15
56	Rich Garces	.15
57	Carlos Pena	.15
58	Paul LoDuca	.15
59	Mike Lieberthal	.15
60	Barry Larkin	.15
61	Jon Lieber	.15
62	Jose Cruz	.15
63	Mo Vaughn	.15
64	Ivan Rodriguez	.60
65	Jorge Posada	.25
66	Magglio Ordonez	.15
67	Juan Encarnacion	.15
68	Shawn Estes	.15
69	Kevin Appier	.15
70	Jeff Bagwell	.75
71	Tim Wakefield	.15
72	Shannon Stewart	.15
73	Scott Rolen	.65
74	Bobby Higginson	.15
75	Jim Edmonds	.15
76	Adam Dunn	.50
77	Eric Chavez	.30
78	Adrian Beltre	.30
79	Jason Varitek	.15
80	Barry Bonds	2.50
81	Edgar Renteria	.15
82	Raul Mondesi	.15
83	Eric Karros	.15
84	Ken Griffey Jr.	1.50
85	Jermaine Dye	.15
86	Carlos Beltran	.40
87	Mark Quinn	.15
88	Terrence Long	.15
89	Shawn Green	.40
90	Nomar Garciaparra	1.50
91	Sean Casey	.25
92	Homer Bush	.15
93	Bobby Abreu	.15
94	Jamey Wright	.15
95	Tony Womack	.15
96	Larry Walker	.15
97	Doug Mientkiewicz	.15
98	Jimmy Rollins	.40
99	Brady Anderson	.15
100	Derek Jeter	2.50
101	Kevin Young	.15
102	Juan Pierre	.15
103	Edgar Martinez	.15
104	Corey Koskie	.15
105	Jeffrey Hammonds	.15
106	Luis Gonzalez	.25
107	Travis Fryman	.15
108	Kerry Wood	.50
109	Rafael Palmeiro	.60
110	Ichiro Suzuki	1.00
111	Russ Ortiz	.15
112	Jeff Kent	.15
113	Scott Erickson	.15
114	Bruce Chen	.15
115	Craig Biggio	.15
116	Robin Ventura	.15
117	Alex Rodriguez	2.00
118	Roy Oswalt	.25
119	Fred McGriff	.15
120	Juan Gonzalez	.75
121	David Justice	.15
122	Pat Hentgen	.15
123	Hideo Nomo	.65
124	Ramon Ortiz	.15
125	David Ortiz	.25
126	Phil Nevin	.15
127	Ryan Dempster	.15
128	Toby Hall	.15
129	Vladimir Guerrero	.75
130	Chipper Jones	1.00
131	Russell Branyan	.15
132	Jose Vidro	.15
133	Bubba Trammell	.15
134	Tino Martinez	.15
135	Greg Maddux	1.00
136	Derek Lee	.15
137	Troy Glaus	.75
138	Joe Crede	.15
139	Steve Cox	.15
140	Sammy Sosa	1.50
141	Corey Patterson	.15
142	Vernon Wells	.15
143	Matt Lawton	.15
144	Gabe Kapler	.15
145	Johnny Damon	.25
146	Marty Cordova	.15
147	Moises Alou	.15
148	Fernando Tatis	.15
149	Tanyon Sturtze	.15
150	Roger Clemens	1.25
151	Paul Konerko	.15
152	Chan Ho Park	.15
153	Marcus Giles	.15
154	David Eckstein	.15
155	Mike Lowell	.15
156	Preston Wilson	.15
157	John Vander Wal	.15
158	Tim Salmon	.25
159	Andy Pettitte	.35
160	Mike Mussina	.40
161	Doug Davis	.15
162	Peter Bergeron	.15
163	Rich Aurilia	.15
164	Eric Milton	.15
165	Geoff Jenkins	.15
166	Todd Helton	.75
167	Bret Boone	.15
168	Kris Benson	.15
169	Brian Anderson	.15
170	Roberto Alomar	.40
171	Javier Vazquez	.15
172	Scott Schoeneweis	.15
173	Ryan Klesko	.15
174	Jacque Jones	.15
175	Andruw Jones	.75
176	Aubrey Huff	.15
177	Mark Buehrle	.15
178	Josh Beckett	.40
179	Ben Sheets	.15
180	Curt Schilling	.40
181	C.C. Sabathia	.15
182	Denny Neagle	.15
183	Jamie Moyer	.15
184	Jason Kendall	.15
185	Dee Brown	.15
186	Frank Thomas	.75
187	Damian Rolls	.15
188	Carlos Lee	.15
189	Kevin Jarvis	.15
190	Manny Ramirez	.75
191	Cliff Floyd	.15
192	Freddy Garcia	.15
193	Orlando Cabrera	.15
194	Mike Sweeney	.15
195	Gary Sheffield	.35
196	Rafael Furcal	.15
197	Esteban Loaiza	.15
198	Mike Hampton	.15
199	Brian Giles	.15
200	Darin Erstad	.60
201	David Wells	.15
202	Kenny Lofton	.15
203	Aaron Sele	.15
204	Jason Schmidt	.15
205	Javy Lopez	.15
206	Dmitri Young	.15
207	Darryl Kile	.15
208	Matt Williams	.15
209	Joe Kennedy	.15
210	Chuck Knoblauch	.15
211	Brian Jordan	.15
212	Roberto Person	.15
213	Alex Ochoa	.15
214	Steve Finley	.15
215	Ben Petrick	.15
216	Al Leiter	.15
217	Mark Kotsay	.15
218	Miguel Tejada	.35
219	David Segui	.15
220	A.J. Burnett	.15
221	Marlon Anderson	.15
222	Wiki Gonzalez	.15
223	Jeff Suppan	.15
224	Dave Roberts	.15
225	Jose Hernandez	.15
226	Angel Berroa	1.00
227	Sean Burroughs	1.00
228	Luis Martinez RC	1.00
229	Adrian Burnside RC	1.00
230	John Ennis RC	1.00
231	Anastacio Martinez RC	1.00
232	Hank Blalock	2.00
233	Eric Hinske	1.00
234	Chris Booker RC	1.00
235	Colin Young RC	1.00
236	Mark Corey RC	1.00
237	Satoru Komiyama RC	1.00
238	So Taguchi RC	2.50
239	Elio Serrano RC	1.00
240	Reed Johnson RC	2.00
241	Jeremy Lambert RC	1.00
242	Chris Baker RC	1.00
243	Orlando Hudson	1.00
244	Travis Hughes RC	1.00
245	Kevin Frederick RC	1.00
246	Rodrigo Rosario RC	1.00
247	Jeremy Ward RC	1.00
248	Kazuhisa Ishii RC	4.00
249	Austin Kearns	1.00
250	Kyle Kane RC	1.00
251	Cam Esslinger RC	1.00
252	Jeff Austin RC	1.00
253	Brian Mallette RC	1.00
254	Mark Prior	4.00
255	Mark Teixeira	2.00
256	Carlos Valderrama RC	1.00
257	Jason Hart	1.00
258	Takahito Nomura RC	1.00
259	Matt Thornton	1.00
260	Marlon Byrd	1.00

Century
Cards (1-225): 6-10X
Cards (226-260): .75-1.5X
Production 101-199

Jersey Number Parallel
(1-225) print run 26-50: 10-25X
(1-225) p/r 51-75: 8-15X
(1-225) p/r 76-99: 5-10X
Produced to player's jsy #.

Blue Chips

NM/M
Complete Set (15): 10.00
Common Player: .50
Inserted 1:6

1BC	Albert Pujols	3.00
2BC	Sean Burroughs	.50
3BC	Vernon Wells	.50
4BC	Adam Dunn	1.50
5BC	Pat Burrell	1.00
6BC	Juan Pierre	.50
7BC	Russell Branyan	.50
8BC	Carlos Pena	.50
9BC	Toby Hall	.50
10BC	Hank Blalock	1.00
11BC	Alfonso Soriano	1.50
12BC	Jimmy Rollins	.75
13BC	Jose Ortiz	.50
14BC	Eric Hinske	.50
15BC	Nick Johnson	.50

Blue Chips Game-Used
NM/M
Inserted 1:96 Hobby

Russell Branyan/Jsy	8.00
Nick Johnson/Jsy	10.00
Nick Johnson/Patch/100	20.00

International Diamond Co.

NM/M
Complete Set (25): 25.00
Common Player: 1.00
Inserted 1:8

1	Bobby Abreu	1.00
2	Adrian Beltre	1.00
3	Jorge Posada	1.00
4	Vladimir Guerrero	3.00
5	Rafael Palmeiro	2.00
6	Sammy Sosa	4.00
7	Larry Walker	1.00
8	Manny Ramirez	3.00
9	Ichiro Suzuki	4.00
10	Jose Cruz	1.00
11	Juan Gonzalez	3.00
12	Bernie Williams	1.00
13	Ivan Rodriguez	2.00
14	Moises Alou	1.00
15	Cristian Guzman	1.00
16	Andruw Jones	3.00
17	Aramis Ramirez	1.00
18	Raul Mondesi	1.00
19	Edgar Martinez	1.00
20	Magglio Ordonez	1.00
21	Roberto Alomar	1.50
22	Chan Ho Park	1.00
23	Kazuhiro Sasaki	1.00
24	Tsuyoshi Shinjo	1.00
25	Hideo Nomo	3.00

International Diamond Company Game-Used

NM/M
Common Player: 5.00
Inserted 1:144

Jorge Posada/Jsy	15.00
Rafael Palmeiro/Jsy	8.00
Manny Ramirez/Jsy	10.00
Ivan Rodriguez/Jsy	6.00
Andruw Jones/Jsy	6.00
Aramis Ramirez/Jsy	6.00
Raul Mondesi/Jsy	6.00
Edgar Martinez/Jsy	6.00
Chan Ho Park/Jsy	5.00
Kazuhiro Sasaki/Jsy	5.00
Hideo Nomo/Jsy	20.00

International Diamond Company Patch
NM/M
Common Player: 15.00
Production 100

Manny Ramirez	25.00
Ivan Rodriguez	25.00
Raul Mondesi	15.00
Edgar Martinez	20.00
Chan Ho Park	20.00
Hideo Nomo	75.00

K Corps

NM/M
Complete Set (15): 20.00
Common Player: 1.00
Inserted 1:12

1KC	Roger Clemens	5.00
2KC	Randy Johnson	3.00
3KC	Tom Glavine	1.50
4KC	Josh Beckett	1.50
5KC	Matt Morris	1.00
6KC	Curt Schilling	1.50
7KC	Greg Maddux	4.00
8KC	Tim Hudson	1.00
9KC	Roy Oswalt	1.00
10KC	Kerry Wood	2.00
11KC	Barry Zito	1.00
12KC	Kevin Brown	1.00
13KC	Ryan Dempster	1.00
14KC	Ben Sheets	1.00
15KC	Pedro J. Martinez	3.00

K Corps Game-Used
NM/M
Common Player: 5.00
Inserted 1:96

2KC	Randy Johnson/Jsy	15.00
6KC	Curt Schilling/Jsy	15.00
7KC	Greg Maddux/Jsy	15.00
11KC	Barry Zito/Jsy	8.00
12KC	Kevin Brown/Jsy	8.00
15KC	Pedro Martinez/Jsy	10.00

K Corps Patch
NM/M
Production 100

Curt Schilling	20.00
Kevin Brown	20.00
Pedro Martinez	30.00

Kings of Swing
NM/M
Complete Set (20): 80.00
Common Player: 2.00
Inserted 1:48

1KS	Barry Bonds	10.00
2KS	Mike Piazza	6.00
3KS	Albert Pujols	8.00
4KS	Todd Helton	3.00
5KS	Ken Griffey Jr.	6.00
6KS	Alex Rodriguez	8.00
7KS	Sammy Sosa	6.00
8KS	Troy Glaus	3.00
9KS	Derek Jeter	10.00
10KS	Ichiro Suzuki	8.00
11KS	Manny Ramirez	3.00
12KS	Roberto Alomar	2.00
13KS	Juan Gonzalez	3.00
14KS	Shawn Green	2.00
15KS	Vladimir Guerrero	3.00
16KS	Nomar Garciaparra	6.00
17KS	Adam Dunn	3.00
18KS	Jason Giambi	2.50
19KS	Edgar Martinez	2.00
20KS	Chipper Jones	4.00

Kings of Swing Game-Used
NM/M
Common Player: 5.00
Inserted 1:108

Mike Piazza	15.00
Todd Helton	8.00
Alex Rodriguez	15.00
Derek Jeter	30.00
Manny Ramirez	8.00
Shawn Green	5.00
Edgar Martinez	5.00
Chipper Jones	10.00

Kings of Swing Patch
NM/M
Production 100

Todd Helton	25.00
Manny Ramirez	25.00
Shawn Green	20.00
Edgar Martinez	25.00
Mike Piazza	40.00

Larger Than Life

NM/M
Common Player: 4.00
Inserted 1:240

1LL	Jason Giambi	6.00
2LL	Carlos Delgado	5.00
3LL	Alex Rodriguez	20.00
4LL	Preston Wilson	4.00
5LL	Frank Thomas	9.00
6LL	Nomar Garciaparra	15.00
7LL	Jim Edmonds	4.00
8LL	Jim Thome	4.00
9LL	Barry Bonds	25.00
10LL	Mo Vaughn	4.00
11LL	Ichiro Suzuki	20.00
12LL	Ivan Rodriguez	5.00
13LL	Gary Sheffield	4.00
14LL	Derek Jeter	25.00
15LL	Jeff Bagwell	9.00

16LL	Mike Piazza	15.00
17LL	J.D. Drew	4.00
18LL	Sammy Sosa	15.00
19LL	Albert Pujols	20.00
20LL	Luis Gonzalez	4.00

Larger Than Life Game-Used

NM/M

Common Player: 5.00
Inserted 1:144

Alex Rodriguez/Jsy	15.00
Preston Wilson/Jsy	5.00
Frank Thomas/Jsy	10.00
Jim Edmonds/Jsy	6.00
Mo Vaughn/Jsy	5.00
Ivan Rodriguez/Jsy	5.00
Derek Jeter/Jsy	25.00
Jeff Bagwell/Jsy/SP/20	25.00
Mike Piazza/Jsy	15.00
Luis Gonzalez/Jsy	5.00

Larger Than Life Patch

NM/M

Common Player: 15.00
Production 100

Preston Wilson	15.00
Frank Thomas	25.00
Jim Edmonds	15.00
Ivan Rodriguez	25.00
Mike Piazza	40.00
Luis Gonzalez	15.00

Lettermen

No Pricing
Production One Set

Materialistic Away

NM/M

Complete Set (15): 75.00
Common Player: 4.00
Inserted 1:24
Home: 1.5-3X
Production 50 Sets
Away Oversized: .5-1X
One per hobby box.
Home Oversized: 2-4X
Production 50 Sets

1MA	Derek Jeter	12.00
2MA	Alex Rodriguez	10.00
3MA	Mike Piazza	8.00
4MA	Ivan Rodriguez	4.00
5MA	Chipper Jones	6.00
6MA	Todd Helton	5.00
7MA	Nomar Garciaparra	8.00
8MA	Barry Bonds	12.00
9MA	Ichiro Suzuki	8.00
10MA	Ken Griffey Jr.	8.00
11MA	Jason Giambi	4.00
12MA	Sammy Sosa	8.00
13MA	Albert Pujols	10.00
14MA	Pedro J. Martinez	5.00
15MA	Vladimir Guerrero	5.00

2002 Fleer Genuine

NM/M

Complete Set (140):
Common Player: .15
Common (101-140): 3.00
Production 2,002
Pack (5): 3.00
Box (20): 50.00

1	Alex Rodriguez	2.50
2	Manny Ramirez	.75
3	Jim Thome	.15
4	Eric Milton	.15
5	Todd Helton	.75
6	Mike Mussina	.50
7	Ichiro Suzuki	1.50
8	Randy Johnson	1.00
9	Mark Mulder	.15
10	Johnny Damon	.25
11	Sean Casey	.25
12	Albert Pujols	2.50
13	Mark Grace	.25
14	Moises Alou, Mark Mulder	.15
15	Raul Mondesi, Roberto Alomar	.15
16	Cliff Floyd, Scott Rolen	.30
17	Vladimir Guerrero, Tom Glavine	.40
18	Pat Burrell, Bobby Abreu	.25
19	Ryan Klesko, Nomar Garciaparra	.50
20	Mike Hampton, Darin Erstad	.15
21	Shawn Green, Cliff Floyd	.15
22	Rich Aurilia, Tim Hudson	.15
23	Matt Morris, Jim Thome	.15
24	Curt Schilling, Nolan Ryan	1.00
25	Kevin Brown, Reggie Jackson	.25
26	Adrian Beltre, Rafael Palmeiro	.30
27	Joe Mays, Ken Griffey Jr.	.75
28	Luis Gonzalez, Sammy Sosa	.75
29	Barry Larkin, Vladimir Guerrero	.40
30	A.J. Burnett, Ichiro Suzuki	.75
31	Eric Munson	.15
32	Juan Gonzalez	.75
33	Lance Berkman	.15
34	Fred McGriff	.15
35	Paul Konerko	.15
36	Pedro J. Martinez	.75
37	Adam Dunn	.50
38	Jeromy Burnitz	.15
39	Mike Sweeney	.15
40	Bret Boone	.15
41	Ken Griffey Jr.	2.00
42	Eric Chavez	.25
43	Mark Quinn	.15
44	Roberto Alomar	.35
45	Bobby Abreu	.15
46	Bartolo Colon	.15
47	Jimmy Rollins	.25
48	Chipper Jones	1.00
49	Ben Sheets	.15
50	Freddy Garcia	.15
51	Sammy Sosa	2.00
52	Rafael Palmeiro	.65
53	Preston Wilson	.15
54	Troy Glaus	.75
55	Josh Beckett	.15
56	C.C. Sabathia	.15
57	Magglio Ordonez	.15
58	Brian Giles	.15
59	Darin Erstad	.15
60	Gary Sheffield	.35
61	Paul LoDuca	.15
62	Derek Jeter	3.00
63	Greg Maddux	1.50
64	Kerry Wood	.65
65	Toby Hall	.15
66	Barry Bonds	3.00
67	Jeff Bagwell	.75
68	Jason Kendall	.15
69	Richard Hidalgo	.15
70	J.D. Drew	.30
71	Tom Glavine	.25
72	Javier Vazquez	.15
73	Doug Mientkiewicz	.15
74	Jason Giambi	.50
75	Carlos Delgado	.40
76	Aramis Ramirez	.15
77	Torii Hunter	.15
78	Ivan Rodriguez	.65
79	Charles Johnson	.15
80	Jeff Kent	.15
81	Jacque Jones	.15
82	Larry Walker	.15
83	Cristian Guzman	.15
84	Jermaine Dye	.15
85	Roger Clemens	1.75
86	Mike Piazza	2.00
87	Craig Biggio	.15
88	Phil Nevin	.15
89	Jeff Cirillo	.15
90	Barry Zito	.25
91	Ryan Dempster	.15
92	Mark Buehrle	.15
93	Nomar Garciaparra	2.00
94	Frank Thomas	.75
95	Jim Edmonds	.15
96	Geoff Jenkins	.15
97	Scott Rolen	.65
98	Tim Hudson	.25
99	Shannon Stewart	.15
100	Richie Sexson	.15
101	Orlando Hudson	3.00
102	Doug DeVore RC	3.00
103	Rene Reyes RC	3.00
104	Steve Bechler RC	4.00
105	Jorge Nunez RC	3.00
106	Mitch Wylie RC	3.00
107	Jaime Cerda RC	3.00
108	Brandon Puffer RC	3.00
109	Tyler Yates RC	6.00
110	Bill Hall	3.00
111	Peter Zamora RC	3.00
112	Jeff Deardorff RC	3.00
113	J.J. Putz RC	3.00
114	Scotty Layfield RC	3.00
115	Brandon Backe RC	3.00
116	Andy Pratt RC	3.00
117	Mark Prior	3.00
118	Franklyn German RC	3.00
119	Todd Donovan RC	3.00
120	Franklin Nunez RC	3.00
121	Adam Walker RC	3.00
122	Ron Calloway RC	3.00
123	Tim Kalita RC	3.00
124	Kazuhisa Ishii RC	5.00
125	Mark Teixeira RC	5.00
126	Nate Field RC	3.00
127	Nelson Castro RC	3.00
128	So Taguchi RC	8.00
129	Marlon Byrd RC	3.00
130	Drew Henson	3.00
131	Kenny Kelly	3.00
132	John Ennis RC	3.00
133	Anastacio Martinez RC	3.00
134	Matt Guerrier	3.00
135	Tom Wilson RC	3.00
136	Ben Howard RC	4.00
137	Chris Baker RC	3.00
138	Kevin Frederick RC	3.00
159	Wilson Valdez RC	3.00
140	Austin Kearns	4.00

Bat's Incredible

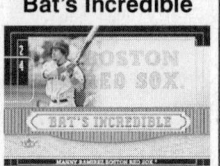

NM/M

Complete Set (25): 60.00
Common Player: 1.50
Inserted 1:10

1BI	Todd Helton	2.00
2BI	Chipper Jones	3.00
3BI	Luis Gonzalez	1.50
4BI	Barry Bonds	8.00
5BI	Jason Giambi	2.00
6BI	Alex Rodriguez	6.00
7BI	Manny Ramirez	2.00
8BI	Jeff Bagwell	2.00
9BI	Shawn Green	1.50
10BI	Albert Pujols	6.00
11BI	Paul LoDuca	1.50
12BI	Mike Piazza	5.00
13BI	Derek Jeter	8.00
14BI	Edgar Martinez	1.50
15BI	Juan Gonzalez	2.00
16BI	Magglio Ordonez	1.50
17BI	Jermaine Dye	1.50
18BI	Larry Walker	1.50
19BI	Phil Nevin	1.50
20BI	Ivan Rodriguez	1.50
21BI	Ichiro Suzuki	5.00
22BI	J.D. Drew	1.50
23BI	Vladimir Guerrero	2.00
24BI	Sammy Sosa	5.00
25BI	Ken Griffey Jr.	5.00

Bat's Incredible Game-Used

NM/M

Common Player: 5.00
Inserted 1:20

Todd Helton	10.00
Chipper Jones	10.00
J.D. Drew	8.00
Alex Rodriguez	15.00
Manny Ramirez	10.00
Shawn Green	6.00
Derek Jeter	20.00
Edgar Martinez	8.00
Juan Gonzalez	8.00
Jermaine Dye	5.00
Phil Nevin	5.00
Ivan Rodriguez	10.00

Genuine Ink

Common Autograph: 15.00
Production Varies

Barry Bonds/150	150.00
Ron Cey/175	15.00
Derek Jeter/200	125.00
Al Kaline/300	60.00
Don Mattingly/50	100.00
Paul Molitor	50.00
Dale Murphy/700	40.00
Phil Rizzuto/700	30.00
Brooks Robinson/140	
Maury Willis/975	15.00

Leaders

NM/M

Complete Set (15): 25.00
Common Player: 1.00
Inserted 1:6

1GL	Sammy Sosa	4.00
2GL	Todd Helton	2.00
3GL	Alex Rodriguez	4.00
4GL	Roger Clemens	3.00
5GL	Barry Bonds	5.00
6GL	Randy Johnson	2.00
7GL	Albert Pujols	4.00
8GL	Curt Schilling	1.00
9GL	Bernie Williams	1.00
10GL	Ken Griffey Jr.	2.00
11GL	Pedro J. Martinez	2.00
12GL	Juan Gonzalez	2.00
13GL	Hideo Nomo	1.50
14GL	Bret Boone	1.00
15GL	Ichiro Suzuki	5.00

Leaders Game-Used

NM/M

Common Player: 8.00
Inserted 1:16

Todd Helton	10.00
Alex Rodriguez	15.00
Roger Clemens	15.00
Barry Bonds	20.00
Randy Johnson	10.00
Curt Schilling	8.00
Bernie Williams	8.00
Pedro J. Martinez	8.00
Hideo Nomo	15.00

Names of the Game

NM/M

Complete Set (30): 60.00
Common Player: 1.00
Inserted 1:10 H, 1:20 R

1	Mike Piazza	5.00
2	Chipper Jones	4.00
3	Jim Edmonds	1.00
4	Barry Larkin	1.00
5	Frank Thomas	3.00
6	Manny Ramirez	3.00
7	Carlos Delgado	1.50
8	Brian Giles	1.00
9	Kerry Wood	2.00
10	Derek Jeter	8.00
11	Adam Dunn	2.00
12	Gary Sheffield	1.50
13	Luis Gonzalez	1.00
14	Mark Mulder	1.00
15	Roberto Alomar	1.50
16	Scott Rolen	2.50
17	Tom Glavine	1.50
18	Bobby Abreu	1.00
19	Nomar Garciaparra	5.00
20	Darin Erstad	2.00
21	Cliff Floyd	1.00
22	Tim Hudson	1.00
23	Jim Thome	1.00
24	Nolan Ryan	8.00
25	Reggie Jackson	3.00
26	Rafael Palmeiro	2.00
27	Ken Griffey Jr.	5.00
28	Sammy Sosa	5.00
29	Vladimir Guerrero	3.00
30	Ichiro Suzuki	5.00

Names of the Game Memorabilia

NM/M

Common Player: 5.00
1:24 H, 1:100 R

1	Roberto Alomar	10.00
2	Carlos Delgado	8.00
3	Jim Edmonds	8.00
4	Darin Erstad	5.00
5	Cliff Floyd	5.00
6	Nomar Garciaparra/SP/90	60.00
7	Brian Giles	5.00
8	Luis Gonzalez	5.00
9	Tim Hudson	5.00
10	Derek Jeter	30.00
11	Chipper Jones	10.00
12	Barry Larkin	8.00
13	Mark Mulder	8.00
14	Rafael Palmeiro	8.00
15	Mike Piazza	15.00
16	Manny Ramirez	8.00
17	Scott Rolen	10.00
18	Nolan Ryan	40.00
19	Jim Thome	10.00

Tip of the Cap

NM/M

Complete Set (25): 40.00
Common Player: .50
Inserted 1:6

1TC	Alex Rodriguez	6.00
2TC	Derek Jeter	8.00
3TC	Kazuhiro Sasaki	.50
4TC	Barry Bonds	8.00
5TC	J.D. Drew	.75
6TC	Tsuyoshi Shinjo	.50
7TC	Alfonso Soriano	1.50
8TC	Albert Pujols	6.00
9TC	Tom Seaver	1.50
10TC	Drew Henson	.75
11TC	Dave Winfield	1.50
12TC	Carlos Delgado	1.00
13TC	Lou Boudreau	.50
14TC	Shawn Green	.75
15TC	Roger Clemens	3.00
16TC	Randy Johnson	1.50
17TC	Sammy Sosa	4.00
18TC	Rafael Palmeiro	1.25
19TC	Ken Griffey Jr.	5.00
20TC	Ichiro Suzuki	5.00
21TC	Eric Chavez	.65
22TC	Andruw Jones	1.50
23TC	Miguel Tejada	.65
24TC	Pedro J. Martinez	1.50
25TC	Tim Salmon	.50

Tip of the Cap Game-Used

NM/M

Common Player:

Alex Rodriguez/670	20.00
Barry Bonds/32	75.00
Tom Seaver/224	25.00
Drew Henson/361	15.00
Dave Winfield/363	15.00
Carlos Delgado/219	15.00
Lou Boudreau/303	15.00
Randy Johnson/74	30.00
Rafael Palmeiro/300	20.00
Andruw Jones/19	40.00
Miguel Tejada/225	15.00

Touch 'Em All

NM/M

Complete Set (25): 60.00
Common Player: 1.50
Inserted 1:10

1	Derek Jeter	8.00
2	Sammy Sosa	5.00
3	Albert Pujols	6.00
4	Vladimir Guerrero	3.00
5	Ken Griffey Jr.	5.00
6	Nomar Garciaparra	5.00
7	Luis Gonzalez	1.50
8	Barry Bonds	8.00
9	Manny Ramirez	2.50
10	Jason Giambi	2.00
11	Chipper Jones	4.00
12	Ichiro Suzuki	5.00
13	Alex Rodriguez	6.00
14	Juan Gonzalez	2.50
15	Todd Helton	2.50
16	Roberto Alomar	1.50
17	Jeff Bagwell	2.50
18	Mike Piazza	5.00
19	Gary Sheffield	1.50
20	Ivan Rodriguez	2.00
21	Frank Thomas	2.50
22	Bobby Abreu	1.50
23	J.D. Drew	1.50
24	Scott Rolen	2.00
25	Darin Erstad	1.50

Touch 'Em All Base

NM/M

Common Player: 4.00
Production 350 Sets

Derek Jeter	15.00
Sammy Sosa	10.00
Albert Pujols	15.00
Vladimir Guerrero	10.00
Ken Griffey Jr.	10.00
Nomar Garciaparra	10.00
Luis Gonzalez	8.00
Barry Bonds	15.00
Manny Ramirez	8.00
Jason Giambi	8.00
Chipper Jones	8.00
Ichiro Suzuki	15.00
Alex Rodriguez	8.00
Juan Gonzalez	8.00
Todd Helton	8.00
Roberto Alomar	8.00
Jeff Bagwell	8.00
Mike Piazza	10.00
Gary Sheffield	6.00
Ivan Rodriguez	8.00
Frank Thomas	8.00

ABBREVIATIONS

SP - Short Print

Bobby Abreu	4.00
J.D. Drew	4.00
Scott Rolen	8.00
Darin Erstad	8.00

2002 Fleer Greats of the Game

		NM/M
Complete Set (100):		45.00
Common Player:		.40
Pack (5):		5.00
Box (24):		100.00
1	Cal Ripken Jr.	6.00
2	Paul Molitor	1.50
3	Roberto Clemente	4.00
4	Cy Young	1.50
5	Tris Speaker	.75
6	Lou Brock	.50
7	Fred Lynn	.40
8	Harmon Killebrew	1.50
9	Ted Williams	6.00
10	Dave Winfield	1.00
11	Orlando Cepeda	.40
12	Johnny Mize	.40
13	Walter Johnson	1.50
14	Roy Campanella	1.50
15	George Sisler	.40
16	Bo Jackson	1.00
17	Rollie Fingers	.40
18	Brooks Robinson	1.50
19	Billy Williams	.40
20	Maury Wills	.40
21	Jimmie Foxx	1.50
22	Alan Trammell	.40
23	Rogers Hornsby	1.50
24	Don Drysdale	1.00
25	Bob Feller	.75
26	Jackie Robinson	5.00
27	Whitey Ford	1.50
28	Enos Slaughter	.40
29	Rod Carew	1.00
30	Eddie Mathews	1.50
31	Ron Cey	.40
32	Thurman Munson	2.00
33	Ty Cobb	3.00
34	Rocky Colavito	.75
35	Satchel Paige	1.50
36	Andre Dawson	.75
37	Phil Rizzuto	.75
38	Roger Maris	3.00
39	Earl Weaver	.40
40	Joe Carter	.40
41	Christy Mathewson	1.50
42	Tony Lazzeri	.40
43	Gil Hodges	.75
44	Gaylord Perry	.40
45	Steve Carlton	1.00
46	George Kell	.40
47	Mickey Cochrane	1.00
48	Joe Morgan	.60
49	Steve Garvey	.40
50	Bob Gibson	1.50
51	Lefty Grove	.40
52	Warren Spahn	1.50
53	Willie McCovey	.75
54	Frank Robinson	1.50
55	Rich "Goose" Gossage	.40
56	Hank Bauer	.40
57	Hoyt Wilhelm	.40
58	Mel Ott	1.00
59	Preacher Roe	.75
60	Yogi Berra	1.50
61	Nolan Ryan	6.00
62	Dizzy Dean	.75
63	Ryne Sandberg	2.00
64	Frank Howard	.40
65	Hack Wilson	.40
66	Robin Yount	1.50
67	Al Kaline	1.50
68	Mike Schmidt	2.00
69	Vida Blue	.40
70	George Brett	3.00
71	Sparky Anderson	.40
72	Tom Seaver	1.50
73	Bill "Moose" Skowron	.40
74	Don Mattingly	2.50
75	Carl Yastrzemski	1.50
76	Eddie Murray	1.00
77	Jim Palmer	1.00
78	Bill Dickey	.75
79	Ozzie Smith	1.50
80	Dale Murphy	1.00
81	Nap Lajoie	1.00
82	Jim "Catfish" Hunter	1.00
83	Duke Snider	1.00
84	Luis Aparicio	.40
85	Reggie Jackson	1.50

86	Honus Wagner	1.50
87	Johnny Bench	2.00
88	Stan Musial	3.00
89	Carlton Fisk	.75
90	Tony Oliva	.75
91	Wade Boggs	2.00
92	Jim Rice	.40
93	Bill Mazeroski	.40
94	Ralph Kiner	.40
95	Tony Perez	.40
96	Kirby Puckett	2.00
97	Bobby Bonds	.75
98	Bill Terry	.40
99	Juan Marichal	.75
100	Hank Greenberg	1.00

Autographs

		NM/M
Common Autograph:		10.00
Inserted 1:24		
SA	Sparky Anderson	15.00
LA	Luis Aparicio	15.00
HB	Hank Bauer	10.00
JB	Johnny Bench	50.00
YB	Yogi Berra	40.00
PB	Paul Blair	10.00
VB	Vida Blue	15.00
WB	Wade Boggs	20.00
BB	Bobby Bonds	15.00
GB	George Brett/150	125.00
LB	Lou Brock/250	25.00
RC	Rod Carew/250	40.00
SC	Steve Carlton	25.00
JC	Joe Carter	15.00
OC	Orlando Cepeda	15.00
CE	Ron Cey	10.00
CO	Rocky Colavito	35.00
AD	Andre Dawson	15.00
BF	Bob Feller	15.00
RF	Rollie Fingers	15.00
CF	Carlton Fisk/100	65.00
WF	Whitey Ford	40.00
SG	Steve Garvey	15.00
BG	Bob Gibson/200	30.00
RG	Rich "Goose" Gossage	10.00
FH	Frank Howard	15.00
RJ	Reggie Jackson/150	70.00
AK	Al Kaline	40.00
GK	George Kell	15.00
HK	Harmon Killebrew	30.00
RK	Ralph Kiner/250	25.00
FL	Fred Lynn	15.00
JM	Juan Marichal	15.00
DM	Don Mattingly/300	75.00
BM	Bill Mazeroski/200	20.00
WM	Willie McCovey	25.00
PM	Paul Molitor	25.00
JM	Joe Morgan	15.00
MU	Dale Murphy	40.00
EM	Eddie Murray/250	70.00
SM	Stan Musial/200	75.00
TO	Tony Oliva	15.00
JP	Jim Palmer	20.00
DP	Dave Parker	10.00
TP	Tony Perez	15.00
GP	Gaylord Perry/4	60.00
KP	Kirby Puckett/250	75.00
JR	Jim Rice	15.00
CR	Cal Ripken Jr./100	180.00
PR	Phil Rizzuto/300	50.00
BR	Brooks Robinson	30.00
FR	Frank Robinson/250	30.00
PR	Preacher Roe	15.00
NR	Nolan Ryan/150	100.00
RS	Ryne Sandberg/200	75.00
MS	Mike Schmidt/150	100.00
TS	Tom Seaver/150	50.00
BS	Bill "Moose" Skowron	15.00
ES	Enos Slaughter	15.00
OS	Ozzie Smith/300	65.00
DS	Duke Snider	25.00
WS	Warren Spahn	50.00
AT	Alan Trammell	20.00
HW	Hoyt Wilhelm	15.00
BW	Billy Williams	15.00
MW	Maury Wills	15.00
DW	Dave Winfield/250	25.00
CY	Carl Yastrzemski/200	75.00
RY	Robin Yount	70.00

Dueling Duos

		NM/M
Complete Set (29):		90.00
Common Player:		2.00

Inserted 1:6		
1DD	Johnny Bench, Carlton Fisk	4.00
2DD	Roy Campanella, Yogi Berra	5.00
3DD	Stan Musial, Ted Williams	8.00
4DD	Carl Yastrzemski, Reggie Jackson	3.00
5DD	Babe Ruth, Jimmie Foxx	8.00
6DD	Steve Carlton, Nolan Ryan	8.00
7DD	Wade Boggs, Don Mattingly	6.00
8DD	Brooks Robinson, Roger Maris	5.00
9DD	Paul Molitor, Don Mattingly	6.00
10DD	Sparky Anderson, Earl Weaver	2.00
11DD	Bob Gibson, Duke Snider	3.00
12DD	Yogi Berra, Gil Hodges	4.00
13DD	Joe Morgan, Ryne Sandberg	3.00
14DD	Tony Perez, Carl Yastrzemski	3.00
15DD	Jimmie Foxx, Bill Dickey	3.00
16DD	Ralph Kiner, Duke Snider	2.00
17DD	Nellie Fox, Rocky Colavito	2.00
18DD	Willie McCovey, Johnny Bench	3.00
19DD	Duke Snider, Eddie Mathews	4.00
20DD	Reggie Jackson, Jim Rice	3.00
21DD	Eddie Murray, Jim Rice	2.00
22DD	Paul Molitor, Dave Winfield	3.00
23DD	Robin Yount, Dave Winfield	3.00
24DD	Enos Slaughter, Ted Kluszewski	2.00
25DD	Wade Boggs, George Brett	4.00
26DD	George Brett, Eddie Murray	4.00
27DD	George Brett, Cal Ripken Jr.	8.00
28DD	Kirby Puckett, Don Mattingly	6.00
29DD	George Brett, Mike Schmidt	5.00

Dueling Duos Autograph

No Pricing	
Production 25 Sets	

Dueling Duos G-U Single

		NM/M
Common Card:		15.00
Inserted 1:24		
	Johnny Bench, Carlton Fisk	20.00
	Roy Campanella, Yogi Berra	25.00
	Carl Yastrzemski, Reggie Jackson	25.00
	Babe Ruth, Jimmie Foxx/75	50.00
	Kirby Puckett, Don Mattingly	25.00
	Steve Carlton, Nolan Ryan	80.00
	Wade Boggs, Don Mattingly	25.00
	Brooks Robinson, Roger Maris	25.00
	Paul Molitor, Don Mattingly	25.00
	Sparky Anderson, Earl Weaver	10.00
	Bob Gibson, Duke Snider/200	20.00
	Yogi Berra, Gil Hodges	25.00

	Joe Morgan, Ryne Sandberg	25.00
	Tony Perez, Carl Yastrzemski	25.00
	Jimmie Foxx, Bill Dickey	20.00
	Ralph Kiner, Duke Snider	20.00
	Nellie Fox, Rocky Colavito	20.00
	Willie McCovey, Johnny Bench	25.00
	Duke Snider, Eddie Mathews	20.00
	Eddie Murray, Jim Rice	15.00
	Paul Molitor, Dave Winfield	15.00
	Robin Yount, Dave Winfield	15.00
	Enos Slaughter, Ted Kluszewski	10.00
	Wade Boggs, George Brett	25.00
	George Brett, Eddie Murray	20.00
	George Brett, Cal Ripken Jr.	40.00
	Eddie Murray, George Brett, Cal Ripken Jr.	40.00

Dueling Duos Game-Used Dual

No Pricing	
Production 25 Sets	

Through the Years Level 1

		NM/M
Common Player:		10.00
Inserted 1:24		
	George Brett	25.00
	Reggie Jackson/A's	15.00
	Reggie Jackson/ Angels	15.00
	Ted Williams/350	100.00
	Robin Yount	20.00
	Willie McCovey	10.00
	Paul Molitor/Brewers	15.00
	Paul Molitor/ Blue Jays	15.00
	Jim Palmer	10.00
	Brooks Robinson	15.00
	Carl Yastrzemski	25.00
	Don Mattingly	25.00
	Carlton Fisk/Htg	15.00
	Carlton Fisk/Fld	15.00
	Nolan Ryan	40.00
	Eddie Murray	10.00
	Wade Boggs	10.00
	Tony Perez	10.00
	Ted Kluszewski	10.00
	Bo Jackson/Royals	15.00
	Bo Jackson/ White Sox	15.00
	Johnny Bench	20.00
	Jackie Robinson	65.00
	Hoyt Wilhelm	10.00
	Vida Blue	10.00
	Dave Winfield	10.00
	Frank Robinson	15.00
	Jim Rice	10.00
	Jim Rice	10.00
	Cal Ripken Hitting	40.00
	Cal Ripken Fielding	40.00

Through the Years Level 2

		NM/M
Common Player:		25.00
Production 100 Sets		
	George Brett	80.00
	Reggie Jackson	30.00
	Ted Williams	120.00
	Robin Yount	40.00
	Willie McCovey	30.00
	Paul Molitor	40.00
	Jim Palmer	25.00
	Carl Yastrzemski	65.00
	Don Mattingly	60.00
	Carlton Fisk	30.00
	Nolan Ryan	75.00
	Eddie Murray	25.00
	Wade Boggs	30.00
	Ted Kluszewski	30.00
	Bo Jackson/Royals	30.00
	Bo Jackson/ White Sox	30.00
	Johnny Bench	40.00
	Dave Winfield	30.00
	Jim Rice	25.00
	Jim Rice	25.00
	Cal Ripken Jr.	60.00
	Cal Ripken Jr.	60.00

	Joe Morgan, Ryne Sandberg	25.00
	Tony Perez, Carl Yastrzemski	25.00
	Jimmie Foxx, Bill Dickey	20.00
	Ralph Kiner, Duke Snider	20.00
	Nellie Fox, Rocky Colavito	20.00
	Willie McCovey, Johnny Bench	25.00
	Duke Snider, Eddie Mathews	20.00
	Reggie Jackson, Jim Rice	20.00
	Eddie Murray, Jim Rice	15.00
	Paul Molitor, Dave Winfield	15.00
	Robin Yount, Dave Winfield	15.00
	Enos Slaughter, Ted Kluszewski	10.00
	Wade Boggs, George Brett	25.00
	George Brett, Eddie Murray	20.00
	George Brett, Eddie Murray	20.00

Through the Years Level 3

No Pricing	
Production 25 Sets	

Through Years Patch Edition

		NM/M
Common Player:		25.00
Production 100 Sets		
	George Brett	80.00
	Reggie Jackson/A's	30.00
	Reggie Jackson/ Angels	30.00
	Ted Williams	120.00
	Robin Yount	50.00
	Willie McCovey	30.00
	Paul Molitor/Brewers	40.00
	Paul Molitor/ Blue Jays	40.00
	Jim Palmer	25.00
	Carl Yastrzemski	75.00
	Don Mattingly	60.00
	Carlton Fisk	30.00
	Nolan Ryan	75.00
	Eddie Murray	30.00
	Wade Boggs	30.00
	Tony Perez	25.00
	Ted Kluszewski	30.00
	Bo Jackson/Royals	40.00
	Bo Jackson/ White Sox	40.00
	Johnny Bench	40.00
	Dave Winfield	30.00
	Frank Robinson	30.00
	Jim Rice	25.00
	Jim Rice	25.00
	Cal Ripken Jr.	80.00
	Cal Ripken Jr.	80.00

2002 Fleer Hot Prospects

		NM/M
Complete Set (125):		
Common Player:		.25
Common (81-105):		8.00
Production 1,000		
Common (106-125):		3.00
Production 1,500		
Pack (5):		4.00
Box (18):		50.00
1	Derek Jeter	3.00
2	Garret Anderson	.25
3	Scott Rolen	.75
4	Bret Boone	.25
5	Lance Berkman	.25
6	Andruw Jones	1.00
7	Ivan Rodriguez	.75
8	Bernie Williams	.35
9	Cristian Guzman	.25
10	Mo Vaughn	.25
11	Troy Glaus	1.00
12	Tim Salmon	.35
13	Jason Giambi	.65
14	Cliff Floyd	.25
15	Tim Hudson	.35
16	Curt Schilling	.40
17	Sammy Sosa	2.00
18	Alex Rodriguez	2.50
19	Chuck Knoblauch	.25
20	Jason Kendall	.25
21	Ben Sheets	.25
22	Nomar Garciaparra	2.00
23	Ryan Klesko	.25
24	Greg Vaughn	.25
25	Rafael Palmeiro	.75
26	Miguel Tejada	.35
27	Shea Hillenbrand	.25
28	Jim Thome	.25
29	Randy Johnson	1.00
30	Barry Larkin	.25
31	Paul LoDuca	.25
32	Pedro J. Martinez	1.00
33	Luis Gonzalez	.35
34	Carlos Delgado	.50
35	Richie Sexson	.25
36	Albert Pujols	2.25
37	Bobby Abreu	.25
38	Gary Sheffield	.40
39	Magglio Ordonez	.25
40	Eric Chavez	.35
41	Jeff Bagwell	1.00
42	Doug Mientkiewicz	.25
43	Moises Alou	.25

44	Todd Helton	1.00
45	Ichiro Suzuki	2.00
46	Jose Cruz Jr.	.25
47	Freddy Garcia	.25
48	Tino Martinez	.25
49	Roger Clemens	1.75
50	Greg Maddux	1.50
51	Mike Piazza	2.00
52	Roberto Alomar	.50
53	Adam Dunn	.50
54	Kerry Wood	.75
55	Edgar Martinez	.25
56	Ken Griffey Jr.	2.00
57	Juan Gonzalez	1.00
58	Pat Burrell	.50
59	Corey Koskie	.25
60	Jose Vidro	.25
61	Ben Grieve	.25
62	Barry Bonds	3.00
63	Raul Mondesi	.25
64	Jimmy Rollins	.50
65	Mike Sweeney	.25
66	Josh Beckett	.25
67	Chipper Jones	1.50
68	Jeff Kent	.25
69	Tony Batista	.25
70	Phil Nevin	.25
71	Brian Jordan	.25
72	Rich Aurilia	.25
73	Brian Giles	.25
74	Frank Thomas	1.00
75	Larry Walker	.25
76	Shawn Green	.40
77	Manny Ramirez	1.00
78	Craig Biggio	.25
79	Vladimir Guerrero	1.00
80	Jeromy Burnitz	.25
81	Mark Teixeira	10.00
82	Corey Thurman **RC**	8.00
83	Mark Prior	15.00
84	Marlon Byrd	8.00
85	Austin Kearns	10.00
86	Satoru Komiyama **RC**	8.00
87	So Taguchi **RC**	12.00
88	Jorge Padilla **RC**	8.00
89	Rene Reyes **RC**	8.00
90	Jorge Nunez **RC**	8.00
91	Ron Calloway **RC**	8.00
92	Kazuhisa Ishii **RC**	10.00
93	Dewon Brazelton	8.00
94	Angel Berroa	8.00
95	Felix Escalona **RC**	8.00
96	Sean Burroughs	8.00
97	Brandon Duckworth	8.00
98	Hank Blalock	10.00
99	Eric Hinske	8.00
100	Carlos Pena	8.00
101	Morgan Ensberg	8.00
102	Ryan Ludwick	8.00
103	Chris Snelling **RC**	8.00
104	Jason Lane	8.00
105	Drew Henson	10.00
106	Bobby Kielty	3.00
107	Earl Snyder **RC**	3.00
108	Nate Field **RC**	3.00
109	Juan Diaz	3.00
110	Ryan Anderson	3.00
111	Esteban German	3.00
112	Takahito Nomura **RC**	3.00
113	David Kelton	3.00
114	Steve Kent **RC**	3.00
115	Colby Lewis	3.00
116	Jason Simontacchi **RC**	3.00
117	Rodrigo Rosario **RC**	3.00
118	Ben Howard **RC**	3.00
119	Hansel Izquierdo **RC**	3.00
120	John Ennis **RC**	3.00
121	Anderson Machado **RC**	3.00
122	Luis Ugueto **RC**	3.00
123	Anastacio Martinez **RC**	3.00
124	Reed Johnson **RC**	6.00
125	Juan Cruz	3.00

Co-Stars

		NM/M
Complete Set (15):		25.00
Common Card:		1.00
Inserted 1:6		
1CS	Barry Bonds, Alex Rodriguez	6.00
2CS	Derek Jeter, Nomar Garciaparra	5.00
3CS	Andruw Jones, Chipper Jones	3.00
4CS	Juan Gonzalez, Jim Thome	2.00

5CS	Pedro J. Martinez, Randy Johnson	2.00
6CS	Adam Dunn, Pat Burrell	1.50
7CS	Frank Thomas, Manny Ramirez	2.00
8CS	Jeff Bagwell, Lance Berkman	2.00
9CS	So Taguchi, Kazuhisa Ishii	4.00
10CS	Jimmy Rollins, Miguel Tejada	2.00
11CS	Morgan Ensberg, Carlos Pena	1.00
12CS	Adam Dunn, Austin Kearns	2.00
13CS	Vladimir Guerrero, Scott Rolen	3.00
14CS	Drew Henson, Xavier Nady	1.00
15CS	Mike Piazza, Ivan Rodriguez	4.00

Future Swatch Autograph
NM/M

Common Auto.
Production 100

83	Mark Prior	40.00
87	So Taguchi	20.00
89	Rene Reyes	10.00
105	Drew Henson	20.00

Inside Barry Bonds
NM/M

Common Bonds: 15.00

1BB	Barry Bonds/Pants/1,000	20.00
2BB	Barry Bonds/Pants/900	20.00
3BB	Barry Bonds/Jsy/800	20.00
4BB	Barry Bonds/Bat/700	20.00
5BB	Barry Bonds/Base/600	15.00
6BB	Barry Bonds/Cleat/500	25.00
7BB	Barry Bonds/Glv/400	25.00
8BB	Barry Bonds/Cap/300	30.00

Jerseygraphs
NM/M

Common Player: 10.00
Inserted 1:186

DJ	Derek Jeter/108	150.00
BB	Barry Bonds/65	250.00
CJ	Chipper Jones/100	80.00
DH	Drew Henson	30.00
ST	So Taguchi/100	25.00
DE	David Espinosa	10.00
DS	Dane Sardinha	10.00
AB	Adrian Beltre/169	35.00

MLB Hot Materials
NM/M

Common Player: 5.00
Inserted 1:9
Red Hots: 1-2X
Production 50 Sets

AD	Adam Dunn	8.00
AR	Alex Rodriguez	10.00
BB	Bret Boone	5.00
BB2	Barry Bonds	20.00
BD	Brandon Duckworth	5.00
BG	Brian Giles	5.00
BW	Bernie Williams	8.00
CD	Carlos Delgado	5.00
CG	Cristian Guzman	5.00
CP	Carlos Pena	6.00
CP	Corey Patterson	6.00
CS	Curt Schilling	5.00
FT	Frank Thomas	10.00
GK	Gabe Kapler	5.00
GM	Greg Maddux	15.00
GS	Gary Sheffield	6.00
IR	Ivan Rodriguez	10.00
JB	Josh Beckett	8.00
JB2	Jeff Bagwell/108	20.00
JG	Juan Gonzalez	8.00
JT	Jim Thome	10.00
JU	Juan Uribe	8.00
LB	Lance Berkman	8.00
MM	Mark Mulder	8.00
MA	Moises Alou	6.00
MP	Mike Piazza	15.00
MS	Mike Sweeney	5.00
NJ	Nick Johnson	5.00
PL	Paul LoDuca	5.00
PM	Pedro J. Martinez	10.00
RF	Rafael Furcal	5.00
RO	Roy Oswalt	5.00
RP	Rafael Palmeiro	5.00
SB	Sean Burroughs/350	10.00
SG	Shawn Green	8.00
TA	Tony Armas Jr.	5.00
TH	Torii Hunter	5.00
TM	Tino Martinez	8.00
VW	Vernon Wells	8.00
TH	Todd Helton	8.00
MO	Magglio Ordonez	5.00
FG	Freddy Garcia	5.00
ST	So Taguchi	8.00

MLB Hot Tandems
NM/M

Common Card: 10.00
Production 100 Sets
Red Hots 10 Sets: No Pricing

Adam Dunn, Lance Berkman	15.00
Alex Rodriguez, Ivan Rodriguez	30.00
Bret Boone, Freddy Garcia	10.00
Barry Bonds, Kazuhisa Ishii	40.00
Brandon Duckworth, Roy Oswalt	10.00
Bernie Williams, Jorge Posada	15.00
Carlos Delgado, Vernon Wells	10.00
Cristian Guzman, Torii Hunter	10.00
Carlos Pena, Corey Patterson	10.00
Curt Schilling, Greg Maddux	25.00
Frank Thomas, Magglio Ordonez	15.00
Gabe Kapler, Rafael Palmeiro	12.00
Gary Sheffield, Rafael Furcal	10.00
Josh Beckett, Roy Oswalt	10.00
Brandon Duckworth, Josh Beckett	15.00
Jeff Bagwell, Lance Berkman	15.00
Juan Gonzalez, Rafael Palmeiro	15.00
Jim Thome, Shawn Green	15.00
Paul LoDuca, Shawn Green	10.00
Juan Uribe, Miguel Tejada	15.00
Mark Mulder, Moises Alou	15.00
Magglio Ordonez, Jorge Posada	10.00
Mike Piazza, Mike Sweeney	25.00
Todd Helton, Carlos Pena	15.00
Nick Johnson, Curt Schilling	10.00
Pedro J. Martinez, Tony Armas Jr., Freddy Garcia	25.00
Tino Martinez, Todd Helton	10.00
Barry Bonds, Derek Jeter	15.00
Kazuhisa Ishii, Derek Jeter	60.00
Juan Uribe, Cristian Guzman	40.00
Kazuhisa Ishii, So Taguchi	10.00
Adam Dunn, Corey Patterson	20.00
Bernie Williams, Nick Johnson	15.00
Bret Boone, Torii Hunter	10.00
Greg Maddux, Pedro J. Martinez	20.00
Sean Burroughs, Drew Henson	10.00
Kazuhisa Ishii, Satoru Komiyama	20.00
Kazuhisa Ishii, Mark Prior	20.00
Hank Blalock, Austin Kearns	15.00
Hank Blalock, Mark Teixeira	15.00
Marlon Byrd, Jorge Padilla	10.00
Marlon Byrd, Austin Kearns	10.00
Gabe Kapler, Juan Gonzalez	15.00
Jeff Bagwell, Mike Piazza	25.00

We're Number One
NM/M

Complete Set (10): 35.00
Common Player: 1.50
Inserted 1:15

1WN	Derek Jeter	8.00
2WN	Barry Bonds	8.00
3WN	Ken Griffey Jr.	5.00
4WN	Roger Clemens	4.50
5WN	Alex Rodriguez	6.00
6WN	J.D. Drew	1.50
7WN	Chipper Jones	3.00
8WN	Manny Ramirez	3.00
9WN	Nomar Garciaparra	5.00
10WN	Todd Helton	3.00

We're Number One Autograph
NM/M

Common Player:
Barry Bonds/85 200.00

We're Number One Memorabilia
NM/M

Common Player: 5.00
Inserted 1:25

Derek Jeter/Jsy	25.00
Barry Bonds/Jsy	20.00
Ken Griffey Jr./Base	20.00
Alex Rodriguez/Jsy	15.00
J.D. Drew/Jsy	5.00
Chipper Jones/Jsy	10.00
Manny Ramirez/Jsy	10.00
Nomar Garciaparra/Jsy	20.00
Todd Helton/Jsy	10.00

2002 Fleer Maximum

Complete Set (270):
Common Player: .15
Common (201-250): 5.00
Production 500
Common (251-270): .50
Inserted 1:Hobby Pack
Pack (15): 2.50
Box (16): 35.00

1	Barry Bonds	2.00
2	Alex Rodriguez	1.50
3	Jim Edmonds	.15
4	Manny Ramirez	.75
5	Jeff Bagwell	.75
6	Kazuhisa Sasaki	.15
7	Jason Giambi	.50
8	J.D. Drew	.25
9	Barry Larkin	.15
10	Chipper Jones	1.00
11	Rafael Palmeiro	.65
12	Roberto Alomar	.35
13	Randy Johnson	.75
14	Juan Gonzalez	.75
15	Gary Sheffield	.15
16	Larry Walker	.15
17	Todd Helton	.75
18	Ivan Rodriguez	.65
19	Greg Maddux	1.00
20	Mike Piazza	1.25
21	Tsuyoshi Shinjo	.15
22	Luis Gonzalez	.15
23	Pedro Martinez	.15
24	Albert Pujols	1.50
25	Jose Canseco	.35
26	Edgar Martinez	.15
27	Moises Alou	.15
28	Vladimir Guerrero	.75
29	Shawn Green	.35
30	Miguel Tejada	.25
31	Bernie Williams	.30
32	Frank Thomas	.75
33	Jim Thome	.15
34	Derek Jeter	2.00
35	Julio Lugo	.15
36	Mo Vaughn	.15
37	Steve Cox	.15
38	Brad Radke	.15
39	Brian Jordan	.15
40	Garret Anderson	.15
41	Ichiro Suzuki	1.25
42	Mike Lieberthal	.15
43	Preston Wilson	.15
44	Bud Smith	.15
45	Curt Schilling	.40
46	Eric Chavez	.25
47	Javier Vazquez	.15
48	Jose Ortiz	.15
49	Mike Sweeney	.15
50	Travis Fryman	.15
51	Brady Anderson	.15
52	Chan Ho Park	.15
53	C.C. Sabathia	.15
54	Jack Wilson	.25
55	Joe Crede	.15
56	Mike Mussina	.40
57	Sean Casey	.30
58	Bobby Abreu	.15
59	Joe Randa	.15
60	Jose Vidro	.15
61	Juan Uribe	.15
62	Mark Grace	.15
63	Matt Morris	.15
64	Omar Vizquel	.15
65	Darryl Kile	.15
66	Dee Brown	.15
67	Fernando Tatis	.15
68	Jeff Cirillo	.15
69	Johnny Damon	.25
70	Milton Bradley	.15
71	Reggie Sanders	.15
72	Al Leiter	.15
73	Andres Galarraga	.15
74	Ellis Burks	.15
75	Jermaine Dye	.15
76	Juan Pierre	.15
77	Junior Spivey	.15
78	Mark Quinn	.15
79	Ben Sheets	.15
80	Brad Fullmer	.15
81	Bubba Trammell	.15
82	Dante Bichette	.15
83	Ken Griffey Jr.	1.25
84	Paul O'Neill	.15
85	Robert Fick	.15
86	Bret Boone	.15
87	Raul Mondesi	.15
88	Josh Beckett	.40
89	Geoff Jenkins	.15
90	Ramon Ortiz	.15
91	Robin Ventura	.15
92	Tom Glavine	.30
93	Jimmy Rollins	.25
94	Jamie Moyer	.15
95	Magglio Ordonez	.15
96	Mike Lowell	.15
97	Ryan Dempster	.15
98	Scott Schoeneweis	.15
99	Todd Zeile	.15
100	A.J. Burnett	.15
101	Aaron Sele	.15
102	Cal Ripken Jr.	2.00
103	Carlos Beltran	.45
104	David Eckstein	.15
105	Jason Marquis	.15
106	Matt Lawton	.15
107	Ben Grieve	.15
108	Brian Giles	.15
109	Josh Towers	.15
110	Lance Berkman	.15
111	Sammy Sosa	1.25
112	Torii Hunter	.15
113	Aubrey Huff	.15
114	Craig Biggio	.15
115	Doug Mientkiewicz	.15
116	Fred McGriff	.15
117	Jason Johnson	.15
118	Pat Burrell	.25
119	Aaron Boone	.15
120	Carlos Delgado	.50
121	Nomar Garciaparra	1.25
122	Richie Sexson	.15
123	Russ Ortiz	.15
124	Tim Hudson	.25
125	Tony Clark	.15
126	Jeromy Burnitz	.15
127	Jose Cruz	.15
128	Juan Encarnacion	.15
129	Mark Mulder	.15
130	Mike Hampton	.15
131	Rich Aurilia	.15
132	Trot Nixon	.15
133	Greg Vaughn	.15
134	Jacque Jones	.15
135	Jason Kendall	.15
136	Jay Gibbons	.15
137	Mark Buehrle	.15
138	Richard Hidalgo	.15
139	Rondell White	.15
140	Cristian Guzman	.15
141	Andy Pettitte	.30
142	Chris Richard	.15
143	Paul LoDuca	.15
144	Phil Nevin	.15
145	Ray Durham	.15
146	Todd Walker	.15
147	Bartolo Colon	.15
148	Ben Petrick	.15
149	Freddy Garcia	.15
150	Jon Lieber	.15
151	Jose Hernandez	.15
152	Matt Williams	.15
153	Shannon Stewart	.15
154	Adrian Beltre	.30
155	Carlos Lee	.15
156	Frank Catalanotto	.15
157	Jorge Posada	.30
158	Pokey Reese	.15
159	Ryan Klesko	.15
160	Ugueth Urbina	.15
161	Adam Dunn	.50
162	Alfonso Soriano	.50
163	Ben Davis	.15
164	Paul Konerko	.25
165	Eric Karros	.15
166	Jeff Weaver	.15
167	Ruben Sierra	.15
168	Bobby Higginson	.15
169	Eric Milton	.15
170	Kerry Wood	.65
171	Roy Oswalt	.30
172	Scott Rolen	.65
173	Tim Salmon	.15
174	Aramis Ramirez	.15
175	Jason Tyner	.15
176	Juan Cruz	.15
177	Keith Foulke	.15
178	Kevin Brown	.25
179	Roger Clemens	1.00
180	Tony Batista	.15
181	Andruw Jones	.75
182	Cliff Floyd	.15
183	Darin Erstad	.15
184	Joe Mays	.15
185	Mike Cameron	.15
186	Robert Person	.15
187	Jeff Kent	.25
188	Gabe Kapler	.25
189	Jason Jennings	.15
190	Jason Varitek	.15
191	Barry Zito	.25
192	Rickey Henderson	.75
193	Tino Martinez	.25
194	Brandon Duckworth	.15
195	Corey Koskie	.15
196	Derrek Lee	.25
197	Javy Lopez	.25
198	John Olerud	.25
199	Terrance Long	.15
200	Troy Glaus	.75
201	Scott MacRae	5.00
202	Scott Chiasson	5.00
203	Bart Miadich	5.00
204	Brian Bowles	5.00
205	David Williams	5.00
206	Victor Zambrano	5.00
207	Joe Beimel	5.00
208	Scott Stewart	5.00
209	Bob File	5.00
210	Ryan Jensen	5.00
211	Jason Karnuth	5.00
212	Brandon Knight	5.00
213	Andy Shibilo RC	5.00
214	Chad Ricketts RC	5.00
215	Mark Prior	5.00
216	Chad Paronto	5.00
217	Corky Miller	5.00
218	Luis Pineda	5.00
219	Ramon Vazquez	5.00
220	Tony Cogan	5.00
221	Roy Smith	5.00
222	Mark Lukasiewicz	5.00
223	Mike Rivera	5.00
224	Brad Voyles	5.00
225	Jamie Burke RC	5.00
226	Justin Duchscherer	5.00
227	Eric Cyr RC	5.00
228	Mark Lukasiewicz	5.00
229	Marlon Byrd	5.00
230	Chris Piersoll RC	5.00
231	Ramon Vazquez	5.00
232	Tony Cogan	5.00
233	Roy Smith	5.00
234	Franklin Nunez RC	5.00
235	Corky Miller	5.00
236	Jorge Nunez RC	5.00
237	Joe Beimel	5.00
238	Eric Knott	5.00
239	Victor Zambrano	5.00
240	Jason Karnuth	5.00
241	Jason Middlebrook	5.00
242	Scott Stewart	5.00
243	Tim Spooneybarger	5.00
244	David Williams	5.00
245	Bart Miadich	5.00
246	Mike Koplove	5.00
247	Ryan Jensen	5.00
248	Jeremy Fikac	5.00
249	Bob File	5.00
250	Craig Monroe	5.00
251	Albert Pujols	2.00
252	Ichiro Suzuki	2.00
253	Nomar Garciaparra	2.00
254	Barry Bonds	3.00
255	Jason Giambi	.75
256	Derek Jeter	3.00
257	Roberto Alomar	.75
258	Roger Clemens	2.00
259	Mike Piazza	1.50
260	Vladimir Guerrero	1.00
261	Todd Helton	.75
262	Shawn Green	.50
263	Chipper Jones	1.00
264	Pedro Martinez	1.00
265	Pat Burrell	.50
266	Sammy Sosa	2.00
267	Ken Griffey Jr.	1.50
268	Cal Ripken Jr.	3.00
269	Kerry Wood	1.00
270	Alex Rodriguez	2.50

To The Max

Stars (1-200):	4-6X
Print Run 200-500	
Stars (1-200):	4-8X
Print Run 121-199	
Stars (1-200):	6-12X
Print Run 75-120	
Stars (1-200):	10-25X
Print Run 40-75	
Stars (1-200):	15-40X
Print Run 20-39	
Rookies (201-250):	.5-1X

Production 100
Impact (251-270): 2-4X
Production 200-400

2002 Fleer Maximum America's Game
NM/M

Complete Set (25): 25.00
Common Player: .50
Inserted 1:10 Retail

1	Pedro Martinez	1.50
2	Miguel Tejada	.75
3	Randy Johnson	1.50
4	Barry Bonds	5.00
5	Rafael Palmeiro	1.00
6	Mike Piazza	3.00
7	Greg Maddux	2.50
8	Jeff Bagwell	1.50
9	Edgar Martinez	.50
10	Albert Pujols	4.00
11	Todd Helton	1.50
12	Chipper Jones	2.50
13	Luis Gonzalez	.50
14	Jason Giambi	1.00
15	Kazuhiro Sasaki	.50
16	Dave Winfield	1.00
17	Reggie Jackson	1.50
18	Tom Glavine	.75
19	Carlos Delgado	.75
20	Bobby Abreu	.50
21	Larry Walker	.50
22	J.D. Drew	.75
23	Alex Rodriguez	4.00
24	Frank Thomas	1.50
25	C.C. Sabathia	.50

Americas Game Jersey
NM/M

Common Player: 8.00
Inserted 1:24 H, 1:72 R

1	Jeff Bagwell	10.00
2	Craig Biggio	8.00
3	Barry Bonds	25.00
4	Carlos Delgado	8.00
5	J.D. Drew	5.00
6	Jason Giambi	10.00
7	Tom Glavine	10.00
8	Luis Gonzalez	5.00
9	Todd Helton	10.00
10	Reggie Jackson	10.00
11	Randy Johnson	10.00
12	Chipper Jones	10.00
13	Greg Maddux	10.00
14	Edgar Martinez	8.00
15	Pedro Martinez	10.00
16	Rafael Palmeiro	10.00
17	Chan Ho Park	5.00
18	Mike Piazza	10.00
19	Albert Pujols	20.00
20	Kazuhiro Sasaki	5.00
21	Miguel Tejada	5.00
22	Frank Thomas	10.00
23	Larry Walker	5.00
24	Dave Winfield	5.00

Americas Game Stars and Stripes
No Pricing
Production 25 Sets

Coverage
NM/M

Common Player: 15.00
Production 100 Sets

1	Roberto Alomar/Bat	25.00
2	Jeff Bagwell/Jsy	20.00
3	Barry Bonds/Bat	50.00
4	Jose Canseco/Bat	25.00
5	J.D. Drew/Bat	25.00
6	Jim Edmonds/Bat	20.00
7	Jason Giambi/Bat	25.00
8	Juan Gonzalez/Bat	25.00
9	Luis Gonzalez/Jsy	15.00
10	Todd Helton/Jsy	25.00
11	Randy Johnson/Jsy	40.00
12	Chipper Jones/Bat	25.00
13	Greg Maddux/Jsy	40.00
14	Pedro Martinez/Jsy	30.00
15	Rafael Palmeiro/Pants	25.00
16	Albert Pujols/Jsy	50.00
17	Manny Ramirez/Bat	25.00
18	Alex Rodriguez/Bat	30.00
19	Ivan Rodriguez/Bat	25.00
20	Kazuhiro Sasaki/Jsy	20.00
21	Gary Sheffield/Bat	25.00
22	Tsuyoshi Shinjo/Bat	15.00

Coverage Autographs
NM/M

Quantity produced listed

1	Barry Bonds/Pants/50	200.00
2	J.D. Drew/Bat/100	25.00
3	Jim Edmonds/Bat/100	25.00
4	Drew Henson/Bat/100	25.00
5	Chipper Jones/Bat/50	60.00

| 6 | Albert Pujols/ Jsy/100 | 150.00 |
| 7 | Gary Sheffield/ Bat/100 | 30.00 |

Derek Jeter Legacy Collection

NM/M
Inserted 1:236

DJ	Derek Jeter/Bat	20.00
DJ	Derek Jeter/ Bat/Auto./222	150.00
DJ	Derek Jeter/Jsy	20.00
DJ	Derek Jeter/ Jsy/Auto.	200.00

Maximum Power Bat

NM/M
Common Player: 5.00
Inserted 1:24 H
Golds: 3-4X
Production 25 Sets

Luis Gonzalez	5.00
Larry Walker	5.00
Frank Thomas	10.00
Manny Ramirez	10.00
Barry Bonds	25.00
Jim Thome	10.00
Tsuyoshi Shinjo	5.00
Bernie Williams/175	25.00
Chipper Jones	5.00
Shawn Green	5.00
Juan Gonzalez	8.00
Jim Edmonds	10.00
Moises Alou	10.00
Roberto Alomar	10.00
Jose Canseco	10.00
Ivan Rodriguez	10.00
Barry Larkin/50	40.00
Mike Piazza	15.00
Gary Sheffield	8.00
J.D. Drew/200	5.00
Alex Rodriguez	15.00
Jason Giambi	10.00
Todd Helton	8.00

Common Player: 5.00
Inserted 1:24 H
Golds: 3-4X
Production 25 Sets

Luis Gonzalez	5.00
Larry Walker	5.00
Frank Thomas	10.00
Manny Ramirez	10.00
Barry Bonds	25.00
Jim Thome	10.00
Tsuyoshi Shinjo	5.00
Bernie Williams/175	25.00
Chipper Jones	5.00
Shawn Green	5.00
Juan Gonzalez	8.00
Jim Edmonds	10.00
Moises Alou	10.00
Roberto Alomar	10.00
Jose Canseco	10.00
Ivan Rodriguez	10.00
Barry Larkin/50	40.00
Mike Piazza	15.00
Gary Sheffield	8.00
J.D. Drew/200	5.00
Alex Rodriguez	15.00
Jason Giambi	10.00
Todd Helton	8.00

Mets All-Amazin' Team

To commemorate the team's 40th anniversary, Fleer produced a set of Mets greats which was given away at Shea on August 17. The cards are printed on heavy stock and fea-

★ JERRY KOOSMAN ★

ture (mostly) color poses, game-action shots and team photos on a textured-look background. The player name, uniform number and years with the Mets appear at bottom. The anniversary logo and Fleer logo are also seen on front. Backs repeat a detail from the front photo in a circle at top. There are a few sentences about the player and stats lines for his Mets days and major league career. Appropriate logos round out the design.

NM/M
Complete Set (21): 15.00
Common Card: .50

1	Gil Hodges	1.00
2	Keith Hernandez	.75
3	Edgardo Alfonzo	.75
4	Howard Johnson	.75
5	Bud Harrelson	.50
6	Mike Piazza	3.00
7	Mookie Wilson	.75
8	Darryl Strawberry	.75
9	Lenny Dykstra	.50
10	Tom Seaver	2.00
11	Jerry Koosman	.50
12	Roger McDowell	.50
13	John Franco	.50
14	Ed Kranepool	.50
15	Rusty Staub	.75
16	Bob Murphy (Broadcaster)	.50
17	Ralph Kiner (Broadcaster)	.50
18	1962 Team Card	1.00
19	1969 Team Card	1.00
20	1986 Team Card	1.00
---	Checklist	.10

2002 Fleer Platinum

NM/M
Complete Set (302): 125.00
Common Player: .15
Common (251-260): 2.00
Common (261-302): 1.50
Inserted 1:3 H, 1:6 Retail
Hobby Pack (10): 2.00
Hobby Box (24): 35.00
Rack Box: 70.00

1	Garrett Anderson	.15
2	Randy Johnson	.65
3	Chipper Jones	.75
4	David Cone	.15
5	Corey Patterson	.15
6	Carlos Lee	.15
7	Barry Larkin	.15
8	Jim Thome	.15
9	Larry Walker	.15
10	Randall Simon	.15
11	Charles Johnson	.15
12	Richard Hidalgo	.15
13	Mark Quinn	.15
14	Paul LoDuca	.15
15	Cristian Guzman	.15
16	Orlando Cabrera	.15
17	Al Leiter	.15
18	Nick Johnson	.15
19	Eric Chavez	.25
20	Miguel Tejada	.25
21	Mike Lieberthal	.15
22	Robert Mackowiak	.15
23	Ryan Klesko	.15
24	Jeff Kent	.15
25	Edgar Martinez	.15
26	Steve Kline	.15
27	Toby Hall	.15
28	Rusty Greer	.15
29	Jose Cruz Jr.	.15
30	Darin Erstad	.50
31	Reggie Sanders	.15
32	Javy Lopez	.15
33	Carl Everett	.15
34	Sammy Sosa	1.00
35	Magglio Ordonez	.15
36	Todd Walker	.15
37	Omar Vizquel	.15
38	Matt Anderson	.15
39	Jeff Weaver	.15
40	Derrek Lee	.15
41	Julio Lugo	.15
42	Joe Randa	.15
43	Chan Ho Park	.15
44	Torii Hunter	.15
45	Vladimir Guerrero	.65
46	Rey Ordonez	.15
47	Tino Martinez	.15
48	Johnny Damon	.25
49	Barry Zito	.25
50	Robert Person	.15
51	Aramis Ramirez	.15
52	Mark Kotsay	.15
53	Jason Schmidt	.15
54	Jamie Moyer	.15
55	David Justice	.15
56	Aubrey Huff	.15
57	Rick Helling	.15
58	Carlos Delgado	.40
59	Troy Glaus	.65
60	Curt Schilling	.40
61	Greg Maddux	.75
62	Nomar Garciaparra	1.00
63	Kerry Wood	.50
64	Frank Thomas	.65
65	Dmitri Young	.15
66	Alex Ochoa	.15
67	Jose Macias	.15
68	Antonio Alfonseca	.15
69	Mike Lowell	.15
70	Wade Miller	.15
71	Mike Sweeney	.15
72	Gary Sheffield	.25
73	Corey Koskie	.15
74	Lee Stevens	.15
75	Jay Payton	.15
76	Mike Mussina	.40
77	Jermaine Dye	.15
78	Bobby Abreu	.15
79	Scott Rolen	.50
80	Todd Ritchie	.15
81	D'Angelo Jimenez	.15
82	Rob Nenn	.15
83	John Olerud	.15
84	Matt Morris	.15
85	Joe Kennedy	.15
86	Gabe Kapler	.15
87	Chris Carpenter	.15
88	David Eckstein	.15
89	Matt Williams	.15
90	John Smoltz	.15
91	Pedro J. Martinez	.65
92	Eric Young	.15
93	Jose Valentin	.15
94	Erubiel Durazo	.15
95	Jeff Cirillo	.15
96	Brandon Inge	.15
97	Josh Beckett	.40
98	Preston Wilson	.15
99	Damian Jackson	.15
100	Adrian Beltre	.25
101	Jeromy Burnitz	.15
102	Joe Mays	.15
103	Michael Barrett	.15
104	Mike Piazza	1.00
105	Brady Anderson	.15
106	Jason Giambi	.40
107	Marlon Anderson	.15
108	Jimmy Rollins	.25
109	Jack Wilson	.15
110	Brian Lawrence	.15
111	Russ Ortiz	.15
112	Kazuhiro Sasaki	.15
113	Placido Polanco	.15
114	Damian Rolls	.15
115	Rafael Palmeiro	.50
116	Brad Fullmer	.15
117	Tim Salmon	.25
118	Tony Womack	.15
119	Tony Batista	.15
120	Trot Nixon	.15
121	Mark Buehrle	.15
122	Derek Jeter	1.50
123	Ellis Burks	.15
124	Mike Hampton	.15
125	Roger Cedeno	.15
126	A.J. Burnett	.15
127	Moises Alou	.15
128	Billy Wagner	.15
129	Kevin Brown	.15
130	Jose Hernandez	.15
131	Doug Mientkiewicz	.15
132	Javier Vazquez	.15
133	Tsuyoshi Shinjo	.15
134	Andy Pettitte	.30
135	Tim Hudson	.25
136	Pat Burrell	.40
137	Brian Giles	.15
138	Kevin Young	.15
139	Xavier Nady	.15
140	J.T. Snow	.15
141	Aaron Sele	.15
142	Albert Pujols	1.25
143	Jason Tyner	.15
144	Ivan Rodriguez	.50
145	Raul Mondesi	.15
146	Matt Lawton	.15
147	Rafael Furcal	.15
148	Jeff Conine	.15
149	Hideo Nomo	.60
150	Jose Canseco	.30
151	Aaron Boone	.15
152	Bartolo Colon	.15
153	Todd Helton	.65
154	Tony Clark	.15
155	Pablo Ozuna	.15
156	Jeff Bagwell	.65
157	Carlos Beltran	.50
158	Shawn Green	.25
159	Geoff Jenkins	.15
160	Eric Milton	.15
161	Jose Vidro	.15
162	Robin Ventura	.15
163	Jorge Posada	.25
164	Terrence Long	.15
165	Brandon Duckworth	.15
166	Chad Hermansen	.15
167	Ben Davis	.15
168	Phil Nevin	.15
169	Bret Boone	.15
170	J.D. Drew	.25
171	Edgar Renteria	.15
172	Randy Winn	.15
173	Alex Rodriguez	1.50
174	Shannon Stewart	.15
175	Steve Finley	.15
176	Marcus Giles	.15
177	Jay Gibbons	.15
178	Manny Ramirez	.65
179	Ray Durham	.15
180	Sean Casey	.25
181	Travis Fryman	.15
182	Denny Neagle	.15
183	Deivi Cruz	.15
184	Luis Castillo	.15
185	Lance Berkman	.15
186	Dee Brown	.15
187	Jeff Shaw	.15
188	Mark Loretta	.15
189	David Ortiz	.25
190	Edgardo Alfonzo	.15
191	Roger Clemens	.75
192	Mariano Rivera	.25
193	Jeremy Giambi	.15
194	Johnny Estrada	.15
195	Craig Wilson	.15
196	Adam Eaton	.15
197	Rich Aurilia	.15
198	Mike Cameron	.15
199	Jim Edmonds	.15
200	Fernando Vina	.15
201	Greg Vaughn	.15
202	Mike Young	.15
203	Vernon Wells	.15
204	Luis Gonzalez	.25
205	Tom Glavine	.30
206	Chris Richard	.15
207	Jon Lieber	.15
208	Keith Foulke	.15
209	Rondell White	.15
210	Bernie Williams	.30
211	Juan Pierre	.15
212	Juan Encarnacion	.15
213	Ryan Dempster	.15
214	Tim Redding	.15
215	Jeff Suppan	.15
216	Mark Grudzielanek	.15
217	Richie Sexson	.15
218	Brad Radke	.15
219	Armando Benitez	.15
220	Orlando Hernandez	.15
221	Alfonso Soriano	.40
222	Mark Mulder	.15
223	Travis Lee	.15
224	Jason Kendall	.15
225	Trevor Hoffman	.15
226	Barry Bonds	1.50
227	Freddy Garcia	.15
228	Darryl Kile	.15
229	Ben Grieve	.15
230	Frank Catalanotto	.15
231	Ruben Sierra	.15
232	Homer Bush	.15
233	Mark Grace	.25
234	Andruw Jones	.60
235	Brian Roberts	.15
236	Fred McGriff	.15
237	Paul Konerko	.15
238	Ken Griffey Jr.	1.00
239	John Burkett	.15
240	Juan Uribe	.15
241	Bobby Higginson	.15
242	Cliff Floyd	.15
243	Craig Biggio	.15
244	Neifi Perez	.15
245	Eric Karros	.15
246	Ben Sheets	.15
247	Tony Armas Jr.	.15
248	Mo Vaughn	.15
249	David Wells	.15
250	Juan Gonzalez	.60
251	Barry Bonds	5.00
252	Sammy Sosa	3.00
253	Ken Griffey Jr.	3.00
254	Roger Clemens	4.00
255	Greg Maddux	2.50
256	Chipper Jones	1.50
257	Alex Rodriguez, Derek Jeter, Nomar Garciaparra	5.00
258	Roberto Alomar	1.50
259	Jeff Bagwell	1.50
260	Mike Piazza	3.00
261	Mark Teixeira	2.00
262	Mark Prior	2.00
263	Alex Escobar	1.50
264	C.C. Sabathia	1.50
265	Drew Henson	1.50
266	Wilson Betemit	1.50
267	Roy Oswalt	1.50
268	Adam Dunn	2.00
269	Bud Smith	1.50
270	Dewon Brazelton	1.50
271	Brandon Backe RC, Jason Standridge	1.50
272	Wilfredo Rodriguez, Carlos Hernandez	1.50
273	Geronimo Gil, Luis Rivera	1.50
274	Carlos Pena, Jovanny Cedeno	1.50
275	Austin Kearns, Ben Broussard	1.50
276	Jorge De La Rosa RC, Kenny Kelly	1.50
277	Ryan Drese, Victor Martinez	1.50
278	Joel Pinero, Nate Cornejo	1.50
279	David Kelton, Carlos Zambrano	1.50
281	Donnie Bridges, Wilkin Ruan	1.50
282	Wily Mo Pena, Brandon Claussen	2.00
283	Jason Jennings, Rene Reyes RC	1.50
284	Steve Green, Alfredo Amezaga	1.50
285	Eric Hinske, Felipe Lopez	1.50
286	Anderson Machado RC, Brad Baisley	1.50
287	Carlos Garcia, Sean Douglass	1.50
288	Pat Strange, Jae Weong Seo	1.50
289	Marcus Thames, Alex Graman	1.50
290	Matt Childers RC, Hansel Izquierdo RC	1.50
291	Ron Calloway RC, Adam Walker RC	1.50
292	J.R. House, J.J. Davis	1.50
293	Ryan Anderson, Rafael Soriano	1.50
294	Mike Bynum, Dennis Tankersley	1.50
295	Kurt Ainsworth, Carlos Valderrama	1.50
296	Billy Hall, Cristian Guerrero	1.50
297	Miguel Olivo, Danny Wright	1.50
298	Marlon Byrd, Jorge Padilla RC	1.50
299	Juan Cruz, Ben Christensen	1.50
300	Adam Johnson, Michael Restovich	1.50
301	So Taguchi RC	2.00
302	Kazuhisa Ishii RC	3.00

Edition

| Stars (1-250) | 4-8X |

Production 202

| Cards 251-302: | No Pricing |

Production 22

Buy Back Autographs

Common Player:

Barry Bonds RC Autograph

NM/M
73 cards autographed

| Barry Bonds | 450.00 |

Clubhouse Collection - Dual

DARIN ERSTAD • Anaheim Angels

NM/M
Common Card: 10.00
Inserted 1:96

Edgardo Alfonzo	10.00
Rick Ankiel	8.00
Adrian Beltre	10.00
Barry Bonds	40.00
Sean Casey	10.00
Eric Chavez	10.00
Roger Clemens	30.00
Carlos Delgado	10.00
J.D. Drew	10.00
Darin Erstad	10.00
Jim Thome	20.00
Juan Gonzalez	15.00
Nomar Garciaparra	30.00
Derek Jeter	40.00
Randy Johnson	20.00
Andruw Jones	10.00
Johnny Damon	10.00
Paul LoDuca	10.00
Greg Maddux	20.00
Pedro J. Martinez	20.00
Magglio Ordonez	10.00
Mike Piazza	30.00
Manny Ramirez	15.00
Mariano Rivera	15.00
Ivan Rodriguez	20.00
Alex Rodriguez	25.00
Scott Rolen	20.00
Kazuhiro Sasaki	10.00
Curt Schilling	20.00
Gary Sheffield	10.00
Frank Thomas	20.00
Jim Thome	20.00
Omar Vizquel	10.00

Clubhouse Collection Memorabilia

CRAIG BIGGIO • Houston Astros

NM/M
Common Player: 5.00
Inserted 1:32

Edgardo Alfonzo/Jsy	5.00
Rick Ankiel/Jsy	5.00
Craig Biggio/Bat	8.00
Adrian Beltre/Jsy	5.00
Sean Casey/Jsy	8.00
Barry Bonds/Jsy	25.00
Scott Rolen/Jsy	10.00
Eric Chavez/Jsy	8.00
Roger Clemens/Jsy	25.00
Carlos Delgado/Jsy	8.00
J.D. Drew/Jsy	8.00
Darin Erstad/Jsy	8.00
Jim Thome/Bat	10.00
Juan Gonzalez/Bat	8.00
Nomar Garciaparra/ Jsy	15.00
Todd Helton/Jsy	8.00
Derek Jeter/Pants	25.00
Randy Johnson/Jsy	10.00
Andruw Jones/Jsy	8.00
Tim Hudson/Jsy	5.00
Jason Kendall/Jsy	5.00
Johnny Damon/Bat	5.00
Paul LoDuca/Jsy	5.00
Greg Maddux/Jsy	10.00
Pedro Martinez/Jsy	10.00
Raul Mondesi/Jsy	5.00
Magglio Ordonez/Jsy	5.00
Mike Piazza/Jsy	10.00
Manny Ramirez/Jsy	8.00
Mariano Rivera/Jsy	8.00
Ivan Rodriguez/Jsy	10.00
Alex Rodriguez/Jsy	15.00
Kazuhiro Sasaki/Jsy	5.00
Frank Thomas/Jsy	8.00
Curt Schilling/Jsy	8.00
Gary Sheffield/Bat	6.00
Omar Vizquel/Jsy	5.00

Cornerstones

NM/M
Complete Set (40): 120.00
Inserted 1:12 Jumbo

1	Bill Terry, Johnny Mize	1.50
2	Cal Ripken Jr., Eddie Murray	10.00
3	Eddie Mathews, Chipper Jones	3.00
4	Albert Pujols, George Sisler	6.00
5	Sean Casey, Tony Perez	1.50
6	Jimmie Foxx, Scott Rolen	4.00
7	Wade Boggs, George Brett	8.00
8	Rod Carew, Troy Glaus	1.50
9	Jeff Bagwell, Rafael Palmeiro	2.00
10	Willie Stargell, Pie Traynor	2.00
11	Cal Ripken Jr., Brooks Robinson	10.00

	NM/M
12 Tony Perez, Ted Kluszewski	1.50
13 Jason Giambi, Don Mattingly	8.00
14 Hank Greenberg, Jimmie Foxx	4.00
15 Ernie Banks, Willie McCovey	3.00
16 Jim Thome, Travis Fryman	3.00
17 Ted Kluszewski, Sean Casey	1.50
18 Gil Hodges, Johnny Mize	3.00
19 Brooks Robinson, Boog Powell	3.00
20 Bill Terry, George Sisler	2.00
21 Wade Boggs, Don Mattingly	8.00
22 Jason Giambi, Carlos Delgado	2.50
23 Willie Stargell, Bill Madlock	2.00
24 Mark Grace, Matt Williams	2.00
25 Paul Molitor, George Brett	8.00
26 Carlos Delgado, Mo Vaughn	1.50
27 Bill Terry, Willie McCovey	1.50
28 Mike Sweeney, George Brett	8.00
29 Eddie Mathews, Ernie Banks	4.00
30 Eric Karros, Gil Hodges	1.50
31 Paul Molitor, Don Mattingly	8.00
32 Brooks Robinson, Rod Carew	3.00
33 Chipper Jones, Albert Pujols	8.00
34 Harry Heilmann, Hank Greenberg	1.50
35 Frank Thomas, Carlos Delgado	2.50
36 Jeff Bagwell, Todd Helton	2.00
37 Rafael Palmeiro, Fred McGriff	2.00
38 Cal Ripken Jr., Wade Boggs	10.00
39 Orlando Cepeda, Willie McCovey	2.00
40 John Olerud, Mark Grace	2.00

Cornerstones Memorabilia
No Pricing
Production 25 Sets

Cornerstones Numbered
NM/M
Complete Set (40):
#1-10: Production 250
#11-20: Production 250
#21-30: Production 1,000
#31-40: Production 2,000

1 Bill Terry, Johnny Mize	10.00
2 Cal Ripken Jr., Eddie Murray	30.00
3 Eddie Mathews, Chipper Jones	10.00
4 Albert Pujols, George Sisler	20.00
5 Sean Casey, Tony Perez	8.00
6 Jimmie Foxx, Scott Rolen	10.00
7 Wade Boggs, George Brett	20.00
8 Rod Carew, Troy Glaus	10.00
9 Jeff Bagwell, Rafael Palmeiro	10.00
10 Willie Stargell, Pie Traynor	8.00
11 Cal Ripken Jr., Brooks Robinson	20.00
12 Tony Perez, Ted Kluszewski	5.00
13 Jason Giambi, Don Mattingly	15.00
14 Hank Greenberg, Jimmie Foxx	8.00
15 Ernie Banks, Willie McCovey	8.00
16 Jim Thome, Travis Fryman	6.00
17 Ted Kluszewski, Sean Casey	5.00
18 Gil Hodges, Johnny Mize	5.00
19 Brooks Robinson, Boog Powell	8.00
20 Bill Terry, George Sisler	5.00
21 Wade Boggs, Don Mattingly	10.00
22 Jason Giambi/Yanks, Carlos Delgado	3.00
23 Willie Stargell, Bill Madlock	4.00
24 Mark Grace, Matt Williams	4.00
25 Paul Molitor, George Brett	10.00
26 Carlos Delgado, Mo Vaughn	3.00
27 Bill Terry, Willie McCovey	4.00
28 Mike Sweeney, George Brett	10.00
29 Eddie Mathews, Ernie Banks	4.00
30 Eric Karros, Gil Hodges	3.00
31 Paul Molitor, Don Mattingly	8.00
32 Brooks Robinson, Rod Carew	3.00
33 Chipper Jones, Albert Pujols	6.00
34 Harry Heilmann, Hank Greenburg	3.00
35 Frank Thomas, Carlos Delgado	3.00
36 Jeff Bagwell, Todd Helton	3.00
37 Rafael Palmeiro, Fred McGriff	3.00
38 Cal Ripken Jr., Wade Boggs	8.00
39 Orlando Cepeda, Willie McCovey	3.00
40 John Olerud, Mark Grace	3.00

Fencebusters
NM/M
Common Player: 5.00
Rack Pack Exclusive

Derek Jeter	20.00
J.D. Drew	6.00
Brian Giles	5.00
Moises Alou	5.00
Rafael Palmeiro	6.00
Jeff Bagwell	8.00
Mike Piazza	15.00
Manny Ramirez	8.00
Tino Martinez	5.00
Jim Thome	5.00
Andruw Jones	8.00
Shawn Green	6.00
Frank Thomas	8.00
Miguel Tejada	6.00
Luis Gonzalez	5.00
Alex Rodriguez	12.50
Larry Walker	5.00
Barry Bonds	20.00
Todd Helton	8.00
Chipper Jones	10.00
Roberto Alomar	6.00
Jim Edmonds	5.00

Fencebusters Autographed
NM/M
Numbered to 2001 HR Total.
Barry Bonds/73   275.00

National Patch Time
NM/M
Common Player: 20.00
Inserted 1:12 Jumbo

Barry Bonds/75	100.00
Todd Helton/110	40.00
Ivan Rodriguez/225	40.00
Kazuhiro Sasaki/310	40.00
Derek Jeter/65	100.00
Cal Ripken Jr/350	80.00
Darin Erstad/315	20.00
Jose Canseco/150	40.00
Miguel Tejada/55	35.00
Greg Maddux/775	30.00
Juan Gonzalez/50	50.00
J.D. Drew/210	25.00
Manny Ramirez/100	40.00
Pedro Martinez/45	50.00
Carlos Delgado/70	30.00
Magglio Ordonez/85	30.00
Pat Burrell/285	25.00
Adam Dunn/75	40.00
Alex Rodriguez/325	50.00

Wheelhouse

NM/M
Complete Set (20):   40.00

Common Player: 1.00
Inserted 1:12

1WH Derek Jeter	6.00
2WH Barry Bonds	6.00
3WH Luis Gonzalez	1.00
4WH Jason Giambi	1.00
5WH Ivan Rodriguez	1.50
6WH Mike Piazza	4.00
7WH Troy Glaus	1.50
8WH Nomar Garciaparra	4.00
9WH Juan Gonzalez	1.50
10WH Sammy Sosa	4.00
11WH Albert Pujols	5.00
12WH Ken Griffey Jr.	4.00
13WH Scott Rolen	1.00
14WH Jeff Bagwell	1.50
15WH Ichiro Suzuki	4.00
16WH Todd Helton	1.50
17WH Chipper Jones	3.00
18WH Alex Rodriguez	4.00
19WH Vladimir Guerrero	2.00
20WH Manny Ramirez	1.50

2002 Fleer Premium

NM/M
Complete Set (240): 50.00
Common Player: .15
Common SP (201-240): .50
Inserted 1:2
Pack (8): 2.00
Box (24): 35.00

1 Garret Anderson	.20
2 Derek Jeter	2.50
3 Ken Griffey Jr.	1.50
4 Luis Castillo	.15
5 Richie Sexson	.20
6 Mike Mussina	.40
7 Ricky Henderson	.75
8 Bud Smith	.15
9 David Eckstein	.15
10 Nomar Garciaparra	1.50
11 Barry Larkin	.25
12 Cliff Floyd	.15
13 Ben Sheets	.20
14 Jorge Posada	.30
15 Phil Nevin	.15
16 Fernando Vina	.15
17 Darin Erstad	.65
18 Shea Hillenbrand	.15
19 Todd Walker	.15
20 Charles Johnson	.15
21 Cristian Guzman	.15
22 Mariano Rivera	.30
23 Bubba Trammell	.15
24 Brent Abernathy	.15
25 Troy Glaus	.75
26 Pedro J. Martinez	.75
27 Dmitri Young	.15
28 Derrek Lee	.20
29 Torii Hunter	.20
30 Alfonso Soriano	.65
31 Rich Aurilia	.15
32 Ben Grieve	.15
33 Tim Salmon	.30
34 Trot Nixon	.15
35 Roberto Alomar	.40
36 Mike Lowell	.20
37 Jacque Jones	.15
38 Bernie Williams	.20
39 Barry Bonds	2.50
40 Toby Hall	.15
41 Mo Vaughn	.20
42 Hideo Nomo	.65
43 Travis Fryman	.15
44 Preston Wilson	.15
45 Corey Koskie	.15
46 Eric Chavez	.30
47 Andres Galarraga	.15
48 Greg Vaughn	.15
49 Shawn Wooten	.15
50 Manny Ramirez	.75
51 Juan Gonzalez	.20
52 Moises Alou	.20
53 Joe Mays	.15
54 Johnny Damon	.35
55 Jeff Kent	.20
56 Frank Catalanotto	.15
57 Steve Finley	.15
58 Jason Varitek	.15
59 Kenny Lofton	.20
60 Jeff Bagwell	.75
61 Doug Mientkiewicz	.15
62 Jermaine Dye	.15
63 John Vander Wal	.15
64 Gabe Kapler	.15
65 Luis Gonzalez	.30
66 Jon Lieber	.15
67 C.C. Sabathia	.15
68 Lance Berkman	.20
69 Eric Milton	.15
70 Jason Giambi	.50
71 Ichiro Suzuki	1.50
72 Rafael Palmeiro	.65
73 Mark Grace	.30
74 Fred McGriff	.20
75 Jim Thome	.20
76 Craig Biggio	.15
77 A.J. Pierzynski	.15
78 Ramon Hernandez	.15
79 Paul Abbott	.15
80 Alex Rodriguez	2.00
81 Randy Johnson	.75
82 Corey Patterson	.20
83 Omar Vizquel	.20
84 Richard Hidalgo	.15
85 Luis Rivas	.15
86 Tim Hudson	.30
87 Bret Boone	.20
88 Ivan Rodriguez	.60
89 Junior Spivey	.15
90 Sammy Sosa	1.50
91 Jeff Cirillo	.15
92 Roy Oswalt	.30
93 Orlando Cabrera	.15
94 Terrence Long	.15
95 Mike Cameron	.15
96 Homer Bush	.15
97 Reggie Sanders	.15
98 Rondell White	.20
99 Mike Hampton	.15
100 Carlos Beltran	.50
101 Vladimir Guerrero	.75
102 Miguel Tejada	.30
103 Freddy Garcia	.15
104 Jose Cruz Jr.	.15
105 Curt Schilling	.45
106 Kerry Wood	.65
107 Todd Helton	.75
108 Neifi Perez	.15
109 Javier Vazquez	.15
110 Barry Zito	.30
111 Edgar Martinez	.20
112 Carlos Delgado	.50
113 Matt Williams	.20
114 Eric Young	.15
115 Alex Ochoa	.15
116 Mark Quinn	.15
117 Jose Vidro	.15
118 Bobby Abreu	.15
119 David Bell	.15
120 Brad Fullmer	.15
121 Rafael Furcal	.15
122 Ray Durham	.15
123 Jose Ortiz	.15
124 Joe Randa	.15
125 Edgardo Alfonzo	.15
126 Marlon Anderson	.15
127 Jamie Moyer	.15
128 Alex Gonzalez	.15
129 Marcus Giles	.15
130 Keith Foulke	.15
131 Juan Pierre	.15
132 Mike Sweeney	.15
133 Matt Lawton	.15
134 Pat Burrell	.40
135 John Olerud	.20
136 Raul Mondesi	.20
137 Tom Glavine	.40
138 Paul Konerko	.20
139 Larry Walker	.20
140 Adrian Beltre	.35
141 Al Leiter	.20
142 Mike Lieberthal	.15
143 Kazuhiro Sasaki	.15
144 Shannon Stewart	.15
145 Andruw Jones	.75
146 Carlos Lee	.15
147 Roger Cedeno	.15
148 Kevin Brown	.20
149 Jay Payton	.15
150 Scott Rolen	.65
151 J.D. Drew	.35
152 Chipper Jones	1.00
153 Magglio Ordonez	.20
154 Tony Clark	.15
155 Shawn Green	.35
156 Mike Piazza	1.50
157 Jimmy Rollins	.25
158 Jim Edmonds	.20
159 Javy Lopez	.20
160 Chris Singleton	.15
161 Juan Encarnacion	.15
162 Eric Karros	.15
163 Tsuyoshi Shinjo	.15
164 Brian Giles	.20
165 Darryl Kile	.15
166 Greg Maddux	1.00
167 Frank Thomas	.75
168 Shane Halter	.15
169 Paul LoDuca	.15
170 Robin Ventura	.15
171 Jason Kendall	.15
172 Jason Hart	.15
173 Brady Anderson	.15
174 Jose Valentin	.15
175 Bobby Higginson	.15
176 Gary Sheffield	.40
177 Roger Clemens	1.25
178 Aramis Ramirez	.20
179 Matt Morris	.15
180 Jeff Conine	.15
181 Aaron Boone	.15
182 Jose Macias	.15
183 Jeromy Burnitz	.15
184 Carl Everett	.15
185 Trevor Hoffman	.15
186 Placido Polanco	.15
187 Jay Gibbons	.15
188 Sean Casey	.35
189 Josh Beckett	.40
190 Jeffrey Hammonds	.15
191 Chuck Knoblauch	.15
192 Ryan Klesko	.15
193 Albert Pujols	1.75
194 Chris Richard	.15
195 Adam Dunn	.50
196 A.J. Burnett	.15
197 Geoff Jenkins	.25
198 Tino Martinez	.15
199 Ray Lankford	.15
200 Edgar Renteria	.15
201 Eric Cyr RC	1.00
202 Travis Phelps	.50
203 Rick Bauer	.50
204 Mark Prior	2.00
205 Wilson Betemit	.50
206 Dewon Brazelton	.50
207 Cody Ransom	.50
208 Donnie Bridges	.50
209 Justin Duchscherer	.50
210 Nate Cornejo	.50
211 Jason Romano	.50
212 Juan Cruz	.50
213 Pedro Santana	.50
214 Ryan Drese	.50
215 Bert Snow	.50
216 Nate Frese	.50
217 Rafael Soriano	.50
218 Franklin Nunez RC	.50
219 Tim Spooneybarger	.50
220 Willie Harris	.50
221 Billy Sylvester	.50
222 Carlos Hernandez	.50
223 Mark Teixeira	3.00
224 Adrian Hernandez	.50
225 Andres Torres	.50
226 Marlon Byrd	.50
227 Juan Rivera	.50
228 Adam Johnson	.50
229 Justin Kaye	.50
230 Kyle Kessel	.50
231 Horacio Ramirez	.50
232 Brandon Larson	.50
233 Luis Lopez	.50
234 Robert Mackowiak	.50
235 Henry Mateo	.50
236 Corky Miller	.50
237 Greg Miller	.50
238 Dustan Mohr	.50
239 Bill Ortega	.50
240 Billy Hall	.50

Star Ruby
Stars (1-200): 4-8X
SP's (201-240): 1-2X
Production 125 Sets

Diamond Stars
NM/M
Complete Set (20): 100.00
Common Player: 2.00
Inserted 1:72

1DS Pedro J. Martinez	8.00
2DS Derek Jeter	15.00
3DS Sammy Sosa	8.00
4DS Ken Griffey Jr.	8.00
5DS Chipper Jones	5.00
6DS Roger Clemens	10.00
7DS Ichiro Suzuki	8.00
8DS Jeff Bagwell	4.00
9DS Luis Gonzalez	2.00
10DS Manny Ramirez	4.00
11DS Alex Rodriguez	12.50
12DS Kazuhiro Sasaki	2.00
13DS Mike Piazza	8.00
14DS Vladimir Guerrero	4.00
15DS Randy Johnson	4.00
16DS Ivan Rodriguez	3.00
17DS Nomar Garciaparra	8.00
18DS Barry Bonds	15.00
19DS Todd Helton	4.00
20DS Greg Maddux	5.00

Diamond Stars Autograph
NM/M
Numbered to 100
Derek Jeter   125.00

Diamond Stars Game-Used

NM/M
Common Player: 5.00
Inserted 1:105

Barry Bonds/Jsy	20.00
Manny Ramirez/Jsy	8.00
Ivan Rodriguez/Jsy	8.00
Kazuhiro Sasaki/Jsy	8.00
Roger Clemens	20.00
Alex Rodriguez	15.00
Derek Jeter	25.00
Chipper Jones	10.00
Todd Helton	8.00
Luis Gonzalez	5.00
Mike Piazza	10.00
Nomar Garciaparra	25.00

Diamond Stars Game-Used Premium
NM/M
Production 75 Sets

Barry Bonds	60.00
Roger Clemens	60.00
Todd Helton	30.00
Chipper Jones	30.00
Manny Ramirez	25.00
Alex Rodriguez	50.00
Ivan Rodriguez	25.00
Luis Gonzalez	25.00
Mike Piazza	40.00
Kazuhiro Sasaki	20.00

Diamond Stars Dual Game-Used
NM/M
Numbered to 100.

Barry Bonds	60.00
Todd Helton	20.00
Derek Jeter	60.00
Chipper Jones	30.00
Mike Piazza	35.00
Manny Ramirez	25.00
Alex Rodriguez	40.00

Diamond Stars Dual Game-Used Premium
Production 25 Sets

International Pride

NM/M
Complete Set (15): 10.00
Common Player: .50
Inserted 1:6

1IP Larry Walker	.50
2IP Albert Pujols	3.00
3IP Juan Gonzalez	.75
4IP Ichiro Suzuki	2.00
5IP Rafael Palmeiro	.65
6IP Carlos Delgado	.50
7IP Kazuhiro Sasaki	.50
8IP Vladimir Guerrero	.75
9IP Bobby Abreu	.50
10IP Ivan Rodriguez	.60
11IP Tsuyoshi Shinjo	.50
12IP Pedro J. Martinez	.75
13IP Andruw Jones	.75
14IP Sammy Sosa	2.00
15IP Chan Ho Park	.50

International Pride Game-Used
NM/M
Common Player: 5.00
Inserted 1:90

Carlos Delgado/Jsy	8.00
Juan Gonzalez/Jsy	8.00
Andruw Jones/Jsy	8.00
Pedro Martinez/Jsy	10.00
Rafael Palmeiro/Jsy	5.00
Chan Ho Park/Jsy	5.00
Albert Pujols/Jsy	20.00
Ivan Rodriguez/Bat	10.00
Kazuhiro Sasaki/Jsy	5.00
Tsuyoshi Shinjo/Jsy	5.00

International Pride Premium
NM/M
Production 75 Sets   15.00

Carlos Delgado	25.00
Juan Gonzalez	40.00
Andruw Jones	40.00
Pedro J. Martinez	15.00
Chan Ho Park	15.00
Ivan Rodriguez	25.00
Tsuyoshi Shinjo	15.00
Rafael Palmeiro	25.00
Albert Pujols	75.00
Kazuhiro Sasaki	15.00

Legendary Dynasties

	NM/M
Complete Set (36):	125.00
Common Player:	1.50
Inserted 1:18	
Gold:	1X
Production 300 Sets	
1LD Honus Wagner	4.00
2LD Christy Mathewson	4.00
3LD Lou Gehrig	8.00
4LD Babe Ruth	12.00
5LD Jimmie Foxx	4.00
6LD Lefty Grove	2.00
7LD Al Simmons	1.50
8LD Bill Dickey	1.50
9LD Stan Musial	5.00
10LD Enos Slaughter	1.50
11LD Johnny Mize	2.00
12LD Yogi Berra	3.00
13LD Whitey Ford	3.00
14LD Jackie Robinson	8.00
15LD Duke Snider	3.00
16LD Roger Maris	5.00
17LD Jim Palmer	2.00
18LD Don Drysdale	3.00
19LD Brooks Robinson	3.00
20LD Rollie Fingers	1.50
21LD Reggie Jackson	2.00
22LD Joe Morgan	2.00
23LD Johnny Bench	5.00
24LD Thurman Munson	4.00
25LD Jose Canseco	2.50
26LD Tom Glavine	2.00
27LD Chipper Jones	4.00
28LD Greg Maddux	5.00
29LD Roberto Alomar	3.00
30LD David Cone	1.50
31LD Jim Thome	3.00
32LD Manny Ramirez	5.00
33LD Roger Clemens	6.00
34LD Derek Jeter	8.00
35LD Bernie Williams	2.50
36LD Alfonso Soriano	3.00

Legendary Dynasties Autographs

	NM/M
#'d to World Series Year	
Johnny Bench/76	80.00
Yogi Berra/51	60.00
Reggie Jackson/73	60.00
Derek Jeter/96	125.00

Legendary Dynasties Game-Used

	NM/M
Common Player:	8.00
Inserted 1:120	
Roberto Alomar/Jsy	8.00
Johnny Bench/Jsy	15.00
Yogi Berra/Bat/SP/75	50.00
Roger Clemens/Jsy	25.00
Bill Dickey/Bat	25.00
Rollie Fingers/Jsy	8.00
Reggie Jackson/Bat	25.00
Derek Jeter/Bat	30.00
Chipper Jones/Jsy	10.00
Roger Maris/Pants/SP	50.00
Johnny Mize/Bat	15.00
Joe Morgan/Bat	8.00
Thurman Munson/Bat	35.00
Jim Palmer/Jsy	10.00
Manny Ramirez/Jsy	10.00
Brooks Robinson/Bat	30.00
Jackie Robinson/SP/150	60.00
Babe Ruth/Bat	200.00
Duke Snider/Bat	30.00
Alfonso Soriano/Bat	10.00
Bernie Williams/Jsy	8.00

Legendary Dynasties Premium

	NM/M
Numbered to Highest win total.	
Rollie Fingers/93	15.00
Roger Clemens/114	50.00
Roger Maris/109	70.00
Roberto Alomar/96	25.00
Reggie Jackson/93	30.00
Manny Ramirez/99	25.00
Johnny Bench/108	35.00
Jim Palmer/109	30.00
Derek Jeter/114	80.00
Alfonso Soriano/99	30.00
Chipper Jones/106	30.00
Bernie Williams/114	20.00

On Base!

	NM/M
Complete Set (30):	125.00
Common Player:	2.00
#'d to 2001 OBP	
10B Frank Thomas/316	5.00
20B Ivan Rodriguez/347	5.00
30B Nomar Garciaparra/352	10.00
40B Ken Griffey Jr./365	8.00
50B Juan Gonzalez/370	4.00
60B Shawn Green/372	4.00
70B Vladimir Guerrero/377	5.00
80B Derek Jeter/377	15.00
90B Scott Rolen/378	4.00
100B Ichiro Suzuki/381	10.00
110B Mike Piazza/384	10.00
120B Bernie Williams/395	3.00
130B Moises Alou/396	3.00
140B Jeff Bagwell/397	4.00
150B Alex Rodriguez/399	10.00
160B Albert Pujols/403	8.00
170B Manny Ramirez/405	4.00
180B Carlos Delgado/408	3.00
190B Jim Edmonds/410	3.00
200B Roberto Alomar/415	3.00
210B Jim Thome/416	3.00
220B Gary Sheffield/417	3.00
230B Chipper Jones/427	5.00
240B Luis Gonzalez/429	2.00
250B Lance Berkman/430	3.00
260B Todd Helton/432	4.00
270B Sammy Sosa/437	10.00
280B Larry Walker/449	2.00
290B Jason Giambi/477	4.00
300B Barry Bonds/515	12.00

On Base! Game-Used

	NM/M
Common Player:	5.00
Production 100 Sets	
Roberto Alomar	8.00
Moises Alou	5.00
Jeff Bagwell	8.00
Lance Berkman	5.00
Barry Bonds	20.00
Carlos Delgado	8.00
Jim Edmonds	6.00
Nomar Garciaparra	15.00
Jason Giambi	8.00
Juan Gonzalez	5.00
Luis Gonzalez	5.00
Shawn Green	5.00
Ken Griffey Jr.	20.00
Vladimir Guerrero	8.00
Todd Helton	8.00
Derek Jeter	25.00
Chipper Jones	10.00
Mike Piazza	15.00
Albert Pujols	15.00
Manny Ramirez	10.00
Alex Rodriguez	15.00
Ivan Rodriguez	10.00
Scott Rolen	5.00
Gary Sheffield	6.00
Sammy Sosa	20.00
Ichiro Suzuki	15.00
Frank Thomas	10.00
Jim Thome	8.00
Larry Walker	5.00
Bernie Williams	6.00

Project Liberty N.Y. Mets

"New York is Getting Stronger Every Day" was the theme of this team set distributed at a promotional game in Shea Stadium. Cards feature game-action photos and symbols of the team's efforts to respond to the 9/11/01 attack. An image of the Statue of Liberty is vignetted on front of most cards. Player cards have recent stats and highlights, other cards have information on help lines and other resources.

	NM/M
Complete Set (15):	10.00
Common Card:	.35
1 Mets players	.35
2 Al Leiter	.75
3 Mike Piazza	3.00
4 NYPD baseball cap (Al Leiter)	.75
5 Mo Vaughn	.75
6 Roberto Alomar	1.00
7 Edgardo Alfonzo	.75
8 9-11-01 sleeve patch	.35
9 Rey Ordonez	.75
10 Roger Cedeno	.75
11 Timo Perez	.75
12 NYPD batting helmet (Mike Piazza)	1.50
13 Jeromy Burnitz	.75
14 Bobby Valentine	.75
15 U.S. flag at Shea	.35

2002 Fleer Showcase

	NM/M
Complete Set (166):	225.00
Common Player:	.25
Common (126-141):	5.00
Production 500	
Common (141-166):	4.00
Production 1,500	
Pack (5):	3.00
Box (24):	60.00
1 Albert Pujols	2.00
2 Pedro J. Martinez	.75
3 Frank Thomas	.75
4 Gary Sheffield	.40
5 Roberto Alomar	.40
6 Luis Gonzalez	.35
7 Bobby Abreu	.25
8 Carlos Lee	.25
9 Preston Wilson	.25
10 Todd Helton	.75
11 Juan Gonzalez	.75
12 Chuck Knoblauch	.25
13 Jason Kendall	.25
14 Aaron Sele	.25
15 Greg Vaughn	.25
16 Fred McGriff	.25
17 Doug Mientkiewicz	.25
18 Richard Hidalgo	.25
19 Alfonso Soriano	.50
20 Matt Williams	.25
21 Bobby Higginson	.25
22 Mo Vaughn	.25
23 Andruw Jones	.75
24 Omar Vizquel	.25
25 Bret Boone	.25
26 Bernie Williams	.35
27 Rafael Furcal	.25
28 Jeff Bagwell	.75
29 Marty Cordova	.25
30 Lance Berkman	.25
31 Vernon Wells	.25
32 Garret Anderson	.25
33 Larry Bigbie	.25
34 Steve Finley	.25
35 Barry Bonds	3.00
36 Eric Chavez	.35
37 Tony Clark	.25
38 Roger Clemens	1.50
39 Adam Dunn	.50
40 Roger Cedeno	.25
41 Carlos Delgado	.50
42 Jermaine Dye	.25
43 Brian Jordan	.25
44 Darin Erstad	.65
45 Paul LoDuca	.25
46 Jim Edmonds	.25
47 Tom Glavine	.50
48 Cliff Floyd	.25
49 Jon Lieber	.25
50 Adrian Beltre	.40
51 Joel Pineiro	.25
52 Jim Thome	.25
53 Jimmy Rollins	.40
54 Pat Burrell	.40
55 Jeromy Burnitz	.25
56 Larry Walker	.25
57 Damon Minor	.25
58 John Olerud	.25
59 Carlos Beltran	.50
60 Vladimir Guerrero	.75
61 David Justice	.25
62 Phil Nevin	.25
63 Tino Martinez	.25
64 Curt Schilling	.75
65 Corey Patterson	.25
66 Aubrey Huff	.25
67 Mark Grace	.35
68 Rafael Palmeiro	.65
69 Jorge Posada	.35
70 Craig Biggio	.25
71 Manny Ramirez	.75
72 Mark Quinn	.25
73 Raul Mondesi	.25
74 Shawn Green	.40
75 Brian Giles	.25
76 Paul Konerko	.25
77 Troy Glaus	.25
78 Mike Mussina	.40
79 Greg Maddux	1.00
80 Edgar Martinez	.25
81 Jose Vidro	.25
82 Scott Rolen	.65
83 Ben Grieve	.25
84 Jeff Kent	.25
85 Magglio Ordonez	.25
86 Freddy Garcia	.25
87 Ivan Rodriguez	.65
88 Pokey Reese	.25
89 Shannon Stewart	.25
90 Randy Johnson	.75
91 Cristian Guzman	.25
92 Tsuyoshi Shinjo	.25
93 Steve Cox	.25
94 Mike Sweeney	.25
95 Robert Fick	.25
96 Sean Casey	.40
97 Tim Hudson	.35
98 Bud Smith	.25
99 Corey Koskie	.25
100 Richie Sexson	.25
101 Aramis Ramirez	.25
102 Barry Larkin	.25
103 Rich Aurilia	.25
104 Charles Johnson	.25
105 Ryan Klesko	.25
106 Ben Sheets	.25
107 J.D. Drew	.40
108 Jay Gibbons	.25
109 Kerry Wood	.65
110 C.C. Sabathia	.25
111 Eric Munson	.25
112 Josh Beckett	.40
113 Javier Vasquez	.25
114 Barry Zito	.35
115 Kazuhiro Sasaki	.25
116 Bubba Trammell	.25
117 Russell Branyan	.25
118 Todd Walker	.25
119 Mike Hampton	.25
120 Jeff Weaver	.25
121 Geoff Jenkins	.25
122 Edgardo Alfonzo	.25
123 Mike Lieberthal	.25
124 Mike Lowell	.25
125 Kevin Brown	.25
126 Derek Jeter	8.00
127 Ichiro Suzuki	5.00
128 Nomar Garciaparra	5.00
129 Ken Griffey Jr.	5.00
130 Jason Giambi	5.00
131 Alex Rodriguez	6.00
132 Chipper Jones	5.00
133 Mike Piazza	5.00
134 Sammy Sosa	5.00
135 Hideo Nomo	5.00
136 Kazuhisa Ishii RC	8.00
137 Satoru Komiyama RC	5.00
138 So Taguchi RC	6.00
139 Jorge Padilla RC	5.00
140 Rene Reyes RC	5.00
141 Jorge Nunez RC	5.00
142 Nelson Castro RC	4.00
143 Anderson Machado RC	4.00
144 Edwin Almonte RC	4.00
145 Luis Ugueto RC	4.00
146 Felix Escalona RC	4.00
147 Ron Calloway RC	4.00
148 Hansel Izquierdo RC	4.00
149 Mark Teixeira RC	6.00
150 Orlando Hudson RC	4.00
151 Aaron Cook RC	4.00
152 Aaron Taylor RC	4.00
153 Takahito Nomura RC	4.00
154 Matt Thornton RC	4.00
155 Mark Prior RC	6.00
156 Reed Johnson RC	6.00
157 Doug DeVore RC	4.00
158 Ben Howard RC	4.00
159 Francis Beltran RC	4.00
160 Brian Mallette RC	4.00
161 Sean Burroughs	4.00
162 Michael Restovich	4.00
163 Austin Kearns	4.00
164 Marlon Byrd	4.00
165 Hank Blalock	5.00
166 Mike Rivera	4.00

Legacy

Stars (1-125):	3-5X
Legacy (126-166):	1X
Production 175 Sets	

Baseball's Best

	NM/M
Complete Set (20):	40.00
Common Player:	1.00
Inserted 1:8	
1 Derek Jeter	5.00
2 Barry Bonds	5.00
3 Mike Piazza	3.00
4 Alex Rodriguez	4.00
5 Pat Burrell	1.00
6 Rafael Palmeiro	1.00
7 Nomar Garciaparra	3.00
8 Todd Helton	1.50
9 Roger Clemens	2.50
10 Shawn Green	1.00
11 Chipper Jones	2.00
12 Pedro J. Martinez	1.50
13 Luis Gonzalez	1.00
14 Randy Johnson	1.50
15 Ichiro Suzuki	3.00
16 Ken Griffey Jr.	3.00
17 Vladimir Guerrero	1.50
18 Sammy Sosa	3.00
19 Jason Giambi	1.00
20 Albert Pujols	2.00

Baseball's Best Memorabilia

	NM/M
Common Player:	5.00
Inserted 1:24	
Golds:	1-2X
Production 100 Sets	
Derek Jeter/Jsy	20.00
Barry Bonds/Jsy	20.00
Mike Piazza/Jsy	15.00
Alex Rodriguez/Bat	15.00
Rafael Palmeiro/Jsy	8.00
Nomar Garciaparra/Jsy	10.00
Todd Helton/Bat	10.00
Roger Clemens/Jsy	15.00
Shawn Green/Jsy	5.00
Chipper Jones/Jsy	10.00
Pedro Martinez/Jsy	8.00
Luis Gonzalez/Jsy	5.00
Randy Johnson/Jsy	10.00
Ichiro Suzuki/Jsy	10.00
Ken Griffey Jr./Base	10.00
Vladimir Guerrero/Base	8.00
Sammy Sosa/Base	10.00
Jason Giambi/Base	8.00
Albert Pujols/Base	10.00

Baseball's Best Silver Autograph

	NM/M
Serial numbered to 400.	
Derek Jeter	125.00
Barry Bonds	200.00

Baseball's Best Gold Autograph

	NM/M
Serial numbered to 100.	
Derek Jeter	150.00
Barry Bonds	225.00

Derek Jeter's Legacy Collection

Common Jeter:	5.00
Production 1,000 Sets	
1-22 Derek Jeter	5.00

Derek Jeter's Legacy Collection Memorabilia

	NM/M
Quantity produced listed	
Derek Jeter/Jsy/300	75.00
Derek Jeter/Combo/Jsy/175	90.00
Derek Jeter/World Series Ball/50	100.00
Derek Jeter/Glv/425	60.00

Sweet Sigs Leather

	NM/M
Common Player:	8.00
2 Russell Branyan/90	10.00
6 Rafael Furcal/92	15.00
8 Brandon Inge/122	10.00
10 Xavier Nady/301	8.00
11 Jose Ortiz/50	10.00
12 Ben Sheets/60	25.00
13 Mike Sweeney/103	15.00

Sweet Sigs Lumber

	NM/M
Common Player:	5.00
1 Bobby Abreu/231	10.00
2 Russell Branyan/425	10.00
3 Pat Burrell/115	10.00
4 Sean Casey/64	20.00
6 Eric Chavez/256	10.00
8 Rafael Furcal/530	10.00
9 Brandon Inge/528	5.00
9 Jackson Melian/636	5.00
10 Xavier Nady/589	8.00
11 Jose Ortiz/515	8.00
12 Ben Sheets/458	15.00
13 Mike Sweeney/495	10.00

Sweet Sigs Wall

	NM/M
Common Player:	8.00
1 Bobby Abreu/70	20.00
2 Russell Branyan/200	8.00
5 Eric Chavez/108	15.00
6 Rafael Furcal/207	10.00
8 Brandon Inge/187	8.00
9 Jackson Melian/146	8.00
10 Xavier Nady/286	8.00
11 Jose Ortiz/116	8.00
12 Ben Sheets/150	20.00
13 Mike Sweeney/371	10.00

2002 Fleer Tradition

	NM/M
Complete Set (500):	175.00
Common Player:	.15
Common SP (1-100):	1.50
Inserted 1:2	
Pack (10):	2.00
Box (36):	50.00
1 Barry Bonds	10.00
2 Cal Ripken Jr.	10.00
3 Tony Gwynn	5.00
4 Brad Radke	1.50
5 Jose Ortiz	1.50
6 Mark Mulder	1.50
7 Jon Lieber	1.50
8 John Olerud	1.50
9 Phil Nevin	1.50
10 Craig Biggio	1.50
11 Pedro Martinez	4.00
12 Fred McGriff	1.50
13 Vladimir Guerrero	4.00
14 Jason Giambi	3.00
15 Mark Kotsay	1.50
16 Bud Smith	1.50
17 Kevin Brown	1.50
18 Darin Erstad	3.00
19 Julio Franco	1.50
20 C.C. Sabathia	1.50
21 Larry Walker	1.50
22 Doug Mientkiewicz	1.50
23 Luis Gonzalez	2.00
24 Albert Pujols	8.00
25 Brian Lawrence	1.50
26 Al Leiter	1.50

No.	Player	Price
27	Mike Sweeney	1.50
28	Jeff Weaver	1.50
29	Matt Morris	1.50
30	Hideo Nomo	4.00
31	Tom Glavine	2.50
32	Magglio Ordonez	1.50
33	Roberto Alomar	2.50
34	Roger Cedeno	1.50
35	Greg Vaughn	1.50
36	Chan Ho Park	1.50
37	Rich Aurilia	1.50
38	Tsuyoshi Shinjo	1.50
39	Eric Young	1.50
40	Bobby Higginson	1.50
41	Marlon Anderson	1.50
42	Mark Grace	2.00
43	Steve Cox	1.50
44	Cliff Floyd	1.50
45	Brian Roberts	1.50
46	Paul Konerko	1.50
47	Brandon Duckworth	1.50
48	Josh Beckett	2.50
49	David Ortiz	2.50
50	Geoff Jenkins	1.50
51	Ruben Sierra	1.50
52	John Franco	1.50
53	Einar Diaz	1.50
54	Luis Castillo	1.50
55	Mark Quinn	1.50
56	Shea Hillenbrand	1.50
57	Rafael Palmeiro	3.00
58	Paul O'Neill	1.50
59	Andruw Jones	4.00
60	Lance Berkman	1.50
61	Jimmy Rollins	2.00
62	Jose Hernandez	1.50
63	Rusty Greer	1.50
64	Wade Miller	1.50
65	David Eckstein	1.50
66	Jose Valentin	1.50
67	Javier Vazquez	1.50
68	Roger Clemens	6.00
69	Omar Vizquel	1.50
70	Roy Oswalt	1.50
71	Shannon Stewart	1.50
72	Byung-Hyun Kim	1.50
73	Jay Gibbons	1.50
74	Barry Larkin	1.50
75	Brian Giles	1.50
76	Andres Galarraga	1.50
77	Sammy Sosa	6.00
78	Manny Ramirez	4.00
79	Carlos Delgado	2.50
80	Jorge Posada	1.50
81	Todd Ritchie	1.50
82	Russ Ortiz	1.50
83	Brent Mayne	1.50
84	Mike Mussina	3.00
85	Raul Mondesi	1.50
86	Mark Loretta	1.50
87	Tim Raines	1.50
88	Ichiro Suzuki	6.00
89	Juan Pierre	1.50
90	Adam Dunn	2.50
91	Jason Tyner	1.50
92	Miguel Tejada	1.50
93	Elpidio Guzman	1.50
94	Freddy Garcia	1.50
95	Marcus Giles	1.50
96	Junior Spivey	1.50
97	Aramis Ramirez	1.50
98	Jose Rijo	1.50
99	Paul LoDuca	1.50
100	Mike Cameron	1.50
101	Alex Hernandez	.15
102	Benji Gil	.15
103	Benito Santiago	.15
104	Bobby Abreu	.15
105	Brad Penny	.15
106	Calvin Murray	.15
107	Chad Durbin	.15
108	Chris Singleton	.15
109	Chris Carpenter	.15
110	David Justice	.15
111	Eric Chavez	.25
112	Fernando Tatis	.15
113	Frank Castillo	.15
114	Jason LaRue	.15
115	Jim Edmonds	.15
116	Joe Kennedy	.15
117	Jose Jimenez	.15
118	Josh Towers	.15
119	Junior Herndon	.15
120	Luke Prokopec	.15
121	Mac Suzuki	.15
122	Mark DeRosa	.15
123	Marty Cordova	.15
124	Michael Tucker	.15
125	Michael Young	.15
126	Robin Ventura	.15
127	Shane Halter	.15
128	Shane Reynolds	.15
129	Tony Womack	.15
130	A.J. Pierzynski	.15
131	Aaron Rowand	.15
132	Antonio Alfonseca	.15
133	Arthur Rhodes	.15
134	Bob Wickman	.15
135	Brady Clark	.15
136	Chad Hermansen	.15
137	Marlon Byrd	.15
138	Dan Wilson	.15
139	David Cone	.15
140	Dean Palmer	.15
141	Denny Neagle	.15
142	Derek Jeter	2.50
143	Erubiel Durazo	.15
144	Felix Rodriguez	.15
145	Jason Hart	.15
146	Jay Bell	.15
147	Jeff Suppan	.15
148	Jeff Zimmerman	.15
149	Kerry Wood	.65
150	Kerry Robinson	.15
151	Kevin Appier	.15
152	Michael Barrett	.15
153	Mo Vaughn	.15
154	Rafael Furcal	.15
155	Sidney Ponson	.15
156	Terry Adams	.15
157	Tim Redding	.15
158	Toby Hall	.15
159	Aaron Sele	.15
160	Bartolo Colon	.15
161	Brad Ausmus	.15
162	Carlos Pena	.15
163	Jace Brewer	.15
164	David Wells	.15
165	David Segui	.15
166	Derek Lowe	.15
167	Derek Bell	.15
168	Jason Grabowski	.15
169	Johnny Damon	.25
170	Jose Mesa	.15
171	Juan Encarnacion	.15
172	Ken Caminiti	.15
173	Ken Griffey Jr.	1.50
174	Luis Rivas	.15
175	Mariano Rivera	.25
176	Mark Grudzielanek	.15
177	Mark McGwire	2.00
178	Mike Bordick	.15
179	Mike Hampton	.15
180	Nick Bierbrodt	.15
181	Paul Byrd	.15
182	Robb Nen	.15
183	Ryan Dempster	.15
184	Ryan Klesko	.15
185	Scott Spiezio	.15
186	Scott Strickland	.15
187	Todd Zeile	.15
188	Tom Gordon	.15
189	Troy Glaus	.75
190	Matt Williams	.15
191	Wes Helms	.15
192	Jerry Hairston Jr.	.15
193	Brook Fordyce	.15
194	Nomar Garciaparra	1.50
195	Kevin Tapani	.15
196	Mark Buehrle	.15
197	Dmitri Young	.15
198	John Rocker	.15
199	Juan Uribe	.15
200	Matt Anderson	.15
201	Alex Gonzalez	.15
202	Julio Lugo	.15
203	Roberto Hernandez	.15
204	Richie Sexson	.15
205	Corey Koskie	.15
206	Tony Armas Jr.	.15
207	Rey Ordonez	.15
208	Orlando Hernandez	.15
209	Pokey Reese	.15
210	Mike Lieberthal	.15
211	Kris Benson	.15
212	Jermaine Dye	.15
213	Livan Hernandez	.15
214	Bret Boone	.15
215	Dustin Hermanson	.15
216	Placido Polanco	.15
217	Jesus Colome	.15
218	Alex Gonzalez	.15
219	Adam Everett	.15
220	Adam Piatt	.15
221	Brad Fullmer	.15
222	Brian Buchanan	.15
223	Chipper Jones	1.00
224	Chuck Finley	.15
225	David Bell	.15
226	Jack Wilson	.25
227	Jason Bere	.15
228	Jeff Conine	.15
229	Jeff Bagwell	.75
230	Joe McEwing	.15
231	Kip Wells	.15
232	Mike Lansing	.15
233	Neifi Perez	.15
234	Omar Daal	.15
235	Reggie Sanders	.15
236	Shawn Wooten	.15
237	Shawn Chacon	.15
238	Shawn Estes	.15
239	Steve Sparks	.15
240	Steve Kline	.15
241	Tino Martinez	.15
242	Tyler Houston	.15
243	Xavier Nady	.15
244	Bengie Molina	.15
245	Ben Davis	.15
246	Casey Fossum	.15
247	Chris Stynes	.15
248	Danny Graves	.15
249	Pedro Feliz	.15
250	Darren Oliver	.15
251	Dave Veres	.15
252	Deivi Cruz	.15
253	Desi Relaford	.15
254	Devon White	.15
255	Edgar Martinez	.15
256	Eric Munson	.15
257	Eric Karros	.15
258	Homer Bush	.15
259	Jason Kendall	.15
260	Javy Lopez	.15
261	Keith Foulke	.15
262	Keith Ginter	.15
263	Nick Johnson	.15
264	Pat Burrell	.35
265	Ricky Gutierrez	.15
266	Russ Johnson	.15
267	Steve Finley	.15
268	Terrence Long	.25
269	Tony Batista	.15
270	Torii Hunter	.15
271	Vinny Castilla	.15
272	A.J. Burnett	.15
273	Adrian Beltre	.35
274	Alex Rodriguez	2.00
275	Armando Benitez	.15
276	Billy Koch	.15
277	Brady Anderson	.15
278	Brian Jordan	.15
279	Carlos Febles	.15
280	Daryle Ward	.15
281	Eli Marrero	.15
282	Garret Anderson	.15
283	Jack Cust	.15
284	Jacque Jones	.15
285	Jamie Moyer	.15
286	Jeffrey Hammonds	.15
287	Jim Thome	.15
288	Jon Garland	.15
289	Jose Offerman	.15
290	Matt Stairs	.15
291	Orlando Cabrera	.15
292	Ramiro Mendoza	.15
293	Ray Durham	.15
294	Rickey Henderson	.75
295	Rob Mackowiak	.15
296	Scott Rolen	.65
297	Tim Hudson	.25
298	Todd Helton	.75
299	Tony Clark	.15
300	B.J. Surhoff	.15
301	Bernie Williams	.30
302	Bill Mueller	.15
303	Chris Richard	.15
304	Craig Paquette	.15
305	Curt Schilling	.40
306	Damian Jackson	.15
307	Derek Lee	.15
308	Eric Milton	.15
309	Frank Catalanotto	.15
310	J.T. Snow	.15
311	Jared Sandberg	.15
312	Jason Varitek	.15
313	Jeff Cirillo	.15
314	Jeromy Burnitz	.15
315	Joe Crede	.15
316	Joel Pineiro	.15
317	Jose Cruz Jr.	.15
318	Kevin Young	.15
319	Marquis Grissom	.15
320	Moises Alou	.15
321	Randall Simon	.15
322	Royce Clayton	.15
323	Tim Salmon	.25
324	Travis Fryman	.15
325	Travis Lee	.15
326	Vance Wilson	.15
327	Jarrod Washburn	.15
328	Ben Petrick	.15
329	Ben Grieve	.15
330	Carl Everett	.15
331	Eric Byrnes	.15
332	Doug Glanville	.15
333	Edgardo Alfonzo	.15
334	Ellis Burks	.15
335	Gabe Kapler	.15
336	Gary Sheffield	.25
337	Greg Maddux	1.00
338	J.D. Drew	.25
339	Jamey Wright	.15
340	Jeff Kent	.15
341	Jeremy Giambi	.15
342	Joe Randa	.15
343	Joe Mays	.15
344	Jose Macias	.15
345	Kazuhiro Sasaki	.15
346	Mike Kinkade	.15
347	Mike Lowell	.15
348	Randy Johnson	.75
349	Randy Wolf	.15
350	Richard Hidalgo	.15
351	Ron Coomer	.15
352	Sandy Alomar	.15
353	Sean Casey	.25
354	Trevor Hoffman	.15
355	Adam Eaton	.15
356	Alfonso Soriano	.50
357	Barry Zito	.25
358	Billy Wagner	.15
359	Brent Abernathy	.15
360	Bret Prinz	.15
361	Carlos Beltran	.40
362	Carlos Guillen	.15
363	Charles Johnson	.15
364	Cristian Guzman	.15
365	Damion Easley	.15
366	Darryl Kile	.15
367	Delino DeShields	.15
368	Eric Davis	.15
369	Frank Thomas	.75
370	Ivan Rodriguez	.65
371	Jay Payton	.15
372	Jeff D'Amico	.15
373	John Burkett	.15
374	Melvin Mora	.15
375	Ramon Ortiz	.15
376	Robert Person	.15
377	Russell Branyan	.15
378	Shawn Green	.25
379	Todd Hollandsworth	.15
380	Tony McKnight	.15
381	Trot Nixon	.15
382	Vernon Wells	.15
383	Troy Percival	.15
384	Albie Lopez	.15
385	Alex Ochoa	.15
386	Andy Pettitte	.25
387	Brandon Inge	.15
388	Bubba Trammell	.15
389	Corey Patterson	.15
390	Damian Rolls	.15
391	Dee Brown	.15
392	Edgar Renteria	.15
393	Eric Gagne	.35
394	Jason Johnson	.15
395	Jeff Nelson	.15
396	John Vander Wal	.15
397	Johnny Estrada	.15
398	Jose Canseco	.40
399	Juan Gonzalez	.75
400	Kevin Millwood	.15
401	Lee Stevens	.15
402	Matt Lawton	.15
403	Mike Lamb	.15
404	Octavio Dotel	.15
405	Ramon Hernandez	.15
406	Ruben Quevedo	.15
407	Todd Walker	.15
408	Troy O'Leary	.15
409	Wascar Serrano	.15
410	Aaron Boone	.15
411	Aubrey Huff	.15
412	Ben Sheets	.15
413	Carlos Lee	.15
414	Chuck Knoblauch	.15
415	Steve Karsay	.15
416	Dante Bichette	.15
417	David Dellucci	.15
418	Esteban Loaiza	.15
419	Fernando Vina	.15
420	Ismael Valdes	.15
421	Jason Isringhausen	.15
422	Jeff Shaw	.15
423	John Smoltz	.15
424	Jose Vidro	.15
425	Kenny Lofton	.15
426	Mark Little	.15
427	Mark McLemore	.15
428	Marvin Benard	.15
429	Mike Piazza	1.50
430	Pat Hentgen	.15
431	Preston Wilson	.15
432	Rick Helling	.15
433	Robert Fick	.15
434	Rondell White	.15
435	Adam Kennedy	.15
436	David Espinosa	.15
437	Dewon Brazelton	.15
438	Drew Henson	.25
439	Juan Cruz	.15
440	Jason Jennings	.15
441	Carlos Garcia	.15
442	Carlos Hernandez	.15
443	Wilkin Ruan	.15
444	Wilson Betemit	.15
445	Horacio Ramirez	.15
446	Danys Baez	.15
447	Abraham Nunez	.15
448	Josh Hamilton	.25
449	Chris George	.15
450	Rick Bauer	.15
451	Donnie Bridges	.15
452	Erick Almonte	.15
453	Cory Aldridge	.15
454	Ryan Drese	.15
455	Jason Romano	.15
456	Corky Miller	.15
457	Rafael Soriano	.15
458	Mark Prior	.75
459	Mark Teixeira	.50
460	Adrian Hernandez	.15
461	Tim Spooneybarger	.15
462	Bill Ortega	.15
463	D'Angelo Jimenez	.15
464	Andres Torres	.15
465	Alexis Gomez	.15
466	Angel Berroa	.15
467	Henry Mateo	.15
468	Endy Chavez	.15
469	Billy Sylvester	.15
470	Nate Frese	.15
471	Luis Gonzalez	.25
472	Barry Bonds	2.50
473	Rich Aurilia	.15
474	Albert Pujols	2.00
475	Todd Helton	.75
476	Moises Alou	.15
477	Lance Berkman	.15
478	Brian Giles	.15
479	Cliff Floyd	.15
480	Sammy Sosa	1.50
481	Shawn Green	.30
482	Jon Lieber	.15
483	Matt Morris	.15
484	Curt Schilling	.40
485	Randy Johnson	.75
486	Manny Ramirez	.75
487	Ichiro Suzuki	1.50
488	Juan Gonzalez	.75
489	Derek Jeter	2.50
490	Alex Rodriguez	2.00
491	Bret Boone	.15
492	Roberto Alomar	.30
493	Jason Giambi	.50
494	Rafael Palmeiro	.65
495	Doug Mientkiewicz	.15
496	Jim Thome	.15
497	Freddy Garcia	.15
498	Mark Buehrle	.15
499	Mark Mulder	.15
500	Roger Clemens	1.25

Diamond Tributes

	NM/M
Complete Set (15):	15.00
Common Player:	.50
Inserted 1:6	
1DT Cal Ripken Jr.	3.00
2DT Tony Gwynn	1.00
3DT Derek Jeter	3.00
4DT Pedro Martinez	.75
5DT Mark McGwire	2.50
6DT Sammy Sosa	2.00
7DT Barry Bonds	3.00
8DT Roger Clemens	1.50
9DT Mike Piazza	2.00
10DT Alex Rodriguez	2.50
11DT Randy Johnson	.75
12DT Chipper Jones	1.00
13DT Nomar Garciaparra	2.00
14DT Ichiro Suzuki	2.00
15DT Jason Giambi	.50

Grass Roots

	NM/M
Complete Set (10):	15.00
Common Player:	.75
Inserted 1:18	
1GR Barry Bonds	5.00
2GR Alex Rodriguez	4.00
3GR Derek Jeter	5.00
4GR Greg Maddux	2.50
5GR Ivan Rodriguez	1.00
6GR Cal Ripken Jr.	5.00
7GR Bernie Williams	.75
8GR Jeff Bagwell	1.50
9GR Scott Rolen	1.00
10GR Larry Walker	.75

Grass Roots Patch

	NM/M
Production 50 Sets	
Barry Bonds	100.00
Alex Rodriguez	75.00
Greg Maddux	50.00
Ivan Rodriguez	25.00
Cal Ripken Jr.	100.00
Bernie Williams	25.00
Jeff Bagwell	40.00
Scott Rolen	30.00
Larry Walker	20.00

Heads Up

MARK McGWIRE / 1B

	NM/M
Complete Set (10):	45.00
Common Player:	1.00
Inserted 1:36	
1HU Derek Jeter	8.00
2HU Ichiro Suzuki	8.00
3HU Sammy Sosa	5.00
4HU Mike Piazza	5.00
5HU Ken Griffey Jr.	5.00
6HU Alex Rodriguez	6.00
7HU Barry Bonds	8.00
8HU Nomar Garciaparra	5.00
9HU Mark McGwire	6.00
10HU Cal Ripken Jr.	8.00

Lumber Co.

	NM/M
Complete Set (30):	40.00
Common Player:	1.00
Inserted 1:12	
1LC Moises Alou	1.00
2LC Luis Gonzalez	1.00
3LC Todd Helton	2.50
4LC Mike Piazza	4.00
5LC J.D. Drew	1.50
6LC Albert Pujols	5.00
7LC Chipper Jones	3.00
8LC Manny Ramirez	2.50
9LC Miguel Tejada	1.00
10LC Curt Schilling	1.50
11LC Alex Rodriguez	5.00
12LC Barry Larkin	1.00
13LC Nomar Garciaparra	4.00
14LC Cliff Floyd	1.00
15LC Alfonso Soriano	1.50
16LC Sean Casey	1.00
17LC Scott Rolen	2.00
18LC Jose Ortiz	1.00
19LC Corey Patterson	1.00
20LC Joe Crede	1.00
21LC Jace Brewer	1.00
22LC Derek Jeter	6.00
23LC Jim Thome	1.00
24LC Frank Thomas	2.50
25LC Shawn Green	1.00
26LC Drew Henson	1.00
27LC Jimmy Rollins	1.50
28LC Dave Justice	1.00
29LC Roberto Alomar	1.50
30LC Bernie Williams	1.00

Lumber Company Game-Used

	NM/M
Common Player:	5.00
Inserted 1:72	
Moises Alou	5.00
Luis Gonzalez	5.00
Todd Helton	8.00
Mike Piazza	12.00
J.D. Drew	6.00
Albert Pujols	15.00
Chipper Jones	10.00
Manny Ramirez	8.00
Miguel Tejada	6.00
Curt Schilling	6.00
Alex Rodriguez	15.00
Barry Larkin	5.00
Nomar Garciaparra	12.00
Cliff Floyd	5.00
Alfonso Soriano	8.00
Sean Casey	6.00
Scott Rolen	8.00
Jose Ortiz	5.00
Corey Patterson	5.00
Joe Crede	5.00
Jace Brewer	5.00
Derek Jeter	25.00
Jim Thome	5.00
Frank Thomas	8.00
Shawn Green	5.00
Drew Henson	5.00
Jimmy Rollins	5.00
Dave Justice	5.00
Roberto Alomar	6.00
Bernie Williams	5.00

This Day in History

	NM/M
Complete Set (29):	120.00
Common Player:	1.50
Inserted 1:18	
1 Cal Ripken Jr.	10.00
2 Barry Bonds	10.00
3 George Brett	4.00
4 Tony Gwynn	3.00
5 Nolan Ryan	10.00
6 Reggie Jackson	3.00
7 Paul Molitor	2.00
8 Ichiro Suzuki	5.00
9 Alex Rodriguez	6.00
10 Don Mattingly	6.00
11 Sammy Sosa	5.00
12 Mark McGwire	5.00
13 Derek Jeter	10.00
14 Roger Clemens	4.00
15 Jim "Catfish" Hunter	1.50

#	Player	Price
16	Greg Maddux	3.00
17	Ken Griffey Jr.	5.00
18	Gil Hodges	1.50
19	Edgar Martinez	1.50
20	Mike Piazza	5.00
21	Jimmie Foxx	1.50
22	Albert Pujols	6.00
23	Chipper Jones	3.00
25	Jeff Bagwell	2.00
26	Nomar Garciaparra	5.00
27	Randy Johnson	2.00
28	Todd Helton	2.00
29	Ted Kluszewski	1.50
30	Ivan Rodriguez	1.75

This Day in History Autographs

NM/M

Common Player:

#	Player	Price
3	Derek Jeter/100	100.00
4	Randy Johnson/75	50.00
5	Don Mattingly/50	90.00
7	Albert Pujols/50	200.00
8	Cal Ripken Jr./50	125.00

This Day in History Game-Used

NM/M

Common Player:

Player	Price
Jeff Bagwell/Bat/100	15.00
Barry Bonds/Jsy/250	40.00
Roger Clemens/Jsy/150	30.00
Jimmie Foxx/Bat/250	40.00
Todd Helton/Bat/150	15.00
Jim "Catfish" Hunter/Jsy/250	15.00
Derek Jeter/Jsy/250	40.00
Greg Maddux/Jsy/100	20.00
Mike Piazza/Bat/150	20.00
Alex Rodriguez/Hat/250	30.00

Update

TINO MARTINEZ

NM/M

	Price
Complete Set (400):	75.00
Common Player:	.15
Common SP (1-100):	.50
Inserted 1:1	
Pack (10):	1.50
Box (36):	35.00

#	Player	Price
1	P.J. Bevis RC	.50
2	Michael Crudale RC	.50
3	Ben Howard RC	.75
4	Travis Driskill RC	.50
5	Reed Johnson RC	.50
6	Kyle Kane RC	.50
7	Deivis Santos	.50
8	Tim Kalita RC	.50
9	Brandon Puffer RC	.50
10	Chris Snelling RC	1.00
11	Juan Brito RC	.50
12	Tyler Yates RC	.50
13	Victor Alvarez RC	.50
14	Takahito Nomura RC	.50
15	Ron Calloway RC	.50
16	Satoru Komiyama RC	.50
17	Julius Matos RC	.50
18	Jorge Nunez RC	.50
19	Anderson Machado RC	.50
20	Scotty Layfield RC	.50
21	Aaron Cook RC	.50
22	Alex Pelaez RC	.50
23	Corey Thurman RC	.50
24	Nelson Castro RC	.50
25	Jeff Austin RC	.50
26	Felix Escalona RC	.50
27	Luis Ugueto RC	.50
28	Jaime Cerda RC	.50
29	J.J. Trujillo RC	.50
30	Rodrigo Rosario RC	.50
31	Jorge Padilla RC	.50
32	Shawn Sedlacek RC	.50
33	Nate Field RC	.50

#	Player	Price
34	Earl Snyder RC	.75
35	Miguel Asencio RC	.50
36	Ken Huckaby RC	.50
37	Valentino Pascucci	.50
38	So Taguchi RC	1.00
39	Brian Mallette RC	.50
40	Kazuhisa Ishii RC	2.00
41	Matt Thornton	.50
42	Mark Corey	.50
43	Kirk Saarloos RC	.50
44	Brandon Bracke	.50
45	Hansel Izquierdo RC	.50
46	Rene Reyes RC	.50
47	Luis Garcia	.50
48	Jason Simontacchi RC	.50
49	John Ennis RC	.75
50	Franklyn German RC	.50
51	Aaron Guiel RC	.50
52	Howie Clark RC	.50
53	David Ross RC	.50
54	Walt McKeel RC	.50
55	Francis Beltran RC	.50
56	Barry Wesson RC	.50
57	Runelvys Hernandez RC	.50
58	Oliver Perez RC	2.00
59	Ryan Bukvich RC	.50
60	Steve Kent RC	.50
61	Julio Mateo RC	.50
62	Jason Jimenez	.50
63	Jayson Durocher RC	.75
64	Kevin Frederick RC	.50
65	Kevin Gryboski RC	.50
66	Edwin Almonte RC	.50
67	John Foster RC	.50
68	Doug DeVore RC	1.00
69	Tom Shearn RC	.50
70	Colin Young RC	.50
71	Jon Adkins RC	.50
72	Wilbert Nieves RC	.50
73	Matt Duff	.50
74	Carl Sadler RC	.50
75	Jason Kershner	.50
76	Brandon Backe RC	.50
77	Wilson Valdez RC	.50
78	Chris Baker RC	.50
79	Ryan Jamison	.50
80	Steve Bechler RC	.75
81	Allan Simpson RC	.50
82	Aaron Taylor RC	.50
83	Kevin Cash RC	.50
84	Chone Figgins RC	1.00
85	Clay Condrey RC	.50
86	Shane Nance RC	.50
87	Freddy Sanchez RC	.50
88	Jim Rushford RC	.50
89	Jeriome Robertson RC	.50
90	Trey Lunsford RC	.50
91	Cody McKay RC	.50
92	Trey Hodges RC	.50
93	Hee Seop Choi	1.00
94	Joe Borchard	.50
95	Orlando Hudson	.50
96	Carl Crawford	.50
97	Mark Prior	2.00
98	Brett Myers	.50
99	Kenny Lofton	.50
100	Cliff Floyd	.50
101	Randy Winn	.15
102	Ryan Dempster	.15
103	Josh Phelps	.15
104	Marcus Giles	.15
105	Rickey Henderson	.15
106	Jose Leon	.15
107	Tino Martinez	.15
108	Greg Norton	.15
109	Odalis Perez	.15
110	J.C. Romero	.15
111	Gary Sheffield	.35
112	Ismael Valdes	.15
113	Juan Acevedo	.15
114	Ben Broussard	.15
115	Deivi Cruz	.15
116	Geronimo Gil	.15
117	Eric Hinske	.15
118	Ted Lilly	.15
119	Quinton McCracken	.15
120	Antonio Alfonseca	.15
121	Brent Abernathy	.15
122	Johnny Damon	.25
123	Francisco Cordova	.15
124	Sterling Hitchcock	.15
125	Vladimir Nunez	.15
126	Andres Galarraga	.15
127	Timoniel Perez	.15
128	Tsuyoshi Shinjo	.15
129	Joe Girardi	.15
130	Roberto Alomar	.35
131	Ellis Burks	.15
132	Mike DeJean	.15
133	Alex Gonzalez	.15
134	Johan Santana	.35
135	Kenny Lofton	.15
136	Juan Encarnacion	.15
137	Dewon Brazelton	.15
138	Jeromy Burnitz	.15
139	Elmer Dessens	.15
140	Juan Gonzalez	.75
141	Todd Hundley	.15
142	Tomokazu Ohka	.15
143	Robin Ventura	.15
144	Rodrigo Lopez	.15
145	Ruben Sierra	.15
146	Jason Phillips	.15
147	Ryan Rupe	.15
148	Kevin Appier	.15
149	Sean Burroughs	.15
150	Masato Yoshii	.15
151	Juan Diaz	.15

#	Player	Price
152	Tony Graffanino	.15
153	Raul Ibanez	.15
154	Kevin Mench	.15
155	Pedro Astacio	.15
156	Brent Butler	.15
157	Kirk Rueter	.15
158	Eddie Guardado	.15
159	Hideki Irabu	.15
160	Wendell Magee	.15
161	Antonio Osuna	.15
162	Jose Vizcaino	.15
163	Danny Bautista	.15
164	Vinny Castilla	.15
165	Chris Singleton	.15
166	Mark Redman	.15
167	Olmedo Saenz	.15
168	Scott Erickson	.15
169	Ty Wigginton	.15
170	Jason Isringhausen	.15
171	Lou Merloni	.15
172	Chris Magruder	.15
173	Brandon Berger	.15
174	Roger Cedeno	.15
175	Kelvim Escobar	.15
176	Jose Guillen	.15
177	Damian Jackson	.15
178	Eric Owens	.15
179	Angel Berroa	.15
180	Alex Cintron	.15
181	Jeff Weaver	.15
182	Damon Minor	.15
183	Bobby Estalella	.15
184	David Justice	.15
185	Roy Halladay	.25
186	Brian Jordan	.15
187	Mike Maroth	.15
188	Pokey Reese	.15
189	Rey Sanchez	.15
190	Hank Blalock	.50
191	Jeff Cirillo	.15
192	Dmitri Young	.15
193	Carl Everett	.15
194	Joey Hamilton	.15
195	Jorge Julio	.15
196	Pablo Ozuna	.15
197	Jason Marquis	.15
198	Dustan Mohr	.15
199	Joe Borowski	.15
200	Tony Clark	.15
201	David Wells	.15
202	Josh Fogg	.15
203	Aaron Harang	.15
204	John McDonald	.15
205	John Stephens	.15
206	Chris Reitsma	.15
207	Alex Sanchez	.15
208	Milton Bradley	.15
209	Matt Clement	.15
210	Brad Fullmer	.15
211	Shigetoshi Hasegawa	.15
212	Austin Kearns	.50
213	Damaso Marte	.15
214	Vicente Padilla	.15
215	Raul Mondesi	.15
216	Russell Branyan	.15
217	Bartolo Colon	.15
218	Moises Alou	.15
219	Scott Hatteberg	.15
220	Bobby Kielty	.15
221	Kip Wells	.15
222	Scott Stewart	.15
223	Victor Martinez	.40
224	Marty Cordova	.15
225	Desi Relaford	.15
226	Reggie Sanders	.15
227	Jason Giambi	.50
228	Jimmy Haynes	.15
229	Billy Koch	.15
230	Damian Moss	.15
231	Chan Ho Park	.15
232	Cliff Floyd	.15
233	Todd Zeile	.15
234	Jeremy Giambi	.15
235	Rick Helling	.15
236	Matt Lawton	.15
237	Ramon Martinez	.15
238	Rondell White	.15
239	Scott Sullivan	.15
240	Hideo Nomo	.60
241	Todd Ritchie	.15
242	Ramon Santiago	.15
243	Jake Peavy	.15
244	Brad Wilkerson	.15
245	Reggie Taylor	.15
246	Carlos Pena	.15
247	Willis Roberts	.15
248	Jason Schmidt	.15
249	Mike Williams	.15
250	Alan Zinter	.15
251	Michael Tejera	.15
252	Dave Roberts	.15
253	Scott Schoeneweis	.15
254	Woody Williams	.15
255	John Thomson	.15
256	Ricardo Rodriguez	.15
257	Aaron Sele	.15
258	Paul Wilson	.15
259	Brett Tomko	.15
260	Kenny Rogers	.15
261	Mo Vaughn	.15
262	John Burkett	.15
263	Dennis Stark	.15
264	Ray Durham	.15
265	Scott Rolen	.65
266	Gabe Kapler	.15
267	Todd Hollandsworth	.15
268	Bud Smith	.15
269	Jay Payton	.15

#	Player	Price
270	Tyler Houston	.15
271	Brian Moehler	.15
272	David Espinosa	.15
273	Placido Polanco	.15
274	John Patterson	.15
275	Adam Hyzdu	.15
276	Albert Pujols	2.00
277	Larry Walker	.15
278	Magglio Ordonez	.15
279	Ryan Klesko	.15
280	Darin Erstad	.60
281	Jeff Kent	.15
282	Paul LoDuca	.15
283	Jim Edmonds	.15
284	Chipper Jones	1.00
285	Bernie Williams	.30
286	Pat Burrell	.40
287	Cliff Floyd	.15
288	Troy Glaus	.75
289	Brian Giles	.15
290	Jim Thome	.15
291	Greg Maddux	1.00
292	Roberto Alomar	.30
293	Jeff Bagwell	.75
294	Rafael Furcal	.15
295	Josh Beckett	.25
296	Carlos Delgado	.35
297	Ken Griffey Jr.	1.50
298	Jason Giambi	.50
299	Paul Konerko	.15
300	Mike Sweeney	.15
301	Alfonso Soriano	.50
302	Shea Hillenbrand	.15
303	Tony Batista	.15
304	Robin Ventura	.15
305	Alex Rodriguez	2.00
306	Nomar Garciaparra	1.50
307	Derek Jeter	2.50
308	Miguel Tejada	.30
309	Omar Vizquel	.15
310	Jorge Posada	.25
311	A.J. Pierzynski	.15
312	Ichiro Suzuki	1.50
313	Manny Ramirez	.75
314	Torii Hunter	.15
315	Garret Anderson	.15
316	Robert Fick	.15
317	Randy Winn	.15
318	Mark Buehrle	.15
319	Freddy Garcia	.15
320	Eddie Guardado	.15
321	Roy Halladay	.25
322	Derek Lowe	.15
323	Pedro J. Martinez	.75
324	Mariano Rivera	.25
325	Kazuhiro Sasaki	.15
326	Barry Zito	.25
327	Johnny Damon	.25
328	Ugueth Urbina	.15
329	Todd Helton	.75
330	Richie Sexson	.15
331	Jose Vidro	.15
332	Luis Castillo	.15
333	Junior Spivey	.15
334	Scott Rolen	.65
335	Mike Lowell	.15
336	Jimmy Rollins	.25
337	Jose Hernandez	.15
338	Mike Piazza	1.50
339	Benito Santiago	.15
340	Sammy Sosa	1.50
341	Barry Bonds	2.50
342	Vladimir Guerrero	.75
343	Lance Berkman	.15
344	Adam Dunn	.40
345	Shawn Green	.25
346	Luis Gonzalez	.25
347	Eric Gagne	.25
348	Tom Glavine	.30
349	Trevor Hoffman	.15
350	Randy Johnson	.75
351	Byung-Hyun Kim	.15
352	Matt Morris	.15
353	Odalis Perez	.15
354	Curt Schilling	.40
355	John Smoltz	.15
356	Mike Williams	.15
357	Andruw Jones	.75
358	Vicente Padilla	.15
359	Mike Remlinger	.15
360	Robb Nen	.15
361	Shawn Green	.25
362	Derek Jeter	2.50
363	Troy Glaus	.75
364	Ken Griffey Jr.	1.50
365	Mike Piazza	1.50
366	Jason Giambi	.50
367	Greg Maddux	1.00
368	Albert Pujols	2.00
369	Pedro J. Martinez	.75
370	Barry Zito	.25
371	Ichiro Suzuki	1.50
372	Nomar Garciaparra	1.50
373	Vladimir Guerrero	.75
374	Randy Johnson	.75
375	Barry Bonds	2.50
376	Sammy Sosa	1.50
377	Hideo Nomo	.75
378	Jeff Bagwell	.75
379	Curt Schilling	.35
380	Jim Thome	.75
381	Todd Helton	.75
382	Roger Clemens	1.25
383	Chipper Jones	1.00
384	Alex Rodriguez	2.00
385	Manny Ramirez	.40
386	Barry Bonds	2.50
387	Jim Thome	.15

#	Player	Price
388	Adam Dunn	.40
389	Alex Rodriguez	2.00
390	Shawn Green	.25
391	Jason Giambi	.15
392	Lance Berkman	.15
393	Pat Burrell	.40
394	Eric Chavez	.25
395	Mike Piazza	1.50
396	Vladimir Guerrero	.75
397	Paul Konerko	.15
398	Sammy Sosa	1.50
399	Richie Sexson	.15
400	Torii Hunter	.15

Update Glossy

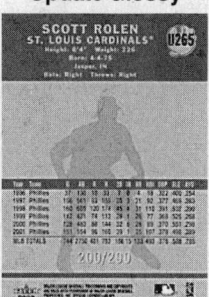

SCOTT ROLEN ST. LOUIS CARDINALS U265

	Price
Stars (1-100):	1-2X
Cards (101-400):	4-8X
Production 200 Sets	

Update Diamond Debuts

NM/M

	Price
Complete Set (15):	10.00
Common Player:	.50
Inserted 1:6	

#	Player	Price
1DD	Mark Prior	1.50
2DD	Eric Hinske	.50
3DD	Kazuhisa Ishii	.50
4DD	Ben Broussard	.50
5DD	Sean Burroughs	.50
6DD	Austin Kearns	1.00
7DD	Hee Seop Choi	1.00
8DD	Kirk Saarloos	.50
9DD	Orlando Hudson	.50
10DD	So Taguchi	.50
11DD	Kevin Mench	.50
12DD	Carl Crawford	.50
13DD	John Patterson	.50
14DD	Hank Blalock	1.50
15DD	Brett Myers	.50

Update Grass Patch

NM/M

	Price
Common Player:	20.00
Production 50 Sets	

Player	Price
Alfonso Soriano	30.00
Torii Hunter	20.00
Andruw Jones	30.00
Jim Edmonds	20.00
Shawn Green	20.00
Nomar Garciaparra	50.00
Roberto Alomar	25.00

Update Grass Roots

NM/M

	Price
Complete Set (10):	15.00
Common Player:	1.00
Inserted 1:24	

#	Player	Price
1GR	Alfonso Soriano	1.50
2GR	Torii Hunter	1.00
3GR	Andruw Jones	1.50
4GR	Jim Edmonds	1.00
5GR	Shawn Green	1.00
6GR	Todd Helton	1.50
7GR	Nomar Garciaparra	4.00
8GR	Roberto Alomar	1.00
9GR	Vladimir Guerrero	1.50
10GR	Ichiro Suzuki	4.00

Update Heads Up

RANDY JOHNSON / P

NM/M

	Price
Complete Set (10):	25.00
Common Player:	2.00
Inserted 1:48	

#	Player	Price
1HU	Roger Clemens	6.00
2HU	Adam Dunn	2.00
3HU	Kazuhisa Ishii	1.50
4HU	Barry Zito	1.50
5HU	Pedro J. Martinez	4.00
6HU	Alfonso Soriano	3.00
7HU	Mark Prior	2.00
8HU	Chipper Jones	5.00
9HU	Randy Johnson	4.00
10HU	Lance Berkman	1.50

Update Heads Up Game-Used

RANDY JOHNSON / P

NM/M

	Price
Common Player:	5.00
Production 150 Sets	

Player	Price
Roger Clemens	25.00
Adam Dunn	10.00
Kazuhisa Ishii	5.00
Barry Zito	5.00
Alfonso Soriano	10.00
Mark Prior	10.00
Chipper Jones	15.00
Randy Johnson	15.00
Lance Berkman	5.00
Mike Piazza	20.00
Barry Bonds	50.00

Update New York's Finest

PIAZZA NEW YORK METS C 31

NEW YORK'S FINEST

NM/M

	Price
Complete Set (15):	60.00
Common Player:	3.00
Inserted 1:83	

#	Player	Price
1	Edgardo Alfonzo	3.00

2	Roberto Alomar	4.00
3	Jeromy Burnitz	3.00
4	Satoru Komiyama	3.00
5	Rey Ordonez	3.00
6	Mike Piazza	10.00
7	Mo Vaughn	3.00
8	Roger Clemens	10.00
9	Jason Giambi	5.00
10	Derek Jeter	15.00
11	Mike Mussina	5.00
12	Jorge Posada	3.00
13	Alfonso Soriano	5.00
14	Robin Ventura	3.00
15	Bernie Williams	4.00

Update N.Y.'s Finest Single Swatch

NM/M
Common Card: 5.00
Inserted 1:112

Derek Jeter/Jsy, Rey Ordonez	25.00
Alfonso Soriano/Jsy, Roberto Alomar	10.00
Roger Clemens/Jsy, Mike Piazza	15.00
Mike Mussina/Jsy, Mo Vaughn	8.00
Bernie Williams/Jsy, Jeromy Burnitz	8.00
Derek Jeter/Jsy, Satoru Komiyama	25.00
Robin Ventura/Jsy, Edgardo Alfonzo	8.00
Jorge Posada/Jsy, Mike Piazza	8.00
Jason Giambi/Base, Mo Vaughn	8.00
Alfonso Soriano/Jsy, Edgardo Alfonzo	10.00
Derek Jeter, Rey Ordonez/Jsy	5.00
Alfonso Soriano, Roberto Alomar/Jsy	8.00
Roger Clemens, Mike Piazza/Jsy	15.00
Mike Mussina, Mo Vaughn/Jsy	6.00
Bernie Williams, Jeromy Burnitz/Jsy	5.00
Derek Jeter, Satoru Komiyama/Bat	8.00
Robin Ventura, Edgardo Alfonzo/Jsy	5.00
Jorge Posada, Mike Piazza/Jsy	15.00
Jason Giambi, Mo Vaughn/Jsy	6.00
Alfonso Soriano, Edgardo Alfonzo/Jsy	5.00

Update N.Y.'s Finest Dual Swatch

NM/M
Common Card: 10.00
Production 100 Sets

Derek Jeter, Rey Ordonez	75.00
Alfonso Soriano, Roberto Alomar	40.00
Roger Clemens, Mike Piazza	65.00
Mike Mussina, Mo Vaughn	30.00
Bernie Williams, Jeromy Burnitz	20.00
Robin Ventura, Edgardo Alfonzo	10.00

Update Plays of the Week

NM/M
Complete Set (30): 35.00

Common Player: 1.00
Inserted 1:12

1PW	Troy Glaus	1.50
2PW	Andruw Jones	1.50
3PW	Curt Schilling	1.25
4PW	Manny Ramirez	1.50
5PW	Sammy Sosa	2.50
6PW	Magglio Ordonez	1.00
7PW	Ken Griffey Jr.	2.50
8PW	Jim Thome	1.00
9PW	Larry Walker	1.00
10PW	Robert Fick	1.00
11PW	Josh Beckett	1.00
12PW	Roy Oswalt	1.00
13PW	Mike Sweeney	1.00
14PW	Shawn Green	1.00
15PW	Torii Hunter	1.00
16PW	Vladimir Guerrero	1.50
17PW	Mike Piazza	2.50
18PW	Jason Giambi	1.25
19PW	Eric Chavez	1.00
20PW	Pat Burrell	1.25
21PW	Brian Giles	1.00
22PW	Ryan Klesko	1.00
23PW	Barry Bonds	5.00
24PW	Mike Cameron	1.00
25PW	Albert Pujols	4.00
26PW	Alex Rodriguez	4.00
27PW	Carlos Delgado	1.00
28PW	Richie Sexson	1.00
29PW	Jay Gibbons	1.00
30PW	Randy Winn	1.00

Update This Day in History

NM/M
Complete Set (25): 40.00
Common Player: 1.00

1	Shawn Green	1.00
2	Ozzie Smith	2.50
3	Derek Lowe	1.00
4	Ken Griffey Jr.	3.00
5	Barry Bonds	5.00
6	Juan Gonzalez	1.50
7	Wade Boggs	2.00
8	Mark Prior	1.50
9	Thurman Munson	2.00
10	Curt Schilling	1.25
11	Jason Giambi	1.25
12	Cal Ripken Jr.	5.00
13	Craig Biggio	1.00
14	Drew Henson	1.00
15	Steve Carlton	1.00
16	Greg Maddux	2.50
17	Adam Dunn	1.00
18	Vladimir Guerrero	2.00
19	Alex Rodriguez	4.00
20	Carlton Fisk	1.50
21	Ichiro Suzuki	3.00
22	Johnny Bench	3.00
23	Kazuhisa Ishii	1.00
24	Derek Jeter	3.00
25	Jim Thome	1.00

Update This Day in History Autograph

NM/M
Inserted 1:582

Barry Bonds/150	200.00
Mark Prior/64	40.00
Drew Henson	20.00
Greg Maddux/99	150.00
Derek Jeter	100.00

Update This Day in History Memorabilia

NM/M
Common Player: 5.00
Inserted 1:24

Shawn Green/Jsy	5.00
Ozzie Smith/Jsy	10.00
Barry Bonds/Bat	15.00
Barry Bonds/Jsy	15.00
Juan Gonzalez/Bat	6.00
Wade Boggs/Jsy	6.00
Wade Boggs/Pants	6.00
Curt Schilling/Jsy	6.00
Craig Biggio/Jsy	6.00
Adam Dunn/Jsy	8.00
Alex Rodriguez/Bat	10.00
Alex Rodriguez/Jsy	10.00
Carlton Fisk/Bat	8.00
Kazuhisa Ishii/Bat	5.00
Derek Jeter/Pants	20.00
Jim Thome/Jsy	8.00
Greg Maddux/Jsy	10.00

2002 Fleer Triple Crown

Complete Set (270): 30.00
Common Player: .15
Pack (10): 1.50
Box (24): 30.00

1	Mo Vaughn	.15
2	Derek Jeter	2.00
3	Ken Griffey Jr.	1.25
4	Charles Johnson	.15
5	Geoff Jenkins	.15
6	Chuck Knoblauch	.15
7	Jason Kendall	.15
8	Jim Edmonds	.15
9	David Eckstein	.15
10	Carl Everett	.15
11	Barry Larkin	.15
12	Cliff Floyd	.15
13	Ben Sheets	.15
14	Jeff Conine	.15
15	Brian Giles	.15
16	Darryl Kile	.15
17	Troy Glaus	.65
18	Trot Nixon	.15
19	Jim Thome	.15
20	Preston Wilson	.15
21	Roger Clemens	1.00
22	Chad Hermansen	.15
23	Matt Morris	.15
24	Shawn Wooten	.15
25	Manny Ramirez	.65
26	Roberto Alomar	.30
27	Josh Beckett	.25
28	Jose Hernandez	.15
29	Mike Mussina	.35
30	Jack Wilson	.15
31	Bud Smith	.15
32	Garret Anderson	.15
33	Pedro J. Martinez	.65
34	Travis Fryman	.15
35	Jeff Bagwell	.65
36	Doug Mientkiewicz	.15
37	Andy Pettitte	.25
38	Ryan Klesko	.15
39	Edgar Renteria	.15
40	Mariano Rivera	.25
41	Darin Erstad	.50
42	Hideo Nomo	.50
43	Ellis Burks	.15
44	Craig Biggio	.15
45	Corey Koskie	.15
46	Jason Varitek	.15
47	Xavier Nady	.15
48	Aubrey Huff	.15
49	Tim Salmon	.25
50	Nomar Garciaparra	1.25
51	Juan Gonzalez	.65
52	Moises Alou	.15
53	A.J. Pierzynski	.15
54	Bernie Williams	.30
55	Phil Nevin	.15
56	Ben Grieve	.15
57	Mark Grace	.25
58	Mike Lansing	.15
59	Kenny Lofton	.15
60	Lance Berkman	.15
61	David Ortiz	.25
62	Jason Giambi	.40
63	Mark Kotsay	.15
64	Greg Vaughn	.15
65	Junior Spivey	.15
66	Fred McGriff	.15
67	C.C. Sabathia	.15
68	Richard Hidalgo	.15
69	Torii Hunter	.15
70	Jason Hart	.15
71	Bubba Trammell	.15
72	Jace Brewer	.15
73	Matt Williams	.15
74	Matt Stairs	.15
75	Omar Vizquel	.15
76	Daryle Ward	.15
77	Joe Mays	.15
78	Eric Chavez	.15
79	Andres Galarraga	.15
80	Rafael Palmeiro	.50
81	Steve Finley	.15
82	Eric Young	.15
83	Todd Helton	.65
84	Roy Oswalt	.25
85	Eric Milton	.15
86	Ramon Hernandez	.15
87	Jeff Kent	.15
88	Ivan Rodriguez	.50
89	Luis Gonzalez	.25
90	Corey Patterson	.15
91	Jose Ortiz	.15
92	Mike Sweeney	.15
93	Cristian Guzman	.15
94	Johnny Damon	.25
95	Barry Bonds	2.00
96	Rusty Greer	.15
97	Reggie Sanders	.15
98	Sammy Sosa	1.25
99	Jeff Cirillo	.15
100	Carlos Febles	.15
101	Jose Vidro	.15
102	Jermaine Dye	.15
103	Rich Aurilia	.15
104	Gabe Kapler	.15
105	Randy Johnson	.65
106	Rondell White	.15
107	Ben Petrick	.15
108	Joe Randa	.15
109	Fernando Tatis	.15
110	Tim Hudson	.25
111	John Olerud	.15
112	Alex Rodriguez	1.50
113	Curt Schilling	.40
114	Kerry Wood	.40
115	Alex Ochoa	.15
116	Carlos Beltran	.40
117	Vladimir Guerrero	.65
118	Mark Mulder	.15
119	Bret Boone	.15
120	Carlos Delgado	.35
121	Marcus Giles	.15
122	Paul Konerko	.15
123	Juan Pierre	.15
124	Mark Quinn	.15
125	Edgardo Alfonzo	.15
126	Barry Zito	.25
127	Dan Wilson	.15
128	Jose Cruz Jr.	.15
129	Chipper Jones	.75
130	Ray Durham	.15
131	Larry Walker	.15
132	Neifi Perez	.15
133	Robin Ventura	.15
134	Miguel Tejada	.25
135	Edgar Martinez	.15
136	Raul Mondesi	.15
137	Javy Lopez	.15
138	Jose Canseco	.25
139	Mike Hampton	.15
140	Eric Karros	.15
141	Mike Piazza	1.25
142	Travis Lee	.15
143	Ichiro Suzuki	1.25
144	Shannon Stewart	.15
145	Andruw Jones	.65
146	Frank Thomas	.65
147	Tony Clark	.15
148	Adrian Beltre	.25
149	Matt Lawton	.15
150	Marlon Anderson	.15
151	Freddy Garcia	.15
152	Brian Jordan	.15
153	Carlos Lee	.15
154	Eric Munson	.15
155	Paul LoDuca	.15
156	Jay Payton	.15
157	Scott Rolen	.50
158	Jamie Moyer	.15
159	Tom Glavine	.30
160	Magglio Ordonez	.15
161	Brandon Inge	.15
162	Shawn Green	.25
163	Tsuyoshi Shinjo	.15
164	Mike Lieberthal	.15
165	Kazuhiro Sasaki	.15
166	Greg Maddux	.75
167	Chris Singleton	.15
168	Juan Encarnacion	.15
169	Gary Sheffield	.25
170	Nick Johnson	.15
171	Bobby Abreu	.15
172	Aaron Boone	.15
173	Rafael Furcal	.15
174	Mark Buehrle	.15
175	Bobby Higginson	.15
176	Kevin Brown	.15
177	Tino Martinez	.15
178	Pat Burrell	.30
179	Fernando Vina	.15
180	Jay Gibbons	.15
181	Jose Valentin	.15
182	Derrek Lee	.15
183	Richie Sexson	.15
184	Alfonso Soriano	.50
185	Jimmy Rollins	.25
186	Albert Pujols	1.50
187	Brady Anderson	.15
188	Sean Casey	.25
189	Luis Castillo	.15
190	Jeromy Burnitz	.15
191	Jorge Posada	.25
192	Kevin Young	.15
193	Eli Marrero	.15
194	Shea Hillenbrand	.15
195	Adam Dunn	.40
196	Mike Lowell	.15
197	Jeffrey Hammonds	.15
198	David Justice	.25
199	Aramis Ramirez	.15
200	J.D. Drew	.25
201	Pedro Santana	.15
202	Endy Chavez	.15
203	Donnie Bridges	.15
204	Travis Phelps	.15
205	Drew Henson	.25
206	Angel Berroa	.15
207	George Perez	.15
208	Billy Sylvester	.15
209	Juan Cruz	.15
210	Horacio Ramirez	.15
211	J.J. Davis	.15
212	Cody Ransom	.15
213	Mark Teixeira	.50
214	Nate Frese	.15
215	Brian Rogers	.15
216	Dewon Brazelton	.15
217	Carlos Hernandez	.15
218	Juan Rivera	.15
219	Luis Lopez	.15
220	Benito Baez	.15
221	Bill Ortega	.15
222	Dustan Mohr	.15
223	Corky Miller	.15
224	Tyler Walker	.15
225	Rick Bauer	.15
226	Mark Prior	.50
227	Rafael Soriano	.15
228	Greg Miller	.15
229	Dave Williams	.15
230	Bert Snow	.15
231	Barry Bonds	1.50
232	Rickey Henderson	.50
233	Alex Rodriguez	1.25
234	Luis Gonzalez	.25
235	Derek Jeter	1.50
236	Bud Smith	.15
237	Sammy Sosa	.75
238	Jeff Bagwell	.50
239	Jim Thome	.50
240	Hideo Nomo	.50
241	Greg Maddux	.75
242	Ken Griffey Jr.	1.00
243	Curt Schilling	.25
244	Arizona Diamondbacks	.15
245	Ichiro Suzuki	.75
246	Albert Pujols	.75
247	Ichiro Suzuki	.75
248	Barry Bonds	1.50
249	Roger Clemens	.65
250	Randy Johnson	.50
251	Todd Helton	.50
252	Rafael Palmeiro	.40
253	Mike Piazza	1.00
254	Alex Rodriguez	1.25
255	Manny Ramirez	.50
256	Ken Griffey Jr.	1.00
257	Jason Giambi	.40
258	Chipper Jones	.65
259	Larry Walker	.15
260	Sammy Sosa	.50
261	Vladimir Guerrero	.50
262	Nomar Garciaparra	.75
263	Randy Johnson	.50
264	Roger Clemens	.65
265	Ichiro Suzuki	1.00
266	Barry Bonds	1.50
267	Paul LoDuca	.15
268	Albert Pujols	1.00
269	Derek Jeter	1.50
270	Adam Dunn	.40

Batting Average Parallel

Stars: 4-8X
Numbered to 2001 batting avg.

Home Run Parallel

Stars Print Run 50-75:	10-20X
Stars P/R 31-50:	15-25X
Stars P/R 21-30:	20-40X

Numbered to 2001 HR total

RBI Parallel

Stars P/R 101-200:	4-8X
Stars P/R 76-100:	5-10X
Stars P/R 51-75:	6-12X
Stars P/R 25-50:	10-20X

Numbered to 2001 RBI total.

Diamond Immortality

NM/M
Complete Set (10): 25.00
Common Player: 1.00
Inserted 1:12

1DI	Derek Jeter	5.00
2DI	Barry Bonds	5.00
3DI	Ricky Henderson	1.00

4DI	Roger Clemens	2.50
5DI	Alex Rodriguez	4.00
6DI	Albert Pujols	4.00
7DI	Nomar Garciaparra	3.00
8DI	Ichiro Suzuki	3.00
9DI	Chipper Jones	2.00
10DI	Ken Griffey Jr.	3.00

Diamond Immortality Game-Used

NM/M
Inserted 1:129

Barry Bonds/Jsy	25.00
Roger Clemens/Jsy	20.00
Nomar Garciaparra/Jsy/SP	40.00
Ricky Henderson/Bat	15.00
Derek Jeter/Bat	25.00
Chipper Jones/Bat	10.00
Albert Pujols/Jsy	25.00
Alex Rodriguez/Jsy	20.00

Home Run Kings

NM/M
Complete Set (25): 100.00
Common Player: 2.00
Inserted 1:24

1	Ted Williams	10.00
2	Todd Helton	4.00
3	Eddie Murray	2.00
4	Jeff Bagwell	4.00
5	Babe Ruth	15.00
6	Eddie Mathews	5.00
7	Alex Rodriguez	10.00
8	Juan Gonzalez	4.00
9	Chipper Jones	4.00
10	Luis Gonzalez	2.00
11	Johnny Bench	5.00
12	Frank Thomas	4.00
13	Ernie Banks	3.00
14	Jimmie Foxx	4.00
15	Ken Griffey Jr.	8.00
16	Rafael Palmeiro	3.00
17	Sammy Sosa	8.00
18	Reggie Jackson	4.00
19	Barry Bonds	10.00
20	Willie McCovey	2.00
21	Manny Ramirez	4.00
22	Larry Walker	2.00
23	Jason Giambi	4.00
24	Mike Piazza	8.00
25	Jose Canseco	2.00

Home Run Kings Autograph

NM/M
Common Player:

Barry Bonds/73	300.00
Alex Rodriguez/52	100.00

Home Run Kings Game-Used

NM/M
Common Player: 5.00
Inserted 1:155

Jeff Bagwell/Jsy	10.00
Johnny Bench/Bat/SP	50.00
Barry Bonds/Jsy	25.00
Jimmie Foxx/Bat	40.00
Jason Giambi/Jsy	10.00
Reggie Jackson/Bat	10.00

		NM/M
	Eddie Mathews/Bat	15.00
	Eddie Murray/Bat	10.00
	Rafael Palmeiro/Bat	10.00
	Mike Piazza/Jsy	15.00
	Manny Ramirez/Bat/SP	50.00
	Todd Helton/Bat	10.00
	Alex Rodriguez/Bat	15.00
	Larry Walker/Bat	5.00
	Ted Williams/Jsy	100.00

RBI Kings

		NM/M
	Complete Set (15):	140.00
	Common Player:	4.00
	Inserted 1:144	
1	Sammy Sosa	15.00
2	Todd Helton	8.00
3	Albert Pujols	20.00
4	Manny Ramirez	8.00
5	Luis Gonzalez	4.00
6	Shawn Green	4.00
7	Barry Bonds	20.00
8	Ken Griffey Jr.	15.00
9	Alex Rodriguez	20.00
10	Jason Giambi	8.00
11	Jeff Bagwell	8.00
12	Vladimir Guerrero	8.00
13	Juan Gonzalez	8.00
14	Chipper Jones	8.00
15	Mike Piazza	15.00

RBI Kings Game-Used

		NM/M
	Common Player:	5.00
	Inserted 1:70	
	Jeff Bagwell/Jsy	10.00
	Barry Bonds/Jsy	25.00
	Jason Giambi/Jsy	8.00
	Luis Gonzalez/Bat	5.00
	Juan Gonzalez/Bat	8.00
	Shawn Green/Jsy	6.00
	Todd Helton/Jsy	10.00
	Mike Piazza/Jsy	15.00
	Albert Pujols/Bat/SP	70.00
	Manny Ramirez/Bat	10.00
	Alex Rodriguez/Shoe	25.00

Season Crowns

		NM/M
	Complete Set (10):	25.00
	Common Card:	2.00
	Inserted 1:12	
1SC	Barry Bonds, Sammy Sosa, Luis Gonzalez	4.00
2SC	Larry Walker, Nomar Garciaparra, Todd Helton	4.00
3SC	Sammy Sosa, Todd Helton, Manny Ramirez	4.00
4SC	Pedro J. Martinez, Derek Jeter, Cal Ripken Jr.	6.00
5SC	Jose Canseco, Barry Bonds, Alex Rodriguez	5.00
6SC	Barry Bonds, Jeff Kent, Chipper Jones	4.00
7SC	Ichiro Suzuki, Jason Giambi, Ivan Rodriguez	3.00
8SC	Curt Schilling, Tom Glavine, Pedro J. Martinez	2.00
9SC	Randy Johnson, Pedro J. Martinez, Greg Maddux	3.00
10SC	Randy Johnson, Curt Schilling, John Smoltz	2.00

Season Crowns Autograph

		NM/M
	Jeter #'d to 160.	
	Derek Jeter/160	150.00
	Barry Bonds/77	250.00

Season Crowns Game-Used

		NM/M
	Common Player:	5.00
	Inserted 1:90	
	Barry Bonds/Jsy	25.00
	Sammy Sosa/Jsy	15.00
	Larry Walker/Bat	5.00
	Nomar Garciaparra/Jsy	20.00
	Todd Helton/Jsy	10.00
	Sammy Sosa/Base	15.00
	Todd Helton/Jsy	10.00
	Manny Ramirez/Jsy	10.00
	Pedro Martinez/Jsy	10.00
	Derek Jeter/Pants	25.00
	Cal Ripken Jr/Bat	60.00
	Jose Canseco/Jsy	8.00
	Barry Bonds/Jsy	25.00
	Alex Rodriguez/Jsy	20.00
	Barry Bonds/Jsy	25.00
	Jeff Kent/Jsy	5.00
	Ichiro Suzuki/Base	25.00
	Jason Giambi/Jsy	10.00
	Ivan Rodriguez/Jsy	10.00
	Curt Schilling/Jsy	10.00
	Tom Glavine/Jsy	10.00
	Pedro Martinez/Jsy	10.00
	Randy Johnson/Jsy	10.00
	Greg Maddux/Jsy	15.00
	Randy Johnson/Jsy	10.00
	Curt Schilling/Jsy	10.00
	John Smoltz/Jsy	10.00

Season Crowns Triple Swatch

		NM/M
	Production 100 Sets	
	Barry Bonds, Sammy Sosa, Luis Gonzalez	100.00
	Larry Walker, Nomar Garciaparra, Todd Helton	40.00
	Sammy Sosa, Todd Helton, Manny Ramirez	50.00
	Barry Bonds, Jeff Kent, Chipper Jones	80.00
	Ichiro Suzuki, Jason Giambi, Ivan Rodriguez	80.00
	Curt Schilling, Tom Glavine, Pedro J. Martinez	50.00
	Randy Johnson, Pedro J. Martinez, Greg Maddux	50.00
	Randy Johnson, Curt Schilling, John Smoltz	50.00

Turn Two Foundation Derek Jeter

In conjunction with Jeter's charitable foundation, Fleer produced a three-card set that was given to youngsters entering an essay contest at after-school recreation centers in New York City. The 2-1/2" x 3-1/2" cards have pictures of Jeter on front and back and information about the contest and the foundation. Fleer reported production as 10,000 sets.

		NM/M
	Complete Set (3):	13.50
	Common Card:	5.00
1	Derek Jeter (Foundation's mission.)	
2	Derek Jeter (w/firefighters)	5.00
3	Derek Jeter (stats)	5.00

Utz Yankees Starting Five

The starting rotation of the Yankees is featured on this stadium giveaway set sponsored by Utz snacks and produced by Fleer. The 3-1/2" x 2-1/2" horizontal cards have vignetted action photos. The player name is bracketed by the famed Yankee Stadium facade, with the set title in red at bottom. Backs have player biographical data, career highlights and recent stats, along with a serial number from within the edition of 25,000 sets given out to fans 14 and under on June 12. A cover card was included with the set. Autographed versions of the cards were produced for charitable purposes.

		NM/M
	Complete Set (6):	7.50
	Common Player:	1.00
1	Roger Clemens	3.00
1	Roger Clemens/Auto.	100.00
2	David Wells	1.00
2	David Wells/Auto.	15.00
3	Mike Mussina	2.00
3	Mike Mussina/Auto.	15.00
4	Orlando Hernandez	1.00
4	Orlando Hernandez/Auto.	25.00
5	Andy Pettitte	1.00
5	Andy Pettitte/Auto.	15.00
--	Cover card	.25

2003 Fleer Authentix

		NM/M
	Complete Set (160):	
	Common Player:	.25
	Common (111-125):	3.00
	Production 1,850	
	Common (126-160):	1.50
	Exclusive to Home Team boxes.	
	Pack (5):	3.00
	Box (24):	50.00
1	Derek Jeter	3.00
2	Tom Glavine	.40
3	Jason Jennings	.25
4	Craig Biggio	.40
5	Miguel Tejada	.40
6	Barry Bonds	3.00
7	Juan Gonzalez	1.00
8	Luis Gonzalez	.40
9	Johnny Damon	.40
10	Ellis Burks	.25
11	Frank Thomas	1.00
12	Richie Sexson	.25
13	Roger Clemens	1.50
14	Matt Morris	.25
15	Troy Glaus	1.00
16	Tony Batista	.25
17	Magglio Ordonez	.25
18	Jose Vidro	.25
19	Barry Zito	.40
20	Chipper Jones	1.50
21	Moises Alou	.25
22	Lance Berkman	.25
23	Jacque Jones	.25
24	Alfonso Soriano	.75
25	Sean Burroughs	.25
26	Scott Rolen	1.00
27	Mark Grace	.35
28	Manny Ramirez	.75
29	Ken Griffey Jr.	2.00
30	Josh Beckett	.25
31	Kazuhisa Ishii	.25
32	Pat Burrell	1.00
33	Edgar Martinez	.25
34	Tim Salmon	.35
35	Raul Ibanez	.25
36	Vladimir Guerrero	.75
37	Jermaine Dye	.25
38	Rich Aurilia	.25
39	Rafael Palmeiro	.75
40	Kerry Wood	.75
41	Omar Vizquel	.25
42	Fred McGriff	.25
43	Ben Sheets	.25
44	Bernie Williams	.40
45	Brian Giles	.25
46	Jim Edmonds	.25
47	Garret Anderson	.25
48	Pedro J. Martinez	1.00
49	Adam Dunn	.75
50	A.J. Burnett	.25
51	Eric Gagne	.25
52	Mo Vaughn	.25
53	Bobby Abreu	.25
54	Bret Boone	.25
55	Carlos Delgado	.40
56	Gary Sheffield	.40
57	Sammy Sosa	2.00
58	Jim Thome	.25
59	Jeff Bagwell	1.00
60	David Eckstein	.25
61	Jason Kendall	.25
62	Albert Pujols	2.50
63	Curt Schilling	.40
64	Nomar Garciaparra	.75
65	Sean Casey	.35
66	Shawn Green	.40
67	Mike Piazza	2.00
68	Ichiro Suzuki	2.00
69	Eric Hinske	.25
70	Greg Maddux	1.50
71	Larry Walker	.40
72	Roy Oswalt	.40
73	Alex Rodriguez	2.50
74	Austin Kearns	.75
75	Cliff Floyd	.25
76	Kevin Brown	.25
77	Jason Giambi	.75
78	Jorge Julio	.25
79	Carlos Lee	.25
80	Mike Sweeney	.25
81	Edgardo Alfonzo	.25
82	Eric Chavez	.40
83	Andruw Jones	1.00
84	Mark Prior	.75
85	Todd Helton	1.00
86	Torii Hunter	.25
87	Ryan Klesko	.25
88	Aubrey Huff	.25
89	Randy Johnson	1.00
90	Barry Larkin	.25
91	Mike Lowell	.25
92	Jimmy Rollins	.40
93	Darin Erstad	.65
94	Jay Gibbons	.25
95	Paul Konerko	.40
96	Bobby Higginson	.25
97	Carlos Beltran	.60
98	Bartolo Colon	.25
99	Jeff Kent	.25
100	Ivan Rodriguez	.65
101	Joe Borchard	.25
102	Mark Teixeira	.50
103	Francisco Rodriguez	.25
104	Chris Snelling	.25
105	Hee Seop Choi	.25
106	Hank Blalock	.50
107	Marlon Byrd	.25
108	Michael Restovich	.25
109	Victor Martinez	.25
110	Lyle Overbay	.25
111	Brian Stokes RC	3.00
112	Josh Hall RC	4.00
113	Chris Waters RC	3.00
114	Lew Ford RC	5.00
115	Ian Ferguson RC	3.00
116	Josh Willingham RC	4.00
117	Josh Stewart RC	3.00
118	Pete LaForest RC	4.00
119	Jose Contreras RC	5.00
120	Terrmel Sledge RC	3.00
121	Guillermo Quiroz RC	4.00
122	Alejandro Machado RC	3.00
123	Nook Logan RC	4.00
124	Rontrez Johnson RC	4.00
125	Hideki Matsui RC	10.00
126	Phil Rizzuto	3.00
127	Robin Ventura	1.50
128	Andy Pettitte	4.00
129	Mike Mussina	3.00
130	Mariano Rivera	3.00
131	Jeff Weaver	1.50
132	David Wells	1.50
133	Tommy Lasorda	2.00
134	Pee Wee Reese	2.00
135	Hideo Nomo	4.00
136	Adrian Beltre	2.00
137	Chin-Feng Chen	4.00
138	Odalis Perez	1.50
139	Dave Roberts	1.50
140	Bobby Doerr	3.00
141	Jason Varitek	1.50
142	Trot Nixon	1.50
143	Tim Wakefield	1.50
144	John Burkett	1.50
145	Jeremy Giambi	1.50
146	Casey Fossum	1.50
147	Phil Niekro	1.50
148	Warren Spahn	4.00
149	Rafael Furcal	2.00
150	Vinny Castilla	1.50
151	Javy Lopez	1.50
152	Jason Marquis	1.50
153	Mike Hampton	1.50
154	Gaylord Perry	1.50
155	Ruben Sierra	1.50
156	Mike Cameron	1.50
157	Freddy Garcia	1.50
158	Joel Pineiro	1.50
159	Jamie Moyer	1.50
160	Carlos Guillen	1.50

Balcony

Stars (1-110)	3-6X
SP's (111-125)	.5-1.5X
Production 250 Sets	
Club Box (1-110)	5-10X
SP's (111-125)	.75-2X
Production 100 Sets	
Standing Room Only:	No Pricing
Production 25 Sets	

Autographed Authentix

		NM/M
	Quantity produced listed	
DJ	Derek Jeter/50	150.00
DJ	Derek Jeter/150	125.00
DJ	Derek Jeter/250	125.00
BB	Barry Bonds/50	200.00
BB	Barry Bonds/150	200.00
BB	Barry Bonds/250	200.00

Autographed Jersey Authentix

		NM/M
	Quantity produced listed	
DJ	Derek Jeter/100	150.00
DJ	Derek Jeter/200	150.00
DJ	Derek Jeter/300	125.00
NR	Nolan Ryan/100	185.00
NR	Nolan Ryan/200	150.00
NR	Nolan Ryan/300	125.00

Ballpark Classics

		NM/M
	Complete Set (10):	25.00
	Common Player:	1.50
	Inserted 1:12	
1	Derek Jeter	6.00
2	Randy Johnson	2.00
3	Nomar Garciaparra	4.00
4	Barry Bonds	6.00
5	Alfonso Soriano	2.00
6	Alex Rodriguez	5.00
7	Jim Thome	1.50
8	Chipper Jones	3.00
9	Mike Piazza	4.00
10	Ichiro Suzuki	4.00

Bat Authentix

		NM/M
	Common Player:	8.00
	Inserted 1:78	
	Unripped:	1.5-3X
	Production 50 Sets	
AD	Adam Dunn	8.00
NG	Nomar Garciaparra	15.00
JG	Jason Giambi	15.00
VG	Vladimir Guerrero	15.00
DJ	Derek Jeter	30.00
CJ	Chipper Jones	10.00
SS	Sammy Sosa	15.00
JT	Jim Thome	15.00

Hometown Heroes Memorabilia

		NM/M
	Common Player:	8.00
	Home Team Box Exclusive	
BB	Bret Boone/Jsy/200	8.00
KB	Kevin Brown/Jsy/150	10.00
CC	Chin-Feng Chen/Jsy/150	35.00
RC	Roger Clemens/Jsy	25.00
JD	Johnny Damon/Jsy/100	8.00
FG	Freddy Garcia/Jsy/200	8.00
NG	Nomar Garciaparra	25.00
JG	Jason Giambi/Bat/300	8.00
SG	Shawn Green/Jsy/100	8.00
KI	Kazuhisa Ishii/Jsy/100	8.00
DJ	Derek Jeter	40.00
AJ	Andruw Jones/Jsy/150	10.00
CJ	Chipper Jones	15.00
GM	Greg Maddux/Jsy	10.00
EM	Edgar Martinez/Jsy/200	10.00
PM	Pedro Martinez/Jsy/100	10.00
MR	Manny Ramirez	10.00
GS	Gary Sheffield/Jsy/100	8.00
AS	Alfonso Soriano	15.00
I	Ichiro Suzuki/Base/100	30.00

Jersey Authentix

		NM/M
	Common Player:	5.00
	Inserted 1:10	
	Unripped:	1.5-3X
	Production 50 Sets	
JB	Jeff Bagwell	8.00
JB2	Josh Beckett	5.00
LB	Lance Berkman	5.00
MB	Mark Buehrle	5.00
PB	Pat Burrell	10.00
SB	Sean Burroughs	5.00
RC	Roger Clemens	15.00
CD	Carlos Delgado	5.00
AD	Adam Dunn	8.00
NG	Nomar Garciaparra	15.00
VG	Vladimir Guerrero	8.00
EH	Eric Hinske	5.00
TH	Torii Hunter	6.00
DJ	Derek Jeter	25.00
RJ	Randy Johnson	8.00
CJ	Chipper Jones	8.00
GM	Greg Maddux	15.00
MP	Mike Piazza	12.00
MR	Manny Ramirez	8.00
AR	Alex Rodriguez	12.00
AS	Alfonso Soriano	10.00
SS	Sammy Sosa	12.00
MT	Miguel Tejada	5.00
KW	Kerry Wood	8.00

Jersey Authentix Game of the Week

		NM/M
	Common Card:	10.00
	Inserted 1:240	
	Unripped:	1.5-3X
	Production 50 Sets	
	Derek Jeter, Nomar Garciaparra, Mike Piazza,	45.00
	Sammy Sosa, Chipper Jones, Pat Burrell	25.00
	Greg Maddux, Randy Johnson, Alex Rodriguez,	20.00
	Miguel Tejada, Adam Dunn, Lance Berkman	20.00
	Torii Hunter, Alfonso Soriano	10.00
	Derek Jeter, Miguel Tejada, Eric Hinske,	15.00
	Torii Hunter, Alfonso Soriano, Sammy Sosa	25.00
		10.00
		15.00

Ticket Studs

		NM/M
	Complete Set (15):	25.00
	Common Player:	1.00
	Inserted 1:6	
1TS	Curt Schilling	1.00
2TS	Greg Maddux	2.50
3TS	Torii Hunter	1.00
4TS	Mike Piazza	3.00
5TS	Pedro J. Martinez	2.00
6TS	Nomar Garciaparra	3.00
7TS	Derek Jeter	5.00
8TS	Alex Rodriguez	4.00
9TS	Alfonso Soriano	3.00
10TS	Pat Burrell	1.50

11TS	Barry Bonds	5.00
12TS	Jason Giambi	2.50
13TS	Sammy Sosa	2.50
14TS	Vladimir Guerrero	1.50
15TS	Ichiro Suzuki	3.00

2003 Fleer Avant

		NM/M
Complete Set (90):		240.00
Common Player:		
Common Retired SP (66-75): 5.00
Production 799		
Common Rk (76-90):		3.00
Production 699		
Pack (4):		4.00
Box (18):		60.00
1	Adam Dunn	.50
2	Barry Zito	.50
3	Preston Wilson	.50
4	Barry Bonds	4.00
5	Hank Blalock	1.00
6	Omar Vizquel	.50
7	Brian Giles	.50
8	Kerry Wood	.75
9	Miguel Tejada	.75
10	Magglio Ordonez	.75
11	Randy Johnson	1.00
12	Jeff Bagwell	1.00
13	Pat Burrell	.75
14	Jason Giambi	.75
15	Mark Prior	2.00
16	Roger Clemens	2.00
17	Sammy Sosa	2.50
18	Jay Gibbons	.50
19	Torii Hunter	.75
20	Ichiro Suzuki	4.00
21	Derek Jeter	4.00
22	Tom Glavine	.50
23	Alfonso Soriano	1.00
24	Manny Ramirez	1.00
25	Frank Thomas	1.50
26	Carlos Pena	.50
27	Alex Rodriguez	3.00
28	Edgar Martinez	.50
29	Larry Walker	.50
30	Rafael Palmeiro	.75
31	Mike Piazza	2.00
32	Nomar Garciaparra	2.50
33	Lance Berkman	.75
34	Vladimir Guerrero	1.00
35	Troy Glaus	.75
36	Ivan Rodriguez	.75
37	Mark Mulder	.50
38	Curt Schilling	.75
39	Mike Sweeney	.50
40	Albert Pujols	3.00
41	Tim Hudson	.50
42	Greg Maddux	1.50
43	Shawn Green	.50
44	Scott Rolen	1.00
45	Gary Sheffield	.75
46	Richie Sexson	.75
47	Aubrey Huff	.50
48	Luis Gonzalez	.50
49	Todd Helton	1.00
50	Xavier Nady	.50
51	Juan Gonzalez	1.00
52	Pedro J. Martinez	1.00
53	Garret Anderson	.50
54	Craig Biggio	.50
55	Bret Boone	.50
56	Ken Griffey Jr.	2.00
57	Kevin Millwood	.50
58	Carlos Delgado	.50
59	Chipper Jones	1.50
60	Hideo Nomo	.50
61	Jim Edmonds	.50
62	Austin Kearns	.75
63	Jim Thome	.50
64	Vernon Wells	.50
65	Mike Lowell	.50
66	Whitey Ford	5.00
67	Bob Gibson	5.00
68	Reggie Jackson	5.00
69	Willie McCovey	5.00
70	Phil Rizzuto	5.00
71	Al Kaline	6.00
72	Brooks Robinson	5.00
73	Nolan Ryan	15.00
74	Mike Schmidt	10.00
75	Tom Seaver	6.00
76	Hideki Matsui RC	15.00
77	Rocco Baldelli	4.00
78	Jose Contreras RC	6.00
79	Hee Seop Choi	3.00
80	Jeremy Bonderman	6.00
81	Bo Hart RC	3.00

82	Brandon Webb RC	10.00
83	Ron Calloway	3.00
84	Jesse Foppert	3.00
85	Kyle Snyder	3.00
86	Mark Teixeira	5.00
87	Jose Reyes	5.00
88	Dontrelle Willis	4.00
89	Reed Johnson	3.00
90	Rickie Weeks RC	10.00

Black/White

		NM/M
Common Player:		
Production 50 Sets		
Stars (1-65):		4-6X
SP's (66-90):		1-2X
Production 199 Sets		

Autographs

		NM/M
Common Autograph:		10.00
Varying quantities produced		
Parallel SP's:		1-1.5X
Production 75 or 150		
DJ	Derek Jeter/75	140.00
MR	Manny Ramirez/100	35.00
VW	Vernon Wells/250	10.00
HB	Hank Blalock/150	25.00
DW	Dontrelle Willis/300	30.00
AK	Al Kaline/200	35.00
BR	Brooks Robinson/300	20.00
BG	Bob Gibson/250	20.00
JR	Jose Reyes/300	30.00
BZ	Barry Zito/150	20.00
EM	Edgar Martinez/246	25.00
BH	Bo Hart/300	15.00
AH	Aubrey Huff/300	15.00
CP	Carlos Pena/150	15.00
MT	Miguel Tejada/150	20.00
ML	Mike Lowell/150	10.00
CB	Craig Biggio/250	15.00
BW	Brandon Webb/300	25.00
RB	Rocco Baldelli/250	30.00

Candid Collection

		NM/M
Complete Set (15):		50.00
Common Player:		2.00
Production 500 Sets		
1CC	Derek Jeter	6.00
2CC	Mike Piazza	4.00
3CC	Albert Pujols	6.00
4CC	Randy Johnson	3.00
5CC	Alex Rodriguez	6.00
6CC	Vladimir Guerrero	3.00
7CC	Troy Glaus	2.00
8CC	Ichiro Suzuki	4.00
9CC	Barry Zito	2.00
10CC	Jim Thome	2.00
11CC	Sammy Sosa	5.00
12CC	Greg Maddux	4.00
13CC	Barry Bonds	8.00
14CC	Jason Giambi	3.00
15CC	Nomar Garciaparra	6.00

Candid Collection Memorabilia

		NM/M
Common Player:		
Production 150 Sets		
	Derek Jeter	30.00
	Mike Piazza	12.00
	Randy Johnson	8.00
	Alex Rodriguez	25.00
	Barry Zito	8.00
	Jim Thome	15.00
	Sammy Sosa	15.00
	Greg Maddux	15.00
	Jason Giambi	10.00
	Nomar Garciaparra	15.00

Hall of Frame

		NM/M
Complete Set (14):		80.00
Common Player:		6.00
Production 299 Sets		

1	Richie Ashburn	6.00
2	Rod Carew	8.00
3	Whitey Ford	8.00
4	Bob Gibson	8.00
5	Reggie Jackson	8.00
6	Harmon Killebrew	8.00
7	Willie McCovey	8.00
8	Phil Rizzuto	8.00
9	Al Kaline	10.00
10	Brooks Robinson	8.00
11	Nolan Ryan	15.00
12	Mike Schmidt	10.00
13	Tom Seaver	8.00
14	Warren Spahn	8.00

Hall of Frame Memorabilia

		NM/M
Production 99 sets		
	Reggie Jackson	25.00
	Willie McCovey	20.00
	Al Kaline	35.00
	Nolan Ryan	65.00
	Mike Schmidt	40.00

Material

		NM/M
Common Player:		
Production 50 Sets		
RB	Rocco Baldelli	25.00
AR	Alex Rodriguez	25.00
AS	Alfonso Soriano	20.00
SS	Sammy Sosa	20.00
NG	Nomar Garciaparra	20.00
MT	Miguel Tejada	10.00
CJ	Chipper Jones	15.00
RJ	Randy Johnson	15.00
JT	Jim Thome	15.00
GM	Greg Maddux	25.00
JG	Jason Giambi	15.00
VG	Vladimir Guerrero	15.00

On Display

		NM/M
Complete Set (10):		50.00
Common Player:		3.00
Production 399 Sets		
1OD	Derek Jeter	6.00
2OD	Barry Bonds	8.00
3OD	Rocco Baldelli	4.00
4OD	Alex Rodriguez	6.00
5OD	Alfonso Soriano	4.00
6OD	Sammy Sosa	6.00
7OD	Nomar Garciaparra	6.00
8OD	Hideki Matsui	20.00
9OD	Miguel Tejada	3.00
10OD	Chipper Jones	6.00

On Display Memorabilia

		NM/M
Common Player:		5.00
Production 250 Sets		
	Derek Jeter	20.00
	Barry Bonds	15.00
	Rocco Baldelli	25.00
	Alex Rodriguez	10.00
	Alfonso Soriano	10.00
	Sammy Sosa	12.00
	Nomar Garciaparra	15.00
	Hideki Matsui	40.00
	Miguel Tejada	5.00
	Chipper Jones	10.00

2003 Fleer Box Score

		NM/M
Complete Set (245):		
Common Player:		.15
Common Box Score Debut		
(101-110):		4.00
Production 599		
Common Rookie (111-125): 1.00
Inserted 1:6		
Complete Rising Stars (30): 25.00
Common (126-155):		1.00
Complete All-Stars (30):		20.00
Common (156-185):		.50
Comp. Intl. Road Trip (30): 20.00
Common (186-215):		.50
Comp. Bronx Bombers (30): 30.00
Common (216-245):		.50
Pack (7):		3.00
Box (18 + 1 Supplemental
Box):		40.00
1	Troy Glaus	.75
2	Derek Jeter	3.00
3	Alex Rodriguez	2.50
4	Barry Zito	.40
5	Darin Erstad	.60
6	Tim Hudson	.40
7	Josh Beckett	.15
8	Adam Dunn	.60
9	Tim Salmon	.25
10	Ivan Rodriguez	.50
11	Mark Buehrle	.15
12	Sammy Sosa	2.00
13	Vicente Padilla	.15
14	Randy Johnson	1.00
15	Lance Berkman	.15
16	Jim Thome	.15
17	Luis Gonzalez	.25
18	Craig Biggio	.15
19	Cliff Floyd	.15
20	Pat Burrell	.50
21	Matt Morris	.15
22	Torii Hunter	.15
23	Curt Schilling	.40
24	Paul Konerko	.15
25	Jeff Bagwell	.75
26	Mike Piazza	2.00
27	A.J. Burnett	.15
28	Jimmy Rollins	.25
29	Greg Maddux	1.50
30	Jeff Kent	.15
31	Bobby Abreu	.15
32	Chipper Jones	1.50
33	Mike Sweeney	.15
34	Jason Kendall	.15
35	Gary Sheffield	.30
36	Carlos Beltran	.50
37	Brian Giles	.15
38	Jim Edmonds	.15
39	Roger Clemens	1.75
40	Andruw Jones	.75
41	Paul LoDuca	.15
42	Ryan Klesko	.15
43	Jay Gibbons	.15
44	Shawn Green	.40
45	Sean Burroughs	.15
46	Magglio Ordonez	.15
47	Tony Batista	.15
48	J.D. Drew	.45
49	Hideo Nomo	.50
50	Edgardo Alfonzo	.15
51	Nomar Garciaparra	2.00
52	Frank Thomas	.75
53	Kazuhisa Ishii	.15
54	Rich Aurilia	.15
55	Shea Hillenbrand	.15
56	Tom Glavine	.40
57	Richie Sexson	.15
58	Mo Vaughn	.15
59	Barry Bonds	3.00
60	Carlos Delgado	.50
61	Pedro J. Martinez	1.00
62	Jacque Jones	.15
63	Edgar Martinez	.15
64	Manny Ramirez	.75
65	Bret Boone	.15
66	Kerry Wood	.50
67	Roy Oswalt	.40
68	Cristian Guzman	.15
69	Moises Alou	.15
70	Bartolo Colon	.15
71	Ichiro Suzuki	1.50
72	Jose Vidro	.15
73	Scott Rolen	.50
74	Mark Prior	1.00
75	Vladimir Guerrero	.75
76	Albert Pujols	1.50

77	Aubrey Huff	.15
78	Ken Griffey Jr.	2.00
79	Roberto Alomar	.30
80	Ben Grieve	.15
81	Miguel Tejada	.40
82	Austin Kearns	.50
83	Jason Giambi	.75
84	John Olerud	.15
85	Omar Vizquel	.15
86	Juan Gonzalez	.75
87	Larry Walker	.15
88	Jorge Posada	.25
89	Rafael Palmeiro	.65
90	Todd Helton	.75
91	Bernie Williams	.30
92	Garret Anderson	.15
93	Eric Hinske	.15
94	Mike Lowell	.15
95	Jason Jennings	.15
96	Eric Chavez	.30
97	Alfonso Soriano	1.00
98	David Eckstein	.15
99	Bobby Higginson	.15
100	Roy Halladay	.15
101	Robby Hammock RC	4.00
102	Hideki Matsui RC	12.00
103	Chase Utley	4.00
104	Oscar Villarreal RC	4.00
105	Jose Contreras RC	8.00
106	Rocco Baldelli	4.00
107	Rontrez Johnson RC	4.00
108	Jeremy Bonderman	8.00
109	Shane Victorino RC	4.00
110	Ron Calloway	4.00
111	Brandon Webb RC	4.00
112	Guillermo Quiroz RC	2.00
113	Clint Barmes RC	2.00
114	Pete LaForest RC	2.00
115	Craig Brazell RC	2.00
116	Todd Wellemeyer RC	1.00
117	Bernie Castro RC	1.00
118	Alejandro Machado RC	1.50
119	Terrmel Sledge RC	1.00
120	Ian Ferguson RC	1.00
121	Lew Ford RC	3.00
122	Nook Logan RC	1.50
123	Mike Nicolas RC	1.00
124	Jeff Duncan RC	1.50
125	Tim Olson RC	1.00
126	Michael Hessman RC	1.50
127	Francisco Rosario RC	1.00
128	Felix Sanchez RC	1.00
129	Andrew Brown RC	1.50
130	Matt Bruback RC	2.00
131	Diegomar Markwell RC	2.00
132	Josh Willingham RC	1.50
133	Wes Obermueller RC	1.50
134	Phil Seibel RC	2.00
135	Arnie Munoz RC	1.50
136	Matt Kata RC	3.00
137	Joe Valentine RC	1.00
138	Ricardo Rodriguez RC	1.00
139	Lyle Overbay	2.00
140	Brian Stokes RC	1.50
141	Josh Hall RC	1.50
142	Kevin Hooper RC	1.50
143	Chien-Ming Wang RC	10.00
144	Prentice Redman RC	1.50
145	Chris Waters RC	1.50
146	Jon Leicester RC	1.50
147	Daniel Cabrera RC	3.00
148	Alfredo Gonzalez RC	1.50
149	Doug Waechter RC	1.50
150	Brandon Larson	1.00
151	Beau Kemp RC	1.50
152	Cory Stewart RC	1.00
153	Francisco Rodriguez	1.00
154	Hee Seop Choi	1.50
155	Mike Neu RC	1.00
156	Derek Jeter	3.00
157	Alex Rodriguez	2.50
158	Nomar Garciaparra	2.00
159	Barry Bonds	2.50
160	Sammy Sosa	1.50
161	Vladimir Guerrero	.75
162	Roger Clemens	2.00
163	Randy Johnson	1.50
164	Greg Maddux	1.50
165	Ken Griffey Jr.	1.50
166	Mike Piazza	2.00
167	Ichiro Suzuki	1.50
168	Barry Larkin	.50
169	Lance Berkman	.50
170	Jim Thome	.75
171	Jason Giambi	1.00
172	Gary Sheffield	.50
173	Ivan Rodriguez	.50
174	Miguel Tejada	.50
175	Manny Ramirez	.75
176	Mike Sweeney	.50
177	Larry Walker	.50
178	Jeff Bagwell	.75
179	Chipper Jones	1.50
180	Craig Biggio	.50
181	Curt Schilling	.50
182	Pedro J. Martinez	1.00
183	Roberto Alomar	.50
184	Bernie Williams	.50
185	Magglio Ordonez	.50
186	Jose Contreras	.50
187	Rafael Palmeiro	1.00
188	Andruw Jones	.75
189	Bartolo Colon	.50
190	Vladimir Guerrero	.75
191	Pedro Martinez	.50
192	Albert Pujols	1.50
193	Manny Ramirez	.75

194	Felix Rodriguez	.50
195	Alfonso Soriano	1.00
196	Sammy Sosa	1.50
197	Miguel Tejada	.50
198	Kazuhisa Ishii	.50
199	Hideki Matsui	5.00
200	Hideo Nomo	1.00
201	Tomokazu Ohka	.50
202	Kazuhiro Sasaki	.50
203	Tsuyoshi Shinjo	.50
204	Ichiro Suzuki	1.50
205	Vicente Padilla	.50
206	Carlos Beltran	.50
207	Jose Cruz Jr.	.50
208	Carlos Delgado	.50
209	Juan Gonzalez	.75
210	Jorge Posada	.50
211	Ivan Rodriguez	.50
212	Hee Seop Choi	.50
213	Bobby Abreu	.50
214	Magglio Ordonez	.50
215	Francisco Rodriguez	.50
216	Juan Acevedo	.50
217	Erick Almonte	.50
218	Yogi Berra	1.50
219	Brandon Claussen	1.00
220	Roger Clemens	2.00
221	Jose Contreras	1.00
222	Whitey Ford	1.00
223	Jason Giambi	1.00
224	Michel Hernandez RC	.50
225	Sterling Hitchcock	.50
226	Jim "Catfish" Hunter	.75
227	Reggie Jackson	1.00
228	Derek Jeter	3.00
229	Nick Johnson	.50
230	Hideki Matsui	5.00
231	Raul Mondesi	.50
232	Mike Mussina	.50
233	Andy Pettitte	.50
234	Jorge Posada	.50
235	Mariano Rivera	.50
236	Phil Rizzuto	1.00
237	Enos Slaughter	.50
238	Alfonso Soriano	1.00
239	Robin Ventura	.50
240	Chien-Ming Wang	2.00
241	Jeff Weaver	.50
242	David Wells	.50
243	Bernie Williams	.50
244	Todd Zeile	.50

First Edition

Stars (1-100):		4-8X
Rookies (101-125):		1.5-3X
Production 150 Sets		

All-Star Lineup

| | | NM/M |
| Common Card: | | 15.00 |
| Inserted 1:All-Stars Set |
Derek Jeter, Alex Rodriguez, Nomar Garciaparra		35.00
Barry Bonds, Sammy Sosa, Vladimir Guerrero		15.00
Roger Clemens, Randy Johnson, Greg Maddux		30.00
Jason Giambi, Alfonso Soriano, Derek Jeter		30.00
Craig Biggio, Jeff Bagwell, Lance Berkman		20.00
Chipper Jones, Gary Sheffield, Greg Maddux		30.00
Ivan Rodriguez, Mike Piazza, Randy Johnson, Roger Clemens		40.00
Roberto Alomar, Mike Piazza, Alfonso Soriano, Jason Giambi		45.00
Jim Thome, Roberto Alomar, Alex Rodriguez, Nomar Garciaparra		40.00

Bat Rack

| | | NM/M |
| Common Card: | | 20.00 |
| Production 250 Sets |
| Derek Jeter, Alfonso Soriano, Jason Giambi | | 35.00 |

Scott Rolen, Miguel Tejada,
Troy Glaus 20.00
Jim Thome, Torii Hunter,
Mike Piazza 25.00
Troy Glaus,
Nomar Garciaparra,
Alfonso Soriano 30.00
Lance Berkman,
Vladimir Guerrero,
Sammy Sosa 20.00
Chipper Jones,
Lance Berkman,
Vladimir Guerrero 20.00
Torii Hunter, Jason Giambi,
Nomar Garciaparra 25.00
Derek Jeter, Miguel Tejada,
Alex Rodriguez 25.00
Scott Rolen, Sammy Sosa,
Alex Rodriguez 25.00

Bat Rack Quad
NM/M
Production 50 Sets
Derek Jeter, Torii Hunter,
Troy Glaus,
Miguel Tejada 40.00
Derek Jeter, Mike Piazza,
Nomar Garciaparra,
Chipper Jones 60.00
Alex Rodriguez,
Jim Thome, Sammy Sosa,
Barry Bonds 50.00

Bronx Bombers Jersey
NM/M
Common Player: 4.00
Inserted 1:Bronx Bombers Set
Roger Clemens 15.00
Jason Giambi 12.00
Derek Jeter 20.00
Nick Johnson 4.00
Mike Mussina 10.00
Jorge Posada 8.00
Alfonso Soriano 10.00
Robin Ventura 5.00
Bernie Williams 8.00

Classic Minatures

NM/M
Complete Set (30): 10.00
Common Player: .25
1CM Jim Thome .40
2CM Jason Giambi .50
3CM Miguel Tejada .25
4CM Alfonso Soriano 1.00
5CM Ivan Rodriguez .40
6CM Troy Glaus .40
7CM Mike Piazza 1.00
8CM Barry Bonds 1.50
9CM Sammy Sosa 1.00
10CM Lance Berkman .25
11CM Pat Burrell .25
12CM Chipper Jones .75
13CM Shawn Green .25
14CM Manny Ramirez .50
15CM Ichiro Suzuki .75
16CM Vladimir Guerrero .50
17CM Albert Pujols .75
18CM Ken Griffey Jr. 1.00
19CM Bernie Williams .40
20CM Austin Kearns .40
21CM Randy Johnson .50
22CM Greg Maddux .75
23CM Roger Clemens 1.00
24CM Hideo Nomo .25
25CM Pedro J. Martinez .50
26CM Kerry Wood .40
27CM Mark Prior .50
28CM Derek Jeter 1.50
29CM Alex Rodriguez 1.00
30CM Nomar Garciaparra 1.00

Classic Miniatures Mini Jersey
NM/M
Common Jersey: 4.00
1:Classic Miniatures Box
NG Nomar Garciaparra 10.00
JG Jason Giambi 8.00
VG Vladimir Guerrero 5.00
DJ Derek Jeter 15.00
AK Austin Kearns 8.00
GM Greg Maddux 10.00
HN Hideo Nomo 10.00

MP Mark Prior 10.00
MT Miguel Tejada 4.00
JT Jim Thome 8.00

Jersey Rack
NM/M
Common Card: 15.00
Production 350 Sets
Derek Jeter,
Alfonso Soriano,
Jason Giambi 40.00
Curt Schilling,
Randy Johnson,
Greg Maddux 25.00
Roger Clemens,
Pedro J. Martinez,
Barry Zito 30.00
Alex Rodriguez,
Vladimir Guerrero,
Sammy Sosa 25.00
Derek Jeter,
Nomar Garciaparra,
Alex Rodriguez 30.00
Lance Berkman,
Sammy Sosa,
Torii Hunter 20.00
Vladimir Guerrero,
Jim Thome,
Alex Rodriguez 20.00
Derek Jeter, Miguel Tejada,
Nomar Garciaparra 30.00
Alfonso Soriano,
Eric Chavez,
Jim Thome 20.00
Miguel Tejada, Eric Chavez,
Barry Zito 15.00

Jersey Rack Quad
NM/M
Common Card:
Production 150 Sets
Derek Jeter,
Alex Rodriguez,
Nomar Garciaparra,
Miguel Tejada 60.00
Jim Thome, Jason Giambi,
Sammy Sosa,
Vladimir Guerrero 50.00
Randy Johnson,
Greg Maddux,
Roger Clemens,
Pedro J. Martinez 60.00
Curt Schilling,
Vladimir Guerrero,
Randy Johnson,
Alex Rodriguez 40.00
Alfonso Soriano,
Jim Thome, Sammy Sosa,
Eric Chavez 40.00
Eric Chavez, Miguel Tejada,
Barry Zito,
Nomar Garciaparra 20.00

Press Clippings

NM/M
Complete Set (20): 40.00
Common Player: 1.00
Inserted 1:18
1PC Derek Jeter 6.00
2PC Nomar Garciaparra 5.00
3PC Miguel Tejada 1.00
4PC Barry Bonds 5.00
5PC Alex Rodriguez 5.00
6PC Sammy Sosa 3.00
7PC Lance Berkman 1.00
8PC Torii Hunter 1.00
9PC Troy Glaus 1.50
10PC Eric Chavez 1.00
11PC Tim Hudson 1.00
12PC Randy Johnson 2.00
13PC Mike Piazza 4.00
14PC Roberto Alomar 1.50
15PC Jim Thome 1.50
16PC Alfonso Soriano 3.00
17PC Roger Clemens 4.00
18PC Pedro J. Martinez 2.00
19PC Mark Prior 1.50
20PC Curt Schilling 1.00

Press Clippings Game-Used
NM/M
Common Player: 4.00
Inserted 1:12
Derek Jeter 15.00

Nomar Garciaparra 15.00
Miguel Tejada 4.00
Alex Rodriguez 10.00
Sammy Sosa 12.00
Lance Berkman 4.00
Torii Hunter 6.00
Troy Glaus 5.00
Eric Chavez 4.00
Tim Hudson 4.00
Randy Johnson 8.00
Mike Piazza 12.00
Roberto Alomar 4.00
Jim Thome 10.00
Alfonso Soriano 10.00
Roger Clemens 12.00
Pedro J. Martinez 8.00
Mark Prior 6.00
Curt Schilling 4.00

Press Clippings Dual
NM/M
Complete Set (10): 35.00
Common Player: 2.00
Production 250 Sets
1 Derek Jeter,
Nomar Garciaparra 8.00
2 Miguel Tejada,
Barry Bonds 6.00
3 Alex Rodriguez,
Sammy Sosa 6.00
4 Lance Berkman,
Torii Hunter 2.00
5 Troy Glaus,
Eric Chavez 2.00
6 Tim Hudson,
Randy Johnson 3.00
7 Mike Piazza,
Roberto Alomar 5.00
8 Jim Thome,
Alfonso Soriano 4.00
9 Roger Clemens,
Pedro J. Martinez 5.00
10 Mark Prior,
Curt Schilling 2.00

Press Clippings Dual Patch
NM/M
Common Card: 25.00
Derek Jeter,
Nomar Garciaparra/100 60.00
Miguel Tejada,
Troy Glaus/150 25.00
Alex Rodriguez,
Sammy Sosa/150 80.00
Lance Berkman,
Torii Hunter/150 30.00
Troy Glaus,
Eric Chavez/150 30.00
Tim Hudson,
Randy Johnson/150 30.00
Mike Piazza,
Roberto Alomar/150 40.00
Jim Thome,
Alfonso Soriano/100 40.00
Roger Clemens,
Pedro Martinez/100 50.00
Mark Prior,
Curt Schilling/150 25.00

Wave of the Future
NM/M
Common Player: 4.00
Inserted 1:Rising Stars Set
Jeremy Bonderman/Bat 12.00
Ron Calloway/Jsy 4.00
Hee Seop Choi/Jsy 10.00
Brandon Larson/Bat 8.00
Lyle Overbay/Bat 6.00
Francisco Rodriguez/Jsy 6.00
Chase Utley/Jsy 6.00

World Piece
NM/M
Common Player: 4.00
Inserted 1:Intl. Road Trip Set
Vladimir Guerrero 6.00
Pedro Martinez 10.00
Sammy Sosa 12.00
Miguel Tejada 4.00

Hideo Nomo 10.00
Jose Cruz Jr. 4.00
Ivan Rodriguez 6.00
Hee Seop Choi 10.00
Francisco Rodriguez 4.00
Kazuhiro Sasaki 4.00

2003 Fleer Double Header

NM/M
Complete Set (300): 60.00
Common Player: .20
Common (181-300): .40
Pack (8): 2.00
Box (20): 35.00
1 Ramon Vazquez .20
2 Derek Jeter 2.00
3 Orlando Hudson .20
4 Miguel Tejada .30
5 Steve Finley .20
6 Brad Wilkerson .20
7 Craig Biggio .20
8 Marlon Anderson .20
9 Phil Nevin .20
10 Hideo Nomo .50
11 Barry Larkin .20
12 Alfonso Soriano .75
13 Rodrigo Lopez .20
14 Paul Konerko .25
15 Carlos Beltran .50
16 Kazuhisa Ishii .20
17 Garret Anderson .20
18 Eddie Guardado .20
19 Juan Gonzalez .50
20 Mark Mulder .20
21 Sammy Sosa 1.25
22 Kazuhisa Sasaki .20
23 Jose Cruz Jr. .20
24 Tomokazu Ohka .20
25 Barry Bonds 2.00
26 Carlos Delgado .50
27 Scott Rolen .50
28 Steve Cox .20
29 Mike Sweeney .20
30 Ryan Klesko .20
31 Greg Maddux 1.00
32 Derek Lowe .20
33 David Wells .20
34 Kerry Wood .40
35 Randall Simon .20
36 Ben Howard .20
37 Jeff Suppan .20
38 Curt Schilling .40
39 Eric Gagne .20
40 Raul Mondesi .20
41 Jeffrey Hammonds .20
42 Mo Vaughn .20
43 Sidney Ponson .20
44 Adam Dunn .20
45 Pedro J. Martinez .75
46 Jason Simontacchi .20
47 Tom Glavine .40
48 Torii Hunter .20
49 Gabe Kapler .20
50 Andy Van Hekken .20
51 Ichiro Suzuki 1.25
52 Andruw Jones .50
53 Bobby Abreu .20
54 Junior Spivey .20
55 Ray Durham .20
56 Mark Buehrle .20
57 Drew Henson .20
58 Brandon Duckworth .20
59 Robert Mackowiak .20
60 Josh Beckett .20
61 Chan Ho Park .20
62 John Smoltz .20
63 Jimmy Rollins .40
64 Orlando Cabrera .20
65 Johnny Damon .20
66 Austin Kearns .40
67 Tsuyoshi Shinjo .20
68 Tim Hudson .30
69 Coco Crisp .20
70 Darin Erstad .60
71 Jacque Jones .20
72 Vicente Padilla .20
73 Hee Seop Choi .20
74 Shea Hillenbrand .20
75 Edgardo Alfonzo .20
76 Pat Burrell .50
77 Ben Sheets .20
78 Ivan Rodriguez .40
79 Josh Phelps .20
80 Adam Kennedy .20
81 Eric Chavez .30
82 Bobby Higginson .20
83 Nomar Garciaparra 1.50
84 J.D. Drew .30
85 Carl Crawford .20
86 Matt Morris .20
87 Chipper Jones 1.00
88 Luis Gonzalez .30
89 Richie Sexson .20
90 Eric Milton .20
91 Andres Galarraga .20
92 Paul LoDuca .30
93 Mark Grace .30
94 Ben Grieve .20
95 Mike Lowell .20
96 Roberto Alomar .35
97 Wade Miller .20
98 Sean Casey .20
99 Roger Clemens 1.25
100 Matt Williams .20
101 Brian Giles .20
102 Jim Thome .50
103 Troy Glaus .75
104 Joe Borchard .20
105 Vladimir Guerrero .75
106 Kevin Mench .20
107 Omar Vizquel .20
108 Magglio Ordonez .20
109 Ken Griffey Jr. 1.50
110 Mike Piazza 1.50
111 Mark Teixeira .40
112 Jason Jennings .20
113 Ellis Burks .20
114 Jason Varitek .20
115 Larry Walker .20
116 Frank Thomas .75
117 Ramon Ortiz .20
118 Mark Quinn .20
119 Preston Wilson .20
120 Carlos Lee .20
121 Brian Lawrence .20
122 Tim Salmon .20
123 Shawn Green .30
124 Randy Johnson .75
125 Jeff Bagwell .75
126 C.C. Sabathia .20
127 Bernie Williams .35
128 Roy Oswalt .30
129 Albert Pujols .75
130 Reggie Sanders .20
131 Jeff Conine .20
132 John Olerud .20
133 Lance Berkman .20
134 Geoff Jenkins .20
135 Jim Edmonds .20
136 Todd Helton .65
137 Jason Kendall .20
138 Robin Ventura .20
139 Randy Winn .20
140 Carl Everett .20
141 Jose Vidro .20
142 Pokey Reese .20
143 Edgar Renteria .20
144 Alex Rodriguez 1.75
145 Doug Mientkiewicz .20
146 Aramis Ramirez .20
147 Bobby Hill .20
148 Jorge Posada .35
149 Sean Burroughs .20
150 Jeff Kent .20
151 Tino Martinez .20
152 Mark Prior .50
153 Brad Radke .20
154 Al Leiter .20
155 Eric Karros .20
156 Manny Ramirez .20
157 Jason Lane .20
158 Mike Lieberthal .20
159 Shannon Stewart .20
160 Robert Fick .20
161 Derrek Lee .20
162 Jason Giambi .50
163 Rafael Palmeiro .65
164 Jay Payton .20
165 Adrian Beltre .20
166 Marlon Byrd .20
167 Bret Boone .20
168 Roy Halladay .20
169 Freddy Garcia .20
170 Rich Aurilia .20
171 Jared Sandberg .20
172 Paul Byrd .20
173 Gary Sheffield .30
174 Edgar Martinez .20
175 Eric Hinske .20
176 Milton Bradley .20
177 David Eckstein .20
178 Jay Gibbons .20
179 Corey Patterson .20
180 Barry Zito .20
181-182 Darin Erstad,
Troy Glaus .50
183-184 Curt Schilling,
Randy Johnson .75
185-186 Andruw Jones,
Chipper Jones 1.00
187-188 Tony Batista,
Jay Gibbons .40
189-190 Pedro Martinez,
Nomar Garciaparra 1.25
191-192 Sammy Sosa,
Kerry Wood 1.00
193-194 Paul Konerko,
Joe Borchard .40
195-196 Austin Kearns,
Adam Dunn .50
197-198 Omar Vizquel,
Jim Thome .50
199-200 Larry Walker,
Todd Helton .40
201-202 Josh Beckett,
Luis Castillo .40
203-204 Craig Biggio,
Jeff Bagwell .50
205-206 Paul Byrd,
Mike Sweeney .40
207-208 Adrian Beltre,
Shawn Green .40
209-210 Jose Hernandez,
Richie Sexson .40
211-212 Jacque Jones,
Torii Hunter .40
213-214 Vladimir Guerrero,
Jose Vidro .75
215-216 Edgardo Alfonzo,
Mike Piazza 1.50
217-218 Roger Clemens,
Derek Jeter 2.00
219-220 Eric Chavez,
Miguel Tejada .40
221-222 Marlon Byrd,
Pat Burrell .50
223-224 Jason Kendall,
Brian Giles .40
225-226 Phil Nevin,
Sean Burroughs .40
227-228 Jeff Kent,
Barry Bonds 2.00
229-230 Kazuhiro Sasaki,
Ichiro Suzuki 1.25
231-232 Albert Pujols,
J.D. Drew .75
233-234 Juan Gonzalez,
Ivan Rodriguez .50
235-236 Eric Hinske,
Orlando Hudson .20
237-238 Lance Berkman,
Chipper Jones 1.00
239-240 Alex Rodriguez,
Derek Jeter 2.00
241-242 Ichiro Suzuki,
Hideo Nomo 1.25
243-244 Manny Ramirez,
Bernie Williams .50
245-246 Tom Glavine,
Roger Clemens 1.00
247-248 Ken Griffey Jr.,
Barry Larkin 1.25
249-250 Mark Teixeira,
Mark Prior .75
251-252 Albert Pujols,
Drew Henson .75
253-254 Jason Kendall,
Todd Helton 1.00
255-256 Jose Vidro,
Alfonso Soriano .75
257-258 Shea Hillenbrand,
Scott Rolen .50
259-260 Jimmy Rollins,
Alex Rodriguez 2.00
261-262 Torii Hunter,
Vladimir Guerrero .75
263-264 Ichiro Suzuki,
Sammy Sosa 1.25
265-266 Barry Bonds,
Manny Ramirez 2.00
267-268 Mike Piazza,
Jorge Posada 1.25
269-270 Robin Yount,
Ozzie Smith 1.00
271-272 Josh Hancock,
Freddy Sanchez .40
273-274 Ryan Bukvich,
Shawn Sedlacek .40
275-276 Doug DeVore,
Rene Reyes .40
277-278 Hank Blalock,
Travis Hafner .50
279-280 Eric Junge,
Brett Myers .40
281-282 Brad Lidge,
Jeriome Robertson .40
283-284 Miguel Asencio,
Runelvys Hernandez .40
285-286 Fernando Rodney,
Barry Wesson .40
287-288 Victor Alvarez,
David Ross .40
289-290 Tony Torcato,
Chris Snelling .50
291-292 Kirk Saarloos,
Morgan Ensberg .40
293-294 Josh Bard,
Wilbert Nieves .40
295-296 Jung Bong,
Trey Hodges .40
297-298 Kevin Nash,
Reed Johnson .40
299-300 Chone Figgins,
John Lackey .40

Flip Card Memorabilia
NM/M
Common Player: 4.00

Inserted 1:20
Golds: .75-2X
Production 100 Sets
1 Roberto Alomar/Bat/200 10.00
2 Jeff Bagwell/Jsy 8.00
3 Adrian Beltre/Jsy 4.00
4 Barry Bonds/Bat/200 15.00
5 Roger Clemens/Jsy/200 12.00
6 J.D. Drew/Jsy 6.00
7 Adam Dunn/Jsy/200 10.00
8 Nomar Garciaparra/Jsy/200 15.00
9 Mark Grace/Jsy 8.00
10 Todd Helton/Jsy/200 8.00
11 Derek Jeter/Jsy/200 20.00
12 Randy Johnson/Jsy/200 10.00
13 Chipper Jones/Jsy 8.00
14 Eric Karros/Jsy 4.00
15 Barry Larkin/Jsy/200 8.00
16 Greg Maddux/Jsy/200 10.00
17 Hideo Nomo/Jsy/200 10.00
18 Kazuhisa Ishii/Jsy 6.00
19 Mike Piazza/Jsy/200 10.00
20 Jorge Posada/Jsy/200 8.00
21 Mark Prior/Jsy/200 5.00
22 Alex Rodriguez/Jsy 10.00
23 Kazuhiro Sasaki/Jsy/200 6.00
24 Curt Schilling/Jsy/200 8.00
25 Alfonso Soriano/Jsy 8.00
26 Miguel Tejada/Jsy 8.00
27 Jim Thome/Jsy/200 10.00
28 Robin Ventura/Jsy 4.00
29 Bernie Williams/Jsy/200 8.00
30 Kerry Wood/Jsy/200 10.00

Keystone Combination

NM/M
Complete Set (10): 25.00
Common Card: 1.00
Inserted 1:10
1KC Derek Jeter, Bret Boone 6.00
2KC Miguel Tejada, Jeff Kent 1.00
3KC Nomar Garciaparra, Ray Durham 4.00
4KC Omar Vizquel, Roberto Alomar
5KC Pee Wee Reese, Joe Morgan 1.00
6KC Alex Rodriguez, Craig Biggio 5.00
7KC Orlando Hudson, Jose Vidro 1.00
8KC Phil Rizzuto, Alfonso Soriano 3.00
9KC Alex Rodriguez, Miguel Tejada 5.00
10KC Nomar Garciaparra, Derek Jeter 6.00

Keystone Combination Memorabilia

NM/M
Common Card: 4.00
Inserted 1:40
Derek Jeter, Bret Boone/Jsy 8.00
Miguel Tejada, Jeff Kent/Jsy 4.00
N.Garciaparra/Jsy/175, Ray Durham 12.00
Omar Vizquel, Roberto Alomar/Jsy 6.00
Alex Rodriguez, Craig Biggio/Jsy 6.00
Orlando Hudson, Jose Vidro/Jsy 4.00
Phil Rizzuto, Alfonso Soriano/Jsy/75 15.00
Alex Rodriguez/Bat, Miguel Tejada 10.00
N.Garciaparra/Jsy/175, Derek Jeter 12.00
Derek Jeter/Jsy/175, Bret Boone 20.00
Derek Jeter/Jsy/175, Nomar Garciaparra 20.00
Alex Rodriguez/Jsy/200, Craig Biggio 10.00
Miguel Tejada/Jsy, Jeff Kent 8.00
Miguel Tejada/Jsy, Alex Rodriguez 8.00

Let's Play, Too!

NM/M
Complete Set (15): 8.00
Common Player: .50
Inserted 1:5
1LPT Chris Snelling 1.00
2LPT Kevin Mench .50
3LPT Brett Myers .50
4LPT Julius Matos .50
5LPT Drew Henson 1.00
6LPT Joe Borchard .50
7LPT Felix Escalona .50
8LPT Kirk Saarloos .50
9LPT Ben Howard .50
10LPT Hee Seop Choi 1.00
11LPT Rene Reyes .50
12LPT Josh Bard .50
13LPT Marlon Byrd .50
14LPT Coco Crisp .50
15LPT Reed Johnson .50

Matinee Idols

NM/M
Complete Set (15): 50.00
Common Player: 2.00
Inserted 1:20
1MI Yogi Berra 3.00
2MI Richie Ashburn 3.00
3MI Whitey Ford 3.00
4MI Eddie Mathews 3.00
5MI Jim Palmer 2.00
6MI Al Kaline 6.00
7MI Brooks Robinson 3.00
8MI Willie McCovey 3.00
9MI Billy Williams 2.00
10MI Willie Stargell 3.00
11MI Nolan Ryan 15.00
12MI Rod Carew 3.00
13MI Reggie Jackson 3.00
14MI Tom Seaver 4.00
15MI Mike Schmidt 6.00

Twin Bill

NM/M
Complete Set (20): 45.00
Common Player: 1.00
Inserted 1:10
1a Barry Bonds 5.00
1b Lance Berkman 1.00
2a Derek Jeter 6.00
2b Alex Rodriguez 5.00
3a Roger Clemens 3.00
3b Pedro Martinez 2.00
4a Roberto Alomar 1.25
4b Chipper Jones 3.00
5a Barry Zito 1.00
5b Ichiro Suzuki 4.00
6a Sammy Sosa 3.00
6b Ken Griffey Jr. 4.00
7a Bernie Williams 1.00
7b Manny Ramirez 1.50
8a Nomar Garciaparra 4.00
8b Derek Jeter 6.00
9a Randy Johnson 2.00
9b Greg Maddux 3.00
10a Albert Pujols 2.00
10b Adam Dunn 1.50

Twin Bill Single Swatch

NM/M
Common Player: 1.00
Barry Bonds/Cap/100 25.00
Alex Rodriguez/Cap/100 15.00
Roger Clemens/Cap/100 15.00
Pedro Martinez/Cap/100 12.00
Roberto Alomar/Cap 10.00
Barry Zito/Cap/100 15.00
Bernie Williams/Cap/100 10.00
Manny Ramirez/Cap/75 12.00
Nomar Garciaparra/Cap/100 25.00
Derek Jeter/Cap/100 30.00
Randy Johnson/Cap/100 15.00
Adam Dunn/Cap/100 12.00

Twin Bill Dual Swatch

NM/M
Common Card:
Production 50 Sets
Barry Bonds, Adam Dunn 40.00
Randy Johnson, Barry Zito 35.00

2003 Fleer E-X

NM/M
Complete Set (102): 125.00
Common Player: .50
Common SP (83-102): 3.00
Pack (3): 4.00
Box (20): 60.00
1 Troy Glaus .75
2 Darin Erstad .75
3 Garret Anderson .50
4 Curt Schilling .75
5 Randy Johnson 1.00
6 Luis Gonzalez .50
7 Greg Maddux 1.50
8 Chipper Jones 1.50
9 Andruw Jones 1.00
10 Melvin Mora .50
11 Jay Gibbons .50
12 Nomar Garciaparra 2.00
13 Pedro J. Martinez 1.00
14 Manny Ramirez 1.00
15 Sammy Sosa 2.00
16 Kerry Wood .75
17 Magglio Ordonez .50
18 Frank Thomas 1.00
19 Roberto Alomar .60
20 Barry Larkin .50
21 Adam Dunn 1.00
22 Austin Kearns .50
23 Omar Vizquel .50
24 Larry Walker .50
25 Todd Helton 1.00
26 Preston Wilson .50
27 Dmitri Young .50
28 Ivan Rodriguez .75
29 Mike Lowell .50
30 Jeff Kent .50
31 Jeff Bagwell 1.00
32 Roy Oswalt .75
33 Craig Biggio .50
34 Mike Sweeney .50
35 Carlos Beltran .75
36 Shawn Green .60
37 Kazuhisa Ishii .50
38 Richie Sexson .50
39 Torii Hunter .50
40 Jacque Jones .50
41 Jose Vidro .50
42 Vladimir Guerrero 1.00
43 Mike Piazza 2.00
44 Tom Glavine .60
45 Roger Clemens 1.75
46 Jason Giambi .75
47 Bernie Williams .60
48 Alfonso Soriano 1.00
49 Mike Mussina .60
50 Barry Zito .60
51 Miguel Tejada .60
52 Eric Chavez .60
53 Eric Byrnes .50
54 Jim Thome .50
55 Kevin Millwood .50
56 Brian Giles .50
57 Xavier Nady .50
58 Barry Bonds 3.00
59 Bret Boone .50
60 Edgar Martinez .50
61 Kazuhiro Sasaki .50
62 Edgar Renteria .50
63 J.D. Drew .50
64 Scott Rolen 1.00
65 Jim Edmonds .50
66 Aubrey Huff .50
67 Alex Rodriguez 2.50
68 Juan Gonzalez 1.00
69 Hank Blalock .75
70 Mark Teixeira .75
71 Carlos Delgado .75
72 Vernon Wells .50
73 Shea Hillenbrand .50
74 Gary Sheffield .50
75 Mark Prior .50
76 Ken Griffey Jr. 2.00
77 Lance Berkman .50
78 Hideo Nomo .75
79 Derek Jeter 3.00
80 Ichiro Suzuki 2.00
81 Albert Pujols 2.50
82 Rafael Palmeiro .75
83 Jose Reyes 4.00
84 Rocco Baldelli 4.00
85 Hee Seop Choi 3.00
86 Dontrelle Willis 4.00
87 Robby Hammock RC 3.00
88 Brandon Webb RC 8.00
89 Matt Kata RC 3.00
90 Todd Wellemeyer RC 3.00
91 Francisco Cruceta RC 3.00
92 Clint Barmes RC 6.00
93 Jeremy Bonderman 8.00
94 Dave Matranga RC 3.00
95 Ryan Wagner RC 5.00
96 Jeremy Griffiths RC 3.00
97 Hideki Matsui RC 15.00
98 Jose Contreras RC 6.00
99 Chien-Ming Wang RC 25.00
100 Bo Hart RC 4.00
101 Dan Haren RC 5.00
102 Rickie Weeks RC 10.00

Essential Credentials Now/Future

Cards serial numbered
26-50: 6-12X
Cards s/n 51-75: 4-8X
Cards s/n 76-102: 3-5X
SP's (83-102) s/n 83-102: 1-2X
Now is consecutively #'d from 1 to 102.
Future is consect. #'d from 102 to 1.

Behind the Numbers

NM/M
Complete Set (15): 50.00
Common Player: 1.50
Inserted 1:80
1 Derek Jeter 8.00
2 Alex Rodriguez 8.00
3 Randy Johnson 3.00
4 Chipper Jones 5.00
5 Jim Thome 3.00
6 Alfonso Soriano 4.00
7 Adam Dunn 2.00
8 Nomar Garciaparra 6.00
9 Roger Clemens 6.00
10 Gary Sheffield 1.50
11 Vladimir Guerrero 3.00
12 Greg Maddux 5.00
13 Sammy Sosa 6.00
14 Mike Piazza 6.00
15 Troy Glaus 2.00

Behind the Numbers Autograph

No pricing due to scarcity.
Numbered to jersey number.

Behind the Numbers Game-Used

NM/M
Common Player: 5.00
Inserted 1:10
Patch Version: 1.5-2.5X
DJ Derek Jeter 15.00
AR Alex Rodriguez 10.00
RJ Randy Johnson 8.00
CJ Chipper Jones 8.00
JT Jim Thome 8.00
AS Alfonso Soriano 8.00
AD Adam Dunn 6.00
NG Nomar Garciaparra 8.00
RC Roger Clemens 10.00
GS Gary Sheffield 5.00
VG Vladimir Guerrero 8.00
GM Greg Maddux 8.00
SS Sammy Sosa 10.00
MP Mike Piazza 8.00
TG Troy Glaus 5.00
HB Hank Blalock 6.00
TG Tom Glavine 5.00
BM Brett Myers 5.00
LB Lance Berkman 5.00
RB Rocco Baldelli 10.00
BZ Barry Zito 6.00
DW Dontrelle Willis 10.00
RP Rafael Palmeiro 5.00
RA Roberto Alomar 5.00
MB Marlon Byrd 5.00

Diamond Essentials

NM/M
Common Player: 5.00
Inserted 1:480
1DE Randy Johnson 15.00
2DE Ichiro Suzuki 25.00
3DE Albert Pujols 30.00
4DE Barry Bonds 40.00
5DE Hideki Matsui 30.00
6DE Derek Jeter 40.00
7DE Chipper Jones 20.00
8DE Sammy Sosa 25.00
9DE Jeff Bagwell 10.00
10DE Mike Piazza 20.00
11DE Pedro J. Martinez 15.00
12DE Mark Prior 20.00
13DE Jason Giambi 10.00
14DE Jose Reyes 5.00
15DE Alfonso Soriano 15.00

Diamond Essentials Autograph

NM/M
Common Player:
Dontrelle Willis 30.00
Ryan Wagner 20.00
Rocco Baldelli 25.00
Albert Pujols 150.00

Diamond Essentials Game-Used

NM/M
Common Player: 8.00
Same price for cards #'d 145, 245 & 345.
Patch Versions: 1.5-2.5X
Production 55
RJ Randy Johnson 8.00
DJ Derek Jeter 15.00
CJ Chipper Jones 8.00
SS Sammy Sosa 12.00
JB Jeff Bagwell 8.00
MP Mike Piazza 10.00
PM Pedro J. Martinez 8.00
MP Mark Prior 10.00
JG Jason Giambi 8.00
JR Jose Reyes 8.00

Emerald Essentials

NM/M
Complete Set (10): 60.00
Common Player: 4.00
Inserted 1:240
1 Austin Kearns 4.00
2 Alfonso Soriano 8.00
3 Miguel Tejada 4.00
4 Troy Glaus 4.00
5 Adam Dunn 4.00
6 Hideo Nomo 6.00
7 Kerry Wood 6.00
8 Nomar Garciaparra 15.00
9 Roger Clemens 15.00
10 Derek Jeter 15.00

Emerald Essentials Autograph

NM/M
Common Player:
Brandon Webb 40.00
Hank Blalock 20.00

Emerald Essentials Game-Used

NM/M
Common Player: 4.00
Same price for levels #'d 175, 250 & 375.
Patch Versions: 1.5-2.5X
Production 60
AK Austin Kearns 6.00
AS Alfonso Soriano 8.00
MT Miguel Tejada 4.00
TG Troy Glaus 6.00
AD Adam Dunn 6.00
HN Hideo Nomo 15.00
KW Kerry Wood 8.00
NG Nomar Garciaparra 12.00
RC Roger Clemens 12.00
AR Alex Rodriguez 10.00

X-tra Innings

NM/M
Complete Set (10): 25.00
Common Player: 1.00
Inserted 1:32
1XI Ichiro Suzuki 3.00
2XI Albert Pujols 4.00
3XI Barry Bonds 5.00
4XI Jason Giambi 1.50
5XI Pedro J. Martinez 2.00
6XI Mark Prior 3.00
7XI Derek Jeter 5.00
8XI Curt Schilling 1.00
9XI Jeff Bagwell 1.50
10XI Alex Rodriguez 5.00

2003 Fleer Fall Classic

NM/M
Complete Set (87): 30.00
Common Player: .25
Common SP:
Hobby Pack (5): 4.00
Hobby Box (24): 75.00
1 Rod Carew .50
2 Bobby Doerr .25
3 Eddie Mathews 1.00
  Eddie Mathews/SP/Tigers 4.00
4 Tom Seaver 1.50
5 Lou Brock .75
6 Nolan Ryan 3.00
  Nolan Ryan/SP/Astros 10.00
7 Pee Wee Reese .25
8 Robin Yount .50
9 Bob Feller .50
10 Harmon Killebrew 3.00

ABBREVIATIONS

SP - Short Print

11	Hal Newhouser	.25
12	Al Kaline	1.00
13	Hoyt Wilhelm	.25
14	Early Wynn	.25
15	Yogi Berra	1.00
15	Yogi Berra/SP/Mets	4.00
16	Billy Williams	.25
17	Rollie Fingers	.25
18	Sparky Anderson	.25
18	Sparky Anderson/SP/Reds	3.00
19	Lou Boudreau	.25
20	Warren Spahn	1.00
21	Enos Slaughter	.25
22	Luis Aparicio	.50
23	Phil Rizzuto	.75
24	Willie McCovey	.75
25	Joe Morgan	.50
26	Alan Trammell	.25
27	Eddie Plank	.25
28	Lefty Grove	.25
29	Walter Johnson	1.00
30	Roy Campanella	1.00
31	Carlton Fisk	.75
32	Bill Dickey	.25
33	Rogers Hornsby	1.00
33	Rogers Hornsby/SP/Cubs	5.00
34	Wade Boggs	.75
35	Chick Stahl	.25
36	Don Drysdale	.75
36	Don Drysdale/SP/Dodgers	4.00
37	Jose Canseco	.75
38	Roger Maris	2.00
38	Roger Maris/SP/Yankees	8.00
39	Cal Ripken Jr.	3.00
40	Kiki Cuyler	.25
40	Kiki Cuyler/SP/Cubs	3.00
41	Hank Greenberg	.25
42	Don Larsen	.50
43	Eddie Murray	.75
43	Eddie Murray/SP/Indians	4.00
44	Jimmy Sebring	.25
45	Ozzie Smith	1.50
46	Darryl Strawberry	.25
46	Darryl Strawberry/SP/Yankees	3.00
47	Dave Parker	.25
48	Gil Hodges	.25
48	Gil Hodges/SP/Mets	3.00
49	Joe Carter	.50
50	Leo Durocher	.25
50	Leo Durocher/SP/Giants	3.00
51	Christy Mathewson	.75
52	Elston Howard	.25
53	Hughie Jennings	.25
54	Nellie Fox	.50
55	Carl Yastrzemski	1.00
56	Frank Robinson	1.00
56	Frank Robinson/SP/Reds	4.00
57	Dennis Eckersley	.50
58	Grover Alexander	.50
58	Grover Alexander/SP/Cards	4.00
59	Carl Hubbell	.25
60	Dave Winfield	.75
61	Honus Wagner	1.50
62	Duke Snider	1.00
62	Duke Snider/SP/Dodgers	5.00
63	Frankie Frisch	.25
63	Frankie Frisch/SP/Cards	3.00
64	Dizzy Dean	.75
65	Bob Gibson	1.00
66	Johnny Bench	1.50
67	Ty Cobb	2.00
68	Lou Gehrig	2.50
69	Jim "Catfish" Hunter	.50
70	Willie Stargell	.75
71	Reggie Jackson	1.00
71	Reggie Jackson/SP/Yankees	5.00
72	George Brett	2.50
73	Babe Ruth	3.00
73	Babe Ruth/SP/Yankees	10.00
74	Cy Young	1.00
75	Jim Palmer	.50
76	Mickey Lolich	.25
77	Stan Musial	1.50
78	Steve Carlton	.75
79	Roberto Clemente	2.50
80	John McGraw	.25
81	Paul Molitor	.75
82	Red Ruffing	.25
83	Connie Mack	.25
84	Mike Schmidt	2.00
85	Mickey Cochrane	.50
85	Mickey Cochrane/SP/Tigers	4.00
86	Brooks Robinson	1.00
87	Whitey Ford	1.00

Championship Gold

Cards 1-87:	3-6X
Production 50 Sets	

All-American Collection

NM/M

	Common Player:	8.00
OS	Ozzie Smith/100	20.00
TS	Tom Seaver/100	15.00
SM	Stan Musial/100	30.00
CR	Cal Ripken Jr./100	60.00
EM	Eddie Mathews/100	10.00
NR	Nolan Ryan	30.00
YB	Yogi Berra	15.00
EM	Eddie Murray/100	15.00
FR	Frank Robinson	8.00
DS	Duke Snider	8.00
RJ	Reggie Jackson	8.00
LA	Luis Aparicio/100	10.00
GH	Gil Hodges	8.00
AK	Al Kaline	10.00
BM	Bill Mazeroski/100	10.00
BR	Brooks Robinson/100	15.00
WB	Wade Boggs/100	12.00
AT	Alan Trammell/100	12.00

All American Collection Autograph

NM/M

	Common Autograph:	
	Varying quantities produced	
	SP version #'d to 100:	1-1.5X
	SP version #'d to 50:	1-2X
LA	Luis Aparicio/150	10.00
VB	Vida Blue/450	8.00
RB	Rick Burleson/250	8.00
SC	Steve Carlton/100	20.00
BF	Bob Feller/300	15.00
CF	Carlton Fisk/75	30.00
AL	Al Kaline/325	20.00
HK	Harmon Killebrew/150	30.00
FL	Fred Lynn/275	8.00
BM	Bill Mazeroski/75	20.00
JP	Jim Palmer/100	15.00
BR	Brooks Robinson/325	20.00
PR	Preacher Roe/450	12.00
MS	Mike Schmidt/50	60.00
BS	"Moose" Skowron/150	10.00
OS	Ozzie Smith/50	65.00
DS	Duke Snider/100	25.00
WS	Warren Spahn/75	40.00
AT	Alan Trammell/150	15.00

All American Collection Jersey Autograph

NM/M

	Production 25 Sets	
GB	George Brett	160.00
SC	Steve Carlton	50.00

Legendary Collection

NM/M

	Common Player:	
	Inserted 1:Legendary Star Pack	
EM	Eddie Mathews/SP	15.00
NR	Nolan Ryan	30.00
YB	Yogi Berra	15.00
EMY	Eddie Murray	8.00
FR	Frank Robinson	6.00
DS	Duke Snider/SP	10.00
DSy	Darryl Strawberry	5.00
RJ	Reggie Jackson	8.00
RM	Roger Maris/SP	30.00
GH	Gil Hodges/SP	10.00

Pennant Aggression

	Common Player:	3.00
	Numbered to pennant year.	
1PA	Ty Cobb/1,908	4.00
2PA	Honus Wagner/1,909	3.00
3PA	Walter Johnson/1,924	3.00
4PA	Jimmie Foxx/1,930	3.00
5PA	Frankie Frisch/1,931	3.00
6PA	Pee Wee Reese/1,947	3.00
7PA	Yogi Berra/1,951	4.00
8PA	Roy Campanella/1,953	4.00
9PA	Whitey Ford/1,961	4.00
10PA	Frank Robinson/1,966	3.00
11PA	Carl Yastrzemski/1,967	3.00
12PA	Brooks Robinson/1,970	3.00
13PA	Johnny Bench/1,972	4.00
14PA	Reggie Jackson/1,973	3.00
15PA	Jim "Catfish" Hunter/1,974	3.00
16PA	Joe Morgan/1,975	3.00
17PA	Thurman Munson/1,976	3.00
18PA	Willie Stargell/1,979	3.00
19PA	Mike Schmidt/1,980	4.00
20PA	George Brett/1,985	4.00

Pennant Aggression Game-Used

NM/M

	Common Player:	8.00
	Production 100	
	Patches:	1.5-2X
	Production 50	
YB	Yogi Berra	15.00
FB	Frank Robinson	10.00
CY	Carl Yastrzemski	20.00
BR	Brooks Robinson	15.00
JB	Johnny Bench	15.00
RJ	Reggie Jackson	12.00
CH	Jim "Catfish" Hunter	8.00
JM	Joe Morgan	8.00
TM	Thurman Munson	15.00
WS	Willie Stargell	10.00
MS	Mike Schmidt	25.00
GB	George Brett	35.00

Postseason Glory

NM/M

	Complete Set (30):	125.00
	Common Player:	2.00
	#1-15 numbered to 1,500	
	16-25 numbered to 750	
	26-30 numbered to 100	
1	Carlton Fisk, Carl Yastrzemski	2.00
2	Enos Slaughter, Stan Musial	4.00
3	Reggie Jackson, Thurman Munson	4.00
4	Eddie Plank, Christy Mathewson	3.00
5	Cy Young, Jimmy Sebring	3.00
6	Yogi Berra, Whitey Ford	4.00
7	Mickey Lolich, Alan Trammell	2.00
8	Eddie Mathews, Al Schoendienst	3.00
9	Roy Campanella, Pee Wee Reese	3.00
10	Joe Carter, Bill Mazeroski	2.00
11	Brooks Robinson, Frank Robinson	3.00
12	Tom Seaver, Gil Hodges	3.00
13	Robin Yount, Paul Molitor	2.50
14	Dave Parker, Willie Stargell	2.00
15	Cal Ripken Jr., Jim Palmer	6.00
16	Babe Ruth, Whitey Ford	8.00
18	Lou Brock, Bob Gibson	4.00
19	Mike Schmidt, Brooks Robinson	5.00
20	Johnny Bench, Thurman Munson	5.00
21	Nolan Ryan, Walter Johnson	10.00
22	Don Drysdale, Duke Snider	4.00
23	Joe Carter, Paul Molitor	2.00
24	Hughie Jennings, Ty Cobb	4.00
25	Cal Ripken Jr., Eddie Murray	10.00
26	Mike Schmidt, Steve Carlton	5.00
27	Roberto Clemente, Willie Stargell	15.00
28	Jim Palmer, Nolan Ryan	25.00
29	Joe Morgan, Johnny Bench	10.00
	Lou Gehrig, Babe Ruth	25.00

Postseason Glory Dual Game-Used

NM/M

Production 100	
Single Jerseys:	.5X
Production 150	
Carlton Fisk, Carl Yastrzemski, Reggie Jackson, Thurman Munson	25.00
Yogi Berra, Whitey Ford	30.00
Brooks Robinson, Frank Robinson	20.00
Robin Yount, Paul Molitor	25.00
Dave Parker, Willie Stargell/Single/150	8.00
Lou Brock, Bob Gibson/Single/150	10.00
Joe Carter, Paul Molitor/Single/150	8.00
Don Drysdale, Duke Snider	25.00
Cal Ripken Jr., Eddie Murray	50.00
Mike Schmidt, Steve Carlton	25.00
Jim Palmer, Nolan Ryan	40.00
Joe Morgan, Johnny Bench	25.00
Babe Ruth/Single/150, Lou Gehrig	125.00

Postseason Glory Dual Patch

NM/M

Production 50	
Single Patch:	.5-.75X
Production 75	
Carlton Fisk, Carl Yastrzemski	70.00
Robin Yount, Paul Molitor	50.00
Lou Brock, Bob Gibson	50.00
Cal Ripken Jr., Eddie Murray	120.00
Mike Schmidt, Steve Carlton	50.00
Jim Palmer, Nolan Ryan	80.00
Joe Morgan, Johnny Bench	50.00
Brooks Robinson, Frank Robinson	40.00

Series Contender

NM/M

	Common Player:	
	Inserted 1:50 Retail	
	Bat Knobs:	No Pricing
	Production 9 or 10	
SK	Al Kaline	15.00
BD	Bill Dickey	15.00
DS	Darryl Strawberry	5.00
DM	Don Mattingly	30.00
PR	Phil Rizzuto/SP	10.00
WM	Willie McCovey/SP	10.00
HK	Harmon Killebrew	25.00
CF	Carlton Fisk	6.00
JC	Jose Canseco	10.00

Yankee Penstripes

NM/M

	Production 100	
	World Series Edition:	No Pricing
	Production 26	
RJ	Reggie Jackson	40.00
BSP	Bill "Moose" Skowron	15.00
WB	Wade Boggs	50.00
DM	Don Mattingly	75.00
DW	Dave Winfield	35.00

2003 Fleer Focus Jersey Edition

NM/M

	Complete Set (180)	45.00
	Common Player:	.15
	Common Prospect (161-180):	.75
	Inserted 1:4	
	Pack (7):	1.50
	Box (24):	30.00
1	Derek Jeter	2.50
2	Preston Wilson	.15
3	Trevor Hoffman	.15
4	Moises Alou	.15
5	Roberto Alomar	.35
6	Tim Salmon	.25
7	Mike Lowell	.15
8	Barry Bonds	2.50
9	Fred McGriff	.15
10	Mo Vaughn	.15
11	Junior Spivey	.15
12	Roy Oswalt	.25
13	Ichiro Suzuki	1.50
14	Magglio Ordonez	.25
15	Adam Kennedy	.15
16	Randy Johnson	.75
17	Carlos Beltran	.15
18	John Olerud	.15
19	Joe Borchard	.15
20	Alfonso Soriano	.75
21	Curt Schilling	.50
22	Mike Sweeney	.15
23	Tino Martinez	.15
24	Barry Larkin	.15
25	Miguel Tejada	.40
26	Chipper Jones	1.00
27	Kevin Brown	.15
28	J.D. Drew	.15
29	Sean Casey	.15
30	Bernie Williams	.35
31	Troy Percival	.15
32	Jeff Bagwell	.75
33	Kenny Lofton	.15
34	Kerry Wood	.50
35	Armando Benitez	.15
36	David Eckstein	.15
37	Wade Miller	.15
38	Edgar Martinez	.15
39	Mark Prior	.75
40	Mike Piazza	1.50
41	Shea Hillenbrand	.15
42	Bartolo Colon	.15
43	Darin Erstad	.50
44	A.J. Burnett	.15
45	Jeff Kent	.15
46	Corey Patterson	.15
47	Derek Wigginton	.15
48	Troy Glaus	.75
49	Josh Beckett	.75
50	Brian Lawrence	.15
51	Frank Thomas	.75
52	Jason Giambi	.60
53	Luis Gonzalez	.25
54	Raul Ibanez	.15
55	Kazuhiro Sasaki	.15
56	Mark Buehrle	.15
57	Roger Clemens	1.25
58	Matt Williams	.15
59	Joe Randa	.15
60	Jamie Moyer	.15
61	Paul Konerko	.15
62	Mike Mussina	.50
63	Javy Lopez	.15
64	Brian Jordan	.15
65	Scott Rolen	.75
66	Aaron Boone	.15
67	Eric Chavez	.25
68	Mark Grace	.25
69	Shawn Green	.25
70	Albert Pujols	1.25
71	Sammy Sosa	1.50
72	Edgardo Alfonzo	.15
73	Garret Anderson	.15
74	Lance Berkman	.15
75	Bret Boone	.15
76	Joe Crede	.15
77	Al Leiter	.15
78	Jarrod Washburn	.15
79	Craig Biggio	.15
80	Rich Aurilia	.15
81	Adam Dunn	.60
82	Jermaine Dye	.15
83	Tom Glavine	.40
84	Eric Gagne	.15
85	Jared Sandberg	.15
86	Jim Thome	.75
87	Barry Zito	.35
88	Gary Sheffield	.25
89	Paul LoDuca	.15
90	Matt Morris	.15
91	Juan Pierre	.15
92	Randy Wolf	.15
93	Jay Gibbons	.15
94	Brad Radke	.15
95	Carlos Delgado	.35
96	Carlos Pena	.15
97	Brian Giles	.15
98	Rodrigo Lopez	.15
99	Jacque Jones	.15
100	Juan Gonzalez	.75
101	Randall Simon	.15
102	Mike Williams	.15
103	Derek Lowe	.15
104	Brad Wilkerson	.15
105	Eric Hinske	.15
106	Luis Castillo	.15
107	Phil Nevin	.15
108	Manny Ramirez	.75
109	Vladimir Guerrero	.75
110	Roy Halladay	.15
111	Ellis Burks	.15
112	Bobby Abreu	.15
113	Tony Batista	.15
114	Richie Sexson	.15
115	Rafael Palmeiro	.65
116	Todd Helton	.65
117	Pat Burrell	.60
118	John Smoltz	.15
119	Ben Sheets	.15
120	Aubrey Huff	.15
121	Andruw Jones	.75
122	Kazuhisa Ishii	.15
123	Jim Edmonds	.15
124	Austin Kearns	.60
125	Mark Mulder	.25
126	Greg Maddux	1.00
127	Jose Hernandez	.15
128	Ben Grieve	.15
129	Ken Griffey Jr.	1.50
130	Tim Hudson	.35
131	Jorge Julio	.15
132	Torii Hunter	.15
133	Ivan Rodriguez	.65
134	Jason Jennings	.15
135	Jason Kendall	.15
136	Nomar Garciaparra	1.50
137	Michael Cuddyer	.15
138	Shannon Stewart	.15
139	Larry Walker	.15
140	Aramis Ramirez	.15
141	Johnny Damon	.15
142	Orlando Cabrera	.15
143	Vernon Wells	.15
144	Bobby Higginson	.15
145	Sean Burroughs	.15
146	Pedro J. Martinez	.75
147	Jose Vidro	.15
148	Orlando Hudson	.15
149	Robert Fick	.15
150	Ryan Klesko	.15
151	Kevin Millwood	.15
152	Alex Sanchez	.15
153	Randy Winn	.15
154	Omar Vizquel	.15
155	Mike Lieberthal	.15
156	Marty Cordova	.15
157	Cristian Guzman	.15
158	Alex Rodriguez	2.00
159	C.C. Sabathia	.15
160	Jimmy Rollins	.25
161	Josh Willingham RC	2.00
162	Lance Niekro	.75
163	Nook Logan RC	.75
164	Chase Utley	.75
165	Pete LaForest RC	.75
166	Victor Martinez	.75
167	Adam LaRoche	.75
168	Ian Ferguson RC	.75
169	Mark Teixeira	.75
170	Chris Waters RC	.75
171	Hideki Matsui RC	5.00
172	Alejandro Machado RC	.75
173	Francisco Rosario RC	.75
174	Terrmel Sledge RC	1.00
175	Guillermo Quiroz RC	.75
176	Lew Ford RC	3.00
177	Hank Blalock	.75
178	Lyle Overbay	.75
179	Matt Bruback RC	.75
180	Jose Contreras RC	3.00

Century Jersey Number

Stars (1-160):	5-10X
Prospects (161-180):	2-4X
Numbered to jsy number + 100	

Franchise Focus

		NM/M
Complete Set (20):		15.00
Common Player:		.50
Inserted 1:4		
1	Troy Glaus	.75
2	Randy Johnson	1.00
3	Chipper Jones	1.50
4	Nomar Garciaparra	2.00
5	Sammy Sosa	1.50
6	Ken Griffey Jr.	1.50
7	Jeff Bagwell	.75
8	Mike Sweeney	.50
9	Shawn Green	.50
10	Torii Hunter	.50
11	Vladimir Guerrero	1.00
12	Mike Piazza	2.00
13	Jason Giambi	1.00
14	Barry Zito	.50
15	Pat Burrell	.75
16	Barry Bonds	3.00
17	Ichiro Suzuki	1.50
18	Albert Pujols	1.00
19	Alex Rodriguez	2.50
20	Carlos Delgado	.50

Home and Aways

		NM/M
Common Player:		10.00
Inserted 1:288		
	Lance Berkman	10.00
	J.D. Drew	10.00
	Nomar Garciaparra	20.00
	Derek Jeter	40.00
	Chipper Jones	20.00
	Greg Maddux	20.00
	Roy Oswalt	10.00
	Alex Rodriguez	30.00
	Alfonso Soriano	10.00

Materialistic

		NM/M
Common Player:		3.00
Inserted 1:192		
Action Home:		1.5-2.5X
Production 50 Sets		
Portrait Away:		.75-1.5X
Inserted 1:576		
Plus (Memorabilia):		1.5-2.5X
Production 250 Sets		
Portrait Home:		No Pricing
Production One Set		
1M	Greg Maddux	5.00
2M	Roger Clemens	5.00
3M	Nomar Garciaparra	6.00
4M	Derek Jeter	10.00
5M	Mike Piazza	6.00
6M	Pat Burrell	3.00
7M	Alfonso Soriano	5.00
8M	Chipper Jones	5.00
9M	Adam Dunn	3.00
10M	Alex Rodriguez	8.00
11M	Jason Giambi	4.00
12M	Sammy Sosa	5.00
13M	Albert Pujols	4.00
14M	Ken Griffey Jr.	5.00
15M	Ichiro Suzuki	5.00

Materialistic Flannels

	NM/M
Complete Set (15):	

Materialistic Oversize

		NM/M
Complete Set (16):		60.00
Common Player:		2.00
5-1/4" x 3-3/4" Box Topper		
(1)	Pat Burrell	2.00
(2)	Roger Clemens	6.00
(3)	Adam Dunn	2.00
(4)	Nomar Garciaparra	4.00
(5)	Jason Giambi	2.00
(6)	Ken Griffey Jr.	6.00
(7)	Reggie Jackson	5.00
(8)	Derek Jeter	12.50
(9)	Chipper Jones	5.00
(10)	Greg Maddux	5.00
(11)	Mike Piazza	6.00
(12)	Albert Pujols	5.00
(13)	Alex Rodriguez	10.00
(14)	Alfonso Soriano	2.00
(15)	Sammy Sosa	6.00
(16)	Ichiro Suzuki	7.50

Materialistic Oversize Autographs

		NM/M
Complete Set (3):		200.00
(1)	Reggie Jackson/360	50.00
(2)	Derek Jeter/360	100.00
(3)	Chipper Jones/80	75.00

Shirtified

		NM/M
Complete Set (15):		35.00
Common Player:		1.00
Inserted 1:24		
1	Manny Ramirez	2.00
2	Jarrod Washburn	1.00
3	Greg Maddux	4.00
4	Austin Kearns	2.00
5	Jim Thome	2.00
6	Kazuhisa Ishii	1.00
7	Mike Piazza	5.00
8	Alfonso Soriano	3.00
9	Pat Burrell	2.00
10	Derek Jeter	8.00
11	Miguel Tejada	1.50
12	Roger Clemens	4.00
13	Alex Rodriguez	6.00
14	Barry Bonds	8.00
15	Scott Rolen	2.00

Shirtified Game-Used

		NM/M
Common Player:		
Inserted 1:35		
Patches:		2-3X
Production 200		
	Manny Ramirez	8.00
	Greg Maddux	12.00
	Mike Piazza	10.00
	Alfonso Soriano	15.00
	Derek Jeter	25.00
	Miguel Tejada	6.00
	Roger Clemens	12.00
	Alex Rodriguez	12.00

Team Colors

		NM/M
Complete Set (20):		20.00
Common Player:		.50
Inserted 1:12		
1TC	Alex Rodriguez	3.50
2TC	Mark Prior	1.00
3TC	Derek Jeter	4.00
4TC	Curt Schilling	1.00
5TC	Pat Burrell	1.00
6TC	Josh Beckett	.50
7TC	Sean Burroughs	.50
8TC	Troy Glaus	1.00
9TC	Torii Hunter	.75
10TC	Jeff Bagwell	1.00
11TC	Pedro J. Martinez	1.50
12TC	Mike Piazza	3.00
13TC	Lance Berkman	.75
14TC	Nomar Garciaparra	2.50
15TC	Chipper Jones	2.00
16TC	Eric Chavez	.75
17TC	Barry Zito	.75
18TC	Barry Bonds	4.00
19TC	Adam Dunn	1.00
20TC	Randy Johnson	1.50

Team Colors Game-Used

		NM/M
Common Player:		4.00
Inserted 1:28		
Multi-Color:		1.5X
Production 250		
	Derek Jeter	25.00
	Curt Schilling	5.00
	Josh Beckett	4.00
	Troy Glaus	8.00
	Jeff Bagwell	8.00
	Pedro J. Martinez	8.00
	Lance Berkman	8.00
	Nomar Garciaparra	15.00
	Chipper Jones	10.00
	Eric Chavez	6.00
	Adam Dunn	8.00
	Randy Johnson	8.00

2003 Fleer Genuine

		NM/M
Complete Set (130):		150.00
Common Player:		.25
Common Gen. Upside		
(101-130):		3.00
Production 799		
Pack (5):		2.00
Box (24):		40.00
1	Derek Jeter	3.00
2	Mo Vaughn	.25
3	Adam Dunn	.75
4	Aubrey Huff	.25
5	Jacque Jones	.25
6	Kerry Wood	.60
7	Barry Bonds	3.00
8	Kevin Brown	.25
9	Sammy Sosa	2.00
10	Ray Durham	.25
11	Carlos Beltran	.50
12	Tony Batista	.25
13	Bobby Abreu	.25
14	Craig Biggio	.25
15	Gary Sheffield	.45
16	Jermaine Dye	.25
17	Carlos Pena	.25
18	Tim Salmon	.35
19	Mike Piazza	2.00
20	Moises Alou	.25
21	Edgardo Alfonzo	.25
22	Mike Sweeney	.25
23	Jay Gibbons	.25
24	Kevin Millwood	.25
25	A.J. Burnett	.25
26	Austin Kearns	.75
27	Rafael Palmeiro	.75
28	Vladimir Guerrero	1.00
29	Paul Konerko	.25
30	Scott Rolen	.75
31	Fred McGriff	.25
32	Frank Thomas	1.00
33	John Olerud	.25
34	Eric Gagne	.25
35	Nomar Garciaparra	2.00
36	Ryan Klesko	.25
37	Lance Berkman	.75
38	Andruw Jones	.75
39	Pat Burrell	.60
40	Juan Encarnacion	.25
41	Curt Schilling	.50
42	Jason Giambi	.65
43	Barry Larkin	.25
44	Alex Rodriguez	2.50
45	Kazuhisa Ishii	.25
46	Pedro J. Martinez	.75
47	Sean Burroughs	.25
48	Roy Oswalt	.40
49	Chipper Jones	1.50
50	Barry Zito	.40
51	Jeff Kent	.25
52	Rodrigo Lopez	.25
53	Jim Thome	.75
54	Ivan Rodriguez	.60
55	Luis Gonzalez	.40
56	Alfonso Soriano	1.00
57	Josh Beckett	.25
58	Junior Spivey	.25
59	Bernie Williams	.40
60	Omar Vizquel	.25
61	Eric Hinske	.25
62	Jose Vidro	.25
63	Bartolo Colon	.25
64	Jim Edmonds	.25
65	Ben Sheets	.25
66	Mark Prior	1.00
67	Edgar Martinez	.25
68	Raul Ibanez	.25
69	Darin Erstad	.40
70	Roger Clemens	1.75
71	C.C. Sabathia	.25
72	Carlos Delgado	.50
73	Tom Glavine	.40
74	Magglio Ordonez	.40
75	Ichiro Suzuki	1.50
76	Johnny Damon	.40
77	Brian Giles	.25
78	Jeff Bagwell	1.00
79	Greg Maddux	1.50
80	Eric Chavez	.40
81	Larry Walker	.25
82	Randy Johnson	1.00
83	Miguel Tejada	.50
84	Todd Helton	.75
85	Jarrod Washburn	.25
86	Troy Glaus	.75
87	Ken Griffey Jr.	2.00
88	Albert Pujols	2.00
89	Torii Hunter	.25
90	Joe Crede	.25
91	Matt Morris	.25
92	Shawn Green	.40
93	Manny Ramirez	1.00
94	Jason Kendall	.25
95	Preston Wilson	.25
96	Garret Anderson	.25
97	Cliff Floyd	.25
98	Sean Casey	.25
99	Juan Gonzalez	.75
100	Richie Sexson	.25
101	Joe Borchard	3.00
102	Josh Stewart RC	3.00
103	Francisco Rodriguez	4.00
104	Jeremy Bonderman	8.00
105	Walter Young	3.00
106	Brandon Webb RC	6.00
107	Lyle Overbay	3.00
108	Jose Contreras RC	6.00
109	Victor Martinez	3.00
110	Hideki Matsui RC	10.00
111	Brian Stokes RC	3.00
112	Daniel Cabrera RC	6.00
113	Josh Willingham RC	3.00
114	Mark Teixeira	4.00
115	Pete LaForest RC	3.00
116	Chris Waters RC	3.00
117	Chien-Ming Wang RC	30.00
118	Ian Ferguson RC	3.00
119	Rocco Baldelli	4.00
120	Terrmel Sledge RC	4.00
121	Hank Blalock	4.00
122	Alejandro Machado RC	3.00
123	Hee Seop Choi	3.00
124	Guillermo Quiroz RC	4.00
125	Chase Utley	4.00
126	Nook Logan RC	3.00
127	Josh Hall RC	3.00
128	Ryan Church RC	3.00
129	Lew Ford RC	6.00
130	Francisco Rosario RC	3.00

Reflection

Cards 1-100 print run	
25-50:	8-15X
Cards 101-130 p/r	
101-130:	.5-1.5X
Cards 1-100 p/r 51-80:	4-8X
Cards 1-100 p/r 81-130:	3-5X
Ascending consecutively #'d	
from 1-130.	
Descending consecutively #'d	
from 130-1.	

Article Insider

		NM/M
Common Player:		4.00
Inserted 1:24		
	Adam Dunn	5.00
	Andruw Jones	6.00
	Alex Rodriguez	10.00
	Alfonso Soriano	8.00
	Chipper Jones	8.00
	Curt Schilling	5.00
	Derek Jeter	15.00
	Don Mattingly	25.00
	Greg Maddux	10.00
	Jeff Bagwell	6.00
	Jason Giambi	10.00
	Lance Berkman	4.00
	Magglio Ordonez	4.00
	Mike Piazza	10.00
	Miguel Tejada	4.00
	Nomar Garciaparra	15.00
	Pat Burrell	4.00
	Pedro J. Martinez	8.00
	Randy Johnson	6.00
	Shawn Green	4.00
	Sammy Sosa	10.00
	Troy Glaus	5.00
	Torii Hunter	5.00
	Todd Helton	6.00
	Vladimir Guerrero	6.00

Article Insider Autograph

		NM/M
Quantity produced listed		
	Lance Berkman/165	25.00
	Lance Berkman/100	25.00
	Lance Berkman/50	40.00
	Derek Jeter/100	125.00
	Don Mattingly/170	85.00
	Don Mattingly/100	100.00

Long Ball Threats

		NM/M
Complete Set (15):		15.00
Common Card:		.50
Inserted 1:8		
1	Derek Jeter, Nomar Garciaparra	3.00
2	Jim Thome, Pat Burrell	1.00
3	Alex Rodriguez, Rafael Palmeiro	3.00
4	Alfonso Soriano, Hideki Matsui	3.00
5	Torii Hunter, Vladimir Guerrero	1.00
6	Mike Sweeney, Phil Nevin	.50
7	Mike Piazza, Sammy Sosa	2.00
8	Shawn Green, Jason Giambi	1.00
9	Magglio Ordonez, Andruw Jones	1.00
10	Eric Chavez, Carlos Delgado	.75
11	Manny Ramirez, Jeff Bagwell	1.00
12	Scott Rolen, Troy Glaus	1.00

Long Ball Threats Single Jersey

		NM/M
Common Player:		3.00
Inserted 1:13		
	Derek Jeter/Jsy	
	Nomar Garciaparra	15.00
	Derek Jeter, Nomar Garciaparra/Jsy	10.00
	Jim Thome/Jsy, Pat Burrell	6.00
	Jim Thome, Pat Burrell/Jsy	6.00
	Alfonso Soriano/Jsy, Hideki Matsui	8.00
	Torii Hunter/Jsy, Vladimir Guerrero	6.00
	Torii Hunter, Vladimir Guerrero/Jsy	6.00
	Mike Sweeney/Jsy, Phil Nevin	3.00
	Mike Sweeney, Phil Nevin/Jsy	3.00
	Mike Piazza/Jsy, Sammy Sosa	8.00
	Mike Piazza, Sammy Sosa/Jsy	10.00
	Jason Giambi	4.00
	Magglio Ordonez/Jsy, Andruw Jones	4.00
	Eric Chavez, Carlos Delgado/Jsy	5.00
	Manny Ramirez/Jsy, Jeff Bagwell	8.00
	Manny Ramirez, Jeff Bagwell/Jsy	8.00
	Scott Rolen/Jsy, Troy Glaus	6.00
	Scott Rolen, Troy Glaus/Jsy	6.00
	Barry Bonds, Miguel Tejada/Jsy	5.00
	Albert Pujols, Lance Berkman/Jsy	4.00
	Chipper Jones/Jsy, Todd Helton	8.00
	Chipper Jones, Todd Helton/Jsy	6.00

Long Ball Threats Dual Jersey

		NM/M
Common Card:		5.00
Inserted 1:72		
	Derek Jeter, Nomar Garciaparra	30.00
	Jim Thome, Pat Burrell	15.00
	Alex Rodriguez, Rafael Palmeiro	15.00
	Torii Hunter, Vladimir Guerrero	10.00
	Mike Sweeney, Phil Nevin	5.00
	Mike Piazza, Sammy Sosa	20.00
	Magglio Ordonez, Andruw Jones	10.00
	Scott Rolen, Troy Glaus	10.00
	Chipper Jones, Todd Helton	12.00

Long Ball Threats Dual Patch

		NM/M
#'d to combined 2002 HR total		
	Derek Jeter, Nomar Garciaparra/42	80.00
	Jim Thome, Pat Burrell/89	30.00
	Alex Rodriguez, Rafael Palmeiro/100	50.00
	Mike Piazza, Sammy Sosa/82	75.00
	Shawn Green, Jason Giambi/83	40.00
	Magglio Ordonez, Andruw Jones/73	40.00
	Manny Ramirez, Jeff Bagwell/64	40.00
	Scott Rolen, Troy Glaus/61	50.00

Tools of the Game

	NM/M
Complete Set (15):	20.00
Common Player:	.75
Inserted 1:20	
1 Adam Dunn	1.00
2 Chipper Jones	2.00
3 Torii Hunter	.75
4 Mike Piazza	1.50
5 Hideki Matsui	8.00
6 Nomar Garciaparra	3.00
7 Derek Jeter	4.00
8 Alex Rodriguez	3.00
9 Alfonso Soriano	2.00
10 Pat Burrell	.75
11 Barry Bonds	4.00
12 Jason Giambi	1.50
13 Sammy Sosa	2.00
14 Vladimir Guerrero	1.00
15 Ichiro Suzuki	2.00

Tools of the Game 1-Piece

	NM/M
Common Player:	
Inserted 1:42	
2-Piece:	1.5-3X
Production 250	
3-Piece:	3-6X
Production 100	
Adam Dunn	6.00
Mike Piazza	8.00
Derek Jeter	15.00
Alex Rodriguez	10.00
Alfonso Soriano	10.00
Jason Giambi	8.00
Sammy Sosa	10.00
Vladimir Guerrero	6.00

2003 Fleer Hardball

MARK GRACE

	NM/M
Complete Set (280):	85.00
Common Player:	.15
Common (241-280):	.75
Inserted 1:2 Hobby	
Pack (7):	1.75
Box (24):	30.00
1 Barry Bonds	2.00
2 Derek Jeter	2.00
3 Jason Varitek	.15
4 Magglio Ordonez	.25
5 Ryan Dempster	.15
6 Adam Everett	.15
7 Paul LoDuca	.15
8 Brad Wilkerson	.15
9 Al Leiter	.15
10 Jermaine Dye	.15
11 Robert Mackowiak	.15
12 J.T. Snow	.15
13 Juan Gonzalez	.60
14 Eric Hinske	.15
15 Greg Maddux	1.00
16 Moises Alou	.15
17 Carlos Lee	.15
18 Richard Hidalgo	.15
19 Jorge Posada	.25
20 Mike Lieberthal	.15
21 Jeff Cirillo	.15
22 Corey Patterson	.15
23 C.C. Sabathia	.15
24 Brian Giles	.15
25 Edgar Martinez	.15
26 Trot Nixon	.15
27 Kerry Wood	.50
28 Austin Kearns	.40
29 Lance Berkman	.15
30 Hideo Nomo	.50
31 Brad Radke	.15
32 John Valentin	.15
33 Tim Hudson	.35
34 Aramis Ramirez	.15
35 Kevin Mench	.15
36 Kevin Appier	.15
37 Chris Richard	.15
38 Ruben Mateo	.15
39 Juan Pierre	.15
40 Nick Neugebauer	.15
41 Mike Mussina	.50
42 Rich Aurilia	.15
43 Albert Pujols	1.00
44 Carlos Delgado	.50

45 Junior Spivey	.15
46 Marcus Giles	.15
47 Johnny Damon	.25
48 Mark Prior	.50
49 Omar Vizquel	.15
50 Craig Biggio	.15
51 Chuck Knoblauch	.15
52 Eric Milton	.15
53 Jeromy Burnitz	.15
54 Jim Thome	.15
55 Steve Finley	.15
56 Kevin Millwood	.15
57 Alex Gonzalez	.15
58 Ben Broussard	.15
59 Derrek Lee	.15
60 Joe Randa	.15
61 Doug Mientkiewicz	.15
62 Jason L. Phillips	.15
63 Brett Myers	.15
64 Josh Fogg	.15
65 Reggie Sanders	.15
66 Chipper Jones	1.00
67 Roosevelt Brown	.15
68 Matt Lawton	.15
69 Charles Johnson	.15
70 Mark Quinn	.15
71 Jacque Jones	.15
72 Armando Benitez	.15
73 Bobby Abreu	.15
74 Jason Kendall	.15
75 Jeff Kent	.15
76 Mark Teixeira	.50
77 Garret Anderson	.15
78 Jerry Hairston Jr.	.15
79 Tony Graffanino	.15
80 Josh Beckett	.15
81 Eric Gagne	.15
82 Fernando Tatis	.15
83 Brett Tomko	.15
84 Fernando Vina	.15
85 Rafael Palmeiro	.15
86 Luis Gonzalez	.35
87 Javy Lopez	.15
88 Shea Hillenbrand	.15
89 Hee Seop Choi	.15
90 Preston Wilson	.15
91 Neifi Perez	.15
92 Ray Lankford	.15
93 Tsuyoshi Shinjo	.15
94 Ben Grieve	.15
95 Jarrod Washburn	.15
96 Gary Sheffield	.35
97 Derek Lowe	.15
98 Tony Womack	.15
99 Milton Bradley	.15
100 Brad Penny	.15
101 Mike Sweeney	.15
102 A.J. Pierzynski	.15
103 Edgardo Alfonzo	.15
104 Marlon Byrd	.15
105 Sean Burroughs	.15
106 Kazuhiro Sasaki	.15
107 Damian Rolls	.15
108 Troy Glaus	.60
109 Rafael Furcal	.15
110 Nomar Garciaparra	1.25
111 Josh Bard	.15
112 Alex Gonzalez	.15
113 Cristian Guzman	.15
114 Roger Cedeno	.15
115 Freddy Garcia	.15
116 Travis Phelps	.15
117 Juan Cruz	.15
118 Frank Thomas	.60
119 Jaret Wright	.15
120 Carlos Beltran	.45
121 Ronnie Belliard	.15
122 Roger Clemens	1.00
123 Vicente Padilla	.15
124 Joel Pineiro	.15
125 Jared Sandberg	.15
126 Tom Glavine	.35
127 Matt Clement	.15
128 Aaron Rowand	.15
129 Alex Escobar	.15
130 Randy Wolf	.15
131 Ichiro Suzuki	1.00
132 Toby Hall	.15
133 Scott Spiezio	.15
134 Bobby Higginson	.15
135 A.J. Burnett	.15
136 Cesar Izturis	.15
137 Roberto Alomar	.40
138 Trevor Hoffman	.15
139 Edgar Renteria	.15
140 Rusty Greer	.15
141 David Eckstein	.15
142 Pedro J. Martinez	.75
143 Joe Crede	.15
144 Robert Fick	.15
145 Mike Lowell	.15
146 Brian Jordan	.15
147 Mark Mulder	.25
148 Scott Rolen	.60
149 Ivan Rodriguez	.60
150 Adam Kennedy	.15
151 Ken Griffey Jr.	1.25
152 Larry Walker	.15
153 Carlos Pena	.15
154 Geoff Jenkins	.15
155 Bartolo Colon	.15
156 Mariano Rivera	.25
157 Robb Nen	.15
158 Bret Boone	.15
159 Shannon Stewart	.15
160 Chris Singleton	.15
161 Todd Walker	.15
162 Jay Payton	.15

163 Zach Day	.15
164 Bernie Williams	.40
165 Bubba Trammell	.15
166 Matt Morris	.15
167 Jose Cruz Jr.	.15
168 Mark Grace	.40
169 Andruw Jones	.75
170 Cliff Floyd	.15
171 Antonio Alfonseca	.15
172 Jeff Bagwell	.75
173 Shawn Green	.40
174 Joe Mays	.15
175 Mike Piazza	1.25
176 Adam Piatt	.15
177 Pokey Reese	.15
178 Carl Everett	.15
179 Tim Salmon	.35
180 Rodrigo Lopez	.15
181 Brandon Inge	.15
182 Kazuhisa Ishii	.15
183 Jose Vidro	.15
184 Barry Zito	.40
185 Phil Nevin	.15
186 J.D. Drew	.35
187 Vernon Wells	.15
188 Darin Erstad	.50
189 Barry Larkin	.15
190 Jason Jennings	.15
191 Luis Castillo	.15
192 Adrian Beltre	.35
193 Tony Armas	.15
194 Terrence Long	.15
195 Mark Kotsay	.15
196 Tino Martinez	.15
197 Jayson Werth	.15
198 Eric Chavez	.25
199 Matt Williams	.15
200 Jon Lieber	.15
201 Eddie Taubensee	.15
202 Shane Reynolds	.15
203 Alex Sanchez	.15
204 Jason Giambi	.60
205 Jimmy Rollins	.25
206 Jamie Moyer	.15
207 Francisco Rodriguez	.15
208 Marty Cordova	.15
209 Aaron Boone	.15
210 Mike Hampton	.15
211 Mark Redman	.15
212 Richie Sexson	.15
213 Andy Pettitte	.15
214 Livan Hernandez	.15
215 Jason Isringhausen	.15
216 Curt Schilling	.40
217 Manny Ramirez	.75
218 Jose Valentin	.15
219 Brent Butler	.15
220 Billy Wagner	.15
221 Ben Sheets	.15
222 Jeff Weaver	.15
223 Brent Abernathy	.15
224 Jay Gibbons	.15
225 Sean Casey	.15
226 Greg Norton	.15
227 Andy Van Hekken	.15
228 Kevin Brown	.15
229 Orlando Cabrera	.15
230 Scott Hatteberg	.15
231 Ryan Klesko	.15
232 Roy Halladay	.15
233 Randy Johnson	.75
234 Mark Buehrle	.15
235 Todd Helton	.60
236 Jeffrey Hammonds	.15
237 Sidney Ponson	.15
238 Kip Wells	.15
239 John Olerud	.15
240 Aubrey Huff	.15
241 Derek Jeter	4.00
242 Barry Bonds	4.00
243 Ichiro Suzuki	2.00
244 Troy Glaus	1.00
245 Alex Rodriguez	3.00
246 Sammy Sosa	2.00
247 Lance Berkman	.75
248 Jason Giambi	2.00
249 Nomar Garciaparra	2.50
250 Miguel Tejada	.75
251 Albert Pujols	1.50
252 Mike Piazza	1.50
253 Vladimir Guerrero	1.50
254 Shawn Green	.75
255 Todd Helton	.75
256 Ken Griffey Jr.	2.00
257 Torii Hunter	.75
258 Chipper Jones	2.00
259 Alfonso Soriano	1.50
260 Luis Gonzalez	.75
261 Pedro J. Martinez	1.50
262 Tim Hudson	.75
263 Roger Clemens	2.00
264 Greg Maddux	1.50
265 Randy Johnson	1.50
266 Vinnie Chulk	.15
267 Jose Castillo	1.50
268 Craig Brazell RC	1.50
269 Felix Sanchez RC	.50
270 John Webb	.50
271 Josh Hall RC	.50
272 Alexis Rios	.50
273 Phil Seibel RC	.50
274 Prentice Redman RC	1.50
275 Walter Young	1.00
276 Nic Jackson	.50
277 Adam Morrissey	.50
278 Bobby Jenks	.75
279 Rodrigo Rosario	.50
280 Chin-Feng Chen	1.00

Gold

Gold (1-240):	2-3X
Gold (241-280):	1-2X
Inserted 1:4 Hobby	

Platinum

Cards (1-240):	8-15X
Cards (241-280):	3-5X
Production 50 Sets	

Discs

	NM/M
Complete Set (20):	50.00
Common Player:	1.00
Inserted 1:24	
1D Derek Jeter	8.00
2D Barry Bonds	8.00
3D Ichiro Suzuki	4.00
4D Sammy Sosa	4.00
5D Nomar Garciaparra	4.00
6D Lance Berkman	1.50
7D Jason Giambi	4.00
8D Mike Piazza	3.00
9D Shawn Green	1.50
10D Barry Zito	1.50
11D Albert Pujols	3.00
12D Alex Rodriguez	6.00
13D Tim Salmon	1.00
14D Eric Chavez	1.00
15D Ken Griffey Jr.	4.00
16D Alfonso Soriano	3.00
17D Vladimir Guerrero	2.50
18D Francisco Rodriguez	1.50
19D Miguel Tejada	1.50
20D Randy Johnson	2.50

On the Ball

	NM/M
Complete Set (15):	20.00
Common Player:	1.00
Inserted 1:12	
1 Derek Jeter	4.00
2 Barry Bonds	4.00
3 Nomar Garciaparra	2.50
4 Alfonso Soriano	1.50
5 Mike Piazza	2.50
6 Alex Rodriguez	3.00
7 Chipper Jones	2.00
8 Randy Johnson	1.50
9 Pedro J. Martinez	1.50
10 Albert Pujols	1.50
11 Vladimir Guerrero	1.50
12 Sammy Sosa	2.00
13 Ichiro Suzuki	2.00
14 Troy Glaus	1.00
15 Jason Giambi	2.00

On the Ball Memorabilia

	NM/M
Common Player:	5.00
Inserted 1:18	
Derek Jeter/Bat	15.00
Barry Bonds/Jsy	15.00
Nomar Garciaparra/ Jsy	10.00
Alfonso Soriano/Jsy	10.00
Mike Piazza/Jsy	10.00
Alex Rodriguez/Jsy	10.00
Chipper Jones/Bat	8.00
Randy Johnson/Jsy	8.00
Pedro J. Martinez/Jsy	8.00

Round Numbers

	NM/M
Complete Set (14):	50.00
Common Player:	3.00
Production 1,000 Sets	
1 Nolan Ryan	10.00
2 Al Kaline	6.00
3 Mike Schmidt	6.00
4 Yogi Berra	4.00
5 Brooks Robinson	4.00
6 Tom Seaver	4.00
7 Willie McCovey	3.00
8 Harmon Killebrew	3.00
9 Richie Ashburn	3.00
10 Lou Brock	3.00
11 Jim Palmer	4.00
12 Willie Stargell	4.00
13 Whitey Ford	4.00
14 Robin Yount	5.00

Troy Glaus/Jsy 5.00

Round Numbers Memorabilia

	NM/M
Inserted 1:288	
Al Kaline/Jsy	20.00
Mike Schmidt/Jsy	15.00
Harmon Killebrew/ Bat	
Lou Brock/Jsy	30.00

Round Trippers

	NM/M
Complete Set (20):	15.00
Common Player:	.50
Inserted 1:8	
1 Alfonso Soriano	1.50
2 Alex Rodriguez	3.00
3 Lance Berkman	.75
4 Shawn Green	.75
5 Pat Burrell	1.00
6 Andruw Jones	.75
7 Garret Anderson	.50
8 Miguel Tejada	.50
9 Mike Piazza	2.50
10 Eric Chavez	.50
11 Rafael Palmeiro	.50
12 Chipper Jones	2.00
13 Manny Ramirez	.75
14 Jeff Bagwell	1.00
15 Torii Hunter	.75
16 Nomar Garciaparra	1.50
17 Sammy Sosa	2.00
18 Vladimir Guerrero	1.50
19 Troy Glaus	.75
20 Jason Giambi	2.00

Round Trippers Rounding First

	NM/M
Common Player:	5.00
Quantity produced listed	
Rounding Second:	No Pricing
Production 10 Sets	
Rounding Third:	No Pricing
Production 3 Sets	
Alfonso Soriano/ Jsy/228	10.00
Alex Rodriguez/ Jsy/536	12.00

Lance Berkman/ Jsy/557	5.00
Shawn Green/Bat/249	5.00
Pat Burrell/Bat/502	10.00
Andruw Jones/ Jsy/569	5.00
Garret Anderson/ Bat/40	20.00
Miguel Tejada/ Jsy/524	5.00
Mike Piazza/Bat/289	12.00
Eric Chavez/Jsy/572	5.00
Rafael Palmeiro/ Jsy/515	6.00
Chipper Jones/ Jsy/570	10.00
Manny Ramirez/ Jsy/530	8.00
Jeff Bagwell/Bat/344	6.00
Nomar Garciaparra/ Bat/529	12.00

Signatures

	NM/M
Bonds 600 HR inscription: 1-1.5X	
Barry Bonds/255	200.00
Derek Jeter	110.00

2003 Fleer Hot Prospects

	NM/M
Complete Set (120):	
Common Player:	.25
Common SP (81-120):	5.00
Production 1,250 unless noted.	
Pack (5):	4.00
Box (15):	50.00
1 Derek Jeter	3.00
2 Ryan Klesko	.25
3 Troy Glaus	.75
4 Jeff Kent	.40
5 Frank Thomas	.75
6 Gary Sheffield	.50
7 Jim Edmonds	.40
8 Pat Burrell	.50
9 Jacque Jones	.25
10 Jason Jennings	.25
11 Pedro J. Martinez	1.00
12 Rafael Palmeiro	.50
13 Jason Kendall	.25
14 Tom Glavine	.40
15 Josh Beckett	.25
16 Luis Gonzalez	.40
17 Edgar Martinez	.25
18 Miguel Tejada	.50
19 Fred McGriff	.40
20 Adam Dunn	.50
21 Lance Berkman	.50
22 Magglio Ordonez	.40
23 Darin Erstad	.40
24 Rich Aurilia	.25
25 Mike Piazza	1.50
26 Shawn Green	.50
27 Larry Walker	.40
28 Manny Ramirez	.75
29 Juan Gonzalez	.75
30 Eric Chavez	.50
31 Torii Hunter	.50
32 A.J. Burnett	.25
33 Sammy Sosa	1.50
34 Eric Hinske	.25
35 Brian Giles	.25
36 Mike Sweeney	.25
37 Sean Casey	.25
38 Chipper Jones	1.50
39 Scott Rolen	.75
40 Jason Giambi	1.00
41 Mo Vaughn	.25
42 Roy Oswalt	.25
43 Paul Konerko	.25
44 Tim Salmon	.40
45 Edgardo Alfonzo	.25

46	Jermaine Dye	.25
47	Ben Sheets	.25
48	Todd Helton	.75
49	Greg Maddux	1.50
50	Albert Pujols	2.00
51	Jim Thome	.75
52	Vladimir Guerrero	.75
53	Ivan Rodriguez	.50
54	Nomar Garciaparra	2.00
55	Alex Rodriguez	2.50
56	Alfonso Soriano	1.50
57	Kazuhisa Ishii	.25
58	Austin Kearns	.50
59	Curt Schilling	.50
60	Bret Boone	.40
61	Mark Prior	1.50
62	Garret Anderson	.40
63	Barry Bonds	2.50
64	Roger Clemens	2.00
65	Jeff Bagwell	.75
66	Omar Vizquel	.40
67	Jay Gibbons	.25
68	Aubrey Huff	.25
69	Bobby Abreu	.25
70	Richie Sexson	.50
71	Bobby Higginson	.25
72	Kerry Wood	.50
73	Carlos Delgado	.50
74	Sean Burroughs	.25
75	Jose Vidro	.25
76	Ken Griffey Jr.	1.50
77	Randy Johnson	1.00
78	Ichiro Suzuki	1.50
79	Barry Zito	.50
80	Carlos Beltran	.25
81	Joe Borchard	5.00
82	Mark Teixeira	5.00
83	Brandon Webb RC	8.00
84	Shane Victorino/ Auto./400 RC	8.00
85	Hee Seop Choi	6.00
86	Hank Blalock	6.00
87	Brett Myers	6.00
88	Mike Ryan RC	5.00
89	Jesse Foppert	8.00
90	Lyle Overbay	6.00
91	Brian Stokes/ Auto./400 RC	10.00
92	Josh Hall/ Auto./400 RC	10.00
93	Chris Waters/ Auto./400 RC	10.00
94	Lew Ford/ Auto./500 RC	25.00
95	Ian Ferguson/ Auto./500 RC	8.00
96	Josh Willingham RC	5.00
97	Josh Stewart/ Auto./500 RC	8.00
98	Pete LaForest/ Auto./500 RC	8.00
99	J.Contreras/ Auto./Jsy/300 RC	40.00
100	Terrmel Sledge/ Auto./500 RC	8.00
101	Guillermo Quiroz/ Auto./500 RC	15.00
102	Alejandro Machado/ Auto./500 RC	8.00
103	Nook Logan/ Auto./Jsy/400 RC	10.00
104	Robby Hammock/ Auto./Jsy/400 RC	10.00
105	Hideki Matsui/ Base RC	15.00
106	Wilfredo Ledezma RC	5.00
107	Rocco Baldelli/Jsy	
108	Oscar Villarreal RC	5.00
109	Todd Wellemeyer/ Auto./400 RC	8.00
110	Michael Hessman/ Auto./400 RC	8.00
111	Jeremy Bonderman/ Auto./Jsy/400 RC	35.00
112	Craig Brazell/ Auto./Jsy/400 RC	10.00
113	Francisco Rosario/ Auto./Jsy/400 RC	10.00
114	Jeff Duncan/ Auto./Jsy/400 RC	10.00
115	Daniel Cabrera/ Auto./Jsy/400 RC	25.00
116	Dontrelle Willis/ Auto./Jsy/400	40.00
117	Cory Stewart/ Auto./500 RC	10.00
118	Tim Olson/ Auto./Jsy/400 RC	10.00
119	Chien-Ming Wang/ Auto./Jsy/500 RC	200.00

Class Of...

	NM/M
Common Duo:	10.00
Inserted 1:15	

	Barry Zito, Josh Beckett	10.00
	Pat Burrell, J.D. Drew	12.00
	Mark Prior, Mark Teixeira	15.00
	Austin Kearns, Sean Burroughs	10.00
	Troy Glaus, Lance Berkman	10.00
	Darin Erstad, Todd Helton	10.00

	Manny Ramirez, Shawn Green	10.00
	Matt Morris, Kerry Wood	10.00
	Nomar Garciaparra, Paul Konerko	15.00
	Alex Rodriguez, Torii Hunter	20.00

Cream of the Crop

	NM/M
Complete Set (15):	35.00
Common Player:	1.50
Inserted 1:5	
1 Barry Bonds	5.00
2 Derek Jeter	5.00
3 Ichiro Suzuki	3.00
4 Nomar Garciaparra	3.00
5 Roger Clemens	3.00
6 Alex Rodriguez	4.00
7 Greg Maddux	2.50
8 Mike Piazza	2.50
9 Sammy Sosa	2.50
10 Jason Giambi	2.00
11 Hideki Matsui	6.00
12 Albert Pujols	4.00
13 Vladimir Guerrero	1.50
14 Jim Thome	1.50
15 Pedro J. Martinez	1.50

Hot Materials

	NM/M
Common Player:	5.00
Production 499 Sets	
Red-Hots:	1-2X
Production 50	
1HM Derek Jeter	20.00
2HM Torii Hunter	8.00
3HM Mark Prior	8.00
4HM Nomar Garciaparra	15.00
5HM Sammy Sosa	15.00
6HM Rafael Palmeiro	6.00
7HM Hee Seop Choi	10.00
8HM Mark Teixeira	5.00
9HM Mike Piazza	10.00
10HM Pat Burrell	8.00
11HM Jim Thome	8.00
12HM Lance Berkman	5.00
13HM Vladimir Guerrero	8.00
14HM Troy Glaus	5.00
15HM Chipper Jones	8.00
16HM Lyle Overbay	5.00
17HM Jason Giambi	8.00
18HM Alex Rodriguez	10.00
19HM Miguel Tejada	5.00
20HM Adam Dunn	5.00
21HM Randy Johnson	8.00
22HM Josh Beckett	5.00
23HM Alfonso Soriano	10.00
24HM Greg Maddux	10.00
25HM Shawn Green	5.00
26HM Carlos Delgado	5.00
27HM Todd Helton	5.00
28HM Mike Sweeney	5.00
29HM Manny Ramirez	6.00
30HM Tom Glavine	5.00

Hot Tandems

	NM/M
Common Duo:	8.00
Production 100 Sets	
Red-Hots numbered to 10.	
Derek Jeter, Chipper Jones	25.00
Derek Jeter, Mike Piazza	25.00

	Derek Jeter, Miguel Tejada	25.00
	Torii Hunter, Lance Berkman	10.00
	Mark Prior, Sammy Sosa	25.00
	Sammy Sosa, Pat Burrell	20.00
	Rafael Palmeiro, Mark Teixeira	10.00
	Hee Seop Choi, Lyle Overbay	15.00
	Alex Rodriguez, Mark Teixeira	20.00
	Mike Piazza, Chipper Jones	15.00
	Pat Burrell, Jim Thome	10.00
	Lance Berkman, Adam Dunn	8.00
	Nomar Garciaparra, Miguel Tejada	15.00
	Randy Johnson, Greg Maddux	12.00
	Mark Prior, Josh Beckett	10.00
	Miguel Tejada, Alex Rodriguez	15.00
	Jason Giambi, Jim Thome	10.00

Hot Triple Patch

	NM/M
Production 50 Sets	
Some not priced yet.	
Derek Jeter, Nomar Garciaparra, Alex Rodriguez	125.00
Mark Prior, Josh Beckett, Greg Maddux	80.00
Mike Piazza, Pat Burrell, Jim Thome	50.00
Lance Berkman, Troy Glaus, Chipper Jones	50.00
Randy Johnson, Alfonso Soriano, Shawn Green	50.00
Derek Jeter, Torii Hunter, Mark Prior	75.00
Nomar Garciaparra, Sammy Sosa, Mike Piazza	90.00
Pat Burrell, Jim Thome, Lance Berkman	40.00
Vladimir Guerrero, Troy Glaus, Chipper Jones	60.00
Alfonso Soriano, Greg Maddux, Shawn Green	60.00

Playergraphs

	NM/M
Common Player:	10.00
Production 400 Sets	
Red-Hots:	1-1.5X
Production 100	
Hank Blalock	20.00
Brett Myers	10.00
Mark Prior	35.00
Carlos Zambrano	20.00
Mark Teixeira	20.00
Francisco Rodriguez	10.00
Roy Oswalt	15.00
Xavier Nady	10.00
Jose Reyes	25.00
Aubrey Huff	10.00

MLB 3-D Stars

Eighteen players are included in this novelty card issue from Fleer Entertainment division. Each player is printed on a 2-1/4" x 3-1/2" card that is die-cut to allow the pieces to be punched out and assembled in a variety of action poses. Each 5-5/8" x 7-3/8" blister pack contains five 3-D cards, one assembled and four unassembled. Values shown are for unpunched cards.

	NM/M
Complete Set (18):	7.50

Common Player:		.25
1	Derek Jeter	1.00
2	Barry Bonds	1.00
3	Greg Maddux	.40
4	Nomar Garciaparra	.65
5	Curt Schilling	.25
6	Jason Giambi	.25
7	Pedro Martinez	.25
8	Alfonso Soriano	.25
9	Alex Rodriguez	.75
10	Ken Griffey Jr.	.60
11	Sammy Sosa	.60
12	Albert Pujols	.50
13	Roger Clemens	.50
14	Chipper Jones	.40
15	Ichiro	.50
16	Miguel Tejada	.25
17	Mark Prior	.50
18	Mariano Rivera	.25

2003 Fleer Mystique

	NM/M
Complete Set (130):	
Common Player:	.25
Common SP (81-130):	3.00
Production 699	
Pack (4):	3.00
Box (20):	40.00
1 Alex Rodriguez	2.50
2 Derek Jeter	3.00
3 Jose Vidro	.25
4 Miguel Tejada	.40
5 Albert Pujols	2.50
6 Rocco Baldelli	.25
7 Jose Reyes	.50
8 Hideo Nomo	.75
9 Hank Blalock	.75
10 Chipper Jones	1.50
11 Barry Larkin	.25
12 Alfonso Soriano	1.00
13 Aramis Ramirez	.25
14 Darin Erstad	.65
15 Jim Edmonds	.25
16 Garret Anderson	.25
17 Todd Helton	1.00
18 Jason Kendall	.25
19 Aubrey Huff	.25
20 Troy Glaus	.75
21 Sammy Sosa	2.00
22 Roger Clemens	1.75
23 Mark Teixeira	.50
24 Barry Bonds	3.00
25 Jim Thome	.25
26 Carlos Delgado	.50
27 Vladimir Guerrero	.75
28 Austin Kearns	.50
29 Pat Burrell	.75
30 Ken Griffey Jr.	2.00
31 Greg Maddux	1.50
32 Corey Patterson	.25
33 Larry Walker	.25
34 Kerry Wood	.65
35 Frank Thomas	1.00
36 Dontrelle Willis	.25
37 Randy Johnson	1.00
38 Curt Schilling	.25
39 Jay Gibbons	.25
40 Dmitri Young	.25
41 Edgar Martinez	.25
42 Kevin Brown	.25
43 Scott Rolen	.25
44 Adam Dunn	.75
45 Pedro J. Martinez	1.00
46 Corey Koskie	.25
47 Tom Glavine	.40
48 Torii Hunter	.40
49 Shawn Green	.40
50 Nomar Garciaparra	.40
51 Bernie Williams	.40
52 Milton Bradley	.25
53 Jason Giambi	.75
54 Mike Lieberthal	.25
55 Jeff Bagwell	.50
56 Carlos Pena	.25
57 Lance Berkman	.25
58 Jose Cruz Jr.	.25
59 Josh Beckett	.25
60 Mark Mulder	.40
61 Mike Piazza	2.00
62 Mark Prior	.75
63 Sean Burroughs	.25
64 Angel Berroa	.25
65 Geoff Jenkins	.25
66 Magglio Ordonez	.25
67 Craig Biggio	.25
68 Roberto Alomar	.40
69 Hee Seop Choi	.25
70 J.D. Drew	.25
71 Richie Sexson	.25
72 Brian Giles	.25
73 Gary Sheffield	.50
74 Manny Ramirez	1.00
75 Barry Zito	.45
76 Andruw Jones	1.00
77 Ivan Rodriguez	.65
78 Ichiro Suzuki	.75
79 Mike Sweeney	.25
80 Vernon Wells	.25
81 Craig Brazell RC	5.00
82 Wilfredo Ledezma RC	3.00
83 Josh Willingham RC	3.00
84 Chien-Ming Wang RC	35.00
85 Mike Ryan RC	3.00
86 Mike Gallo RC	3.00
87 Rickie Weeks RC	15.00
88 Brian Stokes RC	3.00
89 Humberto Quintero RC	3.00
90 Ramon Nivar RC	3.00
91 Jeremy Griffiths	3.00
92 Terrmel Sledge RC	4.00
93 Brandon Webb RC	5.00
94 David DeJesus RC	5.00
95 Doug Waechter RC	3.00
96 Jeremy Bonderman	10.00
97 Felix Sanchez RC	3.00
98 Colin Porter RC	3.00
99 Francisco Cruceta RC	3.00
100 Hideki Matsui RC	15.00
101 Chris Waters RC	6.00
102 Dan Haren RC	6.00
103 Lew Ford RC	6.00
104 Oscar Villarreal RC	3.00
105 Ryan Wagner RC	3.00
106 Prentice Redman RC	3.00
107 Josh Stewart RC	3.00
108 Carlos Mendez RC	3.00
109 Michael Hessman RC	6.00
110 Josh Hall RC	6.00
111 Daniel Garcia RC	6.00
112 Matt Kata RC	6.00
113 Michel Hernandez RC	3.00
114 Sergio Mitre RC	6.00
115 Pete LaForest RC	6.00
116 Edwin Jackson RC	10.00
117 Matt Diaz RC	6.00
118 Greg Aquino RC	3.00
119 Jose Contreras RC	8.00
120 Jeff Duncan RC	6.00
121 Richard Fischer RC	6.00
122 Todd Wellemeyer RC	6.00
123 Robby Hammock RC	6.00
124 Delmon Young RC	15.00
125 Clint Barmes RC	8.00
126 Phil Seibel RC	3.00
127 Bo Hart RC	6.00
128 Jon Leicester RC	6.00
129 Chad Gaudin RC	6.00
130 Guillermo Quiroz RC	6.00

Gold

Stars (1-80):	4-8X
Production 150	
SP's (81-130):	1-2X
Production 50	

Awe Pairs

	NM/M
Complete Set (20):	60.00
Common Duo:	2.00
Production 250 Sets	
Golds:	1.5X
#'d to team win total for 2003	
1 Nomar Garciaparra, Pedro J. Martinez	8.00
2 Derek Jeter, Alfonso Soriano	8.00
3 Rocco Baldelli, Aubrey Huff	2.00
4 Carlos Delgado, Vernon Wells	2.00

5	Troy Glaus, Garret Anderson	2.00
6	Ichiro Suzuki, Bret Boone	5.00
7	Alex Rodriguez, Hank Blalock	8.00
8	Chipper Jones, Andruw Jones	5.00
9	Dontrelle Willis, Mike Lowell	3.00
10	Vladimir Guerrero, Orlando Cabrera	4.00
11	Tom Glavine, Mike Piazza	5.00
12	Jim Thome, Mike Lieberthal	3.00
13	Sammy Sosa, Corey Patterson	6.00
14	Jeff Bagwell, Lance Berkman	3.00
15	Geoff Jenkins, Richie Sexson	2.00
16	Albert Pujols, Jim Edmonds	6.00
17	Todd Helton, Larry Walker	3.00
18	Paul LoDuca, Shawn Green	2.00
19	Ryan Klesko, Sean Burroughs	2.00
20	Barry Bonds, Rich Aurilia	8.00

Awe Pairs Game-Used

	NM/M
Common Duo:	10.00
Production 100 Sets	
Golds:	No Pricing
Production 10 Sets	
Nomar Garciaparra, Pedro J. Martinez	25.00
Derek Jeter, Alfonso Soriano	30.00
Rocco Baldelli, Aubrey Huff	15.00
Carlos Delgado, Vernon Wells	10.00
Troy Glaus, Garret Anderson	10.00
Chipper Jones, Andruw Jones	15.00
Dontrelle Willis, Mike Lowell	25.00
Vladimir Guerrero, Orlando Cabrera	10.00
Tom Glavine, Mike Piazza	20.00
Jim Thome, Mike Lieberthal	15.00
Sammy Sosa, Corey Patterson	10.00
Jeff Bagwell, Lance Berkman	15.00
Geoff Jenkins, Richie Sexson	10.00
Albert Pujols, Jim Edmonds	20.00
Todd Helton, Larry Walker	10.00
Paul LoDuca, Shawn Green	10.00
Ryan Klesko, Sean Burroughs	10.00

Diamond Dominators

	NM/M
Complete Set (10):	50.00
Common Player:	3.00
Production 100 Sets	
1 Mike Piazza	8.00
2 Greg Maddux	8.00
3 Alfonso Soriano	5.00
4 Barry Zito	5.00
5 Alex Rodriguez	10.00
6 Roger Clemens	10.00
7 Sammy Sosa	10.00
8 Adam Dunn	3.00
9 Randy Johnson	5.00
10 Pedro J. Martinez	5.00

Diamond Dominators Gold

	NM/M
Some not priced due to scarcity. Numbered to jersey number.	
1DD Mike Piazza/31	25.00
2DD Greg Maddux/31	25.00
4DD Barry Zito/75	5.00
8DD Adam Dunn/44	8.00
9DD Randy Johnson/51	8.00
10DD Pedro Martinez/45	10.00

Diamond Dominators Game-Used

		NM/M
Common Player:		6.00
Production 75 Sets		
Golds:		No Pricing
Production 10 Sets		
RC	Roger Clemens	20.00
AD	Adam Dunn	6.00
RJ	Randy Johnson	10.00
GM	Greg Maddux	25.00
PM	Pedro Martinez	12.00
MP	Mike Piazza	15.00
AR	Alex Rodriguez	15.00
AS	Alfonso Soriano	12.00
SS	Sammy Sosa	20.00
BZ	Barry Zito	8.00

Ink Appeal Autographs

Common Player:		15.00
Production 50 Sets		
RB	Rocco Baldelli	40.00
HB	Hank Blalock	35.00
BH	Bo Hart	25.00
AH	Aubrey Huff	15.00
TH	Torii Hunter	20.00
CP	Corey Patterson	15.00
JR	Jose Reyes	30.00
MR	Mike Ryan	15.00
JW	Josh Willingham	15.00

Ink Appeal Gold Autographs

NM/M
Numbered to jersey number.
Some not priced due to scarcity.

BH	Bo Hart/31	50.00
TH	Torii Hunter/48	20.00
MR	Mike Ryan/54	15.00
JW	Josh Willingham/70	12.00

Ink Appeal Dual Autographs

No pricing due to scarcity.
Production 20 Sets
Golds: No Pricing
Production 5 Sets

Rare Finds

	NM/M
Complete Set (10):	40.00
Common Trio:	3.00
Production 250 Sets	
1 Jason Giambi, Roger Clemens, Derek Jeter	8.00
2 Randy Johnson, Curt Schilling, Brandon Webb	4.00
3 Nomar Garciaparra, Pedro J. Martinez, Manny Ramirez	8.00
4 Mark Prior, Kerry Wood, Sammy Sosa	5.00
5 Jeff Bagwell, Craig Biggio, Lance Berkman	3.00
6 Austin Kearns, Adam Dunn, Barry Larkin	3.00
7 Jim Edmonds, Scott Rolen, J.D. Drew	3.00
8 Chipper Jones, Andruw Jones, Greg Maddux	5.00
9 Barry Zito, Miguel Tejada, Mark Mulder	3.00
10 Alex Rodriguez, Mark Teixeira, Rafael Palmeiro	8.00

Rare Finds Autographs

No Pricing:
Production 15 Sets
Auto/Game-Used: No Pricing
Production 5 Sets

Rare Finds Single Swatch

	NM/M
Common Player:	6.00
Production 150 Sets	
Golds:	No Pricing
Production 15 Sets	
JG Jason Giambi, Roger Clemens, Derek Jeter	10.00

RC	Jason Giambi, Roger Clemens, Derek Jeter	15.00
DJ	Jason Giambi, Roger Clemens, Derek Jeter	20.00
RJ	Randy Johnson, Curt Schilling, Brandon Webb	8.00
BW	Randy Johnson, Curt Schilling, Brandon Webb	10.00
NG	Nomar Garciaparra, Pedro J. Martinez, Manny Ramirez	15.00
PM	Nomar Garciaparra, Pedro J. Martinez, Manny Ramirez	8.00
MP	Mark Prior, Kerry Wood, Sammy Sosa	10.00
SS	Mark Prior, Kerry Wood, Sammy Sosa	8.00
JB	Jeff Bagwell, Craig Biggio, Lance Berkman	6.00
AK	Austin Kearns, Adam Dunn, Barry Larkin	6.00
BL	Austin Kearns, Adam Dunn, Barry Larkin	6.00
SR	Jim Edmonds, Scott Rolen, J.D. Drew	10.00
JD	Jim Edmonds, Scott Rolen, J.D. Drew	6.00
CJ	Chipper Jones, Andruw Jones, Greg Maddux	10.00
GM	Chipper Jones, Andruw Jones, Greg Maddux	15.00
MT	Barry Zito, Miguel Tejada, Mark Mulder	6.00
MM	Barry Zito, Miguel Tejada, Mark Mulder	6.00
AR	Alex Rodriguez, Mark Teixeira, Rafael Palmeiro	15.00
MT	Alex Rodriguez, Mark Teixeira, Rafael Palmeiro	8.00

Finds Dual Swatch

	NM/M
Common Dual:	10.00
Production 75 Sets	
Golds:	No Pricing
Production 10 Sets	
Jason Giambi, Roger Clemens, Derek Jeter	35.00
Jason Giambi, Roger Clemens, Derek Jeter	40.00
Randy Johnson, Curt Schilling, Brandon Webb	15.00
Randy Johnson, Curt Schilling, Brandon Webb	10.00
Nomar Garciaparra, Pedro J. Martinez, Manny Ramirez	20.00
Nomar Garciaparra, Pedro J. Martinez, Manny Ramirez	15.00
Mark Prior, Kerry Wood, Sammy Sosa	15.00
Mark Prior, Kerry Wood, Sammy Sosa	20.00
Jeff Bagwell, Craig Biggio, Lance Berkman	20.00
Austin Kearns, Adam Dunn, Barry Larkin	20.00
Jim Edmonds, Scott Rolen, J.D. Drew	15.00
Chipper Jones, Andruw Jones, Greg Maddux	20.00
Chipper Jones, Andruw Jones, Greg Maddux	20.00
Barry Zito, Miguel Tejada, Mark Mulder	10.00
Alex Rodriguez, Mark Teixeira, Rafael Palmeiro	20.00

Rare Finds Triple Swatch

	NM/M
Production 50 Sets	
Golds:	No Pricing
Production 5 Sets	
Jason Giambi, Roger Clemens, Derek Jeter	50.00
Randy Johnson, Curt Schilling, Brandon Webb	25.00
Nomar Garciaparra, Pedro J. Martinez, Manny Ramirez	60.00
Mark Prior, Kerry Wood, Sammy Sosa	40.00
Jeff Bagwell, Craig Biggio, Lance Berkman	20.00
Austin Kearns, Adam Dunn, Barry Larkin	20.00
Jim Edmonds, Scott Rolen, J.D. Drew	25.00
Chipper Jones, Andruw Jones, Greg Maddux	40.00
Barry Zito, Miguel Tejada, Mark Mulder	15.00
Alex Rodriguez, Mark Teixeira, Rafael Palmeiro	40.00

Secret Weapons

NM/M
Complete Set (10): 25.00
Common Player: 2.00
Production 250 Sets
Golds: 1X
#'d to career batting average

1	Hank Blalock	3.00
2	Dontrelle Willis	3.00
3	Jose Reyes	3.00
4	Bo Hart	4.00
5	Corey Patterson	2.00
6	Hideki Matsui	8.00
7	Mark Teixeira	3.00
8	Brandon Webb	3.00
9	Rocco Baldelli	3.00
10	Mark Prior	5.00

Shining Stars

		NM/M
Complete Set (15):		50.00
Common Player:		2.00
Production 300 Sets		
1SS	Derek Jeter	8.00
2SS	Barry Bonds	8.00
3SS	Nomar Garciaparra	6.00
4SS	Austin Kearns	2.00
5SS	Vladimir Guerrero	3.00
6SS	Jim Thome	3.00
7SS	Ichiro Suzuki	5.00
8SS	Jason Giambi	3.00
9SS	Albert Pujols	5.00
10SS	Ken Griffey Jr.	5.00
11SS	Chipper Jones	5.00
12SS	Scott Rolen	3.00
13SS	Manny Ramirez	3.00
14SS	Jeff Bagwell	3.00
15SS	Torii Hunter	2.00

Shining Stars Gold

NM/M
Numbered to career HR total

1SS	Derek Jeter/127	10.00
2SS	Barry Bonds/658	5.00
3SS	Nomar Garciaparra/173	10.00
4SS	Austin Kearns/28	10.00
5SS	Vladimir Guerrero/234	4.00
6SS	Jim Thome/381	3.00
7SS	Ichiro Suzuki/29	30.00
8SS	Jason Giambi/269	3.00
9SS	Albert Pujols/114	8.00
10SS	Ken Griffey Jr./481	4.00
11SS	Chipper Jones/280	5.00
12SS	Scott Rolen/192	4.00
13SS	Manny Ramirez/347	3.00
14SS	Jeff Bagwell/419	3.00
15SS	Torii Hunter/96	4.00

Shining Stars Game-Used

NM/M
Common Player: 6.00
Production 100 Sets
Patch: 1.5X
Production 50 Sets

JB	Jeff Bagwell	8.00
CD	Carlos Delgado	6.00
NG	Nomar Garciaparra	15.00
JG	Jason Giambi	8.00
TH	Todd Helton	8.00
TH	Torii Hunter	8.00
DJ	Derek Jeter	20.00
AJ	Andruw Jones	6.00
CJ	Chipper Jones	10.00
AK	Austin Kearns	6.00
AP	Albert Pujols	15.00
MR	Manny Ramirez	8.00
SR	Scott Rolen	10.00
JT	Jim Thome	8.00

N.Y. Mets

While the basic format of Fleer Tradition was preserved in this stadium give-away set, different photos were used than those found in regular-issue packs. Persons attending a special Baseball Card Pack promotional game received a cello-wrapped set of seven player cards and a header card.

		NM/M
Complete Set (8):		4.00
Common Player:		.25
1	Mike Piazza	3.00
2	Tom Glavine	.50
3	Cliff Floyd	.25
4	Al Leiter	.25
5	Jae Seo	.25
6	John Franco	.25
7	Ty Wigginton	.25
---	Header Card	.10

2003 Fleer Patchworks

		NM/M
Complete Set (115):		
Common Player:		.15
Common Prospect (91-115):		3.00
Production 1,500		
Pack (5):		3.00
Box (24):		60.00
1	Luis Castillo	.15
2	Derek Jeter	2.00
3	Vladimir Guerrero	.75
4	Bobby Higginson	.15
5	Pat Burrell	.40
6	Ivan Rodriguez	.60
7	Craig Biggio	.15
8	Troy Glaus	.60
9	Barry Bonds	2.00
10	Hideo Nomo	.60
11	Barry Larkin	.15
12	Roberto Alomar	.35
13	Rodrigo Lopez	.15
14	Eric Chavez	.25
15	Shawn Green	.25
16	Joe Randa	.15
17	Mark Grace	.25
18	Jason Kendall	.15
19	Hee Seop Choi	.15
20	Luis Gonzalez	.15
21	Sammy Sosa	1.25
22	Larry Walker	.15
23	Phil Nevin	.15
24	Manny Ramirez	.75
25	Jim Thome	.15
26	Randy Johnson	.75
27	Jose Vidro	.15
28	Austin Kearns	.35
29	Mike Sweeney	.15
30	Magglio Ordonez	.15
31	Mike Piazza	1.25
32	Eric Hinske	.15
33	Alex Rodriguez	1.50
34	Kerry Wood	.60
35	Matt Morris	.15
36	Lance Berkman	.15
37	Michael Cuddyer	.15
38	Curt Schilling	.40
39	Sean Burroughs	.15
40	Ken Griffey Jr.	1.25
41	Edgardo Alfonzo	.15
42	Carlos Pena	.15
43	Adam Dunn	.50
44	Pedro J. Martinez	.75
45	Miguel Tejada	.35
46	Tom Glavine	.35
47	Torii Hunter	.15
48	Jason Giambi	.50
49	Tony Batista	.15
50	Ben Grieve	.15
51	Ichiro Suzuki	1.25
52	Bobby Abreu	.15
53	Todd Helton	.75
54	Kazuhiro Sasaki	.15
55	Nomar Garciaparra	1.25
56	Francisco Rodriguez	.15
57	Ellis Burks	.15
58	Frank Thomas	.75
59	Greg Maddux	1.00
60	Josh Beckett	.25
61	Brad Wilkerson	.15
62	Joe Borchard	.15
63	Carlos Delgado	.40
64	Alfonso Soriano	.75
65	Chipper Jones	1.00
66	J.D. Drew	.15
67	Mark Prior	.75
68	Rafael Palmeiro	.60
69	Jeff Kent	.15
70	Adrian Beltre	.25
71	Marlon Byrd	.15
72	Orlando Hudson	.15
73	Junior Spivey	.15
74	Jeff Bagwell	.75
75	Barry Zito	.35
76	Roger Clemens	1.00
77	Aubrey Huff	.15
78	Geoff Jenkins	.15
79	Andruw Jones	.75
80	Scott Rolen	.75
81	Omar Vizquel	.15
82	Darin Erstad	.50
83	Bernie Williams	.35
84	Freddy Garcia	.15
85	Richie Sexson	.15
86	Josh Phelps	.15
87	Albert Pujols	1.50
88	Aramis Ramirez	.15
89	Shea Hillenbrand	.15
90	Cristian Guzman	.15
91	Adam LaRoche	3.00
92	David Pember RC	3.00
93	Terrmel Sledge RC	3.00
94	Hideki Matsui	10.00
95	Nook Logan RC	3.00
96	Jose Contreras RC	4.00
97	Pete LaForest RC	3.00
98	Richard Fischer RC	3.00
99	Francisco Rosario RC	3.00
100	Josh Willingham RC	3.00
101	Alejandro Machado RC	3.00
102	Lew Ford RC	4.00
103	Joe Valentine RC	3.00
104	Guillermo Quiroz RC	4.00
105	Chien-Ming Wang RC	20.00
106	Jhonny Peralta RC	3.00
107	Shane Victorino RC	3.00
108	Prentice Redman RC	3.00
109	Matt Bruback RC	3.00
110	Lance Niekro	3.00
111	Travis Hughes	3.00
112	Nic Jackson	3.00
113	Hector Luna RC	4.00
114	Cliff Lee	3.00
115	Tim Olson RC	3.00

Star Ruby

Stars (1-90):	4-8X
Prospects (91-115):	1-3X
Production 100 Sets	

Diamond Ink

NM/M
Quantity signed listed

Derek Jeter/210	90.00
Derek Jeter/101	125.00
Derek Jeter/50	175.00
Mark Prior/88	40.00
Troy Glaus/351	25.00
Mike Schmidt/194	75.00

Licensed Apparel - Jersey

NM/M
Common Player: 4.00
Production 500 Sets

J.D. Drew	8.00
Magglio Ordonez	6.00
Todd Helton	8.00
Paul Konerko	4.00
Shawn Green	4.00
Carlos Beltran	4.00
Kevin Brown	4.00
Shannon Stewart	4.00
Mike Mussina	8.00
Adam Dunn	10.00
Jimmy Rollins	6.00
Darin Erstad	6.00
Chipper Jones	10.00
Mike Piazza	10.00
Derek Jeter	20.00

Licensed Apparel - Patch

NM/M
Common Player: 10.00
Production 300 Sets

J.D. Drew	12.00
Magglio Ordonez	15.00
Todd Helton	10.00
Paul Konerko	10.00
Shawn Green	15.00
Carlos Beltran	10.00
Kevin Brown	10.00
Shannon Stewart	10.00
Mike Mussina	15.00
Adam Dunn	20.00
Jimmy Rollins	15.00
Darin Erstad	25.00
Chipper Jones	20.00
Mike Piazza	25.00
Derek Jeter	40.00

National Pastime

		NM/M
Complete Set (25):		40.00
Common Player:		1.00
Inserted 1:12		
1NP	Barry Bonds	6.00
2NP	Kazuhiro Sasaki	1.00
3NP	Mike Piazza	4.00
4NP	Barry Zito	1.50
5NP	Sammy Sosa	3.00
6NP	Pedro J. Martinez	2.00
7NP	Craig Biggio	1.00
8NP	Rafael Palmeiro	1.50
9NP	Greg Maddux	3.00
10NP	Manny Ramirez	2.00
11NP	Adam Dunn	1.50
12NP	Omar Vizquel	1.00
13NP	Hideo Nomo	1.00
14NP	Alex Rodriguez	5.00
15NP	Pat Burrell	1.00
16NP	Nomar Garciaparra	4.00
17NP	Randy Johnson	2.00
18NP	Juan Gonzalez	1.50
19NP	Chipper Jones	3.00
20NP	Frank Thomas	1.50
21NP	Vladimir Guerrero	3.00
22NP	Troy Glaus	2.00
23NP	Albert Pujols	3.00
24NP	Ichiro Suzuki	3.00
25NP	Ken Griffey Jr.	3.00

National Pastime - MLB Logo

Production One Set:

National Patchtime- Commemorative

Production 25 Sets: No Pricing

National Patchtime - Nameplate

NM/M
Production 50 Sets

Vladimir Guerrero	40.00
Rafael Palmeiro	40.00
Nomar Garciaparra	40.00
Greg Maddux	30.00
Sammy Sosa	60.00
Mike Piazza	35.00
Barry Zito	50.00
Hideo Nomo	50.00
Alex Rodriguez	50.00
Pat Burrell	25.00
Randy Johnson	50.00
Chipper Jones	35.00
Frank Thomas	40.00
Troy Glaus	30.00

National Patchtime - Number

NM/M
Common Player: 15.00
Production 75 Sets

Vladimir Guerrero	20.00
Manny Ramirez	25.00
Craig Biggio	15.00
Rafael Palmeiro	20.00
Nomar Garciaparra	40.00
Greg Maddux	25.00
Sammy Sosa	25.00
Mike Piazza	30.00
Pedro J. Martinez	25.00
Hideo Nomo	25.00
Alex Rodriguez	30.00
Pat Burrell	25.00
Randy Johnson	45.00
Chipper Jones	35.00
Frank Thomas	30.00

National Patchtime - Team Name

NM/M
Common Player: 15.00
Production 100 Sets

Vladimir Guerrero	15.00

Rafael Palmeiro	20.00
Nomar Garciaparra	35.00
Sammy Sosa	40.00
Mike Piazza	30.00
Barry Zito	20.00
Hideo Nomo	30.00
Alex Rodriguez	30.00
Pat Burrell	20.00
Randy Johnson	45.00
Chipper Jones	35.00
Troy Glaus	30.00
Omar Vizquel	20.00

National Patchtime - Trim

	NM/M
Common Player:	12.00
Production 200 Sets	
Vladimir Guerrero	12.00
Manny Ramirez	15.00
Rafael Palmeiro	12.00
Nomar Garciaparra	25.00
Greg Maddux	20.00
Mike Piazza	20.00
Pedro J. Martinez	20.00
Hideo Nomo	20.00
Alex Rodriguez	25.00
Chipper Jones	20.00
Frank Thomas	20.00

Numbers Game

	NM/M
Complete Set (15):	30.00
Common Player:	1.00
Inserted 1:24	
1 Ichiro Suzuki	3.00
2 Derek Jeter	6.00
3 Alex Rodriguez	5.00
4 Miguel Tejada	1.00
5 Nomar Garciaparra	4.00
6 Jason Giambi	3.00
7 J.D. Drew	1.00
8 Barry Bonds	6.00
9 Alfonso Soriano	2.00
10 Jeff Bagwell	1.50
11 Barry Larkin	1.00
12 Roberto Alomar	1.00
13 Larry Walker	1.00
14 Roger Clemens	3.00
15 Ken Griffey Jr.	3.00

Numbers Game - Jersey

	NM/M
Common Player:	4.00
Inserted 1:25	
Barry Larkin	6.00
Roberto Alomar	4.00
Jeff Bagwell	8.00
Jason Giambi	8.00
Larry Walker	4.00
Derek Jeter	15.00
Alex Rodriguez	10.00
Alfonso Soriano	10.00
Roger Clemens	12.00
Miguel Tejada	4.00

Numbers Game - Patch

	NM/M
Common Player:	10.00
Production 300 Sets	
Barry Larkin	15.00
Roberto Alomar	15.00
Jeff Bagwell	25.00
Jason Giambi	15.00
Larry Walker	10.00
Derek Jeter	40.00
Alex Rodriguez	25.00
Alfonso Soriano	25.00
Roger Clemens	30.00
Miguel Tejada	10.00

Past, Present, Future

	NM/M
Complete Set (10):	40.00
Common Card:	4.00
Inserted 1:72	
1 Eddie Mathews, Rafael Palmeiro, Alex Rodriguez	5.00

2 Phil Rizzuto, Derek Jeter, Alfonso Soriano	5.00
3 Reggie Jackson, Barry Bonds, Sammy Sosa	6.00
4 Billy Williams, Sammy Sosa, Hee Seop Choi	4.00
5 Joe Morgan, Roberto Alomar, Alfonso Soriano	3.00
6 Yogi Berra, Mike Piazza, Josh Phelps	4.00
7 Nolan Ryan, Roger Clemens, Kerry Wood	6.00
8 Mike Schmidt, Scott Rolen, Eric Hinske	4.00
9 Barry Bonds, Alex Rodriguez, Alfonso Soriano	5.00
10 Yogi Berra, Derek Jeter, Hideki Matsui	6.00

Patch, Present, Future Dual

Production 100 Sets

Patch, Present, Future Single

	NM/M
Common Player:	10.00
Production 200 Sets	
Rafael Palmeiro	15.00
Alex Rodriguez	20.00
Derek Jeter	50.00
Alfonso Soriano	50.00
Barry Bonds	50.00
Sammy Sosa	25.00
Sammy Sosa	25.00
Roberto Alomar	25.00
Alfonso Soriano	25.00
Mike Piazza	25.00
Roger Clemens	40.00
Kerry Wood	40.00
Eric Hinske	10.00
Alex Rodriguez	20.00
Alfonso Soriano	50.00
Derek Jeter	50.00

Patchworks

	NM/M
Common Player:	8.00
Production 250 Sets	
2 Frank Thomas	12.00
8 Lance Berkman	15.00
9 Kazuhiro Sasaki	15.00
10 Roy Oswalt	15.00
11 Bernie Williams	15.00
12PW Bob Abreu	15.00
14PW Greg Maddux	20.00
15PW Josh Beckett	8.00
16PW Mark Grace	20.00
17PW Eric Chavez	10.00
18PW Andruw Jones	15.00
19PW Adrian Beltre	8.00

Patchworks - Dual Color

	NM/M
Common Player:	10.00
Production 100 Sets	
Alex Rodriguez	35.00
Frank Thomas	20.00
Vladimir Guerrero	20.00
Roberto Alomar	20.00
Kerry Wood	35.00
Curt Schilling	15.00
Lance Berkman	20.00
Kazuhiro Sasaki	35.00
Roy Oswalt	20.00
Bernie Williams	25.00
Bob Abreu	10.00
Carlos Delgado	12.00
Greg Maddux	25.00
Josh Beckett	10.00
Mark Grace	15.00
Eric Chavez	15.00
Andruw Jones	15.00
Adrian Beltre	10.00

Patchworks - Multi-Color

	NM/M
Common Player:	20.00
Production 50 Sets	
Alex Rodriguez	60.00
Frank Thomas	30.00
Vladimir Guerrero	35.00
Roberto Alomar	35.00
Kerry Wood	40.00
Curt Schilling	20.00
Lance Berkman	25.00
Kazuhiro Sasaki	50.00
Roy Oswalt	40.00
Bernie Williams	35.00
Bob Abreu	25.00
Carlos Delgado	20.00
Greg Maddux	35.00
Josh Beckett	20.00
Mark Grace	30.00
Eric Chavez	30.00
Andruw Jones	30.00
Adrian Beltre	20.00

2003 Fleer Platinum

	NM/M
Complete Set (250):	40.00
Common Player:	.15
Common SP (221-250):	.50
Hobby Pack (10):	1.50
Hobby Box (14 + 4 Jumbo + 1 Rack):	35.00
Jumbo Pack:	3.00
Rack Pack:	5.00
1 Barry Bonds	2.50
2 Sean Casey	.25
3 Todd Walker	.15
4 Tony Batista	.15
5 Todd Zeile	.15
6 Ruben Sierra	.15
7 Jose Cruz Jr.	.15
8 Ben Grieve	.15
9 Robert Mackowiak	.15
10 Gary Sheffield	.25
11 Armando Benitez	.15
12 Tim Hudson	.15
13 Eric Milton	.15
14 Andy Pettitte	.40
15 Jeff Bagwell	.75
16 Jeff Kent	.15
17 Joe Randa	.15
18 Benito Santiago	.15
19 Russell Branyan	.15
20 Cliff Floyd	.15
21 Chris Richard	.15
22 Randy Winn	.15
23 Freddy Garcia	.15
24 Derek Lowe	.15
25 Ben Sheets	.15
26 Fred McGriff	.15
27 Bret Boone	.15
28 Jose Hernandez	.15
29 Phil Nevin	.15
30 Mike Piazza	1.50
31 Bobby Abreu	.15
32 Darin Erstad	.50
33 Andruw Jones	.75
34 Brad Wilkerson	.15
35 Brian Lawrence	.15
36 Vladimir Nunez	.15
37 Kazuhiro Sasaki	.15
38 Carlos Delgado	.45
39 Steve Cox	.15
40 Adrian Beltre	.25
41 Josh Bard	.15
42 Randall Simon	.15
43 Johnny Damon	.25
44 Ken Griffey Jr.	1.50
45 Sammy Sosa	1.50
46 Kevin Brown	.15
47 Kazuhisa Ishii	.15
48 Matt Morris	.15
49 Mark Prior	.75
50 Kip Wells	.15
51 Hee Seop Choi	.15
52 Craig Biggio	.15
53 Derek Jeter	2.50
54 Albert Pujols	1.25
55 Joe Borchard	.15
56 Robert Fick	.15
57 Jacque Jones	.15
58 Juan Pierre	.15
59 Bernie Williams	.35
60 Elmer Dessens	.15
61 Al Leiter	.15
62 Curt Schilling	.40
63 Carlos Pena	.15
64 Tino Martinez	.15
65 Fernando Vina	.15
66 Aaron Boone	.15
67 Michael Barrett	.15
68 Frank Thomas	.75
69 J.D. Drew	.25
70 Vladimir Guerrero	.75
71 Shannon Stewart	.15
72 Mark Buehrle	.15
73 Jamie Moyer	.15
74 Brad Radke	.15
75 Mike Williams	.15
76 Ryan Klesko	.15
77 Roberto Alomar	.35
78 Edgardo Alfonzo	.15
79 Matt Williams	.15
80 Edgar Martinez	.15
81 Shawn Green	.25
82 Kenny Lofton	.15
83 Josh Beckett	.15
84 Trevor Hoffman	.15
85 Kevin Millwood	.15
86 Odalis Perez	.15
87 Jarrod Washburn	.15
88 Jason Giambi	.60
89 Eric Young	.15
90 Barry Larkin	.15
91 Aramis Ramirez	.15
92 Ivan Rodriguez	.50
93 Steve Finley	.15
94 Brian Jordan	.15
95 Manny Ramirez	.75
96 Preston Wilson	.15
97 Rodrigo Lopez	.15
98 Ramon Ortiz	.15
99 Jim Thome	.15
100 Luis Castillo	.15
101 Alex Rodriguez	2.00
102 Jared Sandberg	.15
103 Ellis Burks	.15
104 Pat Burrell	.60
105 Brian Giles	.15
106 Mark Kotsay	.15
107 Dave Roberts	.15
108 Roy Halladay	.15
109 Chan Ho Park	.15
110 Erubiel Durazo	.15
111 Bobby Hill	.15
112 Cristian Guzman	.15
113 Troy Glaus	.60
114 Lance Berkman	.15
115 Juan Encarnacion	.15
116 Chipper Jones	1.00
117 Corey Patterson	.15
118 Vernon Wells	.15
119 Matt Clement	.15
120 Billy Koch	.15
121 Hideo Nomo	.50
122 Derrek Lee	.15
123 Todd Helton	.75
124 Sean Burroughs	.15
125 Jason Kendall	.15
126 Dmitri Young	.15
127 Adam Dunn	.60
128 Bobby Higginson	.15
129 Raul Mondesi	.15
130 Bubba Trammell	.15
131 A.J. Burnett	.15
132 Randy Johnson	.75
133 Mark Mulder	.15
134 Mariano Rivera	.25
135 Kerry Wood	.50
136 Mo Vaughn	.15
137 Jimmy Rollins	.25
138 Jose Valentin	.15
139 Brad Fullmer	.15
140 Mike Cameron	.15
141 Luis Gonzalez	.25
142 Kevin Appier	.15
143 Mike Hampton	.15
144 Pedro J. Martinez	.75
145 Javier Vazquez	.15
146 Doug Mientkiewicz	.15
147 Adam Kennedy	.15
148 Rafael Furcal	.15
149 Eric Chavez	.25
150 Mike Lieberthal	.15
151 Moises Alou	.15
152 Jermaine Dye	.15
153 Torii Hunter	.15
154 Trot Nixon	.15
155 Larry Walker	.15
156 Jorge Julio	.15
157 Mike Mussina	.40
158 Kirk Rueter	.15
159 Rafael Palmeiro	.65
160 Pokey Reese	.15
161 Miguel Tejada	.35
162 Robin Ventura	.15
163 Raul Ibanez	.15
164 Roger Cedeno	.15
165 Juan Gonzalez	.65
166 Carlos Lee	.15
167 Tim Salmon	.25
168 Orlando Hernandez	.15
169 Wade Miller	.15
170 Troy Percival	.15
171 Billy Wagner	.15
172 Jeff Conine	.15
173 Junior Spivey	.15
174 Edgar Renteria	.15
175 Scott Rolen	.65
176 Jason Varitek	.15
177 Ben Broussard	.15
178 Jeremy Giambi	.15
179 Gabe Kapler	.15
180 Armando Rios	.15
181 Ichiro Suzuki	2.00
182 Tom Glavine	.35
183 Greg Maddux	1.00
184 Roy Oswalt	.25
185 John Smoltz	.15
186 Eric Karros	.15
187 Alfonso Soriano	.75
188 Nomar Garciaparra	1.50
189 Joe Crede	.15
190 Javy Lopez	.15
191 Carlos Beltran	.15
192 Jim Edmonds	.15
193 Geoff Jenkins	.15
194 Magglio Ordonez	.25
195 Daryle Ward	.15
196 Roger Clemens	1.25
197 Byung-Hyun Kim	.15
198 Robb Nen	.15
199 C.C. Sabathia	.15
200 Barry Zito	.35
201 Mark Grace	.25
202 Paul Konerko	.25
203 Mike Sweeney	.15
204 John Olerud	.15
205 Jose Vidro	.15
206 Ray Durham	.15
207 Omar Vizquel	.15
208 Shea Hillenbrand	.15
209 Mike Lowell	.15
210 Aubrey Huff	.15
211 Eric Hinske	.15
212 Paul LoDuca	.15
213 Jay Gibbons	.15
214 Austin Kearns	.50
215 Richie Sexson	.15
216 Garret Anderson	.15
217 Eric Gagne	.15
218 Jason Jennings	.15
219 Damian Moss	.15
220 David Eckstein	.15
221 Mark Teixeira	1.00
222 Bill Hall	.50
223 Bobby Jenks	.75
224 Adam Morrisey	.50
225 Rodrigo Rosario	.50
226 Brett Myers	.75
227 Tony Alvarez	.50
228 Willie Bloomquist	2.00
229 Ben Howard	.50
230 Nic Jackson	.50
231 Carl Crawford	.50
232 Omar Infante	.50
233 Francisco Rodriguez	1.00
234 Andy Van Hekken	.50
235 Kirk Saarloos	.50
236 Dusty Wathan RC	.75
237 Jamey Carroll	1.50
238 Jason L. Phillips	1.50
239 Jose Castillo	4.00
240 Arnaldo Munoz RC	.50
241 Orlando Hudson	.50
242 Drew Henson	.75
243 Jason Lane	.75
244 Vinnie Chulk	1.50
245 Prentice Redman RC	2.00
246 Marlon Byrd	1.00
247 Chin-Feng Chen	1.00
248 Craig Brazell RC	2.00
249 John Webb	1.50
250 Adam LaRoche	1.00

Platinum Finish

Stars (1-220):	5-10X
SP (221-250):	2-4X
Production 100 Sets	

Barry Bonds Chasing History

	NM/M
Production 250 Sets	
Five Player card #'d to 25.	
Barry Bonds, Bobby Bonds,	35.00
Barry Bonds, Roger Maris,	40.00
Barry Bonds, Willie McCovey,	35.00
Barry Bonds, Babe Ruth,	200.00
Barry Bonds,	35.00
Barry Bonds, Babe Ruth, Roger Maris, Willie McCovey, Bobby Bonds	200.00

Guts and Glory

	NM/M
Complete Set (20):	12.00
Common Player:	.40
Inserted 1:4	
1GG Jason Giambi	.75
2GG Alfonso Soriano	.75
3GG Scott Rolen	.50
4GG Ivan Rodriguez	.50
5GG Barry Bonds	1.50
6GG Jim Edmonds	.40
7GG Darin Erstad	.40
8GG Brian Giles	.40
9GG Luis Gonzalez	.40
10GG Adam Dunn	.50
11GG Torii Hunter	.40
12GG Andruw Jones	.40
13GG Sammy Sosa	1.00
14GG Ichiro Suzuki	1.50
15GG Miguel Tejada	.40
16GG Roger Clemens	1.00
17GG Curt Schilling	.40
18GG Nomar Garciaparra	1.50
19GG Derek Jeter	2.00
20GG Alex Rodriguez	1.50

Heart of the Order

	NM/M
Complete Set (20):	20.00
Common Card:	.75
Inserted 1:12	
1 Jason Giambi, Derek Jeter, Alfonso Soriano	3.00
2 Todd Helton, Preston Wilson, Larry Walker	.75
3 Rafael Palmeiro, Alex Rodriguez, Ivan Rodriguez	3.00
4 Adam Dunn, Ken Griffey Jr., Austin Kearns	3.00
5 Jeff Bagwell, Craig Biggio, Lance Berkman	1.00
6 Eric Chavez, Miguel Tejada, Jermaine Dye	.75
7 Troy Glaus, Garrett Anderson, Darin Erstad	1.00
8 Mike Piazza, Mo Vaughn, Roberto Alomar	2.00
9 Torii Hunter, Jacque Jones, Corey Koskie	.75
10 Barry Bonds, Jeff Kent, Rich Aurilia	1.50
11 Pat Burrell, Bobby Abreu, Jimmy Rollins	1.50
12 Shawn Green, Adrian Beltre, Paul LoDuca	.75
13 Vladimir Guerrero, Brad Wilkerson, Jose Vidro	1.50
14 Chipper Jones, Andruw Jones, Gary Sheffield	2.00
15 Ichiro Suzuki, Bret Boone, Edgar Martinez	2.50
16 Albert Pujols, Scott Rolen, J.D. Drew	2.00
17 Sammy Sosa, Fred McGriff, Moises Alou	2.00
18 Nomar Garciaparra, Shea Hillenbrand, Manny Ramirez	2.50
19 Frank Thomas, Magglio Ordonez, Paul Konerko	1.00
20 Jason Kendall, Brian Giles, Aramis Ramirez	.75

Heart of the Order Memorabilia

	NM/M
Common Card:	5.00
Production 400 Sets	
Jason Giambi, Derek Jeter, Alfonso Soriano/Bat	15.00
Todd Helton/Jsy, Preston Wilson, Larry Walker	8.00
Rafael Palmeiro/Jsy, Alex Rodriguez, Ivan Rodriguez	6.00
Adam Dunn, Ken Griffey Jr., Austin Kearns/Pants	12.00
Troy Glaus, Garrett Anderson, Darin Erstad/Jsy	8.00
Mike Piazza/Jsy, Mo Vaughn, Roberto Alomar	10.00
Barry Bonds, Jeff Kent/Jsy, Rich Aurilia	8.00
Pat Burrell, Bobby Abreu, Jimmy Rollins/Jsy	6.00

Shawn Green,
Adrian Beltre/Jsy,
Paul LoDuca,   5.00
Vladimir Guerrero,
Brad Wilkerson,
Jose Vidro/Jsy   5.00
Chipper Jones/Jsy,
Andruw Jones,
Gary Sheffield   10.00
Ichiro Suzuki,
Bret Boone/Jsy,
Edgar Martinez   5.00
Albert Pujols, Scott Rolen,
J.D. Drew/Jsy   8.00
Sammy Sosa/Jsy,
Fred McGriff,
Moises Alou   12.00
Nomar Garciaparra,
Shea Hillenbrand,
Manny Ramirez/Jsy   8.00
Frank Thomas,
Magglio Ordonez/Jsy,
Paul Konerko   5.00
Jason Kendall,
Brian Giles/Bat,
Aramis Ramirez   5.00

MLB Scouting Report

		NM/M
Complete Set (32):		55.00
Common Player:		1.00
Production 400 Sets		
1	Jason Giambi	3.00
2	Paul Konerko	1.00
3	Jim Thome	1.50
4	Alfonso Soriano	2.00
5	Troy Glaus	1.50
6	Eric Hinske	1.00
7	Paul LoDuca	1.00
8	Mike Piazza	4.00
9	Marlon Byrd	1.00
10	Garrett Anderson	1.00
11	Barry Bonds	5.00
12	Pat Burrell	1.50
13	Joe Crede	1.00
14	J.D. Drew	1.00
15	Ken Griffey Jr.	4.00
16	Vladimir Guerrero	2.00
17	Torii Hunter	1.00
18	Chipper Jones	3.00
19	Austin Kearns	1.00
20	Albert Pujols	2.00
21	Manny Ramirez	1.50
22	Gary Sheffield	2.00
23	Sammy Sosa	3.00
24	Ichiro Suzuki	4.00
25	Bernie Williams	1.25
26	Randy Johnson	2.00
27	Greg Maddux	3.00
28	Hideo Nomo	1.00
29	Nomar Garciaparra	4.00
30	Derek Jeter	6.00
31	Alex Rodriguez	5.00
32	Miguel Tejada	1.00

MLB Scouting Report Game-Used

		NM/M
Common Player:		6.00
Production 250 Sets		
3	Jim Thome/Jsy	10.00
4	Alfonso Soriano/Bat	10.00
8	Mike Piazza/Jsy	15.00
11	Barry Bonds/Jsy	20.00
14	J.D. Drew/Jsy	6.00
18	Chipper Jones/Jsy	10.00
19	Austin Kearns/Pants	10.00
21	Manny Ramirez/Jsy	8.00
23	Sammy Sosa/Jsy	15.00
26	Randy Johnson/Jsy	10.00
27	Greg Maddux/Jsy	10.00
28	Hideo Nomo/Jsy	20.00
30	Derek Jeter/Jsy	20.00

Nameplates

		NM/M
Common Player:		
Jumbo Pack Exclusive		
Barry Larkin/97		30.00
Kazuhiro Sasaki/82		20.00
Greg Maddux/248		25.00
Craig Biggio/152		25.00
Pedro J. Martinez/		
244		35.00
Barry Zito/248		25.00
Nomar Garciaparra/		
258		40.00
John Olerud/180		25.00
Ivan Rodriguez/189		20.00
Jeff Bagwell/121		45.00
Chipper Jones/251		40.00
Frank Thomas/58		45.00
Roger Clemens/141		40.00
Mike Piazza/200		35.00
Mark Prior/123		45.00
Manny Ramirez/94		30.00
Kerry Wood/49		45.00
Rafael Palmeiro/245		20.00
Jimmy Rollins/74		20.00
Barry Bonds/251		50.00
Adam Dunn/117		25.00
Alex Rodriguez/248		40.00
Miguel Tejada/225		20.00
Chin-Feng Chen/110		100.00

Portraits

		NM/M
Complete Set (20):		25.00
Common Player:		.75
Inserted 1:20		
1	Josh Beckett	.75
2	Roberto Alomar	1.00
3	Alfonso Soriano	2.00
4	Mike Piazza	3.00
5	Ivan Rodriguez	1.00
6	Edgar Martinez	.75
7	Barry Bonds	4.00
8	Adam Dunn	1.25
9	Juan Gonzalez	1.00
10	Chipper Jones	2.50
11	Albert Pujols	1.50
12	Magglio Ordonez	.75
13	Shea Hillenbrand	.75
14	Larry Walker	.75
15	Pedro J. Martinez	1.00
16	Kerry Wood	1.00
17	Barry Zito	1.00
18	Nomar Garciaparra	3.00
19	Derek Jeter	5.00
20	Alex Rodriguez	4.00

Portraits Game Jersey

		NM/M
Common Player:		5.00
Inserted 1:86		
4	Mike Piazza	10.00
5	Ivan Rodriguez	6.00
7	Barry Bonds	15.00
8	Adam Dunn	8.00
10	Chipper Jones	8.00
15	Pedro J. Martinez	8.00
16	Kerry Wood	8.00
17	Barry Zito	5.00
18	Nomar Garciaparra	8.00
19	Derek Jeter SP/150	25.00

Portraits Game Patch

	NM/M
Common Player:	25.00

Production 100 Sets		
4	Mike Piazza	35.00
5	Ivan Rodriguez	25.00
7	Barry Bonds	40.00
8	Adam Dunn	25.00
10	Chipper Jones	25.00
15	Pedro J. Martinez	25.00
16	Kerry Wood	25.00
17	Barry Zito	25.00
18	Nomar Garciaparra	40.00
19	Derek Jeter	45.00

2003 Fleer Rookies & Greats

		NM/M
Complete Set (75):		30.00
Common Player:		.25
Pack (5):		6.00
Box (20):		100.00
1	Troy Glaus	.65
2	Gary Sheffield	.40
3	Sammy Sosa	.75
4	Mark Prior	.75
5	Dontrelle Willis	.25
6	Shawn Green	.50
7	Vladimir Guerrero	.75
8	Jose Reyes	.50
9	Miguel Tejada	.40
10	Bret Boone	.25
11	Rocco Baldelli	.40
12	Rafael Palmeiro	.65
13	Ichiro Suzuki	1.50
14	Carlos Delgado	.50
15	Garret Anderson	.25
16	Richie Sexson	.25
17	Roger Clemens	1.75
18	Barry Zito	.40
19	Jim Thome	.50
20	Alex Rodriguez	2.50
21	Randy Johnson	.75
22	Chipper Jones	1.00
23	Kerry Wood	.40
24	Ken Griffey Jr.	1.50
25	Ivan Rodriguez	.60
26	Jeff Kent	.25
27	Todd Helton	.40
28	Jeff Bagwell	.75
29	Hideo Nomo	.25
30	Torii Hunter	.25
31	Brian Giles	.25
32	Albert Pujols	2.00
33	Vernon Wells	.25
34	Nomar Garciaparra	2.00
35	Magglio Ordonez	.25
36	C.C. Sabathia	.25
37	Preston Wilson	.25
38	Mike Sweeney	.25
39	Jose Vidro	.25
40	Jason Giambi	.60
41	Derek Jeter	3.00
42	Mike Piazza	1.50
43	Rich Harden	.25
44	Jason Kendall	.25
45	Barry Bonds	3.00
46	Barry Larkin	.25
47	Dmitri Young	.25
48	Craig Biggio	.25
49	Angel Berroa	.25
50	Alfonso Soriano	.75
51	Kevin Millwood	.25
52	Edgar Martinez	.25
53	Jim Edmonds	.25
54	Curt Schilling	.40
55	Jay Gibbons	.25
56	Pedro J. Martinez	.75
57	Greg Maddux	1.00
58	Manny Ramirez	.75
59	Frank Thomas	.75
60	Adam Dunn	.60
61	Babe Ruth	2.00
62	Bob Gibson	1.00
63	Willie Stargell	.75
64	Mike Schmidt	1.50
65	Nolan Ryan	3.00
66	Tom Seaver	1.00
67	Brooks Robinson	1.00
68	Willie McCovey	.50
69	Harmon Killebrew	1.00
70	Al Kaline	1.00
71	Reggie Jackson	1.50
72	Eddie Mathews	.75
73	Ralph Kiner	.25
74	Cal Ripken Jr.	3.00
75	Phil Rizzuto	.75

Ultra

Production 1,500		
U-251	Chien-Ming Wang RC	8.00
U-252	Rickie Weeks RC	6.00
U-253	Brandon Webb RC	4.00
U-254	Hideki Matsui RC	8.00
U-255	Michael Hessman RC	4.00
U-256	Ryan Wagner RC	3.00
U-257	Matt Kata RC	3.00
U-258	Edwin Jackson RC	6.00
U-259	Jose Contreras RC	3.00
U-260	Delmon Young RC	8.00
U-261	Bo Hart RC	3.00
U-262	Jeff Duncan RC	3.00
U-263	Robby Hammock RC	2.00
U-264	Jeremy Bonderman	5.00
U-265	Clint Barmes RC	3.00

Authentix

Production 1,250		
A-161	Chien-Ming Wang	
	RC	10.00
A-162	Rickie Weeks RC	8.00
A-163	Brandon Webb RC	4.00
A-164	Craig Brazell RC	3.00
A-165	Michael Hessman RC	3.00
A-166	Ryan Wagner RC	5.00
A-167	Matt Kata RC	4.00
A-168	Edwin Jackson RC	8.00
A-169	Mike Ryan RC	4.00
A-170	Delmon Young RC	10.00
A-171	Bo Hart RC	4.00
A-172	Jeff Duncan RC	4.00
A-173	Robby Hammock RC	3.00
A-174	Jeremy Bonderman	5.00
A-175	Clint Barmes RC	3.00

Genuine

Production 1,000		
G-131	Dan Haren RC	5.00
G-132	Rickie Weeks RC	4.00
G-133	Prentice Redman RC	4.00
G-134	Craig Brazell RC	4.00
G-135	Jon Leicester RC	4.00
G-136	Ryan Wagner RC	6.00
G-137	Matt Kata RC	4.00
G-138	Edwin Jackson RC	8.00
G-139	Mike Ryan RC	4.00
G-140	Delmon Young RC	10.00
G-141	Bo Hart RC	5.00
G-142	Jeff Duncan RC	4.00
G-143	Robby Hammock RC	4.00
G-144	Michael Hessman RC	4.00
G-145	Clint Barmes RC	4.00

Showcase

Production 750		
S-136	Chien-Ming Wang	
	RC	12.00
S-137	Rickie Weeks RC	10.00
S-138	Brandon Webb RC	10.00
S-139	Hideki Matsui RC	10.00
S-140	Michael Hessman RC	8.00
S-141	Ryan Wagner RC	6.00
S-142	Bo Hart RC	5.00
S-143	Edwin Jackson RC	8.00
S-144	Jose Contreras RC	6.00
S-145	Delmon Young RC	10.00

Flair

Production 500		
F-126	Jeff Duncan RC	6.00
F-127	Rickie Weeks RC	12.00
F-128	Brandon Webb RC	8.00
F-129	Robby Hammock RC	5.00
F-130	Jon Leicester RC	6.00
F-131	Ryan Wagner RC	8.00
F-132	Bo Hart RC	5.00
F-133	Edwin Jackson RC	10.00
F-134	Sergio Mitre RC	5.00
F-135	Delmon Young RC	15.00

Hot Prospects

Production 250		
H-120	Josh Willingham RC	10.00
H-121	Rickie Weeks RC	15.00
H-122	Prentice Redman RC	8.00
H-123	Mike Ryan RC	8.00
H-124	Oscar Villarreal RC	8.00
H-125	Ryan Wagner RC	10.00
H-126	Bo Hart RC	8.00
H-127	Edwin Jackson RC	12.00

Boyhood Idols

		NM/M
Common Player:		5.00
Production 615 Sets		
	Carlton Fisk	8.00
	Joe Carter	5.00
	Cal Ripken Jr.	20.00
	Mike Schmidt	15.00
	Robin Yount	8.00
	Joe Morgan	5.00
	Jim Palmer	5.00
	Harmon Killebrew	8.00
	Brooks Robinson	5.00
	Frank Howard	5.00
	Bill "Moose" Skowron	5.00
	Bucky Dent	5.00
	Nolan Ryan	20.00
	Don Mattingly	20.00

Boyhood Idols Autograph

	NM/M
Production 50 unless noted.	
Carlton Fisk	30.00
Brooks Robinson	35.00
Bucky Dent	20.00

Dynamic Debuts

		NM/M
Complete Set (10):		10.00
Common Player:		.50
Inserted 1:10		
1DD	Rickie Weeks	4.00
2DD	Brandon Webb	1.00
3DD	Jose Reyes	1.00
4DD	Bo Hart	1.00
5DD	Dontrelle Willis	1.00
6DD	Rich Harden	1.00
7DD	Ryan Wagner	.50
8DD	Rocco Baldelli	1.00
9DD	Mark Teixeira	1.00
10DD	Hideki Matsui	1.00

Dynamic Debuts Autograph

	NM/M
Common Player:	10.00
Production 100	
Rickie Weeks	50.00
Jose Reyes	35.00

Looming Large

		NM/M
Complete Set (15):		30.00
Common Player:		1.50
Production 500 Sets		
Uncommon:		1-2X
Production 150		
Rare:		No Pricing
Production 15		
1LL	Chien-Ming Wang	4.00
2LL	Rickie Weeks	6.00
3LL	Brandon Webb	3.00
4LL	Hideki Matsui	6.00
5LL	Michael Hessman	1.50
6LL	Ryan Wagner	1.50
7LL	Matt Kata	1.50
8LL	Edwin Jackson	1.50
9LL	Jose Contreras	1.50
10LL	Delmon Young	6.00
11LL	Bo Hart	3.00
12LL	Jeff Duncan	1.50
13LL	Robby Hammock	1.50
14LL	Jeremy Bonderman	1.50
15LL	Clint Barmes	1.50

The Naturals

		NM/M
Complete Set (25):		45.00
Common Player:		.50
Inserted 1:5		
Uncommons:		2-4X
Production 75 Sets		
1	Cal Ripken Jr.	5.00
2	Mike Schmidt	3.00
3	Derek Jeter	5.00
4	Joe Carter	.50
5	Nomar Garciaparra	3.00
6	Frank Howard	.50
7	Al Kaline	2.00
8	Albert Pujols	4.00
9	Nolan Ryan	5.00
10	Duke Snider	1.50
11	Alex Rodriguez	4.00
12	Brooks Robinson	1.50
13	Roger Clemens	4.00
14	Sammy Sosa	3.00
15	Jim Palmer	1.00
16	Alfonso Soriano	2.00
17	Don Mattingly	3.00
18	Harmon Killebrew	1.50
19	Bob Feller	.50
20	Reggie Jackson	1.50
21	Ichiro Suzuki	2.50
22	Barry Bonds	5.00
23	Hideki Matsui	4.00
24	Willie Stargell	.50
25	Pee Wee Reese	.50

The Naturals Autograph

		NM/M
Common Player:		
Production 50		
	Joe Carter	15.00
	Bob Feller	25.00
	Frank Howard	25.00
	Al Kaline	40.00
	Harmon Killebrew	35.00
	Jim Palmer	15.00
	Cal Ripken Jr.	140.00
	Brooks Robinson	35.00
	Nolan Ryan	100.00
	Duke Snider	25.00

The Naturals Jersey Autograph

		NM/M
Production 30		
	Joe Carter	25.00
	Frank Howard	25.00
	Al Kaline	60.00
	Harmon Killebrew	50.00
	Jim Palmer	25.00
	Cal Ripken Jr.	150.00
	Brooks Robinson	50.00
	Nolan Ryan	120.00
	Duke Snider	40.00

The Naturals Memorabilia

		NM/M
Common Player:		5.00
Production 250 unless noted.		
CR	Cal Ripken Jr.	30.00
MS	Mike Schmidt	15.00
DJ	Derek Jeter	20.00
JC	Joe Carter	5.00
NG	Nomar Garciaparra	15.00
FH	Frank Howard/400	5.00
AK	Al Kaline	15.00
AP	Albert Pujols	12.00
NR	Nolan Ryan/400	15.00
DS	Duke Snider	10.00
AR	Alex Rodriguez	10.00
BR	Brooks Robinson/	
	400	10.00
RC	Roger Clemens/400	10.00
JP	Jim Palmer	8.00
AS	Alfonso Soriano	8.00

	Bo Hart	10.00
	Dontrelle Willis	30.00
	Ryan Wagner	10.00

The Naturals Patch

No Pricing
Production 25
Patch Autos: No Pricing
Production 5

Through the Years

		NM/M
Common Duo:		10.00
Production 360		
Patches:		No Pricing
Production 25		
	Sammy Sosa,	
	Mark Prior	20.00
	Mark Prior,	
	Jose Reyes	10.00
	Nolan Ryan,	
	Hank Blalock	25.00
	Roger Clemens,	
	Chien-Ming Wang	35.00
	Jim Thome,	
	Mike Schmidt	25.00
	Alex Rodriguez,	
	Mark Teixeira	25.00
	Randy Johnson,	
	Brandon Webb	15.00
	Phil Rizzuto,	
	Jose Reyes	15.00
	Nomar Garciaparra,	
	Bobby Doerr	20.00
	Jason Giambi,	
	Reggie Jackson	15.00
	Derek Jeter,	
	Phil Rizzuto	45.00
	Barry Larkin,	
	Joe Morgan	10.00
	Harmon Killebrew,	
	Torii Hunter	20.00
	Willie McCovey,	
	Barry Bonds	15.00
	Bo Hart, Lou Brock	15.00
	Jose Contreras,	
	Mike Mussina	10.00
	Michael Hessman,	
	Chipper Jones	12.00
	Steve Carlton,	
	Kevin Millwood	12.00
	Robin Yount,	
	Scott Podsednik	20.00
	Eddie Mathews,	
	Chipper Jones	15.00

2003 Fleer Showcase

		NM/M
Complete Set (135):		50.00
Common Player:		.25
Common SP (106-135):		1.00
Inserted 1:4		
Pack (5):		3.00
Box (24):		60.00
1	David Eckstein	.25
2	Curt Schilling	.75
3	Jay Gibbons	.25
4	Kerry Wood	.75
5	Jeff Bagwell	.75
6	Hideo Nomo	.25
7	Tim Hudson	.40
8	J.D. Drew	.50
9	Josh Phelps	.25
10	Bartolo Colon	.25
11	Bobby Abreu	.25
12	Matt Morris	.25
13	Kazuhiro Sasaki	.25
14	Sean Burroughs	.25
15	Vicente Padilla	.25
16	Jorge Posada	.35
17	Torii Hunter	.25
18	Richie Sexson	.25
19	Lance Berkman	.25
20	Todd Helton	1.00
21	Paul Konerko	.25
22	Pedro J. Martinez	1.00
23	Rodrigo Lopez	.25
24	Gary Sheffield	.35
25	Darin Erstad	.50
26	Nomar Garciaparra	2.50
27	Adam Dunn	.75
28	Jason Giambi	.75
29	Miguel Tejada	.40
30	Chipper Jones	1.50

DM	Don Mattingly	20.00
HK	Harmon Killebrew/	
	400	10.00
RJ	Reggie Jackson/400	10.00

#	Player	Price
31	Alex Rodriguez	3.00
32	Barry Bonds	4.00
33	Roger Clemens	2.00
34	Sammy Sosa	2.50
35	Randy Johnson	1.00
36	Tim Salmon	.35
37	Shea Hillenbrand	.25
38	Larry Walker	.25
39	A.J. Burnett	.25
40	Shawn Green	.50
41	Cristian Guzman	.25
42	Bernie Williams	.35
43	Mark Mulder	.25
44	Brian Giles	.25
45	Bret Boone	.25
46	Juan Gonzalez	.75
47	Roy Halladay	.25
48	Wade Miller	.25
49	Jeff Kent	.25
50	Carlos Delgado	.50
51	Mike Lowell	.25
52	Jim Edmonds	.25
53	Ivan Rodriguez	.75
54	Aubrey Huff	.25
55	Ryan Klesko	.25
56	Paul LoDuca	.25
57	Roy Oswalt	.50
58	Omar Vizquel	.25
59	Manny Ramirez	1.00
60	Andruw Jones	1.00
61	Troy Glaus	1.00
62	Ichiro Suzuki	2.50
63	Albert Pujols	2.50
64	Derek Jeter	4.00
65	Mark Prior	1.00
66	Ken Griffey Jr.	2.50
67	Vladimir Guerrero	1.00
68	Mike Piazza	2.50
69	Alfonso Soriano	1.00
70	Greg Maddux	1.50
71	Adam Kennedy	.25
72	Junior Spivey	.25
73	Tom Glavine	.40
74	Derek Lowe	.25
75	Magglio Ordonez	.25
76	Jim Thome	.25
77	Robert Fick	.25
78	Josh Beckett	.25
79	Mike Sweeney	.25
80	Kazuhisa Ishii	.25
81	Roberto Alomar	.40
82	Barry Zito	.40
83	Pat Burrell	.65
84	Scott Rolen	1.00
85	John Olerud	.25
86	Eric Hinske	.25
87	Rafael Palmeiro	.75
88	Edgar Martinez	.40
89	Eric Chavez	.40
90	Jose Vidro	.25
91	Craig Biggio	.25
92	Rich Aurilia	.25
93	Austin Kearns	.75
94	Luis Gonzalez	.40
95	Garrett Anderson	.25
96	Yogi Berra	1.50
97	Al Kaline	1.50
98	Robin Yount	1.00
99	Reggie Jackson	1.00
100	Harmon Killebrew	1.50
101	Eddie Mathews	1.50
102	Willie McCovey	.50
103	Nolan Ryan	4.00
104	Mike Schmidt	2.50
105	Tom Seaver	1.00
106	Francisco Rodriguez	1.00
107	Carl Crawford	1.00
108	Ben Howard	1.00
109	Hank Blalock	2.00
110	Hee Seop Choi	2.00
111	Kirk Saarloos	1.00
112	Lew Ford RC	3.00
113	Andy Van Hekken	1.00
114	Drew Henson	1.50
115	Marlon Byrd	1.00
116	Jayson Werth	1.00
117	Willie Bloomquist	1.00
118	Joe Borchard	1.00
119	Mark Teixeira	2.00
120	Bobby Hill	1.00
121	Jason Lane	1.00
122	Omar Infante	1.00
123	Victor Martinez	1.50
124	Jorge Padilla	1.00
125	John Lackey	1.00
126	Anderson Machado	1.00
127	Rodrigo Rosario	1.00
128	Freddy Sanchez	1.00
129	Tony Alvarez	1.00
130	Matt Thornton	1.00
131	Joe Thurston	1.00
132	Brett Myers	1.00
133	Antonio Perez	1.00
134	Chris Snelling	1.00
135	Termmel Sledge RC	2.00

Legacy

Legacy Stars (1-105): 3-6X
SP's (106-135): 1-3X
Production 150 Sets

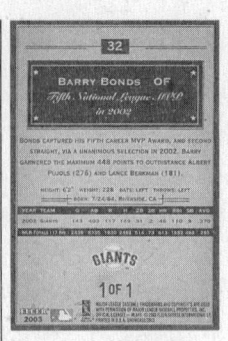

Masterpiece 1 of 1 also exists.

Baseball's Best

NM/M
Complete Set (15): 40.00
Common Player: 1.50
Inserted 1:24

#	Player	Price
1	Curt Schilling	2.00
2	Barry Zito	2.00
3	Torii Hunter	2.00
4	Pedro J. Martinez	4.00
5	Bernie Williams	2.00
6	Magglio Ordonez	1.50
7	Alfonso Soriano	4.00
8	Hideo Nomo	2.00
9	Jason Giambi	5.00
10	Sammy Sosa	5.00
11	Vladimir Guerrero	4.00
12	Ken Griffey Jr.	5.00
13	Troy Glaus	3.00
14	Ichiro Suzuki	6.00
15	Albert Pujols	4.00

Baseball's Best Memorabilia

NM/M
Common Player: 5.00
Inserted 1:24

Code	Player	Price
CS	Curt Schilling	6.00
BZ	Barry Zito	6.00
TH	Torii Hunter	8.00
PM	Pedro J. Martinez	10.00
BW	Bernie Williams	8.00
MO	Magglio Ordonez	8.00
AS	Alfonso Soriano	15.00
HN	Hideo Nomo	8.00
JG	Jason Giambi	8.00
SS	Sammy Sosa	15.00

Hot Gloves

NM/M
Complete Set (10): 15.00
Common Player: 1.00
Inserted 1:8

#	Player	Price
1	Greg Maddux	2.00
2	Ivan Rodriguez	1.00
3	Derek Jeter	4.00
4	Mike Piazza	2.50
5	Nomar Garciaparra	2.50
6	Andruw Jones	1.00
7	Scott Rolen	1.00
8	Barry Bonds	3.00
9	Roger Clemens	2.00
10	Alex Rodriguez	3.00

Hot Gloves Memorabilia

NM/M
Common Player: 5.00
Inserted 1:24

Code	Player	Price
GM	Greg Maddux	12.00
IR	Ivan Rodriguez	5.00
DJ	Derek Jeter	25.00
MP	Mike Piazza	15.00
NG	Nomar Garciaparra	15.00
AJ	Andruw Jones	6.00
SR	Scott Rolen	8.00
BB	Barry Bonds	25.00
RC	Roger Clemens	15.00
AR	Alex Rodriguez	15.00

Sweet Sigs

NM/M
Quantity produced listed

Code	Player	Price
DJ	Derek Jeter/250	130.00
DJ	Derek Jeter/50/Red	185.00
BB	Barry Bonds/90 MVP/150	200.00
BB	Barry Bonds/92 MVP/100	200.00
BB	Barry Bonds/93 MVP/75	200.00

Sweet Stitch

NM/M
Complete Set (10): 12.00
Common Player: .75
Inserted 1:8

Code	Player	Price
1SS	Derek Jeter	4.00
2SS	Randy Johnson	1.50
3SS	Jeff Bagwell	1.00
4SS	Nomar Garciaparra	2.50
5SS	Roger Clemens	2.00
6SS	Todd Helton	.75
7SS	Barry Bonds	3.00
8SS	Alfonso Soriano	1.50
9SS	Miguel Tejada	.75
10SS	Mark Prior	.75

Sweet Stitch Memorabilia

NM/M
Varying quantities produced

Code	Player	Price
DJ	Derek Jeter	25.00
RJ	Randy Johnson	8.00
JB	Jeff Bagwell	8.00
NG	Nomar Garciaparra	12.00
RC	Roger Clemens	12.00
TH	Todd Helton	5.00
BB	Barry Bonds	20.00
AS	Alfonso Soriano	12.00
MT	Miguel Tejada	5.00
MP	Mark Prior	10.00

Sweet Stitch Patch

NM/M
Common Player: 20.00
Inserted 1:24

Code	Player	Price
DJ	Derek Jeter/50	60.00
RJ	Randy Johnson/150	40.00
JB	Jeff Bagwell/150	35.00
NG	Nomar Garciaparra/150	45.00
RC	Roger Clemens/50	45.00
TH	Todd Helton/50	30.00
BB	Barry Bonds/150	75.00
AS	Alfonso Soriano/50	40.00
MT	Miguel Tejada/150	20.00
MP	Mark Prior/150	25.00

Thundersticks

NM/M
Complete Set (10): 12.00
Common Player: .75
Inserted 1:8

Code	Player	Price
1TS	Adam Dunn	1.00
2TS	Alex Rodriguez	3.00
3TS	Barry Bonds	4.00
4TS	Jim Thome	1.00
5TS	Chipper Jones	2.00
6TS	Manny Ramirez	1.00
7TS	Carlos Delgado	.75
8TS	Mike Piazza	2.50
9TS	Shawn Green	.75
10TS	Pat Burrell	.75

Thundersticks Bat

NM/M
Common Player: 5.00

Golds: 1-2.5X
Production 99 Sets

Code	Player	Price
AD	Adam Dunn	10.00
AR	Alex Rodriguez	15.00
BB	Barry Bonds	20.00
JT	Jim Thome	8.00
CJS	Chipper Jones	8.00
MR	Manny Ramirez	8.00
SG	Shawn Green	5.00
PB	Pat Burrell	10.00

2003 Fleer Splendid Splinters

NM/M
Complete Set (150):
Common Player: .20
Common Wood (91-110): 6.00
Production 499
Common SP (111-140): 1.50
Inserted 1:6
Common (141-150): 3.00
Production 999
Pack (5): 3.00
Box (24): 50.00

#	Player	Price
1	David Eckstein	.20
2	Barry Larkin	.40
3	Edgardo Alfonzo	.20
4	Darin Erstad	.50
5	Ellis Burks	.20
6	Omar Vizquel	.40
7	Bartolo Colon	.20
8	Roberto Alomar	.50
9	Garret Anderson	.20
10	Al Leiter	.20
11	Tim Salmon	.40
12	Larry Walker	.40
13	Jorge Posada	.50
14	Curt Schilling	.50
15	Jason Jennings	.20
16	Jason Giambi	1.00
17	Robert Fick	.20
18	Kazuhiro Sasaki	.20
19	Bernie Williams	.50
20	Junior Spivey	.20
21	Mike Lowell	.20
22	Luis Gonzalez	.40
23	Josh Beckett	.20
24	John Smoltz	.50
25	Mike Mussina	.50
26	Gary Sheffield	.40
27	Tom Glavine	.40
28	Tim Hudson	.40
29	Austin Kearns	.75
30	Andruw Jones	.40
31	Roger Clemens	1.50
32	Mark Mulder	.40
33	Jay Gibbons	.20
34	Jeff Kent	.40
35	Barry Zito	.40
36	Rodrigo Lopez	.20
37	Jeff Bagwell	.75
38	Eric Chavez	.40
39	Pedro J. Martinez	1.00
40	Lance Berkman	.40
41	Bobby Abreu	.40
42	Wade Miller	.20
43	Bret Boone	.20
44	Vicente Padilla	.20
45	Shea Hillenbrand	.20
46	Roy Oswalt	.40
47	Pat Burrell	.75
48	Manny Ramirez	.75
49	Craig Biggio	.40
50	Randy Wolf	.20
51	Kerry Wood	.50
52	Mike Sweeney	.40
53	Brian Giles	.40
54	Kazuhisa Ishii	.20
55	Jason Kendall	.20
56	Hideo Nomo	.40
57	Josh Phelps	.20
58	Sean Burroughs	.20
59	Paul Konerko	.40
60	Shawn Green	.40
61	Ryan Klesko	.40
62	Magglio Ordonez	.40
63	Paul LoDuca	.20
64	Edgar Martinez	.40
65	J.D. Drew	.30
66	Phil Nevin	.20
67	Jim Edmonds	.40
68	Matt Morris	.20
69	Aubrey Huff	.20
70	Adam Dunn	.75
71	John Olerud	.40
72	Juan Gonzalez	.50
73	Scott Rolen	.50
74	Rafael Palmeiro	.50
75	Roy Halladay	.20
76	Kevin Brown	.20
77	Ivan Rodriguez	.50
78	Eric Hinske	.20
79	Frank Thomas	.75
80	Carlos Delgado	.40
81	Bobby Higginson	.20
82	Trevor Hoffman	.20
83	Cliff Floyd	.20
84	Derek Lowe	.20
85	Richie Sexson	.50
86	Rich Aurilia	.20
87	Sean Casey	.20
88	Cristian Guzman	.20
89	Randy Winn	.20
90	Jose Vidro	.20
91	Mark Prior	15.00
92	Derek Jeter	15.00
93	Alex Rodriguez	12.00
94	Greg Maddux	9.00
95	Troy Glaus	7.50
96	Vladimir Guerrero	7.50
97	Todd Helton	7.50
98	Albert Pujols	10.00
99	Torii Hunter	6.00
100	Mike Piazza	10.00
101	Ichiro Suzuki	10.00
102	Sammy Sosa	10.00
103	Ken Griffey Jr.	10.00
104	Nomar Garciaparra	10.00
105	Barry Bonds	15.00
106	Chipper Jones	9.00
107	Jim Thome	6.00
108	Miguel Tejada	6.00
109	Randy Johnson	7.50
110	Alfonso Soriano	7.50
111	Guillermo Quiroz RC	3.00
112	Josh Willingham RC	3.00
113	Alejandro Machado RC	1.50
114	Chris Waters RC	1.50
115	Adam LaRoche	1.50
116	Prentice Redman RC	3.00
117	Jhonny Peralta	1.50
118	Francisco Rosario RC	1.50
119	Shane Victorino RC	1.50
120	Chien-Ming Wang RC	15.00
121	Matt Bruback RC	2.00
122	Rontrez Johnson RC	3.00
123	Josh Hall RC	2.00
124	Matt Kata RC	2.00
125	Hector Luna RC	2.00
126	Josh Stewart RC	2.00
127	Craig Brazell RC	2.00
128	Tim Olson RC	2.00
129	Michel Hernandez RC	1.50
130	Michael Hessman RC	2.00
131	Clint Barmes RC	2.00
132	Justin Morneau	1.50
133	Chris Snelling	1.50
134	Bobby Jenks	1.50
135	Tim Hummel RC	1.50
136	Adam Morrissey	1.50
137	Carl Crawford	1.50
138	Garrett Atkins	1.50
139	Jung Bong	1.50
140	Ken Harvey	1.50
141	Chin-Feng Chen	2.00
142	Hee Seop Choi	2.00
143	Lance Niekro	2.00
144	Mark Teixeira	2.00
145	Nook Logan RC	3.00
146	Terrmel Sledge RC	3.00
147	Lew Ford RC	6.00
148	Ian Ferguson RC	3.00
149	Hideki Matsui/499 RC	15.00
150	Jose Contreras RC	6.00

Bat Chips

NM/M
Common Player: 4.00
Production 425 Sets

#	Player	Price
1	Jason Giambi	8.00
2	Jeff Bagwell	8.00
3	Manny Ramirez	8.00
4	Adam Dunn	8.00
5	Derek Jeter	25.00
6	Alex Rodriguez	15.00
7	Troy Glaus	5.00
8	Mike Piazza	15.00
9	Sammy Sosa	12.00
10	Nomar Garciaparra	18.00
11	Barry Bonds	18.00
12	Jim Thome	10.00
13	Miguel Tejada	5.00
14	Alfonso Soriano	10.00
15	Ryan Klesko	4.00
16	Sean Casey	4.00
17	Bernie Williams	8.00
18	Vladimir Guerrero	8.00
19	Gary Sheffield	5.00

Family Tree

NM/M
Complete Set (10): 10.00
Common Player: .50
Inserted 1:8

#	Players	Price
1	Lance Niekro, Phil Niekro	.50
2	Bob Boone, Bret Boone	.50
3	Sandy Alomar Jr., Roberto Alomar	.50
4	Ken Griffey Sr., Ken Griffey Jr.	2.00
5	Jason Giambi, Jeremy Giambi	1.50
6	Bobby Bonds, Barry Bonds	3.00
7	Tony Perez, Eduardo Perez	.50
8	Brian Giles, Marcus Giles	.75
9	Felipe Alou, Moises Alou	.75
10	Pedro J. Martinez, Ramon Martinez	1.50

Home Run Club

NM/M
Complete Set (12): 50.00
Common Player: 2.00
Inserted 1:72

#	Player	Price
1	Barry Bonds	10.00
2	Jason Giambi	5.00
3	Sammy Sosa	6.00
4	Jim Thome	4.00
5	Lance Berkman	2.00
6	Alfonso Soriano	5.00
7	Vladimir Guerrero	4.00
8	Shawn Green	2.00
9	Troy Glaus	3.00
10	Pat Burrell	3.00
11	Alex Rodriguez	10.00
12	Mike Piazza	8.00

Home Run Club Autographs

NM/M
Quantity produced listed

Code	Player	Price
BB1	Barry Bonds/Black ink/150	150.00
CR1	Cal Ripken Jr/Black ink/300	100.00
CR2	Cal Ripken Jr/Blue ink/150	125.00
CR3	Cal Ripken Jr/Red ink/50	200.00
DJ1	Derek Jeter/Black ink/400	80.00
DJ2	Derek Jeter/Blue ink/250	100.00
DJ3	Derek Jeter/Red ink/50	125.00

Home Run Club Memorabilia

NM/M
Common Player: 5.00
Production 599 Sets

Player	Price
Barry Bonds/Jsy	20.00
Jason Giambi/Bat	8.00
Sammy Sosa/Jsy	12.00
Jim Thome/Bat	8.00
Lance Berkman/Bat	8.00
Alfonso Soriano/Jsy	15.00
Vladimir Guerrero/Jsy	8.00
Shawn Green/Jsy	5.00
Troy Glaus/Bat	8.00
Pat Burrell/Bat	10.00
Alex Rodriguez/Jsy	15.00
Mike Piazza/Jsy	12.00

Todd Helton/Jsy	8.00
Rafael Palmeiro/Jsy	6.00

Knot Hole Gang

	NM/M
Complete Set (15):	40.00
Common Player:	1.00
Inserted 1:24	
1 Derek Jeter	6.00
2 Barry Bonds	6.00
3 Sammy Sosa	3.00
4 Jason Giambi	3.00
5 Alfonso Soriano	2.00
6 Roger Clemens	3.00
7 Miguel Tejada	1.00
8 Greg Maddux	3.00
9 Randy Johnson	2.00
10 Chipper Jones	3.00
11 Nomar Garciaparra	4.00
12 Alex Rodriguez	5.00
13 Ichiro Suzuki	4.00
14 Vladimir Guerrero	2.00
15 Albert Pujols	2.00

Knot Hole Gang Game-Used

	NM/M
Common Player:	4.00
Inserted 1:40	
Derek Jeter	20.00
Barry Bonds	15.00
Sammy Sosa	10.00
Vladimir Guerrero	8.00
Alfonso Soriano	8.00
Roger Clemens	10.00
Miguel Tejada	5.00
Greg Maddux	10.00
Randy Johnson	8.00
Chipper Jones	8.00
Nomar Garciaparra	12.00
Alex Rodriguez	12.00
Magglio Ordonez	4.00
Lance Berkman	6.00

Knot Hole Gang Patch

	NM/M
Common Player:	15.00
Production 99 Sets	
Derek Jeter	45.00
Barry Bonds	45.00
Sammy Sosa	35.00
Vladimir Guerrero	25.00
Alfonso Soriano	25.00
Roger Clemens	25.00
Miguel Tejada	15.00
Greg Maddux	30.00
Randy Johnson	20.00
Chipper Jones	30.00
Nomar Garciaparra	35.00
Alex Rodriguez	35.00

Knot Hole Gang Triple

Common Player:	
Production 29 Sets:	No Pricing

Splendid Splinters

	NM/M
Complete Set (10):	15.00
Common Player:	1.00
Inserted 1:12	
1 Derek Jeter	4.00
2 Barry Bonds	4.00
3 Scott Rolen	1.00
4 Nomar Garciaparra	2.50
5 Sammy Sosa	2.00
6 Alfonso Soriano	1.50
7 Alex Rodriguez	3.00
8 Mike Piazza	2.50
9 Manny Ramirez	1.00
10 Jeff Bagwell	1.00

Splendid Splinters G-U

	NM/M
Common Player:	8.00
Production 349 Sets	
Derek Jeter	20.00
Barry Bonds	20.00
Nomar Garciaparra	15.00
Sammy Sosa	10.00
Alfonso Soriano	10.00

Alex Rodriguez	12.00
Mike Piazza	12.00
Manny Ramirez	8.00
Jeff Bagwell	8.00

Splendid Splinters Dual

	NM/M
Production 99 Sets	
Derek Jeter, Alfonso Soriano	40.00
Barry Bonds, Sammy Sosa	50.00
Alex Rodriguez, Nomar Garciaparra	40.00
Mike Piazza, Jeff Bagwell	25.00

2003 Fleer Tradition

JASON GIAMBI
New York Yankees® - First Base

	NM/M
Complete Set (485):	150.00
Common Player:	.15
Common SP (1-100):	1.00
Inserted 1:1	
Hobby Pack (10):	1.50
Hobby Box (40):	40.00
1 Jarrod Washburn, Troy Glaus, Garret Anderson, Ramon Ortiz	1.50
2 Luis Gonzalez, Randy Johnson, Andruw Jones	1.50
3 Andruw Jones, Chipper Jones, Tom Glavine, Kevin Millwood	2.00
4 Tony Batista, Rodrigo Lopez	1.00
5 Manny Ramirez, Nomar Garciaparra, Derek Lowe, Pedro J. Martinez	3.00
6 Sammy Sosa, Matt Clement, Kerry Wood	3.00
7 Mark Buehrle, Magglio Ordonez, Danny Wright	1.00
8 Adam Dunn, Aaron Boone, Jimmy Haynes	1.00
9 C.C. Sabathia, Jim Thome	1.50
10 Todd Helton, Jason Jennings	1.50
11 Randall Simon, Steve Sparks, Mark Redman	1.00
12 Derek Lee, Mike Lowell, A.J. Burnett	1.00
13 Lance Berkman, Roy Oswalt	1.50
14 Paul Byrd, Carlos Beltran	1.00
15 Shawn Green, Hideo Nomo	1.50
16 Richie Sexson, Ben Sheets	1.00
17 Torii Hunter, Kyle Lohse, Johan Santana	1.00
18 Vladimir Guerrero, Tomokazu Ohka, Javier Vazquez	2.00
19 Mike Piazza, Al Leiter	3.00
20 Jason Giambi, David Wells, Roger Clemens	4.00
21 Eric Chavez, Miguel Tejada, Barry Zito	1.50
22 Pat Burrell, Vicente Padilla, Randy Wolf	1.50
23 Brian Giles, Josh Fogg, Kip Wells	1.00
24 Ryan Klesko, Brian Lawrence	1.00
25 Barry Bonds, Russ Ortiz, Jason Schmidt	5.00
26 Mike Cameron, Bret Boone, Freddy Garcia	1.00
27 Albert Pujols, Matt Morris	3.00
28 Aubrey Huff, Randy Winn, Joe Kennedy, Tanyon Sturtze	1.00
29 Alex Rodriguez, Kenny Rogers, Chan Ho Park	5.00

30	Carlos Delgado,	
31	Roy Halladay	1.00
32	Greg Maddux	6.00
33	Nick Neugebauer	1.00
34	Larry Walker	1.50
35	Freddy Garcia	1.00
36	Rich Aurilia	1.00
37	Craig Wilson	1.00
38	Jeff Suppan	1.00
39	Joel Pineiro	1.00
40	Pedro Feliz	1.00
41	Bartolo Colon	1.50
42	Pete Walker	1.00
43	Mo Vaughn	1.50
44	Sidney Ponson	1.00
45	Jason Isringhausen	1.00
46	Hideki Irabu	1.00
47	Pedro J. Martinez	4.00
48	Tom Glavine	2.50
49	Matt Lawton	1.00
50	Kyle Lohse	1.00
51	Corey Patterson	1.00
52	Ichiro Suzuki	6.00
53	Wade Miller	1.00
54	Ben Diggins	1.00
55	Jayson Werth	1.00
56	Masato Yoshii	1.00
57	Mark Buehrle	1.00
58	Drew Henson	1.50
59	Dave Williams	1.00
60	Juan Rivera	1.00
61	Scott Schoeneweis	1.00
62	Josh Beckett	1.50
63	Vinny Castilla	1.00
64	Barry Zito	2.00
65	Jose Valentin	1.00
66	Jon Lieber	1.00
67	Jorge Padilla	1.00
68	Luis Aparicio	1.00
69	Boog Powell	1.00
70	Dick Radatz	1.00
71	Frank Malzone	1.00
72	Lou Brock	1.50
73	Billy Williams	1.00
74	Early Wynn	1.00
75	Jim Bunning	1.00
76	Al Kaline	5.00
77	Eddie Mathews	5.00
78	Harmon Killebrew	5.00
79	Gil Hodges	1.00
80	Duke Snider	3.00
81	Yogi Berra	4.00
82	Whitey Ford	3.00
83	Willie Stargell	1.50
84	Willie McCovey	1.50
85	Gaylord Perry	1.00
86	Red Schoendienst	1.00
87	Derek Jeter	8.00
88	Orlando Hudson	1.00
89	Bobby Higginson	1.00
90	Brent Butler	1.00
91	Brad Wilkerson	1.00
92	Craig Biggio	1.50
93	Marlon Anderson	1.00
94	Ty Wigginton	1.00
95	Hideo Nomo	3.00
96	Barry Larkin	2.00
97	Roberto Alomar	3.00
98	Omar Vizquel	1.50
99	Andres Galarraga	1.00
100	Shawn Green	1.50
101	Rafael Furcal	.15
102	Bill Selby	.15
103	Brent Abernathy	.15
104	Nomar Garciaparra	1.50
105	Michael Barrett	.15
106	Travis Hafner	.15
107	Carl Crawford	.15
108	Jeff Cirillo	.15
109	Mike Hampton	.15
110	Kip Wells	.15
111	Luis Alicea	.15
112	Ellis Burks	.15
113	Matt Anderson	.15
114	Carlos Beltran	.50
115	Paul LoDuca	.15
116	Lance Berkman	.15
117	Moises Alou	.15
118	Roger Cedeno	.15
119	Brad Fullmer	.15
120	Sean Burroughs	.15
121	Eric Byrnes	.15
122	Milton Bradley	.15
123	Jason Giambi	.75
124	Brook Fordyce	.15
125	Kevin Appier	.15
126	Steve Cox	.15
127	Danny Bautista	.15
128	Edgardo Alfonzo	.15
129	Matt Clement	.15
130	Robb Nen	.15
131	Roy Halladay	.15
132	Brian Jordan	.15
133	A.J. Burnett	.15
134	Aaron Cook	.15
135	Paul Byrd	.15
136	Ramon Ortiz	.15
137	Adam Hyzdu	.15
138	Rafael Soriano	.15
139	Marty Cordova	.15
140	Nelson Cruz	.15
141	Jamie Moyer	.15
142	Raul Mondesi	.15
143	Josh Bard	.15
144	Elmer Dessens	.15
145	Rickey Henderson	.75
146	Joe McEwing	.15

147	Luis Rivas	.15
148	Armando Benitez	.15
149	Keith Foulke	.15
150	Zach Day	.15
151	Troy Lunsford	.15
152	Bobby Abreu	.15
153	Juan Cruz	.15
154	Ramon Hernandez	.15
155	Brandon Duckworth	.15
156	Matt Ginter	.15
157	Robert Mackowiak	.15
158	Josh Pearce	.15
159	Marlon Byrd	.15
160	Todd Walker	.15
161	Chad Hermansen	.15
162	Felix Escalona	.15
163	Ruben Mateo	.15
164	Mark Johnson	.15
165	Juan Pierre	.15
166	Gary Sheffield	.30
167	Edgar Martinez	.15
168	Randy Winn	.15
169	Pokey Reese	.15
170	Kevin Mench	.15
171	Albert Pujols	1.50
172	J.T. Snow	.15
173	Dean Palmer	.15
174	Jay Payton	.15
175	Abraham Nunez	.15
176	Richie Sexson	.15
177	Jose Vidro	.15
178	Geoff Jenkins	.15
179	Dan Wilson	.15
180	John Olerud	.15
181	Javy Lopez	.15
182	Carl Everett	.15
183	Vernon Wells	.15
184	Juan Gonzalez	.75
185	Jorge Posada	.35
186	Mike Sweeney	.15
187	Cesar Izturis	.15
188	Jason Schmidt	.15
189	Chris Richard	.15
190	Jason Phillips	.15
191	Fred McGriff	.15
192	Shea Hillenbrand	.15
193	Ivan Rodriguez	.50
194	Mike Lowell	.15
195	Neifi Perez	.15
196	Kenny Lofton	.15
197	A.J. Pierzynski	.15
198	Larry Bigbie	.15
199	Juan Uribe	.15
200	Jeff Bagwell	.75
201	Timoniel Perez	.15
202	Jeremy Giambi	.15
203	Deivi Cruz	.15
204	Marquis Grissom	.15
205	Chipper Jones	1.00
206	Alex Gonzalez	.15
207	Steve Finley	.15
208	Ben Davis	.15
209	Mike Bordick	.15
210	Casey Fossum	.15
211	Aramis Ramirez	.15
212	Aaron Boone	.15
213	Orlando Cabrera	.15
214	Hee Seop Choi	.15
215	Jeromy Burnitz	.15
216	Todd Hollandsworth	.15
217	Rey Sanchez	.15
218	Jose Cruz Jr.	.15
219	Roosevelt Brown	.15
220	Odalis Perez	.15
221	Carlos Delgado	.40
222	Orlando Hernandez	.15
223	Adam Everett	.15
224	Adrian Beltre	.25
225	Ken Griffey Jr.	1.50
226	Brad Penny	.15
227	Carlos Lee	.15
228	J.C. Romero	.15
229	Ramon Martinez	.15
230	Matt Morris	.15
231	Ben Howard	.15
232	Damon Minor	.15
233	Jason Marquis	.15
234	Paul Wilson	.15
235	Ryan Dempster	.15
236	Jeffrey Hammonds	.15
237	Jaret Wright	.15
238	Carlos Pena	.15
239	Toby Hall	.15
240	Rick Helling	.15
241	Alex Escobar	.15
242	Trevor Hoffman	.15
243	Bernie Williams	.35
244	Jorge Julio	.15
245	Byung-Hyun Kim	.15
246	Mike Redmond	.15
247	Tony Armas	.15
248	Aaron Rowand	.15
249	Rusty Greer	.15
250	Aaron Harang	.15
251	Jeremy Fikac	.15
252	Jay Gibbons	.15
253	Brandon Puffer	.15
254	Dewayne Wise	.15
255	Chan Ho Park	.15
256	David Bell	.15
257	Kenny Rogers	.15
258	Mark Quinn	.15
259	Greg LaRocca	.15
260	Reggie Taylor	.15
261	Brett Tomko	.15
262	Jack Wilson	.15
263	Billy Wagner	.15
264	Greg Norton	.15

265	Tim Salmon	.25
266	Joe Randa	.15
267	Geronimo Gil	.15
268	Johnny Damon	.25
269	Robin Ventura	.15
270	Frank Thomas	.75
271	Terrence Long	.15
272	Mark Redman	.15
273	Mark Kotsay	.15
274	Ben Sheets	.15
275	Reggie Sanders	.15
276	Mark Grace	.25
277	Eddie Guardado	.15
278	Julio Mateo	.15
279	Bengie Molina	.15
280	Bill Hall	.15
281	Eric Chavez	.30
282	Joe Kennedy	.15
283	John Valentin	.15
284	Ray Durham	.15
285	Trot Nixon	.15
286	Rondell White	.15
287	Alex Gonzalez	.15
288	Tomas Perez	.15
289	Jared Sandberg	.15
290	Jacque Jones	.15
291	Cliff Floyd	.15
292	Ryan Klesko	.15
293	Morgan Ensberg	.15
294	Jerry Hairston Jr.	.15
295	Doug Mientkiewicz	.15
296	Darin Erstad	.50
297	Jeff Conine	.15
298	Johnny Estrada	.15
299	Mark Mulder	.15
300	Jeff Kent	.15
301	Roger Clemens	1.25
302	Endy Chavez	.15
303	Joe Crede	.15
304	J.D. Drew	.30
305	David Dellucci	.15
306	Eli Marrero	.15
307	Josh Fogg	.15
308	Mike Crudale	.15
309	Bret Boone	.15
310	Mariano Rivera	.30
311	Mike Piazza	1.50
312	Jason Jennings	.15
313	Jason Varitek	.15
314	Vicente Padilla	.15
315	Kevin Millwood	.15
316	Nick Johnson	.15
317	Shane Reynolds	.15
318	Joe Thurston	.15
319	Mike Lamb	.15
320	Aaron Sele	.15
321	Fernando Tatis	.15
322	Randy Wolf	.15
323	David Justice	.15
324	Andy Pettitte	.30
325	Freddy Sanchez	.15
326	Scott Spiezio	.15
327	Randy Johnson	.75
328	Karim Garcia	.15
329	Eric Milton	.15
330	Jermaine Dye	.15
331	Kevin Brown	.15
332	Adam Pettyjohn	.15
333	Jason Lane	.15
334	Mark Prior	.60
335	Mike Lieberthal	.15
336	Matt White	.15
337	John Patterson	.15
338	Marcus Giles	.15
339	Kazuhisa Ishii	.15
340	Willie Harris	.15
341	Travis Phelps	.15
342	Randall Simon	.15
343	Manny Ramirez	.75
344	Kerry Wood	.60
345	Shannon Stewart	.15
346	Mike Mussina	.40
347	Joe Borchard	.15
348	Tyler Walker	.15
349	Preston Wilson	.15
350	Damian Moss	.15
351	Eric Karros	.15
352	Bobby Kielty	.15
353	Jason LaRue	.15
354	Phil Nevin	.15
355	Tony Graffanino	.15
356	Antonio Alfonseca	.15
357	Eddie Taubensee	.15
358	Luis Ugueto	.15
359	Greg Vaughn	.15
360	Corey Thurman	.15
361	Omar Infante	.15
362	Alex Cintron	.15
363	Esteban Loaiza	.15
364	Tino Martinez	.15
365	David Eckstein	.15
366	David Pember RC	.15
367	Damian Rolls	.15
368	Richard Hidalgo	.15
369	Brad Radke	.15
370	Alex Sanchez	.15
371	Ben Grieve	.15
372	Brandon Inge	.15
373	Adam Piatt	.15
374	Charles Johnson	.15
375	Rafael Palmeiro	.65
376	Joe Mays	.15
377	Derek Lee	.15
378	Fernando Vina	.15
379	Andruw Jones	.75
380	Troy Glaus	.15
381	Bobby Hill	.15
382	C.C. Sabathia	.15

383	Jose Hernandez	.15
384	Al Leiter	.15
385	Jarrod Washburn	.15
386	Cody Ransom	.15
387	Matt Stairs	.15
388	Edgar Renteria	.15
389	Tsuyoshi Shinjo	.15
390	Matt Williams	.15
391	Bubba Trammell	.15
392	Jason Kendall	.15
393	Scott Rolen	.65
394	Chuck Knoblauch	.15
395	Jimmy Rollins	.25
396	Gary Bennett	.15
397	David Wells	.15
398	Ronnie Belliard	.15
399	Austin Kearns	.50
400	Tim Hudson	.30
401	Andy Van Hekken	.15
402	Ray Lankford	.15
403	Todd Helton	.75
404	Jeff Weaver	.15
405	Gabe Kapler	.15
406	Luis Gonzalez	.40
407	Sean Casey	.15
408	Kazuhiro Sasaki	.15
409	Mark Teixeira	.50
410	Brian Giles	.15
411	Robert Fick	.15
412	Wilkin Ruan	.15
413	Jose Rijo	.15
414	Ben Broussard	.15
415	Aubrey Huff	.15
416	Magglio Ordonez	.25
417	Barry Bonds	2.00
418	Miguel Tejada	.40
419	Randy Johnson	.75
420	Barry Zito	.30
421	Jason Jennings	.15
422	Eric Hinske	.15
423	Benito Santiago	.15
424	Adam Kennedy	.15
425	Troy Glaus	.65
426	Brandon Phillips	.15
427	Jake Peavy	.15
428	Jason Romano	.15
429	Jeriome Robertson	.15
430	Aaron Guiel	.15
431	Hank Blalock	.15
432	Brad Lidge	.15
433	Francisco Rodriguez	.15
434	Jaime Cerda	.15
435	Jung Bong	.15
436	Reed Johnson	.15
437	Rene Reyes	.15
438	Chris Snelling	.15
439	Miguel Olivo	.15
440	Brian Banks	.15
441	Eric Junge	.15
442	Kirk Saarloos	.15
443	Jamey Carroll	.15
444	Josh Hancock	.15
445	Michael Restovich	.15
446	William Bloomquist	.15
447	John Lackey	.15
448	Marcus Thames	.15
449	Victor Martinez	.15
450	Brett Myers	.15
451	Wes Obermueller	.15
452	Hansel Izquierdo	.15
453	Brian Tallet	.15
454	Craig Monroe	.15
455	Doug DeVore	.15
456	John Buck	.15
457	Tony Alvarez	.15
458	Wily Mo Pena	.15
459	John Stephens	.15
460	Tony Torcato	.15
461	Adam Kennedy	.15
462	Alex Rodriguez	.15
463	Derek Lowe	.15
464	Garret Anderson	.15
465	Pat Burrell	.50
466	Eric Gagne	.15
467	Tomokazu Ohka	.15
468	Josh Phelps	.15
469	Sammy Sosa	1.50
470	Jim Thome	.15
471	Vladimir Guerrero	.75
472	Jason Simontacchi	.15
473	Adam Dunn	.50
474	Jim Edmonds	.15
475	Barry Bonds	2.00
476	Paul Konerko	.25
477	Alfonso Soriano	.75
478	Curt Schilling	.40
479	John Smoltz	.15
480	Torii Hunter	.15
481	Rodrigo Lopez	.15
482	Miguel Tejada	.35
483	Eric Hinske	.15
484	Roy Oswalt	.25
485	Junior Spivey	.15

Glossy

SP's (1-100):	1-2X
Cards (101-485):	5-10X
Production 100 Sets	
Randomly inserted in Update packs.	

B/W Goudey

	NM/M
Complete Set (25):	80.00
Common Player:	1.50
Production 1,936 Sets	
Golds:	4-8X

Chicago Cubs

Production 36 Sets

1BWG	Jim Thome	2.50
2BWG	Derek Jeter	10.00
3BWG	Alex Rodriguez	8.00
4BWG	Mark Prior	1.00
5BWG	Nomar Garciaparra	6.00
6BWG	Curt Schilling	2.00
7BWG	Pat Burrell	2.00
8BWG	Frank Thomas	2.50
9BWG	Roger Clemens	5.00
10BWG	Chipper Jones	5.00
11BWG	Barry Larkin	1.50
12BWG	Hideo Nomo	2.00
13BWG	Pedro J. Martinez	3.00
14BWG	Jeff Bagwell	2.50
15BWG	Greg Maddux	5.00
16BWG	Vladimir Guerrero	3.00
17BWG	Ichiro Suzuki	6.00
18BWG	Mike Piazza	8.00
19BWG	Drew Henson	1.50
20BWG	Albert Pujols	3.00
21BWG	Sammy Sosa	5.00
22BWG	Jason Giambi	5.00
23BWG	Randy Johnson	3.00
24BWG	Ken Griffey Jr.	6.00
25BWG	Barry Bonds	8.00

Checklist

		NM/M
Complete Set (18):		6.00
Common Card:		.50
Inserted 1:4		
1CL	Derek Jeter	.50
2CL	Derek Jeter	.50
3CL	Derek Jeter	.50
4CL	Derek Jeter	.50
5CL	Derek Jeter	.50
6CL	Derek Jeter	.50
7CL	Derek Jeter	.50
8CL	Derek Jeter	.50
9CL	Derek Jeter	.50
10CL	Barry Bonds	.50
11CL	Barry Bonds	.50
12CL	Barry Bonds	.50
13CL	Barry Bonds	.50
14CL	Barry Bonds	.50
15CL	Barry Bonds	.50
16CL	Barry Bonds	.50
17CL	Barry Bonds	.50
18CL	Barry Bonds	.50

Game-Used Parallel

FRANK THOMAS
Chicago White Sox - Designated Hitter

	NM/M
Common Player:	5.00
Inserted 1:35	
Golds:	1-2X
Production 100 Sets	
Derek Jeter/Jsy/150	35.00
Craig Biggio/Bat	8.00
Hideo Nomo/Jsy/200	20.00
Barry Larkin/Jsy/200	10.00
Kazuhiro Sasaki/	
Jsy/200	10.00
Greg Maddux/Jsy	15.00
Mo Vaughn/Jsy/60	10.00
Pedro Martinez/	
Jsy/200	12.00
Barry Zito/Jsy	10.00
Luis Aparicio/Jsy/150	10.00
Willie Stargell/	
Pants/150	15.00
Nomar Garciaparra/	
Jsy/200	20.00
Edgardo Alfonzo/	
Jsy/200	8.00
John Olerud/Jsy	6.00
Juan Gonzalez/	
Bat/200	10.00
Jorge Posada/Bat	8.00
Shea Hillenbrand/Bat	10.00

Ivan Rodriguez/Jsy	8.00
Mike Lowell/Bat	5.00
Jeff Bagwell/Jsy/200	12.00
Chipper Jones/Jsy	15.00
Jeromy Burnitz/	
Jsy	6.00
Adrian Beltre/Jsy	6.00
Robin Ventura/Jsy	8.00
Frank Thomas/Jsy	10.00
Mark Grace/Jsy	10.00
Darin Erstad/Jsy	8.00
Roger Clemens/	
Jsy	20.00
J.D. Drew/Jsy	8.00
Mike Piazza/Jsy/150	20.00
Randy Johnson/	
Jsy/150	12.00
Mark Prior/Jsy/200	15.00
Kazuhisa Ishii/Jsy	10.00
Manny Ramirez/	
Jsy/150	10.00
Kerry Wood/Jsy/200	15.00
Mike Mussina/Jsy	10.00
Eric Karros/Jsy	5.00
Rafael Palmeiro/Jsy	8.00
Andruw Jones/	
Bat/150	10.00
Jason Kendall/Jsy	6.00
Jimmy Rollins/Jsy	8.00
Barry Bonds/Jsy/50	40.00
Miguel Tejada/Bat/150	8.00
Jason Jennings/Jsy	6.00

Hardball Preview

		NM/M
Complete Set (10):		125.00
Common Player:		5.00
Inserted 1:400		
1	Miguel Tejada	5.00
2	Derek Jeter	25.00
3	Mike Piazza	20.00
4	Barry Bonds	20.00
5	Mark Prior	4.00
6	Ichiro Suzuki	20.00
7	Alex Rodriguez	20.00
8	Nomar Garciaparra	15.00
9	Alfonso Soriano	12.00
10	Ken Griffey Jr.	15.00

Lumber Co.

		NM/M
Complete Set (30):		70.00
Common Player:		1.00
Inserted 1:10		
1	Mike Piazza	6.00
2	Derek Jeter	8.00
3	Alex Rodriguez	6.00
4	Miguel Tejada	1.00
5	Nomar Garciaparra	5.00
6	Andruw Jones	1.50
7	Pat Burrell	1.50
8	Albert Pujols	3.00
9	Jeff Bagwell	2.00
10	Chipper Jones	4.00
11	Ichiro Suzuki	6.00
12	Alfonso Soriano	3.00
13	Eric Chavez	1.50
14	Brian Giles	1.00
15	Shawn Green	1.50
16	Jim Thome	2.00
17	Lance Berkman	1.50
18	Bernie Williams	1.50
19	Manny Ramirez	2.00
20	Vladimir Guerrero	3.00
21	Carlos Delgado	1.25
22	Scott Rolen	1.50
23	Sammy Sosa	4.00
24	Ken Griffey Jr.	5.00
25	Barry Bonds	6.00
26	Todd Helton	1.50
27	Jason Giambi	4.00
28	Austin Kearns	1.50
29	Jeff Kent	1.50
30	Magglio Ordonez	1.00

Lumber Co. Bat

		NM/M
Common Player:		6.00
Inserted 1:108		
	Jeff Bagwell/200	15.00
	Lance Berkman/200	10.00
	Barry Bonds/150	25.00
	Pat Burrell/75	25.00
	Eric Chavez/125	8.00
	Carlos Delgado/200	6.00
	Nomar Garciaparra/	
	200	25.00
	Brian Giles/200	8.00
	Shawn Green/200	8.00
	Todd Helton	8.00
	Derek Jeter/96	35.00
	Andruw Jones	8.00
	Chipper Jones	15.00
	Austin Kearns/75	18.00

Jeff Kent/200	6.00
Magglio Ordonez	6.00
Mike Piazza/200	20.00
Manny Ramirez	10.00
Alex Rodriguez	15.00
Scott Rolen/80	8.00
Alfonso Soriano/200	12.00
Miguel Tejada	10.00
Jim Thome/200	12.00
Bernie Williams	10.00

Lumber Co. Bat Gold

		NM/M
Numbered to 2002 HR total.		
Lance Berkman/42	25.00
Barry Bonds/46	70.00
Pat Burrell/37	50.00
Eric Chavez/34	20.00
Carlos Delgado/33	35.00
Nomar Garciaparra/	
24	60.00
Brian Giles/38	25.00
Shawn Green/42	35.00
Todd Helton/30	35.00
Derek Jeter/18	200.00
Andruw Jones/35	25.00
Chipper Jones/26	45.00
Austin Kearns/13	35.00
Jeff Kent/37	20.00
Magglio Ordonez/38	25.00
Mike Piazza/33	65.00
Alex Rodriguez/57	40.00
Miguel Tejada/34	35.00
Jim Thome/52	30.00

Milestones

		NM/M
Complete Set (25):		40.00
Common Player:		1.00
Inserted 1:5		
1	Eddie Mathews	1.50
2	Rickey Henderson	1.50
3	Harmon Killebrew	1.50
4	Al Kaline	2.50
5	Willie McCovey	1.00
6	Tom Seaver	2.00
7	Reggie Jackson	2.00
8	Mike Schmidt	3.00
9	Nolan Ryan	5.00
10	Mike Piazza	4.00
11	Randy Johnson	2.00
12	Bernie Williams	1.50
13	Rafael Palmeiro	1.50
14	Juan Gonzalez	1.50
15	Ken Griffey Jr.	3.00
16	Derek Jeter	5.00
17	Roger Clemens	3.00
18	Roberto Alomar	1.50
19	Manny Ramirez	1.50
20	Luis Gonzalez	1.00
21	Barry Bonds	4.00
22	Nomar Garciaparra	3.00
23	Fred McGriff	1.00
24	Greg Maddux	2.50
25	Barry Bonds	4.00

Milestones Game-Used

	NM/M
Common Player:	8.00
Inserted 1:143	
Golds:	1-2X
Production 100 Sets	
Roberto Alomar/	
Bat/200	8.00
Barry Bonds/600 HR/	
Bat/100	30.00
Barry Bonds/5 MVP/	
Jsy/200	25.00
Roger Clemens/	
Jsy/150	20.00
Nomar Garciaparra/	
Jsy/200	20.00
Juan Gonzalez/	
Bat/250	10.00
Derek Jeter/Jsy/150	35.00
Randy Johnson/	
Jsy/100	15.00
Greg Maddux/200	20.00
Fred McGriff	5.00
Rafael Palmeiro/	
Jsy/200	8.00
Mike Piazza/Jsy/100	20.00

Manny Ramirez/	
Jsy/150	10.00
Bernie Williams/	
Jsy/200	10.00

Standouts

ALEX RODRIGUEZ
SHORTSTOP   TEXAS RANGERS*

		NM/M
Complete Set (15):		60.00
Common Player:		1.50
Inserted 1:40		
1SO	Greg Maddux	5.00
2SO	Derek Jeter	10.00
3SO	Alex Rodriguez	8.00
4SO	Miguel Tejada	2.00
5SO	Nomar Garciaparra	6.00
6SO	Barry Bonds	8.00
7SO	Pat Burrell	2.00
8SO	Ken Griffey Jr.	6.00
9SO	Alfonso Soriano	4.00
10SO	Mike Piazza	8.00
11SO	Sammy Sosa	5.00
12SO	Ichiro Suzuki	6.00
13SO	Vladimir Guerrero	3.00
14SO	Roger Clemens	5.00
15SO	Adam Dunn	2.50

Update

ROOKIE
'03
DELMON YOUNG
Tampa Bay Devil Rays™ - Outfield

		NM/M
Complete Set (398):		175.00
Common Player:		.15
Common Rookie (286-398):		.50
Cards (286-299):		
Inserted 1:4		
Pack (10):		2.00
Box (32 + 25 count		
update box):		50.00
1	Aaron Boone	.15
2	Carl Everett	.15
3	Eduardo Perez	.15
4	Jason Michaels	.15
5	Karim Garcia	.15
6	Rainier Olmedo	.15
7	Scott Williamson	.15
8	Adam Kennedy	.15
9	Carl Pavano	.15
10	Eli Marrero	.15
11	Jason Simontacchi	.15
12	Keith Foulke	.15
13	Preston Wilson	.15
14	Scott Hatteberg	.15
15	Adam Dunn	.50
16	Carlos Baerga	.15
17	Elmer Dessens	.15
18	Javier Vazquez	.15
19	Kenny Rogers	.15
20	Quinton McCracken	.15
21	Shane Reynolds	.15
22	Adam Eaton	.15
23	Carlos Zambrano	.15
24	Enrique Wilson	.15
25	Jeff DaVanon	.15
26	Kenny Lofton	.15
27	Ramon Castro	.15
28	Shannon Stewart	.15
29	Al Martin	.15
30	Carlos Guillen	.15
31	Eric Karros	.15
32	Tim Worrell	.15
33	Kevin Millwood	.25
34	Randall Simon	.15
35	Shawn Chacon	.15
36	Alex Rodriguez	1.50
37	Casey Blake	.15
38	Eric Munson	.15
39	Jeff Kent	.25
40	Kris Benson	.15
41	Randy Winn	.15
42	Shea Hillenbrand	.15

43	Alfonso Soriano	1.00
44	Chris George	.15
45	Eric Bruntlett	.15
46	Jeromy Burnitz	.15
47	Kyle Farnsworth	.15
48	Torii Hunter	.40
49	Sidney Ponson	.15
50	Andres Galarraga	.25
51	Chris Singleton	.15
52	Eric Gagne	.25
53	Jesse Foppert	.15
54	Lance Carter	.15
55	Ray Durham	.15
56	Tanyon Sturtze	.15
57	Andy Ashby	.15
58	Cliff Floyd	.15
59	Eric Young	.15
60	Jhonny Peralta	.50
61	Livan Hernandez	.15
62	Reggie Sanders	.15
63	Tim Spooneybarger	.15
64	Angel Berroa	.15
65	Coco Crisp	.15
66	Eric Hinske	.15
67	Jim Edmonds	.25
68	Luis Matos	.15
69	Rickey Henderson	.40
70	Todd Walker	.15
71	Antonio Alfonseca	.15
72	Corey Koskie	.15
73	Erubiel Durazo	.15
74	Jim Thome	.50
75	Lyle Overbay	.15
76	Robert Fick	.15
77	Todd Hollandsworth	.15
78	Aramis Ramirez	.15
79	Cristian Guzman	.15
80	Esteban Loaiza	.15
81	Jody Gerut	.15
82	Mark Grudzielanek	.15
83	Roberto Alomar	.40
84	Todd Hundley	.15
85	Mike Hampton	.15
86	Curt Schilling	.40
87	Francisco Rodriguez	.15
88	John Lackey	.15
89	Mark Redman	.15
90	Robin Ventura	.25
91	Todd Zeile	.15
92	B.J. Surhoff	.15
93	Raul Mondesi	.15
94	Frank Catalanotto	.15
95	John Smoltz	.25
96	Mark Ellis	.15
97	Rocco Baldelli	.50
98	Todd Pratt	.15
99	Barry Bonds	2.00
100	Danny Graves	.15
101	Fred McGriff	.25
102	John Burkett	.15
103	Marquis Grissom	.15
104	Rocky Biddle	.15
105	Tom Glavine	.25
106	Bartolo Colon	.25
107	Darren Bragg	.15
108	Gabe Kapler	.15
109	John Franco	.15
110	Matt Mantei	.15
111	Rod Beck	.15
112	Tomokazu Ohka	.15
113	Ben Petrick	.15
114	Darren Dreifort	.15
115	Garret Anderson	.25
116	John Vander Wal	.15
117	Melvin Mora	.15
118	Rodrigo Lopez	.15
119	Raul Ibanez	.15
120	Benito Santiago	.15
121	David Ortiz	.25
122	Gary Bennett	.15
123	Jon Garland	.15
124	Michael Young	.15
125	Rodrigo Rosario	.15
126	Travis Lee	.15
127	Bill Mueller	.15
128	Derek Lowe	.15
129	Gil Meche	.15
130	Jose Guillen	.15
131	Miguel Cabrera	.40
132	Ron Calloway	.15
133	Troy Percival	.15
134	Billy Koch	.15
135	Dmitri Young	.15
136	Glendon Rusch	.15
137	Jose Jimenez	.15
138	Miguel Tejada	.40
139	John Thomson	.15
140	Troy O'Leary	.15
141	Bobby Kielty	.15
142	Dontrelle Willis	.50
143	Greg Myers	.15
144	Jose Vizcaino	.15
145	Mike MacDougal	.15
146	Ronnie Belliard	.15
147	Tyler Houston	.15
148	Brady Clark	.15
149	Edgardo Alfonzo	.15
150	Guillermo Mota	.15
151	Jose Lima	.15
152	Mike Williams	.15
153	Roy Oswalt	.25
154	Scott Podsednik	.15
155	Brandon Lyon	.15
156	Henry Mateo	.15
157	Jose Macias	.15
158	Mike Bordick	.15
159	Royce Clayton	.15
160	Vance Wilson	.15

161	Brent Abernathy	.15
162	Horacio Ramirez	.15
163	Jose Reyes	.50
164	Nick Punto	.15
165	Ruben Sierra	.15
166	Victor Zambrano	.15
167	Brett Tomko	.15
168	Ivan Rodriguez	.75
169	Jose Mesa	.15
170	Octavio Dotel	.15
171	Russ Ortiz	.15
172	Vladimir Guerrero	.75
173	Brian Lawrence	.15
174	Jae Weong Seo	.15
175	Jose Cruz Jr.	.15
176	Pat Burrell	.40
177	Russell Branyan	.15
178	Warren Morris	.15
179	Brian Boehringer	.15
180	Jason Johnson	.15
181	Josh Phelps	.15
182	Paul Konerko	.15
183	Ryan Franklin	.15
184	Wes Helms	.15
185	Brooks Kieschnick	.15
186	Jason Davis	.15
187	Juan Pierre	.15
188	Paul Wilson	.15
189	Sammy Sosa	1.50
190	Wil Cordero	.15
191	Byung-Hyun Kim	.15
192	Juan Encarnacion	.15
193	Placido Polanco	.15
194	Sandy Alomar	.15
195	Julio Lugo	.15
196	Junior Spivey	.15
197	Woody Williams	.15
198	Xavier Nady	.15
199	Mark Loretta	.15
200	Deivi Cruz	.15
201	Jorge Posada	.25
202	Carlos Delgado	.25
203	Alfonso Soriano	.50
204	Alex Rodriguez	1.00
205	Troy Glaus	.25
206	Garret Anderson	.15
207	Hideki Matsui	2.00
208	Ichiro Suzuki	.75
209	Esteban Loaiza	.15
210	Manny Ramirez	.25
211	Roger Clemens	.75
212	Roy Halladay	.15
213	Jason Giambi	.25
214	Edgar Martinez	.15
215	Bret Boone	.15
216	Hank Blalock	.15
217	Nomar Garciaparra	.75
218	Vernon Wells	.15
219	Melvin Mora	.15
220	Magglio Ordonez	.25
221	Mike Sweeney	.15
222	Barry Zito	.25
223	Carl Everett	.15
224	Shigetoshi Hasegawa	.15
225	Jamie Moyer	.15
226	Mark Mulder	.15
227	Eddie Guardado	.15
228	Ramon Hernandez	.15
229	Keith Foulke	.15
230	Javy Lopez	.15
231	Todd Helton	.25
232	Marcus Giles	.15
233	Edgar Renteria	.25
234	Scott Rolen	.25
235	Barry Bonds	1.00
236	Albert Pujols	.75
237	Gary Sheffield	.25
238	Jim Edmonds	.25
239	Jason Schmidt	.15
240	Mark Prior	1.00
241	Dontrelle Willis	.25
242	Kerry Wood	.25
243	Kevin Brown	.15
244	Woody Williams	.15
245	Paul LoDuca	.15
246	Richie Sexson	.15
247	Jose Vidro	.15
248	Luis Castillo	.15
249	Aaron Boone	.15
250	Mike Lowell	.25
251	Rafael Furcal	.15
252	Andruw Jones	.25
253	Preston Wilson	.15
254	John Smoltz	.25
255	Eric Gagne	.25
256	Randy Wolf	.15
257	Billy Wagner	.15
258	Luis Gonzalez	.25
259	Russ Ortiz	.15
260	Jim Thome,	
	Pedro J. Martinez	.40
261	Alfonso Soriano,	
	Jeff Bagwell	.25
262	Dontrelle Willis,	
	Rocco Baldelli	
263	Carlos Delgado,	
	Vladimir Guerrero	.25
264	Sammy Sosa,	
	Magglio Ordonez	.50
265	Jason Giambi,	
	Adam Dunn	.25
266	Mike Sweeney,	
	Albert Pujols	.50
267	Barry Bonds,	
	Torii Hunter	.75
268	Ichiro Suzuki,	
	Andruw Jones	.15

269 Chipper Jones, Hank Blalock .50
270 Mark Prior, Vernon Wells .75
271 Nomar Garciaparra, Scott Rolen .75
272 Alex Rodriguez, Lance Berkman .75
273 Roger Clemens, Kerry Wood .75
274 Derek Jeter, Jose Reyes .75
275 Greg Maddux, Barry Zito .50
276 Carlos Delgado .25
277 J.D. Drew .15
278 Barry Bonds 1.00
279 Albert Pujols .75
280 Jim Thome .25
281 Sammy Sosa .75
282 Alfonso Soriano .50
283 Hideki Matsui 1.00
284 Mike Piazza .50
285 Vladimir Guerrero .40
286 Rich Harden .50
287 Chin-Hui Tsao .50
288 Edwin Jackson RC 4.00
289 Chien-Ming Wang RC 6.00
290 Josh Willingham RC 2.00
291 Matt Kata RC 2.00
292 Jose Contreras 2.00
293 Chris Bootcheck .50
294 Javier Lopez 1.00
295 Delmon Young RC 8.00
296 Pedro Liriano .50
297 Noah Lowry .50
298 Khalil Greene 3.00
299 Rob Bowen .50
300 Bo Hart RC 2.00
301 Beau Kemp RC .25
302 Gerald Laird .15
303 Miguel Ojeda RC .40
304 Todd Wellemeyer RC .75
305 Ryan Wagner RC 2.00
306 Jeff Duncan RC 1.50
307 Wilfredo Ledezma RC .15
308 Wes Obermueller .15
309 Bernie Castro RC .25
310 Tim Olson RC .25
311 Colin Porter RC 2.00
312 Francisco Cruceta RC 1.50
313 Guillermo Quiroz RC 1.50
314 Brian Stokes RC .50
315 Robby Hammock RC .50
316 Lew Ford RC 2.00
317 Todd Linden .15
318 Mike Gallo RC .50
319 Francisco Rosario RC 1.50
320 Rosman Garcia RC .50
321 Felix Sanchez RC .50
322 Chad Gaudin RC 1.00
323 Phil Seibel RC .50
324 Jason Gilfillan RC .50
325 Terrmel Sledge RC .75
326 Alfredo Gonzalez RC .50
327 Josh Stewart RC 1.00
328 Jeremy Griffiths .15
329 Cory Stewart RC .50
330 Josh Hall RC 1.00
331 Arnie Munoz RC .50
332 Garrett Atkins .15
333 Neal Cotts .15
334 Dan Haren 2.00
335 Shane Victorino RC .50
336 David Sanders RC .50
337 Oscar Villarreal RC .50
338 Michael Hessman RC .50
339 Andrew Brown RC .50
340 Kevin Hooper .50
341 Prentice Redman RC .50
342 Brandon Webb RC 3.00
343 Jimmy Gobble .15
344 Pete LaForest RC .50
345 Chris Waters RC .75
346 Hideki Matsui RC 8.00
347 Chris Capuano RC 1.00
348 Jon Leicester RC .50
349 Mike Nicolas RC .50
350 Nook Logan RC .50
351 Craig Brazell RC 1.00
352 Aaron Looper RC .50
353 D.J. Carrasco RC .50
354 Clint Barmes RC 1.00
355 Doug Waechter RC .75
356 Julio Manon RC .50
357 Jeremy Bonderman 3.00
358 Diegomar Markwell RC .50
359 Dave Matranga RC .75
360 Luis Ayala RC .50
361 Jason Stanford RC .50
362 Roger Deago RC .50
363 Geoff Geary RC .50
364 Edgar Gonzalez RC .50
365 Michel Hernandez RC .50
366 Aquilino Lopez RC .50
367 David Manning RC 1.00
368 Carlos Mendez RC .50
369 Matt Miller RC .15
370 Micheal Nakamura RC 1.00
371 Mike Neu RC .50
372 Ramon Nivar RC .50
373 Kevin Ohme RC .50
374 Alex Prieto RC 1.00
375 Stephen Randolph RC .50
376 Brian Sweeney RC 1.00
377 Matt Diaz RC .50
378 Mike Gonzalez .15
379 Daniel Cabrera RC 2.00

380 Fernando Cabrera RC .50
381 David DeJesus RC .50
382 Mike Ryan RC 1.00
383 Rick Roberts RC .50
384 Seung Jun Song .15
385 Rickie Weeks RC 6.00
386 Humberto Quintero RC .50
387 Alexis Rios .15
388 Aaron Miles RC 2.00
389 Tom Gregorio RC .50
390 Anthony Ferrari RC .75
391 Kevin Correia RC .50
392 Rafael Betancourt RC .75
393 Rett Johnson RC .50
394 Richard Fischer RC .50
395 Greg Aquino RC .50
396 Daniel Garcia RC 1.00
397 Sergio Mitre RC 1.00
398 Edwin Almonte .15

Update Glossy

ELI MARRERO
Cardinals - Outfield

Stars (1-285): 5-10X
Rookies (286-398): .5-1.5X
Production 100 Sets

Update Diamond Debuts

NM/M
Complete Set (25): 40.00
Common Player: 1.00
Inserted 1:10
1 Dontrelle Willis 4.00
2 Bo Hart 1.00
3 Jose Reyes 4.00
4 Chin-Hui Tsao 1.00
5 Brandon Webb 3.00
6 Rich Harden 2.00
7 Jesse Foppert 1.00
8 Rocco Baldelli 2.00
9 Hideki Matsui 5.00
10 Ron Calloway 1.00
11 Jeremy Bonderman 1.50
12 Mark Teixeira 3.00
13 Ryan Wagner 2.00
14 Jose Contreras 2.00
15 Miguel Cabrera 4.00
16 Lew Ford 1.00
17 Jeff Duncan 1.50
18 Matt Kata 1.00
19 Jeremy Griffiths 1.00
20 Todd Wellemeyer 1.00
21 Robby Hammock 1.00
22 Dave Matranga 1.00
23 Laynce Nix 1.00
24 Jhonny Peralta 1.00
25 Oscar Villarreal 1.00

Update Long GONE!

NM/M
Complete Set (20): 60.00
Common Player:
Quantity produced listed
1 Barry Bonds/475 8.00
2 Jason Giambi/440 2.00
3 Albert Pujols/452 6.00
4 Chipper Jones/420 2.00
5 Manny Ramirez/430 2.00
6 Sammy Sosa/536 5.00
7 Alfonso Soriano/440 3.00
8 Alex Rodriguez/430 6.00
9 Jim Thome/445 3.00
10 Vladimir Guerrero/502 3.00
11 Austin Kearns/430 2.00
12 Jeff Bagwell/420 2.00
13 Andruw Jones/430 2.00
14 Carlos Delgado/451 2.00
15 Nomar Garciaparra/440 6.00
16 Adam Dunn/464 2.00
17 Mike Piazza/450 4.00
18 Derek Jeter/410 6.00
19 Ken Griffey Jr./420 4.00
20 Hank Blalock/424 3.00

Update Milestones

ALFONSO SORIANO

NM/M
Complete Set (20): 25.00
Common Player: 1.00
Inserted 1:8
1 Roger Clemens 3.00
2 Rafael Palmeiro 1.00
3 Jeff Bagwell 1.00
4 Barry Bonds 4.00
5 Sammy Sosa 2.50
6 Albert Pujols 3.00
7 Ichiro Suzuki 2.00
8 Alfonso Soriano 1.00
9 Alex Rodriguez 3.00
10 Randy Johnson 1.50
11 Manny Ramirez 1.00
12 Chipper Jones 2.00
13 Todd Helton 1.00
14 Ken Griffey Jr. 2.00
15 Jim Thome 1.00
16 Frank Thomas 1.00
17 Pedro J. Martinez 1.50
18 Hideo Nomo 1.00
19 Jason Schmidt 1.00
20 Carlos Delgado 1.00

Update Milestones Memorabilia

NM/M
Common Player: 5.00
Inserted 1:20
Golds: 1-2X
Production 100 Sets
Roger Clemens 15.00
Rafael Palmeiro 5.00
Jeff Bagwell 8.00
Sammy Sosa 10.00
Alfonso Soriano 10.00
Alex Rodriguez 10.00
Randy Johnson 8.00
Manny Ramirez 5.00
Chipper Jones 5.00
Todd Helton 6.00
Jim Thome 8.00
Frank Thomas 8.00
Pedro J. Martinez 8.00
Hideo Nomo 8.00
Jason Schmidt 8.00
Carlos Delgado 5.00

Update Milestones Memorabilia Gold

Complete Set (16):
Common Player:

Update Throwback Threads

AL LEITER

NM/M
Common Player: 4.00
Inserted 1:64
Kevin Millwood 6.00
Vladimir Guerrero 8.00
Troy Glaus 6.00
Mike Piazza 10.00
Al Leiter 4.00

Update Throwback Threads Dual

NM/M
Production 100
Vladimir Guerrero, Troy Glaus 15.00
Mike Piazza, Al Leiter 15.00

Update Throwback Threads Patch

NM/M
Common Player: 10.00
Production 100 Sets
Kevin Millwood 15.00
Vladimir Guerrero 20.00
Troy Glaus 15.00
Mike Piazza 25.00
Al Leiter 10.00

Update Turn Back the Clock

NM/M
Complete Set (10): 75.00
Common Player: 4.00
Inserted 1:160
1 Yogi Berra 8.00
2 Mike Schmidt 15.00
3 Tom Seaver 6.00
4 Reggie Jackson 5.00
5 Pee Wee Reese 4.00
6 Phil Rizzuto 4.00
7 Jim Palmer 4.00
8 Robin Yount 15.00
9 Nolan Ryan 20.00
10 Al Kaline 10.00

Cub Foods

OMAR VIZQUEL INDIANS / SS

In an unusual 2" x 2-3/4" format, these cards were distributed in 24-can cubes of soda, reportedly only at Cub Foods stores in the Upper Midwest. Fronts have player portraits over team logos on a white background. Cub Foods and Pepsi logos are at bottom. Backs have personal data, recent stats, career highlights and a team logo.

NM/M
Complete Set (10): 7.50
Common Player: .50
1 Ichiro 2.00
2 Kerry Wood .75
3 Mike Piazza 1.00
4 Randy Johnson .75
5 Magglio Ordonez .50
6 Brad Radke .50
7 Omar Vizquel .50
8 Ben Sheets .50
9 Barry Zito .50
10 Ken Griffey Jr. 2.00

Pepsi-Cola

MIKE PIAZZA Mets

2004 Fleer America's National Pastime

MIGUEL CABRERA / FLORIDA MARLINS

NM/M
Common Player (1-60): .25
Minor Stars (1-60): .60
Unlisted Stars (1-60): .75
Common Star (61-90): 3.00
Production 699 Sets
Pack (5): 10.00
Box (10): 100.00
1 Hideki Matsui 2.50
2 Khalil Greene 1.00
3 Pedro J. Martinez 1.00
4 Sammy Sosa 2.00
5 Mark Teixeira .40
6 Orlando Cabrera .25
7 Scott Podsednik .25
8 Miguel Tejada .60
9 Andruw Jones .75
10 Manny Ramirez .75
11 Jose Reyes .25
12 Bobby Abreu .40
13 Alex Rodriguez 2.50
14 Ivan Rodriguez .60
15 Jason Schmidt .40
16 Mike Piazza 1.50
17 Eric Chavez .40
18 Mark Prior 1.50
19 Adam Dunn .60
20 Richard Hidalgo .25
21 Todd Helton 1.00
22 Rocco Baldelli .60
23 Roy Oswalt .40
24 Angel Berroa .25
25 Jason Giambi 1.00
26 Jim Thome 1.00
27 Javy Lopez .40
28 Derek Jeter 3.00
29 Tom Glavine .40
30 Magglio Ordonez .40
31 Austin Kearns .60
32 Scott Rolen 1.00
33 Miguel Cabrera .75
34 Vernon Wells .40
35 Frank Thomas .75
36 Jeff Bagwell .75
37 Shannon Stewart .25
38 Richie Sexson .60
39 Hideo Nomo .40
40 Nomar Garciaparra 2.50
41 C.C. Sabathia .25
42 Albert Pujols 2.50
43 Barry Zito .60
44 Hank Blalock .60
45 Carlos Delgado .40
46 Greg Maddux 1.50
47 Randy Johnson 1.00
48 Josh Beckett .75
49 Kerry Wood .75
50 Roger Clemens 1.50
51 Garret Anderson .40
52 Ichiro Suzuki 2.00
53 Kip Wells .25
54 Vladimir Guerrero 1.00
55 Shawn Green .40
56 Chipper Jones 1.50
57 Aubrey Huff .25
58 Ken Griffey Jr. 1.50
59 Torii Hunter .50
60 Alfonso Soriano 1.00
61 Chris Shelton RC 8.00
62 Graham Koonce RC 4.00
63 Kazuo Matsui RC 8.00
64 Alfredo Simon RC 4.00
65 Mike Gosling RC 4.00
66 Mike Rouse RC 4.00
67 Mariano Gomez RC 4.00
68 Justin Leone RC 3.00
69 Jose Capellan RC 3.00
70 Donald Kelly RC 4.00
71 Merkin Valdez RC 4.00
72 Greg Dobbs RC 4.00
73 Shingo Takatsu RC 4.00
74 Chris Aguila RC 3.00
75 Jerome Gamble RC 4.00
76 Onil Joseph RC 4.00
77 Ramon Ramirez RC 4.00
78 Angel Chavez RC 3.00
79 Hector Gimenez RC 4.00
80 Ivan Ochoa RC 4.00
81 Aarom Baldiris RC 4.00
82 Akinori Otsuka RC 4.00
83 Ruddy Yan RC 4.00
84 Jerry Gil RC 3.00
85 Shawn Hill RC 3.00
86 John Gall RC 4.00
87 Jason Bartlett RC 4.00
88 Jorge Sequea RC 4.00
89 Luis Gonzalez RC 4.00
90 Sean Henn 3.00

Red

VLADIMIR GUERRERO / ANAHEIM ANGELS

(1-60): 1-4X
(61-90): .75-1.25X
Production 150 Sets

White

MARK TEIXEIRA / TEXAS RANGERS

(1-60): 2-6X
(61-90): .75-2X
Production 50 Sets

Blue

No Pricing
Production One Set

American Flag Box Topper

No Pricing
Numbered to indicated quantity.

American GAME

NM/M
Common Player: 1.00
Inserted 1:10 (Hobby)
Inserted 1:12 (Retail)
1 Greg Maddux 2.50
2 Randy Johnson 2.00
3 Roger Clemens 4.00
4 Mark Prior 3.00
5 Mike Piazza 2.50
6 Alex Rodriguez 4.00
7 Adam Dunn 1.00
8 Jim Thome 2.00
9 Derek Jeter 5.00
10 Scott Rolen 4.00
11 Nomar Garciaparra 4.00
12 Kerry Wood 1.50
13 Chipper Jones 2.50
14 Frank Thomas 1.50
15 Jeff Bagwell 1.50

American Game Retired - Dual

Numbered between 10 & 25.
No Pricing

American Game Retired - Single

Numbered between 6 & 31.
No Pricing

American GAME - Jersey

NM/M
Common Player: 8.00
Inserted 1:96
Patch #'d between 25 & 50: 2-6X
Patch #'d less than 25: No Pricing
Masterpiece: No Pricing
Production One Set
AM-JB Jeff Bagwell/50 8.00
AM-RCL Roger Clemens/47 10.00
AM-AD Adam Dunn/30 8.00

AM-DJ Derek Jeter/10 15.00
AM-RJO Randy Johnson/42 8.00
AM-CJ Chipper Jones/37 10.00
AM-GM Greg Maddux/46 12.00
AM-MP Mike Piazza/29 10.00
AM-MPR Mark Prior/45 10.00
AM-AR Alex Rodriguez/13 15.00
AM-SR Scott Rolen/49 8.00
AM-FT Frank Thomas/35 8.00
AM-JT Jim Thome/47 8.00
AM-KW Kerry Wood/43 8.00

History in the Making

NM/M
Common Player: .75
Inserted 1:5 (Hobby)
Inserted 1:4 (Retail)
1 Pedro J. Martinez 1.50
2 Alex Rodriguez 3.00
3 Sammy Sosa 2.50
4 Mike Piazza 2.00
5 Jason Giambi 1.50
6 Jim Thome 1.50
7 Derek Jeter 4.00
8 Hideo Nomo .75
9 Nomar Garciaparra 3.00
10 Albert Pujols 3.00
11 Greg Maddux 2.00
12 Randy Johnson 1.50
13 Roger Clemens 2.00
14 Ichiro Suzuki 2.50
15 Vladimir Guerrero 1.50
16 Chipper Jones 2.00
17 Ken Griffey Jr. 2.00
18 Manny Ramirez 1.00
19 Ivan Rodriguez .75
20 Mark Prior 2.00
21 Austin Kearns .75
22 Alfonso Soriano 1.50
23 Barry Zito .75
24 Josh Beckett 1.00
25 Angel Berroa .75
26 Jose Reyes .75
27 Adam Dunn .75
28 Todd Helton 1.00
29 Hank Blalock .75
30 Kazuo Matsui 6.00

History in the Making - Jersey

NM/M
Common Player: 5.00
Inserted 1:36
Patch: 2-6X
Numbered between 20 & 50.
Masterpiece: No Pricing
Production One Set
HM-JB Josh Beckett/45 8.00
HM-AB Angel Berroa/20 5.00
HM-MB Hank Blalock/48 8.00
HM-RC Roger Clemens/26 10.00
HM-AD Adam Dunn/49 8.00
HM-JG Jason Giambi/24 8.00
HM-VG Vladimir Guerrero/50 8.00
HM-TH Todd Helton/32 8.00
HM-DJ Derek Jeter/22 15.00
HM-RJ Randy Johnson/50 8.00
HM-CJ Chipper Jones/48 10.00
HM-AK Austin Kearns/41 8.00
HM-GM Greg Maddux/47 12.00
HM-PM Pedro J. Martinez/45 8.00
HM-KM Kazuo Matsui/20 20.00
HM-HN Hideo Nomo/50 5.00
HM-MP Mike Piazza/106 10.00
HM-MPR Mark Prior/49 10.00
HM-AP Albert Pujols/46 15.00
HM-MR Manny Ramirez/46 8.00
HM-JR Jose Reyes/37 5.00
HM-AR Alex Rodriguez/21 15.00
HM-AS Alfonso Soriano/48 8.00
HM-SS Sammy Sosa/39 12.00
HM-JT Jim Thome/49 8.00
HM-BZ Barry Zito/44 8.00

History in the Making Dual Swatch

No Pricing
Production Five Sets

National Treasures

NM/M
Common Card: 3.00
Production 500 Sets
Gold: Numbered to notable year
#75-99: 1-3X
#25-74: 1-5X
Less than 25: No Pricing
2NT Kenesaw Landis 3.00

5NT Leo Durocher 3.00
9NT Peter Gammons 3.00
10NT Ernie Harwell 3.00
11NT Billy Martin 4.00
12NT John McGraw 3.00
13NT Red Barber 3.00
15NT Casey Stengel 3.00
16NT Sparky Anderson 3.00
17NT Harry Caray 4.00
18NT Ban Johnson 3.00
20NT Ralph Kiner 3.00

National Treasures - Red

NM/M
Peter Gammons/50 20.00
Ernie Harwell/50 20.00
Ralph Kiner/50 20.00

National Treasures - White

NM/M
Ernie Harwell/30 15.00

National Treasures - Blue

No Pricing

2004 Fleer ANP National Treasures - Masterpiece

No Pricing

2004 Fleer ANP Signature Swing - Red

NM/M
Numbered to indicated quantity.
Carlos Beltran/109 25.00
Lance Berkman/98 20.00
Hank Blalock/109 20.00
George Brett/42 120.00
Sean Casey/108 15.00
Eric Chavez/85 20.00
Bucky Dent/35 20.00
David Eckstein/76 15.00
Carlton Fisk/51 40.00
Lew Ford/109 20.00
Jay Gibbons/33 20.00
Luis Gonzalez/109 10.00
Chipper Jones/88 40.00
Al Kaline/43 50.00
Javy Lopez/65 20.00
Don Mattingly/73 50.00
Bill Mazeroski/56 30.00
Stan Musial/36 60.00
Jim Palmer/25 25.00
Dave Parker/79 15.00
Mike Piazza/31 125.00
Albert Pujols/76 150.00
Gary Sheffield/26 60.00
Bill "Moose" Skowron/59 15.00
Warren Spahn/106 40.00
Alan Trammell/89 15.00

Signature Swing - White

NM/M
Numbered to indicated quantity.
Carlos Beltran/29 25.00
Lance Berkman/42 25.00
Hank Blalock/29 30.00
George Brett/30 120.00
Joe Carter/35 20.00
Sean Casey/25 25.00
Eric Chavez/34 25.00
Jim Edmonds/42 20.00
Carlton Fisk/37 40.00
Jay Gibbons/28 20.00
Luis Gonzalez/57 20.00
Vladimir Guerrero/44 30.00
Frank Howard/48 25.00
Aubrey Huff/34 15.00
Chipper Jones/45 50.00
Al Kaline/29 50.00
Javy Lopez/43 20.00
Edgar Martinez/37 30.00
Don Mattingly/35 80.00
Stan Musial/39 60.00
Rafael Palmeiro/47 50.00

Dave Parker/34 15.00
Mike Piazza/40 125.00
Albert Pujols/43 175.00
Cal Ripken Jr./25 200.00
Ivan Rodriguez/35 50.00
Scott Rolen/28 80.00
Gary Sheffield/43 60.00
Bill "Moose" Skowron/28 20.00
Frank Thomas/43 80.00
Alan Trammell/28 20.00

Signature Swing - Blue

NM/M
Numbered to indicated quantity.
Sean Casey/31 40.00
Adam Dunn/31 20.00
David Eckstein/44 15.00
Jim Edmonds/37 20.00
Lew Ford/44 40.00
Bill Mazeroski/39 50.00
Jim Palmer/44 25.00
Dave Parker/29 15.00
Scott Podsednik/38 20.00
Warren Spahn/26 50.00

Signature Swing - Gold

NM/M
Numbered to indicated quantity.
Carlos Beltran/176 25.00
Lance Berkman/173 15.00
Hank Blalock/265 15.00
Joe Carter/95 12.00
Sean Casey/169 12.00
Eric Chavez/138 15.00
David Eckstein/161 10.00
Carlton Fisk/36 40.00
Lew Ford/183 20.00
Luis Gonzalez/61 15.00
Frank Howard/20 20.00
Derek Jeter/35 125.00
Chipper Jones/116 40.00
Al Kaline/79 40.00
Javy Lopez/220 15.00
Edgar Martinez/85 20.00
Bill Mazeroski/61 25.00
Jim Palmer/33 25.00
Dave Parker/57 15.00
Mike Piazza/64 100.00
Albert Pujols/110 125.00
Gary Sheffield/25 60.00
Warren Spahn/188 30.00
Alan Trammell/138 10.00

Signature Swing - Masterpiece

No Pricing

Signs of the Future - Red

NM/M
Numbered to indicated quantity.
Aarom Baldiris/64 10.00
Jeremy Bonderman/120 10.00
A.J. Burnett/58 20.00
Miguel Cabrera/133 25.00
Bobby Crosby/114 20.00
Adam Everett/106 12.00
Luis Gonzalez/132 10.00
Mike Gosling/132 10.00
Khalil Greene/121 50.00
Rich Harden/133 15.00
Sean Henn/128 10.00
Koyie Hill/58 12.00
Edwin Jackson/125 15.00
Graham Koonce/55 10.00
Josh Labandeira/55 8.00
Adam LaRoche/124 8.00
Justin Leone/68 8.00
Micheal Nakamura/133 10.00
Bubba Nelson/99 8.00
Jose Reyes/93 25.00
Mike Rouse/124 8.00
Alfredo Simon/112 10.00
Ryan Wagner/98 12.00
Kerry Wood/55 30.00
Kevin Youkilis/133 20.00

Signs of the Future - White

NM/M
Numbered to indicated quantity.
Garrett Atkins/25 15.00
Miguel Cabrera/34 40.00
Bobby Crosby/52 30.00
Adam Everett/36 15.00
Luis Gonzalez/50 15.00
Mike Gosling/41 12.00

Khalil Greene/52 80.00
Rich Harden/52 20.00
Sean Henn/48 12.00
Koyie Hill/27 15.00
Tim Hudson/28 40.00
Adam LaRoche/50 12.00
Micheal Nakamura/33 15.00
Jose Reyes/52 30.00
Alexis Rios/39 15.00
Mike Rouse/40 10.00
Alfredo Simon/28 15.00
Ryan Wagner/46 15.00
Kevin Youkilis/52 25.00

Signs of the Future - Blue

NM/M
Numbered to indicated quantity.
Javier Vazquez/98 15.00
Kerry Wood/98 25.00

Signs of the Future - Gold

NM/M
Numbered to indicated quantity.
Jeremy Bonderman/300 8.00
Miguel Cabrera/300 20.00
Bobby Crosby/299 20.00
Adam Everett/285 10.00
Luis Gonzalez/264 8.00
Mike Gosling/195 8.00
Khalil Greene/300 50.00
Rich Harden/304 10.00
Sean Henn/300 8.00
Koyie Hill/340 8.00
Ryan Howard/53 60.00
Tim Hudson/72 20.00
Adam LaRoche/78 8.00
Micheal Nakamura/231 8.00
Alexis Rios/45 15.00
Alfredo Simon/258 8.00
Javier Vazquez/21 20.00
Ryan Wagner/251 10.00
Dontrelle Willis/47 40.00
Kevin Youkilis/317 15.00

1959 Fleer Ted Williams Reprint Set

May 16, 1954 — Ted Is Patched Up

NM/M
Ted Williams Card (1-81): 6.00
Production 406 Sets
Masterpiece: No Pricing
Production One Set
1-80 Ted Williams 6.00

Ted Williams Reprint Game-Used

No Pricing
Production 9 Sets

2004 Fleer Authentix

NM/M
Complete Set (130):
Common Player: .25
Common SP (101-130): 2.50
Production 999
Pack (5): 4.00
Box (24): 80.00
1 Albert Pujols 2.50
2 Derek Jeter 3.00
3 Jody Gerut .25
4 Mark Teixeira .40
5 Tom Glavine .50
6 Kerry Wood 1.00
7 Ichiro Suzuki .75
8 Jose Vidro .25
9 Mark Prior 1.50

10 Jim Edmonds .50
11 Richie Sexson .50
12 Jay Gibbons .25
13 Jason Kendall .25
14 Lance Berkman .50
15 Andruw Jones .75
16 Jim Thome 1.00
17 Josh Beckett .75
18 Troy Glaus .50
19 Jason Giambi 1.00
20 Sammy Sosa 2.00
21 Bret Boone .40
22 Eric Gagne .40
23 Nomar Garciaparra 2.00
24 Geoff Jenkins .50
25 Ivan Rodriguez .50
26 Preston Wilson .40
27 Alex Rodriguez 2.50
28 Jorge Posada .50
29 Ken Griffey Jr. 1.50
30 Rocco Baldelli .25
31 Shannon Stewart .25
32 Frank Thomas .75
33 Edgar Renteria .25
34 Torii Hunter .50
35 Corey Patterson .25
36 Edgar Martinez .75
37 Jeff Bagwell .75
38 Greg Maddux 1.50
39 Mike Lieberthal .25
40 Craig Biggio .40
41 Randy Johnson 1.00
42 Marlon Byrd .25
43 Jay Payton .25
44 Carlos Delgado .40
45 Scott Podsednik .50
46 Pedro J. Martinez .40
47 Carlos Beltran .40
48 Mike Sweeney .25
49 Gary Sheffield .50
50 Pat Burrell .50
51 Shawn Green .25
52 Tony Batista .25
53 Brian Giles .40
54 Roy Oswalt .40
55 Brandon Webb .40
56 Miguel Tejada .50
57 Miguel Cabrera .75
58 Luis Gonzalez .25
59 Billy Wagner .25
60 Craig Monroe .25
61 Vernon Wells .40
62 Bernie Williams .50
63 Austin Kearns .50
64 Aubrey Huff .25
65 Mike Piazza 1.50
66 Magglio Ordonez .50
67 Bo Hart .25
68 Hideo Nomo .50
69 Curt Schilling .50
70 Barry Zito .50
71 Todd Helton .75
72 Roy Halladay .50
73 Alfonso Soriano 1.00
74 Roberto Alomar .50
75 Scott Rolen 1.00
76 Manny Ramirez .75
77 Sean Burroughs .25
78 Angel Berroa .25
79 Javy Lopez .25
80 Reggie Sanders .25
81 Juan Pierre .25
82 Chipper Jones 1.50
83 Bobby Abreu .40
84 Dontrelle Willis .40
85 Tim Salmon .40
86 Eric Chavez .40
87 Adam Dunn .50
88 Rafael Palmeiro .50
89 Hideki Matsui 2.50
90 Esteban Loaiza .25
91 Darin Erstad .25
92 Vladimir Guerrero 1.00
93 David Ortiz .50
94 Jason Schmidt .40
95 Dmitri Young .25
96 Garret Anderson .50
97 Mark Mulder .25
98 Omar Vizquel .25
99 Hank Blalock .25
100 Jose Reyes .25
101 Rickie Weeks 8.00
102 Chad Gaudin 2.50
103 Ryan Wagner 3.00
104 Koyie Hill 2.50
105 Rich Harden 2.50
106 Edwin Jackson 4.00
107 Khalil Greene 3.00
108 Chien-Ming Wang 3.00
109 Matt Kata 2.50
110 Chin-Hui Tsao 2.50
111 Dan Haren 2.50
112 Delmon Young 8.00
113 Mike Hessman 2.50
114 Bobby Crosby 2.50
115 Cory Sullivan RC 2.50
116 Brandon Watson 2.50
117 Aaron Miles 2.50
118 Jonny Gomes 2.50
119 Graham Koonce 2.50
120 Shawn Hill RC 2.50
121 Garrett Atkins 2.50
122 John Gall RC 2.50
123 Chad Bentz RC 2.50
124 Alfredo Simon RC 2.50
125 Josh Labandeira RC 2.50
126 Ryan Howard 3.00
127 Jason Bartlett RC 2.50

128 Dallas McPherson 2.50
129 Greg Dobbs RC 2.50
130 Jerry Gil RC 2.50

Balcony

Stars (1-100): 4-8X
SP's (101-130): 1-2X
Production 100 Sets

Club Box

Stars (1-100): 10-15X
SP's (101-130): 2-4X
Production 25 Sets

Standing Room Only

No Pricing
Production 5 Sets

Autographed Authentix

NM/M
Common Autograph: 15.00
Production 75
Championship: No Pricing
Production 25
Rocco Baldelli 40.00
Angel Berroa 15.00
Marlon Byrd 15.00
Miguel Cabrera 40.00
Eric Gagne 40.00
Roy Halladay 20.00
Trot Nixon 35.00
Juan Pierre 15.00
Albert Pujols 120.00
Vernon Wells 20.00

Ballpark Classics

NM/M
Complete Set (10): 15.00
Common Player: 1.00
Inserted 1:12
1BC Nomar Garciaparra 3.00
2BC Alfonso Soriano 1.50
3BC Chipper Jones 1.50
4BC Albert Pujols 3.00
5BC Jason Giambi 1.00
6BC Mark Prior 2.00
7BC Sammy Sosa 2.50
8BC Derek Jeter 4.00
9BC Greg Maddux 3.00
10BC Alex Rodriguez 3.00

Ballpark Classics Game-Used

NM/M
Common Player: 8.00
Inserted 1:37
Nomar Garciaparra 10.00
Jason Giambi 8.00
Derek Jeter 15.00
Chipper Jones 8.00
Greg Maddux 10.00
Mark Prior 10.00
Albert Pujols 15.00
Alex Rodriguez 10.00
Alfonso Soriano 8.00
Sammy Sosa 12.00

Jersey Authentix Autograph

NM/M
Common Autograph: 15.00
Production 100
All-Star Autographs: 1-1.25X
Production 50
Championship Autos.: No Pricing
Production 10
Albert Pujols 125.00
Juan Pierre 15.00
Miguel Cabrera 40.00
Eric Gagne 40.00
Marlon Byrd 15.00
Rocco Baldelli 40.00
Roy Halladay 25.00
Vernon Wells 20.00
Trot Nixon 35.00

Jersey Authentix Game of the Week

NM/M
Common Duo: 10.00
Inserted 1:120
Unripped: 1-1.5X
Production 50
1 Dontrelle Willis, Kerry Wood 20.00
2 Miguel Cabrera, Mark Teixeira 15.00
3 Nomar Garciaparra, Alfonso Soriano 15.00

4	Jim Thome,	
	Ivan Rodriguez	10.00
5	Josh Beckett,	
	Mark Prior	15.00
6	Alex Rodriguez,	
	Derek Jeter	35.00
7	Jeff Bagwell,	
	Austin Kearns	15.00
8	Jason Giambi,	
	Barry Zito	10.00
9	Jose Reyes,	
	Juan Pierre	10.00
10	Chipper Jones,	
	Albert Pujols	20.00

Jersey Authentix Ripped

	NM/M
Common Player:	4.00
Inserted 1:16	
Unripped:	2-3X
Production 50 Sets	
All-Star Unripped:	No Pricing
Production One Set	
Jeff Bagwell	8.00
Josh Beckett	6.00
Miguel Cabrera	8.00
Hee Seop Choi	4.00
Nomar Garciaparra	10.00
Jason Giambi	8.00
Torii Hunter	5.00
Derek Jeter	15.00
Randy Johnson	8.00
Chipper Jones	8.00
Austin Kearns	6.00
Greg Maddux	8.00
Juan Pierre	4.00
Mark Prior	10.00
Albert Pujols	15.00
Jose Reyes	8.00
Alex Rodriguez	10.00
Ivan Rodriguez	6.00
Alfonso Soriano	8.00
Sammy Sosa	12.00
Mark Teixeira	6.00
Jim Thome	8.00
Dontrelle Willis	6.00
Kerry Wood	8.00
Barry Zito	6.00

Ticket for Four

		NM/M
Common Quad Jersey:		20.00
Production 100 Sets		
1	Dontrelle Willis,	
	Josh Beckett, Mark Prior,	
	Kerry Wood	20.00
2	Nomar Garciaparra,	
	Alex Rodriguez,	
	Derek Jeter,	
	Jose Reyes	50.00
4	Jason Giambi, Jim Thome,	
	Mark Teixeira,	
	Jeff Bagwell	25.00
5	Chipper Jones,	
	Albert Pujols,	
	Sammy Sosa,	
	Torii Hunter	40.00
6	Greg Maddux,	
	Randy Johnson,	
	Kerry Wood,	
	Barry Zito	20.00
7	Nomar Garciaparra,	
	Alfonso Soriano,	
	Chipper Jones,	
	Albert Pujols	40.00
8	Sammy Sosa, Derek Jeter,	
	Alex Rodriguez,	
	Jim Thome	50.00
9	Mark Prior, Greg Maddux,	
	Austin Kearns,	
	Ivan Rodriguez	15.00
10	Jason Giambi,	
	Randy Johnson,	
	Jeff Bagwell,	
	Torii Hunter	20.00

Ticket Studs

	NM/M
Complete Set (15):	20.00
Common Player:	.75
Inserted 1:6	
1TS Nomar Garciaparra	3.00
2TS Josh Beckett	1.00
3TS Derek Jeter	4.00
4TS Mark Prior	2.00
5TS Albert Pujols	2.00
6TS Alfonso Soriano	1.50
7TS Jim Thome	1.50
8TS Ichiro Suzuki	2.00
9TS Hideki Matsui	3.00
10TS Dontrelle Willis	.75
11TS Mike Schmidt	2.00
12TS Nolan Ryan	4.00
13TS Reggie Jackson	1.00
14TS Tom Seaver	1.00
15TS Brooks Robinson	1.00

2004 Fleer Classic Clippings

	NM/M
Common Player (1-75):	.25
Minor Stars (1-75):	.40
Unlisted Stars (1-75):	.60
Common Player (76-110):	5.00
Production 500 Sets	
Pack (5):	5.00
Box (18):	90.00
1 Juan Pierre	.25
2 Derek Jeter	3.00
3 Jose Reyes	.40
4 Eric Chavez	.40
5 Alex Rodriguez	2.50
6 Mark Prior	.40
7 Carlos Beltran	.40
8 Ichiro Suzuki	2.00
9 Shawn Green	.40
10 Richie Sexson	.60
11 Andruw Jones	.75
12 Geoff Jenkins	.40
13 Luis Gonzalez	.40
14 Garret Anderson	.40
15 Adam Dunn	.60
16 Nomar Garciaparra	2.50
17 Albert Pujols	2.50
18 Jeff Bagwell	.75
19 Rocco Baldelli	.60
20 Preston Wilson	.25
21 Gary Sheffield	.60
22 Magglio Ordonez	.60
23 Kerry Wood	.75
24 Manny Ramirez	.75
25 Randy Johnson	1.00
26 Ken Griffey Jr.	1.50
27 Rafael Palmeiro	.40
28 Vernon Wells	.25
29 Mike Piazza	1.50
30 Hank Blalock	.60
31 Miguel Cabrera	.75
32 Jason Giambi	.60
33 Troy Glaus	.60
34 Angel Berroa	.40
35 Greg Maddux	1.50
36 Lance Berkman	.60
37 Austin Kearns	.60
38 Hideo Nomo	.40
39 Sammy Sosa	2.00
40 Jose Vidro	.25
41 Curt Schilling	.60
42 Melvin Mora	.25
43 Scott Podsednik	.40
44 Dontrelle Willis	.40
45 Roy Halladay	.40
46 Hideki Matsui	2.50
47 Tom Glavine	.40
48 Torii Hunter	.60
49 Chipper Jones	1.50
50 Barry Zito	.60
51 Vladimir Guerrero	1.00
52 Jim Thome	1.00
53 Shannon Stewart	.40
54 Miguel Tejada	.60
55 Roy Oswalt	.40
56 Jason Kendall	.40
57 Brian Giles	.40
58 Jason Schmidt	.40
59 Pedro J. Martinez	1.00
60 Bret Boone	.40
61 Josh Beckett	.75
62 Scott Rolen	1.00
63 Aubrey Huff	.25
64 Pat Burrell	.40
65 Mark Teixeira	.40
66 Alfonso Soriano	1.00
67 Carlos Delgado	.75
68 Ivan Rodriguez	.60
69 Brandon Webb	.25
70 Eric Gagne	.75
71 Frank Thomas	.75
72 Jody Gerut	.25
73 Todd Helton	.75
74 Andy Pettitte	.60
75 Roger Clemens	1.50
76 Rickie Weeks	8.00

77 Chien-Ming Wang	8.00
78 Edwin Jackson	6.00
79 Dallas McPherson	8.00
80 John Gall RC	6.00
81 Ryan Wagner	6.00
82 Clint Barmes	8.00
83 Khalil Greene	6.00
84 Chin-Hui Tsao	6.00
85 Alexis Rios	6.00
86 Merkin Valdez RC	5.00
87 Aarom Baldiris RC	5.00
88 Onil Joseph RC	5.00
89 Ruddy Yan RC	5.00
90 Chad Bentz RC	5.00
91 Shawn Hill RC	5.00
92 Delmon Young	5.00
93 Hector Gimenez RC	5.00
94 William Bergolla RC	5.00
95 Ronny Cedeno RC	5.00
96 Angel Chavez RC	5.00
97 Justin Leone RC	5.00
98 Ivan Ochoa RC	5.00
99 Ian Snell RC	10.00
100 Rich Harden	6.00
101 Joe Mauer	8.00
102 Akinori Otsuka RC	10.00
103 Bobby Crosby	6.00
104 Garrett Atkins	5.00
105 Dan Haren	5.00
106 Koyie Hill	5.00
107 Kazuo Matsui RC	20.00
108 Adam LaRoche	5.00
109 Terrmel Sledge	5.00
110 Shingo Takatsu RC	5.00

First Edition

	NM/M
(1-75):	1-5X
(76-110):	.5-1.25X
Production 150 Sets	

All-Star Lineup Triple Jersey Silver

		NM/M
Common Card:		15.00
Production 75 Sets		
Gold Triple Patch:		2-4X
Production 75 Sets		
No Gold Card For ASL-SMA.		
S/C/G	Alfonso Soriano,	
	Roger Clemens,	
	Jason Giambi	25.00
R/G/R	Alex Rodriguez,	
	Nomar Garciaparra,	
	Manny Ramirez	25.00
W/P/W	Kerry Wood, Mark Prior,	
	Dontrelle Willis	25.00
S/P/W	Gary Sheffield,	
	Albert Pujols,	
	Preston Wilson	20.00
C/H/R	Luis Castillo, Todd Helton,	
	Scott Rolen	15.00
D/S/G	Carlos Delgado,	
	Alfonso Soriano,	
	Troy Glaus	15.00
W/D/H	Vernon Wells,	
	Carlos Delgado,	
	Roy Halladay	15.00
S/M/A	Ichiro Suzuki,	
	Hideki Matsui,	
	Garret Anderson	30.00
R/R/P	Edgar Renteria,	
	Scott Rolen,	
	Albert Pujols	50.00
S/J/L	Gary Sheffield,	
	Andruw Jones,	
	Javy Lopez	15.00
C/Z/H	Roger Clemens,	
	Barry Zito,	
	Roy Halladay	20.00
C/W/L	Luis Castillo,	
	Dontrelle Willis,	
	Mike Lowell	10.00
O/B/G	Magglio Ordonez,	
	Hank Blalock,	
	Troy Glaus	15.00
G/R/G	Nomar Garciaparra,	
	Alex Rodriguez,	
	Jason Giambi	40.00
H/S/P	Todd Helton,	
	Richie Sexson,	
	Albert Pujols	20.00

Bat Rack (3 Bat) - Green

	NM/M
Common Card:	10.00

Production 175 Sets	
Red:	.5-1.5X
Production 50 Sets	
Gold:	1-2X
Production 25 Sets	
Derek Jeter,	
Alex Rodriguez,	
Gary Sheffield	40.00
Sammy Sosa, Derek Lee,	
Mark Prior	25.00
Miguel Cabrera,	
Juan Pierre,	
Josh Beckett	15.00
Nomar Garciaparra,	
Manny Ramirez,	
Curt Schilling	20.00
Alfonso Soriano,	
Hank Blalock,	
Mark Teixeira	15.00
Mike Piazza, Jose Reyes,	
Kazuo Matsui	20.00
Richie Sexson,	
Brandon Webb,	
Roberto Alomar	10.00
Mark Prior, Josh Beckett,	
Curt Schilling	20.00
Carlos Delgado,	
Aubrey Huff,	
Jason Giambi	10.00
Albert Pujols, Scott Rolen	30.00
Rocco Baldelli,	
Aubrey Huff,	
Carlos Delgado	10.00
Jeff Bagwell, Jim Thome,	
Todd Helton	20.00
Gary Sheffield,	
Manny Ramirez,	
Rocco Baldelli	20.00
Troy Glaus, Scott Rolen,	
Hank Blalock	15.00
Roberto Alomar,	
Jose Reyes,	
Alfonso Soriano	15.00
Alex Rodriguez,	
Miguel Tejada,	
Miguel Cabrera	15.00
Vladimir Guerrero,	
Juan Pierre,	
Chipper Jones	10.00
Jason Giambi, Jim Thome,	
Todd Helton	15.00
Vladimir Guerrero,	
Albert Pujols,	
Sammy Sosa	25.00
Derek Jeter, Hideki Matsui,	
Nomar Garciaparra	40.00

Bat Rack (4 Bat) - Green

	NM/M
Common Card:	15.00
Production 75 Sets	
Red:	1-2X
Production 25 Sets	
Gold:	No Pricing
Production 10 Sets	
Derek Jeter,	
Alex Rodriguez,	
Gary Sheffield,	
Jason Giambi	50.00
Sammy Sosa, Mark Prior,	
Josh Beckett	30.00
Derek Jeter,	
Alex Rodriguez,	
Kazuo Matsui,	
Nomar Garciaparra	60.00
Juan Pierre, Gary Sheffield,	
Miguel Cabrera,	
Rocco Baldelli	15.00
Jim Thome, Jeff Bagwell,	
Mark Teixeira,	
Carlos Delgado	20.00
Albert Pujols, Mark Prior,	
Alex Rodriguez,	
Curt Schilling	40.00
Todd Helton, Jose Reyes,	
Kazuo Matsui,	
Scott Rolen	40.00
Sammy Sosa,	
Vladimir Guerrero,	
Jim Edmonds,	
Chipper Jones	25.00
Alfonso Soriano,	
Roberto Alomar,	
Hank Blalock,	
Troy Glaus	15.00
Rocco Baldelli,	
Chipper Jones, Juan Pierre,	
Manny Ramirez	15.00
Jim Thome, Jeff Bagwell,	
Todd Helton,	
Derek Lee	20.00
Curt Schilling,	
Nomar Garciaparra,	
Brandon Webb,	
Richie Sexson	25.00
Mike Piazza, Jose Reyes,	
Albert Pujols,	
Scott Rolen	30.00
Vladimir Guerrero,	
Miguel Tejada,	
Jason Giambi,	
Mike Piazza	25.00

Jeff Bagwell, Derek Lee,	
Aubrey Huff,	
Carlos Delgado	20.00

Bat Rack Autographs-Bronze

	NM/M
Common Player:	12.00
Production 75 Sets	
Roberto Alomar	40.00
Josh Beckett	40.00
Hank Blalock	30.00
Miguel Cabrera	30.00
Jim Edmonds	40.00
Aubrey Huff	12.00
Edgar Martinez	20.00
Jose Reyes	25.00
Gary Sheffield	20.00
Mark Teixeira	20.00

Classic Clippings

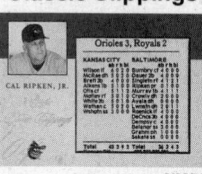

	NM/M
Common Player (1-20):	4.00
Production 750 Sets	
Common Player (21-25):	8.00
Production 100 Sets	
1CC Nolan Ryan	15.00
2CC Mike Schmidt	10.00
3CC Cal Ripken Jr.	10.00
4CC Don Mattingly	8.00
5CC Roger Clemens	5.00
6CC Randy Johnson	4.00
7CC Mark Prior	3.00
8CC Jim Thome	4.00
9CC Sammy Sosa	5.00
10CC Pedro J. Martinez	4.00
11CC Chipper Jones	4.00
12CC Vladimir Guerrero	4.00
13CC Albert Pujols	6.00
14CC Ichiro Suzuki	6.00
15CC Derek Jeter	10.00
16CC Alex Rodriguez	8.00
17CC Greg Maddux	6.00
18CC Nomar Garciaparra	8.00
19CC Mike Piazza	8.00
20CC Ken Griffey Jr.	8.00
21CC Pie Traynor	8.00
22CC Bill Dickey	8.00
23CC George Sisler	12.00
24CC Ted Williams	20.00
25CC Enos Slaughter	8.00

C.C. Signature Edition

	NM/M
Common Player:	15.00
Production 50 Sets	
Masterpiece:	No Pricing
Production 1 Set	
1 Nolan Ryan	125.00
2 Mike Schmidt	75.00
3 Cal Ripken Jr.	175.00
4 Don Mattingly	75.00
5 Albert Pujols	125.00
6 Randy Johnson	60.00
7 Khalil Greene	40.00
8 Rickie Weeks	30.00
9 Edwin Jackson	15.00
10 Rich Harden	15.00
16 Vladimir Guerrero	40.00
17 Mark Prior	40.00

Jersey Rack (3 Jersey)-Blue

	NM/M
Common Card:	15.00
Production 225 Sets	
Bronze Jersey:	.5-1.25X
Production 99 Sets	
Silver Jersey:	.75-1.5X
Production To Player's Jersey No.	
Patch Pack Gold:	No Pricing
Production 125 Sets	

Derek Jeter,	
Alex Rodriguez,	
Jason Giambi	50.00
Sammy Sosa, Kerry Wood,	
Mark Prior	25.00
Miguel Cabrera,	
Dontrelle Willis,	
Josh Beckett	15.00
Nomar Garciaparra,	
Pedro J. Martinez,	
Curt Schilling	15.00
Alex Rodriguez,	
Derek Jeter,	
Nomar Garciaparra	40.00
Mike Piazza,	
Ivan Rodriguez	20.00
Javy Lopez,	
Roger Clemens,	
Mark Prior,	
Josh Beckett	15.00
Roger Clemens,	
Andy Pettitte,	
Roy Oswalt	40.00
Dontrelle Willis,	
Kerry Wood,	
Curt Schilling	20.00
Albert Pujols,	
Sammy Sosa,	
Manny Ramirez	20.00
Rocco Baldelli,	
Miguel Cabrera,	
Albert Pujols	20.00
Barry Zito, Tim Hudson,	
Mark Mulder	15.00
Randy Johnson,	
Richie Sexson,	
Brandon Webb	15.00
Dontrelle Willis,	
Brandon Webb,	
Angel Berroa	15.00
Carlos Delgado,	
Miguel Tejada,	
Alfonso Soriano	15.00

Jersey Rack Autograph - Bronze

	NM/M
Common Player:	12.00
Production 149 Sets	
Silver Jersey:	.5-1.5X
Production 50 Sets	
Patch Rack Gold:	No Pricing
Production To Player's Jersey No.	
Garret Anderson	15.00
Garrett Atkins	12.00
Rocco Baldelli	20.00
Josh Beckett	20.00
Angel Berroa	15.00
Marlon Byrd	12.00
Miguel Cabrera	40.00
Carlos Delgado	20.00
Jody Gerut	12.00
Roy Halladay	15.00
Dan Haren	12.00
Torii Hunter	20.00
Edwin Jackson	20.00
Barry Larkin	20.00
Mark Mulder	15.00
Mike Mussina	25.00
Andy Pettitte	40.00
Albert Pujols	120.00
Ivan Rodriguez	50.00
Scott Rolen	50.00
Ryan Wagner	12.00
Brandon Webb	15.00
Dontrelle Willis	20.00
Kerry Wood	30.00

Phenom Lineup Autograph - Red

	NM/M
Common Card:	10.00
Production 150 Sets	
Silver:	.5-1.25X
Production 99 Sets	
Gold:	.5-1.5X
Production 50 Sets	
Cards contain autograph of the first player listed.	
Ryan Howard, Jim Thome,	
Todd Helton	10.00
John Gall, Albert Pujols,	
Scott Rolen	10.00
Jose Reyes, Kazuo Matsui,	
Rickie Weeks	20.00
Hank Blalock, Troy Glaus,	
Alex Rodriguez	20.00
Rich Harden, Roy Halladay,	
Barry Zito	10.00
Alexis Rios,	
Carlos Delgado,	
Vernon Wells	10.00
Laynce Nix,	
Alex Rodriguez,	
Garret Anderson	10.00
Khalil Greene,	
Edgar Renteria,	
Mike Lowell	25.00

Dontrelle Willis,
Mark Prior,
Kerry Wood — 15.00
Rickie Weeks, Luis Castillo,
Jose Reyes, — 20.00
Dallas McPherson,
Troy Glaus,
Garret Anderson — 15.00
Chien-Ming Wang,
Hideki Matsui,
Jason Giambi — 20.00
Scott Podsednik,
Albert Pujols,
Andruw Jones — 15.00
Bobby Crosby,
Nomar Garciaparra,
Alex Rodriguez — 18.00
Ryan Wagner,
Dontrelle Willis,
Mark Prior — 8.00
Delmon Young,
Ichiro Suzuki,
Hideki Matsui — 30.00
Grady Sizemore,
Manny Ramirez,
Garret Anderson — 20.00
Adam LaRoche,
Albert Pujols,
Jim Thome — 10.00
Edwin Jackson, Mark Prior,
Kerry Wood — 10.00
Miguel Cabrera,
Luis Castillo,
Mike Lowell — 40.00
Merkin Valdez,
Edwin Jackson,
Dontrelle Willis — 10.00
Angel Berroa,
Nomar Garciaparra,
Alex Rodriguez — 10.00

Press Clippings

	NM/M
Common Player:	1.25
Inserted 1:6	
1PC Josh Beckett	1.75
2PC Albert Pujols	4.00
3PC Derek Jeter	5.00
4PC Alex Rodriguez	5.00
5PC Jim Thome	2.00
6PC Angel Berroa	1.00
7PC Dontrelle Willis	1.25
8PC Roy Halladay	1.25
9PC Kerry Wood	1.75
10PC Mark Prior	3.00
11PC Roger Clemens	3.00
12PC Hideki Matsui	4.00
13PC Ichiro Suzuki	3.50
14PC Eric Gagne	1.25
15PC Miguel Cabrera	1.75
16PC Nomar Garciaparra	4.00
17PC Hank Blalock	1.25
18PC Chipper Jones	3.00
19PC Sammy Sosa	3.50
20PC Alfonso Soriano	2.00

Press Proof Black

(1-100): No Pricing
Production One Set

Press Proof Cyan
(1-100): No Pricing
Production One Set

Press Proof Magenta
(1-100): No Pricing
Production One Set

Press Proof Yellow
(1-100): No Pricing
Production One Set

2004 Fleer EX
	NM/M
Common Player (1-40):	1.50
Minor Stars (1-40):	2.00
Unlisted Stars (1-40):	2.50
Common Player (41-65):	5.00

Production 500 Sets
Die-Cut (41-65): .75-1.25X
First 150 seq. #'d cards are die-cut.

1	Vladimir Guerrero	3.50
2	Randy Johnson	3.50
3	Chipper Jones	4.00
4	Miguel Tejada	2.50
5	Pedro J. Martinez	3.50
6	Nomar Garciaparra	6.00
7	Sammy Sosa	5.00
8	Greg Maddux	4.00
9	Frank Thomas	3.00
10	Ken Griffey Jr.	4.00
11	Omar Vizquel	2.00
12	Todd Helton	3.00
13	Ivan Rodriguez	2.50
14	Miguel Cabrera	3.00
15	Dontrelle Willis	2.00
16	Jeff Bagwell	3.00
17	Roger Clemens	4.00
18	Carlos Beltran	2.00
19	Hideo Nomo	2.00
20	Scott Podsednik	1.50
21	Torii Hunter	2.50
22	Jose Vidro	1.50
23	Mike Piazza	4.00
24	Hideki Matsui	6.00
25	Alex Rodriguez	6.00
26	Derek Jeter	8.00
27	Tim Hudson	2.00
28	Jim Thome	3.50
29	Craig Wilson	1.50
30	Brian Giles	2.00
31	Jason Schmidt	2.00
32	Ichiro Suzuki	5.00
33	Scott Rolen	3.50
34	Albert Pujols	6.00
35	Rocco Baldelli	2.50
36	Alfonso Soriano	3.50
37	Carlos Delgado	3.00
38	Curt Schilling	2.50
39	Mark Prior	4.00
40	Josh Beckett	3.00
41	Merkin Valdez RC	5.00
42	Akinori Otsuka RC	8.00
43	Ian Snell RC	8.00
44	Kazuo Matsui RC	10.00
45	Jason Bartlett RC	8.00
46	Dennis Sarfate RC	5.00
47	Sean Henn	5.00
48	David Aardsma	5.00
49	Casey Kotchman	8.00
50	John Gall RC	5.00
51	William Bergolla RC	5.00
52	Angel Chavez RC	5.00
53	Hector Gimenez RC	5.00
54	Aarom Baldiris RC	5.00
55	Justin Leone RC	8.00
56	Onil Joseph RC	5.00
57	Freddy Guzman RC	5.00
58	Andres Blanco RC	5.00
59	Greg Dobbs RC	5.00
60	Joe Mauer	5.00
61	Luis Gonzalez RC	8.00
62	Chris Saenz RC	5.00
63	Zack Greinke	5.00
64	Jose Capellan RC	8.00
65	Brad Halsey RC	10.00

Essential Credentials Future
Cards 1-25: .75-2X
Cards 26-40: 2-4X
Cards 41-65: No Pricing
Production 65 - One Set

Essential Credentials Now

Cards 51-65: 1-2X
Cards 41-50: 1.25-2.25X
Cards 25-40: 3-5X
Cards 1-24: No Pricing
Production 65 - One Set

Check Mates
NM/M
Production 1 or 25 Sets

1	Albert Pujols, Stan Musial/25	500.00
2	Eddie Murray, Rafael Palmeiro/25	200.00
4	Ernie Banks, Ryne Sandberg/25	300.00
9	Manny Ramirez, Pedro J. Martinez/25	300.00
10	Wade Boggs, Tony Gwynn/25	175.00
11	Reggie Jackson, Don Mattingly/25	200.00
14	Robin Yount/ Kirby Puckett/25	150.00

Classic ConnEXions Doubles

No Pricing
Production 22 Sets
Emerald: No Pricing
Production One Set

Classic ConnEXions Triples
No Pricing
Production 13 Sets
Emerald: No Pricing
Production One Set

Clearly Authentics Signature Black Jersey
NM/M
Sequentially #'d to varying quantities.
Burgundy Buttons: No Pricing
Production 6 Sets
Emerald MLB Logo: No Pricing
Production One Set

Josh Beckett/50	30.00
Hank Blalock/50	50.00
Miguel Cabrera/50	30.00
Roger Clemens/50	150.00
J.D. Drew	30.00
Troy Glaus/50	50.00
Vladimir Guerrero/50	50.00
Todd Helton/50	40.00
Chipper Jones/50	60.00
Roy Oswalt/49	30.00
Rafael Palmeiro/50	60.00
Albert Pujols/50	225.00
Manny Ramirez/50	60.00
Mariano Rivera/50	80.00
Gary Sheffield/50	50.00
Frank Thomas/50	60.00
Bernie Williams/42	75.00
Dontrelle Willis/50	25.00
Kerry Wood/34	50.00

Clearly Authentics Black Patch
NM/M
Common Player: 10.00
Production 75 Sets

Jeff Bagwell	20.00
Rocco Baldelli	15.00
Josh Beckett	20.00
Lance Berkman	15.00
Hank Blalock	15.00
Pat Burrell	15.00
Miguel Cabrera	20.00
Rod Carew	30.00
Roger Clemens	30.00
Adam Dunn	15.00
Eric Gagne	15.00
Jason Giambi	25.00
Brian Giles	15.00
Troy Glaus	15.00
Shawn Green	15.00
Vladimir Guerrero	25.00
Tony Gwynn	30.00
Todd Helton	20.00
Rickey Henderson	30.00
Tim Hudson	15.00
Torii Hunter	15.00
Randy Johnson	25.00
Andruw Jones	15.00
Chipper Jones	30.00
Greg Maddux	30.00
Pedro J. Martinez	25.00
Hideki Matsui	40.00
Kazuo Matsui	40.00
Don Mattingly	40.00
Paul Molitor	30.00
Eddie Murray	50.00
Hideo Nomo	15.00
Magglio Ordonez	15.00
Rafael Palmeiro	20.00
Mike Piazza	30.00
Mark Prior	30.00
Albert Pujols	40.00
Manny Ramirez	20.00
Cal Ripken Jr.	75.00
Alex Rodriguez	40.00
Ivan Rodriguez	15.00
Scott Rolen	25.00
Curt Schilling	15.00
Ozzie Smith	25.00
Alfonso Soriano	25.00
Sammy Sosa	35.00
Mark Teixeira	15.00
Miguel Tejada	15.00
Frank Thomas	20.00
Jim Thome	25.00
Rickie Weeks	15.00
Dontrelle Willis	15.00
Kerry Wood	20.00
Barry Zito	15.00

Clearly Authentics Bronze Patch/Jersey

.75-1.5X Black Patch Version
Production 35 Sets

Clearly Authentics Burgundy Triple Patch
No Pricing
Production 13 Sets

Clearly Authentics - Double MLB Logo

No Pricing
Production One Set

Clearly Authentics Pewter
Sequentially #'d to varying quantities.

Clearly Authentics Pewter Patch/Bat
.75-1.5X Black Patch Version
Production 44 Sets

Clearly Authentics Royal Patch/Bat/Jersey
No Pricing
Production 8 Sets

Clearly Authentics Signature Tan Patch
Sequentially #'d to varying quantities.

Clearly Authentics Tan Double Patch
No Pricing
Production 22 Sets

Clearly Authentics Tan Double Patches
No Pricing
Production 22 Sets

Clearly Authentics Turquoise Nameplate
No Pricing
Sequentially #'d to varying quantities.

ConnEXions
NM/M
Production 25 or 50 Sets

6	Casey Kotchman, Joe Mauer/50	100.00
7	Shannon Stewart, Torii Hunter/25	90.00
9	Johnny Damon, Trot Nixon/25	90.00
10	Carlos Lee, Magglio Ordonez/25	30.00
12	Scott Podsednik, Lyle Overbay/25	60.00
13	Barry Zito, Tim Hudson/25	125.00
14	Bucky Dent, Mike Torrez/50	40.00
15	Brian Giles, Marcus Giles/25	60.00
17	Dontrelle Willis, Miguel Cabrera/25	60.00
18	Michael Young, Khalil Greene/50	80.00
19	Mark Teixeira, Hank Blalock/25	100.00

Double Barrel
No Pricing
Production One Set

2004 Fleer EX Signings of the Times Best Year
NM/M
Sequentially #'d to player's best year.
Emerald: No Pricing
Production One Set

Ernie Banks/58/Bat	60.00
Johnny Bench/72/Jsy	60.00
Wade Boggs/87/Bat	40.00
George Brett/80/Jsy	80.00
Jose Canseco/88/Jsy	30.00
Will Clark/91/Jsy	40.00
Tony Gwynn/94/Jsy	50.00
Rickey Henderson/90/Jsy	75.00
Bo Jackson/89/Jsy	60.00
Don Mattingly/85/Jsy	60.00
Eddie Murray/83/Jsy	60.00
Stan Musial/48/Bat	75.00
Nolan Ryan/73/Jsy	150.00
Ryne Sandberg/90/Bat	60.00
Mike Schmidt/80/Jsy	80.00
Tom Seaver/85/Jsy	75.00
Ozzie Smith/87/Jsy	50.00
Duke Snider/55/Bat	50.00
Carl Yastrzemski/67/Bat	60.00

Signings of the Times Debut Year
NM/M
Sequentially #'d to player's debut year.

Ernie Banks/53/Bat	60.00
Johnny Bench/67/Jsy	60.00
Yogi Berra/46/Bat	60.00
Wade Boggs/82/Bat	40.00
Jose Canseco/85/Jsy	30.00
Will Clark/86/Jsy	40.00
Tony Gwynn/82/Jsy	50.00
Rickey Henderson/79/Jsy	75.00
Bo Jackson/86/Jsy	60.00
Reggie Jackson/67/Jsy	50.00
Don Mattingly/82/Jsy	80.00
Eddie Murray/77/Jsy	60.00
Stan Musial/41/Bat	75.00
Kirby Puckett/84/Bat	50.00
Nolan Ryan/66/Jsy	150.00
Ryne Sandberg/81/Bat	60.00
Deion Sanders/89/Jsy	40.00
Mike Schmidt/72/Jsy	80.00
Ozzie Smith/78/Jsy	50.00
Duke Snider/47/Bat	50.00
Carl Yastrzemski/61/Bat	75.00
Robin Yount/74/Jsy	40.00

Signings of the Times HOF Year
NM/M
Sequentially #'d to player's HOF year.

Ernie Banks/77/Bat	60.00
Johnny Bench/89/Jsy	60.00
Yogi Berra/72/Bat	50.00
George Brett/99/Jsy	80.00
Reggie Jackson/93/Jsy	50.00
Stan Musial/69/Bat	75.00
Mike Schmidt/95/Jsy	75.00
Tom Seaver/92/Jsy	50.00
Duke Snider/80/Bat	30.00
Carl Yastrzemski/89/Bat	60.00

Signings of the Times Pewter
NM/M
Sequentially #'d to varying quantities.

Wade Boggs/32/Bat	50.00
Jose Canseco/27/Jsy	75.00
Rickey Henderson/32/Jsy	75.00
Bo Jackson/60/Jsy	50.00
Don Mattingly/33/Jsy	80.00
Eddie Murray/50/Jsy	80.00
Stan Musial/51/Bat	80.00
Kirby Puckett/31/Bat	50.00
Ryne Sandberg/28/Jsy	60.00
Ozzie Smith/36/Jsy	80.00

2004 Fleer Flair

	NM/M
Common Player (1-60):	1.00
Minor Star (1-60):	1.25
Unlisted Star (1-60):	1.75
Common Rookie (61-82):	5.00
Rookie Production 799 Sets	
Collection Row 1:	1-3X
Common Rookie (61-82):	.5-2X
Row 1 Production 125 Sets	
Collection Row 2:	No Pricing
Production One Set	
Box (1):	100.00
1 Brandon Webb	1.00
2 Todd Helton	2.00
3 Jeff Bagwell	2.00
4 Shawn Green	1.25
5 Vladimir Guerrero	3.00
6 Tom Glavine	1.25
7 Jason Giambi	3.00
8 Barry Zito	1.75
9 Jason Kendall	1.25
10 Carlos Delgado	2.00
11 Curt Schilling	1.75
12 Ken Griffey Jr.	3.50
13 Mike Piazza	3.50
14 Alfonso Soriano	1.75
15 Albert Pujols	5.00
16 Chipper Jones	3.50
17 Alex Rodriguez	5.00
18 Miguel Tejada	1.75
19 Pedro J. Martinez	3.00
20 Mark Prior	4.00
21 Magglio Ordonez	1.25
22 Scott Podsednik	1.75
23 Shannon Stewart	1.00
24 Rocco Baldelli	1.75
25 Darin Erstad	1.25
26 Omar Vizquel	1.00
27 Angel Berroa	1.00
28 Jose Vidro	1.00
29 Rich Harden	1.00
30 Andruw Jones	2.00
31 Troy Glaus	1.75
32 Sammy Sosa	4.00
33 Dontrelle Willis	1.25
34 Ivan Rodriguez	1.75
35 Nomar Garciaparra	5.00
36 Josh Beckett	2.00
37 Jose Reyes	1.00
38 Scott Rolen	3.00
39 Greg Maddux	3.50
40 Andy Pettitte	1.75
41 Jason Schmidt	1.25
42 Edgar Martinez	1.25
43 Manny Ramirez	2.00
44 Torii Hunter	1.75
45 Mark Teixeira	1.25
46 Hideo Nomo	1.25
47 Brian Giles	1.75
48 Adam Dunn	1.75
49 Fernando Vina	1.00
50 Hideki Matsui	5.00
51 Jim Thome	3.00
52 Hank Blalock	1.75
53 Miguel Cabrera	2.00
54 Randy Johnson	3.00
55 Javy Lopez	1.25
56 Frank Thomas	2.00
57 Roger Clemens	3.50

58	Marlon Byrd	1.00
59	Derek Jeter	6.00
60	Ichiro Suzuki	4.00
61	Kazuo Matsui RC	25.00
62	Chad Bentz RC	8.00
63	Greg Dobbs RC	5.00
64	John Gall RC	5.00
65	Cory Sullivan RC	5.00
66	Hector Gimenez RC	5.00
67	Graham Koonce RC	5.00
68	Jason Bartlett RC	5.00
69	Angel Chavez RC	5.00
70	Ronny Cedeno RC	5.00
71	Donald Kelly RC	5.00
72	Ivan Ochoa RC	5.00
73	Ruddy Yan RC	5.00
74	Mike Gosling RC	5.00
75	Alfredo Simon RC	5.00
76	Jerome Gamble RC	5.00
77	Chris Aguila RC	5.00
78	Mike Rouse RC	5.00
79	Justin Leone RC	5.00
80	Merkin Valdez RC	5.00
81	Aarom Baldiris RC	5.00
82	Chris Shelton RC	10.00

Autograph Collection

	NM/M
Common Player:	10.00

Production between 65-200 Sets
Crown: .5-1X
Production 100 Sets
Parchment: 1-1.75X
Production 25 Sets
Platinum: No Pricing
Production 10 Sets
Masterpiece: No Pricing
Production One Set

Garrett Atkins/195	10.00
Rocco Baldelli/180	25.00
Aarom Baldiris/180	10.00
Jason Bartlett/95	15.00
Josh Beckett/65	15.00
Angel Berroa/178	15.00
Miguel Cabrera/172	40.00
Bobby Crosby/87	30.00
Jim Edmonds/73	25.00
John Gall/94	30.00
Khalil Greene/40	195.00
Dan Haren/195	15.00
Ryan Howard/185	75.00
Edwin Jackson/183	15.00
Andruw Jones/163	25.00
Graham Koonce/175	10.00
Josh Labandeira/166	10.00
Adam LaRoche/280	15.00
Justin Leone/180	15.00
Ryan Meaux/180	10.00
Mike Mussina/69	50.00
Micheal Nakamura/180	10.00
Bubba Nelson/185	10.00
Corey Patterson/172	15.00
Juan Pierre/94	15.00
Scott Podsednik/96	25.00
Mark Prior/60	60.00
Alexis Rios/185	20.00
Michael Rouse/195	10.00
Chris Shelton/170	30.00
Grady Sizemore/197	30.00
Merkin Valdez/187	15.00
Javier Vazquez/187	30.00
Ryan Wagner/175	15.00
Chien-Ming Wang/178	50.00
Brandon Webb/122	15.00
Rickie Weeks/169	30.00
Dontrelle Willis/73	30.00
Kerry Wood/73	40.00
Delmon Young/177	25.00

Cuts and Glory

	NM/M
Common Player:	25.00

Production 100 Sets
Silver: .75-1.25X
Production 50 Sets
Gold: No Pricing
Production 15 Sets
Platinum: No Pricing
Production 3 Sets
Masterpiece: No Pricing
Production One Set

Garret Anderson	30.00
Hank Blalock	25.00
Marlon Byrd	25.00
Carlos Delgado	30.00
Adam Dunn	40.00
Eric Gagne	40.00
Luis Gonzalez	25.00
Vladimir Guerrero	50.00
Ricky Henderson	100.00
Torii Hunter	25.00
Randy Johnson	60.00
Chipper Jones	60.00
Austin Kearns	25.00
Greg Maddux	75.00
Edgar Martinez	40.00
Magglio Ordonez	25.00
Albert Pujols	150.00
Jose Reyes	30.00
Scott Rolen	40.00
Mark Teixeira	25.00
Frank Thomas	75.00

Diamond Cuts Game-Used Blue

	NM/M
Common Player:	5.00

Production 250 Sets
Blue Die-Cut: 1-3X
Production 25 Sets
Red: .5-1.25X
Production 175 Sets
Red Die-Cut: No Pricing
Production 18 Sets
Pewter: .5-1.5X
Production 125 Sets
Pewter Die-Cut: No Pricing
Production 13 Sets
Copper: .5-1.5X
Production 75 Sets
Die-Cut Copper: No Pricing
Production 8 Sets
Silver: .5-1.5X
Production 50 Sets
Silver Die-Cut: No Pricing
Production 5 Sets
Gold: 1-5X
Numbered to player's jersey No.
Gold Die-Cut: No Pricing
Production 3 Sets
Platinum: 2-5X
Numbered to 2003 HR/Win total.
Platinum Die-Cut: No Pricing
Production One Set
Purple: No Pricing
Production One Set

JB	Josh Beckett	8.00
HB	Hank Blalock	5.00
RC	Roger Clemens	10.00
NG	Nomar Garciaparra	12.00
DJ	Derek Jeter	15.00
AJ	Andruw Jones	8.00
CJ	Chipper Jones	8.00
PM	Pedro J. Martinez	8.00
HM	Hideki Matsui	12.00
ANP	Andy Pettitte	8.00
MIP	Mike Piazza	8.00
MAP	Mark Prior	8.00
ALP	Albert Pujols	12.00
JR	Jose Reyes	5.00
SR	Scott Rolen	8.00
SS	Curt Schilling	5.00
SS	Sammy Sosa	10.00
IS	Ichiro Suzuki	10.00
MT	Mark Teixeira	5.00
DW	Dontrelle Willis	5.00

Dual Patch

No Pricing
Production 10 Sets

Hot Numbers Game-Used Blue

	NM/M
Common Player:	5.00

Production 250 Sets
Blue Die-Cut: 1X-3X
Production 25 Sets
Red: .5X-1.25X
Production 175 Sets
Red Die-Cut: No Pricing
Production 18 Sets
Pewter: .5X-1.5X
Production 125 Sets
Pewter Die-Cut: No Pricing
Production 13 Sets
Copper: .5X-1.5X
Production 75 Sets
Die-Cut Copper: No Pricing
Production 8 Sets
Silver: .5X-1.5X
Production 50 Sets
Silver Die-Cut: No Pricing
Production 5 Sets
Gold: 1X-5X
Numbered to player's jersey No.
Gold Die-Cut: No Pricing
Production 3 Sets
Platinum: 2X-5X
Numbered to 2003 HR/Win total.
Platinum Die-Cut: No Pricing
Production One Set
Purple: No Pricing
Production One Set

Jeff Bagwell	8.00
Rocco Baldelli	8.00
Josh Beckett	8.00
Hank Blalock	5.00
Nomar Garciaparra	12.00
Jason Giambi	8.00
Troy Glaus	5.00
Tom Glavine	5.00
Vladimir Guerrero	8.00
Todd Helton	8.00
Derek Jeter	15.00
Randy Johnson	8.00
Chipper Jones	8.00
Barry Larkin	5.00
Greg Maddux	8.00
Pedro J. Martinez	8.00
Mike Mussina	5.00
Hideo Nomo	5.00
Mike Piazza	8.00
Mark Prior	8.00
Albert Pujols	12.00
Manny Ramirez	8.00
Alex Rodriguez	12.00
Curt Schilling	5.00
Sammy Sosa	10.00
Mark Teixeira	5.00
Frank Thomas	8.00
Jim Thome	8.00
Brandon Webb	5.00
Kerry Wood	8.00

Lettermen

No Pricing
Numbered to number of letters in player's last name.

Power Tools Game-Used Blue

	NM/M
Common Player:	5.00

Production 250 Sets
Blue Die-Cut: 1X-3X
Production 25 Sets
Red: .5X-1.25X
Production 175 Sets
Red Die-Cut: No Pricing
Production 18 Sets
Pewter: .5X-1.5X
Production 125 Sets
Pewter Die-Cut: No Pricing
Production 13 Sets
Copper: .5X-1.5X
Production 75 Sets
Die-Cut Copper: No Pricing
Production 8 Sets
Silver: .5X-1.5X
Production 50 Sets
Silver Die-Cut: No Pricing
Production 5 Sets
Gold: 1X-5X
Numbered to player's jersey No.
Gold Die-Cut: No Pricing
Production 3 Sets
Platinum: 2X-5X
Numbered to 2003 HR total.
Platinum Die-Cut: No Pricing
Production One Set
Purple: No Pricing
Production One Set

Rocco Baldelli	5.00
Adam Dunn	5.00
Nomar Garciaparra	12.00
Jason Giambi	8.00
Vladimir Guerrero	8.00
Derek Jeter	15.00
Chipper Jones	8.00
Mike Piazza	10.00
Jorge Posada	8.00
Albert Pujols	12.00
Manny Ramirez	8.00
Alex Rodriguez	12.00
Alfonso Soriano	8.00
Sammy Sosa	8.00
Jim Thome	8.00

SIGnificant Cuts

	NM/M
Serially Numbered	
RA Roberto Alomar/50	60.00

JB2	Johnny Bench/25	100.00
VC	Vince Carter/200	50.00
TC	Ty Cobb	2,650
DE	Dennis Eckersley/75	30.00
RH	Roy Halladay/50	40.00
BL	Barry Larkin/75	50.00
PM	Paul Molitor/75	50.00
AP1	Andy Pettitte/50	40.00
JR	Jose Reyes/25	40.00
MR	Mariano Rivera/50	75.00
IR	Ivan Rodriguez/50	50.00
NR	Nolan Ryan/25	200.00
MS	Mike Schmidt/25	125.00
GS	Gary Sheffield/50	40.00

2004 Fleer Genuine Insider

	NM/M
Common Player (1-90):	.25
Minor Stars:	.40
Unlisted Stars:	.60
Common Rookie Insider (91-100):	4.00

Production 499 Sets

Common Upside (101-120):	4.00

Production 799 Sets

Common Mini Rookie:	4.00

Production 350 Sets

Pack (5):	4.00
Box (18):	75.00

1	Troy Glaus	.60
2	Eric Chavez	.40
3	Lance Berkman	.40
4	Pedro J. Martinez	1.00
5	Jim Edmonds	.40
6	Tom Glavine	.40
7	Ken Griffey Jr.	1.50
8	Vernon Wells	.40
9	Hideki Matsui	2.50
10	Jeff Bagwell	.75
11	Rafael Palmeiro	.40
12	Edgar Martinez	.40
13	Bernie Williams	.60
14	Josh Beckett	.75
15	Javy Lopez	.40
16	Ichiro Suzuki	2.00
17	Scott Podsednik	.40
18	Sammy Sosa	2.00
19	Mark Teixeira	.40
20	Jorge Posada	.60
21	Miguel Cabrera	.75
22	Chipper Jones	1.50
23	Sean Burroughs	.25
24	Dmitri Young	.25
25	Brandon Webb	.40
26	Bobby Abreu	.40
27	Hideo Nomo	.40
28	Frank Thomas	.75
29	Alex Rodriguez	2.50
30	Derek Jeter	3.00
31	Todd Helton	.75
32	Andruw Jones	.75
33	Jason Kendall	.40
34	Eric Gagne	.40
35	Omar Vizquel	.40
36	Vladimir Guerrero	1.00
37	Jim Thome	.75
38	Mike Sweeney	.25
39	Manny Ramirez	.75
40	Scott Rolen	1.00
41	Jose Vidro	.25
42	Adam Dunn	.60
43	Garret Anderson	.40
44	Mike Lieberthal	.25
45	Roy Oswalt	.40
46	Geoff Jenkins	.25
47	Magglio Ordonez	.40
48	Hank Blalock	.60
49	Barry Zito	.40
50	Dontrelle Willis	.60
51	Greg Maddux	1.50
52	Brian Giles	.40
53	Shawn Green	.40
54	Carlos Lee	.25
55	Carlos Delgado	.40
56	Alfonso Soriano	1.00
57	Angel Berroa	.25
58	Kerry Wood	.75
59	Rocco Baldelli	.60
60	Gary Sheffield	.60
61	Ivan Rodriguez	.60
62	Richie Sexson	.60
63	Marlon Byrd	.25
64	Carlos Beltran	.40
65	Mark Prior	2.00
66	Aubrey Huff	.40
67	Jason Giambi	1.00
68	Curt Schilling	.60
69	Reggie Sanders	.25
70	Mike Piazza	1.50
71	Craig Monroe	.25
72	Randy Johnson	1.00
73	Pat Burrell	.40
74	Craig Biggio	.40
75	Nomar Garciaparra	2.50
76	Albert Pujols	2.50
77	Jose Reyes	.25
78	Preston Wilson	.25
79	Miguel Tejada	.60
80	Bret Boone	.40
81	Shannon Stewart	.25
82	Jody Gerut	.25
83	Tim Salmon	.40
84	Tim Hudson	.40
85	Juan Pierre	.25
86	Jay Gibbons	.40
87	Jason Schmidt	.40
88	Torii Hunter	.60
89	Austin Kearns	.25
90	Roy Halladay	.40
91	John Gall RC	8.00
92	Hideki Matsui RC	25.00
93	Merkin Valdez RC	5.00
94	William Bergolla RC	8.00
95	Angel Chavez RC	5.00
96	Hector Gimenez RC	5.00
97	Aarom Baldiris RC	5.00
98	Justin Leone RC	6.00
99	Onil Joseph RC	5.00
100	Freddy Guzman RC	4.00
101	Rickie Weeks	6.00
102	Chad Bentz RC	5.00
103	Bobby Crosby	6.00
104	Dallas McPherson	5.00
105	Brandon Watson	4.00
106	Garrett Atkins	6.00
107	Graham Koonce	4.00
108	Chien-Ming Wang	4.00
109	Jonny Gomes	5.00
110	Edwin Jackson	5.00
111	Alfredo Simon RC	5.00
112	Delmon Young	6.00
113	Angel Guzman	4.00
114	Ryan Howard	4.00
115	Scott Nairon	10.00
116	Edwin Encarnacion	8.00
117	Byron Gettis	4.00
118	Kevin Youkilis	8.00
119	Grady Sizemore	8.00
120	Corey Hart	4.00
121	Greg Dobbs RC	5.00
122	Jerry Gil RC	4.00
123	Shawn Hill RC	4.00
124	John Labandeira RC	4.00
125	Jason Bartlett RC	4.00
126	Ronny Cedeno RC	4.00
127	Donald Kelly RC	8.00
128	Ivan Ochoa RC	4.00
129	Mariano Gomez RC	5.00
130	Ruddy Yan RC	5.00

Genuine Reflection

	NM/M
(1-90):	.5-2X
(101-120):	.5-1.25X

Production 99 Sets

Autograph Insider

	NM/M
Common Player:	10.00

Production as indicated.

RA	Roberto Alomar/150	30.00
MB	Marlon Byrd/550	10.00
MC	Miguel Cabrera/250	40.00
DE	David Eckstein/350	10.00
JG	Jody Gerut/550	10.00
JG2	Jay Gibbons/550	10.00
OH	Orlando Hudson/550	15.00
AH	Aubrey Huff/550	10.00
AK	Austin Kearns/350	10.00
MO	Magglio Ordonez/250	20.00
RP	Rafael Palmeiro/150	50.00
SP	Scott Podsednik/550	15.00
JR	Jose Reyes/350	25.00
MR	Mariano Rivera/150	60.00
IR	Ivan Rodriguez/150	40.00
JR2	Jimmy Rollins/350	15.00
JS	Jason Schmidt/300	300.00
JS2	John Smoltz/150	30.00
MT	Mark Teixeira/350	20.00
BW	Brandon Webb/450	10.00

Autograph Insider - Ball

No Pricing
Production 10 Sets

Autograph Insider - Bat

	NM/M
Common Card:	20.00

Production 50 Sets

RA	Roberto Alomar	40.00
MB	Marlon Byrd	20.00
MC	Miguel Cabrera	60.00
DE	David Eckstein	30.00
JG	Jody Gerut	25.00
JG2	Jay Gibbons	20.00
OH	Orlando Hudson	20.00
AH	Aubrey Huff	25.00
AK	Austin Kearns	25.00
RP	Rafael Palmeiro	50.00
SP	Scott Podsednik	20.00
JR	Jose Reyes	35.00
IR	Ivan Rodriguez	50.00
JR2	Jimmy Rollins	25.00
MT	Mark Teixeira	25.00

Autograph Insider- Cut Sigs

No Pricing

Autograph Insider - Jersey

	NM/M
Common Player:	10.00

Production 100 Sets

RA	Roberto Alomar	30.00
MB	Marlon Byrd	10.00
MC	Miguel Cabrera	40.00
DE	David Eckstein	15.00
JG	Jody Gerut	25.00
JG2	Jay Gibbons	10.00
OH	Orlando Hudson	10.00
AH	Aubrey Huff	10.00
AK	Austin Kearns	20.00
MO	Magglio Ordonez	20.00
RP	Rafael Palmeiro	50.00
SP	Scott Podsednik	20.00
AP	Albert Pujols	100.00
JR	Jose Reyes	35.00
MR	Mariano Rivera	75.00
IR	Ivan Rodriguez	50.00
JR2	Jimmy Rollins	20.00
JS	Jason Schmidt	20.00
JS2	John Smoltz	50.00
MT	Mark Teixeira	25.00
BW	Brandon Webb	10.00

Classic Confrontations

	NM/M
Common Card:	3.00
Inserted 1:18	

1CC	Mike Piazza, Roger Clemens	4.00
2CC	Pedro J. Martinez, Derek Jeter	6.00
3CC	Randy Johnson, Jeff Bagwell	3.00
4CC	Mark Prior, Albert Pujols	4.00
5CC	Josh Beckett, Sammy Sosa	4.00
6CC	Eric Gagne, Hank Blalock	4.00
7CC	Mariano Rivera, Nomar Garciaparra	5.00
8CC	Curt Schilling, Chipper Jones	4.00
9CC	Kerry Wood, Jim Edmonds	3.00
10CC	Barry Zito, Alfonso Soriano	3.00
11CC	Randy Johnson, Ken Griffey Jr.	4.00
12CC	Derek Jeter, John Smoltz	6.00
13CC	Roy Oswalt, Ken Griffey Jr.	4.00

14CC Dontrelle Willis, Hideki Matsui 4.00
15CC Hideo Nomo, Ichiro Suzuki 4.00

Classic Confrontations Jersey

NM/M
Common Card: 5.00
Production 400 Sets

JB	Jeff Bagwell with Randy Johnson	6.00
JB2	Josh Beckett with Sammy Sosa	6.00
HB	Hank Blalock with Eric Gagne	8.00
RC	Roger Clemens with Mike Piazza	.15.00
JE	Jim Edmonds with Kerry Wood	5.00
EG	Eric Gagne with Hank Blalock	5.00
NG	Nomar Garciaparra with Mariano Rivera	8.00
DJ	Derek Jeter with Pedro J. Martinez	15.00
RJ1	Randy Johnson with Jeff Bagwell	8.00
RJ2	Randy Johnson with Ken Griffey Jr.	8.00
CJ	Chipper Jones with Curt Schilling	8.00
PM	Pedro J. Martinez with Derek Jeter	10.00
HN	Hideo Nomo with Ichiro Suzuki	12.00
RO	Roy Oswalt with Ken Griffey Jr.	5.00
MP	Mike Piazza with Roger Clemens	8.00
MP2	Mark Prior with Albert Pujols	8.00
AP	Albert Pujols with Mark Prior	12.00
MR	Mariano Rivera with Nomar Garciaparra	8.00
CS	Curt Schilling with Chipper Jones	5.00
JS	John Smoltz with Derek Jeter	5.00
AS	Alfonso Soriano with Barry Zito	8.00
SS	Sammy Sosa with Josh Beckett	8.00
DW	Dontrelle Willis with Matsui	5.00
KW	Kerry Wood with Jim Edmonds	8.00
BZ	Barry Zito with Alfonso Soriano	5.00

Classic Confrontations Dual Jersey

NM/M
Common Card: 12.00
Production 100 Sets
Dual Patch: No Pricing
Production 10 Sets

Barry Zito, Alfonso Soriano	12.00
Curt Schilling, Chipper Jones	12.00
Eric Gagne, Hank Blalock	12.00
Josh Beckett, Sammy Sosa	12.00
Kerry Wood, Jim Edmonds	15.00
Mark Prior, Albert Pujols	15.00
Mike Piazza, Roger Clemens	15.00
Mariano Rivera, Nomar Garciaparra	20.00
Pedro J. Martinez, Derek Jeter	20.00
Randy Johnson, Jeff Bagwell	12.00

Genuine Article Insider-Jersey

NM/M
Common Player: 5.00
Production 250 Sets
Bat: .75-1.25X

Production 100 Sets
Jersey/Bat: .75-1.5X
Production 50 Sets
Jersey Tags: No Pricing
Production 5 Sets

RB	Rocco Baldelli	5.00
LB	Lance Berkman	5.00
HB	Hank Blalock	5.00
MC	Miguel Cabrera	8.00
CD	Carlos Delgado	6.00
AD	Adam Dunn	5.00
NG	Nomar Garciaparra	12.00
JG	Jason Giambi	6.00
TG	Troy Glaus	5.00
VG	Vladimir Guerrero	8.00
TH	Todd Helton	5.00
DJ	Derek Jeter	18.00
CJ	Chipper Jones	8.00
MO*	Magglio Ordonez	5.00
RP	Rafael Palmeiro	5.00
MP	Mike Piazza	8.00
AP	Albert Pujols	12.00
MR	Manny Ramirez	6.00
JR	Jose Reyes	6.00
AR	Alex Rodriguez	15.00
CS	Gary Sheffield	6.00
AS	Alfonso Soriano	8.00
SS	Sammy Sosa	10.00
MT	Mark Teixeira	6.00
JT	Jim Thome	6.00

Tools of the Game

NM/M
Common Player: 1.00
Inserted 1:6

1TG	Jason Giambi	1.50
2TG	Torii Hunter	1.00
3TG	Derek Jeter	4.00
4TG	Nomar Garciaparra	3.00
5TG	Albert Pujols	3.00
6TG	Jim Thome	1.50
7TG	Alex Rodriguez	4.00
8TG	Chipper Jones	2.00
9TG	Sammy Sosa	2.50
10TG	Jose Reyes	1.00
11TG	Pedro J. Martinez	1.50
12TG	Greg Maddux	2.00
13TG	Randy Johnson	1.50
14TG	Curt Schilling	1.00
15TG	Mark Prior	2.00
16TG	Ichiro Suzuki	2.50
17TG	Hideki Matsui	3.00
18TG	Kazuo Matsui	2.50
19TG	Ken Griffey Jr.	2.00
20TG	Josh Beckett	1.00

Tools of Game-Game Jersey

NM/M
Common Player: 5.00
Production 250 Sets
Jersey/Bat: .75-2X
Production 125
Jersey/Bat/Cap: 1-2.5X
Production 75

NG	Nomar Garciaparra	12.00
JG	Jason Giambi	8.00
TH	Torii Hunter	5.00
DJ	Derek Jeter	15.00
RJ	Randy Johnson	6.00
CJ	Chipper Jones	8.00
GM	Greg Maddux	6.00
PM	Pedro J. Martinez	5.00
MP	Mark Prior	10.00
AP	Albert Pujols	12.00
JR	Jose Reyes	8.00
AR	Alex Rodriguez	15.00
CS	Curt Schilling	5.00
SS	Sammy Sosa	10.00
JT	Jim Thome	6.00

2004 Fleer Greats of the Game

NM/M
Common Player: .40
Minor Stars: .75
Pack (5): 10.00
Box (15): 130.00

1	Lou Gehrig	4.00
2	Ty Cobb	3.00
3	Dizzy Dean	1.50
4	Jimmie Foxx	1.50
5	Hank Greenberg	1.00
6	Babe Ruth	6.00
7	Honus Wagner	1.50
8	Mickey Cochrane	1.50
9	Pepper Martin	.40
10	Charlie Gehringer	.75
11	Carl Hubbell	.40
12	Bill Terry	.40
13	Mel Ott	.75
14	Bill Dickey	1.50
15	Ted Williams	6.00
16	Roger Maris	3.00
17	Thurman Munson	2.00
18	Phil Rizzuto	2.00
19	Stan Musial	3.00
20	Duke Snider	2.50
21	Reggie Jackson	1.50
22	Don Mattingly	1.50
23	Vida Blue	.75
24	Harmon Killebrew	1.50
25	Lou Brock	.75
26	Al Kaline	1.00
27	Dave Parker	.40
28	Nolan Ryan	6.00
29	Jim Rice	.40
30	Paul Molitor	2.00
31	Dwight Evans	.40
32	Brooks Robinson	1.50
33	Jose Canseco	.40
34	Alan Trammell	.40
35	Johnny Bench	2.00
36	Carlton Fisk	1.00
37	Jim Palmer	1.50
38	George Brett	2.00
39	Mike Schmidt	2.00
40	Tony Perez	.75
41	Paul Blair	.40
42	Fred Lynn	.40
43	Carl Yastrzemski	1.50
44	Steve Carlton	1.00
45	Dennis Eckersley	1.50
46	Tom Seaver	1.50
47	Juan Marichal	.75
48	Tony Gwynn	2.00
49	Bill "Moose" Skowron	.40
50	Bob Gibson	1.50
51	Luis Tiant	.75
52	Eddie Murray	1.00
53	Frank Robinson	2.00
54	Rocky Colavito	.75
55	Bobby Shantz	.40
56	Ernie Banks	2.00
57	Rod Carew	1.00
58	Gorman Thomas	.40
59	Bernie Carbo	.40
60	Joe Rudi	.40
61	Graig Nettles	.75
62	Ron Guidry	.75
63	Whitey Ford	1.50
64	George Kell	1.00
65	Cal Ripken Jr.	6.00
66	Willie McCovey	.75
67	Bo Jackson	1.00
68	Kirby Puckett	2.00
69	Ted Kluszewski	.75
70	Johnny Podres	.40
71	Davey Lopes	.40
72	Chris Short	.40
73	Jeff Torborg	.40
74	Bill Freehan	.40
75	Frank Tanana	.40
76	Jack Morris	.75
77	Rick Dempsey	.40
78	Yogi Berra	1.50
79	Tim McCarver	.40
80	Rusty Staub	.40
81	Tony Lazzeri	.40
82	Al Rosen	.40
83	Willie McGee	.75
84	Preacher Roe	.75
85	Dave Kingman	.40
86	Luis Aparicio	1.00
87	John Kruk	.40
88	Bing Miller	.40
89	Joe Charboneau	.40
90	Mark Fidrych	.40
91	Jim "Catfish" Hunter	2.00
92	Nap Lajoie	2.00
93	Eddie Murray	2.00
94	Johnny Pesky	1.00
95	Tom Seaver	2.00
96	Frank Robinson	2.00
97	Enos Slaughter	1.00
98	Cecil Travis	.40
99	Robin Yount	2.00
100	Don Zimmer	.75
101	Babe Herman	.40
102	Ron Santo	.40
103	Willie Stargell	2.00
104	Jimmy Piersall	.75
106	Johnny Sain	.40
107	Joe Pepitone	.75
108	Ryne Sandberg	3.00
109	Jim Thorpe	3.00
110	Steve Garvey	1.50
111	Ray Knight	.75
112	Fernando Valenzuela	1.00
113	Will Clark	1.00
114	Tony Kubek	.75
115	Jim Bouton	.40
116	Jerry Koosman	.75
117	Steve Carlton	3.00
118	Richie Ashburn	.75
119	Roberto Clemente	6.00
120	Paul O'Neill	.40
121	Reggie Jackson	3.00
122	Andre Dawson	1.50
123	Hoyt Wilhelm	1.00
124	Dale Murphy	1.50
125	Dwight Gooden	1.50
126	Roger Maris	1.50
127	Bill Mazeroski	1.00
128	Don Newcombe	.75
129	Robin Roberts	.75
130	Duke Snider	2.00
131	Eddie Mathews	3.00
132	Wade Boggs	2.00
133	Rollie Fingers	1.50
134	Frankie Frisch	.40
135	Billy Williams	.75
136	Rod Carew	1.50
137	Dom DiMaggio	1.50
138	Orel Hershiser	.40
139	Gary Carter	1.00
140	Keith Hernandez	.75
141	Bob Lemon	.75
142	Nolan Ryan	6.00
143	Ozzie Smith	1.50
144	Rick Sutcliffe	.40
145	Carlton Fisk	1.50

Blue

Cards 81-145
Cards #'d to 51-96: 3-5X
Cards #'d to 26-50: 5-10X
Cards #'d to less than 25: No Pricing

Announcing Greats

NM/M
Common Card: 6.00
Inserted 1:12 Retail

1AG	Harry Kalas, Mike Schmidt	8.00
2AG	Vin Scully, Steve Garvey	12.00
3AG	Harry Caray, Ryne Sandberg	12.00
4AG	Ned Martin, Carlton Fisk	6.00
5AG	Ernie Harwell, Kirk Gibson	6.00
6AG	Ken Harrelson, Carl Yastrzemski	6.00
7AG	Don Mattingly, Phil Rizzuto	10.00
8AG	Yogi Berra, Mel Allen	10.00
9AG	Jonathan Miller, Cal Ripken Jr.	10.00
10AG	Marty Brennaman, Johnny Bench	8.00

Announcing Greats Autographs

NM/M
Sequentially #'d between 1 & 50.

Ken Harrelson, Carl Yastrzemski/50	75.00
Phil Rizzuto, Don Mattingly/26	225.00
Johnny Bench, Marty Brennaman/50	60.00

Battery Mates

NM/M
Common Card: 5.00
Serially Numbered

1BM	Steve Carlton, Tim McCarver/1972	5.00
2BM	Don Drysdale, Roy Campanella/1957	5.00
3BM	Tom Seaver, Johnny Bench/1979	8.00
4BM	Whitey Ford, Yogi Berra/1956	8.00
5BM	Ron Guidry, Thurman Munson/1978	8.00
6BM	Nolan Ryan, Jeff Torborg/1973	10.00
7BM	Denny McLain, Bill Freehan/1968	5.00
8BM	Lefty Gomez, Bill Dickey/1934	5.00
9BM	Jim Palmer, Rick Dempsey/1977	5.00
10BM	Luis Tiant, Carlton Fisk	5.00

Single Panel: Battery Mates

NM/M
Common Card: 15.00
Serially Numbered

TM	Steve Carlton, Tim McCarver/72	30.00
TS-JB	Tom Seaver, Johnny Bench/79	60.00
WF-YB	Whitey Ford, Yogi Berra/56	40.00
RG-TM	Ron Guidry, Thurman Munson/78	25.00
NR-JT	Nolan Ryan, Jeff Torborg/73	15.00
DM-BF	Denny McLain, Bill Freehan/68	60.00
JP-RD	Jim Palmer, Rick Dempsey/77	25.00

Dual Panel: Battery Mates

No Pricing
Production 10 Sets

Comparison Cuts: Dual Cut

No Pricing
Production One Set

Forever

NM/M
Common Player: 4.00
Sequentially #'d to player's rookie year.

1	Fernando Valenzuela/1980	4.00
2	Steve Garvey/1969	4.00
3	Zach Wheat/1909	4.00
4	Orel Hershiser/1983	4.00
5	Duke Snider/1947	6.00
6	Jim Rice/1974	5.00
7	Carlton Fisk/1969	5.00
8	Wade Boggs/1982	6.00
9	Ted Williams/1939	10.00
10	Carl Yastrzemski/1961	8.00
11	Dom DiMaggio/1940	5.00
12	Ron Santo/1960	5.00
13	Billy Williams/1959	5.00
14	Ryne Sandberg/1981	8.00
15	Ernie Banks/1953	8.00
16	Gabby Hartnett/1922	4.00
17	Hack Wilson/1923	6.00
18	Dwight Gooden/1984	5.00
19	Ray Knight/1974	4.00
20	Tom Seaver/1967	8.00
21	Nolan Ryan/1966	10.00
22	Keith Hernandez/1974	5.00
23	Darryl Strawberry/1983	5.00
24	Bob Gibson/1959	8.00
25	Pepper Martin/1928	4.00
26	Stan Musial/1941	8.00
27	Frankie Frisch/1919	4.00
28	Steve Carlton/1965	8.00
29	Ozzie Smith/1978	6.00

Forever Game-Used Jersey

NM/M
Common Player: 10.00
Production 149 Sets
Jersey: .75-1.5X
Production 99 Sets
Patch Number: 1-2X
Production 49 Sets
Patch Logo: No Pricing
Production 10 Sets

EB	Ernie Banks	20.00
WB	Wade Boggs	12.00
SC	Steve Carlton	12.00
DD	Dom DiMaggio	20.00
CF	Carlton Fisk	15.00
SG	Steve Garvey	15.00
BG	Bob Gibson	15.00
DG	Dwight Gooden	10.00
KH	Keith Hernandez	10.00
OH	Orel Hershiser	10.00
RK	Ray Knight	10.00
SM	Stan Musial	30.00
JR	Jim Rice	12.00
NR	Nolan Ryan	50.00
RS	Ryne Sandberg	25.00
RST	Ron Santo	10.00
TS	Tom Seaver	15.00
OS	Ozzie Smith	10.00
DS	Darryl Strawberry	12.00
FV	Fernando Valenzuela	10.00
BW	Billy Williams	10.00
TW	Ted Williams	75.00
CY	Carl Yastrzemski	20.00

Gold Border Autographs

NM/M
Common Player: 10.00
Randomly Inserted

Ernie Banks	60.00
Johnny Bench	50.00
Yogi Berra	60.00
Paul Blair	10.00
Vida Blue	10.00
George Brett	125.00
Lou Brock	20.00
Jose Canseco	30.00
Bernie Carbo	10.00
Rod Carew	30.00
Steve Carlton	30.00
Rocky Colavito	100.00
Rick Dempsey	15.00
Dennis Eckersley	50.00
Dwight Evans	15.00
Carlton Fisk	40.00
Whitey Ford	40.00
Bill Freehan	10.00
Bob Gibson	25.00
Ron Guidry	20.00
Tony Gwynn	50.00
Bo Jackson	50.00
Reggie Jackson	100.00
Al Kaline	25.00
George Kell	15.00
Harmon Killebrew	30.00
Davey Lopes	10.00
Fred Lynn	10.00
Juan Marichal	20.00
Don Mattingly	80.00
Tim McCarver	15.00
Willie McCovey	40.00
Paul Molitor	40.00
Jack Morris	10.00
Eddie Murray	80.00
Stan Musial	100.00
Graig Nettles	15.00
Jim Palmer	20.00
Dave Parker	10.00
Tony Perez	30.00
Johnny Podres	10.00
Kirby Puckett	50.00
Jim Rice	20.00
Cal Ripken Jr.	150.00
Phil Rizzuto	40.00
Brooks Robinson	20.00
Frank Robinson	30.00
Joe Rudi	10.00
Nolan Ryan	150.00
Mike Schmidt	60.00
Tom Seaver	80.00
Bobby Shantz	10.00
Bill "Moose" Skowron	10.00
Duke Snider	30.00
Rusty Staub	10.00
Frank Tanana	10.00
Gorman Thomas	10.00
Luis Tiant	10.00
Jeff Torborg	10.00
Alan Trammell	10.00
Carl Yastrzemski	60.00

Gold Border Autograph Series 2

NM/M
Common Player: 15.00
Inserted 1:75

LA	Luis Aparicio	20.00
WB	Wade Boggs	40.00
JBO	Jim Bouton	15.00
RC2	Rod Carew/Twins	40.00
SC2	Steve Carlton/Cards	30.00
GC	Gary Carter	25.00
JCH	Joe Charboneau	15.00
WC	Will Clark	40.00
DC	David Cone	40.00
AD	Andre Dawson	20.00
DD	Dom DiMaggio	50.00

RF	Rollie Fingers	15.00
CF2	Carlton Fisk/White Sox	40.00
SG	Steve Garvey	15.00
DG	Dwight Gooden	20.00
KH	Keith Hernandez	15.00
OH	Orel Hershiser	15.00
RJ2	Reggie Jackson/Angels	60.00
DK	Dave Kingman	15.00
RK	Ray Knight	15.00
JK	Jerry Koosman	20.00
JKR	John Kruk	15.00
TK	Tony Kubek	25.00
BM	Bill Mazeroski	30.00
WMG	Willie McGee	25.00
PM2	Paul Molitor/Jays	40.00
DMU	Dale Murphy	25.00
DN	Don Newcombe	15.00
PO	Paul O'Neill	30.00
JPP	Joe Pepitone	15.00
JPS	Johnny Pesky	25.00
JPI	Jimmy Piersall	20.00
RR	Robin Roberts	25.00
FR2	Frank Robinson/O's	30.00
PRO	Preacher Roe	20.00
AR	Al Rosen	15.00
NR2	Nolan Ryan/Angels	120.00
RS	Ryne Sandberg	75.00
DS	Deion Sanders	30.00
RST	Ron Santo	20.00
TS2	Tom Seaver/Reds	75.00
OS	Ozzie Smith	40.00
DS2	Duke Snider	40.00
BW	Billy Williams	20.00
RY	Robin Yount	40.00
DZ	Don Zimmer	25.00

Personality Cuts
No Pricing
Production One Set

Personality Cuts Series 2
No Pricing
Production 1 or 2 Sets

Single Cuts: Etched in Time
NM/M
No Pricing
ET-RC Roberto Clemente/1 (7/04 auction) 6,100

Etched In Time Series 2
NM/M
Sequentially #'d to indicated quantity.
Cards #'d 25 or less: No Pricing

EA	Ethan Allen/50	150.00
EAV	Earl Averill/50	125.00
DC	Dolph Camilli/40	250.00
BH	Babe Herman/35	250.00
HK	Harvey Kuenn/32	120.00
SM	Sal Maglie/40	100.00
ER	Edd Roush/95	100.00
PR	Pete Runnels/35	200.00
CS	Chris Short/30	120.00

The Glory of Their Time

NM/M
Common Player: 4.00
Serially Numbered

1GOT	Harmon Killebrew/1961	4.00
2GOT	Johnny Bench/1974	5.00
3GOT	George Brett/1980	8.00
4GOT	Tony Gwynn/1987	5.00
5GOT	Paul Molitor/1987	5.00
6GOT	Don Mattingly/1986	8.00
7GOT	Reggie Jackson/1980	8.00
8GOT	Carlton Fisk/1985	5.00
9GOT	Cal Ripken Jr./1983	10.00
10GOT	Brooks Robinson/1964	4.00
11GOT	Eddie Murray/1980	5.00
12GOT	Bill "Moose" Skowron/1960	4.00
13GOT	Lou Brock/1974	5.00
14GOT	Don Drysdale/1962	5.00
15GOT	Tony Gwynn/1997	4.00
16GOT	Mike Schmidt/1980	8.00
17GOT	Carl Yastrzemski/1967	4.00
18GOT	Babe Ruth/1927	10.00
19GOT	Nolan Ryan/1989	10.00
20GOT	Yogi Berra/1950	5.00
21GOT	Al Kaline/1955	5.00
22GOT	Ty Cobb/1911	5.00
23GOT	Duke Snider/1955	5.00
24GOT	Stan Musial/1948	8.00
25GOT	Jose Canseco/1988	5.00
26GOT	Rocky Colavito/1958	5.00
27GOT	Dave Winfield/1979	4.00
28GOT	Nolan Ryan/1982	10.00
29GOT	Thurman Munson/1977	8.00
30GOT	Jackie Robinson/1949	8.00
31GOT	Kirby Puckett/1988	8.00
32GOT	Ted Kluszewski/1954	5.00
33GOT	Warren Spahn/1953	5.00
34GOT	Willie McCovey/1969	4.00
35GOT	Phil Rizzuto/1950	5.00

The Glory/Time: Game-Used

JOSE CANSECO

NM/M
Common Player: 10.00
Production 250 Sets
Hobby Only
Gold: 1.5-2X
Retail Only (Not Numbered)
No Rizzuto Retail Version

JB	Johnny Bench/Jsy	15.00
YB	Yogi Berra/Pants	15.00
GB	George Brett/Jsy	15.00
LB	Lou Brock/Jsy	15.00
JC1	Jose Canseco/Jsy	10.00
JC2	Jose Canseco/Bat	10.00
RC	Rocky Colavito/Bat	25.00
DD	Don Drysdale/Jsy	15.00
CF1	Carlton Fisk/Jsy	10.00
CF2	Carlton Fisk/Bat	10.00
TG1	Tony Gwynn/Jsy	10.00
TG2	Tony Gwynn/Bat	10.00
RJ	Reggie Jackson/Pants	20.00
AK	Al Kaline/Pants	15.00
HK	Harmon Killebrew/Bat	10.00
TK	Ted Kluszewski/Pants	15.00
DM	Don Mattingly/Pants	20.00
WM	Willie McCovey/Pants	10.00
PM	Paul Molitor/Jsy	15.00
TM	Thurman Munson/Pants	10.00
EM	Eddie Murray/Jsy	10.00
KP	Kirby Puckett/Bat	20.00
CR	Cal Ripken Jr./Jsy	20.00
PR	Phil Rizzuto/Pants	15.00
BR	Brooks Robinson/Jsy	10.00
NR1	Nolan Ryan/Jsy	20.00
NR2	Nolan Ryan/Bat	20.00
MS	Mike Schmidt/Jsy	15.00
MS	Bill "Moose" Skowron/Jsy	10.00
WS	Warren Spahn/Jsy	20.00
DW	Dave Winfield/Jsy	10.00
CY	Carl Yastrzemski/Jsy	20.00

The Glory/Time: G-U Patch
No Pricing
Production 25 Sets

Yankee Clippings
NM/M
Common Player: 25.00
Inserted 1:45

YB	Yogi Berra	60.00
WB	Wade Boggs	40.00
RJ	Reggie Jackson	40.00
LG	Roger Maris	400.00
DM	Don Mattingly	100.00
PO	Paul O'Neill	30.00
PR	Phil Rizzuto	325.00
BS	Bill "Moose" Skowron	25.00

Yankee Clippings Autographs
No Pricing
Sequentially #'d between 3 & 26.

2004 Fleer Hot Prospects Draft Edition

NM/M
Common Player (1-60): .25
Minor Stars (1-60): .40
Unlisted Stars (1-60): .60
Common Rookie (61-70): 3.00
Common Rookie (71-120): 15.00
Production 1,000 Sets
Cards 112 & 113 do not exist.
Production 299 Sets
Pack (5): 6.00
Box (15): 75.00

1	Miguel Tejada	.50
2	Jose Vidro	.25
3	Hideki Matsui	2.00
4	Roger Clemens	2.50
5	Craig Wilson	.25
6	Bobby Crosby	.25
7	Pat Burrell	.40
8	Mike Sweeney	.25
9	Craig Biggio	.40
10	Scott Rolen	1.00
11	Roy Halladay	.40
12	Lyle Overbay	.25
13	Rocco Baldelli	.50
14	Mike Piazza	1.50
15	Rafael Palmeiro	.75
16	Hank Blalock	.50
17	Sammy Sosa	1.50
18	Dontrelle Willis	.40
19	Alfonso Soriano	1.00
20	Gary Sheffield	.75
21	Jim Thome	1.00
22	Ivan Rodriguez	.75
23	Adam Dunn	.50
24	Kerry Wood	.50
25	Khalil Greene	.50
26	Richie Sexson	.40
27	Nomar Garciaparra	1.00
28	Andruw Jones	.75
29	Tom Glavine	.40
30	Carlos Beltran	.75
31	Chipper Jones	1.00
32	Jeff Bagwell	.75
33	Tim Hudson	.40
34	Alex Rodriguez	2.00
35	Omar Vizquel	.40
36	Albert Pujols	2.50
37	Frank Thomas	.75
38	Ben Sheets	.40
39	Jason Schmidt	.40
40	Miguel Cabrera	.75
41	Carlos Delgado	.75
42	Ichiro Suzuki	2.00
43	Curt Schilling	.75
44	Todd Helton	.75
45	Ken Griffey Jr.	1.50
46	Mark Prior	.75
47	Vladimir Guerrero	1.00
48	Pedro Martinez	1.00
49	Manny Ramirez	1.00
50	Joe Mauer	.50
51	Jorge Posada	.75
52	Troy Glaus	.50
53	Randy Johnson	1.00
54	Adrian Beltre	.40
55	Eric Gagne	.50
56	Josh Beckett	.50
57	Jason Giambi	.75
58	Barry Zito	.50
59	Lance Berkman	.50
60	Derek Jeter	2.00
61	Kazuo Matsui **RC**	5.00
62	Jason Bartlett **RC**	5.00
63	John Gall **RC**	3.00
64	Chris Saenz **RC**	3.00
65	Merkin Valdez **RC**	3.00
66	Akinori Otsuka **RC**	3.00
67	Joey Gathright **RC**	5.00
68	Brad Halsey **RC**	5.00
69	David Aardsma **RC**	3.00
70	Scott Kazmir	10.00
71	Matt Bush AU **RC**	30.00
72	John Bowker AU **RC**	15.00
73	Mike Ferris AU **RC**	15.00
74	Brian Bixler AU **RC**	15.00
75	Scott Elbert AU **RC**	40.00
76	Josh Fields AU **RC**	50.00
77	Bill Bray AU **RC**	25.00
78	Greg Golson AU **RC**	30.00
79	Neil Walker AU **RC**	30.00
80	Phillip Hughes AU **RC**	200.00
81	Chris Nelson AU **RC**	40.00
82	Mark Rogers AU **RC**	30.00
83	Trevor Plouffe AU **RC**	25.00
84	Christian Garcia AU **RC**	15.00
85	Thomas Diamond AU **RC**	30.00
86	B.J. Szymanski AU **RC**	25.00
87	Richie Robnett AU **RC**	25.00
88	Seth Smith AU **RC**	25.00
89	Kyle Waldrop AU **RC**	25.00
90	Curtis Thigpen AU **RC**	15.00
91	J.P. Howell AU **RC**	15.00
92	Blake DeWitt AU **RC**	30.00
93	Taylor Tankersley AU **RC**	15.00
94	Zach Jackson AU **RC**	15.00
95	Justin Orenduff AU **RC**	15.00
96	Tyler Lumsden AU **RC**	15.00
97	Danny Putnam **RC**	20.00
98	Jon Poterson AU **RC**	15.00
99	Matt Fox AU **RC**	15.00
100	Gio Gonzalez AU **RC**	35.00
101	Huston Street AU **RC**	25.00
102	Jay Rainville AU **RC**	25.00
103	Matt Durkin AU **RC**	15.00
104	Brett Smith AU **RC**	15.00
105	Justin Hoyman AU **RC**	20.00
106	Erick San Pedro AU **RC**	15.00
107	Jeff Marquez AU **RC**	15.00
108	Hunter Pence AU **RC**	90.00
109	Dustin Pedroia AU **RC**	40.00
110	Kurt Suzuki AU **RC**	25.00
111	Billy Buckner AU **RC**	15.00
114	J.C. Holt AU **RC**	15.00
115	Homer Bailey AU **RC**	100.00
116	David Purcey AU **RC**	20.00
117	Jeremy Sowers AU **RC**	50.00
118	Chris Lambert AU **RC**	15.00
119	Eric Hurley AU **RC**	25.00
120	Grant Johnson AU **RC**	15.00

Red Hot
Veterans (1-60): 2-4X
Rookies (61-70): 1-2X
Production 150
Rookies (71-120): No Pricing
Production 25 Sets

White Hot
Cards (1-120): No Pricing
Production One Set

Alumni Ink
No Pricing
Production 15 Sets
Red Hot: No Pricing
Production 5 Sets
White Hot: No Pricing
Production One Set

Double Team Autograph Patch Red Hot
No Pricing
Production 22 Sets
White Hot: No Pricing
Production One Set

Double Team Jersey
NM/M
Common Player: 10.00
Production 100 Sets
Red Hot: No Pricing
Production 25 Sets
White Hot: No Pricing
Production 1 Set
Patch: .75-1.5X
Production 50 Sets
Patch Red Hot: No Pricing
Production 10 Sets
Patch White Hot: No Pricing
Production One Set

CB	Carlos Beltran	15.00
RCA	Rod Carew	20.00
RCL	Roger Clemens	20.00
JG	Jason Giambi	12.00
TG	Tom Glavine	15.00
VG	Vladimir Guerrero	15.00
RH	Rickey Henderson	15.00
RJ	Reggie Jackson	25.00
GM	Greg Maddux	15.00
PM	Pedro Martinez	15.00
EM	Eddie Murray	20.00
HN	Hideo Nomo	10.00
RP	Rafael Palmeiro	12.00
MP	Mike Piazza	20.00
MR	Manny Ramirez	15.00
IR	Ivan Rodriguez	15.00
SR	Scott Rolen	10.00
NR	Nolan Ryan	50.00
AS	Alfonso Soriano	12.00
MT	Miguel Tejada	10.00

Draft Rewind

NM/M
Common Player: 2.00
Inserted 1:5

1	Joe Mauer	2.00
2	Derek Jeter	6.00
3	Chipper Jones	3.50
4	Greg Maddux	3.50
5	Alex Rodriguez	5.00
6	Nomar Garciaparra	3.00
7	Curt Schilling	3.00
8	Kerry Wood	3.00
9	Troy Glaus	3.00
10	Pat Burrell	2.00
11	Mark Mulder	2.00
12	Josh Beckett	3.00
13	Barry Zito	3.00
14	Mark Prior	4.00
15	Rickie Weeks	3.00
16	Khalil Greene	3.00
17	Ken Griffey Jr.	3.50
18	Gary Sheffield	3.00
19	Todd Helton	3.00
20	Barry Larkin	2.00
21	Kevin Brown	2.00
22	Frank Thomas	3.00
23	Manny Ramirez	3.00
24	Roger Clemens	5.00
25	Lance Berkman	3.00
26	Randy Johnson	3.00
27	Jason Giambi	3.00
28	Ben Sheets	2.00
29	Scott Rolen	3.00
30	Tom Glavine	2.00

Draft Rewind Jersey
NM/M
Common Player: 8.00
Sequentially #'d to indicated qty.
Red Hot: No Pricing
Production 10 Sets
White Hot: No Pricing
Production One Set
Patch
Cards #'d 41-68: .75-1.5X
Cards #'d 29 or less: No Pricing
Patch Red Hot: No Pricing
Production 5 Sets
Patch White Hot: No Pricing
Production One Set

RB	Rocco Baldelli/119	8.00
JB	Josh Beckett/102	10.00
LB	Lance Berkman/116	8.00
KB	Kevin Brown/104	8.00
PB	Pat Burrell/101	8.00
EC	Eric Chavez/110	8.00
RC	Roger Clemens/119	15.00
JG	Jason Giambi/158	8.00
TG	Troy Glaus/103	8.00
TG	Tom Glavine/147	8.00
KG	Khalil Greene/113	15.00
ZG	Zack Greinke/106	8.00
TH	Todd Helton/108	10.00
RJ	Randy Johnson/136	10.00
CJ	Chipper Jones/101	12.00
CK	Casey Kotchman/113	8.00
BL	Barry Larkin/104	10.00
GM	Greg Maddux/131	12.00
JM	Joe Mauer/101	10.00
MM	Mark Mulder/102	8.00
MP	Mark Prior/102	8.00
MR	Manny Ramirez/113	10.00
SR	Scott Rolen/146	10.00
CS	Curt Schilling/139	10.00
BS	Ben Sheets/110	8.00
GS	Gary Sheffield/106	8.00
FT	Frank Thomas/117	15.00
RW	Rickie Weeks/102	8.00
KW	Kerry Wood/102	10.00
BZ	Barry Zito/109	8.00

Hot Tandems
NM/M
Common Card: 3.00

HOT TANDEMS

Inserted 1:15

1HT	Mark Prior, Greg Maddux	4.00
2HT	Jim Thome, Pat Burrell	3.50
3HT	Ken Griffey Jr., Adam Dunn	4.00
4HT	Mike Piazza, Tom Glavine	4.00
5HT	Alex Rodriguez, Derek Jeter	10.00
6HT	Roger Clemens, Andy Pettitte	6.00
7HT	Hideki Matsui, Jason Giambi	6.00
8HT	Hank Blalock, Alfonso Soriano	3.50
9HT	Manny Ramirez, David Ortiz	3.50
10HT	Miguel Cabrera, Dontrelle Willis	3.50
11HT	Hideki Matsui, Ichiro Suzuki	6.00
12HT	Albert Pujols, Scott Rolen	6.00
13HT	Curt Schilling, Pedro J. Martinez	3.50
14HT	Nomar Garciaparra, Sammy Sosa	3.50
15HT	Kazuo Matsui, Derek Jeter	8.00

MLB Hot Materials
NM/M
Common Player: 5.00
Production 325 Sets
Red Hot: 1-2X
Production 50 Sets
White Hot Patch: No Pricing
Production One Set

JB	Jeff Bagwell/Jsy	6.00
LB	Lance Berkman/Jsy	5.00
HB	Hank Blalock/Jsy	6.00
MC	Miguel Cabrera/Jsy	8.00
RC	Roger Clemens/Jsy	12.00
CD	Carlos Delgado/Jsy	6.00
JD	J.D. Drew/Jsy	6.00
AD	Adam Dunn/Jsy	6.00
JE	Jim Edmonds/Jsy	6.00
EG	Eric Gagne/Jsy	6.00
VG	Vladimir Guerrero/Jsy	8.00
THE	Todd Helton/Jsy	5.00
THU	Tim Hudson/Jsy	5.00
THN	Torii Hunter/Jsy	5.00
RJ	Randy Johnson/Jsy	8.00
AJ	Andruw Jones/Jsy	6.00
CJ	Chipper Jones/Jsy	8.00
HM	Hideki Matsui/Jsy	20.00
KM	Kazuo Matsui/Jsy	8.00
JM	Joe Mauer/Jsy	8.00
MM	Mike Mussina/Jsy	8.00
HN	Hideo Nomo/Jsy	8.00
LO	Lyle Overbay/Jsy	5.00
APE	Andy Pettitte/Jsy	8.00
MPI	Mike Piazza/Jsy	8.00
JP	Jorge Posada/Jsy	6.00
MPR	Mark Prior/Jsy	8.00
APU	Albert Pujols/Jsy	12.00
MR	Manny Ramirez/Jsy	8.00
IR	Ivan Rodriguez/Jsy	6.00
CS	Curt Schilling/Jsy	8.00
JS	Jason Schmidt/Jsy	5.00
AS	Alfonso Soriano/Jsy	8.00
SS	Sammy Sosa/Jsy	10.00
MTX	Mark Teixeira/Jsy	6.00
MTJ	Miguel Tejada/Jsy	8.00
FT	Frank Thomas/Jsy	8.00
JT	Jim Thome/Jsy	8.00
DW	Dontrelle Willis/Jsy	5.00
KW	Kerry Wood/Jsy	5.00

Past, Present, Future Triple Autograph
NM/M
Production 33 Sets
Red Hot: No Pricing
Production 3 Sets
White Hot: No Pricing
Production One Set
Matt Durkin, Mookie Wilson, Mike Piazza 150.00
Hideo Nomo, Scott Elbert, Kirk Gibson 250.00

Josh Fields, Carlton Fisk, Ryan Meaux	80.00
Greg Golson, Steve Carlton, Jim Thome	100.00
Jack Wilson, Neil Walker, Ralph Kiner	80.00
Ryne Sandberg, Mark Prior, Grant Johnson	250.00
Homer Bailey, Johnny Bench, Adam Dunn	150.00
Albert Pujols, Chris Lambert, Stan Musial	300.00
Richie Robnett, Reggie Jackson, Eric Chavez	80.00
Dustin Pedroia, Bill Buckner, Manny Ramirez	60.00

2004 Fleer InScribed

ALBERT PUJOLS

	NM/M
Common Player (1-75):	.25
Minor Stars (1-75):	.40
Unlisted Stars (1-75):	.60
Common Player (76-85):	3.00

Production 1,000 Sets
Numbered to 750
Not all 750 of each card not released.

Pack (5):	10.00
Box (12):	85.00
1 Vladimir Guerrero	1.00
2 Bartolo Colon	.40
3 Troy Glaus	.60
4 Richie Sexson	.60
5 Randy Johnson	1.00
6 Luis Gonzalez	.40
7 J.D. Drew	.40
8 Chipper Jones	1.50
9 Andruw Jones	.75
10 Melvin Mora	.25
11 Miguel Tejada	.60
12 Curt Schilling	.60
13 Pedro J. Martinez	1.00
14 Nomar Garciaparra	2.50
15 Kerry Wood	.75
16 Mark Prior	2.00
17 Sammy Sosa	2.00
18 Frank Thomas	.75
19 Magglio Ordonez	.40
20 Sean Casey	.25
21 Ken Griffey Jr.	1.50
22 Adam Dunn	.60
23 Jody Gerut	.25
24 Omar Vizquel	.25
25 Todd Helton	.75
26 Vinny Castilla	.25
27 Alex Sanchez	.25
28 Ivan Rodriguez	.60
29 Dontrelle Willis	.40
30 Josh Beckett	.75
31 Miguel Cabrera	.75
32 Roger Clemens	1.50
33 Andy Pettitte	.60
34 Jeff Bagwell	.75
35 Ken Harvey	.25
36 Carlos Beltran	.60
37 Shawn Green	.40
38 Hideo Nomo	.40
39 Scott Podsednik	.25
40 Ben Sheets	.40
41 Torii Hunter	.60
42 Jacque Jones	.25
43 Jose Vidro	.25
44 Mike Piazza	1.50
45 Tom Glavine	.40
46 Derek Jeter	3.00
47 Alex Rodriguez	2.50
48 Jason Giambi	1.00
49 Hideki Matsui	2.50
50 Eric Chavez	.40
51 Barry Zito	.60
52 Tim Hudson	.40
53 Mark Mulder	.40
54 Jim Thome	1.00
55 Pat Burrell	.25
56 Chase Utley	.25
57 Jason Kendall	.40
58 Jack Wilson	.25
59 Khalil Greene	.75
60 Brian Giles	.40
61 Jason Schmidt	.40
62 Marquis Grissom	.25
63 Ichiro Suzuki	2.00
64 Bret Boone	.40
65 Albert Pujols	2.50
66 Scott Rolen	1.00
67 Jim Edmonds	.40
68 Tino Martinez	.25
69 Rocco Baldelli	.60
70 Alfonso Soriano	1.00
71 Michael Young	.25
72 Hank Blalock	.40
73 Roy Halladay	.40
74 Carlos Delgado	.75
75 Vernon Wells	.40
76 Johnny Bench	3.00
77 Reggie Jackson	5.00
78 Al Kaline	3.00
79 Nolan Ryan	10.00
80 Tom Seaver	3.00
81 Robin Yount	6.00
82 Mike Schmidt	5.00
83 Jim Palmer	5.00
84 Harmon Killebrew	5.00
85 Joe Morgan	5.00
86 Kazuo Matsui RC	5.00
87 Luis Gonzalez RC	3.00
88 Yadier Molina RC	4.00
89 Jon Knott RC	3.00
90 Kevin Youkilis RC	5.00
91 Chris Saenz RC	3.00
92 Andres Blanco RC	3.00
93 David Aardsma	3.00
94 Merkin Valdez RC	3.00
95 Jason Bartlett RC	3.00
96 John Gall RC	3.00
97 Zack Greinke	3.00
98 Scott Hairston	3.00
99 Matt Holliday	4.00
100 Casey Kotchman	5.00

Red
No Pricing
Production 5 Sets

Gold
Veterans (1-75):	2-5X
Rookies (76-100):	.75-2X

Production 199 Sets

Autographs Silver
	NM/M
Common Player:	10.00

Numbered to indicated quantity.
Red: No Pricing
Production 25 Sets
Purple: .5-2X
Numbered to jersey number.

RB Rocco Baldelli/34	25.00
CB Carlos Beltran/296	25.00
JB Jeremy Bonderman/ 287	10.00
EC Eric Chavez/322	15.00
EG Eric Gagne/57	40.00
BG Brian Giles/134	15.00
LG Luis Gonzalez/55	15.00
RHL Roy Halladay/139	15.00
RHR Rich Harden/235	10.00
TH Trevor Hoffman/174	15.00
BL Barry Larkin/140	20.00
JL Javy Lopez/257	15.00
TN Trot Nixon/318	10.00
LO Lyle Overbay/240	10.00
SP Scott Podsednik/280	10.00
BR Brad Radke/168	15.00

Facsimile Signature Gold

JASON SCHMIDT
047/199

Current (1-75):	3-5X
Retired (76-85):	1-2X
Rookies (86-100):	.75-1.5X

Production 199 Sets

Award Winners
	NM/M
Common Player:	

Production 150 Sets
1 Alex Rodriguez	10.00
2 Eric Gagne	3.00
3 Miguel Tejada	4.00
4 Roy Halladay	3.00
5 Randy Johnson	5.00
6 Barry Zito	4.00
7 Chipper Jones	3.00
8 Ivan Rodriguez	4.00
9 Pedro J. Martinez	5.00
10 Barry Larkin	3.00
11 Dontrelle Willis	3.00
12 Angel Berroa	3.00
13 Kerry Wood	5.00
14 Albert Pujols	8.00
15 Hideo Nomo	3.00

Award Winners Jersey Silver
	NM/M
Common Player:	

Production 175 Sets
Copper: .75-1.5X
Production 99 Sets
Purple: 1-3X
Production 49 Sets

AB Angel Berroa	5.00
EG Eric Gagne	8.00
RH Roy Halladay	8.00
RJ Randy Johnson	10.00
CJ Chipper Jones	10.00
BL Barry Larkin	5.00
PM Pedro J. Martinez	10.00
HN Hideo Nomo	5.00
AP Albert Pujols	15.00
IR Ivan Rodriguez	8.00
MT Miguel Tejada	8.00
DW Dontrelle Willis	5.00
KW Kerry Wood	10.00
BZ Barry Zito	8.00

Award Winners Autographs
	NM/M
Common Player:	15.00

Numbered to award year.
All cards not released for some cards.

AB Angel Berroa/103	15.00
RH Roy Halladay/102	20.00
BL Barry Larkin 95/50	30.00
DW Dontrelle Willis/103	25.00

Induction Ceremony
	NM/M
Common Player:	6.00

Numbered to year of Induction.

1 Carlton Fisk/100	8.00
2 Tony Perez/100	6.00
3 Nolan Ryan/99	20.00
4 Robin Yount/99	10.00
5 Orlando Cepeda/99	8.00
6 Bill Mazeroski/101	8.00
7 Larry Doby/98	6.00
8 Phil Niekro/97	6.00
9 Jim Bunning/96	6.00
10 Sparky Anderson/100	6.00
11 Phil Rizzuto/94	8.00
12 Rollie Fingers/92	6.00
13 Hal Newhouser/92	6.00
14 Rod Carew/91	8.00
15 Reggie Jackson/93	8.00
16 Tom Seaver/92	8.00
17 Bob Gibson/81	8.00
18 Jim Palmer/90	6.00
19 Joe Morgan/90	6.00
20 Al Kaline/80	10.00

Induction Ceremony Autograph Bronze
	NM/M
Common Player:	20.00

Numbered to 50
Silver: No Pricing
Production 15 Sets
Gold: No Pricing
Production 5 Sets

JB Jim Bunning	20.00
OC Orlando Cepeda/40	20.00
RF Rollie Fingers	30.00
CF Carlton Fisk	30.00
BG Bob Gibson	40.00
AK Al Kaline	50.00
TP Tony Perez	30.00

Induction Ceremony Material Silver
	NM/M
Common Player:	10.00

Numbered (2-Digit) to Induction Year.
Masterpiece: No Pricing
Production One Set

SA Sparky Anderson/100	10.00
RC Rod Carew/91	15.00
OC Orlando Cepeda/99	10.00
LD Larry Doby/98	20.00
RF Rollie Fingers/92	10.00
CF Carlton Fisk/100	15.00
RJ Reggie Jackson/93	10.00
AK Al Kaline/80	20.00
BM Bill Mazeroski/101	10.00
JM Joe Morgan/90	15.00
PN Phil Niekro/97	10.00
JP Jim Palmer/90	10.00
TP Tony Perez/100	15.00
PR Phil Rizzuto/94	20.00
NR Nolan Ryan/99	25.00
TS Tom Seaver/92	10.00
RY Robin Yount/99	10.00

Names of the Game

299/299

	NM/M
Common Player:	2.00

Production 299 Sets

1 Nomar Garciaparra	8.00
2 Randy Johnson	3.00
3 Hideki Matsui	8.00
4 Frank Thomas	2.00
5 Ivan Rodriguez	2.00
6 Roger Clemens	5.00
7 Chipper Jones	5.00
8 Dontrelle Willis	5.00
9 Luis Gonzalez	2.00
10 Alex Rodriguez	8.00
11 Eric Gagne	2.00
12 Juan Gonzalez	2.00
13 Hideo Nomo	2.00
14 Sean Casey	2.00
15 Greg Maddux	5.00
16 Cal Ripken Jr.	15.00
17 Carl Yastrzemski	5.00
18 Tony Perez	3.00
19 Joe Morgan	3.00
20 Carlton Fisk	3.00
21 Willie McCovey	5.00
22 Al Kaline	5.00
23 Dennis Eckersley	3.00
24 Ted Williams	10.00
25 Willie Stargell	5.00
26 Rollie Fingers	3.00
27 Yogi Berra	2.00
28 Reggie Jackson	5.00
29 Harmon Killebrew	5.00
30 Nolan Ryan	10.00

Names of the Game Autograph Silver
	NM/M
Common Player:	15.00

Stated Production 99 Sets
All 99 not released for some cards.
Gold: No Pricing
Stated Production 25 Sets.
All 25 not released for some cards.

SC Sean Casey	5.00
DE Dennis Eckersley/90	25.00
RF Rollie Fingers/90	25.00
CF Carlton Fisk/50	30.00
LG Luis Gonzalez/75	15.00
CJ Chipper Jones/40	40.00
AK Al Kaline/90	40.00
DW Dontrelle Willis	25.00

Names of the Game Material Copper

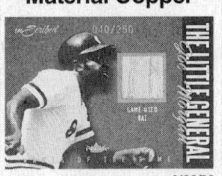

040/250
THE LITTLE GENERAL

	NM/M
Common Player:	5.00

Production 250 Sets
Gold: .5-1.25X
Production 150 Sets
Red: .75-1.5X
Production 79 Sets
Purple: 1-2X
Production 33 Sets

YB Yogi Berra	10.00
SC Sean Casey	5.00
RC Roger Clemens	10.00
DE Dennis Eckersley	8.00
RF Rollie Fingers	8.00
CF Carlton Fisk	8.00
EG Eric Gagne	10.00
JG Juan Gonzalez	10.00
LG Luis Gonzalez	8.00
RJA Reggie Jackson	10.00
RJO Randy Johnson	8.00
CJ Chipper Jones	8.00
AK Al Kaline	10.00
HK Harmon Killebrew	10.00
GM Greg Maddux	15.00
HM Hideki Matsui	15.00
WM Willie McCovey	10.00
JM Joe Morgan	8.00
HN Hideo Nomo	5.00
TP Tony Perez	8.00
CR Cal Ripken Jr.	30.00
IR Ivan Rodriguez	8.00
NR Nolan Ryan	20.00
WS Willie Stargell	10.00
FT Frank Thomas	5.00
TW Ted Williams	25.00
DW Dontrelle Willis	5.00
CY Carl Yastrzemski	10.00

Rookie Autographs Notation
	NM/M
Common Player:	15.00

Stated Production 750 Sets
75 Notation Cards for each player

87 Luis A. Gonzalez 4/6/04	15.00
89 Jon Knott 5/30/04	15.00
90 Kevin Youkilis 5/15/04	20.00
91 Chris Saenz 4/24/04	15.00
92 Andres Blanco 4/17/04	15.00
94 Merkin Valdez Go Giants	20.00
95 Jason Bartlett Go Twins	20.00
96B John Gall Go Cards/50	20.00
98 Scott Hairston 5/17/04	15.00
100 Casey Kotchman 5/9/04	25.00

L.A. Dodgers

Paul Lo Duca — Catcher — Dodgers

Persons attending April 11 (#1-7), May 30 (#8-14) and July 10 (#15-21) special Baseball Card Pack promotional games received a cellowrapped series of seven Tradition cards and a checklist card. Fronts have game-action photos with blue borders. Backs have major/minor league stats.

	NM/M
Complete Set (22):	7.50
Common Player:	.25
1 Hideo Nomo	1.50
2 Paul LoDuca	.50
3 Alex Cora	.25
4 Paul Shuey	.25
5 Juan Encarnacion	.25
6 Steve Colyer	.25
7 Joe Thurston	.25
8 Shawn Green	.35
9 Edwin Jackson	.50
10 Dave Roberts	.25
11 Guillermo Mota	.25
12 Jolbert Cabrera	.25
13 Darren Dreifort	.25
14 David Ross	.25
15 Eric Gagne	.35
16 Adrian Beltre	.35
17 Cesar Izturis	.25
18 Robin Ventura	.25
19 Wilson Alvarez	.25
20 Bubba Trammell	.25
21 Wilkin Ruan	.25
--- Checklist	.25

2004 Fleer Legacy

THOME

	NM/M
Common Player (1-60):	1.50
Minor Stars (1-60):	2.00
Unlisted Stars (1-60):	2.50
Common Rookie (61-75):	4.00

Box (1 Pack, 1 Autographed Baseball): 150.00

1 Angel Berroa	1.50
2 Derek Jeter	8.00
3 Jody Gerut	1.50
4 Curt Schilling	2.50
5 Khalil Greene	3.00
6 Manny Ramirez	3.00
7 Rocco Baldelli	2.50
8 Sammy Sosa	3.00
9 Shawn Green	2.00
10 Austin Kearns	2.50
11 Frank Thomas	3.00
12 Alfonso Soriano	3.50
13 Alex Rodriguez	6.00
14 Carlos Delgado	3.00
15 Chipper Jones	4.00
16 Edgar Martinez	2.00
17 Ivan Rodriguez	2.50
18 Mark Prior	4.00
19 Mike Piazza	4.00
20 Orlando Cabrera	1.50
21 Adam Dunn	3.00
22 Andruw Jones	3.00
23 Eric Chavez	2.00
24 Mark Teixeira	2.00
25 Scott Podsednik	2.50
26 Torii Hunter	2.50
27 Miguel Cabrera	3.00
28 Hideki Matsui	4.00
29 Jose Reyes	1.50
30 Vladimir Guerrero	3.50
31 Albert Pujols	6.00
32 Greg Maddux	3.50
33 Jason Giambi	3.50
34 Randy Johnson	3.50
35 Roger Clemens	4.00
36 Casey Kotchman	2.00
37 Ken Griffey Jr.	3.00
38 Todd Helton	3.00
39 Javy Lopez	1.50
40 Jim Thome	3.50
41 Josh Beckett	3.00
42 Kerry Wood	4.00
43 Scott Rolen	3.50
44 Pat Burrell	2.00
45 Pedro J. Martinez	3.50
46 Barry Zito	2.50
47 Hank Blalock	2.50
48 Hideo Nomo	2.00
49 Jeff Bagwell	2.00
50 Magglio Ordonez	2.00
51 Ichiro Suzuki	5.00
52 Joe Mauer	4.00
53 Richie Sexson	2.00
54 Shannon Stewart	1.50
55 Craig Wilson	1.50
56 Miguel Tejada	2.50
57 Sean Casey	1.50
58 Tom Glavine	2.00
59 Jason Schmidt	2.00
60 Nomar Garciaparra	6.00
61 Kazuo Matsui RC	6.00
62 Justin Leone RC	4.00
63 Merkin Valdez RC	6.00
64 Shingo Takatsu RC	6.00
65 Andres Blanco RC	4.00
66 Angel Chavez RC	4.00
67 Hector Gimenez RC	4.00
68 Akinori Otsuka RC	4.00
69 Jason Bartlett RC	4.00
70 Luis Gonzalez RC	4.00
71 Sean Henn	4.00
72 Mike Rouse	4.00
73 Chris Aguila RC	4.00
74 Aarom Baldiris RC	4.00
75 Jerry Gil RC	4.00

Gold Legacy

Veterans (1-60):	2-4X
Rookies (61-75):	.75-1.5X

Production 50 Sets

Ultimate Legacy
No Pricing
Production One Set

Franchise Legacy Patch
	NM/M
Common Player:	10.00

Production 99 Sets
Patch 50: .5-1.5X
Production 50 Sets
Patch 25: No Pricing
Production 25 Sets
Masterpiece: No Pricing
Production One Set

JBA Jeff Bagwell	15.00
JBE Josh Beckett	15.00
RC Roger Clemens	25.00
VG Vladimir Guerrero	15.00
RJ Randy Johnson	20.00
CJ Chipper Jones	20.00
JL Javy Lopez	10.00
GM Greg Maddux	30.00
PM Pedro Martinez	15.00
HM Hideki Matsui	60.00
KM Kazuo Matsui	20.00
DM Don Mattingly	40.00
HN Hideo Nomo	20.00
MP Mike Piazza	20.00
MPR Mark Prior	10.00
AP Albert Pujols	50.00
CR Cal Ripken Jr.	60.00
IR Ivan Rodriguez	15.00

NR	Nolan Ryan	50.00
SS	Sammy Sosa	15.00
MT	Miguel Tejada	10.00
JT	Jim Thome	15.00
KW	Kerry Wood	15.00

Franchise Dual Patch

No Pricing
Sequentially #'d between 5 & 31.

Franchise Legacy Quad Patch

No Pricing
Sequentially #'d between 2 & 22.

Hit Kings Patch Silver

		NM/M
Common Player:		15.00
Production 99 Sets		
Gold:		.5-1.5X
Production 50 Sets		
Masterpiece:		No Pricing
Production One Set		
JB	Jeff Bagwell	15.00
LB	Lance Berkman	15.00
HB	Hank Blalock	20.00
MC	Miguel Cabrera	20.00
CD	Carlos Delgado	20.00
AD	Adam Dunn	30.00
JG	Jason Giambi	15.00
VG	Vladimir Guerrero	20.00
CJ	Chipper Jones	20.00
AK	Austin Kearns	15.00
HM	Hideki Matsui	50.00
MP	Mike Piazza	25.00
AP	Albert Pujols	50.00
MR	Manny Ramirez	25.00
SR	Scott Rolen	20.00
MS	Mike Schmidt	40.00
RS	Richie Sexson	15.00
GS	Gary Sheffield	20.00
SS	Sammy Sosa	20.00
MT	Mark Teixeira	15.00
FT	Frank Thomas	15.00
JT	Jim Thome	25.00

Hit Kings Dual Patch

No Pricing
Sequentially numbered between 7 & 21.

Kaz Matsui Special Edition

This card was produced in an edition of 25,000. It was available to customers presenting a sheet of the Fleer/N.Y. Post Mets cards at any Mets Team Store and purchasing a Fleer pack. The back is labeled "1 OF 1 SPECIAL EDITION."

		NM/M
1	Kaz Matsui	3.00

National Trading Card Day

As part of its participation in NTCD on April 3, Fleer issued a foil pack with four baseball player cards, two football and three basketball, plus a header. Only the baseball players are listed here. Fronts have game-action photos on a ghosted background; backs have recent stats and biographical data. The NTCD logo appears on both sides.

		NM/M
Unopened Pack:		3.00
Common Player:		.25
1	Derek Jeter	.50
2	Alex Rodriguez	.50
3	Nomar Garciaparra	.35
4	Jose Reyes	.25

N.Y. Mets

Persons attending a special Baseball Card Pack promotional game received a cello-wrapped set of seven player cards and a header card. Fronts have game-action photos on a blue graph background. Backs have portrait and action photos and career highlights.

		NM/M
Complete Set (8):		4.00
Common Player:		.50
1	Mike Cameron	.50
2	Cliff Floyd	.50
3	Al Leiter	.50
4	Kaz Matsui	1.00
5	Mike Piazza	1.00
6	Jose Reyes	1.00
7	Shea Stadium	.50
---	Checklist	.05

2004 Fleer Patchworks

	NM/M
Common Player (1-90):	.15
Minor Stars:	.40
Unlisted Stars:	.60
Common Rookie (91-110):	2.00
Minor Rookies:	.75
Unlisted Rookies:	5.00
Production 799 Sets	
Pack (5):	4.00
Box (18):	70.00

1	Kerry Wood	1.00
2	Brian Giles	.40
3	Tino Martinez	.40
4	Mark Mulder	.40
5	Andy Pettitte	.60
6	Gary Sheffield	.60
7	Mark Teixeira	.40
8	Garret Anderson	.40
9	Craig Biggio	.40
10	Alfonso Soriano	1.50
11	Bret Boone	.40
12	Mike Piazza	2.00
13	Todd Helton	1.00
14	Jay Gibbons	.40
15	Eric Chavez	.40
16	Andruw Jones	1.00
17	Adam Dunn	.60
18	Corey Koskie	.15
19	Rafael Palmeiro	.60
20	Ivan Rodriguez	.60
21	Tom Glavine	.40
22	Luis Gonzalez	.40
23	Miguel Tejada	.60
24	Jose Vidro	.40
25	Richie Sexson	.60
26	Roy Halladay	.40

27	Vladimir Guerrero	1.50
28	Randy Johnson	1.50
29	Vernon Wells	.40
30	Pat Burrell	.40
31	Jason Schmidt	.40
32	Casey Blake	.15
33	Greg Maddux	2.00
34	Mike Lowell	.15
35	Hideo Nomo	.40
36	Carlos Delgado	1.00
37	Dontrelle Willis	.40
38	Shawn Green	.40
39	Pedro Martinez	1.50
40	Josh Beckett	1.00
41	Eric Gagne	.40
42	Manny Ramirez	1.00
43	Jim Edmonds	.40
44	Curt Schilling	.60
45	Mike Sweeney	.15
46	Albert Pujols	3.00
47	Nomar Garciaparra	3.00
48	Alex Rodriguez	3.00
49	Angel Berroa	.15
50	Jim Thome	1.50
51	Edgardo Alfonzo	.15
52	Jeremy Bonderman	.15
53	Miguel Cabrera	1.00
54	Bobby Higginson	.15
55	John Smoltz	.40
56	Jason Kendall	.40
57	Torii Hunter	.60
58	Troy Glaus	.60
59	Rafael Furcal	.40
60	Austin Kearns	.60
61	Esteban Loaiza	.15
62	Darin Erstad	.15
63	Jose Reyes	.15
64	Preston Wilson	.15
65	Rocco Baldelli	.60
66	Barry Zito	.40
67	Ken Griffey Jr.	2.00
68	Frank Thomas	1.00
69	Roger Clemens	2.00
70	Brett Myers	.15
71	Billy Wagner	.15
72	Scott Podsednik	.15
73	Jody Gerut	.15
74	Bartolo Colon	.15
75	Jeff Bagwell	1.00
76	Jason Giambi	1.50
77	Edgar Martinez	.40
78	Chipper Jones	2.00
79	Jason Bay	.15
80	Doug Mientkiewicz	.15
81	Hank Blalock	.60
82	Sammy Sosa	2.00
83	Derek Jeter	4.00
84	Ichiro Suzuki	2.00
85	Ben Sheets	.40
86	Magglio Ordonez	.40
87	Carlos Beltran	.40
88	Mark Prior	2.00
89	Sean Burroughs	.15
90	Tim Hudson	.40
91	Hector Gimenez **RC**	8.00
92	Khalil Greene **RC**	5.00
93	Rickie Weeks	8.00
94	Delmon Young	10.00
95	Donald Kelly **RC**	3.00
96	Chad Bentz **RC**	5.00
97	Greg Dobbs **RC**	3.00
98	John Gall **RC**	5.00
99	Cory Sullivan **RC**	5.00
100	Kazuo Matsui **RC**	25.00
101	Graham Koonce	3.00
102	Jason Bartlett **RC**	8.00
103	Angel Chavez **RC**	2.00
104	Ronny Cedeno **RC**	3.00
105	Jerry Gil **RC**	3.00
106	Ivan Ochoa **RC**	3.00
107	Ruddy Yan **RC**	8.00
108	Mike Gosling **RC**	3.00
109	Alfredo Simon **RC**	2.00
110	Koyie Hill **RC**	2.00

Ruby

Ruby (1-90):	3-10X
Ruby (91-110):	.5-2X
Production 50 Sets	

Autoworks

	NM/M
Common Player:	10.00
Inserted 1:54	
Parallel:	.5-1.25X
Production 100 Sets	
Patch	
Production 10 Sets	
1	Garret Anderson/145	15.00
2	Josh Beckett/148	25.00
3	Angel Berroa/145	10.00
4	Eric Gagne/193	20.00
5	Jody Gerut/376	10.00
6	Roy Halladay/286	10.00
7	Mark Mulder/190	10.00
8	Andy Pettitte/148	30.00
9	Scott Podsednik/146	20.00
10	Albert Pujols/193	120.00
11	Grady Sizemore/263	25.00
12	Miguel Tejada/164	20.00

By The Numbers

		NM/M
Common Player:		3.00
Inserted 1:24		
Patch:		3-8X
Production 100 Sets		
1	Albert Pujols	8.00
2	Derek Jeter	10.00
3	Mike Piazza	6.00
4	Nomar Garciaparra	8.00
5	Eric Gagne	4.00
6	Sammy Sosa	6.00
7	Josh Beckett	4.00
8	Vladimir Guerrero	5.00
9	Jose Reyes	3.00
10	Bret Boone	3.00
11	Alex Rodriguez	6.00
12	Randy Johnson	6.00
13	Chipper Jones	6.00
14	Tim Hudson	4.00
15	Rocco Baldelli	4.00

Game-Used Level 1

		NM/M
Common Player:		6.00
Production 200 Sets		
Level 2:		1-1.5X
Production 100 Sets		
Patch:		1-2X
Production 50 Sets		
1	Albert Pujols	15.00
2	Andy Pettitte	6.00
3	Dontrelle Willis	6.00
4	Mike Piazza	10.00
5	Barry Zito	6.00
6	Troy Glaus	6.00
7	Carlos Delgado	8.00
8	Torii Hunter	6.00
9	Roy Halladay	8.00
10	Andruw Jones	8.00
11	Garret Anderson	6.00
12	Larry Walker	6.00
13	Shawn Green	6.00
14	Bernie Williams	6.00
15	Alfonso Soriano	10.00
16	Bret Boone	6.00
17	Hank Blalock	6.00
18	Jose Reyes	6.00
19	Mark Prior	10.00

Licensed Apparel

		NM/M
Common Player:		5.00
Production 300 Sets		
Team Name:		1-2X
Production 150 Sets		
Number:		1-2X
Production 100 Sets		
Nameplate:		1-3X
Production 50 Sets		
Jersey Tags:		
Production 10 Sets		
MLB Logo		
Production One Set		
1	Albert Pujols	15.00
2	Derek Jeter	18.00
3	Alex Rodriguez	15.00
4	Jim Thome	8.00
5	Mike Piazza	10.00
6	Dontrelle Willis	5.00
7	Torii Hunter	5.00
8	Tim Hudson	5.00
9	Sammy Sosa	12.00
10	Troy Glaus	5.00
11	Andruw Jones	8.00
12	Austin Kearns	5.00
13	Jeff Bagwell	8.00
14	Mark Prior	10.00
15	Bret Boone	5.00

National Pastime

		NM/M
Common Player:		5.00
Production 250 Sets		
Jersey:		1-1.5X
Production 350 Sets		
Gold Jersey:		2X
Production 200 Sets		
Patch:		1-3X
Production 100 Sets		
1	Albert Pujols	15.00
2	Alex Rodriguez	15.00
3	Derek Jeter	18.00
4	Nomar Garciaparra	15.00

5	Jim Thome	8.00
6	Chipper Jones	10.00
7	Mark Prior	10.00
8	Ichiro Suzuki	12.00
9	Jeff Bagwell	6.00
10	Troy Glaus	5.00
11	Randy Johnson	8.00
12	Sammy Sosa	12.00
13	Austin Kearns	5.00
14	Miguel Cabrera	6.00
15	Vladimir Guerrero	8.00

Stitches In Time

		NM/M
Common Player:		2.00
Inserted 1:12		
Jersey:		
Production 350 Sets		
Patch:		
Production 150 Sets		
1	Albert Pujols	5.00
2	Alex Rodriguez	5.00
3	Derek Jeter	6.00
4	Nomar Garciaparra	5.00
5	Jim Thome	3.00
6	Chipper Jones	3.00
7	Mark Prior	4.00
8	Eric Gagne	2.00
9	Jeff Bagwell	3.00
10	Troy Glaus	2.00
11	Randy Johnson	3.00
12	Sammy Sosa	3.00
13	Austin Kearns	2.00
14	Miguel Cabrera	2.00
15	Vladimir Guerrero	3.00
16	Mike Piazza	3.00
17	Jason Giambi	2.00
18	Tim Hudson	2.00
19	Carlos Delgado	2.00
20	Rocco Baldelli	2.00
21	Ichiro Suzuki	4.00
22	Barry Zito	2.00
23	Pedro Martinez	3.00
24	Torii Hunter	2.00
25	Andruw Jones	3.00

2004 Fleer Platinum

Vladimir Guerrero
MONTREAL EXPOS™ • OUTFIELD

		NM/M
Complete Set (200):		35.00
Common Player:		.15
Common SP (136-151):		.50
Inserted 1:3		
Pack (7):		2.00
Jumbo Pack (20):		5.00
Box (18 + 4 Jumbo):		55.00
1	Luis Castillo	.15
2	Preston Wilson	.15
3	Johan Santana	.15

4	Fred McGriff	.25
5	Albert Pujols	1.50
6	Reggie Sanders	.15
7	Ivan Rodriguez	.40
8	Roy Halladay	.25
9	Brian Giles	.25
10	Bernie Williams	.40
11	Barry Larkin	.25
12	Marlon Anderson	.15
13	Ramon Ortiz	.15
14	Luis Matos	.15
15	Esteban Loaiza	.15
16	Orlando Cabrera	.15
17	Jamie Moyer	.15
18	Tino Martinez	.25
19	Josh Beckett	.50
20	Derek Jeter	2.00
21	Derek Lowe	.15
22	Jack Wilson	.15
23	Bret Boone	.25
24	Matt Morris	.15
25	Javier Vazquez	.25
26	Joe Crede	.15
27	Jose Vidro	.15
28	Mike Piazza	1.00
29	Curt Schilling	.40
30	Alex Rodriguez	1.50
31	John Olerud	.25
32	Dontrelle Willis	.25
33	Larry Walker	.25
34	Joe Randa	.15
35	Paul LoDuca	.15
36	Marlon Byrd	.15
37	Bo Hart	.15
38	Rafael Palmeiro	.50
39	Garret Anderson	.40
40	Tom Glavine	.25
41	Ichiro Suzuki	1.25
42	Derek Lee	.25
43	Lance Berkman	.25
44	Nomar Garciaparra	1.50
45	Mike Sweeney	.15
46	A.J. Burnett	.15
47	Sean Casey	.15
48	Eric Gagne	.25
49	Joel Pineiro	.15
50	Russ Ortiz	.15
51	Placido Polanco	.15
52	Sammy Sosa	1.25
53	Mark Teixeira	.25
54	Randy Wolf	.15
55	Vladimir Guerrero	.75
56	Tim Hudson	.25
57	Lew Ford	.15
58	Carlos Delgado	.50
59	Darin Erstad	.25
60	Mike Lieberthal	.15
61	Craig Biggio	.25
62	Ryan Klesko	.25
63	C.C. Sabathia	.15
64	Carlos Lee	.15
65	Al Leiter	.15
66	Brandon Webb	.15
67	Jacque Jones	.15
68	Kerry Wood	.25
69	Omar Vizquel	.25
70	Jeremy Bonderman	.15
71	Kevin Brown	.25
72	Richie Sexson	.40
73	Zach Day	.15
74	Mike Mussina	.40
75	Sidney Ponson	.15
76	Andruw Jones	.50
77	Woody Williams	.15
78	Kazuhiro Sasaki	.15
79	Matt Clement	.15
80	Shea Hillenbrand	.15
81	Bartolo Colon	.25
82	Ken Griffey Jr.	1.00
83	Todd Helton	.50
84	Dmitri Young	.15
85	Richard Hidalgo	.15
86	Carlos Beltran	.25
87	Brad Wilkerson	.15
88	Andy Pettitte	.40
89	Miguel Tejada	.40
90	Edgar Martinez	.25
91	Vernon Wells	.25
92	Magglio Ordonez	.25
93	Tony Batista	.15
94	Jose Reyes	.25
95	Matt Stairs	.15
96	Manny Ramirez	.50
97	Carlos Pena	.15
98	A.J. Pierzynski	.15
99	Jim Thome	.75
100	Aubrey Huff	.15
101	Roberto Alomar	.40
102	Luis Gonzalez	.25
103	Chipper Jones	1.00
104	Jay Gibbons	.25
105	Adam Dunn	.25
106	Jay Payton	.15
107	Scott Podsednik	.40
108	Roy Oswalt	.25
109	Milton Bradley	.25
110	Shawn Green	.25
111	Ryan Wagner	.15
112	Eric Chavez	.25
113	Pat Burrell	.25
114	Frank Thomas	.50
115	Jason Kendall	.25
116	Jake Peavy	.25
117	Mike Cameron	.15
118	Jim Edmonds	.25
119	Hank Blalock	.25
120	Troy Glaus	.40
121	Jeff Kent	.25
122	Jason Schmidt	.25
123	Corey Patterson	.15

124	Austin Kearns	.40
125	Edwin Jackson	.15
126	Alfonso Soriano	.75
127	Bobby Abreu	.25
128	Scott Rolen	.75
129	Jeff Bagwell	.50
130	Shannon Stewart	.15
131	Rich Aurilia	.15
132	Ty Wigginton	.15
133	Randy Johnson	.75
134	Rocco Baldelli	.40
135	Hideo Nomo	.25
136	Greg Maddux	2.00
137	Johnny Damon	1.50
138	Mark Prior	.75
139	Corey Koskie	.15
140	Miguel Cabrera	1.50
141	Hideki Matsui	2.00
142	Jose Cruz	.50
143	Barry Zito	1.00
144	Javy Lopez	.50
145	Jason Varitek	1.00
146	Moises Alou	1.00
147	Torii Hunter	1.00
148	Juan Encarnacion	.15
149	Jorge Posada	1.00
150	Marquis Grissom	.50
151	Rich Harden	1.00
152	Gary Sheffield	4.00
153	Pedro J. Martinez	5.00
154	Brad Radke	3.00
155	Mike Lowell	3.00
156	Jason Giambi	4.00
157	Mark Mulder	4.00
158	Ben Weber	.15
159	Mark DeRosa	.15
160	Melvin Mora	.15
161	Bill Mueller	.15
162	Jon Garland	.15
163	Jody Gerut	.15
164	Javier Lopez	.15
165	Craig Monroe	.15
166	Juan Pierre	.15
167	Morgan Ensberg	.15
168	Angel Berroa	.15
169	Geoff Jenkins	.25
170	Matt LeCroy	.15
171	Livan Hernandez	.15
172	Jason L. Phillips	.15
173	Mariano Rivera	.25
174	Erubiel Durazo	.15
175	Jason Michaels	.15
176	Kip Wells	.15
177	Ray Durham	.15
178	Randy Winn	.15
179	Edgar Renteria	.15
180	Carl Crawford	.15
181	Laynce Nix	.15
182	Greg Myers	.15
183	Delmon Young, Chad Gaudin	1.00
184	Humberto Quintero, Bernie Castro	.50
185	Craig Brazell, Daniel Garcia	.50
186	Ryan Wing, Francisco Cruceta	.50
187	William Bergolla RC, Josh Hall	.50
188	Clint Barmes, Garrett Atkins	.50
189	Chris Bootcheck, Richard Fischer	.50
190	Edgar Gonzalez, Matt Kata	.50
191	Andrew Brown, Koyie Hill	.50
192	John Gall RC, Dan Haren	.50
193	Chad Bentz RC, Luis Ayala	.50
194	Hector Gimenez RC, Eric Bruntlett	.50
195	Boof Bonser, Rob Bowen	.50
196	Chris Snelling, Rett Johnson	.50
197	Rickie Weeks, Adam Morrissey	1.00
198	Noah Lowry, Todd Linden	.50
199	Chris Waters, Brett Evert	.50
200	Jorge DePaula, Chien-Ming Wang	.50

Finish

Barry Zito
OAKLAND ATHLETICS • PITCHER

Stars (1-200): 4-6X
Production 100 Sets

Big Signs

RANGERS
RODRIGUEZ

	NM/M
Complete Set (15):	25.00
Common Player:	.75
Inserted 1:9	

1	Albert Pujols	3.00
2	Derek Jeter	4.00
3	Mike Piazza	2.00
4	Jason Giambi	1.50
5	Ichiro Suzuki	2.50
6	Nomar Garciaparra	3.00
7	Mark Prior	2.00
8	Randy Johnson	1.50
9	Greg Maddux	2.00
10	Sammy Sosa	2.50
11	Ken Griffey Jr.	2.00
12	Dontrelle Willis	.75
13	Alex Rodriguez	2.00
14	Chipper Jones	2.00
15	Hank Blalock	.75

Big Signs Autographs

	NM/M
Production 100	

	Hank Blalock	25.00
	Albert Pujols	150.00
	Dontrelle Willis	25.00

Classic Combinations

	NM/M
Complete Set (10):	50.00
Common Player:	3.00
Inserted 1:108	

1	Ivan Rodriguez, Mike Piazza	6.00
2	Alex Rodriguez, Sammy Sosa	8.00
3	Dontrelle Willis, Angel Berroa	3.00
4	Nomar Garciaparra, Derek Jeter	10.00
5	Ichiro Suzuki, Hideo Nomo	6.00
6	Josh Beckett, Kerry Wood	4.00
7	Albert Pujols, Carlos Delgado	8.00
8	Alfonso Soriano, Joe Morgan	4.00
9	Jason Giambi, Reggie Jackson	4.00
10	Nolan Ryan, Tom Seaver	10.00

Clubhouse Memorabilia

	NM/M
Common Player:	5.00
Inserted 1:24	

	Rocco Baldelli	10.00
	Josh Beckett	8.00
	Hank Blalock	6.00
	Nomar Garciaparra	12.00
	Jason Giambi	8.00
	Vladimir Guerrero	8.00
	Todd Helton	6.00
	Torii Hunter	6.00
	Derek Jeter	15.00
	Chipper Jones	8.00
	Austin Kearns	6.00
	Greg Maddux	10.00
	Hideo Nomo	8.00
	Mike Piazza	8.00
	Mark Prior	10.00
	Albert Pujols	12.00
	Alex Rodriguez	10.00
	Richie Sexson	5.00
	Alfonso Soriano	5.00
	Sammy Sosa	12.00
	Miguel Tejada	5.00

	Jim Thome	8.00
	Dontrelle Willis	8.00

Clubhouse Memorabilia Dual

	NM/M
Common Player:	10.00
Production 50 Sets	

	Hank Blalock	15.00
	Nomar Garciaparra	30.00
	Jason Giambi	15.00
	Vladimir Guerrero	20.00
	Todd Helton	15.00
	Torii Hunter	15.00
	Derek Jeter	35.00
	Chipper Jones	25.00
	Austin Kearns	15.00
	Greg Maddux	30.00
	Hideo Nomo	25.00
	Mark Prior	20.00
	Albert Pujols	30.00
	Alex Rodriguez	25.00
	Sammy Sosa	25.00
	Jim Thome	20.00

Nameplates

NAME PLATES
JOSE REYES

	NM/M
Common Player:	8.00
Inserted 1:4 Jumbo	
Varying quantities produced	

1	Austin Kearns	10.00
2	Juan Pierre	10.00
3	Albert Pujols	30.00
4	Manny Ramirez	15.00
5	Kerry Wood	20.00
6	Alex Rodriguez	20.00
7	Barry Zito	10.00
8	Hee Seop Choi	15.00
9	Kevin Brown	10.00
10	Jose Reyes	15.00
11	Marlon Byrd	10.00
12	Nomar Garciaparra	20.00
14	Josh Beckett	15.00
16	Hideo Nomo	15.00
19	Randy Johnson	15.00
20	Hank Blalock	12.00
21	Tom Glavine/25	15.00
22	Luis Castillo	8.00
23	Mark Teixeira	12.00
24	Gary Sheffield	15.00
25	Richie Sexson	10.00
26	Miguel Cabrera	20.00
27	Sammy Sosa	25.00
28	Curt Schilling	15.00
30	Chipper Jones	20.00

Portraits

CUBS

	NM/M
Complete Set (10):	25.00
Common Player:	1.50
Inserted 1:18	

1	Jason Giambi	1.50
2	Nomar Garciaparra	4.00
3	Vladimir Guerrero	1.50
4	Mark Prior	3.00
5	Jim Thome	1.50
6	Derek Jeter	5.00
7	Sammy Sosa	3.00
8	Alex Rodriguez	4.00
9	Greg Maddux	2.50
10	Albert Pujols	4.00

Portraits Jersey

	NM/M
Common Player:	8.00
Inserted 1:48	

	Nomar Garciaparra	15.00
	Jason Giambi	8.00
	Vladimir Guerrero	8.00
	Derek Jeter	15.00
	Greg Maddux	8.00
	Mark Prior	6.00
	Albert Pujols	15.00
	Alex Rodriguez	10.00
	Sammy Sosa	12.00
	Jim Thome	8.00

Portraits Patch

	NM/M
Common Player:	10.00
Production 100 Sets	

	Nomar Garciaparra	20.00
	Jason Giambi	10.00
	Vladimir Guerrero	10.00
	Derek Jeter	25.00
	Mark Prior	20.00
	Albert Pujols	30.00
	Alex Rodriguez	15.00
	Sammy Sosa	20.00
	Jim Thome	12.00

Scouting Report

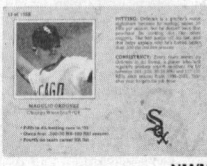

	NM/M
Complete Set (15):	35.00
Common Player:	1.50
Production 400 Sets	

1	Josh Beckett	2.00
2	Todd Helton	2.00
3	Rocco Baldelli	2.00
4	Pedro J. Martinez	3.00
5	Jeff Bagwell	2.00
6	Mark Prior	4.00
7	Ichiro Suzuki	4.00
8	Barry Zito	2.00
9	Manny Ramirez	2.00
10	Miguel Cabrera	2.00
11	Richie Sexson	1.50
12	Hideki Matsui	8.00
13	Magglio Ordonez	1.50
14	Brandon Webb	1.50
15	Kerry Wood	2.00

Scouting Report Memorabilia

	NM/M
Common Player:	6.00
Production 250 Sets	

	Jeff Bagwell	8.00
	Rocco Baldelli	8.00
	Josh Beckett	8.00
	Todd Helton	6.00
	Pedro J. Martinez	8.00
	Mark Prior	10.00
	Manny Ramirez	6.00
	Brandon Webb	6.00
	Kerry Wood	8.00

2004 Fleer Showcase

	NM/M
Complete Set (130):	25.00
Common Player:	.25
Common SP (101-130):	1.00
Inserted 1:6	
Pack (5):	4.50
Box (24):	90.00

1	Corey Patterson	.25
2	Ken Griffey Jr.	1.50
3	Preston Wilson	.40
4	Juan Pierre	.25
5	Jose Reyes	.50
6	Jason Schmidt	.40
7	Rocco Baldelli	.50
8	Carlos Delgado	.75
9	Hideki Matsui	2.50
10	Nomar Garciaparra	2.00
11	Brian Giles	.40
12	Darin Erstad	.40
13	Larry Walker	.50
14	Bernie Williams	.50
15	Laynce Nix	.25

16	Manny Ramirez	.75
17	Magglio Ordonez	.50
18	Khalil Greene	.25
19	Jim Edmonds	.40
20	Troy Glaus	.50
21	Curt Schilling	.50
22	Chipper Jones	1.50
23	Sammy Sosa	2.00
24	Frank Thomas	.75
25	Todd Helton	.75
26	Craig Biggio	.40
27	Shannon Stewart	.25
28	Mark Mulder	.40
29	Mike Lieberthal	.25
30	Reggie Sanders	.25
31	Edgar Martinez	.25
32	Bo Hart	.25
33	Mark Teixeira	.25
34	Jay Gibbons	.25
35	Roberto Alomar	.50
36	Kip Wells	.25
37	J.D. Drew	.25
38	Jason Varitek	.25
39	Craig Monroe	.25
40	Roy Oswalt	.40
41	Edgardo Alfonzo	.25
42	Roy Halladay	.50
43	Gary Sheffield	.50
44	Lance Berkman	.50
45	Torii Hunter	.50
46	Vladimir Guerrero	1.00
47	Marlon Byrd	.25
48	Austin Kearns	.50
49	Angel Berroa	.25
50	Geoff Jenkins	.50
51	Aubrey Huff	.25
52	Dontrelle Willis	.50
53	Tony Batista	.25
54	Shawn Green	.40
55	Jason Kendall	.25
56	Garret Anderson	.50
57	Andruw Jones	.75
58	Dmitri Young	.25
59	Richie Sexson	.50
60	Jorge Posada	.50
61	Bobby Abreu	.40
62	Vernon Wells	.40
63	Javy Lopez	.40
64	Josh Beckett	.75
65	Eric Chavez	.40
66	Tim Salmon	.40
67	Brandon Webb	.40
68	Pedro J. Martinez	1.00
69	Kerry Wood	1.00
70	Jose Vidro	.25
71	Alfonso Soriano	1.00
72	Barry Zito	.50
73	Sean Burroughs	.25
74	Jamie Moyer	.25
75	Luis Gonzalez	.40
76	Adam Dunn	.50
77	Mike Piazza	1.50
78	Pat Burrell	.50
79	Scott Rolen	1.00
80	Milton Bradley	.25
81	Mike Sweeney	.25
82	Hank Blalock	.25
83	Esteban Loaiza	.25
84	Hideo Nomo	.40
85	Derek Jeter	3.00
86	Albert Pujols	2.50
87	Greg Maddux	1.50
88	Mark Prior	1.50
89	Mike Lowell	.25
90	Jeff Bagwell	.75
91	Scott Podsednik	.25
92	Tom Glavine	.50
93	Jason Giambi	1.00
94	Jim Thome	1.00
95	Ichiro Suzuki	2.00
96	Randy Johnson	1.00
97	Omar Vizquel	.25
98	Ivan Rodriguez	.50
99	Miguel Tejada	.50
100	Alex Rodriguez	2.50
101	Rickie Weeks	3.00
102	Chad Gaudin	1.00
103	Rich Harden	1.00
104	Edwin Jackson	1.50
105	Chien-Ming Wang	1.00
106	Matt Kata	1.00
107	Delmon Young	3.00
108	Ryan Wagner	1.00
109	Jeff Duncan	1.00
110	Prentice Redman	1.00
111	Clint Barmes	1.00
112	Jeremy Guthrie	1.00
113	Brian Stokes	1.00
114	David DeJesus	1.00
115	Felix Sanchez	1.00
116	Josh Stewart	1.00
117	Daniel Garcia	1.00
118	Jon Leicester	1.00
119	Francisco Cruceta	1.00
120	Oscar Villarreal	1.00
121	Michael Hessman	1.00
122	Michel Hernandez	1.00
123	Richard Fischer	1.00
124	Robby Hammock	1.00
125	Guillermo Quiroz	1.00
126	Craig Brazell	1.00
127	Wilfredo Ledezma	1.00
128	Josh Willingham	1.00
129	Ramon Nivar	1.00
130	Matt Diaz	1.00

Legacy

Stars (1-100):	4-8X
SP's (101-130):	1-3X
Production 99 Sets	

Masterpiece

tim SALMON

No Pricing
Production One Set

Albert Pujols Legacy Collection

ALBERT PUJOLS

	NM/M
Complete Set (10):	60.00
Common Pujols:	8.00
Production 1,000 Sets	
1-10 Albert Pujols	8.00

Albert Pujols Legacy Collection Autograph

Varying quantities produced
No Pricing

Albert Pujols Legacy Collection Jersey

	NM/M
Varying quantities produced	

3	Albert Pujols/30	40.00
4	Albert Pujols/40	30.00
5	Albert Pujols/50	30.00
6	Albert Pujols/60	30.00
7	Albert Pujols/70	25.00
8	Albert Pujols/80	25.00
9	Albert Pujols/90	25.00
10	Albert Pujols/100	25.00

Baseball's Best

COLORADO ROCKIES
TODD HELTON
FIRST BASE

	NM/M
Complete Set (15):	20.00
Common Player:	.75
Inserted 1:24	

1	Derek Jeter	4.00
2	Mark Prior	2.00
3	Mike Piazza	2.50
4	Jeff Bagwell	1.00
5	Kerry Wood	1.00
6	Ivan Rodriguez	1.00
7	Albert Pujols	3.00
8	Jim Thome	1.50
9	Sammy Sosa	2.50
10	Vladimir Guerrero	1.50
11	Eric Gagne	.75
12	Randy Johnson	1.50
13	Todd Helton	1.00
14	Chipper Jones	2.00
15	Alex Rodriguez	4.00

Baseball's Best Memorabilia

TODD HELTON
ROCKIES

	NM/M
Common Player:	5.00

Inserted 1:72
Parallel 150: .75-1.5X
Production 150
Parallel 50: 1.5-2X
Patch Versions: 2-4X
Production 50
	Derek Jeter	15.00
	Mark Prior	10.00
	Mike Piazza	10.00
	Jeff Bagwell	8.00
	Kerry Wood	8.00
	Ivan Rodriguez	5.00
	Albert Pujols	15.00
	Jim Thome	8.00
	Sammy Sosa	10.00
	Vladimir Guerrero	8.00
	Eric Gagne	8.00
	Randy Johnson	8.00
	Todd Helton	8.00
	Chipper Jones	8.00
	Alex Rodriguez	10.00

Grace

NM/M
Complete Set (20): 20.00
Common Player: .75
Inserted 1:12
1	Kerry Wood	1.50
2	Derek Jeter	4.00
3	Nomar Garciaparra	3.00
4	Mike Piazza	2.50
5	Mark Prior	2.00
6	Jose Reyes	1.00
7	Dontrelle Willis	.75
8	Pedro J. Martinez	1.50
9	Tim Hudson	.75
10	Troy Glaus	.75
11	Hank Blalock	1.00
12	Albert Pujols	3.00
13	Juan Pierre	.75
14	Angel Berroa	.75
15	Rocco Baldelli	1.00
16	Carlos Delgado	1.00
17	Manny Ramirez	1.00
18	Alex Rodriguez	3.00
19	Andruw Jones	1.00
20	Luis Gonzalez	1.00

Grace Memorabilia
NM/M
Common Player: 5.00
Inserted 1:48
Parallel 150: 1-1.5X
Production 150
Patch: 1.5-2.5X
Production 50
	Derek Jeter	15.00
	Nomar Garciaparra	10.00
	Mike Piazza	10.00
	Mark Prior	10.00
	Dontrelle Willis	5.00
	Pedro J. Martinez	8.00
	Albert Pujols	15.00
	Rocco Baldelli	8.00
	Manny Ramirez	8.00
	Alex Rodriguez	10.00

Hot Gloves
NM/M
Common Player: 8.00
Inserted 1:288
1	Derek Jeter	40.00
2	Nomar Garciaparra	30.00
3	Alex Rodriguez	30.00
4	Chipper Jones	15.00
5	Torii Hunter	8.00
6	Ichiro Suzuki	35.00
7	Mark Prior	20.00
8	Vladimir Guerrero	15.00
9	Albert Pujols	30.00
10	Ivan Rodriguez	10.00
11	Hideki Matsui	30.00
12	Sammy Sosa	25.00
13	Jim Thome	15.00
14	Rocco Baldelli	10.00
15	Jeff Bagwell	10.00

Hot Gloves Memorabilia
NM/M
Common Player: 20.00
All jerseys unless noted.
Production 50 Sets
	Derek Jeter	60.00
	Nomar Garciaparra	50.00
	Alex Rodriguez	40.00
	Chipper Jones	40.00
	Ichiro Suzuki/Base	65.00
	Mark Prior	25.00
	Vladimir Guerrero	30.00
	Albert Pujols	50.00
	Ivan Rodriguez	20.00
	Hideki Matsui/Base	60.00
	Sammy Sosa	40.00
	Jim Thome	20.00

	Rocco Baldelli	20.00
	Jeff Bagwell	20.00

Sweet Sigs
NM/M
Common Player: 6.00
Inserted 1:24
Sweet Sigs Game-Used: No Pricing
Production 5
	Hank Blalock/824	20.00
	Taylor Bucholz/Redemp.	6.00
	John Gall/Redemp.	8.00
	Bo Hart/667	5.00
	Torii Hunter/294	15.00
	Austin Kearns/224	20.00
	Wilfredo Ledezma/376	6.00
	Mike Lowell/44	15.00
	Corey Patterson/176	15.00
	Carlos Pena/48	10.00
	Albert Pujols/Redemp.	120.00
	Jose Reyes/115	40.00
	Scott Rolen/200	25.00
	Michael Ryan/288	12.00
	Miguel Tejada/52	20.00
	Ryan Wagner/Redemp.	
	Brandon Webb/1,000	15.00
	Rickie Weeks/416	30.00
	Josh Willingham/180	6.00
	Dontrelle Willis/26	60.00
	Delmon Young/1,000	25.00
	Barry Zito/248	25.00

2004 Fleer Sweet Sigs

NM/M
Common Player (1-75): .20
Minor Stars (1-75): .40
Unlisted Star (1-75): .60
Common Future Sig-cess (76-100): 3.00
Future Sig-cess Production 999 Sets
Pack (6): 5.00
Box (12): 80.00
1	Manny Ramirez	1.00
2	Frank Thomas	1.00
3	Josh Beckett	1.00
4	Shawn Green	.40
5	Tom Glavine	.40
6	Marquis Grissom	.20
7	Nomar Garciaparra	3.00
8	Magglio Ordonez	.40
9	Alex 1odriguez	3.00
10	Chipper Jones	2.00
11	Jody Gerut	.20
12	Dontrelle Willis	.40
13	Lance Berkman	.40
14	Jose Vidro	.40
15	Barry Zito	.60
16	Jason Kendall	.20
17	Scott Rolen	1.50
18	Troy Glaus	.60
19	Brandon Webb	.40
20	Tim Hudson	.40
21	Shannon Stewart	.40
22	Darin Erstad	.40
23	Curt Schilling	.60
24	Bret Boone	.40
25	Richie Sexson	.60
26	Hideki Matsui	3.00
27	Albert Pujols	3.00
28	Greg Maddux	2.00
29	Austin Kearns	.60
30	Todd Helton	1.00
31	Miguel Cabrera	1.00
32	Jeff Bagwell	1.00
33	Marlon Byrd	.20
34	Ichiro Suzuki	2.50
35	Rocco Baldelli	.60
36	Garret Anderson	.40
37	Javy Lopez	.40
38	Kerry Wood	1.00
39	Adam Dunn	.60
40	Geoff Jenkins	.40
41	Derek Jeter	4.00
42	Rich Harden	.20
43	Alfonso Soriano	1.50
44	Ken Griffey Jr.	.60
45	Ivan Rodriguez	.60
46	Pedro J. Martinez	1.50
47	Andy Pettitte	.60
48	Gary Sheffield	.60
49	Brian Giles	.40
50	Carlos Delgado	1.00
51	Mike Piazza	2.00
52	Hank Blalock	.60
53	Roger Clemens	2.00
54	Scott Podsednik	.20
55	Torii Hunter	.60
56	Jose Reyes	.20
57	Jim Thome	1.50
58	Jason Schmidt	.40
59	Jose Cruz	.20
60	Mark Teixeira	.40
61	Randy Johnson	1.50
62	Miguel Tejada	.60
63	Sammy Sosa	2.50
64	Larry Walker	.40
65	Carl Everett	.20
66	Luis Castillo	.20
67	Jason Giambi	1.50
68	Mike Sweeney	.20
69	Andruw Jones	1.00
70	Vladimir Guerrero	1.50
71	J.D. Drew	.40
72	Mark Prior	2.00
73	Angel Berroa	.40
74	Hideo Nomo	.40
75	Roy Halladay	.40
76	John Gall RC	3.00
77	Angel Chavez RC	3.00
78	Alfredo Simon RC	3.00
79	Merkin Valdez RC	3.00
80	Chad Bentz RC	6.00
81	Justin Leone RC	6.00
82	Mike Rouse RC	3.00
83	Aarom Baldiris RC	3.00
84	Chris Shelton RC	6.00
85	Akinori Otsuka RC	6.00
86	Ruddy Yan RC	3.00
87	Ramon Ramirez RC	6.00
88	Hector Gimenez RC	6.00
89	Mike Gosling RC	3.00
90	Greg Dobbs RC	3.00
91	Kazuo Matsui RC	8.00
92	Donald Kelly RC	3.00
93	Shingo Takatsu RC	6.00
94	Ivan Ochoa RC	5.00
95	Chris Aguila RC	5.00
96	Jason Bartlett RC	5.00
97	Graham Koonce RC	5.00
98	Ronny Cedeno RC	3.00
99	Jerome Gamble RC	6.00
100	Onil Joseph RC	3.00

Sweet Sigs Black
(1-100): No Pricing
Production 5 Sets

Sweet Sigs Gold

(1-75): 1-5X
(76-100): .5-2X
Production 99 Sets

Ballpark Heroes

NM/M
Common Player: 1.25
Inserted 1:6
1	Rocco Baldelli	1.75
2	Adam Dunn	1.75
3	Nomar Garciaparra	1.75
4	Ken Griffey Jr.	3.50
5	Vladimir Guerrero	1.75
6	Torii Hunter	1.75
7	Andruw Jones	3.50
8	Mike Piazza	3.50
9	Alfonso Soriano	3.00
10	Frank Thomas	3.00
11	Dontrelle Willis	1.25
12	Barry Zito	1.75
13	Javy Lopez	1.25
14	Miguel Cabrera	3.50
15	Kazuo Matsui	3.50
16	Josh Beckett	2.00
17	Derek Jeter	6.00
18	Greg Maddux	3.50
19	Pedro J. Martinez	3.00
20	Hideo Nomo	1.25
21	Mark Prior	4.00
22	Albert Pujols	5.00
23	Alex Rodriguez	5.00
24	Scott Rolen	3.00
25	Ichiro Suzuki	4.00

Ballpark Heroes Duals
No Pricing
Sequentially Numbered

Ballpark Heroes Quad
NM/M
Sequentially Numbered
1	Josh Beckett, Greg Maddux, Pedro J. Martinez, Mark Prior/42	150.00
2	Dontrelle Willis, Kazuo Matsui, Miguel Cabrera, Rocco Baldelli/26	75.00
4	Dontrelle Willis, Josh Beckett, Derek Jeter, Alex Rodriguez/32	150.00
5	Albert Pujols, Vladimir Guerrero, Mike Piazza, Alex Rodriguez/37	150.00

Ballpark Heroes Black Patch
NM/M
Sequentially Numbered
MP	Mike Piazza/31	50.00

Ballpark Heroes Copper Jersey
NM/M
Common Player: 5.00
Production 110 Sets
Gold Patch: 1-3X
Production 50 Sets
Masterpiece Patch: No Pricing
Production One Set
RB	Rocco Baldelli/110	5.00
MC	Miguel Cabrera/110	6.00
AD	Adam Dunn/110	5.00
VG	Vladimir Guerrero/110	8.00
GM	Greg Maddux/110	10.00
PM	Pedro J. Martinez/110	8.00
HN	Hideo Nomo/110	5.00
MP	Mike Piazza/110	10.00
AP	Albert Pujols/110	15.00
SR	Scott Rolen/110	6.00
AS	Alfonso Soriano/110	8.00
FT	Frank Thomas/110	8.00
DW	Dontrelle Willis/110	5.00
BZ	Barry Zito/110	5.00

Ballpark Heroes Silver Jersey
NM/M
Common Player: 4.00
Sequentially Numbered
RB	Rocco Baldelli/250	4.00
MC	Miguel Cabrera/196	6.00
AD	Adam Dunn/215	4.00
VG	Vladimir Guerrero/200	6.00
GM	Greg Maddux/224	8.00
PM	Pedro J. Martinez/239	6.00
HN	Hideo Nomo/210	4.00
MP	Mike Piazza/163	8.00
AP	Albert Pujols/199	12.00
SR	Scott Rolen/221	6.00
AS	Alfonso Soriano/235	6.00
FT	Frank Thomas/242	6.00
DW	Dontrelle Willis/186	5.00
BZ	Barry Zito/195	4.00

Sweet Sigs Copper
NM/M
Common Player: 10.00
Sequentially Numbered
Gold: .75-1.5X
Production 30 Sets
Hideo Nomo #'d to 10.
No Roger Clemens or Ted Williams Gold card.
Masterpiece: No Pricing
Production One Set
GA	Garret Anderson/100	20.00
RB	Rocco Baldelli/75	25.00
JB	Josh Beckett/75	30.00
CB	Carlos Beltran/75	30.00
LB	Lance Berkman/150	20.00
AB	Angel Berroa/75	20.00
JB	Jeremy Bonderman/150	15.00
MC	Miguel Cabrera/150	30.00
MC	Mike Cameron/150	20.00
RC	Roger Clemens/52	400.00
CC	Carl Crawford/150	15.00
JD	Johnny Damon/100	30.00
JD	J.D. Drew/98	40.00
DE	Dennis Eckersley/75	40.00
AE	Adam Everett/150	10.00
JF	Julio Franco/150	15.00
LG	Luis Gonzalez/150	15.00
KG	Khalil Greene/150	15.00
VG	Vladimir Guerrero/75	75.00
TH	Torii Hunter/150	15.00
EJ	Edwin Jackson/75	15.00
RJ	Randy Johnson/28	150.00
CJ	Chipper Jones/50	100.00
MK	Matt Kata/150	10.00
BL	Barry Larkin/50	50.00
CL	Carlos Lee/150	15.00
AL	Al Leiter/75	25.00
KL	Kenny Lofton/50	25.00
JL	Javy Lopez/75	25.00
GM	Greg Maddux/50	75.00
PM	Pedro J. Martinez/75	125.00
JM	Joe Mauer/150	40.00
WM	Wade Miller/150	20.00
KM	Kevin Millwood/100	15.00
PM	Paul Molitor/75	25.00
SM	Stan Musial/25	80.00
MM	Mike Mussina/50	40.00
LN	Lance Niekro/150	10.00
JO	John Olerud/75	30.00
MO	Magglio Ordonez/150	20.00
RO	Russ Ortiz/150	15.00
RO	Roy Oswalt/150	20.00
AO	Akinori Otsuka/150	20.00
BP	Brad Penny/150	15.00
AP	Andy Pettitte/50	40.00
MP	Mike Piazza/50	120.00
AP	Albert Pujols/73	300.00
BR	Brad Radke/100	20.00
JR	Jose Reyes/163	30.00
AR	Alexis Rios/150	15.00
NR	Nolan Ryan/300	300.00
CS	C.C. Sabathia/150	15.00
TS	Tim Salmon/100	40.00
DS	Deion Sanders/50	50.00
JS	Johan Santana/150	80.00
MS	Mike Schmidt/50	60.00
SS	Shannon Stewart/75	20.00
FT	Frank Thomas/75	75.00
JV	Jason Varitek/75	20.00
TW	Tim Wakefield/150	30.00
VW	Vernon Wells/150	20.00
BW	Bernie Williams/50	30.00
DW	Dontrelle Willis/150	20.00
KW	Kerry Wood/75	60.00
CY	Carl Yastrzemski/100	100.00
BZ	Barry Zito/44	150.00

2004 Fleer Sweet Sigs Sweet Sigs Jersey Number
NM/M
No. 3-25: 1-3X Copper
No. 26-57: .75-1.5X Copper
Numbered to player's jersey #
No Hideo Nomo card
MC	Mike Cameron/44	30.00

2004 Fleer Sweet Sigs Sweet Stitches Black Patch
NM/M
Sequentially Numbered
SS-GM	Greg Maddux/32	25.00

2004 Fleer Sweet Sigs Sweet Stitches Copper Jersey
NM/M
Common Player: 5.00
Production 125 Sets
Gold Patch: 1-3X
Production 50 Sets
Masterpiece Patch: No Pricing
Production One Set
HB	Hank Blalock/125	5.00
MC	Miguel Cabrera/125	8.00
RC	Roger Clemens/125	8.00
JG	Jason Giambi/125	8.00
VG	Vladimir Guerrero/125	8.00
AJ	Andruw Jones/125	10.00
GM	Greg Maddux/125	8.00
MO	Magglio Ordonez/125	8.00
MP	Mike Piazza/125	8.00
MP;	Mark Prior/125	8.00
AP	Albert Pujols/125	15.00
MR	Manny Ramirez/125	8.00
JR	Jose Reyes/125	8.00
SR	Scott Rolen/125	8.00
GS	Gary Sheffield/125	8.00
AS	Alfonso Soriano/125	8.00
SS	Sammy Sosa/125	10.00
MT	Mark Teixeira/125	8.00
MT	Miguel Tejada/125	8.00
FT	Frank Thomas/125	8.00
JT	Jim Thome/125	8.00
KW	Kerry Wood/125	8.00

Sweet Stitches Silver Jersey

NM/M
Common Player: 5.00
Sequentially Numbered
HB	Hank Blalock/166	8.00
MC	Miguel Cabrera/169	8.00
RC	Roger Clemens/165	8.00
JG	Jason Giambi/125	8.00
VG	Vladimir Guerrero/172	8.00
AJ	Andruw Jones/175	8.00
GM	Greg Maddux/156	8.00
MO	Magglio Ordonez/113	5.00
MP	Mike Piazza/174	8.00
MP	Mark Prior/172	8.00
AP	Albert Pujols/170	12.00
MR	Manny Ramirez/163	8.00
JR	Jose Reyes/171	8.00
SR	Scott Rolen/166	8.00
GS	Gary Sheffield/88	8.00
AS	Alfonso Soriano/162	8.00
SS	Sammy Sosa/158	10.00
MT	Mark Teixeira/158	8.00
MT	Miguel Tejada/162	8.00
FT	Frank Thomas/159	8.00
JT	Jim Thome/8	8.00
KW	Kerry Wood/134	8.00

Sweet Stitches Quad Patches
NM/M
Sequentially Numbered
No pricing for quantities less than 25.
4	Andruw Jones/31, Miguel Cabrera/31, Albert Pujols/31, Sammy Sosa/31	80.00
10	Greg Maddux/33, Sammy Sosa/33, Mark Prior/33, Kerry Wood/33	150.00

Sweet Swing

NM/M
Common Player: 2.50
Inserted 1:12
1SS	Sammy Sosa	5.00
2SS	Vladimir Guerrero	3.50
3SS	Jason Giambi	3.50
4SS	Chipper Jones	4.00
5SS	Alfonso Soriano	3.50
6SS	Manny Ramirez	3.00
7SS	Todd Helton	3.00
8SS	Alex Rodriguez	6.00
9SS	Albert Pujols	6.00
10SS	Jeff Bagwell	3.00
11SS	Mike Piazza	4.00
12SS	Hank Blalock	2.50
13SS	Jim Thome	3.50
14SS	Carlos Delgado	3.00
15SS	Nomar Garciaparra	6.00

Sweet Swing Black Bat/Patch
Numbered to most home runs.

Sweet Swing Copper Jersey
NM/M
Common Player: 4.00
Production 200 Sets
Gold Bat/Jersey: 1.5-4X
Production 50 Sets
Masterpiece Bat/Patch
Production One Set
HB	Hank Blalock/200	4.00
JG	Jason Giambi/200	6.00
VG	Vladimir Guerrero/200	6.00
CJ	Chipper Jones/200	8.00
MP	Mike Piazza/200	8.00
AP	Albert Pujols/200	12.00
MR	Manny Ramirez/200	5.00

AR	Alex Rodriguez/200	12.00
AS	Alfonso Soriano/200	6.00
SS	Sammy Sosa/200	10.00
JT	Jim Thome/200	6.00

Sweet Swing Silver Bat

NM/M

Common Player: 5.00
Sequentially Numbered

JG	Jason Giambi/247	6.00
VG	Vladimir Guerrero/250	6.00
CJ	Chipper Jones/235	8.00
MP	Mike Piazza/231	8.00
AP	Albert Pujols/237	12.00
MR	Manny Ramirez/224	5.00
AR	Alex Rodriguez/213	12.00
AS	Alfonso Soriano/216	6.00
SS	Sammy Sosa/221	10.00
JT	Jim Thome/245	6.00

Sweet Swing Quad

NM/M

Sequentially Numbered

1	Jason Giambi, Alex Rodriguez, Jeff Bagwell, Manny Ramirez/35	80.00
3	Mike Piazza, Alfonso Soriano, Todd Helton, Hank Blalock/32	125.00

2004 Fleer Tradition

NM/M

Complete Set (500):		100.00
Common Player:		.15
Common SP (401-500):		.25
Pack (10):		1.75
Hobby Box (36):		50.00
1	Juan Pierre	.15
2	Josh Beckett	.50
3	Ivan Rodriguez	.50
4	Miguel Cabrera	.50
5	Dontrelle Willis	.15
6	Derek Jeter	2.00
7	Jason Giambi	.75
8	Bernie Williams	.40
9	Alfonso Soriano	.75
10	Hideki Matsui	2.00
11	Garret Anderson, Ramon Ortiz, John Lackey	.15
12	Luis Gonzalez, Brandon Webb, Curt Schilling	.25
13	Javy Lopez, Gary Sheffield, Russ Ortiz	.25
14	Tony Batista, Jay Gibbons, Sidney Ponson, Jason Johnson	.15
15	Manny Ramirez, Nomar Garciaparra, Derek Lowe, Pedro J. Martinez	.50
16	Sammy Sosa, Mark Prior, Kerry Wood	.75
17	Frank Thomas, Carlos Lee, Esteban Loaiza	.25
18	Adam Dunn, Sean Casey, Chris Reitsma, Paul Wilson	.15
19	Jody Gerut, C.C. Sabathia	.15
20	Preston Wilson, Darren Oliver, Jason Jennings	.15
21	Dmitri Young, Mike Maroth, Jeremy Bonderman	.13
22	Mike Lowell, Dontrelle Willis, Josh Beckett	.25
23	Jeff Bagwell, Jeriome Robertson, Wade Miller	.25
24	Carlos Beltran, Darrell May	.15
25	Adrian Beltre, Shawn Green, Hideo Nomo, Kevin Brown	.15
26	Richie Sexson, Ben Sheets	.15
27	Torii Hunter, Brad Radke, Johan Santana	.15
28	Vladimir Guerrero, Orlando Cabrera, Livan Hernandez, Javier Vazquez	.25
29	Cliff Floyd, Ty Wigginton, Steve Trachsel, Al Leiter	.15
30	Jason Giambi, Andy Pettitte, Mike Mussina	.40
31	Eric Chavez, Miguel Tejada, Tim Hudson	.25
32	Jim Thome, Randy Wolf	.25
33	Reggie Sanders, Josh Fogg, Kip Wells	.15
34	Ryan Klesko, Mark Loretta, Jake Peavy	.15
35	Jose Cruz, Edgardo Alfonzo, Jason Schmidt	.25
36	Bret Boone, Jamie Moyer, Joel Pineiro	.15
37	Albert Pujols, Woody Williams	.75
38	Aubrey Huff, Victor Zambrano	.15
39	Alex Rodriguez, John Thomson	.75
40	Carlos Delgado, Roy Halladay	.25
41	Greg Maddux	1.00
42	Ben Grieve	.15
43	Darin Erstad	.15
44	Ruben Sierra	.15
45	Byung-Hyun Kim	.15
46	Freddy Garcia	.15
47	Richard Hidalgo	.15
48	Tike Redman	.15
49	Kevin Millwood	.25
50	Marquis Grissom	.15
51	Jae Weong Seo	.15
52	Wil Cordero	.15
53	LaTroy Hawkins	.15
54	Jolbert Cabrera	.15
55	Kevin Appier	.15
56	John Lackey	.15
57	Garret Anderson	.25
58	R.A. Dickey	.15
59	David Segui	.15
60	Erubiel Durazo	.15
61	Bobby Abreu	.25
62	Travis Hafner	.15
63	Victor Zambrano	.15
64	Randy Johnson	.75
65	Bernie Williams	.40
66	J.T. Snow	.15
67	Sammy Sosa	1.50
68	Al Leiter	.15
69	Jason Jennings	.15
70	Matt Morris	.15
71	Mike Hampton	.15
72	Juan Encarnacion	.15
73	Alex Gonzalez	.15
74	Bartolo Colon	.25
75	Brett Myers	.15
76	Michael Young	.15
77	Ichiro Suzuki	1.50
78	Jason Johnson	.15
79	Brad Ausmus	.15
80	Ted Lilly	.15
81	Ken Griffey Jr.	1.00
82	Chone Figgins	.15
83	Edgar Martinez	.25
84	Adam Eaton	.15
85	Ken Harvey	.15
86	Francisco Rodriguez	.25
87	Bill Mueller	.15
88	Mike Maroth	.15
89	Charles Johnson	.15
90	Jhonny Peralta	.15
91	Kip Wells	.15
92	Cesar Izturis	.15
93	Matt Clement	.15
94	Lyle Overbay	.15
95	Kirk Rueter	.15
96	Cristian Guzman	.15
97	Garrett Stephenson	.15
98	Lance Berkman	.25
99	Brett Tomko	.15
100	Chris Stynes	.15
101	Nate Cornejo	.15
102	Aaron Rowand	.15
103	Javier Vazquez	.15
104	Jason Kendall	.25
105	Mark Redman	.15
106	Benito Santiago	.15
107	C.C. Sabathia	.15
108	David Wells	.15
109	Mark Ellis	.15
110	Casey Blake	.15
111	Sean Burroughs	.15
112	Carlos Beltran	.25
113	Ramon Hernandez	.15
114	Eric Hinske	.15
115	Luis Gonzalez	.25
116	Jarrod Washburn	.15
117	Ronnie Belliard	.15
118	Troy Percival	.15
119	Jose Valentine	.15
120	Chase Utley	.15
121	Odalis Perez	.15
122	Steve Finley	.15
123	Bret Boone	.25
124	Jeff Conine	.15
125	Jason Fogg	.15
126	Neifi Perez	.15
127	Ben Sheets	.25
128	Randy Winn	.15
129	Matt Stairs	.15
130	Carlos Delgado	.50
131	Morgan Ensberg	.15
132	Vinny Castilla	.15
133	Matt Mantei	.15
134	Alex Rodriguez	1.50
135	Matthew LeCroy	.15
136	Woody Williams	.15
137	Frank Catalanotto	.15
138	Rondell White	.15
139	Scott Rolen	.75
140	Cliff Floyd	.15
141	Chipper Jones	.75
142	Robin Ventura	.15
143	Mariano Rivera	.25
144	Brady Clark	.15
145	Ramon Ortiz	.15
146	Omar Infante	.15
147	Mike Matheny	.15
148	Pedro J. Martinez	.75
149	Carlos Baerga	.15
150	Shannon Stewart	.15
151	Travis Lee	.15
152	Eric Byrnes	.15
153	Rafael Furcal	.25
154	B.J. Surhoff	.15
155	Zach Day	.15
156	Marlon Anderson	.15
157	Mark Hendrickson	.15
158	Mike Mussina	.50
159	Randall Simon	.15
160	Jeff DaVanon	.15
161	Joel Pineiro	.15
162	Vernon Wells	.25
163	Adam Kennedy	.15
164	Trot Nixon	.15
165	Rodrigo Lopez	.15
166	Curt Schilling	.50
167	Horacio Ramirez	.15
168	Gerald Laird	.15
169	Magglio Ordonez	.25
170	Scott Schoeneweis	.15
171	Andruw Jones	.50
172	Tino Martinez	.25
173	Moises Alou	.25
174	Kelvim Escobar	.15
175	Xavier Nady	.15
176	Ramon Martinez	.15
177	Pat Hentgen	.15
178	Austin Kearns	.40
179	D'Angelo Jimenez	.15
180	Deivi Cruz	.15
181	John Smoltz	.25
182	Toby Hall	.15
183	Mark Buehrle	.15
184	Howie Clark	.15
185	David Ortiz	.15
186	Raul Mondesi	.15
187	Milton Bradley	.15
188	Jorge Julio	.15
189	Victor Martinez	.15
190	Gabe Kapler	.15
191	Julio Franco	.15
192	Ryan Freel	.15
193	Brad Fullmer	.15
194	Joe Borowski	.15
195	Darren Oliver	.15
196	Jason Varitek	.25
197	Greg Myers	.15
198	Eric Munson	.15
199	Tim Wakefield	.15
200	Kyle Farnsworth	.15
201	John Vander Wal	.15
202	Alex Escobar	.15
203	Sean Casey	.15
204	John Thomson	.15
205	Carlos Zambrano	.15
206	Kenny Lofton	.25
207	Marcus Giles	.15
208	Wade Miller	.15
209	Geoff Blurn	.15
210	Jason LaRue	.15
211	Omar Vizquel	.25
212	Carlos Pena	.15
213	Adam Dunn	.40
214	Oscar Villarreal	.15
215	Paul Konerko	.15
216	Hideo Nomo	.40
217	Mike Sweeney	.15
218	Coco Crisp	.15
219	Shawn Chacon	.15
220	Brook Fordyce	.15
221	Josh Beckett	.50
222	Paul Wilson	.15
223	Josh Towers	.15
224	Geoff Jenkins	.25
225	Shawn Green	.25
226	Derek Lee	.15
227	Karim Garcia	.15
228	Preston Wilson	.15
229	Dane Sardinha	.15
230	Aramis Ramirez	.15
231	Doug Mientkiewicz	.15
232	Jay Gibbons	.15
233	Adam Everett	.15
234	Brooks Kieschnick	.15
235	Dmitri Young	.15
236	Brad Penny	.15
237	Todd Zeile	.15
238	Eric Gagne	.25
239	Esteban Loaiza	.15
240	Billy Wagner	.15
241	Nomar Garciaparra	1.50
242	Desi Relaford	.15
243	Luis Rivas	.15
244	Andy Pettitte	.40
245	Ty Wigginton	.15
246	Edgar Gonzalez	.15
247	Brian Anderson	.15
248	Richie Sexson	.40
249	Russell Branyan	.15
250	Jose Guillen	.15
251	Chin-Hui Tsao	.15
252	Jose Hernandez	.15
253	Kevin Brown	.25
254	Pete LaForest	.15
255	Adrian Beltre	.15
256	Jacque Jones	.15
257	Jimmy Rollins	.25
258	Brandon Phillips	.15
259	Derek Jeter	2.00
260	Carl Everett	.15
261	Wes Helms	.15
262	Kyle Lohse	.15
263	Jason L. Phillips	.15
264	Jake Peavy	.15
265	Orlando Hernandez	.15
266	Keith Foulke	.15
267	Brad Wilkerson	.15
268	Corey Koskie	.15
269	Josh Hall	.15
270	Bobby Higginson	.15
271	Andres Galarraga	.15
272	Alfonso Soriano	.75
273	Carlos Rivera	.15
274	Steve Trachsel	.15
275	David Bell	.15
276	Endy Chavez	.15
277	Jay Payton	.15
278	Mark Mulder	.25
279	Terrence Long	.15
280	A.J. Burnett	.15
281	Pokey Reese	.15
282	Phil Nevin	.15
283	Jose Contreras	.25
284	Jim Thome	.75
285	Pat Burrell	.40
286	Luis Castillo	.15
287	Juan Uribe	.15
288	Raul Ibanez	.15
289	Sidney Ponson	.15
290	Shane Hatteberg	.15
291	Jack Wilson	.15
292	Reggie Sanders	.15
293	Brian Giles	.25
294	Craig Biggio	.25
295	Kazuhisa Ishii	.15
296	Jim Edmonds	.25
297	Trevor Hoffman	.15
298	Ray Durham	.15
299	Mike Lieberthal	.15
300	Todd Worrell	.15
301	Chris George	.15
302	Jamie Moyer	.15
303	Mike Cameron	.15
304	Matt Kinney	.15
305	Aubrey Huff	.15
306	Brian Lawrence	.15
307	Carlos Guillen	.15
308	J.D. Drew	.25
309	Paul LoDuca	.15
310	Tim Salmon	.25
311	Jason Schmidt	.15
312	A.J. Pierzynski	.15
313	Lance Carter	.15
314	Julio Lugo	.15
315	Johan Santana	.15
316	Laynce Nix	.15
317	John Olerud	.25
318	Robb Quinlan	.15
319	Scott Spiezio	.15
320	Tony Clark	.15
321	Jose Vidro	.15
322	Shea Hillenbrand	.15
323	Doug Glanville	.15
324	Orlando Palmeiro	.15
325	Juan Gonzalez	.40
326	Jason Giambi	.75
327	Junior Spivey	.15
328	Tom Glavine	.25
329	Reed Johnson	.15
330	David Eckstein	.15
331	Damian Jackson	.15
332	Orlando Hudson	.15
333	Barry Zito	.40
334	Robert Fick	.15
335	Aaron Boone	.15
336	Rafael Palmeiro	.50
337	Bobby Kielty	.15
338	Tony Batista	.15
339	Ryan Dempster	.15
340	Derek Lowe	.15
341	Alex Cintron	.15
342	Jermaine Dye	.15
343	John Burkett	.15
344	Javy Lopez	.25
345	Eric Karros	.15
346	Corey Patterson	.25
347	Josh Phelps	.15
348	Ryan Klesko	.25
349	Craig Wilson	.15
350	Brian Roberts	.15
351	Roberto Alomar	.40
352	Frank Thomas	.50
353	Gary Sheffield	.40
354	Alex Gonzalez	.15
355	Jose Cruz	.15
356	Jerome Williams	.15
357	Mark Kotsay	.15
358	Chris Reitsma	.15
359	Carlos Lee	.15
360	Todd Helton	.50
361	Gil Meche	.15
362	Ryan Franklin	.15
363	Josh Bard	.15
364	Juan Pierre	.15
365	Barry Larkin	.25
366	Edgar Renteria	.15
367	Alex Sanchez	.15
368	Jeff Bagwell	.50
369	Ben Broussard	.15
370	Chan Ho Park	.15
371	Darrell May	.15
372	Roy Oswalt	.25
373	Craig Monroe	.15
374	Fred McGriff	.25
375	Bengie Molina	.15
376	Aaron Guiel	.15
377	Jeriome Robertson	.15
378	Kenny Rogers	.15
379	Colby Lewis	.15
380	Jeromy Burnitz	.15
381	Orlando Cabrera	.15
382	Joe Randa	.15
383	Miguel Batista	.15
384	Brad Radke	.15
385	Jason Giambi	.25
386	Vladimir Guerrero	.75
387	Melvin Mora	.15
388	Royce Clayton	.15
389	Danny Garcia	.15
390	Manny Ramirez	.50
391	Dave McCarty	.15
392	Mark Grudzielanek	.15
393	Mike Piazza	1.00
394	Jorge Posada	.40
395	Tim Hudson	.25
396	Placido Polanco	.15
397	Mark Loretta	.15
398	Jesse Foppert	.15
399	Albert Pujols	1.50
400	Jeremi Gonzalez	.15
401	Paul Bako	.25
402	Luis Matos	.25
403	Johnny Damon	.50
404	Kerry Wood	1.00
405	Joe Crede	.25
406	Jason Davis	.25
407	Larry Walker	.50
408	Ivan Rodriguez	1.00
409	Nick Johnson	.25
410	Jose Lima	.25
411	Brian Jordan	.25
412	Eddie Guardado	.25
413	Ron Calloway	.25
414	Aaron Heilman	.25
415	Eric Chavez	.50
416	Randy Wolf	.25
417	Jason Bay	.25
418	Edgardo Alfonzo	.25
419	Kazuhiro Sasaki	.25
420	Eduardo Perez	.25
421	Carl Crawford	.25
422	Troy Glaus	1.00
423	Joaquin Benoit	.25
424	Russ Ortiz	.25
425	Larry Bigbie	.25
426	Todd Walker	.25
427	Kris Benson	.25
428	Sandy Alomar	.25
429	Jody Gerut	.25
430	Rene Reyes	.25
431	Mike Lowell	.25
432	Jeff Kent	.25
433	Mike MacDougal	.25
434	Dave Roberts	.25
435	Torii Hunter	.75
436	Tomokazu Ohka	.25
437	Jeremy Griffiths	.25
438	Miguel Tejada	.75
439	Vicente Padilla	.25
440	Bobby Hill	.25
441	Rich Aurilia	.25
442	Shigetoshi Hasegawa	.25
443	So Taguchi	.25
444	Damian Rolls	.25
445	Roy Halladay	.75
446	Rocco Baldelli	.75
447	Dontrelle Willis	.75
448	Mark Prior	2.00
449	Jason Lane	.25
450	Angel Berroa	.25
451	Jose Reyes	.25
452	Ryan Wagner	.25
453	Marlon Byrd	.25
454	Hee Seop Choi	.25
455	Brandon Webb	.25
456	Bo Hart	.75
457	Hank Blalock	1.00
458	Mark Teixeira	.75
459	Hideki Matsui	4.00
460	Scott Podsednik	.25
461	Miguel Cabrera	1.00
462	Josh Beckett	.75
463	Mariano Rivera	.50
464	Ivan Rodriguez	1.00
465	Alex Rodriguez	3.00
466	Albert Pujols	3.00
467	Roy Halladay	.75
468	Eric Gagne	.50
469	Angel Berroa	.25
470	Dontrelle Willis	.50
471	Chris Bootcheck, Tom Gregorio, Richard Fischer	.25
472	Matt Kata, Tim Olson, Robby Hammock	.25
473	Michael Hessman, Chris Waters, Humberto Quintero	.25
474	Carlos Mendez, Daniel Cabrera, Jeremy Guthrie	.25
475	Edwin Almonte, Phil Seibel, Felix Sanchez	.25
476	Todd Wellemeyer, Jon Leicester, Sergio Mitre	.25
477	Josh Stewart, Neal Cotts, Aaron Miles	.25
478	Terrmel Sledge, Josh Hall, Brandon Claussen	.25
479	Francisco Cruceta, Jason Stanford, Rafael Betancourt	.25
480	Javier Lopez, Garrett Atkins, Clint Barmes	.25
481	Wilfredo Ledezma, Nook Logan, Jeremy Bonderman	.25
482	Josh Willingham, Kevin Hooper, Rick Roberts	.25
483	Colin Porter, Mike Gallo, Dave Matranga	.25
484	David DeJesus, Jason Gilfillan, Jimmy Gobble	.25
485	Koyie Hill, Alfredo Gonzalez, Andrew Brown	.25
486	Rickie Weeks, Pedro Liriano, Wes Obermueller	1.00
487	Alex Prieto, Mike Ryan, Lew Ford	.25
488	Julio Manon, Luis Ayala, Seung Jun Song	.25
489	Jeff Duncan, Prentice Redman, Craig Brazell	.25
490	Chien-Ming Wang, Michel Hernandez, Mike Gonzalez	.25
491	Rich Harden, Mike Neu, Geoff Geary	.25
492	Diegomar Markwell, Chad Gaudin, David Sanders	.25
493	Beau Kemp, Micheal Nakamura, D.J. Carrasco	.25
494	Khalil Greene, Miguel Ojeda, Bernie Castro	.25
495	Noah Lowry, Todd Linden, Kevin Correia	.25
496	Aaron Looper, Brian Sweeney, Rett Johnson	.25
497	Bo Hart, Dan Haren, Kevin Ohme	.50
498	Delmon Young, Doug Waechter, Matt Diaz	1.00
499	Gerald Laird, Rosman Garcia, Ramon Nivar	.25
500	Alexis Rios, Guillermo Quiroz, Francisco Rosario	.25

Career Tributes

NM/M

Complete Set (10): 30.00
Common Player: 3.00
Numbered to last season.
Die-Cut: 2-3X
#'d to last two digits of last season.

1CT	Mike Schmidt/1,989	5.00
2CT	Nolan Ryan/1,993	5.00
3CT	Tom Seaver/1,986	4.00
4CT	Reggie Jackson/1,987	3.00
5CT	Bob Gibson/1,975	4.00
6CT	Harmon Killebrew/1,975	3.00
7CT	Phil Rizzuto/1,956	3.00
8CT	Lou Brock/1,979	3.00
9CT	Eddie Mathews/1,968	3.00
10CT	Al Kaline/1,974	4.00

Diamond Tributes

NM/M

Complete Set (20): 18.00
Common Player: .50
Inserted 1:6

1DT	Derek Jeter	3.00
2DT	Chipper Jones	1.50
3DT	Vladimir Guerrero	1.00
4DT	Kerry Wood	.75
5DT	Jim Thome	1.00

6DT	Nomar Garciaparra	2.00
7DT	Alex Rodriguez	3.00
8DT	Mike Piazza	1.50
9DT	Jason Giambi	1.00
10DT	Barry Zito	.50
11DT	Dontrelle Willis	.50
12DT	Albert Pujols	2.50
13DT	Todd Helton	.75
14DT	Richie Sexson	.50
15DT	Randy Johnson	1.00
16DT	Pedro J. Martinez	1.00
17DT	Josh Beckett	.75
18DT	Manny Ramirez	.75
19DT	Roy Halladay	.50
20DT	Mark Prior	1.50

Diamond Tributes Game-Used

	NM/M
Common Player:	5.00
Inserted 1:36	
Patch versions:	2-3X
Production 50 Sets	
Josh Beckett	8.00
Nomar Garciaparra	10.00
Jason Giambi	8.00
Vladimir Guerrero	8.00
Roy Halladay	5.00
Todd Helton	8.00
Derek Jeter	15.00
Randy Johnson	8.00
Chipper Jones	8.00
Pedro J. Martinez	10.00
Mike Piazza	8.00
Mark Prior	10.00
Albert Pujols	15.00
Manny Ramirez	8.00
Alex Rodriguez	10.00
Richie Sexson	6.00
Jim Thome	8.00
Dontrelle Willis	8.00
Kerry Wood	8.00
Barry Zito	8.00

Retrospection Collection

	NM/M
Complete Set (10):	60.00
Common Player:	4.00
Inserted 1:360	
1RC	Rickie Weeks	10.00
2RC	Delmon Young	12.00
3RC	Torii Hunter	5.00
4RC	Aubrey Huff	4.00
5RC	Rocco Baldelli	6.00
6RC	Mike Lowell	4.00
7RC	Dontrelle Willis	6.00
8RC	Albert Pujols	10.00
9RC	Bo Hart	8.00
10RC	Brandon Webb	4.00

Retrospection Collection Autograph

	NM/M
Common Autograph:	10.00
Production 60	
Hank Blalock	25.00
Bo Hart	25.00
Aubrey Huff	10.00
Torii Hunter	30.00
Austin Kearns	20.00
Corey Patterson	25.00
Albert Pujols	75.00
Jose Reyes	25.00
Scott Rolen	30.00
Mike Ryan	15.00
Ryan Wagner	15.00
Brandon Webb	20.00
Rickie Weeks	50.00
Josh Willingham	20.00
Dontrelle Willis	35.00
Delmon Young	50.00

Retrospection Collection Dual Autograph

No Pricing
Production 19 Sets

Standouts Game-Used

	NM/M
Common Player:	4.00
Inserted 1:41	
Rocco Baldelli	8.00
Angel Berroa	5.00
Hank Blalock	6.00
Marlon Byrd	5.00
Miguel Cabrera	8.00
Hee Seop Choi	4.00
Bo Hart	8.00
Jose Reyes	8.00
Mark Teixeira	6.00
Brandon Webb	5.00
Dontrelle Willis	6.00

Standouts Game-Used Gold

Numbered to player's age.

This Day in History

		NM/M
Complete Set (15):		12.00
Common Player:		.50
Inserted 1:18		
1	Josh Beckett	1.00
2	Carlos Delgado	1.00
3	Javy Lopez	.50
4	Greg Maddux	2.00
5	Rafael Palmeiro	1.00
6	Sammy Sosa	2.50
7	Jeff Bagwell	1.00
8	Frank Thomas	1.00
9	Kevin Millwood	.50
10	Jose Reyes	.75
11	Rafael Furcal	.50
12	Alfonso Soriano	1.50
13	Eric Gagne	.50
14	Hideki Matsui	4.00
15	Hank Blalock	.75

This Day in History Memorabilia

	NM/M
Common Player:	5.00
Inserted 1:288	
Jeff Bagwell	8.00
Carlos Delgado	5.00
Javy Lopez	5.00
Greg Maddux	15.00
Rafael Palmeiro	8.00
Alfonso Soriano	8.00
Sammy Sosa	12.00
Frank Thomas	8.00

This Day/History Dual Memorabilia

	NM/M
Production 25 Sets	
Frank Thomas, Jeff Bagwell	25.00

N.Y. Daily News Yankees

Ten popular Yankees stars are featured on this promotional issue. The April 25 Sunday Daily News included a nine-card sheet produced in an edition of 1.1 million. The 7-1/2" x 12" sheet has nine standard-size player cards. Fronts have game-action photos on a dark blue background. Backs are in blue and black on white, presenting personal data and stats. A 10th card, Alex Rodriguez, in a special edition of

50,000 was available at the Yankees Clubhouse Store with the purchase of a Fleer product and a coupon found in the newspaper. Cards on the sheet are not perforated and must be hand-cut to seperate.

	NM/M
Uncut Sheet:	2.00
Alex Rodriguez:	7.50

N.Y. Post Mets

The opening day lineup of the N.Y. Mets was featured in this promotional issue. The April 19 issue of the Post included a nine-card sheet produced in an edition of 800,000. The 7-1/2" x 12" sheet has nine standard-size player cards. Fronts have game-action photos superimposed on a background resembling the team's jersey. Backs are in team colors and reproduce part of the photo while presenting personal data, stats and career highlights. A 10th card, a Kaz Matsui special edition of 25,000 was available with the purchase of a Fleer product at Mets Team Store outlets. Cards on the sheet are not perforated and must be hand-cut to seperate.

	NM/M
Complete Sheet:	2.00

2005 Fleer

	NM/M
Common Player (1-50):	1.00
Minor Stars (1-50):	1.25
Unlisted Stars (1-50):	1.75
Common Star '05 (51-80):	3.00
Minor Class '05 (51-80):	4.00
Production 699 Sets	
Common Veteran (81-90):	3.00
Production 699 Sets	
Box (1):	90.00
1	Curt Schilling	1.75
2	Jim Thome	3.00
3	Miguel Cabrera	2.00
4	Randy Johnson	3.50
5	David Ortiz	1.75
6	Vladimir Guerrero	3.00
7	Nomar Garciaparra	5.00
8	Ivan Rodriguez	1.75
9	Jason Schmidt	1.25
10	Khalil Greene	2.00
11	Jose Vidro	1.00
12	Lyle Overbay	1.00
13	Todd Helton	2.00
14	Vernon Wells	1.25
15	B.J. Upton	1.25
16	Hideki Matsui	5.00
17	Pedro Martinez	3.00
18	Victor Martinez	1.00
19	Adam Dunn	1.75
20	Andruw Jones	2.00
21	Jeff Bagwell	2.00
22	Mike Sweeney	1.00
23	Mike Piazza	3.50
24	Ben Sheets	1.25
25	Adrian Beltre	1.25
26	Chipper Jones	3.50
27	Greg Maddux	3.50
28	Manny Ramirez	2.00
29	Roger Clemens	5.00
30	Johan Santana	1.25
31	Derek Jeter	6.00
32	Jason Bay	1.00
33	Ken Griffey Jr.	3.50
34	Miguel Tejada	1.75
35	Richie Sexson	1.75
36	Scott Rolen	3.00
37	Alfonso Soriano	3.00
38	Ichiro Suzuki	4.00
39	Sammy Sosa	4.00
40	Barry Zito	1.75
41	Kazuo Matsui	3.00
42	Mark Teixeira	1.25
43	Carlos Beltran	1.75
44	Mark Prior	4.00
45	Travis Hafner	1.00
46	Alex Rodriguez	5.00
47	Lew Ford	1.00
48	Albert Pujols	5.00
49	Frank Thomas	2.00
50	Juan Pierre	1.00
51	David Aardsma	5.00
52	J.D. Durbin	3.00
53	Zack Greinke	4.00
54	Dioner Navarro	4.00
55	Edwin Encarnacion	4.00
56	Luis Hernandez **RC**	4.00
57	Jeff Baker	4.00
58	Victor Diaz	5.00
59	Joey Gathright	3.00
60	Casey Kotchman	4.00
61	David Wright	5.00
62	Jon Knott	3.00
63	Charlton Jimerson	4.00
64	Nick Swisher	5.00
65	Ryan Raburn	3.00
66	Josh Kroeger	3.00
67	Kelly Johnson	4.00
68	Justin Verlander **RC**	6.00
69	Taylor Buchholz	4.00
70	Ubaldo Jimenez **RC**	5.00
71	Russ Adams	4.00
72	Ronny Cedeno	4.00
73	Bobby Jenks	5.00
74	Dan Meyer	4.00
75	Jeff Francis	3.00
76	Scott Kazmir	5.00
77	Sean Burnett	3.00
78	Jose Lopez	4.00
79	Andres Blanco	3.00
80	Gavin Floyd	4.00
81	Tom Seaver	3.00
82	Steve Carlton	3.00
83	Al Kaline	4.00
84	Cal Ripken Jr.	10.00
85	Willie McCovey	5.00
86	Johnny Bench	5.00
87	Nolan Ryan	10.00
88	Mike Schmidt	4.00
89	Carlton Fisk	3.00
90	Don Mattingly	4.00

Row 1

Stars (1-50):	
Class of '05 (51-80):	.5-2X
Veterans:	.5-2X
Production 100 Sets	

Row 2

Cards 1-90:	No Pricing
Production One Set	

Cuts and Glory Jersey

	NM/M
Common Card:	15.00
Production 100 Sets	
Patch:	2-4X
Production 50 Sets	
Jersey and Patch:	No Pricing
Production 15 Sets	
Masterpiece Logo:	No Pricing
Production One Set	
JB	Johnny Bench	60.00
CC	Carl Crawford	20.00
JL	Javy Lopez	20.00
JP	Josh Phelps	15.00
BS	Ben Sheets	20.00
SS	Shannon Stewart	20.00

Cuts and Glory Dual Patch

Production 35 Sets

Diamond Cuts Jersey

	NM/M
Common Player:	5.00
Production 150 Sets	
Die-Cut:	.75-1.5X
Production 75 Sets	
Patch:	1-3X
Production 50 Sets	
Super Patch:	No Pricing
Production 20 Sets	
Die-Cut Patch:	No Pricing
Production 10 Sets	
MLB Logo Masterpiece:	No Pricing
Production One Set	
JB	Jeff Bagwell	8.00
CB	Carlos Beltran	6.00
HB	Hank Blalock	6.00
MC	Miguel Cabrera	8.00
RC	Roger Clemens	12.00
AD	Adam Dunn	6.00
VG	Vladimir Guerrero	8.00
TH	Todd Helton	8.00
RJ	Randy Johnson	8.00
AJ	Andruw Jones	8.00
CJ	Chipper Jones	8.00
AK	Austin Kearns	6.00
PM	Pedro Martinez	8.00
VM	Victor Martinez	5.00
HM	Hideki Matsui	15.00
HN	Hideo Nomo	8.00
DO	David Ortiz	6.00
MP	Mike Piazza	8.00
MP2	Mark Prior	8.00
AP	Albert Pujols	12.00
MR	Manny Ramirez	8.00
SR	Scott Rolen	8.00
CS	Curt Schilling	6.00
GS	Gary Sheffield	6.00
AS	Alfonso Soriano	8.00
SS	Sammy Sosa	10.00
MT	Mark Teixeira	5.00
JT	Jim Thome	8.00
BU	B.J. Upton	5.00
KW	Kerry Wood	8.00

Diamond Cuts Dual Jersey

	NM/M
Common Card:	8.00
Production 99 Sets	
Die-Cut:	.5-1.5X
Production 50 Sets	
Patch:	No Pricing
Production 15 Sets	
Patch Die-Cut:	No Pricing
Production 5 Sets	
BC	Jeff Bagwell, Roger Clemens	15.00
BM	Carlos Beltran, Pedro Martinez	10.00
BS	Hank Blalock, Alfonso Soriano	10.00
CH	Miguel Cabrera, Todd Helton	10.00
DK	Adam Dunn, Austin Kearns	8.00
JJ	Chipper Jones, Andruw Jones	12.00
JS	Randy Johnson, Curt Schilling	10.00
MS	Hideki Matsui, Gary Sheffield	20.00
MT	Victor Martinez, Mark Teixeira	8.00
NU	Hideo Nomo, B.J. Upton	10.00
OR	David Ortiz, Manny Ramirez	10.00
PR	Albert Pujols, Scott Rolen	15.00
PT	Mike Piazza, Jim Thome	12.00
PW	Mark Prior, Kerry Wood	10.00
SG	Sammy Sosa, Vladimir Guerrero	15.00

Dynasty Cornerstones Signatures

Sequentially Numbered

		NM/M
JB	Jeremy Bonderman/75	20.00
DG	Dwight Gooden/25	30.00
DO	David Ortiz/75	40.00

Dynasty Cornerstones Dual Signatures

Sequentially Numbered

Dynasty Foundations Dual Player Jersey

	NM/M
Common Card:	10.00
Production 150 Sets	
Patch:	1-3X
Production 50 Sets	
BO	Miguel Tejada, Javy Lopez	15.00
BR	Manny Ramirez, David Ortiz	10.00
CI	Victor Martinez, Travis Hafner	10.00
CR1	Adam Dunn, Austin Kearns	12.00
CR2	Todd Helton, Preston Wilson	12.00
FM	Miguel Cabrera, Juan Pierre	10.00
HA	Jeff Bagwell, Lance Berkman	12.00
LA	Vladimir Guerrero, Garret Anderson	12.00
MT	Johan Santana, Torii Hunter	12.00
NM	Mike Piazza, Tom Glavine	10.00
OA	Barry Zito, Eric Chavez	10.00
PP	Jim Thome, Bobby Abreu	10.00
SC	Scott Rolen, Albert Pujols	25.00
TD	B.J. Upton, Scott Kazmir	10.00
TR	Mark Teixeira, Michael Young	10.00

Dynasty Foundations Three Player Jersey

	NM/M
Common Card:	15.00
Production 99 Sets	
Patch:	No Pricing
Production 25 Sets	
CR1	Adam Dunn, Austin Kearns, Joe Morgan	15.00
FM	Miguel Cabrera, Josh Beckett, Juan Pierre	15.00
HA	Jeff Bagwell, Lance Berkman, Roger Clemens	40.00
LA	Vladimir Guerrero, Garret Anderson, Darin Erstad	20.00
MT	Johan Santana, Torii Hunter, Shannon Stewart	15.00
NM	Mike Piazza, Pedro Martinez, Tom Glavine	20.00
SC	Scott Rolen, Albert Pujols, Jim Edmonds	40.00
TR	Alfonso Soriano, Mark Teixeira, Michael Young	15.00

Dynasty Foundations Four Player Jersey

	NM/M
Production 40 Sets	
Patch:	No Pricing
Production 15 Sets	
NM	Mike Piazza, Nolan Ryan, Pedro Martinez, Tom Glavine	100.00

Dynasty Foundations Five Player Jersey

No Pricing
Production 25 Sets
Patch: No Pricing
Production 9 Sets
MLB Logo Masterpiece: No Pricing
Production One Set

Head of the Class Triple Player Jersey

	NM/M
Common Card:	15.00
Numbered to Debut Year.	
No pricing for quantities 3 or less.	
Patch:	1-3X
Production 33 Sets	
MLB Logo Masterpiece: No Pricing	
Production One Set	
AGJ	Bobby Abreu, Vladimir Guerrero, Andruw Jones/96	20.00
BGB	Carlos Beltran, Troy Glaus, Adrian Beltre/98	15.00
BTR	Jeff Bagwell, Jim Thome, Ivan Rodriguez/91	15.00
GBH	Eric Gagne, A.J. Burnett, Tim Hudson/99	15.00
JDR	Chipper Jones, Carlos Delgado, Manny Ramirez/93	20.00
OHS	David Ortiz, Torii Hunter, Richie Sexson/97	15.00
SNP	Jason Schmidt, Hideo Nomo, Andy Pettitte/95	20.00

Letterman

Sequentially numbered between 4-8.
No Pricing

Significant Signings Blue

NM/M

Common Player: 10.00
Sequentially #'d to indicated quantity.
Silver Die-Cut: 1-3X
Cards #'d 50 or less: .25-1X
Production 50 Sets
Gold Jersey: No Pricing
Production 25 Sets
Patch: No Pricing
Production 15 Sets
Masterpiece Jersey Tag: No Pricing
Production One Set

JB	Jason Bay/250	15.00
AB	Adrian Beltre/30	50.00
MC	Miguel Cabrera/250	20.00
SC	Steve Carlton/59	30.00
BC	Bobby Crosby/93	15.00
GF	Gavin Floyd/221	8.00
LF	Lew Ford/230	10.00
ZG	Zack Greinke/250	10.00
TH	Travis Hafner/250	10.00
SK	Scott Kazmir/250	10.00
CK	Casey Kotchman/250	10.00
PM	Pedro Martinez/101	40.00
VM	Victor Martinez/224	10.00
DM	Don Mattingly/103	40.00
JM	Justin Morneau/225	25.00
JR	Jeremy Reed/250	40.00
NR	Nolan Ryan/92	100.00
BU	B.J. Upton/250	10.00
KW	Kerry Wood/200	25.00
DW	David Wright/250	40.00

Significant Dual

NM/M

Common Player: 30.00
Production 40 Sets
Dual Jersey: No Pricing
Production 15 Sets
Dual Patch: No Pricing
Production 5 Sets

BR	Adrian Beltre, Jeremy Reed	60.00
CF	Steve Carlton, Gavin Floyd	40.00
FM	Lew Ford, Justin Morneau	40.00
MH	Victor Martinez, Travis Hafner	30.00
SR	Mike Schmidt, Cal Ripken Jr.	250.00

Dynasty Foundations

NM/M

Common Card: 6.00
Production 500 Sets

1DF	Rod Carew, Nolan Ryan, Vladimir Guerrero, Garret Anderson, Darin Erstad	8.00
2DF	Cal Ripken Jr., Brooks Robinson, Miguel Tejada, Javy Lopez, Jim Palmer	15.00
3DF	Ted Williams, Manny Ramirez, Johnny Damon, Carl Yastrzemski, David Ortiz	15.00
4DF	Ryne Sandberg, Sammy Sosa, Ernie Banks, Greg Maddux, Mark Prior	8.00
5DF	Adam Dunn, Johnny Bench, Tony Perez, Austin Kearns, Joe Morgan	8.00
6DF	Victor Martinez, Travis Hafner, Bob Feller, C.C. Sabathia, Larry Doby	6.00
7DF	Aaron Miles, Matt Holliday, Todd Helton, Garrett Atkins, Preston Wilson	6.00
8DF	Miguel Cabrera, Dontrelle Willis, Juan Pierre, Al Leiter, Josh Beckett	6.00
9DF	Lance Berkman, Jeff Bagwell, Craig Biggio, Roger Clemens, Roy Oswalt	8.00
10DF	Ben Sheets, Lyle Overbay, Robin Yount, Geoff Jenkins, Paul Molitor	8.00
11DF	Johan Santana, Shannon Stewart, Harmon Killebrew, Torii Hunter, Lee Ford	6.00
12DF	Tom Glavine, Mike Piazza, Tom Seaver, Nolan Ryan, Pedro Martinez	8.00
13DF	Eric Chavez, Reggie Jackson, Bobby Crosby, Dennis Eckersley, Barry Zito	6.00
14DF	Jim Thome, Bobby Abreu, Gavin Floyd, Robin Roberts, Mike Schmidt	6.00
15DF	Craig Wilson, Willie Stargell, Bill Mazeroski, Jason Bay, Jack Wilson	6.00
16DF	Willie McCovey, Jason Schmidt, Juan Marichal, Orlando Cepeda, Ray Durham	6.00
17DF	Scott Rolen, Mark Mulder, Albert Pujols, Jim Edmonds, Stan Musial	10.00
18DF	Rocco Baldelli, Scott Kazmir, Aubrey Huff, B.J. Upton, Carl Crawford	8.00
19DF	Alfonso Soriano, Mark Teixeira, Hank Blalock, Nolan Ryan, Michael Young	8.00
20DF	Alexis Rios, Paul Molitor, Roy Halladay, Vernon Wells, Orlando Hudson	6.00

National Pastime

NM/M

Common Player (1-50): .25
Minor Stars (1-50): .40
Unlisted Stars (1-50): .60
Common Player (51-70): 3.00
Production 699 Sets
Common Player (71-80): 3.00
Production 699 Sets
Pack (5): 7.00
Box (10): 60.00

1	Khalil Greene	.75
2	Pedro Martinez	1.00
3	Mark Teixeira	.40
4	Jim Thome	1.00
5	Jack Wilson	.25
6	Johan Santana	.40
7	Jason Bay	.25
8	Adam Dunn	.60
9	Lyle Overbay	.25
10	Jason Schmidt	.40
11	Bobby Crosby	.25
12	J.D. Drew	.40
13	Ken Griffey Jr.	1.50
14	Sammy Sosa	2.00
15	Hank Blalock	.60
16	Victor Martinez	.25
17	Randy Johnson	1.00
18	Vernon Wells	.40
19	Todd Helton	.40
20	Javy Lopez	.40
21	Kazuo Matsui	.40
22	Ben Sheets	.40
23	Brad Wilkerson	.25
24	Miguel Cabrera	.75
25	Mike Sweeney	.25
26	Roger Clemens	2.50
27	Chipper Jones	1.50
28	Hideki Matsui	2.50
29	Manny Ramirez	.75
30	Scott Rolen	1.00
31	Lance Berkman	.40
32	Jim Edmonds	.40
33	Derek Jeter	3.00
34	B.J. Upton	.40
35	Carlos Delgado	.75
36	Ichiro Suzuki	2.00
37	Nomar Garciaparra	2.50
38	Albert Pujols	.60
39	Ivan Rodriguez	.60
40	Gary Sheffield	.60
41	Alfonso Soriano	1.00
42	Carlos Beltran	.40
43	Magglio Ordonez	.40
44	Alex Rodriguez	2.50
45	Curt Schilling	.60
46	Greg Maddux	1.50
47	Vladimir Guerrero	1.00
48	Mike Piazza	1.50
49	Miguel Tejada	.40
50	Adrian Beltre	.40
51	Scott Kazmir	5.00
52	Gavin Floyd	4.00
53	Zack Greinke	4.00
54	David Wright	5.00
55	David Aardsma	4.00
56	Ryan Raburn	3.00
57	Joey Gathright	3.00
58	J.D. Durbin	3.00
59	Sean Burnett	3.00
60	Jose Lopez	3.00
61	Nick Swisher	4.00
62	Bobby Jenks	3.00
63	Kelly A. Johnson	3.00
65	Ronny Cedeno	4.00
66	Edwin Encarnacion	3.00
67	Jeff Baker	3.00
68	Taylor Buchholz	3.00
69	Justin Verlander RC	5.00
70	Luis Hernandez RC	5.00
71	Mike Schmidt	5.00
72	Al Kaline	3.00
73	Yogi Berra	4.00
74	Robin Yount	4.00
75	Nolan Ryan	8.00
76	Johnny Bench	5.00
77	Eddie Murray	4.00
78	Tom Seaver	4.00
79	Willie McCovey	3.00
80	Cal Ripken Jr.	8.00

Blue Foil

No Pricing
Production One Set

Red Foil

Cards 1-50:	1-3X
Cards 51-70:	.75-1.5X
Cards 71-80:	.75-1.5X

Production 150 Sets

White Foil

Cards 1-50 #'d to 41-57:	2-6X
Cards 1-50 #'d to 26-40:	4-8X
Cards #'d 25 or less:	No Pricing
Cards 71-80 #'d to 26-44:	1-3X
Cards 71-80 #'d 25 or less:	No Pricing

Numbered to player's jersey number.

Beltway Baseball

NM/M

Common Card: 6.00
Production 202 Sets

1	Ed Delahanty	8.00
2	Benjamin Harrison	8.00
3	William Howard Taft	8.00
4	Clark Griffith	6.00
5	Bobby Burke	8.00
6	Roy Seivers	8.00
7	Tom Cheney	8.00
8	Woodrow Wilson	8.00
9	Franklin D. Roosevelt	8.00
10	John F. Kennedy	10.00
11	Frank Howard	8.00
12	Griffith Stadium	10.00
13	RFK Stadium	8.00
14	All-Star Game	8.00
15	Ted Williams	15.00
16	Harmon Killebrew	12.00
17	Jeff Burroughs	8.00
18	All-Star Game	6.00
19	Unveiling the Nationals	10.00
20	New Logo	8.00

First Name Bases Autograph Gold

NM/M

Cards #'d 25 or less: No Pricing
Sequentially #'d to indicated quantity.

AB	Adrian Beltre/96	25.00
MCAM	Mike Cameron/126	15.00
SH	Shea Hillenbrand/99	15.00
JL	Javy Lopez/73	15.00
AP	Albert Pujols/73	200.00
MT	Mark Teixeira/147	25.00
JV	Justin Verlander/149	20.00

First Name Bases Autograph Red

NM/M

Cards #'d 25 or less: No Pricing
Sequentially #'d to indicated quantity.

MCAM	Mike Cameron/90	15.00
BL	Barry Larkin/27	40.00
MT	Mark Teixeira/95	30.00
JV	Justin Verlander/99	20.00

First Name Bases Autograph Silver

NM/M

Sequentially #'d to indicated quantity.
Blue: No Pricing
Production One Set

MCAM	Mike Cameron/375	10.00
SH	Shea Hillenbrand/316	10.00
JL	Javy Lopez/158	15.00
MT	Mark Teixeira/225	20.00
JV	Justin Verlander/401	15.00

First Name Bases Autograph White

NM/M

Cards #'d 25 or less: No Pricing
Sequentially #'d to indicated quantity.

AB	Adrian Beltre/48	25.00

Grand Old Gamers

NM/M

Common Player: .75
Inserted 1:5

1	Pedro Martinez	1.50
2	Jim Thome	1.50
3	Ken Griffey Jr.	2.00
4	Sammy Sosa	2.00
5	Hank Blalock	1.00
6	Randy Johnson	1.50
7	Roger Clemens	3.00
8	Chipper Jones	2.00
9	Hideki Matsui	3.00
10	Manny Ramirez	1.25
11	Derek Jeter	4.00
12	Ichiro Suzuki	2.50
13	Nomar Garciaparra	3.00
14	Albert Pujols	3.00
15	Gary Sheffield	1.00

16	Alfonso Soriano	1.50
17	Alex Rodriguez	3.00
18	Curt Schilling	1.00
19	Vladimir Guerrero	1.50
20	Mike Piazza	2.00
21	Greg Maddux	2.00
22	Frank Thomas	1.25
23	Adrian Beltre	.75
24	Barry Larkin	.75
25	Todd Helton	1.25
26	Kerry Wood	1.25
27	Kazuo Matsui	1.00
28	Scott Rolen	1.50
29	Ivan Rodriguez	1.00
30	Miguel Tejada	.75
31	Mark Teixeira	.75
32	Rafael Palmeiro	1.25
33	Andruw Jones	1.25
34	Carlos Beltran	1.00
35	Jeff Bagwell	1.25

Grand Old Gamers Jersey

NM/M

Common Player: 6.00
Inserted 1:36 Retail

JB	Jeff Bagwell	8.00
CB	Carlos Beltran	8.00
AB	Adrian Beltre	8.00
HB	Hank Blalock	8.00
RC	Roger Clemens/SP/50	15.00
VG	Vladimir Guerrero	8.00
TH	Todd Helton	8.00
RJ	Randy Johnson	8.00
AJ	Andruw Jones	8.00
CJ	Chipper Jones	8.00
BL	Barry Larkin	6.00
GM	Greg Maddux/SP/75	12.00
PM	Pedro Martinez	8.00
HM	Hideki Matsui/SP/50	15.00
KM	Kazuo Matsui	8.00
RP	Rafael Palmeiro	8.00
MP	Mike Piazza	8.00
AP	Albert Pujols	12.00
MR	Manny Ramirez	8.00
IR	Ivan Rodriguez	8.00
SR	Scott Rolen	8.00
CS	Curt Schilling	8.00
GS	Gary Sheffield	8.00
AS	Alfonso Soriano	8.00
SS	Sammy Sosa	12.00
MT	Mark Teixeira	6.00
FT	Frank Thomas	8.00
JT	Jim Thome	8.00
KW	Kerry Wood	8.00

Grand Old Gamers Patch Blue

NM/M

Numbered to player's jersey number.
Cards numbered 25 or less: No Pricing
Masterpiece: No Pricing
Production One Set

VG	Vladimir Guerrero/27	25.00
RJ	Randy Johnson/51	20.00
GM	Greg Maddux/31	25.00
PM	Pedro Martinez/45	20.00
HM	Hideki Matsui/55	50.00
MP	Mike Piazza/31	25.00
SR	Scott Rolen/27	25.00
CS	Curt Schilling/38	15.00
FT	Frank Thomas/35	15.00
KW	Kerry Wood/34	20.00

Grand Old Gamers Dual Patch

NM/M

Cards #'d to 25 or less: No Pricing
Production 5-33 Sets

	Ivan Rodriguez, Mike Piazza/31	75.00
	Hank Blalock, Mark Teixeira/33	30.00

Historical Record

NM/M

Common Card: 2.00
Inserted 1:6

1	Ichiro Suzuki/2004	2.50
2	Greg Maddux/2004	3.00
3	Alex Rodriguez/1998	3.00
4	Mike Piazza/2004	2.00
5	Nolan Ryan/1991	5.00
6	Albert Pujols/2001	3.00
7	Mike Schmidt/1987	4.00
8	Randy Johnson/2004	2.00
9	Sammy Sosa/2003	2.50
10	Cal Ripken Jr./1996	5.00
11	Roger Clemens/2004	3.00
12	Hideki Matsui/2003	3.00
13	Hideo Nomo/1994	2.00
14	Gene Autry/1961	2.00
15	Walter O'Malley/1944	2.00

Historical Record Jersey

NM/M

Common Player: 6.00

Abbreviations

SP - Short Print

Historical Record Patch Blue

No Pricing
Numbered to player's jersey number.
Masterpiece: No Pricing
Production One Set

Historical Record Dual Patch

No Pricing
Production 8-25 Sets

Signature Swings Bat Red

NM/M

Common Player: 20.00
Production 30-99 Sets

BAY	Jason Bay/99	20.00
JB	Johnny Bench/42	80.00
LB	Lance Berkman/99	20.00
CC	Carl Crawford/99	20.00
LF	Lew Ford/76	20.00
CK	Casey Kotchman/99	20.00
BR	Brooks Robinson/64	40.00
MS	Mike Schmidt/30	100.00
SS	Shannon Stewart/99	20.00
DW	David Wright/99	60.00

Signnature Swings Jersey White

NM/M

Production 3-29 Sets
Cards #'d less than 25: No Pricing

LB	Lance Berkman/29	30.00
CC	Carl Crawford/29	30.00
JP	Josh Phelps/27	15.00

Signature Swings Patch Blue

NM/M

Numbered to player's jersey number.
Cards #'d less than 25: No Pricing
Masterpiece: No Pricing
Production One Set

BAY	Jason Bay/38	60.00
JP	Josh Phelps/45	20.00

Signature Swings Silver

NM/M

Common Player: 10.00
Gold: .75-1.5X
Sequentially #'d between 50 & 199.

BAY	Jason Bay	20.00
CC	Carl Crawford	10.00
AE	Adam Everett	10.00
CF	Chone Figgins	10.00
LF	Lew Ford	10.00
JG	Joey Gathright	10.00
KG	Khalil Greene	30.00
TH	Travis Hafner	10.00
AH	Aubrey Huff	10.00
CK	Casey Kotchman	10.00
VAL	Val Majewski	10.00
JM	Joe Mauer	25.00
DM	Dallas McPherson	15.00
JMO	Justin Morneau	40.00
WMP	Wily Mo Pena	25.00
JP	Josh Phelps	10.00
RR	Ryan Raburn	10.00
SS	Shannon Stewart	10.00
NS	Nick Swisher	10.00
BJU	B.J. Upton	15.00
CU	Chase Utley	12.00
DW	David Wright	50.00
MY	Michael Young	10.00

2005 Fleer Authentix

NM/M

Inserted 1:96 Retail

RC	Roger Clemens	10.00
RJ	Randy Johnson	8.00
GM	Greg Maddux	8.00
HM	Hideki Matsui	12.00
HN	Hideo Nomo	6.00
MP	Mike Piazza	8.00
AP	Albert Pujols	10.00
CR	Cal Ripken Jr.	30.00
NRO	Nolan Ryan	20.00
MS	Mike Schmidt	25.00
SS	Sammy Sosa	10.00

NM/M

Common Player (1-100): .25
Minor Stars (1-100): .40
Unlisted Stars (1-100): .60
Common Player Autograph (101-125): 10.00
Minor Stars Autograph (101-125): 15.00
Production 250 Sets
Pack (5):
Box ( ):

1	Albert Pujols	2.50
2	Bernie Williams	.60
3	Vinny Castilla	.25
4	Rocco Baldelli	.60
5	Mike Piazza	1.50
6	Sean Casey	.25
7	Oliver Perez	.25
8	Tony Batista	.25
9	Paul Konerko	.25
10	Scott Rolen	1.00
11	Justin Morneau	.25
12	Nomar Garciaparra	2.50
13	Lance Berkman	.25
14	Mike Sweeney	.25
15	Miguel Tejada	.25
16	Craig Wilson	.25
17	Craig Biggio	.40
18	Shea Hillenbrand	.25
19	Mark Mulder	.40
20	Juan Pierre	.25
21	Troy Glaus	.60
22	Eric Chavez	.25
23	Jeromy Burnitz	.25
24	Carl Crawford	.75
25	Kazuo Matsui	.75
26	Ivan Rodriguez	.60
27	Aubrey Huff	.25
28	Derek Jeter	3.00
29	Casey Blake	.25
30	Mark Teixeira	.40
31	Brad Wilkerson	.25
32	Austin Kearns	.60
33	Jim Edmonds	.40
34	Johan Santana	.40
35	Kerry Wood	.75
36	Ichiro Suzuki	2.00
37	Lyle Overbay	.25
38	Melvin Mora	.25
39	Jason Bay	.25
40	Jake Westbrook	.25
41	Andruw Jones	.25
42	Chase Utley	.25
43	Carl Pavano	.25
44	Luis Gonzalez	.40
45	Bobby Crosby	.25
46	Carlos Guillen	.25
47	Carlos Delgado	.75
48	Alex Rodriguez	2.50
49	Todd Helton	.75
50	Michael Young	.25
51	Geoff Jenkins	.40
52	Pedro Martinez	1.00
53	Brian Giles	.25
54	Ken Harvey	.25
55	Johnny Estrada	.25
56	Billy Wagner	.25
57	Roger Clemens	2.50
58	Chipper Jones	1.50
59	Jim Thome	1.00
60	Miguel Cabrera	.75
61	Vladimir Guerrero	1.00
62	Gary Sheffield	.60
63	Travis Hafner	.25
64	Alfonso Soriano	1.00
65	Richard Hidalgo	.25
66	Adam Dunn	.60
67	Garret Anderson	.40
68	Lew Ford	.25
69	Mark Prior	1.50
70	Bret Boone	.40
71	Ben Sheets	.40
72	David Ortiz	.60
73	Mark Loretta	.25
74	Eric Gagne	.25
75	Curt Schilling	.60
76	Jason Schmidt	.40
77	Adrian Beltre	.40
78	Javy Lopez	.25
79	Jack Wilson	.25
80	Carlos Beltran	.60
81	J.D. Drew	.40
82	Bobby Abreu	.40
83	Jeff Bagwell	.75
84	Randy Johnson	1.00
85	Tim Hudson	.40
86	Carlos Pena	.40
87	Vernon Wells	.40
88	Tom Glavine	.40
89	Victor Martinez	.25
90	Hank Blalock	.60
91	Jose Vidro	.25
92	Magglio Ordonez	.40
93	Jake Peavy	.25
94	Torii Hunter	.60
95	Sammy Sosa	2.00
96	Hideki Matsui	2.50
97	Shawn Green	.40
98	Manny Ramirez	.75
99	Khalil Greene	.75
100	Jason Marquis	.25
101	B.J. Upton/Auto.	20.00
102	Scott Kazmir/Auto.	20.00
103	Gavin Floyd/Auto.	20.00
104	Jeff Francis/Auto.	20.00
105	Russ Adams/ Auto./EXch	10.00

106	Zack Greinke/Auto.	15.00
107	David Wright/Auto.	60.00
108	David Aardsma/Auto.	20.00
109	Josh Kroeger/Auto.	10.00
110	Ryan Raburn/Auto.	30.00
111	Jason Kubel/Auto.	10.00
112	Casey Kotchman/ Auto.	20.00
113	Joey Gathright/Auto.	15.00
114	Jon Knott/Auto.	10.00
115	J.D. Durbin/Auto.	25.00
116	Andres Blanco/Auto.	10.00
117	Charlton Jimerson/ Auto.	10.00
118	Sean Burnett/Auto.	15.00
119	Joe Mauer/Auto.	30.00
120	Justin Verlander/ Auto. RC	30.00
121	Mike Gosling/Auto.	10.00
122	Jeff Keppinger/Auto.	10.00
123	David Krynzel/Auto.	10.00
124	Jose Lopez/Auto.	15.00
125	Ruben Gotay/Auto.	15.00

General Admission

Cards 1-100:	1-2.5X
Cards 101-125:	.75-1.5X
Production 100 Sets	

Autographed General Admission

	NM/M
Common Player:	15.00
Production 100 Sets	
Mezzanine:	1-2X
Production 40 Sets	
Club Box:	No Pricing
Production 5 Sets	
Standing Room Only:	No Pricing
Production One Set	
AA-JB Jason Bay	15.00
AA-JE Johnny Estrada	15.00
AA-CF Chone Figgins	20.00
AA-LF Lew Ford	15.00
AA-KG Khalil Greene	50.00
AA-TH Travis Hafner	15.00
AA-JM Justin Morneau	40.00
AA-JS Johan Santana	25.00
AA-BS Ben Sheets	20.00
AA-CU Chase Utley	15.00
AA-JW Jack Wilson	15.00

Authentix Mezzanine

Cards 1-100:	1-3X
Cards 101-125:	.75-2X
Production 75 Sets	

Club Box

Cards 1-100:	1-3.25X
Cards 101-125:	1-2X
Production 50 Sets	

Standing Room Only

Cards 1-125:	No Pricing
Production 10 Sets	

Hot Ticket

	NM/M
Common Player:	2.00

Inserted 1:12

1	Derek Jeter	6.00
2	Roger Clemens	5.00
3	Vladimir Guerrero	3.00
4	Manny Ramirez	2.00
5	Alex Rodriguez	5.00
6	Albert Pujols	5.00
7	Mike Piazza	3.50
8	Hideki Matsui	5.00
9	Sammy Sosa	4.00
10	Chipper Jones	3.50

Hot Ticket Jersey

	NM/M
Common Player:	8.00
Inserted 1:87	
Patch	
Cards #'d to 55:	1-3X
Cards #'d to 27:	2-4X
Cards #'d to 25 or less:	No Pricing
Sequentially #'d to player's jersey #.	
MLB Logo:	No Pricing
Production One Set	
HT-RC Roger Clemens	15.00
HT-VG Vladimir Guerrero	8.00
HT-CJ Chipper Jones	10.00
HT-HM Hideki Matsui	25.00
HT-MP Mike Piazza	10.00
HT-AP Albert Pujols	20.00
HT-MR Manny Ramirez	8.00
HT-SS Sammy Sosa	12.00

Jersey Game of the Week

	NM/M
Common Player:	10.00
Sequentially #'d between 10 & 200.	
No pricing for cards #'d to 20 or less.	
Patch:	No Pricing
Production 10 Sets	
BR	Carlos Beltran, Scott Rolen/120	15.00
BT	Tony Batista, Miguel Tejada/170	10.00
CG	Eric Chavez, Troy Glaus/150	12.00
CJ	Roger Clemens, Randy Johnson/70	15.00
CJ2	Miguel Cabrera, Chipper Jones/90	12.00
CP	Carl Crawford, Juan Pierre/190	10.00
DT	Adam Dunn, Jim Thome/110	20.00
GG	Shawn Green, Vladimir Guerrero/180	12.00
GS	Vladimir Guerrero, Alfonso Soriano/100	15.00
KG	Scott Kazmir, Zack Greinke/80	10.00
MM	Kazuo Matsui, Hideki Matsui/30	100.00
MM2	Joe Mauer, Victor Martinez/130	10.00
MR	Pedro Martinez, Mariano Rivera/60	12.00
OP	David Ortiz, Albert Pujols/200	15.00
OS	Magglio Ordonez, Sammy Sosa/160	15.00
RH	Manny Ramirez, Torii Hunter/140	10.00
SS	Johan Santana, Curt Schilling/40	30.00
WO	Kerry Wood, Roy Oswalt/50	30.00

Jersey General Admission

	NM/M
Common Player:	5.00
Inserted 1:16	
Jersey Mezzanine:	1-3X
Production 75 Sets	
Jersey Club Box:	No Pricing
Production 25 Sets	
Jersey Standing Room Only:	No Pricing
Production One Set	
Patch General Admission:	2-4X
Production 75 Sets	
Patch Mezzanine:	No Pricing
Production 15 Sets	
Patch Club Box:	No Pricing

Production 5 Sets
Patch Standing Room Only: No Pricing
Production One Set

JA-CB	Carlos Beltran	10.00
JA-AB	Adrian Beltre	5.00
JA-LB	Lance Berkman	5.00
JA-HB	Hank Blalock	5.00
JA-MC	Miguel Cabrera	8.00
JA-RC	Roger Clemens	12.00
JA-AD	Adam Dunn	5.00
JA-EG	Eric Gagne	5.00
JA-KG	Khalil Greene	10.00
JA-VG	Vladimir Guerrero	8.00
JA-TH	Todd Helton	5.00
JA-RJ	Randy Johnson	8.00
JA-CJ	Chipper Jones	8.00
JA-PM	Pedro Martinez	8.00
JA-HM	Hideki Matsui	20.00
JA-KM	Kazuo Matsui	10.00
JA-JM	Joe Mauer	8.00
JA-HN	Hideo Nomo	8.00
JA-DO	David Ortiz	10.00
JA-MP	Mike Piazza	8.00
JA-AP	Albert Pujols	15.00
JA-MR	Manny Ramirez	8.00
JA-MR2	Mariano Rivera	8.00
JA-IR	Ivan Rodriguez	8.00
JA-SR	Scott Rolen	8.00
JA-JS	Johan Santana	5.00
JA-CS	Curt Schilling	5.00
JA-GS	Gary Sheffield	5.00
JA-AS	Alfonso Soriano	8.00
JA-SS	Sammy Sosa	10.00
JA-JT	Jim Thome	8.00
JA-BU	B.J. Upton	5.00
JA-BW	Bernie Williams	5.00
JA-KW	Kerry Wood	5.00
JA-DW	David Wright	15.00

Autograph Jersey General Admission

	NM/M
Common Player:	20.00
Production 75 Sets	
Mezzanine:	No Pricing
Production 15 Sets	
Club Box:	No Pricing
Production 5 Sets	
Standing Room Only:	No Pricing
Production One Set	
JB	Jason Bay	20.00
MC	Miguel Cabrera	30.00
JE	Johnny Estrada	20.00
CF	Chone Figgins	25.00
LF	Lew Ford	20.00
KG	Khalil Greene	60.00
TH	Travis Hafner	20.00
JM	Justin Morneau	50.00
JS	Johan Santana	25.00
MS	Mike Schmidt	75.00
BS	Ben Sheets	25.00
CU	Chase Utley	20.00
JW	Jack Wilson	20.00

Autograph Patch General Admission

	NM/M
Production 40 Sets	
Mezzanine:	No Pricing
Production 10 Sets	
Club Box:	No Pricing
Production 5 Sets	
Standing Room Only	
Production One Set	
CF	Chone Figgins	25.00
MP	Mike Piazza	150.00
CR	Cal Ripken Jr.	400.00
MS	Mike Schmidt	150.00
JT	Jim Thome	80.00

Showstoppers

	NM/M
Common Player:	2.00
Inserted 1:8	
1	Nomar Garciaparra	4.00
2	Ichiro Suzuki	3.50
3	Ken Griffey Jr.	3.00
4	Alex Rodriguez	4.00
5	Albert Pujols	4.00
6	Derek Jeter	5.00
7	Roger Clemens	4.00
8	Randy Johnson	2.50
9	Hideo Nomo	2.50
10	Jim Thome	2.50
11	Mike Piazza	3.00
12	Hideki Matsui	3.00
13	Sammy Sosa	3.50
14	Kerry Wood	2.50
15	Eric Gagne	2.50

Teammate Trios

	NM/M
Common Card:	12.00
Production 75 Sets	
Hometown 1:	2-3X
Production 25 Sets	
Hometown 2:	No Pricing
Production 5 Sets	
TT-BR	David Ortiz, Manny Ramirez, Pedro Martinez	25.00
TT-NY	Hideki Matsui, Bernie Williams, Gary Sheffield	30.00
TT-AB	J.D. Drew, Chipper Jones, Andruw Jones	15.00
TT-CC	Sammy Sosa, Mark Prior, Nomar Garciaparra	15.00
TT-CI	Victor Martinez, Travis Hafner, Casey Blake	12.00
TT-HA	Lance Berkman, Roger Clemens, Carlos Beltran	25.00
TT-MT	Johan Santana, Torii Hunter, Corey Koskie	12.00
TT-WN	Tony Batista, Jose Vidro, Brad Wilkerson	12.00
TT-NM	Mike Piazza, David Wright, Kazuo Matsui	40.00
TT-OA	Barry Zito, Tim Hudson, Mark Mulder	12.00
TT-PP	Bobby Abreu, Jim Thome, Pat Burrell	15.00
TT-SC	Scott Rolen, Albert Pujols, Jim Edmonds	30.00
TT-TD	Scott Kazmir, Rocco Baldelli, B.J. Upton	25.00
TT-TR	Hank Blalock, Mark Teixeira, Alfonso Soriano	15.00
TT-LD	Shawn Green, Adrian Beltre, Steve Finley	12.00

2005 Fleer Classic Clippings

	NM/M
Common Player (1-75):	.25
Minor Stars (1-75):	.40
Unlisted Stars (1-75):	.60
Common Legends (76-105):	2.00
Production 999 Sets	
Common Player (106-125):	3.00
Inserted 1:6	

1	Frank Thomas	.75
2	Vladimir Guerrero	1.00
3	Ken Griffey Jr.	1.50
4	Derek Jeter	3.00
5	Rafael Palmeiro	.75
6	Adrian Beltre	.40
7	Khalil Greene	.75
8	Richie Sexson	.60
9	Roger Clemens	2.50
10	Mike Piazza	1.50
11	Chipper Jones	1.50
12	Juan Pierre	.25
13	Todd Helton	.75
14	Ben Sheets	.40
15	John Smoltz	.40
16	Steve Finley	.25
17	Jim Thome	1.00
18	Vernon Wells	.40
19	Melvin Mora	.25
20	Dontrelle Willis	.40
21	Eric Gagne	.40
22	Craig Wilson	.25
23	Curt Schilling	.60
24	Justin Morneau	.25
25	Jason Schmidt	.40
26	Kerry Wood	.75
27	Ivan Rodriguez	.60
28	Rocco Baldelli	.60
29	Mark Prior	2.00
30	Josh Beckett	.75
31	Scott Rolen	1.00
32	Nomar Garciaparra	2.50
33	Carl Crawford	.25
34	Paul Konerko	.40
35	Miguel Cabrera	.75
36	Hank Blalock	.60
37	Sammy Sosa	2.00
38	Jim Edmonds	.40
39	David Ortiz	.60
40	Lance Berkman	.40
41	Ichiro Suzuki	2.00
42	Adam Dunn	.60
43	Carlos Guillen	.25
44	Alfonso Soriano	1.00
45	Victor Martinez	.25
46	Torii Hunter	.60
47	Kazuo Matsui	.60
48	Andruw Jones	.75
49	Matt Holliday	.25
50	Eric Chavez	.40
51	Randy Johnson	1.00
52	Lew Ford	.25
53	Hideki Matsui	.75
54	Manny Ramirez	.75
55	Mark Teixeira	.40
56	Jose Vidro	.25
57	Mike Sweeney	.25
58	Jack Wilson	.25
59	Greg Maddux	1.50
60	Tony Batista	.25
61	Albert Pujols	2.50
62	Miguel Tejada	.60
63	Carlos Beltran	.60
64	Bobby Abreu	.40
65	Carlos Delgado	.75
66	Travis Hafner	.25
67	Scott Podsednik	.25
68	Gary Sheffield	.60
69	Johan Santana	.40
70	Barry Zito	.25
71	Pedro Martinez	1.00
72	Brian Giles	.40
73	Garret Anderson	.40
74	Jeff Bagwell	.75
75	Alex Rodriguez	2.50
76	Johnny Bench	4.00
77	Yogi Berra	3.00
78	Lou Brock	3.00
79	Rod Carew	3.00
80	Orlando Cepeda	2.00
81	Carlton Fisk	3.00
82	Bob Gibson	3.00
83	Reggie Jackson	3.00
84	Al Kaline	4.00
85	Harmon Killebrew	3.00
86	Ralph Kiner	4.00
87	Willie McCovey	3.00
88	Eddie Murray	4.00
89	Phil Rizzuto	4.00
90	Brooks Robinson	3.00
91	Nolan Ryan	5.00
92	Mike Schmidt	4.00
93	Tom Seaver	3.00
94	Willie Stargell	2.00
95	Rollie Fingers	2.00
96	Dennis Eckersley	2.00
97	Enos Slaughter	2.00
98	Jim Palmer	2.00
99	Warren Spahn	3.00
100	Joe Morgan	2.00
101	Richie Ashburn	3.00
102	Robin Yount	3.00
103	Bob Feller	3.00
104	Pee Wee Reese	2.00
105	Eddie Mathews	3.00
106	David Wright	6.00
107	David Aardsma	3.00
108	B.J. Upton	3.00
109	Scott Kazmir	4.00
110	Gavin Floyd	3.00
111	Jeff Francis	3.00
112	Dioner Navarro	3.00
113	Zack Greinke	3.00
114	Nick Swisher	5.00
115	Josh Kroeger	3.00
116	Ryan Raburn	3.00
117	Victor Diaz	3.00
118	Casey Kotchman	4.00
119	Joey Gathright	3.00
120	Jon Knott	3.00
121	J.D. Durbin	3.00
122	Andres Blanco	3.00
123	Charlton Jimerson	3.00
124	Russ Adams	3.00
125	Justin Verlander RC	5.00

First Edition

(1-75):	2-5X
(76-105):	1-1.5X
(106-125):	1-2X
Production 150 Sets	

Final Edition

No Pricing
Production One Set

Bat Rack Quad Blue

	NM/M
Inserted 1:118	
Silver:	No Pricing
Production 10 Sets	
Purple:	No Pricing
Production One Set	
Gary Sheffield, Vladimir Guerrero, Manny Ramirez, Sammy Sosa	20.00
Manny Ramirez, Wade Boggs, Carl Yastrzemski, Bobby Doerr	40.00
Kirby Puckett, Jacque Jones, Harmon Killebrew, Torii Hunter	40.00
Brandon Webb, Randy Johnson, Curt Schilling, Roger Clemens	40.00
Willie Stargell, Bill Madlock, Bill Mazeroski, Roberto Clemente	100.00
Al Kaline, Tony Gwynn, Frank Howard, Rocky Colavito	50.00
Jose Reyes, Gary Carter, Mike Piazza, Kazuo Matsui	25.00
Bobby Abreu, Adam Dunn, Rocco Baldelli, Hideki Matsui	30.00
Jim Thome, Albert Pujols, Jeff Bagwell, Todd Helton	40.00
Hank Blalock, Miguel Tejada, Troy Glaus, Ivan Rodriguez	25.00
Carlos Delgado, Jason Giambi, Rafael Palmeiro, Mark Teixeira	25.00

Classic Clippings

	NM/M
Common Player:	3.00
Gold:	2-5X
Production 51-95 Sets	
1	Nolan Ryan/1991	6.00
2	Cal Ripken Jr./1995	8.00
3	Joe Carter/1993	3.00
4	Bucky Dent/1978	3.00
5	Kirk Gibson/1988	3.00
6	Reggie Jackson/1977	5.00
7	Carlton Fisk/1975	4.00
8	Bobby Thomson/1951	3.00
9	Bill Mazeroski/1960	3.00
10	Don Larsen/1956	4.00

Cut of History Single Autograph Blue

	NM/M
Common Player:	20.00
Inserted 1:161	
Silver:	No Pricing
Production 25 Sets	
Purple:	No Pricing
Production One Set	
JB	Johnny Bench	50.00
BB	Bill Buckner	20.00
BF	Bob Feller	20.00
KG	Kirk Gibson	20.00
DG	Dwight Gooden	30.00
DL	Don Larsen	20.00
DM	Don Mattingly	50.00
JP	Jim Palmer	30.00
BR	Brooks Robinson	40.00
DS	Darryl Strawberry	25.00
MW	Mookie Wilson	20.00

Cut of History Dual Autograph Blue

	NM/M
Production 49 Sets	
Silver:	No Pricing
Production 22 Sets	
Purple:	No Pricing
Production One Set	
GE	Kirk Gibson, Dennis Eckersley	50.00
GS	Dwight Gooden, Darryl Strawberry	40.00
WB	Mookie Wilson, Bill Buckner	40.00

Cut of History Triple Autograph Blue

No Pricing	
Production 15 Sets	
Silver:	No Pricing
Production 5 Sets	
Purple:	No Pricing
Production One Set	

Cut of History Single Jersey Blue

	NM/M
Common Player:	6.00
Inserted 1:21	
Silver Patch:	No Pricing
Production 25 Sets	
Purple Patch:	No Pricing
Production One Set	
SA	Sparky Anderson	6.00
JB	Johnny Bench	15.00

OC	Orlando Cepeda	8.00
CF	Carlton Fisk	10.00
BG	Bob Gibson	8.00
DG	Dwight Gooden	6.00
RJ	Reggie Jackson	12.00
DM	Don Mattingly	15.00
WM	Willie Mccovey	6.00
JM	Joe Morgan/SP/82	12.00
EM	Eddie Murray	10.00
CR	Cal Ripken Jr.	20.00
BR	Brooks Robinson	8.00
NR	Nolan Ryan	20.00
MS	Mike Schmidt	12.00
TS	Tom Seaver	10.00
OS	Ozzie Smith	15.00
WS	Willie Stargell	6.00
DS	Darryl Strawberry	6.00
CY	Carl Yastrzemski	10.00

Cut of History Dual Jersey Blue

NM/M
Common Card: 15.00
Inserted 1:112
Silver Patch: No Pricing
Production 15 Sets
Purple Patch: No Pricing
Production One Set

BF	Johnny Bench, Carlton Fisk	20.00
BS	Lou Brock, Mike Schmidt	25.00
CM	Orlando Cepeda, Willie McCovey	15.00
GS	Dwight Gooden, Darryl Strawberry	15.00
JY	Reggie Jackson, Carl Yastrzemski	20.00
RS	Cal Ripken Jr., Ozzie Smith	30.00
RS	Nolan Ryan, Tom Seaver	30.00
SJ	Willie Stargell, Reggie Jackson	20.00

Cut of History Triple Jersey Blue

NM/M
Inserted 1:67
Silver Patch: No Pricing
Production 25 Sets
Purple Patch: No Pricing
Production One Set

ACW	Hank Aaron, Roberto Clemente, Ted Williams	160.00
BSG	Lou Brock, Kirk Gibson, Ozzie Smith	50.00
JKM	Reggie Jackson, Harmon Killebrew, Willie McCovey	40.00
MMC	Eddie Murray, Orlando Cepeda, Willie McCovey	25.00
MRS	Don Mattingly, Cal Ripken Jr., Mike Schmidt	75.00
OJM	Paul O'Neill, Don Mattingly, Reggie Jackson	50.00
RCJ	Nolan Ryan, Roger Clemens, Randy Johnson	50.00

Diamond Signings Single Blue

NM/M
Inserted 1:29
Silver: No Pricing
Production 25 Sets
Purple: No Pricing
Production One Set

JB	Jason Bay	20.00
AB	Andres Blanco	15.00
CF	Chone Figgins	15.00
GF	Gavin Floyd	15.00
KG	Khalil Greene/150	25.00
ZG	Zack Greinke	15.00
TH	Travis Hafner	10.00
CJ	Charlton Jimerson	15.00
SK	Scott Kazmir	20.00
CK	Casey Kotchman	10.00
BL	Brad Lidge/97	40.00
JM	Justin Morneau/98	25.00
DN	Dioner Navarro	10.00
JP	Jake Peavy	20.00
NS	Nick Swisher	15.00
BU	B.J. Upton	15.00
JV	Justin Verlander/150	35.00
DW	David Wright/97	50.00

Diamond Signings Dual Blue

NM/M
Production 49 Sets
Silver: No Pricing
Production 22 Sets
Purple: No Pricing
Production One Set

BC	Jason Bay, B. Crosby/ExCh	30.00
FU	Gavin Floyd, Chase Utley	40.00

Diamond Signings Triple Blue

NM/M
Sequentially Numbered
Silver: No Pricing
Production 5 Sets
Purple: No Pricing
Production One Set

Khalil Greene, B.J. Upton, Bobby Crosby/99	50.00
Justin Verlander, Gavin Floyd, Scott Kazmir/99	75.00
Nick Swisher, Charlton Jimerson, Chone Figgins/99	30.00
Casey Kotchman, Justin Morneau, Jason Bay/86	40.00

Jersey Rack Dual Jersey Blue

NM/M
Common Card: 10.00
Inserted 1:100
Silver Patch: No Pricing
Production 25 Sets
Purple Patch: No Pricing
Production One Set

BW	Josh Beckett, Kerry Wood	10.00
CJ	Miguel Cabrera, Andruw Jones	12.00
DB	Adam Dunn, Lance Berkman	10.00
GS	Vladimir Guerrero, Sammy Sosa	15.00
GT	Khalil Greene, Miguel Tejada	10.00
HB	Todd Helton, Jeff Bagwell	10.00
HE	Torii Hunter, Jim Edmonds	10.00
JC	Randy Johnson, Roger Clemens	20.00
JW	Chipper Jones, David Wright	15.00
MM	Hideki Matsui, Kazuo Matsui	25.00
OG	David Ortiz, Jason Giambi	12.00
RB	Scott Rolen, Adrian Beltre	12.00
RS	Manny Ramirez, Gary Sheffield	12.00
SG	John Smoltz, Eric Gagne	10.00
SM	Jason Schmidt, Pedro Martinez	12.00
SM1	Alfonso Soriano, Kazuo Matsui	10.00
SP	Curt Schilling, Mark Prior	8.00
TP	Jim Thome, Mike Piazza	12.00
WS	Dontrelle Willis, Johan Santana	12.00

Jersey Rack Triple Jersey Blue

NM/M
Common Card: 12.00
Inserted 1:54
Silver Patch: No Pricing
Production 25 Sets
Purple Patch: No Pricing
Production One Set

CJS	Roger Clemens, Randy Johnson, Jason Schmidt	20.00
CSJ	Roger Clemens, Curt Schilling, Randy Johnson	20.00
EHJ	Jim Edmonds, Torii Hunter, Andruw Jones	12.00
GRS	Vladimir Guerrero, Manny Ramirez, Gary Sheffield	15.00
GSR	Eric Gagne, John Smoltz, Mariano Rivera	15.00
HSB	Todd Helton, Alfonso Soriano, Adrian Beltre	12.00
MGT	Kazuo Matsui, Khalil Greene, Miguel Tejada	15.00
MRG	Hideki Matsui, Mariano Rivera, Jason Giambi	25.00
ORM	David Ortiz, Manny Ramirez, Pedro Martinez	15.00
PRE	Albert Pujols, Scott Rolen, Jim Edmonds	25.00
PTB	Albert Pujols, Jim Thome, Jeff Bagwell	20.00
RBJ	Scott Rolen, Adrian Beltre, Chipper Jones	15.00
SDC	Sammy Sosa, Adam Dunn, Miguel Cabrera	12.00
SJJ	John Smoltz, Chipper Jones, Andruw Jones	20.00
SPB	Jason Schmidt, Mark Prior, Josh Beckett	10.00
STB	Sammy Sosa, Miguel Tejada, Adrian Beltre	15.00
WPM	David Wright, Mike Piazza, Kazuo Matsui	20.00
WSW	Dontrelle Willis, Johan Santana, Kerry Wood	15.00

Press Clippings

NM/M
Common Player: 2.00
Inserted 1:6
Gold: No Pricing
Production 4 Sets

1	Ichiro Suzuki	4.00
2	Manny Ramirez	5.00
3	Albert Pujols	5.00
4	David Ortiz	2.00
5	Greg Maddux	3.00
6	Ken Griffey Jr.	3.00
7	Vladimir Guerrero	3.00
8	Randy Johnson	3.00
9	Johan Santana	5.00
10	Roger Clemens	2.00
11	Bobby Crosby	2.00
12	Jason Bay	2.00

2005 Fleer Patchworks

NM/M
Complete Set (100):
Common (1-70): .40
Common (71-90): 1.50
Production 499 Sets
Common (91-100): 2.00
Production 999 Sets
Pack (5): 4.00
Box (18): 60.00

1	Bobby Abreu	.50
2	Miguel Cabrera	1.00
3	J.D. Drew	.40
4	Justin Morneau	.40
5	David Ortiz	1.00
6	Ivan Rodriguez	.75
7	Jason Schmidt	.40
8	Frank Thomas	.75
9	Travis Hafner	.50
10	Curt Schilling	1.00
11	Jim Edmonds	.75
12	Randy Johnson	1.00
13	Jose Vidro	.40
14	Vernon Wells	.40
15	Lance Berkman	.50
16	Khalil Greene	.50
17	Andruw Jones	.75
18	Mark Prior	.75
19	Mark Teixeira	.50
20	Jack Wilson	.40
21	Adrian Beltre	.50
22	Lew Ford	.40
23	Shawn Green	.40
24	Juan Pierre	.40
25	Alfonso Soriano	.75
26	Mike Sweeney	.40
27	Chipper Jones	1.00
28	Javy Lopez	.40
29	Victor Martinez	.40
30	Kazuo Matsui	.40
31	Bernie Williams	.50
32	Kerry Wood	.50
33	Barry Zito	.50
34	Austin Kearns	.40
35	Todd Helton	.75
36	B.J. Upton	.40
37	Jeff Bagwell	.75
38	Pedro Martinez	1.00
39	Lyle Overbay	.40
40	Ichiro Suzuki	2.00
41	Jason Bay	.50
42	Bobby Crosby	.40
43	Vladimir Guerrero	1.00
44	Richie Sexson	.50
45	Johan Santana	1.00
46	Magglio Ordonez	.40
47	Derek Jeter	3.00
48	Eric Gagne	.40
49	Albert Pujols	3.00
50	Jim Thome	.75
51	Hideki Matsui	1.00
52	Torii Hunter	.40
53	Greg Maddux	2.00
54	Michael Young	.40
55	Carlos Beltran	.75
56	Carl Crawford	.40
57	Adam Dunn	.75
58	Nomar Garciaparra	1.00
59	Mike Piazza	1.00
60	Alex Rodriguez	3.00
61	Scott Rolen	.75
62	Ben Sheets	.50
63	Sammy Sosa	1.00
64	Hank Blalock	.50
65	Carlos Delgado	.50
66	Ken Griffey Jr.	2.00
67	Manny Ramirez	1.00
68	Miguel Tejada	.75
69	Roger Clemens	3.00
70	Gary Sheffield	.75
71	Jon Knott	1.50
72	Ryan Raburn	1.50
73	Zack Greinke	1.50
74	David Aardsma	1.50
75	Justin Verlander RC	4.00
76	Andres Blanco	1.50
77	David Wright	1.50
78	Jeff Baker	1.50
79	Charlton Jimerson	1.50
80	Sean Burnett	1.50
81	Joey Gathright	1.50
82	Victor Diaz	1.50
83	Scott Kazmir	1.50
84	Edwin Encarnacion	1.50
85	J.D. Durbin	1.50
86	Nick Swisher	1.50
87	Casey Kotchman	1.50
88	Gavin Floyd	1.50
89	Josh Kroeger	1.50
90	Taylor Buchholz	1.50
91	Reggie Jackson	2.00
92	Nolan Ryan	6.00
93	Eddie Murray	2.00
94	Carlton Fisk	2.00
95	Mike Schmidt	4.00
96	Joe Morgan	2.00
97	Rod Carew	2.00
98	Harmon Killebrew	3.00
99	Tom Seaver	3.00
100	Brooks Robinson	3.00

Gold

Gold (1-70): 3-6X
Gold (71-100): 1-2X
Production 99 Sets

Autoworks Silver

NM/M
Production 99 Sets

RB	Rocco Baldelli	12.00
JB	Jason Bay	20.00
JBO	Jeremy Bonderman	15.00
SB	Sean Burnett	8.00
MC	Miguel Cabrera	25.00
MCA	Mike Cameron	12.00
CC	Carl Crawford	15.00
JD	J.D. Durbin	8.00
LF	Lew Ford	10.00
ZG	Zack Greinke	10.00
TH	Travis Hafner	15.00
BL	Brad Lidge	15.00
VM	Victor Martinez	15.00
JM	Justin Morneau	20.00
JP	Josh Phelps	10.00
BS	Ben Sheets	15.00
BU	B.J. Upton	15.00
JV	Justin Verlander	20.00
DW	David Wright	20.00

Autoworks Gold

NM/M
Production 49 Sets

HA	Hank Aaron	200.00
RB	Rocco Baldelli	15.00
EB	Ernie Banks	50.00
JB	Jason Bay	20.00
LB	Lance Berkman	20.00
JBO	Jeremy Bonderman	20.00
SB	Sean Burnett	10.00
MC	Miguel Cabrera	30.00
MCA	Mike Cameron	12.00
CC	Carl Crawford	20.00
JD	J.D. Durbin	10.00
GF	Gavin Floyd	10.00
LF	Lew Ford	10.00
ZG	Zack Greinke	12.00
TH	Travis Hafner	20.00
BL	Brad Lidge	20.00
VM	Victor Martinez	20.00
JM	Justin Morneau	25.00
JP	Josh Phelps	10.00
BS	Ben Sheets	20.00
BU	B.J. Upton	20.00
DW	David Wright	60.00
MY	Michael Young	15.00

Autoworks Copper

NM/M
Production 75-250
Masterpiece: No Pricing
Production One Set

RB	Rocco Baldelli/100	12.00
JB	Jason Bay/150	20.00
JBO	Jeremy Bonderman/100	15.00
SB	Sean Burnett/100	8.00
MC	Miguel Cabrera/75	25.00
CC	Carl Crawford/175	15.00
JD	J.D. Durbin/100	8.00
ZG	Zack Greinke/200	10.00
TH	Travis Hafner/150	15.00
BL	Brad Lidge/75	15.00
VM	Victor Martinez/100	15.00
JM	Justin Morneau/175	20.00
BU	B.J. Upton/150	15.00
JV	Justin Verlander/100	20.00
DW	David Wright/250	50.00

Autoworks Dual

Production 25 Sets

Autoworks Quad

Production 10 Sets

By the Numbers

BY THE NUMBERS
ADRIAN BELTRE • SEATTLE MARINERS

NM/M
Common Player: 1.00
Inserted 1:18

1	Roy Oswalt	1.00
2	Hideki Matsui	3.00
3	Curt Schilling	1.50
4	Mike Piazza	2.00
5	Alex Rodriguez	4.00
6	Vladimir Guerrero	1.50
7	Victor Martinez	1.00
8	Adrian Beltre	1.00
9	Johnny Estrada	1.00
10	Ken Griffey Jr.	3.00
11	Sammy Sosa	2.00
12	Ichiro Suzuki	3.00
13	Roger Clemens	4.00
14	David Ortiz	1.50
15	Johan Santana	1.50
16	Pedro Martinez	1.50
17	Austin Kearns	1.50
18	Randy Johnson	1.50
19	Nomar Garciaparra	1.50
20	Albert Pujols	4.00

By the Numbers Jersey

NM/M
Common Player: 4.00

AB	Adrian Beltre	4.00
RC	Roger Clemens/SP	10.00
JE	Johnny Estrada	4.00
VG	Vladimir Guerrero/SP	8.00
RJ	Randy Johnson	8.00
PM	Pedro Martinez	8.00
HM	Hideki Matsui	20.00
RO	Roy Oswalt	4.00
AP	Albert Pujols	15.00
JS	Johan Santana	6.00
CS	Curt Schilling	8.00
SS	Sammy Sosa	8.00

By the Numbers Jersey Die-Cut

NM/M
Production 199 Sets
Jersey Tag: No Pricing
Production One Set

AB	Adrian Beltre	4.00
RC	Roger Clemens	10.00
JE	Johnny Estrada	4.00
VG	Vladimir Guerrero	8.00
RJ	Randy Johnson	8.00
AK	Austin Kearns	4.00
PM	Pedro Martinez	8.00
HM	Hideki Matsui	20.00
DO	David Ortiz	8.00
RO	Roy Oswalt	4.00
MP	Mike Piazza/116	10.00
AP	Albert Pujols	15.00
JS	Johan Santana	6.00
CS	Curt Schilling	8.00
SS	Sammy Sosa	8.00

By the Numbers Patch

NM/M
Production 99 Sets
Patch Die-Cut: No Pricing
Production 25 Sets

AB	Adrian Beltre	10.00
JE	Johnny Estrada	8.00
VG	Vladimir Guerrero	15.00
AK	Austin Kearns/78	10.00
HM	Hideki Matsui	30.00
DO	David Ortiz/46	15.00
RO	Roy Oswalt	10.00
MP	Mike Piazza	20.00
AP	Albert Pujols	30.00
JS	Johan Santana	15.00
CS	Curt Schilling	15.00
SS	Sammy Sosa	20.00

By the Numbers Patch Autographs

No Pricing
Production 25 Sets

Heart of the Team

HEART OF THE TEAM

NM/M
Inserted 1:108

1	Braves/Marlins	8.00
2	Red Sox/Yankees	15.00
3	Cardinals/Astros	10.00
4	Angels/A's	8.00
5	Phillies/Mets	8.00
6	Twins/White Sox	8.00
7	Reds/Cubs	10.00
8	Mariners/Rangers	10.00
9	Orioles/Nationals	8.00
10	Blue Jays/Devil Rays	6.00

Heart of the Team Jersey

Production 199 Sets
Patch: No Pricing
Production 15 Sets

Jersey

NM/M
Common Player: 4.00

JB	Josh Beckett	4.00
TH	Torii Hunter	4.00
MARK	Mark Prior	4.00
MR	Manny Ramirez	8.00
GS	Gary Sheffield	6.00
AS	Alfonso Soriano	4.00
SS	Shannon Stewart	4.00
BW	Bernie Williams	6.00
DW	Dontrelle Willis	4.00
KW	Kerry Wood	4.00
DWR	David Wright	15.00
MY	Michael Young	4.00

Dual Jersey

NM/M
Common Duo: 6.00
Die-Cut: 1-1.5X
Production 199 Sets
Dual MLB Logo: No Pricing
Production One Set
Dual Patch: No Pricing
Production 25 Sets
Dual Patch Die-Cut: No Pricing
Production 15 Sets

DWJB	Dontrelle Willis, Josh Beckett	6.00
DWMP	David Wright, Mike Piazza	15.00
GSBW	Gary Sheffield, Bernie Williams/SP	8.00
KWMP	Kerry Wood, Mark Prior/SP	8.00
MRDO	Manny Ramirez, David Ortiz	15.00
MYAS	Michael Young, Alfonso Soriano	8.00
SSTH	Shannon Stewart, Torii Hunter	6.00

Patch

NM/M
Production 99 Sets
Die-Cut: 1-1.5X
Production 49 Sets

JB	Josh Beckett	8.00
TH	Torii Hunter	10.00
DO	David Ortiz/51	20.00
MIKE	Mike Piazza	20.00
MARK	Mark Prior	15.00
MR	Manny Ramirez	20.00
AS	Alfonso Soriano/73	12.00
SS	Shannon Stewart	12.00
BW	Bernie Williams	12.00
DW	Dontrelle Willis	15.00
KW	Kerry Wood	12.00
DWR	David Wright	35.00
MY	Michael Young	10.00

Property of

NM/M
Common Player: 1.00
Inserted 1:6

1	Vladimir Guerrero	1.50
2	Luis Gonzalez	1.00
3	Chipper Jones	1.50
4	Miguel Tejada	1.50
5	David Ortiz	1.50
6	Kerry Wood	1.00
7	Frank Thomas	1.00
8	Adam Dunn	1.00
9	Victor Martinez	1.00
10	Todd Helton	1.00
11	Ivan Rodriguez	1.00
12	Miguel Cabrera	1.50
13	Jeff Bagwell	1.50

14	Mike Sweeney	1.00
15	Eric Gagne	1.00
16	Lyle Overbay	1.00
17	Johan Santana	1.50
18	Mike Piazza	2.00
19	Derek Jeter	5.00
20	Bobby Crosby	1.00
21	Jim Thome	1.50
22	Jason Bay	1.00
23	Khalil Greene	1.00
24	Jason Schmidt	1.00
25	Ichiro Suzuki	1.00
26	Albert Pujols	5.00
27	B.J. Upton	1.00
28	Hank Blalock	1.00
29	Vernon Wells	1.00
30	Jose Vidro	1.00

Property of Jersey
NM/M

JB	Jeff Bagwell	6.00
JBA	Jason Bay	4.00
HB	Hank Blalock	4.00
MC	Miguel Cabrera	8.00
EG	Eric Gagne	4.00
LG	Luis Gonzalez	4.00
VG	Vladimir Guerrero/SP	8.00
CJ	Chipper Jones	4.00
AP	Albert Pujols	15.00
IR	Ivan Rodriguez	6.00
JS	Johan Santana/SP	8.00
JSC	Jason Schmidt	4.00
MT	Miguel Tejada	6.00
FT	Frank Thomas	6.00
JT	Jim Thome	6.00
BU	B.J. Upton	4.00
VW	Vernon Wells	4.00
KW	Kerry Wood	4.00

Property of Jersey Die-Cut
NM/M

Production 199 Sets
MLB Logo: No Pricing
Production One Set

JB	Jeff Bagwell	6.00
JBA	Jason Bay	4.00
HB	Hank Blalock	4.00
MC	Miguel Cabrera	8.00
EG	Eric Gagne	4.00
LG	Luis Gonzalez	4.00
KG	Khalil Greene	4.00
VG	Vladimir Guerrero	8.00
CJ	Chipper Jones	4.00
DO	David Ortiz	8.00
LO	Lyle Overbay/86 UER	8.00
MP	Mike Piazza	8.00
AP	Albert Pujols	15.00
IR	Ivan Rodriguez	6.00
JS	Johan Santana	6.00
JSC	Jason Schmidt	6.00
MT	Miguel Tejada	6.00
FT	Frank Thomas	6.00
JT	Jim Thome	6.00
BU	B.J. Upton	4.00
VW	Vernon Wells	4.00
KW	Kerry Wood	4.00

Property of Patch

NM/M

Production 99 Sets
Die-Cut: No Pricing
Production 25 Sets
Nameplate: 1-2X
Production 49 Sets

JB	Jeff Bagwell	15.00
JBA	Jason Bay/84	10.00
HB	Hank Blalock	12.00
MC	Miguel Cabrera	15.00
AD	Adam Dunn/42	10.00
EG	Eric Gagne	10.00
LG	Luis Gonzalez	10.00
KG	Khalil Greene	10.00
VG	Vladimir Guerrero	15.00
CJ	Chipper Jones	15.00
DO	David Ortiz/45	20.00
MP	Mike Piazza	20.00
AP	Albert Pujols	30.00
IR	Ivan Rodriguez	15.00
JS	Johan Santana	15.00

ABBREVIATIONS
SP - Short Print

JSC	Jason Schmidt	12.00
MS	Mike Sweeney/77	10.00
MT	Miguel Tejada	15.00
JT	Jim Thome	15.00
BU	B.J. Upton	10.00
VW	Vernon Wells/30	10.00
KW	Kerry Wood/89	10.00

2005 Fleer Platinum
NM/M

Common Players (1-100): .25
Minor Players (1-100): .40
Unlisted Stars (1-100): .50
Common Players (101-125): 3.00
Production 1,000 Sets
Pack (5): 2.00
Box (24): 40.00

1	Nomar Garciaparra	1.50
2	Matt Holliday	.25
3	Rickie Weeks	.25
4	Jim Thome	.75
5	Roy Halladay	.40
6	Paul Konerko	.25
7	Lance Berkman	.40
8	Ichiro Suzuki	1.25
9	Kerry Wood	.60
10	Lew Ford	.25
11	Omar Vizquel	.40
12	Manny Ramirez	.60
13	Carlos Beltran	.50
14	Lyle Overbay	.25
15	Billy Wagner	.40
16	Jose Vidro	.25
17	Vladimir Guerrero	.75
18	Miguel Tejada	.50
19	Alex Rodriguez	1.50
20	Rocco Baldelli	.50
21	David Ortiz	.50
22	Victor Martinez	.25
23	Shawn Green	.40
24	Jason Bay	.25
25	Pedro Martinez	.75
26	Travis Hafner	.25
27	Eric Gagne	.40
28	Jack Wilson	.25
29	Ivan Rodriguez	.50
30	Jody Gerut	.25
31	Adrian Beltre	.40
32	Craig Wilson	.25
33	J.D. Drew	.40
34	Craig Biggio	.40
35	Mark Mulder	.40
36	Mark Teixeira	.50
37	Melvin Mora	.25
38	Ken Griffey Jr.	1.00
39	Mike Sweeney	.25
40	Khalil Greene	.60
41	Rafael Palmeiro	.60
42	Austin Kearns	.50
43	Garret Anderson	.40
44	Trevor Hoffman	.25
45	Andruw Jones	.60
46	Adam Dunn	.50
47	Angel Berroa	.25
48	Ryan Klesko	.40
49	Sean Casey	.25
50	Kazuo Matsui	.50
51	Jim Edmonds	.40
52	Magglio Ordonez	.40
53	Tom Glavine	.40
54	Larry Walker	.40
55	Johnny Estrada	.25
56	Brad Lidge	.25
57	Barry Zito	.50
58	Michael Young	.40
59	Chipper Jones	1.00
60	Andy Pettitte	.50
61	Eric Chavez	.40
62	Carlos Delgado	.60
63	David Eckstein	.25
64	Dmitri Young	.25
65	Mike Piazza	1.00
66	Albert Pujols	1.50
67	Luis Gonzalez	.40
68	Hideki Matsui	1.50
69	Gary Sheffield	.50
70	Carl Crawford	.25
71	Curt Schilling	.50
72	Todd Helton	.60
73	Ben Sheets	.40
74	Bobby Abreu	.40
75	Jose Guillen	.25
76	Richie Sexson	.50
77	Miguel Cabrera	.60
78	Bernie Williams	.50
79	Aubrey Huff	.25
80	John Smoltz	.40
81	Jeff Bagwell	.60
82	Tim Hudson	.40
83	Alfonso Soriano	.75
84	Freddy Garcia	.25
85	Johan Santana	.40
86	Bret Boone	.40
87	Troy Glaus	.50
88	Carlos Guillen	.25
89	Derek Jeter	2.00
90	Scott Rolen	.75
91	Sammy Sosa	1.25
92	Jacque Jones	.25
93	Jason Schmidt	.25
94	Randy Johnson	.75
95	Dontrelle Willis	.40
96	Mariano Rivera	.50
97	Hank Blalock	.50
98	Mark Prior	1.50
99	Torii Hunter	.50
100	Roger Clemens	1.50
101	David Wright	6.00
102	Justin Morneau	4.00
103	Scott Kazmir	4.00
104	Gavin Floyd	4.00
105	Justin Verlander RC	8.00
106	Zack Greinke	4.00
107	David Aardsma	3.00
108	Ryan Raburn	3.00
109	Joey Gathright	3.00
110	J.D. Durbin	3.00
111	Sean Burnett	3.00
112	Jose Lopez	5.00
113	Nick Swisher	4.00
114	Bobby Jenks	3.00
115	Kelly Johnson	8.00
116	B.J. Upton	5.00
117	Ronny Cedeno	3.00
118	Edwin Encarnacion	6.00
119	Jeff Baker	3.00
120	Taylor Buchholz	3.00
121	Livan Hernandez RC	4.00
122	Dioner Navarro	4.00
123	Victor Diaz	4.00
124	Jon Knott	4.00
125	Russ Adams	4.00

Finish
Cards 1-100: 3-6X
Cards 101-125: .75-1.25X
Production 199 Sets

Extreme
Cards 1-125: No Pricing
Production 20 Sets

Autograph Die-Cuts
NM/M

Numbered to indicated quantities.

2	Lew Ford/99	10.00
3	Jason Bay/50	15.00
4	Travis Hafner/99	15.00
6	Brad Lidge/99	30.00
7	Michael Young/99	15.00
8	David Eckstein/99	20.00
9	Carl Crawford/50	15.00
10	Miguel Cabrera/50	25.00
11	David Wright/50	50.00
13	Scott Kazmir/99	15.00
14	Gavin Floyd/99	10.00
15	Justin Verlander/99	40.00
18	Joey Gathright/50	10.00

Decade of Excellence
NM/M

Common Player: 2.00
Inserted 1:199

1	Albert Pujols	6.00
2	Derek Jeter	8.00
3	Randy Johnson	4.00
4	Ichiro Suzuki	5.00
5	Alex Rodriguez	6.00
6	Mike Piazza	4.00
7	Greg Maddux	4.00
8	Curt Schilling	3.00
9	Frank Thomas	3.00
10	Torii Hunter	3.00
11	Al Kaline	6.00
12	Travis Hafner	2.00
13	Ivan Rodriguez	3.00
14	Rafael Palmeiro	3.00
15	Mike Schmidt	8.00
16	Johnny Bench	8.00
17	Jim Edmonds	2.00
18	Pedro Martinez	4.00
19	Robin Yount	6.00
20	Sammy Sosa	5.00

Decade of Excellence Jersey Silver
NM/M

Common Player: 5.00
Inserted 1:54
Gold: .75-1.25X
Production 99 Sets
Patch Platinum: No Pricing
Production 10 Sets

JB	Johnny Bench	15.00
JE	Jim Edmonds	5.00
TF	Travis Hafner	5.00
TH	Torii Hunter	5.00
RJ	Randy Johnson	8.00
AK	Al Kaline	10.00
GM	Greg Maddux	8.00
PM	Pedro Martinez	8.00
RP	Rafael Palmeiro	8.00
MP	Mike Piazza	12.00
AP	Albert Pujols	12.00
IR	Ivan Rodriguez	5.00
CS	Curt Schilling	5.00
MS	Mike Schmidt	15.00
SS	Sammy Sosa	10.00
FT	Frank Thomas	8.00
RY	Robin Yount	10.00

Decade of Excellence Autograph Jersey Platinum
No Pricing
Production 5 Sets

Diamond Dominators
NM/M

Common Player: 2.00
Inserted 1:12 Retail

1	Albert Pujols	6.00
2	Curt Schilling	3.00
3	Adrian Beltre	2.00
4	Randy Johnson	4.00
5	Ivan Rodriguez	3.00
6	Mike Piazza	4.00
7	Chipper Jones	4.00
8	Sammy Sosa	5.00
9	Tim Hudson	2.00
10	Rocco Baldelli	3.00
11	Alfonso Soriano	4.00
12	David Ortiz	3.00
13	Mariano Rivera	2.00
14	Kazuo Matsui	3.00
15	Khalil Greene	3.00
16	Eric Gagne	2.00
17	Vladimir Guerrero	4.00
18	Jason Giambi	4.00
19	Scott Rolen	4.00
20	Miguel Cabrera	3.00

Diamond Dominators Jersey Silver
NM/M

Common Player:
Inserted 1:45
Gold: .75-1.25X
Production 199 Sets (Hobby)
Red: .5-1X
Inserted 1:50 (Retail)

RB	Rocco Baldelli	5.00
AB	Adrian Beltre	5.00
MC	Miguel Cabrera	8.00
EG	Eric Gagne	5.00
JG	Jason Giambi	8.00
KG	Khalil Greene	8.00
VG	Vladimir Guerrero	8.00
TH	Tim Hudson	5.00
RJ	Randy Johnson	8.00
CJ	Chipper Jones	4.00
KM	Kazuo Matsui	5.00
DO	David Ortiz	5.00
MP	Mike Piazza	8.00
AP	Albert Pujols	12.00
IR	Ivan Rodriguez	5.00
SR	Scott Rolen	8.00
CS	Curt Schilling	5.00
AS	Alfonso Soriano	8.00
SS	Sammy Sosa	10.00

Diamond Dominators Metal
NM/M

Common Player: 2.00
Inserted 1:18 Hobby

1	Albert Pujols	6.00
2	Curt Schilling	3.00
3	Adrian Beltre	2.00
4	Randy Johnson	4.00
5	Ivan Rodriguez	3.00
6	Mike Piazza	4.00
7	Chipper Jones	4.00
8	Sammy Sosa	5.00
9	Tim Hudson	3.00
10	Rocco Baldelli	3.00
11	Alfonso Soriano	4.00
12	David Ortiz	3.00
13	Kazuo Matsui	3.00
14	Khalil Greene	3.00
15	Eric Gagne	2.00
16	Vladimir Guerrero	4.00
17	Jason Giambi	4.00
18	Scott Rolen	4.00
19	Miguel Cabrera	3.00

Diamond Dominators Metal Autograph
No Pricing
Production 10 Sets

Diamond Dominators Metal Patch
NM/M

1-2X Diamond Dominators Jersey Silver
Sequentially #'d to 30.

HA	Hank Aaron	100.00

Lumberjacks
NM/M

Common Player: .75
Inserted 1:6
Bat Silver: 2-3X
Inserted 1:9
Bat Gold: 2-4X
Production 250 Sets
Bat Patch: No Pricing
Production 20 Sets

1	Albert Pujols	2.50
2	Jim Thome	1.25
3	Andruw Jones	1.00
4	Kazuo Matsui	.75
5	Adam Dunn	.75
6	Bernie Williams	.75
7	Hank Blalock	.75
8	Bobby Abreu	.75
9	Rocco Baldelli	.75
10	Jacque Jones	.75
11	Mark Teixeira	.75
12	Ichiro Suzuki	2.00
13	Gary Sheffield	.75
14	Sean Casey	.75
15	Carl Crawford	.75

Lumberjacks Autograph Platinum
No Pricing
Production 20 Sets

Nameplates Patch Platinum
No Pricing
Production 25 Sets
Masterpiece: No Pricing
Production One Set

2005 Fleer Platinum Nameplates Dual Patch Platinum

No Pricing
Production 25 Sets
Masterpiece: No Pricing
Production One Set

Nameplates Patch Autograph Platinum
No Pricing
Production 25 Sets

2005 Fleer Platinum Nameplates Dual Patch Autograph Platinum
No Pricing
Production One Set

2005 Fleer Showcase

NM/M

Common Player (1-100): .25
Minor Stars (1-100): .40
Unlisted Stars (1-100): .60
Common Showcasing Talent (101-110): 2.00
Inserted 1:5
Common Showcasing History (111-135): .40
Inserted 1:20
Pack (5): 3.00
Box (20): 50.00

1	Albert Pujols	2.50
2	Rocco Baldelli	.60
3	Bernie Williams	.60
4	Shawn Green	.40
5	Garret Anderson	.40
6	Paul Konerko	.25
7	Mike Sweeney	.25
8	Jim Thome	1.00
9	Mark Teixeira	.40
10	Mark Prior	.60
11	Angel Berroa	.25
12	Barry Zito	.40
13	Carlos Delgado	.75
14	Troy Glaus	.40
15	Travis Hafner	.25
16	Lyle Overbay	.25
17	David Ortiz	.60
18	Ivan Rodriguez	.60
19	Jack Wilson	.40
20	Jason Schmidt	.40
21	Mike Piazza	1.50
22	David Eckstein	.25
23	Ben Sheets	.40
24	Randy Johnson	1.00
25	Jacque Jones	.25
26	Jody Gerut	.25
27	Kris Benson	.25
28	Luis Gonzalez	.40
29	Victor Martinez	.25
30	Torii Hunter	.60
31	Gary Sheffield	.60
32	Miguel Tejada	.60
33	Dontrelle Willis	.60
34	Bret Boone	.40
35	Hideki Matsui	.60
36	Shea Hillenbrand	.25
37	Wily Mo Pena	.25
38	Johan Santana	.40
39	Derek Jeter	3.00
40	Chipper Jones	1.50
41	Sean Casey	.25
42	Corey Koskie	.25
43	Alex Rodriguez	2.50
44	Andruw Jones	.75
45	Austin Kearns	.60
46	Jose Vidro	.25
47	Adam Dunn	.60
48	Adrian Beltre	.40
49	Bobby Abreu	.40
50	Michael Young	.25
51	Freddy Garcia	.25
52	Eric Gagne	.40
53	Chase Utley	.25
54	Alfonso Soriano	1.00
55	Nick Johnson	.25
56	Johnny Estrada	.25
57	Jeff Bagwell	.75
58	Randy Winn	.25
59	Roy Halladay	.40
60	J.D. Drew	.40
61	Craig Biggio	.40
62	Scott Rolen	1.00
63	Nomar Garciaparra	2.50
64	Matt Holliday	.25
65	Billy Wagner	.25
66	Carl Crawford	.25
67	Pedro J. Martinez	1.00
68	Jeremy Bonderman	.25
69	Jason Bay	.25
70	A.J. Pierzynski	.25
71	Vladimir Guerrero	1.00
72	Rickie Weeks	.60
73	Mark Loretta	.25
74	Todd Helton	.75
75	Manny Ramirez	.75
76	Carlos Guillen	.25
77	Khalil Greene	.75
78	Javy Lopez	.40
79	Josh Beckett	.75
80	Ichiro Suzuki	2.00
81	Magglio Ordonez	.40
82	Ken Harvey	.25
83	Mark Mulder	.40
84	Hank Blalock	.60
85	Richard Hidalgo	.25
86	Curt Schilling	.60
87	Jeromy Burnitz	.25
88	Craig Wilson	.25
89	Aubrey Huff	.25
90	Kerry Wood	.75
91	Andy Pettitte	.60
92	Tim Hudson	.40
93	Jim Edmonds	.40
94	Melvin Mora	.25
95	Miguel Cabrera	.75
96	Trevor Hoffman	.25
97	J.T. Snow	.25
98	Sammy Sosa	2.00
99	Roger Clemens	2.50
100	Eric Chavez	4.00
101	B.J. Upton	5.00
102	Gavin Floyd	3.00
103	Casey Kotchman	3.00
104	David Wright	3.00
105	Dioner Navarro	3.00
106	Scott Kazmir	3.00
107	Andres Blanco	2.00
108	Joey Gathright	2.00
109	Jon Knott	2.00
110	Charlton Jimerson	3.00
111	Larry Doby	.75
112	Reggie Jackson	2.00
113	Enos Slaughter	.60
114	Bill "Moose" Skowron	.60
115	Duke Snider	.75
116	Harmon Killebrew	1.00
117	Willie McCovey	.75
118	Rollie Fingers	.75
119	Preacher Roe	.40
120	Carlton Fisk	.60
121	Andre Dawson	.60
122	Orlando Cepeda	.60
123	Bucky Dent	.40
124	Cal Ripken Jr.	1.50
125	Nolan Ryan	3.00
126	Tony Perez	.60
127	Mike Schmidt	1.50
128	Johnny Bench	1.50
129	Sparky Anderson	.40
130	Ted Williams	2.50
131	Al Kaline	1.00
132	Carl Yastrzemski	1.00
133	Eddie Murray	.60
134	Roberto Clemente	1.50
135	Yogi Berra	1.50

Masterpiece Legacy

Cards (1-135): No Pricing
Production One Set

Masterpiece Showpiece Patch

Cards (1-135): No Pricing
Production One Set
Autograph Patch: No Pricing
Production One Set
Patch Showdown: No Pricing
Production One Set
Patch Showtime: No Pricing
Production One Set

Autographed Legacy

		NM/M
Common Player:		15.00

Sequentially Numbered
8 Jim Thome/34 60.00
10 Mark Prior/43 30.00
12 Barry Zito/45 35.00
18 Ivan Rodriguez/217 40.00
19 Jack Wilson/298 15.00
20 Jason Schmidt/127 15.00
21 Mike Piazza/26 100.00
22 David Eckstein/40 35.00
23 Ben Sheets/427 15.00
40 Chipper Jones/41 50.00
45 Austin Kearns/460 10.00
47 Adam Dunn/52 35.00
48 Adrian Beltre/180 15.00
50 Michael Young/80 15.00
52 Eric Gagne/310 25.00
53 Chase Utley/446 25.00
65 Roy Halladay/99 15.00
68 Jeremy Bonderman/97 20.00
72 Rickie Weeks/453 15.00
75 Manny Ramirez/31 75.00
77 Khalil Greene/299 25.00
88 Craig Wilson/40 20.00
89 Aubrey Huff/453 15.00
90 Kerry Wood/28 25.00
92 Tim Hudson/183 25.00
95 Miguel Cabrera/32 35.00
99 Roger Clemens/64 100.00
100 Eric Chavez/204 15.00
103 Casey Kotchman/454 15.00
104 David Wright/298 40.00
106 Scott Kazmir/458 20.00
107 Andres Blanco/23 15.00
109 Jon Knott/402 10.00
114 Bill "Moose" Skowron/64 20.00
119 Preacher Roe/304 20.00
120 Carlton Fisk/86 30.00
123 Bucky Dent/99 15.00
135 Yogi Berra/25 75.00

Showdown

Cards (1-135): No Pricing
Production 15 Sets
Masterpiece: No Pricing
Production One Set

Showtime

Veterans (1-100): 3-6X
Showcasing Talent (101-110): 2-4X
Showcasing History (111-135): 1-3X
Production 99 Sets
Masterpiece: No Pricing
Production One Set

Measures of Greatness

	NM/M
Common Player:	.75

Inserted 1:5
Jersey Red: 2-4X

Production 340 Sets
Patch: No Pricing
Production 10 Sets
Masterpiece: No Pricing
Production One Set
1 Albert Pujols 4.00
2 Mike Piazza 2.50
3 Vladimir Guerrero 2.00
4 Jim Thome 2.00
5 Pedro J. Martinez 2.00
6 Rafael Palmeiro .75
7 Adrian Beltre .75
8 Sammy Sosa 3.00
9 Todd Helton 1.50
10 Randy Johnson 2.00
11 Jeff Bagwell 1.50
12 Jason Giambi 2.00
13 Scott Rolen 2.00
14 Greg Maddux 2.50
15 Alfonso Soriano 2.00
16 Mariano Rivera .75
17 Curt Schilling 1.00
18 Derek Jeter 5.00
19 Chipper Jones 2.50
20 Roger Clemens 4.00

Swing Time

	NM/M
Common Player:	2.50

Inserted 1:45
Jersey Red: 1-3X
Production 610 Sets
Patch: 2-5X
Production 50 Sets
Masterpiece: No Pricing
Production One Set
1 Ivan Rodriguez 2.50
2 Gary Sheffield 2.50
3 Bernie Williams 2.50
4 Vladimir Guerrero 3.50
5 Jim Edmonds 2.50
6 Manny Ramirez 3.00
7 Todd Helton 2.50
8 Hank Blalock 2.50
9 Hideki Matsui 6.00
10 David Ortiz 2.50
11 Albert Pujols 6.00
12 Miguel Tejada 2.50
13 Miguel Cabrera 3.00
14 Alex Rodriguez 6.00
15 Ichiro Suzuki 5.00

Timepiece Extreme

No Pricing
Production One Set

Timepiece Ink

No Pricing
Production 10 Sets

Timepiece Teammates

No Pricing
Production One Set

Timepiece Unique

No Pricing
Production 5 Sets

Wave of the Future

	NM/M
Common Player:	1.00

Inserted 1:15
Jersey Red: 1-3X
Production 610 Sets
Patch: 2-5X
Production 50 Sets
Masterpiece: No Pricing
Production One Set
1 Kazuo Matsui 5.00
2 Johan Santana 1.50
3 Khalil Greene 2.00
4 Dontrelle Willis 1.50
5 Mark Teixeira 1.50
6 Travis Hafner 1.50
7 Jason Bay 1.50
8 Angel Berroa 1.50
9 Miguel Cabrera 2.00
10 Joe Mauer 1.50
11 Adam Dunn 2.00
12 B.J. Upton 3.00
13 Victor Martinez 1.00
14 Michael Young 1.00
15 David Wright 3.00

2005 Fleer Tradition

	NM/M
Common Player (1-300):	.15
Minor Stars (1-300):	.25
Unlisted Stars (1-300):	.40
Common Card (301-330):	3.00
Unlisted Card (301-330):	4.00

Inserted 1:2
Common Player (331-350): .15
Minor Stars (331-350): .25
Unlisted Stars (331-350): .40
Cards 1-12; 331-350 Inserted 1:2
Pack (10): 1.25
Box (36): 35.00

1 Johan Santana, Curt Schilling, Jake Westbrook .40
2 Ben Sheets, Jake Peavy, Randy Johnson .75
3 Johan Santana, Bartolo Colon, Curt Schilling .40
4 Carl Pavano, Roy Oswalt, Roger Clemens 1.50
5 Johan Santana, Pedro Martinez, Curt Schilling .75
6 Jason Schmidt, Randy Johnson, Ben Sheets .75
7 Melvin Mora, Vladimir Guerrero, Ichiro Suzuki 1.25
8 Adrian Beltre, Todd Helton, Mark Loretta .50
9 Manny Ramirez, Paul Konerko, David Ortiz .50
10 Albert Pujols, Adrian Beltre, Adam Dunn 1.50
11 David Ortiz, Manny Ramirez, Miguel Tejada .50
12 Albert Pujols, Vinny Castilla, Scott Rolen 1.50
13 Jason Bay .75
14 Greg Maddux 1.00
15 Melvin Mora .15
16 Matt Stairs .15
17 Scott Podsednik .25
18 Bartolo Colon .15
19 Roger Clemens 1.50
20 Eric Hinske .15
21 Johnny Estrada .15
22 Brett Tomko .15
23 John Buck .15
24 Nomar Garciaparra 1.50
25 Milton Bradley .15
26 Craig Biggio .25
27 Kyle Denney .50
28 Brad Penny .15
29 Todd Helton .50
30 Luis Gonzalez .25
31 Bill Hall .15
32 Ruben Sierra .15
33 Zack Greinke .15
34 Sandy Alomar Jr. .15
35 Jason Giambi .75
36 Ben Sheets .25
37 Edgardo Alfonzo .15
38 Kenny Rogers .15
39 Coco Crisp .15
40 Randy Choate .50
41 Braden Looper .15
42 Adam Dunn .40
43 Adam Eaton .15
44 Luis Castillo .25
45 Casey Fossum .15
46 Mike Piazza 1.00
47 Juan Pierre .15
48 Doug Davis .15
49 Manny Ramirez .50
50 Travis Hafner .15
51 Jack Wilson .15
52 Mike Maroth .15
53 Ken Harvey .15
54 Brooks Kieschnick .15
55 Brad Fullmer .15
56 Octavio Dotel .15
57 Mike Matheny .15
58 Andruw Jones .50
59 Alfonso Soriano .75
60 Royce Clayton .15
61 Jon Garland .15
62 John Mabry .15
63 Rafael Palmeiro .25
64 Garrett Atkins .15
65 Brian Meadows .15
66 Tony Armas Jr. .15
67 Toby Hall .15
68 Carlos Baerga .15
69 Barry Larkin .25
70 Jody Gerut .15
71 Brent Mayne .15
72 Shigetoshi Hasegawa .15
73 Jose Cruz Jr. .15
74 Dan Wilson .15
75 Sidney Ponson .15
76 Jason Jennings .15
77 A.J. Burnett .15
78 Tony Batista .15
79 Kris Benson .15
80 Sean Burroughs .15
81 Eric Young .15
82 Casey Kotchman .40
83 Derrek Lee .25
84 Mariano Rivera .25
85 Julio Franco .15
86 Corey Patterson .15
87 Carlos Beltran .40
88 Trevor Hoffman .15
89 Danny Garcia .15
90 Marco Scutaro .15
91 Marquis Grissom .15
92 Aubrey Huff .15
93 Tony Womack .15
94 Placido Polanco .15
95 Bengie Molina .15
96 Roger Cedeno .15
97 Geoff Jenkins .25
98 Kip Wells .15
99 Derek Jeter 2.00
100 Omar Infante .15
101 Phil Nevin .15
102 Edgar Renteria .15
103 B.J. Surhoff .15
104 David DeJesus .15
105 Raul Ibanez .15
106 Hank Blalock .40
107 Shawn Estes .15
108 Wily Mo Pena .15
109 Shawn Green .25
110 David Wright .50
111 Kenny Lofton .15
112 Matt Clement .15
113 Cesar Izturis .15
114 John Lackey .15
115 Torii Hunter .40
116 Charles Johnson .15
117 Ray Durham .15
118 Luke Hudson .15
119 Jeremy Bonderman .15
120 Sean Casey .15
121 Johnny Damon .25
122 Eric Milton .15
123 Shea Hillenbrand .15
124 Jim Edmonds .25
125 Jim Edmonds .15
126 Javier Vazquez .15
127 Jon Adkins .15
128 Mike Lowell .15
129 Khalil Greene .50
130 Quinton McCracken .15
131 Edgar Martinez .25
132 Matt Lawton .15
133 Jeff Weaver .15
134 Marlon Byrd .15
135 John Smoltz .25
136 Grady Sizemore .25
137 Brian Roberts .15
138 Dee Brown .15
139 Joel Pineiro .15
140 David Dellucci .15
141 Bobby Higginson .15
142 Ryan Madson .15
143 Scott Hatteberg .15
144 Gregg Zaun .15
145 Brian Jordan .15
146 Jason Isringhausen .15
147 Vinnie Chulk .15
148 Al Leiter .15
149 Pedro Martinez .50
150 Carlos Guillen .15
151 Randy Wolf .15
152 Vernon Wells .25
153 Barry Zito .40
154 Pedro Feliz .15
155 Omar Vizquel .15
156 Chone Figgins .15
157 David Ortiz .40
158 Sun-Woo Kim RC 1.00
159 Adam Kennedy .15
160 Carlos Lee .15
161 Rick Ankiel .15
162 Roy Oswalt .25
163 Armando Benitez .15
164 Erubiel Durazo .15
165 Adam Hyzdu .15
166 Esteban Yan .15
167 Victor Santos .15
168 Kevin Millwood .15
169 Andy Pettitte .60
170 Mike Cameron .15
171 Scott Rolen .75
172 Trot Nixon .15
173 Eric Munson .15
174 Roy Halladay .25
175 Juan Encarnacion .15
176 Eric Chavez .25
177 Termel Sledge .15
178 Jason Schmidt .25
179 Endy Chavez .15
180 Carlos Zambrano .15
181 Carlos Delgado .50
182 Dewon Brazelton .15
183 J.D. Drew .25
184 Orlando Cabrera .15
185 Craig Wilson .15
186 Chin-Hui Tsao .15
187 Jolbert Cabrera .15
188 Rod Barajas .15
189 Craig Monroe .15
190 Dave Berg .15
191 Carlos Silva .15
192 Eric Gagne .25
193 Marcus Giles .15
194 Nick Johnson .15
195 Kelvim Escobar .15
196 Wade Miller .15
197 David Bell .15
198 Rondell White .15
199 Brian Giles .25
200 Jeromy Burnitz .15
201 Carl Pavano .15
202 Alex Rios .15
203 Ryan Freel .15
204 R.A. Dickey .15
205 Miguel Cairo .15
206 Kerry Wood .50
207 C.C. Sabathia .15
208 Jaime Cerda .15
209 Jerome Williams .15
210 Ryan Wagner .15
211 Javy Lopez .25
212 Tike Redman .15
213 Richie Sexson .40
214 Shannon Stewart .15
215 Ben Davis .15
216 Jeff Bagwell .50
217 David Wells .15
218 Justin Leone .15
219 Brad Radke .15
220 Ramon Santiago .15
221 Richard Hidalgo .15
222 Aaron Miles .15
223 Mark Loretta .15
224 Aaron Boone .15
225 Steve Trachsel .15
226 Geoff Blum .15
227 Shingo Takatsu .15
228 Kevin Youkilis .15
229 Laynce Nix .15
230 Daniel Cabrera .15
231 Kyle Lohse .15
232 Todd Pratt .15
233 Reed Johnson .15
234 Lance Berkman .25
235 Hideki Matsui 1.50
236 Randy Winn .15
237 Joe Randa .15
238 Bob Howry .15
239 Jason LaRue .15
240 Jose Valentin .15
241 Livan Hernandez .15
242 Jamie Moyer .15
243 Garret Anderson .25
244 Brad Ausmus .15
245 Russell Branyan .15
246 Paul Wilson .15
247 Tim Wakefield .15
248 Roberto Alomar .40
249 Kazuhisa Ishii .15
250 Tino Martinez .15
251 Tomokazu Ohka .15
252 Mark Redman .15
253 Paul Byrd .15
254 Greg Aquino .15
255 Adrian Beltre .25
256 Ricky Ledee .15
257 Josh Fogg .15
258 Derek Lowe .15
259 Lew Ford .15
260 Bobby Crosby .15
261 Jim Thome .75
262 Jaret Wright .15
263 Chin-Feng Chen .15
264 Troy Glaus .40
265 Jorge Sosa .15
266 Mike Lamb .15
267 Russ Ortiz .15
268 Reggie Sanders .15
269 Orlando Hudson .15
270 Rodrigo Lopez .15
271 Jose Vidro .15
272 Akinori Otsuka .15
273 Victor Martinez .15
274 Carl Crawford .15
275 Roberto Novoa .25
276 Brian Lawrence .15
277 Angel Berroa .15
278 Josh Beckett .50
279 Lyle Overbay .15
280 Dustin Hermanson .15
281 Jeff Conine .15
282 Mark Prior 1.00
283 Kevin Brown .25
284 Magglio Ordonez .25
285 Dontrelle Willis .25
286 Dallas McPherson .25
287 Rafael Furcal .25
288 Ty Wigginton .15
289 Moises Alou .25
290 A.J. Pierzynski .15
291 Todd Walker .15
292 Hideo Nomo .15
293 Larry Walker .25
294 Choo Freeman .15
295 Eduardo Perez .15
296 Miguel Tejada .40
297 Corey Koskie .15
298 Jermaine Dye .15
299 John Riedling .15
300 John Olerud .25
301 Tim Bittner, Jake Woods, Bobby Jenks 5.00
302 Josh Kroeger, Casey Daigle, Brandon Medders 5.00
303 Kelly Johnson, Charles Thomas, Dan Meyer 4.00
304 Eddy Rodriguez, Ryan Hannaman, John Maine 6.00
305 Anastacio Martinez, Jerome Gamble, Lenny Dinardo 8.00
306 Ronny Cedeno, Carlos Vasquez, Renyel Pinto 6.00
307 Arnie Munoz, Ryan Wing, Felix Diaz 6.00
308 William Bergolla, Ray Olmedo RC, Edwin Encarnacion 4.00
309 Mariano Gomez, Ivan Ochoa, Kazuhito Tadano 3.00
310 Toby Miller RC, Jeff Baker, Matt Holliday 6.00
311 Preston Larrison, Curtis Granderson, Ryan Raburn 8.00
312 Josh Wilson, Logan Kensing, Kevin Cave 5.00
313 Hector Gimenez, Willy Taveras, Taylor Buchholz 3.00
314 Ruben Gotay, Brian Bass, Andres Blanco 4.00
315 Joel Hanrahan, Willy Aybar, Yhency Brazoban 3.00
316 David Krynzel, Ben Hendrickson, Corey Hart 3.00
317 Colby Miller, Jason Kubel, J.D. Durban 5.00
318 Maicer Izturis, Chad Cordero, Brandon Watson 3.00
319 Victor Diaz, Aarom Baldiris, Wayne Lydon 8.00
320 Edwardo Sierra, Dioner Navarro, Sean Henn 3.00
321 Nick Swisher, Joe Blanton, Dan Johnson 6.00
322 Ryan Howard, Gavin Floyd, Keith Bucktrot 6.00
323 Ryan Doumit, Sean Burnett, Bobby Bradley 6.00
324 Justin Germano, Rusty Tucker, Freddy Guzman 6.00
325 David Aardsma, Justin Knoedler, Alfredo Simon 4.00
326 Jose Lopez, Rene Rivera, Cha Seung Baek 4.00
327 Yadier Molina, Evan Rust, Adam Wainwright 6.00
328 Jorge Cantu, Scott Kazmir, B.J. Upton 5.00
329 Adrian Gonzalez, Ramon Nivar, Jason Bourgeois 6.00
330 Russ Adams, Dustin McGowan, Gustavo Chacin 8.00
331 Alfonso Soriano .75
332 Albert Pujols 1.50
333 David Ortiz .40
334 Manny Ramirez .50
335 Jason Bay .15
336 Bobby Crosby .15
337 Roger Clemens 1.50
338 Johan Santana .25
339 Jim Thome .75
340 Vladimir Guerrero .75
341 David Ortiz .40
342 Alex Rodriguez 1.50
343 Albert Pujols 1.50
344 Carlos Beltran .40

345	Johnny Damon	.25
346	Scott Rolen	.75
347	Larry Walker	.25
348	Curt Schilling	.40
349	Pedro Martinez	.75
350	David Ortiz	.40

Gray Backs
Cards 13-300: .75-1.5X
Cards 1-10; 301-350: .5-1.25X
Inserted 1:2

Club 3,000/500/300
NM/M
Inserted 1:360

1	Ernie Banks/500	30.00
2	Stan Musial/3000	40.00
3	Steve Carlton/3000	15.00
4	Greg Maddux/300	25.00
5	Dave Winfield/3000	15.00
6	Rafael Palmeiro/500	15.00
7	Rickey Henderson/ 3000	15.00
8	Roger Clemens/3000	30.00
9	Don Sutton/300	10.00
10	George Brett/3000	25.00
11	Reggie Jackson/500	20.00
12	Wade Boggs/3000	20.00
13	Bob Gibson/3000	20.00
14	Eddie Murray/3000	20.00
15	Tom Seaver/3000	20.00
16	Willie McCovey/500	20.00
17	Rod Carew/3000	20.00
18	Fergie Jenkins/300	15.00
19	Phil Niekro/300	10.00
20	Frank Robinson/500	20.00

Cooperstown Tribute
NM/M
Common Player: 4.00
Sequentially #'d to HOF Induction Year.
Gold: .5-1X
Inserted 1:24
Jersey: 1-2X
Inserted 1:200
There are 20 total jersey cards for Joe.
Morgan & Yogi Berra.
No Pricing for Morgan & Berra jers. card.
Patch: No Pricing
Production 10 Sets

1	Mike Schmidt/1995	5.00
2	Al Kaline/1980	4.00
3	Yogi Berra/1972	6.00
4	Robin Yount/1999	4.00
5	Joe Morgan/1990	4.00
6	Willie Stargell/1988	4.00
7	Harmon Killebrew/ 1984	5.00
8	Nolan Ryan/1999	10.00
9	Carlton Fisk/2000	5.00
10	Johnny Bench/1989	6.00

Diamond Tributes

NM/M
Common Player: 2.00
Inserted 1:6

1	Albert Pujols	5.00
2	Alex Rodriguez	5.00
3	Ken Griffey Jr.	3.50
4	Sammy Sosa	4.00
5	Chipper Jones	3.50
6	Johan Santana	2.00
7	Roger Clemens	5.00
8	Pedro Martinez	3.00
9	Jim Thome	3.00
10	Greg Maddux	3.50
11	Alfonso Soriano	2.00
12	Derek Jeter	6.00
13	Randy Johnson	3.00
14	Miguel Cabrera	2.00
15	Adrian Beltre	2.00
16	Ivan Rodriguez	2.00
17	Manny Ramirez	2.00
18	Mark Teixeira	2.00
19	Adam Dunn	2.00
20	Scott Rolen	2.00
21	Mike Piazza	3.50
22	J.D. Drew	2.00
23	Hideki Matsui	4.00
24	Nomar Garciaparra	5.00
25	Kazuo Matsui	3.00

Diamond Tribute Jersey

NM/M
Common Player: 6.00
Inserted 1:30
Patch: 1-3X
Production 50 Sets

AB	Adrian Beltre/Bat	6.00
RC	Roger Clemens/Jsy	12.00
JD	J.D. Drew/Bat	6.00
NG	Nomar Garciaparra/ Bat	12.00
RJ	Randy Johnson/Jsy	8.00
CJ	Chipper Jones/Bat	8.00
GM	Greg Maddux/Jsy	10.00
PM	Pedro Martinez/Jsy	8.00
HM	Hideki Matsui/Bat	15.00
KM	Kazuo Matsui/Bat	8.00
MP	Mike Piazza/Bat	10.00
AP	Albert Pujols/Bat	15.00
MR	Manny Ramirez/Bat	8.00
JS	Johan Santana/Jsy	8.00
AS	Alfonso Soriano/Bat	8.00
SS	Sammy Sosa/Bat	10.00
MT	Mark Teixeira/Bat	8.00
JT	Jim Thome/Bat	8.00

Diamond Tributes Dual Patch
NM/M
Common Player: 75.00
Production 50 Sets

APSR	Albert Pujols, Scott Rolen	100.00
ASMT	Alfonso Soriano, Mark Teixeira	75.00
CJJD	Chipper Jones, J.D. Drew	80.00
HMKM	Hideki Matsui, Kazuo Matsui	125.00
JTAB	Jim Thome, Adrian Beltre	75.00
MPIR	Mike Piazza, Ivan Rodriguez	75.00
PMMR	Pedro Martinez, Manny Ramirez	120.00
RCJS	Roger Clemens, Johan Santana	100.00
RJGM	Randy Johnson, Greg Maddux	75.00
SSMC	Miguel Cabrera, Sammy Sosa	80.00

Standouts
NM/M
Common Player: 3.50
Inserted 1:18

1	Albert Pujols	6.00
2	Ichiro Suzuki	5.00
3	Derek Jeter	8.00
4	Randy Johnson	3.50
5	Greg Maddux	4.00
6	Hideki Matsui	6.00
7	Mike Piazza	4.00
8	Vladimir Guerrero	3.50
9	Sammy Sosa	5.00
10	Jim Thome	3.50
11	Chipper Jones	4.00
12	Alex Rodriguez	6.00
13	Roger Clemens	6.00
14	Nomar Garciaparra	6.00
15	Lance Berkman	3.50

Standouts Jersey

NM/M
Common Player: 10.00

Diamond Tribute Jersey (continued)
Inserted 1:18
Patch: 1-3X
Production 50 Sets

LB	Lance Berkman	6.00
RC	Roger Clemens	18.00
VG	Vladimir Guerrero	10.00
RJ	Randy Johnson	10.00
CJ	Chipper Jones	12.00
GM	Greg Maddux	12.00
HM	Hideki Matsui	20.00
MP	Mike Piazza	12.00
AP	Albert Pujols	18.00
SS	Sammy Sosa	15.00
JT	Jim Thome	15.00

2006 Fleer

NM/M
Complete Set (400): 40.00
Complete Factory Set (430): 50.00
#'s 401-430 available in Factory Set
Common Player: .15
Pack (10): 1.75
Box (36): 55.00

1	Adam Kennedy	.15
2	Bartolo Colon	.25
3	Bengie Molina	.15
4	Chone Figgins	.15
5	Dallas McPherson	.15
6	Darin Erstad	.15
7	Francisco Rodriguez	.15
8	Garret Anderson	.25
9	Jarrod Washburn	.15
10	John Lackey	.15
11	Orlando Cabrera	.15
12	Ryan Theriot (RC)	.50
13	Steve Finley	.15
14	Vladimir Guerrero	.75
15	Adam Everett	.15
16	Andy Pettitte	.40
17	Charlton Jimerson	.15
18	Brad Lidge	.15
19	Chris Burke	.15
20	Craig Biggio	.25
21	Jason Lane	.15
22	Jeff Bagwell	.40
23	Lance Berkman	.50
24	Morgan Ensberg	.25
25	Roger Clemens	2.00
26	Roy Oswalt	.25
27	Willy Taveras	.15
28	Barry Zito	.25
29	Bobby Crosby	.15
30	Bobby Kielty	.15
31	Dan Johnson	.15
32	Danny Haren	.15
33	Eric Chavez	.25
34	Huston Street	.15
35	Jason Kendall	.15
36	Jay Payton	.15
37	Joe Blanton	.15
38	Mark Kotsay	.15
39	Nick Swisher	.15
40	Rich Harden	.25
41	Ron Flores RC	.15
42	Alex Rios	.15
43	John-Ford Griffin (RC)	.15
44	David Bush	.15
45	Eric Hinske	.15
46	Frank Catalanotto	.15
47	Gustavo Chacin	.15
48	Josh Towers	.15
49	Miguel Batista	.15
50	Orlando Hudson	.15
51	Roy Halladay	.25
52	Shea Hillenbrand	.15
53	Shaun Marcum (RC)	.15
54	Vernon Wells	.25
55	Adam LaRoche	.15
56	Andruw Jones	.50
57	Chipper Jones	.75
58	Anthony Lerew (RC)	.15
59	Jeff Francoeur	.25
60	John Smoltz	.40
61	Johnny Estrada	.15
62	Julio Franco	.15
63	Joey Devine RC	1.00
64	Marcus Giles	.15
65	Mike Hampton	.15
66	Rafael Furcal	.25
67	Chuck James (RC)	.15
68	Tim Hudson	.25
69	Ben Sheets	.25
70	Bill Hall	.15
71	Brady Clark	.15
72	Carlos Lee	.25
73	Chris Capuano	.15
74	Nelson Cruz (RC)	.15
75	Derrick Turnbow	.15
76	Doug Davis	.15
77	Geoff Jenkins	.15
78	J.J. Hardy	.15
79	Lyle Overbay	.15
80	Prince Fielder (RC)	.50
81	Rickie Weeks	.25
82	Albert Pujols	2.00
83	Chris Carpenter	.25
84	David Eckstein	.15
85	Jason Isringhausen	.15
86	Tyler Johnson (RC)	.15
87	Adam Wainwright (RC)	.15
88	Jim Edmonds	.25
89	Chris Duncan	.15
90	Mark Grudzielanek	.15
91	Mark Mulder	.25
92	Matt Morris	.15
93	Reggie Sanders	.15
94	Scott Rolen	.50
95	Yadier Molina	.15
96	Aramis Ramirez	.40
97	Carlos Zambrano	.25
98	Corey Patterson	.15
99	Derrek Lee	.50
100	Glendon Rusch	.15
101	Greg Maddux	1.00
102	Jeromy Burnitz	.15
103	Kerry Wood	.25
104	Mark Prior	.50
105	Michael Barrett	.15
106	Geovany Soto (RC)	.15
107	Nomar Garciaparra	.50
108	Ryan Dempster	.15
109	Todd Walker	.15
110	Alex Gonzalez	.15
111	Aubrey Huff	.15
112	Victor Diaz	.15
113	Carl Crawford	.25
114	Danys Baez	.15
115	Joey Gathright	.15
116	Jonny Gomes	.25
117	Jorge Cantu	.15
118	Julio Lugo	.15
119	Rocco Baldelli	.15
120	Scott Kazmir	.15
121	Toby Hall	.15
122	Tim Corcoran RC	.40
123	Alex Cintron	.15
124	Brandon Webb	.25
125	Chad Tracy	.15
126	Dustin Nippert (RC)	.15
127	Claudio Vargas	.15
128	Craig Counsell	.15
129	Javier Vazquez	.25
130	Jose Valverde	.15
131	Luis Gonzalez	.25
132	Royce Clayton	.15
133	Russ Ortiz	.15
134	Shawn Green	.15
135	Tony Clark	.15
136	Troy Glaus	.25
137	Brad Penny	.15
138	Cesar Izturis	.15
139	Derek Lowe	.15
140	Eric Gagne	.25
141	Hee Seop Choi	.15
142	J.D. Drew	.25
143	Jason Phillips	.15
144	Jayson Werth	.15
145	Jeff Kent	.25
146	Jeff Weaver	.15
147	Milton Bradley	.15
148	Odalis Perez	.15
149	Hong-Chih Kuo	.15
150	Brian Myrow RC	.25
151	Armando Benitez	.15
152	Edgardo Alfonzo	.15
153	J.T. Snow	.15
154	Jason Schmidt	.25
155	Lance Niekro	.15
156	Doug Clark	.15
157	Daniel Ortmeier (RC)	.15
158	Moises Alou	.25
159	Noah Lowry	.15
160	Omar Vizquel	.25
161	Pedro Feliz	.15
162	Randy Winn	.15
163	Jeremy Accardo RC	.15
164	Aaron Boone	.15
165	Ryan Garko (RC)	.25
166	C.C. Sabathia	.25
167	Casey Blake	.15
168	Cliff Lee	.15
169	Coco Crisp	.25
170	Grady Sizemore	.40
171	Jake Westbrook	.15
172	Jhonny Peralta	.15
173	Kevin Millwood	.15
174	Scott Elarton	.15
175	Travis Hafner	.50
176	Victor Martinez	.25
177	Adrian Beltre	.15
178	Eddie Guardado	.15
179	Felix Hernandez	.40
180	Gil Meche	.15
181	Ichiro Suzuki	1.50
182	Jamie Moyer	.15
183	Jeremy Reed	.15
184	Jaime Bubela (RC)	.15
185	Raul Ibanez	.15
186	Richie Sexson	.40
187	Ryan Franklin	.15
188	Jeff Harris RC	.15
189	A.J. Burnett	.15
190	Josh Wilson (RC)	.15
191	Josh Johnson (RC)	.15
192	Carlos Delgado	.25
193	Dontrelle Willis	.25
194	Bernie Castro	.15
195	Josh Beckett	.25
196	Juan Encarnacion	.15
197	Juan Pierre	.15
198	Robert Andino RC	.25
199	Miguel Cabrera	.75
200	Ryan Jorgensen RC	.25
201	Paul LoDuca	.15
202	Todd Jones	.15
203	Braden Looper	.15
204	Carlos Beltran	.50
205	Cliff Floyd	.15
206	David Wright	1.00
207	Doug Mientkiewicz	.15
208	Jae Weong Seo	.15
209	Jose Reyes	.50
210	Anderson Hernandez (RC)	.15
211	Miguel Cairo	.15
212	Mike Cameron	.15
213	Mike Piazza	.50
214	Pedro Martinez	.75
215	Tom Glavine	.25
216	Tim Hamulack	.15
217	Brad Wilkerson	.15
218	Darrell Rasner (RC)	.15
219	Chad Cordero	.15
220	Cristian Guzman	.15
221	Jason Bergmann RC	.50
222	John Patterson	.15
223	Jose Guillen	.15
224	Jose Vidro	.15
225	Livan Hernandez	.15
226	Nick Johnson	.15
227	Preston Wilson	.15
228	Ryan Zimmerman (RC)	.25
229	Vinny Castilla	.15
230	B.J. Ryan	.15
231	B.J. Surhoff	.15
232	Brian Roberts	.25
233	Walter Young	.15
234	Daniel Cabrera	.15
235	Erik Bedard	.15
236	Javy Lopez	.15
237	Jay Gibbons	.15
238	Luis Matos	.15
239	Melvin Mora	.25
240	Miguel Tejada	.50
241	Rafael Palmeiro	.25
242	Alejandro Freire RC	.25
243	Sammy Sosa	.75
244	Adam Eaton	.15
245	Brian Giles	.25
246	Brian Lawrence	.15
247	Dave Roberts	.15
248	Jake Peavy	.25
249	Khalil Greene	.15
250	Mark Loretta	.15
251	Ramon Hernandez	.15
252	Ryan Klesko	.15
253	Trevor Hoffman	.15
254	Woody Williams	.15
255	Craig Breslow RC	.25
256	Billy Wagner	.25
257	Bobby Abreu	.25
258	Brett Myers	.15
259	Chase Utley	.40
260	David Bell	.15
261	Jim Thome	.50
262	Jimmy Rollins	.40
263	Jon Lieber	.15
264	Danny Sandoval RC	.25
265	Mike Lieberthal	.15
266	Pat Burrell	.25
267	Randy Wolf	.15
268	Ryan Howard	1.00
269	J.J. Furmaniak (RC)	.15
270	Ronny Paulino (RC)	.15
271	Craig Wilson	.15
272	Bryan Bullington	.15
273	Jack Wilson	.15
274	Jason Bay	.25
275	Matt Capps (RC)	.15
276	Oliver Perez	.15
277	Robert Mackowiak	.15
278	Tom Gorzelanny (RC)	.15
279	Zachary Duke	.15
280	Alfonso Soriano	.50
281	Chris Young	.15
282	David Dellucci	.15
283	Francisco Cordero	.15
284	Jason Botts (RC)	.15
285	Hank Blalock	.25
286	Josh Rupe	.15
287	Kevin Mench	.15
288	Laynce Nix	.15
289	Mark Teixeira	.50
290	Michael Young	.25
291	Richard Hidalgo	.15
292	Scott Feldman RC	.25
293	Bill Mueller	.15
294	Hanley Ramirez (RC)	.25
295	Curt Schilling	.75
296	David Ortiz	.75
297	Alejandro Machado (RC)	.15
298	Edgar Renteria	.25
299	Jason Varitek	.40
300	Johnny Damon	.75
301	Keith Foulke	.15
302	Manny Ramirez	.75
303	Matt Clement	.15
304	Craig Hansen RC	2.00
305	Tim Wakefield	.15
306	Trot Nixon	.15
307	Aaron Harang	.15
308	Adam Dunn	.50
309	Austin Kearns	.25
310	Brandon Claussen	.15
311	Chris Booker	.15
312	Edwin Encarnacion	.15
313	Chris Denorfia (RC)	.15
314	Felipe Lopez	.15
315	Miguel Perez (RC)	.15
316	Ken Griffey Jr.	1.50
317	Ryan Freel	.15
318	Sean Casey	.15
319	Wily Mo Pena	.15
320	Mike Esposito	.15
321	Aaron Miles	.15
322	Brad Hawpe	.15
323	Brian Fuentes	.15
324	Clint Barmes	.15
325	Cory Sullivan	.15
326	Garrett Atkins	.15
327	J.D. Closser	.15
328	Jeff Francis	.15
329	Luis Gonzalez	.15
330	Matt Holliday	.15
331	Todd Helton	.50
332	Angel Berroa	.15
333	David DeJesus	.15
334	Emil Brown	.15
335	Jeremy Affeldt	.15
336	Chris Demaria RC	.50
337	Mark Teahen	.15
338	Matt Stairs	.15
339	Steve Stemle RC	.25
340	Mike Sweeney	.15
341	Runelvys Hernandez	.15
342	Jonah Bayliss RC	.25
343	Zack Greinke	.15
344	Brandon Inge	.15
345	Carlos Guillen	.25
346	Carlos Pena	.15
347	Chris Shelton	.25
348	Craig Monroe	.15
349	Dmitri Young	.15
350	Ivan Rodriguez	.40
351	Jeremy Bonderman	.15
352	Magglio Ordonez	.25
353	Mark Woodyard (RC)	.15
354	Omar Infante	.15
355	Placido Polanco	.15
356	Rondell White	.15
357	Brad Radke	.15
358	Carlos Silva	.15
359	Jacque Jones	.15
360	Joe Mauer	.25
361	Chris Heintz RC	.25
362	Joe Nathan	.15
363	Johan Santana	.50
364	Justin Morneau	.25
365	Francisco Liriano (RC)	.50
366	Travis Bowyer	.15
367	Michael Cuddyer	.15
368	Scott Baker	.15
369	Shannon Stewart	.15
370	Torii Hunter	.25
371	A.J. Pierzynski	.15
372	Aaron Rowand	.15
373	Carl Everett	.15
374	Dustin Hermanson	.15
375	Frank Thomas	.40
376	Freddy Garcia	.15
377	Jermaine Dye	.15
378	Joe Crede	.15
379	Jon Garland	.15
380	Jose Contreras	.15
381	Juan Uribe	.15
382	Mark Buehrle	.25
383	Orlando Hernandez	.25
384	Paul Konerko	.25
385	Scott Podsednik	.15
386	Tadahito Iguchi	.25
387	Alex Rodriguez	2.00
388	Bernie Williams	.25
389	Chien-Ming Wang	.40
390	Derek Jeter	2.00
391	Gary Sheffield	.40
392	Hideki Matsui	1.00
393	Jason Giambi	.40
394	Jorge Posada	.25
395	Michael Vento	.15
396	Mariano Rivera	.25
397	Mike Mussina	.25
398	Randy Johnson	.75
399	Robinson Cano	.25
400	Tino Martinez	.25
401	Alay Soler RC	.40
402	Boof Bonser (RC)	.40
403	Cole Hamels (RC)	1.50
404	Ian Kinsler (RC)	.40
405	Jason Kubel (RC)	.40
406	Joel Zumaya (RC)	1.00
407	Jonathan Papelbon (RC)	2.50
408	Jered Weaver (RC)	2.50
409	Kendry Morales (RC)	1.00
410	Lastings Milledge (RC)	1.00
411	Matthew Kemp (RC)	1.00
412	Taylor Buchholz (RC)	.40
413	Andre Ethier (RC)	2.50
414	Dan Uggla (RC)	1.00
415	Jeremy Sowers (RC)	.40
416	Chad Billingsley (RC)	.40
417	Josh Barfield (RC)	.40
418	Matt Cain (RC)	.40
419	Fausto Carmona (RC)	.40
420	Josh Willingham (RC)	.40
421	Jeremy Hermida (RC)	.75
422	Conor Jackson (RC)	.75
423	Dave Gassner (RC)	.40
424	Brian Bannister (RC)	.40
425	Fernando Nieve (RC)	.40

426	Justin Verlander (RC)	2.50
427	Scott Olsen (RC)	.40
428	Takashi Saito RC	.50
429	Willie Eyre (RC)	.40
430	Travis Ishikawa (RC)	.40

Glossy

Glossy:	2-3X
Inserted 1:12	

Glossy Gold

Glossy Gold:	4-8X
Inserted 1:144	

Autographics

Inserted 1:432

		NM/M
AN	Garret Anderson	15.00
GA	Garrett Atkins	10.00
JB	Joe Blanton	15.00
EC	Eric Chavez	20.00
KG	Ken Griffey Jr.	85.00
TI	Tadahito Iguchi	50.00
CS	Chris Shelton	30.00
NS	Nick Swisher	20.00
KY	Kevin Youkilis	15.00

Award Winners

		NM/M
Complete Set (6):		5.00
Common Player:		.50
1	Albert Pujols	3.00
2	Alex Rodriguez	3.00
3	Chris Carpenter	.50
4	Bartolo Colon	.50
5	Ryan Howard	1.00
6	Huston Street	.50

Fabrics

		NM/M
Inserted 1:36		
BA	Bobby Abreu	6.00
CB	Carlos Beltran	8.00
MC	Miguel Cabrera	8.00
EC	Eric Chavez	4.00
RC	Roger Clemens	15.00
JD	Johnny Damon	8.00
JE	Jim Edmonds	6.00
EG	Eric Gagne	4.00
LG	Luis Gonzalez	4.00
GR	Khalil Greene	4.00
KG	Ken Griffey Jr.	15.00
VG	Vladimir Guerrero	8.00
RH	Roy Halladay	4.00
TH	Todd Helton	6.00
DJ	Derek Jeter	20.00
RJ	Randy Johnson	8.00
AJ	Andruw Jones	6.00
CJ	Chipper Jones	8.00
DL	Derek Lee	8.00
GM	Greg Maddux	15.00
PM	Pedro Martinez	8.00
JM	Joe Mauer	4.00
DO	David Ortiz	8.00
JP	Jake Peavy	6.00
MP	Mark Prior	6.00
AP	Albert Pujols	20.00
AR	Aramis Ramirez	6.00
MR	Manny Ramirez	8.00
IR	Ivan Rodriguez	6.00
SR	Scott Rolen	6.00
JS	Johan Santana	8.00
CS	Curt Schilling	8.00
GS	Gary Sheffield/SP	10.00
SM	John Smoltz	6.00
AS	Alfonso Soriano	6.00
MT	Mark Teixeira	6.00
TE	Miguel Tejada	6.00
JT	Jim Thome	6.00

ABBREVIATIONS

SP - Short Print

RW	Rickie Weeks	4.00
DW	Dontrelle Willis/SP	8.00
WR	David Wright	12.00
MY	Michael Young	4.00

Lumber Company

MARK TEIXEIRA - 1B

		NM/M
1	Adam Dunn	1.00
2	Albert Pujols	3.00
3	Alex Rodriguez	3.00
4	Alfonso Soriano	.75
5	Andruw Jones	.75
6	Aramis Ramirez	.75
7	Bobby Abreu	.75
8	Carlos Delgado	.75
9	Carlos Lee	.50
10	David Ortiz	1.00
11	David Wright	1.00
12	Derrek Lee	1.00
13	Eric Chavez	.50
14	Gary Sheffield	.75
15	Jeff Kent	.50
16	Ken Griffey Jr.	2.00
17	Manny Ramirez	1.00
18	Mark Teixeira	1.00
19	Miguel Cabrera	1.00
20	Miguel Tejada	.75
21	Paul Konerko	.75
22	Richie Sexson	.50
23	Todd Helton	.75
24	Troy Glaus	.50
25	Vladimir Guerrero	1.00

Smoke 'n Heat

SMOKE 'n HEAT

		NM/M
1	Carlos Zambrano	.50
2	Chris Carpenter	.50
3	Curt Schilling	1.00
4	Dontrelle Willis	1.00
5	Felix Hernandez	1.00
6	Jake Peavy	.75
7	Johan Santana	1.00
8	John Smoltz	.75
9	Mark Prior	.75
10	Pedro Martinez	1.00
11	Randy Johnson	1.00
12	Roger Clemens	3.00
13	Roy Halladay	.50
14	Roy Oswalt	.50
15	Scott Kazmir	.50

Smooth Leather

ICHIRO MARINERS-OF

		NM/M
Complete Set (14):		10.00
Common Player:		.50
1	Alex Rodriguez	3.00
2	Andruw Jones	1.00

3	Derek Jeter	3.00
4	Derrek Lee	1.00
5	Eric Chavez	.50
6	Greg Maddux	2.00
7	Ichiro Suzuki	2.00
8	Ivan Rodriguez	.75
9	Jim Edmonds	.75
10	Mike Mussina	.75
11	Omar Vizquel	.50
12	Scott Rolen	1.00
13	Todd Helton	.75
14	Torii Hunter	.50

Stars of Tomorrow

		NM/M
Complete Set (10):		5.00
Common Player:		.50
Inserted 1:10		
1	David Wright	1.50
2	Ryan Howard	1.00
3	Felix Hernandez	1.00
4	Jeff Francoeur	.50
5	Joe Mauer	.75
6	Mark Prior	.75
7	Mark Teixeira	1.00
8	Miguel Cabrera	1.00
9	Prince Fielder (RC)	1.00
10	Rickie Weeks	.50

Team Fleer

		NM/M
Inserted 1:Case		
1	Albert Pujols	40.00
2	Alex Rodriguez	30.00
3	Alfonso Soriano	10.00
4	Andruw Jones	10.00
5	Bobby Abreu	10.00
6	David Ortiz	15.00
7	David Wright	25.00
8	Eric Gagne	8.00
9	Ichiro Suzuki	30.00
10	Jason Varitek	8.00
11	Jeff Kent	8.00
12	Johan Santana	10.00
13	Jose Reyes	10.00
14	Manny Ramirez	15.00
15	Mariano Rivera	10.00
16	Miguel Cabrera	15.00
17	Miguel Tejada	8.00
18	Mike Piazza	15.00
19	Roger Clemens	30.00
20	Torii Hunter	8.00

Team Leaders

		NM/M
Complete Set (30):		15.00
Common Player:		.50
1	Troy Glaus, Brandon Webb	.50
2	John Smoltz, Andruw Jones	.50
3	Miguel Tejada, Erik Bedard	.50
4	David Ortiz, Curt Schilling	.75
5	Derrek Lee, Mark Prior	.75
6	Mark Buehrle, Paul Konerko	.50
7	Ken Griffey Jr., Aaron Harang	1.50
8	Cliff Lee, Travis Hafner	.50
9	Todd Helton, Jeff Francis	.50
10	Jeremy Bonderman, Ivan Rodriguez	.50
11	Miguel Cabrera, Dontrelle Willis	.75
12	Lance Berkman, Roger Clemens	2.00
13	Mike Sweeney, Zack Greinke	.50
14	Derek Lowe, Jeff Kent	.90
15	Carlos Lee, Ben Sheets	.50
16	Johan Santana, Torii Hunter	.50
17	Pedro Martinez, David Wright	1.00
18	Derek Jeter, Randy Johnson	2.00
19	Barry Zito, Eric Chavez	.50
20	Bobby Abreu, Brett Myers	.50
21	Jason Bay, Zachary Duke	.50
22	Jake Peavy, Brian Giles	.50

23	Moises Alou, Jason Schmidt	.50
24	Felix Hernandez, Ichiro Suzuki	1.00
25	Chris Carpenter, Albert Pujols	2.00
26	Scott Kazmir, Carl Crawford	.50
27	Mark Teixeira, Kenny Rogers	.50
28	Vernon Wells, Roy Halladay	.50
29	Livan Hernandez, Jose Guillen	.50
30	Bartolo Colon, Vladimir Guerrero	.50

2006 Fleer Greats of the Game

Kirby Puckett
MINNESOTA TWINS

		NM/M
Complete Set (100):		35.00
Common Player:		.40
Pack (5):		8.00
Box (15):		100.00
1	Al Kaline	1.50
2	Alan Trammell	.50
3	Andre Dawson	.75
4	Barry Larkin	.75
5	Bill Buckner	.40
6	Bill Freehan	.40
7	Bill Madlock	.40
8	Bill Mazeroski	.40
9	Billy Williams	.50
10	Bo Jackson	1.00
11	Bob Feller	1.00
12	Bob Gibson	.50
13	Bobby Doerr	.50
14	Bobby Murcer	.50
15	Boog Powell	.40
16	Brooks Robinson	1.50
17	Bruce Sutter	.40
18	Bucky Dent	.40
19	Cal Ripken Jr.	4.00
20	Rico Petrocelli	.40
21	Carlton Fisk	.75
22	Chris Chambliss	.40
23	Dave Concepcion	.40
24	Dave Parker	.40
25	Dave Winfield	1.00
26	David Cone	.50
27	Denny McLain	.50
28	Don Mattingly	3.00
29	Don Newcombe	.50
30	Don Sutton	.50
31	Dusty Baker	.50
32	Dwight Evans	.50
33	Eric Davis	.50
34	Ernie Banks	2.00
35	Fergie Jenkins	.75
36	Frank Robinson	1.00
37	Fred Lynn	.40
38	Fred McGriff	.50
39	Andre Thornton	.40
40	Garry Maddox	.40
41	Gary Matthews	.40
42	Gaylord Perry	.40
43	George Foster	.40
44	George Kell	.40
45	Graig Nettles	.40
46	Greg Luzinski	.40
47	Harmon Killebrew	1.50
48	Jack Clark	.50
49	Jack Morris	.50
50	Jim Palmer	.75
51	Jim Rice	.75
52	Joe Morgan	.75
53	John Kruk	.50
54	Johnny Bench	2.00
55	Jose Canseco	.75
56	Kirby Puckett	2.00
57	Kirk Gibson	.50
58	Lee Mazzilli	.40
59	Lou Brock	.75
60	Lou Piniella	.50
61	Luis Aparicio	.50
62	Luis Tiant	.50
63	Mark Fidrych	.50
64	Mark Grace	.75
65	Maury Wills	.50
66	Mike Schmidt	2.00
67	Nolan Ryan	3.00
68	Ozzie Smith	1.00
69	Paul Molitor	1.00
70	Paul O'Neill	.50
71	Phil Niekro	.50
72	Ralph Kiner	.75
73	Randy Hundley	.40

74	Red Schoendienst	.50
75	Reggie Jackson	1.00
76	Robin Yount	1.00
77	Rod Carew	.75
78	Rollie Fingers	.50
79	Ron Cey	.50
80	Ron Guidry	.50
81	Ron Santo	.75
82	Rusty Staub	.40
83	Ryne Sandberg	2.00
84	Sparky Lyle	.40
85	Stan Musial	2.00
86	Steve Carlton	.75
87	Steve Garvey	.50
88	Steve Sax	.40
89	Tommy Herr	.40
90	Tim McCarver	.50
91	Tim Raines	.50
92	Tom Seaver	1.00
93	Tony Gwynn	1.00
94	Tony Perez	.75
95	Wade Boggs	.75
96	Whitey Ford	1.00
97	Will Clark	.75
98	Willie Horton	.40
99	Willie McCovey	1.00
100	Yogi Berra	1.50

Copper

Copper:	2-4X
Production 299 Sets	

Pewter

Pewter:	2X
Inserted 1:15	

AUTOGRAPHics

Inserted 1:180
Cards are not serial numbered.

		NM/M
LA	Luis Aparicio/25	20.00
LB	Lou Brock/25	25.00
RC	Rod Carew/25	30.00
SC	Steve Carlton/50	25.00
WC	Will Clark/25	40.00
AD	Andre Dawson	25.00
BF	Bob Feller/50	30.00
GF	George Foster/50	20.00
SG	Steve Garvey/50	25.00
BG	Bob Gibson/25	40.00
KG	Kirk Gibson/25	25.00
MG	Mark Grace/50	30.00
RG	Ron Guidry/99	50.00
BJ	Bo Jackson/25	75.00
FJ	Fergie Jenkins/25	30.00
AK	Al Kaline/99	35.00
HK	Harmon Killebrew/25	50.00
BL	Barry Larkin/50	40.00
BI	Bill Mazeroski/25	35.00
FM	Fred McGriff/99	30.00
PM	Paul Molitor/50	25.00
JM	Joe Morgan/25	35.00
BM	Bobby Murcer/99	30.00
DN	Don Newcombe/99	15.00
PN	Phil Niekro/50	20.00
JP	Jim Palmer/99	20.00
DP	Dave Parker/99	20.00
TP	Tony Perez/99	30.00
JR	Jim Rice/99	20.00
BR	Brooks Robinson/50	40.00
RS	Ron Santo/99	20.00
OS	Ozzie Smith/25	60.00
BS	Bruce Sutter/50	15.00
SU	Don Sutton/50	20.00
BW	Billy Williams/99	25.00
MW	Maury Wills/99	20.00

Bat Barrel Autograph

No Pricing
Production 1-5

Cardinals Greats

		NM/M
Complete Set (10):		8.00
LB	Lou Brock	1.00
SC	Steve Carlton	.50
DD	Dizzy Dean	1.00
BG	Bob Gibson	1.00
TH	Tommy Herr	.25
RH	Rogers Hornsby	1.00
TM	Tim McCarver	.50
SM	Stan Musial	2.00
RS	Red Schoendienst	.50
OS	Ozzie Smith	1.00

Cubs Greats

		NM/M
Complete Set (10):		8.00
EB	Ernie Banks	2.00
AD	Andre Dawson	1.00
MG	Mark Grace	1.00
RH	Randy Hundley	.50
FJ	Fergie Jenkins	.50

GM Gary Mathews 1984-1987
CUBS GREATS

GM	Gary Mathews	.50
SA	Ryne Sandberg	2.00
RS	Ron Santo	1.00
BS	Bruce Sutter	.50
BW	Billy Williams	.50

Decade Greats

'90s
DECADE GREATS

		NM/M
Complete Set (30):		20.00
EA	Earl Averill	.50
RO	Rod Carew	1.00
SC	Steve Carlton	.75
CC	Chris Chambliss	.50
JC	Jack Clark	.50
WC	Will Clark	1.00
RC	Roberto Clemente	3.00
MC	Mickey Cochrane	1.00
BF	Bob Feller	1.00
TG	Tony Gwynn	1.00
BJ	Bo Jackson	1.00
JK	John Kruk	.50
BI	Bill Madlock	.50
EM	Eddie Mathews	1.00
BM	Bill Mazeroski	1.00
WM	Willie McCovey	1.00
JM	Johnny Mize	1.00
PM	Paul Molitor	1.00
MO	Mel Ott	1.00
DP	Dave Parker	.50
KP	Kirby Puckett	1.00
TR	Tim Raines	.50
CR	Cal Ripken Jr.	3.00
BR	Brooks Robinson	1.00
NR	Nolan Ryan	2.00
TS	Tom Seaver	1.00
MS	Mike Schmidt	1.00
WS	Willie Stargell	1.00
PT	Paul Traynor	1.00
RY	Robin Yount	1.00

Dodgers Greats

Dodgers GREATS 1940-1958

		NM/M
Complete Set (10):		6.00
DB	Dusty Baker	.50
CA	Roy Campanella	1.00
RC	Ron Cey	.50
DD	Don Drysdale	1.00
SG	Steve Garvey	.50
PR	Pee Wee Reese	.50
JR	Jackie Robinson	2.00
SS	Steve Sax	.50
DS	Don Sutton	.50
MW	Maury Wills	.50

Nickname Greats

NICKNAME GREATS
"Pudge"

		NM/M
LA	Luis Aparicio	.50
SB	Steve Balboni	.50
DB	Don Baylor	.50
BE	Steve Bedrosian	.50
JB	Jim Bouton	.50
TB	Tom Brunansky	.50
RB	Rick Burleson	.50
RC	Ron Cey	.50
CH	Joe Charboneau	.50
JC	Jack Clark	.50
WC	Will Clark	1.00
DD	Darren Daulton	.50
DE	Dwight Evans	.50
BF	Bob Feller	1.00
SF	Sid Fernandez	.50
MF	Mark Fidrych	.50
CF	Carlton Fisk	.75
DF	Dan Ford	.50

GF	George Foster	.50
AG	Andres Galarraga	.50
RG	Ron Guidry	.50
MH	Mike Hargrove	.50
KH	Ken Harrelson	.50
TH	Tom Henke	.50
HE	Tommy Herr	.50
BH	Burt Hooton	.50
AH	Al Hrabosky	.50
GH	Glenn Hubbard	.50
HJ	Howard Johnson	.50
JJ	Jay Johnstone	.50
ML	Mike LaValliere	.50
BL	Bill Lee	.50
SL	Sparky Lyle	.50
GM	Garry Maddox	.50
BM	Bill Madlock	.50
MZ	Dennis Martinez	.50
MA	Gary Matthews	.50
DM	Don Mattingly	2.00
LM	Lee Mazzilli	.50
WM	Willie McCovey	1.00
SM	Sam McDowell	.50
JM	John Montefusco	.50
DP	Dave Parker	.50
JP	Joe Pepitone	.50
LP	Lou Piniella	.50
RA	Doug Rader	.50
TR	Tim Raines	.50
RR	Rick Reuschel	.50
DR	Dave Righetti	.50
MR	Mickey Rivers	.50
FR	Frank Robinson	1.00
GS	George Scott	.50
JS	John Shelby	.50
FS	Fred Stanley	.50
RS	Rusty Staub	.50
AT	Andre Thornton	.50
ST	Steve Trout	.50
EV	Ellis Valentine	.50
MW	Mitch Williams	.50
JW	Jimmy Wynn	.50

Red Sox Greats

		NM/M
	Complete Set (10):	8.00
WB	Wade Boggs	1.00
BD	Bobby Doerr	.50
DE	Dwight Evans	.50
CF	Carlton Fisk	1.00
JF	Jimmie Foxx	2.00
FL	Fred Lynn	.50
RP	Rico Petrocelli	.50
JR	Jim Rice	.75
LT	Luis Tiant	.50
TW	Ted Williams	2.00

Reds Greats

		NM/M
	Complete Set (10):	8.00
JB	Johnny Bench	1.50
DC	Dave Concepcion	.50
ED	Eric Davis	.50
GF	George Foster	.50
KG	Ken Griffey Sr.	.50
BL	Barry Larkin	1.00
JM	Joe Morgan	1.00
TP	Tony Perez	1.00
FR	Frank Robinson	1.00
TS	Tom Seaver	1.00

Tigers Greats

		NM/M
	Complete Set (10):	6.00
TC	Ty Cobb	2.00
MF	Mark Fidrych	.50
BF	Bill Freehan	.50
KG	Kirk Gibson	1.00
WH	Willie Horton	.50
AK	Al Kaline	1.00
GK	George Kell	1.00
DM	Denny McLain	1.00
JM	Jack Morris	.50
AT	Alan Trammell	.50

Yankee Clippings

Autographs

		NM/M
	Common Autograph:	10.00
1	Al Kaline	25.00
2	Alan Trammell	15.00
3	Andre Dawson	20.00
4	Barry Larkin	35.00
5	Bill Buckner	12.00
6	Bill Freehan	12.00
7	Bill Madlock	15.00
8	Bill Mazeroski	35.00
9	Billy Williams	20.00
10	Bo Jackson	60.00
11	Bob Feller	25.00
12	Bob Gibson	40.00
13	Bobby Doerr	20.00
14	Bobby Murcer	20.00
15	Boog Powell	15.00
16	Brooks Robinson	25.00
17	Bruce Sutter	15.00
18	Bucky Dent	15.00
19	Cal Ripken Jr./SP	140.00
20	Rico Petrocelli	15.00
21	Carlton Fisk	30.00
22	Chris Chambliss	15.00
23	Dave Concepcion	15.00
24	Dave Parker	20.00
25	Dave Winfield	30.00
26	Dave Cone	15.00
27	Denny McLain	20.00
28	Don Mattingly	50.00
29	Don Newcombe	20.00
30	Don Sutton	15.00
31	Dusty Baker	25.00
32	Dwight Evans	20.00
33	Eric Davis	20.00
34	Ernie Banks	50.00
35	Fergie Jenkins	20.00
36	Frank Robinson	30.00
37	Fred Lynn	15.00
38	Fred McGriff	30.00
39	Andre Thornton	15.00
40	Garry Maddox	20.00
41	Gary Matthews	10.00
42	Gaylord Perry	15.00
43	George Foster	15.00
44	George Kell	15.00
45	Graig Nettles	20.00
46	Greg Luzinski	15.00
47	Harmon Killebrew	30.00
48	Jack Clark/SP	20.00
49	Jack Morris	15.00
50	Jim Palmer	20.00
51	Jim Rice	20.00
52	Joe Morgan	25.00
53	John Kruk	20.00
54	Johnny Bench	60.00
55	Kirby Puckett	100.00
56	Kirk Gibson	25.00
57	Lee Mazzilli	15.00
58	Lou Brock	30.00
59	Lou Piniella	15.00
60	Luis Aparicio	15.00
61	Luis Tiant	15.00
62	Mark Fidrych	25.00
63	Mark Grace	25.00
64	Maury Wills	20.00
65	Mike Schmidt	50.00
66	Nolan Ryan/SP	100.00
67	Ozzie Smith	40.00
68	Paul Molitor	25.00
69	Paul O'Neill	25.00
70	Phil Niekro	20.00
71	Ralph Kiner	20.00
72	Randy Hundley	8.00
73	Red Schoendienst	25.00
74	Reggie Jackson	35.00
75	Robin Yount	50.00
76	Rod Carew	25.00
77	Rollie Fingers	20.00
78	Ron Cey	10.00
79	Ron Guidry/SP	15.00
80	Ron Santo	25.00
81	Ryne Sandberg/SP	50.00
82	Sparky Lyle	15.00
83	Stan Musial	65.00
84	Steve Carlton	25.00
85	Steve Garvey	25.00
86	Steve Sax	10.00
87	Tommy Herr	15.00
88	Tim McCarver	20.00
89	Tim Raines/SP	20.00
90	Tom Seaver	50.00
91	Tony Gwynn	40.00
92	Tony Perez	25.00
93	Wade Boggs	25.00
94	Whitey Ford	50.00
95	Will Clark/SP	35.00

Abbreviations
SP - Short Print

		NM/M
	Complete Set (10):	12.00
YB	Yogi Berra	1.50
JD	Joe DiMaggio	2.00
WF	Whitey Ford	1.00
RG	Ron Guidry	.50
RJ	Reggie Jackson	1.00
DM	Don Mattingly	2.00
TM	Thurman Munson	1.50
BM	Bobby Murcer	.50
GN	Graig Nettles	.50
BR	Babe Ruth	3.00

Cardinals Greats Memorabilia Autograph

		NM/M
	Production 30 Sets	
LB	Lou Brock	50.00
SC	Steve Carlton	35.00
BG	Bob Gibson	60.00
TH	Tommy Herr	20.00
TM	Tim McCarver	30.00
SM	Stan Musial	75.00
RS	Red Schoendienst	25.00
OS	Ozzie Smith	50.00

Cardinals Greats Autograph

		NM/M
	Production 30 Sets	
LB	Lou Brock	40.00
SC	Steve Carlton	30.00
BG	Bob Gibson	50.00
TH	Tommy Herr	20.00
TM	Tim McCarver	30.00
SM	Stan Musial	75.00
RS	Red Schoendienst	25.00
OS	Ozzie Smith	50.00

Cardinals Greats Memorabilia

		NM/M
	Common Player:	5.00
LB	Lou Brock	5.00
SC	Steve Carlton	5.00
DD	Dizzy Dean/SP	50.00
BG	Bob Gibson	15.00
TH	Tommy Herr	5.00
RH	Rogers Hornsby	40.00
TM	Tim McCarver	5.00
SM	Stan Musial	20.00
RS	Red Schoendienst	10.00
OS	Ozzie Smith	15.00

Cubs Greats Memorabilia Autograph

		NM/M
	Production 30 Sets	
EB	Ernie Banks	60.00
AD	Andre Dawson	30.00
FJ	Fergie Jenkins	25.00
GM	Gary Matthews	25.00
SA	Ryne Sandberg	60.00
RS	Ron Santo	40.00
BS	Bruce Sutter	20.00
BW	Billy Williams	30.00

Cubs Greats Autograph

		NM/M
	Production 30 Sets	
EB	Ernie Banks	60.00
AD	Andre Dawson	30.00
MG	Mark Grace	30.00
FJ	Fergie Jenkins	25.00
GM	Gary Matthews	25.00
SA	Ryne Sandberg	60.00
RS	Ron Santo	40.00
BS	Bruce Sutter	20.00
BW	Billy Williams	30.00

Cubs Greats Memorabilia

		NM/M
EB	Ernie Banks	20.00
AD	Andre Dawson	8.00
MG	Mark Grace	8.00
FJ	Fergie Jenkins	8.00
GM	Gary Matthews	15.00
SA	Ryne Sandberg	15.00
RS	Ron Santo	10.00
BS	Brian Sutter	5.00
BW	Billy Williams	8.00

Decade Greats Memorabilia Autograph

		NM/M
	Production 30 Sets	
RO	Rod Carew	35.00
SC	Steve Carlton	35.00
CC	Chris Chambliss	25.00
JC	Jack Clark	25.00
WC	Will Clark	35.00
BF	Bob Feller	50.00
TG	Tony Gwynn	60.00
BJ	Bo Jackson	65.00
JK	John Kruk	25.00
BI	Bill Madlock	20.00
BM	Bill Mazeroski	35.00
WM	Willie McCovey	40.00
PM	Paul Molitor	35.00
DP	Dave Parker	20.00
KP	Kirby Puckett	100.00
TR	Tim Raines	20.00
CR	Cal Ripken Jr.	150.00

Decade Greats Autograph

		NM/M
	Production 30 Sets	
LB	Lou Brock	50.00
SC	Steve Carlton	35.00
BG	Bob Gibson	60.00
TH	Tommy Herr	20.00
TM	Tim McCarver	30.00
SM	Stan Musial	75.00
OS	Ozzie Smith	50.00

		NM/M
	Production 30 Sets	
RO	Rod Carew	35.00
SC	Steve Carlton	35.00
CC	Chris Chambliss	25.00
JC	Jack Clark	25.00
WC	Will Clark	35.00
BF	Bob Feller	50.00
TG	Tony Gwynn	60.00
BJ	Bo Jackson	65.00
JK	John Kruk	25.00
BI	Bill Madlock	20.00
BM	Bill Mazeroski	35.00
WM	Willie McCovey	40.00
PM	Paul Molitor	35.00
DP	Dave Parker	20.00
KP	Kirby Puckett	100.00
TR	Tim Raines	20.00
CR	Cal Ripken Jr.	150.00

Decade Greats Memorabilia

		NM/M
	Common Player:	5.00
EA	Earl Averill	20.00
RO	Rod Carew	8.00
SC	Steve Carlton	5.00
CC	Chris Chambliss	5.00
JC	Jack Clark	5.00
WC	Will Clark	8.00
RC	Roberto Clemente	60.00
BF	Bob Feller	15.00
BJ	Bo Jackson	15.00
JK	John Kruk	8.00
BI	Bill Madlock	5.00
EM	Eddie Matthews	10.00
BM	Bill Mazeroski	8.00
WM	Willie McCovey	10.00
JM	Johnny Mize	15.00
PM	Paul Molitor	15.00
MO	Mel Ott SP	50.00
DP	Dave Parker	5.00
KP	Kirby Puckett	15.00
TR	Tim Raines	5.00
CR	Cal Ripken Jr.	20.00
BR	Brooks Robinson	10.00
NR	Nolan Ryan	20.00
MS	Mike Schmidt	10.00
TS	Tom Seaver	10.00
WS	Willie Stargell	15.00
RY	Robin Yount	8.00

Dodgers Greats Memorabilia Autograph

		NM/M
	Production 30 Sets	
DB	Dusty Baker	40.00
RC	Ron Cey	30.00
SG	Steve Garvey	35.00
SS	Steve Sax	35.00
DS	Don Sutton	35.00
MW	Maury Wills	35.00

Dodgers Greats Autograph

		NM/M
	Production 30 Sets	
DB	Dusty Baker	40.00
RC	Ron Cey	30.00
SG	Steve Garvey	35.00
SS	Steve Sax	25.00
DS	Don Sutton	35.00
MW	Maury Wills	35.00

Dodgers Greats Memorabilia

		NM/M
	Common Player:	5.00

98	Willie Horton	15.00
99	Willie McCovey	35.00
100	Yogi Berra	60.00

Decade Greats Autograph

		NM/M
	Production 30 Sets	
RO	Rod Carew	35.00
SC	Steve Carlton	35.00
CC	Chris Chambliss	25.00
JC	Jack Clark	25.00
WC	Will Clark	35.00
BF	Bob Feller	50.00
TG	Tony Gwynn	60.00
BJ	Bo Jackson	65.00
JK	John Kruk	25.00
BI	Bill Madlock	20.00
BM	Bill Mazeroski	35.00
WM	Willie McCovey	40.00
PM	Paul Molitor	35.00
DP	Dave Parker	20.00
KP	Kirby Puckett	100.00
TR	Tim Raines	20.00
CR	Cal Ripken Jr.	150.00

Decade Greats Memorabilia

		NM/M
	Common Player:	5.00
EA	Earl Averill	20.00

BR	Brooks Robinson	40.00
NR	Nolan Ryan	100.00
MS	Mike Schmidt	75.00
TS	Tom Seaver	50.00
RY	Robin Yount	50.00

Nickname Greats Autograph

DB	Dusty Baker	8.00
CA	Roy Campanella	35.00
RC	Ron Cey	5.00
DD	Don Drysdale	25.00
SG	Steve Garvey	8.00
PR	Pee Wee Reese	10.00
JR	Jackie Robinson	40.00
SS	Steve Sax	5.00
DS	Don Sutton	5.00
MW	Maury Wills	5.00

		NM/M
SB	Steve Balboni	15.00
BE	Steve Bedrosian	15.00
JB	Jim Bouton	35.00
TB	Tom Brunansky	15.00
RB	Rick Burleson	15.00
CH	Joe Charboneau	15.00
JC	Jack Clark	20.00
WC	Will Clark	30.00
DD	Darren Daulton	20.00
DE	Dwight Evans	20.00
BF	Bob Feller	50.00
SF	Sid Fernandez	15.00
MF	Mark Fidrych	35.00
CF	Carlton Fisk	50.00
DF	Dan Ford	15.00
GF	George Foster	20.00
RG	Ron Guidry	40.00
MH	Mike Hargrove	15.00
TH	Tom Henke	15.00
HE	Tommy Herr	15.00
BH	Burt Hooton	20.00
AH	Al Hrabosky	20.00
GH	Glenn Hubbard	15.00
HJ	Howard Johnson	20.00
JJ	Jay Johnstone	20.00
ML	Mike LaValliere	15.00
BL	Bill Lee	15.00
SL	Sparky Lyle	15.00
GM	Garry Maddox	15.00
BM	Bill Madlock	15.00
MZ	Dennis Martinez	15.00
MA	Gary Matthews	15.00
LM	Lee Mazzilli	15.00
WM	Willie McCovey	50.00
SM	Sam McDowell	20.00
JM	John Montefusco	20.00
DP	Dave Parker	20.00
JP	Joe Pepitone	20.00
LP	Lou Piniella	25.00
RA	Doug Rader	15.00
TR	Tim Raines	15.00
RR	Rick Reuschel	20.00
DR	Dave Righetti	20.00
MR	Mickey Rivers	20.00
FR	Frank Robinson	50.00
GS	George Scott	20.00
JS	John Shelby	15.00
FS	Fred Stanley	15.00
RS	Rusty Staub	15.00
AT	Andre Thornton	15.00
ST	Steve Trout	20.00
EV	Ellis Valentine	15.00
MW	Mitch Williams	15.00
JW	Jimmy Wynn	15.00

Red Sox Greats Memorabilia Autograph

		NM/M
	Production 30 Sets	
WB	Wade Boggs	50.00
BD	Bobby Doerr	20.00
DE	Dwight Evans	20.00
CF	Carlton Fisk	35.00
FL	Fred Lynn	20.00
RP	Rico Petrocelli	20.00
JR	Jim Rice	25.00
LT	Luis Tiant	20.00

Red Sox Greats Autograph

		NM/M
	Production 30 Sets	
WB	Wade Boggs	50.00
BD	Bobby Doerr	20.00
DE	Dwight Evans	20.00
CF	Carlton Fisk	35.00
FL	Fred Lynn	20.00
RP	Rico Petrocelli	20.00
JR	Jim Rice	25.00
LT	Luis Tiant	20.00

Red Sox Greats Memorabilia

		NM/M
	Common Player:	5.00
WB	Wade Boggs	10.00
BD	Bobby Doerr	8.00
DE	Dwight Evans	8.00

CF	Carlton Fisk	8.00
JF	Jimmie Foxx	50.00
FL	Fred Lynn	5.00
RP	Rico Petrocelli	5.00
JR	Jim Rice	8.00
LT	Luis Tiant	5.00
TW	Ted Williams	50.00

Reds Greats Memorabilia Autograph

		NM/M
	Production 30 Sets	
JB	Johnny Bench	65.00
DC	Dave Concepcion	25.00
ED	Eric Davis	30.00
GF	George Foster	25.00
KG	Ken Griffey Sr.	30.00
BL	Barry Larkin	40.00
JM	Joe Morgan	40.00
TP	Tony Perez	40.00
FR	Frank Robinson	50.00
TS	Tom Seaver	50.00

Reds Greats Autograph

		NM/M
	Production 30 Sets	
JB	Johnny Bench	65.00
DC	Dave Concepcion	25.00
ED	Eric Davis	30.00
GF	George Foster	25.00
KG	Ken Griffey Sr.	30.00
BL	Barry Larkin	40.00
JM	Joe Morgan	40.00
TP	Tony Perez	40.00
FR	Frank Robinson	50.00
TS	Tom Seaver	50.00

Reds Greats Memorabilia

		NM/M
	Common Player:	5.00
JB	Johnny Bench	15.00
DC	Dave Concepcion	5.00
ED	Eric Davis	10.00
GF	George Foster	5.00
KG	Ken Griffey Sr.	5.00
BL	Barry Larkin	8.00
JM	Joe Morgan	8.00
TP	Tony Perez	5.00
FR	Frank Robinson	10.00
TS	Tom Seaver	10.00

Tigers Greats Memorabilia Autograph

		NM/M
	Production 30 Sets	
MF	Mark Fidrych	35.00
BF	Bill Freehan	30.00
KG	Kirk Gibson	35.00
WH	Willie Horton	20.00
AK	Al Kaline	50.00
GK	George Kell	40.00
JM	Jack Morris	25.00
AT	Alan Trammell	35.00

Tigers Greats Autograph

		NM/M
	Production 30 Sets	
MF	Mark Fidrych	35.00
BF	Bill Freehan	30.00
KG	Kirk Gibson	35.00
WH	Willie Horton	20.00
AK	Al Kaline	50.00
GK	George Kell	40.00
DM	Denny McLain	35.00
JM	Jack Morris	25.00
AT	Alan Trammell	35.00

Tigers Greats Memorabilia

		NM/M
	Common Player:	5.00
TC	Ty Cobb	85.00
MF	Mark Fidrych	10.00
BF	Bill Freehan	5.00
KG	Kirk Gibson	5.00
WH	Willie Horton	5.00
AK	Al Kaline	12.00
GK	George Kell	8.00
JM	Jack Morris	5.00
AT	Alan Trammell	5.00

Yankee Clippings Memorabilia Autograph

		NM/M
	Production 30 Sets	
YB	Yogi Berra	80.00
WF	Whitey Ford	60.00
RG	Ron Guidry	65.00
RJ	Reggie Jackson	50.00
DM	Don Mattingly	100.00
BM	Bobby Murcer	25.00
GN	Graig Nettles	40.00

Yankee Clippings Autograph

		NM/M
Production 30 Sets		
YB	Yogi Berra	80.00
WF	Whitey Ford	60.00
RG	Ron Guidry	65.00
RJ	Reggie Jackson	50.00
DM	Don Mattingly	100.00
BM	Bobby Murcer	25.00
GN	Graig Nettles	40.00

Yankee Clippings Memorabilia

		NM/M
Common Player:		8.00
YB	Yogi Berra	25.00
JD	Joe DiMaggio	75.00
WF	Whitey Ford	15.00
RG	Ron Guidry	15.00
RJ	Reggie Jackson	12.00
DM	Don Mattingly	15.00
TM	Thurman Munson	20.00
BM	Bobby Murcer	10.00
GN	Graig Nettles	8.00
BR	Babe Ruth	200.00

2006 Fleer Tradition

		NM/M
Complete Set (200):		35.00
Common Player:		.15
Hobby Pack (10):		2.00
Hobby Box (36):		60.00
1	Andruw Jones	.50
2	Chipper Jones	.75
3	John Smoltz	.25
4	Tim Hudson	.25
5	Joey Devine RC	.25
6	Chuck James (RC)	.25
7	Alay Soler RC	.50
8	Conor Jackson (RC)	.25
9	Luis Gonzalez	.15
10	Brandon Webb	.15
11	Chad Tracy	.15
12	Orlando Hudson	.15
13	Shawn Green	.15
14	Vladimir Guerrero	.75
15	Bartolo Colon	.15
16	Chone Figgins	.15
17	Garret Anderson	.15
18	Francisco Rodriguez	.25
19	Casey Kotchman	.15
20	Lance Berkman	.25
21	Craig Biggio	.25
22	Andy Pettitte	.15
23	Morgan Ensberg	.15
24	Brad Lidge	.15
25	Jered Weaver (RC)	1.00
26	Roy Oswalt	.25
27	Eric Chavez	.25
28	Rich Harden	.15
29	Cole Hamels (RC)	.25
30	Huston Street	.25
31	Bobby Crosby	.15
32	Nick Swisher	.25
33	Vernon Wells	.25
34	Roy Halladay	.25
35	A.J. Burnett	.25
36	Troy Glaus	.25
37	B.J. Ryan	.15
38	Bengie Molina	.15
39	Alex Rios	.15
40	Prince Fielder (RC)	2.00
41	Jose Capellan (RC)	.15
42	Rickie Weeks	.15
43	Ben Sheets	.25
44	Carlos Lee	.25
45	J.J. Hardy	.15
46	Albert Pujols	2.00
47	Skip Schumaker (RC)	.25
48	Adam Wainwright (RC)	.25
49	Jim Edmonds	.25
50	Scott Rolen	.75

51	Chris Carpenter	.25
52	David Eckstein	.15
53	Derrek Lee	.50
54	Jon Lester (RC)	3.00
55	Mark Prior	.40
56	Aramis Ramirez	.25
57	Juan Pierre	.15
58	Greg Maddux	1.50
59	Michael Barrett	.15
60	Carl Crawford	.15
61	Scott Kazmir	.25
62	Jorge Cantu	.15
63	Jonny Gomes	.15
64	Julio Lugo	.15
65	Aubrey Huff	.15
66	Jeff Kent	.25
67	Nomar Garciaparra	.75
68	Rafael Furcal	.15
69	Tim Hamulack (RC)	.25
70	Chad Billingsley (RC)	.25
71	Hong-Chih Kuo (RC)	.25
72	J.D. Drew	.15
73	Moises Alou	.15
74	Randy Winn	.15
75	Jason Schmidt	.25
76	Jeremy Accardo RC	.25
77	Matt Cain (RC)	.50
78	Joel Zumaya (RC)	.50
79	Travis Hafner	.50
80	Victor Martinez	.25
81	Grady Sizemore	.40
82	C.C. Sabathia	.15
83	Jhonny Peralta	.15
84	Jason Michaels	.15
85	Jeremy Sowers (RC)	.25
86	Ichiro Suzuki	1.50
87	Richie Sexson	.25
88	Adrian Beltre	.25
89	Felix Hernandez	.25
90	Kenji Johjima RC	3.00
91	Jeff Harris RC	.25
92	Taylor Buchholz (RC)	.25
93	Miguel Cabrera	.75
94	Dontrelle Willis	.25
95	Jeremy Hermida (RC)	.25
96	Mike Jacobs (RC)	.25
97	Josh Johnson (RC)	.25
98	Hanley Ramirez (RC)	.25
99	Josh Willingham (RC)	.25
100	Dan Uggla (RC)	.25
101	David Wright	1.00
102	Jose Reyes	.50
103	Pedro Martinez	.75
104	Carlos Beltran	.50
105	Carlos Delgado	.40
106	Billy Wagner	.15
107	Lastings Milledge (RC)	.75
108	Alfonso Soriano	.75
109	Jose Vidro	.15
110	Livan Hernandez	.15
111	Matthew Kemp (RC)	.25
112	Brandon Watson (RC)	.25
113	Ryan Zimmerman (RC)	2.00
114	Miguel Tejada	.50
115	Ramon Hernandez	.15
116	Brian Roberts	.15
117	Melvin Mora	.15
118	Erik Bedard	.15
119	Jay Gibbons	.15
120	Aaron Rakers (RC)	.25
121	Jake Peavy	.25
122	Brian Giles	.25
123	Khalil Greene	.15
124	Trevor Hoffman	.25
125	Josh Barfield (RC)	.25
126	Ben Johnson (RC)	.25
127	Ryan Howard	1.50
128	Bobby Abreu	.25
129	Chase Utley	.50
130	Pat Burrell	.25
131	Jimmy Rollins	.50
132	Brett Myers	.15
133	Mike Thompson RC	.25
134	Jason Bay	.40
135	Oliver Perez	.15
136	Matt Capps (RC)	.25
137	Paul Maholm (RC)	.25
138	Nate McLouth (RC)	.25
139	John Van Benschoten (RC)	.25
140	Mark Teixeira	.50
141	Michael Young	.25
142	Hank Blalock	.25
143	Kevin Millwood	.15
144	Laynce Nix	.15
145	Francisco Cordero	.15
146	Ian Kinsler (RC)	.25
147	David Ortiz	.75
148	Manny Ramirez	.75
149	Jason Varitek	.25
150	Curt Schilling	.75
151	Josh Beckett	.25
152	Coco Crisp	.15
153	Jonathan Papelbon (RC)	2.00
154	Ken Griffey Jr.	1.50
155	Adam Dunn	.50
156	Felipe Lopez	.15
157	Bronson Arroyo	.15
158	Ryan Freel	.15
159	Chris Denorfia (RC)	.25
160	Todd Helton	.50
161	Garrett Atkins	.15
162	Matt Holliday	.25
163	Clint Barmes	.15
164	Kendry Morales (RC)	.25
165	Ryan Shealy (RC)	.25

166	Josh Wilson (RC)	.25
167	Reggie Sanders	.15
168	Angel Berroa	.15
169	Mike Sweeney	.15
170	Mark Grudzielanek	.15
171	Jeremy Affeldt	.15
172	Steve Stemle RC	.50
173	Justin Verlander (RC)	2.00
174	Ivan Rodriguez	.50
175	Chris Shelton	.15
176	Jeremy Bonderman	.25
177	Magglio Ordonez	.25
178	Carlos Guillen	.15
179	Placido Polanco	.15
180	Johan Santana	.75
181	Torii Hunter	.25
182	Joe Nathan	.15
183	Joe Mauer	.50
184	David Gassner (RC)	.25
185	Jason Kubel (RC)	.25
186	Francisco Liriano (RC)	2.00
187	Jim Thome	.50
188	Paul Konerko	.40
189	Scott Podsednik	.25
190	Tadahito Iguchi	.25
191	A.J. Pierzynski	.15
192	Jose Contreras	.15
193	Brian Anderson (RC)	.25
194	Hideki Matsui	1.50
195	Wilbert Nieves (RC)	.25
196	Alex Rodriguez	1.00
197	Gary Sheffield	.25
198	Randy Johnson	.25
199	Johnny Damon	.40
200	Derek Jeter	1.00

Griffey Jr. 1989 Fleer Buyback Autograph

	NM/M
Production 50	
Ken Griffey Jr.	250.00

Black & White

B&W (1-200):	2-3X

Printing Plates

No Pricing
Production one set per color.

Sepia Tone

Sepia (1-200):	2-3X

1934 Goudey Greats

		NM/M
Common Player:		2.00
GG-1	Andruw Jones	5.00
GG-2	Chipper Jones	8.00
GG-3	John Smoltz	4.00
GG-4	Tim Hudson	3.00
GG-5	Conor Jackson	2.00
GG-6	Luis Gonzalez	2.00
GG-7	Brandon Webb	3.00
GG-8	Vladimir Guerrero	8.00
GG-9	Bartolo Colon	2.00
GG-10	Lance Berkman	3.00
GG-11	Craig Biggio	4.00
GG-12	Andy Pettitte	3.00
GG-13	Morgan Ensberg	2.00
GG-14	Roy Oswalt	3.00
GG-15	Eric Chavez	3.00
GG-16	Rich Harden	3.00
GG-17	Huston Street	3.00
GG-18	Vernon Wells	3.00
GG-19	Roy Halladay	3.00
GG-20	Troy Glaus	3.00
GG-21	Prince Fielder	10.00
GG-22	Rickie Weeks	3.00
GG-23	Ben Sheets	3.00
GG-24	Carlos Lee	3.00
GG-25	Albert Pujols	20.00
GG-26	Jim Edmonds	4.00
GG-27	Scott Rolen	8.00
GG-28	Chris Carpenter	5.00
GG-29	Derrek Lee	5.00
GG-30	Mark Prior	5.00
GG-31	Greg Maddux	15.00
GG-32	Carl Crawford	4.00
GG-33	Scott Kazmir	3.00
GG-34	Jorge Cantu	2.00
GG-35	Jeff Kent	3.00
GG-36	Nomar Garciaparra	8.00
GG-37	J.D. Drew	2.00
GG-38	Randy Winn	2.00
GG-39	Jason Schmidt	3.00
GG-40	Travis Hafner	5.00
GG-41	Victor Martinez	3.00
GG-42	Grady Sizemore	4.00
GG-43	Jhonny Peralta	2.00
GG-44	Ichiro Suzuki	15.00
GG-45	Richie Sexson	4.00
GG-46	Felix Hernandez	4.00
GG-47	Kenji Johjima	10.00
GG-48	Miguel Cabrera	8.00
GG-49	Dontrelle Willis	4.00
GG-50	Josh Willingham	3.00
GG-51	David Wright	15.00
GG-52	Jose Reyes	5.00
GG-53	Pedro Martinez	8.00
GG-54	Carlos Beltran	5.00
GG-55	Alfonso Soriano	8.00
GG-56	Ryan Zimmerman	8.00
GG-57	Miguel Tejada	4.00
GG-58	Brian Roberts	3.00
GG-59	Jake Peavy	3.00
GG-60	Brian Giles	2.00
GG-61	Khalil Greene	2.00
GG-62	Ryan Howard	15.00
GG-63	Bobby Abreu	4.00
GG-64	Chase Utley	8.00
GG-65	Jimmy Rollins	3.00
GG-66	Jason Bay	5.00
GG-67	Mark Teixeira	5.00
GG-68	Michael Young	3.00
GG-69	Hank Blalock	3.00
GG-70	David Ortiz	8.00
GG-71	Manny Ramirez	8.00
GG-72	Curt Schilling	8.00
GG-73	Josh Beckett	3.00
GG-74	Jonathan Papelbon	10.00
GG-75	Ken Griffey Jr.	15.00
GG-76	Adam Dunn	5.00
GG-77	Todd Helton	4.00
GG-78	Garrett Atkins	2.00
GG-79	Matt Holliday	2.00
GG-80	Reggie Sanders	2.00
GG-81	Justin Verlander	10.00
GG-82	Ivan Rodriguez	5.00
GG-83	Chris Shelton	2.00
GG-84	Jeremy Bonderman	3.00
GG-85	Magglio Ordonez	3.00
GG-86	Johan Santana	6.00
GG-87	Torii Hunter	3.00
GG-88	Joe Nathan	2.00
GG-89	Joe Mauer	5.00
GG-90	Francisco Liriano	8.00
GG-91	Jim Thome	5.00
GG-92	Paul Konerko	4.00
GG-93	Scott Podsednik	3.00
GG-94	Tadahito Iguchi	4.00
GG-95	A.J. Pierzynski	2.00
GG-96	Hideki Matsui	12.00
GG-97	Alex Rodriguez	20.00
GG-98	Gary Sheffield	4.00
GG-99	Derek Jeter	25.00
GG-100	Jason Giambi	6.00

Blue Chip Prospects

		NM/M
Common Player:		.50
BC-1	Ryan Zimmerman	3.00
BC-2	Conor Jackson	.75
BC-3	Justin Verlander	3.00
BC-4	Justin Verlander	3.00
BC-5	Jeremy Hermida	.75
BC-6	Josh Willingham	.75
BC-7	Hanley Ramirez	1.00
BC-8	Prince Fielder	3.00
BC-9	Francisco Liriano	3.00
BC-10	Lastings Milledge	2.00
BC-11	Jon Lester	2.00
BC-12	Matt Cain	1.50
BC-13	Adam Wainwright	.75
BC-14	Chuck James	1.00
BC-15	Kenji Johjima	3.00
BC-16	Josh Johnson	.75
BC-17	Jason Kubel	.50
BC-18	Brian Anderson	.50
BC-19	Cole Hamels	2.00
BC-20	Mike Jacobs	.50
BC-21	Jered Weaver	3.00
BC-22	Kendry Morales	.50
BC-23	Alay Soler	.50
BC-24	Chris Denorfia	.50
BC-25	Chad Billingsley	1.00

Diamond Tribute

		NM/M
Common Player:		.50
DT-1	Derek Jeter	3.00
DT-2	Ken Griffey Jr.	3.00
DT-3	Vladimir Guerrero	1.50
DT-4	Albert Pujols	3.00
DT-5	Derrek Lee	1.00
DT-6	David Ortiz	1.50
DT-7	Miguel Tejada	1.00
DT-8	Jim Thome	1.00
DT-9	Travis Hafner	1.00
DT-10	Grady Sizemore	1.00
DT-11	Chris Shelton	.50
DT-12	Dontrelle Willis	1.00
DT-13	Craig Biggio	1.00
DT-14	Roy Oswalt	1.00
DT-15	Prince Fielder	2.00
DT-16	David Wright	2.50
DT-17	Jose Reyes	1.00
DT-18	Hideki Matsui	2.00
DT-19	Rich Harden	.75
DT-20	Bobby Abreu	.75
DT-21	Jason Bay	1.00
DT-22	Jake Peavy	.75
DT-23	Felix Hernandez	.75
DT-24	Carl Crawford	.75
DT-25	Vernon Wells	.75

Grass Roots

		NM/M
Common Player:		.50
GR-1	Ken Griffey Jr.	2.50
GR-2	Albert Pujols	3.00
GR-3	Derek Jeter	3.00
GR-4	Derrek Lee	1.00
GR-5	Vladimir Guerrero	1.00
GR-6	Andruw Jones	1.00
GR-7	Manny Ramirez	1.00
GR-8	Johan Santana	1.00
GR-9	Victor Martinez	.75
GR-10	Todd Helton	1.00
GR-11	Ivan Rodriguez	1.00
GR-12	Miguel Cabrera	1.00
GR-13	Lance Berkman	.75
GR-14	Bartolo Colon	.50
GR-15	Jeff Kent	.50
GR-16	Carlos Lee	.50
GR-17	Torii Hunter	.50
GR-18	Carlos Beltran	1.00
GR-19	Alex Rodriguez	3.00
GR-20	Randy Johnson	.75
GR-21	Eric Chavez	.50
GR-22	Ryan Howard	2.50
GR-23	Ichiro Suzuki	2.00
GR-24	Chris Carpenter	1.00
GR-25	Mark Teixeira	1.00

Signature Tradition

		NM/M
Inserted 1:1,269 Hobby		
CH	Craig Hansen	35.00
JM	Joe Mauer/SP	30.00

Traditional Threads

		NM/M
Common Player:		4.00
JB	Josh Barfield	4.00
BA	Jason Bay	8.00
EB	Erik Bedard	4.00
HB	Hank Blalock	6.00
SC	Sean Casey	4.00
JD	Johnny Damon	10.00
ZD	Zachary Duke	4.00
PF	Prince Fielder	15.00
CF	Chone Figgins	4.00
BG	Brian Giles	4.00
MG	Marcus Giles	4.00
GR	Khalil Greene	4.00
KG	Ken Griffey Jr.	15.00
VG	Vladimir Guerrero	6.00
JH	Jeremy Hermida	6.00
FH	Felix Hernandez	6.00
LH	Livan Hernandez	4.00
GJ	Geoff Jenkins	4.00
DJ	Derek Jeter	20.00
CK	Casey Kotchman/SP	4.00
CL	Carlos Lee	6.00
DL	Derrek Lee	8.00
JL	Javy Lopez	4.00
GM	Greg Maddux	10.00
MM	Melvin Mora	4.00
DO	David Ortiz	10.00
RO	Roy Oswalt	6.00
JP	Jake Peavy	6.00
AP	Albert Pujols	20.00
AR	Aramis Ramirez	4.00
AS	Alfonso Soriano	8.00
BR	Brian Roberts	4.00
BS	Ben Sheets	6.00
TE	Mark Teixeira	8.00
MT	Miguel Tejada	6.00
JV	Jose Vidro	4.00
OV	Omar Vizquel	4.00
RW	Rickie Weeks	6.00
MY	Michael Young	6.00
CZ	Carlos Zambrano	4.00
RZ	Ryan Zimmerman	15.00

Triple Crown Contenders

		NM/M
Common Player:		.75
TC-1	Albert Pujols	3.00
TC-2	Derrek Lee	.75
TC-3	Manny Ramirez	1.00
TC-4	David Ortiz	1.00
TC-5	Mark Teixeira	.75
TC-6	Alex Rodriguez	3.00
TC-7	Andruw Jones	.75
TC-8	Todd Helton	.75
TC-9	Vladimir Guerrero	1.00
TC-10	Miguel Cabrera	1.00
TC-11	Hideki Matsui	.75
TC-12	Travis Hafner	.75
TC-13	David Wright	2.00
TC-14	Ken Griffey Jr.	2.50
TC-15	Jason Bay	.75

2007 Fleer

		NM/M
Complete Set (400):		75.00
Common Player:		.15
Hobby Pack (10):		1.50
Hobby Box (36):		50.00
Rack Pack (52):		4.50
Rack Box (18):		75.00
1	Chad Cordero	.15
2	Alfonso Soriano	.50
3	Nick Johnson	.15
4	Austin Kearns	.15
5	Ramon Ortiz	.15
6	Brian Schneider	.15

ABBREVIATIONS

SP - Short Print

No	Player	Price
7	Ryan Zimmerman	.40
8	Jose Vidro	.15
9	Felipe Lopez	.15
10	Cristian Guzman	.15
11	B.J. Ryan	.15
12	Alex Rios	.25
13	Vernon Wells	.25
14	Roy Halladay	.25
15	A.J. Burnett	.15
16	Lyle Overbay	.15
17	Troy Glaus	.25
18	Bengie Molina	.15
19	Gustavo Chacin	.15
20	Aaron Hill	.15
21	Vicente Padilla	.15
22	Kevin Millwood	.15
23	Akinori Otsuka	.15
24	Adam Eaton	.15
25	Hank Blalock	.15
26	Mark Teixeira	.40
27	Michael Young	.15
28	Mark DeRosa	.15
29	Gary Matthews	.15
30	Ian Kinsler	.25
31	Carlos Lee	.25
32	James Shields	.25
33	Scott Kazmir	.15
34	Carl Crawford	.25
35	Jonny Gomes	.15
36	Tim Corcoran	.15
37	B.J. Upton	.25
38	Rocco Baldelli	.25
39	Jae Weong Seo	.15
40	Jorge Cantu	.15
41	Ty Wigginton	.15
42	Chris Carpenter	.40
43	Albert Pujols	1.50
44	Scott Rolen	.50
45	Jim Edmonds	.40
46	Jason Isringhausen	.15
47	Yadier Molina	.15
48	Adam Wainwright	.25
49	Mark Mulder	.25
50	Jason Marquis	.15
51	Juan Encarnacion	.15
52	Aaron Miles	.15
53	Ichiro Suzuki	1.00
54	Felix Hernandez	.40
55	Kenji Johjima	.25
56	Richie Sexson	.15
57	Yuniesky Betancourt	.15
58	J.J. Putz	.15
59	Jarrod Washburn	.15
60	Ben Broussard	.15
61	Adrian Beltre	.25
62	Raul Ibanez	.15
63	Jose Lopez	.15
64	Matt Cain	.25
65	Noah Lowry	.15
66	Jason Schmidt	.25
67	Pedro Feliz	.15
68	Matt Morris	.15
69	Ray Durham	.15
70	Steve Finley	.15
71	Randy Winn	.15
72	Moises Alou	.15
73	Eliezer Alfonzo	.15
74	Armando Benitez	.15
75	Omar Vizquel	.25
76	Chris Young	.15
77	Adrian Gonzalez	.25
78	Khalil Greene	.15
79	Mike Piazza	.75
80	Josh Barfield	.25
81	Brian Giles	.15
82	Jake Peavy	.25
83	Trevor Hoffman	.25
84	Mike Cameron	.15
85	Dave Roberts	.15
86	David Wells	.15
87	Zachary Duke	.15
88	Ian Snell	.15
89	Jason Bay	.40
90	Freddy Sanchez	.15
91	Jack Wilson	.15
92	Tom Gorzelanny	.15
93	Chris Duffy	.15
94	Jose Castillo	.15
95	Matt Capps	.15
96	Mike Gonzalez	.15
97	Chase Utley	.50
98	Jimmy Rollins	.50
99	Aaron Rowand	.15
100	Ryan Howard	1.00
101	Cole Hamels	.50
102	Pat Burrell	.25
103	Shane Victorino	.15
104	Jamie Moyer	.15
105	Mike Lieberthal	.15
106	Tom Gordon	.15
107	Brett Myers	.25
108	Nick Swisher	.25
109	Barry Zito	.25
110	Jason Kendall	.15
111	Milton Bradley	.15
112	Bobby Crosby	.15
113	Huston Street	.15
114	Eric Chavez	.25
115	Frank Thomas	.40
116	Danny Haren	.15
117	Jay Payton	.15
118	Randy Johnson	.50
119	Mike Mussina	.40
120	Bobby Abreu	.40
121	Jason Giambi	.40
122	Derek Jeter	1.50
123	Alex Rodriguez	1.50
124	Jorge Posada	.40
125	Robinson Cano	.40
126	Mariano Rivera	.40
127	Chien-Ming Wang	.40
128	Hideki Matsui	1.00
129	Gary Sheffield	.40
130	Lastings Milledge	.25
131	Tom Glavine	.25
132	Billy Wagner	.25
133	Pedro Martinez	.50
134	Paul LoDuca	.15
135	Carlos Delgado	.40
136	Carlos Beltran	.40
137	David Wright	.75
138	Jose Reyes	.50
139	Julio Franco	.15
140	Michael Cuddyer	.15
141	Justin Morneau	.40
142	Johan Santana	.50
143	Francisco Liriano	.25
144	Joe Mauer	.25
145	Torii Hunter	.25
146	Luis Castillo	.15
147	Joe Nathan	.15
148	Carlos Silva	.15
149	Boof Bonser	.15
150	Ben Sheets	.25
151	Prince Fielder	.40
152	Bill Hall	.25
153	Rickie Weeks	.25
154	Geoff Jenkins	.15
155	Kevin Mench	.15
156	Francisco Cordero	.15
157	Chris Capuano	.15
158	Brady Clark	.15
159	Tony Gwynn Jr.	.15
160	Chad Billingsley	.25
161	Russell Martin	.25
162	Wilson Betemit	.15
163	Nomar Garciaparra	.50
164	Kenny Lofton	.15
165	Rafael Furcal	.25
166	Julio Lugo	.15
167	Brad Penny	.25
168	Jeff Kent	.25
169	Greg Maddux	1.00
170	Derek Lowe	.15
171	Andre Ethier	.25
172	Chone Figgins	.15
173	Francisco Rodriguez	.25
174	Garret Anderson	.15
175	Orlando Cabrera	.25
176	Adam Kennedy	.15
177	John Lackey	.25
178	Vladimir Guerrero	.50
179	Bartolo Colon	.25
180	Jered Weaver	.25
181	Juan Rivera	.15
182	Howie Kendrick	.25
183	Ervin Santana	.15
184	Mark Redman	.15
185	David DeJesus	.15
186	Joey Gathright	.15
187	Mike Sweeney	.15
188	Mark Teahen	.15
189	Angel Berroa	.15
190	Ambiorix Burgos	.15
191	Luke Hudson	.15
192	Mark Grudzielanek	.15
193	Roger Clemens	1.50
194	Willy Taveras	.15
195	Craig Biggio	.25
196	Andy Pettitte	.25
197	Roy Oswalt	.40
198	Lance Berkman	.40
199	Morgan Ensberg	.25
200	Brad Lidge	.15
201	Chris Burke	.15
202	Miguel Cabrera	.50
203	Dontrelle Willis	.25
204	Josh Johnson	.15
205	Ricky Nolasco	.15
206	Dan Uggla	.15
207	Jeremy Hermida	.15
208	Scott Olsen	.15
209	Josh Willingham	.15
210	Joe Borowski	.15
211	Hanley Ramirez	.40
212	Mike Jacobs	.15
213	Kenny Rogers	.15
214	Justin Verlander	.40
215	Ivan Rodriguez	.40
216	Magglio Ordonez	.25
217	Todd Jones	.15
218	Joel Zumaya	.25
219	Jeremy Bonderman	.40
220	Nate Robertson	.15
221	Brandon Inge	.15
222	Craig Monroe	.15
223	Carlos Guillen	.15
224	Jeff Francis	.15
225	Brian Fuentes	.15
226	Todd Helton	.40
227	Matt Holliday	.25
228	Garrett Atkins	.25
229	Clint Barmes	.15
230	Jason Jennings	.15
231	Aaron Cook	.15
232	Brad Hawpe	.25
233	Cory Sullivan	.15
234	Aaron Boone	.15
235	C.C. Sabathia	.25
236	Grady Sizemore	.50
237	Travis Hafner	.25
238	Jhonny Peralta	.15
239	Jake Westbrook	.15
240	Jeremy Sowers	.15
241	Andy Marte	.15
242	Victor Martinez	.25
243	Jason Michaels	.15
244	Cliff Lee	.15
245	Bronson Arroyo	.15
246	Aaron Harang	.15
247	Ken Griffey Jr.	1.00
248	Adam Dunn	.40
249	Rich Aurilia	.15
250	Eric Milton	.15
251	David Ross	.15
252	Brandon Phillips	.15
253	Ryan Freel	.15
254	Eddie Guardado	.15
255	Jose Contreras	.15
256	Freddy Garcia	.15
257	Jon Garland	.15
258	Mark Buehrle	.25
259	Bobby Jenks	.15
260	Paul Konerko	.25
261	Jermaine Dye	.15
262	Joe Crede	.15
263	Jim Thome	.40
264	Javier Vazquez	.15
265	A.J. Pierzynski	.15
266	Tadahito Iguchi	.15
267	Carlos Zambrano	.40
268	Derrek Lee	.40
269	Aramis Ramirez	.40
270	Ryan Theriot	.15
271	Juan Pierre	.25
272	Rich Hill	.15
273	Ryan Dempster	.15
274	Jacque Jones	.15
275	Mark Prior	.25
276	Kerry Wood	.25
277	Josh Beckett	.25
278	David Ortiz	.50
279	Kevin Youkilis	.15
280	Jason Varitek	.40
281	Manny Ramirez	.50
282	Curt Schilling	.50
283	Jon Lester	.25
284	Jonathan Papelbon	.50
285	Alex Gonzalez	.15
286	Mike Lowell	.15
287	Kyle Snyder	.15
288	Miguel Tejada	.40
289	Erik Bedard	.25
290	Ramon Hernandez	.15
291	Melvin Mora	.15
292	Nicholas Markakis	.25
293	Brian Roberts	.25
294	Corey Patterson	.15
295	Kris Benson	.15
296	Jay Gibbons	.15
297	Rodrigo Lopez	.15
298	Chris Ray	.15
299	Andruw Jones	.50
300	Brian McCann	.40
301	Jeff Francoeur	.25
302	Chuck James	.25
303	John Smoltz	.40
304	Bob Wickman	.15
305	Edgar Renteria	.25
306	Adam LaRoche	.25
307	Marcus Giles	.15
308	Tim Hudson	.25
309	Chipper Jones	.50
310	Miguel Batista	.15
311	Claudio Vargas	.15
312	Brandon Webb	.25
313	Luis Gonzalez	.15
314	Livan Hernandez	.15
315	Stephen Drew	.25
316	Johnny Estrada	.15
317	Orlando Hudson	.15
318	Conor Jackson	.15
319	Chad Tracy	.15
320	Carlos Quentin	.25
321	Alvin Colina RC	.50
322	Miguel Montero (RC)	.25
323	Jeff Fiorentino (RC)	.25
324	Jeff Baker (RC)	.25
325	Brian Burres (RC)	.25
326	David Murphy (RC)	.25
327	Francisco Cruceta (RC)	.25
328	Beltran Perez (RC)	.25
329	Scott Moore (RC)	.25
330	Sean Henn (RC)	.25
331	Ryan Sweeney (RC)	.25
332	Josh Fields (RC)	.25
333	Jerry Owens (RC)	.25
334	Vinny Rottino (RC)	.25
335	Kevin Kouzmanoff (RC)	.50
336	Alexi Casilla RC	.50
337	Justin Hampson (RC)	.25
338	Troy Tulowitzki (RC)	.50
339	Jose Garcia RC	.50
340	Andrew Miller RC	2.00
341	Glen Perkins (RC)	.25
342	Ubaldo Jimenez (RC)	.50
343	Doug Slaten RC	.50
344	Angel Sanchez RC	.50
345	Mitch Maier RC	.50
346	Ryan Braun RC	.50
347	Joselo Diaz (RC)	.25
348	Delwyn Young (RC)	.25
349	Kevin Hooper (RC)	.25
350	Dennis Sarfate (RC)	.25
351	Andy Cannizaro RC	.50
352	Devern Hansack RC	1.00
353	Michael Bourn (RC)	.25
354	Carlos Maldonado (RC)	.25
355	Shane Youman RC	.50
356	Philip Humber (RC)	.50
357	Hector Gimenez (RC)	.25
358	Fred Lewis (RC)	.25
359	Ryan Feierabend (RC)	.25
360	Juan Morillo (RC)	.25
361	Travis Chick (RC)	.25
362	Oswaldo Navarro RC	.50
363	Cesar Jimenez RC	.50
364	Brian Stokes (RC)	.50
365	Delmon Young (RC)	.50
366	Juan Salas (RC)	.25
367	Shawn Riggans (RC)	.50
368	Adam Lind (RC)	.50
369	Joaquin Arias (RC)	.50
370	Eric Stults RC	.50
371	Brandon Webb	.50
372	John Smoltz	.50
373	Miguel Tejada	.50
374	David Ortiz	1.00
375	Carlos Zambrano	.50
376	Jermaine Dye	.50
377	Ken Griffey Jr.	1.50
378	Victor Martinez	.50
379	Todd Helton	.50
380	Ivan Rodriguez	.50
381	Miguel Cabrera	.50
382	Lance Berkman	.50
383	Mike Sweeney	.50
384	Vladimir Guerrero	.50
385	Derek Lowe	.25
386	Bill Hall	.25
387	Johan Santana	.75
388	Carlos Beltran	.75
389	Derek Jeter	2.00
390	Nick Swisher	.50
391	Ryan Howard	1.50
392	Jason Bay	.50
393	Trevor Hoffman	.25
394	Omar Vizquel	.50
395	Ichiro Suzuki	1.00
396	Albert Pujols	2.00
397	Carl Crawford	.50
398	Mark Teixeira	.50
399	Roy Halladay	.50
400	Ryan Zimmerman	.50

Printing Plates

No Pricing
Production one set per color.

Mini Die-Cuts

Mini:	1.5-2X
Inserted 1:2	
Mini Gold:	No Pricing
Inserted 1:576	

1992 Flopps Promos

Prior to the 1992 season, Pro Set announced plans to produce a set of 66 cards parodying contemporary baseball stars and teams. The name "Flopps" was used instead of Pro Set, which does not appear anywhere on the cards. While the announced checklist included players such as Craig Piggio, George Brat and Cal Ripped-One, only five promo cards were produced before the players' union whined and the idea was dropped. Pro Set didn't want to offend the union at the time because they were attempting to get a baseball card license. Cards pictured caricatures of the players on front and funny biographies on back, all in color in the standard 2-1/2" x 3-1/2" format.

		NM/M
Complete Set (5):		6.00
Common Player:		.50
(1)	Barry Bones	4.00
(2)	Wade Bugs	2.50
(3)	Ken Groovy, Jr.	3.00
(4)	Stickey Henderson	1.50
(5)	Lance Infishable	.50

1993 Florida Agriculture Dept. Braves/Marlins

A pair of eight-card team panels of the Atlanta Braves and Florida Marlins was issued by

the Florida Department of Agriculture and Consumer Services to promote the state's fruit and vegetable products. Individual cards show the player posing - sometimes comically - with one of the state's agricultural products. The photos are bordered in team colors and have a "Fresh 2 U" logo in the upper-left consisting of a fruit or vegetable superimposed on a ball diamond and crossed bats. Backs have the player's name, uniform number, and a short career summary at top. In center is a baseball with the result of an at-bat. In the bottom panel is a statistic about one of the state's crops. A card number is at top. Individual cards measure the standard 2-1/2" x 3-1/2," with the eight-card perforated sheets measuring 10" x 7". The card sheets were distributed during the Sunshine State Games in Tallahassee.

		NM/M
Complete Set (16):		18.00
Common Player:		1.00
Atlanta Braves Team Set:		10.00
1	Team logo card	1.00
2	Steve Avery	1.00
3	Jeff Blauser	1.00
4	Sid Bream	1.00
5	Tom Glavine	4.00
6	Mark Lemke	1.00
7	Greg Olson	1.00
8	Terry Pendleton	1.00
Florida Marlins Team Set:		9.00
1	Team logo card	1.00
2	Billy the Marlin/Mascot	1.00
3	Ryan Bowen	1.00
4	Benito Santiago	1.00
5	Richie Lewis	1.00
6	Bret Barbarie	1.00
7	Rich Renteria	1.00
8	Jeff Conine	1.00

1987 Red Foley Stickers

Individual player stickers were inserted in sheets within the pages of "Red Foley's Best Baseball Book Ever." The 8-1/2" x 11", 96-page softbound book offered games, quizzes and trivia, with a space to put each sticker. Individual stickers measure about 1-3/8" x 1-3/4". Stickers have color photos on front with a number in the white border at bottom. Player identification does not appear on the sticker. Cover price of the book in 1987 was about $7.

	NM/M
Complete Book:	9.00
Complete Sticker Set (130):	7.50

No	Player	Price
	Common Player:	.05
1	Julio Franco	.05
2	Willie Randolph	.05
3	Jesse Barfield	.05
4	Mike Witt	.05
5	Orel Hershiser	.05
6	Dwight Gooden	.05
7	Dan Quisenberry	.05
8	Vince Coleman	.05
9	Rich Gossage	.05
10	Kirk Gibson	.05
11	Joaquin Andujar	.05
12	Dave Concepcion	.05
13	Andre Dawson	.25
14	Tippy Martinez	.05
15	Bob James	.05
16	Ryne Sandberg	1.00
17	Bob Knepper	.05
18	Bob Stanley	.05
19	Jim Presley	.05
20	Greg Gross	.05
21	Bob Horner	.05
22	Paul Molitor	.75
23	Kirby Puckett	1.00
24	Scott Garrelts	.05
25	Tony Pena	.05
26	Charlie Hough	.05
27	Joe Carter	.25
28	Dave Winfield	.75
29	Tony Fernandez	.05
30	Bobby Grich	.05
31	Mike Marshall	.05
32	Keith Hernandez	.05
33	Dennis Leonard	.05
34	John Tudor	.05
35	Kevin McReynolds	.05
36	Lance Parrish	.05
37	Carney Lansford	.05
38	Buddy Bell	.05
39	Tim Raines	.05
40	Mike Boddicker	.05
41	Carlton Fisk	.75
42	Lee Smith	.05
43	Glenn Davis	.05
44	Jim Rice	.25
45	Mark Langston	.05
46	Mike Schmidt	1.50
47	Dale Murphy	.45
48	Cecil Cooper	.05
49	Kent Hrbek	.05
50	Will Clark	.10
51	Johnny Ray	.05
52	Darrell Porter	.05
53	Brook Jacoby	.05
54	Ron Guidry	.05
55	Lloyd Moseby	.05
56	Donnie Moore	.05
57	Fernando Valenzuela	.05
58	Darryl Strawberry	.05
59	Hal McRae	.05
60	Tommy Herr	.05
61	Steve Garvey	.35
62	Alan Trammell	.05
63	Jose Canseco	.50
64	Pete Rose	1.75
65	Jeff Reardon	.05
66	Eddie Murray	.75
67	Ozzie Guillen	.05
68	Jody Davis	.05
69	Bill Doran	.05
70	Roger Clemens	1.25
71	Alvin Davis	.05
72	Von Hayes	.05
73	Zane Smith	.05
74	Ted Higuera	.05
75	Tom Brunansky	.05
76	Chili Davis	.05
77	R.J. Reynolds	.05
78	Oddibe McDowell	.05
79	Brett Butler	.05
80	Rickey Henderson	.75
81	Dave Steib	.05
82	Wally Joyner	.05
83	Pedro Guerrero	.05
84	Jesse Orosco	.05
85	Steve Balboni	.05
86	Willie McGee	.05
87	Graig Nettles	.05
88	Lou Whitaker	.05
89	Jay Howell	.05
90	Dave Parker	.05
91	Hubie Brooks	.05
92	Rick Dempsey	.05
93	Neil Allen	.05
94	Shawon Dunston	.05
95	Jose Cruz	.05
96	Wade Boggs	1.00
97	Danny Tartabull	.05
98	Steve Bedrosian	.05
99	Ken Oberkfell	.05
100	Ben Oglivie	.05
101	Bert Blyleven	.05
102	Jeff Leonard	.05
103	Rick Rhoden	.05
104	Larry Parrish	.05
105	Tony Bernazard	.05
106	Don Mattingly	1.50
107	Willie Upshaw	.05
108	Reggie Jackson	1.00
109	Bill Madlock	.05
110	Gary Carter	.75
111	George Brett	1.50
112	Ozzie Smith	1.00
113	Tony Gwynn	1.00
114	Jack Morris	.05
115	Dave Kingman	.05
116	John Franco	.05
117	Tim Wallach	.05

118	Cal Ripken Jr.	2.00
119	Harold Baines	.05
120	Leon Durham	.05
121	Nolan Ryan	2.00
122	Dennis (Oil Can) Boyd	.05
123	Matt Young	.05
124	Shane Rawley	.05
125	Bruce Sutter	.65
126	Robin Yount	.75
127	Frank Viola	.05
128	Vida Blue	.05
129	Rick Reuschel	.05
130	Pete Incaviglia	.05

1988 Red Foley Stickers

Identical in format to the previous year's issues, the 104 player and 26 team logo stickers in this set were bound into a 96-page, 8-1/2" x 11" softbound book titled "Red Foley's Best Baseball Book Ever." Each 1-3/8" x 1-3/4" sticker could be placed in the book as an answer to trivia questions, quizzes, games, etc. Stickers have color player photos with a number in the white border at bottom. There is no player identification on the stickers. Original issue price was about $8.

		NM/M
Complete Book:		9.00
Complete Sticker Set (130):		6.00
Common Player:		.05
1	Mike Aldrete	.05
2	Andy Ashby	.05
3	Harold Baines	.05
4	Floyd Bannister	.05
5	Buddy Bell	.05
6	George Bell	.05
7	Barry Bonds	2.00
8	Scott Bradley	.05
9	Bob Brower	.05
10	Ellis Burks	.05
11	Casey Candaele	.05
12	Jack Clark	.05
13	Roger Clemens	1.25
14	Kal Daniels	.05
15	Eric Davis	.05
16	Mike Davis	.05
17	Andre Dawson	.25
18	Rob Deer	.05
19	Brian Downing	.05
20	Doug Drabek	.05
21	Dwight Evans	.05
22	Sid Fernandez	.05
23	Carlton Fisk	.75
24	Scott Fletcher	.05
25	Julio Franco	.05
26	Gary Gaetti	.05
27	Ken Gerhardt	.05
28	Ken Griffey	.05
29	Pedro Guerrero	.05
30	Billy Hatcher	.05
31	Mike Heath	.05
32	Neal Heaton	.05
33	Tom Henke	.05
34	Larry Herndon	.05
35	Brian Holton	.05
36	Glenn Hubbard	.05
37	Bruce Hurst	.05
38	Bo Jackson	.10
39	Michael Jackson	.05
40	Howard Johnson	.05
41	Wally Joyner	.05
42	Jimmy Key	.05
43	Ray Knight	.05
44	John Kruk	.05
45	Mike Krukow	.05
46	Mark Langston	.05
47	Gene Larkin	.05
48	Jeff Leonard	.05
49	Bill Long	.05
50	Fred Lynn	.05
51	Dave Magadan	.05
52	Joe Magrane	.05
53	Don Mattingly	1.50
54	Fred McGriff	.05
55	Mark McGwire	1.75
56	Kevin McReynolds	.05
57	Dave Meads	.05
58	Keith Moreland	.05
59	Dale Murphy	.30
60	Juan Nieves	.05
61	Paul Noce	.05
62	Matt Nokes	.05
63	Pete O'Brien	.05
64	Paul O'Neill	.05
65	Lance Parrish	.05
66	Larry Parrish	.05
67	Tony Pena	.05
68	Terry Pendleton	.05
69	Ken Phelps	.05
70	Dan Plesac	.05
71	Luis Polonia	.05
72	Kirby Puckett	1.00
73	Jeff Reardon	.05
74	Rick Rhoden	.05
75	Dave Righetti	.05
76	Cal Ripken Jr.	2.00
77	Bret Saberhagen	.05
78	Benito Santiago	.05
79	Mike Schmidt	1.50
80	Dick Schofield	.05
81	Mike Scott	.05
82	John Smiley	.05
83	Cory Snyder	.05
84	Franklin Stubbs	.05
85	B.J. Surhoff	.05
86	Rick Sutcliffe	.05
87	Pat Tabler	.05
88	Jose Tartabull (Danny)	.05
89	Garry Templeton	.05
90	Walt Terrell	.05
91	Andre Thornton	.05
92	Andy Van Slyke	.05
93	Ozzie Virgil	.05
94	Tim Wallach	.05
95	Gary Ward	.05
96	Mark Wasinger	.05
97	Mitch Webster	.05
98	Bob Welch	.05
99	Devon White	.05
100	Frank White	.05
101	Ed Whitson	.05
102	Bill Wilkinson	.05
103	Glenn Wilson	.05
104	Curt Young	.05
105	Braves logo	.05
106	Phillies logo	.05
107	Padres logo	.05
108	Giants logo	.05
109	Orioles logo	.05
110	Tigers logo	.05
111	Pirates logo	.05
112	Royals logo	.05
113	Astros logo	.05
114	Indians logo	.05
115	Brewers logo	.05
116	Cardinals logo	.05
117	White Sox logo	.05
118	Blue Jays logo	.05
119	Red Sox logo	.05
120	Athletics logo	.05
121	Cubs logo	.05
122	Mariners logo	.05
123	Rangers logo	.05
124	Dodgers logo	.05
125	Yankees logo	.05
126	Mets logo	.05
127	Twins logo	.05
128	Expos logo	.05
129	Angels logo	.05
130	Reds logo	.05

1989 Red Foley Stickers

In its third consecutive year of publication, "Red Foley's Best Baseball Book Ever" retained its 96-page softbound 8-1/2" x 11" format of trivia, quizzes and games to be illustrated by placing one of 130 player stickers in the book. Individual stickers are 1-3/8" x 1-3/4" and feature color photos with a white border. Sticker number appears in the bottom-right. There is no player identification on the sticker. Original price of the book was about $8.

		NM/M
Complete Book:		9.00
Complete Sticker Set (130):		7.50
Common Player:		.05
1	Doyle Alexander	.05
2	Luis Alicea	.05
3	Roberto Alomar	.15
4	Andy Ashby	.05
5	Floyd Bannister	.05
6	Jesse Barfield	.05
7	George Bell	.05
8	Wade Boggs	1.00
9	Barry Bonds	2.00
10	Bobby Bonilla	.05
11	Chris Bosio	.05
12	George Brett	1.50
13	Hubie Brooks	.05
14	Tom Brunansky	.05
15	Tim Burke	.05
16	Ivan Calderon	.05
17	Tom Candiotti	.05
18	Jose Canseco	.50
19	Gary Carter	.75
20	Joe Carter	.05
21	Jack Clark	.05
22	Will Clark	.10
23	Roger Clemens	1.25
24	David Cone	.05
25	Ed Correa	.05
26	Kal Daniels	.05
27	Al Davis	.05
28	Chili Davis	.05
29	Eric Davis	.05
30	Glen Davis	.05
31	Jody Davis	.05
32	Mark Davis	.05
33	Andre Dawson	.25
34	Rob Deer	.05
35	Jose DeLeon	.05
36	Bo Diaz	.05
37	Bill Doran	.05
38	Shawon Dunston	.05
39	Dennis Eckersley	.60
40	Dwight Evans	.05
41	Tony Fernandez	.05
42	Brian Fisher	.05
43	Carlton Fisk	.75
44	Mike Flanagan	.05
45	John Franco	.05
46	Gary Gaetti	.05
47	Andres Galarraga	.05
48	Scott Garrelts	.05
49	Kirk Gibson	.05
50	Dan Gladden	.05
51	Dwight Gooden	.05
52	Pedro Guerrero	.05
53	Ozzie Guillen	.05
54	Tony Gwynn	1.00
55	Mel Hall	.05
56	Von Hayes	.05
57	Keith Hernandez	.05
58	Orel Hershiser	.05
59	Ted Higuera	.05
60	Charlie Hough	.05
61	Jack Howell	.05
62	Kent Hrbek	.05
63	Pete Incaviglia	.05
64	Bo Jackson	.10
65	Brook Jacoby	.05
66	Chris James	.05
67	Lance Johnson	.05
68	Wally Joyner	.05
69	John Kruk	.05
70	Mike LaCoss	.05
71	Mark Langston	.05
72	Carney Lansford	.05
73	Barry Larkin	.05
74	Mike LaValliere	.05
75	Jose Lind	.05
76	Fred Lynn	.05
77	Greg Maddux	1.00
78	Candy Maldonado	.05
79	Don Mattingly	1.50
80	Mark McGwire	1.75
81	Paul Molitor	.75
82	Jack Morris	.05
83	Lloyd Moseby	.05
84	Dale Murphy	.30
85	Eddie Murray	.75
86	Matt Nokes	.05
87	Pete O'Brien	.05
88	Rafael Palmeiro	.65
89	Melido Perez	.05
90	Gerald Perry	.05
91	Tim Raines	.05
92	Willie Randolph	.05
93	Johnny Ray	.05
94	Jeff Reardon	.05
95	Jody Reed	.05
96	Harold Reynolds	.05
97	Dave Righetti	.05
98	Billy Ripken	.05
99	Cal Ripken Jr.	2.00
100	Nolan Ryan	2.00
101	Juan Samuel	.05
102	Benito Santiago	.05
103	Steve Sax	.05
104	Mike Schmidt	1.50
105	Rick Schu	.05
106	Mike Scott	.05
107	Kevin Seitzer	.05
108	Ruben Sierra	.05
109	Lee Smith	.05
110	Ozzie Smith	1.00
111	Zane Smith	.05
112	Dave Stewart	.05
113	Darryl Strawberry	.05
114	Bruce Sutter	.65
115	Bill Swift	.05
116	Greg Swindell	.05
117	Frank Tanana	.05
118	Danny Tartabull	.05
119	Milt Thompson	.05
120	Rob Thompson	.05
121	Alan Trammell	.05
122	John Tudor	.05
123	Fernando Valenzuela	.05
124	Dave Valle	.05
125	Frank Viola	.05
126	Ozzie Virgil	.05
127	Tim Wallach	.05
128	Dave Winfield	.75
129	Mike Witt	.05
130	Robin Yount	.75

1990 Red Foley Stickers

In its fourth consecutive year of publication, "Red Foley's Best Baseball Book Ever" retained its 96-page softbound 8-1/2" x 11" format of trivia, quizzes and games to be illustrated by placing one of 104 player or 26 team logo stickers in the book. Individual stickers are 1-3/8" x 1-3/4" and feature color photos with a white border. Sticker number appears in the bottom-right. There is no player identification on the sticker.

		NM/M
Complete Book:		9.00
Complete Sticker Set (130):		7.00
Common Player:		.05
1	Allan Anderson	.05
2	Scott Bailes	.05
3	Jeff Ballard	.05
4	Jesse Barfield	.05
5	Bert Blyleven	.05
6	Wade Boggs	1.00
7	Barry Bonds	2.00
8	Chris Bosio	.05
9	George Brett	1.50
10	Tim Burke	.05
11	Ellis Burks	.05
12	Brett Butler	.05
13	Ivan Calderon	.05
14	Jose Canseco	.50
15	Joe Carter	.05
16	Jack Clark	.05
17	Will Clark	.10
18	Roger Clemens	1.25
19	Vince Coleman	.05
20	Eric Davis	.05
21	Glenn Davis	.05
22	Mark Davis	.05
23	Andre Dawson	.05
24	Rob Deer	.05
25	Jose DeLeon	.05
26	Jim Deshaies	.05
27	Doug Drabek	.05
28	Lenny Dykstra	.05
29	Dennis Eckersley	.65
30	Steve Farr	.05
31	Tony Fernandez	.05
32	Carlton Fisk	.75
33	John Franco	.05
34	Julio Franco	.05
35	Andres Galarraga	.05
36	Tom Glavine	.25
37	Dwight Gooden	.05
38	Mark Grace	.10
39	Mike Greenwell	.05
40	Ken Griffey Jr.	1.25
41	Kelly Gruber	.05
42	Pedro Guerrero	.05
43	Tony Gwynn	1.00
44	Bryan Harvey	.05
45	Von Hayes	.05
46	Willie Hernandez	.05
47	Tommy Herr	.05
48	Orel Hershiser	.05
49	Jay Howell	.05
50	Kent Hrbek	.05
51	Bo Jackson	.05
52	Steve Jeltz	.05
53	Jimmy Key	.05
54	Ron Kittle	.05
55	Mark Langston	.05
56	Carney Lansford	.05
57	Barry Larkin	.05
58	Jeffrey Leonard	.05
59	Don Mattingly	1.50
60	Fred McGriff	.05
61	Mark McGwire	1.75
62	Kevin McReynolds	.05
63	Randy Myers	.05
64	Kevin Mitchell	.05
65	Paul Molitor	.75
66	Mike Morgan	.05
67	Dale Murphy	.30
68	Eddie Murray	.75
69	Matt Nokes	.05
70	Greg Olson	.05
71	Paul O'Neill	.05
72	Rafael Palmeiro	.65
73	Lance Parrish	.05
74	Dan Plesac	.05
75	Kirby Puckett	1.00
76	Jeff Reardon	.05
77	Rick Reuschel	.05
78	Cal Ripken Jr.	2.00
79	Dave Righetti	.05
80	Jeff Russell	.05
81	Nolan Ryan	2.00
82	Benito Santiago	.05
83	Steve Sax	.05
84	Mike Schooler	.05
85	Mike Scott	.05
86	Kevin Seitzer	.05
87	Dave Smith	.05
88	Lonnie Smith	.05
89	Ozzie Smith	1.00
90	John Smoltz	.05
91	Cory Snyder	.05
92	Darryl Strawberry	.05
93	Greg Swindell	.05
94	Mickey Tettleton	.05
95	Bobby Thigpen	.05
96	Alan Trammell	.05
97	Dave Valle	.05
98	Andy Van Slyke	.05
99	Tim Wallach	.05
100	Jerome Walton	.05
101	Lou Whitaker	.05
102	Devon White	.05
103	Mitch Williams	.05
104	Glen Wilson	.05
105	Indians logo	.05
106	Rangers logo	.05
107	Reds logo	.05
108	Orioles logo	.05
109	Red Sox logo	.05
110	White Sox logo	.05
111	Dodgers logo	.05
112	Tigers logo	.05
113	Mariners logo	.05
114	Blue Jays logo	.05
115	Expos logo	.05
116	Pirates logo	.05
117	Astros logo	.05
118	Cardinals logo	.05
119	Padres logo	.05
120	Angels logo	.05
121	Yankees logo	.05
122	Cubs logo	.05
123	Brewers logo	.05
124	Twins logo	.05
125	Giants logo	.05
126	Royals logo	.05
127	A's logo	.05
128	Mets logo	.05
129	Phillies logo	.05
130	Braves logo	.05

1991 Red Foley Stickers

In its fifth consecutive year of publication, "Red Foley's Best Baseball Book Ever" retained its 96-page softbound 8-1/2" x 11" format of trivia, quizzes and games to be illustrated by placing one of 112 regular player or 18 All-Star (#113-130) stickers in the book. Individual stickers are 1-3/8" x 1-3/4" and feature color photos with a white border. Sticker number appears in the bottom-right. There is no player identification on the sticker.

		NM/M
Complete Book:		10.00
Comlete Sticker Set (130):		8.00
Common Player:		.05
1	Jim Abbott	.05
2	Rick Aguilera	.05
3	Roberto Alomar	.30
4	Rob Dibble	.05
5	Wally Backman	.05
6	Harold Baines	.05
7	Steve Bedrosian	.05
8	Craig Biggio	.05
9	Wade Boggs	1.00
10	Bobby Bonilla	.05
11	George Brett	1.25
12	Greg Brock	.05
13	Hubie Brooks	.05
14	Tom Brunansky	.05
15	Tim Burke	.05
16	Tom Candiotti	.05
17	Jose Canseco	.50
18	Jack Clark	.05
19	Will Clark	.10
20	Roger Clemens	1.25
21	Vince Coleman	.05
22	Kal Daniels	.05
23	Glenn Davis	.05
24	Mark Davis	.05
25	Andre Dawson	.25
26	Rob Deer	.05
27	Delino DeShields	.05
28	Doug Drabek	.05
29	Shawon Dunston	.05
30	Lenny Dykstra	.05
31	Dennis Eckersley	.35
32	Kevin Elster	.05
33	Tony Fernandez	.05
34	Cecil Fielder	.05
35	Chuck Finley	.05
36	Carlton Fisk	.75
37	Greg Gagne	.05
38	Ron Gant	.05
39	Dan Gladden	.05
40	Dwight Gooden	.05
41	Ken Griffey Jr.	1.50
42	Kelly Gruber	.05
43	Pedro Guerrero	.05
44	Ozzie Guillen	.05
45	Pete Harnisch	.05
46	Billy Hatcher	.05
47	Von Hayes	.05
48	Rickey Henderson	.75
49	Mike Henneman	.05
50	Kent Hrbek	.05
51	Pete Incaviglia	.05
52	Howard Johnson	.05
53	Randy Johnson	.75
54	Doug Jones	.05
55	Ricky Jordan	.05
56	Wally Joyner	.05
57	Roberto Kelly	.05
58	Barry Larkin	.05
59	Craig Lefferts	.05
60	Candy Maldonado	.05
61	Don Mattingly	1.25
62	Oddibe McDowell	.05
63	Roger McDowell	.05
64	Willie McGee	.05
65	Fred McGriff	.05
66	Kevin Mitchell	.05
67	Mike Morgan	.05
68	Eddie Murray	.75
69	Gregg Olson	.05
70	Joe Orsulak	.05
71	Dan Petry	.05
72	Dan Plesac	.05
73	Jim Presley	.05
74	Kirby Puckett	1.00
75	Tim Raines	.05
76	Jeff Reardon	.05
77	Dave Righetti	.05
78	Cal Ripken Jr.	2.00
79	Nolan Ryan	2.00
80	Bret Saberhagen	.05
81	Chris Sabo	.05
82	Ryne Sandberg	1.00
83	Benito Santiago	.05
84	Steve Sax	.05
85	Mike Schooler	.05
86	Mike Scott	.05
87	Ruben Sierra	.05
88	Cory Snyder	.05
89	Dave Steib	.05
90	Dave Stewart	.05
91	Kurt Stillwell	.05
92	Bobby Thigpen	.05
93	Alan Trammell	.05
94	John Tudor	.05
95	Dave Valle	.05
96	Andy Van Slyke	.05
97	Robin Ventura	.05
98	Frank Viola	.05
99	Tim Wallach	.05
100	Matt Williams	.05
101	Mitch Williams	.05
102	Dave Winfield	.75
103	Eric Yelding	.05
104	Robin Yount	.75
105	Steve Avery	.05
106	Travis Fryman	.05
107	Juan Gonzalez	.40
108	Todd Hundley	.05
109	Ben McDonald	.05
110	Jose Offerman	.05
111	Frank Thomas	.75
112	Bernie Williams	.10
113	Sandy Alomar Jr.	.05
114	Jack Armstrong	.05
115	Wade Boggs	.40
116	Jose Canseco	.05
117	Will Clark	.10
118	Andre Dawson	.05
119	Lenny Dykstra	.05
120	Ken Griffey Jr.	.65
121	Rickey Henderson	.40

122	Mark McGwire	1.75
123	Kevin Mitchell	.05
124	Cal Ripken Jr.	1.00
125	Chris Sabo	.05
126	Ryne Sandberg	.50
127	Steve Sax	.05
128	Mike Scoscia	.05
129	Ozzie Smith	.50
130	Bob Welch	.05

1992 Red Foley Stickers

The format was unchanged when "Red Foley's Best Baseball Book Ever" was published in 1992. The 96-page, 8-1/2" x 11" softcover book features 96 pages of quizzes, trivia and games, along with 130 player stickers (#105-130 are All-Star stickers) to be placed on the proper pages. Single stickers measure 1-3/8" x 1-3/4" and have color photos with a white border. A sticker number is in the bottom-right. No player identification appears on the stickers. Issue price of the book was about $9.

		NM/M
Complete Book:		12.00
Complete Sticker Set (130):		10.00
Common Player:		.05
1	Jim Abbott	.05
2	Roberto Alomar	.15
3	Sandy Alomar Jr.	.05
4	Eric Anthony	.05
5	Kevin Appier	.05
6	Jack Armstrong	.05
7	Steve Avery	.05
8	Carlos Baerga	.05
9	Scott Bankhead	.05
10	George Bell	.05
11	Albert Belle	.05
12	Andy Benes	.05
13	Craig Biggio	.05
14	Wade Boggs	1.00
15	Barry Bonds	2.00
16	Bobby Bonilla	.05
17	Sid Bream	.05
18	George Brett	1.25
19	Hubie Brooks	.05
20	Ellis Burks	.05
21	Brett Butler	.05
22	Jose Canseco	.40
23	Joe Carter	.05
24	Jack Clark	.05
25	Will Clark	.05
26	Roger Clemens	1.25
27	Vince Coleman	.05
28	Eric Davis	.05
29	Glenn Davis	.05
30	Andre Dawson	.25
31	Rob Deer	.05
32	Delino DeShields	.05
33	Lenny Dykstra	.05
34	Scott Erickson	.05
35	Cecil Fielder	.05
36	Carlton Fisk	.75
37	Travis Fryman	.05
38	Greg Gagne	.05
39	Juan Gonzalez	.40
40	Tommy Greene	.05
41	Ken Griffey Jr.	1.50
42	Kent Hrbek	.05
43	Kelly Gruber	.05
44	Tony Gwynn	1.00
45	Dave Henderson	.05
46	Rickey Henderson	.75
47	Orel Hershiser	.05
48	Marquis Grissom	.05
49	Howard Johnson	.05
50	Felix Jose	.05
51	Wally Joyner	.05
52	David Justice	.05
53	Roberto Kelly	.05
54	Ray Lankford	.05
55	Barry Larkin	.05
56	Mark Lewis	.05
57	Kevin Maas	.05
58	Greg Maddux	1.00
59	Dennis Martinez	.05
60	Edgar Martinez	.05
61	Don Mattingly	1.50
62	Ben McDonald	.05
63	Jack McDowell	.05
64	Willie McGee	.05
65	Fred McGriff	.05
66	Brian McRae	.05
67	Mark McGwire	1.75
68	Kevin Mitchell	.05
69	Terry Mulholland	.05
70	Dale Murphy	.25
71	Eddie Murray	.75
72	John Olerud	.05
73	Rafael Palmeiro	.65
74	Terry Pendleton	.05
75	Luis Polonia	.05
76	Mark Portugal	.05
77	Kirby Puckett	1.00
78	Tim Raines	.05
79	Harold Reynolds	.05
80	Billy Ripken	.05
81	Cal Ripken Jr.	2.00
82	Nolan Ryan	2.00
83	Chris Sabo	.05
84	Ryne Sandberg	1.00
85	Benito Santiago	.05
86	Kevin Seitzer	.05
87	Gary Sheffield	.30
88	Ruben Sierra	.05
89	John Smiley	.05
90	Ozzie Smith	1.00
91	Darryl Strawberry	.05
92	B.J. Surhoff	.05
93	Frank Thomas	.75
94	Alan Trammell	.05
95	Andy Van Slyke	.05
96	Greg Vaughn	.05
97	Frank Viola	.05
98	Tim Wallach	.05
99	Matt Williams	.05
100	Dave Winfield	.75
101	Mike Witt	.05
102	Eric Yelding	.05
103	Robin Yount	.75
104	Todd Zeile	.05
105	Roberto Alomar	.10
106	Sandy Alomar, Jr.	.05
107	Wade Boggs	.50
108	Bobby Bonilla	.05
109	Ivan Calderon	.05
110	Will Clark	.05
111	Andre Dawson	.05
112	Cecil Fielder	.05
113	Carlton Fisk	.30
114	Tom Glavine	.25
115	Ken Griffey Jr.	.65
116	Tony Gwynn	.50
117	Dave Henderson	.05
118	Rickey Henderson	.05
119	Felix Jose	.05
120	Jimmy Key	.05
121	Tony LaRussa	.05
122	Jack Morris	.05
123	Lou Piniella	.05
124	Cal Ripken Jr.	1.00
125	Chris Sabo	.05
126	Juan Samuel	.05
127	Ryne Sandberg	.50
128	Benito Santiago	.05
129	Ozzie Smith	.50
130	Danny Tartabull	.05

1993 Red Foley Stickers

The format was unchanged when "Red Foley's Best Baseball Book Ever" was published in 1993. The 96-page, 8-1/2" x 11" softcover book features 96 pages of quizzes, trivia and games, along with 130 player stickers (#105-130 are All-Star stickers) to be placed on the proper pages. Single stickers measure 1-3/8" x 1-3/4" and have color photos with a white border. A sticker number is in the bottom-right. No player identification appears on the stickers.

		NM/M
Complete Book:		10.00
Complete Sticker Set (130):		9.00
Common Player:		.05
1	Jim Abbott	.05
2	Roberto Alomar	.15
3	Sandy Alomar Jr.	.05
4	Steve Avery	.05
5	Jeff Bagwell	.75
6	Harold Baines	.05
7	Bret Barberie	.05
8	Derek Bell	.05
9	Jay Bell	.05
10	Albert Belle	.05
11	Andy Benes	.05
12	Craig Biggio	.05
13	Wade Boggs	1.00
14	Barry Bonds	2.00
15	Bobby Bonilla	.05
16	Jose Canseco	.40
17	Joe Carter	.05
18	Wes Chamberlain	.05
19	Will Clark	.10
20	Roger Clemens	1.25
21	Milt Cuyler	.05
22	Eric Davis	.05
23	Delino DeShields	.05
24	Rob Dibble	.05
25	Doug Drabek	.05
26	Shawon Dunston	.05
27	Lenny Dykstra	.05
28	Scott Erickson	.05
29	Cecil Fielder	.05
30	Steve Finley	.05
31	Tom Glavine	.25
32	Dwight Gooden	.05
33	Mark Grace	.10
34	Ken Griffey Jr.	1.50
35	Marquis Grissom	.05
36	Kelly Gruber	.05
37	Mark Gubicza	.05
38	Tony Gwynn	1.00
39	Mel Hall	.05
40	Pete Harnisch	.05
41	Brian Harper	.05
42	Bryan Harvey	.05
43	Rickey Henderson	.75
44	Orel Hershiser	.05
45	Gregg Jefferies	.05
46	Howard Johnson	.05
47	Felix Jose	.05
48	Wally Joyner	.05
49	David Justice	.05
50	Roberto Kelly	.05
51	Chuck Knoblauch	.05
52	John Kruk	.05
53	Barry Larkin	.05
54	Kenny Lofton	.05
55	Greg Maddux	1.00
56	Dennis Martinez	.05
57	Edgar Martinez	.05
58	Tino Martinez	.05
59	Don Mattingly	1.25
60	Jack McDowell	.05
61	Willie McGee	.05
62	Fred McGriff	.05
63	Mark McGwire	1.75
64	Brian McRae	.05
65	Randy Milligan	.05
66	Kevin Mitchell	.05
67	Paul Molitor	.75
68	Dale Murphy	.25
69	Mike Mussina	.40
70	Charles Nagy	.05
71	Gregg Olson	.05
72	Rafael Palmeiro	.65
73	Dean Palmer	.05
74	Phil Plantier	.05
75	Luis Polonia	.05
76	Kirby Puckett	1.00
77	Tim Raines	.05
78	Cal Ripken Jr.	2.00
79	Bip Roberts	.05
80	Ivan Rodriguez	.65
81	Nolan Ryan	2.00
82	Bret Saberhagen	.05
83	Ryne Sandberg	1.00
84	Deion Sanders	.10
85	Reggie Sanders	.05
86	Benito Santiago	.05
87	Mike Scoscia	.05
88	Lee Smith	.05
89	Ozzie Smith	1.00
90	Lee Stevens	.05
91	Darryl Strawberry	.05
92	B.J. Surhoff	.05
93	Danny Tartabull	.05
94	Mickey Tettleton	.05
95	Frank Thomas	.75
96	Robby Thompson	.05
97	Alan Trammell	.05
98	Greg Vaughn	.05
99	Mo Vaughn	.05
100	Andy Van Slyke	.05
101	Robin Ventura	.05
102	Matt Williams	.05
103	Robin Yount	.75
104	Todd Zeile	.05
105	Roberto Alomar	.15
106	Sandy Alomar Jr.	.05
107	Wade Boggs	.50
108	Kevin Brown	.05
109	Joe Carter	.05
110	Will Clark	.05
111	Bobby Cox	.05
112	Dennis Eckersley	.40
113	Tony Fernandez	.05
114	Tom Glavine	.05
115	Ken Griffey Jr.	.65
116	Tony Gwynn	.50
117	Tom Kelly	.05
118	John Kruk	.05
119	Fred McGriff	.05
120	Mark McGwire	.75
121	Kirby Puckett	.50
122	Cal Ripken Jr.	1.00
123	Bip Roberts	.05
124	Ivan Rodriguez	.20
125	Gary Sheffield	.25
126	Ruben Sierra	.05
127	Ozzie Smith	.50
128	Andy Van Slyke	.05
129	Robin Ventura	.05
130	Larry Walker	.05

1994 Red Foley

SUPERSTAR

Beginning in 1994, major changes were seen in "Red Foley's Best Baseball Book Ever." The book remained in 8-1/2" x 11" format, but was downsized to 64 pages. The previous years' stickers were replaced with four nine-card sheets of perforated baseball cards. When separated from the sheets, cards measure the standard 2-1/2" x 3-1/2". The unnumbered cards appear in two types. "Superstar" cards feature a single player in a color action photo on front. "Team Leaders" cards have two teammates on front. Red and black printing on backs give personal data and career highlights. Original retail cost of the book was $8.95.

		NM/M
Complete Book:		15.00
Complete Set (36):		12.00
Common Card:		.25
(1)	Barry Bonds	2.00
(2)	Joe Carter	.25
(3)	Roger Clemens	1.25
(4)	Juan Gonzalez	.60
(5)	Ken Griffey Jr.	1.50
(6)	Fred McGriff	.25
(7)	Jose Rijo	.25
(8)	Ryne Sandberg	1.00
(9)	Angels (Tim Salmon, Mark Langston)	.25
(10)	Astros (Jeff Bagwell, Doug Drabek)	.50
(11)	Athletics (Mark McGwire, Dennis Eckersley)	.75
(12)	Blue Jays (Roberto Alomar, John Olerud)	.30
(13)	Braves (Greg Maddux, Tom Glavine)	.60
(14)	Brewers (Robin Yount, Cal Eldred)	.50
(15)	Cardinals (Ray Lankford, Ozzie Smith)	.60
(16)	Cubs (Mark Grace, Randy Myers)	.30
(17)	Dodgers (Mike Piazza, Orel Hershiser)	.65
(18)	Expos (Larry Walker, Marquis Grissom)	.25
(19)	Giants (Will Clark, Matt Williams)	.25
(20)	Indians (Albert Belle, Carlos Baerga)	.25
(21)	Mariners (Jay Buhner, Randy Johnson)	.40
(22)	Marlins (Gary Sheffield, Bryan Harvey)	.25
(23)	Mets (Bobby Bonilla, Dwight Gooden)	.25
(24)	Orioles (Cal Ripken Jr., Mike Mussina)	1.00
(25)	Padres (Andy Benes, Tony Gwynn)	.60
(26)	Phillies (John Kruk, Tommy Greene)	.25
(27)	Pirates (Jay Bell, Andy Van Slyke)	.25
(28)	Rangers (Jose Canseco, Kevin Brown)	.35
(29)	Reds (Barry Larkin, Reggie Sanders)	.25
(30)	Red Sox (Mo Vaughn, Frank Viola)	.25
(31)	Rockies (Charlie Hayes, Andres Galarraga)	.25
(32)	Royals (Brian McRae, David Cone)	.25
(33)	Tigers (Cecil Fielder, Mike Henneman)	.25
(34)	Twins (Kirby Puckett, Rick Aguilera)	.60
(35)	White Sox (Frank Thomas, Jack McDowell)	.50
(36)	Yankees (Don Mattingly, Jim Abbott)	.75

1995 Red Foley

The Red Foley book of children's games, quizzes, trivia and other baseball related entertainment reprised its 1994 format for 1995. The 36 perforated insert cards, 2-1/2" x 3-1/2", were again divided into single-player "Superstar" and two-player "Team Leaders" types. Designs were identical to the previous year, with color action photos on front and career highlights on back. The unnumbered cards are checklisted here in alphabetical order by type.

		NM/M
Complete Book:		15.00
Complete Set (36):		12.00
Common Card:		.25
(1)	Barry Bonds	2.00
(2)	Joe Carter	.25
(3)	Roger Clemens	1.00
(4)	Juan Gonzalez	.60
(5)	Ken Griffey Jr.	1.50
(6)	Fred McGriff	.25
(7)	Cal Ripken Jr.	2.00
(8)	Frank Thomas	.75
(9)	Angels (Tim Salmon, Steve Finley)	.35
(10)	Astros (Jeff Bagwell, Craig Biggio)	.50
(11)	Athletics (Mark McGwire, Dennis Eckersley)	.75
(12)	Blue Jays (Roberto Alomar, John Olerud)	.35
(13)	Braves (Greg Maddux, David Justice)	.60
(14)	Brewers (Cal Eldred, Dave Nillson)	.25
(15)	Cardinals (Ozzie Smith, Gregg Jefferies)	.60
(16)	Cubs (Mark Grace, Randy Myers)	.35
(17)	Dodgers (Mike Piazza, Orel Hershiser)	.65
(18)	Expos (Larry Walker, Ken Hill)	.25
(19)	Giants (Matt Williams, Rod Beck)	.25
(20)	Indians (Albert Belle, Carlos Baerga)	.25
(21)	Mariners (Jay Buhner, Randy Johnson)	.40
(22)	Marlins (Gary Sheffield, Benito Santiago)	.25
(23)	Mets (Bret Saberhagen, Bobby Bonilla)	.25
(24)	Orioles (Rafael Palmeiro, Mike Mussina)	.40
(25)	Padres (Tony Gwynn, Andy Benes)	.60
(26)	Phillies (John Kruk, Lenny Dykstra)	.25
(27)	Pirates (Andy Van Slyke, Al Martin)	.25
(28)	Rangers (Jose Canseco, Will Clark)	.35
(29)	Reds (Barry Larkin, Jose Rijo)	.25
(30)	Red Sox (Mo Vaughn, Aaron Sele)	.25
(31)	Rockies (Andres Galarraga, Dante Bichette)	.25
(32)	Royals (Brian McRae, David Cone)	.25
(33)	Tigers (Cecil Fielder, Travis Fryman)	.25
(34)	Twins (Kirby Puckett, Rick Aguilera)	.60
(35)	White Sox (Robin Ventura, Wilson Alvarez)	.25
(36)	Yankees (Don Mattingly, Jimmy Key)	.65

1996 Red Foley

WALLY JOYNER — FIRST BASE

The Red Foley book of children's games, quizzes, trivia and other baseball related entertainment changed little for its 1996 edition. The number of cards was decreased to 32 and the size to a 2" x 2-3/4" perforated format. Only single-player cards were produced. Designs were nearly identical to the previous year, with color action photos on front and career highlights on back. The unnumbered cards are checklisted here in alphabetical order.

		NM/M
Complete Book:		12.00
Complete Set (32):		9.00
Common Player:		.25
(1)	Roberto Alomar	.30
(2)	Moises Alou	.25
(3)	Carlos Baerga	.25
(4)	Jay Bell	.25
(5)	Craig Biggio	.25
(6)	Barry Bonds	1.50
(7)	Jeff Conine	.25
(8)	Lenny Dykstra	.25
(9)	Cecil Fielder	.25
(10)	Ken Griffey Jr.	1.00
(11a)	Tony Gwynn/Red	.75
(11b)	Tony Gwynn/Purple	.75
(12)	Rickey Henderson	.65
(13)	Wally Joyner	.25
(14)	Barry Larkin	.25
(15)	Mark McGwire	1.25
(16)	Eddie Murray	.65
(17)	Rafael Palmeiro	.50
(18)	Mike Piazza	1.00
(19)	Greg Maddux	.75
(20)	Paul O'Neill	.25
(21)	Kirby Puckett	.75
(22)	Bill Pulsipher	.25
(23)	Cal Ripken Jr.	1.50
(24)	Ivan Rodriguez	.50
(25)	Kenny Rogers	.25
(26)	Tim Salmon	.30
(27)	Kevin Seitzer	.25
(28)	Ozzie Smith	.75
(29)	Sammy Sosa	.90
(30)	Frank Thomas	.25
(31)	Mo Vaughn	.25
(32)	Larry Walker	.25

1988 Foot Locker Slam Fest

Two baseball players are among the athletes pictured in this Foot Locker set issued in conjunction with the shoe store chain's Slam Fest competition. Cards were given away at local stores. The 2-1/2" x 3-1/2" cards have color player portrait photos on a semi-gloss front. All athletes are pictured in Slam Dunk basketball jerseys. A sponsor's banner is at top; the chain's referee logo at lower-left. Backs are printed in blue with information about the televised competition and the player's career.

		NM/M
Complete Set (9):		6.00
Common Player:		.50
(1)	Carl Banks/Football	.50
(2)	Mike Conley/SP/Track	.50
(3)	Thomas Hearns/Boxing	2.00
(4)	Bo Jackson	2.00
(5)	Keith Jackson/Football	.50
(6)	Karch Kiraly/Volleyball	.50
(7)	Ricky Sanders/Football	.50
(8)	Dwight Stones/Track	.50
(9)	Devon White	1.00

1989 Foot Locker Slam Fest

VINCE COLEMAN

One baseball player is among the athletes pictured in this Foot Locker set issued in conjunction with the shoe store chain's Slam Fest competition. Cards were given away at local stores. The 2-1/2" x 3-1/2" cards have color player portrait photos on a semi-gloss front. All athletes are pictured in Slam Dunk basketball jerseys. A sponsor's banner is at top. Backs have information about the televised competition and the player's career.

	NM/M
Complete Set (10):	3.00
Common Player:	.35
1 Mike Conley/Track	.40
2 Keith Jackson/Football	.75
3 Vince Coleman	1.00
4 Eric Dickerson/ Football	2.00
5 Steve Timmons/ Volleyball	.40
6 Matt Biondi/Swimming	.50
7 Carl Lewis/Track	.75
8 Mike Quick/Football	.50
9 Mike Powell/Track	.50
10 Checklist	.05

1991 Foot Locker Slam Fest

BARRY BONDS

A number of baseball players were included among the various current and former athletes in this set of three 10-card series produced in conjunction with the sporting gear retailer's Slam Fest charity event. Players are pictured in color on the 2-1/2" x 3-1/2" cards wearing Nike basketball uniforms.

	NM/M
Complete Set (30):	5.00
Common Player:	.03
1-1 Ken Griffey Jr.	1.50
1-2 Delino DeShields	.10
1-3 Barry Bonds	4.00
1-4 Jack Armstrong	.10
1-5 Dave Justice	.25
1-6 Deion Sanders	.50
1-7 Michael Dean Perry/ Football	.10
1-8 Tim Brown/Football	.10
1-9 Mike Conley/Track	.10
1-10 Mike Powell/Track	.10
10-1 Wilt Chamberlain/ Basketball	1.00
10-2 Carl Ramsey/ Basketball	.10
10-3 Bobby Jones/ Basketball	.10
10-4 John Havlicek/ Basketball	.10
10-5 Calvin Murphy/ Basketball	.10

10-6 Nate Thurmond/ Basketball	.10
10-7 John Havlicek/ Basketball	.10
10-8 Checklist Series 1	.05
10-9 Checklist Series 2	.05
10-10 Checklist Series 3	.05
20-1 Jerry Lucas/Basketball	.25
20-2 Bo Jackson	.25
20-3 Elvin Hayes/Basketball	.10
20-4 Thomas Hearns/Boxing	.25
20-5 Matt Biondi/Swimming	.10
20-6 Earl Monroe/Basketball	.10
20-7 Eric Dickerson/Football	.50
20-8 Carl Lewis/Track	.25
20-9 Wilt and Company/ Basketball	.10
20-10 TV Schedule	.05

1989 Foxes Holsum Super Stars Discs

(See 1989 Holsum for checklist and price guide. Distributed in Carolinas.)

1981 Franchise 1966 Baltimore Orioles

One of the lesser-known producers of collectors' issues in the early 1980s was "The Franchise." Most of their card sets featured subjects of special interest to their home (Maryland) area. This set, for example, features the 1966 Baltimore Orioles World Champions. In 2-1/2" x 3-1/2" size, cards have black-and-white player photos on front surrounded by orange borders. Black-and-white backs are somewhat in the style of 1953 Bowman, with personal data, career highlights and 1966/Lifetime stats.

	NM/M
Complete Set (32):	13.50
Common Player:	.50
1 World Champs 1966	.50
2 Team photo	.50
3 Luis Aparicio	2.50
4 Steve Barber	.50
5 Hank Bauer	.50
6 Paul Blair	.50
7 Curt Blefary	.50
8 Sam Bowens	.50
9 Gene Brabender	.50
10 Harry Brecheen	.50
11 Wally Bunker	.50
12 Moe Drabowsky	.50
13 Andy Etchebarren	.50
14 Eddie Fisher	.50
15 Dick Hall	.50
16 Larry Haney	.50
17 Woody Held	.50
18 Billy Hunter	.50
19 Bob Johnson	.50
20 Dave Johnson	.50
21 Sherman Lollar	.50
22 Dave McNally	.50
23 John Miller	.50
24 Stu Miller	.50
25 Jim Palmer	2.50
26 Boog Powell	1.50
27 Brooks Robinson	3.00
28 Frank Robinson	3.00
29 Vic Roznovsky	.50
30 Russ Snyder	.50
31 Eddie Watt	.50
32 Gene Woodling	.50

1983 Franchise Brooks Robinson

This collectors' issue was produced by a Maryland company which specialized in sets of local interest. Cards detail the career of the Orioles Hall of Famer. Fronts of the 2-1/2" x 3-1/2" cards have a black-and-white photo with orange

graphics. Backs are printed in black, white and orange and provide a title and details about the front photo.

	NM/M
Complete Set (40):	35.00
Common Card:	1.00
1 Professional record	1.00
2 Youngest on team	1.00
3 All-state performer	1.00
4 Teen-ager in Texas	1.00
5 First spring training	1.00
6 Another uniform	1.00
7 First solid infield	1.00
8 Celebration time	1.00
9 Instinctive baserunner	1.00
10 Wedding day	1.00
11 First business partner	1.00
12 Second solid infield	1.00
13 Two Baltimore heroes	1.00
14 Enjoying the kids	1.00
15 Playing every game	1.00
16 Upsetting the Yankees	1.00
17 Tag out at third	1.00
18 Getting net results	1.00
19 The future MVPs	1.50
20 The original Rocky	1.00
21 Bauer's gloveman	1.00
22 World Series infield	1.00
23 Orioles' power parade	1.00
24 All-star trio	1.50
25 Lethal lumber	1.00
26 Belanger joins infield	1.00
27 Respect for Oliva	1.00
28 Out of Harm's way	1.00
29 Master trader	1.00
30 Eastern Shore visit	1.00
31 Gloves of gold	1.00
32 Ripping the Reds	1.00
33 Rappin' with Willie	2.00
34 Using the body	1.00
35 Getting the umps' attention	1.00
36 Respect from teammate	1.00
37 Touch of class	1.00
38 Bubble never burst	1.00
39 Honored by Yankees	1.00
40 Two greats at third	1.00

2002 Franz Bread Seattle Mariners

This team set was produced by Upper Deck and issued regionally with individually cello-wrapped cards inserted into loaves of bread. The cards have game-action photos which are borderless at top and sides. In a wide white strip at bottom are the team name, player name, position and uniform number and a Franz logo. In the upper corners are UD and Mariners 25th Anniversary logos. Backs have a portrait photo, a few words about the player, previous season's stats and various logos and copyright information.

	NM/M
Complete Set (16):	10.00
Common Player:	.50

1	Ichiro	5.00
2	Edgar Martinez	1.00
3	John Olerud	.75
4	Bret Boone	.75
5	Jeff Cirillo	.50
6	Carlos Guillen	.50
7	Mike Cameron	.50
8	Ruben Sierra	.50
9	Ben Davis	.50
10	Freddy Garcia	.50
11	Kazuhiro Sasaki	1.00
12	Jamie Moyer	.50
13	James Baldwin	.50
14	Jeff Nelson	.50
15	Dan Wilson	.50
16	Mark McLemore	.50

1987 French/ Bray Orioles

8 CAL RIPKEN, IF
Compliments of
FRENCH/BRAY, INC.

The Baltimore Orioles and French Bray, Inc. issued a baseball card set to be handed out to fans in attendance at Memorial Stadium on July 26th. Thirty perforated, detachable cards were printed within a three-panel fold-out piece measuring 9-1/2" x 11-1/4". The card fronts feature full-color player photos surrounded by an orange border. The French/Bray logo appears on the card front. The backs are of simple design, containing only the player's name, uniform number, position and professional record.

	NM/M
Complete Set, Panel:	45.00
Complete Set, Singles (30):	40.00
Common Player:	1.00
2 Alan Wiggins	1.00
3 Bill Ripken	1.00
6 Floyd Rayford	1.00
7 Cal Ripken, Sr.	1.00
8 Cal Ripken, Jr.	25.00
9 Jim Dwyer	1.00
12 Terry Crowley	1.00
15 Terry Kennedy	1.00
16 Scott McGregor	1.00
18 Larry Sheets	1.00
19 Fred Lynn	1.00
20 Frank Robinson	4.00
24 Dave Schmidt	1.00
25 Ray Knight	1.00
27 Lee Lacy	1.00
31 Mark Wiley	1.00
32 Mark Williamson	1.00
33 Eddie Murray	12.50
38 Ken Gerhart	1.00
39 Ken Dixon	1.00
40 Jimmy Williams	1.00
42 Mike Griffin	1.00
43 Mike Young	1.00
44 Elrod Hendricks	1.00
45 Eric Bell	1.00
46 Mike Flanagan	1.00
49 Tom Niedenfuer	1.00
52 Mike Boddicker	1.00
54 John Habyan	1.00
57 Tony Arnold	1.00

1988 French/ Bray Orioles

52 MIKE BODDICKER, RHS
Compliments of
FRENCH BRAY, INC.

French Bray sponsored a full-color brochure that was distributed to fans during an in-stadium promotion. A blue and orange front cover features inset photos of the Orioles in action on the upper left in a filmstrip motif. To the right is the Orioles logo and their 1988 slogan, "You Gotta Be There" above a baseball glove and ball. The 3-panel foldout measures approximately 9-1/2" x 11-1/4" and includes a team photo on the inside cover, with two perforated pages of individual cards featuring players, coaches and the team manager. Individual cards measure 2-1/4" x 3-1/8", with close-ups framed in white with an orange accent line. The player name and sponsor logo are printed beneath the photo. The black-and-white backs are numbered by player uniform and provide career stats. Additional copies of the brochure were made available from the Orioles Baseball Store following the free giveaway.

	NM/M
Complete Set, Panel:	70.00
Complete Set, Singles (31):	60.00
Common Player:	1.00
2 Don Buford	1.00
6 Joe Orsulak	1.00
7 Bill Ripken	1.00
8 Cal Ripken, Jr.	40.00
9 Jim Dwyer	1.00
10 Terry Crowley	1.00
12 Mike Morgan	1.00
14 Mickey Tettleton	1.00
15 Terry Kennedy	1.00
17 Pete Stanicek	1.00
18 Larry Sheets	1.00
19 Fred Lynn	1.00
20 Frank Robinson	5.00
23 Ozzie Peraza	1.00
24 Dave Schmidt	1.00
25 Rich Schu	1.00
28 Jim Traber	1.00
31 Herm Starrette	1.00
33 Eddie Murray	15.00
34 Jeff Ballard	1.00
38 Ken Gerhart	1.00
40 Minnie Mendoza	1.00
41 Don Aase	1.00
44 Elrod Hendricks	1.00
47 John Hart	1.00
48 Jose Bautista	1.00
49 Tom Niedenfuer	1.00
52 Mike Boddicker	1.00
53 Jay Tibbs	1.00
88 Rene Gonzales	1.00
— Team photo	5.00

1989 French/ Bray Orioles

16 PHIL BRADLEY, OF
Compliments of
French-Bray, Incorporated
Wilcox Walter Furlong Paper Co.

This 32-card team set was co-sponsored by French-Bray and the Wilcox Walter Furlong Paper Co., and was distributed as an in-stadium promotion to fans attending the May 12 game. Smaller than standard size, the cards measure 2-1/4" x 3" and feature a full-color player photo with number, name and position below. The backs, done in black-and-white, include brief player data and complete major and minor league stats.

	NM/M
Complete Set (32):	20.00
Common Player:	.50
3 Bill Ripken	.50
6 Joe Orsulak	.50

7	Cal Ripken, Sr.	.50
8	Cal Ripken, Jr.	15.00
9	Brady Anderson	1.50
10	Steve Finley	.50
11	Craig Worthington	.50
12	Mike Devereaux	.50
14	Mickey Tettleton	.50
15	Randy Milligan	.50
17	Phil Bradley	.50
18	Bob Milacki	.50
19	Larry Sheets	.50
20	Frank Robinson	4.50
21	Mark Thurmond	.50
22	Kevin Hickey	.50
24	Dave Schmidt	.50
28	Jim Traber	.50
29	Jeff Ballard	.50
30	Gregg Olson	.50
31	Al Jackson	.50
32	Mark Williamson	.50
36	Bob Melvin	.50
37	Brian Holton	.50
42	Tom McCraw	.50
42	Pete Harnisch	.50
43	Fransisco Melendez	.50
44	Elrod Hendricks	.50
48	Johnny Oates	.50
48	Jose Bautista	.50
88	Rene Gonzales	.50
—	Sponsor's card	.50

1992 French's Mustard

In 1992 French's gave away a promotional card with the purchase of its mustard products. Each of the cards displays photographs of two players. The cards, which have team insignias airbrushed out, feature a green border, color photos and the players' statistics on the back.

	NM/M
Complete Set (18):	4.00
Common Card:	.10
1 Jeff Bagwell, Chuck Knoblauch	.50
2 Roger Clemens, Tom Glavine	.65
3 Julio Franco, Terry Pendleton	.10
4 Howard Johnson, Jose Canseco	.35
5 John Smiley, Scott Erickson	.10
6 Bryan Harvey, Lee Smith	.10
7 Kirby Puckett, Barry Bonds	1.00
8 Robin Ventura, Matt Williams	.10
9 Tony Pena, Tom Pagnozzi	.10
10 Benito Santiago, Sandy Alomar, Jr.	.10
11 Don Mattingly, Will Clark	.75
12 Ryne Sandberg, Roberto Alomar	.60
13 Cal Ripken, Jr., Ozzie Smith	1.00
14 Wade Boggs, Chris Sabo	.60
15 Ken Griffey Jr., David Justice	.75
16 Joe Carter, Tony Gwynn	.60
17 Rickey Henderson, Darryl Strawberry	.50
18 Jack Morris, Steve Avery	.10

2003 French's Mustard N.Y. Yankees

Nothing cuts the mustard like French's

This six-card set sponsored by Yankee Stadium's long-time condiments concessionaire was distirubted to fans 14 and under. Produced by Donruss, the standard-sized cards have game-action photos on front with the sponsor's ad message at bottom. Backs have player personal data, career highlights and career stats.

		NM/M
Complete Set (6):		5.00
Common Player:		.25
1	Derek Jeter	4.00
2	Alfonso Soriano	1.00
3	Jorge Posada	.25
4	Jose Contreras	.50
5	Jeff Weaver	.25
6	Steve Karsay	.25
--	Header Card	.05

1983 Fritsch One-Year Winners

Benny Valenzuela

Larry Fritsch Cards continued its series of collector's issues under the banner of "One-Year Winners" with a 64-card color issue in 1983. Most of the player photos featured are unused Topps pictures. As in previous issues, the set features players with short major league careers, few of whom appear on any contemporary baseball card. In the style of 1966 Topps cards, the set has large player photos bordered in white with a diagonal blue strip in an upper corner containing the initials OYW. A blue strip beneath the photo has the player name in black. Backs are in red, black and white with personal data, stats and career highlights.

		NM/M
Complete Set (64):		35.00
Common Player:		2.00
55	Don Prince	2.00
56	Tom Gramly	2.00
57	Roy Heiser	2.00
58	Hank Izquierdo	2.00
59	Rex Johnston	2.00
60	Jack Damaska	2.00
61	John Flavin	2.00
62	John Glenn	2.00
63	Stan Johnson	2.00
64	Don Choate	2.00
65	Bill Kern	2.00
66	Dick Luebke	2.00
67	Glen Clark	2.00
68	Lamar Jacobs	2.00
69	Rick Herrscher	2.00
70	Jim McManus	2.00
71	Len Church	2.00
72	Larry Stubing	2.00
73	Cal Emery	2.00
74	Lee Gregory	2.00
75	Mike Page	2.00
76	Benny Valenzuela	2.00
77	John Papa	2.00
78	Jim Stump	2.00
79	Brian McCall	2.00
80	Al Kenders	2.00
81	Corky Withrow	2.00
82	Verle Tiefenthaler	2.00
83	Dave Wissman	2.00
84	Tom Fletcher	2.00
85	Dale Willis	2.00
86	Larry Foster	2.00
87	Johnnie Seale	2.00
88	Jim Lehew	2.00
89	Charlie Shoemaker	2.00
90	Don Arlick	2.00
91	George Gerberman	2.00
92	John Pregenzer	2.00
93	Merlin Nippert	2.00
94	Steve Demeter	2.00
95	John Paciorek	2.00
96	Larry Loughlin	2.00
97	Alan Brice	2.00
98	Chet Boak	2.00
99	Alan Koch	2.00
100	Dan Thomas	2.00
101	Elder White	2.00
102	Jim Snyder	2.00
103	Ted Schreiber	2.00
104	Evans Killeen	2.00
105	Ray Daviault	2.00
106	Larry Foss	2.00
107	Wayne Graham	2.00
108	Santiago Rosario	2.00
109	Bob Sprout	2.00
110	Tom Hughes	2.00
111	Em Lindbeck	2.00
112	Ray Blemker	2.00
113	Shaun Fitzmaurice	2.00
114	Ron Stillwell	2.00
115	Carl Thomas	2.00
116	Mike DeGerick	2.00
117	Jay Dahl	2.00
118	Al Lary	2.00

1983 Fritsch 1953 Boston/ Milwaukee Braves

Bucky Walters coach

This collectors' issue commemorates the 30th anniversary of the move of the Boston Braves to Milwaukee. The black-and-white photos on the front of the cards (bordered in blue) were taken in spring training, with players still wearing Boston caps. Card backs have personal data and detailed career highlights. Cards measure about 2-5/8" x 3-3/4", which was the standard prior to 1957.

		NM/M
Complete Set (32):		8.00
Common Player:		.25
1	Joe Adcock	.35
2	John Antonelli	.25
3	Billy Bruton	.25
4	Bob Buhl	.25
5	Lew Burdette	.35
6	Paul Burris	.25
7	Dave Cole	.25
8	Johnny Cooney	.25
9	Walker Cooper	.25
10	Del Crandall	.35
11	George Crowe	.25
12	Jack Dittmer	.25
13	Dick Donovan	.25
14	Sid Gordon	.25
15	Virgil Jester	.25
16	Ernie Johnson	.25
17	Dave Jolly	.25
18	Billy Klaus	.25
19	Don Liddle	.25
20	Johnny Logan	.25
21	Luis Marquez	.25
21s	Luis Marquez (Sample overprint.)	.25
22	Eddie Mathews	1.00
22s	Eddie Mathews (Sample overprint.)	.25
23	Andy Pafko	.35
24	Jim Pendleton	.25
25	Ebba St. Claire	.25
26	Sibby Sisti	.25
27	Warren Spahn	1.00
28	Max Surkont	.25
29	Bob Thorpe	.25
30	Murray Wall	.25
31	Bucky Walters	.25
32	Jim Wilson	.25
33	1953 Braves Team	.25

1986 Fritsch Negro League Baseball Stars

One of the most comprehensive collectors' issues to feature the stars of the Negro Leagues, the Fritsch set features black-and-white photos of varying quality; most of the photos are contemporary with

Negro League Baseball Stars

★ Satchel Paige ★

the players' careers from the 1920s into the 1950s, with a few of the segregated leagues' earlier pioneers also included. Fronts are highlighted with red graphics. Backs are printed in blue and present a brief summary of the player's career and a list of the teams on which he played. Cards are in standard 2-1/2" x 3-1/2" format.

		NM/M
Complete Set (119):		15.00
Common Player:		.10
1	Buck Leonard	.15
2	Ted Page	.10
3	Cool Papa Bell	.15
4	Oscar Charleston, Josh Gibson, Ted Page, Judy Johnson	.15
5	Judy Johnson	.15
6	Monte Irvin	.15
7	Ray Dandridge	.15
8	Oscar Charleston	.15
9	Josh Gibson	.15
10	Satchel Paige	.25
10s	Satchel Paige (SAMPLE on back.)	2.50
11	Jackie Robinson	.50
12	Piper Davis	.10
13	Josh Johnson	.10
14	Lou Dials	.15
15	Andy Porter	.10
16	Pop Lloyd	.15
17	Andy Watts	.10
18	Rube Foster	.15
19	Martin Dihigo	.15
20	Lou Dials	.10
21	Satchel Paige	.25
22	Crush Holloway	.10
23	Josh Gibson	.15
24	Oscar Charleston	.15
25	Jackie Robinson	.50
26	Larry Brown	.10
27	Hilton Smith	.15
28	Moses Fleetwood Walker	.25
29	Jimmie Crutchfield	.10
30	Josh Gibson	.15
30s	Josh Gibson (SAMPLE on back.)	2.00
31	Josh Gibson	.15
32	Bullet Rogan	.10
33	Clint Thomas	.10
34	Rats Henderson	.10
35	Pat Scantlebury	.10
36	Sidney Morton	.10
37	Larry Kimbrough	.10
38	Sam Jethroe	.10
39	Normal "Tweed" Webb	.10
40	Mahlon Duckett	.10
41	Andy Anderson	.10
42	Buster Haywood	.10
43	Bob Trice	.10
44	Bus Clarkson	.10
45	Buck O'Neil	.15
46	Jim Zapp	.10
47	Piper Davis	.10
48	Ed Steel	.10
49	Bob Boyd	.10
50	Marlin Carter	.10
51	George Giles	.10
52	Bill Byrd	.10
53	Art Pennington	.10
54	Max Manning	.10
55	Ron Teasley	.10
56	Ziggy Marcell	.10
57	Bill Cash	.10
58	Joe Scott	.10
59	Joe Fillmore	.10
60	Bob Thurman	.10
61	Larry Kimbrough	.10
62	Verdell Mathis	.10
63	Josh Johnson	.10
64	Double Duty Radcliffe	.15
65	William Bobby Robinson	.10
66	Bingo DeMoss	.15
67	John Beckwith	.10
68	Bill Jackman	.10
69	Bill Drake	.10
70	Charles Grant	.15
71	Willie Wells	.25
72	Jose Fernandez	.10
73	Isidro Fabri	.10
74	Frank Austin	.10
75	Richard Lundy	.10
76	Junior Gilliam	.10
77	John Donaldson	.10
78	Herb Dixon	.10
79	Slim Jones	.10
80	Sam Jones	.10
81	Dave Hoskins	.10
82	Jerry Benjamin	.10
83	Luke Easter	.10
84	Ramon Herrera	.10
85	Matthew Carlisle	.10
86	Smoky Joe Williams	.25
87	Marv Williams	.10
88	William Yancey	.10
89	Monte Irvin	.15
89s	Monte Irvin (SAMPLE on back.)	1.00
90	Cool Papa Bell	.15
91	Biz Mackey	.25
92	Harry Simpson	.10
93	Lazario Salazar	.10
94	Bill Perkins	.10
95	Johnny Davis	.10
96	Jelly Jackson	.10
97	Sam Bankhead	.10
98	Hank Thompson	.10
99	William Bell	.10
100	Cliff Bell	.10
101	Dave Barnhill	.10
102	Dan Bankhead	.10
103	Lloyd Bassett	.10
104	Newt Allen	.10
105	George Jefferson	.10
106	Pat Paterson	.10
107	Goose Tatum	.15
108	Dave Malarcher	.10
109	Home Run Johnson	.10
110	Bill Monroe	.10
111	Sammy Hughes	.10
112	Dick Redding	.10
113	Fats Jenkins	.10
114	Jimmie Lyons	.10
115	Mule Suttles	.15
116	Ted Trent	.10
117	George Sweatt	.10
118	Frank Duncan	.10
119	Checklist	.05

1991 Front Row Ken Griffey Jr.

KEN GRIFFEY JR.

Production of this collectors' set and related promo cards was reported at 25,000 sets each. Cards trace the three-year career of Junior in photos, stats, highlights and biographic details. Fronts have various posed and color action photos, complete with team logos, and a white border. Horizontal backs are printed in black on a light blue background. Promo cards have a large "PROMO" printed on a baseball at center. Size is 2-1/2" x 3-1/2".

		NM/M
Complete Set (10):		2.00
Complete Promo Set (5):		1.00
Common Card:		.25
Common Promo:		.25
1	Ken Griffey Jr./AS	.25
1	Ken Griffey Jr./AS (Promo)	.25
2	Ken Griffey Jr. (The Breakdown)	.25
2	Ken Griffey Jr. (The Breakdown) (Promo)	.25
3	Ken Griffey Jr. (Homers)	.25
3	Ken Griffey Jr. (Homers) (Promo)	.25
4	Ken Griffey Jr. (Gold Glv)	.25
4	Ken Griffey Jr. (Gold Glv) (Promo)	.25
5	Ken Griffey Jr. (Drafted)	.25

ABBREVIATIONS

AS - All-Star

5	Ken Griffey Jr. (Drafted) (Promo)	.25
6	Ken Griffey Jr. (Up Close and Personal)	.25
7	Ken Griffey Jr. (Background)	.25
8	Ken Griffey Jr. (The Majors)	.25
9	Ken Griffey Jr. (Career Highlights)	.25
10	Ken Griffey Jr. (The American League)	.25

1992-95 Front Row All-Time Great Series

GRAYS
BUCK LEONARD

Some of baseball's greatest living former stars were featured in this run of five-card sets. Originally intended to encompass 100 players, the issue was cut considerably short. Each single-player set contains five cards featuring black-and-white and/or color photos on front. Backs have a photo in the background, overprinted with statistical, biographical or career information. Major league uniform logos have been removed from photos for lack of licensing by MLB. Each set was issued in an edition of 25,000, with an illustrated, numbered certificate of authenticity included. Each set was also produced with the top card authentically autographed. The Perry and Spahn sets were issued some time after the first 37 players. Sets are checklisted here alphabetically; single cards are not listed because the cards are usually sold only as sets.

		NM/M
Common Player Set:		.25
(1)	Hank Aaron (5-card set)	1.00
(1a)	Hank Aaron/Auto.	40.00
(2)	Ernie Banks (5-card set)	.75
(2a)	Ernie Banks/Auto.	15.00
(3)	Al Barlick (5-card set)	.25
(3a)	Al Barlick/Auto.	25.00
(4)	Johnny Bench (5-card set)	.75
(4a)	Johnny Bench/Auto.	20.00
(5)	Yogi Berra (5-card set)	.75
(5a)	Yogi Berra/Auto.	20.00
(6)	Lou Boudreau (5-card set)	.25
(6a)	Lou Boudreau/Auto.	16.00
(7)	Lou Brock (5-card set)	.25
(7a)	Lou Brock/Auto.	12.50
(8)	Roy Campanella (5-card set)	.75
(8a)	Roy Campanella/Auto.	150.00
(9)	Rod Carew (5-card set)	.35
(9a)	Rod Carew/Auto.	20.00
(10)	Ray Dandridge (5-card set)	.25
(10a)	Ray Dandridge/Auto.	17.50
(11)	Bobby Doerr (5-card set)	.25
(11a)	Bobby Doerr/Auto.	12.50
(12)	Rick Ferrell (5-card set)	.25
(12a)	Rick Ferrell/Auto.	30.00
(13)	Rollie Fingers (5-card set)	.25
(13a)	Rollie Fingers/Auto.	12.50
(14)	Whitey Ford (5-card set)	.50
(14a)	Whitey Ford/Auto.	22.50
(15)	George Foster (5-card set)	.25
(15a)	George Foster/Auto.	10.00
(16)	Catfish Hunter (5-card set)	.25
(16a)	Catfish Hunter/Auto.	15.00
(17)	Monte Irvin (5-card set)	.25
(17a)	Monte Irvin/Auto.	5.00
(18)	Al Kaline (5-card set)	.50
(18a)	Al Kaline/Auto.	15.00
(19)	George Kell (5-card set)	.25
(19a)	George Kell/Auto.	12.50
(20)	Ralph Kiner (5-card set)	.25
(20a)	Ralph Kiner/Auto.	30.00
(21)	Don Larsen (5-card set)	.25
(21a)	Don Larsen/Auto.	15.00
(22)	Bob Lemon (5-card set)	.25
(22a)	Bob Lemon/Auto.	25.00
(23)	Buck Leonard (5-card set)	.25
(23a)	Buck Leonard/Auto.	22.50
(23p)	Buck Leonard ("PROMO" on back.)	1.00
(24)	Juan Marichal (5-card set)	.35
(24a)	Juan Marichal/Auto.	15.00
(25)	Joe Morgan (5-card set)	.25
(25a)	Joe Morgan/Auto.	25.00
(26)	Stan Musial (5-card set)	.50
(26a)	Stan Musial/Auto.	40.00
(27)	Hal Newhouser (5-card set)	.25
(27a)	Hal Newhouser/Auto.	15.00
(28)	Jim Palmer (5-card set)	.25
(28a)	Jim Palmer/Auto.	12.50
(29)	Tony Perez (5-card set)	.25
(29a)	Tony Perez/Auto.	12.50
(30)	Gaylord Perry (5-card set)	.50
(30a)	Gaylord Perry/Auto.	12.50
(31)	Pee Wee Reese (5-card set)	.35
(32a)	Pee Wee Reese/Auto.	40.00
(32)	Phil Rizzuto (5-card set)	.50
(32a)	Phil Rizzuto/Auto.	20.00
(33)	Brooks Robinson (5-card set)	.35
(33a)	Brooks Robinson/Auto.	12.50
(34)	Frank Robinson (5-card set)	.35
(34a)	Frank Robinson/Auto.	15.00
(35)	Red Schoendienst (5-card set)	.25
(35a)	Red Schoendienst/Auto.	40.00
(36)	Tom Seaver (5-card set)	.35
(36a)	Tom Seaver/Auto.	17.50
(37)	Warren Spahn (5-card set)	.50
(37a)	Warren Spahn/Auto.	30.00
(38)	Willie Stargell (5-card set)	.25
(38a)	Willie Stargell/Auto.	15.00
(39)	Carl Yastrzemski (5-card set)	.35
(39a)	Carl Yastrzemski/Auto.	30.00

1992 Front Row Club House Series Ken Griffey, Jr.

Club House Series

Ten cards tracing the life and career of Ken Griffey, Jr. comprise this collectors' issue. Cards are standard 2-1/2" x 3-1/2" with borderless color action and posed photos. Uniform logos have been removed from the photos since the set is not licensed by MLB. A Club House Series logo is on front at bottom-right. Horizontal backs have a color photo of Griffey ghosted in the background. Printed over that are personal data, career highlights and stats.

		NM/M
Complete Set (10):		1.00
Common Player:		.15
1	Ken Griffey Jr. (Background)	.15
2	Ken Griffey Jr. (Drafted)	.15

3	Ken Griffey Jr. (The Majors)	.15
4	Ken Griffey Jr. (The Breakdown)	.15
5	Ken Griffey Jr. (The American League)	.15
6	Ken Griffey Jr./AS	.15
7	Ken Griffey Jr. (Gold Glv)	.15
8	Ken Griffey Jr. (Homers)	.15
9	Ken Griffey Jr. (Career Highlights)	.15
10	Ken Griffey Jr. (A Closer Look)	.15

Ken Griffey Jr. Holograms

This set of collectors' edition cards was produced in an issue of 50,000, with each set including a numbered certificate of authenticity. In standard 2-1/2" x 3-1/2" size, the cards have a borderless hologram picture on front. Conventionally printed backs have a color photo of the player and a few sentences about his career. Team logos have been removed from the pictures because the cards were not licensed by MLB.

		NM/M
Complete Set (3):		3.00
Common Card:		1.00
1	Ken Griffey Jr. (Making History)	1.00
2	Ken Griffey Jr. (Rewriting the Record Book)	1.00
3	Ken Griffey Jr. (Turning Up Gold)	1.00

Ken Griffey Jr. Pure Gold

This set of collectors' edition cards was produced in an issue of 20,000, with each set including a numbered certificate of authenticity. In standard 2-1/2" x 3-1/2" size, the cards have wide gold-foil borders on front. Backs have stats or a few sentences about his career. Team logos have been removed from the pictures because the cards were not licensed by MLB.

		NM/M
Complete Set (3):		3.00
Uncut Strip:		5.00
Common Card:		1.00
1	Ken Griffey Jr./ Gold Glv	1.00
2	Ken Griffey Jr./ Background	1.00
3	Ken Griffey Jr./Drafted	1.00

Holograms

The "career" seasons of three Hall of Famers are remembered in this series of cards. In

standard 2-1/2" x 3-1/2" format, fronts have a borderless hologram featuring a vintage action photo. Conventionally printed backs have a color photo, a recap and stats from the named season, and a foil holographic serial number tag designating the card's place in an edition of 100,000 each.

		NM/M
Complete Set (3):		1.50
Common Player:		.50
(1)	Hank Aaron	.70
(2)	Roy Campanella	.50
(3)	Tom Seaver	.50

Pure Gold

Each of these 2-1/2" x 3-1/2" cards features 23-K gold borders on front, surrounding a color action photo on which uniform details have been airbrushed away. Backs have player information.

		NM/M
Complete Set (6):		15.00
Common Player:		3.00
(1)	Hank Aaron	3.00
(2)	Roy Campanella	3.00
(3)	Tom Seaver	3.00
	Frank Thomas strip (3):	10.00
(4)	Frank Thomas/Btg	3.00
(5)	Frank Thomas/ Standing	3.00
(6)	Frank Thomas/Fielding	3.00

Frank Thomas

Budding super slugger Frank Thomas is featured in this collectors' issue. The 2-1/2" x 3-1/2" cards have color photos on front, from which team logos have been airbrushed because the set was licensed only by the player, and not by MLB. Horizontally formatted backs have a second color photo along with a headline and a few sentences about his career to that point. The set was released in an edition of 30,000 and each was sold with a serial-numbered certificate of authenticity.

		NM/M
Complete Set (7):		3.00
Common Card:		1.00
Autographed (# to 4,000):		15.00
1	Frank Thomas (A Good Start)	.50
nno	Frank Thomas (A Good Start- promo overprint on back.)	.50
2	Frank Thomas (Multi-Talented)	.50
3	Frank Thomas (Auburn Career)	.50
4	Frank Thomas (Accomplishments)	.50

5	Frank Thomas (Individual Honors)	.50
6	Frank Thomas (Minor League Stats)	.50
7	Frank Thomas (Major League Stats)	.50

1993 Front Row Gold Collection

Five borderless color photos (uniform logos removed) of Rollie Fingers are featured on the cards in this set. At bottom in a dark green stripe is the player name and, at left, the Front Row logo and the word "PREMIUM." Vertically at left is "The Gold Collection." All front printing is in gold foil. Backs have dark green borders with a ghost-image action photo and a few sentences about the player. A baseball at top carries the legend, "All Time Great / Series." Production was reported as 5,000 sets.

		NM/M
Complete Set (5):		2.00
Common Card:		.50
1-5	Rollie Fingers	.50

1999 FroZsnack's High-Screamers Lids

These 3-1/4" plastic lids were found on ice cream snacks sold at ballparks and possibly other outlets. A player photo with uniform logos covered is featured at center with personal data and 1998 stats on the side. The player name is in a banner at top, his team, position and career highlights are in a banner at bottom.

		NM/M
Complete Set (40):		30.00
Common Player:		.75
(1)	Roberto Alomar	.75
(2)	Jeff Bagwell	1.25
(3)	Albert Belle	.75
(4)	Dante Bichette	.75
(5)	Craig Biggio	.75
(6)	Barry Bonds	2.50
(7)	Kevin Brown	.75
(8)	Jose Canseco	1.00
(9)	Vinny Castilla	.75
(10)	Tony Clark	.75
(11)	Francisco Cordova	.75
(12)	Eric Davis	.75
(13)	Nomar Garciaparra	1.75
(14)	Tom Glavine	1.00
(15)	Ben Grieve	.75
(16)	Ken Griffey Jr.	2.00
(17)	Tony Gwynn	1.50
(18)	Rickey Henderson	1.25
(19)	Livan Hernandez	.75
(20)	Derek Jeter	2.50
(21)	Jason Kendall	.75
(22)	Randy Johnson	1.25
(23)	Barry Larkin	.75
(24)	Greg Maddux	1.50
(25)	Tino Martinez	.75
(26)	Mark McGwire	2.25
(27)	Robb Nen	.75
(28)	Mike Piazza	2.00
(29)	Manny Ramirez	1.25
(30)	Cal Ripken Jr.	2.50
(31)	Alex Rodriguez	2.25
(32)	Scott Rolen	1.00
(33)	Sammy Sosa	1.75
(34)	Frank Thomas	1.25
(35)	Greg Vaughn	.75
(36)	Fernando Vina	.75
(37)	Omar Vizquel	.75
(38)	Larry Walker	.75
(39)	Matt Williams	.75
(40)	Kerry Wood	1.00

1998 Fruit Roll-Ups All-Stars

Perforated panels of eight small (1-1/2" x 2") cards bearing the Topps logo were found on 38-count boxes of Fruit Roll-Ups snacks early in the 1998 season. The blank-back cards are printed on a 6" x 4" panel which can be removed from the box back. The front of the box pictures Rodriguez, Thomas and McGwire.

		NM/M
Complete Box:		5.00
Complete Panel:		4.00
Complete Set, Singles (8):		3.50
Common Player:		.50
(1)	Tony Gwynn	1.00
(2)	Derek Jeter	1.50
(3)	Kenny Lofton	.50
(4)	Mark McGwire	1.25
(5)	Mike Piazza	1.25
(6)	Cal Ripken Jr.	1.50
(7)	Ivan Rodriguez	.65
(8)	Frank Thomas	.75

1985 Fun Food Buttons

Fun Foods of Little Silver, N.J., issued a set of 133 full-color metal pins in 1985. The buttons, which are 1-1/4" in diameter and have a "safety pin" back, have bright borders which correspond to the player's team colors. The button backs are numbered and contain the player's 1984 batting or earned run average. The buttons were available as complete sets through hobby dealers and were also distributed in packs of three through retail stores. Cardboard 1-1/2" x 1-1/2" square proofs of the buttons' fronts are also seen in the hobby; their value is 2-3X that of the corresponding button, with production reported to be only 2,000 cardboard proofs.

		NM/M
Complete Set (133):		20.00
Common Player:		.10
Wax Pack (3):		.50
Wax Box (36):		9.00
1	Dave Winfield	1.00
2	Lance Parrish	.10
3	Gary Carter	1.00
4	Pete Rose	2.00
5	Jim Rice	.35
6	George Brett	1.00
7	Fernando Valenzuela	.10
8	Darryl Strawberry	.10
9	Steve Garvey	.45
10	Rollie Fingers	.75
11	Mike Schmidt	1.75
12	Kent Tekulve	.10
13	Ryne Sandberg	1.50
14	Bruce Sutter	.75
15	Tom Seaver	1.00
16	Reggie Jackson	1.50
17	Rickey Henderson	1.00
18	Mark Langston	.10
19	Jack Clark	.10
20	Willie Randolph	.10
21	Kirk Gibson	.10
22	Andre Dawson	.35
23	Dave Concepcion	.10
24	Tony Armas	.10
25	Dan Quisenberry	.10
26	Pedro Guerrero	.10
27	Dwight Gooden	.10
28	Tony Gwynn	1.50
29	Robin Yount	1.00
30	Steve Carlton	1.00
31	Bill Madlock	.10
32	Rick Sutcliffe	.10
33	Willie McGee	.10
34	Greg Luzinski	.10
35	Rod Carew	1.00
36	Dave Kingman	.10
37	Alvin Davis	.10
38	Chili Davis	.10
39	Don Baylor	.10
40	Alan Trammell	.10
41	Tim Raines	.10
42	Cesar Cedeno	.10
43	Wade Boggs	1.50
44	Frank White	.10
45	Steve Sax	.10
46	George Foster	.10
47	Terry Kennedy	.10
48	Cecil Cooper	.10
49	John Denny	.10
50	John Candelaria	.10
51	Jody Davis	.10
52	George Hendrick	.10
53	Ron Kittle	.10
54	Fred Lynn	.10
55	Carney Lansford	.10
56	Gorman Thomas	.10
57	Manny Trillo	.10
58	Steve Kemp	.10
59	Jack Morris	.10
60	Dan Petry	.10
61	Mario Soto	.10
62	Dwight Evans	.10
63	Hal McRae	.10
64	Mike Marshall	.10
65	Mookie Wilson	.10
66	Graig Nettles	.10
67	Ben Oglivie	.10
68	Juan Samuel	.10
69	Johnny Ray	.10
70	Gary Matthews	.10
71	Ozzie Smith	1.50
72	Carlton Fisk	1.00
73	Doug DeCinces	.10
74	Joe Morgan	1.00
75	Dave Stieb	.10
76	Buddy Bell	.10
77	Don Mattingly	1.75
78	Lou Whitaker	.10
79	Willie Hernandez	.10
80	Dave Parker	.10
81	Bob Stanley	.10
82	Willie Wilson	.10
83	Orel Hershiser	.10
84	Rusty Staub	.10
85	Goose Gossage	.10
86	Don Sutton	.75
87	Al Holland	.10
88	Tony Pena	.10
89	Ron Cey	.10
90	Joaquin Andujar	.10
91	LaMarr Hoyt	.10
92	Tommy John	.10
93	Dwayne Murphy	.10
94	Willie Upshaw	.10
95	Gary Ward	.10
96	Ron Guidry	.10
97	Chet Lemon	.10
98	Aurelio Lopez	.10
99	Tony Perez	.75
100	Bill Buckner	.10
101	Mike Hargrove	.10
102	Scott McGregor	.10
103	Dale Murphy	.50
104	Keith Hernandez	.10
105	Paul Molitor	1.00
106	Bert Blyleven	.10
107	Leon Durham	.10
108	Lee Smith	.10
109	Nolan Ryan	3.00
110	Harold Baines	.10
111	Kent Hrbek	.10
112	Ron Davis	.10
113	George Bell	.10
114	Charlie Hough	.10
115	Phil Niekro	.75
116	Dave Righetti	.10
117	Darrell Evans	.10
118	Cal Ripken, Jr.	3.00
119	Eddie Murray	1.00
120	Storm Davis	.10
121	Mike Boddicker	.10
122	Bob Horner	.10
123	Chris Chambliss	.10
124	Ted Simmons	.10
125	Andre Thornton	.10
126	Larry Bowa	.10
127	Bob Dernier	.10
128	Joe Niekro	.10
129	Jose Cruz	.10
130	Tom Brunansky	.10
131a	Garry Gaetti	50.00
131b	Gary Gaetti	.10
132	Lloyd Moseby	.10
133	Frank Tanana	.10

G

1982 Renata Galasso 20 Years of Met Baseball

The original New York Mets team of 1962 is featured on this 20-year anniversary set. The 2-1/2" x 3-1/2" cards have black-and-white photos with blue borders. The player name and position is in orange at bottom. Backs repeat the team colors with blue and orange printing on white cardboard. Card and uniform numbers appear in the top corners, there is a career summary, 1962 and career stats and a trivia question. Production was reported as 2,500 sets.

		NM/M
Complete Set (30):		10.00
Common Player:		.50
1	Marv Throneberry	.75
2	Richie Ashburn	2.00
3	Charlie Neal	.50
4	Cliff Cook	.50
5	Elio Chacon	.50
6	Chris Cannizzaro	.50
7	Jim Hickman	.50
8	Rod Kanehl	.50
9	Gene Woodling	.50
10	Gil Hodges	2.00
11	Al Jackson	.50
12	Sammy Taylor	.50
13	Felix Mantilla	.50
14	Ken MacKenzie	.50
15	Craig Anderson	.50
16	Bob Moorhead	.50
17	Joe Christopher	.50
18	Bob Miller	.50
19	Frank Thomas	.50
20	Vinegar Bend Mizell	.50
21	Bill Hunter	.50
22	Roger Craig	.50
23	Jay Hook	.50
24	Meet The Mets (Team card.)	.75
25	Choo Choo Coleman	.50
26	Casey Stengel	2.00
28	Solly Hemus	.50
29	Rogers Hornsby	2.00
31	Red Ruffing	.50
32	George Weiss	.50

1983 Renata Galasso 1933 All-Stars

CHUCK KLEIN
OUTFIELDER - NATIONAL LEAGUE

The premiere All-Star Game in 1933 is commemorated in this 50th anniversary collectors' issue. In standard 2-1/2" x 3-1/2" format (though not uniformly cut to exact size), the cards feature black-and-white portrait photos on front. Many of the National League All-Stars are pictured in their special NL uniforms. In the wide white border at bottom is the player's name, position and league. Backs are printed in red, white and blue with a large Galasso ad and a short career summary; there is little mention of the 1933 All-Star Game. Two unnumbered cards issued with the set have N.L. and A.L. team photos on front and blue-tone backs showing A-S managers Connie Mack and John McGraw "choosing up sides."

		NM/M
Complete Set (45):		15.00
Common Player:		1.00
1	Tony Cuccinello	1.00
2	Lon Warenke (Warneke)	1.00
3	Hal Schumacher	1.00
4	Wally Berger	1.00
5	Lefty O'Doul	1.00
6	Chuck Klein	1.00
7	Chick Hafey	1.00
8	Jimmie Wilson	1.00
9	John McGraw	1.00
10	Max Carey	1.00
11	Bill McKechnie	1.00
12	Dick Bartell	1.00
13	Bill Hallahan	1.00
14	Woody English	1.00
15	Paul Waner	1.00
16	Carl Hubbell	1.50
17	Frank Frisch	1.00
18	Gabby Hartnett	1.00
19	Pie Traynor	1.00
20	Bill Terry	1.00
21	Pepper Martin	1.00
22	Earl Averill	1.00
23	Jimmy Dykes	1.00
24	Charlie Gehringer	1.50
25	Rich Ferrell (Rick)	1.00
26	Joe Cronin	1.00
27	Ben Chapman	1.00
28	Eddie Rommel	1.00
29	Lefty Grove	1.50
30	Connie Mack	1.00
31	Babe Ruth	5.00
32	Sam West	1.00
33	Tony Lazzeri	1.00
34	Al Simmons	1.00
35	Wes Ferrell	1.00
36	Bill Dickey	1.00
37	General Crowder	1.00
38	Oral Hildebrand	1.00
39	Lefty Gomez	1.50
40	Jimmie Foxx	1.50
41	Art Fletcher	1.00
42	Eddie Collins	1.00
43	Lou Gehrig	3.00
(44)	1933 N.L. All-Star Team	2.00
(45)	1933 A.L. All-Star Team	2.00

1969 Seattle Pilots

The one-year American League franchise in Seattle is recalled with this collectors' issue. Full-color photos of the peripatetic Pilots are framed in team-color blue and gold on a beige background in standard 2-1/2" x 3-1/2" size. Backs are printed in red and blue on white and feature a career summary and 1969 stats. For some players, this represents their only baseball card appearance and for many more, it is their only card in a Pilots' uniform. Many of the sets were originally sold with the #1 Jim Bouton card personally autographed.

		NM/M
Complete Set (43)		12.50
Common Player:		.50
1	Jim Bouton	2.00
1(a)	Jim Bouton/Auto.	15.00
2	Joe Schultz	.50
3	Bill Edgerton	.70
4	Gary Timberlake	.70
5	Dick Baney	.50
6	Mike G. Marshall	1.00
7	Jim Gosger	.50
8	Mike Hegan	.50
9	Steve Hovley	.50
10	Don Mincher	.50
11	Miguel Fuentes	.50
12	Charlie Bates	.50
13	John O'Donoghue	.50
14	Tommy Davis	.75
15	Jerry McNertney	.50
16	Rich Rollins	.50
17	Fred Talbot	.50
18	John Gelnar	.50
19	Bob Locker	.50
20	Frank Crosetti	.75
21	Sal Maglie	.75
22	Sibby Sisti	.50
23	Ron Plaza	.50
24	Federico Velazquez	.50
25	Diego Segui	.50
26	Steve Barber	.50
27	Jack Aker	.50
28	Marty Pattin	.50
29	Ray Oyler	.50
30	Danny Walton	.75
31	Merritt Ranew	.50
32	John Donaldson	.50
33	Greg Goossen	.50
34	Gary Bell	.50
35	Jim Pagliaroni	.50
36	Mike Ferraro	.50
37	Tommy Harper	.75
38	John Morris	.50
39	Larry Haney	.50
40	Ron Clark	.50
41	Steve Whitaker	.50
42	Wayne Comer	.50
43	Gene Brabender	.50

1984 Renata Galasso Baseball Collector Series

Some of baseball's best are presented in this glossy-front black-and-white, 2-3/8" x 3-1/2", collectors' set patterned after the 1953 Bowmans. Backs are in red and black with a career summary and lifetime stats.

		NM/M
Complete Set (20):		15.00
Common Player:		.50
1	Roberto Clemente	1.50
2	Duke Snider	.75
3	Sandy Koufax	1.50
4	Carl Hubbell	.50
5	Ty Cobb	1.00
6	Willie Mays	1.50
7	Jackie Robinson	1.50
8	Joe DiMaggio	3.00
9	Stan Musial	1.00
10	Pie Traynor	.50
11	Yogi Berra	.75
12	Babe Ruth	3.00
13	Brooks Robinson	.50
14	Walter Johnson	.50
15	Ted Williams	1.50
16	Bill Dickey	.50
17	Lou Gehrig	2.00
18	Hank Aaron	1.50
19	Eddie Mathews	.50
20	Mickey Mantle	5.00

Hall of Fame Art Card Series

Painting on these 2-7/8" x 5" deckle-edge cards are by Ron Lewis and depict Hall of Famers' induction between 1936-46. There are no graphics or player identification on the front. Backs are printed in red and black and have player personal data, career highlights and lifetime stats within a decorative shield.

		NM/M
Complete Set (45):		15.00
Common Player:		.50
1	Ty Cobb	3.00
2	Babe Ruth	5.00
3	Walter Johnson	1.50
4	Christy Mathewson	1.50
5	Honus Wagner	1.50
6	Napoleon Lajoie	.75
7	Tris Speaker	.75
8	Cy Young	1.50
9	Morgan Bulkeley	.50
10	Ban Johnson	.50
11	John McGraw	.50
12	Connie Mack	.50
13	George Wright	.50
14	Grover Alexander	.65
15	Alexander Cartwright	.50
16	Henry Chadwick	.50
17	Eddie Collins	.50
18	Lou Gehrig	4.00
19	Willie Keeler	.50
20	George Sisler	.50
21	Cap Anson	.50
22	Charles Comiskey	.50
23	Candy Cummings	.50
24	Buck Ewing	.50
25	Charlie Radbourne	.50
26	A.G. Spalding	.50
27	Roger (Rogers) Hornsby	.75
28	Kenesaw M. Landis	.50
29	Roger Bresnahan	.50
30	Dan Brouthers	.50
31	Fred Clarke	.50
32	Jimmy Collins	.50
33	Ed Delahanty	.50
34	Hugh Duffy	.50
35	Mike "King" Kelly	.50
36	Hughie Jennings	.50
37	Jim O'Rourke	.50
38	Wilbert Robinson	.50
39	Jesse Burkett	.50
40	Frank Chance	.50
41	Jack Chesbro	.50
42	Johnny Evers	.50
43	Joe Tinker	.50
44	Eddie Plank	.50
45	Checklist	.50

Reggie Jackson

This collectors' issue chronicling the career of "Mr. October" was produced in two sizes - the standard 2-1/2" x 3-1/2" and the Topps' "mini" format of 2-1/4" x 3-1/8". Both sizes share the same design of a color or black-and-white photo on a blue border with "Reggie 44" at bottom, along with a photo of his classic swing. Backs have statistical data, career summary or part of a puzzle showing all of Jackson's Topps cards to that point. The full-size set was limited to 10,000, with 500 featuring a genuine autograph on card #1; the mini set was issued in an edition of 5,000.

	NM/M
Complete Standard-size Set (30):	7.50
Complete Set w/Autographed #1:	45.00
Complete Mini Set (30):	10.00
Common Card:	.40

Willie Mays Story

Color and black-and-white photos from the Hall of Famer's career and off-field life are featured in this collectors' set. Each photo is surrounded by a red frame and white border. Many of the photos will be familiar to collectors as having earlier appeared on Topps cards. Backs of the first 45 cards are in red, black and white, with biographical information or a description of the front photo. Backs of cards #46-90 can be assembled into a full-color puzzle of Mays' baseball cards from Topps, Bowman and others. Card #1 in each set is authentically autographed by Mays. Retail price at issue was $20.

	NM/M
Complete Set (90):	35.00
Common Card:	.50

1927 N.Y. Yankees

Paintings by Ron Lewis adorn this collectors' issue honoring what may have been baseball's best team ever. The 2-1/2" x 3-1/2" cards have blue borders with the player's name in a banner at bottom. Backs have typical player data plus 1927 and career stats. The set was originally issued at about $5.

		NM/M
Complete Set (30):		18.00
Common Player:		.50
1	Lou Gehrig	5.00
2	Babe Ruth	7.50
3	Earle Combs	1.00
4	Ed Barrow	.50
5	Bob Shawkey	.50
6	Bob Meusel	.50
7	Urban Shocker	.50
8	Ben Paschal	.50
9	John Grabowski	.50
10	Jacob Ruppert	.50
11	Herb Pennock	1.00
12	Miller Huggins	1.00
13	Wilcy Moore	.50
14	Walter Beall	.50
15	Cedric Durst	.50
16	Tony Lazzeri	.50
17	Mark Koenig	.50
18	Waite Hoyt	1.00
19	Myles Thomas	.50
20	Joe Dugan	.50
21	Art Fletcher	.50
22	Charlie O'Leary	.50
23	Ray Morehart	.50
24	Benny Bengough	.50
25	Pat Collins	.50
26	Dutch Reuther (Ruether)	.50
27	George Pipgras	.50
28	Mike Gazella	.50
29	Julian Wera	.50
30	Joe Giard	.50

1985 Renata Galasso Dwight Gooden

This collectors' issue was produced by Brooklyn dealer Renata Galasso as one of several to capitalize on Gooden's early fame. Card #1 features a Ron Lewis painting of Gooden, the others feature color photos from his boyhood and early career. (Card #16 pictures him shaking hands with Henry Aaron.) Photos are surrounded on front with a border of blue squares. A pink "DR. K" logo is at bottom-right. Backs are in blue and white and feature a question and answer session with the pitcher, stats, or part of a nine-piece puzzle. Five thousand sets were produced, with 500 of them featuring Gooden's autograph on Card #1. Issue price was about $11.

	NM/M
Complete Set (30):	4.00
Complete Autographed Set:	15.00
Single Card:	.15

1986 Renata Galasso Dwight Gooden

Dr. K's Cy Young Season in 1985 is recalled in this collectors' set. Numbered from 31-60, picking up where the 1985 set had left off, the series share a similar format. Fronts have black-and-white or color photos surrounded by a frame of blue dots and larger orange squares. A blue "Dr. K" appears in the lower-right corner. Backs are in blue and orange on white and narrate the 1985 season. The final nine cards in the set have pieces forming a puzzle picture of Gooden.

	NM/M
Complete Set (30):	4.00
Single Card:	.15

Don Mattingly

The life and career of the Yankees superstar is traced in this collectors' issue. The

2-1/2" x 3-1/2" cards have a mix of black-and-white and color photos on a white background with blue pinstripes. A yellow circle in a bottom corner of each card front has "THE HIT MAN" in red. Backs are printed in blue, with 21 of them featuring a question-and-answer format and nine forming a puzzle picture of Mattingly.

	NM/M
Complete Set (30):	6.00
Single Card:	.50

Yankees Black-and-White

Illustrating one of the problems with collectors' issues, a person holding one of these cards might assume it is of 1961 or 1962 vintage because there is no date of actual issue, which occurred around 1986, anywhere on the cards. In a format similar to Topps' 1961 cards, this set features large black-and-white player photos on a 2-1/2" x 3-1/2" glossy stock. The player name and position are in a pair of color bars at bottom. Backs are in red and black and have personal data, season and career stats, a 1961 season summary and a trivia question. Reported production was 2,500.

		NM/M
Complete Set (30):		20.00
Common Player:		.50
1	Roger Maris	3.00
2	Bobby Richardson	.75
3	Tony Kubek	.75
4	Elston Howard	.75
5	Bill Skowron	.75
6	Clete Boyer	.50
7	Mickey Mantle	7.50
8	Yogi Berra	2.00
9	Johnny Blanchard	.50
10	Hector Lopez	.50
11	Whitey Ford	2.00
12	Ralph Terry	.50
13	Bill Stafford	.50
14	Bud Daley	.50
15	Billy Gardner	.50
16	Jim Coates	.50
17	Luis Arroyo	.50
18	Tex Clevenger	.50
19	Bob Cerv	.50
20	Art Ditmar	.50
21	Bob Turley	.50
22	Joe DeMaestri	.50
23	Rollie Sheldon	.50
24	Earl Torgeson	.50
25	Hal Reniff	.50
26	Ralph Houk	.50
27	Jim Hegan	.50
28	Johnny Sain	.60
29	Frank Crosetti	.50
30	Wally Moses	.50

Yankees Color

MICKEY MANTLE — Outfielder

The World Champion N.Y. Yankees of 1961 are remembered in this collectors' set. The 2-1/2" x 3-1/2" cards borrow the design of Topps' 1961 issue, with a large color photo at top and red and yellow boxes below with player name and position in contrasting color. Backs are printed in blue and red with a few biographical details, 1961 and career stats and a career summary.

		NM/M
Complete Set (37):		15.00
Common Player:		.25
1	Roger Maris	3.00
2	Yogi Berra	1.50
3	Whitey Ford	1.50
4	Hector Lopez	.25
5	Bob Turley	.25
6	Frank Crosetti	.25
7	Bob Cerv	.25
8	Jack Reed	.25
9	Luis Arroyo	.25
10	Danny McDevitt	.25
11	Duke Maas	.25
12	Jesse Gonder	.25
13	Ralph Terry	.25
14	Deron Johnson	.25
15	Johnny Blanchard	.25
16	Bill Stafford	.25
17	Earl Torgeson	.25
18	Tony Kubek	.40
19	Rollie Sheldon	.25
20	Tex Clevenger	.25
21	Art Ditmar	.25
22	Bud Daley	.25
23	Jim Coates	.25
24	Al Downing	.25
25	Johnny Sain	.25
26	Jim Hegan	.25
27	Wally Moses	.25
28	Ralph Houk	.25
29	Bill Skowron	.40
30	Bobby Richardson	.40
31	Johnny James	.25
32	Hal Reniff	.25
33	Mickey Mantle	6.00
34	Clete Boyer	.25
35	Elston Howard	.35
36	Joe DeMaestri	.25
37	Billy Gardner	.25

1983 Gardner's Brewers

PETE VUCKOVICH — Brewers

Topps produced in 1983 for Gardner's Bakery of Madison, WI, a 22-card set featuring the American League champion Milwaukee Brewers. The cards, which measure 2-1/2" x 3-1/2", have colorful fronts which contain the player's name, team and position plus the Brewers and Gardner's logos. The card backs are identical to the regular Topps issue but are numbered 1-22. The cards were inserted in specially marked packages of Gardner's bread products and were susceptible to grease stains.

		NM/M
Complete Set (22):		8.00
Common Player:		.25
1	Harvey Kuenn	.25
2	Dwight Bernard	.25
3	Mark Brouhard	.25
4	Mike Caldwell	.25
5	Cecil Cooper	.25
6	Marshall Edwards	.25
7	Rollie Fingers	1.00
8	Jim Gantner	.25
9	Moose Haas	.25
10	Bob McClure	.25
11	Paul Molitor	4.00
12	Don Money	.25
13	Charlie Moore	.25
14	Ben Oglivie	.25
15	Ed Romero	.25
16	Ted Simmons	.25
17	Jim Slaton	.25
18	Don Sutton	1.00
19	Gorman Thomas	.25
20	Pete Vuckovich	.25
21	Ned Yost	.25
22	Robin Yount	4.00

1984 Gardner's Brewers

DON SUTTON — Brewers — P — 1984 SERIES II

For the second straight year, Gardner's Bakery inserted baseball cards featuring the Milwaukee Brewers with its bread products. The 22-card set, entitled "1984 Series II," have multi-colored fronts that include the Brewers and Gardner's logos. The card backs are identical to the regular 1984 Topps issue except for the 1-22 numbering system. The Topps-produced cards are the standard 2-1/2" x 3-1/2" size. The cards are sometimes found with grease stains, resulting from contact with the bread.

		NM/M
Complete Set (22):		5.00
Common Player:		.25
1	Rene Lachemann	.25
2	Mark Brouhard	.25
3	Mike Caldwell	.25
4	Bobby Clark	.25
5	Cecil Cooper	.25
6	Rollie Fingers	.50
7	Jim Gantner	.25
8	Moose Haas	.25
9	Roy Howell	.25
10	Pete Ladd	.25
11	Rick Manning	.25
12	Bob McClure	.25
13	Paul Molitor	3.00
14	Charlie Moore	.25
15	Ben Oglivie	.25
16	Ed Romero	.25
17	Ted Simmons	.25
18	Jim Sundberg	.25
19	Don Sutton	.50
20	Tom Tellmann	.25
21	Pete Vuckovich	.25
22	Robin Yount	3.00

1985 Gardner's Brewers

PETE LADD — Pitcher — 27

Gardner's Bakery issued a 22-card set featuring the Milwaukee Brewers for the third consecutive year in 1985. The set was produced by Topps and is designed in a horizontal format. The card fronts feature color photos inside blue, red and yellow frames. The player's name and position are placed in orange boxes to the right of the photo and are accompanied by the Brewers and Gardner's logos. The card backs are identical to the regular 1985 Topps set but are blue rather than green and are numbered 1-22. The cards, which were inserted in specially marked bread products, are often found with grease stains.

		NM/M
Complete Set (22):		5.00
Common Player:		.25
1	George Bamberger	.25
2	Mark Brouhard	.25
3	Bob Clark	.25
4	Jaime Cocanower	.25
5	Cecil Cooper	.25
6	Rollie Fingers	.50
7	Jim Gantner	.25
8	Moose Haas	.25
9	Dion James	.25
10	Pete Ladd	.25
11	Rick Manning	.25
12	Bob McClure	.25
13	Paul Molitor	3.00
14	Charlie Moore	.25
15	Ben Oglivie	.25
16	Chuck Porter	.25
17	Ed Romero	.25
18	Bill Schroeder	.25
19	Ted Simmons	.25
20	Tom Tellmann	.25
21	Pete Vuckovich	.25
22	Robin Yount	3.00

1989 Gardner's Brewers

ROBIN YOUNT — MILWAUKEE BREWERS — OUTFIELD

Returning after a three-year hiatus, Gardner's Bread of Madison, WI., issued a 15-card Milwaukee Brewers set in 1989. The blue and white-bordered cards are the standard size and feature posed portrait photos with all Brewer logos airbrushed from the players' caps. The Gardner's logo appears at the top of the card, while the player's name is below the photo. The set, which was produced in conjunction with Mike Schechter Associates, was issued with loaves of bread or packages of buns, one card per package.

		NM/M
Complete Set (15):		5.00
Common Player:		.25
1	Paul Molitor	2.50
2	Robin Yount	2.50
3	Jim Gantner	.25
4	Rob Deer	.25
5	B.J. Surhoff	.25
6	Dale Sveum	.25
7	Ted Higuera	.25
8	Dan Plesac	.25
9	Bill Wegman	.25
10	Juan Nieves	.25
11	Greg Brock	.25
12	Glenn Braggs	.25
13	Joey Meyer	.25
14	Ernest Riles	.25
15	Don August	.25

1986 Gatorade Cubs

Gatorade sponsored this set which was given away at the July 17, 1986 Cubs game.

CHICAGO (19) MANNY TRILLO, IF

Cards measure 2-7/8" x 4-1/4" and feature color photos inside red and white frames. The Cubs logo appears at the top of the card. Backs include statistical information and the Gatorade logo. This set marked the fifth consecutive year the Cubs had held a baseball card giveaway promotion.

		NM/M
Complete Set (28):		12.00
Common Player:		.25
4	Gene Michael	.25
6	Keith Moreland	.25
7	Jody Davis	.25
10	Leon Durham	.25
11	Ron Cey	.25
12	Shawon Dunston	.25
15	Davey Lopes	.25
16	Terry Francona	.25
18	Steve Christmas	.25
19	Manny Trillo	.25
20	Bob Dernier	.25
22	Scott Sanderson	.25
23	Jerry Mumphrey	.25
23	Ryne Sandberg	9.00
27	Thad Bosley	.25
28	Chris Speier	.25
29	Steve Lake	.25
31	Ray Fontenot	.25
34	Steve Trout	.25
36	Gary Matthews	.25
39	George Frazier	.25
40	Rick Sutcliffe	.35
43	Dennis Eckersley	1.50
46	Lee Smith	.35
48	Jay Baller	.25
49	Jamie Moyer	.25
50	Guy Hoffman	.25
---	The Coaching Staff (Ruben Amaro, Billy Connors, Johnny Oates, John Vukovich, Billy Williams)	.25

1987 Gatorade Indians

(28) CORY SNYDER, IF — COMPLIMENTS OF Gatorade

For the second year in a row, the Indians gave out a perforated set of baseball cards to fans attending the Team Photo/Baseball Card Day promotion. Sponsored by Gatorade, the individual cards measure 2-1/2" x 3-1/8". Fronts contain a color photo surrounded by a red frame inside a white border. The player's name, uniform number and the Gatorade logo are also on front. Backs are printed in black, blue and red and carry a facsimile autograph and the player's stats.

		NM/M
Complete Set, Foldout:		6.00
Complete Set, Singles (31):		6.00
Common Player:		.25
2	Brett Butler	.25
4	Tony Bernazard	.25
6	Andy Allanson	.25
7	Pat Corrales	.25
8	Carmen Castillo	.25
10	Pat Tabler	.25
11	Jamie Easterly	.25
12	Dave Clark	.25
13	Ernie Camacho	.25
14	Julio Franco	.35
17	Junior Noboa	.25
18	Ken Schrom	.25
20	Otis Nixon	.25
21	Greg Swindell	.25
22	Frank Wills	.25
23	Chris Bando	.25
24	Rick Dempsey	.25
26	Brook Jacoby	.25
27	Mel Hall	.25
28	Cory Snyder	.25
29	Andre Thornton	.35
30	Joe Carter	.75
35	Phil Niekro	.75
36	Ed Vande Berg	.25
42	Rich Yett	.25
43	Scott Bailes	.25
46	Doug Jones	.25
49	Tom Candiotti	.25
54	Tom Waddell	.25
---	Manager and Coaching Staff (Jack Aker, Bobby Bonds, Pat Corrales, Doc Edwards, Johnny Goryl)	.25
---	Team photo	.25

1988 Gatorade Indians

(52) JOHN FARRELL, P — COMPLIMENTS OF Gatorade

This three-panel foldout was sponsored by Gatorade for distribution during an in-stadium giveaway. The cover includes four game-action photos. One panel of the 9-1/2" x 11-1/4" glossy color foldout features a team photo (with checklist), two panels consist of 30 perforated baseball cards (2-1/4" x 3") featuring team members. Posed portrait photos are framed in red on a white background. The player's name and uniform number are printed below the photo. Backs are printed in red, blue and black. A facsimile autograph appears at the top-right of the card back, opposite the player uniform number, name and position. Both major and minor league stats are listed.

		NM/M
Complete Set, Foldout:		5.00
Complete Set, Singles (31):		5.00
Common Player:		.25
2	Tom Spencer	.25
6	Andy Allanson	.25
7	Luis Issac	.25
8	Carmen Castillo	.25
9	Charlie Manuel	.25
10	Pat Tabler	.25
14	Doug Jones	.25
14	Julio Franco	.50
16	Ron Washington	.25
16	Jay Bell	.75
17	Bill Laskey	.25
20	Willie Upshaw	.25
21	Greg Swindell	.25
23	Chris Bando	.25
25	Dave Clark	.25
26	Brook Jacoby	.25
27	Mel Hall	.25
28	Cory Snyder	.25
30	Joe Carter	.75
31	Dan Schatzeder	.25
32	Doc Edwards	.25
33	Ron Kittle	.25
35	Mark Wiley	.25
42	Rich Yett	.25
43	Scott Bailes	.25
46	Johnny Goryl	.25
47	Jeff Kaiser	.25
50	Tom Candiotti	.25
52	Jeff Dedmon	.25
52	John Farrell	.25
---	Team photo	2.00

1993 Gatorade Detroit Tigers

ALAN TRAMMELL

Color action photos are featured on these oversized (2-7/8" x 4-1/4") cards. The pictures are framed in team-color navy and orange pinstripes with a white border. Player name is in white in a navy border below the photo, with the position printed in orange at bottom. A large team logo appears in the upper-right corner. Backs are printed in orange and black and include a Gatorade logo, player identification and stats. Cards are listed here by uniform number.

		NM/M
Complete Set (28):		4.00
Common Player:		.25
1	Lou Whitaker	.75
3	Alan Trammell	1.00
4	Tony Phillips	.25
7	Scott Livingstone	.25
9	Skeeter Barnes	.25
11	Sparky Anderson	.75
15	Gary Thurman	.25
16	David Wells	.25
18	David Haas	.25
19	Chad Kreuter	.25
20	Mickey Tettleton	.25
21	Mike Moore	.25
22	Milt Cuyler	.25
23a	Kirk Gibson	.50
23b	Mark Leiter	.25
24	Travis Fryman	.50
27	Kurt Knudsen	.25
29	Rob Deer	.25
30	Bill Krueger	.25
32	Dan Gladden	.25
36	Bill Gullickson	.25
38	Bob MacDonald	.25
39	Mike Henneman	.25
44	Buddy Groom	.25
44	John Doherty	.25
45	Cecil Fielder	.50
49	Tom Bolton	.25
---	Coaches (Dick Tracewksi, Billy Muffett, Larry Herndon, Gene Roof, Dan Whitmer)	.25

1995 Gatorade Cubs

SHAWON DUNSTON-12 — INFIELDER

Fans attending the August 24 game at Wrigley Field received a set of oversized (2-7/8" x 4-1/4") cards of the Chicago Cubs, sponsored by Gatorade. Cards feature a color action photo at top, with the player's name, position and uniform number in a blue box at bottom. Backs have a small black-and-white portrait photo, complete minor and major league stats and the team and sponsor logos. Cards are checklisted here by player uniform number.

		NM/M
Complete Set (27):		5.00
Common Player:		.25
5	Jim Riggleman	.25
9	Scott Servais	.25
10	Scott Bullett	.25
11	Rey Sanchez	.25
12	Shawon Dunston	.25
13	Turk Wendell	.25
16	Anthony Young	.25
17	Mark Grace	.50
18	Jose Hernandez	.25
20	Howard Johnson	.25
21	Sammy Sosa	4.00
25	Luis Gonzalez	.50
27	Todd Zeile	.25
28	Randy Myers	.25
29	Jose Guzman	.25
30	Ozzie Timmons	.25
32	Kevin Foster	.25
38	Jaime Navarro	.25
46	Steve Trachsel	.25
47	Mike Perez	.25
49	Frank Castillo	.25
52	Jim Bullinger	.25
53	Chris Nabholz	.25
55	Larry Casian	.25
56	Brian McRae	.25
57	Rich Garces	.25
---	Cubs coaches (Dave Bialas, Fergie Jenkins, Tony Muser, Max Oliveras, Dan Radison, Billy Williams)	.25

1997 Gatorade Cubs

This postcard-size set was a stadium give-away. Fronts have game-action photos on a green ivy background. Backs have player data and stats. The set is arranged here alphabetically.

		NM/M
Complete Set (26):		8.00
Common Player:		.25
(1)	Terry Adams	.25
(2)	Kent Bottenfield	.25
(3)	Brant Brown	.25
(4)	Dave Clark	.25
(5)	Shawon Dunston	.25
(6)	Kevin Foster	.25
(7)	Doug Glanville	.25
(8)	Jeremi Gonzalez	.25
(9)	Mark Grace	.50
(10)	Dave Hansen	.25
(11)	Jose Hernandez	.25
(12)	Tyler Houston	.25
(13)	Brian McRae	.25
(14)	Kevin Orie	.25
(15)	Bob Patterson	.25
(16)	Jim Riggleman	.25
(17)	Mel Rojas	.25
(18)	Rey Sanchez	.25
(19)	Ryne Sandberg	4.00
(20)	Scott Servais	.25
(21)	Sammy Sosa	4.00
(22)	Kevin Tapani	.25
(23)	Ramon Tatis	.25
(24)	Steve Traschel	.25
(25)	Turk Wendell	.25
(26)	Cubs Coaches (Rick Kranitz, Jeff Pentland, Mako Oliveras, Dan Radison, Phil Regan, Billy Williams)	.25

1985 General Mills Stickers

General Mills of Canada inserted a panel of two cellophane-wrapped baseball stickers in each box of Cheerios in 1985. The full-color sticker panels, measuring 2-3/8" x 3-3/4", are blank-backed and unnumbered and contain the player's name, team and position in both English and French. The General Mills logo appears at the top of each sticker. All team insignia on the players' uniforms and caps have been airbrushed off.

	NM/M
Complete Panel Set (15):	10.00
Complete Singles Set (26):	7.00

		NM/M
Common Panel:		.50
Common Player:		.25
	Panel (1)	1.25
(1)	Gary Carter	.50
(2)	Tom Brunansky	.25
	Panel (2)	1.25
(1)	Gary Carter	.50
(3)	Dave Stieb	.25
	Panel (3)	1.00
(4)	Andre Dawson	.35
(5)	Alvin Davis	.25
	Panel (4)	1.00
(4)	Andre Dawson	.35
(3)	Dave Stieb	.25
	Panel (5)	1.00
(6)	Steve Garvey	.35
(7)	Buddy Bell	.25
	Panel (6)	1.25
(6)	Steve Garvey	.35
(8)	Jim Rice	.30
	Panel (7)	1.00
(9)	Jeff Leonard	.25
(10)	Eddie Murray	.50
	Panel (8)	1.50
(11)	Dale Murphy	.35
(12)	Robin Yount	.50
	Panel (9)	1.50
(13)	Terry Puhl	.25
(14)	Reggie Jackson	.60
	Panel (10)	.50
(15)	Johnny Ray	.25
(16)	Lou Whitaker	.25
	Panel (11)	1.00
(17)	Ryne Sandberg	.75
(18)	Mike Hargrove	.25
	Panel (12)	2.00
(19)	Mike Schmidt	.75
(20)	George Brett	.75
	Panel (13)	1.25
(21)	Ozzie Smith	.60
(22)	Dave Winfield	.50
	Panel (14)	1.25
(23)	Mario Soto	.25
(24)	Carlton Fisk	.50
	Panel (15)	1.00
(25)	Fernando Valenzuela	.25
(26)	Dwayne Murphy	.25

1986 General Mills Booklets

In 1986, General Mills of Canada inserted six different "Baseball Players Booklets" in specially marked boxes of Cheerios. Ten different players are featured in each booklet, with statistics for the 1985 season in both English and French. The booklet, when opened fully, measures 3-3/4" x 15". Also included in the booklet is a contest sponsored by Petro-Canada service stations to win a day with a major league player at his 1987 spring training site in Florida. Team insignias have been airbrushed off the players' uniforms and caps.

		NM/M
Complete Set (6):		12.50
Common Booklet:		1.25
1	A.L. East (Wade Boggs, Kirk Gibson, Rickey Henderson, Don Mattingly, Jack Morris, Lance Parrish, Jim Rice, Dave Righetti, Cal Ripken, Lou Whitaker)	4.00
2	A.L. West (Harold Baines, Phil Bradley, George Brett, Carlton Fisk, Ozzie Guillen, Kent Hrbek, Reggie Jackson, Dan Quisenberry, Bret Saberhagen, Frank White)	2.50
3	Toronto Blue Jays (Jesse Barfield, George Bell, Bill Caudill, Tony Fernandez, Damaso Garcia,	

		NM/M
	Lloyd Moseby, Rance Mulliniks, Dave Stieb, Willie Upshaw, Ernie Whitt)	2.00
4	N.L. East (Gary Carter, Jack Clark, George Foster, Dwight Gooden, Gary Matthews, Willie McGee, Ryne Sandberg, Mike Schmidt, Lee Smith, Ozzie Smith)	2.50
5	N.L. West (Dave Concepcion, Pedro Guerrero, Terry Kennedy, Dale Murphy, Graig Nettles, Dave Parker, Tony Perez, Steve Sax, Bruce Sutter, Fernando Valenzuela)	1.25
6	Montreal Expos (Hubie Brooks, Andre Dawson, Mike Fitzgerald, Vance Law, Tim Raines, Jeff Reardon, Bryn Smith, Jason Thompson, Tim Wallach, Mitch Webster)	2.00

1987 General Mills Booklets

For a second straight year, General Mills of Canada inserted one of six different "Baseball Super-Stars Booklets" in specially marked boxes of Cheerios and Honey Nut Cheerios cereal. Each booklet contains ten full-color photos for a total of 60 players. The booklets, when completely unfolded, measure 15" x 3-3/4". Written in both English and French, the set was produced by Mike Schechter and Associates. All team insignias have been airbrushed off the photos.

		NM/M
Complete Set (6):		9.00
Common Booklet:		2.00
1	Toronto Blue Jays (Jesse Barfield, George Bell, Tony Fernandez, Kelly Gruber, Tom Henke, Jimmy Key, Lloyd Moseby, Dave Stieb, Willie Upshaw, Ernie Whitt)	2.00
2	A.L. East (Wade Boggs, Roger Clemens, Kirk Gibson, Rickey Henderson, Don Mattingly, Jack Morris, Eddie Murray, Pat Tabler, Dave Winfield, Robin Yount)	4.00
3	A.L. West (Phil Bradley, George Brett, Jose Canseco, Carlton Fisk, Reggie Jackson, Wally Joyner, Kirk McCaskill, Larry Parrish, Kirby Puckett, Dan Quisenberry)	2.50
4	Montreal Expos (Hubie Brooks, Mike Fitzgerald, Andres Galarraga, Vance Law, Andy McGaffigan, Bryn Smith, Jason Thompson, Tim Wallach, Mitch Webster, Floyd Youmans)	2.00
5	N.L. East (Gary Carter, Dwight Gooden, Keith Hernandez, Willie McGee, Tim Raines, R.J. Reynolds,	

		NM/M
	Ryne Sandberg, Mike Schmidt, Ozzie Smith, Darryl Strawberry)	2.50
6	N.L. West (Kevin Bass, Chili Davis, Bill Doran, Pedro Guerrero, Tony Gwynn, Dale Murphy, Dave Parker, Steve Sax, Mike Scott, Fernando Valenzuela)	2.00

1990 Giant Eagle Roberto Clemente Stickers

The Giant Eagle food stores around Pittsburgh issued a collectors' poster and set of 18 stickers circa 1990. Each of the 2-1/2" x 3-1/2" stickers features one of Roberto Clemente's regular-issue Topps cards 1955-72. The stickers were originally issued in strips of three. Backs are blank. The issue was almost certainly not authorized by Topps or the Clemente estate.

	NM/M
Complete Set, Strips (6):	20.00
Common Sticker:	2.00
Poster:	16.00

1981 Granny Goose Potato Chips A's

The 1981 Granny Goose set features the Oakland A's. The 2-1/2" x 3-1/2" cards were issued in bags of potato chips and are sometimes found

---

with grease stains. The cards have full color fronts with the graphics done in the team's green and yellow colors. The backs contain the A's logo and a short player biography. The Revering card was withdrawn from the set shortly after he was traded and is in shorter supply than the rest of the cards in the set. The cards are numbered in the checklist that follows by the player's uniform number.

		NM/M
Complete Set (15):		100.00
Common Player:		2.00
1	Billy Martin	8.00
2	Mike Heath	2.00
5	Jeff Newman	2.00
6	Mitchell Page	2.00
8	Rob Picciolo	2.00
10	Wayne Gross	2.00
13	Dave Revering	40.00
17	Mike Norris	2.00
20	Tony Armas	2.00
21	Dwayne Murphy	2.00
22	Rick Langford	2.00
27	Matt Keough	2.00
35	Rickey Henderson	35.00
39	Dave McKay	2.00
54	Steve McCatty	2.00

1982 Granny Goose Potato Chips A's

Granny Goose repeated its promotion from the previous year and issued another set featuring the Oakland A's. The 2-1/2" x 3-1/2" cards were distributed in two fashions - in bags of potato chips and at Fan Appreciation Day at Oakland-Alameda Coliseum. The cards are identical in design to the 1981 set and can be distinguished from it by the date on the copyright on the bottom of the card reverse. The cards are numbered in the checklist that follows by the player's uniform number.

		NM/M
Complete Set (15):		7.50
Common Player:		.50
1	Billy Martin	1.00
2	Mike Heath	.50
5	Jeff Newman	.50
8	Rob Picciolo	.50
10	Wayne Gross	.50
11	Fred Stanley	.50
15	Davey Lopes	.50
17	Mike Norris	.50
20	Tony Armas	.50
21	Dwayne Murphy	.50
22	Rick Langford	.50
27	Matt Keough	.50
35	Rickey Henderson	6.00
44	Cliff Johnson, Jr.	.50
54	Steve McCatty	.50

Signature Set

The cards from this very scarce 15-card set are identical to the regular Granny Goose cards, but contain a facsimile autograph on the front. The cards were initially intended as special prize-redemption inserts from Granny Goose potato chips, but were never released in any quantity.

		NM/M
Complete Set (15):		125.00
Common Player:		5.00
1	Billy Martin	30.00
2	Mike Heath	5.00
5	Jeff Newman	5.00

8	Rob Picciolo	5.00
10	Wayne Gross	5.00
11	Fred Stanley	5.00
15	Davey Lopes	7.50
17	Mike Norris	5.00
20	Tony Armas	5.00
21	Dwayne Murphy	5.00
22	Rick Langford	5.00
27	Matt Keough	5.00
35	Rickey Henderson	45.00
44	Cliff Johnson, Jr.	5.00
54	Steve McCatty	5.00

1983 Granny Goose Potato Chips A's

For the third consecutive year, Granny Goose issued a set of baseball cards featuring the Oakland A's. The cards were issued with or without a detachable coupon found at the bottom of each card. Issued in bags of potato chips were the coupon cards, which contain a scratch-off section offering prizes. The cards without the coupon section were given away to fans at Oakland-Alameda Coliseum on July 3, 1983. Cards with the detachable coupon command a 50 per cent premium over the coupon-less variety. The cards in the following checklist are numbered by the player's uniform number.

		NM/M
Complete Set (15):		8.00
Common Player:		.50
2	Mike Heath	.50
4	Carney Lansford	.50
10	Wayne Gross	.50
14	Steve Boros	.50
15	Davey Lopes	.50
16	Mike Davis	.50
17	Mike Norris	.50
21	Dwayne Murphy	.50
22	Rick Langford	.50
27	Matt Keough	.50
31	Tom Underwood	.50
33	Dave Beard	.50
35	Rickey Henderson	6.00
39	Tom Burgmeier	.50
54	Steve McCatty	.50

1999 GTE Tampa Bay Devil Rays

This team set was a stadium giveaway. Fronts have game-action color photos. On back are complete minor and major league stats along with team and sponsor logos.

	NM/M
Complete Set (30):	10.00
Common Player:	.25

1 Scott Aldred .25
2 Wilson Alvarez .25
3 Rolando Arrojo .25
4 Wade Boggs 3.00
5 Miguel Cairo .25
6 Jose Canseco .25
7 Coaches (Orlando Gomez, Billy Hatcher, Frank Howard, Greg Riddoch, Leon Roberts, Rick Williams) .25
8 Mike DiFelice .25
9 John Flaherty .25
10 Roberto Hernandez .25
11 David Lamb .25
12 Aaron Ledesma .25
13 Albie Lopez .25
14 Dave Martinez .25
15 Quinton McCracken .35
16 Fred McGriff .35
17 Herbert Perry .25
18 Bryan Rekar .25
19 Larry Rothschild .25
20 Ryan Rupe .25
21 Julio Santana .25
22 Tony Saunders .25
23 Paul Sorrento .25
24 Kevin Stocker .25
25 Rick White .25
26 Randy Winn .25
27 Bobby Witt .25
28 Esteban Yan .25
--- Literacy Champion (Quinton McCracken) .25
--- Sponsor's Card .25

H

1981-89 Hall of Fame Metallic Plaque-cards

Between 1981-89, the National Baseball Hall of Fame & Museum issued a set of metallic baseball cards reproducing the plaques of the baseball greats inducted. The plaques are pictured on 2-1/2" x 3-1/2" blank-backed gold anodized aluminum. Every detail of the plaque is fully and faithfully reproduced. The set was sold in series through the Hall of Fame's gift shop. The series was discontinued for economic reasons in 1989. Only 1,000 plaques of each player were produced. Values are, to some extent, based not only on player popularity, but on year of issue; later plaques tend to be more expensive because fewer were sold.

NM/M
Complete Set (204): 650.00
Common Player: 3.00
(1) Hank Aaron/1983 20.00
(2) Grover Alexander/1982 5.00
(3) Walter Alston/1984 4.00
(4) Cap Anson/1981 4.00
(5) Luis Aparicio/1984 6.50
(6) Luke Appling/1982 3.50
(7) Earl Averill/1983 3.00
(8) "Home Run" Baker/1983 3.00
(9) David Bancroft/1982 3.00
(10) Ernie Banks/1982 8.00
(11) Al Barlick/1989 4.50
(12) Ed Barrow/1982 3.00
(13) Jacob Beckley/1982 3.00
(14) Cool Papa Bell/1981 6.00
(15) Johnny Bench/1989 15.00
(16) "Chief" Bender/1982 3.50
(17) Yogi Berra/1982 12.00
(18) Jim Bottomley/1982 4.00
(19) Lou Boudreau/1982 3.00
(20) Roger Bresnahan/1982 3.00
(21) Lou Brock/1986 12.00
(22) Dan Brouthers/1982 3.00
(23) Mordecai Brown/1981 4.00
(24) Morgan Burkeley/1981 3.00
(25) Jesse Burkett/1982 3.00
(26) Roy Campanella/1981 12.50
(27) Max Carey/1982 3.00
(28) Alexander Cartwright/1981 3.00
(29) Henry Chadwick/1982 3.00
(30) Frank Chance/1983 4.50
(31) Happy Chandler/1983 3.00
(32) Oscar Charleston/1982 4.00
(33) Jack Chesbro/1982 3.50
(34) Fred Clarke/1983 3.00
(35) John Clarkson/1982 3.00
(36) Roberto Clemente/1982 30.00
(37) Ty Cobb/1982 30.00
(38) Mickey Cochrane/1983 5.00
(39) Eddie Collins/1981 3.00
(40) James Collins/1982 3.00
(41) Earle Combs/1983 3.00
(42) Charles Comiskey/1982 3.00
(43) Jocko Conlan/1981 3.00
(44) Thomas Connolly/1982 3.00
(45) Roger Connor/1982 3.00
(46) Stan Coveleski/1982 3.00
(47) Sam Crawford/1983 3.50
(48) Joe Cronin/1981 5.00
(49) Candy Cummings/1982 3.00
(50) Kiki Cuyler/1983 4.00
(51) Ray Dandridge/1989 6.00
(52) Dizzy Dean/1983 10.00
(53) Ed Delahanty/1983 3.00
(54) Bill Dickey/1981 5.00
(55) Martin Dihigo/1982 6.50
(56) Joe DiMaggio/1983 35.00
(57) Bobby Doerr/1986 4.00
(58) Don Drysdale/1983 10.00
(59) Hugh Duffy/1982 3.00
(60) Bill Evans/1983 3.00
(61) John Evers/1982 4.50
(62) Buck Ewing/1981 3.00
(63) Urban Faber/1983 3.00
(64) Bob Feller/1981 6.50
(65) Rick Ferrell/1984 4.00
(66) Elmer Flick/1982 3.00
(67) Whitey Ford/1982 10.00
(68) Rube Foster/1983 3.00
(69) Jimmie Foxx/1982 7.50
(70) Ford Frick/1981 3.00
(71) Frank Frisch/1981 3.00
(72) Pud Galvin/1983 3.00
(73) Lou Gehrig/1982 35.00
(74) Charles Gehringer/1983 6.50
(75) Bob Gibson/1982 6.50
(76) Josh Gibson/1981 6.50
(77) Warren Giles/1983 3.00
(78) Lefty Gomez/1981 4.00
(79) Goose Goslin/1982 4.00
(80) Hank Greenberg/1981 8.00
(81) Clark Griffith/1982 3.00
(82) Burleigh Grimes/1982 3.00
(83) Lefty Grove/1981 4.50
(84) Chick Hafey/1982 3.00
(85) Pop Haines/1982 3.00
(86) William Hamilton/1982 3.00
(87) William Harridge/1982 3.00
(88) Bucky Harris/1982 3.00
(89) Gabby Hartnett/1982 3.50
(90) Harry Heilmann/1983 3.00
(91) Bill Herman/1982 3.00
(92) Harry Hooper/1982 3.00
(93) Rogers Hornsby/1981 8.00
(94) Schoolboy Hoyt/1983 3.00
(95) Cal Hubbard/1982 3.00
(96) Carl Hubbell/1981 3.00
(97) Miller Huggins/1982 3.50
(98) Catfish Hunter/1983 6.00
(99) Monte Irvin/1981 3.50
(100) Travis Jackson/1983 3.00
(101) Hugh Jennings/1983 3.00
(102) Ban Johnson/1981 3.00
(103) Judy Johnson/1981 3.00
(104) Walter Johnson/1982 10.00
(105) Addie Joss/1982 3.00
(106) Al Kaline/1981 8.00
(107) Timothy Keefe/1983 3.00
(108) Willie Keeler (1982) 3.00
(109) George Kell/1984 4.00
(110) Joe Kelley/1983 3.00
(111) Highpockets Kelly (?) 4.00
(112) King Kelly/1981 4.00
(113) Harmon Killebrew/1984 6.50
(114) Ralph Kiner/1982 3.00
(115) Chuck Klein/1983 3.00
(116) Bill Klem/1981 3.00
(117) Sandy Koufax/1982 25.00
(118) Nap Lajoie/1983 5.00
(119) Kenesaw Landis/1983 3.00
(120) Buck Leonard/1982 3.50
(121) Bob Lemon/1982 3.00
(122) Fred Linstrom/1982 3.00
(123) Pop Lloyd/1981 3.00
(124) Ernie Lombardi/1986 3.00
(125) Al Lopez/1981 3.00
(126) Ted Lyons/1983 3.00
(127) Connie Mack/1981 3.00
(128) Larry MacPhail/1983 3.00
(129) Mickey Mantle/1983 40.00
(130) Heinie Manush/1981 3.00
(131) Rabbit Maranville/1981 4.00
(132) Juan Marichal/1984 5.00
(133) Rube Marquard/1983 3.50
(134) Eddie Mathews/1983 3.50
(135) Christy Mathewson/1981 10.00
(136) Willie Mays/1981 20.00
(137) Joe McCarthy/1983 3.00
(138) Thomas McCarthy/1983 3.00
(139) Willie McCovey/1986 3.50
(140) Iron Man McGinnity/1982 3.00
(141) John McGraw/1982 3.00
(142) Bill McKechnie/1982 3.00
(143) Joe Medwick/1983 3.00
(144) Johnny Mize/1982 3.00
(145) Stan Musial/1981 15.00
(146) Kid Nichols/1983 4.00
(147) James O'Rourke/1982 3.00
(148) Mel Ott/1981 4.00
(149) Satchel Paige/1982 12.50
(150) Herb Pennock/1983 3.00
(151) Eddie Plank/1982 3.00
(152) Hoss Radbourne/1983 3.00
(153) Pee Wee Reese/1984 3.50
(154) Sam Rice/1983 3.00
(155) Branch Rickey/1981 3.00
(156) Eppa Rixey/1983 3.00
(157) Robin Roberts/1982 5.00
(158) Brooks Robinson/1984 6.00
(159) Frank Robinson/1983 6.50
(160) Jackie Robinson/1981 20.00
(161) Wilbert Robinson/1982 3.50
(162) Edd Roush/1982 3.00
(163) Red Ruffing/1982 4.00
(164) Amos Rusie/1983 3.00
(165) Babe Ruth/1981 40.00
(166) Ray Schalk/1982 3.00
(167) Red Schoendienst/1989 8.00
(168) Joe Sewell/1982 3.00
(169) Al Simmons/1982 5.00
(170) George Sisler/1981 3.00
(171) Enos Slaughter/1986 3.00
(172) Duke Snider/1981 8.00
(173) Warren Spahn/1982 8.00
(174) Al Spalding/1982 4.00
(175) Tris Speaker/1982 6.50
(176) Willie Stargell/1989 3.00
(177) Casey Stengel/1981 6.50
(178) Bill Terry/1981 3.00
(179) Sam Thompson/1983 3.00
(180) Joe Tinker/1982 6.00
(181) Pie Traynor/1982 6.00
(182) Dazzy Vance/1983 4.00
(183) Arky Vaughan/1986 3.00
(184) Rube Waddell/1983 4.00
(185) Honus Wagner/1982 15.00
(186) Roderick Wallace/1982 3.00
(187) Ed Walsh/1982 3.00
(188) Lloyd Waner/1981 4.00
(189) Paul Waner/1981 5.00
(190) John Ward/1982 3.00
(191) George Weiss/1983 3.00
(192) Mickey Welch/1983 3.00
(193) Zack Wheat/1982 4.00
(194) Hoyt Wilhelm/1986 6.50
(195) Billy Williams/1989 8.00
(196) Ted Williams/1981 27.50
(197) Hack Wilson/1982 4.00
(198) George Wright/1982 3.00
(199) Harry Wright/1983 3.00
(200) Early Wynn/1982 4.00
(201) Carl Yastrzemski/1989 12.00
(202) Tom Yawkey/1982 3.00
(203) Cy Young/1981 10.00
(204) Ross Youngs/1982 3.00

1995 Baseball's Hall of Famers Creating History

Colorized artist's renderings of 19th Century Old Judge cabinet cards are the basis for this set of postcards produced for the Hall of Fame by R.F. Ball, who produced a similar set of lithographs in 1987. The postcards are 5" x 7" and have the central color painting bordered in black. Postcard-format backs have a few words about the player. The cards were produced in a serial-numbered edition of 2,000 each, packaged with a like-numbered checklist. Issue price at the Hall of Fame's gift shop was $12.95. A 21-1/2" x 38" uncut poster of the cards was sold for $49.95.

NM/M
Complete Set (10): 13.00
Common Player: 1.50
1 Cap Anson 2.00
2 Dan Brouthers 1.50
3 John Clarkson 1.50
4 Ed Delahanty 1.50
5 Buck Ewing 1.50
6 Tim Keefe 1.50
7 Mike Kelly 2.00
8 Kid Nichols 1.50
9 Jim O'Rourke 1.50
10 Sam Thompson 1.50

This boxed set of large-format (2-7/8" x 4-1/2") round-cornered cards was designated "Flash-Pack / Knowledge in a Nutshell." It was described as the first in a series. Card fronts feature borderless black-and-white or color photos with no player identification or other graphics. Black-and-white backs identify the player, provide a career summary and date of selection to the Hall of Fame. The unnumbered cards are listed here alphabetically. The boxed set originally retailed for $9.95.

NM/M
Complete Set (36): 20.00
Common Player: .50
(1) Cap Anson .50
(2) Ernie Banks 2.00
(3) Edward G. Barrow .50
(4) Roger Bresnahan .50
(5) Lou Brock 1.00
(6) Roy Campanella 2.00
(7) Alexander Cartwright .50
(8) Henry Chadwick .50
(9) Oscar Charleston .50
(10) Jack Chesbro .50
(11) Roberto Clemente 4.00
(12) Charles Comiskey .50
(13) Candy Cummings .50
(14) Andrew "Rube" Foster .50
(15) Ford Frick .50
(16) Josh Gibson 1.00
(17) Burleigh Grimes .50
(18) Cal Hubbard .50
(19) Carl Hubbell .50
(20) Willie Keeler .50
(21) Bill Klem .50
(22) Kenesaw M. Landis .50
(23) Larry MacPhail .50
(24) Juan Marichal 1.00
(25) Willie Mays 3.00
(26) John McGraw .50
(27) Stan Musial 2.00
(28) Charles Radbourne .50
(29) Branch Rickey .50
(30) Robin Roberts 1.00
(31) Brooks Robinson 1.00
(32) Warren Spahn 1.00
(33) Albert Spalding .50
(34) Willie Stargell 1.00
(35) Rube Waddell .50
(36) Harry Wright .50

2001 Hall of Fame Postcards

NM/M
Complete Set, Boxes (8): 15.00

2005 Hall of Fame Education Program

Each of the National Baseball Hall of Fame's educational programs is featured on a card in this special issue. Cards were issued in two 10-card cello packs.

NM/M
Complete Set (20): 7.50
Common Card: .50
(1) Header Card .05
(2) American History (Joe Jackson) 1.50
(3) Artifacts and Education (The Doubleday Ball) .50
(4) Civil Rights (Satchel Paige) .75
(5) Cultural Diversity (Jim Thorpe) 1.00
(6) Economics (T206 Honus Wagner) .50
(7) Fine Art (Babe Ruth painting) .50
(8) Leadership (Jackie Robinson) .50
(9) Popular Culture (Ichiro Suzuki bobblehead) .50
(10) Women's History (Mickey Maguire) .50
(11) Header Card .05
(12) Artifacts and Education (Roberto Clemente artifacts.) .50
(13) Character Education (Lou Gehrig) .75
(14) Communication Arts (Dizzy Dean) .50
(15) Geography (1958 N.Y. Yankees) .50
(16) Industrial Technology (Roger Bresnahan) .50
(17) Labor History (John Montgomery Ward) .50
(18) Mathematics (Hank Aaron) .50
(19) Science (Ozzie Smith) .50
(20) Special Abilities (Pete Gray) .75

1998 Hamburger Helper Home Run Heroes

Eight top sluggers are featured in this box-back set from Hamburger Helper. The 2-1/2" x 3-1/2" cards are printed on the backs of various flavors of the skillet meal boxes. Unlike many similar issues these are fully licensed by Major League Baseball, as well as the Players Association, and the player photos have uniform logos. Also unusual is that the cards have a printed back in black-and-white offering personal data, career highlights and stats.

NM/M
Complete Set, Boxes (8): 15.00
Complete Set, Singles (8): 15.00
Common Player: .50
1 Mark McGwire 3.00
2 Rafael Palmeiro 1.25
3 Tino Martinez .50
4 Barry Bonds 4.00
5 Larry Walker .50
6 Juan Gonzalez 1.25
7 Mike Piazza 2.00
8 Frank Thomas 1.50

1988 Hardee's/Coke Conlon

Regionally issued in a promotion sponsored by Hardee's restaurants and Coca-Cola, this six-card set features the photos of Charles Martin Conlon and is closely related to the Sporting News-Wide World Conlon issues of the time. The cards feature sepia photos on front and career stats and summary on back. The unnumbered cards are checklisted here alphabetically.

NM/M
Complete Set (6): 3.00
Common Player: .40
(1) Cool Papa Bell .40
(2) Ty Cobb 1.25
(3) Lou Gehrig 1.50
(4) Connie Mack .40
(5) Casey Stengel .40
(6) Rube Waddell .40

1996 Hebrew National Detroit Tigers

One of the team's hot dog concessionaires sponsored a set of Tiger cards given away at the September 1 game. Originally intended to be 28 cards, only 26 were issued due to late-season trades. Cards are in a larger than normal 2-7/8" x 4-1/4" format with game-action photo on front. Down one side in team colors are the player name and position, with the stalking tiger logo at bottom. Backs have a large light blue gothic "D" in the background with player personal data and major/minor league stats and team/sponsor logos.

NM/M
Complete Set (26): 12.00
Common Player: .50
1 Kimera Bartee .50
3 Jose Lima .50
5 Tony Clark .50
6 Travis Fryman .50
7 Bobby Higginson .50
8 Greg Keagle .50
9 Mark Lewis .50
10 Richie Lewis .50
11 Felipe Lira .50

12	Mike Myers	.50
13	Melvin Nieves	.50
14	Alan Trammell	1.00
15	Tom Urbani	.50
16	Brian Williams	.50
17	Eddie Williams	.50
18	Curtis Pride	.50
19	Mark Parent	.50
20	Raul Casanova	.50
21	Omar Olivares	.50
22	Gregg Olson	.50
23	Justin Thompson	.50
24	Brad Ausmus	.50
25	Andujar Cedeno	.50
26	Buddy Bell	.50
27	Paws/Mascot	.50
28	Detroit Tigers Coaches (Glenn Ezell, Terry Francona, Larry Herndon, Fred Kendall, John (Jon) Matlack, Ron Oester)	.50

1997 Hebrew National Detroit Tigers

The hot dog concession-aire at Tiger Stadium produced a second annual team set in 1997, giving the cards away at the June 22 game. Cards feature borderless color action photos on front, with a tiny black-and-white portrait photo at bottom-right. Backs are printed in blue and yellow and have player data, complete major and minor league stats and the team and sponsor logos.

		NM/M
	Complete Set (28):	12.00
	Common Player:	.50
1	Jose Bautista	.50
2	Willie Blair	.50
3	Doug Brocail	.50
4	Raul Casanova	.50
5	Tony Clark	.50
6	Deivi Cruz	.50
7	John Cummings	.50
8	Damion Easley	.50
9	Travis Fryman	.50
10	Bobby Higginson	.50
11	Brian Hunter	.50
12	Todd Johnson	.50
13	Todd Jones	.50
14	Felipe Lira	.50
15	Dan Miceli	.50
16	Brian Moehler	.50
17	Mike Myers	.50
18	Phil Nevin	.50
19	Melvin Nieves	.50
20	Omar Oliveras	.50
21	Curtis Pride	.50
22	A.J. Sager	.50
23	Justin Thompson	.50
24	Matt Walbeck	.50
25	Jody Reed	.50
26	Bob Hamelin	.50
27	Buddy Bell	.50
28	Tigers coaches (Rick Adair, Larry Herndon, Perry Hill, Fred Kendall, Larry Parrish, Jerry White)	.50

2005 Helmar Brewing Co.

These cards were inserted three per foil pack in packages of snack foods from a Michigan company. The product was sold only in parts of Michigan, Ohio and Pennsylvania. Fronts have color artwork. Besides major leaguers, Negro Leagues and Japanese Leagues players, the set included House of David players, wrestlers and boxers. The

1-5/8" x 2-3/4" cards are printed on thick cardboard. Backs have a scratch-off circle for prize redemptions. No checklist was ever issued for the unnumbered cards, so it is possible additions to this list may be forthcoming. Gaps have been left in the assigned numbering for that reason.

		NM/M
	Common Player:	.50
(1)	Frank "Home Run" Baker	1.00
(2)	Moe Berg	2.50
(3)	Mordecai Brown	1.00
(4)	Slim Caldwell	.50
(5)	Ray Chapman	1.00
(6)	Kiki Cuyler	.50
(7)	Bill Donovan	.50
(8)	Johnny "The Crab" Evers	1.00
(9)	Happy Felsch	1.00
(10)	Elmer Flick	.50
(11)	Chick Gandil	1.00
(12)	Sy Gragg (Gregg)	.50
(13)	Miller Huggins	.50
(14)	Joe Jackson (Chicago)	2.50
(15)	Joe Jackson (Cleveland)	2.50
(16)	Hughie Jennings	.50
(17)	Davy Jones	.50
(18)	Jimmy McAleer	.50
(19)	John McGraw	1.00
(20)	Herb Pennock	.50
(21)	Eppa Rixey	.50
(22)	Billy Rogell	.50
(23)	Rube Waddell	.50
(24)	Buck Weaver	1.50
(25)	Ross Youngs	.50
(30)	Joe Hauser	.50
(31)	Walter Ball	.50
(32)	James "Cool Papa" Bell	1.00
(33)	Dennis Biddle	.50
(34)	Sherwood Brewer	.50
(35)	Jim Cobbin	.50
(36)	Jimmie Crutchfield	.50
(37)	Leon (Pepper) Daniels	.50
(38)	Martin DiHigo	1.00
(39)	Rube Foster	1.00
(40)	Arthur Hamilton	.50
(41)	Pete Hill	1.00
(42)	Dave Malarcher	.50
(43)	"Double Duty" Radcliffe	.50
(44)	Turkey Stearns (Stearnes)	.50
(45)	Moses Walker	1.00
(48)	George Anderson	.50
(49)	Barnstorming Team	.50
(50)	Lloyd Dalager	.50
(51)	Eddie Deal	.50
(52)	Judge Dewhurst	.50
(53)	David Harrison	.50
(54)	Jesse Lee Tally	.50
(55)	John Tucker	.50
(56)	Percy Walker	.50
(58)	Kaoru Betto	.50
(59)	Sadayushi Fujimoto	.50
(60)	Taketoshi Goto	.50
(61)	Tetsuhara Kawakami	1.00
(62)	Tokuji Iida	.50
(63)	Jiro Noguchi	.50
(64)	Tokyo Team (Tetsuhara Kawakami, Shigeru Chiba, Noboru Aota, Jiro Noguchi)	.50

1998 Hershey's Baltimore Orioles

This team set was a stadium giveaway at a late-season game. The 2-1/2" x 3-1/2" cards have portrait or game-action photos bordered in black. An orange stripe verti-

cally at left has the player name. Backs have a red border around complete major and minor league stats. Team and Hershey's logos are at bottom.

		NM/M
	Complete Set (25):	15.00
	Common Player:	.50
(1)	Roberto Alomar	.75
(2)	Brady Anderson	.75
(3)	Harold Baines	.75
(4)	Rich Becker	.50
(5)	Armando Benitez	.50
(6)	Mike Bordick	.50
(7)	Eric Davis	.60
(8)	Doug Drabek	.50
(9)	Scott Erickson	.50
(10)	Chris Hoiles	.50
(11)	Doug Johns	.50
(12)	Scott Kamieniecki	.50
(13)	Jimmy Key	.50
(14)	Alan Mills	.50
(15)	Mike Mussina	2.00
(16)	Jesse Orosco	.50
(17)	Rafael Palmeiro	2.00
(18)	Sidney Ponson	.50
(19)	Jeff Reboulet	.50
(20)	Arthur Rhodes	.50
(21)	Cal Ripken	4.00
(22)	Pete Smith	.50
(23)	B.J. Surhoff	.50
(24)	Lenny Webster	.50
(25)	Orioles Coaches (Carlos Bernhardt, Rick Down, Mike Flanagan, Elrod Hendricks, Eddie Murray, Sam Perlozzo)	.50

1993 Highland Mint Mint-Cards

The Highland Mint produced replicas of several Topps rookie cards and other prominent cards in bronze and silver. Limited to 1,000 in silver and 5,000 in bronze, the company produced cards of many current stars along with a replica of Brooks Robinson's 1957 rookie card. The cards carried a suggested retail price of $235 for the silver and $50 for the bronze. Cards measure 2-1/2" x 3-1/2" and are 1/10" thick. Each Mint-Card has a serial number engraved on the edge and is sold in a heavy lucite holder, packaged with a certificate of authenticity in a plastic book-style folder.

		NM/M
	Common Player, Silver:	70.00
	Common Player, Bronze:	12.50
(1s)	Brooks Robinson (1957 Topps, silver edition of 796)	110.00
(1b)	Brooks Robinson (1957 Topps, bronze edition of 2,043)	20.00
(2s)	Dave Winfield (1974 Topps, silver edition of 266)	200.00
(2b)	Dave Winfield (1974 Topps, bronze edition of 1,216)	20.00
(3s)	George Brett (1975 Topps, silver edition of 999)	100.00
(3b)	George Brett (1975 Topps, bronze edition of 3,560)	20.00
(4s)	Robin Yount (1975 Topps silver edition of 349)	110.00
(4b)	Robin Yount (1975 Topps, bronze edition of 1,564)	40.00
(5s)	Ozzie Smith (1979 Topps, silver edition of 211)	245.00
(5b)	Ozzie Smith (1979 Topps, bronze edition of 1,088)	35.00
(6s)	Don Mattingly (1984 Topps, silver edition of 414)	75.00
(6b)	Don Mattingly (1984 Topps, bronze edition of 1,550)	40.00
(7s)	Roger Clemens (1985 Topps, silver edition of 432)	140.00
(7b)	Roger Clemens (1985 Topps, bronze edition of 1,789)	25.00
(8s)	Kirby Puckett (1985 Topps, silver edition of 359)	85.00
(8b)	Kirby Puckett (1985 Topps, bronze edition of 1,723)	20.00
(9s)	Barry Bonds (1986 Topps Traded, silver edition of 596)	125.00
(9b)	Barry Bonds (1986 Topps Traded, bronze edition of 2,677)	50.00
(10s)	Will Clark (1986 Topps Traded, silver edition of 150)	225.00
(10b)	Will Clark (1986 Topps Traded, bronze edition of 1,0444)	20.00
(11s)	Roberto Alomar (1988 Topps Traded, silver edition of 214)	90.00
(11b)	Roberto Alomar (1988 Topps Traded, bronze edition of 928)	20.00
(12s)	Juan Gonzalez (1990 Topps, silver edition of 365)	65.00
(12b)	Juan Gonzalez (1990 Topps, bronze edition of 1,899)	15.00
(13s)	Ken Griffey Jr. (1992 Topps, silver edition of 1,000)	100.00
(13b)	Ken Griffey Jr. (1992 Topps, bronze edition of 5,000)	15.00
(13g)	Ken Griffey Jr. (1992 Topps, gold edition of 500)	200.00
(14s)	Cal Ripken, Jr. (1992 Topps, silver edition of 1,000)	100.00
(14b)	Cal Ripken, Jr. (1992 Topps, bronze edition of 4,065)	15.00
(15s)	Nolan Ryan (1992 Topps silver edition of 999)	150.00
(15b)	Nolan Ryan (1992 Topps, bronze edition of 5,000)	25.00
(16s)	Ryne Sandberg (1992 Topps, silver edition of 430)	145.00
(16b)	Ryne Sandberg (1992 Topps, bronze edition of 1,932)	15.00
(17s)	Frank Thomas (1992 Topps, silver edition of 1,000)	85.00
(17b)	Frank Thomas (1992 Topps, bronze edition of 5,000)	12.50
(17g)	Frank Thomas (1992 Topps, gold edition of 500)	150.00

1994 Highland Mint Mint-Cards

In 1994 the Highland Mint continued its production of Mint-Cards, licensed metal replicas of Topps baseball, football and hockey cards. Maximum production of baseball players in the series was reduced to 750 in silver and halved to 2,500 in bronze. Suggested retail prices remained at

$235 and $50, respectively. Once again cards were produced in the same 2-1/2" x 3-1/2" format as original Topps cards and were minted to a thickness of 1/10", with a serial number engraved on the edge. Mint-cards were sold in a heavy lucite holder, packaged with a certificate of authenticity in a plastic book-style holder. In mid-year, the company announced it was ceasing production of Topps-replica baseball cards and that henceforth all baseball Mint-Cards would reproduce the designs of Pinnacle brand cards.

		NM/M
	Common Player, Silver:	50.00
	Common Player, Bronze:	12.00
	Common Player, Gold:	200.00
(1a)	Ernie Banks (1954 Topps, silver edition of 437)	65.00
(1b)	Ernie Banks (1954 Topps, bronze edition of 920)	25.00
(2a)	Carl Yastrzemski (1960 Topps, silver edition of 500)	75.00
(2b)	Carl Yastrzemski (1960 Topps, bronze edition of 1,072)	30.00
(3a)	Johnny Bench (1969 Topps, silver edition of 500)	75.00
(3b)	Johnny Bench (1969 Topps, bronze edition of 1,384)	22.50
(4a)	Mike Schmidt (1974 Topps, silver edition of 500)	75.00
(4b)	Mike Schmidt (1974 Topps, bronze edition of 1,641)	20.00
(5a)	Paul Molitor (1979 Topps, silver edition of 260)	175.00
(5b)	Paul Molitor (1979 Topps, bronze edition of 639)	17.50
(6a)	Deion Sanders (1989 Topps, silver edition of 187)	60.00
(6b)	Deion Sanders (1989 Topps, bronze edition of 668)	12.50
(7a)	Dave Justice (1990 Topps, silver edition of 265)	75.00
(7b)	Dave Justice (1990 Topps, bronze edition of 1,396)	12.50
(8a)	Jeff Bagwell (1992 Pinnacle, silver edition of 750)	50.00
(8b)	Jeff Bagwell (1992 Pinnacle, bronze edition of 2,500)	15.00
(9a)	Greg Maddux (1992 Pinnacle, silver edition of 750)	175.00
(9b)	Greg Maddux (1992 Pinnacle, bronze edition of 2,500)	25.00
(10a)	Mike Piazza (1992 Topps, silver edition of 750)	75.00
(10b)	Mike Piazza (1992 Topps, bronze edition of 2,500)	20.00
(10c)	Mike Piazza (1992 Topps, gold edition of 374)	300.00
(12a)	Nolan Ryan (1992 Pinnacle Then and Now, silver edition of 1,000)	75.00
(12b)	Nolan Ryan (1992 Pinnacle Then and Now, bronze edition of 5,000)	15.00
(12c)	Nolan Ryan (1992 Pinnacle Then & Now, gold edition 500)	200.00
(13a)	Tim Salmon (1993 Topps silver edition of 264)	110.00
(13b)	Tim Salmon (1993 Topps, bronze edition of 768)	10.00

1995 Highland Mint Mint-Cards

For 1995, the Highland Mint continued its series of precious-metal editions of cards in all major team sports. The 2-1/2" x 3-1/2" cards contain 4-1/4 oz. of bronze or silver or 24-K gold plating on silver. Each Mint-card is sold in a heavy plastic holder within a numbered album and with a certificate of authenticity. Only the firm's baseball cards are listed here.

		NM/M
38b	Michael Jordan (Upper Deck Rare Air, bronze, edition of 5,000.)	15.00
38s	Michael Jordan (Upper Deck Rare Air, silver, edition of 1,000.)	100.00
38g	Michael Jordan (Upper Deck Rare Air, gold, edition of 500.)	300.00
	Mickey Mantle (1992 Pinnacle, bronze edition of 1,000.)	20.00
	Mickey Mantle (1992 Pinnacle, silver edition of 1,000.)	75.00
	Mickey Mantle (1992 Pinnacle, gold edition of 500.)	300.00

1992 High 5 Decals

This issue of peelable, reusable "decals" was sold in both team sets and superstar panels. Each $2.99 panel contains five player decals and a team logo decal. The backing paper has a color 5" x 7" photo of a superstar that can be cut out and framed. Overall dimensions of the decal sheet are 7-1/2" x 7". The unnumbered decals are checklisted here in alphabetical order within team.

		NM/M
	Complete Set (156):	30.00
	Common Player:	.25
(1)	Baltimore Orioles Logo	.25
(2)	Mike Devereaux	.25
(3)	Ben McDonald	.25
(4)	Gregg Olson	.25
(5)	Joe Orsulak	.25
(6)	Cal Ripken Jr.	3.00
(7)	Boston Red Sox Logo	.25
(8)	Wade Boggs	2.00
(9)	Roger Clemens	2.25
(10)	Phil Plantier	.25
(11)	Jeff Reardon	.25
(12)	Mo Vaughn	.25
(13)	California Angels Logo	.25
(14)	Jim Abbott	.25
(15)	Chuck Finley	.25
(16)	Bryan Harvey	.25
(17)	Mark Langston	.25
(18)	Dave Winfield	1.50
(19)	Chicago White Sox Logo	.25
(20)	Carlton Fisk	1.50

(21)	Jack McDowell	.25
(22)	Bobby Thigpen	.25
(23)	Frank Thomas	1.50
(24)	Robin Ventura	.25
(25)	Cleveland Indians logo	.25
(26)	Sandy Alomar Jr.	.25
(27)	Carlos Baerga	.25
(28)	Albert Belle	.25
(29)	Alex Cole	.25
(30)	Charles Nagy	.25
(31)	Detroit Tigers logo	.25
(32)	Cecil Fielder	.25
(33)	Travis Fryman	.25
(34)	Tony Phillips	.25
(35)	Alan Trammell	.25
(36)	Lou Whitaker	.25
(37)	Kansas City Royals logo	.25
(38)	George Brett	2.50
(39)	Jim Eisenreich	.25
(40)	Brian McRae	.25
(41)	Jeff Montgomery	.25
(42)	Bret Saberhagen	.25
(43)	Milwaukee Brewers logo	.25
(44)	Chris Bosio	.25
(45)	Paul Molitor	1.50
(46)	B.J. Surhoff	.25
(47)	Greg Vaughn	.25
(48)	Robin Yount	1.50
(49)	Minnesota Twins logo	.25
(50)	Rick Aguilera	.25
(51)	Scott Erickson	.25
(52)	Kent Hrbek	.25
(53)	Kirby Puckett	2.00
(54)	Kevin Tapani	.25
(55)	New York Yankees logo	.25
(56)	Mel Hall	.25
(57)	Roberto Kelly	.25
(58)	Kevin Maas	.25
(59)	Don Mattingly	2.50
(60)	Steve Sax	.25
(61)	Oakland A's logo	.25
(62)	Harold Baines	.25
(63)	Jose Canseco	.75
(64)	Dennis Eckersley	1.25
(65)	Dave Henderson	.25
(66)	Rickey Henderson	1.50
(67)	Seattle Mariners logo	.25
(68)	Jay Buhner	.25
(69)	Ken Griffey Jr.	2.75
(70)	Randy Johnson	1.50
(71)	Edgar Martinez	.25
(72)	Harold Reynolds	.25
(73)	Texas Rangers logo	.25
(74)	Julio Franco	.25
(75)	Juan Gonzalez	1.25
(76)	Rafael Palmeiro	1.25
(77)	Nolan Ryan	3.00
(77p)	Nolan Ryan (prototype)	6.50
(78)	Ruben Sierra	.25
(79)	Toronto Blue Jays logo	.25
(80)	Roberto Alomar	.50
(81)	Joe Carter	.25
(82)	Kelly Gruber	.25
(83)	John Olerud	.25
(84)	Devon White	.25
(85)	Atlanta Braves logo	.25
(86)	Steve Avery	.25
(87)	Ron Gant	.25
(88)	Tom Glavine	.40
(89)	David Justice	.25
(90)	Terry Pendleton	.25
(91)	Chicago Cubs logo	.25
(92)	George Bell	.25
(93)	Andre Dawson	.30
(94)	Mark Grace	.25
(95)	Greg Maddux	2.00
(96)	Ryne Sandberg	2.00
(97)	Cincinnati Reds logo	.25
(98)	Eric Davis	.25
(99)	Barry Larkin	.25
(100)	Hal Morris	.25
(101)	Jose Rijo	.25
(102)	Chris Sabo	.25
(103)	Houston Astros logo	.25
(104)	Jeff Bagwell	1.50
(105)	Craig Biggio	.25
(106)	Ken Caminiti	.25
(107)	Luis Gonzalez	.50
(108)	Pete Harnisch	.25
(109)	Los Angeles Dodgers logo	.25
(110)	Brett Butler	.25
(111)	Lenny Harris	.25
(112)	Ramon Martinez	.25
(113)	Eddie Murray	1.50
(114)	Darryl Strawberry	.25
(115)	Montreal Expos logo	.25
(116)	Ivan Calderon	.25
(117)	Delino DeShields	.25
(118)	Marquis Grissom	.25
(119)	Dennis Martinez	.25
(120)	Larry Walker	.25
(121)	New York Mets logo	.25
(122)	David Cone	.25
(123)	Dwight Gooden	.25
(124)	Gregg Jefferies	.25
(125)	Howard Johnson	.25
(126)	Kevin McReynolds	.25
(127)	Philadelphia Phillies logo	.25
(128)	Wes Chamberlain	.25
(129)	Lenny Dykstra	.25
(130)	John Kruk	.25
(131)	Terry Mulholland	.25
(132)	Mitch Williams	.25

(133)	Pittsburgh Pirates logo	.25
(134)	Barry Bonds	3.00
(135)	Doug Drabek	.25
(136)	John Smiley	.25
(137)	Zane Smith	.25
(138)	Andy Van Slyke	.25
(139)	St. Louis Cardinals logo	.25
(140)	Felix Jose	.25
(141)	Ray Lankford	.25
(142)	Lee Smith	.25
(143)	Ozzie Smith	2.00
(144)	Todd Zeile	.25
(145)	San Diego Padres logo	.25
(146)	Tony Fernandez	.25
(147)	Tony Gwynn	2.00
(148)	Bruce Hurst	.25
(149)	Fred McGriff	.25
(150)	Gary Sheffield	.50
(151)	San Francisco Giants logo	.25
(152)	Will Clark	.30
(152p)	Will Clark (Prototype)	1.50
(153)	Willie McGee	.25
(154)	Kevin Mitchell	.25
(155)	Robby Thompson	.25
(156)	Matt Williams	.25

1989 Hills Team MVP's

This high-gloss, boxed set of superstars was produced by Topps for the Hills department store chain. The words "Hills Team MVP's" appear above the player photos, while the player's name and team are printed below. The front of the card carries a red, white and blue color scheme with yellow and gold accents. The horizontal backs include player data set against a green playing field background.

	NM/M
Complete Set (33):	4.00
Common Player:	.10

1	Harold Baines	.10
2	Wade Boggs	.75
3	George Brett	1.00
4	Tom Brunansky	.10
5	Jose Canseco	.35
6	Joe Carter	.15
7	Will Clark	.15
8	Roger Clemens	.85
9	Dave Cone	.10
10	Glenn Davis	.10
11	Andre Dawson	.25
12	Dennis Eckersley	.40
13	Andres Galarraga	.10
14	Kirk Gibson	.10
15	Mike Greenwell	.10
16	Tony Gwynn	.75
17	Orel Hershiser	.10
18	Danny Jackson	.10
19	Mark Langston	.10
20	Fred McGriff	.10
21	Dale Murphy	.25
22	Eddie Murray	.50
23	Kirby Puckett	.75
24	Johnny Ray	.10
25	Juan Samuel	.10
26	Ruben Sierra	.25
27	Dave Stewart	.10
28	Darryl Strawberry	.10
29	Alan Trammell	.10
30	Andy Van Slyke	.25
31	Frank Viola	.10
32	Dave Winfield	.25
33	Robin Yount	.50

1990 Hills Hit Men

The 33 slugging percentage leaders are featured in this high-gloss boxed set. The cards were produced by Topps for the Hills department store chain. Fronts feature "Hit Men" in a bat design above the photo. The player's name appears on a band below the photo. Horizontal backs fea-

PEDRO GUERRERO

ture a breakdown of the player's slugging percentage and also display career statistics.

	NM/M
Complete Set (33):	5.00
Common Player:	.10

1	Eric Davis	.10
2	Will Clark	.15
3	Don Mattingly	.75
4	Darryl Strawberry	.10
5	Kevin Mitchell	.10
6	Pedro Guerrero	.10
7	Jose Canseco	.35
8	Jim Rice	.15
9	Danny Tartabull	.10
10	George Brett	.75
11	Kent Hrbek	.10
12	George Bell	.10
13	Eddie Murray	.50
14	Fred Lynn	.10
15	Andre Dawson	.25
16	Dale Murphy	.15
17	Dave Winfield	.50
18	Jack Clark	.10
19	Wade Boggs	.65
20	Ruben Sierra	.10
21	Dave Parker	.10
22	Glenn Davis	.10
23	Dwight Evans	.10
24	Jesse Barfield	.10
25	Kirk Gibson	.10
26	Alvin Davis	.10
27	Kirby Puckett	.65
28	Joe Carter	.10
29	Carlton Fisk	.50
30	Harold Baines	.10
31	Andres Galarraga	.10
32	Cal Ripken, Jr.	1.50
33	Howard Johnson	.10

1993 Hills Pirates Kids Club

DENNY NEAGLE

Stars of the Eastern Division N.L. champions are pictured on this 12-card issue. The set was issued in the form of a perforated 10" x 10-1/2" panel. Fronts have player action photos with orange frames, white borders and a team logo. Black-and-white backs have a player portrait, personal data and stats, and the Hills Pirates Kids Club logo. Cards are numbered by uniform number.

	NM/M
Complete Set, Sheet:	7.00
Complete Set, Singles (12):	6.00
Common Player:	.50

6	Orlando Merced	.50
9	Jeff King	.50
10	Jim Leyland	.50
14	Tom Prince	.50
23	Lloyd McClendon	.50
26	Steve Cooke	.50
28	Al Martin	.50
32	Denny Neagle	.50
36	Kevin Young	.50
45	John Candelaria	.50
50	Stan Belinda	.50
55	Blas Minor	.50

1999 Hillshire Farm Home Run Heroes

ERNIE BANKS

Via a special offer on packages of Hillshire Farm meats, collectors could order an autographed card of several star sluggers of the 1960s. Cards were available by sending in a package coupon and $4 for handling. The 2-1/2" x 3-1/2" cards have color player photos on which uniform logos have been removed. Borders are black and enhanced with gold foil. Black and gold backs offer lifetime stats and career highlights.

	NM/M
Complete Set (4):	30.00
Common Player:	7.50

(1)	Ernie Banks	10.00
(2)	Harmon Killebrew	7.50
(3)	Frank Robinson	7.50
(4)	Willie Stargell	12.00

1988 Historic Limited Editions Brooklyn Dodgers

This set of Brooklyn Dodgers postcards features the artwork of Susan Rini, combining on most cards a player portrait and an action pose with Ebbets Field as the background. Fronts of the 5-1/2" x 3-1/2" cards have the artwork at left, bordered in bright blue. In the wide right border, the team name and logo, and the player name, are printed in white. Postcard-style backs are printed in blue. The cards were issued in three series of 12 each, but are checklisted here in alphabetical order. Two different cards each exist for Erskine and Lavagetto. Production of the series was limited to 5,000 sets; 2,000 sets were produced with a low-gloss finish to facilitate autographing, while the remaining 3,000 sets were high-gloss. Either sold for $20 at time of issue. Two hundred uncut sheets of each series were sold for $30 apiece. A special album was also made available.

	NM/M
Complete Set (36):	10.00
Common Player:	.50

(1)	Cal Abrams	.50
(2)	Sandy Amoros	.50
(3)	Red Barber/Announcer	.50
(4)	Ralph Branca	.50
(5)	Chuck Connors	.75
(6)	Roger Craig	.50
(7)	Roy Campanella	1.50
(8)	Don Drysdale	1.00
(9)	Leo Durocher	.50
(10)	Carl Erskine	.50
(11)	Carl Erskine	.50
(12)	Carl Furillo	.50
(13)	Gene Hermanski	.50
(14)	Gil Hodges	1.00
(15)	Clyde King	.50
(16)	Clem Labine	.50
(17)	Tommy Lasorda	.75
(18)	Cookie Lavagetto	.50
(19)	Cookie Lavagetto	.50
(20)	Larry MacPhail/GM	.50
(21)	Sal Maglie	.50
(22)	Eddie Miksis	.50
(23)	Don Newcombe	.60
(24)	Walter O'Malley/Owner	.50
(25)	Mickey Owen	.50
(26)	Andy Pafko	.50
(27)	Johnny Podres	.50
(28)	Pee Wee Reese	1.00
(29)	Preacher Roe	.50
(30)	Jackie Robinson	2.50
(31)	George Shuba	.50
(32)	Duke Snider	1.50
(33)	Red Barber, Leo Durocher	.50
(34)	Jackie Robinson, Branch Rickey	1.00
(35)	Ebbets Field	.50
(36)	Dodgers Sym-Phony Band	.50

1989 Historic Limited Editions Lou Gehrig Postcards

LOU GEHRIG

This set of postcards combines portrait and action art with a Yankee Stadium backdrop in paintings by Susan Rini. The art is set towards the top of the 3-1/2" x 5-1/2" cards which have a pinstripe background, player name beneath the art and team name and logo at bottom. Horizontal backs are postcard-style and printed in blue with appropriate credit lines, copyright notice and logos. Original issue price was $10 per set, with uncut sheets available for $15.

	NM/M
Complete Set (8):	6.00
Common Card:	1.00

Don Mattingly Series 1

DON MATTINGLY

One of the most popular Yankees of the past 25 years is honored on this set of postcards. The 3-1/2" x 5-1/2" cards feature the artwork of Susan Rini on each card. Mattingly is shown in portrait and action art on most of the cards, though sometimes the picture of another Yankee great takes the place of the action picture. Background on the front is white with blue pinstripes. Postcard-style backs are printed in blue and announce an edition of 5,000 sets. Price at

issue was about $10, with uncut sheets of the cards available for $24.

	NM/M
Complete Set (12):	6.00
Common Card:	.50

Negro Leagues Postcards

WILLIE WELLS

NEGRO LEAGUE

Both well-known and obscure players of the segregated Negro Leagues are included in this series of color postcards. Fronts of the 3-1/2" x 5-1/2" cards have portrait and action paintings of the players on a peach-colored background. Postcard-style backs are printed in blue and indicate a limit of 5,000 sets were produced. An edition of 200 uncut sheets was also produced.

	NM/M
Complete Set (12):	7.00
Common Player:	.50
Uncut Sheet:	10.00

1	Monte Irvin	1.00
2	Martin Dihigo	.85
3	Clint Thomas	.50
4	Buster Haywood	.50
5	George Giles	.50
6	Isidro Fabri	.50
7	James (Cool Papa) Bell	.65
8	Josh Gibson	1.50
9	Lou Dials	.50
10	Willie Wells	.75
11	Walter (Buck) Leonard	.75
12	Jose Fernandez	.50

1990 Historic Limited Editions Roberto Clemente

ROBERTO CLEMENTE

PITTSBURGH PIRATES

This set of 3-1/2" x 5-1/2" postcards details the career of the Pirates outfielder. Background of each card is beige. At top is an approximately 3" x 3-1/2" color painting of Clemente in both portrait and action poses, created by sports artist Susan Rini. Player and team name, and team logo are at bottom. Postcard-style backs are printed in blue with appropriate credit lines and copyright data. Production was reported at 5,000 sets.

	NM/M
Complete Set (12):	12.50
Common Card:	1.50

Thurman Munson Postcards

The late, great Yankees catcher is memorialized in this set of color postcards

THURMAN MUNSON

New York Yankees

from sports artist Susan Rini. Fronts of the 3-1/2" x 5-1/2" cards have a combination portrait/action painting toward the top, on a background of pinstripes. Player and team names and the Yankees logo are at bottom. Horizontal backs are in postcard style, printed in blue with appropriate licensing, copyright and credit data, and logos. Production was limited to 5,000 sets and 200 complete-set uncut sheets.

	NM/M
Complete Set (12):	10.00
Common Card:	1.25
Uncut Sheet:	55.00
1-12 Thurman Munson	1.25

Nolan Ryan Series 1

NOLAN RYAN

Texas Rangers

The Mets and Rangers years are graphically depicted on this set of postcards in combined portrait and action paintings by sports artist Susan Rini. The 3-1/2" x 5-1/2" cards have a light blue background on front, with the player and team name, and the team logo at bottom. Postcard-style backs are printed in blue and offer copyright and licensing information, along with a notice that the set is limited to an edition of 10,000.

	NM/M
Complete Set (12):	10.00
Common Card:	1.00

Nolan Ryan Series 2

NOLAN RYAN

Astros

The Astros and Angels years are graphically depicted on this set of postcards in combined portrait and action paintings by sports artist Susan Rini. The 3-1/2" x 5-1/2" cards have a beige background on front, with the player and team name, and the team logo at bottom. Postcard-style backs are printed in blue and offer copyright and licensing information, along with a notice that the set is limited to an edition of 10,000.

	NM/M
Complete Set (12):	10.00
Common Card:	1.00

Yankees Monuments

BABE RUTH

New York Yankees

Those honored with plaques in Monument Park behind the center field wall at Yankee Stadium are presented in this series of postcards. On a pinstriped background, the fronts of the 3-1/2" x 5-1/2" cards have a portrait of the person with his plaque in the background, the work of Susan Rini. The team name and logo are at bottom. Postcard-style backs are printed in blue with various copyright and creator notices, MLB logo and an indication that the cards were produced in an edition of 5,000. At time of issue, complete sets sold for about $10; uncut sheets were available for $20.

	NM/M
Complete Set (12):	12.00
Common Player:	.70
1 Lou Gehrig	2.25
2 Babe Ruth	3.00
3 Thurman Munson	1.50
4 Elston Howard	.70
5 Phil Rizzuto	.70
6 Mickey Mantle	4.50
7 Bill Dickey	.70
8 Lefty Gomez	.70
9 Pope Paul VI	2.25
10 Jacob Ruppert	.70
11 Roger Maris	2.25
12 Joe DiMaggio	3.00

1969 Mets Postcards

This set commemorates the Amazin' Mets World Championship team of 1969. The 5-1/2" x 3-1/2" cards have bright blue front borders. At left is a portrait/action painting of the players by sports artist Susan Rini. Postcard-style backs are printed in blue with copyright and credit data, card number, logos, etc. The issue was limited to 5,000 sets and originally sold for about $20. Uncut sheets were available for $25.

	NM/M
Complete Set (36):	11.00
Common Player:	.50
1 Championship Trophy	.50
2 Shea Stadium	.50
3 Tommie Agee	.50
4 Ken Boswell	.50
5 Ed Charles	.50
6 Don Cardwell	.50
7 Donn Clendenon	.65
8 Jack DiLauro	.50
9 Duffy Dyer	.50
10 Wayne Garrett	.50
11 Jerry Grote	.50
12 Rod Gaspar	.50
13 Gary Gentry	.50
14 Bud Harrelson	.65
15 Gil Hodges	1.00
16 Cleon Jones	.65
17 Ed Kranepool	.65
18 Cal Koonce	.50
19 Jerry Koosman	.65
20 Jim McAndrew	.50
21 Tug McGraw	.75
22 J.C. Martin	.50
23 Bob Pfeil	.50
24 Nolan Ryan	4.00
25 Ron Swoboda	.50
26 Tom Seaver	1.50
27 Art Shamsky	.50
28 Ron Taylor	.50
29 Al Weis	.50
30 Joe Pignatano	.50
31 Eddie Yost	.50
32 Ralph Kiner/Announcer	.50
33 Bob Murphy/Writer	.50
34 Lindsey Nelson/ Announcer	.50
35 Yogi Berra	1.00
36 Rube Walker	.50

1991 Historic Limited Editions Brooklyn Dodgers

Three additional series of 12-card player postcard sets in 1991 were issued as a follow-up to the company's debut issue of 1988. Identical in format, the 5-1/2" x 3-1/2" cards have a Dodger blue background on front. At the left end is artwork by Susan Rini combining portrait and action pictures of the player against a background of Ebbets Field. Player and team identification are in white at right. Postcard backs are printed in blue with credits, copyright data, logos and series and card numbers.

	NM/M
Complete Set (36):	20.00
Common Player:	.50
SERIES 2	5.00
1 Charley Dressen	.50
2 John Roseboro	.50
3 Eddie Stanky	.50
4 Goody Rosen	.50
5 Ed Head	.50
6 Dick Williams	.50
7 Clarence (Bud) Podbielan	.50
8 Erv Palica	.50
9 Augie Galan	.50
10 Billy Loes	.50
11 Billy Cox	.50
12 Phil Phifer	.50
SERIES 3	5.00
1 Joe Black	.75
2 Jack Banta	.50
3 Whitlow Wyatt	.50
4 Gino Cimoli	.50
5 Dolph Camilli (Dolf)	.50
6 Dan Bankhead	.50
7 Henry Behrman	.50
8 Pete Reiser	.50
9 Chris Van Cuyk	.50
10 James (Junior) Gilliam	.75
11 Don Zimmer	.75
12 Ed Roebuck	.50
SERIES 4	5.00
1 Billy Herman	.50
2 Rube Walker	.50
3 Tommy Brown	.50
4 Charlie Neal	.50
5 Kirby Higbe	.50
6 Bruce Edwards	.50
7 Joe Hatten	.50

8 Rex Barney	.50
9 Al Gionfriddo	.50
10 Luis Olmo	.50
11 Dixie Walker	.50
12 Walter Alston	1.00

Don Mattingly Series 2

DON MATTINGLY

New York Yankees

Two years after the release of the first series, another 12 Mattingly postcards were issued. The 3-1/2" x 5-1/2" cards feature the artwork of Susan Rini on each card. Mattingly is shown in portrait and action art on each of the cards. Background on the front is white with blue pinstripes. Postcard-style backs are printed in blue and announce an edition of 5,000 sets. Price at issue was about $10, with uncut sheets of the cards available for $24.

	NM/M
Complete Set (12):	6.00
Common Card:	.50
1-12 Don Mattingly	.50

1961 Yankees Postcards

New York Yankees

Three series of 12 postcards each were issued to commemorate the '61 Yanks. All cards are 5-1/2" x 3-1/2", with a pinstriped border design. At left front are combination portrait/action paintings by Susan Rini. Team name and logo are at right, along with player identification. Backs are printed in blue, in postcard style, with copyright, credits, logos, etc.

	NM/M
Complete Set (36):	16.00
Common Player:	.25
SERIES 1	3.00
1 Yogi Berra	1.00
2 Tom Tresh	.45
3 Bill Skowron	.45
4 Al Downing	.25
5 Jim Coates	.25
6 Luis Arroyo	.25
7 Johnny Blanchard	.25
8 Hector Lopez	.25
9 Tony Kubek	.50
10 Ralph Houk	.25
11 Bobby Richardson	.50
12 Clete Boyer	.35
SERIES 2	8.00
1 Roger Maris	6.00
2 Jesse Gonder	.25
3 Danny McDevitt	.25
4 Leroy Thomas	.25
5 Billy Gardner	.25
6 Ralph Terry	.25
7 Hal Reniff	.25
8 Earl Torgeson	.25
9 Art Ditmar	.25
10 Jack Reed	.25
11 Johnny James	.25
12 Elston Howard	.75
SERIES 3	6.00
1 Mickey Mantle	5.00
2 Deron Johnson	.25
3 Bob Hale	.25
4 Bill Stafford	.25
5 Duke Maas	.25

6 Bob Cerv	.25
7 Roland Sheldon	.25
8 Ryne Duren	.35
9 Bob Turley	.25
10 Whitey Ford	1.00
11 Bud Daley	.25
12 Joe DeMaestri	.25

1989 Holsum/ Schafer's Super Stars Discs

WALLY JOYNER

This version of the 1989 MSA bakeries disc set was issued in Canada by Ben's bakeries. The discs are nearly identical to the other regional variations except for the appearance of a red "Schafer's" logo at top.

	NM/M
Complete Set (20):	9.00
Common Player:	.25
1 Wally Joyner	.25
2 Wade Boggs	1.00
3 Ozzie Smith	1.00
4 Don Mattingly	1.25
5 Jose Canseco	.50
6 Tony Gwynn	1.00
7 Eric Davis	.25
8 Kirby Puckett	1.00
9 Kevin Seitzer	.25
10 Darryl Strawberry	.25
11 Gregg Jefferies	.25
12 Mark Grace	.25
13 Matt Nokes	.25
14 Mark McGwire	2.00
15 Don Mattingly	1.25
16 Roger Clemens	1.25
17 Frank Viola	.25
18 Orel Hershiser	.25
19 Dave Cone	.25
20 Kirk Gibson	.25

1989 Holsum Bakeries Super Stars Discs

This set of 2-3/4" diameter discs was manufactured by Mike Schechter Associates for Holsum bakeries' inclusion in various bread brands. Because the cards are licensed only by the players' association and not MLB, the player photos have been airbrushed to remove cap and uniform logos. Cards feature white borders with red, yellow and blue decorations. Backs are printed in dark blue and include a few 1988 and career stats and some player vitals. The set was distributed in Michigan.

	NM/M
Complete Set (20):	12.00
Common Player:	.50
1 Wally Joyner	.50
2 Wade Boggs	2.00
3 Ozzie Smith	2.00
4 Don Mattingly	2.50
5 Jose Canseco	1.00
6 Tony Gwynn	2.00
7 Eric Davis	.50
8 Kirby Puckett	2.00
9 Kevin Seitzer	.50
10 Darryl Strawberry	.50
11 Gregg Jefferies	.50
12 Mark Grace	.50
13 Matt Nokes	.50
14 Mark McGwire	3.00
15 Bobby Bonilla	.50
16 Roger Clemens	2.50
17 Frank Viola	.50
18 Orel Hershiser	.50
19 Dave Cone	.50
20 Kirk Gibson	.50

1990 Holsum Bakeries Super Stars Discs

Players in this disc set are featured in round portrait photos on which uniform logos have been painted over for lack

MARK DAVIS

SUPERSTARS

of a license from Major League Baseball (the set is licensed by the players' union and bears their logo on back). Most of the front border on these 2-3/4" diameter discs is in red, with yellow stars and white baseballs around the portrait and the bakery's logo at top. A yellow banner beneath the photo has the "Superstars" logo. At bottom, in the white portion of the border, the player's name is presented in red, with his team and position in blue. Backs are printed in blue and include 1989 and career stats, a few biographical details, the card number and appropriate copyrights.

	NM/M
Complete Set (20):	4.00
Common Player:	.25
1 George Bell	.25
2 Tim Raines	.25
3 Tom Henke	.25
4 Andres Galarraga	.25
5 Bret Saberhagen	.25
6 Mark Davis	.25
7 Robin Yount	.75
8 Rickey Henderson	.75
9 Kevin Mitchell	.25
10 Howard Johnson	.25
11 Will Clark	.30
12 Orel Hershiser	.25
13 Fred McGriff	.25
14 Dave Stewart	.25
15 Vince Coleman	.25
16 Steve Sax	.25
17 Kirby Puckett	1.00
18 Tony Gwynn	1.00
19 Jerome Walton	.25
20 Gregg Olson	.25

1991 Holsum Bakeries Super Stars Discs

TIM WALLACH

Montreal Expos

Similar to the previous year's issue, the 20 discs in the 1991 bakery set feature a color player photo (uniform logos airbrushed off) at center, with a wide white border to the edge of the 2-3/4" diameter cardboard. The player's name appears in a yellow stripe at bottom, along with his team and position. Backs are printed in dark blue and include a few stats from the previous season. The issue was distributed in Canada for Ben's Bakeries.

	NM/M
Complete Set (20):	45.00
Common Player:	.75
1 Darryl Strawberry	.75
2 Eric Davis	.75
3 Tim Wallach	.75
4 Kevin Mitchell	.75
5 Tony Gwynn	4.50
6 Ryne Sandberg	4.50
7 Doug Drabek	.75
8 Randy Myers	.75
9 Ken Griffey Jr.	6.50
10 Alan Trammell	.75
11 Ken Griffey Sr.	.75
12 Rickey Henderson	3.00
13 Roger Clemens	5.50
14 Bob Welch	.75
15 Kelly Gruber	.75
16 Mark McGwire	7.50
17 Cecil Fielder	.75

18	Dave Steib	.75
19	Nolan Ryan	9.00
20	Cal Ripken, Jr.	9.00

1983 Homeplate Sports Cards Al Kaline Story

Commemorating Al Kaline's 30th anniversary with the Detroit Tigers, this set chronicles his life and career. The 2-1/2" x 3-1/2" cards have either black-and-white front photos with orange borders or color photos with black borders. Backs reverse the color scheme and provide details about the photo on front. The first card in each set has been personally autographed by Kaline.

		NM/M
	Complete Set (73):	15.00
	Common Card:	.25
1a	30 Years a Tiger/ Auto.	12.00
1b	I'd play baseball for nothing	.25
2	Sandlot days in Baltimore	.25
3	MVP trophy winner	.25
4	Learning the ropes	.25
5	Working for a living	.25
6	Pleasing a young fan	.25
7	Al and Louise - the newlyweds	.25
8	Al and Pat Mullin	.25
9	How Al does it #1	.25
10	How Al does it #2	.25
11	Silver Bat for the Champ	.25
12	Al and George Stark	.25
13	Al watches Gordie Howe swing a bat	2.00
14	Kaline and Mantle - batting champs	1.00
15	Kaline	.25
16	Martin, Kaline, Kuenn, Mantle, Ford	.50
17	Crossing the plate	.25
18	1959 All-Star Game (w/ Bill Skowron)	.25
19	Cash, Colavito, Kaline	.50
20	Kaline slides under Nellie Fox	.25
21	One of many awards	.25
22	Kaline, Jim Campbell, Norm Cash - 1962	.25
23	Costly catch - 1962	.25
24	Jim Bunning, Al, Norm Cash in Japan	.25
25	Perfect form	.25
26	Ernie Harwell, Al, George Kell	.25
27	Life isn't always easy	.25
28	Al, Michael and Mark Kaline	.25
29	Al and Charlie Dressen - 1965	.25
30	George Kell and Al - Fielding masters	.25
31	Al and Hal Newhouser	.25
32	Michael, Louise, Al and Mark Kaline	.25
33	Al, Charlie Gehringer, Bill Freehan	.25
34	Rapping a hit in 1967	.25
35	Veteran rivals Mantle and Kaline	1.00
36	Al homers against Boston - 1968	.25
37	1968 World Series homer	.25
38	Premier fielder	.25
39	All-Time All-Stars (w/ Hank Greenberg, etc.)	.50
40	Part of the game	.25
41	Family portrait	.25
42	Spring training tribute	.25
43	Billy Martin and Al	.25
44	First $100,000 Tiger	.25
45	On deck - 1972	.25
46	A close call	.25
47	On deck in Baltimore - 1974	.25

48	Hit number 3,000 - 1974	.25
49	April 17, 1955 - 3 Homers	.25
50	All-Star Game record	.25
51	1968 Series action - Cepeda	.25
52	Celebrating 1968	.25
53	Al Kaline Day	.25
54	3,000 Hit Day	.25
55	Thank you - Sept. 29, 1974	.25
56	Silver salute - Sept. 29, 1974	.25
57	Al and Kell - a new career	.25
58	Voices of the Tigers	.25
59	Tiger record setter	.25
60	1970 AL All-Star team	.25
61	Pat Mullin and Al	.25
62	Al and Lolich - Aug., 1980	.25
63	Hall of Fame plaque	.25
64	Al and Bowie Kuhn - Aug. 4, 1980	.25
65	Al and parents - Aug., 1980	.25
66	Fame	.25
67	"The Man" and the Boy (w/ Stan Musial)	.50
68	Two Kids - Ted Williams and Kaline	.50
69	Master glovemen (w/ Brooks Robinson)	.45
70	Coach and Pupil - Al and Pat Underwood	.25
71	Kaline career records	.25
72	A Tiger Forever	.25

1990 Homers Cookies Pittsburgh Pirates

This set of 4" x 6" color cards was a stadium giveaway. Fronts have borderless game-action photos. Backs are in black, white and green and have player biographical data, major and minor league stats, career highlights and a sponsor's logo.

		NM/M
	Complete Set (31):	20.00
	Common Player:	.50
(1)	Wally Backman	.50
(2)	Doug Bair	.50
(3)	Jay Bell	.50
(4)	Rafael Belliard	.50
(5)	Barry Bonds	8.00
(6)	Bobby Bonilla	.50
(7)	Sid Bream	.50
(8)	John Cangelosi	.50
(9)	Rich Donnelly	.50
(10)	Doug Drabek	.50
(11)	Billy Hatcher	.50
(12)	Neal Heaton	.50
(13)	Jeff King	.50
(14)	Bob Kipper	.50
(15)	Randy Kramer	.50
(16)	Gene Lamont	.50
(17)	Bill Landrum	.50
(18)	Mike LaValliere	.50
(19)	Jim Leyland	.50
(20)	Jose Lind	.50
(21)	Milt May	.50
(22)	Ray Miller	.50
(23)	Ted Power	.50
(24)	Gary Redus	.50
(25)	R.J. Reynolds	.50
(26)	Tommy Sandt	.50
(27)	Don Slaught	.50
(28)	John Smiley	.50
(29)	Walt Terrell	.50
(30)	Andy Van Slyke	.50
(31)	Bob Walk	.50

1991 Homers Cookies

One Hall of Famer's card was inserted in each box of Homers Cookies. The cards

measure 2-1/2" x 3-1/2" and feature sepia-toned photos. The card backs feature lifetime statistics and career highlights. The cards are also numbered on the back and a checklist is featured on the back of each card.

		NM/M
	Complete Set (9):	5.00
	Common Player:	.50
1	Babe Ruth	2.00
2	Satchel Paige	.75
3	Lefty Gomez	.50
4	Ty Cobb	1.00
5	Cy Young	.50
6	Bob Feller	.50
7	Roberto Clemente	2.00
8	Dizzy Dean	.50
9	Lou Gehrig	1.50

1999 Homers Cookies

Former stars are featured in this set of cards inserted into specially marked boxes of cookies (suggested retail about $1). The 2-1/2" x 3-1/2" cards have color player photos (without uniform logos) with a white border. At top is player identification, at bottom is a red stripe with "HOMERS." Horizontal backs have a cartoon, career data, biographical information and a checklist.

		NM/M
	Complete Set (9):	7.50
	Common Player:	1.00
1	Vida Blue	1.00
2	Orlando Cepeda	1.00
3	Darrell Evans	1.00
4	Harmon Killebrew	1.00
5	Dave Kingman	1.00
6	Eddie Murray	1.50
7	Frank Robinson	1.50
8	Willie Stargell	1.00
9	Carl Yastrzemski	1.50

1985 Hostess Braves

After a five-year hiatus, Hostess returned to the production of baseball cards in 1985 with an Atlanta Braves team set. The 22 cards in the set were printed by Topps and inserted into packages of snack cake products, three cello-wrapped player cards and a header card per box. The 2-1/2" x 3-1/2" cards share a common back design with the regular-issue Topps cards of 1985.

		NM/M
	Complete Set (22):	4.00
	Common Player:	.35
1	Eddie Haas	.35
2	Len Barker	.35
3	Steve Bedrosian	.35
4	Bruce Benedict	.35
5	Rick Camp	.35
6	Rick Cerone	.35
7	Chris Chambliss	.35
8	Terry Forster	.35
9	Gene Garber	.35
10	Albert Hall	.35
11	Bob Horner	.50
12	Glenn Hubbard	.35
13	Brad Komminsk	.35
14	Rick Mahler	.35
15	Craig McMurtry	.35
16	Dale Murphy	3.00
17	Ken Oberkfell	.35
18	Pascual Perez	.35
19	Gerald Perry	.35
20	Rafael Ramirez	.35
21	Bruce Sutter	2.50
22	Claudell Washington	.35
---	Header Card	.05

1987 Hostess Stickers

Hostess of Canada issued a 30-card set of stickers in specially marked bags of potato chips. One sticker, measuring 1-3/4" x 1-3/8" in size, was found in each bag. The stickers have full-color fronts with the player's name appearing in black type in a white band. The Hostess logo and the sticker number are also included on the fronts. The backs are written in both English and French and contain the player's name, position and team.

		NM/M
	Complete Set (30):	12.00
	Common Player:	.25
1	Jesse Barfield	.25
2	Ernie Whitt	.25
3	George Bell	.25
4	Hubie Brooks	.25
5	Tim Wallach	.25
6	Floyd Youmans	.25
7	Dale Murphy	.50
8	Ryne Sandberg	2.25
9	Eric Davis	.25
10	Mike Scott	.25
11	Fernando Valenzuela	.25
12	Gary Carter	1.50
13	Mike Schmidt	2.50
14	Tony Pena	.25
15	Ozzie Smith	2.00
16	Tony Gwynn	2.00
17	Mike Krukow	.25
18	Eddie Murray	1.50
19	Wade Boggs	2.00
20	Wally Joyner	.25
21	Harold Baines	.25
22	Brook Jacoby	.25
23	Lou Whitaker	.25
24	George Brett	2.50
25	Robin Yount	1.50
26	Kirby Puckett	2.00
27	Don Mattingly	2.50
28	Jose Canseco	.75
29	Phil Bradley	.25
30	Pete O'Brien	.25

1988 Hostess Potato Chips Expos/Blue Jays

The Expos and Blue Jays are showcased in this set of 24 discs (1-1/2" diameter). Full-color portraits are framed in white, surrounded by red stars. A yellow-banner "1988 Collectors Edition" label is printed (English and French) beneath the photo, followed by the player's name in black. Numbered disc backs are bilingual, blue and white, and include player name and stats. This set was distributed inside Hostess potato chip packages sold in Canada.

		NM/M
	Complete Panel Set (12):	6.50
	Complete Singles Set (24):	4.50
	Common Panel:	.50
	Common Player:	.35
	Panel 1	.50
1	Mitch Webster	.35
20	Lloyd Moseby	.35
	Panel 2	.50
2	Tim Burke	.35
23	Tom Henke	.35
	Panel 3	.50
3	Tom Foley	.35
13	Jim Clancy	.35
	Panel 4	.50
4	Herm Winningham	.35
14	Rance Mulliniks	.35
	Panel 5	.75
5	Hubie Brooks	.35
24	Jimmy Key	.35
	Panel 6	.75
6	Mike Fitzgerald	.35
17	Dave Steib	.35
	Panel 7	1.50
7	Tim Wallach	.50
15	Fred McGriff	.50
	Panel 8	1.50
8	Andres Galarraga	.45
21	Tony Fernandez	.50
	Panel 9	.50
9	Floyd Youmans	.35
18	Mark Eichhorn	.35
	Panel 10	.50
10	Neal Heaton	.35
19	Jesse Barfield	.35
	Panel 11	1.00
11	Tim Raines	.45
16	Ernie Whitt	.35
	Panel 12	.75
12	Casey Candaele	.35
22	George Bell	.35

1990 Hostess Blue Jays Highlight Stickers

Team history highlights through the 1980 season are featured in this set of stickers. The set was produced in strips of three 2-1/4" x 3-1/4" stickers, some oriented horizontally, some vertically. Fronts have color photos with a light blue box beneath containing the

highlight printed in both English and French. Black-and-white Hostess and team logos are at the left and right, respectively. Backs are blank. The set is checklisted here alphabetically based on the title of the sticker at top or left of the strip.

		NM/M
	Complete Set (18):	15.00
	Common Sticker:	.50
	Panel 1	2.00
(1)	First AL East Pennant (Dave Steib)	.50
(2)	Killer Bees Born (George Bell, Lloyd Moseby, Jesse Barfield)	1.00
(3)	AL Home Run Champ (Jesse Barfield)	1.00
	Panel 2	3.00
(4)	First Home Run in Skydome (Fred McGriff)	1.50
(5)	Club Save Leader (Tom Henke)	.50
(6)	Three Winning Openers in a Row (Jimmy Key)	.50
	Panel 3	2.00
(7)	First 100 Wins (Jim Clancy)	.50
(8)	ML Home Run Record (Ernie Whitt)	.50
(9)	AL East Champs Again (Tom Henke)	.50
	Panel 4	2.00
(10)	Home Run on First Pitch (Junior Felix)	.50
(11)	Almost Perfect (Dave Steib)	.50
(12)	First Game at Skydome	.50
	Panel 5	2.00
(13)	Most Double Plays (Damaso Garcia)	.50
(14)	M.V.P. (George Bell)	.50
(15)	Hits the Cycle (Kelly Gruber)	.50
	Panel 6	2.00
(16)	Stolen Bases (Dave Collins)	.50
(17)	Gold Glove Winners (Jesse Barfield, Tony Fernandez)	.50
(18)	Goodbye to Exhibition Stadium	.50

1993 Hostess Twinkies

The Continental Baking Co., makers of Hostess Twinkies and cupcakes, returned to the baseball card market in 1993 with a 32-card set issued in two series. The promotion began around opening day with the first series; the second series was made available after the All-Star break. The cards were packaged in multipacks with cupcakes that look like baseballs, with three cards in a box of eight cupcakes.

		NM/M
	Complete Set (32):	4.00
	Common Player:	.10
	Uncut Sheet:	9.00
1	Andy Van Slyke	.10
2	Ryne Sandberg	.65
3	Bobby Bonilla	.10
4	John Kruk	.10
5	Ray Lankford	.10
6	Gary Sheffield	.25
7	Darryl Strawberry	.10
8	Barry Larkin	.25
9	Terry Pendleton	.10
10	Jose Canseco	.40
11	Dennis Eckersley	.50
12	Brian McRae	.10
13	Frank Thomas	.60
14	Roberto Alomar	.25
15	Cecil Fielder	.10
16	Carlos Baerga	.10
17	Will Clark	.15

18	Andres Galarraga	.10
19	Jeff Bagwell	.60
20	Brett Butler	.10
21	Benito Santiago	.10
22	Tom Glavine	.25
23	Rickey Henderson	.60
24	Wally Joyner	.10
25	Ken Griffey Jr.	.85
26	Cal Ripken, Jr.	1.00
27	Roger Clemens	.75
28	Don Mattingly	.75
29	Kirby Puckett	.65
30	Larry Walker	.10
31	Jack McDowell	.10
32	Pat Listach	.10

1986 Houston Astros Police

This full-color police safety set was issued by the Houston Police Department and sponsored by Kool-Aid. The set was distributed at the Astrodome on June 14, when 15,000 sets of the first 12 cards were given away. The balance of the set was distributed throughout the summer by police. The cards feature player photos on the fronts and a safety tip on the back. The cards measure 4-1/8" x 2-5/8".

		NM/M
Complete Set (26):		4.00
Common Player:		.25
1	Jim Pankovits	.25
2	Nolan Ryan	3.00
3	Mike Scott	.25
4	Kevin Bass	.25
5	Bill Doran	.25
6	Hal Lanier	.25
7	Denny Walling	.25
8	Alan Ashby	.25
9	Phil Garner	.25
10	Charlie Kerfeld	.25
11	Dave Smith	.25
12	Jose Cruz	.25
13	Craig Reynolds	.25
14	Mark Bailey	.25
15	Bob Knepper	.25
16	Julio Solano	.25
17	Dickie Thon	.25
18	Mike Madden	.25
19	Jeff Calhoun	.25
20	Tony Walker	.25
21	Terry Puhl	.25
22	Glenn Davis	.25
23	Billy Hatcher	.25
24	Jim Deshaies	.25
25	Frank DiPino	.25
26	Coaching Staff (Yogi Berra, Matt Galante, Denis Menke, Les Moss, Gene Tenace)	.25

1987 Houston Astros Police

The 1987 Astros safety set was produced through the combined efforts of the team, Deer Park Hospital and Sportsmedia Presentations. Cards #1-12 were handed out to youngsters 14 and under at the Astrodome on July 14. The balance of the distribution was handled by Deer Park Hospital. The cards, which measure 2-5/8" x 4-1/8", contain full-color photos. The backs offer a brief team/player history and a "Tips From The Dugout" anti-drug message.

		NM/M
Complete Set (26):		5.00
Common Player:		.25
1	Larry Andersen	.25
2	Mark Bailey	.25
3	Jose Cruz	.25
4	Danny Darwin	.25
5	Bill Doran	.25
6	Billy Hatcher	.25
7	Hal Lanier	.25
8	Davey Lopes	.25
9	Dave Meads	.25
10	Craig Reynolds	.25
11	Mike Scott	.25
12	Denny Walling	.25
13	Aurelio Lopez	.25
14	Dickie Thon	.25
15	Terry Puhl	.25
16	Nolan Ryan	4.00
17	Dave Smith	.25
18	Julio Solano	.25
19	Jim Deshaies	.25
20	Bob Knepper	.25
21	Alan Ashby	.25
22	Kevin Bass	.25
23	Glenn Davis	.25
24	Phil Garner	.25
25	Jim Pankovits	.25
26	Coaching Staff (Yogi Berra, Matt Galante, Denis Menke, Les Moss, Gene Tenace)	.25

1988 Houston Astros Police

This set of full-color cards highlighting the Houston Astros was produced by the team, in conjunction with Deer Park Hospital and Sportsmedia Promotions for distribution to fans 14 years and younger at a ballpark giveaway. The 2-5/8" x 4-1/8" cards feature full-color player photos framed by a narrow blue border with an orange player/team name block below the photo. Blue-and-white backs have orange borders with player information, career highlights and anti-drug tips.

		NM/M
Complete Set (26):		5.00
Common Player:		.25
1	Juan Agosto	.25
2	Larry Andersen	.25
3	Joaquin Andujar	.25
4	Alan Ashby	.25
5	Mark Bailey	.25
6	Kevin Bass	.25
7	Danny Darwin	.25
8	Glenn Davis	.25
9	Jim Deshaies	.25
10	Bill Doran	.25
11	Billy Hatcher	.25
12	Jeff Heathcock	.25
13	Steve Henderson	.25
14	Chuck Jackson	.25
15	Bob Knepper	.25
16	Jim Pankovits	.25
17	Terry Puhl	.25
18	Rafael Ramirez	.25
19	Craig Reynolds	.25

20	Nolan Ryan	4.00
21	Mike Scott	.25
22	Dave Smith	.25
23	Denny Walling	.25
24	Gerald Young	.25
25	Hal Lanier	.25
26	Coaching Staff (Yogi Berra, Gene Clines, Matt Galante, Marc Hill, Denis Menke, Les Moss)	.25

2005 Houston Astros Card Deck

This stadium giveaway was sponsored by Academy Sports+ Outdoors. Cards are 2-1/2" x 3-1/2" with rounded corners. Backs have a baseball in the background with team and sponsor's logos. Fronts have game-action photos. Many players have two cards in the deck, most with the same photo.

		NM/M
Complete Set (56):		12.00
Common Player:		.25
AS	Roger Clemens	3.00
2S	Russ Springer	.25
3S	Chad Harville	.25
4S	Brad Lidge	.35
5S	Jeff Bagwell	1.00
6S	Jason Lane	.25
7S	Luke Scott	.25
8S	Brad Lidge	.35
9S	Roger Clemens	3.00
10S	Jason Lane	.25
JS	Luke Scott	.25
QS	Minute Maid Park	.25
KS	Jeff Bagwell	1.00
AD	Roy Oswalt	.50
2D	Brad Ausmus	.25
3D	Russ Springer	.25
4D	Raul Chavez	.25
5D	Morgan Ensberg	.25
6D	Brandon Duckworth	.25
7D	Orlando Palmeiro	.25
8D	Brandon Duckworth	.25
9D	Roy Oswalt	.50
10D	Orlando Palmeiro	.25
JD	Morgan Ensberg	.25
QD	Minute Maid Park	.25
KD	Brad Ausmus	.25
AC	Brandon Backe	.25
2C	Chris Burke	.25
3C	Dan Wheeler	.25
4C	Eric Bruntlett	.25
5C	Jose Vizcaino	.25
6C	Dan Wheeler	.25
7C	Craig Biggio	.50
8C	Willy Taveras	.25
9C	Brandon Backe	.25
10C	Jose Vizcaino	.25
JC	Willy Taveras	.25
QC	Minute Maid Park	.25
KC	Craig Biggio	.50
AH	Andy Pettitte	.35
2H	Raul Chavez	.25
3H	Chad Qualls	.25
4H	John Franco	.25
5H	Mike Lamb	.25
6H	Adam Everett	.25
7H	John Franco	.25
8H	Lance Berkman	.50
9H	Andy Pettitte	.35
10H	Mike Lamb	.25
JH	Adam Everett	.25
QH	Minute Maid Park	.25
KH	Lance Berkman	.50
---	Phil Garner	.25
---	Phil Garner	.25
---	NL Wild Cardb 04	.05
---	NL Wild Card 04	.05

1989 Houston Colt .45s Fire Safety

The expansion Houston Colt .45s of 1962 are featured in this 1989 fire safety issue. The 2-1/2" x 3-1/2" cards have sepia player photos on front, with blue pistol frames and team logo, an orange name

banner and brown Smokey logo. Backs are in black-and-white with a fire prevention cartoon, Forest Service logos and the player name, position and uniform number. Cards numbers are at upper-right.

		NM/M
Complete Set (29):		12.50
Common Player:		.50
1	Bob Bruce	.50
2	Al Cicotte	.50
3	Dave Giusti	.50
4	Jim Golden	.50
5	Ken Johnson	.50
6	Tom Borland	.50
7	Bobby Shantz	.50
8	Dick Farrell	.50
9	Jim Umbricht	.50
10	Hal Woodeshick	.50
11	Merritt Ranew	.50
12	Hal Smith	.50
13	Jim Campbell	.50
14	Norm Larker	.75
15	Joe Amalfitano	.50
16	Bob Aspromonte	.75
17	Bob Lillis	.50
18	Dick Gernert	.50
19	Don Buddin	.50
20	Pidge Browne	.50
21	Von McDaniel	.50
22	Don Taussig	.50
23	Al Spangler	.50
24	Al Heist	.50
25	Jim Pendleton	.50
26	Johnny Weekly	.50
27	Harry Craft	.50
28	.45s coaches (Lum Harris, Bobby Bragan, Jim Busby, Cot Deal, Jim Adair)	.50
29	Team photo	.50

1993 Hoyle Legends of Baseball

SATCHEL PAIGE

Specially marked decks of Hoyle playing cards contained one of nine Hall of Famer's cards. In the 2-1/2" x 3-1/2" round-cornered poker-size format, the cards have oft-seen black-and-white photos on a glossy front. Backs have a facsimile autograph, biographical data, some stats and career highlights.

		NM/M
Complete Set (9):		12.00
Common Player:		1.00
(1)	Ty Cobb	2.00
(2)	Dizzy Dean	1.00
(3)	Lou Gehrig	2.00
(4)	Walter Johnson	1.00
(5)	Satchel Paige	1.00
(6)	Babe Ruth	3.00
(7)	Casey Stengel	1.00
(8)	Honus Wagner	1.50
(9)	Cy Young	1.00

1993 Humpty Dumpty

The Canadian potato chip company Humpty Dumpty is-

sued a 50-card set of miniature cards in 1993. The UV coated cards measure 1-7/16" x 1-15/16", with a full-bleed color photo on the front along with the team logo. The backs have three-year statistics and biographical information about the player, along with appropriate product and baseball logos and a card number. Besides being packed one per bag in chips, the complete set was also available via a mail-in offer with a plastic album.

		NM/M
Complete Set (50):		10.00
Complete Set, W/Album:		15.00
Common Player:		.25
1	Cal Ripken, Jr.	3.00
2	Mike Mussina	.50
3	Roger Clemens	2.25
4	Chuck Finley	.25
5	Sandy Alomar	.25
6	Frank Thomas	1.00
7	Robin Ventura	.25
8	Cecil Fielder	.25
9	George Brett	2.00
10	Cal Eldred	.25
11	Kirby Puckett	1.50
12	Dave Winfield	1.00
13	Jim Abbott	.25
14	Rickey Henderson	1.00
15	Ken Griffey Jr.	2.50
16	Nolan Ryan	3.00
17	Ivan Rodriguez	.75
18	Paul Molitor	1.00
19	John Olerud	.25
20	Joe Carter	.25
21	Jack Morris	.25
22	Roberto Alomar	.40
23	Pat Borders	.25
24	Devon White	.25
25	Juan Guzman	.25
26	Steve Avery	.25
27	John Smoltz	.25
28	Mark Grace	.25
29	Jose Rijo	.25
30	Dave Nied	.25
31	Benito Santiago	.25
32	Jeff Bagwell	1.00
33	Tim Wallach	.25
34	Eric Karros	.25
35	Delino DeShields	.25
36	Wilfredo Cordero	.25
37	Marquis Grissom	.25
38a	Ken Hill (Weight: 1915)	.50
38b	Ken Hill (Weight: 195)	.25
39	Moises Alou	.25
40	Chris Nabholz	.25
41	Dennis Martinez	.25
42	Larry Walker	.25
43	Bobby Bonilla	.25
44	Lenny Dykstra	.25
45	Tim Wakefield	.25
46	Andy Van Slyke	.25
47	Tony Gwynn	1.50
48	Fred McGriff	.25
49	Barry Bonds	3.00
50	Ozzie Smith	1.50
---	Checklist	.10

1982 Hygrade Expos

Gary Carter 8

This Montreal Expos team set was the object of intense collector speculation when it was first issued. Single cello-wrapped cards were included in packages of Hy-grade luncheon meat in the province of Quebec only. A mail-in offer for the complete set appeared later in the season. It remains a relatively scarce issue today. The 2" x 3" cards are printed on heavy paper, with round corners. Backs are printed in French, and contain an offer for an album to house the set.

		NM/M
Complete Set (24):		15.00
Common Player:		1.00
Album:		5.00
0	Al Oliver	2.00
4	Chris Speier	1.00
5	John Milner	1.00
6	Jim Fanning	1.00
8	Gary Carter	7.50
10	Andre Dawson	5.00
11	Frank Tavaras (Taveras)	1.00
16	Terry Francona	1.00
17	Tim Blackwell	1.00
18	Jerry White	1.00
20	Bob James	1.00
21	Scott Sanderson	1.00
24	Brad Mills	1.00
29	Tim Wallach	1.00
30	Tim Raines	3.00
34	Bill Gullickson	1.00
37	Woodie Fryman	1.00
38	Bryn Smith	1.00
44	Jeff Reardon	1.00
44	Dan Norman	1.00
45	Steve Rogers	1.00
48	Ray Burris	1.00
49	Warren Cromartie	1.00
53	Charlie Lea	1.00

I

1994 Innovative Confections Sucker Savers

BARRY BONDS
SAN FRANCISCO GIANTS

These 2-3/8" diameter discs were included in a plastic snap-top lollipop holder. A yellow strip which intersects the red border at the top contains the player name and team, while a yellow diamond graphic surrounds the player photo. Produced by Michael Schechter Assoc., the discs are licensed by the players' union but not MLB, so team uniform logos are airbrushed off the photos. Backs are printed in blue and have 1993 and career stats. Square "proof" versions are common in the hobby and carry little or no premium.

		NM/M
Complete Set (20):		25.00
Common Player:		1.00
1	Rickey Henderson	2.00
2	Ken Caminiti	1.00
3	Terry Pendleton	1.00
4	Tim Raines	1.00
5	Joe Carter	1.00
6	Benito Santiago	1.00
7	Jim Abbott	1.00
8	Ozzie Smith	2.50
9	Don Slaught	1.00
10	Tony Gwynn	2.50
11	Mark Langston	1.00
12	Darryl Strawberry	1.00
13	David Justice	1.00
14	Cecil Fielder	1.00

15	Cal Ripken Jr.	4.00
16	Jeff Bagwell	2.00
17	Mike Piazza	3.00
18	Bobby Bonilla	1.00
19	Barry Bonds	4.00
20	Roger Clemens	2.75

1991 International Playing Card Co. All-Stars

(See 1991 U.S. Playing Card All-Stars for checklist and price guide.)

1994 International Playing Cards Toronto Blue Jays

ROBERTO ALOMAR • 2B

Virtually identical to the team and mixed stars playing card sets issued by U.S. Playing Card Co., this Toronto team set was issued for the Canadian market. In playing card format at 2-1/2" x 3-1/2" with rounded corners, the set features Blue Jays players on front with their name and position in white in a blue stripe beneath the photo. Backs are bright blue with the team logo at top-center and sponsors' logos along the bottom. The set was sold in a colorful cardboard box.

		NM/M
Complete Set (55):		4.00
Common Player:		.05
AC	John Olerud	.15
2C	Al Leiter	.05
3C	Dave Stewart	.10
4C	Pat Borders	.05
5C	Devon White	.10
6C	Joe Carter	.10
7C	Roberto Alomar	.35
8C	Woody Williams	.05
9C	Eddie Zosky	.05
10C	Willie Canate	.05
JC	Danny Cox	.05
QC	Todd Stottlemyre	.10
KC	Ed Sprague	.05
AS	Paul Molitor	1.00
2S	Michael Timlin	.05
3S	Randy Knorr	.05
4S	Pat Hentgen	.05
5S	Darnell Coles	.05
6S	Juan Guzman	.05
7S	Roberto Alomar	.35
8S	Joe Carter	.10
9S	Scott Brow	.05
10S	Dick Schofield	.05
JS	Rob Butler	.05
QS	Tony Castillo	.05
KS	Duane Ward	.05
AH	Joe Carter	.10
2H	Woody Williams	.05
3H	Danny Cox	.05
4H	Todd Stottlemyre	.10
5H	Ed Sprague	.05
6H	John Olerud	.15
7H	Paul Molitor	1.00
8H	Scott Brow	.05
9H	Pat Hentgen	.05
10H	Al Leiter	.05
JH	Dave Stewart	.10
QH	Pat Borders	.05
KH	Devon White	.10
AD	Roberto Alomar	.35
2D	Eddie Zosky	.05
3D	Rob Butler	.05
4D	Tony Castillo	.05
5D	Duane Ward	.05
6D	Paul Molitor	1.00
7D	John Olerud	.15
8D	Carlos Delgado	.75
9D	Michael Timlin	.05
10D	Randy Knorr	.05
JD	Pat Hentgen	.05
QD	Darnell Coles	.05
KD	Juan Guzman	.05
Joker	Team name	.05
Joker	A.L. logo	.05
---	Checklist	.05

1995 International Playing Cards Toronto Blue Jays

For a second year the Canadian affiliate of the U.S. Playing Card Co. issued a team set of Blue Jays. Fronts have color portrait and action photos - up to three for popular players - with player identification and traditional playing card suit and value indicators in opposite corners. Backs have a large team logo. Cards are in 2-1/2" x 3-1/2" round-cornered format and were sold in a colorful flip-top box.

		NM/M
Complete Set (56):		4.00
Common Player:		.05
AC	John Olerud	.15
2C	Pat Hentgen	.05
3C	Juan Guzman	.05
4C	Cecil Fielder	.10
5C	Roberto Alomar	.35
6C	Joe Carter	.10
7C	Mark Eichhorn	.05
8C	Carlos Delgado	.75
9C	Tom Candiotti	.05
10C	Dave Stewart	.10
JC	Tony Fernandez	.05
QC	Pat Borders	.05
KC	Dave Winfield	1.00
AS	Paul Molitor	1.00
2S	Todd Stottlemyre	.10
3S	Rickey Henderson	1.00
4S	Tom Henke	.05
5S	Fred McGriff	.10
6S	Devon White	.10
7S	Duane Ward	.05
8S	David Wells	.05
9S	David Cone	.10
10S	Mike Timlin	.05
JS	Ed Sprague	.05
QS	Jack Morris	.05
KS	Jimmy Key	.10
AH	Roberto Alomar	.35
2H	Candy Maldonado	.05
3H	Mike Timlin	.05
4H	Ed Sprague	.05
5H	Pat Borders	.05
6H	Jimmy Key	.10
7H	Paul Molitor	1.00
8H	Candy Maldonado	.05
9H	Danny Cox	.05
10H	Todd Stottlemyre	.05
JH	Rickey Henderson	1.00
QH	Tom Henke	.05
KH	Cecil Fielder	.10
AD	Joe Carter	.05
2D	Duane Ward	.05
3D	Dave Stewart	.10
4D	Tony Fernandez	.05
5D	Jack Morris	.05
6D	Dave Winfield	1.00
7D	John Olerud	.15
8D	Manny Lee	.05
9D	Pat Hentgen	.05
10D	Randy Knorr	.05
JD	Juan Guzman	.05
QD	Fred McGriff	.10
KD	Devon White	.05
---	Toronto Blue Jays	.05
---	Team logo card	.05
---	A.L. logo card	.05
---	Checklist	.05

J

1984 Jarvis Press Rangers

BILLY SAMPLE OF
Rangers

For its second annual "Baseball Card Day" game promotional set, the Rangers picked up a new sponsor, Jarvis Press of Dallas. The 30 cards in the set include 27 players, the manager, trainer and a group card of the coaches. Cards measure 2-3/8" x 3-1/2". Color game-action photos make up the card fronts. Backs, printed in black and white, include a portrait photo of the player. A source close to the promotion indicated 10,000 sets were produced.

		NM/M
Complete Set (30):		4.00
Common Player:		.35
1	Bill Stein	.35
2	Alan Bannister	.35
3	Wayne Tolleson	.35
5	Billy Sample	.35
6	Bobby Jones	.35
9	Ned Yost	.35
10	Pete O'Brien	.35
11	Doug Rader	.35
13	Tommy Dunbar	.35
14	Jim Anderson	.35
15	Larry Parrish	.35
16	Mike Mason	.35
17	Mickey Rivers	.35
19	Curtis Wilkerson	.35
21	Jeff Kunkel	.35
23	Odell Jones	.35
24	Dave Schmidt	.35
25	Buddy Bell	.35
26	George Wright	.35
27	Frank Tanana	.35
30	Marv Foley	.35
31	Dave Stewart	.50
32	Gary Ward	.35
36	Dickie Noles	.35
43	Donnie Scott	.35
24	Danny Darwin	.35
49	Charlie Hough	.35
53	Joey McLaughlin	.35
---	Coaching Staff (Rich Donnelly, Glenn Ezell, Merv Rettenmund, Dick Such, Wayne Terwilliger)	.35
---	Trainer (Bill Zeigler)	.35

1986 Jays Potato Chips

Jays

TEDDY HIGUERA
MILWAUKEE BREWERS PITCHER

One of a handful of round baseball cards produced for inclusion in boxes of potato chips on a regional basis in 1986, the Jays set of 2-7/8" discs is believed to be the scarcest of the type. The 20 cards in the issue include the most popular Milwaukee Brewers and Chicago Cubs and White Sox players; the set having been distributed in the southern Wisconsin- northern Illinois area. Like many contemporary sets produced by Mike Schechter Associates, the '86 Jays cards feature player photos on which the team logos have been airbrushed off the caps.

		NM/M
Complete Set (20):		17.50
Common Player:		.50
(1)	Harold Baines	.50
(2)	Cecil Cooper	.50
(3)	Jody Davis	.50
(4)	Bob Dernier	.50
(5)	Richard Dotson	.50
(6)	Shawon Dunston	.50
(7)	Carlton Fisk	3.00
(8)	Jim Gantner	.50
(9)	Ozzie Guillen	.50
(10)	Teddy Higuera	.50
(11)	Ron Kittle	.50
(12)	Paul Molitor	3.00
(13)	Keith Moreland	.50
(14)	Ernie Riles	.50
(15)	Ryne Sandberg	6.00
(16)	Tom Seaver	3.00
(17)	Lee Smith	.50
(18)	Rick Sutcliffe	.50
(19)	Greg Walker	.50
(20)	Robin Yount	3.00

1984 Jewel Food Chicago Cubs/ White Sox

Similar in format to previous issues by the Midwestern food company, these 16-piece sets of Chicago's National and American League teams are printed on 6"x 9" paper. Fronts feature a chest-to-cap color player photo with a black facsimile autograph. A logo and copyright notice by the players' association is at upper-left. Backs are blank. Cards were distributed four per week with the purchase of specific sale products.

		NM/M
Complete Cubs Set (16):		12.00
Complete White Sox Set (16):		12.50
Common Player:		.50
(1)	Larry Bowa	.50
(2)	Ron Cey	.50
(3)	Jody Davis	.50
(4)	Bob Dernier	.50
(5)	Leon Durham	.50
(6)	Dennis Eckersley	2.50
(7)	Richie Hebner	.50
(8)	Gary Matthews	.50
(9)	Keith Moreland	.50
(10)	Ryne Sandberg	6.00
(11)	Scott Sanderson	.50
(12)	Lee Smith	.75
(13)	Tom Stoddard	.50
(14)	Rick Sutcliffe	.50
(15)	Steve Trout	.50
(16)	Gary Woods	.50
(1)	Harold Baines	.50
(2)	Alan Bannister	.50
(3)	Julio Cruz	.50
(4)	Richard Dotson	.50
(5)	Jerry Dybzinski	.50
(6)	Carlton Fisk	4.00
(7)	Scott Fletcher	.50
(8)	LaMarr Hoyt	.50
(9)	Ron Kittle	.50
(10)	Rudy Law	.50
(11)	Vance Law	.50
(12)	Greg Luzinski	.50
(13)	Tom Paciorek	.50
(14)	Tom Seaver	4.00
(15)	Mike Squires	.50
(16)	Greg Walker	.50

2003 Jewish Major Leaguers

Jewish Major Leaguers
CINCINNATI
Art Shamsky

Produced by Fleer for the American Jewish Historical Society, this set is a first-ever compilation of cards of every American Jew who played in Major League Baseball between 1871 and the All-Star break of 2003. Cards are standard 2-1/2" x 3-1/2", uv-coated on both front and back. Fronts have color or black-and-white photos, bordered in black. Backs have personal data, a career summary, an indication of what other baseball cards the player appeared on and photo/text credits. The issue was sold only as a complete boxed set with an initial price of about $100. A more limited silver-stamped version was available for $200.

		NM/M
Complete Set (149):		100.00
Common Player:		.75
Silver Edition:		3X
1	Sandy Koufax	15.00
2	Harry Danning	.75
3	Hank Greenberg	7.50
4	Andy Cohen	.75
5	Al Rosen	2.50
6	Buddy Myer	.75
7	Sid Gordon	.75
8	Shawn Green	3.00
9	Morrie Arnovich	.75
10	"Lip" Pike	2.00
11	Nate Berkenstock	.75
12	Jacob Pike (?)	.75
13	Jake Goodman	.75
14	Ike Samuls'	
	1895 St. Louis Team	.75
15	Leo Fishel	.75
16	Bill Cristall	.75
17	Harry Kane	.75
18	Barney Pelty	.75
19	Moxie Manuel	.75
20	Phil Cooney	.75
21	Guy Zinn	.75
22	Ed Mensor	.75
23	Erskine Mayer	.75
24	Henry Bostick	.75
25	Sam Mayer	.75
26	Sammy Bohne	.75
27	Jake Pitler	.75
28	Bob Berman	.75
29	Eddie Corey	.75
30	Jesse Baker	.75
31	Al Schacht	.75
32	Sam Fishburn	.75
33	Reuben Ewing	.75
34	Heinie Scheer	.75
35	Lou Rosenberg	.75
36	Moe Berg	7.50
37	Joe Bennett	.75
38	Moe Solomon	.75
39	Happy Foreman	.75
40	Simon Rosenthal	.75
41	Ike Danning	.75
42	Jonah Goldman	.75
43	Ed Wineapple	.75
44	Jimmie Reese	.75
45	Harry Rosenberg	.75
46	Jim Levey	.75
47	Alta Cohen	.75
48	Max Rosenfeld	.75
49	Lou Brower	.75
50	Izzy Goldstein	.75
51	Milt Galatzer	.75
52	Phil Weintraub	.75
53	Cy Malis	.75
54	Syd Cohen	.75
55	Fred Sington	.75
56	Harry Eisenstat	.75
57	Chick Starr	.75
58	Goody Rosen	.75
59	Harry Chozen	.75
60	Eddie Feinberg	.75
61	Sam Nahem	.75
62	Dick Conger	.75
63	Murray Franklin	.75
64	Harry Feldman	.75
65	Harry Shuman	.75
66	Eddie Turchin	.75
67	Cy Block	.75
68	Hal Schacker	.75
69	Mike Schemer	.75
70	Herb Karpel	.75
71	Bud Swartz	.75
72	Mickey Rutner	.75
73	Marv Rotblatt	.75
74	Joe Ginsberg	.75
75	Cal Abrams	.75
76	Saul Rogovin	.75
77	Sid Schacht	.75
78	Lou Limmer	.75
79	Duke Markell	.75
80	Al Richter	.75
81	Al Federoff	.75
82	Herb Gorman	.75
83	Moe Savransky	.75
84	Hy Cohen	.75
85	Al Silvera	.75
86	Barry Latman	.75
87	Ed Mayer	.75
88	Larry Sherry	1.00
89	Don Taussig	.75
90	Norm Sherry	1.00
91	Randy Cardinal	.75
92	Alan Koch	.75
93	Larry Yellen	.75
94	Steve Hertz	.75
95	Art Shamsky	.75
96	Richie Scheinblum	.75
97	Greg Goossen	.75
98	Norm Miller	.75
99	Ken Holtzman	.75
100	Mike Epstein	.75
101	Ron Blomberg	.75
102	Lloyd Allen	.75
103	Dave Roberts	.75
104	Elliott Maddox	.75
105	Steve Stone	2.00
106	Steve Yeager	.75
107	Skip Jutze	.75
108	Dick Sharon	.75
109	Jeff Newman	.75
110	Ross Baumgarten	.75
111	Jeff Stember	.75
112	Steve Ratzer	.75
113	Bob Tufts	.75
114	Larry Rothschild	.75
115	Mark Gilbert	.75
116	Steve Rosenberg	.75
117	Roger Samuels	.75
118	Steve Wapnick	.75
119	Scott Radinsky	.75
120	Ruben Amaro, Jr.	.75
121	Wayne Rosenthal	.75
122	Eddie Zosky	.75
123	Jesse Levis	.75
124	Brad Ausmus	.75
125	Eric Helfand	.75
126	Mike Lieberthal	2.00
127	Andrew Lorraine	.75
128	Brian Kowitz	.75
129	Brian Bark	.75
130	Mike Milchin	.75
131	Al Levine	.75
132	Micah Franklin	.75
133	Mike Saipe	.75
134	Keith Glauber	.75
135	Gabe Kapler	2.00
136	Scott Schoeneweis	.75
137	David Newhan	.75
138	Jason Marquis	.75
139	Frank Charles	.75
140	Tony Cogan	.75
141	Justin Wayne	.75
142	Matt Ford	.75
---	Career Batting Leaders	.75
---	Career Pitching Leaders	.10
---	Alphabetical Listing A-M	.10
---	Alphabetical Listing M-Z	.10
---	Header Card/Credits	.05
---	Credits	.05
149	George Brace (photographer)	.25

2006 Jewish Major Leaguers Update Edition

Jewish Major Leaguers
Solomon Israel

Produced by the American Jewish Historical Society, this set updates the premiere edition of 2003. Cards are standard 2-1/2" x 3-1/2". Fronts have color or black-and-white photos, bordered in blue. Backs have personal data, a career summary, and photo/text credits. Ther update includes players who debuted after 2003, as well as female players, minor leaguers and many specialty cards.

		NM/M
Complete Set (55):		40.00
Common Player:		.50
(1)	Header Card	.50
(2)	All-time Roster, A-F	.50
(3)	All-time Roster, G-Rad	.50
(4)	All-time Roster, Rat-Z	.50
(5)	Career Leaders: Batting	.50
(6)	Career Leaders: Pitching	.50
7	Shawn Green	.75
8	Brad Ausmus	.75
9	Mike Lieberthal	.75
10	Al Levine	.75
11	Scott Schoeneweis	.75
12	Jason Marquis	.75
13	Gabe Kapler	.75

14	John Grabow	.75
15	Kevin Youkilis	.75
16	Adam Stern	.75
17	Craig Breslow	.75
18	Adam Greenberg	.75
19	Scott Feldman	.75
20	Prospects (Aaron Rifkin, Scott Schneider, Tony Schrager, Jeff Pickler)	.75
21	1901 Giants Team (Jacob Livingston)	.50
22	Jacob Atz	.75
23	Lefty Weinert	.75
24	Lou Boudreau	1.50
25	Bob Davis	.75
26	Jose Bautista	.75
27	Sam Nahem	.50
28	Thelma Eisen	.50
29	Anita Foss	.50
30	Blanche Schachter	.50
31	Margaret Wigiser/SP (Withdrawn)	.50
31A	Error! (Replacement)	.50
32	Cy Block	.50
33	Harry Danning	.50
34	Lipman Pike	1.50
35	Abe Yager	.50
36	Barney Dreyfuss	.50
37	Dolly Stark	.50
38	Hank Greenberg	1.50
39	Allen Roth	.75
40	Mel Allen	.75
41	Ron Blomberg	.50
42	Richie Scheinblum	.50
43	Allan H. "Bud" Selig	.75
44	Israel's National Baseball Team	.50
45	Marvin Miller, Donald Fehr	.50
46	Moe Berg, Heinie Scheer	.50
47	Saul Rogovin, Lou Limmer, Joe Ginsberg	.50
48	"The Cooperstown Eight"	.50
49	Half a "Minyan": 1946 Giants	.50
50	Clown Princes (Al Schacht, Max Patkin)	.50
51	Mickey Rutner, Lou Limmer	.50
52	Jake Levy, Hal Saltzman	.50
53	Solomon Israel	.50
54	Marty Abramowitz	.50
55	Gabe Kapler, Adam Stern, Kevin Youkilis	.50

1986 Jiffy Pop/ MSA Promos

This 20-card set was produced by Mike Schecter Associates in 1986 to provide attendees at a restaurant and food trade show with examples of his card promotions. The promos have the same fronts as the 1986 Jiffy Pop discs on a 2-7/8" diameter format. The backs have an advertisement for MSA's services. Like the regular issues, the uniform logos have been airbrushed from the discs due to lack of a license from Major League Baseball (the issue is licensed by the players' union). The unnumbered promo discs are checklisted here alphabetically.

		NM/M
Complete Set (20):		175.00
Common Player:		6.00
(1)	Wade Boggs	10.00
(2)	George Brett	15.00
(3)	Gary Carter	10.00
(4)	Steve Garvey	6.00
(5)	Dwight Gooden	4.00
(6)	Reggie Jackson	12.50
(7)	Don Mattingly	15.00
(8)	Willie McGee	4.00
(9)	Dale Murphy	6.00
(10)	Eddie Murray	10.00
(11)	Lance Parrish	4.00
(12)	Jim Rice	6.00
(13)	Cal Ripken, Jr.	25.00
(14)	Pete Rose	20.00
(15)	Nolan Ryan	25.00
(16)	Ryne Sandberg	12.50

(17)	Mike Schmidt	15.00
(18)	Fernando Valenzuela	4.00
(19)	Dave Winfield	10.00
(20)	Robin Yount	10.00

1986 Jiffy Pop

One of the scarcer of the 1986 regionals, the Jiffy Pop discs were inserted in packages of heat-and-eat popcorn. A production of Mike Schechter Associates, the 2-7/8" diameter discs feature 20 popular stars, many in the same pictures found in other '86 regionals. Like other MSA issues, caps have had the team logos erased, allowing Jiffy Pop to avoid paying a licensing fee to the teams. Backs have a few biographical details and stats.

		NM/M
Complete Set (20):		15.00
Common Player:		.50
1	Jim Rice	.65
2	Wade Boggs	1.00
3	Lance Parrish	.50
4	George Brett	2.00
5	Robin Yount	1.00
6	Don Mattingly	2.00
7	Dave Winfield	1.00
8	Reggie Jackson	1.50
9	Cal Ripken	3.50
10	Eddie Murray	1.00
11	Pete Rose	2.50
12	Ryne Sandberg	1.50
13	Nolan Ryan	3.50
14	Fernando Valenzuela	.50
15	Willie McGee	.50
16	Dale Murphy	.75
17	Mike Schmidt	2.00
18	Steve Garvey	.50
19	Gary Carter	1.00
20	Dwight Gooden	.50

1987 Jiffy Pop

For a second year, Jiffy Pop inserted player discs in its packages of popcorn. The full-color discs measure 2-7/8" in diameter and were produced by Mike Schechter Associates. Titled "2nd Annual Collectors' Edition," the card fronts feature player photos with all team insignias airbrushed away. Information on the backs of the discs is printed in bright red on white stock. Die-cut 16-1/4" x 14" press sheets containing all 20 discs were available via a mail-in offer.

		NM/M
Complete Set (20):		20.00
Uncut Sheet:		25.00
Common Player:		.75
1	Ryne Sandberg	2.00
2	Dale Murphy	1.25
3	Jack Morris	.75
4	Keith Hernandez	.75
5	George Brett	2.50
6	Don Mattingly	2.50
7	Ozzie Smith	2.00
8	Cal Ripken, Jr.	3.50
9	Dwight Gooden	.75
10	Pedro Guerrero	.75
11	Lou Whitaker	.75
12	Roger Clemens	2.50
13	Lance Parrish	.75
14	Rickey Henderson	2.00
15	Fernando Valenzuela	.75
16	Mike Schmidt	2.50

1988 Jiffy Pop

This 20-disc set is the third Jiffy Pop issue spotlighting leading players. Discs are 2-1/2" in diameter with a semi-gloss finish and feature full-color closeups on white stock. Team logos have been airbrushed off the player's caps. Fronts have a curved label "3rd Annual Collector's Edition." Disc backs are white, with dark blue lettering, and contain player information, stats and disc number. An uncut sheet (16" x 14-1/2") with all 20 discs was available in a mail-in redemption offer.

		NM/M
Complete Set (20):		9.00
Uncut Sheet:		10.00
Common Player:		.35
1	Buddy Bell	.35
2	Wade Boggs	1.25
3	Gary Carter	1.25
4	Jack Clark	.35
5	Will Clark	.45
6	Roger Clemens	2.00
7	Vince Coleman	.35
8	Andre Dawson	.50
9	Keith Hernandez	.35
10	Kent Hrbek	.35
11	Wally Joyner	.35
12	Paul Molitor	1.25
13	Eddie Murray	1.25
14	Tim Raines	.35
15	Bret Saberhagen	.35
16	Alan Trammell	.35
17	Ozzie Virgil	.35
18	Tim Wallach	.35
19	Dave Winfield	1.25
20	Robin Yount	1.25

1998 Ronnie Joyner St. Louis Browns Heads-Up

Though there is nothing on the cards themselves to identify their origins, this set is the work of sports artist Ronnie Joyner, produced in co-operation with the St. Louis Browns Historical Society. They approximate the 1938 Goudey Heads-Up format in 2-1/2" x 2-7/8" size with sepia portraits and orange backgrounds. Backs have a vintage look with player personal data, a career summary and trivia question. Cards were sold as complete sets.

		NM/M
Complete Set (20):		10.00
Common Player:		.50
1	Hank Arft	.50
2	Ellis Clary	.50
3	Jim Delsing	.50
4	Ned Garver	.65
5	Don Gutteridge	.50
6	Red Hayworth	.50
7	Bill Jennings	.50
8	Dick Kryhoski	.50
9	Don Lenhardt	.50

17	Darryl Strawberry	.75
18	Mike Scott	.75
19	Jim Rice	1.00
20	Wade Boggs	2.00

2003 Ronnie Joyner 1953 St. Louis Browns

Though there is nothing on the cards themselves to identify their origins, or even that they do not actually date from 1953, this set is the work of sports artist Ronnie Joyner, who produced two other Brownies sets in previous years in co-operation with the St. Louis Browns Historical Society. The cards are in the modern 2-1/2" x 3-1/2" format with colorful fronts featuring Joyner portraits of the players and cartoon-style names. Backs have a vintage look with player personal data, a cartoon about the player, a career summary and 1953 and lifetime stats. Cards were sold as complete sets.

		NM/M
Complete Set (40):		15.00
Common Player:		.50
1	Satchel Paige	5.00
2	Les Moss	.50
3	Roy Sievers	.65
4	Bobby Young	.50
5	Marlin Stuart	.50
6	Billy Hunter	.50
7	Don Lenhardt	.50
8	Johnny Groth	.50
9	Vic Wertz	.50
10	Don Larsen	1.00
11	Clint Courtney	.50
12	Dick Kryhoski	.50
13	Neil Berry	.50
14	Bob Cain	.50
15	Willie Miranda	.50
16	Hank Edwards	.50
17	Dick Kokos	.50
18	Jim Pisoni	.50
19	Harry Brecheen	.50
20	Browns 1953 Season Summary	.50
21	Checklist	.50
22	Lou Kretlow	.50
23	Babe Martin	.50
24	Ed Mickelson	.50
25	Frank Kellert	.50
26	Virgil Trucks	.65
27	Dick Littlefield	.50
28	Jim Dyck	.50
29	Mike Blyzka	.50
30	Bob Habenicht	.75
31	Max Lanier	.50
32	Bob Elliott	.50
33	Duane Pillette	.50
34	Johnny Lipon	.50
35	Bob Turley	.65
36	Vern Stephens	.50
37	Hal White	.50
38	Dixie Upright	.75
39	Bobo Holloman	.50
40	Marty Marion	.65

1990 Jumbo Sunflower Seeds

The 1990 "Autograph Series" of 24 cards came in packages of sunflower seeds and were produced by Mike Schecter Associates for Stagi & Scriv-

10	Bob Mahoney	.50
11	Frank Mancuso	.50
12	Babe Martin	.50
13	Ed Mickelson	.50
14	J.W. Porter	.50
15	Roy Sievers	.65
16	Virgil Trucks	.50
17	Al Widmar	.50
18	Jerry Witte	.50
19	Arthur Richman (Number One Fan)	.50
20	Stan Musial (Cross Town Rival)	5.00

en Farms Inc. The cards were found in specially-marked packages of Jumbo California Sunflower Seeds, three cards per package. Standard size with MLB logos airbrushed out, the cards are blue with a white frame. The numbered backs contain yearly statistics and biographical information along with a facsimile autograph.

		NM/M
Complete Set (24):		10.00
Common Player:		.25
(1)	Kevin Mitchell	.25
(2)	Ken Griffey Jr.	1.75
(3)	Howard Johnson	.25
(4)	Bo Jackson	.35
(5)	Kirby Puckett	1.25
(6)	Robin Yount	1.00
(7)	Dave Stieb	.25
(8)	Don Mattingly	1.50
(9)	Barry Bonds	2.00
(10)	Pedro Guerrero	.25
(11)	Tony Gwynn	1.25
(12)	Von Hayes	.25
(13)	Rickey Henderson	1.00
(14)	Tim Raines	.25
(15)	Alan Trammell	.25
(16)	Dave Stewart	.25
(17)	Will Clark	.50
(18)	Roger Clemens	1.50
(19)	Wally Joyner	.25
(20)	Ryne Sandberg	1.25
(21)	Eric Davis	.25
(22)	Mike Scott	.25
(23)	Cal Ripken, Jr.	2.00
(24)	Eddie Murray	1.00

1991 Jumbo Sunflower Seeds

In its second year of baseball card production, Jumbo California Sunflower Seeds maintained the same basic format for its cards. Player photos, with uniform logos airbrushed away, in a white frame are surrounded by a red border with yellow pinstripe. At top left is the issuer's logo; above the photo in white is "Autograph Series II." A facsimile autograph is printed over the photo. Beneath the picture are the player's name, team and position. Backs are printed in red and include major league stats and a career summary.

		NM/M
Complete Set (24):		7.50
Common Player:		.25
1	Ozzie Smith	1.00
2	Wade Boggs	1.00
3	Bobby Bonilla	.50
4	George Brett	1.25
5	Kal Daniels	.25
6	Glenn Davis	.25
7	Chuck Finley	.25
8	Cecil Fielder	.25

9	Len Dykstra	.25
10	Dwight Gooden	.25
11	Ken Griffey Jr.	1.50
12	Kelly Gruber	.25
13	Kent Hrbek	.25
14	Andre Dawson	.35
15	Dave Justice	.25
16	Barry Larkin	.25
17	Ben McDonald	.25
18	Mark McGwire	1.75
19	Roberto Alomar	.50
20	Nolan Ryan	2.00
21	Sandy Alomar, Jr.	.25
22	Bobby Thigpen	.25
23	Tim Wallach	.25
24	Mitch Williams	.25

1992 Jumbo Sunflower Seeds

The basic format used in 1990-91 was returned for 1992 when Michael Schecter Associates produced another 24-card set for inclusion in packages of Jumbo Sunflower Seeds (the "California" identifier was dropped in 1992). Cards feature a player photo on which the uniform logos have been eliminated. Across the photo in black is a facsimile autograph. Around the photo are borders of, successively, white, blue, yellow and white. In the upper-left corner is the issuer's logo. "Autograph Series III" appears in red at upper-right. Beneath the picture, the player's name is printed in red, with his team and position in white. Backs are printed in blue, with major league stats and a career summary, along with a few personal data and the appropriate logos.

		NM/M
Complete Set (24):		6.00
Common Player:		.25
1	Jeff Reardon	.25
2	Bill Gullickson	.25
3	Todd Zeile	.25
4	Terry Mulholland	.25
5	Kirby Puckett	1.00
6	Howard Johnson	.25
7	Terry Pendleton	.25
8	Will Clark	.35
9	Cal Ripken, Jr.	2.00
10	Chris Sabo	.25
11	Jim Abbott	.25
12	Joe Carter	.25
13	Paul Molitor	.75
14	Ken Griffey Jr.	1.50
15	Randy Johnson	.75
16	Bobby Bonilla	.25
17	John Smiley	.25
18	Jose Canseco	.50
19	Tom Glavine	.50
20	Darryl Strawberry	.25
21	Brett Butler	.25
22	Devon White	.25
23	Scott Erickson	.25
24	Willie McGee	.25

K

1987 Kahn's Reds

After a nearly 20-year layoff, Kahn's Wieners sponsored a baseball card set in 1987. The hot dog concessionaire sponsored a Reds team set that was distributed to fans attending

(44) ERIC DAVIS, OF

the August 2 game at Riverfront Stadium. Cards are the standard 2-1/2" x 3-1/2" size. The fronts offer a full-color player photo bordered in red and white. Backs carry the Kahn's logo, a portrait photo of the player and career stats.

		NM/M
Complete Set (26):		9.00
Common Player:		.25
6	Bo Diaz	.25
10	Terry Francona	.25
11	Kurt Stillwell	.25
12	Nick Esasky	.25
13	Dave Concepcion	.25
15	Barry Larkin	3.00
16	Ron Oester	.25
21	Paul O'Neill	1.00
23	Lloyd McClendon	.25
25	Buddy Bell	.25
28	Kal Daniels	.25
29	Tracy Jones	.25
30	Guy Hoffman	.25
31	John Franco	.25
32	Tom Browning	.25
33	Ron Robinson	.25
34	Bill Gullickson	.25
35	Pat Pacillo	.25
39	Dave Parker	.25
43	Bill Landrum	.25
44	Eric Davis	.50
46	Rob Murphy	.25
47	Frank Williams	.25
48	Ted Power	.25
---	Pete Rose/Manager	3.00
	Reds coaches (Scott Breeden, Billy DeMars, Tommy Helms, Bruce Kimm, Jim Lett, Tony Perez)	.25

1988 Kahn's Mets

DAVID CONE 44 PITCHER

Approximately 50,000 Mets fans received this complimentary card set during a ballpark promotion sponsored by Kahn's Wieners. Twenty-five players are featured in the set, along with manager Davey Johnson, four coaches and a team photo. Card fronts have a dark blue border with an orange rectangle framing the color player photo; players' uniform numbers are printed in white in the upper-right corner, beside the team logo. Backs are black-and-white with red accents. In addition to player acquisition date, birthday and residence, a paragraph-style career summary is included. Cards measure 2-1/2" x 3-1/2".

		NM/M
Complete Set (31):		4.00
Common Player:		.25
1	Mookie Wilson	.25
2	Mackey Sasser	.25

3	Bud Harrelson	.25
4	Lenny Dykstra	.35
5	Davey Johnson	.25
6	Wally Backman	.25
8	Gary Carter	3.00
11	Tim Teufel	.25
12	Ron Darling	.25
13	Lee Mazzilli	.25
15	Rick Aguilera	.25
16	Dwight Gooden	.50
17	Keith Hernandez	.35
18	Darryl Strawberry	.50
19	Bob Ojeda	.25
20	Howard Johnson	.30
21	Kevin Elster	.25
22	Kevin McReynolds	.25
26	Terry Leach	.25
28	Bill Robinson	.25
29	Dave Magadan	.25
30	Mel Stottlemyre	.25
31	Gene Walter	.25
33	Barry Lyons	.25
34	Sam Perlozzo	.25
42	Roger McDowell	.25
44	David Cone	.50
48	Randy Myers	.25
50	Sid Fernandez	.25
52	Greg Pavlick	.25
---	Team Photo	.25

Reds

(17) CHRIS SABO, IF

This 26-card team set was a giveaway during the Aug. 14, 1988 Cincinnati Reds game. The glossy cards (2-1/2" x 3-1/2") feature color action photos inside red and white borders. The Reds logo, player uniform number, name and position is printed below the photo. The backs are black and white, with small player close-ups and career stats. A promotional 25-cent coupon for Kahn's Wieners was included with each set.

		NM/M
Complete Set (26):		6.00
Common Player:		.25
6	Bo Diaz	.25
8	Terry McGriff	.25
9	Eddie Milner	.25
10	Leon Durham	.25
11	Barry Larkin	.50
12	Nick Esasky	.25
13	Dave Concepcion	.25
14	Pete Rose	3.00
15	Jeff Treadway	.30
17	Chris Sabo	.30
20	Danny Jackson	.25
21	Paul O'Neill	.30
22	Dave Collins	.25
27	Jose Rijo	.25
28	Kal Daniels	.25
29	Tracy Jones	.25
31	Lloyd McClendon	.25
31	John Franco	.25
32	Tom Browning	.25
33	Ron Robinson	.25
44	Jack Armstrong	.25
44	Eric Davis	.30
46	Rob Murphy	.25
47	Frank Williams	.25
48	Tim Birtsas	.25
---	Coaches (Danny Breeden, Tommy Helms, Bruce Kimm, Jim Lett, Lee May, Tony Perez)	

Cooperstown Collection

This 11-player card set was available through a mail-in offer. One dollar and three proofs of purchase from Hillshire Farms were needed to obtain the set. The card fronts feature paintings of recent Hall of Fame inductees. A coupon card was also included with each set.

	NM/M
Complete Set (11):	3.00

COOPERSTOWN COLLECTION — JOHNNY BENCH

Common Player:		.50
(1)	Cool Papa Bell	.50
(2)	Johnny Bench	.75
(3)	Lou Brock	.60
(4)	Whitey Ford	.75
(5)	Bob Gibson	.65
(6)	Billy Herman	.50
(7)	Harmon Killebrew	.75
(8)	Eddie Mathews	.65
(9)	Brooks Robinson	.65
(10)	Willie Stargell	.65
(11)	Carl Yastrzemski	.75

1989 Kahn's Mets

Mookie Wilson 1

This team set was sponsored by Kahn's Wieners and given to fans attending the July 6 game at Shea Stadium. Standard-size cards feature a color photo surrounded by a blue and orange border with the player's name and uniform number across the top. Backs include the Kahn's logo, along with player information and complete Major League stats. Four update cards were later added to the set.

		NM/M
Complete Set (35):		4.00
Common Player:		.20
1	Mookie Wilson	.25
2	Mackey Sasser	.20
3	Bud Harrelson	.20
4	Davey Johnson	.20
7	Juan Samuel	.20
8	Gary Carter	1.00
9	Gregg Jefferies	.50
11	Tim Teufel	.20
12	Ron Darling	.20
13	Lee Mazzilli	.20
16	Dwight Gooden	.30
17	Keith Hernandez	.30
18	Darryl Strawberry	.30
19	Bob Ojeda	.20
20	Howard Johnson	.30
21	Kevin Elster	.20
22	Kevin McReynolds	.20
28	Bill Robinson	.20
29	Dave Magadan	.20
30	Mel Stottlemyre	.20
32	Mark Carreon	.20
33	Barry Lyons	.20
34	Sam Perlozzo	.20
38	Rick Aguilera	.20
44	David Cone	.25
46	Dave West	.20
48	Randy Myers	.20
49	Don Aase	.20
50	Sid Fernandez	.20
52	Greg Pavlick	.20
---	Team Card	.20
13	Jeff Musselman	.50
25	Keith Miller	.50
44	Frank Viola	.50
40	Jeff Innis	.50

1989 Kahn's Reds

This team set, sponsored by Kahn's Wieners, was distributed to fans attending the August 6 Reds game at Riverfront Stadium. The standard-

size, red-bordered cards feature action photos with the player's name in the upper-left corner, his uniform number in the upper-right and the Reds logo in the middle. Backs include a black-and-white portrait, player data and complete major and minor league stats. The Kahn's logo appears in the upper-right corner of the back.

		NM/M
Complete Set (26):		6.00
Common Player:		.20
6	Bo Diaz	.20
7	Lenny Harris	.25
11	Barry Larkin	.50
12	Joel Youngblood	.20
14	Pete Rose	3.00
16	Ron Oester	.20
17	Chris Sabo	.20
20	Danny Jackson	.20
21	Paul O'Neill	.40
25	Todd Benzinger	.20
27	Jose Rijo	.20
28	Kal Daniels	.20
29	Herm Winningham	.20
30	Ken Griffey	.25
31	John Franco	.20
32	Tom Browning	.20
33	Ron Robinson	.20
34	Jeff Reed	.20
36	Rolando Roomes	.20
37	Norm Charlton	.20
42	Rick Mahler	.20
43	Kent Tekulve	.20
44	Eric Davis	.30
48	Tim Birtsas	.20
49	Rob Dibble	.25
---	Coaches (Danny Breeden, Dave Bristol, Tommy Helms, Jim Lett, Lee May, Tony Perez)	.20

1990 Kahn's Mets

Mets — DAVID CONE 44

For the third consecutive year, Kahn's issued a team set of Mets baseball cards. The sets were distributed at Shea Stadium on May 3, prior to the Mets/Reds game. Cards feature blue and orange (team colors) graphics and are numbered according to uniform number. Two coupon cards were also included with each set.

		NM/M
Complete Set (34):		3.00
Common Player:		.20
1	Lou Thornton	.20
2	Mackey Sasser	.20
3	Bud Harrelson	.20
4	Mike Cubbage	.20
5	Davey Johnson	.20
6	Mike Marshall	.20
9	Gregg Jefferies	.50
10	Dave Magadan	.20
11	Tim Teufel	.20
13	Jeff Musselman	.20
15	Ron Darling	.20
16	Dwight Gooden	.30

18	Darryl Strawberry	.30
19	Bob Ojeda	.20
20	Howard Johnson	.20
21	Kevin Elster	.20
22	Kevin McReynolds	.20
25	Keith Miller	.20
26	Alejandro Pena	.20
27	Tom O'Malley	.20
29	Frank Viola	.20
30	Mel Stottlemyre	.20
31	John Franco	.20
32	Doc Edwards	.20
33	Barry Lyons	.20
35	Orlando Mercado	.20
40	Jeff Innis	.20
44	David Cone	.35
45	Mark Carreon	.20
47	Wally Whitehurst	.20
48	Julio Machado	.20
50	Sid Fernandez	.20
52	Greg Pavlick	.20
---	Team Card	.20

Reds

CINCINNATI REDS — (44) Eric Davis, OF

This team set marks the fourth consecutive year in which Kahn's released a modern Reds issue. The cards feature color photos, red and white borders and the player's name, number, and position on the card front. The flip sides feature biographical information, statistics, a posed photo and the Kahn's logo. The set is numbered by uniform.

		NM/M
Complete Set (27):		4.00
Common Player:		.25
7	Mariano Duncan	.25
9	Joe Oliver	.25
10	Luis Quinones	.25
11	Barry Larkin	.50
15	Glenn Braggs	.25
16	Ron Oester	.25
17	Chris Sabo	.25
20	Danny Jackson	.25
21	Paul O'Neill	.40
22	Billy Hatcher	.25
23	Hal Morris	.25
25	Todd Benzinger	.25
27	Jose Rijo	.25
29	Randy Myers	.25
29	Herm Winningham	.25
30	Ken Griffey	.25
32	Tom Browning	.25
34	Jeff Reed	.25
37	Norm Charlton	.25
40	Jack Armstrong	.25
41	Lou Pinella	.30
42	Rick Mahler	.25
43	Tim Layana	.25
44	Eric Davis	.35
48	Tim Birtsas	.25
49	Rob Dibble	.25
	Coaches (Jackie Moore, Tony Perez, Sam Perlozzo, Larry Rothschild, Stan Williams)	.25

1991 Kahn's Mets

Mets — Howard Johnson IF 20

Kahn's kept its tradition in 1991 with the release of this set featuring members of the New

York Mets. Cards measure 2-1/2" x 3-1/2" and the fronts feature a pinstripe design. The backs are printed horizontally and feature complete statistics. The cards are numbered according to uniform number. The complete set was distributed at a 1991 home game.

		NM/M
Complete Set (33):		4.00
Common Player:		.20
1	Vince Coleman	.20
2	Mackey Sasser	.20
3	Bud Harrelson	.20
4	Mike Cubbage	.20
5	Charlie O'Brien	.20
7	Hubie Brooks	.20
8	Daryl Boston	.20
9	Gregg Jefferies	.30
10	Dave Magadan	.20
11	Tim Teufel	.20
13	Rick Cerone	.20
15	Ron Darling	.20
16	Dwight Gooden	.30
	David Cone	.50
20	Howard Johnson	.20
21	Kevin Elster	.20
22	Kevin McReynolds	.20
25	Keith Miller	.20
26	Alejandro Pena	.20
28	Tom Herr	.20
29	Frank Viola	.20
30	Mel Stottlemyre	.20
31	John Franco	.20
32	Doc Edwards	.20
40	Jeff Innis	.20
43	Doug Simons	.20
45	Mark Carreon	.20
47	Wally Whitehurst	.20
48	Pete Schourek	.20
50	Sid Fernandez	.20
51	Tom Spencer	.20
52	Greg Pavlick	.20
---	Team Card	.20

Reds

BARRY LARKIN INFIELDER (11) — WORLD CHAMPION CINCINNATI REDS

The World Champion Cincinnati Reds are showcased in this 28-card set. The card fronts feature small color action photos on white stock. Backs feature statistics, biographical information and the Kahn's logo. A special card of team mascot Schottzie is included in this set.

		NM/M
Complete Set (28):		4.00
Common Player:		.25
7	Mariano Duncan	.25
9	Joe Oliver	.25
10	Luis Quinones	.25
11	Barry Larkin	.50
15	Glenn Braggs	.25
17	Chris Sabo	.25
19	Bill Doran	.25
21	Paul O'Neill	.30
22	Billy Hatcher	.25
23	Hal Morris	.25
25	Todd Benzinger	.25
27	Jose Rijo	.25
29	Randy Myers	.25
29	Herm Winningham	.25
32	Tom Browning	.25
34	Jeff Reed	.25
36	Don Carman	.25
37	Norm Charlton	.25
40	Jack Armstrong	.25
41	Lou Pinella	.30
44	Eric Davis	.25
45	Chris Hammond	.25
47	Scott Scudder	.25
48	Ted Power	.25
49	Rob Dibble	.25
57	Freddie Benavides	.25
---	Schottzie (mascot)	.25
	Coaches (Jackie Moore, Tony Perez, Sam Perlozzo, Larry Rothschild, Stan Williams)	.25

1992 Kahn's Mets

TODD HUNDLEY

A Mets' blue border surrounds the game-action photos in this team set. Backs are horizontally formatted and present full major league stats and the '92 Mets team slogan, "Hardball is Back." A baseball on front carries the uniform number by which the set is checklisted here. Cents-offs coupons for Kahn's hot dogs and corn dogs were packaged with the set when it was distributed at a home game, but are not considered part of the set.

		NM/M
Complete Set (33):		4.00
Common Player:		.20
1	Vince Coleman	.20
2	Mackey Sasser	.20
3	Junior Noboa	.20
4	Mike Cubbage	.20
6	Daryl Boston	.20
8	Dave Gallagher	.20
9	Todd Hundley	.35
10	Jeff Torborg	.20
11	Dick Schofield	.20
12	Willie Randolph	.20
15	Kevin Elster	.20
16	Dwight Gooden	.20
17	David Cone	.40
18	Bret Saberhagen	.35
19	Anthony Young	.20
20	Howard Johnson	.20
22	Charlie O'Brien	.20
25	Bobby Bonilla	.20
26	Barry Foote	.20
27	Tom McGraw	.20
28	Dave LaRoche	.20
29	Dave Magadan	.20
30	Mel Stottlemyre	.20
31	John Franco	.20
32	Bill Pecota	.20
33	Eddie Murray	1.00
40	Jeff Innis	.20
44	Tim Burke	.20
45	Paul Gibson	.20
47	Wally Whitehurst	.20
50	Sid Fernandez	.20
51	John Stephenson	.20
---	Mets Team	.20

Reds

(37) NORM CHARLTON P

This 27-card set (two coupon cards distributed with the team set are not considered part of the set) was given to fans at a promotional home date. The 2-1/2" x 3-1/2" cards have a red border with the team name at top and player name at bottom in white. The player's uniform number and position in black flank his name. A team logo appears in the lower-left corner of the photo. Backs are printed in red and black and have complete pro stats, a few biographical details and the logo of the Riverfront Stadium hot dog concessionaire. The checklist presented here is in order of uniform number.

		NM/M
Complete Set (27):		4.00
Common Player:		.25
2	Schottzie/Mascot	.25
9	Joe Oliver	.25
10	Bip Roberts	.25
11	Barry Larkin	.45
12	Freddie Benavides	.25
15	Glenn Braggs	.25
16	Reggie Sanders	.25
17	Chris Sabo	.25
19	Bill Doran	.25
21	Paul O'Neill	.35
23	Hal Morris	.25
24	Scott Bankhead	.25
26	Darnell Coles	.25
27	Jose Rijo	.25
28	Scott Ruskin	.25
29	Greg Swindell	.25
30	Dave Martinez	.25
31	Tim Belcher	.25
32	Tom Browning	.25
34	Jeff Reed	.25
37	Norm Charlton	.25
38	Troy Afenir	.25
41	Lou Piniella	.30
45	Chris Hammond	.25
48	Dwayne Henry	.25
49	Rob Dibble	.25
---	Coaches (Jackie Moore, John McLaren, Sam Perlozzo, Tony Perez, Larry Rothschild)	.25

1993 Kahn's Mets

1F EDDIE MURRAY 33

The Mets distributed the 1993 Kahn's team set to fans on May 23 at Shea Stadium. Cards feature color photos and a white border. The Mets logo is at the bottom center and the player's name, position and uniform number at the top. Backs include career statistics and biography inside a red border. Also included in the set is a team photo card and a title card which features the New York skyline and the stadium. Apparently not all cards, such as those of coaches, were issued in all sets.

		NM/M
Complete Set (36):		7.50
Common Player:		.25
4	Tony Fernandez	.25
4	Mike Cubbage	.50
6	Joe Orsulak	.25
7	Jeff McKnight	.25
8	Dave Gallagher	.25
9	Todd Hundley	.50
10	Jeff Torborg	.50
12	Vince Coleman	.50
12	Jeff Kent	1.00
16	Dwight Gooden	.25
18	Bret Saberhagen	.35
19	Anthony Young	.25
20	Howard Johnson	.25
21	Darren Reed	.25
22	Charlie O'Brien	.25
23	Tim Bogar	.25
25	Bobby Bonilla	.30
26	Barry Foote	.50
27	Tom McGraw	.50
28	Dave LaRoche	.50
29	Frank Tanana	.50
30	Mel Stottlemyre	.50
31	John Franco	.25
33	Eddie Murray	1.50
34	Chico Walker	.25
40	Jeff Innis	.25
44	Ryan Thompson	.25
47	Mike Draper	.25
48	Pete Schourek	.25
50	Sid Fernandez	.25
51	Mike Maddux	.25
---	John Stephenson	.50
---	Team Photo	.25
---	Header Card	.10

--- Corn dog coupon .05
--- Hot dog coupon .05

Reds

BIP ROBERTS

Kahn's produced a Reds team set which was given away to fans at Riverfront Stadium on August 1. The cards, organized by player's uniform number, show a photo of the player on the front with the player's name at the top and the Reds logo in the lower corner, surrounded by a pinstripe border. Card backs have the player's lifetime statistics and biography. Card #2 in the set portrays team owner Marge Schott and her dog Schottzie II. Coupon cards good for discounts on packages of Kahn's hot dogs and corn dogs were packaged with the set but are not considered part of the set.

		NM/M
Complete Set (28):		6.00
Common Player:		.25
2	Schottzie/Mascot (Marge Schott)	.25
7	Kevin Mitchell	.25
8	Juan Samuel	.25
9	Joe Oliver	.25
10	Bip Roberts	.25
11	Barry Larkin	.40
15	Davey Johnson	.25
16	Reggie Sanders	.25
17	Chris Sabo	.25
19	Randy Milligan	.25
20	Jeff Branson	.25
23	Hal Morris	.25
25	Greg Cadaret	.25
27	Jose Rijo	.25
30	Bobby Kelly	.25
31	Tim Belcher	.25
32	Tom Browning	.25
40	Tim Pugh	.25
41	Jeff Reardon	.25
42	Gary Varsho	.25
44	Bill Landrum	.25
46	Jacob Brumfield	.25
48	Rob Dibble	.25
53	Kevin Wickander	.25
57	John Smiley	.25
59	Bobby Ayala	.25
---	Coaches (Jose Cardenal, Don Gullett, Ray Knight, Bobby Valentine, Dave Miley)	.25
---	Broadcasters (Marty Brennaman, Joe Nuxhall)	.25

Reds

RON GANT
OUTFIELDER

Distributed at a promotional game and sponsored by the hot dog concessionaire at Riverfront Stadium this was the eighth consecutive Reds team set produced by Kahn's. Cards feature a player action photo with a red stripe superimposed near the left border. The stripe contains the player name and position at top and the team logo at bottom. Backs are printed in red and black and include full minor and major league stats. Cards are numbered by uniform number printed on back.

		NM/M
Complete Set (31):		4.00
Common Player:		.20
2	Schottzie/Mascot	.20
4	Jacob Brumfield	.20
7	Kevin Mitchell	.20
9	Joe Oliver	.20
10	Eddie Taubensee	.20
11	Barry Larkin	.35
12	Deion Sanders	.50
15	Davey Johnson	.20
16	Reggie Sanders	.20
19	Jerome Walton	.20
20	Jeff Branson	.20
21	Tony Fernandez	.20
22	Thomas Howard	.20
23	Hal Morris	.20
27	Jose Rijo	.20
29	Lenny Harris	.20
29	Brett Boone	.50
31	Chuck McElroy	.20
32	Tom Browning	.20
33	Brian Dorsett	.20
39	Erik Hanson	.20
40	Tim Pugh	.20
43	John Roper	.20
45	Jeff Brantley	.20
46	Pete Schourek	.20
47	Johnny Ruffin	.20
49	Rob Dibble	.20
52	Tim Fortugno	.20
57	John Smiley	.20
58	Hector Carrasco	.20
---	Reds Coaching Staff (Bob Boone, Don Gullett, Grant Jackson, Ray Knight, Joel Youngblood)	.20

1995 Kahn's Mets

BUTLER

Game-action photos are featured in this edition of the annual tradition of cards sponsored by the Mets hot dog concessionaire. In standard 2-1/2" x 3-1/2" format the cards have a gray background with navy pinstripes. The player's name, uniform number and position are in team colors of blue and orange at bottom. Backs are in red, black and white with personal data, previous-year or career stats and team and sponsor logos. The cards are checklisted here by uniform number.

		NM/M
Complete Set (36):		4.00
Common Player:		.25
1	Ricky Otero	.25
4	Mike Cubbage	.25
5	Chris Jones	.25
6	Joe Orsulak	.25
7	Bobby Wine	.25
8	Steve Swisher	.25
9	Todd Hundley	.30
10	Tom McGraw	.25
11	Aaron Ledesma	.25
12	Jeff Kent	.75
13	Edgardo Alfonzo	.60
15	Jose Vizcaino	.25
17	Bret Saberhagen	.35
18	Jeff Barry	.25
19	Bill Spiers	.25
20	Ryan Thompson	.25
21	Bill Pulsipher	.25
22	Brett Butler	.25
23	Tim Bogar	.25
25	Bobby Bonilla	.25
26	Rico Brogna	.25
27	Pete Harnisch	.25
28	Bobby Jones	.25
31	John Franco	.25
33	Kelly Stinnett	.25

34	Blas Minor	.25
35	Doug Henry	.25
38	Dave Mlicki	.25
40	Eric Gunderson	.25
44	Jason Isringhausen	.25
45	Jerry DiPoto	.25
46	Dallas Green	.25
52	Greg Pavlick	.25
55	Frank Howard	.25
---	50-cent hot dog coupon	.05
---	50-cent corn dog coupon	.05

Reds

CINCINNATI REDS
1995

RON GANT · OUTFIELDER

This team set continues the tradition of baseball card sponsorship by Kahn's Meats. The set was given away at the August 6 game. Team name and the year are printed in the white border above the photo; the player's name and position are in white in a red strip at bottom. A Reds logo appears in the upper-right corner of the photo, with the player's uniform number below in white. Backs have complete minor and major league stats, along with a few biographical details and the Reds and Kahn's logos. The checklist is presented here by uniform number. Two Kahn's coupons were included in each cello-wrapped set.

		NM/M
Complete Set (34):		4.50
Common Player:		.15
02	Schottzie (02)	.15
6	Ron Gant	.30
8	Damon Berryhill	.15
9	Eric Anthony	.15
10	Eddie Taubensee	.15
11	Barry Larkin	.40
12	Willie Greene	.15
15	Davey Johnson	.15
16	Reggie Sanders	.15
17	Mark Lewis	.15
18	Benito Santiago	.15
19	Jerome Walton	.15
20	Jeff Branson	.15
22	Deion Sanders	.30
22	Thomas Howard	.15
23	Hal Morris	.15
26	Johnny Ruffin	.15
27	Jose Rijo	.15
28	Lenny Harris	.15
29	Bret Boone	.40
30	Brian Hunter	.15
31	Chuck McElroy	.15
33	Kevin Jarvis	.15
37	Xavier Hernandez	.15
40	Tim Pugh	.15
41	Brad Pennington	.15
42	Mike Jackson	.15
43	John Roper	.15
45	Jeff Brantley	.15
46	Pete Schourek	.15
49	C.J. Nitkowski	.15
57	John Smiley	.15
58	Hector Carrasco	.15
---	Reds coaches (Ray Knight, Don Gullett, Grant Jackson, Hal McRae, Joel Youngblood)	.15

1996 Kahn's Mets

This team set was handed out to attendees at the August 3 game at Shea Stadium. Sponsored by the Mets' hot dog concessionaire, the set features the players, coaches and manager in color action photos. Borders are in dark shades and include a Mets logo at lower-right. The player name and uniform number are in white. Backs are in black, red

ROBERT PERSON 29

and white with personal data, 1995 stats and sponsors logos. The uniform number is repeated at lower-left. Cards are checklisted here in alphabetical order. The set was distributed cello-wrapped with two 50-cent hot dogs coupons.

		NM/M
Complete Set (32):		5.00
Common Player:		.25
(1)	Edgardo Alfonzo	.25
(2)	Tim Bogar	.25
(3)	Rico Brogna	.25
(4)	Paul Byrd	.25
(5)	Mark Clark	.25
(6)	Mike Cubbage	.25
(7)	Jerry Dipoto	.25
(8)	Carl Everett	.25
(9)	John Franco	.25
(10)	Bernard Gilkey	.25
(11)	Dallas Green	.25
(12)	Pete Harnisch	.25
(13)	Doug Henry	.25
(14)	Frank Howard	.25
(15)	Todd Hundley	.25
(16)	Butch Huskey	.25
(17)	Jason Isringhausen	.25
(18)	Lance Johnson	.25
(19)	Bobby Jones	.25
(20)	Chris Jones	.25
(21)	Brent Mayne	.25
(22)	Tom McGraw	.25
(23)	Dave Mlicki	.25
(24)	Alex Ochoa	.25
(25)	Rey Ordonez	.25
(26)	Greg Pavlick	.25
(27)	Robert Person	.25
(28)	Bill Pulsipher	.25
(29)	Steve Swisher	.25
(30)	Andy Tomberlin	.25
(31)	Paul Wilson	.25
(32)	Bobby Wine	.25

Reds

29 BRET BOONE
INFIELDER

1996 CINCINNATI REDS

The players, manager, coaches and mascot are once again featured in a Cincinnati Reds team set sponsored by the team's hot dog concessionaire and given away to fans at the August 4 game. The 2-1/2" x 3-1/2" cards have color game-action photos on front. A red stripe at top has the team logo, player name, position and uniform number. A stripe beneath the photo has team name and year. Backs are printed in black and red on white and include personal data and complete major and minor league stats. Cards are checklisted here by uniform number.

		NM/M
Complete Set (34):		5.00
Common Player:		.25
02	Schottzie/Mascot	.25
7	Curtis Goodwin	.25
9a	Eric Anthony	.25
9b	Joe Oliver	.25

10	Eddie Taubensee	.25
11	Barry Larkin	.45
12	Willie Greene	.25
15	Mike Kelly	.25
16	Reggie Sanders	.25
17	Chris Sabo	.25
18	Eric Owens	.25
20	Jeff Branson	.25
21	Mark Portugal	.25
22	Thomas Howard	.25
23	Hal Morris	.25
25	Ray Knight	.25
26	Johnny Ruffin	.25
27	Jose Rijo	.25
28	Lenny Harris	.25
29	Bret Boone	.50
30	Eduardo Perez	.25
32	Kevin Jarvis	.25
34	Dave Burba	.25
36	Scott Service	.25
41	Jeff Shaw	.25
42	Roger Salkeld	.25
44	Eric Davis	.30
45	Jeff Brantley	.25
46	Pete Schourek	.25
57	John Smiley	.25
58	Hector Carrasco	.25
69	Tim Belk	.25
---	Coaches (Marc Bombard, Don Gullett, Tom Hume, Jim Lett, Hal McRae)	.25
	Bernie Stowe (equipment manager)	.25

1997 Kahn's Reds

This team set was given away to fans at the August 3 game, sponsored by the Reds' hot dog concessionaire. The 2-1/2" x 3-1/2" cards have game action player photos at right and the player's name, position and uniform number in a two-toned red stripe vertically at left. Backs are printed in red and black and include complete major and minor league stats. Cards are listed here according to uniform number.

		NM/M
Complete Set (34):		5.00
Common Player:		.25
00	Curtis Goodwin	.25
02	Schottzie/Mascot	.25
3	Pokey Reese	.25
6	Brook Fordyce	.25
7	Joe Oliver	.25
9	Terry Pendleton	.25
10	Eddie Taubensee	.25
11	Barry Larkin	.35
12	Willie Greene	.25
15	Mike Kelly	.25
16	Reggie Sanders	.25
17	Aaron Boone	.50
20	Jeff Branson	.25
21	Deion Sanders	.35
23	Hal Morris	.25
25	Ray Knight	.25
27	Jose Rijo	.25
28	Lenny Harris	.25
29	Bret Boone	.50
33	Steve Gibraltar	.25
34	Dave Burba	.25
36	Mike Morgan	.25
37	Stan Belinda	.25
38	Kent Mercker	.25
39	Eduardo Perez	.25
40	Brett Tomko	.25
41	Jeff Shaw	.25
43	Mike Remlinger	.25
45	Jeff Brantley	.25
46	Pete Schourek	.25
56	Scott Sullivan	.25
57	John Smiley	.25
67	Felix Rodriguez	.25
---	Ken Griffey Sr., Don Gullett, Tom Hume, Denis Menke, Joel Youngblood	.25

1998 Kahn's Reds

For the 12th consecutive year, the Reds hot dog concessionaire issued a team set, given

away at an August 9 promotional game. The 2-1/2" x 3-1/2" cards have game-action photos at right, borderless at top, bottom and right. At left is a vertical red stripe with player name and uniform number. Horizontal backs have player data and complete major and minor league stats overprinted on a Kahn's logo. Backs are printed in red, black and white.

		NM/M
Complete Set (34):		5.00
Common Player:		.25
3	Pokey Reese	.25
4	Damian Jackson	.25
6	Brook Fordyce	.25
9	Pat Watkins	.25
10	Ed Taubensee	.25
11	Barry Larkin	.35
12	Willie Greene	.25
15	Jack McKeon	.25
16	Reggie Sanders	.25
17	Aaron Boone	.25
21	Sean Casey	.75
22	Jon Nunnally	.25
23	Chris Stynes	.25
25	Dmitri Young	.25
26	Steve Cooke	.25
28	Paul Konerko	.75
29	Bret Boone	.50
31	Scott Sullivan	.25
33	Danny Graves	.25
33	John Hudek	.25
34	Mike Frank	.25
36	Gabe White	.25
37	Stan Belinda	.25
38	Pete Harnisch	.25
39	Eduardo Perez	.25
43	Brett Tomko	.25
43	Mike Remlinger	.25
44	Scott Winchester	.25
46	Melvin Nieves	.25
48	Rick Krivda	.25
53	Todd Williams	.25
58	Steve Parris	.25
---	Reds coaches (Harry Dunlop, Ken Griffey, Don Gullett, Tom Hume, Ron Oester)	.25
02	Schottzie/Mascot	.25

1999 Kahn's Reds

Distribution of a Kahn's team set for the Reds attained its 13th annual celebration July 31 when the cards were handed out to fans at Cinergy Field. Cards have player action photos which are borderless at top and right. At left is a ragged-edged red strip with player identification. Team identification is in a red strip at bottom. Backs are in red and black on white with a large Kahn's logo ghosted at center. Player data and complete professional stats are provided. Cards are checklisted here by uniform number.

		NM/M
Complete Set (34):		5.00
Common Player:		.25
02	Schottzie/Mascot	.25
3	Pokey Reese	.25
4	Jeffrey Hammonds	.25
9	Hal Morris	.25
10	Eddie Taubensee	.25
11	Barry Larkin	.35
12	Chris Stynes	.25
15	Denny Neagle	.25
17	Aaron Boone	.25
21	Sean Casey	.50
23	Greg Vaughn	.25
25	Dmitri Young	.25
26	Jason LaRue	.25
28	Mark Lewis	.25
31	Brian Johnson	.25
32	Jack McKeon	.25
33	Danny Graves	.25
33	Steve Avery	.25
36	Michael Tucker	.25
36	Gabe White	.25
37	Stan Belinda	.25
38	Pete Harnisch	.25
40	Brett Tomko	.25
43	Ron Villone	.25
43	Mark Wohlers	.25
44	Mike Cameron	.25
46	Jason Bere	.25
48	Scott Williamson	.25
49	Dennis Reyes	.25
56	Scott Sullivan	.25
58	Steve Parris	.25
---	Marty Brennaman, Joe Nuxhall/ Broadcasters	.25
---	Ken Griffey Sr., Ron Oester, Denis Menke, Dave Collins (Reds coaches.)	.25

2000 Kahn's Reds

Some 42,500 sets of Reds cards were distributed to fans at the July 22 game at Cinergy Field. Sponsored for the 14th consecutive year by Kahn's meats, the cards do not have a Kahn's logo. Fronts have game action photos with the team logo at top-left, the player name at top-right, his position and uniform number at lower-right and "2000 Cincinnati Reds" vertically in a red stripe at left. Backs have a ghosted team logo, player data and stats. The checklist here is presented by uniform number.

		NM/M
Complete Set (34):		5.00
Common Player:		.25
3	Pokey Reese	.25
6	Chris Stynes	.25
6	Benito Santiago	.25
8	Alex Ochoa	.25
10	Dante Bichette	.25
10	Eddie Taubensee	.25
11	Barry Larkin	.45
12	Juan Castro	.25
15	Denny Neagle	.25
17	Aaron Boone	.25
21	Sean Casey	.65
23	Hal Morris	.25
25	Dmitri Young	.25
28	Rob Bell	.25
30	Ken Griffey Jr.	3.00
31	Jack McKeon	.25
32	Danny Graves	.25
34	Michael Tucker	.25
36	Manny Aybar	.25
38	Pete Harnisch	.25
43	Ron Villone	.25
43	Osvaldo Fernandez	.25
48	Elmer Dessens	.25
48	Scott Williamson	.25
49	Dennis Reyes	.25
56	Scott Sullivan	.25
58	Steve Parris	.25
---	Coaching staff (Ken Griffey Sr., Denis Menke, Ron Oester, Dave Collins)	.25

Coaching staff (Don Gullett, Harry Dunlop, Tom Hume, Mark Berry) .25

---	Marty Brennaman, Joe Nuxhall/ Broadcasters	
---	Red/Mascot	.25
---	Kahnlee/Mascot	.25
	Coupon	.05
	Coupon	.05

2001 Kahn's Reds

This team set was distributed to fans attending the August 11 game at Cinergy Field. The 2-1/2" x 3-1/2" cards have borderless game-action photos on front. Backs have brief biographical data along with minor and major league stats. The set is checklisted here by uniform number which appears on both front and back.

		NM/M
Complete Set (33):		7.50
Common Player:		.25
3	Pokey Reese	.25
9	Bob Boone	.35
11	Barry Larkin	.45
12	Juan Castro	.25
17	Aaron Boone	.25
21	Sean Casey	.50
22	Brady Clark	.25
25	Jason LaRue	.25
28	Dmitri Young	.25
28	Ruben Rivera	.25
29	Jose Acevedo	.25
30	Ken Griffey Jr.	3.00
31	Kelly Stinnett	.25
32	Danny Graves	.25
34	Michael Tucker	.25
38	Pete Harnisch	.25
41	Chris Reitsma	.25
43	Osvaldo Fernandez	.25
45	Adam Dunn	3.00
48	Elmer Dessens	.25
46	John Riedling	.25
48	Scott Williamson	.25
49	Dennys Reyes	.25
52	Hector Mercado	.25
53	Jim Brower	.25
54	Bill Selby	.25
56	Scott Sullivan	.25
57	Chris Nichting	.25
59	Lance Davis	.25
	Coaches (Don Gullett, Mark Berry, Tom Hume)	
---	Coaches (Ken Griffey Sr., Ron Oester, Tim Foli, Bill Doran)	.25
---	Broadcasters (Marty Brennaman, Joe Nuxhall)	
---	Mr. Red/Mascot	.25

2002 Kahn's Reds

Team sets sponsored by the Reds' hot dog concessionaire were given to fans attending the August 16 game at Cinergy Field. The 2-1/2" x 3-1/2" cards have game-action photos that are borderless at top,

bottom and right. At left is a vertical blue stripe with the date, team name and a 1970-2002 Riverfront Stadium logo. The player name is at bottom-right in black and red; his uniform number is in red at top-right. Horizontal backs are printed in red and black and have personal data and complete professional stats, over-printed on a large Kahn's logo.

		NM/M
Complete Set (33):		10.00
Common Player:		.25
(1)	Aaron Boone	.25
(2)	Bob Boone	.35
(3)	Russell Branyan	.25
(4)	Sean Casey	.50
(5)	Juan Castro	.25
(6)	Bruce Chen	.25
(7)	Ryan Dempster	.25
(8)	Elmer Dessens	.25
(9)	Adam Dunn	3.00
(10)	Jared Fernandez	.25
(11)	Danny Graves	.25
(12)	Ken Griffey Jr.	3.00
(13)	Joey Hamilton	.25
(14)	Jimmy Haynes	.25
(15)	Austin Kearns	1.50
(16)	Barry Larkin	.35
(17)	Jason LaRue	.25
(18)	Corky Miller	.25
(19)	Luis Pineda	.25
(20)	Chris Reitsma	.25
(21)	John Riedling	.25
(22)	Jose Rijo	.25
(23)	Jose Silva	.25
(24)	Kelly Stinnett	.25
(25)	Scott Sullivan	.25
(26)	Reggie Taylor	.25
(27)	Todd Walker	.25
(28)	Gabe White	.25
(29)	Scott Williamson	.25
(30)	Coaching Staff (Jim Lefebvre, Ray Knight, Tim Foli, Jose Cardenal)	.25
(31)	Coaching Staff (Don Gullett, Tom Hume, Mark Berry)	.25
(32)	Marty Brennaman, Joe Nuxhall/ Broadcasters	.25
(33)	Riverfront Stadium	.25

2003 Kahn's Cincinnati Reds

Team sets sponsored by the Reds' hot dog concessionaire were given to fans attending the August 15 game at Cinergy Field. The 2-1/2" x 3-9/16" cards have game-action photos that are borderless at top and right. At left is a vertical black stripe with the team name. At bottom-left is a Great American Ball Park inaugural season logo. The player name and uniform number are at bottom in white on black. Horizontal backs are printed in red, yellow and black and have personal data and complete professional stats, along with a color Kahn's logo.

		NM/M
Complete Set (28):		7.50
Common Player:		.25
(1)	Aaron Boone	.50
(2)	Bob Boone	.50
(3)	Russell Branyan	.25
(4)	Sean Casey	.50
(5)	Juan Castro	.25
(6)	Coaching Staff (Tom Robson, Tim Foli, Ray Knight, Jose Cardenal)	.25

(7)	Coaching Staff (Don Gullett, Tom Hume, Mark Berry)	.25
(8)	Ryan Dempster	.25
(9)	Adam Dunn	1.00
(10)	Danny Graves	.25
(11)	Ken Griffey Jr.	3.00
(12)	Jose Guillen	.35
(13)	Jimmy Haynes	.25
(14)	Felix Heredia	.25
(15)	Austin Kearns	.75
(16)	Barry Larkin	.35
(17)	Jason LaRue	.25
(18)	Kent Mercker	.25
(19)	Wily Mo Pena	.25
(20)	Brian Reith	.25
(21)	Chris Reitsma	.25
(22)	John Riedling	.25
(23)	Kelly Stinnett	.25
(24)	Scott Sullivan	.25
(25)	Reggie Taylor	.25
(26)	Gabe White	.25
(27)	Scott Williamson	.25
(28)	Paul Wilson	.25

2004 Kahn's Cincinnati Reds

This set, sponsored by the Reds' hot dog concessionaire, was given to fans attending the August 15 game at Great American Ball Park. The 2-1/2" x 3-1/2" cards have game-action photos that are borderless at top, left and right. At left is a vertical black stripe with the team name. At bottom-left is a team logo. The player name, position and uniform number are at bottom in white on black or red. Horizontal backs are printed in red, yellow and black and have personal data and complete professional stats, along with a color Kahn's logo.

		NM/M
Complete Set (29):		7.50
Common Player:		.25
3	D'Angelo Jimenez	.25
6	Ryan Freel	.25
7	Juan Castro	.25
9	Jacob Cruz	.25
11	Barry Larkin	.35
13	Dave Miley	.25
15	Cory Lidle	.25
16	Brandon Larson	.25
19	Javier Valentin	.25
21	Sean Casey	.50
23	Jason Larue	.25
25	John Vander Wal	.25
26	Wily Mo Pena	.50
28	Austin Kearns	.50
29	Jose Acevedo	.25
30	Ken Griffey Jr.	3.00
32	Danny Graves	.25
34	Brandon Claussen	.25
36	Gabe White	.25
38	Ryan Wagner	.40
39	Aaron Harang	.25
40	Paul Wilson	.25
44	Adam Dunn	1.50
45	Todd Van Poppel	.25
46	John Riedling	.25
51	Phil Norton	.25
60	Tim Hummel	.25
	Mark Berry, Chris Chambliss, Don Gullett, Tom Hume	.25
---	Coaching Staff (Jerry Narron, Randy Whisler, Mike Stefanski, Mark Mann)	.25

2005 Kahn's Cincinnati Reds

This set, sponsored by the Reds' hot dog concessionaire, was given to fans attending the August 7 game at Great American Ball Park. The 2-1/2" x 3-1/2" cards have game-action photos that are borderless at top, left and right. At bottom, are a team logo, player name, position and uniform number. Horizontal backs are printed in red, yellow and black and have personal data and complete professional stats, along with a color Kahn's logo.

		NM/M
Complete Set (28):		10.00
Common Player:		.25
2	Felipe Lopez	.25
6	Ryan Freel	.25
9	Jacob Cruz	.25
12	Edwin Encarnacion	.50
16	Joe Randa	.25
17	Javier Valentin	.25
21	Sean Casey	.60
22	Eric Milton	.25
23	Jason LaRue	.25
25	David Weathers	.25
26	Wily Mo Pena	.25
28	Austin Kearns	.50
30	Ken Griffey Jr.	3.00
31	Matt Belisle	.25
33	Rich Aurilia	.25
34	Brandon Claussen	.25
36	Ramon Ortiz	.25
38	Ryan Wagner	.25
39	Aaron Harang	.25
40	Paul Wilson	.25
41	Jerry Narron	.25
44	Adam Dunn	1.00
50	Kent Mercker	.25
56	Luke Hudson	.25
56	Todd Coffey	.25
57	Randy Keisler	.25
77	Ben Weber	.25
---	Coaching Staff (Mark Berry, Chris Chambliss, Tom Hume, John Moses, Vern Ruhle, Randy Whisler)	.25

1981 Kansas City Royals Police

CLINT HURDLE

Outfielder
6'-3"
195 lbs.

Ten of the most popular Royals players are featured in this 2-1/2" x 4-1/8" set. Card fronts feature full-color photos with player name, position, facsimile autograph and team logo. Backs include player statistics, a tip from the Royals and list the four sponsoring organizations. The set was issued by the Ft. Myers, Fla., Police Department near the Royals' spring training headquarters.

		NM/M
Complete Set (10):		20.00
Common Player:		1.00
(1)	Willie Mays Aikens	1.00
(2)	George Brett	15.00
(3)	Rich Gale	1.00
(4)	Clint Hurdle	1.00
(5)	Dennis Leonard	1.00
(6)	Hal McRae	1.00
(7)	Amos Otis	1.00
(8)	U.L. Washington	1.00
(9)	Frank White	1.00
(10)	Willie Wilson	1.50

1983 Kansas City Royals Police

JOHN WATHAN

Catcher
6' 2"
205 lbs.

After skipping the 1982 season, the Ft. Myers, Fla., Police Department issued a Royals safety set in 1983 that is almost identical to their 1981 set. Cards are again 2-1/2" x 4-1/8" and include just 10 players. Cards are unnumbered, with vertical fronts and horizontal backs. Fronts have team logos, player name and position and facsimile autographs. Backs list the four sponsoring organizations, a "Tip from the Royals" and a "Kids and Cops Fact" about each player.

		NM/M
Complete Set (10):		15.00
Common Player:		.50
(1)	Willie Mays Aikens	.50
(2)	George Brett	13.50
(3)	Dennis Leonard	.50
(4)	Hal McRae	.50
(5)	Amos Otis	.50
(6)	Dan Quisenberry	.50
(7)	U.L. Washington	.50
(8)	John Wathan	.50
(9)	Frank White	.50
(10)	Willie Wilson	.75

1988 Kansas City Royals Fire Safety

BO JACKSON

This set featuring full-color player caricatures by K.K. Goodale was produced for an in-stadium promotion August 14. The 3" x 5" cards depict players, manager and coaches in action poses against a white background with a Royals logo at upper-left, opposite the Smokey Bear logo. Backs are black-and-white and contain brief player data and a Smokey cartoon.

		NM/M
Complete Set (28):		7.50
Common Player:		.25
1	John Wathan	.25
2	Coaches (Frank Funk, Adrian Garrett, Mike Lum, Ed Napolean, Bob Schaefer, Jim Schaefer)	.25
3	Willie Wilson	.35
4	Danny Tartabull	.25
5	Bo Jackson	1.50
6	Gary Thurman	.25
7	Jerry Don Gleaton	.25
8	Floyd Bannister	.25
9	Buddy Black	.25

10	Steve Farr	.25
11	Gene Garber	.25
12	Mark Gubicza	.25
13	Charlie Liebrandt	.25
14	Ted Power	.25
15	Dan Quisenberry	.25
16	Bret Saberhagen	.35
17	Mike Macfarlane	.25
18	Scotti Madison	.25
19	Jamie Quirk	.25
20	George Brett	5.00
21	Kevin Seitzer	.25
22	Bill Pecota	.25
23	Kurt Stillwell	.25
24	Brad Wellman	.25
25	Frank White	.25
26	Jim Eisenreich	.25
27	Smokey Bear	.10
---	Checklist	.10

1991 Kansas City Royals Police

#16 Bo Jackson

Bo Jackson's release by the Royals in spring training caused his card to be withdrawn from distribution with the other 26 cards in this set. The 2-5/8" x 4-1/8" cards feature a color action photo on front, with the team name in royal blue and the player name and uniform number in black in the bottom border. Backs are printed in blue on white and feature a large cartoon safety message at center, career stats and bio at top, and the logos of the set's sponsors, Kansas City Life Insurance Co., and the Metro Chiefs and Sheriffs Assn., at bottom. Complete sets were distributed in a white paper envelope with team and sponsor logos.

		NM/M
Complete Set (27) (w/Bo Jackson):		5.00
Complete Set (26) (no Bo Jackson):		3.00
Common Player:		.10
1	Kurt Stillwell	.10
3	Terry Shumpert	.10
4	Danny Tartabull	.10
5	George Brett	3.00
8	Jim Eisenreich	.10
12	John Wathan	.10
14	Storm Davis	.10
15	Mike MacFarlane	.10
16	Bo Jackson	3.00
18	Bret Saberhagen	.25
21	Jeff Montgomery	.10
23	Mark Gubicza	.10
25	Gary Thurman	.10
27	Luis Aquino	.10
28	Steve Crawford	.10
30	Kirk Gibson	.15
32	Bill Pecota	.10
33	Kevin Seitzer	.10
36	Tom Gordon	.10
36	Andy McGaffigan	.10
48	Mark Davis	.10
52	Mike Boddicker	.10
55	Kevin Appier	.15
56	Brian McRae	.10
---	Royals coaches (Pat Dobson, Adrian Garrett)	.10
---	Royals coaches (Glenn Ezell, Lynn Jones, Bob Schaefer)	
---	Header Card - Royals Stadium	.10

1992 Kansas City Royals Police

Sponsored by K.C. Life Insurance and distributed by the Metropolitan Chiefs and Sheriffs Association, this 27-card

#5 George Brett

set was distributed at a promotional game. Though they are checklisted, it is rumored that the cards of Kevin Seitzer (traded) and Kirk Gibson (released) were withdrawn early in the promotion, though both names appear on the checklist. The cards are numbered to match the player's uniform numbers. Cards are in the popular police-set format of 2-5/8" x 4-1/8" with white borders around color action photos. Backs have player data, stats, a fire safety message and sponsor's information.

		NM/M
Complete Set (27):		5.00
Common Player:		.25
2	Bob Melvin	.25
3	Terry Shumpert	.25
5	George Brett	3.00
8	Jim Eisenreich	.25
9	Gregg Jefferies	.35
11	Hal McRae	.25
12	Wally Joyner	.35
13	David Howard	.25
15	Mike McFarlane	.25
16	Keith Miller	.25
21	Jeff Montgomery	.25
22	Kevin McReynolds	.25
23	Mark Gubicza	.25
24	Brent Mayne	.25
27	Gary Thomas	.25
27	Luis Aquino	.25
29	Chris Gwynn	.25
30	Kirk Gibson	.35
33	Kevin Seitzer	.25
36	Tom Gordon	.25
37	Joel Johnson	.25
48	Mark Davis	.25
52	Mike Boddicker	.25
55	Kevin Appier	.25
56	Brian McRae	.25
57	Mike Magnante	.25
---	Coaches (Glenn Ezell, Adrian Garrett, Guy Hansen, Lynn Jones, Bruce Kison, Lee May)	.25

1993 Kansas City Royals Police

GEORGE BRETT
INF/DH • 5

One of the longest-running police/fire safety issues continued in 1993 with a set marking the team's 25th anniversary season. The 2-5/8" x 4" cards have a light blue border, a color photo at center, an anniversary logo at lower-left and the player's name, position and uniform number at lower-right. All typography is in royal blue. Backs are printed in blue on white and feature career stats and highlights, a few bio-

graphical notes and a large safety message. Logos of the set's sponsors, Kansas City Life Insurance and the Metro Police Chiefs and Sheriffs Assn. are featured at bottom.

		NM/M
Complete Set (27):		4.00
Common Player:		.15
5	George Brett	3.00
7	Greg Gagne	.15
9	Craig Wilson	.15
11	Hal McRae	.15
12	Wally Joyner	.25
13	Jose Lind	.15
14	Chris Gwynn	.15
15	Mike MacFarlane	.15
16	Keith Miller	.15
17	David Cone	.25
19	Curtis Wilkerson	.15
21	Jeff Montgomery	.15
22	Kevin McReynolds	.15
23	Mark Gubicza	.15
24	Brent Mayne	.15
27	Luis Aquino	.15
28	Rusty Meacham	.15
33	Chris Haney	.15
34	Felix Jose	.15
35	Hipolito Pichardo	.15
36	Tom Gordon	.15
37	Mark Gardner	.15
40	Kevin Koslofski	.15
52	Mike Boddicker	.15
55	Kevin Appier	.15
56	Brian McRae	.15
---	Royals coaches (Steve Boros, Glenn Ezell, Guy Hansen, Bruce Kison, Lee May)	.15

1994 Kansas City Royals Police

Gary Gaetti
3rd Base

The team's long run of police/fire safety issues continued in 1994. The 2-5/8" x 4" cards have a pale yellow background with vertical light blue stripe, a color photo at center, team logo at top and the player's name, position and uniform number at bottom. Backs are printed in blue on white and feature career stats and highlights, a few biographical notes and a large safety message. Logos of the set's sponsors, Kansas City Life Insurance and the Metro Police Chiefs and Sheriffs Assn. are featured at bottom.

		NM/M
Complete Set (27):		8.00
Common Player:		.25
3	Bob Hamelin	.25
6	David Howard	.25
7	Greg Gagne	.25
8	Gary Gaetti	.25
11	Hal McRae	.25
12	Wally Joyner	.25
13	Jose Lind	.25
15	Mike MacFarlane	.25
16	Keith Miller	.25
21	Jeff Montgomery	.25
22	David Cone	.25
23	Mark Gubicza	.25
24	Brent Mayne	.25
29	Vince Coleman	.25
33	Chris Haney	.25
34	Felix Jose	.25
35	Hipolito Pichardo	.25
36	Tom Gordon	.25
40	Kevin Koslofski	.25
41	Billy Brewer	.25
43	Dave Henderson	.25
50	Stan Belinda	.25
55	Kevin Appier	.25
56	Brian McRae	.25
'94	Royals coaches (Steve Boros, Glenn Ezell, Bruce Kison, Lee May, Jamie Quirk)	.25

---	George Brett (Royals Hall of Fame)	3.00
---	Frank White (Royals Hall of Fame)	.50

1995 Kansas City Royals Police

In 1995, the Royals safety set was sponsored by Kansas City Life Insurance Co., and distributed by law enforcement agencies in the greater Kansas City area. The cards measure about 2-5/8" x 4" and feature action photos on front. The team name is scripted at bottom with logo and the player's last name and "1995" are vertically at right. Backs have a few vital data, a career stats line, a safety message and sponsor's logo. Cards are listed here in alphabetical order.

		NM/M
Complete Set (12):		4.00
Common Player:		.50
(1)	Kevin Appier	.50
(2)	Bob Boone	.65
(3)	Vince Coleman	.50
(4)	Gary Gaetti	.50
(5)	Greg Gagne	.50
(6)	Tom Gordon	.50
(7)	Mark Gubicza	.50
(8)	Chris Haney	.50
(9)	Wally Joyner	.65
(10)	Brent Mayne	.50
(11)	Jeff Montgomery	.50
(12)	Hipolito Pichardo	.50

1996 Kansas City Royals Police

Nunnally • 22

The 1997 Royals safety set issue is a 23-card presentation given to young fans at a promotional game. The 2-5/8" x 4" cards have game-action color photo bordered in white. Backs are in blue on white with a few personal data, career highlights and record, a cartoon safety message and the logo of sponsoring Kansas City Life Insurance, which provided the cards for distribution by the Metropolitan Chiefs and Sheriffs Assn. Cards are checklisted here alphabetically.

		NM/M
Complete Set (27):		4.00
Common Player:		.25
1	Bip Roberts	.25
3	Bob Hamelin	.25
4	Keith Lockhart	.25
6	David Howard	.25
8	Bob Boone	.45
15	Mike Macfarlane	.25
16	Joe Randa	.25
17	Kevin Appier	.25
18	Johnny Damon	1.50
21	Jeff Montgomery	.25
22	David Cone	.25
22	Jon Nunnally	.25
23	Mark Gubicza	.25
24	Terry Clark	.25
25	Les Norman	.25
28	Rusty Meacham	.25
30	Jose Offerman	.25
31	Michael Tucker	.25
33	Chris Haney	.25
35	Hipolito Pichardo	.25
37	Rick Huisman	.25
38	Jim Converse	.25
41	Tim Belcher	.25
42	Tom Goodwin	.25
44	Joe Vitiello	.25
45	Jason Jacome	.25
50	Melvin Bunch	.25
57	Mike Magnante	.25

1997 Kansas City Royals Police

In 1996, the Royals returned to safety set issue with this 27-card presentation given to fans 14 and under at the April 20 game. The 2-5/8" x 4" cards have game-action color photo bordered in white. Backs are in blue on white with a few personal data, career highlights and record, a cartoon safety message and the logo of sponsoring Kansas City Life Insurance, which provided the cards for distribution by the Metropolitan Chiefs and Sheriffs Assn. Cards are checklisted here by uniform number.

		NM/M
Complete Set (23):		4.00
Common Player:		.25
(1)	Kevin Appier	.25
(2)	Tim Belcher	.25
(3)	Jay Bell	.25
(4)	Jaime Bluma	.25
(5)	Bob Boone	.50
(6)	Johnny Damon	1.50
(7)	Chili Davis	.25
(8)	Tom Goodwin	.25
(9)	Chris Haney	.25
(10)	David Howard	.25
(11)	Rick Huisman	.25
(12)	Jason Jacome	.25
(13)	Jeff King	.25
(14)	Mike Macfarlane	.25
(15)	Jeff Montgomery	.25
(16)	Jose Offerman	.25
(17)	Craig Paquette	.25
(18)	Hipolito Pichardo	.25
(19)	Bip Roberts	.25
(20)	Jose Rosado	.25
(21)	Sluggerrr/Mascot	.25
(22)	Mike Sweeney	.25
(23)	Joe Vitiello	.25

1998 Kansas City Royals Police

In 1998, the Royals issued this safety set to fans 14 and under at a promotional game. The 2-5/8" x 4" cards have game-action color photo bordered in white. Backs are in blue on white with a few bits of personal data, a cartoon safety message and the logo of sponsoring Kansas City Life Insurance, which provided the cards for distribution by the Metropolitan Chiefs and Sheriffs Association Cards are checklisted here by uniform number.

		NM/M
Complete Set (26):		4.00
Common Player:		.25
2	Jed Hansen	.25
4	Shane Halter	.25
7	Jeff King	.35
14	Felix Martinez	.25
15	Mike Macfarlane	.25
16	Dean Palmer	.25
17	Kevin Appier	.25
18	Johnny Damon	1.50
19	Jeff Conine	.50
21	Jeff Montgomery	.25
22	Larry Sutton	.25
23	Hal Morris	.25
24	Jermaine Dye	.25
27	Joe Vitiello	.25
29	Mike Sweeney	.25
30	Jose Offerman	.25
33	Chris Haney	.25
35	Hipolito Pichardo	.25
40	Tony Muser	.25
41	Tim Belcher	.25
43	Roderick Myers	.25

47	Brian Bevil	.25
50	Jose Rosado	.25
53	Glendon Rusch	.25
56	Matt Whisenant	.25
	Sluggerrr/Mascot	.25

2000 Kansas City Royals Police

The Royals issued this safety set to the first 10,000 fans 14 and under at an April 30 promotional game. The 2-5/8" x 4" cards have game-action color photo bordered in white. Backs are in blue on white with a few bits of personal data, a cartoon safety message and the logo of sponsoring Kansas City Life Insurance, which provided the cards for distribution by the Metropolitan Chiefs and Sheriffs Association Cards are checklisted here by uniform number.

		NM/M
Complete Set (25):		4.00
Common Player:		.25
1	Rey Sanchez	.25
3	Carlos Febles	.50
4	Ray Holbert	.25
6	Todd Dunwoody	.25
12	Jeff Reboulet	.25
14	Mark Quinn	.25
15	Carlos Beltran	3.00
16	Joe Randa	.25
18	Johnny Damon	1.00
19	Brian Johnson	.25
24	Jermaine Dye	.25
28	Jay Witasick	.25
29	Mike Sweeney	.25
33	Chad Durbin	.25
34	Blake Stein	.25
37	Jeff Suppan	.25
38	Scott Pose	.25
40	Tony Muser	.25
41	Dan Reichert	.25
46	Jose Santiago	.25
48	Jerry Spradlin	.25
49	Chris Fussell	.25
50	Jose Rosado	.25
52	Ricky Bottalico	.25
	Sluggerrr/Mascot	.25

2001 Kansas City Royals Police

The Royals issued this safety set to fans attending a promotional game. The 2-5/8" x 4" cards have a game-action color photo on front. The same photo is enlarged, posterized and rendered in blue as a background. A gold stripe at left and top has player identification. Backs have a few bits of personal data, a cartoon safety message and the logo of sponsoring Kansas City Life Insur-

ance, which provided the cards for distribution by the Metropolitan Chiefs and Sheriffs Association Cards are checklisted here alphabetically.

		NM/M
Complete Set (27):		4.00
Common Player:		.25
(1)	Luis Alicea	.25
(2)	Carlos Beltran	2.00
(3)	Dee Brown	.25
(4)	Chad Durbin	.25
(5)	Jermaine Dye	.25
(6)	Carlos Febles	.40
(7)	Doug Henry	.25
(8)	Roberto Hernandez	.25
(9)	Dave McCarty	.25
(10)	Brian Meadows	.25
(11)	Scott Mullen	.25
(12)	Tony Muser	.25
(13)	Luis Ordaz	.25
(14)	Hector Ortiz	.25
(15)	Mark Quinn	.25
(16)	Joe Randa	.25
(17)	Dan Reichert	.25
(18)	Jose Rosado	.25
(19)	Rey Sanchez	.25
(20)	Jose Santiago	.25
(21)	Blake Stein	.25
(22)	Jeff Suppan	.25
(23)	Mac Suzuki	.25
(24)	Mike Sweeney	.25
(25)	Kris Wilson	.25
(26)	Gregg Zaun	.25
(27)	Slugger/Mascot	.25

2002 Kansas City Royals Police

This safety set was a stadium give-away to fans attending an early-season promotional game. The 2-5/8" x 4" cards have a game-action color photo on front, with the background rendered in blue and an arc of blue at left. Backs have a few bits of personal data, a cartoon, safety message and the logo of sponsoring Kansas City Life Insurance, which provided the cards for distribution by the Metropolitan Chiefs and Sheriffs Association Cards are checklisted here alphabetically.

		NM/M
Complete Set (26):		4.00
Common Player:		.25
(1)	Luis Alicea	.25
(2)	Cory Bailey	.25
(3)	Carlos Beltran	2.00
(4)	Dee Brown	.25
(5)	Paul Byrd	.25
(6)	Chad Durbin	.25
(7)	Carlos Febles	.50
(8)	Jason Grimsley	.25
(9)	Roberto Hernandez	.25
(10)	A.J. Hinch	.25
(11)	Raul Ibanez	.25
(12)	Chuck Knoblauch	.25
(13)	Darrell May	.25
(14)	Brent Mayne	.25
(15)	Dave McCarty	.25
(16)	Tony Muser	.25
(17)	Neifi Perez	.25
(18)	Mark Quinn	.25
(19)	Joe Randa	.35
(20)	Dan Reichert	.25
(21)	Donnie Sadler	.25
(22)	Sluggerrr/Mascot	.25
(23)	Blake Stein	.25
(24)	Jeff Suppan	.25
(25)	Mike Sweeney	.50
(26)	Michael Tucker	.25

2003 Kansas City Royals Police

The Royals issued this safety set to fans attending an early-season promotional game. The 2-5/8" x 4" cards have a game-action color photo on front. Backs have a few bits of personal data, a cartoon, safety message and the logo of sponsoring Kansas City Life Insurance, which provided the cards for distribution by the Metropolitan Chiefs and Sheriffs Association Cards are checklisted here by uniform number.

		NM/M
Complete Set (27):		6.00
Common Player:		.50
2	Brent Mayne	.50
3	Carlos Febles	.50
4	Angel Berroa	1.00
9	Tony Pena	.50
12	Desi Relaford	.50
15	Carlos Beltran	2.00
16	Joe Randa	.50
18	Raul Ibanez	.50
24	Michael Tucker	.50
26	Mike DiFelice	.50
28	Ken Harvey	.50
29	Mike Sweeney	.60
30	Brandon Berger	.50
31	Albie Lopez	.50
32	Chris George	.50
33	James Baldwin	.50
34	Darrell May	.50
35	Ryan Bukvich	.50
40	Jason Grimsley	.50
40	Runelvys Hernandez	.50
45	Aaron Guiel	.50
48	Jeremy Affeldt	.50
51	Kris Wilson	.50
53	Miguel Asencio	.50
54	Mike MacDougal	.50
57	Scott Mullen	.50
---	Sluggerrr/Mascot	.50

2004 Kansas City Royals Police

The Royals issued this safety set to fans attending an early-season promotional game. The 2-5/8" x 4" cards have a game-action color photo on front, on a dot-matrix background. Backs have a few bits of personal data, a cartoon, safety message and the logo of sponsoring Kansas City Life Insurance, which provided the cards for distribution by the Metropolitan Chiefs and Sheriffs Association Cards are checklisted here by uniform number.

		NM/M
Complete Set (27):		10.00

2003 Kansas City Royals Police

Common Player:		.50
00	Sluggerrr/Mascot	.50
4	Angel Berroa	1.00
9	Tony Pena	.50
9	David DeJesus	.50
11	Matt Stairs	.50
12	Desi Relaford	.50
17	Tony Graffanino	.50
15	Carlos Beltran	2.00
16	Joe Randa	.50
18	Kelly Stinnett	.50
19	Brian Anderson	.50
22	Juan Gonzalez	1.00
24	Rich Thompson	.50
28	Ken Harvey	.50
29	Mike Sweeney	.65
30	Benito Santiago	.50
33	Curtis Leskanic	.50
34	Darrell May	.50
38	Jason Grimsley	.50
41	Jimmy Gobble	.50
45	Aaron Guiel	.50
47	Scott Sullivan	.50
48	Jeremy Affeldt	.50
54	Mike MacDougal	.50
55	Kevin Appier	.50
59	D.J. Carrasco	.50
62	Jaime Cerda	.50

2005 Kansas City Royals Police

The Royals issued this safety set to fans attending an early-season promotional game. The 2-5/8" x 4" cards have a game-action color photo on front, on a marbled background. Backs are printed in blue and have a few bits of personal data, a cartoon, safety message and the logo of sponsoring Kansas City Life Insurance, which provided the cards for distribution by the Metropolitan Chiefs and Sheriffs Association Cards are checklisted here by uniform number.

		NM/M
Complete Set (27):		8.00
Common Player:		.50
00	Sluggerrr/Mascot	.50
2	John Buck	.50
3	Terrence Long	.50
4	Angel Berroa	.75
6	Tony Pena	.50
9	David DeJesus	.50
11	Eli Marrero	.50
12	Matt Stairs	.50
17	Tony Graffanino	.50
19	Brian Anderson	.50
23	Zack Greinke	1.50
24	Mark Teahen	.50
27	Denny Bautista	.50
28	Ken Harvey	.50
29	Mike Sweeney	.65
30	Ruben Gotay	.50
33	Jose Lima	.50
40	Runelvys Hernandez	.50
41	Jimmy Gobble	.50
45	Aaron Guiel	.50
46	Mike Wood	.50
48	Jeremy Affeldt	.50
51	Andy Sisco	.50
54	Mike MacDougal	.50
56	Jaime Cerda	.50
57	Nate Field	.50
58	Shawn Camp	.50

1993 Kansas City Star Royals All-Time Team

On the occasion of the team's 25th anniversary the Kansas City Star newspaper issued a sheet honoring the All-Time Team. The 10-3/8" x 14-3/8" sheet is perforated to allow separation of the individual 2-1/2" x 3-1/2" cards.

Fronts have color photos at center with royal blue borders at the sides and gold at top and bottom. A Royals 25th anniversary logo is at lower-right. Backs are printed in black and blue on white with a career summary and the player's K.C. stats. The unnumbered cards are checklisted here alphabetically.

		NM/M
Uncut Sheet:		12.00
Complete Set (16):		10.00
Common Player:		.50
(1)	George Brett	6.00
(2)	Steve Busby	.50
(3)	Al Cowens	.50
(4)	Dick Howser	.50
(5)	Dennis Leonard	.50
(6)	John Mayberry	.50
(7)	Hal McRae	.75
(8)	Amos Otis	.50
(9)	Fred Patek	.50
(10)	Darrell Porter	.50
(11)	Dan Quisenberry	.75
(12)	Bret Saberhagen	1.00
(13)	Paul Splittorff	.50
(14)	Frank White	.75
(15)	Willie Wilson	1.00
(16)	25th Anniversary Logo	.50

1985 Kas Potato Chips Discs

One of a pair of nearly identical (see Kitty Clover) sets issued by midwestern potato chip companies, this issue features top stars of the day on 2-3/4" cardboard discs. The discs have a player portrait at center, with uniform logos airbrushed away because the producer was licensed only by the MLB Players Association and not Major League Baseball. The player's name, team and position are printed in a white diamond around the photo. The sponsor's logo is in the orange border. Backs are in black-and-white and have a few biographical data, a 1984 stats line and a Snack Time logo. The unnumbered discs are checklisted here in alphabetical order. Square versions of the discs, which have been cut from press sheets are known within the hobby and carry a small premium. KAS was based in St. Louis.

		NM/M
Complete Set (20):		75.00
Common Player:		1.50
(1)	Steve Carlton	4.50
(2)	Jack Clark	1.50
(3)	Rich Gossage	1.50
(4)	Tony Gwynn	7.50
(5)	Bob Horner	1.50
(6)	Keith Hernandez	1.50
(7)	Kent Hrbek	1.50
(8)	Willie McGee	1.50
(9)	Dan Quisenberry	1.50

(10)	Cal Ripken Jr.	20.00
(11)	Ryne Sandberg	7.50
(12)	Mike Schmidt	12.50
(13)	Tom Seaver	5.00
(14)	Ozzie Smith	7.50
(15)	Rick Sutcliffe	1.50
(16)	Bruce Sutter	4.00
(17)	Alan Trammell	1.50
(18)	Fernando Valenzuela	1.50
(19)	Willie Wilson	1.50
(20)	Dave Winfield	4.50

1986 Kas Potato Chips Cardinals

One of several of 2-7/8" round baseball card discs created by Mike Schecter Associates for inclusion in packages of potato chips, the 20-card Kas set features players of the defending National League Champion St. Louis Cardinals. Fronts feature color photos on which the team logos have been removed from the caps by airbrushing the photos' uniform logos. Card backs have minimal personal data and 1985 stats.

		NM/M
Complete Set (20):		16.00
Common Player:		.50
1	Vince Coleman	1.00
2	Ken Dayley	.50
3	Tito Landrum	.50
4	Steve Braun	.50
5	Danny Cox	.50
6	Bob Forsch	.50
7	Ozzie Smith	9.00
8	Brian Harper	.50
9	Jack Clark	.50
10	Todd Worrell	.50
11	Joaquin Andujar	.50
12	Tom Nieto	.50
13	Kurt Kepshire	.50
14	Terry Pendleton	.50
15	Tom Herr	.50
16	Darrell Porter	.50
17	John Tudor	.50
18	Jeff Lahti	.50
19	Andy Van Slyke	1.00
20	Willie McGee	1.00

1986 Kay Bee Young Superstars

One of the most-widely distributed of the specialty boxed sets of 1986, the Kay Bee toy store chain set of "Young Superstars of Baseball" was produced by Topps. The 2-1/2" x 3-1/2" cards are printed on white stock with a glossy surface finish. Backs, printed in red and black, are strongly reminiscent of the 1971 Topps cards. While the set concentrated on "young" stars of the game, few of the year's top rookies were included.

		NM/M
Complete Set (33):		2.00
Common Player:		.05
1	Rick Aguilera	.05
2	Chris Brown	.05
3	Tom Browning	.05
4	Tom Brunansky	.05
5	Vince Coleman	.05

6	Ron Darling	.05
7	Alvin Davis	.05
8	Mariano Duncan	.05
9	Shawon Dunston	.05
10	Sid Fernandez	.05
11	Tony Fernandez	.05
12	Brian Fisher	.05
13	John Franco	.05
14	Julio Franco	.05
15	Dwight Gooden	.05
16	Ozzie Guillen	.05
17	Tony Gwynn	.75
18	Jimmy Key	.05
19	Don Mattingly	1.50
20	Oddibe McDowell	.05
21	Roger McDowell	.05
22	Dan Pasqua	.05
23	Terry Pendleton	.05
24	Jim Presley	.05
25	Kirby Puckett	.75
26	Earnie Riles	.05
27	Bret Saberhagen	.05
28	Mark Salas	.05
29	Juan Samuel	.05
30	Jeff Stone	.05
31	Darryl Strawberry	.05
32	Andy Van Slyke	.05
33	Frank Viola	.05

1987 Kay Bee Superstars of Baseball

For a second year, Topps produced a boxed set for the Kay Bee toy store chain. Called "Superstars of Baseball," cards in the set measure 2-1/2" x 3-1/2". The glossy-coated fronts carry a color player photo plus the Kay Bee logo. Backs, reminiscent of those found in the 1971 Topps set, offer a black-and-white portrait of the player along with his name, postion, personal information, playing record and a brief biography.

		NM/M
Complete Set (33):		3.00
Common Player:		.05
1	Harold Baines	.05
2	Jesse Barfield	.05
3	Don Baylor	.05
4	Wade Boggs	.65
5	George Brett	.75
6	Hubie Brooks	.05
7	Jose Canseco	.30
8	Gary Carter	.50
9	Joe Carter	.05
10	Roger Clemens	.75
11	Vince Coleman	.05
12	Glenn Davis	.05
13	Dwight Gooden	.05
14	Pedro Guerrero	.05
15	Tony Gwynn	.65
16	Rickey Henderson	.50
17	Keith Hernandez	.05
18	Wally Joyner	.05
19	Don Mattingly	.75
20	Jack Morris	.05
21	Dale Murphy	.15
22	Eddie Murray	.50
23	Dave Parker	.05
24	Kirby Puckett	.65
25	Tim Raines	.05
26	Jim Rice	.05
27	Dave Righetti	.05
28	Ryne Sandberg	.65
29	Mike Schmidt	.05
30	Mike Scott	.05
31	Darryl Strawberry	.05
32	Fernando Valenzuela	.05
33	Dave Winfield	.50

1988 Kay Bee Superstars of Baseball

This boxed set was produced by Topps for exclusive distribution via Kay Bee toy stores nationwide. Card fronts are super glossy and feature

---

color player action photos below a bright red and yellow player name banner. Photos are framed in green above a large, cartoon-style Kay Bee logo. Backs feature player closeups in a horizontal layout in blue ink on a green and white background. Backs are numbered and carry biographical information, career data and major league batting stats.

		NM/M
Complete Set (33):		3.00
Common Player:		.05
1	George Bell	.05
2	Wade Boggs	.65
3	Jose Canseco	.30
4	Joe Carter	.05
5	Jack Clark	.05
6	Alvin Davis	.05
7	Eric Davis	.05
8	Andre Dawson	.25
9	Darrell Evans	.05
10	Dwight Evans	.05
11	Gary Gaetti	.05
12	Pedro Guerrero	.05
13	Tony Gwynn	.65
14	Howard Johnson	.05
15	Wally Joyner	.05
16	Don Mattingly	.75
17	Willie McGee	.05
18	Mark McGwire	.85
19	Paul Molitor	.50
20	Dale Murphy	.25
21	Dave Parker	.05
22	Lance Parrish	.05
23	Kirby Puckett	.65
24	Tim Raines	.05
25	Cal Ripken, Jr.	1.00
26	Juan Samuel	.05
27	Mike Schmidt	.75
28	Ruben Sierra	.05
29	Darryl Strawberry	.05
30	Danny Tartabull	.05
31	Alan Trammell	.05
32	Tim Wallach	.05
33	Dave Winfield	.50

1988 Kay Bee Team Leaders

This boxed edition of 44 player and six team logo cards was produced by Fleer for distribution to Kay Bee toy stores nationwide. Color player photos are framed in black against a bright red border. "Fleer Team Leaders 1988" and Kay Bee logos appear on the front. Backs, (red, white and pink) repeat the Team Leaders logo, followed by stats, personal data, team and MLB logos. The player's name, card number and position are listed on the lower border. The set includes six team logo sticker cards that feature black-and-white stadium photos on the backs.

		NM/M
Complete Set (44):		3.00

Common Player:		.05
1	George Bell	.05
2	Wade Boggs	.65
3	Jose Canseco	.40
4	Will Clark	.10
5	Roger Clemens	.75
6	Eric Davis	.05
7	Andre Dawson	.25
8	Julio Franco	.05
9	Andres Galarraga	.05
10	Dwight Gooden	.05
11	Tony Gwynn	.65
12	Tom Henke	.05
13	Orel Hershiser	.05
14	Kent Hrbek	.05
15	Ted Higuera	.05
16	Wally Joyner	.05
17	Jimmy Key	.05
18	Mark Langston	.05
19	Don Mattingly	.75
20	Willie McGee	.05
21	Mark McGwire	.85
22	Paul Molitor	.50
23	Jack Morris	.05
24	Dale Murphy	.25
25	Larry Parrish	.05
26	Kirby Puckett	.65
27	Tim Raines	.05
28	Jeff Reardon	.05
29	Dave Righetti	.05
30	Cal Ripken, Jr.	1.00
31	Don Robinson	.05
32	Bret Saberhagen	.05
33	Juan Samuel	.05
34	Mike Schmidt	.75
35	Mike Scott	.05
36	Kevin Seitzer	.05
37	Dave Smith	.05
38	Ozzie Smith	.65
39	Zane Smith	.05
40	Darryl Strawberry	.05
41	Rick Sutcliffe	.05
42	Bobby Thigpen	.05
43	Alan Trammell	.05
44	Andy Van Slyke	.05

1989 Kay Bee Superstars of Baseball

The top stars of baseball are featured in this boxed set produced by Topps for the Kay Bee Toy store chain. The glossy, standard-size cards display the Kay Bee logo below the player photo on the front. The top of the card is headlined "Superstars of Baseball," with the player's name underneath. Backs include a small black-and-white player photo and personal data.

		NM/M
Complete Set (33):		3.00
Common Player:		.05
1	Wade Boggs	.65
2	George Brett	.75
3	Jose Canseco	.30
4	Gary Carter	.50
5	Jack Clark	.05
6	Will Clark	.10
7	Roger Clemens	.75
8	Eric Davis	.05
9	Andre Dawson	.25
10	Dwight Evans	.05
11	Carlton Fisk	.50
12	Andres Galarraga	.05
13	Kirk Gibson	.05
14	Dwight Gooden	.05
15	Mike Greenwell	.05
16	Pedro Guerrero	.05
17	Tony Gwynn	.65
18	Rickey Henderson	.50
19	Orel Hershiser	.05
20	Don Mattingly	.75
21	Mark McGwire	.85
22	Dale Murphy	.25
23	Eddie Murray	.50
24	Kirby Puckett	.65
25	Tim Raines	.05
26	Ryne Sandberg	.65
27	Mike Schmidt	.75
28	Ozzie Smith	.65
29	Darryl Strawberry	.05
30	Alan Trammell	.05

31	Frank Viola	.05
32	Dave Winfield	.50
33	Robin Yount	.50

1990 Kay Bee Kings

This boxed set was the fifth annual issue produced by Topps for the Kay Bee toy store chain. The 2-1/2" x 3-1/2" cards feature color action photos on the front and complete statistics on the flip sides. The cards are numbered alphabetically.

		NM/M
Complete Set (33):		4.00
Common Player:		.05
1	Doyle Alexander	.05
2	Bert Blyleven	.05
3	Wade Boggs	.65
4	George Brett	.75
5	John Candelaria	.05
6	Gary Carter	.50
7	Vince Coleman	.05
8	Andre Dawson	.25
9	Dennis Eckersley	.40
10	Darrell Evans	.05
11	Dwight Evans	.05
12	Carlton Fisk	.50
13	Ken Griffey	.05
14	Tony Gwynn	.65
15	Rickey Henderson	.50
16	Keith Hernandez	.05
17	Charlie Hough	.05
18	Don Mattingly	.75
19	Jack Morris	.05
20	Dale Murphy	.25
21	Eddie Murray	.50
22	Dave Parker	.05
23	Kirby Puckett	.65
24	Tim Raines	.05
25	Rick Reuschel	.05
26	Jerry Reuss	.05
27	Jim Rice	.15
28	Nolan Ryan	1.00
29	Ozzie Smith	.65
30	Frank Tanana	.05
31	Willie Wilson	.05
32	Dave Winfield	.50
33	Robin Yount	.50

1993 Keebler Texas Rangers

Over a series of eight home dates in Arlington Stadium's final season, the Keebler baking company along with a group of rotating co-sponsors produced and distributed a team set featuring "all players, manager and coaches who have ever appeared in a Rangers game." Besides the player cards there were checklists, team photo cards, team-leader cards, logo cards and other specials. The cards were made up into 8-1/2" x 11" booklets, with the cards perforated for removal. Series 2 and 3 booklets had 72

---

cards; the other series had 54 cards each. Single cards measure 2-1/2" x 3-1/2". Sepiatoned player portraits are featured with red frames. A blue banner at top has the team name. The player name is printed in black in the white bottom border. The Keebler logo is at the photo's lower-left, while the player's position is in a baseball diamond diagram at lower-right. Backs are printed in black, include a few biographical details and the player's Rangers' and major league career stats. The Keebler logo is repreated on the back, along with the logo of the co-sponsor of that particular series. A total of 42,000 of the first series booklets were distributed; 35,000 each of the other seven series were produced.

		NM/M
Complete Set (468):		35.00
Common Player:		.10
1	Ted Williams	5.00
2	Larry Biittner	.10
3	Rich Billings	.10
4	Dick Bosman	.10
5	Pete Broberg	.10
6	Jeff Burroughs	.10
7	Casey Cox	.10
8	Jim Drixcoll	.10
9	Jan Dukes	.10
10	Bill Fahey	.10
11	Ted Ford	.10
12	Bill Gogolewski	.10
13	Tom Grieve	.10
14	Rich Hand	.10
15	Toby Harrah	.25
16	Vic Harris	.10
17	Rich Hinton	.10
18	Frank Howard	.25
19	Gerry Janeski	.10
20	Dalton Jones	.10
21	Hal King	.10
22	Ted Kubiak	.10
23	Steve Lawson	.10
24	Paul Lindblad	.10
25	Joe Lovitto	.10
26	Elliott Maddox	.10
27	Marty Martinez	.10
28	Jim Mason	.10
29	Don Mincher	.10
30	Dave Nelson	.10
31	Jim Panther	.10
32	Mike Paul	.10
33	Horacio Pina	.10
34	Tom Ragland	.10
35	Lenny Randle	.10
36	Jim Roland	.10
37	Jim Shellenback	.10
38	Don Stanhouse	.10
39	Ken Suarez	.10
40	Joe Camacho	.10
41	Nellie Fox	2.00
42	Sid Hudson	.10
43	George Susce	.10
44	Wayne Terwilliger	.10
45	Darrel Akerfelds	.10
46	Doyle Alexander	.10
47	Gerald Alexander	.10
48	Brian Allard	.10
49	Lloyd Allen	.10
50	Sandy Alomar	.10
51	Wilson Alvarez	.10
52	Jim Anderson	.10
53	Scott Anderson	.10
54	Brad Arnsberg	.10
55	Tucker Ashford	.10
56	Doug Ault	.10
57	Bob Babcock	.10
58	Mike Bacsik	.10
59	Harold Baines	.10
60	Alan Bannister	.10
61	Floyd Bannister	.10
62	John Barfield	.10
63	Len Barker	.10
64	Steve Barr	.10
65	Randy Bass	.10
66	Lew Beasley	.10
67	Kevin Belcher	.10
68	Buddy Bell	.10
69	Juan Beniquez	.10
70	Kurt Bevacqua	.10
71	Jim Bibby	.10
72	Joe Bitker	.10
73	Larvell Blanks	.10
74	Bert Blyleven	.25
75	Terry Bogener	.10
76	Tommy Boggs	.10
77	Dan Boitano	.10
78	Bobby Bonds	.25
79	Thad Bosley	.10
80	Dennis Boyd	.10
81	Nelson Briles	.10
82	Ed Brinkman	.10
83	Bob Brower	.10
84	Jackie Brown	.10
85	Larry Brown	.10

#	Player	Price
86	Jerry Browne	.10
87	Glenn Brummer	.10
88	Kevin Buckley	.10
89	Steve Buechele	.10
90	Ray Burris	.10
91	John Butcher	.10
92	Bert Campaneris	.10
93	Mike Campbell	.10
94	John Cangelosi	.10
95	Nick Capra	.10
96	Leo Cardenas	.10
97	Don Carman	.10
98	Rico Carty	.10
99	Don Castle	.10
100	Jose Cecena	.10
101	Dave Chalk	.10
102	Scott Chiamparino	.10
103	Ken Clay	.10
104	Reggie Cleveland	.10
105	Gene Clines	.10
106	David Clyde	.10
107	Cris Colon	.10
108	Merrill Combs	.10
109	Steve Comer	.10
110	Glen Cook	.10
111	Scott Coolbaugh	.10
112	Pat Corrales	.10
113	Edwin Correa	.10
114	Larry Cox	.10
115	Keith Creel	.10
116	Victor Cruz	.10
117	Mike Cubbage	.10
118	Bobby Cuellar	.10
119	Danny Darwin	.10
120	Jack Daugherty	.10
121	Doug Davis	.10
122	Odie Davis	.10
123	Willie Davis	.10
124	Bucky Dent	.10
125	Adrian Devine	.10
126	Mario Diaz	.10
127	Rich Donnelly	.10
128	Brian Downing	.10
129	Tommy Dunbar	.10
130	Steve Dunning	.10
131	Dan Duran	.10
132	Don Durham	.10
133	Dick Egan	.10
134	Dock Ellis	.10
135	John Ellis	.10
136	Mike Epstein	.10
137	Cecil Espy	.10
138	Chuck Estrada	.10
139	Glenn Ezell	.10
140	Hector Fajardo	.10
141	Monty Fariss	.10
142	Ed Farmer	.10
143	Jim Farr	.10
144	Joe Ferguson	.10
145	Ed Figueroa	.10
146	Steve Fireovid	.10
147	Scott Fletcher	.10
148	Doug Flynn	.10
149	Marv Foley	.10
150	Tim Foli	.10
151	Tony Fossas	.10
152	Steve Foucault	.10
153	Art Fowler	.10
154	Jim Fregosi	.10
155	Pepe Frias	.10
156	Oscar Gamble	.10
157	Barbaro Garbey	.10
158	Dick Gernert	.10
159	Jim Gideon	.10
160	Jerry Don Gleaton	.10
161	Orlando Gomez	.10
162	Rich Gossage	.25
163	Gary Gray	.10
164	Gary Green	.10
165	John Grubb	.10
166	Cecilio Guante	.10
167	Jose Guzman	.10
168	Drew Hall	.10
169	Bill Hands	.10
170	Steve Hargan	.10
171	Mike Hargrove	.10
172	Toby Harrah	.10
173	Bud Harrelson	.10
174	Donald Harris	.10
175	Greg Harris	.10
176	Mike Hart	.10
177	Bill Haselman	.10
178	Ray Hayward	.10
179	Tommy Helms	.10
180	Ken Henderson	.10
181	Rick Henninger	.10
182	Dwayne Henry	.10
183	Jose Hernandez	.10
184	Whitey Herzog	.10
185	Chuck Hiller	.10
186	Joe Hoerner	.10
187	Guy Hoffman	.10
188	Gary Holle	.10
189	Rick Honeycutt	.10
190	Burt Hooton	.10
191	John Hoover	.10
192	Willie Horton	.10
193	Dave Hostetler	.10
194	Charlie Hough	.10
195	Tom House	.10
196	Art Howe	.10
197	Steve Howe	.10
198	Roy Howell	.10
199	Charles Hudson	.10
200	Billy Hunter	.10
201	Pete Incaviglia	.25
202	Mike Jeffcoat	.10
203	Ferguson Jenkins	2.00
204	Alex Johnson	.10
205	Bobby Johnson	.10
206	Cliff Johnson	.10
207	Darrell Johnson	.10
208	John Henry Johnson	.10
209	Lamar Johnson	.10
210	Bobby Jones	.10
211	Odell Jones	.10
212	Mike Jorgensen	.10
213	Don Kainer	.10
214	Mike Kekich	.10
215	Steve Kemp	.10
216	Jim Kern	.10
217	Paul Kilgus	.10
218	Ed Kirkpatrick	.10
219	Darold Knowles	.10
220	Fred Koenig	.10
221	Jim Kremmel	.10
222	Chad Kreuter	.10
223	Jeff Kunkel	.10
224	Bob Lacey	.10
225	Al Lachowicz	.10
226	Joe Lahoud	.10
227	Rick Leach	.10
228	Danny Leon	.10
229	Dennis Lewallyn	.10
230	Rick Lisi	.10
231	Davey Lopes	.10
232	John Lowenstein	.10
233	Mike Loynd	.10
234	Frank Lucchesi	.10
235	Sparky Lyle	.10
236	Pete Mackanin	.10
237	Bill Madlock	.25
238	Greg Mahlberg	.10
239	Mickey Mahler	.10
240	Bob Malloy	.10
241	Ramon Manon	.10
242	Fred Manrique	.10
243	Barry Manuel	.10
244	Mike Marshall	.10
245	Billy Martin	.50
246	Mike Mason	.10
247	Terry Mathews	.10
248	Jon Matlack	.10
249	Rob Maurer	.10
250	Dave May	.10
251	Scott May	.10
252	Lee Mazzilli	.10
253	Larry McCall	.10
254	Lance McCullers	.10
255	Oddibe McDowell	.10
256	Russ McGinnis	.10
257	Joey McLaughlin	.10
258	Craig McMurtry	.10
259	Doc Medich	.10
260	Dave Meier	.10
261	Mario Mendoza	.10
262	Orlando Mercado	.10
263	Mark Mercer	.10
264	Ron Meridith	.10
265	Jim Merritt	.10
266	Gary Mielke	.10
267	Eddie Miller	.10
268	Paul Mirabella	.10
269	Dave Moates	.10
270	Dale Mohorcic	.10
271	Willie Montanez	.10
272	Tommy Moore	.10
273	Roger Moret	.10
274	Jamie Moyer	.10
275	Dale Murray	.10
276	Al Newman	.10
277	Dickie Noles	.10
278	Eric Nolte	.10
279	Nelson Norman	.10
280	Jim Norris	.10
281	Edwin Nunez	.10
282	Pete O'Brien	.10
283	Al Oliver	.25
284	Tom O'Malley	.10
285	Tom Paciorek	.10
286	Ken Pape	.10
287	Mark Parent	.10
288	Larry Parrish	.10
289	Gaylord Perry	2.00
290	Stan Perzanowski	.10
291	Fritz Peterson	.10
292	Mark Petkovsek	.10
293	Gary Pettis	.10
294	Jim Piersall	.25
295	John Poloni	.10
296	Jim Poole	.10
297	Tom Poquette	.10
298	Darrell Porter	.10
299	Ron Pruitt	.10
300	Greg Pryor	.10
301	Luis Pujols	.10
302	Pat Putnam	.10
303	Doug Rader	.10
304	Dave Rajsich	.10
305	Kevin Reimer	.10
306	Merv Rettenmund	.10
307	Mike Richardt	.10
308	Mickey Rivers	.10
309	Dave Roberts	.10
310	Leon Roberts	.10
311	Jeff Robinson	.10
312	Tom Robson	.10
313	Wayne Rosenthal	.10
314	Dave Rozema	.10
315	Jeff Russell	.10
316	Connie Ryan	.10
317	Billy Sample	.10
318	Jim Schaffer	.10
319	Calvin Schiraldi	.10
320	Dave Schmidt	.10
321	Donnie Scott	.10
322	Tony Scruggs	.10
323	Bob Sebra	.10
324	Larry See	.10
325	Sonny Siebert	.10
326	Ruben Sierra	.10
327	Charlie Silvera	.10
328	Duke Sims	.10
329	Bill Singer	.10
330	Craig Skok	.10
331	Don Slaught	.10
332	Roy Smalley	.10
333	Dan Smith	.10
334	Keith Smith	.10
335	Mike Smithson	.10
336	Eric Soderholm	.10
337	Sammy Sosa	4.00
338	Jim Spencer	.10
339	Dick Such	.10
340	Eddie Stanky	.10
341	Mike Stanley	.10
342	Rusty Staub	.35
343	James Steels	.10
344	Bill Stein	.10
345	Rick Stelmaszek	.10
346	Ray Stephens	.10
347	Dave Stewart	.10
348	Jeff Stone	.10
349	Bill Sudakis	.10
350	Jim Sundberg	.10
351	Rich Surhoff	.10
352	Greg Tabor	.10
353	Frank Tanana	.10
354	Jeff Terpko	.10
355	Stan Thomas	.10
356	Bobby Thompson	.10
357	Danny Thompson	.10
358	Dickie Thon	.10
359	Dave Tobik	.10
360	Wayne Tolleson	.10
361	Cesar Tovar	.10
362	Jim Umbarger	.10
363	Bobby Valentine	.10
364	Ellis Valentine	.10
365	Ed Vande Berg	.10
366	Dewayne Vaughn	.10
367	Mark Wagner	.10
368	Rick Waits	.10
369	Duane Walker	.10
370	Mike Wallace	.10
371	Denny Walling	.10
372	Danny Walton	.10
373	Gary Ward	.10
374	Claudell Washington	.10
375	Larue Wasington	.10
376	Chris Welsh	.10
377	Don Werner	.10
378	Len Whitehouse	.10
379	Del Wilber	.10
380	Curtis Wilkerson	.10
381	Matt Williams	.10
382	Mitch Williams	.10
383	Bump Wills	.10
384	Paul Wilmet	.10
385	Steve Wilson	.10
386	Bobby Witt	.10
387	Clyde Wright	.10
388	George Wright	.10
389	Ricky Wright	.10
390	Ned Yost	.10
391	Don Zimmer	.10
392	Richie Zisk	.10
393	Kevin Kennedy	.10
394	Steve Balboni	.10
395	Brian Bohanon	.10
396	Jeff Bronkey	.10
397	Kevin Brown	.10
398	Todd Burns	.10
399	Jose Canseco	.75
400	Cris Carpenter	.10
401	Doug Dascenzo	.10
402	Butch Davis	.10
403	Steve Dreyer	.10
404	Rob Ducey	.10
405	Julio Franco	.10
406	Jeff Frye	.10
407	Benji Gil	.10
408	Juan Gonzalez	3.00
409	Tom Henke	.10
410	David Hulse	.10
411	Jeff Huson	.10
412	Chris James	.10
413	Manuel Lee	.10
414	Craig Lefferts	.10
415	Charlie Leibrandt	.10
416	Gene Nelson	.10
417	Robb Nen	.10
418	Darren Oliver	.10
419	Rafael Palmeiro	2.00
420	Dean Palmer	.10
421	Bob Patterson	.10
422	Roger Pavlik	.10
423	Dan Peltier	.10
424	Geno Petralli	.10
425	Gary Redus	.10
426	Rick Reed	.10
427	Bill Ripken	.10
428	Ivan Rodriguez	3.00
429	Kenny Rogers	.10
430	John Russell	.10
431	Nolan Ryan	6.00
432	Mike Schooler	.10
433	Jon Shave	.10
434	Doug Strange	.10
435	Matt Whiteside	.10
436	Mickey Hatcher	.10
437	Perry Hill	.10
438	Jackie Moore	.10
439	Dave Oliver	.10
440	Claude Osteen	.10
441	Willie Upshaw	.10
442	Checklist 1-112	.10
443	Checklist 113-224	.10
444	Checklist 225-336	.10
445	Checklist 337-446	.10
446	Arlington Stadium	.10

1999 Keebler Los Angeles Dodgers

In a promotion similar to those of Mother's Cookies in the past, Keebler sponsored a kids' trading card day August 15 distributing 28-card packs to fans 14 and under. Each pack contained 21 different cards and seven duplicates to trade in an effort to complete the set. The 2-1/2" x 3-1/2" cards have borderless player photos on front with a Dodgers logo ad team-color red and blue stripes at bottom in which the player's name appears. Color backs have a team logo, a Keebler's elf logo and a few bits of player biographical data.

		NM/M
Complete Set (28):		10.00
Common Player:		.50
1	Davey Johnson	.50
2	Eric Karros	.50
3	Gary Sheffield	.75
4	Raul Mondesi	.50
5	Kevin Brown	.60
6	Mark Grudzielanek	.50
7	Todd Hollandsworth	.50
8	Todd Hundley	.50
9	Jeff Shaw	.50
10	Pedro Borbon	.50
11	Chan Ho Park	.75
12	Jose Vizcaino	.50
13	Devon White	.50
14	Darren Dreifort	.50
15	Onan Masaoka	.50
16	Dave Hansen	.50
17	Adrian Beltre	1.50
18	Ismael Valdes	.50
19	Alan Mills	.50
20	Eric Young	.50
21	Mike Maddux	.50
22	Carlos Perez	.50
23	Tripp Cromer	.50
24	Jamie Arnold	.50
25	Angel Pena	.50
26	Trenidad Hubbard	.50
27	Doug Bochtler	.50
28	Coaches/checklist (Rick Dempsey, Rich Down, Glenn Hoffman, Manny Mota, Claude Osteen, John Shelby, Jim Tracy)	.50

San Diego Padres

In a promotion similar to those of Mother's Cookies in the past, Keebler sponsored a kids' trading card day August 1 distributing 28-card packs to fans 14 and under. Each pack contained 21 different cards and seven duplicates to trade in an effort to complete the set. The 2-1/2" x 3-1/2" cards have borderless player photos on front with a Padres logo and team-color orange and blue stripes at bottom in which the player's name appears. Color backs have a Padres 1969-1999 logo, a Keebler's elf logo and a few bits of player biographical data.

		NM/M
Complete Set (28):		10.00
Common Player:		.50
1	Bruce Bochy	.50
2	Tony Gwynn	4.00
3	Wally Joyner	.50
4	Sterling Hitchcock	.50
5	Jim Leyritz	.50
6	Trevor Hoffman	.75
7	Quilvio Veras	.50
8	Dave Magadan	.50
9	Andy Ashby	.50
10	Damian Jackson	.50
11	Dan Miceli	.50
12	Reggie Sanders	.50
13	Chris Gomez	.50
14	Ruben Rivera	.50
15	Greg Myers	.50
16	Ed Vosberg	.50
17	John Vander Wal	.50
18	Donne Wall	.50
19	Eric Owens	.50
20	Brian Boehringer	.50
21	Woody Williams	.50
22	Matt Clement	.50
23	Carlos Reyes	.50
24	Stan Spencer	.50
25	George Arias	.50
26	Carlos Almanzar	.50
27	Phil Nevin	.50
28	Greg Booker, Tim Flannery, Davey Lopes, Rob Picciolo, Merv Rettenmund, Dave Smith (Padres Coaches)	.50

S.F. Giants

In a promotion similar to those of Mother's Cookies in the past, Keebler sponsored a kids' trading card day distributing 28-card packs to fans 14 and under. Each pack contained 21 different cards and seven duplicates to trade in an effort to complete the set. The 2-1/2" x 3-1/2" cards have borderless player photos on front with a farewell to Candlestick Park logo and team-color orange and black stripes at bottom in which the player's name appears. Color backs have a Keebler's elf logo and a few bits of player biographical data.

		NM/M
Complete Set (28):		12.50
Common Player:		.50
1	Dusty Baker	.50
2	Barry Bonds	7.50
3	Jeff Kent	.75
4	Robb Nen	.50
5	Bill Mueller	.50
6	Russ Ortiz	.50
7	Ellis Burks	.50
8	Marvin Benard	.50
9	Kirk Rueter	.50
10	J.T. Snow	.50
11	Stan Javier	.50
12	Chris Brock	.50
13	Charlie Hayes	.50
14	Joe Nathan	.50
15	Rich Rodriguez	.50
16	Brent Mayne	.50
17	Shawn Estes	.50
18	Rich Aurilia	.50
19	Mark Gardner	.50
20	Scott Servais	.50
21	John Johnstone	.50
22	Felix Rodriguez	.50
23	Armando Rios	.50
24	Alan Embree	.50
25	F.P. Santangelo	.50
26	Jerry Spradlin	.50
27	Lon Simmons/ Broadcaster	.50
28	Giants coaches (Carlos Alfonso, Gene Clines, Sonny Jackson, Juan Lopez, Ron Perranoski, Ron Wotus)	.50

2000 Keebler Arizona Diamondbacks

Keebler cookies sponsored a kids' trading card day, distributing 28-card packs to fans 14 and under. Each pack contained 21 different cards and seven duplicates to trade in an effort to complete the set. Round-cornered cards have borderless portrait photos with a stripe at bottom featuring player identification and team logo. Backs have player data, uniform number, biographical information and Keebler's logo.

		NM/M
Complete Set (28):		10.00
Common Player:		.50
1	Buck Showalter	.50
2	Randy Johnson	3.00
3	Luis Gonzalez	.65
4	Todd Stottlemyre	.50
5	Matt Williams	.75
6	Curt Schilling	1.50
7	Jay Bell	.50
8	Steve Finley	.50
9	Brian Anderson	.50
10	Tony Womack	.50
11	Mike Morgan	.50
12	Damian Miller	.50
13	Greg Swindell	.50
14	Greg Colbrunn	.50
15	Dan Plesac	.50
16	Craig Counsell	.50
17	Russ Springer	.50
18	Kelly Stinnett	.50
19	Alex Cabrera	.50
20	Matt Mantei	.50
21	Danny Klassen	.50
22	Hanley Frias	.50
23	Byung-Hyun Kim	.50
24	Jason Conti	.50
25	Danny Bautista	.50
26	Erubiel Durazo	.50
27	Armando Reynoso	.50
28	Coaches/checklist	.50

L.A. Dodgers

Keebler cookies sponsored a kids' trading card day August 20, distributing 28-card packs to fans 14 and under. Each pack contained 21 different cards and seven duplicates to trade in an effort to complete the set. Round-cornered cards have borderless portrait photos with a red stripe at bottom featuring player identification and team logo. Backs have player data, uniform number, biographical information and Keebler's logo.

		NM/M
Complete Set (28):		10.00
Common Player:		.50
1	Davey Johnson	.50
2	Eric Karros	.50
3	Gary Sheffield	.75
4	Kevin Brown	.60

5	Shawn Green	2.50
6	Mark Grudzielanek	.50
7	Todd Hollandsworth	.50
8	Todd Hundley	.50
9	Jeff Shaw	.50
10	Adrian Beltre	1.00
11	Chan Ho Park	.60
12	Jose Vizcaino	.50
13	Devon White	.50
14	Darren Dreifort	.50
15	Onan Masaoka	.50
16	Dave Hansen	.50
17	Kevin Elster	.50
18	Antonio Osuna	.50
19	Geronimo Berroa	.50
20	Orel Hershiser	.65
21	Chad Kreuter	.50
22	Carlos Perez	.50
23	F.P. Santangelo	.50
24	Terry Adams	.50
25	Alex Cora	.50
26	Matt Herges	.50
27	Mike Fetters	.50
28	Coaches/Checklist (Rick Dempsey, Claude Osteen, Rick Down, Manny Mota, Jim Tracy, Glenn Hoffman, John Shelby)	.50

San Diego Padres

Keebler cookies sponsored a kids' trading card day July 16 distributing 28-card packs to fans 14 and under. Each pack contained 21 different cards and seven duplicates to trade in an effort to complete the set. Fronts of the round-cornered 2-1/2" x 3-1/2" cards have posed photos with team-color orange and blue bars at bottom with player name and team logo. Backs have player ID, jersey number and team logo.

NM/M
Complete Set (28): 10.00
Common Player: .50

1	Bruce Bochy	.50
2	Tony Gwynn	4.00
3	Ryan Klesko	.50
4	Sterling Hitchcock	.50
5	Al Martin	.50
6	Trevor Hoffman	.75
7	Bret Boone	.65
8	Dave Magadan	.50
9	Steve Montgomery	.50
10	Damian Jackson	.50
11	Woody Williams	.50
12	Wiki Gonzalez	.50
13	Chris Gomez	.50
14	Ruben Rivera	.50
15	Ed Sprague	.50
16	Carlton Loewer	.50
17	Kory DeHaan	.50
18	Donne Wall	.50
19	Eric Owens	.50
20	Brian Boehringer	.50
21	Phil Nevin	.50
22	Matt Clement	.50
23	Brian Meadows	.50
24	Vincente Palacios	.50
25	Carlos Hernandez	.50
26	Carlos Almanzar	.50
27	Kevin Walker	.50
28	Coaches/Checklist (Greg Booker, Tim Flannery, Ben Oglivie, Rob Picciolo, Dave Smith, Alan Trammell)	.50

S.F. Giants

Keebler cookies sponsored a trading card day August 6, distributing 25,000 28-card packs to fans. Each pack contained 21 different cards and seven duplicates to trade in an effort to complete the set.

NM/M
Complete Set (28): 10.00
Common Player: .50

1	Dusty Baker	.50
2	Barry Bonds	5.00
3	Jeff Kent	.75
4	Robb Nen	.50
5	J.T. Snow	.50
6	Russ Ortiz	.50
7	Ellis Burks	.50
8	Bill Mueller	.50
9	Shawn Estes	.50
10	Marvin Benard	.50
11	Kirk Rueter	.50
12	Bobby Estalella	.50
13	Livan Hernandez	.50
14	Rich Aurilia	.50
15	Alan Embree	.50
16	Armando Rios	.50
17	Felix Rodriguez	.50
18	Doug Mirabelli	.50
19	John Johnstone	.50
20	Russ Davis	.50
21	Joe Nathan	.50
22	Aaron Fultz	.50
23	Felipe Crespo	.50
24	Mark Gardner	.50
25	Ramon Martinez	.50
26	Calvin Murray	.50
27	Carlos Alfonso	.50
28	Giants coaches (Gene Clines, Sonny Jackson, Juan Lopez, Dave Righetti, Robby Thompson, Ron Wotus)	.50

Seattle Mariners

Keebler cookies sponsored a trading card day at a home game August 13, distributing 20,000 28-card packs to fans. Each pack contained 21 different cards and seven duplicates to trade in an effort to complete the set. Cards are 2-1/2" x 3-1/2" with rounded corners. Fronts have borderless posed photos with a team logo at lower-left and the player name in white in a dark blue strip. Backs have a color Keebler logo and basic player information.

NM/M
Complete Set (28): 15.00
Common Player: .50

1	Lou Piniella	.50
2	Alex Rodriguez	6.00
3	Jamie Moyer	.50
4	Edgar Martinez	.50
5	Kazuhiro Sasaki	.75
6	Jay Buhner	.50
7	Rickey Henderson	2.50
8	John Olerud	.50
9	Aaron Sele	.50
10	Charles Gipson	.50
11	Arthur Rhodes	.50
12	Dan Wilson	.50
13	Jose Mesa	.50
14	Mike Cameron	.50
15	John Halama	.50
16	Mark McLemore	.50
17	Brett Tomko	.50
18	Tom Lampkin	.50
19	Freddy Garcia	.50
20	John Mabry	.50
21	Paul Abbott	.50
22	Stan Javier	.50
23	Gil Meche	.50
24	David Bell	.50
25	Frankie Rodriguez	.50
26	Raul Ibanez	.50
27	Jose Paniagua	.50
28	Coaches/checklist	.50

2001 Keebler Arizona Diamondbacks

Keebler cookies sponsored a trading card day on July 29, distributing 20,000 28-card packs to fans. Each pack contained 21 different cards and seven duplicates to trade in an effort to complete the set. Round-cornered cards have borderless portrait photos with a stripe at bottom featuring player name and team logo. Backs have player data, uniform number, biographical information and Keebler's logo.

NM/M
Complete Set (28): 10.00
Common Player: .50

1	Bob Brenly	.50
2	Randy Johnson	3.00
3	Luis Gonzalez	.60
4	Curt Schilling	1.50
5	Matt Williams	.65
6	Todd Stottlemyre	.50
7	Jay Bell	.50
8	Steve Finley	.50
9	Mark Grace	.60
10	Brian Anderson	.50
11	Tony Womack	.50
12	Damian Miller	.50
13	Russ Springer	.50
14	Greg Colbrunn	.50
15	Craig Counsell	.50
16	Greg Swindell	.50
17	Reggie Sanders	.50
18	Matt Mantei	.50
19	Danny Bautista	.50
20	Mike Morgan	.50
21	Erubiel Durazo	.50
22	Troy Brohawn	.50
23	Byung-Hyun Kim	.50
24	David Dellucci	.50
25	Robert Ellis	.50
26	Rod Barajas	.50
27	Armando Reynoso	.50
28	Coaches/Checklist (Bob Melvin, Dwayne Murphy, Eddie Rodriguez, Glenn Sherlock, Chris Speier, Bob Welch)	.50

L.A. Dodgers

Keebler cookies sponsored a kids' trading card day, on August 19, distributing 28-card packs to fans 14 and under. Each pack contained 21 different cards and seven duplicates to trade in an effort to complete the set. Round-cornered cards have borderless portrait photos with a stripe at bottom featuring player name and team logo. Backs have player data, uniform number, biographical information and Keebler's logo.

NM/M
Complete Set (28): 10.00
Common Player: .50

1	Jim Tracy	.50
2	Eric Karros	.50
3	Shawn Green	2.00
4	Kevin Brown	.60
5	Gary Sheffield	.75
6	Mark Grudzielanek	.50
7	Darren Dreifort	.50
8	Dave Hansen	.50
9	Jeff Shaw	.50
10	Chad Kreuter	.50
11	Chan Ho Park	.60
12	Adrian Beltre	1.00
13	Marquis Grissom	.50
14	Alex Cora	.50
15	Tom Goodwin	.50
16	Gregg Olson	.50
17	Andy Ashby	.50
18	Paul LoDuca	.60
19	Luke Prokopec	.50
20	Mike Fetters	.50
21	Giovanni Carrara	.50
22	Chris Donnels	.50
23	Matt Herges	.50
24	Jeff Reboulet	.50
25	Terry Adams	.50
26	Hiram Bocachica	.50
27	Jesse Orosco	.50
28	Dodgers coaches/checklist (Travis Barbary, Jack Clark, Jim Colborn, Glenn Hoffman, Jim Lett, Manny Mota, Jim Riggleman, John Shelby)	.50

San Diego Padres

Keebler cookies sponsored a kids' trading card day July 22, distributing 15,000 28-card packs to fans 14 and under. Each pack contained 21 different cards and seven duplicates to trade in an effort to complete the set. Fronts of the round-cornered 2-1/2" x 3-1/2" cards have posed photos with a dark blue bar at bottom with player name and team logo. Backs have player data, jersey number and color team and sponsor's logos.

NM/M
Complete Set (28): 10.00
Common Player: .50

1	Bruce Bochy	.50
2	Tony Gwynn	4.00
3	Trevor Hoffman	.60
4	Rickey Henderson	2.00
5	Ryan Klesko	.50
6	Phil Nevin	.50
7	Ben Davis	.50
8	Woody Williams	.50
9	Chris Gomez	.50
10	Dave Magadan	.50
11	Wiki Gonzalez	.50
12	Bobby J. Jones	.50
13	Damian Jackson	.50
14	Kevin Jarvis	.50
15	Bubba Trammell	.50
16	Kevin Walker	.50
17	Mark Kotsay	.50
18	Alex Arias	.50
19	Jay Witasick	.50
20	Mike Darr	.50
21	Adam Eaton	.75
22	Wascar Serrano	.50
23	Jose Nunez	.50
24	Brian Tollberg	.50
25	Donaldo Mendez	.50
26	Tom Davey	.50
27	Rodney Myers	.50
28	Coaches/Checklist (Greg Booker, Duane Espy, Tim Flannery, Rob Picciolo, Dave Smith, Alan Trammell)	.50

San Francisco Giants

Keebler cookies sponsored a trading card day, on September 2, distributing 28-card packs to the first 25,000 fans. Each pack contained 20 different cards and eight duplicates to trade in an effort to complete the set. Round-cornered cards have borderless portrait photos with a stripe at bottom featuring player name and team logo. Backs have player data, uniform number, biographical information and Keebler's logo.

NM/M
Complete Set (28): 10.00
Common Player: .50

1	Dusty Baker	.50
2	Jeff Kent	.75
3	Barry Bonds	6.00
4	Robb Nen	.50
5	J.T. Snow	.50
6	Russ Ortiz	.50
7	Rich Aurilia	.50
8	Benito Santiago	.50
9	Shawn Estes	.50
10	Marvin Benard	.50
11	Kirk Rueter	.50
12	Calvin Murray	.50
13	Livan Hernandez	.50
14	Eric Davis	.50
15	Aaron Fultz	.50
16	Armando Rios	.50
17	Felix Rodriguez	.50
18	Shawon Dunston	.50
19	Mark Gardner	.50
20	Ramon Martinez	.50
21	Pedro Feliz	.50
22	Chad Zerbe	.50
23	Felipe Crespo	.50
24	Tim Worrell	.50
25	Edwards Guzman	.50
26	Ryan Vogelsong	.50
27	Brian Boehringer	.50
28	Coaches/Checklist (Carlos Alfonso, Gene Clines, Sonny Jackson, Juan Lopez, Dave Righetti, Robby Thompson, Ron Wotus)	.50

Seattle Mariners

Keebler cookies sponsored a kids' trading card day at Safeco Field July 15, distributing 20,000 28-card packs to fans. Each pack contained 21 different cards and seven duplicates to trade in an effort to complete the set. Cards are 2-1/2" x 3-1/2" with rounded corners. Fronts have borderless posed photos with a team logo at lower-left and the player name in white in a dark blue strip. Backs have a color Keebler logo and basic player information.

NM/M
Complete Set (28): 10.00
Common Player: .50

1	Lou Piniella	.50
2	Edgar Martinez	.50
3	Mike Cameron	.50
4	Jamie Moyer	.50
5	Ichiro Suzuki	6.00
6	Jay Buhner	.50
7	Kazuhiro Sasaki	.50
8	John Olerud	.50
9	Aaron Sele	.50
10	Bret Boone	.65
11	Arthur Rhodes	.50
12	Al Martin	.50
13	Jeff Nelson	.50
14	Dan Wilson	.50
15	John Halama	.50
16	Stan Javier	.50
17	Brett Tomko	.50
18	Carlos Guillen	.50
19	Freddy Garcia	.50
20	David Bell	.50
21	Paul Abbott	.50
22	Mark McLemore	.50
23	Tom Lampkin	.50
24	Charles Gipson	.50
25	Ryan Franklin	.50
26	Anthony Sanders	.50
27	Jose Paniagua	.50
28	Coaches/Checklist (Lee Elia, John McLaren, John Moses, Dave Myers, Gerald Perry, Bryan Price, Matt Sinatro)	.50

2002 Keebler Arizona Diamondbacks

Keebler cookies sponsored a kids' trading card day July 28, distributing 20,000 28-card packs to fans 14 and under. Each pack contained 20 different cards and eight duplicates to trade in an effort to complete the set. Fronts of the round-cornered 2-1/2" x 3-1/2" cards have posed photos with a purple stripe at bottom with player name and team logo. Color-printed backs have player data, jersey number and team and sponsor's logos.

NM/M
Complete Set (28): 10.00
Common Player: .50

1	Bob Brenly	.50
2	Luis Gonzalez	.60
3	Randy Johnson	3.00
4	Curt Schilling	1.50
5	Matt Williams	.65
6	Todd Stottlemyre	.50
7	Jay Bell	.50
8	Steve Finley	.50
9	Mark Grace	.60
10	Brian Anderson	.50
11	Tony Womack	.50
12	Damian Miller	.50
13	Erubiel Durazo	.50
14	Craig Counsell	.50
15	David Dellucci	.50
16	Greg Swindell	.50
17	Greg Colbrunn	.50
18	Rick Helling	.50
19	Danny Bautista	.50
20	Mike Morgan	.50
21	Rod Barajas	.50
22	Byung-Hyun Kim	.50
23	Mike Myers	.50
24	Jose Guillen	.50
25	Miguel Batista	.50
26	Junior Spivey	.50
27	Quinton McCracken	.50
28	Coaches/Checklist (Chuck Kniffin, Bob Melvin, Dwayne Murphy, Eddie Rodriguez, Glenn Sherlock, Robin Yount)	.50

L.A. Dodgers

Keebler cookies sponsored a kids' trading card day in August, distributing 28-card packs to fans 14 and under. Each pack contained 20 different cards and eight duplicates to trade in an effort to complete the set. Fronts of the round-cornered 2-1/2" x 3-1/2" cards have posed photos with a red stripe at bottom with player name and team logo. Color-printed backs have player data, jersey number and team and sponsor's logos.

NM/M
Complete Set (28): 10.00
Common Player: .50

1	Jim Tracy	.50
2	Eric Karros	.50
3	Shawn Green	1.50
4	Kevin Brown	.65
5	Paul LoDuca	.50
6	Mark Grudzielanek	.50
7	Brian Jordan	.50
8	Kazuhisa Ishii	1.00
9	Hideo Nomo	1.50
10	Dave Hansen	.50
11	Chad Kreuter	.50
12	Adrian Beltre	1.00
13	Marquis Grissom	.50
14	Eric Gagne	.65
15	Odalis Perez	.50

16	Dave Roberts	.50
17	Omar Daal	.50
18	Alex Cora	.50
19	Andy Ashby	.50
20	Hiram Bocachica	.50
21	Darren Dreifort	.50
22	Jesse Orosco	.50
23	Cesar Izturis	.50
24	Terry Mulholland	.50
25	Jeff Reboulet	.50
26	Paul Quantrill	.50
27	Giovanni Carrara	.50
28	Checklist/Coaches (Robert Flippo, Jack Clark, Jim Colborn, Glenn Hoffman, Jim Lett, Manny Mota, Jim Riggleman, John Shelby)	.50

San Diego Padres

Keebler cookies sponsored a kids' trading card day July 21, distributing 28-card packs to fans 14 and under. Each pack contained 21 different cards and seven duplicates to trade in an effort to complete the set. Fronts of the round-cornered 2-1/2" x 3-1/2" cards have posed photos with an orange and dark blue stripe at bottom with player name and team logo. Color-printed backs have player data, jersey number and color team and sponsor's logos.

		NM/M
Complete Set (28):		7.50
Common Player:		.50
1	Bruce Bochy	.50
2	Trevor Hoffman	.50
3	Sean Burroughs	1.50
4	Ryan Klesko	.50
5	Phil Nevin	.50
6	Kevin Jarvis	.50
7	Ron Gant	.50
8	Ramon Vazquez	.50
9	Alan Embree	.50
10	Wiki Gonzalez	.50
11	Bobby J. Jones	.50
12	Mark Kotsay	.50
13	Brett Tomko	.50
14	Bubba Trammell	.50
15	Tom Lampkin	.50
16	Steve Reed	.50
17	Deivi Cruz	.50
18	Brian Tollberg	.50
19	Trenidad Hubbard	.50
20	Jose Nunez	.50
21	Ray Lankford	.50
22	Kevin Walker	.50
23	Dennis Tankersley	.50
24	Jeremy Fikac	.50
25	D'Angelo Jimenez	.50
26	Brian Lawrence	.50
27	Adam Eaton	.50
28	Coaches/Checklist Greg Booker, Darrel Akerfelds, Duane Espy, Tim Flannery, Rob Picciolo, Alan Trammell	.50

San Francisco Giants

Keebler cookies sponsored a kids' trading card day August 25, distributing 28-card packs to fans 14 and under. Each pack contained 21 different cards and seven duplicates to trade in an effort to complete the set. Fronts of the round-cornered 2-1/2" x 3-1/2" cards have posed photos with an orange and dark black stripe at bottom with player name and team logo. Color-printed backs have player data, jersey number and team and sponsor's logos.

		NM/M
Complete Set (28):		10.00
Common Player:		.50
1	Dusty Baker	.50
2	Barry Bonds	6.00
3	Jeff Kent	.75
4	Robb Nen	.50
5	J.T. Snow	.50
6	Russ Ortiz	.50
7	Rich Aurilia	.50
8	Marvin Benard	.50
9	Kirk Reuter	.50
10	Benito Santiago	.50
11	Jason Schmidt	.50
12	Reggie Sanders	.50
13	Livan Hernandez	.50
14	Tsuyoshi Shinjo	.50
15	Aaron Fultz	.50
16	Ramon Martinez	.50
17	Felix Rodriguez	.50
18	Shawon Dunston	.50
19	Tim Worrell	.50
20	David Bell	.50
21	Pedro Feliz	.50
22	Chad Zerbe	.50
23	Damon Minor	.50
24	Yorvit Torrealba	.50
25	Jay Witasick	.50
26	Ryan Jensen	.50
27	Jason Christiansen	.50
28	Coaches/Checklist (Carlos Alfonso, Gene Clines, Sonny Jackson, Joe Lefebvre, Juan Lopez, Dave Righetti, Ron Wotus)	.50

Seattle Mariners

Keebler cookies sponsored a kids' trading card day August 4, distributing 28-card packs to fans 14 and under. Each pack contained 21 different cards and seven duplicates to trade in an effort to complete the set. Fronts of the round-cornered 2-1/2" x 3-1/2" cards have posed photos with a dark blue strip at bottom with player name and team logo. Color-printed backs have player data, jersey number and color team and sponsor's logos.

		NM/M
Complete Set (28):		10.00
Common Player:		.50
1	Lou Piniella	.50
2	Ichiro Suzuki	5.00
3	Edgar Martinez	.50
4	Jamie Moyer	.50
5	Mike Cameron	.50
6	Bret Boone	.75
7	Kazuhiro Sasaki	.65
8	Mark McLemore	.50
9	John Olerud	.50
10	Arthur Rhodes	.50
11	Ruben Sierra	.50
12	Freddy Garcia	.50
13	Dan Wilson	.50
14	Jeff Nelson	.50
15	John Halama	.50
16	Carlos Guillen	.50
17	Ben Davis	.50
18	James Baldwin	.50
19	Jeff Cirillo	.50
20	Shigetoshi Hasegawa	.50
21	Paul Abbott	.50
22	Desi Relaford	.50
23	Ryan Franklin	.50
24	Luis Ugueto	.50
25	Charles Gipson	.50
26	Joel Pineiro	.50
27	Rafael Soriano	.50
28	M's coaches	.50

2003 Keebler Arizona Diamondbacks

Keebler cookies sponsored a kids' trading card day July 27, distributing 20,000 28-card packs to fans 14 and under. Each pack contained 20 different cards and eight duplicates to trade in an effort to complete the set. Fronts of the round-cornered 2-1/2" x 3-1/2" cards have posed photos with a purple stripe at bottom with player name and team logo. Color-printed backs have player data, jersey number and team and sponsor's logos.

		NM/M
Complete Set (28):		12.00
Common Player:		.50
1	Bob Brenly	.50
2	Luis Gonzalez	.60
3	Randy Johnson	3.00
4	Curt Schilling	1.50
5	Danny Bautista	.50
6	Matt Mantei	.50
7	Craig Counsell	.50
8	Steve Finley	.50
9	Mark Grace	.60
10	Alex Cintron	.50
11	Tony Womack	.50
12	Chad Moeller	.50
13	Shea Hillenbrand	.50
14	Miguel Batista	.50
15	David Dellucci	.50
16	Elmer Dessens	.50
17	Lyle Overbay	.75
18	Mike Myers	.50
19	Quinton McCracken	.50
20	Rod Barajas	.50
21	Junior Spivey	.50
22	Stephen Randolph	.50
23	Carlos Baerga	.50
24	Mike Koplove	.50
25	Brandon Webb	1.00
26	Oscar Villarreal	.50
27	Bret Prinz	.50
28	Coaches/Checklist (Mark Davis, Chuck Kniffin, Dwayne Murphy, Eddie Rodriguez, Glenn Sherlock, Robin Yount)	.50

L.A. Dodgers

Keebler cookies sponsored a kids' trading card night August 24, distributing 20,000 28-card packs to fans 14 and under. Each pack contained 20 different cards and eight dupli-cates to trade in an effort to complete the set. Fronts of the round-cornered 2-1/2" x 3-1/2" cards have posed photos with an orange stripe at bottom with player name and team logo. Color-printed backs have player data, jersey number and team and sponsor's logos.

		NM/M
Complete Set (28):		7.50
Common Player:		.50
1	Jim Tracy	.50
2	Shawn Green	1.00
3	Paul LoDuca	.60
4	Kevin Brown	.60
5	Adrian Beltre	1.00
6	Eric Gagne	.50
7	Brian Jordan	.50
8	Kazuhisa Ishii	.50
9	Fred McGriff	.50
10	Dave Roberts	.50
11	Hideo Nomo	1.00
12	Alex Cora	.50
13	Paul Quantrill	.50
14	Darren Dreifort	.50
15	Odalis Perez	.50
16	Cesar Izturis	.50
17	Todd Hundley	.50
18	Daryle Ward	.50
19	Paul Shuey	.50
20	Guillermo Mota	.50
21	Andy Ashby	.50
22	Tom Martin	.50
23	Jason Romano	.50
24	Jolbert Cabrera	.50
25	Mike Kinkade	.50
26	Ron Coomer	.50
27	David Ross	.50
28	Coaches	.50

San Diego Padres

Keebler cookies sponsored a kids' trading card day distributing 28-card packs to fans 14 and under. Each pack contained 21 different cards and seven duplicates to trade in an effort to complete the set. Fronts of the round-cornered 2-1/2" x 3-1/2" cards have posed photos with an orange and dark blue stripe at bottom with player name and team logo. Color-printed backs have player data, jersey number and color team and sponsor's logos.

		NM/M
Complete Set (28):		5.00
Common Player:		.50
1	Bruce Bochy	.50
2	Trevor Hoffman	.50
3	Phil Nevin	.50
4	Ryan Klesko	.50
5	Sean Burroughs	.75
6	Brian Lawrence	.50
7	Rondell White	.50
8	Ramon Vazquez	.50
9	Mark Kotsay	.50
10	Dave Hansen	.50
11	Jaret Wright	.50
12	Gary Bennett	.50
13	Brandon Villafuerte	.50
14	Lou Merloni	.50
15	Jesse Orosco	.50
16	Keith Lockhart	.50
17	Kevin Walker	.50
18	Mark Loretta	.50
19	Kevin Jarvis	.50
20	Xavier Nady	.50
21	Jake Peavy	.50
22	Mike Matthews	.50
23	Brian Buchanan	.50
24	Luther Hackman	.50
25	Adam Eaton	.50
26	Matt Herges	.50
27	Jay Witasick	.50
28	Coaches/Checklist (Darrel Akerfelds, Darren Balsley, Davey Lopes, Dave Magadan, Mark Merila, Tony Muser, Rob Picciolo)	.50

S.F. Giants

Keebler cookies sponsored a kids' trading card day August 10, distributing 28-card packs to fans 14 and under. Each pack contained 21 different cards and seven duplicates to trade in an effort to complete the set. Fronts of the round-cornered 2-1/2" x 3-1/2" cards have posed photos with an orange stripe at bottom with player name and team logo. Color-printed backs have player data, jersey number and color team and sponsor's logos.

		NM/M
Complete Set (28):		10.00
Common Player:		.50
1	Felipe Alou	.50
2	Barry Bonds	4.00
3	Rich Aurilia	.50
4	Robb Nen	.50
5	J.T. Snow	.50
6	Kirk Reuter	.50
7	Benito Santiago	.50
8	Jose Cruz Jr.	.50
9	Damian Moss	.50
10	Ray Durham	.50
11	Jason Schmidt	.50
12	Marquis Grissom	.50
13	Kurt Ainsworth	.50
14	Andres Galarraga	.50
15	Scott Eyre	.50
16	Yorvit Torrealba	.50
17	Felix Rodriguez	.50
18	Edgardo Alfonzo	.50
19	Tim Worrell	.50
20	Pedro Feliz	.50
21	Jesse Foppert	.50
22	Chad Zerbe	.50
23	Neifi Perez	.50
24	Jason Christiansen	.50
25	Marvin Benard	.50
26	Jim Brower	.50
27	Joe Nathan	.50
28	Coaches (Carlos Alfonzo, Mark Gardner, Gene Glynn, Bill Hayes, Joe Lefebvre, Luis Pujols, Dave Righetti, Ron Wotus)	.50

Seattle Mariners

Keebler cookies sponsored a kids' trading card day July 13, distributing 28-card packs to fans 14 and under. Each pack contained 21 different cards and seven duplicates to trade in an effort to complete the set. Fronts of the round-cornered 2-1/2" x 3-1/2" cards have posed photos with a dark blue stripe at bottom with player name and team logo. Color-printed backs have player data, jersey number and color team and sponsor's logos.

		NM/M
Complete Set (28):		10.00
Common Player:		.50
1	Bob Melvin	.50
2	Ichiro Suzuki	4.00
3	Edgar Martinez	.50
4	Jamie Moyer	.50
5	Mike Cameron	.50
6	Bret Boone	.75
7	Kazuhiro Sasaki	.60
8	John Olerud	.50
9	Mark McLemore	.50
10	Arthur Rhodes	.50
11	Randy Winn	.50
12	Freddy Garcia	.50
13	Dan Wilson	.50
14	Jeff Nelson	.50
15	Carlos Guillen	.50
16	Ryan Franklin	.50
17	Ben Davis	.50
18	Joel Pineiro	.50
19	Jeff Cirillo	.50
20	Shigetoshi Hasegawa	.50
21	Greg Colbrunn	.50
22	John Mabry	.50
23	Julio Mateo	.50
24	Willie Bloomquist	.75
25	Gil Meche	.50
26	Giovanni Carrara	.50
27	Chris Snelling	.50
28	M's coaches	.50

1986 Keller's Butter Phillies

It's a good thing the Keller's Butter set of six Philadelphia Phillies players is downright unattractive or their value would be sky high. One card was printed on each one pound package of butter, The 2-1/2" x 2-3/4" cards feature crude drawings of the players, the backs are blank.

		NM/M
Complete Set (6):		15.00
Common Player:		1.00
(1)	Steve Carlton	4.00
(2)	Von Hayes	1.00
(3)	Gary Redus	1.00
(4)	Juan Samuel	1.00
(5)	Mike Schmidt	8.00
(6)	Glenn Wilson	1.00

1981 Kellogg's

"Bigger" is the word to best describe Kellogg's 1981 card set. Not only were the cards themselves larger than ever before at 2-1/2" x 3-1/2", but the size of the set was increased to 66, the largest since the 75-card issues of 1970-71. The '81 Kellogg's set was available only as complete sets by mail. It is thought that the wider format of the 1981s may help prevent the problems of curling and cracking from which other years of Kellogg's issues suffer.

		NM/M
Complete Set (66):		15.00
Common Player:		.50
1	George Foster	.50
2	Jim Palmer	1.50
3	Reggie Jackson	2.50
4	Al Oliver	.50

5	Mike Schmidt	3.00
6	Nolan Ryan	7.50
7	Bucky Dent	.50
8	George Brett	3.00
9	Jim Rice	.75
10	Steve Garvey	.75
11	Willie Stargell	1.50
12	Phil Niekro	1.00
13	Dave Parker	.50
14	Cesar Cedeno	.50
15	Don Baylor	.50
16	J.R. Richard	.50
17	Tony Perez	1.00
18	Eddie Murray	1.50
19	Chet Lemon	.50
20	Ben Oglivie	.50
21	Dave Winfield	1.50
22	Joe Morgan	1.50
23	Vida Blue	.50
24	Willie Wilson	.50
25	Steve Henderson	.50
26	Rod Carew	1.50
27	Garry Templeton	.50
28	Dave Concepcion	.50
29	Davey Lopes	.50
30	Ken Landreaux	.50
31	Keith Hernandez	.50
32	Cecil Cooper	.50
33	Rickey Henderson	3.00
34	Frank White	.50
35	George Hendrick	.50
36	Reggie Smith	.50
37	Tug McGraw	.50
38	Tom Seaver	1.50
39	Ken Singleton	.50
40	Fred Lynn	.50
41	Rich "Goose" Gossage	.50
42	Terry Puhl	.50
43	Larry Bowa	.50
44	Phil Garner	.50
45	Ron Guidry	.50
46	Lee Mazzilli	.50
47	Dave Kingman	.50
48	Carl Yastrzemski	2.00
49	Rick Burleson	.50
50	Steve Carlton	1.50
51	Alan Trammell	.75
52	Tommy John	.50
53	Paul Molitor	1.50
54	Joe Charboneau	1.00
55	Rick Langford	.50
56	Bruce Sutter	1.00
57	Robin Yount	1.50
58	Steve Stone	.50
59	Larry Gura	.50
60	Mike Flanagan	.50
61	Bob Horner	.50
62	Bruce Bochte	.50
63	Pete Rose	6.00
64	Buddy Bell	.50
65	Johnny Bench	2.00
66	Mike Hargrove	.50

1982 Kellogg's

For the second straight year in 1982, Kellogg's cards were not inserted into cereal boxes, but had to be obtained by sending cash and box tops to the company for complete sets. The '82 cards were downsized both in number of cards in the set - 64 - and in physical dimensions, 2-1/8" x 3-1/4".

		NM/M
Complete Set (64):		15.00
Common Player:		.25
1	Richie Zisk	.25
2	Bill Buckner	.25
3	George Brett	3.00
4	Rickey Henderson	1.50
5	Jack Morris	.25
6	Ozzie Smith	2.00
7	Rollie Fingers	1.00
8	Tom Seaver	2.00
9	Fernando Valenzuela	.25
10	Hubie Brooks	.25
11	Nolan Ryan	7.50
12	Dave Winfield	1.50
13	Bob Horner	.25
14	Reggie Jackson	2.50
15	Burt Hooton	.25
16	Mike Schmidt	3.00

17	Bruce Sutter	1.00
18	Pete Rose	6.00
19	Dave Kingman	.25
20	Neil Allen	.25
21	Don Sutton	1.00
22	Dave Concepcion	.25
23	Keith Hernandez	.25
24	Gary Carter	1.50
25	Carlton Fisk	1.50
26	Ron Guidry	.25
27	Steve Carlton	1.50
28	Robin Yount	1.50
29	John Castino	.25
30	Johnny Bench	2.00
31	Bob Knepper	.25
32	Rich "Goose" Gossage	.25
33	Buddy Bell	.25
34	Art Howe	.25
35	Tony Armas	.25
36	Phil Niekro	1.00
37	Len Barker	.25
38	Bobby Grich	.25
39	Steve Kemp	.25
40	Kirk Gibson	.25
41	Carney Lansford	.25
42	Jim Palmer	1.50
43	Carl Yastrzemski	2.00
44	Rick Burleson	.25
45	Dwight Evans	.25
46	Ron Cey	.25
47	Steve Garvey	.50
48	Dave Parker	.25
49	Mike Easler	.25
50	Dusty Baker	.25
51	Rod Carew	1.50
52	Chris Chambliss	.25
53	Tim Raines	.25
54	Chet Lemon	.25
55	Bill Madlock	.25
56	George Foster	.25
57	Dwayne Murphy	.25
58	Ken Singleton	.25
59	Mike Norris	.25
60	Cecil Cooper	.25
61	Al Oliver	.25
62	Willie Wilson	.25
63	Vida Blue	.25
64	Eddie Murray	1.50

1983 Kellogg's

In its 14th consecutive year of baseball card issue, Kellogg's returned to the policy of inserting single cards into cereal boxes, as well as offering complete sets by a mail-in box top redemption offer. The 3-D cards themselves returned to a narrow 1-7/8" x 3-1/4" format, while the set size was reduced to 60 cards.

		NM/M
Complete Set (60):		15.00
Common Player:		.40
1	Rod Carew	1.50
2	Rollie Fingers	1.50
3	Reggie Jackson	2.50
4	George Brett	3.00
5	Hal McRae	.40
6	Pete Rose	6.00
7	Fernando Valenzuela	.40
8	Rickey Henderson	1.50
9	Carl Yastrzemski	2.00
10	Rich "Goose" Gossage	.40
11	Eddie Murray	1.50
12	Buddy Bell	.40
13	Jim Rice	.60
14	Robin Yount	1.50
15	Dave Winfield	1.50
16	Harold Baines	.40
17	Garry Templeton	.40
18	Bill Madlock	.40
19	Pete Vuckovich	.40
20	Pedro Guerrero	.40
21	Ozzie Smith	2.00
22	George Foster	.40
23	Willie Wilson	.40
24	Johnny Ray	.40
25	George Hendrick	.40
26	Andre Thornton	.40

27	Leon Durham	.40
28	Cecil Cooper	.40
29	Don Baylor	.40
30	Lonnie Smith	.40
31	Nolan Ryan	7.50
32	Dan Quisenberry (Quisenberry)	.40
33	Len Barker	.40
34	Neil Allen	.40
35	Jack Morris	.40
36	Dave Stieb	.40
37	Bruce Sutter	1.00
38	Jim Sundberg	.40
39	Jim Palmer	1.50
40	Lance Parrish	.40
41	Floyd Bannister	.40
42	Larry Gura	.40
43	Britt Burns	.40
44	Toby Harrah	.40
45	Steve Carlton	1.50
46	Greg Minton	.40
47	Gorman Thomas	.40
48	Jack Clark	.40
49	Keith Hernandez	.40
50	Greg Luzinski	.40
51	Fred Lynn	.40
52	Dale Murphy	.75
53	Kent Hrbek	.40
54	Bob Horner	.40
55	Gary Carter	1.50
56	Carlton Fisk	1.50
57	Dave Concepcion	.40
58	Mike Schmidt	3.00
59	Bill Buckner	.40
60	Bobby Grich	.40

1991 Kellogg's Baseball Greats

Six Hall of Famers are featured on the backs of 7- and 12-ounce Corn Flakes boxes. The photos are designed to be cut out and assembled as a stand-up figure. A career summary also appears on the box back.

		NM/M
Complete Set (6):		12.00
Common Player:		2.00
(1)	Hank Aaron	4.00
(2)	Ernie Banks	2.50
(3)	Yogi Berra	2.50
(4)	Lou Brock	2.00
(5)	Steve Carlton	2.00
(6)	Bob Gibson	2.00

1991 Kellogg's Leyendas

These bilingual (English/Spanish) cards honoring past Hispanic stars were inserted in several brands of Kellogg's cereal in selected geographic areas. Fronts have an action player photo, while backs have a black-and-white portrait photo, biographical details, career stats and highlights.

		NM/M
Complete Set (11):		9.00
Common Player:		.50
(1)	Bert Campaneris	.50
(2)	Rod Carew	1.00
(3)	Rico Carty	.50
(4)	Cesar Cedeno	.50
(5)	Orlando Cepeda	1.00
(6)	Roberto Clemente	6.00
(7)	Mike Cuellar	.50
(8)	Ed Figueroa	.50
(9)	Minnie Minoso	.75
(10)	Manny Sanguillen	.50
(11)	Header Card	.25

1991 Kellogg's 3-D

In 1991, specially-marked packages of Kellogg's Corn Flakes included 3-D baseball cards, resuming a tradition that began in 1970 and continued without interruption until 1983. In the 1991 edition, there are 15 cards to collect, featuring many of the greatest living retired stars in the game. Most of the players are in the Hall of Fame. The card fronts show two pictures of the player, while the backs include career highlights and a portrait. The cards are 2-1/2" x 3-5/16", numbered and were made by Sportflics. A complete set was available via a mail-in offer for $4.95 plus proofs of purchase.

		NM/M
Complete Set (15):		4.50
Common Player:		.25
1	Gaylord Perry	.25
2	Hank Aaron	1.00
3	Willie Mays	1.00
4	Ernie Banks	.75
5	Bob Gibson	.50
6	Harmon Killebrew	.50
7	Rollie Fingers	.25
8	Steve Carlton	.50
9	Billy Williams	.50
10	Lou Brock	.25
11	Yogi Berra	.75
12	Warren Spahn	.50
13	Boog Powell	.25
14	Don Baylor	.25
15	Ralph Kiner	.25

1992 Kellogg's 3-D

Kellogg's cereal company created a 10-card 1992 All Star set of retired stars, with one card inserted in specially-marked boxes of corn flakes, and complete sets available by mail. The cards, produced by Sportflics, feature two sequential action images on each front. Red, white and blue designs comprise the border, with yellow bands above and beneath the photo. On back is a black-and-white portrait photo, plus a career summary and a few stats, and the logos of the cereal company, the Major League Baseball Players Alumni and Sportflics. As in the previous year, cards are slightly longer, at 2-1/2" x 2-5/16", than standard size. Also available by mail was a large, colorful cardboard display in which the cards could be placed.

		NM/M
Complete Set (10):		2.00
Common Player:		.25
1	Willie Stargell	.50
2	Tony Perez	.50
3	Jim Palmer	.50
4	Rod Carew	.50
5	Tom Seaver	.65
6	Phil Niekro	.50
7	Bill Madlock	.25
8	Jim Rice	.35
9	Dan Quisenberry	.25
10	Mike Schmidt	1.00

1992 Kellogg's 3-D Canadian

Very similar in format to the American version, 3-D cards of 10 baseball stars of the past were found in packages of Kellogg's Frosted Flakes. Backs of the Canadian cards are printed in both English and French, which left no room for a card number, so the checklist provided here is alphabetical.

		NM/M
Complete Set (10):		8.00
Common Player:		.75
(1)	Rod Carew	1.00
(2)	Bill Madlock	.75
(3)	Phil Niekro	1.00
(4)	Jim Palmer	1.00
(5)	Tony Perez	1.00
(6)	Dan Quisenberry	.75
(7)	Jim Rice	.75
(8)	Mike Schmidt	3.00
(9)	Tom Seaver	1.50
(10)	Willie Stargell	1.00

1994 Kellogg's Clemente Collection

To commemorate the life and career of its greatest sports hero, special boxes of Kellogg's Corn Flakes sold in Puerto Rico for a time in 1994 contained one of three special cards in a cello pack. The 2-1/2" x 3-1/2" cards have color photos on front bordered in bright colors. A home plate design at top-left reads: "Kellogg's Clemente Coleccion Classico." Black-and-white backs are printed in Spanish, have personal data, career stats, highlights and a portrait photo.

		NM/M
Complete Set (3):		35.00
Common Card:		12.50
1	Roberto Clemente (Bat on shoulder.)	12.50
2	Roberto Clemente/ Running (Black helemt.)	12.50
3	Roberto Clemente/ Running (Yellow helmet.)	12.50

1987 Key Food Discs

(See 1987 Super Stars Discs for checklist and price guide.)

1988 Key Food Discs

(See 1988 Super Stars Discs for checklist and price guide.)

1988 King-B

Created by Mike Schechter Associates, this set consists of 24 numbered discs, 2-3/4" in diameter. The cards were inserted in specially marked 7/16 ounce tubs of Jerky Stuff (shredded beef jerky). Fronts feature full-color photos surrounded by a blue border. The King-B logo appears in the upper left portion of the disc. Backs are printed in blue on white stock and carry player personal and playing information. Team insignias have been airbrushed from the players' caps and jerseys.

		NM/M
Complete Set (24):		15.00
Common Player:		.50
Uncut Sheet:		20.00
1	Mike Schmidt	1.50
2	Dale Murphy	.65
3	Kirby Puckett	1.00
4	Ozzie Smith	1.00
5	Tony Gwynn	1.00
6	Mark McGwire	2.50
7	George Brett	1.50
8	Darryl Strawberry	.50
9	Wally Joyner	.50
10	Cory Snyder	.50
11	Barry Bonds	3.00
12	Darrell Evans	.50
13	Mike Scott	.50
14	Andre Dawson	.65
15	Don Mattingly	1.50
16	Candy Maldonado	.50
17	Alvin Davis	.50
18	Carlton Fisk	.75
19	Fernando Valenzuela	.50
20	Roger Clemens	1.50
21	Larry Parrish	.50
22	Eric Davis	.50
23	Paul Molitor	.75
24	Cal Ripken, Jr.	3.00

1989 King-B

The second King-B set created by Mike Schechter Associates again consists of 24 circular baseball cards measuring 2-3/4" in diameter. The cards were inserted into specially-marked tubs of "Jerky Stuff." Fronts feature full-color photos bordered in red. The King-B logo appears in the upper left portion of the disc. Like the 1988 set, the team insignias have airbrushed from uniforms and caps. The backs are printed in red and display personal information and stats.

		NM/M
Complete Set (24):		15.00
Common Player:		.50
1	Kirk Gibson	.50
2	Eddie Murray	1.50
3	Wade Boggs	2.00
4	Mark McGwire	3.00
5	Ryne Sandberg	2.00
6	Ozzie Guillen	.50
7	Chris Sabo	.50
8	Joe Carter	.50
9	Alan Trammell	.50
10	Nolan Ryan	4.00
11	Bo Jackson	.75
12	Orel Hershiser	.50
13	Robin Yount	1.50
14	Frank Viola	.50
15	Darryl Strawberry	.50
16	Dave Winfield	1.50
17	Jose Canseco	.75
18	Von Hayes	.50
19	Andy Van Slyke	.50
20	Pedro Guerrero	.50
21	Tony Gwynn	2.00
22	Will Clark	.50
23	Danny Jackson	.50
24	Pete Incaviglia	.50

1990 King-B

King-B meat products offered baseball player discs inside specially-marked packages in 1990, the third year in a row the company inserted the discs with shredded beef jerky. Each disc measures 2-3/4" across and uses full-color pictures on the front. The backs have biographical information and statistics. Team insignias have been airbrushed from caps and uniforms. As in the first two years of the promotion, there are 24 cards in the set.

		NM/M
Complete Set (24):		8.00
Common Player:		.50
1	Mike Scott	.50
2	Kevin Mitchell	.50
3	Tony Gwynn	.75
4	Ozzie Smith	.75
5	Kirk Gibson	.50
6	Tim Raines	.50
7	Von Hayes	.50
8	Bobby Bonilla	.50
9	Wade Boggs	.75
10	Chris Sabo	.50
11	Dale Murphy	.65
12	Cory Snyder	.50
13	Fred McGriff	.50
14	Don Mattingly	1.00
15	Jerome Walton	.50
16	Ken Griffey Jr.	2.50
17	Bo Jackson	.65
18	Robin Yount	.65
19	Rickey Henderson	.65
20	Jim Abbott	.50
21	Kirby Puckett	.75
22	Nolan Ryan	3.00
23	Gregg Olson	.50
24	Lou Whitaker	.50

1991 King-B

The 1991 release of baseball player discs in cans of shredded beef snack was labeled "Fourth Annual Collectors' Edition." Once again the

discs are 2-3/8" in diameter and feature player photos on which uniform logos have been removed for lack of an MLB license. Front border is in green; backs are printed in blue and include 1990 and major league cumulative stats. One player from each major league team is included in the set.

		NM/M
Complete Set (24):		15.00
Common Player:		.50
1	Willie McGee	.50
2	Kevin Seitzer	.50
3	Kevin Maas	.50
4	Ben McDonald	.50
5	Rickey Henderson	1.00
6	Ken Griffey Jr.	2.00
7	John Olerud	.50
8	Dwight Gooden	.50
9	Ruben Sierra	.50
10	Luis Polonia	.50
11	Wade Boggs	1.50
12	Ramon Martinez	.50
13	Craig Biggio	.50
14	Cecil Fielder	.50
15	Will Clark	.50
16	Matt Williams	.50
17	Sandy Alomar Jr.	.50
18	David Justice	.50
19	Ryne Sandberg	1.50
20	Benito Santiago	.50
21	Barry Bonds	3.00
22	Carlton Fisk	1.00
23	Kirby Puckett	1.50
24	Jose Rijo	.50

1992 King-B

Labeled the "Fifth Annual Collectors Edition," the 1992 King-B discs were again packaged in plastic containers of shredded beef snack. The 2-3/8" diameter discs have a color player portrait at center. Uniform logos have been removed from the photos for lack of an MLB licensing agreement. The player's name and team are in white in a blue banner above his photo. Backs are printed in blue and include previous year and career stats along with a few biographical details and appropriate logos.

		NM/M
Complete Set (24):		15.00
Common Player:		.50
1	Terry Pendleton	.50
2	Chris Sabo	.50
3	Frank Thomas	1.00
4	Todd Zeile	.50
5	Bobby Bonilla	.50
6	Howard Johnson	.50
7	Nolan Ryan	3.00
8	Ken Griffey Jr.	2.00
9	Roger Clemens	1.75
10	Tony Gwynn	1.50
11	Steve Avery	.50
12	Cal Ripken Jr.	3.00
13	Danny Tartabull	.50
14	Paul Molitor	1.00
15	Willie McGee	.50
16	Wade Boggs	1.50
17	Cecil Fielder	.50
18	Jack Morris	.50
19	Ryne Sandberg	1.50
20	Kirby Puckett	1.50
21	Craig Biggio	.50
22	Harold Baines	.50
23	Scott Erickson	.50
24	Joe Carter	.50

1993 King-B

The sixth annual edition of baseball player discs inserted into packages of King-B meat snacks followed the format of previous issues. Measuring 2-3/8" in diameter, the cards have a photo (with uniform logos airbrushed away) in a yellow baseball diamond design at center. The disc is bordered in black. Backs are printed in red and contain 1992 and career stats.

		NM/M
Complete Set (24):		9.00
Common Player:		.50
1	Barry Bonds	2.00
2	Ken Griffey Jr.	1.50
3	Cal Ripken, Jr.	2.00
4	Frank Thomas	.75
5	Steve Avery	.50
6	Benito Santiago	.50
7	Luis Polonia	.50
8	Jose Rijo	.50
9	George Brett	1.25
10	Darren Daulton	.50
11	Cecil Fielder	.50
12	Ozzie Smith	1.00
13	Joe Carter	.50
14	Dwight Gooden	.50
15	Tom Henke	.50
16	Brett Butler	.50
17	Nolan Ryan	2.00
18	Sandy Alomar, Jr.	.50
19	Tom Glavine	.60
20	Rafael Palmeiro	.75
21	Roger Clemens	1.25
22	Ryne Sandberg	1.00
23	Doug Drabek	.50
24	Chuck Knoblauch	.50

1994 King-B

King-B once again created and inserted discs of 24 major league stars with its products in 1994. The entire set was also available in uncut sheet form which was found in each case. Discs measure 2-3/8" diameter and have a broad purple border with yellow and white typography surrounding the player photo at center. A black glove holds a King-B logo at bottom. Uniform logos have been airbrushed from the photos. Backs are printed in purple and include 1993 and career stats.

		NM/M
Complete Set (24):		6.00
Common Player:		.50
1	Fred McGriff	.50
2	Paul Molitor	.75
3	Jack McDowell	.50
4	Darren Daulton	.50
5	Wade Boggs	1.00
6	Ken Griffey Jr.	2.00
7	Tim Salmon	.50
8	Dennis Eckersley	.65
9	Albert Belle	.50
10	Travis Fryman	.50
11	Chris Hoiles	.50
12	Kirby Puckett	1.00
13	John Olerud	.50
14	Frank Thomas	.75
15	Lenny Dykstra	.50
16	Andres Galarraga	.50
17	Barry Larkin	.50
18	Greg Maddux	1.00
19	Mike Piazza	1.50
20	Roberto Alomar	.50
21	Robin Ventura	.50
22	Ryne Sandberg	1.00
23	Andy Van Slyke	.50
24	Barry Bonds	3.00

1995 King-B

A wood-grain background distinguishes the eighth annual baseball disc issue packaged inside shredded beef snack tins. Because they are licensed only by the Players Association, and not MLB, cards in the set have had team logos removed from the color player photos at the center of the 2-3/8" diameter discs. Backs are printed in black and have a few personal bits of data, previous season and career stats and the logos of King-B and the MLBPA.

		NM/M
Complete Set (24):		15.00
Common Player:		.35
1	Roberto Alomar	.35
2	Jeff Bagwell	.75
3	Wade Boggs	1.50
4	Barry Bonds	3.00
5	Joe Carter	.35
6	Mariano Duncan	.35
7	Lenny Dykstra	.35
8	Andres Galarraga	.35
9	Matt Williams	.35
10	Raul Mondesi	.35
11	Ken Griffey Jr.	2.00
12	Gregg Jefferies	.35
13	Fred McGriff	.35
14	Paul Molitor	.75
15	Dave Justice	.35
16	Mike Piazza	1.75
17	Kirby Puckett	1.50
18	Cal Ripken Jr.	3.00
19	Ivan Rodriguez	.65
20	Ozzie Smith	1.50
21	Gary Sheffield	.50
22	Frank Thomas	.75
23	Greg Maddux	1.50
24	Jimmy Key ("JIIMY" on back)	.35

1996 King-B

The "9th Annual Collectors Edition" of King-B discs once again features player photos on which uniform insignia have been airbrushed away. The cards are licensed by Michael Schechter Associates only with the players' union, not MLB, and so cannot display team logos. The 2-5/8" cardboard discs are packaged in plastic cannisters of shredded dried meat. Fronts have the 1996 date at left in a black and gold pinstriped area. The backs are in black and white with 1995 and career stats, along with a few vital data and appropriate logos and copyright information.

		NM/M
Complete Set (24):		15.00
Common Player:		.50
1	Roger Clemens	1.75
2	Mo Vaughn	.50
3	Dante Bichette	.50
4	Jeff Bagwell	1.00
5	Randy Johnson	1.00
6	Ken Griffey Jr.	2.00

		NM/M
7	Kirby Puckett	1.50
8	Orel Hershiser	.50
9	Albert Belle	.50
10	Tony Gwynn	1.50
11	Tom Glavine	.65
12	Jim Abbott	.50
13	Andres Galarraga	.50
14	Frank Thomas	1.00
15	Barry Larkin	.50
16	Mike Piazza	1.75
17	Matt Williams	.50
18	Greg Maddux	1.50
19	Hideo Nomo	.75
20	Roberto Alomar	.50
21	Ivan Rodriguez	.75
22	Cal Ripken Jr.	3.00
23	Barry Bonds	3.00
24	Mark McGwire	2.50

1997 King-B

The shredded beef product issued its 10th Anniversary set of player discs in 1997. The discs are packed inside the plastic canisters of the snack food and measure 2-3/8" in diameter. The '97 discs have a player action photo on front against a gold and black marbled background. Backs are in black-and-white and repeat the photo in the background, along with a few stats and personal data, logos and a disc number. One player from each team is represented in the checklist.

		NM/M
Complete Set (28):		15.00
Common Player:		.50
1	Brady Anderson	.50
2	Barry Bonds	3.00
3	Travis Fryman	.50
4	Rey Ordonez	.50
5	Kenny Lofton	.50
6	Mark McGwire	2.50
7	Jeff Bagwell	1.00
8	Roger Clemens	1.75
9	Juan Gonzalez	.75
10	Mike Piazza	1.75
11	Tim Salmon	.50
12	Jeff Montgomery	.50
13	Joe Carter	.50
14	David Cone	.50
15	Frank Thomas	1.00
16	Mickey Morandini	.50
17	Ray Lankford	.50
18	Pedro Martinez	1.00
19	Tom Glavine	.65
20	Chuck Knoblauch	.50
21	Dan Wilson	.50
22	Gary Sheffield	.65
23	Dante Bichette	.50
24	Al Martin	.50
25	Barry Larkin	.50
26	Ryne Sandberg	.50
27	Steve Finley	.50
28	Matt Mieske	.50

1998 King-B

Except for the expansion teams, each Major League team has one player in this issue of player discs which were packed inside plastic canisters of the snack food. The cards measure 2-3/8" in diameter with a color player action photo on front (uniform logos have been removed). Backs have a few stats and personal data, logos plus a disc number.

		NM/M
Complete Set (28):		12.50

21	Robin Ventura	.50
22	Ryne Sandberg	1.00
23	Andy Van Slyke	.50
24	Barry Bonds	3.00

1	Brady Anderson	.50
2	Barry Bonds	3.00
3	Tony Clark	.50
4	Rey Ordonez	.50
5	Travis Fryman	.50
6	Jason Giambi	.75
7	Jeff Bagwell	1.00
8	Tim Naehring	.50
9	Juan Gonzalez	.75
10	Mike Piazza	1.50
11	Tim Salmon	.50
12	Jeff Montgomery	.50
13	Tom Glavine	.65
14	Chuck Knoblauch	.50
15	Dan Wilson	.50
16	Gary Sheffield	.65
17	Dante Bichette	.50
18	Al Martin	.50
19	Roger Clemens	1.50
20	David Cone	.50
21	Frank Thomas	1.00
22	Mike Lieberthal	.50
23	Ray Lankford	.50
24	Rondell White	.50
25	Barry Larkin	.50
26	Matt Mieske	.50
27	Steve Finley	.50
28	Fernando Vina	.50

1999 King-B

The shredded beef product issued its 12th set of cardboard player discs in 1999. The discs are packed inside plastic canisters of the snack food and measure 2-3/8" in diameter. The cards have a color player action photo on front. Uniform logos are removed and team names are nowhere to be seen on the cards. Backs repeat the front photo in black-and-white in the background, along with a few stats and personal data, logos and a disc number. One player from each team is represented in the checklist.

		NM/M
Complete Set (30):		15.00
Common Player:		.50
1	Brady Anderson	.50
2	Barry Bonds	3.00
3	Scott Rolen	.75
4	Tony Clark	.50
5	Jeff Bagwell	1.00
6	Roberto Alomar	.50
7	Mark Kotsay	.50
8	Juan Gonzalez	.75
9	Tim Salmon	.50
10	Tom Glavine	.65
11	Frank Thomas	1.00
12	Dan Wilson	.50
13	Dante Bichette	.50
14	Mickey Morandini	.50
15	Fred McGriff	.50
16	Andy Benes	.50
17	Jeff Montgomery	.50
18	Pedro Martinez	1.00
19	Barry Larkin	.50
20	Carlos Delgado	.75
21	Mike Myers	.50
22	Ray Lankford	.50
23	Brad Radke	.50
24	Al Martin	.50
25	Raul Mondesi	.50
26	Ugueth Urbina	.50
27	Derek Jeter	3.00
28	Ben Grieve	.50
29	Mike Piazza	1.75
30	Wally Joyner	.50

2000 King-B

The shredded beef product issued its 13th annual set of cardboard player discs in 2000. The discs are packed inside plastic canisters of the snack food and measure 2-3/8" in diameter. The cards have a color player action photo on front. Uniform logos are removed and team names are nowhere to be seen on the cards. Backs have a black-and-white portrait photo, along with a few stats and personal data, logos and a disc number. One player from each team is represented in the checklist.

		NM/M
Complete Set (30):		15.00
Common Player:		.50
1	Nomar Garciaparra	1.50
2	Larry Walker	.50
3	Manny Ramirez	.75
4	Carlos Beltran	.65
5	Mark McGwire	2.00
6	Jeromy Burnitz	.50
7	Carlos Delgado	.60
8	Tom Glavine	.60
9	Shawn Green	.60
10	Mark Kotsay	.50
11	Warren Morris	.50
12	Fred McGriff	.50
13	Brady Anderson	.50
14	Jeff Bagwell	.75
15	Tony Clark	.50
16	Ben Grieve	.50
17	Vladimir Guerrero	.75
18	Tony Gwynn	1.00
19	Derek Jeter	3.00
20	Barry Larkin	.50
21	Rafael Palmeiro	.65
22	Mike Piazza	1.50
23	Brad Radke	.50
24	Scott Rolen	.65
25	Tim Salmon	.50
26	Frank Thomas	.75
27	Mark Grace	.50
28	Jeff Kent	.50
29	Dan Wilson	.50
30	Jay Bell	.50

2001 King-B

The cardboard discs for the shredded-beef snack's 14th annual issue were produced by Playoff, whose logo is among those appearing on back. The 2-3/8" diameter discs have a color action photo and black-and-white portrait on a pinstriped ball diamond background on front. Backs have another black-and-white portrait photo, along with 2000 and career stats and a few biographical bits. All photos have had team logos removed. Each disc is numbered "1 of 30" on back, so the checklist presented here is in alphabetical order.

		NM/M
Complete Set (30):		15.00
Common Player:		.50
(1)	Brady Anderson	.50
(2)	Jeff Bagwell	.75
(3)	Jay Bell	.50
(4)	Carlos Beltran	.50
(5)	Jeromy Burnitz	.50
(6)	Tony Clark	.50
(7)	Carlos Delgado	.60
(8)	Nomar Garciaparra	1.50
(9)	Tom Glavine	.65
(10)	Mark Grace	.50
(11)	Shawn Green	.60
(12)	Ben Grieve	.50
(13)	Vladimir Guerrero	.75
(14)	Tony Gwynn	1.00
(15)	Derek Jeter	2.50
(16)	Jeff Kent	.50
(17)	Mark Kotsay	.50
(18)	Barry Larkin	.50
(19)	Fred McGriff	.50
(20)	Mark McGwire	2.00
(21)	Warren Morris	.50
(22)	Rafael Palmeiro	.65

(23)	Mike Piazza	1.50
(24)	Brad Radke	.50
(25)	Manny Ramirez	.75
(26)	Scott Rolen	.65
(27)	Tim Salmon	.50
(28)	Frank Thomas	.75
(29)	Larry Walker	.50
(30)	Dan Wilson	.50

2001 King-B League Legends

For the first time in its 14 years of producing baseball player discs as a premium with its beef snacks, King B produced a set in 2001 featuring non-current players. Issued one per package of King B jerkey, the 2-3/8" diameter discs have a color portrait (with uniform logos removed) on front, against a ballpark photo background. Backs are in white and green and have a baseball design background with player data and a repeat of the "League Legends" logo.

		NM/M
Complete Set (18):		12.00
Common Player:		.50
1	Frank Robinson	1.00
2	Steve Carlton	1.00
3	Harmon Killebrew	1.00
4	Frank Torre	.50
5	Rollie Fingers	.50
6	Robin Roberts	1.00
7	Ernie Banks	1.50
8	Steve Sax	.50
9	Duke Snider	1.50
10	Gaylord Perry	.50
11	Andre Dawson	.50
12	Dave Kingman	.50
13	Reggie Jackson	2.00
14	Willie McCovey	1.00
15	Gary Carter	.50
16	Orlando Cepeda	.50
17	Willie Randolph	.50
18	Bob Gibson	1.00

2002 King-B

For the shredded-beef snack's 15th annual issue, Donruss produced the 2-3/8" diameter discs. Fronts have a large "15" over which is printed a color action photo. Backs have a portrait photo, along with 2001 and career stats and a few biographical bits. All photos have had team logos removed.

		NM/M
Complete Set (28):		12.50
Common Player:		.50
1	Randy Johnson	.75
2	Curt Schilling	.65
3	Chipper Jones	1.00
4	Greg Maddux	1.00
5	John Burkett	.50
6	Manny Ramirez	.75
7	Barry Larkin	.50
8	Roberto Alomar	.50
9	Chuck Finley	.50
10	Jim Thome	.65
11	Juan Gonzalez	.65
12	Larry Walker	.50
13	Charles Johnson	.50
14	Moises Alou	.50
15	Gary Sheffield	.65
16	Chan Ho Park	.50
17	Vladimir Guerrero	.75
18	Roger Clemens	1.25
19	Mariano Rivera	.60

20	Jason Giambi	.65
21	Rich Aurilia	.50
22	Jeff Kent	.50
23	Edgar Martinez	.50
24	Kazuhiro Sasaki	.50
25	Bret Boone	.50
26	John Olerud	.50
27	Greg Vaughn	.50
28	Ivan Rodriguez	.65

1985 Kitty Clover Potato Chips Discs

One of a pair of nearly identical (see KAS) sets issued by midwestern potato chip companies, this issue features top stars of the day on 2-3/4" cardboard discs. The discs have a player portrait at center, with uniform logos airbrushed away because the producer was licensed only by the Players Association and not Major League Baseball. The player's name, team and position are printed in a white diamond around the photo. The sponsor's logo is in the yellow border. Backs are in black-and-white and have a few biographical data, a 1984 stats line and a Snack Time logo. The unnumbered discs are checklisted here in alphabetical order. Square versions of the discs, which have been cut from press sheets are known within the hobby and carry a small premium. Kitty Clover was based in Omaha.

		NM/M
Complete Set (20):		15.00
Common Player:		.75
1	Lonnie Smith	.75
2	Buddy Biancalana	.75
3	Bret Saberhagen	1.00
4	Hal McRae	.75
5	Onix Concepcion	.75
6	Jorge Orta	.75
7	Bud Black	.75
8	Dan Quisenberry	.75
9	Dane Iorg	.75
10	Charlie Leibrandt	.75
11	Pat Sheridan	.75
12	John Wathan	.75
13	Frank White	.75
14	Darryl Motley	.75
15	Willie Wilson	1.00
16	Danny Jackson	.75
17	Steve Balboni	.75
18	Jim Sundberg	.75
19	Mark Gubicza	.75
20	George Brett	6.00

1996 Klosterman Baking Big Red Machine

Twenty years after The Big Red Machine captured the World's Championship, the 1976 Cincinnati Reds were honored on a card set issued by this Queen City bakery. One card was included with each 20-oz. loaf of bread during the run of the promotion. Cards are 2-3/8" x 3-1/2". Fronts feature color game-action photos with a large headline above and the player's name and position in white on a red strip at bottom. The Reds logo is in an upper corner of the photo, with the player's uniform number beneath. Backs have career summary and stats for the 1976 season and M.L. career, along with sponsors' logos and copyright information.

		NM/M
Complete Set (20):		60.00
Common Player:		1.50
(1)	Steve Carlton	6.00
(2)	Jack Clark	1.50
(3)	Rich Gossage	1.50
(4)	Tony Gwynn	7.50
(5)	Bob Horner	1.50
(6)	Keith Hernandez	1.50
(7)	Kent Hrbek	1.50
(8)	Willie McGee	1.50
(9)	Dan Quisenberry	1.50
(10)	Cal Ripken Jr.	25.00
(11)	Ryne Sandberg	7.50
(12)	Mike Schmidt	20.00
(13)	Tom Seaver	6.00
(14)	Ozzie Smith	7.50
(15)	Rick Sutcliffe	1.50
(16)	Bruce Sutter	4.00
(17)	Alan Trammell	1.50
(18)	Fernando Valenzuela	1.50
(19)	Willie Wilson	1.50
(20)	Dave Winfield	6.00

1986 Kitty Clover Potato Chips Royals

Twenty players of the 1985 World's Champion Kansas City Royals are featured in a round card inserted into packages of potato chips in the K.C. area. The 2-7/8" discs were similar to other contemporary snack issues produced by Mike Schechter Associates in that team logos have been airbrushed off the players'

caps. The photos of some of the players can be found on other regional issues of 1986.

		NM/M
Complete Set (20):		15.00
Common Player:		.75
1	Lonnie Smith	.75
2	Buddy Biancalana	.75
3	Bret Saberhagen	1.00
4	Hal McRae	.75
5	Onix Concepcion	.75
6	Jorge Orta	.75
7	Bud Black	.75
8	Dan Quisenberry	.75
9	Dane Iorg	.75
10	Charlie Leibrandt	.75
11	Pat Sheridan	.75
12	John Wathan	.75
13	Frank White	.75
14	Darryl Motley	.75
15	Willie Wilson	1.00
16	Danny Jackson	.75
17	Steve Balboni	.75
18	Jim Sundberg	.75
19	Mark Gubicza	.75
20	George Brett	6.00

2000 Klosterman Bakery Big Red Machine

The 25th anniversary of Cincinnati's 1975 World Series championship is marked with this issue by a regional bakery. The cards are printed on thin stock in a 2-3/8" x 3-1/2" format. Fronts have vintage game-action photos with red borders and a Big Red Machine 25th anniversary logo. Backs recap the player's 1975 season in words and stats. The cards were distributed singly in

loaves of bread. The unnumbered cards are listed here in alphabetical order.

		NM/M
Complete Set (10):		5.00
Common Player:		.50
(1)	Sparky Anderson	.65
(2)	Johnny Bench	1.00
(3)	Jack Billingham	.50
(4)	Dave Concepcion	.50
(5)	George Foster	.50
(6)	Cesar Geronimo	.50
(7)	Ken Griffey	.50
(8)	Joe Morgan	.75
(9)	Tony Perez	.65
(10)	Pete Rose, Joe Morgan, Johnny Bench	1.00

1982 K-Mart

The first of what became dozens of boxed sets specially produced for retail chain stores by the major card producers, the 1982 K-Mart set has enjoyed little collector popularity. The theme of the set is Most Valuable Players and selected record-breaking performances of the 1962-1981 seasons. The design used miniature reproductions of Topps cards of the era, except in a few cases where designs had to be created because original cards were never issued (1962 Maury Wills, 1975 Fred Lynn). Originally sold for about $2 per boxed set of 44, large quantities were bought up by speculators who got burned when over-production and lack of demand caused the set to drop as low as 10¢. The 2-1/2" x 3-1/2" cards were printed by Topps.

		NM/M
Complete Set (44):		3.00
Common Player:		.10
1	Mickey Mantle	2.00
2	Maury Wills	.10
3	Elston Howard	.10
4	Sandy Koufax	.50
5	Brooks Robinson	.50
6	Ken Boyer	.10
7	Zoilo Versalles	.10
8	Willie Mays	.50
9	Frank Robinson	.10
10	Bob Clemente	.50
11	Carl Yastrzemski	.25
12	Orlando Cepeda	.10
13	Denny McLain	.10
14	Bob Gibson	.10
15	Harmon Killebrew	.10
16	Willie McCovey	.10
17	Boog Powell	.10
18	Johnny Bench	.50
19	Vida Blue	.10
20	Joe Torre	.10
21	Rich Allen	.10
22	Johnny Bench	.10
23	Reggie Jackson	.25
24	Pete Rose	.45

25	Jeff Burroughs	.10
26	Steve Garvey	.10
27	Fred Lynn	.10
28	Joe Morgan	.10
29	Thurman Munson	.10
30	Joe Morgan	.10
31	Rod Carew	.10
32	George Foster	.10
33	Jim Rice	.10
34	Dave Parker	.10
35	Don Baylor	.10
36	Keith Hernandez	.10
37	Willie Stargell	.10
38	George Brett	.50
39	Mike Schmidt	.50
40	Rollie Fingers	.10
41	Mike Schmidt	.50
42	Don Drysdale	.10
43	Hank Aaron	.50
44	Pete Rose	.45

1987 K-Mart

Produced by Topps for K-Mart, the 1987 K-Mart set was distributed by the department stores to celebrate their 25th anniversary. Entitled "Baseball's Stars of the Decades," the 33-card set was issued in a special cardboard box with one stick of bubblegum. Fronts feature a full-color photo set diagonally against a red background. The backs contain career highlights plus pitching or batting statistics for the decade in which the player enjoyed his greatest success. Cards are the standard 2-1/2" x 3-1/2".

		NM/M
Complete Set (33):		3.00
Common Player:		.10
1	Hank Aaron	.60
2	Roberto Clemente	.75
3	Bob Gibson	.10
4	Harmon Killebrew	.10
5	Mickey Mantle	2.00
6	Juan Marichal	.10
7	Roger Maris	.25
8	Willie Mays	.60
9	Brooks Robinson	.10
10	Frank Robinson	.10
11	Carl Yastrzemski	.25
12	Johnny Bench	.10
13	Lou Brock	.10
14	Rod Carew	.10
15	Steve Carlton	.10
16	Reggie Jackson	.25
17	Jim Palmer	.10
18	Jim Rice	.10
19	Pete Rose	.60
20	Nolan Ryan	.75
21	Tom Seaver	.10
22	Willie Stargell	.10
23	Wade Boggs	.25
24	George Brett	.50
25	Gary Carter	.10
26	Dwight Gooden	.10
27	Rickey Henderson	.10
28	Don Mattingly	.50
29	Dale Murphy	.10
30	Eddie Murray	.10
31	Mike Schmidt	.50
32	Darryl Strawberry	.10
33	Fernando Valenzuela	.10

1988 K-Mart

This 33-card boxed set, titled "Memorable Moments," was produced by Topps for distribution via K-Mart. The 1988 cards are standard-size with red, white and blue borders and a super glossy coating. Numbered card backs are printed in red and blue on white and highlight special events in the featured players' careers. The set was marketed in a bright yellow and green checklist box (gum included).

		NM/M
Complete Set (33):		2.00
Common Player:		.10
1	George Bell	.10
2	Wade Boggs	.45
3	George Brett	.50
4	Jose Canseco	.25
5	Jack Clark	.10
6	Will Clark	.10
7	Roger Clemens	.50
8	Vince Coleman	.10
9	Andre Dawson	.15
10	Dwight Gooden	.10
11	Pedro Guerrero	.10
12	Tony Gwynn	.45
13	Rickey Henderson	.35
14	Keith Hernandez	.10
15	Don Mattingly	.75
16	Mark McGwire	.75
17	Paul Molitor	.15
18	Dale Murphy	.15
19	Tim Raines	.10
20	Dave Righetti	.10
21	Cal Ripken, Jr.	1.00
22	Pete Rose	.60
23	Nolan Ryan	1.00
24	Benny Santiago	.10
25	Mike Schmidt	.50
26	Mike Scott	.10
27	Kevin Seitzer	.10
28	Ozzie Smith	.45
29	Darryl Strawberry	.10
30	Rick Sutcliffe	.10
31	Fernando Valenzuela	.10
32	Todd Worrell	.10
33	Robin Yount	.35

1989 K-Mart

This 33-card, glossy set was produced by Topps for K-Mart, where it was sold in stores nationwide. The standard-size cards feature mostly action shots on the front, and include the Topps "Dream Team" logo at the top, with the K-Mart logo in the lower right corner. The first 11 cards in the set picture the top rookies of 1988, while the next 11 picture the top A.L. rookies of the '80s, and the final 11 cards highlight the top N.L. rookies of the decade.

		NM/M
Complete Set (33):		2.00
Common Player:		.10
1	Mark Grace	.10
2	Ron Gant	.10
3	Chris Sabo	.10
4	Walt Weiss	.10
5	Jay Buhner	.10
6	Cecil Espy	.10
7	Dave Gallagher	.10
8	Damon Berryhill	.10
9	Tim Belcher	.10
10	Paul Gibson	.10
11	Gregg Jefferies	.10
12	Don Mattingly	.75
13	Harold Reynolds	.10
14	Wade Boggs	.60

15	Cal Ripken, Jr.	1.00
16	Kirby Puckett	.60
17	George Bell	.10
18	Jose Canseco	.25
19	Terry Steinbach	.10
20	Roger Clemens	.65
21	Mark Langston	.10
22	Harold Baines	.10
23	Will Clark	.10
24	Ryne Sandberg	.60
25	Tim Wallach	.10
26	Shawon Dunston	.10
27	Tim Raines	.10
28	Darryl Strawberry	.10
29	Tony Gwynn	.60
30	Tony Pena	.10
31	Doc Gooden	.10
32	Fernando Valenzuela	.10
33	Pedro Guerrero	.10

1990 K-Mart

This 33-card glossy set was produced by Topps for K-Mart, where it was available nationwide. The set is subtitled "Superstars" and features sixteen A.L. players, sixteen N.L. stars and a managers' card featuring both Tony LaRussa and Roger Craig. A special Superstars logo is featured on the card fronts. The 1990 issue marks the fourth consecutive year that Topps has produced a set in cooperation with K-Mart.

		NM/M
Complete Set (33):		3.00
Common Player:		.10
1	Will Clark	.10
2	Ryne Sandberg	.50
3	Howard Johnson	.10
4	Ozzie Smith	.50
5	Tony Gwynn	.50
6	Kevin Mitchell	.10
7	Jerome Walton	.10
8	Craig Biggio	.10
9	Mike Scott	.10
10	Dwight Gooden	.10
11	Sid Fernandez	.10
12	Joe Magrane	.10
13	Jay Howell	.10
14	Mark Davis	.10
15	Pedro Guerrero	.10
16	Glenn Davis	.10
17	Don Mattingly	.65
18	Julio Franco	.10
19	Wade Boggs	.50
20	Cal Ripken, Jr.	1.00
21	Jose Canseco	.25
22	Kirby Puckett	.50
23	Rickey Henderson	.35
24	Mickey Tettleton	.10
25	Nolan Ryan	1.00
26	Bret Saberhagen	.10
27	Jeff Ballard	.10
28	Chuck Finley	.10
29	Dennis Eckersley	.30
30	Dan Plesac	.10
31	Fred McGriff	.10
32	Mark McGwire	.75
33	Managers (Tony LaRussa, Roger Craig)	.10

1988 Kodak White Sox

These blank-back large format (8" x 12") cards feature borderless color action photos of team stars, overprinted with team and sponsor logos and a facsimile autograph. At top is a line of type with the card number and a "1988 Kodak Collectible Series" title.

		NM/M
Complete Set (5):		10.00
Common Player:		2.00
1	Ozzie Guillen	2.00
2	Carlton Fisk	4.00
3	Rick Horton	2.00
4	Ivan Calderon	2.00
5	Harold Baines	2.00

1989 Kodak White Sox

A series of six collectible pictures was given to fans over the course of the 1989 season. Sponsored by Kodak and Osco drug stores, the 8" x 12" sheets combine pictures of a current White Sox star with those of two former stars who played the same position. Ads for the sponsors appear on the photos' fronts, while there is a modicum of information about the former stars accompanying their portraits, including the years they played for the Sox.

		NM/M
Complete Set (6):		10.00
Common Card:		2.00
1	Greg Walker, Dick Allen, Ted Kluszewski	2.50
2	Steve Lyons, Eddie Collins, Nellie Fox	2.50
3	Carlton Fisk, Sherm Lollar, Ray Schalk	2.50
3	Harold Baines, Minnie Minoso, Jim Landis	2.00
5	Bobby Thigpen, Gerry Staley, Hoyt Wilhelm	2.00
6	Ozzie Guillen, Luke Appling, Luis Aparicio	2.00

1990 Kodak White Sox

Again utilizing a large format (7" x 11") with borderless color action photos, the "1990 Kodak Collectible Series" features top stars of the South Siders. Player name and position, along with team and sponsor's logos, are superimposed over the photo, along with the title line and card number. The blank-back cards were distributed over the course of the season at various home games.

		NM/M
Complete Set (6):		10.00
Common Player:		2.00
1	Carlton Fisk	4.00
2	Melido Perez	2.00
3	Ozzie Guillen	2.00
4	Ron Kittle	2.00
5	Scott Fletcher	2.00
6	Comiskey Park	2.00

1991 Kodak White Sox

For a fourth year in a row, Kodak sponsored a White Sox

team set in 1991. Fronts feature a full-bleed color action photo with the player's name and uniform number at the bottom and a commemorative logo for new Comiskey Park's inaugural season at top. Black-and-white backs have a few stats, personal details and career highlights along with the Kodak logo.

		NM/M
Complete Set (30):		24.00
Common Player:		.50
1	Lance Johnson	.50
5	Matt Merullo	.50
7	Scott Fletcher	.50
8	Bo Jackson	1.50
10	Jeff Torborg	.50
13	Ozzie Guillen	.50
14	Craig Grebeck	.50
20	Ron Karkovice	.50
21	Joey Cora	.50
22	Donn Pall	.50
23	Robin Ventura	1.00
27	Sammy Sosa	10.00
27	Greg Hibbard	.50
28	Cory Snyder	.50
29	Jack McDowell	.50
30	Tim Raines	.50
31	Scott Radinsky	.50
32	Alex Fernandez	.50
33	Melido Perez	.50
34	Ken Patterson	.50
35	Frank Thomas	5.00
37	Bobby Thigpen	.50
44	Dan Pasqua	.50
45	Wayne Edwards	.50
49	Charlie Hough	.50
50	Brian Drahman	.50
72	Carlton Fisk	3.00
---	White Sox Coaches (Terry Bevington, Sammy Ellis, Barry Foote, Walt Hriniak, Dave Laroche, Joe Nossek, John Stephenson)	.50
---	Co-captains (Ozzie Guillen, Carlton Fisk)	.50
---	No. 1 Draft Choices (Alex Fernandez, Jack McDowell, Frank Thomas, Robin Ventura)	1.00

1992 Kodak White Sox

With the theme of "Good Guys Wear Black," this set depicts the Chicago southsiders in photos featuring the team's Sunday-best black uniform jerseys. Photos on the cards are full-bleed with the GGWB logo in the upper-left corner of each card. At bottom is a black strip with the player's last name and uniform number. On back are the player's 1991 and career stats, a few biographical details, a trivia question and Kodak logo. At 2-5/8" x 3-1/2", the cards are slightly wider than current standard.

		NM/M
Complete Set (30):		10.00
Common Player:		.25
1	Lance Johnson	.25
7	Steve Sax	.25
8	Bo Jackson	.75
10	Mike LaValliere	.25
12	Mike Huff	.25
13	Ozzie Guillen	.25
14	Craig Grebeck	.25
20	Ron Karkovice	.25
21	George Bell	.25
22	Donn Pall	.25
23	Robin Ventura	.50
25	Kirk McCaskill	.25
26	Ellis Burks	.25
28	Joey Cora	.25
29	Jack McDowell	.25
30	Tim Raines	.25
31	Scott Radinsky	.25
32	Alex Fernandez	.25
33	Gene Lamont	.25
34	Terry Leach	.25
35	Frank Thomas	4.00
37	Bobby Thigpen	.25
39	Roberto Hernandez	.25
40	Wilson Alvarez	.25
42	Rod Bolton	.25
44	Dan Pasqua	.25
45	Chuck Cary	.25
49	Jeff Schwartz	.25
51	Jason Bere	.25

		NM/M
Complete Set (30):		10.00
Common Player:		.25
1	Lance Johnson	.25
5	Matt Merullo	.25
7	Steve Sax	.25
12	Mike Huff	.25
13	Ozzie Guillen	.25
14	Craig Grebeck	.25
20	Ron Karkovice	.25
21	George Bell	.25
22	Donn Pall	.25
23	Robin Ventura	.50
24	Warren Newson	.25
25	Kirk McCaskill	.25
27	Greg Hibbard	.25
28	Joey Cora	.25
29	Jack McDowell	.25
30	Tim Raines	.25
31	Scott Radinsky	.25
32	Alex Fernandez	.25
33	Gene Lamont	.25
34	Terry Leach	.25
35	Frank Thomas	4.00
38	Bobby Thigpen	.25
39	Roberto Hernandez	.25
40	Wilson Alvarez	.25
44	Dan Pasqua	.25
45	Shawn Abner	.25
49	Charlie Hough	.25
72	Carlton Fisk	2.50
00	Waldo (Cartoon mascot)	.25
---	Mike Squires, Terry Bevington, Gene Lamont, Joe Nossek, Jackie Brown, Walt Hriniak, Doug Mansolino, Dave Huppert	.25

1993 Kodak White Sox

Kodak produced a White Sox set of 30 cards in 1993 that was given away prior to the July 23 game between Chicago and Milwaukee. The full color cards are slightly oversized at 2-5/8" x 3-1/2" and are printed on a very heavy card stock. The photo on the front is full bleed, with the White Sox logo appearing in the upper corner and a metallic blue stripe at the card bottom displaying the player's uniform number, name and position. The backs are white with gray borders and a Kodak logo, with year and career statistics and biographical information. The cards are unnumbered.

		NM/M
Complete Set (30):		10.00
Common Player:		.25
1	Lance Johnson	.25
7	Steve Sax	.25
8	Bo Jackson	.75
10	Mike LaValliere	.25
12	Mike Huff	.25
13	Ozzie Guillen	.25
14	Craig Grebeck	.25
20	Ron Karkovice	.25
21	George Bell	.25
22	Donn Pall	.25
23	Robin Ventura	.50
25	Kirk McCaskill	.25
26	Ellis Burks	.25
28	Joey Cora	.25
29	Jack McDowell	.25
30	Tim Raines	.25
31	Scott Radinsky	.25
32	Alex Fernandez	.25
33	Gene Lamont	.25
34	Terry Leach	.25
35	Frank Thomas	4.00
37	Bobby Thigpen	.25
39	Roberto Hernandez	.25
40	Wilson Alvarez	.25
42	Rod Bolton	.25
44	Dan Pasqua	.25
45	Chuck Cary	.25
49	Jeff Schwartz	.25
51	Jason Bere	.25

---	1993 Coaching Staff (Gene Lamont, Jackie Brown, Terry Bevington, Joe Nossek, Walt Hriniak, Doug Mansolino, Dewey Robinson, Jose Antigua)	.25

1994 Kodak White Sox

Slightly wider than standard cards, at 2-5/8" x 3-1/2" cards, this team set features borderless game-action photos on front with a silver facsimile autograph. Backs are bordered in silver and have a few stats, player personal data, career highlights and logos of the team and sponsor.

		NM/M
Complete Set (30):		12.00
Common Player:		.50
(1)	Wilson Alvarez	.50
(2)	Paul Assenmacher	.50
(3)	Jason Bere	.50
(4)	Dennis Cook	.50
(5)	Joey Cora	.50
(6)	Jose DeLeon	.50
(7)	Alex Fernandez	.50
(8)	Julio Franco	.50
(9)	Craig Grebeck	.50
(10)	Ozzie Guillen	.50
(11)	Joe Hall	.50
(12)	Roberto Hernandez	.50
(13)	Dann Howitt	.50
(14)	Darrin Jackson	.50
(15)	Dane Johnson	.50
(16)	Lance Johnson	.50
(17)	Ron Karkovice	.50
(18)	Gene Lamont	.50
(19)	Mike LaValliere	.50
(20)	Norberto Martin	.50
(21)	Kirk McCaskill	.50
(22)	Jack McDowell	.50
(23)	Warren Newson	.50
(24)	Dan Pasqua	.50
(25)	Tim Raines	.50
(26)	Scott Sanderson	.50
(27)	Frank Thomas	4.00
(28)	Robin Ventura	.75
(29)	Bob Zupcic	.50
(30)	Coaches (Terry Bevington, Jackie Brown, Roly de Armas, Walt Hriniak, Gene Lamont, Doug Mansolino, Joe Nossek, Rick Peterson)	.50

1995 Kodak Pittsburgh Pirates

This 13-1/2" x 20-1/4" perforated sheet containing 30 player and staff cards and sponsor advertising was issued to persons attending a July 23 promotional game. Individual cards measure 2-1/4" x 3-1/4". Player photos at center are flanked by the team name in gold with the player name in yellow in a red banner above. Backs are in black-and-white with just a few biographical notes and team and sponsor logos. The unnumbered cards are checklisted here alphabetically.

		NM/M
Complete Set, Sheet:		6.00
Complete Set, Singles (30):		6.00
Common Player:		.25
(1)	Rich Aude	.25
(2)	Jay Bell	.50
(3)	Jacob Brumfield	.25
(4)	Jason Christianson	.25
(5)	Dave Clark	.25
(6)	Steve Cooke	.25
(7)	Midre Cummings	.25

(8) Mike Dyer .25
(9) Angelo Encarnacion .25
(10) Carlos Garcia .25
(11) Freddy García .25
(12) Jim Gott .25
(13) Mark Johnson .25
(14) Jeff King .25
(15) Jim Leyland .25
(16) Jon Lieber .25
(17) Nelson Liriano .25
(18) Esteban Loaiza .25
(19) Al Martin .25
(20) Jeff McCurry .25
(21) Orlando Merced .25
(22) Dan Miceli .25
(23) Denny Neagle .25
(24) Mark Parent .25
(25) Steve Pegues .25
(26) Dan Plesac .25
(27) Don Slaught .25
(28) Paul Wagner .25
(29) Rick White .25
(30) Gary Wilson .25

1995 Kodak White Sox

Fans attending the July 21 game at Comiskey Park received a cello-wrapped 30-card team set. Fronts of the 2-5/8" x 3-1/2" cards have color player photos that are borderless at top and sides. At bottom the player's name appears in black-and-white. Backs are in black-and-white and feature the sponsor's logo and the team's 95-year anniversary logo. There are also a few biographical details, 1994 and career stats and a player trivia question. Cards are numbered by player uniform number.

NM/M
Complete Set (30): 9.00
Common Player: .15
1 Lance Johnson .15
2 Ray Durham .30
7 Norberto Martin .15
8 Mike Devereaux .15
10 Mike Lavalliere .15
12 Craig Grebeck .15
13 Ozzie Guillen .15
14 Dave Martinez .15
15 Kirk McCaskill .15
18 Terry Bevington .15
20 Ron Karkovice .15
23 Robin Ventura .15
24 Warren Newson .15
25 Jim Abbott .15
26 Brian Keyser .15
29 John Kruk .15
30 Tim Raines .15
31 Scott Radinsky .15
33 Alex Fernandez .15
35 Frank Thomas 4.00
39 Roberto Hernandez .15
40 Wilson Alvarez .15
46 Jason Bere .15
48 Jose DeLeon .15
49 Rob Dibble .15
51 Tim Fortugno .15
--- Frank Thomas (1995 All-Star) 2.00
--- White Sox Coaching Staff (Terry Bevington, Don Cooper, Roly DeArmas, Walt Hriniak, Ron Jackson, Doug Mansolino, Joe Nossek, Mark Salas) .15
--- Trainers (Herm Schneider, Mark Anderson) .15
--- Director of Conditioning (Steve Odgers) .15

1985 Kondritz Vince Coleman

The debut season of 1985 N.L. Rookie of the Year Vince Coleman is traced in this 20-card set issued by Illinois dealer

Kondritz Trading Cards. Fronts of the 2-1/2" x 3-1/2" cards have player posed or action photos surrounded by a wide red border. Backs are in black-and-white with a few sentences about Coleman, a card number, large "Invincible" and copyright data. Sets were originally sold for about $10.

NM/M
Complete Set (20): 5.00
Common Back: .25

1986 Kondritz Ozzie Smith

The career of future Hall of Fame Cardinals shortstop Ozzie Smith is traced in this 20-card set issued by Illinois dealer Kondritz Trading Cards. Fronts of the 2-1/2" x 3-1/2" cards have player posed or action photos surrounded by a wide red border. Backs are in black-and-white with a few sentences about Smith, a card number, a large "THE WIZARD" and copyright data. Sets were originally sold for about $10.

NM/M
Complete Set (20): 20.00
Common Card: 1.50
1-20 Ozzie Smith 1.50

1987 Kraft Home Plate Heroes

Kraft Foods issued a 48-card set on specially marked packages of macaroni & cheese dinners. Titled "Home Plate Heroes," 24 two-card panels measuring 3-1/2" x 7-1/8" make up the set. Individual cards measure 2-1/4" x 3-1/2". The blank-backed cards feature fronts with full-color photos, although all

team insignias have been erased. In conjunction with the card set, Kraft offered a contest to "Win A Day With A Major Leaguer." Mike Schechter Associates produced the set for Kraft. A total of 120 different panel combinations (five with each player) can be found.

NM/M
Complete Set, Panels: 20.00
Complete Set, Singles (48): 16.00
Common Player: .25
1 Eddie Murray .50
2 Dale Murphy .40
3 Cal Ripken, Jr. 1.00
4 Mike Scott .25
5 Jim Rice .35
6 Jody Davis .25
7 Wade Boggs .60
8 Ryne Sandberg .60
9 Wally Joyner .25
10 Eric Davis .25
11 Ozzie Guillen .25
12 Tony Pena .25
13 Harold Baines .25
14 Johnny Ray .25
15 Joe Carter .25
16 Ozzie Smith .60
17 Cory Snyder .25
18 Vince Coleman .25
19 Kirk Gibson .25
20 Steve Garvey .35
21 George Brett .75
22 John Tudor .25
23 Robin Yount .50
24 Von Hayes .25
25 Kent Hrbek .25
26 Darryl Strawberry .25
27 Kirby Puckett .60
28 Ron Darling .25
29 Don Mattingly .75
30 Mike Schmidt .75
31 Rickey Henderson .50
32 Fernando Valenzuela .25
33 Dave Winfield .50
34 Pete Rose .85
35 Jose Canseco .40
36 Glenn Davis .25
37 Alvin Davis .25
38 Steve Sax .25
39 Pete Incaviglia .25
40 Jeff Reardon .25
41 Jesse Barfield .25
42 Hubie Brooks .25
43 George Bell .25
44 Tony Gwynn .60
45 Roger Clemens .65
46 Chili Davis .25
47 Mike Witt .25
48 Nolan Ryan 1.00

1993 Kraft Pop-Up Action

Kraft released a set of Pop-Up Action baseball cards in 1993 that was available in specially-marked packages of Kraft Singles. The cards are similar to the 1992 Canadian Post Cereal cards with a pop-up tab. The set is made up of 15 players each from the American and National Leagues.

NM/M
Complete Set (30): 12.00
Common Player: .35
American League
(1) Jim Abbott .35
(2) Roberto Alomar .35
(3) Sandy Alomar Jr. .35
(4) George Brett .75
(5) Roger Clemens .75
(6) Dennis Eckersley .50
(7) Cecil Fielder .35
(8) Ken Griffey Jr. 1.00
(9) Don Mattingly .75
(10) Mark McGwire 1.50
(11) Kirby Puckett .65
(12) Cal Ripken, Jr. 2.00
(13) Nolan Ryan 2.00
(14) Robin Ventura .35
(15) Robin Yount .60
National League
(1) Bobby Bonilla .35
(2) Ken Caminiti .35
(3) Will Clark .35
(4) Darren Daulton .35
(5) Doug Drabek .35
(6) Delino DeShields .35
(7) Tom Glavine .45
(8) Tony Gwynn .65
(9) Orel Hershiser .35
(10) Barry Larkin .35
(11) Terry Pendleton .35
(12) Ryne Sandberg .65
(13) Gary Sheffield .50
(14) Lee Smith .35
(15) Andy Van Slyke .35

1994 Kraft Pop-Ups

Kraft offered a 30-card set in 1994 featuring major stars in a pop-up format. The cards show the players in action shots front and back, with the front picture "popping up." Kraft Singles consumers could find one 2-1/2" x 3-3/8" card in each package of cheese, with 15 players from each league. The cards were licensed by the Major League Baseball Players Association, but not by Major League Baseball, so the team logos were airbrushed from player's caps and uniforms. Through an on-pack and in-store mail-in offer, collectors could order complete sets of the cards for $1.95 per league (15 cards), plus the appropriate proofs of purchase. In a somewhat unusual move, officials of Kraft USA announced that the print run would be eight million cards, which works out to about 266,000 sets.

NM/M
Complete Set (30): 7.50
Common Player: .25
1 Carlos Baerga .25
2 Dennis Eckersley .50
3 Cecil Fielder .25
4 Juan Gonzalez .50
5 Ken Griffey Jr. 1.00
6 Mark Langston .25
7 Brian McRae .25
8 Paul Molitor .60
9 Kirby Puckett .75
10 Cal Ripken Jr. 1.50
11 Danny Tartabull .25
12 Frank Thomas .60
13 Greg Vaughn .25
14 Mo Vaughn .25
15 Dave Winfield .60
16 Jeff Bagwell .60
17 Barry Bonds 1.50
18 Bobby Bonilla .25
19 Delino DeShields .25
20 Lenny Dykstra .25
21 Andres Galarraga .25
22 Tom Glavine .25
23 Mark Grace .25
24 Tony Gwynn .75
25 David Justice .25
26 Barry Larkin .25
27 Mike Piazza .90
28 Gary Sheffield .40
29 Ozzie Smith .75
30 Andy Van Slyke .25

1995 Kraft Singles Superstars

Once again incorporating a pop-up center action figure, these cards were available both in packages of cheese slices and via a mail-in offer.

The 2-1/2" x 3-1/2" cards have a second player photo in the center which is revealed by pushing down the hinged front and back of the card, creating a stand. All photos have had uniform logos removed. A baseball design is at the bottom of each player photo. Back of the card has abbreviated stats and career highlights. The back of the pop-up figure has a paragraph about the player titled, "What Singles Him Out." Besides being packaged with cheese, the cards were available by sending in proofs of purchase and $1.95 for each 15-player A.L. or N.L. set.

NM/M
Complete Set (30): 7.50
Common Player: .25
1 Roberto Alomar .25
2 Joe Carter .25
3 Cecil Fielder .25
4 Juan Gonzalez .50
5 Ken Griffey Jr. 1.25
6 Jimmy Key .25
7 Chuck Knoblauch .25
8 Kenny Lofton .25
9 Mike Mussina .40
10 Paul O'Neill .25
11 Kirby Puckett .75
12 Cal Ripken Jr. 1.50
13 Ivan Rodriguez .50
14 Frank Thomas .60
15 Mo Vaughn .25
16 Moises Alou .25
17 Jeff Bagwell .60
18 Barry Bonds 1.50
19 Jeff Conine .25
20 Lenny Dykstra .25
21 Andres Galarraga .25
22 Tony Gwynn .75
23 Gregg Jefferies .25
24 Barry Larkin .25
25 Greg Maddux .75
26 Mike Piazza 1.00
27 Bret Saberhagen .25
28 Ozzie Smith .75
29 Sammy Sosa 1.00
30 Matt Williams .25

1994 KVTU-TV San Francisco Giants

This short set was sponsored by the Giants' television broadcasting partner. Eight of the team's top names are featured on the 2-1/2" x 3-1/2" cards. Fronts have action photos framed in orange and brown with white borders. Black-and-white backs have a few career highlights and the TV station's logo.

NM/M
Complete Set (9): 12.00
Common Player: 1.00
(1) Dusty Baker 1.00
(2) Rod Beck 1.00
(3) Barry Bonds 7.50
(4) Bobby Bonds 1.00
(5) John Burkett 1.00
(6) Billy Swift 1.00
(7) Robby Thompson 1.00
(8) Matt Williams 1.00
(9) Header Card .50

L

1981 L.A. Dodgers Police

Similar in format to the previous year's set, the Dodgers 1981 police set grew to 32 cards due to the acquisitions of Ken Landreaux and Dave Stewart shortly before printing of the sets. These two cards may even have been added after the initial printing run, making them slightly more difficult to obtain. The full-color cards are again 2-13/16" x 4-1/8", with a safety tip on the card back. Each card front has the line "LAPD Salutes the 1981 Dodgers."

NM/M
Complete Set (32): 6.00
Common Player: .25
2 Tom Lasorda .50
4 Rudy Law .25
6 Steve Garvey 3.00
7 Steve Yeager .25
8 Reggie Smith .25
10 Ron Cey .25
12 Dusty Baker .35
13 Joe Ferguson .25
14 Mike Scioscia .25
15 Davey Lopes .25
16 Rick Monday .25
18 Bill Russell .25
21 Jay Johnstone .25
26 Don Stanhouse .25
27 Joe Beckwith .25
28 Pete Guerrero .25
30 Derrel Thomas .25
34 Fernando Valenzuela 1.50
35 Bob Welch .25
36 Pepe Frias .25
37 Robert Castillo .25
38 Dave Goltz .25
41 Jerry Reuss .25
43 Rick Sutcliffe .25
44a Mickey Hatcher .25
44b Ken Landreaux 1.25
46 Burt Hooton .25
48 Dave Stewart 1.50
51 Terry Forster .25
57 Steve Howe .25
--- Coaching Staff (Monty Basgall, Mark Cresse, Tom Lasorda, Manny Mota, Danny Ozark, Ron Perranoski) .25
--- Team Photo/Checklist .25

1982 L.A. Dodgers Police

Again issued in the same 2-13/16" x 4-1/8" size of the '80 and '81 sets, the 1982 Los Angeles set commemorates the team's 1981 World Championship. In addition to the 26 cards numbered by uniform for players and manager Tom Lasorda, there are four unnumbered cards which feature the team winning the di-

FERNANDO VALENZUELA
No. 34 — PITCHER
The Los Angeles Police Department
presents the World Champion
Dodgers

vision, league and World Series titles, plus one of the World Series trophy. The full-color card photos are once again vivid portraits on a clean white card stock. Card backs offer brief biographies and stadium information in addition to a safety tip.

		NM/M
Complete Set (30):		5.00
Common Player:		.25
2	Tom Lasorda	.50
6	Steve Garvey	2.00
7	Steve Yeager	.25
8	Mark Belanger	.25
10	Ron Cey	.25
12	Dusty Baker	.35
14	Mike Scioscia	.25
16	Rick Monday	.25
18	Bill Russell	.25
21	Jay Johnstone	.25
26	Alejandro Pena	.25
28	Pedro Guerrero	.25
30	Derrel Thomas	.25
31	Jorge Orta	.25
34	Fernando Valenzuela	.75
35	Bob Welch	.25
38	Dave Goltz	.25
40	Ron Roenicke	.25
41	Jerry Reuss	.25
44	Ken Landreaux	.25
46	Burt Hooton	.25
48	Dave Stewart	.35
49	Tom Niedenfuer	.25
51	Terry Forster	.25
52	Steve Sax	.35
57	Steve Howe	.25
---	Division Championship	.25
---	League Championship	.25
---	World Series Championship	.25
---	Trophy Card/Checklist	.25

1983 L.A. Dodgers Police

FERNANDO VALENZUELA 34
Dodgers
1983

While these full-color cards remained 2-13/16" x 4-1/8" and card fronts were similar to those of previous years, the card backs are quite different. Card backs are in a horizontal design for the first time, and include a small head portrait photo of the player in the upper left corner. Fairly complete player statistics are included but there is no safety tip. The 30 cards are numbered by uniform number, with an unnumbered coaches card also included. Fronts include the year, team logo, player name and number.

		NM/M
Complete Set (30):		6.00
Common Player:		.25
2	Tom Lasorda	.50
3	Steve Sax	.25
5	Mike Marshall	.25
7	Steve Yeager	.25

12	Dusty Baker	.35
14	Mike Scioscia	.25
16	Rick Monday	.25
17	Greg Brock	.25
18	Bill Russell	.25
20	Candy Maldonado	.25
21	Ricky Wright	.25
22	Mark Bradley	.25
23	Dave Sax	.25
26	Alejandro Pena	.25
27	Joe Beckwith	.25
28	Pedro Guerrero	.25
30	Derrel Thomas	.25
34	Fernando Valenzuela	.75
35	Bob Welch	.25
38	Pat Zachry	.25
40	Ron Roenicke	.25
41	Jerry Reuss	.25
43	Jose Morales	.25
44	Ken Landreaux	.25
46	Burt Hooton	.25
47	Larry White	.25
48	Dave Stewart	.35
49	Tom Niedenfuer	.25
57	Steve Howe	.25
---	Coaches Card (Joe Amalfitano, Monty Basgall, Mark Cresse, Manny Mota, Ron Perranoski)	.25

1984 L.A. Dodgers Fire Safety

S   A   X

Dodgers

Unlike the California Angels and San Diego Padres sets issued in conjunction with the Forestry Service in 1984, the Los Angeles Dodgers set contains only three players, pictured on much larger 5" x 7" cards. Each player is pictured with Smokey in a forest scene on the full-color fronts. Backs of the unnumbered cards have brief biographical information and lifetime statistics. The cards were distributed at a Dodgers home game.

		NM/M
Complete Set (4):		7.00
Common Player:		2.50
(1)	Ken Landreaux	2.50
(2)	Tom Niedenfuer	2.50
(3)	Steve Sax	2.50
(4)	Smokey Bear	.50

1984 L.A. Dodgers Police

MIKE MARSHALL
Dodgers 1984 5

This was the fifth yearly effort of the Dodgers and the Los Angeles Police Department. There are 30 cards in the set, which remains 2-13/16" x 4-1/8". Card fronts are designed somewhat differently than previous years, with more posed photos, bolder player names and numbers and a different team logo. Card backs again feature a small portrait photo in

the upper left corner, along with brief biographical information and an anti-drug tip. Card backs are in Dodger blue. Cards are numbered by uniform number, with an unnumbered coaches card also included.

		NM/M
Complete Set (30):		4.00
Common Player:		.25
2	Tom Lasorda	.50
3	Steve Sax	.25
5	Mike Marshall	.25
7	Steve Yeager	.25
9	Greg Brock	.25
10	Dave Anderson	.25
14	Mike Scioscia	.25
16	Rick Monday	.25
17	Rafael Landestoy	.25
18	Bill Russell	.25
20	Candy Maldonado	.25
21	Bob Bailor	.25
26	German Rivera	.25
26	Alejandro Pena	.25
27	Carlos Diaz	.25
28	Pedro Guerrero	.25
31	Jack Fimple	.25
34	Fernando Valenzuela	.75
35	Bob Welch	.25
38	Pat Zachry	.25
40	Rick Honeycutt	.25
41	Jerry Reuss	.25
43	Jose Morales	.25
44	Ken Landreaux	.25
45	Terry Whitfield	.25
46	Burt Hooton	.25
49	Tom Niedenfuer	.25
55	Orel Hershiser	3.00
56	Richard Rodas	.25
---	Coaches Card (Joe Amalfitano, Monty Basgall, Mark Cresse, Manny Mota, Ron Perranoski)	.25

1986 L.A. Dodgers Police

Dodgers 1986
MIKE MARSHALL 5

After skipping the 1985 season, the Los Angeles Dodgers once again issued baseball cards related to police safety. The 1986 set features 30 full-color glossy cards measuring 2-1/4" x 4-1/8", numbered according to player uniforms. The backs feature brief player data and a safety tip from the Los Angeles Police Department. The sets were given away May 18 during Baseball Card Day at Dodger Stadium.

		NM/M
Complete Set (30):		4.00
Common Player:		.20
2	Tom Lasorda	.40
3	Steve Sax	.20
5	Mike Marshall	.20
9	Greg Brock	.20
10	Dave Anderson	.20
12	Bill Madlock	.20
14	Mike Scioscia	.20
17	Len Matuszek	.20
18	Bill Russell	.20
22	Franklin Stubbs	.20
23	Enos Cabell	.20
25	Mariano Duncan	.20
26	Alejandro Pena	.20
27	Carlos Diaz	.20
29	Pedro Guerrero	.20
31	Alex Trevino	.20
32	Ed Vande Berg	.20
34	Fernando Valenzuela	.50
35	Bob Welch	.20
40	Rick Honeycutt	.20
41	Jerry Reuss	.20
43	Ken Howell	.20
44	Ken Landreaux	.20
45	Terry Whitfield	.20
48	Dennis Powell	.20
49	Tom Niedenfuer	.20
51	Reggie Williams	.20

55	Orel Hershiser	.50
---	Team photo/checklist	.20
---	Coaching Staff (Joe Amalfitano, Monty Basgall, Mark Cresse, Ben Hines, Don McMahon, Manny Mota, Ron Perranoski)	.20

1987 L.A. Dodgers All-Stars Fire Safety

SANDY KOUFAX
25 Years of Dodger All-Stars

This fire safety set features "25 Years of Dodger All-Stars." The cards, which measure 2-1/2" x 3-3/4", were given out to fans age 14 and younger at the September 18 dame at Dodgers Stadium. Fronts have full-color photos set in the shape of Dodger Stadium and have attractive silver borders. Backs carry the player's All-Star Game record plus a fire prevention message. Many of the photos used in the set were from team-issued picture packs sold by the Dodgers in the past.

		NM/M
Complete Set (40):		7.50
Common Player:		.25
(1)	Walt Alston	.45
(2)	Dusty Baker	.30
(3)	Jim Brewer	.25
(4)	Ron Cey	.25
(5)	Tommy Davis	.25
(6)	Willie Davis	.25
(7)	Don Drysdale	2.00
(8)	Steve Garvey	1.50
(9)	Bill Grabarkewitz	.25
(10)	Pedro Guerrero	.25
(11)	Tom Haller	.25
(12)	Orel Hershiser	.45
(13)	Burt Hooton	.25
(14)	Steve Howe	.25
(15)	Tommy John	.30
(16)	Sandy Koufax	5.00
(17)	Tom Lasorda	.45
(18)	Jim Lefebvre	.25
(19)	Davey Lopes	.25
(20)	Mike Marshall/Outfielder	.25
(21)	Mike Marshall/Pitcher	.25
(22)	Andy Messersmith	.25
(23)	Rick Monday	.25
(24)	Manny Mota	.25
(25)	Claude Osteen	.25
(26)	Johnny Podres	.30
(27)	Phil Regan	.25
(28)	Jerry Reuss	.25
(29)	Rick Rhoden	.25
(30)	John Roseboro	.25
(31)	Bill Russell	.25
(32)	Steve Sax	.25
(33)	Bill Singer	.25
(34)	Reggie Smith	.25
(35)	Don Sutton	1.00
(36)	Fernando Valenzuela	.50
(37)	Bob Welch	.25
(38)	Maury Wills	.45
(39)	Jim Wynn	.25
(40)	Logo Card/Checklist	.10

1987 L.A. Dodgers Police

Producing a police set for the seventh time in eight years, the 1987 edition contains 30 cards which measure 2-13/16" x 4-1/8". The set includes a special Dodger Stadium 25th Anniversary card. The card fronts contain a full-color photo plus the Dodger Stadium 25th Anniversay logo. The photos are a mix of

JOSE GONZALEZ 47

action and posed shots. The backs contain personal player data plus a police safety tip. The cards were given out April 24th at Dodger Stadium and were distributed by the Los Angeles police department at a rate of two cards per week.

		NM/M
Complete Set (30):		4.00
Common Player:		.20
2	Tom Lasorda	.50
3	Steve Sax	.25
5	Mike Marshall	.25
10	Dave Anderson	.25
12	Bill Madlock	.25
14	Mike Scioscia	.25
15	Gilberto Reyes	.25
17	Len Matuszek	.25
21	Reggie Williams	.25
22	Franklin Stubbs	.25
23	Tim Leary	.25
26	Mariano Duncan	.25
26	Alejandro Pena	.25
29	Alex Trevino	.25
33	Jeff Hamilton	.25
34	Fernando Valenzuela	.50
35	Bob Welch	.25
40	Matt Young	.25
40	Rick Honeycutt	.25
41	Jerry Reuss	.25
43	Ken Howell	.25
44	Ken Landreaux	.25
47	Ralph Bryant	.25
47	Jose Gonzalez	.25
49	Tom Niedenfuer	.25
51	Brian Holton	.25
55	Orel Hershiser	.60
---	Coaching Staff (Joe Amalfitano, Mark Cresse, Tom Lasorda, Don McMahon, Manny Mota, Ron Perranoski, Bill Russell)	.25
---	Dodger Stadium/Checklist	.25

1988 L.A. Dodgers Fire Safety

STEVE SAX
L.A. Dodgers Record-Breakers
Dodgers

Record-breaking Dodgers from the past three decades are featured on this perforated sheet. Individual cards measure 2-1/2" x 4" and are printed on a light blue background in a design similar to the previous year's All-Star set. Black-and-white card backs contain the player name, a summary of the player's record-breaking performance and a reproduction of one of a number of Smokey Bear fire prevention posters printed during the 1950s-1980s. The sheets were distributed to fans in Dodger Stadium.

		NM/M
Complete Set, Foldout:		9.00
Complete Set, Singles (32):		7.50
Common Player:		.25
1	Walter Alston	.30
2	John Roseboro	.25
3	Frank Howard	.30
4	Sandy Koufax	5.00
5	Manny Mota	.25
6	Record Pitchers (Sandy Koufax, Jerry Reuss, Bill Singer)	.35
7	Maury Wills	.30
8	Tommy Davis	.25
9	Phil Regan	.25
10	Wes Parker	.25
11	Don Drysdale	1.50
12	Willie Davis	.25
13	Bill Russell	.25
14	Jim Brewer	.25
15	Record Fielders (Ron Cey, Steve Garvey, Davey Lopes, Bill Russell)	.25
16	Mike Marshall/Pitcher	.25
17	Steve Garvey	.75
18	Davey Lopes	.25
19	Burt Hooton	.25
20	Jim Wynn	.25
21	Record Hitters (Dusty Baker, Ron Cey, Steve Garvey, Reggie Smith)	.25
22	Dusty Baker	.30
23	Tom Lasorda	.40
24	Fernando Valenzuela	.25
25	Steve Sax	.25
26	Dodger Stadium	.25
27	Ron Cey	.25
28	Pedro Guerrero	.25
29	Mike Marshall/Outfielder	.25
30	Don Sutton	.75
---	Logo Card/Checklist	.10
---	Smokey Bear	.10

1988 L.A. Dodgers Police

DON SUTTON 20
Dodgers

The Los Angeles Police Department sponsored this 30-card set (2-3/4" x 4-1/8") for use in a local crime prevention promotion. The sets include an unnumbered manager/coaches photo and three double-photo cards. The double cards feature posed closeups; the rest are action photos. The card fronts have white borders, with the team logo lower right and a bold black player name lower left. Card backs are black and white with a small closeup photo of the player, followed by personal and career info, a crime prevention tip and a LAPD badge logo. Card numbers refer to players' uniform numbers (the double-photo cards carry two numbers on both front and back).

		NM/M
Complete Set (30):		6.00
Common Player:		.15
2	Tom Lasorda	.30
3	Steve Sax	.15
5	Mike Marshall	.15
7	Alfredo Griffin	.15
9	Mickey Hatcher	.15
10	Dave Anderson	.15
12	Danny Heep	.15
14	Mike Scioscia	.15
17/21	Tito Landrum, Len Matuszek	.15
20	Don Sutton	.60
22	Franklin Stubbs	.15
23	Kirk Gibson	.40
25	Mariano Duncan	.15
26	Alejandro Pena	.15
27/52	Tim Crews, Mike Sharperson	.15
28	Pedro Guerrero	.15
29	Alex Trevino	.15
31	John Shelby	.15

33	Jeff Hamilton	.15
34	Fernando Valenzuela	.50
37	Mike Davis	.15
41	Brad Havens	.15
43	Ken Howell	.15
47	Jesse Orosco	.15
49/57	Tim Belcher, Shawn Hillegas	.15
50	Jay Howell	.15
51	Brian Holton	.15
54	Tim Leary	.15
55	Orel Hershiser	.40
---	Manager/Coaches (Joe Amalfitano, Steve Boros, Mark Cresse, Joe Ferguson, Tom Lasorda, Manny Mota, Ron Perranoski, Bill Russell)	.15

1989 L.A. Dodgers Greats Fire Safety

The largest baseball card set ever issued in conjunction with the U.S. Forest Service's Smokey the Bear fire prevention campaign was this 104-card issue featuring great players of the Brooklyn and L.A. Dodgers. Issued on perforated sheets, individual cards measure 2-1/2" x 3-1/2". White-bordered fronts have a sepia-toned photo of the player, with Dodger blue rules on the top and sides. Beneath the photo is a baseball-and-banner logo, "A Century of Dodger Greats." The player's name is beneath the ball with Smokey at left and the team logo at right. Backs are printed in blue, feature career stats and highlights and include a Smokey fire safety cartoon.

		NM/M
Complete Set (104):		20.00
Common Player:		.10
1	Tommy Lasorda, Walter Alston, Burt Shotton	.50
2	David Bancroft	.10
3	Dan Brouthers	.10
4	Roy Campanella	2.00
5	Max Carey	.10
6	Hazen "Kiki" Cuyler	.10
7	Don Drysdale	1.00
8	Burleigh Grimes	.10
9	Billy Herman	.10
10	Waite Hoyt	.10
11	Hughie Jennings	.10
12	Willie Keeler	.10
13	Joseph Kelley	.10
14	George Kelly	.10
15	Sandy Koufax	3.00
16	Heinie Manush	.10
17	Juan Marichal	.75
18	Walter Maranville	.10
19	Rube Marquard	.10
20	Thomas McCarthy	.10
21	Joseph McGinnity	.10
22	Joe Medwick	.10
23	Pee Wee Reese	2.00
24	Frank Robinson	1.00
25	Jackie Robinson	3.50
26	Babe Ruth	4.00
27	Duke Snider	2.00
28	Casey Stengel	.25
29	Dazzy Vance	.10
30	Arky Vaughan	.10
31	Mike Scioscia	.10
32	Lloyd Waner, Paul Waner	.10
33	John Monte Ward	.10
34	Zack Wheat	.10
35	Hoyt Wilhelm	.10
36	Hack Wilson	.10
37	Tony Cuccinello	.10
38	Al Lopez	.10
39	Leo Durocher	.25
40	Cookie Lavagetto	.10
41	Babe Phelps	.10
42	Dolf Camilli	.10
43	Whit Wyatt	.10
44	Mickey Owen	.10
45	Van Mungo	.10
46	Pete Coscarart	.10
47	Pete Reiser	.10
48	Augie Galan	.10
49	Dixie Walker	.10
50	Kirby Higbe	.10
51	Ralph Branca	.10
52	Bruce Edwards	.10
53	Eddie Stanky	.10
54	Gil Hodges	1.50
55	Don Newcombe	.50
56	Preacher Roe	.25
57	Willie Randolph	.10
58	Carl Furillo	.50
59	Charles Dressen	.10
60	Carl Erskine	.25
61	Clem Labine	.15
62	Gino Cimoli	.10
63	Johnny Podres	.25
64	Johnny Roseboro	.10
65	Wally Moon	.10
66	Charlie Neal	.10
67	Norm Larker	.10
68	Stan Williams	.10
69	Maury Wills	.20
70	Tommy Davis	.15
71	Jim Lefebvre	.10
72	Phil Regan	.10
73	Claude Osteen	.10
74	Tom Haller	.10
75	Bill Singer	.10
76	Bill Grabarkewitz	.10
77	Willie Davis	.15
78	Don Sutton	.50
79	Jim Brewer	.10
80	Manny Mota	.15
81	Bill Russell	.10
82	Ron Cey	.15
83	Steve Garvey	.50
84	Mike G. Marshall	.10
85	Andy Messersmith	.10
86	Jimmy Wynn	.10
87	Rick Rhoden	.10
88	Reggie Smith	.15
89	Jay Howell	.10
90	Rick Monday	.10
91	Tommy John	.15
92	Bob Welch	.10
93	Dusty Baker	.20
94	Pedro Guerrero	.10
95	Burt Hooton	.10
96	Davey Lopes	.10
97	Fernando Valenzuela	.20
98	Steve Howe	.10
99	Steve Sax	.10
100	Orel Hershiser	.40
101	Mike A. Marshall	.10
102	Wilbert Robinson	.10
103	Fred Lindstrom	.10
104	Ernie Lombardi	.10

1989 L.A. Dodgers Police

The Los Angeles Dodgers and the L.A. Police Department teamed up in 1989 to produce a 30-card police set. The cards, which measure 4-1/4" x 2-5/8", feature color action photos with the player's name and uniform number below. The Dodgers logo and "1989" appear in the upper left. The backs include player information plus a safety message.

		NM/M
Complete Set (30):		3.00
Common Player:		.15
2	Tom Lasorda	.30
3	Jeff Hamilton	.15
7	Mike Marshall	.15
9	Alfredo Griffin	.15
10	Mickey Hatcher	.15
12	Dave Anderson	.15
14	Willie Randolph	.15
15	Mike Scioscia	.15
17	Rick Dempsey	.15
18	Mike Davis	.15
21	Tracy Woodson	.15
22	Franklin Stubbs	.15
23	Kirk Gibson	.30
25	Mariano Duncan	.15
26	Alejandro Pena	.15
27	Mike Sharperson	.15
29	Ricky Horton	.15
30	John Tudor	.15
31	John Shelby	.15
33	Eddie Murray	2.00
34	Fernando Valenzuela	.35
38	Mike Morgan	.15
48	Ramon Martinez	.35
50	Tim Belcher	.15
52	Jay Howell	.15
54	Tim Crews	.15
55	Tim Leary	.15
57	Orel Hershiser	.35
59	Ray Searage	.15
---	Dodger coaches (Joe Amalfitano, Mark Cresse, Joe Ferguson, Ben Hines, Tommy Lasorda, Manny Mota, Ron Perranoski, Bill Russell)	.15

1990 L.A. Dodgers Police

This set honors the centennial celebration of the Los Angeles Dodgers. A special 100 Anniversary logo appears on the card fronts. The cards measure 2-3/4" x 4-1/4" and feature full-color photos. The card backs are printed horizontally and contain a special safety tip or anti-drug message along with player information. The L.A.P.D. logo is featured on the bottom of the card back.

		NM/M
Complete Set (30):		3.00
Common Player:		.15
2	Tommy Lasorda	.30
3	Jeff Hamilton	.15
7	Alfredo Griffin	.15
9	Mickey Hatcher	.15
12	Juan Samuel	.15
14	Willie Randolph	.15
15	Mike Scioscia	.15
16	Chris Gwynn	.15
17	Rick Dempsey	.15
21	Hubie Brooks	.15
22	Franklin Stubbs	.15
23	Kirk Gibson	.25
26	Mike Sharperson	.15
28	Kal Daniels	.15
29	Lenny Harris	.15
31	John Shelby	.15
33	Eddie Murray	2.00
34	Fernando Valenzuela	.40
35	Jim Gott	.15
38	Mike Morgan	.15
39	Jose Gonzalez	.15
45	Mike Hartley	.15
48	Ramon Martinez	.15
49	Tim Belcher	.15
50	Jay Howell	.15
52	Tim Crews	.15
57	Orel Hershiser	.35
---	Dodgers coaches (Joe Amalfitano, Mark Cresse, Joe Ferguson, Ben Hines, Tommy Lasorda, Manny Mota, Ron Perranoski, Bill Russell)	.15

1991 L.A. Dodgers Police

One of the longest-running police/fire safety sets continued in 1991 with this 30-card set. Players are featured in color action photos set in a tombstone shape against a white background. The date is in a banner at top with the player name, team logo and uniform number at bottom. All typography is printed in Dodger blue. Backs are printed in black-and-white and include biographical data, an anti-drug message and an LAPD badge. Cards measure 2-13/16" x 4-1/8".

		NM/M
Complete Set (30):		4.00
Common Player:		.15
3	Jeff Hamilton	.15
5	Stan Javier	.15
10	Alfredo Griffin	.15
12	Juan Samuel	.15
14	Gary Carter	1.50
15	Mike Scioscia	.15
17	Chris Gwynn	.15
22	Bob Ojeda	.15
25	Brett Butler	.15
27	Mike Sharperson	.15
29	Kal Daniels	.15
30	Lenny Harris	.15
31	Jose Offerman	.15
32	Jim Neidlinger	.15
33	Eddie Murray	1.50
35	Jim Gott	.15
36	Mike Morgan	.15
38	Jose Gonzalez	.15
40	Barry Lyons	.15
44	Darryl Strawberry	.45
45	Kevin Gross	.15
46	Mike Hartley	.15
48	Ramon Martinez	.15
49	Tim Belcher	.15
50	Jay Howell	.15
52	Tim Crews	.15
54	John Candelaria	.15
55	Orel Hershiser	.35
---	Dodgers coaches (Ben Hines, Ron Perranoski, Mark Cresse, Manny Mota, Tommy Lasorda, Joe Amalfitano, Joe Ferguson, Bill Russell)	.15

1992 L.A. Dodgers Police

The 1992 Dodgers Police set consists of 30 cards numbered to correspond to the player's uniform number. The set includes a card of manager Tommy Lasorda and Dodgers coaches. They were given out at promotional dates at Dodger Stadium.

		NM/M
Complete Set (30):		4.00
Common Player:		.25
2	Tommy Lasorda	.35
3	Jeff Hamilton	.25
5	Stan Javier	.25
10	Juan Samuel	.25
14	Mike Scioscia	.25
15	Dave Hansen	.25
17	Bob Ojeda	.25
20	Mitch Webster	.25
22	Brett Butler	.25
23	Eric Karros	.50
27	Mike Sharperson	.25
28	Kal Daniels	.25
29	Lenny Harris	.25
30	Jose Offerman	.25
31	Roger McDowell	.25
33	Eric Davis	.25
35	Jim Gott	.25
36	Todd Benzinger	.25
38	Steve Wilson	.25
41	Carlos Hernandez	.25
44	Darryl Strawberry	.35
46	Kevin Gross	.25
48	Ramon Martinez	.25
49	Tom Candiotti	.25
50	Jay Howell	.25
52	Tim Crews	.25
54	John Candelaria	.25
55	Orel Hershiser	.40
57	Kip Gross	.25
---	Coaches (Joe Amalfitano, Mark Cresse, Joe Ferguson, Ben Hines, Tommy Lasorda, Manny Mota, Ron Perranoski, Ron Roenicke)	.25

1993 L.A. Dodgers Police

The 1993 Los Angeles Dodgers Police Set consisted of 29 cards, including cards of manager Tommy Lasorda and his coaches. The fronts of the cards have a photo surrounded by a blue border, with the Dodgers logo and the player's name on the bottom. The set is not numbered, but the player's uniform number does appear on the front of the cards.

		NM/M
Complete Set (29):		6.00
Common Player:		.25
2	Tommy Lasorda	.35
3	Jody Reed	.25
5	Dave Hansen	.25
12	Lance Parrish	.25
17	Roger McDowell	.25
20	Mitch Webster	.25
22	Brett Butler	.25
23	Eric Karros	.25
25	Tim Wallach	.25
26	Henry Rodriguez	.25
27	Mike Sharperson	.25
28	Cory Snyder	.25
29	Lenny Harris	.25
30	Jose Offerman	.25
31	Mike Piazza	3.00
33	Eric Davis	.25
35	Jim Gott	.25
38	Todd Worrell	.25
41	Carlos Hernandez	.25
45	Pedro Martinez	2.00
46	Kevin Gross	.25
47	Tom Goodwin	.25
48	Ramon Martinez	.25
49	Tom Candiotti	.25
50	Steve Wilson	.25
55	Orel Hershiser	.45
56	Pedro Astacio	.25
57	Kip Gross	.25
---	Coaches (Joe Amalfitano, Mark Cresse, Joe Ferguson, Ben Hines, Tommy Lasorda, Manny Mota, Ron Perranoski, Ron Roenicke)	.25

1994 L.A. Dodgers Police

This 30-card set was distributed to all fans attending the Dodgers May 27 home game. Cards were produced in the form of a perforated sheet. Fronts have mostly game-action photos surrounded by a Dodger-blue border. The player's uniform number is in red in a baseball in the upper-left corner. At bottom is the team logo and the player's name in black on a yellow strip. Backs are in black on white, have a few career and biographical notes and an anti-drug message from the L.A.P.D. and the D.A.R.E. program. When removed from the sheet, cards measure the standard 2-1/2" x 3-1/2". They are checklisted here by uniform number.

		NM/M
Uncut Sheet:		6.00
Complete Set (30):		5.00
Common Player:		.25
2	Tommy Lasorda	.35
5	Dave Hansen	.25
7	Billy Ashley	.25
10	Chris Gwynn	.25
12	Jeff Treadway	.25
14	Delino DeShields	.25
15	Tom Prince	.25
17	Roger McDowell	.25
20	Mitch Webster	.25
21	Rafael Bournigal	.25
22	Brett Butler	.25
23	Eric Karros	.25
26	Carlos Hernandez	.25
28	Cory Snyder	.25
29	Tim Wallach	.25
30	Jose Offerman	.25
31	Mike Piazza	2.50
33	Jim Gott	.25
37	Darren Dreifort	.25
38	Todd Worrell	.25
40	Henry Rodriguez	.25
43	Raul Mondesi	.50
46	Kevin Gross	.25
47	Garey Wayne	.25
48	Ramon Martinez	.25
49	Tom Candiotti	.25
55	Orel Hershiser	.35
56	Pedro Astacio	.25
61	Chan Ho Park	.75
---	Coaches (Mark Cresse, Manny Mota, Bill Russell, Reggie Smith, Joe Ferguson, Ron Perranoski, Tommy Lasorda, Joe Amalfitano)	.25

1995 L.A. Dodgers Limited Edition

This special high-tech set of Brooklyn/Los Angeles Dodgers rookie of the year winners between 1947-94 was given to Dodger season ticket purchasers prior to the strike-shortened 1995 baseball season. Produced in a technique similar to Topps Finest, the cards have on front metallic backgrounds in red, green, blue or purple. A color player action photo is featured. Faux granite strips at bottom have the player's name and year of his ROY award in gold. Backs have a color portrait photo in a gold frame with career stats and highlights and a few personal details. The primary front background color is repeated on the back. A header card printed in blue on white linen-texture paper accompanies the set.

		NM/M
Complete Set (14):		50.00
Common Player:		2.00
1	Jackie Robinson	15.00
2	Don Newcombe	4.00
3	Joe Black	4.00
4	Jim Gilliam	4.00
5	Frank Howard	2.00
6	Jim Lefebvre	2.00
7	Ted Sizemore	2.00
8	Rick Sutcliffe	3.00
9	Steve Howe	2.00
10	Fernando Valenzuela	5.00
11	Steve Sax	3.00
12	Eric Karros	3.00
13	Mike Piazza	15.00
14	Raul Mondesi	2.00
---	Header Card	.10

1995 L.A. Dodgers Police

BILLY ASHLEY

Action photos of the L.A. Dodgers are featured on this 30-card safety set which was given away to some 40,000 fans attending an early-season game. The set was produced as a perforated sheet measuring 14-13/16" x 17-1/2", with individual cards measuring 2-1/2" x 3-1/2". Fronts feature a Dodger-blue border with the player name in black in a yellow stripe at bottom. The player's uniform number is in red in a baseball in the upper-right. Backs are in black-and-white and have a few player biographical details along with an anti-drug safety message and the logos of the LAPD and D.A.R.E.

		NM/M
Uncut Sheet:		6.00
Complete Set (30):		6.00
Common Player:		.25
2	Tommy Lasorda	.35
3	Eddie Pye	.25
5	Dave Hansen	.25
7	Billy Ashley	.25
12	Jeff Treadway	.25
14	Delino DeShields	.25
16	Hideo Nomo	2.00
21	Rafael Bournigal	.25
23	Eric Karros	.25
25	Ron Coomer	.25
26	Carlos Hernandez	.25
28	Todd Hollandsworth	.25
29	Tim Wallach	.25
30	Jose Offerman	.25
31	Mike Piazza	2.00
38	Todd Worrell	.25
40	Henry Rodriguez	.25
43	Raul Mondesi	.35
45	Al Osuna	.25
48	Ramon Martinez	.25
49	Tom Candiotti	.25
50	Antonio Osuna	.25
52	Greg Hansell	.25
54	Omar Daal	.25
56	Pedro Astacio	.25
57	Rudy Seanez	.25
59	Ismael Valdes	.25
61	Chan Ho Park	.50
66	Todd Williams	.25
---	Coaches (Mark Cresse, Manny Mota, Bill Russell, Reggie Smith,	

Tommy Lasorda, Joe Amalfitano, Dave Wallace, Ralph Avila) .25

1996 L.A. Dodgers Police

BRETT BUTLER

For the 16th time in 17 years (they skipped 1985), the Dodgers issued a safety set to fans attending the April 11 game. As in recent years, the set was issued in the form of a perforated 30-card sheet. Each card measures just under 2-1/2" wide and is 3-1/2" tall; sheet dimensions are 14-7/8" x 17-1/2". Game-action photos are bordered in Dodger blue with the uniform number in red at upper-left. Backs are in black-and-white with a few vital stats and an anti-drug abuse, anti-gang message from D.A.R.E.

		NM/M
Uncut Sheet:		6.50
Complete Set (30):		6.00
Common Player:		.10
2	Tommy Lasorda	.25
3	Chad Fonville	.10
5	Dave Hansen	.10
7	Greg Gagne	.10
12	Karim Garcia	.25
13	Antonio Osuna	.10
14	Delino DeShields	.10
16	Hideo Nomo	2.00
20	Mike Blowers	.10
21	Billy Ashley	.10
22	Brett Butler	.10
23	Eric Karros	.10
25	Mike Busch	.10
26	Carlos Hernandez	.10
27	Roger Cedeno	.10
28	Todd Hollandsworth	.10
29	Milt Thompson	.10
31	Mike Piazza	2.00
33	Garey Ingram	.10
38	Todd Worrell	.10
41	John Cummings	.10
43	Raul Mondesi	.10
44	Mark Guthrie	.10
48	Ramon Martinez	.10
49	Tom Candiotti	.10
51	Joey Eischen	.10
53	Darren Hall	.10
56	Pedro Astacio	.10
59	Ismael Valdes	.10
---	Dodgers coaches (Joe Amalfitano, Mark Cresse, Tommy Lasorda, Manny Mota, Bill Russell, Reggie Smith, Dave Wallace)	.10

1996 L.A. Dodgers Rookies of the Year

This card was inserted into a die-cut space in the 1996 holiday greetings card sent out by the L.A. Dodgers.

In 2-1/2" x 3-1/2 format it features portrait photos of the 1992-96 National League Rookies of the Year - all Dodgers. Overall background of the front is green. Back has information on previous Dodgers ROYs and the rookie season stats of the 1992-96 winners.

	NM/M
Dodger Rookies of the Year: Eric Karros/1992 Mike Piazza/1993 Raul Mondesi/1994 Hideo Nomo/1995 Todd Hollandsworth/ 1996	15.00

1997 L.A. Dodgers Fan Appreciation Days

Fans attending the September 21 game were given this 11" x 8-1/2" sheet announcing a one-day sale of Dodgers souvenirs. At bottom are three differently styled cards of some of the team's most popular players. All are in color and standard 2-1/2" x 3-1/2" size, perforated for easy separation from the sheet. Card backs are in black-and-white with drawings of the players in the upper-left, biographical data and trivia. Cards are numbered by uniform number.

		NM/M
Complete Sheet:		6.00
Complete Set, Singles (3):		6.00
16	Hideo Nomo	3.00
31	Mike Piazza	4.00
61	Chan Ho Park	1.50

1997 L.A. Dodgers Police

ANTONIO OSUNA

Action photos of the 1997 Dodgers are featured on this set distributed at the April 23 game to nearly 30,500 fans. The 14-3/4" x 17-1/2" sheet has 30 cards, perforated on two, three or four sides, depending on position on the sheet. Individual cards measure 2-1/2" x 3-1/2". A central photo is surrounded with a white border. A ball with the player's uniform number in red is at top-left. At bottom is the team logo and player name. Backs are in black-and-white with biographical notes, an anti-drug message from each player and the logos of LAPD and DARE. Cards are checklisted here by uniform number.

		NM/M
Uncut Sheet:		7.00
Complete Set (30):		6.00
Common Player:		.20
3	Chad Fonville	.20
4	Chip Hale	.20
5	Greg Gagne	.20
12	Karim Garcia	.20

13	Anthony Osuna	.20
15	Tom Prince	.20
16	Hideo Nomo	1.50
18	Bill Russell	.20
21	Billy Ashley	.20
22	Brett Butler	.20
23	Eric Karros	.20
25	Juan Castro	.20
27	Todd Zeile	.20
28	Todd Hollandsworth	.20
29	Wilton Guerrero	.20
31	Mike Piazza	2.50
35	Wayne Kirby	.20
37	Scott Radinsky	.20
37	Darren Dreifort	.20
38	Todd Worrell	.20
43	Raul Mondesi	.20
44	Mark Guthrie	.20
46	Nelson Liriano	.20
48	Ramon Martinez	.20
52	Tom Candiotti	.20
52	Darren Hall	.20
56	Pedro Astacio	.20
59	Ismael Valdes	.20
61	Chan Ho Park	.20
---	Coaches (Joe Amalfitano, Mark Cresse, Manny Mota, Mike Scioscia, Reggie Smith, Dave Wallace)	.20

1998 L.A. Dodgers Fan Appreciation Days

Fans attending the Dodgers' final homestand were given this 11" x 8-1/2" sheet announcing a sale of Dodgers souvenirs. At bottom are three cards of some of the team's most popular players. All are in color and standard 2-1/2" x 3-1/2" size, perforated for easy separation from the sheet. Card backs are in black-and-white with personal data, a facsimile autograph and trivia. Cards are numbered by uniform number.

		NM/M
Complete Sheet:		6.00
Complete Set (3):		4.00
Common Player:		2.00
10	Gary Sheffield	2.50
23	Eric Karros	2.00
43	Raul Mondesi	2.00

1998 L.A. Dodgers Police

ISMAEL VALDES

Repeating the format used in recent years, a 30-card perforated sheet, the Dodgers issued their annual D.A.R.E. drug-awareness set in April. Individual cards are the standard 2-1/2" x 3-1/2" on the 15" x 17-1/2" sheet. Fronts have action photos with blue borders. A baseball at top-left has the player's uniform number, by which the set is checklisted here.

		NM/M
Uncut Sheet:		7.00
Complete Set (30):		6.00
Common Player:		.25
7	Paul Konerko	.50
10	Jose Vizcaino	.25

12	Mike Devereaux	.25
13	Antonio Osuna	.25
15	Tom Prince	.25
16	Hideo Nomo	2.00
18	Bill Russell	.25
22	Thomas Howard	.25
23	Eric Karros	.25
25	Juan Castro	.25
26	Eric Young	.25
27	Todd Zeile	.25
28	Todd Hollandsworth	.25
30	Wilton Guerrero	.25
31	Mike Piazza	3.00
36	Scott Radinsky	.25
37	Darren Dreifort	.25
40	Matt Luke	.25
41	Tripp Cromer	.25
43	Raul Mondesi	.25
44	Mark Guthrie	.25
46	Roger Cedeno	.25
46	Jim Bruske	.25
47	Trenidad Hubbard	.25
48	Ramon Martinez	.25
49	Frank Lankford	.25
52	Darren Hall	.25
59	Ismael Valdes	.25
61	Chan Ho Park	.25
---	Joe Amalfitano, Mark Cresse, Glenn Gregson, Manny Mota, Mike Scioscia, Reggie Smith	.25

1998 L.A. Dodgers Record Breakers

This set of motion cards was distributed one per month to members of the Dodgers Kids Clubhouse when they attended a game. The 3-1/2" x 2-1/2" cards have a borderless front with an action scene viewed by changing the angle of the card. The team logo appears in an upper corner. Backs repeat the logo and have personal data and details of the record performance. The cards are unnumbered. Distribution of the Nomo and Piazza cards was cut short when those players were traded in mid-season.

		NM/M
Complete Set (5):		17.50
Common Player:		2.00
(1)	Ramon Martinez	2.00
(2)	Raul Mondesi/Action	2.00
(3)	Raul Mondesi/Portrait (Membership card.)	2.00
(4)	Hideo Nomo	6.00
(5)	Mike Piazza	7.50

1999 L.A. Dodgers Concession Stand Cards

During the first five home games of the 1999 season, fans visiting the concession stands at Dodgers Stadium could receive a free player card. Fronts have color action photos on a white background with blue borders. The player's first name is printed at bottom, and a catchword at top. Backs are horizontal in black-and-white with a por-

trait photo career highlights and personal data, plus team and Dodger Stadium logos.

		NM/M
Complete Set (5):		4.00
Common Player:		1.00
1	Kevin Brown	1.50
2	Chan Ho Park	1.00
3	Ismael Valdes	1.00
4	Carlos Perez	1.00
5	Darren Dreifort	1.00

1999 L.A. Dodgers Fan Appreciation Days

Fans attending the Dodgers' final homestand were given this 11" x 8-1/2" sheet announcing special sales of Dodgers souvenirs. At bottom are three cards of some of the team's most popular players. All are in color and standard 2-1/2" x 3-1/2" size, perforated for easy separation from the sheet. The card fronts are in the style of 1953 Topps while backs are in black-and-white 1951-Bowman format with personal data, and a career summary.

		NM/M
Complete Sheet:		5.00
Complete Set (3):		4.00
1	Adrian Beltre	2.00
2	Kevin Brown	1.00
3	Eric Karros	1.00

1999 L.A. Dodgers Library Card

As part of a promotion to draw youngsters to the library to receive a free baseball bat, these sheets were given away at a promotional game at Dodger Stadium. The 8-1/2" x 4-3/4" sheet has a standard-size card perforated for easy removal. Front has an action photo. On back is another photo overprinted with stats.

		NM/M
(1)	Eric Karros	3.00

1999 L.A. Dodgers Police

PAUL LODUCA

Repeating the format used in recent years, a 30-card perforated sheet, the Dodgers issued their annual D.A.R.E. drug-awareness set in April. Individual cards are the standard 2-1/2" x 3-1/2" on the 15" x 17-1/2" sheet. Fronts have action photos with blue borders. A baseball at top-left has the player's uniform number, by which the set is checklisted here. Backs are in black-and-white with LAPD and D.A.R.E. logos, player data and a safety message.

		NM/M
Uncut Sheet:		7.00
Complete Set (30):		6.00
Common Player:		.25
5	Jose Vizcaino	.25
7	Tripp Cromer	.25
8	Mark Grudzielanek	.25
9	Todd Hundley	.25
10	Gary Sheffield	.75
13	Antonio Osuna	.25
14	Adam Riggs	.25
15	Davey Johnson	.25
16	Paul LoDuca	.75
17	Juan Castro	.25
21	Eric Young	.25
22	Devon White	.25
23	Eric Karros	.25
25	Dave Hansen	.25
27	Kevin Brown	.45
28	Todd Hollandsworth	.25
29	Adrian Beltre	2.00
33	Carlos Perez	.25
37	Darren Dreifort	.25
41	Jeff Shaw	.25
43	Raul Mondesi	.25
46	Rick Wilkins	.25
48	Jacob Brumfield	.25
50	Pedro Borbon	.25
55	Onan Masaoka	.25
59	Ismael Valdes	.25
61	Chan Ho Park	.20
63	Angel Pena	.25
75	Alan Mills	.25
	Coaches (Rick Dempsey, Rick Down, Glenn Hoffman, Charlie Hough, Manny Mota, John Shelby, Jim Tracy)	.25

2000 L.A. Dodgers Fan Appreciation Days

Shawn Green

Fans attending late-season Dodgers' games were given this 11" x 8-1/2" sheet announcing special sales of Dodgers souvenirs. At bottom are three cards of some of the team's most popular players. All are in color and standard 2-1/2" x 3-1/2" size, perforated for easy separation from the sheet. Card fronts have portrait and action photos with backs have 1/3 of a color team photo.

		NM/M
Complete Sheet:		5.00
Complete Set (3):		4.00
10	Gary Sheffield	1.00
15	Shawn Green	2.00
23	Eric Karros	1.00

2000 L.A. Dodgers Library Cards

As part of a promotion to draw youngsters to the library to receive a free baseball, this sheet was given away at a promotional game at Dodger Stadium. The 8-1/2" x 4-3/4" sheet has a standard-size card perforated for easy removal. Front has both

portrait and action photos. On back is another photo overprinted with stats.

		NM/M
Complete Set (2):		4.00
Common Player:		2.00
(1)	Kevin Brown	2.00
(2)	Gary Sheffield	2.00

2000 L.A. Dodgers Police

SHAWN GREEN

Repeating the format used in recent years, a 30-card 14-7/8" x 17-1/2" perforated sheet, the Dodgers issued their annual D.A.R.E. drug-awareness set in April. Individual cards are the standard 2-1/2" x 3-1/2". Fronts have game-action photos with blue borders. A baseball at top-left has the player's uniform number, by which the set is checklisted here. Backs are in black-and-white with LAPD and D.A.R.E. logos, player data and a safety message.

		NM/M
Uncut Sheet:		7.00
Complete Set (30):		6.00
Common Player:		.25
3	Alex Cora	.25
7	Jose Vizcaino	.25
8	Mark Grudzielanek	.25
9	Todd Hundley	.25
10	Gary Sheffield	.75
13	Antonio Osuna	.25
14	F.P. Santangelo	.25
15	Shawn Green	1.00
16	Paul LoDuca	.75
21	Chad Kreuter	.25
22	Devon White	.25
23	Eric Karros	.25
25	Dave Hansen	.25
27	Kevin Brown	.60
28	Todd Hollandsworth	.25
29	Adrian Beltre	1.00
30	Gregg Olson	.25
33	Carlos Perez	.25
36	Angel Pena	.25
37	Darren Dreifort	.25
40	Onan Masaoka	.25
41	Jeff Shaw	.25
43	Kevin Elster	.25
48	Eric Gagne	.75
51	Terry Adams	.25
55	Orel Hershiser	.50
56	Mike Fetters	.25
61	Chan Ho Park	.25
75	Alan Mills	.25
	Coaches (Rick Down, Glenn Hoffman, Davey Johnson, Manny Mota, Claude Osteen, John Shelby, Jim Tracy)	.25

2001 L.A. Dodgers Fan Appreciation Days

PAUL LODUCA

Fans attending late-season Dodgers' games were given this 8-1/2" x 11" tri-fold

sheet announcing special sales of Dodgers souvenirs. At bottom are three cards of some of the team's most popular players. All are in color and standard 2-1/2" x 3-1/2" size, perforated for easy separation from the sheet. Card fronts action photos set on an embossed steel design background. Backs have a color portrait photo along with 2000 and 2001 highlights and stats.

		NM/M
Complete Sheet:		4.00
Complete Set (3):		3.00
1	Paul LoDuca	1.50
2	Chan Ho Park	1.00
3	Gary Sheffield	1.00

2001 L.A. Dodgers Police

ANDY ASHBY

All fans attending the April 29 game at Dodger Stadium received the team's annual police-sponsored drug awareness safety set. The 30-card set was produced in the format of an 14-3/4" x 17-1/2" perforated sheet. Virtually identical in design to previous years' issues, there is no 2001 identifier on the cards. Fronts have game-action photos bordered in blue with the uniform number in a baseball at top-left. Black-and-white backs have some personal data, an anti-drug message and sponsors' logos.

		NM/M
Uncut Sheet:		9.00
Complete Set (30):		6.00
Common Player:		.25
3	Alex Cora	.25
8	Mark Grudzielanek	.25
9	Marquis Grissom	.25
10	Gary Sheffield	.75
14	Jeff Reboulet	.25
15	Shawn Green	1.00
16	Paul LoDuca	.75
18	Tim Bogar	.25
21	Chad Kreuter	.25
23	Eric Karros	.25
25	Dave Hansen	.25
27	Kevin Brown	.60
28	Tom Goodwin	.25
29	Adrian Beltre	1.00
30	Gregg Olson	.25
36	Angel Pena	.25
37	Darren Dreifort	.25
38	Eric Gagne	.50
40	Onan Masaoka	.25
41	Jeff Shaw	.25
43	Andy Ashby	.25
45	Jose Antonio Nunez	.25
46	Hiram Bocachica	.25
47	Bruce Aven	.25
49	Matt Herges	.25
50	Chris Donnels	.25
51	Terry Adams	.25
56	Mike Fetters	.25
61	Chan Ho Park	.25
	Coaches (Travis Barbary, Jack Clark, Jim Colborn, Glenn Hoffman, Jim Lett, Manny Mota, Jim Riggleman, John Shelby, Jim Tracy)	.25

2002 L.A. Dodgers Police

Once again in 2002, at the April 21 game, children 14 and under received the team's annual police-sponsored drug awareness safety set, produced in the format of a 14-7/8" x 17-1/2" perforated sheet. Vir-

KAZUHISA ISHII

tually identical in design to previous years' issues, there is no 2002 identifier on the cards. Fronts have game-action photos bordered in blue with the uniform number in a baseball at top-left. Black-and-white backs have some personal data, an anti-drug message and sponsors' logos.

		NM/M
Uncut Sheet:		10.00
Complete Set (30):		8.00
Common Player:		.25
3	Cesar Izturis	.25
7	Jeff Branson	.25
8	Mark Grudzielanek	.25
9	Marquis Grissom	.25
10	Hideo Nomo	1.50
13	Alex Cora	.25
14	Jeff Reboulet	.25
15	Shawn Green	1.00
16	Paul LoDuca	.75
17	Kazuhisa Ishii	1.50
21	Chad Kreuter	.25
23	Eric Karros	.25
25	Dave Hansen	.25
26	Hiram Bocachica	.25
27	Kevin Brown	.60
29	Adrian Beltre	1.00
30	Dave Roberts	.35
33	Brian Jordan	.25
36	Omar Daal	.25
37	Darren Dreifort	.25
38	Eric Gagne	.60
43	Odalis Perez	.25
43	Andy Ashby	.25
44	Phil Hiatt	.25
45	Terry Mulholland	.25
46	Paul Quantrill	.25
47	Jesse Orosco	.25
55	Giovanni Carrara	.25
74	Mike Kinkade	.35
---	Manager & Coaches (Jack Clark, Jim Colborn, Rob Flippo, Glenn Hoffman, Jim Lett, Manny Mota, Jim Riggleman, John Shelby, Jim Tracy)	.25

2003 L.A. Dodgers Fan Appreciation Days

GAME OVER

Fans attending late-season Dodgers' games were given this 8-1/2" x 11" tri-fold sheet announcing special sales of Dodgers souvenirs. At bottom are three cards of some of the team's most popular players. All are in color and standard 2-1/2" x 3-1/2" size, perforated for easy separation from the sheet. Card fronts action photos and player-themed pennants. Black-and-white backs have another photo along with personal data and highlights.

		NM/M
Complete Sheet:		6.00

2003 L.A. Dodgers Police

		NM/M
Complete Set (3):		5.00
10	Hideo Nomo	2.50
16	Paul Lo Duca	1.50
38	Eric Gagne	1.50

MIKE KINKADE

At the April 20 game, children 14 and under received the team's annual police-sponsored drug awareness safety set, produced in the format of a 14-3/4" x 17-3/4" perforated sheet. Virtually identical in design to previous years' issues, there is no 2002 identifier on the cards. Fronts have game-action photos bordered in blue with the uniform number in a baseball at top-left. Black-and-white backs have some personal data, an anti-drug message and sponsors' logos.

		NM/M
Uncut Sheet:		10.00
Complete Set (30):		9.00
Common Player:		.25
3	Cesar Izturis	.25
6	Jolbert Cabrera	.25
7	Mike Kinkade	.35
8	Ron Coomer	.25
9	Todd Hundley	.25
10	Hideo Nomo	1.50
13	Alex Cora	.25
15	Shawn Green	1.00
16	Paul LoDuca	.50
17	Kazuhisa Ishii	1.00
26	Wilkin Ruan	.25
27	Kevin Brown	.45
28	Fred McGriff	.25
29	Adrian Beltre	1.00
30	Dave Roberts	.25
33	Brian Jordan	.25
36	Daryle Ward	.25
37	Darren Dreifort	.25
38	Eric Gagne	.60
40	David Ross	.25
43	Chad Hermansen	.25
43	Andy Ashby	.25
44	Paul Shuey	.25
45	Odalis Perez	.25
46	Paul Quantrill	.25
52	Chin-Feng Chen	.75
54	Troy Brohawn	.25
57	Victor Alvarez	.25
59	Guillermo Mota	.25
---	Manager & Coaches (Jack Clark, Jim Colborn, Rob Flippo, Glenn Hoffman, Jim Lett, Manny Mota, Jim Riggleman, John Shelby, Jim Tracy)	.25

2005 L.A./Brooklyn Dodgers Medallion Collection

A set of 21 commemorative medallions was sponsored by the Los Angeles Newspaper Group in this promotion. Coupons found in the newspapers between June 6-

29 could be redeemed at convenience stores (along with $2.99) for that day's medallion. Larger and thicker than a quarter, the 1-3/16" diameter medals are struck in bronze (Brooklyn players) or nickel (current players) and have on their fronts an enameled portrait photo. A team logo dominates the back. A colorful, photo-filled album was available to house the pieces. The medals are listed here alphabetically.

		NM/M
Complete Set (21):		75.00
Common Player:		3.00
	Album:	3.00
(1)	Wilson Alvarez	3.00
(2)	Milton Bradley	3.00
(3)	Yhency Brazoban	3.00
(4)	Roy Campanella	6.00
(5)	Hee Seop Choi	3.50
(6)	J.D. Drew	3.50
(7)	Eric Gagne	4.50
(8)	Cesar Izturis	3.00
(9)	Jeff Kent	4.50
(10)	Tommy Lasorda	3.00
(11)	Derek Lowe	3.00
(12)	Don Newcombe	3.00
(13)	Brad Penny	3.00
(14)	Odalis Perez	3.00
(15)	Jason Phillips	3.00
(16)	Jackie Robinson	10.00
(17)	Duke Snider	6.00
(18)	Jose Valentin	3.00
(19)	Jeff Weaver	3.00
(20)	Jayson Werth	3.00
(21)	50th Anniversary 1955 World Champions	3.00

1997 LaSalle Bank Ryne Sandberg

RYNE SANDBERG #23
FOR 15 YEARS, A CLASSIC CUB

This card was part of a souvenir tribute distributed to more than 30,000 persons attending Ryne Sandberg's final game at Wrigley Field on September 20. A commemorative program and this card marked Ryno's 15 years as a Chicago Cub. The 2-1/2" x 3-1/2" card is printed on heavy, UV-coated cardboard. The front features a borderless color action photo. On the full-color back are portrait and action photos, career highlights and stats through September 14.

	NM/M
Ryne Sandberg	7.50

1985 Leaf-Donruss

KENT HRBEK

In an attempt to share in the Canadian baseball card market, Donruss issued a 264-card version of its regular set to be sold in Canada. Fronts of the 2-1/2" x 3-1/2" cards are virtually identical to the regular '85 Donruss cards of the same players, except that a green stylized leaf has been added to the logo in the upper-left. On back, player biographies have been re-written to accomodate both English and French versions, and new card numbers have been assigned. The 264 cards in this shortened set concentrate on star-caliber players, as well as those of Canada's two major league teams. A special two-card subset, "Canadian Greats," featured paintings of Dave Stieb and Tim Raines. The Leaf-Donruss cards were widely distributed in the U.S. through hobby dealers.

		NM/M
Complete Set (264):		35.00
Common Player:		.05
Wax Pack (12):		2.50
Wax Box (36):		75.00
1	Ryne Sandberg/DK	1.25
2	Doug DeCinces/DK	.05
3	Rich Dotson/DK	.05
4	Bert Blyleven/DK	.05
5	Lou Whitaker/DK	.05
6	Dan Quisenberry/DK	.05
7	Don Mattingly/DK	2.00
8	Carney Lansford/DK	.05
9	Frank Tanana/DK	.05
10	Willie Upshaw/DK	.05
11	Claudell Washington/DK	.05
12	Mike Marshall/DK	.05
13	Joaquin Andujar/DK	.05
14	Cal Ripken, Jr./DK	5.00
15	Jim Rice/DK	.25
16	Don Sutton/DK	.60
17	Frank Viola/DK	.05
18	Alvin Davis/DK	.05
19	Mario Soto/DK	.05
20	Jose Cruz/DK	.05
21	Charlie Lea/DK	.05
22	Jesse Orosco/DK	.05
23	Juan Samuel/DK	.05
24	Tony Pena/DK	.05
25	Tony Gwynn/DK	1.25
26	Bob Brenly/DK	.05
27	Steve Kiefer/RR	.05
28	Joe Morgan	.60
29	Luis Leal	.05
30	Dan Gladden	.05
31	Shane Rawley	.05
32	Mark Clear	.05
33	Terry Kennedy	.05
34	Hal McRae	.05
35	Mickey Rivers	.05
36	Tom Brunansky	.05
37	LaMarr Hoyt	.05
38	Orel Hershiser	1.00
39	Chris Bando	.05
40	Lee Lacy	.05
41	Lance Parrish	.05
42	George Foster	.05
43	Kevin McReynolds	.05
44	Robin Yount	.60
45	Craig McMurtry	.05
46	Mike Witt	.05
47	Gary Redus	.05
48	Dennis Rasmussen	.05
49	Gary Woods	.05
50	Phil Bradley	.05
51	Steve Bedrosian	.05
52	Duane Walker	.05
53	Geoff Zahn	.05
54	Dave Stieb	.05
55	Pascual Perez	.05
56	Mark Langston	.25
57	Bob Dernier	.05
58	Joe Cowley	.05
59	Dan Schatzeder	.05
60	Ozzie Smith	1.25
61	Bob Knepper	.05
62	Keith Hernandez	.05
63	Rick Rhoden	.05
64	Alejandro Pena	.05
65	Damaso Garcia	.05
66	Chili Davis	.05
67	Al Oliver	.05
68	Alan Wiggins	.05
69	Darryl Motley	.05
70	Gary Ward	.05
71	John Butcher	.05
72	Scott McGregor	.05
73	Bruce Hurst	.05
74	Dwayne Murphy	.05
75	Greg Luzinski	.05
76	Pat Tabler	.05
77	Chet Lemon	.05
78	Jim Sundberg	.05
79	Wally Backman	.05
80	Terry Puhl	.05
81	Storm Davis	.05
82	Jim Wohlford	.05
83	Willie Randolph	.05
84	Ron Cey	.05
85	Jim Beattie	.05
86	Rafael Ramirez	.05

87	Cesar Cedeno	.05
88	Bobby Grich	.05
89	Jason Thompson	.05
90	Steve Sax	.05
91	Tony Fernandez	.15
92	Jeff Leonard	.05
93	Von Hayes	.05
94	Steve Garvey	.30
95	Steve Balboni	.05
96	Larry Parrish	.05
97	Tim Teufel	.05
98	Sammy Stewart	.05
99	Roger Clemens	30.00
100	Steve Kemp	.05
101	Tom Seaver	1.00
102	Andre Thornton	.05
103	Kirk Gibson	.05
104	Ted Simmons	.05
105	David Palmer	.05
106	Roy Lee Jackson	.05
107	Kirby Puckett	4.00
108	Charlie Hough	.05
109	Mike Boddicker	.05
110	Willie Wilson	.05
111	Tim Lollar	.05
112	Tony Armas	.05
113	Steve Carlton	.60
114	Gary Lavelle	.05
115	Cliff Johnson	.05
116	Ray Burris	.05
117	Rudy Law	.05
118	Mike Scioscia	.05
119	Kent Tekulve	.05
120	George Vukovich	.05
121	Barbaro Garbey	.05
122	Mookie Wilson	.05
123	Ben Oglivie	.05
124	Jerry Mumphrey	.05
125	Willie McGee	.05
126	Jeff Reardon	.05
127	Dave Winfield	1.00
128	Lee Smith	.10
129	Ken Phelps	.05
130	Rick Camp	.05
131	Dave Concepcion	.05
132	Rod Carew	.60
133	Andre Dawson	.25
134	Doyle Alexander	.05
135	Miguel Dilone	.05
136	Jim Gott	.05
137	Eric Show	.05
138	Phil Niekro	.45
139	Rick Sutcliffe	.05
140	Two For The Title (Don Mattingly, Dave Winfield)	3.00
141	Ken Oberkfell	.05
142	Jack Morris	.05
143	Lloyd Moseby	.05
144	Pete Rose	2.00
145	Gary Gaetti	.05
146	Don Baylor	.05
147	Bobby Meacham	.05
148	Frank White	.05
149	Mark Thurmond	.05
150	Dwight Evans	.05
151	Al Holland	.05
152	Joel Youngblood	.05
153	Rance Mulliniks	.05
154	Bill Caudill	.05
155	Carlton Fisk	.60
156	Rick Honeycutt	.05
157	John Candelaria	.05
158	Alan Trammell	.05
159	Darryl Strawberry	.05
160	Aurelio Lopez	.05
161	Enos Cabell	.05
162	Dion James	.05
163	Bruce Sutter	.75
164	Razor Shines	.05
165	Butch Wynegar	.05
166	Rich Bordi	.05
167	Spike Owen	.05
168	Chris Chambliss	.05
169	Dave Parker	.05
170	Reggie Jackson	1.00
171	Bryn Smith	.05
172	Dave Collins	.05
173	Dave Engle	.05
174	Buddy Bell	.05
175	Mike Flanagan	.05
176	George Brett	1.50
177	Graig Nettles	.05
178	Jerry Koosman	.05
179	Wade Boggs	1.25
180	Jody Davis	.05
181	Ernie Whitt	.05
182	Dave Kingman	.05
183	Vance Law	.05
184	Fernando Valenzuela	.05
185	Bill Madlock	.05
186	Brett Butler	.05
187	Doug Sisk	.05
188	Dan Petry	.05
189	Joe Niekro	.05
190	Rollie Fingers	.45
191	David Green	.05
192	Steve Rogers	.05
193	Ken Griffey	.05
194	Scott Sanderson	.05

195	Barry Bonnell	.05
196	Bruce Benedict	.05
197	Keith Moreland	.05
198	Fred Lynn	.05
199	Tim Wallach	.20
200	Kent Hrbek	.05
201	Pete O'Brien	.05
202	Bud Black	.05
203	Eddie Murray	.60
204	Goose Gossage	.05
205	Mike Schmidt	1.50
206	Mike Easler	.05
207	Jack Clark	.05
208	Rickey Henderson	1.00
209	Jesse Barfield	.15
210	Ron Kittle	.05
211	Pedro Guerrero	.05
212	Johnny Ray	.05
213	Julio Franco	.05
214	Hubie Brooks	.05
215	Darrell Evans	.05
216	Nolan Ryan	5.00
217	Jim Gantner	.05
218	Tim Raines	.20
219	Dave Righetti	.05
220	Gary Matthews	.05
221	Jack Perconte	.05
222	Dale Murphy	.30
223	Brian Downing	.05
224	Mickey Hatcher	.05
225	Lonnie Smith	.05
226	Jorge Orta	.05
227	Milt Wilcox	.05
228	John Denny	.05
229	Marty Barrett	.05
230	Alfredo Griffin	.05
231	Harold Baines	.05
232	Bill Russell	.05
233	Marvell Wynne	.05
234	Dwight Gooden	.50
235	Willie Hernandez	.05
236	Bill Gullickson	.05
237	Ron Guidry	.05
238	Leon Durham	.05
239	Al Cowens	.05
240	Bob Horner	.05
241	Gary Carter	1.00
242	Glenn Hubbard	.05
243	Steve Trout	.05
244	Jay Howell	.05
245	Terry Francona	.05
246	Cecil Cooper	.05
247	Larry McWilliams	.05
248	George Bell	.15
249	Larry Herndon	.05
250	Ozzie Virgil	.05
251	Dave Stieb (Canadian Great)	.50
252	Tim Raines (Canadian Great)	2.00
253	Ricky Horton	.05
254	Bill Buckner	.05
255	Dan Driessen	.05
256	Ron Darling	.05
257	Doug Flynn	.05
258	Darrell Porter	.05
259	George Hendrick	.05
653	Lou Gehrig Puzzle Card	.05
----	Checklist 1-26 DK	.05
----	Checklist 27-102	.05
----	Checklist 103-178	.05
----	Checklist 179-259	.05

1986 Leaf

For its second Canadian card set the Donruss name was removed from the front of the company's 264-card issue, identifying the cards as "Leaf '86." Again concentrating on big-name stars and players from the Expos and Blue Jays, the 2-1/2" x 3-1/2" cards feature a design identical to the 1986 Donruss cards. Backs were altered to allow the publication of career highlights in both English and French, and card numbers were changed. The "Canadian Greats" cards in the 1986 Leaf set, painted portraits rather than photos, were Jesse Barfield and Jeff Reardon. Be-

sides being sold in its intended market in Canada, the set was widely distributed in the U.S. through hobby vendors.

		NM/M
Complete Set (264):		12.00
Common Player:		.05
Wax Pack:		1.00
Wax Box (36):		20.00
1	Kirk Gibson/DK	.05
2	Goose Gossage/DK	.05
3	Willie McGee/DK	.05
4	George Bell/DK	.10
5	Tony Armas/DK	.05
6	Chili Davis/DK	.05
7	Cecil Cooper/DK	.05
8	Mike Boddicker/DK	.05
9	Davey Lopes/DK	.05
10	Bill Doran/DK	.05
11	Bret Saberhagen/DK	.05
12	Brett Butler/DK	.05
13	Harold Baines/DK	.05
14	Mike Davis/DK	.05
15	Tony Perez/DK	.35
16	Willie Randolph/DK	.05
17	Bob Boone/DK	.05
18	Orel Hershiser/DK	.05
19	Johnny Ray/DK	.05
20	Gary Ward/DK	.05
21	Rick Mahler/DK	.05
22	Phil Bradley/DK	.05
23	Jerry Koosman/DK	.05
24	Tom Brunansky/DK	.05
25	Andre Dawson/DK	.35
26	Dwight Gooden/DK	.05
27	Andres Galarraga/RR	2.00
28	Fred McGriff/RR	4.00
29	Dave Shipanoff/RR	.05
30	Danny Jackson	.05
31	Robin Yount	.50
32	Mike Fitzgerald	.05
33	Lou Whitaker	.05
34	Alfredo Griffin	.05
35	"Oil Can" Boyd	.05
36	Ron Guidry	.05
37	Rickey Henderson	.75
38	Jack Morris	.05
39	Brian Downing	.05
40	Mike Marshall	.05
41	Tony Gwynn	1.00
42	George Brett	1.25
43	Jim Gantner	.05
44	Hubie Brooks	.05
45	Tony Fernandez	.10
46	Oddibe McDowell	.05
47	Ozzie Smith	1.00
48	Ken Griffey	.05
49	Jose Cruz	.05
50	Mariano Duncan	.05
51	Mike Schmidt	1.25
52	Pat Tabler	.05
53	Pete Rose	1.50
54	Frank White	.05
55	Carney Lansford	.05
56	Steve Garvey	.15
57	Vance Law	.05
58	Tony Pena	.05
59	Wayne Tolleson	.05
60	Dale Murphy	.20
61	LaMarr Hoyt	.05
62	Ryne Sandberg	1.00
63	Gary Carter	1.00
64	Lee Smith	.05
65	Alvin Davis	.05
66	Edwin Nunez	.05
67	Kent Hrbek	.05
68	Dave Stieb	.05
69	Kirby Puckett	1.00
70	Paul Molitor	.75
71	Glenn Hubbard	.05
72	Lloyd Moseby	.05
73	Mike Smithson	.05
74	Jeff Leonard	.05
75	Danny Darwin	.05
76	Kevin McReynolds	.05
77	Bill Buckner	.05
78	Ron Oester	.05
79	Tommy Herr	.05
80	Mike Pagliarulo	.05
81	Ron Romanick	.05
82	Brook Jacoby	.05
83	Eddie Murray	.50
84	Gary Pettis	.05
85	Chet Lemon	.05
86	Toby Harrah	.05
87	Mike Scioscia	.05
88	Bert Blyleven	.05
89	Dave Righetti	.05
90	Bob Knepper	.05
91	Fernando Valenzuela	.05
92	Dave Dravecky	.05
93	Julio Franco	.05
94	Keith Moreland	.05
95	Darryl Motley	.05
96	Jack Clark	.05
97	Tim Wallach	.05
98	Steve Balboni	.05
99	Storm Davis	.05
100	Jay Howell	.05
101	Alan Trammell	.05
102	Willie Hernandez	.05
103	Don Mattingly	1.25
104	Lee Lacy	.05
105	Pedro Guerrero	.05
106	Willie Wilson	.05
107	Craig Reynolds	.05

108	Tim Raines	.15
109	Shane Rawley	.05
110	Larry Parrish	.05
111	Eric Show	.05
112	Mike Witt	.05
113	Dennis Eckersley	.35
114	Mike Moore	.05
115	Vince Coleman	.05
116	Damaso Garcia	.05
117	Steve Carlton	.50
118	Floyd Bannister	.05
119	Mario Soto	.05
120	Fred Lynn	.05
121	Bob Horner	.05
122	Rick Sutcliffe	.05
123	Walt Terrell	.05
124	Keith Hernandez	.05
125	Dave Winfield	.75
126	Frank Viola	.05
127	Dwight Evans	.05
128	Willie Upshaw	.05
129	Andre Thornton	.05
130	Donnie Moore	.05
131	Darryl Strawberry	.05
132	Nolan Ryan	2.00
133	Garry Templeton	.05
134	John Tudor	.05
135	Dave Parker	.05
136	Larry McWilliams	.05
137	Terry Pendleton	.05
138	Terry Puhl	.05
139	Bob Dernier	.05
140	Ozzie Guillen	.05
141	Jim Clancy	.05
142	Cal Ripken, Jr.	2.00
143	Mickey Hatcher	.05
144	Dan Petry	.05
145	Rich Gedman	.05
146	Jim Rice	.10
147	Butch Wynegar	.05
148	Donnie Hill	.05
149	Jim Sundberg	.05
150	Joe Hesketh	.05
151	Chris Codiroli	.05
152	Charlie Hough	.05
153	Herman Winningham	.05
154	Dave Rozema	.05
155	Don Slaught	.05
156	Juan Beniquez	.05
157	Ted Higuera	.05
158	Andy Hawkins	.05
159	Don Robinson	.05
160	Glenn Wilson	.05
161	Earnest Riles	.05
162	Nick Esasky	.05
163	Carlton Fisk	.50
164	Claudell Washington	.05
165	Scott McGregor	.05
166	Nate Snell	.05
167	Ted Simmons	.05
168	Wade Boggs	1.00
169	Marty Barrett	.05
170	Bud Black	.05
171	Charlie Leibrandt	.05
172	Charlie Lea	.05
173	Reggie Jackson	.50
174	Bryn Smith	.05
175	Glenn Davis	.05
176	Von Hayes	.05
177	Danny Cox	.05
178	Sam Khalifa	.05
179	Tom Browning	.05
180	Scott Garrelts	.05
181	Shawon Dunston	.05
182	Doyle Alexander	.05
183	Jim Presley	.05
184	Al Cowens	.05
185	Mark Salas	.05
186	Tom Niedenfuer	.05
187	Dave Henderson	.05
188	Lonnie Smith	.05
189	Bruce Bochte	.05
190	Leon Durham	.05
191	Terry Francona	.05
192	Bruce Sutter	.75
193	Steve Crawford	.05
194	Bob Brenly	.05
195	Dan Pasqua	.05
196	Juan Samuel	.05
197	Floyd Rayford	.05
198	Tim Burke	.05
199	Ben Oglivie	.05
200	Don Carman	.05
201	Lance Parrish	.05
202	Terry Forster	.05
203	Neal Heaton	.05
204	Ivan Calderon	.05
205	Jorge Orta	.05
206	Tom Henke	.05
207	Rick Reuschel	.05
208	Dan Quisenberry	.05
209	Ty-Breaking Hit (Pete Rose)	.25
210	Floyd Youmans	.05
211	Tom Filer	.05
212	R.J. Reynolds	.05
213	Gorman Thomas	.05
214	Canadian Great Jeff Reardon (Canadian Great)	.45
215	Chris Brown	.05
216	Rick Aguilera	.05
217	Ernie Whitt	.05
218	Joe Orsulak	.05
219	Jimmy Key	.05
220	Atlee Hammaker	.05
221	Ron Darling	.05
222	Zane Smith	.05

223	Bob Welch	.05
224	Reid Nichols	.05
225	Fleet Feet (Vince Coleman, Willie McGee)	.10
226	Mark Gubicza	.05
227	Tim Birtsas	.05
228	Mike Hargrove	.05
229	Randy St. Claire	.05
230	Larry Herndon	.05
231	Dusty Baker	.05
232	Mookie Wilson	.05
233	Jeff Lahti	.05
234	Tom Seaver	.50
235	Mike Scott	.05
236	Don Sutton	.35
237	Roy Smalley	.05
238	Bill Madlock	.05
239	Charles Hudson	.05
240	John Franco	.05
241	Frank Tanana	.05
242	Sid Fernandez	.05
243	Knuckle Brothers (Joe Niekro, Phil Niekro)	.10
244	Dennis Lamp	.05
245	Gene Nelson	.05
246	Terry Harper	.05
247	Vida Blue	.05
248	Roger McDowell	.05
249	Tony Bernazard	.05
250	Cliff Johnson	.05
251	Hal McRae	.05
252	Garth Iorg	.05
253	Mitch Webster	.05
254	Jesse Barfield (Canadian Great)	.35
255	Dan Driessen	.05
256	Mike Brown	.05
257	Ron Kittle	.05
258	Bo Diaz	.05
259	Hank Aaron Puzzle Card	.05
260	Pete Rose (King of Kings)	1.50
----	Checklist 1-26 DK	.05
----	Checklist 27-106	.05
----	Checklist 107-186	.05
----	Checklist 187-260	.05

1987 Leaf

For the third consecutive season, Leaf-Donruss issued a Canadian baseball card set. These cards are nearly identical to the American set except for the name "Leaf" which appears on the front in place of "Donruss." The set contains 264 cards, each measuring 2-1/2" x 3-1/2", with a special emphasis being placed on players from the Montreal and Toronto teams. Backs feature career highlights in both English and French. As in the previous years, two "Canadian Greats" cards appear in the set. These painted portraits feature Mark Eichhorn and Floyd Youmans.

		NM/M
Unopened Factory Set (264):		25.00
Complete Set (264):		17.50
Common Player:		.05
Wax Pack:		1.50
Wax Box (36):		30.00
1	Wally Joyner/DK	.05
2	Roger Clemens/DK	1.00
3	Dale Murphy/DK	.15
4	Darryl Strawberry/DK	.35
5	Ozzie Smith/DK	.65
6	Jose Canseco/DK	.40
7	Charlie Hough/DK	.05
8	Brook Jacoby/DK	.05
9	Fred Lynn/DK	.05
10	Rick Rhoden/DK	.05
11	Chris Brown/DK	.05
12	Von Hayes/DK	.05
13	Jack Morris/DK	.10
14	Kevin McReynolds/DK	.05
15	George Brett/DK	.75
16	Ted Higuera/DK	.05
17	Hubie Brooks/DK	.05
18	Mike Scott/DK	.05
19	Kirby Puckett/DK	.65
20	Dave Winfield/DK	.75

ABBREVIATIONS

DK - Diamond King
RR - Rated Rookie

21	Lloyd Moseby/DK	.10
22	Eric Davis/DK	.05
23	Jim Presley/DK	.05
24	Keith Moreland/DK	.05
25	Greg Walker/DK	.05
26	Steve Sax/DK	.05
27	Checklist 1-27	.05
28	B.J. Surhoff/RR	.05
29	Randy Myers/RR	.05
30	Ken Gerhart/RR	.05
31	Benito Santiago/RR	.05
32	Greg Swindell/RR	.05
33	Mike Birkbeck/RR	.05
34	Terry Steinbach/RR	.05
35	Bo Jackson/RR	.25
36	Greg Maddux/RR	2.00
37	Jim Lindeman/RR	.05
38	Devon White/RR	.75
39	Eric Bell/RR	.05
40	Will Fraser/RR	.05
41	Jerry Browne/RR	.05
42	Chris James/RR	.05
43	Rafael Palmeiro/RR	1.00
44	Pat Dodson/RR	.05
45	Duane Ward/RR	.25
46	Mark McGwire/RR	4.00
47	Bruce Fields/RR (Photo actually Darnell Coles)	.05
48	Jody Davis	.05
49	Roger McDowell	.05
50	Jose Guzman	.05
51	Oddibe McDowell	.05
52	Harold Baines	.05
53	Dave Righetti	.05
54	Moose Haas	.05
55	Mark Langston	.05
56	Kirby Puckett	.65
57	Dwight Evans	.05
58	Willie Randolph	.05
59	Wally Backman	.05
60	Bryn Smith	.05
61	Tim Wallach	.05
62	Joe Hesketh	.05
63	Garry Templeton	.05
64	Rob Thompson	.05
65	Canadian Greats (Floyd Youmans)	.10
66	Ernest Riles	.05
67	Robin Yount	.50
68	Darryl Strawberry	.05
69	Ernie Whitt	.05
70	Dave Winfield	.65
71	Paul Molitor	.75
72	Dave Stieb	.05
73	Tom Henke	.05
74	Frank Viola	.05
75	Scott Garrelts	.05
76	Mike Boddicker	.05
77	Keith Moreland	.05
78	Lou Whitaker	.05
79	Dave Parker	.05
80	Lee Smith	.05
81	Tom Candiotti	.05
82	Greg Harris	.05
83	Fred Lynn	.05
84	Dwight Gooden	.05
85	Ron Darling	.05
86	Mike Krukow	.05
87	Spike Owen	.05
88	Len Dykstra	.05
89	Rick Aguilera	.05
90	Jim Clancy	.05
91	Joe Johnson	.05
92	Damaso Garcia	.05
93	Sid Fernandez	.05
94	Bob Ojeda	.05
95	Ted Higuera	.05
96	George Brett	.75
97	Willie Wilson	.05
98	Cal Ripken	1.50
99	Kent Hrbek	.05
100	Bert Blyleven	.05
101	Ron Guidry	.05
102	Andy Allanson	.05
103	Dave Henderson	.05
104	Kirk Gibson	.05
105	Lloyd Moseby	.05
106	Tony Fernandez	.05
107	Lance Parrish	.05
108	Ozzie Smith	.75
109	Gary Carter	.75
110	Eddie Murray	.50
111	Mike Witt	.05
112	Bobby Witt	.05
113	Willie McGee	.05
114	Steve Garvey	.10
115	Glenn Davis	.05
116	Jose Cruz	.05
117	Ozzie Guillen	.05
118	Alvin Davis	.05
119	Jose Rijo	.05
120	Bill Madlock	.05
121	Tommy Herr	.05
122	Mike Schmidt	.75
123	Mike Scioscia	.05
124	Terry Pendleton	.05
125	Leon Durham	.05
126	Alan Trammell	.05
127	Jesse Barfield	.05
128	Shawon Dunston	.05
129	Pete Rose	1.25
130	Von Hayes	.05
131	Julio Franco	.05
132	Juan Samuel	.05
133	Joe Carter	.10
134	Brook Jacoby	.05
135	Jack Morris	.05
136	Bob Horner	.05

137	Calvin Schiraldi	.05
138	Tom Browning	.05
139	Shane Rawley	.05
140	Mario Soto	.05
141	Dale Murphy	.15
142	Hubie Brooks	.05
143	Jeff Reardon	.05
144	Will Clark	.15
145	Ed Correa	.05
146	Glenn Wilson	.05
147	Johnny Ray	.05
148	Fernando Valenzuela	.05
149	Tim Raines	.10
150	Don Mattingly	.75
151	Jose Canseco	.40
152	Gary Pettis	.05
153	Don Sutton	.05
154	Jim Presley	.05
155	Checklist 28-105	.05
156	Dale Sveum	.05
157	Cory Snyder	.05
158	Jeff Sellers	.05
159	Denny Walling	.05
160	Danny Cox	.05
161	Bob Forsch	.05
162	Joaquin Andujar	.05
163	Roberto Clemente Puzzle Card	.10
164	Paul Assenmacher	.05
165	Marty Barrett	.05
166	Ray Knight	.05
167	Rafael Santana	.05
168	Bruce Ruffin	.05
169	Buddy Bell	.05
170	Kevin Mitchell	.05
171	Ken Oberkfell	.05
172	Gene Garber	.05
173	Canadian Greats (Mark Eichhorn)	.15
174	Don Carman	.05
175	Jesse Orosco	.05
176	Mookie Wilson	.05
177	Gary Ward	.05
178	John Franco	.05
179	Eric Davis	.05
180	Walt Terrell	.05
181	Phil Niekro	.30
182	Pat Tabler	.05
183	Brett Butler	.05
184	George Bell	.10
185	Pete Incaviglia	.05
186	Pete O'Brien	.05
187	Jimmy Key	.05
188	Frank White	.05
189	Mike Pagliarulo	.05
190	Roger Clemens	1.00
191	Rickey Henderson	.75
192	Mike Easler	.05
193	Wade Boggs	.75
194	Vince Coleman	.05
195	Charlie Kerfeld	.05
196	Dickie Thon	.05
197	Bill Doran	.05
198	Alfredo Griffin	.05
199	Carlton Fisk	.50
200	Phil Bradley	.05
201	Reggie Jackson	.65
202	Bob Boone	.05
203	Steve Sax	.05
204	Tom Niedenfuer	.05
205	Tim Burke	.05
206	Floyd Youmans	.05
207	Jay Tibbs	.05
208	Chili Davis	.05
209	Larry Parrish	.05
210	John Cerutti	.05
211	Kevin Bass	.05
212	Andre Dawson	.25
213	Bob Sebra	.05
214	Kevin McReynolds	.05
215	Jim Morrison	.05
216	Candy Maldonado	.05
217	John Kruk	.05
218	Todd Worrell	.05
219	Barry Bonds	10.00
220	Andy McGaffigan	.05
221	Andres Galarraga	.10
222	Mike Fitzgerald	.05
223	Kirk McCaskill	.05
224	Dave Smith	.05
225	Ruben Sierra	.05
226	Scott Fletcher	.05
227	Chet Lemon	.05
228	Dan Petry	.05
229	Mark Eichhorn	.05
230	Cecil Cooper	.05
231	Willie Upshaw	.05
232	Don Baylor	.05
233	Keith Hernandez	.05
234	Ryne Sandberg	.75
235	Tony Gwynn	.65
236	Chris Brown	.05
237	Pedro Guerrero	.05
238	Mark Gubicza	.05
239	Sid Bream	.05
240	Joe Cowley	.05
241	Bill Buckner	.05
242	John Candelaria	.05
243	Scott McGregor	.05
244	Tom Brunansky	.05

ABBREVIATIONS

DK - Diamond King
RR - Rated Rookie

245	Gary Gaetti	.05
246	Orel Hershiser	.05
247	Jim Rice	.10
248	Oil Can Boyd	.05
249	Bob Knepper	.05
250	Danny Tartabull	.05
251	John Cangelosi	.05
252	Wally Joyner	.05
253	Bruce Hurst	.05
254	Rich Gedman	.05
255	Jim Deshaies	.05
256	Tony Pena	.05
257	Nolan Ryan	1.50
258	Mike Scott	.05
259	Checklist 106-183	.05
260	Dennis Rasmussen	.05
261	Bret Saberhagen	.05
262	Steve Balboni	.05
263	Tom Seaver	.50
264	Checklist 184-264	.05

1987 Leaf Candy City Team

Leaf produced this set as part of its endorsement for the Special Olympics. Twelve cards feature Baseball Hall of Famers. The cards measure 2-1/2" x 3-1/2" and are numbered H1-H12. The remaining six cards in the set are numbered S1-S6 and feature unnamed Special Olympics champions. All cards feature the artwork of Dick Perez. The cards were available through a mail-in offer advertised at special store displays. Only the baseball-related subjects are listed in the checklist.

		NM/M
	Complete Set (12):	3.00
	Common Player:	.15
H1	Mickey Mantle	1.00
H2	Yogi Berra	.35
H3	Roy Campanella	.35
H4	Stan Musial	.50
H5	Ted Williams	.60
H6	Duke Snider	.35
H7	Hank Aaron	.60
H8	Pee Wee Reese	.35
H9	Brooks Robinson	.25
H10	Al Kaline	.25
H11	Willie McCovey	.25
H12	Cool Papa Bell	.15

1988 Leaf

This 264-card set features color player photos from among the 1988 Donruss 660-card standard issue, with emphasis on players from Montreal and Toronto. A border of red, blue and black stripes duplicates the design of the Donruss set, with the exception of a "Leaf '88" logo in the upper-left corner that replaces the Donruss logo. Two special Canadian Greats cards are included in this set: Perez-Steele portraits of Tim Wallach and George Bell. The set also includes the portrait-style Diamond Kings cards (the set's first 26 cards, one for each team). The DK's carry the Donruss logo above the gold DK banner. All card backs are bilingual (French/English), numbered, and printed in black on white stock with a light blue border. This set was sold in 10-card wax packs with one triple-piece puzzle card per pack and was distributed via larger hobby and retail shops in the U.S. and Canada.

		NM/M
	Complete Set (264):	6.00
	Common Player:	.05
	Wax Pack (15):	.50
	Wax Box (36):	9.00
1	Mark McGwire/DK	1.25
2	Tim Raines/DK	.20
3	Benito Santiago/DK	.05
4	Alan Trammell/DK	.05
5	Danny Tartabull/DK	.05
6	Ron Darling/DK	.05
7	Paul Molitor/DK	.75
8	Devon White/DK	.20
9	Andre Dawson/DK	.25
10	Julio Franco/DK	.05
11	Scott Fletcher/DK	.05
12	Tony Fernandez /DK	.10
13	Shane Rawley/DK	.05
14	Kal Daniels/DK	.05
15	Jack Clark/DK	.05
16	Dwight Evans/DK	.05
17	Tommy John/DK	.05
18	Andy Van Slyke/DK	.05
19	Gary Gaetti/DK	.05
20	Mark Langston/DK	.05
21	Will Clark/DK	.15
22	Glenn Hubbard/DK	.05
23	Billy Hatcher/DK	.05
24	Bob Welch/DK	.05
25	Ivan Calderon/DK	.05
26	Cal Ripken, Jr./DK	1.50
27	Checklist 1-27	.05
28	Mackey Sasser/RR	.05
29	Jeff Treadway/RR	.05
30	Mike Campbell/RR	.05
31	Lance Johnson/RR	.05
32	Nelson Liriano/RR	.05
33	Shawn Abner/RR	.05
34	Roberto Alomar/RR	2.50
35	Shawn Hillegas/RR	.05
36	Joey Meyer/RR	.05
37	Kevin Elster/RR	.05
38	Jose Lind/RR	.05
39	Kirt Manwaring/RR	.05
40	Mark Grace/RR	.75
41	Jody Reed/RR	.05
42	John Farrell/RR	.05
43	Al Leiter/RR	.25
44	Gary Thurman/RR	.05
45	Vincente Palacios/RR	.05
46	Eddie Williams/RR	.05
47	Jack McDowell/RR	.20
48	Dwight Gooden	.05
49	Mike Witt	.05
50	Wally Joyner	.05
51	Brook Jacoby	.05
52	Bert Blyleven	.05
53	Ted Higuera	.05
54	Mike Scott	.05
55	Jose Guzman	.05
56	Roger Clemens	1.25
57	Dave Righetti	.05
58	Benito Santiago	.05
59	Ozzie Guillen	.05
60	Matt Nokes	.05
61	Fernando Valenzuela	.05
62	Orel Hershiser	.05
63	Sid Fernandez	.05
64	Ozzie Virgil	.05
65	Wade Boggs	.50
66	Floyd Youmans	.05
67	Jimmy Key	.05
68	Bret Saberhagen	.05
69	Jody Davis	.05
70	Shawon Dunston	.05
71	Julio Franco	.05
72	Danny Cox	.05
73	Jim Clancy	.05
74	Mark Eichhorn	.05
75	Scott Bradley	.05
76	Charlie Liebrandt	.05
77	Nolan Ryan	1.50
78	Ron Darling	.05
79	John Franco	.05
80	Dave Stieb	.05
81	Mike Fitzgerald	.05
82	Steve Bedrosian	.05
83	Dale Murphy	.20
84	Tim Burke	.05
85	Jack Morris	.05
86	Greg Walker	.05
87	Kevin Mitchell	.05
88	Doug Drabek	.05
89	Charlie Hough	.05
90	Tony Gwynn	.75
91	Rick Sutcliffe	.05
92	Shane Rawley	.05

93	George Brett	1.00
94	Frank Viola	.05
95	Tony Pena	.05
96	Jim Deshaies	.05
97	Mike Scioscia	.05
98	Rick Rhoden	.05
99	Terry Kennedy	.05
100	Cal Ripken	1.50
101	Pedro Guerrero	.05
102	Andy Van Slyke	.05
103	Willie McGee	.05
104	Mike Kingery	.05
105	Kevin Seitzer	.05
106	Robin Yount	.50
107	Tracy Jones	.05
108	Dave Magadan	.05
109	Mel Hall	.05
110	Billy Hatcher	.05
111	Todd Benzinger	.05
112	Mike LaValliere	.05
113	Barry Bonds	1.50
114	Tim Raines	.20
115	Ozzie Smith	.75
116	Dave Winfield	.75
117	Keith Hernandez	.05
118	Jeffrey Leonard	.05
119	Larry Parrish	.05
120	Rob Thompson	.05
121	Andres Galarraga	.15
122	Mickey Hatcher	.05
123	Mark Langston	.05
124	Mike Schmidt	1.00
125	Cory Snyder	.05
126	Andre Dawson	.15
127	Devon White	.15
128	Vince Coleman	.05
129	Bryn Smith	.05
130	Lance Parrish	.05
131	Willie Upshaw	.05
132	Pete O'Brien	.05
133	Tony Fernandez	.10
134	Billy Ripken	.05
135	Len Dykstra	.05
136	Kirk Gibson	.05
137	Kevin Bass	.05
138	Jose Canseco	.50
139	Kent Hrbek	.05
140	Lloyd Moseby	.05
141	Marty Barrett	.05
142	Carmelo Martinez	.05
143	Tom Foley	.05
144	Kirby Puckett	.75
145	Rickey Henderson	.75
146	Juan Samuel	.05
147	Pete Incaviglia	.05
148	Greg Brock	.05
149	Eric Davis	.05
150	Kal Daniels	.05
151	Bob Boone	.05
152	John Cerutti	.05
153	Mike Greenwell	.05
154	Oddibe McDowell	.05
155	Scott Fletcher	.05
156	Gary Carter	.75
157	Harold Baines	.05
158	Greg Swindell	.05
159	Mark McLemore	.05
160	Keith Moreland	.05
161	Jim Gantner	.05
162	Willie Randolph	.05
163	Fred Lynn	.05
164	B.J. Surhoff	.05
165	Ken Griffey	.05
166	Chet Lemon	.05
167	Alan Trammell	.05
168	Paul Molitor	.75
169	Lou Whitaker	.05
170	Will Clark	.10
171	Dwight Evans	.05
172	Eddie Murray	.50
173	Darrell Evans	.05
174	Ellis Burks	.05
175	Ivan Calderon	.05
176	John Kruk	.05
177	Don Mattingly	1.00
178	Dick Schofield	.05
179	Bruce Hurst	.05
180	Ron Guidry	.05
181	Jack Clark	.05
182	Franklin Stubbs	.05
183	Bill Doran	.05
184	Joe Carter	.05
185	Steve Sax	.05
186	Glenn Davis	.05
187	Bo Jackson	.10
188	Bobby Bonilla	.05
189	Willie Wilson	.05
190	Danny Tartabull	.05
191	Bo Diaz	.05
192	Buddy Bell	.05
193	Tim Wallach	.05
194	Mark McGwire	1.25
195	Carney Lansford	.05
196	Alvin Davis	.05
197	Von Hayes	.05
198	Mitch Webster	.05
199	Casey Candaele	.05
200	Gary Gaetti	.05
201	Tommy Herr	.05
202	Wally Backman	.05
203	Brian Downing	.05
204	Rance Mulliniks	.05
205	Craig Reynolds	.05
206	Ruben Sierra	.05
207	Ryne Sandberg	.75
208	Carlton Fisk	.50
209	Checklist 28-107	.05
210	Gerald Young	.05

211	MVP (Tim Raines)	.25
212	John Tudor	.05
213	Canadian Greats (George Bell)	.60
214	MVP (George Bell)	.25
215	Jim Rice	.10
216	Gerald Perry	.05
217	Dave Stewart	.05
218	Jose Uribe	.05
219	Rick Rueschel	.05
220	Darryl Strawberry	.05
221	Chris Brown	.05
223	Lee Mazzilli	.05
224	Denny Walling	.05
225	Jesse Barfield	.05
226	Barry Larkin	.05
227	Harold Reynolds	.05
228	Kevin McReynolds	.05
229	Todd Worrell	.05
230	Tommy John	.05
231	Rick Aguilera	.05
232	Bill Madlock	.05
233	Roy Smalley	.05
234	Jeff Musselman	.05
235	Mike Dunne	.05
236	Jerry Browne	.05
237	Sam Horn	.05
238	Howard Johnson	.05
239	Candy Maldonado	.05
240	Nick Esasky	.05
241	Geno Petralli	.05
242	Herm Winningham	.05
243	Roger McDowell	.05
244	Brian Fisher	.05
245	John Marzano	.05
246	Terry Pendleton	.05
247	Rick Leach	.05
248	Pascual Perez	.05
249	Mookie Wilson	.05
250	Ernie Whitt	.05
251	Ron Kittle	.05
252	Oil Can Boyd	.05
253	Jim Gott	.05
254	George Bell	.10
255	Canadian Greats (Tim Wallach)	.60
256	Luis Polonia	.05
257	Hubie Brooks	.05
258	Mickey Brantley	.05
259	Gregg Jefferies	.25
260	Johnny Ray	.05
261	Checklist 108-187	.05
262	Dennis Martinez	.05
263	Stan Musial Puzzle Card	.05
264	Checklist 188-264	.05

1989 Leaf Blue Chip Cards

Unknown until 2001, these cards are a variation of the 1989 Donruss Grand Slammers insert set and share the back design with that issue. Instead of the GS logo in the lower-left corner of the photo, these cards have a black, white and blue logo reading "Blue Chip / CARDS / Leaf." The Blue Chip cards are printed on heavier stock and have a blue background on the back. Why they were produced and apparently not distributed is not known. It is presumed, though not confirmed, that all 12 Grand Slammers cards can also be found in the Blue Chip version.

		NM/M
	Complete Set (12):	1,200
	Common Player:	60.00
1	Jose Canseco	125.00
2	Mike Marshall	60.00
3	Walt Weiss	60.00
4	Kevin McReynolds	60.00
5	Mike Greenwell	60.00
6	Dave Winfield	150.00
7	Mark McGwire	400.00
8	Keith Hernandez	75.00
9	Franklin Stubbs	60.00
10	Danny Tartabull	60.00
11	Jesse Barfield	60.00
12	Ellis Burks	60.00

1990 Leaf Previews

JOE CARTER OF

This 12-card set was produced for dealer distribution to introduce Leaf as Donruss' premium-quality brand in mid-1990. Cards have the same format as the regular-issue versions with metallic silver ink highlights on front and back. The preview cards have a white undertype on back over the stats and career highlights. It reads "Special Preview Card."

		NM/M
Complete Set (12):		275.00
Common Player:		12.50
1	Steve Sax	12.50
2	Joe Carter	12.50
3	Dennis Eckersley	20.00
4	Ken Griffey Jr.	200.00
5	Barry Larkin	12.50
6	Mark Langston	12.50
7	Eric Anthony	12.50
8	Robin Ventura	12.50
9	Greg Vaughn	12.50
10	Bobby Bonilla	12.50
11	Gary Gaetti	12.50
12	Ozzie Smith	75.00

1990 Leaf

BOB TEWKSBURY P

This 528-card set was issued in two 264-card series. The cards were printed on heavy quality stock and both the card fronts and backs have full color player photos. Cards also have an ultra-glossy finish on both the fronts and the backs. A high-tech foil Hall of Fame puzzle features former Yankee great Yogi Berra.

		NM/M
Complete Set (528):		75.00
Series 1 (264):		50.00
Series 2 (264):		25.00
Common Player:		.10
Series 1 Foil Pack (15):		4.00
Series 1 Foil Box (36):		80.00
Series 2 Foil Pack (15):		2.50
Series 2 Foil Box (36):		60.00
1	Introductory card	.10
2	Mike Henneman	.10
3	Steve Bedrosian	.10
4	Mike Scott	.10
5	Allan Anderson	.10
6	Rick Sutcliffe	.10
7	Gregg Olson	.10
8	Kevin Elster	.10
9	Pete O'Brien	.10
10	Carlton Fisk	1.00
11	Joe Magrane	.10
12	Roger Clemens	2.50
13	Tom Glavine	.35
14	Tom Gordon	.10
15	Todd Benzinger	.10
16	Hubie Brooks	.10
17	Roberto Kelly	.10
18	Barry Larkin	.10
19	Mike Boddicker	.10
20	Roger McDowell	.10
21	Nolan Ryan	5.00

22	John Farrell	.10
23	Bruce Hurst	.10
24	Wally Joyner	.10
25	Greg Maddux	2.00
26	Chris Bosio	.10
27	John Cerutti	.10
28	Tim Burke	.10
29	Dennis Eckersley	.75
30	Glenn Davis	.10
31	Jim Abbott	.10
32	Mike LaValliere	.10
33	Andres Thomas	.10
34	Lou Whitaker	.10
35	Alvin Davis	.10
36	Melido Perez	.10
37	Craig Biggio	.10
38	Rick Aguilera	.10
39	Pete Harnisch	.10
40	David Cone	.10
41	Scott Garrelts	.10
42	Jay Howell	.10
43	Eric King	.10
44	Pedro Guerrero	.10
45	Mike Bielecki	.10
46	Bob Boone	.10
47	Kevin Brown	.10
48	Jerry Browne	.10
49	Mike Scioscia	.10
50	Chuck Cary	.10
51	Wade Boggs	2.00
52	Von Hayes	.10
53	Tony Fernandez	.10
54	Dennis Martinez	.10
55	Tom Candiotti	.10
56	Andy Benes	.10
57	Rob Dibble	.10
58	Chuck Crim	.10
59	John Smoltz	.10
60	Mike Heath	.10
61	Kevin Gross	.10
62	Mark McGwire	3.50
63	Bert Blyleven	.10
64	Bob Walk	.10
65	Mickey Tettleton	.10
66	Sid Fernandez	.10
67	Terry Kennedy	.10
68	Fernando Valenzuela	.10
69	Don Mattingly	2.50
70	Paul O'Neill	.10
71	Robin Yount	1.00
72	Bret Saberhagen	.10
73	Geno Petralli	.10
74	Brook Jacoby	.10
75	Roberto Alomar	.25
76	Devon White	.10
77	Jose Lind	.10
78	Pat Combs	.10
79	Dave Steib	.10
80	Tim Wallach	.10
81	Dave Stewart	.10
82	Eric Anthony RC	.10
83	Randy Bush	.10
84	Checklist	.10
85	Jaime Navarro	.10
86	Tommy Gregg	.10
87	Frank Tanana	.10
88	Omar Vizquel	.10
89	Ivan Calderon	.10
90	Vince Coleman	.10
91	Barry Bonds	5.00
92	Randy Milligan	.10
93	Frank Viola	.10
94	Matt Williams	.10
95	Alfredo Griffin	.10
96	Steve Sax	.10
97	Gary Gaetti	.10
98	Ryne Sandberg	2.00
99	Danny Tartabull	.10
100	Rafael Palmeiro	1.00
101	Jesse Orosco	.10
102	Garry Templeton	.10
103	Frank DiPino	.10
104	Tony Pena	.10
105	Dickie Thon	.10
106	Kelly Gruber	.10
107	Marquis Grissom RC	2.00
108	Jose Canseco	.60
109	Mike Blowers	.10
110	Tom Browning	.10
111	Greg Vaughn	.10
112	Oddibe McDowell	.10
113	Gary Ward	.10
114	Jay Buhner	.10
115	Eric Show	.10
116	Bryan Harvey	.10
117	Andy Van Slyke	.10
118	Jeff Ballard	.10
119	Barry Lyons	.10
120	Kevin Mitchell	.10
121	Mike Gallego	.10
122	Dave Smith	.10
123	Kirby Puckett	2.00
124	Jerome Walton	.10
125	Bo Jackson	.20
126	Harold Baines	.10
127	Scott Bankhead	.10
128	Ozzie Guillen	.10
129	Jose Oquendo	.10
130	John Dopson	.10
131	Charlie Hayes	.10
132	Fred McGriff	.10
133	Chet Lemon	.10
134	Gary Carter	1.00
135	Rafael Ramirez	.10
136	Shane Mack	.10
137	Mark Grace	.10
138	Phil Bradley	.10
139	Dwight Gooden	.10

140	Harold Reynolds	.10
141	Scott Fletcher	.10
142	Ozzie Smith	2.00
143	Mike Greenwell	.10
144	Pete Smith	.10
145	Mark Gubicza	.10
146	Chris Sabo	.10
147	Ramon Martinez	.10
148	Tim Leary	.10
149	Randy Myers	.10
150	Jody Reed	.10
151	Bruce Ruffin	.10
152	Jeff Russell	.10
153	Doug Jones	.10
154	Tony Gwynn	2.00
155	Mark Langston	.10
156	Mitch Williams	.10
157	Gary Sheffield	.60
158	Tom Henke	.10
159	Oil Can Boyd	.10
160	Rickey Henderson	1.00
161	Bill Doran	.10
162	Chuck Finley	.10
163	Jeff King	.10
164	Nick Esasky	.10
165	Cecil Fielder	.10
166	Dave Valle	.10
167	Robin Ventura	.10
168	Jim Deshaies	.10
169	Juan Berenguer	.10
170	Craig Worthington	.10
171	Gregg Jefferies	.10
172	Will Clark	.10
173	Kirk Gibson	.10
174	Checklist	.10
175	Bobby Thigpen	.10
176	John Tudor	.10
177	Andre Dawson	.35
178	George Brett	2.50
179	Steve Buechele	.10
180	Albert Belle	.10
181	Eddie Murray	1.00
182	Bob Geren	.10
183	Rob Murphy	.10
184	Tom Herr	.10
185	George Bell	.10
186	Spike Owen	.10
187	Cory Snyder	.10
188	Fred Lynn	.10
189	Eric Davis	.10
190	Dave Parker	.10
191	Jeff Blauser	.10
192	Matt Nokes	.10
193	Delino DeShields RC	.50
194	Scott Sanderson	.10
195	Lance Parrish	.10
196	Bobby Bonilla	.10
197	Cal Ripken, Jr.	5.00
198	Kevin McReynolds	.10
199	Robby Thompson	.10
200	Tim Belcher	.10
201	Jesse Barfield	.10
202	Mariano Duncan	.10
203	Bill Spiers	.10
204	Frank White	.10
205	Julio Franco	.10
206	Greg Swindell	.10
207	Benito Santiago	.10
208	Johnny Ray	.10
209	Gary Redus	.10
210	Jeff Parrett	.10
211	Jimmy Key	.10
212	Tim Raines	.10
213	Carney Lansford	.10
214	Gerald Young	.10
215	Gene Larkin	.10
216	Dan Plesac	.10
217	Lonnie Smith	.10
218	Alan Trammell	.10
219	Jeffrey Leonard	.10
220	Sammy Sosa	20.00
221	Todd Zeile	.10
222	Bill Landrum	.10
223	Mike Devereaux	.10
224	Mike Marshall	.10
225	Jose Uribe	.10
226	Juan Samuel	.10
227	Mel Hall	.10
228	Kent Hrbek	.10
229	Shawon Dunston	.10
230	Kevin Seitzer	.10
231	Pete Incaviglia	.10
232	Sandy Alomar	.10
233	Bip Roberts	.10
234	Scott Terry	.10
235	Dwight Evans	.10
236	Ricky Jordan	.10
237	John Olerud RC	5.00
238	Zane Smith	.10
239	Walt Weiss	.10
240	Alvaro Espinoza	.10
241	Billy Hatcher	.10
242	Paul Molitor	1.00
243	Dale Murphy	.30
244	Dave Bergman	.10
245	Ken Griffey Jr.	3.00
246	Ed Whitson	.10
247	Kirk McCaskill	.10
248	Jay Bell	.10
249	Ben McDonald RC	.50
250	Darryl Strawberry	.10
251	Brett Butler	.10
252	Terry Steinbach	.10
253	Ken Caminiti	.10
254	Dan Gladden	.10
255	Dwight Smith	.10
256	Kurt Stillwell	.10
257	Ruben Sierra	.10

258	Mike Schooler	.10
259	Lance Johnson	.10
260	Terry Pendleton	.10
261	Ellis Burks	.10
262	Len Dykstra	.10
263	Mookie Wilson	.10
264	Checklist (Nolan Ryan)	.10
265	Nolan Ryan (No-Hit King)	2.00
266	Brian DuBois	.10
267	Don Robinson	.10
268	Glenn Wilson	.10
269	Kevin Tapani RC	.25
270	Marvell Wynne	.10
271	Billy Ripken	.10
272	Howard Johnson	.10
273	Brian Holman	.10
274	Dan Pasqua	.10
275	Ken Dayley	.10
276	Jeff Reardon	.10
277	Jim Presley	.10
278	Jim Eisenreich	.10
279	Danny Jackson	.10
280	Orel Hershiser	.10
281	Andy Hawkins	.10
282	Jose Rijo	.10
283	Luis Rivera	.10
284	John Kruk	.10
285	Jeff Huson	.10
286	Joel Skinner	.10
287	Jack Clark	.10
288	Chili Davis	.10
289	Joe Girardi	.10
290	B.J. Surhoff	.10
291	Luis Sojo	.10
292	Tom Foley	.10
293	Mike Moore	.10
294	Ken Oberkfell	.10
295	Luis Polonia	.10
296	Doug Drabek	.10
297	Dave Justice RC	2.00
298	Paul Gibson	.10
299	Edgar Martinez	.10
300	Frank Thomas RC	20.00
301	Eric Yelding	.10
302	Greg Gagne	.10
303	Brad Komminsk	.10
304	Ron Darling	.10
305	Kevin Bass	.10
306	Jeff Hamilton	.10
307	Ron Karkovice	.10
308	Milt Thompson	.10
309	Mike Harkey	.10
310	Mel Stottlemyre	.10
311	Kenny Rogers	.10
312	Mitch Webster	.10
313	Kal Daniels	.10
314	Matt Nokes	.10
315	Dennis Lamp	.10
316	Ken Howell	.10
317	Glenallen Hill	.10
318	Dave Martinez	.10
319	Chris James	.10
320	Mike Pagliarulo	.10
321	Hal Morris	.10
322	Rob Deer	.10
323	Greg Olson	.10
324	Tony Phillips	.10
325	Larry Walker RC	8.00
326	Ron Hassey	.10
327	Jack Howell	.10
328	John Smiley	.10
329	Steve Finley	.10
330	Dave Magadan	.10
331	Greg Litton	.10
332	Mickey Hatcher	.10
333	Lee Guetterman	.10
334	Norm Charlton	.10
335	Edgar Diaz	.10
336	Willie Wilson	.10
337	Bobby Witt	.10
338	Candy Maldonado	.10
339	Craig Lefferts	.10
340	Dante Bichette	.10
341	Wally Backman	.10
342	Dennis Cook	.10
343	Pat Borders	.10
344	Wallace Johnson	.10
345	Willie Randolph	.10
346	Danny Darwin	.10
347	Al Newman	.10
348	Mark Knudson	.10
349	Joe Boever	.10
350	Larry Sheets	.10
351	Mike Jackson	.10
352	Wayne Edwards	.10
353	Bernard Gilkey RC	.50
354	Don Slaught	.10
355	Joe Orsulak	.10
356	John Franco	.10
357	Jeff Brantley	.10
358	Mike Morgan	.10
359	Deion Sanders	.10
360	Terry Leach	.10
361	Les Lancaster	.10
362	Storm Davis	.10
363	Scott Coolbaugh	.10
364	Checklist	.10
365	Cecilio Guante	.10
366	Joey Cora	.10
367	Willie McGee	.10
368	Jerry Reed	.10
369	Darren Daulton	.10
370	Manny Lee	.10
371	Mark Gardner	.10
372	Rick Honeycutt	.10
373	Steve Balboni	.10
374	Jack Armstrong	.10

375	Charlie O'Brien	.10
376	Ron Gant	.10
377	Lloyd Moseby	.10
378	Gene Harris	.10
379	Joe Carter	.10
380	Scott Bailes	.10
381	R.J. Reynolds	.10
382	Bob Melvin	.10
383	Tim Teufel	.10
384	John Burkett	.10
385	Felix Jose	.10
386	Larry Andersen	.10
387	David West	.10
388	Luis Salazar	.10
389	Mike Macfarlane	.10
390	Charlie Hough	.10
391	Greg Briley	.10
392	Donn Pall	.10
393	Bryn Smith	.10
394	Carlos Quintana	.10
395	Steve Lake	.10
396	Mark Whiten RC	.15
397	Edwin Nunez	.10
398	Rick Parker	.10
399	Mark Portugal	.10
400	Roy Smith	.10
401	Hector Villanueva	.10
402	Bob Milacki	.10
403	Alejandro Pena	.10
404	Scott Bradley	.10
405	Ron Kittle	.10
406	Bob Tewksbury	.10
407	Wes Gardner	.10
408	Ernie Whitt	.10
409	Terry Shumpert	.10
410	Tim Layana	.10
411	Chris Gwynn	.10
412	Jeff Robinson	.10
413	Scott Scudder	.10
414	Kevin Romine	.10
415	Jose DeJesus	.10
416	Mike Jeffcoat	.10
417	Rudy Seanez	.10
418	Mike Dunne	.10
419	Dick Schofield	.10
420	Steve Wilson	.10
421	Bill Krueger	.10
422	Junior Felix	.10
423	Drew Hall	.10
424	Curt Young	.10
425	Franklin Stubbs	.10
426	Dave Winfield	1.00
427	Rick Reed	.10
428	Charlie Leibrandt	.10
429	Jeff Robinson	.10
430	Erik Hanson	.10
431	Barry Jones	.10
432	Alex Trevino	.10
433	John Moses	.10
434	Dave Johnson	.10
435	Mackey Sasser	.10
436	Rick Leach	.10
437	Lenny Harris	.10
438	Carlos Martinez	.10
439	Rex Hudler	.10
440	Domingo Ramos	.10
441	Gerald Perry	.10
442	John Russell	.10
443	Carlos Baerga RC	.50
444	Checklist	.10
445	Stan Javier	.10
446	Kevin Maas RC	.10
447	Tom Brunansky	.10
448	Carmelo Martinez	.10
449	Willie Blair RC	.10
450	Andres Galarraga	.10
451	Bud Black	.10
452	Greg Harris	.10
453	Joe Oliver	.10
454	Greg Brock	.10
455	Jeff Treadway	.10
456	Lance McCullers	.10
457	Dave Schmidt	.10
458	Todd Burns	.10
459	Max Venable	.10
460	Neal Heaton	.10
461	Mark Williamson	.10
462	Keith Miller	.10
463	Mike LaCoss	.10
464	Jose Offerman RC	.25
465	Jim Leyritz RC	.50
466	Glenn Braggs	.10
467	Ron Robinson	.10
468	Mark Davis	.10
469	Gary Pettis	.10
470	Keith Hernandez	.10
471	Dennis Rasmussen	.10
472	Mark Eichhorn	.10
473	Ted Power	.10
474	Terry Mulholland	.10
475	Todd Stottlemyre	.10
476	Jerry Goff	.10
477	Gene Nelson	.10
478	Rich Gedman	.10
479	Brian Harper	.10
480	Mike Felder	.10
481	Steve Avery	.10
482	Jack Morris	.10
483	Randy Johnson	1.00
484	Scott Radinsky	.10
485	Jose DeLeon	.10
486	Stan Belinda RC	.10
487	Brian Holton	.10
488	Mark Carreon	.10
489	Trevor Wilson	.10
490	Mike Sharperson	.10
491	Alan Mills RC	.10
492	John Candelaria	.10

493	Paul Assenmacher	.10
494	Steve Crawford	.10
495	Brad Arnsberg	.10
496	Sergio Valdez	.10
497	Mark Parent	.10
498	Tom Pagnozzi	.10
499	Greg Harris	.10
500	Randy Ready	.10
501	Duane Ward	.10
502	Nelson Santovenia	.10
503	Joe Klink	.10
504	Eric Plunk	.10
505	Jeff Reed	.10
506	Ted Higuera	.10
507	Joe Hesketh	.10
508	Dan Petry	.10
509	Matt Young	.10
510	Jerald Clark	.10
511	John Orton RC	.10
512	Scott Ruskin	.10
513	Chris Hoiles RC	.50
514	Daryl Boston	.10
515	Francisco Oliveras	.10
516	Ozzie Canseco	.10
517	Xavier Hernandez RC	.10
518	Fred Manrique	.10
519	Shawn Boskie	.10
520	Jeff Montgomery	.10
521	Jack Daugherty	.10
522	Keith Comstock	.10
523	Greg Hibbard RC	.10
524	Lee Smith	.10
525	Dana Kiecker	.10
526	Darrel Akerfelds	.10
527	Greg Myers	.10
528	Checklist	.10

1991 Leaf Previews

RYNE SANDBERG 2B

Cello packs of four cards previewing the 1991 Leaf set were included in each 1991 Donruss hobby factory set. The cards are identical in format to the regular 1991 Leafs, except there is a notation, "1991 PREVIEW CARD" in white print beneath the statistics and career information on the back.

		NM/M
Complete Set (26):		20.00
Common Player:		.50
1	Dave Justice	.50
2	Ryne Sandberg	1.50
3	Barry Larkin	.50
4	Craig Biggio	.50
5	Ramon Martinez	.50
6	Tim Wallach	.50
7	Dwight Gooden	.50
8	Len Dykstra	.50
9	Barry Bonds	4.00
10	Ray Lankford	.50
11	Tony Gwynn	1.50
12	Will Clark	.60
13	Leo Gomez	.50
14	Wade Boggs	1.50
15	Chuck Finley	.50
16	Carlton Fisk	1.00
17	Sandy Alomar, Jr.	.50
18	Cecil Fielder	.50
19	Bo Jackson	.75
20	Paul Molitor	1.00
21	Kirby Puckett	1.50
22	Don Mattingly	2.00
23	Rickey Henderson	1.00
24	Tino Martinez	.50
25	Nolan Ryan	4.00
26	Dave Steib	.50

1991 Leaf

Silver borders and black insets surround the color action photos on the 1991 Leaf cards. The set was once again released in two series. Series I consists of cards 1-264. Card backs feature an additional player photo, biographical information, statistics and career highlights. The 1991 issue is not considered as scarce as the 1990 release.

		NM/M
Complete Set (528):		8.00

JOHN OLERUD 1B

Common Player: .05
Series 1 or 2 Pack (15): .50
Series 1 or 2 Box (36): 12.50

#	Player	Price
1	The Leaf Card	.05
2	Kurt Stillwell	.05
3	Bobby Witt	.05
4	Tony Phillips	.05
5	Scott Garrelts	.05
6	Greg Swindell	.05
7	Billy Ripken	.05
8	Dave Martinez	.05
9	Kelly Gruber	.05
10	Juan Samuel	.05
11	Brian Holman	.05
12	Craig Biggio	.05
13	Lonnie Smith	.05
14	Ron Robinson	.05
15	Mike LaValliere	.05
16	Mark Davis	.05
17	Jack Daugherty	.05
18	Mike Henneman	.05
19	Mike Greenwell	.05
20	Dave Magadan	.05
21	Mark Williamson	.05
22	Marquis Grissom	.05
23	Pat Borders	.05
24	Mike Scioscia	.05
25	Shawon Dunston	.05
26	Randy Bush	.05
27	John Smoltz	.05
28	Chuck Crim	.05
29	Don Slaught	.05
30	Mike Macfarlane	.05
31	Wally Joyner	.05
32	Pat Combs	.05
33	Tony Pena	.05
34	Howard Johnson	.05
35	Leo Gomez	.05
36	Spike Owen	.05
37	Eric Davis	.05
38	Roberto Kelly	.05
39	Jerome Walton	.05
40	Shane Mack	.05
41	Kent Mercker	.05
42	B.J. Surhoff	.05
43	Jerry Browne	.05
44	Lee Smith	.05
45	Chuck Finley	.05
46	Terry Mulholland	.05
47	Tom Bolton	.05
48	Tom Herr	.05
49	Jim Deshaies	.05
50	Walt Weiss	.05
51	Hal Morris	.05
52	Lee Guetterman	.05
53	Paul Assenmacher	.05
54	Brian Harper	.05
55	Paul Gibson	.05
56	John Burkett	.05
57	Doug Jones	.05
58	Jose Oquendo	.05
59	Dick Schofield	.05
60	Dickie Thon	.05
61	Ramon Martinez	.05
62	Jay Buhner	.05
63	Mark Portugal	.05
64	Bob Welch	.05
65	Chris Sabo	.05
66	Chuck Cary	.05
67	Mark Langston	.05
68	Joe Boever	.05
69	Jody Reed	.05
70	Alejandro Pena	.05
71	Jeff King	.05
72	Tom Pagnozzi	.05
73	Joe Oliver	.05
74	Mike Witt	.05
75	Hector Villanueva	.05
76	Dan Gladden	.05
77	Dave Justice	.05
78	Mike Gallego	.05
79	Tom Candiotti	.05
80	Ozzie Smith	.60
81	Luis Polonia	.05
82	Randy Ready	.05
83	Greg Harris	.05
84	Checklist (Dave Justice)	.05
85	Kevin Mitchell	.05
86	Mark McLemore	.05
87	Terry Steinbach	.05
88	Tom Browning	.05
89	Matt Nokes	.05
90	Mike Harkey	.05
91	Omar Vizquel	.05
92	Dave Bergman	.05
93	Matt Williams	.05
94	Steve Olin	.05
95	Craig Wilson	.05
96	Dave Stieb	.05
97	Ruben Sierra	.05
98	Jay Howell	.05
99	Scott Bradley	.05
100	Eric Yelding	.05
101	Rickey Henderson	.45
102	Jeff Reed	.05
103	Jimmy Key	.05
104	Terry Shumpert	.05
105	Kenny Rogers	.05
106	Cecil Fielder	.05
107	Robby Thompson	.05
108	Alex Cole	.05
109	Randy Milligan	.05
110	Andres Galarraga	.05
111	Bill Spiers	.05
112	Kal Daniels	.05
113	Henry Cotto	.05
114	Casy Candaele	.05
115	Jeff Blauser	.05
116	Robin Yount	.45
117	Ben McDonald	.05
118	Bret Saberhagen	.05
119	Juan Gonzalez	.35
120	Lou Whitaker	.05
121	Ellis Burks	.05
122	Charlie O'Brien	.05
123	John Smiley	.05
124	Tim Burke	.05
125	John Olerud	.05
126	Eddie Murray	.45
127	Greg Maddux	.60
128	Kevin Tapani	.05
129	Ron Gant	.05
130	Jay Bell	.05
131	Chris Hoiles	.05
132	Tom Gordon	.05
133	Kevin Seitzer	.05
134	Jeff Huson	.05
135	Jerry Don Gleaton	.05
136	Jeff Brantley	.05
137	Felix Fermin	.05
138	Mike Devereaux	.05
139	Delino DeShields	.05
140	David Wells	.05
141	Tim Crews	.05
142	Erik Hanson	.05
143	Mark Davidson	.05
144	Tommy Gregg	.05
145	Jim Gantner	.05
146	Jose Lind	.05
147	Danny Tartabull	.05
148	Geno Petralli	.05
149	Travis Fryman	.05
150	Tim Naehring	.05
151	Kevin McReynolds	.05
152	Joe Orsulak	.05
153	Steve Frey	.05
154	Duane Ward	.05
155	Stan Javier	.05
156	Damon Berryhill	.05
157	Gene Larkin	.05
158	Greg Olson	.05
159	Mark Knudson	.05
160	Carmelo Martinez	.05
161	Storm Davis	.05
162	Jim Abbott	.05
163	Len Dykstra	.05
164	Tom Brunansky	.05
165	Dwight Gooden	.05
166	Jose Mesa	.05
167	Oil Can Boyd	.05
168	Barry Larkin	.05
169	Scott Sanderson	.05
170	Mark Grace	.05
171	Mark Guthrie	.05
172	Tom Glavine	.15
173	Gary Sheffield	.30
174	Checklist (Roger Clemens)	.25
175	Chris James	.05
176	Milt Thompson	.05
177	Donnie Hill	.05
178	Wes Chamberlain	.05
179	John Marzano	.05
180	Frank Viola	.05
181	Eric Anthony	.05
182	Jose Canseco	.30
183	Scott Scudder	.05
184	Dave Eiland	.05
185	Luis Salazar	.05
186	Pedro Munoz	.05
187	Steve Searcy	.05
188	Don Robinson	.05
189	Sandy Alomar	.05
190	Jose DeLeon	.05
191	John Orton	.05
192	Darren Daulton	.05
193	Mike Morgan	.05
194	Greg Briley	.05
195	Karl Rhodes	.05
196	Harold Baines	.05
197	Bill Doran	.05
198	Alvaro Espinoza	.05
199	Kirk McCaskill	.05
200	Jose DeJesus	.05
201	Jack Clark	.05
202	Daryl Boston	.05
203	Randy Tomlin	.05
204	Pedro Guerrero	.05
205	Billy Hatcher	.05
206	Tim Leary	.05
207	Ryne Sandberg	.60
208	Kirby Puckett	.60
209	Charlie Leibrandt	.05
210	Rick Honeycutt	.05
211	Joel Skinner	.05
212	Rex Hudler	.05
213	Bryan Harvey	.05
214	Charlie Hayes	.05
215	Matt Young	.05
216	Terry Kennedy	.05
217	Carl Nichols	.05
218	Mike Moore	.05
219	Paul O'Neill	.05
220	Steve Sax	.05
221	Shawn Boskie	.05
222	Rich DeLucia	.05
223	Lloyd Moseby	.05
224	Mike Kingery	.05
225	Carlos Baerga	.05
226	Bryn Smith	.05
227	Todd Stottlemyre	.05
228	Julio Franco	.05
229	Jim Gott	.05
230	Mike Schooler	.05
231	Steve Finley	.05
232	Dave Henderson	.05
233	Luis Quinones	.05
234	Mark Whiten	.05
235	Brian McRae	.05
236	Rich Gossage	.05
237	Rob Deer	.05
238	Will Clark	.10
239	Albert Belle	.05
240	Bob Melvin	.05
241	Larry Walker	.05
242	Dante Bichette	.05
243	Orel Hershiser	.05
244	Pete O'Brien	.05
245	Pete Harnisch	.05
246	Jeff Treadway	.05
247	Julio Machado	.05
248	Dave Johnson	.05
249	Kirk Gibson	.05
250	Kevin Brown	.05
251	Milt Cuyler	.05
252	Jeff Reardon	.05
253	David Cone	.05
254	Gary Redus	.05
255	Junior Noboa	.05
256	Greg Myers	.05
257	Dennis Cook	.05
258	Joe Girardi	.05
259	Allan Anderson	.05
260	Paul Marak	.05
261	Barry Bonds	2.00
262	Juan Bell	.05
263	Russ Morman	.05
264	Checklist (George Brett)	.25
265	Jerald Clark	.05
266	Dwight Evans	.05
267	Roberto Alomar	.15
268	Danny Jackson	.05
269	Brian Downing	.05
270	John Cerutti	.05
271	Robin Ventura	.05
272	Gerald Perry	.05
273	Wade Boggs	.60
274	Dennis Martinez	.05
275	Andy Benes	.05
276	Tony Fossas	.05
277	Franklin Stubbs	.05
278	John Kruk	.05
279	Kevin Gross	.05
280	Von Hayes	.05
281	Frank Thomas	.45
282	Rob Dibble	.05
283	Mel Hall	.05
284	Rick Mahler	.05
285	Dennis Eckersley	.35
286	Bernard Gilkey	.05
287	Dan Plesac	.05
288	Jason Grimsley	.05
289	Mark Lewis	.05
290	Tony Gwynn	.60
291	Jeff Russell	.05
292	Curt Schilling	.25
293	Pascual Perez	.05
294	Jack Morris	.05
295	Hubie Brooks	.05
296	Alex Fernandez	.05
297	Harold Reynolds	.05
298	Craig Worthington	.05
299	Willie Wilson	.05
300	Mike Maddux	.05
301	Dave Righetti	.05
302	Paul Molitor	.45
303	Gary Gaetti	.05
304	Terry Pendleton	.05
305	Kevin Elster	.05
306	Scott Fletcher	.05
307	Jeff Robinson	.05
308	Jesse Barfield	.05
309	Mike LaCoss	.05
310	Andy Van Slyke	.05
311	Glenallen Hill	.05
312	Bud Black	.05
313	Kent Hrbek	.05
314	Tim Teufel	.05
315	Tony Fernandez	.05
316	Beau Allred	.05
317	Curtis Wilkerson	.05
318	Bill Sampen	.05
319	Randy Johnson	.45
320	Mike Heath	.05
321	Sammy Sosa	1.00
322	Mickey Tettleton	.05
323	Jose Vizcaino	.05
324	John Candelaria	.05
325	David Howard	.05
326	Jose Rijo	.05
327	Todd Zeile	.05
328	Gene Nelson	.05
329	Dwayne Henry	.05
330	Mike Boddicker	.05
331	Ozzie Guillen	.05
332	Sam Horn	.05
333	Wally Whitehurst	.05
334	Dave Parker	.05
335	George Brett	.75
336	Bobby Thigpen	.05
337	Ed Whitson	.05
338	Ivan Calderon	.05
339	Mike Pagliarulo	.05
340	Jack McDowell	.05
341	Dana Kiecker	.05
342	Fred McGriff	.05
343	Mark Lee	.05
344	Alfredo Griffin	.05
345	Scott Bankhead	.05
346	Darrin Jackson	.05
347	Rafael Palmeiro	.35
348	Steve Farr	.05
349	Hensley Meulens	.05
350	Danny Cox	.05
351	Alan Trammell	.05
352	Edwin Nunez	.05
353	Joe Carter	.05
354	Eric Show	.05
355	Vance Law	.05
356	Jeff Gray	.05
357	Bobby Bonilla	.05
358	Ernest Riles	.05
359	Ron Hassey	.05
360	Willie McGee	.05
361	Mackey Sasser	.05
362	Glenn Braggs	.05
363	Mario Diaz	.05
364	Checklist (Barry Bonds)	.35
365	Kevin Bass	.05
366	Pete Incaviglia	.05
367	Luis Sojo	.05
368	Lance Parrish	.05
369	Mark Leonard	.05
370	Heathcliff Slocumb	.05
371	Jimmy Jones	.05
372	Ken Griffey Jr.	1.00
373	Chris Hammond	.05
374	Chili Davis	.05
375	Joey Cora	.05
376	Ken Hill	.05
377	Darryl Strawberry	.05
378	Ron Darling	.05
379	Sid Bream	.05
380	Bill Swift	.05
381	Shawn Abner	.05
382	Eric King	.05
383	Mickey Morandini	.05
384	Carlton Fisk	.45
385	Steve Lake	.05
386	Mike Jeffcoat	.05
387	Darren Holmes	.05
388	Tim Wallach	.05
389	George Bell	.05
390	Craig Lefferts	.05
391	Ernie Whitt	.05
392	Felix Jose	.05
393	Kevin Maas	.05
394	Devon White	.05
395	Otis Nixon	.05
396	Chuck Knoblauch	.05
397	Scott Coolbaugh	.05
398	Glenn Davis	.05
399	Manny Lee	.05
400	Andre Dawson	.20
401	Scott Chiamparino	.05
402	Bill Gullickson	.05
403	Lance Johnson	.05
404	Juan Agosto	.05
405	Danny Darwin	.05
406	Barry Jones	.05
407	Larry Andersen	.05
408	Luis Rivera	.05
409	Jaime Navarro	.05
410	Roger McDowell	.05
411	Brett Butler	.05
412	Dale Murphy	.15
413	Tim Raines	.05
414	Norm Charlton	.05
415	Greg Cadaret	.05
416	Chris Nabholz	.05
417	Dave Stewart	.05
418	Rich Gedman	.05
419	Willie Randolph	.05
420	Mitch Williams	.05
421	Brook Jacoby	.05
422	Greg Harris	.05
423	Nolan Ryan	2.00
424	Dave Rohde	.05
425	Don Mattingly	.75
426	Greg Gagne	.05
427	Vince Coleman	.05
428	Dan Pasqua	.05
429	Alvin Davis	.05
430	Cal Ripken, Jr.	2.00
431	Jamie Quirk	.05
432	Benito Santiago	.05
433	Jose Uribe	.05
434	Candy Maldonado	.05
435	Junior Felix	.05
436	Deion Sanders	.05
437	John Franco	.05
438	Greg Hibbard	.05
439	Floyd Bannister	.05
440	Steve Howe	.05
441	Steve Decker	.05
442	Vicente Palacios	.05
443	Pat Tabler	.05
444	Checklist (Darryl Strawberry)	.05
445	Mike Felder	.05
446	Al Newman	.05
447	Chris Donnels	.05
448	Rich Rodriguez	.05
449	Turner Ward	.05
450	Bob Walk	.05
451	Gilberto Reyes	.05
452	Mike Jackson	.05
453	Rafael Belliard	.05
454	Wayne Edwards	.05
455	Andy Allanson	.05
456	Dave Smith	.05
457	Gary Carter	.45
458	Warren Cromartie	.05
459	Jack Armstrong	.05
460	Bob Tewksbury	.05
461	Joe Klink	.05
462	Xavier Hernandez	.05
463	Scott Radinsky	.05
464	Jeff Robinson	.05
465	Gregg Jefferies	.05
466	Denny Neagle	.05
467	Carmelo Martinez	.05
468	Donn Pall	.05
469	Bruce Hurst	.05
470	Eric Bullock	.05
471	Rick Aguilera	.05
472	Charlie Hough	.05
473	Carlos Quintana	.05
474	Marty Barrett	.05
475	Kevin Brown	.05
476	Bobby Ojeda	.05
477	Edgar Martinez	.05
478	Bip Roberts	.05
479	Mike Flanagan	.05
480	John Habyan	.05
481	Larry Casian	.05
482	Wally Backman	.05
483	Doug Dascenzo	.05
484	Rick Dempsey	.05
485	Ed Sprague	.05
486	Steve Chitren	.05
487	Mark McGwire	1.50
488	Roger Clemens	.75
489	Orlando Merced	.05
490	Rene Gonzales	.05
491	Mike Stanton	.05
492	Al Osuna	.05
493	Rick Cerone	.05
494	Mariano Duncan	.05
495	Zane Smith	.05
496	John Morris	.05
497	Frank Tanana	.05
498	Junior Ortiz	.05
499	Dave Winfield	.45
500	Gary Varsho	.05
501	Chico Walker	.05
502	Ken Caminiti	.05
503	Ken Griffey Sr.	.05
504	Randy Myers	.05
505	Steve Bedrosian	.05
506	Cory Snyder	.05
507	Cris Carpenter	.05
508	Tim Belcher	.05
509	Jeff Hamilton	.05
510	Steve Avery	.05
511	Dave Valle	.05
512	Tom Lampkin	.05
513	Shawn Hillegas	.05
514	Reggie Jefferson	.05
515	Ron Karkovice	.05
516	Doug Drabek	.05
517	Tom Henke	.05
518	Chris Bosio	.05
519	Gregg Olson	.05
520	Bob Scanlan	.05
521	Alonzo Powell	.05
522	Jeff Ballard	.05
523	Ray Lankford	.05
524	Tommy Greene	.05
525	Mike Timlin	.05
526	Juan Berenguer	.05
527	Scott Erickson	.05
528	Checklist (Sandy Alomar Jr.)	.05

Gold Rookies

MO VAUGHN 1B

Special gold rookie and gold bonus cards were randomly inserted in 1991 Leaf packs. Backs have a design similar to the regular-issue cards, but have gold, rather than silver background. Fronts have gold-foil highlights. Card numbers of the issued version have a "BC" prefix, but there is a much rarer

second version of the Series 1 cards, which carry card numbers between 265-276.

		NM/M
Complete Set (26):		10.00
Common Player:		.10
1	Scott Leius	.10
2	Luis Gonzalez	.40
3	Wil Cordero	.10
4	Gary Scott	.10
5	Willie Banks	.10
6	Arthur Rhodes	.10
7	Mo Vaughn	.25
8	Henry Rodriguez	.10
9	Todd Van Poppel	.10
10	Reggie Sanders	.10
11	Rico Brogna	.10
12	Mike Mussina	2.00
13	Kirk Dressendorfer	.10
14	Jeff Bagwell	6.00
15	Pete Schourek	.10
16	Wade Taylor	.10
17	Pat Kelly	.10
18	Tim Costo	.10
19	Roger Salkeld	.10
20	Andujar Cedeno	.10
21	Ryan Klesko	.10
22	Mike Huff	.10
23	Anthony Young	.10
24	Eddie Zosky	.10
25	Nolan Ryan (7th no-hitter)	.50
26	Rickey Henderson (Record Steal)	.25
	Plooey (Babe Ruth)	.01
265	Scott Leius	4.00
266	Luis Gonzalez	6.00
267	Wil Cordero	4.00
268	Gary Scott	4.00
269	Willie Banks	4.00
270	Arthur Rhodes	4.00
271	Mo Vaughn	10.00
272	Henry Rodriguez	4.00
273	Todd Van Poppel	4.00
274	Reggie Sanders	4.00
275	Rico Brogna	4.00
276	Mike Mussina	30.00

1992 Leaf Previews

FRED McGRIFF PADRES

In a format identical to the regular-issue 1992 Leaf cards, this 26-card preview set was issued as a bonus in packs of four cards in each 1992 Donruss hobby factory set.

		NM/M
Complete Set (26):		15.00
Common Player:		.25
1	Steve Avery	.25
2	Ryne Sandberg	1.00
3	Chris Sabo	.25
4	Jeff Bagwell	.75
5	Darryl Strawberry	.25
6	Bret Barberie	.25
7	Howard Johnson	.25
8	John Kruk	.25
9	Andy Van Slyke	.25
10	Felix Jose	.25
11	Fred McGriff	.25
12	Will Clark	.35
13	Cal Ripken, Jr.	3.00
14	Phil Plantier	.25
15	Lee Stevens	.25
16	Frank Thomas	.75
17	Mark Whiten	.25
18	Cecil Fielder	.25
19	George Brett	1.50
20	Robin Yount	.75
21	Scott Erickson	.25
22	Don Mattingly	1.50
23	Jose Canseco	.50
24	Ken Griffey Jr.	2.00
25	Nolan Ryan	3.00
26	Joe Carter	.25

1992 Leaf

Two 264-card series comprise this 528-card set. The cards feature action photos on both the front and the back. Silver borders surround the photo on the card

TRAVIS FRYMAN 3B

front. Each leaf card was also produced in a gold foil version. One gold card was issued per pack and a complete Leaf Gold Edition set can be assembled. Traded players and free agents are shown in uniform with their new teams.

	NM/M
Complete Set (528):	7.50
Common Player:	.05
Series 1 or 2 Pack:	.40
Series 1 or 2 Wax Box:	7.50

#	Player	
1	Jim Abbott	.05
2	Cal Eldred	.05
3	Bud Black	.05
4	Dave Howard	.05
5	Luis Sojo	.05
6	Gary Scott	.05
7	Joe Oliver	.05
8	Chris Gardner	.05
9	Sandy Alomar	.05
10	Greg Harris	.05
11	Doug Drabek	.05
12	Darryl Hamilton	.05
13	Mike Mussina	.30
14	Kevin Tapani	.05
15	Ron Gant	.05
16	Mark McGwire	1.00
17	Robin Ventura	.05
18	Pedro Guerrero	.05
19	Roger Clemens	.65
20	Steve Farr	.05
21	Frank Tanana	.05
22	Joe Hesketh	.05
23	Erik Hanson	.05
24	Greg Cadaret	.05
25	Rex Hudler	.05
26	Mark Grace	.05
27	Kelly Gruber	.05
28	Jeff Bagwell	.45
29	Darryl Strawberry	.05
30	Dave Smith	.05
31	Kevin Appier	.05
32	Steve Chitren	.05
33	Kevin Gross	.05
34	Rick Aguilera	.05
35	Juan Guzman	.05
36	Joe Orsulak	.05
37	Tim Raines	.05
38	Harold Reynolds	.05
39	Charlie Hough	.05
40	Tony Phillips	.05
41	Nolan Ryan	1.50
42	Vince Coleman	.05
43	Andy Van Slyke	.05
44	Tim Burke	.05
45	Luis Polonia	.05
46	Tom Browning	.05
47	Willie McGee	.05
48	Gary DiSarcina	.05
49	Mark Lewis	.05
50	Phil Plantier	.05
51	Doug Dascenzo	.05
52	Cal Ripken, Jr.	1.50
53	Pedro Munoz	.05
54	Carlos Hernandez	.05
55	Jerald Clark	.05
56	Jeff Brantley	.05
57	Don Mattingly	.65
58	Roger McDowell	.05
59	Steve Avery	.05
60	John Olerud	.05
61	Bill Gullickson	.05
62	Juan Gonzalez	.30
63	Felix Jose	.05
64	Robin Yount	.45
65	Greg Briley	.05
66	Steve Finley	.05
67	Checklist	.05
68	Tom Gordon	.05
69	Rob Dibble	.05
70	Glenallen Hill	.05
71	Calvin Jones	.05
72	Joe Girardi	.05
73	Barry Larkin	.05
74	Andy Benes	.05
75	Milt Cuyler	.05
76	Kevin Bass	.05
77	Pete Harnisch	.05
78	Wilson Alvarez	.05
79	Mike Devereaux	.05
80	Doug Henry	.05
81	Orel Hershiser	.05
82	Shane Mack	.05
83	Mike Macfarlane	.05
84	Thomas Howard	.05
85	Alex Fernandez	.05
86	Reggie Jefferson	.05
87	Leo Gomez	.05
88	Mel Hall	.05
89	Mike Greenwell	.05
90	Jeff Russell	.05
91	Steve Buechele	.05
92	David Cone	.05
93	Kevin Reimer	.05
94	Mark Lemke	.05
95	Bob Tewksbury	.05
96	Zane Smith	.05
97	Mark Eichhorn	.05
98	Kirby Puckett	.60
99	Paul O'Neill	.05
100	Dennis Eckersley	.35
101	Duane Ward	.05
102	Matt Nokes	.05
103	Mo Vaughn	.05
104	Pat Kelly	.05
105	Ron Karkovice	.05
106	Bill Spiers	.05
107	Gary Gaetti	.05
108	Mackey Sasser	.05
109	Robby Thompson	.05
110	Marvin Freeman	.05
111	Jimmy Key	.05
112	Dwight Gooden	.05
113	Charlie Leibrandt	.05
114	Devon White	.05
115	Charles Nagy	.05
116	Rickey Henderson	.45
117	Paul Assenmacher	.05
118	Junior Felix	.05
119	Julio Franco	.05
120	Norm Charlton	.05
121	Scott Servais	.05
122	Gerald Perry	.05
123	Brian McRae	.05
124	Don Slaught	.05
125	Juan Samuel	.05
126	Harold Baines	.05
127	Scott Livingstone	.05
128	Jay Buhner	.05
129	Darrin Jackson	.05
130	Luis Mercedes	.05
131	Brian Harper	.05
132	Howard Johnson	.05
133	Checklist	.05
134	Dante Bichette	.05
135	Dave Righetti	.05
136	Jeff Montgomery	.05
137	Joe Grahe	.05
138	Delino DeShields	.05
139	Jose Rijo	.05
140	Ken Caminiti	.05
141	Steve Olin	.05
142	Kurt Stillwell	.05
143	Jay Bell	.05
144	Jaime Navarro	.05
145	Ben McDonald	.05
146	Greg Gagne	.05
147	Jeff Blauser	.05
148	Carney Lansford	.05
149	Ozzie Guillen	.05
150	Milt Thompson	.05
151	Jeff Reardon	.05
152	Scott Sanderson	.05
153	Cecil Fielder	.05
154	Greg Harris	.05
155	Rich DeLucia	.05
156	Roberto Kelly	.05
157	Bryn Smith	.05
158	Chuck McElroy	.05
159	Tom Henke	.05
160	Luis Gonzalez	.05
161	Steve Wilson	.05
162	Shawn Boskie	.05
163	Mark Davis	.05
164	Mike Moore	.05
165	Mike Scioscia	.05
166	Scott Erickson	.05
167	Todd Stottlemyre	.05
168	Alvin Davis	.05
169	Greg Hibbard	.05
170	David Valle	.05
171	Dave Winfield	.45
172	Alan Trammell	.05
173	Kenny Rogers	.05
174	John Franco	.05
175	Jose Lind	.05
176	Pete Schourek	.05
177	Von Hayes	.05
178	Chris Hammond	.35
179	John Burkett	.05
180	Dickie Thon	.05
181	Joel Skinner	.05
182	Scott Cooper	.05
183	Andre Dawson	.25
184	Billy Ripken	.05
185	Kevin Mitchell	.05
186	Brett Butler	.05
187	Tony Fernandez	.05
188	Cory Snyder	.05
189	John Habyan	.05
190	Dennis Martinez	.05
191	John Smoltz	.05
192	Greg Myers	.05
193	Rob Deer	.05
194	Ivan Rodriguez	.45
195	Ray Lankford	.05
196	Bill Wegman	.05
197	Edgar Martinez	.05
198	Darryl Kile	.05
199	Checklist	.05
200	Brent Mayne	.05
201	Larry Walker	.05
202	Carlos Baerga	.05
203	Russ Swan	.05
204	Mike Morgan	.05
205	Hal Morris	.05
206	Tony Gwynn	.60
207	Mark Leiter	.05
208	Kirt Manwaring	.05
209	Al Osuna	.05
210	Bobby Thigpen	.05
211	Chris Hoiles	.05
212	B.J. Surhoff	.05
213	Lenny Harris	.05
214	Scott Leius	.05
215	Gregg Jefferies	.05
216	Bruce Hurst	.05
217	Steve Sax	.05
218	Dave Otto	.05
219	Sam Horn	.05
220	Charlie Hayes	.05
221	Frank Viola	.05
222	Jose Guzman	.05
223	Gary Redus	.05
224	Dave Gallagher	.05
225	Dean Palmer	.05
226	Greg Olson	.05
227	Jose DeLeon	.05
228	Mike LaValliere	.05
229	Mark Langston	.05
230	Chuck Knoblauch	.05
231	Bill Doran	.05
232	Dave Henderson	.05
233	Roberto Alomar	.20
234	Scott Fletcher	.05
235	Tim Naehring	.05
236	Mike Gallego	.05
237	Lance Johnson	.05
238	Paul Molitor	.45
239	Dan Gladden	.05
240	Willie Randolph	.05
241	Will Clark	.10
242	Sid Bream	.05
243	Derek Bell	.05
244	Bill Pecota	.05
245	Terry Pendleton	.05
246	Randy Ready	.05
247	Jack Armstrong	.05
248	Todd Van Poppel	.05
249	Shawon Dunston	.05
250	Bobby Rose	.05
251	Jeff Huson	.05
252	Bip Roberts	.05
253	Doug Jones	.05
254	Lee Smith	.05
255	George Brett	.65
256	Randy Tomlin	.05
257	Todd Benzinger	.05
258	Dave Stewart	.05
259	Mark Carreon	.05
260	Pete O'Brien	.05
261	Tim Teufel	.05
262	Bob Milacki	.05
263	Mark Guthrie	.05
264	Darrin Fletcher	.05
265	Omar Vizquel	.05
266	Chris Bosio	.05
267	Jose Canseco	.30
268	Mike Boddicker	.05
269	Lance Parrish	.05
270	Jose Vizcaino	.05
271	Chris Sabo	.05
272	Royce Clayton	.05
273	Marquis Grissom	.05
274	Fred McGriff	.05
275	Barry Bonds	1.50
276	Greg Vaughn	.05
277	Gregg Olson	.05
278	Dave Hollins	.05
279	Tom Glavine	.25
280	Bryan Hickerson	.05
281	Scott Radinsky	.05
282	Omar Olivares	.05
283	Ivan Calderon	.05
284	Kevin Maas	.05
285	Mickey Tettleton	.05
286	Wade Boggs	.60
287	Stan Belinda	.05
288	Bret Barberie	.05
289	Jose Oquendo	.05
290	Frank Castillo	.05
291	Dave Stieb	.05
292	Tommy Greene	.05
293	Eric Karros	.05
294	Greg Maddux	.60
295	Jim Eisenreich	.05
296	Rafael Palmeiro	.35
297	Ramon Martinez	.05
298	Tim Wallach	.05
299	Jim Thome	.45
300	Chito Martinez	.05
301	Mitch Williams	.05
302	Randy Johnson	.45
303	Carlton Fisk	.45
304	Travis Fryman	.05
305	Bobby Witt	.05
306	Dave Magadan	.05
307	Alex Cole	.05
308	Bobby Bonilla	.05
309	Bryan Harvey	.05
310	Rafael Belliard	.05
311	Mariano Duncan	.05
312	Chuck Crim	.05
313	John Kruk	.05
314	Ellis Burks	.05
315	Craig Biggio	.05
316	Glenn Davis	.05
317	Ryne Sandberg	.60
318	Mike Sharperson	.05
319	Rich Rodriguez	.05
320	Lee Guetterman	.05
321	Benito Santiago	.05
322	Jose Offerman	.05
323	Tony Pena	.05
324	Pat Borders	.05
325	Mike Henneman	.05
326	Kevin Brown	.05
327	Chris Nabholz	.05
328	Franklin Stubbs	.05
329	Tino Martinez	.05
330	Mickey Morandini	.05
331	Checklist	.05
332	Mark Gubicza	.05
333	Bill Landrum	.05
334	Mark Whiten	.05
335	Darren Daulton	.05
336	Rick Wilkins	.05
337	Brian Jordan RC	.25
338	Kevin Ward	.05
339	Ruben Amaro	.05
340	Trevor Wilson	.05
341	Andujar Cedeno	.05
342	Michael Huff	.05
343	Brady Anderson	.05
344	Craig Grebeck	.05
345	Bobby Ojeda	.05
346	Mike Pagliarulo	.05
347	Terry Shumpert	.05
348	Dann Bilardello	.05
349	Frank Thomas	.45
350	Albert Belle	.05
351	Jose Mesa	.05
352	Rich Monteleone	.05
353	Bob Walk	.05
354	Monty Fariss	.05
355	Luis Rivera	.05
356	Anthony Young	.05
357	Geno Petralli	.05
358	Otis Nixon	.05
359	Tom Pagnozzi	.05
360	Reggie Sanders	.05
361	Lee Stevens	.05
362	Kent Hrbek	.05
363	Orlando Merced	.05
364	Mike Bordick	.05
365	Dion James	.05
366	Jack Clark	.05
367	Mike Stanley	.05
368	Randy Velarde	.05
369	Dan Pasqua	.05
370	Pat Listach	.05
371	Mike Fitzgerald	.05
372	Tom Foley	.05
373	Matt Williams	.05
374	Brian Hunter	.05
375	Joe Carter	.05
376	Bret Saberhagen	.05
377	Mike Stanton	.05
378	Hubie Brooks	.05
379	Eric Bell	.05
380	Walt Weiss	.05
381	Danny Jackson°	.05
382	Manuel Lee	.05
383	Ruben Sierra	.05
384	Greg Swindell	.05
385	Ryan Bowen	.05
386	Kevin Ritz	.05
387	Curtis Wilkerson	.05
388	Gary Varsho	.05
389	Dave Hansen	.05
390	Bob Welch	.05
391	Lou Whitaker	.05
392	Ken Griffey Jr.	.75
393	Mike Maddux	.05
394	Arthur Rhodes	.05
395	Chili Davis	.05
396	Eddie Murray	.45
397	Checklist	.05
398	Dave Cochrane	.05
399	Kevin Seitzer	.05
400	Ozzie Smith	.60
401	Paul Sorrento	.05
402	Les Lancaster	.05
403	Junior Noboa	.05
404	Dave Justice	.05
405	Andy Ashby	.05
406	Danny Tartabull	.05
407	Bill Swift	.05
408	Craig Lefferts	.05
409	Tom Candiotti	.05
410	Lance Blankenship	.05
411	Jeff Tackett	.05
412	Sammy Sosa	.65
413	Jody Reed	.05
414	Bruce Ruffin	.05
415	Gene Larkin	.05
416	John Vanderwal	.05
417	Tim Belcher	.05
418	Steve Frey	.05
419	Dick Schofield	.05
420	Jeff King	.05
421	Kim Batiste	.05
422	Jack McDowell	.05
423	Damon Berryhill	.05
424	Gary Wayne	.05
425	Jack Morris	.05
426	Moises Alou	.05
427	Mark McLemore	.05
428	Juan Guerrero	.05
429	Scott Scudder	.05
430	Eric Davis	.05
431	Joe Slusarski	.05
432	Todd Zeile	.05
433	Dwayne Henry	.05
434	Cliff Brantley	.05
435	Butch Henry	.05
436	Todd Worrell	.05
437	Bob Scanlan	.05
438	Wally Joyner	.05
439	John Flaherty	.05
440	Brian Downing	.05
441	Darren Lewis	.05
442	Gary Carter	.45
443	Wally Ritchie	.05
444	Chris Jones	.05
445	Jeff Kent	.05
446	Gary Sheffield	.30
447	Ron Darling	.05
448	Deion Sanders	.05
449	Andres Galarraga	.05
450	Chuck Finley	.05
451	Derek Lilliquist	.05
452	Carl Willis	.05
453	Wes Chamberlain	.05
454	Roger Mason	.05
455	Spike Owen	.05
456	Thomas Howard	.05
457	Dave Martinez	.05
458	Pete Incaviglia	.05
459	Keith Miller	.05
460	Mike Fetters	.05
461	Paul Gibson	.05
462	George Bell	.05
463	Checklist	.05
464	Terry Mulholland	.05
465	Storm Davis	.05
466	Gary Pettis	.05
467	Randy Bush	.05
468	Ken Hill	.05
469	Rheal Cormier	.05
470	Andy Stankiewicz	.05
471	Dave Burba	.05
472	Henry Cotto	.05
473	Dale Sveum	.05
474	Rich Gossage	.05
475	William Suero	.05
476	Doug Strange	.05
477	Bill Krueger	.05
478	John Wetteland	.05
479	Melido Perez	.05
480	Lonnie Smith	.05
481	Mike Jackson	.05
482	Mike Gardiner	.05
483	David Wells	.05
484	Barry Jones	.05
485	Scott Bankhead	.05
486	Terry Leach	.05
487	Vince Horsman	.05
488	Dave Eiland	.05
489	Alejandro Pena	.05
490	Julio Valera	.05
491	Joe Boever	.05
492	Paul Miller	.05
493	Arci Cianfrocco RC	.05
494	Dave Fleming	.05
495	Kyle Abbott	.05
496	Chad Kreuter	.05
497	Chris James	.05
498	Donnie Hill	.05
499	Jacob Brumfield	.05
500	Ricky Bones	.05
501	Terry Steinbach	.05
502	Bernard Gilkey	.05
503	Dennis Cook	.05
504	Len Dykstra	.05
505	Mike Bielecki	.05
506	Bob Kipper	.05
507	Jose Melendez	.05
508	Rick Sutcliffe	.05
509	Ken Patterson	.05
510	Andy Allanson	.05
511	Al Newman	.05
512	Mark Gardner	.05
513	Jeff Schaefer	.05
514	Jim McNamara	.05
515	Peter Hoy	.05
516	Curt Schilling	.30
517	Kirk McCaskill	.05
518	Chris Gwynn	.05
519	Sid Fernandez	.05
520	Jeff Parrett	.05
521	Scott Ruskin	.05
522	Kevin McReynolds	.05
523	Rick Cerone	.05
524	Jesse Orosco	.05
525	Troy Afenir	.05
526	John Smiley	.05
527	Dale Murphy	.25
528	Leaf Set Card	.05

1992 Leaf Gold Previews

CHRIS SABO 3B

In the same format as the chase cards which would be included in the regular 1992 Leaf packs, this preview set was produced for distribution to the Donruss dealer network. Cards feature the same black borders and gold highlights as the regular-issue Leaf Gold cards, but are numbered "X of 33" on the back.

	NM/M
Complete Set (33):	30.00
Common Player:	.50
1	Steve Avery	.50
2	Ryne Sandberg	2.00
3	Chris Sabo	.50
4	Jeff Bagwell	1.50
5	Darryl Strawberry	.50
6	Bret Barbarie	.50
7	Howard Johnson	.50
8	John Kruk	.50
9	Andy Van Slyke	.50
10	Felix Jose	.50
11	Fred McGriff	.50
12	Will Clark	.60
13	Cal Ripken, Jr.	4.00
14	Phil Plantier	.50
15	Lee Stevens	.50
16	Frank Thomas	1.50
17	Mark Whiten	.50
18	Cecil Fielder	.50
19	George Brett	2.50
20	Robin Yount	1.50
21	Scott Erickson	.50
22	Don Mattingly	2.50
23	Jose Canseco	1.00
24	Ken Griffey Jr.	3.00
25	Nolan Ryan	4.00
26	Joe Carter	.50
27	Deion Sanders	.50
28	Dean Palmer	.50
29	Andy Benes	.50
30	Gary DiSarcina	.50
31	Chris Hoiles	.50
32	Mark McGwire	3.00
33	Reggie Sanders	.50

Gold Edition

JOSE VIZCAINO IF

This set is a parallel version of Leaf's regular 1992 set. Card fronts do not have silver borders like the regular cards do; black borders and gold foil highlights are seen instead. A Gold Edition card was inserted in each 15-card 1992 Leaf foil pack.

	NM/M
Complete Set (528):	35.00
Common Player:	.10
Stars/Rookies:	3X

Gold Rookies

PAT MAHOMES RHP

Two dozen of the major leagues' most promising players are featured in this insert set. Cards 1-12 were randomly included in Series 1 foil packs, while cards 13-24 were in Series 2 packs. Cards, numbered with a BC prefix, are standard size and enhanced with gold foil.

	NM/M
Complete Set (24):	4.00

Common Player:		.25
Jumbo:		1.5X
1	Chad Curtis	.25
2	Brent Gates	.25
3	Pedro Martinez	3.00
4	Kenny Lofton	.35
5	Turk Wendell	.25
6	Mark Hutton	.25
7	Todd Hundley	.25
8	Matt Stairs	.25
9	Ed Taubensee	.25
10	David Nied	.25
11	Salomon Torres	.25
12	Bret Boone	.50
13	John Ruffin	.25
14	Ed Martel	.25
15	Rick Trlicek	.25
16	Raul Mondesi	.25
17	Pat Mahomes	.25
18	Dan Wilson	.25
19	Donovan Osborne	.25
20	Dave Silvestri	.25
21	Gary DiSarcina	.25
22	Denny Neagle	.25
23	Steve Hosey	.25
24	John Doherty	.25

1993 Leaf Promo

This unmarked promo of company spokesman Frank Thomas can be distinguished from the issued version of his card #195 by the presence of the Franklin logo on the batting glove he wears. The logo was airbrushed away from the issued card.

		NM/M
195	Frank Thomas	10.00

1993 Leaf

Leaf issued this set in three series: two 220-card series and a 110-card update set. Card fronts have full-bleed action photos and players' names stamped in gold foil. Color-coded slate corners are used to differentiate teams. Backs have player photos against cityscapes or landmarks from the team's home city, a holographic embossed team logo and 1992 and career statistics. Players from the National League's expansion teams, the Colorado Rockies and Florida Marlins, along with the Cincinnati Reds, California Angels and Seattle Mariners were featured in Series II packs so they could be pictured in their new uniforms. The Update series included a specially numbered "DW" insert card honoring Dave Winfield's 3,000-hit landmark, plus 3,500 special Frank Thomas autographed cards.

		NM/M
Complete Set (550):		12.50
Common Player:		.05
Series 1 or 2 Pack (14):		.65
Series 1 or 2 Box (36):		12.50
Update Pack (14):		1.50
Update Box (36):		25.00

#	Player	Price
1	Ben McDonald	.05
2	Sid Fernandez	.05
3	Juan Guzman	.05
4	Curt Schilling	.40
5	Ivan Rodriguez	.65
6	Don Slaught	.05
7	Terry Steinbach	.05
8	Todd Zeile	.05
9	Andy Stankiewicz	.05
10	Tim Teufel	.05
11	Marvin Freeman	.05
12	Jim Austin	.05
13	Bob Scanlan	.05
14	Rusty Meacham	.05
15	Casey Candaele	.05
16	Travis Fryman	.05
17	Jose Offerman	.05
18	Albert Belle	.25
19	John Vander Wahl (Vander Wal)	.05
20	Dan Pasqua	.05
21	Frank Viola	.05
22	Terry Mulholland	.05
23	Gregg Olson	.05
24	Randy Tomlin	.05
25	Todd Stottlemyre	.05
26	Jose Oquendo	.05
27	Julio Franco	.05
28	Tony Gwynn	1.00
29	Ruben Sierra	.25
30	Bobby Thigpen	.05
31	Jim Bullinger	.05
32	Rick Aguilera	.05
33	Scott Servais	.05
34	Cal Eldred	.05
35	Mike Piazza	1.50
36	Brent Mayne	.05
37	Wil Cordero	.05
38	Milt Cuyler	.05
39	Howard Johnson	.05
40	Kenny Lofton	.05
41	Alex Fernandez	.05
42	Denny Neagle	.05
43	Tony Pena	.05
44	Bob Tewksbury	.05
45	Glenn Davis	.05
46	Fred McGriff	.05
47	John Olerud	.05
48	Steve Hosey	.05
49	Rafael Palmeiro	.65
50	Dave Justice	.05
51	Pete Harnisch	.05
52	Sam Militello	.05
53	Orel Hershiser	.05
54	Pat Mahomes	.05
55	Greg Colbrunn	.05
56	Greg Vaughn	.05
57	Vince Coleman	.05
58	Brian McRae	.05
59	Len Dykstra	.05
60	Dan Gladden	.05
61	Ted Power	.05
62	Donovan Osborne	.05
63	Ron Karkovice	.05
64	Frank Seminara	.05
65	Bob Zupcic	.05
66	Kirt Manwaring	.05
67	Mike Devereaux	.05
68	Mark Lemke	.05
69	Devon White	.05
70	Sammy Sosa	1.25
71	Pedro Astacio	.05
72	Dennis Eckersley	.60
73	Chris Nabholz	.05
74	Melido Perez	.05
75	Todd Hundley	.05
76	Kent Hrbek	.05
77	Mickey Morandini	.05
78	Tim McIntosh	.05
79	Andy Van Slyke	.05
80	Kevin McReynolds	.05
81	Mike Henneman	.05
82	Greg Harris	.05
83	Sandy Alomar Jr.	.05
84	Mike Jackson	.05
85	Ozzie Guillen	.05
86	Jeff Blauser	.05
87	John Valentin	.05
88	Rey Sanchez	.05
89	Rick Sutcliffe	.05
90	Luis Gonzalez	.25
91	Jeff Fassero	.05
92	Kenny Rogers	.05
93	Bret Saberhagen	.05
94	Bob Welch	.05
95	Darren Daulton	.05
96	Mike Gallego	.05
97	Orlando Merced	.05
98	Chuck Knoblauch	.05
99	Bernard Gilkey	.05
100	Billy Ashley	.05
101	Kevin Appier	.05
102	Jeff Brantley	.05
103	Bill Gullickson	.05
104	John Smoltz	.05
105	Paul Sorrento	.05
106	Steve Buechele	.05
107	Steve Sax	.05
108	Andujar Cedeno	.05
109	Billy Hatcher	.05
110	Checklist	.05
111	Alan Mills	.05
112	John Franco	.05
113	Jack Morris	.05
114	Mitch Williams	.05
115	Nolan Ryan	2.50
116	Jay Bell	.05
117	Mike Bordick	.05
118	Geronimo Pena	.05
119	Danny Tartabull	.05
120	Checklist	.05
121	Steve Avery	.05
122	Ricky Bones	.05
123	Mike Morgan	.05
124	Jeff Montgomery	.05
125	Jeff Bagwell	.75
126	Tony Phillips	.05
127	Lenny Harris	.05
128	Glenallen Hill	.05
129	Marquis Grissom	.25
130	Gerald Williams (Photo, stats actually Bernie Williams)	.20
131	Greg Harris	.05
132	Tommy Greene	.05
133	Chris Hoiles	.05
134	Bob Walk	.05
135	Duane Ward	.05
136	Tom Pagnozzi	.05
137	Jeff Huson	.05
138	Kurt Stillwell	.05
139	Dave Henderson	.05
140	Darrin Jackson	.05
141	Frank Castillo	.05
142	Scott Erickson	.05
143	Darryl Kile	.05
144	Bill Wegman	.05
145	Steve Wilson	.05
146	George Brett	1.25
147	Moises Alou	.05
148	Lou Whitaker	.05
149	Chico Walker	.05
150	Jerry Browne	.05
151	Kirk McCaskill	.05
152	Zane Smith	.05
153	Matt Young	.05
154	Lee Smith	.05
155	Leo Gomez	.05
156	Dan Walters	.05
157	Pat Borders	.05
158	Matt Williams	.05
159	Dean Palmer	.05
160	John Patterson	.05
161	Doug Jones	.05
162	John Habyan	.05
163	Pedro Martinez	.75
164	Carl Willis	.05
165	Darrin Fletcher	.05
166	B.J. Surhoff	.05
167	Eddie Murray	.75
168	Keith Miller	.05
169	Ricky Jordan	.05
170	Juan Gonzalez	.65
171	Charles Nagy	.05
172	Mark Clark	.05
173	Bobby Thigpen	.05
174	Tim Scott	.05
175	Scott Cooper	.05
176	Royce Clayton	.05
177	Brady Anderson	.05
178	Sid Bream	.05
179	Derek Bell	.05
180	Otis Nixon	.05
181	Kevin Gross	.05
182	Ron Darling	.05
183	John Wetteland	.05
184	Mike Stanley	.05
185	Jeff Kent	.05
186	Brian Harper	.05
187	Mariano Duncan	.05
188	Robin Yount	.75
189	Al Martin	.05
190	Eddie Zosky	.05
191	Mike Munoz	.05
192	Andy Benes	.05
193	Dennis Cook	.05
194	Bill Swift	.05
195	Frank Thomas	.75
196	Damon Berryhill	.05
197	Mike Greenwell	.05
198	Mark Grace	.05
199	Darryl Hamilton	.05
200	Derrick May	.05
201	Ken Hill	.05
202	Kevin Brown	.05
203	Dwight Gooden	.05
204	Bobby Witt	.05
205	Juan Bell	.05
206	Kevin Maas	.05
207	Jeff King	.05
208	Scott Leius	.05
209	Rheal Cormier	.05
210	Darryl Strawberry	.05
211	Tom Gordon	.05
212	Bud Black	.05
213	Mickey Tettleton	.05
214	Pete Smith	.05
215	Felix Fermin	.05
216	Rick Wilkins	.05
217	George Bell	.05
218	Eric Anthony	.05
219	Pedro Munoz	.05
220	Checklist	.05
221	Lance Blankenship	.05
222	Deion Sanders	.10
223	Craig Biggio	.05
224	Ryne Sandberg	1.00
225	Ron Gant	.05
226	Tom Brunansky	.05
227	Chad Curtis	.05
228	Joe Carter	.05
229	Brian Jordan	.05
230	Brett Butler	.05
231	Frank Bolick	.05
232	Rod Beck	.05
233	Carlos Baerga	.05
234	Eric Karros	.05
235	Jack Armstrong	.05
236	Bobby Bonilla	.05
237	Don Mattingly	1.25
238	Jeff Gardner	.05
239	Dave Hollins	.05
240	Steve Cooke	.05
241	Jose Canseco	.35
242	Ivan Calderon	.05
243	Tim Belcher	.05
244	Freddie Benavides	.05
245	Roberto Alomar	.25
246	Rob Deer	.05
247	Will Clark	.10
248	Mike Felder	.05
249	Harold Baines	.05
250	David Cone	.05
251	Mark Guthrie	.05
252	Ellis Burks	.05
253	Jim Abbott	.05
254	Chili Davis	.05
255	Chris Bosio	.05
256	Bret Barberie	.05
257	Hal Morris	.05
258	Dante Bichette	.05
259	Storm Davis	.05
260	Gary DiSarcina	.05
261	Ken Caminiti	.05
262	Paul Molitor	.75
263	Joe Oliver	.05
264	Pat Listach	.05
265	Gregg Jefferies	.05
266	Jose Guzman	.05
267	Eric Davis	.05
268	Delino DeShields	.05
269	Barry Bonds	2.50
270	Mike Bielecki	.05
271	Jay Buhner	.05
272	Scott Pose RC	.05
273	Tony Fernandez	.05
274	Chito Martinez	.05
275	Phil Plantier	.05
276	Pete Incaviglia	.05
277	Carlos Garcia	.05
278	Tom Henke	.05
279	Roger Clemens	1.25
280	Rob Dibble	.05
281	Daryl Boston	.05
282	Greg Gagne	.05
283	Cecil Fielder	.05
284	Carlton Fisk	.75
285	Wade Boggs	1.00
286	Damion Easley	.05
287	Norm Charlton	.05
288	Jeff Conine	.05
289	Roberto Kelly	.05
290	Jerald Clark	.05
291	Rickey Henderson	.75
292	Chuck Finley	.05
293	Doug Drabek	.05
294	Dave Stewart	.05
295	Tom Glavine	.35
296	Jaime Navarro	.05
297	Ray Lankford	.05
298	Greg Hibbard	.05
299	Jody Reed	.05
300	Dennis Martinez	.05
301	Dave Martinez	.05
302	Reggie Jefferson	.05
303	John Cummings RC	.05
304	Orestes Destrade	.05
305	Mike Maddux	.05
306	David Segui	.05
307	Gary Sheffield	.35
308	Danny Jackson	.05
309	Craig Lefferts	.05
310	Andre Dawson	.20
311	Barry Larkin	.05
312	Alex Cole	.05
313	Mark Gardner	.05
314	Kirk Gibson	.05
315	Shane Mack	.05
316	Bo Jackson	.10
317	Jimmy Key	.05
318	Greg Myers	.05
319	Ken Griffey Jr.	1.50
320	Monty Fariss	.05
321	Kevin Mitchell	.05
322	Andres Galarraga	.05
323	Mark McGwire	2.00
324	Mark Langston	.05
325	Steve Finley	.05
326	Greg Maddux	1.00
327	Dave Nilsson	.05
328	Ozzie Smith	1.00
329	Candy Maldonado	.05
330	Checklist	.05
331	Tim Pugh RC	.05
332	Joe Girardi	.05
333	Junior Felix	.05
334	Greg Swindell	.05
335	Ramon Martinez	.05
336	Sean Berry	.05
337	Joe Orsulak	.05
338	Wes Chamberlain	.05
339	Stan Belinda	.05
340	Checklist	.05
341	Bruce Hurst	.05
342	John Burkett	.05
343	Mike Mussina	.40
344	Scott Fletcher	.05
345	Rene Gonzales	.05
346	Roberto Hernandez	.05
347	Carlos Martinez	.05
348	Bill Krueger	.05
349	Felix Jose	.05
350	John Jaha	.05
351	Willie Banks	.05
352	Matt Nokes	.05
353	Kevin Seitzer	.05
354	Erik Hanson	.05
355	David Hulse RC	.05
356	Domingo Martinez RC	.05
357	Greg Olson	.05
358	Randy Myers	.05
359	Tom Browning	.05
360	Charlie Hayes	.05
361	Bryan Harvey	.05
362	Eddie Taubensee	.05
363	Tim Wallach	.05
364	Mel Rojas	.05
365	Frank Tanana	.05
366	John Kruk	.05
367	Tim Laker RC	.05
368	Rich Rodriguez	.05
369	Darren Lewis	.05
370	Harold Reynolds	.05
371	Jose Melendez	.05
372	Joe Grahe	.05
373	Lance Johnson	.05
374	Jose Mesa	.05
375	Scott Livingstone	.05
376	Wally Joyner	.05
377	Kevin Reimer	.05
378	Kirby Puckett	1.00
379	Paul O'Neill	.05
380	Randy Johnson	.05
381	Manuel Lee	.05
382	Dick Schofield	.05
383	Darren Holmes	.05
384	Charlie Hough	.05
385	John Orton	.05
386	Edgar Martinez	.05
387	Terry Pendleton	.05
388	Dan Plesac	.05
389	Jeff Reardon	.05
390	David Nied	.05
391	Dave Magadan	.05
392	Larry Walker	.05
393	Ben Rivera	.05
394	Lonnie Smith	.05
395	Craig Shipley	.05
396	Willie McGee	.05
397	Arthur Rhodes	.05
398	Mike Stanton	.05
399	Luis Polonia	.05
400	Jack McDowell	.05
401	Mike Moore	.05
402	Jose Lind	.05
403	Bill Spiers	.05
404	Kevin Tapani	.05
405	Spike Owen	.05
406	Tino Martinez	.05
407	Charlie Leibrandt	.05
408	Ed Sprague	.05
409	Bryn Smith	.05
410	Benito Santiago	.05
411	Jose Rijo	.05
412	Pete O'Brien	.05
413	Willie Wilson	.05
414	Bip Roberts	.05
415	Eric Young	.05
416	Walt Weiss	.05
417	Milt Thompson	.05
418	Chris Sabo	.05
419	Scott Sanderson	.05
420	Tim Raines	.05
421	Alan Trammell	.05
422	Mike Macfarlane	.05
423	Dave Winfield	.75
424	Bob Wickman	.05
425	David Valle	.05
426	Gary Redus	.05
427	Turner Ward	.05
428	Reggie Sanders	.05
429	Todd Worrell	.05
430	Julio Valera	.05
431	Cal Ripken, Jr.	2.50
432	Mo Vaughn	.05
433	John Smiley	.05
434	Omar Vizquel	.05
435	Billy Ripken	.05
436	Cory Snyder	.05
437	Carlos Quintana	.05
438	Omar Olivares	.05
439	Robin Ventura	.05
440	Checklist	.05
441	Kevin Higgins	.05
442	Carlos Hernandez	.05
443	Dan Peltier	.05
444	Derek Lilliquist	.05
445	Tim Salmon	.05
446	Sherman Obando RC	.05
447	Pat Kelly	.05
448	Todd Van Poppel	.05
449	Mark Whiten	.05
450	Checklist	.05
451	Pat Meares	.05
452	Tony Tarasco RC	.05
453	Chris Gwynn	.05
454	Armando Reynoso	.05
455	Danny Darwin	.05
456	Willie Greene	.05
457	Mike Blowers	.05
458	Kevin Roberson RC	.05
459	Graeme Lloyd RC	.05
460	David West	.05
461	Joey Cora	.05
462	Alex Arias	.05
463	Chad Kreuter	.05
464	Mike Lansing	.05
465	Mike Timlin	.05
466	Paul Wagner	.05
467	Mark Portugal	.05
468	Jim Leyritz	.05
469	Ryan Klesko	.05
470	Mario Diaz	.05
471	Guillermo Velasquez	.05
472	Fernando Valenzuela	.05
473	Raul Mondesi	.05
474	Mike Pagliarulo	.05
475	Chris Hammond	.05
476	Torey Lovullo	.05
477	Trevor Wilson	.05
478	Marcos Armas RC	.05
479	Dave Gallagher	.05
480	Jeff Treadway	.05
481	Jeff Branson	.05
482	Dickie Thon	.05
483	Eduardo Perez	.05
484	David Wells	.05
485	Brian Williams	.05
486	Domingo Cedeno	.05
487	Tom Candiotti	.05
488	Steve Frey	.05
489	Greg McMichael	.05
490	Marc Newfield	.05
491	Larry Andersen	.05
492	Damon Buford	.05
493	Ricky Gutierrez	.05
494	Jeff Russell	.05
495	Vinny Castilla	.05
496	Wilson Alvarez	.05
497	Scott Bullett	.05
498	Larry Casian	.05
499	Jose Vizcaino	.05
500	J.T. Snow RC	.75
501	Bryan Hickerson	.05
502	Jeremy Hernandez	.05
503	Jeromy Burnitz	.05
504	Steve Farr	.05
505	J. Owens	.05
506	Craig Paquette	.05
507	Jim Eisenreich	.05
508	Matt Whiteside	.05
509	Luis Aquino	.05
510	Mike LaValliere	.05
511	Jim Gott	.05
512	Mark McLemore	.05
513	Randy Milligan	.05
514	Gary Gaetti	.05
515	Lou Frazier	.05
516	Rich Amaral	.05
517	Gene Harris	.05
518	Aaron Sele	.05
519	Mark Wohlers	.05
520	Scott Kamieniecki	.05
521	Kent Mercker	.05
522	Jim Deshaies	.05
523	Kevin Stocker	.05
524	Jason Bere	.05
525	Tim Bogar	.05
526	Brad Pennington	.05
527	Curt Leskanic RC	.05
528	Wayne Kirby	.05
529	Tim Costo	.05
530	Doug Henry	.05
531	Trevor Hoffman	.05
532	Kelly Gruber	.05
533	Mike Harkey	.05
534	John Doherty	.05
535	Erik Pappas	.05
536	Brent Gates	.05
537	Roger McDowell	.05
538	Chris Haney	.05
539	Blas Minor	.05
540	Pat Hentgen	.05
541	Chuck Carr	.05
542	Doug Strange	.05
543	Xavier Hernandez	.05
544	Paul Quantrill	.05
545	Anthony Young	.05
546	Bret Boone	.05
547	Dwight Smith	.05
548	Bobby Munoz	.05
549	Russ Springer	.05
550	Roger Pavlik	.05
----	Dave Winfield (3000 Hits)	2.00

Fasttrack

This 20-card insert set was released in two series; cards 1-10 were randomly included in Leaf Series I retail packs, while 11-20 were in Series II packs. Card fronts and backs are similar with a player photo and a diagonal white strip with "on the Fasttrack" printed in black and red. Fronts have the gold embossed Leaf logo, backs have the silver holographic team logo.

		NM/M
Complete Set (20):		15.00
Common Player:		.60
1	Frank Thomas	3.00
2	Tim Wakefield	.60
3	Kenny Lofton	1.00
4	Mike Mussina	1.00
5	Juan Gonzalez	2.50
6	Chuck Knoblauch	.60
7	Eric Karros	.60
8	Ray Lankford	.60
9	Juan Guzman	.60

10	Pat Listach	.60
11	Carlos Baerga	.60
12	Felix Jose	.60
13	Steve Avery	.60
14	Robin Ventura	.60
15	Ivan Rodriguez	2.50
16	Cal Eldred	.60
17	Jeff Bagwell	3.00
18	Dave Justice	.60
19	Travis Fryman	.60
20	Marquis Grissom	.60

Gold All-Stars

Cards 1-10 in this insert set were randomly inserted one per Leaf Series I jumbo packs, while cards 11-20 were in Series II jumbo packs. Cards feature two players per card, one on each side. Only one side is numbered, but both sides have gold foil.

		NM/M
Complete Set (20):		15.00
Common Player:		.25
1	Ivan Rodriguez, Darren Daulton	.75
2	Don Mattingly, Fred McGriff	1.50
3	Cecil Fielder, Jeff Bagwell	.75
4	Carlos Baerga, Ryne Sandberg	1.00
5	Chuck Knoblauch, Delino DeShields	.25
6	Robin Ventura, Terry Pendleton	.25
7	Ken Griffey Jr., Andy Van Slyke	2.00
8	Joe Carter, Dave Justice	.25
9	Jose Canseco, Tony Gwynn	1.00
10	Dennis Eckersley, Rob Dibble	.60
11	Mark McGwire, Will Clark	2.50
12	Frank Thomas, Mark Grace	.75
13	Roberto Alomar, Craig Biggio	.50
14	Barry Larkin, Cal Ripken, Jr.	3.00
15	Gary Sheffield, Edgar Martinez	.50
16	Juan Gonzalez, Barry Bonds	3.00
17	Kirby Puckett, Marquis Grissom	1.00
18	Jim Abbott, Tom Glavine	.40
19	Nolan Ryan, Greg Maddux	3.00
20	Roger Clemens, Doug Drabek	1.50

Gold Rookies

These cards, numbered 1 of 20 etc., feature 1993 rookies and were randomly inserted into hobby foil packs, 10 players per series. Card fronts feature action photos, while the backs show a player photo against a landmark from his team's city. Jumbo versions in 3-1/2" x 5" format were produced as special retail box toppers, in a numbered edition of 5,000 each.

		NM/M
Complete Set (20):		5.00
Common Player:		.25
1	Kevin Young	.25
2	Wil Cordero	.25
3	Mark Kiefer	.25
4	Gerald Williams	.25
5	Brandon Wilson	.25
6	Greg Gohr	.25
7	Ryan Thompson	.25
8	Tim Wakefield	.25
9	Troy Neel	.25
10	Tim Salmon	.50
11	Kevin Rogers	.25
12	Rod Bolton	.25
13	Ken Ryan	.25
14	Phil Hiatt	.25
15	Rene Arocha	.25
16	Nigel Wilson	.25
17	J.T. Snow	.50
18	Benji Gil	.25
19	Chipper Jones	3.00
20	Darrell Sherman	.25

Heading for the Hall

Ten players on the way to the Baseball Hall of Fame are featured in this insert set. Series I Leaf packs had cards 1-5 randomly included; Series II packs had cards 6-10.

		NM/M
Complete Set (10):		10.00
Common Player:		.75
1	Nolan Ryan	2.50
2	Tony Gwynn	1.00
3	Robin Yount	1.00
4	Eddie Murray	1.00
5	Cal Ripken, Jr.	2.50
6	Roger Clemens	2.00
7	George Brett	2.00
8	Ryne Sandberg	1.00
9	Kirby Puckett	1.00
10	Ozzie Smith	1.00

Frank Thomas

Leaf signed Frank Thomas as its spokesman for 1993, and honored him with a 10-card insert set. Cards 1-5 were randomly included in Series I packs; cards 6-10 were in Series II packs. A large "Frank" logo in a holographic foil stamp is featured on each card front along with a one-word character trait. On back is a color portrait photo of Thomas superimposed on a Chicago skyline. A paragraph on back describes how the character trait on front applies to Thomas.

		NM/M
Complete Set (10):		4.50
Common Card:		.75
Autographed Card:		30.00

1	Aggressive (Frank Thomas)		.75
2	Serious (Frank Thomas)		.75
3	Intense (Frank Thomas)		.75
4	Confident (Frank Thomas)		.75
5	Assertive (Frank Thomas)		.75
6	Power (Frank Thomas)		.75
7	Control (Frank Thomas)		.75
8	Strength (Frank Thomas)		.75
9	Concentration (Frank Thomas)		.75
10	Preparation (Frank Thomas)		.75

Update Gold All-Stars

These 10 cards, featuring 20 all-stars, were randomly inserted in Leaf Update packs. Each card features two players, one on each side. Cards are distinguished from the regular Gold All-Stars by indicating on the front the card is number X of 10, with a tiny white "Update" in the red stripe above the card number.

		NM/M
Complete Set (10):		7.50
Common Player:		.25
1	Mark Langston, Terry Mulholland	.25
2	Ivan Rodriguez, Darren Daulton	.50
3	John Olerud, John Kruk	.25
4	Roberto Alomar, Ryne Sandberg	1.00
5	Wade Boggs, Gary Sheffield	.75
6	Cal Ripken, Jr., Barry Larkin	3.00
7	Kirby Puckett, Barry Bonds	2.50
8	Marquis Grissom, Ken Griffey Jr.	2.00
9	Joe Carter, Dave Justice	.25
10	Mark Grace, Paul Molitor	.75

Update Gold Rookies

These five cards were randomly inserted in Leaf Update packs. Cards are similiar in design to the regular Gold Rookies cards, except the logo on the back indicates they are from the Update series. Jumbo 3-1/2" x 5" versions were produced as special retail box toppers in a numbered edition of 5,000 each.

		NM/M
Complete Set (5):		3.50
Common Player:		.25
Jumbos:		1.5X
1	Allen Watson	.25
2	Jeffrey Hammonds	.25

3	David McCarty	.25
4	Mike Piazza	3.00
5	Roberto Meija	.25

Update Frank Thomas Autograph

This card was a random insert in '93 Leaf Update packs and features a genuine Frank Thomas autograph on front. Unlike the other cards in the set, this has a silver-gray border on front and back. Front has a gold-foil seal in upper-left. Back has a photo of Thomas in his batting follow-through. At bottom on back is a white strip bearing the card's individual serial number from an edition of 3,500.

		NM/M
FT	Frank Thomas	35.00

Update Frank Thomas Super

This 10-card insert set features Leaf's 1993 spokesman, Frank Thomas. Cards, which measure 5" x 7", were included one per every Leaf Update foil box and are identical to the inserts found in Series I and II except in size. Cards are individually numbered. Thomas autographed 3,500 cards.

		NM/M
Complete Set (10):		17.50
Common Card:		2.00
1	Aggressive (Frank Thomas)	2.00
2	Serious (Frank Thomas)	2.00
3	Intense (Frank Thomas)	2.00
4	Confident (Frank Thomas)	2.00
5	Assertive (Frank Thomas)	2.00
6	Power (Frank Thomas)	2.00
7	Control (Frank Thomas)	2.00
8	Strength (Frank Thomas)	2.00
9	Concentration (Frank Thomas)	2.00
10	Preparation (Frank Thomas)	2.00

1994 Leaf Promos

Identical in format to the regular issue, this nine-card set was produced as a preview for the 1994 Leaf cards. The only differences on the promo cards are a large, black "Promotional Sample" notice

overprinted diagonally on both the front and back of the cards. Instead of the regular card numbers, the promos are numbered "X of" at top to the left of the team logo hologram.

		NM/M
Complete Set (9):		7.50
Common Player:		.25
1	Roberto Alomar	.75
2	Darren Daulton	.25
3	Ken Griffey Jr.	2.00
4	David Justice	.25
5	Don Mattingly	1.50
6	Mike Piazza	2.00
7	Cal Ripken, Jr.	3.00
8	Ryne Sandberg	1.25
9	Frank Thomas	1.00

1994 Leaf

Donruss returned its premium-brand Leaf set in 1994 with an announced 25 percent production cut from the previous season - fewer than 20,000 20-box cases of each 220-card series. Game-action photos dominate the fronts of the cards, borderless at the top and sides. At bottom are team color-coded faux-marble borders with the player's name (last name in gold foil) and team. Backs have a background of the player's home stadium with another action photo superimposed. In a ticket-stub device at upper-left is a portrait photo and a few personal numbers. Previous season and career stats are in white stripes at bottom. The team logo is presented in holographic foil at upper-right. To feature 1994's new stadiums and uniforms, cards of the Indians, Rangers, Brewers and Astros were included only in the second series. Seven different types of insert cards were produced and distributed among the various types of Leaf packaging.

		NM/M
Complete Set (440):		10.00
Series 1 or 2 Pack (12):		.75
Series 1 or 2 Box (36):		12.50
1	Cal Ripken, Jr.	2.50
2	Tony Tarasco	.05
3	Joe Girardi	.05
4	Bernie Williams	.20
5	Chad Kreuter	.05
6	Troy Neel	.05
7	Tom Pagnozzi	.05
8	Kirk Rueter	.05
9	Chris Bosio	.05
10	Dwight Gooden	.05
11	Mariano Duncan	.05
12	Jay Bell	.05
13	Lance Johnson	.05
14	Richie Lewis	.05
15	Dave Martinez	.05
16	Orel Hershiser	.05
17	Rob Butler	.05
18	Glenallen Hill	.05
19	Chad Curtis	.05
20	Mike Stanton	.05
21	Tim Wallach	.05
22	Milt Thompson	.05
23	Kevin Young	.05
24	John Smiley	.05
25	Jeff Montgomery	.05
26	Robin Ventura	.05
27	Scott Lydy	.05
28	Todd Stottlemyre	.05
29	Mark Whiten	.05
30	Robby Thompson	.05
31	Bobby Bonilla	.05
32	Andy Ashby	.05
33	Greg Myers	.05
34	Billy Hatcher	.05
35	Brad Holman	.05
36	Mark McLemore	.05
37	Scott Sanders	.05
38	Jim Abbott	.05
39	David Wells	.05
40	Roberto Kelly	.05
41	Jeff Conine	.05
42	Sean Berry	.05
43	Mark Grace	.05
44	Eric Young	.05
45	Rick Aguilera	.05
46	Chipper Jones	1.00
47	Mel Rojas	.05
48	Ryan Thompson	.05
49	Al Martin	.05
50	Cecil Fielder	.05
51	Pat Kelly	.05
52	Kevin Tapani	.05
53	Tim Costo	.05
54	Dave Hollins	.05
55	Kirt Manwaring	.05
56	Gregg Jefferies	.05
57	Ron Darling	.05
58	Bill Haselman	.05
59	Phil Plantier	.05
60	Frank Viola	.05
61	Todd Zeile	.05
62	Bret Barberie	.05
63	Roberto Mejia	.05
64	Chuck Knoblauch	.05
65	Jose Lind	.05
66	Brady Anderson	.05
67	Ruben Sierra	.05
68	Jose Vizcaino	.05
69	Joe Grahe	.05
70	Kevin Appier	.05
71	Wilson Alvarez	.05
72	Tom Candiotti	.05
73	John Burkett	.05
74	Anthony Young	.05
75	Scott Cooper	.05
76	Nigel Wilson	.05
77	John Valentin	.05
78	Dave McCarty	.05
79	Archi Cianfrocco	.05
80	Lou Whitaker	.05
81	Dante Bichette	.05
82	Mark Dewey	.05
83	Danny Jackson	.05
84	Harold Baines	.05
85	Todd Benzinger	.05
86	Damion Easley	.05
87	Danny Cox	.05
88	Jose Bautista	.05
89	Mike Lansing	.05
90	Phil Hiatt	.05
91	Tim Pugh	.05
92	Tino Martinez	.05
93	Raul Mondesi	.05
94	Greg Maddux	1.00
95	Al Leiter	.05
96	Benito Santiago	.05
97	Len Dykstra	.05
98	Sammy Sosa	1.25
99	Tim Bogar	.05
100	Checklist	
101	Deion Sanders	.10
102	Bobby Witt	.05
103	Wil Cordero	.05
104	Rich Amaral	.05
105	Mike Mussina	.50
106	Reggie Sanders	.05
107	Ozzie Guillen	.05
108	Paul O'Neill	.05
109	Tim Salmon	.05
110	Rheal Cormier	.05
111	Billy Ashley	.05
112	Jeff Kent	.05
113	Derek Bell	.05
114	Danny Darwin	.05
115	Chip Hale	.05
116	Tim Raines	.05
117	Ed Sprague	.05
118	Darrin Fletcher	.05
119	Darren Holmes	.05
120	Alan Trammell	.05
121	Don Mattingly	1.25
122	Greg Gagne	.05
123	Jose Offerman	.05
124	Joe Orsulak	.05
125	Jack McDowell	.05
126	Barry Larkin	.05
127	Ben McDonald	.05
128	Mike Bordick	.05
129	Devon White	.05
130	Mike Perez	.05

131	Jay Buhner	.05
132	Phil Leftwich	.05
133	Tommy Greene	.05
134	Charlie Hayes	.05
135	Don Slaught	.05
136	Mike Gallego	.05
137	Dave Winfield	.75
138	Steve Avery	.05
139	Derrick May	.05
140	Bryan Harvey	.05
141	Wally Joyner	.05
142	Andre Dawson	.20
143	Andy Benes	.05
144	John Franco	.05
145	Jeff King	.05
146	Joe Oliver	.05
147	Bill Gullickson	.05
148	Armando Reynoso	.05
149	Dave Fleming	.05
150	Checklist	.05
151	Todd Van Poppel	.05
152	Bernard Gilkey	.05
153	Kevin Gross	.05
154	Mike Devereaux	.05
155	Tim Wakefield	.05
156	Andres Galarraga	.05
157	Pat Meares	.05
158	Jim Leyritz	.05
159	Mike Macfarlane	.05
160	Tony Phillips	.05
161	Brent Gates	.05
162	Mark Langston	.05
163	Allen Watson	.05
164	Randy Johnson	.75
165	Doug Brocail	.05
166	Rob Dibble	.05
167	Roberto Hernandez	.05
168	Felix Jose	.05
169	Steve Cooke	.05
170	Darren Daulton	.05
171	Eric Karros	.05
172	Geronimo Pena	.05
173	Gary DiSarcina	.05
174	Marquis Grissom	.05
175	Joey Cora	.05
176	Jim Eisenreich	.05
177	Brad Pennington	.05
178	Terry Steinbach	.05
179	Pat Borders	.05
180	Steve Buechele	.05
181	Jeff Fassero	.05
182	Mike Greenwell	.05
183	Mike Henneman	.05
184	Ron Karkovice	.05
185	Pat Hentgen	.05
186	Jose Guzman	.05
187	Brett Butler	.05
188	Charlie Hough	.05
189	Terry Pendleton	.05
190	Melido Perez	.05
191	Orestes Destrade	.05
192	Mike Morgan	.05
193	Joe Carter	.05
194	Jeff Blauser	.05
195	Chris Hoiles	.05
196	Ricky Gutierrez	.05
197	Mike Moore	.05
198	Carl Willis	.05
199	Aaron Sele	.05
200	Checklist	.05
201	Tim Naehring	.05
202	Scott Livingstone	.05
203	Luis Alicea	.05
204	Torey Lovullo RC	.05
205	Jim Gott	.05
206	Bob Wickman	.05
207	Greg McMichael	.05
208	Scott Brosius	.05
209	Chris Gwynn	.05
210	Steve Sax	.05
211	Dick Schofield	.05
212	Robb Nen	.05
213	Ben Rivera	.05
214	Vinny Castilla	.05
215	Jamie Moyer	.05
216	Wally Whitehurst	.05
217	Frank Castillo	.05
218	Mike Blowers	.05
219	Tim Scott	.05
220	Paul Wagner	.05
221	Jeff Bagwell	.75
222	Ricky Bones	.05
223	Sandy Alomar Jr.	.05
224	Rod Beck	.05
225	Roberto Alomar	.20
226	Jack Armstrong	.05
227	Scott Erickson	.05
228	Rene Arocha	.05
229	Eric Anthony	.05
230	Jeromy Burnitz	.05
231	Kevin Brown	.05
232	Tim Belcher	.05
233	Bret Boone	.05
234	Dennis Eckersley	.05
235	Tom Glavine	.30
236	Craig Biggio	.05
237	Pedro Astacio	.05
238	Ryan Bowen	.05
239	Brad Ausmus	.05
240	Vince Coleman	.05
241	Jason Bere	.05
242	Ellis Burks	.05
243	Wes Chamberlain	.05
244	Ken Caminiti	.05
245	Willie Banks	.05
246	Sid Fernandez	.05
247	Carlos Baerga	.05
248	Carlos Garcia	.05

249	Jose Canseco	.50
250	Alex Diaz	.05
251	Albert Belle	.05
252	Moises Alou	.05
253	Bobby Ayala	.05
254	Tony Gwynn	1.00
255	Roger Clemens	1.25
256	Eric Davis	.05
257	Wade Boggs	1.00
258	Chili Davis	.05
259	Rickey Henderson	.75
260	Andujar Cedeno	.05
261	Cris Carpenter	.05
262	Juan Guzman	.05
263	Dave Justice	.05
264	Barry Bonds	2.50
265	Pete Incaviglia	.05
266	Tony Fernandez	.05
267	Cal Eldred	.05
268	Alex Fernandez	.05
269	Kent Hrbek	.05
270	Steve Farr	.05
271	Doug Drabek	.05
272	Brian Jordan	.05
273	Xavier Hernandez	.05
274	David Cone	.05
275	Brian Hunter	.05
276	Mike Harkey	.05
277	Delino DeShields	.05
278	David Hulse	.05
279	Mickey Tettleton	.05
280	Kevin McReynolds	.05
281	Darryl Hamilton	.05
282	Ken Hill	.05
283	Wayne Kirby	.05
284	Chris Hammond	.05
285	Mo Vaughn	.05
286	Ryan Klesko	.05
287	Rick Wilkins	.05
288	Bill Swift	.05
289	Rafael Palmeiro	.65
290	Brian Harper	.05
291	Chris Turner	.05
292	Luis Gonzalez	.25
293	Kenny Rogers	.05
294	Kirby Puckett	1.00
295	Mike Stanley	.05
296	Carlos Reyes	.05
297	Charles Nagy	.05
298	Reggie Jefferson	.05
299	Bip Roberts	.05
300	Darrin Jackson	.05
301	Mike Jackson	.05
302	Dave Nilsson	.05
303	Ramon Martinez	.05
304	Bobby Jones	.05
305	Johnny Ruffin	.05
306	Brian McRae	.05
307	Bo Jackson	.10
308	Dave Stewart	.05
309	John Smoltz	.05
310	Dennis Martinez	.05
311	Dean Palmer	.05
312	David Nied	.05
313	Eddie Murray	.75
314	Darryl Kile	.05
315	Rick Sutcliffe	.05
316	Shawon Dunston	.05
317	John Jaha	.05
318	Salomon Torres	.05
319	Gary Sheffield	.45
320	Curt Schilling	.05
321	Greg Vaughn	.05
322	Jay Howell	.05
323	Todd Hundley	.05
324	Chris Sabo	.05
325	Stan Javier	.05
326	Willie Greene	.05
327	Hipolito Pichardo	.05
328	Doug Strange	.05
329	Dan Wilson	.05
330	Checklist	.05
331	Omar Vizquel	.05
332	Scott Servais	.05
333	Bob Tewksbury	.05
334	Matt Williams	.05
335	Tom Foley	.05
336	Jeff Russell	.05
337	Scott Leius	.05
338	Ivan Rodriguez	.65
339	Kevin Seitzer	.05
340	Jose Rijo	.05
341	Eduardo Perez	.05
342	Kirk Gibson	.05
343	Randy Milligan	.05
344	Edgar Martinez	.05
345	Fred McGriff	.05
346	Kurt Abbott	.05
347	John Kruk	.05
348	Mike Felder	.05
349	Dave Staton	.05
350	Kenny Lofton	.05
351	Graeme Lloyd	.05
352	David Segui	.05
353	Danny Tartabull	.05
354	Bob Welch	.05
355	Duane Ward	.05
356	Tuffy Rhodes	.05
357	Lee Smith	.05
358	Chris James	.05
359	Walt Weiss	.05
360	Pedro Munoz	.05
361	Paul Sorrento	.05
362	Todd Worrell	.05
363	Bob Hamelin	.05
364	Julio Franco	.05
365	Roberto Petagine	.05
366	Willie McGee	.05

367	Pedro Martinez	.75
368	Ken Griffey Jr.	1.50
369	B.J. Surhoff	.05
370	Kevin Mitchell	.05
371	John Doherty	.05
372	Manuel Lee	.05
373	Terry Mulholland	.05
374	Zane Smith	.05
375	Otis Nixon	.05
376	Jody Reed	.05
377	Doug Jones	.05
378	John Olerud	.05
379	Greg Swindell	.05
380	Checklist	.05
381	Royce Clayton	.05
382	Jim Thome	.65
383	Steve Finley	.05
384	Ray Lankford	.05
385	Henry Rodriguez	.05
386	Dave Magadan	.05
387	Gary Redus	.05
388	Orlando Merced	.05
389	Tom Gordon	.05
390	Luis Polonia	.05
391	Mark McGwire	2.00
392	Mark Lemke	.05
393	Doug Henry	.05
394	Chuck Finley	.05
395	Paul Molitor	.75
396	Randy Myers	.05
397	Larry Walker	.05
398	Pete Harnisch	.05
399	Darren Lewis	.05
400	Frank Thomas	.75
401	Jack Morris	.05
402	Greg Hibbard	.05
403	Jeffrey Hammonds	.05
404	Will Clark	.10
405	Travis Fryman	.05
406	Scott Sanderson	.05
407	Gene Harris	.05
408	Chuck Carr	.05
409	Ozzie Smith	1.00
410	Kent Mercker	.05
411	Andy Van Slyke	.05
412	Jimmy Key	.05
413	Pat Mahomes	.05
414	John Wetteland	.05
415	Todd Jones	.05
416	Greg Harris	.05
417	Kevin Stocker	.05
418	Juan Gonzalez	.65
419	Pete Smith	.05
420	Pat Listach	.05
421	Trevor Hoffman	.05
422	Scott Fletcher	.05
423	Mark Lewis	.05
424	Mickey Morandini	.05
425	Ryne Sandberg	1.00
426	Erik Hanson	.05
427	Gary Gaetti	.05
428	Harold Reynolds	.05
429	Mark Portugal	.05
430	David Valle	.05
431	Mitch Williams	.05
432	Howard Johnson	.05
433	Hal Morris	.05
434	Tom Henke	.05
435	Shane Mack	.05
436	Mike Piazza	1.50
437	Bret Saberhagen	.05
438	Jose Mesa	.05
439	Jaime Navarro	.05
440	Checklist	.05

Clean-Up Crew

The number four spot in the line-up is featured on this 12-card insert set (six per series) found only in magazine distributor packaging. Fronts are gold-foil enhanced; backs feature an action photo set against a background of a line-up card on which the player is penciled into the #4 spot. His 1993 stats when batting clean-up are presented.

		NM/M
Complete Set (12):		8.00
Common Player:		1.00
1	Larry Walker	1.00
2	Andres Galarraga	1.00
3	Dave Hollins	1.00
4	Bobby Bonilla	1.00

5	Cecil Fielder	1.00
6	Danny Tartabull	1.00
7	Juan Gonzalez	2.00
8	Joe Carter	1.00
9	Fred McGriff	1.00
10	Matt Williams	1.00
11	Albert Belle	1.00
12	Harold Baines	1.00

Gamers

Leaf jumbo packs are the exclusive venue for the six cards of this insert set which were issued in each series.

		NM/M
Complete Set (12):		30.00
Common Player:		1.00
1	Ken Griffey Jr.	6.00
2	Len Dykstra	1.00
3	Juan Gonzalez	3.00
4	Don Mattingly	6.00
5	Dave Justice	1.00
6	Mark Grace	1.00
7	Frank Thomas	4.00
8	Barry Bonds	7.50
9	Kirby Puckett	4.50
10	Will Clark	1.00
11	John Kruk	1.00
12	Mike Piazza	6.00

Gold Rookies

A gold-foil rendered stadium background and huge black "94 Gold Leaf Rookie" serve as a backdrop for a player photo on these insert cards found at the rate of about one per 18 foil packs. The player's name and team are in silver at bottom. Horizontal backs have a ghosted action photo of the player in the background. A portrait photo is in the upper-right corner, above some personal data and stats. Cards are numbered "X of 20."

		NM/M
Complete Set (20):		6.00
Common Player:		.25
1	Javier Lopez	.25
2	Rondell White	.25
3	Butch Huskey	.25
4	Midre Cummings	.25
5	Scott Ruffcorn	.25
6	Manny Ramirez	3.50
7	Danny Bautista	.25
8	Russ Davis	.25
9	Steve Karsay	.25
10	Carlos Delgado	2.50
11	Bob Hamelin	.25
12	Marcus Moore	.25
13	Miguel Jimenez	.25
14	Matt Walbeck	.25
15	James Mouton	.25
16	Rich Becker	.25
17	Brian Anderson	.25
18	Cliff Floyd	.25
19	Steve Trachsel	.25
20	Hector Carrasco	.25

Gold Stars

The "Cadillac" of 1994 Leaf inserts, this 15-card series (#1-8 in Series 1; 9-15 in

Series 2) is found on average of one card per 90 packs. The edition of 10,000 of each player's card is serially numbered. Fronts feature a rather small photo in a diamond-shaped frame against a green marble-look background. The border, facsimile autograph and several other graphic elements are presented in prismatic foil. The back repeats the basic front design with a few sentences about the player and a serial number strip at bottom.

		NM/M
Complete Set (15):		60.00
Common Player:		3.00
1	Roberto Alomar	4.00
2	Barry Bonds	12.00
3	Dave Justice	3.00
4	Ken Griffey Jr.	9.00
5	Len Dykstra	3.00
6	Don Mattingly	7.50
7	Andres Galarraga	3.00
8	Greg Maddux	6.00
9	Carlos Baerga	3.00
10	Paul Molitor	5.00
11	Frank Thomas	5.00
12	John Olerud	3.00
13	Juan Gonzalez	4.00
14	Fred McGriff	3.00
15	Jack McDowell	3.00

MVP Contenders

Found on an average of about once per 36-pack foil box, these inserts were produced in an edition of 10,000 each. Cards found in packs were marked "Silver Collection" on the horizontal fronts, and featured a silver-foil Leaf seal and other enhancements. Persons holding cards of the players selected as N.L. and A.L. MVPs could trade in their Contender card for an individually numbered 5" x 7" card of Leaf spokesman Frank Thomas and be entered in a drawing for one of 5,000 Gold Collection MVP Contender 28-card sets. Winning cards were punch-cancelled and returned to the winner along with his prize.

		NM/M
Complete Set, Silver (30):		20.00
Complete Set, Gold (30):		40.00
Common Player, Silver:		.25
Common Player, Gold:		.50
AMERICAN LEAGUE		2.00
1a	Albert Belle/Silver	.25
1b	Albert Belle/Gold	.50
2a	Jose Canseco/Silver	1.25
2b	Jose Canseco/Gold	2.00
3a	Joe Carter/Silver	.25
3b	Joe Carter/Gold	.50
4a	Will Clark/Silver	.35
4b	Will Clark/Gold	.60
5a	Cecil Fielder/Silver	.25
5b	Cecil Fielder/Gold	.50
6a	Juan Gonzalez/Silver	1.50
6b	Juan Gonzalez/Gold	2.50
7a	Ken Griffey Jr./Silver	4.00
7b	Ken Griffey Jr./Gold	7.50
8a	Paul Molitor/Silver	2.00
8b	Paul Molitor/Gold	4.00
9a	Rafael Palmeiro/Silver	1.50
9b	Rafael Palmeiro/Gold	2.50

10a	Kirby Puckett/Silver	2.50
10b	Kirby Puckett/Gold	5.00
11a	Cal Ripken, Jr./Silver	6.00
11b	Cal Ripken, Jr./Gold	12.50
12a	Frank Thomas/Silver	2.00
12b	Frank Thomas/Gold	4.00
13a	Mo Vaughn/Silver	.25
13b	Mo Vaughn/Gold	.50
14a	Carlos Baerga/Silver	.25
14b	Carlos Baerga/Gold	.50
15	AL Bonus Card/Silver	.60
NATIONAL LEAGUE		.60
1a	Gary Sheffield/Silver	.25
1b	Gary Sheffield/Gold	.65
2a	Jeff Bagwell/Silver	2.00
2b	Jeff Bagwell/Gold	4.00
3a	Dante Bichette/Silver	.25
3b	Dante Bichette/Gold	.50
4a	Barry Bonds/Silver	6.00
4b	Barry Bonds/Gold	12.50
5a	Darren Daulton/Silver	.50
5b	Darren Daulton/Gold	.50
6a	Andres Galarraga/Silver	.25
6b	Andres Galarraga/Gold	.50
7a	Gregg Jefferies/Silver	.50
7b	Gregg Jefferies/Gold	.50
8a	Dave Justice/Silver	.50
8b	Dave Justice/Gold	.50
9a	Ray Lankford/Silver	.25
9b	Ray Lankford/Gold	.50
10a	Fred McGriff/Silver	.25
10b	Fred McGriff/Gold	.50
11a	Barry Larkin/Silver	.25
11b	Barry Larkin/Gold	.50
12a	Mike Piazza/Silver	4.00
12b	Mike Piazza/Gold	7.50
13a	Deion Sanders/Silver	.50
13b	Deion Sanders/Gold	.50
14a	Matt Williams/Silver	.50
14b	Matt Williams/Gold	.50
15	NL Bonus Card/Silver	.25

Power Brokers

This insert set was unique to Leaf Series 2 and features top sluggers. Horizontal fronts have a player photo at left, depicting his power stroke. A fireworks display is featured in the large letters of "POWER" at top. Other gold and silver foil highlights are featured on the black background. Backs have pie charts showing home run facts along with another player photo and a few stats. Stated odds of finding a Power Brokers insert card were one per dozen packs, on average.

		NM/M
Complete Set (10):		8.00
Common Player:		.40
1	Frank Thomas	.75
2	Dave Justice	.40
3	Barry Bonds	3.00
4	Juan Gonzalez	.65
5	Ken Griffey Jr.	2.00
6	Mike Piazza	2.00
7	Cecil Fielder	.40
8	Fred McGriff	.40
9	Joe Carter	.40
10	Albert Belle	.40

Slide Show

A new level of high-tech insert card production values was reached with the creation of Leaf's "Slide Show" cards, featuring a printed acetate center sandwiched between cardboard front and back. The see-through portion of the card is bordered in white to give it the appearance of a slide. The player's name, location and date of the photo are printed on the front of the "slide," with the card number on back. The pseudo-slide is bordered in black (Series 1) or white (Series 2), with a blue "Slide Show" logo at bottom and a silver-foil Leaf logo. Backs of the Slide Show inserts have a few sentences about the featured player from Frank Thomas, Leaf's official spokesman again in 1994. The first five cards were released in Series 1; cards 6-10 in Series 2. Stated odds of finding a Slide Show insert are one per 54 packs.

		NM/M
Complete Set (10):		9.00
Common Player:		.25
1	Frank Thomas	1.00
2	Mike Piazza	2.00
3	Darren Daulton	.25
4	Ryne Sandberg	1.50
5	Roberto Alomar	.50
6	Barry Bonds	3.00
7	Juan Gonzalez	.75
8	Tim Salmon	.25
9	Ken Griffey Jr.	2.00
10	Dave Justice	.25

Statistical Standouts

Significant statistical achievements of the 1993 season are marked in this insert set found in both retail and hobby packs at a rate of about once every 12 packs. Fronts feature player action photos set against a foil background of silver at right and a team color at left. A gold embossed Leaf seal is at upper-left. Backs are bordered in the complementary team color at right, silver at left and have a vertical player photo along with the statistical achievement. Cards are numbered "X-10."

		NM/M
Complete Set (10):		10.00
Common Player:		.40
1	Frank Thomas	.75
2	Barry Bonds	2.50
3	Juan Gonzalez	.65
4	Mike Piazza	2.00
5	Greg Maddux	1.00
6	Ken Griffey Jr.	2.00
7	Joe Carter	.40
8	Dave Winfield	.75
9	Tony Gwynn	1.00
10	Cal Ripken, Jr.	2.50

Frank Thomas Super

An edition of 20,000 super-size versions of Frank Thomas' 1994 Leaf card was produced for inclusion in Series II hobby boxes as a bonus. Except for its 5" x 7" format and a white strip on back bearing a serial number, the card is identical to the normal-size issue.

		NM/M
400	Frank Thomas	5.00

5th Anniversary

FRANK THOMAS 1B

The card which insured the success of the Leaf brand name when it was re-introduced in 1990, the Frank Thomas rookie card, was re-issued in a 5th anniversary commemorative form as an insert in the 1994 set. On the chase card, silver foil rays emanate from the White Sox logo at lower-left, while a silver-foil 5th anniversary logo at upper-right replaces the Leaf script on the 1990 version. The card back carries a 1994 copyright. The Thomas anniversary card is found on average of once every 36 Series I hobby packs.

		NM/M
300	Frank Thomas	2.50

1994 Leaf/Limited Promo

A single, unlabeled promo card was issued by Leaf to preview its Limited brand. The front is printed on a matte finish background as opposed to the shiny silver of the issued versions, but is otherwise identical. On back there are subtle differences in the cropping of the background photo, and a Total Bases stat is provided instead of Slugging Percentage as on the issued card. The principal difference is the use of card number 1 on the promo; the issued card is #24.

		NM/M
1	Frank Thomas	100.00

1994 Leaf/Limited

Leaf Limited is a 160-card super-premium set printed on the highest quality board stock ever used by Donruss. Production was limited to 3,000 20-box case equiva-

Joe Girardi

lents, making this the most limited product up to that point from Donruss. Fronts feature silver holographic Spectra Tech foiling and a silhouetted player action photo over full silver foil. The team name and logo in silver and player name in black are at the bottom of the card. Leaf Limited appears in silver at the top. Backs are dull gray with a quote from a baseball personality and a player picture in the top-right corner.

		NM/M
Complete Set (160):		35.00
Common Player:		.25
Pack (5):		2.50
Wax Box (20):		40.00
1	Jeffrey Hammonds	.25
2	Ben McDonald	.25
3	Mike Mussina	.75
4	Rafael Palmeiro	1.50
5	Cal Ripken, Jr.	6.00
6	Lee Smith	.25
7	Roger Clemens	3.00
8	Scott Cooper	.25
9	Andre Dawson	.40
10	Mike Greenwell	.25
11	Aaron Sele	.25
12	Mo Vaughn	.25
13	Brian Anderson RC	.25
14	Chad Curtis	.25
15	Chili Davis	.25
16	Gary DiSarcina	.25
17	Mark Langston	.25
18	Tim Salmon	.25
19	Wilson Alvarez	.25
20	Jason Bere	.25
21	Julio Franco	.25
22	Jack McDowell	.25
23	Tim Raines	.25
24	Frank Thomas	2.00
25	Robin Ventura	.25
26	Carlos Baerga	.25
27	Albert Belle	.25
28	Kenny Lofton	.25
29	Eddie Murray	2.00
30	Manny Ramirez	2.00
31	Cecil Fielder	.25
32	Travis Fryman	.25
33	Mickey Tettleton	.25
34	Alan Trammell	.25
35	Lou Whitaker	.25
36	David Cone	.25
37	Gary Gaetti	.25
38	Greg Gagne	.25
39	Bob Hamelin	.25
40	Wally Joyner	.25
41	Brian McRae	.25
42	Ricky Bones	.25
43	Brian Harper	.25
44	John Jaha	.25
45	Pat Listach	.25
46	Dave Nilsson	.25
47	Greg Vaughn	.25
48	Kent Hrbek	.25
49	Chuck Knoblauch	.25
50	Shane Mack	.25
51	Kirby Puckett	2.50
52	Dave Winfield	2.00
53	Jim Abbott	.25
54	Wade Boggs	2.50
55	Jimmy Key	.25
56	Don Mattingly	3.00
57	Paul O'Neill	.25
58	Danny Tartabull	.25
59	Dennis Eckersley	1.50
60	Rickey Henderson	2.00
61	Mark McGwire	5.00
62	Troy Neel	.25
63	Ruben Sierra	.25
64	Eric Anthony	.25
65	Jay Buhner	.25
66	Ken Griffey Jr.	4.00
67	Randy Johnson	2.00
68	Edgar Martinez	.25
69	Tino Martinez	.25
70	Jose Canseco	.75
71	Will Clark	.25
72	Juan Gonzalez	1.50
73	Dean Palmer	.25
74	Ivan Rodriguez	1.50
75	Roberto Alomar	.40

76	Joe Carter	.25
77	Carlos Delgado	1.00
78	Paul Molitor	2.00
79	John Olerud	.25
80	Devon White	.25
81	Steve Avery	.25
82	Tom Glavine	.50
83	Dave Justice	.25
84	Roberto Kelly	.25
85	Ryan Klesko	.25
86	Javier Lopez	.25
87	Greg Maddux	2.50
88	Fred McGriff	.25
89	Shawon Dunston	.25
90	Mark Grace	.25
91	Derrick May	.25
92	Sammy Sosa	3.00
93	Rick Wilkins	.25
94	Bret Boone	.25
95	Barry Larkin	.25
96	Kevin Mitchell	.25
97	Hal Morris	.25
98	Deion Sanders	.25
99	Reggie Sanders	.25
100	Dante Bichette	.25
101	Ellis Burks	.25
102	Andres Galarraga	.25
103	Joe Girardi	.25
104	Charlie Hayes	.25
105	Chuck Carr	.25
106	Jeff Conine	.25
107	Bryan Harvey	.25
108	Benito Santiago	.25
109	Gary Sheffield	.60
110	Jeff Bagwell	2.00
111	Craig Biggio	.25
112	Ken Caminiti	.25
113	Andujar Cedeno	.25
114	Doug Drabek	.25
115	Luis Gonzalez	.40
116	Brett Butler	.25
117	Delino DeShields	.25
118	Eric Karros	.25
119	Raul Mondesi	.25
120	Mike Piazza	4.00
121	Henry Rodriguez	.25
122	Tim Wallach	.25
123	Moises Alou	.25
124	Cliff Floyd	.25
125	Marquis Grissom	.25
126	Ken Hill	.25
127	Larry Walker	.25
128	John Wetteland	.25
129	Bobby Bonilla	.25
130	John Franco	.25
131	Jeff Kent	.25
132	Bret Saberhagen	.25
133	Ryan Thompson	.25
134	Darren Daulton	.25
135	Mariano Duncan	.25
136	Len Dykstra	.25
137	Danny Jackson	.25
138	John Kruk	.25
139	Jay Bell	.25
140	Jeff King	.25
141	Al Martin	.25
142	Orlando Merced	.25
143	Andy Van Slyke	.25
144	Bernard Gilkey	.25
145	Gregg Jefferies	.25
146	Ray Lankford	.25
147	Ozzie Smith	2.50
148	Mark Whiten	.25
149	Todd Zeile	.25
150	Derek Bell	.25
151	Andy Benes	.25
152	Tony Gwynn	2.50
153	Phil Plantier	.25
154	Bip Roberts	.25
155	Rod Beck	.25
156	Barry Bonds	6.00
157	John Burkett	.25
158	Royce Clayton	.25
159	Bill Swift	.25
160	Matt Williams	.25

Gold

Marcano Duncan

Leaf Limited Gold was an 18-card insert set randomly packed into Leaf Limited. All cards are individually numbered and feature the starting lineups at each position in both the National League and American League for the 1994 All-

Star Game. There were only 10,000 cards of each player produced in this insert set.

		NM/M
Complete Set (18):		20.00
Common Player:		.25
1	Frank Thomas	1.50
2	Gregg Jefferies	.25
3	Roberto Alomar	.50
4	Mariano Duncan	.25
5	Wade Boggs	2.00
6	Matt Williams	.25
7	Cal Ripken, Jr.	4.00
8	Ozzie Smith	2.00
9	Kirby Puckett	2.00
10	Barry Bonds	4.00
11	Ken Griffey Jr.	3.00
12	Tony Gwynn	2.00
13	Joe Carter	.25
14	Dave Justice	.25
15	Ivan Rodriguez	1.25
16	Mike Piazza	3.00
17	Jimmy Key	.25
18	Greg Maddux	2.00

Rookies

Similar in format to the super-premium Leaf Limited issue, this separate issue features 80 of baseball's brightest young talents. Total production was reported as 30,000 serial numbered 20-pack foil boxes.

		NM/M
Complete Set (80):		17.50
Common Player:		.25
Pack (5):		3.00
Box (20):		60.00
1	Charles Johnson	.25
2	Rico Brogna	.25
3	Melvin Nieves	.25
4	Rich Becker	.25
5	Russ Davis	.25
6	Matt Mieske	.25
7	Paul Shuey	.25
8	Hector Carrasco	.25
9	J.R. Phillips	.25
10	Scott Ruffcorn	.25
11	Kurt Abbott	.25
12	Danny Bautista	.25
13	Rick White	.25
14	Steve Dunn	.25
15	Joe Ausanio	.25
16	Salomon Torres	.25
17	Rick Bottalico	.25
18	Johnny Ruffin	.25
19	Kevin Foster	.25
20	W. Van Landingham RC	.25
21	Troy O'Leary	.25
22	Mark Acre	.25
23	Norberto Martin	.25
24	Jason Jacome RC	.25
25	Steve Trachsel	.25
26	Denny Hocking	.25
27	Mike Lieberthal	.25
28	Gerald Williams	.25
29	John Mabry	.25
30	Greg Blosser	.25
31	Carl Everett	.25
32	Steve Karsay	.25
33	Jose Valentin	.25
34	Jon Lieber	.25
35	Chris Gomez	.25
36	Jesus Tavarez	.25
37	Tony Longmire	.25
38	Luis Lopez	.25
39	Matt Walbeck	.25
40	Rikkert Faneyte	.25
41	Shane Reynolds	.25
42	Joey Hamilton	.25
43	Ismael Valdes	.25
44	Danny Miceli	.25
45	Darren Bragg	.25
46	Alex Gonzalez	.25
47	Rick Helling	.25
48	Jose Oliva	.25
49	Jim Edmonds	4.00
50	Miguel Jimenez	.25
51	Tony Eusebio	.25
52	Shawn Green	4.00
53	Billy Ashley	.25
54	Rondell White	.25
55	Cory Bailey	.25
56	Tim Davis	.25

57	John Hudek	.25
58	Darren Hall	.25
59	Darren Dreifort	.25
60	Mike Kelly	.25
61	Marcus Moore	.25
62	Garret Anderson	.25
63	Brian Hunter	.25
64	Mark Smith	.25
65	Garey Ingram	.25
66	Rusty Greer RC	.25
67	Marc Newfield	.25
68	Gar Finnvold	.25
69	Paul Spoljaric	.25
70	Ray McDavid	.25
71	Orlando Miller	.25
72	Jorge Fabregas	.25
73	Ray Holbert	.25
74	Armando Benitez	.25
75	Ernie Young	.25
76	James Mouton	.25
77	Robert Perez RC	.25
78	Chan Ho Park RC	1.00
79	Roger Salkeld	.25
80	Tony Tarasco	.25

Rookies Rookie Phenoms

Similar in format to the other Leaf Limited cards for 1994, these Phenom inserts feature gold-foil background and graphics, rather than silver. Each card is numbered from within an edition of 5,000 of each player.

		NM/M
Complete Set (10):		260.00
Common Player:		1.00
Production 5,000 Sets		
1	Raul Mondesi	1.00
2	Bob Hamelin	1.00
3	Midre Cummings	1.00
4	Carlos Delgado	8.00
5	Cliff Floyd	1.00
6	Jeffrey Hammonds	1.00
7	Ryan Klesko	1.00
8	Javier Lopez	1.00
9	Manny Ramirez	10.00
10	Alex Rodriguez	250.00

1995 Leaf Promos

The lack of a "Sample" or "Promotional Card" notice makes these promos difficult to spot. They can be detected by the placement of the Registered symbol farther down and to the right compared to regular-issue cards. Also the thin line inside the gold-foil stamping enclosing the Leaf logo and inner "95" diamond is missing on the promos.

		NM/M
Complete Set (9):		35.00
Common Player:		2.00
1	Frank Thomas	4.00
10	Joe Carter	2.00
28	Matt Williams	2.00
49	Wade Boggs	6.00
60	Raul Mondesi	2.00
115	Greg Maddux	6.00
119	Jeff Bagwell	4.00
134	Cal Ripken Jr.	12.00
183	Kirby Puckett	6.00

1995 Leaf

Two series of 200 basic cards each, plus numerous insert sets, are featured in 1995 Leaf. The basic card design has a borderless action photo on front, with a small portrait photo printed at upper-left on holographic silver foil. The team name is printed in the same foil in large letters down the left side. A script rendition of the player's name is at bottom-right, with the Leaf logo under the portrait photo; both elements are in gold foil. Backs have a couple more player photos. The card number is in white in a silver-foil seal at upper-right. Previous season and career stats are at lower-left. Several of the insert sets are unique to various package configurations, while others are found in all types of packs.

	NM/M
Complete Set (400):	12.50
Common Player:	.05
Series 1 or 2 Pack (12):	.75
Series 1 or 2 Wax Box (36):	15.00

No.	Player	Price
1	Frank Thomas	.75
2	Carlos Garcia	.05
3	Todd Hundley	.05
4	Damion Easley	.05
5	Roberto Mejia	.05
6	John Mabry	.05
7	Aaron Sele	.05
8	Kenny Lofton	.05
9	John Doherty	.05
10	Joe Carter	.05
11	Mike Lansing	.05
12	John Valentin	.05
13	Ismael Valdes	.05
14	Dave McCarty	.05
15	Melvin Nieves	.05
16	Bobby Jones	.05
17	Trevor Hoffman	.05
18	John Smoltz	.05
19	Leo Gomez	.05
20	Roger Pavlik	.05
21	Dean Palmer	.05
22	Rickey Henderson	.75
23	Eddie Taubensee	.05
24	Damon Buford	.05
25	Mark Wohlers	.05
26	Jim Edmonds	.05
27	Wilson Alvarez	.05
28	Matt Williams	.05
29	Jeff Montgomery	.05
30	Shawon Dunston	.05
31	Tom Pagnozzi	.05
32	Jose Lind	.05
33	Royce Clayton	.05
34	Cal Eldred	.05
35	Chris Gomez	.05
36	Henry Rodriguez	.05
37	Dave Fleming	.05
38	Jon Lieber	.05
39	Scott Servais	.05
40	Wade Boggs	1.00
41	John Olerud	.05
42	Eddie Williams	.05
43	Paul Sorrento	.05
44	Ron Karkovice	.05
45	Kevin Foster	.05
46	Miguel Jimenez	.05
47	Reggie Sanders	.05
48	Rondell White	.05
49	Scott Leius	.05
50	Jose Valentin	.05
51	William Van Landingham	.05
52	Denny Hocking	.05
53	Jeff Fassero	.05
54	Chris Hoiles	.05
55	Walt Weiss	.05
56	Geronimo Berroa	.05
57	Rich Rowland	.05
58	Dave Weathers	.05
59	Sterling Hitchcock	.05
60	Raul Mondesi	.05
61	Rusty Greer	.05
62	Dave Justice	.05
63	Cecil Fielder	.05
64	Brian Jordan	.05
65	Mike Lieberthal	.05
66	Rick Aguilera	.05
67	Chuck Finley	.05
68	Andy Ashby	.05
69	Alex Fernandez	.05
70	Ed Sprague	.05
71	Steve Buechele	.05
72	Willie Greene	.05
73	Dave Nilsson	.05
74	Bret Saberhagen	.05
75	Jimmy Key	.05
76	Darren Lewis	.05
77	Steve Cooke	.05
78	Kirk Gibson	.05
79	Ray Lankford	.05
80	Paul O'Neill	.05
81	Mike Bordick	.05
82	Wes Chamberlain	.05
83	Rico Brogna	.05
84	Kevin Appier	.05
85	Juan Guzman	.05
86	Kevin Seitzer	.05
87	Mickey Morandini	.05
88	Pedro Martinez	.75
89	Matt Mieske	.05
90	Tino Martinez	.05
91	Paul Shuey	.05
92	Bip Roberts	.05
93	Chili Davis	.05
94	Deion Sanders	.05
95	Darrell Whitmore	.05
96	Joe Orsulak	.05
97	Bret Boone	.05
98	Kent Mercker	.05
99	Scott Livingstone	.05
100	Brady Anderson	.05
101	James Mouton	.05
102	Jose Rijo	.05
103	Bobby Munoz	.05
104	Ramon Martinez	.05
105	Bernie Williams	.10
106	Troy Neel	.05
107	Ivan Rodriguez	.65
108	Salomon Torres	.05
109	Johnny Ruffin	.05
110	Darryl Kile	.05
111	Bobby Ayala	.05
112	Ron Darling	.05
113	Jose Lima	.05
114	Joey Hamilton	.05
115	Greg Maddux	1.00
116	Greg Colbrunn	.05
117	Ozzie Guillen	.05
118	Brian Anderson	.05
119	Jeff Bagwell	.75
120	Pat Listach	.05
121	Sandy Alomar	.05
122	Jose Vizcaino	.05
123	Rick Helling	.05
124	Allen Watson	.05
125	Pedro Munoz	.05
126	Craig Biggio	.05
127	Kevin Stocker	.05
128	Wil Cordero	.05
129	Rafael Palmeiro	.65
130	Gar Finnvold	.05
131	Darren Hall	.05
132	Heath Slocumb	.05
133	Darrin Fletcher	.05
134	Cal Ripken Jr.	2.50
135	Dante Bichette	.05
136	Don Slaught	.05
137	Pedro Astacio	.05
138	Ryan Thompson	.05
139	Greg Gohr	.05
140	Javier Lopez	.05
141	Lenny Dykstra	.05
142	Pat Rapp	.05
143	Mark Kiefer	.05
144	Greg Gagne	.05
145	Eduardo Perez	.05
146	Felix Fermin	.05
147	Jeff Frye	.05
148	Terry Steinbach	.05
149	Jim Eisenreich	.05
150	Brad Ausmus	.05
151	Randy Myers	.05
152	Rick White	.05
153	Mark Portugal	.05
154	Delino DeShields	.05
155	Scott Cooper	.05
156	Pat Hentgen	.05
157	Mark Gubicza	.05
158	Carlos Baerga	.05
159	Joe Girardi	.05
160	Rey Sanchez	.05
161	Todd Jones	.05
162	Luis Polonia	.05
163	Steve Trachsel	.05
164	Roberto Hernandez	.05
165	John Patterson	.05
166	Rene Arocha	.05
167	Will Clark	.10
168	Jim Leyritz	.05
169	Todd Van Poppel	.05
170	Robb Nen	.05
171	Midre Cummings	.05
172	Jay Buhner	.05
173	Kevin Tapani	.05
174	Mark Lemke	.05
175	Marcus Moore	.05
176	Wayne Kirby	.05
177	Rich Amaral	.05
178	Lou Whitaker	.05
179	Jay Bell	.05
180	Rick Wilkins	.05
181	Paul Molitor	.75
182	Gary Sheffield	.35
183	Kirby Puckett	1.00
184	Cliff Floyd	.05
185	Darren Oliver	.05
186	Tim Naehring	.05
187	John Hudek	.05
188	Eric Young	.05
189	Roger Salkeld	.05
190	Kirt Manwaring	.05
191	Kurt Abbott	.05
192	David Nied	.05
193	Todd Zeile	.05
194	Wally Joyner	.05
195	Dennis Martinez	.05
196	Billy Ashley	.05
197	Ben McDonald	.05
198	Bob Hamelin	.05
199	Chris Turner	.05
200	Lance Johnson	.05
201	Willie Banks	.05
202	Juan Gonzalez	.50
203	Scott Sanders	.05
204	Scott Brosius	.05
205	Curt Schilling	.25
206	Alex Gonzalez	.05
207	Travis Fryman	.05
208	Tim Raines	.05
209	Steve Avery	.05
210	Hal Morris	.05
211	Ken Griffey Jr.	1.50
212	Ozzie Smith	1.00
213	Chuck Carr	.05
214	Ryan Klesko	.05
215	Robin Ventura	.05
216	Luis Gonzalez	.05
217	Ken Ryan	.05
218	Mike Piazza	1.50
219	Matt Walbeck	.05
220	Jeff Kent	.05
221	Orlando Miller	.05
222	Kenny Rogers	.05
223	J.T. Snow	.05
224	Alan Trammell	.05
225	John Franco	.05
226	Gerald Williams	.05
227	Andy Benes	.05
228	Dan Wilson	.05
229	Dave Hollins	.05
230	Vinny Castilla	.05
231	Devon White	.05
232	Fred McGriff	.05
233	Quilvio Veras	.05
234	Tom Candiotti	.05
235	Jason Bere	.05
236	Mark Langston	.05
237	Mel Rojas	.05
238	Chuck Knoblauch	.05
239	Bernard Gilkey	.05
240	Mark McGwire	2.00
241	Kirk Rueter	.05
242	Pat Kelly	.05
243	Ruben Sierra	.05
244	Randy Johnson	.75
245	Shane Reynolds	.05
246	Danny Tartabull	.05
247	Darryl Hamilton	.05
248	Danny Bautista	.05
249	Tom Gordon	.05
250	Tom Glavine	.25
251	Orlando Merced	.05
252	Eric Karros	.05
253	Benji Gil	.05
254	Sean Bergman	.05
255	Roger Clemens	1.25
256	Roberto Alomar	.20
257	Benito Santiago	.05
258	Robby Thompson	.05
259	Marvin Freeman	.05
260	Jose Offerman	.05
261	Greg Vaughn	.05
262	David Segui	.05
263	Geronimo Pena	.05
264	Tim Salmon	.05
265	Eddie Murray	.75
266	Mariano Duncan	.05
267	Hideo Nomo RC	2.50
268	Derek Bell	.05
269	Mo Vaughn	.05
270	Jeff King	.05
271	Edgar Martinez	.05
272	Sammy Sosa	1.25
273	Scott Ruffcorn	.05
274	Darren Daulton	.05
275	John Jaha	.05
276	Andres Galarraga	.05
277	Mark Grace	.05
278	Mike Moore	.05
279	Barry Bonds	2.50
280	Manny Ramirez	.75
281	Ellis Burks	.05
282	Greg Swindell	.05
283	Barry Larkin	.05
284	Albert Belle	.05
285	Shawn Green	.35
286	John Roper	.05
287	Scott Erickson	.05
288	Moises Alou	.05
289	Mike Blowers	.05
290	Brent Gates	.05
291	Sean Berry	.05
292	Mike Stanley	.05
293	Jeff Conine	.05
294	Tim Wallach	.05
295	Bobby Bonilla	.05
296	Bruce Ruffin	.05
297	Chad Curtis	.05
298	Mike Greenwell	.05
299	Tony Gwynn	1.00
300	Russ Davis	.05
301	Danny Jackson	.05
302	Pete Harnisch	.05
303	Don Mattingly	1.25
304	Rheal Cormier	.05
305	Larry Walker	.05
306	Hector Carrasco	.05
307	Jason Jacome	.05
308	Phil Plantier	.05
309	Harold Baines	.05
310	Mitch Williams	.05
311	Charles Nagy	.05
312	Ken Caminiti	.05
313	Alex Rodriguez	2.00
314	Chris Sabo	.05
315	Gary Gaetti	.05
316	Andre Dawson	.25
317	Mark Clark	.05
318	Vince Coleman	.05
319	Brad Clontz	.05
320	Steve Finley	.05
321	Doug Drabek	.05
322	Mark McLemore	.05
323	Stan Javier	.05
324	Ron Gant	.05
325	Charlie Hayes	.05
326	Carlos Delgado	.50
327	Ricky Bottalico	.05
328	Rod Beck	.05
329	Mark Acre	.05
330	Chris Bosio	.05
331	Tony Phillips	.05
332	Garret Anderson	.05
333	Pat Meares	.05
334	Todd Worrell	.05
335	Marquis Grissom	.05
336	Brent Mayne	.05
337	Lee Tinsley	.05
338	Terry Pendleton	.05
339	David Cone	.05
340	Tony Fernandez	.05
341	Jim Bullinger	.05
342	Armando Benitez	.05
343	John Smiley	.05
344	Dan Miceli	.05
345	Charles Johnson	.05
346	Lee Smith	.05
347	Brian McRae	.05
348	Jim Thome	.65
349	Jose Oliva	.05
350	Terry Mulholland	.05
351	Tom Henke	.05
352	Dennis Eckersley	.65
353	Sid Fernandez	.05
354	Paul Wagner	.05
355	John Dettmer	.05
356	John Wetteland	.05
357	John Burkett	.05
358	Marty Cordova	.05
359	Norm Charlton	.05
360	Mike Devereaux	.05
361	Alex Cole	.05
362	Brett Butler	.05
363	Mickey Tettleton	.05
364	Al Martin	.05
365	Tony Tarasco	.05
366	Pat Mahomes	.05
367	Gary DiSarcina	.05
368	Bill Swift	.05
369	Chipper Jones	1.00
370	Orel Hershiser	.05
371	Kevin Gross	.05
372	Dave Winfield	.75
373	Andujar Cedeno	.05
374	Jim Abbott	.05
375	Glenallen Hill	.05
376	Otis Nixon	.05
377	Roberto Kelly	.05
378	Chris Hammond	.05
379	Mike Macfarlane	.05
380	J.R. Phillips	.05
381	Luis Alicea	.05
382	Bret Barberie	.05
383	Tom Goodwin	.05
384	Mark Whiten	.05
385	Jeffrey Hammonds	.05
386	Omar Vizquel	.05
387	Mike Mussina	.35
388	Rickey Bones	.05
389	Steve Ontiveros	.05
390	Jeff Blauser	.05
391	Jose Canseco	.35
392	Bob Tewksbury	.05
393	Jacob Brumfield	.05
394	Doug Jones	.05
395	Ken Hill	.05
396	Pat Borders	.05
397	Carl Everett	.05
398	Gregg Jefferies	.05
399	Jack McDowell	.05
400	Denny Neagle	.05

Checklists

Honoring the major 1994 award winners in the American (Series I) and National (Series II) Leagues, checklists for the 1995 Leaf set are not numbered among the regular issue. Horizontal cards have a player action photo at left with his name and team in gold foil at bottom. The award is printed vertically at left with the checklist beginning on the right. Backs continue the checklist on a grad-uated purple background with the checklist number in a silver-foil seal at top-right.

		NM/M
Complete Set (8):		1.50
Common Player:		.25
1	Checklist 1-67 Bob Hamelin (Rookie of the Year)	.25
2	Checklist 68-134 David Cone (Cy Young)	.25
3	Checklist 135-200 (Frank Thomas/MVP)	.45
4	Series II inserts checklist Paul O'Neill (Batting title)	.25
5	Checklist 201-267 Raul Mondesi (Rookie of the Year)	.25
6	Checklist 268-334 Greg Maddux (Cy Young)	.50
7	Checklist 335-400 (Jeff Bagwell/MVP)	.45
8	Series 2 inserts checklist Tony Gwynn (Batting title)	.50

Cornerstones

Cornerstones, six of the best first baseman-third baseman combos in baseball, is a six-card insert series found, on average, once every 18 packs in Series I Leaf. Card fronts are horizontally oriented and have a silver prismatic border and player names. Player defensive action photos are set against a background resembling their team logo chiseled into a stone block. Backs have player batting photos at each end with offensive and defensive stats from 1994, and a few words about the duo.

		NM/M
Complete Set (6):		3.50
Common Player:		.40
1	Frank Thomas, Robin Ventura	.75
2	Cecil Fielder, Travis Fryman	.40
3	Don Mattingly, Wade Boggs	2.00
4	Jeff Bagwell, Ken Caminiti	.75
5	Will Clark, Dean Palmer	.40
6	J.R. Phillips, Matt Williams	.40

Gold Stars

Once again the toughest pull among the Leaf inserts are the Gold Leaf Stars found in both series. Found on average of one card per 90-270 packs, depending on pack card count, each of these chase cards is numbered on back within an edition of 10,000. Cards have fronts printed on metallic foil with the player name at top, the series title at bottom and a vertical stars and stripe device at right all printed in gold foil. A die-cut star appears at bottom-left. Backs are conventionally printed with another player photo and a few sentences about the star. The serial number is in gold foil in a white strip at top.

	NM/M
Complete Set (14):	35.00
Common Player:	1.00
1 Jeff Bagwell	2.50
2 Albert Belle	1.00
3 Tony Gwynn	3.50
4 Ken Griffey Jr.	4.50
5 Barry Bonds	6.00
6 Don Mattingly	4.00
7 Raul Mondesi	1.00
8 Joe Carter	1.00
9 Greg Maddux	3.50
10 Frank Thomas	2.50
11 Mike Piazza	4.50
12 Jose Canseco	1.50
13 Kirby Puckett	3.50
14 Matt Williams	1.00

Gold Rookies

Every other pack of Series I Leaf Series I is seeded with a Gold Leaf Rookie card. Fronts have a largely white background with a large player photo at left-center and a smaller picture in a rectangle at upper-right. A team-color stripe is at left, while a smaller gray stripe is at top-right. The team name is printed in large gray letters across the center of the card, with the player name in a team color beneath that and above the gold-foil Leaf logo at lower-left. "Gold Leaf Rookies" is printed in gold foil down the right side. Backs repeat the team-color motif with a large action photo of the player in a single color and a smaller color portrait. Full career stats are at bottom.

	NM/M
Complete Set (16):	3.00
Common Player:	.10
1 Alex Rodriguez	2.50
2 Garret Anderson	.10
3 Shawn Green	.50
4 Armando Benitez	.10
5 Darren Dreifort	.10
6 Orlando Miller	.10
7 Jose Oliva	.10
8 Ricky Bottalico	.10
9 Charles Johnson	.10
10 Brian Hunter	.10
11 Ray McDavid	.10
12 Chan Ho Park	.10
13 Mike Kelly	.10
14 Cory Bailey	.10
15 Alex Gonzalez	.10
16 Andrew Lorraine	.10

Great Gloves

While the stated emphasis is on fielding prowess in this Series II chase set, players who don't also swing a big stick are ignored. Found as frequently as one per two packs, cards have a detail photo of a glove at left, with an action photo at right. The player name in the Great Gloves logo at bottom-right is in gold foil, as are the Leaf logo at top-left and the team name vertically at right. Backs repeat the glove photo and series logo as background for another player photo and a few words and stats about the player's defense.

		NM/M
Complete Set (16):		3.00
Common Player:		.15
1	Jeff Bagwell	.35
2	Roberto Alomar	.20
3	Barry Bonds	1.00
4	Wade Boggs	.45
5	Andres Galarraga	.15
6	Ken Griffey Jr.	.60
7	Marquis Grissom	.15
8	Kenny Lofton	.15
9	Barry Larkin	.15
10	Don Mattingly	.50
11	Greg Maddux	.45
12	Kirby Puckett	.45
13	Ozzie Smith	.45
14	Cal Ripken Jr.	1.00
15	Matt Williams	.15
16	Ivan Rodriguez	.30

Heading For The Hall

Series 2 hobby packs were the home of this scarce (one per 75 packs, average) chase set. Eight players deemed to be sure shots for Cooperstown are pictured in a semblance of the famed tombstone-shaped plaque they will someday adorn at the Hall of Fame; in fact the cards are die-cut to that shape. Backs have a sepia-toned photo, career stats and a serial number placing the card within an edition of 5,000.

		NM/M
Complete Set (8):		50.00
Common Player:		4.50
1	Frank Thomas	4.50
2	Ken Griffey Jr.	9.00
3	Jeff Bagwell	4.50
4	Barry Bonds	15.00
5	Kirby Puckett	6.00
6	Cal Ripken Jr.	15.00
7	Tony Gwynn	6.00
8	Paul Molitor	4.50

Slideshow

The hold-to-light technology which Leaf debuted with its 1994 Slideshow inserts continued in 1995 with a cross-series concept. The same eight players are featured on these cards in both Series 1 and 2. Each card has three clear photos at center, between the spokes of a silver-foil wheel. When both the player's cards are placed side-by-side, the six-picture see-through photo device is complete. Slideshow inserts are found on average of just over one per box among all types

of pack configurations. Cards were issued with a peelable plastic protector on the front.

		NM/M
Complete Set (16):		35.00
Complete Series 1 (1a-8a):		20.00
Complete Series 2 (1b-8b):		20.00
Same prices for both series.		
Common Player:		1.50
1a	Raul Mondesi	1.50
1b	Raul Mondesi	1.50
2a	Frank Thomas	3.00
2b	Frank Thomas	3.00
3a	Fred McGriff	1.50
3b	Fred McGriff	1.50
4a	Cal Ripken Jr.	6.00
4b	Cal Ripken Jr.	6.00
5a	Jeff Bagwell	3.00
5b	Jeff Bagwell	3.00
6a	Will Clark	1.50
6b	Will Clark	1.50
7a	Matt Williams	1.50
7b	Matt Williams	1.50
8a	Ken Griffey Jr.	4.50
8b	Ken Griffey Jr.	4.50

Statistical Standouts

Embossed red stitches on the large baseball background make the Statistical Standouts chase cards stand out among the inserts in Series 1 hobby packs (one per 70, average). The leather surface of the ball is also lightly textured, as is the player action photo at center. Printed in gold foil on front are the series name at top, the player's facsimile autograph at lower-center and the Leaf logo and team name at bottom. Backs have a graduated black background with a large team logo at bottom, and a circular player portrait at center. A few words explain why the player's stats stand out among his peers. Each card is serially numbered on back to 5,000. A promo card version of each was issued without the specific serial number on back and with the upper-right corner cut off.

		NM/M
Complete Set (9):		95.00
Common Player:		3.00
Promos: 25-50%		
1	Joe Carter	3.00
2	Ken Griffey Jr.	25.00
3	Don Mattingly	15.00
4	Fred McGriff	3.00
5	Paul Molitor	9.00
6	Kirby Puckett	12.50
7	Cal Ripken Jr.	30.00
8	Frank Thomas	9.00
9	Matt Williams	3.00

Special Edition Jumbos

As a dealer incentive, each case of 1995 Leaf Series I cards contained one of two 3" x 5" jumbos. Similar in format to the players' regular Leaf cards, each is individually serially numbered within an edition of 5,000.

		NM/M
Complete Set (2):		7.00
1	Frank Thomas	3.00
2	Barry Bonds	5.00

Frank Thomas

The Big Hurt's six seasons in the major leagues are chronicled in this flashy insert set. Silver and gold foil squares are the background for a photo of Thomas on front. Backs repeat the motif with standard print technology and another photo, along with a few words about Thomas' season. The Frank Thomas inserts are found in all types of Series II packs, with odds varying from one in 42 packs to one in 14 packs, depending on card count per pack.

		NM/M
Complete Set (6):		7.50
Common Card:		1.50
1	The Rookie	1.50
2	Sophomore Stardom	1.50
3	Super Star	1.50
4	AL MVP	1.50
5	Back-To-Back	1.50
6	The Big Hurt	1.50

300 Club

Issued in both Series I and II Leaf, but only in the retail and magazine packs, at a rate of one per 12-30 packs, depending on pack configuration, 300 Club inserts feature the 18 active players with lifetime .300+ batting averages in a minimum of 1,000 AB. Fronts have color player photos with a large white "300" in the background and "club" in gold foil near the bottom. The player name is in gold foil in an arc above the silver Leaf logo at bottom-center. Large embossed silver triangles in each bottom corner have the team name and player position (left) and career BA (right). Backs have another player photo and highlight his place on the list of .300+ batters.

		NM/M
Complete Set (18):		12.50
Common Player:		.25
1	Frank Thomas	1.00
2	Paul Molitor	1.00
3	Mike Piazza	3.00

4	Moises Alou	.25
5	Mike Greenwell	.25
6	Will Clark	.25
7	Hal Morris	.25
8	Edgar Martinez	.25
9	Carlos Baerga	.25
10	Ken Griffey Jr.	3.00
11	Wade Boggs	1.50
12	Jeff Bagwell	1.00
13	Tony Gwynn	1.50
14	John Kruk	.25
15	Don Mattingly	2.00
16	Mark Grace	.25
17	Kirby Puckett	1.50
18	Kenny Lofton	.25

1995 Leaf/Limited

Issued in two series of 96 basic cards each, plus inserts, Leaf Limited was a hobby-only product limited to 90,000 numbered 20-pack boxes. Five-card packs had a suggested retail price of $4.99. Fronts of the basic cards have a player action photo on a background of silver holographic foil highlighted with team colors and a gold-foil Leaf Limited logo. Horizontal-format backs have two more player photos, career stats and holographic foil team logos and card numbers.

		NM/M
Complete Set (192):		20.00
Common Player:		.10
Series 1 or 2 Pack (5):		2.00
Series 1 or 2 Wax Box (20):		30.00
1	Frank Thomas	.75
2	Geronimo Berroa	.10
3	Tony Phillips	.10
4	Roberto Alomar	.25
5	Steve Avery	.10
6	Darryl Hamilton	.10
7	Scott Cooper	.10
8	Mark Grace	.10
9	Billy Ashley	.10
10	Wil Cordero	.10
11	Barry Bonds	5.00
12	Kenny Lofton	.10
13	Jay Buhner	.10
14	Alex Rodriguez	3.00
15	Bobby Bonilla	.10
16	Brady Anderson	.10
17	Ken Caminiti	.10
18	Charlie Hayes	.10
19	Jay Bell	.10
20	Will Clark	.15
21	Jose Canseco	.35
22	Bret Boone	.10
23	Dante Bichette	.10
24	Kevin Appier	.10
25	Chad Curtis	.10
26	Marty Cordova	.10
27	Jason Bere	.10
28	Jimmy Key	.10
29	Rickey Henderson	.75
30	Tim Salmon	.10
31	Joe Carter	.10
32	Tom Glavine	.35
33	Pat Listach	.10
34	Brian Jordan	.10
35	Brian McRae	.10
36	Eric Karros	.10
37	Pedro Martinez	.75
38	Royce Clayton	.10
39	Eddie Murray	.75
40	Randy Johnson	.75
41	Jeff Conine	.10
42	Brett Butler	.10
43	Jeffrey Hammonds	.10
44	Andujar Cedeno	.10
45	Dave Hollins	.10
46	Jeff King	.10
47	Benji Gil	.10
48	Roger Clemens	2.00
49	Barry Larkin	.25
50	Joe Girardi	.10
51	Bob Hamelin	.10
52	Travis Fryman	.10
53	Chuck Knoblauch	.10
54	Ray Durham	.10
55	Don Mattingly	2.00

56	Ruben Sierra	.10
57	J.T. Snow	.10
58	Derek Bell	.10
59	David Cone	.10
60	Marquis Grissom	.10
61	Kevin Seitzer	.10
62	Ozzie Smith	1.50
63	Rick Wilkins	.10
64	Hideo Nomo RC	3.00
65	Tony Tarasco	.10
66	Manny Ramirez	.75
67	Charles Johnson	.10
68	Craig Biggio	.10
69	Bobby Jones	.10
70	Mike Mussina	.60
71	Alex Gonzalez	.10
72	Gregg Jefferies	.10
73	Rusty Greer	.10
74	Mike Greenwell	.10
75	Hal Morris	.10
76	Paul O'Neill	.10
77	Luis Gonzalez	.25
78	Chipper Jones	1.50
79	Mike Piazza	2.50
80	Rondell White	.10
81	Glenallen Hill	.10
82	Shawn Green	.50
83	Bernie Williams	.10
84	Jim Thome	.65
85	Terry Pendleton	.10
86	Rafael Palmeiro	.65
87	Tony Gwynn	1.50
88	Mickey Tettleton	.10
89	John Valentin	.10
90	Deion Sanders	.10
91	Larry Walker	.10
92	Michael Tucker	.10
93	Alan Trammell	.10
94	Tim Raines	.10
95	Dave Justice	.10
96	Tino Martinez	.10
97	Cal Ripken Jr.	5.00
98	Deion Sanders	.10
99	Darren Daulton	.10
100	Paul Molitor	.75
101	Randy Myers	.10
102	Wally Joyner	.10
103	Carlos Perez	.10
104	Brian Hunter	.10
105	Wade Boggs	.10
106	Bobby Higginson RC	.50
107	Jeff Kent	.10
108	Jose Offerman	.10
109	Dennis Eckersley	.65
110	Dave Nilsson	.10
111	Chuck Finley	.10
112	Devon White	.10
113	Bip Roberts	.10
114	Ramon Martinez	.10
115	Greg Maddux	1.50
116	Curtis Goodwin	.10
117	John Jaha	.10
118	Ken Griffey Jr.	2.50
119	Geronimo Pena	.10
120	Shawon Dunston	.10
121	Ariel Prieto	.10
122	Kirby Puckett	1.50
123	Carlos Baerga	.10
124	Todd Hundley	.10
125	Tim Naehring	.10
126	Gary Sheffield	.45
127	Dean Palmer	.10
128	Rondell White	.10
129	Greg Gagne	.10
130	Jose Rijo	.10
131	Ivan Rodriguez	.65
132	Jeff Bagwell	.75
133	Greg Vaughn	.10
134	Chili Davis	.10
135	Al Martin	.10
136	Kenny Rogers	.10
137	Aaron Sele	.10
138	Raul Mondesi	.10
139	Cecil Fielder	.10
140	Tim Wallach	.10
141	Andres Galarraga	.10
142	Lou Whitaker	.10
143	Jack McDowell	.10
144	Matt Williams	.10
145	Ryan Klesko	.10
146	Carlos Garcia	.10
147	Albert Belle	.10
148	Ryan Thompson	.10
149	Roberto Kelly	.10
150	Edgar Martinez	.10
151	Robby Thompson	.10
152	Mo Vaughn	.10
153	Todd Zeile	.10
154	Harold Baines	.10
155	Phil Plantier	.10
156	Mike Stanley	.10
157	Ed Sprague	.10
158	Moises Alou	.10
159	Quilvio Veras	.10
160	Reggie Sanders	.10
161	Delino DeShields	.10
162	Rico Brogna	.10
163	Greg Colbrunn	.10
164	Steve Finley	.10
165	Orlando Merced	.10
166	Mark McGwire	3.00
167	Garret Anderson	.10
168	Paul Sorrento	.10
169	Mark Langston	.10
170	Danny Tartabull	.10
171	Vinny Castilla	.10
172	Javier Lopez	.10
173	Bret Saberhagen	.10

174	Eddie Williams	.10
175	Scott Leius	.10
176	Juan Gonzalez	.50
177	Gary Gaetti	.10
178	Jim Edmonds	.10
179	John Olerud	.10
180	Lenny Dykstra	.10
181	Ray Lankford	.10
182	Ron Gant	.10
183	Doug Drabek	.10
184	Fred McGriff	.10
185	Andy Benes	.10
186	Kurt Abbott	.10
187	Bernard Gilkey	.10
188	Sammy Sosa	2.00
189	Lee Smith	.10
190	Dennis Martinez	.10
191	Ozzie Guillen	.10
192	Robin Ventura	.10

Bat Patrol

Yet another insert of the game's top veteran hitters was featured as chase cards in Series 2 Leaf Limited. The cards have player action photos on front with large silver-foil "BAT / PATROL" lettering at lower-left. Backs are printed on a silver background and include career stats plus another color player photo. The cards were seeded at the rate of one per pack.

		NM/M
Complete Set (24):		7.50
Common Player:		.15
1	Frank Thomas	.75
2	Tony Gwynn	1.00
3	Wade Boggs	1.00
4	Larry Walker	.25
5	Ken Griffey Jr.	1.50
6	Jeff Bagwell	.75
7	Manny Ramirez	.75
8	Mark Grace	.25
9	Kenny Lofton	.15
10	Mike Piazza	1.50
11	Will Clark	.25
12	Mo Vaughn	.25
13	Carlos Baerga	.15
14	Rafael Palmeiro	.65
15	Barry Bonds	2.50
16	Kirby Puckett	1.00
17	Roberto Alomar	.35
18	Barry Larkin	.15
19	Eddie Murray	.75
20	Tim Salmon	.25
21	Don Mattingly	1.25
22	Fred McGriff	.15
23	Albert Belle	.25
24	Dante Bichette	.15

Gold

Seeded one per pack in Series I only, this insert set follows the format of the basic Leaf Limited cards, but is distinguished by the presence of gold, rather than silver, holographic foil.

		NM/M
Complete Set (24):		10.00
Common Player:		.25

1	Frank Thomas	.60
2	Jeff Bagwell	.60
3	Raul Mondesi	.25
4	Barry Bonds	1.50
5	Albert Belle	.25
6	Ken Griffey Jr.	1.00
7	Cal Ripken (Ripken) Jr.	1.50
8	Will Clark	.25
9	Jose Canseco	.45
10	Larry Walker	.25
11	Kirby Puckett	.75
12	Don Mattingly	1.00
13	Tim Salmon	.25
14	Roberto Alomar	.35
15	Greg Maddux	.75
16	Mike Piazza	1.00
17	Matt Williams	.25
18	Kenny Lofton	.25
19	Alex Rodriguez (Rodriguez)	1.25
20	Tony Gwynn	.75
21	Mo Vaughn	.25
22	Chipper Jones	.75
23	Manny Ramirez	.60
24	Deion Sanders	.25

Lumberjacks

Lumberjacks inserts are found in both Series 1 and 2 Leaf Limited at a rate of one per 23 packs on average (less than one per box). Fronts are printed on woodgrain veneer with a large team logo behind a batting action photo of the game's top sluggers. Backs have another photo against a background of tree trunks. A white stripe at bottom carries each card's unique serial number within an edition of 5,000.

		NM/M
Complete Set (16):		55.00
Common Player:		2.00
1	Albert Belle	2.00
2	Barry Bonds	12.00
3	Juan Gonzalez	3.50
4	Ken Griffey Jr.	7.50
5	Fred McGriff	2.00
6	Mike Piazza	7.50
7	Kirby Puckett	6.00
8	Mo Vaughn	2.00
9	Frank Thomas	4.50
10	Jeff Bagwell	4.50
11	Matt Williams	2.00
12	Jose Canseco	3.00
13	Raul Mondesi	2.00
14	Manny Ramirez	4.50
15	Cecil Fielder	2.00
16	Cal Ripken Jr.	12.00

Opening Day

Issued in celebration of the 1995's season's delayed debut, this set was only available via a mail-in offer for $2 and eight wrappers. Cards were advertised as featuring front and back photos shot on opening day. Fronts have a player photo bordered on the left with a vertical "1995 Opening Day" stripe fea-

turing exploding fireworks at the bottom. The player's name and position appear in a silver-foil strip at bottom; a silver-foil Leaf logo is at upper-right. Backs have a player action photo set against a background of exploding fireworks and a re-cap of the player's 1995 Opening Day performance.

		NM/M
Complete Set (8):		6.00
Common Player:		.25
1	Frank Thomas	.50
2	Jeff Bagwell	.50
3	Barry Bonds	2.00
5	Ken Griffey Jr.	1.00
5	Mike Piazza	1.00
6	Cal Ripken Jr.	2.00
7	Jose Canseco	.35
8	Larry Walker	.25

1996 Leaf

Reverting to a single-series issue of 220 basic cards, plus numerous insert set bells and whistles, this was the final Leaf set under Donruss' ownership. Regular cards offer large action photos on front and back with a side and bottom border subdued through darkening (front) or lightening (back). Fronts feature silver prismatic-foil graphic highlights while the back includes a circular portrait photo with vital data around. Leaf was sold in both hobby and retail versions, each with some unique inserts. Basic unit was the 12-card foil pack, with suggested retail of $2.49.

	NM/M
Complete Set (220):	10.00
Common Player:	.05
Complete Gold Set (220):	100.00
Common Golds:	1.00
Gold Press Proofs:	15X
Complete Silver Set (220):	50.00
Common Silvers:	.50
Silver Press Proofs:	6X
Complete Bronze Set (220):	40.00
Common Bronze:	.25
Bronze Press Proofs:	4X
Pack (12):	1.00
Wax Box (30):	25.00

1	John Smoltz	.10
2	Dennis Eckersley	.60
3	Delino DeShields	.05
4	Cliff Floyd	.05
5	Chuck Finley	.05
6	Cecil Fielder	.05
7	Tim Naehring	.05
8	Carlos Perez	.05
9	Brad Ausmus	.05
10	Matt Lawton **RC**	.15
11	Alan Trammell	.05
12	Steve Finley	.05
13	Paul O'Neill	.05
14	Gary Sheffield	.40
15	Mark McGwire	1.50
16	Bernie Williams	.05
17	Jeff Montgomery	.05
18	Chan Ho Park	.05
19	Greg Vaughn	.05
20	Jeff Kent	.05
21	Cal Ripken Jr.	2.00
22	Charles Johnson	.05
23	Eric Karros	.05
24	Alex Rodriguez	1.50
25	Chris Snopek	.05
26	Jason Isringhausen	.05
27	Chili Davis	.05
28	Chipper Jones	.75
29	Bret Saberhagen	.05
30	Tony Clark	.05
31	Marty Cordova	.05
32	Dwayne Hosey	.05
33	Fred McGriff	.25
34	Deion Sanders	.05

35	Orlando Merced	.05
36	Brady Anderson	.05
37	Ray Lankford	.05
38	Manny Ramirez	.65
39	Alex Fernandez	.05
40	Greg Colbrunn	.05
41	Ken Griffey Jr.	1.00
42	Mickey Morandini	.05
43	Chuck Knoblauch	.05
44	Quinton McCracken	.05
45	Tim Salmon	.05
46	Jose Mesa	.05
47	Marquis Grissom	.05
48	Checklist	.05
49	Raul Mondesi	.05
50	Mark Grudzielanek	.05
51	Ray Durham	.05
52	Matt Williams	.05
53	Bob Hamelin	.05
54	Lenny Dykstra	.05
55	Jeff King	.05
56	LaTroy Hawkins	.05
57	Terry Pendleton	.05
58	Kevin Stocker	.05
59	Ozzie Timmons	.05
60	David Justice	.05
61	Ricky Bottalico	.05
62	Andy Ashby	.05
63	Larry Walker	.05
64	Jose Canseco	.40
65	Bret Boone	.05
66	Shawn Green	.35
67	Chad Curtis	.05
68	Travis Fryman	.05
69	Roger Clemens	1.00
70	David Bell	.05
71	Rusty Greer	.05
72	Bob Higginson	.05
73	Joey Hamilton	.05
74	Kevin Seitzer	.05
75	Julian Tavarez	.05
76	Troy Percival	.05
77	Kirby Puckett	.75
78	Barry Bonds	2.00
79	Michael Tucker	.05
80	Paul Molitor	.65
81	Carlos Garcia	.05
82	Johnny Damon	.35
83	Mike Hampton	.05
84	Ariel Prieto	.05
85	Tony Tarasco	.05
86	Pete Schourek	.05
87	Tom Glavine	.30
88	Rondell White	.05
89	Jim Edmonds	.05
90	Robby Thompson	.05
91	Wade Boggs	.75
92	Pedro Martinez	.65
93	Gregg Jefferies	.05
94	Albert Belle	.05
95	Benji Gil	.05
96	Denny Neagle	.05
97	Mark Langston	.05
98	Sandy Alomar	.05
99	Tony Gwynn	.75
100	Todd Hundley	.05
101	Dante Bichette	.05
102	Eddie Murray	.65
103	Lyle Mouton	.05
104	John Jaha	.05
105	Checklist	.05
106	Jon Nunnally	.05
107	Juan Gonzalez	.50
108	Kevin Appier	.05
109	Brian McRae	.05
110	Lee Smith	.05
111	Tim Wakefield	.05
112	Sammy Sosa	1.00
113	Jay Buhner	.05
114	Garret Anderson	.05
115	Edgar Martinez	.05
116	Edgardo Alfonzo	.05
117	Billy Ashley	.05
118	Joe Carter	.05
119	Javy Lopez	.05
120	Bobby Bonilla	.05
121	Ken Caminiti	.05
122	Barry Larkin	.05
123	Shannon Stewart	.05
124	Orel Hershiser	.05
125	Jeff Conine	.05
126	Mark Grace	.05
127	Kenny Lofton	.05
128	Luis Gonzalez	.25
129	Rico Brogna	.05
130	Mo Vaughn	.05
131	Brad Radke	.05
132	Jose Herrera	.05
133	Rick Aguilera	.05
134	Gary DiSarcina	.05
135	Andres Galarraga	.05
136	Carl Everett	.05
137	Steve Avery	.05
138	Vinny Castilla	.05
139	Dennis Martinez	.05
140	John Wetteland	.05
141	Alex Gonzalez	.05
142	Brian Jordan	.05
143	Todd Hollandsworth	.05
144	Terrell Wade	.05
145	Wilson Alvarez	.05
146	Reggie Sanders	.05
147	Will Clark	.10
148	Hideo Nomo	.50
149	J.T. Snow	.05
150	Frank Thomas	.65
151	Ivan Rodriguez	.60
152	Jay Bell	.05

153	Checklist	.05
154	David Cone	.05
155	Roberto Alomar	.20
156	Carlos Delgado	.40
157	Carlos Baerga	.05
158	Geronimo Berroa	.05
159	Joe Vitiello	.05
160	Terry Steinbach	.05
161	Doug Drabek	.05
162	David Segui	.05
163	Ozzie Smith	.75
164	Kurt Abbott	.05
165	Randy Johnson	.65
166	John Valentin	.05
167	Mickey Tettleton	.05
168	Ruben Sierra	.05
169	Jim Thome	.60
170	Mike Greenwell	.05
171	Quilvio Veras	.05
172	Robin Ventura	.05
173	Bill Pulsipher	.05
174	Rafael Palmeiro	.05
175	Hal Morris	.05
176	Ryan Klesko	.05
177	Eric Young	.05
178	Shane Andrews	.05
179	Brian Hunter	.05
180	Brett Butler	.05
181	John Olerud	.05
182	Moises Alou	.05
183	Glenallen Hill	.05
184	Ismael Valdes	.05
185	Andy Pettitte	.25
186	Yamil Benitez	.05
187	Jason Bere	.05
188	Dean Palmer	.05
189	Jimmy Haynes	.05
190	Trevor Hoffman	.05
191	Mike Mussina	.40
192	Greg Maddux	.75
193	Ozzie Guillen	.05
194	Pat Listach	.05
195	Derek Bell	.05
196	Darren Daulton	.05
197	John Mabry	.05
198	Ramon Martinez	.05
199	Jeff Bagwell	.65
200	Mike Piazza	1.00
201	Al Martin	.05
202	Aaron Sele	.05
203	Ed Sprague	.05
204	Rod Beck	.05
205	Checklist	.05
206	Mike Lansing	.05
207	Craig Biggio	.05
208	Jeffrey Hammonds	.05
209	Dave Nilsson	.05
210	Checklist, Inserts (Dante Bichette, Albert Belle)	.05
211	Derek Jeter	2.00
212	Alan Benes	.05
213	Jason Schmidt	.05
214	Alex Ochoa	.05
215	Ruben Rivera	.05
216	Roger Cedeno	.05
217	Jeff Suppan	.05
218	Billy Wagner	.05
219	Mark Loretta	.05
220	Karim Garcia	.10

Press Proofs

Carrying the parallel edition concept to its inevitable next level, '96 Leaf offered the Press Proof insert cards in three degrees of scarcity, each highlighted with appropriate holographic foil. At the top of the line are Gold Press Proofs in an edition of only 500 of each card. Silver and Bronze versions were produced in editions of 1,000 and 2,000, respectively. Press Proofs are inserted into both hobby and retail packs at an average rate of one card per 10 packs.

	NM/M
Complete Set, Gold (220):	200.00
Complete Set, Silver (220):	100.00
Complete Set, Bronze (220):	75.00
Common Player, Gold:	1.00
Common Player, Silver:	.50
Common Player, Bronze:	.25

All-Star MVP Contenders

A surprise insert in Leaf boxes was this interactive redemption issue. Twenty leading candidates for MVP honors at the 1996 All-Star Game in Philadelphia were presented in a silver-foil highlighted horizontal format. The player's league logo serves as a background to the color action photo on front. Backs have details of the redemption offer which expired Aug. 15, 1996. The first 5,000 persons who sent in the Mike Piazza card for redemption received a gold version of the set and had their Piazza card punch-cancelled and returned.

		NM/M
Complete Set (20):		12.50
Common Card:		.25
Golds:		1.5X
1	Frank Thomas	.75
2	Mike Piazza	1.50
2c	Mike Piazza (Redeemed and punch-cancelled.)	1.00
3	Sammy Sosa	1.50
4	Cal Ripken Jr.	2.00
5	Jeff Bagwell	.75
6	Reggie Sanders	.25
7	Mo Vaughn	.25
8	Tony Gwynn	1.00
9	Dante Bichette	.25
10	Tim Salmon	.25
11	Chipper Jones	1.00
12	Kenny Lofton	.25
13	Manny Ramirez	.75
14	Barry Bonds	2.00
15	Raul Mondesi	.25
16	Kirby Puckett	1.00
17	Albert Belle	.25
18	Ken Griffey Jr.	1.50
19	Greg Maddux	1.00
20	Bonus card	.10

Gold Leaf Stars

A vignetted background of embossed gold metallic cardboard and a Gold Leaf Stars logo in 22-K gold foil are featured on this limited (2,500 of each) edition insert. Backs include a second color photo of the player and a serial number from within the edition. Gold Leaf Stars were included in both hobby and retail packaging, with an average insertion rate of one per 210 packs.

		NM/M
Complete Set (15):		125.00
Common Player:		3.00
1	Frank Thomas	9.00
2	Dante Bichette	3.00
3	Sammy Sosa	3.00
4	Ken Griffey Jr.	15.00
5	Mike Piazza	15.00
6	Tim Salmon	3.00
7	Hideo Nomo	3.00
8	Cal Ripken Jr.	20.00
9	Chipper Jones	12.00
10	Albert Belle	3.00
11	Tony Gwynn	12.00
12	Mo Vaughn	3.00
13	Barry Larkin	3.00
14	Manny Ramirez	9.00
15	Greg Maddux	12.00

Hats Off

The most technically innovative inserts of 1996 have to be the Hats Off series exclusive to Leaf retail packs. Front player photos are on a background that is both flocked to simulate the cloth of a baseball cap, plus enhanced with a stiched team logo. The graphics are all in raised textured gold foil. Backs are conventionally printed and include a gold-foil serial number placing each card within an edition of 5,000 per player.

		NM/M
Complete Set (8):		30.00
Common Player:		3.00
1	Cal Ripken Jr.	12.00
2	Barry Larkin	3.00
3	Frank Thomas	4.50
4	Mo Vaughn	3.00
5	Ken Griffey Jr.	7.50
6	Hideo Nomo	4.00
7	Albert Belle	3.00
8	Greg Maddux	6.00

Picture Perfect

Leaf calls the glossy central area of these inserts "pearlized foil," which allows the player action photo to stand out in contrast to the actual wood veneer background. Gold-foil highlights complete the design. Backs are conventionally printed and include a gold-foil serial number from within the edition of 5,000 of each player's card. Cards #1-6 are hobby-only inserts, while #7-12 are found in retail packs. Average insertion rate is one per 140 packs. A promo version of each card was also issued.

		NM/M
Complete Set (12):		22.50
Common Player:		1.00
Promos:		2X
1	Frank Thomas	2.00
2	Cal Ripken Jr.	5.00
3	Greg Maddux	2.50
4	Manny Ramirez	2.00
5	Chipper Jones	2.50
6	Tony Gwynn	2.50
7	Ken Griffey Jr.	3.00
8	Albert Belle	1.00
9	Jeff Bagwell	2.00
10	Mike Piazza	3.00
11	Mo Vaughn	1.00
12	Barry Bonds	5.00

Statistical Standouts

The feel of leather complements the game-used baseball background on these hobby-only inserts featuring the game's top names. Backs offer statistical data and a gold-foil serial number placing the card within an edition of 2,500 for each player. Average insertion rate is one per 210 packs.

		NM/M
Complete Set (8):		60.00
Common Player:		3.00
1	Cal Ripken Jr.	20.00
2	Tony Gwynn	10.00
3	Frank Thomas	7.50
4	Ken Griffey Jr.	13.50
5	Hideo Nomo	6.00
6	Greg Maddux	10.00
7	Albert Belle	3.00
8	Chipper Jones	10.00

Frank Thomas' Greatest Hits

Die-cut plastic with a background of prismatic foil to simulate a segment of a compact disc is the format for this insert issue chronicling the career-to-date of Frank Thomas. Backs include a few stats and a portrait photo, plus a gold-foil serial number from within an edition of 5,000. Cards #1-4 are found only in hobby packs; cards #5-7 are exclusive to retail packs (average insertion rate one per 210 packs) and card #8 could be had only through a wrapper redemption.

		NM/M
Complete Set (8):		12.50
Common Card:		2.00
1	1990	2.00
2	1991	2.00
3	1992	2.00
4	1993	2.00
5	1994	2.00
6	1995	2.00
7	Career	2.00
8	MVP	2.00

Total Bases

Total-base leaders from 1991-95 are featured in this hobby-only insert set. Card fronts are printed on textured canvas to simulate a base. Fronts are highlighted with gold foil. Backs have stats ranking the player in this category plus a gold-foil serial number from an edition of 5,000 of each player. Total Bases inserts are seeded at an average rate of one per 72 packs. Each player can also be found in a promo card version, marked as such on each side.

		NM/M
Complete Set (12):		25.00
Common Player:		1.00
Promos:		2X
1	Frank Thomas	2.50
2	Albert Belle	1.00
3	Rafael Palmeiro	2.00
4	Barry Bonds	6.00
5	Kirby Puckett	3.00
6	Joe Carter	1.00
7	Paul Molitor	2.50
8	Fred McGriff	1.00
9	Ken Griffey Jr.	4.00
10	Carlos Baerga	1.00
11	Juan Gonzalez	2.00
12	Cal Ripken Jr.	6.00

1996 Leaf/Limited

Leaf Limited contains 90 of the top rookies and stars. There is also a 100-card Limited Gold parallel set which includes the 90 base cards, plus 10 Limited Rookies inserts. The gold parallel cards are seeded one per 11 packs. Regular Limited Rookies inserts were seeded one per seven packs. Other insert sets were two versions of Lumberjacks and Pennant Craze.

		NM/M
Complete Set (90):		15.00
Common Player:		.10
Gold Set (90):		50.00
Gold Stars/Rookies:		3X
Pack (5):		1.50
Wax Box (14):		20.00
1	Ivan Rodriguez	.60
2	Roger Clemens	1.50
3	Gary Sheffield	.40
4	Tino Martinez	.10
5	Sammy Sosa	1.50
6	Reggie Sanders	.10
7	Ray Lankford	.10
8	Manny Ramirez	.75
9	Jeff Bagwell	.75
10	Greg Maddux	1.00
11	Ken Griffey Jr.	1.50
12	Rondell White	.10
13	Mike Piazza	1.50
14	Marc Newfield	.10
15	Cal Ripken Jr.	3.00
16	Carlos Delgado	.40
17	Tim Salmon	.10
18	Andres Galarraga	.10
19	Chuck Knoblauch	.10
20	Matt Williams	.10
21	Mark McGwire	2.00
22	Ben McDonald	.10
23	Frank Thomas	.75
24	Johnny Damon	.35
25	Gregg Jefferies	.10
26	Travis Fryman	.10
27	Chipper Jones	1.00
28	David Cone	.10
29	Kenny Lofton	.10
30	Mike Mussina	.30
31	Alex Rodriguez	2.00
32	Carlos Baerga	.10
33	Brian Hunter	.10
34	Juan Gonzalez	.60
35	Bernie Williams	.10
36	Wally Joyner	.10
37	Fred McGriff	.10
38	Randy Johnson	.75
39	Marty Cordova	.10
40	Garret Anderson	.10
41	Albert Belle	.10
42	Edgar Martinez	.10
43	Barry Larkin	.10
44	Paul O'Neill	.10
45	Cecil Fielder	.10
46	Rusty Greer	.10
47	Mo Vaughn	.10
48	Dante Bichette	.10
49	Ryan Klesko	.10
50	Roberto Alomar	.25
51	Raul Mondesi	.10
52	Robin Ventura	.10
53	Tony Gwynn	1.00
54	Mark Grace	.10
55	Jim Thome	.60
56	Jason Giambi	.50
57	Tom Glavine	.25
58	Jim Edmonds	.10
59	Pedro Martinez	.75
60	Charles Johnson	.10
61	Wade Boggs	1.00
62	Orlando Merced	.10
63	Craig Biggio	.10
64	Brady Anderson	.10
65	Hideo Nomo	.60
66	Ozzie Smith	1.00
67	Eddie Murray	.75
68	Will Clark	.15
69	Jay Buhner	.10
70	Kirby Puckett	1.00
71	Barry Bonds	3.00
72	Ray Durham	.10
73	Sterling Hitchcock	.10
74	John Smoltz	.10
75	Andre Dawson	.35
76	Joe Carter	.10
77	Ryne Sandberg	1.00
78	Rickey Henderson	.75
79	Brian Jordan	.10
80	Greg Vaughn	.10
81	Andy Pettitte	.25
82	Dean Palmer	.10
83	Paul Molitor	.75
84	Rafael Palmeiro	.60
85	Henry Rodriguez	.10
86	Larry Walker	.10
87	Ismael Valdes	.10
88	Derek Bell	.10
89	J.T. Snow	.10
90	Jack McDowell	.10

Lumberjacks

Lumberjacks inserts returned to Leaf Limited, but the 1996 versions feature an improved maple stock that puts wood grains on both sides of the card. Ten different Lumberjacks are available in two different versions. Regular versions are serial numbered to 5,000, while a special black-bordered Limited Edition version is numbered to 500. Each Lumberjacks card was also produced in a promo card version, appropriately marked on each side.

		NM/M
Complete Set (10):		40.00
Common Player:		1.50
Lumberjack Blacks (500):		2X
Promos:		2X
1	Ken Griffey Jr.	5.00
2	Sammy Sosa	5.00
3	Cal Ripken Jr.	7.50
4	Frank Thomas	3.00
5	Alex Rodriguez	6.00
6	Mo Vaughn	1.50
7	Chipper Jones	4.00
8	Mike Piazza	5.00
9	Jeff Bagwell	3.00
10	Mark McGwire	6.00

Pennant Craze

Each card in this insert set is sequentially numbered to 2,500 in silver foil on the back. The top-front of the cards have a die-cut pennant shape and is felt-textured. Appropriately marked promotional versions of each card can also be found.

		NM/M
Complete Set (10):		20.00
Common Player:		1.00
Promos:		2X
1	Juan Gonzalez	1.25
2	Cal Ripken Jr.	4.00
3	Frank Thomas	1.50
4	Ken Griffey Jr.	2.50
5	Albert Belle	1.00
6	Greg Maddux	2.00
7	Paul Molitor	1.50
8	Alex Rodriguez	3.00
9	Barry Bonds	4.00
10	Chipper Jones	2.00

Rookies

There are two versions of this 1996 Limited insert set. The cards are reprinted as part of a Limited Gold parallel set, which also includes the regular issue's 90 cards. The gold cards are seeded one per every 11 packs. The top young players are also featured on regular Limited Rookies inserts; these versions are seeded one per every seven packs.

		NM/M
Complete Set (10):		7.50
Common Player:		.50
Limited Gold:		3X
1	Alex Ochoa	.50
2	Darin Erstad	1.00
3	Ruben Rivera	.50
4	Derek Jeter	5.00
5	Jermaine Dye	.50
6	Jason Kendall	.50
7	Mike Grace	.50
8	Andruw Jones	2.50
9	Rey Ordonez	.50
10	George Arias	.50

1996 Leaf/Preferred

Leaf Preferred consists of 150 cards, a Press Proof parallel set and three insert sets, one of which has its own parallel set, too. While no individual odds are given for insert sets, the overall odds of getting an insert card are one per 10 packs. The Press Proof inserts replace the silver foil name and strip down the left side of the card with gold foil. Press Proof parallels were limited to 250 sets. Another insert set, Silver Leaf Steel, has a card seeded one per pack. This insert set is paralleled by a Gold Leaf Steel set, which appears in much more limited numbers. The two other insert sets are Steel Power and Staremaster.

		NM/M
Complete Set (150):		15.00
Common Player:		.05
Press Proofs:		12X
Pack (6):		1.00
Wax Box (24):		20.00
1	Ken Griffey Jr.	1.25
2	Rico Brogna	.05
3	Gregg Jefferies	.05
4	Reggie Sanders	.05
5	Manny Ramirez	.75
6	Shawn Green	.40
7	Tino Martinez	.05
8	Jeff Bagwell	.75
9	Marc Newfield	.05
10	Ray Lankford	.05
11	Jay Bell	.05
12	Greg Maddux	1.00
13	Frank Thomas	.75
14	Travis Fryman	.05
15	Mark McGwire	1.50
16	Chuck Knoblauch	.05
17	Sammy Sosa	1.25
18	Matt Williams	.05
19	Roger Clemens	1.25
20	Rondell White	.05
21	Ivan Rodriguez	.65
22	Cal Ripken Jr.	2.00
23	Ben McDonald	.05
24	Kenny Lofton	.05
25	Mike Piazza	1.25
26	David Cone	.05
27	Gary Sheffield	.40
28	Tim Salmon	.05
29	Andres Galarraga	.05
30	Johnny Damon	.35
31	Ozzie Smith	1.00
32	Carlos Baerga	.05
33	Raul Mondesi	.05
34	Moises Alou	.05
35	Alex Rodriguez	1.50
36	Mike Mussina	.40
37	Jason Isringhausen	.05
38	Barry Larkin	.05
39	Bernie Williams	.05
40	Chipper Jones	1.00
41	Joey Hamilton	.05
42	Charles Johnson	.05
43	Juan Gonzalez	.50
44	Greg Vaughn	.05
45	Robin Ventura	.05
46	Albert Belle	.05
47	Rafael Palmeiro	.65
48	Brian Hunter	.05
49	Mo Vaughn	.05
50	Paul O'Neill	.05
51	Mark Grace	.05
52	Randy Johnson	.75
53	Pedro Martinez	.05
54	Marty Cordova	.05
55	Garret Anderson	.05
56	Joe Carter	.05
57	Jim Thome	.60
58	Edgardo Alfonzo	.05
59	Dante Bichette	.05
60	Darryl Hamilton	.05
61	Roberto Alomar	.20
62	Fred McGriff	.05
63	Kirby Puckett	1.00
64	Hideo Nomo	.60
65	Alex Fernandez	.05
66	Ryan Klesko	.05
67	Wade Boggs	1.00
68	Eddie Murray	.75
69	Eric Karros	.05
70	Jim Edmonds	.05
71	Edgar Martinez	.05
72	Andy Pettitte	.30
73	Mark Grudzielanek	.05
74	Tom Glavine	.25
75	Ken Caminiti	.05
76	Will Clark	.10
77	Craig Biggio	.05
78	Brady Anderson	.05
79	Tony Gwynn	1.00
80	Larry Walker	.05
81	Brian Jordan	.05
82	Lenny Dykstra	.05
83	Butch Huskey	.05
84	Jack McDowell	.05
85	Cecil Fielder	.05
86	Jose Canseco	.40
87	Jason Giambi	.05
88	Rickey Henderson	.75
89	Kevin Seitzer	.05
90	Carlos Delgado	.40
91	Ryne Sandberg	1.00
92	Dwight Gooden	.05
93	Michael Tucker	.05
94	Barry Bonds	2.00
95	Eric Young	.05
96	Dean Palmer	.05
97	Henry Rodriguez	.05
98	John Mabry	.05
99	J.T. Snow	.05
100	Andre Dawson	.25
101	Ismael Valdes	.05
102	Charles Nagy	.05
103	Jay Buhner	.05
104	Derek Bell	.05
105	Paul Molitor	.75
106	Hal Morris	.05
107	Ray Durham	.05
108	Bernard Gilkey	.05
109	John Valentin	.05
110	Melvin Nieves	.05
111	John Smoltz	.05
112	Terrell Wade	.05
113	Chad Mottola	.05
114	Tony Clark	.05
115	John Wasdin	.05
116	Derek Jeter	2.00
117	Rey Ordonez	.05
118	Jason Thompson	.05
119	Robin Jennings RC	.05
120	Rocky Coppinger RC	.05
121	Billy Wagner	.05
122	Steve Gibralter	.05
123	Jermaine Dye	.05
124	Jason Kendall	.05
125	Mike Grace RC	.05
126	Jason Schmidt	.05
127	Paul Wilson	.05
128	Alan Benes	.05
129	Justin Thompson	.05
130	Brooks Kieschnick	.05
131	George Arias	.05
132	Osvaldo Fernandez RC	.20
133	Todd Hollandsworth	.05
134	Eric Owens	.05
135	Chan Ho Park	.05
136	Mark Loretta	.05
137	Ruben Rivera	.05
138	Jeff Suppan	.05
139	Ugueth Urbina	.05
140	LaTroy Hawkins	.05
141	Chris Snopek	.05
142	Edgar Renteria	.05
143	Raul Casanova	.05
144	Jose Herrera	.05
145	Matt Lawton RC	.05
146	Ralph Milliard RC	.05
147	Checklist	
	(Frank Thomas)	.05
148	Checklist (Jeff Bagwell)	.05
149	Checklist	
	(Ken Griffey Jr.)	.05
150	Checklist (Mike Piazza)	.05

Press Proofs

Inserted at a rate of about one per 48 packs, Press Proof parallels of the 150 cards in Leaf Preferred are identifiable only by the use of gold foil, rather than silver, on the card fronts, and gold ink on back. The cards are not otherwise marked or numbered. It is believed the issue was limited to 250-500 of each card.

		NM/M
Complete Set (150):		100.00
Common Player:		.50
Stars/Rookies:		12X

Leaf Steel Promos

Each of the 77 gold cards in the Preferred Steel set can also be found in gold, silver and bronze promo card versions. The samples differ from the issued versions only in an overprint diagonally on the back which reads "PROMOTIONAL CARD." This parallel promo edition represents one of the largest promo card issues of the mid-1990s. Cards were reportedly distributed to dealers on the basis of one gold promo per three-case order. The silver and bronze versions were reportedly never officially released, though examples have found their way into the market in some quantity.

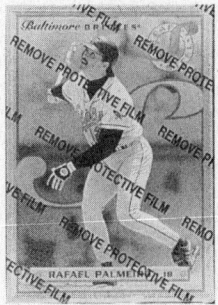

	NM/M
Complete Gold Set (77):	625.00
Common Gold Player:	4.00
Silver: Values Undetermined	
Bronze: Values Undetermined	
1 Frank Thomas	15.00
2 Paul Molitor	15.00
3 Kenny Lofton	4.00
4 Travis Fryman	4.00
5 Jeff Conine	4.00
6 Barry Bonds	50.00
7 Gregg Jefferies	4.00
8 Alex Rodriguez	40.00
9 Wade Boggs	20.00
10 David Justice	4.00
11 Hideo Nomo	12.50
12 Roberto Alomar	6.00
13 Todd Hollandsworth	4.00
14 Mark McGwire	40.00
15 Rafael Palmeiro	12.50
16 Will Clark	4.00
17 Cal Ripken Jr.	50.00
18 Derek Bell	4.00
19 Gary Sheffield	7.50
20 Juan Gonzalez	12.50
21 Garret Anderson	4.00
22 Mo Vaughn	4.00
23 Robin Ventura	4.00
24 Carlos Baerga	4.00
26 Tim Salmon	4.00
27 Fred McGriff	4.00
28 Rondell White	4.00
29 Ray Lankford	4.00
30 Lenny Dykstra	4.00
31 J.T. Snow	4.00
32 Sammy Sosa	25.00
33 Chipper Jones	20.00
34 Bobby Bonilla	4.00
35 Paul Wilson	4.00
36 Darren Daulton	4.00
37 Larry Walker	4.00
38 Raul Mondesi	4.00
39 Jeff Bagwell	15.00
40 Derek Jeter	50.00
41 Kirby Puckett	20.00
42 Jason Isringhausen	4.00
43 Vinny Castilla	4.00
44 Jim Edmonds	4.00
45 Ron Gant	4.00
46 Carlos Delgado	7.50
47 Jose Canseco	7.50
48 Tony Gwynn	20.00
49 Mike Mussina	7.50
50 Charles Johnson	4.00
51 Mike Piazza	25.00
52 Ken Griffey Jr.	25.00
53 Greg Maddux	20.00
54 Mark Grace	4.00
55 Ryan Klesko	4.00
56 Dennis Eckersley	12.50
57 Rickey Henderson	15.00
58 Michael Tucker	4.00
59 Joe Carter	4.00
60 Randy Johnson	15.00
61 Brian Jordan	4.00
62 Shawn Green	7.50
63 Roger Clemens	22.50
64 Andres Galarraga	4.00
65 Johnny Damon	7.50
66 Ryne Sandberg	20.00
67 Alan Benes	4.00
68 Albert Belle	4.00
69 Barry Larkin	4.00
70 Marty Cordova	4.00
71 Dante Bichette	4.00
72 Craig Biggio	4.00
73 Reggie Sanders	4.00
74 Moises Alou	4.00
75 Chuck Knoblauch	4.00
76 Cecil Fielder	4.00
77 Manny Ramirez	15.00

Leaf Steel

This 77-card insert set has two versions - a silver one and a much more limited gold one. A Silver Leaf Steel card

is included in every pack; the parallel versions appear about one per 24 packs.

	NM/M
Complete Set (77):	25.00
Common Player:	.15
Gold:	2X
1 Frank Thomas	1.00
2 Paul Molitor	1.00
3 Kenny Lofton	.15
4 Travis Fryman	.15
5 Jeff Conine	.15
6 Barry Bonds	3.00
7 Gregg Jefferies	.15
8 Alex Rodriguez	2.50
9 Wade Boggs	1.50
10 David Justice	.15
11 Hideo Nomo	.75
12 Roberto Alomar	.30
13 Todd Hollandsworth	.15
14 Mark McGwire	2.50
15 Rafael Palmeiro	.75
16 Will Clark	.25
17 Cal Ripken Jr.	3.00
18 Derek Bell	.15
19 Gary Sheffield	.50
20 Juan Gonzalez	.65
21 Garret Anderson	.15
22 Mo Vaughn	.15
23 Robin Ventura	.15
24 Carlos Baerga	.15
25 Tim Salmon	.15
26 Matt Williams	.15
27 Fred McGriff	.15
28 Rondell White	.15
29 Ray Lankford	.15
30 Lenny Dykstra	.15
31 J.T. Snow	.15
32 Sammy Sosa	2.00
33 Chipper Jones	1.50
34 Bobby Bonilla	.15
35 Paul Wilson	.15
36 Darren Daulton	.15
37 Larry Walker	.15
38 Raul Mondesi	.15
39 Jeff Bagwell	1.00
40 Derek Jeter	3.00
41 Kirby Puckett	1.50
42 Jason Isringhausen	.15
43 Vinny Castilla	.15
44 Jim Edmonds	.15
45 Ron Gant	.15
46 Carlos Delgado	.50
47 Jose Canseco	.40
48 Tony Gwynn	1.00
49 Mike Mussina	.50
50 Charles Johnson	.15
51 Mike Piazza	2.00
52 Ken Griffey Jr.	2.00
53 Greg Maddux	1.50
54 Mark Grace	.15
55 Ryan Klesko	.15
56 Dennis Eckersley	.75
57 Rickey Henderson	1.00
58 Michael Tucker	.15
59 Joe Carter	.15
60 Randy Johnson	1.00
61 Brian Jordan	.15
62 Shawn Green	.50
63 Roger Clemens	2.00
64 Andres Galarraga	.15
66 Johnny Damon	.40
66 Ryne Sandberg	1.50
67 Alan Benes	.15
68 Albert Belle	.75
69 Barry Larkin	.15
70 Marty Cordova	.15
71 Dante Bichette	.15
72 Craig Biggio	.15
73 Reggie Sanders	.15
74 Moises Alou	.15
75 Chuck Knoblauch	.15
76 Cecil Fielder	.15
77 Manny Ramirez	1.00

Staremaster

These 1996 Leaf Preferred inserts provide a photographic tribute to the stares of 12 top players. Each card is printed on silver holographic card stock and is numbered up to 2,500.

	NM/M
Complete Set (12):	50.00

	NM/M
Common Player:	3.00
1 Chipper Jones	5.00
2 Alex Rodriguez	7.50
3 Derek Jeter	10.00
4 Tony Gwynn	3.00
5 Frank Thomas	4.00
6 Ken Griffey Jr.	6.00
7 Cal Ripken Jr.	10.00
8 Greg Maddux	5.00
9 Albert Belle	3.00
10 Barry Bonds	10.00
11 Jeff Bagwell	4.00
12 Mike Piazza	6.00

Steel Power

This eight-card Leaf Steel insert set combines micro-etched foil with interior die-cutting to honor the game's top power hitters. Each insert card carries a serial number up to 5,000.

	NM/M
Complete Set (8):	17.50
Common Player:	1.00
1 Albert Belle	1.00
2 Mo Vaughn	1.00
3 Ken Griffey Jr.	3.50
4 Cal Ripken Jr.	5.00
5 Mike Piazza	3.50
6 Barry Bonds	5.00
7 Jeff Bagwell	2.50
8 Frank Thomas	2.50

1996 Leaf/Signature Series

The base set which rode along with the autographed cards of more than 250 Major League players in Leaf's Signature Series (at least one authentic signature is guaranteed in every pack) features action photos with silver-foil highlights. Horizontal backs have a large photo along with a few stats and bits of personal data. One out of every 48 packs is a super pack containing nothing but autographed cards. The 150-card base set is paralleled in Gold and Plat-

inum Press Proof insert sets. The gold version is seeded one per 12 packs in Series 1 and one per eight in the Extended Series. Platinums were issued in an edition of 150 of each of the 150 cards and are found only in the Extended Series at the rate of one per 24 packs. Four-card packs of Leaf Signature Series carried a suggested retail price at issue of $9.99.

	NM/M
Complete Set (150):	30.00
Complete 1st Series (100):	20.00
Complete Extended Series (50):	10.00
Common Player:	.05
Gold PP Stars/Rookies:	8X
Platinum PP Stars/Rookies:	20X
Pack (4):	3.50
Wax Box (12):	35.00
1 Mike Piazza	1.25
2 Juan Gonzalez	.65
3 Greg Maddux	1.00
4 Marc Newfield	.05
5 Wade Boggs	1.00
6 Ray Lankford	.05
7 Frank Thomas	.75
8 Rico Brogna	.05
9 Tim Salmon	.05
10 Ken Griffey Jr.	1.25
11 Manny Ramirez	.75
12 Cecil Fielder	.05
13 Gregg Jefferies	.05
14 Rondell White	.05
15 Cal Ripken Jr.	2.00
16 Alex Rodriguez	1.50
17 Bernie Williams	.05
18 Andres Galarraga	.05
19 Mike Mussina	.50
20 Chuck Knoblauch	.05
21 Joe Carter	.05
22 Jeff Bagwell	.75
23 Mark McGwire	1.50
24 Sammy Sosa	1.00
25 Reggie Sanders	.05
26 Chipper Jones	1.00
27 Jeff Cirillo	.05
28 Roger Clemens	1.25
29 Craig Biggio	.05
30 Gary Sheffield	.45
31 Paul O'Neill	.05
32 Johnny Damon	.35
33 Jason Isringhausen	.05
34 Jay Bell	.05
35 Henry Rodriguez	.05
36 Matt Williams	.05
37 Randy Johnson	.75
38 Fred McGriff	.05
39 Jason Giambi	.60
40 Ivan Rodriguez	.65
41 Raul Mondesi	.05
42 Barry Larkin	.05
43 Ryan Klesko	.05
44 Joey Hamilton	.05
45 Todd Hundley	.05
46 Jim Edmonds	.05
47 Dante Bichette	.20
48 Roberto Alomar	.20
49 Mark Grace	.05
50 Brady Anderson	.05
51 Hideo Nomo	.65
52 Ozzie Smith	1.00
53 Robin Ventura	.05
54 Andy Pettitte	.35
55 Kenny Lofton	.05
56 John Mabry	.05
57 Paul Molitor	.75
58 Rey Ordonez	.05
59 Albert Belle	.05
60 Charles Johnson	.05
61 Edgar Martinez	.05
62 Derek Bell	.05
63 Carlos Delgado	.50
64 Raul Casanova	.05
65 Ismael Valdes	.05
66 J.T. Snow	.05
67 Derek Jeter	2.00
68 Jason Kendall	.05
69 John Smoltz	.05
70 Chad Mottola	.05
71 Jim Thome	.60
72 Will Clark	.10
73 Mo Vaughn	.05
74 John Wasdin	.05
75 Rafael Palmeiro	.65
76 Mark Grudzielanek	.05
77 Larry Walker	.05
78 Alan Benes	.05
79 Michael Tucker	.05
80 Billy Wagner	.05
81 Paul Wilson	.05
82 Greg Vaughn	.05
83 Dean Palmer	.05
84 Ryne Sandberg	1.00
85 Eric Young	.05
86 Jay Buhner	.05
87 Tony Clark	.05
88 Jermaine Dye	.05
89 Barry Bonds	2.00
90 Ugueth Urbina	.05
91 Charles Nagy	.05
92 Ruben Rivera	.05
93 Todd Hollandsworth	.05
94 Darin Erstad RC	1.50
95 Brooks Kieschnick	.05
96 Edgar Renteria	.05
97 Lenny Dykstra	.05
98 Tony Gwynn	1.00
99 Kirby Puckett	1.00
100 Checklist	.05
101 Andruw Jones	.75
102 Alex Ochoa	.05
103 David Cone	.05
104 Rusty Greer	.05
105 Jose Canseco	.45
106 Ken Caminiti	.05
107 Mariano Rivera	.15
108 Ron Gant	.05
109 Darryl Strawberry	.05
110 Vladimir Guerrero	.75
111 George Arias	.05
112 Jeff Conine	.05
113 Bobby Higginson	.05
114 Eric Karros	.05
115 Brian Hunter	.05
116 Eddie Murray	.75
117 Todd Walker	.05
118 Chan Ho Park	.05
119 John Jaha	.05
120 David Justice	.05
121 Makoto Suzuki	.05
122 Scott Rolen	.65
123 Tino Martinez	.05
124 Kimera Bartee	.05
125 Garret Anderson	.05
126 Brian Jordan	.05
127 Andre Dawson	.30
128 Javier Lopez	.05
129 Bill Pulsipher	.05
130 Dwight Gooden	.05
131 Al Martin	.05
132 Terrell Wade	.05
133 Steve Gibralter	.05
134 Tom Glavine	.35
135 Kevin Appier	.05
136 Tim Raines	.05
137 Curtis Pride	.05
138 Todd Greene	.05
139 Bobby Bonilla	.05
140 Trey Beamon	.05
141 Marty Cordova	.05
142 Rickey Henderson	.75
143 Ellis Burks	.05
144 Dennis Eckersley	.65
145 Kevin Brown	.05
146 Carlos Baerga	.05
147 Brett Butler	.05
148 Marquis Grissom	.05
149 Karim Garcia	.05
150 Checklist	.05

Press Proofs

The 150-card base set of Leaf/Signature was paralleled in a pair of Press Proof versions. Identical in format to the regular issue, the Press Proofs have an embossed gold- or platinum-foil oval seal at left and "PRESS PROOF" vertically at right in the same color foil. Backs are identical to the regular version. Gold Press Proofs were inserted one per 12 packs of Series 1 and one per eight packs of Extended. Platinum Proofs are found only in Extended Series packs, at an average rate of one per 24. Total production of Platinum Press proofs was 150 of each card.

	NM/M
Common Gold:	2.00
Gold Stars:	8X
Common Platinum:	4.00
Platinum Stars:	20X

Autographs Promos

To introduce its Autograph Series, Leaf sent dealers one of two promo card versions of the Frank Thomas card. Most received a card with a pre-printed facsimile autograph, duly noted in small type beneath the signature. Others (500) received a genuine Frank Thomas autograph on their promo. All of the cards are marked "PROMOTIONAL CARD" diagonally on both front and back.

	NM/M
Frank Thomas (Facsimile signature.)	4.00
Frank Thomas (Genuine autograph.)	50.00

Autographs

Every pack of 1996 Leaf Signature Series includes at least one authentically signed card from one of over 250 players. There were 240 players who signed three versions in these quantities: 500 Gold, 1,000 Silver and 3,500 Bronze. There are also short-printed autographs for 10 players in quantities of 100 Gold, 200 Silver and 700 Bronze. The short-printed players are designated with an "SP" in the checklist. Cards are numbered alphabetically in the checklist since the autographed cards are unnumbered. Each major leaguer signed a notarized affidavit to guarantee each signature was authentic. Series 1 cards of Carlos Delgado, Brian Hunter, Phil Plantier, Jim Thome, Terrell Wade and Ernie Young were signed too late for inclusion in Series 1 packs, and were inserted with Extended. No Bronze cards of Thome were signed.

	NM/M
Common Bronze Player:	4.00
Silver:	1.5X
Gold:	2X
SPs: 100 Gold, 200 Silver, 700 Bronze	
(1) Kurt Abbott	4.00
(2) Juan Acevedo	4.00
(3) Terry Adams	4.00
(4) Manny Alexander	4.00
(5) Roberto Alomar/SP	35.00
(6) Moises Alou	12.00
(7) Wilson Alvarez	4.00
(8) Garret Anderson	10.00
(9) Shane Andrews	4.00
(10) Andy Ashby	4.00

(11) Pedro Astacio 4.00
(12) Brad Ausmus 4.00
(13) Bobby Ayala 4.00
(14) Carlos Baerga 4.00
(15) Harold Baines 10.00
(16) Jason Bates 4.00
(17) Allen Battle 4.00
(18) Rich Becker 4.00
(19) David Bell 4.00
(20) Rafael Belliard 4.00
(21) Andy Benes 4.00
(22) Armando Benitez 4.00
(23) Jason Bere 4.00
(24) Geronimo Berroa 4.00
(25) Willie Blair 4.00
(26) Mike Blowers 4.00
(27) Wade Boggs/SP 50.00
(28) Ricky Bones 4.00
(29) Mike Bordick 4.00
(30) Toby Borland 4.00
(31) Ricky Bottalico 4.00
(32) Darren Bragg 4.00
(33) Jeff Branson 4.00
(34) Tilson Brito 4.00
(35) Rico Brogna 4.00
(36) Scott Brosius 7.50
(37) Damon Buford 4.00
(38) Mike Busby 4.00
(39) Tom Candiotti 4.00
(40) Frank Castillo 4.00
(41) Andujar Cedeno 4.00
(42) Domingo Cedeno 4.00
(43) Roger Cedeno 4.00
(44) Norm Charlton 4.00
(45) Jeff Cirillo 4.00
(46) Will Clark 10.00
(47) Jeff Conine 4.00
(48) Steve Cooke 4.00
(49) Joey Cora 4.00
(50) Marty Cordova 4.00
(51) Rheal Cormier 4.00
(52) Felipe Crespo 4.00
(53) Chad Curtis 4.00
(54) Johnny Damon 15.00
(55) Russ Davis 4.00
(56) Andre Dawson 10.00
(57a) Carlos Delgado (Black autograph.) 15.00
(57b) Carlos Delgado (Blue autograph.) 15.00
(58) Doug Drabek 4.00
(59) Darren Dreifort 4.00
(60) Shawon Dunston 4.00
(61) Ray Durham 4.00
(62) Jim Edmonds 12.00
(63) Joey Eischen 4.00
(64) Jim Eisenreich 4.00
(65) Sal Fasano 4.00
(66) Jeff Fassero 4.00
(67) Alex Fernandez 4.00
(68) Darrin Fletcher 4.00
(69) Chad Fonville 4.00
(70) Kevin Foster 4.00
(71) John Franco 4.00
(72) Julio Franco 10.00
(73) Marvin Freeman 4.00
(74) Travis Fryman 4.00
(75) Gary Gaetti 4.00
(76) Carlos Garcia 4.00
(77) Jason Giambi 10.00
(78) Benji Gil 4.00
(79) Greg Gohr 4.00
(80) Chris Gomez 4.00
(81) Leo Gomez 4.00
(82) Tom Goodwin 4.00
(83) Mike Grace 4.00
(84) Mike Greenwell 6.00
(85) Rusty Greer 4.00
(86) Mark Grudzielanek 4.00
(87) Mark Gubicza 4.00
(88) Juan Guzman 4.00
(89) Darryl Hamilton 4.00
(90) Joey Hamilton 4.00
(91) Chris Hammond 4.00
(92) Mike Hampton 7.50
(93) Chris Haney 4.00
(94) Todd Haney 4.00
(95) Erik Hanson 4.00
(96) Pete Harnisch 4.00
(97) LaTroy Hawkins 4.00
(98) Charlie Hayes 4.00
(99) Jimmy Haynes 4.00
(100) Roberto Hernandez 4.00
(101) Bobby Higginson 4.00
(102) Glenallen Hill 4.00
(103) Ken Hill 4.00
(104) Sterling Hitchcock 4.00
(105) Trevor Hoffman 10.00
(106) Dave Hollins 4.00
(107) Dwayne Hosey 4.00
(108) Thomas Howard 4.00
(109) Steve Howe 6.00
(110) John Hudek 4.00
(111) Rex Hudler 4.00
(112) Brian Hunter 4.00
(113) Butch Huskey 4.00
(114) Mark Hutton 4.00
(115) Jason Jacome 4.00
(116) John Jaha 4.00
(117) Reggie Jefferson 4.00
(118) Derek Jeter/SP 150.00
(119) Bobby Jones 4.00
(120) Todd Jones 4.00
(121) Brian Jordan 5.00
(122) Kevin Jordan 4.00
(123) Jeff Juden 4.00
(124) Ron Karkovice 4.00
(125) Roberto Kelly 4.00

(126) Mark Kiefer 4.00
(127) Brooks Kieschnick 4.00
(128) Jeff King 4.00
(129) Mike Lansing 4.00
(130) Matt Lawton 7.50
(131) Al Leiter 6.00
(132) Mark Leiter 4.00
(133) Curtis Leskanic 4.00
(134) Darren Lewis 4.00
(135) Mark Lewis 4.00
(136) Felipe Lira 4.00
(137) Pat Listach 4.00
(138) Keith Lockhart 4.00
(139) Kenny Lofton/SP 25.00
(140) John Mabry 4.00
(141) Mike Macfarlane 4.00
(142) Kirt Manwaring 4.00
(143) Al Martin 4.00
(144) Norberto Martin 4.00
(145) Dennis Martinez 5.00
(146) Pedro Martinez 40.00
(147) Sandy Martinez 4.00
(148) Mike Matheny 4.00
(149) T.J. Mathews 4.00
(150) David McCarty 4.00
(151) Ben McDonald 4.00
(152) Pat Meares 4.00
(153) Orlando Merced 4.00
(154) Jose Mesa 4.00
(155) Matt Mieske 4.00
(156) Orlando Miller 4.00
(157) Mike Mimbs 4.00
(158) Paul Molitor/SP 40.00
(159) Raul Mondesi/SP 20.00
(160) Jeff Montgomery 4.00
(161) Mickey Morandini 4.00
(162) Lyle Mouton 4.00
(163) James Mouton 4.00
(164) Jamie Moyer 4.00
(165) Rodney Myers 4.00
(166) Denny Neagle 4.00
(167) Robb Nen 4.00
(168) Marc Newfield 4.00
(169) Dave Nilsson 4.00
(170) Jon Nunnally 4.00
(171) Chad Ogea 4.00
(172) Troy O'Leary 4.00
(173) Rey Ordonez 4.00
(174) Jayhawk Owens 4.00
(175) Tom Pagnozzi 4.00
(176) Dean Palmer 4.00
(177) Roger Pavlik 4.00
(178) Troy Percival 4.00
(179) Carlos Perez 4.00
(180) Robert Perez 4.00
(181) Andy Pettitte 30.00
(182) Phil Plantier 4.00
(183) Mike Potts 4.00
(184) Curtis Pride 4.00
(185) Ariel Prieto 4.00
(186) Bill Pulsipher 4.00
(187) Brad Radke 4.00
(188) Manny Ramirez/SP 35.00
(189) Joe Randa 4.00
(190) Pat Rapp 4.00
(191) Bryan Rekar 4.00
(192) Shane Reynolds 4.00
(193) Arthur Rhodes 4.00
(194) Mariano Rivera 45.00
(195a) Alex Rodriguez/SP (Black autograph.) 120.00
(195b) Alex Rodriguez/SP (Blue autograph.) 120.00
(196) Frank Rodriguez 4.00
(197) Mel Rojas 4.00
(198) Ken Ryan 4.00
(199) Bret Saberhagen 4.00
(200) Tim Salmon 5.00
(201) Rey Sanchez 4.00
(202) Scott Sanders 4.00
(203) Steve Scarsone 4.00
(204) Curt Schilling 25.00
(205) Jason Schmidt 20.00
(206) David Segui 4.00
(207) Kevin Seitzer 4.00
(208) Scott Servais 4.00
(209) Don Slaught 4.00
(210) Zane Smith 4.00
(211) Paul Sorrento 4.00
(212) Scott Stahoviak 4.00
(213) Mike Stanley 4.00
(214) Terry Steinbach 4.00
(215) Kevin Stocker 4.00
(216) Jeff Suppan 4.00
(217) Bill Swift 4.00
(218) Greg Swindell 4.00
(219) Kevin Tapani 4.00
(220) Danny Tartabull 4.00
(221) Julian Tavarez 4.00
(222a) Frank Thomas/SP (Blue autograph.) 40.00
(222b) Frank Thomas/SP (Black autograph.) 40.00
(223) Jim Thome/SP/Silver 40.00
(224) Ozzie Timmons 4.00
(225a) Michael Tucker (Black autograph.) 4.00
(225b) Michael Tucker (Blue autograph.) 4.00
(226) Ismael Valdez 4.00
(227) Jose Valentin 4.00
(228) Todd Van Poppel 4.00
(229) Quilvio Veras 4.00
(230) Fernando Vina 4.00
(231) Joe Vitiello 4.00
(232) Jose Vizcaino 4.00
(233) Jose Vizcaino 4.00
(234) Omar Vizquel 12.00

(235) Terrell Wade 4.00
(236) Paul Wagner 4.00
(237) Matt Walbeck 4.00
(238) Jerome Walton 4.00
(239) Turner Ward 4.00
(240) Allen Watson 4.00
(241) David Weathers 4.00
(242) Walt Weiss 4.00
(243) Turk Wendell 4.00
(244) Rondell White 5.00
(245) Brian Williams 4.00
(246) George Williams 4.00
(247) Paul Wilson 4.00
(248) Bobby Witt 4.00
(249) Bob Wolcott 4.00
(250) Eric Young 4.00
(251) Ernie Young 4.00
(252) Gregg Zaun 4.00
--- Frank Thomas (Autographed jumbo edition of 1,500.) 25.00

Extended Autographs

Signature Series Extended Autograph cards comprise 30 short-printed stars and top prospects, and 187 other major leaguers. Most players signed 5,000 cards each, while other signees' totals are listed in parentheses. Signature cards for Alex Rodriguez, Juan Gonzalez and Andruw Jones were only available through mail-in redemption. Autographed cards were a different design from Series 1 and were seeded two per pack in Extended. The unnumbered cards are checklisted here in alphabetical order.

NM/M
Common Player: 4.00
Extended Pack: 20.00
Extended Box: 150.00
(1) Scott Aldred 4.00
(2) Mike Aldrete 4.00
(3) Rich Amaral 4.00
(4) Alex Arias 4.00
(5) Paul Assenmacher 4.00
(6) Roger Bailey 4.00
(7) Erik Bennett 4.00
(8) Sean Bergman 4.00
(9) Doug Bochtler 4.00
(10) Tim Bogar 4.00
(11) Pat Borders 4.00
(12) Pedro Borbon 4.00
(13) Shawn Boskie 4.00
(14) Rafael Bournigal 4.00
(15) Mark Brandenburg 4.00
(16) John Briscoe 4.00
(17) Jorge Brito 4.00
(18) Doug Brocail 4.00
(19) Jay Buhner/SP/1000 17.50
(20) Scott Bullett 4.00
(21) Dave Burba 4.00
(22) Ken Caminiti/SP/1000 25.00
(23) John Cangelosi 4.00
(24) Cris Carpenter 4.00
(25) Chuck Carr 4.00
(26) Larry Casian 4.00
(27) Tony Castillo 4.00
(28) Jason Christianson 4.00
(29) Archi Cianfrocco 4.00
(30) Mark Clark 4.00
(31) Terry Clark 4.00
(32) Roger Clemens/SP/1000 150.00
(33) Jim Converse 4.00
(34) Dennis Cook 4.00
(35) Francisco Cordova 4.00
(36) Jim Corsi 4.00
(37) Tim Crabtree 4.00
(38) Doug Creek/SP/1950 8.00
(39) John Cummings 4.00
(40) Omar Daal 4.00

(41) Rich DeLucia 4.00
(42) Mark Dewey 4.00
(43) Alex Diaz 4.00
(44) Jermaine Dye/SP/2500 12.00
(45) Ken Edenfield 4.00
(46) Mark Eichhorn 4.00
(47) John Ericks 4.00
(48) Darin Erstad 10.00
(49) Alvaro Espinoza 4.00
(50) Jorge Fabregas 4.00
(51) Mike Fetters 4.00
(52) John Flaherty 4.00
(53) Bryce Florie 4.00
(54) Tony Fossas 4.00
(55) Lou Frazier 4.00
(56) Mike Gallego 4.00
(57) Karim Garcia/SP/2500 6.00
(58) Jason Giambi 12.00
(59) Ed Giovanola 4.00
(60) Tom Glavine/SP/1250 40.00
(61) Juan Gonzalez/1000 30.00
(61) Juan Gonzalez (Redemption card.) 5.00
(62) Craig Grebeck 4.00
(63) Buddy Groom 4.00
(64) Kevin Gross 4.00
(65) Eddie Guardado 4.00
(66) Mark Guthrie 4.00
(67) Tony Gwynn/SP/1000 60.00
(68) Chip Hale 4.00
(69) Darren Hall 4.00
(70) Lee Hancock 4.00
(71) Dave Hansen 4.00
(72) Bryan Harvey 4.00
(73) Bill Haselman 4.00
(74) Mike Henneman 4.00
(75) Doug Henry 4.00
(76) Gil Heredia 4.00
(77) Carlos Hernandez 4.00
(78) Jose Hernandez 4.00
(79) Darren Holmes 4.00
(80) Mark Holzemer 4.00
(81) Rick Honeycutt 4.00
(82) Chris Hook 4.00
(83) Chris Howard 4.00
(84) Jack Howell 4.00
(85) David Hulse 4.00
(86) Edwin Hurtado 4.00
(87) Jeff Huson 4.00
(88) Mike James 4.00
(89) Derek Jeter/SP/1000 160.00
(90) Brian Johnson 4.00
(91) Randy Johnson/SP/1000 125.00
(92) Mark Johnson 4.00
(93) Andruw Jones/SP/2000 30.00
(93) Andruw Jones (Redemption card.) 5.00
(94) Chris Jones 4.00
(95) Ricky Jordan 4.00
(96) Matt Karchner 4.00
(97) Scott Karl 4.00
(98) Jason Kendall/SP/2500 10.00
(99) Brian Keyser 4.00
(100) Mike Kingery 4.00
(101) Wayne Kirby 4.00
(102) Ryan Klesko/SP/1000 17.50
(103) Chuck Knoblauch/SP/1000 15.00
(104) Chad Kreuter 4.00
(105) Tom Lampkin 4.00
(106) Scott Leius 4.00
(107) Jon Lieber 4.00
(108) Nelson Liriano 4.00
(109) Scott Livingstone 4.00
(110) Graeme Lloyd 4.00
(111) Kenny Lofton/SP/1000 10.00
(112) Luis Lopez 4.00
(113) Torey Lovullo 4.00
(114) Greg Maddux/SP/500 250.00
(115) Mike Maddux 4.00
(116) Dave Magadan 4.00
(117) Mike Magnante 4.00
(118) Joe Magrane 4.00
(119) Pat Mahomes 4.00
(120) Matt Mantei 4.00
(121) John Marzano 4.00
(122) Terry Matthews 4.00
(123) Chuck McElroy 4.00
(124) Fred McGriff/SP/1000 35.00
(125) Mark McLemore 4.00
(126) Greg McMichael 4.00
(127) Blas Minor 4.00
(128) Dave Mlicki 4.00
(129) Mike Mohler 4.00
(130) Paul Molitor/SP/1000 25.00
(131) Steve Montgomery 4.00
(132) Mike Mordecai 4.00
(133) Mike Morgan 4.00
(134) Mike Munoz 4.00
(135) Greg Myers 4.00
(136) Jimmy Myers 4.00
(137) Mike Myers 4.00
(138) Bob Natal 4.00
(139) Dan Naulty 4.00
(140) Jeff Nelson 4.00

(141) Warren Newson 4.00
(142) Chris Nichting 4.00
(143) Melvin Nieves 4.00
(144) Charlie O'Brien 4.00
(145) Alex Ochoa 4.00
(146) Omar Olivares 4.00
(147) Joe Oliver 4.00
(148) Lance Painter 4.00
(149) Rafael Palmeiro/SP/2000 35.00
(150) Mark Parent 4.00
(151) Steve Parris/SP/1800 7.50
(152) Bob Patterson 4.00
(153) Tony Pena 7.50
(154) Eddie Perez 4.00
(155) Yorkis Perez 4.00
(156) Robert Person 4.00
(157) Mark Petkovsek 4.00
(158) Andy Pettitte/SP/1000 60.00
(159) J.R. Phillips 4.00
(160) Hipolito Pichardo 4.00
(161) Eric Plunk 4.00
(162) Jimmy Poole 4.00
(163) Kirby Puckett/SP/1000 80.00
(164) Paul Quantrill 4.00
(165) Tom Quinlan 4.00
(166) Jeff Reboulet 4.00
(167) Jeff Reed 4.00
(168) Steve Reed 4.00
(169) Carlos Reyes 4.00
(170) Bill Risley 4.00
(171) Kevin Ritz 4.00
(172) Kevin Roberson 4.00
(173) Rich Robertson 4.00
(174) Alex Rodriguez/SP/100 180.00
(174) Alex Rodriguez (Redemption card.) 15.00
(175) Ivan Rodriguez/SP/1250 40.00
(176) Bruce Ruffin 4.00
(177) Juan Samuel 4.00
(178) Tim Scott 4.00
(179) Kevin Sefcik 4.00
(180) Jeff Shaw 4.00
(181) Danny Sheaffer 4.00
(182) Craig Shipley 4.00
(183) Dave Silvestri 4.00
(184) Aaron Small 4.00
(185) John Smoltz/SP/1000 90.00
(186) Luis Sojo 4.00
(187) Sammy Sosa/SP/1000 160.00
(188) Steve Sparks 4.00
(189) Tim Spehr 4.00
(190) Russ Springer 4.00
(191) Matt Stairs 4.00
(192) Andy Stankiewicz 4.00
(193) Mike Stanton 4.00
(194) Kelly Stinnett 4.00
(195) Doug Strange 4.00
(196) Mark Sweeney 4.00
(197) Jeff Tabaka 4.00
(198) Jesus Tavarez 4.00
(199) Frank Thomas/SP/1000 45.00
(200) Larry Thomas 4.00
(201) Mark Thompson 4.00
(202) Mike Timlin 4.00
(203) Steve Trachsel 4.00
(204) Tom Urbani 4.00
(205) Julio Valera 4.00
(206) Dave Valle 4.00
(207) William Van Landingham 4.00
(208) Mo Vaughn/SP/1000 10.00
(209) Dave Veres 4.00
(210) Ed Vosberg 4.00
(211) Don Wengert 4.00
(212) Matt Whiteside 4.00
(213) Bob Wickman 4.00
(214) Matt Williams/SP/1250 12.00
(215) Mike Williams 4.00
(216) Woody Williams 4.00
(217) Craig Worthington 4.00
--- Frank Thomas (Autographed jumbo edition of 1,500.) 30.00

Extended Autographs - Century Marks

Century Marks represent the first 100 autographs by the 30 short-printed stars and prospects, plus Alex Ochoa. These are designated with a blue holographic foil "Century Marks" logo. Cards of Gonzalez, Jeter, Andruw Jones, Palmeiro and Alex Rodriguez were available only via mail-in redemption cards.

NM/M
Common Player: 15.00
(1) Jay Buhner 30.00
(2) Ken Caminiti 30.00
(3) Roger Clemens 250.00
(4) Jermaine Dye 30.00
(5) Darin Erstad 45.00
(6) Karim Garcia 30.00
(7) Jason Giambi 75.00
(8) Tom Glavine 90.00
(9) Juan Gonzalez 90.00
(9) Juan Gonzalez (Redemption card.) 7.50
(10) Tony Gwynn 150.00
(11) Derek Jeter 350.00
(11) Derek Jeter (Redemption card.) 15.00
(12) Randy Johnson 185.00
(13) Andruw Jones 150.00
(13) Andruw Jones (Redemption card.) 7.50
(14) Jason Kendall 30.00
(15) Ryan Klesko 30.00
(16) Chuck Knoblauch 30.00
(17) Kenny Lofton 30.00
(18) Greg Maddux 200.00
(19) Fred McGriff 30.00
(20) Paul Molitor 110.00
(21) Alex Ochoa 15.00
(22) Rafael Palmeiro 110.00
(22) Rafael Palmeiro (Redemption card.) 7.50
(23) Andy Pettitte 75.00
(24) Kirby Puckett 185.00
(25) Alex Rodriguez 350.00
(25) Alex Rodriguez (Redemption card.) 15.00
(26) Ivan Rodriguez 100.00
(27) John Smoltz 100.00
(28) Sammy Sosa 350.00
(29) Frank Thomas 135.00
(30) Mo Vaughn 30.00
(31) Matt Williams 30.00

Frank Thomas The Big Heart

In one of several specialty card charitable endeavors, Frank Thomas and Leaf teamed up to issue this set as a fund raiser for "The Big Hurt's" charitable foundation. Each of the cards was available in an edition limited to 3,500 each for a $20 donation. Cards are standard 2-1/2" x 3-1/2" with posed photos on front and "THE BIG HEART," a play on his nickname. Backs have information on the foundation.

NM/M
Complete Set (4): 35.00
Common Card: 10.00
(1) Frank Thomas (Bat on shoulder.) 10.00
(2) Frank Thomas (Holding glove.) 10.00
(3) Frank Thomas/Horizontal 10.00
(4) Frank Thomas/Seated 10.00

1997 Leaf

Leaf produced a 400-card set in two series in 1997. The cards feature a grey border with the player photo vignetted at center. The player's name, team and a Leaf logo are displayed at bottom in silver foil. A team logo is in the upper-right corner. Besides the base cards, 10-card packs retailing for $2.99 could contain one of the following inserts: Banner Season, Dress for Success, Get-A-Grip, Knot-hole Gang, Statistical Standouts, Fractal Matrix or Fractal Matrix Die-cut.

	NM/M
Complete Set (400):	25.00
Common Player:	.05
Jackie Robinson 1948	
Leaf Reprint:	10.00
Series 1 Pack (12):	2.00
Series 1 Wax Box (18):	30.00
Series 2 Pack (12):	1.50
Series 2 Wax Box (24):	30.00

1 Wade Boggs 1.50
2 Brian McRae .05
3 Jeff D'Amico .05
4 George Arias .05
5 Billy Wagner .05
6 Ray Lankford .05
7 Will Clark .10
8 Edgar Renteria .05
9 Alex Ochoa .05
10 Roberto Hernandez .05
11 Joe Carter .05
12 Gregg Jefferies .05
13 Mark Grace .05
14 Roberto Alomar .10
15 Joe Randa .05
16 Alex Rodriguez 2.50
17 Tony Gwynn 1.50
18 Steve Gibralter .05
19 Scott Stahoviak .05
20 Matt Williams .05
21 Quinton McCracken .05
22 Ugueth Urbina .05
23 Jermaine Allensworth .05
24 Paul Molitor .75
25 Carlos Delgado .50
26 Bob Abreu .05
27 John Jaha .05
28 Rusty Greer .05
29 Kimera Bartee .05
30 Ruben Rivera .05
31 Jason Kendall .05
32 Lance Johnson .05
33 Robin Ventura .05
34 Kevin Appier .05
35 John Mabry .05
36 Ricky Otero .05
37 Mike Lansing .05
38 Mark McGwire 2.50
39 Tim Naehring .05
40 Tom Glavine .30
41 Rey Ordonez .05
42 Tony Clark .05
43 Rafael Palmeiro .65
44 Pedro Martinez .75
45 Keith Lockhart .05
46 Dan Wilson .05
47 John Wetteland .05
48 Chan Ho Park .05
49 Gary Sheffield .40
50 Shawn Estes .05
51 Royce Clayton .05
52 Jaime Navarro .05
53 Raul Casanova .05
54 Jeff Bagwell 1.00
55 Barry Larkin .05
56 Charles Nagy .05
57 Ken Caminiti .05
58 Todd Hollandsworth .05
59 Pat Hentgen .05
60 Jose Valentin .05
61 Frank Rodriguez .05
62 Mickey Tettleton .05
63 Marty Cordova .05
64 Cecil Fielder .05
65 Barry Bonds 3.00
66 Scott Servais .05
67 Ernie Young .05
68 Wilson Alvarez .05
69 Mike Grace .05
70 Shane Reynolds .05
71 Henry Rodriguez .05
72 Eric Karros .05
73 Mark Langston .05
74 Scott Karl .05
75 Trevor Hoffman .05
76 Orel Hershiser .05
77 John Smoltz .05
78 Raul Mondesi .05
79 Jeff Brantley .05
80 Donne Wall .05
81 Joey Cora .05
82 Mel Rojas .05
83 Chad Mottola .05
84 Omar Vizquel .05
85 Greg Maddux 1.50
86 Jamey Wright .05
87 Chuck Finley .05
88 Brady Anderson .05
89 Alex Gonzalez .05
90 Andy Benes .05
91 Reggie Jefferson .05
92 Paul O'Neill .05
93 Javier Lopez .05
94 Mark Grudzielanek .05
95 Marc Newfield .05
96 Kevin Ritz .05
97 Fred McGriff .05
98 Dwight Gooden .05
99 Hideo Nomo .65
100 Steve Finley .05
101 Juan Gonzalez .65
102 Jay Buhner .05
103 Paul Wilson .05
104 Alan Benes .05
105 Manny Ramirez 1.00
106 Kevin Elster .05
107 Frank Thomas 1.00
108 Orlando Miller .05
109 Ramon Martinez .05
110 Kenny Lofton .05
111 Bernie Williams .05
112 Robby Thompson .05
113 Bernard Gilkey .05
114 Ray Durham .05
115 Jeff Cirillo .05
116 Brian Jordan .05
117 Rich Becker .05
118 Al Leiter .05
119 Mark Johnson .05
120 Ellis Burks .05
121 Sammy Sosa 2.00
122 Willie Greene .05
123 Michael Tucker .05
124 Eddie Murray .75
125 Joey Hamilton .05
126 Antonio Osuna .05
127 Bobby Higginson .05
128 Tomas Perez .05
129 Tim Salmon .05
130 Mark Wohlers .05
131 Charles Johnson .05
132 Randy Johnson .75
133 Brooks Kieschnick .05
134 Al Martin .05
135 Dante Bichette .05
136 Andy Pettitte .30
137 Jason Giambi .60
138 James Baldwin .05
139 Ben McDonald .05
140 Shawn Green .35
141 Geronimo Berroa .05
142 Jose Offerman .05
143 Curtis Pride .05
144 Terrell Wade .05
145 Ismael Valdes .05
146 Mike Mussina .40
147 Mariano Rivera .15
148 Ken Hill .05
149 Darin Erstad .05
150 Jay Bell .05
151 Mo Vaughn .05
152 Ozzie Smith 1.50
153 Jose Mesa .05
154 Osvaldo Fernandez .05
155 Vinny Castilla .05
156 Jason Isringhausen .05
157 B.J. Surhoff .05
158 Robert Perez .05
159 Ron Coomer .05
160 Darren Oliver .05
161 Mike Mohler .05
162 Russ Davis .05
163 Bret Boone .05
164 Ricky Bottalico .05
165 Derek Jeter 3.00
166 Orlando Merced .05
167 John Valentin .05
168 Andruw Jones 1.00
169 Angel Echevarria .05
170 Todd Walker .05
171 Desi Relaford .05
172 Trey Beamon .05
173 Brian Giles RC .75
174 Scott Rolen .60
175 Shannon Stewart .05
176 Dmitri Young .05
177 Justin Thompson .05
178 Trot Nixon .05
179 Josh Booty .05
180 Robin Jennings .05
181 Marvin Benard .05
182 Luis Castillo .05
183 Wendell Magee .05
184 Vladimir Guerrero 1.00
185 Nomar Garciaparra 2.00
186 Ryan Hancock .05
187 Mike Cameron .05
188 Cal Ripken Jr.
  (Legacy) 1.50
189 Chipper Jones
  (Legacy) .75
190 Albert Belle (Legacy) .75
191 Mike Piazza (Legacy) 1.00
192 Chuck Knoblauch
  (Legacy) .05
193 Ken Griffey Jr.
  (Legacy) 1.00
194 Ivan Rodriguez
  (Legacy) .30
195 Jose Canseco (Legacy) .25
196 Ryne Sandberg
  (Legacy) .75
197 Jim Thome (Legacy) .30
198 Andy Pettitte
  (Checklist) .05
199 Andruw Jones
  (Checklist) .50
200 Derek Jeter
  (Checklist)
201 Chipper Jones 1.50
202 Albert Belle .05
203 Mike Piazza 2.00
204 Ken Griffey Jr. 2.00
205 Ryne Sandberg 1.50
206 Jose Canseco .40
207 Chili Davis .05
208 Roger Clemens 2.00
209 Deion Sanders .05
210 Darryl Hamilton .05
211 Jermaine Dye .05
212 Matt Williams .05
213 Kevin Elster .05
214 John Wetteland .05
215 Garret Anderson .05
216 Kevin Brown .05
217 Matt Lawton .05
218 Cal Ripken Jr. 3.00
219 Moises Alou .05
220 Chuck Knoblauch .05
221 Ivan Rodriguez .65
222 Travis Fryman .05
223 Jim Thome .65
224 Eddie Murray .75
225 Eric Young .05
226 Ron Gant .05
227 Tony Phillips .05
228 Reggie Sanders .05
229 Johnny Damon .35
230 Bill Pulsipher .05
231 Jim Edmonds .05
232 Melvin Nieves .05
233 Ryan Klesko .05
234 David Cone .05
235 Derek Bell .05
236 Julio Franco .05
237 Juan Guzman .05
238 Larry Walker .05
239 Delino DeShields .05
240 Troy Percival .05
241 Andres Galarraga .05
242 Rondell White .05
243 John Burkett .05
244 J.T. Snow .05
245 Alex Fernandez .05
246 Edgar Martinez .05
247 Craig Biggio .05
248 Todd Hundley .05
249 Jimmy Key .05
250 Cliff Floyd .05
251 Jeff Conine .05
252 Curt Schilling .05
253 Jeff King .05
254 Tino Martinez .05
255 Carlos Baerga .05
256 Jeff Fassero .05
257 Dean Palmer .05
258 Robb Nen .05
259 Sandy Alomar Jr. .05
260 Carlos Perez .05
261 Rickey Henderson .75
262 Bobby Bonilla .05
263 Darren Daulton .05
264 Jim Leyritz .05
265 Dennis Martinez .05
266 Butch Huskey .05
267 Joe Vitiello .05
268 Steve Trachsel .05
269 Glenallen Hill .05
270 Terry Steinbach .05
271 Mark McLemore .05
272 Devon White .05
273 Jeff Kent .05
274 Tim Raines .05
275 Carlos Garcia .05
276 Hal Morris .05
277 Gary Gaetti .05
278 John Olerud .05
279 Wally Joyner .05
280 Brian Hunter .05
281 Steve Karsay .05
282 Denny Neagle .05
283 Jose Herrera .05
284 Todd Stottlemyre .05
285 Bip Roberts .05
286 Kevin Seitzer .05
287 Benji Gil .05
288 Dennis Eckersley .65
289 Brad Ausmus .05
290 Otis Nixon .05
291 Darryl Strawberry .05
292 Marquis Grissom .05
293 Darryl Kile .05
294 Quilvio Veras .05
295 Tom Goodwin .05
296 Benito Santiago .05
297 Mike Bordick .05
298 Roberto Kelly .05
299 David Justice .05
300 Carl Everett .05
301 Mark Whiten .05
302 Aaron Sele .05
303 Darren Dreifort .05
304 Bobby Jones .05
305 Fernando Vina .05
306 Ed Sprague .05
307 Andy Ashby .05
308 Tony Fernandez .05
309 Roger Pavlik .05
310 Mark Clark .05
311 Mariano Duncan .05
312 Tyler Houston .05
313 Eric Davis .05
314 Greg Vaughn .05
315 David Segui .05
316 Dave Nilsson .05
317 F.P. Santangelo .05
318 Wilton Guerrero .05
319 Jose Guillen .05
320 Kevin Orie .05
321 Derrek Lee .05
322 Bubba Trammell RC .50
323 Pokey Reese .05
324 Hideki Irabu RC .25
325 Scott Spiezio .05
326 Bartolo Colon .05
327 Damon Mashore .05
328 Ryan McGuire .05
329 Chris Carpenter .05
330 Jose Cruz Jr. RC .50
331 Todd Greene .05
332 Brian Moehler .05
333 Mike Sweeney .05
334 Neifi Perez .05
335 Matt Morris .05
336 Marvin Benard .05
337 Karim Garcia .05
338 Jason Dickson .05
339 Brant Brown .05
340 Jeff Suppan .05
341 Deivi Cruz RC .25
342 Antone Williamson .05
343 Curtis Goodwin .05
344 Brooks Kieschnick .05
345 Tony Womack RC .25
346 Rudy Pemberton .05
347 Todd Dunwoody .05
348 Frank Thomas (Legacy) .50
349 Andruw Jones (Legacy) .50
350 Alex Rodriguez
  (Legacy) 1.25
351 Greg Maddux (Legacy) .75
352 Jeff Bagwell (Legacy) .50
353 Juan Gonzalez (Legacy) .35
354 Barry Bonds (Legacy) 1.50
355 Mark McGwire
  (Legacy) 1.25
356 Tony Gwynn (Legacy) .75
357 Gary Sheffield (Legacy) .25
358 Derek Jeter (Legacy) 1.50
359 Manny Ramirez
  (Legacy) .50
360 Hideo Nomo (Legacy) .30
361 Sammy Sosa (Legacy) 1.00
362 Paul Molitor (Legacy) .40
363 Kenny Lofton (Legacy) .05
364 Eddie Murray (Legacy) .40
365 Barry Larkin (Legacy) .05
366 Roger Clemens
  (Legacy) 1.00
367 John Smoltz (Legacy) .05
368 Alex Rodriguez
  (Gamers) 1.50
369 Frank Thomas
  (Gamers) .40
370 Cal Ripken Jr.
  (Gamers) 1.50
371 Ken Griffey Jr.
  (Gamers) 1.50
372 Greg Maddux
  (Gamers) 1.00
373 Mike Piazza (Gamers) 1.25
374 Chipper Jones
  (Gamers) 1.00
375 Albert Belle (Gamers) .05
376 Chuck Knoblauch
  (Gamers) .05
377 Brady Anderson
  (Gamers) .05
378 David Justice (Gamers) .05
379 Randy Johnson
  (Gamers) .40
380 Wade Boggs (Gamers) .75
381 Kevin Brown (Gamers) .05
382 Tom Glavine (Gamers) .05
383 Raul Mondesi (Gamers) .05
384 Ivan Rodriguez
  (Gamers) .30
385 Larry Walker (Gamers) .05
386 Bernie Williams
  (Gamers) .05
387 Rusty Greer (Gamers) .05
388 Rafael Palmeiro
  (Gamers) .05
389 Matt Williams (Gamers) .05
390 Eric Young (Gamers) .05
391 Fred McGriff (Gamers) .05
392 Ken Caminiti (Gamers) .05
393 Roberto Alomar
  (Gamers) .05
394 Brian Jordan (Gamers) .05
395 Mark Grace (Gamers) .05
396 Jim Edmonds (Gamers) .05
397 Deion Sanders
  (Gamers) .05
398 Checklist
  (Vladimir Guerrero) .50
399 Checklist (Darin Erstad) .10
400 Checklist
  (Nomar Garciaparra) 1.00

Fractal Matrix

Leaf introduced Fractal Matrix inserts, a 400-card parallel set broken down into three colors and three unique die-cuts. One "fracture" breaks the insert set down by foil background color (80 Gold, 120 Silver and 200 Bronze). A second fracture breaks those cards down into X, Y and Z "axis" variations. There are no markings on the cards to segregate the X, Y and Z groups, though that information was printed on the box bottoms. No production numbers or insert ratios were released for either fracture. Each player is available in only one color/axis combination. The incredibly convoluted nature of the issue insured that virtually nobody understood the concept, putting a damper on collector interest.

	NM/M
Common Bronze:	.35
Common Silver:	.50
Common Gold:	1.25

1 Wade Boggs G/Y 8.00
2 Brian McRae B/Y .35
3 Jeff D'Amico B/Y .35
4 George Arias S/Y .50
5 Billy Wagner S/Y .35
6 Ray Lankford B/Z .35
7 Will Clark S/Y .60
8 Edgar Renteria S/Y .50
9 Alex Ochoa S/Y .50
10 Roberto Hernandez B/X .35
11 Joe Carter S/Y .50
12 Gregg Jefferies B/X .35
13 Mark Grace S/Y .75
14 Roberto Alomar G/Y 2.00
15 Joe Randa B/X .35
16 Alex Rodriguez G/Y 10.00
17 Tony Gwynn G/Z 6.00
18 Steve Gibralter B/Y .35
19 Scott Stahoviak B/X .35
20 Matt Williams S/Z .50
21 Quinton McCracken B/Y .35
22 Ugueth Urbina B/X .35
23 Jermaine Allensworth
  S/X .50
24 Paul Molitor G/X 5.00
25 Carlos Delgado S/Y 1.00
26 Bob Abreu B/X .50
27 John Jaha S/Y .50
28 Rusty Greer S/Z .50
29 Kimera Bartee B/Y .35
30 Ruben Rivera S/Y .50
31 Jason Kendall S/Y .50
32 Lance Johnson B/X .35
33 Robin Ventura B/X .35
34 Kevin Appier S/Y .50
35 John Mabry S/Y .50
36 Ricky Otero B/X .35
37 Mike Lansing B/X .35
38 Mark McGwire G/Z 10.00
39 Tim Naehring B/X .35
40 Tom Glavine S/Z 1.00
41 Rey Ordonez B/Y .35
42 Tony Clark S/Y .50
43 Rafael Palmeiro G/Z 2.00
44 Pedro Martinez B/X 2.00
45 Keith Lockhart B/X .35
46 Dan Wilson B/Y .35
47 John Wetteland B/Y .35
48 Chan Ho Park B/X .35
49 Gary Sheffield G/Z 3.00
50 Shawn Estes B/X .35
51 Royce Clayton B/X .35
52 Jaime Navarro B/X .35
53 Raul Casanova B/X .35
54 Jeff Bagwell G/Z 5.00
55 Barry Larkin G/X 1.25
56 Charles Nagy B/Y .35
57 Ken Caminiti B/Y 1.25
58 Todd Hollandsworth
  S/Z .50
59 Pat Hentgen S/X .50
60 Jose Valentin B/X .35
61 Frank Rodriguez B/X .35
62 Mickey Tettleton B/X .35
63 Marty Cordova G/X 1.25
64 Cecil Fielder S/X .50
65 Barry Bonds G/Z 13.50
66 Scott Servais B/X .35
67 Ernie Young B/X .35
68 Wilson Alvarez B/X .35
69 Mike Grace B/X .35
70 Shane Reynolds S/X .50
71 Henry Rodriguez S/Y .50
72 Eric Karros B/X .35
73 Mark Langston B/X .35
74 Scott Karl B/X .35
75 Trevor Hoffman S/X .50
76 Orel Hershiser S/X .50
77 John Smoltz G/Y 1.50
78 Raul Mondesi G/Z 1.25
79 Jeff Brantley B/X .35
80 Donne Wall B/X .35
81 Joey Cora B/X .35
82 Mel Rojas B/X .35
83 Chad Mottola B/X .35
84 Omar Vizquel B/X .35
85 Greg Maddux G/Z 6.00
86 Jamey Wright S/Y .35
87 Chuck Finley B/X .35
88 Brady Anderson G/Y 1.25
89 Alex Gonzalez S/X .50
90 Andy Benes B/X .35
91 Reggie Jefferson B/X .35
92 Paul O'Neill B/X .35
93 Javier Lopez S/X .50
94 Mark Grudzielanek S/X .50
95 Marc Newfield B/X .35
96 Kevin Ritz B/X .35
97 Fred McGriff G/Y 1.25
98 Dwight Gooden S/X .35
99 Hideo Nomo S/Y 1.50
100 Steve Finley B/Y .35
101 Juan Gonzalez G/Z 4.00
102 Jay Buhner S/Z .50
103 Paul Wilson S/Y .35
104 Alan Benes B/Y .35
105 Manny Ramirez B/X 5.00
106 Kevin Elster B/X .35
107 Frank Thomas B/X 5.00
108 Orlando Miller B/X .35
109 Ramon Martinez B/X .35
110 Kenny Lofton G/Y 1.25
111 Bernie Williams G/Y 1.25
112 Robby Thompson B/X .35
113 Bernard Gilkey B/X .35
114 Ray Durham B/X .35
115 Jeff Cirillo S/Z .50
116 Brian Jordan G/Z 1.25
117 Rich Becker S/Y .50
118 Al Leiter B/X .35
119 Mark Johnson B/X .35
120 Ellis Burks B/Y .35
121 Sammy Sosa G/Z 7.50
122 Willie Greene B/X .35
123 Michael Tucker B/X .35
124 Eddie Murray G/Y 6.00
125 Joey Hamilton S/Y .50
126 Antonio Osuna B/X .35
127 Bobby Higginson S/Y .50
128 Tomas Perez B/X .35
129 Tim Salmon G/Z 1.25
130 Mark Wohlers B/X .35
131 Charles Johnson S/X .50
132 Randy Johnson S/Y 2.00
133 Brooks Kieschnick S/X .35
134 Al Martin S/Y .50
135 Dante Bichette B/X .35
136 Andy Pettitte S/Y 2.00
137 Jason Giambi G/Y 4.00
138 James Baldwin S/X .35
139 Ben McDonald B/X .35
140 Shawn Green S/X 1.00
141 Geronimo Berroa B/Y .35
142 Jose Offerman B/X .35
143 Curtis Pride B/X .35
144 Terrell Wade B/X .35
145 Ismael Valdes B/X .35
146 Mike Mussina S/Y 1.25
147 Mariano Rivera S/X .75
148 Ken Hill S/X .50
149 Darin Erstad G/Z 4.00
150 Jay Bell B/X .35
151 Mo Vaughn G/Z 1.25
152 Ozzie Smith S/X 8.00
153 Jose Mesa B/X .35
154 Osvaldo Fernandez B/X .35
155 Vinny Castilla B/Y .35
156 Jason Isringhausen S/Y .50
157 B.J. Surhoff B/X .35
158 Robert Perez B/X .35
159 Ron Coomer B/X .35
160 Darren Oliver B/X .35
161 Mike Mohler B/X .35
162 Russ Davis B/X .35
163 Bret Boone B/X .35
164 Ricky Bottalico B/X .35
165 Derek Jeter G/Z 13.50
166 Orlando Merced B/X .35
167 John Valentin B/X .35
168 Andruw Jones G/Z 5.00
169 Angel Echevarria B/X .35
170 Todd Walker G/X 1.25
171 Desi Relaford B/X .35
172 Trey Beamon S/X .50
173 Brian Giles S/Y .50
174 Scott Rolen S/Z 3.50
175 Shannon Stewart S/Z .50
176 Dmitri Young G/Z .50
177 Justin Thompson B/X .35
178 Trot Nixon S/Y .50
179 Josh Booty B/X .35
180 Robin Jennings B/X .35
181 Marvin Benard B/X .35
182 Luis Castillo B/Y .35
183 Wendell Magee B/X .35
184 Vladimir Guerrero G/X 5.00
185 Nomar Garciaparra 12.50
186 Ryan Hancock .35
187 Mike Cameron .35
188 Cal Ripken Jr. B/Z
  (Legacy) 5.00
189 Chipper Jones S/Z
  (Legacy) 4.00
190 Albert Belle S/Z
  (Legacy) 1.00
191 Mike Piazza B/Z
  (Legacy) 4.00
192 Chuck Knoblauch S/Y
  (Legacy) .50
193 Ken Griffey Jr. B/Z
  (Legacy) 3.50

#	Card	Price
194	Ivan Rodriguez G/Z (Legacy)	4.00
195	Jose Canseco S/X (Legacy)	1.25
196	Ryne Sandberg S/X (Legacy)	3.00
197	Jim Thome G/Y (Legacy)	1.50
198	Checklist (Andy Pettitte B/Y)	.75
199	Checklist (Andruw Jones B/Y)	2.00
200	Checklist (Derek Jeter S/Y)	2.00
201	Chipper Jones G/X	10.00
202	Albert Belle G/Y	1.25
203	Mike Piazza G/Y	12.00
204	Ken Griffey Jr. G/X	15.00
205	Ryne Sandberg G/X	6.00
206	Jose Canseco S/Y	.75
207	Chili Davis B/X	.35
208	Roger Clemens G/Z	6.50
209	Deion Sanders G/Z	1.50
210	Darryl Hamilton B/X	.35
211	Jermaine Dye S/X	.35
212	Matt Williams G/Y	1.25
213	Kevin Elster B/X	.35
214	John Wetteland S/X	.50
215	Garret Anderson G/Z	1.25
216	Kevin Brown G/Y	1.25
217	Matt Lawton S/Y	.35
218	Cal Ripken Jr. G/X	16.50
219	Moises Alou G/Y	1.25
220	Chuck Knoblauch	1.25
221	Ivan Rodriguez G/Y	5.50
222	Travis Fryman B/Y	.35
223	Jim Thome G/Z	2.00
224	Eddie Murray S/Z	3.00
225	Eric Young G/Y	1.25
226	Ron Gant S/X	.50
227	Tony Phillips B/X	.35
228	Reggie Sanders B/Y	.35
229	Johnny Damon S/Z	1.00
230	Bill Pulsipher B/X	.35
231	Jim Edmonds B/X	1.25
232	Melvin Nieves B/X	.35
233	Ryan Klesko G/Z	1.25
234	David Cone S/X	.50
235	Derek Bell B/Y	.35
236	Julio Franco S/X	.50
237	Juan Guzman B/X	.35
238	Larry Walker G/Y	.35
239	Delino DeShields B/X	.35
240	Troy Percival S/X	.35
241	Andres Galarraga G/Z	1.25
242	Rondell White G/Z	1.25
243	John Burkett B/X	.35
244	J.T. Snow B/Y	.35
245	Alex Fernandez S/Y	.50
246	Edgar Martinez G/Z	1.25
247	Craig Biggio G/Z	1.25
248	Todd Hundley G/Y	1.25
249	Jimmy Key S/X	.50
250	Cliff Floyd B/Y	.35
251	Jeff Conine B/Y	.35
252	Curt Schilling B/X	.65
253	Jeff King B/X	.35
254	Tino Martinez G/Z	1.25
255	Carlos Baerga S/Y	.50
256	Jeff Fassero B/Y	.35
257	Dean Palmer S/Y	.35
258	Robb Nen B/X	.35
259	Sandy Alomar Jr. S/Y	.50
260	Carlos Perez B/X	.35
261	Rickey Henderson S/Y	2.00
262	Bobby Bonilla S/Y	.50
263	Darren Daulton B/X	.35
264	Jim Leyritz B/X	.35
265	Dennis Martinez S/Y	.50
266	Butch Huskey B/X	.35
267	Joe Vitiello S/Y	.50
268	Steve Trachsel B/X	.35
269	Glenallen Hill B/X	.35
270	Terry Steinbach B/X	.35
271	Mark McLemore B/X	.35
272	Devon White B/X	.35
273	Jeff Kent B/X	.35
274	Tim Raines B/X	.35
275	Carlos Garcia B/X	.35
276	Hal Morris B/X	.35
277	Gary Gaetti B/X	.35
278	John Olerud S/Y	.50
279	Wally Joyner B/X	.35
280	Brian Hunter S/Y	.50
281	Steve Karsay B/X	.35
282	Denny Neagle S/Y	.35
283	Jose Herrera B/X	.35
284	Todd Stottlemyre B/X	.35
285	Bip Roberts S/X	.50
286	Kevin Seitzer B/X	.35
287	Benji Gil B/X	.35
288	Dennis Eckersley S/X	.50
289	Brad Ausmus B/X	.35
290	Otis Nixon B/X	.35
291	Darryl Strawberry B/X	.35
292	Marquis Grissom S/Y	.50
293	Darryl Kile B/X	.35
294	Quilvio Veras B/X	.35
295	Tom Goodwin B/X	.35
296	Benito Santiago B/X	.35
297	Mike Bordick B/X	.35
298	Roberto Kelly B/X	.35
299	David Justice G/Z	1.25
300	Carl Everett B/X	.35
301	Mark Whiten B/X	.35
302	Aaron Sele B/X	.35
303	Darren Dreifort B/X	.35
304	Bobby Jones B/X	.35
305	Fernando Vina B/X	.35
306	Ed Sprague B/X	.35
307	Andy Ashby S/X	.35
308	Tony Fernandez B/X	.35
309	Roger Pavlik B/X	.35
310	Mark Clark B/X	.35
311	Mariano Duncan B/X	.35
312	Tyler Houston B/X	.35
313	Eric Davis S/Y	.50
314	Greg Vaughn B/X	.35
315	David Segui S/Y	.50
316	Dave Nilsson S/X	.50
317	F.P. Santangelo S/X	.50
318	Wilton Guerrero G/Z	1.25
319	Jose Guillen S/X	1.25
320	Kevin Orie S/Y	.50
321	Derek Lee G/Z	2.50
322	Bubba Trammell S/Y	.50
323	Pokey Reese G/X	1.25
324	Hideki Irabu G/X	1.25
325	Scott Spiezio S/Z	.50
326	Bartolo Colon B/X	1.25
327	Damon Mashore S/Y	.50
328	Ryan McGuire S/Y	.50
329	Chris Carpenter B/X	.35
330	Jose Cruz, Jr. G/X	1.25
331	Todd Greene S/Z	.50
332	Brian Moehler B/X	.35
333	Mike Sweeney B/Y	.35
334	Neifi Perez G/Z	1.25
335	Matt Morris S/Y	.50
336	Marvin Benard B/Y	.35
337	Karim Garcia S/Z	.75
338	Jason Dickson S/Y	.50
339	Brant Brown S/Y	.50
340	Jeff Suppan S/Z	.50
341	Deivi Cruz B/X	.35
342	Antone Williamson G/Z	1.25
343	Curtis Goodwin B/X	.50
344	Brooks Kieschnick S/Y	.50
345	Tony Womack B/X	.35
346	Rudy Pemberton B/X	.35
347	Todd Dunwoody B/X	.35
348	Frank Thomas B/X (Legacy)	2.25
349	Andruw Jones S/X (Legacy)	2.00
350	Alex Rodriguez B/Y (Legacy)	4.00
351	Greg Maddux S/Y (Legacy)	3.00
352	Jeff Bagwell B/Y (Legacy)	2.25
353	Juan Gonzalez S/Y (Legacy)	1.50
354	Barry Bonds G/Y (Legacy)	5.00
355	Mark McGwire S/X (Legacy)	4.00
356	Tony Gwynn S/X (Legacy)	3.00
357	Gary Sheffield B/X (Legacy)	.75
358	Derek Jeter S/X (Legacy)	4.00
359	Manny Ramirez S/Y (Legacy)	2.00
360	Hideo Nomo G/Z (Legacy)	4.00
361	Sammy Sosa B/X (Legacy)	3.50
362	Paul Molitor S/Y (Legacy)	3.00
363	Kenny Lofton G/Z (Legacy)	.35
364	Eddie Murray B/X (Legacy)	2.00
365	Barry Larkin S/Z (Legacy)	.50
366	Roger Clemens S/Y (Legacy)	3.50
367	John Smoltz B/Z (Legacy)	.35
368	Alex Rodriguez S/X (Gamers)	3.25
369	Frank Thomas B/X (Gamers)	2.25
370	Cal Ripken Jr. S/Y (Gamers)	4.00
371	Ken Griffey Jr. S/Y (Gamers)	3.25
372	Greg Maddux B/X (Gamers)	3.00
373	Mike Piazza S/X (Gamers)	3.00
374	Chipper Jones B/Y (Gamers)	3.00
375	Albert Belle B/X (Gamers)	.50
376	Chuck Knoblauch B/X (Gamers)	.35
377	Brady Anderson B/Z (Gamers)	.50
378	David Justice S/X (Gamers)	.50
379	Randy Johnson B/Z (Gamers)	2.00
380	Wade Boggs B/X (Gamers)	3.00
381	Kevin Brown S/Y (Gamers)	.35
382	Tom Glavine G/Y (Gamers)	3.00
383	Raul Mondesi S/Y (Gamers)	.50
384	Ivan Rodriguez B/X (Gamers)	1.25
385	Larry Walker B/Y (Gamers)	.35
386	Bernie Williams B/Z (Gamers)	.45
387	Rusty Greer G/Y (Gamers)	1.25
388	Rafael Palmeiro G/Y (Gamers)	4.50
389	Matt Williams B/X (Gamers)	.35
390	Eric Young B/X (Gamers)	.35
391	Fred McGriff B/X (Gamers)	.35
392	Ken Caminiti B/X (Gamers)	.35
393	Roberto Alomar B/Z (Gamers)	.75
394	Brian Jordan B/X (Gamers)	.35
395	Mark Grace G/Z (Gamers)	1.25
396	Jim Edmonds B/Y (Gamers)	.35
397	Deion Sanders S/Y (Gamers)	.50
398	Checklist (Vladimir Guerrero S/Z)	1.25
399	Checklist (Darin Erstad S/Y)	1.00
400	Checklist (Nomar Garciaparra Z)	2.00

Fractal Matrix Die-Cut

A second parallel set to the Leaf product, the Fractal Matrix Die-Cuts offer three different die-cut designs with three colors for each. The Axis-X die-cuts comprise 200 players (150 Bronze, 40 Silver and 10 Gold), the Axis-Y die-cuts has 120 players (60 Silver, 40 Bronze, 20 Gold), and the Axis-Z die-cuts consist of 80 players (50 Gold, 20 Silver, 10 Bronze). Odds of finding any of these inserts are 1:6 packs. Each player was issued in only one color/cut combination.

#	Card	NM/M
	Common X- or Y-Axis:	.75
	Common Z-Axis:	1.25
1	Wade Boggs G/Y	6.00
2	Brian McRae B/Y	.75
3	Jeff D'Amico B/Y	.75
4	George Arias S/Y	.75
5	Billy Wagner S/Y	.75
6	Ray Lankford B/Z	1.25
7	Will Clark S/Y	.75
8	Edgar Renteria S/Y	.75
9	Alex Ochoa S/Y	.75
11	Joe Carter S/Y	.75
12	Gregg Jefferies B/Y	.75
13	Mark Grace S/Y	.75
14	Roberto Alomar A/Y	1.50
15	Joe Randa S/Y	.75
16	Alex Rodriguez G/Z	12.50
17	Tony Gwynn S/Y	7.50
18	Steve Gibralter B/Y	.75
19	Scott Stahoviak B/X	.75
20	Matt Williams S/Z	1.25
21	Quinton McCracken B/Y	.75
22	Ugueth Urbina B/Y	.75
23	Jermaine Allensworth S/X	.75
24	Paul Molitor S/X	5.00
25	Carlos Delgado S/Y	2.00
26	Bob Abreu S/Y	.75
27	John Jaha S/Y	.75
28	Rusty Greer S/Z	1.25
29	Kimera Bartee B/Y	.75
30	Ruben Rivera S/Y	.75
31	Jason Kendall S/Y	.75
32	Lance Johnson S/Y	.75
33	Robin Ventura B/Y	.75
34	Kevin Appier S/X	.75
35	John Mabry S/Y	.75
36	Ricky Otero B/X	.75
37	Mike Lansing S/X	.75
38	Mark McGwire G/Z	12.50
39	Tim Naehring B/X	.75
40	Tom Glavine S/Z	3.00
41	Rey Ordonez S/Y	.75
42	Tony Clark S/Y	.75
43	Rafael Palmeiro	4.00
44	Pedro Martinez S/X	5.00
45	Keith Lockhart B/X	.75
46	Dan Wilson B/Y	.75
47	John Wetteland B/Y	.75
48	Chan Ho Park B/X	.75
49	Gary Sheffield S/Z	2.50
50	Shawn Estes B/X	.75
51	Royce Clayton B/X	.75
52	Jaime Navarro B/X	.75
53	Raul Casanova B/X	.75
54	Jeff Bagwell G/X	6.00
55	Barry Larkin G/X	.75
56	Charles Nagy B/Y	.75
57	Ken Caminiti G/Y	.75
58	Todd Hollandsworth S/Z	1.25
59	Pat Hentgen S/X	.75
60	Jose Valentin B/X	.75
61	Frank Rodriguez B/X	.75
62	Mickey Tettleton B/X	.75
63	Marty Cordova B/X	.75
64	Cecil Fielder S/X	.75
65	Barry Bonds G/Z	15.00
66	Scott Servais B/X	.75
67	Ernie Young B/X	.75
68	Wilson Alvarez B/X	.75
69	Mike Grace B/X	.75
70	Shane Reynolds S/X	.75
71	Henry Rodriguez S/Y	.75
72	Eric Karros B/X	.75
73	Mark Langston B/X	.75
74	Scott Karl B/X	.75
75	Trevor Hoffman B/X	.75
76	Orel Hershiser S/X	.75
77	John Smoltz G/Y	.75
78	Raul Mondesi B/X	1.25
79	Jeff Brantley B/X	.75
80	Donne Wall B/X	.75
81	Joey Cora B/X	.75
82	Mel Rojas B/X	.75
83	Chad Mottola B/X	.75
84	Omar Vizquel B/X	.75
85	Greg Maddux B/Z	7.50
86	Jamey Wright S/Y	.75
87	Chuck Finley B/X	.75
88	Brady Anderson G/Y	.75
89	Alex Gonzalez S/X	.75
90	Andy Benes B/X	.75
91	Reggie Jefferson B/X	.75
92	Paul O'Neill B/Y	.75
93	Javier Lopez S/X	.75
94	Mark Grudzielanek S/X	.75
95	Marc Newfield B/X	.75
96	Kevin Ritz B/X	.75
97	Fred McGriff G/Y	.75
98	Dwight Gooden S/X	.75
99	Hideo Nomo S/X	4.00
100	Steve Finley B/X	.75
101	Juan Gonzalez G/X	4.00
102	Jay Buhner S/Z	1.25
103	Paul Wilson B/X	.75
104	Alan Benes B/X	.75
105	Manny Ramirez G/X	6.00
106	Kevin Elster B/X	.75
107	Frank Thomas B/X	6.00
108	Orlando Miller B/X	.75
109	Ramon Martinez B/X	.75
110	Kenny Lofton G/Z	1.25
111	Bernie Williams G/Y	.75
112	Robby Thompson B/X	.75
113	Bernard Gilkey B/X	1.25
114	Ray Durham B/X	.75
115	Jeff Cirillo S/Z	1.25
116	Brian Jordan B/X	1.25
117	Rich Becker S/Y	.75
118	Al Leiter B/X	.75
119	Mark Johnson B/X	.75
120	Ellis Burks B/Y	.75
121	Sammy Sosa G/Z	9.00
122	Willie Greene B/X	.75
123	Michael Tucker B/X	.75
124	Eddie Murray G/Y	5.00
125	Joey Hamilton S/Y	.75
126	Antonio Osuna B/X	.75
127	Bobby Higginson S/Y	.75
128	Tomas Perez B/X	.75
129	Tim Salmon B/Z	1.25
130	Mark Wohlers B/X	.75
131	Charles Johnson B/X	.75
132	Randy Johnson S/Y	5.00
133	Brooks Kieschnick S/X	.75
134	Al Martin S/Y	.75
135	Dante Bichette S/X	.75
136	Andy Pettitte G/Z	3.00
137	Jason Giambi S/Y	2.00
138	James Baldwin S/Y	.75
139	Ben McDonald B/X	.75
140	Shawn Green S/X	1.25
141	Geronimo Berroa B/Y	.75
142	Jose Offerman B/X	.75
143	Curtis Pride S/Y	.75
144	Terrell Wade B/X	.75
145	Ismael Valdes S/Y	.75
146	Mike Mussina S/X	2.00
147	Mariano Rivera S/X	1.00
148	Ken Hill B/Y	.75
149	Darin Erstad G/Z	2.50
150	Jay Bell B/X	.75
151	Mo Vaughn G/Z	1.25
152	Ozzie Smith G/X	6.00
153	Jose Mesa B/X	.75
154	Osvaldo Fernandez B/X	.75
155	Vinny Castilla B/Y	.75
156	Jason Isringhausen S/Y	.75
157	B.J. Surhoff B/X	.75
158	Robert Perez B/X	.75
159	Ron Coomer B/X	.75
160	Darren Oliver B/X	.75
161	Mike Mohler B/X	.75
162	Russ Davis B/X	.75
163	Bret Boone B/X	.75
164	Ricky Bottalico B/X	.75
165	Derek Jeter G/Z	15.00
166	Orlando Merced B/X	.75
167	John Valentin B/X	.75
168	Andruw Jones G/Z	6.00
169	Angel Echevarria B/X	.75
170	Todd Walker G/Z	1.25
171	Desi Relaford B/Y	.75
172	Trey Beamon B/X	.75
173	Brian Giles S/Y	.75
174	Scott Rolen G/Z	4.00
175	Shannon Stewart S/Z	1.25
176	Dmitri Young S/Z	1.25
177	Justin Thompson B/X	.75
178	Trot Nixon S/X	1.00
179	Josh Booty S/Y	.75
180	Robin Jennings B/X	.75
181	Marvin Benard B/X	.75
182	Luis Castillo B/Y	.75
183	Wendell Magee B/X	.75
184	Vladimir Guerrero G/X	5.00
185	Nomar Garciaparra G/X	7.50
186	Ryan Hancock B/X	.75
187	Mike Cameron B/X	.75
188	Cal Ripken Jr. B/Z (Legacy)	15.00
189	Chipper Jones S/Z (Legacy)	7.50
190	Albert Belle S/Z (Legacy)	1.25
191	Mike Piazza B/Z (Legacy)	12.50
192	Chuck Knoblauch B/X (Legacy)	.75
193	Ken Griffey Jr. B/Z (Legacy)	10.00
194	Ivan Rodriguez G/Z (Legacy)	5.00
195	Jose Canseco S/X (Legacy)	1.50
196	Ryne Sandberg S/X (Legacy)	5.00
197	Jim Thome G/Y (Legacy)	.75
198	Checklist (Andy Pettitte B/Y)	1.00
199	Checklist (Andruw Jones B/Y)	5.00
200	Checklist (Derek Jeter S/Y)	7.50
201	Chipper Jones G/X	6.00
202	Albert Belle G/Y	.75
203	Mike Piazza G/Y	10.00
204	Ken Griffey Jr. G/X	7.50
205	Ryne Sandberg G/Z	6.00
206	Jose Canseco S/X	1.50
207	Chili Davis B/X	.75
208	Roger Clemens G/Z	9.00
209	Deion Sanders G/Z	1.50
210	Darryl Hamilton B/X	.75
211	Jermaine Dye S/X	.75
212	Matt Williams G/Y	.75
213	Kevin Elster B/X	.75
214	John Wetteland S/X	.75
215	Garret Anderson G/Z	1.25
216	Kevin Brown G/Y	.75
217	Matt Lawton S/Y	.75
218	Cal Ripken Jr. G/X	12.50
219	Moises Alou G/Y	.75
220	Chuck Knoblauch G/Z	1.25
221	Ivan Rodriguez G/Y	4.00
222	Travis Fryman B/Y	.75
223	Jim Thome G/Z	2.50
224	Eddie Murray S/Z	6.00
225	Eric Young G/Y	1.25
226	Ron Gant S/X	.75
227	Tony Phillips B/X	.75
228	Reggie Sanders B/Y	.75
229	Johnny Damon S/Z	1.25
230	Bill Pulsipher B/X	.75
231	Jim Edmonds B/X	1.25
232	Melvin Nieves B/X	.75
233	Ryan Klesko G/Z	1.25
234	David Cone S/X	.75
235	Derek Bell B/Y	.75
236	Julio Franco S/X	.75
237	Juan Guzman B/X	.75
238	Larry Walker G/Y	1.25
239	Delino DeShields B/X	.75
240	Troy Percival B/Y	.75
241	Andres Galarraga G/Z	1.25
242	Rondell White G/Z	1.25
243	John Burkett B/X	.75
244	J.T. Snow B/Y	.75
245	Alex Fernandez S/Y	.75
246	Edgar Martinez G/Z	1.25
247	Craig Biggio G/Z	1.25
248	Todd Hundley G/Y	.75
249	Jimmy Key S/X	.75
250	Cliff Floyd B/Y	.75
251	Jeff Conine B/Y	.75
252	Curt Schilling B/X	1.50
253	Jeff King B/X	.75
254	Tino Martinez G/Z	1.25
255	Carlos Baerga S/Y	.75
256	Jeff Fassero B/Y	.75
257	Dean Palmer S/Y	.75
258	Robb Nen B/X	.75
259	Sandy Alomar Jr. S/Y	.75
260	Carlos Perez B/X	.75
261	Rickey Henderson S/Y	5.00
262	Bobby Bonilla S/Y	.75
263	Darren Daulton B/X	.75
264	Jim Leyritz B/X	.75
265	Dennis Martinez S/Y	.75
266	Butch Huskey B/X	.75
267	Joe Vitiello S/Y	.75
268	Steve Trachsel B/X	.75
269	Glenallen Hill B/X	.75
270	Terry Steinbach B/X	.75
271	Mark McLemore B/X	.75
272	Devon White B/X	.75
273	Jeff Kent B/X	.75
274	Tim Raines B/X	.75
275	Carlos Garcia B/X	.75
276	Hal Morris B/X	.75
277	Gary Gaetti B/X	.75
278	John Olerud S/Y	.75
279	Wally Joyner B/X	.75
280	Brian Hunter S/X	.75
281	Steve Karsay B/X	.75
282	Denny Neagle S/Y	.75
283	Jose Herrera B/X	.75
284	Todd Stottlemyre B/X	.75
285	Bip Roberts S/X	.75
286	Kevin Seitzer B/X	.75
287	Benji Gil B/X	.75
288	Dennis Eckersley S/X	.75
289	Brad Ausmus B/X	.75
290	Otis Nixon B/X	.75
291	Darryl Strawberry B/X	.75
292	Marquis Grissom S/Y	.75
293	Darryl Kile B/X	.75
294	Quilvio Veras B/X	.75
295	Tom Goodwin B/X	.75
296	Benito Santiago B/X	.75
297	Mike Bordick B/X	.75
298	Roberto Kelly B/X	.75
299	David Justice G/Z	1.25
300	Carl Everett B/X	.75
301	Mark Whiten B/X	.75
302	Aaron Sele B/X	.75
303	Darren Dreifort B/X	.75
304	Bobby Jones B/X	.75
305	Fernando Vina B/X	.75
306	Ed Sprague B/X	.75
307	Andy Ashby S/X	.75
308	Tony Fernandez B/X	.75
309	Roger Pavlik B/X	.75
310	Mark Clark B/X	.75
311	Mariano Duncan B/X	.75
312	Tyler Houston B/X	.75
313	Eric Davis S/Y	.75
314	Greg Vaughn B/X	.75
315	David Segui S/Y	.75
316	Dave Nilsson S/X	.75
317	F.P. Santangelo S/X	.75
318	Wilton Guerrero G/Z	1.25
319	Jose Guillen S/X	1.25
320	Kevin Orie S/Y	.75
321	Derek Lee G/Z	2.50
322	Bubba Trammell S/Y	1.25
323	Pokey Reese G/Z	1.25
324	Hideki Irabu G/X	1.25
325	Scott Spiezio S/Z	1.25
326	Bartolo Colon G/Z	1.25
327	Damon Mashore S/Y	.75
328	Ryan McGuire S/Y	.75
329	Chris Carpenter B/X	.75
330	Jose Cruz, Jr. G/X	.75
331	Todd Greene S/Z	1.25
332	Brian Moehler B/X	.75
333	Mike Sweeney B/Y	.75
334	Neifi Perez G/Z	1.25
335	Matt Morris S/Y	.75
336	Marvin Benard B/Y	.75
337	Karim Garcia S/Z	1.25
338	Jason Dickson S/Y	.75
339	Brant Brown S/Y	.75
340	Jeff Suppan S/Z	1.25
341	Deivi Cruz B/X	.75
342	Antone Williamson G/Z	1.25
343	Curtis Goodwin B/X	.75
344	Brooks Kieschnick S/Y	.75
345	Tony Womack B/X	.75
346	Rudy Pemberton B/X	.75
347	Todd Dunwoody B/X	.75
348	Frank Thomas S/Y (Legacy)	5.00
349	Andruw Jones S/X (Legacy)	5.00
350	Alex Rodriguez B/Z (Legacy)	10.00
351	Greg Maddux S/Y (Legacy)	6.00
352	Jeff Bagwell B/Y (Legacy)	5.00
353	Juan Gonzalez S/Y (Legacy)	4.00
354	Barry Bonds G/Y (Legacy)	12.50
355	Mark McGwire S/X (Legacy)	10.00
356	Tony Gwynn S/X (Legacy)	6.00
357	Gary Sheffield B/X (Legacy)	1.50
358	Derek Jeter S/X (Legacy)	12.50
359	Manny Ramirez S/Y (Legacy)	5.00
360	Hideo Nomo G/Z (Legacy)	4.00
361	Sammy Sosa B/X (Legacy)	6.50
362	Paul Molitor S/Z (Legacy)	6.00

#	Player	Price
363	Kenny Lofton B/Y (Legacy)	.75
364	Eddie Murray B/X (Legacy)	5.00
365	Barry Larkin S/Z (Legacy)	1.25
366	Roger Clemens S/Y (Legacy)	6.50
367	John Smoltz B/Z (Legacy)	1.25
368	Alex Rodriguez S/X (Gamers)	10.00
369	Frank Thomas B/X (Gamers)	5.00
370	Cal Ripken Jr. S/Y (Gamers)	12.50
371	Ken Griffey Jr. S/Y (Gamers)	7.50
372	Greg Maddux B/X (Gamers)	6.00
373	Mike Piazza S/X (Gamers)	10.00
374	Chipper Jones B/Y (Gamers)	6.00
375	Albert Belle B/X (Gamers)	.75
376	Chuck Knoblauch B/X (Gamers)	.75
377	Brady Anderson B/Z (Gamers)	1.25
378	David Justice S/X (Gamers)	.75
379	Randy Johnson B/Z (Gamers)	6.00
380	Wade Boggs B/X (Gamers)	6.00
381	Kevin Brown B/X (Gamers)	.75
382	Tom Glavine G/Y (Gamers)	2.00
383	Raul Mondesi S/X (Gamers)	.75
384	Ivan Rodriguez S/X (Gamers)	4.00
385	Larry Walker B/Y (Gamers)	.75
386	Bernie Williams B/Z (Gamers)	1.25
387	Rusty Greer G/Y (Gamers)	.75
388	Rafael Palmeiro G/Y (Gamers)	4.00
389	Matt Williams B/X (Gamers)	.75
390	Eric Young B/X (Gamers)	.75
391	Fred McGriff B/X (Gamers)	.75
392	Ken Caminiti B/X (Gamers)	.75
393	Roberto Alomar B/Z (Gamers)	2.00
394	Brian Jordan B/X (Gamers)	.75
395	Mark Grace G/Z (Gamers)	1.25
396	Jim Edmonds B/Y (Gamers)	.75
397	Deion Sanders S/Y (Gamers)	.75
398	Checklist (Vladimir Guerrero S/Z)	3.00
399	Checklist (Darin Erstad S/Y)	1.00
400	Checklist (Nomar Garciaparra S/Z)	4.00

Banner Season

Banner Season was a 15-card insert set that was die-cut and printed on a canvas card stock. Only 2,500 individually numbered sets were produced, with cards only found in pre-priced packs.

		NM/M
Complete Set (15):		30.00
Common Player:		.50
1	Jeff Bagwell	2.50
2	Ken Griffey Jr.	5.00
3	Juan Gonzalez	1.50
4	Frank Thomas	2.50
5	Alex Rodriguez	6.00
6	Kenny Lofton	.50
7	Chuck Knoblauch	.50
8	Mo Vaughn	.50

#	Player	Price
9	Chipper Jones	4.00
10	Ken Caminiti	.50
11	Craig Biggio	.50
12	John Smoltz	.50
13	Pat Hentgen	.50
14	Derek Jeter	7.50
15	Todd Hollandsworth	.50

Dress for Success

Exclusive to retail packs was an insert called Dress for Success. It included 18 players printed on nylon and flocking card stock. Dress for Success was limited to 3,500 individually numbered sets.

		NM/M
Complete Set (18):		17.50
Common Player:		.25
1	Greg Maddux	1.50
2	Cal Ripken Jr.	3.00
3	Albert Belle	.25
4	Frank Thomas	1.00
5	Dante Bichette	.25
6	Gary Sheffield	.25
7	Jeff Bagwell	1.00
8	Mike Piazza	2.00
9	Mark McGwire	2.25
10	Ken Caminiti	.25
11	Alex Rodriguez	2.50
12	Ken Griffey Jr.	2.00
13	Juan Gonzalez	.75
14	Brian Jordan	.25
15	Mo Vaughn	.25
16	Ivan Rodriguez	.75
17	Andruw Jones	1.00
18	Chipper Jones	1.50

Get-A-Grip

Get a Grip included 16 double-sided cards, with a star hitter on one side and a star pitcher on the other. The card slated the two stars against each other and explained how the hitter would hit against the pitcher, while featuring the pitcher's top pitch. This insert was printed on silver foilboard with the right side die-cut, and limited to 3,500 numbered sets found only in hobby packs.

		NM/M
Complete Set (16):		30.00
Common Card:		1.00
1	Ken Griffey Jr., Greg Maddux	3.00
2	John Smoltz, Frank Thomas	1.50
3	Mike Piazza, Andy Pettitte	3.00
4	Randy Johnson, Chipper Jones	2.50
5	Tom Glavine, Alex Rodriguez	4.00
6	Pat Hentgen, Jeff Bagwell	1.50
7	Kevin Brown, Juan Gonzalez	1.25
8	Barry Bonds, Mike Mussina	5.00
9	Hideo Nomo, Albert Belle	1.25

#	Player	Price
10	Troy Percival, Andruw Jones	1.50
11	Roger Clemens, Brian Jordan	3.00
12	Paul Wilson, Ivan Rodriguez	1.25
13	Andy Benes, Mo Vaughn	1.00
14	Al Leiter, Derek Jeter	5.00
15	Bill Pulsipher, Cal Ripken Jr.	5.00
16	Mariano Rivera, Ken Caminiti	1.00

Knot-Hole Gang

Knot-Hole Gang pictures 12 hitters viewed through a wood picket fence. Cards are die-cut along the top of the fence and printed on a wood stock. Production was limited to 5,000 numbered sets. A "SAMPLE" marked promo card exists for each.

		NM/M
Complete Set (12):		18.00
Common Player:		.50
	Promos:	2X
1	Chuck Knoblauch	.50
2	Ken Griffey Jr.	3.50
3	Frank Thomas	1.50
4	Tony Gwynn	2.50
5	Mike Piazza	3.50
6	Jeff Bagwell	1.50
7	Rusty Greer	.50
8	Cal Ripken Jr.	5.00
9	Chipper Jones	2.50
10	Ryan Klesko	.50
11	Barry Larkin	.50
12	Paul Molitor	1.50

Leagues of the Nation

A 15-card insert set featuring a double-sided die-cut design. The players on each card represent matchups from the initial rounds of interleague play. Cards were numbered to 2,500 and feature a flocked texture.

		NM/M
Complete Set (15):		60.00
Common Card:		1.50
1	Juan Gonzalez, Barry Bonds	10.00
2	Cal Ripken Jr., Chipper Jones	10.00
3	Mark McGwire, Ken Caminiti	7.00
4	Derek Jeter, Kenny Lofton	10.00
5	Ivan Rodriguez, Mike Piazza	6.00
6	Ken Griffey Jr., Larry Walker	6.00
7	Frank Thomas, Sammy Sosa	5.00
8	Paul Molitor, Barry Larkin	3.00
9	Albert Belle, Deion Sanders	1.50
10	Matt Williams, Jeff Bagwell	3.00
11	Mo Vaughn, Gary Sheffield	1.50
12	Alex Rodriguez, Tony Gwynn	7.50
13	Tino Martinez, Scott Rolen	2.00
14	Darin Erstad, Wilton Guerrero	2.00
15	Tony Clark, Vladimir Guerrero	3.00

Statistical Standouts

Statistical Standouts were limited to only 1,000 individually numbered sets. Inserts were printed on leather and die-cut. The set included 15 top stars who excelled beyond their competition in many statistical categories.

		NM/M
Complete Set (15):		175.00
Common Player:		4.00
1	Albert Belle	4.00
2	Juan Gonzalez	9.00
3	Ken Griffey Jr.	20.00
4	Alex Rodriguez	25.00
5	Frank Thomas	12.00
6	Chipper Jones	15.00
7	Greg Maddux	15.00
8	Mike Piazza	20.00
9	Cal Ripken Jr.	30.00
10	Mark McGwire	25.00
11	Barry Bonds	30.00
12	Derek Jeter	30.00
13	Ken Caminiti	4.00
14	John Smoltz	4.00
15	Paul Molitor	12.00

Thomas Collection

This six-card insert from Series 2 features pieces of various game-used Frank Thomas items built into the texture of each card. Jerseys, bats, hats, batting gloves and sweatbands are all featured on the various cards, which are numbered to 100 each.

		NM/M
Complete Set (6):		360.00
Common Card:		60.00
1	Frank Thomas/Hat	60.00
2	Frank Thomas/Home Jsy	80.00
3	Frank Thomas/Btg Glv	60.00
4	Frank Thomas/Bat	60.00
5	Frank Thomas/Sweatband	60.00
6	Frank Thomas/Away Jsy	80.00

Warning Track

A 12-card insert printed on embossed canvas depicting players who are known for making tough catches. Cards were numbered to 3,500.

	NM/M
Complete Set (18):	40.00

#	Player	Price
	Common Player:	1.00
1	Ken Griffey Jr.	6.00
2	Albert Belle	1.00
3	Barry Bonds	7.50
4	Andruw Jones	4.00
5	Kenny Lofton	1.00
6	Tony Gwynn	5.00
7	Manny Ramirez	4.00
8	Rusty Greer	1.00
9	Bernie Williams	1.00
10	Gary Sheffield	2.00
11	Juan Gonzalez	2.50
12	Raul Mondesi	1.00
13	Brady Anderson	1.00
14	Rondell White	1.00
15	Sammy Sosa	6.00
16	Deion Sanders	1.00
17	David Justice	1.00
18	Jim Edmonds	1.00

22kt Gold Stars

A 36-card insert from Series II Leaf, each card features a special 22-K. gold foil embossed stamp on front which is printed on gold foil cardboard. Horizontal backs have a portrait photo on a dark background and are serially numbered to a limit of 2,500 each.

		NM/M
Complete Set (36):		115.00
Common Player:		1.00
1	Frank Thomas	4.00
2	Alex Rodriguez	8.00
3	Ken Griffey Jr.	6.50
4	Andruw Jones	5.50
5	Chipper Jones	5.50
6	Jeff Bagwell	3.50
7	Derek Jeter	10.00
8	Deion Sanders	1.00
9	Ivan Rodriguez	3.50
10	Juan Gonzalez	3.00
11	Greg Maddux	5.50
12	Andy Pettitte	2.50
13	Roger Clemens	6.00
14	Hideo Nomo	3.00
15	Tony Gwynn	5.50
16	Barry Bonds	10.00
17	Kenny Lofton	1.00
18	Paul Molitor	1.00
19	Jim Thome	3.00
20	Albert Belle	1.00
21	Cal Ripken Jr.	10.00
22	Mark McGwire	8.00
23	Barry Larkin	1.00
24	Mike Piazza	6.50
25	Darin Erstad	2.00
26	Chuck Knoblauch	1.00
27	Vladimir Guerrero	4.00
28	Tony Clark	1.00
29	Scott Rolen	3.00
30	Nomar Garciaparra	6.50
31	Eric Young	1.00
32	Ryne Sandberg	5.50
33	Roberto Alomar	2.00
34	Eddie Murray	4.00
35	Rafael Palmeiro	3.50
36	Jose Guillen	1.00

1998 Leaf

The 50th Anniversary edition of Leaf Baseball consists of a 200-card base set with three subsets, three parallels and four inserts. The base set has 148 regular cards, a 10-card Curtain Calls subset, Gold Leaf Stars subset (20 cards), Gold Leaf Rookies subset (20 cards) and three checklists. The subsets cards #148-197 are short-printed in relation to the rest of the set. Card #42 does not exist because Leaf retired the number in honor of Jackie Robinson. The base set was paralleled in Fractal Matrix, Fractal Matrix Die-Cuts and Fractal Diamond Axis. Inserts include Crusade, Heading for the Hall, State Representatives and Statistical Standouts.

		NM/M
Complete Set (200):		40.00
Common Player:		.05
Common SP (#148-197):		.40
Pack (10):		2.00
Wax Box (24):		40.00
1	Rusty Greer	.05
2	Tino Martinez	.05
3	Bobby Bonilla	.05
4	Jason Giambi	.50
5	Matt Morris	.05
6	Craig Counsell	.05
7	Reggie Jefferson	.05
8	Brian Rose	.05
9	Ruben Rivera	.05
10	Shawn Estes	.05
11	Tony Gwynn	1.00
12	Jeff Abbott	.05
13	Jose Cruz Jr.	.05
14	Francisco Cordova	.05
15	Ryan Klesko	.05
16	Tim Salmon	.05
17	Brett Tomko	.05
18	Matt Williams	.05
19	Joe Carter	.05
20	Harold Baines	.05
21	Gary Sheffield	.50
22	Charles Johnson	.05
23	Aaron Boone	.05
24	Eddie Murray	.75
25	Matt Stairs	.05
26	David Cone	.05
27	Jon Nunnally	.05
28	Chris Stynes	.05
29	Enrique Wilson	.05
30	Randy Johnson	.75
31	Garret Anderson	.05
32	Manny Ramirez	.75
33	Jeff Suppan	.05
34	Rickey Henderson	.75
35	Scott Spiezio	.05
36	Rondell White	.05
37	Todd Greene	.05
38	Deline DeShields	.05
39	Kevin Brown	.05
40	Chili Davis	.05
41	Jimmy Key	.05
43	Mike Mussina	.40
44	Joe Randa	.05
45	Chan Ho Park	.05
46	Brad Radke	.05
47	Geronimo Berroa	.05
48	Wade Boggs	1.00
49	Kevin Appier	.05
50	Moises Alou	.05
51	David Justice	.05
52	Ivan Rodriguez	.65
53	J.T. Snow	.05
54	Brian Giles	.05
55	Will Clark	.10
56	Justin Thompson	.05
57	Javier Lopez	.05
58	Hideki Irabu	.05
59	Mark Grudzielanek	.05
60	Abraham Nunez	.05
61	Todd Hollandsworth	.05
62	Jay Bell	.05
63	Nomar Garciaparra	1.25
64	Vinny Castilla	.05
65	Lou Collier	.05
66	Kevin Orie	.05
67	John Valentin	.05
68	Robin Ventura	.05
69	Denny Neagle	.05
70	Tony Womack	.05
71	Dennis Reyes	.05
72	Wally Joyner	.05
73	Kevin Brown	.05
74	Ray Durham	.05
75	Mike Cameron	.05
76	Dante Bichette	.05
77	Jose Guillen	.05
78	Carlos Delgado	.50
79	Paul Molitor	.75
80	Jason Kendall	.05
81	Mark Belhorn	.05
82	Damian Jackson	.05
83	Bill Mueller	.05
84	Kevin Young	.05
85	Curt Schilling	.25
86	Jeffrey Hammonds	.05
87	Sandy Alomar Jr.	.05
88	Bartolo Colon	.05
89	Wilton Guerrero	.05
90	Bernie Williams	.05
91	Deion Sanders	.05

#	Player	NM/M
92	Mike Piazza	1.25
93	Butch Huskey	.05
94	Edgardo Alfonzo	.05
95	Alan Benes	.05
96	Craig Biggio	.05
97	Mark Grace	.05
98	Shawn Green	.25
99	Derrek Lee	.60
100	Ken Griffey Jr.	1.25
101	Tim Raines	.05
102	Pokey Reese	.05
103	Lee Stevens	.05
104	Shannon Stewart	.05
105	John Smoltz	.05
106	Frank Thomas	.75
107	Jeff Fassero	.05
108	Jay Buhner	.05
109	Jose Canseco	.50
110	Omar Vizquel	.05
111	Travis Fryman	.05
112	Dave Nilsson	.05
113	John Olerud	.05
114	Larry Walker	.05
115	Jim Edmonds	.05
116	Bobby Higginson	.05
117	Todd Hundley	.05
118	Paul O'Neill	.05
119	Bip Roberts	.05
120	Ismael Valdes	.05
121	Pedro Martinez	.75
122	Jeff Cirillo	.05
123	Andy Benes	.05
124	Bobby Jones	.05
125	Brian Hunter	.05
126	Darryl Kile	.05
127	Pat Hentgen	.05
128	Marquis Grissom	.05
129	Eric Davis	.05
130	Chipper Jones	1.00
131	Edgar Martinez	.05
132	Andy Pettitte	.20
133	Cal Ripken Jr.	2.00
134	Scott Rolen	.65
135	Ron Coomer	.05
136	Luis Castillo	.05
137	Fred McGriff	.05
138	Neifi Perez	.05
139	Eric Karros	.05
140	Alex Fernandez	.05
141	Jason Dickson	.05
142	Lance Johnson	.05
143	Ray Lankford	.05
144	Sammy Sosa	1.25
145	Eric Young	.05
146	Bubba Trammell	.05
147	Todd Walker	.05
148	Mo Vaughn/CC	.40
149	Jeff Bagwell/CC	1.00
150	Kenny Lofton/CC	.40
151	Raul Mondesi/CC	.40
152	Mike Piazza/CC	2.00
153	Chipper Jones/CC	1.50
154	Larry Walker/CC	.40
155	Greg Maddux/CC	1.50
156	Ken Griffey Jr./CC	2.00
157	Frank Thomas/CC	1.00
158	Darin Erstad/GLS	.75
159	Roberto Alomar/GLS	.60
160	Albert Belle/GLS	.40
161	Jim Thome/GLS	.75
162	Tony Clark/GLS	.40
163	Chuck Knoblauch/GLS	.40
164	Derek Jeter/GLS	3.00
165	Alex Rodriguez/GLS	2.50
166	Tony Gwynn/GLS	1.50
167	Roger Clemens/GLS	2.00
168	Barry Larkin/GLS	.40
169	Andres Galarraga/GLS	.40
170	Vladimir Guerrero/GLS	1.00
171	Mark McGwire/GLS	2.50
172	Barry Bonds/GLS	3.00
173	Juan Gonzalez/GLS	.75
174	Andruw Jones/GLS	1.00
175	Paul Molitor/GLS	.75
176	Hideo Nomo/GLS	.75
177	Cal Ripken Jr./GLS	3.00
178	Brad Fullmer/GLR	.40
179	Jaret Wright/GLR	.40
180	Bobby Estalella/GLR	.40
181	Ben Grieve/GLR	.60
182	Paul Konerko/GLR	.60
183	David Ortiz/GLR	1.00
184	Todd Helton/GLR	1.00
185	Juan Encarnacion/GLR	.40
186	Miguel Tejada/GLR	.60
187	Jacob Cruz/GLR	.40
188	Mark Kotsay/GLR	.40
189	Fernando Tatis/GLR	.40
190	Ricky Ledee/GLR	.40
191	Richard Hidalgo/GLR	.40
192	Richie Sexson/GLR	.40
193	Luis Ordaz/GLR	.40
194	Eli Marrero/GLR	.40
195	Livan Hernandez/GLR	.40
196	Homer Bush/GLR	.40
197	Raul Ibanez/GLR	.40
198	Checklist (Nomar Garciaparra)	
199	Checklist (Scott Rolen)	.30
200	Checklist (Jose Cruz Jr.)	.05
201	Al Martin	.05

Crusade

Thirty cards from the cross-brand Crusade insert appear in 1998 Leaf. The cards

had Green (250 sets), Purple (100 sets) and Red (25 sets) versions. Forty Crusade cards were in 1998 Donruss and 30 each in 1998 Donruss Update and Leaf Rookies & Stars.

		NM/M
Complete Set (30):		400.00
Common Player:		6.00
Purples:		3X
Reds:		12X
3	Jim Edmonds	7.50
4	Darin Erstad	7.50
11	Mike Mussina	15.00
15	Albert Belle	6.00
18	Manny Ramirez	25.00
19	Jim Thome	6.00
25	Bubba Trammell	6.00
26	Bobby Higginson	6.00
28	Paul Molitor	25.00
30	Todd Walker	6.00
34	Andy Pettitte	10.00
35	Wade Boggs	30.00
40	Alex Rodriguez	60.00
41	Randy Johnson	25.00
46	Ivan Rodriguez	20.00
48	Roger Clemens	40.00
54	John Smoltz	6.00
56	Andruw Jones	25.00
58	Javier Lopez	6.00
59	Fred McGriff	6.00
64	Pokey Reese	6.00
66	Andres Galarraga	6.00
70	Eric Young	6.00
73	Moises Alou	6.00
76	Ben Grieve	6.00
79	Mike Piazza	50.00
91	Jason Kendall	6.00
95	Alan Benes	6.00
97	Tony Gwynn	30.00
98	Ken Caminiti	6.00

Heading for the Hall

This 20-card insert features players destined for the Hall of Fame. The set is sequentially numbered to 3,500. Each card is also found in a "SAMPLE" marked edition with no serial number.

		NM/M
Complete Set (20):		35.00
Common Player:		.75
Samples:		1X
1	Roberto Alomar	1.00
2	Jeff Bagwell	1.50
3	Albert Belle	.75
4	Wade Boggs	2.00
5	Barry Bonds	5.00
6	Roger Clemens	2.50
7	Juan Gonzalez	1.50
8	Ken Griffey Jr.	3.00
9	Tony Gwynn	2.00
10	Barry Larkin	.75
11	Kenny Lofton	.75
12	Greg Maddux	2.00
13	Mark McGwire	4.00
14	Paul Molitor	1.50
15	Eddie Murray	1.00
16	Mike Piazza	3.00
17	Cal Ripken Jr.	5.00
18	Ivan Rodriguez	1.25
19	Ryne Sandberg	2.00
20	Frank Thomas	1.50

State Representatives/Provincial Powers

This 30-card insert features top players. The background has a picture of the state or, in the case of Canadian teams, the province in which he plays. "State Representatives" or "Provincial Powers" is printed at the top with the player's name at the bottom. This set is sequentially numbered to 5,000.

		NM/M
Complete Set (30):		40.00
Common Player:		.50
1	Ken Griffey Jr.	3.00
2	Frank Thomas	2.00
3	Alex Rodriguez	4.00
4	Cal Ripken Jr.	5.00
5	Chipper Jones	2.50
6	Andruw Jones	2.00
7	Scott Rolen	1.50
8	Nomar Garciaparra	3.00
9	Tim Salmon	.50
10	Manny Ramirez	2.00
11	Jose Cruz Jr.	.50
12	Vladimir Guerrero	2.00
13	Tino Martinez	.50
14	Larry Walker	.50
15	Mo Vaughn	.50
16	Jim Thome	1.50
17	Tony Clark	.50
18	Derek Jeter	5.00
19	Juan Gonzalez	1.00
20	Jeff Bagwell	2.00
21	Ivan Rodriguez	1.50
22	Mark McGwire	4.00
23	David Justice	.50
24	Chuck Knoblauch	.50
25	Andy Pettitte	.75
26	Raul Mondesi	.50
27	Randy Johnson	2.00
28	Greg Maddux	2.50
29	Bernie Williams	.50
30	Rusty Greer	.50

Statistical Standouts

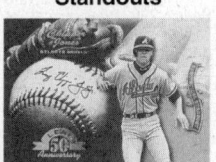

This 24-card insert features players with impressive statistics. The cards have a horizontal layout and the feel of leather. The background has a ball and glove with the player's facsimile signature on the ball. Statistical Standouts is numbered to 2,500. A parallel die-cut version of each card comprises the first 250 numbered cards.

		NM/M
Complete Set (24):		55.00
Common Player:		1.00
Die-Cut:		2X
1	Frank Thomas	2.50
2	Ken Griffey Jr.	4.00
3	Alex Rodriguez	5.00
4	Mike Piazza	4.00
5	Greg Maddux	3.00
6	Cal Ripken Jr.	6.00
7	Chipper Jones	3.00
8	Juan Gonzalez	2.00
9	Jeff Bagwell	2.50
10	Mark McGwire	5.00
11	Tony Gwynn	3.00
12	Mo Vaughn	1.00
13	Nomar Garciaparra	4.00
14	Jose Cruz Jr.	1.00
15	Vladimir Guerrero	2.50
16	Scott Rolen	2.00
17	Andy Pettitte	1.50
18	Randy Johnson	2.50
19	Larry Walker	1.00
20	Kenny Lofton	1.00
21	Tony Clark	1.00
22	David Justice	1.00
23	Derek Jeter	6.00
24	Barry Bonds	6.00

Fractal Foundation

Fractal Foundation is a stand-alone product but it parallels the 1998 Leaf set. It contains the Curtain Calls, Gold Leaf Stars and Gold Leaf Rookies subsets and is missing card #42 which Leaf retired in honor of Jackie Robinson. The set was printed on foil board and each card is numbered to 3,999. The set is paralleled in Fractal Materials, Fractal Materials Die-Cuts and Fractal Materials Z2 Axis.

		NM/M
Complete Set (200):		60.00
Common Player:		.20
Semistars:		.60
Unlisted Stars:		1.00
Pack (3):		2.00
Wax Box (18):		35.00
1	Rusty Greer	.20
2	Tino Martinez	.20
3	Bobby Bonilla	.20
4	Jason Giambi	.60
5	Matt Morris	.20
6	Craig Counsell	.20
7	Reggie Jefferson	.20
8	Brian Rose	.20
9	Ruben Rivera	.20
10	Shawn Estes	.20
11	Tony Gwynn	1.50
12	Jeff Abbott	.20
13	Jose Cruz Jr.	.20
14	Francisco Cordova	.20
15	Ryan Klesko	.20
16	Tim Salmon	.20
17	Brett Tomko	.20
18	Matt Williams	.20
19	Joe Carter	.20
20	Harold Baines	.20
21	Gary Sheffield	.50
22	Charles Johnson	.20
23	Aaron Boone	.20
24	Eddie Murray	1.00
25	Matt Stairs	.20
26	David Cone	.20
27	Jon Nunnally	.20
28	Chris Stynes	.20
29	Enrique Wilson	.20
30	Randy Johnson	1.00
31	Garret Anderson	.20
32	Manny Ramirez	1.00
33	Jeff Suppan	.20
34	Rickey Henderson	1.00
35	Scott Spiezio	.20
36	Rondell White	.20
37	Todd Greene	.20
38	Delino DeShields	.20
39	Kevin Brown	.20
40	Chili Davis	.20
41	Jimmy Key	.20
42	Mike Mussina	.40
43	Joe Randa	.20
44	Chan Ho Park	.20
45	Brad Radke	.20
46	Geronimo Berroa	.20
47	Wade Boggs	1.50
48	Kevin Appier	.20
49	Moises Alou	.20
50	David Justice	.20
51	Ivan Rodriguez	.75
52	J.T. Snow	.20
53	Brian Giles	.20
55	Will Clark	.20
56	Justin Thompson	.20
57	Javier Lopez	.20
58	Hideki Irabu	.20
59	Mark Grudzielanek	.20
60	Abraham Nunez	.20
61	Todd Hollandsworth	.20
62	Jay Bell	.20
63	Nomar Garciaparra	1.75
64	Vinny Castilla	.20
65	Lou Collier	.20
66	Kevin Orie	.20
67	John Valentin	.20
68	Robin Ventura	.20
69	Denny Neagle	.20
70	Tony Womack	.20
71	Dennis Reyes	.20
72	Wally Joyner	.20
73	Kevin Brown	.20
74	Ray Durham	.20
75	Mike Cameron	.20
76	Dante Bichette	.20
77	Jose Guillen	.20
78	Carlos Delgado	.50
79	Paul Molitor	1.00
80	Jason Kendall	.20
81	Mark Belhorn	.20
82	Damian Jackson	.20
83	Bill Mueller	.20
84	Kevin Young	.20
85	Curt Schilling	.40
86	Jeffrey Hammonds	.20
87	Sandy Alomar Jr.	.20
88	Bartolo Colon	.20
89	Wilton Guerrero	.20
90	Bernie Williams	.20
91	Deion Sanders	.20
92	Mike Piazza	2.00
93	Butch Huskey	.20
94	Edgardo Alfonzo	.20
95	Alan Benes	.20
96	Craig Biggio	.20
97	Mark Grace	.20
98	Shawn Green	.20
99	Derrek Lee	.50
100	Ken Griffey Jr.	2.00
101	Tim Raines	.20
102	Pokey Reese	.20
103	Lee Stevens	.20
104	Shannon Stewart	.20
105	John Smoltz	.20
106	Frank Thomas	1.00
107	Jeff Fassero	.20
108	Jay Buhner	.20
109	Jose Canseco	.40
110	Omar Vizquel	.20
111	Travis Fryman	.20
112	Dave Nilsson	.20
113	John Olerud	.20
114	Larry Walker	.20
115	Jim Edmonds	.20
116	Bobby Higginson	.20
117	Todd Hundley	.20
118	Paul O'Neill	.20
119	Bip Roberts	.20
120	Ismael Valdes	.20
121	Pedro Martinez	1.00
122	Jeff Cirillo	.20
123	Andy Benes	.20
124	Bobby Jones	.20
125	Brian Hunter	.20
126	Darryl Kile	.20
127	Pat Hentgen	.20
128	Marquis Grissom	.20
129	Eric Davis	.20
130	Chipper Jones	1.50
131	Edgar Martinez	.20
132	Andy Pettitte	.35
133	Cal Ripken Jr.	3.00
134	Scott Rolen	.75
135	Ron Coomer	.20
136	Luis Castillo	.20
137	Fred McGriff	.20
138	Neifi Perez	.20
139	Eric Karros	.20
140	Alex Fernandez	.20
141	Jason Dickson	.20
142	Lance Johnson	.20
143	Ray Lankford	.20
144	Sammy Sosa	1.75
145	Eric Young	.20
146	Bubba Trammell	.20
147	Todd Walker	.20
148	Mo Vaughn/CC	.20
149	Jeff Bagwell/CC	1.00
150	Kenny Lofton/CC	.20
151	Raul Mondesi/CC	.20
152	Mike Piazza/CC	2.00
153	Chipper Jones/CC	1.50
154	Larry Walker/CC	.20
155	Greg Maddux/CC	1.50
156	Ken Griffey Jr./CC	2.00
157	Frank Thomas/CC	1.00
158	Darin Erstad/GLS	.20
159	Roberto Alomar/GLS	.40
160	Albert Belle/GLS	.20
161	Jim Thome/GLS	.75
162	Tony Clark/GLS	.20
163	Chuck Knoblauch/GLS	.20
164	Derek Jeter/GLS	3.00
165	Alex Rodriguez/GLS	2.50
166	Tony Gwynn/GLS	1.50
167	Roger Clemens/GLS	1.75
168	Barry Larkin/GLS	.20
169	Andres Galarraga/GLS	.20
170	Vladimir Guerrero/GLS	1.00
171	Mark McGwire/GLS	2.50
172	Barry Bonds/GLS	3.00
173	Juan Gonzalez/GLS	.75
174	Andruw Jones/GLS	1.00
175	Paul Molitor/GLS	1.00
176	Hideo Nomo/GLS	.75
177	Cal Ripken Jr./GLS	3.00
178	Brad Fullmer/GLR	.20
179	Jaret Wright/GLR	.20
180	Bobby Estalella/GLR	.20
181	Ben Grieve/GLR	.40
182	Paul Konerko/GLR	.40
183	David Ortiz/GLR	.75
184	Todd Helton/GLR	1.00
185	Juan Encarnacion/GLR	.20
186	Miguel Tejada/GLR	.40
187	Jacob Cruz/GLR	.20
188	Mark Kotsay/GLR	.20
189	Fernando Tatis/GLR	.20
190	Ricky Ledee/GLR	.20
191	Richard Hidalgo/GLR	.20
192	Richie Sexson/GLR	.20
193	Luis Ordaz/GLR	.20
194	Eli Marrero/GLR	.20
195	Livan Hernandez/GLR	.20
196	Homer Bush/GLR	.20
197	Raul Ibanez/GLR	.20
198	Checklist (Nomar Garciaparra)	1.00
199	Checklist (Scott Rolen)	.30
200	Checklist (Jose Cruz Jr.)	.20

1998 Leaf Fractal Materials Samples

Each of the 50 Leather cards in Fractal Materials can be found in a sample version, prominently marked as such on back.

		NM/M
Complete Set (50):		100.00
Common Player:		2.00
5	Matt Morris	2.00
9	Ruben Rivera	2.00
10	Shawn Estes	2.00
15	Ryan Klesko	2.00
17	Brett Tomko	2.00
22	Charles Johnson	2.00
33	Jeff Suppan	2.00
36	Rondell White	2.00
39	Kevin Brown	2.00
52	J.T. Snow	2.00
55	Will Clark	2.00
58	Hideki Irabu	2.00
66	Kevin Orie	2.00
70	Tony Womack	2.00
76	Dennis Reyes	2.00
76	Dante Bichette	2.00
78	Carlos Delgado	3.50
81	Mark Belhorn	2.00
87	Sandy Alomar Jr.	2.00
89	Wilton Guerrero	2.00
93	Butch Huskey	2.00
95	Edgardo Alfonzo	2.00
95	Alan Benes	2.00
97	Mark Grace	2.00
98	Shawn Green	3.00
99	Derrek Lee	4.00
105	John Smoltz	2.00
108	Jay Buhner	2.00
109	Jose Canseco	3.50
116	Bobby Higginson	2.00
117	Todd Hundley	2.00
136	Luis Castillo	2.00
137	Fred McGriff	2.00
138	Neifi Perez	2.00
146	Bubba Trammell	2.00
147	Todd Walker	2.00
158	Darin Erstad/GLS	3.50
160	Albert Belle/GLS	2.00
161	Jim Thome/GLS	4.00
162	Tony Clark/GLS	2.00
163	Chuck Knoblauch/GLS	2.00
167	Roger Clemens/GLS	6.50
170	Vladimir Guerrero/GLS	2.00
171	Mark McGwire/GLS	7.50
172	Barry Bonds/GLS	10.00
176	Hideo Nomo/GLS	4.00
189	Fernando Tatis/GLR	2.00
194	Eli Marrero/GLR	2.00
195	Livan Hernandez/GLR	2.00
201	Al Martin	2.00

ABBREVIATIONS

CC - Curtain Calls
GLR - Gold Leaf Rookies
GLS - Gold Leaf Stars

1998 Leaf Fractal Materials

The Fractal Materials set fully parallels Fractal Foundations. Each of the inserts is sequentially numbered. The 200 card chase set was printed on four different materials: 100 plastic cards (numbered to 3,250), 50 leather (1,000), 30 nylon (500) and 20 wood (250). These parallels were inserted one per pack of Fractal Foundations. Each of the Leather cards can be found in a sample version marked as such on back.

	NM/M
Complete Set (200):	375.00
Complete Plastic Set (100):	65.00
Common Plastic (3,250):	.35
Complete Leather Set (50):	55.00
Common Leather (1,000):	.75
Complete Nylon Set (30):	60.00
Common Nylon (500):	1.25
Complete Wood Set (20):	200.00
Common Wood (250):	5.00
Wax Box:	120.00

No.	Card	Price
1	Rusty Greer/N	.35
2	Tino Martinez/W	5.00
3	Bobby Bonilla/P	1.25
4	Jason Giambi/N	4.00
5	Matt Morris/L	.75
6	Craig Counsell/P	.35
7	Reggie Jefferson/P	.35
8	Brian Rose/P	.35
9	Ruben Rivera/L	.75
10	Shawn Estes/L	.75
11	Tony Gwynn/W	20.00
12	Jeff Abbott/P	.35
13	Jose Cruz Jr./W	5.00
14	Francisco Cordova/P	.35
15	Ryan Klesko/L	.75
16	Tim Salmon/W	5.00
17	Brett Tomko/L	.75
18	Matt Williams/N	1.25
19	Joe Carter/P	.35
20	Harold Baines/P	.35
21	Gary Sheffield/P	2.50
22	Charles Johnson/L	.75
23	Aaron Boone/P	.35
24	Eddie Murray/N	5.00
25	Matt Stairs/P	.35
26	David Cone/P	.35
27	Jon Nunnally/P	.35
28	Chris Stynes/P	.35
29	Enrique Wilson/P	.35
30	Randy Johnson/W	15.00
31	Garret Anderson/N	1.25
32	Manny Ramirez/W	15.00
33	Jeff Suppan/L	.75
34	Rickey Henderson/N	5.00
35	Scott Spiezio/L	.35
36	Rondell White/L	1.25
37	Todd Greene/L	1.25
38	Delino DeShields/P	.35
39	Kevin Brown/L	.75
40	Chili Davis/P	.35
41	Jimmy Key/P	.35
42	Mike Mussina/N	4.00
43	Joe Randa/P	.35
44	Chan Ho Park/N	1.25
45	Brad Radke/P	.35
46	Geronimo Berroa/P	.35
47	Wade Boggs/N	6.00
48	Kevin Appier/N	.35
49	Moises Alou/N	1.25
50	David Justice/N	.35
51	Ivan Rodriguez/W	12.50
52	J.T. Snow/L	.75
53	Brian Giles/P	.35
54	Will Clark/L	.75
55	Justin Thompson/L	1.25
56	Javier Lopez/L	.75
57	Hideki Irabu/L	.75
58	Mark Grudzielanek/P	.35
59	Abraham Nunez/N	.35
60	Todd Hollandsworth/P	.35
61	Jay Bell/P	.35
62	Nomar Garciaparr/W	20.00
63	Vinny Castilla/P	.35
64	Lou Collier/L	.35
65	Kevin Orie/L	.35
66	John Valentin/P	.35
67	Robin Ventura/P	.35
69	Denny Neagle/P	.35
70	Tony Womack/L	.75
71	Dennis Reyes/L	.75
72	Wally Joyner/P	.35
73	Kevin Brown/P	.35
74	Ray Durham/P	.35
75	Mike Cameron/N	1.25
76	Dante Bichette/L	.75
77	Jose Guillen/N	1.25
78	Carlos Delgado/L	1.25
79	Paul Molitor/W	15.00
80	Jason Kendall/P	.35
81	Mark Belhorn/P	.75
82	Damian Jackson/P	.35
83	Bill Mueller/P	.35
84	Kevin Young/P	.35
85	Curt Schilling/P	.60
86	Jeffrey Hammonds/P	.35
87	Sandy Alomar Jr./L	.75
88	Bartolo Colon/P	.35
89	Wilton Guerrero/L	.75
90	Bernie Williams/N	1.25
91	Deion Sanders/N	1.25
92	Mike Piazza/W	25.00
93	Butch Huskey/L	.75
94	Edgardo Alfonzo/L	.75
95	Alan Benes/L	.75
96	Craig Biggio/L	1.25
97	Mark Grace/L	.75
98	Shawn Green/L	1.25
99	Derrek Lee/L	2.00
100	Ken Griffey Jr./W	25.00
101	Tim Raines/P	.35
102	Pokey Reese/P	.35
103	Lee Stevens/N	1.25
104	Shannon Stewart/N	1.25
105	John Smoltz/L	.75
106	Frank Thomas/W	15.00
107	Jeff Fassero/L	.35
108	Jay Buhner/L	.75
109	Jose Canseco/L	1.50
110	Omar Vizquel/P	.35
111	Travis Fryman/P	.35
112	Dave Nilsson/P	.35
113	John Olerud/P	.35
114	Larry Walker/W	5.00
115	Jim Edmonds/N	1.25
116	Bobby Higginson/L	.75
117	Todd Hundley/P	.35
118	Paul O'Neill/P	.35
119	Bip Roberts/P	.35
120	Ismael Valdes/P	.35
121	Pedro Martinez/N	5.00
122	Jeff Cirillo/P	.35
123	Andy Benes/P	.35
124	Bobby Jones/P	.35
125	Brian Hunter/P	.35
126	Darryl Kile/P	.35
127	Pat Hentgen/P	.35
128	Marquis Grissom/P	.35
129	Eric Davis/P	.35
130	Chipper Jones/W	20.00
131	Edgar Martinez/N	1.25
132	Andy Pettitte/W	10.00
133	Cal Ripken Jr./W	35.00
134	Scott Rolen/W	12.50
135	Ron Coomer/L	.35
136	Luis Castillo/L	.35
137	Fred McGriff/L	.75
138	Neifi Perez/L	.75
139	Eric Karros/P	.35
140	Alex Fernandez/P	.35
141	Jason Dickson/P	.35
142	Lance Johnson/P	.35
143	Ray Lankford/P	.35
144	Sammy Sosa/W	7.00
145	Eric Young/P	.35
146	Bubba Trammell/L	.75
147	Todd Walker/L	.75
148	Mo Vaughn/P/CC	.75
149	Jeff Bagwell/P/CC	3.00
150	Kenny Lofton/P/CC	.35
151	Raul Mondesi/P/CC	.35
152	Mike Piazza/P/CC	5.00
153	Chipper Jones/P/CC	4.00
154	Larry Walker/P/CC	.35
155	Greg Maddux/P/CC	4.00
156	Ken Griffey Jr./P/CC	5.00
157	Frank Thomas/P/CC	3.00
158	Darin Erstad/L/GLS	2.00
159	Roberto Alomar/P/GLS	.65
160	Albert Belle/L/GLS	1.00
161	Jim Thome/L/GLS	2.00
162	Tony Clark/L/GLS	.75
163	Chuck Knoblauch/L/GLS	.75
164	Derek Jeter/P/GLS	7.50
165	Alex Rodriguez/P/GLS	6.00
166	Tony Gwynn/P/GLS	5.00
167	Roger Clemens/L/GLS	5.00
168	Barry Larkin/P/GLS	.35
169	Andres Galarraga/P/GLS	.35
170	Vladimir Guerrero/L/GLS	4.00
171	Mark McGwire/L/GLS	6.00
172	Barry Bonds/L/GLS	7.50
173	Juan Gonzalez/L/GLS	2.00
174	Andruw Jones/P/GLS	2.00
175	Paul Molitor/P/GLS	3.00
176	Hideo Nomo/L/GLS	2.00
177	Cal Ripken Jr./P/GLS	7.50
178	Brad Fullmer/P/GLS	2.00
179	Jaret Wright/N/GLR	1.25
180	Bobby Estalella/W/GLR	.35
181	Ben Grieve/W/GLR	5.00
182	Paul Konerko/W/GLR	6.00
183	David Ortiz/N/GLR	2.50
184	Todd Helton/W/GLR	10.00
185	Juan Encarnacion N/GLR	1.25
186	Miguel Tejada/N/GLR	1.50
187	Jacob Cruz/P/GLR	.35
188	Mark Kotsay/N/GLR	1.25
189	Fernando Tatis/L/GLR	.75
190	Ricky Ledee/P/GLR	.35
191	Richard Hidalgo/P/GLR	.35
192	Richie Sexson/P/GLR	.35
193	Luis Ordaz/P/GLR	.35
194	Eli Marrero/L/GLR	.75
195	Livan Hernandez/L/GLR	.35
196	Homer Bush/P/GLR	.35
197	Raul Ibanez/P/GLR	.35
198	Checklist (Nomar Garciaparra/P)	3.00
199	Checklist (Scott Rolen/P)	.40
200	Checklist (Jose Cruz Jr./P)	.35
201	Al Martin/L	.75

Die-Cut

This parallel set adds a die-cut to the Fractal Materials set. The first 200 of 75 plastic, 15 leather, 5 nylon and 5 wood cards have an x-axis die-cut. The first 100 of 20 plastic, 25 leather, 10 nylon and 5 wood cards have a y-axis die-cut. The first 50 of 5 plastic, 10 leather, 15 nylon and 10 wood cards have a z-axis die-cut. The serial numbers on the backs of the die-cut cards are meaningless because they were printed prior to the die-cut fracture. This compounds the confusion engendered among collectors which has had a significant dampening effect on demand and, thus, market values.

	NM/M
Common X (200 of each):	1.50
Common Y (100):	3.00
Common Z (50):	6.00

No.	Card	Price
1	Rusty Greer/Z	6.00
2	Tino Martinez/Y	3.00
3	Bobby Bonilla/Y	3.00
4	Jason Giambi/Z	20.00
5	Matt Morris/Y	3.00
6	Craig Counsell/X	1.50
7	Reggie Jefferson/X	1.50
8	Brian Rose/X	1.50
9	Ruben Rivera/Y	3.00
10	Shawn Estes/Y	3.00
11	Tony Gwynn/Z	12.50
12	Jeff Abbott/Y	3.00
13	Jose Cruz Jr./Z	6.00
14	Francisco Cordova/Y	3.00
15	Ryan Klesko/Y	1.50
16	Tim Salmon/Y	3.00
17	Brett Tomko/Y	1.50
18	Matt Williams/Y	3.00
19	Joe Carter/Y	3.00
20	Harold Baines/Y	1.50
21	Gary Sheffield/Z	12.00
22	Charles Johnson/Y	3.00
23	Aaron Boone/Y	1.50
24	Eddie Murray/Y	10.00
25	Matt Stairs/X	1.50
26	David Cone/X	1.50
27	Jon Nunnally/X	1.50
28	Chris Stynes/X	1.50
29	Enrique Wilson/X	1.50
30	Randy Johnson/Y	10.00
31	Garret Anderson/Y	3.00
32	Manny Ramirez/Y	10.00
33	Jeff Suppan/Y	3.00
34	Rickey Henderson/X	10.00
35	Scott Spiezio/Y	3.00
36	Rondell White/Y	3.00
37	Todd Greene/Z	6.00
38	Delino DeShields/Y	3.00
39	Kevin Brown/Y	1.50
40	Chili Davis/Y	1.50
41	Jimmy Key/Z	20.00
42	Mike Mussina/Z	20.00
43	Joe Randa/X	1.50
44	Chan Ho Park/Y	3.00
45	Brad Radke/X	1.50
46	Geronimo Berroa/X	1.50
47	Wade Boggs/Y	12.50
48	Kevin Appier/X	1.50
49	Moises Alou/X	1.50
50	David Justice/Z	6.00
51	Ivan Rodriguez/X	7.50
52	J.T. Snow/X	1.50
53	Brian Giles/Y	3.00
54	Will Clark/Y	3.00
55	Justin Thompson/Y	3.00
56	Javier Lopez/Y	3.00
57	Hideki Irabu/X	1.50
58	Mark Grudzielanek/X	1.50
59	Abraham Nunez/X	6.00
60	Todd Hollandsworth/X	1.50
61	Jay Bell/X	1.50
62	Nomar Garciaparra/Z	45.00
63	Vinny Castilla/Y	3.00
64	Lou Collier/Y	1.50
65	Kevin Orie/X	1.50
66	John Valentin/X	1.50
67	Robin Ventura/X	1.50
68	Denny Neagle/X	1.50
69	Tony Womack/X	3.00
70	Dennis Reyes/X	3.00
71	Wally Joyner/X	1.50
72	Kevin Brown/X	1.50
73	Ray Durham/X	1.50
74	Mike Cameron/Y	3.00
75	Dante Bichette/X	1.50
76	Jose Guillen/Y	6.00
77	Carlos Delgado/X	5.00
78	Paul Molitor/X	10.00
79	Jason Kendall/X	1.50
80	Mark Belhorn/X	1.50
81	Damian Jackson/X	3.00
82	Bill Mueller/X	1.50
83	Kevin Young/X	1.50
84	Curt Schilling/X	3.00
85	Jeffrey Hammonds/Y	1.50
86	Sandy Alomar Jr./Y	3.00
87	Bartolo Colon/X	3.00
88	Wilton Guerrero/Y	6.00
89	Bernie Williams/Y	6.00
90	Deion Sanders/Y	6.00
91	Mike Piazza/Z	55.00
92	Butch Huskey/Z	1.50
93	Edgardo Alfonzo/X	3.00
94	Alan Benes/Z	6.00
95	Craig Biggio/X	1.50
96	Mark Grace/X	3.00
97	Shawn Green/Y	5.00
98	Derrek Lee/X	6.00
99	Ken Griffey/Z	55.00
100	Tim Raines/X	1.50
101	Pokey Reese/X	3.00
102	Lee Stevens/X	1.50
103	Shannon Stewart/Y	1.50
104	John Smoltz/Y	3.00
105	Frank Thomas/Z	30.00
106	Jeff Fassero/Y	1.50
107	Jay Buhner/X	3.00
108	Jose Canseco/X	3.00
109	Omar Vizquel/X	1.50
110	Travis Fryman/X	1.50
111	Dave Nilsson/X	1.50
112	John Olerud/X	1.50
113	Larry Walker/X	1.50
114	Jim Edmonds/Z	6.00
115	Bobby Higginson/X	3.00
116	Todd Hundley/X	1.50
117	Paul O'Neill/X	1.50
118	Bip Roberts/X	1.50
119	Ismael Valdes/X	1.50
120	Pedro Martinez/X	10.00
121	Jeff Cirillo/X	1.50
122	Andy Benes/X	1.50
123	Bobby Jones/X	1.50
124	Brian Hunter/X	1.50
125	Darryl Kile/X	1.50
126	Pat Hentgen/X	1.50
127	Marquis Grissom/X	1.50
128	Eric Davis/X	1.50
129	Chipper Jones/Z	45.00
130	Edgar Martinez/Z	6.00
131	Andy Pettitte/Y	3.00
132	Cal Ripken Jr./Z	75.00
133	Scott Rolen/Z	7.50
134	Ron Coomer/X	1.50
135	Luis Castillo/X	1.50
136	Fred McGriff/X	1.50
137	Neifi Perez/Y	3.00
138	Eric Karros/X	1.50
139	Alex Fernandez/X	1.50
140	Jason Dickson/X	1.50
141	Lance Johnson/Y	3.00
142	Ray Lankford/Y	3.00
143	Eric Young/X	1.50
144	Bubba Trammell/Z	6.00
145	Todd Walker/Z	6.00
146	Mo Vaughn/X/CC	1.50
147	Jeff Bagwell/X/CC	10.00
148	Kenny Lofton/X/CC	1.50
149	Raul Mondesi/X/CC	1.50
150	Mike Piazza/X/CC	15.00
151	Chipper Jones/X/CC	12.50
152	Larry Walker/X/CC	1.50
153	Greg Maddux/X/CC	12.50
154	Ken Griffey Jr./CC	15.00
157	Frank Thomas/X/CC	10.00
158	Darin Erstad/Y/GLS	4.00
159	Roberto Alomar X/GLS	2.00
160	Albert Belle/X/GLS	1.50
161	Jim Thome/X/GLS	6.00
162	Tony Clark/Z/GLS	6.00
163	Chuck Knoblauch Z/GLS	6.00
164	Derek Jeter/X/GLS	25.00
165	Alex Rodriguez Y/GLS	30.00
166	Tony Gwynn/X/GLS	12.50
167	Roger Clemens Y/GLS	17.50
168	Barry Larkin/Y/GLS	3.00
169	Andres Galarraga Y/GLS	3.00
170	Vladimir Guerrero Y/GLS	10.00
171	Mark McGwire Z/GLS	65.00
172	Barry Bonds/Y/GLS	35.00
173	Juan Gonzalez/Y/GLS	7.50
174	Andruw Jones/X/GLS	10.00
175	Paul Molitor/X/GLS	10.00
176	Hideo Nomo/X/GLS	25.00
177	Cal Ripken Jr./X/GLS	25.00
178	Brad Fullmer/Z/GLR	6.00
179	Jaret Wright/Z/GLR	6.00
180	Bobby Estalella/Y/GLR	3.00
181	Ben Grieve/Z/GLR	6.00
182	Paul Konerko/Z/GLR	7.50
183	David Ortiz/Z/GLR	10.00
184	Todd Helton/Z/GLR	20.00
185	Juan Encarnacion Z/GLR	6.00
186	Miguel Tejada/Z/GLR	12.00
187	Jacob Cruz/Z/GLR	1.50
188	Mark Kotsay/Z/GLR	6.00
189	Fernando Tatis/X/GLR	3.00
190	Ricky Ledee/X/GLR	1.50
191	Richard Hidalgo Z/GLR	6.00
192	Richie Sexson/Z/GLR	6.00
193	Luis Ordaz/X/GLR	1.50
194	Eli Marrero/Z/GLR	6.00
195	Livan Hernandez	
196	Homer Bush/X/GLR	1.50
197	Raul Ibanez/X/GLR	1.50
198	Checklist (Nomar Garciaparra/X)	7.50
199	Checklist (Scott Rolen/Z)	7.50
200	Checklist (Jose Cruz Jr./X)	1.50
201	Al Martin/Y	3.00

Z2 Axis

This 200-card set parallels Leaf Fractal Materials and was numbered to 20 sets.

	NM/M
Common Player:	
Z2 Stars:	10X
Production 20 Sets	

1998 Leaf Fractal Matrix

Fractal Matrix is a parallel insert set to 1998 Leaf. Cards have a metallic finish, with 100 done in bronze, 60 in silver and 40 in gold, and each color having some cards in X, Y and Z axis. Stated print runs are: Bronze: X - 1,600; Y - 1,800; Z - 1,900. Silver: X - 600; Y - 800; Z - 900. Gold: X - 100; Y - 300; Z - 400. Each player is found only in a single color/axis combination.

	NM/M
Complete Set (200):	250.00
Common Bronze:	.25
Common Silver:	.75
Common Gold:	2.00

No.	Card	Price
1	Rusty Greer G/Z	2.00
2	Tino Martinez G/Z	2.00
3	Bobby Bonilla S/Y	.75
4	Jason Giambi S/Y	1.25
5	Matt Morris B/X	.25
6	Craig Counsell B/X	.25
7	Reggie Jefferson S/Y	.25
8	Brian Rose S/Y	.75
9	Ruben Rivera S/Y	.75
10	Shawn Estes S/Y	.75
11	Tony Gwynn G/Z	10.00
12	Jeff Abbott B/Y	.25
13	Jose Cruz Jr. G/Z	2.00
14	Francisco Cordova B/X	.25
15	Ryan Klesko B/X	.25
16	Tim Salmon G/Y	2.00
17	Brett Tomko B/X	.25
18	Matt Williams S/Y	.75
19	Joe Carter B/X	.25
20	Harold Baines B/X	.25
21	Gary Sheffield S/Z	1.25
22	Charles Johnson S/X	.75
23	Aaron Boone B/X	.25
24	Eddie Murray B/Y	7.50
25	Matt Stairs B/X	.25
26	David Cone B/X	.25
27	Jon Nunnally B/X	.25
28	Chris Stynes B/X	.25
29	Enrique Wilson B/Y	.25
30	Randy Johnson S/Z	2.00
31	Garret Anderson B/X	.25
32	Manny Ramirez G/Z	7.50
33	Jeff Suppan B/X	.25
34	Rickey Henderson B/X	1.00
35	Scott Spiezio B/X	.25
36	Rondell White S/Y	.75
37	Todd Greene S/Z	.25
38	Delino DeShields B/X	.25
39	Kevin Brown S/X	.75
40	Chili Davis B/X	.25
41	Jimmy Key B/X	.25
42	Mike Mussina G/Y	5.00
43	Joe Randa S/Z	.25
44	Chan Ho Park S/Z	.75
45	Brad Radke B/X	.25
46	Geronimo Berroa B/X	.25
47	Wade Boggs B/X	2.50
48	Kevin Appier B/X	.25
49	Moises Alou S/Y	.75
50	David Justice G/Y	2.00
51	Ivan Rodriguez G/Z	6.00
52	J.T. Snow B/X	.25
53	Brian Giles B/X	.25
54	Will Clark B/Y	.25
55	Justin Thompson S/Y	.75
56	Javier Lopez S/X	.75
57	Hideki Irabu B/Z	.25
58	Mark Grudzielanek B/X	.25
59	Abraham Nunez S/X	.25
60	Todd Hollandsworth B/X	.25
61	Jay Bell B/X	.25
62	Nomar Garciaparra G/Z	10.00
63	Vinny Castilla B/Y	.25
64	Lou Collier S/X	.25
65	Kevin Orie S/X	.75
66	John Valentin B/X	.25
67	Robin Ventura B/X	.25
68	Denny Neagle B/Y	.25
69	Tony Womack S/Y	.75
70	Dennis Reyes B/Y	.25
71	Wally Joyner B/X	.25
72	Kevin Brown B/Y	.25
73	Ray Durham B/X	.25
74	Mike Cameron S/Z	.75
75	Dante Bichette S/Z	.75
76	Jose Guillen G/Y	2.00
77	Carlos Delgado B/Y	.50
78	Paul Molitor G/Z	7.50
79	Jason Kendall B/X	.25
80	Mark Belhorn B/X	.25
81	Damian Jackson B/X	.25
82	Bill Mueller B/X	.25
83	Kevin Young B/X	.25
84	Curt Schilling B/X	.40
85	Jeffrey Hammonds B/X	.25
86	Sandy Alomar Jr. S/Y	.75
87	Bartolo Colon B/Y	.50
88	Wilton Guerrero B/X	.25
89	Bernie Williams G/Y	2.00
90	Deion Sanders S/Y	.75
91	Mike Piazza B/Z	12.50
92	Butch Huskey B/X	.25
93	Edgardo Alfonzo S/X	.75
94	Alan Benes S/Y	.75
95	Craig Biggio S/Y	.75
96	Mark Grace S/Y	.75
97	Shawn Green S/Y	1.50
98	Derrek Lee S/Y	2.00
99	Ken Griffey Jr. G/Z	12.50
100	Tim Raines B/X	.25
101	Pokey Reese S/X	.75

103	Lee Stevens B/X	.25
104	Shannon Stewart S/Y	.75
105	John Smoltz S/Y	.75
106	Frank Thomas G/X	7.50
107	Jeff Fassero B/X	.25
108	Jay Buhner B/Y	.25
109	Jose Canseco B/X	.50
110	Omar Vizquel B/X	.25
111	Travis Fryman B/X	.25
112	Dave Nilsson B/X	.25
113	John Olerud B/X	.25
114	Larry Walker G/Z	2.00
115	Jim Edmonds S/Y	.75
116	Bobby Higginson S/X	.75
117	Todd Hundley S/Y	.75
118	Paul O'Neill B/X	.25
119	Bip Roberts B/X	.25
120	Ismael Valdes B/X	.25
121	Pedro Martinez S/Y	2.00
122	Jeff Cirillo B/X	.25
123	Andy Benes B/X	.25
124	Bobby Jones B/X	.25
125	Brian Hunter B/X	.25
126	Darryl Kile B/X	.25
127	Pat Hentgen B/X	.25
128	Marquis Grissom B/X	.25
129	Eric Davis B/X	.25
130	Chipper Jones G/Z	10.00
131	Edgar Martinez S/Z	.75
132	Andy Pettitte G/Z	3.00
133	Cal Ripken Jr. G/X	20.00
134	Scott Rolen G/Z	6.00
135	Ron Coomer B/X	.25
136	Luis Castillo B/Y	.25
137	Fred McGriff B/Y	.25
138	Neifi Perez S/Y	.25
139	Eric Karros B/X	.25
140	Alex Fernandez B/X	.25
141	Jason Dickson B/X	.25
142	Lance Johnson B/X	.25
143	Ray Lankford B/Y	.25
144	Sammy Sosa G/Y	10.00
145	Eric Young B/Y	.25
146	Bubba Trammell S/Y	.75
147	Todd Walker S/Y	.75
148	Mo Vaughn S/X/CC	.75
149	Jeff Bagwell S/X/CC	.75
150	Kenny Lofton S/X/CC	.75
151	Raul Mondesi S/X/CC	.75
152	Mike Piazza S/X/CC	4.00
153	Chipper Jones S/X/CC	3.00
154	Larry Walker S/X/CC	.75
155	Greg Maddux S/X/CC	3.00
156	Ken Griffey Jr. S/X/CC	4.00
157	Frank Thomas S/X/CC	2.00
158	Darin Erstad B/Z/GLS	.50
159	Roberto Alomar B/Y/GLS	.35
160	Albert Belle G/Y/GLS	2.00
161	Jim Thome G/Y/GLS	4.00
162	Tony Clark G/Y/GLS	2.00
163	Chuck Knoblauch B/Y/GLS	.25
164	Derek Jeter G/Z/GLS	20.00
165	Alex Rodriguez G/Z/GLS	15.00
166	Tony Gwynn B/X/GLS	1.25
167	Roger Clemens G/Z/GLS	12.00
168	Barry Larkin B/Y/GLS	.25
169	Andres Galarraga B/Y/GLS	.25
170	Vladimir Guerrero G/Z/GLS	7.50
171	Mark McGwire B/Z/GLS	2.00
172	Barry Bonds B/Z/GLS	3.00
173	Juan Gonzalez G/Z/GLS	4.00
174	Andruw Jones G/Z/GLS	7.50
175	Paul Molitor B/X/GLS	1.00
176	Hideo Nomo B/Z/GLS	.75
177	Cal Ripken Jr. B/X/GLS	2.25
178	Brad Fullmer S/Z/GLR	.75
179	Jaret Wright G/X/GLR	2.00
180	Bobby Estalella B/Y/GLR	.25
181	Ben Grieve G/X/GLR	2.00
182	Paul Konerko G/Z/GLR	3.00
183	David Ortiz G/Z/GLR	6.00
184	Todd Helton G/X/GLR	5.00
185	Juan Encarnacion G/Z/GLR	4.00
186	Miguel Tejada G/Z/GLR	4.00
187	Jacob Cruz B/Y/GLR	.25
188	Mark Kotsay G/Z/GLR	2.00
189	Fernando Tatis S/Z/GLR	.75
190	Ricky Ledee S/Y/GLR	.75
191	Richard Hidalgo S/Y/GLR	.75
192	Richie Sexson S/Y/GLR	.75
193	Luis Ordaz B/X/GLR	.25
194	Eli Marrero S/Z/GLR	.75
195	Livan Hernandez S/Z/GLR	.75
196	Homer Bush B/X/GLR	.25
197	Raul Ibanez B/X/GLR	.25
198	Checklist (Nomar Garciaparra B/X)	.75
199	Checklist (Scott Rolen B/X)	.35
200	Checklist (Jose Cruz Jr. B/X)	.25
201	Al Martin B/X	.25

Die-Cut

This parallel set adds a die-cut to the Fractal Matrix set. Three different die-cut versions were created: X-axis, Y-axis and Z-axis. An X-axis die-cut was added to 75 bronze, 20 silver and 5 gold cards. A Y-axis die-cut was added to 20 bronze, 30 silver and 10 gold cards. Of the 40 Z-axis cards, 5 are bronze, 10 silver and 25 gold. Stated print runs were 400 of each X-axis card; 200 Y and 100 Z.

		NM/M
Complete Set (200):		950.00
Common X-Axis:		2.00
Common Y-Axis:		3.00
Common Z-Axis:		5.00
1	Rusty Greer G/Z	5.00
2	Tino Martinez G/Z	5.00
3	Bobby Bonilla S/Y	3.00
4	Jason Giambi S/Y	7.50
5	Matt Morris S/Y	3.00
6	Craig Counsell B/X	2.00
7	Reggie Jefferson B/X	2.00
8	Brian Rose S/Y	3.00
9	Ruben Rivera B/X	2.00
10	Shawn Estes S/Y	3.00
11	Tony Gwynn G/Z	35.00
12	Jeff Abbott B/Y	3.00
13	Jose Cruz Jr. G/Z	5.00
14	Francisco Cordova B/X	2.00
15	Ryan Klesko B/X	2.00
16	Tim Salmon G/Y	4.00
17	Brett Tomko B/X	2.00
18	Matt Williams S/Y	3.00
19	Joe Carter B/X	2.00
20	Harold Baines B/X	2.00
21	Gary Sheffield S/Z	15.00
22	Charles Johnson S/X	2.00
23	Aaron Boone B/X	2.00
24	Eddie Murray G/Y	10.00
25	Matt Stairs B/X	2.00
26	David Cone B/X	2.00
27	Jon Nunnally B/X	2.00
28	Chris Stynes B/X	2.00
29	Enrique Wilson B/Y	3.00
30	Randy Johnson S/Z	30.00
31	Garret Anderson S/Y	3.00
32	Manny Ramirez G/Z	30.00
33	Jeff Suppan S/X	2.00
34	Rickey Henderson B/X	6.00
35	Scott Spiezio B/X	2.00
36	Rondell White S/Y	3.00
37	Todd Greene S/Z	5.00
38	Delino DeShields B/X	2.00
39	Kevin Brown S/Y	2.00
40	Chili Davis B/X	2.00
41	Jimmy Key B/X	2.00
42	Mike Mussina G/Y	7.50
43	Joe Randa B/X	2.00
44	Chan Ho Park S/Z	5.00
45	Brad Radke B/X	2.00
46	Geronimo Berroa B/X	2.00
47	Wade Boggs S/Y	12.00
48	Kevin Appier B/X	2.00
49	Moises Alou S/Y	3.00
50	David Justice G/Y	3.00
51	Ivan Rodriguez G/Z	25.00
52	J.T. Snow B/X	2.00
53	Brian Giles B/X	2.00
54	Will Clark S/Y	4.00
55	Justin Thompson S/Y	3.00
56	Javier Lopez S/X	2.00
57	Hideki Irabu S/Y	5.00
58	Mark Grudzielanek B/X	2.00
59	Abraham Nunez S/X	2.00
60	Todd Hollandsworth B/X	2.00
61	Jay Bell B/Y	2.00
62	Nomar Garciaparra G/Z	40.00
63	Vinny Castilla B/Y	3.00

ABBREVIATIONS

CC - Curtain Calls
GLR - Gold Leaf Rookies
GLS - Gold Leaf Stars

65	Lou Collier B/Y	3.00
66	Kevin Orie S/X	2.00
67	John Valentin B/X	2.00
68	Robin Ventura B/X	2.00
69	Denny Neagle B/X	2.00
70	Tony Womack S/Y	3.00
71	Dennis Reyes S/Y	3.00
72	Wally Joyner B/X	2.00
73	Kevin Brown B/Y	2.00
74	Ray Durham B/X	2.00
75	Mike Cameron S/Z	2.00
76	Dante Bichette B/X	2.00
77	Jose Guillen G/Y	3.00
78	Carlos Delgado B/Y	5.00
79	Paul Molitor G/Y	30.00
80	Jason Kendall B/X	2.00
81	Mark Belhorn B/X	2.00
82	Damian Jackson B/X	2.00
83	Bill Mueller B/X	2.00
84	Kevin Young B/X	2.00
85	Curt Schilling B/X	3.00
86	Jeffrey Hammonds B/X	2.00
87	Sandy Alomar Jr. S/Y	3.00
88	Bartolo Colon B/Y	3.00
89	Wilton Guerrero B/Y	3.00
90	Bernie Williams S/Y	4.00
91	Deion Sanders S/Y	3.00
92	Mike Piazza G/X	20.00
93	Butch Huskey B/X	2.00
94	Edgardo Alfonzo S/X	2.00
95	Alan Benes S/Y	3.00
96	Craig Biggio S/Y	3.00
97	Mark Grace S/Y	4.00
98	Shawn Green S/Y	5.00
99	Derrek Lee S/Y	3.00
100	Ken Griffey Jr. G/Z	40.00
101	Tim Raines B/X	2.00
102	Pokey Reese S/Y	3.00
103	Lee Stevens B/X	2.00
104	Shannon Stewart S/Y	3.00
105	John Smoltz S/Y	3.00
106	Frank Thomas G/X	6.00
107	Jeff Fassero B/X	2.00
108	Jay Buhner B/Y	3.00
109	Jose Canseco B/X	4.50
110	Omar Vizquel B/X	2.00
111	Travis Fryman B/X	2.00
112	Dave Nilsson B/X	2.00
113	John Olerud B/X	2.00
114	Larry Walker G/Z	5.00
115	Jim Edmonds S/Y	3.00
116	Bobby Higginson S/X	2.00
117	Todd Hundley S/X	2.00
118	Paul O'Neill B/X	2.00
119	Bip Roberts B/X	2.00
120	Ismael Valdes B/X	2.00
121	Pedro Martinez B/X	10.00
122	Jeff Cirillo B/X	2.00
123	Andy Benes B/X	2.00
124	Bobby Jones B/X	2.00
125	Brian Hunter B/X	2.00
126	Darryl Kile B/X	2.00
127	Pat Hentgen B/X	2.00
128	Marquis Grissom B/X	2.00
129	Eric Davis B/X	2.00
130	Chipper Jones G/Z	35.00
131	Edgar Martinez S/Z	3.00
132	Andy Pettitte G/Z	10.00
133	Cal Ripken Jr. G/X	25.00
134	Scott Rolen G/Z	25.00
135	Ron Coomer B/X	2.00
136	Luis Castillo B/Y	3.00
137	Fred McGriff B/Y	3.00
138	Neifi Perez S/Y	3.00
139	Eric Karros B/X	2.00
140	Alex Fernandez B/X	2.00
141	Jason Dickson B/X	2.00
142	Lance Johnson B/X	2.00
143	Ray Lankford B/Y	3.00
144	Sammy Sosa G/Y	20.00
145	Eric Young B/Y	3.00
146	Bubba Trammell S/Y	3.00
147	Todd Walker S/Y	3.00
148	Mo Vaughn S/X/CC	3.00
149	Jeff Bagwell S/X/CC	6.00
150	Kenny Lofton S/X/CC	2.00
151	Raul Mondesi S/X/CC	2.00
152	Mike Piazza S/X/CC	20.00
153	Chipper Jones S/X/CC	10.00
154	Larry Walker S/X/CC	2.00
155	Greg Maddux S/X/CC	10.00
156	Ken Griffey Jr. S/X/CC	15.00
157	Frank Thomas S/X/CC	6.00
158	Darin Erstad B/Z/GLS	20.00
159	Roberto Alomar B/Y/GLS	4.00
160	Albert Belle G/Y/GLS	3.50
161	Jim Thome G/Y/GLS	3.00
162	Tony Clark G/Y/GLS	3.00
163	Chuck Knoblauch B/Y/GLS	3.00
164	Derek Jeter G/Z/GLS	50.00
165	Alex Rodriguez G/Z/GLS	45.00
166	Tony Gwynn B/X/GLS	37.50
167	Roger Clemens G/Z/GLS	37.50
168	Barry Larkin B/Y/GLS	3.00
169	Andres Galarraga B/Y/GLS	3.00
170	Vladimir Guerrero G/Z/GLS	30.00
171	Mark McGwire B/Z/GLS	45.00

172	Barry Bonds B/Z/GLS	50.00
173	Juan Gonzalez G/Z/GLS	30.00
174	Andruw Jones G/Z/GLS	30.00
175	Paul Molitor B/X/GLS	6.00
176	Hideo Nomo B/Z/GLS	30.00
177	Cal Ripken Jr. B/X/GLS	20.00
178	Brad Fullmer S/Z/GLR	5.00
179	Jaret Wright G/Z/GLR	5.00
180	Bobby Estalella B/Y/GLR	3.00
181	Ben Grieve G/X/GLR	5.00
182	Paul Konerko G/Z/GLR	6.00
183	David Ortiz G/Z/GLR	7.50
184	Todd Helton G/X/GLR	6.00
185	Juan Encarnacion G/Z/GLR	5.00
186	Miguel Tejada G/Z/GLR	10.00
187	Jacob Cruz B/Y/GLR	3.00
188	Mark Kotsay G/Z/GLR	5.00
189	Fernando Tatis S/Z/GLR	3.00
190	Ricky Ledee S/Y/GLR	3.00
191	Richard Hidalgo S/Y/GLR	3.00
192	Richie Sexson S/Y/GLR	3.00
193	Luis Ordaz B/X/GLR	2.00
194	Eli Marrero S/Z/GLR	2.00
195	Livan Hernandez S/Z/GLR	5.00
196	Homer Bush B/X/GLR	2.00
197	Raul Ibanez B/X/GLR	2.00
198	Checklist (Nomar Garciaparra B/X)	
199	Checklist (Scott Rolen B/X)	
200	Checklist (Jose Cruz Jr. B/X)	2.00
201	Al Martin B/X	2.00

Diamond Axis

Production of this blue-foil finished top-shelf parallel within the 1998 Leaf set was limited to 50 serially numbered examples of each card.

	NM/M
Common Player:	7.50
Stars/Rookies:	20X
SP (148-177):	12X

1998 Leaf Limited Star Factor Sample

This sample card was intended to preview the 1998 Leaf Limited issue which was never released due to Pinnacle's bankruptcy. The card is printed with a refractive foil background and hundreds of embossed stars front and back. The back has a large "SAMPLE" overprint and is numbered "000."

		NM/M
000	Frank Thomas	4.00

1998 Leaf Rookies & Stars

This 339-card set consists of three subsets: Power Tools, Lineup Card and Rookies. Fronts feature full-bleed photos and silver-foil graphics. Backs have complete year-by-year statistics and a small photo. The base set has short-printed base cards, numbers 131-230, 301-339, which are seeded 1:2 packs. Rookies and Stars has two parallels to the base set: True Blue and Longevity. True Blue's feature blue foil stamping and are each numbered "1 Of 500" on the card back. Longevity's are printed on a full-foiled card front with gold foil stamping and limited to 50 serially numbered sets.

		NM/M
Complete Set (339):		200.00
Common Player:		.10
Common SP (131-230):		.20
Common SP (301-339):		.50
Inserted 1:2		
True Blues:		12X
SP True Blues:		2X
Production 500 sets		
Longevitys:		50X
SP Longevitys:		15X
Production 50 sets		
Pack (9):		7.50
Wax Box (24):		150.00
1	Andy Pettitte	.30
2	Roberto Alomar	.20
3	Randy Johnson	.75
4	Manny Ramirez	.75
5	Paul Molitor	.50
6	Mike Mussina	.50
7	Jim Thome	.65
8	Tino Martinez	.50
9	Gary Sheffield	.50
10	Chuck Knoblauch	.10
11	Bernie Williams	.10
12	Tim Salmon	.10
13	Sammy Sosa	1.25
14	Wade Boggs	1.00
15	Andres Galarraga	.10
16	Pedro Martinez	.75
17	David Justice	.10
18	Chan Ho Park	.10
19	Jay Buhner	.10
20	Ryan Klesko	.10
21	Barry Larkin	.10
22	Will Clark	.15
23	Raul Mondesi	.10
24	Rickey Henderson	.75
25	Jim Edmonds	.10
26	Ken Griffey Jr.	1.25
27	Frank Thomas	.75
28	Cal Ripken Jr.	2.00
29	Alex Rodriguez	1.50
30	Mike Piazza	1.25
31	Greg Maddux	1.00
32	Chipper Jones	1.00
33	Tony Gwynn	1.00
34	Derek Jeter	2.00
35	Jeff Bagwell	.75
36	Juan Gonzalez	1.00
37	Nomar Garciaparra	1.00
38	Andruw Jones	.75
39	Hideo Nomo	.60
40	Roger Clemens	1.25
41	Mark McGwire	1.50
42	Scott Rolen	.60
43	Vladimir Guerrero	.75
44	Barry Bonds	2.00
45	Darin Erstad	.25
46	Albert Belle	.10
47	Kenny Lofton	.10
48	Mo Vaughn	.10
49	Ivan Rodriguez	.60
50	Jose Cruz Jr.	.10
51	Tony Clark	.10
52	Larry Walker	.10
53	Mark Grace	.10
54	Edgar Martinez	.10
55	Fred McGriff	.10
56	Rafael Palmeiro	.60
57	Matt Williams	.10

58	Craig Biggio	.10
59	Ken Caminiti	.10
60	Jose Canseco	.40
61	Brady Anderson	.10
62	Moises Alou	.10
63	Justin Thompson	.10
64	John Smoltz	.50
65	Carlos Delgado	.50
66	J.T. Snow	.10
67	Jason Giambi	.50
68	Garret Anderson	.10
69	Rondell White	.10
70	Eric Karros	.10
71	Javier Lopez	.10
72	Pat Hentgen	.10
73	Dante Bichette	.10
74	Charles Johnson	.10
75	Tom Glavine	.30
76	Rusty Greer	.10
77	Travis Fryman	.10
78	Todd Hundley	.10
79	Ray Lankford	.10
80	Denny Neagle	.10
81	Henry Rodriguez	.10
82	Sandy Alomar Jr.	.10
83	Robin Ventura	.10
84	John Olerud	.10
85	Omar Vizquel	.10
86	Darren Dreifort	.10
87	Kevin Brown	.10
88	Curt Schilling	.35
89	Francisco Cordova	.10
90	Brad Radke	.10
91	David Cone	.10
92	Paul O'Neill	.10
93	Vinny Castilla	.10
94	Marquis Grissom	.10
95	Brian Hunter	.10
96	Kevin Appier	.10
97	Bobby Bonilla	.10
98	Eric Young	.10
99	Jason Kendall	.10
100	Shawn Green	.40
101	Edgardo Alfonzo	.10
102	Alan Benes	.10
103	Bobby Higginson	.10
104	Todd Greene	.10
105	Jose Guillen	.15
106	Neifi Perez	.10
107	Edgar Renteria	.10
108	Chris Stynes	.10
109	Todd Walker	.10
110	Brian Jordan	.10
111	Joe Carter	.10
112	Ellis Burks	.10
113	Brett Tomko	.10
114	Mike Cameron	.10
115	Shannon Stewart	.10
116	Kevin Orie	.10
117	Brian Giles	.10
118	Hideki Irabu	.10
119	Delino DeShields	.10
120	David Segui	.10
121	Dustin Hermanson	.10
122	Kevin Young	.10
123	Jay Bell	.10
124	Doug Glanville	.10
125	John Roskos RC	.10
126	Damon Hollins RC	.10
127	Matt Stairs	.10
128	Cliff Floyd	.10
129	Derek Bell	.10
130	Darryl Strawberry	.10
131	Ken Griffey Jr. (Power Tools)	1.25
132	Tim Salmon (Power Tools)	.20
133	Manny Ramirez (Power Tools)	.75
134	Paul Konerko (Power Tools)	.30
135	Frank Thomas (Power Tools)	.75
136	Todd Helton (Power Tools)	.75
137	Larry Walker (Power Tools)	.20
138	Mo Vaughn (Power Tools)	.20
139	Travis Lee (Power Tools)	.20
140	Ivan Rodriguez (Power Tools)	.60
141	Ben Grieve (Power Tools)	.20
142	Brad Fullmer (Power Tools)	.20
143	Alex Rodriguez (Power Tools)	1.50
144	Mike Piazza (Power Tools)	1.25
145	Greg Maddux (Power Tools)	1.00
146	Chipper Jones (Power Tools)	1.00
147	Kenny Lofton (Power Tools)	.20
148	Albert Belle (Power Tools)	.20
149	Barry Bonds (Power Tools)	2.00
150	Vladimir Guerrero (Power Tools)	.75
151	Tony Gwynn (Power Tools)	1.00
152	Derek Jeter (Power Tools)	2.00

#	Player	Price
153	Jeff Bagwell (Power Tools)	.75
154	Juan Gonzalez (Power Tools)	.60
155	Nomar Garciaparra (Power Tools)	1.00
156	Andruw Jones (Power Tools)	.75
157	Hideo Nomo (Power Tools)	.60
158	Roger Clemens (Power Tools)	1.25
159	Mark McGwire (Power Tools)	1.50
160	Scott Rolen (Power Tools)	.60
161	Travis Lee (Team Line-Up)	.20
162	Ben Grieve (Team Line-Up)	.20
163	Jose Guillen (Team Line-Up)	.20
164	John Olerud (Team Line-Up)	.20
165	Kevin Appier (Team Line-Up)	.20
166	Marquis Grissom (Team Line-Up)	.20
167	Rusty Greer (Team Line-Up)	.20
168	Ken Caminiti (Team Line-Up)	.20
169	Craig Biggio (Team Line-Up)	.20
170	Ken Griffey Jr. (Team Line-Up)	1.25
171	Larry Walker (Team Line-Up)	.20
172	Barry Larkin (Team Line-Up)	.20
173	Andres Galarraga (Team Line-Up)	.20
174	Wade Boggs (Team Line-Up)	1.00
175	Sammy Sosa (Team Line-Up)	1.25
176	Mike Piazza (Team Line-Up)	1.50
177	Jim Thome (Team Line-Up)	.60
178	Paul Molitor (Team Line-Up)	.75
179	Tony Clark (Team Line-Up)	.20
180	Jose Cruz Jr. (Team Line-Up)	.20
181	Darin Erstad (Team Line-Up)	.25
182	Barry Bonds (Team Line-Up)	2.00
183	Vladimir Guerrero (Team Line-Up)	.75
184	Scott Rolen (Team Line-Up)	.60
185	Mark McGwire (Team Line-Up)	1.50
186	Nomar Garciaparra (Team Line-Up)	1.00
187	Gary Sheffield (Team Line-Up)	.50
188	Cal Ripken Jr. (Team Line-Up)	2.00
189	Frank Thomas (Team Line-Up)	.75
190	Andy Petitte	.30
191	Paul Konerko	.35
192	Todd Helton	1.50
193	Mark Kotsay	.20
194	Brad Fullmer	.20
195	Kevin Millwood RC	8.00
196	David Ortiz	3.00
197	Kerry Wood	1.50
198	Miguel Tejada	.40
199	Fernando Tatis	.20
200	Jaret Wright	.20
201	Ben Grieve	.20
202	Travis Lee	.20
203	Wes Helms	.20
204	Geoff Jenkins	.20
205	Russell Branyan	.20
206	Esteban Yan RC	.20
207	Ben Ford RC	.20
208	Rich Butler RC	.75
209	Ryan Jackson RC	.50
210	A.J. Hinch	.20
211	Magglio Ordonez RC	15.00
212	David Dellucci RC	.50
213	Billy McMillon	.20
214	Mike Lowell RC	6.00
215	Todd Erdos RC	.20
216	Carlos Mendoza RC	.25
217	Frank Catalanotto RC	.75
218	Julio Ramirez RC	.20
219	John Halama RC	.50
220	Wilson Delgado	.20
221	Mike Judd RC	.20
222	Rolando Arrojo RC	1.00
223	Jason LaRue RC	.50
224	Manny Aybar RC	.20
225	Jorge Velandia	.20
226	Mike Kinkade RC	.75
227	Carlos Lee RC	20.00
228	Bobby Hughes	.20
229	Ryan Christenson RC	.50
230	Masato Yoshii RC	1.00
231	Richard Hidalgo	.10
232	Rafael Medina	.10
233	Damian Jackson	.10
234	Derek Lowe	.15
235	Mario Valdez	.10
236	Eli Marrero	.10
237	Juan Encarnacion	.10
238	Livan Hernandez	.10
239	Bruce Chen	.10
240	Eric Milton	.10
241	Jason Varitek	.10
242	Scott Elarton	.10
243	Manuel Barrios RC	.10
244	Mike Caruso	.10
245	Tom Evans	.10
246	Pat Cline	.10
247	Matt Clement	.15
248	Karim Garcia	.15
249	Richie Sexson	.10
250	Sidney Ponson	.10
251	Randall Simon	.10
252	Tony Saunders	.10
253	Javier Valentin	.10
254	Danny Clyburn	.10
255	Michael Coleman	.10
256	Hanley Frias RC	.10
257	Miguel Cairo	.10
258	Rob Stanifer RC	.10
259	Lou Collier	.10
260	Abraham Nunez	.10
261	Ricky Ledee	.10
262	Carl Pavano	.10
263	Derrek Lee	.50
264	Jeff Abbott	.10
265	Bob Abreu	.10
266	Bartolo Colon	.10
267	Mike Drumright	.10
268	Daryle Ward	.10
269	Gabe Alvarez	.10
270	Josh Booty	.10
271	Damian Moss	.10
272	Brian Rose	.10
273	Jarrod Washburn	.10
274	Bobby Estalella	.10
275	Enrique Wilson	.10
276	Derrick Gibson	.10
277	Ken Cloude	.10
278	Kevin Witt	.10
279	Donnie Sadler	.10
280	Sean Casey	.20
281	Jacob Cruz	.10
282	Ron Wright	.10
283	Jeremi Gonzalez	.10
284	Desi Relaford	.10
285	Bobby Smith	.10
286	Javier Vazquez	.10
287	Steve Woodard RC	.20
288	Greg Norton	.10
289	Cliff Politte	.10
290	Felix Heredia	.10
291	Braden Looper	.10
292	Felix Martinez	.10
293	Brian Meadows	.10
294	Edwin Diaz	.10
295	Pat Watkins	.10
296	Marc Pisciotta RC	.10
297	Rick Gorecki	.10
298	DaRond Stovall	.10
299	Andy Larkin	.10
300	Felix Rodriguez	.10
301	Blake Stein	.50
302	John Rocker RC	1.00
303	Justin Baughman RC	.50
304	Jesus Sanchez RC	.50
305	Randy Winn	.50
306	Lou Merloni	.50
307	Jim Parque RC	1.00
308	Dennis Reyes	.50
309	Orlando Hernandez RC	10.00
310	Jason Johnson	.50
311	Torii Hunter	.50
312	Mike Piazza	2.50
313	Mike Frank RC	.50
314	Troy Glaus RC	60.00
315	Jin Cho RC	.75
316	Ruben Mateo RC	1.00
317	Ryan Minor RC	1.00
318	Aramis Ramirez RC	.75
319	Adrian Beltre	1.00
320	Matt Anderson RC	1.00
321	Gabe Kapler RC	2.00
322	Jeremy Giambi RC	1.00
323	Carlos Beltran	.50
324	Dermal Brown	.50
325	Ben Davis	.50
326	Eric Chavez	1.00
327	Bob Howry RC	1.00
328	Roy Halladay	1.00
329	George Lombard	.50
330	Michael Barrett	.50
331	Fernando Seguignol RC	1.00
332	J.D. Drew RC	25.00
333	Odalis Perez RC	4.00
334	Alex Cora RC	1.00
335	Placido Polanco RC	8.00
336	Armando Rios RC	.50
337	Sammy Sosa (HR commemorative)	3.00
338	Mark McGwire (HR commemorative)	4.00
339	Sammy Sosa, Mark McGwire (Checklist)	4.00

Longevity

Only 50 sets of this parallel edition were issued. Each card is serially numbered on back. Fronts are printed with gold foil background and have LONGEVITY printed at top. Special Longevity holographic 1 of 1 cards exist, but cannot be priced due to rarity.

	NM/M
Common Player:	3.00
Stars:	50X
SP Stars (131-230):	15X
SP Stars (301-339):	5X

True Blue

This parallel edition of the Rookies & Stars base set is labeled at top-back "1 of 500." The parallels feature blue foil graphic highlights on front with TRUE BLUE at top.

	NM/M
Common Player:	1.00
Stars:	12X
SP Stars (131-230; 301-339):	2X

Cross Training

This 10-card insert set highlights players who excel at multiple aspects of the game. Card fronts are full-foiled and sequentially numbered on the card back to 1,000.

		NM/M
Complete Set (10):		30.00
Common Player:		1.50
Production 1,000 Sets		
1	Kenny Lofton	1.50
2	Ken Griffey Jr.	5.00
3	Alex Rodriguez	6.00
4	Greg Maddux	4.00
5	Barry Bonds	7.50
6	Ivan Rodriguez	2.50
7	Chipper Jones	4.00
8	Jeff Bagwell	3.00
9	Nomar Garciaparra	4.00
10	Derek Jeter	7.50

Crusade

This 30-card set is a continuation of this cross-brand insert. Cards are printed on a holographic green foil front and limited to 250 serial numbered sets. Two parallels are also randomly seeded: Purple and Red. Purples have purple holographic foil fronts and limited to 100 serial numbered sets. Reds are printed on red holographic foil fronts and limited to 25 serial numbered sets.

		NM/M
Complete Green Set (30):		225.00
Common Player:		7.50
Production 250 Sets		
Purples (100 Sets):		3X
Reds (25 Sets):		10X
101	Richard Hidalgo	7.50
102	Paul Konerko	15.00
103	Miguel Tejada	15.00
104	Fernando Tatis	7.50
105	Travis Lee	7.50
106	Wes Helms	7.50
107	Rich Butler	7.50
108	Mark Kotsay	7.50
109	Eli Marrero	7.50
110	David Ortiz	15.00
111	Juan Encarnacion	7.50
112	Jaret Wright	7.50
113	Livan Hernandez	7.50
114	Ron Wright	7.50
115	Ryan Christenson	7.50
116	Eric Milton	7.50
117	Brad Fullmer	7.50
118	Karim Garcia	10.00
119	Abraham Nunez	7.50
120	Ricky Ledee	7.50
121	Carl Pavano	7.50
122	Derrek Lee	15.00
123	A.J. Hinch	7.50
124	Brian Rose	7.50
125	Bobby Estalella	7.50
126	Kevin Millwood	10.00
127	Kerry Wood	30.00
128	Sean Casey	12.50
129	Russell Branyan	7.50
130	Magglio Ordonez	20.00

Extreme Measures

These inserts are printed on a full-foiled card front. Each card highlights an outstanding statistic for the featured player and is sequentially numbered to 1,000, minus the number of die-cut versions produced for each.

		NM/M
Complete Set (10):		50.00
Common Player:		3.00
1	Ken Griffey Jr./944	7.50
2	Frank Thomas/653	5.00
3	Tony Gwynn/628	6.00
4	Mark McGwire/942	9.00
5	Larry Walker/280	3.00
6	Mike Piazza/960	7.50
7	Roger Clemens/708	6.50
8	Greg Maddux/980	5.00
9	Jeff Bagwell/873	4.50
10	Nomar Garciaparra/989	6.50

Extreme Measures Die-Cuts

Each card highlights an outstanding statistic for each featured player, is die-cut and

serially numbered to the limit of the particular statistic as shown.

		NM/M
Complete Set (10):		375.00
Common Player:		2.50
1	Ken Griffey Jr./56	65.00
2	Frank Thomas/347	11.00
3	Tony Gwynn/372	13.50
4	Mark McGwire/58	80.00
5	Larry Walker/720	2.50
6	Mike Piazza	75.00
7	Roger Clemens/292	16.00
8	Greg Maddux/20	100.00
9	Jeff Bagwell/127	20.00
10	Nomar Garciaparra/11	125.00

Freshman Orientation

Card fronts are printed on holographic foil with silver foil stamping and feature top prospects. Card backs highlight the date of the featured player's Major League debut, have a small photo and are serially numbered to 5,000 sets. Each card was also issued in an appropriately labeled sample version.

		NM/M
Complete Set (20):		20.00
Common Player:		.75
Production 5,000 Sets		
Samples:		1X
1	Todd Helton	4.00
2	Ben Grieve	.75
3	Travis Lee	.75
4	Paul Konerko	1.50
5	Jaret Wright	.75
6	Livan Hernandez	.75
7	Brad Fullmer	.75
8	Carl Pavano	.75
9	Richard Hidalgo	.75
10	Miguel Tejada	1.50
11	Mark Kotsay	.75
12	David Ortiz	1.50
13	Juan Encarnacion	.75
14	Fernando Tatis	.75
15	Kevin Millwood	1.50
16	Kerry Wood	2.50
17	Magglio Ordonez	1.50
18	Derrek Lee	1.50
19	Jose Cruz Jr.	.75
20	A.J. Hinch	.75

Great American Heroes

Card fronts are stamped with a holographic silver foil and done on a horizontal format. Card backs have a photo and are serially numbered to 2,500. Each card was also produced in an appropriately marked sample version.

		NM/M
Complete Set (20):		35.00
Common Player:		.75
Production 2,500 Sets		
Samples:		1X
1	Frank Thomas	1.75
2	Cal Ripken Jr.	5.00
3	Ken Griffey Jr.	3.00
4	Alex Rodriguez	4.00
5	Greg Maddux	2.25
6	Mike Piazza	3.00
7	Chipper Jones	2.25
8	Tony Gwynn	2.25
9	Jeff Bagwell	1.75
10	Juan Gonzalez	1.25
11	Hideo Nomo	1.25
12	Roger Clemens	2.50
13	Mark McGwire	4.00
14	Barry Bonds	5.00
15	Kenny Lofton	.75
16	Larry Walker	.75
17	Paul Molitor	1.75
18	Wade Boggs	2.25
19	Barry Larkin	.75
20	Andres Galarraga	.75

Greatest Hits

These inserts feature holographic silver foil stamping on the card front done on a horizontal format. Card backs have a photo and are serially numbered to 2,500.

		NM/M
Complete Set (20):		30.00
Common Player:		.50
Production 2,500 Sets		
1	Ken Griffey Jr.	2.50
2	Frank Thomas	1.50
3	Cal Ripken Jr.	4.00
4	Alex Rodriguez	3.00
5	Ben Grieve	.50
6	Mike Piazza	2.50
7	Chipper Jones	2.00
8	Tony Gwynn	2.00
9	Derek Jeter	4.00
10	Jeff Bagwell	1.50
11	Tino Martinez	.50
12	Juan Gonzalez	.75
13	Nomar Garciaparra	2.00
14	Mark McGwire	3.00
15	Scott Rolen	.75
16	David Justice	.50
17	Darin Erstad	.75
18	Mo Vaughn	.50
19	Ivan Rodriguez	1.00
20	Travis Lee	.50

Home Run Derby

This 20-card set spotlights the top home run hitters on a bronze full-foiled card front. Card backs have a portrait photo and are serially numbered to 2,500.

		NM/M
Complete Set (20):		30.00
Common Player:		.75
Production 2,500 Sets		
1	Tino Martinez	.75
2	Jim Thome	1.25
3	Larry Walker	.75
4	Tony Clark	.75
5	Jose Cruz Jr.	.75
6	Barry Bonds	5.00
7	Scott Rolen	1.00
8	Paul Konerko	1.25
9	Travis Lee	.75
10	Todd Helton	1.25
11	Mark McGwire	4.00
12	Andruw Jones	1.50
13	Nomar Garciaparra	2.50
14	Juan Gonzalez	1.00
15	Jeff Bagwell	1.50
16	Chipper Jones	2.50
17	Mike Piazza	3.00
18	Frank Thomas	1.50
19	Ken Griffey Jr.	3.00
20	Albert Belle	.75

ML Hard Drives

Card fronts are stamped with silver holographic foil. Card backs detail to which field (left, center and right) the featured player hit each of his singles, doubles, triples and home runs. Each card is serially numbered to 2,500. Each card was also produced in an appropriately marked sample version.

	NM/M
Complete Set (20):	30.00
Common Player:	.70
Production 2,500 Sets	
Samples:	1X
1 Jeff Bagwell	1.50
2 Juan Gonzalez	1.00
3 Nomar Garciaparra	2.00
4 Ken Griffey Jr.	3.00
5 Frank Thomas	1.50
6 Cal Ripken Jr.	4.50
7 Alex Rodriguez	3.50
8 Mike Piazza	3.00
9 Chipper Jones	2.00
10 Tony Gwynn	2.00
11 Derek Jeter	4.50
12 Mo Vaughn	.75
13 Ben Grieve	.75
14 Manny Ramirez	1.50
15 Vladimir Guerrero	1.50
16 Scott Rolen	1.00
17 Darin Erstad	.75
18 Kenny Lofton	.75
19 Brad Fullmer	.75
20 David Justice	.75

MVPs

This 20-card set is printed on a full silver-foil card stock and sequentially numbered to 5,000. The first 500 of each card is treated with a "Pennant Edition" logo and unique color coating.

	NM/M
Complete Set (20):	35.00
Common Player:	.50
Production 4,500 Sets	
Pennant Editions:	2X
Production 500 Sets	
1 Frank Thomas	2.00
2 Chuck Knoblauch	.50
3 Cal Ripken Jr.	5.00
4 Alex Rodriguez	4.00
5 Ivan Rodriguez	1.50
6 Albert Belle	.50
7 Ken Griffey Jr.	3.00
8 Juan Gonzalez	1.50
9 Roger Clemens	2.75
10 Mo Vaughn	.50
11 Jeff Bagwell	2.00
12 Craig Biggio	.50
13 Chipper Jones	2.50
14 Barry Larkin	.50
15 Mike Piazza	3.00
16 Barry Bonds	5.00
17 Andruw Jones	2.50
18 Tony Gwynn	2.50
19 Greg Maddux	2.50
20 Mark McGwire	4.00

Standing Ovation

Card fronts are stamped with silver holographic foil and card backs have a small

photo of the featured player and are serially numbered to 5,000. Each card was also produced in an appropriately labeled sample version.

	NM/M
Complete Set (10):	12.50
Common Player:	.75
Production 5,000 Sets	
Samples:	1X
1 Barry Bonds	3.00
2 Mark McGwire	2.50
3 Ken Griffey Jr.	2.00
4 Frank Thomas	1.00
5 Tony Gwynn	1.50
6 Cal Ripken Jr.	3.00
7 Greg Maddux	1.50
8 Roger Clemens	1.75
9 Paul Molitor	1.00
10 Ivan Rodriguez	.75

Ticket Masters

Card fronts are printed on a full-foiled card stock with silver foil stamping and have a photo of one of the two players featured from the same team. Card backs have a photo of the other featured player and are serially numbered to 2,500. The first 250 of each card are die-cut.

	NM/M
Complete Set (20):	32.50
Common Card:	.50
Production 2,250 Sets	
Die-Cut:	1.5X
Production 250 Sets	
1 Ken Griffey Jr., Alex Rodriguez	4.00
2 Frank Thomas, Albert Belle	1.50
3 Cal Ripken Jr., Roberto Alomar	5.00
4 Greg Maddux, Chipper Jones	2.00
5 Tony Gwynn, Ken Caminiti	2.00
6 Derek Jeter, Andy Pettitte	5.00
7 Jeff Bagwell, Craig Biggio	1.50
8 Juan Gonzalez, Ivan Rodriguez	1.25
9 Nomar Garciaparra, Mo Vaughn	2.00
10 Vladimir Guerrero, Brad Fullmer	1.50
11 Andruw Jones, Andres Galarraga	1.50
12 Tino Martinez, Chuck Knoblauch	.50
13 Raul Mondesi, Paul Konerko	.75
14 Roger Clemens, Jose Cruz Jr.	2.25
15 Mark McGwire, Brian Jordan	4.00
16 Kenny Lofton, Manny Ramirez	1.50
17 Larry Walker, Todd Helton	1.25
18 Darin Erstad, Tim Salmon	.75

19 Travis Lee, Matt Williams	.50
20 Ben Grieve, Jason Giambi	1.00

2001 Leaf Certified Materials

	NM/M
Complete Set (160):	.40
Common Player:	.40
Common SP (111-160):	10.00
Production 200	
Pack (5):	12.00
Box (12):	125.00
1 Alex Rodriguez	5.00
2 Barry Bonds	6.00
3 Cal Ripken Jr.	6.00
4 Chipper Jones	3.00
5 Derek Jeter	6.00
6 Troy Glaus	2.00
7 Frank Thomas	2.00
8 Greg Maddux	3.00
9 Ivan Rodriguez	2.00
10 Jeff Bagwell	2.00
11 Eric Karros	.40
12 Todd Helton	2.00
13 Ken Griffey Jr.	4.00
14 Manny Ramirez	2.00
15 Mark McGwire	5.00
16 Mike Piazza	4.00
17 Nomar Garciaparra	4.00
18 Pedro Martinez	2.00
19 Randy Johnson	2.00
20 Rick Ankiel	.75
21 Rickey Henderson	1.50
22 Roger Clemens	3.50
23 Sammy Sosa	4.00
24 Tony Gwynn	3.00
25 Vladimir Guerrero	2.00
26 Kazuhiro Sasaki	.40
27 Roberto Alomar	.75
28 Barry Zito	.60
29 Pat Burrell	1.00
30 Harold Baines	.40
31 Carlos Delgado	1.00
32 J.D. Drew	1.00
33 Jim Edmonds	.60
34 Darin Erstad	.50
35 Jason Giambi	1.00
36 Tom Glavine	.75
37 Juan Gonzalez	2.00
38 Mark Grace	.60
39 Shawn Green	1.00
40 Tim Hudson	.60
41 Andruw Jones	1.50
42 Jeff Kent	.40
43 Barry Larkin	.40
44 Rafael Furcal	.40
45 Mike Mussina	1.00
46 Hideo Nomo	1.50
47 Rafael Palmeiro	1.25
48 Scott Rolen	1.00
49 Gary Sheffield	.60
50 Bernie Williams	.60
51 Bobby Abreu	.40
52 Edgardo Alfonzo	.40
53 Edgar Martinez	.40
54 Magglio Ordonez	.60
55 Kerry Wood	1.25
56 Adrian Beltre	.75
57 Lance Berkman	.40
58 Kevin Brown	.40
59 Sean Casey	.60
60 Eric Chavez	.60
61 Bartolo Colon	.60
62 Johnny Damon	.60
63 Jermaine Dye	.40
64 Juan Encarnacion	.40
65 Carl Everett	.40
66 Brian Giles	.40
67 Mike Hampton	.40
68 Richard Hidalgo	.40
69 Geoff Jenkins	.40
70 Jacque Jones	.40
71 Jason Kendall	.40
72 Ryan Klesko	.40
73 Chan Ho Park	.40
74 Richie Sexson	.40
75 Mike Sweeney	.40
76 Fernando Tatis	.40
77 Miguel Tejada	.60
78 Jose Vidro	.40
79 Larry Walker	.40
80 Preston Wilson	.40
81 Craig Biggio	.40
82 Fred McGriff	.40
83 Jim Thome	1.50

84 Garret Anderson	.40
85 Russell Branyan	.40
86 Tony Batista	.40
87 Terrence Long	.40
88 Deion Sanders	.40
89 Rusty Greer	.40
90 Orlando Hernandez	.40
91 Gabe Kapler	.40
92 Paul Konerko	.40
93 Carlos Lee	.40
94 Kenny Lofton	.40
95 Raul Mondesi	.40
96 Jorge Posada	.60
97 Tim Salmon	.40
98 Greg Vaughn	.40
99 Mo Vaughn	.40
100 Omar Vizquel	.40
101 Ray Durham	.40
102 Jeff Cirillo	.40
103 Dean Palmer	.40
104 Ryan Dempster	.40
105 Carlos Beltran	.40
106 Timo Perez	.40
107 Robin Ventura	.40
108 Andy Pettitte	.60
109 Aramis Ramirez	.40
110 Phil Nevin	.40
111 Alex Escobar	10.00
112 Johnny Estrada RC	20.00
113 Pedro Feliz	10.00
114 Nate Frese RC	10.00
115 Joe Kennedy RC	10.00
116 Brandon Larson RC	10.00
117 Alexis Gomez RC	10.00
118 Jason Hart	10.00
119 Jason Michaels RC	10.00
120 Marcus Giles	10.00
121 Christian Parker RC	10.00
122 Jackson Melian RC	10.00
123 Donaldo Mendez RC	10.00
124 Adrian Hernandez RC	10.00
125 Bud Smith RC	10.00
126 Jose Mieses RC	10.00
127 Roy Oswalt	10.00
128 Eric Munson	10.00
129 Xavier Nady	10.00
130 Horacio Ramirez RC	20.00
131 Abraham Nunez	10.00
132 Jose Ortiz	10.00
133 Jeremy Owens RC	10.00
134 Claudio Vargas RC	10.00
135 Ricardo Rodriguez RC	10.00
136 Aubrey Huff	10.00
137 Ben Sheets	10.00
138 Adam Dunn	10.00
139 Andres Torres RC	10.00
140 Elpidio Guzman RC	10.00
141 Jay Gibbons RC	20.00
142 Wilkin Ruan RC	10.00
143 Tsuyoshi Shinjo RC	10.00
144 Alfonso Soriano	15.00
145 Josh Towers RC	10.00
146 Ichiro Suzuki RC	140.00
147 Juan Uribe RC	15.00
148 Joe Crede	10.00
149 Carlos Valderrama RC	10.00
150 Matt White RC	10.00
151 Dee Brown	10.00
152 Juan Cruz RC	10.00
153 Cory Aldridge RC	10.00
154 Wilmy Caceres	10.00
155 Josh Beckett	10.00
156 Wilson Betemit RC	10.00
157 Corey Patterson	10.00
158 Albert Pujols RC	220.00
159 Rafael Soriano RC	10.00
160 Jack Wilson RC	10.00

Mirror Red/Gold

These randomly inserted parallels of both the base low-numbers and the short-printed Rookie Freshman Fabric high-numbers are printed on "holographic dual-sided metallized film board" with appropriate color tinting and foil highlights. Mirror red cards are individually serial numbered to 75; golds to 25. All of the mirror red SPs can be found autographed except Kennedy, Melian, Munson, Shinjo and Ichi-

ro. Because no information was released about the number of each autographed, values cannot be attributed.

	NM/M
Common Mirror Red (1-110):	2.00
Stars (1-110):	3-5X
Common Mirror Red (111-160):	6.00
Stars (111-160):	1-2X
Production 75	
Mirror Gold:	6-8X
Production 25	

Fabric of the Game

	NM/M
Common Player:	5.00
1 Lou Gehrig/184	200.00
1 Lou Gehrig/23	375.00
2 Babe Ruth/136	250.00
2 Babe Ruth/60	400.00
3 Stan Musial/177	40.00
3 Stan Musial/39	100.00
4 Nolan Ryan	40.00
4 Nolan Ryan/61	60.00
4 Nolan Ryan/34	80.00
5 Roberto Clemente/166	100.00
5 Roberto Clemente/29	250.00
6 Al Kaline/137	25.00
7 Brooks Robinson	25.00
7 Brooks Robinson/68	30.00
8 Mel Ott	30.00
8 Mel Ott/72	50.00
9 Dave Winfield/88	15.00
10 Eddie Mathews/115	25.00
10 Eddie Mathews/72	40.00
11 Ernie Banks/50	40.00
11 Ernie Banks/47	40.00
12 Frank Robinson	15.00
13 George Brett/137	40.00
14 Hank Aaron	40.00
14 Hank Aaron/98	50.00
14 Hank Aaron/47	100.00
15 Harmon Killebrew	25.00
15 Harmon Killebrew/49	50.00
16 Joe Morgan	10.00
16 Joe Morgan/96	15.00
17 Johnny Bench	20.00
17 Johnny Bench/68	30.00
18 Kirby Puckett/134	40.00
19 Mike Schmidt	40.00
19 Mike Schmidt/59	60.00
20 Phil Rizzuto/149	15.00
21 Reggie Jackson	15.00
21 Reggie Jackson/44	30.00
22 Catfish Hunter	15.00
22 Catfish Hunter/42	25.00
23 Rod Carew/92	20.00
23 Rod Carew/100	20.00
24 Bob Feller	15.00
24 Bob Feller/44	30.00
25 Lou Brock	10.00
25 Lou Brock/141	15.00
26 Tom Seaver	15.00
26 Tom Seaver/61	30.00
27 Paul Molitor	15.00
27 Paul Molitor/114	25.00
28 Willie McCovey/126	15.00
29 Yogi Berra	20.00
29 Yogi Berra/49	40.00
30 Don Drysdale	15.00
30 Don Drysdale/49	30.00
31 Duke Snider	20.00
31 Duke Snider/99	30.00
33 Orlando Cepeda/46	20.00
34 Casey Stengel	10.00
34 Casey Stengel/103	15.00
35 Robin Yount	20.00
35 Robin Yount/126	40.00
36 Eddie Murray	15.00
36 Eddie Murray/35	40.00
37 Jim Palmer	10.00
38 Juan Marichal	15.00
38 Juan Marichal/52	20.00
39 Willie Stargell	15.00
39 Willie Stargell/55	20.00
40 Ted Williams	150.00
40 Ted Williams/71	100.00
40 Ted Williams/43	150.00
41 Cal Ripken Jr.	30.00
41 Cal Ripken/75	50.00
41 Cal Ripken/277	40.00

42 Vladimir Guerrero/322	15.00
42 Vladimir Guerrero/44	25.00
43 Greg Maddux	15.00
43 Greg Maddux/240	20.00
44 Barry Bonds	30.00
44 Barry Bonds/49	75.00
44 Barry Bonds/289	30.00
45 Pedro Martinez	15.00
45 Pedro Martinez/268	15.00
46 Ivan Rodriguez	10.00
46 Ivan Rodriguez/304	15.00
47 Roger Maris	50.00
47 Roger Maris/275	50.00
48 Randy Johnson	15.00
48 Randy Johnson/179	20.00
49 Roger Clemens	20.00
49 Roger Clemens/260	20.00
50 Todd Helton	10.00
50 Todd Helton/334	10.00
51 Tony Gwynn	15.00
51 Tony Gwynn/119	25.00
51 Tony Gwynn/134	20.00
52 Troy Glaus	8.00
52 Troy Glaus/47	15.00
52 Troy Glaus/256	8.00
53 Phil Niekro	8.00
53 Phil Niekro/245	10.00
54 Don Sutton	8.00
54 Don Sutton/178	8.00
55 Frank Thomas	10.00
55 Frank Thomas/321	15.00
56 Jeff Bagwell	10.00
56 Jeff Bagwell/305	15.00
57 Rickey Henderson	15.00
57 Rickey Henderson/282	15.00
58 Darin Erstad/301	10.00
59 Andruw Jones	10.00
59 Andruw Jones/272	10.00
60 Roberto Alomar	10.00
60 Roberto Alomar/120	15.00
60 Roberto Alomar/170	15.00
61 Mike Piazza	20.00
61 Mike Piazza/328	20.00
62 Chipper Jones	15.00
62 Chipper Jones/189	15.00
63 Shawn Green	8.00
63 Shawn Green/143	8.00
64 Don Mattingly	50.00
64 Don Mattingly/145	50.00
64 Don Mattingly/222	40.00
66 Rafael Palmeiro	8.00
66 Wade Boggs	10.00
66 Wade Boggs/116	15.00
66 Wade Boggs/89	20.00
67 Hoyt Wilhelm	8.00
67 Hoyt Wilhelm/143	10.00
68 Andre Dawson	8.00
68 Andre Dawson/49	15.00
68 Andre Dawson/314	10.00
69 Ryne Sandberg	30.00
69 Ryne Sandberg/282	35.00
70 Nomar Garciaparra/333	25.00
71 Tom Glavine	8.00
71 Tom Glavine/208	10.00
71 Tom Glavine/247	10.00
72 Magglio Ordonez	8.00
72 Magglio Ordonez/301	8.00
72 Magglio Ordonez/126	10.00
73 Bernie Williams	8.00
73 Bernie Williams/304	10.00
74 Jim Edmonds	8.00
74 Jim Edmonds/108	10.00
74 Jim Edmonds/291	10.00
75 Hideo Nomo	20.00
75 Hideo Nomo/69	30.00
76 Barry Larkin	10.00
76 Barry Larkin/300	10.00
77 Scott Rolen	10.00
77 Scott Rolen/284	10.00
78 Miguel Tejada	8.00
78 Miguel Tejada/253	8.00
79 Freddy Garcia	5.00
79 Freddy Garcia/170	5.00
79 Freddy Garcia/249	5.00
80 Edgar Martinez	10.00
80 Edgar Martinez/320	10.00
81 Edgardo Alfonzo	5.00
81 Edgardo Alfonzo/108	5.00
81 Edgardo Alfonzo/296	5.00
82 Steve Garvey	8.00
82 Steve Garvey/272	8.00
83 Larry Walker	5.00
83 Larry Walker/311	5.00
83 Larry Walker/49	10.00
84 A.J. Burnett	5.00
84 A.J. Burnett/90	8.00
85 Richie Sexson	8.00
85 Richie Sexson/242	5.00
85 Richie Sexson/116	8.00
86 Mark Mulder	8.00
87 Mark Mulder/88	8.00
87 Kerry Wood	10.00
87 Kerry Wood/233	10.00
88 Sean Casey	5.00
88 Sean Casey/312	5.00
89 Jermaine Dye	5.00
89 Jermaine Dye/118	5.00
89 Jermaine Dye/286	5.00
90 Kevin Brown	5.00
90 Kevin Brown/170	5.00
90 Kevin Brown/257	5.00
91 Craig Biggio	5.00
91 Craig Biggio/88	8.00
91 Craig Biggio/291	5.00
92 Mike Sweeney	

#	Player	Price
92	Mike Sweeney/302	5.00
92	Mike Sweeney/144	5.00
93	Jim Thome	10.00
93	Jim Thome/233	10.00
93	Jim Thome/40	20.00
94	Al Leiter	5.00
94	Al Leiter/247	5.00
94	Al Leiter/106	5.00
95	Barry Zito	8.00
95	Barry Zito/272	8.00
95	Barry Zito/78	15.00
96	Rafael Furcal	5.00
96	Rafael Furcal/295	5.00
97	J.D. Drew	5.00
97	J.D. Drew/276	5.00
98	Andres Galarraga	5.00
98	Andres Galarraga/150	5.00
98	Andres Galarraga/291	5.00
99	Kazuhiro Sasaki	5.00
99	Kazuhiro Sasaki/266	5.00
100	Chan Ho Park	5.00
100	Chan Ho Park/65	5.00
100	Chan Ho Park/217	5.00
101	Eric Milton	5.00
101	Eric Milton/163	5.00
102	Carlos Lee	5.00
102	Carlos Lee/297	5.00
103	Preston Wilson	5.00
103	Preston Wilson/266	5.00
104	Adrian Beltre	5.00
104	Adrian Beltre/85	5.00
104	Adrian Beltre/272	5.00
105	Luis Gonzalez	5.00
105	Luis Gonzalez/281	5.00
105	Luis Gonzalez/114	5.00
106	Kenny Lofton	5.00
106	Kenny Lofton/306	5.00
107	Shannon Stewart	5.00
107	Shannon Stewart/297	5.00
108	Javy Lopez	5.00
108	Javy Lopez/290	5.00
108	Javy Lopez/106	5.00
109	Raul Mondesi	5.00
109	Raul Mondesi/286	5.00
110	Mark Grace	10.00
110	Mark Grace/51	20.00
110	Mark Grace/308	15.00
111	Curt Schilling	8.00
111	Curt Schilling/235	8.00
111	Curt Schilling/110	10.00
112	Cliff Floyd	5.00
112	Cliff Floyd/275	5.00
113	Moises Alou	5.00
113	Moises Alou/124	5.00
113	Moises Alou/303	5.00
114	Aaron Sele	5.00
114	Aaron Sele/92	5.00
115	Jose Cruz Jr.	5.00
115	Jose Cruz Jr/245	5.00
116	John Olerud	5.00
116	John Olerud/186	5.00
116	John Olerud/107	5.00
117	Jose Vidro	5.00
117	Jose Vidro/296	5.00
118	John Smoltz	5.00
118	John Smoltz/334	5.00

2001 Leaf Limited

		NM/M
Complete Set (375):		
Common Player:		.75
Common Lumberjack (151-200):		5.00
#'d to 100, 250 or 500		
Common Rk (201-300):		5.00
Production 1,500		
Common Auto (301-325):		10.00
Production 1,000		
Pack (3):		10.00
Box (18):		140.00
1	Curt Schilling	1.00
2	Craig Biggio	.75
3	Brian Giles	.75
4	Scott Brosius	.75
5	Barry Larkin	.75
6	Bartolo Colon	.75
7	John Olerud	.75
8	Cal Ripken Jr.	6.00
9	Moises Alou	.75
10	Barry Zito	4.00
11	Ken Griffey Jr.	4.00
12	Garret Anderson	.75
13	Andy Pettitte	1.00
14	Jim Edmonds	1.00
15	Tom Glavine	1.00
16	Jose Canseco	.75
17	Fred McGriff	.75
18	Robin Ventura	.75
19	Tony Gwynn	3.00
20	Jeff Cirillo	.75
21	Brad Radke	.75
22	Ellis Burks	.75
23	Scott Rolen	1.50
24	Rickey Henderson	2.00
25	Edgar Martinez	.75
26	Kerry Wood	1.50
27	Al Leiter	.75
28	Jose Cruz Jr.	.75
29	Sean Casey	.75
30	Eric Chavez	.75
31	Jarrod Washburn	.75
32	Gary Sheffield	1.00
33	Jermaine Dye	.75
34	Bernie Williams	1.00
35	Tony Armas Jr.	.75
36	Carlos Beltran	1.50
37	Geoff Jenkins	.75
38	Shawn Green	1.50
39	Ryan Klesko	.75
40	Richie Sexson	.75
41	Pat Burrell	1.00
42	J.D. Drew	1.00
43	Larry Walker	.75
44	Andres Galarraga	.75
45	Tino Martinez	.75
46	Rafael Furcal	.75
47	Cristian Guzman	.75
48	Omar Vizquel	.75
49	Bret Boone	.75
50	Wade Miller	.75
51	Eric Milton	.75
52	Gabe Kapler	.75
53	Johnny Damon	.75
54	Shannon Stewart	.75
55	Kenny Lofton	.75
56	Raul Mondesi	.75
57	Jorge Posada	1.00
58	Mark Grace	1.00
59	Robert Fick	.75
60	Phil Nevin	1.00
61	Mike Mussina	1.00
62	Joe Mays	.75
63	Todd Helton	2.00
64	Tim Hudson	2.00
65	Manny Ramirez	2.00
66	Sammy Sosa	4.00
67	Darin Erstad	1.00
68	Roberto Alomar	1.00
69	Jeff Bagwell	2.00
70	Mark McGwire	5.00
71	Jason Giambi	1.50
72	Cliff Floyd	.75
73	Barry Bonds	6.00
74	Juan Gonzalez	2.00
75	Jeremy Giambi	.75
76	Carlos Lee	.75
77	Randy Johnson	2.00
78	Frank Thomas	2.00
79	Carlos Delgado	1.00
80	Pedro Martinez	2.00
81	Rusty Greer	.75
82	Brian Jordan	.75
83	Vladimir Guerrero	2.00
84	Juan Gonzalez	.75
85	Jose Vidro	.75
86	Paul LoDuca	.75
87	Matt Morris	.75
88	Adrian Beltre	.75
89	Aramis Ramirez	.75
90	Derek Jeter	6.00
91	Rich Aurilia	.75
92	Freddy Garcia	.75
93	Preston Wilson	.75
94	Greg Maddux	3.00
95	Miguel Tejada	1.00
96	Luis Gonzalez	.75
97	Torii Hunter	.75
98	Nomar Garciaparra	4.00
99	Jamie Moyer	.75
100	Javier Vazquez	.75
101	Ben Grieve	.75
102	Mike Piazza	4.00
103	Paul O'Neill	.75
104	Terrence Long	.75
105	Charles Johnson	.75
106	Rafael Palmeiro	1.50
107	David Cone	.75
108	Alex Rodriguez	5.00
109	John Burkett	.75
110	Chipper Jones	3.00
111	Ryan Dempster	.75
112	Bobby Abreu	.75
113	Brad Fullmer	.75
114	Kazuhiro Sasaki	.75
115	Mariano Rivera	1.00
116	Edgardo Alfonzo	.75
117	Ray Durham	.75
118	Richard Hidalgo	.75
119	Jeff Weaver	.75
120	Paul Konerko	.75
121	Jon Lieber	.75
122	Mike Hampton	.75
123	Mike Cameron	.75
124	Kevin Brown	.75
125	Doug Mientkiewicz	.75
126	Jim Thome	.75
127	Corey Koskie	.75
128	Trot Nixon	.75
129	Darryl Kile	.75
130	Ivan Rodriguez	1.50
131	Carl Everett	.75
132	Jeff Kent	.75
133	Rondell White	.75
134	Chan Ho Park	.75
135	Robert Person	.75
136	Troy Glaus	2.00
137	Aaron Sele	.75
138	Roger Clemens	3.50
139	Tony Clark	.75
140	Mark Buehrle	.75
141	David Justice	.75
142	Magglio Ordonez	.75
143	Bobby Higginson	.75
144	Hideo Nomo	2.00
145	Tim Salmon	.75
146	Mark Mulder	.75
147	Troy Percival	.75
148	Lance Berkman	.75
149	Russ Ortiz	.75
150	Mike Piazza	25.00
151	Manny Ramirez	8.00
152	Bernie Williams	8.00
153	Nomar Garciaparra	25.00
154	Andres Galarraga	5.00
155	Kenny Lofton	5.00
156	Scott Rolen	8.00
157	Jim Thome	6.00
158	Darin Erstad	5.00
159	Garret Anderson	5.00
160	Andruw Jones	8.00
161	Juan Gonzalez	8.00
162	Rafael Palmeiro	8.00
163	Magglio Ordonez	5.00
164	Jeff Bagwell	8.00
165	Eric Chavez	5.00
166	Brian Giles	5.00
167	Adrian Beltre	5.00
168	Tony Gwynn	15.00
169	Shawn Green	5.00
170	Todd Helton	8.00
171	Troy Glaus	8.00
172	Lance Berkman	5.00
173	Ivan Rodriguez	8.00
174	Sean Casey	5.00
175	Aramis Ramirez	5.00
176	J.D. Drew	5.00
177	Barry Bonds	40.00
178	Barry Larkin	5.00
179	Cal Ripken Jr.	40.00
180	Frank Thomas	8.00
181	Craig Biggio	5.00
182	Carlos Lee	5.00
183	Chipper Jones	10.00
184	Miguel Tejada	5.00
185	Jose Vidro	5.00
186	Terrence Long	5.00
187	Moises Alou	5.00
188	Trot Nixon	5.00
189	Shannon Stewart	5.00
190	Ryan Klesko	5.00
191	Carlos Beltran	7.00
192	Vladimir Guerrero	8.00
193	Edgar Martinez	5.00
194	Luis Gonzalez	5.00
195	Richard Hidalgo	5.00
196	Roberto Alomar	6.00
197	Mike Sweeney	5.00
198	Bobby Abreu	5.00
199	Cliff Floyd	5.00
200	Jackson Melian RC	5.00
201	Jason Jennings	5.00
202	Toby Hall	5.00
203	Jason Karnuth RC	5.00
204	Jason Smith RC	5.00
205	Mike Maroth RC	5.00
206	Sean Douglass RC	5.00
207	Adam Johnson	5.00
208	Luke Hudson RC	5.00
209	Nick Maness RC	5.00
210	Les Walrond RC	5.00
211	Travis Phelps RC	5.00
212	Carlos Garcia RC	5.00
213	Bill Ortega	5.00
214	Gene Altman RC	5.00
215	Nate Frese	5.00
216	Bob File RC	5.00
217	Steve Green RC	5.00
218	Kris Keller RC	5.00
219	Matt White RC	5.00
220	Nate Teut RC	5.00
221	Nick Johnson	5.00
222	Jeremy Fikac RC	5.00
223	Abraham Nunez	5.00
224	Mike Penney RC	5.00
225	Roy Smith RC	5.00
226	Tim Christman RC	5.00
227	Carlos Pena	5.00
228	Joe Beimel RC	5.00
229	Mike Koplove RC	5.00
230	Scott MacRae RC	5.00
231	Kyle Lohse RC	10.00
232	Jerrod Riggan RC	5.00
233	Scott Podsednik RC	12.00
234	Winston Abreu RC	5.00
235	Ryan Freel RC	5.00
236	Ken Vining RC	5.00
237	Bret Prinz RC	5.00
238	Paul Phillips RC	5.00
239	Josh Fogg RC	5.00
240	Saul Rivera RC	5.00
241	Esix Snead RC	5.00
242	John Grabow RC	5.00
243	Tony Cogan RC	5.00
244	Pedro Santana RC	5.00
245	Jack Cust RC	5.00
246	Joe Crede	5.00
247	Juan Moreno RC	5.00
248	Kevin Joseph RC	5.00
249	Scott Stewart RC	5.00
250	Rob Mackowiak RC	5.00
251	Luis Pineda RC	5.00
252	Bert Snow RC	5.00
253	Bert Snow RC	5.00
254	Dustan Mohr RC	5.00
255	Justin Kaye RC	5.00
256	Chad Paronto RC	5.00
257	Nick Punto RC	5.00
258	Brian Roberts RC	15.00
259	Eric Hinske RC	8.00
260	Victor Zambrano RC	5.00
261	Juan Pena	5.00
262	Rick Bauer RC	5.00
263	Jorge Julio RC	5.00
264	Craig Monroe RC	5.00
265	Stubby Clapp RC	5.00
266	Martin Vargas RC	5.00
267	Josue Perez RC	5.00
268	Cody Ransom RC	5.00
269	Will Ohman RC	5.00
270	Juan Diaz RC	5.00
271	Ramon Vazquez RC	5.00
272	Grant Balfour RC	5.00
273	Ryan Jensen RC	5.00
274	Benito Baez RC	5.00
275	Angel Santos RC	5.00
276	Brian Reith RC	5.00
277	Brandon Lyon RC	5.00
278	Erik Hiljus RC	5.00
279	Brandon Knight RC	5.00
280	Jose Acevedo RC	5.00
281	Cesar Crespo RC	5.00
282	Kevin Olsen RC	5.00
283	Duaner Sanchez RC	5.00
284	Endy Chavez RC	5.00
285	Blaine Neal RC	5.00
286	Brett Jodie RC	5.00
287	Brad Voyles RC	5.00
288	Doug Nickle RC	5.00
289	Junior Spivey RC	8.00
290	Henry Mateo RC	5.00
291	Xavier Nady RC	5.00
292	Lance Davis RC	5.00
293	Willie Harris RC	5.00
294	Mark Lukasiewicz RC	5.00
295	Ryan Drese RC	5.00
296	Morgan Ensberg RC	10.00
297	Jose Mieses RC	5.00
298	Jason Michaels RC	5.00
299	Kris Foster RC	5.00
300	Justin Duchscherer RC	5.00
301	Elpidio Guzman RC	5.00
302	Cory Aldridge RC	5.00
303	Angel Berroa RC	15.00
304	Travis Hafner RC	125.00
305	Horacio Ramirez RC	15.00
306	Juan Uribe RC	10.00
307	Mark Prior RC	80.00
308	Brandon Larson RC	10.00
309	Nick Neugebauer RC	10.00
310	Zach Day RC	10.00
311	Jeremy Owens RC	5.00
312	Dewon Brazelton RC	10.00
313	Brandon Duckworth RC	10.00
314	Adrian Hernandez RC	10.00
315	Mark Teixeira RC	160.00
316	Brian Rogers RC	10.00
317	David Brous RC	10.00
318	Geronimo Gil RC	10.00
319	Erick Almonte RC	10.00
320	Claudio Vargas RC	10.00
321	Wilkin Ruan RC	10.00
322	David Williams RC	10.00
323	Alexis Gomez RC	10.00
324	Mike Rivera RC	10.00
325	Brandon Berger RC	10.00
326	Keith Ginter RC	10.00
327	Brandon Inge/700	10.00
328	Brent Abernathy/700	10.00
329	Billy Sylvester/700 RC	10.00
330	Bart Miadich/500 RC	10.00
331	Tsuyoshi Shinjo/500 RC	15.00
332	Eric Valent	10.00
333	Dee Brown/500	10.00
334	Andres Torres/125 RC	10.00
335	Timo Perez/700	10.00
336	Cesar Izturis/650	10.00
337	Pedro Feliz	10.00
338	Jason Hart/200	10.00
339	Greg Miller/700	10.00
340	Eric Munson/700	10.00
341	Aubrey Huff/450	10.00
342	Wilmy Caceres/700 RC	10.00
343	Alex Escobar/650	10.00
344	Brian Lawrence/700 RC	10.00
345	Adam Pettyjohn/650 RC	10.00
346	Donaldo Mendez/700 RC	10.00
347	Carlos Valderrama/RC	10.00
348	Christian Parker/650 RC	10.00
349	Corky Miller/500 RC	10.00
350	Michael Cuddyer/500	10.00
351	Adam Dunn/500	20.00
352	Josh Beckett/650 RC	10.00
353	Juan Cruz/500 RC	10.00
354	Ben Sheets/400	10.00
355	Roy Oswalt/100	15.00
356	Rafael Soriano/650 RC	10.00
357	Ricardo Rodriguez/650 RC	10.00
358	Jimmy Rollins/300	10.00
359	C.C. Sabathia	10.00
360	Bud Smith/500 RC	10.00
361	Jose Ortiz	10.00
362	Marcus Giles/400	10.00
363	Jack Wilson RC	20.00
364	Wilson Betemit/100 RC	10.00
365	Corey Patterson/650	10.00
366	Jay Gibbons/Spikes/125 RC	35.00
367	Albert Pujols/250 RC	300.00
368	Joe Kennedy/100 RC	10.00
369	Alfonso Soriano/Hat/100	40.00
370	Delvin James/650 RC	10.00
371	Josh Towers/500 RC	10.00
372	Jeremy Affeldt/650 RC	10.00
373	Tim Redding/500 RC	10.00
374	Ichiro Suzuki/100 RC	400.00
375	Johnny Estrada/100 RC	30.00

2001 Leaf Rookies & Stars Samples

Each January 2002 issue of Beckett Baseball Card Monthly included a sample 2002 Leaf R&S card rubber-cemented inside. The cards differ from the issued version only in the appearance on back of a (usually) silver-foil "SAMPLE" notation. Some cards were produced with the overprint in gold-foil, in much more limited quantities. The number of different players' cards involved in the promotion is unknown.

	NM/M
Common Player:	.10
Stars:	1.5-2X
Gold:	20X

2001 Leaf Rookies & Stars

		NM/M
Complete Set (300):		
Common Player:		.15
Common (101-200):		1.50
Inserted 1:4		
Common (201-300):		4.00
Inserted 1:24		
Pack (5):		7.50
Box (24):		160.00
1	Alex Rodriguez	2.50
2	Derek Jeter	3.00
3	Aramis Ramirez	.15
4	Cliff Floyd	.15
5	Nomar Garciaparra	2.00
6	Craig Biggio	.15
7	Ivan Rodriguez	.75
8	Cal Ripken Jr.	3.00
9	Fred McGriff	.15
10	Chipper Jones	1.50
11	Roberto Alomar	.50
12	Moises Alou	.15
13	Freddy Garcia	.15
14	Bobby Abreu	.15
15	Shawn Green	.50
16	Jason Giambi	.50
17	Todd Helton	1.00
18	Robert Fick	.15
19	Tony Gwynn	1.50
20	Luis Gonzalez	.35
21	Sean Casey	.25
22	Roger Clemens	1.75
23	Brian Giles	.15
24	Manny Ramirez	1.00
25	Barry Bonds	3.00
26	Richard Hidalgo	.15
27	Vladimir Guerrero	1.00
28	Kevin Brown	.15
29	Mike Sweeney	.15
30	Ken Griffey Jr.	2.00
31	Mike Piazza	2.00
32	Richie Sexson	.15
33	Matt Morris	.15
34	Jorge Posada	.25
35	Eric Chavez	.25
36	Mark Buehrle	.15
37	Jeff Bagwell	1.00
38	Curt Schilling	.35
39	Bartolo Colon	.15
40	Mark Quinn	.15
41	Tony Clark	.15
42	Brad Radke	.15
43	Gary Sheffield	.35
44	Doug Mientkiewicz	.15
45	Pedro Martinez	1.00
46	Carlos Lee	.15
47	Troy Glaus	1.00
48	Preston Wilson	.15
49	Phil Nevin	.15
50	Chan Ho Park	.15
51	Randy Johnson	1.00
52	Jermaine Dye	.15
53	Terrence Long	.15
54	Joe Mays	.15
55	Scott Rolen	.75
56	Miguel Tejada	.25
57	Jim Thome	.15
58	Jose Vidro	.15
59	Gabe Kapler	.15
60	Darin Erstad	.75
61	Jim Edmonds	.15
62	Jarrod Washburn	.15
63	Tom Glavine	.40
64	Adrian Beltre	.50
65	Sammy Sosa	2.00
66	Juan Gonzalez	1.00
67	Rafael Furcal	.15
68	Mike Mussina	.50
69	Mark McGwire	2.50
70	Ryan Klesko	.15
71	Raul Mondesi	.15
72	Trot Nixon	.15
73	Barry Larkin	.15
74	Rafael Palmeiro	.75
75	Mark Mulder	.25
76	Carlos Delgado	.60
77	Mike Hampton	.15
78	Carl Everett	.15
79	Paul Konerko	.15
80	Larry Walker	.15
81	Kerry Wood	.60
82	Frank Thomas	1.00
83	Andruw Jones	1.00
84	Eric Milton	.15
85	Ben Grieve	.15
86	Carlos Beltran	.15
87	Tim Hudson	.25
88	Hideo Nomo	1.00
89	Greg Maddux	1.50
90	Edgar Martinez	.15
91	Lance Berkman	.15
92	Pat Burrell	.45
93	Jeff Kent	.15
94	Magglio Ordonez	.15
95	Cristian Guzman	.15
96	Jose Canseco	.30
97	J.D. Drew	.60
98	Bernie Williams	.40
99	Kazuhiro Sasaki	.15
100	Rickey Henderson	1.00
101	Wilson Guzman	1.50
102	Nick Neugebauer	1.50
103	Lance Davis RC	1.50
104	Felipe Lopez	1.50
105	Toby Hall	1.50
106	Jack Cust	1.50
107	Jason Karnuth	1.50
108	Bart Miadich RC	1.50
109	Brian Roberts RC	10.00
110	Brandon Larson RC	2.00
111	Sean Douglass RC	1.50
112	Joe Crede	1.50
113	Tim Redding	1.50
114	Adam Johnson	1.50
115	Marcus Giles	1.50
116	Jose Ortiz	1.50
117	Jose Mieses RC	1.50
118	Nick Maness RC	1.50
119	Les Walrond RC	1.50
120	Travis Phelps RC	1.50
121	Troy Mattes RC	1.50
122	Carlos Garcia	1.50
123	Bill Ortega	1.50
124	Gene Altman RC	1.50
125	Nate Frese	1.50
126	Jose Nunez	1.50
127	Bob File RC	1.50
128	Dan Wright	1.50
129	Nick Johnson	1.50
130	Brent Abernathy	1.50
131	Steve Green RC	1.50
132	Billy Sylvester RC	1.50
133	Scott MacRae RC	1.50
134	Kris Keller RC	1.50
135	Scott Stewart RC	1.50
136	Henry Mateo RC	1.50
137	Timoniel Perez	1.50
138	Nate Teut RC	1.50
139	Jason Michaels RC	1.50
140	Junior Spivey RC	4.00
141	Carlos Pena	1.50
142	Wilmy Caceres RC	1.50
143	David Lundquist	1.50
144	Jack Wilson RC	6.00
145	Jeremy Fikac RC	1.50
146	Alex Escobar	1.50
147	Abraham Nunez	1.50
148	Xavier Nady	1.50
149	Michael Cuddyer	1.50
150	Greg Miller RC	1.50
151	Eric Munson	1.50
152	Aubrey Huff	1.50
153	Tim Christman RC	1.50
154	Erick Almonte	1.50
155	Erick Almonte RC	1.50

156	Mike Penny	1.50
157	Delvin James RC	1.50
158	Ben Sheets	1.50
159	Jason Hart	1.50
160	Jose Acevedo RC	1.50
161	Will Ohman RC	1.50
162	Erik Hiljus RC	1.50
163	Juan Moreno RC	1.50
164	Mike Koplove RC	1.50
165	Pedro Santana RC	1.50
166	Jimmy Rollins RC	1.50
167	Matt White RC	1.50
168	Cesar Crespo RC	1.50
169	Carlos Hernandez	1.50
170	Chris George RC	1.50
171	Brad Voyles RC	1.50
172	Luis Pineda RC	1.50
173	Carlos Zambrano RC	1.50
174	Nate Cornejo	1.50
175	Jason Smith RC	1.50
176	Craig Monroe RC	1.50
177	Cody Ransom RC	1.50
178	John Grabow RC	1.50
179	Pedro Feliz	1.50
180	Jeremy Owens RC	1.50
181	Kurt Ainsworth	1.50
182	Luis Lopez	1.50
183	Stubby Clapp RC	1.50
184	Ryan Freel RC	1.50
185	Duaner Sanchez RC	1.50
186	Jason Jennings	1.50
187	Kyle Lohse RC	3.00
188	Jerrod Riggan RC	1.50
189	Joe Beimel RC	1.50
190	Nick Punto RC	1.50
191	Willie Harris RC	1.50
192	Ryan Jensen RC	1.50
193	Adam Pettyjohn RC	1.50
194	Donaldo Mendez RC	1.50
195	Bret Prinz RC	1.50
196	Paul Phillips RC	1.50
197	Brian Lawrence RC	2.00
198	Cesar Izturis	1.50
199	Blaine Neal RC	1.50
200	Josh Fogg RC	1.50
201	Josh Towers RC	4.00
202	Tim Spooneybarger RC	4.00
203	Mike Rivera RC	4.00
204	Juan Cruz RC	4.00
205	Albert Pujols RC	220.00
206	Josh Beckett	4.00
207	Roy Oswalt	4.00
208	Elpidio Guzman RC	4.00
209	Horacio Ramirez RC	8.00
210	Corey Patterson	4.00
211	Geronimo Gil RC	4.00
212	Jay Gibbons RC	10.00
213	Orlando Woodwards	4.00
214	David Espinosa	4.00
215	Angel Berroa RC	8.00
216	Brandon Duckworth RC	4.00
217	Brian Reith RC	4.00
218	David Brous RC	4.00
219	Bud Smith RC	4.00
220	Ramon Vazquez RC	4.00
221	Mark Teixeira RC	35.00
222	Justin Atchley RC	4.00
223	Tony Cogan RC	4.00
224	Grant Balfour RC	4.00
225	Ricardo Rodriguez RC	4.00
226	Brian Rogers RC	4.00
227	Adam Dunn	4.00
228	Wilson Betemit RC	4.00
229	Juan Diaz RC	4.00
230	Jackson Melian RC	4.00
231	Claudio Vargas RC	4.00
232	Wilkin Ruan RC	4.00
233	Justin Duchscherer RC	4.00
234	Kevin Olsen RC	4.00
235	Tony Fiore	4.00
236	Jeremy Affeldt RC	4.00
237	Mike Maroth RC	4.00
238	C.C. Sabathia	4.00
239	Cory Aldridge RC	4.00
240	Zach Day RC	6.00
241	Brett Jodie RC	4.00
242	Winston Abreu RC	4.00
243	Travis Hafner RC	20.00
244	Joe Kennedy RC	4.00
245	Rick Bauer RC	4.00
246	Mike Young RC	8.00
247	Ken Vining RC	4.00
248	Doug Nickle RC	4.00
249	Pablo Ozuno RC	4.00
250	Dustan Mohr RC	4.00
251	Ichiro Suzuki RC	50.00
252	Ryan Drese RC	4.00
253	Morgan Ensberg RC	10.00
254	George Perez RC	4.00
255	Roy Smith RC	4.00
256	Juan Uribe RC	6.00
257	Dewon Brazelton RC	4.00
258	Endy Chavez RC	4.00
259	Kris Foster RC	4.00
260	Eric Knott RC	4.00
261	Corky Miller RC	4.00
262	Larry Bigbie	4.00
263	Andres Torres RC	4.00
264	Adrian Hernandez RC	4.00
265	Johnny Estrada RC	6.00
266	David Williams RC	4.00
267	Steve Lomasney	4.00
268	Victor Zambrano RC	6.00
269	Keith Ginter	4.00
270	Casey Fossum RC	6.00
271	Josue Perez RC	4.00

272	Josh Phelps	4.00
273	Mark Prior RC	25.00
274	Brandon Berger RC	4.00
275	Scott Podsednik RC	10.00
276	Jorge Julio RC	6.00
277	Esix Snead RC	4.00
278	Brandon Knight RC	4.00
279	Saul Rivera RC	4.00
280	Benito Baez RC	4.00
281	Robert Mackowiak RC	4.00
282	Eric Hinske RC	8.00
283	Juan Rivera	4.00
284	Kevin Joseph RC	4.00
285	Juan Pena	4.00
286	Brandon Lyon RC	4.00
287	Adam Everett	4.00
288	Eric Valent	4.00
289	Ken Harvey	4.00
290	Bert Snow RC	4.00
291	Wily Mo Pena	4.00
292	Rafael Soriano RC	4.00
293	Carlos Valderrama RC	4.00
294	Christian Parker	4.00
295	Tsuyoshi Shinjo RC	4.00
296	Martin Vargas RC	4.00
297	Luke Hudson RC	4.00
298	Dee Brown	4.00
299	Alexis Gomez RC	4.00
300	Angel Santos RC	4.00

Longevity

Stars (1-100): 10-20X
Production 50
#'s 101-300 Production 25

Autographs

		NM/M
Common Player:		8.00
107	Jason Karnuth	8.00
110	Brandon Larson/100	10.00
117	Jose Mieses	8.00
118	Nick Maness	8.00
119	Les Walrond	8.00
122	Carlos Garcia	8.00
123	Bill Ortega	8.00
124	Gene Altman	8.00
125	Nate Frese	8.00
130	Nick Johnson/100	15.00
133	Billy Sylvester	8.00
135	Kris Keller	8.00
139	Nate Teut	8.00
140	Jason Michaels	8.00
143	Wilmy Caceres	8.00
145	Jack Wilson/100	25.00
151	Greg Miller	8.00
155	Erick Almonte	8.00
156	Mike Penney	8.00
157	Delvin James	8.00
161	Will Ohman	8.00
167	Matt White	8.00
180	Jeremy Owens	8.00
184	Ryan Freel	10.00
185	Duaner Sanchez	8.00
193	Adam Pettyjohn/100	8.00
194	Donaldo Mendez/100	10.00
196	Paul Phillips	8.00
197	Brian Lawrence/100	15.00
199	Blaine Neal	8.00
201	Josh Towers/100	15.00
203	Michael Rivera	8.00
204	Juan Cruz/100	10.00
207	Roy Oswalt/50	50.00
208	Elpidio Guzman/100	8.00
209	Horacio Ramirez	15.00
210	Corey Patterson SP	25.00
211	Geronimo Gil	8.00
212	Jay Gibbons/100	30.00
213	Orlando Woodwards	8.00

215	Angel Berroa/100	25.00
216	Brandon Duckworth/100	10.00
218	David Brous	8.00
219	Bud Smith/50	10.00
221	Mark Teixeira/100	250.00
223	Tony Cogan	8.00
225	Ricardo Rodriguez	8.00
226	Brian Rogers	8.00
227	Adam Dunn/50	50.00
228	Wilson Betemit/100	25.00
231	Claudio Vargas	8.00
232	Wilkin Ruan	8.00
234	Kevin Olsen	8.00
236	Jeremy Affeldt	10.00
237	Mike Maroth	8.00
238	C.C. Sabathia/50	25.00
239	Cory Aldridge	8.00
240	Zach Day	10.00
243	Travis Hafner	100.00
244	Joe Kennedy/100	15.00
254	George Perez	8.00
256	Juan Uribe	8.00
257	Dewon Brazelton/100	10.00
261	Corky Miller/100	8.00
263	Andres Torres/100	8.00
265	Johnny Estrada/100	15.00
266	David Williams	10.00
270	Casey Fossum	8.00
273	Mark Prior/100	150.00
274	Brandon Berger	8.00
277	Esix Snead	8.00
282	Eric Hinske	15.00
292	Rafael Soriano	10.00
293	Carlos Valderrama	8.00
299	Alexis Gomez	8.00

Dress For Success

		NM/M
Common Player:		8.00
Inserted 1:96		
Prime Cuts:		2X
Numbered to 50 each.		
1	Cal Ripken Jr.	40.00
2	Mike Piazza	35.00
3	Barry Bonds	40.00
4	Frank Thomas	20.00
5	Nomar Garciaparra	35.00
6	Richie Sexson	8.00
7	Brian Giles	8.00
8	Todd Helton	20.00
9	Ivan Rodriguez	15.00
10	Andruw Jones	20.00
11	Juan Gonzalez	20.00
12	Vladimir Guerrero	20.00
13	Greg Maddux	25.00
14	Tony Gwynn	25.00
15	Randy Johnson	20.00
16	Jeff Bagwell	20.00
17	Kerry Wood	15.00
18	Roberto Alomar	8.00
19	Chipper Jones	20.00
20	Pedro Martinez	20.00
21	Shawn Green	8.00
22	Magglio Ordonez	10.00
23	Darin Erstad	12.00
24	Rafael Palmeiro	15.00
25	Edgar Martinez	8.00

Dress For Success Autographs

Values Undetermined

Freshman Orientation

	NM/M
Common Player:	8.00
Inserted 1:96	
Class Officers:	2X
Numbered to 50 each.	
1 Adam Dunn	15.00
2 Josh Towers	8.00
3 Vernon Wells	10.00
4 Corey Patterson	8.00
6 Ben Sheets	8.00

7	Pedro Feliz	8.00
8	Keith Ginter	8.00
9	Luis Rivas	8.00
11	Andres Torres	8.00
12	Carlos Valderrama	8.00
13	Brandon Inge	8.00
13	Jay Gibbons	15.00
14	Cesar Izturis	8.00
15	Marcus Giles	8.00
16	Tsuyoshi Shinjo	12.00
17	Eric Valent	8.00
18	David Espinosa	8.00
19	Aubrey Huff	8.00
20	Wilmy Caceres	8.00
21	Bud Smith	8.00
22	Ricardo Rodriguez	8.00
23	Wes Helms	8.00
24	Jason Hart	8.00
25	Dee Brown	8.00

Freshman Orientation Autograph

No Pricing

Great American Treasures

		NM/M
Inserted 1:1,120		
1	Barry Bonds/Jsy	100.00
2	Magglio Ordonez/Bat	40.00
3	Derek Jeter/Ball	150.00
4	Nolan Ryan/Ball	600.00
5	Sammy Sosa/Ball	125.00
6	Tom Glavine/Jsy	50.00
7	Ivan Rodriguez/Bat	40.00
8	Pedro Martinez/Ball	100.00
9	Mark McGwire/Ball	250.00
10	Ted Williams/Ball	350.00
11	Ryne Sandberg/Ball	60.00
12	Barry Bonds/Ball	300.00
13	Hideo Nomo/Ball	450.00
14	Roger Maris/Ball	300.00
15	Ty Cobb/Ball	750.00
16	Harmon Killebrew/Bat	150.00
17	Magglio Ordonez/Cap	30.00
18	Wade Boggs/Bat	40.00
19	Hank Aaron/Cap	400.00
20	David Cone/Ball	100.00

Great American Treasures Autograph

		NM/M
GT-6	Tom Glavine 96 WS/Jsy	125.00
GT-11	Ryne Sandberg 91 AS/Bat	300.00
GT-16	Harmon Killebrew 570 HR/Bat	200.00
GT-18	Wade Boggs WS/Bat	150.00

Player's Collection

		NM/M
Singles #'d to 100.		
1	Tony Gwynn/Bat	30.00
2	Tony Gwynn/Jsy	30.00
3	Tony Gwynn/Pants	30.00
4	Tony Gwynn/Shoe	30.00
6	Cal Ripken/Jsy	75.00
7	Cal Ripken/Bat	75.00
8	Cal Ripken/Glv	75.00
9	Cal Ripken/Jsy	75.00
11	Barry Bonds/Jsy	60.00
12	Barry Bonds/Shoe	60.00
13	Barry Bonds/Pants	60.00
14	Barry Bonds/Bat	60.00

Player's Collection Autograph

No Pricing

Slideshow

		NM/M
Common Player:		10.00
Production 100 Sets		
View Masters:		1.5X
Numbered to 25 each.		
1	Cal Ripken Jr.	40.00
2	Chipper Jones	20.00
3	Jeff Bagwell	15.00
4	Larry Walker	10.00
5	Greg Maddux	25.00
6	Ivan Rodriguez	15.00
7	Andruw Jones	15.00
8	Lance Berkman	10.00
9	Luis Gonzalez	15.00
10	Tony Gwynn	25.00
11	Troy Glaus	15.00
12	Todd Helton	20.00
13	Roberto Alomar	10.00
14	Barry Bonds	40.00
15	Vladimir Guerrero	20.00
16	Sean Casey	10.00
17	Curt Schilling	15.00
18	Frank Thomas	20.00
19	Pedro Martinez	20.00
20	Juan Gonzalez	15.00
21	Randy Johnson	20.00
22	Kerry Wood	10.00
23	Mike Sweeney	10.00
24	Magglio Ordonez	10.00
25	Kazuhiro Sasaki	10.00
26	Manny Ramirez	20.00
27	Roger Clemens	25.00
28	Albert Pujols	120.00
29	Hideo Nomo	25.00
30	Miguel Tejada	10.00

Slideshow Autographs

No Pricing

Statistical Standouts

		NM/M
Common Player:		5.00
Inserted 1:96		
1	Ichiro Suzuki	35.00
2	Barry Bonds	40.00
3	Ivan Rodriguez	10.00
4	Jeff Bagwell	10.00
5	Vladimir Guerrero	10.00
6	Mike Sweeney	5.00
7	Miguel Tejada	5.00
8	Mike Piazza	30.00
9	Darin Erstad	5.00
10	Alex Rodriguez	35.00
11	Jason Giambi	8.00
12	Cal Ripken Jr.	40.00
13	Albert Pujols	35.00
14	Carlos Delgado	8.00
15	Rafael Palmeiro	8.00
16	Lance Berkman	5.00
17	Luis Gonzalez	5.00
18	Sammy Sosa	30.00
19	Andruw Jones	10.00
20	Derek Jeter	40.00
21	Edgar Martinez	5.00
22	Troy Glaus	10.00
23	Magglio Ordonez	5.00
24	Mark McGwire	35.00
25	Manny Ramirez	10.00

Statistical Standouts Autograph

No Pricing

Triple Threads

		NM/M
Common Card:		50.00
Numbered to 100.		
TT-1	Pedro Martinez, Manny Ramirez, Nomar Garciaparra	100.00
TT-2	Frank Robinson, Cal Ripken Jr., Brooks Robinson	200.00
TT-3	Yogi Berra, Lou Gehrig, Babe Ruth	500.00
TT-4	Andre Dawson, Ryne Sandberg, Ernie Banks	140.00
TT-5	Warren Spahn, Hank Aaron, Eddie Mathews	150.00
TT-6	Greg Maddux, Chipper Jones, Andruw Jones	75.00
TT-7	Nolan Ryan, Ivan Rodriguez, Juan Gonzalez	100.00
TT-8	Lance Berkman, Jeff Bagwell, Craig Biggio	50.00
TT-9	Rod Carew, Harmon Killebrew, Kirby Puckett	75.00
TT-10	Luis Gonzalez, Curt Schilling, Randy Johnson	60.00

2002 Leaf Samples

Each April 2002 issue of Beckett Baseball Card Monthly included a sample Leaf card rubber-cemented inside. The cards differ from the issued version only in the appearance on back of a (usually) silver-foil "SAMPLE" notation. Some cards were produced with the back overprint in gold-foil in much more limited quantities. The number of different players' cards involved in the promotion is unknown.

	NM/M
Common Player:	.10
Stars:	1.5-2X
Gold:	20X

2002 Leaf

	NM/M
Complete Set (1-200):	80.00
Common Player:	.15
Common (151-200):	1.50
Inserted 1:6	
Pack (4):	1.50
Box (24):	30.00
1 Tim Salmon	.25
2 Troy Glaus	.65
3 Curt Schilling	.40
4 Luis Gonzalez	.25
5 Mark Grace	.25

#	Player	Price
6	Matt Williams	.15
7	Randy Johnson	.65
8	Tom Glavine	.40
9	Brady Anderson	.15
10	Hideo Nomo	.15
11	Pedro Martinez	.65
12	Corey Patterson	.15
13	Paul Konerko	.25
14	Jon Lieber	.15
15	Carlos Lee	.15
16	Magglio Ordonez	.15
17	Adam Dunn	.40
18	Ken Griffey Jr.	1.00
19	C.C. Sabathia	.15
20	Jim Thome	.50
21	Juan Gonzalez	.15
22	Kenny Lofton	.15
23	Juan Encarnacion	.15
24	Tony Clark	.15
25	A.J. Burnett	.15
26	Josh Beckett	.25
27	Lance Berkman	.15
28	Eric Karros	.15
29	Shawn Green	.30
30	Brad Radke	.15
31	Joe Mays	.15
32	Javier Vazquez	.15
33	Alfonso Soriano	.50
34	Jorge Posada	.25
35	Eric Chavez	.15
36	Mark Mulder	.15
37	Miguel Tejada	.25
38	Tim Hudson	.15
39	Bobby Abreu	.15
40	Pat Burrell	.40
41	Ryan Klesko	.15
42	John Olerud	.15
43	Ellis Burks	.15
44	Mike Cameron	.15
45	Jim Edmonds	.15
46	Ben Grieve	.15
47	Carlos Pena	.15
48	Alex Rodriguez	1.50
49	Raul Mondesi	.15
50	Billy Koch	.15
51	Manny Ramirez	.65
52	Darin Erstad	.15
53	Troy Percival	.15
54	Andruw Jones	.65
55	Chipper Jones	.75
56	David Segui	.15
57	Chris Stynes	.15
58	Trot Nixon	.15
59	Sammy Sosa	1.00
60	Kerry Wood	.50
61	Frank Thomas	.65
62	Barry Larkin	.15
63	Bartolo Colon	.15
64	Kazuhiro Sasaki	.15
65	Roberto Alomar	.35
66	Mike Hampton	.15
67	Roger Cedeno	.15
68	Cliff Floyd	.15
69	Mike Lowell	.15
70	Billy Wagner	.15
71	Craig Biggio	.15
72	Jeff Bagwell	.65
73	Carlos Beltran	.50
74	Mark Quinn	.15
75	Mike Sweeney	.15
76	Gary Sheffield	.25
77	Kevin Brown	.15
78	Paul LoDuca	.15
79	Ben Sheets	.15
80	Jeromy Burnitz	.15
81	Richie Sexson	.15
82	Corey Koskie	.15
83	Eric Milton	.15
84	Jose Vidro	.15
85	Mike Piazza	1.00
86	Robin Ventura	.15
87	Andy Pettitte	.25
88	Mike Mussina	.40
89	Orlando Hernandez	.15
90	Roger Clemens	.85
91	Barry Zito	.25
92	Jermaine Dye	.15
93	Jimmy Rollins	.25
94	Jason Kendall	.15
95	Rickey Henderson	.65
96	Andres Galarraga	.15
97	Bret Boone	.15
98	Freddy Garcia	.15
99	J.D. Drew	.25
100	Jose Cruz Jr.	.15
101	Greg Maddux	.75
102	Javy Lopez	.15
103	Nomar Garciaparra	1.00

#	Player	Price
105	Fred McGriff	.15
106	Keith Foulke	.15
107	Ray Durham	.15
108	Sean Casey	.15
109	Todd Walker	.15
110	Omar Vizquel	.15
111	Travis Fryman	.15
112	Larry Walker	.15
113	Todd Helton	.65
114	Bobby Higginson	.15
115	Charles Johnson	.15
116	Moises Alou	.15
117	Richard Hidalgo	.15
118	Roy Oswalt	.25
119	Neifi Perez	.15
120	Adrian Beltre	.30
121	Chan Ho Park	.15
122	Geoff Jenkins	.15
123	Doug Mientkiewicz	.15
124	Torii Hunter	.15
125	Vladimir Guerrero	.65
126	Matt Lawton	.15
127	Tsuyoshi Shinjo	.15
128	Bernie Williams	.40
129	Derek Jeter	2.00
130	Mariano Rivera	.25
131	Tino Martinez	.15
132	Jason Giambi	.45
133	Scott Rolen	.50
134	Brian Giles	.15
135	Phil Nevin	.15
136	Trevor Hoffman	.15
137	Barry Bonds	2.00
138	Jeff Kent	.15
139	Shannon Stewart	.15
140	Shawn Estes	.15
141	Edgar Martinez	.15
142	Ichiro Suzuki	1.00
143	Albert Pujols	1.50
144	Bud Smith	.15
145	Matt Morris	.15
146	Frank Catalanotto	.15
147	Gabe Kapler	.15
148	Ivan Rodriguez	.45
149	Rafael Palmeiro	.45
150	Carlos Delgado	.40
151	Marlon Byrd	2.00
152	Alex Herrera	1.50
153	Brandon Backe RC	1.50
154	Jorge De La Rosa RC	2.00
155	Corky Miller	1.50
156	Dennis Tankersley	1.50
157	Kyle Kane RC	2.00
158	Justin Duchscherer	1.50
159	Brian Mallette RC	2.00
160	Eric Hinske	1.50
161	Jason Lane	1.50
162	Hee Seop Choi	3.00
163	Juan Cruz	1.50
164	Rodrigo Rosario RC	2.00
165	Matt Guerrier	1.50
166	Anderson Machado RC	2.00
167	Geronimo Gil	1.50
168	Dewon Brazelton	1.50
169	Mark Prior	4.00
170	Bill Hall	1.50
171	Jorge Padilla RC	1.50
172	Josh Pearce	1.50
173	Allan Simpson RC	2.00
174	Doug DeVore RC	1.50
175	Morgan Ensberg	1.50
176	Angel Berroa	1.50
177	Steve Bechler RC	2.00
178	Antonio Perez	1.50
179	Mark Teixeira	3.00
180	Mark Ellis	1.50
181	Michael Cuddyer	1.50
182	Mike Rivera	1.50
183	Raul Chavez RC	1.50
184	Juan Pena	1.50
185	Austin Kearns	1.50
186	Ryan Ludwick	1.50
187	Ed Rogers	1.50
188	Wilson Betemit	1.50
189	Nick Neugebauer	1.50
190	Tom Shearn RC	2.00
191	Eric Cyr RC	2.00
192	Victor Martinez	1.50
193	Brandon Berger	1.50
194	Erik Bedard	1.50
195	Franklin German RC	2.00
196	Joe Thurston	1.50
197	John Buck	1.50
198	Jeff Deardorff RC	2.00
199	Ryan Jamison RC	1.50
200	Alfredo Amezaga	1.50
201	So Taguchi/500 RC	6.00
202	Kazuhisa Ishii/250 RC	8.00

Lineage

1999 Lineage (1-50):	2-5X
Inserted 1:12	
2000 Lineage (51-100):	2-5X
Inserted 1:12	
2001 Lineage (101-150):	2-5X
Inserted 1:12	
Silver Holofoils:	8-15X
Production 100	

Press Proof Blue

Stars (1-150):	5-10X
Inserted 1:24 Retail	

Press Proof Red

Stars (1-150):	4-6X
Inserted 1:12 Retail	

Autograph

Quantity produced listed

Burn n' Turn

NM/M

Complete Set (10):	50.00
Common Player:	4.00
Inserted 1:96	
1 Fernando Vina, Edgar Renteria	4.00
2 Alex Rodriguez, Mike Young	10.00
3 Derek Jeter, Alfonso Soriano	15.00
4 Carlos Guillen, Bret Boone	4.00
5 Jose Vidro, Orlando Cabrera	4.00
6 Barry Larkin, Todd Walker	4.00
7 Carlos Febles, Neifi Perez	4.00
8 Jeff Kent, Rich Aurilia	4.00
9 Craig Biggio, Julio Lugo	5.00
10 Miguel Tejada, Mark Ellis	4.00

Clean Up Crew

NM/M

Complete Set (15):	90.00
Common Player:	4.00
Inserted 1:192	
1 Barry Bonds	20.00
2 Sammy Sosa	12.00
3 Luis Gonzalez	4.00
4 Richie Sexson	4.00
5 Jim Thome	6.00
6 Chipper Jones	8.00
7 Alex Rodriguez	15.00
8 Troy Glaus	6.00
9 Rafael Palmeiro	6.00
10 Lance Berkman	4.00
11 Mike Piazza	12.00
12 Jason Giambi	5.00
13 Todd Helton	6.00
14 Shawn Green	5.00
15 Carlos Delgado	5.00

Clubhouse Signatures Bronze

NM/M

Common Player:	5.00
(1) Wilson Betemit/150	6.00
(2) Marlon Byrd/200	6.00
(3) Joe Crede/200	8.00
(4) Andre Dawson/100	30.00
(5) J.D. Drew/25	35.00
(6) Adam Dunn/200	25.00
(7) Jermaine Dye/125	8.00
(8) Mark Ellis/300	8.00
(9) Johnny Estrada/250	8.00
(10) Bob Feller/250	15.00
(11) Robert Fick/300	5.00
(12) Steve Garvey/200	15.00
(13) Austin Kearns/300	10.00
(14) Jason Lane/250	8.00
(15) Paul LoDuca/300	8.00
(16) Terrence Long/250	8.00
(17) Edgar Martinez/50	30.00
(18) Don Mattingly/25	100.00
(19) Joe Mays/200	6.00
(20) Mark Mulder/200	25.00
(21) Xavier Nady/200	8.00
(22) Roy Oswalt/300	10.00
(23) Aramis Ramirez/250	10.00
(24) Tim Redding/300	5.00
(25) Phil Rizzuto/25	45.00
(26) Ryne Sandberg/25	100.00
(27) Ron Santo/300	15.00
(28) Bud Smith/200	5.00
(29) Ozzie Smith/25	85.00
(30) Alfonso Soriano/75	15.00
(31) Alan Trammell/75	15.00
(32) Billy Williams/150	10.00
(33) Barry Zito/100	25.00

Clubhouse Signatures Silver

NM/M

Common Player:	10.00
(1) Rich Aurilia/100	15.00
(2) Wilson Betemit/100	15.00
(3) Marlon Byrd/100	15.00
(4) Sean Casey/50	20.00
(5) Eric Chavez/100	20.00
(6) Roger Clemens/25	150.00
(7) Joe Crede/50	20.00
(8) Andre Dawson/100	30.00
(9) Adam Dunn/75	40.00
(10) Jermaine Dye/100	15.00
(11) Mark Ellis/100	15.00
(12) Johnny Estrada/100	15.00
(13) Bob Feller/100	20.00
(14) Robert Fick/100	15.00
(15) Steve Garvey/100	20.00
(16) Vladimir Guerrero/25	60.00
(17) Todd Helton/50	50.00
(18) Austin Kearns/100	20.00
(19) Jason Lane/100	15.00
(20) Paul LoDuca/100	15.00
(21) Terrence Long/100	10.00
(22) Edgar Martinez/100	25.00
(23) Joe Mays/50	20.00
(24) Mark Mulder/100	30.00
(25) Xavier Nady/100	15.00
(26) Roy Oswalt/100	20.00
(27) Aramis Ramirez/100	20.00
(28) Tim Redding/100	10.00
(29) Cal Ripken Jr./25	225.00
(30) Phil Rizzuto/25	50.00
(31) Ron Santo/100	40.00
(32) Mike Schmidt/75	75.00
(33) Bud Smith/100	10.00
(34) Miguel Tejada/100	20.00
(35) Javier Vazquez/100	15.00
(36) Billy Williams/100	20.00
(37) Barry Zito/100	30.00

Clubhouse Signatures Gold

NM/M

Common Player:	15.00
Numbered to 25	
(1) Rich Aurilia	15.00
(2) Josh Beckett	60.00
(3) Wilson Betemit	15.00
(4) Marlon Byrd	15.00
(5) Sean Casey	25.00
(6) Eric Chavez	30.00
(7) Roger Clemens	150.00
(8) Joe Crede	50.00
(9) Andre Dawson	40.00
(10) J.D. Drew	40.00
(11) Adam Dunn	65.00
(12) Jermaine Dye	20.00
(13) Mark Ellis	15.00
(14) Johnny Estrada	20.00
(15) Bob Feller	45.00
(16) Robert Fick	15.00
(17) Steve Garvey	40.00
(18) Luis Gonzalez	35.00
(19) Vladimir Guerrero	75.00
(20) Todd Helton	35.00
(21) Orel Hershiser	35.00
(22) Austin Kearns	15.00
(23) Jason Lane	15.00
(24) Paul LoDuca	25.00
(25) Terrence Long	15.00
(26) Edgar Martinez	30.00
(27) Don Mattingly	125.00
(28) Joe Mays	25.00
(29) Mark Mulder	40.00
(30) Xavier Nady	15.00
(31) Roy Oswalt	30.00
(32) Chan Ho Park	15.00
(33) Kirby Puckett	125.00
(34) Aramis Ramirez	15.00
(35) Tim Redding	15.00
(36) Cal Ripken Jr.	225.00
(37) Phil Rizzuto	60.00
(38) Ryne Sandberg	125.00
(39) Ron Santo	65.00
(40) Mike Schmidt	90.00
(41) Bud Smith	15.00
(42) Ozzie Smith	100.00
(43) Alfonso Soriano	40.00
(44) Miguel Tejada	30.00
(45) Alan Trammell	20.00
(46) Javier Vazquez	15.00
(47) Billy Williams	35.00
(48) Barry Zito	50.00

Cornerstones

NM/M

Production 50 Sets
Some not priced yet

1	Andruw Jones, Chipper Jones	40.00
4	Curt Schilling, Randy Johnson	40.00
6	Larry Walker, Todd Helton	25.00
7	Carlos Delgado, Shannon Stewart	25.00
10	Bernie Williams, Roger Clemens	60.00

Future 500 Club

NM/M

Complete Set (10):	40.00
Common Player:	2.00
Inserted 1:64	
1 Sammy Sosa	8.00
2 Mike Piazza	8.00
3 Alex Rodriguez	10.00
4 Chipper Jones	6.00
5 Jeff Bagwell	4.00
6 Carlos Delgado	2.00
7 Shawn Green	2.00
8 Ken Griffey Jr.	8.00
9 Rafael Palmeiro	3.00
10 Vladimir Guerrero	4.00

Game Collection

NM/M

Common Player:	5.00
Inserted 1:62 R	
SP's indicated	
AB B Adrian Beltre/Bat	5.00
AD BG Adam Dunn/Btg Glv/25	25.00
AG B Andres Galarraga/Bat	
AJ B Andruw Jones/Bat/300	8.00
BG B Brian Giles/Bat	5.00
BH B Bobby Higginson/Bat	5.00
BS H Ben Sheets/Hat/25	35.00
BW S Bernie Williams/Shoe/25	30.00
BZ FG Barry Zito/Fielding Glv/25	25.00
CB B Carlos Beltran/Bat	8.00
CBI B Craig Biggio/Bat	6.00
CF B Carlton Fisk/Bat	10.00
CK B Chuck Knoblauch/Bat	5.00
CP S Corey Patterson/Shoe/25	25.00
EM B Eddie Murray/Bat/250	15.00
GJ P Geoff Jenkins/Pants	5.00
IR BG Ivan Rodriguez/Btg Glv/25	30.00
JB B Jeff Bagwell/Bat/100	15.00
JD H Johnny Damon/Hat/25	25.00
JE B Juan Encarnacion/Bat	5.00
JG B Juan Gonzalez/Bat	5.00
KL B Kenny Lofton/Bat	5.00
KW S Kerry Wood/Shoe/25	40.00
LB BG Lance Berkman/Btg Glv/25	25.00
LW B Larry Walker/Bat/50	15.00
MB BG Marlon Byrd/Btg Glv/25	20.00
MG B Mark Grace/Bat/200	5.00
MM FG Mike Mussina/Fielding Glv/25	55.00
MO B Magglio Ordonez/Bat/150	6.00
MP B Mike Piazza/Bat/100	15.00
PB B Pat Burrell/Bat/100	15.00
RA B Roberto Alomar/Bat	5.00
RD B Ray Durham/Bat	5.00
RG B Rusty Greer/Bat	5.00
RJ FG Randy Johnson/Fielding Glv	80.00
RP B Rafael Palmeiro/Bat	10.00
RP BG Rafael Palmeiro/Btg Glv/25	30.00
RV B Robin Ventura/Bat	5.00
SC B Sean Casey/Bat	5.00
SR B Scott Rolen/Bat/250	15.00
SS H Shannon Stewart/Hat/25	20.00
TC B Tony Clark/Bat	5.00
TG BG Tony Gwynn/Btg Glv/25	90.00
TH B Todd Helton/Bat	10.00
TN B Trot Nixon/Bat	5.00
WB B Wade Boggs/Bat	8.00

Gold Leaf Rookies

NM/M

Complete Set (10):	20.00
Common Player:	2.00
Inserted 1:24	
1 Josh Beckett	4.00
2 Marlon Byrd	2.00
3 Dennis Tankersley	2.00
4 Jason Lane	2.00
5 Dewon Brazelton	2.00
6 Mark Prior	4.00
7 Bill Hall	2.00
8 Angel Berroa	2.00
9 Mark Teixeira	4.00
10 John Buck	2.00

Heading for the Hall Autographs

NM/M

Common Player:	25.00
Production 50 each.	
1 Greg Maddux	125.00
2 Ozzie Smith	100.00
3 Andre Dawson	40.00
4 Dennis Eckersley	45.00
5 Roberto Alomar	25.00
6 Cal Ripken Jr.	200.00
7 Roger Clemens	150.00
8 Tony Gwynn	100.00
9 Alex Rodriguez	150.00
10 Jeff Bagwell	40.00

League of Nations

NM/M

Complete Set (10):	20.00
Common Player:	2.00
Inserted 1:60	
1 Ichiro Suzuki	8.00
2 Tsuyoshi Shinjo	2.00
3 Chan Ho Park	2.00
4 Larry Walker	2.00
5 Andruw Jones	4.00
6 Hideo Nomo	4.00
7 Byung-Hyun Kim	2.00
8 Sun-Woo Kim	2.00
9 Orlando Hernandez	2.00
10 Luke Prokopec	2.00

Retired Numbers

#'d to jersey number
No Pricing

Rookie Reprints

NM/M

Complete Set (6):	35.00

Common Player:		3.00
#'d to year of issue		
1	Roger Clemens/1,985	
	1,985	10.00
2	Kirby Puckett/1,985	9.00
3	Andres Galarraga/1,986	
	1,986	3.00
4	Fred McGriff/1,986	3.00
5	Sammy Sosa/1,990	10.00
6	Frank Thomas/1,990	8.00

Shirt Off My Back

		NM/M
Common Player:		5.00
Inserted 1:29		
Patch Variations:		2-4X
RA	Roberto Alomar	8.00
JB	Jeff Bagwell/SP	20.00
MB	Michael Barrett	5.00
CB	Carlos Beltran	15.00
LB	Lance Berkman	5.00
GB	George Brett/SP	50.00
KB	Kevin Brown	5.00
MB	Mark Buehrle	5.00
AB	A.J. Burnett	5.00
JBU	Jeromy Burnitz	5.00
CD	Carlos Delgado	5.00
RD	Ryan Dempster	5.00
DE	Darin Erstad/SP	15.00
CF	Cliff Floyd	5.00
FG	Freddy Garcia/SP	8.00
NG	Nomar Garciaparra/SP	40.00
TGL	Troy Glaus/SP	20.00
TGL	Tom Glavine	8.00
LG	Luis Gonzalez	5.00
TG	Tony Gwynn	25.00
MH	Mike Hampton	5.00
TH	Todd Helton	20.00
THU	Tim Hudson	6.00
BJA	Bo Jackson/SP	25.00
RJ	Randy Johnson	20.00
CJ	Chipper Jones/SP	30.00
AK	Al Kaline/SP	20.00
EK	Eric Karros	5.00
BL	Barry Larkin	5.00
CL	Carlos Lee	5.00
JL	Javy Lopez	5.00
GM	Greg Maddux/SP	30.00
EM	Edgar Martinez/SP	20.00
PM	Pedro Martinez/SP	20.00
DM	Don Mattingly/SP	50.00
KM	Kevin Millwood	5.00
HN	Hideo Nomo/SP	25.00
JO	John Olerud	5.00
MO	Magglio Ordonez	5.00
RP	Rafael Palmeiro	10.00
CHP	Chan Ho Park/SP	8.00
TP	Troy Percival	5.00
AP	Andy Pettitte/SP	12.00
MP	Mike Piazza	30.00
KP	Kirby Puckett	25.00
BR	Brad Radke	5.00
MR	Manny Ramirez	20.00
CR	Cal Ripken Jr./SP/50	100.00
AR	Alex Rodriguez	35.00
SR	Scott Rolen/SP	15.00
KS	Kazuhiro Sasaki/SP	8.00
CS	Curt Schilling/SP	15.00
RS	Richie Sexson	5.00
TS	Tsuyoshi Shinjo/SP	8.00
JS	John Smoltz	5.00
MS	Mike Sweeney	5.00
MT	Miguel Tejada	6.00
LW	Larry Walker/SP	8.00
MW	Matt Williams	5.00
DW	Dave Winfield/SP	20.00

2002 Leaf Certified Samples

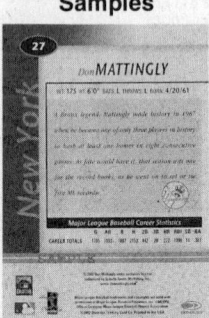

Abbreviations

SP - Short Print

Each October 2002 issue of Beckett Baseball Card Monthly included a sample Leaf Certified card rubber-cemented inside. The cards differ from the issued version only in the appearance on back of a (usually) silver-foil "SAMPLE" notation. Some cards were produced with the back overprint in gold foil in much more limited quantities. The number of different players' cards involved in the promotion is unknown.

	NM/M
Common Player:	.10
Stars:	1.5X
Gold:	20X

2002 Leaf Certified

		NM/M
Complete Set (200):		
Common Player:		.50
Common (151-200):		5.00
Production 500		
Pack (5):		6.00
Box (16):		75.00
1	Alex Rodriguez	4.00
2	Luis Gonzalez	.65
3	Javier Vazquez	.50
4	Juan Uribe	.50
5	Ben Sheets	.50
6	George Brett	4.00
7	Magglio Ordonez	.50
8	Randy Johnson	1.00
9	Joe Kennedy	.50
10	Richie Sexson	.50
11	Larry Walker	.50
12	Lance Berkman	.50
13	Jose Cruz Jr.	.50
14	Doug Davis	.50
15	Cliff Floyd	.50
16	Ryan Klesko	.50
17	Troy Glaus	1.00
18	Robert Person	.50
19	Bartolo Colon	.50
20	Adam Dunn	.75
21	Kevin Brown	.50
22	John Smoltz	.50
23	Edgar Martinez	.50
24	Eric Karros	.50
25	Tony Gwynn	2.00
26	Mark Mulder	.50
27	Don Mattingly	4.00
28	Brandon Duckworth	.50
29	C.C. Sabathia	.50
30	Nomar Garciaparra	3.00
31	Adam Johnson	.50
32	Miguel Tejada	.65
33	Ryne Sandberg	2.00
34	Roger Clemens	2.50
35	Edgardo Alfonzo	.50
36	Jason Jennings	.50
37	Todd Helton	1.00
38	Nolan Ryan	5.00
39	Paul LoDuca	.50
40	Cal Ripken Jr.	5.00
41	Terrence Long	.50
42	Mike Sweeney	.50
43	Carlos Lee	.50
44	Ben Grieve	.50
45	Tony Armas Jr.	.50
46	Joe Mays	.50
47	Jeff Kent	.50
48	Andy Pettitte	.65
49	Kirby Puckett	2.00
50	Aramis Ramirez	.50
51	Tim Redding	.50
52	Freddy Garcia	.50
53	Javy Lopez	.50
54	Mike Schmidt	4.00
55	Wade Miller	.50
56	Ramon Ortiz	.50
57	Ray Durham	.50
58	J.D. Drew	.75
59	Bret Boone	.50
60	Mark Buehrle	.50
61	Geoff Jenkins	.50
62	Greg Maddux	2.00
63	Mark Grace	.65
64	Toby Hall	.50
65	A.J. Burnett	.50
66	Bernie Williams	.65
67	Roy Oswalt	.65
68	Shannon Stewart	.50
69	Barry Zito	.65
70	Juan Pierre	.50
71	Preston Wilson	.50
72	Rafael Furcal	.50
73	Sean Casey	.65
74	John Olerud	.50
75	Paul Konerko	.75
76	Vernon Wells	.50
77	Juan Gonzalez	1.00
78	Ellis Burks	.50
79	Jim Edmonds	.75
80	Robert Fick	.50
81	Michael Cuddyer	.50
82	Tim Hudson	.65
83	Phil Nevin	.50
84	Curt Schilling	.75
85	Juan Cruz	.50
86	Jeff Bagwell	1.00
87	Raul Mondesi	.50
88	Bud Smith	.50
89	Omar Vizquel	.50
90	Vladimir Guerrero	1.00
91	Garret Anderson	.50
92	Mike Piazza	3.00
93	Josh Beckett	.65
94	Carlos Delgado	1.00
95	Kazuhiro Sasaki	.50
96	Chipper Jones	2.00
97	Jacque Jones	.50
98	Pedro J. Martinez	1.00
99	Marcus Giles	.50
100	Craig Biggio	.50
101	Orlando Cabrera	.50
102	Al Leiter	.50
103	Michael Barrett	.50
104	Hideo Nomo	1.00
105	Mike Mussina	.75
106	Jeremy Giambi	.50
107	Cristian Guzman	.50
108	Frank Thomas	1.00
109	Carlos Beltran	1.00
110	Jorge Posada	.65
111	Roberto Alomar	.65
112	Bobby Abreu	.50
113	Robin Ventura	.50
114	Pat Burrell	.75
115	Kenny Lofton	.50
116	Adrian Beltre	.75
117	Gary Sheffield	.75
118	Jermaine Dye	.50
119	Manny Ramirez	1.00
120	Brian Giles	.50
121	Tsuyoshi Shinjo	.50
122	Rafael Palmeiro	.85
123	Mo Vaughn	.50
124	Kerry Wood	.75
125	Moises Alou	.50
126	Rickey Henderson	1.00
127	Corey Patterson	.50
128	Jim Thome	1.00
129	Richard Hidalgo	.50
130	Darin Erstad	.75
131	Johnny Damon	.75
132	Juan Encarnacion	.50
133	Scott Rolen	1.00
134	Tom Glavine	.75
135	Ivan Rodriguez	.85
136	Jay Gibbons	.50
137	Trot Nixon	.50
138	Nick Neugebauer	.50
139	Barry Larkin	.50
140	Andruw Jones	1.00
141	Shawn Green	.75
142	Jose Vidro	.50
143	Derek Jeter	5.00
144	Ichiro Suzuki	3.00
145	Ken Griffey Jr.	3.00
146	Barry Bonds	5.00
147	Albert Pujols	4.00
148	Sammy Sosa	3.00
149	Jason Giambi	.75
150	Alfonso Soriano	.75
151	Drew Henson/Bat	8.00
152	Luis Garcia/Bat	5.00
153	Geronimo Gil/Jsy	5.00
154	Corky Miller/Bat	5.00
155	Mike Rivera/Bat	5.00
156	Mark Ellis/Jsy	5.00
157	Josh Pearce/Bat	5.00
158	Ryan Ludwick/Bat	5.00
159	So Taguchi/Bat RC	12.00
160	Cody Ransom/Jsy	5.00
161	Jeff Deardorff/Bat RC	5.00
162	Franklyn German/Bat RC	5.00
163	Ed Rogers/Jsy	5.00
164	Eric Cyr/Jsy RC	5.00
165	Victor Alvarez/Jsy RC	5.00
166	Victor Martinez/Jsy	15.00
167	Brandon Berger/Jsy	5.00
168	Juan Diaz/Jsy	5.00
169	Kevin Frederick/Jsy RC	5.00
170	Earl Snyder/Bat RC	5.00
171	Morgan Ensberg/Bat	8.00
172	Ryan Jamison/Jsy RC	5.00
173	Rodrigo Rosario/Jsy RC	5.00
174	Willie Harris/Bat	5.00
175	Ramon Vazquez/Bat	5.00
176	Kazuhisa Ishii/Bat RC	12.00
177	Hank Blalock/Bat	10.00
178	Mark Prior/Bat	15.00
179	Dewon Brazelton/Jsy RC	5.00
180	Doug DeVore/Jsy RC	5.00
181	Jorge Padilla/Bat RC	5.00
182	Mark Teixeira/Jsy	10.00
183	Orlando Hudson/Bat	5.00
184	John Buck/Jsy	5.00
185	Erik Bedard/Jsy	5.00
186	Allan Simpson/Jsy RC	5.00
187	Travis Hafner/Jsy	10.00
188	Jason Lane/Jsy	5.00
189	Marlon Byrd/Jsy	5.00
190	Joe Thurston/Jsy	5.00
191	Brandon Backe/Jsy RC	5.00
192	Josh Phelps/Jsy	5.00
193	Bill Hall/Bat	5.00
194	Chris Snelling/Bat RC	8.00
195	Austin Kearns/Bat	8.00
196	Antonio Perez/Bat	5.00
197	Angel Berroa/Bat	5.00
198	Anderson Machado/Jsy RC	5.00
199	Alfredo Amezaga/Jsy	5.00
200	Eric Hinske/Bat	8.00

Mirror Red

		NM/M
Common (1-200):		5.00
Cards (151-200):		.5-1X base
Mirror Blues (1-200):		.5-1.5X
Production 150 Sets		
Mirror Blues 75 Sets		
Mirror Golds not priced.		
Production 25 Sets		
Mirror Emerald five sets produced.		
Mirror Black one set produced.		
1	Alex Rodriguez	25.00
2	Luis Gonzalez	5.00
3	Javier Vazquez/Bat	5.00
4	Juan Uribe/Jsy	5.00
5	Ben Sheets/Jsy	8.00
6	George Brett/Jsy	40.00
7	Magglio Ordonez/Jsy	8.00
8	Randy Johnson/Jsy	15.00
9	Joe Kennedy/Jsy	5.00
10	Richie Sexson/Jsy	10.00
11	Larry Walker/Jsy	8.00
12	Lance Berkman/Jsy	8.00
13	Jose Cruz Jr/Jsy	5.00
14	Doug Davis/Jsy	5.00
15	Cliff Floyd/Jsy	5.00
16	Ryan Klesko/Jsy	8.00
17	Troy Glaus/Jsy	10.00
18	Robert Person/Jsy	5.00
19	Bartolo Colon/Jsy	5.00
20	Adam Dunn/Jsy	15.00
21	Kevin Brown/Jsy	8.00
22	John Smoltz/Jsy	8.00
23	Edgar Martinez/Jsy	8.00
24	Eric Karros/Jsy	5.00
25	Tony Gwynn/Jsy	20.00
26	Mark Mulder/Jsy	8.00
27	Don Mattingly/Jsy	40.00
28	Brandon Duckworth/Jsy	5.00
29	C.C. Sabathia/Jsy	5.00
30	Nomar Garciaparra/Jsy	20.00
31	Adam Johnson/Jsy	5.00
32	Miguel Tejada/Jsy	8.00
33	Ryne Sandberg/Jsy	40.00
34	Roger Clemens/Jsy	25.00
35	Edgardo Alfonzo/Jsy	5.00
36	Jason Jennings/Jsy	5.00
37	Todd Helton/Jsy	10.00
38	Nolan Ryan/Jsy	60.00
39	Paul LoDuca/Jsy	5.00
40	Cal Ripken Jr./Jsy	55.00
41	Terrence Long/Jsy	5.00
42	Mike Sweeney/Jsy	5.00
43	Carlos Lee/Jsy	5.00
44	Ben Grieve/Jsy	5.00
45	Tony Armas Jr/Jsy	5.00
46	Joe Mays/Jsy	5.00
47	Jeff Kent/Jsy	8.00
48	Andy Pettitte/Jsy	8.00
49	Kirby Puckett/Jsy	15.00
50	Aramis Ramirez/Jsy	8.00
51	Tim Redding/Jsy	5.00
52	Freddy Garcia/Jsy	5.00
53	Javy Lopez/Jsy	6.00
54	Mike Schmidt/Jsy	35.00
55	Wade Miller/Jsy	5.00
56	Ramon Ortiz/Jsy	5.00
57	Ray Durham/Jsy	5.00
58	J.D. Drew/Jsy	5.00
59	Bret Boone/Jsy	5.00
60	Mark Buehrle/Jsy	5.00
61	Geoff Jenkins/Jsy	5.00
62	Greg Maddux/Jsy	20.00
63	Mark Grace/Jsy	10.00
64	Toby Hall/Jsy	5.00
65	A.J. Burnett/Jsy	5.00
66	Bernie Williams/Jsy	8.00
67	Roy Oswalt/Jsy	8.00
68	Shannon Stewart/Jsy	5.00
69	Barry Zito/Jsy	8.00
70	Juan Pierre/Jsy	5.00
71	Preston Wilson/Jsy	5.00
72	Rafael Furcal/Jsy	5.00
73	Sean Casey/Jsy	8.00
74	John Olerud/Jsy	5.00
75	Paul Konerko/Jsy	8.00
76	Vernon Wells/Jsy	5.00
77	Juan Gonzalez/Jsy	8.00
78	Ellis Burks/Jsy	5.00
79	Jim Edmonds/Jsy	8.00
80	Robert Fick/Jsy	5.00
81	Michael Cuddyer/Jsy	5.00
82	Tim Hudson/Jsy	8.00
83	Phil Nevin/Jsy	5.00
84	Curt Schilling/Jsy	8.00
85	Juan Cruz/Jsy	5.00
86	Jeff Bagwell/Jsy	10.00
87	Raul Mondesi/Jsy	5.00
88	Bud Smith/Jsy	5.00
89	Omar Vizquel/Jsy	5.00
90	Vladimir Guerrero/Jsy	20.00
91	Garret Anderson/Jsy	8.00
92	Mike Piazza/Jsy	15.00
93	Josh Beckett/Jsy	8.00
94	Carlos Delgado/Jsy	8.00
95	Kazuhiro Sasaki/Jsy	5.00
96	Chipper Jones/Jsy	10.00
97	Jacque Jones/Jsy	5.00
98	Pedro Martinez/Jsy	15.00
99	Marcus Giles/Jsy	5.00
100	Craig Biggio/Jsy	6.00
101	Orlando Cabrera/Jsy	5.00
102	Al Leiter/Jsy	5.00
103	Michael Barrett/Jsy	5.00
104	Hideo Nomo/Jsy	8.00
105	Mike Mussina/Jsy	12.00
106	Jeremy Giambi/Jsy	5.00
107	Cristian Guzman/Jsy	5.00
108	Frank Thomas/Jsy	10.00
109	Carlos Beltran/Bat	8.00
110	Jorge Posada/Bat	8.00
111	Roberto Alomar/Bat	12.00
112	Bobby Abreu/Bat	5.00
113	Robin Ventura/Bat	10.00
114	Pat Burrell/Bat	18.00
115	Kenny Lofton/Bat	6.00
116	Adrian Beltre/Bat	5.00
117	Gary Sheffield/Bat	6.00
118	Jermaine Dye/Bat	5.00
119	Manny Ramirez/Bat	8.00
120	Brian Giles/Bat	5.00
121	Tsuyoshi Shinjo/Bat	5.00
122	Rafael Palmeiro/Bat	10.00
123	Mo Vaughn/Bat	5.00
124	Kerry Wood/Bat	15.00
125	Moises Alou/Bat	8.00
126	Rickey Henderson/Bat	15.00
127	Corey Patterson/Bat	8.00
128	Jim Thome/Bat	15.00
129	Richard Hidalgo/Bat	5.00
130	Darin Erstad/Bat	8.00
131	Johnny Damon/Bat	8.00
132	Juan Encarnacion/Bat	5.00
133	Scott Rolen/Bat	10.00
134	Tom Glavine/Bat	8.00
135	Ivan Rodriguez/Bat	10.00
136	Jay Gibbons/Bat	5.00
137	Trot Nixon/Bat	5.00
138	Nick Neugebauer/Bat	5.00
139	Barry Larkin/Jsy	10.00
140	Andruw Jones/Bat	8.00
141	Shawn Green/Bat	8.00
142	Jose Vidro/Jsy	5.00
143	Derek Jeter/Base	25.00
144	Ichiro Suzuki/Base	20.00
145	Ken Griffey Jr./Base	15.00
146	Barry Bonds/Base	15.00
147	Albert Pujols/Base	15.00
148	Sammy Sosa/Base	15.00
149	Jason Giambi/Base	5.00
150	Alfonso Soriano/Base	10.00
151	Drew Henson/Bat	5.00
152	Luis Garcia/Bat	5.00
153	Geronimo Gil/Jsy	5.00
154	Corky Miller/Bat	5.00
155	Mike Rivera/Bat	5.00
156	Mark Ellis/Jsy	5.00
157	Josh Pearce/Bat	5.00
158	Ryan Ludwick/Bat	5.00
159	So Taguchi/Bat	12.00
160	Cody Ransom/Jsy	5.00
161	Jeff Deardorff/Bat	5.00
162	Franklyn German/Bat	5.00
163	Ed Rogers/Jsy	5.00
164	Eric Cyr/Jsy	5.00
165	Victor Alvarez/Jsy	5.00
166	Victor Martinez/Jsy	10.00
167	Brandon Berger/Jsy	5.00
168	Juan Diaz/Jsy	5.00
169	Kevin Frederick/Jsy	5.00
170	Earl Snyder/Bat	5.00
171	Morgan Ensberg/Bat	5.00
172	Ryan Jamison/Jsy	5.00
173	Rodrigo Rosario/Jsy	5.00
174	Willie Harris/Bat	5.00
175	Ramon Vazquez/Bat	5.00
176	Kazuhisa Ishii/Jsy	15.00
177	Hank Blalock/Bat	10.00
178	Mark Prior/Bat	10.00
179	Dewon Brazelton/Jsy	5.00
180	Doug DeVore/Jsy	5.00
181	Jorge Padilla/Bat	5.00
182	Mark Teixeira/Jsy	10.00
183	Orlando Hudson/Bat	5.00
184	John Buck/Jsy	5.00
185	Erik Bedard/Jsy	5.00
186	Allan Simpson/Jsy	5.00
187	Travis Hafner/Jsy	8.00
188	Jason Lane/Jsy	5.00
189	Marlon Byrd/Jsy	5.00
190	Joe Thurston/Jsy	5.00
191	Brandon Backe/Jsy	5.00
192	Josh Phelps/Jsy	5.00
193	Bill Hall/Bat	5.00
194	Chris Snelling/Bat	5.00
195	Austin Kearns/Bat	8.00
196	Antonio Perez/Bat	5.00
197	Angel Berroa/Bat	6.00
198	Anderson Machado/Jsy	5.00
199	Alfredo Amezaga/Jsy	5.00
200	Eric Hinske/Bat	6.00

All Certified Team

		NM/M
Complete Set (25):		75.00
Common Player:		1.50
Inserted 1:17		
Mirror Blues:		2-4X
Production 50 Sets		
Mirror Reds:		1.5-3X
Production 75 Sets		
Golds not priced 25 sets produced.		
1	Ichiro Suzuki	5.00
2	Alex Rodriguez	6.00
3	Sammy Sosa	5.00
4	Jeff Bagwell	3.00
5	Greg Maddux	4.00
6	Todd Helton	3.00
7	Nomar Garciaparra	5.00
8	Ken Griffey Jr.	4.50
9	Roger Clemens	4.50
10	Adam Dunn	2.00
11	Chipper Jones	4.00
12	Hideo Nomo	3.00
13	Lance Berkman	1.50
14	Barry Bonds	8.00
15	Manny Ramirez	3.00
16	Jason Giambi	2.00
17	Rickey Henderson	3.00
18	Randy Johnson	3.00
19	Derek Jeter	5.00
20	Kazuhisa Ishii	1.50
21	Frank Thomas	3.00
22	Mike Piazza	5.00
23	Albert Pujols	6.00
24	Pedro J. Martinez	5.00
25	Vladimir Guerrero	3.00

Certified Skills

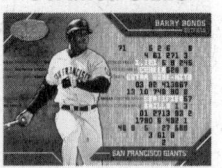

		NM/M
Complete Set (20):		65.00
Common Player:		2.00
Inserted 1:17		
Mirror Blues:		1.5-2.5X
Production 75 Sets		
Mirror Reds:		1-2X
Production 150 Sets		
Mirror Golds not priced 25 sets.		
1	Barry Bonds	8.00
2	Greg Maddux	4.00
3	Rickey Henderson	3.00
4	Ichiro Suzuki	5.00
5	Pedro J. Martinez	2.00
6	Kazuhisa Ishii	1.50
7	Alex Rodriguez	5.00
8	Mike Piazza	5.00
9	Sammy Sosa	5.00
10	Derek Jeter	5.00
11	Albert Pujols	6.00
12	Roger Clemens	4.50
13	Mark Prior	1.50
14	Chipper Jones	3.00
15	Ken Griffey Jr.	4.00
16	Frank Thomas	2.00
17	Randy Johnson	2.00

#	Player	NM/M
18	Vladimir Guerrero	2.00
19	Nomar Garciaparra	5.00
20	Jeff Bagwell	2.00

Fabric of the Game

#	Player	NM/M
	Common Player:	
1	Bobby Doerr/37	20.00
2	Ozzie Smith/78	40.00
3	Pee Wee Reese/40	35.00
4	Tommy Lasorda/80	8.00
4	Tommy Lasorda/54	15.00
4	Tommy Lasorda/15	15.00
5	Red Schoendienst/45	20.00
7	Harmon Killebrew/54	35.00
8	Roger Maris A's/57	75.00
8	Mel Ott/26	75.00
11	Paul Molitor/100	20.00
11	Paul Molitor/78	20.00
11	Paul Molitor/50	30.00
12	Duke Snider/47	40.00
13	Brooks Robinson/55	40.00
14	George Brett/40	75.00
14	George Brett/73	50.00
15	Johnny Bench/80	40.00
15	Johnny Bench/67	30.00
15	Johnny Bench/50	30.00
16	Lou Boudreau/38	20.00
17	Stan Musial/41	60.00
18	Al Kaline/53	30.00
19	Steve Garvey/100	8.00
19	Steve Garvey/69	15.00
19	Steve Garvey/45	15.00
20	Nomar Garciaparra/100	25.00
20	Nomar Garciaparra/96	25.00
20	Nomar Garciaparra/50	35.00
21	Joe Morgan/80	10.00
21	Joe Morgan/63	20.00
21	Joe Morgan/50	20.00
22	Willie Stargell/62	25.00
23	Andre Dawson/80	40.00
23	Andre Dawson/76	15.00
23	Andre Dawson/50	20.00
24	Gary Carter/100	10.00
24	Gary Carter/74	20.00
24	Gary Carter/50	20.00
25	Reggie Jackson A's/67	30.00
27	Phil Rizzuto/41	30.00
28	Luis Aparicio/56	20.00
29	Robin Yount/80	30.00
29	Robin Yount/74	30.00
29	Robin Yount/50	30.00
30	Tony Gwynn/100	20.00
30	Tony Gwynn/82	20.00
30	Tony Gwynn/50	30.00
31	Ernie Banks/53	40.00
32	Joe Torre/50	15.00
32	Joe Torre/60	15.00
33	Bo Jackson/100	20.00
33	Bo Jackson/86	20.00
33	Bo Jackson/35	50.00
34	Alfonso Soriano/80	20.00
34	Alfonso Soriano/99	20.00
34	Alfonso Soriano/50	25.00
35	Cal Ripken Jr./80	60.00
35	Cal Ripken Jr./81	60.00
35	Cal Ripken Jr./50	80.00
36	Miguel Tejada/100	10.00
36	Miguel Tejada/97	10.00
36	Miguel Tejada/50	20.00
37	Alex Rodriguez M's/100	20.00
37	Alex Rodriguez M's/94	20.00
37	Alex Rodriguez M's/50	35.00
38	Mike Schmidt/80	40.00
38	Mike Schmidt/72	40.00
38	Mike Schmidt/50	50.00
39	Lou Brock/61	25.00
40	Don Sutton/80	8.00
40	Don Sutton/76	10.00
40	Don Sutton/50	15.00
41	Roberto Clemente/55	125.00
42	Jim Palmer/65	20.00
43	Don Mattingly/40	75.00
43	Don Mattingly/82	50.00
44	Ryne Sandberg/40	60.00
44	Ryne Sandberg/81	20.00
45	Early Wynn/39	20.00
46	Mike Piazza Dodgers/100	20.00
46	Mike Piazza Dodgers/92	20.00
46	Mike Piazza Dodgers/31	40.00
46	Mike Piazza Dodgers/50	25.00
47	Wade Boggs/100	15.00
47	Wade Boggs/82	15.00
47	Wade Boggs/26	40.00
47	Wade Boggs/45	30.00
48	Jim "Catfish" Hunter/65	25.00
48	Jim "Catfish" Hunter/27	40.00
49	Juan Marichal/60	40.00
49	Juan Marichal/27	40.00
50	Carlton Fisk/Red Sox/80	25.00
50	Carlton Fisk/Red Sox/69	40.00
50	Carlton Fisk/Red Sox/27	50.00
50	Carlton Fisk/Red Sox/50	30.00
51	Curt Schilling/100	15.00
51	Curt Schilling/88	15.00
51	Curt Schilling/38	25.00
51	Curt Schilling/50	20.00
52	Rod Carew Angels/80	15.00
52	Rod Carew Angels/67	25.00
52	Rod Carew Angels/50	25.00
53	Rod Carew Twins/67	25.00
54	Joe Carter/100	8.00
54	Joe Carter/83	8.00
54	Joe Carter/29	10.00
54	Joe Carter/50	10.00
55	Nolan Ryan Angels/66	60.00
56	Orlando Cepeda/80	8.00
56	Orlando Cepeda/55	10.00
56	Orlando Cepeda/25	20.00
56	Orlando Cepeda/50	10.00
57	Dave Winfield/80	15.00
57	Dave Winfield/73	20.00
57	Dave Winfield/31	30.00
57	Dave Winfield/50	20.00
58	Hoyt Wilhelm/80	8.00
58	Hoyt Wilhelm/52	10.00
58	Hoyt Wilhelm/31	20.00
58	Hoyt Wilhelm/50	15.00
59	Steve Carlton/80	15.00
59	Steve Carlton/65	20.00
59	Steve Carlton/32	30.00
59	Steve Carlton/50	15.00
60	Eddie Murray/100	15.00
60	Eddie Murray/77	15.00
60	Eddie Murray/33	30.00
60	Eddie Murray/50	20.00
61	Nolan Ryan Rangers/40	75.00
61	Nolan Ryan Rangers/66	60.00
61	Nolan Ryan Rangers/34	75.00
62	Nolan Ryan Astros/40	75.00
62	Nolan Ryan Astros/66	60.00
62	Nolan Ryan Astros/34	75.00
63	Kirby Puckett/40	40.00
63	Kirby Puckett/84	20.00
63	Kirby Puckett/34	40.00
64	Yogi Berra/46	40.00
64	Yogi Berra/35	40.00
65	Phil Niekro/80	8.00
65	Phil Niekro/64	10.00
65	Phil Niekro/35	15.00
65	Phil Niekro/50	10.00
66	Gaylord Perry/80	8.00
66	Gaylord Perry/62	10.00
66	Gaylord Perry/36	10.00
66	Gaylord Perry/50	10.00
67	Pedro Martinez/Expos/100	15.00
67	Pedro Martinez/Expos/92	15.00
67	Pedro Martinez/Expos/45	25.00
67	Pedro Martinez/Expos/50	20.00
68	Alex Rodriguez/Rgr/100	20.00
68	Alex Rodriguez/Rgr/94	20.00
68	Alex Rodriguez/Rgr/50	30.00
69	Dave Parker/100	8.00
69	Dave Parker/73	10.00
69	Dave Parker/39	15.00
69	Dave Parker/50	10.00
70	Darin Erstad/100	8.00
70	Darin Erstad/96	8.00
70	Darin Erstad/50	15.00
71	Eddie Matthews/52	30.00
71	Eddie Matthews/41	35.00
72	Tom Seaver Mets/67	30.00
72	Tom Seaver Mets/41	40.00
73	Tom Seaver Reds/67	30.00
73	Tom Seaver Reds/41	40.00
74	Jackie Robinson/47	100.00
74	Jackie Robinson/42	100.00
75	Randy Johnson M's/80	15.00
75	Randy Johnson M's/88	15.00
75	Randy Johnson M's/51	25.00
75	Randy Johnson M's/50	25.00
76	Reggie Jackson Yanks/57	30.00
76	Reggie Jackson/Yanks/44	40.00
77	Reggie Jackson/Angels/80	20.00
77	Reggie Jackson/Angels/67	30.00
77	Reggie Jackson/Angels/44	40.00
77	Reggie Jackson/Angels/50	
78	Willie McCovey/80	10.00
78	Willie McCovey/59	15.00
78	Willie McCovey/44	20.00
78	Willie McCovey/20	20.00
79	Eric Davis/100	5.00
79	Eric Davis/84	5.00
79	Eric Davis/34	10.00
79	Eric Davis/50	8.00
80	Carlos Delgado/95	6.00
80	Carlos Delgado/93	6.00
81	Dale Murphy/100	20.00
81	Dale Murphy/76	20.00
81	Dale Murphy/50	30.00
82	Brian Giles/100	5.00
82	Brian Giles/95	5.00
82	Brian Giles/50	8.00
83	Kazuhiro Sasaki/100	8.00
83	Kazuhiro Sasaki/93	8.00
83	Kazuhiro Sasaki/50	10.00
84	Phil Nevin/100	8.00
84	Phil Nevin/95	8.00
84	Phil Nevin/50	8.00
85	Frank Thomas/80	15.00
85	Frank Thomas/90	15.00
85	Frank Thomas/35	25.00
85	Frank Thomas/50	15.00
86	Raul Mondesi/100	5.00
86	Raul Mondesi/93	5.00
86	Raul Mondesi/43	8.00
86	Raul Mondesi/50	8.00
87	Don Drysdale/56	25.00
87	Don Drysdale/53	25.00
88	Gary Sheffield/100	6.00
88	Gary Sheffield/88	5.00
88	Gary Sheffield/50	10.00
89	Andy Pettitte/100	15.00
89	Andy Pettitte/95	15.00
89	Andy Pettitte/46	30.00
89	Andy Pettitte/50	15.00
90	Lance Berkman/45	20.00
90	Lance Berkman/99	15.00
91	Paul LoDuca/100	5.00
91	Paul LoDuca/98	5.00
91	Paul LoDuca/50	8.00
92	Kevin Brown/86	5.00
92	Kevin Brown/27	15.00
93	Jim Thome/100	15.00
93	Jim Thome/91	15.00
93	Jim Thome/25	25.00
94	Mike Sweeney/100	5.00
94	Mike Sweeney/95	5.00
94	Mike Sweeney/29	15.00
94	Mike Sweeney/50	8.00
95	Pedro J. Martinez/Red Sox/100	15.00
95	Pedro J. Martinez/Red Sox/92	15.00
95	Pedro J. Martinez/Red Sox/45	25.00
95	Pedro J. Martinez/Red Sox/50	25.00
96	Cliff Floyd/100	5.00
96	Cliff Floyd/93	5.00
96	Cliff Floyd/30	10.00
96	Cliff Floyd/50	10.00
97	Larry Walker/100	8.00
97	Larry Walker/89	5.00
97	Larry Walker/33	30.00
97	Larry Walker/50	10.00
98	Ivan Rodriguez/100	10.00
98	Ivan Rodriguez/91	10.00
98	Ivan Rodriguez/50	20.00
99	Aramis Ramirez/100	8.00
99	Aramis Ramirez/98	8.00
99	Aramis Ramirez/50	12.00
100	Roberto Alomar/100	10.00
100	Roberto Alomar/88	10.00
100	Roberto Alomar/50	20.00
101	Ben Sheets/100	8.00
101	Ben Sheets/101	5.00
101	Ben Sheets/50	15.00
102	Adam Dunn/101	20.00
102	Adam Dunn/39	40.00
103	Hideo Nomo/95	30.00
104	C.C. Sabathia/50	10.00
104	C.C. Sabathia/101	5.00
104	C.C. Sabathia/52	10.00
104	C.C. Sabathia/50	10.00
105	Rickey Henderson/A's/100	20.00
105	Rickey Henderson/A's/79	20.00
105	Rickey Henderson/A's/30	50.00
105	Rickey Henderson/A's/50	30.00
106	Carlton Fisk/White Sox/80	20.00
106	Carlton Fisk/White Sox/69	30.00
106	Carlton Fisk/White Sox/72	30.00
106	Carlton Fisk/White Sox/50	30.00
107	Chan Ho Park/100	5.00
107	Chan Ho Park/94	5.00
107	Chan Ho Park/61	8.00
107	Chan Ho Park/50	8.00
108	Mike Mussina/100	20.00
108	Mike Mussina/91	20.00
108	Mike Mussina/35	50.00
108	Mike Mussina/50	30.00
109	Mark Mulder/100	8.00
109	Mark Mulder/76	8.00
109	Mark Mulder/20	20.00
109	Mark Mulder/35	20.00
110	Tsuyoshi Shinjo/100	5.00
110	Tsuyoshi Shinjo/101	5.00
110	Tsuyoshi Shinjo/30	20.00
111	Pat Burrell/100	10.00
111	Pat Burrell/50	15.00
112	Edgar Martinez/100	10.00
112	Edgar Martinez/87	10.00
112	Edgar Martinez/50	15.00
113	Barry Larkin/100	10.00
113	Barry Larkin/86	10.00
113	Barry Larkin/50	15.00
114	Jeff Kent/100	6.00
114	Jeff Kent/92	6.00
114	Jeff Kent/50	8.00
115	Chipper Jones/100	15.00
115	Chipper Jones/93	15.00
115	Chipper Jones/50	30.00
116	Magglio Ordonez/100	8.00
116	Magglio Ordonez/97	8.00
116	Magglio Ordonez/30	30.00
116	Magglio Ordonez/50	15.00
117	Jim Edmonds/100	8.00
117	Jim Edmonds/93	8.00
117	Jim Edmonds/50	10.00
118	Andruw Jones/100	10.00
118	Andruw Jones/96	10.00
118	Andruw Jones/45	20.00
119	Jose Canseco/100	15.00
119	Jose Canseco/85	15.00
119	Jose Canseco/50	10.00
120	Manny Ramirez/100	10.00
120	Manny Ramirez/93	10.00
120	Manny Ramirez/50	20.00
121	Sean Casey/100	10.00
121	Sean Casey/97	10.00
121	Sean Casey/50	15.00
122	Bret Boone/100	6.00
122	Bret Boone/92	6.00
122	Bret Boone/29	15.00
122	Bret Boone/50	10.00
123	Tim Hudson/100	8.00
123	Tim Hudson/99	8.00
123	Tim Hudson/50	10.00
124	Craig Biggio/100	10.00
124	Craig Biggio/88	10.00
124	Craig Biggio/50	15.00
125	Mike Piazza/Mets/100	15.00
125	Mike Piazza Mets/92	20.00
125	Mike Piazza Mets/31	40.00
125	Mike Piazza Mets/51	25.00
126	Jack Morris/100	5.00
126	Jack Morris/77	5.00
126	Jack Morris/47	10.00
127	Roy Oswalt/100	8.00
127	Roy Oswalt/101	5.00
127	Roy Oswalt/39	15.00
127	Roy Oswalt/50	15.00
128	Shawn Green/100	8.00
128	Shawn Green/50	15.00
129	Carlos Beltran/100	8.00
129	Carlos Beltran/98	8.00
129	Carlos Beltran/50	10.00
130	Todd Helton/100	10.00
130	Todd Helton/97	10.00
130	Todd Helton/50	20.00
131	Barry Zito/75	15.00
131	Barry Zito/100	10.00
131	Barry Zito/75	15.00
131	Barry Zito/50	30.00
132	J.D. Drew/100	15.00
132	J.D. Drew/98	15.00
132	J.D. Drew/50	20.00
133	Mark Grace/100	10.00
133	Mark Grace/88	10.00
133	Mark Grace/50	20.00
134	Rickey Henderson/Mets/100	20.00
134	Rickey Henderson/Mets/79	20.00
134	Rickey Henderson/Mets/50	30.00
135	Greg Maddux/100	20.00
135	Greg Maddux/86	20.00
135	Greg Maddux/50	30.00
136	Garret Anderson/100	8.00
136	Garret Anderson/94	8.00
136	Garret Anderson/50	15.00
137	Rafael Palmeiro/100	15.00
137	Rafael Palmeiro/86	15.00
137	Rafael Palmeiro/50	20.00
138	Luis Gonzalez/50	10.00
138	Luis Gonzalez/90	8.00
138	Luis Gonzalez/45	15.00
139	Nick Johnson/50	5.00
139	Nick Johnson/101	5.00
139	Nick Johnson/26	15.00
140	Vladimir Guerrero/80	15.00
140	Vladimir Guerrero/96	15.00
140	Vladimir Guerrero/50	25.00
141	Mark Buehrle/100	5.00
141	Mark Buehrle/56	8.00
142	Troy Glaus/100	15.00
142	Troy Glaus/98	15.00
142	Troy Glaus/50	25.00
143	Juan Gonzalez/100	10.00
143	Juan Gonzalez/89	10.00
143	Juan Gonzalez/50	15.00
144	Kerry Wood/100	15.00
144	Kerry Wood/98	15.00
144	Kerry Wood/34	40.00
144	Kerry Wood/50	15.00
145	Roger Clemens/100	25.00
145	Roger Clemens/84	25.00
145	Roger Clemens/50	40.00
146	Bob Abreu/100	8.00
146	Bob Abreu/96	8.00
146	Bob Abreu/53	15.00
146	Bob Abreu/50	15.00
147	Bernie Williams/95	10.00
147	Bernie Williams/91	10.00
147	Bernie Williams/51	20.00
148	Tom Glavine/100	10.00
148	Tom Glavine/87	10.00
148	Tom Glavine/47	25.00
148	Tom Glavine/50	25.00
149	Jorge Posada/100	10.00
149	Jorge Posada/95	10.00
149	Jorge Posada/50	25.00
150	Randy Johnson/D'Backs/80	15.00
150	Randy Johnson/D'Backs/88	15.00
150	Randy Johnson/D'Backs/51	30.00
150	Randy Johnson/D'Backs/50	30.00

2002 Leaf Rookies & Stars Samples

Each December 2002 issue of Beckett Baseball Card Monthly included a sample Leaf R&S card rubber-cemented inside. The cards differ from the issued version only in the appearance on back of a (usually) silver-foil "SAMPLE" notation. Some cards were produced with the back overprint in gold foil in much more limited quantities. The number of different players' cards involved in the promotion is unknown.

	NM/M
Common Player:	.10
Stars:	1.5-2X
Gold:	20X

2002 Leaf Rookies & Stars

MIKE PIAZZA

#	Player	NM/M
	Complete Set (400):	
	Common Player:	.15
	Common SP (1-300):	.75
	Common (301-400):	.40
	Inserted 1:2	
	Pack (6):	1.50
	Box (24):	30.00
1	Darin Erstad	.25
2	Garret Anderson	.15
3	Troy Glaus	.15
4	David Eckstein	.15
5	Adam Kennedy	.15
6	Kevin Appier	.15
6	Kevin Appier/SP/Mets	.75
6	Kevin Appier/SP/Royals	.75
7	Jarrod Washburn	.15
8	David Segui	.15
9	Jay Gibbons	.15
10	Tony Batista	.15
11	Scott Erickson	.15
12	Jeff Conine	.15
13	Melvin Mora	.15
14	Shea Hillenbrand	.15
14	Manny Ramirez	.65
15	Manny Ramirez/SP/Indians	2.00
16	Pedro J. Martinez	.65
16	Pedro J. Martinez/SP/Dodgers	2.50
16	Pedro J. Martinez/SP/Expos	2.50
17	Nomar Garciaparra	1.00
18	Rickey Henderson	.65
18	Rickey Henderson/SP/Angels	3.00
18	Rickey Henderson/SP/A's	3.00
18	Rickey Henderson/SP/Blue Jays	3.00
18	Rickey Henderson/SP/M's	3.00
18	Rickey Henderson/SP/Mets	3.00
18	Rickey Henderson/SP/Padres	3.00
18	Rickey Henderson/SP/Yankees	3.00
19	Johnny Damon	.25
19	Johnny Damon/SP/A's	1.00
19	Johnny Damon/SP/Royals	1.00
20	Trot Nixon	.15
21	Derek Lowe	.15
22	Jason Varitek	.15
23	Tim Wakefield	.15
24	Frank Thomas	.65
25	Kenny Lofton	.15
25	Kenny Lofton/SP/Indians	.75
26	Magglio Ordonez	.15
27	Ray Durham	.15
28	Mark Buehrle	.25
29	Paul Konerko	.15
29	Paul Konerko/SP/Dodgers	1.00
29	Paul Konerko/SP/Reds	1.00
30	Jose Valentin	.15
31	C.C. Sabathia	.15
32	Ellis Burks	.15
32	Ellis Burks/SP/Giants	.75
32	Ellis Burks/SP/Red Sox	.75
32	Ellis Burks/SP/Rockies	.75
33	Omar Vizquel	.15
33	Omar Vizquel/SP/Mariners	1.00
34	Jim Thome	.50
35	Matt Lawton	.15
36	Travis Fryman	.15
36	Travis Fryman/SP/Tigers	.75
37	Robert Fick	.15
38	Bobby Higginson	.15
39	Steve Sparks	.15
40	Mike Rivera	.15
41	Wendell Magee	.15
42	Randall Simon	.15
43	Carlos Pena	.15
43	Carlos Pena/SP/A's	.75
43	Carlos Pena/SP/Rangers	.75
44	Mike Sweeney	.15
45	Chuck Knoblauch	.15
46	Carlos Beltran	.50
47	Joe Randa	.15
48	Paul Byrd	.15
49	Mac Suzuki	.15
50	Torii Hunter	.15
51	Jacque Jones	.15
52	David Ortiz	.35
53	Corey Koskie	.15
54	Brad Radke	.15
55	Doug Mientkiewicz	.15
56	A.J. Pierzynski	.15
57	Dustan Mohr	.15
58	Derek Jeter	2.00
59	Bernie Williams	.30
60	Roger Clemens	.85
60	Roger Clemens/SP/Blue Jays	4.00
60	Roger Clemens/SP/Red Sox	4.00
61	Mike Mussina	.40
61	Mike Mussina/SP/Orioles	1.50
62	Jorge Posada	.25
63	Alfonso Soriano	.50
64	Jason Giambi	.40
64	Jason Giambi/SP/A's	2.50
65	Robin Ventura	.15
65	Robin Ventura/SP/Mets	.75
65	Robin Ventura/SP/White Sox	.75
66	Andy Pettitte	.25
67	David Wells	.15
67	David Wells/SP/Blue Jays	.75
67	David Wells/SP/Tigers	.75

ABBREVIATIONS

SP - Short Print

68 Nick Johnson .15
69 Jeff Weaver .15
69 Jeff Weaver/SP/Tigers .75
70 Raul Mondesi .15
70 Raul Mondesi/SP/Blue Jays .75
70 Raul Mondesi/SP/Dodgers .75
71 Tim Hudson .25
72 Barry Zito .25
73 Mark Mulder .25
74 Miguel Tejada .25
75 Eric Chavez .25
76 Billy Koch .15
76 Billy Koch/SP/Blue Jays .75
77 Jermaine Dye .15
77 Jermaine Dye/SP/Royals .75
78 Scott Hatteberg .15
79 Ichiro Suzuki 1.00
80 Edgar Martinez .15
81 Mike Cameron .15
81 Mike Cameron/SP/White Sox .75
82 John Olerud .15
82 John Olerud/SP/Blue Jays .75
82 John Olerud/SP/Mets .75
83 Bret Boone .15
84 Dan Wilson .15
85 Freddy Garcia .15
86 Jamie Moyer .15
87 Carlos Guillen .15
88 Ruben Sierra .15
89 Kazuhiro Sasaki .15
90 Mark McLemore .15
91 Ben Grieve .15
92 Aubrey Huff .15
93 Steve Cox .15
94 Toby Hall .15
95 Randy Winn .15
96 Brent Abernathy .15
97 Chan Ho Park .15
97 Chan Ho Park/SP/Dodgers .75
98 Alex Rodriguez 1.50
98 Alex Rodriguez/SP/Mariners 4.00
99 Juan Gonzalez .40
99 Juan Gonzalez/SP/Indians 1.50
99 Juan Gonzalez/SP/Tigers 1.50
100 Rafael Palmeiro .60
100 Rafael Palmeiro/SP/Cubs 1.00
100 Rafael Palmeiro/SP/Orioles 1.00
101 Ivan Rodriguez .50
102 Rusty Greer .15
103 Kenny Rogers .15
103 Kenny Rogers/SP/A's .75
103 Kenny Rogers/SP/Yankees .75
104 Hank Blalock .40
105 Mark Teixeira .25
106 Carlos Delgado .40
107 Shannon Stewart .15
108 Eric Hinske .15
109 Roy Halladay .25
110 Felipe Lopez .15
111 Vernon Wells .15
112 Curt Schilling .40
112 Curt Schilling/SP/Phillies 1.50
113 Randy Johnson .65
113 Randy Johnson/SP/Astros 3.00
113 Randy Johnson/SP/Expos 3.00
113 Randy Johnson/SP/Mariners 3.00
114 Luis Gonzalez .25
114 Luis Gonzalez/SP/Astros 1.00
114 Luis Gonzalez/SP/Cubs 1.00
115 Mark Grace .25
115 Mark Grace/SP/Cubs 1.50
116 Junior Spivey .15
117 Tony Womack .15
118 Matt Williams .15
118 Matt Williams/SP/Giants 1.00
118 Matt Williams/SP/Indians 1.00
119 Danny Bautista .15
120 Byung-Hyun Kim .15
121 Craig Counsell .15
122 Greg Maddux .75
122 Greg Maddux/SP/Cubs 4.00
123 Tom Glavine .25
124 John Smoltz .15
124 John Smoltz/SP/Tigers .75
125 Chipper Jones .75
126 Gary Sheffield .25
127 Andruw Jones .65
128 Vinny Castilla .15
129 Damian Moss .15
130 Rafael Furcal .15
131 Kerry Ligtenberg .50
132 Fred McGriff .15
132 Fred McGriff/SP/Blue Jays 1.00
132 Fred McGriff/SP/Braves 1.00
132 Fred McGriff/SP/Devil Rays 1.00

132 Fred McGriff/SP/Padres 1.00
133 Sammy Sosa 1.00
133 Sammy Sosa/SP/Rangers 4.00
133 Sammy Sosa/SP/White Sox 4.00
134 Alex Gonzalez .15
135 Corey Patterson .15
136 Moises Alou .15
137 Mark Prior .50
138 Jon Lieber .15
139 Matt Clement .15
140 Ken Griffey Jr. 1.00
140 Ken Griffey Jr./SP/Mariners 4.00
141 Barry Larkin .15
142 Adam Dunn .40
143 Sean Casey .15
143 Sean Casey/SP/Indians .75
144 Jose Rijo .15
145 Elmer Dessens .15
146 Austin Kearns .15
147 Corky Miller .15
148 Todd Walker .15
148 Todd Walker/SP/Rockies .75
148 Todd Walker/SP/Expos .75
149 Chris Reitsma .15
150 Ryan Dempster .15
151 Larry Walker .15
152 Todd Helton .65
153 Juan Uribe .15
154 Juan Pierre .15
155 Mike Hampton .15
156 Todd Zeile .15
157 Josh Beckett .25
158 Mike Lowell .15
158 Mike Lowell/SP/Yankees .75
159 Derrek Lee .15
160 A.J. Burnett .15
161 Luis Castillo .15
162 Tim Raines .15
163 Preston Wilson .15
164 Juan Encarnacion .15
165 Jeff Bagwell .65
166 Craig Biggio .15
167 Lance Berkman .15
168 Wade Miller .15
169 Roy Oswalt .25
170 Richard Hidalgo .15
171 Carlos Hernandez .15
172 Daryle Ward .15
173 Shawn Green .30
173 Shawn Green/SP/Blue Jays 1.00
174 Adrian Beltre .35
175 Paul LoDuca .15
176 Eric Karros .15
177 Kevin Brown .15
178 Hideo Nomo .65
178 Hideo Nomo/SP/Brewers 1.50
178 Hideo Nomo/SP/Mets 1.50
178 Hideo Nomo/SP/Red Sox 1.50
178 Hideo Nomo/SP/Tigers 1.50
179 Odalis Perez .15
180 Eric Gagne .35
181 Brian Jordan .15
182 Cesar Izturis .15
183 Geoff Jenkins .15
184 Richie Sexson .15
184 Richie Sexson/SP/Indians 1.00
185 Jose Hernandez .15
186 Ben Sheets .15
187 Ruben Quevedo .15
188 Jeffrey Hammonds .15
189 Alex Sanchez .15
190 Vladimir Guerrero .65
191 Jose Vidro .15
192 Orlando Cabrera .15
193 Michael Barrett .15
194 Javier Vazquez .15
195 Tony Armas Jr. .15
196 Andres Galarraga .15
197 Tomokazu Ohka .15
198 Bartolo Colon .15
198 Bartolo Colon/SP/Indians .75
199 Cliff Floyd .15
199 Cliff Floyd/SP/Marlins .75
200 Mike Piazza 1.00
200 Mike Piazza/SP/Dodgers 4.00
200 Mike Piazza/SP/Marlins 4.00
201 Jeromy Burnitz .15
202 Roberto Alomar .35
202 Roberto Alomar/SP/Blue Jays 1.50
202 Roberto Alomar/SP/Indians 1.50
202 Roberto Alomar/SP/Orioles 1.50
202 Roberto Alomar/SP/Padres 1.50
203 Mo Vaughn .15
203 Mo Vaughn/SP/Angels 1.00

203 Mo Vaughn/SP/Red Sox 1.00
204 Al Leiter .15
204 Al Leiter/SP/Blue Jays .75
205 Pedro Astacio .15
206 Edgardo Alfonzo .15
207 Armando Benitez .15
208 Scott Rolen .50
209 Pat Burrell .35
210 Bobby Abreu .15
210 Bobby Abreu/SP/Astros 1.00
211 Mike Lieberthal .15
212 Brandon Duckworth .15
213 Jimmy Rollins .40
214 Jeremy Giambi .15
215 Vicente Padilla .15
216 Travis Lee .15
217 Jason Kendall .15
218 Brian Giles .15
218 Brian Giles/SP/Indians 1.00
219 Aramis Ramirez .15
220 Pokey Reese .15
221 Kip Wells .15
222 Josh Fogg .15
222 Josh Fogg/SP/White Sox .75
223 Mike Williams .15
224 Ryan Klesko .15
224 Ryan Klesko/SP/Braves .75
225 Phil Nevin .15
225 Phil Nevin/SP/Tigers .75
226 Brian Lawrence .15
227 Mark Kotsay .15
228 Brett Tomko .15
229 Trevor Hoffman .15
229 Trevor Hoffman/SP/Marlins .75
230 Barry Bonds 2.00
230 Barry Bonds/SP/Pirates 6.00
231 Jeff Kent .15
231 Jeff Kent/SP/Blue Jays 1.00
232 Rich Aurilia .15
233 Tsuyoshi Shinjo .15
233 Tsuyoshi Shinjo/SP/Mets 1.00
234 Benito Santiago .15
234 Benito Santiago/SP/Padres .75
235 Kirk Rueter .15
236 Kurt Ainsworth .15
237 Livan Hernandez .15
238 Russ Ortiz .15
239 David Bell .15
240 Jason Schmidt .15
241 Reggie Sanders .15
242 Jim Edmonds .25
242 Jim Edmonds/SP/Angels 1.00
243 J.D. Drew .25
244 Albert Pujols 1.50
245 Fernando Vina .15
246 Tino Martinez .15
246 Tino Martinez/SP/Mariners 1.00
246 Tino Martinez/SP/Yankees 1.00
247 Edgar Renteria .15
248 Matt Morris .15
249 Woody Williams .15
250 Jason Isringhausen .15
250 Jason Isringhausen/SP/A's .75
251 Cal Ripken Jr. 2.00
252 Cal Ripken Jr. 2.00
253 Cal Ripken Jr. 2.00
254 Cal Ripken Jr. 2.00
255 Ryne Sandberg .75
256 Don Mattingly 1.00
257 Don Mattingly 1.00
258 Roger Clemens .85
259 Roger Clemens .85
260 Roger Clemens .85
261 Roger Clemens .85
262 Roger Clemens .85
263 Roger Clemens .85
264 Roger Clemens .85
265 Rickey Henderson .65
266 Rickey Henderson .65
267 Jose Canseco .40
268 Barry Bonds 2.00
269 Barry Bonds 2.00
270 Barry Bonds 2.00
271 Barry Bonds 2.00
272 Jeff Bagwell .65
273 Kirby Puckett .75
274 Kirby Puckett .75
275 Greg Maddux .75
276 Greg Maddux .75
277 Greg Maddux .75
278 Greg Maddux .75
279 Ken Griffey Jr. 1.00
280 Mike Piazza 1.00
281 Kirby Puckett .75
282 Mike Piazza 1.00
283 Frank Thomas .65
284 Hideo Nomo .65
285 Randy Johnson .65
286 Juan Gonzalez .65
287 Derek Jeter 2.00
288 Derek Jeter 2.00
289 Derek Jeter 2.00
290 Nomar Garciaparra 1.00
291 Pedro J. Martinez .65
292 Kerry Wood .50
293 Sammy Sosa 1.00
294 Chipper Jones .75

295 Ivan Rodriguez .50
296 Ivan Rodriguez .50
297 Albert Pujols 1.50
298 Ichiro Suzuki 1.00
299 Ichiro Suzuki 1.00
300 Ichiro Suzuki 1.00
301 So Taguchi RC 1.00
302 Kazuhisa Ishii RC 2.00
303 Jeremy Lambert RC .40
304 Sean Burroughs .40
305 P.J. Bevis RC .40
306 Jon Rauch .40
307 Scotty Layfield RC .50
308 Miguel Ascencio .40
309 Franklyn German RC .50
310 Luis Ugueto RC .50
311 Jorge Sosa RC .50
312 Felix Escalona RC .50
313 Jose Valverde RC .50
314 Jeremy Ward RC .50
315 Kevin Gryboski RC .50
316 Francis Beltran RC .50
317 Joe Thurston .40
318 Cliff Lee RC 1.00
319 Takahito Nomura RC .50
320 Bill Hall .50
321 Marlon Byrd .50
322 Andy Shibilo RC .50
323 Edwin Almonte RC .40
324 Brandon Backe RC .40
325 Chone Figgins RC 1.50
326 Brian Mallette RC .50
327 Rodrigo Rosario RC .50
328 Anderson Machado RC .50
329 Jorge Padilla RC .50
330 Allan Simpson RC .50
331 Doug DeVore RC .50
332 Drew Henson .50
333 Raul Chavez RC .50
334 Tom Shearn RC .50
335 Ben Howard RC .50
336 Chris Baker RC .50
337 Travis Hughes RC .50
338 Kevin Mench .40
339 Brian Tallet .40
340 Mike Moriarty RC .50
341 Corey Thurman RC .50
342 Terry Pearson RC .50
343 Steve Kent RC .50
344 Satoru Komiyama RC .50
345 Jason Lane .40
346 Freddy Sanchez RC .50
347 Brandon Puffer RC .50
348 Clay Condrey RC .50
349 Rene Reyes RC .50
350 Hee Seop Choi .50
351 Rodrigo Lopez .40
352 Colin Young RC .50
353 Jason Simontacchi RC .50
354 Oliver Perez RC 2.00
355 Kirk Saarloos .50
356 Marcus Thames .40
357 Jeff Austin RC .50
358 Justin Kaye RC .50
359 Julio Mateo RC .50
360 Mike Smith RC .50
361 Chris Snelling RC .75
362 Dennis Tankersley .40
363 Runelvys Hernandez RC .50
364 Aaron Cook RC .50
365 Joe Borchard .40
366 Earl Snyder RC .50
367 Shane Nance RC .50
368 Aaron Guiel RC .50
369 Steve Bechler RC .50
370 Tim Kalita RC .50
371 Shawn Sedlacek RC .50
372 Eric Good RC .50
373 Eric Junge RC .50
374 Matt Thornton .40
375 Travis Driskill RC .50
376 Mitch Wylie RC .50
377 John Ennis RC .50
378 Reed Johnson RC .75
379 Juan Brito RC .50
380 Ron Calloway RC .50
381 Adrian Burnside RC .50
382 Josh Bard RC .50
383 Matt Childers RC .50
384 Gustavo Chacin RC .50
385 Luis Martinez RC .50
386 Trey Hodges RC .50
387 Hansel Izquierdo RC .50
388 Jeriome Robertson RC .50
389 Victor Alvarez RC .50
390 David Ross RC .50
391 Ron Chiavacci .40
392 Adam Walker RC .50
393 Mike Gonzalez RC .50
394 John Foster RC .50
395 Kyle Kane RC .50
396 Cam Esslinger RC .50
397 Kevin Frederick RC .50
398 Franklin Nunez RC .50
399 Todd Donovan RC .50
400 Kevin Cash RC .50

Longevity

Stars (1-300): 5-10X
SP's (1-300): 1-3X
Production 100

Rookies (301-400): No Pricing
Production 25

BLC Homers

	NM/M
Common Player:	20.00

Production 25 Sets

1	Luis Gonzalez	20.00
2	Luis Gonzalez	20.00
3	Luis Gonzalez	20.00
4	Todd Helton	35.00
5	Todd Helton	35.00
6	Todd Helton	35.00
7	Todd Helton	35.00
8	Todd Helton	35.00
9	Todd Helton	35.00
10	Todd Helton	35.00
11	Todd Helton	35.00
12	Jim Thome	35.00
13	Jim Thome	35.00
14	Jim Thome	35.00
15	Rafael Palmeiro	30.00
16	Rafael Palmeiro	30.00
17	Rafael Palmeiro	30.00
18	Rafael Palmeiro	30.00
19	Rafael Palmeiro	30.00
20	Troy Glaus	35.00
21	Troy Glaus	35.00
22	Troy Glaus	35.00
23	Gary Sheffield	20.00
24	Gary Sheffield	20.00
25	Gary Sheffield	20.00
26	Mike Piazza	50.00
27	Mike Piazza	50.00
28	Mike Piazza	50.00
29	Mike Piazza	50.00
30	Mike Piazza	50.00

Dress For Success

	NM/M
Common Player:	5.00

Production 250 Sets
Prime Cuts: No Pricing
Production 25 Sets

1	Mike Piazza	25.00
2	Cal Ripken Jr.	40.00
3	Carlos Delgado	8.00
4	Chipper Jones	20.00
5	Bernie Williams	8.00
6	Carlos Beltran	10.00
7	Curt Schilling	10.00
8	Greg Maddux	20.00
9	Ivan Rodriguez	12.00
10	Alex Rodriguez	20.00
11	Roger Clemens	20.00
12	Todd Helton	15.00
13	Jim Edmonds	8.00
14	Manny Ramirez	15.00
15	Mark Buehrle	8.00

Freshman Orientation

	NM/M
Common Player:	5.00

Inserted 1:142
Class Officer Parallel: 1.5X
Production 50 Sets

1	Andres Torres/Bat	8.00
2	Mark Ellis/Jsy	8.00
3	Erik Bedard/Bat	8.00
4	Delvin James/Jsy	5.00
5	Austin Kearns/Bat	10.00
6	Josh Pearce/Bat	5.00
7	Rafael Soriano/Jsy	8.00
8	Jason Lane/Bat	8.00
9	Mark Prior/Jsy	15.00
10	Alfredo Amezaga/Bat	5.00
11	Ryan Ludwick/Bat	5.00
12	So Taguchi/Bat	5.00
13	Duaner Sanchez/Bat	5.00
14	Kazuhisa Ishii/Jsy	15.00
15	Zach Day/Jsy	8.00
16	Eric Cyr/Bat	5.00
17	Francis Beltran/Jsy	5.00
18	Joe Borchard/Jsy	10.00
19	Jeremy Affeldt/shoe	5.00
20	Alexis Gomez/Jsy	10.00

Great American Signings

	NM/M
Common Autograph:	5.00

Inserted 1:56

Brent Abernathy/175	5.00
Brandon Backe/175	5.00
Chris Baker/175	5.00
Francis Beltran/175	5.00
Raul Chavez/175	5.00
Doug DeVore/175	5.00
Felix Escalona/100	8.00
Franklyn German/175	5.00
Jay Gibbons/150	10.00
Bill Hall/175	8.00
Drew Henson/50	35.00
Eric Hinske/175	5.00
Ben Howard/175	5.00
Aubrey Huff/175	8.00
Travis Hughes/175	5.00
Cesar Izturis/175	8.00
Nick Johnson/175	8.00
Austin Kearns/175	5.00
Satoru Komiyama/75	20.00
Jason Lane/150	8.00
Brian Lawrence/175	5.00
Anderson Machado/175	5.00
Roy Oswalt/100	15.00
Jorge Padilla/175	5.00
Oliver Perez/175	25.00
Rene Reyes/175	5.00
Mike Rivera/175	5.00
Rodrigo Rosario/175	5.00
Tom Shearn/175	5.00
Chris Snelling/175	10.00
Mac Suzuki/100	30.00
So Taguchi/50	40.00
Dennis Tankersley/175	8.00
Corey Thurman/175	5.00
Luis Ugueto/175	5.00
Kip Wells/175	5.00

Statistical Standouts

	NM/M
Complete Set (50):	120.00
Common Player:	1.50

Inserted 1:12

1	Adam Dunn	2.50
2	Alex Rodriguez	8.00
3	Andruw Jones	4.00
4	Brian Giles	1.50
5	Chipper Jones	5.00
6	Cliff Floyd	1.50
7	Craig Biggio	1.50
8	Frank Thomas	4.00
9	Fred McGriff	1.50
10	Garret Anderson	1.50
11	Greg Maddux	5.00
12	Luis Gonzalez	1.50

ABBREVIATIONS

SP - Short Print

13	Magglio Ordonez	1.50
14	Ivan Rodriguez	3.00
15	Ken Griffey Jr.	6.00
16	Ichiro Suzuki	6.00
17	Jason Giambi	2.50
18	Derek Jeter	10.00
19	Sammy Sosa	6.00
20	Albert Pujols	8.00
21	J.D. Drew	4.00
22	Jeff Bagwell	4.00
23	Jim Edmonds	1.50
24	Jose Vidro	1.50
25	Juan Encarnacion	1.50
26	Kerry Wood	3.00
27	Al Leiter	1.50
28	Curt Schilling	2.50
29	Manny Ramirez	4.00
30	Lance Berkman	1.50
31	Miguel Tejada	1.50
32	Mike Piazza	6.00
33	Nomar Garciaparra	6.00
34	Omar Vizquel	1.50
35	Pat Burrell	2.00
36	Paul Konerko	1.50
37	Rafael Palmeiro	3.00
38	Randy Johnson	4.00
39	Richie Sexson	1.50
40	Roger Clemens	5.50
41	Shawn Green	2.00
42	Todd Helton	4.00
43	Tom Glavine	1.50
44	Troy Glaus	1.50
45	Vladimir Guerrero	4.00
46	Mike Sweeney	1.50
47	Alfonso Soriano	3.00
48	Barry Zito	1.50
49	John Smoltz	1.50
50	Ellis Burks	1.50

Statistical Standouts Materials

		NM/M
Common Player:		5.00
Inserted 1:69		
Super Materials:		2-3X
Production 25 Sets		
1	Adam Dunn/Bat/200	15.00
2	Alex Rodriguez/Bat/200	15.00
3	Andruw Jones/Bat/200	10.00
4	Brian Giles/Bat	8.00
5	Chipper Jones/Bat/200	15.00
6	Cliff Floyd/Jsy	5.00
7	Craig Biggio/Jsy	8.00
8	Frank Thomas/Jsy/125	12.00
9	Fred McGriff/Bat	10.00
10	Garret Anderson/Bat	8.00
11	Greg Maddux/Jsy/200	20.00
12	Luis Gonzalez/Jsy	8.00
13	Magglio Ordonez/Bat/150	10.00
14	Ivan Rodriguez/Jsy/100	15.00
15	Ken Griffey Jr./Base/150	15.00
16	Ichiro Suzuki/Base/100	30.00
17	Jason Giambi/Base	15.00
18	Derek Jeter/Base/100	25.00
19	Sammy Sosa/Base/100	15.00
20	Albert Pujols/Base/100	15.00
21	J.D. Drew/Bat/150	10.00
22	Jeff Bagwell/Jsy/150	10.00
23	Jim Edmonds/Bat	8.00
24	Jose Vidro/Bat	5.00
25	Juan Encarnacion/Bat	5.00
26	Kerry Wood/Jsy/200	15.00
27	Al Leiter/Jsy	
28	Curt Schilling/Jsy/225	12.00
29	Manny Ramirez/Bat/150	15.00
30	Lance Berkman/Bat/150	
31	Miguel Tejada/Jsy	10.00
32	Mike Piazza/Bat/200	20.00
33	Nomar Garciaparra/Bat/200	20.00
34	Omar Vizquel/Jsy	8.00
35	Pat Burrell/Bat	6.00
36	Paul Konerko/Bat	6.00
37	Rafael Palmeiro/Bat	10.00
38	Randy Johnson/Jsy/200	15.00
39	Richie Sexson/Jsy	10.00
40	Roger Clemens/Jsy/200	20.00
41	Shawn Green/Jsy	10.00
42	Todd Helton/Jsy/175	15.00

43	Tom Glavine/Jsy/125	10.00
44	Troy Glaus/Jsy	10.00
45	Vladimir Guerrero/Jsy	15.00
46	Mike Sweeney/Bat	5.00
47	Alfonso Soriano/Jsy/200	15.00
48	Barry Zito/Jsy/100	8.00
49	John Smoltz/Jsy	8.00
50	Ellis Burks/Jsy	5.00

Triple Threads

		NM/M
Common Card:		25.00
Production 100 Sets		
1	Reggie Jackson, Alfonso Soriano, Don Mattingly	80.00
2	Alex Rodriguez, Rafael Palmeiro, Ivan Rodriguez	30.00
3	Mike Piazza, Gary Carter, Rickey Henderson	40.00
4	Dale Murphy, Andruw Jones, Chipper Jones	40.00
5	Mike Schmidt, Steve Carlton, Scott Rolen	85.00
6	Rickey Henderson	40.00
7	Johnny Bench, Joe Morgan, Tom Seaver	50.00
8	Randy Johnson, Pedro J. Martinez, Vladimir Guerrero	35.00
9	Nolan Ryan, Rod Carew, Troy Glaus	75.00
10	Lou Brock, J.D. Drew, Stan Musial	65.00

View Masters

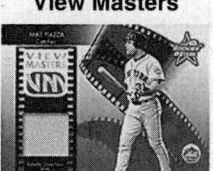

		NM/M
Common Player:		10.00
Production 100 Sets		
Slideshows:		No Pricing
Production 25 Sets		
1	Carlos Delgado	12.00
2	Todd Helton	20.00
3	Tony Gwynn	25.00
4	Bernie Williams	10.00
5	Luis Gonzalez	10.00
6	Larry Walker	10.00
7	Troy Glaus	20.00
8	Alfonso Soriano	15.00
9	Curt Schilling	12.00
10	Chipper Jones	25.00
11	Vladimir Guerrero	20.00
12	Adam Dunn	15.00
13	Rickey Henderson	20.00
14	Miguel Tejada	15.00
15	Kazuhisa Ishii	10.00
16	Greg Maddux	25.00
17	Pedro J. Martinez	30.00
18	Nomar Garciaparra	30.00
19	Mike Piazza	30.00
20	Lance Berkman	10.00

2003 Leaf Samples

Each March 2003 issue of Beckett Baseball Card Monthly and April issue of Beckett Vintage Sports Collectibles included a sample Leaf card rubber-cemented inside. The cards differ from the issued version only in the appearance on back of a (usually) silver-foil "SAMPLE" notation. Some cards were produced with the back overprint in gold-foil in much more limited quantities.

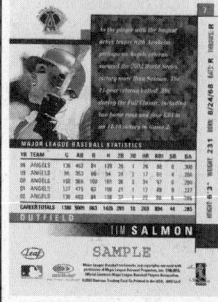

The number of different players' cards involved in the promotion is unknown.

		NM/M
Common Player:		.10
Stars:		1.5-2X
Gold:		20X

2003 Leaf

		NM/M
Complete Set (320):		40.00
Common Player:		.15
Pack (10):		1.50
Box (24):		30.00
1	Brad Fullmer	.15
2	Darin Erstad	.25
3	David Eckstein	.15
4	Garret Anderson	.15
5	Jarrod Washburn	.15
6	Kevin Appier	.15
7	Tim Salmon	.25
8	Troy Glaus	.75
9	Troy Percival	.15
10	Buddy Groom	.15
11	Jay Gibbons	.15
12	Jeff Conine	.15
13	Marty Cordova	.15
14	Melvin Mora	.15
15	Rodrigo Lopez	.15
16	Tony Batista	.15
17	Jorge Julio	.15
18	Cliff Floyd	.15
19	Derek Lowe	.15
20	Jason Varitek	.15
21	Johnny Damon	.25
22	Manny Ramirez	.75
23	Nomar Garciaparra	1.25
24	Pedro J. Martinez	.75
25	Rickey Henderson	.75
26	Shea Hillenbrand	.15
27	Trot Nixon	.15
28	Carlos Lee	.15
29	Frank Thomas	.75
30	Jose Valentin	.15
31	Magglio Ordonez	.15
32	Mark Buehrle	.15
33	Paul Konerko	.25
34	C.C. Sabathia	.15
35	Danys Baez	.15
36	Ellis Burks	.15
37	Jim Thome	.75
38	Omar Vizquel	.15
39	Ricky Gutierrez	.15
40	Travis Fryman	.15
41	Bobby Higginson	.15
42	Carlos Pena	.15
43	Juan Acevedo	.15
44	Mark Redman	.15
45	Randall Simon	.15
46	Robert Fick	.15
47	Steve Sparks	.15
48	Carlos Beltran	.50
49	Joe Randa	.15
50	Michael Tucker	.15
51	Mike Sweeney	.15
52	Paul Byrd	.15
53	Raul Ibanez	.15
54	Runelvys Hernandez	.15
55	A.J. Pierzynski	.15
56	Brad Radke	.15
57	Corey Koskie	.15
58	Cristian Guzman	.15
59	David Ortiz	.50
60	Doug Mientkiewicz	.15
61	Dustan Mohr	.15
62	Eddie Guardado	.15

63	Jacque Jones	.15
64	Torii Hunter	.15
65	Alfonso Soriano	.50
66	Andy Pettitte	.35
67	Bernie Williams	.30
68	David Wells	.15
69	Derek Jeter	2.00
70	Jason Giambi	.40
71	Jeff Weaver	.15
72	Jorge Posada	.25
73	Mike Mussina	.30
74	Nick Johnson	.15
75	Raul Mondesi	.15
76	Robin Ventura	.15
77	Roger Clemens	1.00
78	Barry Zito	.25
79	Billy Koch	.15
80	David Justice	.15
81	Eric Chavez	.25
82	Jermaine Dye	.15
83	Mark Mulder	.15
84	Miguel Tejada	.30
85	Ray Durham	.15
86	Scott Hatteberg	.15
87	Ted Lilly	.15
88	Tim Hudson	.25
89	Bret Boone	.15
90	Carlos Guillen	.15
91	Chris Snelling	.15
92	Dan Wilson	.15
93	Edgar Martinez	.15
94	Freddy Garcia	.15
95	Ichiro Suzuki	1.25
96	Jamie Moyer	.15
97	Joel Pineiro	.15
98	John Olerud	.15
99	Mark McLemore	.15
100	Mike Cameron	.15
101	Kazuhiro Sasaki	.15
102	Aubrey Huff	.15
103	Ben Grieve	.15
104	Joe Kennedy	.15
105	Paul Wilson	.15
106	Randy Winn	.15
107	Steve Cox	.15
108	Alex Rodriguez	1.50
109	Chan Ho Park	.15
110	Hank Blalock	.50
111	Herbert Perry	.15
112	Ivan Rodriguez	.65
113	Juan Gonzalez	.75
114	Kenny Rogers	.15
115	Kevin Mench	.15
116	Rafael Palmeiro	.65
117	Carlos Delgado	.40
118	Eric Hinske	.15
119	Jose Cruz	.15
120	Josh Phelps	.15
121	Roy Halladay	.25
122	Shannon Stewart	.15
123	Vernon Wells	.15
124	Curt Schilling	.40
125	Junior Spivey	.15
126	Luis Gonzalez	.25
127	Mark Grace	.25
128	Randy Johnson	.75
129	Steve Finley	.15
130	Tony Womack	.15
131	Andruw Jones	.75
132	Chipper Jones	1.00
133	Gary Sheffield	.30
134	Greg Maddux	1.00
135	John Smoltz	.25
136	Kevin Millwood	.15
137	Rafael Furcal	.15
138	Tom Glavine	.40
139	Alex Gonzalez	.15
140	Corey Patterson	.15
141	Fred McGriff	.15
142	Jon Lieber	.15
143	Kerry Wood	.65
144	Mark Prior	.75
145	Matt Clement	.15
146	Moises Alou	.15
147	Sammy Sosa	1.25
148	Aaron Boone	.15
149	Adam Dunn	.50
150	Austin Kearns	.40
151	Barry Larkin	.25
152	Danny Graves	.15
153	Elmer Dessens	.15
154	Ken Griffey Jr.	1.25
155	Sean Casey	.25
156	Todd Walker	.15
157	Gabe Kapler	.15
158	Jason Jennings	.15
159	Jay Payton	.15
160	Larry Walker	.25
161	Mike Hampton	.15
162	Todd Helton	.75
163	Todd Zeile	.15
164	A.J. Burnett	.15
165	Derrek Lee	.15
166	Josh Beckett	.50
167	Juan Encarnacion	.15
168	Luis Castillo	.15
169	Mike Lowell	.15
170	Preston Wilson	.15
171	Billy Wagner	.15
172	Craig Biggio	.25
173	Daryle Ward	.15
174	Jeff Bagwell	.75
175	Lance Berkman	.25
176	Octavio Dotel	.15
177	Richard Hidalgo	.15
178	Roy Oswalt	.25
179	Adrian Beltre	.40
180	Eric Gagne	.40

181	Eric Karros	.15
182	Hideo Nomo	.65
183	Kazuhisa Ishii	.15
184	Kevin Brown	.15
185	Mark Grudzielanek	.15
186	Odalis Perez	.15
187	Paul LoDuca	.15
188	Shawn Green	.40
189	Alex Sanchez	.15
190	Ben Sheets	.15
191	Jeffrey Hammonds	.15
192	Jose Hernandez	.15
193	Takahito Nomura	.15
194	Richie Sexson	.15
195	Andres Galarraga	.15
196	Bartolo Colon	.15
197	Brad Wilkerson	.15
198	Javier Vazquez	.15
199	Jose Vidro	.15
200	Michael Barrett	.15
201	Tomokazu Ohka	.15
202	Vladimir Guerrero	.75
203	Al Leiter	.15
204	Armando Benitez	.15
205	Edgardo Alfonzo	.15
206	Mike Piazza	1.25
207	Mo Vaughn	.15
208	Pedro Astacio	.15
209	Roberto Alomar	.35
210	Roger Cedeno	.15
211	Timoniel Perez	.15
212	Bobby Abreu	.15
213	Jimmy Rollins	.25
214	Mike Lieberthal	.15
215	Pat Burrell	.25
216	Randy Wolf	.15
217	Travis Lee	.15
218	Vicente Padilla	.15
219	Aramis Ramirez	.15
220	Brian Giles	.15
221	Craig Wilson	.15
222	Jason Kendall	.15
223	Josh Fogg	.15
224	Kevin Young	.15
225	Kip Wells	.15
226	Mike Williams	.15
227	Brett Tomko	.15
228	Brian Lawrence	.15
229	Mark Kotsay	.15
230	Oliver Perez	.15
231	Phil Nevin	.15
232	Ryan Klesko	.15
233	Sean Burroughs	.15
234	Trevor Hoffman	.15
235	Barry Bonds	2.00
236	Benito Santiago	.15
237	Jeff Kent	.15
238	Kirk Rueter	.15
239	Livan Hernandez	.15
240	Kenny Lofton	.15
241	Rich Aurilia	.15
242	Russ Ortiz	.15
243	Albert Pujols	1.50
244	Edgar Renteria	.15
245	J.D. Drew	.40
246	Jason Isringhausen	.15
247	Jim Edmonds	.40
248	Matt Morris	.15
249	Tino Martinez	.15
250	Scott Rolen	.75
251	Curt Schilling	.25
252	Ivan Rodriguez	.35
253	Mike Piazza	.75
254	Sammy Sosa	.75
255	Matt Williams	.15
256	Frank Thomas	.25
257	Barry Bonds	1.00
258	Roger Clemens	.65
259	Rickey Henderson	.25
260	Ken Griffey Jr.	.60
261	Greg Maddux	.50
262	Randy Johnson	.40
263	Jeff Bagwell	.25
264	Roberto Alomar	.25
265	Tom Glavine	.25
266	Juan Gonzalez	.25
267	Mark Grace	.25
268	Mike Mussina	.25
269	Ryan Klesko	.15
270	Fred McGriff	.15
271	Joe Borchard	.15
272	Chris Snelling	.15
273	Brian Tallet	.15
274	Cliff Lee	.15
275	Freddy Sanchez	.15
276	Chone Figgins	.15
277	Kevin Cash	.15
278	Josh Bard	.15
279	Jeriome Robertson	.15
280	Jeremy Hill	.15
281	Shane Nance	.15
282	Jeff Baker	.15
283	Trey Hodges	.15
284	Eric Eckenstahler	.15
285	Jim Rushford	.15
286	Carlos Rivera	.15
287	Josh Bonifay	.15
288	Garrett Atkins	.15
289	Nic Jackson	.15
290	Corwin Malone	.15
291	Jimmy Gobble	.15
292	Josh Wilson	.15
293	Clint Barmes RC	.50
294	Jon Adkins	.15
295	Tim Kalita	.15
296	Nelson Castro	.15
297	Colin Young	.15
298	Adrian Burnside	.15

299	Luis Martinez	.15
300	Terrmel Sledge RC	.50
301	Todd Donovan	.15
302	Jeremy Ward	.15
303	Wilson Valdez	.15
304	Jose Contreras RC	.75
305	Marshall McDougall	.15
306	Mitch Wylie	.15
307	Ron Calloway	.15
308	Jose Valverde	.15
309	Jason Davis	.15
310	Scotty Layfield	.15
311	Matt Thornton	.15
312	Adam Walker	.15
313	Gustavo Chacin	.15
314	Ron Chiavacci	.15
315	Wilbert Nieves	.15
316	Clifford Bartosh	.15
317	Mike Gonzalez	.15
318	Jeremy Guthrie	.15
319	Eric Junge	.15
320	Ben Kozlowski	.15

Green

No Pricing
Production 25 Sets

Blue Press Proofs

| Stars: | 8-15X |
| Production 50 Sets | |

Red Press Proofs

| Stars: | 3-5X |
| Inserted 1:12 | |

Clean Up Crew

		NM/M
Complete Set (10):		30.00
Common Card:		1.50
Inserted 1:49		
1	Alex Rodriguez, Rafael Palmeiro, Ivan Rodriguez	6.00
2	Nomar Garciaparra, Manny Ramirez, Cliff Floyd	5.00
3	Jason Giambi, Bernie Williams, Jorge Posada	4.00
4	Rich Aurilia, Jeff Kent, Barry Bonds	6.00
5	Larry Walker, Todd Helton, Jay Payton	1.50
6	Lance Berkman, Jeff Bagwell, Daryle Ward	2.00
7	Scott Rolen, Albert Pujols, Jim Edmonds	5.00
8	Gary Sheffield, Chipper Jones, Andruw Jones	4.00
9	Miguel Tejada, Eric Chavez, Jermaine Dye	1.50
10	Sammy Sosa, Moises Alou, Fred McGriff	4.00

Clean Up Crew Memorabilia

		NM/M
Production 50 Sets		
1	Alex Rodriguez, Rafael Palmeiro, Ivan Rodriguez	30.00
2	Nomar Garciaparra, Manny Ramirez, Cliff Floyd	25.00
3	Jason Giambi, Bernie Williams, Jorge Posada	25.00
4	Rich Aurilia, Jeff Kent, Barry Bonds	35.00
5	Larry Walker, Todd Helton, Jay Payton	20.00

6	Lance Berkman, Jeff Bagwell, Daryle Ward	25.00
7	Scott Rolen, Albert Pujols, Jim Edmonds	40.00
8	Gary Sheffield, Chipper Jones, Andruw Jones	30.00
9	Miguel Tejada, Eric Chavez, Jermaine Dye	20.00
10	Sammy Sosa, Moises Alou, Fred McGriff	30.00

Clubhouse Signatures Bronze

NM/M

Common Bronze Auto:		8.00
Inserted 1:300		
Silvers:		1-2X
Production 100 Sets		
Golds:		No Pricing
Production 25 Sets		
Edwin Almonte		8.00
Jeff Baker		10.00
Josh Bard		10.00
Angel Berroa		8.00
Joe Crede/SP/25		15.00
Andre Dawson/SP/50		25.00
Bobby Doerr/SP/100		20.00
Dwight "Doc" Gooden		25.00
Drew Henson/SP/50		20.00
Eric Hinske		8.00
Torii Hunter/SP/75		35.00
Omar Infante		8.00
Brian Lawrence		8.00
Kevin Mench		8.00
Jack Morris/SP/100		15.00
Franklin Nunez		8.00
Magglio Ordonez/SP/50		25.00
Corey Patterson/SP/100		15.00
Jhonny Peralta		20.00
J.C. Romero		10.00
Chris Snelling/SP/100		10.00
Alfonso Soriano/SP/25		40.00
Brian Tallet/SP/100		8.00

Game Collection

NM/M

Common Player:		8.00
Production 150 Sets		
1	Miguel Tejada/Cap	10.00
2	Shannon Stewart/Cap	6.00
3	Mike Schmidt/Jkt	40.00
4	Nolan Ryan/Jkt	75.00
5	Rafael Palmeiro/Glv	15.00
6	Andruw Jones/Shoe	10.00
7	Bernie Williams/Shoe	15.00
8	Ivan Rodriguez/Shoe	10.00
9	Lance Berkman/Shoe	10.00
10	Magglio Ordonez/Shoe	10.00
11	Roy Oswalt/Glv	10.00
12	Andy Pettitte/Shoe	10.00
13	Vladimir Guerrero/Glv	30.00
14	Jason Jennings/Glv	8.00
15	Mike Sweeney/Shoe	8.00
16	Joe Borchard/Shoe	10.00
17	Mark Prior/Shoe	10.00
18	Gary Carter/Jkt	10.00
19	Austin Kearns/Glv	10.00
20	Ryan Klesko/Glv	10.00

Gold Leaf Rookies

NM/M

Complete Set (10):		10.00
Common Player:		1.00
Inserted 1:24		
Mirror Golds:		10-20X
Production 25 Sets		
1	Joe Borchard	1.00
2	Chone Figgins	1.00
3	Alexis Gomez	1.00
4	Chris Snelling	1.00
5	Cliff Lee	1.00

ABBREVIATIONS

SP - Short Print

6	Victor Martinez	2.00
7	Hee Seop Choi	1.50
8	Michael Restovich	1.00
9	Anderson Machado	1.00
10	Drew Henson	2.00

Hard Hats

NM/M

Complete Set (12):		15.00
Common Player:		1.00
Inserted 1:13		
1	Alex Rodriguez	4.00
2	Bernie Williams	1.00
3	Ivan Rodriguez	1.25
4	Jeff Bagwell	1.50
5	Rafael Furcal	1.50
6	Rafael Palmeiro	1.50
7	Tony Gwynn	2.00
8	Vladimir Guerrero	1.50
9	Adrian Beltre	1.00
10	Shawn Green	1.00
11	Andruw Jones	1.50
12	George Brett	4.00

Hard Hats Batting Helmets

NM/M

Common Player:		15.00
Production 100 Sets		
1	Alex Rodriguez	50.00
2	Bernie Williams	35.00
3	Ivan Rodriguez	30.00
4	Jeff Bagwell	40.00
5	Rafael Furcal	15.00
6	Rafael Palmeiro	35.00
7	Tony Gwynn	35.00
8	Vladimir Guerrero	35.00
9	Adrian Beltre	20.00
10	Shawn Green	20.00
11	Andruw Jones	20.00
12	George Brett	100.00

Home/Away

NM/M

Complete Set (20):		40.00
Common Player:		1.00
Home Inserted 1:34		
1	Andruw Jones/Home	1.50
2	Cal Ripken Jr./Home	6.00
3	Edgar Martinez/Home	1.50
4	Jim Thome/Home	1.50
5	Larry Walker/Home	1.00
6	Nomar Garciaparra/Home	4.00
7	Mark Prior/Home	1.00
8	Mike Piazza/Home	4.00
9	Vladimir Guerrero/Home	1.50
10	Chipper Jones/Home	3.00
Away Inserted 1:34		
1	Andruw Jones	1.50
2	Cal Ripken Jr.	6.00
3	Edgar Martinez	1.00
4	Jim Thome	2.00
5	Larry Walker	1.00
6	Nomar Garciaparra	4.00
7	Mark Prior	1.00
8	Mike Piazza	4.00
9	Vladimir Guerrero	2.00
10	Chipper Jones	3.00

Home/Away Memorabilia

NM/M

Common Player:		6.00
Home Production 250		
1	Andruw Jones/Home	8.00
2	Cal Ripken Jr./Home	45.00
3	Edgar Martinez/Home	8.00
4	Jim Thome/Home	10.00
5	Larry Walker/Home	8.00
6	Nomar Garciaparra/Home	20.00
7	Mark Prior/Home	10.00

8	Mike Piazza/Home	15.00
9	Vladimir Guerrero/Home	12.00
10	Chipper Jones/Home	15.00
Away Production 250		
1	Andruw Jones	8.00
2	Cal Ripken Jr.	45.00
3	Edgar Martinez	8.00
4	Jim Thome	10.00
5	Larry Walker	8.00
6	Nomar Garciaparra	20.00
7	Mark Prior	10.00
8	Mike Piazza	15.00
9	Vladimir Guerrero	12.00
10	Chipper Jones	15.00

Maple & Ash

NM/M

Common Player:		6.00
Production 400 Sets		
1	Jorge Posada	8.00
2	Mike Piazza	12.00
3	Alex Rodriguez	10.00
4	Jeff Bagwell	10.00
5	Joe Borchard	6.00
6	Miguel Tejada	6.00
7	Adam Dunn	8.00
8	Jim Thome	6.00
9	Lance Berkman	6.00
10	Torii Hunter	6.00
11	Carlos Delgado	6.00
12	Reggie Jackson	10.00
13	Juan Gonzalez	6.00
14	Vladimir Guerrero	6.00
15	Richie Sexson	6.00

Number Off My Back

NM/M

Production 50 Sets		
1	Carlos Delgado	15.00
2	Don Mattingly	100.00
3	Todd Helton	30.00
4	Vernon Wells	10.00
5	Bernie Williams	20.00
6	Luis Gonzalez	20.00
7	Kerry Wood	30.00
8	Eric Chavez	10.00
9	Shawn Green	15.00
10	Roy Oswalt	15.00
11	Nomar Garciaparra	40.00
12	Robin Yount	60.00
13	Troy Glaus	20.00
14	C.C. Sabathia	10.00
15	Alex Rodriguez	50.00
16	Mark Mulder	10.00
17	Will Clark	60.00
18	Alfonso Soriano	30.00
19	Andy Pettitte	20.00
20	Curt Schilling	25.00

Shirt Off My Back

NM/M

Common Player:		5.00
Production 500 Sets		
Number Off My Back:		2-4X
Production 50 Sets		
1	Carlos Delgado	6.00
2	Don Mattingly	25.00
3	Todd Helton	10.00
4	Vernon Wells	6.00
5	Bernie Williams	6.00
6	Luis Gonzalez	6.00
7	Kerry Wood	8.00
8	Eric Chavez	6.00
9	Shawn Green	6.00
10	Roy Oswalt	6.00
11	Nomar Garciaparra	12.00
12	Robin Yount	15.00
13	Troy Glaus	6.00
14	C.C. Sabathia	5.00
15	Alex Rodriguez	8.00
16	Mark Mulder	5.00
17	Will Clark	8.00
18	Alfonso Soriano	10.00
19	Andy Pettitte	8.00
20	Curt Schilling	8.00

Slick Leather

NM/M

Complete Set (15):		20.00
Common Player:		1.00
Inserted 1:21		
1	Omar Vizquel	1.00
2	Roberto Alomar	1.50
3	Ivan Rodriguez	2.00
4	Greg Maddux	3.00
5	Scott Rolen	2.00
6	Todd Helton	2.00
7	Andruw Jones	2.00
8	Jim Edmonds	1.50
9	Barry Bonds	6.00
10	Eric Chavez	1.00
11	Ichiro Suzuki	5.00
12	Mike Mussina	1.50
13	John Olerud	1.00
14	Torii Hunter	1.00
15	Larry Walker	1.00

60

SHAWN GREEN
OUTFIELD - Los Angeles Dodgers

NM/M

Complete Set (50):		80.00
Common Player:		.75
Inserted 1:8		
Foil Parallels:		3-5X
Production 60 Sets		
1	Troy Glaus	3.00
2	Curt Schilling	2.00
3	Randy Johnson	3.00
4	Andruw Jones	3.00
5	Chipper Jones	4.00
6	Greg Maddux	4.00
7	Tom Glavine	1.00
8	Manny Ramirez	3.00
9	Nomar Garciaparra	5.00
10	Pedro J. Martinez	3.00
11	Rickey Henderson	3.00
12	Sammy Sosa	5.00
13	Frank Thomas	3.00
14	Magglio Ordonez	.75
15	Mark Buehrle	.75
16	Adam Dunn	1.50
17	Ken Griffey Jr.	5.00
18	Jim Thome	2.00
19	Omar Vizquel	.75
20	Larry Walker	.75
21	Todd Helton	3.00
22	Lance Berkman	.75
23	Roy Oswalt	.75
24	Mike Sweeney	.75
25	Hideo Nomo	3.00
26	Kazuhisa Ishii	1.00
27	Shawn Green	1.00
28	Torii Hunter	.75
29	Vladimir Guerrero	3.00
30	Mike Piazza	5.00
31	Alfonso Soriano	3.00
32	Bernie Williams	1.00
33	Derek Jeter	8.00
34	Jason Giambi	2.00
35	Roger Clemens	4.00
36	Barry Zito	.75
37	Miguel Tejada	.75
38	Pat Burrell	1.00
39	Ryan Klesko	.75
40	Barry Bonds	8.00
41	Jeff Kent	.75
42	Ichiro Suzuki	5.00
43	John Olerud	.75
44	Albert Pujols	5.00
45	Jim Edmonds	1.00
46	Scott Rolen	2.50
47	Alex Rodriguez	6.00
48	Ivan Rodriguez	2.50
49	Rafael Palmeiro	2.50
50	Roy Halladay	.75

2003 Leaf Certified Materials Samples

Each September 2003 issue of Beckett Baseball Card Monthly included a sample Leaf Certified Materials card rubber-cemented inside. The cards differ from the issued version only in the appearance on back of a (usually) silver-foil "SAMPLE" notation. Some cards were produced with the back overprint in gold-foil in much more limited quantities. The number of different players' cards involved in the promotion is unknown.

NM/M

Common Player:	.10
Stars:	1.5X
Gold:	20X

2003 Leaf Certified Materials

NM/M

Complete Set (250):	
Common Player:	.50
Common SP Auto. (206-250):	6.00
Production 400 unless noted.	
Mirror Red Auto. SP's (06-250):	1-1.5X
Production 100	
Mirror Blue Auto. SP's (206-250):	1-2X
Production 50	
Mirror Gold Autos. (206-250):	No Pricing
Production 25	
Pack (5):	20.00
Box (10):	150.00
1	Troy Glaus	1.00
2	Alfredo Amezaga	.50
3	Garret Anderson	1.00
4	Nolan Ryan	6.00
5	Darin Erstad	.75
6	Junior Spivey	.50
7	Randy Johnson	2.00
8	Curt Schilling	1.50
9	Luis Gonzalez	.75
10	Steve Finley	.50
11	Matt Williams	.75
12	Greg Maddux	3.00
13	Chipper Jones	2.00
14	Gary Sheffield	1.00
15	Adam LaRoche	.50
16	Andruw Jones	1.00
17	Robert Fick	.50
18	John Smoltz	1.00
19	Javy Lopez	.75
20	Jay Gibbons	.50
21	Geronimo Gil	.50
22	Cal Ripken Jr.	6.00
23	Nomar Garciaparra	4.00
24	Pedro J. Martinez	2.00
25	Freddy Sanchez	.50
26	Rickey Henderson	1.00
27	Manny Ramirez	1.50
28	Casey Fossum	.50
29	Sammy Sosa	3.00
30	Kerry Wood	2.00
31	Corey Patterson	1.00
32	Nic Jackson	.50

33	Mark Prior	1.50
34	Juan Cruz	.50
35	Steve Smyth	.50
36	Magglio Ordonez	.75
37	Joe Borchard	.50
38	Frank Thomas	1.50
39	Mark Buehrle	.50
40	Joe Crede	.50
41	Carlos Lee	.50
42	Paul Konerko	.50
43	Adam Dunn	1.50
44	Corky Miller	.50
45	Brandon Larson	.50
46	Ken Griffey Jr.	3.00
47	Barry Larkin	1.00
48	Sean Casey	.50
49	Wily Mo Pena	.50
50	Austin Kearns	.75
51	Victor Martinez	1.00
52	Brian Tallet	.50
53	Cliff Lee	.50
54	Jeremy Guthrie	.50
55	C.C. Sabathia	.50
56	Ricardo Rodriguez	.50
57	Omar Vizquel	1.00
58	Travis Hafner	.50
59	Todd Helton	1.50
60	Jason Jennings	.50
61	Jeff Baker	.50
62	Larry Walker	1.00
63	Travis Chapman	.50
64	Mike Maroth	.50
65	Josh Beckett	.50
66	Ivan Rodriguez	1.50
67	Brad Penny	.50
68	A.J. Burnett	1.00
69	Craig Biggio	1.00
70	Roy Oswalt	.50
71	Jason Lane	.50
72	Nolan Ryan	6.00
73	Wade Miller	.50
74	Richard Hidalgo	.50
75	Jeff Bagwell	1.50
76	Lance Berkman	1.00
77	Rodrigo Rosario	.50
78	Jeff Kent	1.00
79	John Buck	.50
80	Angel Berroa	.50
81	Mike Sweeney	.50
82	Mac Suzuki	.50
83	Alexis Gomez	.50
84	Carlos Beltran	1.50
85	Runelvys Hernandez	.50
86	Hideo Nomo	1.00
87	Paul LoDuca	.50
88	Cesar Izturis	.50
89	Kazuhisa Ishii	.50
90	Shawn Green	1.00
91	Joe Thurston	.50
92	Adrian Beltre	1.00
93	Kevin Brown	1.00
94	Richie Sexson	1.00
95	Ben Sheets	1.00
96	Takahito Nomura	.50
97	Geoff Jenkins	.50
98	Bill Hall	.50
99	Torii Hunter	1.00
100	A.J. Pierzynski	.50
101	Michael Cuddyer	.50
102	Jose Morban	.50
103	Brad Radke	.50
104	Jacque Jones	.50
105	Eric Milton	.50
106	Joe Mays	.50
107	Adam Johnson	.50
108	Javier Vazquez	.50
109	Vladimir Guerrero	2.00
110	Jose Vidro	.50
111	Michael Barrett	.50
112	Orlando Cabrera	.50
113	Tom Glavine	1.00
114	Roberto Alomar	1.00
115	Tsuyoshi Shinjo	.50
116	Cliff Floyd	.50
117	Mike Piazza	3.00
118	Al Leiter	.50
119	Don Mattingly	4.00
120	Roger Clemens	4.00
121	Derek Jeter	6.00
122	Alfonso Soriano	2.00
123	Drew Henson	.50
124	Brandon Claussen	.50
125	Christian Parker	.50
126	Jason Giambi	1.00
127	Mike Mussina	1.00
128	Bernie Williams	1.00
129	Jason Anderson	.50
130	Nick Johnson	.50
131	Jorge Posada	1.00
132	Andy Pettitte	1.00
133	Barry Zito	1.00
134	Miguel Tejada	1.00
135	Eric Chavez	1.00
136	Tim Hudson	1.00
137	Mark Mulder	.75
138	Terrence Long	.50
139	Mark Ellis	.50
140	Jim Thome	.75
141	Pat Burrell	.75
142	Marlon Byrd	.75
143	Bobby Abreu	.75
144	Brandon Duckworth	.50
145	Robert Person	.50
146	Anderson Machado	.50
147	Aramis Ramirez	.50
148	Jack Wilson	.50
149	Carlos Rivera	.50
150	Jose Castillo	.50

151	Walter Young	.50
152	Brian Giles	.75
153	Jason Kendall	.50
154	Ryan Klesko	.75
155	Mike Rivera	.50
156	Sean Burroughs	.50
157	Brian Lawrence	.50
158	Xavier Nady	.50
159	Dennis Tankersley	.50
160	Phil Nevin	.50
161	Barry Bonds	6.00
162	Kenny Lofton	.50
163	Rich Aurilia	.50
164	Ichiro Suzuki	4.00
165	Edgar Martinez	.75
166	Chris Snelling	.50
167	Rafael Soriano	.50
168	John Olerud	.75
169	Bret Boone	.75
170	Freddy Garcia	.50
171	Aaron Sele	.50
172	Kazuhiro Sasaki	.50
173	Albert Pujols	4.00
174	Scott Rolen	2.00
175	So Taguchi	.50
176	Jim Edmonds	1.00
177	Edgar Renteria	1.00
178	J.D. Drew	1.00
179	Antonio Perez	.50
180	Dewon Brazelton	.50
181	Aubrey Huff	.50
182	Toby Hall	.50
183	Ben Grieve	.50
184	Joe Kennedy	.50
185	Alex Rodriguez	5.00
186	Rafael Palmeiro	1.50
187	Hank Blalock	1.50
188	Mark Teixeira	1.00
189	Juan Gonzalez	1.50
190	Kevin Mench	.50
191	Nolan Ryan	6.00
192	Doug Davis	.50
193	Eric Hinske	.50
194	Vinnie Chulk	.50
195	Alexis Rios	.50
196	Carlos Delgado	1.00
197	Shannon Stewart	.50
198	Josh Phelps	.50
199	Vernon Wells	.75
200	Roy Halladay	.75
201	Babe Ruth	6.00
202	Lou Gehrig	6.00
203	Jackie Robinson	6.00
204	Ty Cobb	6.00
205	Thurman Munson	4.00
206	Prentice Redman RC	8.00
207	Craig Brazell RC	10.00
208	Nook Logan RC	15.00
209	Hong-Chih Kuo RC	75.00
210	Matt Kata RC	10.00
211	Chien-Ming Wang RC	225.00
212	Alejandro Machado RC	6.00
213	Michael Hessman RC	8.00
214	Francisco Rosario RC	8.00
215	Pedro Liriano RC	
216	Jeremy Bonderman RC	35.00
217	Oscar Villarreal RC	6.00
218	Arnie Munoz RC	6.00
219	Tim Olson RC	10.00
220	Jose Contreras RC/100 RC	40.00
221	Francisco Cruceta RC	10.00
222	John Webb RC	10.00
223	Phil Seibel RC	8.00
224	Aaron Looper RC	10.00
225	Brian Stokes RC	10.00
226	Guillermo Quiroz RC	10.00
227	Fernando Cabrera RC	10.00
228	Josh Hall RC	10.00
229	Diegomar Markwell RC	8.00
230	Andrew Brown RC	10.00
231	Doug Waechter RC	10.00
232	Felix Sanchez RC	10.00
233	Gerardo Garcia RC	8.00
234	Matt Bruback RC	8.00
235	Michel Hernandez RC	8.00
236	Rett Johnson RC	10.00
237	Ryan Cameron RC	8.00
238	Rob Hammock RC	10.00
239	Clint Barmes RC	10.00
240	Brandon Webb RC	40.00
241	Jon Leicester RC	10.00
242	Shane Bazzell RC	10.00
243	Joe Valentine RC	10.00
244	Josh Stewart RC	10.00
245	Pete LaForest RC	8.00
246	Shane Victorino RC	10.00
247	Terrmel Sledge RC	10.00
248	Lew Ford RC	25.00
249	Todd Wellemeyer RC	10.00
250	Hideki Matsui/No Auto. RC	15.00

Production 5 Sets
Mirror Blacks: One set produced.

Mirror Red Materials

NM/M

Common Player: 4.00
Production 250 unless noted.
Mirror Red SP's (206-250): .5X
Mirror Blues: 1-1.5X
Production 100
Mirror Golds: No Pricing
Production 25 sets
Mirror Emeralds: No Pricing
Production 5 Sets
Mirror Blacks: One set produced.

1	Troy Glaus	6.00
2	Alfredo Amezaga	4.00
3	Garret Anderson	8.00
4	Nolan Ryan/35	65.00
5	Darin Erstad	5.00
6	Junior Spivey	4.00
7	Randy Johnson	8.00
8	Curt Schilling	8.00
9	Luis Gonzalez	5.00
10	Steve Finley	4.00
11	Matt Williams	5.00
12	Greg Maddux	10.00
13	Chipper Jones	10.00
14	Gary Sheffield/125	8.00
15	Adam LaRoche	4.00
16	Andruw Jones	8.00
17	Robert Fick	4.00
18	John Smoltz	6.00
19	Javy Lopez	6.00
20	Jay Gibbons	4.00
21	Geronimo Gil	4.00
22	Cal Ripken Jr./35	75.00
23	Nomar Garciaparra	10.00
24	Pedro J. Martinez	10.00
25	Freddy Sanchez	4.00
26	Rickey Henderson	10.00
27	Manny Ramirez	8.00
28	Casey Fossum	4.00
29	Sammy Sosa	15.00
30	Kerry Wood	8.00
31	Corey Patterson	6.00
32	Nic Jackson	4.00
33	Mark Prior	10.00
34	Juan Cruz	4.00
35	Steve Smyth	4.00
36	Magglio Ordonez	6.00
37	Joe Borchard	4.00
38	Frank Thomas	10.00
39	Mark Buehrle	5.00
40	Joe Crede/100	4.00
41	Carlos Lee	4.00
42	Paul Konerko	8.00
43	Adam Dunn	8.00
44	Brandon Larson/150	4.00
45	Ken Griffey Jr.	12.00
46	Barry Larkin	8.00
47	Sean Casey	6.00
48	Wily Mo Pena	6.00
49	Austin Kearns	6.00
50	Victor Martinez/100	8.00
51	C.C. Sabathia	6.00
55	Ricardo Rodriguez	4.00
56	Omar Vizquel	6.00
57	Travis Hafner	6.00
58	Todd Helton	8.00
59	Jason Jennings	4.00
60	Larry Walker	6.00
61	Travis Chapman	4.00
62	Mike Maroth	4.00
63	Josh Beckett	6.00
64	Ivan Rodriguez	8.00

67	Brad Penny	4.00
68	A.J. Burnett	4.00
69	Craig Biggio	6.00
70	Roy Oswalt	4.00
71	Jason Lane	4.00
72	Nolan Ryan/35	65.00
73	Wade Miller	5.00
74	Richard Hidalgo	4.00
75	Jeff Bagwell	10.00
76	Lance Berkman	6.00
77	Rodrigo Rosario	4.00
78	Jeff Kent	6.00
79	John Buck	4.00
80	Angel Berroa	4.00
81	Mike Sweeney	6.00
84	Carlos Beltran	6.00
86	Hideo Nomo	15.00
87	Paul LoDuca	4.00
88	Cesar Izturis	4.00
89	Kazuhisa Ishii	5.00
90	Shawn Green	8.00
91	Joe Thurston	4.00
92	Adrian Beltre	4.00
93	Kevin Brown	6.00
94	Richie Sexson	6.00
95	Ben Sheets	6.00
97	Geoff Jenkins	5.00
98	Bill Hall	4.00
99	Torii Hunter	8.00
101	Michael Cuddyer	4.00
102	Jose Morban	4.00
103	Brad Radke	6.00
104	Jacque Jones	6.00
105	Eric Milton	5.00
106	Joe Mays	5.00
107	Adam Johnson	4.00
108	Javier Vazquez	5.00
109	Vladimir Guerrero	10.00
110	Jose Vidro	4.00
111	Michael Barrett/50	6.00
112	Orlando Cabrera	4.00
113	Tom Glavine	8.00
114	Roberto Alomar	10.00
115	Tsuyoshi Shinjo	4.00
116	Cliff Floyd	4.00
117	Mike Piazza	10.00
118	Al Leiter	4.00
119	Don Mattingly/35	60.00
120	Roger Clemens	25.00
121	Derek Jeter	20.00
122	Alfonso Soriano	8.00
123	Drew Henson	6.00
124	Brandon Claussen/50	10.00
125	Christian Parker	4.00
126	Jason Giambi	8.00
127	Mike Mussina	10.00
128	Bernie Williams	8.00
130	Nick Johnson	4.00
131	Jorge Posada	8.00
132	Andy Pettitte	6.00
133	Barry Zito	6.00
134	Miguel Tejada	6.00
135	Eric Chavez	6.00
136	Tim Hudson	6.00
137	Mark Mulder	6.00
138	Terrence Long	4.00
139	Mark Ellis	4.00
140	Jim Thome	8.00
141	Pat Burrell	6.00
142	Marlon Byrd	4.00
143	Bobby Abreu	6.00
144	Brandon Duckworth	4.00
145	Robert Person	4.00
146	Anderson Machado	6.00
147	Aramis Ramirez	6.00
148	Jack Wilson	4.00
150	Jose Castillo	4.00
151	Walter Young	4.00
152	Brian Giles	5.00
153	Jason Kendall	5.00
155	Mike Rivera	4.00
157	Brian Lawrence	4.00
158	Xavier Nady/60	6.00
159	Dennis Tankersley	4.00
160	Phil Nevin	4.00
161	Barry Bonds	20.00
162	Kenny Lofton	6.00
163	Rich Aurilia	4.00
164	Ichiro Suzuki	25.00
165	Edgar Martinez/100	8.00
166	Chris Snelling	4.00
167	Rafael Soriano	4.00
168	John Olerud	6.00
169	Bret Boone	5.00
170	Freddy Garcia	4.00
171	Aaron Sele	4.00
172	Kazuhiro Sasaki	4.00
173	Albert Pujols	25.00
174	Scott Rolen	10.00
175	So Taguchi	4.00
176	Jim Edmonds	6.00
177	Edgar Renteria	6.00
178	J.D. Drew	6.00
179	Antonio Perez	4.00
180	Dewon Brazelton	4.00
181	Aubrey Huff/50	8.00
182	Toby Hall	4.00
183	Ben Grieve	4.00
184	Joe Kennedy	4.00
185	Alex Rodriguez	15.00
186	Rafael Palmeiro	8.00
187	Hank Blalock	8.00
188	Mark Teixeira	8.00
189	Juan Gonzalez	8.00
190	Kevin Mench	4.00
191	Nolan Ryan/35	65.00
192	Doug Davis	4.00
193	Eric Hinske	8.00
196	Carlos Delgado	6.00
197	Shannon Stewart	5.00
198	Josh Phelps	4.00
199	Vernon Wells	5.00
200	Roy Halladay	8.00

Mirror Red Signatures

NM/M

Common Player:
Production 100 unless noted.
Mirror Blues: 1-1.5X
Production 50
Mirror Golds: 1.5-2X
Production 25 Sets
Mirror Emeralds: No Pricing
Production 5 Sets
Mirror Blacks: One set produced.

2	Alfredo Amezaga	6.00
15	Adam LaRoche	10.00
17	Robert Fick/15	20.00
20	Jay Gibbons	15.00
21	Geronimo Gil/15	15.00
25	Freddy Sanchez	10.00
28	Casey Fossum/50	10.00
32	Nic Jackson	10.00
34	Juan Cruz/15	10.00
35	Steve Smyth/94	8.00
37	Joe Borchard/50	15.00
39	Mark Buehrle/50	20.00
40	Joe Crede/30	15.00
45	Brandon Larson	15.00
49	Wily Mo Pena	20.00
51	Victor Martinez/25	25.00
53	Cliff Lee/50	15.00
54	Jeremy Guthrie/50	15.00
56	Ricardo Rodriguez	8.00
60	Jason Jennings/50	12.00
61	Jeff Baker/50	8.00
63	Travis Chapman	10.00
64	Mike Maroth	10.00
70	Roy Oswalt/50	20.00
71	Jason Lane	10.00
73	Wade Miller/50	15.00
77	Rodrigo Rosario	10.00
80	Angel Berroa/50	15.00
85	Runelvys Hernandez	10.00
88	Cesar Izturis	6.00
91	Joe Thurston	10.00
98	Bill Hall	10.00
102	Jose Morban	8.00
107	Adam Johnson/50	10.00
117	Mike Piazza/20	150.00
124	Brandon Claussen/60	15.00
125	Christian Parker/50	10.00
129	Jason Anderson	10.00
138	Terrence Long/50	15.00
142	Marlon Byrd	10.00
144	Brandon Duckworth/50	10.00
145	Robert Person/50	10.00
146	Anderson Machado	10.00
149	Carlos Rivera	8.00
150	Jose Castillo	8.00
151	Walter Young	8.00
155	Mike Rivera	8.00
157	Brian Lawrence	8.00
166	Chris Snelling	10.00
167	Rafael Soriano/50	12.00
179	Antonio Perez/50	8.00
180	Dewon Brazelton/50	8.00
181	Aubrey Huff/50	15.00
184	Joe Kennedy/50	12.00
187	Hank Blalock/50	40.00
188	Mark Teixeira/50	40.00
190	Kevin Mench	10.00
193	Eric Hinske	15.00
194	Vinnie Chulk	8.00
195	Alexis Rios	25.00

Fabric of the Game

NM/M

Common Player: 4.00
Quantity produced listed

1BA	Bobby Doerr/50	15.00
1JY	Bobby Doerr/39	15.00
1PS	Bobby Doerr/50	15.00
2BA	Ozzie Smith/100	25.00
2IN	Ozzie Smith/50	15.00
2JY	Ozzie Smith/88	20.00
2PS	Ozzie Smith/50	15.00
3DY	Pee Wee Reese/32	30.00
3JY	Pee Wee Reese/58	15.00
4BA	Jeff Bagwell/100	15.00
4DY	Jeff Bagwell/65	10.00
4IN	Jeff Bagwell/50	12.00
4JY	Jeff Bagwell/98	10.00
4PS	Jeff Bagwell/50	10.00
5BA	Tommy Lasorda/100	8.00
5DY	Tommy Lasorda/58	10.00
5JY	Tommy Lasorda/84	8.00
5PS	Tommy Lasorda/50	10.00
6JY	Red Schoendienst/55	10.00
7BA	Harmon Killebrew/50	15.00
7DY	Harmon Killebrew/61	15.00
7IN	Harmon Killebrew/50	15.00
7JY	Harmon Killebrew/71	15.00
7PS	Harmon Killebrew/50	15.00
8DY	Roger Maris/55	40.00
8JY	Roger Maris/58	40.00
8PS	Roger Maris/50	40.00
9BA	Alex Rodriguez/100	15.00
9DY	Alex Rodriguez/77	15.00
9IN	Alex Rodriguez/50	15.00
9JY	Alex Rodriguez/99	15.00
9PS	Alex Rodriguez/50	15.00
10BA	Alex Rodriguez/100	15.00
10DY	Alex Rodriguez/72	15.00
10IN	Alex Rodriguez/50	15.00
10JY	Alex Rodriguez/101	15.00
10PS	Alex Rodriguez/50	15.00
11BA	Dale Murphy/50	15.00
11DY	Dale Murphy/66	15.00
11IN	Dale Murphy/50	15.00
11JY	Dale Murphy/85	15.00
11PS	Dale Murphy/50	15.00
12BA	Alan Trammell/100	10.00
12IN	Alan Trammell/50	10.00
12JY	Alan Trammell/90	10.00
12PS	Alan Trammell/50	10.00
13BA	Babe Ruth/10	250.00
13DY	Babe Ruth/13	250.00
13IN	Babe Ruth/50	250.00
13JY	Babe Ruth/30	200.00
13PS	Babe Ruth/30	250.00
14JY	Lou Gehrig/38	200.00
16JY	Mel Ott/46	30.00
17BA	Paul Molitor/100	15.00
17DY	Paul Molitor/70	15.00
17IN	Paul Molitor/50	15.00
17PS	Paul Molitor/84	15.00
18DY	Duke Snider/58	15.00
18JY	Duke Snider/62	15.00
19BA	Miguel Tejada/50	10.00
19DY	Miguel Tejada/68	8.00
19IN	Miguel Tejada/50	10.00
19JY	Miguel Tejada/99	5.00
19PS	Miguel Tejada/50	10.00
20JY	Lou Gehrig/38	200.00
21BA	Brooks Robinson/54	15.00
21JY	Brooks Robinson/66	15.00
22BA	George Brett/50	30.00
22DY	George Brett/69	25.00
22IN	George Brett/50	30.00
22JY	George Brett/91	25.00
22PS	George Brett/50	30.00
23BA	Johnny Bench/50	15.00
23DY	Johnny Bench/59	15.00
23IN	Johnny Bench/50	15.00
23JY	Johnny Bench/81	15.00
23PS	Johnny Bench/50	15.00
24JY	Lou Boudreau/48	15.00
25BA	Nomar Garciaparra/100	20.00
25IN	Nomar Garciaparra/50	25.00
25JY	Nomar Garciaparra/100	20.00
25PS	Nomar Garciaparra/50	20.00
26BA	Tsuyoshi Shinjo/50	8.00
26DY	Tsuyoshi Shinjo/62	8.00
26JY	Tsuyoshi Shinjo/101	5.00
27BA	Pat Burrell/100	8.00
27DY	Pat Burrell/46	10.00
27JY	Pat Burrell/101	8.00
28BA	Albert Pujols/100	20.00
28JY	Albert Pujols/101	20.00
28PS	Albert Pujols/50	20.00
29JY	Stan Musial/43	30.00
30JY	Al Kaline/64	15.00
31BA	Ivan Rodriguez/100	8.00
31DY	Ivan Rodriguez/72	8.00
31IN	Ivan Rodriguez/50	10.00
31JY	Ivan Rodriguez/101	5.00
32BA	Craig Biggio/100	8.00
32DY	Craig Biggio/65	8.00
32JY	Craig Biggio/101	6.00
32PS	Craig Biggio/50	6.00
33DY	Joe Morgan/74	10.00
33JY	Joe Morgan/74	10.00
34BA	Willie Stargell/100	15.00
34JY	Willie Stargell/68	15.00
34PS	Willie Stargell/50	15.00
35IN	Andre Dawson/100	8.00
35JY	Andre Dawson/87	8.00
35PS	Andre Dawson/50	8.00
36BA	Gary Carter/100	10.00
36DY	Gary Carter/62	10.00
36IN	Gary Carter/50	10.00
36JY	Gary Carter/85	8.00
36PS	Gary Carter/50	10.00
37BA	Cal Ripken Jr./50	50.00
37DY	Cal Ripken Jr./54	50.00
37JY	Cal Ripken Jr./101	40.00
37PS	Cal Ripken Jr./50	50.00
38JY	Enos Slaughter/53	20.00
39BA	Reggie Jackson/50	15.00
39DY	Reggie Jackson/68	15.00
39JY	Reggie Jackson/75	15.00
39PS	Reggie Jackson/50	15.00
40JY	Phil Rizzuto/47	15.00
41BA	Chipper Jones/100	10.00
41DY	Chipper Jones/66	10.00
41IN	Chipper Jones/50	10.00
41JY	Chipper Jones/101	10.00
41PS	Chipper Jones/50	10.00
42BA	Hideo Nomo/100	10.00
42DY	Hideo Nomo/58	15.00
42IN	Hideo Nomo/50	15.00
42JY	Hideo Nomo/95	10.00
42PS	Hideo Nomo/50	15.00
43JY	Luis Aparicio/69	15.00
44BA	Hideo Nomo/100	10.00
44IN	Hideo Nomo/50	15.00
44JY	Hideo Nomo/101	10.00
44PS	Hideo Nomo/50	15.00
45BA	Edgar Martinez/100	8.00
45DY	Edgar Martinez/77	8.00
45JY	Edgar Martinez/100	8.00
45PS	Edgar Martinez/50	8.00
46BA	Barry Larkin/100	6.00
46DY	Barry Larkin/59	6.00
46JY	Barry Larkin/100	6.00
46PS	Barry Larkin/50	6.00
47BA	Alfonso Soriano/100	10.00
47DY	Alfonso Soriano/50	15.00
47JY	Alfonso Soriano/102	10.00
47PS	Alfonso Soriano/50	10.00
47PS	Wade Boggs/100	8.00
48DY	Wade Boggs/98	8.00
48IN	Wade Boggs/50	10.00
48JY	Wade Boggs/99	8.00
48PS	Wade Boggs/50	10.00
49BA	Wade Boggs/50	10.00
49IN	Wade Boggs/50	10.00
49JY	Wade Boggs/94	10.00
49PS	Wade Boggs/50	10.00
50JY	Ernie Banks/68	15.00
51BA	Joe Torre/50	10.00
51DY	Joe Torre/66	10.00
51IN	Joe Torre/50	10.00
51PS	Joe Torre/66	10.00
52BA	Tim Hudson/50	4.00
52DY	Tim Hudson/68	6.00
52JY	Tim Hudson/101	4.00
52PS	Tim Hudson/50	6.00
53BA	Shawn Green/100	4.00
53DY	Shawn Green/58	6.00
53JY	Shawn Green/102	4.00
53PS	Shawn Green/50	6.00
54BA	Carlos Beltran/100	6.00
54DY	Carlos Beltran/69	6.00
54JY	Carlos Beltran/101	6.00
54PS	Carlos Beltran/50	6.00
55BA	Bo Jackson/50	15.00
55DY	Bo Jackson/69	15.00
55JY	Bo Jackson/90	10.00
55PS	Bo Jackson/50	15.00
56BA	Hal Newhouser/50	8.00
56JY	Hal Newhouser/55	8.00
56PS	Hal Newhouser/50	8.00
57BA	Jason Giambi/100	6.00
57DY	Jason Giambi/68	8.00
57IN	Jason Giambi/50	8.00
57JY	Jason Giambi/101	6.00
57PS	Jason Giambi/50	6.00
58BA	Lance Berkman/100	6.00
58DY	Lance Berkman/65	8.00
58IN	Lance Berkman/50	8.00
58JY	Lance Berkman/102	6.00
58PS	Lance Berkman/50	8.00
59BA	Todd Helton/100	8.00
59DY	Todd Helton/93	8.00
59IN	Todd Helton/50	8.00
59PS	Todd Helton/50	8.00
60BA	Mark Grace/100	8.00
60DY	Mark Grace/95	8.00
60JY	Mark Grace/50	15.00
61BA	Fred Lynn/100	8.00
61JY	Fred Lynn/75	8.00
61PS	Fred Lynn/50	8.00
62JY	Bob Feller/52	15.00
63BA	Robin Yount/100	20.00
63DY	Robin Yount/70	25.00
63IN	Robin Yount/50	25.00
63JY	Robin Yount/88	20.00
63PS	Robin Yount/50	25.00
64BA	Tony Gwynn/100	15.00
64DY	Tony Gwynn/69	15.00
64IN	Tony Gwynn/50	15.00
64JY	Tony Gwynn/99	15.00
64PS	Tony Gwynn/50	15.00
65BA	Tony Gwynn/100	15.00
65DY	Tony Gwynn/70	15.00
65IN	Tony Gwynn/50	15.00
65JY	Tony Gwynn/99	15.00
65PS	Tony Gwynn/50	15.00
66DY	Frank Robinson/54	10.00
66JY	Frank Robinson/70	10.00
67BA	Mike Schmidt/50	20.00
67DY	Mike Schmidt/46	20.00
67IN	Mike Schmidt/50	20.00

Mirror Red

Stars (1-205): 2-5X
SP's (206-250): .2-.4X
Production 100 Sets
Mirror Blues (1-205): 4-10X
SP's (206-250): .3-.5X
Production 50 Sets
Mirror Golds: No Pricing
Production 25 Sets
Mirror Emeralds: No Pricing

67JY Mike Schmidt/81 20.00
67PS Mike Schmidt/50 20.00
68JY Lou Brock/66 15.00
69BA Don Sutton/50
69DY Don Sutton/58 8.00
69JY Don Sutton/72
70BA Mark Mulder/100 4.00
70DY Mark Mulder/68 6.00
70JY Mark Mulder/101
70PS Mark Mulder/50 6.00
71BA Luis Gonzalez/100
71DY Luis Gonzalez/98 4.00
71JY Luis Gonzalez/101 4.00
71PS Luis Gonzalez/50 6.00
72BA Jorge Posada/100 6.00
72JY Jorge Posada/101 4.00
72PS Jorge Posada/50 8.00
73BA Sammy Sosa/100 20.00
73IN Sammy Sosa/50 25.00
73JY Sammy Sosa/101 4.00
73PS Sammy Sosa/50 25.00
74BA Roberto Alomar/100
74DY Roberto Alomar/62 10.00
74JY Roberto Alomar/102 8.00
74PS Roberto Alomar/50 10.00
75JY Roberto Clemente/69 80.00
76BA Jeff Kent/100
76DY Jeff Kent/58 6.00
76JY Jeff Kent/101 6.00
76PS Jeff Kent/50 6.00
77DY Sean Casey/59 8.00
77JY Sean Casey/100 4.00
78BA Roger Clemens/50 25.00
78IN Roger Clemens/50 25.00
78JY Roger Clemens/95 20.00
78PS Roger Clemens/50 20.00
79DY Warren Spahn/53 15.00
79JY Warren Spahn/50 15.00
80BA Roger Clemens/100
80IN Roger Clemens/50 25.00
80JY Roger Clemens/102 25.00
80PS Roger Clemens/50 25.00
81BA Jim Palmer/50 10.00
81DY Jim Palmer/54 10.00
81JY Jim Palmer/69 10.00
81PS Jim Palmer/50 10.00
82BA Juan Gonzalez/50 10.00
82JY Juan Gonzalez/101 6.00
82PS Juan Gonzalez/50 10.00
83BA Will Clark/50 15.00
83DY Will Clark/58 15.00
83JY Will Clark/88 15.00
83PS Will Clark/50 15.00
84BA Don Mattingly/50 25.00
84IN Don Mattingly/50 25.00
84JY Don Mattingly/93 25.00
84PS Don Mattingly/50 25.00
85BA Ryne Sandberg/40 30.00
85IN Ryne Sandberg/50 30.00
85JY Ryne Sandberg/85 30.00
85PS Ryne Sandberg/50 30.00
86JY Early Wynn/55 8.00
87BA Manny Ramirez/50 8.00
87JY Manny Ramirez/102 6.00
87PS Manny Ramirez/50 8.00
88BA Rickey Henderson/100 10.00
88DY Rickey Henderson/62 15.00
88IN Rickey Henderson/50 15.00
88JY Rickey Henderson/99 10.00
88PS Rickey Henderson/50 15.00
89BA Rickey Henderson/100 10.00
89DY Rickey Henderson/69 15.00
89JY Rickey Henderson/50 15.00
90BA Jason Giambi/100 8.00
90IN Jason Giambi/50 8.00
90JY Jason Giambi/102 8.00
90PS Jason Giambi/50 10.00
91BA Carlos Delgado/100 8.00
91DY Carlos Delgado/77 4.00
91JY Carlos Delgado/50 4.00
91PS Carlos Delgado/50 6.00
92BA Jim Thome/100 8.00
92JY Jim Thome/102 8.00
92PS Jim Thome/50 10.00
93BA Andruw Jones/100 8.00
93DY Andruw Jones/66 6.00
93JY Andruw Jones/101 8.00
93PS Andruw Jones/50 8.00
94BA Rafael Palmeiro/100 8.00
94DY Rafael Palmeiro/72 4.00
94JY Rafael Palmeiro/102 4.00
94PS Rafael Palmeiro/50 8.00
95BA Troy Glaus/100 6.00
95DY Troy Glaus/97 6.00
95IN Troy Glaus/50 6.00
95JY Troy Glaus/66 6.00
95PS Troy Glaus/50 8.00
96BA Wade Boggs/50 8.00
96IN Wade Boggs/50 10.00
96JY Wade Boggs/34 25.00
96JY Wade Boggs/86 8.00
96PS Wade Boggs/50 10.00
97BA Jim "Catfish" Hunter/50 10.00
97DY Jim "Catfish" Hunter/68 10.00
97JN Jim "Catfish" Hunter/27 15.00

97JY Jim "Catfish" Hunter/68 10.00
97PS Jim "Catfish" Hunter/50 10.00
98BA Juan Marichal/50 10.00
98DY Juan Marichal/58 10.00
98JN Juan Marichal/27 20.00
98JY Juan Marichal/67 10.00
98PS Juan Marichal/50 10.00
99BA Carlton Fisk/50 10.00
99JN Carlton Fisk/27 25.00
99JY Carlton Fisk/80 10.00
99PS Carlton Fisk/50 15.00
100BA Vladimir Guerrero/100 8.00
100DY Vladimir Guerrero/69 15.00
100JN Vladimir Guerrero/27 30.00
100JY Vladimir Guerrero/101 8.00
100PS Vladimir Guerrero/50 15.00
101BA Rod Carew/100 10.00
101DY Rod Carew/65 15.00
101JN Rod Carew/29 20.00
101JY Rod Carew/85 10.00
101PS Rod Carew/50 15.00
102BA Rod Carew/50 10.00
102DY Rod Carew/61 15.00
102JN Rod Carew/29 20.00
102JY Rod Carew/71 10.00
102PS Rod Carew/50 15.00
103BA Joe Carter/50 6.00
103DY Joe Carter/77 8.00
103JN Joe Carter/29 15.00
103JY Joe Carter/94 8.00
104BA Mike Sweeney/100 4.00
104DY Mike Sweeney/69 6.00
104JN Mike Sweeney/29 15.00
104JY Mike Sweeney/101 4.00
104PS Mike Sweeney/50 6.00
105DY Nolan Ryan/65 40.00
105IN Nolan Ryan/30 50.00
105JY Nolan Ryan/70 40.00
105PS Nolan Ryan/50 40.00
106BA Orlando Cepeda/50 8.00
106DY Orlando Cepeda/58 8.00
106IN Orlando Cepeda/50 15.00
106JN Orlando Cepeda/30 15.00
106JY Orlando Cepeda/65 8.00
106PS Orlando Cepeda/50 8.00
107BA Magglio Ordonez/100 4.00
107JN Magglio Ordonez/30 15.00
107JY Magglio Ordonez/100 4.00
107PS Magglio Ordonez/50 6.00
108BA Hoyt Wilhelm/50 8.00
108IN Hoyt Wilhelm/31 15.00
108JY Hoyt Wilhelm/68 8.00
108PS Hoyt Wilhelm/50 8.00
109BA Mike Piazza/100 15.00
109DY Mike Piazza/62 20.00
109IN Mike Piazza/50 25.00
109JN Mike Piazza/31 30.00
109JY Mike Piazza/100 15.00
109PS Mike Piazza/50 15.00
110BA Greg Maddux/100 10.00
110DY Greg Maddux/66 15.00
110IN Greg Maddux/50 15.00
110JN Greg Maddux/31 30.00
110JY Greg Maddux/102 10.00
110PS Greg Maddux/50 15.00
111BA Mark Prior/100 10.00
111IN Mark Prior/50 10.00
111JY Mark Prior/102 8.00
111PS Mark Prior/50 8.00
112BA Torii Hunter/100 6.00
112DY Torii Hunter/61 8.00
112IN Torii Hunter/50 8.00
112JN Torii Hunter/48 6.00
112JY Torii Hunter/101 6.00
112PS Torii Hunter/50 8.00
113BA Steve Carlton/100 8.00
113DY Steve Carlton/46 15.00
113IN Steve Carlton/50 10.00
113JY Steve Carlton/81 8.00
113PS Steve Carlton/50 10.00
114BA Jose Canseco/100 10.00
114DY Jose Canseco/68 8.00
114IN Jose Canseco/33 15.00
114JY Jose Canseco/89 10.00
114PS Jose Canseco/50 15.00
115BA Nolan Ryan/50 30.00
115DY Nolan Ryan/72 30.00
115IN Nolan Ryan/50 30.00
115JY Nolan Ryan/34 40.00
115JY Nolan Ryan/90 30.00
115PS Nolan Ryan/50 30.00
116BA Nolan Ryan/100 30.00
116DY Nolan Ryan/65 30.00
116IN Nolan Ryan/34 40.00
116JY Nolan Ryan/84 30.00
116PS Nolan Ryan/50 30.00
118BA Kerry Wood/100 6.00
118DY Kerry Wood/34 25.00
118JY Kerry Wood/101 6.00
118PS Kerry Wood/50 15.00
119BA Mike Mussina/100 15.00
119DY Mike Mussina/35 25.00
119JY Mike Mussina/101 8.00
119PS Mike Mussina/50 15.00
120JN Yogi Berra/35 25.00
120JY Yogi Berra/47 25.00

121JY Thurman Munson/79 25.00
122BA Frank Thomas/100 8.00
122JN Frank Thomas/35 15.00
122JY Frank Thomas/94 6.00
122PS Frank Thomas/50 8.00
123BA Rickey Henderson/50 15.00
123DY Rickey Henderson/68 10.00
123JN Rickey Henderson/35 20.00
123JY Rickey Henderson/80 10.00
123PS Rickey Henderson/50 15.00
124BA Mike Mussina/100 6.00
124DY Mike Mussina/54 8.00
124IN Mike Mussina/35 20.00
124JN Mike Mussina/97 6.00
124JY Mike Mussina/97 6.00
124PS Mike Mussina/50
125BA Gaylord Perry/100 6.00
125DY Gaylord Perry/77 8.00
125JN Gaylord Perry/36 10.00
125JY Gaylord Perry/82 8.00
125PS Gaylord Perry/50 8.00
126BA Nick Johnson/100 4.00
126JN Nick Johnson/36 4.00
126JY Nick Johnson/102 4.00
126PS Nick Johnson/50 4.00
127BA Curt Schilling/100 8.00
127DY Curt Schilling/98 8.00
127JN Curt Schilling/38 15.00
127JY Curt Schilling/50 8.00
127PS Curt Schilling/50 8.00
128BA Dave Parker/100 6.00
128JN Dave Parker/39 8.00
128JY Dave Parker/80 8.00
128PS Dave Parker/50 8.00
129DY Eddie Mathews/53 15.00
129JN Eddie Mathews/41 25.00
129JY Eddie Mathews/59 20.00
130DY Tom Seaver/62 15.00
130JN Tom Seaver/41 25.00
130JY Tom Seaver/69 15.00
131DY Tom Seaver/59 15.00
131JN Tom Seaver/41 25.00
131JY Tom Seaver/78 15.00
132JN Jackie Robinson/42 80.00
132JY Jackie Robinson/52 60.00
133BA Reggie Jackson/100 10.00
133DY Reggie Jackson/65 15.00
133IN Reggie Jackson/50 15.00
133JN Reggie Jackson/44 20.00
133JY Reggie Jackson/80 10.00
133PS Reggie Jackson/50 15.00
134BA Willie McCovey/100 8.00
134DY Willie McCovey/58 10.00
134JN Willie McCovey/44 10.00
134JY Willie McCovey/77 10.00
134PS Willie McCovey/50 10.00
135BA Eric Davis/100 8.00
135DY Eric Davis/59 8.00
135JN Eddie Davis/44 10.00
135JY Eric Davis/89 8.00
135PS Eric Davis/50 8.00
136BA Adam Dunn/100 8.00
136DY Adam Dunn/59 8.00
136JN Adam Dunn/44 15.00
136JY Adam Dunn/102 8.00
136PS Adam Dunn/50 10.00
137BA Roy Oswalt/100 4.00
137DY Roy Oswalt/65 6.00
137IN Roy Oswalt/50 8.00
137JN Roy Oswalt/44 8.00
137JY Roy Oswalt/102 6.00
137PS Roy Oswalt/50 6.00
138BA Pedro J. Martinez/50 15.00
138DY Pedro J. Martinez/69 15.00
138JN Pedro J. Martinez/45 20.00
138JY Pedro J. Martinez/95 6.00
138PS Pedro J. Martinez/50 10.00
139BA Pedro J. Martinez/100 8.00
139IN Pedro J. Martinez/50 10.00
139JN Pedro J. Martinez/45 10.00
139JY Pedro J. Martinez/102 8.00
139PS Pedro J. Martinez/50 10.00
140BA Andy Pettitte/100 6.00
140JN Andy Pettitte/46 10.00
140JY Andy Pettitte/97 6.00
140PS Andy Pettitte/50 6.00
141BA Jack Morris/50 6.00
141IN Jack Morris/50 10.00
141JY Jack Morris/85 6.00
141PS Jack Morris/50 6.00
142BA Tom Glavine/100 6.00
142DY Tom Glavine/66 8.00
142JY Tom Glavine/40 6.00
143BA Randy Johnson/100 10.00
143DY Randy Johnson/77 15.00
143IN Randy Johnson/50 15.00
143JN Randy Johnson/51 15.00
143JY Randy Johnson/98 15.00
143PS Randy Johnson/50 15.00
144BA Bernie Williams/100 8.00

144IN Bernie Williams/50 10.00
144JN Bernie Williams/51 10.00
144JY Bernie Williams/100 8.00
144PS Bernie Williams/50 8.00
145BA Randy Johnson/50 15.00
145DY Randy Johnson/98 10.00
145IN Randy Johnson/50 15.00
145JN Randy Johnson/51 15.00
145JY Randy Johnson/102 15.00
145PS Randy Johnson/50 10.00
146DY Don Drysdale/58 10.00
146JN Don Drysdale/53 10.00
146JY Don Drysdale/64 10.00
147BA Mark Buehrle/100 4.00
147JN Mark Buehrle/56 6.00
147JY Mark Buehrle/101 4.00
147PS Mark Buehrle/50 6.00
148BA Chan Ho Park/100 4.00
148DY Chan Ho Park/58 6.00
148JN Chan Ho Park/61 8.00
148JY Chan Ho Park/101 4.00
148PS Chan Ho Park/50 6.00
149BA Carlton Fisk/100 8.00
149IN Carlton Fisk/50 15.00
149JN Carlton Fisk/72 15.00
149JY Carlton Fisk/92 15.00
149PS Carlton Fisk/50 15.00
150BA Barry Zito/100 6.00
150DY Barry Zito/68 8.00
150JN Barry Zito/75 8.00
150JY Barry Zito/101 8.00
150PS Barry Zito/50 8.00

2003 Leaf Limited

NM/M

Complete Set (170):
Common Player (1-151): 1.50
Production 999
Common (152-170): 4.00
Production 399
Common Auto. Memor. (171-200): 15.00
Production 99
Common Auto. (171-200): 8.00
Pack (4): 75.00
Box (4): 250.00
1 Derek Jeter 6.00
2 Eric Chavez 1.50
3 Alex Rodriguez 5.00
4 Miguel Tejada 1.50
5 Nomar Garciaparra 4.00
6 Jeff Bagwell 3.00
7 Jim Thome 2.00
8 Pat Burrell 1.50
9 Albert Pujols 5.00
10 Juan Gonzalez 3.00
11 Shawn Green 1.50
12 Craig Biggio 1.50
13 Chipper Jones 3.00
14 Hideo Nomo 2.00
15 Vernon Wells 1.50
16 Gary Sheffield 2.00
17 Barry Larkin 1.50
18 Josh Beckett 1.50
19 Edgar Martinez 1.50
20 Ivan Rodriguez 2.00
21 Jeff Kent 1.50
22 Roberto Alomar 1.50
23 Alfonso Soriano 3.00
24 Jim Thome 2.00
25 Juan Gonzalez 3.00
26 Carlos Beltran 2.00
27 Shawn Green 1.50
28 Tim Hudson 1.50
29 Deion Sanders 2.00
30 Rafael Palmeiro 2.00
31 Todd Helton 3.00
32 Lance Berkman 1.50
33 Mike Mussina 2.00
34 Kazuhisa Ishii 1.50
35 Bill Burrell 1.50
36 Miguel Tejada 1.50
37 Juan Gonzalez 2.00
38 Roberto Alomar 1.50
39 Roberto Alomar 1.50
40 Luis Gonzalez 1.50
41 Jorge Posada 1.50
42 Mark Mulder 1.50
43 Sammy Sosa 4.00
44 Mark Prior 2.00
45 Roger Clemens 4.00
46 Tom Glavine 1.50
47 Mark Teixeira 1.50
48 Manny Ramirez 2.00
49 Frank Thomas 3.00
50 Troy Glaus 3.00

51 Andruw Jones 3.00
52 Jason Giambi 2.00
53 Jim Thome 2.00
54 Barry Bonds 6.00
55 Rafael Palmeiro 2.00
56 Edgar Martinez 1.50
57 Vladimir Guerrero 3.00
58 Roberto Alomar 1.50
59 Mike Sweeney 1.50
60 Magglio Ordonez 1.50
61 Ken Griffey Jr. 4.00
62 Craig Biggio 1.50
63 Greg Maddux 4.00
64 Mike Piazza 4.00
65 Tom Glavine 1.50
66 Kerry Wood 2.00
67 Frank Thomas 3.00
68 Mike Mussina 2.00
69 Nick Johnson 1.50
70 Bernie Williams 1.50
71 Scott Rolen 2.00
72 Curt Schilling 2.00
73 Adam Dunn 2.00
74 Roy Oswalt 1.50
75 Pedro J. Martinez 3.00
76 Tom Glavine 1.50
77 Torii Hunter 1.50
78 Austin Kearns 1.50
79 Randy Johnson 3.00
80 Bernie Williams 1.50
81 Ichiro Suzuki 4.00
82 Kerry Wood 2.00
83 Kazuhisa Ishii 1.50
84 Randy Johnson 3.00
85 Nick Johnson 1.50
86 Josh Beckett 1.50
87 Curt Schilling 2.00
88 Mike Mussina 2.00
89 Pedro J. Martinez 3.00
90 Barry Zito 1.50
91 Jim Edmonds 1.50
92 Rickey Henderson 3.00
93 Rickey Henderson 3.00
94 Rickey Henderson 3.00
95 Rickey Henderson 3.00
96 Rickey Henderson 3.00
97 Randy Johnson 3.00
98 Mark Grace 1.50
99 Pedro J. Martinez 3.00
100 Hee Seop Choi 1.50
101 Ivan Rodriguez 2.00
102 Jeff Kent 1.50
103 Hideo Nomo 3.00
104 Hideo Nomo 3.00
105 Mike Piazza 4.00
106 Tom Glavine 1.50
107 Roberto Alomar 1.50
108 Roger Clemens 5.00
109 Jason Giambi 2.00
110 Jim Thome 2.00
111 Alex Rodriguez 5.00
112 Juan Gonzalez 2.00
113 Torii Hunter 1.50
114 Roy Oswalt 1.50
115 Curt Schilling 2.00
116 Magglio Ordonez 1.50
117 Rafael Palmeiro 2.00
118 Andruw Jones 3.00
119 Manny Ramirez 3.00
120 Mark Teixeira 1.50
121 Mark Mulder 1.50
122 Garret Anderson 1.50
123 Tim Hudson 1.50
124 Todd Helton 3.00
125 Troy Glaus 3.00
126 Derek Jeter 6.00
127 Barry Bonds 6.00
128 Greg Maddux 4.00
129 Roger Clemens 5.00
130 Nomar Garciaparra 4.00
131 Mike Piazza 4.00
132 Alex Rodriguez 5.00
133 Ichiro Suzuki 4.00
134 Randy Johnson 4.00
135 Sammy Sosa 4.00
136 Ken Griffey Jr. 4.00
137 Alfonso Soriano 3.00
138 Jason Giambi 2.00
139 Albert Pujols 5.00
140 Chipper Jones 3.00
141 Adam Dunn 2.00
142 Pedro J. Martinez 3.00
143 Vladimir Guerrero 3.00
144 Mark Prior 2.00
145 Barry Zito 1.50
146 Jeff Bagwell 3.00
147 Lance Berkman 1.50
148 Shawn Green 1.50
149 Jason Giambi 2.00
150 Randy Johnson 3.00
151 Alex Rodriguez 5.00
152 Babe Ruth 10.00
153 Ty Cobb 6.00
154 Jackie Robinson 6.00
155 Lou Gehrig 8.00
156 Thurman Munson 6.00
157 Roberto Clemente 8.00
158 Nolan Ryan 10.00
159 Nolan Ryan 10.00
160 Nolan Ryan 10.00
161 Cal Ripken Jr. 10.00
162 Don Mattingly 6.00
163 Stan Musial 8.00
164 Tony Gwynn 3.00
165 Yogi Berra 3.00
166 Johnny Bench 5.00
167 Mike Schmidt 8.00
168 George Brett 8.00

169 Ryne Sandberg 4.00
170 Ernie Banks 5.00
171 J. Bonderman/ Auto./Jsy 75.00
172 Jose Contreras/ Auto. RC 40.00
173 Chien-Ming Wang/ Auto. 350.00
174 Hideki Matsui/ Base RC 40.00
175 Hong-Chih Kuo/ Auto./Jsy 120.00
176 Brandon Webb/ Auto./Bat RC 60.00
177 Richard Fischer/Auto. 8.00
178 Robby Hammock/ Auto./Bat 20.00
179 Todd Wellemeyer/ Auto./49 RC 15.00
180 Prentice Redman/ Auto./Bat RC 10.00
181 Nook Logan/ Auto. RC 20.00
182 Craig Brazell/ Auto. RC 15.00
183 Tim Olson/Auto./ Bat RC 15.00
184 Matt Kata/Auto./ Bat RC 20.00
185 A. Machado/Auto. 8.00
186 Michael Hessman/ Auto. RC 10.00
187 Oscar Villarreal/ Auto. RC 8.00
188 Guillermo Quiroz/ Auto./Bat RC 10.00
189 Michel Hernandez/ Auto. RC 10.00
190 Clint Barmes/Auto./ Bat RC 40.00
191 Pete LaForest/Auto./ Bat RC 20.00
192 Adam Loewen/ Auto. RC 25.00
193 Terrmel Sledge/ Auto./Bat RC 15.00
194 Lew Ford/Auto./ Bat RC 40.00
195 Todd Wellemeyer/ Auto./49 RC 15.00
196 Clint Barmes/Auto./ Bat RC 40.00
197 J. Bonderman/ Auto./Jsy 50.00
198 Brandon Webb/ Auto./Jsy RC 60.00
199 Hideki Matsui/ Base RC 30.00
200 Jose Contreras/ Auto. RC 40.00

Silver Spotlight

Silvers (1-170): 1-2X
Production 100
Silver Auto. Memor. (171-200):1X
Silver Memor. (171-200): 1X
Silver Auto.: 1X
Production 29 to 50

Gold Spotlight

Golds (1-151): 2-4X
Golds (152-170): 1.5-3X
Production 50
Golds (171-200): No Pricing
Production 10 to 25

Jersey Numbers

NM/M

Common Player:
Production 5-100
Some not priced due to scarcity.
1 Rod Carew/50 20.00
2 Nolan Ryan/50 40.00
3 Reggie Jackson/50 20.00
4 Brooks Robinson/50 25.00
5 Frank Robinson/50 15.00
6 Cal Ripken Jr./100 40.00
7 Carlton Fisk/50 15.00
8 Roger Clemens/100 15.00
10 Lou Boudreau/50 10.00
11 Bob Feller/25 30.00
13 Alan Trammell/50 10.00
14 Harmon Killebrew/50 25.00
15 Rod Carew/50 20.00
16 Kirby Puckett/50 20.00
19 Yogi Berra/50 30.00

20	Thurman Munson/50	30.00
21	Don Mattingly/100	25.00
25	Alex Rodriguez/100	10.00
26	Randy Johnson/50	10.00
27	Nolan Ryan/100	30.00
28	Dale Murphy/50	20.00
29	Warren Spahn/50	20.00
30	Eddie Mathews/50	20.00
32	Ryne Sandberg/100	30.00
33	Johnny Bench/50	30.00
34	Joe Morgan/50	10.00
35	Randy Johnson/50	10.00
36	Nolan Ryan/50	10.00
37	Pee Wee Reese/50	15.00
38	Duke Snider/50	20.00
39	Jackie Robinson/25	65.00
40	Robin Yount/50	30.00
41	Paul Molitor/50	10.00
42	Pedro Martinez/50	10.00
43	Randy Johnson/50	10.00
44	Tom Seaver/25	25.00
45	Gary Carter/50	10.00
46	Mike Schmidt/50	30.00
47	Steve Carlton/50	20.00
48	Willie Stargell/50	20.00
50	Ozzie Smith/50	35.00
51	Stan Musial/100	30.00
52	Enos Slaughter/50	10.00
53	Orlando Cepeda/50	10.00
54	Willie McCovey/50	15.00
57	Harmon Killebrew, Rod Carew/50	50.00
58	Harmon Killebrew, Kirby Puckett/50	50.00
68	Thurman Munson, Yogi Berra/50	50.00
69	Don Mattingly, Yogi Berra/25	60.00
71	Dale Murphy, Warren Spahn/25	50.00
72	Dale Murphy, Eddie Mathews/25	45.00
73	Eddie Mathews, Warren Spahn/25	60.00
74	Joe Morgan, Johnny Bench/25	40.00
75	Duke Snider, Pee Wee Reese/25	40.00
78	Paul Molitor, Robin Yount/25	75.00
81	Ozzie Smith, Stan Musial/25	60.00
82	Enos Slaughter, Stan Musial/25	60.00
83	Orlando Cepeda, Willie McCovey/25	40.00
84	Nolan Ryan, Reggie Jackson/25	60.00
90	Alex Rodriguez, Randy Johnson/25	25.00
91	Pedro J. Martinez, Randy Johnson/25	35.00
94	Reggie Jackson/25	35.00
95	Nolan Ryan/25	60.00
96	Nolan Ryan/25	60.00
97	Nolan Ryan/25	60.00
98	Nolan Ryan/25	60.00
99	Cal Ripken Jr., Rafael Palmeiro/25	90.00
100	Dale Murphy, Deion Sanders/25	50.00

Jersey Numbers Retired
NM/M
Many not priced due to scarcity.

1	Rod Carew/29	30.00
2	Nolan Ryan/30	50.00
5	Frank Robinson/20	20.00
7	Carlton Fisk/27	30.00
9	Carlton Fisk/27	15.00
16	Kirby Puckett/34	35.00
21	Don Mattingly/23	15.00
27	Nolan Ryan/34	50.00
30	Eddie Mathews/41	20.00
36	Nolan Ryan/34	50.00
39	Jackie Robinson/42	50.00
41	Tom Seaver/41	20.00
46	Mike Schmidt/20	50.00
47	Steve Carlton/32	15.00
49	Roberto Clemente/21	100.00
53	Orlando Cepeda/30	15.00
54	Willie McCovey/44	50.00

2003 Leaf Limited Leather
NM/M
Common Player:
Production 10-25
Golds: No Pricing
Production 5-10
Leather & Lace: No Pricing
Production 10
Leather & Lace Gold: No Pricing
Production 5

1	Alex Rodriguez/25	40.00
2	Chipper Jones/25	30.00
4	Jimmie Foxx/25	65.00
5	Kirby Puckett/25	25.00
6	Mike Schmidt/25	30.00
7	Roger Clemens/25	45.00
8	Tony Gwynn/25	30.00
10	Vladimir Guerrero/25	25.00
11	Adam Dunn/25	20.00
12	Andruw Jones/25	25.00

13	Curt Schilling/25	20.00
14	Randy Johnson/25	25.00
15	Mark Prior/25	40.00

Lineups - Bats
NM/M
Common Player:
Production 25-50

1	Paul Molitor, Robin Yount/50	35.00
2	Bernie Williams, Don Mattingly/50	40.00
3	Derek Jeter, Hideki Matsui/25	60.00
4	Andre Dawson, Ryne Sandberg/50	40.00
5	Bo Jackson, George Brett/50	40.00
6	Jose Canseco, Reggie Jackson/50	25.00
7	Mark Grace, Ryne Sandberg/50	40.00
8	Jose Canseco, Rickey Henderson/50	30.00
10	Hideo Nomo, Mike Piazza/50	30.00

Lineups - Buttons
No Pricing
Production One Set

Lineups - Jerseys
NM/M
Production 5-50

1	Paul Molitor, Robin Yount/50	35.00
2	Bernie Williams, Don Mattingly/50	40.00
3	Hee Seop Choi, Sammy Sosa/50	30.00
4	Derek Jeter, Hideki Matsui 50/Base	60.00
5	Andre Dawson, Ryne Sandberg/50	35.00
6	Bo Jackson, George Brett/50	50.00
7	Jose Canseco, Reggie Jackson/50	25.00
8	Mark Grace, Ryne Sandberg/50	35.00
9	Jose Canseco, Rickey Henderson/50	25.00
10	Hideo Nomo, Mike Piazza/50	25.00

Lineups Tag Team
No Pricing
Production 5

Lumberjacks
NM/M
Some not priced due to scarcity.
Production 1-25
Black: No Pricing
Production 1-5
Silver: No Pricing
Production 1-10

1	Babe Ruth/25	200.00
2	Lou Gehrig/25	150.00
3	Roberto Clemente/25	120.00
4	Stan Musial/25	40.00
5	Rogers Hornsby/25	50.00
6	Don Mattingly/25	50.00
7	Rickey Henderson/25	20.00
8	Cal Ripken Jr./25	75.00
9	Yogi Berra/25	30.00
10	Reggie Jackson/25	35.00
11	George Brett/25	60.00
12	Mel Ott/25	40.00
13	Roger Maris/25	60.00
14	Ryne Sandberg/25	50.00
16	Richie Ashburn/25	40.00
17	Mike Schmidt/25	40.00
18	Tony Gwynn/25	25.00
19	Ty Cobb/25	110.00
20	Thurman Munson/25	35.00
21	Jimmie Foxx/25	60.00
22	Duke Snider/25	50.00
24	Alex Rodriguez/25	30.00
25	Nomar Garciaparra/25	30.00
26	Hideki Matsui/25/Base	50.00
27	Ichiro Suzuki/25/Base	50.00
28	Barry Bonds/25/Base	35.00
29	Mike Piazza/25	35.00
30	Alfonso Soriano/25	25.00
31	Al Kaline/25	30.00
33	Dale Murphy/25	30.00
34	Orlando Cepeda/25	30.00
35	Willie McCovey/25	30.00
37	Brooks Robinson/25	30.00

Lumberjacks - Barrel
NM/M
1/1 except where indicated
No pricing due to scarcity.

21	Jimmie Foxx (7/05 auction)	1,525

Lumberjacks - Jerseys
NM/M
Production 1-25
Black: No Pricing
Production 1-5
Silver: No Pricing
Production 1-10

4	Stan Musial/25	40.00
6	Don Mattingly/25	50.00
8	Cal Ripken Jr./25	80.00
9	Yogi Berra/25	25.00
11	George Brett/25	60.00
12	Mel Ott/25	40.00
14	Ryne Sandberg/25	25.00
15	Eddie Mathews/25	25.00
17	Mike Schmidt/25	50.00
18	Tony Gwynn/25	25.00
20	Thurman Munson/25	25.00
22	Duke Snider/25	20.00
24	Alex Rodriguez/25	30.00
25	Nomar Garciaparra/25	30.00
26	Hideki Matsui/25/Ball	50.00
27	Ichiro Suzuki/25/Ball	50.00
28	Barry Bonds/25/Ball	40.00
29	Mike Piazza/25	40.00
30	Alfonso Soriano/25	20.00
32	Harmon Killebrew/25	25.00
33	Dale Murphy/25	25.00
34	Orlando Cepeda/25	15.00
35	Willie McCovey/25	20.00
36	Willie Stargell/25	20.00
37	Brooks Robinson/25	20.00

Lumberjacks - Jerseys/Bats
NM/M
Production 1-25
Some not priced due to scarcity.
Black: No Pricing
Production 1-5
Silver: No Pricing
Production 1-10

4	Stan Musial/25	60.00
6	Don Mattingly/25	75.00
8	Cal Ripken Jr./25	140.00
9	Yogi Berra/25	30.00
11	George Brett/25	80.00
13	Roger Maris/25	100.00
14	Ryne Sandberg/25	65.00
15	Eddie Mathews/25	65.00
17	Mike Schmidt/25	65.00
18	Tony Gwynn/25	40.00
20	Thurman Munson/25	40.00
24	Alex Rodriguez/25	40.00
25	Nomar Garciaparra/25	40.00
26	Hideki Matsui/25/Base/Ball	65.00
27	Ichiro Suzuki/25/Base/Ball	60.00
28	Barry Bonds/25/Base/Ball	60.00
29	Mike Piazza/25	40.00
30	Alfonso Soriano/25	25.00
33	Dale Murphy/25	40.00
35	Willie McCovey/25	35.00
36	Willie Stargell/25	30.00
37	Brooks Robinson/25	30.00

Lumberjacks Combos
NM/M
Production 1-25
Black: No Pricing
Production 1-5
Silver: No Pricing
Production 1-10

38	Hideki Matsui, Ichiro Suzuki/25/Base	80.00
40	Don Mattingly, Lou Gehrig/25	240.00
41	Thurman Munson, Yogi Berra/25	50.00
42	Mike Schmidt, Richie Ashburn/25	60.00
43	Rogers Hornsby, Stan Musial/25	80.00
44	Don Mattingly, Roger Maris/25	100.00

Lumberjacks Combos - Jerseys
NM/M
Production 1-25
Some not priced due to scarcity.
Black: No Pricing
Production 1-5
Silver: No Pricing
Production 1-10

38	Hideki Matsui, Ichiro Suzuki/25/Ball	100.00
41	Thurman Munson, Yogi Berra/25	60.00

Lumberjacks Combos - Jerseys/Bats
NM/M
Production 1-25
Some not priced due to scarcity.
Black: No Pricing
Production 1-5
Silver: No Pricing
Production 1-10

38	Hideki Matsui, Ichiro Suzuki/25/Ball	100.00
41	Thurman Munson, Yogi Berra/25	50.00
42	Mike Schmidt, Richie Ashburn/25	60.00

Material Monikers Bats

NM/M
Production 1-25
No pricing for many, due to scarcity.

2	Eric Chavez/25	35.00
12	Craig Biggio/25	40.00
15	Vernon Wells/25	30.00
19	Edgar Martinez/25	50.00
26	Carlos Beltran/25	40.00
28	Tim Hudson/25	40.00
44	Mark Prior/25	50.00
47	Mark Teixeira/25	40.00
69	Nick Johnson/25	25.00
73	Adam Dunn/25	30.00
77	Torii Hunter/25	30.00
85	Nick Johnson/25	25.00
113	Torii Hunter/25	30.00
114	Roy Oswalt/25	30.00
120	Mark Teixeira/25	40.00

Material Monikers Jerseys
NM/M
Common Player:

2	Eric Chavez/25	25.00
4	Miguel Tejada/25	35.00
12	Craig Biggio/25	35.00
15	Vernon Wells/25	40.00
26	Carlos Beltran/25	50.00
28	Tim Hudson/25	40.00
44	Mark Prior/25	40.00
47	Mark Teixeira/25	25.00
69	Nick Johnson/25	20.00
73	Adam Dunn/25	40.00
74	Roy Oswalt/25	25.00
77	Torii Hunter/25	25.00
85	Nick Johnson/25	20.00
113	Torii Hunter/25	25.00
114	Roy Oswalt/25	25.00
120	Mark Teixeira/25	40.00

2003 Leaf Limited Material Monikers Jersey Numbers
NM/M
Production 1-25
Many not priced due to scarcity.

2	Eric Chavez/25	25.00
4	Miguel Tejada/25	30.00
12	Craig Biggio/25	35.00
15	Vernon Wells/25	30.00
19	Edgar Martinez/25	30.00
26	Carlos Beltran/25	50.00
28	Tim Hudson/25	25.00
44	Mark Prior/25	40.00
47	Mark Teixeira/25	40.00
69	Nick Johnson/25	15.00
73	Adam Dunn/25	40.00
74	Roy Oswalt/25	20.00
77	Torii Hunter/25	25.00
85	Nick Johnson/25	15.00
113	Torii Hunter/25	25.00
114	Roy Oswalt/25	20.00
120	Mark Teixeira/25	40.00

Material Monikers Jersey Position
NM/M
Production 1-25
Many not priced due to scarcity.

2	Eric Chavez/25	25.00
4	Miguel Tejada/25	30.00
12	Craig Biggio/25	30.00
15	Vernon Wells/25	20.00
19	Edgar Martinez/25	20.00
26	Carlos Beltran/25	50.00
28	Tim Hudson/25	25.00
29	Deion Sanders/25	50.00
44	Mark Prior/25	40.00
47	Mark Teixeira/25	40.00
69	Nick Johnson/25	20.00
73	Adam Dunn/25	40.00
74	Roy Oswalt/25	25.00
77	Torii Hunter/25	25.00
85	Nick Johnson/25	20.00
113	Torii Hunter/25	25.00
114	Roy Oswalt/25	25.00
120	Mark Teixeira/25	40.00

Player Threads
NM/M
Production 5-50
Some not priced due to scarcity.
Primes: No Pricing
Production 5-10

1	Roger Clemens/50	15.00
2	Alex Rodriguez/50	15.00
3	Pedro Martinez/50	10.00
4	Randy Johnson/50	10.00
5	Curt Schilling/50	8.00
7	Nolan Ryan/50	35.00
8	Hideo Nomo/50	12.00
9	Mike Piazza/50	15.00
11	Rickey Henderson/50	15.00
12	Ivan Rodriguez/50	10.00
13	Gary Sheffield/50	8.00
14	Jeff Kent/50	10.00
15	Roberto Alomar/50	10.00
16	Rafael Palmeiro/50	10.00
17	Juan Gonzalez/50	8.00
18	Shawn Green/50	8.00
19	Jason Giambi/50	8.00
20	Jim Thome/50	10.00
21	Scott Rolen/50	12.00
22	Mike Mussina/50	10.00
23	Tom Glavine/50	8.00
24	Sammy Sosa/50	15.00

Player Threads Double
NM/M
Production 5-50
Some not priced due to scarcity.
Double Primes: No Pricing
Production 5-10

1	Roger Clemens/50	25.00
2	Alex Rodriguez/50	25.00
3	Pedro Martinez/50	20.00
4	Randy Johnson/50	15.00
5	Curt Schilling/50	10.00
7	Nolan Ryan/50	50.00
8	Hideo Nomo/50	20.00
9	Mike Piazza/50	25.00
11	Rickey Henderson/50	20.00
12	Ivan Rodriguez/50	15.00
13	Gary Sheffield/50	15.00
14	Jeff Kent/50	10.00
15	Roberto Alomar/50	15.00
16	Rafael Palmeiro/50	15.00
17	Juan Gonzalez/50	15.00
18	Shawn Green/50	15.00
19	Jason Giambi/50	15.00
20	Jim Thome/50	15.00
21	Scott Rolen/50	20.00
22	Mike Mussina/50	15.00
23	Tom Glavine/50	10.00
24	Sammy Sosa/50	25.00

Player Threads Triple
NM/M
Production 50
Some not priced due to scarcity.
Triple Primes: No Pricing
Production 5-10

4	Randy Johnson/50	20.00
7	Nolan Ryan/50	75.00
8	Hideo Nomo/50	60.00
11	Rickey Henderson/50	30.00
13	Gary Sheffield/50	15.00
14	Jeff Kent/50	15.00
15	Roberto Alomar/25	25.00

Swatch
Complete Set (40):
Common Player:

Team Threads
NM/M
Production 10-50
Some not priced due to scarcity.
Primes: No Pricing
Production 5-10

26	Alex Rodriguez, Nolan Ryan/50	50.00
27	Hideo Nomo, Mike Piazza/50	20.00
28	Cal Ripken Jr., Mike Mussina/50	50.00
29	Hideo Nomo, Kazuhisa Ishii/50	15.00
30	Nolan Ryan, Randy Johnson/50	40.00

Team Trademarks Autographs
NM/M
Some not priced due to scarcity.

1	Alan Trammell/25	40.00
3	Jim Palmer/25	30.00

29	Deion Sanders/25	50.00
44	Mark Prior/25	40.00
47	Mark Teixeira/25	40.00
69	Nick Johnson/25	20.00
73	Adam Dunn/25	40.00
74	Roy Oswalt/25	25.00
77	Torii Hunter/25	25.00
85	Nick Johnson/25	20.00
113	Torii Hunter/25	25.00
114	Roy Oswalt/25	25.00
120	Mark Teixeira/25	40.00

Team Trademarks Jersey Autograph
NM/M
Some not priced due to scarcity.

12	Eric Davis/44	30.00
12	Jack Morris/47	25.00
23	Rod Carew/29	50.00
25	Willie McCovey/44	25.00
27	Nolan Ryan/34	140.00
31	Rod Carew/29	50.00
32	Nolan Ryan/34	140.00
34	Nolan Ryan/30	140.00
37	Greg Maddux/31	150.00

Team Trademarks Threads Jersey Number
NM/M
Some not priced due to scarcity.
Primes: 1-1.5X
Production 1-25
Some not priced due to scarcity.

3	Jim Palmer/22	20.00
12	Eric Davis/44	8.00
15	Jack Morris/47	8.00
17	Deion Sanders/24	25.00
19	Orlando Cepeda/30	10.00
23	Rod Carew/29	20.00
24	Will Clark/22	50.00
25	Willie McCovey/44	10.00
27	Nolan Ryan/34	50.00
31	Rod Carew/29	20.00
32	Nolan Ryan/34	50.00
34	Nolan Ryan/30	50.00
37	Greg Maddux/31	30.00

2003 Leaf Limited Threads

NM/M
Common Player: 8.00
Varying quantities produced

1	Derek Jeter/Base/50	20.00
2	Eric Chavez/50	10.00
3	Alex Rodriguez/100	15.00
4	Miguel Tejada/50	8.00
5	Nomar Garciaparra/100	15.00
6	Jeff Bagwell/50	10.00
7	Jim Thome/50	10.00
8	Pat Burrell/50	10.00
9	Albert Pujols/100	20.00
10	Juan Gonzalez/25	20.00
11	Shawn Green/50	10.00
12	Craig Biggio/50	10.00
13	Chipper Jones/50	20.00
14	Hideo Nomo/100	12.00
15	Vernon Wells/50	10.00
16	Gary Sheffield/25	10.00
17	Barry Larkin/25	15.00
18	Josh Beckett/25	10.00
19	Edgar Martinez/25	15.00
20	Ivan Rodriguez/25	20.00
21	Jeff Kent/25	10.00
22	Roberto Alomar/25	15.00
23	Alfonso Soriano/100	8.00
24	Jim Thome/50	10.00
25	Juan Gonzalez/25	10.00
26	Carlos Beltran/25	20.00
27	Shawn Green/50	8.00
28	Tim Hudson/25	10.00
29	Deion Sanders/25	20.00
30	Rafael Palmeiro/25	10.00
31	Todd Helton/50	10.00
32	Lance Berkman/25	10.00
33	Mike Mussina/50	10.00
34	Kazuhisa Ishii/50	8.00
35	Pat Burrell/25	10.00
36	Miguel Tejada/50	8.00
37	Juan Gonzalez/25	10.00
38	Roberto Alomar/25	15.00

39 Roberto Alomar/25 15.00
40 Luis Gonzalez/25 10.00
41 Jorge Posada/50 15.00
42 Mark Mulder/25 15.00
43 Sammy Sosa/100 15.00
44 Mark Prior/50 15.00
45 Roger Clemens/100 15.00
46 Tom Glavine/25 15.00
47 Mark Teixeira/25 10.00
48 Manny Ramirez/50 12.00
49 Frank Thomas/25 15.00
50 Troy Glaus/50 8.00
51 Andruw Jones/50 8.00
52 Jason Giambi/100 8.00
53 Jim Thome/50 10.00
54 Barry Bonds/50/Base 25.00
55 Rafael Palmeiro/25 10.00
56 Edgar Martinez/25 10.00
57 Vladimir Guerrero/50 10.00
58 Roberto Alomar/25 15.00
59 Mike Sweeney/25 10.00
60 Magglio Ordonez/25 10.00
62 Craig Biggio/25 10.00
63 Greg Maddux/100 10.00
64 Mike Piazza/100 10.00
65 Tom Glavine/25 15.00
66 Kerry Wood/25 20.00
67 Frank Thomas/25 15.00
68 Mike Mussina/50 10.00
69 Nick Johnson/25 8.00
70 Bernie Williams/50 10.00
71 Scott Rolen/25 15.00
72 Curt Schilling/25 10.00
73 Adam Dunn/50 10.00
74 Roy Oswalt/25 10.00
75 Pedro Martinez/25 20.00
76 Tom Glavine/25 15.00
77 Torii Hunter/25 10.00
78 Austin Kearns/25 10.00
79 Randy Johnson/100 10.00
80 Bernie Williams/50 10.00
81 Ichiro Suzuki/50 25.00
82 Kerry Wood/50 20.00
83 Kazuhisa Ishii/50 8.00
84 Randy Johnson/50 10.00
85 Nick Johnson/25 8.00
86 Josh Beckett/25 10.00
87 Curt Schilling/25 15.00
88 Mike Mussina/50 10.00
89 Pedro Martinez/25 15.00
90 Barry Zito/75 8.00
91 Jim Edmonds/100 6.00
92 Rickey Henderson/100 8.00
93 Rickey Henderson/50 12.00
94 Rickey Henderson/50 12.00
95 Rickey Henderson/50 12.00
96 Rickey Henderson/50 12.00
97 Randy Johnson/50 8.00
98 Mark Grace/50 10.00
99 Pedro Martinez/25 15.00
100 Hee Seop Choi/25 8.00
101 Ivan Rodriguez/25 15.00
102 Jeff Kent/25 10.00
104 Hideo Nomo/25 10.00
105 Mike Piazza/100 10.00
106 Tom Glavine/25 15.00
107 Roberto Alomar/25 10.00
108 Roger Clemens/100 10.00
109 Jason Giambi/25 10.00
110 Jim Thome/25 10.00
111 Alex Rodriguez/100 10.00
112 Juan Gonzalez/25 10.00
113 Torii Hunter/25 10.00
114 Roy Oswalt/25 10.00
115 Curt Schilling/25 15.00
116 Magglio Ordonez/25 10.00
117 Rafael Palmeiro/25 10.00
118 Andruw Jones/25 8.00
119 Manny Ramirez/50 10.00
120 Mark Teixeira/25 10.00
121 Mark Mulder/25 10.00
123 Tim Hudson/25 10.00
124 Todd Helton/25 10.00
125 Troy Glaus/50 6.00
126 Derek Jeter/Base/50 20.00
127 Barry Bonds/Base/25 25.00
128 Greg Maddux/100 10.00
129 Roger Clemens/100 10.00
130 Nomar Garciaparra/100 10.00
131 Mike Piazza/100 10.00
132 Alex Rodriguez/100 10.00
133 Ichiro Suzuki/Base/50 25.00
134 Randy Johnson/100 10.00
135 Sammy Sosa/100 15.00
137 Alfonso Soriano/100 8.00
138 Jason Giambi/100 10.00
139 Albert Pujols/25 20.00
140 Chipper Jones/25 10.00
141 Adam Dunn/50 8.00
142 Pedro Martinez/50 10.00
143 Vladimir Guerrero/50 10.00
144 Mark Prior/50 15.00
145 Barry Zito/50 10.00
146 Jeff Bagwell/25 12.00
147 Lance Berkman/Socks/25 10.00
148 Shawn Green/25 10.00
149 Jason Giambi/25 10.00
150 Randy Johnson/25 10.00
151 Alex Rodriguez/100 10.00
153 Ty Cobb/25 100.00
154 Jackie Robinson/50 50.00
156 Thurman Munson/100 10.00
158 Nolan Ryan/100 30.00
159 Nolan Ryan/100 30.00
160 Nolan Ryan/100 30.00
161 Cal Ripken Jr./100 60.00
162 Don Mattingly/100 25.00
163 Stan Musial/100 25.00
164 Tony Gwynn/100 12.00
165 Yogi Berra/100 12.00
166 Johnny Bench/100 25.00
167 Mike Schmidt/100 25.00
168 George Brett/100 30.00
169 Ryne Sandberg/100 25.00
170 Ernie Banks/50 30.00

Button Up
Production 2-6
No Pricing

Double
NM/M
Common Player:
Production 5 to 25
Some not priced due to scarcity.
Primes: No Pricing
Production 1 to 10

3 Alex Rodriguez/25 40.00
4 Miguel Tejada/25 25.00
10 Juan Gonzalez/25 20.00
12 Craig Biggio/25 20.00
14 Hideo Nomo/25 40.00
15 Vernon Wells/25 15.00
26 Carlos Beltran/25 25.00
28 Tim Hudson/25 20.00
31 Todd Helton/25 20.00
32 Lance Berkman/25 15.00
34 Kazuhisa Ishii/25 20.00
37 Juan Gonzalez/25 20.00
43 Sammy Sosa/25 50.00
44 Mark Prior/25 25.00
51 Andruw Jones/25 20.00
54 Barry Bonds/25 60.00
60 Magglio Ordonez/25 30.00
73 Adam Dunn/25 20.00
75 Pedro Martinez/25 30.00
78 Austin Kearns/25 20.00
81 Ichiro Suzuki/25 60.00
90 Barry Zito/25 20.00
94 Rickey Henderson/25 25.00
101 Ivan Rodriguez/25 25.00
109 Jason Giambi/25 25.00
117 Magglio Ordonez/25 20.00
118 Rafael Palmeiro/25 20.00
120 Andruw Jones/25 20.00
123 Mark Teixeira/25 20.00
124 Todd Helton/25 25.00
127 Barry Bonds/25 50.00
132 Alex Rodriguez/25 40.00
133 Ichiro Suzuki/25 60.00
141 Sammy Sosa/25 50.00
142 Adam Dunn/25 30.00
144 Pedro Martinez/25 35.00
145 Barry Zito/25 20.00
146 Jeff Bagwell/25 15.00
147 Lance Berkman/25 15.00
149 Jason Giambi/25 25.00
158 Nolan Ryan/25 80.00
162 Don Mattingly/25 65.00
164 Tony Gwynn/25 40.00
165 Mike Schmidt/25 65.00
168 George Brett/25 75.00
169 Ryne Sandberg/25 65.00

Number
NM/M
Common Player:

7 Jim Thome/25 20.00
18 Josh Beckett/61 10.00
24 Jim Thome/25 20.00
29 Deion Sanders/21 35.00
30 Rafael Palmeiro/20 20.00
33 Mike Mussina/35 15.00
40 Luis Gonzalez/20 15.00
41 Jorge Posada/20 15.00
42 Mark Mulder/20 15.00
43 Sammy Sosa/21 50.00
44 Mark Prior/22 25.00
45 Roger Clemens/22 50.00
46 Tom Glavine/47 8.00
47 Mark Teixeira/23 15.00
48 Manny Ramirez/30 30.00
49 Frank Thomas/35 15.00
50 Troy Glaus/25 15.00
51 Andruw Jones/25 15.00
52 Jason Giambi/52 10.00
53 Jim Thome/25 15.00
55 Rafael Palmeiro/25 20.00
57 Vladimir Guerrero/27 20.00
59 Mike Sweeney/29 10.00
60 Magglio Ordonez/30 10.00
63 Greg Maddux/31 25.00
64 Mike Piazza/31 30.00
65 Tom Glavine/47 8.00
66 Kerry Wood/52 15.00
67 Frank Thomas/35 15.00
68 Mike Mussina/35 15.00
69 Nick Johnson/25 15.00
70 Bernie Williams/51 15.00
71 Scott Rolen/27 20.00
72 Curt Schilling/38 15.00
73 Adam Dunn/44 8.00
74 Roy Oswalt/44 6.00
75 Pedro Martinez/45 10.00
76 Tom Glavine/47 8.00
77 Torii Hunter/48 10.00
78 Austin Kearns/28 10.00
79 Randy Johnson/51 10.00
80 Bernie Williams/51 10.00
82 Kerry Wood/34 20.00
84 Randy Johnson/51 10.00
85 Nick Johnson/36 8.00
86 Josh Beckett/61 8.00
87 Curt Schilling/38 10.00
88 Mike Mussina/35 15.00
89 Pedro Martinez/45 10.00
90 Barry Zito/75 8.00
93 Rickey Henderson/24 25.00
94 Rickey Henderson/35 20.00
95 Rickey Henderson/24 25.00
96 Rickey Henderson/24 25.00
97 Randy Johnson/51 10.00
99 Pedro Martinez/45 10.00
105 Mike Piazza/31 30.00
106 Tom Glavine/47 8.00
108 Roger Clemens/21 50.00
110 Jim Thome/25 15.00
112 Juan Gonzalez/22 20.00
113 Torii Hunter/48 8.00
114 Roy Oswalt/44 6.00
115 Curt Schilling/38 10.00
116 Magglio Ordonez/30 8.00
118 Rafael Palmeiro/25 20.00
119 Andruw Jones/25 10.00
120 Manny Ramirez/24 25.00
123 Mark Teixeira/23 20.00
125 Mark Mulder/20 15.00
125 Troy Glaus/25 12.00
128 Greg Maddux/31 25.00
129 Roger Clemens/22 50.00
131 Mike Piazza/31 30.00
134 Randy Johnson/51 12.00
135 Sammy Sosa/21 50.00
138 Jason Giambi/25 10.00
141 Adam Dunn/44 8.00
142 Pedro Martinez/45 10.00
143 Vladimir Guerrero/27 20.00
144 Mark Prior/22 25.00
145 Barry Zito/75 8.00
150 Randy Johnson/51 10.00
154 Jackie Robinson/42 50.00
157 Roberto Clemente/21 140.00
158 Nolan Ryan/34 50.00
159 Nolan Ryan/30 50.00
160 Nolan Ryan/34 50.00
162 Don Mattingly/23 50.00
165 Yogi Berra/42 15.00
167 Mike Schmidt/20 60.00
169 Ryne Sandberg/23 60.00

Position
NM/M
Common (2-151): 8.00
#'s 2-151
Production 25
#'s 152-170
Production 5-25
Primes: 1-1.5X
Production 25 for #'s 2-151

2 Eric Chavez 8.00
3 Alex Rodriguez 25.00
4 Miguel Tejada 10.00
5 Nomar Garciaparra 30.00
6 Jeff Bagwell 15.00
7 Jim Thome 15.00
8 Pat Burrell 10.00
9 Albert Pujols 35.00
10 Juan Gonzalez 10.00
11 Shawn Green 15.00
12 Craig Biggio 8.00
13 Chipper Jones 25.00
14 Hideo Nomo 30.00
15 Vernon Wells 8.00
16 Gary Sheffield 10.00
17 Barry Larkin 10.00
18 Josh Beckett 15.00
19 Edgar Martinez 15.00
20 Ivan Rodriguez 15.00
21 Jeff Kent 8.00
22 Roberto Alomar 15.00
23 Alfonso Soriano 20.00
24 Juan Gonzalez 15.00
26 Carlos Beltran 8.00
27 Shawn Green 10.00
28 Tim Hudson 10.00
29 Deion Sanders 30.00
30 Rafael Palmeiro 15.00
31 Todd Helton 15.00
32 Lance Berkman 10.00
33 Mike Mussina 15.00
34 Kazuhisa Ishii 10.00
35 Pat Burrell 10.00
36 Miguel Tejada 15.00
37 Juan Gonzalez 15.00
38 Roberto Alomar 15.00
39 Roberto Alomar 15.00
40 Luis Gonzalez 15.00
41 Jorge Posada 15.00
42 Mark Mulder 15.00
43 Sammy Sosa 40.00
44 Mark Prior 25.00
45 Roger Clemens 25.00
46 Tom Glavine 15.00
47 Mark Teixeira 15.00
48 Manny Ramirez 15.00
49 Frank Thomas 15.00
50 Troy Glaus 10.00
51 Andruw Jones 15.00
52 Jason Giambi 15.00
53 Jim Thome 15.00
54 Kazuhisa Ishii 10.00
55 Rafael Palmeiro 15.00
56 Edgar Martinez 15.00
57 Vladimir Guerrero 15.00
58 Roberto Alomar 15.00
60 Magglio Ordonez 10.00
62 Craig Biggio 10.00
63 Greg Maddux 30.00
64 Mike Piazza 25.00
66 Tom Glavine 15.00
67 Kerry Wood 15.00
68 Frank Thomas 15.00
69 Nick Johnson 10.00
71 Bernie Williams 15.00
72 Scott Rolen 15.00
73 Curt Schilling 15.00
74 Adam Dunn 15.00
75 Pedro J. Martinez 15.00
76 Tom Glavine 15.00
77 Torii Hunter 15.00
78 Austin Kearns 15.00
79 Randy Johnson 15.00
80 Bernie Williams 15.00
82 Kerry Wood 15.00
83 Kazuhisa Ishii 15.00
84 Randy Johnson 15.00
85 Nick Johnson 10.00
86 Josh Beckett 15.00
87 Curt Schilling 15.00
88 Mike Mussina 15.00
89 Pedro J. Martinez 15.00
90 Barry Zito 15.00
91 Jim Edmonds 15.00
93 Rickey Henderson 25.00
94 Rickey Henderson 25.00
95 Rickey Henderson 25.00
96 Rickey Henderson 25.00
97 Randy Johnson 15.00
98 Mark Grace 15.00
99 Pedro J. Martinez 15.00
100 Hee Seop Choi 10.00
101 Ivan Rodriguez 15.00
102 Jeff Kent 15.00
104 Hideo Nomo 30.00
105 Mike Piazza 25.00
106 Tom Glavine 15.00
107 Roberto Alomar 15.00
108 Roger Clemens 40.00
109 Jason Giambi 15.00
110 Jim Thome 15.00
111 Alex Rodriguez 25.00
112 Juan Gonzalez 15.00
113 Torii Hunter 15.00
114 Roy Oswalt 10.00
115 Curt Schilling 15.00
116 Magglio Ordonez 10.00
117 Rafael Palmeiro 15.00
118 Andruw Jones 15.00
119 Manny Ramirez 15.00
120 Mark Teixeira 15.00
121 Mark Mulder 15.00
123 Tim Hudson 10.00
124 Todd Helton 15.00
125 Troy Glaus 15.00
128 Greg Maddux 30.00
129 Roger Clemens 40.00
130 Nomar Garciaparra 30.00
131 Mike Piazza 25.00
132 Alex Rodriguez 25.00
134 Randy Johnson 15.00
135 Sammy Sosa 40.00
137 Alfonso Soriano 20.00
138 Jason Giambi 15.00
139 Albert Pujols 35.00
140 Chipper Jones 25.00
141 Adam Dunn 15.00
142 Pedro J. Martinez 15.00
143 Vladimir Guerrero 15.00
144 Mark Prior 25.00
145 Barry Zito 15.00
146 Jeff Bagwell 15.00
147 Lance Berkman 10.00
148 Shawn Green 10.00
149 Jason Giambi 15.00
150 Randy Johnson 15.00
151 Alex Rodriguez 25.00
153 Ty Cobb 125.00
156 Thurman Munson 30.00
158 Nolan Ryan 50.00
159 Nolan Ryan 50.00
160 Nolan Ryan 50.00
161 Cal Ripken Jr. 85.00
162 Don Mattingly 60.00
163 Stan Musial 60.00
164 Tony Gwynn 30.00
165 Yogi Berra 30.00
168 George Brett 60.00
169 Ryne Sandberg 60.00

Timber
NM/M
Common Player: 10.00
Production 25 Sets

2 Eric Chavez 10.00
3 Alex Rodriguez 25.00
4 Miguel Tejada 10.00
5 Nomar Garciaparra 30.00
6 Jeff Bagwell 15.00
7 Jim Thome 15.00
8 Pat Burrell 15.00
9 Albert Pujols 35.00
10 Juan Gonzalez 10.00
11 Shawn Green 15.00
12 Craig Biggio 10.00
13 Chipper Jones 20.00
14 Hideo Nomo 30.00
15 Vernon Wells 10.00
16 Gary Sheffield 10.00
17 Barry Larkin 10.00
18 Josh Beckett 15.00
19 Edgar Martinez 15.00
20 Ivan Rodriguez 15.00
21 Jeff Kent 10.00
22 Roberto Alomar 15.00
23 Alfonso Soriano 20.00
24 Jim Thome 15.00
25 Juan Gonzalez 15.00
26 Carlos Beltran 15.00
27 Shawn Green 15.00
28 Tim Hudson 10.00
30 Rafael Palmeiro 15.00
31 Todd Helton 15.00
32 Lance Berkman 15.00
33 Mike Mussina 15.00
34 Kazuhisa Ishii 10.00
35 Pat Burrell 15.00
36 Miguel Tejada 10.00
37 Juan Gonzalez 15.00
38 Roberto Alomar 15.00
39 Roberto Alomar 15.00
41 Jorge Posada 15.00
42 Mark Mulder 10.00
43 Sammy Sosa 40.00
44 Mark Prior 25.00
45 Roger Clemens 40.00
46 Tom Glavine 15.00
47 Mark Teixeira 15.00
48 Manny Ramirez 15.00
49 Frank Thomas 15.00
51 Andruw Jones 10.00
52 Jason Giambi 15.00
53 Jim Thome 15.00
55 Rafael Palmeiro 15.00
56 Edgar Martinez 15.00
57 Vladimir Guerrero 15.00
58 Roberto Alomar 15.00
59 Mike Sweeney 10.00
60 Magglio Ordonez 15.00
62 Craig Biggio 10.00
63 Greg Maddux 30.00
64 Mike Piazza 25.00
65 Tom Glavine 15.00
66 Kerry Wood 15.00
67 Frank Thomas 15.00
68 Mike Mussina 15.00
69 Nick Johnson 10.00
70 Bernie Williams 15.00
71 Scott Rolen 15.00
72 Curt Schilling 15.00
73 Adam Dunn 15.00
74 Roy Oswalt 10.00
75 Pedro J. Martinez 15.00
76 Tom Glavine 15.00
77 Torii Hunter 15.00
78 Austin Kearns 15.00
79 Randy Johnson 15.00
80 Bernie Williams 15.00
82 Kerry Wood 15.00
83 Kazuhisa Ishii 15.00
84 Randy Johnson 15.00
85 Nick Johnson 10.00
86 Josh Beckett 15.00
87 Curt Schilling 15.00
88 Mike Mussina 15.00
89 Pedro J. Martinez 15.00
90 Barry Zito 15.00
91 Jim Edmonds 15.00
92 Rickey Henderson 15.00
93 Rickey Henderson 15.00
94 Rickey Henderson 15.00
95 Rickey Henderson 15.00
96 Rickey Henderson 15.00
97 Randy Johnson 15.00
98 Mark Grace 15.00
99 Pedro J. Martinez 15.00
101 Ivan Rodriguez 15.00
102 Jeff Kent 10.00
103 Hideo Nomo 30.00
104 Hideo Nomo 30.00
105 Mike Piazza 25.00
106 Tom Glavine 15.00
107 Roberto Alomar 15.00
108 Roger Clemens 40.00
109 Jason Giambi 15.00
110 Jim Thome 15.00
111 Alex Rodriguez 25.00
112 Juan Gonzalez 15.00
113 Torii Hunter 15.00
114 Roy Oswalt 10.00
115 Curt Schilling 15.00
116 Magglio Ordonez 15.00
117 Rafael Palmeiro 15.00
118 Andruw Jones 15.00
119 Manny Ramirez 15.00
120 Mark Teixeira 15.00
122 Garret Anderson 10.00
123 Tim Hudson 10.00
124 Todd Helton 15.00
125 Troy Glaus 15.00
128 Greg Maddux 30.00
129 Roger Clemens 40.00
130 Nomar Garciaparra 30.00
131 Mike Piazza 25.00
132 Alex Rodriguez 25.00
134 Randy Johnson 15.00
135 Sammy Sosa 40.00
137 Alfonso Soriano 20.00
138 Jason Giambi 15.00
139 Albert Pujols 35.00
140 Chipper Jones 25.00
141 Adam Dunn 15.00
142 Pedro J. Martinez 15.00
143 Vladimir Guerrero 15.00
144 Mark Prior 25.00
145 Barry Zito 15.00
146 Jeff Bagwell 15.00
147 Lance Berkman 10.00
148 Jason Giambi 15.00
149 Jason Giambi 15.00
150 Randy Johnson 15.00
151 Alex Rodriguez 25.00
152 Babe Ruth 180.00
153 Ty Cobb 125.00
155 Lou Gehrig 150.00
156 Thurman Munson 30.00
157 Roberto Clemente 140.00
158 Nolan Ryan 50.00
159 Nolan Ryan 50.00
160 Nolan Ryan 50.00
161 Cal Ripken Jr. 85.00
162 Don Mattingly 60.00
163 Stan Musial 60.00
164 Tony Gwynn 30.00
165 Yogi Berra 30.00
166 Johnny Bench 35.00
167 Mike Schmidt 60.00
168 George Brett 60.00
169 Ryne Sandberg 60.00
170 Ernie Banks/1 10.00

TNT

NM/M
Production 25 unless noted.
Some not priced due to scarcity.
Primes: 1X
Production 1-25
No pricing production 15 or less.

2 Eric Chavez 15.00
3 Alex Rodriguez 45.00
4 Miguel Tejada 15.00
5 Nomar Garciaparra 45.00
6 Jeff Bagwell 25.00
7 Jim Thome 30.00
8 Pat Burrell 30.00
9 Albert Pujols 60.00
10 Juan Gonzalez 25.00
11 Shawn Green 15.00
12 Craig Biggio 15.00
13 Chipper Jones 40.00
14 Hideo Nomo 50.00
15 Vernon Wells 15.00
16 Gary Sheffield 25.00
17 Barry Larkin 20.00
18 Josh Beckett 25.00
19 Edgar Martinez 25.00
20 Ivan Rodriguez 20.00
21 Jeff Kent 10.00
22 Roberto Alomar 25.00
23 Alfonso Soriano 30.00
24 Jim Thome 30.00
25 Juan Gonzalez 25.00
26 Carlos Beltran 20.00
27 Shawn Green 25.00
28 Tim Hudson 20.00
30 Rafael Palmeiro 20.00
31 Todd Helton 20.00
32 Lance Berkman 20.00
33 Mike Mussina 25.00
34 Kazuhisa Ishii 10.00
35 Pat Burrell 30.00
36 Miguel Tejada 15.00
37 Juan Gonzalez 20.00
38 Roberto Alomar 20.00
39 Roberto Alomar 20.00
40 Luis Gonzalez 15.00
41 Jorge Posada 25.00
42 Mark Mulder 20.00
43 Sammy Sosa 40.00
44 Mark Prior 25.00
45 Roger Clemens 50.00
46 Tom Glavine 25.00
47 Mark Teixeira 20.00
48 Manny Ramirez 25.00
49 Frank Thomas 35.00
50 Troy Glaus 15.00
51 Andruw Jones 20.00
52 Jason Giambi 25.00
53 Jim Thome 30.00
55 Rafael Palmeiro 20.00
56 Edgar Martinez 20.00
57 Vladimir Guerrero 20.00
59 Mike Sweeney 10.00
60 Magglio Ordonez 15.00
62 Craig Biggio 15.00
63 Greg Maddux 40.00
64 Mike Piazza 25.00
66 Tom Glavine 15.00
67 Kerry Wood 25.00
68 Mike Mussina 25.00
69 Nick Johnson 15.00

#	Player	Price
70	Bernie Williams	15.00
71	Scott Rolen	30.00
72	Curt Schilling	20.00
73	Adam Dunn	25.00
74	Roy Oswalt	15.00
75	Pedro J. Martinez	35.00
76	Tom Glavine	20.00
77	Torii Hunter	15.00
78	Austin Kearns	15.00
79	Randy Johnson	30.00
80	Bernie Williams	20.00
82	Kerry Wood	30.00
83	Kazuhisa Ishii	10.00
84	Randy Johnson	30.00
85	Nick Johnson	15.00
86	Josh Beckett	20.00
87	Curt Schilling	25.00
88	Mike Mussina	25.00
89	Pedro J. Martinez	35.00
90	Barry Zito	15.00
91	Jim Edmonds	20.00
92	Rickey Henderson	35.00
93	Rickey Henderson	35.00
94	Rickey Henderson	35.00
95	Rickey Henderson	35.00
96	Rickey Henderson	35.00
97	Randy Johnson	30.00
98	Mark Grace	20.00
99	Pedro J. Martinez	35.00
101	Ivan Rodriguez	20.00
102	Jeff Kent	10.00
103	Hideo Nomo	40.00
104	Hideo Nomo	40.00
105	Mike Piazza	40.00
106	Tom Glavine	20.00
107	Roberto Alomar	25.00
108	Roger Clemens	50.00
109	Jason Giambi	20.00
110	Jim Thome	30.00
111	Alex Rodriguez	45.00
112	Juan Gonzalez	25.00
113	Torii Hunter	15.00
114	Roy Oswalt	15.00
115	Curt Schilling	25.00
116	Magglio Ordonez	15.00
117	Rafael Palmeiro	25.00
118	Andruw Jones	15.00
119	Manny Ramirez	35.00
120	Mark Teixeira	25.00
121	Mark Mulder	20.00
123	Tim Hudson	20.00
124	Todd Helton	20.00
125	Troy Glaus	15.00
128	Greg Maddux	40.00
129	Roger Clemens	50.00
130	Nomar Garciaparra	40.00
131	Mike Piazza	40.00
132	Alex Rodriguez	40.00
134	Randy Johnson	30.00
135	Sammy Sosa	40.00
137	Alfonso Soriano	30.00
138	Jason Giambi	20.00
139	Albert Pujols	60.00
140	Chipper Jones	30.00
141	Adam Dunn	25.00
142	Pedro J. Martinez	35.00
143	Vladimir Guerrero	30.00
144	Mark Prior	25.00
145	Barry Zito	15.00
146	Jeff Bagwell	25.00
147	Lance Berkman	20.00
148	Shawn Green	15.00
149	Jason Giambi	20.00
150	Randy Johnson	30.00
151	Alex Rodriguez	40.00
156	Thurman Munson	50.00
158	Nolan Ryan	65.00
159	Nolan Ryan	65.00
160	Nolan Ryan	65.00
161	Cal Ripken Jr.	100.00
162	Don Mattingly	65.00
163	Stan Musial	65.00
164	Tony Gwynn	40.00
165	Yogi Berra	40.00
166	Johnny Bench	40.00
167	Mike Schmidt	65.00
168	George Brett	75.00
169	Ryne Sandberg	65.00

7th Inning Stretch

NM/M
Production 50 unless noted.

#	Player	Price
1	Alex Rodriguez	20.00
3	Sammy Sosa	25.00
4	Juan Gonzalez	10.00
5	Albert Pujols	30.00
6	Chipper Jones	15.00
7	Alfonso Soriano/40	
8	Jim Thome	15.00
9	Mike Piazza	20.00
10	Rafael Palmeiro	15.00

2004 Leaf

NM/M
Complete Set (300): 50.00
Common Player: .15
Common (202-301): .25
Second Edition (1-301): 1X
Pack (8): 5.00
Box (24): 90.00

#	Player	Price
1	Darin Erstad	.25
2	Garret Anderson	.25
3	Jarrod Washburn	.15
4	Kevin Appier	.15
5	Tim Salmon	.25
6	Troy Glaus	.40

Barry ZITO

#	Player	Price
7	Troy Percival	.15
8	Jason Johnson	.15
9	Jay Gibbons	.25
10	Melvin Mora	.15
11	Sidney Ponson	.15
12	Tony Batista	.15
13	Derek Lowe	.25
14	Robert Person	.15
15	Manny Ramirez	.50
16	Nomar Garciaparra	1.50
17	Pedro J. Martinez	.75
18	Jorge de la Rosa	.25
19	Bartolo Colon	.25
20	Carlos Lee	.25
21	Esteban Loaiza	.15
22	Frank Thomas	.50
23	Joe Crede	.25
24	Magglio Ordonez	.25
25	Ryan Ludwick	.15
26	Luis Garcia	.15
27	Brandon Phillips	.15
28	C.C. Sabathia	.15
29	Jhonny Peralta	.15
30	Josh Bard	.15
31	Omar Vizquel	.25
32	Fernando Rodney	.15
33	Mike Maroth	.15
34	Bobby Higginson	.15
35	Omar Infante	.15
36	Dmitri Young	.15
37	Eric Munson	.15
38	Jeremy Bonderman	.15
39	Carlos Beltran	.25
40	Jeremy Affeldt	.15
41	Dee Brown	.15
42		.15
43	Mike Sweeney	.15
44	Brent Abernathy	.15
45	Runelvys Hernandez	.15
46	A.J. Pierzynski	.15
47	Corey Koskie	.15
48	Cristian Guzman	.15
49	Jacque Jones	.15
50	Kenny Rogers	.15
51	J.C. Romero	.15
52	Torii Hunter	.40
53	Alfonso Soriano	.75
54	Bernie Williams	.50
55	David Wells	.15
56	Derek Jeter	2.00
57	Hideki Matsui	1.50
58	Jason Giambi	.75
59	Jorge Posada	.40
60	Jose Contreras	.25
61	Mike Mussina	.50
62	Nick Johnson	.15
63	Roger Clemens	1.50
64	Barry Zito	.40
65	Justin Duchscherer	.15
66	Eric Chavez	.25
67	Erubiel Durazo	.15
68	Miguel Tejada	.40
69	Mark Mulder	.25
70	Terrence Long	.15
71	Tim Hudson	.25
72	Bret Boone	.15
73	Dan Wilson	.15
74	Edgar Martinez	.15
75	Freddy Garcia	.15
76	Rafael Soriano	.15
77	Ichiro Suzuki	1.25
78	Jamie Moyer	.15
79	John Olerud	.15
80	Kazuhiro Sasaki	.15
81	Aubrey Huff	.15
82	Carl Crawford	.15
83	Joe Kennedy	.15
84	Rocco Baldelli	.40
85	Toby Hall	.15
86	Alex Rodriguez	1.50
87	Kevin Mench	.15
88	Hank Blalock	.15
89	Juan Gonzalez	.50
90	Mark Teixeira	.25
91	Rafael Palmeiro	.25
92	Carlos Delgado	.50
93	Eric Hinske	.15
94	Josh Phelps	.15
95	Brian Bowles	.15
96	Roy Halladay	.40
97	Shannon Stewart	.15
98	Vernon Wells	.25
99	Curt Schilling	.40
100	Junior Spivey	.15
101	Luis Gonzalez	.15
102	Lyle Overbay	.15
103	Mark Grace	.40
104	Randy Johnson	.75
105	Shea Hillenbrand	.15
106	Andruw Jones	.50
107	Chipper Jones	.75
108	Gary Sheffield	.40
109	Greg Maddux	1.00
110	Javy Lopez	.25
111	John Smoltz	.25
112	Marcus Giles	.15
113	Rafael Furcal	.25
114	Corey Patterson	.15
115	Juan Cruz	.15
116	Kerry Wood	.50
117	Mark Prior	1.00
118	Moises Alou	.25
119	Sammy Sosa	1.00
120	Aaron Boone	.15
121	Adam Dunn	.50
122	Austin Kearns	.50
123	Barry Larkin	.40
124	Ken Griffey Jr.	1.00
125	Brian Reith	.15
126	Wily Mo Pena	.15
127	Jason Jennings	.15
128	Jay Payton	.15
129	Larry Walker	.25
130	Preston Wilson	.15
131	Todd Helton	.50
132	Dontrelle Willis	.40
133	Ivan Rodriguez	.50
134	Josh Beckett	.50
135	Juan Encarnacion	.15
136	Mike Lowell	.15
137	Craig Biggio	.25
138	Jeff Bagwell	.50
139	Jeff Kent	.25
140	Lance Berkman	.25
141	Richard Hidalgo	.15
142	Roy Oswalt	.25
143	Eric Gagne	.25
144	Fred McGriff	.25
145	Hideo Nomo	.40
146	Kazuhisa Ishii	.15
147	Kevin Brown	.25
148	Paul LoDuca	.15
149	Shawn Green	.25
150	Ben Sheets	.25
151	Geoff Jenkins	.25
152	Rey Sanchez	.15
153	Richie Sexson	.40
154	Wes Helms	.15
155	Shane Nance	.15
156	Fernando Tatis	.15
157	Javier Vazquez	.15
158	Jose Vidro	.15
159	Orlando Cabrera	.15
160	Henry Mateo	.15
161	Vladimir Guerrero	.75
162	Zach Day	.15
163	Edwin Almonte	.15
164	Al Leiter	.15
165	Cliff Floyd	.15
166	Jae Weong Seo	.15
167	Mike Piazza	1.00
168	Roberto Alomar	.50
169	Tom Glavine	.25
170	Bobby Abreu	.25
171	Brandon Duckworth	.15
172	Jim Thome	.75
173	Kevin Millwood	.25
174	Pat Burrell	.25
175	Aramis Ramirez	.15
176	Jack Wilson	.15
177	Brian Giles	.25
178	Jason Kendall	.15
179	Kenny Lofton	.25
180	Kip Wells	.15
181	Kris Benson	.15
182	Albert Pujols	1.50
183	J.D. Drew	.15
184	Jim Edmonds	.25
185	Matt Morris	.15
186	Scott Rolen	.75
187	Woody Williams	.15
188	Clifford Bartosh	.15
189	Brian Lawrence	.15
190	Ryan Klesko	.25
191	Sean Burroughs	.15
192	Xavier Nady	.15
193	Dennis Tankersley	.15
194	Donaldo Mendez	.15
195	Barry Bonds	2.00
196	Benito Santiago	.15
197	Edgardo Alfonzo	.15
198	Cody Ransom	.15
199	Jason Schmidt	.15
200	Rich Aurilia	.15
201	Ken Harvey	.15
202	Adam Loewen	.25
203	Alfredo Gonzalez	.25
204	Arnie Munoz	.25
205	Andrew Brown	.25
206	Josh Hall	.25
207	Josh Stewart	.25
208	Clint Barmes	.25
209	Brandon Webb	.25
210	Chien-Ming Wang	.40
211	Edgar Gonzalez	.25
212	Alejandro Machado	.25
213	Jeremy Griffiths	.25
214	Craig Brazell	.25
215	Daniel Cabrera	.25
216	Fernando Cabrera	.25
217	Terrmel Sledge	.25
218	Rob Hammock	.25
219	Francisco Rosario	.25
220	Francisco Cruceta	.25
221	Rett Johnson	.25
222	Guillermo Quiroz	.25
223	Hong-Chih Kuo	.25
224	Ian Ferguson	.25
225	Tim Olson	.25
226	Todd Wellemeyer	.25
227	Rich Fischer	.25
228	Phil Seibel	.25
229	Joe Valentine	.25
230	Matt Kata	.25
231	Michael Hessman	.25
232	Michel Hernandez	.25
233	Doug Waechter	.25
234	Prentice Redman	.25
235	Nook Logan	.25
236	Oscar Villarreal	.25
237	Pete LaForest	.25
238	Matt Bruback	.25
239	Josh Willingham	.25
240	Greg Aquino	.25
241	Lew Ford	.25
242	Jeff Duncan	.25
243	Chris Waters	.25
244	Miguel Ojeda	.25
245	Rosman Garcia	.25
246	Felix Sanchez	.25
247	Jon Leicester	.25
248	Roger Deago	.25
249	Mike Ryan	.25
250	Chris Capuano	.25
251	Matt White	.25
252	Bernie Williams	.50
253	Mark Grace	.50
254	Chipper Jones	1.00
255	Greg Maddux	1.50
256	Sammy Sosa	2.00
257	Mike Mussina	.75
258	Tim Salmon	.50
259	Barry Larkin	.50
260	Randy Johnson	1.00
261	Jeff Bagwell	.75
262	Roberto Alomar	.50
263	Tom Glavine	.50
264	Roger Clemens	2.50
265	Barry Bonds	3.00
266	Ivan Rodriguez	.75
267	Pedro J. Martinez	1.00
268	Ken Griffey Jr.	1.50
269	Jim Thome	1.00
270	Frank Thomas	.75
271	Mike Piazza	1.50
272	Troy Glaus	.40
273	Melvin Mora	.25
274	Nomar Garciaparra	2.00
275	Magglio Ordonez	.40
276	Omar Vizquel	.40
277	Dmitri Young	.25
278	Mike Sweeney	.25
279	Torii Hunter	.50
280	Derek Jeter	2.00
281	Barry Zito	.50
282	Ichiro Suzuki	1.50
283	Rocco Baldelli	.50
284	Alex Rodriguez	2.00
285	Carlos Delgado	.50
286	Randy Johnson	.75
287	Greg Maddux	1.00
288	Sammy Sosa	1.50
289	Ken Griffey Jr.	1.00
290	Todd Helton	.50
291	Ivan Rodriguez	.50
292	Jeff Bagwell	.50
293	Hideo Nomo	.50
294	Richie Sexson	.50
295	Vladimir Guerrero	.75
296	Mike Piazza	1.00
297	Jim Thome	.75
298	Jason Kendall	.40
299	Albert Pujols	1.50
300	Ryan Klesko	.40
301	Barry Bonds	2.00

Black Press Proof

NM/M
Stars (1-301): 5-10X
Production 50 Sets
Hot Pack Exclusive

Blue Press Proof

Josh BECKETT

Stars (1-301): 4-8X
Production 100 Sets

Gold Press Proof

Cards (1-301): 12-25X
Production 25 Sets

Red Press Proof

Curt SCHILLING

Stars (1-301): 1-2X
Inserted 1:8

Autographs

Jorge DE LA ROSA

NM/M

#	Player	Price
	Common Autograph	6.00
14	Robert Person	6.00
18	Jorge De La Rosa	6.00
25	Ryan Ludwick	6.00
26	Luis Garcia	6.00
29	Jhonny Peralta	6.00
30	Josh Bard	6.00
32	Fernando Rodney	6.00
33	Mike Maroth	6.00
35	Omar Infante	6.00
41	Dee Brown	6.00
44	Brent Abernathy/SP	10.00
51	J.C. Romero	6.00
65	Justin Duchscherer	10.00
70	Terrence Long/SP	15.00
85	Rafael Soriano	8.00
85	Toby Hall/SP	10.00
87	Kevin Mench	6.00
95	Brian Bowles	6.00
115	Juan Cruz	6.00
126	Brian Reith	6.00
126	Wily Mo Pena	8.00
127	Jason Jennings	6.00
155	Shane Nance	6.00
160	Henry Mateo/SP	8.00
164	Edwin Almonte	6.00
171	Brandon Duckworth	6.00
176	Jack Wilson	6.00
180	Kip Wells	6.00
188	Clifford Bartosh	6.00
189	Brian Lawrence	6.00
193	Dennis Tankersley	6.00
194	Donaldo Mendez	6.00
198	Cody Ransom/SP	8.00
247	Jon Leicester/SP	8.00

Away

NM/M
Complete Set (10): 20.00
Common Player: 1.00
Inserted 1:35

#	Player	Price
1	Greg Maddux	2.50
2	Sammy Sosa	3.00
3	Alex Rodriguez	4.00
4	Albert Pujols	4.00
5	Jason Giambi	1.50
6	Chipper Jones	2.00
7	Vladimir Guerrero	1.50
8	Mike Piazza	2.50
9	Nomar Garciaparra	3.00
10	Austin Kearns	1.00

Away Jersey

NM/M
Common Player: 5.00
Inserted 1:119
Prime: 1.5-2X
Production 50

#	Player	Price
1	Greg Maddux	8.00
2	Sammy Sosa	12.00
3	Alex Rodriguez	10.00
4	Albert Pujols	15.00
5	Jason Giambi	8.00
6	Chipper Jones	8.00

Abbreviations

SP - Short Print

SAMMY SOSA

#	Player	Price
7	Vladimir Guerrero	8.00
8	Mike Piazza	10.00
9	Nomar Garciaparra	12.00
10	Austin Kearns	5.00

Clean Up Crew

NM/M
Complete Set (10): 20.00
Common Player: 1.00
Inserted 1:49

#	Players	Price
1	Sammy Sosa, Moises Alou, Hee Seop Choi	3.00
2	Jason Giambi, Alfonso Soriano, Hideki Matsui	5.00
3	Vernon Wells, Carlos Delgado, Josh Phelps	1.00
4	Alex Rodriguez, Juan Gonzalez, Hank Blalock	4.00
5	Gary Sheffield, Andruw Jones, Chipper Jones	2.50
6	Ken Griffey Jr., Austin Kearns, Aaron Boone	3.00
7	Albert Pujols, Jim Edmonds, Scott Rolen	4.00
8	Jeff Bagwell, Jeff Kent, Lance Berkman	1.50
9	Todd Helton, Preston Wilson, Larry Walker	1.50
10	Miguel Tejada, Erubiel Durazo, Eric Chavez	1.00

Clean Up Crew Materials

NM/M
Common Card: 15.00
Production 50 Sets

#	Players	Price
1	Sammy Sosa, Moises Alou, Hee Seop Choi	35.00
2	Jason Giambi, Alfonso Soriano, Hideki Matsui	60.00
3	Vernon Wells, Carlos Delgado, Josh Phelps	15.00
4	Alex Rodriguez, Juan Gonzalez, Hank Blalock	35.00
5	Gary Sheffield, Andruw Jones, Chipper Jones	20.00
6	Ken Griffey Jr., Austin Kearns, Aaron Boone	25.00
7	Albert Pujols, Jim Edmonds, Scott Rolen	40.00
8	Jeff Bagwell, Jeff Kent, Lance Berkman	25.00
9	Todd Helton, Preston Wilson, Larry Walker	20.00
10	Miguel Tejada, Erubiel Durazo, Eric Chavez	15.00

Cornerstones

NM/M
Complete Set (10): 20.00
Common Player: 1.00
Inserted 1:78

#	Players	Price
1	Alex Rodriguez, Hank Blalock	4.00
2	Kerry Wood, Mark Prior	3.00
3	Roger Clemens, Alfonso Soriano	4.00
4	Nomar Garciaparra, Manny Ramirez	4.00
5	Austin Kearns, Adam Dunn	1.00
6	Tom Glavine, Mike Piazza	2.50
7	Andruw Jones, Chipper Jones	2.50
8	Albert Pujols, Scott Rolen	4.00
9	Curt Schilling, Randy Johnson	2.00
10	Hideo Nomo, Kazuhisa Ishii	1.00

Cornerstones Materials

NM/M
Common Duo: 15.00
Production 50 Sets

#	Player	NM/M
1	Alex Rodriguez, Hank Blalock	25.00
2	Kerry Wood, Mark Prior	40.00
3	Roger Clemens, Alfonso Soriano	40.00
4	Nomar Garciaparra, Manny Ramirez	30.00
5	Austin Kearns, Adam Dunn	15.00
7	Andruw Jones, Chipper Jones	20.00
8	Albert Pujols, Scott Rolen	40.00
9	Curt Schilling, Randy Johnson	20.00
10	Hideo Nomo, Kazuhisa Ishii	20.00

Exhibits

NM/M
Common Player: 2.50
Production 66 Sets
Variations #'d to 63: 1X
Variations #'d to 46: 1X
Variations #'d 21 to 27: 1.5X

#	Player	Price
1	Adam Dunn	2.50
2	Albert Pujols	8.00
3	Alex Rodriguez	8.00
4	Alfonso Soriano	4.00
5	Andruw Jones	3.00
6	Barry Bonds	10.00
7	Barry Larkin	2.50
8	Barry Zito	2.50
9	Cal Ripken Jr.	10.00
10	Chipper Jones	5.00
11	Dale Murphy	2.50
12	Derek Jeter	10.00
13	Don Mattingly	8.00
14	Ernie Banks	5.00
15	Frank Thomas	5.00
16	George Brett	6.00
17	Greg Maddux	5.00
18	Hank Blalock	2.50
19	Hideo Nomo	2.50
20	Ichiro Suzuki	6.00
21	Jason Giambi	3.00
22	Jim Thome	4.00
23	Juan Gonzalez	2.50
24	Ken Griffey Jr.	5.00
25	Kirby Puckett	4.00
26	Mark Prior	5.00
27	Mike Mussina	2.50
28	Mike Piazza	5.00
29	Mike Schmidt	6.00
30	Nolan Ryan	8.00
31	Nolan Ryan	8.00
32	Nolan Ryan	8.00
33	Nomar Garciaparra	8.00
34	Ozzie Smith	5.00
35	Pedro J. Martinez	4.00
36	Randy Johnson	3.00
37	Reggie Jackson	2.50
38	Reggie Jackson	2.50
39	Rickey Henderson	2.50
40	Roberto Alomar	2.50
41	Roberto Clemente	8.00
42	Rod Carew	3.00
43	Roger Clemens	8.00
44	Sammy Sosa	6.00
45	Stan Musial	6.00
46	Tom Glavine	2.50
47	Tom Seaver	4.00
48	Tony Gwynn	4.00
49	Vladimir Guerrero	4.00
50	Yogi Berra	4.00

Gamers

NM/M
Complete Set (20): 40.00
Common Player: 1.00
Quantum: 2-4X
Production 100 Sets

#	Player	Price
1	Albert Pujols	4.00
2	Alex Rodriguez	4.00
3	Alfonso Soriano	1.50
4	Barry Bonds	5.00
5	Barry Zito	1.00
6	Chipper Jones	2.00
7	Derek Jeter	5.00
8	Greg Maddux	2.50
9	Ichiro Suzuki	3.00
10	Jason Giambi	1.50
11	Jeff Bagwell	1.50
12	Ken Griffey Jr.	2.50
13	Manny Ramirez	1.50
14	Mark Prior	3.00
15	Mike Piazza	2.50
16	Nomar Garciaparra	3.00
17	Pedro J. Martinez	2.00
18	Randy Johnson	3.00
19	Roger Clemens	3.00
20	Sammy Sosa	3.00

Gold Leaf Rookies

GOLD LEAF ROOKIES

Complete Set (10): 6.00
Common Player: .50
Inserted 1:23
Mirror Gold: No Pricing
Production 25 Sets

#	Player	Price
1	Adam Loewen	2.00
2	Rickie Weeks	5.00
3	Khalil Greene	5.00
4	Chad Tracy	.50
5	Alexis Rios	.50
6	Craig Brazell	.50
7	Clint Barmes	.50
8	Pete LaForest	.50
9	Alfredo Gonzalez	.50
10	Arnie Munoz	.50

Home

VLADIMIR GUERRERO

NM/M
Complete Set (10): 20.00
Common Player: 1.00
Inserted 1:35

#	Player	Price
1	Greg Maddux	2.50
2	Sammy Sosa	3.00
3	Alex Rodriguez	4.00
4	Albert Pujols	4.00
5	Jason Giambi	1.50
6	Chipper Jones	2.00
7	Vladimir Guerrero	1.50
8	Mike Piazza	2.50
9	Nomar Garciaparra	3.00
10	Austin Kearns	1.00

Home Jersey

NM/M
Common Player: 5.00
Inserted 1:119
Primes: 1.5-2X
Production 50

#	Player	Price
1	Greg Maddux	8.00
2	Sammy Sosa	12.00
3	Alex Rodriguez	10.00
4	Albert Pujols	15.00
5	Jason Giambi	8.00
6	Chipper Jones	8.00
7	Vladimir Guerrero	10.00
8	Mike Piazza	10.00
9	Nomar Garciaparra	12.00
10	Austin Kearns	4.00

Limited Previews

NM/M
Common Player: 2.00
Production 999 Sets
Silver: 1-2X
Production 100 Sets
Gold: 2-3X
Production 50 Sets

#	Player	Price
1	Derek Jeter	8.00
2	Barry Zito	2.00
3	Ichiro Suzuki	6.00
4	Pedro J. Martinez	3.00
5	Alfonso Soriano	3.00
6	Alex Rodriguez	6.00
7	Greg Maddux	4.00
8	Mike Piazza	4.00
9	Mark Prior	2.00
10	Albert Pujols	8.00
11	Sammy Sosa	4.00
12	Ken Griffey Jr.	4.00
13	Nomar Garciaparra	4.00
14	Randy Johnson	3.00
15	Jason Giambi	2.00
16	Barry Bonds	8.00
17	Manny Ramirez	3.00
18	Chipper Jones	3.00
19	Jeff Bagwell	3.00
20	Roger Clemens	6.00

MVP Winners

NM/M
Complete Set (20): 50.00
Common Player: 1.00
Gold: 1-2X
Production 500 Sets

#	Player	Price
1	Stan Musial/1948 NL	3.00
2	Ernie Banks/1958 NL	2.00
3	Roberto Clement/1966 NL	4.00
4	George Brett/1980 AL	4.00
5	Mike Schmidt/1980 NL	4.00
6	Cal Ripken Jr./1983 AL	5.00
7	Dale Murphy/1983 NL	1.50
8	Ryne Sandberg/1984 NL	3.00
9	Don Mattingly/1985 AL	3.00
10	Roger Clemens/1986 AL	4.00
11	Rickey Henderson/1990 AL	1.00
12	Cal Ripken Jr./1991 AL	5.00
13	Barry Bonds/1992 NL	5.00
14	Barry Bonds/1993 NL	5.00
15	Frank Thomas/1994 AL	1.50
16	Ken Griffey Jr./1997 AL	2.50
17	Sammy Sosa/1998 NL	3.00
18	Chipper Jones/1999 NL	2.00
19	Jason Giambi/2000 AL	1.50
20	Ichiro Suzuki/2001 AL	3.00

Picture Perfect

NM/M
Complete Set (15): 25.00
Common Player: 1.00
Inserted 1:37

#	Player	Price
1	Albert Pujols	5.00
2	Alex Rodriguez	5.00
3	Alfonso Soriano	2.00
4	Austin Kearns	1.00
5	Carlos Delgado	1.50
6	Chipper Jones	2.50
7	Hank Blalock	1.50
8	Jason Giambi	2.00
9	Jeff Bagwell	1.50
10	Jim Thome	2.00
11	Manny Ramirez	1.50
12	Mike Piazza	3.00
13	Nomar Garciaparra	4.00
14	Sammy Sosa	4.00
15	Todd Helton	1.50

Picture Perfect Materials

NM/M
Common Player: 6.00
Inserted 1:437

#	Player	Price
1	Albert Pujols	15.00
2	Alex Rodriguez	10.00
3	Alfonso Soriano	8.00
4	Austin Kearns	6.00
5	Carlos Delgado	6.00
6	Chipper Jones	8.00
7	Hank Blalock	6.00
8	Jason Giambi	8.00
9	Jeff Bagwell	8.00
10	Jim Thome	10.00
11	Manny Ramirez	6.00
12	Mike Piazza	10.00
13	Nomar Garciaparra	10.00
14	Sammy Sosa	10.00
15	Todd Helton	8.00

Recollection Autographs

All are 1990 Leaf cards.

Shirt Off My Back

NM/M
Common Player: 4.00
Inserted 1:47

#	Player	Price
1	Shawn Green	4.00
2	Andruw Jones	4.00
3	Ivan Rodriguez	6.00
4	Hideo Nomo	6.00
5	Don Mattingly	20.00
6	Mark Prior	10.00
7	Alfonso Soriano	4.00
8	Richie Sexson	5.00
9	Vernon Wells	4.00
10	Nomar Garciaparra	8.00
11	Jason Giambi	6.00
12	Austin Kearns	6.00
13	Chipper Jones	6.00
14	Rickey Henderson	5.00
15	Alex Rodriguez	12.00
16	Garret Anderson	4.00
17	Vladimir Guerrero	8.00
18	Sammy Sosa	10.00
19	Mike Piazza	8.00
20	David Wells	4.00
21	Scott Rolen	6.00
22	Adam Dunn	5.00
23	Carlos Delgado	5.00
24	Greg Maddux	8.00
25	Hank Blalock	6.00

Shirt Off My Back Team Logo Patch

NM/M
Common Player: 4.00
Autographs: No Pricing
Production 5 Sets
Jersey Number Patch: .75-1X
Production 50 Sets
Sosa #'d to 42.
Jersey Number Patch Auto.: No Pricing
Production 5 Sets

#	Player	Price
1	Shawn Green/41	15.00
2	Andruw Jones/75	15.00
3	Ivan Rodriguez/75	15.00
4	Hideo Nomo/74	20.00
5	Mark Prior/46	20.00
6	Alfonso Soriano/28	25.00
7	Richie Sexson/38	15.00
8	Vernon Wells/74	10.00
10	Nomar Garciaparra/75	25.00
11	Jason Giambi/26	10.00
12	Austin Kearns/32	10.00
13	Chipper Jones/75	15.00
14	Rickey Henderson/40	20.00
15	Alex Rodriguez/75	30.00
16	Garret Anderson/71	10.00
17	Vladimir Guerrero/55	20.00
18	Sammy Sosa/39	25.00
19	Mike Piazza/75	20.00
20	David Wells/74	10.00
21	Scott Rolen/29	30.00
22	Adam Dunn/32	15.00
23	Carlos Delgado/56	15.00
24	Greg Maddux/75	20.00
25	Hank Blalock/62	15.00

Sunday Dress

NM/M
Complete Set (10): 10.00
Common Player: .75
Inserted 1:17

#	Player	Price
1	Frank Thomas	1.00
2	Barry Zito	.75
3	Mike Piazza	2.00
4	Mark Prior	2.00
5	Jeff Bagwell	1.00
6	Roy Oswalt	.75
7	Todd Helton	1.00
8	Magglio Ordonez	.75
9	Alex Rodriguez	3.00
10	Manny Ramirez	1.00

Sunday Dress Jersey

NM/M
Common Player: 5.00
Inserted 1:119
Prime Jersey: 1-1.5X
Production 100

#	Player	Price
1	Frank Thomas	8.00
2	Barry Zito	6.00
3	Mike Piazza	10.00
4	Mark Prior	10.00
5	Jeff Bagwell	8.00
6	Roy Oswalt	5.00
7	Todd Helton	8.00
8	Magglio Ordonez	6.00
9	Alex Rodriguez	10.00
10	Manny Ramirez	6.00

2004 Leaf Certified Cuts

NM/M
Complete Set (300):
Common Player (1-200): .75
Common (201-250): 2.00
Production 599
Common (251-300): 5.00
Production 499
Auto. production 99-499
Pack (5): 20.00
Box (10): 160.00

#	Player	Price
1	Vladimir Guerrero	1.50
2	Garret Anderson	.75
3	John Lackey	.75
4	Bartolo Colon	.75
5	Troy Glaus	.75
6	Tim Salmon	.75
7	Shea Hillenbrand	.75
8	Brandon Webb	.75
9	Roberto Alomar	.75
10	Randy Johnson	2.00
11	Alex Cintron	.75
12	Richie Sexson	.75
13	Luis Gonzalez	.75
14	Adam LaRoche	.75
15	Rafael Furcal	.75
16	Chipper Jones	2.00
17	Marcus Giles	.75
18	Andruw Jones	1.00
19	Russ Ortiz	.75
20	Rafael Palmeiro	1.00
21	Melvin Mora	.75
22	Luis Matos	.75
23	Jay Gibbons	.75
24	Adam Loewen	.75
25	Larry Bigbie	.75
26	Rodrigo Lopez	.75
27	Javy Lopez	.75
28	Miguel Tejada	1.00
29	Trot Nixon	.75
30	Curt Schilling	1.00
31	Jason Varitek	.75
32	Manny Ramirez	1.00
33	Keith Foulke	.75
34	Derek Lowe	.75
35	Pedro J. Martinez	1.50
36	Nomar Garciaparra	2.50
37	Bill Mueller	.75
38	Johnny Damon	.75
39	David Ortiz	1.50
40	Mark Prior	1.00
41	Kerry Wood	1.50
42	Sammy Sosa	2.50
43	Derrek Lee	.75
44	Greg Maddux	2.00
45	Aramis Ramirez	.75
46	Matt Clement	.75
47	Carlos Zambrano	.75
48	Todd Walker	.75
49	Moises Alou	.75
50	Corey Patterson	.75
51	Frank Thomas	1.00
52	Magglio Ordonez	.75
53	Carlos Lee	.75
54	Mark Buehrle	.75
55	Esteban Loaiza	.75
56	Joe Crede	.75
57	Paul Konerko	.75
58	Adam Dunn	1.00
59	Austin Kearns	.75
60	Barry Larkin	.75
61	Ryan Wagner	.75
62	Danny Graves	.75
63	Sean Casey	.75
64	Ken Griffey Jr.	2.00
65	Jody Gerut	.75
66	Cliff Lee	.75
67	Victor Martinez	.75
68	C.C. Sabathia	.75
69	Omar Vizquel	.75
70	Travis Hafner	.75
71	Todd Helton	1.00
72	Preston Wilson	.75
73	Jeromy Burnitz	.75
74	Larry Walker	.75
75	Ivan Rodriguez	1.00
76	Rondell White	.75
77	Miguel Cabrera	1.50
78	Luis Castillo	.75
79	Josh Beckett	.75
80	Mike Lowell	.75
81	Dontrelle Willis	.75
82	Brad Penny	.75
83	Hee Seop Choi	.75
84	Juan Pierre	.75
85	Andy Pettitte	.75
86	Jeff Bagwell	1.00
87	Roy Oswalt	.75
88	Lance Berkman	.75
89	Morgan Ensberg	.75
90	Craig Biggio	.75
91	Octavio Dotel	.75
92	Wade Miller	.75
93	Jeff Kent	.75
94	Richard Hidalgo	.75
95	Roger Clemens	3.00
96	Carlos Beltran	1.00
97	Angel Berroa	.75
98	Jeremy Affeldt	.75
99	Juan Gonzalez	.75
100	Mike Sweeney	.75
101	Kazuhisa Ishii	.75
102	Shawn Green	.75
103	Milton Bradley	.75
104	Paul LoDuca	.75
105	Hideo Nomo	.75
106	Eric Gagne	.75
107	Adrian Beltre	.75
108	Scott Podsednik	.75
109	Rickie Weeks	.75
110	Ben Sheets	.75
111	Geoff Jenkins	.75
112	Jacque Jones	.75
113	Johan Santana	1.00
114	Shannon Stewart	.75
115	Corey Koskie	.75
116	Lew Ford	.75
117	Torii Hunter	.75
118	Chad Cordero	.75
119	Orlando Cabrera	.75
120	Jose Vidro	.75
121	Nick Johnson	.75
122	Brad Wilkerson	.75
123	Mike Piazza	2.00
124	Jae Weong Seo	.75
125	Jose Reyes	.75
126	Tom Glavine	.75
127	Jorge Posada	.75
128	Gary Sheffield	1.00
129	Bernie Williams	.75
130	Mike Mussina	1.00
131	Mariano Rivera	.75
132	Bubba Crosby	.75
133	Kevin Brown	.75
134	Javier Vazquez	.75
135	Jason Giambi	.75
136	Derek Jeter	4.00
137	Alex Rodriguez	4.00
138	Hideki Matsui	3.00
139	Mark Mulder	.75
140	Jermaine Dye	.75
141	Tim Hudson	.75
142	Barry Zito	.75
143	Eric Chavez	.75
144	Bobby Crosby	.75
145	Eric Byrnes	.75
146	Marlon Byrd	.75
147	Billy Wagner	.75
148	Mike Lieberthal	.75
149	Jimmy Rollins	1.00
150	Jim Thome	1.50
151	Bobby Abreu	.75
152	Pat Burrell	.75
153	Jose Castillo	.75
154	Craig Wilson	.75
155	Jason Bay	.75
156	Jason Kendall	.75
157	Raul Mondesi	.75
158	Jay Payton	.75
159	Trevor Hoffman	.75
160	Jake Peavy	.75
161	Sean Burroughs	.75
162	Phil Nevin	.75
163	Brian Giles	.75
164	Ryan Klesko	.75
165	Todd Linden	.75
166	Jerome Williams	.75
167	Jason Schmidt	1.00
168	Ray Durham	.75
169	Marquis Grissom	.75
170	Shigetoshi Hasegawa	.75
171	Edgar Martinez	.75
172	Freddy Garcia	.75
173	Bret Boone	.75
174	Raul Ibanez	.75
175	Ichiro Suzuki	3.00
176	Randy Winn	.75
177	Scott Rolen	1.50
178	Jim Edmonds	.75
179	Albert Pujols	3.00
180	Matt Morris	.75
181	Edgar Renteria	.75
182	Aubrey Huff	.75
183	Delmon Young	.75
184	Dewon Brazelton	.75
185	Rocco Baldelli	.75
186	Carl Crawford	.75
187	Mark Teixeira	1.00
188	Hank Blalock	1.00
189	Michael Young	.75
190	Laynce Nix	.75
191	Alfonso Soriano	1.50
192	Kevin Mench	.75
193	Adrian Gonzalez	.75

194 Alexis Rios .75
195 Roy Halladay .75
196 Vernon Wells .75
197 Carlos Delgado .75
198 Bill Hall .75
199 Jose Guillen .75
200 Jeremy Bonderman .75
201 Roger Clemens/SP 6.00
202 Alex Rodriguez/SP 6.00
203 Greg Maddux/SP 4.00
204 Miguel Tejada/SP 3.00
205 Alfonso Soriano/SP 3.00
206 Andy Pettitte/SP 2.00
207 Curt Schilling/SP 2.00
208 Gary Sheffield/SP 2.00
209 Ivan Rodriguez/SP 2.00
210 Jim Thome/SP 2.00
211 Mike Mussina/SP 2.00
212 Mike Piazza/SP 4.00
213 Randy Johnson/SP 4.00
214 Roger Clemens/SP 6.00
215 Sammy Sosa/SP 4.00
216 Alex Rodriguez/SP 6.00
217 Randy Johnson/SP 4.00
218 Vladimir Guerrero/SP 3.00
219 Rafael Palmeiro/SP 2.00
220 Manny Ramirez/SP 2.00
221 Mike Piazza/SP 4.00
222 Cal Ripken Jr. 10.00
223 Ted Williams 8.00
224 Duke Snider 2.00
225 Ernie Banks 4.00
226 Ryne Sandberg 8.00
227 Mark Grace 2.00
228 Andre Dawson 2.00
229 Bob Feller 2.00
230 Bob Feller 6.00
231 George Brett 8.00
232 Bo Jackson 3.00
233 Robin Yount 4.00
234 Harmon Killebrew 4.00
235 Gary Carter 2.00
236 Don Mattingly 8.00
237 Phil Rizzuto 2.00
238 Babe Ruth 8.00
239 Lou Gehrig 8.00
240 Reggie Jackson 3.00
241 Rickey Henderson 3.00
242 Mike Schmidt 8.00
243 Roberto Clemente 4.00
244 Tony Gwynn 3.00
245 Will Clark 3.00
246 Lou Brock 2.00
247 Bob Gibson 3.00
248 Stan Musial 5.00
249 Nolan Ryan 10.00
250 Dale Murphy 2.00
251 Aarom Baldiris/ Auto./499 RC 8.00
252 Akinori Otsuka/ Auto./99 RC 40.00
253 Andres Blanco/ Auto./499 RC 8.00
254 Angel Chavez/ Auto./499 RC 5.00
255 Carlos Hines/ Auto./199 RC 8.00
256 Carlos Vasquez/ Auto./499 RC 10.00
257 Casey Daigle/499 RC 10.00
258 Chris Oxspring/ Auto./499 RC 8.00
259 Colby Miller/ Auto./499 RC 5.00
260 David Crouthers/ Auto./199 8.00
261 Donald Kelly/ Auto./499 RC 5.00
262 Eddy Rodriguez/ Auto./499 RC 10.00
263 Edwardo Sierra/ Auto./299 RC 8.00
264 Edwin Moreno/ Auto./499 RC 10.00
265 Fernando Nieve/ Auto./499 RC 5.00
266 Freddy Guzman/ Auto./499 RC 5.00
267 Greg Dobbs/ Auto./499 RC 5.00
268 Brad Halsey/ Auto./499 RC 5.00
269 Hector Gimenez/ Auto./499 RC 5.00
270 Ivan Ochoa/ Auto./499 RC 5.00
271 Jake Woods/ Auto./499 8.00
272 Jamie Brown/ Auto./499 RC 5.00
273 Jason Bartlett/ Auto./499 RC 8.00
274 Jason Szuminski/ Auto./499 RC 5.00
275 John Gall/499 RC 5.00
276 Jorge Vasquez/ Auto./499 RC 5.00
277 Josh Labandeira/ Auto./499 RC 8.00
278 Justin Hampson/ Auto./499 RC 5.00
279 Kazuo Matsui/499 RC 15.00
280 Kevin Cave/ Auto./499 RC 8.00
281 Lance Cormier/ Auto./499 RC 5.00
282 Lincoln Holdzkom/ Auto./199 RC 8.00

283 Merkin Valdez/ Auto./199 RC 15.00
284 Mike Wuertz/ Auto./499 RC 8.00
285 Mike Johnston/ Auto./499 RC 5.00
286 Mike Rouse/Auto./329 8.00
287 Onil Joseph/ Auto./499 RC 5.00
288 Phil Stockman/ Auto./499 RC 5.00
289 Roberto Novoa/ Auto./499 RC 8.00
290 Ronald Belisario/ Auto./499 RC 5.00
291 Ronny Cedeno/ Auto./499 RC 5.00
292 Ryan Meaux/ Auto./499 RC 5.00
293 Scott Proctor/499 RC 5.00
294 Sean Henn/Auto./199 10.00
295 Shawn Camp/ Auto./499 RC 5.00
296 Shawn Hill/ Auto./499 RC 5.00
297 Shingo Takatsu/ Auto./99 RC 40.00
298 Tim Bittner/ Auto./499 RC 8.00
299 William Bergolla/ 499 RC 5.00
300 Yadier Molina/ Auto./499 RC 15.00

Marble Black
No Pricing
Production One Set

Marble Blue
Blue 1-200: 3-5X
Blue 201-250: 2-3X
Blue 251-300: .5-1X
Production 50 Sets

Marble Emerald
No Pricing
Production 5 Sets

Marble Gold
Gold 1-200: 6-8X
Gold 201-250: 2-4X
Gold 251-300: No Pricing
Production 25 Sets

Marble Red
Red 1-200: 2-3X
Red 201-250: 1-2X
Red 251-300: .4-1X
Production 100 Sets

Check Signature Blue
NM/M
Quantity produced listed
1 Al Kaline/22 60.00
2 Andre Dawson/22 25.00
22 Duke Snider/20 40.00
31 George Kell/60 35.00

Check Signature Green
No Pricing
Production 1-15

Check Signature Red
No Pricing

Check Signature Material Blue

NM/M
Quantity produced listed
1 Al Kaline/Bat/50 50.00
2 Andre Dawson/ Jsy/50 20.00
4 Bob Gibson/Hat/50 30.00
6 Brooks Robinson/ Bat/50 50.00
7 Cal Ripken Jr./ Jsy/25 200.00
8 Cal Ripken Jr./ Jsy/25 200.00
9 Cal Ripken Jr./ Bat/25 200.00
10 Cal Ripken Jr./ Jkt/25 200.00
13 Carlton Fisk/Jkt/35 40.00
14 Carlton Fisk/Jsy/35 40.00
16 Dale Murphy/Jsy/50 30.00
17 Dale Murphy/Jsy/50 30.00

18 Don Mattingly/ Jsy/25 80.00
19 Don Mattingly/Gray/ Jsy/25 80.00
20 Don Mattingly/Bat/25 80.00
21 Don Mattingly/Jkt/25 80.00
22 Duke Snider/ Pants/100 40.00
23 Ozzie Smith/Jsy/40 60.00
24 Ozzie Smith/Jsy/40 60.00
25 Ozzie Smith/Bat/40 60.00
26 Frank Robinson/ Bat/50 30.00
27 George Brett White/ Jsy/30 80.00
28 George Brett Blue/ Jsy/30 80.00
29 George Brett/Bat/30 80.00
32 Hal Newhouser/ Jsy/15 30.00
33 Harmon Killebrew/ Shoe/35 60.00
34 Harmon Killebrew/ Bat/35 60.00
38 Kirby Puckett/ Fld Glv/25 60.00
39 Kirby Puckett/Bat/25 60.00
40 Lou Boudreau/ Jsy/15. 100.00
41 Lou Brock/Jsy/50 50.00
43 Luis Aparicio/ Pants/25 20.00
44 Mark Grace/ Fld Glv/25 30.00
46 Mike Schmidt/ Fld Glv/25 80.00
47 Mike Schmidt/Jsy/25 80.00
48 Mike Schmidt/Jkt/25 80.00
49 Mike Schmidt/Bat/25 80.00
50 Nolan Ryan/Astros/ Jkt/30 150.00
51 Nolan Ryan/Rgr/ Pants/30 150.00
52 Nolan Ryan/Angels/ Jkt/30 150.00
53 Paul Molitor/Bat/50 35.00
57 Red Schoendienst/ Bat/50 25.00
63 Ron Santo/Bat/25 40.00
65 Ryne Sandberg/ Jsy/50 65.00
67 Stan Musial/White/ Jsy/30 80.00
68 Stan Musial/Gray/ Jsy/30 80.00
69 Stan Musial/Bat/30 80.00
70 Steve Carlton/ Pants/25 40.00
71 Steve Carlton/Jsy/25 40.00
73 Tony Gwynn/White/ Jsy/50 50.00
74 Tony Gwynn/Navy/ Jsy/50 50.00
77 Whitey Ford/ Pants/25 30.00
78 Will Clark/Jsy/50 50.00
79 Will Clark/Bat/50 50.00

Check Signature Material Green
NM/M
Quantity produced listed
1 Al Kaline/Bat/33 65.00
2 Andre Dawson/ Jsy/33 25.00
4 Bob Gibson/Hat/15 50.00
6 Brooks Robinson/ Bat/15 80.00
22 Duke Snider/ Pants/25 50.00
26 Frank Robinson/ Bat/15 40.00
41 Lou Brock/Jsy/15 50.00
43 Luis Aparicio/ Pants/15 30.00
44 Mark Grace/ Fld Glv/15 50.00
53 Paul Molitor/Bat/15 40.00
77 Whitey Ford/ Pants/15 75.00

Check Signature Material Red
NM/M
Quantity produced listed
4 Bob Gibson/Hat/25 50.00
5 Bobby Doerr/Jsy/25 30.00
6 Brooks Robinson/ Bat/25 65.00
13 Carlton Fisk/Jkt/25 50.00
14 Carlton Fisk/Jsy/25 50.00
16 Dale Murphy/Jsy/25 40.00
17 Dale Murphy/Jsy/25 40.00
22 Duke Snider/ Pants/50 40.00
26 Frank Robinson/ Bat/25 40.00
27 George Brett/Jsy/15 100.00
28 George Brett/Jsy/15 100.00
29 George Brett/Bat/15 100.00
33 Harmon Killebrew/ Shoe/25 65.00
34 Harmon Killebrew/ Bat/25 65.00
41 Lou Brock/Jsy/25 40.00

43 Luis Aparicio/ Pants/25 25.00
44 Mark Grace/ Fld Glve/25 40.00
53 Paul Molitor/Bat/25 40.00
57 Red Schoendienst/ Bat/25 25.00
65 Ryne Sandberg/ Jsy/25 75.00
73 Tony Gwynn/Jsy/25 70.00
74 Tony Gwynn/Jsy/25 70.00
77 Whitey Ford/ Pants/25 60.00
78 Will Clark/Jsy/25 40.00
79 Will Clark/Bat/25 40.00

Hall of Fame Souvenirs

NM/M
Quantity produced listed
1 Ernie Banks/84 8.00
2 Stan Musial/93 15.00
3 Nolan Ryan/99 25.00
4 Duke Snider/87 8.00
5 Bob Feller/94 8.00
6 George Brett/98 20.00
7 Robin Yount/78 15.00
8 Harmon Killebrew/83 10.00
9 Gary Carter/78 4.00
10 Phil Rizzuto/75 8.00
11 Reggie Jackson/94 8.00
12 Mike Schmidt/97 20.00
13 Lou Brock/80 6.00
14 Bob Gibson/84 6.00
15 Bobby Doerr/75 6.00
16 Tony Perez/77 4.00
17 Whitey Ford/78 4.00
18 Juan Marichal/84 4.00
19 Monte Irvin/75 4.00
20 Fergie Jenkins/75 4.00
21 Ralph Kiner/75 8.00
22 Eddie Murray/85 10.00
23 George Kell/75 4.00
24 Hoyt Wilhelm/84 4.00
25 Carlton Fisk/80 8.00
26 Rod Carew/91 8.00
27 Frank Robinson/89 6.00
28 Gaylord Perry/77 4.00
29 Red Schoendienst/75 4.00
30 Brooks Robinson/92 8.00
31 Al Kaline/88 10.00
32 Orlando Cepeda/75 4.00
33 Steve Carlton/50 8.00
34 Luis Aparicio/85 4.00
35 Warren Spahn/83 8.00
36 Kirby Puckett/85 10.00
37 Phil Niekro/80 4.00
38 Jim Bunning/75 4.00
39 Tom Seaver/99 8.00
40 Paul Molitor/85 4.00
41 Johnny Bench/96 4.00
42 Don Sutton/82 4.00
43 Robin Roberts/87 6.00
44 Jim Palmer/93 4.00
45 Joe Morgan/82 4.00
46 Roberto Clemente/93 25.00
47 Lou Gehrig/100 10.00
48 Babe Ruth/95 20.00
49 Ty Cobb/98 10.00
50 Ted Williams/94 20.00

Hall of Fame Souvenirs Signature
NM/M
Quantity produced listed
3 Nolan Ryan/34 150.00
4 Duke Snider/50 30.00
5 Bob Feller/50 30.00
8 Harmon Killebrew/25 50.00
9 Gary Carter/50 15.00
10 Phil Rizzuto/50 30.00
12 Mike Schmidt/20 60.00
13 Lou Brock/50 25.00
14 Bob Gibson/45 25.00
15 Bobby Doerr/50 15.00
16 Tony Perez/50 15.00
17 Whitey Ford/16 40.00
18 Juan Marichal/50 25.00
19 Monte Irvin/50 25.00
20 Fergie Jenkins/50 25.00
21 Ralph Kiner/50 25.00
22 Eddie Murray/33 60.00
23 George Kell/50 25.00
24 Hoyt Wilhelm/25 15.00
25 Carlton Fisk/27 50.00
26 Rod Carew/30 30.00
28 Gaylord Perry/50 25.00
29 Red Schoendienst/50 15.00
30 Brooks Robinson/50 40.00
31 Al Kaline/50 40.00
32 Orlando Cepeda/50 25.00
33 Steve Carlton/50 25.00
34 Luis Aparicio/50 15.00
35 Warren Spahn/21 50.00

36 Kirby Puckett/34 50.00
37 Phil Niekro/50 15.00
38 Jim Bunning/50 15.00
40 Paul Molitor/25 30.00
42 Don Sutton/50 15.00
43 Robin Roberts/50 15.00
44 Jim Palmer/22 20.00
45 Joe Morgan/25 20.00

HOF Souvenirs Material
NM/M
Production 25 Sets
1 Ernie Banks/Jsy 30.00
2 Stan Musial/Jsy 50.00
3 Nolan Ryan/Jsy 60.00
4 Duke Snider/Pants 40.00
5 Bob Feller/Jsy 20.00
6 George Brett/Jsy 50.00
7 Robin Yount/Jsy 40.00
8 Harmon Killebrew/ Jsy 25.00
9 Gary Carter/Jkt 15.00
10 Phil Rizzuto/Pants 20.00
11 Reggie Jackson/Jsy 25.00
12 Mike Schmidt/Jsy 50.00
13 Lou Brock/Jsy 20.00
14 Bob Gibson/Jsy 20.00
15 Bobby Doerr/Jsy 15.00
16 Tony Perez/Bat 10.00
17 Whitey Ford/Pants 25.00
18 Juan Marichal/Jsy 10.00
20 Fergie Jenkins/Jsy 10.00
21 Ralph Kiner/Bat 25.00
24 Eddie Murray/Jsy 25.00
25 Hoyt Wilhelm/Jsy 10.00
26 Rod Carew/Jsy 20.00
27 Frank Robinson/Jsy 15.00
29 Red Schoendienst/ Jsy 15.00
30 Brooks Robinson/ Bat 30.00
31 Al Kaline/Pants 10.00
32 Orlando Cepeda/Bat 10.00
33 Steve Carlton/Pants 10.00
34 Luis Aparicio/Jsy 10.00
35 Warren Spahn/Pants 25.00
36 Kirby Puckett/Jsy 25.00
37 Phil Niekro/Jsy 10.00
39 Tom Seaver/Jsy 25.00
40 Paul Molitor/Jsy 20.00
41 Johnny Bench/Jsy 25.00
42 Don Sutton/Jsy 10.00
43 Robin Roberts/Hat 15.00
44 Jim Palmer/Jsy 15.00
45 Joe Morgan/Jsy 15.00
46 Roberto Clemente/ Jsy 80.00
47 Lou Gehrig/Pants 150.00
48 Babe Ruth/Pants 275.00
49 Ty Cobb/Pants 150.00
50 Ted Williams/Jsy 125.00

HOF Souvenirs Signature Material

NM/M
Quantity produced listed
3 Nolan Ryan/Jsy/34 180.00
5 Bob Feller/Jsy/19 50.00
12 Mike Schmidt/Jsy/20 80.00
13 Lou Brock/Jsy/20 40.00
14 Bob Gibson/Jsy/45 30.00
16 Tony Perez/Bat/24 25.00
17 Whitey Ford/ Pants/16 25.00
18 Juan Marichal/Jsy/27 30.00
20 Fergie Jenkins/ Pants/31 30.00
22 Eddie Murray/Jsy/33 85.00
25 Carlton Fisk/Jsy/27 50.00
26 Rod Carew/Jsy/29 25.00
32 Orlando Cepeda/ Bat/30 30.00
33 Steve Carlton/ Pants/32 40.00
35 Warren Spahn/ Pants/21 75.00
36 Kirby Puckett/Jsy/34 65.00
37 Phil Niekro/Jsy/25 25.00
42 Don Sutton/Jsy/40 25.00
43 Robin Roberts/ Hat/25 25.00
44 Jim Palmer/Jsy/22 30.00
45 Joe Morgan/Jsy/16 35.00

K-Force
NM/M
Quantity produced listed
1 Nolan Ryan/500 8.00
2 Steve Carlton/500 2.00
3 Roger Clemens/500 6.00
4 Randy Johnson/500 3.00
5 Bert Blyleven/500 1.50

6 Tom Seaver/500 3.00
7 Don Sutton/500 1.50
8 Gaylord Perry/500 1.50
9 Phil Niekro/500 1.50
10 Fergie Jenkins/500 1.50
11 Bob Gibson/500 3.00
12 Nolan Ryan/383 8.00
13 Randy Johnson/308 3.00
14 Bob Feller/348 3.00
15 Curt Schilling/319 3.00
16 Pedro J. Martinez/313 3.00
17 Dwight Gooden/276 1.50
18 John Smoltz/276 2.00
19 Curt Schilling/316 3.00
20 Randy Johnson/319 3.00
21 Pedro Martinez/305 3.00
22 Roger Clemens/291 6.00
23 Roger Clemens/292 6.00
24 Tom Seaver/289 3.00
25 Hal Newhouser/275 2.00
26 Jim Bunning/201 2.00
27 Robin Roberts/198 3.00
28 Warren Spahn/191 4.00
29 Jack Morris/232 2.00
30 Nolan Ryan/270 3.00
31 Hideo Nomo/236 3.00
32 Barry Zito/205 2.00
33 Mike Mussina/214 3.00
34 Roy Oswalt/208 2.00
35 Mark Prior/245 3.00
36 Kerry Wood/266 4.00
37 Roy Halladay/204 2.00
38 Esteban Loaiza/207 1.50
39 Whitey Ford/94 6.00
40 Bob Gibson/17 12.00
41 Ben Sheets/18 8.00
42 Hoyt Wilhelm/139 3.00
43 Satchel Paige/91 10.00
44 Burleigh Grimes/136 3.00
45 Mark Prior, Kerry Wood,
46 Nolan Ryan, Roger Clemens/500 10.00
47 Steve Carlton, Randy Johnson/500 3.00
48 Nolan Ryan, Roger Clemens/500 8.00
49 Nolan Ryan, Steve Carlton/500 8.00
50 Kerry Wood, Roger Clemens/20 30.00

K-Force Material
NM/M
Quantity produced listed
1 Nolan Ryan/Jsy/100 25.00
2 Steve Carlton/Jsy/32 12.00
3 Roger Clemens/ Jsy/25 25.00
4 Randy Johnson/ Jsy/51 15.00
5 Bert Blyleven/Jsy/28 10.00
6 Tom Seaver/Jsy/25 25.00
7 Gaylord Perry/Jsy/36 8.00
9 Phil Niekro/Jsy/35 10.00
10 Fergie Jenkins/ Pants/31 10.00
11 Bob Gibson/Jsy/45 15.00
12 Nolan Ryan/Jkt/100 25.00
13 Randy Johnson/ Jsy/51 15.00
14 Bob Feller/Jsy/25 20.00
15 Curt Schilling/Jsy/25 12.00
16 Pedro J. Martinez/ Jsy/45 15.00
17 Dwight Gooden/ Jsy/25 10.00
18 John Smoltz/Jsy/25 15.00
19 Curt Schilling/Jsy/25 12.00
20 Randy Johnson/ Jsy/51 15.00
21 Pedro Martinez/ Jsy/45 15.00
22 Roger Clemens/ Jsy/100 15.00
25 Hal Newhouser/ Jsy/25 20.00
28 Warren Spahn/ Jsy/50 15.00
29 Jack Morris/Jsy/47 15.00
30 Nolan Ryan/Jkt/100 25.00
31 Hideo Nomo/Jsy/25 20.00
32 Barry Zito/Jsy/25 10.00
33 Mike Mussina/ Jsy/25 20.00
34 Roy Oswalt/Jsy/44 6.00
35 Mark Prior/Jsy/50 8.00
36 Kerry Wood/Jsy/34 20.00
39 Whitey Ford/Jsy/50 15.00
40 Bob Gibson/Jsy/25 10.00
41 Ben Sheets/Jsy/25 10.00
43 Satchel Paige/ Jsy/100 60.00
44 Burleigh Grimes/ Pants/100 75.00

45 Mark Prior/Jsy, Kerry Wood/ Pants/50 15.00
46 Nolan Ryan/Jsy, Roger Clemens/ Jsy/50 40.00
47 Steve Carlton/Jsy, Randy Johnson/ Jsy/50 25.00
48 Nolan Ryan/Pants, Roger Clemens/ Jsy/50 40.00
49 Nolan Ryan/Jsy, Carlton Fisk/Pants/50 35.00
50 Kerry Wood/Jsy, Roger Clemens/ Jsy/50 25.00

K-Force Signature
NM/M
Quantity produced listed
2 Steve Carlton/50 30.00
5 Bert Blyleven/50 15.00
6 Don Sutton/50 15.00
8 Gaylord Perry/50 15.00
9 Phil Niekro/50 25.00
10 Fergie Jenkins/50 15.00
14 Bob Feller/50 30.00
17 Dwight Gooden/50 15.00
26 Jim Bunning/50 25.00
27 Robin Roberts/50 15.00
29 Jack Morris/50 15.00
34 Roy Oswalt/50 15.00
38 Esteban Loaiza/50 10.00

K-Force Signature Material

FORCE 5/14

NM/M
Quantity produced listed
1 Nolan Ryan/Jsy/34 150.00
2 Steve Carlton/Jsy/32 50.00
5 Bert Blyleven/Jsy/28 25.00
8 Gaylord Perry/Jsy/36 25.00
9 Phil Niekro/Jsy/35 40.00
10 Fergie Jenkins/ Pants/31 25.00
11 Bob Gibson/Jsy/45 40.00
12 Nolan Ryan/Jkt/34 150.00
14 Bob Feller/Jsy/19 50.00
17 Dwight Gooden/ Jsy/16 30.00
28 Warren Spahn/ Jsy/21 65.00
29 Jack Morris/Jsy/47 20.00
30 Nolan Ryan/Jkt/34 150.00
34 Roy Oswalt/Jsy/44 20.00
36 Kerry Wood/Jsy/34 50.00
37 Roy Halladay/Jsy/32 15.00
39 Whitey Ford/Jsy/16 50.00
40 Bob Gibson/Jsy/45 30.00

Marble Material Black
No Pricing
Production One Set

Marble Material Blue Number
NM/M
Quanity produced listed
1 Vladimir Guerrero/ Jsy/27 25.00
2 Garret Anderson/ Jsy/16 15.00
5 Troy Glaus/Jsy/25 10.00
6 Tim Salmon/Jsy/15 20.00
8 Brandon Webb/Jsy/55 5.00
10 Randy Johnson/ Jsy/51 12.00
13 Luis Gonzalez/Jsy/20 10.00
17 Marcus Giles/Jsy/22 10.00
18 Andruw Jones/ Jsy/25 10.00
20 Rafael Palmeiro/ Jsy/25 15.00
22 Luis Matos/Jsy/32 10.00
23 Jay Gibbons/Jsy/31 10.00
26 Rodrigo Lopez/ Jsy/19 10.00
27 Javy Lopez/Jsy/18 15.00
30 Curt Schilling/Jsy/38 12.00
31 Jason Varitek/Jsy/33 10.00
32 Manny Ramirez/ Jsy/29 20.00
35 Pedro Martinez/Jsy/45 15.00
39 David Ortiz/Jsy/34 20.00
40 Mark Prior/Jsy/22 15.00
41 Kerry Wood/ Pants/34 20.00
42 Sammy Sosa/Jsy/21 30.00
44 Greg Maddux/Jsy/31 25.00
45 Aramis Ramirez/ Jsy/16 15.00

49 Moises Alou/Jsy/18 15.00
51 Frank Thomas/ Jsy/35 20.00
52 Magglio Ordonez/ Jsy/30 10.00
53 Carlos Lee/Jsy/45 5.00
54 Mark Buehrle/Jsy/56 5.00
58 Adam Dunn/Jsy/44 12.00
59 Austin Kearns/Jsy/28 10.00
63 Sean Casey/Jsy/21 10.00
66 Cliff Lee/Jsy/34 8.00
67 Victor Martinez/Jsy/41 8.00
68 C.C. Sabathia/Jsy/52 5.00
70 Travis Hafner/Jsy/48 8.00
71 Todd Helton/Jsy/17 20.00
72 Preston Wilson/ Jsy/44 5.00
73 Jeromy Burnitz/ Jsy/35 5.00
74 Larry Walker/Jsy/33 10.00
77 Miguel Cabrera/ Jsy/24 20.00
79 Josh Beckett/Jsy/21 12.00
81 Dontrelle Willis/ Jsy/35 10.00
82 Brad Penny/Jsy/31 8.00
85 Andy Pettitte/Jsy/21 15.00
87 Roy Oswalt/Jsy/44 5.00
88 Lance Berkman/ Jsy/17 10.00
95 Roger Clemens/ Jsy/22 25.00
100 Mike Sweeney/ Jsy/29 10.00
101 Kazuhisa Ishii/Jsy/17 15.00
113 Adrian Beltre/Jsy/29 15.00
113 Johan Santana/ Jsy/15 15.00
114 Shannon Stewart/ Jsy/23 10.00
117 Torii Hunter/Jsy/48 5.00
119 Orlando Cabrera/ Jsy/18 5.00
123 Mike Piazza/Jsy/31 30.00
124 Jae Weong Seo/ Jsy/26 10.00
126 Tom Glavine/Jsy/47 10.00
127 Jorge Posada/Jsy/20 15.00
129 Bernie Williams/ Jsy/51 10.00
130 Mike Mussina/ Jsy/35 15.00
131 Mariano Rivera/ Jsy/42 10.00
138 Jason Giambi/Jsy/25 10.00
139 Hideki Matsui/Jsy/55 40.00
139 Mark Mulder/Jsy/20 10.00
142 Barry Zito/Jsy/75 5.00
146 Marlon Byrd/Jsy/29 10.00
150 Jim Thome/Jsy/25 20.00
151 Bobby Abreu/Jsy/53 5.00
154 Craig Wilson/Jsy/36 5.00
161 Sean Burroughs/ Jsy/32 10.00
163 Brian Giles/Jsy/24 8.00
164 Ryan Klesko/Jsy/30 10.00
166 Jerome Williams/ Jsy/57 5.00
172 Freddy Garcia/Jsy/34 8.00
177 Scott Rolen/Jsy/27 20.00
178 Jim Edmonds/Jsy/15 15.00
180 Matt Morris/Jsy/35 10.00
181 Edgar Renteria/ Jsy/15 10.00
182 Aubrey Huff/Jsy/19 10.00
184 Dewon Brazelton/ Jsy/45 5.00
187 Mark Teixeira/Jsy/23 15.00
192 Kevin Mench/Jsy/28 8.00
195 Roy Halladay/Jsy/32 10.00
197 Carlos Delgado/ Jsy/25 10.00
200 Jeremy Bonderman/ Jsy/38 5.00
201 Roger Clemens/ Jsy/22 30.00
203 Greg Maddux/Jsy/31 25.00
206 Andy Pettitte/Jsy/46 10.00
207 Curt Schilling/Jsy/38 12.00
210 Jim Thome/Jsy/25 20.00
211 Mike Mussina/Jsy/35 15.00
212 Mike Piazza/Jsy/31 30.00
213 Randy Johnson/ Jsy/51 15.00
214 Roger Clemens/ Jsy/21 30.00
215 Sammy Sosa/Jsy/21 30.00
217 Randy Johnson/ Jsy/51 15.00
218 Vladimir Guerrero/ Jsy/27 25.00
219 Rafael Palmeiro/ Jsy/25 15.00
221 Mike Piazza/Jsy/25 30.00
226 Ryne Sandberg/ Jsy/23 30.00
227 Mark Grace/Jsy/17 25.00
229 Bob Feller/Jsy/19 25.00
232 Bo Jackson/Jsy/16 40.00
233 Robin Yount/Jsy/19 40.00
234 Don Mattingly/ Jsy/23 40.00
241 Rickey Henderson/ Jsy/35 25.00
242 Mike Schmidt/Jsy/20 40.00
243 Roberto Clemente/ Jsy/21 100.00
245 Will Clark/Jsy/22 30.00

246 Lou Brock/Jsy/20 20.00
247 Bob Gibson/Jsy/45 15.00
249 Nolan Ryan/Jsy/34 40.00

Marble Material Emerald Prime
No Pricing
Production 5 Sets

Marble Material Red Position
NM/M
Quantity produced listed
1 Vladimir Guerrero/ Jsy/100 10.00
2 Garret Anderson/ Jsy/100 4.00
5 Troy Glaus/Jsy/75 4.00
6 Tim Salmon/Jsy/75 4.00
10 Randy Johnson/ Jsy/100 8.00
13 Luis Gonzalez/Jsy/100 4.00
15 Rafael Furcal/Jsy/100 4.00
16 Chipper Jones/ Jsy/100 8.00
17 Marcus Giles/Jsy/100 4.00
18 Andruw Jones/ Jsy/100 6.00
20 Rafael Palmeiro/ Jsy/100 8.00
21 Melvin Mora/Jsy/50 6.00
22 Luis Matos/Jsy/100 6.00
23 Jay Gibbons/Jsy/100 4.00
25 Larry Bigbie/Jsy/50 6.00
26 Rodrigo Lopez/Jsy/50 6.00
27 Javy Lopez/Jsy/25 10.00
28 Miguel Tejada/ Jsy/100 6.00
30 Curt Schilling/Jsy/100 8.00
31 Jason Varitek/Jsy/100 6.00
32 Manny Ramirez/ Jsy/100 8.00
35 Pedro J. Martinez/ Jsy/100 10.00
39 David Ortiz/Jsy/100 8.00
40 Mark Prior/Jsy/100 8.00
41 Kerry Wood/ Pants/100 8.00
42 Sammy Sosa/ Jsy/100 8.00
44 Greg Maddux/Jsy/100 15.00
45 Aramis Ramirez/ Jsy/100 6.00
51 Frank Thomas/ Jsy/100 8.00
52 Magglio Ordonez/ Jsy/100 4.00
53 Carlos Lee/Jsy/100 4.00
54 Mark Buehrle/Jsy/100 4.00
57 Paul Konerko/Jsy/50 6.00
58 Adam Dunn/Jsy/100 8.00
59 Austin Kearns/ Jsy/100 4.00
60 Barry Larkin/Jsy/100 6.00
65 Jody Gerut/Jsy/100 4.00
66 Cliff Lee/Jsy/100 4.00
67 Victor Martinez/ Jsy/100 6.00
68 C.C. Sabathia/Jsy/100 4.00
69 Omar Vizquel/Jsy/100 4.00
70 Travis Hafner/Jsy/100 4.00
71 Todd Helton/Jsy/100 8.00
72 Preston Wilson/ Jsy/100 4.00
75 Ivan Rodriguez/ Jsy/50 10.00
77 Miguel Cabrera/ Jsy/100 8.00
79 Josh Beckett/Jsy/100 6.00
81 Dontrelle Willis/ Jsy/100 4.00
82 Brad Penny/Jsy/100 4.00
86 Jeff Bagwell/Jsy/100 8.00
87 Roy Oswalt/Jsy/100 4.00
88 Lance Berkman/ Jsy/100 4.00
89 Morgan Ensberg/ Jsy/100 4.00
90 Craig Biggio/Jsy/100 6.00
93 Jeff Kent/Jsy/100 4.00
94 Richard Hidalgo/ Pants/100 4.00
95 Roger Clemens/ Jsy/25 30.00
96 Carlos Beltran/ Jsy/100 6.00
97 Angel Berroa/ Pants/100 4.00
98 Mike Sweeney/ Jsy/100 4.00
101 Kazuhisa Ishii/ Jsy/100 4.00
102 Shawn Green/Jsy/100 4.00
104 Paul LoDuca/Jsy/100 4.00
105 Hideo Nomo/Jsy/100 4.00
107 Adrian Beltre/Jsy/100 4.00
110 Ben Sheets/Jsy/100 4.00
111 Geoff Jenkins/ Jsy/100 4.00
112 Jacque Jones/ Jsy/100 4.00
113 Johan Santana/ Jsy/100 4.00
114 Shannon Stewart/ Jsy/100 4.00
117 Torii Hunter/Jsy/75 4.00

123 Mike Piazza/Jsy/100 10.00
125 Jose Reyes/Jsy/75 4.00
126 Tom Glavine/Jsy/75 6.00
127 Jorge Posada/ Jsy/100 8.00
129 Bernie Williams/ Jsy/100 6.00
130 Mike Mussina/ Jsy/25 20.00
131 Mariano Rivera/ Jsy/25 20.00
138 Hideki Matsui/ Jsy/100 25.00
139 Mark Mulder/Jsy/100 4.00
142 Barry Zito/Jsy/100 4.00
146 Eric Chavez/Jsy/100 4.00
146 Marlon Byrd/Jsy/100 4.00
150 Jim Thome/Jsy/100 8.00
151 Bobby Abreu/Jsy/100 4.00
152 Pat Burrell/Jsy/100 4.00
154 Craig Wilson/Jsy/100 4.00
156 Jason Kendall/ Jsy/100 4.00
161 Sean Burroughs/ Jsy/100 4.00
164 Ryan Klesko/Jsy/100 4.00
166 Jerome Williams/ Jsy/25 10.00
171 Edgar Martinez/ Jsy/100 8.00
172 Freddy Garcia/ Jsy/100 6.00
177 Scott Rolen/Jsy/100 10.00
178 Jim Edmonds/ Jsy/100 6.00
179 Albert Pujols/ Jsy/100 20.00
180 Matt Morris/Jsy/75 4.00
181 Edgar Renteria/ Jsy/100 10.00
182 Aubrey Huff/Jsy/100 4.00
185 Rocco Baldelli/ Jsy/100 4.00
186 Carl Crawford/ Jsy/100 8.00
187 Mark Teixeira/Jsy/25 8.00
188 Hank Blalock/ Jsy/100 8.00
191 Alfonso Soriano/ Jsy/100 8.00
192 Kevin Mench/Jsy/100 4.00
195 Roy Halladay/Jsy/100 4.00
196 Vernon Wells/Jsy/100 4.00
197 Carlos Delgado/ Jsy/100 4.00
200 Jeremy Bonderman/ Jsy/100 4.00
201 Roger Clemens/ Jsy/100 10.00
202 Alex Rodriguez/ Jsy/100 10.00
203 Greg Maddux/ Jsy/100 10.00
204 Miguel Tejada/ Jsy/100 6.00
205 Alfonso Soriano/ Jsy/100 4.00
206 Andy Pettitte/Jsy/100 6.00
207 Curt Schilling/Jsy/100 8.00
208 Gary Sheffield/Jsy/50 8.00
209 Ivan Rodriguez/ Jsy/100 8.00
210 Jim Thome/Jsy/25 20.00
211 Mike Mussina/Jsy/50 10.00
212 Mike Piazza/Jsy/100 10.00
213 Randy Johnson/ Jsy/100 8.00
214 Roger Clemens/ Jsy/100 6.00
215 Sammy Sosa/Jsy/50 15.00
216 Alex Rodriguez/ Jsy/100 10.00
217 Randy Johnson/ Jsy/100 8.00
218 Vladimir Guerrero/ Jsy/100 8.00
219 Rafael Palmeiro/ Jsy/100 8.00
221 Mike Piazza/Jsy/100 10.00
222 Cal Ripken Jr./ Jsy/50 50.00
223 Ted Williams/ Jsy/25 100.00
225 Ernie Banks/Jsy/50 15.00
226 Ryne Sandberg/ Jsy/25 15.00
227 Mark Grace/Jsy/25 20.00
228 Andre Dawson/ Jsy/50 6.00
229 Bob Feller/Jsy/50 20.00
231 George Brett/ Jsy/100 15.00
232 Bo Jackson/Jsy/100 10.00
233 Robin Yount/Jsy/100 12.00
234 Harmon Killebrew/ Jsy/25 40.00
235 Gary Carter/Jkt/100 10.00
236 Don Mattingly/ Jsy/50 25.00
237 Phil Rizzuto/ Pants/25 20.00
238 Babe Ruth/ Pants/50 200.00
239 Lou Gehrig/ Pants/50 150.00
240 Reggie Jackson/ Jsy/100 8.00

241 Rickey Henderson/ Jsy/100 10.00
242 Mike Schmidt/ Jsy/50 25.00
243 Roberto Clemente/ Jsy/50 75.00
244 Tony Gwynn/ Jsy/100 10.00
245 Will Clark/Jsy/100 8.00
246 Lou Brock/Jsy/25 8.00
247 Bob Gibson/Jsy/25 20.00
248 Stan Musial/Jsy/25 60.00
249 Nolan Ryan/Jsy/50 40.00
250 Dale Murphy/ Jsy/100 10.00

Marble Signature Black
No Pricing
Production One Set

Marble Signature Blue
NM/M
Quantity produced listed
2 Garret Anderson/50 20.00
3 John Lackey/75 15.00
7 Shea Hillenbrand/75 15.00
8 Brandon Webb/75 10.00
11 Alex Cintron/75 10.00
14 Adam LaRoche/75 15.00
15 Rafael Furcal/50 20.00
17 Marcus Giles/50 15.00
19 Russ Ortiz/75 10.00
21 Melvin Mora/75 15.00
23 Luis Matos/75 10.00
23 Jay Gibbons/75 15.00
24 Adam Loewen/50 15.00
25 Larry Bigbie/75 15.00
26 Rodrigo Lopez/75 10.00
29 Trot Nixon/50 35.00
33 Keith Foulke/75 8.00
39 David Ortiz/50 40.00
40 Mark Prior/25 40.00
41 Kerry Wood/25 50.00
45 Derrek Lee/25 30.00
45 Aramis Ramirez/50 20.00
46 Matt Clement/25 15.00
47 Carlos Zambrano/25 35.00
48 Todd Walker/75 15.00
52 Magglio Ordonez/25 20.00
53 Carlos Lee/75 15.00
54 Mark Buehrle/50 15.00
55 Esteban Loaiza/25 15.00
59 Adam Dunn/25 40.00
59 Austin Kearns/25 20.00
63 Sean Casey/25 25.00
65 Jody Gerut/25 8.00
66 Cliff Lee/75 10.00
67 Victor Martinez/25 20.00
68 C.C. Sabathia/75 15.00
70 Travis Hafner/75 15.00
72 Preston Wilson/75 15.00
77 Miguel Cabrera/35 35.00
80 Mike Lowell/25 20.00
82 Brad Penny/75 10.00
85 Roy Oswalt/75 10.00
89 Morgan Ensberg/75 12.00
90 Craig Biggio/25 30.00
91 Octavio Dotel/75 15.00
92 Wade Miller/75 10.00
96 Carlos Beltran/50 50.00
97 Angel Berroa/50 10.00
98 Jeremy Affeldt/75 10.00
103 Milton Bradley/75 15.00
104 Paul LoDuca/75 15.00
108 Scott Podsednik/75 15.00
108 Rickie Weeks/25 25.00
112 Jacque Jones/75 10.00
113 Johan Santana/50 50.00
114 Shannon Stewart/75 15.00
116 Lew Ford/75 15.00
117 Torii Hunter/25 25.00
118 Chad Cordero/75 10.00
119 Orlando Cabrera/75 20.00
120 Jose Vidro/50 10.00
125 Jose Reyes/25 30.00
132 Bubba Crosby/75 10.00
139 Mark Mulder/25 25.00
140 Jermaine Dye/75 10.00
144 Bobby Crosby/75 40.00
146 Eric Byrnes/75 10.00
146 Marlon Byrd/75 10.00
148 Mike Lieberthal/75 15.00
153 Jose Castillo/75 10.00
154 Craig Wilson/75 10.00
155 Jason Bay/75 25.00
158 Jay Payton/75 10.00
161 Sean Burroughs/75 15.00
165 Todd Linden/75 8.00
170 Shigetoshi Hasegawa/ 50 40.00
171 Edgar Martinez/25 40.00
174 Raul Ibanez/75 10.00
177 Scott Rolen/50 35.00
177 Aubrey Huff/75 15.00
183 Delmon Young/25 25.00
184 Dewon Brazelton/75 10.00
186 Carl Crawford/75 20.00
187 Mark Teixeira/25 40.00
188 Hank Blalock/25 25.00
189 Michael Young/75 15.00
190 Laynce Nix/75 15.00
191 Alfonso Soriano/25 50.00
193 Adrian Gonzalez/75 10.00
194 Alexis Rios/75 20.00

196 Vernon Wells/50 15.00
198 Bill Hall/75 10.00
199 Jose Guillen/75 15.00
200 Jeremy Bonderman/ 75 10.00
222 Cal Ripken Jr./25 150.00
224 Duke Snider/35 35.00
228 Andre Dawson/50 20.00
229 Bob Feller/50 30.00
235 Gary Carter/25 20.00
237 Phil Rizzuto/25 40.00
245 Will Clark/25 50.00
246 Lou Brock/25 35.00
247 Bob Gibson/25 40.00
248 Stan Musial/25 75.00
249 Nolan Ryan/25 150.00
250 Dale Murphy/50 30.00
251 Aarom Baldiris/75 10.00
252 Akinori Otsuka/25 50.00
253 Andres Blanco/75 10.00
254 Angel Chavez/75 8.00
255 Carlos Hines/75 8.00
256 Carlos Vasquez/75 12.00
258 Chris Oxspring/75 10.00
259 Colby Miller/75 8.00
261 Donald Kelly/75 8.00
262 Eddy Rodriguez/75 8.00
263 Edwardo Sierra/65 10.00
264 Edwin Moreno/75 12.00
265 Fernando Nieve/75 8.00
266 Freddy Guzman/75 8.00
267 Greg Dobbs/75 8.00
268 Brad Halsey/75 8.00
269 Hector Gimenez/75 8.00
271 Ivan Ochoa/75 8.00
271 Jake Woods/75 10.00
272 Jamie Brown/75 8.00
273 Jason Bartlett/75 15.00
274 Jason Szuminski/75 10.00
275 John Gall/75 10.00
276 Jorge Vasquez/75 8.00
277 Josh Labandeira/75 8.00
278 Justin Hampson/75 8.00
280 Kevin Cave/75 10.00
281 Lance Cormier/75 8.00
283 Merkin Valdez/75 15.00
284 Mike Wuertz/75 10.00
285 Mike Johnston/75 8.00
287 Onil Joseph/75 8.00
288 Phil Stockman/75 8.00
289 Roberto Novoa/75 10.00
290 Ronald Belisario/75 8.00
291 Ronny Cedeno/75 8.00
292 Ryan Meaux/75 8.00
293 Scott Proctor/75 10.00
295 Shawn Camp/75 8.00
296 Shawn Hill/75 8.00
297 Shingo Takatsu/25 60.00
299 William Bergolla/75 8.00
300 Yadier Molina/75 25.00

Marble Signature Emerald
No Pricing
Production 1-5

Marble Signature Gold
No Pricing
Production 1-25

Marble Signature Material Gold Number
NM/M
Quantity produced listed
1 Vladimir Guerrero/ Jsy/27 60.00
8 Brandon Webb/ Jsy/55 10.00
18 Andruw Jones/ Jsy/25 40.00
23 Luis Matos/Jsy/32 40.00
23 Jay Gibbons/Jsy/31 25.00
32 Manny Ramirez/ Jsy/24 75.00
39 David Ortiz/Jsy/34 50.00
40 Mark Prior/Jsy/22 50.00
41 Kerry Wood/ Pants/34 50.00
42 Sammy Sosa/ Jsy/21 150.00
44 Greg Maddux/ Jsy/31 100.00
51 Frank Thomas/ Jsy/35 50.00
52 Magglio Ordonez/ Jsy/30 25.00
53 Carlos Lee/Jsy/45 20.00
54 Mark Buehrle/Jsy/56 20.00
58 Adam Dunn/Jsy/44 40.00
59 Austin Kearns/ Jsy/28 25.00
66 Cliff Lee/Jsy/34 15.00
67 Victor Martinez/ Jsy/41 25.00
68 C.C. Sabathia/ Jsy/52 20.00
70 Travis Hafner/Jsy/48 20.00
71 Todd Helton/Jsy/17 60.00
72 Preston Wilson/ Jsy/44 20.00
81 Dontrelle Willis/ Jsy/35 30.00

82 Brad Penny/Jsy/31 15.00
85 Andy Pettitte/Jsy/21 50.00
104 Paul LoDuca/Jsy/16 35.00
113 Johan Santana/Jsy/57 50.00
114 Shannon Stewart/Jsy/23 25.00
117 Torii Hunter/Jsy/48 20.00
119 Orlando Cabrera/Jsy/18 30.00
123 Mike Piazza/Jsy/31 100.00
124 Jae Weong Seo/Jsy/26 20.00
127 Jorge Posada/Jsy/20 40.00
130 Mike Mussina/Jsy/35 40.00
139 Mark Mulder/Jsy/25 50.00
141 Tim Hudson/Jsy/15 30.00
146 Marlon Byrd/Jsy/29 15.00
177 Scott Rolen/Jsy/27 50.00
182 Aubrey Huff/Jsy/19 30.00
184 Dewon Brazelton/Jsy/45 15.00
187 Mark Teixeira/Jsy/23 50.00
195 Roy Halladay/Jsy/32 15.00
200 Jeremy Bonderman/Jsy/38 10.00
236 Don Mattingly/Jsy/23 85.00
240 Reggie Jackson/Jsy/44 50.00
241 Rickey Henderson/Jsy/35 50.00
242 Mike Schmidt/Pants/20 100.00
244 Tony Gwynn/Jsy/19 75.00
245 Will Clark/Jsy/22 50.00
246 Lou Brock/Jsy/20 40.00
247 Bob Gibson/Jsy/45 40.00
249 Nolan Ryan/Jsy/34 150.00

Marble Signature Material Gold Position

NM/M
Quantity produced listed
2 Garret Anderson/Jsy/50 20.00
8 Brandon Webb/Jsy/50 15.00
15 Rafael Furcal/Jsy/50 20.00
17 Marcus Giles/Jsy/50 15.00
22 Melvin Mora/Jsy/50 20.00
22 Luis Matos/Jsy/50 15.00
23 Jay Gibbons/Jsy/50 15.00
25 Larry Bigbie/Jsy/50 15.00
26 Rodrigo Lopez/Jsy/50 10.00
45 Aramis Ramirez/Jsy/50 30.00
53 Carlos Lee/Jsy/50 20.00
54 Mark Buehrle/Jsy/50 20.00
59 Austin Kearns/Jsy/50 20.00
65 Jody Gerut/Jsy/50 10.00
66 Cliff Lee/Jsy/50 15.00
67 Victor Martinez/Jsy/50 25.00
68 C.C. Sabathia/Jsy/50 20.00
70 Travis Hafner/Jsy/50 20.00
72 Preston Wilson/Jsy/50 20.00
82 Brad Penny/Jsy/50 10.00
89 Morgan Ensberg/Jsy/50 10.00
96 Carlos Beltran/Jsy/50 50.00
97 Angel Berroa/Pants/50 10.00
104 Paul LoDuca/Jsy/25 25.00
112 Jacque Jones/Jsy/50 20.00
113 Johan Santana/Jsy/50 50.00
114 Shannon Stewart/Jsy/50 20.00
117 Torii Hunter/Jsy/25 25.00
119 Orlando Cabrera/Jsy/50 20.00
120 Jose Vidro/Jsy/50 10.00
139 Mark Mulder/Jsy/25 25.00
146 Marlon Byrd/Jsy/50 15.00
154 Craig Wilson/Jsy/50 15.00
161 Sean Burroughs/Jsy/50 15.00
171 Edgar Martinez/Jsy/25 50.00
182 Aubrey Huff/Jsy/50 20.00
186 Carl Crawford/Jsy/50 30.00
188 Hank Blalock/Jsy/25 40.00
200 Jeremy Bonderman/Jsy/50 10.00
228 Andre Dawson/Jsy/50 50.00
229 Bob Feller/Jsy/50 35.00
234 Harmon Killebrew/Jsy/25 65.00

Marble Signature Red

NM/M
Quantity produced listed

2 Garret Anderson/50 20.00
3 John Lackey/50 15.00
7 Shea Hillenbrand/100 15.00
8 Brandon Webb/100 10.00
11 Alex Cintron/100 8.00
14 Adam LaRoche/100 15.00
15 Rafael Furcal/50 15.00
17 Marcus Giles/50 15.00
19 Russ Ortiz/100 10.00
21 Melvin Mora/100 15.00
22 Luis Matos/100 8.00
23 Jay Gibbons/100 15.00
25 Larry Bigbie/100 10.00
26 Rodrigo Lopez/100 10.00
29 Trot Nixon/50 35.00
33 Keith Foulke/100 8.00
39 David Ortiz/50 40.00
40 Mark Prior/25 40.00
43 Derrek Lee/50 25.00
45 Aramis Ramirez/100 15.00
46 Matt Clement/25 15.00
47 Carlos Zambrano/100 35.00
48 Todd Walker/100 10.00
53 Carlos Lee/100 15.00
54 Mark Buehrle/50 15.00
55 Esteban Loaiza/100 10.00
58 Adam Dunn/25 40.00
63 Sean Casey/25 25.00
65 Jody Gerut/100 8.00
66 Cliff Lee/100 9.00
67 Victor Martinez/100 15.00
68 C.C. Sabathia/100 15.00
70 Travis Hafner/100 15.00
72 Preston Wilson/100 15.00
77 Miguel Cabrera/50 35.00
80 Mike Lowell/25 20.00
82 Brad Penny/100 10.00
89 Morgan Ensberg/100 10.00
90 Craig Biggio/25 30.00
91 Octavio Dotel/100 15.00
92 Wade Miller/100 8.00
96 Carlos Beltran/50 50.00
97 Angel Berroa/50 10.00
98 Jeremy Affeldt/100 10.00
103 Milton Bradley/100 15.00
104 Paul LoDuca/50 15.00
108 Scott Podsednik/100 15.00
109 Rickie Weeks/25 25.00
112 Jacque Jones/100 10.00
113 Johan Santana/50 15.00
114 Shannon Stewart/50 15.00
116 Lew Ford/100 15.00
117 Torii Hunter/25 25.00
118 Chad Cordero/100 10.00
119 Orlando Cabrera/100 20.00
120 Jose Vidro/50 10.00
132 Bubba Crosby/100 10.00
139 Mark Mulder/25 25.00
140 Jermaine Dye/100 10.00
144 Bobby Crosby/100 40.00
145 Eric Byrnes/100 10.00
146 Marlon Byrd/100 10.00
148 Mike Lieberthal/100 15.00
153 Jose Castillo/100 10.00
154 Craig Wilson/100 10.00
155 Jason Bay/100 25.00
158 Jay Payton/100 10.00
161 Sean Burroughs/25 15.00
165 Todd Linden/100 8.00
170 Shigetoshi Hasegawa/50
171 Edgar Martinez/25 40.00
174 Raul Ibanez/100 10.00
177 Scott Rolen/50 35.00
182 Aubrey Huff/100 10.00
183 Delmon Young/25 25.00
184 Dewon Brazelton/100 10.00
186 Carl Crawford/100 20.00
187 Mark Teixeira/25 40.00
188 Hank Blalock/25 40.00
189 Michael Young/100 15.00
190 Laynce Nix/100 10.00
191 Alfonso Soriano/25 50.00
193 Adrian Gonzalez/100 10.00
194 Alexis Rios/100 10.00
196 Vernon Wells/50 15.00
198 Bill Hall/100 8.00
199 Jose Guillen/100 15.00
200 Jeremy Bonderman/100 10.00
222 Cal Ripken Jr./25 150.00
224 Duke Snider/25 40.00
228 Andre Dawson/100 15.00
229 Bob Feller/25 25.00
235 Gary Carter/25 20.00
237 Phil Rizzuto/25 40.00
245 Will Clark/25 50.00
247 Bob Gibson/25 20.00
248 Stan Musial/25 75.00
249 Nolan Ryan/25 150.00
250 Dale Murphy/50 30.00
251 Aarom Baldiris/100 8.00
252 Akinori Otsuka/25 10.00
253 Andres Blanco/100 10.00
254 Angel Chavez/100 8.00
255 Carlos Hines/100 8.00
256 Carlos Vasquez/100 12.00
258 Chris Oxspring/100 8.00
259 Colby Miller/100 8.00
260 David Crouthers/100 8.00
261 Donald Kelly/100 8.00
262 Eddy Rodriguez/100 8.00
263 Edwardo Sierra/100 8.00
264 Edwin Moreno/100 10.00
266 Freddy Guzman/100 8.00
267 Greg Dobbs/100 8.00
268 Brad Halsey/100 8.00

269 Hector Gimenez/100 8.00
270 Ivan Ochoa/100 8.00
271 Jake Woods/100 10.00
272 Jamie Brown/100 8.00
273 Jason Bartlett/100 15.00
274 Jason Szuminski/100 8.00
275 John Gall/100 10.00
276 Jorge Vasquez/100 8.00
277 Josh Labandeira/100 8.00
280 Kevin Cave/100 8.00
281 Lance Cormier/100 8.00
283 Merkin Valdez/100 15.00
284 Mike Wuertz/100 8.00
285 Mike Johnston/100 8.00
287 Onil Joseph/100 8.00
288 Phil Stockman/100 8.00
289 Roberto Novoa/100 10.00
291 Ronny Cedeno/100 8.00
292 Ryan Meaux/100 8.00
293 Scott Proctor/100 8.00
295 Shawn Camp/100 8.00
297 Shingo Takatsu/25 60.00
299 William Bergolla/100 8.00
300 Yadier Molina/100 25.00

Stars Signature Jersey

NM/M
Quantity produced listed
1 Ryne Sandberg/23 75.00
2 Mark Prior/22 40.00
4 Don Mattingly/23 75.00
5 Vladimir Guerrero/27 60.00
6 Garret Anderson/16 35.00
9 Mark Grace/17 50.00
11 Kerry Wood/34 50.00
11 Frank Thomas/35 50.00
12 Magglio Ordonez/30 25.00
13 Adam Dunn/44 50.00
14 Preston Wilson/44 20.00
15 Bo Jackson/16 125.00
16 Carlos Beltran/15 75.00
17 Tony Gwynn/19 75.00
18 Will Clark/22 65.00
20 Scott Rolen/27 60.00
24 Andruw Jones/25 40.00
28 Sammy Sosa/21 150.00
29 Greg Maddux/31 100.00
32 Todd Helton/17 50.00
34 Jorge Posada/20 50.00
37 Miguel Cabrera/24 50.00
41 Fred Lynn/19 20.00
45 Keith Hernandez/37 20.00
48 Luis Tiant/25 25.00
48 George Foster/15 25.00
49 Darryl Strawberry/18 35.00
50 Marty Marion/25 25.00

Stars

NM/M
Production 599 Sets
1 Ryne Sandberg 6.00
2 Mark Prior 2.00
3 Andre Dawson 2.00
4 Don Mattingly 6.00
5 Vladimir Guerrero 3.00
6 Garret Anderson 2.00
7 Dale Murphy 3.00
8 Cal Ripken Jr. 10.00
9 Mark Grace 3.00
10 Kerry Wood 3.00
11 Frank Thomas 3.00
12 Magglio Ordonez 2.00
13 Adam Dunn 3.00
14 Preston Wilson 2.00
15 Bo Jackson 3.00
16 Carlos Beltran 2.00
17 Tony Gwynn 4.00
18 Will Clark 3.00
19 Edgar Martinez 3.00
20 Scott Rolen 3.00
21 Alfonso Soriano 3.00
22 Randy Johnson 3.00
23 Chipper Jones 3.00
24 Andruw Jones 3.00
25 Javy Lopez 3.00
26 Curt Schilling 3.00
27 Manny Ramirez 5.00
28 Sammy Sosa 4.00
29 Greg Maddux 2.00
30 Todd Helton 3.00
31 Jeff Bagwell 3.00
32 Shawn Green 2.00
33 Mike Piazza 3.00
34 Jorge Posada 2.00
35 Gary Sheffield 3.00
36 Mike Mussina 3.00
37 Miguel Cabrera 3.00
38 Rickey Henderson 3.00
39 Albert Pujols 8.00
40 Vernon Wells 2.00
41 Fred Lynn 2.00
42 Alan Trammell 2.00
43 Lenny Dykstra 2.00
44 Dwight Gooden 2.00
45 Keith Hernandez 2.00
46 Luis Tiant 2.00
47 Orel Hershiser 2.00
48 George Foster 2.00
49 Darryl Strawberry 2.00
50 Marty Marion 2.00

Stars Signature

NM/M
Quantity produced listed
3 Andre Dawson/50 20.00
4 Don Mattingly/25 65.00
6 Garret Anderson/50 20.00
7 Dale Murphy/50 30.00
12 Magglio Ordonez/25 40.00
13 Adam Dunn/50 40.00
14 Preston Wilson/50 15.00
16 Carlos Beltran/50 40.00
18 Will Clark/25 40.00
19 Edgar Martinez/50 40.00
20 Scott Rolen/50 40.00
37 Miguel Cabrera/50 40.00
40 Vernon Wells/25 25.00
41 Fred Lynn/50 10.00
42 Alan Trammell/50 20.00
43 Lenny Dykstra/50 20.00
44 Dwight Gooden/50 20.00
45 Keith Hernandez/50 20.00
46 Luis Tiant/50 15.00
47 Orel Hershiser/50 25.00
48 George Foster/50 15.00
49 Darryl Strawberry/50 20.00

2004 Leaf Certified Materials

NM/M
Complete Set (300):
Common Player: .50
Common (201-211): 4.00
Common (212-240): 4.00
Production 500
Common Auto (241-300): 8.00
Pack (5): 10.00
Box (10): 85.00

1 A.J. Burnett .50
2 Adam Dunn 1.00
3 Adam LaRoche .50
4 Adam Loewen .50
5 Adrian Beltre .75
6 Al Leiter .50
7 Albert Pujols 3.00
8 Alex Rodriguez 3.00
9 Alexis Rios .50
10 Alfonso Soriano 1.50
11 Andruw Jones 1.00
12 Andy Pettitte .75
13 Angel Berroa .50
14 Aramis Ramirez .75
15 Aubrey Huff .50
16 Austin Kearns .50
17 Barry Larkin .75
18 Barry Zito .75
19 Ben Sheets .75
21 Bernie Williams .75
21 Bobby Abreu .75
22 Brad Penny .50
23 Brad Wilkerson .50
24 Brandon Webb .50
25 Brendan Harris .50
26 Bret Boone .50
27 Brett Myers .50
28 Bubba Crosby .50
29 Brian Giles .50
30 Chad Cordero .50
31 Bubba Nelson .50
32 Byron Gettis .50
33 C.C. Sabathia .50
34 Carl Crawford .75
35 Carl Everett .50
36 Carlos Beltran .75
37 Carlos Delgado .75
38 Carlos Lee .50
39 Chad Gaudin .50
40 Cliff Lee .50
41 Chipper Jones 1.50

42 Cliff Floyd .50
43 Clint Barmes .50
44 Corey Patterson .75
45 Craig Biggio .75
46 Curt Schilling 1.00
47 Dan Haren .50
48 Darin Erstad .50
49 David Ortiz 1.00
50 Delmon Young .50
51 Derek Jeter 4.00
52 Dewon Brazelton .50
53 Dontrelle Willis .75
54 Edgar Martinez .75
55 Edgar Renteria .75
56 Edwin Almonte .50
57 Edwin Jackson .50
58 Eric Chavez .75
59 Eric Hinske .50
60 Eric Munson .50
61 Erubiel Durazo .50
62 Frank Thomas 1.00
63 Fred McGriff .50
64 Freddy Garcia .50
65 Garret Anderson .75
66 Garrett Atkins .50
67 Gary Sheffield .75
68 Geoff Jenkins .50
69 Greg Maddux 2.00
70 Hank Blalock 1.00
71 Hee Seop Choi .50
72 Hideki Matsui 2.50
73 Hideo Nomo .75
74 Craig Wilson .50
75 Ichiro Suzuki 2.50
76 Ivan Rodriguez 1.00
77 J.D. Drew .50
78 John Lackey .50
79 Jacque Jones .50
80 Jae Weong Seo .50
81 Jamie Moyer .50
82 Jason Giambi .75
83 Jason Jennings .50
84 Jason Kendall .50
85 Jason Varitek .75
86 Javier Vazquez .50
87 Javy Lopez .75
88 Jay Gibbons .50
89 Jay Payton .50
90 Jeff Bagwell 1.00
91 Jeff Baker .50
92 Jeff Kent .50
93 Jeremy Bonderman .50
94 Milton Bradley .50
95 Jerome Williams .50
96 Jim Edmonds .75
97 Jim Thome 1.50
98 Jody Gerut .50
99 Joe Borchard .50
100 Joe Crede .50
101 Johan Santana .50
102 John Olerud .50
103 John Smoltz .75
104 Johnny Damon .75
105 Jorge Posada .75
106 Jose Castillo .50
107 Jose Reyes .75
108 Jose Vidro .50
109 Josh Beckett 1.00
110 Josh Phelps .50
111 Juan Encarnacion .50
112 Juan Gonzalez 1.00
113 Junior Spivey .50
114 Kazuhisa Ishii .50
115 Kenny Lofton .50
116 Kerry Wood 1.50
117 Kevin Millwood .50
118 Kevin Youkilis .50
119 Lance Berkman .50
120 Larry Bigbie .50
121 Larry Walker .75
122 Luis Castillo .50
123 Luis Gonzalez .50
124 Luis Matos .50
125 Lyle Overbay .50
126 Magglio Ordonez .75
127 Manny Ramirez 1.00
128 Marcus Giles .50
129 Mariano Rivera .75
130 Mark Buehrle .50
131 Mark Mulder .75
132 Mark Prior 1.00
133 Mark Teixeira .75
134 Marlon Byrd .50
135 Matt Morris .50
136 Miguel Cabrera 1.00
137 Mike Lowell .50
138 Mike Mussina .75
139 Mike Piazza 2.00
140 Morgan Ensberg .50
141 Mike Sweeney .50
142 Nick Johnson .50
143 Nomar Garciaparra 2.00
144 Omar Vizquel .50
145 Orlando Cabrera .50
146 Orlando Hudson .50
147 Pat Burrell .50
148 Paul Konerko .50
149 Paul LoDuca .50
150 Pedro J. Martinez 1.50
151 Jermaine Dye .50
152 Preston Wilson .50
153 Rafael Furcal .50
154 Rafael Palmeiro 1.00
155 Randy Johnson 1.50
156 Rich Aurilia .50
157 Rich Harden .50
158 Richard Hidalgo .50

160 Richie Sexson .75
161 Rickie Weeks .75
162 Roberto Alomar .75
163 Rocco Baldelli .50
164 Roger Clemens 3.00
165 Roy Halladay .50
166 Roy Oswalt .50
167 Ryan Howard 1.50
168 Ryan Klesko .50
169 Rodrigo Lopez .50
170 Sammy Sosa 2.50
171 Scott Podsednik .50
172 Scott Rolen 1.50
173 Sean Burroughs .50
174 Sean Casey .50
175 Shannon Stewart .50
176 Shawn Green .75
177 Shea Hillenbrand .50
178 Shigetoshi Hasegawa .50
179 Steve Finley .50
180 Tim Hudson .75
181 Todd Helton 1.00
182 Tom Glavine .75
183 Torii Hunter .75
184 Trot Nixon .75
185 Troy Glaus .75
186 Vernon Wells .75
187 Victor Martinez .75
188 Vladimir Guerrero 1.50
189 Wade Miller .50
190 Brandon Larson .50
191 Travis Hafner .50
192 Tim Salmon .75
193 Tim Redding .50
194 Runelvys Hernandez .50
195 Ramon Nivar .50
196 Moises Alou .75
197 Michael Young .50
198 Laynce Nix .50
199 Tino Martinez .50
200 Randall Simon .50
201 Roger Clemens/SP 8.00
202 Greg Maddux/SP 8.00
203 Vladimir Guerrero/SP 6.00
204 Miguel Tejada/SP 4.00
205 Kevin Brown/SP 4.00
206 Jason Giambi/SP 5.00
207 Curt Schilling/SP 5.00
208 Alex Rodriguez/SP 8.00
209 Alfonso Soriano/SP 6.00
210 Ivan Rodriguez/SP 6.00
211 Rafael Palmeiro/SP 6.00
212 Gary Carter 4.00
213 Duke Snider 5.00
214 Whitey Ford 5.00
215 Bob Feller 4.00
216 Reggie Jackson 5.00
217 Ryne Sandberg 10.00
218 Dale Murphy 4.00
219 Tony Gwynn 6.00
220 Don Mattingly 10.00
221 Mike Schmidt 10.00
222 Rickey Henderson 5.00
223 Cal Ripken Jr. 20.00
224 Nolan Ryan 15.00
225 George Brett 10.00
226 Bob Gibson 5.00
227 Lou Brock 4.00
228 Andre Dawson 4.00
229 Rod Carew 4.00
230 Wade Boggs 4.00
231 Roberto Clemente 12.00
232 Roy Campanella 5.00
233 Babe Ruth 15.00
234 Lou Gehrig 10.00
235 Ty Cobb 8.00
236 Roger Maris 6.00
237 Satchel Paige 6.00
238 Ernie Banks 6.00
239 Ted Williams 10.00
240 Stan Musial 6.00
241 Hector Gimenez/Auto./500 RC 8.00
242 Justin Germano/Auto./500 RC 8.00
243 Ian Snell/Auto./500 25.00
244 Graham Koonce/Auto./500 8.00
245 Jose Capellan/Auto./500 RC 25.00
246 Onil Joseph/Auto./200 RC 40.00
247 Shingo Takatsu/Auto./500 RC 8.00
248 Carlos Hines/Auto./500 RC 8.00
249 Lincoln Holdzkom/Auto./500 RC 8.00
250 Mike Gosling/Auto./500 8.00
251 Edwardo Sierra/Auto./500 RC 10.00
252 Renyel Pinto/Auto./500 RC 10.00
253 Merkin Valdez/Auto./500 RC 12.00
254 Angel Chavez/Auto./500 RC 8.00
255 Ivan Ochoa/Auto./1000 RC 8.00
256 Greg Dobbs/Auto./300 RC 8.00
257 William Bergolla/Auto./500 RC 8.00
258 Aarom Baldiris/Auto./500 RC 10.00
259 Kazuo Matsui/500 RC 12.00

260	Carlos Vasquez/Auto./500 RC	8.00
261	Freddy Guzman/Auto./500 RC	8.00
262	Akinori Otsuka/Auto./200 RC	40.00
263	Mariano Gomez/Auto./200 RC	8.00
264	Nick Regilio/Auto./500 RC	8.00
265	Jamie Brown/Auto./500 RC	8.00
266	Shawn Hill/Auto./500 RC	8.00
267	Roberto Novoa/Auto./500 RC	8.00
268	Sean Henn/Auto./500	10.00
269	Ramon Ramirez/Auto./500 RC	8.00
270	Ronny Cedeno/Auto./1000 RC	8.00
271	Ryan Wing/Auto./400	8.00
272	Ruddy Yan/Auto./500 RC	8.00
273	Fernando Nieve/Auto./500 RC	8.00
274	Rusty Tucker/Auto./500 RC	8.00
275	Jason Bartlett/Auto./500 RC	8.00
276	Mike Rouse/Auto./500 RC	8.00
277	Dennis Sarfate/Auto./500 RC	8.00
278	Cory Sullivan/Auto./500 RC	8.00
279	Casey Daigle/Auto./250 RC	8.00
280	Chris Shelton/Auto./400 RC	25.00
281	Jesse Harper/Auto./400 RC	8.00
282	Mike Wuertz/Auto./500 RC	12.00
283	Tim Bausher/Auto./400 RC	8.00
284	Jorge Sequea/Auto./500 RC	8.00
285	Josh Labandeira/Auto./100 RC	12.00
286	Justin Leone/Auto./500 RC	12.00
287	Tim Bittner/Auto./500 RC	8.00
288	Andres Blanco/Auto./500 RC	8.00
289	Kevin Cave/Auto./1000 RC	8.00
290	Mike Johnston/Auto./1000 RC	8.00
291	Jason Szuminski/Auto./500 RC	8.00
292	Shawn Camp/500 RC	8.00
293	Colby Miller/Auto./500 RC	8.00
294	Jake Woods/Auto./500	8.00
295	Ryan Meaux/Auto./500 RC	8.00
296	Donald Kelly/Auto./500 RC	8.00
297	Edwin Moreno/Auto./500 RC	8.00
298	Phil Stockman/Auto./500 RC	8.00
299	Jorge Vasquez/500 RC	8.00
300	Kazuhito Tadano/Auto./500	25.00

Fabric of the Game

		NM/M
	Common Player:	6.00
	Quantity produced listed	
	AL/NL:	.75-1.5X
	Production 1-100	
	Jersey Number:	.75-2X
	Production 1-72	
	Position:	.75-2X
	Production 1-100	
	Prime:	No Pricing
	Production One Set	
	Game Reward:	.75-2X
	Production 1-50	
	Jersey Year:	.75-2X
	Production 1-99	
	Game Stats:	.75-2X
	Production 1-66	
	No Pricing production 20 or less.	
n	Ozzie Smith/Jsy/100	20.00
2	Al Kaline/Pants/100	15.00
3	Alan Trammell/Jsy/100	10.00
4	Albert Pujols/Jsy/100	20.00
5	Alex Rodriguez/Jsy/100	12.00
6	Alex Rodriguez/Jsy/100	12.00
7	Andre Dawson/Jsy/100	8.00
8	Andre Dawson/Pants/100	8.00
11	Billy Williams/Jsy/100	10.00
12	Bo Jackson/Jsy/100	20.00
13	Bob Feller/Jsy/50	15.00
14	Bob Gibson/Jsy/50	15.00
15	Bobby Doerr/Jsy/100	8.00
16	Brooks Robinson/Jsy/25	25.00
17	Cal Ripken Jr./Jsy/100	30.00
18	Carl Yastrzemski/Jsy/100	20.00
19	Carlton Fisk/Jsy/100	10.00
20	Dale Murphy/Jsy/100	12.00
21	Darryl Strawberry/Pants/100	10.00
22	Darryl Strawberry/Jsy/100	10.00
23	Dave Parker/Jsy/100	8.00
24	Dave Parker/Jsy/100	8.00
25	Dave Winfield/Jsy/50	8.00
26	Dave Winfield/Jsy/100	10.00
27	Deion Sanders/Jsy/25	25.00
28	Derek Jeter/Jsy/100	20.00
29	Don Drysdale/Jsy/100	15.00
30	Don Mattingly/Jsy/100	20.00
31	Don Mattingly/Jkt/100	20.00
32	Don Sutton/Jsy/100	8.00
33	Duke Snider/Jsy/100	12.00
34	Dwight Gooden/Jsy/100	8.00
35	Early Wynn/Jsy/100	10.00
36	Eddie Mathews/Jsy/100	20.00
37	Eddie Murray/Jsy/100	15.00
38	Eddie Murray/Jsy/100	15.00
39	Enos Slaughter/Jsy/100	10.00
40	Eric Davis/Jsy/50	10.00
41	Ernie Banks/Jsy/100	15.00
42	Fergie Jenkins/Pants/100	10.00
43	Frank Robinson/Jsy/100	10.00
45	Gary Carter/Jsy/100	10.00
46	Gaylord Perry/Jsy/25	15.00
47	George Brett White/Jsy/100	20.00
48	George Foster/Jsy/100	8.00
49	Hal Newhouser/Jsy/100	8.00
50	Harmon Killebrew/Jsy/25	30.00
51	Harmon Killebrew/Pants/25	30.00
52	Harold Baines/Jsy/100	10.00
53	Hoyt Wilhelm/Jsy/50	10.00
54	Jack Morris/Jsy/100	8.00
56	Jim "Catfish" Hunter/Jsy/100	10.00
57	Jim Palmer/Jsy/100	10.00
58	Jim Rice/Jsy/100	10.00
59	Joe Carter/Jsy/100	8.00
60	Joe Morgan/Jsy/100	10.00
61	Tommy Lasorda/Jsy/100	8.00
62	Johnny Mize/Pants/100	12.00
63	Johnny Bench/Jsy/100	15.00
64	Jose Canseco/Jsy/100	10.00
65	Juan Marichal/Jsy/100	10.00
66	Kirby Puckett/Jsy/100	15.00
67	Lou Boudreau/Jsy/100	10.00
68	Lou Brock/Jsy/100	10.00
71	Luis Aparicio/Jsy/100	10.00
72	Luis Aparicio/Pants/100	10.00
73	Mariano Rivera/Jsy/100	10.00
74	Mark Grace/Jsy/100	12.00
75	Mark Prior/Jsy/100	8.00
76	Mel Ott/Jsy/25	60.00
77	Mel Ott/Pants/25	60.00
78	Mike Schmidt/Jsy/100	20.00
79	Mike Schmidt/Pants/100	20.00
80	Mike Schmidt/Jkt/100	20.00
81	Nolan Ryan Angels/Jsy/100	25.00
82	Nolan Ryan Angels/Jkt/100	25.00
83	Nolan Ryan Astros/Jsy/100	25.00
84	Nolan Ryan Astros/Jkt/100	25.00
85	Nolan Ryan Rgr/Jsy/100	25.00
86	Nolan Ryan Rgr/Pants/100	25.00
88	Ozzie Smith/Jsy/100	15.00
89	Paul Molitor/Jsy/100	12.00
90	Pee Wee Reese/Jsy/100	15.00
91	Phil Niekro/Jsy/100	8.00
92	Phil Rizzuto/Jsy/100	15.00
93	Phil Rizzuto/Pants/100	15.00
94	Red Schoendienst/Jsy/100	10.00
95	Reggie Jackson/Jkt/100	15.00
96	Reggie Jackson/Jsy/100	15.00
97	Richie Ashburn/Jsy/100	20.00
98	Rickey Henderson/Jsy/50	15.00
99	Roberto Clemente/Jsy/100	75.00
100	Robin Yount/Jsy/100	15.00
101	Rod Carew/Jsy/100	10.00
102	Rod Carew/Pants/100	10.00
103	Rod Carew/Jkt/100	10.00
104	Rod Carew/Jsy/100	10.00
105	Roger Clemens/Jsy/100	15.00
106	Roger Clemens/Jsy/100	15.00
107	Roger Maris/Jsy/100	30.00
108	Roger Maris/Pants/100	30.00
109	Roger Maris/Jsy/100	30.00
110	Roy Campanella/Pants/100	15.00
111	Ryne Sandberg/Jsy/100	25.00
112	Stan Musial/Jsy/50	30.00
113	Steve Carlton/Jsy/100	10.00
114	Ted Williams/Jsy/100	75.00
115	Ted Williams/Jkt/100	75.00
116	Thurman Munson/Jsy/100	25.00
117	Thurman Munson/Pants/100	25.00
118	Tony Gwynn/Jsy/100	15.00
119	Wade Boggs/Jsy/100	15.00
120	Wade Boggs/Jsy/100	10.00
121	Warren Spahn/Jsy/100	15.00
122	Warren Spahn/Pants/100	15.00
123	Whitey Ford/Jsy/100	15.00
124	Whitey Ford/Pants/100	15.00
125	Will Clark/Jsy/100	15.00
126	Willie McCovey/Jsy/100	10.00
127	Willie Stargell/Jsy/100	15.00
128	Yogi Berra/Jsy/25	35.00
129	Frankie Frisch/Jkt/100	10.00
130	Marty Marion/Jsy/100	8.00
131	Tommy John/Pants/100	8.00
132	Chipper Jones/Jsy/100	10.00
133	Sammy Sosa/Jsy/100	15.00
134	Rickey Henderson/Jsy/100	10.00
135	Mike Piazza/Jsy/100	12.00
136	Mike Piazza/Jsy/100	12.00
137	Nomar Garciaparra/Jsy/100	15.00
138	Hideo Nomo/Jsy/100	6.00
139	Hideo Nomo/Jsy/50	15.00
140	Randy Johnson/Jsy/100	10.00
141	Randy Johnson/Jsy/100	10.00
142	Randy Johnson/Pants/100	10.00
143	Jason Giambi/Jsy/100	6.00
144	Jason Giambi/Jsy/100	6.00
145	Curt Schilling/Jsy/100	6.00
146	Dennis Eckersley/Jsy/100	10.00
147	Carlton Fisk/Jkt/100	10.00
148	Tom Seaver/Jsy/25	30.00
149	Joe Torre/Jsy/100	10.00
150	Pedro Martinez/Jsy/100	10.00
151	Albert Pujols/Jsy/100	20.00
152	Andre Dawson/Jsy/100	10.00
153	Bert Blyleven/Jsy/100	8.00
154	Bo Jackson/Jsy/100	15.00
155	Cal Ripken Jr./Pants/100	35.00
156	Carlton Fisk/Jsy/100	10.00
157	Curt Schilling/Jsy/100	6.00
158	Darryl Strawberry/Jsy/100	
159	Dave Concepcion/Jsy/100	8.00
160	Dwight Evans/Jsy/100	
161	Ernie Banks/Pants/100	15.00
163	Gary Carter/Pants/100	8.00
164	Gary Sheffield/Jsy/100	6.00
165	George Brett/Jsy/100	20.00
166	Greg Maddux/Jsy/100	10.00
167	Ivan Rodriguez/Jsy/100	10.00
168	Joe Morgan/Jsy/100	10.00
169	Jose Canseco/Jsy/100	10.00
170	Juan Gonzalez/Jsy/100	8.00
171	Juan Gonzalez/Jsy/100	8.00
172	Keith Hernandez/Jsy/100	10.00
173	Ken Boyer/Jsy/100	20.00
174	Kerry Wood/Jsy/100	10.00
175	Lee Smith/Jsy/100	8.00
176	Luis Tiant/Jsy/100	8.00
177	Manny Ramirez/Jsy/100	8.00
178	Mark Grace/Jsy/100	12.00
179	Matt Williams/Jsy/100	
180	Miguel Tejada/Jsy/100	6.00
181	Mike Mussina/Jsy/100	10.00
182	Mike Piazza/Jsy/100	12.00
183	Nomar Garciaparra/Jsy/100	15.00
184	Pedro Martinez/Jsy/100	10.00
185	Rafael Palmeiro/Jsy/100	8.00
186	Reggie Jackson/Pants/100	12.00
187	Rickey Henderson/Jsy/100	10.00
188	Rickey Henderson/Pants/100	10.00
189	Rickey Henderson/Jsy/100	10.00
190	Sammy Sosa/Jsy/100	15.00
191	Satchel Paige/Jsy/100	60.00
192	Shawn Green/Jsy/100	6.00
193	Stan Musial/Jsy/50	35.00
194	Steve Carlton/Jsy/100	10.00
195	Steve Garvey/Jsy/100	8.00
196	Tom Seaver/Jsy/100	12.00
197	Tony Gwynn/Pants/100	12.00
198	Vladimir Guerrero/Jsy/100	8.00
199	Wade Boggs/Jsy/100	10.00
200	Willie Stargell/Jsy/100	10.00

Fabric of the Game Autograph

No Pricing	
Production 1-10	
AL/NL Auto:	No Pricing
Production 1-25	
Jersey Number Auto.:	No Pricing
Production 1-8	
Jersey Year Auto.:	No Pricing
Production 1-8	
Position Auto.:	No Pricing
Production 1-8	
Reward Auto.:	No Pricing
Production 1-8	
Stats Auto.:	No Pricing
Production 1-8	

Mirror Black

No Pricing
Production One Set

Mirror Blue

Stars (1-200):	3-5X
Mirror Blue (201-240):	1-2X
Auto. (241-300):	.5X
No Auto. (241-300):	1X
Production 50 Sets	

Mirror Emerald

No Pricing
Production 5 Sets

Mirror Gold

Mirror Gold (1-200):	4-8X
Mirror Gold (201-240):	1.5-2X
Mirror Gold (241-300):	No Pricing
Production 25 Sets	

Mirror Red

Mirror Red (1-200):	2-4X
Mirror Red (201-240):	.5-1X
Mirror Red (241-300):	.5X
Production 100 Sets	

Mirror White

Mirror White (1-200):	2-4X
Mirror White (201-240):	.5-1X
Mirror White (241-300):	.5X
Production 100 Sets	

Mirror Autograph Black

No Pricing
Production One Set

Mirror Autograph Blue

Mirror Auto Blue: .5-1.5X Red Auto.
Production 1-100
No pricing 25 or less

Mirror Autograph Emerald

No Pricing
Production 1-5

Mirror Autograph Gold

No Pricing
Production 1-25

Mirror Autograph Red

		NM/M
	Quantity produced listed	
3	Adam LaRoche/250	8.00
4	Adam Loewen/250	8.00
9	Alexis Rios/250	15.00
10	Alfonso Soriano/25	50.00
11	Andruw Jones/25	25.00
12	Andy Pettitte/25	35.00
13	Angel Berroa/100	10.00
14	Aramis Ramirez/100	25.00
15	Aubrey Huff/250	10.00
16	Austin Kearns/200	12.00
17	Barry Larkin/25	40.00
22	Brad Penny/25	15.00
25	Brandon Webb/250	8.00
25	Brendan Harris/250	10.00
28	Brett Myers/100	8.00
29	Bubba Crosby/250	8.00
30	Chad Cordero/250	8.00
31	Bubba Nelson/250	8.00
32	Byron Gettis/250	8.00
36	Carlos Beltran/250	25.00
38	Carlos Lee/250	10.00
39	Chad Gaudin/100	8.00
40	Cliff Lee/250	8.00
43	Clint Barmes/100	15.00
47	Dan Haren/250	8.00
49	David Ortiz/250	40.00
50	Delmon Young/50	30.00
52	Dewon Brazelton/250	8.00
53	Dontrelle Willis/100	20.00
56	Edwin Almonte/250	8.00
57	Edwin Jackson/250	8.00
58	Eric Chavez/25	30.00
62	Frank Thomas/50	50.00
65	Garret Anderson/250	15.00
67	Gary Sheffield/50	30.00
74	Hank Blalock/250	30.00
74	Craig Wilson/250	10.00
78	John Lackey/250	8.00
79	Jacque Jones/250	8.00
80	Jae Weong Seo/100	15.00
85	Melvin Mora/250	15.00
86	Jason Varitek/100	40.00
89	Jay Gibbons/250	8.00
90	Jay Payton/250	8.00
91	Jeff Bagwell/50	50.00
92	Jeff Baker/25	20.00
96	Jerome Williams/250	15.00
97	Jim Edmonds/250	35.00
99	Jody Gerut/250	8.00
100	Joe Borchard/250	10.00
101	Joe Crede/50	15.00
102	Johan Santana/250	25.00
106	Jorge Posada/50	50.00
107	Jose Castillo/250	8.00
109	Jose Vidro/250	

110	Josh Beckett/25	50.00
113	Juan Gonzalez/25	40.00
114	Junior Spivey/25	15.00
117	Kerry Wood/50	50.00
119	Kevin Youkilis/250	10.00
120	Lance Berkman/25	30.00
121	Larry Bigbie/250	12.00
123	Luis Castillo/25	15.00
125	Luis Matos/250	8.00
127	Magglio Ordonez/250	15.00
129	Marcus Giles/250	12.00
131	Mark Buehrle/250	12.00
132	Mark Mulder/250	20.00
133	Mark Prior/100	40.00
134	Mark Teixeira/100	25.00
135	Marlon Byrd/250	8.00
137	Miguel Cabrera/250	30.00
140	Mike Piazza/25	125.00
142	Morgan Ensberg/250	8.00
146	Orlando Cabrera/25	20.00
150	Paul LoDuca/25	25.00
152	Jermaine Dye/250	10.00
153	Preston Wilson/250	10.00
154	Rafael Furcal/100	12.00
157	Rich Aurilia/25	15.00
158	Rich Harden/203	15.00
165	Roy Halladay/50	15.00
166	Roy Oswalt/50	15.00
167	Ryan Howard/100	80.00
169	Rodrigo Lopez/250	8.00
170	Sammy Sosa/50	100.00
171	Scott Podsednik/250	15.00
172	Scott Rolen/100	40.00
175	Shannon Stewart/100	8.00
176	Shawn Green/25	30.00
177	Shea Hillenbrand/250	10.00
178	Shigetoshi Hasegawa/250	40.00
179	Steve Finley/100	20.00
183	Torii Hunter/250	15.00
184	Trot Nixon/250	20.00
187	Victor Martinez/250	20.00
188	Vladimir Guerrero/50	75.00
190	Brandon Larson/200	10.00
191	Travis Hafner/250	15.00
197	Michael Young/250	15.00
212	Gary Carter/250	15.00
213	Duke Snider/250	25.00
214	Whitey Ford /50	40.00
215	Bob Feller /250	20.00
216	Reggie Jackson/50	50.00
217	Ryne Sandberg/50	60.00
218	Dale Murphy/50	30.00
219	Tony Gwynn/50	50.00
220	Don Mattingly/50	75.00
221	Mike Schmidt/50	75.00
222	Rickey Henderson/50	50.00
223	Cal Ripken Jr./50	180.00
224	Nolan Ryan/50	100.00
225	George Brett/50	75.00
226	Bob Gibson/100	25.00
227	Lou Brock/100	25.00
228	Andre Dawson/250	15.00
229	Rod Carew/50	25.00
230	Wade Boggs/50	25.00
238	Ernie Banks/50	60.00
240	Stan Musial/100	60.00
241	Hector Gimenez/200	8.00
242	Justin Germano/100	8.00
243	Ian Snell/100	25.00
244	Graham Koonce/200	8.00
245	Jose Capellan/100	40.00
246	Onil Joseph/200	8.00
247	Shingo Takatsu/50	50.00
248	Carlos Hines/200	8.00
249	Lincoln Holdzkom/100	8.00
251	Mike Gosling/100	10.00
251	Edwardo Sierra/200	10.00
252	Renyel Pinto/200	10.00
253	Merkin Valdez/200	12.00
254	Angel Chavez/200	8.00
255	Ivan Ochoa/200	8.00
257	William Bergolla/200	8.00
258	Aarom Baldiris/100	10.00
260	Carlos Vasquez/200	8.00
261	Freddy Guzman/200	8.00
262	Akinori Otsuka/50	50.00
264	Nick Regilio/200	8.00
266	Shawn Hill/200	8.00
268	Sean Henn/200	10.00
269	Ramon Ramirez/200	8.00
270	Ronny Cedeno/200	8.00
273	Fernando Nieve/200	8.00
274	Rusty Tucker/200	8.00
275	Jason Bartlett/200	8.00
276	Mike Rouse/200	8.00
277	Dennis Sarfate/200	8.00
278	Cory Sullivan/200	8.00
282	Mike Wuertz/200	8.00
284	Jorge Sequea/100	8.00
287	Tim Bittner/250	8.00
288	Andres Blanco/250	12.00
289	Kevin Cave/100	10.00
290	Mike Johnston/100	8.00
293	Colby Miller/100	8.00
294	Jake Woods/100	10.00
295	Ryan Meaux/200	8.00
296	Donald Kelly/100	8.00
297	Edwin Moreno/100	8.00
298	Phil Stockman/100	8.00

Mirror Autograph White

White Auto.	
(1-240):	.75-1.5X Red Auto
White Auto	
(241-300):	.5-1X Red Auto

Production 1-100
No pricing 25 or less.

Mirror Bat Blue

NM/M

Blue Bat: 1-1.5X Red price
Production 25-100
Cards listed don't have a red version.
217	Ryne Sandberg/50	40.00
219	Tony Gwynn/50	20.00
221	Mike Schmidt/50	25.00
223	Cal Ripken Jr./50	50.00
224	Nolan Ryan/50	35.00
225	George Brett/50	30.00

Mirror Bat Gold

NM/M

Gold Bat: 1.5-3X Red price
Production 25 Sets
Cards listed don't have a red version.
69	Greg Maddux	25.00
217	Ryne Sandberg	50.00
219	Tony Gwynn	25.00
221	Mike Schmidt	40.00
223	Cal Ripken Jr.	90.00
224	Nolan Ryan	60.00
225	George Brett	40.00
231	Roberto Clemente	90.00
233	Babe Ruth	200.00
234	Lou Gehrig	150.00
235	Ty Cobb	125.00
236	Roger Maris	40.00
239	Ted Williams	80.00

Mirror Bat Red

NM/M

Common Player: 4.00
Quantity produced listed
Black: No Pricing
Production One Set
Emerald: No Pricing
Production 5 Sets
2	Adam Dunn/150	6.00
3	Adam LaRoche/250	4.00
5	Adrian Beltre/150	4.00
7	Albert Pujols/150	15.00
8	Alex Rodriguez/250	10.00
9	Alexis Rios/250	4.00
10	Alfonso Soriano/150	8.00
11	Andruw Jones/150	8.00
12	Andy Pettitte/150	6.00
13	Angel Berroa/150	4.00
15	Aubrey Huff/150	4.00
16	Austin Kearns/150	4.00
17	Barry Larkin/150	6.00
20	Bernie Williams/150	4.00
21	Bobby Abreu/150	6.00
24	Brandon Webb/150	4.00
25	Brendan Harris/250	4.00
26	Bret Boone/250	4.00
29	Brian Giles/250	4.00
35	Carl Everett/250	4.00
36	Carlos Beltran/150	6.00
37	Carlos Delgado/150	6.00
38	Carlos Lee/150	4.00
41	Chipper Jones/150	8.00
42	Cliff Floyd/250	4.00
43	Clint Barmes/250	4.00
44	Corey Patterson/250	6.00
45	Craig Biggio/150	6.00
47	Dan Haren/150	4.00
48	Darin Erstad/150	4.00
49	David Ortiz/250	4.00
50	Delmon Young/250	4.00
51	Derek Jeter/150	20.00
54	Edgar Martinez/150	6.00
55	Edgar Renteria/150	4.00
59	Eric Hinske/150	4.00
60	Eric Munson/250	4.00
61	Erubiel Durazo/250	4.00
62	Frank Thomas/150	8.00
63	Fred McGriff/150	4.00
65	Garret Anderson/150	6.00
67	Gary Sheffield/250	4.00
68	Geoff Jenkins/150	4.00
70	Hank Blalock/150	8.00
71	Hee Seop Choi/250	4.00
73	Hideo Nomo/150	8.00
76	Ivan Rodriguez /250	8.00
77	J.D. Drew/250	6.00
79	Jacque Jones/150	4.00
82	Jason Giambi/150	6.00
83	Jason Jennings/150	4.00
86	Jason Varitek/150	6.00
88	Javy Lopez/250	6.00
89	Jay Gibbons/150	4.00
91	Jeff Bagwell/150	8.00
92	Jeff Baker/250	4.00
93	Jeff Kent/150	4.00
97	Jim Edmonds/150	6.00
98	Jim Thome/150	8.00
100	Joe Borchard/250	4.00
101	Joe Crede/250	4.00
103	John Olerud/250	4.00
105	Johnny Damon/250	4.00
106	Jorge Posada/150	6.00
107	Jose Castillo/250	4.00
108	Jose Reyes/150	6.00
109	Jose Vidro/150	4.00
110	Josh Beckett/150	6.00
111	Josh Phelps/150	4.00
112	Juan Encarnacion/250	4.00
113	Juan Gonzalez/250	6.00
114	Junior Spivey/250	4.00
115	Kazuhisa Ishii/150	4.00
116	Kenny Lofton/250	4.00

117	Kerry Wood/150	8.00
119	Kevin Youkilis/250	4.00
121	Lance Berkman/150	4.00
122	Larry Walker/150	4.00
123	Luis Castillo/150	4.00
124	Luis Gonzalez/150	4.00
126	Lyle Overbay/250	4.00
127	Magglio Ordonez/250	4.00
128	Manny Ramirez/150	8.00
129	Marcus Giles/250	4.00
131	Mark Buehrle/150	4.00
132	Mark Mulder/150	6.00
133	Mark Prior/150	8.00
134	Mark Teixeira/150	6.00
135	Marlon Byrd/150	4.00
137	Miguel Cabrera/250	8.00
138	Mike Lowell/150	4.00
140	Mike Piazza/150	10.00
141	Mike Sweeney/150	4.00
143	Nick Johnson/250	4.00
144	Nomar Garciaparra/150	10.00
145	Omar Vizquel/150	4.00
146	Orlando Cabrera/250	4.00
147	Orlando Hudson/150	4.00
148	Pat Burrell/150	4.00
149	Paul Konerko/150	4.00
150	Paul LoDuca/150	4.00
152	Jermaine Dye/250	4.00
153	Preston Wilson/150	4.00
154	Rafael Furcal/150	4.00
155	Rafael Palmeiro/150	8.00
157	Rich Aurilia/250	4.00
159	Richard Hidalgo/250	4.00
160	Richie Sexson/250	4.00
161	Rickie Weeks/250	6.00
162	Roberto Alomar/250	4.00
163	Rocco Baldelli/150	4.00
164	Roger Clemens/250	12.00
168	Ryan Klesko/150	4.00
170	Sammy Sosa/150	12.00
174	Sean Casey/150	4.00
175	Shannon Stewart/150	4.00
176	Shawn Green/150	4.00
181	Todd Helton/150	8.00
183	Torii Hunter/150	6.00
184	Trot Nixon/150	4.00
185	Troy Glaus/150	6.00
186	Vernon Wells/150	6.00
187	Victor Martinez/250	4.00
188	Vladimir Guerrero/250	8.00
189	Wade Miller/250	4.00
190	Brandon Larson/175	4.00
191	Travis Hafner/150	6.00
192	Tim Salmon/150	6.00
195	Ramon Nivar/150	4.00
196	Moises Alou/250	4.00
197	Michael Young/250	4.00
198	Laynce Nix/250	4.00
199	Tino Martinez/250	4.00
200	Randall Simon/250	4.00
201	Roger Clemens/250	12.00
203	Vladimir Guerrero/150	10.00
204	Miguel Tejada/150	6.00
206	Jason Giambi/250	4.00
208	Alex Rodriguez/150	10.00
209	Alfonso Soriano/150	8.00
210	Ivan Rodriguez/150	6.00
211	Rafael Palmeiro/150	6.00
212	Gary Carter/150	6.00
216	Reggie Jackson/150	10.00
220	Don Mattingly/150	20.00
222	Rickey Henderson/150	8.00
227	Lou Brock/150	6.00
228	Andre Dawson/150	6.00
229	Rod Carew /150	8.00
230	Wade Boggs/150	6.00
240	Stan Musial/100	25.00

Mirror Bat White

NM/M

White Bat: .75-1X Red price
Production 25-200
Cards listed don't have a red version.
219	Tony Gwynn/100	15.00
221	Mike Schmidt/100	20.00
223	Cal Ripken Jr./100	40.00
224	Nolan Ryan/100	30.00
225	George Brett/100	20.00
231	Roberto Clemente/50	65.00
233	Babe Ruth/25	200.00
234	Lou Gehrig/25	150.00
235	Ty Cobb/25	125.00
236	Roger Maris/25	40.00
239	Ted Williams/25	80.00

Mirror Combo Red

		NM/M
	Common (2-211):	6.00
	Production 250	
	Common (212-239):	8.00
	Production 50-250	
	Black Prime: No Pricing	
	Production One Set	
2	Adam Dunn/Bat-Jsy	8.00
5	Adrian Beltre/Bat-Jsy	6.00
7	Albert Pujols/Bat-Jsy	25.00
11	Andruw Jones/Bat-Jsy	8.00
13	Angel Berroa/Bat-Pants	6.00
15	Aubrey Huff/Bat-Jsy	6.00
16	Austin Kearns/Bat-Jsy	6.00
17	Barry Larkin/Bat-Jsy	8.00
18	Barry Zito/Bat-Jsy	6.00
19	Ben Sheets/Bat-Jsy	6.00
20	Bernie Williams/Bat-Jsy	10.00
21	Bobby Abreu/Bat-Jsy	8.00
22	Brad Penny/Bat-Jsy	6.00
24	Brandon Webb/Bat-Jsy	6.00
26	Bret Boone/Bat-Jsy	6.00
36	Carlos Beltran/Bat-Jsy	8.00
37	Carlos Delgado/Bat-Jsy	8.00
38	Carlos Lee/Bat-Jsy	6.00
41	Chipper Jones/Bat-Jsy	10.00
45	Craig Biggio/Bat-Pants	6.00
47	Dan Haren/Bat-Jsy	6.00
51	Derek Jeter/Bat-Jsy	30.00
52	Dewon Brazelton/Glv-Jsy	6.00
54	Edgar Martinez/Bat-Jsy	8.00
55	Edgar Renteria/Bat-Jsy	8.00
58	Eric Chavez/Bat-Jsy	8.00
59	Eric Hinske/Bat-Jsy	6.00
62	Frank Thomas/Bat-Jsy	10.00
63	Fred McGriff/Bat-Jsy	6.00
65	Garret Anderson/Bat-Jsy	8.00
68	Geoff Jenkins/Bat-Jsy	6.00
70	Hank Blalock/Bat-Jsy	10.00
73	Hideo Nomo/Bat-Jsy	6.00
79	Jacque Jones/Bat-Jsy	6.00
82	Jason Giambi/Bat-Jsy	10.00
83	Jason Jennings/Bat-Jsy	6.00
86	Jason Varitek/Bat-Jsy	10.00
89	Jay Gibbons/Bat-Jsy	6.00
91	Jeff Bagwell/Bat-Jsy	10.00
93	Jeff Kent/Bat-Jsy	8.00
97	Jim Edmonds/Bat-Jsy	8.00
98	Jim Thome/Bat-Jsy	10.00
100	Joe Borchard/Bat-Jsy	6.00
103	John Olerud/Bat-Jsy	6.00
106	Jorge Posada/Bat-Jsy	8.00
108	Jose Reyes/Bat-Jsy	6.00
109	Jose Vidro/Bat-Jsy	6.00
110	Josh Beckett/Bat-Jsy	8.00
111	Josh Phelps/Bat-Jsy	6.00
115	Kazuhisa Ishii/Bat-Jsy	6.00
117	Kerry Wood/Bat-Jsy	12.00
120	Lance Berkman/Bat-Jsy	6.00
122	Larry Walker/Bat-Jsy	6.00
123	Luis Castillo/Bat-Jsy	6.00
124	Luis Gonzalez/Bat-Jsy	6.00
127	Magglio Ordonez/Bat-Jsy	6.00
128	Manny Ramirez/Bat-Jsy	10.00
131	Mark Buehrle/Bat-Jsy	6.00
132	Mark Mulder/Bat-Jsy	8.00
133	Mark Prior/Bat-Jsy	8.00
134	Mark Teixeira/Bat-Jsy	8.00
135	Marlon Byrd/Bat-Jsy	6.00
138	Mike Lowell/Bat-Jsy	6.00
140	Mike Piazza/Bat-Jsy	12.00
141	Mike Sweeney/Bat-Jsy	6.00
142	Morgan Ensberg/Bat-Jsy	6.00
144	Nomar Garciaparra/Bat-Jsy	12.00
145	Omar Vizquel/Bat-Jsy	6.00
147	Orlando Hudson/Bat-Jsy	6.00
148	Pat Burrell/Bat-Jsy	6.00
149	Paul Konerko/Bat-Jsy	6.00
150	Paul LoDuca/Bat-Jsy	6.00
151	Pedro J. Martinez/Bat-Jsy	10.00
153	Preston Wilson/Bat-Jsy	6.00
154	Rafael Furcal/Bat-Jsy	6.00
155	Rafael Palmeiro/Bat-Jsy	10.00
156	Randy Johnson/Bat-Jsy	12.00
159	Richard Hidalgo/Bat-Jsy	6.00
163	Rocco Baldelli/Bat-Jsy	6.00
166	Roy Oswalt/Bat-Jsy	6.00
168	Ryan Klesko/Bat-Jsy	6.00
170	Sammy Sosa/Bat-Jsy	15.00
172	Scott Rolen/Bat-Jsy	10.00

175	Shannon Stewart/Bat-Jsy	6.00
176	Shawn Green/Bat-Jsy	6.00
180	Tim Hudson/Bat-Jsy	8.00
181	Todd Helton/Bat-Jsy	10.00
182	Tom Glavine/Bat-Jsy	8.00
183	Torii Hunter/Bat-Jsy	8.00
184	Trot Nixon/Bat-Jsy	6.00
185	Troy Glaus/Bat-Jsy	6.00
186	Vernon Wells/Bat-Jsy	6.00
192	Tim Salmon/Bat-Jsy	6.00
195	Ramon Nivar/Bat-Jsy	6.00
201	Roger Clemens/Bat-Jsy	15.00
203	Vladimir Guerrero/Bat-Jsy	12.00
204	Miguel Tejada/Bat-Jsy	8.00
206	Jason Giambi/Bat-Jsy	8.00
207	Curt Schilling/Bat-Jsy	8.00
208	Alex Rodriguez/Bat-Jsy	12.00
209	Alfonso Soriano/Bat-Jsy	10.00
210	Ivan Rodriguez/Bat-Jsy	10.00
211	Rafael Palmeiro/Bat-Jsy	10.00
212	Gary Carter/Bat-Pants/250	8.00
216	Reggie Jackson/Bat-Jsy	12.00
217	Ryne Sandberg/Bat-Jsy/250	25.00
218	Dale Murphy/Bat-Jsy/250	6.00
219	Tony Gwynn/Bat-Jsy/250	12.00
220	Don Mattingly/Bat-Jsy/250	25.00
221	Mike Schmidt/Bat-Pants/250	25.00
222	Rickey Henderson/Bat-Jsy/250	10.00
223	Cal Ripken Jr./Bat-Jsy/250	35.00
224	Nolan Ryan/Bat-Jsy/250	35.00
225	George Brett/Bat-Jsy/250	35.00
227	Lou Brock/Bat-Jsy/250	8.00
228	Andre Dawson/Bat-Jsy/250	8.00
229	Rod Carew/Bat-Jkt/250	10.00
230	Wade Boggs/Bat-Jsy/250	8.00
231	Roberto Clemente/Bat-Jsy/100	100.00
232	Roy Campanella/Bat-Pants/100	15.00
233	Babe Ruth/Bat-Pants/50	350.00
234	Lou Gehrig/Bat-Pants/50	200.00
235	Ty Cobb/Bat-Pants/50	200.00
236	Roger Maris/Bat-Pants/100	50.00
238	Ernie Banks/Bat-Pants/100	15.00
239	Ted Williams/Bat-Jkt/100	85.00

Mirror Fabric Blue

NM/M

Blue: 1-1.5X Red price
Production 25-100
Cards listed don't have a red version.
217	Ryne Sandberg/25	25.00
219	Tony Gwynn/100	15.00
220	Don Mattingly/100	25.00
221	Mike Schmidt/100	20.00
223	Cal Ripken Jr./100	35.00
224	Nolan Ryan/100	25.00
225	George Brett/100	15.00
231	Roberto Clemente/25	90.00
233	Babe Ruth/25	240.00
234	Lou Gehrig/25	150.00
235	Ty Cobb/25	140.00
236	Roger Maris/25	50.00
237	Satchel Paige/25	90.00
239	Ted Williams/25	100.00

Mirror Fabric Gold

NM/M

Gold: 2-3X Red price

Production 10-25
No pricing 20 or less
Cards listed don't have red version.
217	Ryne Sandberg/25	45.00
219	Tony Gwynn/25	30.00
220	Don Mattingly/25	60.00
221	Mike Schmidt/25	40.00
223	Cal Ripken Jr./25	90.00
224	Nolan Ryan/25	60.00
225	George Brett/25	50.00

Mirror Fabric Red

NM/M

Common Player: 4.00
Quantity produced listed
1	A.J. Burnett/Jsy/150	4.00
2	Adam Dunn/Jsy/150	6.00
5	Adrian Beltre/Jsy/150	4.00
6	Al Leiter/Jsy/150	4.00
7	Albert Pujols/Jsy/150	15.00
11	Andruw Jones/Jsy/150	6.00
13	Angel Berroa/Pants/150	4.00
15	Aubrey Huff/Jsy/150	4.00
16	Austin Kearns/Jsy/150	4.00
17	Barry Larkin/Jsy/150	4.00
18	Barry Zito/Jsy/150	5.00
19	Ben Sheets/Jsy/150	4.00
20	Bernie Williams/Jsy/150	6.00
21	Bobby Abreu/Jsy/150	6.00
22	Brad Penny/Jsy/250	4.00
27	Brett Myers/Jsy/250	4.00
33	C.C. Sabathia/Jsy/150	4.00
34	Carl Crawford/Jsy/250	6.00
36	Carlos Beltran/Jsy/150	6.00
38	Carlos Lee/Jsy/250	4.00
39	Chad Gaudin/Jsy/150	4.00
41	Chipper Jones/Jsy/150	6.00
45	Craig Biggio/Pants/150	4.00
47	Dan Haren/Jsy/150	4.00
48	Darin Erstad/Jsy/250	4.00
51	Derek Jeter/Jsy/150	20.00
53	Dontrelle Willis/Jsy/250	6.00
54	Edgar Martinez/Jsy/150	6.00
55	Edgar Renteria/Jsy/150	6.00
58	Eric Chavez/Jsy/150	4.00
59	Eric Hinske/Jsy/150	4.00
62	Frank Thomas/Jsy/150	6.00
64	Freddy Garcia/Jsy/250	4.00
66	Garrett Atkins/Jsy/250	4.00
68	Geoff Jenkins/Jsy/150	4.00
70	Hank Blalock/Jsy/150	6.00
72	Hideki Matsui/Base/250	15.00
73	Hideo Nomo/Jsy/150	8.00
75	Ichiro Suzuki/Base/250	15.00
79	Jacque Jones/Jsy/150	4.00
81	Jamie Moyer/Jsy/250	4.00
82	Jason Giambi/Jsy/150	6.00
83	Jason Jennings/Jsy/150	4.00
84	Jason Kendall/Jsy/250	4.00
86	Jason Varitek/Jsy/150	6.00
89	Jay Gibbons/Jsy/150	4.00
91	Jeff Bagwell/Jsy/150	8.00
93	Jeff Kent/Jsy/150	4.00
96	Jerome Williams/Jsy/250	4.00
97	Jim Edmonds/Jsy/150	6.00
98	Jim Thome/Jsy/150	8.00
102	Jose Santana/Jsy/250	4.00
103	John Olerud/Jsy/250	4.00
104	John Smoltz/Jsy/150	4.00
108	Jose Reyes/Jsy/150	6.00
109	Jose Vidro/Jsy/150	4.00
110	Josh Beckett/Jsy/150	6.00
111	Josh Phelps/Jsy/150	4.00
115	Kazuhisa Ishii/Jsy/150	4.00
117	Kerry Wood/Jsy/150	6.00
118	Kevin Millwood/Jsy/250	4.00
120	Lance Berkman/Jsy/150	4.00
121	Larry Bigbie/Jsy/250	4.00
122	Larry Walker/Jsy/150	4.00
123	Luis Castillo/Jsy/150	4.00
124	Luis Gonzalez/Jsy/150	4.00
130	Mariano Rivera/Jsy/150	6.00
131	Mark Buehrle/Jsy/150	4.00
133	Mark Prior/Jsy/150	8.00
135	Marlon Byrd/Jsy/150	4.00
136	Matt Morris/Jsy/250	4.00

139	Mike Mussina/Jsy/250	6.00
140	Mike Piazza/Jsy/150	10.00
141	Mike Sweeney/Jsy/150	4.00
142	Morgan Ensberg/Jsy/250	4.00
144	Nomar Garciaparra/Jsy/150	10.00
145	Omar Vizquel/Jsy/150	4.00
147	Orlando Hudson/Jsy/150	4.00
148	Pat Burrell/Jsy/150	4.00
151	Pedro J. Martinez/Jsy/150	8.00
153	Preston Wilson/Jsy/150	4.00
154	Rafael Furcal/Jsy/150	4.00
156	Randy Johnson/Jsy/150	8.00
158	Rich Harden/Jsy/250	4.00
159	Richard Hidalgo/Pants/150	4.00
163	Rocco Baldelli/Jsy/150	4.00
165	Roy Halladay/Jsy/150	4.00
168	Ryan Klesko/Jsy/150	4.00
170	Sammy Sosa/Jsy/150	12.00
172	Scott Rolen/Jsy/150	8.00
173	Sean Burroughs/Jsy/250	4.00
175	Shannon Stewart/Jsy/150	4.00
176	Shawn Green/Jsy/150	4.00
179	Steve Finley/Jsy/250	4.00
180	Tim Hudson/Jsy/150	6.00
181	Todd Helton/Jsy/150	6.00
182	Tom Glavine/Jsy/150	6.00
185	Troy Glaus/Jsy/150	4.00
186	Vernon Wells/Jsy/150	4.00
191	Travis Hafner/Jsy/150	6.00
192	Tim Salmon/Jsy/150	4.00
193	Tim Redding/Jsy/250	4.00
194	Runelvys Hernandez/Jsy/250	4.00
195	Ramon Nivar/Jsy/150	4.00
201	Roger Clemens/Jsy/150	15.00
202	Greg Maddux/Jsy/250	10.00
203	Vladimir Guerrero/Jsy/150	8.00
204	Miguel Tejada/Jsy/150	6.00
205	Kevin Brown/Jsy/250	4.00
206	Jason Giambi/Jsy/150	6.00
207	Curt Schilling/Jsy/150	6.00
208	Alex Rodriguez/Jsy/150	10.00
209	Alfonso Soriano/Jsy/150	8.00
210	Ivan Rodriguez/Jsy/150	8.00
212	Gary Carter/Pants/150	6.00
226	Bob Gibson/Jsy/250	10.00
237	Satchel Paige/Jsy/250	50.00

Mirror Fabric White

NM/M

White: .5-1.5X Red price
Production 25-200
Cards listed don't have red version.
217	Ryne Sandberg/25	45.00
219	Tony Gwynn/25	25.00
220	Don Mattingly/25	50.00
221	Mike Schmidt/25	40.00
223	Cal Ripken Jr./25	90.00
224	Nolan Ryan/25	60.00
225	George Brett/25	50.00
231	Roberto Clemente/25	90.00
233	Babe Ruth/25	240.00
234	Lou Gehrig/25	150.00
235	Ty Cobb/25	140.00
236	Roger Maris/25	50.00
237	Satchel Paige/25	90.00
239	Ted Williams/25	100.00

2004 Leaf Limited

NM/M

Complete Set (275):	
Common Player (1-200):	1.50
Common SP (201-229):	3.00

Production 499
Common SP (251-275): 10.00
Production 99
Pack (4): 60.00
Box (4): 200.00

1 Adam Dunn 2.00
2 Adrian Beltre 2.00
3 Albert Pujols 6.00
4 Alex Rodriguez 6.00
5 Alfonso Soriano 2.50
6 Andruw Jones 1.50
7 Andy Pettitte 1.50
8 Angel Berroa 1.50
9 Aramis Ramirez 1.50
10 Aubrey Huff 1.50
11 Aubrey Huff 1.50
12 Barry Larkin 1.50
13 Barry Zito 1.50
14 Bartolo Colon 1.50
15 Ben Sheets 1.50
16 Bernie Williams 1.50
17 Bobby Abreu 1.50
18 Brandon Webb 1.50
19 Brian Giles 1.50
20 C.C. Sabathia 1.50
21 Carlos Beltran 2.00
22 Carlos Delgado 1.50
23 Chipper Jones 3.00
24 Craig Biggio 1.50
25 Curt Schilling 3.00
26 Darin Erstad 1.50
27 Delmon Young 1.50
28 Derek Jeter 6.00
29 Derek Lee 1.50
30 Dontrelle Willis 1.50
31 Edgar Renteria 1.50
32 Eric Chavez 1.50
33 Esteban Loaiza 1.50
34 Frank Thomas 2.00
35 Fred McGriff 1.50
36 Garret Anderson 1.50
37 Gary Sheffield 1.50
38 Geoff Jenkins 1.50
39 Greg Maddux 3.00
40 Hank Blalock 2.00
41 Hideki Matsui 5.00
42 Hideo Nomo 1.50
43 Ichiro Suzuki 5.00
44 Ivan Rodriguez 2.00
45 J.D. Drew 1.50
46 Jacque Jones 1.50
47 Jae Weong Seo 1.50
48 Jake Peavy 1.50
49 Jamie Moyer 1.50
50 Jason Giambi 1.50
51 Jason Kendall 1.50
52 Jason Schmidt 1.50
53 Jason Varitek 1.50
54 Javier Vazquez 1.50
55 Javy Lopez 1.50
56 Jay Gibbons 1.50
57 Jay Payton 1.50
58 Jeff Bagwell 1.50
59 Jeff Kent 1.50
60 Jeremy Bonderman 1.50
61 Jermaine Dye 1.50
62 Jeromy Burnitz 1.50
63 Jim Edmonds 2.00
64 Jim Thome 1.50
65 Jimmy Rollins 1.50
66 Jody Gerut 1.50
67 Johan Santana 2.00
68 John Olerud 1.50
69 John Smoltz 1.50
70 Johnny Damon 2.00
71 Jorge Posada 1.50
72 Jose Contreras 1.50
73 Jose Reyes 1.50
74 Jose Vidro 1.50
75 Josh Beckett 1.50
76 Juan Gonzalez 1.50
77 Juan Pierre 1.50
78 Junior Spivey 1.50
79 Kazuhisa Ishii 1.50
80 Keith Foulke 1.50
81 Ken Griffey Jr. 3.00
82 Ken Harvey 1.50
83 Kenny Rogers 1.50
84 Kerry Wood 2.50
85 Kevin Brown 1.50
86 Kevin Millwood 1.50
87 Kip Wells 1.50
88 Lance Berkman 1.50
89 Larry Bigbie 1.50
90 Larry Walker 1.50
91 Laynce Nix 1.50
92 Luis Castillo 1.50
93 Luis Gonzalez 1.50
94 Luis Matos 1.50
95 Lyle Overbay 1.50
96 Magglio Ordonez 1.50
97 Manny Ramirez 2.00
98 Marcus Giles 1.50
99 Mark Buehrle 1.50
100 Mark Mulder 1.50
101 Mark Prior 2.00
102 Mark Teixeira 1.50
103 Marlon Byrd 1.50
104 Matt Morris 1.50
105 Melvin Mora 1.50
106 Michael Young 1.50
107 Miguel Cabrera 3.00
108 Miguel Tejada 2.00
109 Mike Lowell 1.50
110 Mike Mussina 2.00
111 Mike Piazza 3.00
112 Mike Sweeney 1.50
113 Milton Bradley 1.50
114 Moises Alou 1.50
115 Morgan Ensberg 1.50
116 Nick Johnson 1.50
117 Nomar Garciaparra 4.00
118 Omar Vizquel 1.50
119 Orlando Cabrera 1.50
120 Pat Burrell 1.50
121 Paul Konerko 1.50
122 Paul LoDuca 1.50
123 Pedro J. Martinez 3.00
124 Preston Wilson 1.50
125 Rafael Furcal 1.50
126 Rafael Palmeiro 2.00
127 Randy Johnson 3.00
128 Rich Harden 1.50
129 Richard Hidalgo 1.50
130 Richie Sexson 1.50
131 Rickie Weeks 1.50
132 Roberto Alomar 1.50
133 Robin Ventura 1.50
134 Rocco Baldelli 1.50
135 Roger Clemens 6.00
136 Roy Halladay 1.50
137 Roy Oswalt 1.50
138 Russ Ortiz 1.50
139 Ryan Klesko 1.50
140 Sammy Sosa 5.00
141 Scott Podsednik 1.50
142 Scott Rolen 3.00
143 Sean Burroughs 1.50
144 Sean Casey 1.50
145 Shannon Stewart 1.50
146 Shawn Green 1.50
147 Shigetoshi Hasegawa 1.50
148 Sidney Ponson 1.50
149 Steve Finley 1.50
150 Tim Hudson 1.50
151 Tim Salmon 1.50
152 Tino Martinez 1.50
153 Todd Helton 2.00
154 Tom Glavine 2.00
155 Torii Hunter 1.50
156 Trot Nixon 1.50
157 Troy Glaus 1.50
158 Vernon Wells 1.50
159 Victor Martinez 1.50
160 Vinny Castilla 1.50
161 Vladimir Guerrero 3.00
162 Alex Rodriguez 6.00
163 Alfonso Soriano 2.50
164 Andy Pettitte 1.50
165 Curt Schilling 3.00
166 Gary Sheffield 1.50
167 Greg Maddux 3.00
168 Hideo Nomo 1.50
169 Ivan Rodriguez 2.00
170 Jason Giambi 1.50
171 Jim Thome 2.00
172 Juan Gonzalez 1.50
173 Ken Griffey Jr. 3.00
174 Kevin Brown 1.50
175 Manny Ramirez 2.00
176 Miguel Tejada 2.00
177 Mike Mussina 2.00
178 Mike Piazza 4.00
179 Pedro Martinez 2.00
180 Rafael Palmeiro 2.00
181 Randy Johnson 3.00
182 Roger Clemens 6.00
183 Scott Rolen 3.00
184 Shawn Green 1.50
185 Tom Glavine 1.50
186 Vladimir Guerrero 3.00
187 Alex Rodriguez 6.00
188 Mike Piazza 3.00
189 Randy Johnson 3.00
190 Roger Clemens 6.00
191 Albert Pujols 6.00
192 Barry Zito 1.50
193 Chipper Jones 3.00
194 Garret Anderson 1.50
195 Jeff Bagwell 1.50
196 Josh Beckett 1.50
197 Magglio Ordonez 1.50
198 Mark Prior 2.00
199 Sammy Sosa 5.00
200 Todd Helton 3.00
201 Andre Dawson 3.00
202 Babe Ruth 8.00
203 Bob Feller 4.00
204 Bob Gibson 3.00
205 Bobby Doerr 3.00
206 Cal Ripken Jr. 10.00
207 Dale Murphy 4.00
208 Don Mattingly 8.00
209 Gary Carter 4.00
210 George Brett 8.00
211 Jackie Robinson 5.00
212 Lou Brock 4.00
213 Lou Gehrig 6.00
214 Mark Grace 4.00
215 Maury Wills 3.00
216 Mike Schmidt 8.00
217 Nolan Ryan 8.00
218 Orel Hershiser 4.00
219 Paul Molitor 4.00
220 Roberto Clemente 8.00
221 Rod Carew 4.00
222 Roy Campanella 4.00
223 Ryne Sandberg 8.00
224 Stan Musial 6.00
225 Ted Williams 8.00
226 Tony Gwynn 6.00
227 Ty Cobb 8.00
228 Whitey Ford 4.00
229 Yogi Berra 4.00
230 Carlos Beltran 3.00
231 David Ortiz 3.00
232 David Ortiz 3.00
233 Carlos Zambrano 1.50
234 Carlos Lee 1.50
235 Travis Hafner 1.50
236 Brad Penny 1.50
237 Wade Miller 1.50
238 Edgar Martinez 1.50
239 Carl Crawford 1.50
240 Roy Oswalt 1.50
241 Kazuo Matsui 8.00
242 Carlos Beltran 1.50
243 Carlos Beltran 1.50
244 Miguel Cabrera 2.00
245 Scott Rolen 3.00
246 Hank Blalock 2.00
247 Vernon Wells 1.50
248 Adam Dunn 1.50
249 Preston Wilson 1.50
250 Victor Martinez 1.50
251 Aarom Baldiris RC 10.00
252 Akinori Otsuka RC 35.00
253 Andres Blanco RC 10.00
254 Brad Halsey RC 10.00
255 Joey Gathright RC 25.00
256 Colby Miller RC 10.00
257 Fernando Nieve RC 10.00
258 Freddy Guzman RC 15.00
259 Hector Gimenez RC 10.00
260 Jake Woods RC 10.00
261 Jason Bartlett RC 10.00
262 John Gall RC 15.00
263 Jose Capellan RC 35.00
264 Josh Labandeira RC 10.00
265 Justin Germano RC 10.00
266 Kazuhito Tadano RC 40.00
267 Lance Cormier RC 10.00
268 Merkin Valdez RC 20.00
269 Mike Gosling RC 10.00
270 Ramon Ramirez RC 10.00
271 Rusty Tucker RC 10.00
272 Shawn Hill RC 10.00
273 Shingo Takatsu RC 40.00
274 William Bergolla RC 10.00
275 Yadier Molina RC 20.00

Bronze Spotlight

Bronze: 1-2X
Production 100 Sets

Silver Spotlight

Silver (1-250): 2-3X
Production 50 Sets

Gold Spotlight

Golds (1-250): 3-5X
Production 25 Sets

Platinum Spotlight

No Pricing
Production One Set

Barrels

No Pricing
Production 1-5

Cuts

NM/M
Quantity produced listed
1 Nolan Ryan/100 125.00
2 Bob Gibson/50 40.00
3 Harmon Killebrew/100 40.00
4 Duke Snider/100 30.00
5 George Brett/100 75.00
6 Stan Musial/100 80.00
7 Alan Trammell/100 20.00
8 Cal Ripken Jr./100 180.00
9 Steve Carlton/50 40.00
10 Phil Rizzuto/100 30.00
11 Mark Prior/50 40.00
12 Will Clark/100 40.00
13 Lou Brock/100 30.00
14 Ozzie Smith/100 60.00
15 Bob Feller/100 30.00
16 Gary Carter/50 25.00
17 Al Kaline/100 40.00
18 Brooks Robinson/100 40.00
19 Tony Gwynn/100 50.00
20 Mike Schmidt/100 75.00
21 Ralph Kiner/50 40.00
22 Jim Palmer/100 40.00
23 Don Mattingly/100 75.00
24 Paul Molitor/100 40.00
25 Dale Murphy/100 30.00

Cuts Gold

NM/M
Quantity produced listed
1 Nolan Ryan/34 200.00
2 Bob Gibson/45 40.00
9 Steve Carlton/32 50.00
11 Mark Prior/22 60.00
12 Will Clark/22 65.00
13 Lou Brock/22 50.00
15 Bob Feller/28 50.00
19 Tony Gwynn/19 100.00
20 Mike Schmidt/20 100.00
22 Jim Palmer/22 100.00
23 Don Mattingly/23 100.00

Legends Material Number

NM/M
Quantity produced listed
1 Al Kaline/Pants/50 15.00
2 Babe Ruth/Pants/50 160.00
3 Bob Feller/Jsy/50 10.00
4 Bob Gibson/Jsy/50 10.00
6 Burleigh Grimes/Pants/100 40.00
7 Carl Yastrzemski/Jsy/25 15.00
8 Harmon Killebrew/Jsy/25 25.00
9 Hoyt Wilhelm/Jsy/100 10.00
10 Johnny Mize/Pants/100 10.00
11 Ernie Banks/Pants/50 15.00
12 Lou Brock/Jsy/50 10.00
13 Luis Aparicio/Pants/100 5.00
14 Pee Wee Reese/Jsy/50 10.00
15 Reggie Jackson/Jsy/100 10.00
16 Red Schoendienst/Jsy/50 8.00
17 Roberto Clemente/Jsy/25 80.00
18 Roger Maris/Pants/100 25.00
19 Stan Musial/Jsy/100 20.00
20 Ted Williams/Jsy/50 75.00
21 Ty Cobb/Pants/50 80.00
22 Warren Spahn/Jsy/100 10.00
23 Whitey Ford/Pants/100 10.00
24 Yogi Berra/Jsy/50 15.00
25 Satchel Paige CO/Jsy/100 50.00

Legends Material Position

NM/M
Quantity produced listed
1 Al Kaline/Pants/50 15.00
2 Babe Ruth/Pants/50 160.00
3 Bob Feller/Jsy/50 10.00
4 Bob Gibson/Jsy/50 10.00
6 Burleigh Grimes/Pants/100 40.00
7 Carl Yastrzemski/Jsy/100 15.00
8 Harmon Killebrew/Jsy/25 25.00
9 Hoyt Wilhelm/Jsy/100 5.00
10 Johnny Mize/Pants/100 10.00
11 Ernie Banks/Pants/50 15.00
12 Lou Brock/Jsy/50 10.00
13 Luis Aparicio/Pants/100 5.00
14 Pee Wee Reese/Jsy/100 10.00
15 Reggie Jackson/Jsy/100 10.00
16 Red Schoendienst/Jsy/100 10.00
17 Roberto Clemente/Jsy/25 80.00
18 Roger Maris/Pants/100 25.00
19 Stan Musial/Jsy/100 20.00
20 Ted Williams/Jsy/50 75.00
21 Ty Cobb/Pants/50 80.00
22 Warren Spahn/Jsy/100 10.00
23 Whitey Ford/Pants/100 10.00
24 Yogi Berra/Jsy/50 15.00
25 Satchel Paige CO/Jsy/100 50.00

Legends Material Autographs Position

NM/M
Quantity produced listed
1 Al Kaline/Pants/50 50.00
3 Bob Feller/Jsy/50 30.00
4 Bob Gibson/Jsy/50 30.00
7 Carl Yastrzemski/Jsy/25 80.00
8 Harmon Killebrew/Jsy/25 65.00
9 Hoyt Wilhelm/Jsy/25 40.00
12 Lou Brock/Jsy/50 30.00
13 Luis Aparicio/Pants/50 20.00
15 Reggie Jackson/Jsy/50 50.00
16 Red Schoendienst/Jsy/50 30.00
19 Stan Musial/Jsy/50 75.00
23 Whitey Ford/Pants/25 50.00
24 Yogi Berra/Jsy/25 75.00

Lumberjacks

NM/M
Common Player: 2.00
Quantity produced listed
Black: 1-3X
Production 16-100
1 Al Kaline/399 4.00
2 Albert Pujols/114 15.00
3 Andre Dawson/438 2.00
4 Babe Ruth/714 8.00
5 Bo Jackson/141 5.00
6 Bobby Doerr/223 3.00
7 Brooks Robinson/268 4.00
8 Cal Ripken Jr./431 10.00
9 Carlton Fisk/376 2.00
10 Dale Murphy/398 2.00
11 Darryl Strawberry/335 2.00
12 Don Mattingly/222 6.00
13 Duke Snider/407 3.00
14 Eddie Mathews/512 3.00
15 Eddie Murray/504 3.00
16 Frank Robinson/586 3.00
17 Frank Thomas/418 3.00
18 Gary Carter/324 2.00
19 George Brett/317 6.00
20 Harmon Killebrew/573 4.00
22 Lou Gehrig/493 5.00
23 Mark Grace/173 2.00
24 Mike Piazza/358 4.00
25 Mike Schmidt/548 5.00
26 Orlando Cepeda/379 2.00
27 Rafael Palmeiro/528 2.00
28 Ralph Kiner/369 2.00
29 Reggie Jackson/563 3.00
30 Rickey Henderson/297 3.00

Legends Material Autographs Number

NM/M
Quanity produced listed
1 Al Kaline/Pants/50 50.00
3 Bob Feller/Jsy/50 30.00
4 Bob Gibson/Jsy/50 30.00
7 Carl Yastrzemski/Jsy/25 80.00
8 Harmon Killebrew/Jsy/25 65.00
9 Hoyt Wilhelm/Jsy/25 40.00
12 Lou Brock/Jsy/50 30.00
13 Luis Aparicio/Pants/50 20.00
15 Reggie Jackson/Jsy/50 50.00
16 Red Schoendienst/Jsy/50 30.00
19 Stan Musial/Jsy/50 75.00
23 Whitey Ford/Pants/25 50.00
24 Yogi Berra/Jsy/25 75.00

31 Roger Maris/275 5.00
32 Ryne Sandberg/282 4.00
33 Sammy Sosa/539 4.00
34 Scott Rolen/192 4.00
35 Stan Musial/475 4.00
36 Ted Williams/521 5.00
37 Thurman Munson/113 5.00
38 Vladimir Guerrero/234 4.00
39 Willie McCovey/521 2.00
40 Willie Stargell/475 2.00
41 Roberto Clemente, Stan Musial 6.00
42 Cal Ripken Jr., Ernie Banks 10.00
43 Babe Ruth, Lou Gehrig 8.00
44 George Brett, Mike Schmidt 8.00
45 Frank Robinson, Jackie Robinson 4.00
46 Don Mattingly, Roger Maris 8.00
47 Nomar Garciaparra, Ted Williams 8.00
48 Johnny Bench, Mike Piazza 4.00
49 Reggie Jackson, Sammy Sosa 4.00
50 Mel Ott, Willie McCovey 4.00

Lumberjacks Autographs

NM/M
Quantity produced listed
1 Al Kaline/100 30.00
3 Andre Dawson/100 15.00
5 Bo Jackson/100 60.00
6 Bobby Doerr/100 20.00
7 Brooks Robinson/100 50.00
8 Cal Ripken Jr./25 180.00
9 Carlton Fisk/25 30.00
10 Dale Murphy/100 20.00
11 Darryl Strawberry/100 15.00
12 Don Mattingly/25 70.00
13 Duke Snider/100 20.00
16 Frank Robinson/100 20.00
17 Frank Thomas/50 50.00
18 Gary Carter/100 15.00
19 George Brett/25 70.00
20 Harmon Killebrew/100 40.00
23 Mark Grace/25 40.00
25 Mike Schmidt/50 65.00
26 Ralph Kiner/100 20.00
29 Reggie Jackson/25 50.00
30 Rickey Henderson/25 50.00
32 Ryne Sandberg/25 90.00
34 Scott Rolen/25 40.00
35 Stan Musial/50 65.00
39 Willie McCovey/25 30.00

Lumberjacks Autographs Bat

NM/M
Quantity produced listed
1 Al Kaline/100 40.00
3 Andre Dawson/50 20.00
5 Bo Jackson/25 70.00
6 Bobby Doerr/50 25.00
7 Brooks Robinson/50 60.00
8 Cal Ripken Jr./25 200.00
9 Carlton Fisk/25 40.00
10 Dale Murphy/100 25.00
11 Darryl Strawberry/25 25.00
12 Don Mattingly/25 80.00
17 Frank Thomas/25 70.00
18 Gary Carter/50 20.00
19 George Brett/25 80.00
20 Harmon Killebrew/50 50.00
23 Mark Grace/17 50.00
25 Mike Schmidt/25 80.00
26 Ralph Kiner/100 25.00
29 Reggie Jackson/25 60.00
32 Ryne Sandberg/25 90.00
34 Scott Rolen/25 50.00
35 Stan Musial/25 75.00
39 Willie McCovey/25 40.00

Lumberjacks Autographs Jersey

NM/M
Quantity produced listed
1 Al Kaline/Pants/100 40.00
3 Andre Dawson/50 20.00
5 Bo Jackson/25 70.00
6 Bobby Doerr/100 15.00
7 Brooks Robinson/25 75.00
8 Cal Ripken Jr./25 200.00
9 Carlton Fisk/50 30.00
10 Dale Murphy/100 25.00

11 Darryl Strawberry/Pants/25 25.00
12 Don Mattingly/25 80.00
15 Eddie Murray/25 70.00
16 Frank Robinson/50 30.00
17 Frank Thomas/25 70.00
18 Gary Carter/50 20.00
19 George Brett/25 80.00
20 Harmon Killebrew/25 60.00
23 Mark Grace/17 50.00
25 Mike Schmidt/25 80.00
26 Orlando Cepeda/Pants/25 20.00
29 Reggie Jackson/25 60.00
32 Ryne Sandberg/25 90.00
34 Scott Rolen/25 50.00
35 Stan Musial/50 75.00
39 Willie McCovey/25 40.00

Lumberjacks Barrel
Quantity produced listed
No Pricing
Production 1-5

Lumberjacks Bat

NM/M
Quantity produced listed
1 Al Kaline/100 15.00
2 Albert Pujols/25 15.00
3 Andre Dawson/25 15.00
4 Babe Ruth/25 125.00
5 Bo Jackson/50 15.00
6 Bobby Doerr/25 12.00
7 Brooks Robinson/100
8 Cal Ripken Jr./100 40.00
9 Carlton Fisk/100 10.00
10 Dale Murphy/50 10.00
11 Darryl Strawberry/25 15.00
12 Don Mattingly/100 20.00
14 Eddie Mathews/100 10.00
15 Eddie Murray/50 15.00
16 Frank Robinson/100 8.00
17 Frank Thomas/25 20.00
18 Gary Carter/50 10.00
19 George Brett/100 20.00
20 Harmon Killebrew/100 15.00
21 Hideki Matsui/100 25.00
22 Lou Gehrig/100 100.00
23 Mark Grace/25 15.00
24 Mike Piazza/50 15.00
25 Mike Schmidt/100 15.00
26 Orlando Cepeda/50 8.00
27 Rafael Palmeiro/50 10.00
28 Ralph Kiner/100 8.00
29 Reggie Jackson/100 10.00
30 Rickey Henderson/100 10.00
31 Roger Maris/100 25.00
32 Ryne Sandberg/100 15.00
33 Sammy Sosa/100 10.00
34 Scott Rolen/25 15.00
35 Stan Musial/100 25.00
36 Ted Williams/100 50.00
37 Thurman Munson/100 20.00
38 Vladimir Guerrero/25 15.00
39 Willie McCovey/100 10.00
40 Willie Stargell/50 10.00
41 Roberto Clemente, Stan Musial/100 85.00
42 Cal Ripken Jr., Ernie Banks/50 100.00
43 Babe Ruth, Lou Gehrig/25 250.00
44 George Brett, Mike Schmidt/50 50.00
46 Don Mattingly, Roger Maris/40 40.00
47 Nomar Garciaparra, Ted Williams/100 75.00
48 Johnny Bench, Mike Piazza/25 35.00
49 Reggie Jackson, Sammy Sosa/50 20.00
50 Mel Ott, Willie McCovey/100 40.00

Lumberjacks Jersey
NM/M
Quantity produced listed
1 Al Kaline/Pants/50 20.00
2 Albert Pujols/25 15.00
3 Andre Dawson/25 15.00
4 Babe Ruth/25 300.00
5 Bo Jackson/50
6 Bobby Doerr/100 5.00
7 Brooks Robinson/25
8 Cal Ripken Jr./100 40.00
9 Carlton Fisk/100 10.00
10 Dale Murphy/100 10.00
11 Darryl Strawberry/Pants/50 8.00

12 Don Mattingly/100 20.00
14 Eddie Mathews/100 10.00
15 Eddie Murray/50 20.00
16 Frank Robinson/50 10.00
17 Frank Thomas/100 10.00
18 Gary Carter/50 10.00
19 George Brett/100 20.00
20 Harmon Killebrew/25 30.00
21 Hideki Matsui/100 25.00
22 Lou Gehrig/25 180.00
23 Mark Grace/100 8.00
24 Mike Piazza/100 10.00
25 Mike Schmidt/100 15.00
26 Orlando Cepeda/Pants/100 5.00
27 Rafael Palmeiro/50 20.00
29 Reggie Jackson/100 10.00
30 Rickey Henderson/100 10.00
31 Roger Maris/100 25.00
32 Ryne Sandberg/100 15.00
33 Sammy Sosa/100 10.00
34 Scott Rolen/50 10.00
35 Stan Musial/50 30.00
36 Ted Williams/100 50.00
37 Thurman Munson/100 20.00
38 Vladimir Guerrero/50 10.00
39 Willie McCovey/100 10.00
40 Willie Stargell/50 8.00
41 Roberto Clemente, Stan Musial/100 120.00
42 Cal Ripken Jr., Ernie Banks/Pants/100 65.00
43 Babe Ruth, Lou Gehrig/25 400.00
44 George Brett, Mike Schmidt/Jkt/100 30.00
45 Frank Robinson, Jackie Robinson/25 30.00
46 Don Mattingly, Roger Maris/Pants/100 25.00
47 Johnny Bench, Mike Piazza/100 10.00
49 Reggie Jackson, Sammy Sosa/100 15.00
50 Mel Ott/Pants, Willie McCovey/25 80.00

Lumberjacks Combos

NM/M
Quantity produced listed
1 Al Kaline/Bat-Pants/100 20.00
2 Albert Pujols/Bat-Jsy/100 20.00
3 Andre Dawson/Bat-Jsy/100 15.00
4 Babe Ruth/Bat-Jsy/25 400.00
5 Bo Jackson/Bat-Jsy/50 20.00
6 Bobby Doerr/Bat-Jsy/100 12.00
7 Brooks Robinson/Bat-Jsy/25 40.00
8 Cal Ripken Jr./Bat-Jsy/25 50.00
9 Carlton Fisk/Bat-Jsy/25 15.00
10 Dale Murphy/Bat-Jsy/100 15.00
11 Darryl Strawberry/Bat-Pants/25 15.00
12 Don Mattingly/Bat-Jsy/25 25.00
14 Eddie Mathews/Bat-Jsy/50 15.00
15 Eddie Murray/Bat-Jsy/50 20.00
16 Frank Robinson/Bat-Jsy/50 15.00
17 Frank Thomas/Bat-Jsy/50 20.00
18 Gary Carter/Bat-Jsy/50 10.00
19 George Brett/Bat-Jsy/50 25.00
20 Harmon Killebrew/Bat-Jsy/50 30.00
21 Hideki Matsui/Bat-Jsy/100 30.00
22 Lou Gehrig/Bat-Jsy/25 250.00
23 Mark Grace/Bat-Jsy/17 30.00
24 Mike Piazza/Bat-Jsy/100 15.00
25 Mike Schmidt/Bat-Jsy/50 20.00
26 Orlando Cepeda/Bat-Pants/50 10.00

27 Rafael Palmeiro/Bat-Jsy/50 15.00
29 Reggie Jackson/Bat-Jsy/50 15.00
30 Rickey Henderson/Bat-Jsy/50 15.00
31 Roger Maris/Bat-Jsy/50 40.00
32 Ryne Sandberg/Bat-Jsy/50 25.00
33 Sammy Sosa/Bat-Jsy/50 15.00
34 Scott Rolen/Bat-Jsy/50 20.00
35 Stan Musial/Bat-Jsy/50 30.00
36 Ted Williams/Bat-Jsy/50 75.00
37 Thurman Munson/Bat-Jsy/100 25.00
38 Vladimir Guerrero/Bat-Jsy/50 15.00
39 Willie McCovey/Bat-Jsy/100 15.00
40 Willie Stargell/Bat-Jsy/100 12.00

Matching Numbers

NM/M
Quantity produced listed
Prime: No Pricing
Production One Set
1 Bobby Doerr/Jsy, Pee Wee Reese/Jsy/100 10.00
2 Lou Gehrig/Pants, Mel Ott/Jsy/50 160.00
3 Albert Pujols/Jsy, George Brett/Jsy/100 30.00
4 Cal Ripken Jr./Jsy, Carl Yastrzemski/Jsy/100 50.00
5 Dwight Gooden/Jsy, Whitey Ford/Pants/50 15.00
6 Mark Grace/Jsy, Todd Helton/Jsy/25 25.00
7 Robin Yount/Jsy, Tony Gwynn/Jsy/50 40.00
8 Frank Robinson/Jsy, Mike Schmidt/Jsy/100 25.00
9 Roberto Clemente/Jsy, Sammy Sosa/Jsy/100 75.00
10 Roger Clemens/Jsy, Warren Spahn/Pant/100 25.00
11 Mark Prior/Jsy, Roger Clemens/Jsy/50 15.00
12 Don Mattingly/Jkt, Ryne Sandberg/Jsy/100 30.00
13 Billy Williams/Jsy, Wade Boggs/Jsy/100 10.00
14 Jim "Catfish" Hunter/Jsy, Juan Marichal/Jsy/50 10.00
15 Fergie Jenkins/Pants, Greg Maddux/Jsy/50 20.00
16 Kerry Wood/Pants, Nolan Ryan/Jsy/100 35.00
17 Rickey Henderson/Jsy, Roger Maris/Pants/100 40.00
18 Dontrelle Willis/Jsy, Mike Mussina/Jsy/100 15.00
19 Reggie Jackson/Jsy, Willie McCovey/Jsy/100 15.00
20 Bob Gibson/Jsy, Pedro Martinez/Jsy/50 15.00
21 Duke Snider/Jsy, Paul Molitor/Jsy/100 10.00
22 Johnny Bench/Jsy, Lou Boudreau/Jsy/100 15.00
23 Andre Dawson/Jsy, Chipper Jones/Jsy/50 15.00
24 Ernie Banks/Jsy, Boyer/Jsy/50 15.00
25 Manny Ramirez/Jsy, Rickey Henderson/Jsy/50 15.00
26 Carlton Fisk/Jsy, Scott Rolen/Jsy/50 15.00
27 Nolan Ryan/Jsy, Orlando Cepeda/Pant/100 25.00
28 Roy Halladay/Jsy, Steve Carlton/Jsy/100 8.00
29 Eddie Mathews/Jsy, Tom Seaver/Jsy/100 15.00
30 Brandon Webb/Jsy, Orel Hershiser/Jsy/100 10.00

Moniker Bat
NM/M
Quanity produced listed
1 Adam Dunn/50 30.00
5 Alfonso Soriano/50 50.00
6 Andruw Jones/25 40.00
8 Angel Berroa/25 15.00
9 Aramis Ramirez/25 25.00
10 Aubrey Huff/25 25.00
15 Ben Sheets/25 25.00
21 Carlos Beltran/50 40.00
24 Craig Biggio/25 40.00
27 Delmon Young/50 30.00
30 Dontrelle Willis/25 30.00
31 Edgar Renteria/25 25.00
34 Frank Thomas/25 70.00
35 Fred McGriff/50 30.00
36 Garret Anderson/50 20.00
37 Gary Sheffield/25 40.00
40 Hank Blalock/50 35.00
61 Jermaine Dye/25 25.00
71 Jorge Posada/25 50.00
84 Kerry Wood/25 50.00
88 Lance Berkman/25 40.00
100 Mark Mulder/50 40.00
101 Mark Prior/50 40.00
102 Mark Teixeira/25 25.00
106 Michael Young/50 15.00
107 Miguel Cabrera/40 40.00
109 Mike Lowell/25 25.00
122 Paul LoDuca/25 25.00
124 Preston Wilson/25 25.00
131 Rickie Weeks/25 25.00
137 Roy Oswalt/25 25.00
145 Shannon Stewart/25 25.00
155 Torii Hunter/25 25.00
158 Trot Nixon/25 25.00
158 Vernon Wells/50 25.00
159 Victor Martinez/50 25.00
163 Alfonso Soriano/50 50.00
166 Gary Sheffield/25 35.00
194 Garret Anderson/25 20.00
198 Mark Prior/50 20.00
205 Andre Dawson/25 20.00
207 Bobby Doerr/25 25.00
208 Dale Murphy/50 25.00
209 Don Mattingly/50 75.00
212 Gary Carter/25 15.00
214 Lou Brock/50 30.00
216 Mark Grace/50 30.00
217 Mike Schmidt/75 75.00
219 Nolan Ryan/50 150.00
221 Paul Molitor/50 30.00
223 Rod Carew/25 35.00
224 Ryne Sandberg/50 80.00
226 Tony Gwynn/50 50.00
230 Carlos Beltran/50 45.00
231 David Ortiz/50 60.00
232 David Ortiz/50 60.00
234 Carlos Lee/50 30.00
235 Travis Hafner/25 25.00
238 Edgar Martinez/25 40.00
240 Roy Oswalt/25 30.00
242 Carlos Beltran/50 45.00
243 Carlos Beltran/50 45.00
246 Miguel Cabrera/25 40.00
246 Hank Blalock/50 35.00
247 Vernon Wells/25 20.00
248 Adam Dunn/50 35.00
249 Preston Wilson/25 25.00
250 Victor Martinez/50 25.00

Moniker Bronze
NM/M
Quanity produced listed
Silver: .5-1.5X
Production 1-50
No pricing 15 or less.
Platinum: No Pricing
Production One Set
1 Adam Dunn/25 30.00
3 Albert Pujols/25 180.00
5 Alfonso Soriano/100 30.00
6 Andruw Jones/25 30.00
8 Angel Berroa/25 15.00
11 Austin Kearns/50 20.00
18 Brandon Webb/21 15.00
21 Carlos Beltran/50 40.00
23 Chipper Jones/25 65.00
24 Craig Biggio/5 40.00
30 Dontrelle Willis/25 30.00
31 Edgar Renteria/25 25.00
34 Frank Thomas/50 60.00
36 Garret Anderson/20 20.00
37 Gary Sheffield/25 40.00
39 Greg Maddux/25 85.00
40 Hank Blalock/25 35.00
46 Jacque Jones/25 25.00
58 Jeff Bagwell/25 75.00
71 Jorge Posada/25 30.00
76 Juan Gonzalez/25 30.00
79 Kazuhisa Ishii/25 35.00
84 Kerry Wood/25 30.00
88 Lance Berkman/50 30.00
98 Marcus Giles/25 25.00
100 Mark Mulder/15 15.00
101 Mark Prior/25 30.00
106 Michael Young/50 15.00
107 Miguel Cabrera/50 40.00
109 Mike Lowell/25 25.00
122 Paul LoDuca/25 25.00
131 Rickie Weeks/25 25.00
137 Roy Oswalt/10 20.00
142 Sammy Sosa/85 85.00
142 Scott Rolen/25 60.00
144 Sean Casey/25 25.00
145 Shannon Stewart/25 25.00
153 Todd Helton/25 40.00
156 Torii Hunter/50 35.00
156 Trot Nixon/25 25.00
163 Vernon Wells/25 25.00
163 Alfonso Soriano/100 30.00
166 Gary Sheffield/10 30.00
166 Greg Maddux/5 80.00
172 Juan Gonzalez/25 40.00
183 Scott Rolen/25 50.00
191 Albert Pujols/5 180.00
194 Chipper Jones/5 65.00
195 Garret Anderson/5 20.00
195 Jeff Bagwell/25 75.00
198 Mark Prior/50 40.00
199 Sammy Sosa/80 80.00
200 Todd Helton/25 40.00
201 Andre Dawson/100 15.00
203 Bob Feller/100 20.00
204 Bob Gibson/100 25.00
205 Bobby Doerr/100 15.00
206 Cal Ripken Jr./25 180.00
207 Dale Murphy/100 25.00
208 Don Mattingly/100 60.00
209 Gary Carter/100 15.00
210 George Brett/25 75.00
212 Lou Brock/50 20.00
214 Mark Grace/100 20.00
216 Maury Wills/100 15.00
216 Mike Schmidt/100 50.00
217 Nolan Ryan/100 120.00
218 Orel Hershiser/25 40.00
219 Paul Molitor/100 25.00
221 Rod Carew/100 25.00
223 Ryne Sandberg/100 100.00
224 Stan Musial/100 60.00
226 Tony Gwynn/100 40.00
231 Carlos Beltran/50 45.00
232 David Ortiz/50 60.00
233 Carlos Zambrano/25 30.00
234 Carlos Lee/25 20.00
238 Edgar Martinez/25 40.00
240 Roy Oswalt/25 20.00
242 Carlos Beltran/50 45.00
243 Carlos Beltran/50 45.00
245 Scott Rolen/25 50.00
246 Hank Blalock/50 35.00
247 Vernon Wells/25 25.00
248 Adam Dunn/50 35.00

Moniker Gold
NM/M
Quanity produced listed
5 Alfonso Soriano/25 40.00
21 Carlos Beltran/25 50.00
100 Mark Mulder/25 25.00
163 Alfonso Soriano/25 40.00
201 Andre Dawson/25 20.00
203 Bob Feller/25 35.00
204 Bob Gibson/25 40.00
205 Bobby Doerr/25 25.00
207 Dale Murphy/25 40.00
208 Don Mattingly/25 90.00
209 Gary Carter/25 25.00
212 Lou Brock/25 20.00
214 Mark Grace/25 25.00
216 Maury Wills/25 15.00
216 Mike Schmidt/25 85.00
217 Nolan Ryan/25 150.00
219 Paul Molitor/25 40.00
221 Rod Carew/25 35.00
223 Ryne Sandberg/25 75.00
224 Stan Musial/25 100.00
226 Tony Gwynn/25 50.00

Moniker Jersey
NM/M
Quanity produced listed
Prime: No Pricing
Production One Set
1 Adam Dunn/50 30.00
5 Alfonso Soriano/50 40.00
6 Andruw Jones/25 40.00
8 Angel Berroa/Pants/25 15.00
9 Aramis Ramirez/25 25.00
10 Aubrey Huff/25 25.00
11 Austin Kearns/25 25.00
15 Ben Sheets/25 25.00
18 Brandon Webb/25 15.00
21 Carlos Beltran/50 40.00
23 Chipper Jones/25 65.00
24 Craig Biggio/25 40.00
30 Dontrelle Willis/25 30.00
32 Eric Chavez/50 20.00
34 Frank Thomas/25 70.00
35 Fred McGriff/25 40.00
40 Garret Anderson/20 20.00
40 Hank Blalock/50 35.00
46 Jacque Jones/25 25.00
66 Jody Gerut/25 15.00
71 Johan Santana/25 40.00
71 Jorge Posada/25 50.00
84 Jose Vidro/25 15.00
84 Kerry Wood/25 50.00
88 Lance Berkman/25 40.00
89 Larry Bigbie/25 15.00
98 Marcus Giles/25 25.00
99 Mark Buehrle/25 25.00
100 Mark Mulder/75 15.00
101 Mark Prior/25 40.00
102 Mark Teixeira/25 40.00
105 Melvin Mora/25 25.00
107 Miguel Cabrera/38 40.00
109 Mike Lowell/25 25.00
109 Morgan Ensberg/25 15.00
122 Paul LoDuca/25 25.00
124 Preston Wilson/25 25.00
137 Roy Oswalt/25 25.00
142 Scott Rolen/50 50.00
143 Sean Burroughs/25 25.00
144 Sean Casey/25 25.00
145 Shannon Stewart/25 25.00
149 Steve Finley/25 25.00
153 Todd Helton/25 40.00
155 Torii Hunter/25 25.00
155 Trot Nixon/25 25.00
158 Vernon Wells/50 25.00
159 Victor Martinez/50 20.00
163 Alfonso Soriano/50 40.00
166 Gary Sheffield/25 40.00
172 Juan Gonzalez/25 40.00
183 Scott Rolen/50 40.00
187 Tom Glavine/25 40.00
193 Chipper Jones/25 65.00
194 Garret Anderson/50 20.00
200 Todd Helton/25 40.00
201 Andre Dawson/25 20.00
204 Bob Gibson/50 30.00
205 Bobby Doerr/50 25.00
207 Dale Murphy/100 25.00
208 Don Mattingly/50 70.00
209 Gary Carter/100 15.00
216 Mike Schmidt/50 75.00
217 Nolan Ryan/50 120.00
218 Orel Hershiser/50 30.00
219 Paul Molitor/50 30.00
221 Rod Carew/25 30.00
223 Ryne Sandberg/25 100.00
224 Stan Musial/100 100.00
226 Tony Gwynn/100 40.00
228 Whitey Ford/Pants/25 40.00
229 Yogi Berra/25 75.00
230 Carlos Beltran/50 45.00
231 David Ortiz/50 60.00
232 David Ortiz/50 60.00
234 Carlos Lee/50 25.00
235 Travis Hafner/25 25.00
236 Brad Penny/25 15.00
237 Wade Miller/25 15.00
238 Edgar Martinez/25 40.00
239 Carl Crawford/25 25.00
240 Roy Oswalt/25 25.00
242 Carlos Beltran/50 45.00
243 Carlos Beltran/50 45.00
244 Miguel Cabrera/50 40.00
245 Scott Rolen/50 40.00
246 Hank Blalock/50 35.00
247 Vernon Wells/50 20.00
247 Adam Dunn/50 35.00
249 Preston Wilson/25 25.00

Moniker Jersey Number

NM/M
Quanity produced listed
Prime: No Pricing
Production One Set
1 Adam Dunn/50 30.00
5 Alfonso Soriano/50 40.00
8 Andruw Jones/25 40.00
8 Angel Berroa/Pants/25 15.00
9 Aramis Ramirez/25 25.00
10 Aubrey Huff/25 25.00
11 Austin Kearns/25 25.00
15 Ben Sheets/25 25.00
18 Brandon Webb/25 15.00
20 C.C. Sabathia/25 25.00
21 Carlos Beltran/50 40.00
23 Chipper Jones/25 65.00
24 Craig Biggio/25 40.00
30 Dontrelle Willis/25 30.00
32 Eric Chavez/50 20.00
34 Frank Thomas/25 70.00
35 Fred McGriff/25 40.00
40 Garret Anderson/20 20.00
40 Hank Blalock/50 35.00
46 Jacque Jones/25 25.00
63 Jim Edmonds/25 40.00
66 Jody Gerut/25 15.00
67 Johan Santana/25 40.00

71 Jorge Posada/25 50.00
74 Jose Vidro/25 15.00
84 Kerry Wood/25 50.00
88 Lance Berkman/25 40.00
90 Larry Walker/25 40.00
98 Marcus Giles/25 25.00
99 Mark Buehrle/25 25.00
100 Mark Mulder/75 15.00
101 Mark Prior/50 40.00
102 Mark Teixeira/25 40.00
105 Melvin Mora/25 25.00
107 Miguel Cabrera/50 30.00
109 Mike Lowell/25 25.00
115 Morgan Ensberg/25 15.00
122 Paul LoDuca/25 25.00
124 Preston Wilson/25 25.00
137 Roy Oswalt/25 25.00
140 Sammy Sosa/25 120.00
142 Scott Rolen/25 50.00
143 Sean Burroughs/25 25.00
145 Shannon Stewart/25 25.00
149 Steve Finley/25 25.00
153 Todd Helton/25 40.00
154 Tom Glavine/25 40.00
155 Torii Hunter/25 25.00
156 Trot Nixon/25 25.00
158 Vernon Wells/25 20.00
159 Victor Martinez/50 40.00
163 Alfonso Soriano/25 40.00
166 Gary Sheffield/25 25.00
172 Juan Gonzalez/25 40.00
183 Scott Rolen/50 40.00
185 Tom Glavine/25 40.00
193 Chipper Jones/25 65.00
194 Garret Anderson/50 40.00
199 Sammy Sosa/25 120.00
200 Todd Helton/25 40.00
201 Andre Dawson/50 20.00
204 Bob Gibson/25 40.00
205 Bobby Doerr/50 25.00
207 Dale Murphy/50 25.00
208 Don Mattingly/50 70.00
209 Gary Carter/25 15.00
216 Mike Schmidt/50 75.00
217 Nolan Ryan/100 120.00
218 Orel Hershiser/50 30.00
219 Paul Molitor/25 30.00
221 Rod Carew/25 30.00
223 Ryne Sandberg/25 100.00
224 Stan Musial/25 100.00
226 Tony Gwynn/100 40.00
228 Whitey Ford/Pants/25 40.00
229 Yogi Berra/25 75.00
230 Carlos Beltran/50 40.00
231 David Ortiz/50 60.00
232 David Ortiz/50 60.00
234 Carlos Lee/50 40.00
235 Travis Hafner/25 25.00
236 Brad Penny/25 15.00
237 Wade Miller/25 15.00
238 Edgar Martinez/25 40.00
239 Carl Crawford/25 25.00
240 Roy Oswalt/25 25.00
242 Carlos Beltran/25 45.00
243 Carlos Beltran/25 45.00
244 Miguel Cabrera/25 40.00
245 Scott Rolen/50 40.00
246 Hank Blalock/25 35.00
247 Vernon Wells/50 25.00
248 Adam Dunn/25 35.00
249 Preston Wilson/25 25.00
250 Victor Martinez/50 20.00

Player Threads Jersey Number
NM/M
Quantity produced listed
Prime: No Pricing
Production One Set
1 Mike Piazza/100 10.00
3 Nolan Ryan/Jkt/100 20.00
4 Reggie Jackson/100 10.00
5 Wade Boggs/100 10.00
6 Steve Carlton/Pants/100 5.00
7 Ivan Rodriguez/25 15.00
8 Pedro Martinez/50 12.00
10 Rickey Henderson/Pants/100 10.00
11 Randy Johnson/100 10.00
12 Curt Schilling/25 15.00
13 Roger Maris/50 50.00
14 Sammy Sosa/100 10.00
15 Gary Carter/Pants/50 8.00
16 Gary Sheffield/25 15.00
17 Eddie Murray/50 15.00
18 Hideo Nomo/50 10.00
19 Rafael Palmeiro/100 10.00
20 Andre Dawson/50 8.00

Player Threads Double
NM/M
Quantity produced listed
1 Mike Piazza/100 15.00
2 Roger Clemens/100 20.00
3 Nolan Ryan/100 30.00
4 Reggie Jackson/100 10.00
5 Wade Boggs/100 10.00
6 Steve Carlton/100 10.00
7 Ivan Rodriguez/100 10.00
8 Pedro Martinez/100 10.00
9 Rickey Henderson/25 25.00
10 Rickey Henderson/100 20.00

11 Randy Johnson/50 20.00
12 Curt Schilling/100 10.00
13 Roger Maris/100 40.00
14 Sammy Sosa/25 15.00
15 Gary Carter/100 8.00
16 Gary Sheffield/50 10.00
17 Eddie Murray/50 20.00
18 Hideo Nomo/50 10.00
19 Rafael Palmeiro/100 10.00
20 Andre Dawson/50 10.00

Player Threads Triple
NM/M
Quantity produced listed
1 Mike Piazza/25 30.00
2 Roger Clemens/25 50.00
3 Nolan Ryan/50 70.00
4 Reggie Jackson/25 40.00
5 Wade Boggs/25 30.00
6 Steve Carlton/25 25.00
7 Ivan Rodriguez/25 30.00
8 Pedro Martinez/25 30.00
10 Rickey Henderson/25 50.00
12 Curt Schilling/25 30.00
13 Roger Maris/25 120.00
14 Sammy Sosa/25 30.00
15 Gary Carter/25 20.00
17 Eddie Murray/25 40.00
18 Hideo Nomo/25 30.00
19 Rafael Palmeiro/25 20.00
20 Andre Dawson/25 20.00

Team Threads Jersey Number
NM/M
Common Card: 15.00
Production 100 Sets
Prime: No Pricing
Production One Set
1 Stan Musial, Albert Pujols 40.00
2 Cal Ripken Jr./Jkt, Mike Mussina 40.00
3 Carlton Fisk, Roger Clemens 25.00
4 Dale Murphy, Chipper Jones 15.00
5 Tony Gwynn, Dave Winfield 25.00
6 Don Mattingly, Hideki Matsui 50.00
7 Lou Boudreau, Early Wynn 15.00
8 Ernie Banks, Sammy Sosa 30.00
9 Nolan Ryan/Jkt, Jeff Bagwell 50.00
10 Mike Schmidt, Jim Thome 25.00

Team Trademarks
NM/M
Common Player: 5.00
Production 100 Sets
Gold: No Pricing
Production 10 Sets
1 Bob Gibson 8.00
2 Cal Ripken Jr. 30.00
3 Carl Yastrzemski 10.00
4 Dale Murphy 8.00
5 Gary Carter 8.00
6 George Brett 15.00
7 Tom Seaver 8.00
8 Kerry Wood 8.00
9 Lou Brock 8.00
10 Luis Aparicio 8.00
11 Mike Piazza 10.00
12 Nolan Ryan 8.00
13 Nolan Ryan 15.00
14 Randy Johnson 8.00
15 Reggie Jackson 8.00
16 Ricky Henderson 8.00
17 Robin Yount 10.00
18 Rod Carew 8.00
19 Ryne Sandberg 15.00
20 Steve Carlton 8.00
21 Steve Garvey 5.00
22 Johnny Bench 8.00
23 Tony Gwynn 10.00
24 Whitey Ford 8.00
25 Will Clark 8.00

Team Trademarks Autographs
NM/M
Quantity produced listed
1 Bob Gibson/100 20.00
2 Cal Ripken Jr./25 150.00
3 Carl Yastrzemski/25 60.00
4 Dale Murphy/100 10.00
5 Gary Carter/100 15.00
6 George Brett/25 65.00
7 Tom Seaver/25 50.00

8 Kerry Wood/25 40.00
9 Lou Brock/100 20.00
10 Luis Aparicio/100 15.00
12 Nolan Ryan/Astros/25 100.00
13 Nolan Ryan/Rgr/25 100.00
15 Reggie Jackson/25 50.00
17 Robin Yount/50 50.00
18 Rod Carew/25 25.00
19 Ryne Sandberg/25 65.00
20 Steve Carlton/25 20.00
21 Steve Garvey/50 25.00
22 Johnny Bench/25 50.00
23 Tony Gwynn/100 35.00
24 Whitey Ford/50 30.00
25 Will Clark/34 50.00

Team Trademarks Jersey Number
NM/M
Quantity produced listed
Prime: No Pricing
Production One Set
1 Bob Gibson/100 10.00
2 Cal Ripken Jr./Pants/100 40.00
3 Carl Yastrzemski/100 15.00
4 Dale Murphy/100 10.00
5 Gary Carter/100 5.00
6 George Brett/100 15.00
7 Tom Seaver/100 10.00
8 Kerry Wood/Pants/100 10.00
9 Lou Brock/100 10.00
10 Luis Aparicio/Pants/100 5.00
11 Mike Piazza/50 15.00
12 Nolan Ryan/Astros/100 20.00
13 Nolan Ryan/Rgr/25 20.00
14 Randy Johnson/50 10.00
15 Reggie Jackson/Pants/100 8.00
16 Ricky Henderson/100 10.00
17 Robin Yount/100 10.00
18 Rod Carew/Jkt/100 8.00
19 Ryne Sandberg/100 15.00
20 Steve Carlton/50 5.00
22 Johnny Bench/100 10.00
23 Tony Gwynn/100 10.00
24 Whitey Ford/100 10.00
25 Will Clark/50 15.00

Team Trademarks Autograph Jersey Numbers
NM/M
Quantity produced listed
Prime: No Pricing
Production One Set
1 Bob Gibson/25 25.00
2 Cal Ripken Jr./Pants/25 200.00
3 Carl Yastrzemski/25 75.00
4 Dale Murphy/100 10.00
5 Gary Carter/25 15.00
6 George Brett/25 80.00
7 Tom Seaver/25 65.00
8 Kerry Wood/Pants/25 50.00
9 Lou Brock/100 25.00
10 Luis Aparicio/Pants/100 15.00
12 Nolan Ryan/Astros/25 120.00
13 Nolan Ryan/Rgr/25 120.00
15 Reggie Jackson/Pants/25 60.00
17 Robin Yount/25 75.00
18 Rod Carew/Jkt/50 30.00
19 Ryne Sandberg/50 65.00
20 Steve Carlton/25 40.00
22 Johnny Bench/50 50.00
23 Tony Gwynn/50 50.00
24 Whitey Ford/50 40.00
25 Will Clark/84 40.00

Threads Jersey
NM/M
Quanity produced listed
Prime: No Pricing
Production One Set
Button: No Pricing
Production 1-6
1 Adam Dunn/25 15.00

3 Albert Pujols/50 20.00
5 Alfonso Soriano/25 15.00
6 Andruw Jones/25 10.00
11 Austin Kearns/25 10.00
12 Barry Larkin/25 15.00
13 Barry Zito/25 8.00
16 Bernie Williams/25 8.00
21 Carlos Beltran/25 15.00
22 Carlos Delgado/25 8.00
23 Chipper Jones/50 10.00
25 Craig Biggio/25 15.00
30 Dontrelle Willis/25 8.00
31 Edgar Renteria/25 8.00
32 Eric Chavez/25 8.00
34 Frank Thomas/25 20.00
36 Garret Anderson/25 10.00
39 Greg Maddux/25 15.00
40 Hank Blalock/25 10.00
41 Hideki Matsui/25 40.00
42 Hideo Nomo/50 10.00
44 Ivan Rodriguez/25 15.00
50 Jason Giambi/50 5.00
55 Javy Lopez/25 10.00
58 Jeff Bagwell/50 10.00
59 Jeff Kent/50 5.00
64 Jim Edmonds/25 10.00
69 John Smoltz/25 15.00
71 Jorge Posada/25 15.00
75 Josh Beckett/25 10.00
76 Juan Gonzalez/25 15.00
84 Kerry Wood/50 12.00
88 Lance Berkman/25 5.00
90 Larry Walker/25 10.00
93 Luis Gonzalez/25 8.00
96 Magglio Ordonez/25 8.00
97 Manny Ramirez/25 10.00
100 Mark Mulder/25 10.00
101 Mark Prior/50 8.00
107 Miguel Cabrera/25 15.00
108 Miguel Tejada/25 10.00
110 Mike Mussina/25 10.00
111 Mike Piazza/50 15.00
112 Mike Sweeney/25 10.00
126 Pedro J. Martinez/50 12.00
126 Rafael Palmeiro/25 15.00
127 Randy Johnson/25 20.00
137 Roy Oswalt/25 10.00
140 Sammy Sosa/25 15.00
142 Scott Rolen/25 20.00
146 Shawn Green/25 8.00
150 Tim Hudson/25 10.00
153 Todd Helton/50 15.00
154 Tom Glavine/25 15.00
155 Torii Hunter/25 10.00
157 Troy Glaus/25 10.00
158 Vernon Wells/25 8.00
161 Vladimir Guerrero/25 20.00
162 Alex Rodriguez/100 10.00
163 Alfonso Soriano/50 10.00
164 Andy Pettitte/25 15.00
165 Curt Schilling/25 10.00
166 Gary Sheffield/25 10.00
167 Greg Maddux/50 15.00
168 Hideo Nomo/25 20.00
169 Ivan Rodriguez/50 12.00
170 Jason Giambi/25 8.00
172 Juan Gonzalez/25 15.00
174 Kevin Brown/25 8.00
176 Miguel Tejada/25 10.00
177 Mike Mussina/50 15.00
178 Mike Piazza/25 15.00
179 Pedro Martinez/25 20.00
180 Rafael Palmeiro/25 15.00
181 Randy Johnson/25 10.00
182 Roger Clemens/100 10.00
183 Scott Rolen/25 20.00
184 Shawn Green/25 8.00
185 Tom Glavine/25 15.00
186 Vladimir Guerrero/25 20.00
187 Alex Rodriguez/100 10.00
189 Randy Johnson/25 8.00
190 Roger Clemens/25 15.00
191 Albert Pujols/25 20.00
192 Barry Zito/25 10.00
193 Chipper Jones/25 15.00
194 Garret Anderson/25 10.00
195 Jeff Bagwell/50 10.00
197 Magglio Ordonez/25 10.00
198 Mark Prior/25 8.00
200 Todd Helton/25 10.00
201 Andre Dawson/25 5.00
202 Babe Ruth/25 350.00
205 Bob Feller/25 20.00
205 Bobby Doerr/50 8.00
206 Cal Ripken Jr./100 40.00
207 Dale Murphy/100 10.00
208 Don Mattingly/25 25.00
209 Gary Carter/50 10.00
210 George Brett/100 15.00
211 Jackie Robinson/50 40.00
212 Lou Brock/25 20.00
213 Lou Gehrig/25 140.00
214 Mark Grace/25 15.00
215 Maury Wills/50 5.00
216 Mike Schmidt/100 15.00
217 Nolan Ryan/100 20.00
218 Orel Hershiser/25 15.00
219 Paul Molitor/50 10.00
221 Roberto Clemente/25 80.00
222 Rod Carew/100 15.00
222 Roy Campanella/Pants/50 15.00
223 Ryne Sandberg/50 25.00
224 Stan Musial/25 40.00

225 Ted Williams/50 75.00
226 Tony Gwynn/100 10.00
227 Ty Cobb/Pants/25 75.00
228 Whitey Ford/Pants/25 20.00
229 Yogi Berra/25 25.00
230 Carlos Beltran/50 15.00
231 David Ortiz/25 20.00
233 David Ortiz/25 20.00
238 Edgar Martinez/25 10.00
240 Roy Oswalt/25 10.00
242 Carlos Beltran/25 15.00
243 Carlos Beltran/25 15.00
244 Miguel Cabrera/25 15.00
245 Scott Rolen/25 20.00
246 Hank Blalock/25 12.00
247 Vernon Wells/25 8.00
248 Adam Dunn/25 15.00

Threads Jersey Number
NM/M
Quanity produced listed
Prime: No Pricing
Production One Set
MLB Logo: No Pricing
Production One Set
1 Adam Dunn/25 15.00
3 Albert Pujols/50 20.00
5 Alfonso Soriano/25 15.00
9 Andruw Jones/25 10.00
11 Austin Kearns/25 8.00
12 Barry Larkin/25 15.00
13 Barry Zito/25 8.00
16 Bernie Williams/50 10.00
21 Carlos Beltran/25 15.00
22 Carlos Delgado/25 8.00
23 Chipper Jones/50 15.00
25 Craig Biggio/25 10.00
29 Curt Schilling/25 10.00
30 Dontrelle Willis/25 8.00
31 Edgar Renteria/25 10.00
32 Eric Chavez/25 10.00
34 Frank Thomas/25 15.00
36 Garret Anderson/25 10.00
39 Greg Maddux/50 15.00
40 Hank Blalock/25 12.00
41 Hideki Matsui/50 40.00
42 Hideo Nomo/50 10.00
44 Ivan Rodriguez/25 20.00
50 Jason Giambi/50 5.00
55 Javy Lopez/25 8.00
58 Jeff Bagwell/50 10.00
59 Jeff Kent/25 10.00
63 Jim Edmonds/25 15.00
69 Jim Thome/50 15.00
71 Jorge Posada/25 15.00
75 Josh Beckett/25 10.00
76 Juan Gonzalez/25 15.00
85 Kerry Wood/50 12.00
88 Lance Berkman/25 5.00
90 Larry Walker/25 10.00
93 Luis Gonzalez/25 8.00
96 Magglio Ordonez/25 8.00
97 Manny Ramirez/25 12.00
100 Mark Mulder/25 10.00
101 Mark Prior/50 15.00
107 Miguel Cabrera/25 15.00
108 Miguel Tejada/25 10.00
110 Mike Mussina/50 15.00
111 Mike Piazza/25 15.00
112 Mike Sweeney/25 10.00
123 Pedro J. Martinez/50 12.00
126 Rafael Palmeiro/25 15.00
127 Randy Johnson/25 20.00
137 Roy Oswalt/25 10.00
140 Sammy Sosa/50 15.00
142 Scott Rolen/25 8.00
146 Shawn Green/25 8.00
150 Tim Hudson/25 10.00
153 Todd Helton/50 10.00
154 Tom Glavine/25 15.00
155 Torii Hunter/25 10.00
157 Troy Glaus/25 8.00
158 Vernon Wells/25 10.00
161 Vladimir Guerrero/25 20.00
162 Alex Rodriguez/100 10.00
163 Alfonso Soriano/50 10.00
164 Andy Pettitte/25 15.00
165 Curt Schilling/25 10.00
166 Gary Sheffield/25 10.00
167 Greg Maddux/50 15.00
168 Hideo Nomo/25 20.00
169 Ivan Rodriguez/50 12.00
170 Jason Giambi/25 8.00
173 Juan Gonzalez/25 12.00
174 Kevin Brown/25 8.00
176 Miguel Tejada/25 10.00
177 Mike Mussina/25 10.00
178 Mike Piazza/25 25.00
179 Pedro Martinez/25 15.00
180 Rafael Palmeiro/25 15.00
181 Randy Johnson/25 10.00
182 Roger Clemens/100 10.00
183 Scott Rolen/25 20.00
184 Shawn Green/25 8.00
185 Tom Glavine/25 15.00
186 Vladimir Guerrero/25 20.00
187 Alex Rodriguez/100 10.00
188 Randy Johnson/25 10.00
190 Roger Clemens/100 10.00
191 Albert Pujols/50 20.00
192 Barry Zito/25 8.00
193 Chipper Jones/50 10.00
194 Garret Anderson/25 10.00
195 Jeff Bagwell/50 10.00

196 Josh Beckett/25 10.00
197 Magglio Ordonez/25 8.00
198 Mark Prior/50 8.00
199 Sammy Sosa/25 15.00
200 Todd Helton/50 10.00
201 Andre Dawson/25 5.00
202 Babe Ruth/25 300.00
203 Bob Feller/25 20.00
205 Bobby Doerr/25 8.00
206 Cal Ripken Jr./100 40.00
207 Dale Murphy/100 10.00
208 Don Mattingly/50 25.00
209 Gary Carter/50 10.00
210 George Brett/50 15.00
211 Jackie Robinson/100 40.00
212 Lou Brock/25 20.00
213 Lou Gehrig/25 150.00
214 Mark Grace/25 15.00
215 Maury Wills/50 8.00
216 Mike Schmidt/100 15.00
217 Nolan Ryan/100 20.00
218 Orel Hershiser/25 10.00
219 Paul Molitor/25 10.00
220 Roberto Clemente/25 80.00
221 Rod Carew/100 15.00
222 Roy Campanella/Pants/50 10.00
223 Ryne Sandberg/50 25.00
224 Stan Musial/50 40.00
225 Ted Williams/50 75.00
226 Tony Gwynn/100 10.00
227 Ty Cobb/Pants/50 60.00
228 Whitey Ford/Pants/25 20.00
229 Yogi Berra/25 25.00
230 Carlos Beltran/25 15.00
231 David Ortiz/25 20.00
232 David Ortiz/25 20.00
238 Edgar Martinez/25 10.00
240 Roy Oswalt H/25 10.00
242 Carlos Beltran/25 15.00
243 Carlos Beltran/25 15.00
244 Miguel Cabrera/25 15.00
245 Scott Rolen/25 10.00
246 Hank Blalock/25 20.00
247 Vernon Wells/25 10.00
248 Adam Dunn/25 15.00

Timber
NM/M
Quanity produced listed
1 Adam Dunn/25 15.00
4 Alex Rodriguez/100 10.00
5 Alfonso Soriano/25 10.00
6 Andruw Jones/25 10.00
7 Andy Pettitte/25 15.00
11 Austin Kearns/25 8.00
12 Barry Larkin/25 15.00
13 Barry Zito/25 8.00
16 Bernie Williams/25 12.00
21 Carlos Beltran/25 5.00
22 Carlos Delgado/25 10.00
23 Chipper Jones/25 20.00
24 Craig Biggio/25 12.00
25 Curt Schilling/25 20.00
30 Dontrelle Willis/25 8.00
32 Eric Chavez/25 8.00
34 Frank Thomas/25 20.00
35 Fred McGriff/25 12.00
36 Garret Anderson/25 10.00
37 Gary Sheffield/25 10.00
39 Greg Maddux/25 25.00
40 Hank Blalock/25 10.00
41 Hideki Matsui/25 60.00
42 Hideo Nomo/25 10.00
44 Ivan Rodriguez/25 20.00
50 Jason Giambi/25 8.00
55 Javy Lopez/25 8.00
58 Jeff Bagwell/25 15.00
59 Jeff Kent/25 8.00
63 Jim Edmonds/25 10.00
69 Jim Thome/25 20.00
71 Jorge Posada/25 15.00
75 Josh Beckett/25 15.00
76 Juan Gonzalez/25 15.00
84 Kerry Wood/25 20.00
85 Kevin Brown/25 8.00
88 Lance Berkman/25 8.00
90 Larry Walker/25 10.00
93 Luis Gonzalez/25 8.00
96 Magglio Ordonez/25 8.00
97 Manny Ramirez/25 15.00
100 Mark Mulder/25 8.00
101 Mark Prior/25 15.00
102 Mark Teixeira/25 10.00
106 Michael Young/25 8.00
107 Miguel Cabrera/25 15.00
108 Miguel Tejada/25 10.00
109 Mike Lowell/25 8.00
110 Mike Mussina/25 15.00
111 Mike Piazza/25 25.00
112 Mike Sweeney/25 8.00
116 Nick Johnson/25 8.00
118 Nomar Garciaparra/25 20.00
122 Paul LoDuca/25 8.00
123 Pedro J. Martinez/25 10.00
126 Rafael Palmeiro/25 15.00
127 Randy Johnson/25 20.00
130 Richie Sexson/25 10.00
134 Rocco Baldelli/25 8.00
135 Roger Clemens/25 25.00
137 Roy Oswalt/25 8.00
140 Sammy Sosa/50 15.00
142 Scott Rolen/25 10.00
146 Shawn Green/25 8.00
150 Tim Hudson/25

153	Todd Helton/25	15.00
154	Tom Glavine/25	15.00
155	Torii Hunter/25	8.00
156	Trot Nixon/25	10.00
157	Troy Glaus/25	8.00
158	Vernon Wells/25	8.00
161	Vladimir Guerrero/25	20.00
162	Alex Rodriguez/100	10.00
163	Alfonso Soriano/25	15.00
164	Andy Pettitte/25	15.00
165	Curt Schilling/25	15.00
166	Gary Sheffield/25	10.00
167	Greg Maddux/25	25.00
168	Hideo Nomo/25	15.00
169	Ivan Rodriguez/25	15.00
170	Jason Giambi/25	8.00
171	Jim Thome/25	15.00
172	Juan Gonzalez/25	10.00
174	Kevin Brown/25	8.00
175	Manny Ramirez/25	15.00
176	Miguel Tejada/25	10.00
177	Mike Mussina/25	15.00
178	Mike Piazza/25	15.00
179	Pedro Martinez/25	20.00
180	Rafael Palmeiro/25	15.00
181	Randy Johnson/25	15.00
182	Roger Clemens/25	15.00
183	Scott Rolen/25	20.00
184	Shawn Green/25	8.00
185	Tom Glavine/25	15.00
186	Vladimir Guerrero/25	20.00
187	Alex Rodriguez/100	10.00
188	Mike Piazza/25	25.00
189	Randy Johnson/25	15.00
190	Roger Clemens/25	25.00
191	Albert Pujols/50	20.00
192	Barry Zito/25	8.00
193	Chipper Jones/25	20.00
194	Garret Anderson/25	8.00
195	Jeff Bagwell/25	15.00
196	Josh Beckett/25	8.00
197	Magglio Ordonez/25	8.00
198	Mark Prior/25	15.00
199	Sammy Sosa/25	15.00
200	Todd Helton/25	15.00
201	Andre Dawson/50	8.00
202	Babe Ruth/100	120.00
206	Cal Ripken Jr./100	40.00
207	Dale Murphy/50	15.00
208	Don Mattingly/50	25.00
209	Gary Carter/25	15.00
210	George Brett/50	25.00
212	Lou Brock/25	15.00
213	Lou Gehrig/100	100.00
214	Mark Grace/25	15.00
216	Mike Schmidt/50	25.00
217	Nolan Ryan/50	30.00
219	Paul Molitor/50	10.00
220	Roberto Clemente/100	75.00
221	Rod Carew/25	25.00
222	Roy Campanella/100	100.00
223	Ryne Sandberg/25	25.00
224	Stan Musial/100	20.00
225	Ted Williams/100	50.00
226	Tony Gwynn/50	20.00
227	Ty Cobb/50	75.00
229	Yogi Berra/100	10.00
230	Carlos Beltran/25	15.00
231	David Ortiz/25	20.00
232	David Ortiz/25	20.00
238	Edgar Martinez/25	10.00
240	Roy Oswalt/25	10.00
242	Carlos Beltran/25	15.00
243	Carlos Beltran/25	15.00
244	Miguel Cabrera/25	15.00
245	Scott Rolen/25	10.00
246	Hank Blalock/25	10.00
248	Adam Dunn/25	15.00

TNT

NM/M

Quanity produced listed
Prime: No Pricing
Production One Set

1	Adam Dunn/ Bat-Jsy/50	10.00
3	Albert Pujols/ Bat-Jsy/100	15.00
5	Alfonso Soriano/ Bat-Jsy/50	10.00
6	Andruw Jones/ Bat-Jsy/50	8.00
11	Austin Kearns/ Bat-Jsy/50	5.00
12	Barry Larkin/ Bat-Jsy/25	20.00
13	Barry Zito/ Bat-Jsy/50	5.00
16	Bernie Williams/ Bat-Jsy/50	10.00
21	Carlos Beltran/ Bat-Jsy/50	10.00
22	Carlos Delgado/ Bat-Jsy/50	5.00
23	Chipper Jones/ Bat-Jsy/50	15.00
24	Craig Biggio/ Bat-Jsy/50	8.00
25	Curt Schilling/ Bat-Jsy/25	25.00
32	Eric Chavez/ Bat-Jsy/50	10.00
34	Frank Thomas/ Bat-Jsy/25	20.00
36	Garret Anderson/ Bat-Jsy/25	10.00

39	Greg Maddux/ Bat-Jsy/50	20.00
40	Hank Blalock/ Bat-Jsy/50	8.00
41	Hideki Matsui/ Bat-Jsy/50	50.00
42	Hideo Nomo/ Bat-Jsy/50	20.00
44	Ivan Rodriguez/ Bat-Jsy/50	20.00
50	Jason Giambi/ Bat-Jsy/50	8.00
55	Javy Lopez/ Bat-Jsy/25	10.00
58	Jeff Bagwell/ Bat-Jsy/25	10.00
59	Jeff Kent/ Bat-Jsy/50	10.00
63	Jim Edmonds/ Bat-Jsy/25	10.00
64	Jim Thome/ Bat-Jsy/50	15.00
71	Jorge Posada/ Bat-Jsy/25	20.00
75	Josh Beckett/ Bat-Jsy/50	10.00
76	Juan Gonzalez/ Bat-Jsy/50	20.00
84	Kerry Wood/ Bat-Jsy/50	15.00
88	Lance Berkman/ Bat-Jsy/50	5.00
90	Larry Walker/ Bat-Jsy/25	
93	Luis Gonzalez/ Bat-Jsy/50	10.00
96	Magglio Ordonez/ Bat-Jsy/25	10.00
97	Manny Ramirez/ Bat-Jsy/50	15.00
100	Mark Mulder/ Bat-Jsy/50	10.00
101	Mark Prior/ Bat-Jsy/50	10.00
102	Mark Teixeira/ Bat-Jsy/50	10.00
107	Miguel Cabrera/ Bat-Jsy/50	20.00
108	Miguel Tejada/ Bat-Jsy/25	10.00
109	Mike Lowell/ Bat-Jsy/25	10.00
110	Mike Mussina/ Bat-Jsy/50	10.00
111	Mike Piazza/ Bat-Jsy/50	20.00
112	Mike Sweeney/ Bat-Jsy/25	10.00
123	Pedro J. Martinez/ Bat-Jsy/50	15.00
126	Rafael Palmeiro/ Bat-Jsy/25	10.00
127	Randy Johnson/ Bat-Jsy/50	15.00
137	Roy Oswalt/ Bat-Jsy/25	10.00
140	Sammy Sosa/ Bat-Jsy/50	20.00
142	Scott Rolen/ Bat-Jsy/25	25.00
146	Shawn Green/ Bat-Jsy/25	10.00
150	Tim Hudson/ Bat-Jsy/25	10.00
153	Todd Helton/ Bat-Jsy/50	10.00
154	Tom Glavine/ Bat-Jsy/25	20.00
155	Torii Hunter/ Bat-Jsy/25	10.00
157	Troy Glaus/ Bat-Jsy/25	10.00
158	Vernon Wells/ Bat-Jsy/25	10.00
161	Vladimir Guerrero/ Bat-Jsy/25	25.00
162	Alex Rodriguez/ Bat-Jsy/100	10.00
163	Alfonso Soriano/ Bat-Jsy/50	10.00
164	Andy Pettitte/ Bat-Jsy/25	20.00
165	Curt Schilling/ Bat-Jsy/25	10.00
166	Gary Sheffield/ Bat-Jsy/25	10.00
167	Greg Maddux/ Bat-Jsy/50	20.00
168	Hideo Nomo/ Bat-Jsy/50	20.00
169	Ivan Rodriguez/ Bat-Jsy/50	15.00
170	Jason Giambi/ Bat-Jsy/50	
172	Juan Gonzalez/ Bat-Jsy/50	15.00
174	Kevin Brown/ Bat-Jsy/25	10.00
176	Miguel Tejada/ Bat-Jsy/50	10.00
177	Mike Mussina/ Bat-Jsy/50	10.00
178	Mike Piazza/ Bat-Jsy/50	20.00
179	Pedro Martinez/ Bat-Jsy/50	15.00
180	Rafael Palmeiro/ Bat-Jsy/50	10.00

181	Randy Johnson/ Bat-Jsy/50	15.00
182	Roger Clemens/ Bat-Jsy/50	10.00
183	Scott Rolen/ Bat-Jsy/25	25.00
184	Shawn Green/ Bat-Jsy/25	10.00
185	Tom Glavine/ Bat-Jsy/25	20.00
186	Vladimir Guerrero/ Bat-Jsy/25	25.00
187	Alex Rodriguez/ Bat-Jsy/100	10.00
189	Randy Johnson/ Bat-Jsy/50	15.00
190	Roger Clemens/ Bat-Jsy/50	10.00
191	Albert Pujols/ Bat-Jsy/50	10.00
192	Barry Zito/ Bat-Jsy/25	10.00
193	Chipper Jones/ Bat-Jsy/50	15.00
194	Garret Anderson/ Bat-Jsy/50	10.00
195	Jeff Bagwell/ Bat-Jsy/50	10.00
196	Josh Beckett/ Bat-Jsy/50	10.00
197	Magglio Ordonez/ Bat-Jsy/50	10.00
198	Mark Prior/ Bat-Jsy/50	10.00
199	Sammy Sosa/ Bat-Jsy/50	20.00
200	Todd Helton/ Bat-Jsy/50	10.00
201	Andre Dawson/ Bat-Jsy/50	8.00
202	Babe Ruth/ Bat-Jsy/50	425.00
206	Cal Ripken Jr./ Bat-Jsy/50	60.00
207	Dale Murphy/ Bat-Jsy/25	10.00
208	Don Mattingly/ Bat-Jsy/100	10.00
209	Gary Carter/ Bat-Jsy/50	10.00
210	George Brett/ Bat-Jsy/100	20.00
212	Lou Brock/ Bat-Jsy/25	25.00
213	Lou Gehrig/ Bat-Jsy/50	250.00
214	Mark Grace/ Bat-Jsy/25	20.00
216	Mike Schmidt/ Bat-Jsy/50	30.00
217	Nolan Ryan/ Bat-Jsy/25	25.00
219	Paul Molitor/ Bat-Jsy/50	20.00
221	Rod Carew/ Bat-Jsy/50	15.00
222	Roy Campanella/ Bat-Pants/50	20.00
223	Ryne Sandberg/ Bat-Jsy/50	30.00
224	Stan Musial/ Bat-Jsy/50	50.00
225	Ted Williams/ Bat-Jsy/50	100.00
226	Tony Gwynn/ Bat-Jsy/25	15.00
227	Ty Cobb/ Bat-Pants/50	120.00
230	Carlos Beltran/ Bat-Jsy/25	20.00
231	David Ortiz/ Bat-Jsy/25	25.00
232	David Ortiz/ Bat-Jsy/25	25.00
238	Edgar Martinez/ Bat-Jsy/25	15.00
240	Roy Oswalt/ Bat-Jsy/25	10.00
242	Carlos Beltran/ Bat-Jsy/25	20.00
243	Carlos Beltran/ Bat-Jsy/25	20.00
244	Miguel Cabrera/ Bat-Jsy/25	20.00
245	Scott Rolen/ Bat-Jsy/25	20.00
246	Hank Blalock/ Bat-Jsy/25	10.00
247	Vernon Wells/ Bat-Jsy/25	10.00
248	Adam Dunn/ Bat-Jsy/25	20.00

2005 Leaf

NM/M

Complete Set (300)	
Common Player (1-200)	.15
Common SP (201-250)	1.00
Inserted 1:3	
Common SP (251-300)	1.00
#251-270 inserted 1:6	
271-300 inserted 1:4	
Hobby Pack (8):	4.00
Hobby Box (24):	80.00

1	Bartolo Colon	.25
2	Casey Kotchman	.15
3	Chone Figgins	.15
4	Darin Erstad	.25
5	Francisco Rodriguez	.25
6	Garret Anderson	.25
7	Jarrod Washburn	.15
8	Troy Glaus	.25
9	Vladimir Guerrero	.50
10	Brandon Webb	.15
11	Casey Fossum	.15
12	Luis Gonzalez	.25
13	Randy Johnson	.50
14	Richie Sexson	.25
15	Andruw Jones	.25
16	Chipper Jones	.50
17	J.D. Drew	.25
18	John Smoltz	.25
19	Johnny Estrada	.15
20	Marcus Giles	.15
21	Rafael Furcal	.25
22	Russ Ortiz	.15
23	Javy Lopez	.25
24	Jay Gibbons	.15
25	Melvin Mora	.15
26	Miguel Tejada	.40
27	Rafael Palmeiro	.40
28	Sidney Ponson	.15
29	Bill Mueller	.15
30	Curt Schilling	.40
31	David Ortiz	.50
32	Doug Mientkiewicz	.15
33	Jason Varitek	.25
34	Johnny Damon	.40
35	Manny Ramirez	.50
36	Pedro J. Martinez	.50
37	Trot Nixon	.15
38	Aramis Ramirez	.25
39	Corey Patterson	.15
40	Derrek Lee	.25
41	Greg Maddux	.75
42	Kerry Wood	.50
43	Mark Prior	.50
44	Moises Alou	.25
45	Nomar Garciaparra	1.00
46	Sammy Sosa	1.00
47	Carlos Lee	.15
48	Kip Wells	.15
49	Magglio Ordonez	.25
50	Mark Buehrle	.15
51	Paul Konerko	.25
52	Roberto Alomar	.25
53	Adam Dunn	.40
54	Austin Kearns	.15
55	Barry Larkin	.25
56	Danny Graves	.15
57	Ken Griffey Jr.	1.00
58	Sean Casey	.15
59	C.C. Sabathia	.15
60	Cliff Lee	.15
61	Jody Gerut	.15
62	Omar Vizquel	.25
63	Travis Hafner	.15
64	Victor Martinez	.25
65	Charles Johnson	.15
66	Jason Jennings	.15
67	Jeromy Burnitz	.15
68	Preston Wilson	.15
69	Todd Helton	.40
70	Bobby Higginson	.15
71	Dmitri Young	.15
72	Eric Munson	.15
73	Ivan Rodriguez	.40
74	Jeremy Bonderman	.15
75	Rondell White	.15
76	A.J. Burnett	.15
77	Carl Pavano	.25
78	Dontrelle Willis	.25
79	Hee Seop Choi	.15
80	Josh Beckett	.25
81	Juan Pierre	.15
82	Miguel Cabrera	.50
83	Mike Lowell	.15
84	Paul LoDuca	.15
85	Andy Pettitte	.25
86	Carlos Beltran	.40
87	Craig Biggio	.25
88	Jeff Bagwell	.40
89	Jeff Kent	.25
90	Lance Berkman	.25
91	Roger Clemens	1.50
92	Roy Oswalt	.25
93	Andres Blanco	.15
94	Jeremy Affeldt	.15
95	Juan Gonzalez	.25
96	Ken Harvey	.15
97	Mike Sweeney	.15
98	Zack Greinke	.25
99	Adrian Beltre	.25
100	Brad Penny	.15
101	Eric Gagne	.25
102	Kazuhisa Ishii	.15
103	Milton Bradley	.15
104	Shawn Green	.25
105	Steve Finley	.15
106	Ben Sheets	.25
107	Bill Hall	.15
108	Danny Kolb	.15
109	Geoff Jenkins	.15
110	Junior Spivey	.15
111	Lyle Overbay	.15
112	Scott Podsednik	.15
113	A.J. Pierzynski	.15
114	Brad Radke	.15
115	Corey Koskie	.15
116	Jacque Jones	.15
117	Joe Mauer	.50
118	Joe Nathan	.15
119	Shannon Stewart	.15
120	Torii Hunter	.25
121	Brad Wilkerson	.15
122	Jeff Fassero	.15
123	Jose Vidro	.15
124	Livan Hernandez	.15
125	Nick Johnson	.15
126	Al Leiter	.25
127	Jose Reyes	.25
128	Kazuo Matsui	.25
129	Mike Cameron	.15
130	Mike Piazza	1.00
131	Richard Hidalgo	.15
132	Tom Glavine	.25
133	Alex Rodriguez	1.50
134	Bernie Williams	.25
135	Derek Jeter	1.50
136	Gary Sheffield	.40
137	Jason Giambi	.25
138	Javier Vazquez	.25
139	Jorge Posada	.25
140	Kevin Brown	.15
141	Mariano Rivera	.25
142	Mike Mussina	.25
143	Barry Zito	.25
144	Bobby Crosby	.25
145	Eric Chavez	.25
146	Erubiel Durazo	.15
147	Jermaine Dye	.15
148	Mark Mulder	.25
149	Tim Hudson	.25
151	Bobby Abreu	.25
152	Eric Milton	.15
153	Jim Thome	.50
155	Kevin Millwood	.15
155	Mike Lieberthal	.15
156	Pat Burrell	.25
157	Randy Wolf	.15
158	Craig Wilson	.15
159	Jack Wilson	.15
160	Jason Bay	.25
161	Jason Kendall	.15
162	Kris Benson	.15
163	Brian Giles	.15
164	Jake Peavy	.15
165	Jay Payton	.15
166	Khalil Greene	.25
167	Mark Loretta	.15
168	Ryan Klesko	.15
169	Sean Burroughs	.15
170	David Aardsma	.15
171	Edgardo Alfonzo	.15
172	Jason Schmidt	.25
173	Merkin Valdez	.15
174	Ray Durham	.15
175	Bret Boone	.15
176	Dan Wilson	.15
177	Ichiro Suzuki	1.25
178	Jamie Moyer	.15
179	Rich Aurilia	.15
180	Albert Pujols	1.50
181	Edgar Renteria	.25
182	Jason Isringhausen	.15
183	Jeff Suppan	.15
184	Jim Edmonds	.25
185	Scott Rolen	.50
186	Woody Williams	.15
187	Aubrey Huff	.15
188	Carl Crawford	.15
189	Dewon Brazelton	.15
190	Jose Cruz Jr.	.15
191	Rocco Baldelli	.25
192	Alfonso Soriano	.40
193	Hank Blalock	.40
194	Kenny Rogers	.15
195	Laynce Nix	.15
196	Mark Teixeira	.25
197	Michael Young	.15
198	Alexis Rios	.15
199	Carlos Delgado	.25
200	Roy Halladay	.15
201	Vernon Wells	.15
202	Josh Kroeger	1.00
203	Angel Guzman	1.00
204	Brad Halsey	1.00
205	Bucky Jacobsen	1.00
206	Carlos Hines	1.00
207	Carlos Vasquez	1.00
208	Billy Traber	1.00
209	Chris Oxspring	1.00
210	Chris Shelton	1.00
211	Colby Miller	1.00
212	David Crouthers	1.00
213	Dennis Sarfate	1.00
214	Donald Kelly	1.00
215	Edwardo Sierra	1.00
216	Edwin Moreno	1.00
218	Fernando Nieve	1.00
218	Freddy Guzman	1.00
219	Greg Dobbs	1.00
220	Hector Gimenez	1.00
221	Andy Green	1.00
222	Jason Bartlett	1.00
223	Jerry Gil	1.00
224	Jesse Crain	2.00
225	Joey Gathright	1.00
226	John Gall	1.00
227	Jorge Sequea	1.00
228	Jorge Vasquez	1.00
229	Josh Labandeira	1.00
230	Justin Leone	1.00
231	Lance Cormier	1.00
232	Lincoln Holdzkom	1.00
233	Miguel Olivo	1.00
234	Mike Rouse	1.00
235	Onil Joseph	1.00
236	Phil Stockman	1.00
237	Ramon Ramirez	1.00
238	Robb Quinlan	1.00
239	Roberto Novoa	1.00
240	Ronald Belisario	1.00
241	Ronny Cedeno	1.00
242	Ruddy Yan	1.00
243	Ryan Meaux	1.00
244	Ryan Wing	1.00
245	Scott Proctor	1.00
246	Sean Henn	1.00
247	Tim Bausher	1.00
248	Tim Bittner	1.00
249	William Bergolla	1.00
250	Yadier Molina	1.00
251	Bernie Williams	1.00
252	Craig Biggio	1.00
253	Chipper Jones	2.00
254	Greg Maddux	3.00
255	Sammy Sosa	3.00
256	Mike Mussina	1.50
257	Tim Salmon	1.00
258	Barry Larkin	1.00
259	Randy Johnson	2.00
260	Jeff Bagwell	1.50
261	Roberto Alomar	1.50
262	Tom Glavine	1.00
263	Roger Clemens	4.00
264	Alex Rodriguez	4.00
265	Ivan Rodriguez	1.50
266	Pedro J. Martinez	2.00
267	Ken Griffey Jr.	3.00
268	Jim Thome	2.00
269	Frank Thomas	1.50
270	Mike Piazza	3.00
271	Garret Anderson	1.00
272	Luis Gonzalez	1.00
273	John Smoltz	1.00
274	Rafael Palmeiro	1.50
275	Curt Schilling	1.50
276	Mark Prior	1.50
277	Magglio Ordonez	1.50
278	Adam Dunn	1.50
279	Travis Hafner	1.00
280	Jeromy Burnitz	1.00
281	Carlos Guillen	1.00
282	Dontrelle Willis	1.00
283	Carlos Beltran	1.50
284	Zack Greinke	1.00
285	Adrian Beltre	1.00
286	Ben Sheets	1.00
287	Johan Santana	1.00
288	Livan Hernandez	1.00
289	Kazuo Matsui	1.00
290	Derek Jeter	4.00
291	Tim Hudson	1.00
292	Eric Milton	1.00
293	Jason Kendall	1.00
294	Jake Peavy	1.00
295	Ray Durham	1.00
296	Ichiro Suzuki	3.00
297	Scott Rolen	2.00
298	Carl Crawford	1.00
299	Hank Blalock	1.50
300	Roy Halladay	1.00

Press Proofs Blue

Blue (1-200):	5-10X
Blue (201-250):	1-2X
Blue (251-300):	2-4X
Production 75 Sets	

Press Proofs Gold

Gold (1-200):	10-20X
Gold (201-250):	2-4X
Blue (251-300):	4-8X
Production 25 Sets	

Press Proofs Red

Red (1-200):	2-4X
Red (201-250):	.5-1X

Red (251-300): 1-2X
Inserted 1:8

Alternate Threads

	NM/M
Complete Set (25):	30.00
Common Player:	1.00
Inserted 1:18	
Holo:	1-2X
Production 150 Sets	
Holo Die-Cut:	2-4X
Production 50 Sets	
1 Adam Dunn	1.50
2 C.C. Sabathia	1.00
3 Curt Schilling	1.50
4 Dontrelle Willis	1.00
5 Greg Maddux	3.00
6 Hank Blalock	1.50
7 Ichiro Suzuki	4.00
8 Jeff Bagwell	1.50
9 Ken Griffey Jr.	3.00
10 Ken Harvey	1.00
11 Magglio Ordonez	1.00
12 Mark Mulder	1.00
13 Mark Teixeira	1.00
14 Michael Young	1.00
15 Miguel Tejada	1.00
16 Mike Piazza	4.00
17 Pedro Martinez	2.00
18 Randy Johnson	2.00
19 Roger Clemens	6.00
20 Sammy Sosa	4.00
21 Tim Hudson	1.00
22 Todd Helton	1.50
23 Torii Hunter	1.00
24 Travis Hafner	1.00
25 Vernon Wells	1.00

Autographs

	NM/M
Common Autograph:	5.00
201 Josh Kroeger	5.00
202 Angel Guzman	15.00
203 Brad Halsey	5.00
204 Bucky Jacobsen	10.00
205 Carlos Hines	5.00
207 Bill Tucker	5.00
208 Bubba Crosby	10.00
210 Chris Shelton	5.00
211 Colby Miller	5.00
212 David Crouthers	5.00
217 Fernando Nieve	10.00
220 Hector Gimenez	5.00
221 Andy Green	5.00
222 Jason Bartlett	5.00
227 Jorge Sequea/84	10.00
228 Jorge Vasquez	8.00
232 Lincoln Holdzkom	8.00
233 Miguel Olivo	8.00
234 Mike Rouse	8.00
236 Phil Stockman	8.00
237 Ramon Ramirez	8.00
242 Ruddy Yan	8.00
245 Scott Proctor	8.00
247 Tim Bausher	8.00
249 William Bergolla	10.00

Autographs Blue

No Pricing
Production 15-25
Golds: No Pricing

Autographs Red

	NM/M
Common Autograph:	
3 Chone Figgins/100	8.00
19 Johnny Estrada/100	15.00
24 Jay Gibbons/100	10.00
47 Carlos Lee/100	10.00
56 Danny Graves/100	8.00
60 Cliff Lee/100	10.00
63 Travis Hafner/50	15.00
74 Jeremy Bonderman/100	10.00
94 Jeremy Affeldt/100	8.00
96 Ken Harvey/100	8.00
103 Milton Bradley/100	8.00
111 Lyle Overbay/50	15.00
118 Joe Nathan/100	8.00
144 Bobby Crosby/100	25.00
154 Mike Lieberthal/50	15.00
157 Craig Wilson/50	15.00
158 Jack Wilson/100	12.00
163 Jake Peavy/100	25.00
172 Merkin Valdez/100	10.00
182 Jeff Suppan/100	10.00

187 Carl Crawford/50	15.00
188 Dewon Brazelton/50	10.00
194 Laynce Nix/100	10.00
202 Angel Guzman/100	15.00
203 Brad Halsey/100	8.00
204 Bucky Jacobsen/100	10.00
205 Carlos Hines/100	8.00
207 Billy Traber/100	8.00
208 Bubba Crosby/100	10.00
210 Chris Shelton/100	8.00
211 Colby Miller/100	8.00
212 David Crouthers/100	8.00
217 Fernando Nieve/100	10.00
218 Freddy Guzman/100	8.00
220 Hector Gimenez/100	8.00
221 Andy Green/100	8.00
222 Jason Bartlett/100	8.00
224 Josh Crain/100	15.00
227 Jorge Sequea/84	10.00
228 Jorge Vasquez/100	8.00
233 Miguel Olivo/100	8.00
234 Mike Rouse/100	8.00
236 Phil Stockman/100	10.00
237 Ramon Ramirez/100	8.00
238 Robb Quinlan/100	8.00
241 Ronny Cedeno/65	10.00
242 Ruddy Yan/100	8.00
243 Ryan Meaux/93	8.00
247 Tim Bausher/100	8.00
249 William Bergolla/100	10.00
250 Yadier Molina/100	15.00

Certified Materials Preview

	NM/M
Complete Set (15):	25.00
Common Player:	1.50
Inserted 1:21	
Blue:	2-3X
Production 100 Sets	
Gold:	4-8X
Production 25 Sets	
Red:	1-2X
Production 200 Sets	
1 Albert Pujols	4.00
2 Alex Rodriguez	3.00
3 Alfonso Soriano	1.50
4 Curt Schilling	1.50
5 Derek Jeter	4.00
6 Greg Maddux	2.00
7 Ichiro Suzuki	3.00
8 Jim Thome	1.50
9 Ken Griffey Jr.	2.00
10 Manny Ramirez	1.50
11 Mark Prior	1.50
12 Randy Johnson	1.50
13 Roger Clemens	4.00
14 Sammy Sosa	2.50
15 Vladimir Guerrero	1.50

Clean Up Crew

	NM/M
Complete Set (15):	45.00
Common Card:	
Inserted 1:49	
Die-Cut:	1X
Production 250 Sets	
1 Albert Pujols, Jim Edmonds, Scott Rolen	6.00
2 Melvin Mora, Miguel Tejada, Rafael Palmeiro	3.00
3 Alfonso Soriano, Michael Young, Hank Blalock	3.00
4 Gary Sheffield, Alex Rodriguez, Hideki Matsui	5.00
5 Moises Alou, Sammy Sosa, Nomar Garciaparra	5.00
6 Paul LoDuca, Mike Lowell, Miguel Cabrera	3.00
7 Carlos Beltran, Lance Berkman, Jeff Bagwell	3.00
8 Paul Konerko, Magglio Ordonez, Frank Thomas	3.00
9 Sean Casey, Ken Griffey Jr., Adam Dunn	5.00
10 Vladimir Guerrero, Garret Anderson, Troy Glaus	3.00

11 Joe Morgan, Johnny Bench, Tony Perez	3.00
12 Keith Hernandez, Darryl Strawberry, Gary Carter	2.00
13 Jim Rice, Carl Yastrzemski, Dwight Evans	5.00
14 Ryne Sandberg, Andre Dawson, Mark Grace	6.00
15 Cal Ripken Jr., Eddie Murray, Rafael Palmeiro	10.00

Cornerstones

	NM/M
Complete Set (20):	50.00
Common Card:	1.50
Inserted 1:37	
1 Albert Pujols, Scott Rolen	6.00
2 Hideki Matsui, Jorge Posada	5.00
3 Nomar Garciaparra, Sammy Sosa	4.00
4 David Ortiz, Manny Ramirez	3.00
5 Miguel Cabrera, Mike Lowell	3.00
6 Hank Blalock, Mark Teixeira	2.00
7 Chipper Jones, J.D. Drew	3.00
8 Craig Biggio, Jeff Bagwell	3.00
9 Kazuo Matsui, Mike Piazza	4.00
10 Shawn Green, Adrian Beltre	1.50
11 Bobby Abreu, Jim Thome	3.00
12 Mike Schmidt, Steve Carlton	6.00
13 Cal Ripken Jr., Eddie Murray	10.00
14 Carl Yastrzemski, Dwight Evans	5.00
15 Joe Morgan, Johnny Bench	3.00
16 Dale Murphy, Phil Niekro	2.00
17 Alan Trammell, Kirk Gibson	2.00
18 Jose Canseco, Rickey Henderson	3.00
19 Paul Molitor, Robin Yount	4.00
20 Bo Jackson, George Brett	6.00

Cornerstones Bats

	NM/M
Common Dual Bat:	8.00
1 Albert Pujols, Scott Rolen	20.00
2 Hideki Matsui, Jorge Posada	35.00
3 Sammy Sosa, Nomar Garciaparra	15.00
4 Manny Ramirez, David Ortiz	20.00
5 Miguel Cabrera, Mike Lowell	10.00
6 Hank Blalock, Mark Teixeira	10.00
7 Chipper Jones, J.D. Drew	15.00
8 Craig Biggio, Jeff Bagwell	10.00
9 Mike Piazza, Kazuo Matsui	15.00
10 Shawn Green, Adrian Beltre	8.00

Cornerstones Jerseys

	NM/M
Common Dual Jersey:	8.00
1 Albert Pujols, Scott Rolen	20.00
2 Hideki Matsui, Jorge Posada	35.00
4 Manny Ramirez, David Ortiz	20.00
6 Miguel Cabrera, Mike Lowell	10.00
7 Hank Blalock, Mark Teixeira	10.00
8 Craig Biggio, Jeff Bagwell	10.00
9 Mike Piazza, Kazuo Matsui	15.00
10 Shawn Green, Adrian Beltre	8.00

Cy Young Winners

	NM/M
Complete Set (15):	30.00
Common Player:	1.50
Inserted 1:31	
Gold:	1X
Production 350 Sets	
Gold Die-Cut:	1.5-2X
Production 100 Sets	
1 Warren Spahn	3.00
2 Whitey Ford	3.00
3 Bob Gibson	3.00
4 Tom Seaver	3.00
5 Steve Carlton	2.00
6 Jim Palmer	2.00
7 Rollie Fingers	1.50
8 Dwight Gooden	1.50
9 Roger Clemens	6.00
10 Orel Hershiser	1.50
11 Greg Maddux	4.00
12 Dennis Eckersley	2.00
13 Randy Johnson	3.00
14 Pedro Martinez	3.00
15 Eric Gagne	2.00

Game Collection

	NM/M
Inserted 1:118	
1 Cal Ripken Jr./Bat	30.00
2 Carl Crawford/Jsy	5.00
3 Dale Murphy/Bat	20.00
4 Don Mattingly/Bat	25.00
5 George Brett/Jsy	25.00
6 Victor Martinez/Bat	8.00
7 Sean Casey/Bat	5.00
8 Torii Hunter/Bat	5.00
9 Magglio Ordonez/Bat	5.00
10 Lance Berkman/Bat	5.00
11 Mike Schmidt/Bat	25.00
12 Nolan Ryan/Jkt	40.00
13 Paul LoDuca/Bat	5.00
14 Preston Wilson/Bat	5.00
15 Rod Carew/Jkt	25.00
16 Reggie Jackson/Bat	10.00
17 Ivan Rodriguez/Bat	5.00
18 Larry Walker Cards/Bat	10.00
19 Miguel Tejada/Bat	8.00
20 Vladimir Guerrero/Bat	10.00

Game Collection Autograph

	NM/M
Common Dual Jersey:	8.00
Production 5-200	
2 Carl Crawford/Jsy/200	15.00
6 Victor Martinez/Bat/200	20.00
7 Sean Casey/Bat/200	20.00
8 Torii Hunter/Bat/50	25.00
13 Paul LoDuca/Bat/100	20.00

Gamers

	NM/M
Complete Set (15):	20.00
Common Player:	1.00
Inserted 1:13	
Quantum:	2-3X
Production 175 Sets	

GAMERS

	NM/M
Quantum Die-Cut:	3-5X
Production 50 Sets	
1 Albert Pujols	4.00
2 Alex Rodriguez	3.00
3 Alfonso Soriano	1.50
4 Chipper Jones	1.50
5 Derek Jeter	4.00
6 Greg Maddux	2.00
7 Ichiro Suzuki	3.00
8 Jim Thome	1.50
9 Ken Griffey Jr.	2.00
10 Lance Berkman	1.00
11 Miguel Tejada	1.00
12 Mike Piazza	2.50
13 Roger Clemens	4.00
14 Scott Rolen	1.50
15 Vladimir Guerrero	1.50

Gold Rookies

	NM/M
Complete Set (10):	15.00
Common Player:	2.00
Inserted 1:24	
Mirror:	3-5X
Production 50 Sets	
1 Dennis Sarfate	2.00
2 Donnie Kelly	2.00
3 Eddy Rodriguez	2.00
4 Edwin Moreno	2.00
5 Greg Dobbs	2.00
6 Josh Labandeira	2.00
7 Kevin Cave	2.00
8 Mariano Gomez	2.00
9 Ronald Belisario	2.00
10 Ruddy Yan	2.00

Gold Rookies Autograph

	NM/M
Common Autograph:	
Mirror:	No Pricing
Production 25 Sets	
1 Dennis Sarfate	10.00
2 Donnie Kelly	8.00
5 Greg Dobbs	8.00
6 Kevin Cave	10.00
9 Ronald Belisario	8.00
10 Ruddy Yan	8.00

Gold Stars

	NM/M
Complete Set (20):	40.00
Common Player:	.75
Inserted 1:27	
Mirror:	4-6X
Production 25 Sets	
1 Albert Pujols	4.00
2 Ichiro Suzuki	3.00
3 Derek Jeter	4.00
4 Alex Rodriguez	3.00
5 Scott Rolen	1.50
6 Randy Johnson	1.50
7 Roger Clemens	4.00
8 Greg Maddux	2.00
9 Alfonso Soriano	1.50
10 Mark Mulder	.75
11 Sammy Sosa	3.00
12 Mike Piazza	3.00
13 Rafael Palmeiro	.75
14 Ivan Rodriguez	.75
15 Miguel Cabrera	.75
16 Stan Musial	3.00
17 Nolan Ryan	6.00
18 Don Mattingly	4.00
19 George Brett	4.00
20 Cal Ripken Jr.	6.00

Home/Road

	NM/M
Common Player:	1.00
Inserted 1:22	
Home & Road price is identical.	
1H Albert Pujols/H	4.00
1R Albert Pujols/R	4.00
2H Alfonso Soriano/H	1.50
2R Alfonso Soriano/R	1.50
3H Carlos Beltran/H	1.00
3R Carlos Beltran/R	1.00
4H Chipper Jones/H	1.50
4R Chipper Jones/R	1.50
5H Frank Thomas/H	1.50
5R Frank Thomas/R	1.50
6H Hank Blalock/H	1.00
6R Hank Blalock/R	1.00
7H Ivan Rodriguez/H	1.50
7R Ivan Rodriguez/R	1.50
8H Manny Ramirez/H	1.50
8R Manny Ramirez/R	1.50
9H Mark Prior/H	1.50
9R Mark Prior/R	1.50
10H Miguel Cabrera/H	1.50
10R Miguel Cabrera/R	1.50
11H Miguel Tejada/H	1.00
11R Miguel Tejada/R	1.00
12H Mike Piazza/H	2.50
12R Mike Piazza/R	2.50
13H Roger Clemens/H	4.00
13R Roger Clemens/R	4.00
14H Todd Helton/H	1.50
14R Todd Helton/R	1.50
15H Vladimir Guerrero/H	1.50
15R Vladimir Guerrero/R	1.50

Home/Road Jersey

	NM/M
Common Player:	
1H Albert Pujols/H	20.00
1R Albert Pujols/R	20.00
2H Alfonso Soriano/H	8.00
3H Carlos Beltran/H	8.00
3R Carlos Beltran/R	8.00
4R Chipper Jones/R	8.00
5H Frank Thomas/H	8.00
5R Frank Thomas/R	8.00
6H Hank Blalock/H	8.00
7H Ivan Rodriguez/H	8.00
7R Ivan Rodriguez/R	8.00
8H Manny Ramirez/H	8.00
9H Mark Prior/H	8.00
11H Miguel Tejada/H	5.00
11R Miguel Tejada/R	5.00
12H Mike Piazza/H	12.00
13H Roger Clemens/H	15.00
13R Roger Clemens/R	15.00
14R Todd Helton/R	8.00
14H Todd Helton/H	8.00
15H Vladimir Guerrero/H	8.00

Patch Off My Back

	NM/M
Common Patch:	15.00
Production 50 Sets	

#	Player	Price
1	Adam Dunn	25.00
2	Aubrey Huff	15.00
3	Austin Kearns	15.00
4	Bobby Crosby	25.00
5	C.C. Sabathia	15.00
7	David Ortiz	25.00
8	Dewon Brazelton	15.00
9	Edgar Martinez	20.00
10	Frankie Francisco	15.00
11	Garret Anderson	20.00
12	Hideki Matsui	50.00
13	Hideo Nomo	20.00
14	Jack Wilson	15.00
15	Javy Lopez	15.00
16	Jay Gibbons	15.00
17	Jim Edmonds	20.00
18	Jody Gerut	15.00
19	Joey Gathright	15.00
20	Johan Santana	20.00
21	Jose Reyes	15.00
22	Jose Vidro	15.00
23	Lance Berkman	20.00
24	Mariano Rivera	20.00
25	Mark Teixeira	20.00
26	Michael Young	15.00
27	Mike Cameron	15.00
28	Mike Sweeney	15.00
29	Omar Vizquel	15.00
30	Preston Wilson	15.00
31	Rocco Baldelli	15.00
32	Scott Rolen	25.00
33	Sean Burroughs	15.00
34	Sean Casey	15.00
35	Tim Hudson	20.00
36	Torii Hunter	20.00
37	Trevor Hoffman	20.00
38	Troy Glaus	20.00
39	Vernon Wells	15.00
40	Victor Martinez	20.00

Patch Off My Back Autograph

NM/M
Production 10-75

#	Player	Price
2	Aubrey Huff/50	35.00
4	Bobby Crosby/75	50.00
5	C.C. Sabathia/75	30.00
7	David Ortiz/50	100.00
8	Dewon Brazelton/75	30.00
9	Jack Wilson/75	30.00
16	Jay Gibbons/50	25.00
18	Jody Gerut/75	25.00
20	Johan Santana/50	60.00
22	Jose Vidro/75	25.00
26	Michael Young/75	35.00
33	Sean Burroughs/25	25.00
40	Victor Martinez/35	35.00

Picture Perfect

NM/M
Complete Set (20): 30.00
Common Player: 1.00
Inserted 1:20
Die-Cut 2-3X
Production 100 Sets

#	Player	Price
1	Albert Pujols	4.00
2	Alex Rodriguez	3.00
3	Alfonso Soriano	1.50
4	Derek Jeter	4.00
5	Greg Maddux	2.00
6	Hideki Matsui	3.00
7	Ichiro Suzuki	4.00
8	Ivan Rodriguez	1.00
9	Jim Thome	1.00
10	Mark Mulder	1.00
11	Mark Prior	1.50
12	Miguel Tejada	1.00
13	Mike Mussina	1.00
14	Mike Piazza	2.50
15	Nomar Garciaparra	2.50
16	Randy Johnson	2.50
17	Roger Clemens	4.00
18	Sammy Sosa	2.50
19	Scott Rolen	1.50
20	Vladimir Guerrero	1.50

Recollection Autographs

No Pricing
Production 1-29

Shirt Off My Back

NM/M
Common Player: 5.00
Inserted 1:48

#	Player	Price
1	Adam Dunn	15.00
4	Bobby Crosby	15.00
5	C.C. Sabathia	8.00
7	David Ortiz	15.00
8	Dewon Brazelton	5.00
9	Edgar Martinez	5.00
10	Frankie Francisco	5.00
11	Garret Anderson	5.00
12	Hideki Matsui	25.00
13	Hideo Nomo	8.00
14	Jack Wilson	5.00
15	Javy Lopez	8.00
16	Jay Gibbons	5.00
17	Jim Edmonds	15.00
18	Jody Gerut SP	5.00
19	Joey Gathright	5.00
20	Johan Santana	10.00
21	Jose Reyes	5.00
22	Jose Vidro	5.00
23	Lance Berkman	5.00
25	Mark Teixeira	5.00
26	Michael Young	5.00
27	Mike Cameron	5.00
28	Mike Sweeney	5.00
29	Omar Vizquel	8.00
30	Preston Wilson	5.00
31	Rocco Baldelli	5.00
32	Scott Rolen	10.00
33	Sean Burroughs	5.00
34	Sean Casey	5.00
35	Tim Hudson	5.00
36	Torii Hunter	5.00
37	Trevor Hoffman	5.00
38	Troy Glaus	5.00
39	Vernon Wells	5.00
40	Victor Martinez	8.00

Sportscasters 70 Green

Baseball

Steve Carlton

NM/M
Common Player: 2.00
Production 70 Sets
Variations #'d 35-65: 1X
Variations #'d 20-30: 1.5X
No pricing 15 or less.

#	Player	Price
1	Adam Dunn	3.00
2	Al Kaline	5.00
3	Albert Pujols	8.00
4	Alex Rodriguez	8.00
5	Alfonso Soriano	3.00
6	Bob Gibson	3.00
7	Cal Ripken Jr.	25.00
8	Carl Yastrzemski	8.00
9	Dale Murphy	3.00
10	Derek Jeter	10.00
11	Don Mattingly	10.00
12	Duke Snider	4.00
13	Eric Gagne	3.00
14	Ernie Banks	6.00
15	Frank Robinson	3.00
16	George Brett	10.00
17	Greg Maddux	5.00
18	Harmon Killebrew	5.00
19	Ichiro Suzuki	6.00
20	Ivan Rodriguez	4.00
21	Jim Edmonds	2.00
22	Jim Palmer	3.00
23	Jim Thome	4.00
24	Johnny Bench	6.00
25	Ken Griffey Jr.	6.00
26	Larry Walker	3.00
27	Mark Mulder	2.00
28	Mark Prior	4.00
29	Miguel Tejada	3.00
30	Mike Mussina	3.00
31	Mike Piazza	4.00
32	Mike Schmidt	10.00
33	Nolan Ryan	15.00
34	Nomar Garciaparra	3.00
35	Pedro Martinez	4.00
36	Rafael Palmeiro	3.00
37	Randy Johnson	4.00
38	Reggie Jackson	6.00
39	Rickey Henderson	4.00
40	Roberto Clemente	15.00
41	Rod Carew	3.00
42	Roger Clemens	8.00
43	Ryne Sandberg	4.00
44	Sammy Sosa	6.00
45	Stan Musial	8.00
46	Steve Carlton	3.00
47	Tony Gwynn	5.00
48	Vladimir Guerrero	6.00
49	Warren Spahn	4.00
50	Willie McCovey	3.00

4 Star Staffs

NM/M
Common Card: 2.00
Inserted 1:48
Die-Cut 1X
Production 250 Sets

#	Players	Price
1	Greg Maddux, John Smoltz, Kevin Millwood, Tom Glavine	4.00
2	A.J. Burnett, Carl Pavano, Dontrelle Willis, Josh Beckett	2.00
3	Andy Pettitte, David Wells, Mike Mussina, Roger Clemens	6.00
4	Carlos Zambrano, Greg Maddux, Kerry Wood, Mark Prior	4.00
5	Andy Pettitte, Mariano Rivera, Mike Mussina, Roger Clemens	3.00
6	Curt Schilling, Derek Lowe, Pedro J. Martinez, Tim Wakefield	4.00
7	Barry Zito, Mark Mulder, Rich Harden, Tim Hudson	2.00
8	Brandon Webb, Byung-Hyun Kim, Curt Schilling, Randy Johnson	3.00
9	Jamie Moyer, Kenny Rogers, Kevin Brown, Nolan Ryan	8.00
10	Kelvim Escobar, Roger Clemens, Roy Halladay, Woody Williams	6.00
11	Andy Pettitte, Roger Clemens, Roy Oswalt, Wade Miller	6.00
12	Barry Zito, Billy Koch, Mark Mulder, Tim Hudson	2.00
13	Eric Gagne, Hideo Nomo, Kazuhisa Ishii, Kevin Brown	3.00
14	Greg Maddux, Jason Schmidt, John Smoltz, Tom Glavine	5.00
15	Derek Lowe, Hideo Nomo, Pedro Martinez, Tim Wakefield	4.00

2005 Leaf Century

NM/M
Complete Set (200): 40.00
Common Player: .25
Pack (5): 12.00
Box (10): 100.00

#	Player	Price
1	Brian Roberts	.25
2	Derek Jeter	2.00
3	Harmon Killebrew	1.00
4	Angel Berroa	.25
5	George Brett	2.00
6	Stan Musial	1.50
7	Ivan Rodriguez	.50
8	Cal Ripken Jr.	3.00
9	Hank Blalock	.50
10	Miguel Tejada	.50
11	Barry Larkin	.40
12	Alfonso Soriano	.75
13	Alex Rodriguez	2.00
14	Paul Konerko	.40
15	Jim Edmonds	.40
16	Garret Anderson	.40
17	Todd Helton	.50
18	Moises Alou	.40
19	Tony Gwynn	.75
20	Mike Schmidt	2.00
21	Sammy Sosa	1.25
22	Roger Clemens	2.00
23	Tony Perez	.25
24	Manny Ramirez	.75
25	Jim Thome	.75
26	Chase Utley	.40
27	Scott Rolen	.75
28	Austin Kearns	.25
29	John Smoltz	.40
30	Ken Griffey Jr.	1.00
31	Mike Piazza	1.00
32	Steve Carlton	.50
33	Larry Walker	.40
34	Nolan Ryan	2.50
35	Mike Mussina	.40
36	Joe Nathan	.25
37	Kenny Rogers	.25
38	Eric Gagne	.40
39	Brett Myers	.25
40	Rich Harden	.25
41	Victor Martinez	.40
42	Mariano Rivera	.40
43	Dennis Eckersley	.50
44	Roy Oswalt	.25
45	Pedro Martinez	.75
46	Jason Bay	.40
47	Tom Glavine	.40
48	Torii Hunter	.25
49	Larry Bigbie	.25
50	Nomar Garciaparra	1.50
51	Ichiro Suzuki	.75
52	C.C. Sabathia	.25
53	Bobby Abreu	.40
54	Doug Mientkiewicz	.25
55	Hideki Matsui	1.50
56	Mark Buehrle	.25
57	Johan Santana	.50
58	Johnny Damon	.75
59	Edgar Martinez	.40
60	Preston Wilson	.25
61	Livan Hernandez	.25
62	Eric Chavez	.25
63	Lyle Overbay	.25
64	Jason Schmidt	.50
65	Cliff Lee	.25
66	Shingo Takatsu	.25
67	Jeff Bagwell	.50
68	Danny Graves	.25
69	Kip Wells	.25
70	Steve Finley	.25
71	Lew Ford	.25
72	Chone Figgins	.25
73	Delmon Young	.40
74	Esteban Loaiza	.25
75	Barry Zito	.40
76	Carlos Delgado	.40
77	Joe Mauer	.50
78	Ryan Wagner	.25
79	John Lackey	.25
80	Adrian Beltre	.40
81	Vernon Wells	.25
82	Sean Burroughs	.25
83	Francisco Cordero	.25
84	Carlos Guillen	.25
85	Eric Byrnes	.25
86	Jose Reyes	.25
87	Rocco Baldelli	.25
88	Josh Beckett	.25
89	Casey Kotchman	.40
90	Scott Podsednik	.25
91	Mike Sweeney	.25
92	Khalil Greene	.50
93	Trot Nixon	.25
94	Chad Cordero	.25
95	Derek Lowe	.25
96	Jason Giambi	.40
97	Jose Guillen	.25
98	Craig Biggio	.40
99	Pat Burrell	.40
100	Kazuo Matsui	.25
101	Rafael Furcal	.25
102	Jack Wilson	.25
103	Edgar Renteria	.50
104	Carlos Beltran	.75
105	Albert Pujols	2.00
106	Melvin Mora	.25
107	J.D. Drew	.40
108	Andre Dawson	.50
109	Jody Gerut	.25
110	Michael Young	.25
111	Gary Sheffield	.50
112	Wade Boggs	.50
113	Carl Crawford	.25
114	Paul LoDuca	.25
115	Tim Hudson	.40
116	Aramis Ramirez	.40
117	Lance Berkman	.40
118	Javy Lopez	.40
119	Robin Yount	1.00
120	Mark Mulder	.25
121	Sean Casey	.25
122	Will Clark	.50
123	Don Mattingly	2.00
124	Miguel Cabrera	.75
125	Rafael Palmeiro	.50
126	David Ortiz	.75
127	Vladimir Guerrero	.75
128	Ken Harvey	.25
129	Rod Carew	.50
130	Magglio Ordonez	.25
131	Greg Maddux	1.00
132	Roy Halladay	.25
133	Javier Vazquez	.25
134	Kerry Wood	.25
135	Frank Thomas	.75
136	Tom Gordon	.25
137	Jake Peavy	.25
138	Curt Schilling	.75
139	Dewon Brazelton	.25
140	Jae Weong Seo	.25
141	Danny Kolb	.25
142	Jeff Kent	.40
143	Juan Encarnacion	.25
144	Adam Dunn	.50
145	Carlos Lee	.40
146	Matt Clement	.25
147	Guillermo Mota	.40
148	Travis Hafner	.40
149	Brad Wilkerson	.25
150	Eric Milton	.25
151	Randy Johnson	.75
152	Joe Crede	.25
153	Mark Kotsay	.25
154	Jason Varitek	.40
155	David Wright	.75
156	Brad Penny	.25
157	Francisco Rodriguez	.25
158	Gary Carter	.50
159	Adrian Gonzalez	.25
160	Derrek Lee	.50
161	Mark Prior	.50
162	Carlos Zambrano	.40
163	Bobby Crosby	.40
164	Jermaine Dye	.25
165	Kris Benson	.25
166	Dontrelle Willis	.40
167	Dallas McPherson	.25
168	Johnny Estrada	.40
169	Milton Bradley	.25
170	Shannon Stewart	.25
171	Ben Sheets	.40
172	Richard Hidalgo	.25
173	Laynce Nix	.25
174	B.J. Upton	.50
175	Craig Wilson	.25
176	Hideo Nomo	.40
177	Troy Glaus	.40
178	Akinori Otsuka	.25
179	Rickie Weeks	.25
180	Mike Lowell	.40
181	Marcus Giles	.25
182	Randy Wolf	.25
183	A.J. Burnett	.25
184	Aubrey Huff	.25
185	Billy Ripken	.25
186	Octavio Dotel	.25
187	Kazuhisa Ishii	.25
188	Mark Teixeira	.50
189	Todd Walker	.25
190	Dale Murphy	.50
191	Alexis Rios	.25
192	Reggie Sanders	.25
193	Orlando Cabrera	.25
194	Shawn Green	.40
195	Andy Pettitte	.25
196	Chipper Jones	.75
197	Jose Vidro	.25
198	Jacque Jones	.25
199	Brian Giles	.25
200	Andruw Jones	.40

Post Marks Silver

Silvers: 3-6X
Production 100 Sets

Post Marks Gold

Golds: 4-8X
Production 50 Sets

Post Marks Platinum

No Pricing
Production One Set

Air Mail Bat

NM/M
Production 50-250

#	Player	Price
1	Babe Ruth/50	150.00
2	Frank Robinson/250	12.00
3	Harmon Killebrew/100	20.00
5	Sammy Sosa/100	8.00
6	Reggie Jackson/250	15.00
7	Mike Schmidt/100	8.00
8	Rafael Palmeiro/100	8.00
9	Ted Williams/50	80.00
10	Willie McCovey/100	10.00
	Ernie Banks/100	20.00

Air Mail Bat Signature

NM/M
Production 1-25

#	Player	Price
2	Frank Robinson/25	40.00
3	Harmon Killebrew/25	60.00
9	Willie McCovey/25	35.00

Material Bat

DERREK LEE Chicago Cubs

NM/M
Common Player: 5.00

#	Player	Price
3	Harmon Killebrew/250	12.00
4	Angel Berroa/50	6.00
5	George Brett/250	15.00
6	Stan Musial/250	8.00
7	Ivan Rodriguez/100	8.00
8	Cal Ripken Jr./250	25.00
9	Hank Blalock/100	5.00
10	Miguel Tejada/100	6.00
11	Barry Larkin/100	8.00
12	Alfonso Soriano/100	8.00
14	Paul Konerko/50	5.00
15	Jim Edmonds/100	8.00
16	Garret Anderson/100	5.00
17	Todd Helton/100	8.00
18	Moises Alou/50	6.00
19	Tony Gwynn/100	10.00
21	Sammy Sosa/100	10.00
22	Roger Clemens/100	15.00
23	Tony Perez/50	5.00
24	Manny Ramirez/100	10.00
25	Jim Thome/100	12.00
27	Scott Rolen/100	10.00
28	Austin Kearns/50	5.00
31	Mike Piazza/100	12.00
32	Steve Carlton/250	8.00
33	Larry Walker/100	8.00
34	Nolan Ryan/250	20.00
35	Mike Mussina/100	8.00
41	Victor Martinez/50	8.00
44	Roy Oswalt/100	5.00
45	Pedro Martinez/100	8.00
47	Tom Glavine/100	6.00
48	Torii Hunter/100	6.00
50	Nomar Garciaparra/100	15.00
53	Bobby Abreu/25	10.00
54	Doug Mientkiewicz/50	5.00
55	Hideki Matsui/100	25.00
56	Mark Buehrle/50	6.00
58	Johnny Damon/100	12.00
59	Edgar Martinez/100	8.00
60	Preston Wilson/50	6.00
62	Eric Chavez/100	5.00
63	Lyle Overbay/50	8.00
67	Jeff Bagwell/100	8.00
71	Lew Ford/50	5.00
73	Delmon Young/100	8.00
75	Barry Zito/100	5.00
76	Carlos Delgado/100	5.00
80	Adrian Beltre/100	5.00
81	Vernon Wells/100	5.00
86	Jose Reyes/100	8.00
87	Rocco Baldelli/100	5.00
88	Josh Beckett/100	5.00
91	Mike Sweeney/50	6.00
93	Trot Nixon/50	5.00
96	Jason Giambi/100	6.00
98	Craig Biggio/100	6.00
99	Pat Burrell/50	6.00
100	Kazuo Matsui/100	8.00
101	Rafael Furcal/50	6.00
102	Jack Wilson/50	5.00
103	Edgar Renteria/100	6.00
104	Carlos Beltran/100	6.00
105	Albert Pujols/100	15.00
106	Melvin Mora/50	5.00
107	J.D. Drew/100	5.00
108	Andre Dawson/250	6.00
109	Jody Gerut/50	5.00
110	Michael Young/100	6.00
111	Gary Sheffield/100	6.00
112	Wade Boggs/250	8.00
114	Paul LoDuca/100	10.00
115	Tim Hudson/100	8.00
116	Aramis Ramirez/50	8.00
117	Lance Berkman/250	5.00
118	Javy Lopez/50	5.00
119	Robin Yount/250	10.00
120	Mark Mulder/50	5.00
121	Sean Casey/50	5.00
122	Will Clark/50	8.00
123	Don Mattingly/250	15.00
124	Miguel Cabrera/50	8.00
125	Rafael Palmeiro/250	8.00
126	David Ortiz/250	12.00
127	Vladimir Guerrero/250	8.00
128	Ken Harvey/250	5.00
129	Rod Carew/250	8.00
130	Magglio Ordonez/250	5.00
131	Greg Maddux/100	10.00

134	Kerry Wood/100	8.00
135	Frank Thomas/100	8.00
138	Curt Schilling/100	8.00
142	Jeff Kent/250	5.00
143	Juan Encarnacion/50	5.00
144	Adam Dunn/250	8.00
145	Carlos Lee/250	5.00
148	Travis Hafner/50	6.00
149	Brad Wilkerson/100	8.00
151	Randy Johnson/100	10.00
152	Joe Crede/50	5.00
154	Jason Varitek/250	10.00
156	Brad Penny/50	5.00
158	Gary Carter/250	8.00
160	Derrek Lee/250	5.00
161	Mark Prior/100	8.00
164	Jermaine Dye/50	5.00
166	Dontrelle Willis/100	6.00
168	Johnny Estrada/50	6.00
170	Shannon Stewart/100	5.00
171	Ben Sheets/50	5.00
172	Richard Hidalgo/50	5.00
173	Laynce Nix/50	5.00
174	B.J. Upton/50	8.00
176	Craig Wilson/100	5.00
176	Hideo Nomo/100	8.00
177	Troy Glaus/250	5.00
179	Rickie Weeks/25	8.00
180	Mike Lowell/100	5.00
183	A.J. Burnett/100	5.00
184	Aubrey Huff/50	5.00
187	Kazuhisa Ishii/100	5.00
188	Mark Teixeira/250	5.00
190	Dale Murphy/250	8.00
191	Alexis Rios/50	5.00
193	Orlando Cabrera/50	6.00
194	Shawn Green/250	5.00
195	Andy Pettitte/100	6.00
196	Chipper Jones/100	5.00
197	Jose Vidro/250	5.00
198	Jacque Jones/100	5.00
199	Brian Giles/250	5.00
200	Andruw Jones/250	6.00

Material Fabric Number

NM/M
Common Player: 5.00

20	Mike Schmidt/Jsy/20	50.00
21	Sammy Sosa/Jsy/21	20.00
22	Roger Clemens/Jsy/22	40.00
23	Tony Perez/Jsy/24	15.00
24	Manny Ramirez/Jsy/24	
25	Jim Thome/Jsy/25	20.00
27	Scott Rolen/Jsy/27	8.00
28	Austin Kearns/Jsy/28	15.00
29	John Smoltz/Jsy/29	20.00
31	Mike Piazza/Jsy/31	25.00
32	Steve Carlton/Pants/32	
34	Nolan Ryan/Jsy/34	50.00
35	Mike Mussina/Jsy/35	15.00
39	Brett Myers/Jsy/39	8.00
41	Victor Martinez/Jsy/41	8.00
42	Mariano Rivera/Jsy/42	15.00
43	Dennis Eckersley/Jsy/43	10.00
44	Roy Oswalt/Jsy/44	5.00
45	Pedro Martinez/Jsy/45	10.00
47	Tom Glavine/Jsy/47	10.00
48	Torii Hunter/Jsy/48	8.00
52	C.C. Sabathia/Jsy/52	5.00
53	Bobby Abreu/Jsy/53	8.00
55	Hideki Matsui/Jsy/55	35.00
56	Mark Buehrle/Jsy/56	8.00
57	Johan Santana/Jsy/57	15.00
60	Preston Wilson/Jsy/44	8.00
61	Livan Hernandez/Jsy/61	5.00
65	Cliff Lee/Jsy/34	8.00
71	Lew Ford/Jsy/20	10.00
75	Barry Zito/Jsy/75	5.00
76	Carlos Delgado/Jsy/25	10.00
78	Ryan Wagner/Jsy/38	5.00
80	Adrian Beltre/Jsy/15	15.00
82	Sean Burroughs/Jsy/32	8.00
83	Francisco Cordero/Jsy/31	5.00
85	Eric Byrnes/Jsy/22	8.00
91	Mike Sweeney/Jsy/29	5.00
96	Jason Giambi/Jsy/25	10.00
100	Kazuo Matsui/Jsy/25	12.00
118	Javy Lopez/Jsy/18	15.00
119	Robin Yount/Jsy/19	30.00
120	Mark Mulder/Jsy/12	12.00
121	Sean Casey/Jsy/21	20.00
122	Will Clark/Jsy/22	20.00
123	Don Mattingly/Pants/23	40.00
124	Miguel Cabrera/Jsy/24	20.00
125	Rafael Palmeiro/Jsy/25	15.00
126	David Ortiz/Jsy/34	20.00
127	Vladimir Guerrero/Jsy/27	20.00
128	Ken Harvey/Jsy/28	10.00
129	Rod Carew/Jsy/29	20.00
130	Magglio Ordonez/Jsy/30	10.00
131	Greg Maddux/Jsy/31	25.00
132	Roy Halladay/Jsy/32	10.00
134	Kerry Wood/Jsy/34	20.00
135	Frank Thomas/Jsy/35	20.00
138	Curt Schilling/Jsy/34	15.00
139	Dewon Brazelton/Jsy/45	5.00
140	Jae Weong Seo/Jsy/40	5.00
141	Danny Kolb/Jsy/41	5.00
144	Adam Dunn/Jsy/44	15.00
145	Carlos Lee/Jsy/45	5.00
146	Matt Clement/Jsy/30	10.00
148	Travis Hafner/Jsy/48	8.00
151	Randy Johnson/Pants/51	15.00
154	Jason Varitek/Jsy/33	20.00
157	Francisco Rodriguez/Jsy/57	5.00
162	Carlos Zambrano/Jsy/38	8.00
164	Jermaine Dye/Jsy/24	10.00
166	Dontrelle Willis/Jsy/35	12.00
168	Johnny Estrada/Jsy/23	10.00
170	Shannon Stewart/Jsy/23	10.00
175	Craig Wilson/Jsy/36	5.00
177	Troy Glaus/Jsy/25	15.00
180	Mike Lowell/Jsy/19	20.00
183	A.J. Burnett/Jsy/34	10.00
188	Mark Teixeira/Jsy/23	15.00
195	Andy Pettitte/Jsy/21	20.00
200	Andruw Jones/Jsy/5	15.00

Material Fabric Position

NM/M
Common Player: 4.00
Prime: No Pricing
Production One Set

1	Brian Roberts/Jsy/250	4.00
3	Harmon Killebrew/Jsy/250	12.00
4	Angel Berroa/Jsy/250	4.00
5	George Brett/Jsy/250	15.00
6	Stan Musial/Pants/250	15.00
7	Ivan Rodriguez/Jsy/250	6.00
8	Cal Ripken Jr./Jkt/250	25.00
9	Hank Blalock/Jsy/250	8.00
10	Miguel Tejada/Jsy/250	6.00
11	Barry Larkin/Jsy/100	6.00
12	Alfonso Soriano/Jsy/250	4.00
14	Paul Konerko/Jsy/250	4.00
15	Jim Edmonds/Jsy/250	6.00
16	Garret Anderson/Jsy/250	4.00
17	Todd Helton/Jsy/250	6.00
18	Tony Gwynn/Jsy/250	10.00
20	Mike Schmidt/Jsy/250	15.00
21	Sammy Sosa/Jsy/250	10.00
22	Roger Clemens/Jsy/250	12.00
23	Tony Perez/Jsy/250	6.00
24	Manny Ramirez/Jsy/250	8.00
25	Jim Thome/Jsy/250	8.00
27	Scott Rolen/Jsy/250	8.00
28	Austin Kearns/Jsy/250	
29	John Smoltz/Jsy/250	6.00
31	Mike Piazza/Jsy/250	10.00
32	Steve Carlton/Pants/250	6.00
34	Nolan Ryan/Jsy/250	20.00
35	Mike Mussina/Jsy/250	6.00
39	Brett Myers/Jsy/250	4.00
41	Victor Martinez/Jsy/250	4.00
42	Mariano Rivera/Jsy/250	6.00
43	Dennis Eckersley/Jsy/250	6.00
44	Roy Oswalt/Jsy/250	4.00
45	Pedro Martinez/Jsy/250	8.00
46	Jason Bay/Jsy/250	4.00
47	Tom Glavine/Jsy/250	6.00
48	Torii Hunter/Jsy/250	4.00
49	Larry Bigbie/Jsy/250	4.00
52	C.C. Sabathia/Jsy/250	4.00
53	Bobby Abreu/Jsy/250	4.00
55	Hideki Matsui/Jsy/250	20.00
56	Mark Buehrle/Jsy/250	4.00
57	Johan Santana/Jsy/250	8.00
59	Edgar Martinez/Jsy/250	6.00
60	Preston Wilson/Jsy/250	4.00
61	Livan Hernandez/Jsy/250	4.00
62	Eric Chavez/Jsy/250	4.00
63	Lyle Overbay/Jsy/250	4.00
65	Cliff Lee/Jsy/250	4.00
67	Jeff Bagwell/Jsy/250	8.00
71	Lew Ford/Jsy/250	4.00
72	Chone Figgins/Jsy/250	4.00
75	Barry Zito/Jsy/250	4.00
76	Carlos Delgado/Jsy/250	4.00
78	Ryan Wagner/Jsy/250	8.00
80	Adrian Beltre/Jsy/250	8.00
81	Vernon Wells/Jsy/250	4.00
82	Sean Burroughs/Jsy/250	4.00
83	Francisco Cordero/Jsy/250	4.00
85	Eric Byrnes/Jsy/250	10.00
86	Jose Reyes/Jsy/250	4.00
87	Rocco Baldelli/Jsy/250	4.00
88	Josh Beckett/Jsy/250	8.00
90	Scott Podsednik/Jsy/250	4.00
91	Mike Sweeney/Jsy/250	4.00
93	Trot Nixon/Jsy/250	4.00
96	Jason Giambi/Jsy/250	4.00
98	Craig Biggio/Jsy/250	6.00
99	Pat Burrell/Jsy/250	4.00
100	Kazuo Matsui/Jsy/250	4.00
101	Rafael Furcal/Jsy/250	4.00
102	Jack Wilson/Jsy/250	4.00
103	Edgar Renteria/Jsy/250	6.00
104	Carlos Beltran/Jsy/250	8.00
105	Albert Pujols/Jsy/250	15.00
106	Melvin Mora/Jsy/100	4.00
108	Andre Dawson/Jsy/250	6.00
109	Jody Gerut/Jsy/250	4.00
110	Michael Young/Jsy/250	4.00
111	Gary Sheffield/Jsy/250	6.00
112	Wade Boggs/Jsy/100	8.00
113	Carl Crawford/Jsy/250	4.00
115	Tim Hudson/Jsy/250	4.00
116	Aramis Ramirez/Jsy/250	6.00
117	Lance Berkman/Jsy/250	4.00
118	Javy Lopez/Jsy/250	4.00
119	Robin Yount/Jsy/250	10.00
120	Mark Mulder/Jsy/250	4.00
121	Sean Casey/Jsy/250	4.00
122	Will Clark/Jsy/250	6.00
123	Don Mattingly/Pants/250	15.00
124	Miguel Cabrera/Jsy/250	8.00
125	Rafael Palmeiro/Jsy/250	8.00
126	David Ortiz/Jsy/250	8.00
127	Vladimir Guerrero/Jsy/250	8.00
128	Ken Harvey/Jsy/250	4.00
129	Rod Carew/Jsy/250	4.00
130	Magglio Ordonez/Jsy/250	4.00
131	Greg Maddux/Jsy/250	10.00
132	Roy Halladay/Jsy/250	4.00
134	Kerry Wood/Jsy/250	8.00
135	Frank Thomas/Jsy/250	8.00
138	Curt Schilling/Jsy/250	4.00
139	Dewon Brazelton/Jsy/100	4.00
140	Jae Weong Seo/Jsy/100	4.00
141	Danny Kolb/Jsy/250	4.00
142	Jeff Kent/Jsy/100	6.00
144	Adam Dunn/Jsy/250	4.00
145	Carlos Lee/Jsy/250	4.00
146	Matt Clement/Jsy/250	4.00
148	Travis Hafner/Jsy/250	4.00
151	Randy Johnson/Pants/250	8.00
154	Jason Varitek/Jsy/100	15.00
157	Francisco Rodriguez/Jsy/100	4.00
158	Gary Carter/Jsy/250	6.00
161	Mark Prior/Jsy/250	8.00
162	Carlos Zambrano/Jsy/250	6.00
163	Bobby Crosby/Jsy/250	8.00
164	Jermaine Dye/Jsy/250	4.00
166	Dontrelle Willis/Jsy/250	4.00
168	Johnny Estrada/Jsy/100	4.00
170	Shannon Stewart/Jsy/100	4.00
171	Ben Sheets/Jsy/250	6.00
173	Laynce Nix/Jsy/100	4.00
175	Craig Wilson/Jsy/100	4.00
176	Hideo Nomo/Jsy/250	8.00
177	Troy Glaus/Jsy/250	4.00
180	Mike Lowell/Jsy/250	4.00
183	A.J. Burnett/Jsy/100	4.00
184	Aubrey Huff/Jsy/250	4.00
187	Kazuhisa Ishii/Jsy/250	4.00
188	Mark Teixeira/Jsy/250	6.00
190	Dale Murphy/Jsy/250	8.00
194	Shawn Green/Jsy/250	4.00
195	Andy Pettitte/Jsy/250	6.00
196	Chipper Jones/Jsy/250	8.00
197	Jose Vidro/Jsy/100	4.00
198	Jacque Jones/Jsy/250	4.00
200	Andruw Jones/Jsy/250	6.00

Pennant Patches

NM/M
Production 5-25

1	Ozzie Smith/25	40.00
2	Keith Hernandez/25	20.00
3	Rickey Henderson/25	30.00
4	Paul Molitor/25	25.00
5	Steve Garvey/25	50.00
7	Randy Johnson/25	25.00
8	Cal Ripken Jr./25	90.00
9	Darryl Strawberry/25	20.00
10	Chipper Jones/25	30.00
11	Steve Carlton/25	20.00
12	Orel Hershiser/25	15.00
13	Carlton Fisk/25	25.00
14	Dave Parker/25	20.00
15	Rollie Fingers/25	20.00
16	Dwight Gooden/25	20.00
17	Dontrelle Willis/25	15.00
19	Dave Righetti/25	15.00

Pennant Patches Signature

NM/M
Production 5-25

2	Keith Hernandez/25	40.00
6	Steve Garvey/25	35.00
9	Darryl Strawberry/25	20.00
11	Steve Carlton/25	25.00
15	Rollie Fingers/25	35.00
16	Dwight Gooden/25	40.00

Shirts

NM/M
Production 25-100

1	Rod Carew/100	10.00
2	Red Schoendienst/50	8.00
3	Harmon Killebrew/50	20.00
4	Joe Cronin/50	35.00
5	Early Wynn/50	8.00
6	Gaylord Perry/100	8.00
7	Willie McCovey/100	15.00
8	Carl Yastrzemski/100	20.00
9	Reggie Jackson/100	10.00
10	Duke Snider/50	15.00
11	Luis Aparicio/100	8.00
12	Bob Gibson/50	15.00
13	Maury Wills/50	8.00
14	Ernie Banks/50	20.00
15	Enos Slaughter/100	10.00
16	Whitey Ford/100	15.00
17	Warren Spahn/100	15.00
18	Roger Maris/100	35.00
19	Hal Newhouser/100	10.00
20	Marty Marion/25	12.00

Shirts Signature

NM/M
Production 5-50
Prime: No Pricing
Production One Set

2	Red Schoendienst/25	25.00
6	Gaylord Perry/50	20.00
7	Willie McCovey/50	20.00
11	Luis Aparicio/25	25.00
13	Maury Wills/50	15.00

Signature Post Marks Gold

NM/M
Production 1-50

36	Joe Nathan/50	20.00
39	Brett Myers/50	12.00
40	Rich Harden/50	15.00
49	Larry Bigbie/50	15.00
61	Livan Hernandez/50	15.00
63	Lyle Overbay/50	15.00
65	Cliff Lee/50	12.00
68	Danny Graves/25	20.00
71	Lew Ford/50	15.00
72	Chone Figgins/50	20.00
74	Esteban Loaiza/50	20.00
78	Ryan Wagner/50	20.00
79	John Lackey/50	15.00
83	Francisco Cordero/25	15.00
85	Eric Byrnes/50	15.00
89	Casey Kotchman/50	15.00
90	Scott Podsednik/50	15.00
94	Chad Cordero/25	15.00
97	Jose Guillen/25	15.00
102	Jack Wilson/50	15.00
106	Melvin Mora/25	20.00
109	Jody Gerut/50	15.00
128	Ken Harvey/50	15.00
136	Tom Gordon/50	15.00
137	Jake Peavy/25	15.00
139	Dewon Brazelton/50	10.00
140	Jae Weong Seo/25	15.00
141	Danny Kolb/50	20.00
145	Carlos Lee/25	15.00
147	Guillermo Mota/50	15.00
148	Travis Hafner/25	15.00
156	Brad Penny/50	15.00
159	Adrian Gonzalez/50	15.00
163	Bobby Crosby/25	30.00
164	Jermaine Dye/25	20.00
168	Johnny Estrada/25	15.00
169	Milton Bradley/25	20.00
170	Shannon Stewart/25	15.00
173	Laynce Nix/50	20.00
175	Craig Wilson/50	15.00
182	Randy Wolf/50	15.00
184	Aubrey Huff/25	15.00
185	Billy Ripken/50	10.00
186	Octavio Dotel/50	15.00
189	Todd Walker/25	15.00
191	Alexis Rios/50	15.00
198	Jacque Jones/25	15.00

Signature Post Marks Silver

NM/M
Production 1-250
Platinum: No Pricing
Production One Set

1	Brian Roberts/250	8.00
4	Angel Berroa/25	15.00
36	Joe Nathan/250	15.00
39	Brett Myers/250	15.00
40	Rich Harden/100	15.00
49	Larry Bigbie/250	15.00
52	C.C. Sabathia/25	20.00
56	Mark Buehrle/50	15.00
61	Livan Hernandez/100	10.00
63	Lyle Overbay/100	10.00
65	Cliff Lee/250	8.00
68	Danny Graves/100	10.00
71	Lew Ford/100	10.00
72	Chone Figgins/250	10.00
74	Esteban Loaiza/250	10.00
78	Ryan Wagner/250	10.00
79	John Lackey/250	10.00
82	Sean Burroughs/25	15.00
83	Francisco Cordero/100	8.00
85	Eric Byrnes/100	10.00
89	Casey Kotchman/100	10.00
90	Scott Podsednik/100	10.00
93	Trot Nixon/25	25.00
94	Chad Cordero/250	8.00
97	Jose Guillen/100	10.00
102	Jack Wilson/100	10.00
106	Melvin Mora/100	10.00
108	Andre Dawson/25	25.00
109	Jody Gerut/250	10.00
116	Aramis Ramirez/250	25.00
128	Ken Harvey/250	10.00
136	Tom Gordon/250	10.00
137	Jake Peavy/250	10.00
139	Dewon Brazelton/250	8.00
140	Jae Weong Seo/100	10.00
141	Danny Kolb/250	12.00
145	Carlos Lee/250	12.00
147	Guillermo Mota/250	10.00
148	Travis Hafner/250	10.00
155	David Wright/25	80.00
156	Brad Penny/250	10.00
157	Francisco Rodriguez/100	15.00
159	Adrian Gonzalez/250	10.00
160	Derrek Lee/25	30.00
162	Carlos Zambrano/250	25.00
163	Bobby Crosby/100	25.00
168	Johnny Estrada/200	15.00
169	Milton Bradley/100	15.00
170	Shannon Stewart/100	15.00
173	Laynce Nix/250	10.00
175	Craig Wilson/250	15.00
181	Marcus Giles/25	15.00
182	Randy Wolf/250	12.00
184	Aubrey Huff/100	15.00
185	Billy Ripken/250	8.00
186	Octavio Dotel/250	15.00
189	Todd Walker/100	15.00
193	Orlando Cabrera/200	15.00
197	Jose Vidro/200	10.00
198	Jacque Jones/100	10.00

Stamps Centennial Autograph

NM/M
Production 1-40

2	Red Schoendienst/39	40.00
6	Bob Feller/39	40.00
11	Dwight Evans/39	30.00
15	Whitey Ford/27	50.00
22	Tony Perez/24	40.00
24	Billy Williams/39	30.00
25	Juan Marichal/39	30.00
27	Maury Wills/39	25.00
28	Fergie Jenkins/39	30.00
29	Steve Carlton/39	30.00
30	Dale Murphy/39	50.00
32	Gaylord Perry/39	25.00
33	Fred Lynn/39	30.00
35	Ron Guidry/39	40.00
38	Jack Morris/39	25.00
39	Torii Hunter/39	25.00
40	Andre Dawson/39	30.00
41	Dave Righetti/39	20.00
43	Lou Brock/20	40.00
46	Sean Casey/21	40.00
48	Ralph Kiner/39	40.00
51	Jim Rice/39	35.00
51	Duke Snider/25	50.00
52	Harold Baines/39	25.00
57	Bobby Doerr/59	30.00
59	Monte Irvin/39	30.00
61	Alan Trammell/40	25.00
62	Al Kaline/39	50.00
64	Bert Blyleven/39	25.00
65	Miguel Cabrera/39	30.00
69	Michael Young/39	25.00
70	Tony Oliva/39	35.00
71	Mark Mulder/25	40.00

Stamps Legendary Fields Autograph

NM/M
Production 1-34

11	Dwight Evans/34	30.00
22	Tony Perez/34	35.00
24	Billy Williams/34	30.00
28	Fergie Jenkins/34	30.00
29	Steve Carlton/34	30.00
33	Fred Lynn/34	30.00
35	Ron Guidry/34	50.00
38	Jack Morris/34	25.00
40	Andre Dawson/34	30.00
41	Dave Righetti/34	25.00
48	Ralph Kiner/34	40.00
51	Jim Rice/34	35.00
52	Harold Baines/34	25.00
57	Bobby Doerr/34	35.00
59	Monte Irvin/34	35.00
66	Luis Tiant/23	30.00

Stamps Masterpiece Signature Centennial

No Pricing
Production 1-2

Stamps Material Centennial

NM/M
Production 1-39

1	Pee Wee Reese/Bat/39	20.00
3	Babe Ruth/Jsy/39	275.00
4	George Brett/Bat/39	40.00
5	Stan Musial/Bat/39	40.00
6	Bob Feller/Pants/39	15.00
7	Cal Ripken Jr./Pants/39	100.00
9	Ted Williams/Jsy/39	100.00
11	Dwight Evans/Jsy/39	25.00
12	Dave Concepcion/Jsy/39	20.00
13	Ernie Banks/Jsy/39	20.00
14	Pedro J. Martinez/Jsy/39	20.00
16	Scott Rolen/Jsy/39	25.00
17	Tony Gwynn/Jsy/39	20.00
18	Mike Schmidt/Jsy/39	60.00
19	Roberto Clemente/Hat/21	200.00
20	Roger Clemens/Jsy/39	35.00
21	Don Mattingly/Jsy/39	50.00
22	Tony Perez/Bat/39	15.00
23	Roger Maris/Jsy/39	75.00
24	Billy Williams/Jsy/39	15.00
25	Juan Marichal/Pants/39	
26	Hank Blalock/Jsy/39	20.00
27	Maury Wills/Jsy/39	15.00
28	Fergie Jenkins/Pants/39	20.00
29	Steve Carlton/Jsy/39	20.00
30	Dale Murphy/Jsy/39	30.00
31	Kerry Wood/Jsy/39	20.00
32	Gaylord Perry/Jsy/39	15.00
33	Fred Lynn/Jsy/39	20.00
34	Tom Seaver/Bat/39	20.00
36	Reggie Jackson/Pants/39	25.00
37	Bob Gibson/Jsy/39	20.00
38	Jack Morris/Jsy/39	20.00
39	Torii Hunter/Jsy/39	15.00

Stamps Material Centennial (continued)

- 40 Andre Dawson/Jsy/39 20.00
- 41 Dave Righetti/Jsy/39 15.00
- 42 Hideki Matsui/Pants/39 65.00
- 43 Lou Brock/Jkt/39 25.00
- 44 Yogi Berra/Bat/39 30.00
- 45 Frankie Frisch/Jkt/39 25.00
- 46 Sean Casey/Jsy/39 15.00
- 47 Sammy Sosa/Jsy/39 30.00
- 48 Ralph Kiner/Bat/39 15.00
- 49 Hoyt Wilhelm/Jsy/39 15.00
- 50 Jim Rice/Jsy/39 20.00
- 51 Duke Snider/Pants/39 25.00
- 52 Harold Baines/Jsy/39 20.00
- 53 Willie Stargell/Jsy/39 20.00
- 54 Johnny Bench/Pants/39 25.00
- 55 Carlton Fisk/Jsy/39 25.00
- 56 Jim Palmer/Jsy/39 40.00
- 57 Bobby Doerr/Jsy/39
- 58 Mark Prior/Jsy/39 30.00
- 60 Lou Boudreau/Jsy/39 25.00
- 61 Alan Trammell/Bat/39 20.00
- 62 Al Kaline/Bat/39 25.00
- 63 Warren Spahn/Pants/39 30.00
- 64 Bert Blyleven/Jsy/39 20.00
- 65 Miguel Cabrera/Jsy/39 25.00
- 66 Luis Tiant/Jsy/39 15.00
- 67 Harmon Killebrew/Jsy/39 30.00
- 68 Richie Ashburn/Pants/39 25.00
- 69 Michael Young/Jsy/39 15.00
- 70 Tony Oliva/Jsy/39 20.00
- 71 Mark Mulder/Jsy/39 15.00
- 72 Nolan Ryan/Jsy/39 75.00
- 73 Willie McCovey/Jsy/39 25.00
- 74 Kirk Gibson/Jsy/39 20.00
- 75 Carl Yastrzemski/Pants/39 40.00

Stamps Material Centennial Autograph
NM/M
Production 1-39

- 2 Red Schoendienst/Jsy/39 40.00
- 6 Bob Feller/Pants/39 25.00
- 11 Dwight Evans/Jsy/39 30.00
- 22 Tony Perez/Bat/24 40.00
- 24 Billy Williams/Jsy/39 35.00
- 25 Juan Marichal/Pants/39 30.00
- 27 Maury Wills/Jsy/39 30.00
- 28 Fergie Jenkins/Pants/39 35.00
- 29 Steve Carlton/Jsy/39 30.00
- 30 Dale Murphy/Jsy/39 50.00
- 32 Gaylord Perry/Jsy/39 50.00
- 33 Fred Lynn/Jsy/39 30.00
- 38 Bob Gibson/Jsy/39 40.00
- 39 Jack Morris/Jsy/39 25.00
- 40 Andre Dawson/Jsy/39 35.00
- 43 Lou Brock/Jkt/39 30.00
- 46 Sean Casey/Jsy/39 30.00
- 48 Ralph Kiner/Jsy/39 35.00
- 51 Jim Rice/Jsy/39 35.00
- Duke Snider/Pants/39 50.00
- 52 Harold Baines/Jsy/39 25.00
- 56 Jim Palmer/Jsy/22 35.00
- 57 Bobby Doerr/Jsy/39 35.00
- 61 Alan Trammell/Bat/39 30.00
- 62 Al Kaline/Bat/39 50.00
- 64 Bert Blyleven/Jsy/39 25.00
- 65 Miguel Cabrera/Jsy/39 50.00
- 66 Luis Tiant/Jsy/39 30.00
- 67 Harmon Killebrew/Jsy/39 60.00
- 70 Tony Oliva/Jsy/39 35.00
- 71 Mark Mulder/Jsy/20 40.00
- 74 Kirk Gibson/Jsy/39 30.00

Stamps Material Legendary Fields
NM/M
Production 1-34

- 1 Pee Wee Reese/Bat/34 30.00
- 11 Dwight Evans/Jsy/34 25.00
- 12 Dave Concepcion/Jsy/34 20.00
- 13 Ernie Banks/Jsy/34 40.00
- 14 Pedro J. Martinez/Jsy/34 25.00
- 15 Whitey Ford/Jsy/34 35.00
- 19 Roberto Clemente/Hat/21 200.00
- 21 Don Mattingly/Jsy/34
- 22 Tony Perez/Bat/34 20.00
- 23 Roger Maris/Jsy/34 85.00
- 24 Billy Williams/Jsy/34 30.00
- 28 Fergie Jenkins/Pants/34 20.00
- 29 Steve Carlton/Jsy/34 25.00
- 31 Kerry Wood/Jsy/34 30.00
- 33 Fred Lynn/Jsy/34 15.00
- 36 Reggie Jackson/Pants/34 25.00
- 38 Jack Morris/Jsy/34 25.00
- 40 Andre Dawson/Jsy/34 20.00
- 41 Dave Righetti/Jsy/34 20.00
- 42 Hideki Matsui/Pants/34 80.00
- 44 Yogi Berra/Bat/34 25.00
- 47 Sammy Sosa/Jsy/34 40.00
- 48 Ralph Kiner/Bat/34 25.00
- 49 Hoyt Wilhelm/Jsy/34 15.00
- 50 Jim Rice/Jsy/34 20.00
- 51 Duke Snider/Jsy/34 30.00
- 52 Harold Baines/Jsy/34 15.00
- 53 Willie Stargell/Jsy/34 30.00
- 54 Johnny Bench/Pants/34 40.00
- 55 Carlton Fisk/Jsy/34 25.00
- 57 Bobby Doerr/Jsy/34 25.00
- 58 Mark Prior/Jsy/34 40.00
- 61 Alan Trammell/Bat/34 30.00
- 62 Al Kaline/Bat/34 40.00
- 66 Luis Tiant/Jsy/34 25.00
- 74 Kirk Gibson/Jsy/34 30.00
- 75 Carl Yastrzemski/Pants/34 50.00

Stamps Material Legendary Fields Autograph
NM/M
Production 1-34

- 11 Dwight Evans/Jsy/34 30.00
- 22 Tony Perez/Bat/34 40.00
- 24 Billy Williams/Jsy/34 30.00
- 28 Fergie Jenkins/Pants/34 35.00
- 29 Steve Carlton/Jsy/34 35.00
- 33 Fred Lynn/Jsy/34 30.00
- 38 Jack Morris/Jsy/34 30.00
- 40 Andre Dawson/Jsy/34 30.00
- 41 Dave Righetti/Jsy/34 20.00
- 50 Jim Rice/Jsy/33 40.00
- 66 Luis Tiant/Jsy/23 35.00
- 74 Kirk Gibson/Jsy/23 30.00

Stamps Material Legendary Players 20
NM/M
Complete Set (2):

- 19 Roberto Clemente/Hat/21 200.00

Stamps Material Legendary Players 33
NM/M
Complete Set (2):

- 19 Roberto Clemente/Hat/21 200.00

Stamps Material Olympic
NM/M
Production 1-92

- 1 Pee Wee Reese/Bat/92 15.00
- 4 George Brett/Jsy/92 30.00
- 6 Bob Feller/Pants/92 15.00
- 7 Cal Ripken Jr./Pants/92 60.00
- 11 Dwight Evans/Jsy/24 30.00
- 13 Ernie Banks/Jsy/92 25.00
- 14 Pedro J. Martinez/Jsy/45 20.00
- 16 Scott Rolen/Jsy/27 30.00
- 17 Tony Gwynn/Jsy/92 30.00
- 18 Mike Schmidt/Jsy/92 40.00
- 19 Roberto Clemente/Hat/21 200.00
- 20 Roger Clemens/Jsy/92 30.00
- 21 Don Mattingly/Jsy/23 40.00
- 22 Tony Perez/Bat/24 30.00
- 24 Billy Williams/Jsy/26 20.00
- 25 Juan Marichal/Pants/92 15.00
- 26 Hank Blalock/Jsy/92 15.00
- 27 Maury Wills/Jsy/30 20.00
- 28 Fergie Jenkins/Pants/92 15.00
- 29 Steve Carlton/Jsy/92 15.00
- 30 Dale Murphy/Jsy/92 30.00
- 31 Kerry Wood/Jsy/92 15.00
- 32 Gaylord Perry/Jsy/92 30.00
- 33 Fred Lynn/Jsy/92 15.00
- 34 Tom Seaver/Bat/92 20.00
- 36 Reggie Jackson/Pants/44 20.00
- 37 Bob Gibson/Jsy/45 25.00
- 38 Jack Morris/Jsy/45 25.00
- 39 Torii Hunter/Jsy/48 15.00
- 41 Dave Righetti/Jsy/92 15.00
- 42 Hideki Matsui/Pants/92 40.00
- 43 Lou Brock/Jkt/92 15.00
- 44 Yogi Berra/Bat/92 25.00
- 45 Frankie Frisch/Jkt/92 15.00
- 46 Sean Casey/Jsy/21 15.00
- 47 Sammy Sosa/Jsy/92 25.00
- 48 Ralph Kiner/Bat/92 15.00
- 49 Hoyt Wilhelm/Jsy/92 15.00
- 50 Jim Rice/Jsy/92 15.00
- 51 Duke Snider/Pants/92 20.00
- 52 Harold Baines/Jsy/92 15.00
- 53 Willie Stargell/Jsy/92 20.00
- 54 Johnny Bench/Pants/92 20.00
- 55 Carlton Fisk/Jsy/92 15.00
- 56 Jim Palmer/Jsy/92 15.00
- 57 Bobby Doerr/Jsy/92 15.00
- 58 Mark Prior/Jsy/92 40.00
- 60 Lou Boudreau/Jsy/92 20.00
- 61 Alan Trammell/Bat/92 15.00
- 62 Al Kaline/Bat/92 20.00
- 63 Warren Spahn/Pants/92 25.00
- 65 Miguel Cabrera/Jsy/24 20.00
- 66 Luis Tiant/Jsy/23 20.00
- 67 Harmon Killebrew/Jsy/92 30.00
- 68 Richie Ashburn/Pants/92 20.00
- 70 Tony Oliva/Jsy/92 20.00
- 71 Mark Mulder/Jsy/20 25.00
- 72 Nolan Ryan/Jsy/30 100.00
- 73 Willie McCovey/Jsy/92 20.00
- 74 Kirk Gibson/Jsy/92 15.00
- 75 Carl Yastrzemski/Pants/92 30.00

Stamps Material Olympic Autograph
NM/M
Production 1-29

- 6 Bob Feller/Pants/29 45.00
- 11 Dwight Evans/Jsy/24 35.00
- 22 Tony Perez/Bat/29 40.00
- 24 Billy Williams/Jsy/29 35.00
- 25 Juan Marichal/Pants/29 35.00
- 27 Maury Wills/Jsy/29 30.00
- 28 Fergie Jenkins/Pants/29 35.00
- 29 Steve Carlton/Jsy/29 35.00
- 30 Dale Murphy/Jsy/29 50.00
- 32 Gaylord Perry/Jsy/29 20.00
- 33 Fred Lynn/Jsy/29 35.00
- 37 Bob Gibson/Jsy/29 35.00
- 38 Jack Morris/Jsy/29 30.00
- 40 Andre Dawson/Jsy/25 35.00
- 43 Lou Brock/Jkt/20 40.00
- 46 Sean Casey/Jsy/21 40.00
- 56 Jim Palmer/Jsy/22 40.00
- 64 Bert Blyleven/Jsy/28 30.00
- 65 Miguel Cabrera/Jsy/24 60.00
- 66 Luis Tiant/Jsy/23 30.00
- 71 Mark Mulder/Jsy/20 40.00
- 74 Kirk Gibson/Jsy/23 30.00

Stamps Material Pro Ball
NM/M
Production 1-69

- 1 Pee Wee Reese/Bat/69 20.00
- 4 George Brett/Jsy/69 40.00
- 5 Stan Musial/Bat/69 30.00
- 6 Bob Feller/Pants/69 20.00
- 7 Cal Ripken Jr./Pants/69 60.00
- 11 Dwight Evans/Jsy/24 30.00
- 13 Ernie Banks/Jsy/69 30.00
- 14 Pedro J. Martinez/Jsy/45 25.00
- 16 Scott Rolen/Jsy/27 40.00
- 17 Tony Gwynn/Jsy/69 35.00
- 18 Mike Schmidt/Jsy/69 60.00
- 19 Roberto Clemente/Hat/21 200.00
- 20 Roger Clemens/Jsy/69 30.00
- 21 Don Mattingly/Jsy/23 50.00
- 22 Tony Perez/Bat/24 50.00
- 24 Billy Williams/Jsy/69 15.00
- 25 Juan Marichal/Pants/69 15.00
- 26 Hank Blalock/Jsy/69 15.00
- 27 Maury Wills/Jsy/69 20.00
- 28 Fergie Jenkins/Pants/69 20.00
- 29 Steve Carlton/Jsy/69 15.00
- 30 Dale Murphy/Jsy/69 15.00
- 31 Kerry Wood/Jsy/69 20.00
- 32 Gaylord Perry/Jsy/69 15.00
- 33 Fred Lynn/Jsy/69 20.00
- 34 Tom Seaver/Bat/69 20.00
- 36 Reggie Jackson/Pants/69 15.00
- 37 Bob Gibson/Jsy/45 25.00
- 38 Jack Morris/Jsy/45 25.00
- 39 Torii Hunter/Jsy/48 15.00
- 40 Andre Dawson/Jsy/69 15.00
- 41 Dave Righetti/Jsy/69 15.00
- 42 Hideki Matsui/Pants/69 40.00
- 43 Lou Brock/Jkt/69 15.00
- 44 Yogi Berra/Bat/69 25.00
- 45 Frankie Frisch/Jkt/69 20.00
- 46 Sean Casey/Jsy/69 15.00
- 47 Sammy Sosa/Jsy/69 20.00
- 48 Ralph Kiner/Bat/69 15.00
- 49 Hoyt Wilhelm/Jsy/69 15.00
- 50 Jim Rice/Jsy/69 15.00
- 51 Duke Snider/Pants/69 20.00
- 52 Harold Baines/Jsy/69 15.00
- 53 Willie Stargell/Jsy/69 20.00
- 54 Johnny Bench/Pants/69 20.00
- 55 Carlton Fisk/Jsy/72 15.00
- 56 Jim Palmer/Jsy/69 15.00
- 57 Bobby Doerr/Jsy/69 15.00
- 58 Mark Prior/Jsy/69 15.00
- 60 Lou Boudreau/Jsy/69 25.00
- 61 Alan Trammell/Bat/69 15.00
- 62 Al Kaline/Bat/69 20.00
- 63 Warren Spahn/Pants/69 25.00
- 65 Miguel Cabrera/Jsy/69 15.00
- 66 Luis Tiant/Jsy/69 15.00
- 67 Harmon Killebrew/Jsy/69 35.00
- 68 Richie Ashburn/Pants/69 15.00
- 69 Michael Young/Jsy/69 15.00
- 70 Tony Oliva/Jsy/69 15.00
- 71 Mark Mulder/Jsy/20 25.00
- 72 Nolan Ryan/Jsy/69 60.00
- 73 Willie McCovey/Jsy/69 25.00
- 74 Kirk Gibson/Jsy/69 15.00
- 75 Carl Yastrzemski/Pants/69 30.00

Stamps Material Pro Ball Autograph
NM/M
Production 1-69

- 6 Bob Feller/Pants/69 30.00
- 11 Dwight Evans/Jsy/24 30.00
- 22 Tony Perez/Bat/24 40.00
- 24 Billy Williams/Jsy/26 35.00
- 25 Juan Marichal/Pants/27 35.00
- 27 Maury Wills/Jsy/69 25.00
- 28 Fergie Jenkins/Pants/69 25.00
- 29 Steve Carlton/Jsy/69 30.00
- 30 Dale Murphy/Jsy/69 40.00
- 32 Gaylord Perry/Jsy/69 20.00
- 33 Fred Lynn/Jsy/69 30.00
- 37 Bob Gibson/Jsy/45 35.00
- 43 Lou Brock/Jkt/20 40.00
- 46 Sean Casey/Jsy/21 30.00
- 57 Bobby Doerr/Jsy/48 30.00
- 65 Miguel Cabrera/Jsy/24 50.00
- 66 Luis Tiant/Jsy/23 30.00
- 71 Mark Mulder/Jsy/20 40.00
- 74 Kirk Gibson/Jsy/23 30.00

Stamps Material USA Flag
NM/M
Production 1-100

- 1 Pee Wee Reese/Bat/100 15.00
- 4 George Brett/Jsy/100 15.00
- 5 Stan Musial/Bat/100 25.00
- 6 Bob Feller/Pants/100 15.00
- 7 Cal Ripken Jr./Pants/100 65.00
- 11 Dwight Evans/Jsy/24 30.00
- 13 Ernie Banks/Jsy/100 30.00
- 14 Pedro J. Martinez/Jsy/45 25.00
- 16 Scott Rolen/Jsy/27 40.00
- 17 Tony Gwynn/Jsy/100 30.00
- 18 Mike Schmidt/Jsy/50 50.00
- 19 Roberto Clemente/Hat/21 200.00
- 20 Roger Clemens/Jsy/100 30.00
- 21 Don Mattingly/Jsy/100 50.00
- 22 Tony Perez/Bat/24 25.00
- 24 Billy Williams/Jsy/100 10.00
- 25 Juan Marichal/Pants/100 15.00
- 26 Hank Blalock/Jsy/100 15.00
- 27 Maury Wills/Jsy/100 10.00
- 28 Fergie Jenkins/Pants/100 15.00
- 29 Steve Carlton/Jsy/100 15.00
- 30 Dale Murphy/Jsy/100 15.00
- 31 Kerry Wood/Jsy/100 20.00
- 32 Gaylord Perry/Jsy/100 10.00
- 33 Fred Lynn/Jsy/100 15.00
- 34 Tom Seaver/Bat/100 15.00
- 36 Reggie Jackson/Pants/44 20.00
- 37 Bob Gibson/Jsy/100 20.00
- 38 Jack Morris/Jsy/100 10.00
- 39 Torii Hunter/Jsy/48 15.00
- 41 Dave Righetti/Jsy/100 10.00
- 42 Hideki Matsui/Pants/100 40.00
- 43 Lou Brock/Jkt/100 15.00
- 44 Yogi Berra/Bat/100 20.00
- 45 Frankie Frisch/Jkt/100 15.00
- 46 Sean Casey/Jsy/100 10.00
- 47 Sammy Sosa/Jsy/100 15.00
- 49 Hoyt Wilhelm/Jsy/100 15.00
- 50 Jim Rice/Jsy/100 12.00
- 51 Duke Snider/Pants/100
- 52 Harold Baines/Jsy/100 10.00
- 53 Willie Stargell/Jsy/100 15.00
- 54 Johnny Bench/Pants/100 20.00
- 55 Carlton Fisk/Jsy/72 15.00
- 56 Jim Palmer/Jsy/100 15.00
- 57 Bobby Doerr/Jsy/100 15.00
- 58 Mark Prior/Jsy/100 15.00
- 62 Al Kaline/Bat/100 15.00
- 63 Warren Spahn/Pants/100 20.00
- 64 Bert Blyleven/Jsy/28 20.00
- 65 Miguel Cabrera/Jsy/24 25.00
- 66 Luis Tiant/Jsy/23 20.00
- 67 Harmon Killebrew/Jsy/100 30.00
- 68 Richie Ashburn/Pants/100 15.00
- 70 Tony Oliva/Jsy/100 15.00
- 71 Mark Mulder/Jsy/100 25.00
- 72 Nolan Ryan/Jsy/100 50.00
- 73 Willie McCovey/Jsy/44 25.00
- 74 Kirk Gibson/Jsy/100 10.00
- 75 Carl Yastrzemski/Pants/100 25.00

Stamps Material USA Flag Autograph
NM/M
Production 1-37

- 2 Red Schoendienst/Jsy/37 40.00
- 6 Bob Feller/Pants/8 40.00
- 11 Dwight Evans/Jsy/37 30.00
- 22 Tony Perez/Bat/37 35.00
- 24 Billy Williams/Jsy/37 30.00
- 25 Juan Marichal/Pants/37 30.00
- 27 Maury Wills/Jsy/37 25.00
- 28 Fergie Jenkins/Pants/37 30.00
- 29 Steve Carlton/Jsy/37 30.00
- 30 Dale Murphy/Jsy/37 50.00
- 32 Gaylord Perry/Jsy/37 25.00
- 33 Fred Lynn/Jsy/37 30.00
- 38 Bob Gibson/Jsy/37 40.00
- 39 Jack Morris/Jsy/37 25.00
- 41 Dave Righetti/Jsy/37 20.00
- 43 Lou Brock/Jkt/37 30.00
- 46 Sean Casey/Jsy/37 30.00
- 48 Ralph Kiner/Jsy/37 25.00
- 51 Jim Rice/Jsy/37
- Duke Snider/Pants/37 40.00
- 52 Harold Baines/Jsy/37 25.00
- 56 Jim Palmer/Jsy/22
- 57 Bobby Doerr/Jsy/37 40.00
- 61 Alan Trammell/Bat/37 50.00
- 62 Al Kaline/Bat/37 50.00
- 64 Bert Blyleven/Jsy/25 25.00
- 65 Miguel Cabrera/Jsy/37 50.00
- 66 Luis Tiant/Jsy/37 25.00
- 67 Harmon Killebrew/Jsy/37 60.00
- 70 Tony Oliva/Jsy/37 35.00
- 71 Mark Mulder/Jsy/23 30.00
- 74 Kirk Gibson/Jsy/23 30.00

Stamps Olympic Autograph
NM/M
Production 1-92

- 2 Red Schoendienst/92 25.00
- 6 Bob Feller/92 25.00
- 11 Dwight Evans/92 20.00
- 22 Tony Perez/24 40.00
- 24 Billy Williams/26 35.00
- 25 Juan Marichal/27 35.00
- 27 Maury Wills/92 20.00
- 28 Fergie Jenkins/92 25.00
- 29 Steve Carlton/92 20.00
- 30 Dale Murphy/92 30.00
- 32 Gaylord Perry/92 20.00
- 33 Fred Lynn/92 20.00
- 35 Ron Guidry/48 35.00
- 38 Jack Morris/92 20.00
- 39 Torii Hunter/48 20.00
- 40 Andre Dawson/92 25.00
- 43 Lou Brock/20 40.00
- 46 Sean Casey/21 40.00
- 50 Jim Rice/92 25.00
- 52 Harold Baines/20 20.00
- 56 Jim Palmer/22 50.00
- 57 Bobby Doerr/92 20.00
- 59 Monte Irvin/92 20.00
- 61 Alan Trammell/92 25.00
- 62 Al Kaline/92 40.00
- 64 Bert Blyleven/92 20.00
- 65 Miguel Cabrera/24 60.00
- 66 Luis Tiant/23 20.00
- 70 Tony Oliva/91 20.00
- 71 Mark Mulder/20 40.00

Stamps Pro Ball Autograph
NM/M
Production 1-69

- 6 Bob Feller/69 30.00
- 11 Dwight Evans/69 25.00
- 22 Tony Perez/24 40.00
- 24 Billy Williams/26 35.00
- 25 Juan Marichal/27 35.00
- 27 Maury Wills/69 20.00
- 28 Fergie Jenkins/69 25.00
- 29 Steve Carlton/69 20.00
- 30 Dale Murphy/69 40.00
- 32 Gaylord Perry/69 20.00
- 33 Fred Lynn/69 25.00
- 35 Ron Guidry/49 40.00
- 38 Jack Morris/47 20.00
- 39 Torii Hunter/48 25.00
- 43 Lou Brock/20 40.00
- 46 Sean Casey/21 40.00
- 57 Bobby Doerr/69 30.00
- 59 Monte Irvin/20 25.00
- 64 Bert Blyleven/28 25.00
- 65 Miguel Cabrera/24 50.00
- 66 Luis Tiant/23 30.00
- 71 Mark Mulder/20 40.00

Stamps USA Flag Autograph
NM/M
Production 1-100

- 2 Red Schoendienst/100 25.00
- 6 Bob Feller/100 25.00
- 11 Dwight Evans/24 35.00
- 22 Tony Perez/24 40.00
- 24 Billy Williams/26 35.00
- 25 Juan Marichal/27 35.00
- 27 Maury Wills/100 20.00
- 28 Fergie Jenkins/100 25.00
- 29 Steve Carlton/100 20.00
- 30 Dale Murphy/100 30.00
- 32 Gaylord Perry/100 20.00
- 33 Fred Lynn/100 20.00
- 35 Ron Guidry/49 20.00
- 38 Jack Morris/100 20.00
- 39 Torii Hunter/48 25.00
- 40 Andre Dawson/100 25.00
- 43 Lou Brock/20 40.00
- 46 Sean Casey/21 40.00
- 48 Ralph Kiner/100 25.00
- 51 Duke Snider/25 45.00
- 52 Harold Baines/100 20.00
- 56 Jim Palmer/22 50.00
- 57 Bobby Doerr/100 20.00
- 59 Monte Irvin/100 20.00
- 61 Alan Trammell/100 25.00
- 62 Al Kaline/100 40.00
- 64 Bert Blyleven/100 20.00
- 65 Miguel Cabrera/24 60.00
- 66 Luis Tiant/100 20.00
- 70 Tony Oliva/100 20.00
- 71 Mark Mulder/20 40.00

Timeline Threads Jersey Number
NM/M
Production 1-43

- 6 Orlando Cepeda/Pants/30 10.00
- 9 Tony Perez/24 10.00
- 11 Tommy John/Jsy/25 15.00
- 15 Carlton Fisk/Jsy/27 20.00
- 17 Bert Blyleven/Jsy/28 10.00
- 20 Lou Brock/Jsy/20 20.00
- 21 Sammy Sosa/Jsy/21 20.00
- 22 Roger Clemens/Jsy/22 40.00

#		
23	Don Mattingly/Jsy/23	40.00
24	Rickey Henderson/Jsy/35	15.00
26	Wade Boggs/Jsy/26	20.00
29	Jim "Catfish" Hunter/Jsy/29	15.00
30	Maury Wills/Jsy/30	10.00
31	Hoyt Wilhelm/Jsy/31	10.00
33	Eddie Murray/Pants/33	
34	Nolan Ryan/Pants/34	50.00
35	Phil Niekro/Jsy/35	15.00
38	Curt Schilling/Jsy/38	15.00
40	Sandy Koufax/Jsy/32	500.00
41	Don Sutton/Jsy/20	15.00
42	Randy Johnson/Jsy/51	15.00
43	Dennis Eckersley/Jsy/43	10.00
44	Frank Thomas/Jsy/35	20.00
45	Mike Mussina/Jsy/35	15.00
46	Greg Maddux/Jsy/31	25.00
47	Jim Palmer/Pants/22	15.00
49	Mike Piazza/Jsy/31	25.00

Timeline Threads Number Autograph

Production 1-19
Position Autograph: No Pricing
Production 1-19
Prime: No Pricing
Production One Set

Timeline Threads Position

NM/M
Common Player: 4.00

#		
1	Bobby Doerr/Jsy/39	10.00
2	Burleigh Grimes/Pants/26	50.00
3	Babe Ruth/Pants/30	200.00
4	Joe Cronin/Pants/38	20.00
5	Johnny Bench/Pants/71	15.00
6	Orlando Cepeda/Pants/62	8.00
7	Ivan Rodriguez/Jsy/103	8.00
8	Cal Ripken Jr./Jsy/78	40.00
9	Tony Perez/Jsy/78	8.00
10	Andre Dawson/Jsy/86	8.00
11	Tommy John/Jsy/86	4.00
12	Alfonso Soriano/Jsy/102	8.00
13	Ozzie Smith/Jsy/78	15.00
14	Ernie Banks/Jsy/70	15.00
15	Carlton Fisk/Jsy/80	8.00
16	Bo Jackson/Jsy/89	10.00
17	Bert Blyleven/Jsy/83	4.00
18	Darryl Strawberry/Jsy/88	6.00
19	Bob Feller/Pants/36	8.00
20	Lou Brock/Jsy/74	8.00
21	Sammy Sosa/Jsy/103	12.00
22	Roger Clemens/Jsy/101	15.00
23	Don Mattingly/Jsy/94	20.00
24	Rickey Henderson/Jsy/83	10.00
25	Albert Pujols/Jsy/103	15.00
26	Wade Boggs/Jsy/87	10.00
27	Joe Morgan/Jsy/82	8.00
28	Gary Carter/Jsy/86	8.00
29	Jim "Catfish" Hunter/Jsy/78	6.00
30	Maury Wills/Jsy/65	4.00
31	Hoyt Wilhelm/Jsy/68	4.00
32	Matt Williams/Jsy/95	4.00
33	Eddie Murray/Pants/88	8.00
34	Nolan Ryan/Pants/90	25.00
35	Phil Niekro/Jsy/80	6.00
36	Paul Molitor/Jsy/96	10.00
37	Dale Murphy/Jsy/83	8.00
38	Curt Schilling/Jsy/99	8.00
39	Fred Lynn/Jsy/75	4.00
40	Sandy Koufax/Jsy/64	260.00
41	Don Sutton/Jsy/76	4.00
42	Randy Johnson/Jsy/98	8.00
43	Dennis Eckersley/Jsy/97	6.00
44	Frank Thomas/Jsy/94	8.00
45	Mike Mussina/Jsy/100	
46	Greg Maddux/Jsy/96	10.00
47	Jim Palmer/Pants/76	6.00
48	Harmon Killebrew/Jsy/62	20.00
49	Mike Piazza/Jsy/99	15.00
50	Billy Martin/Jsy/83	15.00

2005 Leaf Certified Materials

NM/M
Complete Set (250):

Common Player: .50
Common Auto. (201-250): 6.00
Production 499 unless noted.
Hobby Pack (5): 10.00
Hobby Box (10): 90.00

#		
1	A.J. Burnett	.50
2	Adam Dunn	.75
3	Adrian Beltre	.75
4	Bret Boone	.50
5	Albert Pujols	2.50
6	Alex Rodriguez	2.50
7	Alfonso Soriano	1.00
8	Andruw Jones	1.00
9	Andy Pettitte	.75
10	Aramis Ramirez	.75
11	Aubrey Huff	.50
12	Austin Kearns	.50
13	B.J. Upton	.50
14	Brandon Webb	.50
15	Barry Zito	.50
16	Tim Salmon	.50
17	Bobby Abreu	.50
18	Bobby Crosby	.50
19	Brad Penny	.50
20	Preston Wilson	.50
21	C.C. Sabathia	.50
22	Carl Crawford	.50
23	Keith Foulke	.50
24	Carlos Beltran	.50
25	Casey Kotchman	.50
26	Chipper Jones	1.00
27	Chone Figgins	.50
28	Craig Biggio	.75
29	Craig Wilson	.50
30	Curt Schilling	1.00
31	Danny Kolb	.50
32	David Ortiz	1.00
33	Orlando Hudson	.50
34	David Wright	1.50
35	Derek Jeter	2.50
36	Jake Peavy	.50
37	Derrek Lee	.75
38	Dontrelle Willis	.75
39	Edgar Renteria	.50
40	Angel Berroa	.50
41	Eric Chavez	.50
42	Akinori Otsuka	.50
43	Francisco Rodriguez	.50
44	Garret Anderson	.50
45	Gary Sheffield	.75
46	Greg Maddux	1.50
47	Hideki Matsui	2.00
48	Hideo Nomo	.75
49	Ichiro Suzuki	2.00
50	Ivan Rodriguez	1.00
51	J.D. Drew	.50
52	J.T. Snow	.50
53	Jack Wilson	.50
54	Jamie Moyer	.50
55	Jason Bay	.50
56	Jason Giambi	.75
57	Trot Nixon	.50
58	Jason Schmidt	.50
59	Jason Varitek	.50
60	Roy Oswalt	.50
61	Javy Lopez	.50
62	Eric Byrnes	.50
63	Jeff Bagwell	.75
64	Jeff Kent	.75
65	Jeff Suppan	.50
66	Jeremy Bonderman	.50
67	Jermaine Dye	.50
68	Kazuhito Tadano	.50
69	Jim Edmonds	.75
70	Jim Thome	.75
71	Johan Santana	1.00
72	John Smoltz	.75
73	Johnny Damon	1.00
74	Johnny Estrada	.50
75	Brett Myers	.50
76	Jose Guillen	.50
77	Jose Vidro	.50
78	Josh Beckett	.75
79	Edwin Jackson	.50
80	Raul Ibanez	.50
81	Rich Harden	.50
82	Justin Morneau	.75
83	Kazuhisa Ishii	.50
84	Kazuo Matsui	.50
85	Ken Griffey Jr.	1.50
86	Ken Harvey	.50
87	Frank Thomas	.75
88	Kerry Wood	.50
89	Wade Miller	.50
90	Kevin Millwood	.50
91	Jeremy Affeldt	.50
92	Francisco Cordero	.50
93	Lance Berkman	.50
94	Larry Walker	.50
95	Laynce Nix	.50
96	Luis Gonzalez	.50
97	Lyle Overbay	.50
98	Carlos Zambrano	.75
99	Manny Ramirez	1.00
100	Marcus Giles	.50
101	Mark Buehrle	.50
102	Mark Loretta	.50
103	Mark Mulder	.50
104	Mark Prior	1.00
105	Mark Teixeira	.75
106	Marlon Byrd	.50
107	Rafael Furcal	.50
108	Melvin Mora	.50
109	Michael Young	.50
110	Miguel Cabrera	1.00
111	Miguel Tejada	.75
112	Mike Lowell	.50
113	Mike Mussina	.75
114	Mike Piazza	1.50
115	Moises Alou	.50
116	Livan Hernandez	.50
117	Nomar Garciaparra	1.50
118	Omar Vizquel	.50
119	Orlando Cabrera	.50
120	Pat Burrell	.50
121	Paul Konerko	.50
122	Paul LoDuca	.50
123	Pedro Martinez	1.00
124	Rafael Palmeiro	.75
125	Randy Johnson	1.00
126	Richard Hidalgo	.50
127	Richie Sexson	.50
128	Magglio Ordonez	.50
129	Roger Clemens	2.50
130	Russ Ortiz	.50
131	Sammy Sosa	1.50
132	Scott Podsednik	.50
133	Scott Rolen	1.00
134	Sean Burroughs	.50
135	Sean Casey	.50
136	Shawn Green	.50
137	Jorge Posada	.75
138	Roy Halladay	.50
139	Steve Finley	.50
140	Tim Hudson	.50
141	Todd Helton	.75
142	Tom Glavine	.75
143	Torii Hunter	.50
144	Travis Hafner	.50
145	Trevor Hoffman	.50
146	Troy Glaus	.50
147	Vernon Wells	.50
148	Victor Martinez	.50
149	Vladimir Guerrero	1.00
150	Sammy Sosa	1.50
151	Hank Blalock	.75
152	Danny Graves	.50
153	Rocco Baldelli	.50
154	Carlos Delgado	.50
155	Bubba Nelson	.50
156	Kevin Youkilis	.50
157	Jacque Jones	.50
158	Mike Lieberthal	.50
159	Ben Sheets	.50
160	Lew Ford	.50
161	Ervin Santana	.50
162	Jody Gerut	.50
163	Nick Johnson	.50
164	Brian Roberts	.50
165	Joe Nathan	.50
166	Mike Sweeney	.50
167	Ryan Wagner	.50
168	David Dellucci	.50
169	Jae Weong Seo	.50
170	Tom Gordon	.50
171	Carlos Lee	.50
172	Octavio Dotel	.50
173	Jose Castillo	.50
174	Troy Percival	.50
175	Carlos Delgado	.50
176	Curt Schilling	1.00
177	David Ortiz	1.00
178	Greg Maddux	1.50
179	Ivan Rodriguez	.75
180	Jeff Kent	.50
181	Larry Walker	.50
182	Miguel Tejada	.75
183	Pedro J. Martinez	1.00
184	Rafael Palmeiro	.75
185	Roger Clemens	2.50
186	Shawn Green	.50
187	Tim Hudson	.75
188	Tom Glavine	.75
189	Troy Glaus	.50
190	Vladimir Guerrero	1.00
191	Cal Ripken Jr.	4.00
192	Don Mattingly	2.00
193	George Brett	2.00
194	Harmon Killebrew	1.50
195	Mike Schmidt	2.00
196	Nolan Ryan	3.00
197	Stan Musial	2.00
198	Tony Gwynn	2.00
199	Wade Boggs	1.00
200	Willie Mays	2.00
201	Ambiorix Concepcion/Auto.	10.00
202	Agustin Montero/Auto. RC	
203	Carlos Ruiz/Auto. RC	15.00
204	Casey Rogowski/Auto. RC	6.00
205	Chris Resop/Auto. RC	8.00
206	Chris Roberson/Auto. RC	6.00
207	Colter Bean RC	2.00
208	Danny Rueckel/Auto. RC	6.00
209	David Gassner/Auto. RC	8.00
210	Devon Lowery/Auto. RC	8.00
211	Norihiro Nakamura/Auto./115 RC	40.00
212	Erick Threets/Auto./299 RC	6.00
213	Garrett Jones/Auto./299 RC	8.00
214	Geovany Soto/Auto. RC	6.00
215	Jared Gothreaux/Auto./299 RC	
216	Jason Hammel/Auto. RC	10.00
217	Jeff Miller/Auto./299 RC	6.00
218	Jeff Niemann/Auto./299 RC	20.00
219	Huston Street/Auto.	2.00
220	John Hattig Jr./Auto. RC	6.00
221	Justin Verlander/Auto./299 RC	45.00
222	Justin Wechsler/Auto. RC	6.00
223	Luke Scott/Auto. RC	30.00
224	Mark McLemore/Auto. RC	8.00
225	Mark Woodyard/Auto./299 RC	6.00
226	Matt Lindstrom/Auto./299 RC	8.00
227	Miguel Negron/Auto. RC	6.00
228	Mike Morse/Auto. RC	15.00
229	Nate McLouth/Auto. RC	8.00
230	Paulino Reynoso/Auto./299 RC	6.00
231	Philip Humber/Auto./299 RC	15.00
232	Tony Pena/Auto. RC	6.00
233	Randy Messenger/Auto. RC	6.00
234	Raul Tablado/Auto. RC	8.00
235	Russel Rohlicek/Auto. RC	6.00
236	Ryan Speier/Auto. RC	8.00
237	Scott Munter/Auto. RC	8.00
238	Sean Thompson/Auto. RC	6.00
239	Sean Tracey/Auto./299 RC	6.00
240	Marcos Carvajal RC	1.50
241	Travis Bowyer/Auto. RC	10.00
242	Ubaldo Jimenez/Auto. RC	6.00
243	Wladimir Balentien/Auto.	12.00
244	Eude Brito RC	8.00
245	Ambiorix Burgos RC	2.00
246	Tadahito Iguchi RC	5.00
247	Dae-Sung Koo RC	1.00
248	Chris Seddon RC	2.00
249	Keiichi Yabu/Auto. RC	15.00
250	Yuniesky Betancourt/Auto. RC	25.00

Cuts Blue

NM/M
Production 1-80

#		
3	Willie Mays/26	150.00
7	Jim Palmer/50	25.00
12	Steve Carlton/50	25.00
15	Maury Wills/80	20.00
20	Dale Murphy/50	30.00

Cuts Green

NM/M
Production 3-50

#		
7	Jim Palmer/50	25.00
12	Steve Carlton/50	25.00
15	Maury Wills/80	20.00
20	Dale Murphy/50	30.00

Cuts Red

NM/M
Production 1-60

#		
7	Jim Palmer/50	25.00
12	Steve Carlton/50	25.00
15	Maury Wills/60	20.00
20	Dale Murphy/50	30.00

Cuts Materials Blue

NM/M
Production 4-43

#		
2	Hank Aaron/Bat/43	275.00
3	Willie Mays/Pants/24	175.00
4	Sandy Koufax/Jsy/32	400.00
6	Nolan Ryan/Jsy/34	100.00
9	Rod Carew/Jsy/29	25.00
10	Ryne Sandberg/Jsy/23	120.00
12	Steve Carlton/Pants/32	25.00
14	Mike Schmidt/Jsy/20	65.00
19	Don Mattingly/Jsy/23	75.00

Cuts Materials Green

NM/M
Production 4-32

#		
3	Willie Mays/Pants/24	175.00
9	Rod Carew/Jsy/29	25.00
10	Ryne Sandberg/Jsy/23	120.00
12	Steve Carlton/Pants/32	25.00
14	Mike Schmidt/Jsy/20	65.00

Cuts Materials Red

NM/M
Production 4-32

#		
3	Willie Mays/Pants/24	175.00
9	Rod Carew/Jsy/29	25.00
10	Ryne Sandberg/Jsy/23	120.00
12	Steve Carlton/Pants/32	25.00
14	Mike Schmidt/Jsy/20	65.00

Fabric of the Game

NM/M
Common Player: Production 5-100

#		
1	Al Oliver/Jsy/50	6.00
2	Alan Trammell/Jsy/100	6.00
3	Andres Galarraga/Jsy/100	4.00
4	Andres Galarraga/Jsy/100	4.00
6	Babe Ruth/Pants/25	240.00
7	Billy Martin/Pants/100	15.00
8	Billy Williams/Jsy/50	6.00
9	Bo Jackson/Jsy/50	10.00
10	Bo Jackson/Jsy/100	10.00
11	Bob Gibson/Jsy/25	12.00
12	Bobby Doerr/Pants/50	10.00
14	Burleigh Grimes/Pants/25	50.00
15	Cal Ripken Jr./Jsy/50	30.00
16	Cal Ripken Jr./Jsy/50	30.00
17	Carl Yastrzemski/Pants/50	15.00
18	Carlton Fisk/Jkt/50	10.00
19	Jim "Catfish" Hunter/Pants/50	8.00
20	Darryl Strawberry/Jsy/25	8.00
21	Darryl Strawberry/Jsy/100	4.00
22	Dave Concepcion/Jsy/50	6.00
23	Dave Righetti/Jsy/50	8.00
24	Dave Winfield/Pants/100	8.00
25	David Cone/Jsy/100	4.00
26	David Justice/Jsy/100	4.00
27	Deion Sanders/Jsy/50	8.00
28	Deion Sanders/Jsy/100	8.00
29	Dennis Eckersley/Jsy/50	
30	Dennis Eckersley/Pants/50	8.00
31	Don Mattingly/Jsy/100	15.00
32	Don Sutton/Jsy/25	8.00
33	Don Sutton/Jsy/50	6.00
37	Dwight Gooden/Jsy/100	
38	Eddie Murray/Jsy/20	15.00
39	Eddie Murray/Pants/50	10.00
40	Edgar Martinez/Jsy/100	4.00
41	Ernie Banks/Jsy/50	4.00
42	Fergie Jenkins/Jsy/50	8.00
43	Frankie Frisch/Jkt/50	20.00
44	Fred Lynn/Jsy/50	4.00
45	Fred McGriff/Jsy/100	6.00
46	Gary Carter/Jsy/50	6.00
47	Gary Carter/Jsy/50	6.00
48	Gaylord Perry/Jsy/50	6.00
49	Gaylord Perry/Jsy/50	6.00
50	George Brett/Jsy/25	20.00
51	Hal Newhouser/Jsy/50	8.00
54	Harmon Killebrew/Jsy/25	15.00
55	Harmon Killebrew/Jsy/50	12.00
56	Harold Baines/Jsy/50	8.00
57	Hoyt Wilhelm/Jsy/100	4.00
58	Jack Morris/Jsy/50	4.00
59	Jim Thorpe/Jsy/25	300.00
60	Jose Cruz/Jsy/100	4.00
61	Jim Rice/Jsy/50	8.00
62	Joe Cronin/Jsy/50	15.00
63	Joe Cronin/Pants/50	15.00
64	Joe Morgan/Jsy/50	8.00
65	Joe Torre/Jsy/50	10.00
66	John Kruk/Jsy/50	4.00
67	Johnny Bench/Jsy/50	10.00
68	Juan Marichal/Pants/50	6.00
71	Kirk Gibson/Jsy/100	4.00
72	Lee Smith/Jsy/100	4.00
73	Lenny Dykstra/Jsy/100	6.00
74	Lou Boudreau/Jsy/25	15.00
75	Luis Aparicio/Jsy/50	8.00
76	Luis Tiant/Pants/100	4.00
77	Mark Grace/Jsy/50	8.00
78	Hoyt Wilhelm/Jsy/100	6.00
79	Matt Williams/Jsy/100	6.00
80	Matt Williams/Jsy/50	6.00
82	Nolan Ryan/Jsy/50	20.00
84	Nolan Ryan/Jsy/25	25.00
85	Nolan Ryan/Jsy/25	25.00
86	Orlando Cepeda/Pants/50	8.00
87	Ozzie Smith/Pants/25	15.00
88	Paul Molitor/Jsy/25	8.00
89	Paul Molitor/Jsy/50	8.00
90	Paul Molitor/Pants/50	8.00
91	Phil Niekro/Jsy/50	8.00
92	Reggie Jackson/Pants/100	8.00
93	Reggie Jackson/Jkt/100	8.00
94	Reggie Jackson/Jsy/50	8.00
95	Reggie Jackson/Jsy/50	8.00
96	Rickey Henderson/Jkt/100	10.00
97	Rickey Henderson/Jsy/50	10.00
98	Rickey Henderson/Jsy/50	10.00
99	Rickey Henderson/Jsy/50	10.00
100	Rickey Henderson/Jsy/50	10.00
101	Rickey Henderson/Pants/50	10.00
102	Robin Ventura/Jsy/100	6.00
103	Robin Ventura/Jsy/100	6.00
104	Robin Yount/Jsy/50	12.00
105	Rod Carew/Jsy/100	8.00
106	Rod Carew/Jsy/50	8.00
107	Roger Maris/Pants/50	40.00
108	Ron Cey/Jsy/50	8.00
109	Ron Guidry/Pants/100	6.00
110	Ryne Sandberg/Jsy/50	15.00
111	Sandy Koufax/Jsy/25	180.00
112	Stan Musial/Jsy/25	25.00
113	Stan Musial/Pants/25	25.00
114	Steve Garvey/Jsy/100	6.00
115	Ted Williams/Jkt/50	50.00
116	Ted Williams/Jsy/50	50.00
117	Tom Seaver/Jsy/50	10.00
118	Tom Seaver/Pants/50	10.00
119	Tommy John/Jsy/100	4.00
120	Tommy John/Pants/100	4.00
121	Tommy Lasorda/Jsy/100	6.00
122	Tony Gwynn/Jsy/100	10.00
123	Tony Gwynn/Pants/100	10.00
124	Tony Perez/Jsy/50	8.00
125	Wade Boggs/Jsy/100	8.00
126	Warren Spahn/Jsy/25	15.00
127	Whitey Ford/Jsy/25	15.00
128	Will Clark/Jsy/50	6.00
129	Willie Mays/Pants/50	40.00
130	Willie McCovey/Pants/100	10.00
131	Roger Clemens/Jsy/50	15.00
132	Roger Clemens/Jsy/50	15.00
133	Roger Clemens/Jsy/50	15.00
134	Randy Johnson/Jsy/50	15.00
135	Randy Johnson/Jsy/50	15.00
136	Cal Ripken Jr./Jsy/100	30.00
137	Don Mattingly/Jsy/100	15.00
138	George Brett/Jsy/25	20.00

139 Harmon Killebrew/Jsy/25 15.00
140 Mike Schmidt/Jsy/50 20.00
141 Nolan Ryan/Jkt/25 25.00
143 Tony Gwynn/Jsy/100 10.00
144 Wade Boggs/Jsy/50 10.00
145 Willie Mays/Jsy/25 50.00
146 Hideo Nomo/Jsy/100 10.00
147 Dale Murphy/Jsy/100 10.00
148 Dale Murphy/Jsy/100 10.00
149 Bo Jackson/Jsy/50 12.00
150 Darryl Strawberry/Jsy/50 6.00
151 Deion Sanders/Jsy/50 8.00
152 Deion Sanders/Pants/50 8.00
153 Dennis Eckersley/Jsy/50 8.00
154 Dwight Gooden/Jsy/100 6.00
155 Edgar Martinez/Jsy/100 4.00
156 Lou Brock/Jsy/50 8.00
157 Steve Carlton/Pants/50 6.00
158 Albert Pujols/Jsy/50 20.00
159 Tom Glavine/Jsy/100 8.00
160 Hideki Matsui/Pants/50 20.00
161 Babe Ruth/Pants, Jim Thorpe/Jsy/25 500.00
162 Ted Williams/Jkt, Bob Gibson/Jsy/50 50.00
164 Whitey Ford/Jsy, Sandy Koufax/Jsy/25 150.00
165 Roger Maris/Pants, Don Mattingly/Jsy/50 50.00
166 Nolan Ryan/Jsy, Tom Seaver/Jsy/25 25.00
167 Cal Ripken Jr./Jsy, George Brett/Jsy/100 40.00
168 Ryne Sandberg/Jsy, Mike Schmidt/Jsy/50 30.00
169 Tony Gwynn/Jsy, Wade Boggs/Jsy/50 15.00
170 Carlton Fisk/Jsy, Johnny Bench/Pants/50 15.00
172 Reggie Jackson/Pants, Darryl Strawberry/Jsy/50 10.00
173 Robin Yount/Jsy, Paul Molitor/Jsy/50 20.00
174 Warren Spahn/Pants, Juan Marichal/Jsy/50 15.00
175 Bo Jackson/Jsy, Deion Sanders/Pants/100 15.00
176 Tony Gwynn/Jsy, Rickey Henderson/Jsy/100 15.00
177 Hideki Matsui/Jsy, Jim Edmonds/Jsy/100 20.00
178 Rickey Henderson/Pants, Lou Brock/Jsy/100 15.00
179 Roger Clemens/Jsy, Albert Pujols/Jsy/100 25.00
180 Hideo Nomo/Jsy, Kazuhisa Ishii/Jsy/100 12.00

Fabric of the Game Autograph
No Pricing
Production One Set

Fabric of the Game Jersey Number
NM/M
Production 1-72
8 Billy Williams/Jsy/26 8.00
18 Carlton Fisk/Jkt/72 8.00
19 Jim "Catfish" Hunter/Pants/29 10.00
20 Darryl Strawberry/Jsy/39 6.00
21 Darryl Strawberry/Jsy/44 6.00
24 Dave Winfield/Pants/31 10.00
25 David Cone/Jsy/44 8.00
26 David Justice/Jsy/23 10.00
27 Deion Sanders/Jsy/21 12.00
28 Deion Sanders/Jsy/21 12.00
29 Dennis Eckersley/Jsy/43 8.00
30 Dennis Eckersley/Pants/43 8.00
36 Dwight Evans/Jsy/24 10.00
38 Eddie Murray/Jsy/33 15.00
39 Eddie Murray/Pants/33 15.00
42 Fergie Jenkins/Jsy/31 8.00
44 Fred McGriff/Jsy/29 8.00
48 Gaylord Perry/Jsy/36 8.00
49 Gaylord Perry/Jsy/36 8.00
52 Hank Aaron/Jsy/44 40.00
53 Hank Aaron/Jsy/44 40.00
57 Hoyt Wilhelm/Jsy/31 8.00
58 Jack Morris/Jsy/47 4.00

60 Jose Cruz/Jsy/25 6.00
66 John Kruk/Jsy/29 12.00
68 Juan Marichal/Pants/27
71 Kirk Gibson/Jsy/23 10.00
72 Lee Smith/Jsy/47 10.00
76 Luis Tiant/Pants/23 10.00
78 Hoyt Wilhelm/Jsy/31 10.00
82 Nolan Ryan/Jsy/34 25.00
83 Nolan Ryan/Jsy/34 25.00
84 Nolan Ryan/Jsy/30 25.00
85 Nolan Ryan/Jsy/30 25.00
86 Orlando Cepeda/Pants/30 10.00
91 Phil Niekro/Jsy/35 8.00
92 Reggie Jackson/Pants/44 10.00
93 Reggie Jackson/Jkt/44 10.00
94 Reggie Jackson/Jsy/44 10.00
95 Reggie Jackson/Jsy/44 10.00
96 Rickey Henderson/Jkt/24 12.00
97 Rickey Henderson/Jsy/25 12.00
98 Rickey Henderson/Jsy/35 12.00
99 Rickey Henderson/Jsy/35 12.00
100 Rickey Henderson/Pants/24 12.00
101 Rickey Henderson/Pants/24 12.00
105 Rod Carew/Jsy/29 15.00
106 Rod Carew/Jsy/29 15.00
109 Ron Guidry/Pants/49 8.00
110 Ryne Sandberg/Jsy/23 35.00
111 Sandy Koufax/Jsy/32 180.00
117 Tom Seaver/Jsy/41 10.00
118 Tom Seaver/Pants/41 10.00
119 Tommy John/Jsy/25 8.00
120 Tommy John/Pants/44 8.00
124 Tony Perez/Jsy/24 8.00
125 Wade Boggs/Jsy/26 10.00
129 Willie Mays/Pants/24 50.00
130 Willie McCovey/Jsy/44 10.00
131 Roger Clemens/Jsy/22 20.00
132 Roger Clemens/Jsy/22 20.00
133 Roger Clemens/Jsy/21 20.00
134 Randy Johnson/Jsy/51 10.00
135 Randy Johnson/Jsy/51 10.00
137 Don Mattingly/Jsy/23 20.00
144 Wade Boggs/Jsy/26 10.00
145 Willie Mays/Jsy/24 50.00
150 Darryl Strawberry/Jsy/23 6.00
153 Dennis Eckersley/Jsy/43 8.00
159 Tom Glavine/Jsy/47 10.00
160 Hideki Matsui/Pants/55 20.00
166 Nolan Ryan/Jsy, Tom Seaver/Jsy/25 25.00
167 Cal Ripken Jr./Jsy, George Brett/Jsy/25 50.00
168 Ryne Sandberg/Jsy, Mike Schmidt/Jsy/25 35.00
169 Tony Gwynn/Jsy, Wade Boggs/Jsy/50 15.00
170 Carlton Fisk/Jsy, Johnny Bench/Pants/25
172 Reggie Jackson/Pants, Darryl Strawberry/Jsy/50 10.00
173 Robin Yount/Jsy, Paul Molitor/Jsy/25 20.00
174 Warren Spahn/Pants, Juan Marichal/Jsy/50 20.00
175 Bo Jackson/Jsy, Deion Sanders/Pants/25 15.00
176 Tony Gwynn/Jsy, Rickey Henderson/Jsy/25 20.00
177 Hideki Matsui/Jsy, Jim Edmonds/Jsy/50 20.00
178 Rickey Henderson/Pants, Lou Brock/Jsy/50 20.00
179 Roger Clemens/Jsy, Albert Pujols/Jsy/50 25.00
180 Hideo Nomo/Jsy, Kazuhisa Ishii/Jsy/50 15.00

Fabric of the Game Position
NM/M
Production 3-100
1 Al Oliver/Jsy/50 6.00
2 Alan Trammell/Jsy/25 8.00
3 Andres Galarraga/Jsy/25 8.00

4 Andres Galarraga/Jsy/25 8.00
7 Billy Martin/Pants/50 15.00
8 Billy Williams/Jsy/25 8.00
9 Bo Jackson/Jsy/25 12.00
10 Bo Jackson/Jsy/25 12.00
13 Bobby Doerr/Pants/25 12.00
14 Burleigh Grimes/Pants/25 50.00
15 Cal Ripken Jr./Jsy/25 35.00
16 Cal Ripken Jr./Jsy/25 35.00
17 Carl Yastrzemski/Jsy/25 15.00
18 Carlton Fisk/Jkt/25 12.00
19 Jim "Catfish" Hunter/Pants/100 8.00
20 Darryl Strawberry/Jsy/25 8.00
21 Darryl Strawberry/Jsy/25 8.00
22 Dave Concepcion/Jsy/25
23 Dave Righetti/Jsy/50 8.00
24 Dave Winfield/Jsy/25 10.00
25 David Cone/Jsy/50 4.00
26 David Justice/Jsy/100 4.00
27 Deion Sanders/Jsy/50 8.00
28 Deion Sanders/Jsy/50 8.00
29 Dennis Eckersley/Jsy/50 8.00
30 Dennis Eckersley/Pants/50 8.00
32 Don Sutton/Jsy/25 8.00
37 Dwight Gooden/Jsy/100 6.00
40 Edgar Martinez/Jsy/25 6.00
42 Fergie Jenkins/Jsy/25 10.00
43 Frankie Frisch/Jkt/100 15.00
44 Fred Lynn/Jsy/50 4.00
45 Fred McGriff/Jsy/50 6.00
46 Gary Carter/Jsy/50 6.00
47 Gary Carter/Jsy/25 6.00
48 Gaylord Perry/Jsy/25 6.00
49 Gaylord Perry/Jsy/25 8.00
54 Harmon Killebrew/Jsy/25 15.00
56 Harold Baines/Jsy/100 8.00
57 Hoyt Wilhelm/Jsy/100 8.00
60 Jose Cruz/Jsy/100 4.00
61 Jim Rice/Jsy/50 8.00
63 Joe Cronin/Pants/50 15.00
64 Joe Morgan/Jsy/25 10.00
66 John Kruk/Jsy/50 8.00
67 Johnny Bench/Jsy/25 12.00
68 Juan Marichal/Pants/25 10.00
71 Kirk Gibson/Jsy/50 4.00
72 Lee Smith/Jsy/50 4.00
73 Lenny Dykstra/Jsy/50 6.00
75 Luis Aparicio/Jsy/25 8.00
76 Luis Tiant/Pants/25 6.00
77 Mark Grace/Jsy/25 10.00
78 Hoyt Wilhelm/Jsy/50 8.00
79 Matt Williams/Jsy/25 8.00
82 Nolan Ryan/Jsy/25 25.00
85 Nolan Ryan/Jsy/25 25.00
86 Orlando Cepeda/Pants/50 8.00
87 Ozzie Smith/Pants/25 15.00
88 Paul Molitor/Jsy/50 8.00
89 Paul Molitor/Jsy/50 8.00
90 Paul Molitor/Jsy/50 10.00
91 Phil Niekro/Jsy/25 8.00
92 Reggie Jackson/Pants/50 10.00
93 Reggie Jackson/Jkt/25 10.00
94 Reggie Jackson/Jsy/50 8.00
95 Reggie Jackson/Jsy/25 10.00
96 Rickey Henderson/Jkt/100 10.00
97 Rickey Henderson/Jsy/50 10.00
99 Rickey Henderson/Jsy/25 12.00
100 Rickey Henderson/Pants/25 12.00
101 Rickey Henderson/Pants/50 10.00
102 Robin Ventura/Jsy/50 6.00
103 Robin Ventura/Jsy/50 6.00
104 Robin Yount/Jsy/25 8.00
105 Rod Carew/Jsy/25 10.00
106 Rod Carew/Jsy/25 10.00
107 Roger Maris/Pants/25 50.00
108 Ron Cey/Jsy/50 8.00
109 Ron Guidry/Pants/50 8.00
110 Ryne Sandberg/Jsy/50 15.00
111 Sandy Koufax/Jsy/25 180.00
112 Stan Musial/Jsy/25 25.00
113 Stan Musial/Pants/25 25.00
114 Steve Garvey/Jsy/25 8.00

115 Ted Williams/Jkt/50 50.00
118 Tom Seaver/Jsy/50 10.00
119 Tommy John/Jsy/25 4.00
120 Tommy John/Pants/50 4.00
121 Tommy Lasorda/Jsy/25 6.00
122 Tony Gwynn/Jsy/50 10.00
123 Tony Gwynn/Pants/25 10.00
124 Tony Perez/Jsy/50 8.00
125 Wade Boggs/Jsy/50 10.00
129 Willie Mays/Pants/25 50.00
130 Willie McCovey/Pants/50 10.00
131 Roger Clemens/Jsy/25 20.00
132 Roger Clemens/Jsy/50 15.00
133 Roger Clemens/Jsy/50 15.00
134 Randy Johnson/Jsy/50 8.00
135 Randy Johnson/Jsy/50 8.00
136 Cal Ripken Jr./Jsy/50 30.00
137 Don Mattingly/Jsy/50 15.00
138 George Brett/Jsy/25 20.00
139 Harmon Killebrew/Jsy/25 15.00
140 Mike Schmidt/Jsy/50 20.00
143 Tony Gwynn/Jsy/50 10.00
144 Wade Boggs/Jsy/50 10.00
145 Willie Mays/Jsy/25 50.00
146 Hideo Nomo/Jsy/50 10.00
147 Dale Murphy/Jsy/50 10.00
148 Dale Murphy/Jsy/50 10.00
149 Bo Jackson/Jsy/50 12.00
150 Darryl Strawberry/Jsy/50 6.00
151 Deion Sanders/Jsy/50 8.00
152 Deion Sanders/Jsy/50 8.00
153 Dennis Eckersley/Jsy/50 8.00
154 Dwight Gooden/Jsy/50 6.00
155 Edgar Martinez/Jsy/50 4.00
156 Lou Brock/Jsy/50 8.00
157 Steve Carlton/Pants/50 6.00
158 Albert Pujols/Jsy/50 20.00
159 Tom Glavine/Jsy/50 8.00
160 Hideki Matsui/Jsy/50 20.00
161 Babe Ruth/Pants, Jim Thorpe/Jsy/50 500.00
162 Ted Williams/Jkt, Stan Musial/Jsy/50 50.00
164 Whitey Ford/Jsy, Sandy Koufax/Jsy/25 150.00
165 Roger Maris/Pants, Don Mattingly/Jsy/25 50.00
166 Nolan Ryan/Jsy, Tom Seaver/Jsy/100 25.00
167 Cal Ripken Jr./Jsy, George Brett/Jsy/100 40.00
168 Ryne Sandberg/Jsy, Mike Schmidt/Jsy/50 30.00
169 Tony Gwynn/Jsy, Wade Boggs/Jsy/50 15.00
170 Carlton Fisk/Jsy, Johnny Bench/Pants/50 15.00
172 Reggie Jackson/Pants, Darryl Strawberry/Jsy/50 10.00
173 Robin Yount/Jsy, Paul Molitor/Jsy/50 20.00
174 Warren Spahn/Pants, Juan Marichal/Jsy/50 20.00
175 Bo Jackson/Jsy, Deion Sanders/Pants/50 15.00
176 Tony Gwynn/Jsy, Rickey Henderson/Jsy/50 20.00
177 Hideki Matsui/Jsy, Jim Edmonds/Jsy/50 20.00
178 Rickey Henderson/Pants, Lou Brock/Jsy/50 20.00
179 Roger Clemens/Jsy, Albert Pujols/Jsy/50 25.00
180 Hideo Nomo/Jsy, Kazuhisa Ishii/Jsy/50 15.00

Fabric of the Game Reward
NM/M
Production 3-50
1 Al Oliver/Jsy/50 6.00
2 Alan Trammell/Jsy/50 8.00
3 Andres Galarraga/Jsy/50 6.00
4 Andres Galarraga/Jsy/50 6.00
7 Billy Martin/Pants/50 15.00
9 Bo Jackson/Jsy/50 12.00
10 Bo Jackson/Jsy/50 12.00
13 Bobby Doerr/Pants/25 12.00
17 Carl Yastrzemski/Pants/25 15.00

19 Jim "Catfish" Hunter/Pants/50 8.00
21 Darryl Strawberry/Jsy/50 8.00
23 Dave Righetti/Jsy/25 8.00
44 Fred Lynn/Jsy/50 4.00
46 Gary Carter/Jsy/25 6.00
47 Gary Carter/Jsy/25 6.00
48 Gaylord Perry/Jsy/50 6.00
49 Gaylord Perry/Jsy/25 8.00
51 Hal Newhouser/Jsy/25 8.00
58 Jack Morris/Jsy/25 8.00
61 Jim Rice/Jsy/50 8.00
62 Joe Cronin/Jsy/25 20.00
63 Joe Cronin/Pants/25 20.00
64 Joe Morgan/Jsy/25 10.00
66 John Kruk/Jsy/50 10.00
68 Juan Marichal/Pants/25 10.00
71 Kirk Gibson/Jsy/25 8.00
72 Lee Smith/Jsy/50 4.00
75 Luis Aparicio/Jsy/25 8.00
76 Luis Tiant/Pants/25 6.00
78 Hoyt Wilhelm/Jsy/25 10.00
79 Matt Williams/Jsy/25 8.00
82 Nolan Ryan/Jsy/25 25.00
85 Nolan Ryan/Jsy/25 25.00
86 Orlando Cepeda/Pants/25 10.00
87 Ozzie Smith/Pants/25 15.00
88 Paul Molitor/Jsy/25 8.00
89 Paul Molitor/Jsy/25 8.00
90 Paul Molitor/Pants/25 10.00
91 Phil Niekro/Jsy/25 8.00
92 Reggie Jackson/Pants/25 10.00
93 Reggie Jackson/Jkt/25 10.00
95 Reggie Jackson/Jsy/25 10.00
96 Rickey Henderson/Jkt/50 10.00
97 Rickey Henderson/Jsy/50 10.00
99 Rickey Henderson/Jsy/25 12.00
102 Robin Ventura/Jsy/50 6.00
103 Robin Ventura/Jsy/50 6.00
104 Robin Yount/Jsy/50 12.00
105 Rod Carew/Jsy/25 10.00
106 Rod Carew/Jsy/25 10.00
108 Ron Cey/Jsy/50 8.00
109 Ron Guidry/Pants/50 8.00
110 Ryne Sandberg/Jsy/50 15.00
111 Sandy Koufax/Jsy/25 180.00
113 Stan Musial/Pants/25 25.00
114 Steve Garvey/Jsy/25 8.00
115 Ted Williams/Jkt/25 50.00
118 Tom Seaver/Pants/25 10.00
119 Tommy John/Jsy/25 4.00
120 Tommy John/Pants/25 4.00
121 Tommy Lasorda/Jsy/25 6.00
122 Tony Gwynn/Jsy/100 10.00
123 Tony Gwynn/Pants/50 10.00
124 Tony Perez/Jsy/50 8.00
125 Wade Boggs/Jsy/50 10.00
126 Warren Spahn/Pants/50 12.00
128 Will Clark/Jsy/50 8.00
129 Willie Mays/Pants/25 50.00
130 Willie McCovey/Pants/50 10.00
131 Roger Clemens/Jsy/50 20.00
132 Roger Clemens/Jsy/50 15.00
133 Roger Clemens/Jsy/50 15.00
134 Randy Johnson/Jsy/50 10.00
135 Randy Johnson/Jsy/50 10.00
136 Cal Ripken Jr./Jsy/50 30.00
137 Don Mattingly/Jsy/50 15.00
138 George Brett/Jsy/25 20.00
139 Harmon Killebrew/Jsy/25 15.00
140 Mike Schmidt/Jsy/50 20.00
143 Tony Gwynn/Jsy/50 10.00
144 Wade Boggs/Jsy/50 10.00
145 Willie Mays/Jsy/50 50.00
146 Hideo Nomo/Jsy/50 10.00
147 Dale Murphy/Jsy/50 10.00
148 Dale Murphy/Jsy/50 10.00
150 Darryl Strawberry/Jsy/50 6.00
151 Deion Sanders/Jsy/50 8.00
152 Deion Sanders/Pants/50 8.00
153 Dennis Eckersley/Jsy/50 8.00
154 Dwight Gooden/Jsy/50 6.00
155 Edgar Martinez/Jsy/50 4.00
156 Lou Brock/Jsy/50 8.00
157 Steve Carlton/Pants/50 6.00
158 Albert Pujols/Jsy/50 20.00
159 Tom Glavine/Jsy/50 8.00
160 Hideki Matsui/Pants/50 20.00

161 Babe Ruth/Pants, Jim Thorpe/Jsy/25 500.00
162 Ted Williams/Jkt, Stan Musial/Jsy/50 50.00
163 Willie Mays/Jsy, Bob Gibson/Jsy/50 50.00
164 Whitey Ford/Jsy, Sandy Koufax/Jsy/25 150.00
165 Roger Maris/Pants, Don Mattingly/Jsy/25 50.00
166 Nolan Ryan/Jsy, Tom Seaver/Jsy/25 25.00
167 Cal Ripken Jr./Jsy, George Brett/Jsy/50 40.00
168 Ryne Sandberg/Jsy, Mike Schmidt/Jsy/50 30.00
169 Tony Gwynn/Jsy, Wade Boggs/Jsy/50 15.00
170 Carlton Fisk/Jsy, Johnny Bench/Pants/25 20.00
172 Reggie Jackson/Pants, Darryl Strawberry/Jsy/50 10.00
173 Robin Yount/Jsy, Paul Molitor/Jsy/25 20.00
174 Warren Spahn/Pants, Juan Marichal/Jsy/25 20.00
175 Bo Jackson/Jsy, Deion Sanders/Pants/25 15.00
176 Tony Gwynn/Jsy, Rickey Henderson/Jsy/25 20.00
177 Hideki Matsui/Jsy, Jim Edmonds/Jsy/50 20.00
178 Rickey Henderson/Pants, Lou Brock/Jsy/50 20.00
179 Roger Clemens/Jsy, Albert Pujols/Jsy/50 25.00
180 Hideo Nomo/Jsy, Kazuhisa Ishii/Jsy/50 15.00

Fabric of the Game Stats
NM/M
Production 3-75
1 Al Oliver/Jsy/75 6.00
3 Andres Galarraga/Jsy/75 6.00
4 Andres Galarraga/Jsy/75 6.00
7 Billy Martin/Pants/75 15.00
8 Billy Williams/Jsy/75 8.00
9 Bo Jackson/Jsy/75 10.00
10 Bo Jackson/Jsy/25 10.00
13 Bobby Doerr/Jsy/25 12.00
14 Burleigh Grimes/Pants/25 50.00
15 Cal Ripken Jr./Jsy/75 30.00
16 Cal Ripken Jr./Jsy/75 30.00
17 Carl Yastrzemski/Pants/25 15.00
18 Carlton Fisk/Jkt/75 10.00
19 Jim "Catfish" Hunter/Pants/75 8.00
21 Darryl Strawberry/Jsy/75 6.00
22 Dave Concepcion/Jsy/75 4.00
23 Dave Righetti/Jsy/75 4.00
24 Dave Winfield/Pants/75 4.00
25 David Cone/Jsy/75 4.00
26 David Justice/Jsy/75 4.00
27 Deion Sanders/Jsy/75 8.00
28 Deion Sanders/Jsy/75 8.00
29 Dennis Eckersley/Jsy/75 8.00
30 Dennis Eckersley/Pants/75 8.00
39 Eddie Murray/Pants/75 12.00
40 Edgar Martinez/Jsy/75 4.00
43 Frankie Frisch/Jkt/75 15.00
44 Fred Lynn/Jsy/50 4.00
45 Fred McGriff/Jsy/75 6.00
46 Gary Carter/Jsy/75 6.00
47 Gary Carter/Jsy/50 8.00
48 Gaylord Perry/Jsy/50 6.00
49 Gaylord Perry/Jsy/50 8.00
51 Hal Newhouser/Jsy/25 10.00
54 Harmon Killebrew/Jsy/25 15.00
55 Harmon Killebrew/Jsy/50 12.00
56 Harold Baines/Jsy/50 8.00
57 Hoyt Wilhelm/Jsy/50 6.00
62 Joe Cronin/Jsy/25 20.00
63 Joe Cronin/Pants/25 20.00
64 Joe Morgan/Jsy/25 10.00
66 John Kruk/Jsy/25 10.00
71 Kirk Gibson/Jsy/25 8.00
72 Lee Smith/Jsy/25 8.00
73 Lenny Dykstra/Jsy/75 6.00
75 Luis Aparicio/Jsy/25 8.00
76 Luis Tiant/Pants/25 6.00
78 Hoyt Wilhelm/Jsy/25 10.00
79 Matt Williams/Jsy/25 8.00
82 Nolan Ryan/Jsy/25 25.00
85 Nolan Ryan/Jsy/25 25.00

86 Orlando Cepeda/Pants/25 10.00
87 Ozzie Smith/Pants/25 15.00
88 Paul Molitor/Jsy/50 8.00
89 Paul Molitor/Jsy/50 8.00
90 Paul Molitor/Pants/25 10.00
91 Phil Niekro/Jsy/25 8.00
92 Reggie Jackson/Pants/50 10.00
93 Reggie Jackson/Jkt/25 10.00
94 Reggie Jackson/Jsy/75 10.00
95 Reggie Jackson/Jsy/50 10.00
96 Rickey Henderson/Jkt/75 10.00
97 Rickey Henderson/Jsy/75 10.00
98 Rickey Henderson/Jsy/50 10.00
101 Rickey Henderson/Pants/75 10.00
102 Robin Ventura/Jsy/50 6.00
103 Robin Ventura/Jsy/50 6.00
104 Robin Yount/Jsy/50 12.00
105 Rod Carew/Jsy/50 10.00
106 Rod Carew/Jsy/75 8.00
107 Roger Maris/Pants/50 40.00
108 Ron Cey/Jsy/50 8.00
109 Ron Guidry/Pants/50 8.00
111 Sandy Koufax/Jsy/25 180.00
113 Stan Musial/Pants/25 25.00
114 Steve Garvey/Jsy/50 8.00
115 Ted Williams/Jkt/25 50.00
117 Tom Seaver/Jsy/75 10.00
118 Tom Seaver/Pants/50 10.00
119 Tommy John/Jsy/25 6.00
120 Tommy John/Pants/25 6.00
121 Tommy Lasorda/Jsy/25 6.00
124 Tony Perez/Jsy/75 8.00
125 Wade Boggs/Jsy/75 10.00
126 Warren Spahn/Pants/25 12.00
128 Will Clark/Jsy/50 8.00
129 Willie Mays/Pants/50 50.00
130 Willie McCovey/Pants/75 8.00
131 Roger Clemens/Jsy/25 20.00
140 Mike Schmidt/Jsy/25 20.00
144 Wade Boggs/Jsy/50 10.00
145 Willie Mays/Jsy/25 25.00
146 Hideo Nomo/Jsy/75 10.00
147 Dale Murphy/Jsy/25 10.00
148 Dale Murphy/Jsy/50 10.00
153 Dennis Eckersley/Jsy/75 8.00
154 Dwight Gooden/Jsy/75 6.00
155 Edgar Martinez/Jsy/75 4.00
156 Lou Brock/Jsy/75 8.00
157 Steve Carlton/Pants/75 6.00
159 Tom Glavine/Jsy/75 8.00
160 Hideki Matsui/Pants/75 20.00
161 Babe Ruth/Pants, Jim Thorpe/Jsy/25 500.00
162 Ted Williams/Jkt, Stan Musial/Jsy/25 50.00
163 Willie Mays/Jsy, Bob Gibson/Jsy/25 50.00
164 Whitey Ford/Jsy, Sandy Koufax/Jsy/25 150.00
165 Roger Maris/Pants, Don Mattingly/Jsy/25 50.00
166 Nolan Ryan/Jsy, Tom Seaver/Jsy/25 25.00
167 Cal Ripken Jr./Jsy, George Brett/Jsy/50 40.00
168 Ryne Sandberg/Jsy, Mike Schmidt/Jsy/25 30.00
169 Tony Gwynn/Jsy, Wade Boggs/Jsy/50 15.00
170 Carlton Fisk/Jsy, Johnny Bench/Pants/25 20.00
172 Reggie Jackson/Pants, Darryl Strawberry/Jsy/50 10.00
173 Robin Yount/Jsy, Paul Molitor/Jsy/25 20.00
174 Warren Spahn/Pants, Juan Marichal/Jsy/25 20.00
175 Bo Jackson/Jsy, Deion Sanders/Pants/50 15.00
176 Tony Gwynn/Jsy, Rickey Henderson/Jsy/50 20.00
177 Hideki Matsui/Jsy, Jim Edmonds/Jsy/50 20.00
178 Rickey Henderson/Pants, Lou Brock/Jsy/50 20.00
179 Roger Clemens/Jsy, Albert Pujols/Jsy/50 25.00

180 Hideo Nomo/Jsy, Kazuhisa Ishii/Jsy/50 15.00

Gold Team
NM/M
Complete Set (25):
Common Player: 1.00
Inserted 1:7
Mirror: 2-3X
1 Albert Pujols 4.00
2 Alex Rodriguez 3.00
3 Carlos Beltran 1.00
4 Chipper Jones 1.50
5 Curt Schilling 1.50
6 Derek Jeter 3.00
7 Greg Maddux 2.50
8 Hank Blalock 1.00
9 Ichiro Suzuki 3.00
10 Ivan Rodriguez 1.00
11 Jim Thome 1.00
12 Ken Griffey Jr. 3.00
13 Lyle Overbay 1.00
14 Manny Ramirez 1.50
15 Mark Mulder 1.00
16 Mark Prior 1.50
17 Michael Young 1.00
18 Miguel Cabrera 1.50
19 Mike Piazza 2.00
20 Pedro Martinez 1.50
21 Randy Johnson 1.50
22 Roger Clemens 4.00
23 Sammy Sosa 2.00
24 Tim Hudson 1.00
25 Todd Helton 1.50

Gold Team Autograph
No Pricing
Production 5-10

Gold Team Jersey Number
NM/M
Production 100-250
1 Albert Pujols/100 20.00
3 Carlos Beltran/200 5.00
4 Chipper Jones/100 8.00
5 Curt Schilling/250 8.00
7 Greg Maddux/100 10.00
8 Hank Blalock/250 4.00
10 Ivan Rodriguez/120 6.00
11 Jim Thome/250 6.00
13 Lyle Overbay/250 4.00
14 Manny Ramirez/250 8.00
15 Mark Mulder/250 4.00
16 Mark Prior/100 4.00
17 Michael Young/250 4.00
18 Miguel Cabrera/100 8.00
19 Mike Piazza/250 10.00
20 Pedro Martinez/100 4.00
21 Randy Johnson/250 8.00
22 Roger Clemens/250 10.00
23 Sammy Sosa/250 4.00
24 Tim Hudson/250 4.00
25 Todd Helton/100 6.00

Mirror Red
Mirror Red (1-200): 2-4X
Auto. (201-250): .4X
No Auto. (201-250): 1X
Production 100 Sets

Mirror White
Mirror White (1-200): 2-4X
Auto. (201-250): .4X
No Auto. (201-250): 1X
Production 100 Sets

Mirror Blue
Mirror Blue (1-200): 3-6X
Auto. (201-250): .5X
No Auto. (201-250): 1-2X
Production 50 Sets

Mirror Gold
Mirror Gold (1-200): 5-10X
Mirror Gol (201-250): No Pricing
Production 25 Sets

Mirror Emerald
No Pricing
Production 5 Sets

Mirror Black
No Pricing
Production One Set

Mirror Autograph Red
NM/M
Production 1-250
16 Tim Salmon/25 30.00
18 Bobby Crosby/25 15.00
25 Casey Kotchman/50 12.00
33 Orlando Hudson/250 8.00
53 Jack Wilson/50 12.00
62 Eric Byrnes/50 10.00
66 Jeremy Bonderman/50 15.00
67 Jermaine Dye/50 15.00
68 Kazuhito Tadano/100 12.00
79 Edwin Jackson/250 8.00

80 Raul Ibanez/50 12.00
86 Ken Harvey/250 8.00
89 Wade Miller/250 10.00
91 Jeremy Affeldt/250 8.00
92 Francisco Cordero/25 15.00
95 Laynce Nix/100 8.00
106 Marlon Byrd/25 8.00
155 Bubba Nelson/250 6.00
156 Kevin Youkilis/50 20.00
160 Lew Ford/50 12.00
161 Ervin Santana/250 10.00
162 Jody Gerut/50 15.00
164 Brian Roberts/25 30.00
165 Joe Nathan/50 15.00
167 Ryan Wagner/50 10.00
168 David Dellucci/50 15.00
169 Jae Weong Seo/25 15.00
173 Jose Castillo/250 10.00
202 Agustin Montero/99 10.00
211 Norihiro Nakamura/99 50.00
212 Erick Threets/49 10.00
218 Jeff Niemann/49 25.00
221 Justin Verlander/49 40.00
223 Luke Scott/99 30.00
229 Nate McLouth/25 15.00
230 Paulino Reynoso/49 15.00
231 Philip Humber/25 25.00
234 Raul Tablado/99 12.00
239 Sean Tracey/49 10.00
243 Wladimir Balentien/99 15.00

Mirror Autograph White
NM/M
Production 1-50
18 Bobby Crosby/25 25.00
19 Brad Penny/25 15.00
25 Casey Kotchman/25 15.00
33 Orlando Hudson/25 8.00
53 Jack Wilson/25 15.00
62 Eric Byrnes/25 12.00
67 Jermaine Dye/25 15.00
68 Kazuhito Tadano/50 15.00
79 Edwin Jackson/25 10.00
80 Raul Ibanez/25 15.00
81 Rich Harden/25 15.00
86 Ken Harvey/25 8.00
89 Wade Miller/50 8.00
91 Jeremy Affeldt/25 10.00
95 Laynce Nix/50 10.00
106 Marlon Byrd/50 8.00
155 Bubba Nelson/50 8.00
156 Kevin Youkilis/25 25.00
160 Lew Ford/50 15.00
161 Ervin Santana/50 12.00
162 Jody Gerut/25 15.00
167 Ryan Wagner/25 10.00
168 David Dellucci/25 20.00
173 Jose Castillo/50 10.00
202 Agustin Montero/49 12.00
211 Norihiro Nakamura/49 60.00
212 Erick Threets/49 10.00
218 Jeff Niemann/49 25.00
221 Justin Verlander/49 40.00
223 Luke Scott/49 40.00
229 Nate McLouth/49 20.00
230 Paulino Reynoso/49 15.00
231 Philip Humber/25 25.00
234 Raul Tablado/49 15.00
239 Sean Tracey/49 10.00
243 Wladimir Balentien/49 20.00

Mirror Autograph Blue
NM/M
Production 1-100
Black: No Pricing
Production One Set
Emerald: No Pricing
Production 1-5
18 Bobby Crosby/25 25.00
25 Casey Kotchman/25 15.00
33 Orlando Hudson/100 10.00
53 Jack Wilson/25 15.00
62 Eric Byrnes/25 12.00
66 Jeremy Bonderman/25 20.00
67 Jermaine Dye/25 15.00
68 Kazuhito Tadano/25 15.00
79 Edwin Jackson/100 8.00
80 Raul Ibanez/25 15.00
86 Ken Harvey/100 8.00
89 Wade Miller/100 8.00
95 Laynce Nix/25 12.00
106 Marlon Byrd/100 8.00
155 Bubba Nelson/100 8.00
156 Kevin Youkilis/25 25.00
160 Lew Ford/25 15.00
161 Ervin Santana/100 10.00
167 Ryan Wagner/25 10.00
168 David Dellucci/25 20.00
169 Jae Weong Seo/25 15.00
173 Jose Castillo/100 10.00
223 Luke Scott/49 30.00
229 Nate McLouth/49 10.00
234 Raul Tablado/49 10.00
243 Wladimir Balentien/49 25.00

Mirror Autograph Gold
NM/M
Production 1-25
2 Adam Dunn/25 35.00
11 Aubrey Huff/25 15.00
12 Austin Kearns/25 10.00
13 B.J. Upton/25 15.00
16 Brandon Webb/25 15.00
16 Tim Salmon/25 30.00
18 Bobby Crosby/25 25.00
19 Brad Penny/25 15.00
23 C.C. Sabathia/25 15.00
23 Keith Foulke/25 25.00
25 Casey Kotchman/25 15.00
27 Chone Figgins/25 12.00
29 Craig Wilson/25 15.00
31 Danny Kolb/25 10.00
33 Orlando Hudson/25 10.00
34 David Wright/25 70.00
36 Jake Peavy/25 35.00
37 Derek Lee/25 40.00
39 Edgar Renteria/25 10.00
40 Angel Berroa/25 10.00
41 Eric Chavez/25 20.00
42 Akinori Otsuka/25 25.00
43 Francisco Rodriguez/25 25.00
44 Garret Anderson/25 20.00
53 Jack Wilson/25 15.00
54 Jamie Moyer/25 15.00
55 Jason Bay/25 25.00
57 Trot Nixon/25 20.00
60 Roy Oswalt/25 25.00
62 Eric Byrnes/25 12.00
63 Jeff Bagwell/25 40.00
65 Jeff Suppan/25 15.00
66 Jeremy Bonderman/25 20.00
67 Jermaine Dye/25 15.00
68 Kazuhito Tadano/25 15.00
75 Brett Myers/25 20.00
76 Jose Guillen/25 15.00
77 Jose Vidro/25 15.00
79 Edwin Jackson/25 15.00
80 Raul Ibanez/25 15.00
81 Rich Harden/25 20.00
86 Ken Harvey/25 10.00
89 Wade Miller/25 15.00
91 Jeremy Affeldt/25 15.00
92 Francisco Cordero/25 15.00
95 Laynce Nix/25 12.00
97 Lyle Overbay/25 15.00
98 Carlos Zambrano/25 30.00
101 Mark Buehrle/25 25.00
102 Mark Loretta/25 15.00
106 Marlon Byrd/25 10.00
107 Rafael Furcal/25 25.00
108 Michael Young/25 15.00
109 Miguel Cabrera/25 40.00
128 Magglio Ordonez/25 15.00
134 Sean Burroughs/25 15.00
135 Sean Casey/25 15.00
139 Steve Finley/25 15.00
141 Torii Hunter/25 20.00
144 Travis Hafner/25 20.00
147 Vernon Wells/25 15.00
152 Danny Graves/25 12.00
155 Bubba Nelson/25 10.00
156 Kevin Youkilis/25 25.00
157 Jacque Jones/25 15.00
158 Mike Lieberthal/25 15.00
160 Lew Ford/25 15.00
161 Ervin Santana/25 15.00
162 Jody Gerut/25 15.00
163 Nick Johnson/25 20.00
164 Brian Roberts/25 30.00
165 Joe Nathan/25 20.00
167 Ryan Wagner/25 10.00
168 David Dellucci/25 20.00
169 Jae Weong Seo/25 15.00
170 Tom Gordon/25 15.00
171 Carlos Lee/25 20.00
172 Octavio Dotel/25 12.00
173 Jose Castillo/25 15.00
174 Troy Percival/25 15.00
194 Harmon Killebrew/25 40.00

Mirror Bat Red
NM/M
Production 100-250
Gold: 1-2X
Production 25 Sets
2 Adam Dunn/250 6.00
5 Albert Pujols/250 15.00
8 Andruw Jones/250 6.00
11 Aubrey Huff/250 4.00
13 B.J. Upton/250 4.00
14 Brandon Webb/100 4.00
16 Tim Salmon/250 4.00
25 Casey Kotchman/250 4.00
26 Chipper Jones/250 6.00
28 Craig Biggio/250 6.00
29 Craig Wilson/250 4.00
34 David Wright/250 8.00
38 Dontrelle Willis/250 4.00
44 Garret Anderson/250 4.00
45 Gary Sheffield/250 6.00
59 Jason Varitek/250 4.00
61 Javy Lopez/250 4.00
63 Jeff Bagwell/250 4.00
77 Jose Vidro/250 4.00
93 Lance Berkman/250 4.00
105 Mark Teixeira/250 6.00
109 Michael Young/250 4.00

110 Miguel Cabrera/250 8.00
111 Miguel Tejada/250 6.00
121 Paul Konerko/250 4.00
124 Rafael Palmeiro/250 6.00
128 Magglio Ordonez/250 4.00
136 Shawn Green/250 4.00
141 Todd Helton/250 6.00
142 Tom Glavine/250 4.00
143 Torii Hunter/200 4.00
148 Victor Martinez/250 4.00
149 Vladimir Guerrero/250 8.00
150 Sammy Sosa/250 8.00
153 Rocco Baldelli/250 4.00
160 Lew Ford/250 4.00
166 Mike Sweeney/250 4.00
184 Rafael Palmeiro/250 6.00
188 Tom Glavine/250 4.00
190 Vladimir Guerrero/250 8.00

Mirror Bat White
NM/M
Production 75-250
2 Adam Dunn/1 6.00
5 Albert Pujols/1 20.00
7 Alfonso Soriano/1 6.00
11 Aubrey Huff/10 4.00
12 Austin Kearns/5 6.00
13 B.J. Upton/5 6.00
14 Brandon Webb/50 4.00
25 Casey Kotchman/250 8.00
26 Chipper Jones/100 6.00
28 Craig Biggio/250 6.00
29 Craig Wilson/250 10.00
34 David Wright/100 6.00
37 Derek Lee/250 6.00
38 Dontrelle Willis/100 6.00
44 Garret Anderson/100 6.00
45 Gary Sheffield/250 8.00
59 Jason Varitek/100 6.00
61 Javy Lopez/100 4.00
63 Jeff Bagwell/250 4.00
77 Jose Vidro/100 4.00
88 Kerry Wood/100 4.00
93 Lance Berkman/100 6.00
94 Larry Walker/100 8.00
99 Manny Ramirez/250 6.00
105 Mark Teixeira/250 6.00
109 Michael Young/250 6.00
110 Miguel Cabrera/250 6.00
111 Miguel Tejada/250 6.00
121 Paul Konerko/250 4.00
124 Rafael Palmeiro/75 6.00
128 Magglio Ordonez/250 6.00
136 Shawn Green/100 4.00
141 Todd Helton/100 6.00
142 Tom Glavine/100 4.00
143 Torii Hunter/100 4.00
148 Victor Martinez/100 4.00
149 Vladimir Guerrero/100 8.00
150 Sammy Sosa/100 6.00
153 Rocco Baldelli/100 4.00
160 Lew Ford/100 4.00
184 Rafael Palmeiro/75 6.00
188 Tom Glavine/100 4.00
190 Vladimir Guerrero/100 8.00

Mirror Bat Blue
NM/M
Production 75-100
Black: No Pricing
Production One Set
Emerald: No Pricing
Production 5 Sets
2 Adam Dunn/100 6.00
5 Albert Pujols/100 20.00
8 Andruw Jones/100 8.00
11 Aubrey Huff/100 4.00
13 B.J. Upton/100 6.00
14 Brandon Webb/100 4.00
16 Tim Salmon/100 4.00
25 Casey Kotchman/100 4.00
26 Chipper Jones/100 8.00
32 David Ortiz/100 10.00
37 Derek Lee/100 4.00
38 Dontrelle Willis/100 6.00
44 Garret Anderson/100 4.00
45 Gary Sheffield/100 6.00
59 Jason Varitek/100 4.00
61 Javy Lopez/100 4.00
63 Jeff Bagwell/100 6.00
77 Jose Vidro/100 4.00
93 Lance Berkman/100 4.00
99 Manny Ramirez/100 8.00
105 Mark Teixeira/100 4.00
109 Michael Young/100 4.00
110 Miguel Cabrera/100 6.00
111 Miguel Tejada/100 8.00
117 Nomar Garciaparra/100 8.00
121 Paul Konerko/100 4.00
124 Rafael Palmeiro/100 4.00
128 Magglio Ordonez/100 4.00
136 Shawn Green/100 4.00
141 Todd Helton/100 6.00
142 Tom Glavine/100 4.00
143 Torii Hunter/100 4.00
144 Travis Hafner/100 4.00
148 Victor Martinez/100 4.00
149 Vladimir Guerrero/100 8.00
150 Sammy Sosa/100 8.00
153 Rocco Baldelli/100 4.00
160 Lew Ford/100 4.00
166 Mike Sweeney/75 4.00
184 Rafael Palmeiro/100 4.00
188 Tom Glavine/100 4.00
190 Vladimir Guerrero/100 8.00

Mirror Fabric Red
NM/M
Production 100-250
Gold: 1-2X
Production 25 Sets
2 Adam Dunn/Jsy/250 6.00
5 Albert Pujols/Jsy/250 15.00
7 Alfonso Soriano/Jsy/250 6.00
8 Andruw Jones/Jsy/250 6.00
10 Aramis Ramirez/Jsy/250 4.00
11 Aubrey Huff/Jsy/250 4.00
13 B.J. Upton/Jsy/250 4.00
14 Brandon Webb/Pants/100 4.00
15 Barry Zito/Jsy/250 4.00
17 Bobby Abreu/Jsy/250 4.00
20 Preston Wilson/Jsy/250 4.00
25 Casey Kotchman/Jsy/250 4.00
26 Chipper Jones/Jsy/250 8.00
28 Craig Biggio/Jsy/250 4.00
30 Curt Schilling/Jsy/250 4.00
32 David Ortiz/Jsy/250 8.00
37 Derek Lee/Jsy/250 8.00
38 Dontrelle Willis/Jsy/225 4.00
41 Eric Chavez/Jsy/250 4.00
43 Francisco Rodriguez/Jsy/250 4.00
44 Garret Anderson/Jsy/250 4.00
45 Gary Sheffield/Jsy/250 6.00
46 Greg Maddux/Jsy/250 10.00
47 Hideki Matsui/Jsy/250 15.00
48 Hideo Nomo/Jsy/250 6.00
50 Ivan Rodriguez/Jsy/250 4.00
57 Trot Nixon/Jsy/250 4.00
60 Roy Oswalt/Jsy/250 4.00
61 Roy Halladay/Jsy/250 4.00
63 Jeff Bagwell/Jsy/250 6.00
69 Jim Edmonds/Jsy/250 6.00
70 Jim Thome/Jsy/250 4.00
71 Johan Santana/Jsy/250 6.00
82 Justin Morneau/Jsy/250 6.00
84 Kazuo Matsui/Jsy/250 4.00
87 Frank Thomas/Jsy/250 6.00
88 Kerry Wood/Jsy/250 6.00
92 Francisco Cordero/Jsy/250 4.00
93 Lance Berkman/Jsy/250 4.00
94 Larry Walker/Jsy/250 4.00
96 Luis Gonzalez/Jsy/250 4.00
97 Lyle Overbay/Jsy/250 4.00
98 Carlos Zambrano/Jsy/250 4.00
99 Manny Ramirez/Jsy/250 8.00
104 Mark Prior/Jsy/250 8.00
109 Michael Young/Jsy/250 4.00
110 Miguel Cabrera/Jsy/250 8.00
111 Miguel Tejada/Jsy/250 6.00
114 Mike Piazza/Jsy/250 8.00
121 Paul Konerko/Jsy/250 4.00
124 Rafael Palmeiro/Jsy/250 6.00
129 Roger Clemens/Jsy/250 10.00
131 Sammy Sosa/Jsy/250 8.00
133 Scott Rolen/Jsy/250 6.00
135 Sean Casey/Jsy/250 4.00
138 Roy Halladay/Jsy/250 4.00
141 Todd Helton/Jsy/250 6.00
144 Travis Hafner/Jsy/250 4.00
147 Vernon Wells/Jsy/250 4.00
148 Victor Martinez/Jsy/250 4.00
149 Vladimir Guerrero/Jsy/250 8.00
153 Rocco Baldelli/Jsy/250 4.00
159 Ben Sheets/Jsy/250 4.00
160 Lew Ford/Jsy/250 4.00
166 Mike Sweeney/Jsy/250 4.00
178 Greg Maddux/Jsy/250 10.00
179 Ivan Rodriguez/Jsy/250 4.00
183 Pedro J. Martinez/Jsy/250 4.00
184 Rafael Palmeiro/Jsy/250 6.00
185 Roger Clemens/Jsy/250 10.00
188 Tom Glavine/Jsy/250 4.00
190 Vladimir Guerrero/Jsy/250 8.00

Mirror Fabric White
NM/M
Production 50-250

2 Adam Dunn/Jsy/250 6.00
5 Albert Pujols/Jsy/100 15.00
7 Alfonso Soriano/Jsy/100 6.00
8 Andruw Jones/Jsy/100 6.00
10 Aramis Ramirez/Jsy/100 6.00
11 Aubrey Huff/Jsy/150 4.00
13 B.J. Upton/Jsy/250 4.00
15 Barry Zito/Jsy/100 4.00
26 Chipper Jones/Jsy/250 8.00
28 Craig Biggio/Pants/250 4.00
30 Curt Schilling/Jsy/100 8.00
32 David Ortiz/Jsy/100 8.00
34 David Wright/Jsy/100 10.00
38 Dontrelle Willis/Jsy/50 4.00
41 Eric Chavez/Jsy/100 4.00
44 Garret Anderson/Jsy/100 4.00
45 Gary Sheffield/Jsy/50 6.00
46 Greg Maddux/Jsy/50 10.00
47 Hideki Matsui/Pants/100 15.00
48 Hideo Nomo/Jsy/100 6.00
57 Trot Nixon/Jsy/100 4.00
60 Roy Oswalt/Jsy/25 6.00
63 Jeff Bagwell/Jsy/100 6.00
69 Jim Edmonds/Jsy/100 6.00
70 Jim Thome/Jsy/100 6.00
71 Johan Santana/Jsy/100 6.00
78 Josh Beckett/Jsy/250 4.00
82 Justin Morneau/Jsy/100 6.00
84 Kazuo Matsui/Jsy/250 4.00
88 Kerry Wood/Jsy/50 6.00
93 Lance Berkman/Jsy/250 6.00
94 Larry Walker/Jsy/100 6.00
95 Laynce Nix/Jsy/100 4.00
96 Luis Gonzalez/Jsy/250 4.00
98 Carlos Zambrano/Jsy/100 6.00
99 Manny Ramirez/Jsy/100 8.00
104 Mark Prior/Jsy/100 8.00
109 Michael Young/Jsy/100 4.00
110 Miguel Cabrera/Jsy/150 8.00
111 Miguel Tejada/Jsy/100 8.00
113 Mike Mussina/Jsy/100 6.00
114 Mike Piazza/Jsy/100 8.00
121 Paul Konerko/Jsy/150 4.00
124 Rafael Palmeiro/Jsy/150 6.00
129 Roger Clemens/Jsy/100 10.00
131 Sammy Sosa/Jsy/150 8.00
133 Scott Rolen/Jsy/100 4.00
135 Sean Casey/Jsy/100 4.00
138 Roy Halladay/Jsy/100 4.00
141 Todd Helton/Jsy/100 6.00
144 Travis Hafner/Jsy/100 4.00
147 Vernon Wells/Jsy/250 4.00
148 Victor Martinez/Jsy/250 4.00
149 Vladimir Guerrero/Jsy/250 8.00
151 Hank Blalock/Jsy/100 4.00
159 Ben Sheets/Jsy/100 4.00
166 Mike Sweeney/Jsy/50 4.00
178 Greg Maddux/Jsy/200 10.00
179 Ivan Rodriguez/Jsy/250 4.00
184 Rafael Palmeiro/Jsy/250 6.00
185 Roger Clemens/Jsy/100 10.00
188 Tom Glavine/Jsy/250 4.00

Mirror Fabric Blue
NM/M
Production 50-100
Black: No Pricing
Production One Set
Emerald: No Pricing
Production 5 Sets
2 Adam Dunn/Jsy/100 6.00
5 Albert Pujols/Jsy/100 15.00
7 Alfonso Soriano/Jsy/100 6.00
8 Andruw Jones/Jsy/100 6.00
10 Aramis Ramirez/Jsy/100 6.00
11 Aubrey Huff/Jsy/100 4.00
13 B.J. Upton/Jsy/100 4.00
14 Brandon Webb/Pants/100 4.00
15 Barry Zito/Jsy/100 4.00
17 Bobby Abreu/Jsy/100 4.00
18 Bobby Crosby/Jsy/50 6.00
25 Casey Kotchman/Jsy/100 4.00

26 Chipper Jones/Jsy/100 8.00
28 Craig Biggio/Jsy/100 4.00
30 Curt Schilling/Jsy/100 8.00
32 David Ortiz/Jsy/100 8.00
37 Derrek Lee/Jsy/100 8.00
38 Dontrelle Willis/Jsy/100 4.00
41 Eric Chavez/Jsy/100 4.00
43 Francisco Rodriguez/Jsy/100 8.00
44 Garret Anderson/Jsy/100 4.00
46 Greg Maddux/Jsy/100 10.00
47 Hideki Matsui/Pants/100 15.00
50 Ivan Rodriguez/Jsy/100 4.00
57 Trot Nixon/Jsy/100 4.00
60 Roy Oswalt/Jsy/50 4.00
61 Javy Lopez/Jsy/100 4.00
63 Jeff Bagwell/Jsy/100 6.00
69 Jim Edmonds/Jsy/100 6.00
70 Jim Thome/Jsy/100 6.00
71 Johan Santana/Jsy/100 6.00
73 Johnny Damon/Jsy/100 8.00
78 Josh Beckett/Jsy/100 4.00
82 Justin Morneau/Jsy/100 6.00
84 Kazuo Matsui/Jsy/100 4.00
87 Frank Thomas/Jsy/100 6.00
88 Kerry Wood/Jsy/100 6.00
92 Francisco Cordero/Jsy/100 4.00
93 Lance Berkman/Jsy/100 4.00
94 Larry Walker/Jsy/100 6.00
96 Luis Gonzalez/Jsy/100 4.00
98 Lyle Overbay/Jsy/100 4.00
  Carlos Zambrano/Jsy/100 6.00
99 Manny Ramirez/Jsy/100 8.00
104 Mark Prior/Jsy/100 8.00
109 Michael Young/Jsy/100 4.00
110 Miguel Cabrera/Jsy/100 8.00
111 Miguel Tejada/Jsy/100 6.00
113 Mike Mussina/Jsy/50 4.00
114 Mike Piazza/Jsy/100 8.00
121 Paul Konerko/Jsy/100 4.00
124 Rafael Palmeiro/Jsy/100 6.00
129 Roger Clemens/Jsy/100 10.00
131 Sammy Sosa/Jsy/100 6.00
133 Scott Rolen/Jsy/100 6.00
135 Sean Casey/Jsy/100 4.00
138 Roy Halladay/Jsy/100 4.00
141 Todd Helton/Jsy/100 6.00
144 Travis Hafner/Jsy/100 4.00
147 Vernon Wells/Jsy/100 4.00
148 Victor Martinez/Jsy/100 4.00
149 Vladimir Guerrero/Jsy/100 8.00
151 Hank Blalock/Jsy/100 4.00
153 Rocco Baldelli/Jsy/100 4.00
159 Ben Sheets/Jsy/100 4.00
160 Lew Ford/Jsy/100 4.00
166 Mike Sweeney/Jsy/100 4.00
178 Greg Maddux/Jsy/100 10.00
179 Ivan Rodriguez/Jsy/100 4.00
183 Pedro J. Martinez/Jsy/100 8.00
184 Rafael Palmeiro/Pants/100 6.00
185 Roger Clemens/Jsy/100 10.00
188 Tom Glavine/Jsy/100 4.00
190 Vladimir Guerrero/Jsy/100 8.00

Skills
NM/M
Common: 1.50
Inserted 1:7
Mirror: 2-3X
1 Andy Pettitte 1.50
2 Barry Zito 1.50
3 Bobby Crosby 2.00
4 Brandon Webb 1.50
5 Craig Biggio 2.00
6 David Ortiz 3.00
7 Dontrelle Willis 2.00
8 Francisco Rodriguez 1.50
9 Gary Sheffield 2.00
10 Jack Wilson 1.50
11 Jason Bay 1.50
12 Jeff Bagwell 2.00
13 Jim Edmonds 2.00
14 Josh Beckett 1.50
15 Kerry Wood 2.00
16 Lance Berkman 2.00
17 Mark Buehrle 1.50
18 Mark Teixeira 2.00
19 Miguel Tejada 2.00
20 Paul Konerko 1.50
21 Scott Rolen 2.00
22 Sean Burroughs 1.50
23 Vernon Wells 1.50
24 Victor Martinez 1.50
25 Vladimir Guerrero 3.00

Skills Autographs
NM/M
Production 5-25
3 Bobby Crosby/25 25.00
11 Jason Bay/25 25.00

Skills Jersey Position
NM/M
Production 100-250
Prime: No Pricing
Production 5-25
1 Andy Pettitte/250 4.00
2 Barry Zito/250 4.00
3 Bobby Crosby/100 6.00
4 Brandon Webb/Pants/100 4.00
5 Craig Biggio/250 4.00
6 David Ortiz/250 4.00
7 Dontrelle Willis/100 4.00
8 Francisco Rodriguez/250 4.00
9 Gary Sheffield/50 6.00
10 Jack Wilson/50 4.00
11 Jason Bay/100 4.00
12 Jeff Bagwell/250 6.00
13 Jim Edmonds/250 6.00
14 Josh Beckett/250 4.00
15 Kerry Wood/50 6.00
16 Lance Berkman/250 4.00
17 Mark Buehrle/150 4.00
19 Miguel Tejada/250 8.00
20 Paul Konerko/100 4.00
21 Scott Rolen/100 6.00
22 Sean Burroughs/250 4.00
23 Vernon Wells/250 4.00
24 Victor Martinez/250 4.00
25 Vladimir Guerrero/250 8.00

2005 Leaf Limited
NM/M
Complete Set (205): —
Common Player (1-150): 1.00
Production 699
Common (151-175, 197): 4.00
Production 99
Common Auto.
(176-196, 198-200): 12.00
Production 99
Pack (4): 70.00
1 Roger Clemens 5.00
2 Roger Clemens 5.00
3 Ichiro Suzuki 4.00
4 Ichiro Suzuki 4.00
5 Todd Helton 1.50
6 Todd Helton 1.50
7 Vladimir Guerrero 2.00
8 Vladimir Guerrero 2.00
9 Miguel Cabrera 2.00
10 Miguel Cabrera 2.00
11 Albert Pujols 5.00
12 Albert Pujols 5.00
13 Mark Prior 1.50
14 Mark Prior 1.50
15 Chipper Jones 2.00
16 Chipper Jones 2.00
17 Jeff Bagwell 1.50
18 Jeff Bagwell 1.50
19 Kerry Wood 1.00
20 Kerry Wood 1.00
21 Gary Sheffield 1.50
22 Carl Crawford 1.50
23 Mariano Rivera 2.00
24 Curt Schilling 2.00
25 Ben Sheets 1.00
26 Jimmy Rollins 1.00
27 Melvin Mora 1.00
28 Corey Patterson 1.00
29 Rafael Furcal 1.00
30 Jim Thome 1.50
31 Derek Jeter 5.00
32 Jake Peavy 1.50
33 Francisco Cordero 1.00
34 Aramis Ramirez 1.50
35 Javy Lopez 1.00
36 Aaron Rowand 1.00
37 Jason Bay 1.50
38 Michael Young 1.00
39 Ivan Rodriguez 1.50
40 Joe Nathan 1.00
41 Oliver Perez 1.00
42 Adam Dunn 1.50
43 Eric Chavez 1.00
44 Pedro Martinez 2.00
45 Roy Oswalt 1.00
46 Carlos Delgado 1.00
47 Jeff Kent 1.00
48 Johnny Damon 2.00
49 Edgar Renteria 1.00
50 Mark Buehrle 1.00
51 Carl Pavano 1.00
52 J.D. Drew 1.00
53 Hank Blalock 1.00
54 Moises Alou 1.00
55 Brad Radke 1.00
56 Brad Wilkerson 1.00
57 Sean Casey 1.00
58 Mike Lowell 1.00
59 Octavio Dotel 1.00
60 Francisco Rodriguez 1.00
61 Jose Guillen 1.00
62 Greg Maddux 3.00
63 A.J. Burnett 1.00
64 Chris Carpenter 1.50
65 Jose Reyes 1.50
66 Travis Hafner 1.50
67 Rich Harden 1.50
68 Bret Boone 1.00
69 Scott Podsednik 1.00
70 Andruw Jones 1.50
71 Milton Bradley 1.00
72 Zack Greinke 1.00
73 Torii Hunter 1.00
74 Paul Konerko 1.00
75 David Wells 1.00
76 Tim Hudson 1.00
77 Sammy Sosa 2.50
78 Jason Varitek 1.50
79 Lance Berkman 1.50
80 Justin Morneau 1.50
81 Troy Glaus 1.00
82 Jose Vidro 1.00
83 Joe Mauer 1.50
84 Josh Beckett 1.00
85 Craig Biggio 1.00
86 Luis Gonzalez 1.00
87 Larry Walker 1.00
88 Barry Zito 1.00
89 Jacque Jones 1.00
90 Lyle Overbay 1.00
91 Roy Halladay 1.50
92 Orlando Cabrera 1.00
93 Magglio Ordonez 1.00
94 Mike Sweeney 1.00
95 Rafael Palmeiro 1.50
96 Brandon Webb 1.00
97 Preston Wilson 1.00
98 Shannon Stewart 1.00
99 Trot Nixon 1.00
100 Mike Piazza 2.50
101 Dontrelle Willis 1.50
102 Ken Griffey Jr. 3.00
103 Andy Pettitte 1.00
104 Kazuo Matsui 1.00
105 Bobby Crosby 1.00
106 Shawn Green 1.00
107 Alfonso Soriano 2.00
108 Carlos Zambrano 1.00
109 Keith Foulke 1.00
110 Aubrey Huff 1.00
111 Adrian Beltre 1.00
112 Mark Teixeira 1.50
113 Randy Johnson 2.00
114 Miguel Tejada 1.50
115 Alex Rodriguez 4.00
116 Carlos Beltran 1.50
117 Bobby Abreu 1.50
118 Johan Santana 1.50
119 Manny Ramirez 2.00
120 Juan Pierre 1.00
121 Scott Rolen 1.50
122 Livan Hernandez 1.00
123 Carlos Lee 1.00
124 Derrek Lee 1.50
125 Brian Giles 1.00
126 Nomar Garciaparra 1.50
127 John Smoltz 1.50
128 Jim Edmonds 1.50
129 Bartolo Colon 1.00
130 Garret Anderson 1.00
131 Austin Kearns 1.00
132 Shingo Takatsu 1.00
133 Omar Vizquel 1.00
134 Tom Glavine 1.00
135 Mark Mulder 1.00
136 Bernie Williams 1.00
137 Richie Sexson 1.00
138 Mike Mussina 1.50
139 Mark Loretta 1.00
140 Vernon Wells 1.00
141 David Wright 3.00
142 Marcus Giles 1.00
143 David Ortiz 2.00
144 Victor Martinez 1.00
145 Hideki Matsui 4.00
146 C.C. Sabathia 1.00
147 Angel Berroa 1.00
148 Troy Percival 1.00
149 Paul LoDuca 1.00
150 Jorge Posada 1.50
151 Willie Mays 8.00
152 Ryne Sandberg 8.00
153 Rickey Henderson 8.00
154 Ted Williams 10.00
155 Roberto Clemente 10.00
156 George Brett 8.00
157 Whitey Ford 4.00
158 Duke Snider 8.00
159 Don Mattingly 10.00
160 Bob Gibson 4.00
161 Hank Aaron 8.00
162 Al Kaline 6.00
163 Nolan Ryan 10.00
164 Stan Musial 6.00
165 George Kell 4.00
166 Harmon Killebrew 6.00
167 Cal Ripken Jr. 15.00
168 Babe Ruth 10.00
169 Roger Clemens/SP 8.00
170 Curt Schilling/SP 4.00
171 Rafael Palmeiro/SP 4.00
172 Randy Johnson/SP 5.00
173 Mike Piazza/SP 5.00
174 Greg Maddux/SP 6.00
175 Sammy Sosa/SP 5.00
176 Hayden Penn/Auto. RC 15.00
177 Ambiorix Concepcion/Auto. RC 15.00
178 Casey Rogowski/Auto. RC 15.00
179 Prince Fielder/Auto. 100.00
180 Geovany Soto/Auto. RC 15.00
181 Wladimir Balentien/Auto. RC 25.00
182 Jason Hammel/Auto. RC 15.00
183 Keiichi Yabu/Auto. RC 25.00
184 Brandon McCarthy/Auto. RC 40.00
185 Ubaldo Jimenez/Auto. RC 15.00
186 Keiichi Yabu/Auto. RC 25.00
187 Miguel Negron/Auto. RC 15.00
188 Mike Morse/Auto. RC 25.00
189 Nate McLouth/Auto. RC 15.00
190 Norihiro Nakamura/Auto. RC 40.00
191 Bill McCarthy/Auto. RC 50.00
192 Tony Pena/Auto. RC 12.00
193 Ambiorix Concepcion/Auto. RC 15.00
194 Raul Tablado/Auto. RC 15.00
195 Hayden Penn/Auto. RC 15.00
196 Sean Thompson/Auto. RC 15.00
197 Tadahito Iguchi RC 15.00
198 Ubaldo Jimenez/Auto. RC 15.00
199 Wladimir Balentien/Auto. RC 25.00
200 Prince Fielder/Auto. 100.00
201 Philip Humber/Auto./99 RC 60.00
202 Jeff Niemann/Auto./95 RC 40.00
203 Justin Verlander/Auto./70 RC 90.00
205 Yuniesky Betancourt/Auto. RC 50.00

Bronze Spotlight
Bronze (1-150): 1-1.5X
Bronze (151-175): 1X
Bronze (176-200): .25X
Production 99 Sets

Silver Spotlight
Silver (1-150): 1-2X
Silver (151-175): 1-1.5X
Silver (176-200): .25X
Production 50 Sets

Gold Spotlight
Gold (1-150): 2-4X
Gold (151-175): 2-3X
Production 25 Sets
Gold (176-205): No Pricing
Production 5-25

Platinum Spotlight
No Pricing
Production One Set

Cuts Silver
NM/M
Production 7-99
Platinum: No Pricing
Production One Set
1 Orlando Cepeda/44 35.00
2 Hank Aaron/44 275.00
3 Willie Mays/24 175.00
4 Sandy Koufax/32 400.00
5 Cal Ripken Jr./25 150.00
6 Nolan Ryan/34 120.00
7 Jim Palmer/22 60.00
8 Tony Gwynn/19 60.00
9 Rod Carew/29 40.00
10 Ryne Sandberg/23 70.00
11 Stan Musial/28 70.00
12 Steve Carlton/32 60.00
14 Mike Schmidt/20 60.00
15 Harmon Killebrew/25 40.00
17 Duke Snider/53 30.00
18 Don Mattingly/25 40.00
19 Dale Murphy/25 35.00
22 Juan Marichal/99 25.00
23 Greg Maddux/37 25.00
24 Paul Molitor/25 35.00
26 Wade Boggs/25 40.00
27 Mark Prior/27 40.00
28 Al Kaline/28 40.00

Legends
NM/M
Common Player:
Production 50 Sets
Foil: No Pricing
Production 10 Sets
1 Billy Martin 4.00
2 Bobby Doerr 3.00
3 Carlton Fisk 4.00
4 Harmon Killebrew 5.00
5 Duke Snider 5.00
6 George Brett 6.00
7 Johnny Bench 5.00
8 Lou Boudreau 3.00
9 Brooks Robinson 5.00
10 Al Kaline 4.00
11 Stan Musial 5.00
12 Burleigh Grimes 3.00
13 Cal Ripken Jr. 10.00
14 Carl Yastrzemski 6.00
15 Willie Stargell 3.00
16 Yogi Berra 4.00
17 Enos Slaughter 3.00
18 Phil Rizzuto 3.00
19 Luis Aparicio 3.00
20 Ernie Banks 5.00
21 Hal Newhouser 3.00
22 Whitey Ford 3.00
23 Tony Gwynn 4.00
24 Bob Feller 3.00
25 Don Sutton 3.00
26 Lou Brock 5.00
27 Jim Palmer 3.00
28 Billy Williams 3.00
29 Juan Marichal 3.00
30 Rod Carew 3.00
31 Jim "Catfish" Hunter 2.00
32 Maury Wills 2.00
33 Joe Cronin 2.00
34 Fergie Jenkins 2.00
35 Sandy Koufax 5.00
36 Steve Carlton 3.00
37 Eddie Murray 3.00
38 Roger Maris 4.00
39 Gaylord Perry 3.00
40 Bob Gibson 3.00
41 Tom Seaver 3.00
42 Dennis Eckersley 3.00
43 Reggie Jackson 3.00
44 Willie McCovey 3.00
45 Willie Mays 6.00
46 Willie Mays 6.00
47 Rickey Henderson 3.00
48 Rickey Henderson 3.00
49 Nolan Ryan 6.00
50 Nolan Ryan 6.00

Legends Jersey Number
NM/M
Production 1-45
3 Carlton Fisk/50 10.00
25 Don Sutton/20 8.00
26 Lou Brock/20 10.00
27 Jim Palmer/22 8.00
28 Billy Williams/26 8.00
29 Juan Marichal/27 8.00
30 Rod Carew/29 10.00
31 Jim "Catfish" Hunter/Pants/29 8.00
34 Fergie Jenkins/31 6.00
35 Sandy Koufax/32 250.00
36 Steve Carlton/32 8.00
37 Eddie Murray/33 12.00
39 Gaylord Perry/36 6.00
40 Bob Gibson/45 10.00
41 Tom Seaver/41 10.00
42 Dennis Eckersley/45 5.00
43 Reggie Jackson/Pants/44 8.00
44 Willie McCovey/44 10.00
45 Willie Mays/24 40.00
46 Willie Mays/24 40.00
49 Nolan Ryan/30 25.00
50 Nolan Ryan/30 25.00

Production 1-45
3 Carlton Fisk/50 10.00
25 Don Sutton/20 8.00
26 Lou Brock/20 10.00
27 Jim Palmer/22 8.00
28 Billy Williams/26 8.00
29 Juan Marichal/27 8.00
30 Rod Carew/29 10.00
31 Jim "Catfish" Hunter/Pants/29 8.00
34 Fergie Jenkins/31 6.00
35 Sandy Koufax/32 250.00
36 Steve Carlton/32 8.00
37 Eddie Murray/33 12.00
39 Gaylord Perry/36 6.00
40 Bob Gibson/45 10.00
41 Tom Seaver/41 10.00
42 Dennis Eckersley/45 5.00
43 Reggie Jackson/Pants/44 8.00
44 Willie McCovey/44 10.00
45 Willie Mays/24 40.00
46 Willie Mays/24 40.00
49 Nolan Ryan/30 25.00
50 Nolan Ryan/30 25.00

Legends Signature
NM/M
Production 2-50
2 Bobby Doerr/50 15.00

ABBREVIATIONS
SP - Short Print

Cuts Gold
Production 3-30

#	Player	Price
4	Harmon Killebrew/50	30.00
5	Duke Snider/25	35.00
9	Brooks Robinson/50	25.00
10	Al Kaline/50	40.00
18	Phil Rizzuto/50	35.00
19	Luis Aparicio/50	20.00
24	Bob Feller/50	40.00
25	Don Sutton/50	15.00
26	Lou Brock/50	20.00
27	Jim Palmer/50	20.00
28	Billy Williams/25	20.00
29	Juan Marichal/50	25.00
30	Rod Carew/25	35.00
32	Maury Wills/50	15.00
34	Fergie Jenkins/50	15.00
36	Steve Carlton/50	25.00
39	Gaylord Perry/50	15.00
40	Bob Gibson/25	40.00
42	Dennis Eckersley/50	20.00

Legends Signature Jersey Number
NM/M
Production 5-30

#	Player	Price
2	Bobby Doerr/Pants/25	25.00
4	Harmon Killebrew/25	40.00
11	Stan Musial/25	65.00
13	Cal Ripken Jr./25	150.00
18	Phil Rizzuto/Pants/25	40.00
19	Luis Aparicio/25	25.00
23	Tony Gwynn/25	40.00
25	Don Sutton/20	20.00
27	Jim Palmer/22	25.00
34	Fergie Jenkins/25	20.00
36	Steve Carlton/25	30.00
39	Gaylord Perry/25	20.00
40	Bob Gibson/25	40.00
42	Dennis Eckersley/25	25.00
44	Willie McCovey/25	40.00
45	Willie Mays/24	160.00
46	Willie Mays/24	160.00
49	Nolan Ryan/30	90.00
50	Nolan Ryan/30	90.00

Production 5-30

#	Player	Price
2	Bobby Doerr/Pants/25	25.00
4	Harmon Killebrew/25	40.00
11	Stan Musial/25	65.00
13	Cal Ripken Jr./25	150.00
18	Phil Rizzuto/Pants/25	40.00
19	Luis Aparicio/25	25.00
23	Tony Gwynn/25	40.00
25	Don Sutton/20	20.00
27	Jim Palmer/22	25.00
34	Fergie Jenkins/25	20.00
36	Steve Carlton/25	30.00
39	Gaylord Perry/25	20.00
40	Bob Gibson/25	40.00
42	Dennis Eckersley/25	25.00
44	Willie McCovey/25	40.00
45	Willie Mays/24	160.00
46	Willie Mays/24	160.00
49	Nolan Ryan/30	90.00
50	Nolan Ryan/30	90.00

Lettermen
NM/M
Production 4-21

#	Player	Price
DU-H	Dale Murphy H/20	150.00
DU-M	Dale Murphy M/20	150.00
DU-P	Dale Murphy P/20	150.00
DU-R	Dale Murphy R/20	150.00
DU-U	Dale Murphy U/20	150.00
DU-Y	Dale Murphy Y/20	150.00
NR-A	Nolan Ryan A/21	200.00
NR-N	Nolan Ryan N/21	200.00
NR-R	Nolan Ryan R/21	200.00
NR-Y	Nolan Ryan Y/21	200.00

Lumberjacks
NM/M
Common Player:
Production 50 Sets
Foil: No Pricing

#	Player	Price
1	Al Kaline	4.00
2	Albert Pujols	8.00
3	Andre Dawson	3.00
4	Babe Ruth	8.00
5	Cal Ripken Jr.	15.00
6	Chipper Jones	4.00
7	Dale Murphy	3.00
8	Dave Winfield	3.00
9	Don Mattingly	6.00
10	Duke Snider	4.00
11	Eddie Murray	4.00
12	Frank Robinson	4.00
13	Frank Thomas	4.00
14	Gary Carter	3.00
15	Hack Wilson	4.00
16	Hank Aaron	10.00
17	Harmon Killebrew	4.00
18	Joe Morgan	3.00
19	Johnny Bench	4.00
20	Kirby Puckett	4.00
21	Kirk Gibson	4.00
22	Manny Ramirez	4.00
23	Mark Grace	3.00
24	Mike Piazza	5.00
25	Mike Schmidt	6.00
26	Orlando Cepeda	3.00
27	Paul Molitor	4.00
28	Rafael Palmeiro	4.00
29	Ralph Kiner	3.00
30	Reggie Jackson	4.00
31	Richie Ashburn	3.00
32	Rickey Henderson	4.00
33	Robin Yount	5.00
34	Rod Carew	4.00
35	Ryne Sandberg	6.00
36	Stan Musial	5.00
37	Ted Williams	8.00
38	Tony Gwynn	4.00
39	Vladimir Guerrero	4.00
40	Willie Mays	8.00
41	Ernie Banks, Bernie Williams	6.00
42	Ted Williams, Joe Cronin	10.00
43	George Brett, Bo Jackson	8.00
44	John Kruk, Jim Thome	3.00
45	Willie Mays, Jim Thorpe	8.00
46	Wade Boggs, Johnny Damon	6.00
47	M. Williams, W. Clark	3.00
48	Willie Stargell, D. Parker	4.00
49	Ichiro Suzuki, Edgar Martinez	6.00
50	Carl Yastrzemski, Carlton Fisk	6.00

Lumberjacks Barrel
No Pricing
Production 1-5

Lumberjacks Bat
NM/M
Production 1-50

#	Player	Price
1	Al Kaline/50	10.00
4	Babe Ruth/25	180.00
8	Dave Winfield/25	10.00
11	Eddie Murray/25	15.00
12	Frank Robinson/50	15.00
14	Gary Carter/25	10.00
15	Hack Wilson/50	40.00
16	Hank Aaron/25	40.00
18	Joe Morgan/25	8.00
19	Johnny Bench/50	10.00
20	Kirby Puckett/50	10.00
25	Mike Schmidt/50	15.00
26	Orlando Cepeda/25	8.00
27	Paul Molitor/50	8.00
31	Ralph Kiner/25	15.00
33	Richie Ashburn/25	15.00
33	Robin Yount/25	20.00
35	Ryne Sandberg/25	20.00
36	Stan Musial/25	20.00
37	Ted Williams/50	40.00
40	Willie Mays/50	30.00
43	George Brett, Bo Jackson/50	25.00
47	M. Williams, W. Clark/50	15.00
48	Willie Stargell, D. Parker/25	15.00
50	Carl Yastrzemski, Carlton Fisk/50	20.00

Lumberjacks Combos
NM/M
Production 1-50

#	Player	Price
2	Albert Pujols/Bat-Jsy/50	30.00
5	Cal Ripken Jr./Bat-Jsy/50	35.00
6	Chipper Jones/Bat-Jsy/25	15.00
7	Dale Murphy/Bat-Jsy/50	12.00
8	Dave Winfield/Bat-Pants/50	8.00
11	Eddie Murray/Bat-Jsy/25	20.00
13	Frank Thomas/Bat-Jsy/25	15.00
16	Hank Aaron/Bat-Jsy/25	60.00
19	Johnny Bench/Bat-Jsy/25	15.00
20	Kirby Puckett/Bat-Jsy/25	15.00
21	Kirk Gibson/Bat-Jsy/25	8.00
22	Manny Ramirez/Bat-Jsy/25	12.00
23	Mark Grace/Bat-Jsy/25	12.00
24	Mike Piazza/Bat-Jsy/50	15.00
25	Mike Schmidt/Bat-Jsy/25	25.00
26	Orlando Cepeda/Bat-Pants/50	8.00
27	Paul Molitor/Bat-Jsy/50	12.00
31	Richie Ashburn/Bat-Jsy/25	15.00
33	Robin Yount/Bat-Jsy/50	15.00
36	Stan Musial/Bat-Jsy/25	35.00
40	Willie Mays/Bat-Jsy/25	50.00

Lumberjacks Combos Prime
NM/M
Production 1-50

#	Player	Price
2	Albert Pujols/Bat-Jsy/	35.00
3	Andre Dawson/Bat-Jsy/50	8.00
5	Cal Ripken Jr./Bat-Jsy/	50.00
6	Chipper Jones, Bat-Jsy/50	15.00
11	Eddie Murray/Bat-Jsy/	25.00
12	Frank Robinson/Bat-Jsy/50	12.00
13	Frank Thomas/Bat-Jsy/	15.00
14	Gary Carter/Bat-Jsy/50	10.00
18	Joe Morgan/Bat-Jsy/25	15.00
21	Kirk Gibson/Bat-Jsy/50	8.00
22	Manny Ramirez/Bat-Jsy/	20.00
24	Mike Piazza/Bat-Jsy/50	15.00
28	Rafael Palmeiro/Bat-Jsy/50	12.00
32	Rickey Henderson/Bat-Jsy/50	15.00
33	Robin Yount/Bat-Jsy/50	25.00
34	Rod Carew/Bat-Jsy/50	12.00
39	Vladimir Guerrero/Bat-Jsy/50	15.00

Lumberjacks Jersey
NM/M
Production 1-50

#	Player	Price
4	Babe Ruth/25	250.00
8	Dave Winfield/Pants/25	6.00
10	Duke Snider/Pants/50	10.00
11	Eddie Murray/25	15.00
14	Gary Carter/50	5.00
16	Hank Aaron/25	40.00
19	Johnny Bench/25	15.00
20	Kirby Puckett/25	15.00
27	Paul Molitor/50	8.00
30	Reggie Jackson/50	10.00
31	Richie Ashburn/50	10.00
33	Robin Yount/50	12.00
35	Ryne Sandberg/50	12.00
36	Stan Musial/25	25.00
37	Ted Williams/25	50.00
40	Willie Mays/25	35.00
41	Ernie Banks, Bernie Williams/25	30.00
42	Ted Williams, Joe Cronin/25	60.00
43	George Brett, Bo Jackson/50	30.00
44	John Kruk, Jim Thome/25	20.00
45	Willie Mays, Jim Thorpe/25	200.00
46	Wade Boggs, Johnny Damon/50	20.00
47	M. Williams, W. Clark/50	20.00
48	Willie Stargell, D. Parker/25	25.00

Production 1-50

#	Player	Price
4	Babe Ruth/25	250.00
8	Dave Winfield/Pants/25	6.00
10	Duke Snider/Pants/50	10.00
11	Eddie Murray/25	15.00
14	Gary Carter/25	5.00
16	Hank Aaron/25	40.00
19	Johnny Bench/25	15.00
20	Kirby Puckett/25	15.00
27	Paul Molitor/50	8.00
30	Reggie Jackson/25	10.00
31	Richie Ashburn/50	10.00
33	Robin Yount/50	12.00
35	Ryne Sandberg/25	12.00
36	Stan Musial/25	25.00
37	Ted Williams/50	50.00
40	Willie Mays/25	35.00
41	Ernie Banks, Bernie Williams/25	30.00
42	Ted Williams, Joe Cronin/25	60.00
43	George Brett, Bo Jackson/50	30.00
44	John Kruk, Jim Thome/25	20.00
45	Willie Mays, Jim Thorpe/25	200.00
46	Wade Boggs, Johnny Damon/50	20.00
47	M. Williams, W. Clark/25	20.00
48	Willie Stargell, D. Parker/25	25.00

Lumberjacks Signature
NM/M
Production 1-50

#	Player	Price
1	Al Kaline/50	40.00
3	Andre Dawson/25	20.00
5	Cal Ripken Jr./21	120.00
7	Dale Murphy/50	25.00
9	Don Mattingly/50	50.00
10	Duke Snider/50	50.00
12	Frank Robinson/50	30.00
13	Frank Thomas/25	50.00
14	Gary Carter/50	20.00
17	Harmon Killebrew/50	35.00
18	Joe Morgan/25	25.00
19	Johnny Bench/50	40.00
20	Kirby Puckett/50	40.00
23	Mark Grace/25	35.00
25	Mike Schmidt/50	40.00
27	Paul Molitor/50	25.00
29	Ralph Kiner/50	30.00
34	Rod Carew/50	25.00
35	Ryne Sandberg/50	40.00
36	Stan Musial/50	50.00
37	Tony Gwynn/50	35.00
40	Willie Mays/25	140.00

Lumberjacks Signature Bat
NM/M
Production 1-100

#	Player	Price
1	Al Kaline/50	40.00
3	Andre Dawson/100	20.00
5	Cal Ripken Jr./25	140.00
7	Dale Murphy/100	25.00
9	Don Mattingly/50	50.00
12	Frank Robinson/100	35.00
13	Frank Thomas/50	50.00
14	Gary Carter/25	25.00
18	Joe Morgan/25	25.00
19	Johnny Bench/50	50.00
20	Kirby Puckett/25	25.00
23	Mark Grace/25	40.00
26	Orlando Cepeda/100	20.00
27	Paul Molitor/50	25.00
29	Ralph Kiner/100	30.00
33	Robin Yount/50	50.00
34	Rod Carew/50	30.00
36	Stan Musial/50	65.00
38	Tony Gwynn/50	40.00

Lumberjacks Signature Jersey
NM/M
Production 1-100

#	Player	Price
3	Andre Dawson/100	20.00
5	Cal Ripken Jr./25	140.00
7	Dale Murphy/100	25.00
9	Don Mattingly/50	50.00
10	Duke Snider/Pants/	30.00
13	Frank Thomas/50	50.00
14	Gary Carter/50	25.00
17	Harmon Killebrew/25	40.00
19	Johnny Bench/50	50.00
23	Mark Grace/25	40.00
27	Paul Molitor/50	40.00
30	Reggie Jackson/50	40.00
33	Robin Yount/25	50.00
38	Tony Gwynn/50	40.00

Production 1-100

#	Player	Price
3	Andre Dawson/100	20.00
5	Cal Ripken Jr./25	140.00
7	Dale Murphy/100	25.00
9	Don Mattingly/50	50.00
10	Duke Snider/Pants/	30.00
13	Frank Thomas/50	50.00
17	Harmon Killebrew/25	40.00
19	Johnny Bench/25	50.00
23	Mark Grace/25	40.00
27	Paul Molitor/25	40.00
30	Reggie Jackson/25	40.00
33	Robin Yount/25	50.00
38	Tony Gwynn/50	40.00

Lumberjacks Signature Combos
NM/M
Production 1-100

#	Player	Price
3	Andre Dawson/Bat-Jsy/100	20.00
5	Cal Ripken Jr./Bat-Jsy/	140.00
7	Dale Murphy/Bat-Jsy/100	25.00
9	Don Mattingly/Bat-Jsy/50	50.00
13	Frank Thomas/Bat-Jsy/25	25.00
14	Gary Carter/Bat-Jsy/25	25.00
23	Mark Grace/Bat-Jsy/25	40.00
38	Tony Gwynn/Bat-Jsy/25	45.00

Lumberjacks Signature Combos Prime
Production 1-25

Matching Numbers
NM/M
Production 5-50
Prime: No Pricing
Production 1-5

#	Players	Price
1.	Ted Williams, Roger Maris/25	160.00
2.	Nolan Ryan, Kerry Wood/50	35.00
3.	Cal Ripken Jr., Gary Carter/50	40.00
5.	Johnny Bench, Albert Pujols/50	40.00
6.	Roger Clemens, W. Clark/50	35.00
7.	Willie McCovey, Reggie Jackson/25	20.00
8.	Ryne Sandberg, Don Mattingly/35	35.00
9.	Duke Snider, Joe Cronin/25	25.00

Monikers Bronze
NM/M
Production 1-100

#	Player	Price
9	Miguel Cabrera/100	25.00
10	Miguel Cabrera/100	25.00
12	Mark Prior/50	35.00
14	Mark Prior/50	35.00
25	Ben Sheets/100	15.00
27	Melvin Mora/50	15.00
29	Rafael Furcal/25	20.00
32	Jake Peavy/25	15.00
33	Francisco Cordero/25	15.00
38	Michael Young/25	25.00
40	Joe Nathan/25	20.00
43	Eric Chavez/25	25.00
45	Roy Oswalt/50	25.00
49	Edgar Renteria/25	20.00
50	Mark Buehrle/25	30.00
57	Sean Casey/25	15.00
59	Octavio Dotel/25	12.00
60	Francisco Rodriguez/25	30.00
61	Jose Guillen/25	20.00
65	Travis Hafner/25	20.00
67	Rich Harden/50	15.00
71	Milton Bradley/25	15.00
74	Paul Konerko/50	25.00
76	Tim Hudson/25	25.00
80	Justin Morneau/100	25.00
82	Jose Vidro/25	15.00
84	Josh Beckett/25	30.00
85	Craig Biggio/25	30.00
89	Jacque Jones/25	15.00
91	Roy Halladay/25	15.00
95	Magglio Ordonez/100	15.00
96	Brandon Webb/50	15.00
97	Preston Wilson/50	15.00
98	Shannon Stewart/50	10.00
99	Trot Nixon/50	15.00
105	Bobby Crosby/29	15.00
107	Alfonso Soriano/25	15.00
108	Carlos Zambrano/50	25.00
109	Keith Foulke/25	15.00
110	Aubrey Huff/25	15.00
112	Mark Teixeira/100	25.00
116	Carlos Beltran/25	30.00
118	Johan Santana/100	30.00
121	Scott Rolen/25	30.00
123	Carlos Lee/50	20.00
124	Derek Lee/50	25.00
130	Garret Anderson/100	15.00
133	Austin Kearns/100	15.00
135	Omar Vizquel/50	20.00
139	Mark Mulder/50	20.00
141	David Wright/25	60.00
144	Victor Martinez/15	15.00
151	Willie Mays/25	175.00
152	Ryne Sandberg/50	50.00
158	Duke Snider/25	30.00
159	Don Mattingly/25	50.00
162	Al Kaline/25	35.00
163	Nolan Ryan/25	80.00
164	Stan Musial/25	60.00
165	George Kell/50	15.00
166	Harmon Killebrew/50	50.00
167	Cal Ripken Jr./25	120.00
176	Hayden Penn/50	15.00
177	Ambiorix Concepcion/50	15.00
179	Prince Fielder/100	100.00
181	Wladimir Balentien/50	30.00
182	Jason Hammel/50	15.00
183	Keiichi Yabu/50	25.00
184	Brandon McCarthy/50	50.00
185	Ubaldo Jimenez/50	15.00
187	Keiichi Yabu/25	25.00
187	Miguel Negron/50	10.00
188	Mike Morse/30	30.00
189	Nate McLouth/50	15.00
190	Norihiro Nakamura/50	50.00
191	Brandon McCarthy/50	50.00
192	Tony Pena/50	10.00
193	Ambiorix Concepcion/50	15.00
194	Raul Tablado/50	15.00
195	Hayden Penn/50	20.00
196	Sean Thompson/50	12.00
198	Ubaldo Jimenez/50	15.00
199	Wladimir Balentien/50	30.00
200	Prince Fielder/50	100.00

Monikers Silver
NM/M
Production 1-50

#	Player	Price
9	Miguel Cabrera/50	30.00
10	Miguel Cabrera/50	30.00
13	Mark Prior/25	40.00
14	Mark Prior/25	40.00
25	Ben Sheets/50	20.00
27	Melvin Mora/25	20.00
29	Rafael Furcal/25	20.00
32	Jake Peavy/50	25.00
33	Francisco Cordero/25	20.00
38	Michael Young/25	25.00
40	Joe Nathan/25	25.00
43	Eric Chavez/25	25.00
45	Roy Oswalt/25	30.00
49	Edgar Renteria/25	25.00
50	Mark Buehrle/25	30.00
57	Sean Casey/25	25.00
59	Octavio Dotel/25	12.00
61	Jose Guillen/25	20.00
66	Travis Hafner/25	20.00
67	Rich Harden/25	15.00
71	Milton Bradley/25	15.00
80	Justin Morneau/50	15.00
89	Jacque Jones/25	15.00
93	Magglio Ordonez/50	20.00
96	Brandon Webb/25	20.00
97	Preston Wilson/50	15.00
98	Shannon Stewart/50	15.00
99	Trot Nixon/25	25.00
105	Bobby Crosby/29	25.00
108	Carlos Zambrano/25	25.00
109	Keith Foulke/25	30.00
110	Aubrey Huff/25	25.00
112	Mark Teixeira/35	35.00
118	Johan Santana/25	35.00
123	Carlos Lee/25	35.00
130	Garret Anderson/50	25.00
131	Austin Kearns/25	15.00
133	Omar Vizquel/25	25.00
135	Mark Mulder/25	25.00
139	Mark Loretta/25	20.00
141	David Wright/25	70.00
144	Victor Martinez/25	15.00
151	Willie Mays/25	175.00
152	Ryne Sandberg/25	50.00
158	Duke Snider/25	30.00
159	Don Mattingly/25	50.00
162	Al Kaline/25	35.00
163	Nolan Ryan/25	80.00
164	Stan Musial/25	60.00
165	George Kell/25	15.00
166	Harmon Killebrew/25	50.00
167	Cal Ripken Jr./25	120.00

Monikers Material Bat Bronze
NM/M
Production 1-100
Platinum: No Pricing
Production One Set

#	Player	Price
9	Miguel Cabrera/50	35.00
10	Miguel Cabrera/50	35.00
13	Mark Prior/25	40.00
14	Mark Prior/25	40.00
29	Rafael Furcal/75	15.00
34	Aramis Ramirez/100	20.00
37	Jason Bay/100	20.00
38	Michael Young/100	20.00
43	Eric Chavez/50	20.00
45	Roy Oswalt/50	20.00
50	Mark Buehrle/50	25.00
57	Sean Casey/25	15.00
66	Travis Hafner/50	15.00
72	Torii Hunter/50	20.00
74	Paul Konerko/50	25.00
80	Justin Morneau/100	25.00
82	Jose Vidro/100	10.00
85	Craig Biggio/50	30.00
93	Magglio Ordonez/50	20.00
97	Preston Wilson/50	10.00
98	Shannon Stewart/50	10.00
107	Alfonso Soriano/50	30.00
110	Aubrey Huff/100	20.00
111	Adrian Beltre/25	20.00
112	Mark Teixeira/25	30.00
116	Carlos Beltran/25	30.00
121	Scott Rolen/25	30.00
123	Carlos Lee/100	15.00
124	Derek Lee/100	20.00
130	Garret Anderson/100	15.00
131	Austin Kearns/25	15.00
140	Vernon Wells/50	15.00
141	David Wright/50	70.00
143	David Ortiz/50	50.00
144	Victor Martinez/100	15.00
147	Angel Berroa/100	10.00

Monikers Material Button Gold
No Pricing
Production 1-5
Platinum: No Pricing
Production One Set

Monikers Material Jersey Number Silver

Production 1-75
Prime Platinum: No Pricing
Production One Set

		NM/M
9	Miguel Cabrera/50	35.00
10	Miguel Cabrera/50	35.00
13	Mark Prior/25	40.00
25	Ben Sheets/Pants/	20.00
33	Francisco Cordero/25	25.00
34	Aramis Ramirez/75	20.00
38	Michael Young/50	25.00
43	Eric Chavez/75	20.00
45	Roy Oswalt/75	25.00
57	Sean Casey/15	15.00
60	Francisco Rodriguez/75	25.00
66	Travis Hafner/50	20.00
70	Andruw Jones/25	40.00
85	Craig Biggio/25	30.00
89	Jacque Jones/25	15.00
90	Lyle Overbay/75	10.00
98	Shannon Stewart/75	10.00
99	Trot Nixon/50	35.00
101	Dontrelle Willis/24	30.00
107	Alfonso Soriano/50	30.00
112	Mark Teixeira/50	30.00
117	Bobby Abreu/75	20.00
121	Scott Rolen/25	30.00
124	Derrek Lee/25	25.00
128	Jim Edmonds/25	35.00
130	Garret Anderson/20	20.00
131	Austin Kearns/75	15.00
140	Vernon Wells/75	15.00
141	David Wright/75	70.00
143	David Ortiz/75	50.00
152	Victor Martinez/75	15.00
152	Ryne Sandberg/50	40.00
158	Duke Snider/50	40.00
159	Don Mattingly/50	60.00
160	Bob Gibson/50	30.00
163	Nolan Ryan/25	100.00
164	Stan Musial/25	80.00
166	Harmon Killebrew/50	35.00
167	Cal Ripken Jr./25	140.00

Monikers Material Jersey Prime Gold

Production 1-100
Platinum: No Pricing
Production One Set

		NM/M
9	Miguel Cabrera/50	40.00
10	Miguel Cabrera/50	40.00
13	Mark Prior/25	50.00
14	Mark Prior/25	50.00
25	Ben Sheets/50	25.00
34	Aramis Ramirez/100	25.00
38	Michael Young/25	25.00
43	Eric Chavez/75	25.00
45	Roy Oswalt/50	30.00
57	Sean Casey/30	20.00
60	Francisco Rodriguez/75	30.00
66	Travis Hafner/100	25.00
70	Andruw Jones/50	40.00
84	Josh Beckett/25	40.00
88	Barry Zito/25	30.00
89	Jacque Jones/50	15.00
98	Shannon Stewart/75	15.00
107	Alfonso Soriano/50	40.00
112	Mark Teixeira/20	50.00
117	Bobby Abreu/100	25.00
121	Scott Rolen/50	35.00
128	Jim Edmonds/25	40.00
130	Garret Anderson/25	25.00
131	Austin Kearns/75	20.00
140	Vernon Wells/50	20.00
152	Ryne Sandberg/75	75.00
159	Don Mattingly/50	85.00
160	Bob Gibson/50	50.00
163	Nolan Ryan/25	120.00
167	Cal Ripken Jr./25	175.00

Team Trademarks

Common Player: 3.00
Production 50 Sets
Foil: No Pricing
Production 10 Sets

		NM/M
1	Ryne Sandberg	8.00
2	George Brett	8.00
3	Steve Carlton	3.00
4	Reggie Jackson	4.00
5	Edgar Martinez	3.00
6	Barry Larkin	4.00
7	Ozzie Smith	6.00
8	Carlton Fisk	4.00
9	Wade Boggs	5.00
10	Will Clark	4.00
11	Nolan Ryan	8.00
12	Gary Carter	4.00
13	Don Mattingly	8.00
14	Willie Stargell	4.00
15	Don Sutton	3.00
16	Kirk Gibson	3.00
17	Kirby Puckett	4.00
18	Dale Murphy	4.00
19	Rickey Henderson	4.00
20	Willie Mays	8.00
21	Cal Ripken Jr.	10.00
22	Paul Molitor	4.00
23	Tony Gwynn	5.00
24	Andre Dawson	3.00
25	Bob Feller	4.00
26	Alan Trammell	3.00
27	Dave Parker	3.00
28	Dave Righetti	3.00
29	Dwight Gooden	3.00
30	Harold Baines	3.00
31	Jack Morris	3.00
32	John Kruk	3.00
33	Lee Smith	3.00
34	Lenny Dykstra	3.00
35	Luis Tiant	3.00
36	Matt Williams	3.00
37	Ron Guidry	3.00
38	Tony Oliva	3.00

Team Trademarks Jersey Number

Production 1-50

		NM/M
1	Ryne Sandberg/23	20.00
3	Steve Carlton/Pants/32	8.00
4	Reggie Jackson/44	10.00
6	Carlton Fisk/50	8.00
9	Wade Boggs/26	10.00
11	Nolan Ryan/Pants/34	25.00
20	Willie Mays/24	40.00

Team Trademarks Jersey Number Prime

		NM/M
1	Ryne Sandberg/50	25.00
2	George Brett/50	25.00
3	Steve Carlton/50	10.00
4	Reggie Jackson/50	15.00
5	Edgar Martinez/50	15.00
6	Barry Larkin/50	15.00
7	Ozzie Smith/50	20.00
8	Carlton Fisk/50	15.00
9	Wade Boggs/50	15.00
10	Will Clark/50	15.00
11	Nolan Ryan/50	25.00
12	Gary Carter/50	12.00
13	Don Mattingly/40	25.00
14	Willie Stargell/50	15.00
15	Don Sutton/25	12.00
16	Kirk Gibson/50	12.00
18	Dale Murphy/50	15.00
19	Rickey Henderson/50	15.00
21	Cal Ripken Jr./25	50.00
23	Tony Gwynn/50	20.00
24	Andre Dawson/25	15.00
26	Alan Trammell/25	12.00
27	Dave Parker/50	10.00
29	Dwight Gooden/50	15.00
30	Harold Baines/25	15.00
32	John Kruk/25	15.00
33	Lee Smith/47	15.00
34	Lenny Dykstra/25	15.00
38	Tony Oliva/26	15.00

Team Trademarks Signature

Production 5-50

		NM/M
1	Ryne Sandberg/25	50.00
3	Steve Carlton/25	25.00
4	Reggie Jackson/25	30.00
5	Edgar Martinez/50	20.00
6	Barry Larkin/50	20.00
7	Ozzie Smith/50	35.00
8	Carlton Fisk/50	25.00
9	Wade Boggs/50	35.00
10	Will Clark/50	25.00
11	Nolan Ryan/50	75.00
12	Gary Carter/50	15.00
13	Don Mattingly/50	50.00
15	Don Sutton/100	12.00
16	Kirk Gibson/50	20.00
17	Kirby Puckett/25	40.00
18	Dale Murphy/100	20.00
20	Willie Mays/5	160.00
21	Cal Ripken Jr./50	90.00
22	Paul Molitor/25	40.00
23	Tony Gwynn/50	40.00
24	Andre Dawson/100	15.00
25	Bob Feller/50	20.00
26	Alan Trammell/25	25.00
27	Dave Parker/50	15.00
28	Dave Righetti/25	20.00
29	Dwight Gooden/50	15.00
30	Harold Baines/50	15.00
31	Jack Morris/50	12.00
32	John Kruk/25	20.00
33	Lee Smith/50	15.00
34	Lenny Dykstra/25	15.00
35	Luis Tiant/50	15.00
36	Matt Williams/25	15.00
37	Ron Guidry/25	25.00
38	Tony Oliva/50	15.00

Team Trademarks Signature Jersey Number

Production 1-72

		NM/M
4	Reggie Jackson/44	50.00
8	Carlton Fisk/72	35.00
9	Wade Boggs/26	50.00
11	Nolan Ryan/	90.00
17	Kirby Puckett/34	60.00
27	Dave Parker/39	25.00
31	Jack Morris/47	20.00
35	Lee Smith/47	20.00
37	Ron Guidry/Pants/49	20.00

Team Trademarks Signature Jersey Number Prime

		NM/M
3	Steve Carlton/25	30.00
24	Andre Dawson/25	30.00
27	Dave Parker/39	20.00
31	Jack Morris/47	20.00
33	Lee Smith/47	25.00
38	Tony Oliva/26	35.00

Threads Button

No Pricing
Production 1-7

Threads Jersey Number

Production 1-50
Logo: No Pricing
Production One Set

		NM/M
152	Ryne Sandberg/50	15.00
154	Ted Williams/25	60.00
157	Whitey Ford/50	12.00
158	Duke Snider/25	15.00
164	Stan Musial/25	25.00
166	Harmon Killebrew/50	10.00

Threads Jersey Prime

Production 5-100

		NM/M
1	Roger Clemens/25	25.00
5	Todd Helton/100	10.00
7	Todd Helton/100	10.00
7	Vladimir Guerrero/100	12.00
8	Vladimir Guerrero/Jkt/30	20.00
10	Miguel Cabrera/100	10.00
12	Albert Pujols/50	30.00
13	Mark Prior/100	8.00
14	Mark Prior/100	10.00
15	Chipper Jones/100	10.00
16	Chipper Jones/100	10.00
17	Jeff Bagwell/100	8.00
18	Jeff Bagwell/100	8.00
19	Kerry Wood/100	5.00
22	Carl Crawford/100	5.00
23	Mariano Rivera/60	12.00
26	Melvin Mora/25	10.00
27	Corey Patterson/100	5.00
29	Rafael Furcal/100	5.00
30	Jim Thome/100	5.00
34	Aramis Ramirez/50	8.00
37	Javy Lopez/100	5.00
38	Michael Young/100	5.00
39	Ivan Rodriguez/100	8.00
42	Adam Dunn/100	5.00
43	Eric Chavez/100	5.00
45	Roy Oswalt/100	5.00
48	Johnny Damon/50	15.00
50	Mark Buehrle/50	8.00
55	Hank Blalock/100	5.00
56	Brad Radke/50	5.00
57	Sean Casey/50	5.00
58	Mike Lowell/100	5.00
60	Francisco Rodriguez/100	5.00
62	Greg Maddux/25	25.00
63	A.J. Burnett/75	5.00
66	Travis Hafner/100	5.00
68	Bret Boone/100	5.00
70	Andruw Jones/100	10.00
73	Torii Hunter/100	5.00
74	Paul Konerko/100	8.00
79	Lance Berkman/100	5.00
80	Justin Morneau/100	10.00
82	Jose Vidro/100	5.00
84	Josh Beckett/100	5.00
86	Luis Gonzalez/100	5.00
88	Barry Zito/100	5.00
91	Roy Halladay/100	5.00
94	Mike Sweeney/100	5.00
95	Rafael Palmeiro/100	5.00
97	Preston Wilson/100	5.00
98	Shannon Stewart/50	5.00
99	Trot Nixon/25	8.00
100	Mike Piazza/100	12.00
101	Dontrelle Willis/100	8.00
103	Andy Pettitte/50	10.00
104	Kazuo Matsui/100	5.00
107	Alfonso Soriano/100	8.00
110	Aubrey Huff/100	5.00
111	Adrian Beltre/50	5.00
112	Mark Teixeira/60	10.00
114	Miguel Tejada/100	8.00
117	Bobby Abreu/100	5.00
119	Manny Ramirez/60	15.00
121	Scott Rolen/100	10.00
124	Derrek Lee/50	10.00
127	John Smoltz/100	8.00
128	Jim Edmonds/100	8.00
130	Garret Anderson/60	8.00
131	Austin Kearns/100	5.00
138	Mike Mussina/50	10.00
140	Vernon Wells/100	5.00
141	David Wright/100	25.00
142	Marcus Giles/100	5.00
144	Victor Martinez/75	20.00
145	Hideki Matsui/100	40.00
146	C.C. Sabathia/100	5.00
150	Jorge Posada/100	10.00
152	Ryne Sandberg/50	25.00
153	Rickey Henderson/25	20.00
159	George Brett/50	25.00
159	Don Mattingly/50	25.00
160	Bob Gibson/25	20.00
161	Hank Aaron/25	75.00
163	Nolan Ryan/100	30.00
167	Cal Ripken Jr./100	30.00
169	Roger Clemens/50	20.00
170	Curt Schilling/100	8.00
171	Rafael Palmeiro/100	5.00
173	Mike Piazza/100	12.00
174	Greg Maddux/100	15.00
175	Sammy Sosa/100	15.00

Timber Barrel

No Pricing
Production 1-3

TNT

Production 1-50
Prime: .50X-1.5X
Production 5-100

		NM/M
7	Vladimir Guerrero/Bat-Jsy/30	15.00
10	Miguel Cabrera/Bat-Jsy/	12.00
11	Albert Pujols/Bat-Jsy/25	25.00
12	Albert Pujols/Bat-Jsy/25	25.00
13	Mark Prior/Bat-Jsy/50	8.00
14	Mark Prior/Bat-Jsy/50	8.00
15	Chipper Jones/Bat-Jsy/	12.00
16	Chipper Jones/Bat-Jsy/50	12.00
39	Ivan Rodriguez/Bat-Jsy/	12.00
42	Adam Dunn/Bat-Jsy/	5.00
62	Greg Maddux/Bat-Jsy/25	20.00
100	Mike Piazza/Bat-Jsy/	12.00
107	Alfonso Soriano/Bat-Jsy/50	12.00
112	Mark Teixeira/Bat-Jsy/	10.00
119	Manny Ramirez/Bat-Jsy/	12.00
121	Scott Rolen/Bat-Jsy/50	10.00
124	Derrek Lee/Bat-Jsy/50	8.00
143	David Ortiz/Bat-Jsy/50	15.00
151	Willie Mays/Bat-Jsy/25	50.00
153	Rickey Henderson/Bat-Jsy/25	15.00
154	Ted Williams/Bat-Jsy/50	85.00
159	Don Mattingly/Bat-Jsy/50	20.00
161	Hank Aaron/Bat-Jsy/50	50.00
163	Nolan Ryan/Bat-Jsy/25	25.00
164	Stan Musial/Bat-Jsy/25	30.00
166	Harmon Killebrew/Bat-Jsy/25	20.00
167	Cal Ripken Jr./Bat-Jsy/	30.00
169	Roger Clemens/Bat-Jsy/25	15.00
171	Rafael Palmeiro/Bat-Jsy/50	10.00
172	Randy Johnson/Bat-Jsy/25	15.00
174	Greg Maddux/Bat-Jsy/50	15.00
175	Sammy Sosa/Bat-Jsy/50	15.00

1996 Legends of the Negro Leagues Playing Cards

This set of playing cards depicting ballplayers of the pre-integration Negro Leagues was issued as a fundraiser by the International Society of Athletes in conjunction with a reunion of the players. In standard playing card finish and round-corner format; the cards have black-and-white photos at center.

Backs are in black with gold printing. Size is 2-1/2" x 3-1/2". The deck's queens feature notable females of the Negro Leagues and the sponsor.

		NM/M
	Complete Set (56):	10.00
	Common Player:	.15
AS	Satchel Paige	1.00
2S	James "Joe" Greene	.15
3S	James "Red" Moore	.15
4S	Othello "Chico" Renfroe	.15
5S	William "Judy" Johnson	.25
6S	Willie "The Devil" Wells	.25
7S	Gene Benson	.15
8S	Willard "Sunnie" Brown	.25
9S	Martin Dihigo	.25
10S	Don Newcombe	.25
JS	Ray "Hooks" Dandridge	.25
QS	Billie Harden	.15
KS	Roy "Campy" Campanella	.75
AD	Jack "Jackie" Robinson	2.00
2D	Sam Haynes	.15
3D	Bob "The Rope" Boyd	.15
4D	William "Bonnie" Serrell	.15
5D	Orestes "Minnie" Minoso	.20
6D	Pop Lloyd	.25
7D	Art "Superman" Pennington	.15
8D	Francisco "Pancho" Coimbre	.15
9D	Sam "Jet" Jethroe	.20
10D	Joe Black	.25
JD	Monte Irvin	.25
QD	Effa "Effie" Manley	.25
KD	Henry "Hank" Aaron	1.50
AC	Joshua "Josh" Gibson	1.50
2C	William "Bill" Cash	.15
3C	Francis "Fran" Matthews	.15
4C	Fred "Leap" Bankhead	.15
5C	Alex Radcliffe	.15
6C	Authur "Artie" Wilson (Arthur)	.15
7C	James "Jim" Zapp	.15
8C	Henry "Kimmie" Kimbro	.15
9C	Chester "Chet" Brewer	.15
10C	Verdell "Lefty" Mathis	.15
JC	James "Junior" Gilliam	.25
QC	Marcenia "Toni" Stone	.15
KC	Willie Mays	1.50
AH	James "Cool Papa" Bell	.75
2H	Samuel "Harriston" Hairston	.20
3H	John "Buck" O'Neil	.25
4H	Lorenzo "Piper" Davis	.15
5H	Parnell Woods	.15
6H	Thomas "Pee Wee" Butts	.15
7H	Oscar Charleston	.25
8H	Lawrence "Larry" Doby	1.00
9H	Hilton Smith	.25
10H	Leon Day	.25
JH	Walter "Buck" Leonard	.25
QH	Pamela Pryor-Fuller	.15
KH	Ernest "Ernie" Banks	.75
---	Joker (Ted "Double Duty" Radcliffe)	.25
---	Super Joker (Andrew "Rube" Foster)	.25
---	Wilmer "Red" Fields	.15
---	Clifford "Connie" Johnson	.15

2001 Legends European Tour

This two-play, four-card set was issued in conjunction with the 8th annual Baseball Legends European Tour which made a goodwill swing through 11 military bases in Germany in June. Cards feature borderless vintage color photos on front. Team logos have been airbrushed away. A Legends tour logo appears in one corner. Backs have career stats and highlights and some of the tour sponsor's logos. The cards were given away at autograph sessions, baseball clinics, softball games and other events.

		NM/M
	Complete Set (4):	10.00
	Common Player:	2.00
(1)	Vida Blue/Green Jsy	3.00
(2)	Vida Blue/Yellow Jsy	3.00
(3)	Manny Sanguillen/Btg	2.00
(4)	Manny Sanguillen/Catching	2.00

1998 Lemon Chill Chicago White Sox

In standard 2-1/2" x 3-1/2" format, this team set was a stadium giveaway. Fronts feature game-action photos with a stylized flame-like effect at left and bottom. The team logo is at lower-left, with the player name at bottom right. Backs have player personal data, stats, career highlights and a large sponsor's logo. The cards are checklisted here in alphabetical order.

		NM/M
	Complete Set (30):	12.00
	Common Player:	.50
(1)	Jeff Abbott	.50
(2)	Mark Anderson/Trainer, Steve Odgers/Strength Coach), Mark Salas, Herm Schneider/Trainer	
(3)	James Baldwin	.50
(4)	Albert Belle	.50
(5)	Mike Cameron	.50
(6)	Mike Caruso	.50
(7)	Carlos Castillo	.50
(8)	Nardi Contreras, Von Joshua	
(9)	Wil Cordero	.50
(10)	Ray Durham	.50
(11)	Scott Eyre	.50
(12)	Keith Foulke	.50
(13)	Bob Howry	.50
(14)	Wallace Johnson, Bryan Little	.50
(15)	Matt Karchner	.50
(16)	Chad Kreuter	.50
(17)	Art Kusnyer, Joe Nossek	.50
(18)	Jerry Manuel	.50
(19)	Jaime Navarro	.50
(20)	Greg Norton	.50
(21)	Charlie O'Brien	.50
(22)	Magglio Ordonez	2.00
(23)	Jim Parque	.50
(24)	Bill Simas	.50
(25)	Mike Sirotka	.50
(26)	Chris Snopek	.50
(27)	John Snyder	.50
(28)	Frank Thomas	4.00
(29)	Robin Ventura	.50
(30)	Bryan Ward	.50

1999 Lemon Chill Chicago White Sox

In standard 2-1/2" x 3-1/2" format, this team set was a stadium giveaway. Fronts feature game-action photos on a borderless ghost-photo background with the team motto, "The Kids Can Play" and logo at lower-left, with the player name at top-left in red. Backs have a red duotone photo, '98 stats, uniform and card numbers and a large sponsor's logo. A five-card 1959 World Series commemorative subset was also included.

		NM/M
Complete Set (33):		10.00
Common Player:		.25
1	Brook Fordyce	.25
2	Carlos Lee	.50
3	Greg Norton	.25
4	John Snyder	.25
5	Craig Wilson	.25
6	Chris Singleton	.25
7	Liu Rodriguez	.25
8	Magglio Ordonez	1.00
9	Mike Sirotka	.25
10	Jaime Navarro	.25
11	Mark Johnson	.25
12	Jim Parque	.25
13	Jeff Liefer	.25
14	Mike Caruso	.25
15	Ray Durham	.25
16		.25
17	Bob Howry	.25
18	James Baldwin	.25
19	Jerry Manuel	.25
20	Bill Simas	.25
21	Frank Thomas	2.00
22	Bryan Ward	.25
23	Scott Eyre	.25
24	Paul Konerko	1.00
25	Sean Lowe	.25
26	Keith Foulke	.25
---	Von Joshua, Nardi Contreras	.25
---	Joe Nossek, Art Kusnyer	.25
---	Herm Schneider Trainer, Steve Odgers/Conditioning, Mark Salas/Bullpen, Mark Anderson/Trainer	.25
1 of 5	1959 World Series Recap	.25
2 of 5	Billy Pierce	.25
3 of 5	Jim Landis	.25
4 of 5	Al Smith	.25
5 of 5	Al Lopez	.25

2000 Lemon Chill Chicago White Sox

The first 20,000 fans through the gates of Comiskey Park on July 16 received this team set. On front a color action photo stands out from the black-and-white background and is vignetted with black borders. The player name is in purple at bottom. A black-and-white portrait photo is featured on back along with player data, 1999 stats and the sponsor's logo.

	NM/M
Complete Set (31):	10.00

Common Player:		.35
1	James Baldwin	.35
2	Herbert Perry	.35
3	Keith Foulke	.35
4	Tony Graffanino	.35
5	Kip Wells	.35
6	Mark Johnson	.35
7	Chris Singleton	.35
8	Ray Durham	.35
9	Jose-Valentin	.35
10	Kevin Beirne	.35
11	Paul Konerko	1.00
12	Greg Norton	.35
13	Bill Simas	.35
14	Jeff Abbott	.35
15	Frank Thomas	3.00
16	Mike Sirotka	.35
17	Brook Fordyce	.35
18	Cal Eldred	.35
19	Bob Howry	.35
20	Jerry Manuel	.35
21	Kelly Wunsch	.35
22	Bryan Little, Wallace Johnson	.35
23	Joe Nossek, Art Kusnyer	.35
24	Jim Parque	.35
25	Carlos Lee	.50
26	Von Joshua, Nardi Contreras	.35
27	Sean Lowe	.35
28	Magglio Ordonez	1.00
29	Jesus Pena	.35
30	Craig Wilson	.35
31	Mark Anderson, Herm Schneider, Man Soo Lee, Steve Odgers	.35

1989 Lennox/HSE Astros

Formatted similar to a police/fire safety set, this Astros team issue is sponsored instead by a furnace company and the team's cable TV outlet. Cards measure 2-5/8" x 4-1/8" and feature portrait photos on front with orange and black team color pinstripes. Backs have biographical data, career summary and sponsors' logos.

		NM/M
Complete Set (26):		10.00
Common Player:		.25
1	Billy Hatcher	.25
2	Greg Gross	.25
3	Rick Rhoden	.25
4	Mike Scott	.25
5	Kevin Bass	.25
6	Alex Trevino	.25
7	Jim Clancy	.25
8	Bill Doran	.25
9	Dan Schatzeder	.25
10	Bob Knepper	.25
11	Jim Deshaies	.25
12	Eric Yelding	.25
13	Danny Darwin	.25
14	Coaches	.25
15	Craig Reynolds	.25
16	Rafael Ramirez	.25
17	Juan Agosto	.25
18	Larry Andersen	.25
19	Dave Smith	.25
20	Gerald Young	.25
21	Ken Caminiti	.50
22	Terry Puhl	.25
23	Bob Forsch	.25
24	Craig Biggio	6.00
25	Art Howe	.25
26	Glenn Davis	.25

1990 Lennox/HSE Astros

For a second straight year Lennox, the furnace people, and HSE, the Astros cable TV outlet, sponsored a team set in an oversize (3-1/2" x 5") format on thin, semi-gloss stock. Fronts

---

Ken Oberkfell   #10 - Infielder

feature color player portrait photos, backs have a few biographical notes and logos for all parties. Cards are checklisted here by uniform numbers which appear on front and back.

		NM/M
Complete Set (29):		15.00
Common Player:		.50
4	Casey Candaele	.50
6	David Rohde	.50
7	Craig Biggio	5.00
9	Alex Trevino	.50
10	Ken Oberkfell	.50
11	Ken Caminiti	.50
12	Glenn Wilson	.50
13	Gerald Young	.50
15	Eric Yelding	.50
16	Rafael Ramirez	.50
18	Art Howe	.50
19	Bill Doran	.50
20	Dan Schatzeder	.50
21	Terry Puhl	.50
22	Mark Davidson	.50
23	Eric Anthony	.50
24	Franklin Stubbs	.50
27	Glenn Davis	.50
31	Xavier Hernandez	.50
33	Mike Scott	.50
36	Bill Gullickson	.50
38	Jim Clancy	.50
39	Jose Cano	.50
43	Jim Deshaies	.50
44	Danny Darwin	.50
45	Dave Smith	.50
47	Larry Andersen	.50
49	Juan Agosto	.50
51	Mark Portugal	.50

1990 Ron Lewis 1961 N.Y. Yankees

The World's Champion 1961 N.Y. Yankees are featured in this set of cards by sports artist Ron Lewis. The 42-card set contains cards of individual players, coaches and the manager, plus a team picture. The 3-1/2" x 5-1/2" cards were sold only in a complete boxed set edition of 10,000. Cards have oil painted portraits of the players set against a blue background. The card borders are pinstriped in dark blue. At bottom is a blank panel for autographing. Backs are printed in red and blue and have personal data, career summary, 1961 and career stats.

		NM/M
Complete Boxed Set (42):		10.00
Common Player:		.50
1	1961 N.Y. Yankees Team	3.00
2	Bobby Richardson	.75
3	Roger Maris	2.00
4	Elston Howard	.75
5	Bill Skowron	.60
6	Clete Boyer	.50

7	Mickey Mantle	4.00
8	Yogi Berra	1.00
9	Johnny Blanchard	.50
10	Hector Lopez	.50
11	Whitey Ford	1.00
12	Ralph Terry	.50
13	Bill Stafford	.50
14	Bud Daley	.50
15	Billy Gardner	.50
16	Jim Coates	.50
17	Luis Arroyo	.50
18	Tex Clevenger	.50
19	Bob Cerv	.50
20	Art Ditmar	.50
21	Bob Turley	.50
22	Joe DeMaestri	.50
23	Rollie Sheldon	.50
24	Earl Torgeson	.50
25	Hal Reniff	.50
26	Ralph Houk	.50
27	Johnny James	.50
28	Bob Hale	.50
29	Danny McDevitt	.50
30	Duke Maas	.50
31	Jim Hegan	.50
32	Wally Moses	.50
33	Frank Crosetti	.50
34	Lee Thomas	.50
35	Al Downing	.50
36	Jack Reed	.50
37	Ryne Duren	.50
38	Tom Tresh	.50
39	Johnny Sain	.50
40	Jesse Gonder	.50
41	Deron Johnson	.50
42	Tony Kubek	.60

1991 Ron Lewis Negro Leagues Postcards

Willie Mays

The 1991 Negro League Living Legends Postcard Set features paintings by artist Ron Lewis. Cards measure 3-1/2" x 5-1/2" and are stamped with a number within the 10,000 sets produced. Between each player's image and the player's name at the bottom of the card, is ample space for an autograph. The set, originally sold for $27, was created as a fund raiser for the Negro League Baseball Players Association. Two hundred uncut sheets were offered at $100 each.

		NM/M
Complete Set (30):		30.00
Common Player:		.75
1	George Giles	.75
2	Bill Cash	.75
3	Bob Harvey	.75
4	Lyman Bostock Sr.	.90
5	Ray Dandridge	2.50
6	Leon Day	2.00
7	Verdell "Lefty" Mathis	.75
8	Jimmie Crutchfield	.75
9	Clyde McNeal	.75
10	Bill Wright	.75
11	Mahlon Duckett	.75
12	William "Bobby" Robinson	.75
13	Max Manning	.75
14	Armando Vazquez	.75
15	Jehosie Heard	.75
16	Quincy Trouppe	.90
17	Wilmer Fields	.75
18	Lonnie Blair	.75
19	Garnett Blair	.75
20	Monte Irvin	2.50
21	Willie Mays	7.50
22	Buck Leonard	4.00
23	Frank Evans	.75
24	Josh Gibson Jr.	5.00
25	Ted "Double Duty" Radcliffe	1.50
26	Josh Johnson	.75
27	Gene Benson	.75
28	Lester Lockett	.75
29	Cowan "Bubba" Hyde	.75
30	Rufus Lewis	.75

1994 Ron Lewis Negro Leagues Postcards

BUCK O'NEILL

A second series of postcards honoring players of the Negro Leagues was produced by artist Ron Lewis in September 1994. In this set, more emphasis was placed on multi-player cards. Many of the cards also feature detailed backgrounds of street scenes with vintage vehicles, old-time stadiums, etc. Cards measure 3-1/2" x 5-1/2" and have a wide front border with the player(s) name printed at bottom and space above for autographing. Postcard backs are printed in black and include a few career stats, a card number and the card's position among the limited edition of 10,000.

		NM/M
Complete Set (32):		25.00
Common Card:		1.00
1	Willie Mays, Ernie Banks, Hank Aaron	4.00
1p	2-1/2"	2.00
2	Bill Wright, Lester Lockett, Lyman Bostock, Sr.	1.00
3	Josh Gibson, Josh Gibson Jr., Buck Leonard	2.50
4	Max Manning, Monte Irvin, Leon Day	1.50
5	Armando Vazquez, Minnie Minoso, Martin Dihigo	1.50
6	Ted "Double Duty" Radcliffe	1.50
7	Bill Owens, Turkey Stearnes, Bobby Robinson	1.00
8	Wilmer Fields, Edsall Walker, Josh Johnson	1.00
9	Artie Wilson, Lionel Hampton	1.50
10	Earl Taborn	1.00
11	Barney "Bonnie" Serrell	1.00
12	Rodolfo "Rudy" Fernandez	1.00
13	Willie Pope	1.00
14	Ray Noble	1.00
15	Jim "Fireball" Cohen	1.00
16	Henry Kimbro	1.00
17	Charlie Biot	1.00
18	Al Wilmore	1.00
19	Sam Jethroe	1.50
20	Tommy Sampson	1.00
21	Charlie Rivera	1.00
22	Claro Duany	1.00
23	Russell Awkard	1.00
24	Art "Superman" Pennington	1.00
25	Wilmer Harris	1.00
26	Napoleon "Nap" Gulley	1.00
27	Emilio Navarro	1.00
28	Andy Porter	1.00
29	Willie Grace	1.00
30	Red Moore	1.00
31	Buck O'Neill	2.00
32	Stanley Glenn	1.00

1996 Liberty Satellite Sports

This business-to-business promotion for a cable sports network content provider features on card fronts the logo of different cable networks. Space on back is shared by player data and stats and information about a local cable network.

	NM/M
Complete Set (21):	125.00

Common Player:		2.00
1	Cal Ripken Jr.	40.00
2	Paul O'Neill	2.00
3	Mo Vaughn	2.00
4	Travis Fryman	2.00
5	Brian Jordan	2.00
6	Ken Griffey Jr.	20.00
7	Craig Biggio	2.00
8	Chili Davis	2.00
9	Greg Maddux	15.00
10	Gary Sheffield	4.00
11	Frank Thomas	10.00
12	Barry Larkin	2.00
13	John Franco	2.00
14	Albert Belle	2.00
15	Mark McGwire	20.00
16	Barry Bonds	40.00
17	Lenny Dykstra	2.00
(18)	Mickey Lopez	2.00
(19)	Tim Salmon	2.00
(20)	Matt Williams	2.00
(21)	Header Card	.35

1992 Lime Rock Griffey Baseball Holograms

This set of three hologram cards features the Griffey family of pro players. Each card carries a "GRIFFEY BASEBALL" headline at top, with a large central action photo of one of the family and his facsimile autograph. The backs have a color photo, career highlights and stats. The cards were issued in several different versions as noted below.

		NM/M
Complete Set, Silver Holograms (3):		3.00
Complete Set, Gold Holograms (3):		10.00
Complete Set, Autographed (3):		35.00
Complete Set, Blank-backed Promos (3):		6.00
Three-card strip, edition of 5,000:		6.50
1	Ken Griffey Sr. (Silver hologram, edition of 250,000.)	.50
1	Ken Griffey Sr. (Gold hologram, edition of 1,000.)	1.50
1	Ken Griffey Sr. (Autographed edition of 2,500.)	5.00
1	Ken Griffey Sr. (Blank-back promo, edition of 750.)	1.50
2	Ken Griffey Jr./Silver	2.50
2	Ken Griffey Jr./Gold	9.00
2	Ken Griffey Jr./Auto.	30.00
2	Ken Griffey Jr./Promo	3.00
3	Craig Griffey/Silver	.50
3	Craig Griffey/Gold	2.00
3	Craig Griffey/Auto.	2.00
3	Craig Griffey/Promo	1.50

1991 Line Drive

This set of "old-timers" includes many Hall of Famers, as well as stars who had

ROBERTO CLEMENTE

played into the late 1980s. In standard 2-1/2" x 3-1/2", the cards have color or sepia photos framed in blue and bordered in white. Horizontal backs have biographical and career notes and stats.

		NM/M
Complete Set (50):		6.00
Common Player:		.10
1	Don Drysdale	.25
2	Joe Torre	.15
3	Bob Gibson	.25
4	Bobby Richardson	.25
5	Ron Santo	.25
6	Eric Soderholm	.10
7	Yogi Berra	.35
8	Steve Garvey	.15
9	Steve Carlton	.25
10	Toby Harrah	.10
11	Luis Tiant	.10
12	Earl Weaver	.10
13	Bill Mazeroski	.25
14	Don Baylor	.10
15	Lew Burdette	.10
16	Jim Lonborg	.10
17	Jerry Grote	.10
18	Ernie Banks	.35
19	Doug DeCinces	.10
20	Jimmy Piersall	.10
21	Ken Holtzman	.10
22	Manny Mota	.10
23	Alvin Dark	.10
24	Lou Brock	.25
25	Ralph Houk	.15
26	Graig Nettles	.15
27	Bill White	.10
28	Billy Williams	.25
29	Willie Horton	.10
30	Tommie Agee	.10
31	Rico Petrocelli	.10
32	Julio Cruz	.10
33	Robin Roberts	.25
34	Dave Johnson	.10
35	Wilbur Wood	.10
36	Cesar Cedeno	.10
37	George Foster	.10
38	Thurman Munson	.25
39	Roberto Clemente	2.00
40	Eddie Mathews	.25
41	Harmon Killebrew	.25
42	Monte Irvin	.25
43	Bob Feller	2.00
44	Jimmie Foxx	1.00
45	Walter Johnson	1.00
46	Casey Stengel	.25
47	Satchel Paige	1.00
48	Ty Cobb	2.00
49	Mickey Cochrane	.25
50	Dizzy Dean	.35

Mickey Mantle

Mickey Mantle

This 20-card set was part of a collector's kit featuring the Yankees superstar. Fronts of the 2-1/2" x 3-1/2" cards have sepia or color poses or action photos. The player's name appears in white in a blue panel at bottom. Red striping seperates the graphics from the white border. The Line Drive logo appears in an upper corner. Backs are printed in red

and blue and feature a facsimile autograph, a few sentences about Mantle's career, manufacturer's and licensor's logos, and a card number. The same basic cards were included in a Collectors Marketing Corp. (see CMC) in 1989, lacking the Line Drive logo on front and the Impel logo and 1991 dates on back.

		NM/M
Complete Set (20):		15.00
Common Card:		2.00
1-20	Mickey Mantle	2.00

Don Mattingly

Don Mattingly

This 20-card set was part of a collectors kit featuring the Yankees' star. Fronts of the 2-1/2" x 3-1/2" cards have color poses or action photos. The player's name appears in white in a blue panel at bottom along with the Line Drive logo in red and white. Backs are printed in red and blue and feature a facsimile autograph, a few sentences about Mattingly's career, manufacturer's and licensor's logos, and a card number.

		NM/M
Complete Set (20):		3.00
Common Card:		.15
1-20	Don Mattingly	.25

Ryne Sandberg

RYNE SANDBERG

This 20-card set was part of a collectors kit featuring the Cubs Hall of Fame second baseman. Fronts of the 2-1/2" x 3-1/2" cards have color poses or action photos. The player's name appears in blue and red in the white border above the photo. Backs are printed in red and blue and feature a few sentences about Sandberg's career, along with manufacturer's and licensor's logos, and a card number.

		NM/M
Complete Set (20):		10.00
Common Card:		.50
1-20	Ryne Sandberg	.50

1986 Lite Beer Astros

This regional set of the Houston Astros was sponsored by Lite Beer and given away in a special stadium promotion. The 4-1/2" x 6-3/4" cards feature full-color photos surrounded by a wide, white border. Diagonal

Bill Doran

color bands of yellow, orange, red and purple extend throught the upper-right and lower-left corners of the card, which also displays the Astros' 25th Anniversary logo and the Lite Beer logo in opposite corners. The backs include player information and statistics.

		NM/M
Complete Set (22):		25.00
Common Player:		1.00
3	Phil Garner	1.00
6	Mark Bailey	1.00
10	Dickie Thon	1.00
11	Frank DiPino	1.00
12	Craig Reynolds	1.00
14	Alan Ashby	1.00
17	Kevin Bass	1.00
19	Bill Doran	1.00
20	Jim Pankovits	1.00
21	Terry Puhl	1.00
22	Hal Lanier	1.00
25	Jose Cruz	1.00
27	Glenn Davis	1.00
28	Billy Hatcher	1.00
29	Denny Walling	1.00
33	Mike Scott	1.00
34	Nolan Ryan	15.00
37	Charlie Kerfeld	1.00
39	Bob Knepper	1.00
43	Jim Deshaies	1.00
45	Dave Smith	1.00
53	Mike Madden	1.00

Rangers

#5 PETE INCAVIGLIA
Outfielder

This postcard-size (approximately 4" x 6") set of Texas Rangers cards was sponsored by Lite Beer and was available by mail directly from the team. Fronts feature full-color photos surrounded by a wide, white border with the player's name, uniform number and postion appearing below. The Rangers logo is displayed in the lower-left corner, while the Lite Beer logo is in the lower-right. Backs offer personal information and stats.

		NM/M
Complete Set (28):		20.00
Common Player:		1.00
0	Oddibe McDowell	1.00
1	Scott Fletcher	1.00
2	Bobby Valentine	1.00
4	Don Slaught	1.00
5	Pete Incaviglia	2.00
9	Pete O'Brien	1.00
10	Art Howe	1.00
11	Toby Harrah	1.00
12	Geno Petralli	1.00
13	Joe Ferguson	1.00
14	Tim Foli	1.00
15	Larry Parrish	1.00
16	Mike Mason	1.00
17	Darrell Porter	1.00
18	Ed Correa	1.00
19	Curtis Wilkerson	1.00
22	Steve Buechele	1.00

23	Jose Guzman	1.00
24	Ricky Wright	1.00
27	Greg Harris	1.00
31	Tom Robson	1.00
32	Gary Ward	1.00
35	Tom House	1.00
44	Tom Paciorek	1.00
45	Dwayne Henry	1.00
48	Bobby Witt	1.00
49	Charlie Hough	1.00
---	Arlington Stadium	1.00

1994 Lite Beer Milwaukee Brewers

PAUL MOLITOR

The 1994 baseball strike interrupted the issue of this four-series commemorative set advertised as including "Every Player in the Brewers Twenty-Five Year History." The set was produced in four booklets of 94 cards each. Individual 2-1/2" x 3-1/2" cards were perforated for easy detachment from the 13" x 7" booklets. Cards feature black-and-white player photos against a gold border. A blue, green and gold Brewers 25th anniversary logo is in the upper-left corner on front. Half of the cards (Series I, II) have a Lite beer logo at top, while half (Series III, IV) have a Miller Genuine Draft logo. Backs are in black-and-white and include a few biographical bits, a line of career stats, the years played with the Brewers and team and brewery logos. Books I and II were issued as planned to adults attending the April 24 and June 26, 1994 games. The Series IV book, containing 10 special cards honoring the Brewers 25th Anniversary Team, was given away at a June, 1995, game and Book III was distributed in August of 1995. Individual cards are unnumbered and are presented here in alphabetical order within series. Cards of Bobby Clark, Tom Edens, Ken McMullen and Danny Walton, which appear in Series I or III are repeated in Series IV.

		NM/M
Complete Set, Booklets (4):		30.00
Complete Set, Singles		
(376):		24.00
Common Player:		.10
Series I		
	Complete book:	10.00
(1)	Hank Aaron	5.00
(2)	Jim Adduci	.10
(3)	Jay Aldrich	.10
(4)	Andy Allanson	.10
(5)	Dave Baldwin	.10
(6)	Sal Bando	.10
(7)	Len Barker	.10
(8)	Kevin Bass	.10
(9)	Ken Berry	.10
(10)	George Canale	.10
(11)	Tom Candiotti	.10
(12)	Mike Capel	.10
(13)	Bobby Darwin	.10
(14)	Danny Darwin	.10
(15)	Brock Davis	.10
(16)	Dick Davis	.10
(17)	Jamie Easterley	.10
(18)	Tom Edens	.10
(19)	Marshall Edwards	.10
(20)	Cal Eldred	.10
(21)	Bob Ellis	.10
(22)	Ed Farmer	.10
(23)	Mike Felder	.10
(24)	John Felske	.10
(25)	Mike Ferraro	.10

(26)	Mike Fetters	.10
(27)	Danny Frisella	.10
(28)	Bob Galasso	.10
(29)	Jim Gantner	.10
(30)	Pedro Garcia	.10
(31)	Bob Gardner	.10
(32)	John Gelnar	.10
(33)	Moose Haas	.10
(34)	Darryl Hamilton	.10
(35)	Larry Haney	.10
(36)	Jim Hannan	.10
(37)	Bob Hansen	.10
(38)	Mike Ignasiak	.10
(39)	John Jaha	.10
(40)	Dion James	.10
(41)	Deron Johnson	.10
(42)	John Henry Johnson	.10
(43)	Tim Johnson	.10
(44)	Rickey Keeton	.10
(45)	John Kennedy	.10
(46)	Jim Kern	.10
(47)	Pete Ladd	.10
(48)	Joe Lahoud	.10
(49)	Tom Lampkin	.10
(50)	Dave LaPoint	.10
(51)	George Lauzerique	.10
(52)	Julio Machado	.10
(53)	Alex Madrid	.10
(54)	Candy Maldonado	.10
(55)	Carlos Maldonado	.10
(56)	Rick Manning	.10
(57)	Jaime Navarro	.10
(58)	Ray Newman	.10
(59)	Juan Nieves	.10
(60)	Dave Nilsson	.10
(61)	Charlie O'Brien	.10
(62)	Syd O'Brien	.10
(63)	John O'Donoghue	.10
(64)	Jim Paciorek	.10
(65)	Dave Parker	.10
(66)	Bill Parsons	.10
(67)	Marty Pattin	.10
(68)	Jamie Quirk	.10
(69)	Willie Randolph	.10
(70)	Paul Ratliff	.10
(71)	Lance Rautzhan	.10
(72)	Randy Ready	.10
(73)	Ray Sadecki	.10
(74)	Lenn Sakata	.10
(75)	Ken Sanders	.10
(76)	Ted Savage	.10
(77)	Dick Schofield	.10
(78)	Jim Tatum	.10
(79)	Chuck Taylor	.10
(80)	Tom Tellmann	.10
(81)	Frank Tepedino	.10
(82)	Sandy Valdespino	.10
(83)	Jose Valentin	.10
(84)	Greg Vaughn	.10
(85)	Carlos Velazquez	.10
(86)	Rick Waits	.10
(87)	Danny Walton	.10
(88)	Floyd Weaver	.10
(89)	Bill Wegman	.10
(90)	Floyd Wicker	.10
(91)	Al Yates	.10
(92)	Ned Yost	.10
(93)	Mike Young	.10
(94)	Robin Yount	3.00
Series II		
	Complete book:	8.00
(95)	Hank Allen	.10
(96)	Felipe Alou	.25
(97)	Max Alvis	.10
(98)	Larry Anderson	.10
(99)	Rick Auerbach	.10
(100)	Don August	.10
(101)	Billy Bates	.10
(102)	Gary Beare	.10
(103)	Larry Bearnarth	.10
(104)	Andy Beene	.10
(105)	Jerry Bell	.10
(106)	Juan Bell	.10
(107)	Dwight Bernard	.10
(108)	Bernie Carbo	.10
(109)	Jose Cardenal	.10
(110)	Matias Carrillo	.10
(111)	Juan Castillo	.10
(112)	Bill Castro	.10
(113)	Rick Cerone	.10
(114)	Rob Deer	.10
(115)	Rick Dempsey	.10
(116)	Alex Diaz	.10
(117)	Dick Ellsworth	.10
(118)	Narciso Elvira	.10
(119)	Tom Filer	.10
(120)	Rollie Fingers	.75
(121)	Scott Fletcher	.10
(122)	John Flinn	.10
(123)	Rich Folkers	.10
(124)	Tony Fossas	.10
(125)	Chris George	.10
(126)	Bob L. Gibson	.10
(127)	Gus Gil	.10
(128)	Tommy Harper	.10
(129)	Vic Harris	.10
(130)	Paul Hartzell	.10
(131)	Tom Hausman	.10
(132)	Neal Heaton	.10
(133)	Mike Hegan	.10
(134)	Jack Heidemann	.10
(135)	Doug Jones	.10
(136)	Mark Kiefer	.10
(137)	Steve Kiefer	.10
(138)	Ed Kirkpatrick	.10
(139)	Joe Kmak	.10
(140)	Mark Knudson	.10
(141)	Kevin Kobel	.10

(142)	Pete Koegel	.10
(143)	Jack Lazorko	.10
(144)	Tim Leary	.10
(145)	Mark Lee	.10
(146)	Jeffrey Leonard	.10
(147)	Randy Lerch	.10
(148)	Brad Lesley	.10
(149)	Sixto Lezcano	.10
(150)	Josias Manzanillo	.10
(151)	Buck Martinez	.10
(152)	Tom Matchick	.10
(153)	Davey May	.10
(154)	Matt Maysey	.10
(155)	Bob McClure	.10
(156)	Tim McIntosh	.10
(157)	Tim Nordbrook	.10
(158)	Ben Oglivie	.10
(159)	Jim Olander	.10
(160)	Troy O'Leary	.10
(161)	Roberto Pena	.10
(162)	Jeff Peterek	.10
(163)	Ray Peters	.10
(164)	Rob Picciolo	.10
(165)	John Poff	.10
(166)	Gus Polidor	.10
(167)	Dan Plesac	.10
(168)	Kevin Reimer	.10
(169)	Andy Replogle	.10
(170)	Jerry Reuss	.10
(171)	Archie Reynolds	.10
(172)	Bob Reynolds	.10
(173)	Ken Reynolds	.10
(174)	Tommie Reynolds	.10
(175)	Ernest Riles	.10
(176)	Bill Schroeder	.10
(177)	George Scott	.15
(178)	Ray Searage	.10
(179)	Bob Sebra	.10
(180)	Kevin Seitzer	.10
(181)	Dick Selma	.10
(182)	Bill Sharp	.10
(183)	Ron Theobald	.10
(184)	Dan Thomas	.10
(185)	Gorman Thomas	.15
(186)	Randy Veres	.10
(187)	Bill Voss	.10
(188)	Jim Wohlford	.10
Series III		
	Complete book:	8.00
(189)	Jerry Augustine	.10
(190)	James Austin	.10
(191)	Rick Austin	.10
(192)	Kurt Bevacqua	.10
(193)	Tom Bianco	.10
(194)	Dante Bichette	.10
(195)	Mike Birkbeck	.10
(196)	Dan Boitano	.10
(197)	Bobby Bolin	.10
(198)	Mark Bomback	.10
(199)	Ricky Bones	.10
(200)	Chris Bosio	.10
(201)	Thad Bosley	.10
(202)	Steve Bowling	.10
(203)	Gene Brabender	.10
(204)	Glenn Braggs	.10
(205)	Mike Caldwell	.10
(206)	Billy Champion	.10
(207)	Mark Ciardi	.10
(208)	Bobby Clark	.10
(209)	Ron Clark	.10
(210)	Mark Clear	.10
(211)	Reggie Cleveland	.10
(212)	Bryan Clutterbuck	.10
(213)	Jaime Cocanower	.10
(214)	Jim Colborn	.10
(215)	Cecil Cooper	.15
(216)	Edgar Diaz	.10
(217)	Frank DiPino	.10
(218)	Dave Engle	.10
(219)	Ray Fosse	.10
(220)	Terry Francona	.10
(221)	Tito Francona	.10
(222)	LaVel Freeman	.10
(223)	Brian Giles	.10
(224)	Bob Heise	.10
(225)	Doug Henry	.10
(226)	Mike Hershberger	.10
(227)	Teddy Higuera	.10
(228)	Sam Hinds	.10
(229)	Fred Holdsworth	.10
(230)	Darren Holmes	.10
(231)	Paul Householder	.10
(232)	Odell Jones	.10
(233)	Brad Komminsk	.10
(234)	Andy Kosco	.10
(235)	Lew Krausse	.10
(236)	Ray Krawczyk	.10
(237)	Bill Krueger	.10
(238)	Ted Kubiak	.10
(239)	Jack Lind	.10
(240)	Frank Linzy	.10
(241)	Pat Listach	.10
(242)	Graeme Lloyd	.10
(243)	Bob Locker	.10
(244)	Skip Lockwood	.10
(245)	Ken McMullen	.10
(246)	Jerry McNertney	.10
(247)	Doc Medich	.10
(248)	Bob Meyer	.10
(249)	Joey Meyer	.10
(250)	Matt Mieske	.10
(251)	Roger Miller	.10
(252)	Paul Mirabella	.10
(253)	Angel Miranda	.10
(254)	Bobby Mitchell	.10
(255)	Paul Mitchell	.10
(256)	Paul Molitor	3.00
(257)	Rafael Novoa	.10

(258)	Jesse Orosco	.10
(259)	Carlos Ponce	.10
(260)	Chuck Porter	.10
(261)	Darrell Porter	.10
(262)	Billy Jo Robidoux	.10
(263)	Ron Robinson	.10
(264)	Eduardo Rodriguez	.10
(265)	Ellie Rodriguez	.10
(266)	Rich Rollins	.10
(267)	Ed Romero	.10
(268)	Gary Sheffield	1.00
(269)	Bob Sheldon	.10
(270)	Chris Short	.10
(271)	Bob Skube	.10
(272)	Jim Slaton	.10
(273)	Bernie Smith	.10
(274)	Russ Snyder	.10
(275)	Lary Sorenson	.10
(276)	Billy Spiers	.10
(277)	Ed Sprague	.10
(278)	Dickie Thon	.10
(279)	Bill Travers	.10
(280)	Pete Vuckovich	.10
(281)	Clyde Wright	.10
(282)	Jeff Yurak	.10

Series IV
Complete book: 8.00

(283)	Joe Azcue	.10
(284)	Mike Boddicker	.10
(285)	Ken Brett	.10
(286)	John Briggs	.10
(287)	Pete Broberg	.10
(288)	Greg Brock	.10
(289)	Jeff Bronkey	.10
(290)	Mark Brouhard	.10
(291)	Kevin Brown	.10
(292)	Ollie Brown	.10
(293)	Bruce Brubaker	.10
(294)	Tom Brunansky	.10
(295)	Steve Brye	.10
(296)	Bob Burda	.10
(297)	Ray Burris	.10
(298)	Jeff Cirillo	.10
(299)	Bobby Clark	.10
(300)	Bob Coluccio	.10
(301)	Wayne Comer	.10
(302)	Billy Conigliaro	.10
(303)	Cecil Cooper (25th Anniversary Team)	.10
(304)	Barry Cort	.10
(305)	Chuck Crim	.10
(306)	Lafayette Currence	.10
(307)	Kiki Diaz	.10
(308)	Bill Doran	.10
(309)	Al Downing	.10
(310)	Tom Edens	.10
(311)	Andy Etchebarren	.10
(312)	Rollie Fingers (25th)	.50
(313)	Jim Gantner (25th)	.10
(314)	Greg Goossen	.10
(315)	Brian Harper	.10
(316)	Larry Hisle	.10
(317)	Steve Hovley	.10
(318)	Wilbur Howard	.10
(319)	Roy Howell	.10
(320)	Bob Humphreys	.10
(321)	Jim Hunter	.10
(322)	Dave Huppert	.10
(323)	Von Joshua	.10
(324)	Art Kusnyer	.10
(325)	Doug Loman	.10
(326)	Jim Lonborg	.10
(327)	Marcelino Lopez	.10
(328)	Willie Lozado	.10
(329)	Mike Matheny	.10
(330)	Ken McMullen	.10
(331)	Jose Mercedes	.10
(332)	Paul Molitor (25th)	1.50
(333)	Don Money	.10
(334)	Don Money (25th)	.10
(335)	Charlie Moore	.10
(336)	Donnie Moore	.10
(337)	John Morris	.10
(338)	Curt Motton	.10
(339)	Willie Mueller	.10
(340)	Tom Murphy	.10
(341)	Tony Muser	.10
(342)	Edwin Nunez	.10
(343)	Ben Oglivie (25th)	.10
(344)	Pat Osborn (Osburn)	.10
(345)	Dennis Powell	.10
(346)	Jody Reed	.10
(347)	Phil Roof	.10
(348)	Jimmy Rosario	.10
(349)	Bruce Ruffin	.10
(350)	Gary Ryerson	.10
(351)	Bob Scanlan	.10
(352)	Ted Simmons	.10
(353)	Ted Simmons (25th)	.10
(354)	Duane Singleton	.10
(355)	Steve Stanicek	.10
(356)	Fred Stanley	.10
(357)	Dave Stapleton	.10
(358)	Randy Stein	.10
(359)	Earl Stephenson	.10
(360)	Franklin Stubbs	.10
(361)	William Suero	.10
(362)	Jim Sundberg	.10
(363)	B.J. Surhoff	.10
(364)	Gary Sutherland	.10
(365)	Don Sutton	.50
(366)	Dale Sveum	.10
(367)	Gorman Thomas (25th)	.10
(368)	Wayne Twitchell	.10
(369)	Dave Valle	.10
(370)	Greg Vaughn (25th)	.10
(371)	John Vukovich	.10
(372)	Danny Walton	.10
(373)	Turner Ward	.10
(374)	Rick Wrona	.10
(375)	Jim Wynn	.10
(376)	Robin Yount (25th)	1.50

1990 Little Big Leaguers

This set was issued on a series of five nine-card perforated panels at the back of a book titled, "little BIG LEAGUERS / Amazing Boyhood Stories of Today's Baseball Stars." The 96 text pages of the book offer inspiring boyhood baseball tales as well as childhood and major league photos of the players. The tear-out cards measure 2-1/2" x 3-1/2" and are perforated on all four sides. Fronts have a black-and-white childhood photo of the player, nearly all in baseball uniform. The player's name is in white in a red strip at top, with the set name at bottom. Backs have the same red strips. At center in black-and-white are biographical data and career highlights. The unnumbered cards are checklisted here alphabetically.

		NM/M
	Complete Set, Book:	6.00
	Complete Set (45):	6.00
	Common Player:	.25
(1)	Todd Benzinger	.25
(2)	Bud Black	.25
(3)	Wade Boggs	.75
(4)	Chris Bosio	.25
(5)	George Brett	2.00
(6)	Brett Butler	.25
(7)	Jose Canseco	.65
(8)	Gary Carter	.75
(9)	Joe Carter	.25
(10)	Eric Davis	.25
(11)	Glenn Davis	.25
(12)	Storm Davis	.25
(13)	Kevin Elster	.25
(14)	Tony Fernandez	.25
(15)	John Franco	.25
(16)	Gary Gaetti	.25
(17)	Mark Gubicza	.25
(18)	Tony Gwynn	1.00
(19)	Bruce Hurst	.25
(20)	Bo Jackson	.60
(21)	Bob Kipper	.25
(22)	Ron Kittle	.25
(23)	Carney Lansford	.25
(24)	Jeffrey Leonard	.25
(25)	Mike A. Marshall	.25
(26)	Lloyd McClendon	.25
(27)	Andy McGaffigan	.25
(28)	Keith Moreland	.25
(29)	Lloyd Moseby	.25
(30)	Dale Murphy	.50
(31)	Pete O'Brien	.25
(32)	Mike Pagliarulo	.25
(33)	Tim Raines	.25
(34)	Dennis Rasmussen	.25
(35)	Harold Reynolds	.25
(36)	Billy Ripken	.25
(37)	Nolan Ryan	3.00
(38)	Steve Sax	.25
(39)	Ozzie Smith	1.00
(40)	Jim Sundberg	.25
(41)	Rick Sutcliffe	.25
(42)	Dave Valle	.25
(43)	Andy Van Slyke	.25
(44)	Glenn Wilson	.25
(45)	Todd Worrell	.25

1991 Little Big Leaguers

This set was issued on a series of five nine-card perforated panels at the back of a book titled, "little BIG LEAGUERS / Amazing Boyhood Stories of Today's Baseball Stars." The 96 text pages of the

book offer inspiring boyhood baseball tales as well as childhood and major league photos of the players. The tear-out cards measure 2-1/2" x 3-1/2" and are perforated on all four sides. Fronts have a black-and-white childhood photo of the player, nearly all in baseball uniform. The player's name is in white in a green strip at top, with the set name at bottom. Backs have the same green strips. At center in black-and-white are biographical data and career highlights. The unnumbered cards are checklisted here alphabetically.

		NM/M
	Complete Book:	6.00
	Complete Set (45):	6.00
	Common Player:	.25
(1)	Jim Abbott	.25
(2)	Jesse Barfield	.25
(3)	Kevin Bass	.25
(4)	Craig Biggio	.25
(5)	Phil Bradley	.25
(6)	Jeff Brantley	.25
(7)	Tom Brunansky	.25
(8)	Ken Caminiti	.25
(9)	Will Clark	.35
(10)	Vince Coleman	.25
(11)	David Cone	.25
(12)	Alvin Davis	.25
(13)	Andre Dawson	.50
(14)	Bill Doran	.25
(15)	Nick Esasky	.25
(16)	Dwight Gooden	.25
(17)	Tom Gordon	.25
(18)	Ken Griffey Jr.	2.50
(19)	Kevin Gross	.25
(20)	Kelly Gruber	.25
(21)	Lee Guetterman	.25
(22)	Terry Kennedy	.25
(23)	John Kruk	.25
(24)	Bill Landrum	.25
(25)	Mark Langston	.25
(26)	Barry Larkin	.25
(27)	Dave Magadan	.25
(28)	Don Mattingly	2.00
(29)	Mark McGwire	3.00
(30)	Kevin Mitchell	.25
(31)	Bob Ojeda	.25
(32)	Gregg Olson	.25
(33)	Terry Pendleton	.25
(34)	Ted Power	.25
(35)	Kirby Puckett	1.50
(36)	Terry Puhl	.25
(37)	Bret Saberhagen	.25
(38)	Chris Sabo	.25
(39)	Kevin Seitzer	.25
(40)	Don Slaught	.25
(41)	Lonnie Smith	.25
(42)	Darryl Strawberry	.25
(43)	Mickey Tettleton	.25
(44)	Bobby Thigpen	.25
(45)	Frank White	.25

2005 Los Angeles Angels Card Deck

This stadium giveaway was sponsored by ValleyCrest Companies, a golf course design firm. Cards are 2-1/4" x 3-7/16" with rounded corners. Red backs have team and sponsor's logos. Each player appears four times in the deck, with an identical portrait photo on the same value card in each suit. Two wild cards complete the boxed set.

		NM/M
	Complete Set (54):	10.00
	Common Player:	.25
2	Adam Kennedy	.25
3	Darin Erstad	.25
4	Kelvim Escobar	.25
5	Bengie Molina	.25
6	Orlando Cabrera	.25
7	Garret Anderson	.25
8	Steve Finley	.25
9	Bartolo Colon	.25
10	Francisco Rodriguez	.25
J	Chone Figgins	.25
Q	Rally Money/Mascot	.25
K	Mike Scioscia	.25
A	Vladimir Guerrero	.50
WC	Mascot (Brendan Donnelly)	.25
WC	Mascot (Brendan Donnelly)	.25

1981-93 Louisville Slugger

Hillerich & Bradsby, makers of Louisville Slugger bats and gloves, produced these cards to be attached to the company's baseball gloves. A small round hole is punched in the upper-left corner of each standard-size card to enable them to be attached to the gloves. Undamaged cards are hard to find. All cards follow the same basic design - bright blue and green borders, player name and position above the full-color photo (with autograph overprint), yellow Louisville Slugger logo across the bottom border. Beneath the logo are the words "Member Louisville Slugger Bat & Glove Advisory Staff." The card backs are blue and green and include the player name, short biography and a list of personal records and information. Cards were printed with a glossy finish through 1987, when a flat finish was adopted as production moved from Taiwan to the Philippines.

		NM/M
	Common Player:	2.00
(1)	Steve Garvey/Dgr	5.00
(1)	Graig Nettles/Yanks	4.00
(1)	Pedro Guerrero/Dgr	2.00
(2)	Fred Lynn/Angels	2.00
(1)	Ray Knight/Astros	5.00
(2)	Ray Knight/Mets	2.25
(1)	Graig Nettles/Padres	3.25
(1)	Steve Garvey/Padres	3.25
(1)	Gary Matthews/Cubs	2.00
(1)	Orel Hershiser/Dgr	2.00
(1)	Rick Rhoden/Pirates	2.00
(1)	Eric Davis/Reds	2.00
(1)	Eric Davis/Reds	2.00
(1)	Steve Garvey/Padres	4.00
(3)	Orel Hershiser/Dgr	2.00
(1)	Mike Pagliarulo/Yanks	2.00
(1)	Orel Hershiser/Dgr	2.00
(1)	Orel Hershiser/Dgr	2.00
(2)	Andy Van Slyke/Pirates	2.00
(3)	Lou Whitaker/Tigers	3.00
(1)	Wade Boggs/Red Sox	5.00
(1)	Eric Davis/Dgr	2.00
(2)	Jack McDowell/White Sox	2.00

1990s Louisville Slugger TPX Advisory Staff

This series of cards issued sometime, or over a period of time, in the 1990s depicts members of Hillerich & Bradsby's Pro Advisory Staff for its TPX line-up of baseball equipment. Cards are in standard 2-1/2" x 3-1/2" format with game-action or posed color photos and a facsimile autograph on front. Backs picture a bat, glove and bat bag.

		NM/M
	Common Player:	3.00
(1)	Brett Butler/Dgr	3.00
(2)	Bobby Jones/Mets	3.00
(3)	Reggie Sanders/Reds	3.00
(4)	Todd Stottlemyre/Cardinals	3.00
(5)	Robin Ventura/White Sox	3.00

1992 Lykes Braves Team Photo Set

When Lykes Meats was awarded the Braves hot dog contract for 1992 they continued the previous years' baseball card promotions, including this early-May team photo/player card panel. Three 9-1/2" x 10-1/2" panels feature a team photo and 30 player cards. The cards have player portraits against a blue background in a tombstone shape. A blue ball at lower-left has the player's uniform number, while his name is in white in a red strip beneath the photo. Red logos of the team and hot dog vendor are at bottom. Backs are printed in red and dark blue and feature full stats, player data and a facsimile autograph. These cards are much more common than the Lykes singles distributed later in the season. The checklist here is alphabetized.

		NM/M
	Complete Foldout Set:	6.00
	Common Player:	.15
(1)	Steve Avery	.15
(2)	Rafael Belliard	.15
(3)	Juan Berenguer	.15
(4)	Damon Berryhill	.15
(5)	Mike Bielecki	.15
(6)	Jeff Blauser	.15
(7)	Sid Bream	.15
(8)	Francisco Cabrera	.15
(9)	Bobby Cox	.15
(10)	Nick Esasky	.15
(11)	Marvin Freeman	.15
(12)	Ron Gant	.15
(13)	Tom Glavine	1.00
(14)	Tommy Gregg	.15
(15)	Brian Hunter	.15
(16)	David Justice	.25
(17)	Charlie Leibrandt	.15
(18)	Mark Lemke	.15
(19)	Kent Mercker	.15
(20)	Otis Nixon	.15
(21)	Greg Olson	.15
(22)	Alejandro Pena	.15
(23)	Terry Pendleton	.15
(24)	Deion Sanders	.15
(25)	Lonnie Smith	.15
(26)	John Smoltz	1.00
(27)	Mike Stanton	.15
(28)	Jeff Treadway	.15
(29)	Jerry Willard	.15
(30)	Mark Wohlers	.15
(31)	Team Photo	.50

1992 Lykes Braves

Though Braves players no longer appeared at an autograph booth on card giveaway days in 1992, the team's hot dog vendor continued to offer small groups of cards to kids attending Tuesday home games. This distribution makes assembling complete sets very challenging. In standard 2-1/2" x 3-1/2" size, the cards have a player photo border in, successively, white, dark blue, red and white. A red-and-blue Lykes logo is at lower-right. Above is a blue ball with the year of issue, and the team and player name printed in white. Backs are in black with the player's uniform number, full minor and major league stats, and biographical vitae.

		NM/M
	Complete Set (37):	12.00
	Common Player:	.25
(1)	Steve Avery	.25
(2)	Jim Beauchamp	.25
(3)	Rafael Belliard	.25
(4)	Juan Berenguer	.25
(5)	Damon Berryhill	.25
(6)	Mike Bielecki	.25
(7)	Jeff Blauser	.25
(8)	Sid Bream	.25
(9)	Francisco Cabrera	.25
(10)	Pat Corrales	.25
(11)	Bobby Cox	.25
(12)	Marvin Freeman	.25
(13)	Ron Gant	.40
(14)	Tom Glavine	1.50
(15)	Tommy Gregg	.25
(16)	Brian Hunter	.25
(17)	Clarence Jones	.25
(18)	David Justice	.75
(19)	Charlie Leibrandt	.25
(20)	Mark Lemke	.25
(21)	Leo Mazzone	.25
(22)	Kent Mercker	.25
(23)	Otis Nixon	.25
(24)	Greg Olson	.25
(25)	Alejandro Pena	.25
(26)	Terry Pendleton	.25
(27)	Deion Sanders	.50
(28)	Lonnie Smith	.25
(29)	John Smoltz	1.50
(30)	Mike Stanton	.25
(31)	Jeff Treadway	.25
(32)	Jerry Willard	.25
(33)	Jimy Williams	.25
(34)	Mark Wohlers	.25
(35)	Ned Yost	.25
(36)	Homer the Brave/Mascot	.25
(37)	Rally/Mascot	.25

1993 Lykes Braves

Each Tuesday home game during the 1993 season, three player cards were distributed to youngsters, sponsored by the team's hot dog vendor. This style of distribution makes collecting a complete 38-card set very challenging. Standard 2-1/2" x 3-1/2" size cards have a player portrait photo against a blue background. The card's front border is a darker blue separated from the photo by a yellow stripe. Red-white-and-blue team and vendor logos appear at the corners and the player's name and position are in white at lower-left. Backs are printed in black with complete career stats, biographical data and sponsors' logos. The unnumbered cards are checklisted here alphabetically. The final Tuesday's handouts, Lopez, McGriff and Tarasco have slightly different back printing and are somewhat scarcer than other cards.

		NM/M
Complete Set (38):		20.00
Common Player:		.50
(1)	Steve Avery	.50
(2)	Jim Beauchamp	.50
(3)	Steve Bedrosian	.50
(4)	Rafael Belliard	.50
(5)	Damon Berryhill	.50
(6)	Jeff Blauser	.50
(7)	Sid Bream	.50
(8)	Francisco Cabrera	.50
(9)	Pat Corrales	.50
(10)	Bobby Cox	.50
(11)	Marvin Freeman	.50
(12)	Ron Gant	.50
(13)	Tom Glavine	1.50
(14)	Jay Howell	.50
(15)	Brian Hunter	.50
(16)	Clarence Jones	.50
(17)	David Justice	.60
(18)	Mark Lemke	.50
(19)	Javier Lopez	1.00
(20)	Greg Maddux	2.50
(21)	Leo Mazzone	.50
(22)	Fred McGriff	1.00
(23)	Greg McMichael	.50
(24)	Kent Mercker	.50
(25)	Otis Nixon	.50
(26)	Greg Olson	.50
(27)	Bill Pecota	.50
(28)	Terry Pendleton	.50
(29)	Deion Sanders	1.00
(30)	Pete Smith	.50
(31)	John Smoltz	1.50
(32)	Mike Stanton	.50
(33)	Tony Tarasco	1.00
(34)	Jimy Williams	.50
(35)	Mark Wohlers	.50
(36)	Ned Yost	.50
(37)	Homer the Brave/Mascot	.50
(38)	Rally/Mascot	.50

1993 Lykes Braves Team Photo Set

The Atlanta Braves offered a perforated, uncut sheet team set in 1992 that was handed out in an early season game. The set, sponsored by Lykes, includes 30 cards and a team photo and carries the player's name and uniform number on the front of the card along with the Braves and Lykes logos. The backs contain the player's biography, career statistics and a facsimile autograph. The first card of Fred McGriff as a Brave appears in this promotional set issued later in the season than in previous years. The 30 individual player cards also include Ryan Klesko, who was not in the single-card season-long giveaways. Three 9-1/2" x 10-1/2" panels comprise this issue, with each of the player cards perforated at the edges. Also for the first time in 1992, the same photos were used for the team sheet and single card promotions. Single cards measure 2-1/4" x 3-1/2" and are checklisted alphabetically here.

		NM/M
Complete Foldout Set:		5.00
Common Player:		.15
(1)	Steve Avery	.15
(2)	Steve Bedrosian	.15
(3)	Rafael Belliard	.15
(4)	Damon Berryhill	.15
(5)	Jeff Blauser	.15
(6)	Sid Bream	.15
(7)	Francisco Cabrera	.15
(8)	Bobby Cox	.15
(9)	Marvin Freeman	.15
(10)	Ron Gant	.15
(11)	Tom Glavine	1.00
(12)	Jay Howell	.15
(13)	Brian Hunter	.15
(14)	David Justice	.25
(15)	Ryan Klesko	.15
(16)	Mark Lemke	.15
(17)	Greg Maddux	2.00
(18)	Fred McGriff	.15
(19)	Greg McMichael	.15
(20)	Kent Mercker	.15
(21)	Otis Nixon	.15
(22)	Greg Olson	.15
(23)	Bill Pecota	.15
(24)	Terry Pendleton	.15
(25)	Deion Sanders	.15
(26)	Pete Smith	.15
(27)	John Smoltz	1.00
(28)	Mike Stanton	.15
(29)	Tony Tarasco	.15
(30)	Mark Wohlers	.15
(31)	Team Photo	.50

1994 Lykes Braves

While 34 cards were printed, only 27 were publicly released prior to the beginning of the 1994 baseball strike. Sponsored by the Braves' stadium hot dog concessionaire, the cards were given away at the rate of three per Tuesday home game. Because of the strike, the cards of Cox, Hill, Chipper Jones, Mike Kelly, Klesko, McGriff and Sanders were not officially released and are scarcer than the other 27. Card fronts feature a chest-to-cap player portrait photo set agaonst a blue background with an orange border and vertical blue stripe at right bearing the player's name. Backs are printed in black-and-white and have full major and minor league stats along with a few biographical details. There is no card or uniform number on the cards. They are presented here alphabetically.

		NM/M
Complete Set (34):		40.00
Common Player:		.25
(1)	Steve Avery	.25
(2)	Jim Beauchamp	.25
(3)	Steve Bedrosian	.25
(4)	Rafael Belliard	.25
(5)	Mike Bielecki	.25
(6)	Jeff Blauser	.25
(7)	Pat Corrales	.25
(8)	Bobby Cox	2.00
(9)	Dave Gallagher	.25
(10)	Tom Glavine	1.50
(11)	Milt Hill	2.00
(12)	Chipper Jones	10.00
(13)	Clarence Jones	.25
(14)	David Justice	.50
(15)	Mike Kelly	2.00
(16)	Ryan Klesko	6.00
(17)	Mark Lemke	.25
(18)	Javib Lopez	.25
(19)	Greg Maddux	3.00
(20)	Leo Mazzone	.25
(21)	Greg McMichael	.25
(22)	Fred McGriff	6.00
(23)	Kent Mercker	.25
(24)	Charlie O'Brien	.25
(25)	Gregg Olson	.25
(26)	Bill Pecota	.25
(27)	Terry Pendleton	.25
(28)	Deion Sanders	6.00
(29)	John Smoltz	1.50
(30)	Mike Stanton	.25
(31)	Tony Tarasco	.25
(32)	Jimy Williams	.25
(33)	Mark Wohlers	.25
(34)	Ned Yost	.25

1995 Lykes Braves

GREG MADDUX

For the only time since Atlanta's hot dog concessionaires began issuing cards in 1989, the team honored past, as well as current players, as part of its 30th anniversary celebration. The cards were distributed at Tuesday home games, usually three at a time, making assem-

Team Photo Set

Few of these team photo/player card sets have found their way into the hobby because they were intended for distribution at the August 14 Sunday home game which fell after the beginning of the 1994 baseball strike. As in past years, the set was produced as a fold-out containing a team photo and 35 player cards. Unlike previous editions, however, the player cards are identical in format to the single cards given away during the season, except that they are printed in red and blue on the back and are slightly smaller, at 2-1/8" x 3-1/8". The cards are checklisted here alphabeitcally.

		NM/M
Complete Foldout Set:		17.50
Common Player:		.25
(1)	Steve Avery	.25
(2)	Jim Beauchamp	.25
(3)	Steve Bedrosian	.25
(4)	Rafael Belliard	.25
(5)	Mike Bielecki	.25
(6)	Jeff Blauser	.25
(7)	Pat Corrales	.25
(8)	Bobby Cox	.25
(9)	Dave Gallagher	.25
(10)	Tom Glavine	1.50
(11)	Chipper Jones	3.50
(12)	Clarence Jones	.25
(13)	David Justice	.50
(14)	Mike Kelly	.25
(15)	Roberto Kelly	.25
(16)	Ryan Klesko	.25
(17)	Mark Lemke	.25
(18)	Javy Lopez	.25
(19)	Greg Maddux	3.50
(20)	Leo Mazzone	.25
(21)	Greg McMichael	.25
(22)	Fred McGriff	.25
(23)	Kent Mercker	.25
(24)	Mike Mordecai	.25
(25)	Charlie O'Brien	.25
(26)	Jose Oliva	.25
(27)	Gregg Olson	.25
(28)	Bill Pecota	.25
(29)	Terry Pendleton	.25
(30)	John Smoltz	1.50
(31)	Mike Stanton	.25
(32)	Tony Tarasco	.25
(33)	Jimy Williams	.25
(34)	Mark Wohlers	.25
(35)	Ned Yost	.25
(36)	Team Photo	.50

Team Photo Set

javier C LOPEZ

Once again this promotional giveaway by the team's hot dog concessionaire took the form of a three-panel cardboard poster. Overall 10-3/4" x 28", the foldout features a color team photo at top and 30 individual player portrait cards below. Each card is 2-1/8" x 3-1/8" and perforated for separation. Backs are printed in red, white and blue with a few stats and vital data, along with team and sponsor logos. The unnumbered cards are checklisted here alphabetically.

		NM/M
Complete Foldout Set:		8.00
Common Player:		.10
(1)	Steve Avery	.10
(2)	Jim Beauchamp	.10
(3)	Rafael Belliard	.10
(4)	Jeff Blauser	.10
(5)	Pedro Borbon	.10
(6)	Brad Clontz	.10
(7)	Pat Corrales	.10
(8)	Bobby Cox	.10
(9)	Tom Glavine	.75
(10)	Marquis Grissom	.10
(11)	Chipper Jones	2.00
(12)	Clarence Jones	.10
(13)	David Justice	.25
(14)	Mike Kelly	.10
(15)	Ryan Klesko	.10
(16)	Mark Lemke	.10
(17)	Javier Lopez	.10
(18)	Greg Maddux	1.50
(19)	Leo Mazzone	.10
(20)	Fred McGriff	.10
(21)	Greg McMichael	.10
(22)	Kent Mercker	.10
(23)	Mike Mordecai	.10
(24)	Charlie O'Brien	.10
(25)	Jason Schmidt	.10

bly of a complete set difficult. Thus, this checklist may or may not be complete. Fronts have game-action photos with a black strip at bottom bearing the player name. A 30th anniversary logo is at top, the sponsor's logo appears over a baseball in a lower corner. Black-and-white backs have player personal data and career record.

		NM/M
Complete Set (30):		10.00
Common Player:		.25
(1)	Hank Aaron	2.50
(2)	Steve Avery	.25
(3)	Steve Bedrosian	.25
(4)	Jeff Blauser	.25
(5)	Sid Bream	.25
(6)	Francisco Cabrera	.25
(7)	Chris Chambliss	.25
(8)	Bobby Cox	.25
(9)	Ron Gant	.25
(10)	Tom Glavine	1.50
(11)	Marquis Grissom	.25
(12)	Bob Horner	.25
(13)	Glenn Hubbard	.25
(14)	Chipper Jones	2.00
(15)	David Justice	.25
(16)	Ryan Klesko	.25
(17)	Mark Lemke	.25
(18)	Javy Lopez	.25
(19)	Greg Maddux	2.00
(20)	Fred McGriff	.25
(21)	Kent Mercker	.25
(22)	Dale Murphy	1.50
(23)	Phil Niekro	.40
(24)	Otis Nixon	.25
(25)	Charlie O'Brien	.25
(26)	Greg Olson	.25
(27)	Pascual Perez	.25
(28)	Lonnie Smith	.25
(29)	John Smoltz	1.50
(30)	Mark Wohlers	.25

1996 Lykes Braves Team Photo Set

GREG MADDUX

The Braves offered a perforated, four-panel 10-3/4" x 31-1/4" uncut sheet team set in 1996 that was handed out to children 12 and under at an early season game. The set was sponsored by Lykes, the team's hot dog concessionaire. There are 35 individual player and staff portrait cards in 2-1/8" x 3-1/8" format, and a 10-3/4" x 9-1/2" team photo panel. Each card carries the player's name, position and uniform number on the front, along with the Lykes logo. Black, white and blue backs contain biographical data, 1995 and career major and minor league statistics and team and sponsor logos. The cards are checklisted alphabetically here.

		NM/M
Complete Foldout Set:		8.00
Common Player:		.10
(1)	Steve Avery	.10
(2)	Danny Bautista	.10
(3)	Jim Beauchamp	.10
(4)	Rafael Belliard	.10
(5)	Mike Bielecki	.10
(6)	Jeff Blauser	.10
(7)	Pedro Borbon	.10
(8)	Brad Clontz	.10
(9)	Pat Corrales	.10
(10)	Bobby Cox	.10
(11)	Jermaine Dye	.10
(12)	Frank Fultz	.10
(13)	Tom Glavine	1.25
(14)	Marquis Grissom	.10
(15)	Chipper Jones	3.00
(16)	Clarence Jones	.10
(17)	David Justice	.25
(18)	Ryan Klesko	.10
(19)	Mark Lemke	.10
(20)	Javy Lopez	.10
(21)	Greg Maddux	2.50
(22)	Leo Mazzone	.10
(23)	Fred McGriff	.10
(24)	Greg McMichael	.10
(25)	Mike Mordecai	.10
(26)	Eddie Perez	.10
(27)	Jason Schmidt	.10
(28)	Dwight Smith	.10
(29)	John Smoltz	1.25
(30)	Terrell Wade	.10
(31)	Jerome Walton	.10
(32)	Mark Whiten	.10
(33)	Jimy Williams	.10
(34)	Mark Wohlers	.10
(35)	Ned Yost	.10
(36)	Team photo	.50

(26) Dwight Smith .10
(27) John Smoltz .75
(28) Jimy Williams .10
(29) Mark Wohlers .10
(30) Ned Yost .10
(31) Team photo .25

M

1987 M & M's

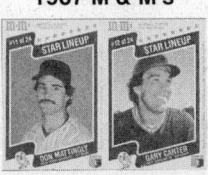

The M&M's "Star Lineup" set consists of 12 two-card panels inserted in specially marked packages of large M&M's candy. The two-card panels measure 5" x 3-1/2" with individual cards measuring 2-1/2" x 3-1/2" in size. The full-color photos are enclosed by a wavy blue frame and a white border. Card backs are printed in red ink on white stock and carry the player's career statistics and highlights. All team insignia have been airbrushed away. The set was designed and produced by Mike Schechter and Associates.

		NM/M
Complete Panel Set (12):		5.00
Complete Singles Set (24):		4.00
Common Panel:		1.00
Common Single Player:		.10
PANEL 1		.25
1	Wally Joyner	.10
2	Tony Pena	.10
PANEL 2		1.25
3	Mike Schmidt	.50
4	Ryne Sandberg	.40
PANEL 3		.65
5	Wade Boggs	.40
6	Jack Morris	.40
PANEL 4		.65
7	Roger Clemens	.45
8	Harold Baines	.10
PANEL 5		.60
9	Dale Murphy	.25
10	Jose Canseco	.20
PANEL 6		.75
11	Don Mattingly	.45
12	Gary Carter	.35
PANEL 7		2.00
13	Cal Ripken Jr.	1.00
14	George Brett	.50
PANEL 8		.65
15	Kirby Puckett	.40
16	Joe Carter	.10
PANEL 9		.25
17	Mike Witt	.10
18	Mike Scott	.10
PANEL 10		.45
19	Fernando Valenzuela	.15
20	Steve Garvey	.15
PANEL 11		1.50
21	Steve Sax	.10
22	Nolan Ryan	1.00
PANEL 12		1.25
23	Tony Gwynn	.40
24	Ozzie Smith	.40

2005 Major League Baseball Superstars Medallions

NEW YORK YANKEES · ALEX RODRIGUEZ · 13 3B

Coupons in USA Today between July 11 and August 19 allowed to collectors to purchase these medallions on a one-per-day basis for $2.99 at 7-Eleven, SuperAmerica and Speedway convenience stores.

		NM/M
Complete Set (30):		100.00
Common Player:		3.00
(1)	Roger Clemens	6.00
(2)	Ichiro Suzuki	7.50
(3)	Derek Jeter	8.00
(4)	Curt Schilling	3.00
(5)	Albert Pujols	8.00
(6)	Randy Johnson	3.00
(7)	Ivan Rodriguez	3.00
(8)	Eric Gagne	3.00
(9)	Kerry Wood	3.00
(10)	Ben Sheets	3.00
(11)	John Smoltz	3.00
(12)	Vladimir Guerrero	3.00
(13)	Torii Hunter	3.00
(14)	David Ortiz	3.00
(15)	Carlos Delgado	3.00
(16)	Scott Rolen	3.00
(17)	Jason Schmidt	3.00
(18)	Sammy Sosa	3.00
(19)	Carlos Beltran	3.00
(20)	Luis Gonzalez	3.00
(21)	Ken Griffey Jr.	4.50
(22)	Todd Helton	3.00
(23)	Alfonso Soriano	3.00

(24)	Pedro Martinez	3.00
(25)	Jim Thome	3.00
(26)	Manny Ramirez	3.00
(27)	Johan Santana	3.00
(28)	Eric Chavez	3.00
(29)	Mark Prior	3.00
(30)	Alex Rodriguez	7.50

1997-2002 Major League Dad

To promote responsible fatherhood the California Department of Child Support Services issued a series of cards picturing big league players and their children. Issued in a variety of designs, all have the phrase "Major League Dad" on front.

		NM/M
Complete Set (10):		20.00
Common Player:		2.00
(1)	Garret Anderson/2000	2.00
(2)	Marvin Benard/2000	2.00
(3)	Mike Fetters/1998	2.00
(4)	Mark Gardner/1998	2.00
(5)	Wally Joyner	2.00
(6)	Chad Kreuter	2.00
(7)	Tim Salmon	2.00
(8)	Jeff Shaw/2000	2.00
(9)	Matt Stairs/2000	2.00
(10)	Greg Vaughn/1998	2.00

1988 Mickey Mantle's Restaurant

To promote the grand opening of Mickey Mantle's restaurant in New York City, this promotional card was issued by an Oklahoma public relations firm to members of the media. In round-cornered 2-1/2" x 3-1/2" format on thin, semi-gloss cardboard, the front has a posed color photo of Mantle. The back has details of the restaurant opening and a design reminiscent of the Yankee Stadium facade, printed in white on a dark blue background.

	NM/M
Mickey Mantle	7.50

1989 Marathon Cubs

This colorful 25-card Cubs team set was sponsored by Marathon and was distributed as a stadium promotion to fans attending the Aug. 10, 1989, game at Chicago's Wrigley Field. The oversize (2-3/4" x 4-1/4") feature an action photo inside a diagonal box on the card front, with the Chicago Cubs logo at the top and the player's uniform number, name and position

along the bottom. The backs include a small black-and-white photo, player data and the Cubs and Marathon logos.

		NM/M
Complete Set (25):		12.00
Common Player:		.50
2	Vance Law	.50
4	Don Zimmer	.50
7	Joe Girardi	.50
8	Andre Dawson	2.50
9	Damon Berryhill	.50
10	Lloyd McClendon	.50
12	Shawon Dunston	.50
15	Domingo Ramos	.50
17	Mark Grace	.75
18	Dwight Smith	.50
19	Curt Wilkerson	.50
20	Jerome Walton	.50
21	Scott Sanderson	.50
23	Ryne Sandberg	6.50
28	Mitch Williams	.50
31	Greg Maddux	6.00
32	Calvin Schiraldi	.50
33	Mitch Webster	.50
36	Mike Bielecki	.50
39	Paul Kilgus	.50
40	Rick Sutcliffe	.50
41	Jeff Pico	.50
44	Steve Wilson	.50
50	Les Lancaster	.50
---	Coaches (Joe Altobelli, Chuck Cottier, Larry Cox, Jose Martinez, Dick Pole)	.50

1989 Marathon Tigers

Marathon sponsored this give-away set for a 1989 Tigers home game. The oversized cards feature thin white stock and full-color player photos. The cards are numbered according to uniform number.

		NM/M
Complete Set (28):		9.00
Common Player:		.50
1	Lou Whitaker	.75
3	Alan Trammell	1.00
8	Mike Heath	.50
9	Fred Lynn	.50
10	Keith Moreland	.50
11	Sparky Anderson	.75
12	Mike Brumley	.50
14	Dave Bergman	.50
15	Pat Sheridan	.50
18	Al Pedrique	.50
19	Ramon Pena	.50
21	Doyle Alexander	.50
22	Guillermo Hernandez	.50
23	Torey Lovullo	.50
24	Gary Pettis	.50
25	Ken Williams	.50
27	Frank Tanana	.50
29	Charles Hudson	.50
33	Gary Ward	.50
34	Matt Nokes	.50
35	Chet Lemon	.50
36	Rick Schu	.50
37	Frank Williams	.50
39	Mike Henneman	.50

44	Jeff Robinson	.50
47	Jack Morris	.50
48	Paul Gibson	.50
---	Coaches (Billy Consolo, Alex Grammas, Billy Muffett, Vada Pinson, Dick Tracewski)	.50

1990 Marathon Cubs

Marathon sponsored its second consecutive Chicago Cubs team set. The oversized cards feature thin white stock and full-color photos. The cards are numbered according to uniform number, and were distributed at a Cubs home game.

		NM/M
Complete Set (28):		6.00
Common Player:		.25
4	Don Zimmer	.35
7	Joe Girardi	.25
8	Andre Dawson	1.50
10	Lloyd McClendon	.25
11	Luis Salazar	.25
12	Shawon Dunston	.25
15	Domingo Ramos	.25
17	Mark Grace	.35
18	Dwight Smith	.25
19	Curtis Wilkerson	.25
20	Jerome Walton	.25
22	Mike Harkey	.25
23	Ryne Sandberg	4.50
25	Marvell Wynne	.25
28	Mitch Williams	.25
29	Doug Dascenzo	.25
30	Dave Clark	.25
31	Greg Maddux	4.00
32	Hector Villanueva	.25
36	Mike Bielecki	.25
37	Bill Long	.25
41	Rick Sutcliffe	.25
41	Jeff Pico	.25
44	Steve Wilson	.25
45	Paul Assenmacher	.25
47	Shawn Boskie	.25
50	Les Lancaster	.25
---	Coaches (Joe Altobelli, Chuck Cottier, Jose Martinez, Dick Pole, Phil Roof)	.25

1991 Marathon Cubs

Marathon Oil once again sponsored a set featuring the Chicago Cubs. This 28-card release features oversized cards measuring 2-7/8" x 4-1/4". The card fronts feature full-color action photos. The flip sides feature complete statistics. The cards are numbered according to uniform number. This number appears on both the front and back of the card.

	NM/M
Complete Set (28):	12.50
Common Player:	.50

8	Joe Girardi	.50
8	Andre Dawson	2.50
9	Damon Berryhill	.50
10	Luis Salazar	.50
11	George Bell	.50
16	Shawon Dunston	.50
16	Jose Vizcaino	.50
17	Mark Grace	.65
18	Dwight Smith	.50
19	Hector Villanueva	.50
20	Jerome Walton	.50
22	Mike Harkey	.50
23	Ryne Sandberg	6.50
24	Chico Walker	.50
29	Doug Dascenzo	.50
30	Bob Scanlan	.50
31	Greg Maddux	6.00
32	Danny Jackson	.50
35	Chuck McElroy	.50
36	Mike Bielecki	.50
40	Rick Sutcliffe	.50
41	Jim Essian	.50
42	Dave Smith	.50
45	Paul Assenmacher	.50
47	Shawn Boskie	.50
50	Les Lancaster	.50
51	Heathcliff Slocumb	.50
---	Coaches (Joe Altobelli, Billy Connors, Chuck Cottier, Jose Martinez, Phil Roof, Richie Zisk)	.50

1992 Marathon Cubs

The fourth consecutive year of a Cubs team set sponsored by Marathon Oil consists of 28 cards, including manager Jim Lefebvre and his coaching staff. The set was originally given away at the July 10, 1993 game at Wrigley Field. Cards are checklisted here by uniform number.

		NM/M
Complete Set (28):		9.00
Common Player:		.25
1	Doug Strange	.30
2	Frank Castillo	.30
3	Jim Lefebvre	.30
6	Rey Sanchez	.30
7	Joe Girardi	.30
8	Andre Dawson	.75
10	Luis Salazar	.30
12	Shawon Dunston	.30
16	Jose Vazcaino	.30
17	Mark Grace	.45
18	Dwight Smith	.30
19	Hector Villanueva	.30
20	Jerome Walton	.30
21	Sammy Sosa	3.50
23	Ryne Sandberg	3.50
27	Derrick May	.30
29	Doug Dascenzo	.30
30	Bob Scanlan	.30
31	Greg Maddux	3.00
32	Danny Jackson	.30
34	Ken Patterson	.30
35	Chuck McElroy	.30
36	Mike Morgan	.30
38	Jeff Robinson	.30
42	Dave Smith	.30
45	Paul Assenmacher	.30
47	Shawn Boskie	.30
---	Coaches (Tom Treblehorn, Jose Martinez, Billy Williams, Sammy Ellis, Chuck Cottier, Billy Connors)	.30

1993 Marathon Cubs

The Cubs distributed the 1993 Marathon Oil set on July 28 in a game against the Padres. The cards, measuring an oversized 4-1/4" x 2-7/8", are unnumbered, with uniform numbers appearing on the back. The cards have a vertical blue stripe down the right side

	NM/M
Complete Set (28):	6.00
Common Player:	.25
2	Rick Wilkins	.25
5	Jim Lefebvre	.25
9	Willie Wilson	.25
10	Steve Lake	.25
11	Rey Sanchez	.25
16	Jose Vizcaino	.25
17	Mark Grace	.35
18	Dwight Smith	.25
20	Eric Yelding	.25
21	Sammy Sosa	3.50
22	Mike Harkey	.25
23	Ryne Sandberg	3.50
24	Steve Buechele	.25
25	Candy Maldonado	.25
27	Derrick May	.25
28	Randy Myers	.25
29	Jose Guzman	.25
30	Bob Scanlan	.25
32	Dan Plesac	.25
36	Mike Morgan	.25
37	Greg Hibbard	.25
38	Jose Bautista	.25
45	Paul Assenmacher	.25
49	Frank Castillo	.25
53	Doug Jennings	.25
---	Coaches (Billy Williams, Jose Martinez, Billy Connors, Tony Muser)	.25
---	Coaches (Dan Simonds, Tom Treblehorn, Chuck Cottier)	.25

2004 Maryland Lottery Golden Ticket Baltimore Orioles

In conjunction with the 50th anniversary of the Baltimore Orioles, the Maryland Lottery issued a set of baseball cards depicting great moments and players from the past. They were issued in a four-card foil pack with the purchase of a $10 Golden Ticket scratch-off card. Cards #1-45 were reported issued in quantities of 50,000 to 100,000 each. The team highlight cards, #45-48 were issued in an edition of 25,000 each. Fifteen thousand of the Ripken Ironman card #49 were produced. Card #50, Babe Ruth (shown on a 1914 Orioles minor league baseball card), was produced in an edition of 10,000. The first 100 persons turning in a complete

with the player's last name in large, white letters. Backs carry complete major and minor league statistics. There are 27 cards in the set. The checklist is presented here by uniform number.

		NM/M
Complete Set (27):		7.50
Common Player:		.25
2	Rick Wilkins	.25
5	Jim Lefebvre	.25
9	Willie Wilson	.25
10	Steve Lake	.25
11	Rey Sanchez	.25
16	Jose Vizcaino	.25
17	Mark Grace	.35
18	Dwight Smith	.25
20	Eric Yelding	.25
21	Sammy Sosa	3.50
22	Mike Harkey	.25
23	Ryne Sandberg	3.50
24	Steve Buechele	.25
25	Candy Maldonado	.25
27	Derrick May	.25
28	Randy Myers	.25
29	Jose Guzman	.25
30	Bob Scanlan	.25
32	Dan Plesac	.25
36	Mike Morgan	.25
37	Greg Hibbard	.25
38	Jose Bautista	.25
45	Paul Assenmacher	.25
49	Frank Castillo	.25
53	Doug Jennings	.25
---	Coaches (Billy Williams, Jose Martinez, Billy Connors, Tony Muser)	.25
---	Coaches (Dan Simonds, Tom Treblehorn, Chuck Cottier)	.25

set won $1,000 and an Orioles prize package. Cards are in the standard 2-1/2" x 3-1/2" format, printed on thin cardboard UV-coated on both sides.

		NM/M
Complete Set (50):		40.00
Common Player:		.50
1	Luis Aparicio	.75
2	Steve Barber	.50
3	Don Baylor	.50
4	Mark Belanger	.50
5	Mike Boddicker	.50
6	Don Buford	.50
7	Al Bumbry	.50
8	Mike Cuellar	.50
9	Rich Dauer	.50
10	Storm Davis	.50
11	Doug DeCinces	.50
12	Pat Dobson	.50
13	Moe Drabowsky	.50
14	Andy Etchebarren	.50
15	Bobby Grich	.50
16	George Kell	.50
17	Tito Landrum	.50
18	Lee MacPhail	.50
19	Tippy Martinez	.50
20	Scott McGregor	.50
21	Dave McNally	.50
22	Milt Pappas	.50
23	Paul Richards	.50
24	Gary Roenicke	.50
25	Dave Schmidt	.50
26	Steve Stone	.50
27	Gus Triandos	.50
28	Gene Woodling	.50
29	Terry Crowley	.50
30	Elrod Hendricks	.50
31	Memorial Stadium	.50
32	Orioles Park	.50
33	Rex Barney	.50
34	Rick Dempsey	.50
35	Mike Flanagan	.50
36	Jim Gentile	.50
37	Reggie Jackson	2.00
38	Frank Robinson	2.00
39	Chuck Thompson	.50
40	Earl Weaver	.50
41	Opening Day 1954	.50
42	Brady Anderson	.50
43	Boog Powell	.65
44	Brooks Robinson	2.00
45	Jim Palmer	1.50
46	1966 World Series	7.50
47	1970 World Series	7.50
48	1983 World Series	7.50
49	2131 Ironman Breaks Record	7.50
50	Babe Ruth	15.00
---	Checklist/Rules	.10

1988 Master Bread Twins

This set of 12 cardboard discs (2-3/4" diameter) features full-color photos of Minnesota Twins team members. Fronts have a bright blue background with red, yellow and black printing. The player photo (with team logos airbrushed off) is centered beneath a "Master Is Good Bread" headliner and a vivid yellow player/team name banner. Backs are black-and-white with five stars printed above the player's name, team, personal data, disc number, stats and "1988 Collector's Edition" banner. The discs were printed in Canada and marketed exclusively in Minnesota in packages of Master Bread, one disc per loaf. Squares cut from sheets are known in the hobby, valued about 50 percent of the issued version.

		NM/M
Complete Set (12):		12.00
Common Player:		1.00
1	Bert Blyleven	1.00
2	Frank Viola	1.00
3	Juan Berenguer	1.00
4	Jeff Reardon	1.00
5	Tim Laudner	1.00

6	Steve Lombardozzi	1.00
7	Randy Bush	1.00
8	Kirby Puckett	5.00
9	Gary Gaetti	1.00
10	Kent Hrbek	1.00
11	Greg Gagne	1.00
12	Tom Brunansky	1.00

1989 Master Bread

For a second year Master Bread packages in the Twin Cities area contained a baseball player disc in 1989. The 2-3/4" discs are in the familiar Mike Schechter Associates format and, unlike the '88 set, featured American League players other than Twins. The issue is among the scarcer of the MSA disc issues. Fronts are trimmed in yellow banners and blue stars. Backs are in blue and have a few stats and player data, along with a disc number.

		NM/M
Complete Set (12):		20.00
Common Player:		1.00
1	Frank Viola	1.00
2	Kirby Puckett	4.00
3	Gary Gaetti	1.00
4	Alan Trammell	1.00
5	Wade Boggs	4.00
6	Don Mattingly	5.00
7	Wally Joyner	1.00
8	Paul Molitor	3.50
9	George Brett	5.00
10	Jose Canseco	2.00
11	Julio Franco	1.00
12	Cal Ripken Jr.	7.50

1989 MasterCard Masters of the Game

The reason for issue and method of distribution for this set is not known. The issue was in the form of a 7-1/2" x 10-1/2" sheet on thin cardboard, picturing eight Hall of Famers around a title card. If cut from the unperforated sheet, single cards measure the standard 2-1/2" x 3-1/2". Fronts have familiar black-and-white photos with a gold border. Backs are in black, white and red with a repeat of the Masters of the Game logo, a few biographical details, lifetime stats and an MLB licensee logo. The unnumbered cards are checklisted here in alphabetical order.

		NM/M
Uncut Sheet:		6.00
Complete Set (9):		6.00
Common Player:		1.00
(1)	Ty Cobb	1.50
(2)	Lou Gehrig	1.50
(3)	Rogers Hornsby	1.00
(4)	Christy Mathewson	1.00
(5)	Satchel Paige	1.00
(6)	Babe Ruth	2.00
(7)	Casey Stengel	1.00
(8)	Cy Young	1.00
(9)	Title Card	.05

1985 Thom McAn Discs

One of the more obscure 1985 issues, this 47-card set of "Pro Player Discs" was issued by Thom McAn as a promotion for its "Jox" tennis shoes, which are advertised on the back of the cards. The discs, which measure 2-3/4" in diameter, feature black-and-white player photos against a background of either gold, yellow, red, pink, green or blue. Although not included in the "official" checklist released by the company, cards of George Brett have also been reported. Many of the Latin players' discs are quite scarce and are believed to have been issued in more limited quantities in Hispanic communities. The discs are unnumbered and checklisted here alphabetically.

		NM/M
Complete Set (47):		50.00
Common Player:		1.00
(1)	Benny Ayala	1.25
(2)	Buddy Bell	1.00
(3)	Juan Beniquez	1.25
(4)	Tony Bernazard	1.25
(5)	Mike Boddicker	1.00
(6)	George Brett	9.00
(7)	Bill Buckner	1.00
(8)	Rod Carew	6.00
(9)	Steve Carlton	6.00
(10)	Caesar Cedeno (Cesar)	1.00
(11)	Onix Concepcion	1.00
(12)	Cecil Cooper	1.00
(13)	Al Cowens	1.00
(14)	Jose Cruz	1.25
(15)	Ivan DeJesus	1.25
(16)	Luis DeLeon	1.25
(17)	Rich Gossage	1.00
(18)	Pedro Guerrero	1.00
(19)	Ron Guidry	1.00
(20)	Tony Gwynn	7.50
(21)	Mike Hargrove	1.00
(22)	Keith Hernandez	1.25
(23)	Bob Horner	1.00
(24)	Kent Hrbek	1.00
(25)	Rick Langford	1.00
(26)	Jeff Leonard	1.00
(27)	Willie McGee	1.00
(28)	Jack Morris	1.25
(29)	Jesse Orosco	1.25
(30)	Junior Ortiz	1.00
(31)	Terry Puhl	1.00
(32)	Dan Quisenberry	1.00
(33)	Johnny Ray	1.00
(34)	Cal Ripken	12.00
(35)	Ed Romero	1.25
(36)	Ryne Sandberg	7.50
(37)	Mike Schmidt	9.00
(38)	Tom Seaver	6.00
(39)	Rick Sutcliffe	1.00
(40)	Bruce Sutter	4.50
(41)	Alan Trammell	1.00
(42)	Fernando Valenzuela	1.25
(43)	Ozzie Virgil	1.25
(44)	Greg Walker	1.00
(45)	Willie Wilson	1.00
(46)	Dave Winfield	6.00
(47)	Geoff Zahn	1.00

1990 McDonald's

This 25-card set was released exclusively at 11 McDonald's restaurants in Idaho and eastern Oregon. Four cards were given with a large fries-soda purchase. Production was reported as 4,000 each. The cards have front borders of graduated purple shades around a game-action photo. Backs are similar in format to regular 1990 Score cards and include a portrait photo. The McDonald's logo appears on front and back. Fifteen World Series trivia cards were part of the promotion.

		NM/M
Complete Set (25):		50.00
Common Player:		1.25
Trivia Card:		.60
1	Will Clark	1.25
2	Sandy Alomar, Jr.	1.25
3	Julio Franco	1.25
4	Carlton Fisk	5.00
5	Rickey Henderson	5.00
6	Matt Williams	1.25
7	John Franco	1.25
8	Ryne Sandberg	6.00
9	Kelly Gruber	1.25
10	Andre Dawson	3.00
11	Barry Bonds	12.00
12	Gary Sheffield	3.00
13	Ramon Martinez	1.25
14	Len Dykstra	1.25
15	Benito Santiago	1.25
16	Cecil Fielder	1.25
17	John Olerud	1.25
18	Roger Clemens	7.50
19	George Brett	10.00
20	George Bell	1.25
21	Ozzie Guillen	1.25
22	Steve Sax	1.25
23	Dave Stewart	1.25
24	Ozzie Smith	6.00
25	Robin Yount	5.00

1991 McDonald's Cleveland Indians

Distributed only at northern Ohio area McDonalds, this set features the players, coaches and manager of the Indians on an oversize (2-7/8" x 4-1/4") format. Color photos on front are framed in white and red with a white border all around. In the upper-left corner is a "Tribe Kids Fan Club" logo, while the McDonald's logo appears at lower-right. The player's uniform number, name and position are in black at lower-left. Backs are printed in black and have complete major and minor league statistics.

		NM/M
Complete Set (30):		5.00
Common Player:		.25
1	John McNamara	.25
2	Alex Cole	.25
4	Joel Skinner	.25
5	Jose Escobar	.25
7	Chris James	.25
8	Albert Belle	.50
9	Carlos Baerga	.25
11	Doug Jones	.25
14	Jerry Browne	.25
15	Sandy Alomar	.25
16	Felix Fermin	.25
17	Turner Ward	.25
21	Greg Swindell	.25
23	Mitch Webster	.25
26	Brook Jacoby	.25
27	Dave Otto	.25
31	Steve Olin	.25
37	Beau Allred	.25
38	Shawn Hillegas	.25
40	Eric King	.25
41	Charles Nagy	.25
43	Mike Huff	.25
44	Jeff Manto	.25
46	Bruce Egloff	.25
47	Jesse Orosco	.25
48	Mike Walker	.25
49	Tom Candiotti	.25
52	John Farrell	.25
54	Rod Nichols	.25
---	Coaches (Billy Williams, Jose Morales, Rich Dauer, Mike Hargrove, Luis Isaac, Mark Wiley)	.25

1992 McDonald's Baseball's Best

Sold in five-card cello packs with a food purchase at McDonald's stores in New York, New Jersey and Connecticut, this 44-card set was produced by Topps and carries the Topps logo, along with the Golden Arches, on front and back. Player photos on front are framed in yellow, surrounded by a black border. A red and blue "Baseball's Best" logo appears at top-right of the photo. Above that is a gold-foil stripe announcing "Limited Edition." At lower-right is another gold-foil stripe with the McDonald's logo and the player's name embossed thereon. On cards #34-44, which were distributed one per pack, there is an additional gold embossed "Rookie" shield at upper-left. Backs have a red border with a yellow stat box at center framed in white.

		NM/M
Complete Set (44):		6.00
Common Player:		.10
1	Cecil Fielder	.10
2	Benito Santiago	.10
3	Rickey Henderson	.60
4	Roberto Alomar	.20
5	Ryne Sandberg	.75
6	George Brett	1.25
7	Terry Pendleton	.10
8	Ken Griffey Jr.	1.25
9	Bobby Bonilla	.10
10	Roger Clemens	1.00
11	Ozzie Smith	.75
12	Barry Bonds	1.50
13	Cal Ripken, Jr.	1.50
14	Ron Gant	.10
15	Carlton Fisk	.60
16	Steve Avery	.10
17	Robin Yount	.60
18	Will Clark	.10
19	Kirby Puckett	.75
20	Jim Abbott	.10
21	Barry Larkin	.10
22	Jose Canseco	.45
23	Howard Johnson	.10
24	Nolan Ryan	1.50
25	Frank Thomas	.60
26	Danny Tartabull	.10
27	Julio Franco	.10
28	David Justice	.10
29	Joe Carter	.10
30	Dale Murphy	.35
31	Andre Dawson	.10
32	Dwight Gooden	.10
33	Bo Jackson	.10
34	Jeff Bagwell	.60
35	Chuck Knoblauch	.10
36	Derek Bell	.10
37	Jim Thome	.10
38	Royce Clayton	.10
39	Ryan Klesko	.10
40	Chito Martinez	.10
41	Ivan Rodriguez	.50
42	Todd Hundley	.10
43	Eric Karros	.10
44	Todd Van Poppel	.10

Cardinals

Pacific Trading Cards and McDonald's combined in 1992 to produce this 55-card (plus checklist) team set for the benefit of Ronald McDonald Children's Charities on the occasion of the St. Louis Cardinals' 100th anniversary. Sets were sold initially for $1.49. Cards are standard 2-1/2" x 3-1/2" size and UV coated on each side. There is a sepia-toned or color photo on both front and back; generally an action photo on front and a portrait on back. Player selection is largely weighted to the last half of the 20th Century, with only a few cards of players pre-dating the Gashouse Gang era. The front design is completed with a Cardinals anniversary logo in the upper-left corner, a McDonald's logo at lower-right and gold stripes top and bottom. The player's name and position appear in red at the bottom of the photo. Besides the portrait photo, backs have a career summary stats for the player's Cardinals year and major league career and all appropriate logos.

		NM/M
Complete Set (55):		6.00
Common Player:		.10
1	Jim Bottomley	.15
2	Rip Collins	.10
3	Johnny Mize	.25
4	Rogers Hornsby	.25
5	Miller Huggins	.10
6	Marty Marion	.25
7	Frank Frisch	.25
8	Whitey Kurowski	.10
9	Joe Medwick	.10
10	Terry Moore	.10
11	Chick Hafey	.10
12	Pepper Martin	.25
13	Bob O'Farrell	.10
14	Walker Cooper	.10
15	Dizzy Dean	.50
16	Grover Cleveland Alexander	.25
17	Jesse Haines	.10
18	Bill Hallahan	.10
19	Mort Cooper	.10
20	Burleigh Grimes	.10
21	Red Schoendienst	.25
22	Stan Musial	3.00
23	Enos Slaughter	.25
24	Keith Hernandez	.25
25	Bill White	.25
26	Orlando Cepeda	.25
27	Julian Javier	.10
28	Dick Groat	.10
29	Ken Boyer	.20
30	Lou Brock	.50
31	Mike Shannon	.25
32	Curt Flood	.25
33	Joe Cunningham	.10
34	Reggie Smith	.10
35	Ted Simmons	.10
36	Tim McCarver	.25
37	Tom Herr	.10
38	Ozzie Smith	2.00
39	Joe Torre	.45
40	Terry Pendleton	.20
41	Ken Reitz	.10
42	Vince Coleman	.10
43	Willie McGee	.25
44	Bake McBride	.10
45	George Hendrick	.10
46	Bob Gibson	1.00
47	Whitey Herzog	.10
48	Harry Brecheen	.10
49	Howard Pollet	.10
50	John Tudor	.10
51	Bob Forsch	.10
52	Bruce Sutter	.50
53	Lee Smith	.15
54	Todd Worrell	.10
55	Al Hrabosky	.10
---	Checklist	.02

Pin/Cards

This set of three card-pin combinations saw limited distribution in the Northwestern U.S., with sales benefitting the Ronald McDonald Children's Charities. Cards measure 2-1/2" x 3-1/2" and have the same color photo of Ken Griffey, Jr. on the front. Fronts also have a McDonald's logo and facsimile autograph. Uniform logos have been removed from the player's photo. Backs have a description of the charity and the logo "Griffey's Golden Moments," along with a 1992 Alrak Enterprises copyright. The pins were fastened through the cardboard of the card, leaving each with a hole. Prices quoted are for card/pin combinations.

		NM/M
Complete Set (3):		7.50
Common Card/Pin:		2.50
1	Ken Griffey Jr.	2.50
2	Ken Griffey Jr.	2.50
3	Ken Griffey Jr.	2.50

MVP

McDonald's restaurants in Ontario released a 26-card All-Star baseball card set in 1992 featuring many of the top players in the game. The cards were sold at Canadian McDonald's in packs of four with the purchase of a meal. Additionally, the company offered a six-card Toronto Blue Jays subset. The cards were produced by Donruss.

		NM/M
Complete Set (33):		8.00
Common Player:		.25
1	Cal Ripken, Jr.	1.50
2	Frank Thomas	.65
3	George Brett	1.00
4	Roberto Kelly	.25
5	Nolan Ryan	1.50
6	Ryne Sandberg	.75
7	Darryl Strawberry	.25
8	Len Dykstra	.25
9	Fred McGriff	.25
10	Roger Clemens	.85
11	Sandy Alomar Jr.	.25
12	Robin Yount	.65
13	Jose Canseco	.45
14	Jimmy Key	.25
15	Barry Larkin	.25
16	Dennis Martinez	.25
17	Andy Van Slyke	.25
18	Will Clark	.25
19	Mark Langston	.25
20	Cecil Fielder	.25
21	Kirby Puckett	.25
22	Ken Griffey Jr.	1.00
23	David Justice	.25

24	Jeff Bagwell	.65
25	Howard Johnson	.25
26	Ozzie Smith	.75
1	Roberto Alomar	.35
2	Joe Carter	.25
3	Kelly Gruber	.25
4	Jack Morris	.25
5	Tom Henke	.25
6	Devon White	.25

WUAB Cleveland Indians

These larger-than-standard (2-7/8" x 4-1/4") cards were given to members of the Tribe Kids Fan Club, sponsored by McDonald's and television station WUAB, whose logos appear on front and back, respectively. Cards have poses or game photos with red frames, white borders and a row of vertical blue diamonds on front. Horizontally formatted backs are in black-and-white with complete career stats. Cards are listed here in order of the uniform numbers which appear on front.

		NM/M
Complete Set (30):		6.00
Common Player:		.25
0	Junior Ortiz	.25
1	Glenallen Hill	.25
2	Alex Cole	.25
4	Bob Skinner	.25
7	Kenny Lofton	.40
8	Albert Belle	.35
9	Carlos Baerga	.25
10	Mark Lewis	.25
11	Paul Sorrento	.25
15	Sandy Alomar Jr.	.25
16	Felix Fermin	.25
20	Tony Perezchica	.25
21	Mike Hargrove	.25
23	Mark Whiten	.25
25	Jim Thome	2.50
26	Brook Jacoby	.25
27	Dave Otto	.25
28	Derek Lilliquist	.25
31	Steve Olin	.25
33	Thomas Howard	.25
36	Brad Arnsberg	.25
39	Dennis Cook	.25
41	Charles Nagy	.25
44	Reggie Jefferson	.25
47	Scott Scudder	.25
48	Ted Power	.25
54	Rod Nichols	.25
63	Eric Bell	.25
77	Jack Armstrong	.25
---	The Coaches (Rick Adair, Ken Bolek, Dom Chiti, Ron Clark, Jose Morales, Dave Nelson, Jeff Newman)	.25

Cy Young

This pair of cards honoring a local hero was issued by McDonald's of Tuscarawas and Coshocton Counties in Ohio. A blue border card shows Young at bat and measures about 3-1/2" x 6". A red-bordered card has a commonly seen pitching pose and is about 3-3/4" x 5-15/16". A banner in front of crossed bats on front has his birth and death dates with a pair of McDonald's logos near the bottom. Backs are identical with biographical and statistical information.

		NM/M
Complete Set (2):		5.00
(1)	Cy Young/Btg	3.00
(2)	Cy Young/Pitching	3.00

1993 McDonald's Blue Jays

This 36-card set was produced by Donruss and distributed by McDonald's of Canada. The set features two distinct styles of cards. The first 26 are "Great Moments" cards which feature team highlights of the 1985-1992 seasons. These cards have gold-foil embossed on front with a team logo/Great Moments seal. Backs have a description of the highlight. Cards #27-35 are individual player cards. They feature full-bleed color action photos on front. Backs have a second photo and recent stats. All cards have the McDonald's and Donruss logos on front. The 36th card in the set is a header card with a checklist on back.

		NM/M
Complete Set (36):		5.00
Common Card:		.15
1	First Title - 1985 (Doyle Alexander)	.15
2	Home Run King - 1986 (Jesse Barfield)	.15
3	Major League Home Run Record - 1987 (Fred McGriff)	.15
4	Opening Bell - 1988 (George Bell)	.35
5	First Cycle - 1989 (Kelly Gruber)	.15
6	Unbelievable Comeback - 1989 (Ernie Whitt)	.15
7	Winners Again - 1989 (Tom Henke)	.15
8	First No-Hitter - 1990 (Dave Stieb)	.15
9	First 20-Gamer (Jack Morris)	.15
10	FANtastic - 1992	.15
11	Sudden Impact - 1992 (Pat Borders, Mark McGwire)	.50
12	The Turning Point - 1992 (Roberto Alomar)	.35
13	On to Atlanta - 1992 (Candy Maldonado)	.15
14	Instant Hero - 1992 (Ed Sprague)	.15
15	Old Friends - 1992 (Cito Gaston, Bobby Cox)	.15
16	The Catch - 1992 (Devon White)	.15
17	Near Triple Play - 1992 (Kelly Gruber, Deion Sanders)	.15
18	Winning Welcome - 1992 (Roberto Alomar)	.35
19	Winning Slide - 1992 (Kelly Gruber)	.15
20	Final Farewell - 1992 (Jimmy Key)	.15
21	Winning RBI - 1992 (Devon White, Candy Maldonado)	.15
22	Clincher - 1992 (Joe Carter)	.35
23	World Chamions - 1992	.15
24	Trophy Presentation - 1992 (Cito Gaston, Bobby Brown)	.15
25	MVP - 1992 (Pat Borders)	.15
26	Heroes' Welcome - 1992 (Roberto Alomar)	.35
	PLAYER CARDS	.15
27	John Olerud	.35
28	Roberto Alomar	.40
29	Ed Sprague	.15
30	Dick Schofield	.15
31	Devon White	.15
32	Joe Carter	.15
33	Darrin Jackson	.15
34	Pat Borders	.15
35	Paul Molitor	1.00
36	Checklist	.05

Expos

Top players and manager's from the team's 25 years were featured in a 33-card set produced by Donruss and distributed by Canadian McDonald's outlets. Card fronts feature a full-color borderless photo with the McDonald's and Donruss logos at top. A blue strip at bottom contains the player name and uniform number. At lower-left is an embossed silver-foil 25th anniversary logo. Fronts of the 2-1/2" x 3-1/2" cards are UV coated. Backs are printed in English and French and include a career summary and the player's stats while with the Expos. Appropriate sponsor, team and licensor logos also appear. Autographed cards of Expos manager Felipe Alou were randomly packaged.

		NM/M
Complete Set (33):		12.00
Common Player:		.25
1	Moises Alou	.75
2	Andre Dawson	1.50
3	Delino DeShields	.25
4	Andres Galarraga	.50
5	Marquis Grissom	.50
6	Tim Raines	.50
7	Larry Walker	1.00
8	Tim Wallach	.25
10	Ken Hill	.25
10	Dennis Martinez	.35
11	Jeff Reardon	.25
12	Gary Carter	4.00
13	Dave Cash	.25
14	Warren Cromartie	.25
15	Mack Jones	.25
16	Al Oliver	.35
17	Larry Parrish	.25
18	Rodney Scott	.25
19	Ken Singleton	.25
20	Rusty Staub	.35
21	Ellis Valentine	.25
22	Woody Fryman	.25
23	Charlie Lea	.25
24	Bill Lee	.25
25	Mike G. Marshall	.25
26	Claude Raymond	.25
27	Steve Renko	.25
28	Steve Rogers	.25
29	Bill Stoneman	.25
30	Gene Mauch	.25
31	Felipe Alou	.45
31a	Felipe Alou/Auto.	20.00
32	Buck Rodgers	.25
33	Checklist	.05

1997 McDonald's N.Y. Yankees

Three popular Yankees stars of the 1996 World Championship team are featured in this issue which raised funds for Ronald McDonald House Charities. The 2-1/2" x 3-1/2" cards have color action photos on front with dark blue borders, a facsimile autograph and McDonald's logo. Uniform and cap logos have been removed from the photos. Backs are printed in blue with a cartoon of Ronald McDonald in baseball gear, a few biographical details about the player and some information about the charity.

		NM/M
Complete Set (3):		10.00
Common Player:		4.00
(1)	Dwight Gooden	4.00
(2)	Tino Martinez	4.00
(3)	Andy Pettitte	4.00

1998 McDonald's Arizona Diamondbacks

Marking the team's first year in the National League, this card set was given away to children 14 and under at an August 14 promotional game. In standard 2-1/2" x 3-1/2" format, the cards feature color portrait photos. Team and sponsor logos are in the left corners, with player identification in a green stripe at bottom. Backs have a desert scene background over which is printed personal data and professional stats. At bottom is a "Diamondbacks' Fact." Cards are listed here according to uniform number appearing on front.

		NM/M
Complete Set (24):		7.50
Common Player:		.50
5	Andy Stankiewicz	.50
6	Andy Fox	.50
9	Matt Williams	.75
10	Tony Batista	.50
11	Buck Showalter	.50
12	Jorge Fabregas	.50
15	Brent Brede	.50
16	Travis Lee	1.00
19	Willie Blair	.50
20	Jeff Suppan	.50
22	Devon White	.50
24	Karim Garcia	.75
25	David Dellucci	.50
26	Damian Miller	.50
30	Gregg Olson	.50
33	Jay Bell	.50
34	Brian Anderson	.50
35	Kelly Stinnett	.50
36	Clint Sodowsky	.50
37	Omar Daal	.50
38	Joel Adamson	.50
40	Andy Benes	.50
43	Yamil Benitez	.50
47	Felix Rodriguez	.50

1999 McDonald's St. Louis Cardinals

A late-season promotion at McDonald's restaurants in the St. Louis area offered six-card packs of Upper Deck Cardinal cards at $2.49, or $1.99 with a purchase. Cards are in the basic style of UD's 1999 MVP issue, but lack the silver-foil highlights on front. Backs

are also nearly identical, but include a McDonald's logo at bottom-right. Both front and back photos on the McDonald's cards differ from those used on UD MVP. Each foil pack contains four of the 15 player cards, plus two of the special Mark McGwire Milestone inserts. Checklist cards are a one-in-nine pack insert.

		NM/M
Complete Set (16):		4.00
Common Player:		.15
1	J.D. Drew	1.00
2	Jose Jiminez	.15
3	Mark McGwire	1.50
4	Fernando Tatis	.15
5	Edgar Renteria	.15
6	Ray Lankford	.15
7	Willie McGee	.15
8	Ricky Bottalico	.15
9	Eli Marrero	.15
10	Kent Bottenfield	.15
11	Eric Davis	.15
12	Darren Bragg	.15
13	Joe McEwing	.15
14	Shawon Dunston	.15
15	Darren Oliver	.15
---	Checklist	.05

1999 McDonald's Mark McGwire Milestones

A late-season promotion at McDonald's restaurants in the St. Louis area offered six-card packs of Upper Deck Cardinal cards at $2.49, or $1.99 with a purchase. Each foil pack contains four of the 15 player cards, plus two special Mark McGwire Milestone inserts. Horizontally formatted, the Milestones inserts have an action photo of McGwire on a silver metallic-foil background with red, blue and black high-tech graphic designs. The cards mark one of McGwire important home runs of 1998. Backs have a portrait photo and recount some of his career highlights. A McDonald's logo appears in the lower-right corner.

		NM/M
Complete Set (9):		7.00
Common Card:		1.00
M1	Mark McGwire (#50)	1.00
M2	Mark McGwire (#60)	1.00
M3	Mark McGwire (#61)	1.00
M4	Mark McGwire (#62)	1.50
M5	Mark McGwire (#63)	1.00
M6	Mark McGwire (#67)	1.00
M7	Mark McGwire (#68)	1.00
M8	Mark McGwire (#69)	1.00
M9	Mark McGwire (#70)	1.50

2000 McDonald's Negro League Baseball

A set of 10 cards of former Negro Leagues ballplayers was issued by McDonald's in Milwaukee. The 2-1/2 x 3-1/2

cards have black-and-white oval photos at center, bordered in blue. A color logo reading "Yesterday's / Negro League Baseball / Players Wall of Fame" appears at top. A red starburst has the card number at upper-right. Below the photo are the McDonald's logo, the player's name and the years he was active in the Negro League. The red-on-white backs have biographical and career information and stats. Cards originally sold in one-card packs for 99 cents, or the set of 10 for about $9.

		NM/M
Complete Set (10):		20.00
Common Player:		2.00
1	William "Bobby" Robinson	2.00
2	Mamie "Peanut" Johnson	2.00
3	Carl Long	2.00
4	John "Mule" Miles	2.00
5	Sherwood Brewer	2.00
6	Ira McKnight	2.00
7	Gordon Hopkins	2.00
8	Johnny Washington	2.00
9	Jim Robinson	2.00
10	Dennis "Bose" Biddle	2.00

St. Louis Cardinals Coin/Cards

At a series of promotional games during the season, the Cardinals distributed these coin/cards. Wrapped in cellophone was a 2-1/2" x 4" card and a 39mm (about 1-1/2") bronze medallion. The card was horizontally perforated so it could be seperated into a 2-1/2" x 2" player card and two 2-1/2" x 1" coupons. The player card has a game action photo on front. On back is the player name and career highlights. The coupons are for $1 off a McDonald's meal and for a free soft drink at Shell gas stations. Coins have the team logo on front, a player image roughly the same as pictured on the card, and the player uniform number. Back of the coin has the team and sponsor logos and the date the coin was distributed.

		NM/M
Complete Set (4):		20.00
Common Player:		4.00
1	Willie McGee (May 13)	4.00
2	Fernando Vina (June 24)	4.00
3	Jim Edmonds (July 9)	6.00
4	Mark McGwire (September 3)	8.00

2003 McDonald's N.Y. Yankees

Beginning July 28, and extending until 8.75 million cards were given away, these Upper Deck-produced cards were available at 600+ McDonald's in the metro New York area with the purchase of a special Yankees-themed Happy Meal. Cards were issued in either singly in a cello pack, or in a pack with a scratch-off game card. Fronts have an action photo with a large ghost-image team logo behind. Also on front are the Yankee's 100th anniversary logo and logos of UD and McDonald's. Backs have another player photo, stats, personal data and the logos.

		NM/M
Complete Set (24):		8.00
Common Player:		.25
1	Juan Acevedo	.25
2	Roger Clemens	1.50
3	John Flaherty	.25
4	Jason Giambi	.50
5	Chris Hammond	.25
6	Sterling Hitchcock	.25
7	Derek Jeter	2.50
8	Nick Johnson	.25
9	Steve Karsay	.25
10	Hideki Matsui	1.50
11	Raul Mondesi	.25
12	Mike Mussina	.35
13	Antonio Osuna	.25
14	Andy Petitte	.35
15	Jorge Posada	.35
16	Mariano Rivera	.35
17	Alfonso Soriano	.35
18	Bubba Trammell	.25
19	Robin Ventura	.25
20	Jeff Weaver	.25
21	David Wells	.25
22	Bernie Williams	.35
23	Enrique Wilson	.25
24	Todd Zeile	.25

2004 McDonald's Philadelphia Phillies

A two-card pack was given away with each Extra Value Meal purchase at Philly area McDonald's in July. Production of 170,000 of each card was reported. Upper Deck created the cards for the promotion.

		NM/M
Complete Set (27):		6.00
Common Player:		.50
1	Jim Thome	1.00
2	Placido Polanco	.50
3	Jimmy Rollins	1.00
4	David Bell	.50
5	Bobby Abreu	.50
6	Pat Burrell	1.00
7	Marlon Byrd	.50
8	Mike Lieberthal	.75
9	Kevin Millwood	.50

10	Randy Wolf	.50
11	Vicente Padilla	.50
12	Eric Milton	.50
13	Brett Myers	.50
14	Billy Wagner	.50
15	Tim Worrell	.50
16	Rheal Cormier	.50
17	Roberto Hernandez	.50
18	Ryan Madson	.50
19	Amaury Telemaco	.50
20	Tomas Perez	.50
21	Shawn Wooten	.50
22	Doug Glanville	.50
23	Ricky Ledee	.50
24	Jason Michaels	.50
25	Todd Pratt	.50
26	Larry Bowa	.50
27	Citizens Bank Park/Checklist	.50

1992 MCI Ambassadors

STEVE GARVEY 1st Base

Issued in conjunction with the MCI-sponsored Ambassadors of Baseball World Tour of overseas military bases, this set features retired players who participated in the tour. Cards feature color photos with a white border, a color tour logo in the lower-left and a banner across the upper-left reading, "Support MWR With MCI." The player's name and position appear in the bottom border. Horizontally oriented backs have career stats and highlights and the logos of MCI and the Major League Baseball Players Alumni in black-and-white.

		NM/M
Complete Set (16):		35.00
Common Player:		2.00
1	Earl Weaver	3.00
2	Steve Garvey	6.00
3	Doug Flynn	2.00
4	Bert Campaneris	2.00
5	Bill Madlock	2.00
6	Graig Nettles	2.00
7	Dave Kingman	3.00
8	Paul Blair	2.00
9	Jeff Burroughs	2.00
10	Rick Waits	2.00
11	Elias Sosa	2.00
12	Tug McGraw	2.00
13	Ferguson Jenkins/ Photo	4.00
14	Bob Feller	6.00
---	Ferguson Jenkins/Art	4.00
---	Header Card	.50

1993 MCI Ambassadors

JOE CHARBONEAU

The Major League Baseball Players Alumni Association produced a set of 13 former players who were featured in 1993's MCI Ambassadors of Baseball World Tour. The card set was available free to military personnel who com-

pleted an MCI application. The tour of military bases worldwide included appearances by the players at base exchanges, clinics for dependent children and a softball game against base all-stars. The cards feature a photo of the player on the front with logos from the Ambassador tour and MCI in opposite corners.

		NM/M
Complete Set (14):		20.00
Common Player:		1.25
1	Vida Blue	1.25
2	Paul Blair	1.25
3	Mudcat Grant	1.25
4	Phil Niekro	2.00
5	Bob Feller	3.00
6	Joe Charboneau	2.00
7	Joe Rudi	1.25
8	Catfish Hunter	2.00
9	Manny Sanguillen	1.25
10	Harmon Killebrew	3.00
11	Al Oliver	1.25
12	Bob Dernier	1.25
13	Graig Nettles, Sparky Lyle	1.75
---	Header Card	.10

1994 MCI Ambassadors

Once again in 1994, the old-timers' tour of overseas military bases sponsored by MCI spawned a card set. The '94 set is similar to previous years' issues except that color player photos have had the uniform logos airbrushed away. MCI and tour logos appear in color on the front; backs are in black-and-white and contain career data and highlights along with MCI and Major League Baseball Players Alumni logos. Besides 11 numbered cards, there are four unnumbered cards in the 1994 set which include a pair honoring major leaguers who served in the military during World War II.

		NM/M
Complete Set (15):		30.00
Common Player:		2.00
1	Sparky Lyle	2.00
2	John Stearns	2.00
3	Bobby Thomson	3.00
4	Jimmy Wynn	2.00
5	Ferguson Jenkins	4.00
6	Tug McGraw	2.00
7	Paul Blair	2.00
8	Ron LeFlore	2.00
9	Manny Sanguillen	2.00
10	Doug Flynn	2.00
11	Bill North	2.00
----	Manny Sanguillen (Signing autographs.)	2.00
----	Doug Flynn (Instructing children.)	2.00
----	American Leaguers in WWII	2.00
----	National Leaguers in WWII	2.00

1995 MCI Ambassadors

BERT BLYLEVEN

For a fourth year, Major League Baseball, the Players' Union and the long distance phone provider issued a card set in conjunction with its series of softball games at military bases. Approximately 2,000 sets were issued. The 2-1/2" x 3-1/2" cards have player photos on front with MCI and the baseball tour logos in opposite cor-

ners. Backs have biographical and career information about the retired stars.

		NM/M
Complete Set (16):		30.00
Common Player:		2.00
1	Vida Blue	2.00
2	Bert Campaneris	2.00
3	Tug McGraw	2.00
4	Doug Flynn	2.00
5	Paul Blair	2.00
6	Harmon Killebrew	5.00
7	Sparky Lyle	2.00
8	Steve Garvey	4.00
9	Bert Blyleven	2.00
10	Omar Moreno	2.00
11	Bill Lee	2.00
12	Maury Wills	2.00
13	Dave Parker	2.00
14	Luis Aparicio	5.00
15	Brooks Robinson	5.00
16	George Foster	2.00

1996 MCI Ambassadors

Tommy Davis

This set of former players cards was issued in conjunction with a tour of overseas U.S. military bases by members of the Major League Baseball Players Alumni Association. Players taking part in the tour are featured on the card fronts in photos contemporary with their major league days. Backs have career summaries and stats along with sponsors logos. The cards were virtually all distributed overseas.

		NM/M
Complete Set (8):		30.00
Common Player:		5.00
(1)	Tommy Davis	5.00
(2)	Darrell Evans	6.00
(3)	Jay Howell	5.00
(4)	John Montefusco	5.00
(5)	Graig Nettles	6.00
(6)	Jim Sundberg	5.00
(7)	Header Card	.50
(8)	American Airlines Sponsor Card	.50

1991 MDA All-Stars

RON SANTO

Though the Muscular Dystrophy Association isn't mentioned on the player cards, it was the beneficiary of this set produced by SmithKline Beecham. Card fronts feature color photos of the players during their active careers. Because the set was not licensed by MLB, team uniform logos have been airbrushed off the photos. Black-and-white backs have a recent portrait photo of the player, along with biographi-

cal and career data. The set was available by mail for $3.99 plus proofs of purchase from Tums antacid.

		NM/M
Complete Set (20):		15.00
Common Player:		.50
1	Steve Carlton	1.00
2	Ted Simmons	.50
3	Willie Stargell	1.00
4	Bill Mazeroski	1.00
5	Ron Santo	.75
6	Dave Concepcion	.50
7	Bobby Bonds	.50
8	George Foster	.50
9	Billy Williams	1.00
10	Whitey Ford	2.00
11	Yogi Berra	2.00
12	Boog Powell	.60
13	Davey Johnson	.50
14	Brooks Robinson	2.00
15	Jim Fregosi	.50
16	Harmon Killebrew	1.00
17	Ted Williams	3.00
18	Al Kaline	1.00
---	MDA Fact Card (Brooks Robinson)	.50
---	Header Card	.25

1992 MVP for MDA

The Muscular Dystrophy Association was the beneficiary of this set sponsored by Smith-Kline Beecham. Card fronts feature color photos of the players during their active careers. Because the set was not licensed by MLB, team uniform logos have been airbrushed off the photos. Black-and-white backs have a portrait photo of the player, along with biographical and career data. A vinyl album to house the set was included in the mail-in offer.

		NM/M
Complete Set (20):		9.00
Common Player:		.50
Album:		4.50
1	Yogi Berra	2.00
2	Dick Groat	1.00
3	Maury Wills	1.00
4	Brooks Robinson	1.50
5	Orlando Cepeda	1.00
6	Harmon Killebrew	1.50
7	Boog Powell	1.00
8	Vida Blue	1.00
9	Jeff Burroughs	1.00
10	George Foster	1.00
11	Rod Carew	1.50
12	Jim Rice	1.00
13	Don Baylor	1.00
14	Willie Stargell	1.50
15	Rollie Fingers	1.00
16	Ray Knight	1.00
17	History of the MVP	.25
18	MVP Trivia	.25
19	Harmon Killebrew (w/1992 MDA Poster Child)	1.00
20	MLB Players Assn. Alumni Info	.25

1986 Meadow Gold Blank Backs

SUPER STARS SERIES

DWIGHT GOODEN NEW YORK METS PITCHER Beatrice

This was the second set to be distributed by Meadow Gold Dairy (Beatrice Foods) in 1986. It was issued on Double Play ice cream cartons, one card per package. Full-color player photos have team logos and insignias airbrushed away. This 16-card set is very similar to the Meadow Gold popsicle set, but the photos are different in some instances. The cards measure 2-3/8"

x 3-1/2". The Willie McGee card is reportedly tougher to find than other cards in the set.

		NM/M
Complete Singles Set (16):		20.00
Complete Carton Set (16):		22.50
Common Player:		.75
(1)	George Brett	2.50
(2)	Wade Boggs	2.00
(3)	Carlton Fisk	1.50
(4)	Steve Garvey	1.00
(5)	Dwight Gooden	.75
(6)	Pedro Guerrero	.75
(7)	Reggie Jackson	2.50
(8)	Don Mattingly	2.50
(9)	Willie McGee	.75
(10)	Dale Murphy	1.00
(11)	Cal Ripken, Jr.	3.00
(12)	Pete Rose	3.00
(13)	Ryne Sandberg	2.50
(14)	Mike Schmidt	2.50
(15)	Fernando Valenzuela	.75
(16)	Dave Winfield	1.50

Statistic Backs

SUPER STARS SERIES

DON MATTINGLY NEW YORK YANKEES INFIELD Beatrice

Beatrice Foods produced this set of 20 cards on specially marked boxes of Meadow Gold Double Play popsicles, fudgesicles and bubble gum coolers. They came in two-card panels and have full-color player pictures with player name, team and position printed below the photo. Card backs are printed in red ink and feature player career highlights. The cards measure 2-3/8" x 3-1/2" and were distributed in the West and Midwest. It is considered one of the toughest 1986 regional sets to complete.

		NM/M
Complete Panel Set (10):		10.00
Complete Singles Set (20):		10.00
Common Panel:		1.00
Common Single:		.30
	PANEL 1	2.00
1	George Brett	1.50
2	Fernando Valenzuela	.30
	PANEL 2	1.00
3	Dwight Gooden	.30
4	Dale Murphy	.75
	PANEL 3	3.50
5	Don Mattingly	1.50
6	Reggie Jackson	1.50
	PANEL 4	3.00
7	Dave Winfield	1.00
8	Pete Rose	2.00
	PANEL 5	1.50
9	Wade Boggs	1.25
10	Willie McGee	.30
	PANEL 6	5.00
11	Cal Ripkin (Ripken)	3.00
12	Ryne Sandberg	1.25
	PANEL 7	1.50
13	Carlton Fisk	1.00
14	Jim Rice	.50
	PANEL 8	2.50
15	Steve Garvey	.50
16	Mike Schmidt	1.50
	PANEL 9	1.00
17	Bruce Sutter	.75
18	Pedro Guerrero	.30
	PANEL 10	1.00
19	Rick Sutcliff (Sutcliffe)	.30
20	Rich Gossage	.30

Milk

The third set from Meadow Gold from 1986 came on milk cartons; on pint, quart and half-gallon size containers. The cards measure 2-1/2" x 3-1/2" and feature drawings instead of photographs. Different dairies distributed the cards in various colors of ink. The cards can be found printed in red, brown or black ink.

SUPER STARS SERIES

DWIGHT GOODEN
NEW YORK METS PITCHER

Beatrice

The crude drawings have prevented this rare set from being higher in price.

		NM/M
Complete Set (11):		75.00
Common Player:		3.50
(1)	Wade Boggs	9.00
(2)	George Brett	12.00
(3)	Steve Carlton	7.50
(4)	Dwight Gooden	3.50
(5)	Willie McGee	3.50
(6)	Dale Murphy	6.00
(7)	Cal Ripken, Jr.	17.50
(8)	Pete Rose	15.00
(9)	Ryne Sandberg	9.00
(10)	Mike Schmidt	12.00
(11)	Fernando Valenzuela	3.50

1992 Megacards Babe Ruth Prototypes

THE BAMBINO – THE MAN
LOU GEHRIG APPRECIATION DAY: JULY 4TH

Basically identical to the regularly issued versions, these sample cards were distributed to hobby dealers to introduce Megacards Babe Ruth Collection. Most of the prototypes have different card numbers than those in the regular set, and all carry a large gray diagonal "PROTOTYPE" on back.

		NM/M
Complete Set (9):		7.50
Common Card:		1.00
14	Year in Review - 1921 (Babe Ruth)	1.00
31	World Series - 1916 (Babe Ruth)	1.00
75	Place in History - 1928 (Babe Ruth)	1.00
106	Career Highlights - 1927 (Babe Ruth)	1.00
124	Trivia - 1926 (Babe Ruth)	1.00
129	Sultan of Swat - 1925 (Babe Ruth)	1.00
134	Being Remembered - 1948 - George Bush (Babe Ruth)	1.00
138	Being Remembered - 1923 - Grantland Rice (Babe Ruth)	1.00
154	The Bambino - The Man (Babe Ruth, Lou Gehrig)	1.25

1992 Megacards Babe Ruth

This 165-card set chronicles the life and times of Babe Ruth. The set was produced by Megacards and is officially entitled "The Babe Ruth Collection." The cards feature classic black and white photos with black borders and captions below the photo. The card backs feature coordinating statistics and information.

	NM/M
Complete Set (165):	15.00

YEAR IN REVIEW
SUSPENDED FOR FIRST 38 GAMES   1922

Complete Set, Tin:		20.00
Common Card:		.10
Wax Box (48):		20.00
1	Lifetime Pitching Statistics	.10
2	Lifetime Batting Statistics	.10
3	Lifetime - World Series Pitching	.10
4	Lifetime World Series Batting	.10
5	22-9 Record in the Minors	.10
6	2-1 Record First Year in the Majors	.10
7	Won 17 of his Last 21 Decisions	.10
8	Led League with 1.75 ERA and 9 Shutouts	.10
9	Defeats Walter Johnson for 6th Time	.10
10	Doubles as Pitcher and a Regular	.10
11	First Season in the Outfield	.10
12	Sold to Yankees for $100,000	.10
13	The Best Year Any Batter Ever Had	.10
14	Suspended for First 38 Games	.10
15	Wins American League MVP	.10
16	Wins Only Batting Title - .378	.10
17	The "Million Dollar Stomachache"	.10
18	Bats .372 with a .737 Slugging Average	.10
19	The Best Baseball Team in History	.20
20	Tops 50 Home Runs - 4th Time	.10
21	Clubs 500th Home Run	.10
22	Bam Bams Nine in a Week	.10
23	.700 Slugging Average for 9th Time	.10
24	Blasts Over 40 Homers for 11th Time	.10
25	Over 100 RBIs for 13th Time	.10
26	Tops 2,000 Career Walks	.10
27	Babe Retires	.10
28	Babe Coaches the Dodgers	.10
29	The Babe in Retirement	.10
30	1915 World Series - Warms Bench	.10
31	1916 World Series - Hurls 14-Inning Win	.10
32	1918 World Series - Scoreless Innings	.10
33	1921 World Series - Yankees' First	.10
34	1922 World Series - Back to the Farm	.10
35	1923 World Series - First Championship	.10
36	1926 World Series - 4 HR in Losing Cause	.15
37	1927 World Series - Destroy Bucs in Four	.15
38	1928 World Series - .625 BA and 1.375 SA	.10
39	1932 World Series - Yanks Sweep Cubs	.15
40	Lifetime - 2,056 Walks	.10
41	First to Fan 1,000 Times	.10
42	Lifetime - 2,174 Runs Scored	.15
43	Lifetime - 5,793 Total Bases	.15
44	Lifetime - 1,356 Extra-Base Hits	.15
45	Lifetime - 714 Home Runs	.10
46	Lifetime - 16 Grand Slams	.10
47	Lifetime - 8.5 Home Run Percentage	.15
48	Lifetime - Most Games, 2 or More HR	.10
49	Lifetime - 11 Seasons with 40+ HRs	.10
50	Lifetime - 2,211 RBIs	.15

51	Lifetime - .342 Batting Average	.15
52	Lifetime - .690 Slugging Average	.15
53	Season - Nine Shutouts	.10
54	Season - 170 Walks	.10
55	Season - 177 Runs Scored	.20
56	Season - .545 On-Base Percentage	.10
57	Season - 457 Total Bases	.15
58	Season - 119 Extra-Base Hits	.15
59	Season - 171 Runs Batted In	.15
60	Season - 60 Home Runs	.10
61	Season - 11.8 Home Run Percentage	.10
62	Season - .847 Slugging Average	.15
63	World Series 3-0 Record	.10
64	World Series - 0.87 ERA	.10
65	World Series - 33 Walks	.10
66	World Series - 37 Runs	.10
67	World Series - 96 Total Bases	.10
68	World Series - 15 Home Runs	.10
69	World Series - 33 RBIs	.10
70	World Series - .744 Slugging Average	.20
71	1914 - First Major League Victory	.10
72	1915 - First Major League Home Run	.10
73	1916 - Babe Derails "Big Train"	.10
74	1919 - Leads League in Fielding	.10
75	1919 First Home Run Record	.10
76	1920 - Babe Becomes a Yankee	.10
77	1923 - First Home Run in Yankee Stadium	.10
78	1923 - American League MVP	.10
79	1924 - Wins Only Batting Title	.15
80	1926 - Hits 3 Home Runs in Series Game	.10
81	1927 - Babe and Lou Smack 107 Home Runs (Lou Gehrig)	.20
82	1927 - The Babe's 60th Home Run	.20
83	1928 - Three HR in World Series Game	.10
84	1932 - Early "Called Shots" by the Bam	.10
85	1932 - The "Called Shot" - The Legend	.10
86	1932 - The "Called Shot" - The Believers	.10
87	1932 - The "Called Shot" - The Doubters	.10
88	1932 - The "Called Shot" - Babe's View	.10
89	1933 - First HR in an All-Star Game	.15
90	1933 - Last Time on the Mound	.10
91	1934 - Babe Hits 700th Home Run	.10
92	1934 - The Babe in Japan	.10
93	1935 - Last Major League Homers	.10
94	1939 - Inaugurated into Hall of Fame	.10
95	1942 - Faces Johnson Again in Exhibition	.10
96	1947 - Babe Ruth Day	.10
97	1948 - Babe's Farewell	.25
98	A Perfect Punch	.10
99	Yankees Best Base Thief	.10
100	Hub Pruett: Babe Buster	.10
101	Babe Caught Stealing, Ends 1926 Series	.10
102	Never Won a Triple Crown	.10
103	Babe Used a 54-Ounce Bat	.10
104	Babe Bats Righty	.10
105	Babe's Greatness	.10
106	The Babe's Best	.10
107	Outslugged Entire Teams	.10
108	First to Hit 30, 40, 50 and 60 Home Runs	.10
109	The Pitkin Study	.10
110	First to Put the Ball Into Orbit	.10
111	Afraid to Kill Somebody	.10
112	The Wonder Years: 1926-31	.10
113	Hit .422 With 7 Homers on Opening Days	.10
114	Babe at Bat	.10
115	"Greatest Ballplayer the Game Has Known"	.10
116	The Babe's Early Childhood	.10

117	St. Mary's Industrial School	.10
118	Babe and Brother Matthias	.10
119	The Babe's Nicknames	.10
120	Babe's First Wife, Helen	.10
121	Babe's Second Wife, Claire	.10
122	Lou Gehrig Appreciation Day	.20
123	Babe's Friendship With Herb Pennock	.10
124	The Babe and Miller Huggins	.10
125	The Babe and Ty Cobb	.15
126	Babe and Walter Johnson	.15
127	Baseball's Biggest Drawing Card	.10
128	Babe's Barnstorming	.10
129	Costly Confrontation	.10
130	He Often Played Hurt	.10
131	Babe's Big Bucks	.10
132	Want to be a Manager	.10
133	The Babe on the Links	.10
134	Babe in the Movies	.10
135	Babe Contributes to War Effort	.10
136	The Babe - Peace Negotiator	.10
137	Everyone Loved the Babe	.10
138	He Brought Children Joy	.10
139	He Always Had Time for Kids	.10
140	The Johnny Sylvester Story	.10
141	Moving with the Great	.10
142	Babe Ruth and the American Dream	.10
143	Being Remembered - Bill James	.10
144	Being Remembered - Bill James	.10
145	Being Remembered - Bill James	.10
146	Being Remembered - Mel Allen	.10
147	Being Remembered - Mel Allen	.10
148	Being Remembered - Wes Ferrell	.10
149	Being Remembered - George Bush	.50
150	Being Remembered - Ethan Allen	.20
151	Being Remembered - Daughter Dorothy	.10
152	Being Remembered - Daughter Julia	.10
153	Being Remembered - Daughter Julia	.10
154	Being Remembered - Mark Koenig	.10
155	Being Remembered - Donald Honig	.10
156	Being Remembered - L. Waner, Waite Hoyt	.10
157	Being Remembered - Waite Hoyt	.10
158	Being Remembered - Bill Dickey	.10
159	Being Remembered - Bob Meusel	.10
160	Being Remembered - Jim Chapman	.10
161	Being Remembered - Christy Walsh	.10
162	Being Remembered - The Babe Passes Away	.10
163	Being Remembered - Grantland Rice	.10
164	Checklist 1-83	.10
165	Checklist 84-165	.10

Ken Griffey, Jr. MegaCaps

Three different "Mega-Caps" picturing Ken Griffey, Jr., were prepared for insertion into blister packs containing full sets of the Ken Griffey, Jr., Wish List Collection. Each of the 1-5/8" diameter cardboard discs has a color photo of Junior on front. Backs have trademark information. Reported print run for each of the three versions was 34,000.

	NM/M
Complete Set:	1.50
Common Cap:	.50
1 Ken Griffey Jr.	.50
2 Ken Griffey Jr.	.50
3 Ken Griffey Jr.	.50

Ken Griffey, Jr. Wish List

1,541 CAREER EXTRA BASE HITS

Sold only as a complete set in a clam-shell plastic blister pack, this set has two areas of focus. The first 14 cards details Griffey's hopes for his baseball career and his life; the second 11 cards feature projections on Junior's possible career stats based on numbers generated by baseball statstician Bill James. Each card has a different action photo of Griffey on the front. Backs have a smaller version of the front photo in the upper-right corner, and a muted background photo of Griffey at bat. Card fronts are gold-foil enhanced. Packed with each set was one of three "Mega-Caps" with Griffey's picture. With a reported print run of 100,000 sets, the issue sold for about $10 retail, with part of the purchase price going to the Make a Wish Foundation for seriously ill children.

		NM/M
Complete Set (27):		7.50
Common Card:		.50
1	Introduction (Ken Griffey Jr.)	.50
2	Make-A-Wish Foundation (Ken Griffey Jr.)	.50
3	To Make Dreams Come True (Ken Griffey Jr.)	.50
4	To Play With Dad Ken Griffey Jr. (w/ Ken Griffey, Sr.)	.50
5	"The Best I Can Be" (Ken Griffey Jr.)	.50
6	To Make the Majors (Ken Griffey Jr.)	.50
7	To Play for a Winner (Ken Griffey Jr.)	.50
8	To Assist B.A.T. (Ken Griffey Jr.)	.50
9	To Enrich Inner-City Baseball (Ken Griffey Jr.)	.50
10	A Lot to Live For (Ken Griffey Jr.)	.50
11	To Be an All-Around Player (Ken Griffey Jr.)	.50
12	To Be #1 in the Draft (Ken Griffey Jr.)	.50
13	To Win the Gold (Ken Griffey Jr.)	.50
14	Most Home Runs by Father/Son (Ken Griffey Jr. (w/ Ken Griffey, Sr.))	.50
15	The Field of Possibilities (Ken Griffey Jr.)	.50
16	The Griffey Forecast (Ken Griffey Jr.)	.50
17	3,598 Career Games (Ken Griffey Jr.)	.50
18	2,361 Career Runs (Ken Griffey Jr.)	.50
19	3,947 Career Hits (Ken Griffey Jr.)	.50
20	777 Career Doubles (Ken Griffey Jr.)	.50
21	699 Career Home Runs (Ken Griffey Jr.)	.50
22	2,234 Career RBIs (Ken Griffey Jr.)	.50
24	1,541 Career Extra Base Hits (Ken Griffey Jr.)	.50
24	40 or More Home Runs 5 Times (Ken Griffey Jr.)	.50
25	28 Career Grand Slams (Ken Griffey Jr.)	.50

---	Contest Card	.05
---	Merchandise Order Card	.05

Babe Ruth 100th Anniversary

Marking the centennial of Babe Ruth's birth, Megacards issued this 25-card set chronicling the life and career of baseball's all-time greatest player. Most of the cards feature on front black-and-white photos of Ruth, although there are several colorized pictures scattered through the set. Fronts have gold-foil frames, captions and Ruth Centennial logo. Reverses have a background photo of Ruth's classic swing and a detailed vignette pertinent to the card's theme. The Babe Ruth 100th Anniversary Collection set was sold in a plastic clamshell package containing one of three Babe Ruth "Mega-caps." The edition was limited to 100,000 sets.

		NM/M
Complete Set (27):		5.00
Common Card:		.25
1	Baseball's Greatest Ever? (Babe Ruth)	.25
2	60 Home Run Club (Babe Ruth)	.25
3	No Slugger Comes Close (Babe Ruth (with Jimmie Foxx, Lou Gehrig, Al Simmons))	.25
4	History's Most Frequent Home Run Threat (Babe Ruth)	.25
5	He Knew the Way Home (Babe Ruth)	.25
6	He Didn't Leave Them Stranded (Babe Ruth (with Lou Gehrig))	.25
7	50 Home Run King (Babe Ruth)	.25
8	Long Ball Legend (Babe Ruth)	.25
9	.342 Plus Power (Babe Ruth (with Lloyd Waner, Paul Waner, Lou Gehrig))	.25
10	No One Hit 'Em More Often (Babe Ruth)	.25
11	Greatest Pitching Prospect (Babe Ruth (colorized, Red Sox pitcher))	.25
12	Career Year (Babe Ruth (colorized, fishing with Lou Gehrig))	.25
13	Mr. Yankee (Babe Ruth (with Lou Gehrig; Don Mattingly superimposed))	.50
14	Babe and "The Kid" (Babe Ruth (Ken Griffey, Jr., superimposed))	.50
15	Everyone Loved the Babe (Babe Ruth)	.25
16	The Babe Played Hurt (Babe Ruth)	.25
17	He Did It His Way (Babe Ruth)	.25
18	The Rewards of Greatness (Babe Ruth)	.25
19	Babe and Today's Rules (Babe Ruth)	.25
20	Babe in Today's Ballparks (Babe Ruth)	.25
21	Babe and Today's Best (Babe Ruth (colorized, Ken Griffey Jr. superimposed))	.75
22	Babe vs. Today's Pitching (Babe Ruth)	.25
23	The Babe and Father Time (Babe Ruth)	.25

24	How He Changed the Game (Babe Ruth (colorized, with Dizzy Dean, Frank Frisch, Mickey Cochrane, Schoolboy Rowe))	.25
25	Will There Be Another Babe? (Babe Ruth)	.25
---	Sweepstakes card	.05
---	Babe Ruth merchandise order card	.05

Babe Ruth MegaCaps

One of three different 1-5/8" "MegaCaps" picturing Babe Ruth was packaged in each set of Babe Ruth 100th Anniversary Collection cards. The discs feature a photo of Ruth on front and trademark information on the back. Each cap was produced in an edition of 34,000.

		NM/M
Complete Set (3):		1.50
Common Cap:		.50
1	Babe Ruth	.50
2	Babe Ruth	.50
3	Babe Ruth	.50

1994 Mellon Bank Phillies

This set sponsored by "The Official Bank of the Phillies" was issued in the form of a perforated fold-out, with individual cards in the standard 2-1/2" x 3-1/2" size. One panel is a 12-1/2" x 7" team photo. Fronts have game-action photos with a border of red pinstripes on white. The team name is in a box at top, the player name is in a banner at bottom. On back are personal data, stats and career highlights, along with the logos of the team, the sponsor and MLB's 125th Anniversary.

		NM/M
Foldout:		12.00
Complete Set, Singles (26):		8.00
Common Player:		.50
(1)	Larry Anderson	.50
(2)	Kim Batiste	.50
(3)	Shawn Boskie	.50
(4)	Darren Daulton	.75
(5)	Mariano Duncan	.50
(6)	Lenny Dykstra	.75
(7)	Jim Eisenreich	.50
(8)	Tommy Greene	.50
(9)	Dave Hollins	.50
(10)	Pete Incaviglia	.50
(11)	Danny Jackson	.50
(12)	Doug Jones	.50
(13)	Ricky Jordan	.50
(14)	John Kruk	.75
(15)	Tony Longmire	.50
(16)	Mickey Morandini	.50
(17)	Bobby Munoz	.50
(18)	Todd Pratt	.50
(19)	Paul Quantrill, Billy Hatcher	.50
(20)	Curt Schilling	.50
(21)	Heathcliff Slocumb	.50
(22)	Kevin Stocker	.50
(23)	Milt Thompson	.50

(24)	David West	.50
(25)	Mike Williams	.50
(26)	Team photo	2.00

1995 Mellon Bank Phillies

This set was issued in the form of a perforated fold-out, with individual cards in the standard 2-1/2" x 3-1/2" size. Fronts have game-action photos with a border of red pinstripes on white. The team name is in a box at top, the player name is in a banner at bottom. On back are personal data and stats, along with the logos of the team, the sponsor and the Phillies "Silver Season." The unnumbered cards are checklisted here alphabetically.

		NM/M
Foldout:		10.00
Complete Set, Singles (25):		8.00
Common Player:		.50
(1)	Kyle Abbott	.50
(2)	Toby Borland	.50
(3)	Ricky Bottalico	.50
(4)	Norm Charlton	.50
(5)	Darren Daulton	.75
(6)	Mariano Duncan	.50
(7)	Lenny Dykstra	.75
(8)	Jim Eisenreich	.50
(9)	Dave Gallagher	.50
(10)	Tyler Green	.50
(11)	Gene Harris	.50
(12)	Charlie Hayes	.50
(13)	Dave Hollins	.50
(14)	Gregg Jefferies	.50
(15)	Tony Longmire	.50
(16)	Michael Mimbs	.50
(17)	Mickey Morandini	.50
(18)	Paul Quantrill	.50
(19)	Randy Ready	.50
(20)	Curt Schilling	1.50
(21)	Heathcliff Slocumb	.50
(22)	Kevin Stocker	.50
(23)	Gary Varsho	.50
(24)	Lenny Webster	.50
(25)	David West	.50

2003 Merrick Mint Laser Line Gold Cards

These 2-1/2" x 3-1/2" cards are produced from 23-K gold foil in an intaglio printing process which gives them an engraved look and feel. Because the set is licensed only by the Players Association, and not MLB, team logos and nicknames are not shown. Fronts have a portrait photo and facsimile autograph. Backs have information on the production process. The unnumbered cards are checklisted here al-

phabetically. Cards were issued in an acrylic case at an original price of about $15.

		NM/M
Complete Set (17):		75.00
Common Player:		3.00
(1)	Roger Clemens	5.00
(2)	Nomar Garciaparra	5.00
(3)	Ken Griffey Jr.	6.00
(4)	Vladimir Guerrero	4.00
(5)	Derek Jeter	10.00
(6)	Randy Johnson	4.00
(7)	Pedro Martinez	4.00
(8)	Hideki Matsui	4.00
(9)	Mike Piazza	6.00
(10)	Mark Prior	3.00
(11)	Albert Pujols	8.00
(12)	Alex Rodriguez	8.00
(13)	Alfonso Soriano	4.00
(14)	Sammy Sosa	5.00
(15)	Ichiro Suzuki	4.00
(16)	Jim Thome	3.00
(17)	Dontrelle Willis	3.00

N.Y. Yankees Stickers/Cards

To commemorate the 100th anniversary of the N.Y. Yankees, this set of stickers and cards was produced. Each player is represented on a self-adhesive 1-3/8" x 1-7/8" sticker and a 3-1/2" x 2-1/2" blank-backed card on which the sticker could be placed. Stickers were issued in sheets of nine or sixteen, and cards on perforated sheets of four or nine. The stickers have portrait photos, a facsimile autograph and uniform number. Cards have an action photo and facsimile autograph. Because the issued was licensed only by the players' union and not MLB, uniform logos have been excised and the team nickname "Yankees" is nowhere to be seen. The issue was sold in sheets in either 5" x 7" or 8" x 10" format.

		NM/M
Set 8x10 Sheets (2):		7.00
Set 5x7 Sheets (4):		6.00
Complete Set Stickers (17):		2.00
Common Sticker:		.25
Complete Set Cards (17):		5.00
Common Card:		.50
2	Derek Jeter	1.00
6	Joe Torre	.25
12	Alfonso Soriano	.50
18	Jeff Weaver	.25
19	Robin Ventura	.25
20	Jorge Posada	.25
25	Jason Giambi	.25
33	Roger Clemens	.75
33	David Wells	.25
35	Mike Mussina	.35
36	Nick Johnson	.35
42	Mariano Rivera	.35
43	Raul Mondesi	.25
46	Andy Pettitte	.35
51	Bernie Williams	.25
55	Hideki Matsui	.50
---	100th Anniversary Logo	.25
2	Derek Jeter	2.00
6	Joe Torre	.50
12	Alfonso Soriano	.75
18	Jeff Weaver	.50
19	Robin Ventura	.50
20	Jorge Posada	.50
25	Jason Giambi	.50
25	Roger Clemens	1.00
33	David Wells	.50
35	Mike Mussina	.60
36	Nick Johnson	.60
42	Mariano Rivera	.60
43	Raul Mondesi	.50
46	Andy Pettitte	.60
51	Bernie Williams	.50
55	Hideki Matsui	1.00
---	100th Anniversary Logo	.50

Stickers/Cards

This issue comprises several types of collectibles in one cello-bagged package. Each pack consists of nine self-ad-

hesive 1-1/2" x 2" stickers, nine 3-1/2" x 2-1/2" blank-backed cards on which the sticker could be placed, one 2-1/2" x 5" "Colossal" sticker and one of seven 2-1/2" x 1-7/8" "Rookie Star" sticker of Hideki Matsui. The stickers have color portrait and black-and-white game action photos and a facsimile autograph. Cards have a color version of the action photo. Because the issued was licensed only by the players' union and not MLB, uniform logos have been excised and team nicknames are nowhere to be seen.

		NM/M
Complete Set, Sheets (7):		20.00
Common Player Sticker + Card:		.50
	Package 1	5.00
(C1)	Derek Jeter (Colossal)	1.00
RS1	Hideki Matsui/Btg (Rookie Star) (One hand visible.)	.50
(1)	Barry Bonds (Facing his right.)	1.50
(2)	Roger Clemens/DP	.75
(3)	Ken Griffey Jr./TP	.75
(4)	Randy Johnson	.65
(5)	Pedro Martinez/DP	.60
(6)	Mike Piazza/DP	1.00
(7)	Mark Prior	.50
(8)	Sammy Sosa/DP	.75
(9)	Ichiro/DP	1.00
	Package 2	3.50
(C2)	Alex Rodriguez (Colossal)	.75
(RS2)	Hideki Matsui/Btg (Rookie Star) (No hands visible.)	.50
(10)	Barry Bonds/DP (Arms up.)	1.00
(11)	Pat Burrell	.50
(12)	Jose Contreras	.50
(13)	Jim Edmonds	.50
(14)	Todd Helton	.65
(15)	Austin Kearns	.50
(16)	Greg Maddux	.75
(17)	Sammy Sosa/DP	.75
(18)	Mike Sweeney	.50
	Package 3	3.75
(C3)	Nomar Garciaparra (Colossal)	.50
(RS3)	Hideki Matsui/Throwing (Rookie Star)	.50
(19)	Jeff Bagwell	.65
(20)	Barry Bonds/DP (Arms up.)	1.00
(21)	Ken Griffey Jr./TP	.75
(22)	Rafael Palmeiro	.60
(23)	Albert Pujols	1.25
(24)	Alfonso Soriano	.50
(25)	Miguel Tedaja (Tejada)	.50
(26)	Larry Walker	.50
(27)	Dontrelle Willis	.50
	Package 4	3.25
(C4)	Sammy Sosa (Colossal)	.50
(RS4)	Hideki Matsui (Rookie Star)(Thumb up.)	.50
(28)	Roger Clemens/DP	.75
(29)	Adam Dunn	.50
(30)	Vladimir Guerrero	.65
(31)	Torii Hunter	.50
(32)	Pedro Martinez/DP	.60
(33)	Magglio Ordonez	.50
(34)	Mike Piazza/DP	1.00
(35)	Ivan Rodriguez	.60
(36)	John Smoltz	.50
	Package 5	3.50
(C5)	Barry Bonds (Colossal)	1.00
(RS5)	Hideki Matsui/Fielding/Running (Rookie Star)	.50
(37)	Lance Berkman	.50
(38)	Eric Chavez	.50
(39)	Troy Glaus	.50
(40)	Shawn Green	.50

(41)	Andruw Jones	.65
(42)	Manny Ramirez	.65
(43)	Curt Schilling	.50
(44)	Ichiro/DP	1.00
(45)	Bernie Williams	.50
	Package 6	3.75
(C6)	Mike Piazza (Colossal)	.50
(RS6)	Hideki Matsui/Fielding/Standing (Rookie Star)	.50
(46)	Garret Anderson	.50
(47)	Rocco Baldelli	.50
(48)	Nomar Garciaparra	1.00
(49)	Juan Gonzalez	.50
(50)	Ken Griffey Jr./TP	.75
(51)	Derek Jeter	1.50
(52)	Gary Sheffield	.50
(53)	Frank Thomas	.65
(54)	Jim Thome	.65
	Package 7	3.25
(C7)	Ichiro (Colossal)	.50
(RS7)	Hideki Matsui/Btg (Rookie Star) (Both hands visible.)	.50
(55)	Carlos Delgado	.50
(56)	Jason Giambi	.60
(57)	Tom Glavine	.50
(58)	Luis Gonzalez	.50
(59)	Chipper Jones	.75
(60)	Mike Mussina	.50
(61)	Alex Rodriguez	1.25
(62)	Scott Rolen	.60
(63)	Barry Zito	.50

1993 Metallic Images Cooperstown Collection

This set of retired players is produced of durable, embossed metal with rolled edges. Limited to 49,900, it came packaged in a collectors' tin with a numbered certificate of authenticity. The cards feature full-color photos on the front and back and statistics on the reverse. Half of the players in the set are members of the Hall of Fame.

		NM/M
Complete Set (20):		5.00
Common Player:		.10
1	Hank Aaron	1.50
2	Vida Blue	.10
3	Yogi Berra	.50
4	Bobby Bonds	.10
5	Lou Brock	.20
6	Lew Burdette	.10
7	Rod Carew	.20
8	Rocky Colavito	.10
9	George Foster	.10
10	Bob Gibson	.20
11	Mickey Lolich	.10
12	Willie Mays	1.50
13	Johnny Mize	.20
14	Don Newcombe	.15
15	Gaylord Perry	.20
16	Boog Powell	.20
17	Bill Skowron	.15
18	Warren Spahn	.35
19	Willie Stargell	.20
20	Luis Tiant	.10
P1	Willie Mays	1.25

1995 Metallic Images Babe Ruth

This five-card set of metal cards honors Babe Ruth in the 100th anniversary of his birth. The cards are 2-5/8" x 3-9/16" and featured gold-toned rolled edges. Fronts have familiar sepia-toned photos of the Babe with colorized backgrounds. "Cooperstown Collection" logos appear on front and back. Backs have an overall background of a ghost-image picture of Ruth at bat, along with a small sepia portrait photo, career summary and, on some cards, a few stats. The set was issued in a black embossed tin box, with cards in a cello wrapper.

		NM/M
Complete Boxed Set (5):		5.00
Common Card:		1.00
1	Babe Ruth (Batting follow-through.)	1.00
2	Babe Ruth (Seated with bat on shoulders.)	1.00
3	Babe Ruth(Batting follow-through.)	1.00
4	Babe Ruth (Standing behind 10 bats.)	1.00
5	Babe Ruth (Batting follow-through.)	1.00

Impressions Willie Mays

As part of its Cooperstown Collection series of embossed metal cards, this set traces Willie Mays' career. The set was originally marketed by Avon cosmetics and sold in a lithographed steel box with pictures of Mays on the top and sides. Each of the cards inside was sealed in a cellophane wrapper. Cards measure about 2-5/8" x 3-5/8" and feature monochrome or color photos lithographed on steel. Borders and other design details are embossed. A second photo of Mays is on back, along with a few sentences about his life and career.

		NM/M
Complete Boxed Set (5):		4.00
Common Card:		1.00
1	Willie Mays (Negro Leagues)	1.00
2	Willie Mays (Minor Leagues)	1.00
3	Willie Mays (Rookie Year)	1.00
4	Willie Mays (New York Mets)	1.00
5	Willie Mays (Willie, Mickey, and the Duke)	1.00

1996 Metallic Impressions Ken Griffey, Jr.

This set of metal cards was sold in a lithographed steel box with pictures of Griffey on the top and sides. Each of the cards inside was sealed in a cellophane wrapper. Cards measure about 2-5/8" x 3-5/8" and feature color photos lithographed on steel. Borders and other design details are embossed. Two more photos of Griffey are on back, along with a few sentences about his life and career.

		NM/M
Complete Boxed Set (5):		3.00
Common Card:		1.00
1	Ken Griffey Jr./At Bat	1.00
2	Ken Griffey Jr./Throwing	1.00
3	Ken Griffey Jr./Running	1.00
4	Ken Griffey Jr./Fielding	1.00
5	Ken Griffey Jr./Swinging	1.00

ABBREVIATIONS

DP - Double Print
TP - Top Performers

Iron Men of Baseball

Originally sold by Avon, this set of embossed metal cards was sold in a lithographed steel box with player pictures on the top and sides. Each of the cards inside was sealed in in a cellophane wrapper. Cards measure about 2-5/8" x 3-5/8" and feature black-and-white or color photos lithographed on steel. Borders and other design details are embossed. A pair of photos is on back, along with details of each player's consecutive games streak.

		NM/M
Complete Boxed Set (5):		6.00
Common Card:		1.50
1	Lou Gehrig	1.50
2	Lou Gehrig	1.50
3	Cal Ripken Jr.	1.50
4	Cal Ripken Jr.	1.50
5	Lou Gehrig,	
	Cal Ripken Jr.	1.50

Cal Ripken, Jr.

Two versions of this set were produced, a five-card set (#1-5) and a 10-card set (#1-10). Highlights of Cal Ripken's career are presented on these metallic baseball cards. Each 2-5/8" x 3-5/8" card has a color photo at center, surrounded by team-colored borders. Embossed at the bottom is a script version of Ripken's name with an oriole atop. In the lower-right corner is a metallic-looking home plate with "Iron Oriole." Backs repeat some of the front graphics and have identical portrait and action photos of Ripken and the magic number "2131" in lights at top. A paragraph at bottom describes a career milestone or highlight. The sets were sold in embossed lithographed metal boxes. The 10-card set is accompanied by a serial numbered certificate from an edition of 29,950.

		NM/M
Complete Boxed Set (10):		7.50
Complete Boxed Set (5):		4.00
Common Card:		1.00
1	Cal Ripken Jr. (Major League debut.)	1.00
2	Cal Ripken Jr. (1982 - Opening Day 3B)	1.00
3	Cal Ripken Jr. (Streak begins)	1.00
4	Cal Ripken Jr. (Rookie of the Year)	1.00
5	Cal Ripken Jr. (1983)	1.00
6	Cal Ripken Jr. (Consecutive innings streak.)	1.00
7	Cal Ripken Jr. (1991 MVP)	1.00
8	Cal Ripken Jr. (Gold Glover.)	1.00
9	Cal Ripken Jr. (Game 2,130)	1.00
10	Cal Ripken Jr. (Game 2,131)	1.00

1936 Hall of Fame Electees

As part of its Cooperstown Collection series of embossed metal cards, this set was released in the 60th anniversary year of the first Hall of Fame selections. The set was sold in a lithographed steel box with player pictures on the top and sides. Each of the cards inside was sealed in a cellophane wrapper. Cards measure about 2-5/8" x 3-5/8" and feature black-and-white photos lithographed on steel. Borders and other design details are embossed. A black-and-white photo is on back, along with "Peak Performance" stats and a career summary. Sets were originally sold through Avon.

		NM/M
Complete Boxed Set (5):		4.50
Common Player:		1.00
1	Babe Ruth	2.00
2	Ty Cobb	1.50
3	Christy Mathewson	1.00
4	Walter Johnson	1.00
5	Honus Wagner	1.00

1997 Metallic Impressions Jackie Robinson

As part of its Cooperstown Collection series of embossed metal cards, this set was released in the 50th anniversary year of Jackie Robinson's entry into the major leagues. The set was sold in a lithographed steel box with pictures of Robinson on the top and sides. Each of the cards inside was sealed in a cellophane wrapper. Cards measure about 2-5/8" x 3-5/8" and feature monochrome or color photos lithographed on steel. Borders and other design details are embossed. A black-and-white photo of Robinson is on back, along with a few sentences about his life and career.

		NM/M
Complete Boxed Set (5):		5.00
Common Card:		1.25
1	Jackie Robinson (Thigh-to-cap portrait.)	1.25
2	Jackie Robinson (Chest-to-cap portrait.)	1.25
3	Jackie Robinson/ Batting-color	1.25
4	Jackie Robinson/ Fielding	1.25
5	Jackie Robinson/ Batting-b/w	1.25

1996 Metal Universe Sample Sheet

To introduce its premiere edition of Metal Universe baseball cards, Fleer sent a nine-card sample sheet to dealers. The 8" x 11" sheet has a black border on each side of each card. The cards are identical in format to the issued version, printed on etched foil and overprinted "PROMOTIONAL SAMPLE" in gold diagonally on front and back.

	NM/M
Complete Sheet:	10.00

1996 Metal Universe

One of the most unusual baseball card issues of its era, Fleer's Metal Universe set is distinguished by its colored, textured metallic-foil backgrounds created by comic book illustrators. The effects range from gaudy to grotesque. Glossy player action photos are featured on front, with a steel-colored metallic strip at bottom carrying set and player ID. Conventionally printed backs have a heavy-metal theme with a color player portrait photo and a few stats and personal data around. The issue was sold in hobby and retail packaging with the basic eight-card pack at a suggested retail price of $2.49. Several insert sets were included, along with a platinum parallel edition of the player cards.

	NM/M
Complete Set (250):	17.50
Common Player:	.10
Platinum Set (250):	75.00
Common Platinum:	.25
Platinums:	5X
Pack (8):	1.50
Wax Box (24):	17.50
1 Roberto Alomar	.20
2 Brady Anderson	.10
3 Bobby Bonilla	.10
4 Chris Holles	.10
5 Ben McDonald	.10
6 Mike Mussina	.40
7 Randy Myers	.10
8 Rafael Palmeiro	.60
9 Cal Ripken Jr.	2.50
10 B.J. Surhoff	.10
11 Luis Alicea	.10
12 Jose Canseco	.50
13 Roger Clemens	1.25
14 Wil Cordero	.10
15 Tom Gordon	.10
16 Mike Greenwell	.10
17 Tim Naehring	.10
18 Troy O'Leary	.10
19 Mike Stanley	.10
20 John Valentin	.10
21 Mo Vaughn	.10
22 Tim Wakefield	.10
23 Garret Anderson	.10
24 Chili Davis	.10
25 Gary DiSarcina	.10
26 Jim Edmonds	.10
27 Chuck Finley	.10
28 Todd Greene	.10
29 Mark Langston	.10
30 Troy Percival	.10
31 Tony Phillips	.10
32 Tim Salmon	.10
33 Lee Smith	.10
34 J.T. Snow	.10
35 Ray Durham	.10
36 Alex Fernandez	.10
37 Ozzie Guillen	.10
38 Roberto Hernandez	.10
39 Lyle Mouton	.10
40 Frank Thomas	.75
41 Robin Ventura	.10
42 Sandy Alomar	.10
43 Carlos Baerga	.10
44 Albert Belle	.10
45 Orel Hershiser	.10
46 Kenny Lofton	.10
47 Dennis Martinez	.10
48 Jack McDowell	.10
49 Jose Mesa	.10
50 Eddie Murray	.75
51 Charles Nagy	.10
52 Manny Ramirez	.75
53 Julian Tavarez	.10
54 Jim Thome	.60
55 Omar Vizquel	.10
56 Chad Curtis	.10
57 Cecil Fielder	.10
58 John Flaherty	.10
59 Travis Fryman	.10
60 Chris Gomez	.10
61 Felipe Lira	.10
62 Kevin Appier	.10
63 Johnny Damon	.35
64 Tom Goodwin	.10
65 Mark Gubicza	.10
66 Jeff Montgomery	.10
67 Jon Nunnally	.10
68 Ricky Bones	.10
69 Jeff Cirillo	.10
70 John Jaha	.10
71 Dave Nilsson	.10
72 Joe Oliver	.10
73 Kevin Seitzer	.10
74 Greg Vaughn	.10
75 Marty Cordova	.10
76 Chuck Knoblauch	.10
77 Pat Meares	.10
78 Paul Molitor	.75
79 Pedro Munoz	.10
80 Kirby Puckett	1.00
81 Brad Radke	.10
82 Scott Stahoviak	.10
83 Matt Walbeck	.10
84 Wade Boggs	1.00
85 David Cone	.10
86 Joe Girardi	.10
87 Derek Jeter	2.50
88 Jim Leyritz	.10
89 Tino Martinez	.10
90 Don Mattingly	1.50
91 Paul O'Neill	.10
92 Andy Pettitte	.25
93 Tim Raines	.10
94 Kenny Rogers	.10
95 Ruben Sierra	.10
96 John Wetteland	.10
97 Bernie Williams	.10
98 Geronimo Berroa	.10
99 Dennis Eckersley	.65
100 Brent Gates	.10
101 Mark McGwire	2.00
102 Steve Ontiveros	.10
103 Terry Steinbach	.10
104 Jay Buhner	.10
105 Vince Coleman	.10
106 Joey Cora	.10
107 Ken Griffey Jr.	1.50
108 Randy Johnson	.75
109 Edgar Martinez	.10
110 Alex Rodriguez	2.00
111 Paul Sorrento	.10
112 Will Clark	.10
113 Juan Gonzalez	.50
114 Rusty Greer	.10
115 Dean Palmer	.10
116 Ivan Rodriguez	.65
117 Mickey Tettleton	.10
118 Joe Carter	.10
119 Alex Gonzalez	.10
120 Shawn Green	.30
121 Erik Hanson	.10
122 Pat Hentgen	.10
123 Sandy Martinez **RC**	.10
124 Otis Nixon	.10
125 John Olerud	.10
126 Steve Avery	.10
127 Tom Glavine	.40
128 Marquis Grissom	.10
129 Chipper Jones	1.00
130 David Justice	.10
131 Ryan Klesko	.10
132 Mark Lemke	.10
133 Javier Lopez	.10
134 Greg Maddux	1.00
135 Fred McGriff	.10
136 John Smoltz	.10
137 Mark Wohlers	.10
138 Frank Castillo	.10
139 Shawon Dunston	.10
140 Luis Gonzalez	.20
141 Mark Grace	.10
142 Brian McRae	.10
143 Jaime Navarro	.10
144 Rey Sanchez	.10
145 Ryne Sandberg	1.00
146 Sammy Sosa	1.25
147 Bret Boone	.10
148 Curtis Goodwin	.10
149 Barry Larkin	.10
150 Hal Morris	.10
151 Reggie Sanders	.10
152 Pete Schourek	.10
153 John Smiley	.10
154 Dante Bichette	.10
155 Vinny Castilla	.10
156 Andres Galarraga	.10
157 Bret Saberhagen	.10
158 Bill Swift	.10
159 Larry Walker	.10
160 Walt Weiss	.10
161 Kurt Abbott	.10
162 John Burkett	.10
163 Greg Colbrunn	.10
164 Jeff Conine	.10
165 Chris Hammond	.10
166 Charles Johnson	.10
167 Al Leiter	.10
168 Pat Rapp	.10
169 Gary Sheffield	.40
170 Quilvio Veras	.10
171 Devon White	.10
172 Jeff Bagwell	.75
173 Derek Bell	.10
174 Craig Biggio	.10
175 Sean Berry	.10
176 Doug Drabek	.10
177 Tony Eusebio	.10
178 Brian Hunter	.10
179 Orlando Miller	.10
180 Shane Reynolds	.10
181 Mike Blowers	.10
182 Roger Cedeno	.10
183 Eric Karros	.10
184 Ramon Martinez	.10
185 Raul Mondesi	.10
186 Hideo Nomo	.60
187 Mike Piazza	1.50
188 Moises Alou	.10
189 Yamil Benitez	.10
190 Darrin Fletcher	.10
191 Cliff Floyd	.10
192 Pedro Martinez	.75
193 Carlos Perez	.10
194 David Segui	.10
195 Tony Tarasco	.10
196 Rondell White	.10
197 Edgardo Alfonzo	.10
198 Rico Brogna	.10
199 Carl Everett	.10
200 Todd Hundley	.10
201 Jason Isringhausen	.10
202 Lance Johnson	.10
203 Bobby Jones	.10
204 Jeff Kent	.10
205 Bill Pulsipher	.10
206 Jose Vizcaino	.10
207 Ricky Bottalico	.10
208 Darren Daulton	.10
209 Lenny Dykstra	.10
210 Jim Eisenreich	.10
211 Gregg Jefferies	.10
212 Mickey Morandini	.10
213 Heathcliff Slocumb	.10
214 Jay Bell	.10
215 Carlos Garcia	.10
216 Jeff King	.10
217 Al Martin	.10
218 Orlando Merced	.10
219 Dan Miceli	.10
220 Denny Neagle	.10
221 Andy Benes	.10
222 Royce Clayton	.10
223 Gary Gaetti	.10
224 Ron Gant	.10
225 Bernard Gilkey	.10
226 Brian Jordan	.10
227 Ray Lankford	.10
228 John Mabry	.10
229 Ozzie Smith	1.00
230 Todd Stottlemyre	.10
231 Andy Ashby	.10
232 Brad Ausmus	.10
233 Ken Caminiti	.10
234 Steve Finley	.10
235 Tony Gwynn	1.00
236 Joey Hamilton	.10
237 Rickey Henderson	.75
238 Trevor Hoffman	.10
239 Wally Joyner	.10
240 Rod Beck	.10
241 Barry Bonds	2.50
242 Glenallen Hill	.10
243 Stan Javier	.10
244 Mark Leiter	.10
245 Deion Sanders	.10
246 William Van Landingham	.10
247 Matt Williams	.10
248 Checklist	.10
249 Checklist	.10
250 Checklist	.10

Platinum Edition

One of the eight cards in each pack of Fleer Metal baseball is a Platinum Edition parallel insert. Each of the 247 player cards (no checklists) in this special version has the textured foil background rendered only in silver. The second line of the logo/ID strip at bottom also identifies the card as part of the Platinum Edition.

	NM/M
Complete Set (247):	75.00
Common Player:	.25
Stars:	5X

Heavy Metal

Some of the game's biggest hitters are included in this insert set. Action photos of players at bat are set on a silver-foil background on front. Backs have a close-up photo down one side, with praise for the player's power potential down the other. The Heavy Metal inserts can be expected to turn up at an average rate of one per eight packs.

		NM/M
Complete Set (10):		5.00
Common Player:		.35
1	Albert Belle	.35
2	Barry Bonds	1.50
3	Juan Gonzalez	.50
4	Ken Griffey Jr.	1.00
5	Mark McGwire	1.25
6	Mike Piazza	1.00
7	Sammy Sosa	.90
8	Frank Thomas	.60
9	Mo Vaughn	.35
10	Matt Williams	.35

Mining for Gold

Available only in retail packs, at an average rate of one per dozen packs, the Mining for Gold insert series focuses on 1995's top rookies. Fronts have player action photos frame and backgrounded with several different gold tones in etched metal foil. Backs are conventionally printed, carrying on the same format with a portrait photo and a few words about the player.

		NM/M
Complete Set (12):		12.50
Common Player:		.75
1	Yamil Benitez	.75
2	Marty Cordova	.75
3	Shawn Green	2.00
4	Todd Greene	.75
5	Brian Hunter	.75
6	Derek Jeter	7.50
7	Charles Johnson	.75
8	Chipper Jones	3.50
9	Hideo Nomo	2.50
10	Alex Ochoa	.75
11	Andy Pettitte	1.00
12	Quilvio Veras	.75

Mother Lode

Medieval designs rendered in textured silver-foil on a plain white background are the setting for the color player photos in this hobby-only insert. Backs also have a silver and white background along with another player photo and some kind words about his skills. The cards are found at an average rate of one per 12 packs.

		NM/M
Complete Set (12):		15.00
Common Player:		.75
1	Barry Bonds	4.50
2	Jim Edmonds	.75
3	Ken Griffey Jr.	3.50
4	Kenny Lofton	.75
5	Raul Mondesi	.75
6	Rafael Palmeiro	1.50
7	Manny Ramirez	2.00
8	Cal Ripken Jr.	4.50
9	Tim Salmon	.75
10	Ryne Sandberg	3.00
11	Frank Thomas	2.00
12	Matt Williams	.75

Platinum Portraits

Close-up color photos on a plain metallic-foil background are featured in this insert set. The checklist is heavy in rookie and sophomore players, who are featured in an action photo on back, with a few career details. Platinum Portraits inserts are found in every fourth pack, on average.

		NM/M
Complete Set (10):		4.00
Common Player:		.40
1	Garret Anderson	.40
2	Marty Cordova	.40
3	Jim Edmonds	.40
4	Jason Isringhausen	.40
5	Chipper Jones	2.25
6	Ryan Klesko	.40
7	Hideo Nomo	1.00
8	Carlos Perez	.40
9	Manny Ramirez	1.50
10	Rondell White	.40

Titanium

A huge purple-highlighted silver baseball in a star-studded night sky is the background for the action photos of the game's biggest names in this insert series. Backs have a second, more up-close, photo and a few words about the player. Titanium inserts are found in Metal Universe packs at an average rate of one per 24 packs.

		NM/M
Complete Set (10):		15.00
Common Player:		.50
1	Albert Belle	.50

2	Barry Bonds	4.00
3	Ken Griffey Jr.	2.50
4	Tony Gwynn	1.50
5	Greg Maddux	1.50
6	Mike Piazza	2.50
7	Cal Ripken Jr.	4.00
8	Frank Thomas	1.00
9	Mo Vaughn	.50
10	Matt Williams	.50

1997 Metal Universe

Metal Universe Baseball arrived in a 250-card set, including three checklists. Each card is printed on 100-percent etched foil with "comic book" art full-bleed backgrounds, with the player's name, team, position and the Metal Universe logo near the bottom of the card. Backs contain another player photo and key statistics. Metal Universe sold in eight-card packs and contained six different insert sets. They included: Blast Furnace, Magnetic Field, Mining for Gold, Mother Lode, Platinum Portraits and Titanium.

		NM/M
Complete Set (250):		17.50
Common Player:		.10
Pack (8):		1.50
Wax Box (24):		18.00
1	Roberto Alomar	.20
2	Brady Anderson	.10
3	Rocky Coppinger	.10
4	Chris Hoiles	.10
5	Eddie Murray	.60
6	Mike Mussina	.40
7	Rafael Palmeiro	.50
8	Cal Ripken Jr.	2.00
9	B.J. Surhoff	.10
10	Brant Brown	.10
11	Mark Grace	.10
12	Brian McRae	.10
13	Jaime Navarro	.10
14	Ryne Sandberg	.75
15	Sammy Sosa	1.00
16	Amaury Telemaco	.10
17	Steve Trachsel	.10
18	Darren Bragg	.10
19	Jose Canseco	.40
20	Roger Clemens	1.00
21	Nomar Garciaparra	1.00
22	Tom Gordon	.10
23	Tim Naehring	.10
24	Mike Stanley	.10
25	John Valentin	.10
26	Mo Vaughn	.40
27	Jermaine Dye	.10
28	Tom Glavine	.30
29	Marquis Grissom	.10
30	Andruw Jones	.60
31	Chipper Jones	.75
32	Ryan Klesko	.10
33	Greg Maddux	.75
34	Fred McGriff	.10
35	John Smoltz	.10
36	Garret Anderson	.10
37	George Arias	.10
38	Gary DiSarcina	.10
39	Jim Edmonds	.10
40	Darin Erstad	.25
41	Chuck Finley	.10
42	Troy Percival	.10
43	Tim Salmon	.10
44	Bret Boone	.10
45	Jeff Brantley	.10
46	Eric Davis	.10
47	Barry Larkin	.10
48	Hal Morris	.10
49	Mark Portugal	.10
50	Reggie Sanders	.10
51	John Smiley	.10
52	Wilson Alvarez	.10
53	Harold Baines	.10
54	James Baldwin	.10
55	Albert Belle	.10
56	Mike Cameron	.10
57	Ray Durham	.10
58	Alex Fernandez	.10

59	Roberto Hernandez	.10
60	Tony Phillips	.10
61	Frank Thomas	.60
62	Robin Ventura	.10
63	Jeff Cirillo	.10
64	Jeff D'Amico	.10
65	John Jaha	.10
66	Scott Karl	.10
67	Ben McDonald	.10
68	Marc Newfield	.10
69	Dave Nilsson	.10
70	Jose Valentin	.10
71	Dante Bichette	.10
72	Ellis Burks	.10
73	Vinny Castilla	.10
74	Andres Galarraga	.10
75	Kevin Ritz	.10
76	Larry Walker	.10
77	Walt Weiss	.10
78	Jamey Wright	.10
79	Eric Young	.10
80	Julio Franco	.10
81	Orel Hershiser	.10
82	Kenny Lofton	.10
83	Jack McDowell	.10
84	Jose Mesa	.10
85	Charles Nagy	.10
86	Manny Ramirez	.60
87	Jim Thome	.50
88	Omar Vizquel	.10
89	Matt Williams	.10
90	Kevin Appier	.10
91	Johnny Damon	.35
92	Chili Davis	.10
93	Tom Goodwin	.10
94	Keith Lockhart	.10
95	Jeff Montgomery	.10
96	Craig Paquette	.10
97	Jose Rosado	.10
98	Michael Tucker	.10
99	Wilton Guerrero	.10
100	Todd Hollandsworth	.10
101	Eric Karros	.10
102	Ramon Martinez	.10
103	Raul Mondesi	.10
104	Hideo Nomo	.60
105	Mike Piazza	1.25
106	Ismael Valdes	.10
107	Todd Worrell	.10
108	Tony Clark	.10
109	Travis Fryman	.10
110	Bob Higginson	.10
111	Mark Lewis	.10
112	Melvin Nieves	.10
113	Justin Thompson	.10
114	Wade Boggs	.75
115	David Cone	.10
116	Cecil Fielder	.10
117	Dwight Gooden	.10
118	Derek Jeter	2.00
119	Tino Martinez	.10
120	Paul O'Neill	.10
121	Andy Pettitte	.20
122	Mariano Rivera	.20
123	Darryl Strawberry	.10
124	John Wetteland	.10
125	Bernie Williams	.10
126	Tony Batista	.10
127	Geronimo Berroa	.10
128	Scott Brosius	.10
129	Jason Giambi	.50
130	Jose Herrera	.10
131	Mark McGwire	1.50
132	John Wasdin	.10
133	Bob Abreu	.10
134	Jeff Bagwell	.60
135	Derek Bell	.10
136	Craig Biggio	.10
137	Brian Hunter	.10
138	Darryl Kile	.10
139	Orlando Miller	.10
140	Shane Reynolds	.10
141	Billy Wagner	.10
142	Donne Wall	.10
143	Jay Buhner	.10
144	Jeff Fassero	.10
145	Ken Griffey Jr.	1.25
146	Sterling Hitchcock	.10
147	Randy Johnson	.60
148	Edgar Martinez	.10
149	Alex Rodriguez	1.50
149p	Alex Rodriguez/OPS	1.50
150	Paul Sorrento	.10
151	Dan Wilson	.10
152	Moises Alou	.10
153	Darrin Fletcher	.10
154	Cliff Floyd	.10
155	Mark Grudzielanek	.10
156	Vladimir Guerrero	.60
157	Mike Lansing	.10
158	Pedro Martinez	.60
159	Henry Rodriguez	.10
160	Rondell White	.10
161	Will Clark	.10
162	Juan Gonzalez	.50
163	Rusty Greer	.10
164	Ken Hill	.10
165	Mark McLemore	.10
166	Dean Palmer	.10
167	Roger Pavlik	.10
168	Ivan Rodriguez	.50
169	Mickey Tettleton	.10
170	Bobby Bonilla	.10
171	Kevin Brown	.10
172	Greg Colbrunn	.10
173	Jeff Conine	.10
174	Jim Eisenreich	.10
175	Charles Johnson	.10

176	Al Leiter	.10
177	Robb Nen	.10
178	Edgar Renteria	.10
179	Gary Sheffield	.40
180	Devon White	.10
181	Joe Carter	.10
182	Carlos Delgado	.40
183	Alex Gonzalez	.10
184	Shawn Green	.35
185	Juan Guzman	.10
186	Pat Hentgen	.10
187	Orlando Merced	.10
188	John Olerud	.10
189	Robert Perez	.10
190	Ed Sprague	.10
191	Mark Clark	.10
192	John Franco	.10
193	Bernard Gilkey	.10
194	Todd Hundley	.10
195	Lance Johnson	.10
196	Bobby Jones	.10
197	Alex Ochoa	.10
198	Rey Ordonez	.10
199	Paul Wilson	.10
200	Ricky Bottalico	.10
201	Gregg Jefferies	.10
202	Wendell Magee Jr.	.10
203	Mickey Morandini	.10
204	Ricky Otero	.10
205	Scott Rolen	.50
206	Benito Santiago	.10
207	Curt Schilling	.25
208	Rich Becker	.10
209	Marty Cordova	.10
210	Chuck Knoblauch	.10
211	Pat Meares	.10
212	Paul Molitor	.60
213	Frank Rodriguez	.10
214	Terry Steinbach	.10
215	Todd Walker	.10
216	Andy Ashby	.10
217	Ken Caminiti	.10
218	Steve Finley	.10
219	Tony Gwynn	.75
220	Joey Hamilton	.10
221	Rickey Henderson	.60
222	Trevor Hoffman	.10
223	Wally Joyner	.10
224	Scott Sanders	.10
225	Fernando Valenzuela	.10
226	Greg Vaughn	.10
227	Alan Benes	.10
228	Andy Benes	.10
229	Dennis Eckersley	.50
230	Ron Gant	.10
231	Brian Jordan	.10
232	Ray Lankford	.10
233	John Mabry	.10
234	Tom Pagnozzi	.10
235	Todd Stottlemyre	.10
236	Jermaine Allensworth	.10
237	Francisco Cordova	.10
238	Jason Kendall	.10
239	Jeff King	.10
240	Al Martin	.10
241	Rod Beck	.10
242	Barry Bonds	2.00
243	Shawn Estes	.10
244	Mark Gardner	.10
245	Glenallen Hill	.10
246	Bill Mueller	.10
247	J.T. Snow	.10
248	Checklist	.10
249	Checklist	.10
250	Checklist	.10

Blast Furnace

Blast Furnace inserts were found only in hobby packs, at a rate of one per 48 packs. The 12-card set was printed on a red-tinted plastic, with the words "Blast Furnace" near the bottom in gold foil with a fire-like border.

		NM/M
Complete Set (12):		40.00
Common Player:		1.50
1	Jeff Bagwell	4.00
2	Albert Belle	1.50
3	Barry Bonds	7.50
4	Andres Galarraga	1.50
5	Juan Gonzalez	2.50
6	Ken Griffey Jr.	5.00
7	Todd Hundley	1.50

8	Mark McGwire	6.00
9	Mike Piazza	5.00
10	Alex Rodriguez	6.00
11	Frank Thomas	4.00
12	Mo Vaughn	1.50

Emerald Autograph Redemption

Six different young stars were featured in this insert, which was found every 480 hobby packs of Metal Universe. The cards are similar to regular-issue cards, but have green foil highlights. Redemption cards are numbered AU1-AU6. The redemption period expired Jan. 15, 1998.

		NM/M
Complete Set (6):		10.00
Common Player:		1.00
1	Darin Erstad	1.50
2	Todd Hollandsworth	1.00
3	Alex Ochoa	1.00
4	Alex Rodriguez	7.50
5	Scott Rolen	1.50
6	Todd Walker	1.00

Emerald Autographs

Six different young stars were featured in this insert, which was found every 480 hobby packs of Metal Universe. The cards are similar to regular-issue cards, but have a green foil finish and autograph on the front. Redemption cards are numbered AU1-AU6, the autographed cards have a notation on back, "Certified Emerald Autograph Card."

		NM/M
Complete Set (6):		75.00
Common Autograph:		4.00
1	Darin Erstad	6.00
2	Todd Hollandsworth	4.00
3	Alex Ochoa	4.00
4	Alex Rodriguez	60.00
5	Scott Rolen	10.00
6	Todd Walker	4.00

Magnetic Field

Magnetic Field inserts are printed in a horizontal format with prismatic foil back-

grounds. This 10-card insert was found every 12 packs of Metal Universe.

		NM/M
Complete Set (10):		15.00
Common Player:		.75
1	Roberto Alomar	.75
2	Jeff Bagwell	1.25
3	Barry Bonds	3.00
4	Ken Griffey Jr.	2.00
5	Derek Jeter	3.00
6	Kenny Lofton	.75
7	Edgar Renteria	.75
8	Cal Ripken Jr.	3.00
9	Alex Rodriguez	2.50
10	Matt Williams	.75

Mining for Gold

Mining for Gold was a 10-card insert that featured some of baseball's brightest stars on a die-cut "ingot" design with pearlized gold coating. This insert was found every nine packs.

		NM/M
Complete Set (10):		12.00
Common Player:		.75
1	Bob Abreu	.75
2	Kevin Brown	.75
3	Nomar Garciaparra	3.50
4	Vladimir Guerrero	3.00
5	Wilton Guerrero	.75
6	Andruw Jones	3.00
7	Curt Lyons	.75
8	Neifi Perez	.75
9	Scott Rolen	2.00
10	Todd Walker	.75

Mother Lode

Mother lode was the most difficult insert out of Metal Universe with a one per 288 pack insertion ratio. Each card in this 10-card inert was printed on etched foil with a plant-type monument in back of the player.

		NM/M
Complete Set (12):		80.00
Common Player:		2.00
1	Roberto Alomar	2.50
2	Jeff Bagwell	6.00
3	Barry Bonds	15.00
4	Ken Griffey Jr.	10.00
5	Andruw Jones	6.00
6	Chipper Jones	8.00
7	Kenny Lofton	6.00
8	Mike Piazza	10.00
9	Cal Ripken Jr.	15.00
10	Alex Rodriguez	12.50
11	Frank Thomas	6.00
12	Matt Williams	2.00

Platinum Portraits

Each card in the Platinum Portraits insert is printed on a background of platinum-colored etched foil. The 10-card set includes some of the top prospects and rising stars in baseball, and is included every 36 packs.

		NM/M
Complete Set (10):		10.00
Common Player:		.60
1	James Baldwin	.60
2	Jermaine Dye	.60
3	Todd Hollandsworth	.60
4	Derek Jeter	5.00
5	Chipper Jones	2.00
6	Jason Kendall	.60
7	Rey Ordonez	.60
8	Andy Pettitte	1.00
9	Edgar Renteria	.60
10	Alex Rodriguez	3.25

Titanium

These retail exclusive inserts include 10 cards and were found every 24 packs. Each card is die-cut on the top-left and bottom-right corner with a silver foil background. Titanium includes some of the most popular players in baseball on cards that are also embossed.

		NM/M
Complete Set (10):		24.00
Common Player:		1.50
1	Jeff Bagwell	2.00
2	Albert Belle	1.50
3	Ken Griffey Jr.	3.00
4	Chipper Jones	2.50
5	Greg Maddux	2.50
6	Mark McGwire	4.00
7	Mike Piazza	3.00
8	Cal Ripken Jr.	5.00
9	Alex Rodriguez	4.00
10	Frank Thomas	2.00

1998 Metal Universe

This 220-card single series release captured players over a foil etched, art background that related in some way to them or the city they played in. Metal Universe included a 15-card Hardball Galaxy subset and dealers and

media were given an Alex Rodriguez promo card that was identical to the base card except for the words "Promotional Sample" written across the back. The set arrived with a parallel called Precious Metal Gems, and included the following insert sets: All-Galactic Team, Diamond Heroes, Platinum Portraits, Titanium and Universal Language.

		NM/M
Complete Set (220):		15.00
Common Player:		.10
Pack (8):		1.50
Wax Box (24):		20.00
1	Jose Cruz Jr.	.10
2	Jeff Abbott	.10
3	Rafael Palmeiro	.65
4	Ivan Rodriguez	.65
5	Jaret Wright	.10
6	Derek Bell	.10
7	Chuck Finley	.10
8	Travis Fryman	.10
9	Randy Johnson	.75
10	Derrek Lee	.50
11	Bernie Williams	.10
12	Carlos Baerga	.10
13	Ricky Bottalico	.10
14	Ellis Burks	.10
15	Russ Davis	.10
16	Nomar Garciaparra	1.00
17	Joey Hamilton	.10
18	Jason Kendall	.10
19	Darryl Kile	.10
20	Edgardo Alfonzo	.10
21	Moises Alou	.10
22	Bobby Bonilla	.10
23	Jim Edmonds	.10
24	Jose Guillen	.10
25	Chuck Knoblauch	.10
26	Javy Lopez	.10
27	Billy Wagner	.10
28	Kevin Appier	.10
29	Joe Carter	.10
30	Todd Dunwoody	.10
31	Gary Gaetti	.10
32	Juan Gonzalez	.60
33	Jeffrey Hammonds	.10
34	Roberto Hernandez	.10
35	Dave Nilsson	.10
36	Manny Ramirez	.75
37	Robin Ventura	.10
38	Rondell White	.10
39	Vinny Castilla	.10
40	Will Clark	.10
41	Scott Hatteberg	.10
42	Russ Johnson	.10
43	Ricky Ledee	.10
44	Kenny Lofton	.10
45	Paul Molitor	.75
46	Justin Thompson	.10
47	Craig Biggio	.10
48	Damion Easley	.10
49	Brad Radke	.10
50	Ben Grieve	.10
51	Mark Bellhorn	.10
52	Henry Blanco RC	.10
53	Mariano Rivera	.20
54	Reggie Sanders	.10
55	Paul Sorrento	.10
56	Terry Steinbach	.10
57	Mo Vaughn	.10
58	Brady Anderson	.10
59	Tom Glavine	.40
60	Sammy Sosa	1.25
61	Larry Walker	.10
62	Rod Beck	.10
63	Jose Canseco	.45
64	Steve Finley	.10
65	Pedro Martinez	.75
66	John Olerud	.10
67	Scott Rolen	.60
68	Ismael Valdes	.10
69	Andrew Vessel	.10
70	Mark Grudzielanek	.10
71	Eric Karros	.10
72	Jeff Shaw	.10
73	Lou Collier	.10
74	Edgar Martinez	.10
75	Vladimir Guerrero	.75
76	Paul Konerko	.25
77	Kevin Orie	.10
78	Kevin Polcovich	.10
79	Brett Tomko	.10
80	Jeff Bagwell	.75
81	Barry Bonds	2.50
82	David Justice	.10
83	Hideo Nomo	.60
84	Ryne Sandberg	1.00
85	Shannon Stewart	.10
86	Derek Wallace	.10
87	Tony Womack	.10
88	Jason Giambi	.50
89	Mark Grace	.10
90	Pat Hentgen	.10
91	Raul Mondesi	.10
92	Matt Morris	.10
93	Matt Perisho	.10
94	Tim Salmon	.10
95	Jeremi Gonzalez	.10
96	Shawn Green	.25
97	Todd Greene	.10
98	Ruben Rivera	.10

99	Deion Sanders	.10
100	Alex Rodriguez	2.00
101	Will Cunnane	.10
102	Ray Lankford	.10
103	Ryan McGuire	.10
104	Charles Nagy	.10
105	Rey Ordonez	.10
106	Mike Piazza	1.50
107	Tony Saunders	.10
108	Curt Schilling	.25
109	Fernando Tatis	.10
110	Mark McGwire	2.00
111	David Dellucci RC	.10
112	Garret Anderson	.10
113	Shane Bowers	.10
114	David Cone	.10
115	Jeff King	.10
116	Matt Williams	.10
117	Aaron Boone	.10
118	Dennis Eckersley	.65
119	Livan Hernandez	.10
120	Richard Hidalgo	.10
121	Bobby Higginson	.10
122	Tino Martinez	.10
123	Tim Naehring	.10
124	Jose Vidro	.10
125	John Wetteland	.10
126	Jay Bell	.10
127	Albert Belle	.75
128	Marty Cordova	.10
129	Chili Davis	.10
130	Jason Dickson	.10
131	Rusty Greer	.10
132	Hideki Irabu	.10
133	Greg Maddux	1.00
134	Billy Taylor	.10
135	Jim Thome	.60
136	Gerald Williams	.10
137	Jeff Cirillo	.10
138	Delino DeShields	.10
139	Andres Galarraga	.10
140	Willie Greene	.10
141	John Jaha	.10
142	Charles Johnson	.10
143	Ryan Klesko	.10
144	Paul O'Neill	.10
145	Robinson Checo	.10
146	Roberto Alomar	.20
147	Wilson Alvarez	.10
148	Bobby Jones	.10
149	Raul Casanova	.10
150	Andruw Jones	.75
151	Mike Lansing	.10
152	Mickey Morandini	.10
153	Neifi Perez	.10
154	Pokey Reese	.10
155	Edgar Renteria	.10
156	Eric Young	.10
157	Darin Erstad	.20
158	Kelvim Escobar	.10
159	Carl Everett	.10
160	Tom Gordon	.10
161	Ken Griffey Jr.	1.50
162	Al Martin	.10
163	Bubba Trammell	.10
164	Carlos Delgado	.30
165	Kevin Brown	.10
166	Ken Caminiti	.10
167	Roger Clemens	1.25
168	Ron Gant	.10
169	Jeff Kent	.10
170	Mike Mussina	.40
171	Dean Palmer	.10
172	Henry Rodriguez	.10
173	Matt Stairs	.10
174	Jay Buhner	.10
175	Frank Thomas	.75
176	Mike Cameron	.10
177	Johnny Damon	.35
178	Tony Gwynn	1.00
179	John Smoltz	.10
180	B.J. Surhoff	.10
181	Antone Williamson	.10
182	Alan Benes	.10
183	Jeromy Burnitz	.10
184	Tony Clark	.10
185	Shawn Estes	.10
186	Todd Helton	.65
187	Todd Hundley	.10
188	Chipper Jones	1.00
189	Mark Kotsay	.10
190	Barry Larkin	.10
191	Mike Lieberthal	.10
192	Andy Pettitte	.25
193	Gary Sheffield	.35
194	Jeff Suppan	.10
195	Mark Wohlers	.10
196	Dante Bichette	.10
197	Trevor Hoffman	.10
198	J.T. Snow	.10
199	Derek Jeter	2.50
200	Cal Ripken Jr.	2.50
201	Steve Woodard RC	.25
202	Ray Durham	.10
203	Barry Bonds (Hardball Galaxy)	1.50
204	Tony Clark (Hardball Galaxy)	.10
205	Roger Clemens (Hardball Galaxy)	.65
206	Ken Griffey Jr. (Hardball Galaxy)	.75
207	Tony Gwynn (Hardball Galaxy)	.50
208	Derek Jeter (Hardball Galaxy)	1.50
209	Randy Johnson (Hardball Galaxy)	.40

210	Mark McGwire (Hardball Galaxy)	1.00
211	Hideo Nomo (Hardball Galaxy)	.30
212	Mike Piazza (Hardball Galaxy)	.75
213	Cal Ripken Jr. (Hardball Galaxy)	1.50
214	Alex Rodriguez (Hardball Galaxy)	1.00
215	Frank Thomas (Hardball Galaxy)	.40
216	Mo Vaughn (Hardball Galaxy)	.10
217	Larry Walker (Hardball Galaxy)	.10
218	Checklist (Ken Griffey Jr.)	.50
219	Checklist (Alex Rodriguez)	.60
220	Checklist (Frank Thomas)	.30

Precious Metal Gems

Precious Metal Gems includes 217 (no checklists) player cards from Metal Universe and are serial numbered to 50 sets. Because there were five Ultimate Metal Gems redemption cards (good for a complete set of Metal Gems) available, only serial numbers 1-45 were found in packs (46-50 were held back for the exchange program).

	NM/M
Common Player:	3.00
Stars:	25X
Production 50 Sets	

All-Galactic Team

This 18-card insert captures players over a planet holofoil background. Cards were inserted one per 192 packs.

		NM/M
Complete Set (18):		140.00
Common Player:		3.00
Inserted 1:192		
1	Ken Griffey Jr.	12.50
2	Frank Thomas	7.50
3	Chipper Jones	10.00
4	Albert Belle	3.00
5	Juan Gonzalez	5.00
6	Jeff Bagwell	7.50
7	Andruw Jones	7.50
8	Cal Ripken Jr.	20.00
9	Derek Jeter	20.00
10	Nomar Garciaparra	10.00
11	Darin Erstad	4.00
12	Greg Maddux	10.00
13	Alex Rodriguez	15.00
14	Mike Piazza	12.50
15	Vladimir Guerrero	7.50
16	Jose Cruz Jr.	3.00
17	Mark McGwire	15.00
18	Scott Rolen	5.00

Diamond Heroes

Diamond Heroes displayed six players in a comic book set-

ting. This insert was seeded one per 18 packs and contained a foil etched image of a Marvel comic in the background.

		NM/M
Complete Set (6):		8.00
Common Player:		.50
Inserted 1:18		
1	Ken Griffey Jr.	2.00
2	Frank Thomas	1.50
3	Andruw Jones	1.50
4	Alex Rodriguez	2.50
5	Jose Cruz Jr.	.50
6	Cal Ripken Jr.	3.00

Platinum Portraits

This 12-card insert set featured color portraits of top players highlighted with a platinum-colored etched foil frame over it. Platinum Portraits are seeded one per 360 packs of Metal Universe.

		NM/M
Complete Set (12):		90.00
Common Player:		4.00
Inserted 1:360		
1	Ken Griffey Jr.	12.00
2	Frank Thomas	7.50
3	Chipper Jones	9.00
4	Jose Cruz Jr.	4.00
5	Andruw Jones	7.50
6	Cal Ripken Jr.	17.50
7	Derek Jeter	17.50
8	Darin Erstad	4.00
9	Greg Maddux	9.00
10	Alex Rodriguez	15.00
11	Mike Piazza	12.00
12	Vladimir Guerrero	7.50

Titanium

This die-cut 15-card insert contained color photos printed on embossed, sculpted cards on etched foil. Titanium inserts were seeded one per 96 packs.

		NM/M
Complete Set (15):		50.00
Common Player:		2.00
Inserted 1:96		
1	Ken Griffey Jr.	5.00
2	Frank Thomas	3.00

3	Chipper Jones	4.00
4	Jose Cruz Jr.	2.00
5	Juan Gonzalez	2.50
6	Scott Rolen	2.50
7	Andruw Jones	3.00
8	Cal Ripken Jr.	7.50
9	Derek Jeter	7.50
10	Nomar Garciaparra	4.00
11	Darin Erstad	2.50
12	Greg Maddux	4.00
13	Alex Rodriguez	6.00
14	Mike Piazza	5.00
15	Vladimir Guerrero	3.00

Universal Language

This 20-card insert features illustration and copy done in the player's native language. Cards were die-cut and inserted one per six packs.

		NM/M
Complete Set (20):		16.00
Common Player:		.40
Inserted 1:6		
1	Ken Griffey Jr.	1.25
2	Frank Thomas	.75
3	Chipper Jones	1.00
4	Albert Belle	.40
5	Juan Gonzalez	.60
6	Jeff Bagwell	.75
7	Andruw Jones	.75
8	Cal Ripken Jr.	2.00
9	Derek Jeter	2.00
10	Nomar Garciaparra	1.00
11	Darin Erstad	.50
12	Greg Maddux	1.00
13	Alex Rodriguez	1.50
14	Mike Piazza	1.25
15	Vladimir Guerrero	.75
16	Jose Cruz Jr.	.40
17	Hideo Nomo	.60
18	Kenny Lofton	.40
19	Tony Gwynn	1.00
20	Scott Rolen	.60

1999 Metal Universe Sample Sheet

To introduce its annual issue of embossed cards this six-card sheet of Metal Universe samples was issued. The 5" x 10-1/2" sheet has five regular cards and an example of the Building Blocks insert set. Cards on the sheet are virtually identical to the issued versions except they have the word "SAMPLE" on back in place of card numbers. At the February Hawaii trade show,

325 sheets with a special gold seal, serial numbered and autographed by J.D. Drew were distributed to attendees.

	NM/M
Complete Sheet:	7.50
Complete Autographed Sheet:	60.00

1999 Metal Universe

The 300-card base set offers 232 player cards and three subsets: Building Blocks, M.L.P.D. and Caught on the Fly. Base cards feature an action photo framed in an etched-foil and metallic, embossed name plate. Packs consist of eight cards with an S.R.P. of $2.69. There are two parallels, Precious Metal Gems and Gem Masters. Metal Gems are numbered to 50 with gold-foil etching. Gem Masters are limited to only one set, with silver foil etching and serial numbered "one of one."

	NM/M
Complete Set (300):	15.00
Common Player:	.10
Pack (8):	1.00
Wax Box (24):	20.00
1 Mark McGwire	1.50
2 Jim Edmonds	.10
3 Travis Fryman	.10
4 Tom Gordon	.10
5 Jeff Bagwell	.65
6 Rico Brogna	.10
7 Tom Evans	.10
8 John Franco	.10
9 Juan Gonzalez	.50
10 Paul Molitor	.65
11 Roberto Alomar	.20
12 Mike Hampton	.10
13 Orel Hershiser	.10
14 Todd Stottlemyre	.10
15 Robin Ventura	.10
16 Todd Walker	.10
17 Bernie Williams	.10
18 Shawn Estes	.10
19 Richie Sexson	.10
20 Kevin Millwood	.10
21 David Ortiz	.50
22 Mariano Rivera	.15
23 Ivan Rodriguez	.60
24 Mike Sirotka	.10
25 David Justice	.10
26 Carl Pavano	.10
27 Albert Belle	.10
28 Will Clark	.10
29 Jose Cruz Jr.	.10
30 Trevor Hoffman	.10
31 Dean Palmer	.10
32 Edgar Renteria	.10
33 David Segui	.10
34 B.J. Surhoff	.10
35 Miguel Tejada	.15
36 Bob Wickman	.10
37 Charles Johnson	.10
38 Andruw Jones	.65
39 Mike Lieberthal	.10
40 Eli Marrero	.10
41 Neifi Perez	.10
42 Jim Thome	.50
43 Barry Bonds	2.00
44 Carlos Delgado	.30
45 Chuck Finley	.10
46 Brian Meadows	.10
47 Tony Gwynn	.75
48 Jose Offerman	.10
49 Cal Ripken Jr.	2.00
50 Alex Rodriguez	1.50
51 Esteban Yan	.10
52 Matt Stairs	.10
53 Fernando Vina	.10
54 Rondell White	.10
55 Kerry Wood	.30
56 Dmitri Young	.10
57 Ken Caminiti	.10
58 Alex Gonzalez	.10
59 Matt Mantei	.10
60 Tino Martinez	.10
61 Hal Morris	.10
62 Rafael Palmeiro	.60
63 Troy Percival	.10
64 Bobby Smith	.10
65 Ed Sprague	.10
66 Brett Tomko	.10
67 Steve Trachsel	.10
68 Ugueth Urbina	.10
69 Jose Valentin	.10
70 Kevin Brown	.10
71 Shawn Green	.30
72 Dustin Hermanson	.10
73 Livan Hernandez	.10
74 Geoff Jenkins	.10
75 Jeff King	.10
76 Chuck Knoblauch	.10
77 Edgar Martinez	.10
78 Fred McGriff	.10
79 Mike Mussina	.40
80 Dave Nilsson	.10
81 Kenny Rogers	.10
82 Tim Salmon	.10
83 Reggie Sanders	.10
84 Wilson Alvarez	.10
85 Rod Beck	.10
86 Jose Guillen	.10
87 Bob Higginson	.10
88 Gregg Olson	.10
89 Jeff Shaw	.10
90 Masato Yoshii	.10
91 Todd Helton	.50
92 David Dellucci	.10
93 Johnny Damon	.35
94 Cliff Floyd	.10
95 Ken Griffey Jr.	1.00
96 Juan Guzman	.10
97 Derek Jeter	2.00
98 Barry Larkin	.10
99 Quinton McCracken	.10
100 Sammy Sosa	.85
101 Kevin Young	.10
102 Jay Bell	.10
103 Jay Buhner	.10
104 Jeff Conine	.10
105 Ryan Jackson	.10
106 Sidney Ponson	.10
107 Jeromy Burnitz	.10
108 Roberto Hernandez	.10
109 A.J. Hinch	.10
110 Hideki Irabu	.10
111 Paul Konerko	.20
112 Henry Rodriguez	.10
113 Shannon Stewart	.10
114 Tony Womack	.10
115 Wilton Guerrero	.10
116 Andy Benes	.10
117 Jeff Cirillo	.10
118 Chili Davis	.10
119 Eric Davis	.10
120 Vladimir Guerrero	.65
121 Dennis Reyes	.10
122 Rickey Henderson	.65
123 Mickey Morandini	.10
124 Jason Schmidt	.10
125 J.T. Snow	.10
126 Justin Thompson	.10
127 Billy Wagner	.10
128 Armando Benitez	.10
129 Sean Casey	.15
130 Brad Fullmer	.10
131 Ben Grieve	.10
132 Robb Nen	.10
133 Shane Reynolds	.10
134 Todd Zeile	.10
135 Brady Anderson	.10
136 Aaron Boone	.10
137 Orlando Cabrera	.10
138 Jason Giambi	.50
139 Randy Johnson	.65
140 Jeff Kent	.10
141 John Wetteland	.10
142 Rolando Arrojo	.10
143 Scott Brosius	.10
144 Mark Grace	.10
145 Jason Kendall	.10
146 Travis Lee	.10
147 Gary Sheffield	.40
148 David Cone	.10
149 Jose Hernandez	.10
150 Todd Jones	.10
151 Al Martin	.10
152 Ismael Valdes	.10
153 Wade Boggs	.75
154 Garret Anderson	.10
155 Bobby Bonilla	.10
156 Darryl Kile	.10
157 Ryan Klesko	.10
158 Tim Wakefield	.10
159 Kenny Lofton	.10
160 Jose Canseco	.40
161 Doug Glanville	.10
162 Todd Hundley	.10
163 Brian Jordan	.10
164 Steve Finley	.10
165 Tom Glavine	.25
166 Al Leiter	.10
167 Raul Mondesi	.10
168 Desi Relaford	.10
169 Bret Saberhagen	.10
170 Omar Vizquel	.10
171 Larry Walker	.10
172 Bobby Abreu	.10
173 Moises Alou	.10
174 Mike Caruso	.10
175 Royce Clayton	.10
176 Bartolo Colon	.10
177 Marty Cordova	.10
178 Darin Erstad	.30
179 Nomar Garciaparra	.75
180 Andy Ashby	.10
181 Dan Wilson	.10
182 Larry Sutton	.10
183 Tony Clark	.10
184 Andres Galarraga	.10
185 Ray Durham	.10
186 Hideo Nomo	.60
187 Steve Woodard	.10
188 Scott Rolen	.35
189 Mike Stanley	.10
190 Jaret Wright	.10
191 Vinny Castilla	.10
192 Jason Christiansen	.10
193 Paul Bako	.10
194 Carlos Perez	.10
195 Mike Piazza	1.00
196 Fernando Tatis	.10
197 Mo Vaughn	.10
198 Devon White	.10
199 Ricky Gutierrez	.10
200 Charlie Hayes	.10
201 Brad Radke	.10
202 Rick Helling	.10
203 John Smoltz	.10
204 Frank Thomas	.65
205 David Wells	.10
206 Roger Clemens	.85
207 Mark Grudzielanek	.10
208 Chipper Jones	.75
209 Ray Lankford	.10
210 Pedro Martinez	.65
211 Manny Ramirez	.65
212 Greg Vaughn	.10
213 Craig Biggio	.10
214 Rusty Greer	.10
215 Greg Maddux	.75
216 Rick Aguilera	.10
217 Andy Pettitte	.20
218 Dante Bichette	.10
219 Damion Easley	.10
220 Matt Morris	.10
221 John Olerud	.10
222 Chan Ho Park	.10
223 Curt Schilling	.25
224 John Valentin	.10
225 Matt Williams	.10
226 Ellis Burks	.10
227 Tom Goodwin	.10
228 Javy Lopez	.10
229 Eric Milton	.10
230 Paul O'Neill	.10
231 Magglio Ordonez	.15
232 Derrek Lee	.45
233 Ken Griffey Jr. (Caught on the Fly)	.60
234 Randy Johnson (Caught on the Fly)	.30
235 Alex Rodriguez (Caught on the Fly)	.75
236 Darin Erstad (Caught on the Fly)	.15
237 Juan Gonzalez (Caught on the Fly)	.20
238 Derek Jeter (Caught on the Fly)	1.00
239 Tony Gwynn (Caught on the Fly)	.40
240 Kerry Wood (Caught on the Fly)	.20
241 Cal Ripken Jr. (Caught on the Fly)	1.00
242 Sammy Sosa (Caught on the Fly)	.50
243 Greg Maddux (Caught on the Fly)	.40
244 Mark McGwire (Caught on the Fly)	.75
245 Chipper Jones (Caught on the Fly)	.40
246 Barry Bonds (Caught on the Fly)	1.00
247 Ben Grieve (Caught on the Fly)	.10
248 Ben Davis (Building Blocks)	.10
249 Robert Fick (Building Blocks)	.10
250 Carlos Guillen (Building Blocks)	.10
251 Mike Frank (Building Blocks)	.10
252 Ryan Minor (Building Blocks)	.10
253 Troy Glaus (Building Blocks)	.65
254 Matt Anderson (Building Blocks)	.10
255 Josh Booty (Building Blocks)	.10
256 Gabe Alvarez (Building Blocks)	.10
257 Gabe Kapler (Building Blocks)	.10
258 Enrique Wilson (Building Blocks)	.10
259 Alex Gonzalez (Building Blocks)	.10
260 Preston Wilson (Building Blocks)	.10
261 Eric Chavez (Building Blocks)	.20
262 Adrian Beltre (Building Blocks)	.30
263 Corey Koskie (Building Blocks)	.10
264 Robert Machado RC (Building Blocks)	.10
265 Orlando Hernandez (Building Blocks)	.10
266 Matt Clement (Building Blocks)	.10
267 Luis Ordaz (Building Blocks)	.10
268 Jeremy Giambi (Building Blocks)	.10
269 J.D. Drew (Building Blocks)	.50
269a J.D. Drew (Building Blocks "Sample" autographed edition of 35.)	30.00
270 Cliff Politte (Building Blocks)	.10
271 Carlton Loewer (Building Blocks)	.10
272 Aramis Ramirez (Building Blocks)	.10
273 Ken Griffey Jr. (M.L.P.D.)	.60
274 Randy Johnson (M.L.P.D.)	.30
275 Alex Rodriguez (M.L.P.D.)	.75
276 Darin Erstad (M.L.P.D.)	.20
277 Scott Rolen (M.L.P.D.)	.25
278 Juan Gonzalez (M.L.P.D.)	.25
279 Jeff Bagwell (M.L.P.D.)	.30
280 Mike Piazza (M.L.P.D.)	.65
281 Derek Jeter (M.L.P.D.)	1.00
282 Travis Lee (M.L.P.D.)	.10
283 Tony Gwynn (M.L.P.D.)	.40
284 Kerry Wood (M.L.P.D.)	.10
285 Albert Belle (M.L.P.D.)	.10
286 Sammy Sosa (M.L.P.D.)	.50
287 Mo Vaughn (M.L.P.D.)	.10
288 Nomar Garciaparra (M.L.P.D.)	.45
289 Frank Thomas (M.L.P.D.)	.30
290 Cal Ripken Jr. (M.L.P.D.)	1.00
291 Greg Maddux (M.L.P.D.)	.40
292 Chipper Jones (M.L.P.D.)	.40
293 Ben Grieve (M.L.P.D.)	.10
294 Andruw Jones (M.L.P.D.)	.30
295 Mark McGwire (M.L.P.D.)	.75
296 Roger Clemens (M.L.P.D.)	.50
297 Barry Bonds (M.L.P.D.)	1.00
298 Ken Griffey Jr.-Checklist (M.L.P.D.)	.60
299 Kerry Wood-Checklist (M.L.P.D.)	.20
300 Alex Rodriguez-Checklist (M.L.P.D.)	.75

Precious Metal Gems

A 300-card parallel of the base set, these cards feature gold-foil etching and are inserted exclusively in hobby packs. Each card is serially numbered to 50. A Gem Master 1 of 1 parallel was also issued, but is too rare to value.

	NM/M
Common Player:	3.00
Stars:	25X
Gem Master 1 of 1: Value Undetermined	

Boyz With The Wood

The top hitters in the game are featured on these folded cards with four sides. These are inserted 1:18.

	NM/M
Complete Set (15):	17.50
Common Player:	.60
Inserted 1:18	
1 Ken Griffey Jr.	2.00
2 Frank Thomas	1.00
3 Jeff Bagwell	1.00
4 Juan Gonzalez	.75
5 Mark McGwire	2.50
6 Scott Rolen	.60
7 Travis Lee	.60
8 Tony Gwynn	2.00
9 Mike Piazza	2.00
10 Chipper Jones	2.00
11 Nomar Garciaparra	2.00
12 Derek Jeter	3.00
13 Cal Ripken Jr.	3.00
14 Andruw Jones	1.00
15 Alex Rodriguez	2.50

Diamond Soul

Utilizing lenticular technology these inserts showcase a soulful "galactic" design. The set consists of 15 cards which are seeded at 1:72 packs.

	NM/M
Complete Set (15):	60.00
Common Player:	1.50
Inserted 1:72	
1 Cal Ripken Jr.	12.00
2 Alex Rodriguez	9.00
3 Chipper Jones	6.00
4 Derek Jeter	12.00
5 Frank Thomas	4.00
6 Greg Maddux	6.00
7 Juan Gonzalez	3.00
8 Ken Griffey Jr.	7.50
9 Kerry Wood	3.00
10 Mark McGwire	9.00
11 Mike Piazza	7.50
12 Nomar Garciaparra	6.00
13 Scott Rolen	2.50
14 Tony Gwynn	6.00
15 Travis Lee	1.50

Linchpins

This 10-card set features a laser die-cut background and highlights key players who hold their teams together on the field and in the clubhouse. These are seeded 1:360 packs.

	NM/M
Complete Set (10):	75.00
Common Player:	5.00
Inserted 1:360	
1 Mike Piazza	10.00
2 Mark McGwire	12.50
3 Kerry Wood	5.00
4 Ken Griffey Jr.	10.00
5 Greg Maddux	7.50
6 Frank Thomas	8.00
7 Derek Jeter	15.00
8 Chipper Jones	7.50
9 Cal Ripken Jr.	15.00
10 Alex Rodriguez	12.50

Neophytes

This 15-card insert set showcases young stars like J.D. Drew and Troy Glaus. The cards feature silver foil stamping on a horizontal format, found on an average of 1:6 packs.

	NM/M
Complete Set (15):	7.50
Common Player:	.35
Inserted 1:6	
1 Troy Glaus	3.00
2 Travis Lee	.75
3 Scott Elarton	.35
4 Ricky Ledee	.35
5 Richard Hidalgo	.35
6 J.D. Drew	1.50
7 Paul Konerko	.75
8 Orlando Hernandez	.75
9 Mike Caruso	.35
10 Mike Frank	.35
11 Miguel Tejada	.50
12 Matt Anderson	.35
13 Kerry Wood	1.00
14 Gabe Alvarez	.35
15 Adrian Beltre	.50

Planet Metal

These die-cut cards feature a metallic view of the planet behind pop-out action photography. The 15-card set features the top players in the game and are seeded 1:36 packs.

	NM/M
Complete Set (15):	45.00
Common Player:	1.50
Inserted 1:36	
1 Alex Rodriguez	9.00
2 Andruw Jones	3.50
3 Cal Ripken Jr.	12.00
4 Chipper Jones	5.00
5 Darin Erstad	2.00
6 Derek Jeter	12.00
7 Frank Thomas	3.50
8 Travis Lee	1.50
9 Scott Rolen	2.50
10 Nomar Garciaparra	5.00
11 Mike Piazza	6.50
12 Mark McGwire	6.50
13 Ken Griffey Jr.	6.50
14 Juan Gonzalez	2.50
15 Jeff Bagwell	3.50

2000 Metal

	NM/M
Complete Set (250):	20.00
Common Player:	.10
Common Prospect (201-250):	.50
Inserted 1:2	
Pack (10):	1.50
Wax Box (28):	25.00

1	Tony Gwynn	1.00
2	Derek Jeter	2.50
3	Johnny Damon	.35
4	Javy Lopez	.10
5	Preston Wilson	.10
6	Derek Bell	.10
7	Richie Sexson	.10
8	Vinny Castilla	.10
9	Billy Wagner	.10
10	Carlos Beltran	.50
11	Chris Singleton	.10
12	Nomar Garciaparra	1.00
13	Carlos Febles	.10
14	Jason Varitek	.10
15	Luis Gonzalez	.20
16	Jon Lieber	.10
17	Mo Vaughn	.10
18	Dave Burba	.10
19	Brady Anderson	.10
20	Carlos Lee	.20
21	Chuck Finley	.10
22	Alex Gonzalez	.10
23	Matt Williams	.10
24	Chipper Jones	1.00
25	Pokey Reese	.10
26	Todd Helton	.65
27	Mike Mussina	.40
28	Butch Huskey	.10
29	Jeff Bagwell	.75
30	Juan Encarnacion	.10
31	A.J. Burnett	.10
32	Micah Bowie	.10
33	Brian Jordan	.10
34	Scott Erickson	.10
35	Sean Casey	.25
36	John Smoltz	.10
37	Edgard Clemente	.10
38	Mike Hampton	.10
39	Tom Glavine	.35
40	Albert Belle	.10
41	Jim Thome	.60
42	Jermaine Dye	.10
43	Sammy Sosa	1.25
44	Pedro Martinez	.75
45	Paul Konerko	.20
46	Damion Easley	.10
47	Cal Ripken Jr.	2.50
48	Jose Lima	.10
49	Mike Lowell	.10
50	Randy Johnson	.75
51	Dean Palmer	.10
52	Tim Salmon	.10
53	Kevin Millwood	.10
54	Mark Grace	.10
55	Aaron Boone	.10
56	Omar Vizquel	.10
57	Moises Alou	.10
58	Travis Fryman	.10
59	Erubiel Durazo	.10
60	Carl Everett	.10
61	Charles Johnson	.10
62	Trot Nixon	.10
63	Andres Galarraga	.10
64	Magglio Ordonez	.10
65	Pedro Astacio	.10
66	Roberto Alomar	.20
67	Pete Harnisch	.10
68	Scott Williamson	.10
69	Alex Fernandez	.10
70	Robin Ventura	.10
71	Chad Allen	.10
72	Darin Erstad	.20
73	Ron Coomer	.10
74	Ellis Burks	.10
75	Kent Bottenfield	.10
76	Ken Griffey Jr.	1.50
77	Mike Piazza	1.50
78	Jorge Posada	.20
79	Dante Bichette	.10
80	Adrian Beltre	.25
81	Andruw Jones	.75
82	Wilson Alvarez	.10
83	Edgardo Alfonzo	.10
84	Brian Giles	.10
85	Gary Sheffield	.25
86	Matt Stairs	.10
87	Bret Boone	.10
88	Kenny Rogers	.10
89	Barry Bonds	2.50
90	Scott Rolen	.60
91	Edgar Renteria	.10
92	Larry Walker	.10
93	Roger Cedeno	.10
94	Kevin Brown	.10
95	Lee Stevens	.10
96	Brad Radke	.10
97	Andy Pettitte	.25
98	Bobby Higginson	.10
99	Eric Chavez	.25
100	Alex Rodriguez	2.00
100s	Alex Rodriguez/OPS	2.00
101	Shannon Stewart	.10
102	Ryan Rupe	.10
103	Freddy Garcia	.10
104	John Jaha	.10
105	Greg Maddux	1.00
106	Hideki Irabu	.10
107	Rey Ordonez	.10
108	Troy O'Leary	.10
109	Frank Thomas	.75

110	Corey Koskie	.10
111	Bernie Williams	.10
112	Barry Larkin	.10
113	Kevin Appier	.10
114	Curt Schilling	.35
115	Bartolo Colon	.10
116	Edgar Martinez	.10
117	Ray Lankford	.10
118	Todd Walker	.10
119	John Wetteland	.10
120	David Nilsson	.10
121	Tino Martinez	.10
122	Phil Nevin	.10
123	Ben Grieve	.10
124	Ron Gant	.10
125	Jeff Kent	.10
126	Rick Helling	.10
127	Russ Ortiz	.10
128	Troy Glaus	.65
129	Chan Ho Park	.10
130	Jeromy Burnitz	.10
131	Aaron Sele	.10
132	Mike Sirotka	.10
133	Brad Ausmus	.10
134	Jose Rosado	.10
135	Mariano Rivera	.25
136	Jason Giambi	.50
137	Mike Lieberthal	.10
138	Chris Carpenter	.10
139	Henry Rodriguez	.10
140	Mike Sweeney	.10
141	Vladimir Guerrero	.75
142	Charles Nagy	.10
143	Jason Kendall	.10
144	Matt Lawton	.10
145	Michael Barrett	.10
146	David Cone	.10
147	Bobby Abreu	.10
148	Fernando Tatis	.10
149	Jose Canseco	.40
150	Craig Biggio	.10
151	Matt Mantei	.10
152	Jacque Jones	.10
153	John Halama	.10
154	Trevor Hoffman	.10
155	Rondell White	.10
156	Reggie Sanders	.10
157	Steve Finley	.10
158	Roberto Hernandez	.10
159	Geoff Jenkins	.10
160	Chris Widger	.10
161	Orel Hershiser	.10
162	Tim Hudson	.20
163	Kris Benson	.10
164	Kevin Young	.10
165	Rafael Palmeiro	.60
166	David Wells	.10
167	Ben Davis	.10
168	Jamie Moyer	.10
169	Randy Wolf	.10
170	Jeff Cirillo	.10
171	Warren Morris	.10
172	Billy Koch	.10
173	Marquis Grissom	.10
174	Geoff Blum	.10
175	Octavio Dotel	.10
176	Orlando Hernandez	.20
177	J.D. Drew	.25
178	Carlos Delgado	.40
179	Sterling Hitchcock	.10
180	Shawn Green	.25
181	Tony Clark	.10
182	Joe McEwing	.10
183	Fred McGriff	.10
184	Tony Batista	.10
185	Al Leiter	.10
186	Roger Clemens	1.25
187	Al Martin	.10
188	Eric Milton	.10
189	Bobby Smith	.10
190	Rusty Greer	.10
191	Shawn Estes	.10
192	Ken Caminiti	.10
193	Eric Karros	.10
194	Manny Ramirez	.75
195	Jim Edmonds	.10
196	Paul O'Neill	.10
197	Rico Brogna	.10
198	Ivan Rodriguez	.60
199	Doug Glanville	.10
200	Mark McGwire	2.00
201	Mark Quinn (Prospect)	.50
202	Norm Hutchins (Prospect)	.50
203	Ramon Ortiz (Prospect)	.50
204	Brett Laxton (Prospect)	.50
205	Jimmy Anderson (Prospect)	.50
206	Calvin Murray (Prospect)	.50
207	Wilton Veras (Prospect)	.50
208	Chad Hermansen (Prospect)	.50
209	Nick Johnson (Prospect)	.50
210	Kevin Barker (Prospect)	.50
211	Casey Blake (Prospect)	.50
212	Chad Meyers (Prospect)	.50
213	Kip Wells (Prospect)	.50
214	Eric Munson (Prospect)	.50
215	Lance Berkman (Prospect)	.50
216	Wily Pena (Prospect)	.50
217	Gary Matthews Jr. (Prospect)	.50
218	Travis Dawkins (Prospect)	.50

219	Josh Beckett (Prospect)	.75
220	Tony Armas Jr. (Prospect)	.50
221	Alfonso Soriano (Prospect)	1.00
222	Pat Burrell (Prospect)	1.00
223	Danys Baez RC (Prospect)	.50
224	Adam Kennedy (Prospect)	.50
225	Ruben Mateo (Prospect)	.50
226	Vernon Wells (Prospect)	.75
227	Brian Cooper (Prospect)	.50
228	Jeff DaVanon RC (Prospect)	.50
229	Glen Barker (Prospect)	.50
230	Robinson Cancel (Prospect)	.50
231	D'Angelo Jimenez (Prospect)	.50
232	Adam Piatt (Prospect)	.50
233	Buddy Carlyle (Prospect)	.50
234	Chad Hutchinson (Prospect)	.50
235	Matt Riley (Prospect)	.50
236	Cole Liniak (Prospect)	.50
237	Ben Petrick (Prospect)	.50
238	Peter Bergeron (Prospect)	.50
239	Cesar King (Prospect)	.50
240	Aaron Myette (Prospect)	.50
241	Eric Gagne (Prospect)	.60
242	Joe Nathan (Prospect)	.50
243	Bruce Chen (Prospect)	.50
244	Rob Bell (Prospect)	.50
245	Juan Sosa RC (Prospect)	.60
246	Julio Ramirez (Prospect)	.50
247	Wade Miller (Prospect)	.50
248	Trace Coquillette RC (Prospect)	.50
249	Robert Ramsay (Prospect)	.50
250	Rick Ankiel (Prospect)	.60

Emerald

A green tone at the top 1/4 of the card fronts, and a small circled "E" at top-right on back differentiate these parallels from the regular-issue cards. The first 200 cards in the set are found in this version about one every four packs. The odds double for the Prospects cards (#201-250) that were short-printed in the regular version as well.

	NM/M
Complete Set (250):	100.00
Common Player:	.25
Stars:	2.5X
Inserted 1:4	
Prospects (201-250):	2.5X
Inserted 1:8	

Fusion

	NM/M
Complete Set (15):	12.50
Common Player:	.50
Inserted 1:4	

1	Ken Griffey Jr., Alex Rodriguez	2.00
2	Mark McGwire, Rick Ankiel	2.00
3	Scott Rolen, Curt Schilling	.50
4	Pedro Martinez, Nomar Garciaparra	1.25
5	Carlos Beltran, Carlos Febles	.60
6	Sammy Sosa, Mark Grace	1.50
7	Vladimir Guerrero, Ugueth Urbina	1.00
8	Roger Clemens, Derek Jeter	3.00
9	Jeff Bagwell, Craig Biggio	1.00
10	Chipper Jones, Andruw Jones	1.50
11	Cal Ripken Jr., Mike Mussina	2.50
12	Manny Ramirez, Roberto Alomar	1.00
13	Sean Casey, Barry Larkin	.50
14	Ivan Rodriguez, Rafael Palmeiro	.75
15	Mike Piazza, Robin Ventura	1.50

Autographics

	NM/M
Common Player:	4.00
Bobby Abreu	8.00
Chad Allen	4.00
Marlon Anderson	4.00
Rick Ankiel	6.00
Glen Barker	4.00
Rob Bell	4.00
Mark Bellhorn	5.00
Peter Bergeron	4.00
Lance Berkman	8.00
Wade Boggs	25.00
Barry Bonds	150.00
Kent Bottenfield	4.00
Pat Burrell	10.00
Miguel Cairo	4.00
Mike Cameron	6.00
Chris Carpenter	6.00
Roger Cedeno	4.00
Mike Darr	6.00
Einar Diaz	4.00
J.D. Drew	15.00
Erubiel Durazo	6.00
Ray Durham	6.00
Damion Easley	4.00
Scott Elarton	4.00
Jeremy Giambi	4.00
Doug Glanville	4.00
Shawn Green	10.00
Jerry Hairston Jr.	4.00
Bob Howry	4.00
Norm Hutchins	4.00
Randy Johnson	40.00
Jacque Jones	4.00
Gabe Kapler	6.00
Cesar King	4.00
Mark Kotsay	4.00
Cole Liniak	4.00
Greg Maddux	50.00
Pedro Martinez	30.00
Ruben Mateo	4.00
Warren Morris	4.00
Heath Murray	4.00
Joe Nathan	4.00
Jim Parque	4.00
Angel Pena	4.00
Cal Ripken Jr.	100.00
Alex Rodriguez	60.00
Ryan Rupe	4.00
Randall Simon	4.00
Chris Singleton	6.00
Mike Sweeney	4.00
Wilton Veras	4.00
Scott Williamson	4.00
Randy Wolf	6.00
Tony Womack	6.00

Base Shredders

	NM/M
Complete Set (18):	160.00
Common Player:	5.00
Inserted 1:288	
(1)	Roberto Alomar	7.50
(2)	Michael Barrett	5.00
(3)	Tony Clark	5.00
(4)	Ben Davis	5.00
(5)	Erubiel Durazo	5.00
(6)	Troy Glaus	12.50
(7)	Ben Grieve	5.00
(8)	Vladimir Guerrero	15.00

Base Shredders

(9)	Tony Gwynn	25.00
(10)	Todd Helton	12.50
(11)	Eric Munson	5.00
(12)	Rafael Palmeiro	10.00
(13)	Manny Ramirez	20.00
(14)	Ivan Rodriguez	10.00
(15)	Miguel Tejada	7.50
(16)	Mo Vaughn	5.00
(17)	Larry Walker	5.00
(18)	Matt Williams	5.00

Heavy Metal

	NM/M
Complete Set (10):	15.00
Common Player:	1.50
Inserted 1:20	
1	Sammy Sosa	2.25
2	Mark McGwire	3.00
3	Ken Griffey Jr.	2.50
4	Mike Piazza	2.50
5	Nomar Garciaparra	2.00
6	Alex Rodriguez	3.00
7	Manny Ramirez	1.50
8	Jeff Bagwell	1.50
9	Chipper Jones	1.50
10	Vladimir Guerrero	1.50

Hit Machines

	NM/M
Complete Set (10):	20.00
Common Player:	1.00
Inserted 1:20	
1	Ken Griffey Jr.	3.00
2	Mark McGwire	4.00
3	Frank Thomas	1.50
4	Tony Gwynn	2.00
5	Rafael Palmeiro	1.25
6	Bernie Williams	1.00
7	Derek Jeter	6.00
8	Sammy Sosa	2.50
9	Mike Piazza	3.00
10	Chipper Jones	2.00

Platinum Portraits

	NM/M
Complete Set (10):	6.00
Common Player:	.25
Inserted 1:8	
1	Carlos Beltran	.50
2	Vladimir Guerrero	.75
3	Manny Ramirez	.75
4	Ivan Rodriguez	.65
5	Sean Casey	.40
6	Alex Rodriguez	1.50
7	Derek Jeter	2.00
8	Nomar Garciaparra	1.00

9	Vernon Wells	.25
10	Shawn Green	.50

Talent Show

	NM/M
Complete Set (15):	6.00
Common Player:	.30
Inserted 1:4	
1	Rick Ankiel	.45
2	Matt Riley	.30
3	Chad Hermansen	.30
4	Ruben Mateo	.30
5	Eric Munson	.30
6	Alfonso Soriano	1.50
7	Wilton Veras	.30
8	Vernon Wells	.75
9	Erubiel Durazo	.30
10	Pat Burrell	1.50
11	Ben Davis	.30
12	A.J. Burnett	.30
13	Peter Bergeron	.30
14	Mark Quinn	.30
15	Ben Petrick	.30

1993 Metz Bakeries

Metz Baking Co. of Sioux City, Iowa, produced this set utilizing drawings of players rather than photos. The company also made available uncut sheets of the sets via a mail-in offer. Cards have either a yellow background with blue pin-stripes or a blue background with yellow pinstripes. Players are shown in a red, white and black porthole at center. Backs are printed in black-and-white with complete major and minor league stats. Because the cards are licensed only by the players' union and not Major League Baseball, the player paintings omit uniform logos. The un-numbered cards are checklisted here in alphabetical order. A special collectors tin to house the set was also available.

	NM/M
Complete Set (40):	35.00
Common Player:	.75
(1)	Dante Bichette	.75

(2)	Wade Boggs	2.00
(3)	Barry Bonds	4.00
(4)	Bobby Bonilla	.75
(5)	Jose Canseco	1.00
(6)	Joe Carter	.75
(7)	Will Clark	.75
(8)	Roger Clemens	2.25
(9)	Doug Drabek	.75
(10)	Shawon Dunston	.75
(11)	Dennis Eckersley	1.25
(12)	Cecil Fielder	.75
(13)	Carlton Fisk	1.50
(14)	Andres Galarraga	.75
(15)	Kirk Gibson	.75
(16)	Dwight Gooden	.75
(17)	Mark Grace	.75
(18)	Ken Griffey Jr.	2.50
(19)	Tony Gwynn	2.00
(20)	Rickey Henderson	1.50
(21)	Kent Hrbek	.75
(22)	Howard Johnson	.75
(23)	Wally Joyner	.75
(24)	Dave Justice	.75
(25)	Barry Larkin	.75
(26)	Don Mattingly	2.50
(27)	Jack McDowell	.75
(28)	Paul Molitor	1.50
(29)	Terry Pendleton	.75
(30)	Kirby Puckett	2.00
(31)	Cal Ripken, Jr.	4.00
(32)	Nolan Ryan	4.00
(33)	Ryne Sandberg	2.00
(34)	Ozzie Smith	2.00
(35)	Darryl Strawberry	.75
(36)	Danny Tartabull	.75
(37)	Mickey Tettleton	.75
(38)	Alan Trammell	.75
(39)	Andy Van Slyke	.75
(40)	Dave Winfield	1.50

1993 Milk Bone Super Stars

Mark McGwire 1B
Ellis & Sam

Milk Bone Flavor Snacks and Dog Treats issued a 20-card Super Stars set in 1993 in a format comparable to the NFL Pro Line cards. The cards show the player at home with his dog, with the player shown in an action photo in the lower left corner of the card. The card backs have the player's stats and biography, along with information about the pet and a quote from the player about his dog. The cards were available, two at a time, in specially-marked packages of the company's products. The set also could be obtained through the mail by following instructions on the boxes.

		NM/M
Complete Set (20):		12.50
Common Player:		.50
(1)	Paul Molitor	1.00
(2)	Tom Glavine	.65
(3)	Barry Larkin	.50
(4)	Mark McGwire	2.50
(5)	Bill Swift	.50
(6)	Ken Caminiti	.50
(7)	Will Clark	.50
(8)	Rafael Palmeiro	.75
(9)	Matt Young	.50
(10)	Todd Zeile	.50
(11)	Wally Joyner	.50
(12)	Cal Ripken Jr.	3.50
(13)	Tom Foley	.50
(14)	Ben McDonald	.50
(15)	Larry Walker	.50
(16)	Rob Dibble	.50
(17)	Brett Butler	.50
(18)	Joe Girardi	.50
(19)	Brady Anderson	.50
(20)	Craig Biggio	.50

1989 Milk Duds Pittsburgh Pirates

This set of Pirates photo-cards carries on its backs advertising for various brands of Leaf candies, principally Milk

John SMILEY

Duds. The 3-3/8" x 5-1/2" cards have color portrait photo on front with the player's name near the bottom and a team logo at bottom center. Backs have a few vital statistics, candy advertising and/or free ticket or contest offers. The cards are numbered by uniform number, but are listed here in alphabetical order.

		NM/M
Complete Set (38):		20.00
Common Player:		.75
(1)	Pirate Parrot/Mascot	.75
(2)	Rafael Belliard	.75
(3)	Dann Bilardello	.75
(4)	Barry Bonds	9.00
(5)	Sid Bream	.75
(6)	Bobby Bonilla	1.00
(7)	John Cangelosi	.75
(8)	Benny Distefano	.75
(9)	Rich Donnelly	.75
(10)	Doug Drabek	.75
(11)	Brian Fisher	.75
(12)	Miguel Garcia	.75
(13)	Jim Gott	.75
(14)	Neal Heaton	.75
(15)	Bruce Kimm	.75
(16)	Jeff King	1.00
(17)	Bob Kipper	.75
(18)	Randy Kramer	.75
(19)	Gene Lamont	.75
(20)	Bill Landrum	.75
(21)	Mike LaValliere	.75
(22)	Jim Leyland	.75
(23)	Jose Lind	.75
(24)	Morris Madden	.75
(25)	Milt May	.75
(26)	Ray Miller	.75
(27)	Junior Ortiz	.75
(28)	Tom Prince	.75
(29)	Rey Quinones	.75
(30)	Gary Redus	.75
(31)	R.J. Reynolds	.75
(32)	Jeff Robinson	.75
(33)	Tommy Sandt	.75
(34)	John Smiley	.75
(35)	Dorn Taylor	.75
(36)	Andy Van Slyke	1.00
(37)	Bob Walk	.75
(38)	Glenn Wilson	.75

1997 Milk Mustache Trading Cards

MILK
ALEX RODRIGUEZ
shortstop SEATTLE MARINERS

Sponsored by the National Fluid Milk Processor Promotion Board (really), this nine-card panel was an advertising insert in the October 1997, issue of Sports Illustrated for Kids. The perforated panel measures about 7-1/2" x 10-1/2", with each card measuring the standard 2-1/2" x 3-1/2" and perforated on two, three or four sides, depending on its placement on the sheet. Player portrait photos are set on a silver-look background. Cap and uniform logos

have been eliminated and a milk moustache added. "MILK" appears in white in a purple stripe at the top of each player's card. Backs have a baseball tip and a milk tip ascribed to each player.

		NM/M
Complete Sheet:		5.00
Complete Set (9):		5.00
Common Player:		.25
1	Alex Rodriguez	2.50
2	Nomar Garciaparra	1.00
3	Andy Pettitte	.35
4	Darin Erstad	.45
5	Jason Kendall	.25
6	Vladimir Guerrero	1.00
7	Scott Rolen	.60
8	Tony Clark	.25
--	Header Card	.05

1990 Miller Beer Milwaukee Brewers

GARY SHEFFIELD
INFIELD

This 32-card set was given away with an album to adults attending an August Brewers game. Cards are standard 2-1/2" x 3-1/2" and feature borderless color photos above gold and black bottom stripes. The beer company's logo is featured in the upper-right corner, with the team logo at lower-left. Black-and-white backs feature player stats. The set has been checklisted below in alphabetical order. Cards are not numbered.

		NM/M
Complete Set w/Album (32):		10.00
Common Player:		.25
(1)	Chris Bosio	.25
(2)	Greg Brock	.25
(3)	Chuck Crim	.25
(4)	Rob Deer	.25
(5)	Edgar Diaz	.25
(6)	Tom Edens	.25
(7)	Mike Felder	.25
(8)	Tom Filer	.25
(9)	Jim Gantner	.25
(10)	Darryl Hamilton	.25
(11)	Teddy Higuera	.25
(12)	Mark Knudson	.25
(13)	Bill Krueger	.25
(14)	Paul Mirabella	.25
(15)	Paul Molitor	4.00
(16)	Jaime Navarro	.25
(17)	Charlie O'Brien	.25
(18)	Dave Parker	.25
(19)	Dan Plesac	.25
(20)	Dennis Powell	.25
(21)	Ron Robinson	.25
(22)	Bob Sebra	.25
(23)	Gary Sheffield	2.00
(24)	Bill Spiers	.25
(25)	B.J. Surhoff	.25
(26)	Dale Sveum	.25
(27)	Tom Trebelhorn	.25
(28)	Greg Vaughn	.25
(29)	Randy Veres	.25
(30)	Bill Wegman	.25
(31)	Robin Yount	4.00
(32)	Coaches (Don Baylor, Ray Burris, Duffy Dyer, Andy Etchebarren, Larry Haney)	.25

1991 Miller Beer Milwaukee Brewers

The Miller High Life Brewing Co., in conjunction with the Milwaukee Brewers, sponsored a 32-card limited edition baseball card set in 1991. The set, which features 30 cards of Brewer players plus additional

'91 BREWERS

PAUL MOLITOR • IF

cards of manager Tom Trebelhorn and his coaching staff, employs a home plate window for the front photo, with the player's name and words "Miller High Life" along the bottom of the card. Complete major and minor league stats are printed on the black-and-white backs, which also include sponsors' logos.

		NM/M
Complete Set w/Album (32):		10.00
Common Player:		.25
(1)	Don August	.25
(2)	James Austin	.25
(3)	Dante Bichette	.35
(4)	Chris Bosio	.25
(5)	Kevin Brown	.25
(6)	Chuck Crim	.25
(7)	Rick Dempsey	.25
(8)	Jim Gantner	.25
(9)	Darryl Hamilton	.25
(10)	Teddy Higuera	.25
(11)	Darren Holmes	.25
(12)	Jim Hunter	.25
(13)	Mark Knudson	.25
(14)	Mark Lee	.25
(15)	Julio Machado	.25
(16)	Candy Maldonado	.25
(17)	Paul Molitor	4.00
(18)	Jaime Navarro	.25
(19)	Edwin Nunez	.25
(20)	Dan Plesac	.25
(21)	Willie Randolph	.25
(22)	Ron Robinson	.25
(23)	Gary Sheffield	1.00
(24)	Bill Spiers	.25
(25)	Franklin Stubbs	.25
(26)	B.J. Surhoff	.25
(27)	Dale Sveum	.25
(28)	Tom Treblehorn	.25
(29)	Greg Vaughn	.25
(30)	Bill Wegman	.25
(31)	Robin Yount	4.00

1994 Miller Genuine Draft Milwaukee Brewers

(See 1994 Lite Beer Milwaukee Breweres.)

1984 Milton Bradley

Championship Baseball BY MILTON BRADLEY

AL SUPER STAR
SHORTSTOP
ROBIN YOUNT
MILWAUKEE BREWERS

In 1984, Milton Bradley printed their baseball game cards in full-color and adopted the standard baseball card size of 2-1/2" x 3-1/2". A total of 30 cards were in the set. The card fronts show the player photos with the team insignias and logos airbrushed away. The game is called Championship Baseball. Card backs varied in style; some had player statistics plus game information, and others only game information.

		NM/M
Complete Boxed Set:		12.00
Complete Card Set (30):		7.50
Common Player:		.25
(1)	Wade Boggs	.75

(2)	George Brett	1.50
(3)	Rod Carew	.50
(4)	Steve Carlton	.50
(5)	Gary Carter	.50
(6)	Dave Concepcion	.25
(7)	Cecil Cooper	.25
(8)	Andre Dawson	.40
(9)	Carlton Fisk	.50
(10)	Steve Garvey	.40
(11)	Pedro Guerrero	.25
(12)	Ron Guidry	.25
(13)	Rickey Henderson	.25
(14)	Reggie Jackson	1.50
(15)	Ron Kittle	.25
(16)	Bill Madlock	.25
(17)	Dale Murphy	.40
(18)	Al Oliver	.25
(19)	Darrell Porter	.25
(20)	Cal Ripken, Jr.	2.50
(21)	Pete Rose	1.50
(22)	Steve Sax	.25
(23)	Mike Schmidt	1.50
(24)	Ted Simmons	.25
(25)	Ozzie Smith	.75
(26)	Dave Stieb	.25
(27)	Fernando Valenzuela	.25
(28)	Lou Whitaker	.25
(29)	Dave Winfield	.50
(30)	Robin Yount	.50

1982 Milwaukee Brewers Police

ROBIN YOUNT
No. 19 – Shortstop
New Berlin Police Department
Salutes The 1982
Milwaukee Brewers

The inaugural Milwaukee Brewers police set contains 30 cards in a 2-13/16" x 4-1/8" format. There are 26 players included in the set, which is numbered by player uniform number. Unnumbered cards were also issued for general manager Harry Dalton, manager Buck Rodgers, the coaches and a team card with checklist. The full-color photos are especially attractive, printed on the cards' crisp white stock. A number of Wisconsin law enforcement agencies distributed the cards and credit lines on the card fronts were changed accordingly.

		NM/M
Complete Set (30):		12.00
Common Player:		.25
4	Paul Molitor	4.00
5	Ned Yost	.25
7	Don Money	.25
9	Larry Hisle	.25
10	Bob McClure	.25
11	Ed Romero	.25
13	Roy Howell	.25
15	Cecil Cooper	.25
17	Jim Gantner	.25
19	Robin Yount	4.00
20	Gorman Thomas	.25
22	Charlie Moore	.25
23	Ted Simmons	.25
24	Ben Oglivie	.25
26	Kevin Bass	.25
28	Jamie Easterly	.25
29	Mark Brouhard	.25
30	Moose Haas	.25
34	Rollie Fingers	2.00
35	Randy Lerch	.25
37	Buck Rodgers	.25
41	Jim Slaton	.25
45	Doug Jones	.25
46	Jerry Augustine	.25
47	Dwight Bernard	.25
48	Mike Caldwell	.25
50	Pete Vuckovich	.25
---	Team photo/checklist	.25
---	Harry Dalton/GM	.25
---	Coaches card (Pat Dobson, Larry Haney, Ron Hansen, Cal McLish, Buck Rogers, Harry Warner)	.25

1983 Milwaukee Brewers Police

Similar to 1982, a number of issuer variations exist for the 1983 Brewers police set, as law

16 MARSHALL EDWARDS – OF
The Milwaukee Police Department
Presents The 1983
Milwaukee Brewers

enforcement agencies throughout the state distributed the set with their own credit lines on the cards. At least 28 variations are known to exist, with those issued by smaller agencies being scarcest. Prices quoted below are for the most common variations, generally the Milwaukee Police Department and a few small-town departments whose entire supply of police cards seem to have fallen into dealers' hands. Some specialists are willing to pay a premium for the scarcer departments' issues. The 30, 2-13/16" x 4-1/8" cards include 29 players and coaches, along with a team card (with a checklist back). The team card and group coaches' card are unnumbered, while the others are numbered by uniform number.

		NM/M
Complete Set (30):		6.00
Common Player:		.25
4	Paul Molitor	3.00
5	Ned Yost	.25
7	Don Money	.25
9	Rob Picciolo	.25
10	Bob McClure	.25
11	Ed Romero	.25
13	Roy Howell	.25
15	Cecil Cooper	.25
16	Marshall Edwards	.25
17	Jim Gantner	.25
19	Robin Yount	3.00
20	Gorman Thomas	.25
21	Don Sutton	1.00
23	Charlie Moore	.25
23	Ted Simmons	.25
24	Ben Oglivie	.25
26	Bob Skube	.25
27	Pete Ladd	.25
28	Jamie Easterly	.25
30	Moose Haas	.25
32	Harvey Kuenn	.25
34	Rollie Fingers	1.00
36	Bob L. Gibson	.25
41	Jim Slaton	.25
42	Tom Tellmann	.25
46	Jerry Augustine	.25
48	Mike Caldwell	.25
50	Pete Vuckovich	.25
---	Team photo/checklist	.25
---	Coaches Card (Pat Dobson, Dave Garcia, Larry Haney, Ron Hansen)	.25

1984 Milwaukee Brewers Police

20 DON SUTTON – P
The Winneconne Police Department
Presents The 1984
MILWAUKEE BREWERS

The king of the variations again in 1984, the Milwaukee Brewers set has been found with 57 different police agencies' credit lines on the front of the cards. Once again, law enforcement agencies statewide participated in distributing the sets. Some departments also include a badge of the participating agency on the card backs. The full-color cards measure 2-13/16" x 4-1/8". There are 28 numbered player and manager cards, along with an unnumbered coaches card and a team card. Player names, uniform numbers and positions are listed on each card front. Prices listed are for the most common variety (Milwaukee Police Department); sets issued by smaller departments may be worth a premium to specialists. Reported print runs varied from 120,000 sets for the Milwaukee P.D., to just 500 sets for the community of Verona.

No.	Player	NM/M
Complete Set (30):		6.00
Common Player:		.15
2	Randy Ready	.15
4	Paul Molitor	2.50
8	Jim Sundberg	.15
9	Rene Lachemann	.15
10	Bob McClure	.15
11	Ed Romero	.15
13	Roy Howell	.15
14	Dion James	.15
15	Cecil Cooper	.15
17	Jim Gantner	.15
19	Robin Yount	2.50
20	Don Sutton	1.00
21	Bill Schroeder	.15
22	Charlie Moore	.15
23	Ted Simmons	.15
24	Ben Oglivie	.15
25	Bobby Clark	.15
27	Pete Ladd	.15
28	Rick Manning	.15
29	Mark Brouhard	.15
30	Moose Haas	.15
34	Rollie Fingers	1.00
42	Tom Tellmann	.15
43	Chuck Porter	.15
46	Jerry Augustine	.15
47	Jaime Cocanower	.15
48	Mike Caldwell	.15
50	Pete Vuckovich	.15
---	Team photo/checklist	.15
---	Coaches Card (Pat Dobson, Dave Garcia, Larry Haney, Tom Trebelhorn)	.15

1985 Milwaukee Brewers Police

49 Ted Higuera P — The Milwaukee Police Department and The Milwaukee Journal present the 1985 Milwaukee Brewers

The Brewers changed the size of their annual police set in 1985, but almost imperceptibly. The full-color cards are 2-3/4" x 4-1/8", a slight 1/16" narrower than the four previous efforts. Player and team name on the card fronts are much bolder than in previous years. Once again, numerous area police groups distributed the sets, leading to nearly 60 variations, as each agency put their own credit line on the cards. Card backs include the Brewers logo, a safety tip and, in some cases, a badge of the participating law enforcement group. There are 27 numbered player cards (by uniform number) and three unnumbered cards - team roster, coaches and a newspaper carrier card. Prices are for the most common departments.

No.	Player	NM/M
Complete Set (30):		6.00
Common Player:		.15
2	Randy Ready	.15
4	Paul Molitor	2.50
5	Doug Loman	.15
7	Paul Householder	.15
10	Bob McClure	.15
11	Ed Romero	.15
14	Dion James	.15
15	Cecil Cooper	.15
17	Jim Gantner	.15
18	Danny Darwin	.15
19	Robin Yount	2.50
21	Bill Schroeder	.15
22	Charlie Moore	.15
23	Ted Simmons	.15
26	Ben Oglivie	.15
26	Brian Giles	.15
27	Pete Ladd	.15
28	Rick Manning	.15
29	Mark Brouhard	.15
30	Moose Haas	.15
31	George Bamberger	.15
34	Rollie Fingers	1.00
40	Bob L. Gibson	.15
42	Ray Searage	.15
47	Jaime Cocanower	.15
48	Ray Burris	.15
49	Ted Higuera	.15
50	Pete Vuckovich	.15
---	Coaches Card (Andy Etchebarren, Larry Haney, Frank Howard, Tony Muser, Herm Starrette)	.15
---	Team Photo/Roster	.15

1986 Milwaukee Brewers Police

45 Rob Deer OF — The Fond du Lac Police Dept., KFIZ Radio, and National Exchange Bank & Trust present the 1986 Milwaukee Brewers

The Milwaukee Brewers, in conjunction with the Milwaukee Police Department, WTMJ Radio and Kinney Shoes, produced this attractive police safety set of 30 cards. The cards measure 2-13/16" x 4-1/2". A thin black border encloses a full-color player photo on the front. The card backs give a safety tip and promos for the sponsor. The cards were distributed throughout the state of Wisconsin by numerous police departments; those of the smaller departments generally being scarcer than those issued in the big cities. Prices quoted below are for the most common departments' issues.

No.	Player	NM/M
Complete Set (30):		4.00
Common Player:		.15
1	Ernest Riles	.15
2	Edgar Diaz	.15
3	Juan Castillo	.15
4	Paul Molitor	2.00
5	B.J. Surhoff	.15
7	Dale Sveum	.15
9	Greg Brock	.15
13	Billy Jo Robidoux	.15
14	Jim Paciorek	.15
15	Cecil Cooper	.15
16	Mike Felder	.15
17	Jim Gantner	.15
19	Robin Yount	2.00
20	Juan Nieves	.15
21	Bill Schroeder	.15
25	Mark Clear	.15
26a	Glenn Braggs	.15
26b	Chris Bosio	.30
28	Rick Manning	.15
29	Chris Bosio	.30
32	Chuck Crim	.15
34	Mark Ciardi	.15
37	Dan Plesac	.15
38	John Henry Johnson	.15
40	Mike Birbeck	.15
42	Tom Trebelhorn	.15
46	Rob Deer	.15
48	Bill Wegman	.15
49	Ted Higuera	.15
---	Coaches Card (Andy Etchebarren, Larry Haney, Frank Howard, Tony Muser, Herm Starrette)	.15
---	Team Photo/Roster	.15

1987 Milwaukee Brewers Police

5 B.J. Surhoff C — The Milwaukee Police Department Kinney Shoes and WTMJ Radio present the 1987 Milwaukee Brewers

The Milwaukee Brewers issued a safety set in 1987 for the sixth consecutive year. As in the past, many local police departments throughout Wisconsin participated in the giveaway program. The Milwaukee version was sponsored by Kinney Shoe Stores and WTMJ Radio and was handed out to youngsters attending the Baseball Card Day at County Stadium on May 9th. The cards, which measure 2-1/4" x 4-1/8", feature full-color photos plus a safety tip on the backs. Chris Bosio can be found with a uniform number of 26 or 29. The card was corrected to #29 in later printings.

No.	Player	NM/M
Complete Set (30):		5.00
Common Player:		.15
1	Ernest Riles	.15
2	Edgar Diaz	.15
3	Juan Castillo	.15
4	Paul Molitor	2.00
5	B.J. Surhoff	.15
7	Dale Sveum	.15
9	Greg Brock	.15
13	Billy Jo Robidoux	.15
14	Jim Paciorek	.15
15	Cecil Cooper	.15
16	Mike Felder	.15
17	Jim Gantner	.15
19	Robin Yount	2.00
20	Juan Nieves	.15
21	Bill Schroeder	.15
25	Mark Clear	.15
26	Glenn Braggs	.15
26	Chris Bosio	.30
28	Rick Manning	.15
29	Chris Bosio	.30
32	Chuck Crim	.15
34	Mark Ciardi	.15
37	Dan Plesac	.15
38	John Henry Johnson	.15
40	Mike Birbeck	.15
42	Tom Trebelhorn	.15
46	Rob Deer	.15
48	Bill Wegman	.15
49	Ted Higuera	.15
---	Coaches Card (Andy Etchebarren, Larry Haney, Chuck Hartenstein, Dave Hilton, Tony Muser)	.15
---	Team photo	.15

1988 Milwaukee Brewers Police

3 Juan Castillo IF — The Marathon County Sheriff's Dept. and Brickner Chrysler Center, 2525 Grand Avenue, Wausau, WI 54401 present the 1988 Milwaukee Brewers

This 30-card set is the 7th annual issue sponsored by the Milwaukee Police Department for local distribution during a crime prevention promotion. The full-color card fronts (2-3/4" x 4-1/8") feature the same design as the 1987 set with white borders and a black frame outlining the player photo and name. Sponsor credits and the team name are listed below the photo. The vertical card backs are blue on white with messages from the player and sponsors. Two group photos - one of the team's five coaches and one of the team (with a checklist back) - are unnumbered and printed horizontally. Card numbers refer to the players' uniform numbers.

No.	Player	NM/M
Complete Set (30):		4.00
Common Player:		.15
1	Ernest Riles	.15
2	Juan Castillo	.15
4	Paul Molitor	2.00
5	B.J. Surhoff	.15
7	Dale Sveum	.15
9	Greg Brock	.15
11	Charlie O'Brien	.15
14	Jim Adduci	.15
16	Mike Felder	.15
17	Jim Gantner	.15
19	Robin Yount	2.00
20	Juan Nieves	.15
21	Bill Schroeder	.15
22	Joey Meyer	.15
25	Mark Clear	.15
26	Glenn Braggs	.15
28	Odell Jones	.15
29	Chris Bosio	.15
30	Steve Kiefer	.15
32	Chuck Crim	.15
37	Jay Aldrich	.15
37	Dan Plesac	.15
40	Mike Birbeck	.15
42	Tom Trebelhorn	.15
43	Dave Stapleton	.15
45	Rob Deer	.15
46	Bill Wegman	.15
49	Ted Higuera	.15
---	Coaches Card (Andy Etchebarren, Larry Haney, Chuck Hartenstein, Dave Hilton, Tony Muser)	.15
---	Team photo	.15

1989 Milwaukee Brewers Police

30 Terry Francona OF — Iola, Manawa & Marion Police Depts. and Wisconsin Power and Light present the 1989 Milwaukee Brewers

The Milwaukee Brewers, in conjunction with various corporate and civic sponsors, issued a 30-card police set in 1989, the eighth consecutive set issued by the club. Some 95 law enforcement agencies in Wisconsin participated in the program, each releasing their own version of the same set. The cards measure 2-13/16" x 4-1/8" and feature full-color action photos with the player's name, uniform number and position below, along with the sponsoring agencies. The backs include the traditional safety messages. The cards were distributed in complete sets at a stadium promotion and also handed out individually over the course of the summer by uniformed police officers in various Wisconsin cities and counties.

No.	Player	NM/M
Complete Set (30):		5.00
Common Player:		.15
1	Gary Sheffield	2.00
4	Paul Molitor	1.50
5	B.J. Surhoff	.15
6	Bill Spiers	.15
7	Dale Sveum	.15
9	Greg Brock	.15
12	Gus Polidor	.15
16	Mike Felder	.15
17	Jim Gantner	.15
19	Robin Yount	1.50
22	Charlie O'Brien	.15
23	Joey Meyer	.15
25	Dave Engle	.15
26	Glenn Braggs	.15
27	Paul Mirabella	.15
29	Chris Bosio	.15
30	Terry Francona	.15
32	Chuck Crim	.15
37	Dan Plesac	.15
40	Mike Birbeck	.15
41	Mark Knudson	.15
42	Tom Trebelhorn	.15
45	Rob Deer	.15
46	Bill Wegman	.15
48	Bryan Clutterbuck	.15
49	Teddy Higuera	.15
---	Team photo	.15
---	Coaching staff	.15

Yearbook Cards

4 Paul Molitor Infielder — Milwaukee Brewers [20]

Included in the team's special 20th anniversary edition yearbook was a set of 18 player cards stapled into the center of the book. Printed on a 16-1/2" x 11" cardboard sheet, there are nine cards per page, perforated on two, three or four sides, depending on sheet position. Cards have a pale yellow background. A blue and bright yellow 20th Anniversary team logo appears in the lower-right corner with the player's uniform number, name and position stacked at left in black. All but one of the photos are game-action shots. Backs are printed in black and include complete major and minor league stats. Cards are checklisted here by uniform number.

No.	Player	NM/M
Complete Set, Singles (18):		8.00
Complete Yearbook:		10.00
Common Player:		.15
1	Gary Sheffield	2.00
4	Paul Molitor	4.00
5	B.J. Surhoff	.25
7	Dale Sveum	.25
9	Greg Brock	.25
17	Jim Gantner	.25
19	Robin Yount	4.00
20	Juan Nieves	.25
26	Glenn Braggs	.25
29	Chris Bosio	.25
32	Chuck Crim	.25
37	Dan Plesac	.25
38	Don August	.25
40	Mike Birbeck	.25
42	Tom Trebelhorn	.25
45	Rob Deer	.25
46	Bill Wegman	.25
49	Teddy Higuera	.25

1990 Milwaukee Brewers Police

Blue borders are featured on the front of the 1990 Brewer Police/Fire Safety set. The cards are numbered according to uniform number and public service messages appear on the card backs. The

4 Paul Molitor IF — The Chilton Police Department Chilton Food Mart & Valley Bank-Chilton present the 1990 Milwaukee Brewers

2-13/16" x 4-1/8" cards were distributed by various Wisconsin police departments.

No.	Player	NM/M
Complete Set (30):		4.00
Common Player:		.15
2	Eddie Diaz	.15
4	Paul Molitor	1.50
5	B.J. Surhoff	.15
6	Bill Spiers	.15
7	Dale Sveum	.15
9	Greg Brock	.15
11	Gary Sheffield	.75
14	Gus Polidor	.15
16	Mike Felder	.15
17	Jim Gantner	.15
19	Robin Yount	1.50
22	Charlie O'Brien	.15
23	Greg Vaughn	.15
26	Glenn Braggs	.15
27	Paul Mirabella	.15
28	Tom Filer	.15
29	Chris Bosio	.15
31	Jaime Navarro	.15
32	Chuck Crim	.15
34	Billy Bates	.15
36	Tony Fossas	.15
37	Dan Plesac	.15
38	Don August	.15
39	Dave Parker	.15
41	Mark Knudson	.15
42	Tom Trebelhorn	.15
45	Rob Deer	.15
49	Ted Higuera	.15
---	Coaches (Don Baylor, Ray Burris, Duffy Dyer, Larry Haney, Andy Etchebarren)	.15
---	Team photo/roster card	.15

Yearbook Cards

Ted Higuera P 49

Printed on cardboard stock and stapled into the center of the team's 1990 yearbook was a set of 18 cards. The sheet is 16-1/2" x 11" overall. Each page has nine 2-5/8" x 3-1/2" cards perforated on two, three or four sides, depending on sheet position. Above-left and below-right of the color player poses are yellow triangles with blue pinstripes. The team's scrip logo is in the same team colors in the lower-left of the photo. The player's name, position abbreviation and uniform number are in yellow in the upper-right corner. Backs are printed in blue and include complete major and minor league stats. The checklist is presented here by uniform number.

No.	Player	NM/M
Complete Set, Singles (18):		8.00
Complete Yearbook:		10.00
Common Player:		.25
4	Paul Molitor	4.00
5	B.J. Surhoff	.25
6	Bill Spiers	.25
7	Dale Sveum	.25

9	Greg Brock	.25
17	Jim Gantner	.25
19	Robin Yount	4.00
26	Glenn Braggs	.25
28	Tom Filer	.25
29	Chris Bosio	.25
31	Jaime Navarro	.25
32	Chuck Crim	.25
37	Dan Plesac	.25
38	Don August	.25
39	Dave Parker	.25
42	Tom Trebelhorn	.25
45	Rob Deer	.25
49	Ted Higuera	.25

1991 Milwaukee Brewers Police

JIM GANTNER • IF

Presented by
The Elm Grove Police Department
& Kanavas Landscape Mgmt. Inc. 1991

The Milwaukee Brewers are featured on a 1991 team set sponsored by several Milwaukee area police departments and Delicious Brand Cookies and Crackers. The 30-card set is in full color with light gray border on the front and the backs are unnumbered and contain safety tips from the players.

		NM/M
Complete Set (30):		4.00
Common Player:		.25
(1)	Robin Yount	1.50
(2)	Rick Dempsey	.25
(3)	Jamie Navarro	.25
(4)	Darryl Hamilton	.25
(5)	Bill Spiers	.25
(6)	Dante Bichette	.25
(7)	Dan Plesac	.25
(8)	Don August	.25
(9)	Willie Randolph	.25
(10)	Franklin Stubbs	.25
(11)	Julio Machado	.25
(12)	Greg Vaughn	.25
(13)	Chris Bosio	.25
(14)	Mark Knudson	.25
(15)	Paul Molitor	1.50
(16)	Kevin Brown	.25
(17)	Ron Robinson	.25
(18)	Bill Wegman	.25
(19)	Teddy Higuera	.25
(20)	Mark Lee	.25
(21)	B.J. Surhoff	.25
(22)	Candy Maldonado	.25
(23)	Chuck Crim	.25
(24)	Dale Sveum	.25
(25)	Jim Gantner	.25
(26)	Greg Brock	.25
(27)	Gary Sheffield	.75
(28)	Edwin Nunez	.25
(29)	Tom Trebelhorn	.25
(30)	Coaches (Don Baylor, Ray Burris, Duffy Dyer, Andy Etchebarren, Larry Haney, Fred Stanley)	.25

1992 Milwaukee Brewers Police

BREWERS '92

DANTE BICHETTE • OF

Presented by
The Waukesha Police Department
& Waukesha Sports Cards

The 1992 Milwaukee Brewers Police set consists of 30-cards in the standard, 2-1/2" x 3-1/2" format. The yellow-bordered cards were

produced by Delicious Brand Cookies and Crackers and distributed by local Wisconsin police departments in cooperation with the Brewers.

		NM/M
Complete Set (30):		4.00
Common Player:		.15
(1)	Andy Allanson	.15
(2)	James Austin	.15
(3)	Dante Bichette	.15
(4)	Ricky Bones	.15
(5)	Chris Bosio	.15
(6)	Mike Fetters	.15
(7)	Scott Fletcher	.15
(8)	Jim Gantner	.15
(9)	Phil Garner	.15
(10)	Darryl Hamilton	.15
(11)	Doug Henry	.15
(12)	Teddy Higuera	.15
(13)	Pat Listach	.15
(14)	Jamie Navarro	.15
(15)	Edwin Nunez	.15
(16)	Tim McIntosh	.15
(17)	Paul Molitor	1.50
(18)	Jesse Orosco	.15
(19)	Dan Plesac	.15
(20)	Ron Robinson	.15
(21)	Bruce Ruffin	.15
(22)	Kevin Seitzer	.15
(23)	Bill Spiers	.15
(24)	Franklin Stubbs	.15
(25)	William Suero	.15
(26)	B.J. Surhoff	.15
(27)	Greg Vaughn	.15
(28)	Bill Wegman	.15
(29)	Robin Yount	1.50
(30)	Coaches (Bill Castro, Duffy Dyer, Mike Easler, Tim Foli, Don Rowe)	.15

1993 Milwaukee Brewers Police

DICKIE THON • IF

Presented by
Brown County Sheriff's Dept.

The 1993 Milwaukee Brewers Police set included 30 cards with a graduated blue border. The left side has a '93 Brewers flag along the border in yellow, with the player's name in the upper right corner in white. The backs, which are white with black print, feature quotes from the player pictured. The cards are not numbered and the set also includes a card commemorating Robin Yount's 3,000th hit.

		NM/M
Complete Set (30):		3.00
Common Player:		.15
(1)	Bernie Brewer/Mascot	.15
(2)	Phil Garner	.15
(3)	Yount's 3,000th Hit (Robin Yount)	1.00
(4)	Mark Kiefer	.15
(5)	Bill Spiers	.15
(6)	John Jaha	.15
(7)	Bill Wegman	.15
(8)	Ted Higuera	.15
(9)	Greg Vaughn	.15
(10)	Kevin Reimer	.15
(11)	Doug Henry	.15
(12)	William Suero	.15
(13)	Dave Nillson	.15
(14)	James Austin	.15
(15)	Mike Fetters	.15
(16)	Ricky Bones	.15
(17)	Jaime Navarro	.15
(18)	Jesse Orosco	.15
(19)	Darryl Hamilton	.15
(20)	Cal Eldred	.15
(21)	Tim McIntosh	.15
(22)	Dickie Thon	.15
(23)	Graeme Lloyd	.15
(24)	Pat Listach	.15
(25)	Joe Kmak	.15
(26)	Alex Diaz	.15
(27)	Robin Yount	1.50
(28)	Tom Brunansky	.15
(29)	B.J. Surhoff	.15
(30)	Bill Doran	.15

1994 Milwaukee Brewers Police

TURNER WARD 27

'94 BREWERS

Pick'n Save SNICKERS
Presented by
The Milwaukee Police Department

All youngsters attending the April 23 Brewers game received this 30-card set sponsored by Pick'n Save supermarkets and Snickers candy bar, whose logos appear on both front and back. Cards featured posed player photos in their new 25th anniversary uniforms, against a lime green fabric backdrop or game action photos. Two green borders surround the photos. Navy blue bars above and below the photo have the player's name, team and uniform number. A 25th anniversary logo is at lower-right. The name of one of the many Wisconsin police agencies which distributed the cards is printed in black at bottom. Backs are printed in black-on-white and feature full major and minor league stats. The traditional safety message or anti-drug warning is not included on this issue. Cards are checklisted here by uniform number. Cards are in the 2-1/2" x 3-1/2" format.

		NM/M
Complete Set (30):		3.00
Common Player:		.25
2	Jose Valentin	.25
3	Phil Garner	.25
5	B.J. Surhoff	.25
8	Jody Reed	.25
9	Bill Spiers	.25
11	Dave Nilsson	.25
12	Brian Harper	.25
16	Pat Listach	.25
18	Tom Brunansky	.25
20	Kevin Seitzer	.25
21	Cal Eldred	.25
23	Greg Vaughn	.25
24	Darryl Hamilton	.25
25	Ricky Bones	.25
27	Turner Ward	.25
28	Doug Henry	.25
29	Jeff Bronkey	.25
30	Matt Mieske	.25
31	Jaime Navarro	.25
33	John Jaha	.25
36	Mike Fetters	.25
37	Graeme Lloyd	.25
39	Bob Scanlan	.25
40	Mike Ignasiak	.25
43	Mark Kiefer	.25
46	Bill Wegman	.25
47	Jesse Orosco	.25
49	Teddy Higuera	.25
63	Jeff D'Amico, Kelly Wunsch	.25
---	Bernie Brewer/Mascot	.25

1995 Milwaukee Brewers Police

Some of the finest portrait photos seen on modern baseball cards are combined with game-action shots in the annual Brewers police set, sponsored by Old Fashioned Foods (makers of Squeeze Cheese). The 2-1/2" x 3-1/2" cards fea-

		NM/M
Complete Set (30):		3.00
Common Player:		.15
1	Fernando Vina	.15
2	Jose Valentin	.15
3	Phil Garner	.15
4	Pat Listach	.15
8	Mark Loretta	.15
14	Dave Nilsson	.15
15	David Hulse	.15

ture forest green borders with the player and team name, and uniform number in white on a deep blue band beneath. A tan panel at bottom has the name of the Milwaukee P.D. Many of the cards are presented in horizontal format. Backs are in black-and-white and include career stats and a safety tip. Cards are checklisted here according to uniform number.

		NM/M
Complete Set (33):		3.00
Common Player:		.25
1	Fernando Vina	.25
2	Jose Valentin	.25
3	Phil Garner	.25
5	B.J. Surhoff	.25
9	Joe Oliver	.25
10	Brewers Coaches (Bill Castro, Duffy Dyer, Tim Foli, Lamar Johnson, Don Rowe)	.25
11	Dave Nilsson	.25
13	Derrick May	.25
15	Dave Hulse	.25
16	Pat Listach	.25
20	Kevin Seitzer	.25
21	Cal Eldred	.25
22	Mike Matheny, Jeff Cirillo	.25
23	Greg Vaughn	.25
24	Darryl Hamilton	.25
25	Ricky Bones	.25
27	Turner Ward	.25
29	Jeff Bronkey	.25
30	Matt Mieske	.25
32	John Jaha	.25
36	Mike Fetters	.25
37	Graeme Lloyd	.25
38	Angel Miranda	.25
39	Bob Scanlan	.25
40	Michael Ignasiak	.25
41	Jose Mercedes, Mark Kiefer	.25
42	Scott Karl, Al Reyes, Steve Sparks	.25
46	Bill Wegman	.25
---	Bob Uecker/ Announcer	1.50
---	Charlie the Mouse/ Sponsor	.05
---	Iris the Cow/Sponsor	.05
---	Squeezasaurus/Sponsor	.05
---	Squeeze Cheese/ Coupon	.05

1996 Milwaukee Brewers Police

Dave Nilsson
INFIELDER

Milwaukee Brewers
Baseball Club

Metallic gold borders are featured on the Brewers' 14th annual safety set issued June 16 as a stadium giveaway. Cards are a mix of horizontal and vertical design with a large color photo at left. In a gold strip at right is the team logotype, player name, position and uniform number. Backs are in black-and-white with a safety message from the pictured player and the team logo. No sponsoring company or police agency is mentioned on the card. A special card in the set illustrates the proposed new Brewers stadium. Cards are listed here by uniform number.

		NM/M
Complete Set (30):		3.00
Common Player:		.15
1	Fernando Vina	.15
2	Jose Valentin	.15
3	Phil Garner	.15
4	Pat Listach	.15
8	Mark Loretta	.15
14	Dave Nilsson	.15
15	David Hulse	.15

16	Jesse Levis	.15
20	Kevin Seitzer	.15
21	Cal Eldred	.15
22	Mike Matheny	.15
23	Greg Vaughn	.15
24	Chuckie Carr	.15
25	Ricky Bones	.15
26	Jeff Cirillo	.15
27	Turner Ward	.15
30	Matt Mieske	.15
32	John Jaha	.15
36	Mike Fetters	.15
37	Graeme Lloyd	.15
38	Angel Miranda	.15
40	Ben McDonald	.15
48	Scott Karl	.15
48	Marshall Boze	.15
49	Mike Potts	.15
50	Steve Sparks	.15
51	Ramon Garcia	.15
52	Kevin Wickander	.15
---	Brewers coaches	.15
---	Miller Park	.15

1997 Milwaukee Brewers Police

LORETTA
13

Milwaukee Brewers Baseball Club

One of the more attractive safety sets of recent years, the 1997 Brewers team issue features action photos of each player in the standard 2-1/2" x 3-1/2" format. Down one side of the photo is the player's name in outline type. A team logo is at bottom-right. Backs are in black-and-white with a few bits of personal data and a cartoon figure presenting a safety tip for youngsters. The set was distributed to children attending the May 30 game at County Stadium. The checklist here is arranged by uniform number.

		NM/M
Complete Set (30):		3.00
Common Player:		.25
1	Fernando Vina	.25
2	Jose Valentin	.25
3	Phil Garner	.25
8	Mark Loretta	.25
9	Tim Unroe	.25
10	Marc Newfield	.25
13	Jeff D'Amico	.25
14	Dave Nillson	.25
15	Jeff Huson	.25
16	Jesse Levis	.25
19	Jeromy Burnitz	.50
21	Cal Eldred	.25
22	Mike Matheny	.25
24	Chuckie Carr	.25
25	Angel Miranda	.25
26	Jeff Cirillo	.25
27	Bob Wickman	.25
29	Gerald Williams	.25
30	Matt Mieske	.25
32	John Jaha	.25
36	Mike Fetters	.25
39	Bryce Florie	.25
40	Ben McDonald	.25
41	Jose Mercedes	.25
42a	Scott Karl	.25
42b	Jackie Robinson/ Tribute	2.00
43	Doug Jones	.25
49	Ron Villone	.25
51	Eddy Diaz	.25
---	Coaches (Chris Bando, Bill Castro, Jim Gantner, Lamar Johnson, Don Rowe)	.25

1998 Milwaukee Brewers Diamond Celebration

Persons attending a January 30 banquet in Milwaukee received a set of these cards highlighting the team's award winners for 1997. The set was

Diamond Celebration
JANUARY 30, 1998

MICHAEL HARRISON
COMMUNITY SERVICE AWARD

sponsored by the Milwaukee Metropolitan Association of Commerce; their logo appears on the back. Fronts have color photos centered on a white background. The players are pictured in action, the staff in portraits. "Diamond Celebration" and the name are in script. The banquet date and specific honor also appear on front. Backs are in black-and-white with season highlights. The unnumbered cards are checklisted here alphabetically.

		NM/M
Complete Set (10):		15.00
Common Card:		.50
(1)	Hank Aaron	6.00
(2)	Jeromy Burnitz	2.00
(3)	Jeff Cirillo	2.00
(4)	Dick Hackett/Staff	.50
(5)	Bill Haig/Staff	.50
(6)	John Jaha	1.00
(7)	Doug Jones/ MV Pitcher	1.00
(8)	Doug Jones/MVP	1.00
(9)	Bob Uecker/MC	3.00
(10)	Bob Wickman	1.00

1998 Milwaukee Brewers Police

ELDRED
Cal

Presented by: Midwest Sports Channel
and The Milwaukee Brewers

For 1998, the Brewers cable television outlet sponsored the team's annual safety set, given away to kids at the June 21 game. Card fronts have player action photos vignetted on a close-up baseball background. Team and sponsor logos appear in opposite corners. Backs have a few bits of player data, a safety tip, sponsor's logo and uniform number.

		NM/M
Complete Set (30):		3.00
Common Player:		.25
1	Fernando Vina	.25
2	Jose Valentin	.25
3	Phil Garner	.25
5	Geoff Jenkins	.60
7	Dave Nillson	.25
8	Mark Loretta	.25
9	Marquis Grissom	.25
10	Marc Newfield	.25
13	Jeff D'Amico	.25
14	Jeff Juden	.25
16	Jesse Levis	.25
19	Jeromy Burnitz	.50
21	Cal Eldred	.25
22	Mike Matheny	.25
24	Darrin Jackson	.25
26	Jeff Cirillo	.25
27	Bob Wickman	.25
28	Mike Myers	.25
30	Bob Hamelin	.25
32	John Jaha	.25
33/39	Bobby Hughes, Eric Owens	.25

37	Steve Woodard	.25
40	Chad Fox	.25
41	Jose Mercedes	.25
42	Scott Karl	.25
43	Doug Jones	.25
46	Paul Wagner	.25
47	Al Reyes	.25
48/30	Brad Woodall, Bronswell Patrick	.25
---	Coaches (Chris Bando, Bill Castro, Lamar Johnson, Doug Mansolino, Don Rowe, Joel Youngblood)	.25

1999 Milwaukee Brewers Diamond Celebration

Robin Yount
Hall of Famer

Persons attending a January 22 banquet in Milwaukee received a set of these cards highlighting the team's award winners for 1997. The set was sponsored by the Milwaukee Metropolitan Association of Commerce, whose logo appears on the back. Fronts have color photos. The players are pictured in action, the staff in portraits. "Diamond Celebration" and team logo are at left. The specific honor also appears on front. Backs are in black-and-white with season highlights. The unnumbered cards are checklisted here alphabetically.

		NM/M
Complete Set (11):		15.00
Common Player:		.50
(1)	Bob Betts (P.A. announcer)	.50
(2)	Jeromy Burnitz (HR Champ)	2.00
(3)	Jeromy Burnitz/MVP	2.00
(4)	Jeff Cirillo	1.00
(5)	Peter Gammons/Writer	.50
(6)	Mark Loretta (Manager's award.)	1.00
(7)	Mark Loretta (Community service.)	1.00
(8)	Bud Selig/Owner	.50
(9)	Bob Wickman	1.00
(10)	Steve Woodard	1.00
(11)	Robin Yount	6.00

1999 Milwaukee Brewers Police

Sean Berry
7

The regional cable station which carries Brewers games was the principal sponsor of the team's safety set given to fans on May 29. Cards feature color player poses against a sepia background showing Milwaukee County Stadium throughout the course of its 46-year history. Sponsor and team logos

are in various corners on front along with the player's name and uniform number. Backs have a few bits of personal data, a safety message and an ad from the sponsor. Cards are checklisted here in order of uniform number.

		NM/M
Complete Set (30):		3.00
Common Player:		.25
1	Fernando Vina	.25
2	Jose Valentin	.25
3	Phil Garner	.25
5	Geoff Jenkins	.60
7	Sean Berry	.25
8	Mark Loretta	.25
9	Marquis Grissom	.25
14	David Nilsson	.25
16	Lou Collier	.25
20	Jeromy Burnitz	.50
21	Cal Eldred	.25
22/48	Rich Becker, Steve Falteisek	.25
23	Brian Banks	.25
24	Alex Ochoa	.25
25	Jim Abbott	.35
26	Jeff Cirillo	.25
27	Bob Wickman	.25
28	Mike Myers	.25
31	Bobby Hughes	.25
37	Steve Woodard	.25
38	Eric Plunk	.25
40	Chad Fox	.25
42	Scott Karl	.25
46	Bill Pulsipher	.25
47	Al Reyes	.25
49	David Weathers	.25
52	Rafael Roque	.25
58	Valerio de los Santos	.25
---	Coaches (Bill Campbell, Bill Castro, Ron Jackson, Jim Lefebvre, Doug Mansolino, Bob Melvin)	.25
---	Milwaukee County Stadium	.25

2000 Milwaukee Brewers Diamond Celebration

26
Jeff Cirillo

Winners of various annual awards by the Milwaukee Brewers are featured in this standard-size card set which was issued at the team's Diamond Celebration dinner on January 21. A large portrait photo is featured along the left or right edge on front. Down the other side is player identification and the name of the award won. Backs have season highlights. The unnumbered cards are checklisted here alphabetically.

		NM/M
Complete Set (10):		15.00
Common Player:		.50
(1)	Kevin Barker	1.50
(2)	Ron Belliard	1.50
(3)	Jeromy Burnitz (HR Champ)	2.50
(4)	Jeromy Burnitz/MVP	2.50
(5)	Jeff Cirillo	1.50
(6)	Marquis Grissom	1.50
(7)	Geoff Jenkins	3.00
(8)	Tim Kurkjian	.50
(9)	Dean Taylor, Davey Lopes	.50
(10)	Bob Wickman	1.00

2000 Milwaukee Brewers Police

In its third season of sponsoring the team's safety set, the Brewers' cable franchise offered the cards to the first 10,000 youngsters at a May

Presented by:
Midwest Sports Channel and The Milwaukee Brewers

5
Geoff Jenkins

promotional game. Other sets were distributed by police agencies. Card fronts have the players posed in their dark blue jerseys against a black background lit by a colorful Milwaukee Brewers neon sign. In a lower corner are the sponsor's logo, player name and uniform number. A Time-Warner Cable logo is in the white border at bottom. Backs have player identification and a safety message. Cards are checklisted here by uniform number.

		NM/M
Complete Set (30):		3.00
Common Player:		.25
00	Curtis Leskanic	.25
1	Luis Lopez	.25
5	Tyler Houston	.25
7	Geoff Jenkins	.50
8	Sean Berry	.25
9	Mark Loretta	.25
10	Marquis Grissom	.25
11	Ron Belliard	.25
12	Henry Blanco	.25
14	Charlie Hayes	.25
18	Jose Hernandez	.25
20	Jeromy Burnitz	.45
22	Kevin Barker	.25
24	James Mouton	.25
27	Bob Wickman	.25
28	Valerio de los Santos	.25
30	Davey Lopes	.25
31	Everett Stull	.25
33	Lyle Mouton	.25
37	Steve Woodard	.25
38	Jaime Navarro	.25
41	Matt Williams	.25
47	Jason Bere	.25
49	David Weathers	.25
51	Jimmy Haynes	.25
53	Juan Acevedo	.25
59	John Snyder	.25
88	Jim Bruske	.25
---	Coaches (Jerry Royster, Rod Carew, Bill Castro, Bob Apodaca, Chris Speier, Gary Allenson)	.25
---	Matt Vasgersian, Bill Schroeder/ Broadcasters	.25

2001 Milwaukee Brewers Diamond Celebration

29
MICHAEL HARRISON
COMMUNITY SERVICE AWARD
ROD CAREW

Winners of various annual awards by the Milwaukee Brewers are featured in this standard-size card set which was issued at the team's Diamond Celebration dinner on January 19. Fronts have a large portrait photo along the left or right edge side. Down the other side is player identification and the name of the award won. Backs have season highlights

and the Miller Park logo. The unnumbered cards are checklisted here alphabetically.

		NM/M
Complete Set (9):		20.00
Common Player:		2.00
(1)	Rod Carew (Community Service Award)	3.00
(2)	Jeff D'Amico (Most Valuable Pitcher)	2.00
(3)	Geoff Jenkins (Harvey Kuenn Award)	2.50
(4)	Geoff Jenkins (Home Run Leader)	2.50
(5)	Geoff Jenkins/MVP	2.50
(6)	Tommy Lasorda/SP (Bud Selig Award)	5.00
(7)	Curtis Leskanic (Newcomer of the Year)	2.00
(8)	Richie Sexson (Manager's Award)	2.00
(9)	Ben Sheets (Minor League Player/Year)	4.00

2001 Milwaukee Brewers Police

2
Tyler Houston
INFIELDER

Presented by:
FOX SPORTS NET and THE MILWAUKEE BREWERS

This team set was given to youngsters attending a special promotional game. The 2-1/2" x 3-1/2" cards have close-up player portraits over a large logo in one of several colors. Also appearing in the photo area are Miller Park and Fox Sports Net logos and the player's name, position and uniform number. There is a white border, at the bottom of which is sponsor credits. Backs have a safety or character-building message from the player. Sets were also distributed locally by more than six dozen Wisconsin police agencies.

		NM/M
Complete Set (30):		4.00
Common Player:		.25
1	Luis Lopez	.25
2	Tyler Houston	.25
5	Geoff Jenkins	.50
7	Tony Fernandez	.25
9	Mark Loretta	.25
10	Ronnie Belliard	.25
11	Richie Sexson	.50
12	Henry Blanco	.25
13	Jeff D'Amico	.25
15	Ben Sheets	.50
18	Jose Hernandez	.25
20	Jeromy Burnitz	.50
21	Jamey Wright	.25
22	Devon White	.35
23	Mark Leiter	.25
25	James Mouton	.25
25	Raul Casanova	.25
30	Davey Lopes	.25
31	Paul Rigdon	.25
33	Will Cunnane	.25
39	Angel Echevarria	.25
40	Chad Fox	.25
47	Jeffrey Hammonds	.25
46	Ray King	.25
48	Mike DeJean	.25
49	David Weathers	.25
51	Jimmy Haynes	.25
00	Curtis Leskanic	.25
---	Brewers Coaches (Bob Apodaca, Gary Allenson, Rod Carew, Bill Castro, Jerry Royster, Luis Salazar)	.25
---	Bill Schroeder, Matt Vasgersian	.25

2002 Milwaukee Brewers Diamond Celebration

Winners of various annual awards by the Milwaukee Brewers are featured in this 2-1/2" x 3-1/2" card set which

11
RICHIE SEXSON
JANUARY 25, 2002

was issued at the team's Diamond Celebration dinner on January 25. Fronts have a photo set against a solid colored background on which the last name is ghosted vertically. An identification strip is vertically at right, including the name of the award won. Backs have season highlights in black-and-white. The unnumbered cards are checklisted here alphabetically.

		NM/M
Complete Set (10):		18.00
Common Player:		2.00
(1)	Bill Castro (Unsung Hero)	2.00
(2)	Cecil Cooper (Walk of Fame)	2.00
(3)	Chad Fox (Most Valuable Pitcher)	2.50
(4)	Ray King (Manager's Award)	2.00
(5)	Ray King (Community Service Award)	2.00
(6)	Mark Loretta (Harvey Kuenn Award)	2.50
(7)	Allan H. (Bud) Selig (Walk of Fame)	2.50
(8)	Richie Sexson (Home Run Champion)	3.00
(9)	Richie Sexson/MVP	3.00
(10)	Ben Sheets (Newcomer of the Year)	3.00

2002 Milwaukee Brewers Police

LOPEZ
INFIELDER

Presented by:
The Milwaukee Brewers Baseball Club

Fans at the May 30 Brewers game received this team set of 2-1/2" x 3-1/2" safety cards. Fronts have action photos with a black-and-white photo of an architectural detail of Miller Park in the top-left corner. Backs repeat the Miller Park photo and have a safety message from the player. Cards are checklisted here by uniform number.

		NM/M
Complete Set (30):		3.00
Common Player:		.25
00	Curtis Leskanic	.25
1	Luis Lopez	.25
2	Tyler Houston	.25
5	Geoff Jenkins	.50
6	Eric Young	.25
9	Mark Loretta	.25
8	Paul Bako	.25
10	Ron Belliard	.25
11	Richie Sexson	.50
12	Matt Stairs	.25
15	Ben Sheets	.35
16	Lenny Harris	.25
18	Jose Hernandez	.25
21	Jamey Wright	.25
23	Alex Sanchez	.25
24	Alex Ochoa	.25
25	Raul Casanova	.25
31	Paul Rigdon	.25
32	Nick Neugebauer	.25

37	Ruben Quevedo	.25
29	Glendon Rusch	.25
40	Chad Fox	.25
41	Jeffrey Hammonds	.25
46	Ray King	.25
47	Mike Buddie	.25
48	Mike DeJean	.25
49	Jose Cabrera	.25
51	Luis Vizcaino	.25
52	Nelson Figueroa	.25
95	Takahito Nomura	.25

2003 Milwaukee Brewers Diamond Celebration

JEFFREY HAMMONDS
MICHAEL HARRISON
COMMUNITY SERVICE AWARD
41
JANUARY 31, 2003

Winners of various annual awards by the Milwaukee Brewers are featured in this 3" x 5" card set which was issued at the team's Diamond Celebration dinner, January 31, one cellowrapped set per place setting. Fronts have a black-and-sepia photo with a black frameline. A dinner logo is at bottom with the honoree's name, award and uniform number (for players) in white. Backs have season highlights in black and red. Production was reported as 1,000 sets. The unnumbered cards are checklisted here alphabetically.

		NM/M
Complete Set (10):		15.00
Common Card:		1.00
(1)	Harry Dalton (Walk of Fame)	1.00
(2)	Mike DeJean (Most Valuable Pitcher)	1.50
(3)	Jeffrey Hammonds (Community Service Award)	2.00
(4)	Ernie Harwell (Bud Selig Award)	1.50
(5)	Alex Sanchez (Harvey Kuenn Award)	1.50
(6)	Richie Sexson (Home Run Champion)	5.00
(7)	Bob Uecker (Walk of Fame)	3.00
(8)	Luis Vizcaino (Newcomer of the Year)	2.00
(9)	Eric Young (Unsung Hero Award)	2.00
(10)	Doug Melvin, Ned Yost, Ulice Payne, Jr. (Dawning of a New Era)	1.00

2003 Milwaukee Brewers Safety

47
SHANE NANCE
pitcher

Presented by:
The Milwaukee Brewers Baseball Club

This team set was a stadium giveaway to the first 10,000 youngsters attending the April 19 game. The 2-1/2" x 3-1/2" cards have neck-to-cap color portraits on front, with player name, position and uniform number. Backs are in gold with a health or safety tip.

		NM/M
Complete Set (29):		3.00
Common Player:		.25
3	Ned Yost	.25
5	Geoff Jenkins	.50
6	Keith Ginter	.25
7	Eric Young	.25
9	Enrique Cruz	.25
10	Royce Clayton	.25
11	Richie Sexson	.50
12	Eddie Perez	.25
15	Ben Sheets	.35
18	Wes Helms	.25
20	Scott Podsednik	.50
21	Keith Osik	.25
22	Alex Sanchez	.25
24	John Vander Wal	.25
26	Wayne Franklin	.25
27	Brady Clark	.25
28	Valerio de los Santos	.25
29	Jason Conti	.25
33	Curtis Leskanic	.25
39	Glendon Rusch	.25
40	John Foster	.25
41	Jeffrey Hammonds	.25
46	Todd Ritchie	.25
47	Shane Nance	.25
48	Mike DeJean	.25
50	Matt Kinney	.25
51	Luis Vizcaino	.25
52	Matt Ford	.25
56	Jayson Durocher	.25
---	Brewers Coaches	.25

2004 Milwaukee Brewers Safety

This team set was a stadium giveaway to youngsters attending the May 1 game. The 2-1/2" x 3-1/2" cards have color portraits on front, with player name, position and uniform number. Backs have a health or safety tip.

		NM/M
Complete Set (30):		5.00
Common Player:		.25
1	Bernie Brewer/Mascot	.25
2	Bill Hall	.25
3	Ned Yost	.25
4	Paul Molitor	2.00
5	Geoff Jenkins	.45
6	Keith Ginter	.25
11	Lyle Overbay	.50
12	Ben Grieve	.25
15	Ben Sheets	.50
18	Wes Helms	.25
20	Scott Podsednik	.50
21	Chad Moeller	.25
22	Trent Durrington	.25
27	Brady Clark	.25
29	Gary Bennett	.25
30	Craig Counsell	.25
31	Adrian Hernandez	.25
33	Wes Obermueller	.25
37	Junior Spivey	.25
39	Chris Capuano	.25
41	Dan Kolb	.25
43	Dave Burba	.25
48	Ben Ford	.25
49	Doug Davis	.25
50	Matt Kinney	.25
51	Luis Vizcaino	.25
55	Brooks Kieschnick	.25
57	Jeff Bennett	.25
---	Brewers Coaches	.25
---	Klements Sausages	.25

2005 Milwaukee Brewers Safety

This team set was a stadium giveaway to the first 10,000 youngsters attending the May 1 game. The 2-1/2" x 3-1/2" cards have color portraits on front, with player name, position and uniform number. Backs have a health or safety tip.

2000 Milwaukee Journal Sentinel 1980s Brewers

As selected by fan balloting, an All-Decade team of 1980s Milwaukee Brewers is honored on this set of cards given to fans at a promotional game August 11. The standard 2-1/2" x 3-1/2" cards have game-action photos on front with a gold-foil diamond naming the player, his position and uniform number. The newspaper sponsor's logo is at bottom. Backs have a team logo, player personal data, stats and career highlights. The unnumbered cards are checklisted here in alphabetical order.

		NM/M
Complete Set (30):		6.00
Common Player:		.25
2	Bill Hall	.25
3	Ned Yost	.25
5	Geoff Jenkins	.50
6	Jeff Cirillo	.25
7	J.J. Hardy	.35
10	David Krynzel	.25
11	Lyle Overbay	.50
15	Ben Sheets	.50
18	Wes Helms	.25
21	Chad Moeller	.25
24	Chris Magruder	.25
26	Damian Miller	.25
27	Brady Clark	.25
31	Russell Branyan	.25
33	Wes Obermueller	.25
37	Junior Spivey	.25
38	Matt Wise	.25
39	Chris Capuano	.25
40	Ben Hendrickson	.25
41	Tommy Phelps	.25
45	Carlos Lee	.50
46	Mike Adams	.25
47	Jorge de la Rosa	.25
49	Doug Davis	.25
52	Ricky Bottalico	.25
53	Victor Santos	.25
57	Jeff Bennett	.25
58	Gary Glover	.25
59	Derrick Turnbow	.25
---	Coaches (Ned Yost, Butch Wynegar, Bill Castro, Marcus Hanel, Dave Nelson, Rich Dauer, Mike Maddux, Rich Donnelly)	.25

2000 Milwaukee Journal Sentinel 1970s Brewers

As selected by fan balloting, an All-Decade team of 1970s Milwaukee Brewers is honored on this set of cards given to fans at a promotional game in July. The standard 2-1/2" x 3-1/2" cards have borderless game-action photos on front with a gold-foil diamond naming the player, his position and uniform number. The newspaper sponsor's logo is at bottom. Backs have a team logo, player personal data, stats and career highlights. The unnumbered cards are checklisted here in alphabetical order.

		NM/M
Complete Set (13):		12.00
Common Player:		.50
(1)	Hank Aaron	6.00
(2)	George Bamberger	.50
(3)	Mike Caldwell	.50
(4)	Cecil Cooper	.75
(5)	Tommy Harper	.50
(6)	Larry Hisle	.50
(7)	Sixto Lezcano	.50
(8)	Don Money	.50
(9)	Charlie Moore	.50
(10)	Ken Sanders	.50
(11)	Jim Slaton	.50
(12)	Gorman Thomas	.50
(13)	Robin Yount	4.00

1990s Brewers

As selected by fan balloting, an All-Decade team of 1990s Milwaukee Brewers is honored on this set of cards given to fans at a promotional game September 8. The standard 2-1/2" x 3-1/2" cards have game-action photos on front with a gold-foil diamond naming the player, his position and uniform number. The newspaper sponsor's logo is at bottom. Backs have a team logo, player personal data, stats and career highlights. The unnumbered cards are checklisted here in alphabetical order.

		NM/M
Complete Set (13):		9.00
Common Player:		.50
(1)	Chris Bosio	.50
(2)	Jeromy Burnitz	1.00
(3)	Jeff Cirillo	.50
(4)	Phil Garner	.50
(5)	John Jaha	.50
(6)	Geoff Jenkins	2.00
(7)	David Nilsson	.50
(8)	B.J. Surhoff	.50
(9)	Jose Valentin	.50
(10)	Fernando Vina	.50
(11)	Bill Wegman	.50
(12)	Bob Wickman	.50
(13)	Robin Yount	3.00

1983 Minnesota Twins Team Issue

The Minnesota Twins produced a 36-card set in 1983 to be sold at concession stands and through the mail. The full-color borderless cards measure 2-1/2" x 3-1/2" and displayed the player's uniform number on a white Twins jersey at the bottom of the card. The backs contain full career statistics.

		NM/M
Complete Set (36):		7.00
Common Player:		.25
1	John Castino	.25
2	Jim Eisenreich	.50
3	Ray Smith	.25
4	Scott Ullger	.25
5	Gary Gaetti	.75
6	Mickey Hatcher	.25
7	Bobby Mitchell	.25
8	Len Faedo	.25
9	Kent Hrbek	2.00
10	Tim Laudner	.25
11	Frank Viola	1.00
12	Bryan Oelkers	.25
13	Rick Lysander	.25
14	Dave Engle	.25
15	Len Whitehouse	.25
16	Pete Filson	.25
17	Tom Brunansky	.25
18	Randy Bush	.25
19	Brad Havens	.25
20	Al Williams	.25
21	Gary Ward	.25
22	Jack O'Connor	.25
23	Bobby Castillo	.25
24	Ron Washington	.25
25	Ron Davis	.25
26	Tom Kelly	.25
27	Billy Gardner	.25
28	Rick Stelmaszek	.25
29	Jim Lemon	.25
30	Johnny Podres	.25
31	Minnesota's Native Sons (Jim Eisenreich, Kent Hrbek, Tim Laudner)	.75
32	Twins' Catchers (Dave Engle, Tim Laudner)	.25
33	The Lumber Company (Tom Brunansky, Gary Gaetti, Kent Hrbek, Gary Ward)	.75
34	Twins' Coaches (Billy Gardner, Tom Kelly, Jim Lemon, Johnny Podres, Rick Stelmaszek)	.25
35	Team Photo	.40
36	Metrodome/Checklist	.25

1984 Minnesota Twins Team Issue

This team-issued set from the Minnesota Twins consists of 36 full-color, borderless cards, each measuring 2-1/2" x 3-1/2". As in the previous year, the player's uniform number appears on a white Twins jersey at the bottom of the card. The backs are printed in red and blue on white stock and include career stats. The set features several special cards, including one of Harmon Killebrew.

		NM/M
Complete Set (36):		7.50
Common Player:		.25
1	John Castino	.25
2	Jim Eisenreich	.35
3	Al Jimenez	.25

4	Dave Meier	.25
5	Gary Gaetti	.50
6	Mickey Hatcher	.25
7	Jeff Reed	.25
8	Tim Teufel	.25
9	Len Faedo	.25
10	Kent Hrbek	1.00
11	Tim Laudner	.25
12	Frank Viola	.50
13	Ken Schrom	.25
14	Larry Pashnick	.25
15	Dave Engle	.25
16	Keith Comstock	.25
17	Pete Filson	.25
18	Tom Brunansky	.25
19	Randy Bush	.25
20	Darrell Brown	.25
21	Al Williams	.25
22	Mike Walters	.25
23	John Butcher	.25
24	Bobby Castillo	.25
25	Ron Washington	.25
26	Ron Davis	.25
27	Tom Kelly	.25
28	Billy Gardner	.25
29	Rick Stelmaszek	.25
30	Jim Lemon	.25
31	Johnny Podres	.25
32	Mike Smithson	.25
33	Harmon Killebrew	4.00
34	Team Photo	.50
35	Logo Card	.25
36	Metrodome/Checklist	.25

1985 Minnesota Twins Team Issue

Similar in format to the previous two years, this 36-card team-issued set features full-color, borderless cards. The player's uniform number is again displayed on a white Twins jersey in the lower right corner, and the 1985 All-Star Game logo is shown in the lower left. The All-Star Game logo also appears on a special card in the set that lists on the back all Twins who have been selected for previous All-Star Games. The set was sold at ballpark concession stands and through the mail.

		NM/M
Complete Set (36):		15.00
Common Player:		.20
1	Alvaro Espinoza	.25
2	Roy Smalley	.25
3	Pedro Oliva	.75
4	Dave Meier	.25
5	Gary Gaetti	.50
6	Mickey Hatcher	.25
7	Jeff Reed	.25
8	Tim Teufel	.25
9	Mark Salas	.25
10	Kent Hrbek	1.00
11	Tim Laudner	.25
12	Frank Viola	.50
13	Ken Schrom	.25
14	Rick Lysander	.25
15	Dave Engle	.25
16	Andre David	.25
17	Len Whitehouse	.25
18	Pete Filson	.25
19	Tom Brunansky	.25
20	Randy Bush	.25
21	Greg Gagne	.75
22	John Butcher	.25
23	Mike Stenhouse	.25
24	Kirby Puckett	10.00
25	Tom Klawitter	.25
26	Curt Wardle	.25
27	Rich Yett	.25
28	Ron Washington	.25
29	Ron Davis	.25
30	Tom Kelly	.25
31	Billy Gardner	.25
32	Rick Stelmaszek	.25
33	Johnny Podres	.40
34	Mike Smithson	.25
35	1985 All-Star Game Logo Card	.25
36	Twins Logo/Checklist	.25

1986 Minnesota Twins Team Issue

This team-issued set contains 36 2-9/16" x 3-1/2" full-color cards. Fronts feature the Twins 25th anniversary logo and a jersey at the bottom of each card with the player's uniform number. All cards, except an action shot of Bert Blyleven, are posed photos, with a facsimile autograph on each. The set also includes a checklist and a team photo.

		NM/M
Complete Set (36):		6.00
Common Player:		.15
1	Chris Pittaro	.15
2	Steve Lombardozzi	.15
3	Roy Smalley	.15
4	Pedro Oliva	.50
5	Gary Gaetti	.30
6	Mickey Hatcher	.15
7	Jeff Reed	.15
8	Mark Salas	.15
9	Kent Hrbek	.50
10	Tim Laudner	.15
11	Frank Viola	.30
12	Dennis Burtt	.15
13	Alex Sanchez	.15
14	Roy Smith	.15
15	Billy Beane	.15
16	Pete Filson	.15
17	Tom Brunansky	.15
18	Randy Bush	.15
19	Frank Eufemia	.15
20	Mark Davidson	.15
21	Bert Blyleven	.40
22	Greg Gagne	.25
23	John Butcher	.15
24	Kirby Puckett	5.00
25	Bill Latham	.15
26	Ron Washington	.15
27	Ron Davis	.15
28	Tom Kelly	.15
29	Dick Such	.15
30	Rick Stelmaszek	.15
31	Ray Miller	.15
32	Wayne Terwilliger	.15
33	Mike Smithson	.15
34	Alvis Woods	.15
35	Team Photo	.25
36	Twins Logo/Checklist	.15

1987 Minnesota Twins Team Issue

The Minnesota Twins produced a 32-card set of 2-1/2" x 3-1/2" full-color baseball cards to be sold at the ballpark and through their souvenir catalog. The card fronts are borderless, containing only the player photo. The backs are printed in blue and red on white card stock and carry the player's personal data and career record. The Twins also produced a post card set that was similar in design to the standard-size card set, but utilized different photos.

		NM/M
Complete Set (33):		12.50
Common Player:		.25
1	Steve Lombardozzi	.25
2	Roy Smalley	.25
3	Pedro Oliva	.50
4	Greg Gagne	.25
5	Gary Gaetti	.30
6	Tom Kelly	.25
7	Tom Nieto	.25
8	Mark Salas	.25
9	Kent Hrbek	.50
10	Tim Laudner	.25
11	Frank Viola	.35
12	Les Straker	.25
13	George Frazier	.25
14	Keith Atherton	.25
15	Tom Brunansky	.25
16	Randy Bush	.25
17	Al Newman	.25
18	Mark Davidson	.25
19	Bert Blyleven	.35
20	Dan Gladden	.25
21	Kirby Puckett	7.50
22	Mark Portugal	.25
23	Juan Berenguer	.25
24	Jeff Reardon	.25
25	Dick Such	.25
26	Rick Stelmaszek	.25
27	Rick Renick	.25
28	Wayne Terwilliger	.25
29	Joe Klink	.25
30	Mike Smithson	.25
31	Team Photo	.25
32	Twins Champions Logo	.25
33	Twins Logo/Checklist	.25

1988 Minnesota Twins Fire Safety

This 8-1/4" x 3-3/4" booklet contains a dozen postcards called Color-Grams featuring caricatures (suitable for coloring) of star players. Postcards are attached along a perforated edge to a baseball card-size stub with a black-and-white photo of the featured player. Backs include the player name and personal information. The card stubs include the same information, along with a fire prevention tip. Twins Color-Grams were produced as a public service by the U.S. Forest Service and Dept. of Agriculture and were distributed to fans at the Metrodome.

		NM/M
Complete Booklet:		10.00
Complete Set, Singles (12):		7.50
Common Player:		.50
(1)	Bert Blyleven	.75
(2)	Randy Bush	.50
(3)	Gary Gaetti	.60
(4)	Greg Gagne	.50
(5)	Dan Gladden	.50
(6)	Kent Hrbek	1.00
(7)	Gene Larkin	.50
(8)	Tim Laudner	.50
(9)	Al Newman	.50
(10)	Kirby Puckett	4.00
(11)	Jeff Reardon	.50
(12)	Frank Viola	.50

1988 Minnesota Twins Team Issue

The Twins issued this set to commemorate the team's 1987 World Series victory. The slightly oversized cards (2-5/8"x 3-7/16") feature color player photos printed on heavy stock with a gold-embossed "1987 World Champions" logo in the lower-left corner. Numbered card backs are red, white and blue and contain player name, personal info and stats. A limited edition of 5000 sets were printed but only a few hundred were sold before the cards were taken off the market due to Major League Baseball licensing restrictions on the use of the World Series logo.

	NM/M
Complete Set (33):	60.00
Common Player:	1.50

1	Steve Lombardozzi	1.50
2	Roy Smalley	1.50
3	Pedro Oliva	4.00
4	Greg Gagne	3.00
5	Gary Gaetti	4.00
6	Gene Larkin	2.00
7	Tom Kelly	2.00
8	Kent Hrbek	6.00
9	Tim Laudner	2.00
10	Frank Viola	4.00
11	Les Straker	1.50
12	Don Baylor	4.00
13	George Frazier	1.50
14	Keith Atherton	1.50
15	Tom Brunansky	1.50
16	Randy Bush	1.50
17	Al Newman	1.50
18	Mark Davidson	1.50
19	Bert Blyleven	4.00
20	Dan Schatzeder	1.50
21	Dan Gladden	2.00
22	Sal Butera	1.50
23	Kirby Puckett	25.00
24	Joe Niekro	1.50
25	Juan Berenguer	1.50
26	Jeff Reardon	3.00
27	Dick Such	1.50
28	Rick Stelmaszek	1.50
29	Rick Renick	1.50
30	Wayne Terwilliger	1.50
31	Team Photo	1.50
32	World Champions Team Logo Card	1.50
33	Team Logo Card/ Checklist	1.50

1997 Minnesota Twins 10th Anniversary

The 10th anniversary of the team's 1987 World Series victory is recalled with this set given to fans on August 8 during the reunion weekend at the Metrodome. The 2-1/2" x 3-1/2" cards have 10-year-old color action photos on front with the anniversary logo and player identification. On back are a black-and-white portrait photo, uniform number, biographical details, the player's 1987 season and post-season performance and the sponsor's logo. The cards are checklisted here in alphabetical order.

		NM/M
Complete Set (25):		10.00
Common Player:		.25
(1)	Keith Atherton	.25
(2)	Don Baylor	.40
(3)	Juan Berenguer	.25
(4)	Bert Blyleven	.35
(5)	Tom Brunansky	.25
(6)	Randy Bush	.25
(7)	Sal Butera	.25
(8)	Mark Davidson	.25
(9)	George Frazier	.25
(10)	Gary Gaetti	.50
(11)	Greg Gagne	.50
(12)	Dan Gladden	.25
(13)	Kent Hrbek	1.00
(14)	Tom Kelly	.25
(15)	Gene Larkin	.25
(16)	Tim Laudner	.25
(17)	Steve Lombardozzi	.25
(18)	Al Newman	.25
(19)	Joe Niekro	.40
(20)	Kirby Puckett	5.00
(21)	Jeff Reardon	.25
(22)	Dan Schatzeder	.25
(23)	Roy Smalley	.25
(24)	Les Straker	.25
(25)	Frank Viola	.40

2002 Minnesota Twins Police

More than 300 agencies comprising the Minnesota Crime Prevention Association distributed this multi-sport set.

#15 • Cristian Guzman • Shortstop

Eight players each from the Twins, Vikings and Wild were included, along with McGruff the Crime Dog. Distribution of the baseball players cards was between August 6-19. The baseball cards have game-action photos which are borderless at top and sides. Two team logos are in the top corners and a blue strip at bottom has player name, uniform number and position. Backs have a black-and-white portrait photo, a safety tip and sponsors logos. Only the baseball players from the issue are listed here.

		NM/M
Complete (Baseball) Set (8):		5.00
Common Player:		.50
1	Eddie Guardado	.50
2	Cristian Guzman	1.00
3	Jacque Jones	1.00
4	Corey Koskie	1.00
5	Doug Mientkiewicz	.50
6	A.J. Pierzynski	.50
7	Luis Rivas	.50
8	Torii Hunter	1.50

2003 Minnesota Twins Police

#47 • Corey Koskie • Third Base

Sponsored by the Minnesota Crime Prevention Association, this set features eight popular players and McGruff the Crime Dog. Standard 2-1/2" x 3-1/2" cards have game-action photos on front, borderless at top and sides. A blue stripe at bottom has uniform number, player name and position. The team's 2002 A.L. Central Division Champions logo and "Gotta See 'Em" 2003 season logo are in the top corners. A facsimile autograph appears on front. Backs are in black, white and blue with a portrait photo, player data and a safety tip, along with the sponsor's and printer's logos.

		NM/M
Complete Set (9):		5.00
Common Player:		.50
1	Torii Hunter	1.00
2	Doug Mientkiewicz	.75
3	Corey Koskie	.75
4	A.J. Pierzynski	.75
5	Brad Radke	.50
6	Jacque Jones	.75
7	Eddie Guardado	.50
8	Eric Milton	.50
9	McGruff the Crime Dog	.50

2004 Minnesota Twins Police

Sponsored by the Minnesota Crime Prevention Associa-

ular players. Standard 2-1/2" x 3-1/2" cards have game-action photos on front, borderless at top and sides. A blue stripe at bottom has uniform number and position. The team's 2003 A.L. Central Division Champions logo is in the top-right corner. A facsimile autograph appears on front. Backs are in black and white with a portrait photo, player data and a safety tip, along with the sponsor's and printer's logos.

		NM/M
Complete Set (8):		5.00
Common Player:		.50
1	Torii Hunter	.75
2	Doug Mientkiewicz	.50
3	Corey Koskie	.50
4	Shannon Stewart	.50
5	Brad Radke	.50
6	Cristian Guzman	.50
7	Johan Santana	2.00
8	Kyle Lohse	.50

2004 Minnesota Twins Team Issue

COREY KOSKIE 47 3B

To build support in its drive to retain Major League Baseball in the Twin Cities and build a new outdoor stadium, the team issued this card set at its winter TwinsFest. Cards are 2-1/2" x 3-1/2" printed on thin semi-gloss stock. There are five player cards and seven depicting artists' views of the proposed ballpark.

		NM/M
Complete Set (12):		6.00
Common Player:		.50
16	Doug Mientkiewicz	.50
22	Brad Radke	.50
23	Shannon Stewart	.75
47	Corey Koskie	.75
48	Torii Hunter	1.00
---	A Ballpark for Minnesota ("As the new home . . .")	.50
---	A Ballpark for Minnesota ("Got off the bench . . .")	.50
---	A Ballpark for Minnesota ("Minnesota's new ballpark will honor . . .")	.50
---	A Ballpark for Minnesota ("Minnesota's new ballpark will mark . . .")	.50
---	A Ballpark for Minnesota ("Much like those . . .")	.50
---	A Ballpark for Minnesota ("The exterior . . .")	.50
---	A Ballpark for Minnesota ("With total seating . . .")	.50

2005 Star Tribune Minnesota Twins Medallion Collection

A set of 21 commemorative medallions was sponsored

by the Star Tribune in this promotion. Coupons found in the newspaper between May 2-25 could be redeemed at newsstands (along with $2.99) for that day's medallion. Larger and thicker than a quarter, the 1-3/16" diameter medals are struck in nickel and have on their fronts an enameled portrait photo. A team logo dominates the back. A colorful, photo-filled 7-3/4" x 13" album was available to house the pieces. The medals are listed here in alphabetical order.

		NM/M
Complete Set (21):		90.00
Common Player:		3.00
Album:		3.00
(1)	Grant Balfour	3.00
(2)	Juan Castro	3.00
(3)	Michael Cuddyer	3.00
(4)	Lew Ford	3.00
(5)	Ron Gardenhire	3.00
(6)	Torii Hunter	4.50
(7)	Jacque Jones	4.50
(8)	Matthew LeCroy	3.00
(9)	Kyle Lohse	3.00
(10)	Joe Mauer	10.00
(11)	Joe Mays	3.00
(12)	Justin Morneau	10.00
(13)	Joe Nathan	3.00
(14)	Brad Radke	4.50
(15)	Juan Rincon	3.00
(16)	Luis Rivas	3.00
(17)	J.C. Romero	3.00
(18)	Johan Santana	12.50
(19)	Carlos Silva	3.00
(20)	Shannon Stewart	3.00
(21)	Twins Back To Back Championships	3.00

2005 Minnesota Twins Police

48 Torii Hunter •Centerfielder

Sponsored by the Minnesota Crime Prevention Association, this set features seven popular players and McGruff the Crime Dog. Standard 2-1/2" x 3-1/2" cards have game-action photos on front, bordered in dark blue. A strip at bottom has uniform number, player name and position. Team logos are in each upper corner. Backs are in black-and-white with a small portrait photo, player information, safety tip, along with the sponsor's and printer's logos. The set was distributed by area police agencies and at a Twins game in May.

		NM/M
Complete Set (8):		8.00
Common Player:		1.00
7	Joe Mauer	2.00
22	Brad Radke	1.00

23	Shannon Stewart	1.00
36	Joe Nathan	1.50
48	Torii Hunter	1.50
49	Kyle Lohse	1.00
57	Johan Santana	1.50
---	McGruff The Crime Dog	1.00

1992 MJB Holoprisms

The Holoprism set consists of two 4-card hologram sets of Rookies of the Year Jeff Bagwell and Chuck Knoblauch. Each player set was packaged in a special plastic case. The production was limited to 250,000 of each set, numbered and with a letter of authenticity. Each player autographed 500 cards, which were randomly inserted.

	NM/M
Complete Bagwell Set (4):	6.00
Common Bagwell Card:	1.50
Complete Knoblauch Set (4):	6.00
Common Knoblauch Card:	1.00
Autographed Bagwell Card:	75.00
Autographed Knoblauch Card:	40.00
R1 Jeff Bagwell/Btg	2.00
R1a Jeff Bagwell/OPS	2.00
R2 Jeff Bagwell/Fielding	2.00
R3 Jeff Bagwell/Btg	2.00
R4 Jeff Bagwell/Btg	2.00
R1 Chuck Knoblauch/Btg	1.00
R1a Chuck Knoblauch/OPS	1.00
R2 Chuck Knoblauch/ Fielding	1.00
R3 Chuck Knoblauch/Btg	1.00
R4 Chuck Knoblauch/Btg	1.00

2000 MLB Showdown Promos

To introduce its baseball card game, Wizards of the Coast produced a series of promo cards that were locally distributed to hobby stores to encourage people to join gaming leagues. The promos differ from the issued cards in the use of silver-foil highlights and the presence of large "FUTURE STAR" or "DIAMOND STAR" in the background, instead of a team logo, or "HOME RUN HITTER" at top. Because of the manner of distribution, some promos are more difficult to find in the hobby market.

		NM/M
Complete Set (43):		10.00
Common Player:		.40
(1)	Sandy Alomar Jr.	.40
(2)	Craig Biggio	.40
(3)	Carlos Delgado	.60
(4)	Damion Easley	.40
(5)	Mark Grace	.40
(6)	Rusty Greer	.40

(7) Tony Gwynn 1.00
(8a) Andruw Jones (8 OB) .60
(8b) Andruw Jones (10 OB) 1.00
(9) Chipper Jones 1.00
(10) Jeff Kent .40
(11) Edgar Martinez .40
(12) Gary Sheffield .60
(13) B.J. Surhoff .40
(14) Jason Varitek .40
(15) Robin Ventura .40
(16) Bernie Williams .40
(1) Bob Abreu .40
(2) Ron Belliard .40
(3) Sean Casey .40
(4) Luis Castillo .40
(5) J.D. Drew .60
(6) Erubiel Durazo .40
(7) Carlos Febles .40
(8) Troy Glaus .65
(9) Ben Grieve .40
(10) Todd Helton .65
(11) Corey Koskie .40
(12) Warren Morris .40
1 Barry Bonds 2.00
2 Jose Canseco .60
3 Nomar Garciaparra 1.00
4 Jason Giambi .60
5 Shawn Green .50
6 Ken Griffey Jr. 1.25
7 Andruw Jones .75
8 Chipper Jones 1.00
9 Mark McGwire 1.50
10 Rafael Palmeiro .65
11 Mike Piazza 1.25
12 Manny Ramirez .75
13 Alex Rodriguez 1.50
14 Sammy Sosa 1.25

2000 MLB Showdown 1st Edition

Yet another attempt to bridge the gap between baseball cards as player-related collectibles and as interactive game, MLB Showdown from veteran gamers Wizards of the Coast enjoyed significant initial interest. Issued as a starter deck and in nine-card booster packs, the debut set has 462 player cards, including 63 premium holofoil star cards and 75 strategy cards. The holo premium foils were inserted in booster packs at a rate of 1:3. Promo cards were locally distributed. While collectors compete with gamers for these cards in the market, relative values placed on the cards by each group of buyers may differ. Cards without the silver-foil "1st Edition" logo were released in booster packs and are worth about half the values shown here.

		NM/M
Complete Set (517):		200.00
Common Player:		.15
Starter Box:		6.00
Starter Deck:		2.00
Booster Box (36):		25.00
Booster Pack (9):		1.00

1 Garret Anderson .15
2 Tim Belcher .15
3 Gary DiSarcina (Photo is Tim Salmon) .15
4 Darin Erstad .30
5 Chuck Finley/Foil 2.00
6 Troy Glaus .65
7 Todd Greene .15
8 Jeff Huson .15
9 Orlando Palmeiro .15
10 Troy Percival .15
11 Mark Petkovsek .15
12 Tim Salmon .15
13 Steve Sparks .15
14 Mo Vaughn .15
15 Matt Walbeck .15
16 Jay Bell/Foil 2.00

17 Andy Benes .15
18 Omar Daal .15
19 Steve Finley .15
20 Andy Fox .15
21 Hanley Frias .15
22 Bernard Gilkey .15
23 Luis Gonzalez/Foil 2.00
24 Randy Johnson/Foil 3.00
25 Travis Lee .15
26 Matt Mantei .15
27 Dan Plesac .15
28 Kelly Stinnett .15
29 Greg Swindell .15
30 Matt Williams/Foil 2.00
31 Tony Womack .15
32 Bret Boone .15
33 Tom Glavine .40
34 Jose Hernandez .15
35 Brian Hunter .15
36 Andruw Jones .15
37 Chipper Jones/Foil 4.00
38 Brian Jordan .15
39 Ryan Klesko .15
40 Keith Lockhart .15
41 Greg Maddux/Foil 4.00
42 Kevin Millwood/Foil 2.00
43 Eddie Perez .15
44 Mike Remlinger .15
45 John Rocker .15
46 John Smoltz .15
47 Walt Weiss .15
48 Gerald Williams .15
49 Rich Amaral .15
50 Brady Anderson .15
51 Albert Belle .15
52 Mike Bordick .15
53 Jeff Conine .15
54 Delino DeShields .15
55 Scott Erickson .15
56 Charles Johnson .15
57 Mike Mussina .35
58 Jesse Orosco .15
59 Sidney Ponson .15
60 Jeff Reboulet .15
61 Cal Ripken Jr./Foil 7.00
62 B.J. Surhoff .15
63 Mike Timlin .15
64 Rod Beck .15
65 Damon Buford .15
66 Rheal Cormier .15
67 Nomar Garciaparra/Foil 4.00
68 Butch Huskey .15
69 Darren Lewis .15
70 Derek Lowe .15
71 Pedro Martinez/Foil 3.00
72 Trot Nixon .15
73 Jose Offerman .15
74 Troy O'Leary .15
75 Mark Portugal .15
76 Pat Rapp .15
77 Mike Stanley .15
78 John Valentin .15
79 Jason Varitek .25
80 Tim Wakefield .15
81 Rick Aguilera .15
82 Jeff Blauser .15
83 Kyle Farnsworth .15
84 Gary Gaetti .15
85 Mark Grace .15
86 Lance Johnson .15
87 Jon Lieber .15
88 Mickey Morandini .15
89 Jose Nieves .15
90 Jeff Reed .15
91 Henry Rodriguez .15
92 Scott Sanders .15
93 Benito Santiago .15
94 Sammy Sosa 4.50
95 Steve Trachsel .15
96 James Baldwin .15
97 Mike Caruso .15
98 Ray Durham .15
99 Brook Fordyce .15
100 Bob Howry .15
101 Paul Konerko .25
102 Carlos Lee .35
103 Greg Norton .15
104 Magglio Ordonez .15
105 Jim Parque .15
106 Bill Simas .15
107 Chris Singleton .15
108 Mike Sirotka .15
109 Frank Thomas/Foil 3.00
110 Craig Wilson .15
111 Aaron Boone .15
112 Mike Cameron .15
113 Sean Casey/Foil 2.00
114 Danny Graves .15
115 Pete Harnisch .15
116 Barry Larkin/Foil 2.00
117 Pokey Reese .15
118 Scott Sullivan .15
119 Eddie Taubensee .15
120 Brett Tomko .15
121 Michael Tucker .15
122 Greg Vaughn .15
123 Ron Villone .15
124 Scott Williamson/Foil 2.00
125 Dmitri Young .15
126 Roberto Alomar/Foil 2.00
127 Harold Baines .15
128 Dave Burba .15
129 Bartolo Colon .15
130 Einar Diaz .15
131 Travis Fryman .15
132 Mike Jackson .15
133 David Justice .15

134 Kenny Lofton/Foil 2.00
135 Charles Nagy .15
136 Manny Ramirez/Foil 3.00
137 Richie Sexson .15
138 Paul Shuey .15
139 Jim Thome/Foil 2.50
140 Omar Vizquel .15
141 Enrique Wilson .15
142 Kurt Abbott .15
143 Pedro Astacio .15
144 Jeff Barry .15
145 Dante Bichette .15
146 Henry Blanco .15
147 Brian Bohanon .15
148 Vinny Castilla .15
149 Jerry Dipoto .15
150 Todd Helton .65
151 Darryl Kile .15
152 Curtis Leskanic .15
153 Neifi Perez .15
154 Terry Shumpert .15
155 Dave Veres .15
156 Larry Walker/Foil 2.00
157 Brad Ausmus .15
158 Frank Catalanotto .15
159 Tony Clark .15
160 Deivi Cruz .15
161 Damion Easley .15
162 Juan Encarnacion .15
163 Karim Garcia .15
164 Bobby Higginson .15
165 Todd Jones .15
166 Gabe Kapler .15
167 Dave Mlicki .15
168 Brian Moehler .15
169 C.J. Nitkowski .15
170 Dean Palmer/Foil 2.00
171 Jeff Weaver .15
172 Antonio Alfonseca .15
173 Bruce Aven .15
174 Dave Berg .15
175 Luis Castillo/Foil 2.00
176 Ryan Dempster .15
177 Brian Edmondson .15
178 Alex Gonzalez .15
179 Mark Kotsay .15
180 Derek Lee .50
181 Braden Looper .15
182 Mike Lowell .15
183 Brian Meadows .15
184 Mike Redmond .15
185 Dennis Springer .15
186 Preston Wilson .15
187 Jeff Bagwell/Foil 3.00
188 Derek Bell .15
189 Craig Biggio .15
190 Tim Bogar .15
191 Ken Caminiti .15
192 Scott Elarton .15
193 Tony Eusebio .15
194 Carl Everett/Foil 2.00
195 Mike Hampton/Foil 2.00
196 Richard Hidalgo .15
197 Stan Javier .15
198 Jose Lima .15
199 Jay Powell .15
200 Shane Reynolds .15
201 Bill Spiers .15
202 Billy Wagner/Foil 2.00
203 Carlos Beltran/Foil 2.50
204 Johnny Damon .35
205 Jermaine Dye .15
206 Carlos Febles .15
207 Jeremy Giambi .15
208 Chad Kreuter .15
209 Jeff Montgomery .15
210 Joe Randa .15
211 Jose Rosado .15
212 Rey Sanchez .15
213 Scott Service .15
214 Tim Spehr .15
215 Jeff Suppan .15
216 Mike Sweeney .15
217 Jay Witasick .15
218 Adrian Beltre .50
219 Pedro Borbon .15
220 Kevin Brown/Foil 2.00
221 Mark Grudzielanek .15
222 Dave Hansen .15
223 Todd Hundley .15
224 Eric Karros .15
225 Raul Mondesi .15
226 Chan Ho Park .15
227 Jeff Shaw .15
228 Gary Sheffield/Foil 2.50
229 Ismael Valdes .15
230 Jose Vizcaino .15
231 Devon White .15
232 Eric Young .15
233 Ron Belliard .15
234 Sean Berry .15
235 Jeromy Burnitz/Foil 2.00
236 Jeff Cirillo .15
237 Marquis Grissom .15
238 Geoff Jenkins .15
239 Scott Karl .15
240 Mark Loretta .15
241 Mike Myers .15
242 David Nilsson/Foil 2.00
243 Hideo Nomo .15
244 Alex Ochoa .15
245 Jose Valentin .15
246 Bob Wickman .15
247 Steve Woodard .15
248 Chad Allen .15
249 Ron Coomer .15
250 Cristian Guzman .15
251 Denny Hocking .15

252 Torii Hunter .15
253 Corey Koskie .15
254 Matt Lawton .15
255 Joe Mays .15
256 Doug Mientkiewicz .15
257 Eric Milton .15
258 Brad Radke/Foil 2.00
259 Terry Steinbach .15
260 Mike Trombley .15
261 Todd Walker .15
262 Bob Wells .15
263 Shane Andrews .15
264 Michael Barrett .15
265 Orlando Cabrera .15
266 Brad Fullmer .15
267 Vladimir Guerrero/Foil 3.00
268 Wilton Guerrero .15
269 Dustin Hermanson .15
270 Steve Kline .15
271 Manny Martinez .15
272 Mike Thurman .15
273 Ugueth Urbina .15
274 Javier Vazquez .15
275 Jose Vidro .15
276 Rondell White .15
277 Chris Widger .15
278 Edgardo Alfonzo/Foil 2.00
279 Armando Benitez .15
280 Roger Cedeno .15
281 Dennis Cook .15
282 Shawon Dunston .15
283 Matt Franco .15
284 Darryl Hamilton .15
285 Rickey Henderson/Foil 3.00
286 Orel Hershiser .15
287 Al Leiter .15
288 John Olerud .15
289 Rey Ordonez .15
290 Mike Piazza/Foil 5.00
291 Kenny Rogers .15
292 Robin Ventura .15
293 Turk Wendell .15
294 Masato Yoshii .15
295 Scott Brosius .15
296 Roger Clemens/Foil 4.50
297 David Cone/Foil 2.00
298 Chad Curtis .15
299 Chili Davis .15
300 Orlando Hernandez .15
301 Derek Jeter/Foil 7.00
302 Chuck Knoblauch .15
303 Ricky Ledee .15
304 Tino Martinez .15
305 Ramiro Mendoza .15
306 Paul O'Neill .15
307 Andy Pettitte .35
308 Jorge Posada .15
309 Mariano Rivera/Foil 2.00
310 Mike Stanton .15
311 Bernie Williams/Foil 2.00
312 Kevin Appier .15
313 Eric Chavez .25
314 Ryan Christenson .15
315 Jason Giambi/Foil 2.50
316 Ben Grieve .15
317 Buddy Groom .15
318 Gil Heredia .15
319 A.J. Hinch .15
320 Jon Jaha .15
321 Doug Jones .15
322 Omar Olivares .15
323 Tony Phillips .15
324 Matt Stairs .15
325 Miguel Tejada .25
326 Randy Velarde/Foil 2.00
327 Bobby Abreu/Foil 2.00
328 Marlon Anderson .15
329 Alex Arias .15
330 Rico Brogna .15
331 Paul Byrd .15
332 Ron Gant .15
333 Doug Glanville .15
334 Wayne Gomes .15
335 Kevin Jordan .15
336 Mike Lieberthal .15
337 Steve Montgomery .15
338 Chad Ogea .15
339 Scott Rolen .60
340 Curt Schilling/Foil 2.50
341 Kevin Sefcik .15
342 Mike Benjamin .15
343 Kris Benson .15
344 Adrian Brown .15
345 Brant Brown .15
346 Brad Clontz .15
347 Brian Giles/Foil 2.00
348 Jason Kendall/Foil 2.00
349 Al Martin .15
350 Warren Morris .15
351 Todd Ritchie .15
352 Scott Sauerbeck .15
353 Jason Schmidt .15
354 Ed Sprague .15
355 Mike Williams .15
356 Kevin Young .15
357 Andy Ashby .15
358 Ben Davis .15
359 Tony Gwynn/Foil 4.00
360 Sterling Hitchcock .15
361 Trevor Hoffman/Foil 2.00
362 Damian Jackson .15
363 Wally Joyner .15
364 Phil Nevin .15
365 Eric Owens .15
366 Ruben Rivera .15
367 Reggie Sanders .15
368 John Vander Wal .15
369 Quilvio Veras .15

370 Matt Whisenant .15
371 Woody Williams .15
372 Rich Aurilia .15
373 Marvin Benard .15
374 Barry Bonds/Foil 7.00
375 Ellis Burks .15
376 Alan Embree .15
377 Shawn Estes .15
378 John Johnstone .15
379 Jeff Kent .15
380 Brent Mayne .15
381 Bill Mueller .15
382 Robb Nen .15
383 Russ Ortiz .15
384 Kirk Rueter .15
385 F.P. Santangelo .15
386 J.T. Snow .15
387 David Bell .15
388 Jay Buhner .15
389 Russ Davis .15
391 Ken Griffey Jr./Foil 5.00
392 John Halama .15
393 Brian L. Hunter .15
394 Raul Ibanez .15
395 Tom Lampkin .15
396 Edgar Martinez/Foil 2.00
397 Jose Mesa .15
398 Jamie Moyer .15
399 Jose Paniagua .15
400 Alex Rodriguez/Foil 6.00
401 Dan Wilson .15
402 Manny Aybar .15
403 Ricky Bottalico .15
404 Kent Bottenfield .15
405 Darren Bragg .15
406 Alberto Castillo .15
407 J.D. Drew .60
408 Jose Jimenez .15
409 Ray Lankford .15
410 Joe McEwing .15
411 Willie McGee .15
412 Mark McGwire/Foil 6.00
413 Darren Oliver .15
414 Lance Painter .15
415 Edgar Renteria .15
416 Fernando Tatis/Foil 2.00
417 Wilson Alvarez .15
418 Rolando Arrojo .15
419 Wade Boggs 1.00
420 Miguel Cairo .15
421 Jose Canseco/Foil 2.50
422 John Flaherty .15
423 Roberto Hernandez .15
424 Dave Martinez .15
425 Fred McGriff .15
426 Paul Sorrento .15
427 Kevin Stocker .15
428 Bubba Trammell .15
429 Rick White .15
430 Randy Winn .15
431 Bobby Witt .15
432 Royce Clayton .15
433 Tim Crabtree .15
434 Juan Gonzalez .45
435 Tom Goodwin .15
436 Rusty Greer .15
437 Rick Helling .15
438 Mark McLemore .15
439 Mike Morgan .15
440 Rafael Palmeiro/Foil 3.00
441 Ivan Rodriguez/Foil 3.00
442 Aaron Sele .15
443 Lee Stevens .15
444 Mike Venafro .15
445 John Wetteland .15
446 Todd Zeile .15
447 Jeff Zimmerman/Foil 2.00
448 Tony Batista .15
449 Homer Bush .15
450 Jose Cruz Jr. .15
451 Carlos Delgado .40
452 Kelvim Escobar .15
453 Tony Fernandez/Foil 2.00
454 Darrin Fletcher .15
455 Shawn Green/Foil 2.00
456 Pat Hentgen .15
457 Billy Koch .15
458 Graeme Lloyd .15
459 Brian McRae .15
460 David Segui .15
461 Shannon Stewart .15
462 David Wells .15
S1 Bad Call/Umpire .10
S2 Big Inning (Mike Stanley) .10
S3 Bobbled in the Outfield (Tony Phillips) .10
S4 Clutch Hitting (Manny Ramirez) .10
S5 Do or Die (Chuck Knoblauch) .10
S6 Down the Middle (?) .10
S7 Ducks on the Pond (Carl Everett) .10
S8 Favorable Matchup (Barry Bonds) .30
S9 Free Steal (Juan Encarnacion) .10
S10 Get Under It (Jose Offerman) .10
S11 Great Lead (Rickey Henderson) .20
S12 Hard Slide (Damian Jackson) .10
S13 High Fives (Derek Jeter) .10

S14 Last Chance (Paul O'Neill) .10
S15 Long Single (Derek Jeter) .30
S16 Out of Gas (Jeff Zimmerman) .10
S17 Out of Position (Rickey Henderson, Ryan Klesko) .10
S18 Play the Percentages (Chipper Jones) .10
S19 Rally Cap (Omar Vizquel) .10
S20 Rattled (Mike Henneman) .10
S21 Runner Not Held (Miguel Tejada) .10
S22 Slow Roller (Brian Bohanon) .10
S23 Stick a Fork in Him (Kevin Millwood) .10
S24 Swing for the Fences (Sammy Sosa) .10
S25 To the Warning Track (Ricky Ledee) .10
S26 Whiplash (Mark McGwire) .25
S27 Wide Throw (Roberto Alomar) .10
S28 Wild Pitch (Eddie Taubensee) .10
S29 By the Book (Walt Weiss) .10
S30 Dominating (Billy Wagner) .10
S31 Full Windup (Orlando Hernandez) .10
S32 Good Fielding (Rey Ordonez, Ryan Klesko) .10
S33 Gun 'Em Down! (Jason Kendall) .10
S34 He's Got a Gun (Sammy Sosa) .10
S35 In the Groove (David Cone) .10
S36 In the Zone (Pedro Martinez) .10
S37 Infield In (S.F. Giants) .10
S38 Intimidation (Randy Johnson) .15
S39 Just Over the Wall (Ken Griffey, Jr.) .25
S40 Knock the Ball Down (?) .10
S41 Lefty Specialist (Jesse Orosco) .10
S42 Nerves of Steel (Mariano Rivera) .10
S43 Nothing but Heat (Randy Johnson) .10
S44 Pitch Out (Bobby Hughes) .10
S45 Pumped Up (John Rocker) .10
S46 Quick Pitch (Greg Maddux) .10
S47 Rally Killer (Carlos Baerga) .10
S48 Short Fly (Chuck Knoblauch, Bernie Williams) .10
S49 Three Up, Three Down (Pedro Martinez) .10
S50 Trick Pitch (Derek Jeter) .30
S51 Belt-High (Sammy Sosa) .15
S52 Change In Strategy (Joe Torre) .10
S53 Grounder to Second (Pokey Reese) .10
S54 Stealing Signals (Mark Grace) .10
S55 Swing at Anything (Cal Ripken, Jr.) .30

2000 MLB Showdown Pennant Run Promos

To promote its forthcoming Pennant Run edition, Wizards of the Coast issued eight specially marked sample cards. The promos have silver-foil player names and a large "W." The promos were issued one per copy of TopDeck magazine (a gamer's publication) which carried a $5.99 cover price.

		NM/M
Complete Set (8):		3.00
Common Player:		.50

1 Peter Bergeron .50
2 Matt Clement .50
3 Ramon Hernandez .50
4 Gabe Kapler .50
5 Adam Kennedy .50
6 Sean Lowe .50
7 Joe Nathan .50
8 Daryle Ward .50

2000 MLB Showdown Pennant Run

Issued just after the 2000 season opened, this is essentially an update to the interactive game MLB Showdown from veteran gamers Wizards of the Coast. Players in the set are generally those who changed teams during the off-season, or promising rookies. The Pennant Run edition was issued in a Booster box of 36 nine-card (seven player, two strategy) packs. The set has 130 "regular" player cards, 20 premium holofoil star cards and 25 strategy cards. The holo premium cards were inserted in packs at a rate of 1:3. While collectors compete with gamers for these cards in the market, relative values placed on the cards by each group of buyers may differ.

		NM/M
Complete Set (175):		30.00
Common Player:		.15
Booster Pack (9):		1.00
Booster Box (36):		20.00
1	Kent Bottenfield	.15
2	Ken Hill	.15
3	Adam Kennedy	.15
4	Ben Molina	.15
5	Scott Spiezio	.15
6	Brian Anderson	.15
7	Erubiel Durazo/Foil	1.00
8	Armando Reynoso	.15
9	Russ Springer	.15
10	Todd Stottlemyre	.15
11	Tony Womack	.15
12	Andres Galarraga/Foil	1.00
13	Javy Lopez/Foil	1.00
14	Kevin McGlinchy	.15
15	Terry Mulholland	.15
16	Reggie Sanders	.15
17	Harold Baines	.15
18	Will Clark	.15
19	Mike Trombley	.15
20	Manny Alexander	.15
21	Carl Everett/Foil	1.00
22	Ramon Martinez/Foil	1.00
23	Bret Saberhagen	.15
24	John Wasdin	.15
25	Joe Girardi	.15
26	Ricky Gutierrez	.15
27	Glenallen Hill	.15
28	Kevin Tapani	.15
29	Kerry Wood/Foil	2.00
30	Eric Young	.15
31	Keith Foulke/Foil	1.00
32	Mark Johnson	.15
33	Sean Lowe	.15
34	Jose Valentin	.15
35	Dante Bichette	.15
36	Ken Griffey Jr./Foil	6.00
37	Denny Neagle	.15
38	Steve Parris	.15
39	Dennis Reyes	.15
40	Sandy Alomar Jr.	.15
41	Chuck Finley/Foil	1.00
42	Steve Karsay	.15
43	Steve Reed	.15
44	Jaret Wright	.15
45	Jeff Cirillo	.15
46	Tom Goodwin	.15
47	Jeffrey Hammonds	.15
48	Mike Lansing	.15
49	Aaron Ledesma	.15
50	Brent Mayne	.15
51	Doug Brocail	.15
52	Robert Fick	.15
53	Juan Gonzalez	.60
54	Hideo Nomo	.60
55	Luis Polonia	.15
56	Brant Brown	.15
57	Alex Fernandez	.15
58	Cliff Floyd	.15
59	Dan Miceli	.15
60	Vladimir Nunez	.15
61	Moises Alou/Foil	1.00

62	Roger Cedeno/Foil	1.00
63	Octavio Dotel	.15
64	Mitch Meluskey	.15
65	Daryle Ward	.15
66	Mark Quinn/Foil	1.00
67	Brad Rigby	.15
68	Blake Stein	.15
69	Mac Suzuki	.15
70	Terry Adams	.15
71	Darren Dreifort	.15
72	Kevin Elster	.15
73	Shawn Green/Foil	1.50
74	Todd Hollandsworth	.15
75	Gregg Olson	.15
76	Kevin Barker	.15
77	Jose Hernandez	.15
78	Dave Weathers	.15
79	Hector Carrasco	.15
80	Eddie Guardado	.15
81	Jacque Jones	.25
82	David Ortiz	.50
83	Peter Bergeron	.15
84	Hideki Irabu	.15
85	Lee Stevens	.15
86	Anthony Telford	.15
87	Derek Bell	.15
88	John Franco	.15
89	Mike Hampton/Foil	1.00
90	Bobby J. Jones	.15
91	Todd Pratt	.15
92	Todd Zeile	.15
93	Jason Grimsley	.15
94	Roberto Kelly	.15
95	Jim Leyritz	.15
96	Ramiro Mendoza	.15
97	Rich Becker	.15
98	Ramon Hernandez	.15
99	Tim Hudson/Foil	2.00
100	Jason Isringhausen	.15
101	Mike Magnante	.15
102	Olmedo Saenz	.15
103	Mickey Morandini	.15
104	Robert Person	.15
105	Desi Relaford	.15
106	Jason Christiansen	.15
107	Wil Cordero	.15
108	Francisco Cordova	.15
109	Chad Hermansen	.15
110	Pat Meares	.15
111	Aramis Ramirez	.15
112	Bret Boone	.15
113	Matt Clement	.15
114	Carlos Hernandez	.15
115	Ryan Klesko	.15
116	Dave Magadan	.15
117	Al Martin	.15
118	Bobby Estalella	.15
119	Livan Hernandez	.15
120	Doug Mirabelli	.15
121	Joe Nathan	.15
122	Mike Cameron	.15
123	Mark McLemore	.15
124	Gil Meche	.15
125	John Olerud	.15
126	Arthur Rhodes	.15
127	Aaron Sele/Foil	1.00
128	Jim Edmonds/Foil	1.00
129	Pat Hentgen	.15
130	Darryl Kile	.15
131	Eli Marrero	.15
132	Dave Veres	.15
133	Fernando Vina	.15
134	Vinny Castilla	.15
135	Juan Guzman	.15
136	Ryan Rupe	.15
137	Greg Vaughn/Foil	1.00
138	Gerald Williams	.15
139	Esteban Yan	.15
140	Tom Evans	.15
141	Gabe Kapler	.15
142	Ruben Mateo/Foil	1.00
143	Kenny Rogers	.15
144	David Segui	.15
145	Tony Batista	.15
146	Chris Carpenter	.15
147	Brad Fullmer	.15
148	Alex Gonzalez	.15
149	Roy Halladay	.15
150	Raul Mondesi/Foil	1.00
S1	Afterburners (Aaron Boone)	.10
S2	Change Sides (Chipper Jones)	.15
S3	Patience is a Virtue (Bob Abreu)	.10
S4	Payoff Pitch (Fernando Tatis)	.15
S5	Pointers (Rod Carew)	.15
S6	Professional Baserunner (J.D. Drew)	.10
S7	Professional Hitter (John VanderWal)	.10
S8	Protect the Runner (Pokey Reese)	.10
S9	Rough Outing (Greg Maddux)	.15
S10	Shelled (Cincinnati Reds)	.10
S11	Take What is Given (Larry Walker)	.15
S12	Tricky Hop (Alex Rodriguez)	.40
S13	Aggressive Coaching (Alex Rodriguez)	.40
S14	Cut Off in the Gap (N.Y. Mets)	.10
S15	Great Start (Kevin Brown)	.15

S16	Insult to Injury (Paul O'Neill)	.10
S17	Job Well Done (Scott Williamson)	.10
S18	Low and Away (Jamie Moyer)	.10
S19	Outfield In (Bernie Williams)	.10
S20	Put Out the Fire (John Franco)	.10
S21	Rotation Play (Pittsburgh Pirates)	.10
S22	Swiss Army Closer (John Rocker)	.10
S23	Whoops (Mike Lansing)	.10
S24	Pep Talk (Roger Clemens, Joe Torre)	.15
S25	Revenue Sharing (Derek Jeter)	.50

2001 MLB Showdown Promos

To introduce its 2001 card game, Wizards of the Coast produced a series of promo cards which were locally distributed to hobby stores to encourage people to join gaming leagues. The promos differ from the issued cards in the use of a designation at top of "ACE PITCHER," "FUTURE STAR" or "DIAMOND STAR" and the absence of the large team logo in the background. Because of the manner of distribution, some promos are more difficult to find in the hobby market.

		NM/M
Complete Set (64):		35.00
Common Player:		.50
(1)	Kris Benson	.50
(2)	Kevin Brown	.50
(3)	Roger Clemens	1.75
(4)	Bartolo Colon	.50
(5)	Jeff D'Amico	.50
(6)	Ryan Dempster	.50
(7)	Adam Eaton	.50
(8)	Scott Elarton	.50
(9)	Livan Hernandez	.50
(10)	Tim Hudson	.65
(11)	Randy Johnson	1.00
(12)	Darryl Kile	.50
(13)	Al Leiter	.50
(14)	Jon Lieber	.50
(15)	Greg Maddux	1.50
(16)	Pedro Martinez	1.00
(17)	Brad Radke	.50
(18)	Javier Vazquez	.50
(19)	Jeff Weaver	.50
(20)	David Wells	.50
(1)	Roberto Alomar	.50
(2)	Carlos Delgado	.65
(3)	Jason Giambi	.75
(4)	Troy Glaus	.75
(5)	Bobby Higginson	.50
(6)	David Justice	.50
(7)	Jeff Kent	.50
(8)	Ivan Rodriguez	.65
(9)	Gary Sheffield	.75
(10)	Frank Thomas	1.00
(11)	Greg Vaughn	.50
(12)	Robin Ventura	.50
(13)	Rondell White	.50
(1)	Peter Bergeron	.50
(2)	Pat Burrell	.75
(3)	Sean Casey	.50
(4)	J.D. Drew	.75
(5)	Richard Hidalgo	.50
(6)	Melvin Mora	.50
(7)	Eric Owens	.50
(8)	Aramis Ramirez	.50
(9)	Preston Wilson	.50
(1)	Joe Crede	.50
(2)	Corey Patterson	.50
(3)	Albert Pujols	15.00
(4)	Ben Sheets	.50
(5)	Alfonso Soriano	.75

2001 MLB Showdown 1st Edition

MLB Showdown returned for a second season in 2001.

Issued as a 50-card starter set, a 60-card "Draft Pack" and in nine-card booster packs, the set has 416 "regular" player cards, 46 premium holofoil star cards and 75 strategy cards. The holo premium cards were inserted in booster packs at a rate of 1:3. Promo cards were locally distributed. While collectors compete with gamers for these cards in the market, relative values placed on the cards by each group of buyers may differ. Cards without the silver-foil "1st Edition" logo were released in booster packs and are worth about half the prices shown here.

		NM/M
Complete Set (537):		195.00
Common Player:		.15
Starter Box:		12.00
Booster Pack (9):		1.50
Booster Box (36):		25.00
1	Garret Anderson	.15
2	Darin Erstad/Foil	2.00
3	Ron Gant	.15
4	Troy Glaus/Foil	3.00
5	Shigetosi Hasegawa	.15
6	Adam Kennedy	.15
7	Al Levine	.15
8	Ben Molina	.15
9	Troy Percival	.15
10	Mark Petkovsek	.15
11	Tim Salmon	.15
12	Scott Schoeneweis	.15
13	Scott Spezio	.15
14	Mo Vaughn	.15
15	Jarrod Washburn	.15
16	Brian Anderson	.15
17	Danny Bautista	.15
18	Jay Bell	.15
19	Greg Colbrunn	.15
20	Steve Finley	.15
21	Luis Gonzalez/Foil	2.00
22	Randy Johnson/Foil	3.50
23	Byung-Hyun Kim	.15
24	Matt Mantei	.15
25	Mike Morgan	.15
26	Curt Schilling	.30
27	Kelly Stinnett	.15
28	Greg Swindell	.15
29	Matt Williams	.15
30	Tony Womack	.15
31	Andy Ashby	.15
32	Bobby Bonilla	.15
33	Rafael Furcal/Foil	2.00
34	Andres Galarraga	.15
35	Tom Glavine/Foil	2.50
36	Andruw Jones	.50
37	Chipper Jones/Foil	4.00
38	Brian Jordan	.15
39	Wally Joyner	.15
40	Keith Lockhart	.15
41	Javy Lopez	.15
42	Greg Maddux/Foil	4.00
43	Kevin Millwood	.15
44	Mike Remlinger	.15
45	John Rocker	.15
46	B.J. Surhoff	.15
47	Quilvio Veras	.15
48	Brady Anderson	.15
49	Albert Belle	.15
50	Jeff Conine	.15
51	Delino DeShields	.15
52	Buddy Groom	.15
53	Trenidad Hubbard	.15
54	Luis Matos	.15
55	Jose Mercedes	.15
56	Melvin Mora	.15
57	Mike Mussina/Foil	2.50
58	Sidney Ponson	.15
59	Pat Rapp	.15
60	Chris Richard	.15
61	Cal Ripken Jr./Foil	7.00
62	Mike Trombley	.15
63	Rolando Arrojo	.15
64	Dante Bichette	.15
65	Rheal Cormier	.15
66	Carl Everett	.15
67	Rich Garces	.15
68	Nomar Garciaparra/Foil	4.00

69	Mike Lansing	.15
70	Darren Lewis	.15
71	Derek Lowe	.15
72	Pedro Martinez/Foil	3.50
73	Ramon Martinez	.15
74	Trot Nixon	.15
75	Jose Offerman	.15
76	Troy O'Leary	.15
77	Jason Varitek	.15
78	Rick Aguilera	.15
79	Damon Buford	.15
80	Joe Girardi	.15
81	Mark Grace	.15
82	Willie Greene	.15
83	Ricky Gutierrez	.15
84	Felix Heredia	.15
85	Jon Lieber	.15
86	Jeff Reed	.15
87	Sammy Sosa/Foil	4.50
88	Kevin Tapani	.15
89	Todd Van Poppel	.15
90	Rondell White	.15
91	Kerry Wood	.35
92	Eric Young	.15
93	James Baldwin	.15
94	Ray Durham	.15
95	Keith Foulke/Foil	2.00
96	Bob Howry	.15
97	Charles Johnson/Foil	2.00
98	Mark L. Johnson	.15
99	Paul Konerko	.25
100	Carlos Lee	.25
101	Magglio Ordonez	.15
102	Jose Valentin	.15
103	Herbert Perry	.15
104	Bill Simas	.15
105	Chris Singleton	.15
106	Mike Sirotka	.15
107	Frank Thomas/Foil	3.50
108	Jose Valentin	.15
109	Kelly Wunsch	.15
110	Aaron Boone	.15
111	Sean Casey	.15
112	Danny Graves	.15
113	Ken Griffey Jr./Foil	5.00
114	Pete Harnisch	.15
115	Barry Larkin/Foil	2.00
116	Alex Ochoa	.15
117	Steve Parris	.15
118	Pokey Reese	.15
119	Chris Stynes	.15
120	Scott Sullivan	.15
121	Eddie Taubensee	.15
122	Michael Tucker	.15
123	Ron Villone	.15
124	Dmitri Young	.15
125	Roberto Alomar/Foil	2.00
126	Sandy Alomar Jr.	.15
127	Jason Bere	.15
128	Dave Burba	.15
129	Bartolo Colon	.15
130	Wil Cordero	.15
131	Chuck Finley	.15
132	Travis Fryman	.15
133	Steve Karsay	.15
134	Kenny Lofton	.15
135	Manny Ramirez/Foil	3.50
136	David Segui	.15
137	Jim Thome	.45
138	Omar Vizquel	.15
139	Bob Wickman	.15
140	Pedro Astacio	.15
141	Brian Bohannon	.15
142	Jeff Cirillo	.15
143	Jeff Frye	.15
144	Jeffrey Hammonds	.15
145	Todd Helton/Foil	3.00
146	Todd Hollandsworth	.15
147	Butch Huskey	.15
148	Jose Jimenez	.15
149	Brent Mayne	.15
150	Neifi Perez	.15
151	Terry Shumpert	.15
152	Larry Walker	.15
153	Gabe White/Foil	2.00
154	Masato Yoshii	.15
155	Matt Anderson	.15
156	Brad Ausmus	.15
157	Rich Becker	.15
158	Tony Clark	.15
159	Deivi Cruz	.15
160	Damion Easley	.15
161	Juan Encarnacion	.15
162	Juan Gonzalez	.30
163	Shane Halter	.15
164	Bobby Higginson	.15
165	Todd Jones/Foil	2.00
166	Brian Moehler	.15
167	Hideo Nomo	.35
168	Dean Palmer	.15
169	Jeff Weaver	.15
170	Antonio Alfonseca	.15
171	Luis Castillo/Foil	2.00
172	Ryan Dempster/Foil	2.00
173	Cliff Floyd	.15
174	Alex Gonzalez	.15
175	Mark Kotsay	.15
176	Derrek Lee	.35
177	Braden Looper	.15
178	Mike Lowell	.15
179	Brad Penny	.15
180	Mike Redmond	.15
181	Henry Rodriguez	.15
182	Jesus Sanchez	.15
183	Mark Smith	.15
184	Preston Wilson	.15
185	Moises Alou	.15
186	Jeff Bagwell/Foil	3.50

187	Lance Berkman	.15
188	Craig Biggio	.15
189	Tim Bogar	.15
190	Jose Cabrera	.15
191	Octavio Dotel	.15
192	Scott Elarton/Foil	2.00
193	Richard Hidalgo	.15
194	Chris Holt	.15
195	Jose Lima	.15
196	Julio Lugo	.15
197	Mitch Meluskey	.15
198	Bill Spiers	.15
199	Daryle Ward	.15
200	Carlos Beltran	.40
201	Ricky Bottalico	.15
202	Johnny Damon/Foil	2.50
203	Jermaine Dye	.15
204	Carlos Febles	.15
205	Dave McCarty	.15
206	Mark Quinn	.15
207	Joe Randa	.15
208	Dan Reichert	.15
209	Rey Sanchez	.15
210	Jose Santiago	.15
211	Jeff Suppan	.15
212	Mac Suzuki	.15
213	Mike Sweeney	.15
214	Gregg Zaun	.15
215	Terry Adams	.15
216	Adrian Beltre	.15
217	Kevin Brown/Foil	2.00
218	Alex Cora	.15
219	Darren Dreifort	.15
220	Tom Goodwin	.15
221	Shawn Green	.25
222	Mark Grudzielanek	.15
223	Dave Hansen	.15
224	Todd Hundley	.15
225	Eric Karros	.15
226	Chad Kreuter	.15
227	Chan Ho Park	.15
228	Jeff Shaw	.15
229	Gary Sheffield/Foil	2.50
230	Juan Acevedo	.15
231	Ron Belliard	.15
232	Henry Blanco	.15
233	Jeromy Burnitz	.15
234	Jeff D'Amico/Foil	2.00
235	Valerio de los Santos	.15
236	Marquis Grissom	.15
237	Charlie Hayes	.15
238	Jimmy Haynes	.15
239	Jose Hernandez	.15
240	Geoff Jenkins	.15
241	Curtis Leskanic	.15
242	Mark Loretta	.15
243	Richie Sexson	.15
244	Dave Weathers	.15
245	Jay Canizaro	.15
246	Ron Coomer	.15
247	Cristian Guzman	.15
248	LaTroy Hawkins	.15
249	Denny Hocking	.15
250	Torii Hunter	.15
251	Jacque Jones	.15
252	Corey Koskie	.15
253	Matt Lawton	.15
254	Matt LeCroy	.15
255	Eric Milton	.15
256	David Ortiz	.40
257	Brad Radke/Foil	2.00
258	Mark Redman	.15
259	Bob Wells	.15
260	Michael Barrett	.15
261	Peter Bergeron	.15
262	Milton Bradley	.15
263	Orlando Cabrera	.15
264	Vladimir Guerrero/Foil	3.50
265	Wilton Guerrero	.15
266	Dustin Hermanson	.15
267	Terry Jones	.15
268	Steve Kline	.15
269	Felipe Lira	.15
270	Mike Mordecai	.15
271	Lee Stevens	.15
272	Anthony Telford	.15
273	Javier Vazquez	.15
274	Jose Vidro/Foil	2.00
275	Edgardo Alfonzo/Foil	2.00
276	Derek Bell	.15
277	Armando Benitez	.15
278	Mike Bordick	.15
279	Mike Hampton/Foil	2.00
280	Lenny Harris	.15
281	Al Leiter	.15
282	Jay Payton	.15
283	Mike Piazza/Foil	5.00
284	Todd Pratt	.15
285	Glendon Rusch	.15
286	Bubba Trammell	.15
287	Robin Ventura	.15
288	Turk Wendell	.15
289	Rick White	.15
290	Todd Zeile	.15
291	Scott Brosius	.15
292	Roger Clemens/Foil	4.50
293	Jason Grimsley	.15
294	Orlando Hernandez	.15
295	Derek Jeter/Foil	7.00
296	Dave Justice	.15
297	Chuck Knoblauch	.15
298	Tino Martinez	.15
299	Denny Neagle	.15
300	Jeff Nelson	.15
301	Paul O'Neill	.15
302	Andy Pettitte	.25
303	Jorge Posada	.15
304	Mariano Rivera/Foil	2.00

305	Jose Vizcaino	.15
306	Bernie Williams/Foil	2.00
307	Kevin Appier	.15
308	Eric Chavez	.15
309	Ryan Christenson	.15
310	Jason Giambi/Foil	3.00
311	Jeremy Giambi	.15
312	Ben Grieve	.15
313	Gil Heredia	.15
314	Ramon Hernandez	.15
315	Tim Hudson/Foil	2.50
316	Jason Isringhausen	.15
317	Terrence Long/Foil	2.00
318	Jim Mecir	.15
319	Mark Mulder	.15
320	Matt Stairs	.15
321	Miguel Tejada	.25
322	Randy Velarde	.15
323	Bobby Abreu	.15
324	Jeff Brantley	.15
325	Pat Burrell	.45
326	Omar Daal	.15
327	Rob Ducey	.15
328	Doug Glanville	.15
329	Wayne Gomes	.15
330	Kevin Jordan	.15
331	Travis Lee	.15
332	Mike Lieberthal	.15
333	Vicente Padilla	.15
334	Robert Person	.15
335	Scott Rolen/Foil	2.50
336	Kevin Sefcik	.15
337	Randy Wolf	.15
338	Jimmy Anderson	.15
339	Mike Benjamin	.15
340	Kris Benson	.15
341	Adrian Brown	.15
342	Brian Giles/Foil	2.00
343	Jason Kendall/Foil	2.00
344	Pat Meares	.15
345	Wayne Morris	.15
346	Aramis Ramirez	.15
347	Todd Ritchie	.15
348	Scott Sauerbeck	.15
349	Jose Silva	.15
350	John Vander Wal	.15
351	Mike Williams	.15
352	Kevin Young	.15
353	Carlos Almanzar	.15
354	Bret Boone	.15
355	Matt Clement	.15
356	Adam Eaton	.15
357	Wiki Gonzalez	.15
358	Trevor Hoffman/Foil	2.00
359	Damian Jackson	.15
360	Ryan Klesko	.15
361	Phil Nevin/Foil	2.00
362	Eric Owens	.15
363	Desi Relaford	.15
364	Ruben Rivera	.15
365	Kevin Walker	.15
366	Woody Williams	.15
367	Jay Witasick	.15
368	Rich Aurilia	.15
369	Marvin Benard	.15
370	Barry Bonds/Foil	7.00
371	Ellis Burks	.15
372	Bobby Estella	.15
373	Doug Henry	.15
374	Livan Hernandez	.15
375	Jeff Kent/Foil	2.00
376	Doug Mirabelli	.15
377	Bill Mueller	.15
378	Calvin Murray	.15
379	Robb Nen/Foil	2.00
380	Russ Ortiz	.15
381	Armando Rios	.15
382	Felix Rodriguez	.15
383	Kirk Rueter	.15
384	J.T. Snow	.15
385	Paul Abbott	.15
386	David Bell	.15
387	Jay Buhner	.15
388	Mike Cameron	.15
389	John Halama	.15
390	Rickey Henderson	.50
391	Al Martin	.15
392	Edgar Martinez/Foil	2.00
393	Mark McLemore	.15
394	John Olerud	.15
395	Jose Paniagua	.15
396	Arthur Rhodes	.15
397	Alex Rodriguez/Foil	6.00
398	Kazuhiro Sasaki/Foil	2.00
399	Aaron Sele	.15
400	Dan Wilson	.15
401	Rick Ankiel/Foil	2.00
402	Will Clark	.15
403	J.D. Drew	.45
404	Jim Edmonds/Foil	2.00
405	Pat Hentgen	.15
406	Darryl Kile	.15
407	Ray Lankford	.15
408	Mike Matheny	.15
409	Mark McGwire/Foil	6.00
410	Craig Paquette	.15
411	Placido Polanco	.15
412	Edgar Renteria	.15
413	Garrett Stephenson	.15
414	Fernando Tatis	.15
415	Mike Timlin	.15
416	Dave Veres	.15
417	Fernando Vina	.15
418	Miguel Cairo	.15
419	Vinny Castilla	.15
420	Steve Cox	.15
421	Doug Creek	.15
422	John Flaherty	.15

423	Jose Guillen	.15
424	Roberto Hernandez/Foil	2.00
425	Russ Johnson	.15
426	Albie Lopez	.15
427	Felix Martinez	.15
428	Fred McGriff	.15
429	Bryan Rekar	.15
430	Greg Vaughn	.15
431	Gerald Williams	.15
432	Esteban Yan	.15
433	Luis Alicea	.15
434	Frank Catalanotto	.15
435	Royce Clayton	.15
436	Tim Crabtree	.15
437	Chad Curtis	.15
438	Rusty Greer	.15
439	Rick Helling	.15
440	Gabe Kapler	.15
441	Mike Lamb	.15
442	Ricky Ledee	.15
443	Rafael Palmeiro	.45
444	Ivan Rodriguez/Foil	3.00
445	Kenny Rogers	.15
446	Mike Venafro	.15
447	John Wetteland	.15
448	Tony Batista/Foil	2.00
449	Jose Cruz, Jr.	.15
450	Carlos Delgado/Foil	2.50
451	Kelvim Escobar	.15
452	Darrin Fletcher	.15
453	Brad Fullmer	.15
454	Alex S. Gonzalez	.15
455	Mark Guthrie	.15
456	Billy Koch	.15
457	Esteban Loaiza	.15
458	Raul Mondesi	.15
459	Mickey Morandini	.15
460	Paul Quantrill	.15
461	Shannon Stewart	.15
462	David Wells/Foil	2.00
S1	Change Sides (Jorge Posada)	.05
S2	Clutch Hitter (Nomar Garciaparra)	.15
S3	Clutch Hitting (Manny Ramirez)	.10
S4	Contact Hitter (Bernie Williams)	.05
S5	Deep in the Gap (Sammy Sosa)	.05
S6	Dog Meat (Brian Buchanon)	.05
S7	Double Steal (Jay Canizaro)	.05
S8	Down the Middle (Michael Tucker)	.05
S9	Drag Bunt (Unidentified)	.05
S10	Drained (Luis Castillo)	.05
S11	Ducks on the Pond (Carl Everett)	.05
S12	Favorable Matchup (Carlos Delgado)	.10
S13	Fight It Off (Unidentified)	.05
S14	Free Swinger (Benji Molina)	.05
S15	Fuel on the Fire (Eric Young)	.05
S16	Hiding an Injury (Unidentified)	.05
S17	In Motion (Nomar Garciaparra)	.15
S18	Last Chance (Alex Ochoa)	.05
S19	Lean Into It (Unidentified)	.05
S20	Nuisance (Rickey Henderson)	.10
S21	Off-Balance (Alex Gonzalez)	.05
S22	Out of Gas (Hideo Nomo)	.10
S23	Overthrow (Sean Casey)	.05
S24	Play the Percentages (Unidentified)	.05
S25	Power Hitter (Unidentified)	.05
S26	Protect the Runner (Chuck Knoblauch)	.05
S27	Pull the Ball (Todd Helton)	.10
S28	Rally Cap (Tim Salmon)	.05
S29	Rough Outing (Randy Johnson)	.10
S30	Runner Not Held (Johnny Damon)	.05
S31	Running on Fumes (Unidentified)	.05
S32	Ruptured Duck (Alex Rodriguez)	.25
S33	Sail Into Center (Pokey Reese)	.05
S34	Say the Magic Word (Mark McGwire)	.25
S35	Shell Shocked (Unidentified)	.05
S36	Singles Hitter (Homer Bush)	.05
S37	Smash up the Middle (Unidentified)	.05
S38	Stick a Fork in Him (Unidentified)	.05
S39	Take What's Given (Unidentified)	.05

S40	To the Warning Track (Brian Giles)	.05
S41	Turn It On (Shawon Dunston)	.05
S42	Anointed Closer (Cutis Leskanic)	.05
S43	By the Book (Unidentified)	.05
S44	Cannon (Bobby Higginson)	.05
S45	Choke (Unidentified)	.05
S46	Fast Worker (Greg Maddux)	.15
S47	Flamethrower (Unidentified)	.05
S48	Full Windup (Kevin Brown)	.05
S49	Goose Egg (Omar Vizquel)	.05
S50	Great Start (Tom Glavine)	.10
S51	Great Throw (Neifi Perez)	.05
S52	Gutsy Play (Mike Lamb)	.05
S53	Highlight Reel (Pokey Reese)	.05
S54	Insult to Injury (Unidentified)	.05
S55	In the Groove (Randy Johnson)	.10
S56	Job Well Done (Unidentified)	.05
S57	Just Foul (Unidentified)	.05
S58	Just Over the Wall (Bernie Williams)	.05
S59	Leaping Catch (Barry Bonds)	.35
S60	Lefty Specialist (Jason Christensen)	.05
S61	Low and Away (Eddie Taubensee)	.05
S62	Mound Conference (Unidentified)	.05
S63	Nerves of Steel (Todd Jones)	.05
S64	Pitchout (Unidentified)	.05
S65	Scuff the Ball (Brian Moehler)	.05
S66	Sloppy Bunt (Livan Hernandez)	.05
S67	Soft Hands (Omar Vizquel)	.05
S68	Submarine Pitch (Byung-Hyun Kim)	.05
S69	Visibly Upset (Unidentified)	.05
S70	What Were You Thinking??? (Benito Santiago)	.05
S71	Air It Out (Kevin Brown)	.05
S72	Bear Down (Pedro Martinez)	.10
S73	Brainstorm (Bobby Cox)	.05
S74	Game of Inches (Dmitri Young)	.05
S75	Second Look (Moises Alou)	.05

2001 MLB Showdown Pennant Run Promos

To promote its Pennant Run update edition, Wizards of the Coast issued eight specially marked sample cards to persons attending All-Star FanFest, the National Sports Collectors Convention and the Origins Gaming Convention (Gen Con) in the summer of 2001. The promos are virtually identical to the issued versions of the same players' cards except for the presence on front of a large logo indicating the show at which the cards were distributed.

NM/M
Complete Set (6): 7.50

Common Player:		1.00
008	C.C. Sabathia	1.00
017	Juan Pierre	1.00
084	Wes Helms	1.00
087	Ben Sheets	1.00
127	Luis Rivas	1.00
169	Ichiro (Suzuki)	3.50

2001 MLB Showdown Pennant Run

Issued after the 2002 season opened, this is essentially an update to the interactive MLB Showdown game. Players in the set are generally those who changed teams during the off-season, or promising rookies. The Pennant Run edition was issued in a Booster box of 36 nine-card (seven player, two strategy) packs. The set has 100 "regular" player cards, 25 SP (1:3) holofoil star cards and 25 strategy cards. Cards #91-125 are a Super Season player subset. While collectors compete with gamers for these cards in the market, relative values placed on the cards by each group of buyers may differ.

NM/M
Complete Set (200): 75.00
Common Player: .15
Booster Pack (9): 1.50
Booster Box (36): 25.00

001	Randy Velarde	.15
002	Dustin Hermanson	.15
003	Jamie Moyer	.15
004	Aaron Fultz	.15
005	Barry Zito/Foil	2.50
006	Adam Piatt	.15
007	Ben Grieve	.15
008	C.C. Sabathia/Foil	2.00
009	Eddie Guardado	.15
010	Matt Kinney	.15
011	Blake Stein	.15
012	Billy Wagner/Foil	2.00
013	Chris Holt	.15
014	Homer Bush	.15
015	Vladimir Nunez	.15
016	C.J. Nitkowski	.15
017	Juan Pierre	.25
018	Jose Valentin	.15
019	Juan Gonzalez	.30
020	Derek Bell	.15
021	Wade Miller	.15
022	Shawn Estes	.15
023	Enrique Wilson	.15
024	Dave Magadan	.15
025	Jason Christiansen	.15
026	Paul Shuey	.15
027	Mark Wohlers	.15
028	John Riedling	.15
029	Francisco Cordova	.15
030	Craig House	.15
031	Scott Strickland	.15
032	Octavio Dotel	.15
033	Jimmy Rollins/Foil	2.00
034	Carl Pavano	.15
035	Sandy Alomar Jr.	.15
036	Hideki Irabu	.15
037	Tom Gordon	.15
038	Roosevelt Brown	.15
039	Alex Rodriguez/Foil	4.00
040	Andres Galarraga	.15
041	Rob Bell	.15
042	Jason Schmidt	.15
043	Rod Beck	.15
044	Paul Rigdon	.15
045	Dan Miceli	.15
046	Ricky Bones	.15
047	Mike Hampton/Foil	2.00
048	Cliff Politte	.15
049	Chris Stynes	.15
050	Ramiro Mendoza	.15
051	Todd Walker	.15
052	Fernando Seguignol	.15
053	Mark Guthrie	.15
054	Tony Armas Jr.	.15
055	Billy McMillon	.15

056	Gary Bennett	.15
057	Corey Patterson/Foil	2.00
058	Juan Guzman	.15
059	Joe Crede	.25
060	A.J. Pierzynski	.15
061	Ben Davis	.15
062	Alan Embree	.15
063	Jon Garland/Foil	2.00
064	Ryan Kohlmeier	.15
065	Andy Benes	.15
066	Ron Gant	.15
067	Jerry Hairston Jr.	.15
068	Odalis Perez	.15
069	Lance Painter	.15
070	David Segui	.15
071	Russ Davis	.15
072	Jeff Zimmerman	.15
073	Dennys Reyes	.15
074	Jamey Wright	.15
075	Rico Brogna	.15
076	Geraldo Guzman	.15
077	Eric Gagne	.15
078	Bruce Chen	.15
079	Justin Speier	.15
080	Randy Keisler	.15
081	Ellis Burks/Foil	2.00
082	Alfonso Soriano	.50
083	Jeff Nelson	.15
084	Wes Helms	.15
085	Freddy Garcia/Foil	2.00
086	Erubiel Durazo	.15
087	Ben Sheets/Foil	2.00
088	Jose Ortiz/Foil	2.00
089	Paul Wilson	.15
090	Onan Masaoka	.15
091	Jose Rosado	.15
092	A.J. Burnett	.15
093	Bubba Trammell	.15
094	Mike Fetters	.15
095	Jacob Cruz	.15
096	John Franco	.15
097	Armando Reynoso	.15
098	Lou Pote	.15
099	D'Angelo Jiminez/Foil	2.00
100	Julio Zuleta	.15
101	Charles Johnson/Foil	2.00
102	Tsuyoshi Shinjo	.15
103	Brett Tomko	.15
104	Marcus Giles	.15
105	Craig Counsell	.15
106	Ruben Mateo	.15
107	Andy Ashby	.15
108	Marlon Anderson	.15
109	Mark Grace	.15
110	Russ Branyan	.15
111	Julian Tavarez	.15
112	Joey Hamilton	.15
113	Jason LaRue	.15
114	Benji Gil	.15
115	Bill Mueller	.15
116	Mike Stanton	.15
117	Ray King	.15
118	Timoniel Perez	.15
119	Johnny Damon/Foil	2.50
120	Matt Morris	.15
121	Kevin Appier	.15
122	Frank Castillo	.15
123	Mike Darr	.15
124	Felipe Crespo	.15
125	John Smoltz/Foil	2.00
126	Ben Weber	.15
127	Luis Rivas	.15
128	Travis Harper	.15
129	Aubrey Huff	.15
130	Paul LoDuca	.15
131	Eric Davis	.15
132	Fernando Tatis	.15
133	Ugueth Urbina	.15
134	Steve Kline	.15
135	Tanyon Sturtze	.15
136	Scott Hatteberg	.15
137	Tomokazu Ohka/Foil	2.00
138	Melvin Mora	.15
139	Kip Wells	.15
140	Ken Caminiti	.15
141	Dave Martinez	.15
142	Robert Fick	.15
143	Mike Bordick	.15
144	Doug Mientkiewicz	.15
145	Darryl Hamilton	.15
146	Shane Reynolds	.15
147	Vernon Wells/Foil	2.00
148	Rey Ordonez	.15
149	Brad Ausmus	.15
150	Jay Powell	.15
151	Todd Hundley	.15
152	Travis Miller	.15
153	Tyler Houston	.15
154	Nelson Cruz	.15
155	Manny Ramirez/Foil	3.00
156	Luis Lopez	.15
157	Luis Sojo	.15
158	Tony Gwynn/Foil	3.50
159	Roger Cedeno	.15
160	Royce Clayton	.15
161	Olmedo Saenz	.15
162	Brook Fordyce	.15
163	Dee Brown	.15
164	David Wells/Foil	2.00
165	Jack Wilson	.15
166	Pedro Feliz	.15
167	Hideo Nomo	.40
168	Albert Pujols/Foil	20.00
169	Ichiro (Suzuki)/Foil	6.00
170	Ramon Ortiz	.15
171	Mike Holtz	.15
172	Chris Woodward	.15
173	Mike Mussina/Foil	2.50

174	Carlos Guillen	.15
175	Ben Petrick	.15
S1	Advance on Throw (Johnny Damon, Shane Halter)	.05
S2	Ball in the Dirt (Roberto Alomar, Ruben Mateo)	.05
S3	Constant Pressure (Sammy Sosa, Mark McGwire)	.35
S4	Emergency Bunt (Jeff Leifer)	.05
S5	First-Pitch Swinging (Cal Ripken, Jr.)	.50
S6	Go Up Hacking (Mike Piazza)	.35
S7	Speedster (Derek Jeter)	.50
S8	Sprint to Second (Jose Valentin)	.05
S9	Wild Thing (Benito Santiago)	.05
S10	Wipeout (J.D. Drew)	.10
S11	Caught Napping (Tony Gwynn)	.20
S12	Comebacker (Greg Maddux)	.20
S13	Confusion (Julio Zuleta, Dmitri Young)	.05
S14	Double-Play Whiz (Ray Durham)	.05
S15	Fired Up (Abraham Nunez)	.05
S16	Focused (Rey Ordonez)	.05
S17	Going the Distance (Roger Clemens)	.25
S18	Great Pickoff Move (Rick Ankiel)	.05
S19	Groundball Pitcher (Greg Maddux)	.20
S20	Hung It (Danny Graves)	.05
S21	Pitch Around (Mark McGwire)	.40
S22	Pour It On (Al Leiter)	.05
S23	Clutch Performance (Barry Bonds)	.50
S24	Dot Racing (Mascots)	.05
S25	It's Crunch Time (Dennys Reyes)	.05
	Checklist 1 (001-066)	.05
	Checklist 2 (067-132)	.05
	Checklist 3 (133-S25)	.05
	Pitcher Usage Card	.05

2002 MLB Showdown Promos

NM/M
Complete Set (10):		20.00
Common Player:		2.00
(1)	Shawn Green	2.00
(2)	Ichiro	4.00
(3)	Derek Jeter	5.00
(4)	Andruw Jones	2.50
(5)	Trot Nixon	2.00
(6)	Andy Pettitte	2.00
(7)	Alex Rodriguez	4.00
(8)	Sammy Sosa	3.00
(9)	Kerry Wood	2.00
(10)	Jeff Zimmerman	2.00

2002 MLB Showdown

MLB Showdown's third season issue in 2002 has 300 "regular" player cards, 56 premium holofoil star cards and 50 strategy cards, including short-prints. The holo premium cards were inserted in booster packs at a rate of 1:3. While collectors compete with gamers for these cards in the market, relative values placed on the cards by each group of buyers may differ.

NM/M
Complete Set (406): 175.00
Common Player: .15
Starter Set: 6.00
Booster Pack: 1.50
Booster Box (36): 20.00

1	Garret Anderson	.15
2	David Eckstein	.15
3	Darin Erstad	.30
4	Troy Glaus/Foil	2.50
5	Adam Kennedy	.15

#	Player	
6	Ben Molina	.15
7	Ramon Ortiz	.15
8	Troy Percival	.15
9	Tim Salmon	.15
10	Scott Schoeneweis	.15
11	Scott Spiezio	.15
12	Jarrod Washburn	.15
13	Miguel Batista	.15
14	Jay Bell	.15
15	Craig Counsell	.15
16	David Dellucci	.15
17	Erubiel Durazo	.15
18	Steve Finley	.15
19	Luis Gonzalez/Foil	2.00
20	Mark Grace	.15
21	Randy Johnson/Foil	3.00
22	Byun-Hun Kim	.15
23	Albie Lopez	.15
24	Curt Schilling/Foil	2.50
25	Matt Williams	.15
26	Tony Womack	.15
27	Marcus Giles/Foil	2.00
28	Tom Glavine	.25
29	Andruw Jones	.45
30	Chipper Jones/Foil	4.00
31	Brian Jordan	.15
32	Steve Karsay	.15
33	Javy Lopez	.15
34	Greg Maddux/Foil	4.00
35	Jason Marquis	.15
36	Mike Remlinger	.15
37	Rey Sanchez	.15
38	B.J. Surhoff	.15
39	Brady Anderson	.15
40	Tony Batista/Foil	2.00
41	Mike Bordick	.15
42	Jeff Conine	.15
43	Buddy Groom	.15
44	Jerry Hairston Jr.	.15
45	Jason Johnson	.15
46	Melvin Mora	.15
47	Chris Richard	.15
48	B.J. Ryan	.15
49	Josh Towers	.15
50	Rolando Arrojo	.15
51	Rod Beck	.15
52	Dante Bichette	.15
53	David Cone	.15
54	Carl Everett	.15
55	Rich Garces	.15
56	Derek Lowe	.15
57	Trot Nixon	.15
58	Hideo Nomo	.35
59	Jose Offerman	.15
60	Troy O'Leary	.15
61	Manny Ramirez/Foil	3.00
62	Delino DeShields	.15
63	Kyle Farnsworth	.15
64	Jeff Fassero	.15
65	Ricky Gutierrez	.15
66	Todd Hundley	.15
67	Jon Lieber	.15
68	Fred McGriff	.15
69	Bill Mueller	.15
70	Corey Patterson	.15
71	Sammy Sosa/Foil	5.00
72	Julian Tavares	.15
73	Kerry Wood	.30
74	Eric Young	.15
75	Mark Buehrle/Foil	2.00
76	Royce Clayton	.15
77	Joe Crede	.15
78	Ray Durham	.15
79	Keith Foulke	.15
80	Bob Howry	.15
81	Mark L. Johnson	.15
82	Paul Konerko	.25
83	Carlos Lee	.25
84	Sean Lowe	.15
85	Magglio Ordonez	.15
86	Jose Valentin	.15
87	Aaron Boone	.15
88	Jim Brower	.15
89	Sean Casey	.15
90	Brady Clark	.15
91	Adam Dunn/Foil	2.00
92	Danny Graves	.15
93	Ken Griffey Jr./Foil	6.00
94	Pokey Reese	.15
95	Chris Reitsma	.15
96	Kelly Stinnett	.15
97	Dmitri Young	.15
98	Roberto Alomar/Foil	2.00
99	Danys Baez	.15
100	Russell Branyan	.15
101	Ellis Burks	.15
102	Bartolo Colon	.15
103	Marty Cordova	.15
104	Einar Diaz	.15
105	Juan Gonzalez	.30
106	Ricardo Rincon	.15
107	C.C. Sabathia/Foil	2.00
108	Paul Shuey	.15
109	Jim Thome/Foil	2.50
110	Omar Vizquel	.15
111	Bob Wickman	.15
112	Shawn Chacon	.15
113	Jeff Cirillo	.15
114	Mike Hampton	.15
115	Todd Helton/Foil	2.50
116	Greg Norton	.15
117	Ben Petrick	.15
118	Juan Pierre	.15
119	Terry Shumpert	.15
120	Larry Walker/Foil	2.00
121	Matt Anderson	.15
122	Roger Cedeno	.15
123	Tony Clark	.15

#	Player	
124	Deivi Cruz	.15
125	Damion Easley	.15
126	Shane Halter	.15
127	Bobby Higginson/Foil	2.00
128	Jose Macias	.15
129	Steve Sparks	.15
130	Jeff Weaver	.15
131	Antonio Alfonseca	.15
132	Josh Beckett/Foil	2.50
133	A.J. Burnett	.15
134	Luis Castillo	.15
135	Ryan Dempster	.15
136	Cliff Floyd	.15
137	Alex Gonzalez	.15
138	Braden Looper	.15
139	Mike Lowell	.15
140	Eric Owens	.15
141	Brad Penny	.15
142	Preston Wilson	.15
143	Moises Alou	.15
144	Brad Ausmus	.15
145	Jeff Bagwell/Foil	3.00
146	Lance Berkman/Foil	2.00
147	Craig Biggio	.15
148	Octavio Dotel	.15
149	Richard Hidalgo	.15
150	Julio Lugo	.15
151	Wade Miller	.15
152	Roy Oswalt/Foil	2.00
153	Shane Reynolds	.15
154	Jose Vizcaino	.15
155	Daryle Ward	.15
156	Carlos Beltran/Foil	2.50
157	Dee Brown	.15
158	Roberto Hernandez	.15
159	Mark Quinn	.15
160	Joe Randa	.15
161	Dan Reichert	.15
162	Jeff Suppan	.15
163	Mike Sweeney	.15
164	Kris Wilson	.15
165	Terry Adams	.15
166	Adrian Beltre	.15
167	Alex Cora	.15
168	Tom Goodwin	.15
169	Shawn Green	.25
170	Marquis Grissom	.15
171	Mark Grudzielanek	.15
172	Eric Karros	.15
173	Paul LoDuca/Foil	2.00
174	Chan Ho Park	.15
175	Luke Prokopec	.15
176	Gary Sheffield	.30
177	Ronnie Belliard	.15
178	Henry Blanco	.15
179	Jeromy Burnitz	.15
180	Mike DeJean	.15
181	Chad Fox	.15
182	Jose Hernandez	.15
183	Geoff Jenkins	.15
184	Mark Loretta	.15
185	Nick Neugebauer	.15
186	Richie Sexson	.15
187	Ben Sheets/Foil	2.00
188	Devon White	.15
189	Cristian Guzman/Foil	2.00
190	Torii Hunter	.15
191	Jacque Jones	.15
192	Corey Koskie	.15
193	Joe Mays	.15
194	Doug Mientkiewicz	.15
195	Eric Milton	.15
196	David Ortiz	.40
197	A.J. Pierzynski	.15
198	Brad Radke	.15
199	Luis Rivas	.15
200	Tony Armas Jr.	.15
201	Michael Barrett	.15
202	Peter Bergeron	.15
203	Orlando Cabrera	.15
204	Vladimir Guerrero/Foil	3.00
205	Graeme Lloyd	.15
206	Scott Strickland	.15
207	Fernando Tatis	.15
208	Mike Thurman	.15
209	Javier Vazquez	.15
210	Jose Vidro	.15
211	Brad Wilkerson	.15
212	Edgardo Alfonzo	.15
213	Kevin Appier	.15
214	Armando Benitez	.15
215	Alex Escobar	.15
216	John Franco	.15
217	Al Leiter	.15
218	Rey Ordonez	.15
219	Mike Piazza/Foil	6.00
220	Glendon Rusch	.15
221	Tsuyoshi Shinjo	.15
222	Steve Trachsel	.15
223	Todd Zeile	.15
224	Roger Clemens/Foil	5.00
225	Derek Jeter/Foil	9.00
226	Nick Johnson	.15
227	David Justice	.15
228	Tino Martinez	.15
229	Ramiro Mendoza	.15
230	Mike Mussina/Foil	2.50
231	Andy Pettitte	.15
232	Jorge Posada	.15
233	Mariano Rivera/Foil	2.00
234	Alfonso Soriano	.40
235	Mike Stanton	.15
236	Bernie Williams/Foil	2.00
237	Eric Chavez	.15
238	Johnny Damon	.30
239	Jermaine Dye	.15
240	Jason Giambi/Foil	2.50
241	Jeremy Giambi	.15

#	Player	
242	Ramon Hernandez	.15
243	Tim Hudson/Foil	2.00
244	Jason Isringhausen	.15
245	Terrence Long	.15
246	Mark Mulder/Foil	2.00
247	Olmedo Saenz	.15
248	Miguel Tejada	.25
249	Barry Zito	.25
250	Bobby Abreu	.15
251	Marlon Anderson	.15
252	Ricky Bottalico	.15
253	Pat Burrell	.35
254	Omar Daal	.15
255	Johnny Estrada	.15
256	Nelson Figueroa	.15
257	Travis Lee	.15
258	Robert Person	.15
259	Scott Rolen/Foil	2.50
260	Jimmy Rollins/Foil	2.00
261	Randy Wolf	.15
262	Brian Giles/Foil	2.00
263	Jason Kendall	.15
264	Josias Manzanillo	.15
265	Warren Morris	.15
266	Aramis Ramirez	.15
267	Todd Ritchie	.15
268	Craig Wilson	.15
269	Jack Wilson	.15
270	Kevin Young	.15
271	Ben Davis	.15
272	Wiki Gonzalez	.15
273	Rickey Henderson	.45
274	Junior Herndon	.15
275	Trevor Hoffman	.15
276	Damian Jackson	.15
277	D'Angelo Jimenez	.15
278	Mark Kotsay	.15
279	Phil Nevin/Foil	2.00
280	Bubba Trammell	.15
281	Rich Aurilia/Foil	2.00
282	Marvin Benard	.15
283	Barry Bonds/Foil	9.00
284	Shawn Estes	.15
285	Pedro Feliz	.15
286	Jeff Kent/Foil	2.00
287	Robb Nen	.15
288	Russ Ortiz	.15
289	Felix Rodriguez	.15
290	Kirk Rueter	.15
291	Benito Santiago	.15
292	J.T. Snow	.15
293	John Vander Wal	.15
294	Bret Boone/Foil	2.00
295	Mike Cameron	.15
296	Freddy Garcia/Foil	2.00
297	Carlos Guillen	.15
298	Edgar Martinez/Foil	2.00
299	Mark McLemore	.15
300	Jamie Moyer	.15
301	Jeff Nelson	.15
302	John Olerud	.15
303	Arthur Rhodes	.15
304	Kazuhiro Sasaki/Foil	2.00
305	Aaron Sele	.15
306	Ichiro/Foil	9.00
307	Dan Wilson	.15
308	J.D. Drew/Foil	2.50
309	Jim Edmonds/Foil	2.00
310	Dustin Hermanson	.15
311	Darryl Kile	.15
312	Steve Kline	.15
313	Mike Matheny	.15
314	Matt Morris	.15
315	Craig Paquette	.15
316	Placido Polanco	.15
317	Albert Pujols/Foil	8.00
318	Edgar Renteria	.15
319	Bud Smith	.15
320	Dave Veres	.15
321	Fernando Vina	.15
322	Brent Abernathy	.15
323	Steve Cox	.15
324	Ben Grieve	.15
325	Aubrey Huff	.15
326	Joe Kennedy/Foil	2.00
327	Tanyon Sturtze	.15
328	Jason Tyner	.15
329	Greg Vaughn	.15
330	Paul Wilson	.15
331	Esteban Yan	.15
332	Frank Catalanotto	.15
333	Chad Curtis	.15
334	Doug Davis	.15
335	Gabe Kapler	.15
336	Mike Lamb	.15
337	Darren Oliver	.15
338	Rafael Palmeiro	.40
339	Alex Rodriguez/Foil	8.00
340	Ivan Rodriguez/Foil	2.50
341	Mike Venafro	.15
342	Michael Young	.15
343	Jeff Zimmerman	.15
344	Chris Carpenter	.15
345	Jose Cruz	.15
346	Carlos Delgado/Foil	2.50
347	Kelvim Escobar	.15
348	Darrin Fletcher	.15
349	Brad Fullmer	.15
350	Alex S. Gonzalez	.15
351	Billy Koch	.15
352	Esteban Loaiza	.15
353	Raul Mondesi	.15
354	Paul Quantrill	.15
355	Shannon Stewart	.15
356	Vernon Wells	.15
S01	Bad Call (Bernie Williams)	.05

#	Card	
S02	Clutch Hitting (Mike Piazza)	.25
S03	Crowd the Plate (Troy Glaus)	.10
S04	Down the Middle/SP (Unidentified)	.50
S05	Drag Bunt/SP (Corey Patterson)	.50
S06	Ducks on the Pond (Unidentified)	.05
S07	Fuel on the Fire/SP (Barry Bonds)	1.50
S08	Last Chance (Craig Biggio)	.05
S09	Nuisance/SP (Unidentified)	.50
S10	Out of Gas (Unidentified)	.05
S11	Payoff Pitch/SP (Manny Ramirez)	.75
S12	Professional Baserunner/SP (Unidentified)	.50
S13	Protect the Runner/SP (Unidentified)	.50
S14	Pull the Ball (Rafael Palmeiro)	.10
S15	Rally Cap (Tom Goodwin)	.05
S16	Rough Outing (Unidentified)	.05
S17	Runner Not Held (Unidentified)	.05
S18	Running on Fumes/SP (Unidentified)	.05
S19	Ruptured Duck/SP (Unidentified)	.50
S20	Sit on the Fastball (Jose Cruz)	.05
S21	Stick a Fork in Him (Kevin Appier)	.05
S22	Sweet Swing (Barry Bonds)	.75
S23	Take What's Given/SP (Johnny Damon)	.60
S24	To the Warning Track (Unidentified)	.05
S25	Turn On It (Lance Berkman)	.05
S26	By the Book (Brad Radke)	.05
S27	Cut Off in the Gap/SP (Unidentified)	.50
S28	Full Windup (Andy Pettitte)	.05
S29	Great Start (Barry Zito)	.05
S30	Great Throw (Ichiro)	.30
S31	Highlight Reel/SP (Brent Abernathy)	.50
S32	Insult to Injury (Curt Schilling)	.05
S33	In the Groove (Mark Mulder)	.05
S34	Intimidation (Mariano Rivera)	.05
S35	Job Well Done/SP (Arthur Rhodes)	.50
S36	Just Over the Wall/SP (Unidentified)	.50
S37	Knock the Ball Down (Abraham Nunez)	.05
S38	Lefty Specialist (Billy Wagner)	.05
S39	Low and Away (Randy Johnson)	.10
S40	Nerves of Steel (Trevor Hoffman)	.05
S41	Pitchout/SP (Unidentified)	.50
S42	Pumped Up (Unidentified)	.05
S43	Put Out the Fire (Kazuhiro Sasaki)	.05
S44	Rally Killer/SP (Unidentified)	.50
S45	Sloppy Bunt/SP (Unidentified)	.50
S46	Submarine Pitch/SP (Byung-Hyun Kim)	.50
S47	Change in Strategy (Unidentified)	.05
S48	Grounder to Second/SP (Unidentified)	.50
S49	It's Crunch Time/SP (Unidentified)	.50
S50	Second Look (Sean Casey)	.05

All-Star Edition

This specially marked edition of the MLB Showdown interactive game cards was produced for distribution at the All-Star FanFest. Cards have an All-Star Game logo on front and most picture the players in All-Star uniforms.

		NM/M
Complete Game Set (50):		20.00
Common Player:		.50
1	Garret Anderson	.50
2	Tony Batista	.50
3	Mark Buehrle	.50
4	Johnny Damon	.65
5	Robert Fick	.50
6	Freddy Garcia	.50
7	Nomar Garciaparra	1.00
8	Jason Giambi	.65
9	Roy Halladay	.50
10	Shea Hillenbrand	.50
11	Torii Hunter	.50
12	Ichiro	1.50
13	Derek Jeter	2.00
14	Paul Konerko	.60
15	Derek Lowe	.50
16	Jorge Posada	.50
17	Manny Ramirez	.75
18	Mariano Rivera	.50
19	Alex Rodriguez	1.50
20	Kazuhiro Sasaki	.60
21	Alfonso Soriano	.60
22	Mike Sweeney	.50
23	Robin Ventura	.50
24	Omar Vizquel	.50
25	Barry Zito	.50
26	Lance Berkman	.50
27	Barry Bonds	2.00
28	Luis Castillo	.50
29	Adam Dunn	.50
30	Eric Gagne	.50
31	Luis Gonzalez	.50
32	Shawn Green	.50
33	Vladimir Guerrero	.75
34	Todd Helton	.60
35	Jose Hernandez	.50
36	Andruw Jones	.75
37	Mike Lowell	.50
38	Robb Nen	.50
39	Vicente Padilla	.50
40	Odalis Perez	.50
41	Mike Piazza	1.25
42	Scott Rolen	.50
43	Jimmy Rollins	.60
44	Benito Santiago	.50
45	Curt Schilling	.60
46	John Smoltz	.50
47	Sammy Sosa	1.25
48	Junior Spivey	.50
49	Jose Vidro	.50
50	Mike Williams	.50

League Prize Cards

		NM/M
Complete Set (15):		15.00
Common Player:		.25
(1)	Bobby Abreu	2.00
(2)	Miguel Batista	2.00
(3)	Armando Benitez	2.00
(4)	Mike Cameron	2.00
(5)	Magglio Ordonez	2.00
(6)	Rafael Palmeiro	3.00
(7)	Brad Penny	2.00
(8)	Aramis Ramirez	2.00
(9)	Miguel Tejada	2.00
(10)	Bad Call	.25
(11)	By the Book	.25
(12)	Change in Strategy	.25
(13)	Ducks on the Pond	.25
(14)	Lefty Specialist	.25
(15)	Rally Cap	.25

Pennant Run

Issued after the 2001 season opened, this is essentially an update to the interactive game MLB Showdown from veteran gamers Wizards of the Coast. Many players in the set changed teams during the off-season, or were promising rookies. The Pennant Run edition was issued in a Booster box of 36 nine-card (seven player, two strategy) packs. The set has 130 "regular" player cards, 25 premium holofoil star cards and 25 strategy cards. The holo premium cards were inserted in packs at a rate of 1:3. While collectors compete with gamers for these cards in the market, relative values placed on the cards by each group of buyers may differ.

		NM/M
Complete Set (150):		60.00
Common Player:		.15
Booster Pack (9):		1.50
Booster Box (36):		20.00
1	J.C. Romero	.15
2	Robb Nen	.15
3	Raul Mondesi	.15
4	Mike Piazza	.65
5	Scott Rolen	.30
6	Shigetoshi Hasegawa	.15
7	Shannon Stewart	.15
8	David Eckstein/Foil	2.00
9	Melvin Mora	.15
10	Jose Rijo	.15
11	Einar Diaz	.15
12	A.J. Burnett	.15
13	Mike Sweeney	.15
14	Jorge Posada/Foil	2.00
15	Mark Kotsay	.15
16	Doug Davis	.15
17	Steve Woodard	.15
18	Sun voo Kim	.15
19	Sean Casey	.15
20	Juan Acevedo	.15
21	Dustan Mohr	.15
22	Mariano Rivera	.15
23	Kip Wells	.15
24	Kenny Lofton/Foil	2.00
25	Steve Cox	.15
26	Josh Fogg/Foil	2.00
27	Ruben Sierra	.15
28	Sandy Alomar Jr.	.15
29	Vicente Padilla/Foil	.15
30	Carlos Beltran	.30
31	Mike Lowell	.15
32	Omar Vizquel	.15
33	Ricky Stone	.15
34	Geoff Jenkins	.15
35	Eric Karros	.15
36	Ryan Drese	.15
37	Adam Dunn	.25
38	Hank Blalock	.40
39	Marcus Giles	.15
40	Joe Randa	.15
41	Bob Wickman	.15
42	Roy Halladay	.15
43	Craig Counsell	.15
44	Derek Lowe	.15
45	Ray Durham	.15
46	Paul Shuey	.15
47	Cliff Floyd	.15
48	Shawn Green	.15
49	Torii Hunter/Foil	2.00
50	Edgardo Alfonzo	.15
51	Carlos Pena	.15
52	Sean Burroughs	.15
53	Placido Polanco	.15
54	Rafael Palmeiro	.45
55	Nate Cornejo	.15
56	Tim Salmon	.15
57	Craig Biggio	.15
58	Eric Hinske/Foil	2.00
59	Rickey Henderson	.45
60	Nick Johnson	.15
61	Rey Ordonez	.15
62	Jose Hernandez	.15
63	Antonio Alfonseca	.15
64	Alfonso Soriano/Foil	2.50
65	Eric Chavez	.25
66	B.J. Surhoff/Foil	2.00
67	Austin Kearns/Foil	2.00
68	Jacob Cruz	.15
69	Armando Benitez	.15
70	Derek Jeter	1.00
71	Ryan Jensen	.15
72	Kevin Mench	.15
73	Mike Remlinger	.15
74	Luis Castillo	.15
75	Kazuhisa Ishii/Foil	2.00
76	Bobby Abreu	.15
77	Dave Veres	.15
78	Tony Batista	.15
79	Rey Sanchez	.15
80	Jason Grimsley	.15
81	Al Leiter/Foil	2.00
82	Kerry Wood/Foil	2.00
83	Ellis Burks	.15
84	Corey Patterson	.15
85	Adrian Beltre	.15
86	Barry Zito	.25
87	Doug Mientkiewicz	.15
88	Jeffrey Hammonds	.15
89	Jeremy Giambi	.15
90	Tsuyoshi Shinjo	.15
91	Roger Clemens/Foil	3.50
92	John Franco	.15
93	Alex Rodriguez/Foil	5.00
94	Barry Bonds/Foil	15.00
95	Fred McGriff	.15
96	Chuck Finley	.15
97	Jose Rijo	.15

98 Jeff Bagwell/Foil 2.50
99 Ron Gant .15
100 Tom Glavine .25
101 Mike Mussina .25
102 Gary Sheffield .30
103 Barry Larkin .15
104 Jim Thome .45
105 Chipper Jones/Foil 3.00
106 Rickey Henderson .50
107 Randy Johnson/Foil 2.50
108 Mike Piazza/Foil 4.00
109 John Smoltz .15
110 Edgar Martinez .15
111 Larry Walker .15
112 Pedro Martinez/Foil 2.00
113 Sammy Sosa/Foil 3.50
114 Roberto Alomar/Foil 2.00
115 Curt Schilling/Foil 2.00
116 Chuck Knoblauch .15
117 Frank Thomas 6.00
118 Jeff Kent .15
119 Kenny Lofton .15
120 Ken Griffey Jr. 7.50
121 Trevor Hoffman/Foil 2.00
122 Mo Vaughn .15
123 Robin Ventura .15
124 Ellis Burks .15
125 Tim Raines .15
S1 Bad Call (Bernie Williams) .05
S2 Clutch Hitting (Mike Piazza) .10
S3 Crowd the Plate (Troy Glaus) .05
S4 Down the Middle (Unidentified) .05
S5 Ducks on the Pond (Unidentified) .05
S6 Free Steal (Alex Rodriguez) .10
S7 Overthrow (Unidentified) .05
S8 Payoff Pitch (Unidentified) .05
S9 Rally Cap (Tom Goodwin) .05
S10 Rattled (Nate Cornejo) .05
S11 Shell Shocked (Rick Ankiel) .05
S12 Shelled (Scott Sullivan) .05
S13 Comebacker (Dave Williams) .05
S14 Fast Worker (Unidentified) .05
S15 Full Windup (Andy Pettitte) .05
S16 Great Thrower (Ichiro Suzuki) .15
S17 Hung It (Unidentified) .05
S18 In the Groove (Mark Mulder) .05
S19 In the Zone (Curt Schilling) .05
S20 Insult to Injury (Trevor Hoffman) .05
S21 Nerves of Steel (Unidentified) .05
S22 Pitchout (Unidentified) .05
S23 Scuff the Ball (Brian Moehler) .05
S24 Bear Down (Brian Giles) .05
S25 Change in Strategy (Unidentified) .05

Stars Promos

These four cards were made available at MLB Showdown Spring Training events. They are similar in format to other cards in the series.

	NM/M
Complete Set (4):	6.00
Common Player:	2.00
1 Eric Chavez	2.00
2 Nick Johnson	2.00
3 Jason Marquis	2.00
4 Bud Smith	2.00

Trading Deadline

Issued after the 2002 season opened, this is an update to the interactive game MLB Showdown from Wizards of the Coast. Players in the set are generally those who changed teams during the off-season, or promising rookies. The Trading Deadline edition was issued in a Booster box of 36 nine-card (seven player, two strategy) packs. The set has 125 "regular" player cards, 25 premium holofoil star cards and 25 strategy cards. The holo premium cards were inserted in packs at a rate of 1:3. While collectors compete with gamers for these cards in the market, relative values placed on the cards by each group of buyers may differ.

	NM/M
Complete Set (175):	55.00
Common Player:	.15
Booster Pack (7+2):	1.50
Booster Box (36):	20.00

1 Jason Giambi/Foil 2.50
2 Chris Singleton .15
3 Ben Davis .15
4 Tsuyoshi Shinjo .15
5 Brian Jordan .15
6 Tony Clark .15
7 Moises Alou/Foil 2.00
8 Todd Walker .15
9 Ricky Gutierrez .15
10 Brad Fullmer .15
11 Jeromy Burnitz .15
12 Gary Sheffield/Foil 2.50
13 Marty Cordova/Foil 2.00
14 Todd Zeile .15
15 Alex Gonzalez .15
16 Kenny Lofton .15
17 Vinny Castilla .15
18 Craig Paquette .15
19 Michael Tucker .15
20 Cesar Izturis .15
21 Eric Young .15
22 Chuck Knoblauch .15
23 Roberto Alomar/Foil 2.00
24 David Bell .15
25 Johnny Damon .35
26 Roger Cedeno .15
27 Robin Ventura .15
28 David Justice/Foil 2.00
29 Brady Anderson .15
30 Pokey Reese .15
31 Reggie Sanders/Foil 2.00
32 Jeff Cirillo/Foil 2.00
33 Juan Encarnacion .15
34 Tino Martinez/Foil 2.00
35 Carl Everett/Foil 2.00
36 Danny Bautista .15
37 Rafael Furcal .15
38 Dmitri Young .15
39 Jay Gibbons .15
40 Brian Buchanan .15
41 David Segui .15
42 Barry Larkin/Foil 2.00
43 John Vander Wal .15
44 Brent Mayne .15
45 Neifi Perez .15
46 Lenny Harris .15
47 Jason LaRue .15
48 Travis Fryman .15
49 Juan Uribe .15
50 Shea Hillenbrand .15
51 Aaron Rowand .15
52 Jose Ortiz .15
53 Robert Fick .15
54 Doug Glanville/Foil 2.00
55 Charles Johnson/Foil 2.00
56 Derrek Lee .45
57 Carlos Febles .15
58 Luis Rivas .15
59 Lee Stevens .15
60 Mike Lieberthal .15
61 Ryan Klesko/Foil 2.00
62 Chris Gomez .15
63 Randy Winn .15
64 Rusty Greer .15
65 Felipe Lopez .15
66 Carlos Pena .15
67 Toby Hall .15
68 Milton Bradley .15
69 Matt Lawton .15
70 Gregg Zaun .15
71 Eric Hinske .15
72 Alex Ochoa .15
73 Rondell White .15
74 Armando Rios .15
75 Desi Relaford .15
76 Nomar Garciaparra/Foil 4.00
77 Frank Thomas/Foil 3.00
78 Mitch Meluskey .15
79 Morgan Ensberg .15
80 Mo Vaughn/Foil 2.00
81 Adrian Brown .15
82 Juan Gonzalez/Foil 2.50
83 Tom Wilson .15
84 Matt Stairs .15
85 Andres Galarraga .15
86 Sidney Ponson .15
87 Jesus Colome .15
88 Juan Cruz .15
89 Eddie Guardado .15
90 Jon Garland .15
91 Denny Neagle .15
92 Chad Durbin .15
93 Kevin Brown/Foil 2.00
94 Elmer Dessens .15
95 Eric Gagne .15
96 Jamey Wright .15
97 Pedro Martinez/Foil 3.00
98 Jason Bere .15
99 Ugueth Urbina .15
100 Carl Pavano .15
101 Kip Wells .15
102 Paul Abbott .15
103 Billy Wagner/Foil 2.00
104 Erik Hiljus .15
105 Brandon Duckworth .15
106 Ruben Quevedo .15
107 Jimmy Anderson .15
108 Bobby Jones .15
109 Livan Hernandez .15
110 Curtis Leskanic .15
111 Tom Gordon .15
112 Jeff Austin .15
113 Joel Pineiro .15
114 Chad Bradford .15
115 Woody Williams .15
116 Victor Zambrano/Foil 2.00
117 Jose Mesa .15
118 Roy Halladay .15
119 Steve Karsay .15
120 Hideo Nomo .50
121 Jeff Farnsworth .15
122 Dave Weathers .15
123 Sean Lowe .15
124 Mike Myers .15
125 Jason Schmidt .15
126 Mike Williams .15
127 Terry Adams .15
128 Chan Ho Park/Foil 2.00
129 Jeff D'Amico .15
130 Kevin Appier/Foil 2.00
131 Glendon Rusch .15
132 Jason Isringhausen .15
133 Todd Ritchie .15
134 Shawn Estes .15
135 Kevin Millwood .15
136 Aaron Sele .15
137 Rick Helling .15
138 Billy Koch .15
139 Paul Quantrill .15
140 Tim Spooneybarger .15
141 Jorge Julio .15
142 Carlos Hernandez .15
143 Rick Ankiel .15
144 Scott Erickson .15
145 Denny Hocking .15
146 Kazuhisa Ishii .15
147 Pedro Astacio .15
148 Satoru Komiyama .15
149 Kurt Ainsworth .15
150 John Smoltz/Foil 2.00
S1 Big Inning (Luis Gonzalez) .05
S2 Do or Die (Jeff Cirillo) .05
S3 Free Steal (Alex Rodriguez) .15
S4 Lean into It (Tsuyoshi Shinjo) .05
S5 Overthrow (Cubs, Mets) .05
S6 Pointers (Corey Patterson) .05
S7 Professional Hitter (David Justice) .05
S8 Rattled (Nate Cornejo) .05
S9 Shelled (Scott Sullivan) .05
S10 Shell Shocked (Rick Ankiel) .05
S11 Swing for the Fences (Unidentified) .05
S12 Tricky Hop (Marlon Anderson) .05
S13 Whiplash (Unidentified) .05
S14 Choke (Aaron Boone) .05
S15 Comebacker (Dave Williams) .05
S16 Fast Worker (Takahito Nomura) .05
S17 Focused (Paul Abbott) .05
S18 Hung It (Unidentified) .05
S19 In the Zone (Rick Helling) .05
S20 Scuff the Ball (Brian Moehler) .05
S21 Swiss Army Closer (Joel Piniero) .05
S22 What Were You Thinking??? (Unidentified) .05
S23 Whoops! (Alex Gonzalez) .05
S24 Bear Down (Brian Giles) .05
S25 Game of Inches (Rich Aurilia) .05

2003 MLB Showdown Promos

	NM/M
Complete Set (50):	35.00
Common Player:	1.00

P01 Aaron Guiel 1.00
P02 Abraham Nunez 1.00
P03 Al Levine 1.00
P04 Armando Rios 1.00
P05 Aubrey Huff 1.00
P06 Brandon Berger 1.00
P07 Carlos Baerga 1.00
P08 Chris Richard 1.00
P09 Corky Miller 1.00
P10 Damaso Marte 1.00
P11 Darren Holmes 1.00
P12 Denny Hocking 1.00
P13 Erubiel Durazo 1.00
P14 Giovanni Carrara 1.00
P15 Joe McEwing 1.00
P16 Kerry Robinson 1.00
P17 Lenny Harris 1.00
P18 Mark Derosa 1.00
P19 Mark Ellis 1.00
P20 Michael Tejera 1.00
P21 Olmedo Saenz 1.00
P22 Pedro Feliz 1.00
P23 Tomas Perez 1.00
P24 Wendell Magee 1.00
P25 Willis Roberts 1.00
P26 Benito Santiago 1.00
P27 Mike Sweeney 1.00
P28 Fernando Vina 1.00
P29 Troy Glaus 1.50
P30 Barry Larkin 1.00
P31 Manny Ramirez 1.50
P32 Steve Finley 1.00
P33 Shannon Stewart 1.00
P34 Frank Thomas 1.50
P35 Jamie Moyer 1.00
P36 Jon Lieber 1.00
P37 Mark Mulder 1.00
P38 Roger Clemens 2.50
P39 Jorge Posada 1.00
P40 Corey Koskie 1.00
P41 Shawn Green 1.00
P42 Phil Nevin 1.00
P43 Gary Sheffield 1.00
P44 Craig Biggio 1.00
P45 Alan Embree 1.00
P46 Jesse Orosco 1.00
P47 Mike Stanton 1.00
P48 Brandon Duckworth 1.00
P49 Troy Percival 1.00
P50 Robb Nen 1.00

2003 MLB Showdown

MLB Showdown's 2003 edition has has 300 "regular" player cards, 56 premium holofoil star cards and 50 strategy cards. The foil premium cards were inserted in booster packs at a rate of 1:3. While collectors compete with gamers for these cards in the market, relative values placed on the cards by each group of buyers may differ.

	NM/M
Complete Set (354):	150.00
Common Player:	.15
Two-Player Starter Set:	9.00
Draft Pack:	7.50
Booster Pack (7+2):	2.00
Booster Box (36):	40.00

1 Garret Anderson/Foil 2.00
2 David Eckstein/Foil 2.00
3 Darin Erstad .30
4 Brad Fullmer .15
5 Troy Glaus .35
6 Adam Kennedy .15
7 Bengie Molina .15
8 Ramon Ortiz .15
9 Orlando Palmeiro .15
10 Troy Percival .15
11 Tim Salmon .15
12 Jarrod Washburn/Foil 2.00
13 Miguel Batista .15
14 Danny Bautista .15
15 Craig Counsell .15
16 Steve Finley .15
17 Luis Gonzalez/Foil 2.00
18 Mark Grace .15
19 Randy Johnson/Foil 7.50
20 Byung-Hyun Kim .15
21 Quinton McCracken .15
22 Curt Schilling/Foil 4.50
23 Junior Spivey/Foil 2.00
24 Tony Womack .15
25 Vinny Castilla .15
26 Julio Franco .15
27 Rafael Furcal/Foil 2.00
28 Marcus Giles .15
29 Tom Glavine/Foil 3.50
30 Andruw Jones/Foil 7.50
31 Keith Lockhart .15
32 Javy Lopez .15
33 Greg Maddux/Foil 8.00
34 Kevin Millwood .15
35 Gary Sheffield .30
36 John Smoltz/Foil 2.00
37 Tony Batista .15
38 Mike Bordick .15
39 Jeff Conine .15
40 Marty Cordova .15
41 Jay Gibbons .15
42 Geronimo Gil .15
43 Jerry Hairston .15
44 Jorge Julio .15
45 Rodrigo Lopez .15
46 Gary Matthews Jr. .15
47 Melvin Mora .15
48 Sidney Ponson .15
49 Chris Singleton .15
50 John Burkett .15
51 Tony Clark .15
52 Johnny Damon .35
53 Alan Embree .15
54 Nomar Garciaparra/Foil 8.00
55 Shea Hillenbrand .15
56 Derek Lowe/Foil 2.00
57 Pedro Martinez/Foil 7.50
58 Trot Nixon .15
59 Manny Ramirez .35
60 Rey Sanchez .15
61 Ugueth Urbina .15
62 Jason Varitek .15
63 Moises Alou .15
64 Mark Bellhorn .15
65 Roosevelt Brown .15
66 Matt Clement .15
67 Joe Girardi .15
68 Alex Gonzalez .15
69 Todd Hundley .15
70 Jon Lieber .15
71 Fred McGriff .15
72 Bill Mueller .15
73 Corey Patterson .15
74 Mark Prior/Foil 6.00
75 Sammy Sosa/Foil 9.00
76 Mark Buehrle/Foil 2.00
77 Jon Garland .15
78 Tony Graffanino .15
79 Paul Konerko/Foil 3.50
80 Carlos Lee .25
81 Magglio Ordonez/Foil 2.00
82 Frank Thomas .35
83 Dan Wright .15
84 Aaron Boone .15
85 Sean Casey .15
86 Elmer Dessens .15
87 Adam Dunn .15
88 Danny Graves .15
89 Joey Hamilton .15
90 Jimmy Haynes .15
91 Austin Kearns/Foil 2.00
92 Barry Larkin .15
93 Jason LaRue .15
94 Reggie Taylor .15
95 Todd Walker .15
96 Danys Baez .15
97 Milton Bradley .15
98 Ellis Burks .15
99 Einar Diaz .15
100 Ricky Gutierrez .15
101 Matt Lawton .15
102 Chris Magruder .15
103 C.C. Sabathia .15
104 Lee Stevens .15
105 Jim Thome/Foil 3.50
106 Omar Vizquel .15
107 Bob Wickman .15
108 Gary Bennett .15
109 Mike Hampton .15
110 Todd Helton .35
111 Jose Jimenez .15
112 Denny Neagle .15
113 Jose Ortiz .15
114 Juan Pierre .15
115 Juan Uribe .15
116 Larry Walker/Foil 2.00
117 Todd Zeile .15
118 Juan Acevedo .15
119 Robert Fick .15
120 Bobby Higginson .15
121 Damian Jackson .15
122 Craig Paquette .15
123 Carlos Pena .15
124 Mark Redman .15
125 Randall Simon .15
126 Steve Sparks .15
127 Dmitri Young .15
128 A.J. Burnett .15
129 Luis Castillo .15
130 Juan Encarnacion .15
131 Alex Gonzalez .15
132 Charles Johnson .15
133 Derrek Lee .40
134 Mike Lowell .15
135 Vladimir Nunez .15
136 Eric Owens .15
137 Preston Wilson .15
138 Brad Ausmus .15
139 Lance Berkman/Foil 2.00
140 Craig Biggio .15
141 Geoff Blum .15
142 Richard Hidalgo .15
143 Julio Lugo .15
144 Orlando Merced .15
145 Billy Wagner .15
146 Carlos Beltran .40
147 Paul Byrd .15
148 Raul Ibanez .15
149 Chuck Knoblauch .15
150 Brent Mayne .15
151 Neifi Perez .15
152 Joe Randa .15
153 Mike Sweeney .15
154 Adrian Beltre .25
155 Eric Gagne/Foil 2.00
156 Shawn Green .25
157 Marquis Grissom .15
158 Mark Grudzielanek .15
159 Kazuhisa Ishii/Foil 2.00
160 Cesar Izturis .15
161 Brian Jordan .15
162 Eric Karros .15
163 Paul LoDuca/Foil 2.00
164 Hideo Nomo .30
165 Jesse Orosco .15
166 Odalis Perez .15
167 Mike DeJean .15
168 Jose Hernandez .15
169 Geoff Jenkins .15
170 Alex Sanchez .15
171 Richie Sexson .15
172 Ben Sheets .15
173 Eric Young .15
174 Eddie Guardado .15
175 Cristian Guzman .15
176 Torii Hunter/Foil 2.00
177 Jacque Jones .15
178 Corey Koskie .15
179 Doug Mientkiewicz .15
180 Eric Milton .15
181 A.J. Pierzynski .15
182 Michael Barrett .15
183 Orlando Cabrera .15
184 Cliff Floyd .15
185 Vladimir Guerrero/Foil 7.50
186 Tomo Ohka .15
187 Fernando Tatis .15
188 Javier Vazquez .15
189 Jose Vidro/Foil 2.00
190 Brad Wilkerson .15
191 Edgardo Alfonzo .15
192 Roberto Alomar .30
193 Pedro Astacio .15
194 Armando Benitez .15
195 Jeromy Burnitz .15
196 Al Leiter .15
197 Rey Ordonez .15
198 Timo Perez .15
199 Mike Piazza/Foil 10.00
200 Steve Trachsel .15
201 Mo Vaughn .15
202 Roger Clemens .50
203 Jason Giambi/Foil 4.50
204 Derek Jeter 1.00
205 Nick Johnson .15
206 Steve Karsay .15
207 Mike Mussina/Foil 2.50
208 Jorge Posada .15
209 Mariano Rivera/Foil 2.00
210 Alfonso Soriano/Foil 4.50
211 Mike Stanton .15
212 Robin Ventura .15
213 Jeff Weaver .15
214 Rondell White .15
215 Bernie Williams/Foil 2.00
216 Eric Chavez .15
217 Jermaine Dye .15
218 Scott Hatteberg .15
219 Tim Hudson .15
220 Billy Koch .15
221 Terrence Long .15
222 Mark Mulder .15
223 Miguel Tejada/Foil 2.00
224 Barry Zito/Foil 2.50
225 Bobby Abreu .15
226 Marlon Anderson .15
227 Pat Burrell .35
228 Brandon Duckworth .15
229 Jeremy Giambi .15
230 Doug Glanville .15
231 Mike Lieberthal .15
232 Jose Mesa .15
233 Vicente Padilla .15
234 Jimmy Rollins .25
235 Adrian Brown .15
236 Josh Fogg .15
237 Brian Giles .15
238 Jason Kendall .15
239 Pokey Reese .15
240 Kip Wells .15
241 Mike Williams/Foil 2.00
242 Craig Wilson .15
243 Jack Wilson .15
244 Kevin Young .15
245 Trevor Hoffman/Foil 2.00
246 Mark Kotsay .15
247 Ray Lankford .15
248 Brian Lawrence .15
249 Phil Nevin .15
250 Kurt Ainsworth .15
251 David Bell .15
252 Barry Bonds/Foil 65.00
253 Ryan Jensen .15
254 Jeff Kent/Foil 2.00
255 Robb Nen .15
256 Reggie Sanders .15
257 Benito Santiago .15
258 Tsuyoshi Shinjo .15
259 J.T. Snow .15
260 Bret Boone .15
261 Mike Cameron .15
262 Jeff Cirillo .15
263 Freddy Garcia .15
264 Carlos Guillen .15
265 Mark McLemore .15
266 Jamie Moyer .15
267 John Olerud .15
268 Joel Pineiro/Foil 2.00

269	Kazuhiro Sasaki/Foil	2.00
270	Ruben Sierra	.15
271	Dan Wilson	.15
272	Ichiro/Foil	12.50
273	J.D. Drew	.30
274	Jim Edmonds/Foil	2.00
275	Jason Isringhausen	.15
276	Matt Morris/Foil	.15
277	Albert Pujols/Foil	12.50
278	Edgar Renteria	.15
279	Scott Rolen/Foil	2.50
280	Jason Simontacchi	.15
281	Fernando Vina	.15
282	Brent Abernathy	.15
283	Steve Cox	.15
284	Chris Gomez	.15
285	Ben Grieve	.15
286	Joe Kennedy	.15
287	Tanyon Sturtze	.15
288	Paul Wilson	.15
289	Randy Winn/Foil	2.00
290	Juan Gonzalez	.30
291	Hideki Irabu	.15
292	Rafael Palmeiro/Foil	6.00
293	Herbert Perry	.15
294	Alex Rodriguez/Foil	10.00
295	Ivan Rodriguez	.40
296	Kenny Rogers	.15
297	Ismael Valdes	.15
298	Mike Young	.15
299	Dave Berg	.15
300	Carlos Delgado	.30
301	Kelvim Escobar	.15
302	Roy Halladay/Foil	2.50
303	Eric Hinske/Foil	2.00
304	Shannon Stewart	.15
S1	Bad Call (Sean Casey)	.10
S2	Clutch Hitting (Ellis Burks)	.10
S3	Down the Middle (Danny Graves)	.10
S4	Drag Bunt (Mark Mulder)	.10
S5	Ducks on the Pond (Unidentified)	.10
S6	Furl on the Fire (Benito Santiago)	.10
S7	Goodbye Baseball! (Ichiro Suzuki)	.40
S8	Great Addition (Ichiro Suzuki)	.40
S9	Last Chance (Ichiro Suzuki)	.40
S10	Nuisance (Barry Larkin)	.10
S11	Protect the Runner (Jacque Jones)	.10
S12	Pull the Ball (Jim Thome)	.10
S13	Rally Cap (Tino Martinez)	.10
S14	Rookie's Big Chance (Eric Hinske)	.10
S15	Runner Not Held (Unidentified)	.10
S16	See It Clearly (Vladimir Guerrero)	.25
S17	Serious Wheels (Deivi Cruz)	.10
S18	Sit on the Fastball (Carlos Guillen)	.10
S19	Take What's Given (David Eckstein)	.10
S20	Turn On It (Derek Jeter)	.50
S21	Valuable Asset (Barry Bonds)	.50
S22	Aces Up (Mark Mulder)	.10
S23	By the Book (Dan Reichert)	.10
S24	Change It Up (Denny Neagle)	.10
S25	Cut Off in the Gap (Juan Encarnacion)	.10
S26	Full Windup (Chris Reitsma)	.10
S27	Good Leather (Juan Encarnacion)	.10
S28	Great Start (Mark Mulder)	.10
S29	Great Throw (Danny Bautista)	.10
S30	Highlight Reel (Jose Hernandez)	.10
S31	In the Groove (Unidentified)	.10
S32	Insult to Injury (David Eckstein)	.10
S33	Job Well Done (Unidentified)	.10
S34	Just Over the Wall (David Justice)	.10
S35	Knock the Ball Down (Luis Gonzalez)	.10
S36	Lefty Specialist (Ricardo Rincon)	.10
S37	Nerves of Steel (Eric Gagne)	.10
S38	Paint the Corner (Carlos Febles)	.10
S39	Pumped Up (Raul Ibanez)	.10
S40	Put Out the Fire (Mark Wohlers)	.10
S41	Rally Killer (Abraham Nunez)	.10
S42	Submarine Pitch (Byung-Hyun Kim)	.10
S43	Throwing Heat (Dave Roberts)	.10
S44	What a Relief! (Unidentified)	.10
S45	Change in Strategy (Unidentified)	.10
S46	Feast of Famine (Giovanni Carrara)	.10
S47	Grounder to Second (Barry Larkin)	.10
S48	It's Crunch Time (Unidentified)	.10
S49	Just Over the Rail (Shane Halter)	.10
S50	Outmanaged (Art Howe, Ray Knight)	.10

Trading Deadline

		NM/M
Complete Set (170):		75.00
Common Player:		.15
Booster Pack (9):		1.50
Booster Box (36):		40.00
1	So Taguchi	.15
2	Ryan Drese	.15
3	Mike Hampton	.15
4	Sandy Alomar Jr.	.15
5	Steve Sparks	.15
6	Chan Ho Park	.15
7	Roger Cedeno	.15
8	Antonio Osuna	.15
9	Ryan Dempster	.15
10	Jesse Orosco	.15
11	Angel Berroa	.15
12	Sean Burroughs	.15
13	Matt Mantei	.15
14	Einar Diaz	.15
15	Ken Griffey Jr.	1.00
16	Rey Sanchez	.15
17	Antonio Alfonseca	.15
18	Carl Crawford	.15
19	Rey Ordonez	.15
20	Brandon Inge	.15
21	Hank Blalock	.40
22	Albie Lopez	.15
23	Aaron Sele	.15
24	Willie Bloomquist	.15
25	Shigetoshi Hasegawa	.15
26	Steve Kline	.15
27	Ramiro Mendoza	.15
28	Mike Stanton	.15
29	Carlos Zambrano	.15
30	Dean Palmer	.15
31	Mark Grudzielanek	.15
32	Matt Williams	.15
33	Michael Cuddyer	.15
34	Glendon Rusch	.15
35	Hee Seop Choi	.15
36	Mike Bordick	.15
37	Ray King	.15
38	Bill Mueller	.15
39	John McDonald	.15
40	Brent Butler	.15
41	Josh Bard	.15
42	Xavier Nady	.15
43	J.C. Romero	.15
44	Paul Shuey	.15
45	Eric Karros	.15
46	Runelvys Hernandez	.15
47	Braden Looper	.15
48	Dave Roberts	.15
49	Deivi Cruz	.15
50	Todd Hollandsworth	.15
51	Billy Koch	.15
52	Brandon Villafuerte	.15
53	Ricardo Rincon	.15
54	Joe Crede	.15
55	Juan Pierre	.15
56	Tsuyoshi Shinjo	.15
57	Ugueth Urbina	.15
58	Luis Vizcaino/Foil	2.00
59	Ben Weber	.15
60	Kerry Wood	.30
61	Tim Worrell	.15
62	Royce Clayton	.15
63	Chone Figgins	.15
64	Ken Huckaby	.15
65	Brian Anderson	.15
66	Aramis Ramirez	.15
67	Edgar Martinez	.15
68	Keith Foulke	.15
69	LaTroy Hawkins	.15
70	Mike Remlinger	.15
71	Lyle Overbay	.15
72	Buddy Groom	.15
73	Orlando Hudson	.15
74	Francisco Rodriguez/Foil	2.00
75	Craig Biggio	.15
76	Todd Zeile	.15
77	Vernon Wells	.15
78	Casey Fossum	.15
79	Wes Helms	.15
80	Robert Fick	.15
81	Scott Spiezio	.15
82	Ty Wigginton	.15
83	Elmer Dessens	.15
84	Arthur Rhodes	.15
85	Matt Stairs	.15
86	Miguel Olivo	.15
87	Tino Martinez	.15
88	Travis Hafner	.15
89	Octavio Dotel	.15
90	Jimmy Rollins	.30
91	Placido Polanco	.15
92	Kevin Brown	.15
93	John Patterson	.15
94	Andy Pettitte	.15
95	Bobby Kielty	.15
96	Jeremy Giambi	.15
97	Brandon Phillips	.15
98	Fred McGriff	.15
99	Damian Moss	.15
100	Russ Ortiz	.15
101	Mark Teixeira	.35
102	Tom Glavine/Foil	2.50
103	Chris Woodward	.15
104	Brad Radke	.15
105	Edgardo Alfonzo	.15
106	Jose Contreras/Foil	2.00
107	Josh Beckett	.30
108	Johan Santana	.30
109	Brandon Larson	.15
110	Randall Simon	.15
111	Randy Winn/Foil	2.00
112	Ray Durham	.15
113	Omar Daal/Foil	2.00
114	David Wells/Foil	2.00
115	Wade Miller	.15
116	Bartolo Colon/Foil	2.00
117	Ryan Klesko/Foil	2.00
118	Jeff Bagwell	.50
119	Roy Oswalt/Foil	2.00
120	Orlando Hernandez/Foil	2.00
121	Ivan Rodriguez/Foil	4.00
122	Tim Wakefield	.15
123	Josh Phelps	.15
124	Woody Williams	.15
125	Chipper Jones/Foil	5.00
126	Randy Wolf	.15
127	Kevin Millwood/Foil	2.00
128	Rocco Baldelli/Foil	4.00
129	Jeff Kent/Foil	2.00
130	Hideki Matsui/Foil	7.00
131	Jim Thome/Foil	3.00
132	Kazuhiro Sasaki	.15
133	Jason Jennings/Foil	2.00
134	Rafael Furcal	.15
135	Derek Jeter/Foil	7.50
136	Benito Santiago	.15
137	Jeff Bagwell	.50
138	Carlos Beltran	.25
139	Scott Rolen/Foil	2.50
140	Kerry Wood/Foil	2.50
141	Tim Salmon	.15
142	Ichiro/Foil	12.00
143	Mike Piazza/Foil	6.00
144	Albert Pujols	6.00
145	Nomar Garciaparra/Foil	5.00
S1	Clutch Hitting	.10
S2	Clutch Rookie	.10
S3	Great Addition	.10
S4	Headed Home	.10
S5	High Fives	.10
S6	Long Gone?	.10
S7	On the Move	.10
S8	Take What's Given	.10
S9	Who is This Guy?	.10
S10	Addition by Subtraction	.10
S11	De-nied!	.10
S12	Digging Deep	.10
S13	Lock it Down	.10
S14	New Arrival	.10
S15	Not So Fast	.10
S16	Pitch Around	.10
S17	Rookie Fireballer	.10
S18	Split-Finger Fastball	.10
S19	Still Learning	.10
S20	Three Up, Three Down	.10
S21	Triple Dip	.10
S22	Brainstorm	.10
S23	Outmanaged	.10
S24	Stealing Signals	.10
S25	Swing at Anything	.10

Pennant Run

Ten-player Super Season and Hall of Fame Heroes subsets were added to the 105 regular player cards and 25 strategy cards in this late-season card gaming issue. As with all MLB Showdown issues, baseball card collectors compete with game players for examples in the market, with each group often placing different values on specific cards.

		NM/M
Complete Set (150):		100.00
Common Player:		.15
Booster Pack (7+2):		2.00
Booster Box (36):		40.00
1	Josh Beckett	.40
2	Jeremy Bonderman	.15
3	Carlos Febles	.15
4	Tom Goodwin	.15
5	Luis Rivas	.15
6	Scott Sullivan	.15
7	John Thomson	.15
8	Lance Carter	.15
9	Terry Mulholland	.15
10	Jake Westbrook	.15
11	Chris George	.15
12	Jake Peavy	.15
13	Felix Rodriguez	.15
14	Marlon Byrd	.15
15	Toby Hall	.15
16	Rocky Biddle	.15
17	Brandon Lyon	.15
18	Roberto Hernandez	.15
19	Carlos Silva	.15
20	Chris Hammond	.15
21	Eric Munson	.15
22	David Dellucci	.15
23	R.A. Dickey	.15
24	Cliff Politte	.15
25	Russ Springer	.15
26	Kirk Reuter	.15
27	Vance Wilson	.15
28	Scott Williamson	.15
29	Ryan Franklin	.15
30	Juan Castro	.15
31	Craig Monroe	.15
32	Joe Beimel	.15
33	Scott Schoeneweis	.15
34	John Halama	.15
35	Eli Marrero	.15
36	Felipe Lopez	.15
37	Casey Blake	.15
38	Mike MacDougal	.15
39	Kris Benson	.15
40	Francisco Cordero	.15
41	Tom Gordon	.15
42	Neifi Perez	.15
43	Chad Bradford	.15
44	Miguel Cairo	.15
45	Mike Matheny	.15
46	Mike Timlin	.15
47	D.J. Carrasco	.15
48	Eddie Perez	.15
49	Gregg Zaun	.15
50	Ronnie Belliard	.15
51	Ricardo Rodriguez	.15
52	B.J. Ryan	.15
53	Michael Tucker	.15
54	Rheal Cormier	.15
55	Felix Heredia	.15
56	Alex Cora	.15
57	Travis Lee	.15
58	Ted Lilly	.15
59	Tom Wilson	.15
60	Jeff D'Amico	.15
61	Adam Eaton	.15
62	Travis Harper	.15
63	Mark Loretta	.15
64	Ricky Stone	.15
65	Wil Cordero	.15
66	Cliff Floyd	.15
67	Livan Hernandez	.15
68	Paul Quantrill	.15
69	Ben Davis	.15
70	Shawn Estes	.15
71	Chris Stynes	.15
72	Jay Payton	.15
73	Ramon Hernandez	.15
74	Jason Johnson	.15
75	John Vander Wal	.15
76	Shawn Chacon/Foil	2.00
77	D'Angelo Jiminez	.15
78	Desi Relaford	.15
79	Rich Aurilia	.15
80	Rod Barajas	.15
81	Jose Cruz/Foil	2.00
82	Kyle Lohse	.15
83	Rondell White	.15
84	Gil Meche/Foil	2.00
85	Jose Guillen	.15
86	Kenny Lofton	.15
87	Zach Day/Foil	2.00
88	Mark Redman	.15
89	Melvin Mora/Foil	2.00
90	Todd Walker	.15
91	Torii Hunter	.15
92	Frank Catalanotto	.15
93	Andres Galarraga	.15
94	Jason Schmidt	.15
95	Eric Byrnes	.15
96	Hank Blalock/Foil	4.00
97	Jacque Jones/Foil	2.00
98	Michael Young	.15
99	Carl Everett	.15
100	Preston Wilson	.15
101	Esteban Loaiza	.15
102	Raul Mondesi/Foil	2.00
103	Carlos Delgado/Foil	2.50
104	Gary Sheffield/Foil	2.50
105	Kevin Appier	.15
106	Jesse Orosco	.15
107	Pat Hentgen	.15
108	Matt Williams	.15
109	David Cone/Foil	2.00
110	Mark Grace/Foil	2.00
111	Carlos Baerga/Foil	.15
112	Greg Maddux/Foil	5.00
113	Kevin Brown/Foil	2.00
114	Ivan Rodriguez/Foil	3.00
115	John Olerud/Foil	2.00
116	Larry Doby	.75
117	Yogi Berra/Foil	7.50
118	Hoyt Wilhelm/Foil	6.00
119	Pee Wee Reese	.75
120	Brooks Robinson/Foil	7.50
121	Robin Yount/Foil	7.50
122	Reggie Jackson/Foil	7.50
123	Harmon Killebrew/Foil	7.50
124	Rod Carew/Foil	6.00
125	Nolan Ryan/Foil	12.00
S1	Change Sides	.10
S2	Emergency Bunt	.10
S3	Get Under It	.10
S4	In Motion	.10
S5	Out of Position	.10
S6	Passed Ball	.10
S7	Say the Magic Word	.10
S8	Suicide Squeeze	.10
S9	To the Warning Track	.10
S10	Block the Plate	.10
S11	Comebacker	.10
S12	Good Matchup	.10
S13	Ground Rule Double	.10
S14	In the Zone	.10
S15	Infield In	.10
S16	Pickoff Attempt	.10
S17	Play the Odds	.10
S18	Playing Shallow	.10
S19	Quick Pitch	.10
S20	Sinker	.10
S21	Up and In	.10
S22	Good Scouting	.10
S23	Looking Ahead	.10
S24	Old Tricks	.10
S25	Think Twice	.10

2004 MLB Showdown Promo

This promo card was inserted into each issue of the September 2004, Beckett Baseball Monthly.

		NM/M
P71	Alex Rodriguez	.50

2004 MLB Showdown

MLB Showdown's 2004 edition has 298 "regular" player cards, 50 premium ho-lofoil star cards and 50 strategy cards. The foil premium cards were inserted in booster packs at a rate of 1:3. While collectors compete with gamers for these cards in the market, relative values placed on the cards by each group of buyers may differ.

		NM/M
Complete Set (398):		200.00
Common Player:		.15
Two-Player Starter Set:		17.50
Draft Pack (60):		10.00
Booster Pack (8+3):		2.00
Booster Box:		75.00
1	Garret Anderson/Foil	2.00
2	David Eckstein	.15
3	Darin Erstad	.25
4	Troy Glaus	.15
5	Bengie Molina	.15
6	Ramon Ortiz	.15
7	Eric Owens	.15
8	Tim Salmon	.15
9	Scot Shields	.15
10	Scott Spezio	.15
11	Jarrod Washburn	.15
12	Rod Barajas	.15
13	Alex Cintron	.15
14	Elmer Dessens	.15
15	Steve Finley	.15
16	Luis Gonzalez/Foil	2.00
17	Mark Grace	.15
18	Shea Hillenbrand	.15
19	Matt Kata	.15
20	Quinton McCracken	.15
21	Curt Schilling/Foil	2.50
22	Vinny Castilla	.15
23	Robert Fick	.15
24	Rafael Furcal	.15
25	Marcus Giles	.15
26	Andruw Jones	.35
27	Chipper Jones/Foil	7.50
28	Ray King	.15
29	Javy Lopez/Foil	2.00
30	Greg Maddux	.50
31	Russ Ortiz	.15
32	Gary Sheffield/Foil	2.50
33	Tony Batista	.15
34	Deivi Cruz	.15
35	Travis Driskill	.15
36	Brook Fordyce	.15
37	Jay Gibbons	.15
38	Pat Hentgen	.15
39	Jorge Julio	.15
40	Rodrigo Lopez	.15
41	Luis Matos/Foil	2.00
42	Melvin Mora	.15
43	Brian Roberts	.15
44	B.J. Surhoff	.15
45	Johnny Damon	.30
46	Alan Embree	.15
47	Nomar Garciaparra/Foil	7.50
48	Byung-Hyun Kim	.15
49	Derek Lowe	.15
50	Pedro Martinez/Foil	6.00
51	Bill Mueller/Foil	2.00
52	Trot Nixon	.15
53	David Ortiz	.35
54	Manny Ramirez	.15
55	Jason Varitek	.15
56	Tim Wakefield	.15
57	Todd Walker	.15
58	Antonio Alfonseca	.15
59	Moises Alou	.15
60	Paul Bako	.15
61	Alex Gonzalez	.15
62	Tom Goodwin	.15
63	Mark Grudzielanek	.15
64	Eric Karros	.15
65	Kenny Lofton	.15
66	Ramon Martinez	.15
67	Corey Patterson	.15
68	Mark Prior/Foil	7.50
69	Aramis Ramirez	.15
70	Mike Remlinger	.15
71	Sammy Sosa/Foil	9.00
72	Kerry Wood/Foil	4.50
73	Carlos Zambrano	.15
74	Mark Buehrle	.15
75	Bartolo Colon	.15
76	Joe Crede	.15
77	Tom Gordon	.15
78	Paul Konerko	.25
79	Carlos Lee	.25
80	Damaso Marte	.15
81	Miguel Olivo	.15
82	Magglio Ordonez/Foil	2.00
83	Frank Thomas	.35
84	Jose Valentin	.15
85	Sean Casey	.15
86	Juan Castro	.15
87	Adam Dunn	.15
88	Denny Graves	.15
89	Ken Griffey Jr.	1.00
90	D'Angelo Jimenez	.15
91	Austin Kearns	.15
92	Barry Larkin	.15
93	Jason LaRue	.15
94	Chris Reitsma	.15
95	Reggie Taylor	.15
96	Paul Wilson	.15
97	Danys Baez	.15
98	Josh Bard	.15
99	Casey Blake	.15
100	Jason Boyd	.15
101	Milton Bradley/Foil	2.00
102	Ellis Burks	.15
103	Coco Crisp	.15
104	Jody Gerut	.15
105	Travis Hafner	.15
106	Matt Lawton	.15
107	John McDonald	.15
108	Terry Mulholland	.15
109	C.C. Sabathia	.15
110	Omar Vizquel	.15
111	Ronnie Belliard	.15
112	Shawn Chacon	.15
113	Todd Helton/Foil	3.00
114	Charles Johnson	.15
115	Darren Oliver	.15
116	Jay Payton	.15
117	Justin Speier	.15
118	Chris Stynes	.15
119	Larry Walker	.15
120	Preston Wilson	.15
121	Jeremy Bonderman	.15
122	Shane Halter	.15
123	Bobby Higginson	.15
124	Brandon Inge	.15
125	Wilfredo Ledezma	.15
126	Chris Mears	.15

#	Player	Price
127	Warren Morris	.15
128	Carlos Pena	.15
129	Ramon Santiago	.15
130	Andres Torres	.15
131	Dmitri Young	.15
132	Josh Beckett	.25
133	Miguel Cabrera	.15
134	Luis Castillo	.15
135	Juan Encarnacion	.15
136	Alex Gonzalez	.15
137	Derrek Lee	.35
138	Braden Looper	.15
139	Mike Lowell	.15
140	Juan Pierre	.15
141	Mark Redman	.15
142	Ivan Rodriguez/Foil	4.50
143	Tim Spooneybarger	.15
144	Dontrelle Willis/Foil	2.00
145	Brad Ausmus	.15
146	Jeff Bagwell	.35
147	Lance Berkman	.15
148	Craig Biggio	.15
149	Geoff Blum	.15
150	Octavio Dotel/Foil	2.00
151	Morgan Ensberg	.15
152	Adam Everett	.15
153	Richard Hidalgo/Foil	2.00
154	Jeff Kent	.15
155	Brad Lidge	.15
156	Roy Oswalt	.15
157	Jeriome Robertson	.15
158	Billy Wagner/Foil	2.00
159	Carlos Beltran/Foil	2.50
160	Angel Berroa	.15
161	Jason Grimsley	.15
162	Aaron Guiel	.15
163	Runelvys Hernandez	.15
164	Raul Ibanez	.15
165	Curtis Leskanic	.15
166	Jose Lima	.15
167	Mike MacDougal	.15
168	Brent Mayne	.15
169	Joe Randa	.15
170	Desi Relaford	.15
171	Mike Sweeney	.15
172	Michael Tucker	.15
173	Adrian Beltre	.25
174	Kevin Brown/Foil	2.00
175	Ron Coomer	.15
176	Alex Cora	.15
177	Eric Gagne/Foil	2.00
178	Shawn Green	.15
179	Cesar Izturis	.15
180	Brian Jordan	.15
181	Paul LoDuca	.15
182	Fred McGriff	.15
183	Hideo Nomo	.25
184	Paul Quantrill	.15
185	Dave Roberts	.15
186	Royce Clayton	.15
187	Keith Ginter	.15
188	Wes Helms	.15
189	Geoff Jenkins	.15
190	Brooks Kieschnick	.15
191	Eddie Perez	.15
192	Scott Podsednik/Foil	2.00
193	Richie Sexson/Foil	2.00
194	Ben Sheets	.15
195	John Vander Wal	.15
196	Chris Gomez	.15
197	Cristian Guzman	.15
198	LaTroy Hawkins	.15
199	Torii Hunter	.15
200	Jacque Jones	.15
201	Corey Koskie	.15
202	Doug Mientkiewicz	.15
203	A.J. Pierzynski	.15
204	Brad Radke	.15
205	Shannon Stewart/Foil	2.00
206	Michael Barrett	.15
207	Orlando Cabrera/Foil	2.00
208	Endy Chavez	.15
209	Zach Day	.15
210	Vladimir Guerrero/Foil	6.00
211	Fernando Tatis	.15
212	Javier Vazquez	.15
213	Jose Vidro	.15
214	Brad Wilkerson	.15
215	Tony Clark	.15
216	Cliff Floyd	.15
217	John Franco	.15
218	Joe McEwing	.15
219	Timo Perez	.15
220	Jason Phillips	.15
221	Mike Piazza	.65
222	Jose Reyes/Foil	3.00
223	Steve Traschel	.15
224	Dave Weathers	.15
225	Ty Wigginton	.15
226	Roger Clemens/Foil	9.00
227	Chris Hammond	.15
228	Derek Jeter/Foil	12.00
229	Nick Johnson	.15
230	Hideki Matsui	.35
231	Mike Mussina/Foil	4.50
232	Andy Pettitte	.15
233	Jorge Posada	.15
234	Mariano Rivera	.15
235	Alfonso Soriano	.25
236	Jeff Weaver	.15
237	Bernie Williams	.15
238	Enrique Wilson	.15
239	Chad Bradford	.15
240	Eric Byrnes	.15
241	Mark Ellis	.15
242	Keith Foulke/Foil	2.00
243	Scott Hatteberg	.15
244	Ramon Hernandez	.15

#	Player	Price
245	Tim Hudson/Foil	3.00
246	Terrence Long	.15
247	Mark Mulder/Foil	2.00
248	Ricardo Rincon	.15
249	Chris Singleton	.15
250	Miguel Tejada	.15
251	Barry Zito	.15
252	Bobby Abreu	.15
253	David Bell	.15
254	Pat Burrell	.30
255	Marlon Byrd	.15
256	Rheal Cormier	.15
257	Vicente Padilla	.15
258	Tomas Perez	.15
259	Placido Polanco	.15
260	Jimmy Rollins	.15
261	Carlos Silva	.15
262	Jim Thome/Foil	3.00
263	Randy Wolf/Foil	2.00
264	Kris Benson	.15
265	Jeff D'Amico	.15
266	Adam Hyzdu	.15
267	Jason Kendall/Foil	2.00
268	Brian Meadows	.15
269	Abraham Nunez	.15
270	Reggie Sanders	.15
271	Matt Stairs	.15
272	Jack Wilson	.15
273	Gary Bennett	.15
274	Sean Burroughs	.15
275	Adam Eaton	.15
276	Luther Hackman	.15
277	Ryan Klesko	.15
278	Brian Lawrence	.15
279	Mark Loretta	.15
280	Phil Nevin	.15
281	Ramon Vazquez	.15
282	Edgardo Alfonzo	.15
283	Rich Aurilia	.15
284	Jim Brower	.15
285	Jose Cruz	.15
286	Ray Durham	.15
287	Andres Galarraga	.15
288	Marquis Grissom	.15
289	Neifi Perez	.15
290	Felix Rodriguez	.15
291	Benito Santiago	.15
292	Jason Schmidt/Foil	2.00
293	J.T. Snow	.15
294	Tim Worrell	.15
295	Bret Boone/Foil	2.00
296	Mike Cameron	.15
297	Ryan Franklin	.15
298	Carlos Guillen	.15
299	Shigetoshi Hasegawa	.15
300	Edgar Martinez	.15
301	Mark McLemore	.15
302	Jamie Moyer/Foil	2.00
303	John Olerud	.15
304	Ichiro/Foil	10.00
305	Dan Wilson	.15
306	Randy Winn	.15
307	J.D. Drew	.30
308	Jeff Fassero	.15
309	Bo Hart	.15
310	Jason Isringhausen	.15
311	Tino Martinez	.15
312	Mike Matheny	.15
313	Orlando Palmeiro	.15
314	Albert Pujols/Foil	10.00
315	Edgar Renteria/Foil	2.00
316	Garrett Stephenson	.15
317	Woody Williams/Foil	2.00
318	Rocco Baldelli	.35
319	Lance Carter	.15
320	Carl Crawford	.15
321	Toby Hall	.15
322	Travis Harper	.15
323	Aubrey Huff/Foil	2.00
324	Travis Lee	.15
325	Julio Lugo	.15
326	Damian Rolls	.15
327	Jorge Sosa	.15
328	Hank Blalock	.35
329	Francisco Cordero	.15
330	Aaron Fultz	.15
331	Juan Gonzalez	.25
332	Rafael Palmeiro	.35
333	Alex Rodriguez/Foil	12.00
334	Mark Teixeira	.35
335	John Thomson	.15
336	Ismael Valdes	.15
337	Michael Young	.15
338	Frank Catalanotto	.15
339	Carlos Delgado	.15
340	Kelvim Escobar	.15
341	Roy Halliday/Foil	2.00
342	Eric Hinske	.15
343	Orlando Hudson	.15
344	Greg Myers	.15
345	Josh Phelps	.15
346	Cliff Politte	.15
347	Vernon Wells/Foil	2.00
348	Chris Woodward	.15
S1	Bad Call	.10
S2	Burned	.10
S3	Check Swing	.10
S4	Deep in the Gap	.10
S5	Drained	.10
S6	Ducks on the Pond	.10
S7	Great Addition	.10
S8	Hard Slide	.10
S9	Inside the Park Home Run	.10
S10	Options	.10
S11	Out of the Frying Pan	.10
S12	Play the Percentages	.10
S13	Pointers	.10

#	Card	Price
S14	Poor Positioning	.10
S15	Pull the Ball	.10
S16	Rough Outing	.10
S17	Slow Roller	.10
S18	Stick a Fork in Him	.10
S19	Sweet Swing	.10
S20	Take What's Given	.10
S21	Think Again	.10
S22	Turn on It	.10
S23	Aces Up	.10
S24	Caught Him Leaning	.10
S25	Caught the Corner	.10
S26	Choke	.10
S27	Cover Second	.10
S28	Dominating	.10
S29	Foul Ball	.10
S30	Good Leather	.10
S31	Hooking Foul	.10
S32	In the Zone	.10
S33	Infield In	.10
S34	Lined out of Play	.10
S35	Locate	.10
S36	Locked In	.10
S37	Nerves of Steel	.10
S38	Paint the Corner	.10
S39	Power Pitching	.10
S40	Short Fly	.10
S41	Sloppy Bunt	.10
S42	Split-Finger Fastball	.10
S43	Top-Level Strategy	.10
S44	Tough As Nails	.10
S45	Change in Strategy	.10
S46	Close Call	.10
S47	New Strategies	.10
S48	Second Look	.10
S49	Swing at Anything	.10
S50	Think Twice	.10

League Promos

#	Player	Price
Complete Set (50):		125.00
Common Player:		3.00
P01	Barry Larkin	3.00
P02	Barry Zito	3.00
P03	C.C. Sabathia	3.00
P04	Carlos Delgado	3.00
P05	Derek Lowe	3.00
P06	Fernando Tatis	3.00
P07	Frank Thomas	4.00
P08	Greg Maddux	6.00
P09	Hideki Matsui	6.00
P10	Jason Isringhausen	3.00
P11	Jeff Kent	3.00
P12	Jimmy Rollins	3.00
P13	Mike Piazza	4.50
P14	Josh Beckett	3.00
P15	Juan Pierre	3.00
P16	Ken Griffey Jr.	5.00
P17	Luis Castillo	3.00
P18	Mike Remlinger	3.00
P19	Moises Alou	3.00
P20	Paul LoDuca	3.00
P21	Preston Wilson	3.00
P22	Rafael Furcal	3.00
P23	Reggie Sanders	3.00
P24	Shigetoshi Hasegawa	3.00
P25	Tony Batista	3.00
P26	Brady Clark	3.00
P27	Carlos Febles	3.00
P28	Damian Jackson	3.00
P29	Darren Bragg	3.00
P30	David Segui	3.00
P31	Jesse Foppert	3.00
P32	Greg Norton	3.00
P33	Hee Seop Choi	3.00
P34	Henry Mateo	3.00
P35	Jake Peavy	3.00
P36	Jeff Reboulet	3.00
P37	Kevin Witt	3.00
P38	Livan Hernandez	3.00
P39	Mike Kinkade	3.00
P40	Paul Shuey	3.00
P41	Ricky Ledee	3.00
P42	Ricky Stone	3.00
P43	Roger Cedeno	3.00
P44	Ron Calloway	3.00
P45	Ryan Wagner	3.00
P46	Shawn Estes	3.00
P47	Todd Pratt	3.00
P48	Tom Wilson	3.00
P49	Tony Graffanino	3.00
P50	Troy O'Leary	3.00

Pennant Run

NM/M

Complete Set (125): 250.00
Common Player: .15

WILLIE McCOVEY

Booster Box (36): 75.00
Booster Pack (9+2): 2.00

#	Player	Price
001	Shawn Chacon	.15
002	Bobby Crosby	.15
003	Russ Ortiz	.15
004	Jason Simontacchi	.15
005	Oscar Villarreal	.15
006	Rocky Biddle	.15
007	Joe Borowski	.15
008	Shawn Estes	.15
009	Adam LaRoche	.15
010	Carl Everett	.15
011	Willie Harris	.15
012	Carlos Silva	.15
013	Aaron Rowand	.15
014	Francisco Cordero	.15
015	Ryan Freel	.15
016	Trevor Hoffman	.15
017	Edgar Renteria	.15
018	Mike Maroth	.15
019	Carlos Pena	.15
020	John Smoltz	.15
021	Carlos Guillen	.15
022	Buddy Groom	.15
023	Aaron Miles	.15
024	Jason Schmidt/Foil	2.00
025	Danny Kolb	.15
026	Marco Scutaro	.15
027	Gary Sheffield	.35
028	Eric Gagne/Foil	4.50
029	Kazuhisa Ishii	.15
030	B.J. Ryan	.15
031	Mark Mulder/Foil	2.00
032	Gerald Laird	.15
033	Joe Mauer	.40
034	Nate Robertson	.15
035	Hideki Matsui	1.50
036	Ray Lankford	.15
037	Jacob Peavy	.15
038	Esteban Loaiza	.15
039	Mike Stanton	.15
040	Kevin Gregg	.15
041	Steve Traschel	.15
042	Albert Pujols/Foil	12.00
043	Shingo Takatsu	.15
044	Ichiro/Foil	10.00
045	Milton Bradley	.15
046	Eric Chavez	.25
047	Paul LoDuca/Foil	2.00
048	Kip Wells	.15
049	Miguel Cabrera/Foil	3.00
050	Johnny Estrada	.15
051	Pedro Martinez/Foil	6.00
052	Jason Giambi	.40
053	Kenny Rogers	.15
054	Alex Rodriguez/Foil	12.00
055	Chone Figgins	.15
056	Ken Harvey	.15
057	Todd Helton	.35
058	Javy Lopez	.15
059	R.A. Dickey	.15
060	J.D. Drew	.15
061	Melvin Mora	.15
062	Denny Bautista	.15
063	Kerry Wood	.30
064	Randy Johnson	.40
065	Scott Rolen/Foil	4.50
066	Roger Clemens/Foil	7.50
067	Brad Penny	.15
068	Matt Clement	.15
069	Ron Belliard/Foil	2.00
070	Alfonso Soriano/Foil	4.00
071	Lew Ford	.15
072	Sean Casey/Foil	2.00
073	Troy Glaus	.30
074	Mike Lowell	.15
075	Juan Uribe	.15
076	Adrian Beltre	.15
077	Jack Wilson	.15
078	Craig Wilson	.15
079	Lyle Overbay/Foil	2.00
080	Jose Contreras	.15
081	Jason Jennings	.15
082	Matt Mantei	.15
083	Luis Vizcaino	.15
084	Luis Ayala	.15
085	Danny Patterson	.15
086	C.J. Nitkowski	.15
087	Larry Bigbie	.15
088	Mike Lieberthal	.15
089	Mike Timlin	.15
090	Robert Mackowiak	.15
091	Kevin Cash	.15
092	Danys Baez	.15
093	J.C. Romero	.15
094	Dan Miceli	.15
095	Armando Benitez	.15
096	Hank Blalock	.40

#	Player	Price
097	Vinny Castilla	.15
098	Danny Graves	.15
099	Derek Jeter	2.50
100	Jim Thome/Foil	4.50
101	Mark Loretta	.15
102	Victor Martinez	.30
103	Ken Griffey Jr.	2.00
104	Miguel Tejada	.25
105	Mike Piazza	1.50
106	Ivan Rodriguez	.35
107	Tom Glavine	.15
108	Carl Crawford/Foil	2.00
109	Jeff Kent	.15
110	Ben Sheets	.15
111	Sammy Sosa	1.25
112	Vladimir Guerrero	.40
113	Curt Schilling	.30
114	Carl Pavano	.15
115	Manny Ramirez/Foil	6.00
116	Billy Williams (Cooperstown)	6.00
117	Ralph Kiner (Cooperstown)	6.00
118	Whitey Ford/Foil (Cooperstown)	8.00
119	Jim Palmer/Foil (Cooperstown)	8.00
120	Willie McCovey/Foil (Cooperstown)	8.00
121	Phil Rizzuto (Cooperstown)	6.00
122	Orlando Cepeda (Cooperstown)	6.00
123	Eddie Mathews/Foil (Cooperstown)	8.00
124	Tom Seaver/Foil (Cooperstown)	8.00
125	Bob Feller/Foil (Cooperstown)	10.00
S1	Down the Middle	.10
S2	Grooved	.10
S3	Lost in the Sun	.10
S4	Protect the Runner	.10
S5	Running on Fumes	.10
S6	Serious Wheels	.10
S7	Smash Up the Middle	.10
S8	Superior Talent	.10
S9	Swat!	.10
S10	Timing	.10
S11	Calculated Risk	.10
S12	Chin Music	.10
S13	Great Start	.10
S14	High and Tight	.10
S15	Intimidation	.10
S16	On Your Toes	.10
S17	Rally Killer	.10
S18	Setup Man	.10
S19	Whiff!	.10
S20	Dugout General	.10
S21	Old Tricks	.10
S22	Out of Sync	.10
S23	Revelation	.10
S24	Stealing Signals	.10
S25	Superstar	.10

Trading Deadline

MIKE SCHMIDT

NM/M

Complete Set (150): 200.00
Common Player: .25
Booster Box (36): 75.00
Booster Pack (9+2): 2.00

#	Player	Price
1	Jose Mesa	.15
2	Pokey Reese	.15
3	Rey Sanchez	.15
4	Jeff Weaver	.15
5	Todd Zeile	.15
6	Carlos Rivera	.15
7	Orlando Palmeiro	.15
8	Roberto Alomar	.15
9	Doug Glanville	.15
10	Khalil Greene	.30
11	Victor Martinez	.25
12	Jeffrey Hammonds	.15
13	Bobby Kielty	.15
14	Brian Schneider	.15
15	Arthur Rhodes	.15
15	David Dellucci	.15
16	Eric Young Jr.	.15
17	Grant Balfour	.15
18	Javy Lopez	.15
19	Jeff Nelson	.15
20	Kelvim Escobar	.15
21	Braden Looper	.15
22	Tino Martinez	.15
23	Laynce Nix	.15
24	Horacio Ramirez	.15
25	Hideki Matsui	.50

#	Player	Price
27	Kevin Mench	.15
28	Scott Sullivan	.15
29	Michael Barrett	.15
30	Jose Cruz	.15
31	Robert Fick	.15
32	Brad Fullmer	.15
33	Eric Karros	.15
34	Mark Kotsay	.15
35	Fernando Vina	.15
36	Tim Worrell	.15
37	Mike Cameron	.15
38	Howie Clark	.15
39	Tom Gordon	.15
40	Adam Kennedy	.15
41	Rafael Palmeiro	.35
42	Reed Johnson	.15
43	Aquilino Lopez	.15
44	Julian Tavarez	.15
45	Ben Broussard	.15
46	Miguel Cabrera	.25
47	Raul Ibanez	.15
48	Randall Simon	.15
49	Ronnie Belliard	.15
50	Scott Spiezio	.15
51	Ellis Burks	.15
52	LaTroy Hawkins	.15
53	Pat Hentgen	.15
54	Eddie Guardado	.15
55	Todd Walker	.15
56	Ivan Rodriguez	.35
57	Raul Mondesi	.15
58	Jeromy Burnitz	.15
59	Rich Aurilia	.15
60	Keith Foulke	.15
61	Ramon Hernandez	.15
62	Kenny Lofton	.15
63	Rafael Soriano/Foil	2.00
64	Jody Gerut	.15
65	Randy Johnson	.40
66	John Burkett	.15
67	Brian Giles/Foil	2.00
68	Matt Morris	.15
69	Derrek Lee	.35
70	Miguel Tejada	.25
71	Ted Lilly	.15
72	David Wells	.15
73	Carl Everett	.15
74	A.J. Pierzynski	.15
75	Gary Sheffield	.25
76	Juan Gonzalez	.20
77	Brandon Webb	.15
78	Joel Pineiro	.15
79	Scott Rolen/Foil	3.00
80	Jim Edmonds/Foil	4.00
81	Curt Schilling/Foil	4.00
82	Kevin Brown/Foil	2.00
83	Chad Cordero	.15
84	Rich Harden	.15
85	Lyle Overbay	.15
86	Paul Quantrill	.15
87	Rondell White	.15
88	Joe Nathan	.15
89	Jose Valverde	.15
90	Francisco Rodriguez	.15
91	Billy Wagner	.15
92	Jason Giambi	.25
93	Jason Lane	.15
94	Frank Thomas	.45
95	Greg Maddux	.50
96	Andy Pettitte	.20
97	Jay Payton	.15
98	Roger Clemens	.50
99	Bartolo Colon/Foil	2.00
100	Vladimir Guerrero	.45
101	Kazuo Matsui/Foil	4.00
102	Javier Vazquez	.15
103	Esteban Loaiza/Foil	2.00
104	Alex Rodriguez/Foil	20.00
105	Javy Lopez/Foil (Super Season)	3.00
106	Tino Martinez (Super Season)	2.00
107	Vladimir Guerrero/Foil (Super Season)	7.50
108	Derek Jeter/Foil (Super Season)	12.00
109	Craig Biggio (Super Season)	3.00
110	Tom Glavine (Super Season)	2.00
111	Nomar Garciaparra/Foil (Super Season)	7.50
112	Mike Mussina/Foil (Super Season)	4.50
113	Todd Helton/Foil (Super Season)	4.50
114	Greg Maddux/Foil (Super Season)	6.00
115	Roger Clemens/Foil (Super Season)	7.50
116	Rollie Fingers/Foil (Cooperstown)	9.00
117	Luis Aparicio (Cooperstown)	9.00
118	Lou Brock (Cooperstown)	9.00
119	Joe Morgan/Foil (Cooperstown)	9.00
120	Richie Ashburn/Foil (Cooperstown)	9.00
121	Al Kaline/Foil (Cooperstown)	9.00
122	Bob Gibson/Foil (Cooperstown)	9.00
123	Willie Stargell (Cooperstown)	9.00
124	Warren Spahn/Foil (Cooperstown)	9.00

125	Mike Schmidt/Foil (Cooperstown)	75.00
S1	Dialed In	.10
S2	En Fuego!	.10
S3	Last Chance	.10
S4	On the Move	.10
S5	Opposite-Field Power	.10
S6	Out of Gas	.10
S7	Quick Thinking	.10
S8	Swing for the Fences	.10
S9	Wheelhouse	.10
S10	Beaned	.10
S11	Broken Bat	.10
S12	Caught Napping	.10
S13	Chopper	.10
S14	Dying Quail	.10
S15	Great Reactions	.10
S16	Insult to Injury	.10
S17	Lefty Shift	.10
S18	Pumped Up	.10
S19	Punched Out	.10
S20	Robbed!	.10
S21	Feast or Famine	.10
S22	Home-Field Advantage	.10
S23	Just Over the Rail	.10
S24	Late Call	.10
S25	Outmanaged	.10

2005 MLB Showdown League Promos

		NM/M
Complete Set (25):		30.00
Common Player:		3.00
P01	Scot Shields	3.00
P02	Mark Derosa	3.00
P03	Larry Bigbie	3.00
P04	Greg Maddux	6.00
P05	Aaron Rowand	3.50
P06	C.C. Sabathia	3.00
P07	Jason Johnson	3.50
P08	Tim Spooneybarger	3.00
P09	Jeff Kent	4.50
P10	Nate Field	3.00
P11	Jimmy Gobble	3.00
P12	Edwin Jackson	3.00
P13	Jose Lima	3.00
P14	Justin Morneau	3.00
P15	Juan Rincon	3.00
P16	Luis Rivas	3.00
P17	Joe McEwing	3.00
P18	Eric Valent	3.00
P19	Billy Wagner	5.00
P20	Jack Wilson	3.00
P21	Pedro Feliz	4.50
P22	Willie Bloomquist	4.00
P23	Geoff Blum	4.00
P24	Mark Teixeira	3.50
P25	Michael Young	3.50

2005 MLB Showdown

MLB Showdown's 2004 edition has 298 "regular" player cards, 50 premium holofoil star cards and 50 strategy cards. The foil premium cards were inserted in booster packs at a rate of 1:3. While collectors compete with gamers for these cards in the market, relative values placed on the cards by each group of buyers may differ.

	NM/M
Complete Set (398):	300.00

Common Player:		.15
Two-Player Starter:		12.50
Booster Box (36):		65.00
Booster Pack (8+3):		2.50
1	Garret Anderson	.15
2	David Eckstein	.15
3	Darin Erstad	.15
4	Chone Figgins	.15
5	Troy Glaus	.15
6	Kevin Gregg	.15
7	Vladimir Guerrero/Foil	5.00
8	Jose Guillen	.15
9	Adam Kennedy	.15
10	Troy Percival	.15
11	Francisco Rodriguez	.15
12	Tim Salmon	.15
13	Danny Bautista	.15
14	Alex Cintron	.15
15	Luis Gonzalez	.15
16	Scott Hairston	.15
17	Shea Hillenbrand	.15
18	Randy Johnson/Foil	7.50
19	Mike Koplove	.15
20	Chad Tracy	.15
21	Brandon Webb	.15
22	Antonio Alfonseca	.15
23	J.D. Drew/Foil	3.00
24	Johnny Estrada/Foil	3.00
25	Julio Franco	.15
26	Rafael Furcal	.15
27	Marcus Giles	.15
28	Andruw Jones	.35
29	Chipper Jones	.35
30	Eli Marrero	.15
31	John Smoltz	.15
32	John Thomson	.15
33	Jaret Wright	.15
34	Buddy Groom	.15
35	Jerry Hairston	.15
36	Jorge Julio	.15
37	Rodrigo Lopez	.15
38	Melvin Mora	.15
39	Rafael Palmeiro	.30
40	Brian Roberts	.25
41	B.J. Ryan	.15
42	B.J. Surhoff	.15
43	Miguel Tejada/Foil	3.00
44	Mark Bellhorn	.15
45	Johnny Damon	.30
46	Alan Embree	.15
47	Keith Foulke	.15
48	Gabe Kapler	.15
49	Pedro Martinez	.35
50	Bill Mueller	.15
51	David Ortiz/Foil	5.00
52	Manny Ramirez/Foil	5.00
53	Pokey Reese	.15
54	Curt Schilling	.30
55	Mike Timlin	.15
56	Jason Varitek	.15
57	Moises Alou	.15
58	Michael Barrett	.15
59	Matt Clement	.15
60	Kyle Farnsworth	.15
61	Nomar Garciaparra	.35
62	LaTroy Hawkins	.15
63	Todd Hollandsworth	.15
64	Derrek Lee	.30
65	Greg Maddux	.35
66	Kent Mercker	.15
67	Corey Patterson	.15
68	Aramis Ramirez	.15
69	Kerry Wood	.25
70	Mark Buehrle	.15
71	Joe Crede	.15
72	Freddy Garcia	.15
73	Paul Konerko/Foil	3.00
74	Carlos Lee	.25
75	Damaso Marte	.15
76	Aaron Rowand	.15
77	Shingo Takatsu	.15
78	Juan Uribe	.15
79	Jose Valentin	.15
80	Sean Casey	.15
81	Juan Castro	.15
82	Adam Dunn/Foil	3.00
83	Ryan Freel	.15
84	Aaron Harang	.15
85	D'Angelo Jimenez	.15
86	Barry Larkin	.15
87	Jason LaRue	.15
88	Wily Mo Pena	.15
89	Phil Norton	.15
90	John Riedling	.15
91	Paul Wilson	.15
92	Ronnie Belliard	.15
93	Casey Blake	.15
94	Ben Broussard	.15
95	Coco Crisp	.30
96	Travis Hafner/Foil	3.00
97	Matt Lawton	.15
98	Cliff Lee	.15
99	Victor Martinez	.15
100	David Riske	.15
101	C.C. Sabathia	.15
102	Omar Vizquel	.15
103	Jake Westbrook	.15
104	Jeromy Burnitz	.15
105	Vinny Castilla	.15
106	Shawn Chacon	.15
107	Royce Clayton	.15
108	Todd Helton/Foil	3.00
109	Jason Jennings	.15
110	Charles Johnson	.15
111	Aaron Miles	.15
112	Steve Reed	.15
113	Mark Sweeney	.15
114	Carlos Guillen	.15

115	Omar Infante	.15
116	Mike Maroth	.15
117	Craig Monroe	.15
118	Carlos Pena	.15
119	Nate Robertson	.15
120	Ivan Rodriguez/Foil	3.00
121	Alex Sanchez	.15
122	Ugueth Urbina	.15
123	Rondell White	.15
124	Esteban Yan	.15
125	Dmitri Young	.15
126	Josh Beckett	.25
127	Armando Benitez	.15
128	Miguel Cabrera/Foil	4.00
129	Luis Castillo	.15
130	Jeff Conine	.15
131	Alex Gonzalez	.15
132	Mike Lowell	.15
133	Carl Pavano	.15
134	Matt Perisho	.15
135	Juan Pierre	.15
136	Tim Spooneybarger	.15
137	Dontrelle Willis	.15
138	Brad Ausmus	.15
139	Jeff Bagwell	.30
140	Carlos Beltran/Foil	5.00
141	Lance Berkman/Foil	2.00
142	Craig Biggio	.15
143	Roger Clemens	.40
144	Morgan Ensberg	.15
145	Adam Everett	.15
146	Mike Gallo	.15
147	Jeff Kent	.15
148	Mike Lamb	.15
149	Brad Lidge	.15
150	Dan Miceli	.15
151	Wade Miller	.15
152	Roy Oswalt	.15
153	Angel Berroa	.15
154	Shawn Camp	.15
155	Tony Graffanino	.15
156	Ken Harvey	.15
157	Darrell May	.15
158	Joe Randa	.15
159	Desi Relaford	.15
160	Matt Stairs	.15
161	Scott Sullivan	.15
162	Mike Sweeney	.15
163	Wilson Alvarez	.15
164	Adrian Beltre/Foil	4.00
165	Milton Bradley	.15
166	Hee Seop Choi	.15
167	Eric Gagne	.15
168	Shawn Green	.15
169	Kazuhisa Ishii	.15
170	Cesar Izturis	.15
171	Jose Lima	.15
172	Jeff Weaver	.15
173	Jeff Bennett	.15
174	Javy Lopez	.15
175	Brady Clark	.15
176	Craig Counsell	.15
177	Doug Davis	.15
178	Bill Hall	.15
179	Geoff Jenkins	.15
180	Brooks Kieschnick	.15
181	Dan Kolb	.15
182	Chad Moeller	.15
183	Lyle Overbay	.15
184	Scott Podsednik	.15
185	Victor Santos	.15
186	Henry Blanco	.15
187	Michael Cuddyer	.15
188	Lew Ford	.15
189	Cristian Guzman	.15
190	Torii Hunter	.15
191	Jacque Jones	.15
192	Corey Koskie	.15
193	Scott Linebrink	.15
194	Brad Radke	.15
195	Johan Santana	20.00
196	Ben Sheets	.15
197	Wes Helms	.15
198	Ken Griffey Jr.	.45
199	Danny Graves	.15
200	Runelvys Hernandez	.15
201	Chris Woodward	.15
202	Paul LoDuca	.15
203	Scot Shields	.15
204	Todd Walker	.15
205	Gregg Zaun	.15
206	Ricky Bottalico	.15
207	Mike Cameron	.15
208	Cliff Floyd	.15
209	Tom Glavine	.15
210	Richard Hidalgo	.15
211	Al Leiter	.15
212	Braden Looper	.15
213	Kazuo Matsui	.15
214	Jason Phillips	.15
215	Mike Piazza/Foil	5.00
216	Jose Reyes	.15
217	David Wright	.50
218	Kevin Brown	.15
219	Miguel Cairo	.15
220	Tom Gordon	.15
221	Derek Jeter	.50
222	Kenny Lofton	.15
223	Jorge Posada/Foil	2.00
224	Paul Quantrill	.15
225	Mariano Rivera	.15
226	Alex Rodriguez/Foil	15.00
227	Gary Sheffield/Foil	3.00
228	Javier Vazquez	.15
229	Enrique Wilson	.15
230	Eric Byrnes	.15
231	Eric Chavez/Foil	3.00
232	Bobby Crosby	.15

233	Erubiel Durazo/Foil	2.00
234	Jermaine Dye	.15
235	Scott Hatteberg	.15
236	Bobby Kielty	.15
237	Mark Kotsay	.15
238	Mark Mulder	.15
239	Ricardo Rincon	.15
240	Marco Scutaro	.15
241	Barry Zito	.15
242	Bobby Abreu/Foil	2.00
243	David Bell	.15
244	Pat Burrell	.30
245	Rheal Cormier	.15
246	Mike Lieberthal	.15
247	Jason Michaels	.15
248	Eric Milton	.15
249	Vicente Padilla	.15
250	Placido Polanco	.15
251	Lance Carter	.15
252	Jimmy Rollins	.15
253	Jim Thome/Foil	4.00
254	Chase Utley	.15
255	Billy Wagner	.15
256	Randy Wolf	.15
257	Jason Bay	.15
258	Jose Castillo	.15
259	Jason Kendall/Foil	2.00
260	Robert Mackowiak	.15
261	Jose Mesa	.15
262	Oliver Perez	.15
263	Tike Redman	.15
264	Salomon Torres	.15
265	Daryle Ward	.15
266	Kip Wells	.15
267	Eric Munson	.15
268	Craig Wilson	.15
269	Jack Wilson	.15
270	Sean Burroughs	.15
271	Brian Giles	.15
272	Khalil Greene	.25
273	Ramon Hernandez	.15
274	Trevor Hoffman	.15
275	Ryan Klesko	.15
276	Mark Loretta/Foil	2.00
277	Phil Nevin	.15
278	Akinori Otsuka	.15
279	Jay Payton	.15
280	Jake Peavy	.15
281	David Wells	.15
282	Edgardo Alfonzo	.15
283	Jim Brower	.15
284	Deivi Cruz	.15
285	Ray Durham	.15
286	Scott Eyre	.15
287	Marquis Grissom	.15
288	Dustan Mohr	.15
289	A.J. Pierzynski	.15
290	Jason Schmidt	.15
291	J.T. Snow/Foil	2.00
292	Brett Tomko	.15
293	Michael Tucker	.15
294	Bret Boone	.15
295	Ryan Franklin	.15
296	Eddie Guardado	.15
297	Shigetoshi Hasegawa	.15
298	Raul Ibanez	.15
299	Edgar Martinez	.15
300	Joel Pineiro	.15
301	Scott Spezio	.15
302	Ichiro Suzuki/Foil	10.00
303	Dan Wilson	.15
304	Randy Winn	.15
305	Chris Carpenter	.15
306	Jim Edmonds/Foil	2.00
307	Jason Isringhausen	.15
308	Ray King	.15
309	Mike Matheny	.15
310	Matt Morris	.15
311	Albert Pujols/Foil	12.50
312	Edgar Renteria	.15
313	Scott Rolen/Foil	4.00
314	Reggie Sanders	.15
315	Julian Tavares	.15
316	Larry Walker	.15
317	Woody Williams	.15
318	Tony Womack	.15
319	Danys Baez	.15
320	Rocco Baldelli	.25
321	Dewan Brazleton	.15
322	Carl Crawford	.15
323	Jose Cruz	.15
324	Toby Hall	.15
325	Travis Harper	.15
326	Aubrey Huff	.15
327	Julio Lugo	.15
328	Tino Martinez	.15
329	Rod Barajas	.15
330	Hank Blalock/Foil	4.00
331	Francisco Cordero	.15
332	Chan Ho Park	.15
333	Kevin Mench	.15
334	Laynce Nix	.15
335	Kenny Rogers	.15
336	Brian Shouse	.15
337	Alfonso Soriano/Foil	4.00
338	Mark Teixeira	.25
339	Michael Young	.25
340	Miguel Batista	.15
341	Frank Catalanotto	.15
342	Carlos Delgado	.15
343	Roy Halliday	.15
344	Eric Hinske	.15
345	Orlando Hudson	.15
346	Reed Johnson	.15
347	Justin Speier	.15
348	Vernon Wells	.15
S01	Goodbye Baseball	.10
S02	Great Addition	.15

S03	Hacker	.10
S04	Helping Himself	.10
S05	High Pitch Count	.10
S06	Hit the Foul Pole	.10
S07	Make Contact	.10
S08	Pull the Ball	.10
S09	Rattled	.10
S10	Role Player	.10
S11	Scuffing	.10
S12	See it Clearly	.10
S13	Serious Wheels	.10
S14	Sprint to Second	.10
S15	Steal the Sign	.10
S16	Turn on It	.10
S17	Upper-Deck Shot	.10
S18	Valuable Asset	.10
S19	Weakest Link	.10
S20	Work the Count	.10
S21	6-4-3	.10
S22	Aces Up	.10
S23	Can of Corn	.10
S24	De-nied!	.10
S25	Fireballer	.10
S26	Full Windup	.10
S27	Good Leather	.10
S28	Hooking Foul	.10
S29	Knuckleball	.10
S30	Lined out of Play	.10
S31	Masterpiece	.10
S32	Out Pitch	.10
S33	Paint the Corner	.10
S34	Playing Shallow	.10
S35	Robbed!	.10
S36	Shut the Door	.10
S37	Up and In	.10
S38	Working the Edge	.10
S39	25th Man	.10
S40	Change in Strategy	.10
S41	Close Call	.10
S42	Fake to Third	.10
S43	Fan Interference	.10
S44	Field General	.10
S45	Intensity	.10
S46	Mind Games	.10
S47	New Strategies	.10
S48	Scouting Report	.10
S49	Second Look	.10
S50	Swing at Anything	.10

Trading Deadline

		NM/M
Complete Set (200):		90.00
Common Player:		.25
Booster Pack (8+3):		3.00
Booster Box (36):		65.00
1	Steve Finley	.25
2	Josh Phelps	.25
3	Magglio Ordonez	.25
4	Nick Johnson	.25
5	Carlos Lee/Foil	3.00
6	Quinton McCracken	.25
7	Shawn Estes	.25
8	J.J. Putz	.25
9	Mike DeJean	.25
10	Juan Gonzalez	.25
11	Eric Young	.25
12	Matt Mantei	.25
13	Neal Cotts	.25
14	Mike Sweeney	.25
15	Glendon Rusch	.25
16	Terrmel Sledge	.25
17	Ron Villone	.25
18	Troy Glaus	.25
19	Wilson Valdez	.25
20	B.J. Surhoff	.25
21	Kazuhisa Ishii	.25
22	Dustin Hermanson	.25
23	Al Leiter	.25
24	Octavio Dotel	.25
25	Henry Blanco	.25
26	J.D. Drew/Foil	5.00
27	Kevin Millwood	.25
28	Sandy Alomar Jr.	.25
29	John Riedling	.25
30	Rich Harden/Foil	3.00
31	Aaron Sele	.25
32	Carlos Beltran/Foil	4.00
33	Jose Lima	.25
34	Richard Hidalgo	.25
35	Placido Polanco	.25
36	Neifi Perez	.25
37	Wilson Alvarez	.25
38	So Taguchi	.25
39	Matt Perisho	.25
40	Roberto Hernandez	.25
41	Todd Walker	.25
42	Jason Kendall	.25
43	Brett Myers	.25
44	Carlos Silva	.25
45	Randy Johnson/Foil	8.00
46	Jeremy Bonderman	.25
47	Orlando Cabrera	.25
48	Carlos Delgado/Foil	4.00
49	A.J. Pierzynski	.25
50	Omar Vizquel	.25
51	Lenny Harris	.25
52	Chris Carpenter	.25
53	Miguel Cairo	.25
54	Sammy Sosa/Foil	8.00
55	Royce Clayton	.25
56	Cal Eldred	.25
57	Rich Aurilia	.25
58	Orlando Palmeiro	.25
59	Bengie Molina	.25
60	Ismael Valdez	.25
61	Nate Bump	.25
62	David Wells	.25

63	Jermaine Dye	.25
64	Carlos Zambrano	.25
65	David Newhan	.25
66	Russ Springer	.25
67	Elmer Dessens	.25
68	Kris Benson	.25
69	Al Reyes	.25
70	Tino Martinez	.25
71	Ruben Sierra	.25
72	Antonio Osuna	.25
73	Moises Alou	.25
74	Brad Wilkerson/Foil	3.00
75	Jason Christiansen	.25
76	Geoff Blum	.25
77	Dennys Reyes	.25
78	Craig Counsell	.25
79	Rey Sanchez	.25
80	Mark Hendrickson	.25
81	Doug Mirabelli	.25
82	Jeromy Burnitz	.25
83	Carl Pavano	.25
84	Richie Sexson	.25
85	Eric Milton	.25
86	Mark DeRosa	.25
87	Bob Wickman	.25
88	Hideo Nomo	.25
89	Tony Armas Jr.	.25
90	Desi Relaford	.25
91	Russ Ortiz	.25
92	Jose Vidro	.25
93	Jeff Kent/Foil	7.00
94	Esteban Yan	.25
95	Tim Hudson/Foil	3.00
96	Jay Payton	.25
97	Tony Womack	.25
98	Gregg Zaun	.25
99	David Weathers	.25
100	Scott Podsednik/Foil	3.00
101	Mark Mulder/Foil	3.00
102	Jose Guillen	.25
103	Grady Sizemore	.25
104	Paul Bako	.25
105	Jeff DaVanon	.25
106	Jeff Nelson	.25
107	Troy Percival	.25
108	Brian Lawrence	.25
109	Mike Redmond	.25
110	Odalis Perez	.25
111	John Franco	.25
112	Doug Brocail	.25
113	Einar Diaz	.25
114	Mark Grudzielanek	.25
115	Jason Marquis	.25
116	Jayson Werth	.25
117	John Mabry	.25
118	Alexis Rios	.25
119	Livan Hernandez	.25
120	Zack Greinke	.25
121	Chris Hammond	.25
122	Kent Mercker	.25
123	Ryan Drese	.25
124	Pedro Martinez/Foil	8.00
125	Alex Cora	.25
126	Kenny Lofton	.25
127	Adrian Beltre/Foil	3.00
128	David Eckstein	.25
129	Derek Lowe	.25
130	Jose Randa	.25
131	Jose Valentin	.25
132	David Bush	.25
133	Brian Schneider	.25
134	Matt Clement	.25
135	Paul Byrd	.25
136	Jose Vizcaino	.25
137	Todd Pratt	.25
138	Jose Offerman	.25
139	Dan Wilson	.25
140	Frank Francisco	.25
141	Woody Williams	.25
142	Juan Castro	.25
143	Jerry Hairston Jr.	.25
144	Jeff Suppan	.25
145	Steve Reed	.25
146	Jon Lieber	.25
147	Cristian Guzman	.25
148	Shawn Green/Foil	5.00
149	Damion Easley	.25
150	Bronson Arroyo	.25
151	Raul Mondesi	.25
152	Roger Cedeno	.25
153	Carlos Baerga	.25
154	Jose Hernandez	.25
155	Antonio Alfonseca	.25
156	Ricky Ledee	.25
157	Armando Benitez	.25
158	Esteban Loaiza	.25
159	Steve Kline	.25
160	Corey Koskie	.25
161	Vinny Castilla/Foil	3.00
162	Tony Clark	.25
163	Edgar Renteria/Foil	3.00
164	Brian Jordan	.25
165	David Dellucci	.25
166	Hoyt Wilhelm/Foil	5.00
167	Pee Wee Reese	.25
168	Larry Doby	.25
169	Yogi Berra/Foil	8.00
170	Robin Yount/Foil	5.00
171	Brooks Robinson/Foil	5.00
172	Reggie Jackson/Foil	8.00
173	Rod Carew/Foil	5.00
174	Harmon Killebrew/Foil	4.00
175	Nolan Ryan/Foil	15.00
S1	Free Steal	.25
S2	Get Under It	.25
S3	Go Yard!	.25
S4	Just Called Up	.25
S5	Leadoof Man	.25

		NM/M
S6	Lofted	.25
S7	Missed the Cutoff	.25
S8	Momentum Swing	.25
S9	Shaken	.25
S10	Shelled	.25
S11	Texas Leaguer	.25
S12	Caught Looking	.25
S13	Great Range	.25
S14	High Heat	.25
S15	Just Over the Wall	.25
S16	Slider	.25
S17	Stranded	.25
S18	Superior Athlete	.25
S19	Taking a Risk	.25
S20	Team Defense	.25
S21	Brainstorm	.25
S22	Change the Scorecard	.25
S23	Good Coaching	.25
S24	Preparation	.25
S25	Shell Game	.25

1992 Modell's Team Mets

Team Mets, the junior fan club, included in its 1992 membership benefits a nine-card perforated sheet sponsored by Modell's Sporting Goods. Cards feature color action photos highlighted by team-color stripes of blue and orange, with a white outer border. The 7-1/2" x 10-1/2" sheet can be separated into standard-size 2-1/2" x 3-1/2" cards. Team Mets and Modell's logos are featured on back, along with 1991 stats and highlights, career numbers and personal data. Cards are checklisted here according to the uniform numbers found on the front.

		NM/M
Complete Set (9):		5.00
Common Player:		.50
1	Vince Coleman	.50
9	Todd Hundley	.50
12	Willie Randolph	.50
16	Dwight Gooden	.50
17	David Cone	.50
18	Bret Saberhagen	.50
20	Howard Johnson	.50
25	Bobby Bonilla	.50
33	Eddie Murray	2.00

1991 MooTown Snackers

Produced by the Sargento Cheese Co., cards were available in Mootown Snacker packages or by sending in a special set redemption coupon from a package to obtain the entire set for $5.95 and three UPCs. Fronts feature action photos with uniform logos airbrushed off. Photos are bordered at top and bottom in red. Backs are in red, black and white and feature statistics and a facsimile autograph. Each player card is attached to a perforated panel on its right which has the checklist and a coupon to order the complete set. Cards without the offer coupon still attached are worth 50 percent of the values quoted here.

		NM/M
Complete Set (24):		10.00
Common Player:		.25
1	Jose Canseco	.50
2	Kirby Puckett	1.00
3	Barry Bonds	2.00
4	Ken Griffey Jr.	1.50
5	Ryne Sandberg	1.00
6	Tony Gwynn	1.00
7	Kal Daniels	.25
8	Ozzie Smith	1.00
9	Dave Justice	.25
10	Sandy Alomar, Jr.	.25
11	Wade Boggs	1.00
12	Ozzie Guillen	.25
13	Dave Magadan	.25
14	Cal Ripken, Jr.	2.00
15	Don Mattingly	1.25
16	Ruben Sierra	.75
17	Robin Yount	.75
18	Len Dykstra	.25
19	George Brett	1.25
20	Lance Parrish	.25
21	Chris Sabo	.25
22	Craig Biggio	.25
23	Kevin Mitchell	.25
24	Cecil Fielder	.25

1992 MooTown Snackers

The unusual venue of cheese snack packs was the source for these cards. Produced as two-piece panels, there is a player card attached by perforations to a card offering a complete set for $7 and proofs of purchase. The player cards have cheese-yellow borders at top and bottom with an action photo at center. Produced by Michael Schecter Assoc., the cards have had uniform and cap logos removed because they are licensed only by the Players Association and not by MLB. Backs are printed in black and yellow on white and include a facsimile autograph. Cards with the complete set offer no longer attached are worth 50 percent of the values shown here.

		NM/M
Complete Set (24):		7.50
Common Player:		.25
1	Albert Belle	.25
2	Jeff Bagwell	.75
3	Jose Rijo	.25
4	Roger Clemens	1.25
5	Kevin Maas	.25
6	Kirby Puckett	1.00
7	Ken Griffey Jr.	1.50
8	Will Clark	.25
9	Felix Jose	.25
10	Cecil Fielder	.25
11	Darryl Strawberry	.25
12	John Smiley	.25
13	Roberto Alomar	.35
14	Paul Molitor	.75
15	Andre Dawson	.25
16	Terry Mulholland	.25
17	Fred McGriff	.25
18	Dwight Gooden	.25
19	Rickey Henderson	.75
20	Nolan Ryan	2.00
21	George Brett	1.25
22	Tom Glavine	.40
23	Cal Ripken Jr.	2.00
24	Frank Thomas	.75

1983 Mother's Cookies Giants

After putting out Pacific Coast League sets in 1952-53, Mother's Cookies distributed this full-color set of 20 San Francisco Giants cards three decades later. The 2-1/2" x 3-1/2" cards were produced by hobbyist Barry Colla and include the Giants logo and player's name on the card fronts. Backs are numbered and contain biographical information, sponsor's logo and a space for the player's autograph. Fifteen cards were given to every fan at the Aug. 7, 1983, Giants game, with each fan also receiving a coupon good for five additional cards.

		NM/M
Complete Set (20):		6.00
Common Player:		.35
1	Frank Robinson	2.00
2	Jack Clark	.50
3	Chili Davis	.45
4	Johnnie LeMaster	.35
5	Greg Minton	.35
6	Bob Brenly	.35
7	Fred Breining	.35
8	Jeff Leonard	.35
9	Darrell Evans	.50
10	Tom O'Malley	.35
11	Duane Kuiper	.35
12	Mike Krukow	.35
13	Atlee Hammaker	.35
14	Gary Lavelle	.35
15	Bill Laskey	.35
16	Max Venable	.35
17	Joel Youngblood	.35
18	Dave Bergman	.35
19	Mike Vail	.35
20	Andy McGaffigan	.35

1984 Mother's Cookies A's

Following the success of their one set in 1983, Mother's Cookies issued five more team sets of cards in 1984. Cards measure 2-1/2" x 3-1/2" with rounded corners. Fronts feature unbordered color photos. Horizontal backs have biographical data, card number, Mother's Cookies logo and space for player autograph. There are 28 cards in the A's set, with 20 of the cards distributed during a stadium promotion. Fans also received a coupon redeemable for eight additional cards. Since those cards did not necessarily complete collectors' sets, Mother's Cookies cards became very popular among card traders. The A's set includes cards for the manager, coaches and a checklist.

		NM/M
Complete Set (28):		9.00
Common Player:		.25
1	Steve Boros	.25
2	Rickey Henderson	5.00
3	Joe Morgan	2.00
4	Dwayne Murphy	.25
5	Mike Davis	.25
6	Bruce Bochte	.25
7	Carney Lansford	.25
8	Steve McCatty	.25
9	Mike Heath	.25
10	Chris Codiroli	.25
11	Bill Almon	.25
12	Bill Caudill	.25
13	Donnie Hill	.25
14	Lary Sorensen	.25
15	Dave Kingman	.50
16	Garry Hancock	.25
17	Jeff Burroughs	.25
18	Tom Burgmeier	.25
19	Jim Essian	.25
20	Mike Warren	.25
21	Davey Lopes	.25
22	Ray Burris	.25
23	Tony Phillips	.25
24	Tim Conroy	.25
25	Jeff Bettendorf	.25
26	Keith Atherton	.25
27	A's Coaches (Clete Boyer, Bob Didier, Jackie Moore, Ron Schueler, Billy Williams)	.25
28	Oakland Coliseum/Checklist	.25

Astros

Mother's Cookies issued a full-color team set for the Astros in 1984. Cards measure 2-1/2" x 3-1/2" with rounded corners. Card fronts feature unbordered color photos. Horizontal backs have biographical data, card number, Mother's Cookies logo and space for player autograph. There are 28 cards in the Astros set, with 20 of the cards distributed during a stadium promotion. Fans also received a coupon redeemable for eight additional cards. Since those cards did not necessarily complete collectors' sets, Mother's Cookies cards became very popular among traders. The Astros set includes one card for the coaches and a checklist.

		NM/M
Complete Set (28):		7.00
Common Player:		.25
1	Nolan Ryan	6.00
2	Joe Niekro	.25
3	Alan Ashby	.25
4	Bill Doran	.25
5	Phil Garner	.25
6	Ray Knight	.25
7	Dickie Thon	.25
8	Jose Cruz	.25
9	Jerry Mumphrey	.25
10	Terry Puhl	.25
11	Enos Cabell	.25
12	Harry Spilman	.25
13	Dave Smith	.25
14	Mike Scott	.25
15	Bob Lillis	.25
16	Bob Knepper	.25
17	Frank DiPino	.25
18	Tom Wieghaus	.25
19	Denny Walling	.25
20	Tony Scott	.25
21	Alan Bannister	.25
22	Bill Dawley	.25
23	Vern Ruhle	.25
24	Mike LaCoss	.25
25	Mike Madden	.25
26	Craig Reynolds	.25
27	Astros Coaches (Cot Deal, Don Leppert, Denis Menke, Les Moss, Jerry Walker)	.25
28	Astros Logo/Checklist	.25

Giants

Mother's Cookies issued a second annual full-color card set for the S.F. Giants in 1984. Cards measure 2-1/2" x 3-1/2" with rounded corners. Fronts feature drawings of former Giant All-Star team selections. Horizontal backs have brief biographical information, card number and Mother's Cookies logo and autograph space. There are 28 cards in the Giants set, with 20 of the cards distributed during a stadium promotion. Fans also received a coupon redeemable for eight additional cards. Since those cards did not necessarily complete collectors' sets, Mother's Cookies cards became very popular among traders. The set includes one card each for the manager, coaches and a checklist.

		NM/M
Complete Set (28):		7.50
Common Player:		.15
1	Willie Mays	4.50
2	Willie McCovey	1.00
3	Juan Marichal	.50
4	Gaylord Perry	.50
5	Tom Haller	.15
6	Jim Davenport	.15
7	Jack Clark	.25
8	Greg Minton	.15
9	Atlee Hammaker	.15
10	Gary Lavelle	.15
11	Orlando Cepeda	.50
12	Bobby Bonds	.25
13	John Antonelli	.15
14	Bob Schmidt (Photo actually Wes Westrum.)	.15
15	Sam Jones	.15
16	Mike McCormick	.15
17	Ed Bailey	.15
18	Stu Miller	.15
19	Felipe Alou	.25
20	Jim Hart	.15
21	Dick Dietz	.15
22	Chris Speier	.15
23	Bobby Murcer	.25
24	John Montefusco	.15
25	Vida Blue	.15
26	Ed Whitson	.15
27	Darrell Evans	.25
28	All-Star Game Logo/Checklist	.15

Mariners

Mother's Cookies issued a full-color set for the Mariners in 1984. Cards measure 2-1/2" x 3-1/2" with rounded corners. Fronts feature unbordered color photos. Horizontal backs have brief biographical data, card number, Mother's Cookies logo and space for player autograph. There are 28 cards in the set with 20 of the cards distributed during a stadium promotion. Fans also received a coupon redeemable for eight additional cards. Since those cards did not necessarily complete collectors' sets, Mother's Cookies cards became very popular among traders. The set includes one card each for the manager, coaches and a checklist.

		NM/M
Complete Set (28):		6.00
Common Player:		.25
1	Del Crandall	.25
2	Barry Bonnell	.25
3	Dave Henderson	.25
4	Bob Kearney	.25
5	Mike Moore	.25
6	Spike Owen	.25
7	Gorman Thomas	.25
8	Ed Vande Berg	.25
9	Matt Young	.25
10	Larry Milbourne	.25
11	Dave Beard	.25
12	Jim Beattie	.25
13	Mark Langston	.25
14	Orlando Mercado	.25
15	Jack Perconte	.25
16	Pat Putnam	.25
17	Paul Mirabella	.25
18	Domingo Ramos	.25
19	Al Cowens	.25
20	Mike Stanton	.25
21	Steve Henderson	.25
22	Bob Stoddard	.25
23	Alvin Davis	.25
24	Phil Bradley	.25
25	Roy Thomas	.25
26	Darnell Coles	.25
27	Mariners Coaches (Chuck Cottier, Frank Funk, Ben Hines, Phil Roof, Rick Sweet)	.25
28	Seattle Kingdome/Checklist	.25

Padres

Mother's Cookies issued a full-color set for the Padres in 1984. Cards measure 2-1/2" x 3-1/2", with rounded corners. Fronts feature unbordered color photos. Horizontal backs have brief biographical data, card number, sponsor's logo and space for player autograph. There are 28 cards in the set, with 20 of the cards distributed during a stadium promotion. Fans also received a coupon redeemable for eight additional cards. Since those cards did not necessarily complete collectors' sets, Mother's Cookies cards became very popular among traders. The Padres set includes one card each for the manager, coaches and a checklist.

		NM/M
Complete Set (28):		9.00
Common Player:		.25
1	Dick Williams	.25
2	Rich Gossage	.50
3	Tim Lollar	.25
4	Eric Show	.25
5	Terry Kennedy	.25
6	Kurt Bevacqua	.25
7	Steve Garvey	1.50
8	Garry Templeton	.25
9	Tony Gwynn	5.00
10	Alan Wiggins	.25
11	Dave Dravecky	.25
12	Tim Flannery	.25
13	Kevin McReynolds	.25
14	Bobby Brown	.25

15 Ed Whitson .25
16 Doug Gwosdz .25
17 Luis DeLeon .25
18 Andy Hawkins .25
19 Craig Lefferts .25
20 Carmelo Martinez .25
21 Sid Monge .25
22 Graig Nettles .25
23 Mario Ramirez .25
24 Luis Salazar .25
25 Champ Summers .25
26 Mark Thurmond .25
27 Padres Coaches (Harry Dunlop, Deacon Jones, Jack Krol, Norm Sherry, Ozzie Virgil) .25
28 Jack Murphy Stadium/Checklist .25

1985 Mother's Cookies A's

Mother's Cookies again issued five full-color sets for Major League teams in 1985. Cards measure 2-1/2" x 3-1/2" with rounded corners. Fronts feature unbordered color photos. Horizontal backs have brief biographical data, card number, Mother's Cookies logo and space for player autograph. The set was distributed in its entirety during a stadium promotion.

NM/M
Complete Set (28): 7.00
Common Player: .25
1 Jackie Moore .25
2 Dave Kingman .40
3 Don Sutton 1.25
4 Mike Heath .25
5 Alfredo Griffin .25
6 Dwayne Murphy .25
7 Mike Davis .25
8 Carney Lansford .25
9 Chris Codiroli .25
10 Bruce Bochte .25
11 Mickey Tettleton .25
12 Donnie Hill .25
13 Rob Picciolo .25
14 Dave Collins .25
15 Dusty Baker .50
16 Tim Conroy .25
17 Keith Atherton .25
18 Jay Howell .25
19 Mike Warren .25
20 Steve McCatty .25
21 Bill Krueger .25
22 Curt Young .25
23 Dan Meyer .25
24 Mike Gallego .25
25 Jeff Kaiser .25
26 Steve Henderson .25
27 A's Coaches (Clete Boyer, Bob Didier, Dave McKay, Wes Stock, Billy Williams) .25
28 Oakland Coliseum/Checklist .25

Astros

Mother's Cookies issued a second annual full-color set for the Astros in 1985. Cards measure 2-1/2" x 3-1/2" with rounded corners. Fronts feature unbordered color photos. Horizontal backs have biographical information, card number, Mother's Cookies logo and space for player autograph. The set was distributed in its entirety during a stadium promotion.

NM/M
Complete Set (28): 8.00
Common Player: .25
1 Bob Lillis .25
2 Nolan Ryan 7.50
3 Phil Garner .25
4 Jose Cruz .25
5 Denny Walling .25
6 Joe Niekro .30
7 Terry Puhl .25
8 Bill Doran .25
9 Dickie Thon .25
10 Enos Cabell .25
11 Frank Dipino (DiPino) .25
12 Julio Solano .25
13 Alan Ashby .25
14 Craig Reynolds .25
15 Jerry Mumphrey .25
16 Bill Dawley .25
17 Mark Bailey .25
18 Mike Scott .25
19 Harry Spilman .25
20 Bob Knepper .25
21 Dave Smith .25
22 Kevin Bass .25
23 Tim Tolman .25
24 Jeff Calhoun .25
25 Jim Pankovits .25
26 Ron Mathis .25
27 Astros Coaches (Cot Deal, Matt Galante, Don Leppert, Denis Menke, Jerry Walker) .25
28 Astros Logo/Checklist .25

Giants

Mother's Cookies issued a third annual full-color set for the Giants in 1985. Cards measure 2-1/2" x 3-1/2" with rounded corners. Fronts feature unbordered color photos. Horizontal backs have brief biographical information, card number, Mother's Cookies logo and space for player autograph. The set was distributed in its entirety during a stadium promotion.

NM/M
Complete Set (28): 6.00
Common Player: .25
1 Jim Davenport .25
2 Chili Davis .25
3 Dan Gladden .25
4 Jeff Leonard .25
5 Manny Trillo .25
6 Atlee Hammaker .25
7 Bob Brenly .25
8 Greg Minton .25
9 Bill Laskey .25
10 Vida Blue .30
11 Mike Krukow .25
12 Frank Williams .25
13 Jose Uribe .25
14 Johnnie LeMaster .25
15 Scot Thompson .25
16 Dave LaPoint .25
17 David Green .25
18 Chris Brown .25
19 Joel Youngblood .25
20 Mark Davis .25
21 Jim Gott .25
22 Doug Gwosdz .25
23 Scott Garrelts .25
24 Gary Rajsich .25
25 Rob Deer .25
26 Brad Wellman .25
27 Coaches (Rocky Bridges, Chuck Hiller, Tom McCraw, Bob Miller, Jack Mull) .25
28 Candlestick Park/Checklist .25

Mariners

Mother's Cookies issued a second annual full-color set for the Mariners in 1985. Cards measure 2-1/2" x 3-1/2" with rounded corners. Fronts feature unbordered color photos. Horizontal backs have biographical information, card number, Mother's Cookies logo and space for player autograph. The set was distributed in its entirety during a stadium promotion.

NM/M
Complete Set (28): 6.00
Common Player: .25
1 Chuck Cottier .25
2 Alvin Davis .25
3 Mark Langston .25
4 Dave Henderson .25
5 Ed Vande Berg .25
6 Al Cowens .25
7 Spike Owen .25
8 Mike Moore .25
9 Gorman Thomas .25
10 Barry Bonnell .25
11 Jack Perconte .25
12 Domingo Ramos .25
13 Bob Kearney .25
14 Matt Young .25
15 Jim Beattie .25
16 Mike Stanton .25
17 David Valle .25
18 Ken Phelps .25
19 Salome Barojas .25
20 Jim Presley .25
21 Phil Bradley .25
22 Dave Geisel .25
23 Harold Reynolds .50
24 Edwin Nunez .25
25 Mike Morgan .25
26 Ivan Calderon .25
27 Mariners Coaches (Deron Johnson, Jim Mahoney, Marty Martinez, Phil Regan, Phil Roof) .25
28 Seattle Kingdome/Checklist .25

Padres

Mother's Cookies issued a second annual full-color Padres team set in 1985. Cards have rounded corners and measure 2-1/2" x 3-1/2". Glossy fronts feature unbordered color photos. Horizontal backs have biographical data, card number, Mother's Cookies logo and space for player autograph. The set was distributed in its entirety during a stadium promotion.

NM/M
Complete Set (28): 6.00
Common Player: .25
1 Dick Williams .25
2 Tony Gwynn 4.50
3 Kevin McReynolds .25
4 Graig Nettles .25
5 Rich Gossage .40
6 Steve Garvey 1.50
7 Garry Templeton .25
8 Dave Dravecky .25
9 Eric Show .25
10 Terry Kennedy .25
11 Luis DeLeon .25
12 Bruce Bochy .25
13 Andy Hawkins .25
14 Kurt Bevacqua .25
15 Craig Lefferts .25
16 Mario Ramirez .25
17 LaMarr Hoyt .25
18 Jerry Royster .25
19 Tim Stoddard .25
20 Tim Flannery .25
21 Mark Thurmond .25
22 Greg Booker .25
23 Bobby Brown .25
24 Carmelo Martinez .25
25 Al Bumbry .25
26 Jerry Davis .25
27 Padres Coaches (Galen Cisco, Harry Dunlop, Deacon Jones, Jack Krol, Ozzie Virgil) .25
28 Jack Murphy Stadium/Checklist .25

1986 Mother's Cookies A's

Mother's Cookies produced four full-color team sets in 1986, with only the San Diego Padres not repeating from the 1985 group. The third annual set for the Oakland A's measures 2-1/2" x 3-1/2" with rounded corners. Glossy fronts feature unbordered color photos. Horizontal backs have brief biographical information, card number and Mother's Cookies logo. There are 28 cards in the A's set, with 20 of the cards distributed during a stadium promotion. Each fan also received a coupon redeemable for eight additional cards which could be traded to complete a set.

NM/M
Complete Set (28): 10.00
Common Player: .25
1 Jackie Moore .25
2 Dave Kingman .40
3 Dusty Baker .40
4 Joaquin Andujar .25
5 Alfredo Griffin .25
6 Dwayne Murphy .25
7 Mike Davis .25
8 Carney Lansford .25
9 Jose Canseco 6.00
10 Bruce Bochte .25
11 Mickey Tettleton .25
12 Donnie Hill .25
13 Jose Rijo .25
14 Rick Langford .25
15 Chris Codiroli .25
16 Moose Haas .25
17 Keith Atherton .25
18 Jay Howell .25
19 Tony Phillips .25
20 Steve Henderson .25
21 Bill Krueger .25
22 Steve Ontiveros .25
23 Bill Bathe .25
24 Rickey Peters .25
25 Tim Birtsas .25
26 Trainers (Frank Ciensczyk, Larry Davis, Steve Vucinich, Barry Weinberg) .25
27 Coaches (Bob Didier, Dave McKay, Jeff Newman, Ron Plaza, Wes Stock, Bob Watson) .25
28 Oakland Coliseum/Checklist .25

Astros

Mother's Cookies produced a third annual Astros team set in 1985. The round-cornered, glossy front 2-1/2" x 3-1/2" cards feature unbordered color paintings of Houston's past All-Star Game performers. Backs have biographical information, card number and Mother's Cookies logo. There are 28 cards in the set, with 20 of the cards distributed during a stadium promotion. Each fan also received a coupon redeemable for eight additional cards that could be traded to complete a set.

NM/M
Complete Set (28): 9.00
Common Player: .25
1 Dick Farrell .25
2 Hal Woodeschick (Woodeshick) .25
3 Joe Morgan 1.00
4 Claude Raymond .25
5 Mike Cuellar .25
6 Rusty Staub .25
7 Jimmy Wynn .25
8 Larry Dierker .25
9 Denis Menke .25
10 Don Wilson .25
11 Cesar Cedeno .25
12 Lee May .25
13 Bob Watson .25
14 Ken Forsch .25
15 Joaquin Andujar .25
16 Terry Puhl .25
17 Joe Niekro .30
18 Craig Reynolds .25
19 Joe Sambito .25
20 Jose Cruz .25
21 J.R. Richard .30
22 Bob Knepper .25
23 Nolan Ryan 7.50
24 Ray Knight .25
25 Bill Dawley .25
26 Dickie Thon .25
27 Jerry Mumphrey .25
28 Astros Logo/Checklist .25

Giants

Mother's Cookies produced a fourth annual set for the Giants in 1985. Round-cornered, glossy front cards measure 2-1/2" x 3-1/2" and feature unbordered color photos. Horizontal backs have biographical data, card number, and Mother's Cookies logo. There are 28 cards in the set, with 20 of the cards distributed during a stadium promotion. Each fan also received a coupon redeemable for eight additional cards which could be traded to complete the set.

NM/M
Complete Set (28): 6.00
Common Player: .25
1 Roger Craig .25
2 Chili Davis .25
3 Dan Gladden .25
4 Jeff Leonard .25
5 Bob Brenly .25
6 Atlee Hammaker .25
7 Will Clark 5.00
8 Greg Minton .25
9 Candy Maldonado .25
10 Vida Blue .25
11 Mike Krukow .25
12 Bob Melvin .25
13 Jose Uribe .25
14 Dan Driessen .25
15 Jeff Robinson .25
16 Rob Thompson .25
17 Mike LaCoss .25
18 Chris Brown .25
19 Scott Garrelts .25
20 Mark Davis .25
21 Jim Gott .25
22 Brad Wellman .25
23 Roger Mason .25
24 Bill Laskey .25
25 Brad Gulden .25
26 Joel Youngblood .25
27 Juan Berenguer .25
28 Coaches/Checklist (Bill Fahey, Bob Lillis, Gordy MacKenzie, Jose Morales, Norm Sherry) .25

Mariners

Mother's Cookies produced a third annual set for the M's in 1985. Round-cornered, glossy front cards measure 2-1/2" x 3-1/2" and feature unbordered color photos. Horizontal backs have brief biographical information, card number and sponsor's logo. There are 28 cards in the set, with 20 distributed during a stadium promotion. Each fan also received a coupon redeemable for eight additional cards which could be traded to complete the set.

NM/M
Complete Set (28): 6.00
Common Player: .25
1 Dick Williams .25
2 Alvin Davis .25
3 Mark Langston .25
4 Dave Henderson .25
5 Steve Yeager .25
6 Al Cowens .25
7 Jim Presley .25
8 Phil Bradley .25
9 Gorman Thomas .25
10 Barry Bonnell .25
11 Milt Wilcox .25
12 Domingo Ramos .25
13 Paul Mirabella .25
14 Matt Young .25
15 Ivan Calderon .25
16 Bill Swift .25
17 Pete Ladd .25
18 Ken Phelps .25
19 Karl Best .25
20 Spike Owen .25
21 Mike Moore .25
22 Danny Tartabull .25
23 Bob Kearney .25
24 Edwin Nunez .25
25 Mike Morgan .25
26 Roy Thomas .25
27 Jim Beattie .25
28 Coaches/Checklist (Deron Johnson, Marty Martinez, Phil Regan, Phil Roof, Ozzie Virgil) .25

1987 Mother's Cookies A's

Continuing with a tradition of producing beautiful baseball cards, Mother's Cookies of Oakland, Calif. issued a 28-card set featuring every Oakland A's player to have been elected to the All-Star Game since 1968. The full-color photos came from the private collection of nationally known photographer Doug McWilliams. Twenty of the 28 cards were given out to fans attending the A's game on July 5. An additional eight cards were available by redeeming a mail-in certificate. The cards measure 2-1/2" x 3-1/2" and feature rounded corners. Backs carry the player's All-Star Game statistics.

		NM/M
Complete Set (28):		12.00
Common Player:		.25
1	Bert Campaneris	.25
2	Rick Monday	.25
3	John Odom	.25
4	Sal Bando	.25
5	Reggie Jackson	2.50
6	Catfish Hunter	1.00
7	Vida Blue	.25
8	Dave Duncan	.25
9	Joe Rudi	.25
10	Rollie Fingers	.75
11	Ken Holtzman	.25
12	Dick Williams	.25
13	Alvin Dark	.25
14	Gene Tenace	.25
15	Claudell Washington	.25
16	Phil Garner	.25
17	Wayne Gross	.25
18	Matt Keough	.25
19	Jeff Newman	.25
20	Rickey Henderson	1.50
21	Tony Armas	.25
22	Mike Norris	.25
23	Billy Martin	.40
24	Bill Caudill	.25
25	Jay Howell	.25
26	Jose Canseco	2.00
27	Jose and Reggie (Jose Canseco, Reggie Jackson)	2.50
28	A's Logo/Checklist	.25

Astros

Twenty of 28 cards featuring Astros players were given out to the first 25,000 fans attending the July 17 game at the Astrodome. An additional eight cards (though not necessarily the exact eight needed to complete a set) were available from the sponsor by redeeming a mail-in certificate. The cards have rounded corners, glossy fronts and measure 2-1/2" x 3-1/2". Backs are printed in purple and orange and contain personal data, the Mother's Cookies logo, card number and a spot for the player's autograph.

		NM/M
Complete Set (28):		10.00
Common Player:		.25
1	Hal Lanier	.25
2	Mike Scott	.25
3	Jose Cruz	.25
4	Bill Doran	.25
5	Bob Knepper	.25
6	Phil Garner	.25
7	Terry Puhl	.25
8	Nolan Ryan	7.50
9	Kevin Bass	.25
10	Glenn Davis	.25
11	Alan Ashby	.25
12	Charlie Kerfeld	.25
13	Denny Walling	.25
14	Danny Darwin	.25
15	Mark Bailey	.25
16	Davey Lopes	.25
17	Dave Meads	.25
18	Aurelio Lopez	.25
19	Craig Reynolds	.25
20	Dave Smith	.25
21	Larry Anderson (Andersen)	.25
22	Jim Pankovits	.25
23	Jim Deshaies	.25
24	Bert Pena	.25
25	Dickie Thon	.25
26	Billy Hatcher	.25
27	Coaches (Yogi Berra, Matt Galante, Denis Menke, Les Moss, Gene Tenace)	.25
28	Houston Astrodome/Checklist	.25

Dodgers

Mother's Cookies produced for the first time in 1987 a team set featuring the L.A. Dodgers. Twenty of the 28 cards were given to youngsters 14 and under at Dodger Stadium on August 9. An additional eight cards were available from Mother's Cookies via a mail-in coupon. The borderless, full-color cards measure 2-1/2" x 3-1/2" and have rounded corners. A special album designed to house the set was available for $3.95 through a mail-in offer.

		NM/M
Complete Set (28):		10.00
Common Player:		.25
1	Tom Lasorda	.40
2	Pedro Guerrero	.25
3	Steve Sax	.25
4	Fernando Valenzuela	.25
5	Mike Marshall	.25
6	Orel Hershiser	.75
7	Mariano Duncan	.25
8	Bill Madlock	.25
9	Bob Welch	.25
10	Mike Scioscia	.25
11	Mike Ramsey	.25
12	Matt Young	.25
13	Franklin Stubbs	.25
14	Tom Niedenfuer	.25
15	Reggie Williams	.25
16	Rick Honeycutt	.25
17	Dave Anderson	.25
18	Alejandro Pena	.25
19	Ken Howell	.25
20	Len Matuszek	.25
21	Tim Leary	.25
22	Tracy Woodson	.25
23	Alex Trevino	.25
24	Ken Landreaux	.25
25	Mickey Hatcher	.25
26	Brian Holton	.25
27	Coaches (Joey Amalfitano, Mark Cresse, Don McMahon, Manny Mota, Ron Perranoski, Bill Russell)	.25
28	Dodger Stadium/Checklist	.25

Giants

Distribution of the 1987 Mother's Cookies Giants cards took place at Candlestick Park on June 27. Twenty of the 28 cards in the set were given to the first 25,000 fans entering the park. The starter packet of 20 cards contained

a mail-in coupon card which was good for an additional eight cards. The glossy-front cards measure 2-1/2" x 3-1/2" with rounded corners. Backs are printed in red and purple and contain personal and statistical information along with the Mother's Cookies logo.

		NM/M
Complete Set (28):		9.00
Common Player:		.25
1	Roger Craig	.25
2	Will Clark	1.00
3	Chili Davis	.25
4	Bob Brenly	.25
5	Chris Brown	.25
6	Mike Krukow	.25
7	Candy Maldonado	.25
8	Jeffrey Leonard	.25
9	Greg Minton	.25
10	Robby Thompson	.25
11	Scott Garrelts	.25
12	Bob Melvin	.25
13	Jose Uribe	.25
14	Mark Davis	.25
15	Eddie Milner	.25
16	Harry Spilman	.25
17	Kelly Downs	.25
18	Chris Speier	.25
19	Jim Gott	.25
20	Joel Youngblood	.25
21	Mike LaCoss	.25
22	Matt Williams	3.00
23	Roger Mason	.25
24	Mike Aldrete	.25
25	Jeff Robinson	.25
26	Mark Grant	.25
27	Coaches (Bill Fahey, Bob Lillis, Gordon MacKenzie, Jose Morales, Norm Sherry, Don Zimmer)	.25
28	Candlestick Park/Checklist	.25

Mariners

For the fourth consecutive year, Mother's Cookies issued a team set featuring the Mariners. Twenty of the 28 cards were distributed to the first 20,000 fans entering the Kingdome on August 9. An additional eight cards (though not necessarily the eight cards needed to complete the set) were available by redeeming a mail-in certificate. Collectors were encouraged to trade to complete a set. The 2-1/2" x 3-1/2" full-color cards feature glossy fronts and rounded corners. A specially designed album to house the set was available.

		NM/M
Complete Set (28):		6.00
Common Player:		.25
1	Dick Williams	.25
2	Alvin Davis	.25
3	Mike Moore	.25
4	Jim Presley	.25
5	Mark Langston	.25
6	Phil Bradley	.25
7	Ken Phelps	.25
8	Mike Morgan	.25
9	David Valle	.25
10	Harold Reynolds	.40
11	Edwin Nunez	.25
12	Bob Kearney	.25
13	Scott Bankhead	.25
14	Scott Bradley	.25
15	Mickey Brantley	.25
16	Mark Huismann	.25
17	Mike Kingery	.25
18	John Moses	.25
19	Donell Nixon	.25
20	Rey Quinones	.25
21	Domingo Ramos	.25
22	Jerry Reed	.25
23	Rich Renteria	.25
24	Rich Monteleone	.25
25	Mike Trujillo	.25
26	Bill Wilkinson	.25
27	John Christensen	.25
28	Coaches/Checklist (Billy Connors, Frank Howard, Phil Roof, Bobby Tolan, Ozzie Virgil)	.25

Rangers

While Mother's Cookies of Oakland had produced high-quality baseball card sets of various teams since 1983, the Rangers participated in the promotion for the first time in 1987. Twenty cards from the 28-card set were handed out to the first 25,000 fans entering Arlington Stadium on July 17. An additional eight cards (though not necessarily the eight needed to complete a set) were available by redeeming a mail-in certificate. The cards measure 2-1/2" x 3-1/2" with rounded corners and glossy finish, like all Mother's Cookies issued in 1987.

		NM/M
Complete Set (28):		9.00
Common Player:		.25
1	Bobby Valentine	.25
2	Pete Incaviglia	.50
3	Charlie Hough	.25
4	Oddibe McDowell	.25
5	Larry Parrish	.25
6	Scott Fletcher	.25
7	Steve Buechele	.25
8	Tom Paciorek	.25
9	Pete O'Brien	.25
10	Darrell Porter	.25
11	Greg Harris	.25
12	Don Slaught	.25
13	Ruben Sierra	.50
14	Curtis Wilkerson	.25
15	Dale Mohorcic	.25
16	Ron Meredith	.25
17	Mitch Williams	.25
18	Bob Brower	.25
19	Edwin Correa	.25
20	Geno Petralli	.25
21	Mike Loynd	.25
22	Jerry Browne	.25
23	Jose Guzman	.25
24	Jeff Kunkel	.25
25	Bobby Witt	.25
26	Jeff Russell	.25
27	Trainers (Danny Wheat, Bill Zeigler)	.25
28	Coaches/Checklist (Joe Ferguson, Tim Foli, Tom House, Art Howe, Dave Oliver, Tom Robson)	.25

Mark McGwire

A four-card set featuring outstanding rookie Mark McGwire of the Oakland A's was produced by Mother's Cookies

in 1987. Cards are 2-1/2" x 3-1/2" and have rounded corners and glossy finish like other Mother's issues. The set was obtainable by sending in eight proof-of-purchase seals or could be secured at the National Sports Collectors Convention held July 9-12 in San Francisco. Convention goers received one card as a bonus for each Mother's Cookies baseball card album purchased.

		NM/M
Complete Set (4):		10.00
Uncut Strip:		10.00
Common Card:		.25
1	Mark McGwire/Portrait	3.00
2	Mark McGwire (Leaning on bat rack.)	3.00
3	Mark McGwire (Beginning batting swing.)	3.00
4	Mark McGwire (Batting follow-through.)	3.00

1988 Mother's Cookies A's

Complete at 28 cards, the 1988 Mother's Cookies A's set features full-color, borderless cards with rounded corners in the standard 2-1/2" x 3-1/2" format. Backs are printed in red and purple and include biographical information, the Mother's Cookies logo and card number. Starter sets of 20 cards were distributed at the stadium along with a promotional card redeemable for another eights cards (not necessarily those needed to complete the set). An album to house the cards was also available.

		NM/M
Complete Set (28):		16.00
Common Player:		.35
1	Tony LaRussa	.50
2	Mark McGwire	6.00
3	Dave Stewart	.35
4	Mickey Tettleton	.35
5	Dave Parker	.35
6	Carney Lansford	.35
7	Jose Canseco	.75
8	Don Baylor	.50
9	Bob Welch	.35
10	Dennis Eckersley	1.25
11	Walt Weiss	.50
12	Tony Phillips	.35
13	Steve Ontiveros	.35
14	Dave Henderson	.35
15	Stan Javier	.35
16	Ron Hassey	.35
17	Curt Young	.35
18	Glenn Hubbard	.35
19	Storm Davis	.35
20	Eric Plunk	.35
21	Matt Young	.35
22	Mike Gallego	.35
23	Rick Honeycutt	.35
24	Doug Jennings	.35
25	Gene Nelson	.35
26	Greg Cadaret	.35
27	Coaches (Dave Duncan, Rene Lachemann, Jim Lefebvre, Dave McKay, Mike Paul, Bob Watson)	.35
28	Jose Canseco, Mark McGwire	2.50

Astros

One of six team sets issued by Mother's Cookies in 1988, the 28-card Astros set is similar in design to other Mother's Cookies sets. Glossy-front cards are 2-1/2" x 3-1/2" size with rounded corners and feature full-color, borderless photos on the fronts. Backs feature red and purple printing and include brief biographical information, the Mother's logo and card number. Twenty of the cards were distributed in a stadium promotion, along with a redemption card that could be exchanged for an additional eight cards (but not necessarily the eight needed to complete the set). An album was also available to house the set.

		NM/M
Complete Set (28):		12.00
Common Player:		.35
1	Hal Lanier	.35
2	Mike Scott	.35
3	Gerald Young	.35
4	Bill Doran	.35
5	Bob Knepper	.35
6	Billy Hatcher	.35
7	Terry Puhl	.35
8	Nolan Ryan	10.00
9	Kevin Bass	.35
10	Glenn Davis	.35
11	Alan Ashby	.35
12	Steve Henderson	.35
13	Denny Walling	.35
14	Danny Darwin	.35
15	Mark Bailey	.35
16	Ernie Camacho	.35
17	Rafael Ramirez	.35
18	Jeff Heathcock	.35
19	Craig Reynolds	.35
20	Dave Smith	.35
21	Larry Andersen	.35
22	Jim Pankovits	.35
23	Jim Deshaies	.35
24	Juan Agosto	.35
25	Chuck Jackson	.35
26	Joaquin Andujar	.35
27	Coaches (Yogi Berra, Gene Clines, Matt Galante, Marc Hill, Denis Menke, Les Moss)	.35
28	Trainers/Checklist (Doc Ewell, Dave Labossiere, Dennis Liborio)	.35

Dodgers

Similar in design to other Mother's Cookies sets, the 1988 Dodgers issue features full-color, borderless photos with backs printed in red and purple. The 28 cards in the set measure 2-1/2" x 3-1/2" with rounded corners. Starter packs of 20 cards were distributed at a ballpark promotion along with a coupon card that could be exchanged for an additional eight cards at a local card show or through the mail. Backs include brief player information, the Mother's Cookies logo and card number. The promotion also included a special album to house the set.

		NM/M
Complete Set (28):		8.00
Common Player:		.35
1	Tom Lasorda	.45
2	Pedro Guerrero	.35
3	Steve Sax	.35
4	Fernando Valenzuela	.35
5	Mike Marshall	.35
6	Orel Hershiser	.50
7	Alfredo Griffin	.35
8	Kirk Gibson	.35
9	Don Sutton	1.25
10	Mike Scioscia	.35
11	Franklin Stubbs	.35
12	Mike Davis	.35
13	Jesse Orosco	.35
14	John Shelby	.35
15	Rick Dempsey	.35
16	Jay Howell	.35
17	Dave Anderson	.35
18	Alejandro Pena	.35
19	Jeff Hamilton	.35
20	Danny Heep	.35
21	Tim Leary	.35
22	Brad Havens	.35
23	Tim Belcher	.35
24	Ken Howell	.35
25	Mickey Hatcher	.35
26	Brian Holton	.35
27	Mike Devereaux	.35
28	Coaches/Checklist (Joe Amalfitano, Mark Cresse, Joe Ferguson, Ben Hines, Manny Mota, Ron Perranoski, Bill Russell)	.35

Giants

BRETT BUTLER
San Francisco Giants

One of six team sets issued in 1988 by Mother's Cookies, this 28-card Giants set featured full-color borderless photos on a standard-size card with rounded corners. Backs, printed in red and purple, include brief player data, the Mother's Cookies logo and card number. Twenty different cards were distributed as a starter set at a stadium promotion along with a coupon card that could be redeemed for an additional eight cards (not necessarily those needed to complete the set). The redemption cards could be exchanged through the mail or redeemed at a local card show.

		NM/M
Complete Set (28):		10.00
Common Player:		.35
1	Roger Craig	.35
2	Will Clark	.75
3	Kevin Mitchell	.35
4	Bob Brenly	.35
5	Mike Aldrete	.35
6	Mike Krukow	.35
7	Candy Maldonado	.35
8	Jeffrey Leonard	.35
9	Dave Dravecky	.35

10	Robby Thompson	.35
11	Scott Garrelts	.35
12	Bob Melvin	.35
13	Jose Uribe	.35
14	Brett Butler	.35
15	Rick Reuschel	.35
16	Harry Spilman	.35
17	Kelly Downs	.35
18	Chris Speier	.35
19	Atlee Hammaker	.35
20	Joel Youngblood	.35
21	Mike LaCoss	.35
22	Don Robinson	.35
23	Mark Wasinger	.35
24	Craig Lefferts	.35
25	Phil Garner	.35
26	Joe Price	.35
27	Coaches (Dusty Baker, Bill Fahey, Bob Lillis, Gordie MacKenzie, Jose Morales, Norm Sherry)	.35
28	Logo Card/Checklist	.35

Mariners

JIM PRESLEY
Seattle Mariners

Similar in design to other Mother's Cookies sets, the 28-card Mariners issue features full-color, borderless photos on a 2-1/2" x 3-1/2" card with rounded corners. Backs, printed in red and purple, include brief biographical information, the Mother's Cookies logo and card number. Twenty-card starter packs were distributed at a stadium promotion, where fans also received a coupon card that could be exchanged for an additional eight cards (not necessarily to complete the set). The coupon card could be redeemed through the mail or exchanged at a local baseball card show. As with the rest of the 1988 Mother's Cookies sets, an album was also available to house the cards.

		NM/M
Complete Set (28):		6.00
Common Player:		.35
1	Dick Williams	.35
2	Alvin Davis	.35
3	Mike Moore	.35
4	Jim Presley	.35
5	Mark Langston	.35
6	Henry Cotto	.35
7	Ken Phelps	.35
8	Steve Trout	.35
9	David Valle	.35
10	Harold Reynolds	.50
11	Edwin Nunez	.35
12	Glenn Wilson	.35
13	Scott Bankhead	.35
14	Scott Bradley	.35
15	Mickey Brantley	.35
16	Bruce Fields	.35
17	Mike Kingery	.35
18	Mike Campbell	.35
19	Mike Jackson	.35
20	Rey Quinones	.35
21	Mario Diaz	.35
22	Jerry Reed	.35
23	Rich Renteria	.35
24	Julio Solano	.35
25	Bill Swift	.35
26	Bill Wilkinson	.35
27	Coaches (Billy Connors, Frank Howard, Phil Roof, Jim Snyder, Ozzie Virgil)	.35
28	Trainers/Checklist (Henry Genzale, Rick Griffin)	.35

Rangers

This 28-card issue was one of six team sets issued in 1988 by Mother's Cookies. The Rangers issue features full-color, borderless cards printed in

standard 2-1/2" x 3-1/2" format with rounded corners. Backs are printed in red and purple and include player information, Mother's Cookies logo and card number. Twenty-card starter packs were distributed as a stadium promotion that included a redemption card good for another eight cards (not necessarily those needed to complete the set) either through the mail or at a local card show.

		NM/M
Complete Set (28):		7.00
Common Player:		.35
1	Bobby Valentine	.35
2	Pete Incaviglia	.35
3	Charlie Hough	.35
4	Oddibe McDowell	.35
5	Larry Parrish	.35
6	Scott Fletcher	.35
7	Steve Buechele	.35
8	Steve Kemp	.35
9	Pete O'Brien	.35
10	Ruben Sierra	.35
11	Mike Stanley	.35
12	Jose Cecena	.35
13	Cecil Espy	.35
14	Curtis Wilkerson	.35
15	Dale Mohorcic	.35
16	Ray Hayward	.35
17	Mitch Williams	.35
18	Bob Brower	.35
19	Paul Kilgus	.35
20	Geno Petralli	.35
21	James Steels	.35
22	Jerry Browne	.35
23	Jose Guzman	.35
24	DeWayne Vaughn	.35
25	Bobby Witt	.35
26	Jeff Russell	.35
27	Coaches (Richard Egan, Tom House, Art Howe, Davey Lopes, David Oliver, Tom Robson)	.35
28	Trainers/Checklist (Danny Wheat, Bill Zeigler)	.35

Will Clark

WILL CLARK
San Francisco Giants

In a baseball spring training-related promotion, Mother's Cookies of Oakland, Calif. produced a full-color four-card set featuring San Francisco Giants first baseman Will Clark. The cards, which have glossy finishes and rounded corners, came cellophane-wrapped in specially marked 18-ounce packages of Mother's Cookies products. The cards are identical in style to the other Mother's Cookies issues.

		NM/M
Complete Set (4):		4.00
4-Card Uncut Panel:		4.00
Common Card:		1.00
1	Will Clark (Bat on shoulder.)	1.00
2	Will Clark/Kneeling	1.00

3	Will Clark (Batting follow-thru.)	1.00
4	Will Clark (Heading for first base.)	1.00

Mark McGwire

MARK McGWIRE
Oakland Athletics

For the second consecutive year, Mother's Cookies devoted a four-card set to Oakland A's slugger Mark McGwire. The full-color cards have rounded corners and measure 2-1/2" x 3-1/2". The cards were issued in specially marked 18-ounce packages of Mother's Cookies products in the northern California area. The cards are identical in design to the team issues produced by Mother's.

		NM/M
Complete Set (4):		7.00
4-Card Uncut Panel:		9.00
Common Card:		2.00
1	Mark McGwire (Holding oversized bat.)	2.00
2	Mark McGwire/ Fielding	2.00
3	Mark McGwire/ Kneeling	2.00
4	Mark McGwire (Bat in air.)	2.00

1989 Mother's Cookies A's

The 1989 Mother's Cookies A's set consists of 28 cards designed in the traditional style: a glossy 2-1/2" x 3-1/2" card with a borderless photo and rounded corners. A starter set of the cards was used as a stadium promotion and distributed to fans attending the July 30 Oakland game.

		NM/M
Complete Set (28):		13.50
Common Player:		.35
1	Tony LaRussa	.35
2	Mark McGwire	5.00
3	Terry Steinbach	.35
4	Dave Parker	.35
5	Carney Lansford	.35
6	Dave Stewart	.35
7	Jose Canseco	1.00
8	Walt Weiss	.35
9	Bob Welch	.35
10	Dennis Eckersley	1.25
11	Tony Phillips	.35
12	Mike Moore	.35
13	Dave Henderson	.35
14	Curt Young	.35
15	Ron Hassey	.35
16	Eric Plunk	.35
17	Luis Polonia	.35
18	Storm Davis	.35
19	Glenn Hubbard	.35
20	Greg Cadaret	.35
21	Stan Javier	.35
22	Felix Jose	.35
23	Mike Gallego	.35
24	Todd Burns	.35
25	Rick Honeycutt	.35
26	Gene Nelson	.35
27	A's Coaches (Dave Duncan, Rene Lacheman, Art Kusnyer, Tommie Reynolds, Merv Rettenmund)	.35
28	Walt Weiss, Mark McGwire, Jose Canseco	2.50

Astros

The 1989 Astros team set issued by Mother's Cookies consists of 28 cards in 2-1/2" x 3-1/2" format in the traditional style of glossy border-

CRAIG BIGGIO
Houston Astros

less photos and rounded corners. Partial sets were distributed to fans attending the July 22 game at the Astrodome. The cards feature the photography of Barry Colla and display the Mother's Cookies logo on the back.

		NM/M
Complete Set (28):		11.00
Common Player:		.35
1	Art Howe	.35
2	Mike Scott	.35
3	Gerald Young	.35
4	Bill Doran	.35
5	Billy Hatcher	.35
6	Terry Puhl	.35
7	Bob Knepper	.35
8	Kevin Bass	.35
9	Glenn Davis	.35
10	Alan Ashby	.35
11	Bob Forsch	.35
12	Greg Gross	.35
13	Danny Darwin	.35
14	Craig Biggio	3.00
15	Jim Clancy	.35
16	Rafael Ramirez	.35
17	Alex Trevino	.35
18	Craig Reynolds	.35
19	Dave Smith	.35
20	Larry Andersen	.35
21	Eric Yelding	.35
22	Jim Deshaies	.35
23	Juan Agosto	.35
24	Rick Rhoden	.35
25	Ken Caminiti	1.00
26	Dave Meads	.35
27	Astros coaches (Yogi Berra, Matt Galante, Phil Garner, Les Moss, Ed Napoleon, Ed Ott)	.35
28	Trainers/checklist (Dave Labossiere, Doc Ewell, Dennis Liborio)	.35

Dodgers

MIKE DAVIS
Los Angeles Dodgers

This 28-card set features the players and coaches of the L.A. Dodgers. The cards follow the traditional Mother's Cookies style featuring rounded corners, borderless color photos, horizontal backs and 2-1/2" x 3-1/2" size. Initially 20 cards were given away as starter sets at Dodger Stadium.

		NM/M
Complete Set (28):		9.00
Common Player:		.35
1	Tom Lasorda	.40
2	Eddie Murray	2.00
3	Mike Scioscia	.35
4	Fernando Valenzuela	.35
5	Mike Marshall	.35
6	Orel Hershiser	.50
7	Alfredo Griffin	.35
8	Kirk Gibson	.35
9	John Tudor	.35
10	Willie Randolph	.35
11	Franklin Stubbs	.35
12	Mike Davis	.35
13	Mike Morgan	.35
14	John Shelby	.35

15	Rick Dempsey	.35
16	Jay Howell	.35
17	Dave Anderson	.35
18	Alejandro Pena	.35
19	Jeff Hamilton	.35
20	Ricky Horton	.35
21	Tim Leary	.35
22	Ray Searage	.35
23	Tim Belcher	.35
24	Tim Crews	.35
25	Mickey Hatcher	.35
26	Mariano Duncan	.35
27	Coaches (Joe Amalfitano, Mark Cresse, Joe Ferguson, Ben Hines, Ron Perranoski, Bill Russell)	.35
28	Checklist	.35

Giants

The 1989 Mother's Cookies Giants set consists of 28 cards, all featuring borderless, color photos with rounded corners. Starter sets of the cards were distributed as a stadium promotion to fans attending the August 6 game at Candlestick Park.

		NM/M
Complete Set (28):		9.00
Common Player:		.35
1	Roger Craig	.35
2	Will Clark	1.00
3	Kevin Mitchell	.35
4	Kelly Downs	.35
5	Brett Butler	.35
6	Mike Krukow	.35
7	Candy Maldonado	.35
8	Terry Kennedy	.35
9	Dave Dravecky	.35
10	Robby Thompson	.35
11	Scott Garrelts	.35
12	Matt Williams	1.00
13	Jose Uribe	.35
14	Tracy Jones	.35
15	Rick Reuschel	.35
16	Ernest Riles	.35
17	Jeff Brantley	.35
18	Chris Speier	.35
19	Atlee Hammaker	.35
20	Ed Jurak	.35
21	Mike LaCoss	.35
22	Don Robinson	.35
23	Kirt Manwaring	.35
24	Craig Lefferts	.35
25	Donnell Nixon	.35
26	Joe Price	.35
27	Rich Gossage	.75
28	Coaches/Checklist (Bill Fahey, Dusty Baker, Bob Lillis, Wendell Kim, Norm Sherry)	.35

Mariners

MICKEY BRANTLEY
Seattle Mariners

For the sixth straight season, Mother's Cookies released a Mariners team set. The 1989 issue features 28 cards. Starter sets of 20 cards were distributed at a Mariners home game. The cards are 2-1/2" x 3-1/2" and feature borderless, glossy full color photos. Card backs are horizontal. Rookie sensation Ken Griffey Jr. was included in the 1989 issue.

		NM/M
Complete Set (28):		12.50
Common Player:		.35
1	Jim Lefebvre	.35
2	Alvin Davis	.35
3	Ken Griffey Jr.	9.00
4	Jim Presley	.35
5	Mark Langston	.35
6	Henry Cotto	.35
7	Mickey Brantley	.35
8	Jeffrey Leonard	.35
9	Dave Valle	.35
10	Harold Reynolds	.50
11	Edgar Martinez	3.00
12	Tom Niedenfuer	.35

ODDIBE McDOWELL
Texas Rangers

13	Scott Bankhead	.35
14	Scott Bradley	.35
15	Omar Vizquel	.35
16	Erik Hanson	.35
17	Bill Swift	.35
18	Mike Campbell	.35
19	Mike Jackson	.35
20	Rich Renteria	.35
21	Mario Diaz	.35
22	Jerry Reed	.35
23	Darnell Coles	.35
24	Steve Trout	.35
25	Mike Schooler	.35
26	Julio Solano	.35
27	Coaches (Gene Clines, Bob Didier, Rusty Kuntz, Mike Paul, Bill Plummer)	
28	Checklist/Trainers (Henry Genzale, Rick Griffin)	.35

Rangers

The 1989 Mother's Cookies Rangers team set features the traditional glossy borderless photos and rounded corners. The 2-1/2" x 3-1/2" set of 28 cards features the photography of Barry Colla. Partial sets were distributed to fans attending the July 30 game at Arlington Stadium.

		NM/M
	Complete Set (28):	8.00
	Common Player:	.35
1	Bobby Valentine	.35
2	Nolan Ryan	6.00
3	Julio Franco	.35
4	Charlie Hough	.35
5	Rafael Palmeiro	4.00
6	Jeff Russell	.35
7	Ruben Sierra	.35
8	Steve Buechele	.35
9	Buddy Bell	.35
10	Pete Incaviglia	.35
11	Geno Petralli	.35
12	Cecil Espy	.35
13	Scott Fletcher	.35
14	Bobby Witt	.35
15	Brad Arnsberg	.35
16	Rick Leach	.35
17	Jamie Moyer	.35
18	Kevin Brown	.35
19	Jeff Kunkel	.35
20	Craig McMurtry	.35
21	Kenny Rogers	.35
22	Mike Stanley	.35
23	Cecilio Guante	.35
24	Jim Sundberg	.35
25	Jose Guzman	.35
26	Jeff Stone	.35
27	Coaches (Dick Egan, Tom Robson, Toby Harrah, Dave Oliver, Tom House, Davey Lopes)	.35
28	Trainers/Checklist (Bill Ziegler, Danny Wheat)	.35

Jose Canseco

This special insert glossy set features Canseco in two posed (one standing, one kneeling) and two action (one batting, one running) shots. Full-color card fronts have rounded corners. Flip sides are numbered, printed in red and purple, and carry 1988 stats and career notes. Cards are individually cello-wrapped and inserted in Mother's Fudge 'N Chips, Oatmeal Raisin and Cocadas cookie bags.

		NM/M
	Complete Set (4):	5.00
	4-Card Uncut Panel:	6.00
	Common Player:	1.50
1	Jose Canseco (Ball in hand.)	1.50
2	Jose Canseco (On one knee grasping bat.)	1.50
3	Jose Canseco (Swinging-in action.)	1.50
4	Jose Canseco (Baserunning)	1.50

Will Clark

Will Clark is featured on a special-edition glossy set inserted in Mother's big bag chocolate chip cookies. The standard-size (2-1/2" x 3-1/2") cards feature Clark in two posed (batting and catching) and two action (batting and running) shots. Purple and red backs list 1986-88 stats.

Ken Griffey, Jr.

This set featuring Ken Griffey, Jr. was issued by Mother's Cookies and was available only in cookie packages in Washington and Oregon. The cards were also available at a Seattle Mariners Kingdome baseball card show on August 20, where the set was introduced. The cards were then packed inside specially marked bags of cookies, one card per bag.

		NM/M
	Complete Set (4):	15.00
	4-Card Uncut Panel:	20.00
	Common Card:	5.00
1	Ken Griffey Jr. (Arms folded.)	5.00
2	Ken Griffey Jr. (Ball in hand.)	5.00
3	Ken Griffey Jr. (Bat over left shoulder.)	5.00
4	Ken Griffey Jr. (Back of jersey showing.)	5.00

Mark McGwire

This special edition features full-color glossy player photos by Barry Colla on standard-size (2-1/2" x 3-1/2") cards with rounded corners. Photos feature four different batting poses. Numbered flip sides, printed in purple and red, carry 1987-88 statistics. Cards are individually cello-wrapped and were inserted in Mother's Cookie Parade variety cookie bags.

		NM/M
	Complete Set (4):	6.00
	Common Player:	1.50
1	Mark McGwire (Bat on shoulder.)	1.50
2	Mark McGwire (Batting stance.)	1.50
3	Mark McGwire (Bat in front.)	1.50
4	Mark McGwire (Batting follow through.)	1.50

Rookies of the Year

This four-card set features the American League Rookies of the Year for 1986, 1987 and 1988, all members of the Oak-

land A's. The 2-1/2" x 3-1/2" cards feature full color photos in the traditional Mother's Cookies format. One card was devoted to each player along with a special card showcasing all three players. The cards were distributed one per box in Mother's Cookies.

		NM/M
	Complete Set (4):	15.00
	4-Card Uncut Panel:	15.00
	Common Card:	.75
1	Jose Canseco	2.25
2	Mark McGwire	7.50
3	Walt Weiss	.75
4	Walt Weiss, Mark McGwire, Jose Canseco	5.50

1990 Mother's Cookies A's

This 28-card set features cards distributed at an A's home game. Cards measure 2-1/2" x 3-1/2" and feature rounded corners. Backs include biographical information and autograph space.

		NM/M
	Complete Set (28):	15.00
	Common Player:	.35
1	Tony LaRussa	.35
2	Mark McGwire	4.00
3	Terry Steinbach	.35
4	Rickey Henderson	2.00
5	Dave Stewart	.35
6	Jose Canseco	.75
7	Dennis Eckersley	1.00
8	Carney Lansford	.35
9	Mike Moore	.35
10	Walt Weiss	.35
11	Scott Sanderson	.35
12	Ron Hassey	.35
13	Rick Honeycutt	.35
14	Ken Phelps	.35
15	Jamie Quirk	.35
16	Bob Welch	.35
17	Felix Jose	.35
18	Dave Henderson	.35
19	Mike Norris	.35
20	Todd Burns	.35
21	Lance Blankenship	.35
22	Gene Nelson	.35
23	Stan Javier	.35
24	Curt Young	.35
25	Mike Gallego	.35
26	Joe Klink	.35
27	Coaches (Dave Duncan, Art Kuysner, Rene Lacheman, Dave McKay, Merv Rettenmund, Tommie Reynolds)	.35
28	Checklist/Trainers (Frank Ciensczyk, Larry Davis, Steve Vucinich, Barry Weinberg)	.35

Astros

This 28-card set features cards styled like past Mother's Cookies releases. The cards were distributed in 20-card packs at an Astros home game. The cards were never distributed in complete set form.

		NM/M
	Complete Set (28):	10.00
	Common Player:	.35
1	Art Howe	.35
2	Glenn Davis	.35
3	Eric Anthony	.35
4	Mike Scott	.35
5	Craig Biggio	2.00
6	Ken Caminiti	.50
7	Bill Doran	.35
8	Gerald Young	.35
9	Terry Puhl	.35
10	Mark Portugal	.35
11	Mark Davidson	.35
12	Jim Deshaies	.35

13	Bill Gullickson	.35
14	Franklin Stubbs	.35
15	Danny Darwin	.35
16	Ken Oberkfell	.35
17	Dave Smith	.35
18	Dan Schatzeder	.35
19	Rafael Ramirez	.35
20	Larry Andersen	.35
21	Alex Trevino	.35
22	Glenn Wilson	.35
23	Jim Clancy	.35
24	Eric Yelding	.35
25	Casey Candaele	.35
26	Juan Agosto	.35
27	Coaches (Bill Bowman, Bob Cluck, Phil Garner, Matt Galante, Rudy Jaramillo, Ed Napoleon)	.35
28	Checklist/Trainers (Doc Ewell, Dave Labossiere, Dennis Liborio)	.35

Dodgers

Distributed as a promotional item, these cards are styled like past Mother's Cookies releases. Fans 14 and under received a 20-card pack at a Dodgers home game. Cards were also available at a Labor Day card show in Anaheim. The cards were not distributed in complete set form.

		NM/M
	Complete Set (28):	10.00
	Common Player:	.35
1	Tom Lasorda	.45
2	Fernando Valenzuela	.45
3	Kal Daniels	.35
4	Mike Scioscia	.35
5	Eddie Murray	3.00
6	Mickey Hatcher	.35
7	Juan Samuel	.35
8	Alfredo Griffin	.35
9	Tim Belcher	.35
10	Hubie Brooks	.35
11	Jose Gonzalez	.35
12	Orel Hershiser	.45
13	Kirk Gibson	.35
14	Chris Gwynn	.35
15	Jay Howell	.35
16	Rick Dempsey	.35
17	Ramon Martinez	.50
18	Lenny Harris	.35
19	John Wetteland	.35
20	Mike Sharperson	.35
21	Mike Morgan	.35
22	Ray Searage	.35
23	Jeff Hamilton	.35
24	Jim Gott	.35
25	John Shelby	.35
26	Tim Crews	.35
27	Don Aase	.35
28	Coaches (Joe Amalfitano, Mark Cresse, Joe Ferguson, Ben Hines, Manny Mota, Ron Perranoski, Bill Russell)	.35

Giants

Like the other Mother's Cookies issues of 1990, Giants cards were distributed as a promotional item. Fans 14 and under were given a 20-card starter set at a Giants game. Cards could also be obtained at the Labor Day card show in San Francisco. The cards were not released in complete set form.

		NM/M
	Complete Set (28):	10.00
	Common Player:	.35
1	Roger Craig	.35
2	Will Clark	1.00
3	Gary Carter	3.00
4	Kelly Downs	.35
5	Kevin Mitchell	.35
6	Steve Bedrosian	.35
7	Brett Butler	.35
8	Rick Reuschel	.35
9	Matt Williams	1.00
10	Robby Thompson	.35

11	Mike LaCoss	.35
12	Terry Kennedy	.35
13	Atlee Hammaker	.35
14	Rick Leach	.35
15	Ernest Riles	.35
16	Scott Garrelts	.35
17	Jose Uribe	.35
18	Greg Litton	.35
19	Dave Anderson	.35
20	Don Robinson	.35
21	Coaches (Dusty Baker, Bill Fahey, Wendell Kim, Bob Lillis, Norm Sherry)	
22	Bill Bathe	.35
23	Randy O'Neal	.35
24	Kevin Bass	.35
25	Jeff Brantley	.35
26	John Burkett	.35
27	Ernie Camacho	.35
28	Checklist	.35

Mariners

This 28-card set features the traditional Mother's Cookies style with borderless full-color photos with rounded corners. Backs feature biographical information and autograph space. The cards were released as a promotion at a Mariners home game and at a Kingdome card show.

		NM/M
	Complete Set (28):	17.50
	Common Player:	.35
1	Jim Lefebvre	.35
2	Alvin Davis	.35
3	Ken Griffey Jr.	7.00
4	Jeffrey Leonard	.35
5	David Valle	.35
6	Harold Reynolds	.35
7	Jay Buhner	.75
8	Erik Hanson	.35
9	Henry Cotto	.35
10	Edgar Martinez	.35
11	Bill Swift	.35
12	Omar Vizquel	.75
13	Randy Johnson	5.00
14	Greg Briley	.35
15	Gene Harris	.35
16	Matt Young	.35
17	Pete O'Brien	.35
18	Brent Knackert	.35
19	Mike Jackson	.35
20	Brian Holman	.35
21	Mike Schooler	.35
22	Darnell Coles	.35
23	Keith Comstock	.35
24	Scott Bankhead	.35
25	Scott Bradley	.35
26	Mike Brumley	.35
27	Coaches (Gene Clines, Bob Didier, Rusty Kuntz, Mike Paul, Bill Plummer)	.35
28	Checklist/Trainers (Henry Genzale, Rick Griffin, Tom Newberg)	.35

Rangers

Putting together a complete set of these cards was not an easy task. The cards were distributed in 20-card packs at a Rangers home game and also could be obtained at a Dallas card convention. The cards were not released in complete set form. The cards feature the traditional Mother's Cookies style of glossy photos and rounded corners.

		NM/M
	Complete Set (28):	12.50
	Common Player:	.35
1	Bobby Valentine	.35
2	Nolan Ryan	6.00
3	Ruben Sierra	.35
4	Pete Incaviglia	.35
5	Charlie Hough	.35
6	Harold Baines	.35

7	Gino Petralli	.35
8	Jeff Russell	.35
9	Rafael Palmeiro	2.00
10	Julio Franco	.35
11	Jack Daugherty	.35
12	Gary Pettis	.35
13	Brian Bohanon	.35
14	Steve Buechele	.35
15	Bobby Witt	.35
16	Thad Bosley	.35
17	Gary Mielke	.35
18	Jeff Kunkel	.35
19	Mike Jeffcoat	.35
20	Mike Stanley	.35
21	Kevin Brown	.35
22	Kenny Rogers	.35
23	Jeff Huson	.35
24	Jamie Moyer	.35
25	Cecil Espy	.35
26	John Russell	.35
27	Coaches (Toby Harrah, Tom House, Davey Lopes, Dave Oliver, Tom Robson)	.35
28	Checklist/Trainers (Joe Macko, Marty Stajduhar, Danny Wheat, Bill Zeigler)	.35

Jose Canseco

This special insert glossy set features Canseco in four posed shots. Full-color card fronts have rounded corners. Flip sides are numbered, printed in red and purple and feature the Mother's Cookies logo. The cards are individually cello-wrapped and inserted one per Mother's Cookies bag.

		NM/M
	Complete Set (4):	4.00
	4-Card Uncut Panel:	5.00
	Common Card:	1.50
1	Jose Canseco (Sitting, bat on shoulder.)	1.50
2	Jose Canseco (Bat behind neck.)	1.50
3	Jose Canseco (Batting stance.)	1.50
4	Jose Canseco (On dugout step.)	1.50

Will Clark

1990 marks the third consecutive year that Mother's Cookies devoted a set to Giants slugger Will Clark. The set features four posed full-color shots. The cards follow the same design as all recent Mother's Cookies cards.

		NM/M
	Complete Set (4):	4.00
	4-Card Uncut Panel:	4.00
	Common Card:	1.00
1	Will Clark (Bat on shoulder.)	1.00
2	Will Clark (Closeup in stance.)	1.00
3	Will Clark (Open in stance.)	1.00
4	Will Clark (Bat behind neck.)	1.00

Mark McGwire

1990 marks the fourth year that A's slugger Mark McGwire was featured on a special four-card Mother's Cookies set. The photos for the cards were once again by Barry Colla. Four different posed shots of McGwire are showcased.

		NM/M
	Complete Set (4):	6.00
	4-Card Uncut Panel:	7.50
	Common Card:	2.00
1	Mark McGwire (Bat on shoulder.)	2.00

2	Mark McGwire (Leaning against bat rack.)	2.00
3	Mark McGwire (Glove in hand.)	2.00
4	Mark McGwire (On dugout step.)	2.00

Nolan Ryan

Unlike other special Mother's Cookies player sets, the Nolan Ryan cards feature "5000 K's" along with his name and team on the card fronts. The set honors the strikeout king's monumental feat. The cards follow the classic Mother's Cookies style.

		NM/M
Complete Set (4):		4.00
4-Card Uncut Panel:		5.00
Common Card:		2.00
1	Nolan Ryan (Facing with ball in hand.)	2.00
2	Nolan Ryan (Standing in dugout.)	2.00
3	Nolan Ryan (Gripping ball behind back.)	2.00
4	Nolan Ryan (Sitting on dugout step.)	2.00

Matt Williams

Matt Williams made his Mother's Cookies single-player card set debut in 1990. Four posed shots of the Giants third baseman are showcased. Williams is featured twice in batting poses and twice as a fielder on the glossy, round-cornered 2-1/2" x 3-1/2" cards.

		NM/M
Complete Set (4):		2.50
4-Card Uncut Panel:		2.50
Common Card:		.75
1	Matt Williams (Bat on shoulder.)	.75
2	Matt Williams (In batting stance.)	.75
3	Matt Williams (Glove in hand.)	.75
4	Matt Williams/Fielding	.75

1991 Mother's Cookies A's

The incomparable photography of Barry Colla captures the Oakland A's in their home-field environs for the 28 cards in this set. Glossy fronts feature borderless posed photos. The player's name and team appear in white in an upper corner. Backs have minimal biographical data, player position, uniform and card numbers and appropriate logos.

		NM/M
Complete Set (28):		12.00
Common Player:		.25
1	Tony LaRussa	.25

2	Mark McGwire	3.50
3	Terry Steinbach	.25
4	Rickey Henderson	1.50
5	Dave Stewart	.25
6	Jose Canseco	.75
7	Dennis Eckersley	1.00
8	Carney Lansford	.25
9	Bob Welch	.25
10	Walt Weiss	.25
11	Mike Moore	.25
12	Vance Law	.25
13	Rick Honeycutt	.25
14	Harold Baines	.25
15	Jamie Quirk	.25
16	Ernest Riles	.25
17	Willie Wilson	.25
18	Dave Henderson	.25
19	Kirk Dressendorfer	.25
20	Todd Burns	.25
21	Lance Blankenship	.25
22	Gene Nelson	.25
23	Eric Show	.25
24	Curt Young	.25
25	Mike Gallego	.25
26	Joe Klink	.25
27	Steve Chitren	.25
28	Coaches/Checklist (Rene Lacheman, Dave Duncan, Dave McKay, Tommie Reynolds, Art Kuysner, Reggie Jackson, Rick Burleson)	.25

Astros

This 28-card set was produced in the now-familiar Mother's Cookies card format. Glossy fronts feature rounded corners and full-bleed posed color photos (apparently taken at San Francisco's Candlestick Park, home base of photographer Barry Colla) with the player's name and team in white in an upper corner. Backs are printed in red and purple and include a few biographical details, along with cookie company and MLB logos, uniform and card numbers and a line for autographing.

		NM/M
Complete Set (28):		10.00
Common Player:		.25
1	Art Howe	.25
2	Steve Finley	.25
3	Pete Harnisch	.25
4	Mike Scott	.25
5	Craig Biggio	.50
6	Ken Caminiti	.25
7	Eric Yelding	.25
8	Jeff Bagwell	6.00
9	Jim Deshaies	.25
10	Mark Portugal	.25
11	Mark Davidson	.25
12	Jimmy Jones	.25
13	Luis Gonzalez	2.00
14	Karl Rhodes	.25
15	Curt Schilling	.25
16	Ken Oberkfell	.25
17	Mark McLemore	.25
18	David Rohde	.25
19	Rafael Ramirez	.25
20	Al Osuna	.25
21	Jim Corsi	.25
22	Carl Nichols	.25
23	Jim Clancy	.25
24	Dwayne Henry	.25
25	Casey Candaele	.25
26	Xavier Hernandez	.25
27	Darryl Kile	.25
28	Coaches/Checklist (CluckGalante, Rudy Jaramillo, Phil Garner, Bob Cluck, Ed Ott)	.25

Dodgers

Dodger Stadium is the background for Barry Colla's portraits of the Los Angeles manager, coaches and players

appearing in this 28-card set. Standard-size cards with rounded corners feature borderless UV-coated fronts on which the only printing is the player's name and team in white in an upper corner. Backs are in red and purple and include a few biographical details, position, uniform and card numbers, a space for an autograph and the logos of the cookie company and MLB.

		NM/M
Complete Set (28):		7.50
Common Player:		.25
1	Tom Lasorda	.40
2	Darryl Strawberry	.25
3	Kal Daniels	.25
4	Mike Scioscia	.25
5	Eddie Murray	2.00
6	Brett Butler	.25
7	Juan Samuel	.25
8	Alfredo Griffin	.25
9	Tim Belcher	.25
10	Ramon Martinez	.25
11	Jose Gonzalez	.25
12	Orel Hershiser	.40
13	Bob Ojeda	.25
14	Chris Gwynn	.25
15	Jay Howell	.25
16	Gary Carter	2.00
17	Kevin Gross	.25
18	Lenny Harris	.25
19	Mike Hartley	.25
20	Mike Sharperson	.25
21	Mike Morgan	.25
22	John Candelaria	.25
23	Jeff Hamilton	.25
24	Jim Gott	.25
25	Barry Lyons	.25
26	Tim Crews	.25
27	Stan Javier	.25
28	Coaches/Checklist (Ron Perranoski, Bill Russell, Manny Mota, Joe Ferguson, Ben Hines, Joe Amalfitano, Mark Cresse)	.25

Giants

For the ninth consecutive year Mother's Cookies sponsored a promotional card set for the Giants. As in the beginning, the cards highlight the work of photographer Barry Colla with posed portraits of the personnel in Candlestick Park. Fronts of the round-cornered borderless cards are UV-coated and have the player's name and team printed in white in an upper corner. Backs are in red and purple and include cookie company and Major League Baseball logos along with a few biographical details and both uniform and card numbers.

	NM/M
Complete Set (28):	7.00

Common Player:		.25
1	Roger Craig	.25
2	Will Clark	.50
3	Steve Decker	.25
4	Kelly Downs	.25
5	Kevin Mitchell	.25
6	Willie McGee	.25
7	Buddy Black	.25
8	Dave Righetti	.25
9	Matt Williams	.50
10	Robby Thompson	.25
11	Mike LaCoss	.25
12	Terry Kennedy	.25
13	Mark Leonard	.25
14	Rick Reuschel	.25
15	Mike Felder	.25
16	Scott Garrelts	.25
17	Jose Uribe	.25
18	Greg Litton	.25
19	Dave Anderson	.25
20	Don Robinson	.25
21	Mike Kingery	.25
22	Trevor Wilson	.25
23	Kirt Manwaring	.25
24	Kevin Bass	.25
25	Jeff Brantley	.25
27	John Burkett	.25
27	Coaches (Norm Sherry, Wendell Kim, Bob Lillis, Dusty Baker, Bill Fahey)	.25
28	Trainers/Checklist (Mark Letendre, Greg Lynn)	.25

Rangers

The unusual venue of the players' locker room provides the backdrop for photos for this 28-card set sponsored by Mother's Cookies. Besides a look at the player's wardrobe, the full-bleed glossy front photos feature the player's name and position vertically along the left side. Backs have uniform and card numbers, some biographical data and logos of the cookie company and Major League Baseball.

		NM/M
Complete Set (28):		12.50
Common Player:		.25
1	Bobby Valentine	.25
2	Nolan Ryan	6.00
3	Ruben Sierra	.25
4	Juan Gonzalez	3.00
5	Steve Buechele	.25
6	Bobby Witt	.25
7	Geno Petralli	.25
8	Jeff Russell	.25
9	Rafael Palmeiro	2.00
10	Julio Franco	.25
11	Jack Daugherty	.25
12	Gary Pettis	.25
13	John Barfield	.25
14	Scott Chiamparino	.25
15	Kevin Reimer	.25
16	Rich Gossage	.25
17	Brian Downing	.25
18	Denny Walling	.25
19	Mike Jeffcoat	.25
20	Mike Stanley	.25
21	Kevin Brown	.25
22	Kenny Rogers	.25
23	Jeff Huson	.25
24	Mario Diaz	.25
25	Brad Arnsberg	.25
26	John Russell	.25
27	Gerald Alexander	.25
28	Coaches/Checklist (Orlando Gomez, Toby Harrah, Tom House, Davey Lopes, Dave Oliver, Tom Robson)	.25

Griffeys

This four-card set was packaged with Mother's Cookies sold in the Pacific Northwest. Each card features a borderless glossy posed photo on front. The traditional rounded

corners of Mother's cards are found on the issue. Backs have a few stats and career notes.

		NM/M
Complete Set, Singles (4):		5.00
Complete Set, Uncut Strip:		5.00
Common Card:		1.00
1	Ken Griffey Jr.	3.00
2	Ken Griffey, Sr.	1.00
3	Ken Griffey Jr., Ken Griffey Sr. (Holding gloves.)	1.00
4	Ken Griffey Jr., Ken Griffey Sr. (Holding bats.)	1.50

Nolan Ryan 300 Wins

Mother's Cookies in 1991 created a four-card Nolan Ryan set honoring baseball's most recent 300-game winner. One card was included in specially marked packages of cookies. Card fronts have the traditional Mother's Cookies look: Barry Colla photography on full-bleed cards with rounded corners. Backs have a few statistics and career notes.

		NM/M
Complete Set (4):		2.00
4-Card Uncut Panel:		2.00
Common Card:		.75
1	Nolan Ryan (Standing, front view.)	.75
2	Nolan Ryan/Kneeling	.75
3	Nolan Ryan (Standing, side view.)	.75
4	Nolan Ryan (Gripping "300" ball.)	.75

1992 Mother's Cookies A's

The commemorative patch marking the Oakland A's 25th season on the West Coast is visible on several of Barry Colla's photos in this 28-card issue. The traditional Mother's Cookies card format of 2-1/2"

x 3-1/2", round-cornered cards with UV-coated borderless front photos is followed in this set. The player's name and team are in white in an upper corner. Backs have cookie company and Major League Baseball logos, along with the player's position, uniform and card numbers, space for an autograph and minimal biographical data. Back printing is in red and purple on white.

		NM/M
Complete Set (28):		7.50
Common Player:		.25
1	Tony LaRussa	.25
2	Mark McGwire	3.50
3	Terry Steinbach	.25
4	Rickey Henderson	1.50
5	Dave Stewart	.25
6	Jose Canseco	.75
7	Dennis Eckersley	1.00
8	Carney Lansford	.25
9	Bob Welch	.25
10	Walt Weiss	.25
11	Mike Moore	.25
12	Goose Gossage	.25
13	Rick Honeycutt	.25
14	Harold Baines	.25
15	Jamie Quirk	.25
16	Jeff Parrett	.25
17	Willie Wilson	.25
18	Dave Henderson	.25
19	Joe Slusarski	.25
20	Mike Bordick	.25
21	Lance Blankenship	.25
22	Gene Nelson	.25
23	Vince Horsman	.25
24	Ron Darling	.25
25	Randy Ready	.25
26	Scott Hemond	.25
27	Scott Brosius	.25
28	Coaches/Checklist (Tommie Reynolds, Dave Duncan, Doug Rader, Rene Lacheman, Art Kusyner, Dave McKay)	.25

Astros

The Astrodome provides the backdrop for Barry Colla's photos of Astros personnel seen on this 28-card set sponsored by Mother's Cookies. Cards are in standard 2-1/2" x 3-1/2" and feature rounded corners. Glossy fronts are borderless and have no graphics except the player's name and team in an upper corner. Backs are printed in red and purple and have a few biographical details along with uniform and card numbers, the player's position, an autograph line and the logos of the cookie company and MLB.

		NM/M
Complete Set (28):		7.50
Common Player:		.25
1	Art Howe	.25
2	Steve Finley	.25
3	Pete Harnisch	.25
4	Pete Incaviglia	.25
5	Craig Biggio	.50
6	Ken Caminiti	.25
7	Eric Anthony	.25
8	Jeff Bagwell	4.00
9	Andujar Cedeno	.25
10	Mark Portugal	.25
11	Eddie Taubensee	.25
12	Jimmy Jones	.25
13	Joe Boever	.25
14	Benny Distefano	.25
15	Juan Guerrero	.25
16	Doug Jones	.25
17	Scott Servais	.25
18	Butch Henry	.25
19	Rafael Ramirez	.25

20	Al Osuna	.25
21	Rob Murphy	.25
22	Chris Jones	.25
23	Rob Mallicoat	.25
24	Darryl Kile	.25
25	Casey Candaele	.25
26	Xavier Hernandez	.25
27	Coaches (Bob Cluck, Matt Galante, Rudy Jaramillo, Ed Ott, Tom Spencer)	.25
28	Trainers / Checklist (Doc Ewell, Dennis Liborio, Dave Labossiere)	.25

Dodgers

A commemorative patch marking Dodger Stadium's 30th anniversary is featured on some of the Barry Colla photos seen on this 28-card set. Cards have the now-traditional round-corner, glossy-front borderless format with player name and team in an upper corner. Printed in red and purple, the backs have a few biographical details along with uniform and card numbers and appropriate logos.

		NM/M
Complete Set (28):		6.00
Common Player:		.25
1	Tom Lasorda	.35
2	Brett Butler	.25
3	Tom Candiotti	.25
4	Eric Davis	.25
5	Lenny Harris	.25
6	Orel Hershiser	.35
7	Ramon Martinez	.25
8	Jose Offerman	.25
9	Mike Scioscia	.25
10	Darryl Strawberry	.25
11	Todd Benzinger	.25
12	John Candelaria	.25
13	Tim Crews	.25
14	Kal Daniels	.25
15	Jim Gott	.25
16	Kevin Gross	.25
17	Dave Hansen	.25
18	Carlos Hernandez	.25
19	Jay Howell	.25
20	Stan Javier	.25
21	Eric Karros	.50
22	Roger McDowell	.25
23	Bob Ojeda	.25
24	Juan Samuel	.25
25	Mike Sharperson	.25
26	Mitch Webster	.25
27	Steve Wilson	.25
28	Coaches/Checklist (Joe Amalfitano, Mark Cresse, Joe Ferguson, Ben Hines, Manny Mota, Ron Perranoski, Ron Roenicke)	.25

Giants

In 1983 Mother's Cookies re-entered the baseball card world with a set of S.F. Giants cards. In 1992, the company sponsored its 10th consecutive Giants team issue. As in the '83 set, the cards feature the photography of Barry Colla. In 2-1/2" x 3-1/2" size with rounded corners and UV-coating on the borderless fronts, the cards continue the format used since 1984. Backs are also in the familiar style, with a bit of biographical data and appropriate logos.

		NM/M
Complete Set (28):		7.50
Common Player:		.25
1	Roger Craig	.25
2	Will Clark	.50
3	Bill Swift	.25
4	Royce Clayton	.25
5	John Burkett	.25
6	Willie McGee	.25
7	Buddy Black	.25
8	Dave Righetti	.25
9	Matt Williams	.50
10	Robby Thompson	.25
11	Darren Lewis	.25
12	Mike Jackson	.25
13	Mark Leonard	.25
14	Rod Beck	.25
15	Mike Felder	.25
16	Bryan Hickerson	.25
17	Jose Uribe	.25
18	Greg Litton	.25
19	Cory Snyder	.25
20	Jim McNamara	.25
21	Kelly Downs	.25
22	Trevor Wilson	.25
23	Kirt Manwaring	.25
24	Kevin Bass	.25
25	Jeff Brantley	.25
26	Dave Burba	.25
27	Chris James	.25
28	Coaches/Checklist (Carlos Alfonso, Dusty Baker, Bob Brenly, Wendell Kim, Bob Lillis)	.25

Mariners

After a one-year absence from the Mother's Cookies lineup, the M's returned in 1992 with a set. Standard-size cards have rounded corners and UV-coated fronts. The only graphics appearing on the borderless photos are the player and team name in white in an upper corner. Backs are printed in red and purple and have basic biographical data, uniform and card numbers, space for an autograph and appropriate sponsor and licensor logos.

		NM/M
Complete Set (28):		12.50
Common Player:		.25
1	Bill Plummer	.25
2	Ken Griffey Jr.	4.00
3	Harold Reynolds	.25
4	Kevin Mitchell	.25
5	David Valle	.25
6	Jay Buhner	.40
7	Erik Hanson	.25
8	Pete O'Brien	.25
9	Henry Cotto	.25
10	Mike Schooler	.25
11	Tino Martinez	1.00
12	Dennis Powell	.25
13	Randy Johnson	2.00
14	Dave Cochrane	.25
15	Greg Briley	.25
16	Omar Vizquel	.40
17	Dave Fleming	.25
18	Matt Sinatro	.25
19	Jeff Nelson	.25
20	Edgar Martinez	.25
21	Calvin Jones	.25
22	Russ Swan	.25
23	Jim Acker	.25
24	Jeff Schaffer	.25

Padres

The Padres ended a six-year hiatus when they re-appeared in the Mother's Cookies lineup for 1992. The 28-card set follows the traditional Mother's format: 2-1/2" x 3-1/2" cards with rounded corners, glossy borderless front photos and the player and team name in white in an upper corner. Backs have appropriate logos, uniform and card numbers, player data and room for an autograph, all printed in red and purple.

		NM/M
Complete Set (28):		10.00
Common Player:		.25
1	Greg Riddoch	.25
2	Greg Harris	.25
3	Gary Sheffield	1.00
4	Fred McGriff	.40
5	Kurt Stillwell	.25
6	Benito Santiago	.25
7	Tony Gwynn	4.00
8	Tony Fernandez	.25
9	Jerald Clark	.25
10	Dave Eiland	.25
11	Randy Myers	.25
12	Oscar Azocar	.25
13	Dann Bilardello	.25
14	Jose Melendez	.25
15	Darrin Jackson	.25
16	Andy Benes	.25
17	Tim Teufel	.25
18	Jeremy Hernandez	.25
19	Kevin Ward	.25
20	Bruce Hurst	.25
21	Larry Andersen	.25
22	Rich Rodriguez	.25
23	Pat Clements	.25
24	Craig Lefferts	.25
25	Craig Shipley	.25
26	Mike Maddux	.25
27	Coaches (Bruce Kimm, Rob Picciolo, Merv Rettenmund, Mike Roarke, Jim Snyder)	.25
28	Team logo/checklist	.25

Rangers

The clubhouse wall provides the universal backdrop for the posed photos in this 28-card set. Standard-size cards have a high-gloss borderless front photo with rounded corners and the player and team name in white in an upper corner. Backs are in red and purple and have a few

25	Clay Parker	.25
26	Brian Holman	.25
27	Coaches (Marty Martinez, Gene Clines, Roger Hansen, Dan Warthen, Russ Nixon, Rusty Kuntz)	.25
28	Mascot/Checklist	.25

player biographical details along with uniform and card numbers, space for an autograph and the logos of the sponsor and licensor.

		NM/M
Complete Set (28):		15.00
Common Player:		.25
1	Bobby Valentine	.25
2	Nolan Ryan	5.00
3	Ruben Sierra	.25
4	Juan Gonzalez	2.00
5	Ivan Rodriguez	4.00
6	Bobby Witt	.25
7	Geno Petralli	.25
8	Jeff Russell	.25
9	Rafael Palmeiro	1.50
10	Julio Franco	.25
11	Jack Daugherty	.25
12	Dickie Thon	.25
13	Floyd Bannister	.25
14	Scott Chiamparino	.25
15	Kevin Reimer	.25
16	Jeff Robinson	.25
17	Brian Downing	.25
18	Brian Bohanon	.25
19	Jose Guzman	.25
20	Terry Mathews	.25
21	Kevin Brown	.25
22	Kenny Rogers	.25
23	Jeff Huson	.25
24	Monty Fariss	.25
25	Al Newman	.25
26	Dean Palmer	.25
27	John Cangelosi	.25
28	Coaches/Checklist (Ray Burris, Orlando Gomez, Toby Harrah, Tom House, Dave Oliver, Tom Robson)	.25

Nolan Ryan 7 No-Hitters

Mother's Cookie Company produced an eight-card set in 1992 commemorating Nolan Ryan's seven no-hitters. Cards were found in specially marked packages of Mother's Cookies. The company also made available uncut sheets of the eight cards through the mail. Fronts feature photos contemporary with Ryan's no-hitters in a borderless, round-cornered format with glossy surface. "Nolan Ryan/7 No-Hitters" appears in white vertically in the upper-left corner. Backs are printed in red and purple and include a bit of biographical data along with details of each no-hitter. The eighth card in the set offers room to write in information about a future no-hitter which never materialized prior to Ryan's retirement following the 1993 season.

		NM/M
Complete Set (8):		6.00
8-Card Uncut Panel:		6.00
Common Card:		1.00
1	Nolan Ryan/Portrait (Angels)	1.00
2	Nolan Ryan/Pitching (Angels)	1.00
3	Nolan Ryan/Waving (Angels)	1.00
4	Nolan Ryan (Angels, holding four "0" balls)	1.00
5	Nolan Ryan (Astros)	1.00
6	Nolan Ryan/Pitching (Rangers)	1.00
7	Nolan Ryan/Pointing (Rangers)	1.00
8	Nolan Ryan/Palms Up (Rangers)	1.00

Jeff Bagwell

The set consists of four standard-size cards with a full-bleed color photo on the fronts of the cards and rounded corners. Bagwell's name appears horizontally in white on the front of the card and the backs are printed in purple and red. Along with the Major League merchandise logo on the bottom of the card there is an area for the player's autograph.

		NM/M
Complete Set (4):		9.00
4-Card Uncut Panel:		10.00
Common Card:		2.50
1	Jeff Bagwell (Head and shoulders.)	2.50
2	Jeff Bagwell (Bat on shoulder.)	2.50
3	Jeff Bagwell (Waist-up.)	2.50
4	Jeff Bagwell (Ball in glove.)	2.50

Chuck Knoblauch

American League 1991 Rookie of the Year Chuck Knoblauch is featured in this four-card set. Similar in format to other Mother's cards, the glossy fronts have rounded corners and feature full-bleed color photos. The red and purple backs have statistical and biographical data along with appropriate logos.

		NM/M
Complete Set (4):		4.00
Common Card:		1.00
1	Chuck Knoblauch (Bat on shoulder.)	1.00
2	Chuck Knoblauch (Head and shoulders.)	1.00
3	Chuck Knoblauch (Waist-up.)	1.00
4	Chuck Knoblauch/ Fielding	1.00

1993 Mother's Cookies Angels

In its 11th year of renewed baseball card production, Mother's Cookies sponsored trading card promotions with seven major league teams including, for the first time, the California Angels. At special promotional games, youngsters entering the ballpark were given packs of 28 cards. Each of the paper envelopes contained 20 different player cards and eight cards of another player. Instructions on the envelope encouraged trading to complete a set of 28. All of the team sets were identical in format. Cards measure the standard 2-1/2" x 3-1/2" with rounded corners. Fronts feature borderless posed photos, the work of photographer Barry Colla. The only graphic elements on the front are the player's name and team in white, generally in an upper corner. In 1993 the Mother's cards featured a somewhat less glossy front finish than in previous years. Backs are printed in red and purple. Data includes the player's position, uniform and card numbers, a few biographical bits, a "How Obtained" statement and a space for an autograph, along with the logos of the cookie company and Major League Baseball.

		NM/M
Complete Set (28):		9.00
Common Player:		.25
1	Buck Rodgers	.25
2	Gary DiSarcina	.25
3	Chuck Finley	.25
4	J.T. Snow	.50
5	Gary Gaetti	.25
6	Chili Davis	.25
7	Tim Salmon	2.50
8	Mark Langston	.25
9	Scott Sanderson	.25
10	John Orton	.25
11	Julio Valera	.25
12	Chad Curtis	.25
13	Kelly Gruber	.25
14	Rene Gonzalez	.25
15	Luis Polonia	.25
16	Greg Myers	.25
17	Gene Nelson	.25
18	Torey Lovullo	.25
19	Scott Lewis	.25
20	Chuck Crim	.25
21	John Farrell	.25
22	Steve Frey	.25
23	Stan Javier	.25
24	Ken Patterson	.25
25	Ron Tingley	.25
26	Damion Easley	.25
27	Joe Grahe	.25
28	Coaches/Checklist (Jimmie Reese, Rod Carew, Bobby Knoop, Chuck Hernandez, Ken Macha, John Wathan, Rick Turner)	.25

A's

		NM/M
Complete Set (28):		6.00
Common Player:		.25
1	Tony LaRussa	.25
2	Mark McGwire	2.00
3	Terry Steinbach	.25
4	Dennis Eckersley	.75
5	Ruben Sierra	.25
6	Rickey Henderson	1.00
7	Mike Bordick	.25
8	Rick Honeycutt	.25
9	Dave Henderson	.25
10	Bob Welch	.25
11	Dale Sveum	.25
12	Ron Darling	.25
13	Jerry Browne	.25
14	Bobby Witt	.25
15	Troy Neel	.25
16	Goose Gossage	.25
17	Brent Gates	.25
18	Storm Davis	.25
19	Scott Hemond	.25
20	Kelly Downs	.25
21	Kevin Seitzer	.25
22	Lance Blankenship	.25
23	Mike Mohler	.25
24	Edwin Nunez	.25
25	Joe Boever	.25
26	Shawn Hillegas	.25

27	Coaches (Dave Duncan, Art Kusynar, Greg Luzinski, Dave McKay, Tommie Reynolds)	.25
28	Checklist (Frank Ciensczyk (equipment manager))	.25

Astros

		NM/M
Complete Set (28):		9.00
Common Player:		.25
1	Art Howe	.25
2	Steve Finley	.25
3	Pete Harnisch	.25
4	Craig Biggio	.50
5	Doug Drabek	.25
6	Scott Servais	.25
7	Jeff Bagwell	2.50
8	Eric Anthony	.25
9	Ken Caminiti	.25
10	Andujar Cedeno	.25
11	Mark Portugal	.25
12	Jose Uribe	.25
13	Rick Parker	.25
14	Doug Jones	.25
15	Luis Gonzalez	.50
16	Kevin Bass	.25
17	Greg Swindell	.25
18	Eddie Taubensee	.25
19	Darryl Kile	.25
20	Brian Williams	.25
21	Chris James	.25
22	Chris Donnels	.25
23	Xavier Hernandez	.25
24	Casey Candaele	.25
25	Eric Bell	.25
26	Mark Grant	.25
27	Tom Edens	.25
28	Coaches/Checklist (Bill Bowman, Bob Cluck, Matt Galante, Rudy Jaramillo, Ed Ott, Tom Spencer)	.25

Dodgers

Complete Set (28): 20.00

		NM/M
Common Player:		.25
1	Tommy Lasorda	.35
2	Eric Karros	.25
3	Brett Butler	.25
4	Mike Piazza	9.00
5	Jose Offerman	.25
6	Tim Wallach	.25
7	Eric Davis	.25
8	Darryl Strawberry	.25
9	Jody Reed	.25
10	Orel Hershiser	.35
11	Tom Candiotti	.25
12	Ramon Martinez	.25
13	Lenny Harris	.25
14	Mike Sharperson	.25
15	Omar Daal	.25
16	Pedro Martinez	6.00
17	Jim Gott	.25
18	Carlos Hernandez	.25
19	Kevin Gross	.25
20	Cory Snyder	.25
21	Todd Worrell	.25
22	Mitch Webster	.25
23	Steve Wilson	.25
24	Dave Hansen	.25
25	Roger McDowell	.25
26	Pedro Astacio	.25
27	Rick Trlicek	.25

28	Coaches/Checklist (Joe Amalfitano, Mark Cresse, Joe Ferguson, Ben Hines, Manny Mota, Ron Perranoski, Ron Roenicke)	.25

Giants

		NM/M
Complete Set (28):		8.00
Common Player:		.25
1	Dusty Baker	.40
2	Will Clark	.50
3	Matt Williams	.50
4	Barry Bonds	7.50
5	Bill Swift	.25
6	Royce Clayton	.25
7	John Burkett	.25
8	Willie McGee	.25
9	Kirt Manwaring	.25
10	Dave Righetti	.25
11	Todd Benzinger	.25
12	Rod Beck	.25
13	Darren Lewis	.25
14	Robby Thompson	.25
15	Mark Carreon	.25
16	Dave Martinez	.25
17	Jeff Brantley	.25
18	Dave Burba	.25
19	Mike Benjamin	.25
20	Mike Jackson	.25
21	Craig Colbert	.25
22	Bud Black	.25
23	Trevor Wilson	.25
24	Kevin Rogers	.25
25	Jeff Reed	.25
26	Bryan Hickerson	.25
27	Gino Minutelli	.25
28	Coaches / Checklist (Bobby Bonds, Bob Brenly, Wendell Kim, Bob Lillis, Dick Pole, Denny Sommers)	.25

Mariners

		NM/M
Complete Set (28):		10.00
Common Player:		.25
1	Lou Piniella	.25
2	Dave Fleming	.25
3	Pete O'Brien	.25
4	Ken Griffey Jr.	6.00
5	Henry Cotto	.25
6	Jay Buhner	.25
7	David Valle	.25
8	Dwayne Henry	.25
9	Mike Felder	.25
10	Norm Charlton	.25
11	Edgar Martinez	.25
12	Erik Hanson	.25
13	Mike Blowers	.25
14	Omar Vizquel	.25
15	Randy Johnson	2.00
16	Russ Swan	.25
17	Tino Martinez	.25
18	Rich DeLucia	.25
19	Jeff Nelson	.25
20	Chris Bosio	.25
21	Tim Leary	.25
22	Mackey Sasser	.25
23	Dennis Powell	.25
24	Mike Hampton	.25
25	Fernando Vina	.25
26	John Cummings	.25
27	Rich Amaral	.25

28	Coaches/Checklist (Sammy Ellis, John McLaren, Ken Griffey Sr., Sam Perlozzo, Sam Mejias, Lee Elia)	.25

Padres

		NM/M
Complete Set (28):		10.00
Common Player:		.25
1	Jim Riggleman	.25
2	Gary Sheffield	1.00
3	Tony Gwynn	6.00
4	Fred McGriff	.25
5	Greg Harris	.25
6	Tim Teufel	.25
7	Dave Eiland	.25
8	Phil Plantier	.25
9	Bruce Hurst	.25
10	Ricky Gutierrez	.25
11	Rich Rodriguez	.25
12	Derek Bell	.25
13	Bob Geren	.25
14	Andy Benes	.25
15	Darrell Sherman	.25
16	Frank Seminara	.25
17	Guillermo Velasquez	.25
18	Gene Harris	.25
19	Dan Walters	.25
20	Craig Shipley	.25
21	Phil Clark	.25
22	Jeff Gardner	.25
23	Mike Scioscia	.25
24	Wally Whitehurst	.25
25	Roger Mason	.25
26	Kerry Taylor	.25
27	Tim Scott	.25
28	Coaches/Checklist (Dave Bialas, Bruce Bochy, Rob Picciolo, Dan Radison, Merv Rettenmund, Mike Roarke)	.25

Nolan Ryan Farewell

Common Card:		.75
1	Nolan Ryan (1984 Astros)	.75
2	Nolan Ryan (1985 Astros)	.75
3	Nolan Ryan (1986 Astros)	.75
4	Nolan Ryan (1987 Astros)	.75
5	Nolan Ryan (1988 Astros)	.75
6	Nolan Ryan (1989 Rangers)	.75
7	Nolan Ryan (1990 Rangers)	.75
8	Nolan Ryan (1991 Rangers)	.75
9	Nolan Ryan (1992 Rangers)	.75
10	Nolan Ryan (All-Star Stats)	.75

Nolan Ryan's final 10 major league seasons with the Astros and Rangers are captured in this set. Cards are in standard Mother's Cookies format: 2-1/2" x 3-1/2" with rounded corners, borderless front photos and UV-coated. Each card has a "Nolan Ryan Farewell Set" diamond logo in an upper corner. Backs are printed in red and purple and have a few biographical details along with the year the picture on front was created. Each card has stats for one year from 1984-1992 or cumulative All-Star stats along with Major League totals. Cards were available either cello-wrapped singly in cookie packages or as a complete set via a mail-in offer.

	NM/M
Complete Set (10):	6.00
Uncut Sheet (10):	6.00

1994 Mother's Cookies Angels

Originally scheduled to be given away at a promotional date during the 1994 season, these cards were caught in the strike and not distributed until the March 30-April 1 home-and-home series between the replacement players of the Angels and those of the Oakland A's. The cards were distributed in a paper envelope containing 20 different cards and eight cards of a 21st player. The idea was to trade to complete a set. The 2-1/2" x 3-1/2" cards have rounded corners and feature borderless color photos on front with the player's name and team in one of the corners. Backs are printed in red and purple and include some biographical data, uniform and card numbers, logos of Mother's Cookies and Major League Baseball and a line for an autograph.

		NM/M
Complete Set (28):		12.50
Common Player:		.25
1	Marcel Lacheman	.25
2	Mark Langston	.25
3	J.T. Snow	.25
4	Chad Curtis	.25
5	Tim Salmon	1.00
6	Gary DiSarcina	.25
7	Bo Jackson	2.50
8	Dwight Smith	.25
9	Chuck Finley	.25
10	Rod Correia	.25
11	Spike Owen	.25
12	Harold Reynolds	.25
13	Chris Turner	.25
14	Chili Davis	.25
15	Bob Patterson	.25
16	Jim Edmonds	4.00
17	Joe Magrane	.25
18	Craig Lefferts	.25
19	Scott Lewis	.25
20	Rex Hudler	.25
21	Mike Butcher	.25
22	Brian Anderson	.25
23	Greg Myers	.25
24	Mark Leiter	.25
25	Joe Grahe	.25
26	Jorge Fabregas	.25
27	John Dopson	.25
28	Angels Coaches/Checklist (Chuck Hernandez, Ken Macha, Bobby Knoop, Joe Maddon, Rod Carew, Max Oliveras)	.25

A's

Departing little from previous years, this 28-card set of the players, manager and coaches of the Oakland A's features the inimitable photography of Barry Colla. Cards are 2-1/2" x 3-1/2" with rounded corners and borderless photos. The player's name and team are in white in one of the corners. Backs are printed in red and purple and feature a few biographical bits, a uniform number and card number, a line for an autograph and the logos of Mother's Cookies and Major League Baseball. Originally intended to be given away at a game during the strike-shortened 1994 season, the cards were instead given out at the March 30-April 1 home-and-home exhibition series between the A's and the California Angels. To promote old-fashioned card trading, each package of cards contained 20 different cards, plus eight cards of a 21st player. Considerable trading was thus required to complete a set.

		NM/M
Complete Set (28):		12.00
Common Player:		.25
1	Tony LaRussa	.25
2	Mark McGwire	5.00
3	Terry Steinbach	.25
4	Dennis Eckersley	1.50
5	Mike Bordick	.25
6	Rickey Henderson	2.00
7	Ruben Sierra	.25
8	Stan Javier	.25
9	Todd Van Poppel	.25
10	Bob Welch	.25
11	Miguel Jiminez	.25
12	Steve Karsay	.25
13	Geronimo Berroa	.25
14	Bobby Witt	.25
15	Troy Neel	.25
16	Ron Darling	.25
17	Scott Hemond	.25
18	Steve Ontiveros	.25
19	Mike Aldrete	.25
20	Carlos Reyes	.25
21	Brent Gates	.25
22	Mark Acre	.25
23	Eric Helfand	.25
24	Vince Horsman	.25
25	Bill Taylor	.25
26	Scott Brosius	.25
27	John Briscoe	.25
28	Athletics Coaches/Checklist (Dave Duncan, Jim Lefebvre, Carney Lansford, Tommie Reynolds, Art Kusynar, Dave McKay)	.25

Astros

Distributed at an early 1995 game because the 1994 strike wiped out the planned promotional date, these cards were handed out in packages that contained 20 different cards and eight cards of a 21st player. The idea was to trade the duplicates to form a team set. The round-cornered 2-1/2" x 3-1/2" cards have a borderless color photo on front. Backs are printed in red and purple and include a few biographical notes, uniform and card numbers, a line for an autograph and logos of Mother's Cookies and Major League Baseball.

		NM/M
Complete Set (28):		10.00
Common Player:		.25
1	Terry Collins	.25
2	Mitch Williams	.25
3	Jeff Bagwell	2.50
4	Luis Gonzalez	.50
5	Craig Biggio	.50
6	Darryl Kile	.25
7	Ken Caminiti	.25
8	Steve Finley	.25
9	Pete Harnisch	.25
10	Sid Bream	.25
11	Mike Felder	.25
12	Tom Edens	.25
13	James Mouton	.25
14	Doug Drabek	.25
15	Greg Swindell	.25
16	Chris Donnels	.25
17	John Hudek	.25
18	Andujar Cedeno	.25
19	Scott Servais	.25
20	Todd Jones	.25
21	Kevin Bass	.25
22	Shane Reynolds	.25
23	Brian Williams	.25
24	Tony Eusebio	.25
25	Mike Hampton	.25
26	Andy Stankiewicz	.25
27	Astros Coaches (Ben Hines, Julio Linares, Matt Galante, Steve Henderson, Mel Stottlemyre, Sr.)	.25
28	Astros Trainers/Checklist (Dave Labossiere, Dennis Liborio, Rex Jones)	.25

Dodgers

Plans to distribute this set were postponed when the players' strike wiped out the latter part of the 1994 season. Instead, the cards were distributed at an early 1995 promotional contest. Each package of 28 cards contained 20 different cards and eight cards of a 21st player. This required extensive trading to complete a team set. Cards feature borderless color photos on a 2-1/2" x 3-1/2" round-cornered format. Backs are printed in red and purple and include uniform and card numbers, biographical data, an autograph line and the logos of Mother's Cookies and Major League Baseball.

		NM/M
Complete Set (28):		9.00
Common Player:		.25
1	Tommy Lasorda	.25
2	Mike Piazza	5.00
3	Delino DeShields	.25
4	Eric Karros	.25
5	Jose Offerman	.25
6	Brett Butler	.25
7	Orel Hershiser	.35
8	Henry Rodriguez	.25
9	Raul Mondesi	.25
10	Tim Wallach	.25
11	Ramon Martinez	.25
12	Mitch Webster	.25
13	Todd Worrell	.25
14	Jeff Treadway	.25
15	Tom Candiotti	.25
16	Pedro Astacio	.25

17	Chris Gwynn	.25
18	Jim Gott	.25
19	Omar Daal	.25
20	Cory Snyder	.25
21	Kevin Gross	.25
22	Dave Hansen	.25
23	Al Osuna	.25
24	Darren Dreifort	.25
25	Roger McDowell	.25
26	Carlos Hernandez	.25
27	Gary Wayne	.25
28	Dodgers Coaches/Checklist (Ron Perranoski, Joe Amalfitano, Reggie Smith, Joe Ferguson, Bill Russell, Mark Cresse)	.25

1994 Mother's Cookies Giants

Unable to distribute these cards in 1994 because the strike wiped out a promotional date, the Giants gave away the cards at an early 1995 game. Cards were distributed in packages containing 20 different players and eight cards of a 21st player; requiring extensive trading to complete a team set. The 2-1/2" x 3-1/2" round-cornered cards feature borderless color photos on front. Backs have red and purple printing and include a few biographical notes, card and uniform numbers, Mother's Cookies and Major League Baseball logos and a line for an autograph.

		NM/M
Complete Set (28):		15.00
Common Player:		.25
1	Dusty Baker	.40
2	Robby Thompson	.25
3	Barry Bonds	7.50
4	Royce Clayton	.25
5	John Burkett	.25
6	Bill Swift	.25
7	Matt Williams	.50
8	Rod Beck	.25
9	Steve Scarsone	.25
10	Mark Portugal	.25
11	John Patterson	.25
12	Darren Lewis	.25
13	Kirt Manwaring	.25
14	Salomon Torres	.25
15	Willie McGee	.25
16	Dave Martinez	.25
17	Darryl Strawberry	.25
18	Steve Frey	.25
19	Rich Monteleone	.25
20	Todd Benzinger	.25
21	Jeff Reed	.25
22	Mike Benjamin	.25
23	Mike Jackson	.25
24	Pat Gomez	.25
25	Dave Burba	.25
26	Bryan Hickerson	.25
27	Mark Carreon	.25
28	Giants Coaches/Checklist (Bobby Bonds, Bob Lillis, Wendell Kim, Bob Brenly, Dick Pole, Denny Sommers)	.25

Mariners

When the players struck on Aug. 12, 1994, it killed the Mariners' plans to distribute these cards at a promotional date. Instead, packages of the cards were given away during the winter as players and management toured the Northwest drumming up fan interest. Cards were issued in a group containing 20 different players and eight cards of a 21st player. It was necessary to trade the duplicates to finish a team set. Cards are 2-1/2" x 3-1/2" with round corners and feature borderless color photos on front. Backs are in red and purple and include biographical bits, uniform and card numbers and the logos of Mother's Cookies and Major League Baseball.

		NM/M
Complete Set (28):		10.00
Common Player:		.25
1	Lou Piniella	.25
2	Randy Johnson	2.00
3	Eric Anthony	.25
4	Ken Griffey Jr.	5.00
5	Felix Fermin	.25
6	Jay Buhner	.25
7	Chris Bosio	.25
8	Reggie Jefferson	.25
9	Greg Hibbard	.25
10	Dave Fleming	.25
11	Rich Amaral	.25
12	Rich Gossage	.25
13	Edgar Martinez	.25
14	Bobby Ayala	.25
15	Darren Bragg	.25
16	Tino Martinez	.25
17	Mike Blowers	.25
18	John Cummings	.25
19	Keith Mitchell	.25
20	Bill Haselman	.25
21	Greg Pirkl	.25
22	Mackey Sasser	.25
23	Tim Davis	.25
24	Dan Wilson	.25
25	Jeff Nelson	.25
26	Kevin King	.25
27	Torey Lovullo	.25
28	Mariners Coaches/Checklist (Sam Perlozzo, Lee Elia, Sammy Ellis, John McLaren, Sam Mejias)	.25

Padres

The cancellation of the latter part of the 1994 season by the players' strike wiped out a planned promotional date on which these cards were to have been given out. Instead, the cards were distributed at an early 1995 game. Packages were given out consisting of 20 different cards plus eight cards of a 21st player, which could be traded to complete a team set. Cards are 2-1/2" x 3-1/2" with rounded corners and a borderless color photo on front. Backs are printed in red and purple and have a few biographical notes, card and uniform numbers, an autograph line and logos of Mother's Cookies and Major League Baseball.

		NM/M
Complete Set (28):		9.00
Common Player:		.25
1	Jim Riggleman	.25
2	Tony Gwynn	5.00
3	Andy Benes	.25
4	Bip Roberts	.25
5	Phil Clark	.25
6	Wally Whitehurst	.25
7	Archi Cianfrocco	.25
8	Derek Bell	.25
9	Ricky Gutierrez	.25
10	Mark Davis	.25
11	Phil Plantier	.25
12	Brian Johnson	.25
13	Billy Bean	.25
14	Craig Shipley	.25
15	Tim Hyers	.25
16	Gene Harris	.25
17	Scott Sanders	.25
18	A.J. Sager	.25
19	Keith Lockhart	.25
20	Tim Mauser	.25
21	Andy Ashby	.25
22	Brad Ausmus	.25
23	Trevor Hoffman	.25
24	Luis Lopez	.25
25	Doug Brocail	.25
26	Dave Staton	.25
27	Pedro A. Martinez	.25
28	Padres Coaches/Checklist (Sonny Siebert, Rob Picciolo, Dave Bialas, Dan Radison, Merv Rettenmund, Bruce Bochy)	.25

Rookies of the Year

In 1994 Mother's Cookies issued three different four-card sets of the 1993 Rookies of the Year. Cards of Mike Piazza of the Dodgers and Tim Salmon of California were available, one per package, in each of six varieties of Mother's Big Cookies. There was also a four-card set featuring both players on each of the four cards. These cards were packaged one per bag of Mother's Major League Double Headers. The specially marked packages with the trading cards inside also carried details about Mother's Commemorative Uncut Strips of each of the three different sets in a mail-in offer. In addition, the company created two chase cards designed to put the real cookie fans to the test. The "One in a Thousand - Rookies of the Year" - foil trading cards were inserted one in every 1,000 packages, with either blue or red foil, and fewer than 10,000 of the foil cards produced.

		NM/M
Complete Set (12):		8.00
4-Card Uncut Piazza Panel:		6.00
4-Card Uncut Salmon Panel:		2.00
4-Card Uncut Piazza-Salmon Panel:		4.00
Common Card:		.50
1	Tim Salmon (Bat on shoulder.)	.50
2	Tim Salmon (Batting stance.)	.50
3	Tim Salmon (Dugout pose.)	.50
4	Tim Salmon/Fielding	.50
5	Mike Piazza (Bat on shoulder.)	1.50
6	Mike Piazza (Batting stance.)	1.50
7	Mike Piazza (Dugout pose.)	1.50
8	Mike Piazza/Catching	1.50
9	Tim Salmon, Mike Piazza (Bats on shoulders.)	.50
10	Tim Salmon, Mike Piazza (Arm around shoulder.)	.50
11	Tim Salmon, Mike Piazza (Shaking hands.)	.50
12	Tim Salmon, Mike Piazza (Back to back.)	.50
BF	Tim Salmon, Mike Piazza (Shaking hands; 1 in 1,000 blue foil.)	9.00
RF	Tim Salmon, Mike Piazza (Kneeling; 1 in 1,000 red foil.)	9.00

Nolan Ryan Final Farewell

A virtual reprint of the 1993 Farewell Set, the 1994 version uses the same photos and, except for card #10, presents the same information on the card backs. Card #10 in the 1994 set offers 1993 season and final Major League stats instead of

the All-Star stats on the 1993 version. Some minor differences in photo cropping between the two sets will be noticed, as well as the fact that many of the back elements which had been printed in red on the 1993 cards are in purple on the 1994 cards, and vice versa. Cards can be distinguished by the presence of a 1993 or 1994 copyright line on the back.

		NM/M
Complete Set (10):		6.00
10-Card Uncut Panel:		10.00
Common Card:		1.00
1	Nolan Ryan (1984 Astros)	1.00
2	Nolan Ryan (1985 Astros)	1.00
3	Nolan Ryan (1986 Astros)	1.00
4	Nolan Ryan (1987 Astros)	1.00
5	Nolan Ryan (1988 Astros)	1.00
6	Nolan Ryan (1989 Rangers)	1.00
7	Nolan Ryan (1990 Rangers)	1.00
8	Nolan Ryan (1991 Rangers)	1.00
9	Nolan Ryan (1992 Rangers)	1.00
10	Nolan Ryan (1993 Rangers)	1.00

1995 Mother's Cookies Angels

Seven teams in the Western U.S. participated in Mother's Cookies 13th season of sponsoring team sets. Virtually identical in format to previous years, the 2-1/2" x 3-1/2" round-cornered cards were given away at promotional dates. To promote old-fashioned card trading, the cards were distributed in a paper envelope containing 20 different cards, plus eight cards of a 21st player. Considerable trading was thus required to complete a team set. As in previous years, Barry Colla's superb photos capture the players, manager and coaches of each team in a 28-card set. Backs are again printed in red and purple with a few bits of biographical data, uniform and card numbers and space for an autograph, along with the sponsor's logo.

		NM/M
Complete Set (28):		9.00
Common Player:		.25
1	Marcel Lachemann	.25
2	Mark Langston	.25
3	J.T. Snow	.25
4	Tim Salmon	1.50
5	Chili Davis	.25
6	Gary DiSarcina	.25
7	Tony Phillips	.25
8	Jim Edmonds	2.50
9	Chuck Finley	.25
10	Mark Dalesandro	.25
11	Greg Myers	.25
12	Spike Owen	.25
13	Lee Smith	.25
14	Eduardo Perez	.25
15	Bob Patterson	.25
16	Mitch Williams	.25
17	Garret Anderson	.50
18	Mike Bielecki	.25
19	Shawn Boskie	.25
20	Damion Easley	.25
21	Mike Butcher	.25
22	Brian Anderson	.25
23	Andy Allanson	.25
24	Scott Sanderson	.25
25	Troy Percival	.25
26	Rex Hudler	.25
27	Mike James	.25
28	Coaches/checklist (Mick Billmeyer, Rick Burleson, Chuck Hernandez, Bobby Knoop, Bill Lachemann, Joe Maddon)	.25

A's

		NM/M
Complete Set (29):		7.50
Common Player:		.25
1	Tony LaRussa	.25
2	Mark McGwire	2.50
3	Terry Steinbach	.25
4	Dennis Eckersley	.75
5	Rickey Henderson	1.00
6	Ron Darling	.25
7	Ruben Sierra	.25
8	Mike Aldrete	.25
9	Stan Javier	.25
10	Mike Bordick	.25
11	Dave Stewart	.25
12	Geronimo Berroa	.25
13	Todd Van Poppel	.25
14	Todd Stottlemyre	.25
15	Eric Helfand	.25
16	Dave Leiper	.25
17	Rick Honeycutt	.25
18	Steve Ontiveros	.25
19	Mike Gallego	.25
20	Carlos Reyes	.25
21	Brent Gates	.25
22	Craig Paquette	.25
23	Mike Harkey	.25
24	Andy Tomberlin	.25
25	Jim Corsi	.25
26	Mark Acre	.25
27	Scott Brosius	.25
28	Coaches/checklist (Dave Duncan, Art Kusnyer, Carney Lansford, Jim Lefebvre, Dave McKay, Tommie Reynolds)	.25
29	Ariel Prieto (late-season update)	2.50
---	Mother's coupon (Spanish)	.05

Astros

		NM/M
Complete Set (28):		9.00
Common Player:		.25
1	Marcel Lachemann	.25
2	Mark Langston	.25

Common Player:

Common Player:		.25
1	Terry Collins	.25
2	Jeff Bagwell	2.50
3	Luis Gonzalez	.50
4	Darryl Kile	.25
5	Derek Bell	.25
6	Scott Servais	.25
7	Craig Biggio	.50
8	Dave Magadan	.25
9	Milt Thompson	.25
10	Derrick May	.25
11	Doug Drabek	.25
12	Tony Eusebio	.25
13	Phil Nevin	.25
14	James Mouton	.25
15	Phil Plantier	.25
16	Pedro Martinez	.25
17	Orlando Miller	.25
18	John Hudek	.25
19	Doug Brocail	.25
20	Craig Shipley	.25
21	Shane Reynolds	.25
22	Mike Hampton	.25
23	Todd Jones	.25
24	Greg Swindell	.25
25	Jim Dougherty	.25
26	Brian Hunter	.25
27	Dave Veres	.25
28	Coaches/checklist (Jesse Barfield, Matt Galante, Steve Henderson, Julio Linares, Mel Stottlemyre)	.25

Dodgers

		NM/M
Complete Set (28):		12.00
Common Player:		.25
1	Tommy Lasorda	.25
2	Mike Piazza	4.00
3	Raul Mondesi	.25
4	Ramon Martinez	.25
5	Eric Karros	.25
6	Roberto Kelly	.25
7	Tim Wallach	.25
8	Jose Offerman	.25
9	Delino DeShields	.25
10	Dave Hansen	.25
11	Pedro Astacio	.25
12	Mitch Webster	.25
13	Hideo Nomo	6.00
14	Billy Ashley	.25
15	Chris Gwynn	.25
16	Todd Hollandsworth	.25
17	Omar Daal	.25
18	Todd Worrell	.25
19	Todd Williams	.25
20	Carlos Hernandez	.25
21	Tom Candiotti	.25
22	Antonio Osuna	.25
23	Ismael Valdes	.25
24	Rudy Seanez	.25
25	Joey Eischen	.25
26	Greg Hansell	.25
27	Rick Parker	.25
28	Coaches/checklist (Joe Amalfitano, Mark Cresse, Manny Mota, Bill Russell, Reggie Smith, Dave Wallace)	.25

Giants

		NM/M
Complete Set (28):		12.00
Common Player:		.25
1	Dusty Baker	.40

2 Robby Thompson .25
3 Barry Bonds 6.00
4 Royce Clayton .25
5 Glenallen Hill .25
7 Terry Mulholland .25
7 Matt Williams .50
8 Mark Portugal .25
9 John Patterson .25
10 Rod Beck .25
11 Mark Leiter .25
12 Kirt Manwaring .25
13 Steve Scarsone .25
14 Darren Lewis .25
15 Tom Lampkin .25
16 William
Van Landingham .25
17 Joe Rosselli .25
18 Chris Hook .25
19 Mark Dewey .25
20 J.R. Phillips .25
21 Jeff Reed .25
22 Pat Gomez .25
23 Mike Benjamin .25
24 Trevor Wilson .25
25 Dave Burba .25
26 Jose Bautista .25
27 Mark Carreon .25
28 Coaches/checklist
(Bobby Bonds, Bob Brenly, Wendell Kim, Bob Lillis, Dick Pole) .25

Mariners

JOEY CORA Mariners

NM/M
Complete Set (28): 12.00
Common Player: .25
1 Lou Piniella .25
2 Randy Johnson 2.00
3 Dave Fleming .25
4 Ken Griffey Jr. 4.00
5 Edgar Martinez .25
6 Jay Buhner .25
7 Alex Rodriguez 7.50
8 Joey Cora .25
9 Tim Davis .25
10 Mike Blowers .25
11 Chris Bosio .25
12 Dan Wilson .25
13 Rich Amaral .25
14 Bobby Ayala .25
15 Darren Bragg .25
16 Bob Wells .25
17 Doug Strange .25
18 Chad Kreuter .25
19 Rafael Carmona .25
20 Luis Sojo .25
21 Tim Belcher .25
22 Steve Frey .25
23 Tino Martinez .25
24 Felix Fermin .25
25 Jeff Nelson .25
26 Alex Diaz .25
27 Bill Risley .25
28 Coaches/checklist
(Bobby Cuellar, Lee Elia, John McLaren, Sam Mejias, Sam Perlozzo, Matt Sinatro) .25

Padres

FERNANDO VALENZUELA Padres

NM/M
Complete Set (28): 9.00
Common Player: .25
1 Bruce Bochy .25
2 Tony Gwynn 4.00
3 Ken Caminiti .25
4 Bip Roberts .25

5 Andujar Cedeno .25
6 Andy Benes .25
7 Phil Clark .25
8 Fernando Valenzuela .25
9 Roberto Petagine .25
10 Brian Johnson .25
11 Scott Livingstone .25
12 Brian Williams .25
13 Jody Reed .25
14 Steve Finley .25
15 Jeff Tabaka .25
16 Ray Holbert .25
17 Tim Worrell .25
18 Eddie Williams .25
19 Brad Ausmus .25
20 Willie Blair .25
21 Trevor Hoffman .25
22 Scott Sanders .25
23 Andy Ashby .25
24 Joey Hamilton .25
25 Andres Berumen .25
26 Melvin Nieves .25
27 Bryce Florie .25
28 Coaches/checklist
(Davey Lopes, Graig Nettles, Rob Picciolo, Merv Rettenmund, Sonny Siebert) .25

1996 Mother's Cookies Angels

GARRET ANDERSON Angels

After a four-year absence, the California Angels returned to participate in Mother's Cookies 14th season of sponsoring team sets. Virtually identical in format to previous years, the 2-1/2" x 3-1/2" round-cornered cards were given away at promotional dates. To promote old-fashioned card trading, the cards were distributed in a paper envelope containing 20 different cards, plus eight cards of a 21st player. Considerable trading was thus required to complete a team set. As in previous years, superb photos capture the players, manager and coaches of each team in a 28-card set. Backs are again printed in red and purple with a few bits of biographical data, uniform and card numbers and space for an autograph, along with the sponsor's logo.

NM/M
Complete Set (28): 7.50
Common Player: .25
1 Marcel Lachemann .25
2 Chili Davis .25
3 Mark Langston .25
4 Tim Salmon .75
5 Jim Abbott .25
6 Jim Edmonds 1.00
7 Gary DiSarcina .25
8 J.T. Snow .25
9 Chuck Finley .25
10 Tim Wallach .25
11 Lee Smith .25
12 George Arias .25
13 Troy Percival .25
14 Randy Velarde .25
15 Garret Anderson .35
16 Jorge Fabregas .25
17 Shawn Boskie .25
18 Mark Eichhorn .25
19 Jack Howell .25
20 Jason Grimsley .25
21 Rex Hudler .25
22 Mike Aldrete .25
23 Mike James .25
24 Scott Sanderson .25
25 Don Slaught .25
26 Mark Holzemer .25
27 Dick Schofield .25
28 Coaches/checklist
(Mick Billmeyer, Rick Burleson, Rod Carew, Chuck Hernandez, Bobby Knoop, Bill Lachemann, Joe Maddon) .25

A's

JASON GIAMBI Athletics

NM/M
Complete Set (28): 7.50
Common Player: .25
1 Art Howe .25
2 Mark McGwire 2.00
3 Jason Giambi 2.50
4 Terry Steinbach .25
5 Mike Bordick .25
6 Brent Gates .25
7 Scott Brosius .25
8 Doug Johns .25
9 Jose Herrera .25
10 John Wasdin .25
11 Ernie Young .25
12 Pedro Munoz .25
13 Steve Wojciechowski .25
14 Geronimo Berroa .25
15 Phil Plantier .25
16 Bobby Chouinard .25
17 George Williams .25
18 Jim Corsi .25
19 Mike Mohler .25
20 Torey Lovullo .25
21 Carlos Reyes .25
22 Buddy Groom .25
23 Don Wengert .25
24 Bill Taylor .25
25 Todd Van Poppel .25
26 Rafael Bournigal .25
27 Damon Mashore .25
28 Coaches/checklist
(Bob Alejo, Bob Cluck, Duffy Dyer, Brad Fischer, Denny Walling, Ron Washington) .25

Astros

DEREK BELL Astros

NM/M
Complete Set (28): 7.50
Common Player: .25
1 Terry Collins .25
2 Jeff Bagwell 2.50
3 Craig Biggio .50
4 Derek Bell .25
5 Darryl Kile .25
6 Sean Berry .25
7 Doug Drabek .25
8 Derrick May .25
9 Orlando Miller .25
10 Mike Hampton .25
11 Rick Wilkins .25
12 Brian Hunter .25
13 Shane Reynolds .25
14 James Mouton .25
15 Greg Swindell .25
16 Bill Spiers .25
17 Alvin Morman .25
18 Tony Eusebio .25
19 John Hudek .25
20 Doug Brocail .25
21 Anthony Young .25
22 John Cangelosi .25
23 Jeff Tabaka .25
24 Mike Simms .25
25 Todd Jones .25
26 Ricky Gutierrez .25
27 Mark Small .25
28 Coaches/checklist
(Matt Galante, Steve Henderson, Julio Linares, Brent Strom, Rick Sweet) .25

Dodgers

NM/M
Complete Set (28): 10.00
Common Player: .25
1 Tommy Lasorda .25
2 Mike Piazza 4.00
3 Hideo Nomo 2.50
4 Raul Mondesi .25
5 Eric Karros .25
6 Delino DeShields .25
7 Greg Gagne .25
8 Brett Butler .25
9 Todd Hollandsworth .25
10 Mike Blowers .25
11 Ismael Valdes .25
12 Pedro Astacio .25
13 Billy Ashley .25
14 Tom Candiotti .25
15 Dave Hansen .25
16 Joey Eischen .25
17 Milt Thompson .25
18 Chan Ho Park 1.50
19 Antonio Osuna .25
20 Carlos Hernandez .25
21 Ramon Martinez .25
22 Scott Radinsky .25
23 Chad Fonville .25
24 Darren Hall .25
25 Todd Worrell .25
26 Mark Guthrie .25
27 Roger Cedeno .25
28 Coaches/checklist
(Joe Amalfitano, Mark Cresse, Manny Mota, Bill Russell, Reggie Smith, Dave Wallace) .25

Giants

ROB BECK Giants

NM/M
Complete Set (28): 9.00
Common Player: .25
1 Dusty Baker .40
2 Barry Bonds 5.00
3 Rod Beck .25
4 Matt Williams .50
5 Robby Thompson .25
6 Glenallen Hill .25
7 Kirt Manwaring .25
8 Mark Carreon .25
9 Osvaldo Fernandez .25
10 J.R. Phillips .25
11 Shawon Dunston .25
12 Mark Leiter .25
13 William
Van Landingham .25
14 Stan Javier .25
15 Allen Watson .25
16 Mel Hall .25
17 Doug Creek .25
18 Steve Scarsone .25
19 Mark Dewey .25
20 Mark Gardner .25
21 David McCarty .25
22 Tom Lampkin .25
23 Jeff Juden .25
24 Steve Decker .25
25 Rich DeLucia .25
26 Kim Batiste .25
27 Steve Bourgeois .25
28 Checklist/coaches
(Carlos Alfonso, Bobby Bonds, Jim Davenport, Wendell Kim, Juan Lopez, Dick Pole, Mike Sadek) .25

Mariners

JAY BUHNER Mariners

NM/M
Complete Set (28): 15.00
Common Player: .25
1 Lou Piniella .25
2 Randy Johnson 1.00
3 Jay Buhner .25
4 Ken Griffey Jr. 3.00
5 Ricky Jordan .25
6 Rich Amaral .25
7 Edgar Martinez .25
8 Joey Cora .25
9 Alex Rodriguez 6.00
10 Sterling Hitchcock .25
11 Chris Bosio .25
12 John Marzano .25
13 Bob Wells .25
14 Rafael Carmona .25
15 Dan Wilson .25
16 Norm Charlton .25
17 Paul Sorrento .25
18 Mike Jackson .25
19 Luis Sojo .25
20 Bobby Ayala .25
21 Alex Diaz .25
22 Doug Strange .25
23 Bob Wolcott .25
24 Darren Bragg .25
25 Paul Menhart .25
26 Edwin Hurtado .25
27 Russ Davis .25
28 Coaches/checklist
(Bobby Cuellar, Lee Elia, John McLaren, Sam Mejias, Matt Sinatro, Steve Smith) .25

Padres

FERNANDO VALENZUELA Padres

NM/M
Complete Set (28): 9.00
Common Player: .25
1 Bruce Bochy .25
2 Tony Gwynn 3.50
3 Wally Joyner .25
4 Rickey Henderson 1.50
5 Ken Caminiti .25
6 Scott Sanders .25
7 Steve Finley .25
8 Fernando Valenzuela .25
9 Brian Johnson .25
10 Jody Reed .25
11 Bob Tewksbury .25
12 Andujar Cedeno .25
13 Sean Bergman .25
14 Marc Newfield .25
15 Craig Shipley .25
16 Scott Livingstone .25
17 Trevor Hoffman .25
18 Doug Bochtler .25
19 Archi Cianfrocco .25
20 Joey Hamilton .25
21 Andy Ashby .25
22 Chris Gwynn .25
23 Luis Lopez .25
24 Tim Worrell .25
25 Brad Ausmus .25
26 Willie Blair .25
27 Bryce Florie .25
28 Coaches/checklist
(Tim Flannery, Grady Little, Davey Lopes, Rob Picciolo, Merv Rettenmund, Dan Warthen) .25

Rangers

NM/M
Complete Set (28): 9.00
Common Player: .25
1 Johnny Oates .25
2 Will Clark .50
3 Juan Gonzalez 2.50
4 Ivan Rodriguez 3.50
5 Darryl Hamilton .25
6 Dean Palmer .25
7 Mickey Tettleton .25
8 Craig Worthington .25
9 Rusty Greer .25
10 Kevin Gross .25
11 Rick Helling .25
12 Kevin Elster .25
13 Bobby Witt .25
14 Mark McLemore .25
15 Warren Newson .25
16 Mike Henneman .25
17 Ken Hill .25
18 Gil Heredia .25
19 Roger Pavlik .25
20 Dave Valle .25
21 Mark Brandenburg .25
22 Kurt Stillwell .25
23 Ed Vosberg .25
24 Dennis Cook .25
25 Damon Buford .25
26 Benji Gil .25
27 Darren Oliver .25
28 Coaches/checklist
(Dick Bosman, Bucky Dent, Larry Hardy, Rudy Jaramillo, Ed Napoleon, Jerry Narron) .25

Angels

TIM SALMON

Fans attending the August 3 game at Anaheim Stadium received a starter set of 21 of the 28 cards in this team set, plus seven duplicates. They were encouraged to trade to fill their sets. The 2-1/2" x 3-1/2" round-corner cards have player portrait photos on front. To the left and bottom are red and blue stripes. The player name is at bottom in white, and the team logo is at bottom-right. Backs have minimal player data, a sponsor's logo and space for an autograph.

NM/M
Complete Set (28): 7.50
Common Player: .25
1 Terry Collins .25
2 Tim Salmon .50
3 Eddie Murray 2.50
4 Mark Langston .25
5 Jim Edmonds .75
7 Tony Phillips .25
8 Gary DiSarcina .25
9 Garret Anderson .25
9 Chuck Finley .25
10 Darin Erstad 2.00
11 Jim Leyritz .25
12 Shigetosi Hasegawa .25
13 Luis Alicea .25
14 Troy Percival .25
15 Allen Watson .25
16 Craig Grebeck .25
17 Mike Holtz .25

18 Chad Kreuter .25
19 Dennis Springer .25
20 Jason Dickson .25
21 Mike James .25
22 Orlando Palmeiro .25
23 Dave Hollins .25
24 Mark Gubicza .25
25 Pep Harris .25
26 Jack Howell .25
27 Rich DeLucia .25
28 Angels coaches/checklist (Larry Bowa, Rod Carew, Joe Coleman, Marcel Lachemann, Joe Maddon, Dave Parker) .25

A's

MARK McGWIRE

Fans attending the August 10 game at the Coliseum received a starter set of 21 of the 28 cards in this team set, plus seven duplicates. They were encouraged to trade to fill their sets. The 2-1/2" x 3-1/2" round-corner cards have player portrait photos on front. To the left and bottom are green and gold stripes. The player name is at bottom in white, and the team logo is at bottom-right. Backs have minimal player data, a sponsor's logo and space for an autograph.

		NM/M
Complete Set (28):		9.00
Common Player:		.25
1	Art Howe	.25
2	Mark McGwire	2.50
3	Jose Canseco	1.00
4	Jason Giambi	1.50
5	Geronimo Berroa	.25
6	Ernie Young	.25
7	Scott Brosius	.25
8	Dave Magadan	.25
9	Mike Mohler	.25
10	George Williams	.25
11	Tony Batista	.25
12	Steve Karsay	.25
13	Rafael Bournigal	.25
14	Ariel Prieto	.25
15	Buddy Groom	.25
16	Matt Stairs	.25
17	Brent Mayne	.25
18	Bill Taylor	.25
19	Scott Spiezio	.25
20	Richie Lewis	.25
21	Mark Acre	.25
22	Dave Telgheder	.25
23	Willie Adams	.25
24	Izzy Molina	.25
25	Don Wengert	.25
26	Damon Mashore	.25
27	Aaron Small	.25
28	A's coaches/checklist (Bob Alejo, Bob Cluck, Duffy Dyer, Brad Fischer, Denny Walling, Ron Washington)	.25

Astros

DARRYL KILE

Children attending a promotional game at the Astrodome received a starter set of 21 of the 28 cards in this team set, plus seven duplicates. They were encouraged to trade to fill their sets. The 2-1/2" x 3-1/2" round-corner cards have portrait photos on front. To the left and bottom are navy and gold stripes. The player name is at bottom in white, and the team logo is at bottom-right. Backs have minimal player data, a sponsor's logo and space for an autograph.

Dodgers

HIDEO NOMO

Children attending the July 13 game at Dodger Stadium received a starter set of 21 of the 28 cards in this team set, plus seven duplicates. They were encouraged to trade to fill their sets. The 2-1/2" x 3-1/2" round-corner cards have player portrait photos on front. To the left and bottom are red and blue stripes. The player name is at bottom in white, and the team logo is at bottom-right. Backs have minimal player data, a sponsor's logo and space for an autograph.

		NM/M
Complete Set (28):		12.00
Common Player:		.25
1	Bill Russell	.25
2	Eric Karros	.25
3	Mike Piazza	4.00
4	Raul Mondesi	.25
5	Hideo Nomo	2.00
6	Todd Hollandsworth	.25
7	Greg Gagne	.25
8	Brett Butler	.25
9	Ramon Martinez	.25
10	Todd Zeile	.25
11	Ismael Valdes	.25
12	Chip Hale	.25
13	Tom Candiotti	.25
14	Billy Ashley	.25
15	Chan Ho Park	.50
16	Wayne Kirby	.25
17	Mark Guthrie	.25
18	Juan Castro	.25
19	Todd Worrell	.25
20	Tom Prince	.25
21	Scott Radinsky	.25
22	Pedro Astacio	.25
23	Wilton Guerrero	.25
24	Darren Hall	.25
25	Darren Dreifort	.25
26	Nelson Liriano	.25
27	Dodgers coaches (Joe Amalfitano, Mark Cresse, Manny Mota, Mike Scioscia, Reggie Smith, Dave Wallace)	.25
28	Robinson 50th anniversary logo/checklist	.25

Giants

MARVIN BENARD GIANTS

Twenty thousand fans attending the July 27 game at 3Com Park received a starter set of 21 of the 28 cards in this team set, plus seven duplicates. They were encouraged to trade to fill their sets. The 2-1/2" x 3-1/2" round-corner cards have player portrait photos on front. To the left and bottom are black and orange stripes. The player name is at bottom in white, and the team logo is at bottom-right. Backs have minimal player data, a sponsor's logo and space for an autograph.

		NM/M
Complete Set (28)		10.00
Common Player:		.25
1	Dusty Baker	.25
2	Barry Bonds	5.00
3	J.T. Snow	.25
4	Rod Beck	.25
5	Glenallen Hill	.25
6	Rick Wilkins	.25
7	Jeff Kent	.50
8	Shawn Estes	.25
9	Darryl Hamilton	.25
10	Jose Vizcaino	.25
11	Julian Tavares	.25
12	Mark Gardner	.25
13	Stan Javier	.25
14	Osvaldo Fernandez	.25
15	Jim Poole	.25
16	Marvin Benard	.25
17	William Van Landingham	.25
18	Bill Mueller	.25
19	Mark Lewis	.25
20	Damon Berryhill	.25
21	Doug Henry	.25
22	Rich Rodriguez	.25
23	Kirk Rueter	.25
24	Rich Aurilia	.25
25	Joe Roa	.25
26	Marcus Jensen	.25
27	Miguel Murphy/Equipment Manager	.25
28	Giants coaches/checklist (Carlos Alfonso, Gene Clines, Sonny Jackson, Juan Lopez, Ron Perranoski, Dick Pole)	.25

Padres

TONY GWYNN PADRES

Partial sets of Mother's Cookies Padres were given to children 14 and under attending the June 22 game at Jack Murphy Stadium. Team colors of royal blue and orange form border strips to the left and bottom of the posed photo. A team logo appears at lower-right.

		NM/M
Complete Set (28):		9.00
Common Player:		.25
1	Bruce Bochy	.25
2	Tony Gwynn	3.00
3	Ken Caminiti	.25
4	Wally Joyner	.25
5	Rickey Henderson	1.50
6	Greg Vaughn	.25
7	Steve Finley	.25
8	Fernando Valenzuela	.25
9	John Flaherty	.25
10	Sterling Hitchcock	.25
11	Quilvio Veras	.25
12	Don Slaught	.25
13	Sean Bergman	.25
14	Chris Gomez	.25
15	Craig Shipley	.25
16	Joey Hamilton	.25
17	Scott Livingstone	.25
18	Trevor Hoffman	.25
19	Doug Bochtler	.25
20	Chris Jones	.25
21	Andy Ashby	.25
22	Archi Cianfrocco	.25
23	Tim Worrell	.25
24	Will Cunnane	.25
25	Carlos Hernandez	.25
26	Tim Scott	.25
27	Dario Veras	.25
28	Coaches/checklist (Greg Booker, Tim Flannery, Davey Lopes, Rob Picciolo, Merv Rettenmund, Dan Warthen)	.25

Rangers

IVAN RODRIGUEZ

Fans attending a promotional game at the Ballpark in Arlington received a starter set of 21 of the 28 cards in this team set, plus seven duplicates. They were encouraged to trade to fill their sets. The 2-1/2" x 3-1/2" round-corner cards have player portrait photos on front. To the left and bottom are red and blue stripes. The player name is at bottom in white, and the team logo is at bottom-right. Backs have minimal player data, a sponsor's logo and space for an autograph.

		NM/M
Complete Set (28):		8.00
Common Player:		.25
1	Johnny Oates	.25
2	Will Clark	.50
3	Juan Gonzalez	2.50
4	Ivan Rodriguez	3.50
5	John Wetteland	.25
6	Mickey Tettleton	.25
7	Dean Palmer	.25
8	Rusty Greer	.25
9	Ed Vosberg	.25
10	Lee Stevens	.25
11	Benji Gil	.25
12	Mike Devereaux	.25
13	Bobby Witt	.25
14	Mark McLemore	.25
15	Warren Newson	.25
16	Eric Gunderson	.25
17	Ken Hill	.25
18	Damon Buford	.25
19	Roger Pavlik	.25
20	Billy Ripken	.25
21	John Burkett	.25
22	Darren Oliver	.25
23	Mike Simms	.25
24	Julio Santana	.25
25	Henry Mercedes	.25
26	Xavier Hernandez	.25
27	Danny Patterson	.25
28	Rangers coaches/checklist (Dick Bosman, Bucky Dent, Larry Hardy, Rudy Jaramillo, Ed Napoleon, Jerry Narron)	.25

1998 Mother's Cookies A's

TOM CANDIOTTI

The first 25,000 fans at the August 2 game in Oakland received a starter set of 21 of the 28 cards in this team set, plus seven duplicates. They were encouraged to trade to fill their sets. The 2-1/2" x 3-1/2" round-corner cards have player portrait photos on front. To the left and bottom are green and gold stripes. The player name is at the bottom in white, and the team logo is at bottom-left. Backs have minimal player data, a sponsor's logo and space for an autograph, all printed in red and purple on a purple background.

		NM/M
Complete Set (28):		8.00
Common Player:		.25
1	Art Howe	.25
2	Rickey Henderson	1.00
3	Jason Giambi	2.00
4	Tom Candiotti	.25
5	Matt Stairs	.25
6	Kenny Rogers	.25
7	Scott Spiezio	.50
8	Ben Grieve	.25
9	Kevin Mitchell	.25
10	A.J. Hinch	.25
11	Bill Taylor	.25
12	Rafael Bournigal	.25
13	Miguel Tejada	3.00
14	Kurt Abbott	.25
15	Buddy Groom	.25
16	Dave Magadan	.25
17	Mike Oquist	.25
18	Mike Macfarlane	.25
19	Mike Fetters	.25
20	Ryan Christenson	.25
21	T.J. Mathews	.25
22	Mike Mohler	.25
23	Jason McDonald	.25
24	Blake Stein	.25
25	Mike Blowers	.25
26	Jimmy Haynes	.25
27	Aaron Small	.25
28	Coaches/checklist (Duffy Dyer, Brad Fischer, Gary Jones, Rick Peterson, Denny Walling, Ron Washington)	.25

Astros

JEFF BAGWELL

The first 25,000 fans at the September 13 game at the Astrodome received a starter set of 21 of the 28 cards in this team set, plus seven duplicates. They were encouraged to trade to fill their sets. The 2-1/2" x 3-1/2" round-corner cards have player portrait photos on front. To the left and bottom are team-color blue and gold stripes. The player name is at the bottom in white, and the team logo is at bottom-left. Backs have minimal player data, a sponsor's logo and space for an autograph, all printed in red and purple on a purple background.

		NM/M
Complete Set (28):		9.00
Common Player:		.25
1	Larry Dierker	.25
2	Jeff Bagwell	3.00
3	Craig Biggio	.50
4	Derek Bell	.25
5	Shane Reynolds	.25
6	Sean Berry	.25
7	Moises Alou	.25
8	Carl Everett	.25
9	Billy Wagner	.25
10	Tony Eusebio	.25
11	Mike Hampton	.25
12	Ricky Gutierrez	.25
13	Jose Lima	.25
14	Brad Ausmus	.25
15	Bill Spiers	.25
16	C.J. Nitkowski	.25
17	Randy Johnson	4.00
18	Mike Magnante	.25
19	Dave Clark	.25
20	Sean Bergman	.25
21	Richard Hidalgo	.25
22	Pete Shourek	.25
23	Jay Powell	.25
24	Trever Miller	.25
25	Tim Bogar	.25
26	Doug Henry	.25
27	Scott Elarton	.25
28	Coaches (Jose Cruz, Mike Cubbage, Dave Engle, Matt Galante, Tom McCraw, Vern Ruhle)	.25

Dodgers

CHARLES JOHNSON

The first 25,000 kids at the August 16 game in Los Angeles received a starter set of 21 of the 28 cards in this team set, plus seven duplicates. They were encouraged to trade to fill their sets. The 2-1/2" x 3-1/2" round-corner cards have player portrait photos on front. To the left and bottom are red and blue stripes. The player name is at the bottom in white, and the team logo is at bottom-left. Backs have minimal player data, a sponsor's logo and space for an autograph, all printed in red and purple on a purple background.

		NM/M
Complete Set (28):		7.50
Common Player:		.25
1	Glenn Hoffman	.25
2	Eric Karros	.25
3	Bobby Bonilla	.25
4	Raul Mondesi	.25
5	Gary Sheffield	1.00
6	Ramon Martinez	.25
7	Charles Johnson	.25
8	Jose Vizcaino	.25
9	Scott Radinsky	.25
10	Jim Eisenreich	.25
11	Ismael Valdes	.25
12	Eric Young	.25
13	Chan Ho Park	.25
14	Roger Cedeno	.25
15	Antonio Osuna	.25
16	Dave Mlicki	.25
17	Mark Guthrie	.25
18	Juan Castro	.25
19	Darren Dreifort	.25
20	Tom Prince	.25
21	Jeff Shaw	.25
22	Alex Cora	.25
23	Matt Luke	.25
24	Darren Hall	.25
25	Trenidad Hubbard	.25
26	Jim Bruske	.25
27	Tripp Cromer	.25

| 28 | Dodgers coaches (Joe Amalfitano, Mickey Hatcher, Charlie Hough, Manny Mota, Mike Scioscia, John Shelby) | .25 |

Giants

The first 25,000 fans at the July 26 game at 3Com Park received a starter set of 21 of the 28 cards in this team set, plus seven duplicates. They were encouraged to trade to fill their sets. The 2-1/2" x 3-1/2" round-corner cards have player portrait photos on front. To the left and bottom are black and orange stripes. The player name is at the bottom in white, and the team logo is at bottom-left. Backs have minimal player data, a sponsor's logo and space for an autograph, all printed in red and purple on a purple background.

		NM/M
Complete Set (28):		9.00
Common Player:		.25
1	Dusty Baker	.25
2	Barry Bonds	5.00
3	Shawn Estes	.25
4	Jeff Kent	.50
5	Orel Hershiser	.25
6	Brian Johnson	.25
7	J.T. Snow	.25
8	Bill Mueller	.25
9	Kirk Rueter	.25
10	Darryl Hamilton	.25
11	Rich Aurilia	.25
12	Mark Gardner	.25
13	Stan Javier	.25
14	Robb Nen	.25
15	Rich Rodriguez	.25
16	Brent Mayne	.25
17	Julian Tavares	.25
18	Rey Sanchez	.25
19	Chris Jones	.25
20	Charlie Hayes	.25
21	Danny Darwin	.25
22	Jim Poole	.25
23	Marvin Benard	.25
24	Steve Reed	.25
25	Alex Diaz	.25
26	John Johnstone	.25
27	Rene De La Rosa, Mike Krukow, Duane Kuiper, Jon Miller, Amaury Pi-Gonzalez, Ted Robinson/ Broadcasters)	.25
28	Giants coaches/checklist (Carlos Alfonso, Gene Clines, Sonny Jackson, Juan Lopez, Ron Perranoski, Ron Wotus)	.25

Padres

Fans at a designated Pads' home game received a starter set of 21 of the 28 cards in this team set, plus seven duplicates. They were encouraged to trade to fill their sets. The 2-1/2" x 3-1/2" round-corner cards have player portrait photos on front. To the left and bottom are blue and orange stripes. The player name is at the bottom in white, and the team logo is at bottom-left. Backs have minimal player data, a sponsor's logo and space for an autograph, all printed in red and purple on a purple background.

	NM/M
Complete Set (28):	9.00

Common Player:		.25
1	Bruce Bochy	.25
2	Tony Gwynn	4.00
3	Ken Caminiti	.25
4	Kevin Brown	.40
5	Wally Joyner	.25
6	Sterling Hitchcock	.25
7	Greg Vaughn	.25
8	Steve Finley	.25
9	Joey Hamilton	.25
10	Carlos Hernandez	.25
11	Quilvio Veras	.25
12	Trevor Hoffman	.25
13	Chris Gomez	.25
14	Andy Ashby	.25
15	Greg Myers	.25
16	Mark Langston	.25
17	Andy Sheets	.25
18	Dan Miceli	.25
19	James Mouton	.25
20	Brian Boehringer	.25
21	Archi Cianfrocco	.25
22	Mark Sweeney	.25
23	Pete Smith	.25
24	Eddie Williams	.25
25	Ed Giovanola	.25
26	Carlos Reyes	.25
27	Donne Wall	.25
28	Padres coaches (Greg Booker, Tim Flannery, Davey Lopes, Rob Picciolo, Merv Rettenmund, Dave Stewart)	.25

1998 Mr. Sub Roger Clemens

The date attributed is speculative, since the cards carry no copyright. This set appears to have been issued by a Canadian sub sandwich chain to honor Roger Clemens first four Cy Young Awards. Borderless fronts of the 2-1/2" x 3-1/2" cards have color portrait and action artwork of Clemens in a Blue Jays uniform, with a sepia multi-exposure image of Cy Young in the background, all four cards in the set share the front design, with the only difference being the card number at top-left. Backs are dominated by a large coin-like design with black-and-white artwork of Clemens. The first three cards have back pictures in a Red Sox uniform, the last card shows him with Toronto. The date of his CY Award is shown on each "coin." Beneath the central design on the graduated blue background are MLB and Mr. Sub logos and "www.RocketRoger.com."

		NM/M
Complete Set (4):		6.00
Common Card:		1.50
1	Roger Clemens/1986	1.50
2	Roger Clemens/1987	1.50
3	Roger Clemens/1991	1.50
4	Roger Clemens/1997	1.50

1992 Mr. Turkey

Mr. Turkey, a division of Sara Lee, offered a set of Major League Superstar cards during the 1992 season. A total of 26 cards, one player representing each team, were included in various Mr. Turkey meat packages. The cardboard packaging allows for the printing directly on the carton instead of inserting the cards inside the package. Collectors were able to collect the cards individually or as an uncut sheet, available by sending to the company.

		NM/M
Complete Set (26):		10.00
Uncut Sheet:		15.00
Common Player:		.35
1	Jim Abbott	.40
2	Roberto Alomar	.50
3	Sandy Alomar, Jr.	.40
4	Craig Biggio	.40
5	George Brett	2.00
6	Will Clark	.40
7	Roger Clemens	2.00
8	Cecil Fielder	.40
9	Carlton Fisk	1.00
10	Andres Galarraga	.40
11	Dwight Gooden	.40
12	Ken Griffey Jr.	3.00
13	Tony Gwynn	1.50
14	Rickey Henderson	.40
15	Dave Justice	.40
16	Don Mattingly	2.00
17	Dale Murphy	.75
18	Kirby Puckett	1.50
19	Cal Ripken, Jr.	3.50
20	Nolan Ryan	3.50
21	Chris Sabo	.40
22	Ryne Sandberg	1.50
23	Ozzie Smith	1.50
24	Darryl Strawberry	.40
25	Andy Van Slyke	.40
26	Robin Yount	1.00

1995 Mr. Turkey

Five retired players are featured in this issue. The 2-1/2" x 3-1/2" cards have a sepia or color photo on front, along with a Baseball Greats logo. Uniform logos have been removed from the photos. Backs have personal and career data, and logos of the sponsor and the players' licensing agent. The cards are unnumbered.

		NM/M
Complete Set (5):		10.00
Common Player:		2.00
(1)	Bob Feller	2.00
(2)	Al Kaline	2.00
(3)	Tug McGraw	2.00
(4)	Boog Powell	2.00
(5)	Warren Spahn	2.00

1983 Mr. Z's Pizza Milwaukee Brewers

These 5" x 7" color cards were given away (bagged in cellophane) with the purchase of frozen pizzas.

		NM/M
Complete Set (3):		7.50
Common Player:		1.00
(1)	Cecil Cooper	1.00
(2)	Paul Molitor	4.00
(3)	Robin Yount	4.00

1984 Mr. Z's Pizza Milwaukee Brewers

These 5"x7" color cards were given away with the purchase of frozen pizza and other Brewer-logo food products.

		NM/M
Complete Set (3):		4.00
Common Player:		1.00
(1)	George Bamberger	1.00
(2)	Rollie Fingers	2.00
(3)	Jim Gantner	1.00

1985 Mr. Z's Pizza Pete Rose

LAY ONE DOWN

These 5" x 7" cards were issued in Mr. Z's pizzas, each one picturing Pete Rose. Fronts have borderless action photos with a headline in black or white and a facsimile autograph. Backs have a red border with photos of Reds team merchandise which could be obtained by saving pizza labels.

		NM/M
Complete Set (11):		35.00
Common Card:		4.00
(1)	Another Hit! (Pete Rose)	4.00
(2)	Classic Rose (Pete Rose)	4.00
(3)	Lay One Down (Pete Rose)	4.00
(4)	Line Up Time (Pete Rose)	4.00
(5)	On Deck (Pete Rose)	4.00
(6)	One Hit Closer! Pete Rose (No facsimile autograph.)	4.00
(7)	Pete's Back (Pete Rose)	4.00
(8)	Play Ball! (Pete Rose)	4.00
(9)	Player-Manager (Pete Rose)	4.00
(10)	Rounding Third Heading for Home (Pete Rose)	4.00
(11)	Send in the Lefty (Pete Rose)	4.00

2001 Mrs. Baird's Breadwinners Texas Rangers

Every third loaf of Mrs. Baird's bread and buns included one of 10 Texas Rangers cards; other packages had ticket dis-

---

count coupons, autographed memorabilia or cards, or one of 500 foil parallel sets. The cards feature game-action photos on a red and white background. The player's name is vertically in white on a blue strip at left. A Mrs. Baird's logo and "BREAD WINNERS" appear in the black band at top. A team logo is at lower-left. Horizontal backs have another photo with the Rangers stadium at top, personal data at left and 2000 season notes at right. Series 1 (#1-5) cards were available from April through June, Series 2 (#6-10) cards were in packages during July-August. Headquartered in the Dallas area, the bakery's products were distributed throughout Texas and Oklahoma and in parts of Louisiana and New Mexico.

		NM/M
Complete Set (11):		7.50
Common Player:		.50
Foil Parallel:		3X
1	Pudge Rodriguez	1.50
2	Gabe Kapler	.50
3	Rusty Greer	.50
4	Rafael Palmeiro	1.50
5	Kenny Rogers	.50
6	Alex Rodriguez	2.50
7	Ruben Mateo	.50
8	Rick Helling	.50
9	Ken Caminiti	.50
10	Andres Galarraga	.50
	Header/checklist	.05

1981 MSA Discs

Unlike the contemporary Peter Pan/Sunbeam blank-back discs, this set of 2-3/4" diameter discs carry on their backs the advertising of Michael Schechter Associates, their producer.

		NM/M
Complete Set (32):		135.00
Common Player:		4.00
(1)	Buddy Bell	4.00
(2)	Johnny Bench	8.00
(3)	Bruce Bochte	4.00
(4)	George Brett	12.50
(5)	Bill Buckner	4.00
(6)	Rod Carew	8.00
(7)	Steve Carlton	8.00
(8)	Cesar Cedeno	4.00
(9)	Jack Clark	4.00
(10)	Cecil Cooper	4.00
(11)	Bucky Dent	4.00
(12)	Carlton Fisk	8.00
(13)	Steve Garvey	6.50
(14)	Goose Gossage	4.00
(15)	Mike Hargrove	4.00
(16)	Keith Hernandez	4.00
(17)	Bob Horner	4.00
(18)	Reggie Jackson	12.50
(19)	Steve Kemp	4.00
(20)	Ron LeFlore	4.00
(21)	Fred Lynn	4.00
(22)	Lee Mazzilli	4.00
(23)	Eddie Murray	8.00
(24)	Mike Norris	4.00
(25)	Dave Parker	4.00
(26)	J.R. Richard	4.00

---

(27)	Pete Rose	15.00
(28)	Mike Schmidt	12.50
(29)	Tom Seaver	9.00
(30)	Roy Smalley	4.00
(31)	Willie Stargell	8.00
(32)	Garry Templeton	4.00

1981 MSA/Peter Pan-Sunbeam Bakery Discs

Only the MSA copyright is found on these 2-3/4" diameter player discs, the names of Peter Pan or Sunbeam Bakery, the sponsors that packed the discs in loaves of bread, are nowhere to be seen. Like other MSA disc issues, the black-and-white player picture appears on a baseball design with side panels in various colors. Player information appears at each side and in the center panel, along with the Players Association logo. Because the discs are not licensed by the leagues, uniform logos have been removed from the photos. Backs are blank. The unnumbered discs are checklisted here in alphabetical order. A 16-3/4" x 22-5/8" red, white and blue display poster with slots for inserting the discs is known bearing the Peter Pan advertising.

		NM/M
Complete Set (32):		75.00
Common Player:		2.00
Pete Pan Poster:		25.00
(1)	Buddy Bell	2.00
(2)	Johnny Bench	4.50
(3)	Bruce Bochte	2.00
(4)	George Brett	7.50
(5)	Bill Buckner	2.00
(6)	Rod Carew	4.50
(7)	Steve Carlton	4.50
(8)	Cesar Cedeno	2.00
(9)	Jack Clark	2.00
(10)	Cecil Cooper	2.00
(11)	Bucky Dent	2.00
(12)	Carlton Fisk	4.50
(13)	Steve Garvey	3.50
(14)	Goose Gossage	2.00
(15)	Mike Hargrove	2.00
(16)	Keith Hernandez	2.00
(17)	Bob Horner	2.00
(18)	Reggie Jackson	7.50
(19)	Steve Kemp	2.00
(20)	Ron LeFlore	2.00
(21)	Fred Lynn	2.00
(22)	Lee Mazzilli	2.00
(23)	Eddie Murray	4.50
(24)	Mike Norris	2.00
(25)	Dave Parker	2.00
(26)	J.R. Richard	2.00
(27)	Pete Rose	9.00
(28)	Mike Schmidt	7.50
(29)	Tom Seaver	5.00
(30)	Roy Smalley	2.00
(31)	Willie Stargell	4.50
(32)	Garry Templeton	2.00

1985 MSA/Subway Sandwiches Discs

Identical in form and format to other Schechter discs of the era, the Subway giveaways are nowhere marked marked as such, only the MSA copyright appears. The 2-3/4" diameter discs have black-and-white player portraits in the white center panel of a baseball design. The variously colored end panels contain player information and a 1985 date. The Players Association logo appears beneath the photo. Because the discs are not licensed by Major League Baseball, team logos have been airbrushed off uniforms. The unnumbered, blank-backed discs are checklisted here in alphabetical order.

		NM/M
Complete Set (36):		95.00
Common Player:		3.00
(1)	Buddy Bell	3.00
(2)	Mike Boddicker	3.00
(3)	George Brett	10.00
(4)	Bill Buckner	3.00
(5)	Rod Carew	6.50
(6)	Steve Carlton	6.50
(7)	Cesar Cedeno	3.00
(8)	Dave Concepcion	3.00
(9)	Cecil Cooper	3.00
(10)	Al Cowens	3.00
(11)	Goose Gossage	3.00
(12)	Pedro Guerrero	3.00
(13)	Ron Guidry	3.00
(14)	Tony Gwynn	9.00
(15)	Mike Hargrove	3.00
(16)	Bob Horner	3.00
(17)	Kent Hrbek	3.00
(18)	Rick Langford	3.00
(19)	Dennis Leonard	3.00
(20)	Willie McGee	3.00
(21)	Jack Morris	3.00
(22)	Terry Puhl	3.00
(23)	Dan Quisenberry	3.00
(24)	Johnny Ray	3.00
(25)	Cal Ripken Jr.	15.00
(26)	Ryne Sandberg	9.00
(27)	Mike Schmidt	10.00
(28)	Tom Seaver	6.50
(29)	Rick Sutcliffe	3.00
(30)	Bruce Sutter	4.50
(31)	Alan Trammell	3.00
(32)	Fernando Valenzuela	3.00
(33)	Greg Walker	3.00
(34)	Willie Wilson	3.00
(35)	Dave Winfield	6.50
(36)	Geoff Zahn	3.00

1992 MTV Rock n' Jock

The third annual softball charity game featuring music and sports personalities was the occasion for issue of this three-card set. Fronts have a multi-colored starred border with the player action photo (presumably taken at the previous year's game). Backs are in black-and-white with the MTV and event logos, the date and place of the game and the notation that the card is from a "Limited Edition of 20,000."

		NM/M
Complete Set (3):		6.00
Common Player:		.50
1	M.C. Hammer	.50
2	Frank Thomas	2.00
3	Ken Griffey Jr.	4.00

1989 Nabisco Don Mattingly

Issued as a mail-in premium for Ritz cracker proofs of

purchase, this sheet measures 10-5/8" x 13-15/16" and includes eight 2-1/2" x 3-1/2" cards and a 5" x 7" card. The individual cards are not perforated and are seldom seen cut from the sheet. For lack of licensing by Major League Baseball, the photos on front have generally had the team logos airbrushed away. Cards are numbered on front and back with a year identifying the photo. Backs are printed in red, white and blue and contain biographical data and career highlights on the small cards, while the large card offers complete major and minor league stats and major awards won. The sheet was produced for Nabisco by Topps.

		NM/M
Complete Sheet:		7.50
Common Card:		1.00
72	Don Mattingly (Boyhood photo.)	1.00
81	Don Mattingly (Minor league photo.)	1.00
84	Don Mattingly/Fielding	1.00
85	Don Mattingly/Btg	1.00
86	Don Mattingly/Btg	1.00
87	Don Mattingly/Btg	1.00
88	Don Mattingly/Btg	1.00
89	Don Mattingly/Btg	1.00
----	Don Mattingly (5" x 7" pose)	1.00

1992 Nabisco Canadian Tradition

Nabisco released a 36-card set of former Toronto Blue Jays and Montreal Expos inside several of its products in 1992. Three cards were included per box. A colorful 9" x 12" album with plastic sheets was available via a mail-in offer. The cards are artist renderings of the players, similar in style to the famous sports drawings that appeared on the pages of the Sporting News over the years. Text on the drawings is in both English and French. Backs are printed in red, white and blue and include the team and Nabisco logos along with English and French descriptions of the Famous Moment.

		NM/M
Complete Set (36):		25.00
Common Player:		.75
Album:		7.50
1	Bill Lee	.75
2	Cliff Johnson	.75
3	Ken Singleton	.75
4	Al Woods	.75
5	Ron Hunt	.75
6	Barry Bonnell	.75

7	Tony Perez	4.00
8	Willie Upshaw	.75
9	Coco Laboy	.75
10	Famous Moments (Blue Jays Win A.L. East - 1985)	.75
11	Bob Bailey	.75
12	Dave McKay	.75
13	Rodney Scott	.75
14	Jerry Garvin	.75
15	Famous Moments (Expos Win N.L. East - 1981)	.75
16	Rick Bosetti	.75
17	Larry Parrish	.75
18	Bill Singer	.75
19	Ron Fairly	.75
20	Damaso Garcia	.75
21	Al Oliver	1.50
22	Famous Moments (Blue Jays Win Eastern Division - 1989)	.75
23	Claude Raymond	.75
24	Buck Martinez	.75
25	Rusty Staub	1.50
26	Otto Velez	.75
27	Mack Jones	.75
28	Garth Iorg	.75
29	Bill Stoneman	.75
30	Doug Ault	.75
31	Famous Moments (Expos Host All-Star Game 1982)	.75
32	Jesse Jefferson	.75
33	Steve Rogers	.75
34	Ernie Whitt	.75
35	John Boccabella	.75
36	Bob Bailor	.75

1993 Nabisco All-Star Autographs

In a promotion with the Major League Baseball Players Alumni, Nabisco produced this six-card set of former stars. For $5 and proofs of purchase, collectors could receive an authentically autographed card. The 2-1/2" x 3-1/2" cards featured color photos on front on which the team logos have been airbrushed away, since Major League Baseball did not license the issue. Backs gave biographical and career information along with a black-and-white childhood photo of the player. The unnumbered cards are checklisted here in alphabetical order. Don Drysdale's death on July 3, in the midst of the promotion, curtailed availability of cards with his autograph. Each card came cased with a certificate of authenticity. Unautographed cards and 12-card uncut sheets are known.

		NM/M
Complete Set (6):		90.00
Common Player:		6.00
(1)	Ernie Banks	13.50
(2)	Don Drysdale	45.00
(3)	Catfish Hunter	20.00
(4)	Phil Niekro	6.00
(5)	Brooks Robinson	7.50
(6)	Willie Stargell	25.00

1994 Nabisco All-Star Legends Autographs

For a second year in 1994, Nabisco continued its program of offering autographed cards of former stars for $5 and proofs of purchase from its snack products. Cards retained the same basic format of using

airbrushed color photos on front and black-and-white childhood photos on back. Fronts have a "Nabisco All-Star Legends" logo in the upper-left. Backs have career and biographical data and the logos of the sponsor and the Major League Baseball Players Alumni. The unnumbered cards are checklisted here alphabetically. Each card came with a certificate of authenticity. The Sparky Lyle card was not part of the mail-in promotion but was distributed in person during the Legends' tour. Unautographed cards and 12-card uncut sheets are also known.

		NM/M
Complete Set (5):		30.00
Common Player:		6.00
(1)	Bob Gibson	9.00
(2)	Sparky Lyle	12.00
(3)	Jim Palmer	6.00
(4)	Frank Robinson	8.00
(5)	Duke Snider	10.00

2000 Team Nabisco All Stars

This series was issued in Nabisco snack and cookie packages. Fronts have color photos on which team logos have been removed. The player figure is set against a background that has a large purple-blue baseball at bottom and red and white rays at top. The sponsor logo is at top-right. Backs have a smaller version of the photo, career stats and highlights. The unnumbered cards are checklisted here alphabetically.

		NM/M
Complete Set (11):		9.00
Common Player:		.50
(1)	Lawrence "Yogi" Berra	1.50
(2)	Gary Carter	1.00
(3)	Orlando Cepeda	1.00
(4)	George Foster	.50
(5)	Steve Garvey	.75
(6)	John Kruk	.50
(7)	Joe Morgan	1.00
(8)	Dot Richardson	.50
(9)	Brooks Robinson	1.00
(10)	Mike Schmidt	2.00
(11)	Ozzie Smith	2.00

2001 Nabisco Latino Legends of Baseball

A trio of popular Latino former stars are featured in this in-store giveaway from Nabisco. Fronts have portrait and action photos of the play-

er in an 8" x 10" format. Because the cards are not licensed by MLB, uniform logos have been removed from the photos. Backs have personal information and career data printed in Spanish.

		NM/M
Complete Set (3):		20.00
Common Player:		4.00
(1)	Roberto Clemente	15.00
(2)	Minnie Minoso	4.00
(3)	Tony Perez	6.00

2002 Nabisco Philadelphia Phillies

At the July 7 game at Veterans Stadium, youngsters 14 and under received this set. On thin card stock, the 2-1/2" x 3-1/2" cards have red, white and blue borders around game-action photos. Nabisco and Acme logos are in the upper corners. At bottom is the team logo and player name. Horizontal backs are also in red, white and blue with a large batter silhouette, biographical data and a line each of minor and major league stats. The checklist is arranged by uniform numbers which appear on back.

		NM/M
Complete Set (35):		9.00
Common Player:		.25
3	Todd Pratt	.25
5	Pat Burrell	1.00
6	Doug Glanville	.25
7	Jeremy Giambi	.25
8	Marlon Anderson	.35
9	Tomas Perez	.25
10	Larry Bowa	.25
11	Jimmy Rollins	.75
13	Turk Wendell	.25
15	Dave Hollins	.25
16	Travis Lee	.35
17	Scott Rolen	.75
18	John Vukovich	.25
19	Dan Plesac	.25
21	Greg Gross	.25
22	Jason Michaels	.25
24	Mike Lieberthal	.35
25	Gary Varsho	.25
27	Ricky Bottalico	.25
30	Tony Scott	.25
31	Robert Person	.25
33	Ricky Ledee	.25
37	Rheal Cormier	.25
40	Jose Santiago	.25
43	Randy Wolf	.25
47	Vicente Padilla	.25
46	Vern Ruhle	.25
48	David Coggin	.25
49	Jose Mesa	.25
50	Doug Nickle	.25
51	Terry Adams	.25
52	Carlos Silva	.25
53	Bobby Abreu	.35
56	Brandon Duckworth	.25
59	Ramon Henderson	.25

1983 Nalley Potato Chips Mariners

These large (8-11/16" x 10-11/16") photo cards were issued only in the area of Washington state by Nalley Potato Chips. The six Seattle Mariners are pictured in full color on the entire back panel of each box. On the side panels, detailed player stats and biographies are listed on one

side, with a Mariners schedule and ticket discount offer on the other side.

		NM/M
Complete Set (6):		45.00
Common Player:		7.50
8	Rick Sweet	7.50
16	Al Cowens	7.50
21	Todd Cruz	7.50
22	Richie Zisk	7.50
36	Gaylord Perry	20.00
37	Bill Caudill	7.50

1995 National Packtime

An unusual joint venture by the six major baseball card licensees resulted in this 18-card set which was available only via a mail-in offer. The set was obtained by sending in $2 and 28 wrappers from any of the companies' 1995 baseball cards prior to June 30, 1995. Most of the card designs were similar to the respective company's regular issues of the same brand. Each card was gold-foil enhanced and each carries the crossed-bats National Packtime logo on front. Cards are numbered on back from 1-18. A reported 130,000 of the sets were exchanged for wrappers.

		NM/M
Complete Set (18):		3.00
Common Player:		.15
1	Frank Thomas (Donruss)	.40
2	Matt Williams (Fleer Ultra)	.15
3	Juan Gonzalez (Pacific Crown)	.35
4	Bob Hamelin (Pinnacle)	.15
5	Mike Piazza (Topps)	.50
6	Ken Griffey Jr. (Upper Deck)	.50
7	Barry Bonds (Donruss)	.75
8	Tim Salmon (Fleer Ultra)	.15
9	Jose Canseco (Pacific Crown)	.25
10	Cal Ripken Jr. (Pinnacle)	.75
11	Raul Mondesi (Topps)	.15
12	Alex Rodriguez (Upper Deck)	.60
13	Will Clark (Donruss)	.20
14	Fred McGriff (Fleer Ultra)	.15
15	Tony Gwynn (Pacific Crown)	.45
16	Kenny Lofton (Pinnacle)	.15
17	Deion Sanders (Topps)	.20
18	Jeff Bagwell (Upper Deck)	.40

1995 National Packtime Welcome to the Show

This special set was another joint venture by the major

card manufacturers, Major League Baseball and the Players Association. Sets of six cards were given to attendees at the National Sports Collectors Convention. In designs similar to the companies' regular-issue cards of 1995, these handouts carry a National Packtime logo on front and a red, white and black "WELCOME TO THE SHOW" logo on back. Cards are various numbered "of" 5, 6 or 8, though only six were issued. A paper accompanying the six-card packs assured collectors they were receiving the entire set.

		NM/M
Complete Set (6):		3.00
Common Player:		.50
1 of 6	Greg Maddux (Leaf)	1.00
1/8	Albert Belle (Upper Deck)	.60
2 of 6	Darren Daulton (Ultra)	.50
2 of 6	Don Mattingly (Topps)	1.50
3 of 5	Hideo Nomo (Pinnacle)	.75
3 of 6	Randy Johnson (Pacific)	.75

1986 National Photo Royals

(10) DICK HOWSER, Manager

These 2-7/8" x 4-1/4" cards were a team issue produced in conjunction with National Photo. The 24-card set includes 21 players, manager Dick Howser, a Royals' 1985 World Championship commemorative card and a discount offer card from National Photo. Card fronts feature full-color action photos with a blue "Kansas City Royals" at the top of each card. Each player's name, number and position are also included. Card backs list complete professional career statistics, along with the National Photo logo.

		NM/M
Complete Set (24):		3.50
Common Player:		.15
1	Buddy Biancalana	.15
2	Jorge Orta	.15
4	Greg Pryor	.15
5	George Brett	3.00
6	Willie Wilson	.25
9	Jim Sundberg	.15
10	Dick Howser	.15
14	Hal McRae	.15
20	Frank White	.15
21	Lonnie Smith	.15
22	Dennis Leonard	.15
23	Mark Gubicza	.15
24	Darryl Motley	.15
25	Danny Jackson	.15
26	Steve Farr	.15
29	Dan Quisenberry	.25
31	Bret Saberhagen	.25

35	Lynn Jones	.15
37	Charlie Leibrandt	.15
38	Mark Huismann	.15
40	Buddy Black	.15
45	Steve Balboni	.15
----	Header Card	.15
----	Discount Card	.15

1988 Negro League Stars

Josh Gibson

Players associated with the segregated Negro Leagues around Pittsburgh are featured on this set sponsored by the Duquesne Light Co. and the Pittsburgh Pirates and handed out at the September 10 Pirates game. The 2-1/2" x 3-1/2" cards were issued on a perforated sheet. Fronts have sepia photos. A yellow banner at top reads "NEGRO LEAGUE STARS," a commemorative circle logo appears at lower-right. Backs are in black-and-white with a career summary, biographical data, and the Pirates logo.

		NM/M
Complete Set (20):		12.00
Uncut Sheet:		12.50
Common Player:		.40
1	Rube Foster	.60
2	1913 Homestead Grays	.40
3	Cum Posey	.75
4	1926 Pittsburgh Crawford	.40
5	Gus Greenlee	.40
6	Pop Lloyd	.60
7	Oscar Charleston	.60
8	Smoky Joe Williams	.60
9	Judy Johnson	.60
10	Martin Dihigo	.60
11	Satchel Paige	1.50
12	Josh Gibson	1.50
13	Sam Streeter	.40
14	Cool Papa Bell	.60
15	Ted Page	.40
16	Buck Leonard	1.00
17	Ray Dandridge	.60
18	Lefty Melix, Willis Moody	.40
19	Harold Tinker	.40
20	Monte Irvin	.80

1984 Nestle

The 792 cards in the 1984 Nestle set are identical to the Topps regular issue except that the candy company's logo replaces the Topps logo in the upper-right corner of the front. The set was offered as a premium in uncut 132-card sheet form (24" x 48"). A few enterprising individuals bought up the majority of the reported 4,000 sets produced and had the sheets cut into single cards. Due to the ease in handling individual cards, as opposed to

---

large press sheets, sets of single cards sell for more than sheet sets.

	NM/M
Complete Set, Sheets (6)	100.00
Complete Set, Singles (792)	130.00
Common Player:	.25
Sheet A:	60.00
Sheet B:	10.00
Sheet C:	10.00
Sheet D:	10.00
Sheet E:	10.00
Sheet F:	10.00

1984 Nestle Don Mattingly "Proof/Test"

This fantasy card has been frequently encountered in the market since the days of Mattingly's dominance in the baseball card world in the late 1980s. The card is seen in several variations, always in black-and-white with a blank-back. Some versions of this unauthorized collectors issues carry notations of proof- or test-card status on front and/or back.

1984 Nestle Dream Team

Cal Ripken
ORIOLES Shortstop

This set was issued by the Nestle candy company in conjunction with Topps. Cards are in standard 2-1/2" x 3-1/2" size and feature the top 22 players of 1984, 11 from each league. This full-color "Dream Team" includes one player at each position, plus right- and left-handed starting pitchers and one reliever. Card fronts and backs each have a Nestle logo An unnumbered checklist was included with the set.

		NM/M
Complete Set (23):		9.00
Common Player:		.35
Uncut Sheet:		10.00
1	Eddie Murray	.75
2	Lou Whitaker	.35
3	George Brett	2.00
4	Cal Ripken	3.50
5	Jim Rice	.50
6	Dave Winfield	.75
7	Lloyd Moseby	.35
8	Lance Parrish	.35
9	LaMarr Hoyt	.35
10	Ron Guidry	.35
11	Dan Quisenberry	.35
12	Steve Garvey	.50
13	Johnny Ray	.35
14	Mike Schmidt	2.00
15	Ozzie Smith	1.50
16	Andre Dawson	.50
17	Tim Raines	.50
18	Dale Murphy	.50
19	Tony Pena	.35

20	John Denny	.35
21	Steve Carlton	.75
22	Al Holland	.35
----	Checklist	.05

1987 Nestle

Ted Williams
OUTFIELD
BOSTON RED SOX

Nestle, in conjunction with Topps, issued a 33-card set in 1987. Cards #1-11 feature black-and-white photos of players from the "Golden Era." Cards #12-33 feature full-color photos of American (12-22) and National League (23-33) players from the "Modern Era" of baseball. The cards measure 2-1/2" x 3-1/2" and have all team emblems airbrushed away. Three cards were inserted in specially marked six-packs of various Nestle candy bars. Two complete sets were available through a mail-in offer for $1.50 and three proofs of purchase.

		NM/M
Complete Set (33):		10.00
Common Player:		.30
1	Lou Gehrig	.75
2	Rogers Hornsby	.30
3	Pie Traynor	.30
4	Honus Wagner	.50
5	Babe Ruth	2.00
6	Tris Speaker	.30
7	Ty Cobb	.65
8	Mickey Cochrane	.30
9	Walter Johnson	.30
10	Carl Hubbell	.30
11	Jimmie Foxx	.30
12	Rod Carew	.30
13	Nellie Fox	.30
14	Brooks Robinson	.30
15	Luis Aparicio	.30
16	Frank Robinson	.30
17	Mickey Mantle	3.00
18	Ted Williams	.75
19	Yogi Berra	.30
20	Bob Feller	.30
21	Whitey Ford	.30
22	Harmon Killebrew	.30
23	Stan Musial	.60
24	Jackie Robinson	.75
25	Eddie Mathews	.30
26	Ernie Banks	.30
27	Roberto Clemente	1.50
28	Willie Mays	.75
29	Hank Aaron	.75
30	Johnny Bench	.30
31	Bob Gibson	.30
32	Warren Spahn	.30
33	Duke Snider	.30

1988 Nestle

Jose Canseco

This 44-card set was produced by Mike Schechter Associates for Nestle. "Dream Team" packets of three player cards and one checklist card were inserted in six-packs of Nestle's candy bars. The issue features current players divided into four Dream Teams (East and West teams for each

---

league). The "1988 Nestle" header appears at the top of the red and yellow-bordered cards. Below the player close-up (in an airbrushed cap) is a blue oval player name banner. Card backs are red, white and blue with personal stats, career highlights and major league totals. The bright red, blue and yellow checklist card outlines two special offers; one for an uncut sheet of all 44 player cards and one for a 1988 replica autographed baseball.

		NM/M
Complete Set, Singles (44):		10.00
Complete Set, Uncut Sheet:		10.00
Common Player:		.25
1	Roger Clemens	2.25
2	Dale Murphy	.50
3	Eric Davis	.25
4	Gary Gaetti	.25
5	Ozzie Smith	2.00
6	Mike Schmidt	2.25
7	Ozzie Guillen	.25
8	John Franco	.25
9	Andre Dawson	.50
10	Mark McGwire	2.50
11	Bret Saberhagen	.25
12	Benny Santiago	.25
13	Jose Uribe	.25
14	Will Clark	.25
15	Don Mattingly	2.25
16	Juan Samuel	.25
17	Jack Clark	.25
18	Darryl Strawberry	.25
19	Bill Doran	.25
20	Pete Incaviglia	.25
21	Dwight Gooden	.25
22	Willie Randolph	.25
23	Tim Wallach	.25
24	Pedro Guerrero	.25
25	Steve Bedrosian	.25
26	Gary Carter	1.00
27	Jeff Reardon	.25
28	Dave Righetti	.25
29	Frank White	.25
30	Buddy Bell	.25
31	Tim Raines	.25
32	Wade Boggs	2.00
33	Dave Winfield	1.00
34	George Bell	.25
35	Alan Trammell	.25
36	Joe Carter	.25
37	Jose Canseco	.75
38	Carlton Fisk	1.00
39	Kirby Puckett	2.00
40	Tony Gwynn	2.00
41	Matt Nokes	.25
42	Keith Hernandez	.25
43	Nolan Ryan	3.00
44	Wally Joyner	.25

2002 Nestle

JONES
CHIPPER JONES

Specially marked boxes of Nestle's ice cream novelties contained one of six Topps-produced cards sealed to the cardboard in a protective plastic pouch. The 2-1/2" x 3-1/2" cards have a color action photo and black-and-white portrait photo on front. Both pictures have had uniform logos removed because the cards are licensed only by the players, and not by MLB. Topps and Nestle's logos appear at top. Backs have another color photo, biographical data, recent stats, career highlights and sponsor/copyright information. Authentically autographed A-Rod and Chipper cards were random inserts.

		NM/M
Complete Set (6):		12.00
Common Player:		2.00
1	Barry Bonds	3.50

2	Chipper Jones	2.00
3	Chipper Jones/Auto.	35.00
3	Mike Piazza	2.50
4	Alex Rodriguez	2.50
4	Alex Rodriguez/Auto.	60.00
5	Sammy Sosa	2.00
6	Ichiro	3.00

1991-1992 NewSport

O. SMITH
Shortstop

This set of glossy player cards was issued in France as four-card panels stapled into issues of a monthly magazine devoted to American sports; hence all of the text is in French. The approximately 4" x 6" cards have a month of issue in tiny type on the back. Fronts have large color game-action photos or poses bordered in white. At top is the player's last name and initial, and his position. The NewSport and MLB logos are at bottom. Backs are in black-and-white with biographical details, major league stats and career summary. The un-numbered cards are checklisted here in alphabetical order. In 2001 a hoard of more than 14,000 of the cards, comprising 175 sets and thousands of four-card panels, was offered in a major hobby auction but did not meet a $5,000 minimum bid.

		NM/M
Complete Set (32):		55.00
Common Player:		1.00
(1)	Roberto Alomar	1.50
(2)	Wade Boggs	4.00
(3)	George Brett	4.50
(4)	Will Clark	1.00
(5)	Eric Davis	1.00
(6)	Rob Dibble	1.00
(7)	Doug Drabek	1.00
(8)	Cecil Fielder	1.00
(9)	Julio Franco	1.00
(10)	Ken Griffey Jr.	5.00
(11)	Rickey Henderson	3.00
(12)	Kent Hrbek	1.00
(13)	Bo Jackson	1.50
(14)	Howard Johnson	1.00
(15)	Barry Larkin	1.00
(16)	Don Mattingly	4.50
(17)	Fred McGriff	1.00
(18)	Mark McGwire	6.00
(19)	Jack Morris	1.00
(20)	Lloyd Moseby	1.00
(21)	Terry Pendleton	1.00
(22)	Kirby Puckett	4.00
(23)	Cal Ripken Jr.	7.50
(24)	Nolan Ryan	7.50
(25)	Bret Saberhagen	1.00
(26)	Ryne Sandberg	4.00
(27)	Benito Santiago	1.00
(28)	Mike Scioscia	1.00
(29)	Ozzie Smith	4.00
(30)	Darryl Strawberry	1.00
(31)	Andy Van Slyke	1.00
(32)	Frank Viola	1.00

1989 J.J. Nissen Super Stars

Distributed with bakery products, these standard-size cards feature central color photos on which uniform logos have been airbrushed away due to lack of a Major League Baseball license by Michael Schechter Associates, the cards' manufacturer. Front graphics are in shades of red, orange and yel-

ROGER CLEMENS
BOSTON RED SOX
PITCHER

low. Backs are printed in black-and-white. The complete set price does not include the Mark Grace card with Vance Law's photo.

		NM/M
Complete Set (20):		7.00
Common Player:		.25
1	Wally Joyner	.25
2	Wade Boggs	1.00
3	Ellis Burks	.25
4	Don Mattingly	1.25
5	Jose Canseco	.75
6	Mike Greenwell	.25
7	Eric Davis	.25
8	Kirby Puckett	1.00
9	Kevin Seitzer	.25
10	Darryl Strawberry	.25
11	Gregg Jefferies	.25
12a	Mark Grace (Photo actually Vance Law.)	3.00
12b	Mark Grace (Correct photo.)	.35
13	Matt Nokes	.25
14	Mark McGwire	1.50
15	Bobby Bonilla	.25
16	Roger Clemens	1.25
17	Frank Viola	.25
18	Orel Hershiser	.25
19	David Cone	.25
20	Ted Williams	2.00

2001 Norstan Milwaukee Brewers Walk of Fame

To commemorate the Walk of Fame in their newly opened ballpark, the Brewers gave this set of inaugural inductees' cards to the first 30,000 fans at the July 12 game. Sponsored by Norstan, whose logo appears in red on front, the 2-1/2" x 3-1/2" cards have sepia toned game-action photos on front with facsimile autograph; at left is a vertical bar with player name and uniform number. Black-and-white backs have another action photo.

		NM/M
Complete Set (4):		8.00
Common Player:		1.00
(1)	Hank Aaron	4.00
(2)	Rollie Fingers	1.00
(3)	Paul Molitor	2.00
(4)	Robin Yount	2.00

1984 N.Y. Mets M.V.P. Club

This nine-card, uncut panel was issued - along with other souvenir items - as a promotion by the New York Mets M.V.P. (Most Valuable Person) Club. Available from the club by mail, the perforated panel fea-

---

tures eight full-color player cards, plus a special promotional card in the center. The full panel measures 7-1/2" x 10-1/2", with individual cards measuring the standard 2-1/2" x 3-1/2". Card backs are numbered in the upper right corner and include player stats and career highlights.

		NM/M
Complete Singles Set (9):		3.00
Common Player:		.25
Panel:		4.50
1	Dave Johnson	.25
2	Ron Darling	.25
3	George Foster	.25
4	Keith Hernandez	.50
5	Jesse Orosco	.25
6	Rusty Staub	.40
7	Darryl Strawberry	1.50
8	Mookie Wilson	.35
----	Membership Card	.05

1985 N.Y. Mets Super Fan Club

KEITH HERNANDEZ   First Base

This nine-card panel was issued as part of a souvenir package by the New York Mets Super Fan Club. The full-color, perforated panel measures 7-1/2" x 10-1/2" and features eight standard-size player cards, plus a special promotional card in the center. The uncut sheet was available by mail directly from the club. The backs are numbered in the upper right corner and include player statistics and career highlights.

		NM/M
Complete Singles Set (9):		3.50
Common Player:		.25
Panel:		4.50
1	Wally Backman	.25
2	Bruce Berenyi	.25
3	Gary Carter	2.00
4	George Foster	.25
5	Dwight Gooden	1.00
6	Keith Hernandez	.50
7	Doug Sisk	.25
8	Darryl Strawberry	.35
----	Membership Card	.05

1985 N.Y. Mets Police

This collectors' issue came out of Florida, where the Mets conducted spring training. The cards were not authorized by the team, the Kiwanis Club or any police agency; they were manufactured strictly for sale to unsuspecting collectors. In format they resemble contemporary safety issues, measuring 2-5/8" x 4-1/4" with color player photos on front and an anti-drug mes-

---

16
Dwight Gooden
PITCHER

sage on back (ironic, considering the percentage of players in the set who had well-publicized substance abuse problems). Cards are checklisted here in alphabetical order. Because of their unlicensed nature no collectible value is quoted.

Complete Set (6):

1986 N.Y. Mets Super Fan Club

This special nine-card panel was issued by the fan club of the 1986 World Champion New York Mets, along with other souvenir items gained with membership in the club. Included in the full-color set are eight top Mets players, with a promotional card in the center of the panel. Individual cards measure 2-1/2" x 3-1/2", and are perforated at the edges to facilitate separation. The full panel measures 70-1/2" x 10-1/2". Card fronts feature posed photos of each player, along with name, position and team logo. Backs feature career and personal data, and are printed in the team's blue and orange colors.

		NM/M
Complete Singles Set (9):		2.00
Common Player:		.15
Panel:		2.00
1	Wally Backman	.25
2	Gary Carter	1.00
3	Ron Darling	.25
4	Dwight Gooden	.35
5	Keith Hernandez	.45
6	Howard Johnson	.25
7	Roger McDowell	.25
8	Darryl Strawberry	.35
----	Membership Card	.05

1992 N.Y. Mets Spring Training Superstars

A series of large-format (13-3/4" x 22-3/4") color pictures of Mets players was issued during spring training 1992 by The Port St. Lucie News and The Stuart News in Florida. The pictures are printed on heavy newspaper stock and feature color action photos with a light blue frame and white border. A box at bottom has the player's major league career stats. Various advertisements appear on back. The unnum-

---

SUPERSTARS
NEW YORK METS SPRING TRAINING 1992
PORT ST. LUCIE, FLORIDA
HARDBALL IS BACK!
The Port St. Lucie News & The Stuart News
METS, MARCH 14

bered pictures are listed here alphabetically and it is possible this list is not complete.

		NM/M
Complete Set (9):		35.00
Common Player:		4.00
(1)	Bobby Bonilla	4.00
(2)	Kevin Elster	4.00
(3)	John Franco	4.00
(4)	Todd Hundley	4.00
(5)	Howard Johnson	4.00
(6)	Dave Magadan	4.00
(7)	Eddie Murray	8.00
(8)	Willie Randolph	4.00
(9)	Bret Saberhagen	6.00

1997 N.Y. Mets Motion Cards

This issue was handed out to fans as a stadium promotion. The 3-1/2" x 2-1/2" cards have a borderless action scene on front, in which the players move when the card is tilted. Backs are conventionally printed with another player action photo, 1996 stats and biographical details.

		NM/M
Complete Set (4):		9.00
Common Player:		2.00
0	Rey Ordonez	3.00
2	Lance Johnson	2.00
9	Todd Hundley	2.50
31	John Franco	2.00

2003 N.Y. Mets Spring Training

Several media outlets at the team's spring training headquarters in Port St. Luice, Fla., sponsored this set of cards as a stadium giveaway on March 12. Several of the cards are the first to show the team's newest stars in their Mets uniforms. Distributed in a paper envelope, the cards are a mix of portrait and action photos in a blank-back 3-1/8" x 4-7/8" format.

		NM/M
Complete Set (7):		15.00
Common Player:		.50
(1)	Roberto Alomar	1.50
(2)	Armando Benitez	.50
(3)	Cliff Floyd	.50
(4)	Tom Glavine	2.50
(5)	Al Leiter	.50
(6)	Mike Piazza	10.00
(7)	Mo Vaughn	1.50

2004 N.Y. Post Yankees Medallion Collection

A set of 16 commemorative medallions was issued by the N.Y. Post in this early-season promotion. Coupons found in the newspaper between April 27 and May 16 could be redeemed at news-

---

NEW YORK POST $2.99
with Coupon

New York Yankees
2004 MEDALLION COLLECTION
16 MEDALLIONS TO COLLECT

KENNY LOFTON · CF

stands (along with $2.99) for that day's medallion. Larger and thicker than a quarter, the 1-3/16" diameter medals are struck in nickel and have on their fronts an enameled portrait photo. Backs have the team logo. A bronze "Next Century" medallion was available with the complete set and a colorful, photo-filled 9-1/2" x 9" album was available to house the pieces. The medals are listed here by uniform number.

		NM/M
Complete Set (16):		60.00
Common Player:		3.00
Album:		3.00
2	Derek Jeter	7.50
11	Gary Sheffield	4.50
12	Kenny Lofton	3.00
13	Alex Rodriguez	6.00
14	Enrique Wilson	3.00
20	Jorge Posada	3.00
22	Jon Lieber	3.00
25	Jason Giambi	4.50
27	Kevin Brown	3.00
33	Javier Vazquez	3.00
35	Mike Mussina	4.50
42	Mariano Rivera	7.00
51	Bernie Williams	3.00
52	Jose Contreras	3.00
55	Hideki Matsui	7.50
----	Next Century	3.00

2005 N.Y. Post Yankees Immortals Medallion Collection

NEW YORK POST $2.99
with Coupon

Yankees

THE IMMORTALS
2005 MEDALLION COLLECTION
20 MEDALLIONS TO COLLECT

A set of 20 commemorative medallions was issued by the N.Y. Post in this promotion. Coupons found in the newspaper between April 18 and May 13 could be redeemed at newsstands (along with $2.99) for that day's medallion. Larger and thicker than a quarter, the 1-3/16" diameter medals are struck in nickel and have on their fronts an enameled portrait photo. Backs have a pinstriped jersey with the player's number. A triple-fold, colorful, photo-filled 14" x 22" album was available to house the medals. The medals are listed here in the order of their issue.

		NM/M
Complete Set (20):		75.00
Common Player:		3.00
Album:		3.00
(1)	Lou Gehrig	7.50
(2)	Mickey Mantle	10.00
(3)	Graig Nettles	3.00

		NM/M
(4)	Jim "Catfish" Hunter	3.00
(5)	Reggie Jackson	5.00
(6)	Yogi Berra	5.00
(7)	Ron Guidry	3.00
(8)	Lefty Gomez	3.00
(9)	Tony Lazzeri	3.00
(10)	Phil Rizzuto	3.00
(11)	Roger Maris	4.50
(12)	Don Mattingly	4.50
(13)	Don Larsen	3.00
(14)	Elston Howard	3.00
(15)	Thurman Munson	4.50
(16)	Joe DiMaggio	7.50
(17)	Whitey Ford	4.50
(18)	Billy Martin	3.00
(19)	Casey Stengel	3.00
(20)	Babe Ruth	9.00

1982 N.Y. Yankees Yearbook

American League stars of the 1940s-1960s are featured in a two-page cardboard panel stapled into the Yankees yearbook in 1982. The cards were the work of TCMA and done in the style of early-1950s Bowman cards, although the size is the standard 2-1/2" x 3-1/2". Like the '51 cards have a color painting of the player on front with his name in a black strip near the bottom. Backs have a career summary and a bit of personal data along with the TCMA copyright notice. The yearbook originally sold for $3.

		NM/M
Complete Yearbook:		18.00
Complete Set, Singles (18):		16.00
Common Player:		1.00
1	Joe DiMaggio	6.00
2	Billy Pierce	1.00
3	Phil Rizzuto	2.00
4	Ted Williams	5.00
5	Billy Martin	1.50
6	Mel Parnell	1.00
7	Harmon Killebrew	1.50
8	Yogi Berra	2.00
9	Roy Sievers	1.00
10	Bill Dickey	1.50
11	Hank Greenberg	2.00
12	Allie Reynolds	1.00
13	Joe Sewell	1.00
14	Virgil Trucks	1.00
15	Mickey Mantle	8.00
16	Boog Powell	1.00
17	Whitey Ford	1.50
18	Lou Boudreau	1.00

1985 N.Y. Yankees Police

30
Willie Randolph
INFIELDER

This collectors' issue came out of Florida, where the Yankees conducted spring training. The cards were not authorized by the team, the Kiwanis Club of any police agency; they were manufactured strictly for sale to unsuspecting collectors. In format they resemble contemporary safety issues, measuring 2-5/8" x 4-1/4" with color player photos on front and an anti-drug message on back. Cards are checklisted here in alphabetical order. Because they were unlicensed, no collector value is attributed.

Complete Set (6):

2004 N.Y. Yankees Collector's Series

Each spring training program sold at 2004 Yankees games at Legends Field in Tampa included one 8" x 10" color card of a current or former Yankees player. Each card was issued only on a single day, making assembly of complete sets difficult. Fronts have a large color game-action photo with the famous Yankee Stadium facade at top. Backs have biographical data, a few stats or, in the case of retired players, a career summary.

		NM/M
	Complete Set (13):	75.00
	Common Player:	5.00
1	Jorge Posada	6.00
2	Ron Guidry	5.00
3	Mike Mussina	5.00
4	Gary Sheffield	5.00
5	Mariano Rivera	5.00
6	Hideki Matsui	7.50
7	Don Mattingly	10.00
8	Jason Giambi	6.00
9	Reggie Jackson	6.00
10	Yogi Berra	6.00
11	Bucky Dent	5.00
12	Derek Jeter	10.00
13	Alex Rodriguez	10.00

1981 O-Pee-Chee

The Canadian version of the 1981 Topps set consists of 374 cards. This O-Pee-Chee set features many cards which note a player team change on front. These notations could be accomplished as the OPC cards were printed after the Topps. The cards measure 2-1/2" x 3-1/2" and have texts that are written in both English and French. The cards were printed on both white and gray stock. Cards with gray stock are valued 2-3X those with white stock.

		NM/M
	Complete Set (374):	40.00
	Common Player:	.10
	Wax Pack (8):	2.50
	Wax Box (36):	60.00
1	Frank Pastore	.10
2	Phil Huffman	.10
3	Len Barker	.10
4	Robin Yount	2.00
5	Dave Stieb	.15
6	Gary Carter	4.00
7	Butch Hobson	.10
8	Lance Parrish	.10
9	Bruce Sutter	1.50
10	Mike Flanagan	.10
11	Paul Mirabella	.10
12	Craig Reynolds	.10
13	Joe Charboneau	.10
14	Dan Driessen	.10
15	Larry Parrish	.10
16	Ron Davis	.10
17	Cliff Johnson	.10
18	Bruce Bochte	.10
19	Jim Clancy	.10
20	Bill Russell	.10
21	Ron Oester	.10
22	Danny Darwin	.10
23	Willie Aikens	.10
24	Don Stanhouse	.10
25	Sixto Lezcano	.10
26	U.L. Washington	.10
27	Champ Summers	.10
28	Enrique Romo	.10
29	Gene Tenace	.10
30	Jack Clark	.10
31	Checklist 1-125	.10
32	Ken Oberkfell	.10
33	Rick Honeycutt	.10
34	Al Bumbry	.10
35	John Tamargo	.10
36	Ed Farmer	.10
37	Gary Roenicke	.10
38	Tim Foli	.10
39	Eddie Murray	2.00
40	Roy Howell	.10
41	Bill Gullickson	.15
42	Jerry White	.10
43	Tim Blackwell	.10
44	Steve Henderson	.10
45	Enos Cabell	.10
46	Rick Bossetti	.10
47	Bill North	.10
48	Rich Gossage	.10
49	Bob Shirley	.10
50	Dave Lopes	.10
51	Shane Rawley	.10
52	Lloyd Moseby	.75
53	Burt Hooton	.10
54	Ivan DeJesus	.10
55	Mike Norris	.10
56	Del Unser	.10
57	Dave Revering	.10
58	Joel Youngblood	.10
59	Steve McCatty	.10
60	Willie Randolph	.10
61	Butch Wynegar	.10
62	Gary Lavelle	.10
63	Willie Montanez	.10
64	Terry Puhl	.10
65	Scott McGregor	.10
66	Buddy Bell	.10
67	Toby Harrah	.10
68	Jim Rice	.45
69	Darrell Evans	.10
70	Al Oliver	.10
71	Hal Dues	.10
72	Barry Evans	.10
73	Doug Bair	.10
74	Mike Hargrove	.10
75	Reggie Smith	.10
76	Mario Mendoza	.10
77	Mike Barlow	.10
78	Garth Iorg	.10
79	Jeff Reardon	1.00
80	Roger Erickson	.10
81	Dave Stapleton	.10
82	Barry Bonnell	.10
83	Dave Concepcion	.10
84	Johnnie LeMaster	.10
85	Mike Caldwell	.10
86	Wayne Gross	.10
87	Rick Camp	.10
88	Joe Lefebvre	.10
89	Darrell Jackson	.10
90	Bake McBride	.10
91	Tim Stoddard	.10
92	Mike Easler	.10
93	Jim Bibby	.10
94	Kent Tekulve	.10
95	Jim Sundberg	.15
96	Tommy John	.15
97	Chris Speier	.10
98	Clint Hurdle	.10
99	Phil Garner	.10
100	Rod Carew	2.00
101	Steve Stone	.10
102	Joe Niekro	.10
103	Jerry Martin	.10
104	Ron LeFlore	.10
105	Jose Cruz	.10
106	Don Money	.10
107	Bobby Brown	.10
108	Larry Herndon	.10
109	Dennis Eckersley	1.50
110	Carl Yastrzemski	2.50
111	Greg Minton	.10
112	Dan Schatzeder	.10
113	George Brett	4.00
114	Tom Underwood	.10
115	Roy Smalley	.10
116	Carlton Fisk	2.00
117	Pete Falcone	.10
118	Dale Murphy	1.00
119	Tippy Martinez	.10
120	Larry Bowa	.10
121	Julio Cruz	.10
122	Jim Gantner	.10
123	Al Cowens	.10
124	Jerry Garvin	.10
125	Andre Dawson	3.00
126	Charlie Leibrandt	.10
127	Willie Stargell	2.00
128	Andre Thornton	.10
129	Art Howe	.10
130	Larry Gura	.10
131	Jerry Remy	.10
132	Rick Dempsey	.10
133	Alan Trammell	.15
134	Mike LaCoss	.10
135	Gorman Thomas	.10
136	Expos Future Stars (Bobby Pate, Tim Raines, Roberto Ramos)	3.00
137	Bill Madlock	.10
138	Rich Dotson	.10
139	Oscar Gamble	.10
140	Bob Forsch	.10
141	Miguel Dilone	.10
142	Jackson Todd	.10
143	Dan Meyer	.10
144	Garry Templeton	.10
145	Mickey Rivers	.10
146	Alan Ashby	.10
147	Dale Berra	.10
148	Randy Jones	.10
149	Joe Nolan	.10
150	Mark Fidrych	.25
151	Tony Armas	.10
152	Steve Kemp	.10
153	Jerry Reuss	.10
154	Rick Langford	.10
155	Chris Chambliss	.10
156	Bob McClure	.10
157	John Wathan	.10
158	John Curtis	.10
159	Steve Howe	.10
160	Garry Maddox	.10
161	Dan Graham	.10
162	Doug Corbett	.10
163	Rob Dressler	.10
164	Bucky Dent	.10
165	Alvis Woods	.10
166	Floyd Bannister	.10
167	Lee Mazzilli	.10
168	Don Robinson	.10
169	John Mayberry	.10
170	Woodie Fryman	.10
171	Gene Richards	.10
172	Rick Burleson	.10
173	Bump Wills	.10
174	Glenn Abbott	.10
175	Dave Collins	.10
176	Mike Krukow	.10
177	Rick Monday	.10
178	Dave Parker	.10
179	Rudy May	.10
180	Pete Rose	6.00
181	Elias Sosa	.10
182	Bob Grich	.10
183	Fred Norman	.10
184	Jim Dwyer	.10
185	Dennis Leonard	.10
186	Gary Matthews	.10
187	Ron Hassey	.10
188	Doug DeCinces	.10
189	Craig Swan	.10
190	Cesar Cedeno	.10
191	Rick Sutcliffe	.10
192	Kiko Garcia	.10
193	Pete Vuckovich	.10
194	Tony Bernazard	.10
195	Keith Hernandez	.10
196	Jerry Mumphrey	.10
197	Jim Kern	.10
198	Jerry Dybzinski	.10
199	John Lowenstein	.10
200	George Foster	.10
201	Phil Niekro	1.50
202	Bill Buckner	.10
203	Steve Carlton	2.00
204	John D'Acquisto	.10
205	Rick Reuschel	.10
206	Dan Quisenberry	.10
207	Mike Schmidt	4.00
208	Bob Watson	.10
209	Jim Spencer	.10
210	Jim Palmer	1.50
211	Derrel Thomas	.10
212	Steve Nicosia	.10
213	Omar Moreno	.10
214	Richie Zisk	.10
215	Larry Hisle	.10
216	Mike Torrez	.10
217	Rich Hebner	.10
218	Britt Burns	.10
219	Ken Landreaux	.10
220	Tom Seaver	2.00
221	Bob Davis	.10
222	Jorge Orta	.10
223	Bobby Bonds	.10
224	Pat Zachry	.10
225	Ruppert Jones	.10
226	Duane Kuiper	.10
227	Rodney Scott	.10
228	Tom Paciorek	.10
229	Rollie Fingers	1.50
230	George Hendrick	.10
231	Tony Perez	2.50
232	Grant Jackson	.10
233	Damaso Garcia	.10
234	Lou Whitaker	.10
235	Scott Sanderson	.10
236	Mike Ivie	.10
237	Charlie Moore	.10
238	Blue Jays Future Stars (Luis Leal, Brian Milner, Ken Schrom)	.45
239	Rick Miller	.10
240	Nolan Ryan	9.00
241	Checklist 126-250	.10
242	Chet Lemon	.10
243	Dave Palmer	.10
244	Ellis Valentine	.10
245	Carney Lansford	.10
246	Ed Ott	.10
248	Glenn Hubbard	.10
248	Joey McLaughlin	.10
249	Jerry Narron	.10
250	Ron Guidry	.10
251	Steve Garvey	.75
252	Victor Cruz	.10
253	Bobby Murcer	.10
254	Ozzie Smith	3.00
255	John Stearns	.10
256	Bill Campbell	.10
257	Rennie Stennett	.10
258	Rick Waits	.10
259	Gary Lucas	.10
260	Ron Cey	.10
261	Rickey Henderson	8.00
262	Sammy Stewart	.10
263	Brian Downing	.10
264	Mark Bomback	.10
265	John Candelaria	.10
266	Renie Martin	.10
267	Stan Bahnsen	.10
268	Expos Team	.50
269	Ken Forsch	.10
270	Greg Luzinski	.10
271	Ron Jackson	.10
272	Wayne Garland	.10
273	Milt May	.10
274	Rick Wise	.10
275	Dwight Evans	.10
276	Sal Bando	.10
277	Alfredo Griffin	.10
278	Rick Sofield	.10
279	Bob Knepper	.10
280	Ken Griffey	.10
281	Ken Singleton	.10
282	Ernie Whitt	.10
283	Billy Sample	.10
284	Jack Morris	.10
285	Dick Ruthven	.10
286	Johnny Bench	2.00
287	Dave Smith	.10
288	Amos Otis	.10
289	Dave Goltz	.10
290	Bob Boone	.10
291	Aurelio Lopez	.10
292	Tom Hume	.10
293	Charlie Lea	.10
294	Bert Blyleven	.10
295	Hal McRae	.10
296	Bob Stanley	.10
297	Bob Bailor	.10
298	Jerry Koosman	.10
299	Eliott Maddox	.10
300	Paul Molitor	2.50
301	Matt Keough	.10
302	Pat Putnam	.10
303	Dan Ford	.10
304	John Castino	.10
305	Barry Foote	.10
306	Lou Piniella	.15
307	Gene Garber	.10
308	Rick Manning	.10
309	Don Baylor	.10
310	Vida Blue	.10
311	Doug Flynn	.10
312	Rick Rhoden	.10
313	Fred Lynn	.10
314	Rich Dauer	.10
315	Kirk Gibson	2.50
316	Ken Reitz	.10
317	Lonnie Smith	.10
318	Steve Yeager	.10
319	Rowland Office	.10
320	Tom Burgmeier	.10
321	Leon Durham	.10
322	Neil Allen	.10
323	Ray Burris	.10
324	Mike Willis	.10
325	Ray Knight	.10
326	Rafael Landestoy	.10
327	Moose Haas	.10
328	Ross Baumgarten	.10
329	Joaquin Andujar	.10
330	Frank White	.10
331	Blue Jays Team	.50
332	Dick Drago	.10
333	Sid Monge	.10
334	Joe Sambito	.10
335	Rick Cerone	.10
336	Eddie Whitson	.10
337	Sparky Lyle	.10
338	Checklist 251-374	.10
339	Jon Matlack	.10
340	Ben Oglivie	.10
341	Dwayne Murphy	.10
342	Terry Crowley	.10
343	Frank Taveras	.10
344	Steve Rogers	.10
345	Warren Cromartie	.10
346	Bill Caudill	.10
347	Harold Baines	1.50
348	Frank LaCorte	.10
349	Glenn Hoffman	.10
350	J.R. Richard	.10
351	Otto Velez	.10
352	Ted Simmons	.10
353	Terry Kennedy	.10
354	Al Hrabosky	.10
355	Bob Horner	.10
356	Cecil Cooper	.10
357	Bob Welch	.10
358	Paul Moskau	.10
359	Dave Rader	.10
360	Willie Wilson	.10
361	Dave Kingman	.10
362	Joe Rudi	.10
363	Rich Gale	.10
364	Steve Trout	.10
365	Graig Nettles	.10
366	Lamar Johnson	.10
367	Denny Martinez	.10
368	Manny Trillo	.10
369	Frank Tanana	.10
370	Reggie Jackson	2.50
371	Bill Lee	.10
372	Jay Johnstone	.10
373	Jason Thompson	.10
374	Tom Hutton	.10

Posters

Inserted inside the regular 1981 O-Pee-Chee wax packs, these full-color posters measure approximately 4-7/8" x 6-7/8". The set is complete at 24 posters and includes 12 players each from the Blue Jays and Expos. The blank-backed posters are numbered in the border below the photo where the caption is written in both French and English. The photos are surrounded by a blue border for Blue Jays players or a red border for Expos. Because they were inserted in wax packs, the posters are usually found quarter-folded; such folds are not considered in grading.

		NM/M
	Complete Set (24):	10.00
	Common Player:	.50
1	Willie Montanez	.50
2	Rodney Scott	.50
3	Chris Speier	.50
4	Larry Parrish	.50
5	Warren Cromartie	.50
6	Andre Dawson	2.00
7	Ellis Valentine	.50
8	Gary Carter	5.00
9	Steve Rogers	.50
10	Woodie Fryman	.50
11	Jerry White	.50
12	Scott Sanderson	.50
13	John Mayberry	.50
14	Damaso Garcia (Damaso)	.50
15	Alfredo Griffin	.50
16	Garth Iorg	.50
17	Alvis Woods	.50
18	Rick Bosetti	.50
19	Barry Bonnell	.50
20	Ernie Whitt	.50
21	Jim Clancy	.50
22	Dave Stieb	1.50
23	Otto Velez	.50
24	Lloyd Moseby	.50

1982 O-Pee-Chee

The 1982 O-Pee-Chee set, complete at 396 cards, is nearly identical in design to the 1982 Topps set, except the Canadian-issued cards display the O-Pee-Chee logo on the front of the card and list the player's position in both French and English. The backs of the cards, which measure the standard 2-1/2" x 3-1/2", are also bilingual. Some of the cards carry an extra line on the front indicating an off-season team change.

		NM/M
	Complete Set (396):	35.00
	Common Player:	.10
	Wax Pack:	1.50
	Wax Box (36):	40.00
1	Dan Spillner	.10
2	Ken Singleton/AS	.10
3	John Candelaria	.10
4	Frank Tanana	.10
5	Reggie Smith	.10
6	Rick Monday	.10
7	Scott Sanderson	.10
8	Rich Dauer	.10
9	Ron Guidry	.15
10	Ron Guidry/IA	.10
11	Tom Brookens	.10
12	Moose Haas	.10
13	Chet Lemon	.10
14	Steve Howe	.10
15	Ellis Valentine	.10
16	Toby Harrah	.10
17	Darrell Evans	.10
18	Johnny Bench	2.00
19	Ernie Whitt	.10
20	Garry Maddox	.10
21	Graig Nettles/IA	.10
22	Al Oliver/IA	.10
23	Bob Boone	.10
24	Pete Rose/IA	2.00
25	Jerry Remy	.10
26	Jorge Orta	.10
27	Bobby Bonds	.10
28	Jim Clancy	.10
29	Dwayne Murphy	.10
30	Tom Seaver	2.00
31	Tom Seaver/IA	1.00
32	Claudell Washington	.10
33	Bob Shirley	.10
34	Bob Forsch	.10
35	Willie Aikens	.10
36	Rod Carew/AS	.60
37	Willie Randolph	.10
38	Charlie Lea	.10
39	Lou Whitaker	.10
40	Dave Parker	.10
41	Dave Parker/IA	.10
42	Mark Belanger	.10
43	Rick Langford	.10
44	Rollie Fingers/IA	.10
45	Rick Cerone	.10
46	Johnny Wockenfuss	.10
47	Jack Morris/AS	.10
48	Cesar Cedeno	.10
49	Alvis Woods	.10
50	Buddy Bell	.10
51	Mickey Rivers/IA	.10
52	Steve Rogers	.10
53	Blue Jays Team	.50
54	Ron Hassey	.10
55	Rick Burleson	.10
56	Harold Baines	.10
57	Craig Reynolds	.10
58	Carlton Fisk/AS	.60
59	Jim Kern	.10
60	Tony Armas	.10
61	Warren Cromartie	.10
62	Graig Nettles	.10
63	Jerry Koosman	.10
64	Pat Zachry	.10
65	Terry Kennedy	.10
66	Richie Zisk	.10
67	Rich Gale	.10
68	Steve Carlton	2.00
69	Greg Luzinski/IA	.10
70	Tim Raines	2.00
71	Roy Lee Jackson	.10
72	Carl Yastrzemski	2.00
73	John Castino	.10
74	Joe Niekro	.10
75	Tommy John	.15
76	Dave Winfield/AS	.75

Abbreviations

AS - All-Star
IA - In Action

#	Player	Price
77	Miguel Dilone	.10
78	Gary Gray	.10
79	Tom Hume	.10
80	Jim Palmer	1.50
81	Jim Palmer/IA	.75
82	Vida Blue/IA	.10
83	Garth Iorg	.10
84	Rennie Stennett	.10
85	Davey Lopes/IA	.10
86	Dave Concepcion	.10
87	Matt Keough	.10
88	Jim Spencer	.10
89	Steve Henderson	.10
90	Nolan Ryan	7.50
91	Carney Lansford	.10
92	Bake McBride	.10
93	Dave Stapleton	.10
94	Expos Team	.50
95	Ozzie Smith	4.00
96	Rich Hebner	.10
97	Tim Foli	.10
98	Darrell Porter	.10
99	Barry Bonnell	.10
100	Mike Schmidt	3.00
101	Mike Schmidt/IA	1.50
102	Dan Briggs	.10
103	Al Cowens	.10
104	Grant Jackson	.10
105	Kirk Gibson	.10
106	Dan Schatzeder	.10
107	Juan Berenguer	.10
108	Jack Morris	.15
109	Dave Revering	.10
110	Carlton Fisk	2.00
111	Carlton Fisk/IA	1.00
112	Billy Sample	.10
113	Steve McCatty	.10
114	Ken Landreaux	.10
115	Gaylord Perry	1.00
116	Elias Sosa	.10
117	Rich Gossage/IA	.10
118	Expos Future Stars (Terry Francona, Brad Mills, Bryn Smith)	.25
119	Billy Almon	.10
120	Gary Lucas	.10
121	Ken Oberkfell	.10
122	Steve Carlton/IA	1.00
123	Jeff Reardon	.50
124	Bill Buckner	.10
125	Danny Ainge	2.50
126	Paul Splittorff	.10
127	Lonnie Smith	.10
128	Rudy May	.10
129	Checklist 1-132	.10
130	Julio Cruz	.10
131	Stan Bahnsen	.10
132	Pete Vuckovich	.10
133	Luis Salazar	.10
134	Dan Ford	.10
135	Denny Martinez	.10
136	Lary Sorensen	.10
137	Fergie Jenkins	1.50
138	Rick Camp	.10
139	Wayne Nordhagen	.10
140	Ron LeFlore	.10
141	Rick Sutcliffe	.10
142	Rick Waits	.10
143	Mookie Wilson	.10
144	Greg Minton	.10
145	Bob Horner	.10
146	Joe Morgan/IA	1.00
147	Larry Gura	.10
148	Alfredo Griffin	.10
149	Pat Putnam	.10
150	Ted Simmons	.10
151	Gary Matthews	.10
152	Greg Luzinski	.10
153	Mike Flanagan	.10
154	Jim Morrison	.10
155	Otto Velez	.10
156	Frank White	.10
157	Doug Corbett	.10
158	Brian Downing	.10
159	Willie Randolph/IA	.10
160	Luis Tiant	.10
161	Andre Thornton	.10
162	Amos Otis	.10
163	Paul Mirabella	.10
164	Bert Blyleven	.10
165	Rowland Office	.10
166	Gene Tenace	.10
167	Cecil Cooper	.10
168	Bruce Benedict	.10
169	Mark Clear	.10
170	Jim Bibby	.10
171	Ken Griffey Sr./IA	.10
172	Bill Gullickson	.10
173	Mike Scioscia	.10
174	Doug DeCinces	.10
175	Jerry Mumphrey	.10
176	Rollie Fingers	1.00
177	George Foster/IA	.10
178	Mitchell Page	.10
179	Steve Garvey	.50
180	Steve Garvey/IA	.25
181	Woodie Fryman	.10
182	Larry Herndon	.10
183	Frank White/IA	.10
184	Alan Ashby	.10
185	Phil Niekro	1.00
186	Leon Roberts	.10
187	Rod Carew	2.00
188	Willie Stargell/IA	1.00
189	Joel Youngblood	.10
190	J.R. Richard	.10
191	Tim Wallach	.50
192	Broderick Perkins	.10

#	Player	Price
193	Johnny Grubb	.10
194	Larry Bowa	.10
195	Paul Molitor	3.00
196	Willie Upshaw	.10
197	Roy Smalley	.10
198	Chris Speier	.10
199	Don Aase	.10
200	George Brett	3.00
201	George Brett/IA	1.50
202	Rick Manning	.10
203	Blue Jays Future Stars (Jesse Barfield, Brian Milner, Boomer Wells)	2.00
204	Rick Reuschel	.10
205	Neil Allen	.10
206	Leon Durham	.10
207	Jim Gantner	.10
208	Joe Morgan	2.00
209	Gary Lavelle	.10
210	Keith Hernandez	.10
211	Joe Charboneau	.10
212	Mario Mendoza	.10
213	Willie Randolph/AS	.10
214	Lance Parrish	.10
215	Mike Krukow	.10
216	Ron Cey	.10
217	Ruppert Jones	.10
218	Dave Lopes	.10
219	Steve Yeager	.10
220	Manny Trillo	.10
221	Dave Concepcion/IA	.10
222	Butch Wynegar	.10
223	Lloyd Moseby	.20
224	Bruce Bochte	.10
225	Ed Ott	.10
226	Checklist 133-264	.10
227	Ray Burris	.10
228	Reggie Smith/IA	.10
229	Oscar Gamble	.10
230	Willie Wilson	.10
231	Brian Kingman	.10
232	John Stearns	.10
233	Duane Kuiper	.10
234	Don Baylor	.10
235	Mike Easler	.10
236	Lou Piniella	.10
237	Robin Yount	2.00
238	Kevin Saucier	.10
239	Jon Matlack	.10
240	Bucky Dent	.10
241	Bucky Dent/IA	.10
242	Milt May	.10
243	Lee Mazzilli	.10
244	Gary Carter	3.00
245	Ken Reitz	.10
246	Scott McGregor/AS	.10
247	Pedro Guerrero	.10
248	Art Howe	.10
249	Dick Tidrow	.10
250	Tug McGraw	.10
251	Fred Lynn	.10
252	Fred Lynn/IA	.10
253	Gene Richards	.10
254	Jorge Bell	4.00
255	Tony Perez	2.50
256	Tony Perez/IA	.10
257	Rich Dotson	.10
258	Bo Diaz	.10
259	Rodney Scott	.10
260	Bruce Sutter	1.50
261	George Brett/AS	1.00
262	Rick Dempsey	.10
263	Mike Phillips	.10
264	Jerry Garvin	.10
265	Al Bumbry	.10
266	Hubie Brooks	.10
267	Vida Blue	.10
268	Rickey Henderson	3.00
269	Rick Peters	.10
270	Rusty Staub	.20
271	Sixto Lezcano	.10
272	Bump Wills	.10
273	Gary Allenson	.10
274	Randy Jones	.10
275	Bob Watson	.10
276	Dave Kingman	.10
277	Terry Puhl	.10
278	Jerry Reuss	.10
279	Sammy Stewart	.10
280	Ben Oglivie	.10
281	Kent Tekulve	.10
282	Ken Macha	.10
283	Ron Davis	.10
284	Bob Grich	.10
285	Sparky Lyle	.10
286	Rich Gossage/AS	.10
287	Dennis Eckersley	1.00
288	Garry Templeton	.10
289	Bob Stanley	.10
290	Ken Singleton	.10
291	Mickey Hatcher	.10
292	Dave Palmer	.10
293	Damaso Garcia	.10
294	Don Money	.10
295	George Hendrick	.10
296	Steve Kemp	.10
297	Dave Smith	.10
298	Bucky Dent/AS	.10
299	Steve Trout	.10

#	Player	Price
300	Reggie Jackson	2.50
301	Reggie Jackson/IA	1.00
302	Doug Flynn	.10
303	Wayne Gross	.10
304	Johnny Bench/IA	1.00
305	Don Sutton	1.00
306	Don Sutton/IA	.40
307	Mark Bomback	.10
308	Charlie Moore	.10
309	Jeff Burroughs	.10
310	Mike Hargrove	.10
311	Enos Cabell	.10
312	Lenny Randle	.10
313	Ivan DeJesus	.10
314	Buck Martinez	.10
315	Burt Hooton	.10
316	Scott McGregor	.10
317	Dick Ruthven	.10
318	Mike Heath	.10
319	Ray Knight	.10
320	Chris Chambliss	.10
321	Chris Chambliss/IA	.10
322	Ross Baumgarten	.10
323	Bill Lee	.10
324	Gorman Thomas	.10
325	Jose Cruz	.10
326	Al Oliver	.10
327	Jackson Todd	.10
328	Ed Farmer	.10
329	U.L. Washington	.10
330	Ken Griffey	.10
331	John Milner	.10
332	Don Robinson	.10
333	Cliff Johnson	.10
334	Fernando Valenzuela	.15
335	Jim Sundberg	.10
336	George Foster	.10
337	Pete Rose/AS	1.50
338	Davey Lopes/AS	.10
339	Mike Schmidt/AS	1.00
340	Dave Concepcion/AS	.10
341	Andre Dawson/AS	.25
342	George Foster/AS	.10
343	Dave Parker/AS	.10
344	Gary Carter/AS	1.00
345	Fernando Valenzuela/AS	.10
346	Tom Seaver/AS	.60
347	Bruce Sutter/AS	.75
348	Darrell Porter/IA	.10
349	Dave Collins	.10
350	Amos Otis/IA	.10
351	Frank Taveras	.10
352	Dave Winfield	3.00
353	Larry Parrish	.10
354	Roberto Ramos	.10
355	Dwight Evans	.10
356	Mickey Rivers	.10
357	Butch Hobson	.10
358	Carl Yastrzemski/IA	1.00
359	Ron Jackson	.10
360	Len Barker	.10
361	Pete Rose	4.00
362	Kevin Hickey	.10
363	Rod Carew/IA	1.00
364	Hector Cruz	.10
365	Bill Madlock	.10
366	Jim Rice	.40
367	Ron Cey/IA	.10
368	Luis Leal	.10
369	Dennis Leonard	.10
370	Mike Norris	.10
371	Tom Paciorek	.10
372	Willie Stargell	2.00
373	Dan Driessen	.10
374	Larry Bowa/IA	.10
375	Dusty Baker	.10
376	Joey McLaughlin	.10
377	Reggie Jackson/AS	.60
378	Mike Caldwell	.10
379	Andre Dawson	1.00
380	Dave Stieb	.20
381	Alan Trammell	.10
382	John Mayberry	.10
383	John Wathan	.10
384	Hal McRae	.10
385	Ken Forsch	.10
386	Jerry White	.10
387	Tom Veryzer	.10
388	Joe Rudi	.10
389	Bob Knepper	.10
390	Eddie Murray	2.00
391	Dale Murphy	.50
392	Bob Boone/IA	.10
393	Al Hrabosky	.10
394	Checklist 265-396	.10
395	Omar Moreno	.10
396	Rich Gossage	.15

Posters

MONTREAL EXPOS

The 24 posters in this Canadian set, which features 12 players from the Expos and 12 from the Blue Jays, were inserted in regular 1982 O-Pee-Chee wax packs. The posters measure approximately 4-7/8" x 6-7/8" and are usually found quarter-folded for pack insertion. Such fold lines are not considered in grading. The blank-backed posters are numbered in the bottom border where the captions appear in both French and English. Red borders surround the photos of Blue Jays players, while blue borders are used for the Expos.

	NM/M
Complete Set (24):	12.00
Common Player:	.50
1 John Mayberry	.50
2 Damaso Garcia	.50
3 Ernie Whitt	.50
4 Lloyd Moseby	.50
5 Alvis Woods	.50
6 Dave Stieb	.75
7 Roy Lee Jackson	.50
8 Joey McLaughlin	.50
9 Luis Leal	.50
10 Aurelio Rodriguez	.50
11 Otto Velez	.50
12 Juan Berenger (Berenguer)	.50
13 Warren Cromartie	.50
14 Rodney Scott	.50
15 Larry Parrish	.50
16 Gary Carter	5.00
17 Tim Raines	2.00
18 Andre Dawson	2.00
19 Terry Francona	.50
20 Steve Rogers	.50
21 Bill Gullickson	.50
22 Scott Sanderson	.50
23 Jeff Reardon	.50
24 Jerry White	.50

Stickers

The Canadian OPC stickers are identical to the Topps version except for the bi-lingual printing on backs.

1983 O-Pee-Chee

CARL YASTRZEMSKI — RED SOX

Again complete at 396 cards, the 1983 O-Pee-Chee set borrows its design from the 1983 Topps set, except the Canadian-issued cards display the O-Pee-Chee logo on the front of the card and show the player's position in both French and English. The backs of the cards are also printed in both languages. The cards measure the standard 2-1/2" x 3-1/2". Some cards carry the extra line on the front indicating an off-season trade.

	NM/M
Complete Set (396):	30.00
Common Player:	.05
Wax Pack:	3.00
Wax Box (36):	60.00
1 Rusty Staub	.15
2 Larry Parrish	.05
3 George Brett	1.75
4 Carl Yastrzemski	1.50
5 Al Oliver (Super Veteran)	.05
6 Bill Virdon	.05
7 Gene Richards	.05
8 Steve Balboni	.05
9 Joey McLaughlin	.05
10 Gorman Thomas	.05
11 Chris Chambliss	.05
12 Ray Burris	.05
13 Larry Herndon	.05
14 Ozzie Smith	1.50

#	Player	Price
15	Ron Cey	.05
16	Willie Wilson	.05
17	Kent Tekulve	.05
18	Kent Tekulve (Super Veteran)	.05
19	Oscar Gamble	.05
20	Carlton Fisk	1.25
21	Dale Murphy/AS	.05
22	Randy Lerch	.05
23	Dale Murphy	.45
24	Steve Mura	.05
25	Hal McRae	.05
26	Dennis Lamp	.05
27	Ron Washington	.05
28	Bruce Bochte	.05
29	Randy Jones	.05
30	Jim Rice	.15
31	Bill Gullickson	.05
32	Dave Concepcion/AS	.05
33	Ted Simmons	.05
34	(Super Veteran)	.05
35	Bobby Cox	.05
36	Rollie Fingers	.60
37	Rollie Fingers (Super Veteran)	.10
38	Mike Hargrove	.05
39	Roy Smalley	.05
40	Terry Puhl	.05
41	Fernando Valenzuela	.05
42	Garry Maddox	.05
43	Dale Murray	.05
44	Bob Dernier	.05
45	Don Robinson	.05
46	John Mayberry	.05
47	Richard Dotson	.05
48	Wayne Nordhagen	.05
49	Lary Sorenson	.05
50	Willie McGee	.15
51	Bob Horner	.05
52	Rusty Staub	.05
53	(Super Veteran)	.05
52	Tom Seaver	1.25
53	Chet Lemon	.05
54	Scott Sanderson	.05
55	Mookie Wilson	.05
56	Reggie Jackson	1.50
57	Tim Blackwell	.05
58	Keith Moreland	.05
59	Alvis Woods	.05
60	Johnny Bench	1.25
61	Johnny Bench (Super Veteran)	.30
62	Jim Gott	.05
63	Rick Monday	.05
64	Gary Matthews	.05
65	Jack Morris	.15
66	Lou Whitaker	.05
67	U.L. Washington	.05
68	Eric Show	.05
69	Lee Lacy	.05
70	Steve Carlton	1.25
71	Steve Carlton (Super Veteran)	.10
72	Tom Paciorek	.05
73	Manny Trillo	.05
74	Tony Perez	.05
	(Super Veteran)	.05
75	Amos Otis	.05
76	Rick Mahler	.05
77	Hosken Powell	.05
78	Bill Caudill	.05
79	Dan Petry	.05
80	George Foster	.05
81	Joe Morgan	.05
82	Burt Hooton	.05
83	Ryne Sandberg	8.00
84	Alan Ashby	.05
85	Ken Singleton	.05
86	Tom Hume	.05
87	Dennis Leonard	.05
88	Jim Gantner	.05
89	Leon Roberts	.05
90	Jerry Reuss	.05
91	Ben Oglivie	.05
92	Sparky Lyle	.05
	(Super Veteran)	.05
93	John Castino	.05
94	Phil Niekro	.60
95	Alan Trammell	.10
96	Gaylord Perry	.05
97	Tom Herr	.05
98	Vance Law	.05
99	Dickie Noles	.05
100	Pete Rose	2.00
101	Pete Rose (Super Veteran)	.50
102	Dave Concepcion	.05
103	Darrell Porter	.05
104	Ron Guidry	.05
105	Don Baylor	.05
106	Steve Rogers/AS	.05
107	Greg Minton	.05
108	Glenn Hoffman	.05
109	Luis Leal	.05
110	Ken Griffey	.05
111	Expos Team	.05
112	Luis Pujols	.05
113	Julio Cruz	.05
114	Jim Slaton	.05
115	Chili Davis	.05
116	Pedro Guerrero	.05
117	Mike Ivie	.05
118	Chris Welsh	.05
119	Frank Pastore	.05
120	Len Barker	.05
121	Chris Speier	.05
122	Bobby Murcer	.05
123	Bill Russell	.05

#	Player	Price
124	Lloyd Moseby	.05
125	Leon Durham	.05
126	Carl Yastrzemski (Super Veteran)	.05
127	John Candelaria	.05
128	Phil Garner	.05
129	Checklist 1-132	.05
130	Dave Stieb	.10
131	Geoff Zahn	.05
132	Todd Cruz	.05
133	Tony Pena	.05
134	Hubie Brooks	.05
135	Dwight Evans	.05
136	Willie Aikens	.05
137	Woodie Fryman	.05
138	Rick Dempsey	.05
139	Bruce Berenyi	.05
140	Willie Randolph	.05
141	Eddie Murray	1.25
142	Mike Caldwell	.05
143	Tony Gwynn	8.00
144	Tommy John (Super Veteran)	.05
145	Don Sutton	.60
146	Don Sutton (Super Veteran)	.10
147	Rick Manning	.05
148	George Hendrick	.05
149	Johnny Ray	.05
150	Bruce Sutter	1.00
151	Bruce Sutter (Super Veteran)	.25
152	Jay Johnstone	.05
153	Jerry Koosman	.05
154	Johnnie LeMaster	.05
155	Dan Quisenberry	.05
156	Luis Salazar	.05
157	Steve Bedrosian	.05
158	Jim Sundberg	.05
159	Gaylord Perry (Super Veteran)	.10
160	Dave Kingman	.05
161	Dave Kingman (Super Veteran)	.05
162	(Super Veteran)	.05
163	Cal Ripken	8.00
164	Dave Palmer	.05
165	Dan Driessen	.05
166	Tug McGraw	.05
167	Denny Martinez	.05
168	Juan Eichelberger	.05
169	Doug Flynn	.05
170	Steve Howe	.05
171	Frank White	.05
172	Mike Flanagan	.05
173	Andre Dawson/AS	.15
174	Manny Trillo/AS	.05
175	Bo Diaz	.05
176	Dave Righetti	.05
177	Harold Baines	.05
178	Vida Blue	.05
179	Luis Tiant (Super Veteran)	.05
180	Rickey Henderson	1.50
181	Rick Rhoden	.05
182	Fred Lynn	.05
183	Ed Vande Berg	.05
184	Dwayne Murphy	.05
185	Tim Lollar	.05
186	Dave Tobik	.05
187	Tug McGraw (Super Veteran)	.05
188	Rick Miller	.05
189	Dan Schatzeder	.05
190	Cecil Cooper	.05
191	Jim Beattie	.05
192	Rich Dauer	.05
193	Al Cowens	.05
194	Roy Lee Jackson	.05
195	Mike Gates	.05
196	Tommy John	.10
197	Bob Forsch	.05
198	Steve Garvey	.15
199	Brad Mills	.05
200	Rod Carew	1.25
201	Rod Carew (Super Veteran)	.05
202	Blue Jays Team	.05
203	Floyd Bannister	.05
204	Bruce Benedict	.05
205	Dave Parker	.05
206	Ken Oberkfell	.05
207	Graig Nettles	.05
208	Sparky Lyle (Super Veteran)	.05
209	Jason Thompson	.05
210	Jack Clark	.05
211	Jim Kaat	.05
212	John Stearns	.05
213	Tom Burgmeier	.05
214	Jerry White	.05
215	Mario Soto	.05
216	Scott McGregor	.05
217	Tim Stoddard	.05
218	Bill Laskey	.05
219	Reggie Jackson (Super Veteran)	.05
220	Dusty Baker	.05
221	Joe Niekro	.05
222	Damaso Garcia	.05
223	John Montefusco	.05
224	Mickey Rivers	.05
225	Enos Cabell	.05
226	LaMarr Hoyt	.05
227	Tim Raines	.25
228	Joaquin Andujar	.05
229	Tim Wallach	.15
230	Fergie Jenkins	.05

ABBREVIATIONS

AS - All-Star
IA - In Action

No.	Player	Price
231	Fergie Jenkins (Super Veteran)	.05
232	Tom Brunansky	.05
233	Ivan DeJesus	.05
234	Bryn Smith	.05
235	Claudell Washington	.05
236	Steve Renko	.05
237	Dan Norman	.05
238	Cesar Cedeno	.05
239	Dave Stapleton	.05
240	Rich Gossage	.10
241	Rich Gossage (Super Veteran)	.05
242	Bob Stanley	.05
243	Rich Gale	.05
244	Sixto Lezcano	.05
245	Steve Sax	.05
246	Jerry Mumphrey	.05
247	Dave Smith	.05
248	Bake McBride	.05
249	Checklist 133-264	.05
250	Bill Buckner	.05
251	Kent Hrbek	.05
252	Gene Tenace	.05
253	Charlie Lea	.05
254	Rick Cerone	.05
255	Gene Garber	.05
256	Gene Garber (Super Veteran)	.05
257	Jesse Barfield	.30
258	Dave Winfield	1.50
259	Don Money	.05
260	Steve Kemp	.05
261	Steve Yeager	.05
262	Keith Hernandez	.05
263	Tippy Martinez	.05
264	Joe Morgan (Super Veteran)	.05
265	Joel Youngblood	.05
266	Bruce Sutter/AS	.25
267	Terry Francona	.05
268	Neil Allen	.05
269	Ron Oester	.05
270	Dennis Eckersley	.60
271	Dale Berra	.05
272	Al Bumbry	.05
273	Lonnie Smith	.05
274	Terry Kennedy	.05
275	Ray Knight	.05
276	Mike Norris	.05
277	Rance Mulliniks	.05
278	Dan Spillner	.05
279	Bucky Dent	.05
280	Bert Blyleven	.05
281	Barry Bonnell	.05
282	Reggie Smith	.05
283	Reggie Smith (Super Veteran)	.05
284	Ted Simmons	.05
285	Lance Parrish	.05
286	Larry Christenson	.05
287	Ruppert Jones	.05
288	Bob Welch	.05
289	John Wathan	.05
290	Jeff Reardon	.05
291	Dave Revering	.05
292	Craig Swan	.05
293	Graig Nettles	.05
294	Alfredo Griffin	.05
295	Jerry Remy	.05
296	Joe Sambito	.05
297	Ron LeFlore	.05
298	Brian Downing	.05
299	Jim Palmer	1.00
300	Mike Schmidt	1.75
301	Mike Schmidt (Super Veteran)	.35
302	Ernie Whitt	.05
303	Andre Dawson	.75
304	Bobby Murcer (Super Veteran)	.05
305	Larry Bowa	.05
306	Lee Mazzilli	.05
307	Lou Piniella	.05
308	Buck Martinez	.05
309	Jerry Martin	.05
310	Greg Luzinski	.05
311	Al Oliver	.05
312	Mike Torrez	.05
313	Dick Ruthven	.05
314	Gary Carter/AS	.05
315	Rick Burleson	.05
316	Phil Niekro (Super Veteran)	.10
317	Moose Haas	.05
318	Carney Lansford	.05
319	Tim Foli	.05
320	Steve Rogers	.05
321	Kirk Gibson	.05
322	Glenn Hubbard	.05
323	Luis DeLeon	.05
324	Mike Marshall	.05
325	Von Hayes	.05
326	Garth Iorg	.05
327	Jose Cruz	.05
328	Jim Palmer (Super Veteran)	.10
329	Darrell Evans	.05
330	Buddy Bell	.05
331	Mike Krukow	.05
332	Omar Moreno	.05
333	Dave LaRoche	.05
334	Dave LaRoche (Super Veteran)	.05
335	Bill Madlock	.05
336	Garry Templeton	.05
337	John Lowenstein	.05
338	Willie Upshaw	.05
339	Dave Hostetler	.05
340	Larry Gura	.05
341	Doug DeCinces	.05
342	Mike Schmidt/AS	.25
343	Charlie Hough	.05
344	Andre Thornton	.05
345	Jim Clancy	.05
346	Ken Forsch	.05
347	Sammy Stewart	.05
348	Alan Bannister	.05
349	Checklist 265-396	.05
350	Robin Yount	1.25
351	Warren Cromartie	.05
352	Tim Raines/AS	.05
353	Tony Armas	.05
354	Tom Seaver (Super Veteran)	.30
355	Tony Perez	1.00
356	Toby Harrah	.05
357	Dan Ford	.05
358	Charlie Puleo	.05
359	Dave Collins	.05
360	Nolan Ryan	6.00
361	Nolan Ryan (Super Veteran)	2.50
362	Bill Almon	.05
363	Eddie Milner	.05
364	Gary Lucas	.05
365	Dave Lopes	.05
366	Bob Boone	.05
367	Biff Pocoroba	.05
368	Richie Zisk	.05
369	Tony Bernazard	.06
370	Gary Carter	1.50
371	Paul Molitor	1.50
372	Art Howe	.05
373	Pete Rose/AS	.50
374	Glenn Adams	.05
375	Pete Vukovich	.05
376	Gary Lavelle	.05
377	Lee May	.05
378	Lee May (Super Veteran)	.05
379	Butch Wynegar	.05
380	Ron Davis	.05
381	Bob Grich	.05
382	Gary Roenicke	.05
383	Jim Kaat	.10
384	Steve Carlton/AS	.05
385	Mike Easler	.05
386	Rod Carew/AS	.05
387	Bobby Grich/AS	.05
388	George Brett/AS	.25
389	Robin Yount/AS	.05
390	Reggie Jackson/AS	.05
391	Rickey Henderson/AS	.25
392	Fred Lynn/AS	.05
393	Carlton Fisk/AS	.05
394	Pete Vuckovich/AS	.05
395	Larry Gura/AS	.05
396	Dan Quisenberry/AS	.05

1984 O-Pee-Chee

Almost identical in design to the 1984 Topps set, the 1984 O-Pee-Chee set contains 396 cards. The O-Pee-Chee cards display the Canadian company's logo in the upper right corner and the backs of the cards are printed in both English and French. The cards measure 2-1/2" x 3-1/2", and some include the extra line on the front of the card to indicate a trade.

		NM/M
	Complete Set (396):	22.50
	Common Player:	.05
	Wax Pack:	1.00
	Wax Box (36):	25.00
1	Pascual Perez	.10
2	Cal Ripken	6.00
3	Lloyd Moseby	.15
4	Mel Hall	.05
5	Willie Wilson	.05
6	Mike Morgan	.05
7	Gary Lucas	.05
8	Don Mattingly	8.00
9	Jim Gott	.05
10	Robin Yount	1.50
11	Joey McLaughlin	.05
12	Billy Sample	.05
13	Oscar Gamble	.05
14	Bill Russell	.05
15	Burt Hooton	.05
16	Omar Moreno	.05
17	Dave Lopes	.05
18	Dale Berra	.05
19	Rance Mulliniks	.05
20	Greg Luzinski	.05
21	Doug Sisk	.05
22	Don Robinson	.05
23	Keith Moreland	.05
24	Richard Dotson	.05
25	Glenn Hubbard	.05
26	Rod Carew	1.50
27	Alan Wiggins	.05
28	Frank Viola	.05
29	Phil Niekro	1.00
30	Wade Boggs	2.50
31	Dave Parker	.05
32	Bobby Ramos	.05
33	Tom Burgmeier	.05
34	Eddie Milner	.05
35	Don Sutton	1.00
36	Glenn Wilson	.05
37	Mike Krukow	.05
38	Dave Collins	.05
39	Garth Iorg	.05
40	Dusty Baker	.05
41	Tony Bernazard	.05
42	Claudell Washington	.05
43	Cecil Cooper	.05
44	Dan Driessen	.05
45	Jerry Mumphrey	.05
46	Rick Rhoden	.05
47	Rudy Law	.05
48	Julio Franco	.05
49	Mike Norris	.05
50	Chris Chambliss	.05
51	Pete Falcone	.05
52	Mike Marshall	.05
53	Amos Otis	.05
54	Jesse Orosco	.05
55	Dave Concepcion	.05
56	Gary Allenson	.05
57	Dan Schatzeder	.05
58	Jerry Remy	.05
59	Carney Lansford	.05
60	Paul Molitor	2.50
61	Chris Codiroli	.05
62	Dave Hostetler	.05
63	Ed Vande Berg	.05
64	Ryne Sandberg	2.50
65	Kirk Gibson	.05
66	Nolan Ryan	6.00
67	Gary Ward	.05
68	Luis Salazar	.05
69	Dan Quisenberry	.05
70	Gary Matthews	.05
71	Pete O'Brien	.05
72	John Wathan	.05
73	Jody Davis	.05
74	Kent Tekulve	.05
75	Bob Forsch	.05
76	Alfredo Griffin	.05
77	Bryn Smith	.05
78	Mike Torrez	.05
79	Mike Hargrove	.05
80	Steve Rogers	.05
81	Bake McBride	.05
82	Doug DeCinces	.05
83	Richie Zisk	.05
84	Randy Bush	.05
85	Atlee Hammaker	.05
86	Chet Lemon	.05
87	Frank Pastore	.05
88	Alan Trammell	.05
89	Terry Francona	.05
90	Pedro Guerrero	.05
91	Dan Spillner	.05
92	Lloyd Moseby	.05
93	Bob Knepper	.05
94	Ted Simmons	.05
95	Aurelio Lopez	.05
96	Bill Buckner	.05
97	LaMarr Hoyt	.05
98	Tom Brunansky	.05
99	Ron Oester	.05
100	Reggie Jackson	1.50
101	Ron Davis	.05
102	Ken Oberkfell	.05
103	Dwayne Murphy	.05
104	Jim Slaton	.05
105	Tony Armas	.05
106	Ernie Whitt	.05
107	Johnnie LeMaster	.05
108	Randy Moffitt	.05
109	Terry Forster	.05
110	Ron Guidry	.05
111	Bill Virdon	.05
112	Doyle Alexander	.05
113	Lonnie Smith	.05
114	Checklist	.05
115	Andre Thornton	.05
116	Jeff Reardon	.15
117	Tom Herr	.05
118	Charlie Hough	.05
119	Phil Garner	.05
120	Keith Hernandez	.05
121	Rich Gossage	.10
122	Ted Simmons	.05
123	Butch Wynegar	.05
124	Damaso Garcia	.05
125	Britt Burns	.05
126	Bert Blyleven	.05
127	Carlton Fisk	1.50
128	Rick Manning	.05
129	Bill Laskey	.05
130	Ozzie Smith	2.50
131	Bo Diaz	.05
132	Tom Paciorek	.05
133	Dave Rozema	.05
134	Dave Stieb	.15
135	Brian Downing	.05
136	Rick Camp	.05
137	Willie Aikens	.05
138	Charlie Moore	.05
139	George Frazier	.05
140	Storm Davis	.05
141	Glenn Hoffman	.05
142	Charlie Lea	.05
143	Mike Vail	.05
144	Steve Sax	.05
145	Gary Lavelle	.05
146	Gorman Thomas	.05
147	Dan Petry	.05
148	Mark Clear	.05
149	Dave Beard	.05
150	Dale Murphy	.75
151	Steve Trout	.05
152	Tony Pena	.05
153	Geoff Zahn	.05
154	Dave Henderson	.05
155	Frank White	.05
156	Dick Ruthven	.05
157	Gary Gaetti	.05
158	Lance Parrish	.05
159	Joe Price	.05
160	Mario Soto	.05
161	Tug McGraw	.05
162	Bob Ojeda	.05
163	George Hendrick	.05
164	Scott Sanderson	.05
165	Ken Singleton	.05
166	Terry Kennedy	.05
167	Gene Garber	.05
168	Juan Bonilla	.05
169	Larry Parrish	.05
170	Jerry Reuss	.05
171	John Tudor	.05
172	Dave Kingman	.05
173	Garry Templeton	.05
174	Bob Boone	.05
175	Graig Nettles	.05
176	Lee Smith	.05
177	LaMarr Hoyt	.05
178	Bill Krueger	.05
179	Buck Martinez	.05
180	Manny Trillo	.05
181	Lou Whitaker	.05
182	Darryl Strawberry	1.00
183	Neil Allen	.05
184	Jim Rice	.25
185	Sixto Lezcano	.05
186	Tom Hume	.05
187	Garry Maddox	.05
188	Bryan Little	.05
189	Jose Cruz	.05
190	Ben Oglivie	.05
191	Cesar Cedeno	.05
192	Nick Esasky	.05
193	Ken Forsch	.05
194	Jim Palmer	1.25
195	Jack Morris	.15
196	Steve Howe	.05
197	Harold Baines	.05
198	Bill Doran	.05
199	Willie Hernandez	.05
200	Andre Dawson	1.25
201	Bruce Kison	.05
202	Bobby Cox	.05
203	Matt Keough	.05
204	Ron Guidry	.05
205	Greg Minton	.05
206	Al Holland	.05
207	Luis Leal	.05
208	Jose Oquendo	.05
209	Leon Durham	.05
210	Joe Morgan	1.50
211	Lou Whitaker/AS	.05
212	George Brett/AS	.75
213	Bruce Hurst	.05
214	Steve Carlton	1.50
215	Tippy Martinez	.05
216	Ken Landreaux	.05
217	Alan Ashby	.05
218	Dennis Eckersley	1.00
219	Craig McMurtry	.05
220	Fernando Valenzuela	.05
221	Cliff Johnson	.05
222	Rick Honeycutt	.05
223	George Bret	3.00
224	Rusty Staub	.20
225	Lee Mazzilli	.05
226	Pat Putnam	.05
227	Bob Welch	.05
228	Rick Cerone	.05
229	Lee Lacy	.05
230	Rickey Henderson	2.50
231	Gary Redus	.05
232	Tim Wallach	.25
233	Checklist	.05
234	Rafael Ramirez	.05
235	Matt Young	.05
236	Ellis Valentine	.05
237	John Castino	.05
238	Eric Show	.05
239	Bob Horner	.05
240	Eddie Murray	1.50
241	Billy Almon	.05
242	Greg Brock	.05
243	Bruce Sutter	1.00
244	Dwight Evans	.05
245	Rick Sutcliffe	.05
246	Terry Crowley	.05
247	Fred Lynn	.05
248	Bill Dawley	.05
249	Dave Stapleton	.05
250	Bill Madlock	.05
251	Jim Sundberg	.05
252	Steve Yeager	.05
253	Jim Wohlford	.05
254	Shane Rawley	.05
255	Bruce Benedict	.05
256	Dave Geisel	.05
257	Julio Cruz	.05
258	Luis Sanchez	.05
259	Von Hayes	.05
260	Scott McGregor	.05
261	Tom Seaver	1.50
262	Doug Flynn	.05
263	Wayne Gross	.05
264	Larry Gura	.05
265	John Montefusco	.05
266	Dave Winfield/AS	1.00
267	Tim Lollar	.05
268	Ron Washington	.05
269	Mickey Rivers	.05
270	Mookie Wilson	.05
271	Moose Haas	.05
272	Rick Dempsey	.05
273	Dan Quisenberry	.05
274	Steve Henderson	.05
275	Len Matuszek	.05
276	Frank Tanana	.05
277	Dave Righetti	.05
278	Jorge Bell	.35
279	Ivan DeJesus	.05
280	Floyd Bannister	.05
281	Dale Murray	.05
282	Andre Robertson	.05
283	Rollie Fingers	1.00
284	Tommy John	.10
285	Darrell Porter	.05
286	Lary Sorensen	.05
287	Warren Cromartie	.05
288	Jim Beattie	.05
289	Blue Jays Team	.25
290	Dave Dravecky	.05
291	Eddie Murray/AS	.50
292	Greg Bargar	.05
293	Tom Underwood	.05
294	U.L. Washington	.05
295	Mike Flanagan	.05
296	Rich Gedman	.05
297	Bruce Berenyi	.05
298	Jim Gantner	.05
299	Bill Caudill	.05
300	Pete Rose	4.00
301	Steve Kemp	.05
302	Barry Bonnell	.05
303	Joel Youngblood	.05
304	Rick Langford	.05
305	Roy Smalley	.05
306	Ken Griffey	.05
307	Al Oliver	.05
308	Ron Hassey	.05
309	Len Barker	.05
310	Willie McGee	.05
311	Jerry Koosman	.05
312	Jorge Orta	.05
313	Pete Vuckovich	.05
314	George Wright	.05
315	Bob Grich	.05
316	Jesse Barfield	.25
317	Willie Upshaw	.05
318	Bill Gullickson	.10
319	Ray Burris	.05
320	Bob Stanley	.05
321	Ray Knight	.05
322	Ken Schrom	.05
323	Johnny Ray	.05
324	Brian Giles	.05
325	Darrell Evans	.05
326	Mike Caldwell	.05
327	Ruppert Jones	.05
328	Chris Speier	.05
329	Bobby Castillo	.05
330	John Candelaria	.05
331	Bucky Dent	.05
332	Expos Team	.25
333	Larry Herndon	.05
334	Chuck Rainey	.05
335	Don Baylor	.05
336	Bob James	.05
337	Jim Clancy	.05
338	Duane Kuiper	.05
339	Roy Lee Jackson	.05
340	Hal McRae	.05
341	Larry McWilliams	.05
342	Tim Foli	.05
343	Fergie Jenkins	2.00
344	Dickie Thon	.05
345	Kent Hrbek	.05
346	Larry Bowa	.05
347	Buddy Bell	.05
348	Toby Harrah	.05
349	Dan Ford	.05
350	George Foster	.05
351	Lou Piniella	.05
352	Dave Stewart	.25
353	Mike Easler	.05
354	Jeff Burroughs	.05
355	Jason Thompson	.05
356	Glenn Abbott	.05
357	Ron Cey	.05
358	Bob Dernier	.05
359	Jim Acker	.05
360	Willie Randolph	.05
361	Mike Schmidt	3.00
362	David Green	.05
363	Cal Ripken Jr./AS	2.00
364	Jim Rice/AS	.05
365	Steve Bedrosian	.05
366	Gary Carter	2.50
367	Chili Davis	.05
368	Hubie Brooks	.05
369	Steve McCatty	.05
370	Tim Raines	.35
371	Joaquin Andujar	.05
372	Gary Roenicke	.05
373	Ron Kittle	.05
374	Rich Dauer	.05
375	Dennis Leonard	.05
376	Rick Burleson	.05
377	Eric Rasmussen	.05
378	Dave Winfield	2.50
379	Checklist	.05
380	Steve Garvey	.50
381	Jack Clark	.05
382	Odell Jones	.05
383	Terry Puhl	.05
384	Joe Niekro	.05
385	Tony Perez	2.00
386	George Hendrick/AS	.05
387	Johnny Ray/AS	.05
388	Mike Schmidt/AS	.75
389	Ozzie Smith/AS	.75
390	Tim Raines/AS	.25
391	Dale Murphy/AS	.25
392	Andre Dawson/AS	.35
393	Gary Carter/AS	1.00
394	Steve Rogers/AS	.15
395	Steve Carlton/AS	.50
396	Jesse Orosco/AS	.05

Stickers

Bi-lingual backs are the only difference between the OPC 1984 sticker set and the Topps issue. The sets share a checklist and, generally, values, although some Blue Jays and Expos stars may command a small premium in the Canadian version.

1985 O-Pee-Chee

This 396-card set is almost identical in design to the 1985 Topps set. Measuring 2-1/2" x 3-1/2", the fronts of the Canadian-issued cards display the O-Pee-Chee logo in the upper left corner, and the backs of the cards are printed in both French and English. A "traded" line appears on the front of some of the cards to indicate a change in teams.

		NM/M
	Complete Set (396):	15.00
	Common Player:	.05
	Wax Pack (15):	1.50
	Wax Box (36):	40.00
1	Tom Seaver	1.50
2	Gary Lavelle	.05
3	Tim Wallach	.15
4	Jim Wohlford	.05
5	Jeff Robinson	.05
6	Willie Wilson	.05
7	Cliff Johnson	.05
8	Willie Randolph	.05
9	Larry Herndon	.05
10	Kirby Puckett	4.00
11	Mookie Wilson	.05
12	Dave Lopes	.05
13	Tim Lollar	.05
14	Chris Bando	.05
15	Jerry Koosman	.05
16	Bobby Meacham	.05
17	Mike Scott	.05
18	Rich Gedman	.05
19	George Frazier	.05
20	Chet Lemon	.05
21	Dave Concepcion	.05
22	Jason Thompson	.05
23	Bret Saberhagen	.15
24	Jesse Barfield	.15
25	Steve Bedrosian	.05
26	Roy Smalley	.05
27	Bruce Berenyi	.05
28	Butch Wynegar	.05
29	Alan Ashby	.05
30	Cal Ripken	4.00
31	Luis Leal	.05
32	Dave Dravecky	.05
33	Tito Landrum	.05
34	Pedro Guerrero	.05
35	Graig Nettles	.05
36	Fred Breining	.05
37	Roy Lee Jackson	.05

#	Player	Price
38	Steve Henderson	.05
39	Gary Pettis	.05
40	Phil Niekro	.75
41	Dwight Gooden	.10
42	Luis Sanchez	.05
43	Lee Smith	.05
44	Dickie Thon	.05
45	Greg Minton	.05
46	Mike Flanagan	.05
47	Bud Black	.05
48	Tony Fernandez	.50
49	Carlton Fisk	1.50
50	John Candelaria	.05
51	Bob Watson	.05
52	Rick Leach	.05
53	Rick Rhoden	.05
54	Cesar Cedeno	.05
55	Frank Tanana	.05
56	Larry Bowa	.05
57	Willie McGee	.05
58	Rich Dauer	.05
59	Jorge Bell	.35
60	George Hendrick	.05
61	Donnie Moore	.05
62	Mike Ramsey	.05
63	Nolan Ryan	4.00
64	Mark Bailey	.05
65	Bill Buckner	.05
66	Jerry Reuss	.05
67	Mike Schmidt	2.50
68	Von Hayes	.05
69	Phil Bradley	.05
70	Don Baylor	.05
71	Julio Cruz	.05
72	Rick Sutcliffe	.05
73	Storm Davis	.05
74	Mike Krukow	.05
75	Willie Upshaw	.05
76	Craig Lefferts	.05
77	Lloyd Moseby	.05
78	Ron Davis	.05
79	Rick Mahler	.05
80	Keith Hernandez	.05
81	Vance Law	.05
82	Joe Price	.05
83	Dennis Lamp	.05
84	Gary Ward	.05
85	Mike Marshall	.05
86	Marvell Wynne	.05
87	David Green	.05
88	Bryn Smith	.05
89	Sixto Lezcano	.05
90	Rich Gossage	.10
91	Jeff Burroughs	.05
92	Bobby Brown	.05
93	Oscar Gamble	.05
94	Rick Dempsey	.05
95	Jose Cruz	.05
96	Johnny Ray	.05
97	Joel Youngblood	.05
98	Eddie Whitson	.05
99	Milt Wilcox	.05
100	George Brett	2.50
101	Jim Acker	.05
102	Jim Sundberg	.05
103	Ozzie Virgil	.05
104	Mike Fitzgerald	.05
105	Ron Kittle	.05
106	Pascual Perez	.05
107	Barry Bonnell	.05
108	Lou Whitaker	.05
109	Gary Roenicke	.05
110	Alejandro Pena	.05
111	Doug DeCinces	.05
112	Doug Flynn	.05
113	Tom Herr	.05
114	Bob James	.05
115	Rickey Henderson	2.00
116	Pete Rose	3.00
117	Greg Gross	.05
118	Eric Show	.05
119	Buck Martinez	.05
120	Steve Kemp	.05
121	Checklist 1-132	.05
122	Tom Brunansky	.05
123	Dave Kingman	.05
124	Garry Templeton	.05
125	Kent Tekulve	.05
126	Darryl Strawberry	.05
127	Mark Gubicza	.05
128	Ernie Whitt	.05
129	Ron Robinson	.05
130	Al Oliver	.05
131	Mario Soto	.05
132	Jeff Leonard	.05
133	Andre Dawson	.35
134	Bruce Hurst	.05
135	Bobby Cox	.05
136	Matt Young	.05
137	Bob Forsch	.05
138	Ron Darling	.05
139	Steve Trout	.05
140	Geoff Zahn	.05
141	Ken Forsch	.05
142	Jerry Willard	.05
143	Bill Gullickson	.05
144	Mike Mason	.05
145	Alvin Davis	.05
146	Gary Redus	.05
147	Willie Aikens	.05
148	Steve Yeager	.05
149	Dickie Noles	.05
150	Jim Rice	.25
151	Moose Haas	.05
152	Steve Balboni	.05
153	Frank LaCorte	.05
154	Argenis Salazar	.05
155	Bob Grich	.05
156	Craig Reynolds	.05
157	Bill Madlock	.05
158	Pat Tabler	.05
159	Don Slaught	.05
160	Lance Parrish	.05
161	Ken Schrom	.05
162	Wally Backman	.05
163	Dennis Eckersley	.75
164	Dave Collins	.05
165	Dusty Baker	.05
166	Claudell Washington	.05
167	Rick Camp	.05
168	Garth Iorg	.05
169	Shane Rawley	.05
170	George Foster	.05
171	Tony Bernazard	.05
172	Don Sutton	.75
173	Jerry Remy	.05
174	Rick Honeycutt	.05
175	Dave Parker	.05
176	Buddy Bell	.05
177	Steve Garvey	.20
178	Miguel Dilone	.05
179	Tommy John	.10
180	Dave Winfield	2.00
181	Alan Trammell	.05
182	Rollie Fingers	.75
183	Larry McWilliams	.05
184	Carmen Castillo	.05
185	Al Holland	.05
186	Jerry Mumphrey	.05
187	Chris Chambliss	.05
188	Jim Clancy	.05
189	Glenn Wilson	.05
190	Rusty Staub	.05
191	Ozzie Smith	2.00
192	Howard Johnson	.05
193	Jimmy Key	1.00
194	Terry Kennedy	.05
195	Glenn Hubbard	.05
196	Pete O'Brien	.05
197	Keith Moreland	.05
198	Eddie Milner	.05
199	Dave Engle	.05
200	Reggie Jackson	1.50
201	Burt Hooton	.05
202	Gorman Thomas	.05
203	Larry Parrish	.05
204	Bob Stanley	.05
205	Steve Rogers	.05
206	Phil Garner	.05
207	Ed Vande Berg	.05
208	Jack Clark	.05
209	Bill Campbell	.05
210	Gary Matthews	.05
211	Dave Palmer	.05
212	Tony Perez	1.50
213	Sammy Stewart	.05
214	John Tudor	.05
215	Bob Brenly	.05
216	Jim Gantner	.05
217	Bryan Clark	.05
218	Doyle Alexander	.05
219	Bo Diaz	.05
220	Fred Lynn	.05
221	Eddie Murray	1.50
222	Hubie Brooks	.05
223	Tom Hume	.05
224	Al Cowens	.05
225	Mike Boddicker	.05
226	Len Matuszek	.05
227	Danny Darwin	.05
228	Scott McGregor	.05
229	Dave LaPoint	.05
230	Gary Carter	2.00
231	Joaquin Andujar	.05
232	Rafael Ramirez	.05
233	Wayne Gross	.05
234	Neil Allen	.05
235	Gary Maddox	.05
236	Mark Thurmond	.05
237	Julio Franco	.05
238	Ray Burris	.05
239	Tim Teufel	.05
240	Dave Stieb	.15
241	Brett Butler	.05
242	Greg Brock	.05
243	Barbaro Garbey	.05
244	Greg Walker	.05
245	Chili Davis	.05
246	Darrell Porter	.05
247	Tippy Martinez	.05
248	Terry Forster	.05
249	Harold Baines	.05
250	Jesse Orosco	.05
251	Brad Gulden	.05
252	Mike Hargrove	.05
253	Nick Esasky	.05
254	Frank Williams	.05
255	Lonnie Smith	.05
256	Daryl Sconiers	.05
257	Terry Francona	.05
258	Bryan Little	.05
259	Mark Langston	.15
260	Dave Righetti	.05
261	Checklist 133-264	.05
262	Bob Horner	.05
263	Mel Hall	.05
264	John Shelby	.05
265	Juan Samuel	.05
266	Frank Viola	.05
267	Jim Fanning	.05
268	Dick Ruthven	.05
269	Bobby Ramos	.05
270	Dan Quisenberry	.05
271	Dwight Evans	.05
272	Andre Thornton	.05
273	Orel Hershiser	.50
274	Ray Knight	.05
275	Bill Caudill	.05
276	Charlie Hough	.05
277	Tim Raines	.25
278	Mike Squires	.05
279	Alex Trevino	.05
280	Ron Romanick	.05
281	Tom Niedenfuer	.05
282	Mike Stenhouse	.05
283	Terry Puhl	.05
284	Hal McRae	.05
285	Dan Driessen	.05
286	Rudy Law	.05
287	Walt Terrell	.05
288	Jeff Kunkel	.05
289	Bob Knepper	.05
290	Cecil Cooper	.05
291	Bob Welch	.05
292	Frank Pastore	.05
293	Dan Schatzeder	.05
294	Tom Nieto	.05
295	Joe Niekro	.05
296	Ryne Sandberg	2.00
297	Gary Lucas	.05
298	John Castino	.05
299	Bill Doran	.05
300	Rod Carew	1.50
301	John Montefusco	.05
302	Johnnie LeMaster	.05
303	Jim Beattie	.05
304	Gary Gaetti	.05
305	Dale Berra	.05
306	Rick Reuschel	.05
307	Ken Oberkfell	.05
308	Kent Hrbek	.05
309	Mike Witt	.05
310	Manny Trillo	.05
311	Jim Gott	.05
312	LaMarr Hoyt	.05
313	Dave Schmidt	.05
314	Ron Oester	.05
315	Doug Sisk	.05
316	John Lowenstein	.05
317	Derrel Thomas	.05
318	Ted Simmons	.05
319	Darrell Evans	.05
320	Dale Murphy	.50
321	Ricky Horton	.05
322	Ken Phelps	.05
323	Lee Mazzilli	.05
324	Don Mattingly	2.50
325	John Denny	.05
326	Ken Singleton	.05
327	Brook Jacoby	.05
328	Greg Luzinski	.05
329	Bob Ojeda	.05
330	Leon Durham	.05
331	Bill Laskey	.05
332	Ben Oglivie	.05
333	Willie Hernandez	.05
334	Bob Dernier	.05
335	Bruce Benedict	.05
336	Rance Mulliniks	.05
337	Rick Cerone	.05
338	Britt Burns	.05
339	Danny Heep	.05
340	Robin Yount	1.50
341	Andy Van Slyke	.05
342	Curt Wilkerson	.05
343	Bill Russell	.05
344	Dave Henderson	.05
345	Charlie Lea	.05
346	Terry Pendleton	.05
347	Carney Lansford	.05
348	Bob Boone	.05
349	Mike Easler	.05
350	Wade Boggs	2.00
351	Atlee Hammaker	.05
352	Joe Morgan	1.50
353	Damaso Garcia	.05
354	Floyd Bannister	.05
355	Bert Blyleven	.05
356	John Butcher	.05
357	Fernando Valenzuela	.05
358	Tony Pena	.05
359	Mike Smithson	.05
360	Steve Carlton	1.50
361	Alfredo Griffin	.05
362	Craig McMurtry	.05
363	Bill Dawley	.05
364	Richard Dotson	.05
365	Carmelo Martinez	.05
366	Ron Cey	.05
367	Tony Scott	.05
368	Dave Bergman	.05
369	Steve Sax	.05
370	Bruce Sutter	1.00
371	Mickey Rivers	.05
372	Kirk Gibson	.05
373	Scott Sanderson	.05
374	Brian Downing	.05
375	Jeff Reardon	.15
376	Frank DiPino	.05
377	Checklist 265-396	.05
378	Alan Wiggins	.05
379	Charles Hudson	.05
380	Ken Griffey	.05
381	Tom Paciorek	.05
382	Jack Morris	.15
383	Tony Gwynn	2.00
384	Jody Davis	.05
385	Jose DeLeon	.05
386	Bob Kearney	.05
387	George Wright	.05
388	Ron Guidry	.05
389	Rick Manning	.05
390	Sid Fernandez	.05
391	Bruce Bochte	.05
392	Dan Petry	.05
393	Tim Stoddard	.05
394	Tony Armas	.05
395	Paul Molitor	2.00
396	Mike Heath	.05

Posters

The 1985 O-Pee-Chee poster set consists of 12 players each from the Expos and Blue Jays. The blank-backed posters measure approximately 4-7/8" x 6-7/8" and generally have fold marks because they were inserted in the OPC wax packs. The card number, written in both French and English, appears in the bottom border. The full-color player photos are surrounded by a red border for Expos and a blue border for Blue Jays.

		NM/M
Complete Set (24):		9.00
Common Player:		.50
1	Mike Fitzgerald	.50
2	Dan Driessen	.50
3	Dave Palmer	.50
4	U.L. Washington	.50
5	Hubie Brooks	.50
6	Tim Wallach	.75
7	Tim Raines	2.50
8	Herm Winningham	.50
9	Andre Dawson	2.50
10	Charlie Lea	.50
11	Steve Rogers	.50
12	Jeff Reardon	.60
13	Buck Martinez	.50
14	Willie Upshaw	.50
15	Damaso Garcia	.50
16	Tony Fernandez	1.00
17	Rance Mulliniks	.50
18	George Bell	1.00
19	Lloyd Moseby	.50
20	Jesse Barfield	.60
21	Doyle Alexander	.50
22	Dave Stieb	.85
23	Bill Caudill	.50
24	Gary Lavelle	.50

Stickers

Bi-lingual backs are the only difference between the OPC 1985 sticker set and the Topps issue. The sets share a checklist and, generally, values, although some Blue Jays and Expos stars may command a small premium in the Canadian version.

1986 O-Pee-Chee

As usual, the 1986 O-Pee-Chee set was issued in close simulation of the Topps cards for the same year. The 396 cards in the set are 2-1/2" x 3-1/2" and use almost all of the same pictures as the Topps set. The O-Pee-Chee cards, being a Canadian issue, list player informa-tion in both English and French. There is an abundance of players from the two Canadian teams - Toronto and Montreal. As the O-Pee-Chee set was issued later in the year than the Topps regular issue, players who changed teams after the printing date are noted with a traded line at the bottom of the player photo. O-Pee-Chee's logo appears in the upper right of each card front.

		NM/M
Complete Set (396):		12.00
Common Player:		.05
Wax Box (36):		16.00
1	Pete Rose	1.50
2	Ken Landreaux	.05
3	Rob Picciolo	.05
4	Steve Garvey	.10
5	Andy Hawkins	.05
6	Rudy Law	.05
7	Lonnie Smith	.05
8	Dwayne Murphy	.05
9	Moose Haas	.05
10	Tony Gwynn	1.00
11	Bob Ojeda	.05
12	Jose Uribe	.05
13	Bob Kearney	.05
14	Julio Cruz	.05
15	Eddie Whitson	.05
16	Rick Schu	.05
17	Mike Stenhouse	.05
18	Lou Thornton	.05
19	Ryne Sandberg	1.00
20	Lou Whitaker	.05
21	Mark Brouhard	.05
22	Gary Lavelle	.05
23	Manny Lee	.05
24	Don Slaught	.05
25	Willie Wilson	.05
26	Mike Marshall	.05
27	Ray Knight	.05
28	Mario Soto	.05
29	Dave Anderson	.05
30	Eddie Murray	.75
31	Dusty Baker	.05
32	Steve Yeager	.05
33	Andy Van Slyke	.05
34	Dave Righetti	.05
35	Jeff Reardon	.05
36	Burt Hooton	.05
37	Johnny Ray	.05
38	Glenn Hoffman	.05
39	Rick Mahler	.05
40	Ken Griffey	.05
41	Brad Wellman	.05
42	Joe Hesketh	.05
43	Mark Salas	.05
44	Jorge Orta	.05
45	Damaso Garcia	.05
46	Jim Acker	.05
47	Bill Madlock	.05
48	Bill Almon	.05
49	Rick Manning	.05
50	Dan Quisenberry	.05
51	Jim Gantner	.05
52	Kevin Bass	.05
53	Len Dykstra	.05
54	John Franco	.05
55	Fred Lynn	.05
56	Jim Morrison	.05
57	Bill Doran	.05
58	Leon Durham	.05
59	Andre Thornton	.05
60	Dwight Evans	.05
61	Larry Herndon	.05
62	Bob Boone	.05
63	Kent Hrbek	.05
64	Floyd Bannister	.05
65	Harold Baines	.05
66	Pat Tabler	.05
67	Carmelo Martinez	.05
68	Ed Lynch	.05
69	George Foster	.05
70	Dave Winfield	1.00
71	Ken Schrom	.05
72	Toby Harrah	.05
73	Jackie Gutierrez	.05
74	Rance Mulliniks	.05
75	Jose DeLeon	.05
76	Ron Romanick	.05
77	Charlie Leibrandt	.05
78	Bruce Benedict	.05
79	Dave Schmidt	.05
80	Darryl Strawberry	.05
81	Wayne Krenchicki	.05
82	Tippy Martinez	.05
83	Phil Garner	.05
84	Darrell Porter	.05
85	Tony Perez	1.00
86	Tom Waddell	.05
87	Tim Hulett	.05
88	Barbaro Garbey	.05
89	Randy St. Claire	.05
90	Garry Templeton	.05
91	Tim Teufel	.05
92	Al Cowens	.05
93	Scot Thompson	.05
94	Tom Herr	.05
95	Ozzie Virgil	.05
96	Jose Cruz	.05
97	Gary Gaetti	.05
98	Roger Clemens	2.00
99	Vance Law	.05
100	Nolan Ryan	2.50
101	Mike Smithson	.05
102	Rafael Santana	.05
103	Darrell Evans	.05
104	Rich Gossage	.05
105	Gary Ward	.05
106	Jim Gott	.05
107	Rafael Ramirez	.05
108	Ted Power	.05
109	Ron Guidry	.05
110	Scott McGregor	.05
111	Mike Scioscia	.05
112	Glenn Hubbard	.05
113	U.L. Washington	.05
114	Al Oliver	.05
115	Jay Howell	.05
116	Brook Jacoby	.05
117	Willie McGee	.05
118	Jerry Royster	.05
119	Barry Bonnell	.05
120	Steve Carlton	.75
121	Alfredo Griffin	.05
122	David Green	.05
123	Greg Walker	.05
124	Frank Tanana	.05
125	Dave Lopes	.05
126	Mike Krukow	.05
127	Jack Howell	.05
128	Greg Harris	.05
129	Herm Winningham	.05
130	Alan Trammell	.05
131	Checklist 1-132	.05
132	Razor Shines	.05
133	Bruce Sutter	.65
134	Carney Lansford	.05
135	Joe Niekro	.05
136	Ernie Whitt	.05
137	Charlie Moore	.05
138	Mel Hall	.05
139	Roger McDowell	.05
140	John Candelaria	.05
141	Bob Rodgers	.05
142	Manny Trillo	.05
143	Dave Palmer	.05
144	Robin Yount	.75
145	Pedro Guerrero	.05
146	Von Hayes	.05
147	Lance Parrish	.05
148	Mike Heath	.05
149	Brett Butler	.05
150	Joaquin Andujar	.05
151	Graig Nettles	.05
152	Pete Vuckovich	.05
153	Jason Thompson	.05
154	Bert Roberge	.05
155	Bob Grich	.05
156	Roy Smalley	.05
157	Ron Hassey	.05
158	Bob Stanley	.05
159	Orel Hershiser	.05
160	Chet Lemon	.05
161	Terry Puhl	.05
162	Dave LaPoint	.05
163	Onix Concepcion	.05
164	Steve Balboni	.05
165	Mike Davis	.05
166	Dickie Thon	.05
167	Zane Smith	.05
168	Jeff Burroughs	.05
169	Alex Trevino	.05
170	Gary Carter	1.00
171	Tito Landrum	.05
172	Sammy Stewart	.05
173	Wayne Gross	.05
174	Britt Burns	.05
175	Steve Sax	.05
176	Jody Davis	.05
177	Joel Youngblood	.05
178	Fernando Valenzuela	.05
179	Storm Davis	.05
180	Don Mattingly	1.25
181	Steve Bedrosian	.05
182	Jesse Orosco	.05
183	Gary Roenicke	.05
184	Don Baylor	.05
185	Rollie Fingers	.50
186	Ruppert Jones	.05
187	Scott Fletcher	.05
188	Bob Dernier	.05
189	Mike Mason	.05
190	George Hendrick	.05
191	Wally Backman	.05
192	Oddibe McDowell	.05
193	Bruce Hurst	.05
194	Ron Cey	.05
195	Dave Concepcion	.05
196	Doyle Alexander	.05
197	Dale Murray	.05
198	Mark Langston	.05
199	Dennis Eckersley	.50
200	Mike Schmidt	1.50
201	Nick Esasky	.05
202	Ken Dayley	.05
203	Rick Cerone	.05
204	Larry McWilliams	.05
205	Brian Downing	.05
206	Danny Darwin	.05
207	Bill Gullickson	.05
208	Dave Rozema	.05
209	Eric Show	.05
210	Brad Komminsk	.05
211	Chris Bando	.05
212	Chris Speier	.05
213	Jim Clancy	.05
214	Randy Bush	.05
215	Frank White	.05
216	Dan Petry	.05

#	Player	Price
217	Tim Wallach	.05
218	Mitch Webster	.05
219	Dennis Lamp	.05
220	Bob Horner	.05
221	Dave Henderson	.05
222	Dave Smith	.05
223	Willie Upshaw	.05
224	Cesar Cedeno	.05
225	Ron Darling	.05
226	Lee Lacy	.05
227	John Tudor	.05
228	Jim Presley	.05
229	Bill Gullickson	.05
230	Terry Kennedy	.05
231	Bob Knepper	.05
232	Rick Rhoden	.05
233	Richard Dotson	.05
234	Jesse Barfield	.10
235	Butch Wynegar	.05
236	Jerry Reuss	.05
237	Juan Samuel	.05
238	Larry Parrish	.05
239	Bill Buckner	.05
240	Pat Sheridan	.05
241	Tony Fernandez	.05
242	Rich Thompson	.05
243	Rickey Henderson	1.00
244	Craig Lefferts	.05
245	Jim Sundberg	.05
246	Phil Niekro	.50
247	Terry Harper	.05
248	Spike Owen	.05
249	Bret Saberhagen	.05
250	Dwight Gooden	.05
251	Rich Dauer	.05
252	Keith Hernandez	.05
253	Bo Diaz	.05
254	Ozzie Guillen	.05
255	Tony Armas	.05
256	Andre Dawson	.25
257	Doug DeCinces	.05
258	Tim Burke	.05
259	Dennis Boyd	.05
260	Tony Pena	.05
261	Sal Butera	.05
262	Wade Boggs	1.00
263	Checklist 133-254	.05
264	Ron Oester	.05
265	Ron Davis	.05
266	Keith Moreland	.05
267	Paul Molitor	1.00
268	John Denny	.05
269	Frank Viola	.05
270	Jack Morris	.10
271	Dave Collins	.05
272	Bert Blyleven	.05
273	Jerry Willard	.05
274	Matt Young	.05
275	Charlie Hough	.05
276	Dave Dravecky	.05
277	Garth Iorg	.05
278	Hal McRae	.05
279	Curt Wilkerson	.05
280	Tim Raines	.20
281	Bill Laskey	.05
282	Jerry Mumphrey	.05
283	Pat Clements	.05
284	Bob James	.05
285	Buddy Bell	.05
286	Tom Brookens	.05
287	Dave Parker	.05
288	Ron Kittle	.05
289	Johnnie LeMaster	.05
290	Carlton Fisk	.75
291	Jimmy Key	.05
292	Gary Matthews	.05
293	Marvell Wynne	.05
294	Danny Cox	.05
295	Kirk Gibson	.05
296	Mariano Duncan	.05
297	Ozzie Smith	1.00
298	Craig Reynolds	.05
299	Bryn Smith	.05
300	George Brett	1.50
301	Walt Terrell	.05
302	Greg Gross	.05
303	Claudell Washington	.05
304	Howard Johnson	.05
305	Phil Bradley	.05
306	R.J. Reynolds	.05
307	Bob Brenly	.05
308	Hubie Brooks	.05
309	Alvin Davis	.05
310	Donnie Hill	.05
311	Dick Schofield	.05
312	Tom Filer	.05
313	Mike Fitzgerald	.05
314	Marty Barrett	.05
315	Mookie Wilson	.05
316	Alan Knicely	.05
317	Ed Romero	.05
318	Glenn Wilson	.05
319	Bud Black	.05
320	Jim Rice	.20
321	Terry Pendleton	.05
322	Dave Kingman	.05
323	Gary Pettis	.05
324	Dan Schatzeder	.05
325	Juan Beniquez	.05
326	Kent Tekulve	.05
327	Mike Pagliarulo	.05
328	Pete O'Brien	.05
329	Kirby Puckett	1.00
330	Rick Sutcliffe	.05
331	Alan Ashby	.05
332	Willie Randolph	.05
333	Tom Henke	.05
334	Ken Oberkfell	.05
335	Don Sutton	.50
336	Dan Gladden	.05
337	George Vuckovich	.05
338	Jorge Bell	.10
339	Jim Dwyer	.05
340	Cal Ripken	2.50
341	Willie Hernandez	.05
342	Gary Redus	.05
343	Jerry Koosman	.05
344	Jim Wohlford	.05
345	Donnie Moore	.05
346	Floyd Youmans	.05
347	Gorman Thomas	.05
348	Cliff Johnson	.05
349	Ken Howell	.05
350	Jack Clark	.05
351	Gary Lucas	.05
352	Bob Clark	.05
353	Dave Stieb	.05
354	Tony Bernazard	.05
355	Lee Smith	.05
356	Mickey Hatcher	.05
357	Ed Vande Berg	.05
358	Rick Dempsey	.05
359	Bobby Cox	.05
360	Lloyd Moseby	.05
361	Shane Rawley	.05
362	Garry Maddox	.05
363	Buck Martinez	.05
364	Ed Nunez	.05
365	Luis Leal	.05
366	Dale Berra	.05
367	Mike Boddicker	.05
368	Greg Brock	.05
369	Al Holland	.05
370	Vince Coleman	.05
371	Rod Carew	.75
372	Ben Oglivie	.05
373	Lee Mazzilli	.05
374	Terry Francona	.05
375	Rich Gedman	.05
376	Charlie Lea	.05
377	Joe Carter	.50
378	Bruce Bochte	.05
379	Bobby Meacham	.05
380	LaMarr Hoyt	.05
381	Jeff Leonard	.05
382	Ivan Calderon	.05
383	Chris Brown	.05
384	Steve Trout	.05
385	Cecil Cooper	.05
386	Cecil Fielder	1.50
387	Tim Flannery	.05
388	Chris Codiroli	.05
389	Glenn Davis	.05
390	Tom Seaver	.75
391	Julio Franco	.05
392	Tom Brunansky	.05
393	Rob Wilfong	.05
394	Reggie Jackson	.75
395	Scott Garrelts	.05
396	Checklist 255-396	.05

Box Panels

The Canadian card company licensed by Topps to distribute cards in Canada is O-Pee-Chee. In 1986, O-Pee-Chee issued wax pack boxes with baseball cards printed on the box bottoms. Four cards appear on four different boxes making a complete set of 16. The cards are identical to the 1986 Topps wax box issue with the exception of the OPC logo replacing Topps' and the addition of French on the card backs. These bilingual cards were issued in Canada but are readily available in the USA. The cards are the standard 2-1/2" x 3-1/2" size, printed in full-color with black and red backs. The panel cards are not numbered but instead are lettered A through P.

	NM/M
Complete Panel Set (4):	12.00
Complete Singles Set (16):	11.00
Common Panel:	3.50
Common Single Player:	.15

Panel		4.50
A	Jorge Bell	
B	Wade Boggs	1.00
C	George Brett	1.50
D	Vince Coleman	.20
Panel		3.50
E	Carlton Fisk	1.00
F	Dwight Gooden	.20
G	Pedro Guerrero	.20
H	Ron Guidry	.20
Panel		4.00
I	Reggie Jackson	1.50
J	Don Mattingly	2.00
K	Oddibe McDowell	.15
L	Willie McGee	.15
Panel		3.00
M	Dale Murphy	.65
N	Pete Rose	2.50
O	Bret Saberhagen	.15
P	Fernando Valenzuela	.15

Stickers

Bi-lingual backs are the only difference between the OPC 1986 sticker set and the Topps issue. The sets share a checklist and, generally, values, although some Blue Jays and Expos stars may command a small premium in the Canadian version.

	NM/M
Complete Set:	15.00
Common Player:	.05
Album:	2.00

Tattoos

Topps and its Canadian shadow O-Pee-Chee returned to tattoos in 1986, marketing a set of 24 different tattoo sheets. Each sheet of tattoos measures 3-7/16" x 14" and includes both player portrait and smaller generic action tattoos. The player tattoos measure about 1-1/2" x 2-1/2". With 24 sheets, eight players per sheet, there are 192 players represented in the set. The sheets are numbered. The OPC version is distinguished from Topps by copyright notice.

1987 O-Pee-Chee

O-Pee-Chee of London, Ont., under license from the Topps Chewing Gum Co., continued a practice started in 1965 by issuing a baseball card set for 1987. The 396-card set is identical in design to the regular Topps set, save the name "O-Pee-Chee" replacing "Topps" in the lower right corner. Because the set is issued after its American counterpart, several cards appear with trade notations and corrected logos on the fronts. The cards, which are printed on white stock and are the standard 2-1/2" x 3-1/2", feature backs written in both English and French.

	NM/M
Complete Set (396):	15.00
Common Player:	.05
Wax Pack:	1.00
Wax Box (36):	17.50

#	Player	Price
1	Ken Oberkfell	.05
2	Jack Howell	.05
3	Hubie Brooks	.05
4	Bob Grich	.05
5	Rick Leach	.05
6	Phil Niekro	.50
7	Rickey Henderson	1.00
8	Terry Pendleton	.05
9	Jay Tibbs	.05
10	Cecil Cooper	.05
11	Mario Soto	.05
12	George Bell	.15
13	Nick Esasky	.05
14	Larry McWilliams	.05
15	Dan Quisenberry	.05
16	Ed Lynch	.05
17	Pete O'Brien	.05
18	Luis Aguayo	.05
19	Matt Young	.05
20	Gary Carter	1.00
21	Tom Paciorek	.05
22	Doug DeCinces	.05
23	Lee Smith	.05
24	Jesse Barfield	.05
25	Bert Blyleven	.05
26	Greg Brock	.05
27	Dan Petry	.05
28	Rick Dempsey	.05
29	Jimmy Key	.05
30	Tim Raines	.15
31	Bruce Hurst	.05
32	Manny Trillo	.05
33	Andy Van Slyke	.05
34	Ed Vande Berg	.05
35	Sid Bream	.05
36	Dave Winfield	1.00
37	Scott Garrelts	.05
38	Dennis Leonard	.05
39	Marty Barrett	.05
40	Dave Righetti	.05
41	Bo Diaz	.05
42	Gary Redus	.05
43	Tom Niedenfuer	.05
44	Greg Harris	.05
45	Jim Presley	.05
46	Danny Gladden	.05
47	Roy Smalley	.05
48	Wally Backman	.05
49	Tom Seaver	.75
50	Dave Smith	.05
51	Mel Hall	.05
52	Tim Flannery	.05
53	Julio Cruz	.05
54	Dick Schofield	.05
55	Tim Wallach	.05
56	Glenn Davis	.05
57	Darren Daulton	.05
58	Chico Walker	.05
59	Garth Iorg	.05
60	Tony Pena	.05
61	Ron Hassey	.05
62	Dave Dravecky	.05
63	Jorge Orta	.05
64	Al Nipper	.05
65	Tom Browning	.05
66	Marc Sullivan	.05
67	Todd Worrell	.05
68	Glenn Hubbard	.05
69	Carney Lansford	.05
70	Charlie Hough	.05
71	Lance McCullers	.05
72	Walt Terrell	.05
73	Bob Kearney	.05
74	Dan Pasqua	.05
75	Ron Darling	.05
76	Robin Yount	.75
77	Pat Tabler	.05
78	Tom Foley	.05
79	Juan Nieves	.05
80	Wally Joyner	.05
81	Wayne Krenchicki	.05
82	Kirby Puckett	1.00
83	Bob Ojeda	.05
84	Mookie Wilson	.05
85	Kevin Bass	.05
86	Kent Tekulve	.05
87	Mark Salas	.05
88	Brian Downing	.05
89	Ozzie Guillen	.05
90	Dave Stieb	.05
91	Rance Mulliniks	.05
92	Mike Witt	.05
93	Charlie Moore	.05
94	Jose Uribe	.05
95	Oddibe McDowell	.05
96	Ray Soff	.05
97	Glenn Wilson	.05
98	Brook Jacoby	.05
99	Darryl Motley	.05
100	Steve Garvey	.10
101	Frank White	.05
102	Mike Moore	.05
103	Rick Aguilera	.05
104	Buddy Bell	.05
105	Floyd Youmans	.05
106	Lou Whitaker	.05
107	Ozzie Smith	1.00
108	Jim Gantner	.05
109	R.J. Reynolds	.05
110	John Tudor	.05
111	Alfredo Griffin	.05
112	Mike Flanagan	.05
113	Neil Allen	.05
114	Ken Griffey	.05
115	Donnie Moore	.05
116	Bob Horner	.05
117	Ron Shepherd	.05
118	Cliff Johnson	.05
119	Vince Coleman	.05
120	Eddie Murray	.75
121	Dwayne Murphy	.05
122	Jim Clancy	.05
123	Ken Landreaux	.05
124	Tom Nieto	.05
125	Bob Brenly	.05
126	George Brett	1.25
127	Vance Law	.05
128	Checklist 1-132	.05
129	Bob Knepper	.05
130	Dwight Gooden	.05
131	Juan Bonilla	.05
132	Tim Burke	.05
133	Bob McClure	.05
134	Scott Bailes	.05
135	Mike Easler	.05
136	Ron Romanick	.05
137	Rich Gedman	.05
138	Bob Dernier	.05
139	John Denny	.05
140	Bret Saberhagen	.05
141	Herm Winningham	.05
142	Rick Sutcliffe	.05
143	Ryne Sandberg	1.00
144	Mike Scioscia	.05
145	Charlie Kerfeld	.05
146	Jim Rice	.15
147	Steve Trout	.05
148	Jesse Orosco	.05
149	Mike Boddicker	.05
150	Wade Boggs	1.00
151	Dane Iorg	.05
152	Rick Burleson	.05
153	Duane Ward	.05
154	Rick Reuschel	.05
155	Nolan Ryan	2.00
156	Bill Caudill	.05
157	Danny Darwin	.05
158	Ed Romero	.05
159	Bill Almon	.05
160	Julio Franco	.05
161	Kent Hrbek	.05
162	Chili Davis	.05
163	Kevin Gross	.05
164	Carlton Fisk	.75
165	Jeff Reardon	.05
166	Bob Boone	.05
167	Rick Honeycutt	.05
168	Dan Schatzeder	.05
169	Jim Wohlford	.05
170	Phil Bradley	.05
171	Ken Schrom	.05
172	Ron Oester	.05
173	Juan Beniquez	.05
174	Tony Armas	.05
175	Bob Stanley	.05
176	Steve Buechele	.05
177	Keith Moreland	.05
178	Cecil Fielder	.50
179	Gary Gaetti	.05
180	Chris Brown	.05
181	Tom Herr	.05
182	Lee Lacy	.05
183	Ozzie Virgil	.05
184	Paul Molitor	1.00
185	Roger McDowell	.05
186	Mike Marshall	.05
187	Ken Howell	.05
188	Rob Deer	.05
189	Joe Hesketh	.05
190	Jim Sundberg	.05
191	Kelly Gruber	.10
192	Cory Snyder	.05
193	Dave Concepcion	.05
194	Kirk McCaskill	.05
195	Mike Pagliarulo	.05
196	Rick Manning	.05
197	Brett Butler	.05
198	Tony Gwynn	1.00
199	Mariano Duncan	.05
200	Pete Rose	1.25
201	John Cangelosi	.05
202	Danny Cox	.05
203	Butch Wynegar	.05
204	Chris Chambliss	.05
205	Graig Nettles	.05
206	Chet Lemon	.05
207	Don Aase	.05
208	Mike Mason	.05
209	Alan Trammell	.05
210	Lloyd Moseby	.05
211	Richard Dotson	.05
212	Mike Fitzgerald	.05
213	Darrell Porter	.05
214	Checklist 133-264	.05
215	Mark Langston	.05
216	Steve Farr	.05
217	Dann Bilardello	.05
218	Gary Ward	.05
219	Cecilio Guante	.05
220	Joe Carter	.15
221	Ernie Whitt	.05
222	Denny Walling	.05
223	Charlie Leibrandt	.05
224	Wayne Tolleson	.05
225	Mike Smithson	.05
226	Zane Smith	.05
227	Terry Puhl	.05
228	Eric Davis	.05
229	Don Mattingly	1.25
230	Don Baylor	.05
231	Frank Tanana	.05
232	Tom Brookens	.05
233	Steve Bedrosian	.05
234	Wallace Johnson	.05
235	Alvin Davis	.05
236	Tommy John	.05
237	Jim Morrison	.05
238	Ricky Horton	.05
239	Shane Rawley	.05
240	Steve Balboni	.05
241	Mike Krukow	.05
242	Rick Mahler	.05
243	Bill Doran	.05
244	Mark Clear	.05
245	Willie Upshaw	.05
246	Hal McRae	.05
247	Jose Canseco	.45
248	George Hendrick	.05
249	Doyle Alexander	.05
250	Teddy Higuera	.05
251	Tom Hume	.05
252	Denny Martinez	.05
253	Eddie Milner	.05
254	Steve Sax	.05
255	Juan Samuel	.05
256	Dave Bergman	.05
257	Bob Forsch	.05
258	Steve Yeager	.05
259	Don Sutton	.50
260	Vida Blue	.05
261	Tom Brunansky	.05
262	Joe Sambito	.05
263	Mitch Webster	.05
264	Checklist 265-396	.05
265	Darrell Evans	.05
266	Dave Kingman	.05
267	Howard Johnson	.05
268	Greg Pryor	.05
269	Tippy Martinez	.05
270	Jody Davis	.05
271	Steve Carlton	.75
272	Andres Galarraga	.15
273	Fernando Valenzuela	.05
274	Jeff Hearron	.05
275	Ray Knight	.05
276	Bill Madlock	.05
277	Tom Henke	.05
278	Gary Pettis	.05
279	Jimmy Williams	.05
280	Jeffrey Leonard	.05
281	Bryn Smith	.05
282	John Cerutti	.05
283	Gary Roenicke	.05
284	Joaquin Andujar	.05
285	Dennis Boyd	.05
286	Tim Hulett	.05
287	Craig Lefferts	.05
288	Tito Landrum	.05
289	Manny Lee	.05
290	Leon Durham	.05
291	Johnny Ray	.05
292	Franklin Stubbs	.05
293	Bob Rodgers	.05
294	Terry Francona	.05
295	Len Dykstra	.05
296	Tom Candiotti	.05
297	Frank DiPino	.05
298	Craig Reynolds	.05
299	Jerry Hairston Sr.	.05
300	Reggie Jackson	1.00
301	Luis Aquino	.05
302	Greg Walker	.05
303	Terry Kennedy	.05
304	Phil Garner	.05
305	John Franco	.05
306	Bill Buckner	.05
307	Kevin Mitchell	.05
308	Don Slaught	.05
309	Harold Baines	.05
310	Frank Viola	.05
311	Dave Lopes	.05
312	Cal Ripken	2.00
313	John Candelaria	.05
314	Bob Sebra	.05
315	Bud Black	.05
316	Brian Fisher	.05
317	Clint Hurdle	.05
318	Ernie Riles	.05
319	Dave LaPoint	.05
320	Barry Bonds	6.00
321	Tim Stoddard	.05
322	Ron Cey	.05
323	Al Newman	.05
324	Jim Royster	.05
325	Garry Templeton	.05
326	Mark Gubicza	.05
327	Andre Thornton	.05
328	Bob Welch	.05
329	Tony Fernandez	.05
330	Mike Scott	.05
331	Jack Clark	.05
332	Danny Tartabull	.05
333	Greg Minton	.05
334	Ed Correa	.05
335	Candy Maldonado	.05
336	Dennis Lamp	.05
337	Sid Fernandez	.05
338	Greg Gross	.05
339	Willie Hernandez	.05
340	Roger Clemens	1.50

341	Mickey Hatcher	.05
342	Bob James	.05
343	Jose Cruz	.05
344	Bruce Sutter	.65
345	Andre Dawson	.25
346	Shawon Dunston	.05
347	Scott McGregor	.05
348	Carmelo Martinez	.05
349	Storm Davis	.05
350	Keith Hernandez	.05
351	Andy McGaffigan	.05
352	Dave Parker	.05
353	Ernie Camacho	.05
354	Eric Show	.05
355	Don Carman	.05
356	Floyd Bannister	.05
357	Willie McGee	.05
358	Atlee Hammaker	.05
359	Dale Murphy	.30
360	Pedro Guerrero	.05
361	Will Clark	.10
362	Bill Campbell	.05
363	Alejandro Pena	.05
364	Dennis Rasmussen	.05
365	Rick Rhoden	.05
366	Randy St. Claire	.05
367	Willie Wilson	.05
368	Dwight Evans	.05
369	Moose Haas	.05
370	Fred Lynn	.05
371	Mark Eichhorn	.05
372	Dave Schmidt	.05
373	Jerry Reuss	.05
374	Lance Parrish	.05
375	Ron Guidry	.05
376	Jack Morris	.05
377	Willie Randolph	.05
378	Joel Youngblood	.05
379	Darryl Strawberry	.05
380	Rich Gossage	.05
381	Dennis Eckersley	.50
382	Gary Lucas	.05
383	Ron Davis	.05
384	Pete Incaviglia	.05
385	Orel Hershiser	.10
386	Kirk Gibson	.05
387	Don Robinson	.05
388	Darnell Coles	.05
389	Von Hayes	.05
390	Gary Matthews	.05
391	Jay Howell	.05
392	Tim Laudner	.05
393	Rod Scurry	.05
394	Tony Bernazard	.05
395	Damaso Garcia	.05
396	Mike Schmidt	1.25

Box Panels

For the second consecutive year, O-Pee-Chee placed baseball cards on the bottoms of its wax pack boxes. The 2-1/8" x 3" cards were issued in panels of four and are slightly smaller in size than the regular issue OPC cards. The card fronts are identical in design to the regular issue, while the backs contain a newspaper-type commentary in both French and English. Collectors may note the 1987 Topps wax box cards were issued on side panels as opposed to box bottoms. Because the OPC wax boxes are smaller in size than their U.S. counterparts, printing cards on side panels was not possible.

		NM/M
Complete Panel Set (2):		5.00
Complete Singles Set (8):		5.00
Common Single Player:		.15
Panel		2.00
A	Don Baylor	.15
B	Steve Carlton	.50
C	Ron Cey	.15
D	Cecil Cooper	.15
Panel		4.00
E	Rickey Henderson	1.00
F	Jim Rice	.35
G	Don Sutton	.50
H	Dave Winfield	1.00

Stickers

Bi-lingual backs are the only difference between the OPC 1987 sticker set and the Topps issue. The sets share a checklist and, generally, values, although some Blue Jays and Expos stars may command a small premium in the Canadian version.

1988 O-Pee-Chee

Under license from Topps, O-Pee-Chee uses the same player photos as the Topps issue, but the Canadian edition includes only 396 cards (one-half the number in the Topps set). The OPC set was printed after the U.S. press run, so several cards carry overprints on the fronts, indicating changes in players' teams. New teams are named in the overprints; card headers bear the former team names. This set follows the same basic design as the 1988 Topps cards. The OPC logo appears in place of the Topps logo, both front and back. A four-card subset consists of #1 and #2 draft choices for the Expos (Nathan Minchey and Delino DeShields) and Blue Jays (Alex Sanchez and Derek Bell). These cards are distinguished by a yellow or orange triangle in the lower-right corner bearing the player's name above the words "Choisi au repecharge." Card backs are bilingual (English-French) and printed in black on orange. This series was marketed primarily in Canada in four separate display boxes, with four cards printed one each box bottom. Individual card packs contain seven cards and one stick of gum.

	NM/M
Unopened Fact. Set (396):	9.00
Complete Set (396):	7.50
Common Player:	.05
Wax Pack (7):	.25
Wax Box (48):	7.50

1	Chris James	.05
2	Steve Buechele	.05
3	Mike Henneman	.05
4	Eddie Murray	.60
5	Bret Saberhagen	.05
6	Nathan Minchey (Draft Pick)	.05
7	Harold Reynolds	.05
8	Bo Jackson	.10
9	Mike Easler	.05
10	Ryne Sandberg	.75
11	Mike Young	.05
12	Tony Phillips	.05
13	Andres Thomas	.05
14	Tim Burke	.05
15	Chili Davis	.05
16	Jim Lindeman	.05
17	Ron Oester	.05
18	Craig Reynolds	.05
19	Juan Samuel	.05
20	Kevin Gross	.05
21	Cecil Fielder	.25
22	Greg Swindell	.05
23	Jose DeLeon	.05
24	Jim Deshaies	.05
25	Andres Galarraga	.10
26	Mitch Williams	.05
27	R.J. Reynolds	.05
28	Jose Nunez	.05
29	Angel Salazar	.05
30	Sid Fernandez	.05

31	Keith Moreland	.05
32	John Kruk	.05
33	Rob Deer	.05
34	Ricky Horton	.05
35	Harold Baines	.05
36	Jamie Moyer	.05
37	Kevin McReynolds	.05
38	Ozzie Smith	.75
39	Ron Darling	.05
40	Orel Hershiser	.05
41	Bob Melvin	.05
42	Alfredo Griffin	.05
43	Dick Schofield	.05
44	Terry Steinbach	.05
45	Kent Hrbek	.05
46	Darnell Coles	.05
47	Jimmy Key	.05
48	Alan Ashby	.05
49	Julio Franco	.05
50	Hubie Brooks	.05
51	Chris Bando	.05
52	Fernando Valenzuela	.05
53	Kal Daniels	.05
54	Jim Clancy	.05
55	Phil Bradley	.05
56	Andy McGaffigan	.05
57	Mike LaValliere	.05
58	Dave Magadan	.05
59	Danny Cox	.05
60	Rickey Henderson	.75
61	Jim Rice	.20
62	Calvin Schiraldi	.05
63	Jerry Mumphrey	.05
64	Ken Caminiti	.05
65	Leon Durham	.05
66	Shane Rawley	.05
67	Ken Oberkfell	.05
68	Keith Hernandez	.05
69	Bob Brenly	.05
70	Roger Clemens	.90
71	Gary Pettis	.05
72	Dennis Eckersley	.50
73	Dave Smith	.05
74	Cal Ripken	1.00
75	Joe Carter	.15
76	Denny Martinez	.05
77	Juan Beniquez	.05
78	Tim Laudner	.05
79	Ernie Whitt	.05
80	Mark Langston	.05
81	Dale Sveum	.05
82	Dion James	.05
83	Dave Valle	.05
84	Bill Wegman	.05
85	Howard Johnson	.05
86	Benito Santiago	.05
87	Casey Candaele	.05
88	Delino DeShields (Draft Pick)	3.00
89	Dave Winfield	.75
90	Dale Murphy	.20
91	Jay Howell	.05
92	Ken Williams	.05
93	Bob Sebra	.05
94	Tim Wallach	.10
95	Lance Parrish	.05
96	Todd Benzinger	.05
97	Scott Garrelts	.05
98	Jose Guzman	.05
99	Jeff Reardon	.05
100	Jack Clark	.05
101	Tracy Jones	.05
102	Barry Larkin	.05
103	Curt Young	.05
104	Juan Nieves	.05
105	Terry Pendleton	.05
106	Rob Ducey	.05
107	Scott Bailes	.05
108	Eric King	.05
109	Mike Pagliarulo	.05
110	Teddy Higuera	.05
111	Pedro Guerrero	.05
112	Chris Brown	.05
113	Kelly Gruber	.05
114	Jack Howell	.05
115	Johnny Ray	.05
116	Mark Eichhorn	.05
117	Tony Pena	.05
118	Bob Welch	.05
119	Mike Kingery	.05
120	Kirby Puckett	.75
121	Charlie Hough	.05
122	Tony Bernazard	.05
123	Tom Candiotti	.05
124	Ray Knight	.05
125	Bruce Hurst	.05
126	Steve Jeltz	.05
127	Ron Guidry	.05
128	Duane Ward	.05
129	Greg Minton	.05
130	Buddy Bell	.05
131	Denny Walling	.05
132	Donnie Hill	.05
133	Wayne Tolleson	.05
134	Bob Rodgers	.05
135	Todd Worrell	.05
136	Brian Dayett	.05
137	Chris Bosio	.05
138	Mitch Webster	.05
139	Jerry Browne	.05
140	Jesse Barfield	.05
141	Doug DeCinces	.05
142	Andy Van Slyke	.05
143	Doug Drabek	.05
144	Jeff Parrett	.05
145	Bill Madlock	.05
146	Larry Herndon	.05
147	Bill Buckner	.05

148	Carmelo Martinez	.05
149	Ken Howell	.05
150	Eric Davis	.05
151	Randy Ready	.05
152	Jeffrey Leonard	.05
153	Dave Steib	.05
154	Jeff Stone	.05
155	Dave Righetti	.05
156	Gary Matthews	.05
157	Gary Carter	.75
158	Bob Boone	.05
159	Glenn Davis	.05
160	Willie McGee	.05
161	Bryn Smith	.05
162	Mark McLemore	.05
163	Dale Mohorcic	.05
164	Mike Flanagan	.05
165	Robin Yount	.60
166	Bill Doran	.05
167	Rance Mulliniks	.05
168	Wally Joyner	.05
169	Cory Snyder	.05
170	Rich Gossage	.05
171	Rick Mahler	.05
172	Henry Cotto	.05
173	George Bell	.15
174	B.J. Surhoff	.05
175	Kevin Bass	.05
176	Jeff Reed	.05
177	Frank Tanana	.05
178	Darryl Strawberry	.05
179	Lou Whitaker	.05
180	Terry Kennedy	.05
181	Mariano Duncan	.05
182	Ken Phelps	.05
183	Bob Dernier	.05
184	Ivan Calderon	.05
185	Rick Rhoden	.05
186	Rafael Palmeiro	.50
187	Kelly Downs	.05
188	Spike Owen	.05
189	Bobby Bonilla	.05
190	Candy Maldonado	.05
191	John Cerutti	.05
192	Devon White	.25
193	Brian Fisher	.05
194	Alex Sanchez (Draft Pick)	.20
195	Dan Quisenberry	.05
196	Dave Engle	.05
197	Lance McCullers	.05
198	Franklin Stubbs	.05
199	Scott Bradley	.05
200	Wade Boggs	.75
201	Kirk Gibson	.05
202	Brett Butler	.05
203	Dave Anderson	.05
204	Donnie Moore	.05
205	Nelson Liriano	.05
206	Danny Gladden	.05
207	Dan Pasqua	.05
208	Robbie Thompson	.05
209	Richard Dotson	.05
210	Willie Randolph	.05
211	Danny Tartabull	.05
212	Greg Brock	.05
213	Albert Hall	.05
214	Dave Schmidt	.05
215	Von Hayes	.05
216	Herm Winningham	.05
217	Mike Davis	.05
218	Charlie Leibrandt	.05
219	Mike Stanley	.05
220	Tom Henke	.05
221	Dwight Evans	.05
222	Willie Wilson	.05
223	Stan Jefferson	.05
224	Mike Dunne	.05
225	Mike Scioscia	.05
226	Larry Parrish	.05
227	Mike Scott	.05
228	Wallace Johnson	.05
229	Jeff Musselman	.05
230	Pat Tabler	.05
231	Paul Molitor	.75
232	Bob James	.05
233	Joe Niekro	.05
234	Oddibe McDowell	.05
235	Gary Ward	.05
236	Ted Power	.05
237	Pascual Perez	.05
238	Luis Polonia	.05
239	Mike Diaz	.05
240	Lee Smith	.05
241	Willie Upshaw	.05
242	Tom Neidenfuer	.05
243	Tim Raines	.20
244	Jeff Robinson	.05
245	Rich Gedman	.05
246	Scott Bankhead	.05
247	Andre Dawson	.05
248	Brook Jacoby	.05
249	Mike Marshall	.05
250	Nolan Ryan	1.00
251	Tom Foley	.05
252	Bob Brower	.05
253	Checklist 1-132	.05
254	Scott McGregor	.05
255	Ken Griffey	.05
256	Ken Schrom	.05
257	Gary Gaetti	.05
258	Ed Nunez	.05
259	Frank Viola	.05
260	Vince Coleman	.05
261	Reid Nichols	.05
262	Tim Flannery	.05
263	Glenn Braggs	.05
264	Garry Templeton	.05

265	Bo Diaz	.05
266	Matt Nokes	.05
267	Barry Bonds	1.00
268	Bruce Ruffin	.05
269	Ellis Burks	.05
270	Mike Witt	.05
271	Ken Gerhart	.05
272	Lloyd Moseby	.05
273	Garth Iorg	.05
274	Mike Greenwell	.05
275	Kevin Seitzer	.05
276	Luis Salazar	.05
277	Shawon Dunston	.05
278	Rick Reuschel	.05
279	Randy St. Claire	.05
280	Pete Incaviglia	.05
281	Mike Boddicker	.05
282	Jay Tibbs	.05
283	Shane Mack	.05
284	Walt Terrell	.05
285	Jim Presley	.05
286	Greg Walker	.05
287	Dwight Gooden	.05
288	Jim Morrison	.05
289	Gene Garber	.05
290	Tony Fernandez	.05
291	Ozzie Virgil	.05
292	Carney Lansford	.05
293	Jim Acker	.05
294	Tommy Hinzo	.05
295	Bert Blyleven	.05
296	Ozzie Guillen	.05
297	Zane Smith	.05
298	Milt Thompson	.05
299	Len Dykstra	.05
300	Don Mattingly	.85
301	Bud Black	.05
302	Jose Uribe	.05
303	Manny Lee	.05
304	Sid Bream	.05
305	Steve Sax	.05
306	Billy Hatcher	.05
307	John Shelby	.05
308	Lee Mazzilli	.05
309	Bill Long	.05
310	Tom Herr	.05
311	Derek Bell (Draft Pick)	3.00
312	George Brett	.85
313	Bob McClure	.05
314	Jimmy Williams	.05
315	Dave Parker	.05
316	Doyle Alexander	.05
317	Dan Plesac	.05
318	Mel Hall	.05
319	Ruben Sierra	.05
320	Alan Trammell	.05
321	Mike Schmidt	.85
322	Wally Ritchie	.05
323	Rick Leach	.05
324	Danny Jackson	.05
325	Glenn Hubbard	.05
326	Frank White	.05
327	Larry Sheets	.05
328	John Cangelosi	.05
329	Bill Gullickson	.05
330	Eddie Whitson	.05
331	Brian Downing	.05
332	Gary Redus	.05
333	Wally Backman	.05
334	Dwayne Murphy	.05
335	Claudell Washington	.05
336	Dave Concepcion	.05
337	Jim Gantner	.05
338	Marty Barrett	.05
339	Mickey Hatcher	.05
340	Jack Morris	.05
341	John Franco	.05
342	Ron Robinson	.05
343	Greg Gagne	.05
344	Steve Bedrosian	.05
345	Scott Fletcher	.05
346	Vance Law	.05
347	Joe Johnson	.05
348	Jim Eisenreich	.05
349	Alvin Davis	.05
350	Will Clark	.10
351	Mike Aldrete	.05
352	Billy Ripken	.05
353	Dave Stewart	.05
354	Neal Heaton	.05
355	Roger McDowell	.05
356	John Tudor	.05
357	Floyd Bannister	.05
358	Rey Quinones	.05
359	Glenn Wilson	.05
360	Tony Gwynn	.75
361	Greg Maddux	.75
362	Juan Castillo	.05
363	Willie Fraser	.05
364	Nick Esasky	.05
365	Floyd Youmans	.05
366	Chet Lemon	.05
367	Matt Young	.05
368	Gerald Young	.05
369	Bob Stanley	.05
370	Jose Canseco	.45
371	Joe Hesketh	.05
372	Rick Sutcliffe	.05
373	Checklist 133-264	.05
374	Checklist 265-396	.05
375	Tom Brunansky	.05
376	Jody Davis	.05
377	Sam Horn	.05
378	Mark Gubicza	.05
379	Rafael Ramirez	.05
380	Joe Magrane	.05
381	Pete O'Brien	.05
382	Lee Guetterman	.05

383	Eric Bell	.05
384	Gene Larkin	.05
385	Carlton Fisk	.60
386	Mike Fitzgerald	.05
387	Kevin Mitchell	.05
388	Jim Winn	.05
389	Mike Smithson	.05
390	Darrell Evans	.05
391	Terry Leach	.05
392	Charlie Kerfeld	.05
393	Mike Krukow	.05
394	Mark McGwire	.90
395	Fred McGriff	.10
396	DeWayne Buice	.05

Box Panels

A Topps licensee, O-Pee-Chee of Canada issued this 16-card set on wax display box bottoms. Cards feature popular current players and are identified by alphabet (A-P) rather than numbers. Player photos are the same ones used on the Topps U.S. issue and cards follow the same design as Topps' regular issue set. The OPC logo replaces the Topps logo on both front and back. Orange and black card backs are bilingual (French/English) and include complete major and minor league career stats.

		NM/M
Complete Panel Set (4):		8.00
Complete Singles Set (16):		8.00
Common Single Player:		.10
Panel		1.00
A	Don Baylor	.10
B	Steve Bedrosian	.10
C	Juan Beniquez	.10
D	Bob Boone	.15
Panel		2.00
E	Darrell Evans	.10
F	Tony Gwynn	1.00
G	John Kruk	.10
H	Marvell Wynne	.10
Panel		1.00
I	Joe Carter	.25
J	Eric Davis	.10
K	Howard Johnson	.10
L	Darryl Strawberry	.10
Panel		5.00
M	Rickey Henderson	1.00
N	Nolan Ryan	3.00
O	Mike Schmidt	1.50
P	Kent Tekulve	.10

Stickers/ Stickercards

This is the Canadian version of Topps' sticker issue for 1988, virtually identical except for the substitution of the OPC logo and copyright notice on the front of the stickercard. The Canadian version shares the Topps' checklists and, essentially, the price structure, although Canadian star players command a small premium in the OPC version.

1989 O-Pee-Chee

At 396 cards, the 1989 O-Pee-Chee issue is half the size of the corresponding Topps set. As in previous years, the design of the OPC cards is virtually identical to the Topps version, though the Topps logo on front has been replaced with an O-Pee-Chee logo in one of the upper corners and the backs are printed in both English and French for the Canadian market. Cards of players who changed teams often contain an overprint indicating the player's new team and date of the transaction.

		NM/M
Complete Set (396):		10.00
Common Player:		.05
Wax Box (48):		12.00
1	Brook Jacoby	.05
2	Atlee Hammaker	.05
3	Jack Clark	.05
4	Dave Steib	.10
5	Bud Black	.05
6	Damon Berryhill	.05
7	Mike Scioscia	.05
8	Jose Uribe	.05
9	Mike Aldrete	.05
10	Andre Dawson	.25
11	Bruce Sutter	.45
12	Dale Sveum	.05
13	Dan Quisenberry	.05
14	Tom Niedenfuer	.05
15	Robby Thompson	.05
16	Ron Robinson	.05
17	Brian Downing	.05
18	Rick Rhoden	.05
19	Greg Gagne	.05
20	Allan Anderson	.05
21	Eddie Whitson	.05
22	Billy Ripken	.05
23	Mike Fitzgerald	.05
24	Shane Rawley	.05
25	Frank White	.05
26	Don Mattingly	.75
27	Fred Lynn	.05
28	Mike Moore	.05
29	Kelly Gruber	.05
30	Dwight Gooden	.05
31	Dan Pasqua	.05
32	Dennis Rasmussen	.05
33	B.J. Surhoff	.05
34	Sid Fernandez	.05
35	John Tudor	.05
36	Mitch Webster	.05
37	Doug Drabek	.05
38	Bobby Witt	.05
39	Mike Maddux	.05
40	Steve Sax	.05
41	Orel Hershiser	.05
42	Pete Incaviglia	.05
43	Guillermo Hernandez	.05
44	Kevin Coffman	.05
45	Kal Daniels	.05
46	Carlton Fisk	.50
47	Carney Lansford	.05
48	Tim Burke	.05
49	Alan Trammell	.05
50	George Bell	.15
51	Tony Gwynn	.60
52	Bob Brenly	.05
53	Ruben Sierra	.05
54	Otis Nixon	.05
55	Julio Franco	.05
56	Pat Tabler	.05
57	Alvin Davis	.05
58	Kevin Seitzer	.05
59	Mark Davis	.05
60	Tom Brunansky	.05
61	Jeff Treadway	.05
62	Alfredo Griffin	.05
63	Keith Hernandez	.05
64	Alex Trevino	.05
65	Rick Reuschel	.05
66	Bob Walk	.05
67	Dave Palmer	.05
68	Pedro Guerrero	.05
69	Jose Oquendo	.05
70	Mark McGwire	.85
71	Mike Boddicker	.05
72	Wally Backman	.05
73	Pascual Perez	.05
74	Joe Hesketh	.05
75	Tom Henke	.05
76	Nelson Liriano	.05
77	Doyle Alexander	.05
78	Tim Wallach	.10
79	Scott Bankhead	.05
80	Cory Snyder	.05
81	Dave Magadan	.05
82	Randy Ready	.05
83	Steve Buechele	.05
84	Bo Jackson	.10
85	Kevin McReynolds	.05
86	Jeff Reardon	.05
87	Tim Raines	.25
88	Melido Perez	.05
89	Dave LaPoint	.05
90	Vince Coleman	.05
91	Floyd Youmans	.05
92	Buddy Bell	.05
93	Andres Galarraga	.15
94	Tony Pena	.05
95	Gerald Young	.05
96	Rick Cerone	.05
97	Ken Oberkfell	.05
98	Larry Sheets	.05
99	Chuck Crim	.05
100	Mike Schmidt	.75
101	Ivan Calderon	.05
102	Kevin Bass	.05
103	Chili Davis	.05
104	Randy Myers	.05
105	Ron Darling	.05
106	Willie Upshaw	.05
107	Jose DeLeon	.05
108	Fred Manrique	.05
109	Johnny Ray	.05
110	Paul Molitor	.60
111	Rance Mulliniks	.05
112	Jim Presley	.05
113	Lloyd Moseby	.05
114	Lance Parrish	.05
115	Jody Davis	.05
116	Matt Nokes	.05
117	Dave Anderson	.05
118	Checklist	.05
119	Rafael Belliard	.05
120	Frank Viola	.05
121	Roger Clemens	.85
122	Luis Salazar	.05
123	Mike Stanley	.05
124	Jim Traber	.05
125	Mike Krukow	.05
126	Sid Bream	.05
127	Joel Skinner	.05
128	Milt Thompson	.05
129	Terry Clark	.05
130	Gerald Perry	.05
131	Bryn Smith	.05
132	Kirby Puckett	.60
133	Bill Long	.05
134	Jim Gantner	.05
135	Jose Rijo	.05
136	Joey Meyer	.05
137	Geno Petralli	.05
138	Wallace Johnson	.05
139	Mike Flanagan	.05
140	Shawon Dunston	.05
141	Eric Plunk	.05
142	Bobby Bonilla	.05
143	Jack McDowell	.05
144	Mookie Wilson	.05
145	Dave Stewart	.10
146	Gary Pettis	.05
147	Eric Show	.05
148	Eddie Murray	.50
149	Lee Smith	.05
150	Fernando Valenzuela	.05
151	Bob Walk	.05
152	Harold Baines	.05
153	Albert Hall	.05
154	Don Carman	.05
155	Marty Barrett	.05
156	Chris Sabo	.05
157	Bret Saberhagen	.05
158	Danny Cox	.05
159	Tom Foley	.05
160	Jeffrey Leonard	.05
161	Brady Anderson	.05
162	Rich Gossage	.05
163	Greg Brock	.05
164	Joe Carter	.10
165	Mike Dunne	.05
166	Jeff Russell	.05
167	Dan Plesac	.05
168	Willie Wilson	.05
169	Mike Jackson	.05
170	Tony Fernandez	.05
171	Jamie Moyer	.05
172	Jim Gott	.05
173	Mel Hall	.05
174	Mark McGwire	.85
175	John Shelby	.05
176	Jeff Parrett	.05
177	Tim Belcher	.05
178	Rich Gedman	.05
179	Ozzie Virgil	.05
180	Mike Scott	.05
181	Dickie Thon	.05
182	Rob Murphy	.05
183	Oddibe McDowell	.05
184	Wade Boggs	.60
185	Claudell Washington	.05
186	Randy Johnson	2.00
187	Paul O'Neill	.05
188	Todd Benzinger	.05
189	Kevin Mitchell	.05
190	Mike Witt	.05
191	Sil Campusano	.05
192	Ken Gerhart	.05
193	Bob Rodgers	.05
194	Floyd Bannister	.05
195	Ozzie Guillen	.05
196	Ron Gant	.05
197	Neal Heaton	.05
198	Bill Swift	.05
199	Dave Parker	.05
200	George Brett	.75
201	Bo Diaz	.05
202	Brad Moore	.05
203	Rob Ducey	.05
204	Bert Blyleven	.05
205	Dwight Evans	.05
206	Roberto Alomar	.60
207	Henry Cotto	.05
208	Harold Reynolds	.05
209	Jose Guzman	.05
210	Dale Murphy	.15
211	Mike Pagliarulo	.05
212	Jay Howell	.05
213	Rene Gonzalez	.05
214	Scott Garrelts	.05
215	Kevin Gross	.05
216	Jack Howell	.05
217	Kurt Stillwell	.05
218	Mike LaValliere	.05
219	Jim Clancy	.05
220	Gary Gaetti	.05
221	Hubie Brooks	.05
222	Bruce Ruffin	.05
223	Jay Buhner	.05
224	Cecil Fielder	.15
225	Willie McGee	.05
226	Bill Doran	.05
227	John Farrell	.05
228	Nelson Santovenia	.05
229	Jimmy Key	.05
230	Ozzie Smith	.60
231	Dave Schmidt	.05
232	Jody Reed	.05
233	Gregg Jefferies	.05
234	Tom Browning	.05
235	John Kruk	.05
236	Charles Hudson	.05
237	Todd Stottlemyre	.10
238	Don Slaught	.05
239	Tim Laudner	.05
240	Greg Maddux	.60
241	Brett Butler	.05
242	Checklist	.05
243	Bob Boone	.05
244	Willie Randolph	.05
245	Jim Rice	.15
246	Rey Quinones	.05
247	Checklist	.05
248	Stan Javier	.05
249	Tim Leary	.05
250	Cal Ripken, Jr.	1.00
251	John Dopson	.05
252	Billy Hatcher	.05
253	Robin Yount	.50
254	Mickey Hatcher	.05
255	Bob Horner	.05
256	Benito Santiago	.05
257	Luis Rivera	.05
258	Fred McGriff	.10
259	Dave Wells	.10
260	Dave Winfield	.60
261	Rafael Ramirez	.05
262	Nick Esasky	.05
263	Barry Bonds	1.00
264	Joe Magrane	.05
265	Kent Hrbek	.05
266	Jack Morris	.10
267	Jeff Robinson	.05
268	Ron Kittle	.05
269	Candy Maldonado	.05
270	Wally Joyner	.05
271	Glenn Braggs	.05
272	Ron Hassey	.05
273	Jose Lind	.05
274	Mark Eichhorn	.05
275	Danny Tartabull	.05
276	Paul Kilgus	.05
277	Mike Davis	.05
278	Andy McGaffigan	.05
279	Scott Bradley	.05
280	Bob Knepper	.05
281	Gary Redus	.05
282	Rickey Henderson	.60
283	Andy Allenson	.05
284	Rick Leach	.05
285	John Candelaria	.05
286	Dick Schofield	.05
287	Bryan Harvey	.05
288	Randy Bush	.05
289	Ernie Whitt	.05
290	John Franco	.05
291	Todd Worrell	.05
292	Teddy Higuera	.05
293	Keith Moreland	.05
294	Juan Berenguer	.05
295	Scott Fletcher	.05
296	Roger McDowell	.05
297	Mark Grace	.10
298	Chris James	.05
299	Frank Tanana	.05
300	Darryl Strawberry	.05
301	Charlie Leibrandt	.05
302	Gary Ward	.05
303	Brian Fisher	.05
304	Terry Steinbach	.05
305	Dave Smith	.05
306	Greg Minton	.05
307	Lance McCullers	.05
308	Phil Bradley	.05
309	Terry Kennedy	.05
310	Rafael Palmeiro	.45
311	Ellis Burks	.05
312	Doug Jones	.05
313	Dennis Martinez	.05
314	Pete O'Brien	.05
315	Greg Swindell	.05
316	Walt Weiss	.05
317	Pete Stanicek	.05
318	Gene Nelson	.05
319	Danny Jackson	.05
320	Lou Whitaker	.05
321	Will Clark	.10
322	John Smiley	.05
323	Mike Marshall	.05
324	Gary Carter	.60
325	Jesse Barfield	.05
326	Dennis Boyd	.05
327	Dave Henderson	.05
328	Chet Lemon	.05
329	Bob Melvin	.05
330	Eric Davis	.05
331	Ted Power	.05
332	Carmelo Martinez	.05
333	Bob Ojeda	.05
334	Steve Lyons	.05
335	Dave Righetti	.05
336	Steve Balboni	.05
337	Calvin Schiraldi	.05
338	Vance Law	.05
339	Zane Smith	.05
340	Kirk Gibson	.05
341	Jim Deshaies	.05
342	Tom Brookens	.05
343	Pat Borders	.10
344	Devon White	.10
345	Charlie Hough	.05
346	Rex Hudler	.05
347	John Cerutti	.05
348	Kirk McCaskill	.05
349	Len Dykstra	.05
350	Andy Van Slyke	.05
351	Jeff Robinson	.05
352	Rick Schu	.05
353	Bruce Benedict	.05
354	Bill Wegman	.05
355	Mark Langston	.05
356	Steve Farr	.05
357	Richard Dotson	.05
358	Andres Thomas	.05
359	Alan Ashby	.05
360	Ryne Sandberg	.60
361	Kelly Downs	.05
362	Jeff Musselman	.05
363	Barry Larkin	.05
364	Rob Deer	.05
365	Mike Henneman	.05
366	Nolan Ryan	1.00
367	Johnny Paredes	.05
368	Bobby Thigpen	.05
369	Mickey Brantley	.05
370	Dennis Eckersley	.45
371	Manny Lee	.05
372	Juan Samuel	.05
373	Tracy Jones	.05
374	Mike Greenwell	.05
375	Terry Pendleton	.05
376	Steve Lombardozzi	.05
377	Mitch Williams	.05
378	Glenn Davis	.05
379	Mark Gubicza	.05
380	Orel Hershiser	.05
381	Jimy Williams	.05
382	Kirk Gibson	.05
383	Howard Johnson	.05
384	Dave Cone	.05
385	Von Hayes	.05
386	Luis Polonia	.05
387	Dan Gladden	.05
388	Pete Smith	.05
389	Jose Canseco	.35
390	Mickey Hatcher	.05
391	Wil Tejada	.05
392	Duane Ward	.05
393	Rick Mahler	.05
394	Rick Sutcliffe	.05
395	Dave Martinez	.05
396	Ken Dayley	.05

Box Panels

Continuing its practice of printing baseball cards on the bottom panels of its wax pack boxes, OPC in 1989 issued a special 16-card set, printing four cards on each of four different box-bottom panels. The cards are identical in design to the regular 1989 OPC cards. They are designated by letter (from A through P) rather than by number.

		NM/M
Complete Panel Set (4):		10.00
Complete Singles Set (16):		10.00
Common Panel:		1.50
Common Single Player:		.10
	Panel	2.50
A	George Brett	1.50
B	Bill Buckner	.10
C	Darrell Evans	.10
D	Rich Gossage	.10
	Panel	1.50
E	Greg Gross	.10
F	Rickey Henderson	1.00
G	Keith Hernandez	.10
H	Tom Lasorda	.25
	Panel	7.50
I	Jim Rice	.50
J	Cal Ripken, Jr.	3.00
K	Nolan Ryan	3.00
L	Mike Schmidt	1.50
	Panel	1.50
M	Bruce Sutter	.75
N	Don Sutton	.50
O	Kent Tekulve	.10
P	Dave Winfield	1.00

Stickers/ Stickercards

Once again sharing a checklist with the 1989 Topps sticker issue, the OPC version differs only in the substitution of the O-Pee-Chee logo and copyright notice on the front of the stickercard. Values are also essentially the same, although Expos and Blue Jays stars carry a small premium in the OPC version.

1990 O-Pee-Chee

Virtually identical to the contemporary 1990 Topps set, the OPC issue features the same 792 cards. On most cards the fronts are indistinguishable, even to the use of a Topps logo on the Canadian product. A number of the OPC cards differ from their Topps counterparts in that there is a notice of team change printed in black on the front. Backs of the OPC cards feature a few lines of French in areas such as the stat headings, the career summary and monthly scoreboard. The OPC cards omit the Topps copyright line and feature an OPC copyright line on back.

	NM/M
Unopened Fact. Set (792):	15.00
Complete Set (792):	12.00
Common Player:	.05
Wax Pack:	.75
Wax Box (36):	20.00

Stickers

Once again sharing a checklist with the 1990 Topps

sticker issue, the OPC version differs only in the substitution of the O-Pee-Chee logo and copyright notice on the sticker-card. Values are also essentially the same, although Expos and Blue Jays stars carry a small premium in the OPC version.

1991 O-Pee-Chee Sample Sheet

This 7-1/2" x 10-1/2" sample sheet debuts the 1991 OPC set. Fronts reproduce the basic design while the back, printed in blue on white, contains an ad for OPC.

	NM/M
Complete Sheet:	5.00

1991 O-Pee-Chee

Once again for 1991, OPC utilized the contemporary Topps set of 792 cards as the basis for its own issue. The OPC cards are again printed on a lighter, whiter stock and differ from the Topps cards in the addition of French to the card backs, along with the OPC copyright. Many card fronts in OPC carry a small black typographical notice concerning team changes by the players.

	NM/M
Complete Set (792):	10.00
Common Player:	.05
Wax Box (36):	9.00

Premier

The O-Pee-Chee Co. of London, Ontario, Canada produced this 132-card set. The card fronts feature action photos, while the flip sides display a posed photo and career statistics. The cards were packaged seven cards per pack in a tamper-proof foil wrap. Several

Expo and Blue Jay players are featured. Two special cards are included in this set. Card #62 honors Rickey Henderson's stolen base record, while card #102 commemorates Nolan Ryan's seventh no-hitter. Traded players and free agents are featured with their new teams.

		NM/M
Unopened Fact. Set (132):		4.00
Complete Set (132):		3.00
Common Player:		.05
Wax Pack (7):		.75
Wax Box (36):		9.00
1	Roberto Alomar	.40
2	Sandy Alomar	.05
3	Moises Alou	.20
4	Brian Barnes	.05
5	Steve Bedrosian	.05
6	George Bell	.10
7	Juan Bell	.05
8	Albert Belle	.05
9	Bud Black	.05
10	Mike Boddicker	.05
11	Wade Boggs	.75
12	Barry Bonds	1.00
13	Denis Boucher	.10
14	George Brett	.85
15	Hubie Brooks	.05
16	Brett Butler	.05
17	Ivan Calderon	.05
18	Jose Canseco	.25
19	Gary Carter	.75
20	Joe Carter	.05
21	Jack Clark	.05
22	Will Clark	.05
23	Roger Clemens	.90
24	Alex Cole	.05
25	Vince Coleman	.05
26	Jeff Conine	.05
27	Milt Cuyler	.05
28	Danny Darwin	.05
29	Eric Davis	.05
30	Glenn Davis	.05
31	Andre Dawson	.25
32	Ken Dayley	.05
33	Steve Decker	.05
34	Delino DeShields	.05
35	Lance Dickson	.05
36	Kirk Dressendorfer	.05
37	Shawon Dunston	.05
38	Dennis Eckersley	.50
39	Dwight Evans	.05
40	Howard Farmer	.05
41	Junior Felix	.05
42	Alex Fernandez	.10
43	Tony Fernandez	.05
44	Cecil Fielder	.15
45	Carlton Fisk	.60
46	Willie Fraser	.05
47	Gary Gaetti	.05
48	Andres Galarraga	.05
49	Ron Gant	.05
50	Kirk Gibson	.05
51	Bernard Gilkey	.05
52	Leo Gomez	.05
53	Rene Gonzalez	.05
54	Juan Gonzalez	.45
55	Doc Gooden	.05
56	Ken Griffey Jr.	.90
57	Kelly Gruber	.05
58	Pedro Guerrero	.05
59	Tony Gwynn	.75
60	Chris Hammond	.05
61	Ron Hassey	.05
62	Rickey Henderson	.75
63	Tom Henke	.05
64	Orel Hershiser	.05
65	Chris Hoiles	.05
66	Todd Hundley	.05
67	Pete Incaviglia	.05
68	Danny Jackson	.05
69	Barry Jones	.05
70	David Justice	.05
71	Jimmy Key	.05
72	Ray Lankford	.05
73	Darren Lewis	.05
74	Kevin Maas	.05
75	Denny Martinez	.10
76	Tino Martinez	.05
77	Don Mattingly	.85
78	Willie McGee	.05
79	Fred McGriff	.15
80	Hensley Meulens	.05
81	Kevin Mitchell	.05
82	Paul Molitor	.75
83	Mickey Morandini	.05
84	Jack Morris	.15
85	Dale Murphy	.15
86	Eddie Murray	.60
87	Chris Nabholz	.05
88	Tim Naehring	.05
89	Otis Nixon	.05
90	Jose Offerman	.05
91	Bob Ojeda	.05
92	John Olerud	.15
93	Gregg Olson	.05
94	Dave Parker	.05
95	Terry Pendleton	.05
96	Kirby Puckett	.75
97	Rock Raines	.10
98	Jeff Reardon	.05
99	Dave Righetti	.05
100	Cal Ripken	1.00
101	Mel Rojas	.10
102	Nolan Ryan	1.00
103	Ryne Sandberg	.75
104	Scott Sanderson	.05
105	Benito Santiago	.05
106	Pete Schourek	.05
107	Gary Scott	.05
108	Terry Shumpert	.05
109	Ruben Sierra	.05
110	Doug Simons	.05
111	Dave Smith	.05
112	Ozzie Smith	.75
113	Cory Snyder	.05
114	Luis Sojo	.05
115	Dave Stewart	.10
116	Dave Stieb	.05
117	Darryl Strawberry	.05
118	Pat Tabler	.05
119	Wade Taylor	.05
120	Bobby Thigpen	.05
121	Frank Thomas	.60
122	Mike Timlin	.05
123	Alan Trammell	.05
124	Mo Vaughn	.05
125	Tim Wallach	.05
126	Devon White	.10
127	Mark Whiten	.05
128	Bernie Williams	.05
129	Willie Wilson	.05
130	Dave Winfield	.75
131	Robin Yount	.60
132	Checklist	.05

1992 O-Pee-Chee

Once again closely following the format of the 1992 Topps set, and for the most part corresponding to its 792-card checklist, the 1992 OPCs differ on the front only in the substitution of an O-Pee-Chee logo for the Topps logo, and in the inclusion of team-change information for many of the players who moved after the Topps cards were printed. On backs, the light blue "Topps" logo printed behind the stats has been removed, and the logo beneath the card number changed from "Topps" to "O-Pee-Chee." The addition of a few lines of French above the stats and in the career summary can be seen on the OPC cards, as well as the substitution of an OPC copyright line for that of Topps. Where the 1992 Topps set features All-Star cards in the number range 386-407, the OPC has a group of player cards who are not represented in the Topps set, including four "Tribute" cards honoring Gary Carter. Card #45 in the OPC set is also a Carter Tribute card, whereas in the Topps set it is a regular card.

		NM/M
Unopened Fact. Set (792):		15.00
Complete Set (792):		10.00
Common Player:		.05
Wax Box (36):		12.00
45	Gary Carter/Tribute	1.00
386	Lance Blankenship	.10
387	Gary Carter/Tribute	1.00
388	Ron Tingley	.10
389	Gary Carter/Tribute	1.00
390	Gene Harris	.10
391	Jeff Schaefer	.10
392	Mark Grant	.10
393	Carl Willis	.10
394	Al Leiter	.25
395	Ron Robinson	.10
396	Tim Hulett	.10
397	Craig Worthington	.10
398	John Orton	.10
399	Gary Carter/Tribute	1.00
400	John Dopson	.10
401	Moises Alou	.60
402	Gary Carter/Tribute	1.00
403	Matt Young	.10
404	Wayne Edwards	.10
405	Nick Esasky	.10
406	Dave Eiland	.10
407	Mike Brumley	.10

Premier

JOSE MELENDEZ

O-Pee-Chee increased the number of cards in its premier set to 198 for 1992. The cards feature white borders surrounding full-color player photos. The O-Pee-Chee banner appears at the top of the card and the player's name and position appear at the bottom. The backs feature an additional player photo, statistics and player information. Traded players and free agents are featured with their new teams.

		NM/M
Factory Set (198):		5.00
Complete Set (198):		4.00
Common Player:		.10
Wax Box (36):		9.00
1	Wade Boggs	.75
2	John Smiley	.10
3	Checklist	.10
4	Ron Gant	.10
5	Mike Bordick	.10
6	Charlie Hayes	.10
7	Kevin Morton	.10
8	Checklist	.10
9	Chris Gwynn	.10
10	Melido Perez	.10
11	Danny Gladden	.10
12	Brian McRae	.10
13	Denny Martinez	.15
14	Bob Scanlan	.10
15	Julio Franco	.10
16	Ruben Amaro	.10
17	Mo Sanford	.10
18	Scott Bankhead	.10
19	Dickie Thon	.10
20	Chris James	.10
21	Mike Huff	.10
22	Orlando Merced	.10
23	Chris Sabo	.10
24	Jose Canseco	.40
25	Reggie Sanders	.10
26	Chris Nabholz	.10
27	Kevin Seitzer	.10
28	Ryan Bowen	.10
29	Gary Carter	.75
30	Wayne Rosenthal	.10
31	Alan Trammell	.10
32	Doug Drabek	.10
33	Craig Shipley	.10
34	Ryne Sandberg	.75
35	Chuck Knoblauch	.10
36	Bret Barberie	.10
37	Tim Naehring	.10
38	Omar Olivares	.10
39	Royce Clayton	.10
40	Brent Mayne	.10
41	Darrin Fletcher	.10
42	Howard Johnson	.10
43	Steve Sax	.10
44	Greg Swindell	.10
45	Andre Dawson	.25
46	Kent Hrbek	.10
47	Doc Gooden	.10
48	Mark Leiter	.10
49	Tom Glavine	.25
50	Mo Vaughn	.10
51	Doug Jones	.10
52	Brian Barnes	.10
53	Rob Dibble	.10
54	Kevin McReynolds	.10
55	Ivan Rodriguez	.50
56	Scott Livingstone	.10
57	Mike Magnante	.10
58	Pete Schourek	.10
59	Frank Thomas	.60
60	Kirk McCaskill	.10
61	Wally Joyner	.10
62	Rick Aguilera	.10
63	Eric Karros	.10
64	Tino Martinez	.10
65	Bryan Hickerson	.10
66	Ruben Sierra	.10
67	Willie Randolph	.10
68	Bill Landrum	.10
69	Bip Roberts	.10
70	Cecil Fielder	.15
71	Pat Kelly	.10
72	Kenny Lofton	.10
73	John Franco	.10
74	Phil Plantier	.10
75	Dave Martinez	.10
76	Warren Newson	.10
77	Chito Martinez	.10
78	Brian Hunter	.10
79	Jack Morris	.10
80	Eric King	.10
81	Nolan Ryan	1.50
82	Bret Saberhagen	.10
83	Roberto Kelly	.10
84	Ozzie Smith	.75
85	Chuck McElroy	.10
86	Carlton Fisk	.60
87	Mike Mussina	.50
88	Mark Carreon	.10
89	Ken Hill	.10
90	Rick Cerone	.10
91	Deion Sanders	.15
92	Don Mattingly	.85
93	Danny Tartabull	.10
94	Keith Miller	.10
95	Gregg Jefferies	.10
96	Barry Larkin	.10
97	Kevin Mitchell	.10
98	Rick Sutcliffe	.10
99	Mark McGwire	1.25
100	Albert Belle	.10
101	Gregg Olson	.10
102	Kirby Puckett	.75
103	Luis Gonzalez	.10
104	Randy Myers	.10
105	Roger Clemens	.90
106	Tony Gwynn	.75
107	Jeff Bagwell	.60
108	John Wetteland	.10
109	Bernie Williams	.10
110	Scott Kamieniecki	.10
111	Robin Yount	.60
112	Dean Palmer	.10
113	Tim Belcher	.10
114	George Brett	.85
115	Frank Viola	.10
116	Kelly Gruber	.10
117	David Justice	.10
118	Scott Leius	.10
119	Jeff Fassero	.10
120	Sammy Sosa	.90
121	Al Osuna	.10
122	Wilson Alvarez	.10
123	Jose Offerman	.10
124	Mel Rojas	.10
125	Shawon Dunston	.10
126	Pete Incaviglia	.10
127	Von Hayes	.10
128	Dave Gallagher	.10
129	Eric Davis	.10
130	Roberto Alomar	.35
131	Mike Gallego	.10
132	Robin Ventura	.10
133	Bill Swift	.10
134	John Kruk	.10
135	Craig Biggio	.10
136	Eddie Taubensee	.10
137	Cal Ripken, Jr.	1.50
138	Charles Nagy	.10
139	Jose Melendez	.10
140	Jim Abbott	.10
141	Paul Molitor	.75
142	Tom Candiotti	.10
143	Bobby Bonilla	.10
144	Matt Williams	.10
145	Brett Butler	.10
146	Will Clark	.10
147	Rickey Henderson	.75
148	Ray Lankford	.10
149	Bill Pecota	.10
150	Dave Winfield	.75
151	Darren Lewis	.10
152	Bob MacDonald	.10
153	David Segui	.10
154	Benny Santiago	.10
155	Chuck Finley	.10
156	Andujar Cedeno	.10
157	Barry Bonds	1.50
158	Joe Grahe	.10
159	Frank Castillo	.10
160	Dave Burba	.10
161	Leo Gomez	.10
162	Orel Hershiser	.10
163	Delino DeShields	.15
164	Sandy Alomar	.10
165	Denny Neagle	.10
166	Fred McGriff	.10
167	Ken Griffey Jr.	1.00
168	Juan Guzman	.10
169	Bobby Rose	.10
170	Steve Avery	.10
171	Rich DeLucia	.10
172	Mike Timlin	.10
173	Randy Johnson	.65
174	Paul Gibson	.10
175	David Cone	.10
176	Marquis Grissom	.15
177	Kurt Stillwell	.10
178	Mark Whiten	.10
179	Darryl Strawberry	.10
180	Mike Morgan	.10
181	Scott Scudder	.10
182	George Bell	.15
183	Alvin Davis	.10
184	Len Dykstra	.10
185	Kyle Abbott	.10
186	Chris Haney	.10
187	Junior Noboa	.10

1993 O-Pee-Chee

For the first time in history, the 1993 O-Pee-Chee set differed significantly from the Topps set; photographs and designs are entirely different. Team names are scripted across the top, but a yellow triangle with a new team name appears on the front for players who have been traded. Two insert sets honoring the 1992 World Champion Toronto Blue Jays were also produced.

		NM/M
Complete Set (396):		15.00
Common Player:		.10
Wax Pack (8):		.75
Wax Box:		15.00
1	Jim Abbott	.10
2	Eric Anthony	.10
3	Harold Baines	.10
4	Roberto Alomar	.45
5	Steve Avery	.10
6	James Austin	.10
7	Mark Wohlers	.10
8	Steve Buechele	.10
9	Pedro Astacio	.10
10	Moises Alou	.20
11	Rod Beck	.10
12	Sandy Alomar	.10
13	Brett Boone	.10
14	Bryan Harvey	.10
15	Bobby Bonilla	.10
16	Brady Anderson	.10
17	Andy Benes	.10
18	Ruben Amaro	.10
19	Jay Bell	.10
20	Kevin Brown	.10
21	Scott Bankhead	.10
22	Denis Boucher	.10
23	Kevin Appier	.10
24	Pat Kelly	.10
25	Rick Aguilera	.10
26	George Bell	.10
27	Steve Farr	.10
28	Chad Curtis	.10
29	Jeff Bagwell	.60
30	Lance Blankenship	.10
31	Derek Bell	.10
32	Damon Berryhill	.10
33	Ricky Bones	.10
34	Rheal Cormier	.10
35	Andre Dawson	.30
36	Brett Butler	.10
37	Sean Berry	.10
38	Bud Black	.10
39	Carlos Baerga	.10
40	Jay Buhner	.10
41	Charlie Hough	.10
42	Sid Fernandez	.10
43	Luis Mercedes	.10
44	Jerald Clark	.10
45	Wes Chamberlain	.10
46	Barry Bonds	1.50
47	Jose Canseco	.30
48	Tim Belcher	.10
49	David Nied	.10
50	George Brett	.85
51	Cecil Fielder	.30
52	Chili Davis	.10
53	Alex Fernandez	.10
54	Charlie Hayes	.10
55	Rob Ducey	.10
56	Craig Biggio	.10
57	Mike Bordick	.10
58	Pat Borders	.10
59	Jeff Blauser	.10
60	Chris Bosio	.10
61	Bernard Gilkey	.10
62	Shawon Dunston	.10
63	Tom Candiotti	.10
64	Darrin Fletcher	.10
65	Jeff Brantley	.10
66	Albert Belle	.10
67	Dave Fleming	.10
68	John Franco	.10
69	Glenn Davis	.10
70	Tony Fernandez	.10
71	Darren Daulton	.10
72	Doug Drabek	.10
73	Julio Franco	.10
74	Tom Browning	.10
75	Tom Gordon	.10
76	Travis Fryman	.10
77	Scott Erickson	.10
78	Carlton Fisk	.60
79	Roberto Kelly	.10
80	Gary DiSarcina	.10
81	Ken Caminiti	.10
82	Ron Darling	.10
83	Joe Carter	.15
84	Sid Bream	.10
85	Cal Eldred	.10
86	Mark Grace	.10
87	Eric Davis	.10
88	Ivan Calderon	.10
89	John Burkett	.10
90	Felix Fermin	.10
91	Ken Griffey Jr.	1.00
92	Doc Gooden	.10
93	Mike Devereaux	.10
94	Tony Gwynn	.75
95	Mariano Duncan	.10
96	Jeff King	.10
97	Juan Gonzalez	.50
98	Norm Charlton	.10
99	Mark Gubicza	.10
100	Danny Gladden	.10
101	Greg Gagne	.10
102	Ozzie Guillen	.10
103	Don Mattingly	.85
104	Damion Easley	.10
105	Casey Candaele	.10
106	Dennis Eckersley	.50
107	David Cone	.10
108	Ron Gant	.10
109	Mike Fetters	.10
110	Mike Harkey	.10
111	Kevin Gross	.10
112	Archi Cianfrocco	.10
113	Will Clark	.10
114	Glenallen Hill	.10
115	Erik Hanson	.10
116	Todd Hundley	.10
117	Leo Gomez	.10
118	Bruce Hurst	.10
119	Len Dykstra	.10
120	Jose Lind	.10
121	Jose Guzman	.10
122	Rob Dibble	.10
123	Gregg Jefferies	.10
124	Bill Gulickson	.10
125	Brian Harper	.10
126	Roberto Hernandez	.10
127	Sam Militello	.10
128	Junior Felix	.10
129	Andujar Cedeno	.10
130	Rickey Henderson	.75
131	Bob MacDonald	.10
132	Tom Glavine	.25
133	Scott Fletcher	.10
134	Brian Jordan	.10
135	Greg Maddux	.75
136	Orel Hershiser	.10
137	Greg Colbrunn	.10
138	Royce Clayton	.10
139	Thomas Howard	.10
140	Randy Johnson	.10
141	Jeff Innis	.10
142	Chris Hoiles	.10
143	Darrin Jackson	.10
144	Tommy Greene	.10
145	Mike LaValliere	.10
146	David Hulse	.10
147	Barry Larkin	.10
148	Wally Joyner	.10
149	Mike Henneman	.10
150	Kent Hrbek	.10
151	Bo Jackson	.15
152	Rich Monteleone	.10
153	Chuck Finley	.10
154	Steve Finley	.10
155	Dave Henderson	.10
156	Kelly Gruber	.10
157	Brian Hunter	.10
158	Darryl Hamilton	.10
159	Derrick May	.10
160	Jay Howell	.10
161	Wil Cordero	.10
162	Bryan Hickerson	.10
163	Reggie Jefferson	.10
164	Edgar Martinez	.10
165	Nigel Wilson	.10
166	Howard Johnson	.10
167	Tim Hulett	.10
168	Mike Maddux	.10
169	Dave Hollins	.10
170	Zane Smith	.10
171	Rafael Palmeiro	.45
172	Dave Martinez	.10
173	Rusty Meacham	.10
174	Mark Leiter	.10
175	Chuck Knoblauch	.10
176	Lance Johnson	.10
177	Matt Nokes	.10
178	Luis Gonzalez	.10
179	Jack Morris	.10
180	David Justice	.10
181	Doug Henry	.10
182	Felix Jose	.10

183	Delino DeShields	.15
184	Rene Gonzales	.10
185	Pete Harnisch	.10
186	Mike Moore	.10
187	Juan Guzman	.10
188	John Olerud	.20
189	Ryan Klesko	.10
190	John Jaha	.10
191	Ray Lankford	.10
192	Jeff Fassero	.10
193	Darren Lewis	.10
194	Mark Lewis	.10
195	Alan Mills	.10
196	Wade Boggs	.75
197	Hal Morris	.10
198	Ron Karkovice	.10
199	John Grahe	.10
200	Butch Henry	.10
201	Mark McGwire	1.25
202	Tom Henke	.10
203	Ed Sprague	.10
204	Charlie Leibrandt	.10
205	Pat Listach	.10
206	Omar Olivares	.10
207	Mike Morgan	.10
208	Eric Karros	.10
209	Marquis Grissom	.15
210	Willie McGee	.10
211	Derek Lilliquist	.10
212	Tino Martinez	.10
213	Jeff Kent	.10
214	Mike Mussina	.35
215	Randy Myers	.10
216	John Kruk	.10
217	Tom Brunansky	.10
218	Paul O'Neill	.10
219	Scott Livingstone	.10
220	John Valentin	.10
221	Eddie Zosky	.10
222	Pete Smith	.10
223	Bill Wegman	.10
224	Todd Zeile	.10
225	Tim Wallach	.10
226	Mitch Williams	.10
227	Tim Wakefield	.10
228	Frank Viola	.10
229	Nolan Ryan	1.50
230	Kirk McCaskill	.10
231	Melido Perez	.10
232	Mark Langston	.10
233	Xavier Hernandez	.10
234	Jerry Browne	.10
235	Dave Stieb	.15
236	Mark Lemke	.10
237	Paul Molitor	.75
238	Geronimo Pena	.10
239	Ken Hill	.10
240	Jack Clark	.10
241	Greg Myers	.10
242	Pete Incaviglia	.10
243	Ruben Sierra	.10
244	Todd Stottlemyre	.10
245	Pat Hentgen	.10
246	Melvin Nieves	.10
247	Jaime Navarro	.10
248	Donovan Osborne	.10
249	Brian Barnes	.10
250	Cory Snyder	.10
251	Kenny Lofton	.10
252	Kevin Mitchell	.10
253	Dave Magadan	.10
254	Ben McDonald	.10
255	Fred McGriff	.20
256	Mickey Morandini	.10
257	Randy Tomlin	.10
258	Dean Palmer	.10
259	Roger Clemens	1.00
260	Joe Oliver	.10
261	Jeff Montgomery	.10
262	Tony Phillips	.10
263	Shane Mack	.10
264	Jack McDowell	.10
265	Mike Macfarlane	.10
266	Luis Polonia	.10
267	Doug Jones	.10
268	Terry Steinbach	.10
269	Jimmy Key	.10
270	Pat Tabler	.10
271	Otis Nixon	.10
272	Dave Nilsson	.10
273	Tom Pagnozzi	.10
274	Ryne Sandberg	.75
275	Ramon Martinez	.10
276	Tim Laker	.10
277	Bill Swift	.10
278	Charles Nagy	.10
279	Harold Reynolds	.10
280	Eddie Murray	.60
281	Gregg Olson	.10
282	Frank Seminara	.10
283	Terry Mulholland	.10
284	Kevin Palmer	.10
285	Mike Greenwell	.10
286	Jose Rijo	.10
287	Brian McRae	.10
288	Frank Tanana	.10
289	Pedro Munoz	.10
290	Tim Raines	.15
291	Andy Stankiewicz	.10
292	Tim Salmon	.10
293	Jimmy Jones	.10
294	Dave Stewart	.15
295	Mike Timlin	.10
296	Greg Olson	.10
297	Dan Plesac	.10
298	Mike Perez	.10
299	Jose Offerman	.10
300	Denny Martinez	.15

World Champs

301	Robby Thompson	.10
302	Bret Saberhagen	.10
303	Joe Orsulak	.10
304	Tim Naehring	.10
305	Bip Roberts	.10
306	Kirby Puckett	.75
307	Steve Sax	.10
308	Danny Tartabull	.10
309	Jeff Juden	.10
310	Duane Ward	.10
311	Alejandro Pena	.10
312	Kevin Seitzer	.10
313	Ozzie Smith	.75
314	Mike Piazza	1.00
315	Chris Nabholz	.10
316	Tony Pena	.10
317	Gary Sheffield	.25
318	Mark Portugal	.10
319	Walt Weiss	.10
320	Manuel Lee	.10
321	David Wells	.15
322	Terry Pendleton	.10
323	Billy Spiers	.10
324	Lee Smith	.10
325	Bob Scanlan	.10
326	Mike Scioscia	.10
327	Spike Owen	.10
328	Mackey Sasser	.10
329	Arthur Rhodes	.10
330	Ben Rivera	.10
331	Ivan Rodriguez	.50
332	Phil Plantier	.10
333	Chris Sabo	.10
334	Mickey Tettleton	.10
335	John Smiley	.10
336	Bobby Thigpen	.10
337	Randy Velarde	.10
338	Luis Sojo	.10
339	Scott Servais	.10
340	Bob Welch	.10
341	Devon White	.15
342	Jeff Reardon	.10
343	B.J. Surhoff	.10
344	Bob Tewksbury	.10
345	Jose Vizcaino	.10
346	Mike Sharperson	.10
347	Mel Rojas	.10
348	Matt Williams	.10
349	Steve Olin	.10
350	Mike Schooler	.10
351	Ryan Thompson	.10
352	Cal Ripken	1.50
353	Benny Santiago	.10
354	Curt Schilling	.25
355	Andy Van Slyke	.10
356	Kenny Rogers	.10
357	Jody Reed	.10
358	Reggie Sanders	.10
359	Kevin McReynolds	.10
360	Alan Trammell	.10
361	Kevin Tapani	.10
362	Frank Thomas	.60
363	Bernie Williams	.10
364	John Smoltz	.10
365	Robin Yount	.60
366	John Wetteland	.10
367	Bob Zupcic	.10
368	Julio Valera	.10
369	Brian Williams	.10
370	Willie Wilson	.10
371	Dave Winfield	.75
372	Deion Sanders	.10
373	Greg Vaughn	.10
374	Todd Worrell	.10
375	Darryl Strawberry	.10
376	John Vander Wal	.10
377	Mike Benjamin	.10
378	Mark Whiten	.10
379	Omar Vizquel	.10
380	Anthony Young	.10
381	Rick Sutcliffe	.10
382	Candy Maldonado	.10
383	Francisco Cabrera	.10
384	Larry Walker	.20
385	Scott Cooper	.10
386	Gerald Williams	.10
387	Robin Ventura	.10
388	Carl Willis	.10
389	Lou Whitaker	.10
390	Hipolito Pichardo	.10
391	Rudy Seanez	.10
392	Greg Swindell	.10
393	Mo Vaughn	.10
394	Checklist 1 of 3	.10
395	Checklist 2 of 3	.10
396	Checklist 3 of 3	.10

World Champs

This 18-card insert set commemorates the Toronto Blue Jays' 1992 World Series victory; 17 players and Manager Cito Gaston are featured. Cards were randomly inserted, one World Champs or World Series Heroes card per every 69-cent, eight-card pack. Fronts and backs each feature the World's Championship logo. Backs include stats from the 1992 ALCS and World Series.

		NM/M
Complete Set (18):		4.00
Common Player:		.25
1	Roberto Alomar	1.00
2	Pat Borders	.25
3	Joe Carter	.65
4	David Cone	.35
5	Kelly Gruber	.25
6	Juan Guzman	.25
7	Tom Henke	.25
8	Jimmy Key	.35
9	Manuel Lee	.25
10	Candy Maldonado	.25
11	Jack Morris	.35
12	John Olerud	.50
13	Ed Sprague	.25
14	Todd Stottlemyre	.25
15	Duane Ward	.25
16	Devon White	.35
17	Dave Winfield	1.50
18	Cito Gaston	.25

World Series Heroes

This insert set honors four of the Toronto Blue Jays' World Series stars. Cards were randomly inserted in every 69-cent, eight-card pack, one World Champs or World Series Heroes card per pack.

		NM/M
Complete Set (4):		1.50
Common Player:		.25
1	Pat Borders	.25
2	Jimmy Key	.25
3	Ed Sprague	.25
4	Dave Winfield	1.50

1993 O-Pee-Chee Premier

For the third consecutive year, O-Pee-Chee produced a set under its Premier brand name. The regular set, issued in three series, has 132 cards and 48 insert cards. The insert sets are titled Star Performers (gold borders), Foil Star Performers (full-bleed photos and gold stamping), and Top Draft Picks (two each featuring the Toronto Blue Jays and Montreal Expos top picks). O-

Pee-Chee announced it produced only 4,000 cases for this set.

		NM/M
Complete Set (132):		4.00
Common Player:		.05
Wax Box:		8.00
1	Barry Bonds	1.50
2	Chad Curtis	.05
3	Chris Bosio	.05
4	Cal Eldred	.05
5	Dan Walter	.05
6	Rene Arocha	.05
7	Delino DeShields	.05
8	Spike Owen	.05
9	Jeff Owen	.05
10	Phil Plantier	.05
11	Mike Christopher	.05
12	Darren Daulton	.05
13	Scott Cooper	.05
14	Paul O'Neill	.05
15	Jimmy Key	.05
16	Dickie Thon	.05
17	Greg Gohr	.05
18	Andre Dawson	.25
19	Steve Cooke	.05
20	Tony Fernandez	.05
21	Mark Gardner	.05
22	Dave Martinez	.05
23	Jose Guzman	.05
24	Chili Davis	.05
25	Randy Knorr	.05
26	Mike Piazza	1.00
27	Benji Gil	.05
28	Dave Winfield	.45
29	Wil Cordero	.05
30	Butch Henry	.05
31	Eric Young	.05
32	Orestes Destrade	.05
33	Randy Myers	.05
34	Tom Brunansky	.05
35	Dan Wilson	.05
36	Juan Guzman	.05
37	Tim Salmon	.05
38	Bill Krueger	.05
39	Larry Walker	.25
40	David Hulse	.05
41	Ken Ryan	.05
42	Jose Lind	.05
43	Benny Santiago	.05
44	Ray Lankford	.05
45	Dave Stewart	.05
46	Don Mattingly	.60
47	Fernando Valenzuela	.05
48	Scott Fletcher	.05
49	Wade Boggs	.50
50	Norm Charlton	.05
51	Carlos Baerga	.05
52	John Olerud	.15
53	Willie Wilson	.05
54	Dennis Moeller	.05
55	Joe Orsulak	.05
56	John Smiley	.05
57	Al Martin	.05
58	Andres Galarraga	.15
59	Billy Ripken	.05
60	Dave Stieb	.05
61	Dave Magadan	.05
62	Todd Worrell	.05
63	Sherman Obando	.05
64	Kent Bottenfield	.05
65	Vinny Castilla	.05
66	Charlie Hayes	.05
67	Mike Hartley	.05
68	Harold Baines	.05
69	John Cummings	.05
70	J.T. Snow	.05
71	Graeme Lloyd	.05
72	Frank Bolick	.05
73	Doug Drabek	.05
74	Milt Thompson	.05
75	Tim Pugh	.05
76	John Kruk	.05
77	Tom Henke	.05
78	Kevin Young	.05
79	Ryan Thompson	.05
80	Mike Hampton	.05
81	Jose Canseco	.30
82	Mike Lansing	.15
83	Candy Maldonado	.05
84	Alex Arias	.05
85	Troy Neel	.05
86	Greg Swindell	.05
87	Tim Wallach	.05
88	Andy Van Slyke	.05
89	Harold Baines	.05
90	Bryan Harvey	.05
91	Jerald Clark	.05
92	David Cone	.05
93	Ellis Burks	.05
94	Scott Bankhead	.05
95	Pete Incaviglia	.05
96	Cecil Fielder	.10
97	Sean Berry	.05
98	Gregg Jefferies	.05
99	Billy Brewer	.05
100	Scott Sanderson	.05
101	Walt Weiss	.05
102	Travis Fryman	.05
103	Barry Larkin	.25
104	Darren Holmes	.05
105	Ivan Calderon	.05
106	Terry Jorgensen	.05
107	David Nied	.05
108	Tim Bogar	.05
109	Roberto Kelly	.05
110	Mike Moore	.05
111	Carlos Garcia	.05
112	Mike Bielecki	.05
113	Trevor Hoffman	.05
114	Rich Amaral	.05
115	Jody Reed	.05
116	Charlie Leibrandt	.05
117	Greg Gagne	.05
118	Darrell Sherman	.05
119	Jeff Conine	.05
120	Tim Laker	.05
121	Kevin Seitzer	.05
122	Jeff Mutis	.05
123	Rico Rossy	.05
124	Paul Molitor	.45
125	Cal Ripken	1.50
126	Greg Maddux	.60
127	Greg McMichael	.05
128	Felix Jose	.05
129	Dick Schofield	.05
130	Jim Abbott	.05
131	Kevin Reimer	.05
132	Checklist	.05

Star Performers

O-Pee-Chee released a 22-card insert set in two forms: Star Performers (featuring a gold border design) and Foil Star Performers (featuring full-bleed photos and gold stamping). The players are identical in both sets, but foil cards are generally worth more. There are 34 Star Performers per 36-card wax box and one Foil Star Performer card per box.

		NM/M
Complete Set (22):		4.50
Common Player:		.10
Foil:		6X
1	Frank Thomas	.50
2	Fred McGriff	.15
3	Roberto Alomar	.40
4	Ryne Sandberg	.65
5	Gary Sheffield	.25
6	Juan Gonzalez	.40
7	Eric Karros	.05
8	Ken Griffey Jr.	.75
9	Deion Sanders	.05
10	Kirby Puckett	.65
11	Will Clark	.10
12	Joe Carter	.15
13	Barry Bonds	1.50
14	Pat Listach	.10
15	Mark McGwire	1.00
16	Kenny Lofton	.05
17	Roger Clemens	.75
18	Greg Maddux	.65
19	Nolan Ryan	1.50
20	Tom Glavine	.20
21	Dennis Eckersley	.40

Top Draft Picks

These randomly inserted cards feature four prospects; two each for Montreal and Toronto. Card fronts are foil-stamped and have a vertical banner with the player's name. The OPC Premier logo is in the corner. On back is an-

other player photo, a team logo and a bi-lingual rationale for the player's draft status.

		NM/M
Complete Set (4):		2.50
Common Player:		.50
1	B.J. Wallace	.50
2	Shannon Stewart	2.00
3	Rod Henderson	.50
4	Todd Steverson	.50

1994 O-Pee-Chee Sample Sheet

The basic '94 OPC card set and all of its chase card sets were previewed on this sample sheet sent to dealers. Measuring 8" x 11", the sheet's cards vary slightly from issued cards in terms of foil highlights. Card fronts on the sample sheet are highlighted in red foil while there is no foil on the backs. Each of the card backs (except the jumbo All-Star) includes the notation "Pre-Production Sample."

	NM/M
Complete Sheet:	6.00

1994 O-Pee-Chee

Limited to 2,500 cases (about 112,000 of each card in the regular 270-card set) the '94 OPC issue features color photos on front and back along with complete major league stats (and some minor league stats) on back. Team names are in a color-coded strip at left. Career summaries and some other data are printed in both English and French.

		NM/M
Complete Set (270):		15.00
Common Player:		.05
Wax Pack (15):		.75
Wax Box (36):		15.00
1	Paul Molitor	.75
2	Kirt Manwaring	.05
3	Brady Anderson	.05
4	Scott Cooper	.05
5	Kevin Stocker	.05
6	Alex Fernandez	.05
7	Jeff Montgomery	.05
8	Danny Tartabull	.05
9	Damion Easley	.05
10	Andujar Cedeno	.05
11	Steve Karsay	.05
12	Dave Stewart	.05
13	Fred McGriff	.05
14	Jaime Navarro	.05
15	Allen Watson	.05
16	Ryne Sandberg	.75
17	Arthur Rhodes	.05
18	Marquis Grissom	.05
19	John Burkett	.05
20	Robby Thompson	.05
21	Denny Martinez	.05

22	Ken Griffey Jr.	1.00
23	Orestes Destrade	.05
24	Dwight Gooden	.05
25	Rafael Palmeiro	.40
26	Pedro Martinez	.05
27	Wes Chamberlain	.05
28	Juan Gonzalez	.50
29	Kevin Mitchell	.05
30	Dante Bichette	.05
31	Howard Johnson	.05
32	Mickey Tettleton	.05
33	Robin Ventura	.05
34	Terry Mulholland	.05
35	Bernie Williams	.05
36	Eduardo Perez	.05
37	Rickey Henderson	.65
38	Terry Pendleton	.05
39	John Smoltz	.05
40	Derrick May	.05
41	Pedro Martinez	.60
42	Mark Portugal	.05
43	Albert Belle	.05
44	Edgar Martinez	.05
45	Gary Sheffield	.35
46	Bret Saberhagen	.05
47	Ricky Gutierrez	.05
48	Orlando Merced	.05
49	Mike Greenwell	.05
50	Jose Rijo	.05
51	Jeff Granger	.05
52	Mike Henneman	.05
53	Dave Winfield	.65
54	Don Mattingly	.85
55	J.T. Snow	.05
56	Todd Van Poppel	.05
57	Chipper Jones	.75
58	Darryl Hamilton	.05
59	Delino DeShields	.05
60	Rondell White	.05
61	Eric Anthony	.05
62	Charlie Hough	.05
63	Sid Fernandez	.05
64	Derek Bell	.05
65	Phil Plantier	.05
66	Curt Schilling	.20
67	Roger Clemens	1.00
68	Jose Lind	.05
69	Andres Galarraga	.05
70	Tim Belcher	.05
71	Ron Karkovice	.05
72	Alan Trammell	.05
73	Pete Harnisch	.05
74	Mark McGwire	1.50
75	Ryan Klesko	.05
76	Ramon Martinez	.05
77	Gregg Jefferies	.05
78	Steve Buechele	.05
79	Bill Swift	.05
80	Matt Williams	.05
81	Randy Johnson	.60
82	Mike Mussina	.50
83	Andy Benes	.05
84	Dave Staton	.05
85	Steve Cooke	.05
86	Andy Van Slyke	.05
87	Ivan Rodriguez	.50
88	Frank Viola	.05
89	Aaron Sele	.05
90	Ellis Burks	.05
91	Wally Joyner	.05
92	Rick Aguilera	.05
93	Kirby Puckett	.75
94	Roberto Hernandez	.05
95	Mike Stanley	.05
96	Roberto Alomar	.25
97	James Mouton	.05
98	Chad Curtis	.05
99	Mitch Williams	.05
100	Carlos Delgado	.40
101	Greg Maddux	.75
102	Brian Harper	.05
103	Tom Pagnozzi	.05
104	Jose Offerman	.05
105	John Wetteland	.05
106	Carlos Baerga	.05
107	Dave Madagan	.05
108	Bobby Jones	.05
109	Tony Gwynn	.75
110	Jeromy Burnitz	.05
111	Bip Roberts	.05
112	Carlos Garcia	.05
113	Jeff Russell	.05
114	Armando Reynoso	.05
115	Ozzie Guillen	.05
116	Bo Jackson	.10
117	Terry Steinbach	.05
118	Deion Sanders	.05
119	Randy Myers	.05
120	Mark Whiten	.05
121	Manny Ramirez	.60
122	Ben McDonald	.05
123	Darren Daulton	.05
124	Kevin Young	.05
125	Barry Larkin	.05
126	Cecil Fielder	.05
127	Frank Thomas	.60
128	Luis Polonia	.05
129	Steve Finley	.05
130	John Olerud	.05
131	John Jaha	.05
132	Darren Lewis	.05
133	Orel Hershiser	.05
134	Chris Bosio	.05
135	Ryan Thompson	.05
136	Chris Sabo	.05
137	Tommy Greene	.05
138	Andre Dawson	.25
139	Bobby Kelly	.05

140	Ken Hill	.05
141	Greg Gagne	.05
142	Julio Franco	.05
143	Chili Davis	.05
144	Dennis Eckersley	.50
145	Joe Carter	.05
146	Mark Grace	.05
147	Mike Piazza	.90
148	J.R. Phillips	.05
149	Rich Amaral	.05
150	Benny Santiago	.05
151	Jeff King	.05
152	Dean Palmer	.05
153	Hal Morris	.05
154	Mike MacFarlane	.05
155	Chuck Knoblauch	.05
156	Pat Kelly	.05
157	Greg Swindell	.05
158	Chuck Finley	.05
159	Devon White	.05
160	Duane Ward	.05
161	Sammy Sosa	.85
162	Javier Lopez	.05
163	Eric Karros	.05
164	Royce Clayton	.05
165	Salomon Torres	.05
166	Jeff Kent	.05
167	Chris Hoiles	.05
168	Len Dykstra	.05
169	Jose Canseco	.35
170	Bret Boone	.05
171	Charlie Hayes	.05
172	Lou Whitaker	.05
173	Jack McDowell	.05
174	Jimmy Key	.05
175	Mark Langston	.05
176	Darryl Kile	.05
177	Juan Guzman	.05
178	Pat Borders	.05
179	Cal Eldred	.05
180	Jose Guzman	.05
181	Ozzie Smith	.75
182	Rod Beck	.05
183	Dave Fleming	.05
184	Eddie Murray	.60
185	Cal Ripken	2.00
186	Dave Hollins	.05
187	Will Clark	.05
188	Otis Nixon	.05
189	Joe Oliver	.05
190	Roberto Mejia	.05
191	Felix Jose	.05
192	Tony Phillips	.05
193	Wade Boggs	.75
194	Tim Salmon	.05
195	Ruben Sierra	.05
196	Steve Avery	.05
197	B.J. Surhoff	.05
198	Todd Zeile	.05
(199)	Raul Mondesi (No card number on back.)	.25
200	Barry Bonds	2.00
201	Sandy Alomar	.05
202	Bobby Bonilla	.05
203	Mike Devereaux	.05
204	Rickey Bottalico	.05
205	Kevin Brown	.05
206	Jason Bere	.05
207	Reggie Sanders	.05
208	David Nied	.05
209	Travis Fryman	.05
210	James Baldwin	.05
211	Jim Abbott	.05
212	Jeff Bagwell	.60
213	Bob Welch	.05
214	Jeff Blauser	.05
215	Brett Butler	.05
216	Pat Listach	.05
217	Bob Tewksbury	.05
218	Mike Lansing	.05
219	Wayne Kirby	.05
220	Chuck Carr	.05
221	Harold Baines	.05
222	Jay Bell	.05
223	Cliff Floyd	.05
224	Rob Dibble	.05
225	Kevin Appier	.05
226	Eric Davis	.05
227	Matt Walbeck	.05
228	Tim Raines	.05
229	Paul O'Neill	.05
230	Craig Biggio	.05
231	Brent Gates	.05
232	Rob Butler	.05
233	Dave Justice	.05
234	Rene Arocha	.05
235	Mike Morgan	.05
236	Denis Boucher	.05
237	Kenny Lofton	.05
238	Jeff Conine	.05
239	Bryan Harvey	.05
240	Danny Jackson	.05
241	Al Martin	.05
242	Tom Henke	.05
243	Erik Hanson	.05
244	Walt Weiss	.05
245	Brian McRae	.05
246	Kevin Tapani	.05
247	David McCarty	.05
248	Doug Drabek	.05
249	Troy Neel	.05
250	Tom Glavine	.20
251	Ray Lankford	.05
252	Wil Cordero	.05
253	Larry Walker	.05
254	Charles Nagy	.05
255	Kirk Rueter	.05
256	John Franco	.05

257	John Kruk	.05
258	Alex Gonzalez	.05
259	Mo Vaughn	.05
260	David Cone	.05
261	Kent Hrbek	.05
262	Lance Johnson	.05
263	Luis Gonzalez	.10
264	Mike Bordick	.05
265	Ed Sprague	.05
266	Moises Alou	.05
267	Omar Vizquel	.05
268	Jay Buhner	.05
269	Checklist	.05
270	Checklist	.05

All-Star Redemption Cards

A series of 25 All-Star redemption cards was one of the several inserts which were found at the rate of one per pack in '94 OPC foil. Fronts feature a color photo floating over a white background. The player's name is displayed in gold script at top and the card number is repeated along the top and left or right of the photo. Backs have information on how to redeem the cards for a super-size version of the set. Approximately 78,000 of each of the 25 cards in the insert set were produced.

		NM/M
Complete Set (25):		9.00
Common Player:		.50
1	Frank Thomas	.65
2	Paul Molitor	1.00
3	Barry Bonds	2.50
4	Juan Gonzalez	.60
5	Jeff Bagwell	.75
6	Carlos Baerga	.50
7	Ryne Sandberg	1.00
8	Ken Griffey Jr.	2.00
9	Mike Piazza	1.50
10	Tim Salmon	.50
11	Marquis Grissom	.50
12	Albert Belle	.50
13	Fred McGriff	.50
14	Jack McDowell	.50
14p	Jack McDowell ("Pre-Production Sample")	.50
15	Cal Ripken, Jr.	2.50
16	John Olerud	.50
17	Kirby Puckett	1.00
18	Roger Clemens	1.50
19	Larry Walker	.60
20	Cecil Fielder	.50
21	Roberto Alomar	.60
22	Greg Maddux	.50
23	Joe Carter	.50
24	Dave Justice	.50
25	Kenny Lofton	.50

Jumbo All-Stars

Each of the 60,000 foil-pack boxes of '94 OPC contained one jumbo (5" x 7") All-Star card from a set of 25. Fronts are identical to the All-Star redemption card inserts found in foil packs, with a UV

coating. Backs are blank. Each of the jumbo All-Stars was produced in a quantity of 2,400. A factory-set version of the jumbo All-Stars was also available by redeeming five of the AS inserts and $20. The factory-set AS jumbos differ from the box-toppers in that they have gold-foil enhancements and are numbered to 5,000 each.

		NM/M
Complete Set (25)		75.00
Common Player:		2.00
Complete Factory Set:		35.00
Factory Set Singles:		.75X
1	Frank Thomas	4.00
2	Paul Molitor	5.00
3	Barry Bonds	9.00
4	Juan Gonzalez	3.00
5	Jeff Bagwell	4.00
6	Carlos Baerga	2.00
7	Ryne Sandberg	5.00
8	Ken Griffey Jr.	7.50
9	Mike Piazza	6.00
10	Tim Salmon	2.00
11	Marquis Grissom	2.50
12	Albert Belle	2.00
13	Fred McGriff	2.50
14	Jack McDowell	2.00
15	Cal Ripken	9.00
16	John Olerud	2.50
17	Kirby Puckett	5.00
18	Roger Clemens	6.00
19	Larry Walker	2.50
20	Cecil Fielder	2.50
21	Roberto Alomar	3.00
22	Greg Maddux	5.00
23	Joe Carter	2.50
24	Dave Justice	2.00
25	Kenny Lofton	2.00

Diamond Dynamos

"Baseball's brightest new stars" was the stated criteria for inclusion in this chase card set. Fronts feature a full-bleed action photo with the player's name and "Diamond Dynamos" logo at bottom in red foil. Backs have a second player photo, personal data, a bi-lingual career summary and gold-foil presentation of the player's name and "Twenty-first Century Stars." An average of 1-2 of the cards was inserted per foil box, creating a production run of 5,000 of each card.

		NM/M
Complete Set (18):		5.00
Common Player:		.25
1	Mike Piazza	4.00
2	Roberto Mejia	.25
3	Wayne Kirby	.25
4	Kevin Stocker	.25
5	Chris Gomez	.25
6	Bobby Jones	.25
7	David McCarty	.25
8	Kirk Rueter	.25
9	J.T. Snow	.25
10	Wil Cordero	.25
11	Tim Salmon	.25
12	Jeff Conine	.25
13	Jason Bere	.25
14	Greg McMichael	.25
15	Brent Gates	.25
16	Allen Watson	.25
17	Aaron Sele	.25
18	Carlos Garcia	.25

Hot Prospects

Nine of 1994's hottest rookies are featured in this insert set. Fronts feature full-bleed photos with the player's name in gold foil at bottom. An "O-Pee-Chee Hot Pros-

pects" logo appears in an upper corner. Backs are in shades of red, yellow and orange and include another player photo, biographical data, a career summary and complete minor league stats.

		NM/M
Complete Set (9):		7.50
Common Player:		.50
1	Cliff Floyd	.50
2	James Mouton	.50
3	Salomon Torres	.50
4	Raul Mondesi	.50
5	Carlos Delgado	3.00
6	Manny Ramirez	3.00
7	Javier Lopez	.50
8	Alex Gonzalez	.50
9	Ryan Klesko	.50

Toronto Blue Jays

The Blue Jays' starting line-up for the final game of the 1993 World Series is honored on this insert set. Fronts have a blue typographic background of "World Series Champions '92 & '93." There is a color player photo with his name in red foil at bottom. Backs repeat the typographic background in black and include 1992 and 1993 World Series stats along with the player's Series highlights in both English and French. A gold-foil seal marking the back-to-back championships is at top center. Stated odds of finding a Blue Jays insert card are one per foil box, indicating a production of about 6,666 of each card.

		NM/M
Complete Set (9):		6.00
Common Player:		.50
1	Rickey Henderson	2.00
2	Devon White	.75
3	Paul Molitor	2.00
4	Joe Carter	.75
5	John Olerud	1.00
6	Roberto Alomar	1.50
7	Ed Sprague	.50
8	Pat Borders	.50
9	Tony Fernandez	.50

1987 Oakland Athletics Fire Safety

The 1987 Smokey Bear A's set is not comparable to earlier Forestry Service issues. The cards are bound together in a book titled "Smokey Bear's Fire Prevention Color-Grams." Each Color-Gram features two cards in one. A near-standard size (2-1/2" x 3-3/4") black-and-white

card is attached to a large perforated (3-3/4" x 6") card, also black-and-white. The large card, which has a postcard back, features a caricature of the player and is intended to be colored and mailed. Backs contain personal and statistical information and carry a Smokey Bear cartoon fire sfaety message. The books were distributed at an A's game during the 1987 season.

		NM/M
Complete Book:		4.50
Complete Singles Set (12):		3.00
Common Player:		.25
(1)	Joaquin Andujar	.25
(2)	Jose Canseco	1.50
(3)	Mike Davis	.25
(4)	Alfredo Griffin	.25
(5)	Moose Haas	.25
(6)	Jay Howell	.25
(7)	Reggie Jackson	1.50
(8)	Carney Lansford	.25
(9)	Dwayne Murphy	.25
(10)	Tony Phillips	.25
(11)	Dave Stewart	.25
(12)	Curt Young	.25

1992 Oakland A's Dream Team

Following fan balloting in 1991, the Oakland A's named an all-time Dream Team for their 25th anniversary season in 1992 and issued a card set of those players. Cards were distributed in two versions. Perforated sheets of eight cards each were included in the second and third editions of the team's magazine. Imperforate four-card strips were also handed out to the first 10,000 fans attending each of four selected home games in 1992. Cards measure 2-9/16" x 3-3/4". Fronts have gray borders. At upper-left is a green and yellow Dream Team pennant; a 25th anniversary logo at lower-right is also in team colors. A red box beneath the color player photo has the name and position in red and white. Black-and-white backs have uniform and card numbers, career stats and highlights and a few biographical bits.

		NM/M
Complete Set (16):		20.00
Common Player:		1.00
1	Mark McGwire	5.00
2	Mike Gallego	1.00
3	Bert Campaneris	1.00
4	Carney Lansford	1.00
5	Reggie Jackson	4.00
6	Rickey Henderson	3.00
7	Jose Canseco	3.00
8	Dave Parker	1.00
9	Terry Steinbach	1.00
10	Dave Stewart	1.00
11	Jim "Catfish" Hunter	2.00
12	Vida Blue	1.00
13	Bob Welch	1.00
14	Dennis Eckersley	2.00
15	Rollie Fingers	2.00
16	Tony LaRussa	1.00

1995 Oakland A's CHP

This safety set was sponsored by the California Highway Patrol. Fronts of the 2-1/2" x 3-1/2" cards have borderless game-action photos with a pair of team logos in the upper corner, a CHiPs badge at bottom-left and the player's name at lower-right. Black-and-white backs have player data and a driving safety tip.

		NM/M
Complete Set (8):		15.00
Common Player:		.50
1	Brent Gates	.50
2	Mark McGwire	10.00
3	Geronimo Berroa	.50
4	Jason Giambi	7.00
5	Terry Steinbach	.50
6	Mike Bordick	.50
7	Todd Van Poppel	.50
8	Ariel Prieto	.50

1999 Plumbers Local 342 Oakland A's

Borrowing from the concept used for many years by Mother's Cookies, this team set was designed to encourage trading when it was distributed to 15,000 fans on May 2. Cards were given away in shrink-wrapped packs of 28, containing 20 single cards and eight of one of the others. Sponsored by a trade union, the Plumbers Steamfitters Refrigeration Local 342, the set has color photos on front, surrounded by borders which morph from yellow to dark green. A "Generation '99 A's" logo is at lower-left. Backs have minimal player data.

		NM/M
Complete Set (28):		12.50
Common Player:		.25
1	Art Howe	.25
2	Ben Grieve	.50
3	Jason Giambi	3.00
4	Kenny Rogers	.25
5	Matt Stairs	.25
6	Tom Candiotti	.25
7	Tony Phillips	.25
8	Eric Chavez	1.50
9	Tim Raines	.50
10	A.J. Hinch	.50
11	Bill Taylor	.25
12	Miguel Tejada	1.50
13	Tim Worrell	.25
14	Scott Spezio	.25
15	Buddy Groom	.25
16	Olmedo Saenz	.25
17	T.J. Mathews	.25
18	Mike Macfarlane	.25
19	Brad Rigby	.25
20	Ryan Christenson	.25
21	Doug Jones	.25
22	Terry Clark	.25
23	Jorge Velandia	.25
24	Gil Heredia	.25
25	John Jaha	.25
26	Jimmy Haynes	.25
27	Jason McDonald	.25
28	A's coaches/checklist (Thad Bosley, Brad Fischer, Dave Hudgens, Ken Macha, Rick Peterson, Ron Washington)	.25

2000 Plumbers Local 342 Oakland A's

This team set was designed to encourage trading when it was distributed to fans at a promotional game. Cards were given away in packs of 28, containing 20 single cards and eight of one of the others. Sponsored by a trade union, the Plumbers Steamfitters Refrigeration Local 342, the set has color photos on front, surrounded by green borders. Backs have minimal player data.

		NM/M
Complete Set (28):		15.00
Common Player:		.50
1	Art Howe	.50
2	Jason Giambi	4.00
3	Tim Hudson	2.00
4	Matt Stairs	.50
5	Kevin Appier	.50
6	Ben Grieve	.50
7	Randy Velarde	.50
8	Eric Chavez	1.50
9	Mark Mulder	.75
10	Sal Fasano	.50
11	Doug Jones	.50
12	Miguel Tejada	1.50
13	Omar Olivares	.50
14	Jeremy Giambi	.50
15	Gil Heredia	.50
16	Olmedo Saenz	.50
17	T.J. Mathews	.50
18	Ramon Hernandez	.50
19	Jeff Tam	.50
20	Ryan Christenson	.50
21	John Jaha	.50
22	Rich Sauveur	.50
23	Terrence Long	.50
24	Mike Magnante	.50
25	Scott Service	.50
26	Frank Menechino	.50
27	Jason Isringhausen	.50
28	Coaches/checklist	.50

2001 Oakland A's Cal Ripken Farewell

To mark his final trip to Oakland as a player, the A's issued these cards to the first 20,000 fans at the September 3-5 games. The cards commemorate career highlights. Fronts have action photos from earlier seasons and a smaller second photo of more current vintage. Red-and-black backs have a ghost-image photo details of the highlight and specifics of the giveaway.

		NM/M
Complete Set (3):		9.00
Common Card:		3.00
1	Cal Ripken Jr. (Rookie Season 1982)	3.00
2	Cal Ripken Jr. (All-Star Game 1987)	3.00
3	Cal Ripken Jr. (2,131 - Record Breaker)	3.00

2002 Plumbers Local 342 Oakland A's

This team set was designed to encourage trading when it was distributed to 15,000 fans on August 18. Cards were given away in shrink-wrapped packs of 28, containing 20 single cards and eight of one of the others. Sponsored by a trade union, the Plumbers Steamfitters Refrigeration Local 342, the set has borderless color photos on front. A team-colors green and gold strip at bottom has the the player name and "BASEBALL A's STYLE." Backs are in black, green and gold with player data and a large union logo.

		NM/M
Complete Set (28):		15.00
Common Player:		.50
1	Art Howe	.50
2	Tim Hudson	2.00
3	David Justice	.50
4	Mark Mulder	.75
5	Jermaine Dye	.50
6	Barry Zito	2.00
7	Miguel Tejada	1.50
8	Eric Chavez	1.50
9	Terrence Long	.50
10	John Mabry	.50
11	Billy Koch	.50
12	Adam Piatt	.50
13	Ramon Hernandez	.50
14	Randy Velarde	.50
15	Scott Hatteberg	.50
16	Mike Magnante	.50
17	Greg Myers	.50
18	Cory Lidle	.50
19	Olmedo Saenz	.50
20	Jim Mecir	.50
21	Eric Byrnes	.50
22	Mark Ellis	.50
23	Mike Venafro	.50
24	Carlos Pena	.50
25	Mike Fyhrie	.50
26	Aaron Harang	.50
27	Chad Bradford	.50
28	A's coaches (Thad Bosley, Brad Fischer, Ken Macha, Rick Peterson, Mike Quade, Ron Washington)	.50

2003 Plumbers Local 342 Oakland A's

This team set was designed to encourage trading when it was distributed to fans at a promotional game. Twenty-eight cards were

MARK MULDER LHP

given away in paper envelopes, containing 20 single cards and eight of one of the others. Sponsored by the Plumbers Steamfitters Refrigeration Local 342, the set has borderless color photos on front. A team-colors green and gold strip at bottom has the player name, position and team logo. Backs are in white, green and gold with player data and a large union logo.

		NM/M
Complete Set (28):		15.00
Common Player:		.50
1	Ken Macha	.50
2	Tim Hudson	2.00
3	Miguel Tejada	1.50
4	Mark Mulder	.75
5	Ramon Hernandez	.50
6	Barry Zito	2.00
7	Jose Guillen	.50
8	Eric Chavez	1.50
9	Terrence Long	.50
10	Ricardo Rincon	.50
11	Erubiel Durazo	.50
12	Mark Ellis	.50
13	Keith Foulke	.50
14	Eric Byrnes	.50
15	Ted Lilly	.50
16	Scott Hatteberg	.50
17	Rich Harden	1.00
18	Chris Singleton	.50
19	Chad Bradford	.50
20	Jermaine Dye	.50
21	Chad Harville	.50
22	Adam Melhuse	.50
23	Jim Mecir	.50
24	John Halama	.50
25	Mike Neu	.50
26	Billy McMillon	.50
27	Frank Menechino	.50
28	A's coaches (Brad Fischer, Terry Francona, Bob Geren, Dave Hudgens, Rick Peterson, Ron Washington)	.50

1983 O'Connell & Son Ink Baseball Greats

AL KALINE — Detroit Tigers

This set of 4-1/2" x 6-1/2" blank-back cards features the artwork of T.S. O'Connell done in the style of 1959 Topps cards. Player portraits are in black-and-white, while backgrounds and team logos are in color. Production was limited to 2,000 sets.

		NM/M
Complete Set (20):		65.00
Common Player:		2.50
(1)	Hank Aaron	6.50
(2)	Johnny Bench	2.50
(3)	Yogi Berra	3.50
(4)	George Brett	4.50
(5)	Roy Campanella	3.50
(6)	Rod Carew	2.50
(7)	Roberto Clemente	10.00
(8)	Bob Gibson	2.50
(9)	Al Kaline	3.00
(10)	Mickey Mantle	12.50
(11)	Joe Morgan	2.50
(12)	Stan Musial	3.50
(13)	Jim Rice	2.50
(14)	Frank Robinson	2.50
(15)	Pete Rose	6.50
(16)	Tom Seaver	2.50
(17)	Duke Snider	3.50
(18)	Honus Wagner	4.50
(19)	Carl Yastrzemski	2.50
(20)	Robin Yount	2.50

1984-91 O'Connell & Son Ink Mini Prints

ryne sandberg

202

This series of 2-1/2" x 3-1/2" blank-backed cards was issued over the period of 1984-91. Cards #1-180 were sold in annual series of 36 each from 1984-88; the 21-card Sixth Series was issued in 1990. The final 43 cards, plus unnumbered checklists for the fist six series were distributed in issues of the company's newsletter, "The Infield Dirt." All cards feature black-and-white pen-and-ink player portraits by T.S. O'Connell and have only the player name and card number on front. Several styles of background, some in color, are found among the various series. Production was limited to 2,000 of each card.

		NM/M
Complete Set (250):		450.00
Common Player:		1.50
	First Series	45.00
1	Ted Williams	7.50
2	Minnie Minoso	1.50
3	Sandy Koufax	9.00
4	Al Kaline	4.50
5	Whitey Ford	3.00
6	Wade Boggs	3.00
7	Nolan Ryan	12.00
8	Greg Luzinski	1.50
9	Cal Ripken	12.00
10	Carl Yastrzemski	4.50
11	Dale Murphy	2.00
12	Rocky Colavito	7.50
13	George Brett	7.50
14	Willie McCovey	3.00
15	Rod Carew	2.50
16	Bob Gibson	2.50
17	Robin Yount	3.00
18	Steve Carlton	2.50
19	Harmon Killebrew	2.50
20	Willie Mays	7.50
21	Reggie Jackson	5.00
22	Eddie Mathews	2.50
23	Eddie Murray	2.50
24	Johnny Bench	2.50
25	Mickey Mantle	18.00
26	Willie Stargell	2.50
27	Rickey Henderson	2.50
28	Roger Maris	6.00
29	Darryl Strawberry	1.50
30	Pete Rose	9.00
31	Jim Rice	1.50
32	Thurman Munson	3.00
33	Brooks Robinson	2.50
34	Fernando Valenzuela	1.50
35	Tony Oliva	1.50
36	Hank Aaron	7.50
	Second Series	45.00
37	Joe Morgan	2.50
38	Kent Hrbek	1.50
39	Yogi Berra	3.00
40	Stan Musial	7.50
41	Gary Matthews	1.50
42	Larry Doby	1.50
43	Steve Garvey	2.50
44	Bob Horner	1.50
45	Ron Guidry	1.50
46	Ernie Banks	3.00
47	Carlton Fisk	2.50
48	"Pee Wee" Reese	2.50
49	Bobby Shantz	1.50
50	Joe DiMaggio	12.00
51	Enos Slaughter	1.50
52	Gary Carter	2.50
53	Bob Feller	2.50
54	Phil Rizzuto	2.50
55	Dave Concepcion	1.50
56	Ron Kittle	1.50
57	Dwight Evans	1.50
58	Johnny Mize	1.50
59	Richie Ashburn	1.50
60	Roberto Clemente	12.00
61	Fred Lynn	1.50
62	Billy Williams	1.50
63	Dave Winfield	2.50
64	Robin Roberts	2.50
65	Billy Martin	1.50
66	Duke Snider	3.00
67	Luis Aparicio	2.50
68	Mickey Vernon	1.50
69	Mike Schmidt	6.00
70	Frank Robinson	2.50
71	Bill Madlock	1.50
72	Rollie Fingers	1.50
	Third Series	45.00
73	Rod Carew	2.50
74	Carl Erskine	1.50
75	Lou Brock	2.50
76	Brooks Robinson	2.50
77	Roberto Clemente	12.00
78	Nellie Fox	1.50
79	Bud Harrelson	1.50
80	Ted Williams	7.50
81	Walter Johnson	2.50
82	Cal Ripken	12.00
83	Lefty Grove	2.00
84	Lou Whitaker	1.50
85	Johnny Bench	2.50
86	Ty Cobb	6.00
87	Mike Schmidt	6.00
88	George Brett	7.50
89	Jim Bunning	1.50
90	Babe Ruth	12.00
91	Satchel Paige	5.00
92	Warren Spahn	1.50
93	Dale Murphy	1.50
94	Early Wynn	1.50
95	Reggie Jackson	2.50
96	Charlie Gehringer	1.50
97	Jackie Robinson	9.00
98	Lou Gehrig	10.00
99	Hank Aaron	7.50
100	Mickey Mantle	18.00
101	Sandy Koufax	9.00
102	Ryne Sandberg	4.00
103	Don Mattingly	6.00
104	Darryl Strawberry	1.50
105	Tom Seaver	2.50
106	Bill Klem	1.50
107	Dwight Gooden	1.50
108	Pete Rose	9.00
	Fourth Series	45.00
109	Elston Howard	2.50
110	Honus Wagner	3.00
111	Waite Hoyt	1.50
112	Bill Bruton	1.50
113	Gil Hodges	1.50
114	Vic Power	1.50
115	Al Kaline	4.50
116	Al Lopez	1.50
117	Rocky Bridges	1.50
118	Jim Gilliam	1.50
119	Christy Mathewson	2.50
120	Hank Greenberg	1.50
121	Eddie Mathews	1.50
122	Van Mungo	1.50
123	Harry Simpson	1.50
124	Carl Yastrzemski	2.50
125	Pete Rose	9.00
126	Dizzy Dean	3.00
127	Chi Chi Olivo	1.50
128	Johnny Vander Meer	1.50
129	Roberto Clemente	12.00
130	Carl Hubbell	1.50
131	Willie Mays	7.50
132	Willie Stargell	2.50
133	Sam Jethroe	1.50
134	Pete Rose	9.00
135	Jackie Robinson	9.00
136	Yogi Berra	3.00
137	Grover Alexander	2.00
138	Joe Morgan	2.50
139	Rube Foster	1.50
140	Mickey Mantle	18.00
141	Ted Williams	7.50
142	Jimmie Foxx	2.50
143	Pepper Martin	1.50
144	Hank Aaron	7.50
	Fifth Series	45.00
145	Vida Blue	1.50
146	Carl Furillo	2.00
147	Lloyd Waner	1.50
148	Eddie Dyer	1.50
149	Casey Stengel	2.50
150	Mickey Mantle	18.00
151	Gil Hodges	2.50
152	Don Mossi	1.50
153	Ron Swoboda	1.50
154	Hoyt Wilhelm	1.50
155	Ed Roush (Edd)	1.50
156	Mickey Lolich	2.00
157	Jim Palmer	2.50
158	Thurman Munson	2.50
159	Don Zimmer	1.50
160	Hank Aaron	7.50
161	Johnny Bench	2.50
162	Orlando Cepeda	1.50
163	Honus Wagner	3.00
164	Tom Seaver	2.50
165	Willie Mays	7.50

166	Elmer Riddle	1.50
167	Tony Oliva	1.50
168	Elmer Flick	1.50
169	Curt Flood	1.50
170	Carl Yastrzemski	2.50
171	Charlie Keller	1.50
172	Christy Mathewson	2.50
173	Eddie Plank	1.50
174	Lou Gehrig	10.00
175	John McGraw	1.50
176	Mule Haas	1.50
177	Paul Waner	1.50
178	Steve Blass	1.50
179	Honus Wagner	3.00
180	Jack Barry	1.50
	Sixth Series	45.00
181	Rocky Colavito	4.50
182	Danny Murtaugh	1.50
183	John Edwards	1.50
184	Pete Rose	9.00
185	Roy Campanella	3.00
186	Jerry Grote	1.50
187	Leo Durocher	1.50
188	Rollie Fingers	2.50
189	Wes Parker	1.50
190	Joe Rudi	1.50
191	Bill Veeck	2.50
192	Mark Fidrych	2.50
193	George Foster	1.50
194	Early Wynn	1.50
195	Frank Howard	1.50
196	Graig Nettles	2.50
197	Juan Pizarro	1.50
198	Jose Cruz	1.50
199	Joe Jackson	12.00
200	Stan Musial	7.50
201	Chuck Klein	1.50
	Seventh Series	45.00
202	Ryne Sandberg	6.00
203	Richie Allen	2.50
204	Bo Jackson	2.50
205	Kevin Mitchell	1.50
206	Al Smith, Early Wynn, Larry Doby	1.50
207	Mickey Mantle	18.00
208	Will Clark	2.50
209	Cecil Fielder	1.50
210	Bobby Richardson	2.50
211	Nolan Ryan	12.00
212	Casey Stengel	2.50
213	Ted Kluszewski	3.00
214	Gaylord Perry	2.50
215	Johnny Vander Meer	1.50
216	Willie Mays	7.50
217	Goose Goslin	1.50
218	Bobby Shantz	1.50
219	Terry Pendleton	1.50
220	Richie Ashburn	2.50
221	Robin Yount	3.00
222	Cal Ripken	12.00
223	Danny Ainge	1.50
224	Bob Friend	1.50
225	Orel Hershiser	2.50
226	Wade Boggs	3.00
227	Bill Mazeroski (1960 World Series home run)	3.00
228	Stan Musial	7.50
229	Chris Short	1.50
230	Johnny Bench	2.50
231	Nellie Fox	2.50
232	Ron Santo	2.50
233	Tony Gwynn	6.00
234	Phil Niekro	2.50
235	Frank Thomas	4.50
236	Greg Gross	1.50
237	Ken Griffey Jr.	9.00
238	Benito Santiago	1.50
239	Dwight Gooden	1.50
240	Darryl Strawberry	1.50
241	Roy Campanella	3.00
242	Roger Clemens	6.00
243	Kirby Puckett	7.50
244	Nolan Ryan	12.00
---	First Series checklist	.25
---	Second Series checklist	.25
---	Third Series checklist	.25
---	Fourth Series checklist	.25
---	Fifth Series checklist	.25
---	Sixth Series checklist	.25

1986 Oh Henry! Cleveland Indians

This 30-card set of Cleveland Indians players was distributed by the team at a special Photo/Baseball Card Day at Municipal Stadium. The cards were printed on an 11" x 29" three-panel, perforated foldout piece which featured four action shots of the Indians on the cover. Unfolded, there are two panels containing the baseball cards and a third which contains a team photo. Cards measure 2-1/4" x 3-1/8". The players' studio portraits are framed in blue with a white border and list player name, number and position. Card fronts also include

a picture of the sponsoring candy bar. Card backs include facsimile autograph and professional records. Each card is perforated for separation.

		NM/M
	Complete Set, Foldout:	9.00
	Common Player:	.40
2	Brett Butler	.40
4	Tony Bernazard	.40
6	Andy Allanson	.40
7	Pat Corrales	.40
8	Carmen Castillo	.40
10	Pat Tabler	.40
13	Ernie Camacho	.40
14	Julio Franco	.50
15	Dan Rohn	.40
18	Ken Schrom	.40
20	Otis Nixon	.40
22	Fran Mullins	.40
23	Chris Bando	.40
24	Ed Williams	.40
26	Brook Jacoby	.40
27	Mel Hall	.40
29	Andre Thornton	.50
30	Joe Carter	.75
35	Phil Niekro	2.00
36	Jamie Easterly	.40
37	Don Schulze	.40
42	Rich Yett	.40
43	Scott Bailes	.40
44	Neal Heaton	.40
46	Jim Kern	.40
48	Dickie Noles	.40
49	Tom Candiotti	.40
52	Reggie Ritter	.40
54	Tom Waddell	.40
	Coaching Staff (Jack Aker, Bobby Bonds, Doc Edwards, John Goryl)	.40
	Team Photo	2.00

1995 Oh Henry! Toronto Blue Jays

The candy bar company, Oh Henry!, sponsored this card set giveaway. The 2-1/2" x 3-1/2" cards have an action photo on a green background with the team name repeated in white diagonally. A large colorful "LET'S PLAY BALL" team logo is at top-left. The player name and uniform number are overprinted at bottom. Backs are printed in black-and-white with personal

data, career highlights, stats, and sponsor's logo. Cards are listed here alphabetically.

		NM/M
	Complete Set (36):	12.00
	Common Player:	.25
(1)	Roberto Alomar	.75
(2)	Bob Bailor	.25
(3)	Howard Battle	.25
(4)	Joe Carter	.45
(5)	Tony Castillo	.25
(6)	Domingo Cedeno	.25
(7)	Galen Cisco	.25
(8)	David Cone	.35
(9)	Brad Cornett	.25
(10)	Danny Cox	.25
(11)	Tim Crabtree	.25
(12)	Carlos Delgado	1.00
(13)	Cito Gaston	.25
(14)	Alex Gonzalez	.50
(15)	Shawn Green	2.00
(16)	Juan Guzman	.25
(17)	Darren Hall	.25
(18)	Pat Hentgen	.25
(19)	Larry Hisle	.25
(20)	Dennis Holmberg	.25
(21)	Michael Huff	.25
(22)	Randy Knorr	.25
(23)	Al Leiter	.25
(24)	Nick Leyva	.25
(25)	Angel Martinez	.25
(26)	Paul Molitor	2.50
(27)	John Olerud	.50
(28)	Tomas Perez	.25
(29)	Aaron Small	.25
(30)	Paul Spoljaric	.25
(31)	Ed Sprague	.25
(32)	Gene Tenace	.25
(33)	Mike Timlin	.25
(34)	Duane Ward	.25
(35)	Devon White	.40
(36)	Woody Williams	.25

1996 Oh Henry! Toronto Blue Jays

In celebration of the team's 20th anniversary, Oh Henry! sponsored a card set giveaway at SkyDome on June 11. The first 25,000 fans received a boxed set of current and former players. The 2-1/2" x 3-1/2" cards have a borderless photo on front. The central portion of the picture is in color, the edges are in black-and-white. The player name and uniform number are overprinted at bottom. The team's anniversary logo is in the upper-left corner. On former players' cards there is a gold "ALUMNI" banner under the logo ball. Backs are printed in blue and white with career summary and stats, a few bits of personal data and logos of the team and sponsor. Cards are listed here alphabetically.

		NM/M
	Complete Set (36):	8.00
	Common Player:	.25
(1)	George Bell	.35
(2)	Brian Bohanon	.25
(3)	Joe Carter	.40
(4)	Tony Castillo	.25
(5)	Domingo Cedeno	.25
(6)	Tim Crabtree	.25
(7)	Felipe Crespo	.25
(8)	Carlos Delgado	1.50
(9)	Cito Gaston	.25
(10)	Alex Gonzalez	.50
(11)	Shawn Green	1.00
(12)	Alfredo Griffin	.25
(13)	Kelly Gruber	.25
(14)	Juan Guzman	.25
(15)	Erik Hanson	.25
(16)	Pat Hentgen	.25
(17)	Marty Janzen	.25
(18)	Nick Leyva	.25
(19)	Sandy Martinez	.25

(20)	Lloyd Moseby	.35
(21)	Otis Nixon	.25
(22)	Charlie O'Brien	.25
(23)	John Olerud	.75
(24)	Robert Perez	.25
(25)	Paul Quantrill	.25
(26)	Mel Queen	.25
(27)	Bill Risley	.25
(28)	Juan Samuel	.25
(29)	Ed Sprague	.25
(30)	Dave Steib	.35
(31)	Gene Tenace	.25
(32)	Mike Timlin	.25
(33)	Willie Upshaw	.25
(34)	Jeffrey Ware	.25
(35)	Ernie Whitt	.25
(36)	Woody Williams	.25

1997 Oh Henry! Toronto Blue Jays

The first 25,000 fans entering SkyDome for the Blue Jays' May 6 game received a team card set sponsored by the candy bar company. In 2-1/2" x 3-1/2" size, fronts feature color action photos with a splash of "infield dirt" vertically at left. The player's name and uniform number appear at top-left. "Oh!" and the team logo are printed in bottom corners. Backs are printed in blue and white with a few personal data, stats and career highlights.

		NM/M
	Complete Set (36):	7.50
	Common Player:	.25
2	Otis Nixon	.25
3	Felipe Crespo	.25
4	Alfredo Griffin	.25
5	Jacob Brumfield	.25
6	Orlando Merced	.25
7	Shannon Stewart	.50
9	Alex Gonzalez	.40
10	Jim Lett	.25
11	Juan Samuel	.25
12	Tilson Brito	.25
13	Carlos Garcia	.25
15	Shawn Green	1.00
16	Nick Leyva	.25
17	Robert Perez	.25
18	Benito Santiago	.25
19	Dan Plesac	.25
21	Roger Clemens	2.50
22	Charlie O'Brien	.25
24	Paul Spoljaric	.25
25	Carlos Delgado	1.50
26	Willie Upshaw	.25
29	Joe Carter	.30
31	Robert Person	.25
32	Ed Sprague	.25
34	Mel Queen	.25
37	Tim Crabtree	.25
38	Erik Hanson	.25
40	Mike Timlin	.25
41	Pat Hentgen	.25
43	Cito Gaston	.25
44	Gene Tenace	.25
48	Paul Quantrill	.25
49	Luis Andujar	.25
54	Woody Williams	.25
55	Bill Risley	.25
57	Juan Guzman	.25

1998 Oh Henry! Toronto Blue Jays

This stadium giveaway card set was issued in a flip-top cardboard box decorated with the team logo and checklist. The 2-1/2" x 3-1/2" cards have (mostly) game action photos on their borderless fronts. Sponsor logo at player name and uniform number are at top, team logo and motto "BRING IT ON." are at bottom. Backs are blue-and-white with

player data, stats and career highlights. The checklist is arranged by uniform number.

		NM/M
	Complete Set (36):	7.50
	Common Player:	.25
1	Tony Fernandez	.25
3	Felipe Crespo	.25
4	Craig Grebeck	.25
5	Mark Dalesandro	.25
7	Eddie Rodriguez	.25
8	Alex Gonzalez	.45
10	Darren Fletcher	.25
10	Jim Lett	.25
11	Juan Samuel	.25
14	Kevin Brown	.25
15	Shawn Green	1.00
16	Jack Hubbard	.25
17	Tim Johnson	.25
18	Benito Santiago	.25
19	Dan Plesac	.25
20	Mike Stanley	.25
21	Roger Clemens	3.00
22	Sal Butera	.25
23	Jose Cruz Jr.	.35
24	Shannon Stewart	.35
25	Carlos Delgado	1.50
26	Chris Carpenter	.25
27	Randy Myers	.25
30	Woody Williams	.25
31	Robert Person	.25
33	Ed Sprague	.25
34	Mel Queen	.25
38	Gary Matthews	.25
39	Erik Hanson	.25
40	Carlos Almanzar	.25
41	Pat Hentgen	.25
42	Jose Canseco	1.00
45	Kelvim Escobar	.25
48	Paul Quantrill	.25
55	Bill Risley	.25
57	Juan Guzman	.25

1999 Oh Henry! Toronto Blue Jays

This boxed set was a stadium give-away. Fronts of the 2-1/2" x 3-1/2" cards have game-action photos on a wood-look background. Backs have personal data, career highlights and stats printed in blue. The checklist is arranged by uniform number.

		NM/M
	Complete Set (36):	7.50
	Common Player:	.25
1	Tony Fernandez	.25
3	Norberto Martin	.25
4	Craig Grebeck	.25
5	Mark Dalesandro	.25
7	Pat Kelly	.25
8	Alex Gonzalez	.25
10	Darrin Fletcher	.25
10	Jim Lett	.25
11	Jim Fregosi	.25
12	Willie Greene	.25
13	Pete Munro	.25
15	Shawn Green	.75
16	Lloyd Moseby	.25
17	Dave Hollins	.25
18	Homer Bush	.25
19	Dan Plesac	.25
22	Mike Matheny	.25

23	Jose Cruz	.25
24a	Paul Spoljaric	.25
24b	Shannon Stewart	.25
25	Carlos Delgado	1.50
26	Chris Carpenter	.25
29	Geronimo Berroa	.25
30	Marty Pevey	.25
32	Roy Halladay	.75
33	David Wells	.25
34	Mel Queen	.25
35	Terry Bevington	.25
36	Gary Matthews	.25
37	Graeme Lloyd	.25
41	Pat Hentgen	.25
43	Tom Davey	.25
47	Kelvim Escobar	.25
48	Paul Quantrill	.25
50	Joey Hamilton	.25
77	Bill Risley	.25

2000 Oh Henry! Toronto Blue Jays

This boxed set was a stadium give-away. Fronts of the 2-1/2" x 3-1/2" cards have game-action photos on a dark blue background. Backs have personal data, career highlights and stats printed in blue.

		NM/M
	Complete Set (36):	10.00
	Common Player:	.25
3	Lee Elia	.25
4	Craig Grebeck	.25
7	Tony Batista	.25
8	Alex Gonzalez	.25
9	Darrin Fletcher	.25
10	Vernon Wells	.50
11	Jim Fregosi	.25
12	Peter Munro	.25
15	Marty Cordova	.25
18	Homer Bush	.25
20	Brad Fullmer	.25
22	Rick Langford	.25
23	Jose Cruz	.25
24	Shannon Stewart	.50
25	Carlos Delgado	1.50
26	Chris Carpenter	.25
28	Lance Painter	.25
29	Bobby Knoop	.25
30	Alberto Castillo	.25
32	Roy Halladay	.75
33	David Wells	.50
34	Clayton Andrews	.25
36	Terry Bevington	.25
37	Frank Castillo	.25
41	Cito Gaston	.25
43	Raul Mondesi	.25
44	Billy Koch	.25
47	Kelvim Escobar	.25
48	Paul Quantrill	.25
49	John Bale	.25
50	Joey Hamilton	.25
52	Pedro Borbon	.25
53	John Frascatore	.25
55	DeWayne Wise	.25
56	Roly de Armas	.25
77/00	Diamond/Ace/Mascots	.25

2001 Oh Henry! Toronto Blue Jays

The team's 25th season is commemorated with this stadium give-away boxed set.

Fronts have action photos on a blue background with team and sponsor logos. Backs have a large 25th anniversary logo, complete stats, personal data and career highlights.

		NM/M
Complete Set (36):		8.00
Common Player:		.25
1	Cookie Rojas	.25
2	Jeff Frye	.25
5	Chris Woodward	.25
7	Tony Batista	.25
8	Alex Gonzalez	.35
9	Darrin Fletcher	.25
13	Buck Martinez	.25
14	Ryan Freel	.25
16	Garth Iorg	.25
17	Chris Michalak	.25
18	Homer Bush	.25
19	Dan Plesac	.25
20	Brad Fullmer	.25
21	Esteban Loaiza	.25
22	Brian Simmons	.25
23	Jose Cruz Jr.	.25
24	Shannon Stewart	.50
25	Carlos Delgado	1.00
26	Chris Carpenter	.25
28	Lance Painter	.25
30	Alberto Castillo	.25
33	Mike Sirotka	.25
35	Terry Bevington	.25
39	Steve Parris	.25
41	Cito Gaston	.25
43	Raul Mondesi	.25
44	Billy Koch	.25
45	Kelvim Escobar	.25
47	Gil Patterson	.25
48	Paul Quantrill	.25
50	Joey Hamilton	.25
51	Pedro Borbon	.25
52	John Frascatore	.25
53	Mark Connor	.25
---	First Pitch (Bill Singer)	
---	Home Run Record (Raul Mondesi, Tony Batista, Jose Cruz Jr., Carlos Delgado)	.25

1982-1988 Ohio Baseball Hall of Fame

Frank Robinson 1975

Ohio natives and players who made their mark playing in the Buckeye State are featured in this collectors issue, along with executives and a few other figures. Fronts of the 3-3/8" x 5-5/8" cards have black-and-white player photos surrounded by red borders. The player's name and year of induction are at bottom. Black-and-white backs have lengthy career summaries. Original production was 2,500 sets which were sold into the hobby at $7 apiece. Later inductees were added to the set through at least 1988, but the checklist after #65 is incomplete and may represent skip-numbering.

		NM/M
Complete Set (93):		100.00
Common Player:		2.00
1	Ohio Baseball Hall of Fame	2.00
2	Checklist	.50
3	Nick Cullop	2.00
4	Dean Chance	2.00
5	Bob Feller	3.00
6	Jesse Haines	2.00
7	Waite Hoyt	2.00
8	Ernie Lombardi	2.00
9	Mike Powers	2.00
10	Edd Roush	2.00

11	Red Ruffing	2.00
12	Luke Sewell	2.00
13	Tris Speaker	2.00
14	Cy Young	3.00
15	Walter Alston	2.00
16	Lou Boudreau	2.00
17	Warren Giles	2.00
18	Ted Kluszewski	3.00
19	William McKinley	2.00
20	Roger Peckinpaugh	2.00
21	Johnny Vander Meer	2.00
22	Early Wynn	2.00
23	Earl Averill	2.00
24	Stan Coveleski	2.00
25	Lefty Grove	2.00
26	Nap Lajoie	2.00
27	Al Lopez	2.00
28	Eddie Onslow	2.00
29	Branch Rickey	2.00
30	Frank Robinson	3.00
31	George Sisler	2.00
32	Bob Lemon	2.00
33	Satchel Paige	3.00
34	Bucky Walters	2.00
35	Gus Bell	2.00
36	Rocky Colavito	3.00
37	Mel Harder	2.00
38	Tommy Henrich	2.00
39	Miller Huggins	2.00
40	Fred Hutchinson	2.00
41	Eppa Rixey	2.00
42	Joe Sewell	2.00
43	George Uhle	2.00
44	Bill Veeck	2.00
45	Estel Crabtree	2.00
46	Harvey Haddix	2.00
47	Noodles Hahn	2.00
48	Joe Jackson	4.00
49	Kenesaw Landis	2.00
50	Thurman Munson	3.00
51	Gabe Paul	2.00
52	Vada Pinson	2.00
53	Wally Post	2.00
54	Vic Wertz	2.00
55	Paul Derringer	2.00
56	John Galbreath	2.00
57	Richard Marquard	2.00
58	Bill McKechnie	2.00
59	Rocky Nelson	2.00
60	Al Rosen	2.00
61	Lew Fonseca	2.00
62	Larry MacPhail	2.00
63	Joe Nuxhall	2.00
64	Birdie Tebbetts	2.00
65	Gene Woodling	2.00
66	Ethan Allen	2.00
67	Mike Garcia	2.00
68	Bob Howsam	2.00
69	Addie Joss	2.00
70	Ken Keltner	2.00
71	"Tot" Pressnell	2.00
72	Roger Bresnahan	2.00
73	Bill Mazeroski	3.00
75a	Frank McCormick	2.00
75b	George H. Sisler	2.00
76	Bill Wambsganss	2.00
79	Woody English	2.00
80	Roy McMillan	2.00
81	Frank Baumholtz	2.00
83	Sam McDowell	2.50
84	James Campbell	2.00
86	Ned Garver	2.00
87	Bob Purkey	2.00
90	Harold Cooper	2.00
91	Dennis Galehouse	2.00
92	Brooks Lawrence	2.50
93	Tony Lucadello	2.00

1992 Old Style Chicago Cubs

1966 - 1973, 1976 - 1977

RANDY HUNDLEY

More than two dozens Cubs stars are featured in this set of 2-1/2" x 3-1/2" cards. Front have sepia player photos with their years at Chicago indicated on top. Backs are printed in black, red and blue on white with a few stats and career highlights, sponsor and team logos and a picture of the Cubs uniform in the player's debut year. The un-numbered cards are checklisted here in alphabetical order.

		NM/M
Complete Set (28):		15.00
Common Player:		.50
(1)	Grover Alexander	.50
(2)	Cap Anson	.50
(3)	Ernie Banks	3.00
(4)	Mordecai Brown	.50
(5)	Phil Cavarretta	.50
(6)	Frank Chance	.50
(7)	Kiki Cuyler	.50
(8)	Johnny Evers	.50
(9)	Charlie Grimm	.50
(10)	Stan Hack	.50
(11)	Gabby Hartnett	.50
(12)	Billy Herman	.50
(13)	Rogers Hornsby	.50
(14)	Ken Hubbs	1.00
(15)	Randy Hundley	.50
(16)	Fergie Jenkins	.75
(17)	Bill Lee	.50
(18)	Andy Pafko	.50
(19)	Rick Reuschel	.50
(20)	Charlie Root	.50
(21)	Ron Santo	.75
(22)	Hank Sauer	.50
(23)	Riggs Stephenson	.50
(24)	Bruce Sutter	.75
(25)	Joe Tinker	.50
(26)	Hippo Vaughn	.50
(27)	Billy Williams	1.00
(28)	Hack Wilson	.50

1993 Old Style Billy Williams

The career of long-time Cubs star, batting coach and Hall of Famer Billy Williams is traced in this four-card set given to fans attending the Aug. 17, 1993 game at Wrigley Field between the Cubs and Expos. Fronts of the first three cards have black-and-white photos, the last card is in color. Backs have biographical and career information along with the sponsor's logo.

		NM/M
Complete Set (4):		8.00
Common Card:		2.00
(1)	Billy Williams/Btg (Personal)	2.00
(2)	Billy Williams/Fielding (Playing career.)	2.00
(3)	Billy Williams/Btg (Playing career.)	2.00
(4)	Billy Williams/Portrait (Coaching career.)	2.00

1999 Old Style Chicago Cubs All-Century Team

#17

MARK GRACE

Cubs greats of the 20th Century are featured in this stadium give-away card set. The set was distributed over the course of three games at Wrigley Field in seven-card cello-wrapped packs. With the exception of all-time manager Frank Chance, the cards were packaged alphabetically; Chance

		NM/M
Complete Set (32):		60.00
Common Player:		1.50
(1)	Buddy Bell	1.50
(2)	Johnny Bench	4.00
(3)	Bruce Bochte	1.50
(4)	George Brett	7.50
(5)	Bill Buckner	1.50
(6)	Rod Carew	4.00
(7)	Steve Carlton	4.00
(8)	Cesar Cedeno	1.50
(9)	Jack Clark	1.50
(10)	Cecil Cooper	1.50
(11)	Bucky Dent	1.50
(12)	Carlton Fisk	4.00
(13)	Steve Garvey	2.50
(14)	Goose Gossage	1.50
(15)	Mike Hargrove	1.50
(16)	Keith Hernandez	1.50
(17)	Bob Horner	1.50
(18)	Reggie Jackson	7.50
(19)	Steve Kemp	1.50
(20)	Ron LeFlore	1.50
(21)	Fred Lynn	1.50
(22)	Lee Mazilli	1.50
(23)	Eddie Murray	4.00
(24)	Mike Norris	1.50
(25)	Dave Parker	1.50
(26)	J.R. Richard	1.50
(27)	Pete Rose	9.00
(28)	Mike Schmidt	7.50

was included in the third "series" pack. Fronts of the 2-1/2" x 3-1/2" cards have black-and-white or color photos in a fancy white frame on a tan background. Color team and sponsor logos appear in the left-hand corners. Black-and-white backs have player data, career highlights and lifetime Cubs stats. The player's uniform number, if any, appears on both front and back. Cards have a glossy surface on both front and back.

		NM/M
Complete Set (21):		20.00
Common Player:		.50
(1)	Grover Alexander	.50
(2)	Ernie Banks	2.50
(3)	Mordecai Brown	.50
(4)	Phil Cavarretta	.50
(5)	Frank Chance	.50
(6)	Andre Dawson	1.00
(7)	Mark Grace	2.00
(8)	Charlie Grimm	.50
(9)	Stan Hack	.50
(10)	Gabby Hartnett	.50
(11)	Billy Herman	.50
(12)	Fergie Jenkins	.75
(13)	Andy Pafko	.50
(14)	Ryne Sandberg	2.00
(15)	Ron Santo	1.50
(16)	Lee Smith	.50
(17)	Sammy Sosa	3.00
(18)	Bruce Sutter	.75
(19)	Joe Tinker	.50
(20)	Billy Williams	.75
(21)	Hack Wilson	.50

1982 On Deck Cookies Discs

These 2-3/4" discs were packaged with a large cookie and sold for 25-29 cents in areas including Florida and New Jersey. The fronts have a 1981 copyright date, but the backs indicate "1982 Collectors Series." Fronts have black-and-white player portraits in the center panel of a baseball design. The end panels can be any one of several pastel colors. Backs are in red and black and repeat the baseball motif and include a copyright for "All sports baking Co., Inc." Each side carries the players' union logo through which the discs were licensed by Michael Schechter Associates. Because they are not licensed through Major League Baseball, player pictures have no uniform logos.

		NM/M
Complete Set (30):		10.00
Common Player:		.50
1	Jim Abbott	.50
2	Kevin Appier	.50
3	Roger Clemens	1.25
4	Cecil Fielder	.50
5	Juan Gonzalez	.60
6	Ken Griffey Jr.	1.50
7	Kenny Lofton	.50
8	Jack McDowell	.50
9	Paul Molitor	.75
10	Kirby Puckett	1.00
11	Cal Ripken Jr.	2.00
12	Tim Salmon	.50
13	Ruben Sierra	.50
14	Frank Thomas	.75
15	Greg Vaughn	.50
16	Jeff Bagwell	.75
17	Barry Bonds	2.00
18	Bobby Bonilla	.50
19	Jeff Conine	.50
20	Lenny Dykstra	.50
21	Andres Galarraga	.50
22	Marquis Grissom	.50
23	Tony Gwynn	1.00
24	Gregg Jefferies	.50
25	John Kruk	.50
26	Greg Maddux	1.00
27	Mike Piazza	1.25
28	Jose Rijo	.50
29	Ryne Sandberg	1.00
30	Andy Van Slyke	.50

1987-89 Our Own Tea Discs

Our Own Tea was one of the regional brands which appears on the series of player disc folders which were packaged with various iced tea mixes and other products between 1987-89.

(29)	Tom Seaver	4.00
(30)	Willie Stargell	4.00
(31)	Roy Smalley	1.50
(32)	Garry Templeton	1.50

1994 Oscar Mayer Superstar Pop-Ups

PAUL MOLITOR

Oscar Mayer Bologna packages in 1994 included one pop-up card in each, but unlike the similar Kraft cards, in this case it was 30 round cards (2-1/2 inches in diameter), with the Oscar Mayer logo on the front and trivia questions on the backs. The promotion ran from April through May, or as long as the supplies lasted. The cards were licensed by the Major League Baseball Players Association, but not by Major League Baseball, so the team logos were airbrushed from player's caps and uniforms. Through an on-pack and in-store mail-in offer, collectors could order complete sets of cards for $1.95 per league (15 cards), plus the appropriate proofs of purchase. Officials of Kraft USA, parent company of Oscar Mayer, announced that they printed 266,000 sets.

P

1988 Pacific Baseball Legends

ROGER MARIS
OUTFIELDER

Pacific Trading Cards rounded up 110 photos of the greatest baseball players from the past 40 years for its 1988 "Baseball Legends" set. All players featured in the set are (or were) members of the Major League Baseball Alumni Association. Card fronts feature silver outer borders and large, clear full-color player photos outlined in black against colorful banner-style inner borders of red, blue, green, orange or gold. The player's name and position are printed in white letters on the lower portion of the banner. Card backs are numbered and carry the Baseball Legends logo, player biography, major league career stats, and personal information. The cards were sold in boxed sets via candy wholesalers, with emphasis on Midwest and New England states. Complete collector sets in clear plastic boxes were made available via dealers or directly from Pacific Trading Cards. Four cards were issued in both error and corrected versions.

		NM/M
Complete Set (110) (no checklist):		15.00
Common Player:		.10
Wax Pack (10):		.75
Wax Box (36):		15.00
1	Hank Aaron	2.00
2	Red Shoendienst (Schoendienst)	.30
3	Brooks Robinson	.30
4	Luke Appling	.30
5	Gene Woodling	.10
6	Stan Musial	1.00
7	Mickey Mantle	6.00
8	Richie Ashburn	.50
9	Ralph Kiner	.40
10	Phil Rizzuto	.50
11	Harvey Haddix	.10
12	Ken Boyer	.20
13	Clete Boyer	.10
14	Ken Harrelson	.10
15	Robin Roberts	.40
16	Catfish Hunter	.40
17	Frank Howard	.20
18	Jim Perry	.10
19a	Elston Howard (Reversed photo.)	.20
19b	Elston Howard (Correct photo.)	.20
20	Jim Bouton	.20
21	Pee Wee Reese	.50
22a	Mel Stottlemyer	.20
22b	Mel Stottlemyre	.20
23	Hank Sauer	.20
24	Willie Mays	1.00
25	Tom Tresh	.20
26	Roy Sievers	.10
27	Leo Durocher	.30
28	Al Dark	.20
29	Tony Kubek	.30
30	Johnny Vander Meer	.20
31	Joe Adcock	.20
32	Bob Lemon	.40
33	Don Newcombe	.40
34	Thurman Munson	.50
35	Earl Battey	.10
36	Ernie Banks	.60
37	Matty Alou	.10
38	Dave McNally	.10
39	Mickey Lolich	.20

40	Jackie Robinson	1.00
41	Allie Reynolds	.30
42a	Don Larson	.20
42b	Don Larsen	.20
43	Fergie Jenkins	.30
44	Jim Gilliam	.20
45	Bobby Thomson	.20
46	Sparky Anderson	.20
47	Roy Campanella	.60
48	Marv Throneberry	.20
49	Bill Virdon	.10
50	Ted Williams	1.00
51	Minnie Minoso	.20
52	Bob Turley	.20
53	Yogi Berra	.60
54	Juan Marichal	.40
55	Duke Snider	.60
56	Harvey Kuenn	.20
57	Nellie Fox	.40
58	Felipe Alou	.10
59	Tony Oliva	.20
60	Bill Mazeroski	.40
61	Bobby Shantz	.20
62	Mark Fidrych	.20
63	Johnny Mize	.30
64	Ralph Terry	.10
65	Gus Bell	.10
66	Jerry Koosman	.20
67	Mike McCormick	.10
68	Lou Burdette	.20
69	George Kell	.30
70	Vic Raschi	.20
71	Chuck Connors	.40
72	Ted Kluszewski	.50
73	Bobby Doerr	.30
74	Bobby Richardson	.30
75	Carl Erskine	.30
76	Hoyt Wilhelm	.40
77	Bob Purkey	.10
78	Bob Friend	.10
79	Monte Irvin	.30
80a	Jim Longborg	.20
80b	Jim Lonborg	.20
81	Wally Moon	.10
82	Moose Skowron	.20
83	Tommy Davis	.20
84	Enos Slaughter	.40
85	Sal Maglie	.20
86	Harmon Killebrew	.50
87	Gil Hodges	.50
88	Jim Kaat	.20
89	Roger Maris	.60
90	Billy Williams	.40
91	Luis Aparicio	.40
92	Jim Bunning	.40
93	Bill Freehan	.10
94	Orlando Cepeda	.30
95	Early Wynn	.40
96	Tug McGraw	.20
97	Ron Santo	.30
98	Del Crandall	.10
99	Sal Bando	.10
100	Joe DiMaggio	2.00
101	Bob Feller	.50
102	Larry Doby	.40
103	Rollie Fingers	.30
104	Al Kaline	.60
105	Johnny Podres	.20
106	Lou Boudreau	.30
107	Zoilo Versalles	.10
108	Dick Groat	.10
109	Warren Spahn	.50
110	Johnny Bench	.60
----	Checklist	2.00

1989 Pacific Legends II

REGGIE JACKSON
OUTFIELDER

Pacific Trading Cards issued its Baseball Legends II set as a carry over of its initial set. The photos are printed on silver background and have colorful inner borders of red, blue, orange or gold. Players' names and positions are printed in white letters below the photos. The card backs once again present the "Baseball Legends" logo, player biography, major league career statistics, and personal information. The Baseball Legends II are numbered 110-220 and were available in wax packs at a limited number of retail chains. The complete set was also made available via dealers or could be ordered directly from Pacific Trading Cards.

		NM/M
Complete Set (110) (no checklist):		12.50
Common Player:		.10
Wax Pack (10):		.75
Wax Box (36):		15.00
111	Reggie Jackson	.50
112	Rich Reese	.10
113	Frankie Frisch	.10
114	Ed Kranepool	.10
115	Al Hrabosky	.10
116	Eddie Mathews	.20
117	Ty Cobb	1.00
118	Jim Davenport	.10
119	Buddy Lewis	.10
120	Virgil Trucks	.10
121	Del Ennis	.10
122	Dick Radatz	.10
123	Andy Pafko	.10
124	Wilbur Wood	.10
125	Joe Sewell	.10
126	Herb Score	.10
127	Paul Waner	.10
128	Lloyd Waner	.10
129	Brooks Robinson	.20
130	Bo Belinsky	.10
131	Phil Cavaretta	.10
132	Claude Osteen	.10
133	Tito Francona	.10
134	Billy Pierce	.10
135	Roberto Clemente	3.00
136	Spud Chandler	.10
137	Enos Slaughter	.10
138	Ken Holtzman	.10
139	John Hopp	.10
140	Tony LaRussa	.20
141	Ryne Duren	.10
142	Glenn Beckert	.10
143	Ken Keltner	.10
144	Hank Bauer	.10
145	Roger Craig	.10
146	Frank Baker	.10
147	Jim O'Toole	.10
148	Rogers Hornsby	.20
149	Jose Cardenal	.10
150	Bobby Doerr	.10
151	Mickey Cochrane	.10
152	Gaylord Perry	.10
153	Frank Thomas	.10
154	Ted Williams	1.00
155	Sam McDowell	.10
156	Bob Feller	.20
157	Bert Campaneris	.10
158	Thornton Lee	.10
159	Gary Peters	.10
160	Joe Medwick	.10
161	Joe Nuxhall	.10
162	Joe Schultz	.10
163	Harmon Killebrew	.20
164	Bucky Walters	.10
165	Bobby Allison	.10
166	Lou Boudreau	.10
167	Joe Cronin	.10
168	Mike Torrez	.10
169	Rich Rollins	.10
170	Tony Cuccinello	.10
171	Hoyt Wilhelm	.10
172	Ernie Harwell	.10
173	George Foster	.10
174	Lou Gehrig	1.50
175	Dave Kingman	.10
176	Babe Ruth	2.00
177	Joe Black	.10
178	Roy Face	.10
179	Earl Weaver	.10
180	Johnny Mize	.10
181	Roger Cramer	.10
182	Jim Piersall	.10
183	Ned Garver	.10
184	Billy Williams	.10
185	Lefty Grove	.10
186	Jim Grant	.10
187	Elmer Valo	.10
188	Ewell Blackwell	.10
189	Mel Ott	.10
190	Harry Walker	.10
191	Bill Campbell	.10
192	Walter Johnson	.40
193	Jim "Catfish" Hunter	.10
194	Charlie Keller	.10
195	Hank Greenberg	.40
196	Bobby Murcer	.10
197	Al Lopez	.10
198	Vida Blue	.10
199	Shag Crawford	.10
200	Arky Vaughan	.10
201	Smoky Burgess	.10
202	Rip Sewell	.10
203	Earl Averill	.10
204	Milt Pappas	.10
205	Mel Harder	.10
206	Sam Jethroe	.10
207	Randy Hundley	.10
208	Jessie Haines	.10
209	Jack Brickhouse	.10
210	Whitey Ford	.20
211	Honus Wagner	1.25
212	Phil Niekro	.10
213	Gary Bell	.10
214	Jon Matlack	.10
215	Moe Drabowsky	.10
216	Edd Roush	.10
217	Joel Horlen	.10
218	Casey Stengel	.20
219	Burt Hooton	.10
220	Joe Jackson	3.00
----	Checklist	2.00

1990 Pacific Legends

Hank Aaron
OUTFIELDER

The cards in this 110-card set feature the same style as the previous Pacific Legends releases. The cards were available in wax packs as well as in complete set form. Several players found in the first two legends releases are also found in this issue along with new players.

		NM/M
Complete Set (110):		10.00
Common Player:		.10
Wax Pack (10):		.50
Wax Box (36):		12.50
1	Hank Aaron	2.00
2	Tommie Agee	.10
3	Luke Appling	.20
4	Sal Bando	.10
5	Ernie Banks	1.00
6	Don Baylor	.10
7	Yogi Berra	.75
8	Vida Blue	.10
9	Lou Boudreau	.10
10	Clete Boyer	.10
11	George Bamberger	.10
12	Lou Brock	.30
13	Ralph Branca	.10
14	Carl Erskine	.10
15	Bert Campaneris	.10
16	Steve Carlton	.50
17	Rod Carew	.50
18	Rocky Colovito	.40
19	Frank Crosetti	.10
20	Larry Doby	.20
21	Bobby Doerr	.10
22	Walt Dropo	.10
23	Rick Ferrell	.10
24	Joe Garagiola	.50
25	Ralph Garr	.10
26	Dick Groat	.10
27	Steve Garvey	.40
28	Bob Gibson	.50
29	Don Drysdale	.40
30	Billy Herman	.10
31	Bobby Grich	.10
32	Monte Irvin	.20
33	Dave Johnson	.10
34	Don Kessinger	.10
35	Harmon Killebrew	.50
36	Ralph Kiner	.20
37	Vern Law	.10
38	Ed Lopat	.20
39	Bill Mazeroski	.40
40	Rick Monday	.10
41	Manny Mota	.10
42	Don Newcombe	.20
43	Gaylord Perry	.20
44	Jim Piersall	.20
45	Johnny Podres	.20
46	Boog Powell	.20
47	Robin Roberts	.20
48	Ron Santo	.30
49	Herb Score	.20
50	Enos Slaughter	.20
51	Warren Spahn	.50
52	Rusty Staub	.20
53	Frank Torre	.10
54	Bob Horner	.10
55	Lee May	.10
56	Bill White	.20
57	Hoyt Wilhelm	.10
58	Billy Williams	.20
59	Ted Williams	1.50
60	Tom Seaver	.40
61	Carl Yastrzemski	.75
62	Marv Throneberry	.10
63	Steve Stone	.10
64	Rico Petrocelli	.10
65	Orlando Cepeda	.30
66	Eddie Mathews	.50
67	Joe Sewell	.10
68	Jim "Catfish" Hunter	.20
69	Alvin Dark	.10
70	Richie Ashburn	.30
71	Dusty Baker	.10
72	George Foster	.10
73	Eddie Yost	.10
74	Buddy Bell	.10
75	Manny Sanguillen	.10
76	Jim Bunning	.20
77	Smoky Burgess	.10
78	Al Rosen	.20
79	Gene Conley	.10
80	Dave Dravecky	.10
81	Charlie Gehringer	.20
82	Billy Pierce	.10
83	Willie Horton	.10
84	Ron Hunt	.10
85	Bob Feller	.40
86	George Kell	.20
87	Dave Kingman	.20
88	Jerry Koosman	.10
89	Clem Labine	.10
90	Tony LaRussa	.20
91	Dennis Leonard	.10
92	Dale Long	.10
93	Sparky Lyle	.10
94	Gil McDougald	.10
95	Don Mossi	.10
96	Phil Niekro	.10
97	Tom Paciorek	.10
98	Mel Parnell	.10
99	Lou Pinella	.20
100	Bobby Richardson	.20
101	Phil Rizzuto	.60
102	Brooks Robinson	.40
103	Pete Runnels	.10
104	Diego Segui	.10
105	Bobby Shantz	.10
106	Bobby Thomson	.10
107	Joe Torre	.30
108	Earl Weaver	.10
109	Willie Wilson	.10
110	Jesse Barfield	.10

1990 Pacific Senior League

An early supporter of the short-lived "old-timers" league, Pacific issued a card set depicting the players of the Senior Professional Baseball Association. Sold in wax packs as well as complete boxed sets, the cards have silver borders on front with yellow stars above and to the right of the player photo. Color team logos are at bottom-left. Red, white and blue backs have appropriate logos, card number, a few biographical details and a short career summary in a horizontal format. The cards were issued with a set of 15 team logo stickers with a puzzle back. Shades of the 1989 Fleer Billy Ripken card, the card of Jim Nettles contains a photo which shows a vulgarity written on the knob of his bat. A cleaned-up version was issued later, and is much scarcer. Many other errors from the regular-edition set were corrected in a glossy edition of 20,000 complete sets, while several new errors were created.

		NM/M
Complete Set (220):		4.00
Common Player:		.05
Glossy:		2X
1	Bobby Tolan	.05
2	Sergio Ferrer	.05
3	David Rajsich	.05
4	Ron LeFlore	.05
5	Steve Henderson	.05
6	Jerry Martin	.05
7	Gary Rajsich	.05
8	Elias Sosa	.05
9	Jon Matlack	.05
10	Steve Kemp	.05
11	Lenny Randle	.05
12	Roy Howell	.05
13	Milt Wilcox	.05
14	Alan Bannister	.05
15	Dock Ellis	.05
16	Mike Williams	.05
17	Luis Gomez	.05
18	Joe Sambito	.05
19	Bake McBride	.05
20a	Pat Zachry (Photo actually Dick Bosman)	
20b	Dick Bosman	.05
21	Dwight Lowry	.05
22	Ozzie Virgil Sr.	.05
23	Randy Lerch	.05
24	Butch Benton	.05
25	Tom Zimmer	.05
26a	Al Holland (Photo actually Nardi Contreras.)	.05
26b	Nardi Contreras	.10
27	Sammy Stewart	.05
28	Bill Lee	.05
29	Ferguson Jenkins	.50
30	Leon Roberts	.05
31	Rick Wise	.05
32	Butch Hobson	.05
33	Pete LaCock	.05
34	Bill Campbell	.05
35	Doug Simunic	.05
36	Mario Guerrero	.05
37	Jim Willoughby	.05
38	Joe Pittman	.05
39	Mark Bomback	.05
40	Tommy McMillian	.05
41	Gary Allanson	.05
42	Cecil Cooper	.10
43	John LaRosa	.05
44	Darrell Brandon	.05
45	Bernie Carbo	.05
46	Mike Cuellar	.10
47	Al Bumbry	.05
48a	Gene Richards (Photo actually Tony Scott.)	.05
49b	Tony Scott	.05
49	Pedro Borbon	.05
50	Julio Solo	.05
51a	Ed Nottle (Back reads Sun Sox.)	.05
51b	Ed Nottle (Back reads Super Sox.)	.10
52	Jim Bibby	.05
53	Doug Griffin	.05
54	Ed Clements	.05
55	Dalton Jones	.05
56	Earl Weaver	.25
57	Jesus DeLaRosa	.05
58	Paul Casanova	.05
59	Frank Riccelli	.05
60	Rafael Landestoy	.05
61	George Hendrick	.05
62	Cesar Cedeno	.10
63	Bert Campaneris	.10
64	Derrel Thomas	.05
65	Bobby Ramos	.05
66	Grant Jackson	.05
67	Steve Whitaker	.05
68	Pedro Ramos	.05
69	Joe Hicks	.05
70	Taylor Duncan	.05
71	Tom Shopay	.05
72	Ken Clay	.05
73	Mike Kekich	.05
74	Ed Halicki	.05
75	Ed Figueroa	.05
76	Paul Blair	.05
77	Luis Tiant	.10
78	Stan Bahnsen	.05
79	Rennie Stennett	.05
80	Bobby Molinaro	.05
81	Jim Gideon	.05
82	Orlando Gonzalez	.05
83	Amos Otis	.05
84	Dennis Leonard	.05
85	Pat Putman	.05
86	Rick Manning	.05
87	Pat Dobson	.05
88	Marty Castillo	.05
89	Steve McCatty	.05
90	Doug Bird	.05
91	Rick Waits	.05
92	Ron Jackson	.05
93	Tim Hosley	.05
94	Steve Luebber	.05
95	Rich Gale	.05
96	Champ Summers	.05
97	Dave LaRoche	.05
98	Bobby Jones	.05
99	Kim Allen	.05
100	Wayne Garland	.05
101	Tom Spencer	.05
102	Dan Driessen	.05
103	Ron Pruitt	.05
104	Tim Ireland	.05
105	Dan Driessen	.05
106	Pepe Frias	.05
107	Eric Rasmussen	.05
108	Don Hood	.05
109a	Joe Coleman (Photo actually Tony Torchia.)	.05
109b	Tony Torchia	.10
110	Jim Slaton	.05
111	Clint Hurdle	.05
112	Larry Milbourne	.05
113	Al Holland	.05
114	George Foster	.10
115	Graig Nettles	.05
116	Oscar Gamble	.05
117	Ross Grimsley	.05
118	Bill Travers	.05
119	Jose Beniquez	.05
120a	Jerry Grote/IA	.05
120b	Jerry Grote/Catcher	.05
121	John D'Acquisto	.05
122	Tom Murphy	.05
123	Walt Williams	.05
124	Roy Thomas	.05
125a	Jerry Grote (Photo actually Fred Stanley.)	.05
125b	Fred Stanley (Jerry Grote back.)	.10
126a	Jim Nettles (Vulgarity on bat knob.)	.50
126b	Jim Nettles (no vulgarity)	3.00
127	Randy Niemann	.05
128a	Bobby Bonds	.10
128b	Bobby Bonds (No name/position on front.)	.50
129	Ed Glynn	.05
130	Ed Hicks	.05
131	Ivan Murrell	.05
132	Graig Nettles	.10
133	Hal McRae	.20
134	Pat Kelly	.05
135	Sammy Stewart	.05
136	Bruce Kison	.05
137	Jim Morrison	.05
138	Omar Moreno	.05
139	Tom Brown	.05
140	Steve Dillard	.05
141	Gary Alexander	.05
142	Al Oliver	.10
143	Rick Lysander	.05
144	Tippy Martinez	.05
145	Al Cowens	.05
146	Gene Clines	.05
147	Willie Aikens	.05
148	Tommy Moore	.05
149	Clete Boyer	.05
150	Stan Cliburn	.05
151	Ken Kravec	.05
152	Garth Iorg	.05
153	Rick Peterson	.05
154	Wayne Nordhagen	.05
155	Danny Meyer	.05
156	Wayne Garrett	.05
157	Wayne Krenchicki	.05
158	Graig Nettles	.10
159	Earl Stephenson	.05
160	Carl Taylor	.05
161	Rollie Fingers	.50
162	Toby Harrah	.10
163	Mickey Rivers	.05
164	Dave Kingman	.10
165	Paul Mirabella	.05
166	Dick Williams	.05
167	Luis Pujols	.05
168	Tito Landrum	.05
169	Tom Underwood	.05
170	Mark Wagner	.05
171	Odell Jones	.05
172	Doug Capilla	.05
173	Alfie Rondon	.05
174	Lowell Palmer	.05
175	Juan Eichelberger	.05
176	Wes Clements	.05
177	Rodney Scott	.05
178	Ron Washington	.05
179	Al Hrabosky	.05
180	Sid Monge	.05
181	Randy Johnson	.05
182	Tim Stoddard	.05
183	Dick Williams	.05
184	Lee Lacy	.05
185	Jerry White	.05
186	Dave Kingman	.10
187	Checklist 1-110	.05
188	Jose Cruz	.10
189	Jamie Easterly	.05
190	Ike Blessit	.05
191	Johnny Grubb	.05
192	Dave Cash	.05
193	Doug Corbett	.05
194	Bruce Bochy	.05
195	Mark Corey	.05
196	Gil Rondon	.05
197	Jerry Martin	.05
198	Gerry Pirtle	.05
199	Gates Brown	.05
200	Bob Galasso	.05
201	Bake McBride	.05
202	Wayne Granger	.05
203	Larry Milbourne	.05
204	Tom Paciorek	.05
205	U.L. Washington	.05
206	Larvell Blanks	.05
207	Bob Shirley	.05
208	Pete Falcone	.05
209	Sal Butera	.05
210	Roy Branch	.05
211	Dyar Miller	.05
212	Paul Siebert	.05
213	Ken Reitz	.05
214	Bill Madlock	.10
215	Vida Blue	.15
216	Dave Hilton	.05
217	Pedro Ramos, Charlie Bree	.05
218	Checklist 111-220	.05
219	Pat Dobson, Earl Weaver	.25
220	Curt Flood	.15

ABBREVIATIONS

IA - In Action

1991 Pacific Senior League

In 1991 Pacific Trading Cards produced its second set of cards of Senior Professional Baseball Association players. The cards feature color photos on the front, with the player's name and position along the bottom, and team nickname and logo on a banner vertically on the left side. There are 160 cards in the glossy set, with some multi-player and in-action cards included. For reasons unknown, some of the cards (including those of Rice, Fingers, Blue, Dave Cash, Dan Norman, Ron LeFlore, Cesar Cedeno, Rafael Landestoy and Dan Driessen) were apparently printed in two versions.

	NM/M
Complete Set (160):	3.00
Common Player:	.05
1 Dan Driessen	.05
2 Marty Castillo	.05
3 Jerry White	.05
4 Bud Anderson	.05
5 Ron Jackson	.05
6 Fred Stanley	.05
7 Steve Luebber	.05
8 Jery Terrell	.05
9 Pat Dobson	.05
10 Ken Kravec	.05
11 Gil Rondon	.05
12 Dyar Miller	.05
13 Bobby Molinaro	.05
14 Jerry Martin	.05
15 Rick Waits	.05
16 Steve McCatty	.05
17 Roger Slagle	.05
18 Mike Ramsey	.05
19 Rich Gale	.05
20 Larry Harlow	.05
21 Dan Rohn	.05
22 Don Cooper	.05
23 Marv Foley	.05
24 Rafael Landestoy	.05
25 Eddie Milner	.05
26a Amos Otis (Green jersey pose.)	.05
26b Amos Otis (White jersey action.)	.05
27 Odell Jones	.05
28 Tippy Martinez	.05
29 Stu Cliburn	.05
30 Stan Cliburn	.05
31 Tony Cloninger	.05
32 Jeff Jones	.05
33 Ken Reitz	.05
34 Dave Sax	.05
35 Orlando Gonzalez	.05
36 Jose Cruz	.10
37 Mickey Mahler	.05
38 Derek Botelho	.05
39 Rick Lysander	.05
40 Cesar Cedeno	.10
41 Garth Iorg	.05
42 Wayne Krenchicki	.05
43 Clete Boyer	.05
44 Dan Boone	.05
45 George Vukovich	.05
46 Omar Moreno	.05
47 Ron Washington	.05
48 Ron Washington/MVP	.05
49 Rick Peterson	.05
50 Tack Wilson	.05
51 Stan Cliburn, Stu Cliburn	.05
52 Rick Lysander (POY)	.05
53 Cesar Cedeno, Pete LaCock	.05
54 Jim Marshall, Clete Boyer	.05
55 Doug Simunic	.05
56 Pat Kelly	.05
57 Roy Branch	.05
58 Dave Cash	.05
59 Bobby Jones	.05
60 Hector Cruz	.05
61 Reggie Cleveland	.05
62 Gary Lance	.05

63 Ron LeFlore	.05
64 Dan Norman	.05
65 Renie Martin	.05
66 Pete Mackanin	.05
67 Frank Riccelli	.05
68 Alfie Rondon	.05
69 Rodney Scott	.05
70 Jim Tracy	.05
71 Ed Dennis	.05
72 Rick Lindell	.05
73 Stu Pepper	.05
74 Jeff Youngbauer	.05
75 Russ Foster	.05
76 Jeff Capriati	.05
77 Art DeFreites	.05
78 Alfie Rondon/Action	.05
79 Reggie Cleveland/Action	.05
80 Dave Cash/Action	.05
81 Vida Blue	.15
82 Ed Glynn	.05
83 Bob Owchinko	.05
84 Bill Fleming	.05
85 Ron Roenicke, Gary Roenicke	.05
86 Tom Thompson	.05
87 Derrell Thomas	.05
88 Jim Willoughby	.05
89 Jim Pankovits	.05
90 Jack Cooley	.05
91 Lenn Sakata	.05
92 Mike Brocki	.05
93 Chuck Fick	.05
94 Tom Benedict	.05
95 Anthony Davis	.05
96 Cardell Camper	.05
97 Leon Roberts	.05
98 Roger Erickson	.05
99 Kim Allen	.05
100 Dave Skaggs	.05
101 Joe Decker	.05
102 U.L. Washington	.05
103 Don Fletcher	.05
104 Gary Roenicke	.05
105 Rich Dauer	.05
106 Ron Roenicke	.05
107 Mike Norris	.05
108 Ferguson Jenkins	.50
109 Ronn Reynolds	.05
110 Pete Falcone	.05
111 Gary Allenson	.05
112 Mark Wagner	.05
113 Jack Lazorko	.05
114 Bob Galasso	.05
115 Ron Davis	.05
116 Lenny Randle	.05
117 Ricky Peters	.05
118 Jim Dwyer	.05
119 Juan Eichelberger	.05
120 Pete LaCock	.05
121 Tony Scott	.05
122 Rick Lancellotti	.05
123 Barry Bonnell	.05
124 Dave Hilton	.05
125 Bill Campbell	.05
126 Rollie Fingers	.50
127 Jim Marshall	.05
128 Razor Shines	.05
129 Guy Sularz	.05
130 Roy Thomas	.05
131 Joel Youngblood	.05
132 Ernie Camacho	.05
133 Dave Hilton, Jim Marshall, Fred Stanley	.05
134 Ken Landreaux	.05
135 Dave Rozema	.05
136 Tom Zimmer	.05
137 Elias Sosa	.05
138 Ozzie Virgil Sr.	.05
139 Al Holland	.05
140 Milt Wilcox	.05
141 Jerry Reed	.05
142 Chris Welch	.05
143 Luis Gomez	.05
144 Steve Henderson	.05
145 Butch Benton	.05
146 Bill Lee	.05
147 Todd Cruz	.05
148 Jim Rice	.45
149 Tito Landrum	.05
150 Ozzie Virgil Jr.	.05
151 Joe Pittman	.05
152 Bobby Tolan	.05
153 Len Barker	.05
154 Dave Rajsich	.05
155 Glenn Gulliver	.05
156 Gary Rajsich	.05
157 Joe Sambito	.05
158 Frank Vito	.05
159 Ozzie Virgil Sr., Ozzie Virgil Jr.	.05
160 Dave Rajsich, Gary Rajsich	.05

1991 Pacific Nolan Ryan

The career and family life of Nolan Ryan (to 1991) were the subject matter of this 110-card set by Pacific Trading Card Co. Sold in both foil packs and factory sets, the cards have a UV-coated front featuring a photo flanked on the left by "Nolan Ryan" print-

ed vertically in a color accent stripe. At lower left is a flaming baseball "Texas Express" logo. A photo caption appears beneath the photo. On back the blazing ball motif is repeated, with a photo or career highlights in its center.

	NM/M
Factory Set (110):	8.00
Complete Set (110):	5.00
Common Card:	.10
Wax Pack (12):	.50
Wax Box (36):	12.00
1 Future Hall of Famer	.10
2 From Little League to the Major Leagues	.10
3 A Dream Come True	.10
4 Signed by the Mets	.10
5 Fireball Pitcher	.10
6 Mets Rookie Pitcher	.10
7 First Major League Win	.10
8 Early in 1969	.10
9 Tensions of a Pennant Race	.10
10 Mets Clinch NL East	.10
11 Keep the Ball Down	.10
12 Playoff Victory	.10
13 World Series Victory	.10
14 The Amazin' Mets	.10
15 Met Strikeout Record	.10
16 One of the Worst Trades in Baseball	.10
17 Slow Start with Mets	.10
18 Pitcher New York Mets	.10
19 Traded to the Angels	.10
20 Meeting New Friends	.10
21 Throwing Fast Balls	.10
22 Move the Ball Around	.10
23 Nolan Heat	.10
24 No-Hitter Number 1	.10
25 Looking Back on Number 1	.10
26 No-Hitter Number 2	.10
27 Single Season Strikeout Record	.10
28 21 Wins in 1973	.10
29 Fastest Pitch Ever Thrown at 100.9 MPH	.10
30 No-Hitter Number 3	.10
31 No-Hitter Number 4	.10
32 Ryan and Tanana	.10
33 Learning Change-Up	.10
34 Pitcher California Angels	.10
35 Nolan Joins Astros	.10
36 Starting Pitcher Nolan Ryan	.10
37 Taking Batting Practice	.10
38 The Game's Greatest Power Pitcher	.10
39 3000 Career Strikeouts	.10
40 A Ryan Home Run	.10
41 The Fast Ball Grip	.10
42 Record 5th No-Hitter	.10
43 No-Hitter Number 5	.10
44 A Dream Fulfilled	.10
45 Nolan Passes Walter Johnson	.10
46 Strikeout 4000	.10
47 Astros Win Western Division Title	.10
48 Pitcher Houston Astros	.10
49 Milestone Strikeouts	.10
50 Post Season Participant	.10
51 Hurling for Houston	.10
52 135 N.L. Wins	.10
53 Through with Chew	.10
54 Signed by Rangers 1989	.10
55 Pleasant Change for Nolan	.10
56 Real Special Moment	.10
57 1989 All-Star Game	.10
58 Pitching in 1989 All-Star Game	.10
59 5000 Strikeouts; A Standing Ovation	.10
60 Great Moments in 1989	.10
61 Nolan with Dan Smith, Rangers First Pic	.10
62 Ranger Club Record 16 Strikeouts	.10
63 Last Pitch No-Hitter Number 6	.10
64 Sweet Number 6	.10

65 Oldest to Throw No-Hitter	.10
66 Another Ryan Win	.10
67 20th Pitcher to Win 300	.10
68 300 Win Battery	.10
69 300 Game Winner	.10
70 Perfect Mechanics	.10
71 22 Seasons with 100 or more Strikeouts	.10
72 11th Strikeout Title	.10
73 232 Strikeouts, 1990	.10
74 The 1990 Season	.10
75 Pitcher Texas Rangers	.10
76 1991, Nolan's 25th Season	.10
77 Throwing Spirals	.10
78 Running the Steps	.10
79 Hard Work and Conditioning	.10
80 The Rigid Workout	.10
81 Ryan's Routine	.10
82 Ryan's Routine Between Starts	.10
83 Running in Outfield	.10
84 B.P. in Texas	.10
85 18 Career Low-Hitters	.10
86 My Job is to Give My Team/Chance to Win	.10
87 The Spring Workout	.10
88 Power versus Power	.10
89 Awesome Power	.10
90 Blazing Speed	.10
91 The Pick Off	.10
92 Real Gamer	.10
93 Ranger Battery Mates	.10
94 The Glare	.10
95 The High Leg Kick	.10
96 Day Off	.10
97 A New Ball	.10
98 Going to Rosin Bag	.10
99 Time for Relief	.10
100 Lone Star Legend	.10
101 Fans' Favorite	.10
102 Watching Nolan Pitch	.10
103 Our Family of Five	.10
104 Texas Beefmaster	.10
105 Gentleman Rancher	.10
106 Texas Cowboy Life	.10
107 The Ryan Family	.10
108 Participating in Cutting Horse Contest	.10
109 Nolan Interviews	.10
110 Lynn Nolan Ryan	.10

Milestones

No-Hitter #1

Issued as inserts in the 1991 Nolan Ryan foil packs was this set of eight career highlight cards. The format is basically the same as the regular-issue cards, except that the inserts are bordered in either silver (edition of 10,000) or gold (edition of 1,000). The unnumbered cards are checklisted here in chronological order. The inserts were found only in foil and wax packs.

	NM/M
Complete Set, Silver (8):	50.00
Complete Set, Gold (8):	65.00
Common Card, Silver:	7.50
Common Card, Gold:	12.00
(1a) Rookie Pitcher/Silver	7.50
(1b) Rookie Pitcher/Gold	12.00
(2a) No-Hitter 1/Silver	7.50
(2b) No-Hitter 1/Gold	12.00
(3a) No-Hitter 2/Silver	7.50
(3b) No-Hitter 2/Gold	12.00
(4a) No-Hitter 3/Silver	7.50
(4b) No-Hitter 3/Gold	12.00
(5a) No-Hitter 4/Silver	7.50
(5b) No-Hitter 4/Gold	12.00
(6a) No-Hitter 5/Silver	7.50
(6b) No-Hitter 5/Gold	12.00
(7a) Sweet 6/Silver	7.50
(7b) Sweet 6/Gold	12.00
(8a) 25th Season/Silver	7.50
(8b) 25th Season/Gold	12.00

7th No-Hitter

Number Seven

On May 1, 1991, before the home crowd at Arlington, Nolan Ryan posted his seventh career no-hitter, blanking the Blue Jays. In commemoration of the event, Pacific produced a seven-card insert set for random inclusion in its Nolan Ryan "Texas Express" foil packs. Each card was produced in an edition of 10,000 silver-foil bordered cards and 1,000 with gold-foil borders. The design follows the basic format of the regular Ryan issue, with the flaming baseball series logo at lower-left on the front, the card's title in a colored stripe beneath the photo, and Ryan's name printed vertically in a colored stripe at left. Backs repeat the flaming ball design at center, containing information about the no-hitter.

	NM/M
Complete Set, Silver (7):	50.00
Complete Set, Gold (7):	125.00
Common Card, Silver:	12.00
Common Card, Gold:	25.00
1a Last Pitch/Silver	12.00
1b Last Pitch/Gold	25.00
2a No-Hitter #7/Silver	12.00
2b No-Hitter-#7/Gold	25.00
3a The Best/Silver	12.00
3b The Best/Gold	25.00
4a Time to Celebrate/Silver	12.00
4b Time to Celebrate/Gold	25.00
5a Congratulations from Rangers Fans/Silver	12.00
5b Congratulations from Rangers Fans/Gold	25.00
6a Catcher Mike Stanley/Silver	12.00
6b Catcher Mike Stanley/Gold	25.00
7a All in a Day's Work/Silver	12.00
7b All in a Day's Work/Gold	25.00

7th No-Hitter Hologram

No-Hitter #7

Even more elusive and exclusive than the gold- and silver-foil bordered "7th No-Hitter" inserts found in wax and foil packs was this edition produced with gold and silver holographic borders (1,000 each in gold and silver. The hologram 7th No-Hitter inserts were found only in 99-cent cello packs.

	NM/M
Complete Set, Silver (7):	300.00
Complete Set, Gold (7):	300.00
Common Card, Silver:	50.00
Common Card, Gold:	50.00
1a Last Pitch/Silver	50.00
1b Last Pitch/Gold	50.00
2a No-Hitter #7/Silver	50.00
2b No-Hitter #7/Gold	50.00
3a The Best/Silver	50.00
3b The Best/Gold	50.00
4a Time to Celebrate/Silver	50.00
4b Time to Celebrate/Gold	50.00
5a Congratulations from Rangers Fans/Silver	50.00
5b Congratulations from Rangers Fans/Gold	50.00
6a Catcher Mike Stanley/Silver	50.00
6b Catcher Mike Stanley/Gold	50.00
7a All in a Day's Work/Silver	50.00
7b All in a Day's Work/Gold	50.00

1992 Pacific Nolan Ryan

The 1992 Nolan Ryan "Texas Express" Series 2 is numbered 111 to 220, featuring the same design as the original 110-card issue of 1991. The set includes photos of Ryan from boyhood to his seventh no-hitter, and two bonus subsets were also randomly inserted in the foil packs.

	NM/M
Complete Set (110):	6.00
Common Player:	.10
111 The Golden Arm	.10
112 Little League All-Star	.10
113 All-State Pitcher	.10
114 Nolan Ryan Field	.10
115 Nolan at Age 20	.10
116 Nolan Ryan Jacksonville Suns	.10
117 Surrounded By Friends	.10
118 Nolan the Cowboy	.10
119 The Simple Life	.10
120 Nolan Loves Animals	.10
121 Growing Up in New York	.10
122 New York Strikeout Record	.10
123 Traded	.10
124 Hall of Fame Victims	.10
125 Number 500	.10
126 California Victory	.10
127 20 Win Season	.10
128 Throwing Heat	.10
129 Strikeout Record	.10
130 Number One	.10
131 1,000th Strikeout	.10
132 Number Two	.10
133 2,000th Strikeout	.10
134 Number Three	.10
135 Pure Speed	.10
136 Independence Day Fireworks	.10
137 Fast Ball Pitcher	.10
138 Number Four	.10
139 Free Agent	.10
140 Houston Bound	.10
141 Big Dollars	.10
142 Strong Houston Staff	.10
143 Number Five	.10
144 Astro MVP	.10
145 Western Division Game	.10
146 National League All-Star	.10
147 Major League Record	.10
148 Nolan Breaks Johnson's Record	.10
149 Reese and Nolan	.10
150 100th National League Win	.10
151 4,000th Strikeout	.10
152 League Leader	.10
153 250th Career Win	.10
154 The Seldom of Swat	.10
155 4,500th Strikeout	.10
156 Like Father Like Son	.10
157 Spoiled in the Ninth	.10
158 Leaving Houston	.10
159 Houston Star	.10
160 Ryan Test Free Agency	.10
161 Awesome Heat	.10
162 Brotherly Love	.10
163 Astros Return	.10
164 Texas Size Decision	.10
165 Texas Legend	.10
166 Drawing a Crowd	.10
167 Great Start	.10
168 5,000th Strikeout	.10
169 Texas All-Star	.10
170 Number Six	.10
171 300th Win	.10
172 1990 League Leader	.10
173 Man of the Year	.10
174 Spring Training 1991	.10
175 Fast Ball Grip	.10
176 Strong Arm	.10
177 Stanley's Delight	.10

178	After Nolan's 7th No-Hitter	.10
179	Stretching Before the Game	.10
180	The Rangers Sign Nolan for 1992 and 199	.10
181	Heading to the Bullpen	.10
182	Nolan Ryan - Banker	.10
183	Time with Fans	.10
184	Solid 1992 Season	.10
185	Ranger Team Leader	.10
186	More Records	.10
187	Number Seven	.10
188	Nolan Passes Niekro	.10
189	Ryan Trails Sutton	.10
190	Ranger Strikeout Mark	.10
191	Consecutive K's	.10
192	5,500th Strikeout	.10
193	Twenty-Five First Timers	.10
194	No-Hitters Ended in the Ninth	.10
195	Constant Work-Outs	.10
196	Nolan in Motion	.10
197	Pitching in Fenway Park	.10
198	Goose and Nolan	.10
199	Talking Over Strategy	.10
200	Don't Mess With Texas	.10
201	314-278 Thru 1991	.10
202	All-Time Leader	.10
203	High Praise	.10
204	Manager's Delight	.10
205	733 Major League Starts	.10
206	Ryan the Quarterback	.10
207	Hard Work Pays Off	.10
208	Passing Along Wisdom	.10
209	Still Dominant	.10
210	Nolan's Fast Ball	.10
211	Seven No-Hitters	.10
212	Training for Perfection	.10
213	Nolan's Edge - Speed	.10
214	This One was for Them	.10
215	Another Day's Work	.10
216	Pick Off at Third	.10
217	Ready to Pitch	.10
218	Spring Training 1992	.10
219	Nolan Receives The Victor Award	.10
220	Nolan's 26th Season	.10

Gold Inserts

Pacific produced this insert set for the 1992 Nolan Ryan "Texas Express" sequel. There are eight different gold-foil bordered cards, one for each of Ryan's no-hitters, plus an additional card combining all seven. Design is similar to the 1991-92 Ryan cards from Pacific. Backs feature box scores of the no-hitters. The cards are unnumbered. According to the manufacturer, 10,000 of each insert were produced.

		NM/M
Complete Set (8):		65.00
Common Ryan:		10.00
(1)	Number One	10.00
(2)	Number Two	10.00
(3)	Number Three	10.00
(4)	Number Four	10.00
(5)	Number Five	10.00
(6)	Number Six	10.00
(7)	Number Seven	10.00
(8)	Seven No-Hitters	10.00

Limited

One of two insert sets included in both regular and jumbo foil packs of 1992 Pacific Nolan Ryan cards was this six-card presentation. Cards have the basic format of the regular issue except the "Texas Express" logo on front has been replaced by a Rangers team logo. Vertically formatted backs have a color photo at left and a few paragraphs of career summary at center. Each card was

printed in an edition of 3,000, and Ryan personally autographed 1,000 of card #1. A second version of these cards, without the words "Limited Edition" on back beneath the Rangers and MLB logos, was produced for inclusion in the July, 1992, issue of "Trading Cards" magazine. The magazine versions of these cards are worth about 10 percent of the inserts.

		NM/M
Complete Set (6):		30.00
Common Card:		7.50
1	Nolan Ryan	7.50
1a	Nolan Ryan/Auto.	90.00
2	Nolan Ryan	7.50
3	The Texas Express	7.50
4	Seventh No-Hitter	7.50
5	Texas Legacy	7.50
6	Quarter Century	7.50

1992 Pacific Tom Seaver

In a style similar to its popular Nolan Ryan sets, Pacific produced a Tom Seaver set of 110 cards in 1992. The company also produced two limited edition subsets as part of the "Tom Terrific" card series. Cards were sold in both foil packs and factory sets. UV-coated fronts have white borders with silver, violet or magenta highlight stripes. A baseball symbol at lower-left has "Tom" above and "Terrific" beneath. This image is duplicated on back, with the ball containing either a photo or career highlights.

		NM/M
Complete Set (110):		4.00
Common Player:		.05
1	Stand-out High School Basketball Player	.05
2	Pro Ball Player	.05
3	Destined to be a Met	.05
4	Brave or Met	.05
5	Mets Luck of the Draw	.05
6	Sent to Jacksonville	.05
7	First Major League Win	.05
8	1967 Rookie of the Year	.05
9	Humble Beginnings	.05
10	Predicting the Future	.05
11	Rookie All-Star	.05
12	16 Wins in 1968	.05
13	1968 N.L. All-Star	.05
14	The Amazing Mets	.05
15	1969 Cy Young Winner	.05
16	Pitcher of the Year	.05
17	Strikeout Leader	.05
18	Ties Major League Record	.05
19	Mr. Consistency	.05
20	Finishing in Style	.05
21	Twenty-Game Winner	.05
22	Second Cy Young Award	.05
23	Batting Star	.05

24	At Bat in the World Series	.05
25	Championship Series Record	.05
26	Injury Plagued Season	.05
27	Comeback	.05
28	Super September	.05
29	Sporting News All-Star	.05
30	Strikeout Record	.05
31	USC Alumni Star	.05
32	Winning Smile	.05
33	One-Hitter	.05
34	Traded to the Reds	.05
35	New York Mets Pitcher	.05
36	Winning with the Reds	.05
37	No-Hitter	.05
38	N.L. Leader	.05
39	Smooth Swing	.05
40	No Decision in the Championship Series	.05
41	Injury Shortened Season	.05
42	Bouncing Back	.05
43	Eighth All-Star Appearance	.05
44	Spring Training 1982	.05
45	Back to New York	.05
46	Cincinnati Reds Pitcher	.05
47	Back in the Big Apple	.05
48	Opening Day Star	.05
49	Not Much Run Support	.05
50	Pair of Shutouts	.05
51	4,000 Inning Mark	.05
52	One Season in New York	.05
53	Chicago Bound	.05
54	Chicago White Sox Pitcher	.05
55	Win 300	.05
56	16 Wins in 1985	.05
57	Blast From the Past	.05
58	Moving Up in the Record Book	.05
59	Cy Young Winners	.05
60	Two Legends of the Game	.05
61	Singing Praise	.05
62	300th Win Tribute	.05
63	The Seaver Family	.05
64	20th Major League Season	.05
65	Traded to the Red Sox	.05
66	Chicago White Sox Career Record	.05
67	Red Sox Man	.05
68	Boston Red Sox Pitcher	.05
69	One Last Try	.05
70	Major League Records	.05
71	Lowest N.L. Career ERA	.05
72	Pitching in Comiskey Park	.05
73	273 N.L. Wins	.05
74	300 Win Honors	.05
75	311 Major League Wins	.05
76	41 Retired	.05
77	Championship Series 2.84 ERA	.05
78	June 1976 Age 32	.05
79	8-Time N.L. All-Star	.05
80	Broadcasting Career	.05
81	300th Win Celebration	.05
82	Tom and Nolan	.05
83	4th Best ERA All-Time	.05
84	15th All-Time in Victories	.05
85	300 Win Club	.05
86	Hall of Fame	.05
87	Pitching in Wrigley Field	.05
88	Power Pitching	.05
89	Spring Training 1980	.05
90	Pitching in Riverfront Stadium 1980	.05
91	Tom Terrific	.05
92	Super Seaver	.05
93	Top 10 All-Time	.05
94	16 Opening Day Starts	.05
95	3,272 Strikeouts	.05
96	Six Opening Day Wins	.05
97	239 Innings Pitched in 1985	.05
98	A Day Off	.05
99	Concentration (You Can't Let Up)	.05
100	Velocity, Movement, and Location	.05
101	Strikeout King	.05
102	The Most Important Pitch	.05
103	Cincinnati Reds Number 41	.05
104	George Thomas Seaver	.05
105	Dazzling Dean of the Reds' Staff	.05
106	Tom Receives the Judge Emil Fuchs Award	.05
107	Boston Mound Ace	.05
108	Fly Ball to Center	.05
109	August 4, 1985 Yankee Stadium	.05
110	Breaking Walter Johnson's Record	.05

Milestones

Inserted into foil packs of its 1992 Seaver set, Pacific produced a gold-foil bordered set limited to 10,000 each of six different cards featuring career milestones. A white-bordered version of 3,000 cards each was also produced. One thousand of the "Rookie Phenomenon" cards were personally autographed by Seaver among the inserts. On each card, an action photo of Seaver is flanked at left with his name vertically printed in a fading color stripe. The "Tom Terrific" baseball logo carried is carried over from the regular set at lower-left. Backs have a second photo at left, and a summary of the career highlight.

		NM/M
Complete Set (6):		12.50
Complete Set, Gold (6):		15.00
Common Card:		2.50
Common Card, Gold:		3.50
1a	Rookie Phenomenon	2.50
1b	Rookie Phenomenon/ Gold	3.50
1c	Rookie Phenomenon (Auto. edition of 1,000.)	25.00
2a	Miracle Mets	2.50
2b	Miracle Mets/Gold	3.50
3a	Strikeout Record	2.50
3b	Strikeout Record/Gold	3.50
4a	No-Hitter	2.50
4b	No-Hitter/Gold	3.50
5a	300th Win	2.50
5b	300th Win/Gold	3.50
6a	Hall of Fame	2.50
6b	Hall of Fame/Gold	3.50

1993 Pacific Nolan Ryan 27th Season

Pacific marked the record-breaking 27th season of Nolan Ryan's career by re-issuing all 220 cards in its popular Nolan Ryan set with a special logo. The first series of the set (110 cards) had been issued in 1991 and the second series was issued in 1992 and numbered 111-220. In 1993 the company released a 30-card update for the pitcher's final season, complete with the special logo. Later the company decided to reissue cards 1-220 with the same logo because of the demand for the cards. Refer to 1991 and 1992 sets for card 1-220 checklists.

		NM/M
Complete Set (250):		10.00
Common Player:		.10
221	Rangers' Opening Night	.10
222	Slow Start in 1992	.10
223	Still Productive	.10

224	Getting Hot	.10
225	Closing Strong	.10
226	No Decision	.10
227	No Run Support	.10
228	Two Complete Games	.10
229	8-2/3 Inning Shutout	.10
230	Multiple Stikeout Games	.10
231	Ejected	.10
232	319 and Counting	.10
233	Strikeout	.10
234	24 of 26 Seasons	.10
235	Smile, Nolan	.10
236	Texas Ranger Marks	.10
237	Ranger Ace	.10
238	Another Record	.10
239	6th Place All-Time Innings Pitched	.10
240	27 Games Started in 1992	.10
241	Seaver & Ryan	.10
242	Angels' Number 30 Retired	.10
243	Angels' Nolan Ryan Night	.10
244	Angels' Hall of Fame	.10
245	Great Friends	.10
246	Cowboys	.10
247	Spring Training	.10
248	Smokin' Fastball	.10
249	The Texas Express	.10
250	Pacific Pride	.10

Limited

Continuing with its "Limited Edition" insert set from the 1992 Nolan Ryan issue, this insert set picks up with numbers 7-12, featuring 1992 highlights in Ryan's career.

	NM/M
Complete Set (6):	20.00
Common Player:	5.00
7-12 Nolan Ryan	5.00

Limited Gold

A gold-foil bordered version of the six 1993 Nolan Ryan "Limited Edition" insert cards was created as a card show give-away and random pack insert. Gold versions of cards #7-9 were given out at a Bellevue, Wash., show, while gold cards of #10-12 were found in foil packs. Just 3,000 of each foil-pack insert was produced.

	NM/M
Complete Set (6):	35.00
Common Player:	7.50
7-12 Nolan Ryan	7.50

Prism

An insert set unique to the 1993 Pacific Nolan Ryan 27th Season set was this issue of 20 prism cards. Fronts feature an action photo of Ryan against a prismatic background. Backs have another photo and a few brief bio-

graphical notes on a marbled background. Each prism card was produced in a silver edition of 10,000, a gold edition of 1,500 and a gold-edition uncut sheet of 20 cards serially numbered to 1,000. The prism cards were inserted into 25-cent foil packs of Pacific's 1993 Nolan Ryan issue.

		NM/M
Complete Set (Silver)(20):		55.00
Common Card (Silver):		3.50
1	Nolan Ryan/Silver	3.50
1a	Nolan Ryan/Gold	6.00
2	Nolan Ryan/Silver	3.50
2a	Nolan Ryan/Gold	6.00
3	Nolan Ryan/Silver	3.50
3a	Nolan Ryan/Gold	6.00
4	Nolan Ryan/Silver	3.50
4a	Nolan Ryan/Gold	6.00
5	Nolan Ryan/Silver	3.50
5a	Nolan Ryan/Gold	6.00
6	Nolan Ryan/Silver	3.50
6a	Nolan Ryan/Gold	6.00
7	Nolan Ryan/Silver	3.50
7a	Nolan Ryan/Gold	6.00
8	Nolan Ryan/Silver	3.50
8a	Nolan Ryan/Gold	6.00
9	Nolan Ryan/Silver	3.50
9a	Nolan Ryan/Gold	6.00
10	Nolan Ryan/Silver	3.50
10a	Nolan Ryan/Gold	6.00
11	Nolan Ryan/Silver	3.50
11a	Nolan Ryan/Gold	6.00
12	Nolan Ryan/Silver	3.50
12a	Nolan Ryan/Gold	6.00
13	Nolan Ryan/Silver	3.50
13a	Nolan Ryan/Gold	6.00
14	Nolan Ryan/Silver	3.50
14a	Nolan Ryan/Gold	6.00
15	Nolan Ryan/Silver	3.50
15a	Nolan Ryan/Gold	6.00
16	Nolan Ryan/Silver	3.50
16a	Nolan Ryan/Gold	6.00
17	Nolan Ryan/Silver	3.50
17a	Nolan Ryan/Gold	6.00
18	Nolan Ryan/Silver	3.50
18a	Nolan Ryan/Gold	6.00
19	Nolan Ryan/Silver	3.50
19a	Nolan Ryan/Gold	6.00
20	Nolan Ryan/Silver	3.50
20a	Nolan Ryan/Gold	6.00
Complete Set (Gold)(20):		85.00
Common Card (Gold):		6.00
Uncut Sheeet (Gold):		110.00

1993 Pacific/ McCormick Nolan Ryan Milestones

No-Hitter #1

Great moments in Nolan Ryan's career are featured in this set produced by Pacific for McCormick & Co., a food products company. Fronts feature similar to several of Pacific's other Ryan issues and include a "Farewell to a Legend" logo in the lower-left corner. The career highlight represented by the photo is named in a red strip at bottom. Backs share an action photo of Ryan over which are printed stats, information about the highlight or other data. Sponsors' logos are in the corners. Cards are UV coated on both sides.

		NM/M
Complete Set (21):		7.50
Common Player:		.50
1	No-Hitter #1 (Nolan Ryan)	.50
2	No-Hitter #2 (Nolan Ryan)	.50
3	No-Hitter #3 (Nolan Ryan)	.50
4	No-Hitter #4 (Nolan Ryan)	.50
5	No-Hitter #5 (Nolan Ryan)	.50
6	Last Pitch No-Hitter #6 (Nolan Ryan)	.50
7	No-Hitter #7 (Nolan Ryan)	.50
8	1st Strikeout (Nolan Ryan)	.50
9	1,000 Strikeout (Nolan Ryan)	.50
10	2,000 Strikeout (Nolan Ryan)	.50
11	3,000 Strikeout (Nolan Ryan)	.50
12	Nolan Breaks Johnson's Record (Nolan Ryan)	.50
13	4,000 Strikeout (Nolan Ryan)	.50
14	5,000 Strikeout (Nolan Ryan)	.50
15	5,500th Strikeout (Nolan Ryan)	.50
16	First Major League Win (Nolan Ryan)	.50
17	250th Career Win (Nolan Ryan)	.50
18	300th Win (Nolan Ryan)	.50
19	100.9 MPH Pitch (Nolan Ryan)	.50
20	Lone Star Legend (Nolan Ryan)	.50
---	Header Card	.10

1993 Pacific

This set marks the first time a major league set was designed entirely for the Spanish-speaking market. Distribution areas included retail markets in the United States, Mexico, South America and the Caribbean. The cards are glossy and feature Spanish text on both sides. Cards are numbered in alphabetical order by team, beginning with Atlanta. Insert sets are: Prism (20 cards featuring Spanish players and their accomplishments), Beisbol De Estralla (Stars of Baseball), Hot Players and Amigos (a 30-card set which features two or more players per card).

		NM/M
Complete Set (660):		20.00
Common Player:		.05
1	Rafael Belliard	.05
2	Sid Bream	.05
3	Francisco Cabrera	.05
4	Marvin Freeman	.05
5	Ron Gant	.05
6	Tom Glavine	.25
7	Brian Hunter	.05
8	Dave Justice	.05
9	Ryan Klesko	.05
10	Melvin Nieves	.05
11	Deion Sanders	.05
12	John Smoltz	.05
13	Mark Wohlers	.05
14	Brady Anderson	.05
15	Glenn Davis	.05
16	Mike Devereaux	.05
17	Leo Gomez	.05
18	Chris Hoiles	.05
19	Chito Martinez	.05
20	Ben McDonald	.05
21	Mike Mussina	.40
22	Gregg Olson	.05
23	Joe Orsulak	.05
24	Cal Ripken, Jr.	1.50
25	David Segui	.05
26	Rick Sutcliffe	.05
27	Wade Boggs	.65
28	Tom Brunansky	.05
29	Ellis Burks	.05
30	Roger Clemens	.75
31	John Dopson	.05
32	John Flaherty	.05
33	Mike Greenwell	.05
34	Tony Pena	.05
35	Carlos Quintana	.05
36	Luis Rivera	.05
37	Mo Vaughn	.05
38	Frank Viola	.05
39	Matt Young	.05
40	Scott Bailes	.05
41	Bert Blyleven	.05
42	Chad Curtis	.05
43	Gary DiSarcina	.05
44	Chuck Finley	.05
45	Mike Fitzgerald	.05
46	Gary Gaetti	.05
47	Rene Gonzales	.05
48	Mark Langston	.05
49	Scott Lewis	.05
50	Luis Polonia	.05
51	Tim Salmon	.50
52	Lee Stevens	.05
53	Steve Buechele	.05
54	Frank Castillo	.05
55	Doug Dascenzo	.05
56	Andre Dawson	.25
57	Shawon Dunston	.05
58	Mark Grace	.05
59	Mike Morgan	.05
60	Luis Salazar	.05
61	Rey Sanchez	.05
62	Ryne Sandberg	.65
63	Dwight Smith	.05
64	Jerome Walton	.05
65	Rick Wilkins	.05
66	Wilson Alvarez	.05
67	George Bell	.05
68	Joey Cora	.05
69	Alex Fernandez	.05
70	Carlton Fisk	.50
71	Craig Grebeck	.05
72	Ozzie Guillen	.05
73	Jack McDowell	.05
74	Scott Radinsky	.05
75	Tim Raines	.05
76	Bobby Thigpen	.05
77	Frank Thomas	.50
78	Robin Ventura	.05
79	Tom Browning	.05
80	Jacob Brumfield	.05
81	Rob Dibble	.05
82	Bill Doran	.05
83	Billy Hatcher	.05
84	Barry Larkin	.05
85	Hal Morris	.05
86	Joe Oliver	.05
87	Jeff Reed	.05
88	Jose Rijo	.05
89	Bip Roberts	.05
90	Chris Sabo	.05
91	Sandy Alomar, Jr.	.05
92	Brad Arnsberg	.05
93	Carlos Baerga	.05
94	Albert Belle	.05
95	Felix Fermin	.05
96	Mark Lewis	.05
97	Kenny Lofton	.05
98	Carlos Martinez	.05
99	Rod Nicholas	.05
100	Dave Rohde	.05
101	Scott Scudder	.05
102	Paul Sorrento	.05
103	Mark Whiten	.05
104	Mark Carreon	.05
105	Milt Cuyler	.05
106	Rob Deer	.05
107	Cecil Fielder	.05
108	Travis Fryman	.05
109	Dan Gladden	.05
110	Bill Gullickson	.05
111	Les Lancaster	.05
112	Mark Leiter	.05
113	Tony Phillips	.05
114	Mickey Tettleton	.05
115	Alan Trammell	.05
116	Lou Whitaker	.05
117	Jeff Bagwell	.50
118	Craig Biggio	.05
119	Joe Boever	.05
120	Casey Candaele	.05
121	Andujar Cedeno	.05
122	Steve Finley	.05
123	Luis Gonzalez	.05
124	Pete Harnisch	.05
125	Jimmy Jones	.05
126	Mark Portugal	.05
127	Rafael Ramirez	.05
128	Mike Simms	.05
129	Eric Yelding	.05
130	Luis Aquino	.05
131	Kevin Appier	.05
132	Mike Boddicker	.05
133	George Brett	.75
134	Tom Gordon	.05
135	Mark Gubicza	.05
136	David Howard	.05
137	Gregg Jefferies	.05
138	Wally Joyner	.05
139	Brian McRae	.05
140	Jeff Montgomery	.05
141	Terry Shumpert	.05
142	Curtis Wilkerson	.05
143	Brett Butler	.05
144	Eric Davis	.05
145	Kevin Gross	.05
146	Dave Hansen	.05
147	Lenny Harris	.05
148	Carlos Hernandez	.05
149	Orel Hershiser	.05
150	Jay Howell	.05
151	Eric Karros	.05
152	Ramon Martinez	.05
153	Jose Offerman	.05
154	Mike Sharperson	.05
155	Darryl Strawberry	.05
156	Jim Gantner	.05
157	Darryl Hamilton	.05
158	Doug Henry	.05
159	John Jaha	.05
160	Pat Listach	.05
161	Jaime Navarro	.05
162	Dave Nilsson	.05
163	Jesse Orosco	.05
164	Kevin Seitzer	.05
165	B.J. Surhoff	.05
166	Greg Vaughn	.05
167	Robin Yount	.50
168	Rick Aguilera	.05
169	Scott Erickson	.05
170	Mark Guthrie	.05
171	Kent Hrbek	.05
172	Chuck Knoblauch	.05
173	Gene Larkin	.05
174	Shane Mack	.05
175	Pedro Munoz	.05
176	Mike Pagliarulo	.05
177	Kirby Puckett	.65
178	Kevin Tapani	.05
179	Gary Wayne	.05
180	Moises Alou	.05
181	Brian Barnes	.05
182	Archie Cianfrocco	.05
183	Delino DeShields	.05
184	Darrin Fletcher	.05
185	Marquis Grissom	.05
186	Ken Hill	.05
187	Dennis Martinez	.05
188	Bill Sampen	.05
189	John VanderWal	.05
190	Larry Walker	.05
191	Tim Wallach	.05
192	Bobby Bonilla	.05
193	Daryl Boston	.05
194	Vince Coleman	.05
195	Kevin Elster	.05
196	Sid Fernandez	.05
197	John Franco	.05
198	Dwight Gooden	.05
199	Howard Johnson	.05
200	Willie Randolph	.05
201	Bret Saberhagen	.05
202	Dick Schofield	.05
203	Pete Schourek	.05
204	Greg Cadaret	.05
205	John Habyan	.05
206	Pat Kelly	.05
207	Kevin Maas	.05
208	Don Mattingly	.75
209	Matt Nokes	.05
210	Melido Perez	.05
211	Scott Sanderson	.05
212	Andy Stankiewicz	.05
213	Danny Tartabull	.05
214	Randy Velarde	.05
215	Bernie Williams	.05
216	Harold Baines	.05
217	Mike Bordick	.05
218	Scott Brosius	.05
219	Jerry Browne	.05
220	Ron Darling	.05
221	Dennis Eckersley	.40
222	Rickey Henderson	.50
223	Rick Honeycutt	.05
224	Mark McGwire	1.25
225	Ruben Sierra	.05
226	Terry Steinbach	.05
227	Bob Welch	.05
228	Willie Wilson	.05
229	Ruben Amaro	.05
230	Kim Batiste	.05
231	Juan Bell	.05
232	Wes Chamberlain	.05
233	Darren Daulton	.05
234	Mariano Duncan	.05
235	Len Dykstra	.05
236	Dave Hollins	.05
237	Stan Javier	.05
238	John Kruk	.05
239	Mickey Morandini	.05
240	Terry Mulholland	.05
241	Mitch Williams	.05
242	Stan Belinda	.05
243	Jay Bell	.05
244	Carlos Garcia	.05
245	Jeff King	.05
246	Mike LaValliere	.05
247	Lloyd McClendon	.05
248	Orlando Merced	.05
249	Paul Miller	.05
250	Gary Redus	.05
251	Don Slaught	.05
252	Zane Smith	.05
253	Andy Van Slyke	.05
254	Tim Wakefield	.05
255	Andy Benes	.05
256	Dann Bilardello	.05
257	Tony Gwynn	.65
258	Greg Harris	.05
259	Darrin Jackson	.05
260	Mike Maddux	.05
261	Fred McGriff	.05
262	Rich Rodriguez	.05
263	Benito Santiago	.05
264	Gary Sheffield	.35
265	Kurt Stillwell	.05
266	Tim Teufel	.05
267	Bud Black	.05
268	John Burkett	.05
269	Will Clark	.05
270	Royce Calyton	.05
271	Bryan Hickerson	.05
272	Chris James	.05
273	Darren Lewis	.05
274	Willie McGee	.05
275	Jim McNamara	.05
276	Francisco Oliveras	.05
277	Robby Thompson	.05
278	Matt Williams	.05
279	Trevor Wilson	.05
280	Bret Boone	.05
281	Greg Briley	.05
282	Jay Buhner	.05
283	Henry Cotto	.05
284	Rich DeLucia	.05
285	Dave Fleming	.05
286	Ken Griffey Jr.	1.00
287	Erik Hanson	.05
288	Randy Johnson	.50
289	Tino Martinez	.05
290	Edgar Martinez	.05
291	Dave Valle	.05
292	Omar Vizquel	.05
293	Luis Alicea	.05
294	Bernard Gilkey	.05
295	Felix Jose	.05
296	Ray Lankford	.05
297	Omar Olivares	.05
298	Jose Oquendo	.05
299	Tom Pagnozzi	.05
300	Geronimo Pena	.05
301	Gerald Perry	.05
302	Ozzie Smith	.65
303	Lee Smith	.05
304	Bob Tewksbury	.05
305	Todd Zeile	.05
306	Kevin Brown	.05
307	Todd Burns	.05
308	Jose Canseco	.35
309	Hector Fajardo	.05
310	Julio Franco	.05
311	Juan Gonzalez	.25
312	Jeff Huson	.05
313	Rob Maurer	.05
314	Rafael Palmeiro	.45
315	Dean Palmer	.05
316	Ivan Rodriguez	.45
317	Nolan Ryan	1.50
318	Dickie Thon	.05
319	Roberto Alomar	.20
320	Derek Bell	.05
321	Pat Borders	.05
322	Joe Carter	.05
323	Kelly Gruber	.05
324	Juan Guzman	.05
325	Manny Lee	.05
326	Jack Morris	.05
327	John Olerud	.05
328	Ed Sprague	.05
329	Todd Stottlemyre	.05
330	Duane Ward	.05
331	Steve Avery	.05
332	Damon Berryhill	.05
333	Jeff Blauser	.05
334	Mark Lemke	.05
335	Greg Maddux	.65
336	Kent Mercker	.05
337	Otis Nixon	.05
338	Greg Olson	.05
339	Bill Pecota	.05
340	Terry Pendleton	.05
341	Mike Stanton	.05
342	Todd Frohwirth	.05
343	Tim Hulett	.05
344	Mark McLemore	.05
345	Luis Mercedes	.05
346	Alan Mills	.05
347	Sherman Obando	.05
348	Jim Poole	.05
349	Harold Reynolds	.05
350	Arthur Rhodes	.05
351	Jeff Tackett	.05
352	Fernando Valenzuela	.05
353	Scott Bankhead	.05
354	Ivan Calderon	.05
355	Scott Cooper	.05
356	Danny Darwin	.05
357	Scott Fletcher	.05
358	Tony Fossas	.05
359	Greg Harris	.05
360	Joe Hesketh	.05
361	Jose Melendez	.05
362	Paul Quantrill	.05
363	John Valentin	.05
364	Mike Butcher	.05
365	Chuck Crim	.05
366	Chili Davis	.05
367	Damion Easley	.05
368	Steve Frey	.05
369	Joe Grahe	.05
370	Greg Myers	.05
371	John Orton	.05
372	J.T. Snow	.05
373	Ron Tingley	.05
374	Julio Valera	.05
375	Paul Assenmacher	.05
376	Jose Bautista	.05
377	Jose Guzman	.05
378	Greg Hibbard	.05
379	Candy Maldonado	.05
380	Derrick May	.05
381	Dan Plesac	.05
382	Tommy Shields	.05
383	Sammy Sosa	.75
384	Jose Vizcaino	.05
385	Greg Walbeck	.05
386	Ellis Burks	.05
387	Roberto Hernandez	.05
388	Mike Huff	.05
389	Bo Jackson	.10
390	Lance Johnson	.05
391	Ron Karkovice	.05
392	Kirk McCaskill	.05
393	Donn Pall	.05
394	Dan Pasqua	.05
395	Steve Sax	.05
396	Dave Stieb	.05
397	Bobby Ayala	.05
398	Tim Belcher	.05
399	Jeff Branson	.05
400	Cesar Hernandez	.05
401	Roberto Kelly	.05
402	Randy Milligan	.05
403	Kevin Mitchell	.05
404	Juan Samuel	.05
405	Reggie Sanders	.05
406	John Smiley	.05
407	Dan Wilson	.05
408	Mike Christopher	.05
409	Dennis Cook	.05
410	Alvaro Espinoza	.05
411	Glenallen Hill	.05
412	Reggie Jefferson	.05
413	Derek Lilliquist	.05
414	Jose Mesa	.05
415	Charles Nagy	.05
416	Junior Ortiz	.05
417	Eric Plunk	.05
418	Ted Power	.05
419	Scott Aldred	.05
420	Andy Ashby	.05
421	Freddie Benavides	.05
422	Dante Bichette	.05
423	Willie Blair	.05
424	Vinny Castilla	.05
425	Jerald Clark	.05
426	Alex Cole	.05
427	Andres Galarraga	.05
428	Joe Girardi	.05
429	Charlie Hayes	.05
430	Butch Henry	.05
431	Darren Holmes	.05
432	Dale Murphy	.20
433	David Nied	.05
434	Jeff Parrett	.05
435	Steve Reed RC	.05
436	Armando Reynoso	.05
437	Bruce Ruffin	.05
438	Bryn Smith	.05
439	Jim Tatum	.05
440	Eric Young	.05
441	Skeeter Barnes	.05
442	Tom Bolton	.05
443	Kirk Gibson	.05
444	Chad Krueter	.05
445	Bill Krueger	.05
446	Scott Livingstone	.05
447	Bob MacDonald	.05
448	Mike Moore	.05
449	Mike Munoz	.05
450	Gary Thurman	.05
451	David Wells	.05
452	Alex Arias	.05
453	Jack Armstrong	.05
454	Bret Barberie	.05
455	Ryan Bowen	.05
456	Cris Carpenter	.05
457	Chuck Carr	.05
458	Jeff Conine	.05
459	Steve Decker	.05
460	Orestes Destrade	.05
461	Monty Fariss	.05
462	Junior Felix	.05
463	Bryan Harvey	.05
464	Trevor Hoffman	.05
465	Charlie Hough	.05
466	Dave Magadan	.05
467	Bob McClure	.05
468	Rob Natal	.05
469	Scott Pose	.05
470	Rich Renteria	.05
471	Benito Santiago	.05
472	Matt Turner	.05
473	Walt Weiss	.05
474	Eric Anthony	.05
475	Chris Donnels	.05
476	Doug Drabek	.05
477	Xavier Hernandez	.05
478	Doug Jones	.05
479	Darryl Kile	.05
480	Scott Servais	.05
481	Greg Swindell	.05
482	Eddie Taubensee	.05
483	Jose Uribe	.05
484	Brian Williams	.05
485	Billy Brewer	.05
486	David Cone	.05
487	Greg Gagne	.05
488	Phil Hiatt	.05
489	Jose Lind	.05
490	Brent Mayne	.05
491	Kevin McReynolds	.05
492	Keith Miller	.05
493	Hipolito Pichardo	.05
494	Harvey Pulliam	.05
495	Rico Rossay	.05
496	Pedro Astacio	.05
497	Tom Candiotti	.05
498	Tom Goodwin	.05
499	Jim Gott	.05
500	Pedro Martinez	.50
501	Roger McDowell	.05
502	Mike Piazza	.75
503	Jody Reed	.05
504	Rick Trlicek	.05
505	Mitch Webster	.05
506	Steve Wilson	.05
507	James Austin	.05
508	Ricky Bones	.05
509	Alex Diaz	.05
510	Mike Fetters	.05
511	Teddy Higuera	.05
512	Graeme Lloyd	.05
513	Carlos Maldonado	.05
514	Josias Manzanillo	.05
515	Kevin Reimer	.05
516	Bill Spiers	.05
517	Bill Wegman	.05
518	Willie Banks	.05
519	J.T. Bruett	.05
520	Brian Harper	.05
521	Terry Jorgensen	.05
522	Scott Leius	.05
523	Pat Mahomes	.05
524	Dave McCarty	.05
525	Jeff Reboulet	.05
526	Mike Trombley	.05
527	Carl Willis	.05
528	Dave Winfield	.50
529	Sean Berry	.05
530	Frank Bolick	.05
531	Kent Bottenfield	.05
532	Wil Cordero	.05
533	Jeff Fassero	.05
534	Tim Laker	.05
535	Mike Lansing	.05
536	Chris Nabholz	.05
537	Mel Rojas	.05
538	John Wetteland	.05
539	Ted Wood (Front photo actually Frank Bollick.)	.05
540	Mike Draper	.05
541	Tony Fernandez	.05
542	Todd Hundley	.05
543	Jeff Innis	.05
544	Jeff McKnight	.05
545	Eddie Murray	.50
546	Charlie O'Brien	.05
547	Frank Tanana	.05
548	Ryan Thompson	.05
549	Chico Walker	.05
550	Anthony Young	.05
551	Jim Abbott	.05
552	Wade Boggs	.75
553	Steve Farr	.05
554	Neal Heaton	.05
555	Steve Howe	.05
556	Dion James	.05
557	Scott Kamieniecki	.05
558	Jimmy Key	.05
559	Jim Leyritz	.05
560	Paul O'Neill	.05
561	Spike Owen	.05
562	Lance Blankenship	.05
563	Joe Boever	.05
564	Storm Davis	.05
565	Kelly Downs	.05
566	Eric Fox	.05
567	Rich Gossage	.05
568	Dave Henderson	.05
569	Shawn Hillegas	.05
570	Mike Mohler RC	.05
571	Troy Neel	.05
572	Dale Sveum	.05
573	Larry Anderson	.05
574	Bob Ayrault	.05
575	Jose DeLeon	.05
576	Jim Eisenreich	.05
577	Pete Incaviglia	.05
578	Danny Jackson	.05
579	Ricky Jordan	.05
580	Ben Rivera	.05
581	Curt Schilling	.25
582	Milt Thompson	.05
583	David West	.05
584	John Candelaria	.05
585	Steve Cooke	.05
586	Tom Foley	.05
587	Al Martin	.05
588	Blas Minor	.05
589	Dennis Moeller	.05
590	Denny Neagle	.05
591	Tom Prince	.05
592	Randy Tomlin	.05
593	Bob Walk	.05
594	Kevin Young	.05
595	Pat Gomez	.05
596	Ricky Gutierrez	.05
597	Gene Harris	.05
598	Jeremy Hernandez	.05
599	Phil Plantier	.05
600	Tim Scott	.05
601	Frank Seminara	.05
602	Darrell Sherman	.05
603	Craig Shipley	.05
604	Guillermo Velasquez	.05
605	Dan Walters	.05
606	Mike Benjamin	.05
607	Barry Bonds	1.50

608 Jeff Brantley .05
609 Dave Burba .05
610 Craig Colbert .05
611 Mike Jackson .05
612 Kirt Manwaring .05
613 Dave Martinez .05
614 Dave Righetti .05
615 Kevin Rogers .05
616 Bill Swift .05
617 Rich Amaral .05
618 Mike Blowers .05
619 Chris Bosio .05
620 Norm Charlton .05
621 John Cummings .05
622 Mike Felder .05
623 Bill Haselman .05
624 Tim Leary .05
625 Pete O'Brien .05
626 Russ Swan .05
627 Fernando Vina .05
628 Rene Arocha .05
629 Rod Brewer .05
630 Ozzie Canseco .05
631 Rheal Cormier .05
632 Brian Jordan .05
633 Joe Magrane .05
634 Donovan Osborne .05
635 Mike Perez .05
636 Stan Royer .05
637 Hector Villanueva .05
638 Tracy Woodson .05
639 Benji Gil .05
640 Tom Henke .05
641 David Hulse .05
642 Charlie Leibrandt .05
643 Robb Nen .05
644 Dan Peltier .05
645 Billy Ripken .05
646 Kenny Rogers .05
647 John Russell .05
648 Dan Smith .05
649 Matt Whiteside .05
650 William Canate .05
651 Darnell Coles .05
652 Al Leiter .05
653 Dominigo Martinez .05
654 Paul Molitor .50
655 Luis Sojo .05
656 Dave Stewart .05
657 Mike Timlin .05
658 Turner Ward .05
659 Devon White .05
660 Eddie Zosky .05

Beisbol Amigos

In groups of two, three or more, and generally from the same team, Latin players are paired in this second series insert set. The cards feature player photos (sometimes posed, sometimes superimposed) on a background of red, white and black baseballs. The players' last names and a card title are printed in Spanish on front and repeated on back. Also on back a few career highlights and stats are printed in red on a marbled background - again all in Spanish.

NM/M
Complete Set (30): 7.50
Common Player: .50
1 Edgar Martinez, .50
2 Luis Polonia,
   Stan Javier .50
3 George Bell,
   Julio Franco .50
4 Ozzie Guillen,
   Ivan Rodriguez .60
5 Carlos Baerga,
   Sandy Alomar Jr. .50
6 Sandy Alomar Jr.,
   Alvaro Espinoza,
   Paul Sorrento,
   Carlos Baerga,
   Felix Fermin, Junior Ortiz,
   Jose Mesa,
   Carlos Martinez .50
7 Sandy Alomar Jr.,
   Roberto Alomar 1.00
8 Jose Lind, Felix Jose .50
9 Ricky Bones,
   Jaime Navarro .50
10 Jaime Navarro,
   Jesse Orosco .50
11 Tino Martinez,
   Edgar Martinez .50
12 Juan Gonzalez,
   Ivan Rodriguez .75
13 Juan Gonzalez,
   Julio Franco .60

14 Julio Franco,
   Jose Canseco,
   Rafael Palmeiro .60
15 Juan Gonzalez,
   Jose Canseco .65
16 Ivan Rodriguez,
   Benji Gil .60
17 Jose Guzman,
   Frank Castillo .50
18 Rey Sanchez,
   Jose Vizcaino .50
19 Derrick May,
   Sammy Sosa 2.00
20 Sammy Sosa,
   Candy Maldonado 2.00
21 Jose Rijo, Juan Samuel .50
22 Freddie Benavides,
   Andres Galarraga .50
23 Guillermo Velasquez,
   Benito Santiago .50
24 Luis Gonzalez,
   Andujar Cedeno .50
25 Wil Cordero,
   Dennis Martinez .50
26 Moises Alou,
   Wil Cordero .50
27 Ozzie Canseco,
   Jose Canseco .75
28 Jose Oquendo,
   Luis Alicea .50
29 Luis Alicea,
   Rene Arocha .50
30 Geronimo Pena,
   Luis Alicea .50

Estrellas de Beisbol

Pacific produced a gold-foil "Stars of Baseball" set of 20 that was randomly inserted as part of the company's first series Spanish language major league set in 1993. Each card features a color action photo on the front surrounded by a gold-foil border. Production was limited to 10,000 of each card.

NM/M
Complete Set (20): 6.00
Common Player: .50
1 Moises Alou .50
2 Bobby Bonilla .50
3 Tony Fernandez .50
4 Felix Jose .50
5 Dennis Martinez .50
6 Orlando Merced .50
7 Jose Oquendo .50
8 Geronimo Pena .50
9 Jose Rijo .50
10 Benito Santiago .50
11 Sandy Alomar Jr. .50
12 Carlos Baerga .50
13 Jose Canseco 1.50
14 Juan "Igor" Gonzalez 2.00
15 Juan Guzman .50
16 Edgar Martinez .50
17 Rafael Palmeiro 2.00
18 Ruben Sierra .50
19 Danny Tartabull .50
20 Omar Vizquel .50

Jugadores Calientes

Three dozen "hot players" with a decidedly Hispanic predominance are featured in this glittery Series 2 insert set. Player action photos appear in front of a silver prismatic foil background. Names appear at bottom in boldly styled, but hard to read, letters in bright colors. Horizontal backs have a pair of player photos and a large team logo, along with a few stats, all printed in Spanish.

NM/M
Complete Set (36): 20.00
Common Player: .50
1 Rich Amaral .50
2 George Brett 1.75
3 Jay Buhner .50
4 Roger Clemens 2.00
5 Kirk Gibson .50
6 Juan Gonzalez 1.00
7 Ken Griffey Jr. 2.00
8 Bo Jackson .50
9 Kenny Lofton .50
10 Mark McGwire 2.25
11 Sherman Obando .50
12 John Olerud .50
13 Carlos Quintana .50
14 Ivan Rodriguez 1.00
15 Nolan Ryan 2.50
16 J.T. Snow .50
17 Fernando Valenzuela .50
18 Dave Winfield 1.25
19 Moises Alou .50
20 Jeff Bagwell 1.25
21 Barry Bonds 2.50
22 Bobby Bonilla .50
23 Vinny Castilla .50
24 Andujar Cedeno .50
25 Orestes Destrade .50
26 Andres Galarraga .50
27 Mark Grace .50
28 Tony Gwynn 1.50
29 Roberto Kelly .50
30 John Kruk .50
31 Dave Magadan .50
32 Derrick May .50
33 Orlando Merced .50
34 Mike Piazza 2.00
35 Armando Reynoso .50
36 Jose Vizcaino .50

Prism Insert

Pacific produced a prism card that was randomly inserted in its Series 1 Spanish-language set in 1993. Each of the 20 cards has a color photo of a star Latino player on the front superimposed over a prismatic silver-foil background. Card backs contain an action photo and a brief player biography on a marbled background. Production was limited to 10,000 of each card.

NM/M
Complete Set (20): 60.00
Common Player: 3.00
1 Francisco Cabrera 3.00
2 Jose Lind 3.00
3 Dennis Martinez 3.00
4 Ramon Martinez 3.00
5 Jose Rijo 3.00
6 Benito Santiago 3.00
7 Roberto Alomar 9.00
8 Sandy Alomar Jr. 3.00
9 Carlos Baerga 3.00
10 George Bell 3.00
11 Jose Canseco 6.00
12 Alex Fernandez 3.00
13 Julio Franco 3.00
14 Igor (Juan) Gonzalez 12.00
15 Ozzie Guillen 3.00
16 Teddy Higuera 3.00
17 Edgar Martinez 3.00
18 Hipolito Pichardo 3.00
19 Luis Polonia 3.00
20 Ivan Rodriguez 7.50

1994 Pacific Crown Promos

Virtually identical in format to the regular 1994 Pacific Crown issue, the eight cards in the promo set have a "P-" prefix to the card number. Each side has a large "For Promotional Use Only" printed diagonally in black. The cards were sent to dealers as a preview to Pacific's 1994 bilingual issue.

NM/M
Complete Set (8): 6.00
Common Player: .75
1 Carlos Baerga .75
2 Joe Carter .75
3 Juan Gonzalez .75
4 Ken Griffey Jr. 2.00
5 Greg Maddux 1.50
6 Mike Piazza 1.75
7 Tim Salmon .75
8 Frank Thomas 1.25

1994 Pacific Crown

Following its 1993 Spanish-language set, Pacific's 1994 "Crown Collection" offering is bilingual, featuring both English and Spanish for most of the back printing. Fronts have an action photo which is borderless at the top and sides. A gold-foil line separates the bottom of the photo from a marbled strip that is color-coded by team. The player's name appears in two lines at the left of the strip, a gold-foil crown logo is at left. A Pacific logo appears in one of the upper corners of the photo. Backs have a photo, again borderless at top and sides, with a Pacific logo in one upper corner and the card number and MLB logos in the lower corners. At bottom is a gray marble strip with a few biographical details, 1993 and career stats and a ghost-image color team logo. The 660 cards in the set were issued in a single series.

NM/M
Complete Set (660): 20.00
Common Player: .05
Pack (12): 1.00
Wax Box (36): 20.00
1 Steve Avery .05
2 Steve Bedrosian .05
3 Damon Beryhill .05
4 Jeff Blauser .05
5 Sid Bream .05
6 Francisco Cabrera .05
7 Ramon Caraballo .05
8 Ron Gant .05
9 Tom Glavine .25
10 Chipper Jones .75

11 Dave Justice .05
12 Ryan Klesko .05
13 Mark Lemke .05
14 Javier Lopez .05
15 Greg Maddux .75
16 Fred McGriff .05
17 Greg McMichael .05
18 Kent Mercker .05
19 Otis Nixon .05
20 Terry Pendleton .05
21 Deion Sanders .05
22 John Smoltz .05
23 Tony Tarasco .05
24 Manny Alexander .05
25 Brady Anderson .05
26 Harold Baines .05
27 Damon Buford
   (Damon) .05
28 Paul Carey .05
29 Mike Devereaux .05
30 Todd Frohwirth .05
31 Leo Gomez .05
32 Jeffrey Hammonds .05
33 Chris Hoiles .05
34 Tim Hulett .05
35 Ben McDonald .05
36 Mark McLemore .05
37 Alan Mills .05
38 Mike Mussina .35
39 Sherman Obando .05
40 Gregg Olson .40
41 Mike Pagliarulo .05
42 Jim Poole .05
43 Harold Reynolds .05
44 Cal Ripken, Jr. 2.00
45 David Segui .05
46 Fernando Valenzuela .05
47 Jack Voight .05
48 Scott Bankhead .05
49 Roger Clemens 1.00
50 Scott Cooper .05
51 Danny Darwin .05
52 Andre Dawson .20
53 John Dopson .05
54 Scott Fletcher .05
55 Tony Fossas .05
56 Mike Greenwell .05
57 Billy Hatcher .05
58 Jeff McNeely .05
59 Jose Melendez .05
60 Tim Naehring .05
61 Tony Pena .05
62 Carlos Quintana .05
63 Paul Quantrill .05
64 Luis Rivera .05
65 Jeff Russell .05
66 Aaron Sele .05
67 John Valentin .05
68 Mo Vaughn .05
69 Frank Viola .05
70 Bob Zupcic .05
71 Mike Butcher .05
72 Ron Correia .05
73 Chad Curtis .05
74 Chili Davis .05
75 Gary DiSarcina .05
76 Damion Easley .05
77 John Farrell .05
78 Chuck Finley .05
79 Joe Grahe .05
80 Stan Javier .05
81 Mark Langston .05
82 Phil Leftwich .05
83 Torey Lovullo .05
84 Joe Magrane .05
85 Greg Myers .05
86 Eduardo Perez .05
87 Luis Polonia .05
88 Tim Salmon .05
89 J.T. Snow .05
90 Kurt Stillwell .05
91 Ron Tingley .05
92 Chris Turner .05
93 Julio Valera .05
94 Jose Bautista .05
95 Shawn Boskie .05
96 Steve Buechele .05
97 Frank Castillo .05
98 Mark Grace .05
99 Jose Guzman .05
100 Mike Harkey .05
101 Greg Hibbard .05
102 Doug Jennings .05
103 Derrick May .05
104 Mike Morgan .05
105 Randy Myers .05
106 Karl Rhodes .05
107 Kevin Robinson .05
108 Rey Sanchez .05
109 Ryne Sandberg .75
110 Tommy Shields .05
111 Dwight Smith .05
112 Sammy Sosa .75
113 Jose Vizcaino .05
114 Turk Wendell .05
115 Rick Wilkins .05
116 Willie Wilson .05
117 Eddie Zambrano .05
118 Wilson Alvarez .05
119 Tim Belcher .05
120 Jason Bere .05
121 Rodney Bolton .05
122 Ellis Burks .05
123 Joey Cora .05
124 Alex Fernandez .05
125 Ozzie Guillen .05
126 Craig Grebeck .05
127 Roberto Hernandez .05

128 Bo Jackson .10
129 Lance Johnson .05
130 Ron Karkovice .05
131 Mike Lavalliere .05
132 Norberto Martin .05
133 Kirk McCaskill .05
134 Jack McDowell .05
135 Scott Radinsky .05
136 Tim Raines .05
137 Steve Sax .05
138 Frank Thomas .60
139 Dan Pasqua .05
140 Robin Ventura .05
141 Jeff Branson .05
142 Tom Browning .05
143 Jacob Brumfield .05
144 Tim Costo .05
145 Rob Dibble .05
146 Brian Dorsett .05
147 Steve Foster .05
148 Cesar Hernandez .05
149 Roberto Kelly .05
150 Barry Larkin .05
151 Larry Luebbers .05
152 Kevin Mitchell .05
153 Joe Oliver .05
154 Tim Pugh .05
155 Jeff Reardon .05
156 Jose Rijo .05
157 Bip Roberts .05
158 Chris Sabo .05
159 Juan Samuel .05
160 Reggie Sanders .05
161 John Smiley .05
162 Jerry Spradlin .05
163 Gary Varsho .05
164 Sandy Alomar Jr. .05
165 Carlos Baerga .05
166 Albert Belle .05
167 Mark Clark .05
168 Alvaro Espinoza .05
169 Felix Fermin .05
170 Reggie Jefferson .05
171 Wayne Kirby .05
172 Tom Kramer .05
173 Jesse Levis .05
174 Kenny Lofton .05
175 Candy Maldonado .05
176 Carlos Martinez .05
177 Jose Mesa .05
178 Jeff Mutis .05
179 Charles Nagy .05
180 Bob Ojeda .05
181 Junior Ortiz .05
182 Eric Plunk .05
183 Manny Ramirez .60
184 Paul Sorrento .05
185 Jeff Treadway .05
186 Bill Wertz .05
187 Freddie Benavides .05
188 Dante Bichette .05
189 Willie Blair .05
190 Daryl Boston .05
191 Pedro Castellano .05
192 Vinny Castilla .05
193 Jerald Clark .05
194 Alex Cole .05
195 Andres Galarraga .05
196 Joe Girardi .05
197 Charlie Hayes .05
198 Darren Holmes .05
199 Chris Jones .05
200 Curt Leskanic .05
201 Roberto Mejia .05
202 David Nied .05
203 J. Owens .05
204 Steve Reed .05
205 Armando Reynoso .05
206 Bruce Ruffin .05
207 Keith Shepherd .05
208 Jim Tatum .05
209 Eric Young .05
210 Skeeter Barnes .05
211 Danny Bautista .05
212 Tom Bolton .05
213 Eric Davis .05
214 Storm Davis .05
215 Cecil Fielder .05
216 Travis Fryman .05
217 Kirk Gibson .05
218 Dan Gladden .05
219 John Doherty .05
220 Chris Gomez .05
221 David Haas .05
222 Bill Krueger .05
223 Chad Kreuter .05
224 Mark Leiter .05
225 Bob MacDonald .05
226 Mike Moore .05
227 Tony Phillips .05
228 Rich Rowland .05
229 Mickey Tettleton .05
230 Alan Trammell .05
231 David Wells .05
232 Lou Whitaker .05
233 Luis Aquino .05
234 Alex Arias .05
235 Jack Armstrong .05
236 Ryan Bowen .05
237 Chuck Carr .05
238 Matias Carrillo .05
239 Jeff Conine .05
240 Henry Cotto .05
241 Orestes Destrade .05
242 Chris Hammond .05
243 Bryan Harvey .05
244 Charlie Hough .05
245 Richie Lewis .05

No.	Player	Price
246	Mitch Lyden	.05
247	Dave Magadan	.05
248	Bob Natal	.05
249	Benito Santiago	.05
250	Gary Sheffield	.30
251	Matt Turner	.05
252	David Weathers	.05
253	Walt Weiss	.05
254	Darrell Whitmore	.05
255	Nigel Wilson	.05
256	Eric Anthony	.05
257	Jeff Bagwell	.60
258	Kevin Bass	.05
259	Craig Biggio	.05
260	Ken Caminiti	.05
261	Andujar Cedeno	.05
262	Chris Donnels	.05
263	Doug Drabek	.05
264	Tom Edens	.05
265	Steve Finley	.05
266	Luis Gonzalez	.05
267	Pete Harnisch	.05
268	Xavier Hernandez	.05
269	Todd Jones	.05
270	Darryl Kile	.05
271	Al Osuna	.05
272	Rick Parker	.05
273	Mark Portugal	.05
274	Scott Servais	.05
275	Greg Swindell	.05
276	Eddie Taubensee	.05
277	Jose Uribe	.05
278	Brian Williams	.05
279	Kevin Appier	.05
280	Billy Brewer	.05
281	David Cone	.05
282	Greg Gagne	.05
283	Tom Gordon	.05
284	Chris Gwynn	.05
285	John Habyan	.05
286	Chris Haney	.05
287	Phil Hiatt	.05
288	David Howard	.05
289	Felix Jose	.05
290	Wally Joyner	.05
291	Kevin Koslofski	.05
292	Jose Lind	.05
293	Brent Mayne	.05
294	Mike Mcfarlane	.05
295	Brian McRae	.05
296	Kevin McReynolds	.05
297	Keith Miller	.05
298	Jeff Montgomery	.05
299	Hipolito Pichardo	.05
300	Rico Rossy	.05
301	Curtis Wilkerson	.05
302	Pedro Astacio	.05
303	Rafael Bournigal	.05
304	Brett Butler	.05
305	Tom Candiotti	.05
306	Omar Daal	.05
307	Jim Gott	.05
308	Kevin Gross	.05
309	Dave Hansen	.05
310	Carlos Hernandez	.05
311	Orel Hershiser	.05
312	Eric Karros	.05
313	Pedro Martinez	.60
314	Ramon Martinez	.05
315	Roger McDowell	.05
316	Raul Mondesi	.05
317	Jose Offerman	.05
318	Mike Piazza	1.00
319	Jody Reed	.05
320	Henry Rodriguez	.05
321	Cory Snyder	.05
322	Darryl Strawberry	.05
323	Tim Wallach	.05
324	Steve Wilson	.05
325	Juan Bell	.05
326	Ricky Bones	.05
327	Alex Diaz	.05
328	Cal Eldred	.05
329	Darryl Hamilton	.05
330	Doug Henry	.05
331	John Jaha	.05
332	Pat Listach	.05
333	Graeme Lloyd	.05
334	Carlos Maldonado	.05
335	Angel Miranda	.05
336	Jaime Navarro	.05
337	Dave Nilsson	.05
338	Rafael Novoa	.05
339	Troy O'Leary	.05
340	Jesse Orosco	.05
341	Kevin Seitzer	.05
342	Bill Spiers	.05
343	William Suero	.05
344	B.J. Surhoff	.05
345	Dickie Thon	.05
346	Jose Valentin	.05
347	Greg Vaughn	.05
348	Robin Yount	.60
349	Willie Banks	.05
350	Bernardo Brito	.05
351	Scott Erickson	.05
352	Mark Guthrie	.05
353	Chip Hale	.05
354	Brian Harper	.05
355	Kent Hrbek	.05
356	Terry Jorgenson	.05
357	Chuck Knoblauch	.05
358	Gene Larkin	.05
359	Scott Leius	.05
360	Shane Mack	.05
361	David McCarty	.05
362	Pat Meares	.05
363	Pedro Munoz	.05
364	Derek Parks	.05
365	Kirby Puckett	.75
366	Jeff Reboulet	.05
367	Kevin Tapani	.05
368	Mike Trombley	.05
369	George Tsamis	.05
370	Carl Willis	.05
371	Dave Winfield	.60
372	Moises Alou	.05
373	Brian Barnes	.05
374	Sean Berry	.05
375	Frank Bolick	.05
376	Wil Cordero	.05
377	Delino DeShields	.05
378	Jeff Fassero	.05
379	Darren Fletcher	.05
380	Cliff Floyd	.05
381	Lou Frazier	.05
382	Marquis Grissom	.05
383	Gil Heredia	.05
384	Mike Lansing	.05
385	Oreste Marrero	.05
386	Dennis Martinez	.05
387	Curtis Pride	.05
388	Mel Rojas	.05
389	Kirk Rueter	.05
390	Joe Siddall	.05
391	John Vander Wal	.05
392	Larry Walker	.05
393	John Wetteland	.05
394	Rondell White	.05
395	Tom Bogar	.05
396	Bobby Bonilla	.05
397	Jeromy Burnitz	.05
398	Mike Draper	.05
399	Sid Fernandez	.05
400	John Franco	.05
401	Dave Gallagher	.05
402	Dwight Gooden	.05
403	Eric Hillman	.05
404	Todd Hundley	.05
405	Butch Huskey	.05
406	Jeff Innis	.05
407	Howard Johnson	.05
408	Jeff Kent	.05
409	Ced Landrum	.05
410	Mike Maddux	.05
411	Josias Manzanillo	.05
412	Jeff McKnight	.05
413	Eddie Murray	.60
414	Tito Navarro	.05
415	Joe Orsulak	.05
416	Bret Saberhagen	.05
417	Dave Telgheder	.05
418	Ryan Thompson	.05
419	Chico Walker	.05
420	Jim Abbott	.05
421	Wade Boggs	.75
422	Mike Gallego	.05
423	Mark Hutton	.05
424	Dion James	.05
425	Domingo Jean	.05
426	Pat Kelly	.05
427	Jimmy Key	.05
428	Jim Leyritz	.05
429	Kevin Maas	.05
430	Don Mattingly	1.00
431	Bobby Munoz	.05
432	Matt Nokes	.05
433	Paul O'Neill	.05
434	Spike Owen	.05
435	Melido Perez	.05
436	Lee Smith	.05
437	Andy Stankiewicz	.05
438	Mike Stanley	.05
439	Danny Tartabull	.05
440	Randy Velarde	.05
441	Bernie Williams	.05
442	Gerald Williams	.05
443	Mike Witt	.05
444	Marcos Armas	.05
445	Lance Blankenship	.05
446	Mike Bordick	.05
447	Ron Darling	.05
448	Dennis Eckersley	.45
449	Brent Gates	.05
450	Goose Gossage	.05
451	Scott Hemond	.05
452	Dave Henderson	.05
453	Shawn Hillegas	.05
454	Rick Honeycutt	.05
455	Scott Lydy	.05
456	Mark McGwire	1.50
457	Henry Mercedes	.05
458	Mike Mohler	.05
459	Troy Neel	.05
460	Edwin Nunez	.05
461	Craig Paquette	.05
462	Ruben Sierra	.05
463	Terry Steinbach	.05
464	Todd Van Poppel	.05
465	Bob Welch	.05
466	Bobby Witt	.05
467	Ruben Amaro	.05
468	Larry Anderson	.05
469	Kim Batiste	.05
470	Wes Chamberlain	.05
471	Darren Daulton	.05
472	Mariano Duncan	.05
473	Len Dykstra	.05
474	Jim Eisenreich	.05
475	Tommy Greene	.05
476	Dave Hollins	.05
477	Pete Incaviglia	.05
478	Danny Jackson	.05
479	John Kruk	.05
480	Tony Longmire	.05
481	Jeff Manto	.05
482	Mike Morandini	.05
483	Terry Mulholland	.05
484	Todd Pratt	.05
485	Ben Rivera	.05
486	Curt Schilling	.25
487	Kevin Stocker	.05
488	Milt Thompson	.05
489	David West	.05
490	Mitch Williams	.05
491	Jeff Ballard	.05
492	Jay Bell	.05
493	Scott Bullett	.05
494	Dave Clark	.05
495	Steve Cooke	.05
496	Midre Cummings	.05
497	Mark Dewey	.05
498	Carlos Garcia	.05
499	Jeff King	.05
500	Al Martin	.05
501	Lloyd McClendon	.05
502	Orlando Merced	.05
503	Blas Minor	.05
504	Denny Neagle	.05
505	Tom Prince	.05
506	Don Slaught	.05
507	Zane Smith	.05
508	Randy Tomlin	.05
509	Andy Van Slyke	.05
510	Paul Wagner	.05
511	Tim Wakefield	.05
512	Bob Walk	.05
513	John Wehner	.05
514	Kevin Young	.05
515	Billy Bean	.05
516	Andy Benes	.05
517	Derek Bell	.05
518	Doug Brocail	.05
519	Jarvis Brown	.05
520	Phil Clark	.05
521	Mark Davis	.05
522	Jeff Gardner	.05
523	Pat Gomez	.05
524	Ricky Gutierrez	.05
525	Tony Gwynn	.75
526	Gene Harris	.05
527	Kevin Higgins	.05
528	Trevor Hoffman	.05
529	Luis Lopez	.05
530	Pedro A. Martinez	.05
531	Melvin Nieves	.05
532	Phil Plantier	.05
533	Frank Seminara	.05
534	Craig Shipley	.05
535	Tim Teufel	.05
536	Guillermo Velasquez	.05
537	Wally Whitehurst	.05
538	Rod Beck	.05
539	Todd Benzinger	.05
540	Barry Bonds	2.00
541	Jeff Brantley	.05
542	Dave Burba	.05
543	John Burkett	.05
544	Will Clark	.05
545	Royce Clayton	.05
546	Brian Hickerson (Bryan)	.05
547	Mike Jackson	.05
548	Darren Lewis	.05
549	Kirt Manwaring	.05
550	Dave Martinez	.05
551	Willie McGee	.05
552	Jeff Reed	.05
553	Dave Righetti	.05
554	Kevin Rogers	.05
555	Steve Scarsone	.05
556	Bill Swift	.05
557	Robby Thompson	.05
558	Salomon Torres	.05
559	Matt Williams	.05
560	Trevor Wilson	.05
561	Rich Amaral	.05
562	Mike Blowers	.05
563	Chris Bosio	.05
564	Jay Buhner	.05
565	Norm Charlton	.05
566	Jim Converse	.05
567	Rich DeLucia	.05
568	Mike Felder	.05
569	Dave Fleming	.05
570	Ken Griffey Jr.	1.00
571	Bill Haselman	.05
572	Dwayne Henry	.05
573	Brad Holman	.05
574	Randy Johnson	.60
575	Greg Litton	.05
576	Edgar Martinez	.05
577	Tino Martinez	.05
578	Jeff Nelson	.05
579	Mark Newfield	.05
580	Roger Salkeld	.05
581	Mackey Sasser	.05
582	Brian Turang	.05
583	Omar Vizquel	.05
584	Dave Valle	.05
585	Luis Alicea	.05
586	Rene Arocha	.05
587	Rheal Cormier	.05
588	Tripp Cromer	.05
589	Bernard Gilkey	.05
590	Lee Guetterman	.05
591	Gregg Jefferies	.05
592	Tim Jones	.05
593	Paul Kilgus	.05
594	Les Lancaster	.05
595	Omar Olivares	.05
596	Jose Oquendo	.05
597	Donovan Osborne	.05
598	Tom Pagnozzi	.05
599	Erik Pappas	.05
600	Geronimo Pena	.05
601	Mike Perez	.05
602	Gerald Perry	.05
603	Stan Royer	.05
604	Ozzie Smith	.75
605	Bob Tewksbury	.05
606	Allen Watson	.05
607	Mark Whiten	.05
608	Todd Zeile	.05
609	Jeff Bronkey	.05
610	Kevin Brown	.05
611	Jose Canseco	.35
612	Doug Dascenzo	.05
613	Butch Davis	.05
614	Mario Diaz	.05
615	Julio Franco	.05
616	Benji Gil	.05
617	Juan Gonzalez	.30
618	Tom Henke	.05
619	Jeff Huson	.05
620	David Hulse	.05
621	Craig Lefferts	.05
622	Rafael Palmeiro	.50
623	Dean Palmer	.05
624	Bob Patterson	.05
625	Roger Pavlik	.05
626	Gary Redus	.05
627	Ivan Rodriguez	.50
628	Kenny Rogers	.05
629	Jon Shave	.05
630	Doug Strange	.05
631	Matt Whiteside	.05
632	Roberto Alomar	.15
633	Pat Borders	.05
634	Scott Brow	.05
635	Rob Butler	.05
636	Joe Carter	.05
637	Tony Castillo	.05
638	Mark Eichhorn	.05
639	Tony Fernandez	.05
640	Huck Flener **RC**	.05
641	Alfredo Griffin	.05
642	Juan Guzman	.05
643	Rickey Henderson	.05
644	Pat Hentgen	.05
645	Randy Knorr	.05
646	Al Leiter	.05
647	Domingo Martinez	.05
648	Paul Molitor	.60
649	Jack Morris	.05
650	John Olerud	.05
651	Ed Sprague	.05
652	Dave Stewart	.05
653	Devon White	.05
654	Woody Williams	.05
655	Barry Bonds/MVP	1.00
656	Greg Maddux (CY)	.40
657	Jack McDowell (CY)	.05
658	Mike Piazza (ROY)	.65
659	Tim Salmon (ROY)	.05
660	Frank Thomas/MVP	.25

Homerun Leaders

A gold prismatic background behind a color action player photo is the featured design on this Pacific insert set. Backs have another player photo against a ballfield backdrop. A huge baseball is overprinted with the player's name and number of 1993 homers. A league designation is among the logos featured on back. A total of 8,000 of these inserts sets was the announced production.

		NM/M
Complete Set (20):		25.00
Common Player:		1.00
1	Juan Gonzalez	1.50
2	Ken Griffey Jr.	3.00
3	Frank Thomas	2.50
4	Albert Belle	1.00
5	Rafael Palmeiro	1.50
6	Joe Carter	1.00
7	Dean Palmer	1.00
8	Mickey Tettleton	1.00
9	Tim Salmon	1.00
10	Danny Tartabull	1.00
11	Barry Bonds	5.00
12	Dave Justice	1.00
13	Matt Williams	1.00
14	Fred McGriff	1.00
15	Ron Gant	1.00
16	Mike Piazza	3.00
17	Bobby Bonilla	1.00
18	Phil Plantier	1.00
19	Sammy Sosa	3.00
20	Rick Wilkins	1.00

All Latino All-Star Team

Latino All-Stars is the theme of the third insert set found randomly packed in Pacific Spanish for 1994. Cards feature a player action photo on front, with a gold foil pinstripe around the sides and top. The player's name appears in gold script at bottom and there is a baseball logo in the corner. On backs a portrait photo of the player is set against a background of his native flag. Season highlights of 1993 are presented in English and Spanish. Eight thousand sets were produced.

		NM/M
Complete Set (20):		4.00
Common Player:		.25
1	Benito Santiago	.25
2	Dave Magadan	.25
3	Andres Galarraga	.25
4	Luis Gonzalez	.25
5	Jose Offerman	.25
6	Bobby Bonilla	.25
7	Dennis Martinez	.25
8	Mariano Duncan	.25
9	Orlando Merced	.25
10	Jose Rijo	.25
11	Danny Tartabull	.25
12	Ruben Sierra	.25
13	Ivan Rodriguez	1.00
14	Juan Gonzalez	1.00
15	Jose Canseco	.50
16	Rafael Palmeiro	1.00
17	Roberto Alomar	.50
18	Eduardo Perez	.25
19	Alex Fernandez	.25
20	Omar Vizquel	.25

Jewels of the Crown

One of three inserts into 1994 Pacific Spanish foil packs. The design features a player action photo set against a silver prismatic background. On back is another color player photo against a background of colored silk and a large jewel. Season highlight stats and awards won are presented in both English and Spanish. The announced production run of these inserts was 8,000 sets.

		NM/M
Complete Set (36):		40.00
Common Player:		1.00
1	Robin Yount	2.50
2	Juan Gonzalez	1.25
3	Rafael Palmeiro	2.00
4	Paul Molitor	2.50
5	Roberto Alomar	1.25
6	John Olerud	.75
7	Randy Johnson	2.50
8	Ken Griffey Jr.	4.00
9	Wade Boggs	3.00
10	Don Mattingly	3.50
11	Kirby Puckett	3.00
12	Tim Salmon	1.00
13	Frank Thomas	2.50
14	Fernando Valenzuela (Comeback Player)	1.00
15	Cal Ripken, Jr.	6.00
16	Carlos Baerga	1.00
17	Kenny Lofton	1.00
18	Cecil Fielder	1.00
19	John Burkett	1.00
20	Andres Galarraga (Comeback Player)	1.00
21	Charlie Hayes	1.00
22	Orestes Destrade	1.00
23	Jeff Conine	1.00
24	Jeff Bagwell	2.50
25	Mark Grace	1.00
26	Ryne Sandberg	3.00
27	Gregg Jefferies	1.00
28	Barry Bonds	6.00
29	Mike Piazza	3.50
30	Greg Maddux	3.00
31	Darren Daulton	1.00
32	John Kruk	1.00
33	Len Dykstra	1.00
34	Orlando Merced	1.00
35	Tony Gwynn	3.00
36	Robby Thompson	1.00

Jewels of the Crown - Retail

Using the same design, photos, graphics and card numbers, the retail version of the Jewels of the Crown insert set varies only in the silver prismatic foil background on front. While the scarcer hobby version has a diamond-shaped pattern to the foil, the retail version has numerous circles as a background pattern. The retail cards were inserted one per pack of retail product and are thus much more common than the hobby version.

		NM/M
Complete Set (36):		40.00
Common Player:		.75
1	Robin Yount	2.50
2	Juan Gonzalez	1.25
3	Rafael Palmeiro	1.25
4	Paul Molitor	2.50
5	Roberto Alomar	1.00
6	John Olerud	.75
7	Randy Johnson	2.50
8	Ken Griffey Jr.	4.00
9	Wade Boggs	3.00
10	Don Mattingly	3.50
11	Kirby Puckett	3.00
12	Tim Salmon	1.00
13	Frank Thomas	2.50
14	Fernando Valenzuela (Comeback Player)	.75
15	Cal Ripken, Jr.	5.00
16	Carlos Baerga	.75
17	Kenny Lofton	.75
18	Cecil Fielder	.75
19	John Burkett	.75
20	Andres Galarraga (Comeback Player)	.75
21	Charlie Hayes	.75
22	Orestes Destrade	.75
23	Jeff Conine	.75
24	Jeff Bagwell	2.50
25	Mark Grace	.75
26	Ryne Sandberg	3.00
27	Gregg Jefferies	.75
28	Barry Bonds	5.00
29	Mike Piazza	3.50
30	Greg Maddux	3.00
31	Darren Daulton	.75
32	John Kruk	.75
33	Len Dykstra	.75
34	Orlando Merced	.75
35	Tony Gwynn	3.00
36	Robby Thompson	.75

1995 Pacific

The base cards in Pacific's Crown Collection baseball issue for 1995 feature borderless color action photos on front, graphically highlighted by the player name at bottom in gold foil and a color team logo in a baseball at lower-left. Backs have a playing field design in the background with a portrait photo at left. At right are 1994 stats, career highlights and a ghosted image of the team logo. Most back printing is in both English and Spanish. The 450 cards in the series are arranged alphabetically within team, with the teams arranged in city-alpha order. Several chase cards series are found in the 12-card foil packs.

	NM/M
Complete Set (450):	20.00
Common Player:	.05
Pack (12):	1.00
Wax Box (36):	20.00

#	Player	Price
1	Steve Avery	.05
2	Rafael Belliard	.05
3	Jeff Blauser	.05
4	Tom Glavine	.25
5	Dave Justice	.05
6	Mike Kelly	.05
7	Roberto Kelly	.05
8	Ryan Klesko	.05
9	Mark Lemke	.05
10	Javier Lopez	.05
11	Greg Maddux	.75
12	Fred McGriff	.05
13	Greg McMichael	.05
14	Jose Oliva	.05
15	John Smoltz	.05
16	Tony Tarasco	.05
17	Brady Anderson	.05
18	Harold Baines	.05
19	Armando Benitez	.05
20	Mike Devereaux	.05
21	Leo Gomez	.05
22	Jeffrey Hammonds	.05
23	Chris Hoiles	.05
24	Ben McDonald	.05
25	Mark McLemore	.05
26	Jamie Moyer	.05
27	Mike Mussina	.40
28	Rafael Palmeiro	.50
29	Jim Poole	.05
30	Cal Ripken Jr.	2.00
31	Lee Smith	.05
32	Mark Smith	.05
33	Jose Canseco	.35
34	Roger Clemens	1.00
35	Scott Cooper	.05
36	Andre Dawson	.25
37	Tony Fossas	.05
38	Mike Greenwell	.05
39	Chris Howard	.05
40	Jose Melendez	.05
41	Nate Minchey	.05
42	Tim Naehring	.05
43	Otis Nixon	.05
44	Carlos Rodriguez	.05
45	Aaron Sele	.05
46	Lee Tinsley	.05
47	Sergio Valdez	.05
48	John Valentin	.05
49	Mo Vaughn	.05
50	Brian Anderson	.05
51	Garret Anderson	.05
52	Rod Correia	.05
53	Chad Curtis	.05
54	Mark Dalesandro	.05
55	Chili Davis	.05
56	Gary DiSarcina	.05
57	Damion Easley	.05
58	Jim Edmonds	.05
59	Jorge Fabregas	.05
60	Chuck Finley	.05
61	Bo Jackson	.10
62	Mark Langston	.05
63	Eduardo Perez	.05
64	Tim Salmon	.05
65	J.T. Snow	.05
66	Willie Banks	.05
67	Jose Bautista	.05
68	Shawon Dunston	.05
69	Kevin Foster	.05
70	Mark Grace	.05
71	Jose Guzman	.05
72	Jose Hernandez	.05
73	Blaise Ilsley	.05
74	Derrick May	.05
75	Randy Myers	.05
76	Karl Rhodes	.05
77	Kevin Roberson	.05
78	Rey Sanchez	.05
79	Sammy Sosa	.75
80	Steve Trachsel	.05
81	Eddie Zambrano	.05
82	Wilson Alvarez	.05
83	Jason Bere	.05
84	Joey Cora	.05
85	Jose DeLeon	.05
86	Alex Fernandez	.05
87	Julio Franco	.05
88	Ozzie Guillen	.05
89	Joe Hall	.05
90	Roberto Hernandez	.05
91	Darrin Jackson	.05
92	Lance Johnson	.05
93	Norberto Martin	.05
94	Jack McDowell	.05
95	Tim Raines	.05
96	Olmedo Saenz	.05
97	Frank Thomas	.60
98	Robin Ventura	.05
99	Bret Boone	.05
100	Jeff Brantley	.05
101	Jacob Brumfield	.05
102	Hector Carrasco	.05
103	Brian Dorsett	.05
104	Tony Fernandez	.05
105	Willie Greene	.05
106	Erik Hanson	.05
107	Kevin Jarvis	.05
108	Barry Larkin	.05
109	Kevin Mitchell	.05
110	Hal Morris	.05
111	Jose Rijo	.05
112	Johnny Ruffin	.05
113	Deion Sanders	.05
114	Reggie Sanders	.05
115	Sandy Alomar Jr.	.05
116	Ruben Amaro	.05
117	Carlos Baerga	.05
118	Albert Belle	.05
119	Alvaro Espinoza	.05
120	Rene Gonzales	.05
121	Wayne Kirby	.05
122	Kenny Lofton	.05
123	Candy Maldonado	.05
124	Dennis Martinez	.05
125	Eddie Murray	.60
126	Charles Nagy	.05
127	Tony Pena	.05
128	Manny Ramirez	.60
129	Paul Sorrento	.05
130	Jim Thome	.40
131	Omar Vizquel	.05
132	Dante Bichette	.05
133	Ellis Burks	.05
134	Vinny Castilla	.05
135	Marvin Freeman	.05
136	Andres Galarraga	.05
137	Joe Girardi	.05
138	Charlie Hayes	.05
139	Mike Kingery	.05
140	Nelson Liriano	.05
141	Roberto Mejia	.05
142	David Nied	.05
143	Steve Reed	.05
144	Armando Reynoso	.05
145	Bruce Ruffin	.05
146	John Vander Wal	.05
147	Walt Weiss	.05
148	Skeeter Barnes	.05
149	Tim Belcher	.05
150	Junior Felix	.05
151	Cecil Fielder	.05
152	Travis Fryman	.05
153	Kirk Gibson	.05
154	Chris Gomez	.05
155	Buddy Groom	.05
156	Chad Kreuter	.05
157	Mike Moore	.05
158	Tony Phillips	.05
159	Juan Samuel	.05
160	Mickey Tettleton	.05
161	Alan Trammell	.05
162	David Wells	.05
163	Lou Whitaker	.05
164	Kurt Abbott	.05
165	Luis Aquino	.05
166	Alex Arias	.05
167	Bret Barberie	.05
168	Jerry Browne	.05
169	Chuck Carr	.05
170	Matias Carrillo	.05
171	Greg Colbrunn	.05
172	Jeff Conine	.05
173	Carl Everett	.05
174	Robb Nen	.05
175	Yorkis Perez	.05
176	Pat Rapp	.05
177	Benito Santiago	.05
178	Gary Sheffield	.35
179	Darrell Whitmore	.05
180	Jeff Bagwell	.60
181	Kevin Bass	.05
182	Craig Biggio	.05
183	Andujar Cedeno	.05
184	Doug Drabek	.05
185	Tony Eusebio	.05
186	Steve Finley	.05
187	Luis Gonzalez	.05
188	Pete Harnisch	.05
189	John Hudek	.05
190	Orlando Miller	.05
191	James Mouton	.05
192	Roberto Petagine	.05
193	Shane Reynolds	.05
194	Greg Swindell	.05
195	Dave Veres	.05
196	Kevin Appier	.05
197	Stan Belinda	.05
198	Vince Coleman	.05
199	David Cone	.05
200	Gary Gaetti	.05
201	Greg Gagne	.05
202	Mark Gubicza	.05
203	Bob Hamelin	.05
204	Dave Henderson	.05
205	Felix Jose	.05
206	Wally Joyner	.05
207	Jose Lind	.05
208	Mike Macfarlane	.05
209	Brian McRae	.05
210	Jeff Montgomery	.05
211	Hipolito Pichardo	.05
212	Pedro Astacio	.05
213	Brett Butler	.05
214	Omar Daal	.05
215	Delino DeShields	.05
216	Darren Dreifort	.05
217	Carlos Hernandez	.05
218	Orel Hershiser	.05
219	Garey Ingram	.05
220	Eric Karros	.05
221	Ramon Martinez	.05
222	Raul Mondesi	.05
223	Jose Offerman	.05
224	Mike Piazza	1.00
225	Henry Rodriguez	.05
226	Ismael Valdes	.05
227	Tim Wallach	.05
228	Jeff Cirillo	.05
229	Alex Diaz	.05
230	Cal Eldred	.05
231	Mike Fetters	.05
232	Brian Harper	.05
233	Ted Higuera	.05
234	John Jaha	.05
235	Graeme Lloyd	.05
236	Jose Mercedes	.05
237	Jaime Navarro	.05
238	Dave Nilsson	.05
239	Jesse Orosco	.05
240	Jody Reed	.05
241	Jose Valentin	.05
242	Greg Vaughn	.05
243	Turner Ward	.05
244	Rick Aguilera	.05
245	Rich Becker	.05
246	Jim Deshaies	.05
247	Steve Dunn	.05
248	Scott Erickson	.05
249	Kent Hrbek	.05
250	Chuck Knoblauch	.05
251	Scott Leius	.05
252	David McCarty	.05
253	Pat Meares	.05
254	Pedro Munoz	.05
255	Kirby Puckett	.75
256	Carlos Pulido	.05
257	Kevin Tapani	.05
258	Matt Walbeck	.05
259	Dave Winfield	.60
260	Moises Alou	.05
261	Juan Bell	.05
262	Freddie Benavides	.05
263	Sean Berry	.05
264	Wil Cordero	.05
265	Jeff Fassero	.05
266	Darrin Fletcher	.05
267	Cliff Floyd	.05
268	Marquis Grissom	.05
269	Gil Heredia	.05
270	Ken Hill	.05
271	Pedro Martinez	.60
272	Mel Rojas	.05
273	Larry Walker	.05
274	John Wetteland	.05
275	Rondell White	.05
276	Tim Bogar	.05
277	Bobby Bonilla	.05
278	Rico Brogna	.05
279	Jeromy Burnitz	.05
280	John Franco	.05
281	Eric Hillman	.05
282	Todd Hundley	.05
283	Jeff Kent	.05
284	Mike Maddux	.05
285	Joe Orsulak	.05
286	Luis Rivera	.05
287	Bret Saberhagen	.05
288	David Segui	.05
289	Ryan Thompson	.05
290	Fernando Vina	.05
291	Jose Vizcaino	.05
292	Jim Abbott	.05
293	Wade Boggs	.75
294	Russ Davis	.05
295	Mike Gallego	.05
296	Xavier Hernandez	.05
297	Steve Howe	.05
298	Jimmy Key	.05
299	Don Mattingly	1.00
300	Terry Mulholland	.05
301	Paul O'Neill	.05
302	Luis Polonia	.05
303	Mike Stanley	.05
304	Danny Tartabull	.05
305	Randy Velarde	.05
306	Bob Wickman	.05
307	Bernie Williams	.05
308	Mark Acre	.05
309	Geronimo Berroa	.05
310	Mike Bordick	.05
311	Dennis Eckersley	.50
312	Rickey Henderson	.60
313	Stan Javier	.05
314	Miguel Jimenez	.05
315	Francisco Matos	.05
316	Mark McGwire	1.50
317	Troy Neel	.05
318	Steve Ontiveros	.05
319	Carlos Reyes	.05
320	Ruben Sierra	.05
321	Terry Steinbach	.05
322	Bob Welch	.05
323	Bobby Witt	.05
324	Larry Andersen	.05
325	Kim Batiste	.05
326	Darren Daulton	.05
327	Mariano Duncan	.05
328	Lenny Dykstra	.05
329	Jim Eisenreich	.05
330	Danny Jackson	.05
331	John Kruk	.05
332	Tony Longmire	.05
333	Tom Marsh	.05
334	Mickey Morandini	.05
335	Bobby Munoz	.05
336	Todd Pratt	.05
337	Tom Quinlan	.05
338	Kevin Stocker	.05
339	Fernando Valenzuela	.05
340	Jay Bell	.05
341	Dave Clark	.05
342	Steve Cooke	.05
343	Carlos Garcia	.05
344	Jeff King	.05
345	Jon Lieber	.05
346	Ravelo Manzanillo	.05
347	Al Martin	.05
348	Orlando Merced	.05
349	Denny Neagle	.05
350	Alejandro Pena	.05
351	Don Slaught	.05
352	Zane Smith	.05
353	Andy Van Slyke	.05
354	Rick White	.05
355	Kevin Young	.05
356	Andy Ashby	.05
357	Derek Bell	.05
358	Andy Benes	.05
359	Phil Clark	.05
360	Donnie Elliott	.05
361	Ricky Gutierrez	.05
362	Tony Gwynn	.75
363	Trevor Hoffman	.05
364	Tim Hyers	.05
365	Luis Lopez	.05
366	Jose Martinez	.05
367	Pedro A. Martinez	.05
368	Phil Plantier	.05
369	Bip Roberts	.05
370	A.J. Sager	.05
371	Jeff Tabaka	.05
372	Todd Benzinger	.05
373	Barry Bonds	2.00
374	John Burkett	.05
375	Mark Carreon	.05
376	Royce Clayton	.05
377	Pat Gomez	.05
378	Erik Johnson	.05
379	Darren Lewis	.05
380	Kirt Manwaring	.05
381	Dave Martinez	.05
382	John Patterson	.05
383	Mark Portugal	.05
384	Darryl Strawberry	.05
385	Salomon Torres	.05
386	Bill Van Landingham	.05
387	Matt Williams	.05
388	Rich Amaral	.05
389	Bobby Ayala	.05
390	Mike Blowers	.05
391	Chris Bosio	.05
392	Jay Buhner	.05
393	Jim Converse	.05
394	Tim Davis	.05
395	Felix Fermin	.05
396	Dave Fleming	.05
397	Goose Gossage	.05
398	Ken Griffey Jr.	1.00
399	Randy Johnson	.60
400	Edgar Martinez	.05
401	Tino Martinez	.05
402	Alex Rodriguez	1.50
403	Dan Wilson	.05
404	Luis Alicea	.05
405	Rene Arocha	.05
406	Bernard Gilkey	.05
407	Gregg Jefferies	.05
408	Ray Lankford	.05
409	Terry McGriff	.05
410	Omar Olivares	.05
411	Jose Oquendo	.05
412	Vicente Palacios	.05
413	Geronimo Pena	.05
414	Mike Perez	.05
415	Gerald Perry	.05
416	Ozzie Smith	.75
417	Bob Tewksbury	.05
418	Mark Whiten	.05
419	Todd Zeile	.05
420	Esteban Beltre	.05
421	Kevin Brown	.05
422	Cris Carpenter	.05
423	Will Clark	.05
424	Hector Fajardo	.05
425	Jeff Frye	.05
426	Juan Gonzalez	.30
427	Rusty Greer	.05
428	Rick Honeycutt	.05
429	David Hulse	.05
430	Manny Lee	.05
431	Junior Ortiz	.05
432	Dean Palmer	.05
433	Ivan Rodriguez	.50
434	Dan Smith	.05
435	Roberto Alomar	.15
436	Pat Borders	.05
437	Scott Brow	.05
438	Rob Butler	.05
439	Joe Carter	.05
440	Tony Castillo	.05
441	Domingo Cedeno	.05
442	Brad Cornett	.05
443	Carlos Delgado	.35
444	Alex Gonzalez	.05
445	Juan Guzman	.05
446	Darren Hall	.05
447	Paul Molitor	.60
448	John Olerud	.05
449	Robert Perez	.05
450	Devon White	.05

Gold Crown Die-Cut

A die-cut gold holographic foil crown in the background is featured in this chase set. The player's name at bottom is rendered in the same foil. Backs have a dark blue background, a portrait photo and a 1994 season recap.

	NM/M
Complete Set (20):	30.00
Common Player:	.45

#	Player	Price
1	Greg Maddux	2.50
2	Fred McGriff	.45
3	Rafael Palmeiro	1.50
4	Cal Ripken Jr.	4.50
5	Jose Canseco	1.00
6	Frank Thomas	4.00
7	Albert Belle	.45
8	Manny Ramirez	2.00
9	Andres Galarraga	.45
10	Jeff Bagwell	2.00
11	Chan Ho Park	.45
12	Raul Mondesi	.45
13	Mike Piazza	3.00
14	Kirby Puckett	2.50
15	Barry Bonds	4.50
16	Ken Griffey Jr.	3.00
17	Alex Rodriguez	3.50
18	Juan Gonzalez	1.00
19	Roberto Alomar	1.00
20	Carlos Delgado	1.25

Hot Hispanics

Acknowledging its bilingual card license and market niche, this insert set of Latinos Destacados (Hot Hispanics) features top Latin players in the majors. The series logo and a gold-foil holographic player name rise from a row of flames at bottom-front. On the reverse is another player photo, on an inferno background, along with 1994 season highlights and a large team logo.

	NM/M
Complete Set (36):	20.00
Common Player:	.25

#	Player	Price
1	Roberto Alomar	1.25
2	Moises Alou	.25
3	Wilson Alvarez	.25
4	Carlos Baerga	.25
5	Geronimo Berroa	.25
6	Jose Canseco	1.00
7	Hector Carrasco	.25
8	Wil Cordero	.25
9	Carlos Delgado	1.50
10	Damion Easley	.25
11	Tony Eusebio	.25
12	Hector Fajardo	.25
13	Andres Galarraga	.25
14	Carlos Garcia	.25
15	Chris Gomez	.25
16	Alex Gonzalez	.25
17	Juan Gonzalez	1.25
18	Luis Gonzalez	.25
19	Felix Jose	.25
20	Javier Lopez	.25
21	Luis Lopez	.25
22	Dennis Martinez	.25
23	Orlando Miller	.25
24	Raul Mondesi	.25
25	Jose Oliva	.25
26	Rafael Palmeiro	2.00
27	Yorkis Perez	.25
28	Manny Ramirez	2.50
29	Jose Rijo	.25
30	Alex Rodriguez	4.00
31	Ivan Rodriguez	2.00
32	Carlos Rodriguez	.25
33	Sammy Sosa	3.00
34	Tony Tarasco	.25
35	Ismael Valdes	.25
36	Bernie Williams	.25

Marquee Prism

Etched gold holographic foil is the background to the action photos in this insert set. Player names at bottom-front are shadowed in team colors. Backs repeat the front photo in miniature version in a box at one side that offers career stats and a highlight. On the other end is a portrait photo on a background of baseballs.

	NM/M
Complete Set (36):	22.50
Common Player:	.35

#	Player	Price
1	Jose Canseco	.65
2	Gregg Jefferies	.35
3	Fred McGriff	.35
4	Joe Carter	.35
5	Tim Salmon	.35
6	Wade Boggs	1.25
7	Dave Winfield	1.00
8	Bob Hamelin	.35
9	Cal Ripken Jr.	3.00
10	Don Mattingly	1.50
11	Juan Gonzalez	.50
12	Carlos Delgado	.65
13	Barry Bonds	3.00
14	Albert Belle	.35
15	Raul Mondesi	.35
16	Jeff Bagwell	1.00
17	Mike Piazza	1.50
18	Rafael Palmeiro	.75
19	Frank Thomas	1.00
20	Matt Williams	.35
21	Ken Griffey Jr.	2.00
22	Will Clark	.35
23	Bobby Bonilla	.35
24	Kenny Lofton	.35
25	Paul Molitor	1.00
26	Kirby Puckett	1.25
27	Dave Justice	.35
28	Jeff Conine	.35
29	Bret Boone	.35
30	Larry Walker	.35
31	Cecil Fielder	.35
32	Manny Ramirez	1.00
33	Javier Lopez	.35
34	Jimmy Key	.35

35	Andres Galarraga	.35
36	Tony Gwynn	1.25

1995 Pacific Prism

The rainbow prismatic foil background on the card fronts provides the visual punch to Pacific's premium brand cards. In a throwback to the 1950s, the cards were sold in single-card packs for $1.75. Production was limited to 2,999 cases of 36-pack boxes. Backs have a large portrait photo on a conventionally printed rainbow background. In keeping with the company's license, the 1994 season summary printed at bottom on back is in both English and Spanish. One checklist, team or Pacific logo was inserted into each pack to protect the Prism card.

		NM/M
Complete Set (144):		65.00
Common Player:		.25
Pack (2):		.60
Wax Box (36):		12.50
1	Dave Justice	.25
2	Ryan Klesko	.25
3	Javier Lopez	.25
4	Greg Maddux	2.00
5	Fred McGriff	.25
6	Tony Tarasco	.25
7	Jeffrey Hammonds	.25
8	Mike Mussina	.75
9	Rafael Palmeiro	1.25
10	Cal Ripken Jr.	5.00
11	Lee Smith	.25
12	Roger Clemens	2.50
13	Scott Cooper	.25
14	Mike Greenwell	.25
15	Carlos Rodriguez	.25
16	Mo Vaughn	2.50
17	Chili Davis	.25
18	Jim Edmonds	.25
19	Jorge Fabregas	.25
20	Bo Jackson	.35
21	Tim Salmon	.25
22	Mark Grace	.25
23	Jose Guzman	.25
24	Randy Myers	.25
25	Rey Sanchez	.25
26	Sammy Sosa	2.50
27	Wilson Alvarez	.25
28	Julio Franco	.25
29	Ozzie Guillen	.25
30	Jack McDowell	.25
31	Frank Thomas	1.50
32	Bret Boone	.25
33	Barry Larkin	.25
34	Hal Morris	.25
35	Jose Rijo	.25
36	Deion Sanders	.25
37	Carlos Baerga	.25
38	Albert Belle	.25
39	Kenny Lofton	.25
40	Dennis Martinez	.25
41	Manny Ramirez	1.50
42	Omar Vizquel	.25
43	Dante Bichette	.25
44	Marvin Freeman	.25
45	Andres Galarraga	.25
46	Mike Kingery	.25
47	Danny Bautista	.25
48	Cecil Fielder	.25
49	Travis Fryman	.25
50	Tony Phillips	.25
51	Alan Trammell	.25
52	Lou Whitaker	.25
53	Alex Arias	.25
54	Bret Barberie	.25
55	Jeff Conine	.25
56	Charles Johnson	.25
57	Gary Sheffield	.65
58	Jeff Bagwell	1.50
59	Craig Biggio	.25
60	Doug Drabek	.25
61	Tony Eusebio	.25
62	Luis Gonzalez	.25
63	David Cone	.25
64	Bob Hamelin	.25
65	Felix Jose	.25

66	Wally Joyner	.25
67	Brian McRae	.25
68	Brett Butler	.25
69	Garey Ingram	.25
70	Ramon Martinez	.25
71	Raul Mondesi	.25
72	Mike Piazza	2.50
73	Henry Rodriguez	.25
74	Ricky Bones	.25
75	Pat Listach	.25
76	Dave Nilsson	.25
77	Jose Valentin	.25
78	Rick Aguilera	.25
79	Denny Hocking	.25
80	Shane Mack	.25
81	Pedro Munoz	.25
82	Kirby Puckett	2.00
83	Dave Winfield	1.50
84	Moises Alou	.25
85	Wil Cordero	.25
86	Cliff Floyd	.25
87	Marquis Grissom	.25
88	Pedro Martinez	1.50
89	Larry Walker	.25
90	Bobby Bonilla	.25
91	Jeromy Burnitz	.25
92	John Franco	.25
93	Jeff Kent	.25
94	Jose Vizcaino	.25
95	Wade Boggs	2.00
96	Jimmy Key	.25
97	Don Mattingly	2.50
98	Paul O'Neill	.25
99	Luis Polonia	.25
100	Danny Tartabull	.25
101	Geronimo Berroa	.25
102	Rickey Henderson	1.50
103	Ruben Sierra	.25
104	Terry Steinbach	.25
105	Darren Daulton	.25
106	Mariano Duncan	.25
107	Lenny Dykstra	.25
108	Mike Lieberthal	.25
109	Tony Longmire	.25
110	Tom Marsh	.25
111	Jay Bell	.25
112	Carlos Garcia	.25
113	Orlando Merced	.25
114	Andy Van Slyke	.25
115	Derek Bell	.25
116	Tony Gwynn	2.00
117	Luis Lopez	.25
118	Bip Roberts	.25
119	Rod Beck	.25
120	Barry Bonds	5.00
121	Darryl Strawberry	.25
122	Bill Van Landingham	.25
123	Matt Williams	.25
124	Jay Buhner	.25
125	Felix Fermin	.25
126	Ken Griffey Jr.	3.00
127	Randy Johnson	1.50
128	Edgar Martinez	.25
129	Alex Rodriguez	4.00
130	Rene Arocha	.25
131	Gregg Jefferies	.25
132	Mike Perez	.25
133	Ozzie Smith	2.00
134	Jose Canseco	.65
135	Will Clark	.25
136	Juan Gonzalez	1.00
137	Ivan Rodriguez	1.25
138	Roberto Alomar	.50
139	Joe Carter	.25
140	Carlos Delgado	.75
141	Alex Gonzalez	.25
142	Juan Guzman	.25
143	Paul Molitor	1.50
144	John Olerud	.25

Team Logos

Inserted one card per pack to provide some protection to the Prism card was a checklist, team or Pacific logo card. The large color logos are on a background of a playing field. Backs have a short English/Spanish history of the team.

		NM/M
Complete Set (31):		2.00
Common Player:		.10
1	Baltimore Orioles	.10
2	Boston Red Sox	.10
3	California Angels	.10
4	Chicago White Sox	.10
5	Cleveland Indians	.10
6	Detroit Tigers	.10
7	Kansas City Royals	.10
8	Milwaukee Brewers	.10
9	Minnesota Twins	.10
10	New York Yankees	.10
11	Oakland Athletics	.10
12	Seattle Mariners	.10
13	Texas Rangers	.10

14	Toronto Blue Jays	.10
15	Atlanta Braves	.10
16	Chicago Cubs	.10
17	Cincinnati Reds	.10
18	Colorado Rockies	.10
19	Florida Marlins	.10
20	Houston Astros	.10
21	Los Angeles Dodgers	.10
22	Montreal Expos	.10
23	New York Mets	.10
24	Philadelphia Phillies	.10
25	Pittsburgh Pirates	.10
26	St. Louis Cardinals	.10
27	San Diego Padres	.10
28	San Francisco Giants	.10
1	Checklist 1-72	.05
2	Checklist 73-144	.05
---	Pacific logo card	.05

Mariners Memories

To commemorate the M's magical 1995 season leading up to the A.L. Western Division pennant and the American League championship series, Pacific issued this boxed set. The first 17 cards in the set depict post-season action, with backs done in newspaper style. The rest of the set features the individual players in borderless action photos on front and smaller color portraits on back. All cards feature silver-foil highlights on front. The set was sold in a team-colors cardboard box. The set was released in late December and includes full 1995 stats for the players.

		NM/M
Complete Set (50):		10.00
Common Player:		.10
1	Griffey slams M's to brink (Ken Griffey Jr.)	.50
2	Mariners clinch tie in Texas (Vince Coleman)	.10
3	Mariners win the West (Luis Sojo)	.10
4	At last, something to celebrate (Randy Johnson)	.25
5	Johnson stands tall (Randy Johnson)	.25
6	Griffey has big debut (Ken Griffey Jr.)	.50
7	Tino ignites Mariners (Edgar Martinez, Tino Martinez)	.10
8	Mariners tie Yankee series (Edgar Martinez)	.10
9	Griffey scores winning run (Ken Griffey Jr.)	.50
10	Thunder in the Kingdome	.10
11	Series win ends years of futility	.10
12	Bob who? beats Cleveland (Bob Wolcott)	.10
13	Buhner rocks Cleveland (Jay Buhner)	.10
14	Johnson salutes Kingdome crowd (Randy Johnson)	.25
15	Fans give their all (Lou Piniella)	.10
16	Cora eludes tag (Joey Cora)	.10
17	Voice of M's calls winner (Dave Niehaus)	.10
18	Rich Amaral	.10
19	Bobby Ayala	.10
20	Tim Belcher	.10
21	Andy Benes	.10
22	Mike Blowers	.10
23	Chris Bosio	.10
24	Darren Bragg	.10
25	Jay Buhner	.25
26	Rafael Carmona	.10
27	Norm Charlton	.10
28	Vince Coleman	.10
29	Joey Cora	.10
30	Alex Diaz	.10

31	Felix Fermin	.10
32	Ken Griffey Jr.	3.00
33	Lee Guetterman	.10
34	Randy Johnson	3.00
35	Edgar Martinez	.25
36	Tino Martinez	.25
37	Jeff Nelson	.10
38	Warren Newson	.10
39	Greg Pirkl	.10
40	Arquimedez Pozo	.10
41	Bill Risley	.10
42	Alex Rodriguez (Rodriguez)	5.00
43	Luis Sojo	.10
44	Doug Strange	.10
45	Salomon Torres	.10
46	Bob Wells	.10
47	Chris Widger	.10
48	Dan Wilson	.10
49	Bob Wolcott	.10
50	Lou Piniella	.25

1996 Pacific Crown

Pacific's base set for 1996 features 450 gold-foil enhanced cards. Fronts have borderless game-action photos with the issuer's logo in an upper corner and the player's name at bottom center in gold. Horizontal backs have a portrait photo at right, career highlights in both English and Spanish at left, and 1995 stats at top. Cards were sold in 12-card foil packs which could include one of six types of insert cards.

		NM/M
Complete Set (450):		17.50
Common Player:		.05
Pack (12):		1.00
Wax Box (36):		25.00
1	Steve Avery	.05
2	Ryan Klesko	.05
3	Pedro Borbon	.05
4	Chipper Jones	1.00
5	Kent Mercker	.05
6	Greg Maddux	1.00
7	Greg McMichael	.05
8	Mark Wohlers	.05
9	Fred McGriff	.05
10	John Smoltz	.05
11	Rafael Belliard	.05
12	Mark Lemke	.05
13	Tom Glavine	.30
14	Javier Lopez	.05
15	Jeff Blauser	.05
16	Dave Justice	.05
17	Marquis Grissom	.05
18	Greg Maddux (NL Cy Young)	.50
19	Randy Myers	.05
20	Scott Servais	.05
21	Sammy Sosa	1.00
22	Kevin Foster	.05
23	Jose Hernandez	.05
24	Jim Bullinger	.05
25	Mike Perez	.05
26	Shawon Dunston	.05
27	Rey Sanchez	.05
28	Frank Castillo	.05
29	Jaime Navarro	.05
30	Brian McRae	.05
31	Mark Grace	.05
32	Roberto Rivera	.05
33	Luis Gonzalez	.05
34	Hector Carrasco	.05
35	Bret Boone	.05
36	Thomas Howard	.05
37	Hal Morris	.05
38	John Smiley	.05
39	Jeff Brantley	.05
40	Barry Larkin	.05
41	Mariano Duncan	.05
42	Xavier Hernandez	.05
43	Pete Schourek	.05
44	Reggie Sanders	.05
45	Dave Burba	.05
46	Jeff Branson	.05
47	Mark Portugal	.05
48	Ron Gant	.05
49	Benito Santiago	.05
50	Barry Larkin (NL MVP)	.05
51	Steve Reed	.05

52	Kevin Ritz	.05
53	Dante Bichette	.05
54	Darren Holmes	.05
55	Ellis Burks	.05
56	Walt Weiss	.05
57	Armando Reynoso	.05
58	Vinny Castilla	.05
59	Jason Bates	.05
60	Mike Kingery	.05
61	Bryan Rekar	.05
62	Curtis Leskanic	.05
63	Bret Saberhagen	.05
64	Andres Galarraga	.05
65	Larry Walker	.05
66	Joe Girardi	.05
67	Quilvio Veras	.05
68	Robb Nen	.05
69	Mario Diaz	.05
70	Chuck Carr	.05
71	Alex Arias	.05
72	Pat Rapp	.05
73	Rich Garces	.05
74	Kurt Abbott	.05
75	Andre Dawson	.25
76	Greg Colbrunn	.05
77	John Burkett	.05
78	Terry Pendleton	.05
79	Jesus Tavarez	.05
80	Charles Johnson	.05
81	Yorkis Perez	.05
82	Jeff Conine	.05
83	Gary Sheffield	.45
84	Brian Hunter	.05
85	Derrick May	.05
86	Greg Swindell	.05
87	Derek Bell	.05
88	Dave Veres	.05
89	Jeff Bagwell	.75
90	Todd Jones	.05
91	Orlando Miller	.05
92	Pedro A. Martinez	.05
93	Tony Eusebio	.05
94	Craig Biggio	.05
95	Shane Reynolds	.05
96	James Mouton	.05
97	Doug Drabek	.05
98	Dave Magadan	.05
99	Ricky Gutierrez	.05
100	Hideo Nomo	.50
101	Delino DeShields	.05
102	Tom Candiotti	.05
103	Mike Piazza	1.50
104	Ramon Martinez	.05
105	Pedro Astacio	.05
106	Chad Fonville	.05
107	Raul Mondesi	.05
108	Ismael Valdes	.05
109	Jose Offerman	.05
110	Todd Worrell	.05
111	Eric Karros	.05
112	Brett Butler	.05
113	Juan Castro	.05
114	Roberto Kelly	.05
115	Omar Daal	.05
116	Antonio Osuna	.05
117	Hideo Nomo (NL Rookie of Year)	.50
118	Mike Lansing	.05
119	Mel Rojas	.05
120	Sean Berry	.05
121	David Segui	.05
122	Tavo Alvarez	.05
123	Pedro Martinez	.75
124	F.P. Santangelo RC	.05
125	Rondell White	.05
126	Cliff Floyd	.05
127	Henry Rodriguez	.05
128	Tony Tarasco	.05
129	Yamil Benitez	.05
130	Carlos Perez	.05
131	Wil Cordero	.05
132	Jeff Fassero	.05
133	Moises Alou	.05
134	John Franco	.05
135	Rico Brogna	.05
136	Dave Mlicki	.05
137	Bill Pulsipher	.05
138	Jose Vizcaino	.05
139	Carl Everett	.05
140	Edgardo Alfonzo	.05
141	Bobby Jones	.05
142	Alberto Castillo	.05
143	Joe Orsulak	.05
144	Jeff Kent	.05
145	Ryan Thompson	.05
146	Jason Isringhausen	.05
147	Todd Hundley	.05
148	Alex Ochoa	.05
149	Charlie Hayes	.05
150	Michael Mimbs	.05
151	Darren Daulton	.05
152	Toby Borland	.05
153	Andy Van Slyke	.05
154	Mickey Morandini	.05
155	Sid Fernandez	.05
156	Tom Marsh	.05
157	Kevin Stocker	.05
158	Paul Quantrill	.05
159	Gregg Jefferies	.05
160	Ricky Bottalico	.05
161	Lenny Dykstra	.05
162	Mark Whiten	.05
163	Tyler Green	.05
164	Jim Eisenreich	.05
165	Heathcliff Slocumb	.05
166	Esteban Loaiza	.05
167	Rich Aude	.05
168	Jason Christiansen	.05

169	Ramon Morel	.05
170	Orlando Merced	.05
171	Paul Wagner	.05
172	Jeff King	.05
173	Jay Bell	.05
174	Jacob Brumfield	.05
175	Nelson Liriano	.05
176	Dan Miceli	.05
177	Carlos Garcia	.05
178	Denny Neagle	.05
179	Angelo Encarnacion	.05
180	Al Martin	.05
181	Midre Cummings	.05
182	Eddie Williams	.05
183	Roberto Petagine	.05
184	Tony Gwynn	1.00
185	Andy Ashby	.05
186	Melvin Nieves	.05
187	Phil Clark	.05
188	Brad Ausmus	.05
189	Bip Roberts	.05
190	Fernando Valenzuela	.05
191	Marc Newfield	.05
192	Steve Finley	.05
193	Trevor Hoffman	.05
194	Andujar Cedeno	.05
195	Jody Reed	.05
196	Ken Caminiti	.05
197	Joey Hamilton	.05
198	Tony Gwynn (NL Batting Champ)	.50
199	Shawn Barton	.05
200	Deion Sanders	.05
201	Rikkert Faneyte	.05
202	Barry Bonds	2.50
203	Matt Williams	.05
204	Jose Bautista	.05
205	Mark Leiter	.05
206	Mark Carreon	.05
207	Robby Thompson	.05
208	Terry Mulholland	.05
209	Rod Beck	.05
210	Royce Clayton	.05
211	J.R. Phillips	.05
212	Kirt Manwaring	.05
213	Glenallen Hill	.05
214	William Van Landingham	.05
215	Scott Cooper	.05
216	Bernard Gilkey	.05
217	Allen Watson	.05
218	Donovan Osborne	.05
219	Ray Lankford	.05
220	Tony Fossas	.05
221	Tom Pagnozzi	.05
222	John Mabry	.05
223	Tripp Cromer	.05
224	Mark Petkovsek	.05
225	Mike Morgan	.05
226	Ozzie Smith	1.00
227	Tom Henke	.05
228	Jose Oquendo	.05
229	Brian Jordan	.05
230	Cal Ripken Jr.	2.50
231	Scott Erickson	.05
232	Harold Baines	.05
233	Jeff Manto	.05
234	Jesse Orosco	.05
235	Jeffrey Hammonds	.05
236	Brady Anderson	.05
237	Manny Alexander	.05
238	Chris Hoiles	.05
239	Rafael Palmeiro	.60
240	Ben McDonald	.05
241	Curtis Goodwin	.05
242	Bobby Bonilla	.05
243	Mike Mussina	.60
244	Kevin Brown	.05
245	Armando Benitez	.05
246	Jose Canseco	.50
247	Erik Hanson	.05
248	Mo Vaughn	.05
249	Tim Naehring	.05
250	Vaughn Eshelman	.05
251	Mike Greenwell	.05
252	Troy O'Leary	.05
253	Tim Wakefield	.05
254	Dwayne Hosey	.05
255	John Valentin	.05
256	Rick Aguilera	.05
257	Mike MacFarlane	.05
258	Roger Clemens	1.50
259	Luis Alicea	.05
260	Mo Vaughn (AL MVP)	.05
261	Mark Langston	.05
262	Jim Edmonds	.05
263	Rod Correia	.05
264	Tim Salmon	.05
265	J.T. Snow	.05
266	Orlando Palmeiro	.05
267	Jorge Fabregas	.05
268	Jim Abbott	.05
269	Eduardo Perez	.05
270	Lee Smith	.05
271	Gary DiSarcina	.05
272	Damion Easley	.05
273	Tony Phillips	.05
274	Garret Anderson	.05
275	Chuck Finley	.05
276	Chili Davis	.05
277	Lance Johnson	.05
278	Alex Fernandez	.05
279	Robin Ventura	.05
280	Chris Snopek	.05
281	Brian Keyser	.05
282	Lyle Mouton	.05
283	Luis Andujar RC	.05
284	Tim Raines	.05

285	Larry Thomas	.05
286	Ozzie Guillen	.05
287	Frank Thomas	.75
288	Roberto Hernandez	.05
289	Dave Martinez	.05
290	Ray Durham	.05
291	Ron Karkovice	.05
292	Wilson Alvarez	.05
293	Omar Vizquel	.05
294	Eddie Murray	.75
295	Sandy Alomar	.05
296	Orel Hershiser	.05
297	Jose Mesa	.05
298	Julian Tavarez	.05
299	Dennis Martinez	.05
300	Carlos Baerga	.05
301	Manny Ramirez	.75
302	Jim Thome	.60
303	Kenny Lofton	.05
304	Tony Pena	.05
305	Alvaro Espinoza	.05
306	Paul Sorrento	.05
307	Albert Belle	.05
308	Danny Bautista	.05
309	Chris Gomez	.05
310	Jose Lima	.05
311	Phil Nevin	.05
312	Alan Trammell	.05
313	Chad Curtis	.05
314	John Flaherty	.05
315	Travis Fryman	.05
316	Todd Steverson	.05
317	Brian Bohanon	.05
318	Lou Whitaker	.05
319	Bobby Higginson	.05
320	Steve Rodriguez	.05
321	Cecil Fielder	.05
322	Felipe Lira	.05
323	Juan Samuel	.05
324	Bob Hamelin	.05
325	Tom Goodwin	.05
326	Johnny Damon	.25
327	Hipolito Pichardo	.05
328	Dilson Torres	.05
329	Kevin Appier	.05
330	Mark Gubicza	.05
331	Jon Nunnally	.05
332	Gary Gaetti	.05
333	Brent Mayne	.05
334	Brent Cookson	.05
335	Tom Gordon	.05
336	Wally Joyner	.05
337	Greg Gagne	.05
338	Fernando Vina	.05
339	Joe Oliver	.05
340	John Jaha	.05
341	Jeff Cirillo	.05
342	Pat Listach	.05
343	Dave Nilsson	.05
344	Steve Sparks	.05
345	Ricky Bones	.05
346	David Hulse	.05
347	Scott Karl	.05
348	Darryl Hamilton	.05
349	B.J. Surhoff	.05
350	Angel Miranda	.05
351	Sid Roberson	.05
352	Matt Mieske	.05
353	Jose Valentin **RC**	.05
354	Matt Lawton **RC**	.25
355	Eddie Guardado	.05
356	Brad Radke	.05
357	Pedro Munoz	.05
358	Scott Stahoviak	.05
359	Erik Schullstrom	.05
360	Pat Meares	.05
361	Marty Cordova	.05
362	Scott Leius	.05
363	Matt Walbeck	.05
364	Rich Becker	.05
365	Kirby Puckett	1.00
366	Oscar Munoz	.05
367	Chuck Knoblauch	.05
368	Marty Cordova (AL Rookie of Year)	.05
369	Bernie Williams	.05
370	Mike Stanley	.05
371	Andy Pettitte	.25
372	Jack McDowell	.05
373	Sterling Hitchcock	.05
374	David Cone	.05
375	Randy Velarde	.05
376	Don Mattingly	1.50
377	Melido Perez	.05
378	Wade Boggs	1.00
379	Ruben Sierra	.05
380	Tony Fernandez	.05
381	John Wetteland	.05
382	Mariano Rivera	.15
383	Derek Jeter	2.50
384	Paul O'Neill	.05
385	Mark McGwire	2.00
386	Scott Brosius	.05
387	Don Wengert	.05
388	Terry Steinbach	.05
389	Brent Gates	.05
390	Craig Paquette	.05
391	Mike Bordick	.05
392	Ariel Prieto	.05
393	Dennis Eckersley	.65
394	Carlos Reyes	.05
395	Todd Stottlemyre	.05
396	Rickey Henderson	.75
397	Geronimo Berroa	.05
398	Steve Ontiveros	.05
399	Mike Gallego	.05
400	Stan Javier	.05
401	Randy Johnson	.75

402	Norm Charlton	.05
403	Mike Blowers	.05
404	Tino Martinez	.05
405	Dan Wilson	.05
406	Andy Benes	.05
407	Alex Diaz	.05
408	Edgar Martinez	.05
409	Chris Bosio	.05
410	Ken Griffey Jr.	1.50
411	Luis Sojo	.05
412	Bob Wolcott	.05
413	Vince Coleman	.05
414	Rich Amaral	.05
415	Jay Buhner	.05
416	Alex Rodriguez	2.00
417	Joey Cora	.05
418	Randy Johnson (AL Cy Young)	.25
419	Edgar Martinez (AL Batting Champ)	.05
420	Ivan Rodriguez	.65
421	Mark McLemore	.05
422	Mickey Tettleton	.05
423	Juan Gonzalez	.40
424	Will Clark	.05
425	Kevin Gross	.05
426	Dean Palmer	.05
427	Kenny Rogers	.05
428	Bob Tewksbury	.05
429	Benji Gil	.05
430	Jeff Russell	.05
431	Rusty Greer	.05
432	Roger Pavlik	.05
433	Esteban Beltre	.05
434	Otis Nixon	.05
435	Paul Molitor	.75
436	Carlos Delgado	.50
437	Ed Sprague	.05
438	Juan Guzman	.05
439	Domingo Cedeno	.05
440	Pat Hentgen	.05
441	Tomas Perez	.05
442	John Olerud	.05
443	Shawn Green	.25
444	Al Leiter	.05
445	Joe Carter	.05
446	Robert Perez	.05
447	Devon White	.05
448	Tony Castillo	.05
449	Alex Gonzalez	.05
450	Roberto Alomar	.20
450p	Roberto Alomar (Unmarked promo card, "Games: 128" on back.)	1.50

Cramer's Choice

One of the most unusually shaped baseball cards of all time is the Cramer's Choice insert set from the 1996 Pacific Crown Collection. The set features the 10 best players as chosen by Pacific founder and president, Mike Cramer. Cards are in a die-cut pyramidal design 3-1/2" tall and 2-1/2" at the base. They player picture on front is set against a silver-foil background, while the player name and other information is in gold foil on a faux marble base at bottom; the effect is a simulation of a trophy. Backs repeat the marbled background and have a bi-lingual justification from Cramer concerning his choice of the player as one of the 10 best. Average insertion rate is one card per case (720 packs). Cards are numbered with a "CC" prefix.

		NM/M
Complete Set (10):		150.00
Common Player:		6.00
1	Roberto Alomar	7.50
2	Wade Boggs	15.00
3	Cal Ripken Jr.	30.00
4	Greg Maddux	15.00
5	Frank Thomas	12.50
6	Tony Gwynn	15.00
7	Mike Piazza	20.00
8	Ken Griffey Jr.	25.00
9	Manny Ramirez	12.50

10	Edgar Martinez	6.00

Estrellas Latinas

Three dozen of the best contemporary Latino ballplayers are honored in this chase set. Cards feature action photos silhouetted on a black background shot through with gold-foil streaks and stars. The player name, set and insert set logos are in gold at left. Backs have a portrait photo and English/Spanish career summary. The Latino Stars insert cards are inserted at an average rate of one per nine packs; about four per foil box. Cards are numbered with an "EL" prefix.

		NM/M
Complete Set (36):		16.00
Common Player:		.25
1	Roberto Alomar	.50
2	Moises Alou	.25
3	Carlos Baerga	.25
4	Geronimo Berroa	.25
5	Ricky Bones	.25
6	Bobby Bonilla	.25
7	Jose Canseco	.65
8	Vinny Castilla	.25
9	Pedro Martinez	1.50
10	John Valentin	.25
11	Andres Galarraga	.25
12	Juan Gonzalez	.75
13	Ozzie Guillen	.25
14	Esteban Loaiza	.25
15	Javier Lopez	.25
16	Dennis Martinez	.25
17	Edgar Martinez	.25
18	Tino Martinez	.25
19	Orlando Merced	.25
20	Jose Mesa	.25
21	Raul Mondesi	.25
22	Jaime Navarro	.25
23	Rafael Palmeiro	.75
24	Carlos Perez	.25
25	Manny Ramirez	1.50
26	Alex Rodriguez	3.50
27	Ivan Rodriguez	1.25
28	David Segui	.25
29	Ruben Sierra	.25
30	Sammy Sosa	2.00
31	Julian Tavarez	.25
32	Ismael Valdes	.25
33	Fernando Valenzuela	.25
34	Quilvio Veras	.25
35	Omar Vizquel	.25
36	Bernie Williams	.25

Gold Crown Die-Cuts

One of Pacific's most popular inserts of the previous year returns in 1996. The Gold Crown die-cuts have the top of the card cut away to form a gold-foil crown design with an action photo below. The player's name is also in gold foil. Backs repeat the gold crown design at top, have a portrait photo at lower-right and a few words about the player, in both English and Spanish. Insertion rate was advertised as one per 37 packs, on average. Cards are numbered with a "DC" prefix.

		NM/M
Complete Set (36):		45.00
Common Player:		.75
1	Roberto Alomar	1.00
2	Will Clark	.75
3	Johnny Damon	1.00
4	Don Mattingly	2.50
5	Edgar Martinez	.75
6	Manny Ramirez	.75
7	Mike Piazza	2.50
8	Quilvio Veras	.75
9	Rickey Henderson	1.50
10	Jeff Bagwell	1.50
11	Andres Galarraga	.75
12	Tim Salmon	.75
13	Ken Griffey Jr.	2.50
14	Sammy Sosa	2.00
15	Cal Ripken Jr.	4.50
16	Raul Mondesi	.75
17	Jose Canseco	1.00
18	Frank Thomas	1.50
19	Hideo Nomo	1.00
20	Wade Boggs	2.00
21	Reggie Sanders	.75
22	Carlos Baerga	.75
23	Mo Vaughn	.75
24	Ivan Rodriguez	1.25
25	Kirby Puckett	2.00
26	Albert Belle	.75
27	Vinny Castilla	.75
28	Greg Maddux	2.00
29	Dante Bichette	.75
30	Deion Sanders	.75
31	Chipper Jones	2.00
32	Cecil Fielder	.75
33	Randy Johnson	1.50
34	Mark McGwire	3.50
35	Tony Gwynn	2.00
36	Barry Bonds	4.50

Hometown of the Players

The hometown roots of 20 top players are examined in this chase set. Fronts have action photos with large areas of the background replaced with textured gold foil, including solid and outline versions of the player's name. Backs have a portrait photo, a representation of the player's native flag and a few words about his hometown. Card numbers have an "HP" prefix and are inserted at an average rate of one per 18 packs; about two per box.

		NM/M
Complete Set (20):		15.00
Common Player:		.50
1	Mike Piazza	1.50
2	Greg Maddux	1.00
3	Tony Gwynn	1.00
4	Carlos Baerga	.50
5	Don Mattingly	1.50
6	Cal Ripken Jr.	2.50
7	Chipper Jones	1.00
8	Andres Galarraga	.50
9	Manny Ramirez	.75
10	Roberto Alomar	.60
11	Ken Griffey Jr.	1.50
12	Jose Canseco	.60
13	Frank Thomas	.75
14	Vinny Castilla	.50
15	Roberto Kelly	.50
16	Dennis Martinez	.50
17	Kirby Puckett	1.00
18	Raul Mondesi	.50
19	Hideo Nomo	.60
20	Edgar Martinez	.50

Milestones

A textured metallic blue-foil background is featured on this insert set. Behind the player

action photo is a spider's web design with flying baseballs, team logo and a number representing the milestone. The player's name is in purple foil, outlined in white, vertically at right. Backs have a portrait photo and bi-lingual description of the milestone. Average insertion rate for this insert series is one per 37 packs. Cards are numbered with an "M" prefix.

		NM/M
Complete Set (10):		12.50
Common Player:		.50
1	Albert Belle	.50
2	Don Mattingly	2.25
3	Tony Gwynn	2.00
4	Jose Canseco	1.00
5	Marty Cordova	.50
6	Wade Boggs	2.00
7	Greg Maddux	2.00
8	Eddie Murray	1.50
9	Ken Griffey Jr.	2.50
10	Cal Ripken Jr.	3.00

October Moments

Post-season baseball has never been better represented on a card than in Pacific's "October Moments" chase set. Action photos are set against a background of a stadium decked in the traditional Fall Classic bunting, all rendered in metallic copper foil. At bottom is a textured silver strip with the player name in copper and a swirl of fallen leaves. Backs have a repeat of the leaves and bunting themes with a player portrait at center and English/Spanish description of his October heroics. These cards are found at an average rate of once per 37 packs. Cards are numbered with an "OM" prefix.

		NM/M
Complete Set (20):		30.00
Common Player:		.60
1	Carlos Baerga	.60
2	Albert Belle	.75
3	Dante Bichette	.60
4	Jose Canseco	1.25
5	Tom Glavine	1.00
6	Ken Griffey Jr.	5.00
7	Randy Johnson	2.50
8	Chipper Jones	3.50
9	Dave Justice	.60
10	Ryan Klesko	.60
11	Kenny Lofton	.60
12	Javier Lopez	.60
13	Greg Maddux	3.50
14	Edgar Martinez	.60
15	Don Mattingly	4.00
16	Hideo Nomo	1.25
17	Mike Piazza	4.00
18	Manny Ramirez	2.50
19	Reggie Sanders	.60
20	Jim Thome	1.50

1996 Pacific Prism

Only the best in baseball make the cut for the Prism checklist. Sold in one-card foil packs the cards feature action photos set against an etched silver-foil background highlighted by slashes approximating team colors. Backs are conventionally printed in a horizontal format with a player portrait photo at left center on a purple background. A short 1995 season recap is feature in both English and Spanish. Card numbers are prefixed with a "P."

		NM/M
Complete Set (144):		50.00
Common Player:		.35
Golds:		1.5X
Pack (2):		.65
Wax Box (36):		20.00
1	Tom Glavine	.75
2	Chipper Jones	2.00
3	David Justice	.35
4	Ryan Klesko	.35
5	Javier Lopez	.35
6	Greg Maddux	2.00
7	Fred McGriff	.35
8	Frank Castillo	.35
9	Luis Gonzalez	.35
10	Mark Grace	.35
11	Brian McRae	.35
12	Jaime Navarro	.35
13	Sammy Sosa	2.00
14	Bret Boone	.35
15	Ron Gant	.35
16	Barry Larkin	.35
17	Reggie Sanders	.35
18	Benito Santiago	.35
19	Dante Bichette	.35
20	Vinny Castilla	.35
21	Andres Galarraga	.35
22	Bryan Rekar	.35
23	Roberto Alomar	1.00
23p	Roberto Alomar ("Azulejos" rather than "Los Azulajos" on back, unmarked promo card.)	1.00
24	Jeff Conine	.35
25	Andre Dawson	.50
26	Charles Johnson	.35
27	Gary Sheffield	1.00
28	Quilvio Veras	.35
29	Jeff Bagwell	1.50
30	Derek Bell	.35
31	Craig Biggio	.35
32	Tony Eusebio	.35
33	Karim Garcia	.35
34	Eric Karros	.35
35	Ramon Martinez	.35
36	Raul Mondesi	.35
37	Hideo Nomo	1.00
38	Mike Piazza	3.00
39	Ismael Valdes	.35
40	Moises Alou	.35
41	Wil Cordero	.35
42	Pedro Martinez	1.50
43	Mel Rojas	.35
44	David Segui	.35
45	Edgardo Alfonzo	.35
46	Rico Brogna	.35
47	John Franco	.35
48	Jason Isringhausen	.35
49	Jose Vizcaino	.35
50	Ricky Bottalico	.35
51	Darren Daulton	.35
52	Lenny Dykstra	.35
53	Tyler Green	.35
54	Gregg Jefferies	.35
55	Jay Bell	.35
56	Jason Christiansen	.35
57	Carlos Garcia	.35
58	Esteban Loaiza	.35
59	Orlando Merced	.35
60	Andujar Cedeno	.35
61	Tony Gwynn	2.00
62	Melvin Nieves	.35
63	Phil Plantier	.35
64	Fernando Valenzuela	.35
65	Barry Bonds	4.50
66	J.R. Phillips	.35
67	Deion Sanders	.35

68	Matt Williams	.35
69	Bernard Gilkey	.35
70	Tom Henke	.35
71	Brian Jordan	.35
72	Ozzie Smith	2.00
73	Manny Alexander	.35
74	Bobby Bonilla	.35
75	Mike Mussina	1.00
76	Rafael Palmeiro	1.00
77	Cal Ripken Jr.	4.50
78	Jose Canseco	1.00
79	Roger Clemens	2.50
80	John Valentin	.35
81	Mo Vaughn	.35
82	Tim Wakefield	.35
83	Garret Anderson	.35
84	Damion Easley	.35
85	Jim Edmonds	.35
86	Tim Salmon	.35
87	Wilson Alvarez	.35
88	Alex Fernandez	.35
89	Ozzie Guillen	.35
90	Roberto Hernandez	.35
91	Frank Thomas	1.50
92	Robin Ventura	.35
93	Carlos Baerga	.35
94	Albert Belle	.35
95	Kenny Lofton	.35
96	Dennis Martinez	.35
97	Eddie Murray	1.50
98	Manny Ramirez	1.50
99	Omar Vizquel	.35
100	Chad Curtis	.35
101	Cecil Fielder	.35
102	Felipe Lira	.35
103	Alan Trammell	.35
104	Kevin Appier	.35
105	Johnny Damon	.35
106	Gary Gaetti	.35
107	Wally Joyner	.35
108	Ricky Bones	.35
109	John Jaha	.35
110	B.J. Surhoff	.35
111	Jose Valentin	.35
112	Fernando Vina	.35
113	Marty Cordova	.35
114	Chuck Knoblauch	.35
115	Scott Leius	.35
116	Pedro Munoz	.35
117	Kirby Puckett	2.00
118	Wade Boggs	2.00
119	Don Mattingly	2.50
120	Jack McDowell	.35
121	Paul O'Neill	.35
122	Ruben Rivera	.35
123	Bernie Williams	.35
124	Geronimo Berroa	.35
125	Rickey Henderson	1.50
126	Mark McGwire	3.50
127	Terry Steinbach	.35
128	Danny Tartabull	.35
129	Jay Buhner	.35
130	Joey Cora	.35
131	Ken Griffey Jr.	3.00
132	Randy Johnson	1.50
133	Edgar Martinez	.35
134	Tino Martinez	.35
135	Will Clark	.35
136	Juan Gonzalez	.75
137	Dean Palmer	.35
138	Ivan Rodriguez	1.25
139	Mickey Tettleton	.35
140	Larry Walker	.35
141	Joe Carter	.35
142	Carlos Delgado	1.00
143	Alex Gonzalez	.35
144	Paul Molitor	1.50

Gold

Exactly paralleling the cards in the regular Prism set, this chase card insert replaces the silver foil on front with gold foil. All else remains the same. Stated odds of picking a Gold Prism parallel card are about one per 18 packs, on average (two per box).

	NM/M
Complete Set (144):	100.00
Common Player:	.50
Stars:	1.5X

Fence Busters

Home run heroes are featured in this insert set. The

player's big swing is photographed in the foreground while a baseball flies out of the etched metallic foil stadium background. The player's name is in blue foil. Backs have another player photo and details of his 1995 season home run output, in both English and Spanish. Cards are numbered with an FB prefix. Stated odds of finding a Fence Busters insert are one per 37 packs, on average.

	NM/M
Complete Set (19):	50.00
Common Player:	1.50
1 Albert Belle	1.50
2 Dante Bichette	1.50
3 Barry Bonds	7.50
4 Jay Buhner	1.50
5 Jose Canseco	2.25
6 Ken Griffey Jr.	5.00
7 Chipper Jones	4.00
8 David Justice	1.50
9 Eric Karros	1.50
10 Edgar Martinez	1.50
11 Mark McGwire	6.00
12 Eddie Murray	3.00
13 Mike Piazza	5.00
14 Kirby Puckett	4.00
15 Cal Ripken Jr.	7.50
16 Tim Salmon	1.50
17 Sammy Sosa	4.00
18 Frank Thomas	3.00
19 Mo Vaughn	1.50

Flame Throwers

Burning baseballs are the background for the game's best pitchers in this die-cut insert set. The gold-foil highlighted flames have their tails die-cut at the card's left end. The featured pitcher is shown in action in the foreground. The name at bottom and company logo are in gold foil. Backs are conventionally printed with another action photo and 1995 highlight printed in both English and Spanish. Card numbers carry an FT prefix. Stated odds of finding a Flame Throwers card are one in 73 packs, about every two boxes.

	NM/M
Complete Set (10):	25.00
Common Player:	1.50
1 Roger Clemens	6.50
2 David Cone	1.50
3 Tom Glavine	2.50
4 Randy Johnson	4.50
5 Greg Maddux	6.00
6 Ramon Martinez	1.50
7 Jose Mesa	1.50
8 Mike Mussina	2.50
9 Hideo Nomo	3.00
10 Jose Rijo	1.50

Red Hot Stars

Bright red metallic foil provides the background for these inserts. Color action photos are in the foreground, while player name and multiple team logos are worked into the background. Backs are conventionally printed with another player photo and a few words - in both English and Spanish - about the player's 1995 season. Card numbers have an RH prefix. Stated odds of finding a Red Hot Stars insert are one per 37 packs.

	NM/M
Complete Set (20):	25.00
Common Player:	.50
1 Roberto Alomar	.75
2 Jeff Bagwell	1.50
3 Albert Belle	.50
4 Wade Boggs	2.00
5 Barry Bonds	4.00
6 Jose Canseco	1.00
7 Ken Griffey Jr.	2.50
8 Tony Gwynn	2.00
9 Randy Johnson	1.50
10 Chipper Jones	2.00
11 Greg Maddux	2.00
12 Edgar Martinez	.50
13 Don Mattingly	2.50
14 Mike Piazza	2.50
15 Kirby Puckett	2.00
16 Manny Ramirez	1.50
17 Cal Ripken Jr.	4.00
18 Tim Salmon	.50
19 Frank Thomas	1.50
20 Mo Vaughn	.50

Carlos Baerga Celebrities Softball

This set was produced for distribution to fans attending the second annual Carlos Baerga Celebrities Softball Game in Puerto Rico. Packs were handed out containing two of the cards from this set, a regular Pacific Crown Collection card, a Pacific logo card and an information card about card shops on the island. The softball celebrities cards have a blue and red marbled border with player names at bottom in gold foil. Players are shown in action during the '95 game. Backs feature a portrait photo of the player and English/Spanish description of his participation in the event.

	NM/M
Complete Set (8):	12.00
Common Player:	1.00
1 Carlos Baerga	1.00
2 Mike Piazza	4.00
3 Bernie Williams	1.00
4 Frank Thomas	2.50
5 Roberto Alomar	1.25
6 Edgar Martinez	1.00
7 Kenny Lofton	1.00
8 Sammy Sosa	4.00

Nolan Ryan Career Highlights

Highlights of Ryan's career with the Texas Rangers are featured in this 11-card set given to fans attending the September 13 game at Arlington during Nolan Ryan Appreciation Week, when the team retired his jersey. Ten cards feature action photos on front with gold-foil graphics. Backs share a background photo of

Ryan's classic windup and describe the action pictured on front. Sponsors' and licensors' logos are at top and bottom. An 11th unnumbered card is a checklist.

	NM/M
Complete Set (11):	9.00
Common Player:	1.00
--- Header Card/Checklist	.25
1 King of K's (Nolan Ryan)	1.00
2 324 Career Wins (Nolan Ryan)	1.00
3 Miracle Man (Nolan Ryan)	1.00
4 Low-Hit Nolan (Nolan Ryan)	1.00
5 Milestone K's (Nolan Ryan)	1.00
6 Pure Heat (Nolan Ryan)	1.00
7 No-Hit Nolan (Nolan Ryan)	1.00
8 Ryan's Farewell (Nolan Ryan)	1.00
9 Legendary Career (Nolan Ryan)	1.00
10 Retiring #34 (Nolan Ryan)	1.00

Advil Nolan Ryan

Nolan Ryan, who starred in TV commericals for Advil pain reliever at the end of his career continued his association with the product via a baseball card set in 1996. A pair of cards marking the all-time strikeout leader's first and last Ks were available in-store with the purchase of a bottle of Advil. A 27-card set of career highlight cards was available by mail for $5.50 and proof of purchase. All of the Ryan cards have full-bleed front photos with gold-foil highlights and the Advil and Pacific logos. Backs have a background photo of Ryan pitching, with a description of the highlight. Cards are UV coated on each side. The mail-in set was issued in a collectors' box.

	NM/M
Complete Set (29):	6.00
Common Card:	.25

IN-STORE CARDS

1a	First Strikeout (Nolan Ryan)	.50
2a	Last strikeout (Nolan Ryan)	.50

MAIL-IN SET

1	New York Mets Rookie Pitcher (Nolan Ryan)	.25
2	California Angels (Nolan Ryan)	.25
3	Houston Astros (Nolan Ryan)	.25

4	Texas Rangers (Nolan Ryan)	.25
5	No-Hitter #1 (Nolan Ryan)	.25
6	No-Hitter #2 (Nolan Ryan)	.25
7	No-Hitter #3 (Nolan Ryan)	.25
8	No-Hitter #4 (Nolan Ryan)	.25
9	No-Hitter #5 (Nolan Ryan)	.25
10	No-Hitter #6 (Nolan Ryan)	.25
11	No-Hitter #7 (Nolan Ryan)	.25
12	First Major League Win (Nolan Ryan)	.25
13	250th Win (Nolan Ryan)	.25
14	300th Win (Nolan Ryan)	.25
15	324th Win (Nolan Ryan)	.25
16	1,000th Strikeout (Nolan Ryan)	.25
17	2,000th Strikeout (Nolan Ryan)	.25
18	3,000th Strikeout (Nolan Ryan)	.25
19	Nolan Breaks Johnson Record (Nolan Ryan)	.25
20	4,000th Strikeout (Nolan Ryan)	.25
21	5,000th Strikeout (Nolan Ryan)	.25
22	World Series Victory (Nolan Ryan)	.25
23	Fastest Pitch Ever Thrown (Nolan Ryan)	.25
24	Ryan Home Run (Nolan Ryan)	.25
25	The Greatest Power Pitcher (Nolan Ryan)	.25
26	1989 All-Star Game (Nolan Ryan)	.25
27	Last Appearance (Nolan Ryan)	.25

1997 Pacific Crown

The 450-card, regular-sized set was available in 12-card packs. The card fronts feature the player's name in gold foil along the left border with the team logo in the bottom right corner. The card backs feature a head shot of the player in the lower left quadrant with a short highlight in both Spanish and English. Inserted in packs were: Card-Supials, Cramer's Choice, Latinos Of The Major Leagues, Fireworks Die-Cuts, Gold Crown Die-Cuts and Triple Crown Die-Cuts. A parallel silver version (67 sets) was available.

	NM/M
Complete Set (450):	30.00
Common Player:	.05
Silver Stars/RC's:	15X
Light Blue:	1X
Pack (12):	1.25
Wax Box (36):	32.50
1 Garret Anderson	.05
2 George Arias	.05
3 Chili Davis	.05
4 Gary DiSarcina	.05
5 Jim Edmonds	.05
6 Darin Erstad	.15
7 Jorge Fabregas	.05
8 Chuck Finley	.05
9 Rex Hudler	.05
10 Mark Langston	.05
11 Orlando Palmeiro	.05
12 Troy Percival	.05
13 Tim Salmon	.05
14 J.T. Snow	.05
15 Randy Velarde	.05
16 Manny Alexander	.05
17 Roberto Alomar	.25
18 Brady Anderson	.05
19 Armando Benitez	.05

20	Bobby Bonilla	.05
21	Rocky Coppinger	.05
22	Scott Erickson	.05
23	Jeffrey Hammonds	.05
24	Chris Hoiles	.05
25	Eddie Murray	.75
26	Mike Mussina	.60
27	Randy Myers	.05
28	Rafael Palmeiro	.65
29	Cal Ripken Jr.	2.50
30	B.J. Surhoff	.05
31	Tony Tarasco	.05
32	Esteban Beltre	.05
33	Darren Bragg	.05
34	Jose Canseco	.05
35	Roger Clemens	1.50
36	Wil Cordero	.05
37	Alex Delgado	.05
38	Jeff Frye	.05
39	Nomar Garciaparra	1.00
40	Tom Gordon	.05
41	Mike Greenwell	.05
42	Reggie Jefferson	.05
43	Tim Naehring	.05
44	Troy O'Leary	.05
45	Heathcliff Slocumb	.05
46	Lee Tinsley	.05
47	John Valentin	.05
48	Mo Vaughn	.05
49	Wilson Alvarez	.05
50	Harold Baines	.05
51	Ray Durham	.05
52	Alex Fernandez	.05
53	Ozzie Guillen	.05
54	Roberto Hernandez	.05
55	Ron Karkovice	.05
56	Darren Lewis	.05
57	Norberto Martin	.05
58	Dave Martinez	.05
59	Lyle Mouton	.05
60	Jose Munoz	.05
61	Tony Phillips	.05
62	Rich Sauveur	.05
63	Danny Tartabull	.05
64	Frank Thomas	.75
65	Robin Ventura	.05
66	Sandy Alomar Jr.	.05
67	Albert Belle	.05
68	Julio Franco	.05
69	Brian Giles **RC**	.50
70	Danny Graves	.05
71	Orel Hershiser	.05
72	Jeff Kent	.05
73	Kenny Lofton	.05
74	Dennis Martinez	.05
75	Jack McDowell	.05
76	Jose Mesa	.05
77	Charles Nagy	.05
78	Manny Ramirez	.75
79	Julian Tavarez	.05
80	Jim Thome	.60
81	Jose Vizcaino	.05
82	Omar Vizquel	.05
83	Brad Ausmus	.05
84	Kimera Bartee	.05
85	Raul Casanova	.05
86	Tony Clark	.05
87	Travis Fryman	.05
88	Bobby Higginson	.05
89	Mark Lewis	.05
90	Jose Lima	.05
91	Felipe Lira	.05
92	Phil Nevin	.05
93	Melvin Nieves	.05
94	Curtis Pride	.05
95	Ruben Sierra	.05
96	Alan Trammell	.05
97	Kevin Appier	.05
98	Tim Belcher	.05
99	Johnny Damon	.35
100	Tom Goodwin	.05
101	Bob Hamelin	.05
102	David Howard	.05
103	Jason Jacome	.05
104	Keith Lockhart	.05
105	Mike Macfarlane	.05
106	Jeff Montgomery	.05
107	Jose Offerman	.05
108	Hipolito Pichardo	.05
109	Joe Randa	.05
110	Bip Roberts	.05
111	Chris Stynes	.05
112	Mike Sweeney	.05
113	Joe Vitiello	.05
114	Jeromy Burnitz	.05
115	Chuck Carr	.05
116	Jeff Cirillo	.05
117	Mike Fetters	.05
118	David Hulse	.05
119	John Jaha	.05
120	Scott Karl	.05
121	Jesse Levis	.05
122	Mark Loretta	.05
123	Mike Matheny	.05
124	Ben McDonald	.05
125	Matt Mieske	.05
126	Angel Miranda	.05
127	Dave Nilsson	.05
128	Jose Valentin	.05
129	Fernando Vina	.05
130	Ron Villone	.05
131	Gerald Williams	.05
132	Rick Aguilera	.05
133	Rich Becker	.05
134	Ron Coomer	.05
135	Marty Cordova	.05
136	Eddie Guardado	.05
137	Denny Hocking	.05

138	Roberto Kelly	.05	256	Rey Sanchez	.05	374	Ricky Bottalico	.05
139	Chuck Knoblauch	.05	257	Ryne Sandberg	1.00	375	David Doster	.05
140	Matt Lawton	.05	258	Scott Servais	.05	376	Lenny Dykstra	.05
141	Pat Meares	.05	259	Sammy Sosa	1.00	377	Jim Eisenreich	.05
142	Paul Molitor	.75	260	Pedro Valdes RC	.05	378	Bobby Estalella	.05
143	Greg Myers	.05	261	Turk Wendell	.05	379	Gregg Jefferies	.05
144	Jeff Reboulet	.05	262	Bret Boone	.05	380	Kevin Jordan	.05
145	Scott Stahoviak	.05	263	Jeff Branson	.05	381	Ricardo Jordan	.05
146	Todd Walker	.05	264	Jeff Brantley	.05	382	Mickey Morandini	.05
147	Wade Boggs	1.00	265	Dave Burba	.05	383	Ricky Otero	.05
148	David Cone	.05	266	Hector Carrasco	.05	384	Benito Santiago	.05
149	Mariano Duncan	.05	267	Eric Davis	.05	385	Gene Schall	.05
150	Cecil Fielder	.05	268	Willie Greene	.05	386	Curt Schilling	.25
151	Dwight Gooden	.05	269	Lenny Harris	.05	387	Kevin Sefcik	.05
152	Derek Jeter	2.50	270	Thomas Howard	.05	388	Kevin Stocker	.05
153	Jim Leyritz	.05	271	Barry Larkin	.05	389	Jermaine Allensworth	.05
154	Tino Martinez	.05	272	Hal Morris	.05	390	Jay Bell	.05
155	Paul O'Neill	.05	273	Joe Oliver	.05	391	Jason Christiansen	.05
156	Andy Pettitte	.25	274	Eric Owens	.05	392	Francisco Cordova	.05
157	Tim Raines	.05	275	Jose Rijo	.05	393	Mark Johnson	.05
158	Mariano Rivera	.15	276	Reggie Sanders	.05	394	Jason Kendall	.05
159	Ruben Rivera	.05	277	Eddie Taubensee	.05	395	Jeff King	.05
160	Kenny Rogers	.05	278	Jason Bates	.05	396	Jon Lieber	.05
161	Darryl Strawberry	.05	279	Dante Bichette	.05	397	Nelson Liriano	.05
162	John Wetteland	.05	280	Ellis Burks	.05	398	Esteban Loaiza	.05
163	Bernie Williams	.05	281	Vinny Castilla	.05	399	Al Martin	.05
164	Tony Batista	.05	282	Andres Galarraga	.05	400	Orlando Merced	.05
165	Geronimo Berroa	.05	283	Quinton McCracken	.05	401	Ramon Morel	.05
166	Mike Bordick	.05	284	Jayhawk Owens	.05	402	Luis Alicea	.05
167	Scott Brosius	.05	285	Jeff Reed	.05	403	Alan Benes	.05
168	Brent Gates	.05	286	Bryan Rekar	.05	404	Andy Benes	.05
169	Jason Giambi	.65	287	Armando Reynoso	.05	405	Terry Bradshaw	.05
170	Jose Herrera	.05	288	Kevin Ritz	.05	406	Royce Clayton	.05
171	Brian Lesher	.05	289	Bruce Ruffin	.05	407	Dennis Eckersley	.65
172	Damon Mashore RC	.05	290	John Vander Wal	.05	408	Gary Gaetti	.05
173	Mark McGwire	2.00	291	Larry Walker	.05	409	Mike Gallego	.05
174	Ariel Prieto	.05	292	Walt Weiss	.05	410	Ron Gant	.05
175	Carlos Reyes	.05	293	Eric Young	.05	411	Brian Jordan	.05
176	Matt Stairs	.05	294	Kurt Abbott	.05	412	Ray Lankford	.05
177	Terry Steinbach	.05	295	Alex Arias	.05	413	John Mabry	.05
178	John Wasdin	.05	296	Miguel Batista	.05	414	Willie McGee	.05
179	Ernie Young	.05	297	Kevin Brown	.05	415	Tom Pagnozzi	.05
180	Rich Amaral	.05	298	Luis Castillo	.05	416	Ozzie Smith	1.00
181	Bobby Ayala	.05	299	Greg Colbrunn	.05	417	Todd Stottlemyre	.05
182	Jay Buhner	.05	300	Jeff Conine	.05	418	Mark Sweeney	.05
183	Rafael Carmona	.05	301	Charles Johnson	.05	419	Andy Ashby	.05
184	Norm Charlton	.05	302	Al Leiter	.05	420	Ken Caminiti	.05
185	Joey Cora	.05	303	Robb Nen	.05	421	Archi Cianfrocco	.05
186	Ken Griffey Jr.	1.50	304	Joe Orsulak	.05	422	Steve Finley	.05
187	Sterling Hitchcock	.05	305	Yorkis Perez	.05	423	Chris Gomez	.05
188	Dave Hollins	.05	306	Edgar Renteria	.05	424	Tony Gwynn	1.00
189	Randy Johnson	.75	307	Gary Sheffield	.30	425	Joey Hamilton	.05
190	Edgar Martinez	.05	308	Jesus Tavarez	.05	426	Rickey Henderson	.75
191	Jamie Moyer	.05	309	Quilvio Veras	.05	427	Trevor Hoffman	.05
192	Alex Rodriguez	2.00	310	Devon White	.05	428	Brian Johnson	.05
193	Paul Sorrento	.05	311	Jeff Bagwell	.75	429	Wally Joyner	.05
194	Salomon Torres	.05	312	Derek Bell	.05	430	Scott Livingstone	.05
195	Bob Wells	.05	313	Sean Berry	.05	431	Jody Reed	.05
196	Dan Wilson	.05	314	Craig Biggio	.05	432	Craig Shipley	.05
197	Will Clark	.05	315	Doug Drabek	.05	433	Fernando Valenzuela	.05
198	Kevin Elster	.05	316	Tony Eusebio	.05	434	Greg Vaughn	.05
199	Rene Gonzales	.05	317	Ricky Gutierrez	.05	435	Rich Aurilia	.05
200	Juan Gonzalez	.40	318	Xavier Hernandez	.05	436	Kim Batiste	.05
201	Rusty Greer	.05	319	Brian L. Hunter	.05	437	Jose Bautista	.05
202	Darryl Hamilton	.05	320	Darryl Kile	.05	438	Rod Beck	.05
203	Mike Henneman	.05	321	Derrick May	.05	439	Marvin Benard	.05
204	Ken Hill	.05	322	Orlando Miller	.05	440	Barry Bonds	2.50
205	Mark McLemore	.05	323	James Mouton	.05	441	Shawon Dunston	.05
206	Darren Oliver	.05	324	Bill Spiers	.05	442	Shawn Estes	.05
207	Dean Palmer	.05	325	Pedro Astacio	.05	443	Osvaldo Fernandez	.05
208	Roger Pavlik	.05	326	Brett Butler	.05	444	Stan Javier	.05
209	Ivan Rodriguez	.65	327	Juan Castro	.05	445	David McCarty	.05
210	Kurt Stillwell	.05	328	Roger Cedeno	.05	446	Bill Mueller RC	.15
211	Mickey Tettleton	.05	329	Delino DeShields	.05	447	Steve Scarsone	.05
212	Bobby Witt	.05	330	Karim Garcia	.10	448	Robby Thompson	.05
213	Tilson Brito	.05	331	Todd Hollandsworth	.05	449	Rick Wilkins	.05
214	Jacob Brumfield	.05	332	Eric Karros	.05	450	Matt Williams	.05
215	Miguel Cairo	.05	333	Oreste Marrero	.05			
216	Joe Carter	.05	334	Ramon Martinez	.05			
217	Felipe Crespo	.05	335	Raul Mondesi	.05			
218	Carlos Delgado	.60	336	Hideo Nomo	.50			
219	Alex Gonzalez	.05	337	Antonio Osuna	.05			
220	Shawn Green	.15	338	Chan Ho Park	.05			
221	Juan Guzman	.05	339	Mike Piazza	1.50			
222	Pat Hentgen	.05	340	Ismael Valdes	.05			
223	Charlie O'Brien	.05	341	Moises Alou	.05			
224	John Olerud	.05	342	Omar Daal	.05			
225	Robert Perez	.05	343	Jeff Fassero	.05			
226	Tomas Perez	.05	344	Cliff Floyd	.05			
227	Juan Samuel	.05	345	Mark Grudzielanek	.05			
228	Ed Sprague	.05	346	Mike Lansing	.05			
229	Mike Timlin	.05	347	Pedro Martinez	.75			
230	Rafael Belliard	.05	348	Sherman Obando	.05			
231	Jermaine Dye	.25	349	Jose Paniagua	.05			
232	Tom Glavine	.05	350	Henry Rodriguez	.05			
233	Marquis Grissom	.05	351	Mel Rojas	.05			
234	Andruw Jones	.75	352	F.P. Santangelo	.05			
235	Chipper Jones	1.00	353	Dave Segui	.05			
236	David Justice	.05	354	Dave Silvestri	.05			
237	Ryan Klesko	.05	355	Ugueth Urbina	.05			
238	Mark Lemke	.05	356	Rondell White	.05			
239	Javier Lopez	.05	357	Edgardo Alfonzo	.05			
240	Greg Maddux	1.00	358	Carlos Baerga	.05			
241	Fred McGriff	.05	359	Tim Bogar	.05			
242	Denny Neagle	.05	360	Rico Brogna	.05			
243	Eddie Perez	.05	361	Alvaro Espinoza	.05			
244	John Smoltz	.05	362	Carl Everett	.05			
245	Mark Wohlers	.05	363	John Franco	.05			
246	Brant Brown	.05	364	Bernard Gilkey	.05			
247	Scott Bullett	.05	365	Todd Hundley	.05			
248	Leo Gomez	.05	366	Butch Huskey	.05			
249	Luis Gonzalez	.05	367	Jason Isringhausen	.05			
250	Mark Grace	.05	368	Bobby Jones	.05			
251	Jose Hernandez	.05	369	Lance Johnson	.05			
252	Brooks Kieschnick	.05	370	Brent Mayne	.05			
253	Brian McRae	.05	371	Alex Ochoa	.05			
254	Jaime Navarro	.05	372	Rey Ordonez	.05			
255	Mike Perez	.05	373	Ron Blazier	.05			

Light Blue

This parallel insert was produced exclusively for insertion in Wal-Mart/Sam's jumbo packs at the rate of one per pack. Following the format of the regular-issue, they use light blue foil, rather than the standard gold. Light blue inserts should not be confused with the much scarcer silver inserts which are visually similar.

	NM/M
Complete Set (450):	60.00
Common Player:	.25
Stars:	1X

Silver

This parallel insert was produced in an edition of only 67 cards per player. Following the format of the regular-issue, they use silver foil, rather than the standard gold. Silver parallels were inserted at an advertised rate of one per 73 packs. Silver inserts should not be confused with the much more common light blue inserts which are visually similar.

	NM/M
Common Player:	1.00
Stars/Rookies:	12X

Card-Supials

The 36-card, regular-sized set was inserted every 37 packs of 1997 Pacific Crown baseball. The card fronts feature a gold-foil spiral with the player's name printed along a curve on the bottom edge. The team logo appears in the lower right corner. The card backs feature an action shot and are numbered "x of 36." The cards come with a mini (1-1/4" x 1-3/4") card that slides into a pocket on the back. The mini cards depict the same action shot as the larger card backs.

		NM/M
Complete Set (72):		80.00
Complete Large Set (36):		60.00
Complete Small Set (36):		45.00
Common Large:		.75
Small Cards: 75%		
1	Roberto Alomar	1.00
2	Brady Anderson	.75
3	Eddie Murray	2.00
4	Cal Ripken Jr.	5.00
5	Jose Canseco	1.00
6	Mo Vaughn	.75
7	Frank Thomas	2.00
8	Albert Belle	.75
9	Omar Vizquel	.75
10	Chuck Knoblauch	.75
11	Paul Molitor	2.00
12	Wade Boggs	2.50
13	Derek Jeter	5.00
14	Andy Pettitte	1.00
15	Mark McGwire	3.50
16	Jay Buhner	.75
17	Ken Griffey Jr.	3.00
18	Alex Rodriguez	3.50
19	Juan Gonzalez	1.00
20	Ivan Rodriguez	1.50
21	Andruw Jones	2.00
22	Chipper Jones	2.50
23	Ryan Klesko	.75
24	Greg Maddux	2.50
25	Ryne Sandberg	2.50
26	Andres Galarraga	.75
27	Gary Sheffield	1.00
28	Jeff Bagwell	2.00
29	Todd Hollandsworth	.75
30	Hideo Nomo	1.00
31	Mike Piazza	3.00
32	Todd Hundley	.75
33	Dennis Eckersley	1.50
34	Ken Caminiti	.75
35	Tony Gwynn	2.50
36	Barry Bonds	5.00

Cramer's Choice Awards

The 10-card, regular-sized set was inserted every 721 packs and features a die-cut pyramid design. A color player photo is imaged over silver foil with the player's name and position in gold foil over a green marble background along the bottom. The card backs feature a headshot with a brief career highlight in both Spanish and English. The cards are numbered with a "CC" prefix.

		NM/M
Complete Set (10):		75.00
Common Player:		4.50
1	Roberto Alomar	5.00
2	Frank Thomas	9.00
3	Albert Belle	4.50
4	Andy Pettitte	4.50
5	Ken Griffey Jr.	17.50
6	Alex Rodriguez	25.00
7	Chipper Jones	12.00
8	John Smoltz	4.50
9	Mike Piazza	15.00
10	Tony Gwynn	12.00

Fireworks Die-Cuts

The 20-card, regular-sized, die-cut set was inserted every 73 packs of 1997 Crown. The card fronts feature a color action shot with generic fireworks over a stadium on the upper half. The horizontal card backs contain close-up shots with highlights in Spanish and English. The cards are numbered with the "FW" prefix.

		NM/M
Complete Set (20):		40.00
Common Player:		.75
1	Roberto Alomar	1.00
2	Brady Anderson	.75
3	Eddie Murray	2.50
4	Cal Ripken Jr.	7.50
5	Frank Thomas	2.50
6	Albert Belle	.75
7	Derek Jeter	7.50
8	Andy Pettitte	1.00
9	Bernie Williams	.75
10	Mark McGwire	6.50
11	Ken Griffey Jr.	5.00
12	Alex Rodriguez	6.50
13	Juan Gonzalez	1.25
14	Andruw Jones	2.50
15	Chipper Jones	3.50
16	Hideo Nomo	1.25
17	Mike Piazza	5.00
18	Henry Rodriguez	.75
19	Tony Gwynn	3.50
20	Barry Bonds	7.50

Gold Crown Die-Cuts

The 36-card, regular-sized, die-cut set was inserted every 37 packs. The card

fronts feature a die-cut, gold-foil crown on the top border and the player's name appears in gold along the bottom edge. The card backs contain a headshot and a Spanish/English highlight and are numbered with the "GC" prefix.

		NM/M
Complete Set (36):		65.00
Common Player:		1.00
1	Roberto Alomar	1.25
2	Brady Anderson	1.00
3	Mike Mussina	1.50
4	Eddie Murray	2.75
5	Cal Ripken Jr.	8.50
6	Jose Canseco	2.00
7	Frank Thomas	2.75
8	Albert Belle	1.00
9	Omar Vizquel	1.00
10	Wade Boggs	3.50
11	Derek Jeter	8.50
12	Andy Pettitte	1.25
13	Mariano Rivera	1.25
14	Bernie Williams	1.00
15	Mark McGwire	6.50
16	Ken Griffey Jr.	5.00
17	Edgar Martinez	1.00
18	Alex Rodriquez	6.50
19	Juan Gonzalez	1.50
20	Ivan Rodriguez	2.50
21	Andruw Jones	2.75
22	Chipper Jones	3.50
23	Ryan Klesko	1.00
24	John Smoltz	1.00
25	Ryne Sandberg	3.50
26	Andres Galarraga	1.00
27	Edgar Renteria	1.00
28	Jeff Bagwell	2.75
29	Todd Hollandsworth	1.00
30	Hideo Nomo	1.50
31	Mike Piazza	5.00
32	Todd Hundley	1.00
33	Brian Jordan	1.00
34	Ken Caminiti	1.00
35	Tony Gwynn	3.50
36	Barry Bonds	8.50

Latinos of the Major Leagues

The 36-card, regular-sized set was inserted twice every 37 packs. The card fronts feature a color action shot over the player's name in gold foil. The card backs have another action shot and a Spanish/English highlight.

		NM/M
Complete Set (36):		45.00
Common Player:		1.00
1	George Arias	1.00
2	Roberto Alomar	1.50
3	Rafael Palmeiro	2.50
4	Bobby Bonilla	1.00
5	Jose Canseco	2.00
6	Wilson Alvarez	1.00
7	Dave Martinez	1.00
8	Julio Franco	1.00
9	Manny Ramirez	3.00
10	Omar Vizquel	1.00
11	Marty Cordova	1.00
12	Roberto Kelly	1.00
13	Tino Martinez	1.00

14	Mariano Rivera	1.50
15	Ruben Rivera	1.00
16	Bernie Williams	1.00
17	Geronimo Berroa	1.00
18	Joey Cora	1.00
19	Edgar Martinez	1.00
20	Alex Rodriguez	6.00
21	Juan Gonzalez	2.00
22	Ivan Rodriguez	2.50
23	Andruw Jones	3.00
24	Javier Lopez	1.00
25	Sammy Sosa	4.50
26	Vinny Castilla	1.00
27	Andres Galarraga	1.00
28	Ramon Martinez	1.00
29	Raul Mondesi	1.00
30	Ismael Valdes	1.00
31	Pedro Martinez	3.00
32	Henry Rodriguez	1.00
33	Carlos Baerga	1.00
34	Rey Ordonez	1.00
35	Fernando Valenzuela	1.00
36	Osvaldo Fernandez	1.00

Triple Crown Die-Cuts

The 20-card, regular-sized, die-cut set was inserted every 145 packs of Crown baseball. The horizontal card fronts feature the same gold-foil, die-cut crown as on the Gold Crown Die-Cut inserts. The card backs feature a headshot, Spanish/English text and are numbered with the "TC" prefix.

		NM/M
Complete Set (20):		75.00
Common Player:		2.00
1	Brady Anderson	2.00
2	Rafael Palmeiro	4.00
3	Mo Vaughn	2.00
4	Frank Thomas	5.00
5	Albert Belle	2.00
6	Jim Thome	4.00
7	Cecil Fielder	2.00
8	Mark McGwire	10.00
9	Ken Griffey Jr.	7.50
10	Alex Rodriguez	10.00
11	Juan Gonzalez	3.00
12	Andruw Jones	5.00
13	Chipper Jones	6.00
14	Dante Bichette	2.00
15	Ellis Burks	2.00
16	Andres Galarraga	2.00
17	Jeff Bagwell	5.00
18	Mike Piazza	7.50
19	Ken Caminiti	2.00
20	Barry Bonds	12.50

1997 Pacific Invincible

The 1997 Pacific Invincible 150-card set was sold in three-card packs. The card fronts feature gold foil parallel lines with a color action shot. The bottom right quadrant contains a transparent cel headshot. The card backs have Spanish/English text and another color action shot. The reverse cel has the player's hat team logo air-brushed off to prevent reverse print. Insert sets are: Sluggers & Hurlers, Sizzling Lumber, Gate Attractions, Gems of the Diamond (2:1) and Light Blue (retail only) and Platinum (hobby) parallel sets of the 150 base cards.

		NM/M
Complete Set (150):		30.00
Common Player:		.25
Light Blues:		1X
Platinums:		2X
Pack (3):		1.00
Wax Box (36):		25.00
1	Chili Davis	.25
2	Jim Edmonds	.25
3	Darin Erstad	.50
4	Orlando Palmeiro	.25
5	Tim Salmon	.25
6	J.T. Snow	.25
7	Roberto Alomar	.50
8	Brady Anderson	.25
9	Eddie Murray	1.50
10	Mike Mussina	1.00
11	Rafael Palmeiro	1.25
12	Cal Ripken Jr.	4.00
13	Jose Canseco	1.00
14	Roger Clemens	2.50
15	Nomar Garciaparra	2.00
16	Reggie Jefferson	.25
17	Mo Vaughn	.25
18	Wilson Alvarez	.25
19	Harold Baines	.25
20	Alex Fernandez	.25
21	Danny Tartabull	.25
22	Frank Thomas	1.50
23	Robin Ventura	.25
24	Sandy Alomar Jr.	.25
25	Albert Belle	.25
26	Kenny Lofton	.25
27	Jim Thome	.75
28	Omar Vizquel	.25
29	Raul Casanova	.25
30	Tony Clark	.25
31	Travis Fryman	.25
32	Bobby Higginson	.25
33	Melvin Nieves	.25
34	Justin Thompson	.25
35	Johnny Damon	.50
36	Tom Goodwin	.25
37	Jeff Montgomery	.25
38	Jose Offerman	.25
39	John Jaha	.25
40	Jeff Cirillo	.25
41	Dave Nilsson	.25
42	Jose Valentin	.25
43	Fernando Vina	.25
44	Marty Cordova	.25
45	Roberto Kelly	.25
46	Chuck Knoblauch	.25
47	Paul Molitor	1.50
48	Todd Walker	.25
49	Wade Boggs	2.00
50	Cecil Fielder	.25
51	Derek Jeter	4.00
52	Tino Martinez	.25
53	Andy Pettitte	.40
54	Mariano Rivera	.40
55	Bernie Williams	.25
56	Tony Batista	.25
57	Geronimo Berroa	.25
58	Jason Giambi	.75
59	Mark McGwire	3.00
60	Terry Steinbach	.25
61	Jay Buhner	.25
62	Joey Cora	.25
63	Ken Griffey Jr.	2.50
64	Edgar Martinez	.25
65	Alex Rodriguez	3.00
66	Paul Sorrento	.25
67	Will Clark	.75
68	Juan Gonzalez	.75
69	Rusty Greer	.25
70	Dean Palmer	.25
71	Ivan Rodriguez	1.25
72	Joe Carter	.25
73	Carlos Delgado	.75
74	Juan Guzman	.25
75	Pat Hentgen	.25
76	Ed Sprague	.25
77	Jermaine Dye	.25
78	Andruw Jones	1.50
79	Chipper Jones	2.00
80	Ryan Klesko	.25
81	Javier Lopez	.25
82	Greg Maddux	2.00
83	John Smoltz	.25
84	Mark Grace	.25
85	Luis Gonzalez	.25
86	Brooks Kieschnick	.25
87	Jaime Navarro	.25
88	Ryne Sandberg	2.00
89	Sammy Sosa	2.00
90	Bret Boone	.25
91	Jeff Brantley	.25
92	Eric Davis	.25
93	Barry Larkin	.25
94	Reggie Sanders	.25
95	Ellis Burks	.25
96	Dante Bichette	.25
97	Vinny Castilla	.25
98	Andres Galarraga	.25
99	Eric Young	.25
100	Kevin Brown	.25
101	Jeff Conine	.25
102	Charles Johnson	.25
103	Edgar Renteria	.25
104	Gary Sheffield	.75
105	Jeff Bagwell	1.50
106	Derek Bell	.25
107	Sean Berry	.25
108	Craig Biggio	.25
109	Shane Reynolds	.25
110	Karim Garcia	.25
111	Todd Hollandsworth	.25
112	Ramon Martinez	.25
113	Raul Mondesi	.25
114	Hideo Nomo	.75
115	Mike Piazza	2.50
116	Ismael Valdes	.25
117	Moises Alou	.25
118	Mark Grudzielanek	.25
119	Pedro Martinez	1.50
120	Henry Rodriguez	.25
121	F.P. Santangelo	.25
122	Carlos Baerga	.25
123	Bernard Gilkey	.25
124	Todd Hundley	.25
125	Lance Johnson	.25
126	Alex Ochoa	.25
127	Rey Ordonez	.25
128	Lenny Dykstra	.25
129	Gregg Jefferies	.25
130	Ricky Otero	.25
131	Benito Santiago	.25
132	Jermaine Allensworth	.25
133	Francisco Cordova	.25
134	Carlos Garcia	.25
135	Jason Kendall	.25
136	Al Martin	.25
137	Dennis Eckersley	1.25
138	Ron Gant	.25
139	Brian Jordan	.25
140	John Mabry	.25
141	Ozzie Smith	2.00
142	Ken Caminiti	.25
143	Steve Finley	.25
144	Tony Gwynn	2.00
145	Wally Joyner	.25
146	Fernando Valenzuela	.25
147	Barry Bonds	4.00
148	Jacob Cruz	.25
149	Osvaldo Fernandez	.25
150	Matt Williams	.25

Gate Attractions

The 32-card, regular-sized set was inserted every 73 packs of Pacific Invincible baseball. The card fronts feature a generic baseball glove background with the player's name and position in a gold-foil circle. The center of the card is a cel action shot within a common baseball image. The player's team logo appears in the upper right corner. The card backs contain a headshot in the upper left corner with highlights in Spanish and English. The player's image in the cel is etched in gray in reverse. The cards are numbered with the "GA" prefix.

		NM/M
Complete Set (32):		80.00
Common Player:		1.00
1	Roberto Alomar	1.00
2	Brady Anderson	1.00
3	Cal Ripken Jr.	8.00
4	Frank Thomas	2.50
5	Kenny Lofton	1.00
6	Omar Vizquel	1.00
7	Paul Molitor	2.50
8	Wade Boggs	3.00
9	Derek Jeter	8.00
10	Andy Pettitte	1.50
11	Bernie Williams	1.00
12	Geronimo Berroa	1.00
13	Mark McGwire	6.00
14	Ken Griffey Jr.	4.50
15	Alex Rodriguez	6.00
16	Juan Gonzalez	1.50
17	Andruw Jones	2.50
18	Chipper Jones	3.00
19	Greg Maddux	3.00
20	Ryne Sandberg	3.00
21	Sammy Sosa	2.00
22	Andres Galarraga	1.00
23	Jeff Bagwell	2.50
24	Todd Hollandsworth	1.00
25	Hideo Nomo	1.50
26	Mike Piazza	4.50
27	Todd Hundley	1.00
28	Lance Johnson	1.00
29	Ozzie Smith	3.00
30	Ken Caminiti	1.00
31	Tony Gwynn	3.00
32	Barry Bonds	8.00

Gems of the Diamond

Essentially the base set for 1997 Pacific Prism Invincible, these cards are found two per three-card pack. Fronts of the 2-1/2" x 3-1/2" cards have action photos with earth-tone borders and a color team logo at bottom. Backs have a large player portrait photos in a diamond at right-center and are numbered with a "GD-" prefix.

		NM/M
Complete Set (220):		20.00
Common Player:		.10
1	Jim Abbott	.10
2	Shawn Boskie	.10
3	Gary DiSarcina	.10
4	Jim Edmonds	.10
5	Todd Greene	.10
6	Jack Howell	.10
7	Jeff Schmidt	.10
8	Shad Williams	.10
9	Roberto Alomar	.35
10	Cesar Devarez	.10
11	Alan Mills	.10
12	Eddie Murray	.75
13	Jesse Orosco	.10
14	Arthur Rhodes	.10
15	Bill Ripken	.10
16	Cal Ripken Jr.	2.50
17	Mark Smith	.10
18	Roger Clemens	1.50
19	Vaughn Eshelman	.10
20	Rich Garces	.10
21	Bill Haselman	.10
22	Dwayne Hosey	.10
23	Mike Maddux	.10
24	Jose Malave	.10
25	Aaron Sele	.10
26	James Baldwin	.10
27	Pat Borders	.10
28	Mike Cameron	.10
29	Tony Castillo	.10
30	Domingo Cedeno	.10
31	Greg Norton	.10
32	Frank Thomas	.75
33	Albert Belle	.10
34	Einar Diaz	.10
35	Alan Embree	.10
36	Albie Lopez	.10
37	Chad Ogea	.10
38	Tony Pena	.10
39	Joe Roa	.10
40	Fausto Cruz	.10
41	Joey Eischen	.10
42	Travis Fryman	.10
43	Mike Myers	.10
44	A.J. Sager	.10
45	Duane Singleton	.10
46	Justin Thompson	.10
47	Jeff Granger	.10
48	Les Norman	.10
49	Jon Nunnally	.10
50	Craig Paquette	.10
51	Michael Tucker	.10
52	Julio Valera	.10
53	Kevin Young	.10
54	Cal Eldred	.10
55	Ramon Garcia	.10
56	Marc Newfield	.10
57	Al Reyes	.10
58	Tim Unroe	.10
59	Tim Vanegmond	.10
60	Turner Ward	.10
61	Bob Wickman	.10
62	Chuck Knoblauch	.10
63	Paul Molitor	.75
64	Kirby Puckett	1.00
65	Tom Quinlan	.10
66	Rich Robertson	.10
67	Dave Stevens	.10
68	Matt Walbeck	.10
69	Wade Boggs	.50
70	Tony Fernandez	.10
71	Andy Fox	.10
72	Joe Girardi	.10
73	Charlie Hayes	.10
74	Pat Kelly	.10
75	Jeff Nelson	.10
76	Melido Perez	.10
77	Mark Acre	.10
78	Allen Battle	.10
79	Rafael Bournigal	.10
80	Mark McGwire	2.00
81	Pedro Munoz	.10
82	Scott Spiezio	.10
83	Don Wengert	.10
84	Steve Wojciechowski	.10
85	Alex Diaz	.10
86	Ken Griffey Jr.	1.50
87	Raul Ibanez	.10
88	Mike Jackson	.10
89	John Marzano	.10
90	Greg McCarthy	.10
91	Alex Rodriguez	2.00
92	Andy Sheets	.10
93	Makoto Suzuki	.10
94	Benji Gil	.10
95	Juan Gonzalez	.40
96	Kevin Gross	.10
97	Gil Heredia	.10
98	Luis Ortiz	.10
99	Jeff Russell	.10
100	Dave Valle	.10
101	Marty Janzen	.10
102	Sandy Martinez	.10
103	Julio Mosquera	.10
104	Otis Nixon	.10
105	Paul Spoljaric	.10
106	Shannon Stewart	.10
107	Woody Williams	.10
108	Steve Avery	.10
109	Mike Bielecki	.10
110	Pedro Borbon	.10
111	Ed Giovanola	.10
112	Chipper Jones	1.00
113	Greg Maddux	1.00
114	Mike Mordecai	.10
115	Terrell Wade	.10
116	Terry Adams	.10
117	Brian Dorsett	.10
118	Doug Glanville	.10
119	Tyler Houston	.10
120	Robin Jennings	.10
121	Ryne Sandberg	1.00
122	Terry Shumpert	.10
123	Amaury Telemaco	.10
124	Steve Trachsel	.10
125	Curtis Goodwin	.10
126	Mike Kelly	.10
127	Chad Mottola	.10
128	Mark Portugal	.10
129	Roger Salkeld	.10
130	John Smiley	.10
131	Lee Smith	.10
132	Roger Bailey	.10
133	Andres Galarraga	.10
134	Darren Holmes	.10
135	Curtis Leskanic	.10
136	Mike Munoz	.10
137	Jeff Reed	.10
138	Mark Thompson	.10
139	Jamey Wright	.10
140	Andre Dawson	.25
141	Craig Grebeck	.10
142	Matt Mantei	.10
143	Billy McMillon	.10
144	Kurt Miller	.10
145	Ralph Milliard	.10
146	Bob Natal	.10
147	Joe Siddall	.10
148	Bob Abreu	.25
149	Doug Brocail	.10
150	Danny Darwin	.10
151	Mike Hampton	.10
152	Todd Jones	.10
153	Kirt Manwaring	.10
154	Alvin Morman	.10
155	Billy Ashley	.10
156	Tom Candiotti	.10
157	Darren Dreifort	.10
158	Greg Gagne	.10
159	Wilton Guerrero	.10
160	Hideo Nomo	.40
161	Mike Piazza	1.50
162	Tom Prince	.10
163	Todd Worrell	.10
164	Moises Alou	.10
165	Shane Andrews	.10
166	Derek Aucoin	.10
167	Raul Chavez	.10
168	Darrin Fletcher	.10
169	Mark Leiter	.10
170	Henry Rodriguez	.10
171	Dave Veres	.10
172	Paul Byrd	.10
173	Alberto Castillo	.10
174	Mark Clark	.10
175	Rey Ordonez	.10
176	Roberto Petagine	.10
177	Andy Tomberlin	.10
178	Derek Wallace	.10
179	Paul Wilson	.10
180	Ruben Amaro Jr.	.10
181	Toby Borland	.10
182	Rich Hunter	.10
183	Tony Longmire	.10
184	Wendell Magee Jr.	.10
185	Bobby Munoz	.10
186	Scott Rolen	.60
187	Mike Williams	.10
188	Trey Beamon	.10
189	Jason Christiansen	.10
190	Elmer Dessens	.10
191	Angelo Encarnacion	.10
192	Carlos Garcia	.10
193	Mike Kingery	.10
194	Chris Peters	.10
195	Tony Womack	.10
196	Brian Barber	.10
197	David Bell	.10
198	Tony Fossas	.10
199	Rick Honeycutt	.10
200	T.J. Mathews	.10
201	Miguel Mejia	.10
202	Donovan Osborne	.10
203	Ozzie Smith	1.00
204	Andres Berumen	.10
205	Ken Caminiti	.10
206	Chris Gwynn	.10
207	Tony Gwynn	1.00
208	Rickey Henderson	.75
209	Scott Sanders	.10
210	Jason Thompson	.10
211	Fernando Valenzuela	.10
212	Tim Worrell	.10
213	Barry Bonds	2.50
214	Jay Canizaro	.10
215	Doug Creek	.10
216	Jacob Cruz	.10
217	Glenallen Hill	.10
218	Tom Lampkin	.10
219	Jim Poole	.10
220	Desi Wilson	.10

Sizzling Lumber

The 36-card, regular-sized, die-cut set was inserted every 37 packs of Invincible. The cards have die-cut flames along the right border with a bat running parallel. The player's name appears in gold foil along the top border with his position in English and Spanish in gold foil along the bottom. The card backs feature a headshot in the upper half and contain Spanish and English text. The cards are numbered with the "SL" prefix.

		NM/M
Complete Set (36):		50.00
Common Player:		.50
1A	Cal Ripken Jr.	6.50
1B	Rafael Palmeiro	2.50
1C	Roberto Alomar	1.00
2A	Frank Thomas	3.00
2B	Robin Ventura	.50
2C	Harold Baines	.50
3A	Albert Belle	.50
3B	Manny Ramirez	3.00
3C	Kenny Lofton	.50
4A	Derek Jeter	6.50
4B	Bernie Williams	.50
4C	Wade Boggs	.50
5A	Mark McGwire	5.00
5B	Jason Giambi	2.00
5C	Geronimo Berroa	.50
6A	Ken Griffey Jr.	4.00
6B	Alex Rodriguez	5.00
6C	Jay Buhner	.50
7A	Juan Gonzalez	1.50
7B	Dean Palmer	.50
7C	Ivan Rodriguez	2.50
8A	Ryan Klesko	.50
8B	Chipper Jones	3.50
8C	Andruw Jones	3.00
9A	Dante Bichette	.50
9B	Andres Galarraga	.50
9C	Vinny Castilla	.50
10A	Jeff Bagwell	3.00
10B	Craig Biggio	.50
10C	Derek Bell	.50
11A	Mike Piazza	4.00
11B	Raul Mondesi	.50
11C	Karim Garcia	.50
12A	Tony Gwynn	3.50
12B	Ken Caminiti	.50
12C	Greg Vaughn	.50

Sluggers & Hurlers

The 24-card, regular-sized set was inserted every 145 packs of Pacific Invincible baseball. The cards are numbered with an "SH-xA" or "SH-xaB." Each "A" card is

4	Sandy Alomar Jr.	1.00
5	Joey Cora	1.00
6	Roberto Alomar	1.50
7	Moises Alou	1.00
8	Rey Ordonez	1.00
9	Derek Jeter	10.00
10	David Justice	1.00

NationsBank Florida Marlins

the left half of a two-card set with the two players from the same team having their logo in the fit-together center. Each card has the player's name printed in gold foil along the bottom border with gold-foil swirls around the team logo. The card backs have a circular headshot with text in English and Spanish.

Certainly one of the nicest team card sets ever given away at a promotional game was this Marlins set produced by Pacific and sponsored by NationsBank. The cello-wrapped set was given out to the first 16,000 children attending the June 27 Marlins game. The 2-1/2" x 3-1/2" cards are UV-coated on both sides with a gold-foil "wave" containing the player names on front. The producer, sponsor and team logos also appear on front. Backs have a swirling teal background with a player color portrait in the upper-right. Personal data, 1996 and career stats and a short career summary - in both English and Spanish - are also found on back.

	NM/M
Complete Set (24):	80.00
Common Player:	2.00
SH-1a Cal Ripken Jr.	10.00
SH-1b Mike Mussina	2.50
SH-2a Jose Canseco	2.50
SH-2b Roger Clemens	6.00
SH-3a Frank Thomas	3.50
SH-3b Wilson Alvarez	2.00
SH-4a Kenny Lofton	2.00
SH-4b Orel Hershiser	2.00
SH-5a Derek Jeter	10.00
SH-5b Andy Pettitte	2.00
SH-6a Ken Griffey Jr.	6.00
SH-6b Randy Johnson	3.50
SH-7a Alex Rodriguez	7.50
SH-7b Jamie Moyer	2.00
SH-8a Andruw Jones	3.50
SH-8b Greg Maddux	4.50
SH-9a Chipper Jones	4.50
SH-9b John Smoltz	2.00
SH-10a Jeff Bagwell	3.50
SH-10b Shane Reynolds	2.00
SH-11a Mike Piazza	6.00
SH-11b Hideo Nomo	2.50
SH-12a Tony Gwynn	4.50
SH-12b Fernando Valenzuela	2.00

Carlos Baerga Celebrities Softball

This set was produced for distribution to fans attending the third annual Carlos Baerga Celebrities Softball Game in Puerto Rico on December 14. Packs were handed out containing two cards from this set, a 1997 Pacific Crown Collection card, a '97 Pacific Invincible card, a Pacific logo card and an information card about card shops on the island. The softball celebrities cards have gold-foil highlighted border-less action photos from the 1996 game. Pacific and the charity game's logos are in upper-right and lower left. Horizontal backs have a player portrait photo at left and English/Spanish description of his participation in the event.

	NM/M
Complete Set (10):	16.00
Common Player:	.25
1 Carlos Baerga	1.00
2 Bernie Williams	1.00
3 Ivan Rodriguez	5.00

Pacific Baseball for 1998 is a 450-card, bilingual set. The base set features full-bleed photos with the Pacific Crown Collection logo in the upper-left and the player's name, position and team at the bottom. Inserts include Cramer's Choice Awards, In The Cage Laser-Cuts, Home Run Hitters, Team Checklist Laser-Cuts, Gold Crown Die-Cuts and Latinos of the Major Leagues. Three foil-color parallels were issued: Reds were found one per Wal-Mart exclusive retail pack; Silvers were found one per Hobby pack. Platinum Blues, numbered to 67 each, were found one per 73 packs.

	NM/M
Complete Set (450):	40.00
Common Player:	.05
Silvers:	3X
Inserted 1:1 H	
Reds:	6X
Inserted 1:1 R	
Platinum Blues:	15X
Inserted 1:73	
Pack (12):	1.00
Wax Box (36):	20.00

1998 Pacific

1	Luis Alicea	.05
2	Garret Anderson	.05
3	Jason Dickson	.05
4	Gary DiSarcina	.05
5	Jim Edmonds	.05
6	Darin Erstad	.15
7	Chuck Finley	.05
8	Shigetosi Hasegawa	.05
9	Rickey Henderson	.75
10	Dave Hollins	.05
11	Mark Langston	.05
12	Orlando Palmeiro	.05
13	Troy Percival	.05
14	Tony Phillips	.05
15	Tim Salmon	.05
16	Allen Watson	.05
17	Roberto Alomar	.25
18	Brady Anderson	.05
19	Harold Baines	.05
20	Armando Benitez	.05
21	Geronimo Berroa	.05
22	Mike Bordick	.05
23	Eric Davis	.05
24	Scott Erickson	.05
25	Chris Hoiles	.05
26	Jimmy Key	.05
27	Aaron Ledesma	.05
28	Mike Mussina	.50
29	Randy Myers	.05
30	Jesse Orosco	.05
31	Rafael Palmeiro	.65
32	Jeff Reboulet	.05
33	Cal Ripken Jr.	2.00
34	B.J. Surhoff	.05
35	Steve Avery	.05
36	Darren Bragg	.05
37	Wil Cordero	.05
38	Jeff Frye	.05
39	Nomar Garciaparra	1.00
40	Tom Gordon	.05
41	Bill Haselman	.05
42	Scott Hatteberg	.05
43	Butch Henry	.05
44	Reggie Jefferson	.05
45	Tim Naehring	.05
46	Troy O'Leary	.05
47	Jeff Suppan	.05
48	John Valentin	.05
49	Mo Vaughn	.25
50	Tim Wakefield	.05
51	James Baldwin	.05
52	Albert Belle	.25
53	Tony Castillo	.05
54	Doug Drabek	.05
55	Ray Durham	.05
56	Jorge Fabregas	.05
57	Ozzie Guillen	.05
58	Matt Karchner	.05
59	Norberto Martin	.05
60	Dave Martinez	.05
61	Lyle Mouton	.05
62	Jaime Navarro	.05
63	Frank Thomas	.75
64	Mario Valdez	.05
65	Robin Ventura	.05
66	Sandy Alomar Jr.	.05
67	Paul Assenmacher	.05
68	Tony Fernandez	.05
69	Brian Giles	.05
70	Marquis Grissom	.05
71	Orel Hershiser	.05
72	Mike Jackson	.05
73	David Justice	.05
74	Albie Lopez	.05
75	Jose Mesa	.05
76	Charles Nagy	.05
77	Chad Ogea	.05
78	Manny Ramirez	.75
79	Jim Thome	.60
80	Omar Vizquel	.05
81	Matt Williams	.05
82	Jaret Wright	.05
83	Willie Blair	.05

84	Raul Casanova	.05
85	Tony Clark	.05
86	Deivi Cruz	.05
87	Damion Easley	.05
88	Travis Fryman	.05
89	Bobby Higginson	.05
90	Brian Hunter	.05
91	Todd Jones	.05
92	Dan Miceli	.05
93	Brian Moehler	.05
94	Melvin Nieves	.05
95	Jody Reed	.05
96	Justin Thompson	.05
97	Bubba Trammell	.05
98	Kevin Appier	.05
99	Jay Bell	.05
100	Yamil Benitez	.05
101	Johnny Damon	.35
102	Chili Davis	.05
103	Jermaine Dye	.05
104	Jed Hansen	.05
105	Jeff King	.05
106	Mike Macfarlane	.05
107	Felix Martinez	.05
108	Jeff Montgomery	.05
109	Jose Offerman	.05
110	Dean Palmer	.05
111	Hipolito Pichardo	.05
112	Jose Rosado	.05
113	Jeromy Burnitz	.05
114	Jeff Cirillo	.05
115	Cal Eldred	.05
116	John Jaha	.05
117	Doug Jones	.05
118	Scott Karl	.05
119	Jesse Levis	.05
120	Mark Loretta	.05
121	Ben McDonald	.05
122	Jose Mercedes	.05
123	Matt Mieske	.05
124	Dave Nilsson	.05
125	Jose Valentin	.05
126	Fernando Vina	.05
127	Gerald Williams	.05
128	Rick Aguilera	.05
129	Rich Becker	.05
130	Ron Coomer	.05
131	Marty Cordova	.05
132	Eddie Guardado	.05
133	LaTroy Hawkins	.05
134	Denny Hocking	.05
135	Chuck Knoblauch	.05
136	Matt Lawton	.05
137	Pat Meares	.05
138	Paul Molitor	.75
139	David Ortiz	.50
140	Brad Radke	.05
141	Terry Steinbach	.05
142	Bob Tewksbury	.05
143	Javier Valentin	.05
144	Wade Boggs	1.00
145	David Cone	.05
146	Chad Curtis	.05
147	Cecil Fielder	.05
148	Joe Girardi	.05
149	Dwight Gooden	.05
150	Hideki Irabu	.05
151	Derek Jeter	2.00
152	Tino Martinez	.05
153	Ramiro Mendoza	.05
154	Paul O'Neill	.05
155	Andy Pettitte	.20
156	Jorge Posada	.05
157	Mariano Rivera	.15
158	Rey Sanchez	.05
159	Luis Sojo	.05
160	David Wells	.05
161	Bernie Williams	.05
162	Rafael Bournigal	.05
163	Scott Brosius	.05
164	Jose Canseco	.50
165	Jason Giambi	.60
166	Ben Grieve	.05
167	Dave Magadan	.05
168	Brent Mayne	.05
169	Jason McDonald	.05
170	Izzy Molina	.05
171	Ariel Prieto	.05
172	Carlos Reyes	.05
173	Scott Spiezio	.05
174	Matt Stairs	.05
175	Bill Taylor	.05
176	Dave Telgheder	.05
177	Steve Wojciechowski	.05
178	Rich Amaral	.05
179	Bobby Ayala	.05
180	Jay Buhner	.05
181	Rafael Carmona	.05
182	Ken Cloude	.05
183	Joey Cora	.05
184	Russ Davis	.05
185	Jeff Fassero	.05
186	Ken Griffey Jr.	1.25
187	Raul Ibanez	.05
188	Randy Johnson	.75
189	Roberto Kelly	.05
190	Edgar Martinez	.05
191	Jamie Moyer	.05
192	Omar Olivares	.05
193	Alex Rodriguez	1.50
194	Heathcliff Slocumb	.05
195	Paul Sorrento	.05
196	Dan Wilson	.05
197	Scott Bailes	.05
198	John Burkett	.05
199	Domingo Cedeno	.05
200	Will Clark	.05
201	Hanley Frias RC	.05

202	Juan Gonzalez	.40
203	Tom Goodwin	.05
204	Rusty Greer	.05
205	Wilson Heredia	.05
206	Darren Oliver	.05
207	Billy Ripken	.05
208	Ivan Rodriguez	.65
209	Lee Stevens	.05
210	Fernando Tatis	.05
211	John Wetteland	.05
212	Bobby Witt	.05
213	Jacob Brumfield	.05
214	Joe Carter	.05
215	Roger Clemens	1.25
216	Felipe Crespo	.05
217	Jose Cruz Jr.	.05
218	Carlos Delgado	.50
219	Mariano Duncan	.05
220	Carlos Garcia	.05
221	Alex Gonzalez	.05
222	Juan Guzman	.05
223	Pat Hentgen	.05
224	Orlando Merced	.05
225	Tomas Perez	.05
226	Paul Quantrill	.05
227	Benito Santiago	.05
228	Woody Williams	.05
229	Rafael Belliard	.05
230	Jeff Blauser	.05
231	Pedro Borbon	.05
232	Tom Glavine	.25
233	Tony Graffanino	.05
234	Andruw Jones	.75
235	Chipper Jones	1.00
236	Ryan Klesko	.05
237	Mark Lemke	.05
238	Kenny Lofton	.05
239	Javier Lopez	.05
240	Fred McGriff	.05
241	Greg Maddux	1.00
242	Denny Neagle	.05
243	John Smoltz	.05
244	Michael Tucker	.05
245	Mark Wohlers	.05
246	Manny Alexander	.05
247	Miguel Batista	.05
248	Mark Clark	.05
249	Doug Glanville	.05
250	Jeremi Gonzalez	.05
251	Mark Grace	.05
252	Jose Hernandez	.05
253	Lance Johnson	.05
254	Brooks Kieschnick	.05
255	Kevin Orie	.05
256	Ryne Sandberg	1.00
257	Scott Servais	.05
258	Sammy Sosa	1.00
259	Kevin Tapani	.05
260	Ramon Tatis	.05
261	Bret Boone	.05
262	Dave Burba	.05
263	Brook Fordyce	.05
264	Willie Greene	.05
265	Barry Larkin	.05
266	Pedro A. Martinez	.05
267	Hal Morris	.05
268	Joe Oliver	.05
269	Eduardo Perez	.05
270	Pokey Reese	.05
271	Felix Rodriguez	.05
272	Deion Sanders	.05
273	Reggie Sanders	.05
274	Jeff Shaw	.05
275	Scott Sullivan	.05
276	Brett Tomko	.05
277	Roger Bailey	.05
278	Dante Bichette	.05
279	Ellis Burks	.05
280	Vinny Castilla	.05
281	Frank Castillo	.05
282	Mike DeJean RC	.05
283	Andres Galarraga	.05
284	Darren Holmes	.05
285	Kirt Manwaring	.05
286	Quinton McCracken	.05
287	Neifi Perez	.05
288	Steve Reed	.05
289	John Thomson	.05
290	Larry Walker	.05
291	Walt Weiss	.05
292	Kurt Abbott	.05
293	Antonio Alfonseca	.05
294	Moises Alou	.05
295	Alex Arias	.05
296	Bobby Bonilla	.05
297	Kevin Brown	.05
298	Craig Counsell	.05
299	Darren Daulton	.05
300	Jim Eisenreich	.05
301	Alex Fernandez	.05
302	Felix Heredia	.05
303	Livan Hernandez	.05
304	Charles Johnson	.05
305	Al Leiter	.05
306	Robb Nen	.05
307	Edgar Renteria	.05
308	Gary Sheffield	.45
309	Devon White	.05
310	Bob Abreu	.10
311	Brad Ausmus	.05
312	Jeff Bagwell	.75
313	Derek Bell	.05
314	Sean Berry	.05
315	Craig Biggio	.05
316	Ramon Garcia	.05
317	Luis Gonzalez	.05
318	Ricky Gutierrez	.05
319	Mike Hampton	.05

320	Richard Hidalgo	.05
321	Thomas Howard	.05
322	Darryl Kile	.05
323	Jose Lima	.05
324	Shane Reynolds	.05
325	Bill Spiers	.05
326	Tom Candiotti	.05
327	Roger Cedeno	.05
328	Greg Gagne	.05
329	Karim Garcia	.05
330	Wilton Guerrero	.05
331	Todd Hollandsworth	.05
332	Eric Karros	.05
333	Ramon Martinez	.05
334	Raul Mondesi	.05
335	Otis Nixon	.05
336	Hideo Nomo	.40
337	Antonio Osuna	.05
338	Chan Ho Park	.05
339	Mike Piazza	1.25
340	Dennis Reyes	.05
341	Ismael Valdes	.05
342	Todd Worrell	.05
343	Todd Zeile	.05
344	Darrin Fletcher	.05
345	Mark Grudzielanek	.05
346	Vladimir Guerrero	.75
347	Dustin Hermanson	.05
348	Mike Lansing	.05
349	Pedro Martinez	.75
350	Ryan McGuire	.05
351	Jose Paniagua	.05
352	Carlos Perez	.05
353	Henry Rodriguez	.05
354	F.P. Santangelo	.05
355	David Segui	.05
356	Ugueth Urbina	.05
357	Marc Valdes	.05
358	Jose Vidro	.05
359	Rondell White	.05
360	Juan Acevedo	.05
361	Edgardo Alfonzo	.05
362	Carlos Baerga	.05
363	Carl Everett	.05
364	John Franco	.05
365	Bernard Gilkey	.05
366	Todd Hundley	.05
367	Butch Huskey	.05
368	Bobby Jones	.05
369	Takashi Kashiwada	.05
370	Greg McMichael	.05
371	Brian McRae	.05
372	Alex Ochoa	.05
373	John Olerud	.05
374	Rey Ordonez	.05
375	Turk Wendell	.05
376	Ricky Bottalico	.05
377	Rico Brogna	.05
378	Lenny Dykstra	.05
379	Bobby Estalella	.05
380	Wayne Gomes	.05
381	Tyler Green	.05
382	Gregg Jefferies	.05
383	Mark Leiter	.05
384	Mike Lieberthal	.05
385	Mickey Morandini	.05
386	Scott Rolen	.60
387	Curt Schilling	.25
388	Kevin Stocker	.05
389	Danny Tartabull	.05
390	Jermaine Allensworth	.05
391	Adrian Brown	.05
392	Jason Christiansen	.05
393	Steve Cooke	.05
394	Francisco Cordova	.05
395	Jose Guillen	.05
396	Jason Kendall	.05
397	Jon Lieber	.05
398	Esteban Loaiza	.05
399	Al Martin	.05
400	Kevin Polcovich RC	.05
401	Joe Randa	.05
402	Ricardo Rincon	.05
403	Tony Womack	.05
404	Kevin Young	.05
405	Andy Benes	.05
406	Royce Clayton	.05
407	Delino DeShields	.05
408	Mike Difelice	.05
409	Dennis Eckersley	.60
410	John Frascatore	.05
411	Gary Gaetti	.05
412	Ron Gant	.05
413	Brian Jordan	.05
414	Ray Lankford	.05
415	Willie McGee	.05
416	Mark McGwire	1.50
417	Matt Morris	.05
418	Luis Ordaz	.05
419	Todd Stottlemyre	.05
420	Andy Ashby	.05
421	Jim Bruske	.05
422	Ken Caminiti	.05
423	Will Cunnane	.05
424	Steve Finley	.05
425	John Flaherty	.05
426	Chris Gomez	.05
427	Tony Gwynn	1.00
428	Joey Hamilton	.05
429	Carlos Hernandez	.05
430	Sterling Hitchcock	.05
431	Trevor Hoffman	.05
432	Wally Joyner	.05
433	Greg Vaughn	.05
434	Quilvio Veras	.05
435	Wilson Alvarez	.05
436	Rod Beck	.05
437	Barry Bonds	2.00

Carlos Baerga Celebrities Softball section complete set table:

	NM/M
Complete Set (33):	6.00
Common Player:	.25
1 Kurt Abbott	.25
2 Moises Alou	.25
3 Alex Arias	.25
4 Bobby Bonilla	.25
5 Kevin Brown	.25
6 John Cangelosi	.25
7 Luis Castillo	.25
8 Jeff Conine	.25
9 Jim Eisenreich	.25
10 Alex Fernandez	.25
11 Cliff Floyd	.25
12 Rick Helling	.25
13 Felix Heredia	.25
14 Mark Hutton	.25
15 Charles Johnson	.25
16 Al Leiter	.25
17 Robb Nen	.25
18 Jay Powell	.25
19 Pat Rapp	.25
20 Edgar Renteria	.25
21 Tony Saunders	.25
22 Gary Sheffield	.75
23 Devon White	.25
24 Gregg Zaun	.25
25 Jim Leyland	.25
26 Rich Donnelly	.25
27 Bruce Kimm	.25
28 Jerry Manuel	.25
29 Milt May	.25
30 Larry Rothschild	.25
31 Tommy Sandt	.25
32 Billy the Marlin/Mascot	.25
(33) Header Card/Checklist	.10

438	Jacob Cruz	.05
439	Shawn Estes	.05
440	Darryl Hamilton	.05
441	Roberto Hernandez	.05
442	Glenallen Hill	.05
443	Stan Javier	.05
444	Brian Johnson	.05
445	Jeff Kent	.05
446	Bill Mueller	.05
447	Kirk Rueter	.05
448	J.T. Snow	.05
449	Julian Tavarez	.05
450	Jose Vizcaino	.05

Red/Silver/Blue

Red, Silver and Platinum Blue parallels were printed for all 450 cards in Pacific, with the gold foil found on base cards being replaced by one of those foils. Red foil versions were inserted one per Wal-Mart pack (retail). Silver versions were inserted one per hobby pack. Platinum Blues, limited to 67 sets, were a one per 73 pack insert.

	NM/M
Common Red:	1.50
Red Stars:	6X
Common Silver:	.75
Silver Stars:	3X
Common Platinum Blue:	3.00
Platinum Blue Stars:	15X

Cramer's Choice

Cramer's Choice Awards is a 10-card die-cut insert. The cards feature the top player at each position as selected by Pacific CEO Mike Cramer. Each card is shaped like a trophy.

		NM/M
Complete Set (10):		150.00
Common Player:		7.50
Inserted 1:721		
1	Greg Maddux	15.00
2	Roberto Alomar	7.50
3	Cal Ripken Jr.	30.00
4	Nomar Garciaparra	15.00
5	Larry Walker	7.50
6	Mike Piazza	17.50
7	Mark McGwire	25.00
8	Tony Gwynn	15.00
9	Ken Griffey Jr.	20.00
10	Roger Clemens	17.50

Gold Crown Die-Cuts

Gold Crown Die-Cuts is a 36-card insert seeded one per 37 packs. Each card has a holographic silver foil background and gold etching. The cards are die-cut around a crown design at the top.

		NM/M
Complete Set (36):		85.00
Common Player:		1.50
1	Chipper Jones	4.00

2	Greg Maddux	4.00
3	Denny Neagle	1.50
4	Roberto Alomar	2.00
5	Rafael Palmeiro	2.50
6	Cal Ripken Jr.	8.00
7	Nomar Garciaparra	4.00
8	Mo Vaughn	1.50
9	Frank Thomas	3.00
10	Sandy Alomar Jr.	1.50
11	David Justice	1.50
12	Manny Ramirez	1.50
13	Andres Galarraga	1.50
14	Larry Walker	1.50
15	Moises Alou	1.50
16	Livan Hernandez	1.50
17	Gary Sheffield	2.00
18	Jeff Bagwell	3.00
19	Raul Mondesi	1.50
20	Hideo Nomo	2.00
21	Mike Piazza	4.50
22	Derek Jeter	8.00
23	Tino Martinez	1.50
24	Bernie Williams	1.50
25	Ben Grieve	1.50
26	Mark McGwire	6.50
27	Tony Gwynn	4.00
28	Barry Bonds	4.00
29	Ken Griffey Jr.	5.00
30	Randy Johnson	3.00
31	Edgar Martinez	1.50
32	Alex Rodriguez	6.50
33	Juan Gonzalez	2.00
34	Ivan Rodriguez	2.50
35	Roger Clemens	4.50
36	Jose Cruz Jr.	1.50

Home Run Hitters

This 20-card set was inserted one per 73 packs. The full-foil cards feature a color player photo with their home run total from 1997 embossed in the background.

		NM/M
Complete Set (20):		50.00
Common Player:		1.00
1	Rafael Palmeiro	1.00
2	Mo Vaughn	1.00
3	Sammy Sosa	4.00
4	Albert Belle	1.00
5	Frank Thomas	3.50
6	David Justice	1.00
7	Jim Thome	3.00
8	Matt Williams	1.00
9	Vinny Castilla	1.00
10	Andres Galarraga	1.00
11	Larry Walker	1.00
12	Jeff Bagwell	3.50
13	Mike Piazza	4.50
14	Tino Martinez	1.00
15	Mark McGwire	6.00
16	Barry Bonds	7.50
17	Jay Buhner	1.00
18	Ken Griffey Jr.	5.00
19	Alex Rodriguez	6.00
20	Juan Gonzalez	2.00

In the Cage

This insert set features top players in a die-cut batting cage. The netting on the cage is laser-cut. In The Cage laser-cuts were inserted one per 145 packs.

		NM/M
Complete Set (20):		175.00
Common Player:		4.00
1	Chipper Jones	12.00
2	Roberto Alomar	4.00
3	Cal Ripken Jr.	25.00
4	Nomar Garciaparra	12.00
5	Frank Thomas	10.00

6	Sandy Alomar Jr.	4.00
7	David Justice	4.00
8	Larry Walker	4.00
9	Bobby Bonilla	4.00
10	Mike Piazza	16.00
11	Tino Martinez	4.00
12	Bernie Williams	4.00
13	Mark McGwire	20.00
14	Tony Gwynn	12.00
15	Barry Bonds	25.00
16	Ken Griffey Jr.	16.00
17	Edgar Martinez	4.00
18	Alex Rodriguez	20.00
19	Juan Gonzalez	6.00
20	Ivan Rodriguez	7.50

Latinos of the Major Leagues

This 36-card set features Major League players of Hispanic descent. The background has a world map on the left, the player's team logo in the center and an American flag on the right.

		NM/M
Complete Set (36):		30.00
Common Player:		.50
Inserted 2:37		
1	Andruw Jones	2.50
2	Javier Lopez	.50
3	Roberto Alomar	1.25
4	Geronimo Berroa	.50
5	Rafael Palmeiro	2.00
6	Nomar Garciaparra	3.00
7	Sammy Sosa	3.00
8	Ozzie Guillen	.50
9	Sandy Alomar Jr.	.50
10	Manny Ramirez	2.50
11	Omar Vizquel	.50
12	Vinny Castilla	.50
13	Andres Galarraga	.50
14	Moises Alou	.50
15	Bobby Bonilla	.50
16	Livan Hernandez	.50
17	Edgar Renteria	.50
18	Wilton Guerrero	.50
19	Raul Mondesi	.50
20	Ismael Valdes	.50
21	Fernando Vina	.50
22	Pedro Martinez	2.50
23	Edgardo Alfonzo	.50
24	Carlos Baerga	.50
25	Rey Ordonez	.50
26	Tino Martinez	1.00
27	Mariano Rivera	1.00
28	Bernie Williams	1.50
29	Jose Canseco	1.50
30	Joey Cora	.50
31	Roberto Kelly	.50
32	Edgar Martinez	.50
33	Alex Rodriguez	3.50
34	Juan Gonzalez	2.00
35	Ivan Rodriguez	2.00
36	Jose Cruz Jr.	.50

Team Checklists

Team Checklists is a 30-card insert in the bilingual Pacific Baseball set. One card was created for each team. A player photo is featured on the right with the team logo laser-cut into a bat barrel design on the left.

		NM/M
Complete Set (30):		60.00
Common Player:		.50
1	Tim Salmon,	
	Jim Edmonds	.50
2	Cal Ripken Jr.,	
	Roberto Alomar	6.00
3	Nomar Garciaparra,	
	Mo Vaughn	3.50
4	Frank Thomas,	
	Albert Belle	2.50
5	Sandy Alomar Jr.,	
	Manny Ramirez	2.50
6	Justin Thompson,	
	Tony Clark	.50
7	Johnny Damon,	
	Jermaine Dye	.75

8	Dave Nilsson,	
	Jeff Cirillo	.50
9	Paul Molitor,	
	Chuck Knoblauch	2.50
10	Tino Martinez,	
	Derek Jeter	6.00
11	Ben Grieve,	
	Jose Canseco	1.00
12	Ken Griffey Jr.,	
	Alex Rodriguez	5.00
13	Juan Gonzalez,	
	Ivan Rodriguez	2.00
14	Jose Cruz Jr.,	
	Roger Clemens	4.00
15	Greg Maddux,	
	Chipper Jones	3.50
16	Sammy Sosa,	
	Mark Grace	3.50
17	Barry Larkin,	
	Deion Sanders	.50
18	Larry Walker,	
	Andres Galarraga	.50
19	Moises Alou,	
	Bobby Bonilla	.50
20	Jeff Bagwell,	
	Craig Biggio	2.50
21	Mike Piazza,	
	Hideo Nomo	4.00
22	Pedro Martinez,	
	Henry Rodriguez	2.50
23	Rey Ordonez,	
	Carlos Baerga	.50
24	Curt Schilling,	
	Scott Rolen	1.50
25	Al Martin,	
	Tony Womack	.50
26	Mark McGwire,	
	Dennis Eckersley	5.00
27	Tony Gwynn,	
	Wally Joyner	3.50
28	Barry Bonds,	
	J.T. Snow	6.00
29	Matt Williams, Jay Bell	.50
30	Fred McGriff,	
	Roberto Hernandez	.50

1998 Pacific Aurora

The Aurora base set consists of 200 cards printed on 24-point board. The cards have a color photo bordered on two sides by a thick green (National League) or red (A.L.) border. A portrait photo appears in the upper-right corner. Back has another portrait photo, 1997 and career stats, career highlights and personal data. Aurora was sold in six-card foil packs. Inserts include Pennant Fever (with three parallels), Hardball Cel-Fusions, Kings of the Major Leagues, On Deck Laser-Cuts and Pacific Cubes.

		NM/M
Complete Set (200):		20.00
Common Player:		.05
Pack (6):		1.00
Wax Box (36):		20.00
1	Garret Anderson	.05
2	Jim Edmonds	.05
3	Darin Erstad	.15
4	Cecil Fielder	.05
5	Chuck Finley	.05
6	Todd Greene	.05
7	Ken Hill	.05
8	Tim Salmon	.05
9	Roberto Alomar	.20
10	Brady Anderson	.05
11	Joe Carter	.05
12	Mike Mussina	.35
13	Rafael Palmeiro	.65
14	Cal Ripken Jr.	2.50
15	B.J. Surhoff	.05
16	Steve Avery	.05
17	Nomar Garciaparra	1.00
18	Pedro Martinez	.75
19	John Valentin	.05
20	Jason Varitek	.05
21	Mo Vaughn	.25
22	Albert Belle	.25
23	Ray Durham	.05
24	Magglio Ordonez **RC**	1.50

25	Frank Thomas	.75
26	Robin Ventura	.05
27	Sandy Alomar Jr.	.05
28	Travis Fryman	.05
29	Dwight Gooden	.05
30	David Justice	.05
31	Kenny Lofton	.05
32	Manny Ramirez	.75
33	Jim Thome	.60
34	Omar Vizquel	.05
35	Enrique Wilson	.05
36	Jaret Wright	.05
37	Tony Clark	.05
38	Bobby Higginson	.05
39	Brian Hunter	.05
40	Bip Roberts	.05
41	Justin Thompson	.05
42	Jeff Conine	.05
43	Johnny Damon	.35
44	Jermaine Dye	.05
45	Jeff King	.05
46	Jeff Montgomery	.05
47	Hal Morris	.05
48	Dean Palmer	.05
49	Terry Pendleton	.05
50	Rick Aguilera	.05
51	Marty Cordova	.05
52	Paul Molitor	.75
53	Otis Nixon	.05
54	Brad Radke	.05
55	Terry Steinbach	.05
56	Todd Walker	.05
57	Chili Davis	.05
58	Derek Jeter	2.50
59	Chuck Knoblauch	.05
60	Tino Martinez	.05
61	Paul O'Neill	.05
62	Andy Pettitte	.20
63	Mariano Rivera	.15
64	Bernie Williams	.50
65	Jason Giambi	.05
66	Ben Grieve	.05
67	Rickey Henderson	.75
68	A.J. Hinch	.05
69	Kenny Rogers	.05
70	Jay Buhner	.05
71	Joey Cora	.05
72	Ken Griffey Jr.	1.50
73	Randy Johnson	.75
74	Edgar Martinez	.05
75	Jamie Moyer	.05
76	Alex Rodriguez	2.00
77	David Segui	.05
78	Rolando Arrojo **RC**	.35
79	Wade Boggs	1.00
80	Roberto Hernandez	.05
81	Dave Martinez	.05
82	Fred McGriff	.05
83	Paul Sorrento	.05
84	Kevin Stocker	.05
85	Will Clark	.05
86	Juan Gonzalez	.40
87	Tom Goodwin	.05
88	Rusty Greer	.05
89	Ivan Rodriguez	.65
90	John Wetteland	.05
91	Jose Canseco	.40
92	Roger Clemens	1.25
93	Jose Cruz Jr.	.50
94	Carlos Delgado	.50
95	Pat Hentgen	.05
96	Jay Bell	.05
97	Andy Benes	.05
98	Karim Garcia	.05
99	Travis Lee	.05
100	Devon White	.05
101	Matt Williams	.05
102	Andres Galarraga	.05
103	Tom Glavine	.30
104	Andruw Jones	.05
105	Chipper Jones	1.00
106	Ryan Klesko	.05
107	Javy Lopez	.05
108	Greg Maddux	1.00
109	Walt Weiss	.05
110	Rod Beck	.05
111	Jeff Blauser	.05
112	Mark Grace	.05
113	Lance Johnson	.05
114	Mickey Morandini	.05
115	Henry Rodriguez	.05
116	Sammy Sosa	1.00
117	Kerry Wood	.05
118	Lenny Harris	.05
119	Damian Jackson	.05
120	Barry Larkin	.05
121	Reggie Sanders	.05
122	Brett Tomko	.05
123	Dante Bichette	.05
124	Ellis Burks	.05
125	Vinny Castilla	.05
126	Todd Helton	.75
127	Darryl Kile	.05
128	Larry Walker	.05
129	Bobby Bonilla	.05
130	Livan Hernandez	.05
131	Charles Johnson	.05
132	Derrek Lee	.05
133	Edgar Renteria	.05
134	Gary Sheffield	.35
135	Moises Alou	.05
136	Jeff Bagwell	.75
137	Derek Bell	.05
138	Craig Biggio	.05
139	John Halama **RC**	.15
140	Mike Hampton	.05
141	Richard Hidalgo	.05
142	Wilton Guerrero	.05

143	Todd Hollandsworth	.05
144	Eric Karros	.05
145	Paul Konerko	.05
146	Raul Mondesi	.05
147	Hideo Nomo	.40
148	Chan Ho Park	.05
149	Mike Piazza	1.25
150	Jeromy Burnitz	.05
151	Todd Dunn	.05
152	Marquis Grissom	.05
153	John Jaha	.05
154	Dave Nilsson	.05
155	Fernando Vina	.05
156	Mark Grudzielanek	.05
157	Vladimir Guerrero	.75
158	F.P. Santangelo	.05
159	Jose Vidro	.05
160	Rondell White	.05
161	Edgardo Alfonzo	.05
162	Carlos Baerga	.05
163	John Franco	.05
164	Todd Hundley	.05
165	Brian McRae	.05
166	John Olerud	.05
167	Rey Ordonez	.05
168	Masato Yoshii **RC**	.25
169	Ricky Bottalico	.05
170	Doug Glanville	.05
171	Gregg Jefferies	.05
172	Desi Relaford	.05
173	Scott Rolen	.60
174	Curt Schilling	.30
175	Jose Guillen	.05
176	Jason Kendall	.05
177	Al Martin	.05
178	Abraham Nunez	.05
179	Kevin Young	.05
180	Royce Clayton	.05
181	Delino DeShields	.05
182	Gary Gaetti	.05
183	Ron Gant	.05
184	Brian Jordan	.05
185	Ray Lankford	.05
186	Willie McGee	.05
187	Mark McGwire	2.00
188	Kevin Brown	.05
189	Ken Caminiti	.05
190	Steve Finley	.05
191	Tony Gwynn	1.00
192	Wally Joyner	.05
193	Ruben Rivera	.05
194	Quilvio Veras	.05
195	Barry Bonds	2.50
196	Shawn Estes	.05
197	Orel Hershiser	.05
198	Jeff Kent	.05
199	Robb Nen	.05
200	J.T. Snow	.05

Cubes

A cardboard cube presenting player photos on top and three sides, plus a side of stats was created for Pacific Aurora. The assembled, shrink-wrapped cubes were packed one per box.

		NM/M
Complete Set (20):		75.00
Common Player:		1.50
Inserted 1:Box		
1	Travis Lee	1.50
2	Chipper Jones	4.00
3	Greg Maddux	4.00
4	Cal Ripken Jr.	10.00
5	Nomar Garciaparra	4.00
6	Frank Thomas	3.00
7	Manny Ramirez	3.00
8	Larry Walker	1.50
9	Hideo Nomo	2.00
10	Mike Piazza	5.00
11	Derek Jeter	10.00
12	Ben Grieve	1.50
13	Mark McGwire	7.50
14	Tony Gwynn	4.00
15	Barry Bonds	10.00
16	Ken Griffey Jr.	6.00
17	Alex Rodriguez	7.50
18	Wade Boggs	4.00
19	Juan Gonzalez	2.00
20	Jose Cruz Jr.	1.50

Hardball Cel-Fusion

Hardball Cel-Fusion features a die-cut celluloid baseball fused to a foiled and etched card.

		NM/M
Complete Set (20):		60.00
Common Player:		2.00
Inserted 1:73		
1	Travis Lee	2.00
2	Chipper Jones	4.00
3	Greg Maddux	6.00
4	Cal Ripken Jr.	15.00
5	Nomar Garciaparra	6.00
6	Frank Thomas	4.50
7	David Justice	2.00
8	Jeff Bagwell	4.50
9	Hideo Nomo	3.00
10	Mike Piazza	7.50
11	Derek Jeter	15.00
12	Ben Grieve	2.00
13	Scott Rolen	3.00
14	Mark McGwire	12.00
15	Tony Gwynn	6.00
16	Ken Griffey Jr.	9.00
17	Alex Rodriguez	12.00
18	Ivan Rodriguez	3.50
19	Roger Clemens	7.50
20	Jose Cruz Jr.	2.00

Kings of the Major Leagues

This 10-card insert features star players on fully-foiled cards. A marble-look semi-circular panel at bottom has the player identification. The action photo at center is set against a bronze orb and concentric circles of gold-foil repeat the "Kings of the Major Leagues" title. Backs have a color portrait on a red and black background along with a few sentences about the player.

		NM/M
Complete Set (10):		75.00
Common Player:		7.50
Inserted 1:361		
1	Chipper Jones	9.00
2	Greg Maddux	9.00
3	Cal Ripken Jr.	20.00
4	Nomar Garciaparra	9.00
5	Frank Thomas	7.50
6	Mike Piazza	10.00
7	Mark McGwire	15.00
8	Tony Gwynn	9.00
9	Ken Griffey Jr.	12.00
10	Alex Rodriguez	15.00

On Deck Laser-Cut

On Deck Laser-Cut is a 20-card insert in packs of 1998 Pacific Aurora. Fronts have an action photo at top, with an intricately die-cut pattern in gold foil below. Backs feature a portrait photo.

		NM/M
Complete Set (20):		30.00
Common Player:		.60
Inserted 1:9		
1	Travis Lee	.60
2	Chipper Jones	2.25

Pennant Fever

Pennant Fever is a 50-card insert seeded one per pack. Each card is fully foiled and etched. The color player image is duplicated in the upper-left corner with an image stamped in gold foil. Pennant Fever has four parallels. Red cards are a 1:4 retail insert. The Silver retail parallel is numbered to 250, Platinum Blue is numbered to 100 and the Copper hobby parallel is numbered to 20. Tony Gwynn signed his card serially numbered one in each insert.

		NM/M
Complete Set (50):		25.00
Common Player:		.20
Inserted 1:1		
Reds (1:4 Retail):		2X
Silvers (250 Sets):		4X
Platinum Blues (100 Sets):		12X
Coppers (20 Sets):		40X
1	Tony Gwynn	3.00
2	Derek Jeter	2.00
3	Alex Rodriguez	1.50
4	Paul Molitor	.75
5	Nomar Garciaparra	1.00
6	Jeff Bagwell	.75
7	Ivan Rodriguez	.65
8	Cal Ripken Jr.	2.00
9	Matt Williams	.20
10	Chipper Jones	1.00
11	Edgar Martinez	.20
12	Wade Boggs	1.00
13	Paul Konerko	.30
14	Ben Grieve	.20
15	Sandy Alomar Jr.	.20
16	Travis Lee	.20
17	Scott Rolen	.65
18	Ryan Klesko	.20
19	Juan Gonzalez	.40
20	Albert Belle	.20
21	Roger Clemens	1.25
22	Javy Lopez	.20
23	Jose Cruz Jr.	.20
24	Ken Griffey Jr.	1.25
25	Mark McGwire	1.50
26	Brady Anderson	.20
27	Jaret Wright	.20
28	Roberto Alomar	.30
29	Joe Carter	.20
30	Hideo Nomo	.40
31	Mike Piazza	1.25
32	Andres Galarraga	.20
33	Larry Walker	.20
34	Tim Salmon	.20
35	Frank Thomas	.75
36	Moises Alou	.20
37	David Justice	.20
38	Manny Ramirez	.75
39	Jim Edmonds	.20
40	Barry Bonds	2.00
41	Jim Thome	.65
42	Mo Vaughn	.20
43	Rafael Palmeiro	.65
44	Darin Erstad	.30
45	Pedro Martinez	.75
46	Greg Maddux	1.00
47	Jose Canseco	.45
48	Vladimir Guerrero	.75
49	Bernie Williams	.20
50	Randy Johnson	.75

1998 Pacific Crown Royale

The Crown Royale base set consists of 144 die-cut cards. The cards have a horizontal layout and are die-cut around a crown design at the top. The cards are double-foiled and etched. Inserts include Diamond Knights, Pillars of the Game, Race to the Record, All-Star Die-Cuts, Firestone on Baseball and Cramer's Choice Awards.

		NM/M
Complete Set (144):		60.00
Common Player:		.20
Pack (6):		1.00
Wax Box (24):		20.00
1	Garret Anderson	.20
2	Jim Edmonds	.20
3	Darin Erstad	.50
4	Tim Salmon	.20
5	Jarrod Washburn	.20
6	David Dellucci	.20
7	Travis Lee	.20
8	Devon White	.20
9	Matt Williams	.20
10	Andres Galarraga	.20
11	Tom Glavine	.35
12	Andruw Jones	2.00
13	Chipper Jones	3.00
14	Ryan Klesko	.20
15	Javy Lopez	.20
16	Greg Maddux	3.00
17	Walt Weiss	.20
18	Roberto Alomar	.75
19	Harold Baines	.20
20	Eric Davis	.20
21	Mike Mussina	1.00
22	Rafael Palmeiro	1.50
23	Cal Ripken Jr.	5.00
24	Nomar Garciaparra	3.00
25	Pedro Martinez	2.00
26	Troy O'Leary	.20
27	Mo Vaughn	.20
28	Tim Wakefield	.20
29	Mark Grace	.20
30	Mickey Morandini	.20
31	Sammy Sosa	3.00
32	Kerry Wood	.50
33	Albert Belle	.20
34	Mike Caruso	.20
35	Ray Durham	.20
36	Frank Thomas	2.00
37	Robin Ventura	.20
38	Bret Boone	.20
39	Sean Casey	.25
40	Barry Larkin	.20
41	Reggie Sanders	.20
42	Sandy Alomar Jr.	.20
43	David Justice	.20
44	Kenny Lofton	.20
45	Manny Ramirez	2.00
46	Jim Thome	1.00
47	Omar Vizquel	.20
48	Jaret Wright	.20
49	Dante Bichette	.20
50	Ellis Burks	.20
51	Vinny Castilla	.20
52	Todd Helton	2.00
53	Larry Walker	.20
54	Tony Clark	.20
55	Damion Easley	.20
56	Bobby Higginson	.20
57	Cliff Floyd	.20
58	Livan Hernandez	.20
59	Derek Lee	.75
60	Edgar Renteria	.20
61	Moises Alou	.20
62	Jeff Bagwell	2.00
63	Derek Bell	.20
64	Craig Biggio	.75
65	Johnny Damon	.35
66	Jeff King	.20
67	Hal Morris	.20
68	Dean Palmer	.20
69	Bobby Bonilla	.20
70	Eric Karros	.20
71	Raul Mondesi	.20
72	Gary Sheffield	.75
73	Jeromy Burnitz	.20
74	Jeff Cirillo	.20
75	Marquis Grissom	.20
76	Fernando Vina	.20
77	Marty Cordova	.20
78	Pat Meares	.20
79	Paul Molitor	2.00
80	Terry Steinbach	.20
81	Todd Walker	.20
82	Brad Fullmer	.20
83	Vladimir Guerrero	2.00
84	Carl Pavano	.20
85	Rondell White	.20
86	Carlos Baerga	.20
87	Hideo Nomo	1.00
88	John Olerud	.20
89	Rey Ordonez	.20
90	Mike Piazza	3.00
91	Masato Yoshii RC	.75
92	Orlando Hernandez RC	.75
93	Hideki Irabu	.20
94	Derek Jeter	5.00
95	Chuck Knoblauch	.20
96	Ricky Ledee	.20
97	Tino Martinez	.20
98	Paul O'Neill	.20
99	Bernie Williams	.20
100	Jason Giambi	1.25
101	Ben Grieve	.20
102	Rickey Henderson	2.00
103	Matt Stairs	.25
104	Bob Abreu	.20
105	Doug Glanville	.20
106	Scott Rolen	1.50
107	Curt Schilling	.35
108	Jose Guillen	.35
109	Jason Kendall	.20
110	Jason Schmidt	.20
111	Kevin Young	.20
112	Delino DeShields	.20
113	Brian Jordan	.20
114	Ray Lankford	.20
115	Mark McGwire	4.00
116	Tony Gwynn	3.00
117	Wally Joyner	.20
118	Ruben Rivera	.20
119	Greg Vaughn	.20
120	Rich Aurilia	.20
121	Barry Bonds	5.00
122	Bill Mueller	.20
123	Robb Nen	.20
124	Jay Buhner	.20
125	Ken Griffey Jr.	3.50
126	Edgar Martinez	.20
127	Shane Monahan	.20
128	Alex Rodriguez	4.00
129	David Segui	.20
130	Rolando Arrojo RC	.75
131	Wade Boggs	3.00
132	Quinton McCracken	.20
133	Fred McGriff	.20
134	Bobby Smith	.20
135	Will Clark	.20
136	Juan Gonzalez	1.00
137	Rusty Greer	.20
138	Ivan Rodriguez	1.50
139	Aaron Sele	.20
140	John Wetteland	.20
141	Jose Canseco	1.00
142	Roger Clemens	3.50
143	Carlos Delgado	1.25
144	Shawn Green	.50

All-Stars

This 20-card insert was seeded one per 25 packs. The featured players all participated in the 1998 All-Star Game. The background features the sun rising over a mountain with a die-cut at the top of the card.

		NM/M
Complete Set (20):		110.00
Common Player:		1.50
Inserted 1:25		
1	Roberto Alomar	2.00
2	Cal Ripken Jr.	15.00
3	Kenny Lofton	1.50
4	Jim Thome	5.00
5	Derek Jeter	15.00
6	David Wells	1.50
7	Ken Griffey Jr.	10.00
8	Alex Rodriguez	12.00
9	Juan Gonzalez	4.00
10	Ivan Rodriguez	5.00
11	Gary Sheffield	2.50
12	Chipper Jones	7.50

		NM/M
13	Greg Maddux	7.50
14	Walt Weiss	1.50
15	Larry Walker	1.50
16	Craig Biggio	1.50
17	Mike Piazza	10.00
18	Mark McGwire	12.00
19	Tony Gwynn	7.50
20	Barry Bonds	15.00

Cramer's Choice Awards

Premium-sized Cramer's Choice Awards were inserted one per box. The 10 players in the set are featured on a die-cut card designed to resemble a trophy. Pacific CEO Mike Cramer signed and hand-numbered 10 sets of Cramer's Choice Awards.

		NM/M
Complete Set (10):		65.00
Common Player:		4.00
Inserted 1:Box		
1	Cal Ripken Jr.	15.00
2	Ken Griffey Jr.	9.00
3	Alex Rodriguez	12.00
4	Juan Gonzalez	5.00
5	Travis Lee	4.00
6	Chipper Jones	7.50
7	Greg Maddux	7.50
8	Kerry Wood	5.00
9	Mark McGwire	12.00
10	Tony Gwynn	7.50

Diamond Knights

Diamond Knights is a 25-card, one per pack insert. Each card features a color action photo and the player's name, team and position listed on a Medieval-type border at the bottom.

		NM/M
Complete Set (25):		20.00
Common Player:		.35
Inserted 1:1		
1	Andres Galarraga	.35
2	Chipper Jones	1.00
3	Greg Maddux	1.00
4	Cal Ripken Jr.	2.50
5	Nomar Garciaparra	1.50
6	Mo Vaughn	.35
7	Kerry Wood	.45
8	Frank Thomas	.75
9	Vinny Castilla	.35
10	Jeff Bagwell	.75
11	Craig Biggio	.35
12	Paul Molitor	.75
13	Mike Piazza	1.50
14	Orlando Hernandez	.35
15	Derek Jeter	2.50
16	Ricky Ledee	.35
17	Mark McGwire	2.00
18	Tony Gwynn	1.00
19	Barry Bonds	2.50
20	Ken Griffey Jr.	1.75
21	Alex Rodriguez	2.00
22	Wade Boggs	1.00
23	Juan Gonzalez	.45
24	Ivan Rodriguez	.65
25	Jose Canseco	.50

Firestone on Baseball

This 26-card insert features star players with commentary by sports personality Roy Firestone. The fronts have a color photo of the player and a portrait of Firestone in the lower-right corner. The card backs have text by Firestone on what makes the featured player great. Firestone signed a total of 300 cards in this insert.

		NM/M
Complete Set (26):		50.00
Common Player:		.35
Firestone Auto. Card:		18.00
Inserted 1:12		
1	Travis Lee	.35
2	Chipper Jones	3.00
3	Greg Maddux	3.00
4	Cal Ripken Jr.	6.00
5	Nomar Garciaparra	3.00
6	Mo Vaughn	.35
7	Kerry Wood	1.00
8	Frank Thomas	2.25
9	Manny Ramirez	2.25
10	Larry Walker	.35
11	Gary Sheffield	1.00
12	Paul Molitor	2.25
13	Hideo Nomo	1.50
14	Mike Piazza	3.50
15	Ben Grieve	.35
16	Mark McGwire	5.00
17	Tony Gwynn	3.00
18	Barry Bonds	6.00
19	Ken Griffey Jr.	4.00
20	Randy Johnson	2.25
21	Alex Rodriguez	5.00
22	Wade Boggs	3.00
23	Juan Gonzalez	1.50
24	Ivan Rodriguez	1.75
25	Roger Clemens	3.50
26	Roy Firestone	.35

Home Run Fever

Home Run Fever features players who had a shot at breaking Roger Maris' home run record in 1998. Fronts have a player photo on the left and a blackboard with numbers from 1 to 60 on the right. Ten circles featuring disappearing ink contained numbers 61 through 70. Collectors could rub the circles to reveal the player's potential record home run total.

		NM/M
Complete Set (10):		30.00
Common Player:		1.50
Inserted 1:73		
1	Andres Galarraga	1.50
2	Sammy Sosa	4.50
3	Albert Belle	1.50
4	Jim Thome	3.00
5	Mark McGwire	7.50
6	Greg Vaughn	1.50
7	Ken Griffey Jr.	6.00
8	Alex Rodriguez	7.50
9	Juan Gonzalez	2.50
10	Jose Canseco	2.50

Pillars of the Game

This 25-card insert was seeded one per pack. Each card features a star player with a background of holographic silver foil.

MARK McGWIRE

		NM/M
Complete Set (25):		20.00
Common Player:		.35
Inserted 1:1		
1	Jim Edmonds	.35
2	Travis Lee	.35
3	Chipper Jones	1.00
4	Tom Glavine, John Smoltz, Greg Maddux	1.00
5	Cal Ripken Jr.	2.50
6	Nomar Garciaparra	1.00
7	Mo Vaughn	.35
8	Sammy Sosa	1.00
9	Kerry Wood	.40
10	Frank Thomas	.75
11	Jim Thome	.65
12	Larry Walker	.35
13	Moises Alou	.35
14	Raul Mondesi	.35
15	Mike Piazza	1.25
16	Hideki Irabu	.35
17	Bernie Williams	.35
18	Ben Grieve	.35
19	Scott Rolen	.65
20	Mark McGwire	2.00
21	Tony Gwynn	1.00
22	Ken Griffey Jr.	1.50
23	Alex Rodriguez	2.00
24	Juan Gonzalez	.40
25	Roger Clemens	1.25

1998 Pacific Invincible

Invincible consists of a 150-card base set with a horizontal format featuring a player photo on the left and a portrait in a cel window on the right. The regular cards were inserted one per five-card pack. Silver (2:37) and Platinum Blue (1:73) parallels were also created. Inserts include Moments in Time, Team Checklists, Photoengravings, Interleague Players, Gems of the Diamond and Cramer's Choice Awards.

		NM/M
Complete Set (150):		60.00
Common Player:		.20
Silvers:		4X
Inserted 2:37		
Platinum Blues:		6X
Inserted 1:73		
Pack (5):		1.25
Wax Box (36):		32.50
1	Garret Anderson	.20
2	Jim Edmonds	.20
3	Darin Erstad	.35
4	Chuck Finley	.20
5	Tim Salmon	.20
6	Roberto Alomar	.35
7	Brady Anderson	.20
8	Geronimo Berroa	.20
9	Eric Davis	.20
10	Mike Mussina	.50
11	Rafael Palmeiro	1.00
12	Cal Ripken Jr.	6.00
13	Steve Avery	.20
14	Nomar Garciaparra	2.50
15	John Valentin	.20
16	Mo Vaughn	.20
17	Albert Belle	.20
18	Ozzie Guillen	.20
19	Norberto Martin	.20
20	Frank Thomas	1.50
21	Robin Ventura	.20
22	Sandy Alomar Jr.	.20
23	David Justice	.20
24	Kenny Lofton	.20
25	Manny Ramirez	1.50
26	Jim Thome	1.00
27	Omar Vizquel	.20
28	Matt Williams	.20
29	Jaret Wright	.20
30	Raul Casanova	.20
31	Tony Clark	.20
32	Deivi Cruz	.20
33	Bobby Higginson	.20
34	Justin Thompson	.20
35	Yamil Benitez	.20
36	Johnny Damon	.35
37	Jermaine Dye	.20
38	Jed Hansen	.20
39	Larry Sutton	.20
40	Jeromy Burnitz	.20
41	Jeff Cirillo	.20
42	Dave Nilsson	.20
43	Jose Valentin	.20
44	Fernando Vina	.20
45	Marty Cordova	.20
46	Chuck Knoblauch	.20
47	Paul Molitor	1.50
48	Brad Radke	.20
49	Terry Steinbach	.20
50	Wade Boggs	2.50
51	Hideki Irabu	.20
52	Derek Jeter	6.00
53	Tino Martinez	.20
54	Andy Pettitte	.30
55	Mariano Rivera	.20
56	Bernie Williams	.20
57	Jose Canseco	.75
58	Jason Giambi	.75
59	Ben Grieve	.20
60	Aaron Small	.20
61	Jay Buhner	.20
62	Ken Cloude	.20
63	Joey Cora	.20
64	Ken Griffey Jr.	3.50
65	Randy Johnson	1.50
66	Edgar Martinez	.20
67	Alex Rodriguez	5.00
68	Will Clark	.20
69	Juan Gonzalez	.75
70	Rusty Greer	.20
71	Ivan Rodriguez	1.00
72	Joe Carter	.20
73	Roger Clemens	3.00
74	Jose Cruz Jr.	.75
75	Carlos Delgado	.75
76	Andruw Jones	1.50
77	Chipper Jones	2.50
78	Ryan Klesko	.20
79	Javier Lopez	.20
80	Greg Maddux	2.50
81	Miguel Batista	.20
82	Jeremi Gonzalez	.20
83	Mark Grace	.20
84	Kevin Orie	.20
85	Sammy Sosa	2.50
86	Barry Larkin	.20
87	Deion Sanders	.20
88	Reggie Sanders	.20
89	Chris Stynes	.20
90	Dante Bichette	.20
91	Vinny Castilla	.20
92	Andres Galarraga	.20
93	Neifi Perez	.20
94	Larry Walker	.20
95	Moises Alou	.20
96	Bobby Bonilla	.20
97	Kevin Brown	.20
98	Craig Counsell	.20
99	Livan Hernandez	.20
100	Edgar Renteria	.20
101	Gary Sheffield	.60
102	Jeff Bagwell	1.50
103	Craig Biggio	.20
104	Luis Gonzalez	.20
105	Darryl Kile	.20
106	Wilton Guerrero	.20
107	Eric Karros	.20
108	Ramon Martinez	.20
109	Raul Mondesi	.20
110	Hideo Nomo	.75
111	Chan Ho Park	.20
112	Mike Piazza	3.00
113	Mark Grudzielanek	.20
114	Vladimir Guerrero	1.50
115	Pedro Martinez	1.50
116	Henry Rodriguez	.20
117	David Segui	.20
118	Edgardo Alfonzo	.20
119	Carlos Baerga	.20
120	John Franco	.20
121	John Olerud	.20
122	Rey Ordonez	.20
123	Ricky Bottalico	.20
124	Gregg Jefferies	.20
125	Mickey Morandini	.20
126	Scott Rolen	1.00
127	Curt Schilling	.45
128	Jose Guillen	.20
129	Esteban Loaiza	.20
130	Al Martin	.20
131	Tony Womack	.20
132	Dennis Eckersley	1.00
133	Gary Gaetti	.20
134	Curtis King	.20
135	Ray Lankford	.20
136	Mark McGwire	5.00
137	Ken Caminiti	.20
138	Steve Finley	.20
139	Tony Gwynn	2.50
140	Carlos Hernandez	.20
141	Wally Joyner	.20
142	Barry Bonds	6.00
143	Jacob Cruz	.20
144	Shawn Estes	.20
145	Stan Javier	.20
146	J.T. Snow	.20
147	Nomar Garciaparra (ROY)	1.00
148	Scott Rolen (ROY)	1.00
149	Ken Griffey Jr./MVP	1.75
150	Larry Walker/MVP	.20

Cramer's Choice

The 10-card Cramer's Choice Awards insert features

top players on cards with a die-cut trophy design. This set has six different foil variations, each with a different production number. Green (99 hand-numbered sets), Dark Blue (80), Light Blue (50), Red (25), Gold (15) and Purple (10) versions were included in Invincible.

		NM/M
Complete Green Set (10):		200.00
Common Green (99 Sets):		10.00
Dark Blues (80 Sets):		1X
Light Blues (50 Sets):		1.5X
Reds (25 Sets):		2X
Golds (15 Sets):		3X
Purples (10 Sets):		5X
1	Greg Maddux	20.00
2	Roberto Alomar	10.00
3	Cal Ripken Jr.	40.00
4	Nomar Garciaparra	20.00
5	Larry Walker	10.00
6	Mike Piazza	22.50
7	Mark McGwire	30.00
8	Tony Gwynn	20.00
9	Ken Griffey Jr.	25.00
10	Roger Clemens	22.50

Gems of the Diamond

Gems of the Diamond is a 220-card insert seeded four per pack. The cards feature a color photo inside a white border.

		NM/M
Complete Set (220):		20.00
Common Player:		.10
1	Jim Edmonds	.10
2	Todd Greene	.10
3	Ken Hill	.10
4	Mike Holtz	.10
5	Mike James	.10
6	Chad Kreuter	.10
7	Tim Salmon	.20
8	Roberto Alomar	.20
9	Brady Anderson	.10
10	David Dellucci	.10
11	Jeffrey Hammonds	.10
12	Mike Mussina	.40
13	Rafael Palmeiro	.65
14	Arthur Rhodes	.10
15	Cal Ripken Jr.	2.50
16	Nerio Rodriguez	.10
17	Tony Tarasco	.10
18	Lenny Webster	.10
19	Mike Benjamin	.10
20	Rich Garces	.10
21	Nomar Garciaparra	1.00
22	Shane Mack	.10
23	Jose Malave	.10
24	Jesus Tavarez	.10
25	Mo Vaughn	.40
26	John Wasdin	.10
27	Jeff Abbott	.10
28	Albert Belle	.60
29	Mike Cameron	.10
30	Al Levine	.10
31	Robert Machado	.10
32	Greg Norton	.10
33	Magglio Ordonez	.20
34	Mike Sirotka	.10
35	Frank Thomas	.75
36	Mario Valdez	.10
37	Sandy Alomar Jr.	.10
38	David Justice	.10
39	Jack McDowell	.10
40	Eric Plunk	.10
41	Manny Ramirez	.75
42	Kevin Seitzer	.10
43	Paul Shuey	.10
44	Omar Vizquel	.10
45	Kimera Bartee	.10
46	Glenn Dishman	.10
47	Orlando Miller	.10
48	Mike Myers	.10
49	Phil Nevin	.10
50	A.J. Sager	.10
51	Ricky Bones	.10
52	Scott Cooper	.10
53	Shane Halter	.10
54	David Howard	.10
55	Glendon Rusch	.10
56	Joe Vitiello	.10
57	Jeff D'Amico	.10
58	Mike Fetters	.10
59	Mike Matheny	.10
60	Jose Mercedes	.10
61	Ron Villone	.10
62	Jack Voigt	.10
63	Brent Brede	.10
64	Chuck Knoblauch	.10
65	Paul Molitor	.75
66	Todd Ritchie	.10
67	Frankie Rodriguez	.10
68	Scott Stahoviak	.10
69	Greg Swindell	.10
70	Todd Walker	.10
71	Wade Boggs	1.00
72	Hideki Irabu	.10
73	Derek Jeter	2.50
74	Pat Kelly	.10
75	Graeme Lloyd	.10
76	Tino Martinez	.10
77	Jeff Nelson	.10
78	Scott Pose	.10
79	Mike Stanton	.10
80	Darryl Strawberry	.10
81	Bernie Williams	.10
82	Tony Batista	.10
83	Mark Bellhorn	.10
84	Ben Grieve	.10
85	Pat Lennon	.10
86	Brian Lesher	.10
87	Miguel Tejada	.20
88	George Williams	.10
89	Joey Cora	.10
90	Rob Ducey	.10
91	Ken Griffey Jr.	1.50
92	Randy Johnson	.75
93	Edgar Martinez	.10
94	John Marzano	.10
95	Greg McCarthy	.10
96	Alex Rodriguez	2.00
97	Andy Sheets	.10
98	Mike Timlin	.10
99	Lee Tinsley	.10
100	Damon Buford	.10
101	Alex Diaz	.10
102	Benji Gil	.10
103	Juan Gonzalez	.40
104	Eric Gunderson	.10
105	Danny Patterson	.10
106	Ivan Rodriguez	.65
107	Mike Simms	.10
108	Luis Andujar	.10
109	Joe Carter	.10
110	Roger Clemens	1.25
111	Jose Cruz Jr.	.10
112	Shawn Green	.30
113	Robert Perez	.10
114	Juan Samuel	.10
115	Ed Sprague	.10
116	Shannon Stewart	.10
117	Danny Bautista	.10
118	Chipper Jones	1.00
119	Ryan Klesko	.10
120	Keith Lockhart	.10
121	Javier Lopez	.10
122	Greg Maddux	1.00
123	Kevin Millwood	.10
124	Mike Mordecai	.10
125	Eddie Perez	.10
126	Randall Simon	.10
127	Miguel Cairo	.10
128	Dave Clark	.10
129	Kevin Foster	.10
130	Mark Grace	.10
131	Tyler Houston	.10
132	Mike Hubbard	.10
133	Kevin Orie	.10
134	Ryne Sandberg	1.00
135	Sammy Sosa	1.00
136	Lenny Harris	.10
137	Kent Mercker	.10
138	Mike Morgan	.10
139	Deion Sanders	.10
140	Chris Stynes	.10
141	Gabe White	.10
142	Jason Bates	.10
143	Vinny Castilla	.10
144	Andres Galarraga	.10
145	Curtis Leskanic	.10
146	Jeff McCurry	.10
147	Mike Munoz	.10
148	Larry Walker	.10
149	Jamey Wright	.10
150	Moises Alou	.10
151	Bobby Bonilla	.10
152	Kevin Brown	.10
153	John Cangelosi	.10
154	Jeff Conine	.10
155	Cliff Floyd	.10
156	Jay Powell	.10
157	Edgar Renteria	.10
158	Tony Saunders	.10
159	Gary Sheffield	.40
160	Jeff Bagwell	.75
161	Tim Bogar	.10
162	Tony Eusebio	.10
163	Chris Holt	.10
164	Ray Montgomery	.10
165	Luis Rivera	.10
166	Eric Anthony	.10
167	Brett Butler	.10
168	Juan Castro	.10
169	Tripp Cromer	.10
170	Raul Mondesi	.10
171	Hideo Nomo	.40
172	Mike Piazza	1.25
173	Tom Prince	.10
174	Adam Riggs	.10
175	Shane Andrews	.10
176	Shayne Bennett	.10
177	Raul Chavez	.10
178	Pedro Martinez	.75
179	Sherman Obando	.10
180	Andy Stankiewicz	.10
181	Alberto Castillo	.10
182	Shawn Gilbert	.10
183	Luis Lopez	.10
184	Roberto Petagine	.10
185	Armando Reynoso	.10
186	Midre Cummings	.10
187	Kevin Jordan	.10
188	Desi Relaford	.10
189	Scott Rolen	.65
190	Ken Ryan	.10
191	Kevin Sefcik	.10
192	Emil Brown	.10
193	Lou Collier	.10
194	Francisco Cordova	.10
195	Kevin Elster	.10
196	Mark Smith	.10
197	Marc Wilkins	.10
198	Manny Aybar	.10
199	Jose Bautista	.10
200	David Bell	.10
201	Rigo Beltran	.10
202	Delino DeShields	.10
203	Dennis Eckersley	.65
204	John Mabry	.10
205	Eli Marrero	.10
206	Willie McGee	.10
207	Mark McGwire	2.00
208	Ken Caminiti	.10
209	Tony Gwynn	1.00
210	Chris Jones	.10
211	Craig Shipley	.10
212	Pete Smith	.10
213	Jorge Velandia	.10
214	Dario Veras	.10
215	Rich Aurilia	.10
216	Damon Berryhill	.10
217	Barry Bonds	2.50
218	Osvaldo Fernandez	.10
219	Dante Powell	.10
220	Rich Rodriguez	.10

Interleague Players

Interleague Players is a 30-card insert featuring 15 sets of players - one National League and one American League player. The dark blue backgrounds have red lightning bolts and the white borders are made of a leather-like material. When a set of players is placed next to each other, they form the MLB Interleague logo in the center. Interleague Players cards were inserted one per 73 packs.

		NM/M
Complete Set (30):		120.00
Common Player:		1.50
Inserted 1:73		
1A	Roberto Alomar	2.50
1N	Craig Biggio	1.50
2A	Cal Ripken Jr.	12.00
2N	Chipper Jones	6.00
3A	Nomar Garciaparra	6.00
3N	Scott Rolen	3.50
4A	Mo Vaughn	1.50
4N	Andres Galarraga	1.50
5A	Frank Thomas	4.50
5N	Tony Gwynn	6.00
6A	Albert Belle	1.50
6N	Barry Bonds	12.00
7A	Hideki Irabu	1.50
7N	Hideo Nomo	2.50
8A	Derek Jeter	12.00
8N	Rey Ordonez	1.50
9A	Tino Martinez	1.50
9N	Mark McGwire	10.00
10A	Alex Rodriguez	10.00
10N	Edgar Renteria	1.50
11A	Ken Griffey Jr.	7.50
11N	Larry Walker	1.50
12A	Randy Johnson	4.50
12N	Greg Maddux	6.00
13A	Ivan Rodriguez	3.50
13N	Mike Piazza	6.50
14A	Roger Clemens	6.50
14N	Pedro Martinez	4.50
15A	Jose Cruz Jr.	1.50
15N	Wilton Guerrero	1.50

Moments in Time

Moments in Time (20 cards, 1:145) is designed as a baseball scoreboard. The cards have a horizontal layout with the date of an important game in the player's career at the top. The player's stats from the game are featured and a picture is located on the scoreboard screen.

		NM/M
Complete Set (20):		100.00
Common Player:		3.00
Inserted 1:145		
1	Chipper Jones	10.00
2	Cal Ripken Jr.	17.50
3	Frank Thomas	7.50
4	David Justice	3.00
5	Andres Galarraga	3.00
6	Larry Walker	3.00
7	Livan Hernandez	3.00
8	Wilton Guerrero	3.00
9	Hideo Nomo	4.50
10	Mike Piazza	12.00
11	Pedro Martinez	7.50
12	Bernie Williams	3.00
13	Ben Grieve	3.00
14	Scott Rolen	6.00
15	Mark McGwire	15.00
16	Tony Gwynn	10.00
17	Ken Griffey Jr.	13.50
18	Alex Rodriguez	15.00
19	Juan Gonzalez	4.50
20	Jose Cruz Jr.	3.00

Photoengravings

Derek Jeter - SS

Photoengravings is an 18-card insert seeded one per 37 packs. Each card has a unique "old-style" design with a player photo in a frame in the center.

		NM/M
Complete Set (18):		50.00
Common Player:		1.00
Inserted 1:37		
1	Greg Maddux	3.50
2	Cal Ripken Jr.	7.50
3	Nomar Garciaparra	3.50
4	Frank Thomas	2.50
5	Larry Walker	1.00
6	Mike Piazza	4.00
7	Hideo Nomo	2.00
8	Pedro Martinez	2.50
9	Derek Jeter	7.50
10	Tino Martinez	1.00
11	Mark McGwire	6.00
12	Tony Gwynn	3.50
13	Barry Bonds	7.50
14	Ken Griffey Jr.	5.00

15 Alex Rodriguez 6.00
16 Ivan Rodriguez 2.25
17 Roger Clemens 4.00
18 Jose Cruz Jr. 1.00

Team Checklists

Team Checklists is a 30-card insert seeded 2:37. The fronts feature a player collage with the team logo in the background. The back has a complete checklist for that team in Invincible and more player photos.

	NM/M
Complete Set (30):	60.00
Common Player:	1.00
Inserted 2:37	

1 Anaheim Angels (Jim Edmonds, Tim Salmon, Darin Erstad, Garret Anderson, Rickey Henderson) 2.50
2 Atlanta Braves (Greg Maddux, Chipper Jones, Javy Lopez, Ryan Klesko, Andruw Jones) 3.00
3 Baltimore Orioles (Cal Ripken Jr., Roberto Alomar, Brady Anderson, Mike Mussina, Rafael Palmeiro) 6.00
4 Boston Red Sox (Nomar Garciaparra, Mo Vaughn, Steve Avery, John Valentin) 3.00
5 Chicago Cubs (Sammy Sosa, Mark Grace, Ryne Sandberg, Jeremi Gonzalez) 3.00
6 Chicago White Sox (Frank Thomas, Albert Belle, Robin Ventura, Ozzie Guillen) 2.50
7 Cincinnati Reds (Barry Larkin, Deion Sanders, Reggie Sanders, Brett Tomko) 1.00
8 Cleveland Indians (Sandy Alomar Jr., Manny Ramirez, David Justice, Jim Thome, Omar Vizquel) 2.50
9 Colorado Rockies (Andres Galarraga, Larry Walker, Vinny Castilla, Dante Bichette, Ellis Burks) 1.00
10 Detroit Tigers (Jason Thompson, Tony Clark, Deivi Cruz, Bobby Higginson) 1.00
11 Florida Marlins (Gary Sheffield, Edgar Renteria, Livan Hernandez, Charles Johnson, Bobby Bonilla) 1.00
12 Houston Astros (Jeff Bagwell, Craig Biggio, Richard Hidalgo, Darryl Kile) 2.50
13 Kansas City Royals (Johnny Damon, Jermaine Dye, Chili Davis, Jose Rosado) 1.00
14 Los Angeles Dodgers (Mike Piazza, Wilton Guerrero, Raul Mondesi, Hideo Nomo, Ramon Martinez) 4.00
15 Milwaukee Brewers (David Nilsson, Fernando Vina, Jeromy Burnitz, Julio Franco, Jeff Cirillo) 1.00
16 Minnesota Twins (Paul Molitor, Chuck Knoblauch, Brad Radke, Terry Steinbach, Marty Cordova) 2.50
17 Montreal Expos (Henry Rodriguez, Vladimir Guerrero, Pedro Martinez, David Segui, Mark Grudzielanek) 2.50
18 New York Mets (Carlos Baerga, Todd Hundley, Rey Ordonez, John Olerud, Edgardo Alfonzo) 1.00
19 New York Yankees (Derek Jeter, Tino Martinez, Bernie Williams, Andy Pettitte, Mariano Rivera) 6.00
20 Oakland Athletics (Jose Canseco, Ben Grieve, Jason Giambi, Matt Stairs) 1.75
21 Philadelphia Phillies (Curt Schilling, Scott Rolen, Gregg Jefferies, Lenny Dykstra, Ricky Bottalico) 1.75
22 Pittsburgh Pirates (Al Martin, Tony Womack, Jose Guillen, Esteban Loiaza) 1.00
23 St. Louis Cardinals (Mark McGwire, Dennis Eckersley, Delino DeShields, Willie McGee, Ray Lankford) 4.50
24 San Diego Padres (Tony Gwynn, Ken Caminiti, Wally Joyner, Steve Finley) 3.00
25 San Francisco Giants (Barry Bonds, J.T. Snow, Stan Javier, Rod Beck, Jose Vizcaino) 6.00
26 Seattle Mariners (Ken Griffey Jr., Alex Rodriguez, Edgar Martinez, Randy Johnson, Jay Buhner) 4.50
27 Texas Rangers (Juan Gonzalez, Ivan Rodriguez, Will Clark, John Wetteland, Rusty Greer) 2.00
28 Toronto Blue Jays (Jose Cruz Jr., Roger Clemens, Pat Hentgen, Joe Carter) 4.00
29 Arizona Diamondbacks (Yamil Benitez, Devon White, Matt Williams, Jay Bell) 1.00
30 Tampa Bay Devil Rays (Wade Boggs, Paul Sorrento, Fred McGriff, Roberto Hernandez) 3.00

1998 Pacific Omega

The Omega base set consists of 250 three-image cards. The horizontal cards feature a color player photo in the center with the image duplicated in foil on the right. Another color photo is on the left. The photos are divided by a baseball seam design. Red-foil parallels were a 1:4 pack insert in Wal-Mart exclusive packaging.

	NM/M
Complete Set (250):	25.00
Common Player:	.10
Reds:	4X
Pack (6):	.10
Wax Box (36):	15.00

1 Garret Anderson .10
2 Gary DiSarcina .10
3 Jim Edmonds .10
4 Darin Erstad .20
5 Cecil Fielder .10
6 Chuck Finley .10
7 Shigetosi Hasegawa .10
8 Tim Salmon .10
9 Brian Anderson .10
10 Jay Bell .10
11 Andy Benes .10
12 Yamil Benitez .10
13 Jorge Fabregas .10
14 Travis Lee .10
15 Devon White .10
16 Matt Williams .10
17 Andres Galarraga .10
18 Tom Glavine .35
19 Andruw Jones .75
20 Chipper Jones 1.00
21 Ryan Klesko .10
22 Javy Lopez .10
23 Greg Maddux .10
24 Kevin Millwood RC .50
25 Denny Neagle .10
26 John Smoltz .10
27 Roberto Alomar .20
28 Brady Anderson .10
29 Joe Carter .10
30 Eric Davis .10
31 Jimmy Key .10
32 Mike Mussina .40
33 Rafael Palmeiro .65
34 Cal Ripken Jr. 2.50
35 B.J. Surhoff .10
36 Dennis Eckersley .65
37 Nomar Garciaparra 1.00
38 Reggie Jefferson .10
39 Derek Lowe .10
40 Pedro Martinez .75
41 Brian Rose .10
42 John Valentin .10
43 Jason Varitek .10
44 Mo Vaughn .65
45 Jeff Blauser .10
46 Jeremi Gonzalez .10
47 Mark Grace .10
48 Lance Johnson .10
49 Kevin Orie .10
50 Henry Rodriguez .10
51 Sammy Sosa 1.00
52 Kerry Wood .35
53 Albert Belle .10
54 Mike Cameron .10
55 Mike Caruso .10
56 Ray Durham .10
57 Jaime Navarro .10
58 Greg Norton .10
59 Magglio Ordonez RC 1.50
60 Frank Thomas .75
61 Robin Ventura .10
62 Bret Boone .10
63 Willie Greene .10
64 Barry Larkin .10
65 Jon Nunnally .10
66 Eduardo Perez .10
67 Reggie Sanders .10
68 Brett Tomko .10
69 Sandy Alomar Jr. .10
70 Travis Fryman .10
71 David Justice .10
72 Kenny Lofton .10
73 Charles Nagy .10
74 Manny Ramirez .75
75 Jim Thome .65
76 Omar Vizquel .10
77 Enrique Wilson .10
78 Jaret Wright .10
79 Dante Bichette .10
80 Ellis Burks .10
81 Vinny Castilla .10
82 Todd Helton .75
83 Darryl Kile .10
84 Mike Lansing .10
85 Neifi Perez .10
86 Larry Walker .10
87 Raul Casanova .10
88 Tony Clark .10
89 Luis Gonzalez .10
90 Bobby Higginson .10
91 Brian Hunter .10
92 Bip Roberts .10
93 Justin Thompson .10
94 Josh Booty .10
95 Craig Counsell .10
96 Livan Hernandez .10
97 Ryan Jackson RC .10
98 Mark Kotsay .10
99 Derrek Lee .50
100 Mike Piazza 1.25
101 Edgar Renteria .10
102 Cliff Floyd .10
103 Moises Alou .10
104 Jeff Bagwell .75
105 Derrick Bell .10
106 Sean Berry .10
107 Craig Biggio .10
108 John Halama RC .15
109 Richard Hidalgo .10
110 Shane Reynolds .10
111 Tim Belcher .10
112 Brian Bevil .10
113 Jeff Conine .10
114 Johnny Damon .25
115 Jeff King .10
116 Jeff Montgomery .10
117 Dean Palmer .10
118 Terry Pendleton .10
119 Bobby Bonilla .10
120 Wilton Guerrero .10
121 Todd Hollandsworth .10
122 Charles Johnson .10
123 Eric Karros .10
124 Paul Konerko .20
125 Ramon Martinez .10
126 Raul Mondesi .10
127 Hideo Nomo .40
128 Gary Sheffield .45
129 Ismael Valdes .10
130 Jeromy Burnitz .10
131 Jeff Cirillo .10
132 Todd Dunn .10
133 Marquis Grissom .10
134 John Jaha .10
135 Scott Karl .10
136 Dave Nilsson .10
137 Jose Valentin .10
138 Fernando Vina .10
139 Rick Aguilera .10
140 Marty Cordova .10
141 Pat Meares .10
142 Paul Molitor .75
143 David Ortiz .50
144 Brad Radke .10
145 Terry Steinbach .10
146 Todd Walker .10
147 Shane Andrews .10
148 Brad Fullmer .10
149 Mark Grudzielanek .10
150 Vladimir Guerrero .75
151 F.P. Santangelo .10
152 Jose Vidro .10
153 Rondell White .10
154 Carlos Baerga .10
155 Bernard Gilkey .10
156 Todd Hundley .10
157 Butch Huskey .10
158 Bobby Jones .10
159 Brian McRae .10
160 John Olerud .10
161 Rey Ordonez .10
162 Masato Yoshii RC .25
163 David Cone .10
164 Hideki Irabu .10
165 Derek Jeter 2.50
166 Chuck Knoblauch .10
167 Tino Martinez .10
168 Paul O'Neill .10
169 Andy Pettitte .30
170 Mariano Rivera .15
171 Darryl Strawberry .15
172 David Wells .10
173 Bernie Williams .10
174 Ryan Christenson RC .15
175 Jason Giambi .60
176 Ben Grieve .10
177 Rickey Henderson .75
178 A.J. Hinch .10
179 Kenny Rogers .10
180 Ricky Bottalico .10
181 Rico Brogna .10
182 Doug Glanville .10
183 Gregg Jefferies .10
184 Mike Lieberthal .10
185 Scott Rolen .65
186 Curt Schilling .35
187 Jermaine Allensworth .10
188 Lou Collier .10
189 Jose Guillen .10
190 Jason Kendall .10
191 Al Martin .10
192 Tony Womack .10
193 Kevin Young .10
194 Royce Clayton .10
195 Delino DeShields .10
196 Gary Gaetti .10
197 Ron Gant .10
198 Brian Jordan .10
199 Ray Lankford .10
200 Mark McGwire 2.00
201 Todd Stottlemyre .10
202 Kevin Brown .10
203 Ken Caminiti .10
204 Steve Finley .10
205 Tony Gwynn 1.00
206 Carlos Hernandez .10
207 Wally Joyner .10
208 Greg Vaughn .10
209 Barry Bonds 2.50
210 Shawn Estes .10
211 Orel Hershiser .10
212 Stan Javier .10
213 Jeff Kent .10
214 Bill Mueller .10
215 Robb Nen .10
216 J.T. Snow .10
217 Jay Buhner .10
218 Ken Cloude .10
219 Joey Cora .10
220 Ken Griffey Jr. 1.50
221 Glenallen Hill .10
222 Randy Johnson .75
223 Edgar Martinez .10
224 Jamie Moyer .10
225 Alex Rodriguez 2.00
226 David Segui .10
227 Dan Wilson .10
228 Rolando Arrojo RC .25
229 Wade Boggs .10
230 Miguel Cairo .10
231 Roberto Hernandez .10
232 Quinton McCracken .10
233 Fred McGriff .10
234 Paul Sorrento .10
235 Kevin Stocker .10
236 Will Clark .10
237 Juan Gonzalez .40
238 Rusty Greer .10
239 Rick Helling .10
240 Roberto Kelly .10
241 Ivan Rodriguez .65
242 Aaron Sele .10
243 John Wetteland .10
244 Jose Canseco .50
245 Roger Clemens 1.25
246 Jose Cruz Jr. .10
247 Carlos Delgado .50
248 Alex Gonzalez .10
249 Ed Sprague .10
250 Shannon Stewart .10

EO Portraits

MARK McGWIRE St. Louis

EO Portraits is a 20-card insert seeded 1:73. Each card has a color action photo with a player portrait laser-cut into the card. A "1-of-1" parallel features a laser-cut number on the card as well. The "EO" stands for "Electro Optical" technology.

	NM/M
Complete Set (20):	70.00
Common Player:	1.25
Inserted 1:73	

1 Cal Ripken Jr. 10.00
2 Nomar Garciaparra 5.00
3 Mo Vaughn 1.25
4 Frank Thomas 4.00
5 Manny Ramirez 4.00
6 Ben Grieve 1.25
7 Ken Griffey Jr. 6.50
8 Alex Rodriguez 7.50
9 Juan Gonzalez 2.00
10 Ivan Rodriguez 3.50
11 Travis Lee 1.25
12 Greg Maddux 5.00
13 Chipper Jones 5.00
14 Kerry Wood 2.00
15 Larry Walker 1.25
16 Jeff Bagwell 4.00
17 Mike Piazza 6.00
18 Mark McGwire 7.50
19 Tony Gwynn 5.00
20 Barry Bonds 10.00

Face to Face

Face to Face features two star players on each card. It is a 10-card insert seeded one per 145 packs.

	NM/M
Complete Set (10):	50.00
Common Player:	2.00
Inserted 1:145	

1 Alex Rodriguez, Nomar Garciaparra 9.00
2 Mark McGwire, Ken Griffey Jr. 9.00
3 Mike Piazza, Sandy Alomar Jr. 6.00
4 Kerry Wood, Roger Clemens 6.00
5 Cal Ripken Jr., Paul Molitor 10.00
6 Tony Gwynn, Wade Boggs 5.00
7 Frank Thomas, Chipper Jones 5.00
8 Travis Lee, Ben Grieve 2.00
9 Hideo Nomo, Hideki Irabu 3.50
10 Juan Gonzalez, Manny Ramirez 3.50

Online

Jaret Wright

Online is a 36-card insert seeded about one per nine packs. The foiled and etched cards feature a color player photo in front of a hi-tech designed background. The card fronts also include the internet address for the player's web site on bigleaguers.com.

	NM/M
Complete Set (36):	35.00
Common Player:	.45
Inserted 1:9	

1 Cal Ripken Jr. 5.00
2 Nomar Garciaparra 2.00
3 Pedro Martinez 1.50
4 Mo Vaughn .45
5 Frank Thomas 1.50
6 Sandy Alomar Jr. .45
7 Manny Ramirez 1.50
8 Jaret Wright .45
9 Paul Molitor 1.50
10 Derek Jeter 5.00
11 Bernie Williams .45
12 Ben Grieve .45
13 Ken Griffey Jr. 3.00
14 Edgar Martinez .45
15 Alex Rodriguez 4.00
16 Wade Boggs 2.00
17 Juan Gonzalez .75
18 Ivan Rodriguez .45
19 Roger Clemens 2.50
20 Travis Lee .45
21 Matt Williams .45
22 Andres Galarraga .45
23 Chipper Jones 2.00
24 Greg Maddux 2.00
25 Sammy Sosa 2.00
26 Kerry Wood .75
27 Barry Larkin .45
28 Larry Walker .45
29 Derrek Lee 1.00
30 Jeff Bagwell 1.50
31 Hideo Nomo .75
32 Mike Piazza 2.50
33 Scott Rolen 1.00
34 Mark McGwire 4.00
35 Tony Gwynn 2.00
36 Barry Bonds 5.00

Prism

MIKE PIAZZA

This 20-card insert was seeded one per 37 packs. Horizontal card fronts feature prismatic foil technology.

	NM/M
Complete Set (20):	30.00
Common Player:	.75
Inserted 1:37	

1 Cal Ripken Jr. 4.50
2 Nomar Garciaparra 2.50
3 Pedro Martinez 1.50
4 Frank Thomas 1.50
5 Manny Ramirez 1.50
6 Brian Giles .75
7 Derek Jeter 4.50
8 Ben Grieve .75
9 Ken Griffey Jr. 3.00
10 Alex Rodriguez 3.50
11 Juan Gonzalez 1.00
12 Travis Lee .75
13 Chipper Jones 2.50
14 Greg Maddux 2.50
15 Kerry Wood .75
16 Larry Walker .75
17 Hideo Nomo 1.00
18 Mike Piazza 3.00
19 Mark McGwire 3.50
20 Tony Gwynn 2.50

Rising Stars

Rising Stars is a multi-tiered hobby-only insert. The 20 base cards are found about 1:9 packs. Each card has two or three prospects from the same team. Five tiers of partial parallels of the insert are sequentially numbered.

	NM/M
Complete Set (30):	15.00
Common Player:	.50
Inserted 1:9	
Tier 1 (# to 100):	3X

Tier 2 (# to 75): 4X
Tier 3 (# to 50): 5X
Tier 4 (# to 25): 10X
Tier 5 (1 of 1): Value Undetermined

1	Nerio Rodriguez, Sidney Ponson,	.50
2	Frank Catalanotto, Roberto Duran, Sean Runyan,	.50
3	Kevin L. Brown, Carlos Almanzar,	.50
4	Aaron Boone, Pat Watkins, Scott Winchester,	.50
5	Brian Meadows, Andy Larkin, Antonio Alfonseca,	.50
6	DaRond Stovall, Trey Moore, Shayne Bennett,	.50
7	Felix Martinez, Larry Sutton, Brian Bevil,	.50
8	Homer Bush, Mike Buddie,	.50
9	Rich Butler, Esteban Yan,	.50
10	Damon Hollins, Brian Edmondson,	.50
11	Lou Collier, Jose Silva, Javier Martinez,	.50
12	Steve Sinclair, Mark Dalesandro,	.50
13	Jason Varitek, Brian Rose, Brian Shouse,	.50
14	Mike Caruso, Jeff Abbott, Tom Fordham,	.50
15	Jason Johnson, Bobby Smith,	.50
16	Dave Berg, Mark Kotsay, Jesus Sanchez,	.50
17	Richard Hidalgo, John Halama, Trever Miller,	.50
18	Geoff Jenkins, Bobby Hughes, Steve Woodard,	.50
19	Eli Marrero, Cliff Politte, Mike Busby,	.50
20	Desi Relaford, Darrin Winston,	.50
21	Todd Helton, Bobby Jones,	1.50
22	Rolando Arrojo, Miguel Cairo, Dan Carlson,	.50
23	David Ortiz, Javier Valentin, Eric Milton,	1.25
24	Magglio Ordonez, Greg Norton,	1.00
25	Brad Fullmer, Javier Vazquez, Rick DeHart,	.50
26	Paul Konerko, Matt Luke,	1.00
27	Derrek Lee, Ryan Jackson, John Roskos,	1.25
28	Ben Grieve, A.J. Hinch, Ryan Christenson,	.50
29	Travis Lee, Karim Garcia, David Dellucci,	.65
30	Kerry Wood, Marc Pisciotta,	1.00

1998 Pacific Online

Online consists of an 800-card base set featuring 750 players on cards that list the internet address of the player's home page on the big-leaguers.com web site. Twenty players have two cards, each with different front and back photos but sharing a card number. Each of the 30 teams has a checklist that lists the team's web site. The Web Cards set parallels the 750 player cards. It has a serial number that can be entered at the bigleaguers.com web site to determine if a prize has been won. Red-foil versions of each card were produced for retail-only jumbo packs; they may carry a modest premium.

	NM/M
Complete Set (800):	60.00
Common Player:	.05
Web Stars/RC's:	2X
Inserted 1:1	
Pack (9):	.75
Wax Box (36):	20.00

1	Garret Anderson	.05
2	Rich DeLucia RC	.05
3	Jason Dickson	.05
4	Gary DiSarcina	.05
5	Jim Edmonds	.05
6	Darin Erstad	.15
7	Cecil Fielder	.05
8	Chuck Finley	.05
9	Carlos Garcia	.05
10	Shigetoshi Hasegawa	.05
11	Ken Hill	.05
12	Dave Hollins	.05
13	Mike Holtz	.05
14	Mike James	.05
15	Norberto Martin	.05
16	Damon Mashore	.05
17	Jack McDowell	.05
18	Phil Nevin	.05
19	Omar Olivares	.05
20	Troy Percival	.05
21	Rich Robertson	.05
22	Tim Salmon	.05
23	Craig Shipley	.05
24	Matt Walbeck	.05
25	Allen Watson	.05
26	Jim Edmonds (Angels Checklist.)	.05
27	Brian Anderson	.05
28	Tony Batista	.05
29	Jay Bell	.05
30	Andy Benes	.05
31	Yamil Benitez	.05
32	Willie Blair	.05
33	Brent Brede	.05
34	Scott Brow	.05
35	Omar Daal	.05
36	David Dellucci	.05
37	Edwin Diaz	.05
38	Jorge Fabregas	.05
39	Andy Fox	.05
40	Karim Garcia	.05
41a	Travis Lee/Btg	.05
41b	Travis Lee/Fielding	.05
42	Barry Manuel	.05
43	Gregg Olson	.05
44	Felix Rodriguez	.05
45	Clint Sodowsky	.05
46	Russ Springer	.05
47	Andy Stankiewicz	.05
48	Kelly Stinnett	.05
49	Jeff Suppan	.05
50	Devon White	.05
51	Matt Williams	.05
52	Travis Lee (Diamondbacks Checklist.)	.05
53	Danny Bautista	.05
54	Rafael Belliard	.05
55	Adam Butler RC	.10
56	Mike Cather	.05
57	Brian Edmonson	.05
58	Alan Embree	.05
59	Andres Galarraga	.05
60	Tom Glavine	.35
61	Tony Graffanino	.05
62	Andruw Jones	.65
63a	Chipper Jones/Btg	.75
63b	Chipper Jones/Fielding	.75
64	Ryan Klesko	.05
65	Keith Lockhart	.05
66	Javy Lopez	.05
67a	Greg Maddux/Btg	.75
67b	Greg Maddux/Pitching	.75
68	Dennis Martinez	.05
69	Kevin Millwood RC	.50
70	Denny Neagle	.05
71	Eddie Perez	.05
72	Curtis Pride	.05
73	John Smoltz	.05
74	Michael Tucker	.05
75	Walt Weiss	.05
76	Gerald Williams	.05
77	Mark Wohlers	.05
78	Chipper Jones (Braves Checklist.)	.40
79	Roberto Alomar	.15
80	Brady Anderson	.05
81	Harold Baines	.05
82	Armando Benitez	.05
83	Mike Bordick	.05
84	Joe Carter	.05
85	Norm Charlton	.05
86	Eric Davis	.05
87	Doug Drabek	.05
88	Scott Erickson	.05
89	Jeffrey Hammonds	.05
90	Chris Hoiles	.05
91	Scott Kamieniecki	.05
92	Jimmy Key	.05
93	Terry Mathews	.05
94	Alan Mills	.05
95	Mike Mussina	.25
96	Jesse Orosco	.05
97	Rafael Palmeiro	.60
98	Sidney Ponson	.05
99	Jeff Reboulet	.05
100	Arthur Rhodes	.05
101a	Cal Ripken Jr./Btg	2.00
101b	Cal Ripken Jr./Btg (Close-up.)	2.00
102	Nerio Rodriguez	.05
103	B.J. Surhoff	.05
104	Lenny Webster	.05
105	Cal Ripken Jr. (Orioles Checklist.)	1.00
106	Steve Avery	.05
107	Mike Benjamin	.05
108	Darren Bragg	.05
109	Damon Buford	.05
110	Jim Corsi	.05
111	Dennis Eckersley	.60
112	Rich Garces	.05
113a	Nomar Garciaparra/Btg	.75
113b	Nomar Garciaparra/Fielding	.75
114	Tom Gordon	.05
115	Scott Hatteberg	.05
116	Butch Henry	.05
117	Reggie Jefferson	.05
118	Mark Lemke	.05
119	Darren Lewis	.05
120	Jim Leyritz	.05
121	Derek Lowe	.05
122	Pedro Martinez	.65
123	Troy O'Leary	.05
124	Brian Rose	.05
125	Bret Saberhagen	.05
126	Donnie Sadler	.05
127	Brian Shouse	.05
128	John Valentin	.05
129	Jason Varitek	.05
130	Mo Vaughn	.05
131	Tim Wakefield	.05
132	John Wasdin	.05
133	Nomar Garciaparra (Red Sox Checklist.)	.45
134	Terry Adams	.05
135	Manny Alexander	.05
136	Rod Beck	.05
137	Jeff Blauser	.05
138	Brant Brown	.05
139	Mark Clark	.05
140	Jeremi Gonzalez	.05
141	Mark Grace	.05
142	Jose Hernandez	.05
143	Tyler Houston	.05
144	Lance Johnson	.05
145	Sandy Martinez	.05
146	Matt Mieske	.05
147	Mickey Morandini	.05
148	Terry Mulholland	.05
149	Kevin Orie	.05
150	Bob Patterson	.05
151	Marc Pisciotta	.05
152	Henry Rodriguez	.05
153	Scott Servais	.05
154	Sammy Sosa	.75
155	Kevin Tapani	.05
156	Steve Trachsel	.05
157a	Kerry Wood/Pitching	.30
157b	Kerry Wood/Pitching (Close-up.)	.30
158	Kerry Wood (Cubs Checklist.)	.20
159	Jeff Abbott	.05
160	James Baldwin	.05
161	Albert Belle	.05
162	Jason Bere	.05
163	Mike Cameron	.05
164	Mike Caruso	.05
165	Carlos Castillo	.05
166	Tony Castillo	.05
167	Ray Durham	.05
168	Scott Eyre	.05
169	Tom Fordham	.05
170	Keith Foulke	.05
171	Lou Frazier	.05
172	Matt Karchner	.05
173	Chad Kreuter	.05
174	Jaime Navarro	.05
175	Greg Norton	.05
176	Charlie O'Brien	.05
177	Magglio Ordonez	.15
178	Ruben Sierra	.05
179	Bill Simas	.05
180	Mike Sirotka	.05
181	Chris Snopek	.05
182a	Frank Thomas (In batter's box.)	.05
182b	Frank Thomas/Swinging	.65
183	Robin Ventura	.05
184	Frank Thomas (White Sox Checklist.)	.40
185	Stan Belinda	.05
186	Aaron Boone	.05
187	Bret Boone	.05
188	Brook Fordyce	.05
189	Willie Greene	.05
190	Pete Harnisch	.05
191	Lenny Harris	.05
192	Mark Hutton	.05
193	Damian Jackson	.05
194	Ricardo Jordan	.05
195	Barry Larkin	.05
196	Eduardo Perez	.05
197	Pokey Reese	.05
198	Mike Remlinger	.05
199	Reggie Sanders	.05
200	Jeff Shaw	.05
201	Chris Stynes	.05
202	Scott Sullivan	.05
203	Eddie Taubensee	.05
204	Brett Tomko	.05
205	Pat Watkins	.05
206	David Weathers	.05
207	Gabe White	.05
208	Scott Winchester	.05
209	Barry Larkin (Reds Checklist.)	.05
210	Sandy Alomar Jr.	.05
211	Paul Assenmacher	.05
212	Geronimo Berroa	.05
213	Pat Borders	.05
214	Jeff Branson	.05
215	Dave Burba	.05
216	Bartolo Colon	.05
217	Shawon Dunston	.05
218	Travis Fryman	.05
219	Brian Giles	.05
220	Dwight Gooden	.05
221	Mike Jackson	.05
222	David Justice	.05
223	Kenny Lofton	.05
224	Jose Mesa	.05
225	Alvin Morman	.05
226	Charles Nagy	.05
227	Chad Ogea	.05
228	Eric Plunk	.05
229	Manny Ramirez	.65
230	Paul Shuey	.05
231	Jim Thome	.65
232	Ron Villone	.05
233	Omar Vizquel	.05
234	Enrique Wilson	.05
235	Jaret Wright	.05
236	Manny Ramirez (Indians Checklist.)	.40
237	Pedro Astacio	.05
238	Jason Bates	.05
239	Dante Bichette	.05
240	Ellis Burks	.05
241	Vinny Castilla	.05
242	Greg Colbrunn	.05
243	Mike DeJean	.05
244	Jerry Dipoto	.05
245	Curtis Goodwin	.05
246	Todd Helton	.65
247	Bobby Jones	.05
248	Darryl Kile	.05
249	Mike Lansing	.05
250	Curtis Leskanic	.05
251	Nelson Liriano	.05
252	Kirt Manwaring	.05
253	Chuck McElroy	.05
254	Mike Munoz	.05
255	Neifi Perez	.05
256	Jeff Reed	.05
257	Mark Thompson	.05
258	John Vander Wal	.05
259	Dave Veres	.05
260a	Larry Walker/Btg	.05
260b	Larry Walker/Btg (Close-up.)	.05
261	Jamey Wright	.05
262	Larry Walker (Rockies Checklist.)	.05
263	Kimera Bartee	.05
264	Doug Brocail	.05
265	Raul Casanova	.05
266	Frank Castillo	.05
267	Frank Catalanotto	.05
268	Tony Clark	.05
269	Deivi Cruz	.05
270	Roberto Duran	.05
271	Damion Easley	.05
272	Bryce Florie	.05
273	Luis Gonzalez	.05
274	Bob Higginson	.05
275	Brian Hunter	.05
276	Todd Jones	.05
277	Greg Keagle	.05
278	Jeff Manto	.05
279	Brian Moehler	.05
280	Joe Oliver	.05
281	Joe Randa	.05
282	Billy Ripken	.05
283	Bip Roberts	.05
284	Sean Runyan	.05
285	A.J. Sager	.05
286	Justin Thompson	.05
287	Tony Clark (Tigers Checklist.)	.05
288	Antonio Alfonseca	.05
289	Dave Berg	.05
290	Josh Booty	.05
291	John Cangelosi	.05
292	Craig Counsell	.05
293	Vic Darensbourg	.05
294	Cliff Floyd	.05
295	Oscar Henriquez	.05
296	Felix Heredia	.05
297	Ryan Jackson RC	.05
298	Mark Kotsay	.05
299	Andy Larkin	.05
300	Derrek Lee	.60
301	Brian Meadows	.05
302	Rafael Medina	.05
303	Jay Powell	.05
304	Edgar Renteria	.05
305	Jesus Sanchez RC	.05
306	Rob Stanifer	.05
307	Gregg Zaun	.05
308	Derrek Lee (Marlins Checklist.)	.30
309	Moises Alou	.05
310	Brad Ausmus	.05
311a	Jeff Bagwell/Btg	.65
311b	Jeff Bagwell/Fielding	.65
312	Derek Bell	.05
313	Sean Bergman	.05
314	Sean Berry	.05
315	Craig Biggio	.05
316	Tim Bogar	.05
317	Jose Cabrera	.05
318	Dave Clark	.05
319	Tony Eusebio	.05
320	Carl Everett	.05
321	Ricky Gutierrez	.05
322	John Halama	.05
323	Mike Hampton	.05
324	Doug Henry	.05
325	Richard Hidalgo	.05
326	Jack Howell	.05
327	Jose Lima	.05
328	Mike Magnante	.05
329	Trever Miller	.05
330	C.J. Nitkowski	.05
331	Shane Reynolds	.05
332	Bill Spiers	.05
333	Billy Wagner	.05
334	Jeff Bagwell (Astros Checklist.)	.40
335	Tim Belcher	.05
336	Brian Bevil	.05
337	Johnny Damon	.35
338	Jermaine Dye	.05
339	Sal Fasano	.05
340	Shane Halter	.05
341	Chris Haney	.05
342	Jed Hansen	.05
343	Jeff King	.05
344	Jeff Montgomery	.05
345	Hal Morris	.05
346	Jose Offerman	.05
347	Dean Palmer	.05
348	Terry Pendleton	.05
349	Hipolito Pichardo	.05
350	Jim Pittsley	.05
351	Pat Rapp	.05
352	Jose Rosado	.05
353	Glendon Rusch	.05
354	Scott Service	.05
355	Larry Sutton	.05
356	Mike Sweeney	.05
357	Joe Vitiello	.05
358	Matt Whisenant	.05
359	Ernie Young	.05
360	Jeff King (Royals Checklist.)	.05
361	Bobby Bonilla	.05
362	Jim Bruske	.05
363	Juan Castro	.05
364	Roger Cedeno	.05
365	Mike Devereaux	.05
366	Darren Dreifort	.05
367	Jim Eisenreich	.05
368	Wilton Guerrero	.05
369	Mark Guthrie	.05
370	Darren Hall	.05
371	Todd Hollandsworth	.05
372	Thomas Howard	.05
373	Trenidad Hubbard	.05
374	Charles Johnson	.05
375	Eric Karros	.05
376	Paul Konerko	.20
377	Matt Luke	.05
378	Ramon Martinez	.05
379	Raul Mondesi	.05
380	Hideo Nomo	.35
381	Antonio Osuna	.05
382	Chan Ho Park	.05
383	Tom Prince	.05
384	Scott Radinsky	.05
385	Gary Sheffield	.40
386	Ismael Valdes	.05
387	Jose Vizcaino	.05
388	Eric Young	.05
389	Gary Sheffield (Dodgers Checklist.)	.10
390	Jeromy Burnitz	.05
391	Jeff Cirillo	.05
392	Cal Eldred	.05
393	Chad Fox	.05
394	Marquis Grissom	.05
395	Bob Hamelin	.05
396	Bobby Hughes	.05
397	Darrin Jackson	.05
398	John Jaha	.05
399	Geoff Jenkins	.05
400	Doug Jones	.05
401	Jeff Juden	.05
402	Scott Karl	.05
403	Jesse Levis	.05
404	Mark Loretta	.05
405	Mike Matheny	.05
406	Jose Mercedes	.05
407	Mike Myers	.05
408	Marc Newfield	.05
409	Dave Nilsson	.05
410	Al Reyes	.05
411	Jose Valentin	.05
412	Fernando Vina	.05
413	Paul Wagner	.05
414	Bob Wickman	.05
415	Steve Woodard	.05
416	Marquis Grissom (Brewers Checklist.)	.05
417	Rick Aguilera	.05
418	Ron Coomer	.05
419	Marty Cordova	.05
420	Brent Gates	.05
421	Eddie Guardado	.05
422	Denny Hocking	.05
423	Matt Lawton	.05
424	Pat Meares	.05
425	Orlando Merced	.05
426	Eric Milton	.05
427	Paul Molitor	.65
428	Mike Morgan	.05
429	Dan Naulty	.05
430	Otis Nixon	.05
431	Alex Ochoa	.05
432	David Ortiz	.40
433	Brad Radke	.05
434	Todd Ritchie	.05
435	Frank Rodriguez	.05
436	Terry Steinbach	.05
437	Greg Swindell	.05
438	Bob Tewksbury	.05
439	Mike Trombley	.05
440	Javier Valentin	.05
441	Todd Walker	.05
442	Paul Molitor (Twins Checklist.)	.40
443	Shane Andrews	.05
444	Miguel Batista	.05
445	Shayne Bennett	.05
446	Rick DeHart	.05
447	Brad Fullmer	.05
448	Mark Grudzielanek	.05
449	Vladimir Guerrero	.65
450	Dustin Hermanson	.05
451	Steve Kline	.05
452	Scott Livingstone	.05
453	Mike Maddux	.05
454	Derrick May	.05
455	Ryan McGuire	.05
456	Trey Moore	.05
457	Mike Mordecai	.05
458	Carl Pavano	.05
459	Carlos Perez	.05
460	F.P. Santangelo	.05
461	DaRond Stovall	.05
462	Anthony Telford	.05
463	Ugueth Urbina	.05
464	Marc Valdes	.05
465	Jose Vidro	.05
466	Rondell White	.05
467	Chris Widger	.05
468	Vladimir Guerrero (Expos Checklist.)	.40
469	Edgardo Alfonzo	.05
470	Carlos Baerga	.05
471	Rich Becker	.05
472	Brian Bohanon	.05
473	Alberto Castillo	.05
474	Dennis Cook	.05
475	John Franco	.05
476	Matt Franco	.05
477	Bernard Gilkey	.05
478	John Hudek	.05
479	Butch Huskey	.05
480	Bobby Jones	.05
481	Al Leiter	.05
482	Luis Lopez	.05
483	Brian McRae	.05
484	Dave Mlicki	.05
485	John Olerud	.05
486	Rey Ordonez	.05
487	Craig Paquette	.05
488a	Mike Piazza/Btg	1.00
488b	Mike Piazza/Btg (Close-up.)	1.00
489	Todd Pratt	.05
490	Mel Rojas	.05
491	Tim Spehr	.05
492	Turk Wendell	.05
493	Masato Yoshii RC	.25
494	Mike Piazza (Mets Checklist.)	.45
495	Willie Banks	.05
496	Scott Brosius	.05
497	Mike Buddie	.05
498	Homer Bush	.05
499	David Cone	.05
500	Chad Curtis	.05
501	Chili Davis	.05
502	Joe Girardi	.05
503	Darren Holmes	.05
504	Hideki Irabu	.05
505a	Derek Jeter/Btg	2.00
505b	Derek Jeter/Fielding	2.00
506	Chuck Knoblauch	.05
507	Graeme Lloyd	.05
508	Tino Martinez	.05
509	Ramiro Mendoza	.05
510	Jeff Nelson	.05
511	Paul O'Neill	.05
512	Andy Pettitte	.20
513	Jorge Posada	.05
514	Tim Raines	.05
515	Mariano Rivera	.15
516	Luis Sojo	.05
517	Mike Stanton	.05
518	Darryl Strawberry	.05
519	Dale Sveum	.05
520	David Wells	.05
521	Bernie Williams	.05
522	Bernie Williams (Yankees Checklist.)	.05
523	Kurt Abbott	.05
524	Mike Blowers	.05
525	Rafael Bournigal	.05
526	Tom Candiotti	.05
527	Ryan Christenson	.05
528	Mike Fetters	.05
529	Jason Giambi	.50
530a	Ben Grieve/Btg	.05
530b	Ben Grieve/Running	.05
531	Buddy Groom	.05
532	Jimmy Haynes	.05
533	Rickey Henderson	.65
534	A.J. Hinch	.05
535	Mike Macfarlane	.05
536	Dave Magadan	.05
537	T.J. Mathews	.05
538	Jason McDonald	.05
539	Kevin Mitchell	.05

540 Mike Mohler	.05	
541 Mike Oquist	.05	
542 Ariel Prieto	.05	
543 Kenny Rogers	.05	
544 Aaron Small	.05	
545 Scott Spiezio	.05	
546 Matt Stairs	.05	
547 Bill Taylor	.05	
548 Dave Telgheder	.05	
549 Jack Voigt	.05	
550 Ben Grieve		
(A's Checklist.)	.05	
551 Bob Abreu	.10	
552 Ruben Amaro	.05	
553 Alex Arias	.05	
554 Matt Beech	.05	
555 Ricky Bottalico	.05	
556 Billy Brewer	.05	
557 Rico Brogna	.05	
558 Doug Glanville	.05	
559 Wayne Gomes	.05	
560 Mike Grace	.05	
561 Tyler Green	.05	
562 Rex Hudler	.05	
563 Gregg Jefferies	.05	
564 Kevin Jordan	.05	
565 Mark Leiter	.05	
566 Mark Lewis	.05	
567 Mike Lieberthal	.05	
568 Mark Parent	.05	
569 Yorkis Perez	.05	
570 Desi Relaford	.05	
571 Scott Rolen	.50	
572 Curt Schilling	.35	
573 Kevin Sefcik	.05	
574 Jerry Spradlin	.05	
575 Garrett Stephenson	.05	
576 Darrin Winston	.05	
577 Scott Rolen		
(Phillies Checklist.)	.20	
578 Jermaine Allensworth	.05	
579 Jason Christiansen	.05	
580 Lou Collier	.05	
581 Francisco Cordova	.05	
582 Elmer Dessens	.05	
583 Freddy Garcia	.05	
584 Jose Guillen	.05	
585 Jason Kendall	.05	
586 Jon Lieber	.05	
587 Esteban Loaiza	.05	
588 Al Martin	.05	
589 Javier Martinez	.05	
590 Chris Peters RC	.05	
591 Kevin Polcovich	.05	
592 Ricardo Rincon	.05	
593 Jason Schmidt	.05	
594 Jose Silva	.05	
595 Mark Smith	.05	
596 Doug Strange	.05	
597 Turner Ward	.05	
598 Marc Wilkins	.05	
599 Mike Williams	.05	
600 Tony Womack	.05	
601 Kevin Young	.05	
602 Tony Womack		
(Pirates Checklist.)	.05	
603 Manny Aybar	.05	
604 Kent Bottenfield	.05	
605 Jeff Brantley	.05	
606 Mike Busby	.05	
607 Royce Clayton	.05	
608 Delino DeShields	.05	
609 John Frascatore	.05	
610 Gary Gaetti	.05	
611 Ron Gant	.05	
612 David Howard	.05	
613 Brian Hunter	.05	
614 Brian Jordan	.05	
615 Tom Lampkin	.05	
616 Ray Lankford	.05	
617 Braden Looper	.05	
618 John Mabry	.05	
619 Eli Marrero	.05	
620 Willie McGee	.05	
621a Mark McGwire/Btg	1.50	
621b Mark McGwire/		
Fielding	1.50	
622 Kent Mercker	.05	
623 Matt Morris	.05	
624 Donovan Osborne	.05	
625 Tom Pagnozzi	.05	
626 Lance Painter	.05	
627 Mark Petkovsek	.05	
628 Todd Stottlemyre	.05	
629 Mark McGwire		
(Cardinals Checklist.)	.75	
630 Andy Ashby	.05	
631 Brian Boehringer	.05	
632 Kevin Brown	.05	
633 Ken Caminiti	.05	
634 Steve Finley	.05	
635 Ed Giovanola	.05	
636 Chris Gomez	.05	
637a Tony Gwynn		
(Blue jersey.)	.75	
637b Tony Gwynn		
(White jersey.)	.75	
SAMPLE Tony Gwynn (SAMPLE		
overprint on back.)	1.00	
638 Joey Hamilton	.05	
639 Carlos Hernandez	.05	
640 Sterling Hitchcock	.05	
641 Trevor Hoffman	.05	
642 Wally Joyner	.05	
643 Dan Miceli	.05	
644 James Mouton	.05	
645 Greg Myers	.05	
646 Carlos Reyes	.05	

647 Andy Sheets	.05
648 Pete Smith	.05
649 Mark Sweeney	.05
650 Greg Vaughn	.05
651 Quilvio Veras	.05
652 Tony Gwynn	
(Padres Checklist.)	.40
653 Rich Aurilia	.05
654 Marvin Benard	.05
655a Barry Bonds/Btg	2.00
655b Barry Bonds/Btg	
(Close-up.)	2.00
656 Danny Darwin	.05
657 Shawn Estes	.05
658 Mark Gardner	.05
659 Darryl Hamilton	.05
660 Charlie Hayes	.05
661 Orel Hershiser	.05
662 Stan Javier	.05
663 Brian Johnson	.05
664 John Johnstone	.05
665 Jeff Kent	.05
666 Brent Mayne	.05
667 Bill Mueller	.05
668 Robb Nen	.05
669 Jim Poole	.05
670 Steve Reed	.05
671 Rich Rodriguez	.05
672 Kirk Rueter	.05
673 Rey Sanchez	.05
674 J.T. Snow	.05
675 Julian Tavarez	.05
676 Barry Bonds	
(Giants Checklist.)	1.00
677 Rich Amaral	.05
678 Bobby Ayala	.05
679 Jay Buhner	.05
680 Ken Cloude	.05
681 Joey Cora	.05
682 Russ Davis	.05
683 Rob Ducey	.05
684 Jeff Fassero	.05
685 Tony Fossas	.05
686a Ken Griffey Jr./Btg	1.25
686b Ken Griffey Jr./Fielding	1.25
687 Glenallen Hill	.05
688 Jeff Huson	.05
689 Randy Johnson	.65
690 Edgar Martinez	.05
691 John Marzano	.05
692 Jamie Moyer	.05
693a Alex Rodriguez/Btg	1.50
693b Alex Rodriguez/	
Fielding	1.50
694 David Segui	.05
695 Heathcliff Slocumb	.05
696 Paul Spoljaric	.05
697 Bill Swift	.05
698 Mike Timlin	.05
699 Bob Wells	.05
700 Dan Wilson	.05
701 Ken Griffey Jr.	
(Mariners Checklist.)	.50
702 Wilson Alvarez	.05
703 Rolando Arrojo RC	.30
704a Wade Boggs/Btg	.75
704b Wade Boggs/Fielding	.75
705 Rich Butler	.05
706 Miguel Cairo	.05
707 Mike Difelice	.05
708 John Flaherty	.05
709 Roberto Hernandez	.05
710 Mike Kelly	.05
711 Aaron Ledesma	.05
712 Albie Lopez	.05
713 Dave Martinez	.05
714 Quinton McCracken	.05
715 Fred McGriff	.05
716 Jim Mecir	.05
717 Tony Saunders	.05
718 Bobby Smith	.05
719 Paul Sorrento	.05
720 Dennis Springer	.05
721 Kevin Stocker	.05
722 Ramon Tatis	.05
723 Bubba Trammell	.05
724 Esteban Yan	.05
725 Wade Boggs	
(Devil Rays Checklist.)	.40
726 Luis Alicea	.05
727 Scott Bailes	.05
728 John Burkett	.05
729 Domingo Cedeno	.05
730 Will Clark	.05
731 Kevin Elster	.05
732a Juan Gonzalez/Bat	.35
732b Juan Gonzalez (No bat.)	.35
733 Tom Goodwin	.05
734 Rusty Greer	.05
735 Eric Gunderson	.05
736 Bill Haselman	.05
737 Rick Helling	.05
738 Roberto Kelly	.05
739 Mark McLemore	.05
740 Darren Oliver	.05
741 Danny Patterson	.05
742 Roger Pavlik	.05
743a Ivan Rodriguez/Btg	.60
743b Ivan Rodriguez/Fielding	.60
744 Aaron Sele	.05
745 Mike Simms	.05
746 Lee Stevens	.05
747 Fernando Tatis	.05
748 John Wetteland	.05
749 Bobby Witt	.05
750 Juan Gonzalez	
(Rangers Checklist.)	.20
751 Carlos Almanzar	.05

752 Kevin Brown	.05
753 Jose Canseco	.40
754 Chris Carpenter	.05
755 Roger Clemens	1.00
756 Felipe Crespo	.05
757 Jose Cruz Jr.	.05
758 Mark Dalesandro	.05
759 Carlos Delgado	.50
760 Kelvim Escobar	.05
761 Tony Fernandez	.05
762 Darrin Fletcher	.05
763 Alex Gonzalez	.05
764 Craig Grebeck	.05
765 Shawn Green	.35
766 Juan Guzman	.05
767 Erik Hanson	.05
768 Pat Hentgen	.05
769 Randy Myers	.05
770 Robert Person	.05
771 Dan Plesac	.05
772 Paul Quantrill	.05
773 Bill Risley	.05
774 Juan Samuel	.05
775 Steve Sinclair	.05
776 Ed Sprague	.05
777 Mike Stanley	.05
778 Shannon Stewart	.05
779 Woody Williams	.05
780 Roger Clemens	
(Blue Jays Checklist.)	.45

Web Cards

This 800-card parallel set allowed collectors to use Pacific's web site to find out the prize they had won. The cards used gold foil on the front instead of the silver foil used on base cards, and contained an eight-digit code on the back that was the claim number.

Web Stars/RC's:	2X
Inserted 1:1	

1998 Pacific Paramount

Paramount was Pacific's first fully-licensed baseball card product. The 250 base cards feature full-bleed photos with the player's name and team listed at the bottom. The base set is paralleled three times. Gold retail (1:1), Copper hobby (1:1) and Platinum Blue (1:73) versions were included. Inserts in the product are Special Delivery Die-Cuts, Team Checklist Die-Cuts, Cooperstown Bound, Fielder's Choice Laser-Cuts and Inaugural Issue.

	NM/M
Complete Set (250):	20.00
Common Player:	.10
Gold (1:1R):	1X
Copper (1:1H):	1X
Red (1:1 ANCO):	2X
Platinum Blue (1:73):	4X
Holographic Silver:	20X
Production 99 Sets	
Pack (6):	1.00
Wax Box (36):	15.00

1 Garret Anderson	.10
2 Gary DiSarcina	.10
3 Jim Edmonds	.10
4 Darin Erstad	.20
5 Cecil Fielder	.10
6 Chuck Finley	.10
7 Todd Greene	.10
8 Shigetosi Hasegawa	.10
9 Tim Salmon	.10
10 Roberto Alomar	.20
11 Brady Anderson	.10
12 Joe Carter	.10
13 Eric Davis	.10
14 Ozzie Guillen	.10
15 Mike Mussina	.40
16 Rafael Palmeiro	.65
17 Cal Ripken Jr.	2.50
18 B.J. Surhoff	.10
19 Steve Avery	.10
20 Nomar Garciaparra	1.00
21 Reggie Jefferson	.10
22 Pedro Martinez	.75
23 Tim Naehring	.10
24 John Valentin	.10
25 Mo Vaughn	.10
26 James Baldwin	.10
27 Albert Belle	.10
28 Ray Durham	.10
29 Benji Gil	.10
30 Jaime Navarro	.10
31 Magglio Ordonez RC	1.50
32 Frank Thomas	.75
33 Robin Ventura	.10
34 Sandy Alomar Jr.	.10
35 Geronimo Berroa	.10
36 Travis Fryman	.10
37 David Justice	.10
38 Kenny Lofton	.10
39 Charles Nagy	.10
40 Manny Ramirez	.10
41 Jim Thome	.65
42 Omar Vizquel	.10
43 Jaret Wright	.10
44 Raul Casanova	.10
45 Frank Catalanotto RC	.20
46 Tony Clark	.10
47 Bobby Higginson	.10
48 Brian Hunter	.10
49 Todd Jones	.10
50 Bip Roberts	.10
51 Justin Thompson	.10
52 Kevin Appier	.10
53 Johnny Damon	.35
54 Jermaine Dye	.10
55 Jeff King	.10
56 Jeff Montgomery	.10
57 Dean Palmer	.10
58 Jose Rosado	.10
59 Larry Sutton	.10
60 Rick Aguilera	.10
61 Marty Cordova	.10
62 Pat Meares	.10
63 Paul Molitor	.75
64 Otis Nixon	.10
65 Brad Radke	.10
66 Terry Steinbach	.10
67 Todd Walker	.10
68 Hideki Irabu	.10
69 Derek Jeter	2.50
70 Chuck Knoblauch	.10
71 Tino Martinez	.10
72 Paul O'Neill	.10
73 Andy Pettitte	.20
74 Mariano Rivera	.15
75 Bernie Williams	.10
76 Mark Bellhorn	.10
77 Tom Candiotti	.10
78 Jason Giambi	.50
79 Ben Grieve	.10
80 Rickey Henderson	.75
81 Jason McDonald	.10
82 Aaron Small	.10
83 Miguel Tejada	.20
84 Jay Buhner	.10
85 Joey Cora	.10
86 Jeff Fassero	.10
87 Ken Griffey Jr.	1.50
88 Randy Johnson	.75
89 Edgar Martinez	.10
90 Alex Rodriguez	2.00
91 David Segui	.10
92 Dan Wilson	.10
93 Wilson Alvarez	.10
94 Wade Boggs	1.00
95 Miguel Cairo	.10
96 John Flaherty	.10
97 Dave Martinez	.10
98 Quinton McCracken	.10
99 Fred McGriff	.10
100 Paul Sorrento	.10
101 Kevin Stocker	.10
102 John Burkett	.10
103 Will Clark	.10
104 Juan Gonzalez	.40
105 Rusty Greer	.10
106 Roberto Kelly	.10
107 Ivan Rodriguez	.65
108 Fernando Tatis	.10
109 John Wetteland	.10
110 Jose Canseco	.40
111 Roger Clemens	1.25
112 Jose Cruz Jr.	.10
113 Carlos Delgado	.50
114 Alex Gonzalez	.10
115 Pat Hentgen	.10
116 Ed Sprague	.10
117 Shannon Stewart	.10
118 Brian Anderson	.10

119 Jay Bell	.10
120 Andy Benes	.10
121 Yamil Benitez	.10
122 Jorge Fabregas	.10
123 Travis Lee	.10
124 Devon White	.10
125 Matt Williams	.10
126 Bob Wolcott	.10
127 Andres Galarraga	.10
128 Tom Glavine	.35
129 Andruw Jones	.75
130 Chipper Jones	1.00
131 Ryan Klesko	.10
132 Javy Lopez	.10
133 Greg Maddux	1.00
134 Denny Neagle	.10
135 John Smoltz	.10
136 Rod Beck	.10
137 Jeff Blauser	.10
138 Mark Grace	.10
139 Lance Johnson	.10
140 Mickey Morandini	.10
141 Kevin Orie	.10
142 Sammy Sosa	1.00
143 Aaron Boone	.10
144 Bret Boone	.10
145 Dave Burba	.10
146 Lenny Harris	.10
147 Barry Larkin	.10
148 Reggie Sanders	.10
149 Brett Tomko	.10
150 Pedro Astacio	.10
151 Dante Bichette	.10
152 Ellis Burks	.10
153 Vinny Castilla	.10
154 Todd Helton	.75
155 Darryl Kile	.10
156 Jeff Reed	.10
157 Larry Walker	.10
158 Bobby Bonilla	.10
159 Todd Dunwoody	.10
160 Livan Hernandez	.10
161 Charles Johnson	.10
162 Mark Kotsay	.10
163 Derrek Lee	.60
164 Edgar Renteria	.10
165 Gary Sheffield	.50
166 Moises Alou	.10
167 Jeff Bagwell	.75
168 Derek Bell	.10
169 Craig Biggio	.10
170 Mike Hampton	.10
171 Richard Hidalgo	.10
172 Chris Holt	.10
173 Shane Reynolds	.10
174 Wilton Guerrero	.10
175 Eric Karros	.10
176 Paul Konerko	.20
177 Ramon Martinez	.10
178 Raul Mondesi	.10
179 Hideo Nomo	.40
180 Chan Ho Park	.10
181 Mike Piazza	1.25
182 Ismael Valdes	.10
183 Jeromy Burnitz	.10
184 Jeff Cirillo	.10
185 Todd Dunn	.10
186 Marquis Grissom	.10
187 John Jaha	.10
188 Doug Jones	.10
189 Dave Nilsson	.10
190 Jose Valentin	.10
191 Fernando Vina	.10
192 Orlando Cabrera	.10
193 Steve Falteisek	.10
194 Mark Grudzielanek	.10
195 Vladimir Guerrero	.75
196 Carlos Perez	.10
197 F.P. Santangelo	.10
198 Jose Vidro	.10
199 Rondell White	.10
200 Edgardo Alfonzo	.10
201 Carlos Baerga	.10
202 John Franco	.10
203 Bernard Gilkey	.10
204 Todd Hundley	.10
205 Butch Huskey	.10
206 Bobby Jones	.10
207 Brian McRae	.10
208 John Olerud	.10
209 Rey Ordonez	.10
210 Ricky Bottalico	.10
211 Bobby Estalella	.10
212 Doug Glanville	.10
213 Gregg Jefferies	.10
214 Mike Lieberthal	.10
215 Desi Relaford	.10
216 Scott Rolen	.65
217 Curt Schilling	.35
218 Adrian Brown	.10
219 Emil Brown	.10
220 Francisco Cordova	.10
221 Jose Guillen	.10
222 Al Martin	.10
223 Abraham Nunez	.10
224 Tony Womack	.10
225 Kevin Young	.10
226 Alan Benes	.10
227 Royce Clayton	.10
228 Gary Gaetti	.10
229 Ron Gant	.10
230 Brian Jordan	.10
231 Ray Lankford	.10
232 Mark McGwire	2.00
233 Todd Stottlemyre	.10
234 Kevin Brown	.10
235 Ken Caminiti	.10
236 Steve Finley	.10

237 Tony Gwynn	1.00
238 Wally Joyner	.10
239 Ruben Rivera	.10
240 Greg Vaughn	.10
241 Quilvio Veras	.10
242 Barry Bonds	2.50
243 Jacob Cruz	.10
244 Shawn Estes	.10
245 Orel Hershiser	.10
246 Stan Javier	.10
247 Brian Johnson	.10
248 Jeff Kent	.10
249 Robb Nen	.10
250 J.T. Snow	.10

Gold/Copper/Red

Gold, Copper and Red foil versions of all 250 cards in Paramount were inserted at a rate of one per pack. Gold versions were retail exclusive, Copper versions were hobby exclusive and Red versions were ANCO pack exclusive. The only difference is these parallels use a different color foil than the base cards.

	NM/M
Common Gold/Copper Player:	.25
Gold/Copper Stars:	1X
Inserted 1:1	
Common Red Player:	.30
Red Stars:	2X

Holographic Silver

Holographics Silver parallel cards were issued for all 250 cards in the Paramount set. These were inserted into hobby packs, with only 99 sets produced.

	NM/M
Common Player:	1.00
Holographic Silver Stars:	20X
Production 99 Sets	

Platinum Blue

This paralled set reprinted all 250 cards in Paramount using blue foil stamping on the card front. These were inserted one per 73 packs.

	NM/M
Common Platinum Blue Player:	1.00
Platinum Blue Stars:	4X
Inserted 1:73	

Cooperstown Bound

Cooperstown Bound is a 10-card insert seeded one per 361 packs. Each card features a color player photo with a silver foil column on the left. The cards are fully foiled and etched.

	NM/M
Complete Set (10):	60.00

3	Cal Ripken Jr.	5.00
4	Nomar Garciaparra	2.50
5	Pedro Martinez	2.00
6	Frank Thomas	2.00
7	David Justice	.50
8	Larry Walker	.50
9	Jeff Bagwell	2.00
10	Hideo Nomo	1.00
11	Mike Piazza	3.00
12	Vladimir Guerrero	2.00
13	Derek Jeter	5.00
14	Ben Grieve	.50
15	Mark McGwire	4.00
16	Tony Gwynn	2.50
17	Barry Bonds	5.00
18	Ken Griffey Jr.	5.00
19	Alex Rodriguez	4.00
20	Jose Cruz Jr.	.50

Common Player: 8.00
Inserted 1:361
Pacific Proofs: 6X
Production 20 Sets

1	Greg Maddux	10.00
2	Cal Ripken Jr.	15.00
3	Frank Thomas	8.00
4	Mike Piazza	8.00
5	Paul Molitor	8.00
6	Mark McGwire	12.00
7	Tony Gwynn	8.00
8	Barry Bonds	15.00
9	Ken Griffey Jr.	10.00
10	Wade Boggs	8.00

Fielder's Choice

Fielder's Choice Laser-Cuts is a 20-card insert seeded one per 73 packs. Each card is die-cut around a baseball glove that appears in the background. The webbing of the glove is laser-cut.

NM/M
Complete Set (20): 45.00
Common Player: .75
Inserted 1:73

1	Chipper Jones	3.00
2	Greg Maddux	3.00
3	Cal Ripken Jr.	6.00
4	Nomar Garciaparra	3.00
5	Frank Thomas	2.50
6	David Justice	.75
7	Larry Walker	.75
8	Jeff Bagwell	2.50
9	Hideo Nomo	1.25
10	Mike Piazza	3.50
11	Derek Jeter	6.00
12	Ben Grieve	.75
13	Mark McGwire	4.50
14	Tony Gwynn	3.00
15	Barry Bonds	6.00
16	Ken Griffey Jr.	4.00
17	Alex Rodriguez	4.50
18	Wade Boggs	3.00
19	Ivan Rodriguez	2.00
20	Jose Cruz Jr.	.75

Special Delivery

Special Delivery cards are die-cut to resemble a postage stamp. Each card front is foiled and etched and features three photos of the player. Special Delivery is a 20-card insert seeded one per 37 packs.

NM/M
Complete Set (20): 30.00
Common Player: .50
Inserted 1:37

1	Chipper Jones	2.50
2	Greg Maddux	2.50

Team Checklists

Team Checklists (30 cards, 2:37) feature a player photo surrounded by two bats. The card is die-cut around the photo and the bats at the top. The bottom has the player's name, position and team.

NM/M
Complete Set (30): 25.00
Common Player: .25
Inserted 1:18

1	Tim Salmon	.25
2	Cal Ripken Jr.	4.00
3	Nomar Garciaparra	1.50
4	Frank Thomas	1.00
5	Manny Ramirez	1.00
6	Tony Clark	.25
7	Dean Palmer	.25
8	Paul Molitor	1.00
9	Derek Jeter	4.00
10	Ben Grieve	.25
11	Ken Griffey Jr.	2.50
12	Wade Boggs	1.50
13	Ivan Rodriguez	.75
14	Roger Clemens	1.50
15	Matt Williams	.25
16	Chipper Jones	1.50
17	Sammy Sosa	1.50
18	Barry Larkin	.25
19	Larry Walker	.25
20	Livan Hernandez	.25
21	Jeff Bagwell	1.00
22	Mike Piazza	2.00
23	John Jaha	.25
24	Vladimir Guerrero	1.00
25	Todd Hundley	.25
26	Scott Rolen	.75
27	Kevin Young	.25
28	Mark McGwire	3.00
29	Tony Gwynn	1.50
30	Barry Bonds	4.00

1998 Pacific Revolution

Pacific Revolution consists of a 150-card base set. The base cards are dual-foiled, etched and embossed. Inserts include Showstoppers, Prime Time Performers Laser-Cuts, Foul Pole Laser-Cuts, Major League Icons and Shadow Series.

NM/M
Complete Set (150): 65.00
Common Player: .25
Pack (3): 1.00
Wax Box (24): 20.00

1	Garret Anderson	.25
2	Jim Edmonds	.25
3	Darin Erstad	.40
4	Chuck Finley	.25
5	Tim Salmon	.25
6	Jay Bell	.25
7	Travis Lee	.25
8	Devon White	.25
9	Matt Williams	.25
10	Andres Galarraga	.25
11	Tom Glavine	.45
12	Andruw Jones	2.50
13	Chipper Jones	3.50
14	Ryan Klesko	.25
15	Javy Lopez	.25
16	Greg Maddux	3.50
17	Walt Weiss	.25
18	Roberto Alomar	.40
19	Joe Carter	.25
20	Mike Mussina	1.25
21	Rafael Palmeiro	2.00
22	Cal Ripken Jr.	6.00
23	B.J. Surhoff	.25
24	Nomar Garciaparra	3.00
25	Reggie Jefferson	.25
26	Pedro Martinez	2.50
27	Troy O'Leary	.25
28	Mo Vaughn	.25
29	Mark Grace	.25
30	Mickey Morandini	.25
31	Henry Rodriguez	.25
32	Sammy Sosa	3.00
33	Kerry Wood	1.25
34	Albert Belle	.25
35	Ray Durham	.25
36	Magglio Ordonez RC	2.00
37	Frank Thomas	2.50
38	Robin Ventura	.25
39	Bret Boone	.25
40	Barry Larkin	.25
41	Reggie Sanders	.25
42	Brett Tomko	.25
43	Sandy Alomar	.25
44	David Justice	.25
45	Kenny Lofton	.25
46	Manny Ramirez	2.50
47	Jim Thome	2.00
48	Omar Vizquel	.25
49	Jaret Wright	.25
50	Dante Bichette	.25
51	Ellis Burks	.25
52	Vinny Castilla	.25
53	Todd Helton	2.50
54	Larry Walker	.25
55	Tony Clark	.25
56	Deivi Cruz	.25
57	Damion Easley	.25
58	Bobby Higginson	.25
59	Brian Hunter	.25
60	Cliff Floyd	.25
61	Livan Hernandez	.25
62	Derek Lee	1.50
63	Edgar Renteria	.25
64	Moises Alou	.25
65	Jeff Bagwell	2.50
66	Derek Bell	.25
67	Craig Biggio	.25
68	Richard Hidalgo	.25
69	Johnny Damon	.40
70	Jeff King	.25
71	Hal Morris	.25
72	Dean Palmer	.25
73	Bobby Bonilla	.25
74	Charles Johnson	.25
75	Paul Konerko	.35
76	Raul Mondesi	.25
77	Gary Sheffield	.75
78	Jeromy Burnitz	.25
79	Marquis Grissom	.25
80	Dave Nilsson	.25
81	Fernando Vina	.25
82	Marty Cordova	.25
83	Pat Meares	.25
84	Paul Molitor	2.50
85	Brad Radke	.25
86	Terry Steinbach	.25
87	Todd Walker	.25
88	Brad Fullmer	.25
89	Vladimir Guerrero	2.50
90	Carl Pavano	.25
91	Rondell White	.25
92	Bernard Gilkey	.25
93	Hideo Nomo	1.25
94	John Olerud	.25
95	Rey Ordonez	.25
96	Mike Piazza	4.00
97	Masato Yoshii RC	.65
98	Hideki Irabu	.25
99	Derek Jeter	6.00
100	Chuck Knoblauch	.25
101	Tino Martinez	.25
102	Paul O'Neill	.25
103	Darryl Strawberry	.25
104	Bernie Williams	1.50
105	Jason Giambi	1.50
106	Ben Grieve	.25
107	Rickey Henderson	2.50
108	Matt Stairs	.25
109	Doug Glanville	.25
110	Desi Relaford	.25
111	Scott Rolen	1.50
112	Curt Schilling	.45
113	Jason Kendall	.25
114	Al Martin	.25
115	Jason Schmidt	.25
116	Kevin Young	.25
117	Delino DeShields	.25
118	Gary Gaetti	.25
119	Brian Jordan	.25
120	Ray Lankford	.25
121	Mark McGwire	5.00
122	Kevin Brown	.25
123	Steve Finley	.25
124	Tony Gwynn	3.50
125	Wally Joyner	.25
126	Greg Vaughn	.25
127	Barry Bonds	6.00
128	Orel Hershiser	.25
129	Jeff Kent	.25
130	Bill Mueller	.25
131	Jay Buhner	.25
132	Ken Griffey Jr.	4.50
133	Randy Johnson	2.50
134	Edgar Martinez	.25
135	Alex Rodriguez	5.00
136	David Segui	.25
137	Rolando Arrojo RC	.75
138	Wade Boggs	3.50
139	Quinton McCracken	.25
140	Fred McGriff	.25
141	Will Clark	.25
142	Juan Gonzalez	1.25
143	Tom Goodwin	.25
144	Ivan Rodriguez	2.00
145	Aaron Sele	.25
146	John Wetteland	.25
147	Jose Canseco	.50
148	Roger Clemens	4.00
149	Jose Cruz Jr.	.25
150	Carlos Delgado	.65

Shadows

Shadows is a full parallel of the Revolution base set. Limited to 99 sequentially numbered sets, each card is embossed with a special "Shadow Series" stamp.

NM/M
Common Player: 2.00
Stars/Rookies: 6X

Foul Pole

Foul Pole Laser-Cuts is a 20-card insert seeded one per 49 packs. Each card features a color player photo on the left and a foul pole on the right. The foul pole design includes netting that is laser cut.

NM/M
Complete Set (20): 100.00
Common Player: 2.00
Inserted 1:49

1	Cal Ripken Jr.	15.00
2	Nomar Garciaparra	7.50
3	Mo Vaughn	2.00
4	Frank Thomas	6.00
5	Manny Ramirez	6.00
6	Bernie Williams	2.00
7	Ben Grieve	2.00
8	Ken Griffey Jr.	10.00
9	Alex Rodriguez	12.00
10	Juan Gonzalez	3.00
11	Ivan Rodriguez	5.00
12	Travis Lee	2.00
13	Chipper Jones	7.50
14	Sammy Sosa	7.50
15	Vinny Castilla	2.00
16	Moises Alou	2.00
17	Gary Sheffield	3.00
18	Mike Piazza	9.00
19	Mark McGwire	12.00
20	Barry Bonds	15.00

Major League Icons

Major League Icons is a 10-card insert seeded one per 121 packs. Each card features a player photo on a die-cut shield, with the shield on a flaming stand.

NM/M
Complete Set (10): 50.00
Common Player: 4.50
Inserted 1:121

1	Cal Ripken Jr.	15.00
2	Nomar Garciaparra	7.50
3	Frank Thomas	6.00
4	Ken Griffey Jr.	10.00
5	Alex Rodriguez	12.50
6	Chipper Jones	7.50
7	Kerry Wood	4.50
8	Mike Piazza	9.00
9	Mark McGwire	12.50
10	Tony Gwynn	7.50

Prime Time Performers

Prime Time Performers is a 20-card insert seeded one per 25 packs. The cards are designed like a TV program guide with the team logo laser-cut on the TV screen. The color player photo is located on the left.

NM/M
Complete Set (20): 25.00
Common Player: .50
Inserted 1:25

1	Cal Ripken Jr.	4.50
2	Nomar Garciaparra	2.00
3	Frank Thomas	1.50
4	Jim Thome	1.25
5	Hideki Irabu	.25
6	Derek Jeter	4.50
7	Ben Grieve	.50
8	Ken Griffey Jr.	3.00
9	Alex Rodriguez	3.50
10	Juan Gonzalez	.75
11	Ivan Rodriguez	1.25
12	Travis Lee	.50
13	Chipper Jones	2.00
14	Greg Maddux	2.00
15	Kerry Wood	.75
16	Larry Walker	.50
17	Jeff Bagwell	1.50
18	Mike Piazza	2.50
19	Mark McGwire	3.50
20	Tony Gwynn	2.00

Rookies and Hardball Heroes

This hobby-only insert combines 20 hot prospects with 10 veteran stars. Horizontal cards have action photos on a flashy metallic-foil background. A portrait photo is on back. The first 20 cards in the set, the youngsters, are paralleled in a gold edition which was limited to just 50 cards of each.

NM/M
Complete Set (30): 20.00
Common Player: .25
Inserted 1:6
Gold (1-20): 10X
Production 50 Sets

1	Justin Baughman	.25
2	Jarrod Washburn	.25
3	Travis Lee	.25
4	Kerry Wood	.50
5	Magglio Ordonez	.50
6	Todd Helton	1.00
7	Derek Lee	.25
8	Richard Hidalgo	.25
9	Mike Caruso	.25
10	David Ortiz	.75
11	Brad Fullmer	.25
12	Masato Yoshii	.25
13	Orlando Hernandez	.25
14	Ricky Ledee	.25
15	Ben Grieve	.25
16	Carlton Loewer	.25
17	Desi Relaford	.25
18	Ruben Rivera	.25
19	Rolando Arrojo	.25
20	Matt Perisho	.25
21	Chipper Jones	2.00
22	Greg Maddux	2.00
23	Cal Ripken Jr.	5.00
24	Nomar Garciaparra	2.00
25	Frank Thomas	1.00
26	Mark McGwire	4.00
27	Tony Gwynn	2.00
28	Ken Griffey Jr.	3.00
29	Alex Rodriguez	4.00
30	Juan Gonzalez	.50

Showstoppers

This 36-card insert was seeded two per 25 packs. The cards feature holographic foil. The color photo is centered above the team logo and the Showstoppers logo.

NM/M
Complete Set (36): 30.00
Common Player: .45
Inserted 1:12

1	Cal Ripken Jr.	5.00
2	Nomar Garciaparra	2.50
3	Pedro Martinez	2.00
4	Mo Vaughn	.45
5	Frank Thomas	2.00
6	Manny Ramirez	2.00
7	Jim Thome	1.75
8	Jaret Wright	.45
9	Paul Molitor	2.00
10	Orlando Hernandez	.60
11	Derek Jeter	5.00
12	Bernie Williams	.45
13	Ben Grieve	.45
14	Ken Griffey Jr.	3.50
15	Alex Rodriguez	4.00
16	Wade Boggs	2.50
17	Juan Gonzalez	1.00
18	Ivan Rodriguez	1.75
19	Jose Canseco	.75
20	Roger Clemens	3.00
21	Travis Lee	.45
22	Andres Galarraga	.45
23	Chipper Jones	2.50
24	Greg Maddux	2.50
25	Sammy Sosa	2.50
26	Kerry Wood	.90
27	Vinny Castilla	.45
28	Larry Walker	.45
29	Moises Alou	.45
30	Raul Mondesi	.45
31	Gary Sheffield	.75
32	Hideo Nomo	1.00
33	Mike Piazza	3.00
34	Mark McGwire	4.00
35	Tony Gwynn	2.50
36	Barry Bonds	3.00

Nestle's Latinos

Produced by Pacific this set of Latino ballplayers' cards

was issued in three-card packs with the purchase of certain Nestle's food products in Los Angeles, Miami, Houston and San Antonio. Cards are found in two styles. Five of the cards have gold-foil graphic highlights on both top and bottom on front. On back the card number is in a white circle. The second style has foil only at bottom front and on back the card number is in a black circle. Both types have Pacific and Nestle logos on front and back.

		NM/M
Complete Set (20):		8.00
Common Player:		.25
1	Ismael Valdes	.25
2	Juan Gonzalez	.50
3	Ivan Rodriguez	.65
4	Joey Cora	.25
5	Livan Hernandez	.25
1	Bernie Williams	.25
2	Tino Martinez	.25
3	Alex Rodriguez	1.50
4	Edgar Martinez	.25
5	Andres Galarraga	.25
6	Manny Ramirez	.75
7	Carlos Baerga	.25
8	Pedro Martinez	.75
9	Vinny Castilla	.25
10	Sammy Sosa	1.00
11	Nomar Garciaparra	1.00
12	Javy Lopez	.25
13	Sandy Alomar	.25
14	Roberto Alomar	.40
15	Jose Canseco	.50

Home Run Heroes

This retail exclusive product was sold as a complete set sealed in a tin lithographed can. The 2-1/2" x 3-1/2" cards have color action photos on front of the players in the followthrough of their home run swing. The figures are set on an artificial background which includes a sign giving the date and distance of their final home run of the 1998 season. Their team logo is in the "turf" at their feet. Fronts are highlighted with gold foil. On back are a portrait photo, a season summary and 1998 stats, along with appropriate licensor and manufacturer logos.

		NM/M
Complete Set (6):		2.50
Common Player:		.25
1	Mark McGwire	1.00
2	Sammy Sosa	.65
3	Ken Griffey Jr.	.75
4	Greg Vaughn	.25
5	Albert Belle	.25
6	Jose Canseco	.50

Home Run History

This boxed set commemorating the great home run

chase of 1998 was an exclusive to one of the television home-shopping shows. Each player is featured on 35 cards, with several depicting both players. Fronts have portraits or action shots which are borderless at the top and sides. At bottom is a gold-foil highlighted panel with the player's name, card title and date. Backs have another photo and details of the highlight. A pair of die-cut bonus cards were included in the boxed set.

		NM/M
Complete Set (70+2):		10.00
Common Card:		.50
1	Mark McGwire (Portrait of a Hero)	.50
2	Sammy Sosa (Portrait of a Hero)	.50
3	Mark McGwire (Fan Favorite)	.50
4	Sammy Sosa (Fan Favorite)	.50
5	Mark McGwire (Well-Rounded Superstar)	.50
6	Sammy Sosa (Well-Rounded Superstar)	.50
7	Mark McGwire (Cardinals Slugger)	.50
8	Sammy Sosa (Cubs Slugger)	.50
9	Mark McGwire (Home Run #48)	.50
10	Sammy Sosa (20 HRs in June)	.50
11	Mark McGwire (Home Run #50)	.50
12	Sammy Sosa (Home Run #50)	.50
13	Mark McGwire (Home Run #57)	.50
14	Sammy Sosa (Home Run #51)	.50
15	Mark McGwire (Home Run #58)	.50
16	Sammy Sosa (Home Run #56)	.50
17	Mark McGwire (Home Run #59)	.50
18	Sammy Sosa (Home Run #59)	.50
19	Mark McGwire (Home Run #60)	.50
20	Sammy Sosa (Home Run #60)	.50
21	Mark McGwire (Home Run #61)	.50
22	Sammy Sosa (Home Run #61)	.50
23	Mark McGwire (Home Run #62)	.50
24	Sammy Sosa (Home Run #62)	.50
25	Mark McGwire (The Record Falls)	.50
26	Sammy Sosa (Tied at 62!)	.50
27	Mark McGwire (The Home Run Ball)	.50
28	Sammy Sosa (Sammy Sosa Day)	.50
29	Mark McGwire (Achievement Award)	.50
30	Sammy Sosa (Achievement Award)	.50
31	Mark McGwire (What a Ride!)	.50
32	Sammy Sosa (A Season of Accolades)	.50
33	Mark McGwire (Home Run #63)	.50
34	Sammy Sosa (Sammy, You're the Man)	.50
35	Mark McGwire (Home Run #64)	.50
36	Sammy Sosa (Home Run #63)	.50
37	Mark McGwire (Home Run #65)	.50
38	Sammy Sosa (Home Run #64)	.50
39	Mark McGwire (Home Run #67)	.50
40	Sammy Sosa (Home Run #65)	.50
41	Mark McGwire (Home Run #68)	.50
42	Sammy Sosa (Home Run #66)	.50
43	Mark McGwire (70!!!)	.50
44	Sammy Sosa (Cubs Win Wild Card)	.50
45	Mark McGwire (Last Swing of the Bat)	.50
46	Sammy Sosa (18 Stolen Bases)	.50
47	Mark McGwire (Power at the Plate)	.50
48	Sammy Sosa (Grand Sam)	.50
49	Mark McGwire (130 Runs Scored)	.50
50	Sammy Sosa (134 Runs Scored)	.50
51	Mark McGwire (32 HRs on the Road)	.50
52	Sammy Sosa (31 HRs on the Road)	.50
53	Mark McGwire (38 HRs at Home)	.50
54	Sammy Sosa (35 HRs at Home)	.50
55	Mark McGwire (11 First-Inning Home Runs)	.50
56	Sammy Sosa (12 First-Inning Home Runs)	.50
57	Mark McGwire (10 Multiple-HR Games)	.50
58	Sammy Sosa (11 Multiple-HR Games)	.50
59	Mark McGwire (545-Foot Blast)	.50
60	Sammy Sosa (500-Foot Blast)	.50
61	Mark McGwire(St. Louis' Favorite Son)	.50
62	Sammy Sosa (Chicago's Favorite Son)	.50
63	Mark McGwire (A Season of Celebration)	.50
64	Sammy Sosa (A Season of Celebration)	.50
65	Mark McGwire (Curtain Call)	.50
66	Sammy Sosa (Curtain Call)	.50
67	Mark McGwire, Sammy Sosa (Awesome Power)	.50
68	Mark McGwire, Sammy Sosa (Ambassadors of the Game)	.50
69	Mark McGwire, Sammy Sosa (Transcending Sports)	.50
70	Mark McGwire, Sammy Sosa (Friends to the End/Checklist)	.50

Home Run History Bonus Cards

Though they are not identified as such, this pair of Gold Crown-style die-cut cards were bonus inserts in the Home Run History boxed set. Fronts have gold-foil highlights with the pivotal number in blue-sky tones. Backs have portrait photos and a few words about the remarkable record.

		NM/M
1	Mark McGwire (Home Run Champ)	1.50
1	Cal Ripken Jr. (Consecutive Games)	2.00

National Convention Redemption

This card of Pacific spokesman Tony Gwynn was given away at the card compa-

ny's booth in a redemption program during the 1998 National Sports Collectors Convention in August 1998. The card front has a color photo of Gwynn on red and yellow rayed background. At lower-right is a gold-foil convention logo. Back has an action photo, copyright information and logos.

		NM/M
1998 Tony Gwynn		3.00

1999 Pacific Sample

This card of Pacific spokesman Tony Gwynn introduces the 1999 series. The sample card follows the format of the issued version but is overprinted "SAMPLE" on back and lacks Gwynn's 1998 season and career stats.

		NM/M
Tony Gwynn		2.00

1999 Pacific

The 450-card base set features full bleed fronts enhanced with silver foil stamping. Card backs have year-by-year statistics, a small photo and a brief career highlight caption. There are two parallels, Platinum Blues and Reds. Platinum Blues have blue foil stamping and are seeded 1:73 packs. Reds are retail exclusive with red foil stamping and are seeded one per retail pack.

		NM/M
Complete Set (500):		30.00
Common Player:		.10
Platinum Blues (1:73):		15X
Reds (1:1R):		2.5X
Pack (10):		1.00
Wax Box (36):		35.00
1	Garret Anderson	.10
2	Jason Dickson	.10
3	Gary DiSarcina	.10
4	Jim Edmonds	.10
5	Darin Erstad	.25
6	Chuck Finley	.10
7	Shigetosi Hasegawa	.10
8	Ken Hill	.10
9	Dave Hollins	.10
10	Phil Nevin	.10
11	Troy Percival	.10
12a	Tim Salmon/Action	.10
12b	Tim Salmon/Portrait	.10
13	Brian Anderson	.10
14	Tony Batista	.10
15	Jay Bell	.10
16	Andy Benes	.10
17	Yamil Benitez	.10
18	Omar Daal	.10
19	David Dellucci	.10
20	Karim Garcia	.10
21	Bernard Gilkey	.10
22a	Travis Lee/Action	.10
22b	Travis Lee/Portrait	.10
23	Aaron Small	.10
24	Kelly Stinnett	.10
25	Devon White	.10
26	Matt Williams	.10
27a	Bruce Chen/Action	.10
27b	Bruce Chen/Portrait	.10
28a	Andres Galarraga/Action	.10
28b	Andres Galarraga/Portrait	.10
29	Tom Glavine	.35
30	Ozzie Guillen	.10
31	Andruw Jones	1.00
32a	Chipper Jones/Action	1.50
32b	Chipper Jones/Portrait	1.50
33	Ryan Klesko	.10
34	George Lombard	.10
35	Javy Lopez	.10
36a	Greg Maddux/Action	1.50
36b	Greg Maddux/Portrait	1.50
37a	Marty Malloy/Action	.10
37b	Marty Malloy/Portrait	.10
38	Dennis Martinez	.10
39	Kevin Millwood	.10
40a	Alex Rodriguez/Action	2.50
40b	Alex Rodriguez/Portrait	2.50
41	Denny Neagle	.10
42	John Smoltz	.10
43	Michael Tucker	.10
44	Walt Weiss	.10
45a	Roberto Alomar/Action	.25
45b	Roberto Alomar/Portrait	.25
46	Brady Anderson	.10
47	Harold Baines	.10
48	Mike Bordick	.10
49a	Danny Clyburn/Action	.10
49b	Danny Clyburn/Portrait	.10
50	Eric Davis	.10
51	Scott Erickson	.10
52	Chris Hoiles	.10
53	Jimmy Key	.10
54a	Ryan Minor/Action	.10
54b	Ryan Minor/Portrait	.10
55	Mike Mussina	.40
56	Jesse Orosco	.10
57a	Rafael Palmeiro/Action	.75
57b	Rafael Palmeiro/Portrait	.75
58	Sidney Ponson	.10
59	Arthur Rhodes	.10
60a	Cal Ripken Jr./Action	3.00
60b	Cal Ripken Jr./Portrait	3.00
61	B.J. Surhoff	.10
62	Steve Avery	.10
63	Darren Bragg	.10
64	Dennis Eckersley	.75
65a	Nomar Garciaparra/Action	1.50
65b	Nomar Garciaparra/Portrait	1.50
66a	Sammy Sosa/Action	1.50
66b	Sammy Sosa/Portrait	1.50
67	Tom Gordon	.10
68	Reggie Jefferson	.10
69	Darren Lewis	.10
70a	Mark McGwire/Action	2.50
70b	Mark McGwire/Portrait	2.50
71	Pedro Martinez	1.00
72	Troy O'Leary	.10
73	Bret Saberhagen	.10
74	Mike Stanley	.10
75	John Valentin	.10
76	Jason Varitek	.10
77	Mo Vaughn	.10
78	Tim Wakefield	.10
79	Manny Alexander	.10
80	Rod Beck	.10
81	Brant Brown	.10
82	Mark Clark	.10
83	Gary Gaetti	.10
84	Mark Grace	.10
85	Jose Hernandez	.10
86	Lance Johnson	.10
87a	Jason Maxwell/Action	.10
87b	Jason Maxwell/Portrait	.10
88	Mickey Morandini	.10
89	Terry Mulholland	.10
90	Henry Rodriguez	.10
91	Scott Servais	.10
92	Kevin Tapani	.10
93	Pedro Valdes	.10
94	Kerry Wood	.40
95	Jeff Abbott	.10
96	James Baldwin	.10
97	Albert Belle	.10
98	Mike Cameron	.10
99	Mike Caruso	.10
100	Wil Cordero	.10
101	Ray Durham	.10
102	Jaime Navarro	.10
103	Greg Norton	.10
104	Magglio Ordonez	.25
105	Mike Sirotka	.10
106a	Frank Thomas/Action	1.00
106b	Frank Thomas/Portrait	1.00
107	Robin Ventura	.10
108	Craig Wilson	.10
109	Aaron Boone	.10
110	Bret Boone	.10
111	Sean Casey	.15
112	Pete Harnisch	.10
113	John Hudek	.10
114	Barry Larkin	.10
115	Eduardo Perez	.10
116	Mike Remlinger	.10
117	Reggie Sanders	.10
118	Chris Stynes	.10
119	Eddie Taubensee	.10
120	Brett Tomko	.10
121	Pat Watkins	.10
122	Dmitri Young	.10
123	Sandy Alomar Jr.	.10
124	Dave Burba	.10
125	Bartolo Colon	.10
126	Joey Cora	.10
127	Brian Giles	.10
128	Dwight Gooden	.10
129	Mike Jackson	.10
130	David Justice	.10
131	Kenny Lofton	.10
132	Charles Nagy	.10
133	Chad Ogea	.10
134a	Manny Ramirez/Action	1.00
134b	Manny Ramirez/Portrait	1.00
135	Richie Sexson	.10
136a	Jim Thome/Action	.75
136b	Jim Thome/Portrait	.75
137	Omar Vizquel	.10
138	Jaret Wright	.10
139	Pedro Astacio	.10
140	Jason Bates	.10
141a	Dante Bichette/Action	.10
141b	Dante Bichette/Portrait	.10
142a	Vinny Castilla/Action	.10
142b	Vinny Castilla/Portrait	.10
143a	Edgar Clemente/Action	.10
143b	Edgar Clemente/Portrait	.10
144a	Derrick Gibson/Action	.10
144b	Derrick Gibson/Portrait	.10
145	Curtis Goodwin	.10
146a	Todd Helton/Action	1.00
146b	Todd Helton/Portrait	1.00
147	Bobby Jones	.10
148	Darryl Kile	.10
149	Mike Lansing	.10
150	Chuck McElroy	.10
151	Neifi Perez	.10
152	Jeff Reed	.10
153	John Thomson	.10
154a	Larry Walker/Action	.10
154b	Larry Walker/Portrait	.10
155	Jamey Wright	.10
156	Kimera Bartee	.10
157	Geronimo Berroa	.10
158	Raul Casanova	.10
159	Frank Catalanotto	.10
160	Tony Clark	.10
161	Deivi Cruz	.10
162	Damion Easley	.10
163	Juan Encarnacion	.10
164	Luis Gonzalez	.10
165	Seth Greisinger	.10
166	Bob Higginson	.10
167	Brian Hunter	.10
168	Todd Jones	.10
169	Justin Thompson	.10
170	Antonio Alfonseca	.10
171	Dave Berg	.10
172	John Cangelosi	.10
173	Craig Counsell	.10
174	Todd Dunwoody	.10
175	Cliff Floyd	.10
176	Alex Gonzalez	.10
177	Livan Hernandez	.10
178	Ryan Jackson	.10
179	Mark Kotsay	.10
180	Derrek Lee	.65
181	Matt Mantei	.10
182	Brian Meadows	.10
183	Edgar Renteria	.10
184a	Moises Alou/Action	.10
184b	Moises Alou/Portrait	.10
185	Brad Ausmus	.10
186a	Jeff Bagwell/Action	1.00
186b	Jeff Bagwell/Portrait	1.00
187	Derek Bell	.10
188	Sean Berry	.10
189	Craig Biggio	.10
190	Carl Everett	.10
191	Ricky Gutierrez	.10
192	Mike Hampton	.10
193	Doug Henry	.10
194	Richard Hidalgo	.10
195	Randy Johnson	1.00
196a	Russ Johnson/Action	.10
196b	Russ Johnson/Portrait	.10
197	Shane Reynolds	.10
198	Bill Spiers	.10
199	Kevin Appier	.10
200	Tim Belcher	.10
201	Jeff Conine	.10
202	Johnny Damon	.35

203	Jermaine Dye	.10
204a	Jeremy Giambi (Batting stance.)	.10
204b	Jeremy Giambi (Follow-through.)	.10
205	Jeff King	.10
206	Shane Mack	.10
207	Jeff Montgomery	.10
208	Hal Morris	.10
209	Jose Offerman	.10
210	Dean Palmer	.10
211	Jose Rosado	.10
212	Glendon Rusch	.10
213	Larry Sutton	.10
214	Mike Sweeney	.10
215	Bobby Bonilla	.10
216	Alex Cora	.10
217	Darren Dreifort	.10
218	Mark Grudzielanek	.10
219	Todd Hollandsworth	.10
220	Trenidad Hubbard	.10
221	Charles Johnson	.10
222	Eric Karros	.10
223	Matt Luke	.10
224	Ramon Martinez	.10
225	Raul Mondesi	.10
226	Chan Ho Park	.10
227	Jeff Shaw	.10
228	Gary Sheffield	.40
229	Eric Young	.10
230	Jeromy Burnitz	.10
231	Jeff Cirillo	.10
232	Marquis Grissom	.10
233	Bobby Hughes	.10
234	John Jaha	.10
235	Geoff Jenkins	.10
236	Scott Karl	.10
237	Mark Loretta	.10
238	Mike Matheny	.10
239	Mike Myers	.10
240	Dave Nilsson	.10
241	Bob Wickman	.10
242	Jose Valentin	.10
243	Fernando Vina	.10
244	Rick Aguilera	.10
245	Ron Coomer	.10
246	Marty Cordova	.10
247	Denny Hocking	.10
248	Matt Lawton	.10
249	Pat Meares	.10
250a	Paul Molitor/Action	1.00
250b	Paul Molitor/Portrait	1.00
251	Otis Nixon	.10
252	Alex Ochoa	.10
253	David Ortiz	.65
254	A.J. Pierzynski	.10
255	Brad Radke	.10
256	Terry Steinbach	.10
257	Bob Tewksbury	.10
258	Todd Walker	.10
259	Shane Andrews	.10
260	Shayne Bennett	.10
261	Orlando Cabrera	.10
262	Brad Fullmer	.10
263	Vladimir Guerrero	1.00
264	Wilton Guerrero	.10
265	Dustin Hermanson	.10
266	Terry Jones	.10
267	Steve Kline	.10
268	Carl Pavano	.10
269	F.P. Santangelo	.10
270a	Fernando Seguignol/Action	
270b	Fernando Seguignol/Portrait	.10
271	Ugueth Urbina	.10
272	Jose Vidro	.10
273	Chris Widger	.10
274	Edgardo Alfonzo	.10
275	Carlos Baerga	.10
276	John Franco	.10
277	Todd Hundley	.10
278	Butch Huskey	.10
279	Bobby Jones	.10
280	Al Leiter	.10
281	Greg McMichael	.10
282	Brian McRae	.10
283	Hideo Nomo	.50
284	John Olerud	.10
285	Rey Ordonez	.10
286a	Mike Piazza/Action	1.75
286b	Mike Piazza/Portrait	1.75
287	Turk Wendell	.10
288	Masato Yoshii	.10
289	David Cone	.10
290	Chad Curtis	.10
291	Joe Girardi	.10
292	Orlando Hernandez	.10
293a	Hideki Irabu/Action	.10
293b	Hideki Irabu/Portrait	.10
294a	Derek Jeter/Action	3.00
294b	Derek Jeter/Portrait	3.00
295	Chuck Knoblauch	.10
296a	Mike Lowell/Action	.10
296b	Mike Lowell/Portrait	.10
297	Tino Martinez	.10
298	Ramiro Mendoza	.10
299	Paul O'Neill	.10
300	Andy Pettitte	.25
301	Jorge Posada	.10
302	Tim Raines	.10
303	Mariano Rivera	.15
304	David Wells	.10
305a	Bernie Williams/Action	.10
305b	Bernie Williams/Portrait	.10
306	Mike Blowers	.10
307	Tom Candiotti	.10
308a	Eric Chavez/Action	.15

308b	Eric Chavez/Portrait	.15
309	Ryan Christenson	.10
310	Jason Giambi	.65
311a	Ben Grieve/Action	.10
311b	Ben Grieve/Portrait	.10
312	Rickey Henderson	1.00
313	A.J. Hinch	.10
314	Jason McDonald	.10
315	Bip Roberts	.10
316	Kenny Rogers	.10
317	Scott Spiezio	.10
318	Matt Stairs	.10
319	Miguel Tejada	.20
320	Bob Abreu	.20
321	Alex Arias	.10
322a	Gary Bennett/Action RC	.10
322b	Gary Bennett/Portrait RC	.10
323	Ricky Bottalico	.10
324	Rico Brogna	.10
325	Bobby Estalella	.10
326	Doug Glanville	.10
327	Kevin Jordan	.10
328	Mark Leiter	.10
329	Wendell Magee	.10
330	Mark Portugal	.10
331	Desi Relaford	.10
332	Scott Rolen	.65
333	Curt Schilling	.35
334	Kevin Sefcik	.10
335	Adrian Brown	.10
336	Emil Brown	.10
337	Lou Collier	.10
338	Francisco Cordova	.10
339	Freddy Garcia	.10
340	Jose Guillen	.10
341	Jason Kendall	.10
342	Al Martin	.10
343	Abraham Nunez	.10
344	Aramis Ramirez	.10
345	Ricardo Rincon	.10
346	Jason Schmidt	.10
347	Turner Ward	.10
348	Tony Womack	.10
349	Kevin Young	.10
350	Juan Acevedo	.10
351	Delino DeShields	.10
352a	J.D. Drew/Action	.40
352b	J.D. Drew/Portrait	.40
353	Ron Gant	.10
354	Brian Jordan	.10
355	Ray Lankford	.10
356	Eli Marrero	.10
357	Kent Mercker	.10
358	Matt Morris	.10
359	Luis Ordaz	.10
360	Donovan Osborne	.10
361	Placido Polanco	.10
362	Fernando Tatis	.10
363	Andy Ashby	.10
364	Kevin Brown	.10
365	Ken Caminiti	.10
366	Steve Finley	.10
367	Chris Gomez	.10
368a	Tony Gwynn/Action	1.50
368b	Tony Gwynn/Portrait	1.50
369	Joey Hamilton	.10
370	Carlos Hernandez	.10
371	Trevor Hoffman	.10
372	Wally Joyner	.10
373	Jim Leyritz	.10
374	Ruben Rivera	.10
375	Greg Vaughn	.10
376	Quilvio Veras	.10
377	Rich Aurilia	.10
378a	Barry Bonds/Action	3.00
378b	Barry Bonds/Portrait	3.00
379	Ellis Burks	.10
380	Joe Carter	.10
381	Stan Javier	.10
382	Brian Johnson	.10
383	Jeff Kent	.10
384	Jose Mesa	.10
385	Bill Mueller	.10
386	Robb Nen	.10
387a	Armando Rios/Action	.10
387b	Armando Rios/Portrait	.10
388	Kirk Rueter	.10
389	Rey Sanchez	.10
390	J.T. Snow	.10
391	David Bell	.10
392	Jay Buhner	.10
393	Ken Cloude	.10
394	Russ Davis	.10
395	Jeff Fassero	.10
396a	Ken Griffey Jr./Action	2.00
396b	Ken Griffey Jr./Portrait	2.00
397	Giomar Guevara RC	.10
398	Carlos Guillen	.10
399	Edgar Martinez	.10
400	Shane Monahan	.10
401	Jamie Moyer	.10
402	David Segui	.10
403	Makoto Suzuki	.10
404	Mike Timlin	.10
405	Dan Wilson	.10
406	Wilson Alvarez	.10
407	Rolando Arrojo	.10
408	Wade Boggs	1.50
409	Miguel Cairo	.10
410	Roberto Hernandez	.10
411	Mike Kelly	.10
412	Aaron Ledesma	.10
413	Albie Lopez	.10
414	Dave Martinez	.10
415	Quinton McCracken	.10
416	Fred McGriff	.10
417	Bryan Rekar	.10

418	Paul Sorrento	.10
419	Randy Winn	.10
420	John Burkett	.10
421	Will Clark	.10
422	Royce Clayton	.10
423a	Juan Gonzalez/Action	.50
423b	Juan Gonzalez/Portrait	.50
424	Tom Goodwin	.10
425	Rusty Greer	.10
426	Rick Helling	.10
427	Roberto Kelly	.10
428	Mark McLemore	.10
429a	Ivan Rodriguez/Action	.75
429b	Ivan Rodriguez/Portrait	.75
430	Aaron Sele	.10
431	Lee Stevens	.10
432	Todd Stottlemyre	.10
433	John Wetteland	.10
434	Tod5 Zeile	.10
435	Jose Canseco	.10
436a	Roger Clemens/Action	1.75
436b	Roger Clemens/Portrait	1.75
437	Felipe Crespo	.10
438a	Jose Cruz Jr./Action	.10
438b	Jose Cruz Jr./Portrait	.10
439	Carlos Delgado	.50
440a	Tom Evans/Action	.10
440b	Tom Evans/Portrait	.10
441	Tony Fernandez	.10
442	Darrin Fletcher	.10
443	Alex Gonzalez	.10
444	Shawn Green	.30
445	Roy Halladay	.10
446	Pat Hentgen	.10
447	Juan Samuel	.10
448	Benito Santiago	.10
449	Shannon Stewart	.10
450	Woody Williams	.10

Cramer's Choice

Pacific CEO Michael Cramer personally chose this 10-card set. Die-cut in a trophy shape, the cards are enhanced with silver holographic etching and gold foil stamping across the card bottom. Cards are serially numbered to 299.

		NM/M
Complete Set (10):		65.00
Common Player:		7.50
Inserted 1:721		
1	Cal Ripken Jr.	20.00
2	Nomar Garciaparra	12.50
3	Frank Thomas	10.00
4	Ken Griffey Jr.	15.00
5	Alex Rodriguez	17.50
6	Greg Maddux	12.50
7	Sammy Sosa	12.50
8	Kerry Wood	7.50
9	Mark McGwire	17.50
10	Tony Gwynn	12.50

Dynagon Diamond

Dynagon Diamond captures 20 of baseball's biggest stars in action against a mirror-patterned multi-foil background. These are seeded about 1:9. A Titanium parallel with each card numbered to 99 was exclusive to hobby packs.

	NM/M
Complete Set (20):	20.00
Common Player:	.40
Inserted 1:9	
Titanium (99 Sets):	8X
1	Cal Ripken Jr.	2.50
2	Nomar Garciaparra	1.00
3	Frank Thomas	.75
4	Derek Jeter	2.50
5	Ben Grieve	.40
6	Ken Griffey Jr.	1.50
7	Alex Rodriguez	2.00
8	Juan Gonzalez	.50
9	Travis Lee	.40
10	Chipper Jones	1.00
11	Greg Maddux	1.00
12	Sammy Sosa	1.00
13	Kerry Wood	.50
14	Jeff Bagwell	.75
15	Hideo Nomo	.50
16	Mike Piazza	12.50
17	J.D. Drew	.50
18	Mark McGwire	2.00
19	Tony Gwynn	1.00
20	Barry Bonds	2.50

Gold Crown Die-Cuts

This 36-card die-cut set is shaped like a crown at the top and features dual foiling, 24-pt. stock and gold foil stamping. These are seeded 1:37 packs.

		NM/M
Complete Set (36):		75.00
Common Player:		.75
Inserted 1:37		
1	Darin Erstad	1.00
2	Cal Ripken Jr.	7.50
3	Nomar Garciaparra	4.00
4	Pedro Martinez	3.00
5	Mo Vaughn	.75
6	Frank Thomas	3.00
7	Kenny Lofton	.75
8	Manny Ramirez	3.00
9	Paul Molitor	3.00
10	Derek Jeter	7.50
11	Bernie Williams	.75
12	Ben Grieve	.75
13	Ken Griffey Jr.	5.00
14	Alex Rodriguez	6.00
15	Wade Boggs	4.00
16	Juan Gonzalez	1.50
17	Ivan Rodriguez	2.50
18	Jose Canseco	1.50
19	Roger Clemens	4.50
20	Travis Lee	.75
21	Chipper Jones	4.00
22	Greg Maddux	4.00
23	Sammy Sosa	4.00
24	Kerry Wood	1.50
25	Todd Helton	3.00
26	Larry Walker	.75
27	Jeff Bagwell	3.00
28	Craig Biggio	.75
29	Raul Mondesi	.75
30	Vladimir Guerrero	3.00
31	Mike Piazza	4.50
32	Scott Rolen	2.00
33	J.D. Drew	1.50
34	Mark McGwire	6.00
35	Tony Gwynn	4.00
36	Barry Bonds	7.50

Hot Cards

This dealer-only 10-card set was awarded to any dealer that had sold any packs/boxes that produced a card for the Pacific Hot Cards Registry Program. Fronts have a metallic foil background. Backs

have a portrait photo and are serial numbered within an edition of 500 each.

		NM/M
Complete Set (10):		75.00
Common Player:		3.00
1	Alex Rodriguez	12.50
2	Tony Gwynn	7.50
3	Ken Griffey Jr.	10.00
4	Sammy Sosa	7.50
5	Ivan Rodriguez	6.00
6	Derek Jeter	15.00
7	Cal Ripken Jr.	15.00
8	Mark McGwire	12.50
9	J.D. Drew	4.50
10	Bernie Williams	3.00

Team Checklists

This 30-card horizontal insert set features a star player from each team on the card front, with each team's complete checklist on the card back. Fronts feature a holographic silver-foiled and embossed logo of the player's respective team. These are seeded 2:37 packs.

		NM/M
Complete Set (30):		30.00
Common Player:		.30
Inserted 1:18		
1	Darin Erstad	.50
2	Cal Ripken Jr.	3.00
3	Nomar Garciaparra	1.50
4	Frank Thomas	1.00
5	Manny Ramirez	1.00
6	Damion Easley	.30
7	Jeff King	.30
8	Paul Molitor	1.00
9	Derek Jeter	3.00
10	Ben Grieve	.30
11	Ken Griffey Jr.	2.00
12	Wade Boggs	1.50
13	Juan Gonzalez	.60
14	Roger Clemens	1.75
15	Travis Lee	.30
16	Chipper Jones	1.50
17	Sammy Sosa	1.50
18	Barry Larkin	.30
19	Todd Helton	1.00
20	Mark Kotsay	.30
21	Jeff Bagwell	1.00
22	Raul Mondesi	.30
23	Jeff Cirillo	.30
24	Vladimir Guerrero	1.00
25	Mike Piazza	1.75
26	Scott Rolen	.75
27	Jason Kendall	.30
28	Mark McGwire	2.50
29	Tony Gwynn	1.50
30	Barry Bonds	3.00

Timelines

Timelines features 20 superstars, giving a chronological history of each player complete with photos from early in their careers. Three photos of the player are on the card front. Inserted exclusively in hobby packs. These are limited to 199 serially numbered sets.

		NM/M
Complete Set (20):		200.00
Common Player:		6.00
Inserted 1:181 H		
1	Cal Ripken Jr.	30.00
2	Frank Thomas	12.00
3	Jim Thome	10.00
4	Paul Molitor	12.00
5	Bernie Williams	6.00
6	Derek Jeter	30.00
7	Ken Griffey Jr.	20.00
8	Alex Rodriguez	25.00
9	Wade Boggs	15.00
10	Jose Canseco	6.00
11	Roger Clemens	17.50
12	Andres Galarraga	6.00
13	Chipper Jones	15.00

14	Greg Maddux	15.00
15	Sammy Sosa	15.00
16	Larry Walker	6.00
17	Randy Johnson	12.00
18	Mike Piazza	17.50
19	Mark McGwire	25.00
20	Tony Gwynn	15.00

1999 Pacific Aurora

The 200-card set features two photos on the card front and one on the back. Card backs also have '98 and career stats along with personal information. The player's name and Aurora logo are stamped with gold foil. A parallel "Opening Day" is-sued is stamped with a gold foil seal and numbered within an edition of 31 each.

	NM/M
Complete Set (200):	20.00
Common Player:	.10
Opening Day:	20X
Production 31 Sets	
Reds:	2X
Retail Only (1:6)	
Pack (6):	1.50
Wax Box (36):	22.50
1	Garret Anderson	.10
2	Jim Edmonds	.10
3	Darin Erstad	.30
4	Matt Luke	.10
5	Tim Salmon	.10
6	Mo Vaughn	.10
7	Jay Bell	.10
8	David Dellucci	.10
9	Steve Finley	.10
10	Bernard Gilkey	.10
11	Randy Johnson	1.00
12	Travis Lee	.10
13	Matt Williams	.10
14	Andres Galarraga	.10
15	Tom Glavine	.35
16	Andruw Jones	1.00
17	Chipper Jones	1.50
18	Brian Jordan	.10
19	Javy Lopez	.10
20	Greg Maddux	1.50
21	Albert Belle	.10
22	Will Clark	.10
23	Scott Erickson	.10
24	Mike Mussina	.40
25	Cal Ripken Jr.	3.00
26	B.J. Surhoff	.10
27	Nomar Garciaparra	1.50
28	Reggie Jefferson	.10
29	Darren Lewis	.10
30	Pedro Martinez	1.00
31	John Valentin	.10
32	Rod Beck	.10
33	Mark Grace	.10
34	Lance Johnson	.10
35	Mickey Morandini	.10
36	Sammy Sosa	1.50
37	Kerry Wood	.40
38	James Baldwin	.10
39	Mike Caruso	.10
40	Ray Durham	.10
41	Magglio Ordonez	.25
42	Frank Thomas	1.00
43	Aaron Boone	.10
44	Sean Casey	.20
45	Barry Larkin	.10
46	Hal Morris	.10
47	Denny Neagle	.10
48	Greg Vaughn	.10
49	Pat Watkins	.10
50	Roberto Alomar	.25
51	Sandy Alomar Jr.	.10
52	David Justice	.10
53	Kenny Lofton	.10
54	Manny Ramirez	1.00
55	Richie Sexson	.10
56	Jim Thome	.75
57	Omar Vizquel	.10
58	Dante Bichette	.10
59	Vinny Castilla	.10
60	Edgard Clemente RC	.10
61	Derrick Gibson	.10
62	Todd Helton	1.00
63	Darryl Kile	.10
64	Larry Walker	.10
65	Tony Clark	.10
66	Damion Easley	.10

67	Bob Higginson	.10
68	Brian Hunter	.10
69	Dean Palmer	.10
70	Justin Thompson	.10
71	Craig Counsell	.10
72	Todd Dunwoody	.10
73	Cliff Floyd	.10
74	Alex Gonzalez	.10
75	Livan Hernandez	.10
76	Mark Kotsay	.10
77	Derrek Lee	.65
78	Moises Alou	.10
79	Jeff Bagwell	1.00
80	Derek Bell	.10
81	Craig Biggio	.10
82	Ken Caminiti	.10
83	Richard Hidalgo	.10
84	Shane Reynolds	.10
85	Jeff Conine	.10
86	Johnny Damon	.35
87	Jermaine Dye	.10
88	Jeff King	.10
89	Jeff Montgomery	.10
90	Mike Sweeney	.10
91	Kevin Brown	.10
92	Mark Grudzielanek	.10
93	Eric Karros	.10
94	Raul Mondesi	.10
95	Chan Ho Park	.10
96	Gary Sheffield	.40
97	Jeromy Burnitz	.10
98	Jeff Cirillo	.10
99	Marquis Grissom	.10
100	Geoff Jenkins	.10
101	Dave Nilsson	.10
102	Jose Valentin	.10
103	Fernando Vina	.10
104	Marty Cordova	.10
105	Matt Lawton	.10
106	David Ortiz	.60
107	Brad Radke	.10
108	Todd Walker	.10
109	Shane Andrews	.10
110	Orlando Cabrera	.10
111	Brad Fullmer	.10
112	Vladimir Guerrero	1.00
113	Wilton Guerrero	.10
114	Carl Pavano	.10
115	Fernando Seguignol	.10
116	Ugueth Urbina	.10
117	Edgardo Alfonzo	.10
118	Bobby Bonilla	.10
119	Rickey Henderson	1.00
120	Hideo Nomo	.60
121	John Olerud	.10
122	Rey Ordonez	.10
123	Mike Piazza	2.00
124	Masato Yoshii	.10
125	Scott Brosius	.10
126	Orlando Hernandez	.10
127	Hideki Irabu	.10
128	Derek Jeter	3.00
129	Chuck Knoblauch	.10
130	Tino Martinez	.10
131	Jorge Posada	.10
132	Bernie Williams	.10
133	Eric Chavez	.10
134	Ryan Christenson	.10
135	Jason Giambi	.65
136	Ben Grieve	.10
137	A.J. Hinch	.10
138	Matt Stairs	.10
139	Miguel Tejada	.20
140	Bob Abreu	.20
141	Gary Bennett **RC**	
142	Desi Relaford	.10
143	Scott Rolen	.75
144	Curt Schilling	.35
145	Kevin Sefcik	.10
146	Brian Giles	.10
147	Jose Guillen	.10
148	Jason Kendall	.10
149	Aramis Ramirez	.10
150	Tony Womack	.10
151	Kevin Young	.10
152	Eric Davis	.10
153	J.D. Drew	.50
154	Ray Lankford	.10
155	Eli Marrero	.10
156	Mark McGwire	2.50
157	Luis Ordaz	.10
158	Edgar Renteria	.10
159	Andy Ashby	.10
160	Tony Gwynn	1.50
161	Trevor Hoffman	.10
162	Wally Joyner	.10
163	Jim Leyritz	.10
164	Ruben Rivera	.10
165	Reggie Sanders	.10
166	Quilvio Veras	.10
167	Rich Aurilia	.10
168	Marvin Benard	.10
169	Barry Bonds	3.00
170	Ellis Burks	.10
171	Jeff Kent	.10
172	Bill Mueller	.10
173	J.T. Snow	.10
174	Jay Buhner	.10
175	Jeff Fassero	.10
176	Ken Griffey Jr.	2.25
177	Carlos Guillen	.10
178	Edgar Martinez	.10
179	Alex Rodriguez	2.50
180	David Segui	.10
181	Dan Wilson	.10
182	Rolando Arrojo	.10
183	Wade Boggs	1.50
184	Jose Canseco	.40

185	Aaron Ledesma	.10
186	Dave Martinez	.10
187	Quinton McCracken	.10
188	Fred McGriff	.10
189	Juan Gonzalez	.60
190	Tom Goodwin	.10
191	Rusty Greer	.10
192	Roberto Kelly	.10
193	Rafael Palmeiro	.75
194	Ivan Rodriguez	.75
195	Roger Clemens	2.00
196	Jose Cruz Jr.	.10
197	Carlos Delgado	.60
198	Alex Gonzalez	.10
199	Roy Halladay	.10
200	Pat Hentgen	.10

Complete Players

The 10 players featured in this serial numbered 20-card set each have two cards, designed to fit together. Card fronts feature a red border on the top and bottom with the rest of the card done in gold foil etching. Each card is serially numbered to 299.

		NM/M
Complete Set (10):		40.00
Common Player:		3.00
Production 299 Sets		
1	Cal Ripken Jr.	9.00
2	Nomar Garciaparra	4.50
3	Sammy Sosa	4.50
4	Kerry Wood	3.00
5	Frank Thomas	4.00
6	Mike Piazza	5.00
7	Mark McGwire	7.50
8	Tony Gwynn	4.50
9	Ken Griffey Jr.	6.00
10	Alex Rodriguez	7.50

Kings of the Major Leagues

The full foiled card fronts also utilize gold foil stamping. Pacific's crown as well as the featured player's team are shadow boxed in the background with the player's image in the foreground. These are seeded 1:361.

		NM/M
Complete Set (10):		80.00
Common Player:		5.00
Inserted 1:361		
1	Cal Ripken Jr.	17.50
2	Nomar Garciaparra	9.00
3	Sammy Sosa	9.00
4	Kerry Wood	5.00
5	Frank Thomas	7.50
6	Mike Piazza	10.00
7	Mark McGwire	15.00
8	Tony Gwynn	9.00
9	Ken Griffey Jr.	12.50
10	Alex Rodriguez	15.00

On Deck

Twenty of the game's hottest players are featured in this laser-cut and silver foil

stamped set. The player's team logo is laser cut into the bottom half of the card beneath the player photo.

		NM/M
Complete Set (20):		17.50
Common Player:		.50
Inserted 1:9		
1	Chipper Jones	1.00
2	Cal Ripken Jr.	3.00
3	Nomar Garciaparra	1.00
4	Sammy Sosa	1.00
5	Frank Thomas	.75
6	Manny Ramirez	.75
7	Todd Helton	.75
8	Larry Walker	.50
9	Jeff Bagwell	.75
10	Vladimir Guerrero	.75
11	Mike Piazza	1.50
12	Derek Jeter	3.00
13	Bernie Williams	.50
14	J.D. Drew	.50
15	Mark McGwire	2.50
16	Tony Gwynn	1.00
17	Ken Griffey Jr.	2.00
18	Alex Rodriguez	2.50
19	Juan Gonzalez	.50
20	Ivan Rodriguez	.65

Pennant Fever

Regular Pennant Fever inserts feature gold foil stamping of 20 of the hottest players in the hobby. These are seeded 4:37 packs. There are also three parallel versions: Platinum Blue, Silver and Copper. Platinum Blues are limited to 100 serial numbered sets, Silvers are retail exclusive and limited to 250 numbered sets and Coppers are hobby exclusive and limited to 20 numbered sets. Pacific spokesman Tony Gwynn autographed 97 regular Pennant Fever cards and one each of the Silver, Blue and Copper.

		NM/M
Complete Set (20):		30.00
Common Player:		.75
Silver (250 Sets):		2X
Platinum Blue (100):		6X
Copper (20):		20X
Tony Gwynn Autograph:		25.00
1	Chipper Jones	2.00
2	Greg Maddux	2.00
3	Cal Ripken Jr.	5.00
4	Nomar Garciaparra	2.00
5	Sammy Sosa	2.00
6	Kerry Wood	.75
7	Frank Thomas	1.50
8	Manny Ramirez	1.50
9	Todd Helton	1.50
10	Jeff Bagwell	1.50
11	Mike Piazza	2.50
12	Derek Jeter	5.00
13	Bernie Williams	.75
14	J.D. Drew	.75
15	Mark McGwire	4.00
16	Tony Gwynn	2.00
17	Ken Griffey Jr.	3.00
18	Alex Rodriguez	4.00

19	Juan Gonzalez	.75
20	Ivan Rodriguez	1.25

Styrotechs

This 20-card set features styrene stock, making the cards more resilient. Fronts have a black border highlighted with gold foil. Backs have a photo and brief career highlights. These are seeded 1:37 packs.

		NM/M
Complete Set (20):		35.00
Common Player:		1.00
Inserted 1:37		
1	Chipper Jones	3.00
2	Greg Maddux	3.00
3	Cal Ripken Jr.	6.00
4	Nomar Garciaparra	3.00
5	Sammy Sosa	3.00
6	Kerry Wood	1.25
7	Frank Thomas	2.00
8	Manny Ramirez	2.00
9	Larry Walker	1.00
10	Jeff Bagwell	2.00
11	Mike Piazza	4.00
12	Derek Jeter	6.00
13	Bernie Williams	1.00
14	J.D. Drew	1.25
15	Mark McGwire	5.00
16	Tony Gwynn	3.00
17	Ken Griffey Jr.	4.50
18	Alex Rodriguez	5.00
19	Juan Gonzalez	1.25
20	Ivan Rodriguez	1.50

1999 Pacific Crown Collection Sample

This card of Pacific spokesman Tony, Gwynn introduces the 1999 Crown series. The sample card follows the format of the issued version but is overprinted "SAMPLE" on back.

	NM/M
Tony Gwynn	2.00

1999 Pacific Crown Collection

Released in one series the 300-card set has white borders and gold-foil highlights

on front. Backs have a small photo along with English and Spanish narrative. A Platinum Blue parallel to the base set utilizes platinum blue holographic foil and is seeded 1:73 packs. A WalMart-exclusive red-foiled parallel is seeded 1:9 packs. Twelve-card packs had an S.R.P. of $2.49.

		NM/M
Complete Set (300):		20.00
Common Player:		.10
Red Stars:		6X
Inserted 1:9		
Platinum Blue Stars:		30X
Inserted 1:73		
Pack (12):		1.00
Wax Box (36):		22.50
1	Garret Anderson	.10
2	Gary DiSarcina	.10
3	Jim Edmonds	.10
4	Darin Erstad	.25
5	Shigetosi Hasegawa	.10
6	Norberto Martin	.10
7	Omar Olivares	.10
8	Orlando Palmeiro	.10
9	Tim Salmon	.10
10	Randy Velarde	.10
11	Tony Batista	.10
12	Jay Bell	.10
13	Yamil Benitez	.10
14	Omar Daal	.10
15	David Dellucci	.10
16	Karim Garcia	.10
17	Travis Lee	.10
18	Felix Rodriguez	.10
19	Devon White	.10
20	Matt Williams	.10
21	Andres Galarraga	.10
22	Tom Glavine	.35
23	Ozzie Guillen	.10
24	Andruw Jones	1.00
25	Chipper Jones	1.50
26	Ryan Klesko	.10
27	Javy Lopez	.10
28	Greg Maddux	1.50
29	Dennis Martinez	.10
30	Odaliz Perez	.10
31	Rudy Seanez	.10
32	John Smoltz	.10
33	Roberto Alomar	.25
34	Armando Benitez	.10
35	Scott Erickson	.10
36	Juan Guzman	.10
37	Mike Mussina	.35
38	Jesse Orosco	.10
39	Rafael Palmeiro	.75
40	Sidney Ponson	.10
41	Cal Ripken Jr.	3.00
42	B.J. Surhoff	.10
43	Lenny Webster	.10
44	Dennis Eckersley	.75
45	Nomar Garciaparra	1.50
46	Darren Lewis	.10
47	Pedro Martinez	1.00
48	Troy O'Leary	.10
49	Bret Saberhagen	.10
50	John Valentin	.10
51	Mo Vaughn	.10
52	Tim Wakefield	.10
53	Manny Alexander	.10
54	Rod Beck	.10
55	Gary Gaetti	.10
56	Mark Grace	.10
57	Felix Heredia	.10
58	Jose Hernandez	.10
59	Henry Rodriguez	.10
60	Sammy Sosa	1.50
61	Kevin Tapani	.10
62	Kerry Wood	.45
63	James Baldwin	.10
64	Albert Belle	.10
65	Mike Caruso	.10
66	Carlos Castillo	.10
67	Wil Cordero	.10
68	Jaime Navarro	.10
69	Magglio Ordonez	.25
70	Frank Thomas	1.00
71	Robin Ventura	.10
72	Bret Boone	.10
73	Sean Casey	.20
74	Guillermo Garcia **RC**	.10
75	Barry Larkin	.25
76	Melvin Nieves	.10
77	Eduardo Perez	.10
78	Roberto Petagine	.10
79	Reggie Sanders	.10
80	Eddie Taubensee	.10
81	Brett Tomko	.10
82	Sandy Alomar Jr.	.10
83	Bartolo Colon	.10
84	Joey Cora	.10
85	Einar Diaz	.10
86	David Justice	.10
87	Kenny Lofton	.10
88	Manny Ramirez	1.00
89	Jim Thome	.75
90	Omar Vizquel	.10
91	Enrique Wilson	.10
92	Pedro Astacio	.10
93	Dante Bichette	.10
94	Vinny Castilla	.10
95	Edgard Clemente **RC**	.10
96	Todd Helton	1.00

97	Darryl Kile	.10
98	Mike Munoz	.10
99	Neifi Perez	.10
100	Jeff Reed	.10
101	Larry Walker	.10
102	Gabe Alvarez	.10
103	Kimera Bartee	.10
104	Frank Castillo	.10
105	Tony Clark	.10
106	Deivi Cruz	.10
107	Damion Easley	.10
108	Luis Gonzalez	.10
109	Marino Santana	.10
110	Justin Thompson	.10
111	Antonio Alfonseca	.10
112	Alex Fernandez	.10
113	Cliff Floyd	.10
114	Alex Gonzalez	.10
115	Livan Hernandez	.10
116	Mark Kotsay	.10
117	Derrek Lee	.65
118	Edgar Renteria	.10
119	Jesus Sanchez	.10
120	Moises Alou	.10
121	Jeff Bagwell	1.00
122	Derek Bell	.10
123	Craig Biggio	.10
124	Tony Eusebio	.10
125	Ricky Gutierrez	.10
126	Richard Hidalgo	.10
127	Randy Johnson	1.00
128	Jose Lima	.10
129	Shane Reynolds	.10
130	Johnny Damon	.40
131	Carlos Febles	.10
132	Jeff King	.10
133	Mendy Lopez	.10
134	Hal Morris	.10
135	Jose Offerman	.10
136	Jose Rosado	.10
137	Jose Santiago	.10
138	Bobby Bonilla	.10
139	Roger Cedeno	.10
140	Alex Cora	.10
141	Eric Karros	.10
142	Raul Mondesi	.10
143	Antonio Osuna	.10
144	Chan Ho Park	.10
145	Gary Sheffield	.30
146	Ismael Valdes	.10
147	Jeromy Burnitz	.10
148	Jeff Cirillo	.10
149	Valerio de los Santos	.10
150	Marquis Grissom	.10
151	Scott Karl	.10
152	Dave Nilsson	.10
153	Al Reyes	.10
154	Rafael Roque	.10
155	Jose Valentin	.10
156	Fernando Vina	.10
157	Rick Aguilera	.10
158	Hector Carrasco	.10
159	Marty Cordova	.10
160	Eddie Guardado	.10
161	Paul Molitor	1.00
162	Otis Nixon	.10
163	Alex Ochoa	.10
164	David Ortiz	.45
165	Frank Rodriguez	.10
166	Todd Walker	.10
167	Miguel Batista	.10
168	Orlando Cabrera	.10
169	Vladimir Guerrero	1.00
170	Wilton Guerrero	.10
171	Carl Pavano	.10
172	Robert Perez	.10
173	F.P. Santangelo	.10
174	Fernando Seguignol	.10
175	Ugueth Urbina	.10
176	Javier Vazquez	.10
177	Edgardo Alfonzo	.10
178	Carlos Baerga	.10
179	John Franco	.10
180	Luis Lopez	.10
181	Hideo Nomo	.50
182	John Olerud	.10
183	Rey Ordonez	.10
184	Mike Piazza	1.75
185	Armando Reynoso	.10
186	Masato Yoshii	.10
187	David Cone	.10
188	Orlando Hernandez	.10
189	Hideki Irabu	.10
190	Derek Jeter	3.00
191	Ricky Ledee	.10
192	Tino Martinez	.10
193	Ramiro Mendoza	.10
194	Paul O'Neill	.10
195	Jorge Posada	.10
196	Mariano Rivera	.15
197	Luis Sojo	.10
198	Bernie Williams	.10
199	Rafael Bournigal	.10
200	Eric Chavez	.20
201	Ryan Christenson	.10
202	Jason Giambi	.60
203	Ben Grieve	.10
204	Rickey Henderson	1.00
205	A.J. Hinch	.10
206	Kenny Rogers	.10
207	Miguel Tejada	.10
208	Jorge Velandia	.10
209	Bobby Abreu	.20
210	Marlon Anderson	.10
211	Alex Arias	.10
212	Bobby Estalella	.10
213	Doug Glanville	.10
214	Scott Rolen	.65

215	Curt Schilling	.35
216	Kevin Sefcik	.10
217	Adrian Brown	.10
218	Francisco Cordova	.10
219	Freddy Garcia	.10
220	Jose Guillen	.10
221	Jason Kendall	.10
222	Al Martin	.10
223	Abraham Nunez	.10
224	Aramis Ramirez	.10
225	Ricardo Rincon	.10
226	Kevin Young	.10
227	J.D. Drew	.40
228	Ron Gant	.10
229	Jose Jimenez	.10
230	Brian Jordan	.10
231	Ray Lankford	.10
232	Eli Marrero	.10
233	Mark McGwire	2.50
234	Luis Ordaz	.10
235	Placido Polanco	.10
236	Fernando Tatis	.10
237	Andy Ashby	.10
238	Kevin Brown	.10
239	Ken Caminiti	.10
240	Steve Finley	.10
241	Chris Gomez	.10
242	Tony Gwynn	1.50
243	Carlos Hernandez	.10
244	Trevor Hoffman	.10
245	Wally Joyner	.10
246	Ruben Rivera	.10
247	Greg Vaughn	.10
248	Quilvio Veras	.10
249	Rich Aurilia	.10
250	Barry Bonds	3.00
251	Stan Javier	.10
252	Jeff Kent	.10
253	Ramon Martinez	.10
254	Jose Mesa	.10
255	Armando Rios	.10
256	Rich Rodriguez	.10
257	Rey Sanchez	.10
258	J.T. Snow	.10
259	Julian Tavarez	.10
260	Jeff Fassero	.10
261	Ken Griffey Jr.	2.00
262	Giomar Guevara **RC**	.10
263	Carlos Guillen	.10
264	Raul Ibanez	.10
265	Edgar Martinez	.10
266	Jamie Moyer	.10
267	Alex Rodriguez	2.50
268	David Segui	.10
269	Makoto Suzuki	.10
270	Wilson Alvarez	.10
271	Rolando Arrojo	.10
272	Wade Boggs	1.50
273	Miguel Cairo	.10
274	Roberto Hernandez	.10
275	Aaron Ledesma	.10
276	Albie Lopez	.10
277	Quinton McCracken	.10
278	Fred McGriff	.10
279	Esteban Yan	.10
280	Luis Alicea	.10
281	Will Clark	.10
282	Juan Gonzalez	.50
283	Rusty Greer	.10
284	Rick Helling	.10
285	Xavier Hernandez	.10
286	Roberto Kelly	.10
287	Esteban Loaiza	.10
288	Ivan Rodriguez	.75
289	Aaron Sele	.10
290	John Wetteland	.10
291	Jose Canseco	.40
292	Roger Clemens	1.75
293	Felipe Crespo	.10
294	Jose Cruz Jr.	.10
295	Carlos Delgado	.60
296	Kelvim Escobar	.10
297	Tony Fernandez	.10
298	Alex Gonzalez	.10
299	Tomas Perez	.10
300	Juan Samuel	.10

In The Cage

These die-cut inserts have a netting like background with laser cutting, giving the look that the player is hitting in a batting cage. These are seeded 1:145 packs.

	NM/M
Complete Set (20):	80.00
Common Player:	2.00

Inserted 1:145

1	Chipper Jones	7.50
2	Cal Ripken Jr.	15.00
3	Nomar Garciaparra	7.50
4	Sammy Sosa	7.50
5	Frank Thomas	5.00
6	Manny Ramirez	5.00
7	Todd Helton	5.00
8	Moises Alou	2.00
9	Vladimir Guerrero	5.00
10	Mike Piazza	9.00
11	Derek Jeter	15.00
12	Ben Grieve	3.00
13	J.D. Drew	3.00
14	Mark McGwire	12.00
15	Tony Gwynn	7.50
16	Ken Griffey Jr.	10.00
17	Edgar Martinez	12.00
18	Alex Rodriguez	12.00
19	Juan Gonzalez	2.50
20	Ivan Rodriguez	4.00

Latinos/Major Leagues

This 36-card set salutes the many Latino players in the major leagues.

	NM/M
Complete Set (36):	25.00
Common Player:	.30

Inserted 1:18

1	Roberto Alomar	.60
2	Rafael Palmeiro	2.00
3	Nomar Garciaparra	3.50
4	Pedro Martinez	2.50
5	Magglio Ordonez	1.50
6	Sandy Alomar Jr.	.30
7	Bartolo Colon	.30
8	Manny Ramirez	2.50
9	Omar Vizquel	.30
10	Enrique Wilson	.30
11	David Ortiz	1.50
12	Orlando Hernandez	.30
13	Tino Martinez	.30
14	Mariano Rivera	.45
15	Bernie Williams	.30
16	Edgar Martinez	.30
17	Alex Rodriguez	5.00
18	David Segui	.30
19	Rolando Arrojo	.30
20	Juan Gonzalez	1.25
21	Ivan Rodriguez	2.00
22	Jose Canseco	1.00
23	Jose Cruz Jr.	.30
24	Andres Galarraga	.30
25	Andruw Jones	2.50
26	Javy Lopez	.30
27	Sammy Sosa	3.50
28	Vinny Castilla	.30
29	Alex Gonzalez	.30
30	Moises Alou	.30
31	Bobby Bonilla	.30
32	Raul Mondesi	.30
33	Fernando Vina	.30
34	Vladimir Guerrero	2.50
35	Carlos Baerga	.30
36	Rey Ordonez	.30

Pacific Cup

These die-cut inserts are shaped like a trophy with the featured player's photo in the foreground. These are seeded 1:721 packs.

	NM/M
Complete Set (10):	80.00
Common Player:	5.00

Inserted 1:721

1	Cal Ripken Jr.	20.00
2	Nomar Garciaparra	8.00
3	Frank Thomas	6.00
4	Ken Griffey Jr.	12.00
5	Alex Rodriguez	16.00
6	Greg Maddux	8.00
7	Sammy Sosa	8.00
8	Kerry Wood	5.00
9	Mark McGwire	16.00
10	Tony Gwynn	8.00

Players Choice

In conjunction with the annual Players Choice Awards ceremonies, Pacific produced a special edition of the cards of some of the players involved. Cards have a "Players Choice" foil stamp on front. Quantities produced were in the range of 25-40 of each.

	NM/M
Complete Set (6):	55.00
Common Player:	5.00

10	Randy Velarde	5.00
41	Cal Ripken Jr.	30.00
47	Pedro Martinez	12.00
88	Manny Ramirez	12.00
112	Alex Fernandez	5.00
128	Jose Lima	5.00

Tape Measure

This 20-card insert set is fully foiled in platinum blue with rainbow highlights in the background of the player photo.

	NM/M
Complete Set (20):	20.00
Common Player:	.60

Inserted 1:73

1	Andres Galarraga	.60
2	Chipper Jones	2.50
3	Nomar Garciaparra	2.50
4	Sammy Sosa	2.50
5	Frank Thomas	1.50
6	Manny Ramirez	1.50
7	Vinny Castilla	.60
8	Moises Alou	.60
9	Jeff Bagwell	1.50
10	Raul Mondesi	.60
11	Vladimir Guerrero	1.50
12	Mike Piazza	2.75
13	J.D. Drew	1.00
14	Mark McGwire	3.50
15	Greg Vaughn	.60
16	Ken Griffey Jr.	3.50
17	Alex Rodriguez	3.50
18	Juan Gonzalez	1.00
19	Ivan Rodriguez	1.25
20	Jose Canseco	1.00

Team Checklists

This features holographic silver-foil stamping and a horizontal format. The backs have a complete team checklist for the featured player's team.

	NM/M
Complete Set (30):	25.00
Common Player:	.50

Inserted 1:37

1	Darin Erstad	.60
2	Travis Lee	.50
3	Chipper Jones	1.75
4	Cal Ripken Jr.	4.00
5	Nomar Garciaparra	1.75
6	Sammy Sosa	1.25
7	Frank Thomas	1.25
8	Barry Larkin	.50
9	Manny Ramirez	1.25
10	Larry Walker	.50
11	Bob Higginson	.50
12	Livan Hernandez	.50
13	Moises Alou	.50
14	Jeff King	.50
15	Raul Mondesi	.50
16	Marquis Grissom	.50
17	David Ortiz	1.00
18	Vladimir Guerrero	1.25
19	Mike Piazza	2.00
20	Derek Jeter	4.00
21	Ben Grieve	.50
22	Scott Rolen	.75
23	Jason Kendall	.50
24	Mark McGwire	3.00
25	Tony Gwynn	1.75
26	Barry Bonds	4.00
27	Ken Griffey Jr.	2.50
28	Wade Boggs	1.75
29	Juan Gonzalez	.75
30	Jose Canseco	.60

1999 Pacific Crown Royale

The Crown Royale 144-card base set has a horizontal format die-cut around a crown design at the top. The cards are double foiled and etched. There are 18 short-printed rookies and prospects cards, which were inserted at a rate of about one per eight packs. There are two parallels: Limited Series and Opening Day. Limited Series is produced on 24-point stock with silver foil and limited to 99 numbered sets. Opening Day is limited to 72 numbered sets.

	NM/M
Complete Set (144):	75.00
Common Player:	.25
Common SP:	.50
Limited Series (99 Sets):	6X
SP's:	2X
Opening Day (72 Sets):	12X
SP's:	2X
Pack (6):	2.00
Wax Box (24):	35.00

1	Jim Edmonds	.25
2	Darin Erstad	.50
3	Troy Glaus	2.00
4	Tim Salmon	.25
5	Mo Vaughn	.25
6	Jay Bell	.25
7	Steve Finley	.25
8	Randy Johnson	2.00
9	Travis Lee	.25
10	Matt Williams	.25
11	Andruw Jones	2.00
12	Chipper Jones	3.00
13	Brian Jordan	.25
14	Ryan Klesko	.25
15	Javy Lopez	.25
16	Greg Maddux	3.00
17	Randall Simon/SP	.50
18	Albert Belle	.25
19	Will Clark	.25
20	Delino DeShields	.25
21	Mike Mussina	.50
22	Cal Ripken Jr.	6.00
23	Nomar Garciaparra	3.00
24	Pedro Martinez	2.00
25	Jose Offerman	.25
26	John Valentin	.25
27	Mark Grace	.25
28	Lance Johnson	.25
29	Henry Rodriguez	.25
30	Sammy Sosa	3.00
31	Kerry Wood	1.00
32	Mike Caruso	.25
33	Ray Durham	.25
34	Magglio Ordonez	.40
35	Brian Simmons/SP	.50
36	Frank Thomas	2.00
37	Mike Cameron	.25
38	Barry Larkin	.25
39	Greg Vaughn	.25
40	Dmitri Young	.25
41	Roberto Alomar	.40
42	Sandy Alomar Jr.	.25
43	David Justice	.25
44	Kenny Lofton	.25
45	Manny Ramirez	2.00
46	Jim Thome	1.50
47	Dante Bichette	.25
48	Vinny Castilla	.25
49	Todd Helton	2.00
50	Larry Walker	.25
51	Tony Clark	.25
52	Damion Easley	.25
53	Bob Higginson	.25
54	Brian Hunter	.25
55	Gabe Kapler/SP	.50
56	Jeff Weaver/SP **RC**	2.50
57	Cliff Floyd	.25
58	Alex Gonzalez/SP	.50
59	Mark Kotsay	.25
60	Derrek Lee	1.00
61	Preston Wilson/SP	.75
62	Moises Alou	.25
63	Jeff Bagwell	2.00
64	Derek Bell	.25
65	Craig Biggio	.25
66	Ken Caminiti	.25
67	Carlos Beltran/SP	2.00
68	Johnny Damon	.45
69	Carlos Febles/SP	.65
70	Jeff King	.25
71	Kevin Brown	.25
72	Todd Hundley	.25
73	Eric Karros	.25
74	Raul Mondesi	.25
75	Gary Sheffield	.75
76	Jeromy Burnitz	.25
77	Jeff Cirillo	.25
78	Marquis Grissom	.25
79	Fernando Vina	.25
80	Chad Allen/SP **RC**	.50
81	Matt Lawton	.25
82	Doug Mientkiewicz/SP	.75
83	Brad Radke	.25
84	Todd Walker	.25
85	Michael Barrett/SP	.50
86	Brad Fullmer	.25
87	Vladimir Guerrero	2.00
88	Wilton Guerrero	.25
89	Ugueth Urbina	.25
90	Bobby Bonilla	.25
91	Rickey Henderson	2.00
92	Rey Ordonez	.25
93	Mike Piazza	3.50
94	Robin Ventura	.25
95	Roger Clemens	3.50
96	Orlando Hernandez	.25
97	Derek Jeter	6.00
98	Chuck Knoblauch	.25
99	Tino Martinez	.25
100	Bernie Williams	.25
101	Eric Chavez/SP	1.50
102	Jason Giambi	1.00
103	Ben Grieve	.25
104	Tim Raines	.25
105	Marlon Anderson/SP	.65
106	Doug Glanville	.25
107	Scott Rolen	1.25
108	Curt Schilling	.40
109	Brian Giles	.25
110	Jose Guillen	.25
111	Jason Kendall	.25
112	Kevin Young	.25
113	J.D. Drew/SP	2.00
114	Jose Jimenez/SP	.50
115	Ray Lankford	.25
116	Mark McGwire	5.00
117	Fernando Tatis	.25
118	Matt Clement/SP	.75
119	Tony Gwynn	3.00
120	Trevor Hoffman	.25
121	Wally Joyner	.25
122	Reggie Sanders	.25
123	Barry Bonds	6.00
124	Ellis Burks	.25
125	Jeff Kent	.25
126	Freddy Garcia/SP **RC**	1.00
127	Ken Griffey Jr.	4.00
128	Edgar Martinez	.25
129	Alex Rodriguez	5.00
130	David Segui	.25
131	Rolando Arrojo	.25
132	Wade Boggs	3.00
133	Jose Canseco	.65
134	Quinton McCracken	.25
135	Fred McGriff	.25
136	Juan Gonzalez	1.00
137	Rusty Greer	.25
138	Rafael Palmeiro	1.50
139	Ivan Rodriguez	1.50
140	Jose Cruz Jr.	.25
141	Carlos Delgado	.75
142	Shawn Green	.75
143	Shawn Green	.75
144	Roy Halladay/SP	1.00

Century 21

This 10-card set features some of baseball's most dominating players, on a full silver foil front. These are seeded 1:25 packs.

	NM/M
Complete Set (10):	30.00
Common Player:	2.00

Inserted 1:25

1	Cal Ripken Jr.	7.50
2	Nomar Garciaparra	4.00
3	Sammy Sosa	4.00
4	Frank Thomas	3.00
5	Mike Piazza	4.50
6	J.D. Drew	2.00
7	Mark McGwire	6.00
8	Tony Gwynn	4.00
9	Ken Griffey Jr.	5.00
10	Alex Rodriguez	6.00

Cramer's Choice Premiums

This enlarged (about 5" x 7") 10-card set is die-cut into a trophy shape. Cards are enhanced with silver holographic fronts with silver holographic etching and gold-foil stamping across the bottom. They are found one per box. Six serially numbered parallels were randomly seeded: Dark Blue (35 each), Green (30), Red (25), Light Blue (20), Gold (10) and Purple (1).

	NM/M
Complete Set (10):	20.00
Common Player:	2.00
Inserted 1:box	
Dark Blue (35 Sets):	5X
Green (30):	6X
Red (25):	8X
Light Blue (20):	10X
Gold (10):	15X
Purple (1):	Value Undetermined

1	Cal Ripken Jr.	6.50
2	Nomar Garciaparra	3.00
3	Sammy Sosa	3.00
4	Frank Thomas	2.50
5	Mike Piazza	3.50
6	Derek Jeter	6.50
7	J.D. Drew	2.00
8	Mark McGwire	5.00
9	Tony Gwynn	3.00
10	Ken Griffey Jr.	

Gold Crown Die-Cut Premiums

This enlarged six-card set was an unannounced premium box-topper. They were limited to 1,036 numbered sets, found less than once every other box.

	NM/M
Complete Set (6):	15.00
Common Player:	2.50

Inserted 6:10 boxes

1	Cal Ripken Jr.	7.00
2	Mike Piazza	4.50
3	Ken Griffey Jr.	5.00
4	Tony Gwynn	3.00
5	Mark McGwire	6.00
6	J.D. Drew	2.50

Abbreviations

SP - Short Print

Living Legends

This 10-card set spotlights baseball's top stars on a fully foiled card front. These are serial numbered to 375 sets.

		NM/M
Complete Set (10):		100.00
Common Player:		7.50
Production 375 Sets		
1	Greg Maddux	10.00
2	Cal Ripken Jr.	20.00
3	Nomar Garciaparra	10.00
4	Sammy Sosa	10.00
5	Frank Thomas	7.50
6	Mike Piazza	12.00
7	Mark McGwire	15.00
8	Tony Gwynn	10.00
9	Ken Griffey Jr.	13.50
10	Alex Rodriguez	15.00

Master Performers

This 20-card set features a full foiled front with the player photo in a frame like border. Master Performers are seeded 2:25 packs.

		NM/M
Complete Set (20):		40.00
Common Player:		1.00
Inserted 2:25		
1	Chipper Jones	2.50
2	Greg Maddux	2.50
3	Cal Ripken Jr.	3.00
4	Nomar Garciaparra	2.50
5	Sammy Sosa	2.50
6	Frank Thomas	2.00
7	Raul Mondesi	1.00
8	Vladimir Guerrero	2.00
9	Mike Piazza	3.00
10	Roger Clemens	3.00
11	Derek Jeter	5.00
12	Scott Rolen	1.75
13	J.D. Drew	1.50
14	Mark McGwire	4.00
15	Tony Gwynn	2.50
16	Barry Bonds	5.00
17	Ken Griffey Jr.	3.50
18	Alex Rodriguez	4.00
19	Juan Gonzalez	1.50
20	Ivan Rodriguez	1.75

Pillars of the Game

This 25-card set features holographic silver foil fronts on a horizontal format.

		NM/M
Complete Set (25):		30.00
Common Player:		.50
Inserted 1:1		
1	Mo Vaughn	.50
2	Chipper Jones	2.00
3	Greg Maddux	2.00
4	Albert Belle	.50

5	Cal Ripken Jr.	4.00
6	Nomar Garciaparra	2.00
7	Sammy Sosa	2.00
8	Frank Thomas	1.50
9	Manny Ramirez	1.50
10	Jeff Bagwell	1.50
11	Raul Mondesi	.50
12	Vladimir Guerrero	1.50
13	Mike Piazza	2.25
14	Roger Clemens	2.25
15	Derek Jeter	4.00
16	Bernie Williams	.50
17	Ben Grieve	.50
18	J.D. Drew	1.00
19	Mark McGwire	3.00
20	Tony Gwynn	2.00
21	Barry Bonds	4.00
22	Ken Griffey Jr.	2.50
23	Alex Rodriguez	3.00
24	Juan Gonzalez	1.00
25	Ivan Rodriguez	1.25

Pivotal Players

This 25-card set features holographic silver foil fronts with a flame in the background of the player photo.

		NM/M
Complete Set (25):		20.00
Common Player:		.50
Inserted 1:1		
1	Mo Vaughn	.50
2	Chipper Jones	2.00
3	Greg Maddux	2.00
4	Albert Belle	.50
5	Cal Ripken Jr.	4.00
6	Nomar Garciaparra	2.00
7	Sammy Sosa	2.00
8	Frank Thomas	1.50
9	Manny Ramirez	1.50
10	Craig Biggio	.50
11	Raul Mondesi	.50
12	Vladimir Guerrero	1.50
13	Mike Piazza	2.25
14	Roger Clemens	2.50
15	Derek Jeter	4.00
16	Bernie Williams	.50
17	Ben Grieve	.50
18	Scott Rolen	.60
19	J.D. Drew	.75
20	Mark McGwire	3.00
21	Tony Gwynn	2.00
22	Ken Griffey Jr.	2.50
23	Alex Rodriguez	3.00
24	Juan Gonzalez	.75
25	Ivan Rodriguez	1.00

Home Run Heroes

These cards were part of an unannounced multi-manufacturer (Fleer, Upper Deck, Topps, Pacific) insert program which was exclusive to Wal-Mart. Each company produced cards of Mark McGwire and Sammy Sosa, along with two other premier sluggers. Each company's cards share a "Power Elite" logo at top and "Home Run Heroes" logo vertically at right.

	NM/M
Complete Set (4):	3.50

1999 Pacific Invincible

The base set consists of 150 cards. Each features an action photo with a portrait in a cel window at bottom. There are two parallels to the base set: Opening Day and Platinum Blue. Both parallels are limited to 67 serial numbered sets.

		NM/M
Complete Set (150):		60.00
Common Player:		.25
Opening Day (69 Sets)		6X
Platinum Blues (67)		6X
Pack (3):		1.50
Wax Box (24):		35.00
1	Jim Edmonds	.25
2	Darin Erstad	.50
3	Troy Glaus	2.50
4	Tim Salmon	.25
5	Mo Vaughn	.25
6	Steve Finley	.25
7	Randy Johnson	2.50
8	Travis Lee	.25
9	Dante Powell	.25
10	Matt Williams	.25
11	Bret Boone	.25
12	Andruw Jones	2.50
13	Chipper Jones	3.00
14	Brian Jordan	.25
15	Ryan Klesko	.25
16	Javy Lopez	.25
17	Greg Maddux	3.00
18	Brady Anderson	.25
19	Albert Belle	.25
20	Will Clark	.25
21	Mike Mussina	.75
22	Cal Ripken Jr.	6.00
23	Nomar Garciaparra	3.00
24	Pedro Martinez	2.50
25	Trot Nixon	.25
26	Jose Offerman	.25
27	Donnie Sadler	.25
28	John Valentin	.25
29	Mark Grace	.25
30	Lance Johnson	.25
31	Henry Rodriguez	.25
32	Sammy Sosa	3.00
33	Kerry Wood	1.25
34	McKay Christensen	.25
35	Ray Durham	.25
36	Jeff Liefer	.25
37	Frank Thomas	2.50
38	Mike Cameron	.25
39	Barry Larkin	.25
40	Greg Vaughn	.25
41	Dmitri Young	.25
42	Roberto Alomar	.50
43	Sandy Alomar Jr.	.25
44	David Justice	.25
45	Kenny Lofton	.25
46	Manny Ramirez	2.50
47	Jim Thome	2.25
48	Dante Bichette	.25
49	Vinny Castilla	.25
50	Darryl Hamilton	.25
51	Todd Helton	2.50
52	Neifi Perez	.25
53	Larry Walker	.25
54	Tony Clark	.25
55	Damion Easley	.25
56	Bob Higginson	.25
57	Brian Hunter	.25
58	Gabe Kapler	.25
59	Cliff Floyd	.25
60	Alex Gonzalez	.25
61	Mark Kotsay	.25
62	Derrek Lee	2.00
63	Braden Looper	.25
64	Moises Alou	.25
65	Jeff Bagwell	2.50
66	Craig Biggio	.25
67	Ken Caminiti	.25
68	Scott Elarton	.25
69	Mitch Meluskey	.25
70	Carlos Beltran	.65
71	Johnny Damon	.50
72	Carlos Febles	.25

73	Jeremy Giambi	.25
74	Kevin Brown	.25
75	Todd Hundley	.25
76	Paul LoDuca	.25
77	Raul Mondesi	.25
78	Gary Sheffield	1.00
79	Geoff Jenkins	.25
80	Jeromy Burnitz	.25
81	Marquis Grissom	.25
82	Jose Valentin	.25
83	Fernando Vina	.25
84	Corey Koskie	.25
85	Matt Lawton	.25
86	Christian Guzman	.25
87	Torii Hunter	.25
88	Doug Mientkiewicz	.25
89	Michael Barrett	.25
90	Brad Fullmer	.25
91	Vladimir Guerrero	2.50
92	Fernando Seguignol	.25
93	Ugueth Urbina	.25
94	Bobby Bonilla	.25
95	Rickey Henderson	2.50
96	Rey Ordonez	.25
97	Mike Piazza	3.50
98	Robin Ventura	.25
99	Roger Clemens	3.50
100	Derek Jeter	6.00
101	Chuck Knoblauch	.25
102	Tino Martinez	.25
103	Paul O'Neill	.25
104	Bernie Williams	.25
105	Eric Chavez	.50
106	Ryan Christenson	.25
107	Jason Giambi	1.25
108	Ben Grieve	.25
109	Miguel Tejada	.50
110	Marlon Anderson	.25
111	Doug Glanville	.25
112	Scott Rolen	2.25
113	Curt Schilling	.50
114	Brian Giles	.25
115	Warren Morris	.25
116	Jason Kendall	.25
117	Kris Benson	.25
118	J.D. Drew	1.25
119	Ray Lankford	.25
120	Mark McGwire	5.00
121	Matt Clement	.25
122	Tony Gwynn	3.00
123	Trevor Hoffman	.25
124	Wally Joyner	.25
125	Reggie Sanders	.25
126	Barry Bonds	6.00
127	Ellis Burks	.25
128	Jeff Kent	.25
129	Stan Javier	.25
130	J.T. Snow	.25
131	Jay Buhner	.25
132	Freddy Garcia RC	.25
133	Ken Griffey Jr.	4.00
134	Russ Davis	.25
135	Edgar Martinez	.25
136	Alex Rodriguez	5.00
137	David Segui	.25
138	Rolando Arrojo	.25
139	Wade Boggs	3.00
140	Jose Canseco	1.00
141	Quinton McCracken	.25
142	Fred McGriff	.25
143	Juan Gonzalez	1.25
144	Tom Goodwin	.25
145	Rusty Greer	.25
146	Ivan Rodriguez	2.25
147	Jose Cruz Jr.	.25
148	Carlos Delgado	1.00
149	Shawn Green	.75
150	Roy Halladay	.25

Diamond Magic

This 10-card set features a horizontal format with silver foil stamping on the front. Diamond Magic's are seeded 1:49 packs.

		NM/M
Complete Set (10):		35.00
Common Player:		3.00
Inserted 1:49		
1	Cal Ripken Jr.	7.50
2	Nomar Garciaparra	4.00
3	Sammy Sosa	4.00
4	Frank Thomas	3.50
5	Mike Piazza	4.50
6	J.D. Drew	3.00
7	Mark McGwire	6.00
8	Tony Gwynn	4.00
9	Ken Griffey Jr.	5.00
10	Alex Rodriguez	6.00

Flash Point

This 20-card set features gold etching and gold foil stamping on the card front. These were seeded 1:25 packs.

		NM/M
Complete Set (20):		50.00
Common Player:		1.25
Inserted 1:25		
1	Mo Vaughn	1.25
2	Chipper Jones	3.50
3	Greg Maddux	3.50
4	Cal Ripken Jr.	9.00
5	Nomar Garciaparra	3.50
6	Sammy Sosa	3.50
7	Frank Thomas	2.50
8	Manny Ramirez	2.50
9	Vladimir Guerrero	2.50
10	Mike Piazza	4.00
11	Roger Clemens	4.00
12	Derek Jeter	9.00
13	Ben Grieve	1.25
14	Scott Rolen	2.00
15	J.D. Drew	1.50
16	Mark McGwire	7.50
17	Tony Gwynn	3.50
18	Ken Griffey Jr.	5.00
19	Alex Rodriguez	7.50
20	Juan Gonzalez	1.50

Giants of the Game

This jumbo mail-in redemption set of baseball's top stars is limited to 10 serially numbered specimens of each card.

		NM/M
Complete Set (10):		300.00
Common Player:		25.00
Production 10 Sets		
1	Cal Ripken Jr.	75.00
2	Nomar Garciaparra	35.00
3	Sammy Sosa	35.00
4	Frank Thomas	30.00
5	Mike Piazza	40.00
6	J.D. Drew	25.00
7	Mark McGwire	60.00
8	Tony Gwynn	35.00
9	Ken Griffey Jr.	50.00
10	Alex Rodriguez	60.00

Sandlot Heroes

Sandlot Heroes salutes baseball's top players on a horizontal format with holographic silver foil stamping on front. These were inserted one per pack. Each player can be found in two versions. A special edition, serially numbered to 10 of each and overprinted with a SportsFest logo, was created for use as a redemption prize at Pacific's booth at the show.

		NM/M
Complete Set (20):		15.00
Common Player:		.50
Inserted 1:1		
SportsFest (10 Sets):		25X
1	Mo Vaughn	.50
2	Chipper Jones	1.00
3	Greg Maddux	1.00
4	Cal Ripken Jr.	3.00
5	Nomar Garciaparra	1.00
6	Sammy Sosa	1.00
7	Frank Thomas	.75
8	Manny Ramirez	.75
9	Vladimir Guerrero	.75
10	Mike Piazza	1.25
11	Roger Clemens	1.25
12	Derek Jeter	3.00

Seismic Force

This 20-card set has a dot pattern behind the featured player with the left side and bottom of the card in a gold border. These were seeded one per pack. A specially marked SportsFest version was created for use as a redemption prize at Pacific's booth at the show. These are serially numbered to just 20 apiece.

		NM/M
Complete Set (20):		15.00
Common Player:		.50
Inserted 1:1		
SportsFest (20 Sets):		15X
1	Mo Vaughn	.50
2	Chipper Jones	1.00
3	Greg Maddux	1.00
4	Cal Ripken Jr.	3.00
5	Nomar Garciaparra	1.00
6	Sammy Sosa	1.00
7	Frank Thomas	.75
8	Manny Ramirez	.75
9	Vladimir Guerrero	.75
10	Mike Piazza	1.25
11	Bernie Williams	.50
12	Derek Jeter	3.00
13	Ben Grieve	.50
14	J.D. Drew	.60
15	Mark McGwire	2.00
16	Tony Gwynn	1.00
17	Ken Griffey Jr.	1.50
18	Alex Rodriguez	2.00
19	Juan Gonzalez	1.00
20	Ivan Rodriguez	.65

Thunder Alley

Thunder Alley focuses on baseball's top power hitters. These were inserted 1:121 packs.

		NM/M
Complete Set (20):		75.00
Common Player:		2.50
Inserted 1:121		
1	Mo Vaughn	2.50
2	Chipper Jones	6.00
3	Cal Ripken Jr.	12.00
4	Nomar Garciaparra	6.00
5	Sammy Sosa	6.00
6	Frank Thomas	5.00
7	Manny Ramirez	5.00
8	Todd Helton	5.00
9	Vladimir Guerrero	5.00
10	Mike Piazza	7.50
11	Derek Jeter	12.00
12	Ben Grieve	2.50
13	Scott Rolen	4.50
14	J.D. Drew	3.00
15	Mark McGwire	10.00
16	Tony Gwynn	6.00
17	Ken Griffey Jr.	9.00
18	Alex Rodriguez	10.00

| 19 | Juan Gonzalez | 3.00 |
| 20 | Ivan Rodriguez | 4.50 |

1999 Pacific Omega Sample

The Omega brand for '99 was launched with this sample card of spokesman Tony Gwynn. The card is in the same format as the regular-issue cards, except for the "SAMPLE" overprint on back and in the card-number circle at bottom-right.

NM/M
SAMPLE Tony Gwynn 2.00

1999 Pacific Omega

This single-series product features both portrait and action photos on front in a horizontal format. Four parallel versions distinguished by the color of foil highlights were random inserts in the six-card packs. Gold parallels are serially numbered to 299 each; Copper to 99; Platinum Blue to 75 and Premiere Date to 50.

NM/M
Complete Set (250): 20.00
Common Player: .10
Gold (299 Sets): 4X
Copper (99): 10X
Platinum Blue (75): 15X
Premire Date (50): 20X
Wax Pack (6): 1.50
Wax Box (36): 35.00

1	Garret Anderson	.10
2	Jim Edmonds	.10
3	Darin Erstad	.20
4	Chuck Finley	.10
5	Troy Glaus	.75
6	Troy Percival	.10
7	Chris Pritchett	.10
8	Tim Salmon	.10
9	Mo Vaughn	.10
10	Jay Bell	.10
11	Steve Finley	.10
12	Luis Gonzalez	.10
13	Randy Johnson	.75
14	Byung-Hyun Kim RC	.75
15	Travis Lee	.10
16	Matt Williams	.10
17	Tony Womack	.10
18	Bret Boone	.10
19	Mark DeRosa	.10
20	Tom Glavine	.35
21	Andruw Jones	.75
22	Chipper Jones	1.00
23	Brian Jordan	.10
24	Ryan Klesko	.10
25	Javy Lopez	.10
26	Greg Maddux	1.00
27	John Smoltz	.10
28	Bruce Chen, Odalis Perez	.10
29	Brady Anderson	.10
30	Harold Baines	.10
31	Albert Belle	.10
32	Will Clark	.10
33	Delino DeShields	.10
34	Jerry Hairston Jr.	.10
35	Charles Johnson	.10
36	Mike Mussina	.40
37	Cal Ripken Jr.	2.50
38	B.J. Surhoff	.10
39	Jin Ho Cho	.10
40	Nomar Garciaparra	1.00
41	Pedro Martinez	.75
42	Jose Offerman	.10
43	Troy O'Leary	.10
44	John Valentin	.10
45	Jason Varitek	.10
46	Juan Pena RC, Brian Rose	.10
47	Mark Grace	.10
48	Glenallen Hill	.10
49	Tyler Houston	.10
50	Mickey Morandini	.10
51	Henry Rodriguez	.10

52	Sammy Sosa	1.00
53	Kevin Tapani	.10
54	Mike Caruso	.10
55	Ray Durham	.10
56	Paul Konerko	.20
57	Carlos Lee	.10
58	Magglio Ordonez	.20
59	Mike Sirotka	.10
60	Frank Thomas	.75
61	Mark L. Johnson, Chris Singleton	.10
62	Mike Cameron	.10
63	Sean Casey	.20
64	Pete Harnisch	.10
65	Barry Larkin	.10
66	Pokey Reese	.10
67	Greg Vaughn	.10
68	Scott Williamson	.10
69	Dmitri Young	.10
70	Roberto Alomar	.25
71	Sandy Alomar Jr.	.10
72	Travis Fryman	.10
73	David Justice	.10
74	Kenny Lofton	.10
75	Manny Ramirez	.75
76	Richie Sexson	.10
77	Jim Thome	.65
78	Omar Vizquel	.10
79	Jaret Wright	.10
80	Dante Bichette	.10
81	Vinny Castilla	.10
82	Todd Helton	.10
83	Darryl Hamilton	.10
84	Darryl Kile	.10
85	Neifi Perez	.10
86	Larry Walker	.10
87	Tony Clark	.10
88	Damion Easley	.10
89	Juan Encarnacion	.10
90	Bobby Higginson	.10
91	Gabe Kapler	.10
92	Dean Palmer	.10
93	Justin Thompson	.10
94	Masao Kida RC, Jeff Weaver RC	1.00
95	Bruce Aven	.10
96	Luis Castillo	.10
97	Alex Fernandez	.10
98	Cliff Floyd	.10
99	Alex Gonzalez	.10
100	Mark Kotsay	.10
101	Preston Wilson	.10
102	Moises Alou	.10
103	Jeff Bagwell	.75
104	Derek Bell	.10
105	Craig Biggio	.10
106	Mike Hampton	.10
107	Richard Hidalgo	.10
108	Jose Lima	.10
109	Billy Wagner	.10
110	Russ Johnson, Daryle Ward	.10
111	Carlos Beltran	.50
112	Johnny Damon	.35
113	Jermaine Dye	.10
114	Carlos Febles	.10
115	Jeremy Giambi	.10
116	Joe Randa	.10
117	Mike Sweeney	.10
118	Orber Moreno RC, Jose Santiago	.10
119	Kevin Brown	.10
120	Todd Hundley	.10
121	Eric Karros	.10
122	Raul Mondesi	.10
123	Chan Ho Park	.10
124	Angel Pena	.10
125	Gary Sheffield	.45
126	Devon White	.10
127	Eric Young	.10
128	Ron Belliard	.10
129	Jeromy Burnitz	.10
130	Jeff Cirillo	.10
131	Marquis Grissom	.10
132	Geoff Jenkins	.10
133	David Nilsson	.10
134	Hideo Nomo	.40
135	Fernando Vina	.10
136	Ron Coomer	.10
137	Marty Cordova	.10
138	Corey Koskie	.10
139	Brad Radke	.10
140	Todd Walker	.10
141	Chad Allen RC, Torii Hunter	.10
142	Cristian Guzman, Jacque Jones	.10
143	Michael Barrett	.10
144	Orlando Cabrera	.10
145	Vladimir Guerrero	.75
146	Wilton Guerrero	.10
147	Ugueth Urbina	.10
148	Rondell White	.10
149	Chris Widger	.10
150	Edgardo Alfonzo	.10
151	Roger Cedeno	.10
152	Octavio Dotel	.10
153	Rickey Henderson	.75
154	John Olerud	.10
155	Rey Ordonez	.10
156	Mike Piazza	1.25
157	Robin Ventura	.10
158	Scott Brosius	.10
159	Roger Clemens	1.25
160	David Cone	.10
161	Chili Davis	.10
162	Orlando Hernandez	.10
163	Derek Jeter	2.50

164	Chuck Knoblauch	.10
165	Tino Martinez	.10
166	Paul O'Neill	.10
167	Bernie Williams	.10
168	Jason Giambi	.60
169	Ben Grieve	.10
170	Chad Harville RC	.10
171	Tim Hudson RC	2.00
172	Tony Phillips	.10
173	Kenny Rogers	.10
174	Matt Stairs	.10
175	Miguel Tejada	.25
176	Eric Chavez	.25
177	Bobby Abreu	.20
178	Ron Gant	.10
179	Doug Glanville	.10
180	Mike Lieberthal	.10
181	Desi Relaford	.10
182	Scott Rolen	.65
183	Curt Schilling	.35
184	Marlon Anderson, Randy Wolf	.10
185	Brant Brown	.10
186	Brian Giles	.10
187	Jason Kendall	.10
188	Al Martin	.10
189	Ed Sprague	.10
190	Kevin Young	.10
191	Kris Benson, Warren Morris	.10
192	Kent Bottenfield	.10
193	Eric Davis	.10
194	J.D. Drew	.45
195	Ray Lankford	.10
196	Joe McEwing RC	.25
197	Mark McGwire	2.00
198	Edgar Renteria	.10
199	Fernando Tatis	.10
200	Andy Ashby	.10
201	Ben Davis	.10
202	Tony Gwynn	1.00
203	Trevor Hoffman	.10
204	Wally Joyner	.10
205	Gary Matthews Jr.	.10
206	Ruben Rivera	.10
207	Reggie Sanders	.10
208	Rich Aurilia	.10
209	Marvin Benard	.10
210	Barry Bonds	2.50
211	Ellis Burks	.10
212	Stan Javier	.10
213	Jeff Kent	.10
214	Robb Nen	.10
215	J.T. Snow	.10
216	David Bell	.10
217	Jay Buhner	.10
218	Freddy Garcia RC	.50
219	Ken Griffey Jr.	1.50
220	Brian Hunter	.10
221	Butch Huskey	.10
222	Edgar Martinez	.10
223	Jamie Moyer	.10
224	Alex Rodriguez	2.00
225	David Segui	.10
226	Rolando Arrojo	.10
227	Wade Boggs	1.00
228	Miguel Cairo	.10
229	Jose Canseco	.60
230	Dave Martinez	.10
231	Fred McGriff	.10
232	Kevin Stocker	.10
233	Mike Duvall RC, David Lamb	.10
234	Royce Clayton	.10
235	Juan Gonzalez	.40
236	Rusty Greer	.10
237	Ruben Mateo	.10
238	Rafael Palmeiro	.65
239	Ivan Rodriguez	.65
240	John Wetteland	.10
241	Todd Zeile	.10
242	Jeff Zimmerman	.10
243	Homer Bush	.10
244	Jose Cruz Jr.	.10
245	Carlos Delgado	.60
246	Tony Fernandez	.10
247	Shawn Green	.35
248	Shannon Stewart	.10
249	David Wells	.10
250	Roy Halladay, Billy Koch	.10

Debut Duos

The careers of two players who made their major league debuts the same season are compared in this scarce (1:145) insert series. Fronts feature action photos of the pair, backs have portraits.

NM/M
Complete Set (10): 45.00
Common Player: 2.50
Inserted 1:145

| 1 | Nomar Garciaparra, Vladimir Guerrero | 6.00 |

2	Derek Jeter, Andy Pettitte	12.00
3	Garret Anderson, Alex Rodriguez	9.00
4	Chipper Jones, Raul Mondesi	6.00
5	Pedro Martinez, Mike Piazza	6.50
6	Mo Vaughn, Bernie Williams	2.50
7	Juan Gonzalez, Ken Griffey Jr.	7.50
8	Sammy Sosa, Larry Walker	6.00
9	Barry Bonds, Mark McGwire	12.00
10	Wade Boggs, Tony Gwynn	6.00

Diamond Masters

NM/M
Complete Set (36): 27.50
Common Player: .25
Inserted 1:9

1	Darin Erstad	.35
2	Mo Vaughn	.25
3	Matt Williams	.25
4	Andruw Jones	.75
5	Chipper Jones	1.00
6	Greg Maddux	1.00
7	Cal Ripken Jr.	3.00
8	Nomar Garciaparra	1.00
9	Pedro Martinez	.75
10	Sammy Sosa	1.00
11	Frank Thomas	.75
12	Kenny Lofton	.25
13	Manny Ramirez	.75
14	Larry Walker	.25
15	Gabe Kapler	.25
16	Jeff Bagwell	.75
17	Craig Biggio	.25
18	Raul Mondesi	.25
19	Vladimir Guerrero	.75
20	Mike Piazza	1.25
21	Roger Clemens	1.25
22	Derek Jeter	3.00
23	Bernie Williams	.25
24	Scott Rolen	.65
25	J.D. Drew	.60
26	Mark McGwire	2.00
27	Fernando Tatis	.25
28	Tony Gwynn	1.00
29	Barry Bonds	3.00
30	Ken Griffey Jr.	1.50
31	Alex Rodriguez	2.00
32	Jose Canseco	.60
33	Juan Gonzalez	.40
34	Ruben Mateo	.25
35	Ivan Rodriguez	.65
36	Rusty Greer	.25

EO Portraits

NM/M
Complete Set (20): 60.00
Common Player: 1.00
Inserted 1:73
1-of-1 Numbered Parallels Exist

1	Mo Vaughn	1.00
2	Chipper Jones	5.00
3	Greg Maddux	5.00
4	Cal Ripken Jr.	10.00
5	Nomar Garciaparra	5.00
6	Sammy Sosa	5.00
7	Frank Thomas	4.00
8	Manny Ramirez	4.00
9	Jeff Bagwell	4.00
10	Mike Piazza	5.50
11	Roger Clemens	5.50
12	Derek Jeter	10.00
13	Scott Rolen	4.00
14	Mark McGwire	8.00
15	Tony Gwynn	4.00
16	Barry Bonds	10.00
17	Ken Griffey Jr.	6.00
18	Alex Rodriguez	8.00
19	Jose Canseco	2.50
20	Juan Gonzalez	2.00

Hit Machine 3000

Within days of Tony Gwynn's 3,000 hit on August 6, Pacific had rushed into production a special insert set honoring the achievement of

---

its long-time spokesman. A total of 3,000 serially numbered sets of 20 cards were issued as random pack inserts in Omega. Fronts feature various game-action and studio photos of Gwynn, and are highlighted in silver foil. Backs have two more color photos of Gwynn and a few sentences about the player. A serial number in printed on front.

NM/M
Complete Set (20): 24.00
Common Card: 1.50

1	The Hitting Machine	1.50
2	The Eyes Have It	1.50
3	The Art of Hitting	1.50
4	Solid as a Rock	1.50
5	Seeing Doubles	1.50
6	Pithcer's Worst Nightmare	1.50
7	Portrait of an All-Star	1.50
8	An American Hero	1.50
9	Fan Favorite	1.50
10	Mr. Batting Title	1.50
11	4-for-5!	1.50
12	Mission Accomplished	1.50
13	One Hit Away	1.50
14	A Tip of the Hat	1.50
15	It's a Base Hit!	1.50
16	2997th - Grand Slam!	1.50
17	2998th Hit	1.50
18	2999th Hit - 2-Run Double	1.50
19	3000th Hit!	1.50
20	3000 Hits, 8874 At-Bats, 18 Years	1.50

HR '99

NM/M
Complete Set (20): 20.00
Common Player: .25
Inserted 1:37

1	Mo Vaughn	.25
2	Matt Williams	.25
3	Chipper Jones	2.00
4	Albert Belle	.25
5	Nomar Garciaparra	2.00
6	Sammy Sosa	2.00
7	Frank Thomas	1.25
8	Manny Ramirez	1.25
9	Jeff Bagwell	1.25
10	Raul Mondesi	.25
11	Vladimir Guerrero	1.25
12	Mike Piazza	2.25
13	Derek Jeter	4.00
14	Mark McGwire	3.00
15	Fernando Tatis	.25
16	Barry Bonds	4.00
17	Ken Griffey Jr.	2.50
18	Alex Rodriguez	3.00
19	Jose Canseco	.75
20	Juan Gonzalez	.65

5-Tool Talents

NM/M
Complete Set (30): 40.00
Common Player: .40
Inserted 4:37

1	Randy Johnson	1.50
2	Greg Maddux	2.00
3	Pedro Martinez	1.50
4	Kevin Brown	.40

5	Roger Clemens	2.50
6	Carlos Lee	.40
7	Gabe Kapler	.40
8	Carlos Beltran	.75
9	J.D. Drew	.75
10	Ruben Mateo	.40
11	Chipper Jones	2.00
12	Sammy Sosa	2.00
13	Manny Ramirez	1.50
14	Vladimir Guerrero	1.50
15	Mark McGwire	4.00
16	Ken Griffey Jr.	3.00
17	Jose Canseco	.75
18	Nomar Garciaparra	2.00
19	Frank Thomas	1.50
20	Larry Walker	.40
21	Jeff Bagwell	1.50
22	Mike Piazza	2.50
23	Tony Gwynn	2.00
24	Juan Gonzalez	.75
25	Cal Ripken Jr.	5.00
26	Derek Jeter	5.00
27	Scott Rolen	1.25
28	Barry Bonds	5.00
29	Alex Rodriguez	4.00
30	Ivan Rodriguez	1.25

5-Tool Talents Tiered

A parallel of the 5-Tool Talents inserts is fractured into five tiers of increasing scarcity, differentiated by the color of foil highlights and the serially numbered limited edition. The breakdown is: Tier 1, blue, 100 sets; Tier 2, red, 75 sets; Tier 3, green, 50 sets; Tier 4, purple, 25 sets; Tier 5, gold, 1 set. The unique gold cards are not priced due to their rarity.

NM/M

1	Randy Johnson	4.00
6	Carlos Lee	2.00
11	Chipper Jones	5.00
18	Nomar Garciaparra	5.00
21	Jeff Bagwell	4.00
28	Barry Bonds	7.50
2	Greg Maddux	7.50
7	Gabe Kapler	2.00
13	Manny Ramirez	6.00
16	Ken Griffey Jr.	10.00
19	Frank Thomas	6.00
30	Ivan Rodriguez	6.00
3	Pedro Martinez	12.50
8	Carlos Beltran	6.00
15	Mark McGwire	20.00
20	Larry Walker	2.00
25	Cal Ripken Jr.	30.00
26	Derek Jeter	30.00
4	Kevin Brown	7.50
9	J.D. Drew	15.00
12	Sammy Sosa	25.00
17	Jose Canseco	20.00
23	Tony Gwynn	25.00
29	Alex Rodriguez	35.00

1999 Pacific Paramount Sample

Pacific spokesman Tony Gwynn is featured on the sample card issued to introduce the brand for 1999. The card carries a large "SAMPLE" overprint diagonally on back.

	NM/M
Tony Gwynn	2.00

1999 Pacific Paramount

The 250-card base set is highlighted by silver foil stamping and a white border. Card backs have a small photo along with 1998 statistics and career totals and a brief career note. There are six parallels to the base set: Copper, Platinum Blue, Holographic Silver, Opening Day Issue, Gold and Holographic Gold. Each parallel is enhanced with the appropriate foil color. Coppers are found exclusively in hobby packs at a rate of one per pack. Platinum Blues are seeded one per 73 packs, Holographic Silvers are hobby only and limited to 99 serial numbered sets. Opening Day Issue is limited to 74 numbered sets. Golds are found one per retail pack. Holographic Golds are limited to 199 numbered sets.

	NM/M
Complete Set (250):	25.00
Common Player:	.10
Copper (1:1H):	2X
Red (1:1R):	2X
Gold (1:1R):	2X
Platinum Blue (1:73):	4X
Holographic Gold (199):	10X
Holographic Silver (99 Sets):	15X
Opening Day (74):	15X
Pack (6):	1.00
Wax Box (36):	25.00

1	Garret Anderson	.10
2	Gary DiSarcina	.10
3	Jim Edmonds	.10
4	Darin Erstad	.25
5	Chuck Finley	.10
6	Troy Glaus	.75
7	Troy Percival	.10
8	Tim Salmon	.10
9	Mo Vaughn	.10
10	Tony Batista	.10
11	Jay Bell	.10
12	Andy Benes	.10
13	Steve Finley	.10
14	Luis Gonzalez	.10
15	Randy Johnson	.75
16	Travis Lee	.10
17	Todd Stottlemyre	.10
18	Matt Williams	.10
19	David Dellucci	.10
20	Bret Boone	.10
21	Andres Galarraga	.10
22	Tom Glavine	.35
23	Andruw Jones	.75
24	Chipper Jones	1.50
25	Brian Jordan	.10
26	Ryan Klesko	.10
27	Javy Lopez	.10
28	Greg Maddux	1.50
29	John Smoltz	.10
30	Brady Anderson	.10
31	Albert Belle	.10
32	Will Clark	.10
33	Delino DeShields	.10
34	Charles Johnson	.10
35	Mike Mussina	.40
36	Cal Ripken Jr.	3.00
37	B.J. Surhoff	.10
38	Nomar Garciaparra	1.50
39	Reggie Jefferson	.10
40	Darren Lewis	.10
41	Pedro Martinez	.75
42	Troy O'Leary	.10
43	Jose Offerman	.10
44	Donnie Sadler	.10
45	John Valentin	.10
46	Rod Beck	.10
47	Gary Gaetti	.10
48	Mark Grace	.10
49	Lance Johnson	.10
50	Mickey Morandini	.10
51	Henry Rodriguez	.10
52	Sammy Sosa	1.50
53	Kerry Wood	.40
54	Mike Caruso	.10
55	Ray Durham	.10
56	Paul Konerko	.20
57	Jaime Navarro	.10
58	Greg Norton	.10
59	Magglio Ordonez	.30
60	Frank Thomas	.75
61	Aaron Boone	.10
62	Mike Cameron	.10
63	Barry Larkin	.10
64	Hal Morris	.10
65	Pokey Reese	.10
66	Brett Tomko	.10
67	Greg Vaughn	.10
68	Dmitri Young	.10
69	Roberto Alomar	.25
70	Sandy Alomar Jr.	.10
71	Bartolo Colon	.10
72	Travis Fryman	.10
73	David Justice	.10
74	Kenny Lofton	.10
75	Manny Ramirez	.75
76	Richie Sexson	.10
77	Jim Thome	.65
78	Omar Vizquel	.10
79	Dante Bichette	.10
80	Vinny Castilla	.10
81	Darryl Hamilton	.10
82	Todd Helton	.75
83	Darryl Kile	.10
84	Mike Lansing	.10
85	Neifi Perez	.10
86	Larry Walker	.10
87	Tony Clark	.10
88	Damion Easley	.10
89	Bob Higginson	.10
90	Brian Hunter	.10
91	Dean Palmer	.10
92	Justin Thompson	.10
93	Todd Dunwoody	.10
94	Cliff Floyd	.10
95	Alex Gonzalez	.10
96	Livan Hernandez	.10
97	Mark Kotsay	.10
98	Derrek Lee	.60
99	Kevin Orie	.10
100	Moises Alou	.10
101	Jeff Bagwell	.75
102	Derek Bell	.10
103	Craig Biggio	.10
104	Ken Caminiti	.10
105	Ricky Gutierrez	.10
106	Richard Hidalgo	.10
107	Billy Wagner	.10
108	Jeff Conine	.10
109	Johnny Damon	.35
110	Carlos Febles	.10
111	Jeremy Giambi	.10
112	Jeff King	.10
113	Jeff Montgomery	.10
114	Joe Randa	.10
115	Kevin Brown	.10
116	Mark Grudzielanek	.10
117	Todd Hundley	.10
118	Eric Karros	.10
119	Raul Mondesi	.10
120	Chan Ho Park	.10
121	Gary Sheffield	.40
122	Devon White	.10
123	Eric Young	.10
124	Jeromy Burnitz	.10
125	Jeff Cirillo	.10
126	Marquis Grissom	.10
127	Geoff Jenkins	.10
128	Dave Nilsson	.10
129	Jose Valentin	.10
130	Fernando Vina	.10
131	Rick Aguilera	.10
132	Ron Coomer	.10
133	Marty Cordova	.10
134	Matt Lawton	.10
135	David Ortiz	.50
136	Brad Radke	.10
137	Terry Steinbach	.10
138	Javier Valentin	.10
139	Todd Walker	.10
140	Orlando Cabrera	.10
141	Brad Fullmer	.10
142	Vladimir Guerrero	.75
143	Wilton Guerrero	.10
144	Carl Pavano	.10
145	Ugueth Urbina	.10
146	Rondell White	.10
147	Chris Widger	.10
148	Edgardo Alfonzo	.10
149	Bobby Bonilla	.10
150	Rickey Henderson	.75
151	Brian McRae	.10
152	Hideo Nomo	.40
153	John Olerud	.10
154	Rey Ordonez	.10
155	Mike Piazza	1.75
156	Robin Ventura	.10
157	Masato Yoshii	.10
158	Roger Clemens	1.75
159	David Cone	.10
160	Orlando Hernandez	.10
161	Hideki Irabu	.10
162	Derek Jeter	3.00
163	Chuck Knoblauch	.10
164	Tino Martinez	.10
165	Paul O'Neill	.10
166	Darryl Strawberry	.10
167	Bernie Williams	.10
168	Eric Chavez	.20
169	Ryan Christenson	.10
170	Jason Giambi	.50
171	Ben Grieve	.10
172	Tony Phillips	.10
173	Tim Raines	.10
174	Scott Spiezio	.10
175	Miguel Tejada	.20
176	Bobby Abreu	.20
177	Rico Brogna	.10
178	Ron Gant	.10
179	Doug Glanville	.10
180	Desi Relaford	.10
181	Scott Rolen	.65
182	Curt Schilling	.35
183	Brant Brown	.10
184	Brian Giles	.10
185	Jose Guillen	.10
186	Jason Kendall	.10
187	Al Martin	.10
188	Ed Sprague	.10
189	Kevin Young	.10
190	Eric Davis	.10
191	J.D. Drew	.40
192	Ray Lankford	.10
193	Eli Marrero	.10
194	Mark McGwire	2.50
195	Edgar Renteria	.10
196	Fernando Tatis	.10
197	Andy Ashby	.10
198	Tony Gwynn	1.50
199	Carlos Hernandez	.10
200	Trevor Hoffman	.10
201	Wally Joyner	.10
202	Jim Leyritz	.10
203	Ruben Rivera	.10
204	Matt Clement	.10
205	Quilvio Veras	.10
206	Rich Aurilia	.10
207	Marvin Benard	.10
208	Barry Bonds	3.00
209	Ellis Burks	.10
210	Jeff Kent	.10
211	Bill Mueller	.10
212	Robb Nen	.10
213	J.T. Snow	.10
214	Jay Buhner	.10
215	Jeff Fassero	.10
216	Ken Griffey Jr.	2.00
217	Carlos Guillen	.10
218	Butch Huskey	.10
219	Edgar Martinez	.10
220	Alex Rodriguez	2.50
221	David Segui	.10
222	Dan Wilson	.10
223	Rolando Arrojo	.10
224	Wade Boggs	1.50
225	Jose Canseco	.50
226	Roberto Hernandez	.10
227	Dave Martinez	.10
228	Quinton McCracken	.10
229	Fred McGriff	.10
230	Kevin Stocker	.10
231	Randy Winn	.10
232	Royce Clayton	.10
233	Juan Gonzalez	.40
234	Tom Goodwin	.10
235	Rusty Greer	.10
236	Rick Helling	.10
237	Rafael Palmeiro	.65
238	Ivan Rodriguez	.65
239	Aaron Sele	.10
240	John Wetteland	.10
241	Todd Zeile	.10
242	Jose Cruz Jr.	.10
243	Carlos Delgado	.50
244	Tony Fernandez	.10
245	Cecil Fielder	.10
246	Alex Gonzalez	.10
247	Shawn Green	.35
248	Roy Halladay	.10
249	Shannon Stewart	.10
250	David Wells	.10

Cooperstown Bound

This 10-card set focuses on players who seem destined for the Hall of Fame. These inserts feature silver foil stamping and are seeded 1:361 packs.

	NM/M
Complete Set (10):	35.00
Common Player:	3.00
Inserted 1:361	

1	Greg Maddux	4.00
2	Cal Ripken Jr.	10.00
3	Nomar Garciaparra	4.00
4	Sammy Sosa	4.00
5	Frank Thomas	3.00
6	Mike Piazza	5.00
7	Mark McGwire	10.00
8	Tony Gwynn	4.00
9	Ken Griffey Jr.	6.00
10	Alex Rodriguez	8.00

Fielder's Choice

Cal Ripken Jr.

This 20-card set is die-cut into a glove shape and enhanced with gold foil stamping. These are seeded 1:73 packs.

	NM/M
Complete Set (20):	60.00
Common Player:	2.50
Inserted 1:73	

1	Chipper Jones	5.00
2	Greg Maddux	5.00
3	Cal Ripken Jr.	10.00
4	Nomar Garciaparra	5.00
5	Sammy Sosa	5.00
6	Kerry Wood	3.00
7	Frank Thomas	4.00
8	Manny Ramirez	4.00
9	Todd Helton	4.00
10	Jeff Bagwell	4.00
11	Mike Piazza	5.50
12	Derek Jeter	10.00
13	Bernie Williams	2.50
14	J.D. Drew	3.00
15	Mark McGwire	7.50
16	Tony Gwynn	5.00
17	Ken Griffey Jr.	6.00
18	Alex Rodriguez	7.50
19	Juan Gonzalez	2.50
20	Ivan Rodriguez	3.50

Personal Bests

Ken Griffey Jr. OF, Seattle Mariners

This 36-card set features holographic silver foil stamping on the card front. Card backs include a close-up photo of the featured player and a career note. These are seeded 1:37 packs.

	NM/M
Complete Set (36):	45.00
Common Player:	.50
Inserted 1:37	

1	Darin Erstad	.65
2	Mo Vaughn	.50
3	Travis Lee	.50
4	Chipper Jones	3.00
5	Greg Maddux	3.00
6	Albert Belle	.50
7	Cal Ripken Jr.	6.00
8	Nomar Garciaparra	3.00
9	Sammy Sosa	3.00
10	Kerry Wood	1.00
11	Frank Thomas	2.00
12	Greg Vaughn	.50
13	Manny Ramirez	2.00
14	Todd Helton	2.00
15	Larry Walker	.50
16	Jeff Bagwell	2.00
17	Craig Biggio	.50
18	Raul Mondesi	.50
19	Vladimir Guerrero	1.00
20	Hideo Nomo	1.00
21	Mike Piazza	3.50
22	Roger Clemens	3.50
23	Derek Jeter	6.00
24	Bernie Williams	.50
25	Eric Chavez	.75
26	Ben Grieve	.50
27	Scott Rolen	1.50
28	J.D. Drew	1.25
29	Mark McGwire	4.50
30	Tony Gwynn	3.00
31	Barry Bonds	6.00
32	Ken Griffey Jr.	4.00
33	Alex Rodriguez	4.50
34	Jose Canseco	1.25
35	Juan Gonzalez	1.00
36	Ivan Rodriguez	1.50

Team Checklists

Marquis Grissom

This 30-card set features gold foil etching and stamping on the card front. Card backs show the featured player's team checklist for the base set. These were seeded 2:37 packs.

	NM/M
Complete Set (30):	40.00
Common Player:	.50
Inserted 2:37	

1	Mo Vaughn	.50
2	Travis Lee	.50
3	Chipper Jones	3.00
4	Cal Ripken Jr.	6.00
5	Nomar Garciaparra	3.00
6	Sammy Sosa	3.00
7	Frank Thomas	2.50
8	Greg Vaughn	.50
9	Manny Ramirez	2.50
10	Larry Walker	.50
11	Damion Easley	.50
12	Mark Kotsay	.50
13	Jeff Bagwell	2.50
14	Jeremy Giambi	.50
15	Raul Mondesi	.50
16	Marquis Grissom	.50
17	Brad Radke	.50
18	Vladimir Guerrero	2.50
19	Mike Piazza	3.50
20	Roger Clemens	3.50
21	Ben Grieve	.50
22	Scott Rolen	2.00
23	Brian Giles	.50
24	Mark McGwire	5.00
25	Tony Gwynn	3.00
26	Barry Bonds	6.00
27	Ken Griffey Jr.	4.00
28	Jose Canseco	1.25
29	Juan Gonzalez	1.25
30	Jose Cruz Jr.	.50

1999 Pacific Prism Sample

Padres Tony Gwynn

This card of Pacific spokesman Tony Gwynn introduces the 1999 Prism series. The sample card follows the format of the issued version but is overprinted "SAMPLE" on back.

	NM/M
Tony Gwynn	2.00

1999 Pacific Prism

This 150-card base set has a full, holographic silver card front. Card backs feature two more player photos along with 1998 and career statistics. Hobby packs consist of five cards. There are also five parallels including Holographic Gold, Holographic Mirror, Holographic Blue, Holographic Purple and Red. Golds are limited to 480 serial numbered sets, Mirrors 160 sets, Blues 80 numbered sets, and, Purples 320 sets. Red parallels are a retail-only insert and are seeded at a rate of one per 12.5 packs.

	NM/M
Complete Set (150):	50.00
Common Player:	.15
Red (2:25R):	3X
HoloGold (480 Sets):	3X
HoloPurple (320):	4X
HoloMirror (160):	8X
HoloBlue (80):	15X
Retail Pack (3):	1.00
Hobby Pack (5):	1.50

1	Garret Anderson	.15
2	Jim Edmonds	.15
3	Darin Erstad	.30
4	Chuck Finley	.15
5	Tim Salmon	.15
6	Jay Bell	.15
7	David Dellucci	.15
8	Travis Lee	.15
9	Matt Williams	.15
10	Andres Galarraga	.15
11	Tom Glavine	.40
12	Andruw Jones	1.50
13	Chipper Jones	2.00
14	Ryan Klesko	.15
15	Javy Lopez	.15
16	Greg Maddux	2.00
17	Roberto Alomar	.50
18	Ryan Minor	.15
19	Mike Mussina	.40
20	Rafael Palmeiro	1.25
21	Cal Ripken Jr.	4.00
22	Nomar Garciaparra	2.00
23	Pedro Martinez	1.50
24	John Valentin	.15
25	Mo Vaughn	.15
26	Tim Wakefield	.15
27	Rod Beck	.15
28	Mark Grace	.15
29	Lance Johnson	.15
30	Sammy Sosa	2.00
31	Kerry Wood	.50
32	Albert Belle	.15
33	Mike Caruso	.15
34	Magglio Ordonez	.30
35	Frank Thomas	1.50
36	Robin Ventura	.15
37	Aaron Boone	.15
38	Barry Larkin	.15
39	Reggie Sanders	.15
40	Brett Tomko	.15
41	Sandy Alomar Jr.	.15
42	Bartolo Colon	.15
43	David Justice	.15
44	Kenny Lofton	.15
45	Manny Ramirez	1.50
46	Richie Sexson	.15
47	Jim Thome	1.00
48	Omar Vizquel	.15
49	Dante Bichette	.15
50	Vinny Castilla	.15
51	Edgard Clemente RC	.15
52	Todd Helton	1.50
53	Quinton McCracken	.15
54	Larry Walker	.15
55	Tony Clark	.15
56	Damion Easley	.15
57	Luis Gonzalez	.15
58	Bob Higginson	.15
59	Brian Hunter	.15
60	Cliff Floyd	.15
61	Alex Gonzalez	.15
62	Livan Hernandez	.15
63	Derrek Lee	.15
64	Edgar Renteria	.15
65	Moises Alou	.15
66	Jeff Bagwell	1.50
67	Derek Bell	.15
68	Craig Biggio	.15
69	Randy Johnson	1.50
70	Johnny Damon	.35
71	Jeff King	.15
72	Hal Morris	.15
73	Dean Palmer	.15
74	Eric Karros	.15
75	Raul Mondesi	.15
76	Chan Ho Park	.15
77	Gary Sheffield	.50

78 Jeromy Burnitz .15
79 Jeff Cirillo .15
80 Marquis Grissom .15
81 Jose Valentin .15
82 Fernando Vina .15
83 Paul Molitor 1.50
84 Otis Nixon .65
85 David Ortiz .15
86 Todd Walker .15
87 Vladimir Guerrero 1.50
88 Carl Pavano .15
89 Fernando Seguignol .15
90 Ugueth Urbina .15
91 Carlos Baerga .15
92 Bobby Bonilla .15
93 Hideo Nomo .75
94 John Olerud .15
95 Rey Ordonez .15
96 Mike Piazza 2.25
97 David Cone .15
98 Orlando Hernandez .15
99 Hideki Irabu .15
100 Derek Jeter 4.00
101 Tino Martinez .15
102 Bernie Williams .15
103 Eric Chavez .25
104 Jason Giambi 1.00
105 Ben Grieve .15
106 Rickey Henderson 1.50
107 Bob Abreu .25
108 Doug Glanville .15
109 Scott Rolen 1.00
110 Curt Schilling .40
111 Emil Brown .15
112 Jose Guillen .15
113 Jason Kendall .15
114 Al Martin .15
115 Aramis Ramirez .15
116 Kevin Young .15
117 J.D. Drew .75
118 Ron Gant .15
119 Brian Jordan .15
120 Eli Marrero .15
121 Mark McGwire 3.00
122 Kevin Brown .15
123 Tony Gwynn 2.00
124 Trevor Hoffman .15
125 Wally Joyner .15
126 Greg Vaughn .15
127 Barry Bonds 4.00
128 Ellis Burks .15
129 Jeff Kent .15
130 Robb Nen .15
131 J.T. Snow .15
132 Jay Buhner .15
133 Ken Griffey Jr. 2.50
134 Edgar Martinez .15
135 Alex Rodriguez 3.00
136 David Segui .15
137 Rolando Arrojo .15
138 Wade Boggs 2.00
139 Aaron Ledesma .15
140 Fred McGriff .15
141 Will Clark .15
142 Juan Gonzalez .75
143 Rusty Greer .15
144 Ivan Rodriguez 1.25
145 Aaron Sele .15
146 Jose Canseco .40
147 Roger Clemens 2.25
148 Jose Cruz Jr. .15
149 Carlos Delgado .15
150 Alex Gonzalez .15

Ahead of the Game

Each card features full gold foil and etching with a close-up photo of baseball's top 20 stars. These are seeded 1:49 packs.

		NM/M
Complete Set (20):		40.00
Common Player:		1.00
Inserted 1:49		
1	Darin Erstad	1.25
2	Travis Lee	1.00
3	Chipper Jones	3.00
4	Cal Ripken Jr.	6.00
5	Nomar Garciaparra	3.00
6	Sammy Sosa	3.00
7	Kerry Wood	1.25
8	Frank Thomas	2.00
9	Manny Ramirez	2.00
10	Todd Helton	2.00
11	Jeff Bagwell	2.00
12	Mike Piazza	3.50

13 Derek Jeter 6.00
14 Bernie Williams 1.00
15 J.D. Drew 1.25
16 Mark McGwire 3.00
17 Tony Gwynn 3.00
18 Ken Griffey Jr. 4.00
19 Alex Rodriguez 5.00
20 Ivan Rodriguez 1.50

Ballpark Legends

This 10 card set salutes baseball's biggest stars. These inserts feature silver foil stamping and etching with an image of a ballpark in the background of the player photo. These are seeded 1:193 packs.

		NM/M
Complete Set (10):		40.00
Common Player:		2.50
Inserted 1:193		
1	Cal Ripken Jr.	10.00
2	Nomar Garciaparra	5.00
3	Frank Thomas	4.00
4	Ken Griffey Jr.	6.00
5	Alex Rodriguez	7.50
6	Greg Maddux	5.00
7	Sammy Sosa	5.00
8	Kerry Wood	2.50
9	Mark McGwire	7.50
10	Tony Gwynn	5.00

1999 Pacific Private Stock

The premiere issue of Private Stock base cards features holographic silver foil on 30-pt. cardboard. Card backs have selected box scores from the '98 season, with a brief commentary on the player. Packs consist of six cards.

		NM/M
Complete Set (150):		25.00
Common Player:		.10
Pack (6):		1.50
Wax Box (24):		20.00
Wax Box (36):		25.00
1	Jeff Bagwell	1.00
2	Roger Clemens	1.75
3	J.D. Drew	.60
4	Nomar Garciaparra	1.50
5	Juan Gonzalez	.50
6	Ken Griffey Jr.	2.00
7	Tony Gwynn	1.50
8	Derek Jeter	3.00
9	Chipper Jones	1.50
10	Travis Lee	.10
11	Greg Maddux	1.50
12	Mark McGwire	2.50
13	Mike Piazza	1.75
14	Manny Ramirez	1.00
15	Cal Ripken Jr.	3.00
16	Alex Rodriguez	2.50
17	Ivan Rodriguez	.75
18	Sammy Sosa	1.50
19	Frank Thomas	1.50
20	Kerry Wood	.40
21	Roberto Alomar	.25
22	Moises Alou	.10
23	Albert Belle	.10
24	Craig Biggio	.10
25	Wade Boggs	1.50
26	Barry Bonds	3.00
27	Jose Canseco	.50
28	Jim Edmonds	.10
29	Darin Erstad	.25
30	Andres Galarraga	.10
31	Tom Glavine	.35
32	Ben Grieve	.10
33	Vladimir Guerrero	1.00
34	Wilton Guerrero	.10
35	Todd Helton	1.00
36	Andruw Jones	1.00
37	Ryan Klesko	.10
38	Kenny Lofton	.10
39	Javy Lopez	.10
40	Pedro Martinez	1.00
41	Paul Molitor	1.00
42	Raul Mondesi	.10
43	Rafael Palmeiro	.75
44	Tim Salmon	.10
45	Jim Thome	.75
46	Mo Vaughn	.10
47	Larry Walker	.10
48	David Wells	.10
49	Bernie Williams	.15
50	Jaret Wright	.10
51	Bobby Abreu	.15
52	Garret Anderson	.10
53	Rolando Arrojo	.10
54	Tony Batista	.10
55	Rod Beck	.10
56	Derek Bell	.10

Diamond Glory

Card fronts feature full copper foil stamping with a star in the background of the player's photo. The 20-card set features 20 of baseball's most exciting players including several top 1999 rookies. These are seeded 2:25 packs.

		NM/M
Complete Set (20):		25.00
Common Player:		.60
Inserted 2:25		
1	Darin Erstad	.60
2	Travis Lee	.60
3	Chipper Jones	2.00
4	Greg Maddux	2.00
5	Cal Ripken Jr.	3.50
6	Nomar Garciaparra	2.00
7	Sammy Sosa	2.00
8	Kerry Wood	.75
9	Frank Thomas	1.50
10	Todd Helton	1.50
11	Jeff Bagwell	1.50
12	Mike Piazza	2.25
13	Derek Jeter	3.50
14	Bernie Williams	.60
15	J.D. Drew	.75
16	Mark McGwire	3.00
17	Tony Gwynn	3.00
18	Ken Griffey Jr.	2.50
19	Alex Rodriguez	3.00
20	Juan Gonzalez	.75

Epic Performers

This hobby-only set features top hobby favorites and is seeded at 1:97 packs.

		NM/M
Complete Set (10):		60.00
Common Player:		4.00
Inserted 1:97 H		
1	Cal Ripken Jr.	15.00
2	Nomar Garciaparra	7.50
3	Frank Thomas	6.00
4	Ken Griffey Jr.	10.00
5	Alex Rodriguez	12.50
6	Greg Maddux	7.50
7	Sammy Sosa	7.50
8	Kerry Wood	4.00
9	Mark McGwire	12.50
10	Tony Gwynn	7.50

57 Marvin Benard .10
58 Dave Berg .10
59 Dante Bichette .10
60 Aaron Boone .10
61 Bret Boone .10
62 Scott Brosius .10
63 Brant Brown .10
64 Kevin Brown .10
65 Jeromy Burnitz .10
66 Ken Caminiti .10
67 Mike Caruso .10
68 Sean Casey .20
69 Vinny Castilla .10
70 Eric Chavez .20
71 Ryan Christenson .10
72 Jeff Cirillo .10
73 Tony Clark .10
74 Will Clark .10
75 Edgard Clemente RC .10
76 David Cone .10
77 Marty Cordova .10
78 Jose Cruz Jr. .10
79 Eric Davis .10
80 Carlos Delgado .50
81 David Dellucci .10
82 Delino DeShields .10
83 Gary DiSarcina .10
84 Damion Easley .10
85 Dennis Eckersley .65
86 Cliff Floyd .10
87 Jason Giambi .65
88 Doug Glanville .10
89 Alex Gonzalez .10
90 Mark Grace .10
91 Rusty Greer .10
92 Jose Guillen .10
93 Carlos Guillen .10
94 Jeffrey Hammonds .10
95 Rick Helling .10
96 Bob Henley .10
97 Livan Hernandez .10
98 Orlando Hernandez .10
99 Bob Higginson .10
100 Trevor Hoffman .10
101 Randy Johnson 1.00
102 Brian Jordan .10
103 Wally Joyner .10
104 Eric Karros .10
105 Jason Kendall .10
106 Jeff Kent .10
107 Jeff King .10
108 Mark Kotsay .10
109 Ray Lankford .10
110 Barry Larkin .10
111 Mark Loretta .10
112 Edgar Martinez .10
113 Tino Martinez .10
114 Quinton McCracken .10
115 Fred McGriff .10
116 Ryan Minor .10
117 Hal Morris .10
118 Bill Mueller .10
119 Mike Mussina .40
120 Dave Nilsson .10
121 Otis Nixon .10
122 Hideo Nomo .50
123 Paul O'Neill .10
124 Jose Offerman .10
125 John Olerud .10
126 Rey Ordonez .10
127 David Ortiz .50
128 Dean Palmer .10
129 Chan Ho Park .10
130 Aramis Ramirez .10
131 Edgar Renteria .10
132 Armando Rios .10
133 Henry Rodriguez .10
134 Scott Rolen .75
135 Curt Schilling .35
136 David Segui .10
137 Richie Sexson .10
138 Gary Sheffield .45
139 John Smoltz .10
140 Matt Stairs .10
141 Justin Thompson .10
142 Greg Vaughn .10
143 Omar Vizquel .10
144 Tim Wakefield .10
145 Todd Walker .10
146 Devon White .10
147 Rondell White .10
148 Matt Williams .10
149 Enrique Wilson RC .25
150 Kevin Young .10

Exclusive Series

This 20-card set is a partial parallel to the base set. Taking the first 20 cards from the set and serially numbering them to 299 sets. These are inserted exclusively in hobby packs.

		NM/M
Complete Set (20):		50.00
Common Player:		1.00
Production: 299 Sets H		
1	Jeff Bagwell	2.00
2	Roger Clemens	3.50
3	J.D. Drew	1.25
4	Nomar Garciaparra	3.00
5	Juan Gonzalez	1.25
6	Ken Griffey Jr.	4.00
7	Tony Gwynn	3.00
8	Derek Jeter	6.00
9	Chipper Jones	3.00
10	Travis Lee	1.00
11	Greg Maddux	3.00
12	Mark McGwire	5.00
13	Mike Piazza	3.50
14	Manny Ramirez	2.00
15	Cal Ripken Jr.	6.00
16	Alex Rodriguez	5.00
17	Ivan Rodriguez	1.50
18	Sammy Sosa	3.00
19	Frank Thomas	2.00
20	Kerry Wood	1.25

Preferred Series

Another partial parallel of the first 20 base cards. Each card is stamped with a holographic Preferred logo and are numbered to 399 sets.

		NM/M
Complete Set (20):		37.50
Common Player:		.60
Production: 399 Sets		
1	Jeff Bagwell	1.50
2	Roger Clemens	2.25
3	J.D. Drew	.75
4	Nomar Garciaparra	2.00
5	Juan Gonzalez	.75
6	Ken Griffey Jr.	2.50
7	Tony Gwynn	2.00
8	Derek Jeter	5.00
9	Chipper Jones	2.00
10	Travis Lee	.60
11	Greg Maddux	2.00
12	Mark McGwire	3.50
13	Mike Piazza	2.25
14	Manny Ramirez	1.50
15	Cal Ripken Jr.	5.00
16	Alex Rodriguez	3.50
17	Ivan Rodriguez	1.25
18	Sammy Sosa	2.00
19	Frank Thomas	1.50
20	Kerry Wood	.75

Platinum Series

Another partial parallel of the first 50 cards in the base set. Cards have a platinum holographic sheen to them with a Platinum stamp on the front. These are limited to 199 numbered sets.

		NM/M
Complete Set (50):		160.00
Common Player:		.75
Production 199 Sets		
1	Jeff Bagwell	5.00
2	Roger Clemens	6.50
3	J.D. Drew	3.00
4	Nomar Garciaparra	6.00
5	Juan Gonzalez	2.50
6	Ken Griffey Jr.	8.00
7	Tony Gwynn	6.00
8	Derek Jeter	12.00
9	Chipper Jones	6.00
10	Travis Lee	.75
11	Greg Maddux	6.00
12	Mark McGwire	10.00
13	Mike Piazza	6.50
14	Manny Ramirez	5.00
15	Cal Ripken Jr.	12.00
16	Alex Rodriguez	10.00
17	Ivan Rodriguez	4.00
18	Sammy Sosa	6.00
19	Frank Thomas	5.00
20	Kerry Wood	2.00
21	Roberto Alomar	1.50
22	Moises Alou	.75
23	Albert Belle	.75
24	Craig Biggio	.75
25	Wade Boggs	6.00
26	Barry Bonds	12.00
27	Jose Canseco	3.00
28	Jim Edmonds	.75
29	Darin Erstad	1.50
30	Andres Galarraga	.75
31	Tom Glavine	2.00
32	Ben Grieve	.75
33	Vladimir Guerrero	5.00
34	Wilton Guerrero	.75
35	Todd Helton	5.00
36	Andruw Jones	5.00
37	Ryan Klesko	.75
38	Kenny Lofton	.75
39	Javy Lopez	.75
40	Pedro Martinez	5.00
41	Paul Molitor	5.00
42	Raul Mondesi	.75
43	Rafael Palmeiro	4.00
44	Tim Salmon	.75
45	Jim Thome	3.50
46	Mo Vaughn	.75
47	Larry Walker	.75
48	David Wells	.75
49	Bernie Williams	.75
50	Jaret Wright	.75

Vintage Series

This insert set is a partial parallel of the first 50 cards in the base set and has a Vintage holographic stamp on the card fronts. These are limited to 99 numbered sets.

		NM/M
Complete Set (50):		375.00
Common Player:		2.50
Production: 99 Sets		
1	Jeff Bagwell	12.50
2	Roger Clemens	17.50
3	J.D. Drew	7.50
4	Nomar Garciaparra	15.00
5	Juan Gonzalez	6.00
6	Ken Griffey Jr.	20.00
7	Tony Gwynn	15.00
8	Derek Jeter	30.00
9	Chipper Jones	15.00
10	Travis Lee	2.50
11	Greg Maddux	15.00
12	Mark McGwire	25.00
13	Mike Piazza	17.50
14	Manny Ramirez	12.50
15	Cal Ripken Jr.	30.00
16	Alex Rodriguez	25.00
17	Ivan Rodriguez	10.00
18	Sammy Sosa	15.00
19	Frank Thomas	12.50
20	Kerry Wood	6.00
21	Roberto Alomar	3.50
22	Moises Alou	2.50
23	Albert Belle	2.50
24	Craig Biggio	2.50
25	Wade Boggs	15.00
26	Barry Bonds	30.00
27	Jose Canseco	5.00
28	Jim Edmonds	2.50
29	Darin Erstad	3.50
30	Andres Galarraga	2.50
31	Tom Glavine	5.00
32	Ben Grieve	2.50
33	Vladimir Guerrero	12.50
34	Wilton Guerrero	2.50
35	Todd Helton	12.50
36	Andruw Jones	12.50
37	Ryan Klesko	2.50
38	Kenny Lofton	2.50
39	Javy Lopez	2.50
40	Pedro Martinez	12.50
41	Paul Molitor	12.50
42	Raul Mondesi	2.50
43	Rafael Palmeiro	10.00
44	Tim Salmon	2.50
45	Jim Thome	10.00
46	Mo Vaughn	2.50
47	Larry Walker	2.50
48	David Wells	2.50
49	Bernie Williams	2.50
50	Jaret Wright	2.50

PS-206

This 150-card set takes reverent reach back into collecting history with its smaller format (1.5" x 2.5"). Card fronts have a white border with silver foil stamping and a blue back, these are found one per pack. A parallel also exists with a red back, which are seeded 1:25 packs.

	NM/M
Complete Set (150):	20.00
Common Player:	.15
Inserted 1:1	
Red Parallels:	4X
Inserted 1:25	

1	Jeff Bagwell	.75
2	Roger Clemens	1.25
3	J.D. Drew	.50
4	Nomar Garciaparra	1.00
5	Juan Gonzalez	.40
6	Ken Griffey Jr.	1.50
7	Tony Gwynn	1.00
8	Derek Jeter	3.00
9	Chipper Jones	1.00
10	Travis Lee	.15
11	Greg Maddux	1.00
12	Mark McGwire	2.00
13	Mike Piazza	1.25
14	Manny Ramirez	.75
15	Cal Ripken Jr.	3.00
16	Alex Rodriguez	2.00
17	Ivan Rodriguez	.65
18	Sammy Sosa	1.00
19	Frank Thomas	.75
20	Kerry Wood	.40
21	Roberto Alomar	.30
22	Moises Alou	.15
23	Albert Belle	.15
24	Craig Biggio	.15
25	Wade Boggs	1.00
26	Barry Bonds	3.00
27	Jose Canseco	.50
28	Jim Edmonds	.15
29	Darin Erstad	.30
30	Andres Galarraga	.15
31	Tom Glavine	.35
32	Ben Grieve	.15
33	Vladimir Guerrero	.75
34	Wilton Guerrero	.15
35	Todd Helton	.75
36	Andruw Jones	.75
37	Ryan Klesko	.15
38	Kenny Lofton	.15
39	Javy Lopez	.15
40	Pedro Martinez	.75
41	Paul Molitor	.75
42	Raul Mondesi	.15
43	Rafael Palmeiro	.65
44	Tim Salmon	.15
45	Jim Thome	.65
46	Mo Vaughn	.15
47	Larry Walker	.15
48	David Wells	.15
49	Bernie Williams	.15
50	Jaret Wright	.15
51	Bobby Abreu	.15
52	Garret Anderson	.15
53	Rolando Arrojo	.15
54	Tony Batista	.15
55	Rod Beck	.15
56	Derek Bell	.15
57	Marvin Benard	.15
58	Dave Berg	.15
59	Dante Bichette	.15
60	Aaron Boone	.15
61	Bret Boone	.15
62	Scott Brosius	.15
63	Brant Brown	.15
64	Kevin Brown	.15
65	Jeromy Burnitz	.15
66	Ken Caminiti	.15
67	Mike Caruso	.15
68	Sean Casey	.25
69	Vinny Castilla	.15
70	Eric Chavez	.25
71	Ryan Christenson	.15
72	Jeff Cirillo	.15
73	Tony Clark	.15

74	Will Clark	.15
75	Edgard Clemente	.15
76	David Cone	.15
77	Marty Cordova	.15
78	Jose Cruz Jr.	.15
79	Eric Davis	.15
80	Carlos Delgado	.60
81	David Dellucci	.15
82	Delino DeShields	.15
83	Gary DiSarcina	.15
84	Damion Easley	.15
85	Dennis Eckersley	.65
86	Cliff Floyd	.15
87	Jason Giambi	.60
88	Doug Glanville	.15
89	Alex Gonzalez	.15
90	Mark Grace	.15
91	Rusty Greer	.15
92	Jose Guillen	.15
93	Carlos Guillen	.15
94	Jeffrey Hammonds	.15
95	Rick Helling	.15
96	Bob Henley	.15
97	Livan Hernandez	.15
98	Orlando Hernandez	.15
99	Bob Higginson	.15
100	Trevor Hoffman	.15
101	Randy Johnson	.75
102	Brian Jordan	.15
103	Wally Joyner	.15
104	Eric Karros	.15
105	Jason Kendall	.15
106	Jeff Kent	.15
107	Jeff King	.15
108	Mark Kotsay	.15
109	Ray Lankford	.15
110	Barry Larkin	.15
111	Mark Loretta	.15
112	Edgar Martinez	.15
113	Tino Martinez	.15
114	Quinton McCracken	.15
115	Fred McGriff	.15
116	Ryan Minor	.15
117	Hal Morris	.15
118	Bill Mueller	.15
119	Mike Mussina	.40
120	Dave Nilsson	.15
121	Otis Nixon	.15
122	Hideo Nomo	.40
123	Paul O'Neill	.15
124	Jose Offerman	.15
125	John Olerud	.15
126	Rey Ordonez	.15
127	David Ortiz	.50
128	Dean Palmer	.15
129	Chan Ho Park	.15
130	Aramis Ramirez	.15
131	Edgar Renteria	.15
132	Armando Rios	.15
133	Henry Rodriguez	.15
134	Scott Rolen	.60
135	Curt Schilling	.35
136	David Segui	.15
137	Richie Sexson	.15
138	Gary Sheffield	.50
139	John Smoltz	.15
140	Matt Stairs	.15
141	Justin Thompson	.15
142	Greg Vaughn	.15
143	Omar Vizquel	.15
144	Tim Wakefield	.15
145	Todd Walker	.15
146	Devon White	.15
147	Rondell White	.15
148	Matt Williams	.15
149	Enrique Wilson	.15
150	Kevin Young	.15

Homerun History

This holographic silver foiled commemorative set honors Mark McGwire and Sammy Sosa's historic '98 seasons. Two cards were added to the end of the set, which are Silver Crown Die-Cuts honoring Ripken Jr.'s consecutive games streak and McGwire's 70 home runs. These are inserted 2:25 packs.

	NM/M
Complete Set (22):	25.00
Common McGwire:	1.50
Common Sosa:	1.00
Inserted 1:12	

1	Home Run #61 (Mark McGwire)	3.00
2	Home Run #59 (Sammy Sosa)	1.00
3	Home Run #62 (Mark McGwire)	1.50
4	Home Run #60 (Sammy Sosa)	1.00
5	Home Run #63 (Mark McGwire)	1.50
6	Home Run #61 (Sammy Sosa)	3.00
7	Home Run #64 (Mark McGwire)	1.50
8	Home Run #62 (Sammy Sosa)	1.00
9	Home Run #65 (Mark McGwire)	1.50
10	Home Run #63 (Sammy Sosa)	1.00
11	Home Run #67 (Mark McGwire)	1.50
12	Home Run #64 (Sammy Sosa)	1.00
13	Home Run #68 (Mark McGwire)	1.50
14	Home Run #65 (Sammy Sosa)	1.00
15	Home Run #70 (Mark McGwire)	5.00
16	Home Run #66 (Sammy Sosa)	3.00
17	A Season of Celebration (Mark McGwire)	1.50
18	A Season of Celebration (Sammy Sosa)	1.00
19	Awesome Power (Sammy Sosa, Mark McGwire)	1.50
20	Transcending Sports (Mark McGwire, Sammy Sosa)	1.50
21	Crown Die-Cut (Mark McGwire)	1.50
22	Crown Die-Cut (Cal Ripken Jr.)	1.00

1999 Pacific Revolution

The 150-card set features dual foiled etching and embossing enhanced by gold-foil stamping. Card backs have year-by-year statistics along with a close-up photo. There are 25 short-printed rookie and prospect cards, which were inserted at a rate of about one per four packs. There are three parallels to the base set: Premiere Date, Red and Shadow. Reds are retail exclusive and are limited to 299 numbered sets. Shadows have light blue foil stamping and are limited to 99 numbered sets. Premiere Date are seeded exclusively in hobby packs at a rate of 1:25 packs.

	NM/M
Complete Set (150):	60.00
Common Player:	.15
Shadow (99 Sets H):	6X
SP:	3X
Red (299 R):	2X
SP:	1.5X
Premiere Date (49 H):	12X
SP:	6X
Wax Pack (3):	2.00
Wax Box (24):	35.00

1	Jim Edmonds	.15
2	Darin Erstad	.30
3	Troy Glaus	1.00
4	Tim Salmon	.15
5	Mo Vaughn	.15
6	Steve Finley	.15
7	Luis Gonzalez	.15
8	Randy Johnson	1.00
9	Travis Lee	.15
10	Matt Williams	.15
11	Andruw Jones	1.00
12	Chipper Jones	1.50
13	Brian Jordan	.15

14	Javy Lopez	.15
15	Greg Maddux	1.50
16	Kevin McGlinchy/SP RC	1.00
17	John Smoltz	.15
18	Brady Anderson	.15
19	Albert Belle	.15
20	Will Clark	.15
21	Willis Otanez/SP RC	.25
22	Calvin Pickering/SP RC	.25
23	Cal Ripken Jr.	4.00
24	Nomar Garciaparra	1.50
25	Pedro Martinez	1.00
26	Troy O'Leary	.15
27	Jose Offerman	.15
28	Mark Grace	.15
29	Mickey Morandini	.15
30	Henry Rodriguez	.15
31	Sammy Sosa	1.50
32	Ray Durham	.15
33	Carlos Lee/SP	.50
34	Jeff Liefer/SP RC	.35
35	Magglio Ordonez	.35
36	Frank Thomas	1.00
37	Mike Cameron	.15
38	Sean Casey	.35
39	Barry Larkin	.15
40	Greg Vaughn	.15
41	Roberto Alomar	.35
42	Sandy Alomar Jr.	.15
43	David Justice	.15
44	Kenny Lofton	.15
45	Manny Ramirez	1.00
46	Richie Sexson	.15
47	Jim Thome	.65
48	Dante Bichette	.15
49	Vinny Castilla	.15
50	Darryl Hamilton	.15
51	Todd Helton	.15
52	Larry Walker	.15
53	Tony Clark	.15
54	Damion Easley	.15
55	Bob Higginson	.15
56	Gabe Kapler/SP	.25
57	Alex Gonzalez/SP RC	.35
58	Mark Kotsay	.15
59	Kevin Orie	.15
60	Preston Wilson/SP	.15
61	Jeff Bagwell	1.00
62	Derek Bell	.15
63	Craig Biggio	.15
64	Ken Caminiti	.15
65	Carlos Beltran/SP	.65
66	Johnny Damon	.35
67	Jermaine Dye	.15
68	Carlos Febles/SP	.35
69	Kevin Brown	.15
70	Todd Hundley	.15
71	Eric Karros	.15
72	Raul Mondesi	.15
73	Gary Sheffield	.45
74	Jeromy Burnitz	.15
75	Jeff Cirillo	.15
76	Marquis Grissom	.15
77	Fernando Vina	.15
78	Chad Allen/SP RC	.25
79	Corey Koskie/SP RC	1.50
80	Doug Mientkiewicz/SP RC	1.00
81	Brad Radke	.15
82	Todd Walker	.15
83	Michael Barrett/SP RC	.15
84	Vladimir Guerrero	1.00
85	Wilton Guerrero	.15
86	Guillermo Mota/SP RC	.35
87	Rondell White	.15
88	Edgardo Alfonzo	.15
89	Rickey Henderson	.15
90	John Olerud	.15
91	Mike Piazza	2.00
92	Robin Ventura	.15
93	Roger Clemens	2.00
94	Chili Davis	.15
95	Derek Jeter	4.00
96	Chuck Knoblauch	.15
97	Tino Martinez	.15
98	Paul O'Neill	.15
99	Bernie Williams	.15
100	Eric Chavez/SP	.35
101	Jason Giambi	.65
102	Ben Grieve	.15
103	John Jaha	.15
104	Olmedo Saenz/SP RC	.25
105	Bobby Abreu	.25
106	Doug Glanville	.15
107	Desi Relaford	.15
108	Scott Rolen	.75
109	Curt Schilling	.35
110	Brian Giles	.15
111	Jason Kendall	.15
112	Pat Meares	.15
113	Kevin Young	.15
114	J.D. Drew/SP	1.00
115	Ray Lankford	.15
116	Eli Marrero	.15
117	Joe McEwing/SP RC	.15
118	Mark McGwire	3.00
119	Fernando Tatis	.15
120	Tony Gwynn	1.50
121	Trevor Hoffman	.15
122	Wally Joyner	.15
123	Reggie Sanders	.15
124	Barry Bonds	4.00
125	Ellis Burks	.15
126	Jeff Kent	.15
127	Ramon Martinez/SP RC	.15
128	Joe Nathan/SP RC	.25
129	Freddy Garcia/SP RC	1.00

130	Ken Griffey Jr.	2.50
131	Brian Hunter	.15
132	Edgar Martinez	.15
133	Alex Rodriguez	3.00
134	David Segui	.15
135	Wade Boggs	1.50
136	Jose Canseco	.45
137	Quinton McCracken	.15
138	Fred McGriff	.15
139	Kelly Dransfeldt/SP RC	.25
140	Juan Gonzalez	.50
141	Rusty Greer	.15
142	Rafael Palmeiro	.75
143	Ivan Rodriguez	.75
144	Lee Stevens	.15
145	Jose Cruz Jr.	.15
146	Carlos Delgado	.60
147	Shawn Green	.15
148	Roy Halladay/SP RC	1.50
149	Shannon Stewart	.15
150	Kevin Witt/SP RC	.35

Shadow

This hobby-only parallel insert features blue metallic-foil background and graphics on front. Backs are identical to the base version except they include a dot-matrix applied serial number at left within an edition of 99.

	NM/M
Common Player:	4.00
Stars:	6X
SP's:	3X

Diamond Legacy

This 36-card set features a holographic patterned foil card front. Card backs have a small close-up photo along with a career note. These were seeded 2:25 packs.

	NM/M
Complete Set (36):	60.00
Common Player:	.50
Inserted 2:25	

1	Troy Glaus	2.00
2	Mo Vaughn	.50
3	Matt Williams	.50
4	Chipper Jones	3.00
5	Andruw Jones	2.00
6	Greg Maddux	3.00
7	Albert Belle	.50
8	Cal Ripken Jr.	6.00
9	Nomar Garciaparra	3.00
10	Sammy Sosa	3.00
11	Frank Thomas	2.00
12	Manny Ramirez	2.00
13	Todd Helton	2.00
14	Larry Walker	.50
15	Gabe Kapler	.50
16	Jeff Bagwell	2.00
17	Craig Biggio	.50
18	Raul Mondesi	.50
19	Vladimir Guerrero	2.00
20	Mike Piazza	3.50
21	Roger Clemens	3.50
22	Derek Jeter	6.00
23	Bernie Williams	.50
24	Ben Grieve	.50
25	Scott Rolen	1.75
26	J.D. Drew	1.50
27	Mark McGwire	5.00

28	Fernando Tatis	.50
29	Tony Gwynn	3.00
30	Barry Bonds	6.00
31	Ken Griffey Jr.	4.00
32	Alex Rodriguez	5.00
33	Jose Canseco	1.25
34	Juan Gonzalez	1.00
35	Ivan Rodriguez	1.75
36	Shawn Green	1.50

Foul Pole

This 20-card set features netting down the right side of each card, with the player photo on the left side. The player name, position and logo are stamped with gold foil. These were seeded 1:49 packs.

	NM/M
Complete Set (20):	100.00
Common Player:	1.50
Inserted 1:49	

1	Chipper Jones	8.00
2	Andruw Jones	6.00
3	Cal Ripken Jr.	16.00
4	Nomar Garciaparra	8.00
5	Sammy Sosa	8.00
6	Frank Thomas	6.00
7	Manny Ramirez	6.00
8	Jeff Bagwell	6.00
9	Raul Mondesi	1.50
10	Vladimir Guerrero	6.00
11	Mike Piazza	9.00
12	Derek Jeter	16.00
13	Bernie Williams	1.50
14	Scott Rolen	5.00
15	J.D. Drew	3.00
16	Mark McGwire	12.00
17	Tony Gwynn	8.00
18	Ken Griffey Jr.	10.00
19	Alex Rodriguez	12.00
20	Juan Gonzalez	3.00

Icons

This 10-card set spotlights the top players, each card is die-cut in the shape of a shield with silver foil etching and stamping. These were seeded 1:121 packs.

	NM/M
Complete Set (10):	50.00
Common Player:	4.00
Inserted 1:121	

1	Cal Ripken Jr.	10.00
2	Nomar Garciaparra	5.00
3	Sammy Sosa	5.00
4	Frank Thomas	4.00
5	Mike Piazza	6.50
6	Derek Jeter	10.00
7	Mark McGwire	8.00
8	Tony Gwynn	5.00
9	Ken Griffey Jr.	7.50
10	Alex Rodriguez	8.00

Thorn in the Side

This 20-card set features full holographic silver foil and is die-cut in the upper right portion. Card backs analyzes the featured player's success against a certain opponent over the years. These were seeded 1:25 packs.

		NM/M
	Complete Set (20):	35.00
	Common Player:	1.00
	Inserted 1:25	
1	Mo Vaughn	1.00
2	Chipper Jones	3.00
3	Greg Maddux	3.00
4	Cal Ripken Jr.	6.00
5	Nomar Garciaparra	3.00
6	Sammy Sosa	3.00
7	Frank Thomas	2.25
8	Manny Ramirez	2.25
9	Jeff Bagwell	2.25
10	Mike Piazza	3.50
11	Derek Jeter	6.00
12	Bernie Williams	1.00
13	J.D. Drew	1.50
14	Mark McGwire	4.50
15	Tony Gwynn	3.00
16	Barry Bonds	6.00
17	Ken Griffey Jr.	4.00
18	Alex Rodriguez	4.50
19	Juan Gonzalez	1.50
20	Ivan Rodriguez	2.00

Tripleheader

This 30-card set features spotted gold foil blotching around the player image with the name, position, team and logo stamped in gold foil. These were seeded 4:25 hobby packs. The set is also broken down into three separate tiers of 10 cards. Tier 1 (cards 1-10) are limited to 99 numbered sets. Tier 2 (11-20) 199 numbered sets and Tier 3 (21-30) 299 numbered sets.

		NM/M
	Complete Set (30):	30.00
	Common Player:	.25
	Inserted 4:25 H	
	Tier 1 (1-10)	
	Production 99 Sets H	
	Tier 2 (11-20)	
	Production 199 Sets H	
	Tier 3 (21-30)	
	Production 299 Sets H	
1	Greg Maddux	1.50
2	Cal Ripken Jr.	3.00
3	Nomar Garciaparra	1.50
4	Sammy Sosa	1.50
5	Frank Thomas	1.00
6	Mike Piazza	1.75
7	Mark McGwire	2.50
8	Tony Gwynn	1.50
9	Ken Griffey Jr.	2.00
10	Alex Rodriguez	2.50
11	Mo Vaughn	.50
12	Chipper Jones	1.50
13	Manny Ramirez	1.00
14	Larry Walker	.25
15	Jeff Bagwell	1.00
16	Vladimir Guerrero	1.00
17	Derek Jeter	1.00
18	J.D. Drew	.60
19	Barry Bonds	3.00
20	Juan Gonzalez	.50
21	Troy Glaus	1.00
22	Andruw Jones	1.00
23	Matt Williams	.25
24	Craig Biggio	.25
25	Raul Mondesi	.25
26	Roger Clemens	1.75
27	Bernie Williams	.25
28	Scott Rolen	.75
29	Jose Canseco	.50
30	Ivan Rodriguez	.75

2000 Pacific Sample

Tony Gwynn was once again the spokesman for Pacific's 2000 line-up of baseball cards products. To showcase its base brand for the year, Pacific produced this sample card, so overprinted and "numbered" on back, but otherwise virtually identical to the issued version.

		NM/M
SAMPLE	Tony Gwynn	3.00

2000 Pacific

The base set consists of 500-cards with the Pacific logo and player name stamped in silver foil on the card front. Card backs have a small photo along with complete career statistics and a brief career highlight. 50 players in the base set also have another version and are priced equally.

		NM/M
	Complete Set (500):	60.00
	Common Player:	.10
	Pack (12):	1.50
	Wax Box (24):	25.00
1	Garret Anderson	.15
2	Tim Belcher	.10
3	Gary DiSarcina	.10
4	Trent Durrington	.10
5	Jim Edmonds	.15
6a	Darin Erstad/Action	.35
6b	Darin Erstad/Portrait	.35
7	Chuck Finley	.10
8	Troy Glaus	.75
9	Todd Greene	.10
10	Bret Hemphill	.10
11	Ken Hill	.10
12	Ramon Ortiz	.10
13	Troy Percival	.10
14	Mark Petkovsek	.10
15	Tim Salmon	.20
16a	Mo Vaughn	.15
16b	Mo Vaughn/Portrait	.15
17	Jay Bell	.10
18	Omar Daal	.10
19	Erubiel Durazo	.10
20	Steve Finley	.10
21	Bernard Gilkey	.10
22	Luis Gonzalez	.20
23	Randy Johnson	.75
24	Byung-Hyun Kim	.10
25	Travis Lee	.10
26	Matt Mantei	.10
27	Armando Reynoso	.10
28	Rob Ryan	.10
29	Kelly Stinnett	.10
30	Todd Stottlemyre	.10
31a	Matt Williams/Action	.15
31b	Matt Williams/Portrait	.15
32	Tony Womack	.10
33	Bret Boone	.10
34	Andres Galarraga	.15
35	Tom Glavine	.35
36	Ozzie Guillen	.10
37a	Andruw Jones/Action	.75
37b	Andruw Jones/Portrait	.75
38a	Chipper Jones/Action	1.00
38b	Chipper Jones/Portrait	1.00
39	Brian Jordan	.10
40	Ryan Klesko	.15
41	Javy Lopez	.10
42a	Greg Maddux/Action	1.00
42b	Greg Maddux/Portrait	1.00
43	Kevin Millwood	.15
44	John Rocker	.10
45	Randall Simon	.10
46	John Smoltz	.15
47	Gerald Williams	.10
48	Brady Anderson	.15
49a	Albert Belle/Action	.15
49b	Albert Belle/Portrait	.15
50	Mike Bordick	.10
51	Will Clark	.25
52	Jeff Conine	.10
53	Delino DeShields	.10
54	Jerry Hairston Jr.	.10
55	Charles Johnson	.10
56	Eugene Kingsale	.10
57	Ryan Minor	.10
58	Mike Mussina	.35
59	Sidney Ponson	.10
60a	Cal Ripken Jr./Action	2.50
60b	Cal Ripken Jr./Portrait	2.50
61	B.J. Surhoff	.10
62	Mike Timlin	.10
63	Rod Beck	.10
64a	Nomar Garciaparra/Action	1.50
64b	Nomar Garciaparra/Portrait	1.50
65	Tom Gordon	.10
66	Butch Huskey	.10
67	Derek Lowe	.10
68a	Pedro Martinez/Action	.75
68b	Pedro Martinez/Portrait	.75
69	Trot Nixon	.10
70	Jose Offerman	.10
71	Troy O'Leary	.10
72	Pat Rapp	.10
73	Donnie Sadler	.10
74	Mike Stanley	.10
75	John Valentin	.10
76	Jason Varitek	.15
77	Wilton Veras	.15
78	Tim Wakefield	.10
79	Rick Aguilera	.10
80	Manny Alexander	.10
81	Roosevelt Brown	.10
82	Mark Grace	.20
83	Glenallen Hill	.10
84	Lance Johnson	.10
85	Jon Lieber	.10
86	Cole Liniak	.10
87	Chad Meyers	.10
88	Mickey Morandini	.10
89	Jose Nieves	.10
90	Henry Rodriguez	.10
91a	Sammy Sosa/Action	1.50
91b	Sammy Sosa/Portrait	1.50
92	Kevin Tapani	.10
93	Kerry Wood	.50
94	Mike Caruso	.10
95	Ray Durham	.10
96	Brook Fordyce	.10
97	Bobby Howry	.10
98	Paul Konerko	.25
99	Carlos Lee	.10
100	Aaron Myette	.10
101	Greg Norton	.10
102	Magglio Ordonez	.25
103	Jim Parque	.10
104	Liu Rodriguez	.10
105	Chris Singleton	.10
106	Mike Sirotka	.10
107a	Frank Thomas/Action	.75
107b	Frank Thomas/Portrait	.75
108	Kip Wells	.10
109	Aaron Boone	.10
110	Mike Cameron	.10
111a	Sean Casey/Action	.20
111b	Sean Casey/Portrait	.20
112	Jeffrey Hammonds	.10
113	Pete Harnisch	.10
114a	Barry Larkin/Action	.15
114b	Barry Larkin/Portrait	.15
115	Jason LaRue	.10
116	Denny Neagle	.10
117	Pokey Reese	.10
118	Scott Sullivan	.10
119	Eddie Taubensee	.10
120	Greg Vaughn	.10
121	Scott Williamson	.10
122	Dmitri Young	.10
123a	Roberto Alomar/Action	.35
123b	Roberto Alomar/Portrait	.35
124	Sandy Alomar Jr.	.10
125	Harold Baines	.10
126	Russell Branyan	.10
127	Dave Burba	.10
128	Bartolo Colon	.10
129	Travis Fryman	.15
130	Mike Jackson	.10
131	David Justice	.15
132a	Kenny Lofton/Action	.15
132b	Kenny Lofton/Portrait	.15
133	Charles Nagy	.10
134a	Manny Ramirez/Action	.75
134b	Manny Ramirez/Portrait	.75
135	Dave Roberts	.10
136	Richie Sexson	.10
137	Jim Thome	.60
138	Omar Vizquel	.10
139	Jaret Wright	.10
140	Pedro Astacio	.10
141	Dante Bichette	.10
142	Brian Bohanon	.10
143a	Vinny Castilla/Action	.10
143b	Vinny Castilla/Portrait	.10
144	Edgard Clemente	.10
145	Derrick Gibson	.10
146	Todd Helton	.75
147	Darryl Kile	.10
148	Mike Lansing	.10
149	Kirt Manwaring	.10
150	Neifi Perez	.10
151	Ben Petrick	.10
152	Juan Sosa RC	.20
153	Dave Veres	.10
154a	Larry Walker/Action	.15
154b	Larry Walker/Portrait	.15
155	Brad Ausmus	.10
156	Dave Borkowski	.10
157	Tony Clark	.15
158	Francisco Cordero	.10
159	Deivi Cruz	.10
160	Damion Easley	.10
161	Juan Encarnacion	.10
162	Robert Fick	.10
163	Bobby Higginson	.10
164	Gabe Kapler	.15
165	Brian Moehler	.10
166	Dean Palmer	.10
167	Luis Polonia	.10
168	Justin Thompson	.10
169	Jeff Weaver	.10
170	Antonio Alfonseca	.10
171	Bruce Aven	.10
172	A.J. Burnett	.15
173	Luis Castillo	.10
174	Ramon Castro	.10
175	Ryan Dempster	.10
176	Alex Fernandez	.10
177	Cliff Floyd	.15
178	Amaury Garcia	.10
179	Alex Gonzalez	.10
180	Mark Kotsay	.10
181	Mike Lowell	.15
182	Brian Meadows	.10
183	Kevin Orie	.10
184	Julio Ramirez	.10
185	Preston Wilson	.15
186	Moises Alou	.15
187a	Jeff Bagwell/Action	.75
187b	Jeff Bagwell/Portrait	.75
188	Glen Barker	.10
189	Derek Bell	.10
190a	Craig Biggio/Action	.15
190b	Craig Biggio/Portrait	.15
191	Ken Caminiti	.10
192	Scott Elarton	.10
193	Carl Everett	.10
194	Mike Hampton	.15
195	Carlos Hernandez	.10
196	Richard Hidalgo	.10
197	Jose Lima	.10
198	Shane Reynolds	.10
199	Bill Spiers	.10
200	Billy Wagner	.15
201a	Carlos Beltran/Action	.50
201b	Carlos Beltran/Portrait	.50
202	Dermal Brown	.10
203	Johnny Damon	.25
204	Jermaine Dye	.10
205	Carlos Febles	.10
206	Jeremy Giambi	.10
207	Mark Quinn	.10
208	Joe Randa	.10
209	Dan Reichert	.10
210	Jose Rosado	.10
211	Rey Sanchez	.10
212	Jeff Suppan	.10
213	Mike Sweeney	.10
214a	Kevin Brown/Action	.15
214b	Kevin Brown/Portrait	.15
215	Darren Dreifort	.10
216	Eric Gagne	.10
217	Mark Grudzielanek	.10
218	Todd Hollandsworth	.10
219	Todd Hundley	.10
220	Eric Karros	.15
221	Raul Mondesi	.15
222	Chan Ho Park	.15
223	Jeff Shaw	.10
224a	Gary Sheffield/Action	.30
224b	Gary Sheffield/Portrait	.30
225	Ismael Valdes	.10
226	Devon White	.10
227	Eric Young	.10
228	Kevin Barker	.10
229	Ron Belliard	.10
230a	Jeromy Burnitz/Action	.10
230b	Jeromy Burnitz/Portrait	.10
231	Jeff Cirillo	.10
232	Marquis Grissom	.10
233	Geoff Jenkins	.10
234	Mark Loretta	.10
235	David Nilsson	.10
236	Hideo Nomo	.75
237	Alex Ochoa	.10
238	Kyle Peterson	.10
239	Fernando Vina	.10
240	Bob Wickman	.10
241	Steve Woodard	.10
242	Chad Allen	.10
243	Ron Coomer	.10
244	Marty Cordova	.10
245	Cristian Guzman	.10
246	Denny Hocking	.10
247	Jacque Jones	.10
248	Corey Koskie	.10
249	Matt Lawton	.10
250	Joe Mays	.10
251	Eric Milton	.10
252	Brad Radke	.10
253	Mark Redman	.10
254	Terry Steinbach	.10
255	Todd Walker	.10
256	Tony Armas Jr.	.10
257	Michael Barrett	.10
258	Peter Bergeron	.10
259	Geoff Blum	.10
260	Orlando Cabrera	.10
261	Trace Coquillette RC	.15
262	Brad Fullmer	.10
263a	Vladimir Guerrero/Action	.75
263b	Vladimir Guerrero/Portrait	.75
264	Wilton Guerrero	.10
265	Dustin Hermanson	.10
266	Manny Martinez	.10
267	Ryan McGuire	.10
268	Ugueth Urbina	.10
269	Jose Vidro	.10
270	Rondell White	.15
271	Chris Widger	.10
272	Edgardo Alfonzo	.15
273	Armando Benitez	.10
274	Roger Cedeno	.10
275	Dennis Cook	.10
276	Octavio Dotel	.10
277	John Franco	.10
278	Darryl Hamilton	.10
279	Rickey Henderson	.75
280	Orel Hershiser	.10
281	Al Leiter	.15
282a	John Olerud/Action	.15
282b	John Olerud/Portrait	.15
283	Rey Ordonez	.10
284a	Mike Piazza/Action	1.50
284b	Mike Piazza/Portrait	1.50
285	Kenny Rogers	.10
286	Jorge Toca	.10
287	Robin Ventura	.10
288	Scott Brosius	.10
289a	Roger Clemens/Action	1.25
289b	Roger Clemens/Portrait	1.25
290	David Cone	.15
291	Chili Davis	.10
292	Orlando Hernandez	.15
293	Hideki Irabu	.10
294a	Derek Jeter/Action	2.50
294b	Derek Jeter/Portrait	2.50
295	Chuck Knoblauch	.10
296	Ricky Ledee	.10
297	Jim Leyritz	.10
298	Tino Martinez	.15
299	Paul O'Neill	.15
300	Andy Pettitte	.15
301	Jorge Posada	.15
302	Mariano Rivera	.25
303	Alfonso Soriano	.75
304a	Bernie Williams/Action	.20
304b	Bernie Williams/Portrait	.20
305	Ed Yarnall	.10
306	Kevin Appier	.10
307	Rich Becker	.10
308	Eric Chavez	.25
309	Jason Giambi	.60
310	Ben Grieve	.10
311	Ramon Hernandez	.10
312	Tim Hudson	.25
313	John Jaha	.10
314	Doug Jones	.10
315	Omar Olivares	.10
316	Mike Oquist	.10
317	Matt Stairs	.10
318	Miguel Tejada	.25
319	Randy Velarde	.10
320	Bobby Abreu	.15
321	Marlon Anderson	.10
322	Alex Arias	.10
323	Rico Brogna	.10
324	Paul Byrd	.10
325	Ron Gant	.10
326	Doug Glanville	.10
327	Wayne Gomes	.10
328	Mike Lieberthal	.10
329	Robert Person	.10
330	Desi Relaford	.10
331a	Scott Rolen/Action	.60
331b	Scott Rolen/Portrait	.60
332a	Curt Schilling/Action	.35
332b	Curt Schilling/Portrait	.35
333	Kris Benson	.10
334	Adrian Brown	.10
335	Brant Brown	.10
336	Brian Giles	.15
337	Chad Hermansen	.10
338	Jason Kendall	.15
339	Al Martin	.10
340	Pat Meares	.10
341a	Warren Morris/Action	.10
341b	Warren Morris/Portrait	.10
342	Todd Ritchie	.10
343	Jason Schmidt	.10
344	Ed Sprague	.10
345	Mike Williams	.10
346	Kevin Young	.10
347	Rick Ankiel	.15
348	Ricky Bottalico	.10
349	Kent Bottenfield	.10
350	Darren Bragg	.10
351	Eric Davis	.15
352a	J.D. Drew/Action	.35
352b	J.D. Drew/Portrait	.35
353	Adam Kennedy	.10
354	Ray Lankford	.10
355	Joe McEwing	.10
356a	Mark McGwire/Action	2.00
356b	Mark McGwire/Portrait	2.00
357	Matt Morris	.10
358	Darren Oliver	.10
359	Edgar Renteria	.10
360	Fernando Tatis	.10
361	Andy Ashby	.10
362	Ben Davis	.10
363a	Tony Gwynn/Action	1.00
363b	Tony Gwynn/Portrait	1.00
364	Sterling Hitchcock	.10
365	Trevor Hoffman	.10
366	Damian Jackson	.10
367	Wally Joyner	.10
368	Dave Magadan	.10
369	Gary Matthews Jr.	.10
370	Phil Nevin	.10
371	Eric Owens	.10
372	Ruben Rivera	.10
373a	Reggie Sanders/Action	.10
373b	Reggie Sanders/Portrait	.10
374	Quilvio Veras	.10
375	Rich Aurilia	.10
376	Marvin Benard	.10
377a	Barry Bonds/Action	2.50
377b	Barry Bonds/Portrait	2.50
378	Ellis Burks	.10
379	Shawn Estes	.10
380	Livan Hernandez	.10
381a	Jeff Kent/Action	.15
381b	Jeff Kent/Portrait	.15
382	Brent Mayne	.10
383	Bill Mueller	.10
384	Calvin Murray	.10
385	Robb Nen	.10
386	Russ Ortiz	.10
387	Kirk Rueter	.10
388	J.T. Snow	.15
389	David Bell	.10
390	Jay Buhner	.15
391	Russ Davis	.10
392a	Freddy Garcia/Action	.10
392b	Freddy Garcia/Portrait	.10
393a	Ken Griffey Jr./Action	1.50
393b	Ken Griffey Jr./Portrait	1.50
394	Carlos Guillen	.10
395	John Halama	.10
396	Brian Hunter	.10
397	Ryan Jackson	.10
398	Edgar Martinez	.15
399	Gil Meche	.10
400	Jose Mesa	.10
401	Jamie Moyer	.10
402a	Alex Rodriguez/Action	2.00
402b	Alex Rodriguez/Portrait	2.00
403	Dan Wilson	.10
404	Wilson Alvarez	.10
405	Rolando Arrojo	.10
406a	Wade Boggs/Action	1.00
406b	Wade Boggs/Portrait	1.00
407	Miguel Cairo	.10
408a	Jose Canseco/Action	.40
408b	Jose Canseco/Portrait	.40
409	John Flaherty	.10
410	Jose Guillen	.10
411	Roberto Hernandez	.10
412	Terrell Lowery	.10
413	Dave Martinez	.10
414	Quinton McCracken	.10
415a	Fred McGriff/Action	.15
415b	Fred McGriff/Portrait	.15
416	Ryan Rupe	.10
417	Kevin Stocker	.10
418	Bubba Trammell	.10
419	Royce Clayton	.10
420a	Juan Gonzalez/Action	.75
420b	Juan Gonzalez/Portrait	.75
421	Tom Goodwin	.10
422	Rusty Greer	.10
423	Rick Helling	.10
424	Roberto Kelly	.10
425	Ruben Mateo	.10
426	Mark McLemore	.10
427	Mike Morgan	.10
428	Rafael Palmeiro	.65
429a	Ivan Rodriguez/Action	.65
429b	Ivan Rodriguez/Portrait	.65
430	Aaron Sele	.10
431	Lee Stevens	.10
432	John Wetteland	.10
433	Todd Zeile	.10
434	Jeff Zimmerman	.10
435	Tony Batista	.10
436	Casey Blake	.10
437	Homer Bush	.10
438	Chris Carpenter	.10
439	Jose Cruz Jr.	.10
440a	Carlos Delgado/Action	.50
440b	Carlos Delgado/Portrait	.50
441	Tony Fernandez	.10
442	Darrin Fletcher	.10
443	Alex Gonzalez	.10
444a	Shawn Green/Action	.35
444b	Shawn Green/Portrait	.35
445	Roy Halladay	.20
446	Billy Koch	.10
447	David Segui	.10
448	Shannon Stewart	.10
449	David Wells	.10
450	Vernon Wells	.15

Copper

Coppers are a parallel set to the 500-card base set and are identical to the base cards besides the copper foil stamping. Inserted exclusively in hobby packs Coppers are limited to 99 serial numbered sets.

	NM/M
Common Copper:	5.00
Stars:	4-8X
Production 99 Sets	

Platinum Blue

A parallel to the 500-card base set these have identical photos as the regular cards besides platinum blue foil stamping. A total of 75 serial numbered sets were produced.

	NM/M
Common Player:	8.00
Stars:	6-10X
Production 75 Sets	

Premiere Date

A parallel to the 500-card base set these are sequentially numbered to 37 sets.

	NM/M
Common Player:	15.00
Stars:	8-15X
Production 37 Sets	

Ruby Red (Seven-11)

This parallel to the base set of 2000 Pacific was available only in 10-card retail "Jewel Collection" packs at Seven-11 convenience stores. Other than the use of red metallic foil for the player name and Pacific logo, the cards are identical to the regular-issue version.

	NM/M
Complete Set (500):	65.00
Common Player:	.15
Stars/Rookies:	1.5X

Command Performers

	NM/M
Complete Set (20):	45.00
Common Player:	1.00
Inserted 1:24 Retail	
1 Chipper Jones	3.00

SEAN CASEY

2	Greg Maddux	3.00
3	Cal Ripken Jr.	6.00
4	Nomar Garciaparra	4.00
5	Sammy Sosa	4.00
6	Sean Casey	1.00
7	Manny Ramirez	2.00
8	Larry Walker	1.00
9	Jeff Bagwell	2.00
10	Vladimir Guerrero	2.00
11	Mike Piazza	4.00
12	Roger Clemens	3.50
13	Derek Jeter	6.00
14	Mark McGwire	5.00
15	Tony Gwynn	3.00
16	Barry Bonds	6.00
17	Ken Griffey Jr.	4.00
18	Alex Rodriguez	5.00
19	Ivan Rodriguez	1.50
20	Shawn Green	1.25

Cramer's Choice Awards

This die-cut set is shaped in a trophy-like design on a holographic silver foil design. Cramer's Choice are seeded 1:721 packs.

		NM/M
Complete Set (10):		300.00
Common Player:		25.00
Inserted 1:721		
1	Chipper Jones	25.00
2	Cal Ripken Jr.	50.00
3	Nomar Garciaparra	30.00
4	Sammy Sosa	30.00
5	Mike Piazza	30.00
6	Derek Jeter	50.00
7	Mark McGwire	40.00
8	Tony Gwynn	25.00
9	Ken Griffey Jr.	30.00
10	Alex Rodriguez	40.00

Diamond Leaders

Designed on a horizontal format each card features three statistical leaders from the 1999 season for each respective team. Card fronts have gold holofoil stamping while card backs give statistical leaders for eight categories for the featured team. These were seeded 2:25 packs.

		NM/M
Complete Set (30):		25.00
Common Card:		.50
Inserted 2:25		
1	Anaheim Angels (Garret Anderson, Chuck Finley, Troy Percival, Mo Vaughn)	.50
2	Baltimore Orioles (Albert Belle, Mike Mussina, B.J. Surhoff)	.50
3	Boston Red Sox (Nomar Garciaparra, Pedro J. Martinez, Troy O'Leary)	3.00
4	Chicago White Sox (Ray Durham, Magglio Ordonez, Frank Thomas)	1.50
5	Cleveland Indians (Bartolo Colon, Manny Ramirez, Omar Vizquel)	1.50
6	Detroit Tigers (Deivi Cruz, Dave Mlicki, David Palmer)	.50
7	Kansas City Royals (Johnny Damon, Jermaine Dye, Jose Rosado, Mike Sweeney)	.50
8	Minnesota Twins (Corey Koskie, Eric Milton, Brad Radke)	.50
9	New York Yankees (Orlando Hernandez, Derek Jeter, Mariano Rivera, Bernie Williams)	4.00
10	Oakland Athletics (Jeremy Giambi, Tim Hudson, Matt Stairs)	1.00
11	Seattle Mariners (Freddy Garcia, Ken Griffey Jr., Edgar Martinez)	3.00
12	Tampa Bay Devil Rays (Jose Canseco, Roberto Hernandez, Fred McGriff)	.75
13	Texas Rangers (Rafael Palmeiro, Ivan Rodriguez, John Wetteland)	1.00
14	Toronto Blue Jays (Carlos Delgado, Shannon Stewart, David Wells)	1.00
15	Arizona Diamondbacks (Luis Gonzalez, Randy Johnson, Matt Williams)	1.50
16	Atlanta Braves (Chipper Jones, Brian Jordan, Greg Maddux)	2.00
17	Chicago Cubs (Mark Grace, Jon Lieber, Sammy Sosa)	3.00
18	Cincinnati Reds (Sean Casey, Pete Harnisch, Greg Vaughn)	.50
19	Colorado Rockies (Pedro Astacio, Dante Bichette, Larry Walker)	.50
20	Florida Marlins (Luis Castillo, Alex Fernandez, Preston Wilson)	.50
21	Houston Astros (Jeff Bagwell, Mike Hampton, Billy Wagner)	1.50
22	Los Angeles Dodgers (Kevin Brown, Mark Grudzielanek, Eric Karros)	.50
23	Milwaukee Brewers (Jeromy Burnitz, Jeff Cirillo, Marquis Grissom, Hideo Nomo)	1.00
24	Montreal Expos (Vladimir Guerrero, Dustin Hermanson, Ugueth Urbina)	1.50
25	New York Mets (Roger Cedeno, Rickey Henderson, Mike Piazza)	3.00
26	Philadelphia Phillies (Bobby Abreu, Mike Lieberthal, Curt Schilling)	.75
27	Pittsburgh Pirates (Brian Giles, Jason Kendall, Kevin Young)	.50
28	St. Louis Cardinals (Kent Bottenfield, Ray Lankford, Mark McGwire)	3.50
29	San Diego Padres (Tony Gwynn, Trevor Hoffman, Reggie Sanders)	2.00
30	San Francisco Giants (Barry Bonds, Jeff Kent, Russ Ortiz)	4.00

Gold Crown Die-Cuts

PALMEIRO — Texas Rangers

Printed on a 24-point stock this set features Pacific's classic crown shaped design on a dual foiled holographic gold and silver stock. These were seeded 1:25 packs.

		NM/M
Complete Set (36):		150.00
Common Player:		1.50
Inserted 1:25		
1	Mo Vaughn	1.50
2	Matt Williams	1.50
3	Andruw Jones	6.00
4	Chipper Jones	8.00
5	Greg Maddux	8.00
6	Cal Ripken Jr.	15.00
7	Nomar Garciaparra	10.00
8	Pedro Martinez	6.00
9	Sammy Sosa	10.00
10	Magglio Ordonez	2.50
11	Frank Thomas	6.00
12	Sean Casey	1.50
13	Roberto Alomar	2.50
14	Manny Ramirez	6.00
15	Larry Walker	1.50
16	Jeff Bagwell	6.00
17	Craig Biggio	1.50
18	Carlos Beltran	4.00
19	Vladimir Guerrero	6.00
20	Mike Piazza	10.00
21	Roger Clemens	9.00
22	Derek Jeter	15.00
23	Bernie Williams	2.00
24	Scott Rolen	5.00
25	Warren Morris	1.50
26	J.D. Drew	2.00
27	Mark McGwire	12.00
28	Tony Gwynn	8.00
29	Barry Bonds	15.00
30	Ken Griffey Jr.	10.00
31	Alex Rodriguez	12.00
32	Jose Canseco	2.00
33	Juan Gonzalez	6.00
34	Rafael Palmeiro	5.00
35	Ivan Rodriguez	5.00
36	Shawn Green	3.00

Reflections

This 20-card die-cut set features a unique sunglasses-on-cap design utilizing cel technology for added effect on the sunglasses portion of the insert. The backs have a small photo of the featured player. These were seeded 1:97 packs.

		NM/M
Common Player:		3.00
Inserted 1:97		
1	Andruw Jones	6.00
2	Chipper Jones	8.00
3	Cal Ripken Jr.	20.00
4	Nomar Garciaparra	12.00
5	Sammy Sosa	12.00
6	Frank Thomas	6.00
7	Manny Ramirez	6.00
8	Jeff Bagwell	6.00
9	Vladimir Guerrero	6.00
10	Mike Piazza	12.00
11	Derek Jeter	20.00
12	Bernie Williams	3.00
13	Scott Rolen	5.00
14	J.D. Drew	3.00
15	Mark McGwire	15.00
16	Tony Gwynn	8.00
17	Ken Griffey Jr.	12.00
18	Alex Rodriguez	15.00
19	Juan Gonzalez	6.00
20	Ivan Rodriguez	5.00

Past & Present

PRESENT — Larry Walker, Colorado Rockies

Inserted exclusively in hobby packs at a rate of 1:49, these inserts have a silver prism front and a cardboard textured back. The fronts have a current photo of the player while the backs have a photo taken years before.

		NM/M
Complete Set (20):		80.00
Common Player:		1.50
Inserted 1:49 H		
1	Chipper Jones	5.00
2	Greg Maddux	5.00
3	Cal Ripken Jr.	10.00
4	Nomar Garciaparra	6.00
5	Pedro Martinez	4.00
6	Sammy Sosa	6.00
7	Frank Thomas	4.00
8	Manny Ramirez	4.00
9	Larry Walker	1.50
10	Jeff Bagwell	4.00
11	Mike Piazza	6.00
12	Roger Clemens	5.50
13	Derek Jeter	10.00
14	Mark McGwire	8.00
15	Tony Gwynn	5.00
16	Barry Bonds	10.00
17	Ken Griffey Jr.	6.00
18	Alex Rodriguez	8.00
19	Wade Boggs	5.00
20	Ivan Rodriguez	3.00

Ornaments

This 20-card set features a number of different Christmas patterned die-cut shapes, including ornaments, wreaths and Christmas trees. Each card comes with a string intended to hang from a tree on a holographic foil design. These were seeded 2:25 packs.

		NM/M
Complete Set (20):		40.00
Common Player:		1.00
Inserted 2:25		
1	Mo Vaughn	1.00
2	Chipper Jones	3.00
3	Greg Maddux	3.00
4	Cal Ripken Jr.	6.00
5	Nomar Garciaparra	4.00
6	Sammy Sosa	4.00
7	Frank Thomas	2.00
8	Manny Ramirez	2.00
9	Larry Walker	1.00
10	Jeff Bagwell	2.00
11	Mike Piazza	4.00
12	Roger Clemens	3.50
13	Derek Jeter	6.00
14	Scott Rolen	1.50
15	J.D. Drew	1.25
16	Mark McGwire	5.00
17	Tony Gwynn	3.00
18	Ken Griffey Jr.	4.00
19	Alex Rodriguez	5.00
20	Ivan Rodriguez	1.50

2000 Pacific Aurora Sample

Nearly identical to the issued version of spokesman

Tony Gwynn's card, this features a large white diagonal "SAMPLE" overprint on back and in the space where a card number usually appears.

	NM/M
Tony Gwynn	3.00

2000 Pacific Aurora

		NM/M
Complete Set (151):		25.00
Common Player:		.15
Pack (10):		2.00
Wax Box (24):		30.00
1	Darin Erstad	.25
2	Troy Glaus	.75
3	Tim Salmon	.25
4	Mo Vaughn	.15
5	Jay Bell	.15
6	Erubiel Durazo	.15
7	Luis Gonzalez	.25
8	Randy Johnson	.75
9	Matt Williams	.15
10	Tom Glavine	.35
11	Andruw Jones	.75
12	Chipper Jones	1.00
13	Brian Jordan	.15
14	Greg Maddux	1.00
15	Kevin Millwood	.15
16	Albert Belle	.25
17	Will Clark	.25
18	Mike Mussina	.35
19	Cal Ripken Jr.	2.50
20	B.J. Surhoff	.15
21	Nomar Garciaparra	1.50
22	Pedro Martinez	.75
23	Troy O'Leary	.15
24	Wilton Veras	.15
25	Mark Grace	.25
26	Henry Rodriguez	.15
27	Sammy Sosa	1.50
28	Kerry Wood	.50
29	Ray Durham	.15
30	Paul Konerko	.25
31	Carlos Lee	.15
32	Magglio Ordonez	.25
33	Chris Singleton	.15
34	Frank Thomas	.75
35	Mike Cameron	.15
36	Sean Casey	.25
37	Barry Larkin	.15
38	Pokey Reese	.15
39	Eddie Taubensee	.15
40	Roberto Alomar	.40
41	David Justice	.15
42	Kenny Lofton	.15
43	Manny Ramirez	.75
44	Richie Sexson	.15
45	Jim Thome	.60
46	Omar Vizquel	.15
47	Todd Helton	.75
48	Mike Lansing	.15
49	Neifi Perez	.15
50	Ben Petrick	.15
51	Larry Walker	.15
52	Tony Clark	.15
53	Damion Easley	.15
54	Juan Encarnacion	.15
55	Juan Gonzalez	.75
56	Dean Palmer	.15
57	Luis Castillo	.15
58	Cliff Floyd	.15
59	Alex Gonzalez	.15
60	Mike Lowell	.15
61	Preston Wilson	.15
62	Jeff Bagwell	.75
63	Craig Biggio	.15
64	Ken Caminiti	.15
65	Jose Lima	.15
66	Billy Wagner	.15
67	Carlos Beltran	.50
68	Johnny Damon	.25
69	Jermaine Dye	.15
70	Mark Quinn	.15
71	Mike Sweeney	.15

72	Kevin Brown	.15
73	Shawn Green	.35
74	Eric Karros	.15
75	Chan Ho Park	.15
76	Gary Sheffield	.40
77	Ron Belliard	.15
78	Jeromy Burnitz	.15
79	Marquis Grissom	.15
80	Geoff Jenkins	.15
81	David Nilsson	.15
82	Ron Coomer	.15
83	Jacque Jones	.15
84	Brad Radke	.15
85	Todd Walker	.15
86	Michael Barrett	.15
87	Peter Bergeron	.15
88	Vladimir Guerrero	.75
89	Jose Vidro	.15
90	Rondell White	.15
91	Edgardo Alfonzo	.15
92	Darryl Hamilton	.15
93	Rey Ordonez	.15
94	Mike Piazza	1.50
95	Robin Ventura	.15
96	Roger Clemens	1.25
97	Orlando Hernandez	.15
98	Derek Jeter	2.50
99	Tino Martinez	.15
100	Mariano Rivera	.25
101	Bernie Williams	.25
102	Eric Chavez	.25
103	Jason Giambi	.60
104	Ben Grieve	.15
105	Tim Hudson	.25
106	John Jaha	.15
107	Matt Stairs	.15
108	Bobby Abreu	.15
109	Doug Glanville	.15
110	Mike Lieberthal	.15
111	Scott Rolen	.60
112	Curt Schilling	.40
113	Brian Giles	.15
114	Chad Hermansen	.15
115	Jason Kendall	.15
116	Warren Morris	.15
117	Kevin Young	.15
118	Rick Ankiel	.25
119	J.D. Drew	.25
120	Ray Lankford	.15
121	Mark McGwire	2.00
122	Edgar Renteria	.15
123	Fernando Tatis	.15
124	Ben Davis	.15
125	Tony Gwynn	1.00
126	Trevor Hoffman	.15
127	Phil Nevin	.15
128	Barry Bonds	2.50
129	Ellis Burks	.15
130	Jeff Kent	.15
131	J.T. Snow	.15
132	Freddy Garcia	.15
133	Ken Griffey Jr.	1.50
133a	Ken Griffey Jr. Reds	2.00
134	Edgar Martinez	.15
135	Alex Rodriguez	2.00
136	Dan Wilson	.15
137	Jose Canseco	.40
138	Roberto Hernandez	.15
139	Dave Martinez	.15
140	Fred McGriff	.15
141	Rusty Greer	.15
142	Ruben Mateo	.15
143	Rafael Palmeiro	.65
144	Ivan Rodriguez	.65
145	Jeff Zimmerman	.15
146	Homer Bush	.15
147	Carlos Delgado	.50
148	Raul Mondesi	.15
149	Shannon Stewart	.15
150	Vernon Wells	.15

Copper
Stars: 2-4X
Production 399 Sets

Platinum Blue
Stars: 5-10X
Production 67 Sets

Silver
Stars: 3-6X
Production 199 Sets

At-Bat Styrotechs

		NM/M
Complete Set (20):		125.00
Common Player:		2.00
Production 299 Sets		
1	Chipper Jones	7.50
2	Cal Ripken Jr.	15.00
3	Nomar Garciaparra	10.00
4	Sammy Sosa	10.00
5	Frank Thomas	6.00
6	Manny Ramirez	6.00
7	Larry Walker	2.00
8	Jeff Bagwell	6.00
9	Carlos Beltran	2.00
10	Vladimir Guerrero	6.00
11	Mike Piazza	10.00
12	Derek Jeter	15.00
13	Bernie Williams	2.00
14	Mark McGwire	12.00
15	Tony Gwynn	7.50
16	Barry Bonds	15.00
17	Ken Griffey Jr.	10.00
18	Alex Rodriguez	12.00
19	Jose Canseco	3.00
20	Ivan Rodriguez	5.00

Dugout View Net-Fusions

		NM/M
Complete Set (20):		110.00
Common Player:		2.50
Inserted 1:37		
1	Mo Vaughn	2.50
2	Chipper Jones	8.00
3	Cal Ripken Jr.	15.00
4	Nomar Garciaparra	10.00
5	Sammy Sosa	10.00
6	Manny Ramirez	6.00
7	Larry Walker	2.50
8	Juan Gonzalez	6.00
9	Jeff Bagwell	6.00
10	Craig Biggio	2.50
11	Shawn Green	3.00
12	Vladimir Guerrero	6.00
13	Mike Piazza	10.00
14	Derek Jeter	15.00
15	Scott Rolen	5.00
16	Mark McGwire	12.00
17	Tony Gwynn	8.00
18	Ken Griffey Jr.	10.00
19	Alex Rodriguez	12.00
20	Rafael Palmeiro	4.00

Pennant Fever

		NM/M
Complete Set (20):		25.00
Common Player:		1.00
Inserted 4:37		
1	Andruw Jones	1.50
2	Chipper Jones	2.00
3	Greg Maddux	2.00
4	Cal Ripken Jr.	4.00
5	Nomar Garciaparra	2.50
6	Pedro Martinez	1.50
7	Sammy Sosa	2.50
8	Manny Ramirez	1.50
9	Jim Thome	1.50
10	Jeff Bagwell	1.50
11	Mike Piazza	2.50
12	Roger Clemens	2.25
13	Derek Jeter	4.00
14	Bernie Williams	1.00
15	Mark McGwire	3.00
16	Tony Gwynn	2.00
17	Ken Griffey Jr.	2.50
18	Alex Rodriguez	3.00
19	Rafael Palmeiro	1.00
20	Ivan Rodriguez	1.00

Pinstripes

		NM/M
Complete Set (50):		30.00
Common Player:		.25
Premiere Date:		3-6X
Production 51 Sets		
4	Mo Vaughn	.25

8	Randy Johnson	1.50
9	Matt Williams	.25
11	Andruw Jones	1.50
12	Chipper Jones	2.00
14	Greg Maddux	2.00
19	Cal Ripken Jr.	4.00
21	Nomar Garciaparra	2.50
22	Pedro Martinez	1.50
27	Sammy Sosa	2.50
32	Magglio Ordonez	.35
34	Frank Thomas	.35
36	Sean Casey	.35
37	Barry Larkin	.25
42	Kenny Lofton	.25
43	Manny Ramirez	1.50
45	Jim Thome	1.50
47	Todd Helton	1.50
51	Larry Walker	.25
55	Juan Gonzalez	1.50
62	Jeff Bagwell	1.50
63	Craig Biggio	.25
67	Carlos Beltran	.50
73	Shawn Green	.40
76	Gary Sheffield	.40
78	Jeromy Burnitz	.25
88	Vladimir Guerrero	1.50
91	Edgardo Alfonzo	.25
94	Mike Piazza	2.50
96	Roger Clemens	2.25
97	Orlando Hernandez	.25
98	Derek Jeter	4.00
101	Bernie Williams	.35
102	Eric Chavez	.35
105	Tim Hudson	.35
111	Scott Rolen	1.25
112	Curt Schilling	.50
113	Brian Giles	.25
114	Rick Ankiel	.25
121	Mark McGwire	3.00
125	Tony Gwynn	2.00
128	Barry Bonds	4.00
130	Jeff Kent	.25
133	Ken Griffey Jr.	2.50
135	Alex Rodriguez	3.00
137	Jose Canseco	.50
140	Fred McGriff	.25
143	Rafael Palmeiro	.75
144	Ivan Rodriguez	.75
147	Carlos Delgado	1.00

Star Factor

		NM/M
Complete Set (10):		200.00
Common Player:		20.00
Inserted 1:361		
1	Chipper Jones	20.00
2	Cal Ripken Jr.	40.00
3	Nomar Garciaparra	25.00
4	Sammy Sosa	25.00
5	Mike Piazza	25.00
6	Derek Jeter	40.00
7	Mark McGwire	30.00
8	Tony Gwynn	20.00
9	Ken Griffey Jr.	25.00
10	Alex Rodriguez	30.00

2000 Pacific Crown Collection Sample

Nearly identical to the is-sued version of spokesman Tony Gwynn's card, this fea-tures a large white diagonal "SAMPLE" overprint on back and in the space where a card number usually appears.

		NM/M
Tony Gwynn		3.00

2000 Pacific Crown Collection

This 300-card base set has a white bordered design with the logo, player name and team stamped in gold foil. Card backs have a small close-up photo, a brief career highlight and 1999 statistics along with career totals.

		NM/M
Complete Set (300):		25.00
Common Player:		.10
Pack (10):		1.50
Wax Box (36):		30.00
1	Garret Anderson	.10
2	Darin Erstad	.25
3	Ben Molina	.10
4	Ramon Ortiz	.10
5	Orlando Palmeiro	.10
6	Troy Percival	.10
7	Tim Salmon	.15
8	Mo Vaughn	.25
9	Checklist (Mo Vaughn)	.10
10	Jay Bell	.10
11	Omar Daal	.10
12	Erubiel Durazo	.10
13	Steve Finley	.10
14	Hanley Frias	.10
15	Luis Gonzalez	.25
16	Randy Johnson	.75
17	Matt Williams	.10
18	Checklist (Matt Williams)	.10
19	Andres Galarraga	.10
20	Tom Glavine	.35
21	Andruw Jones	.75
22	Chipper Jones	1.00
23	Brian Jordan	.10
24	Javy Lopez	.10
25	Greg Maddux	1.00
26	Kevin Millwood	.10
27	Eddie Perez	.10
28	John Smoltz	.10
29	Checklist (Chipper Jones)	.50
30	Albert Belle	.15
31	Jesse Garcia	.10
32	Jerry Hairston Jr.	.10
33	Charles Johnson	.10
34	Mike Mussina	.30
35	Sidney Ponson	.10
36	Cal Ripken Jr.	2.50
37	B.J. Surhoff	.10
38	Checklist (Cal Ripken Jr.)	1.00
39	Nomar Garciaparra	1.50
40	Pedro Martinez	.75
41	Ramon Martinez	.10
42	Trot Nixon	.10
43	Jose Offerman	.10
44	Troy O'Leary	.10
45	John Valentin	.10
46	Wilton Veras	.10
47	Checklist (Nomar Garciaparra)	.75
48	Mark Grace	.15
49	Felix Heredia	.10
50	Jose Molina	.10
51	Jose Nieves	.10
52	Henry Rodriguez	.10
53	Sammy Sosa	1.50
54	Kerry Wood	.65
55	Checklist (Sammy Sosa)	.60
56	Mike Caruso	.10
57	Carlos Castillo	.10
58	Jason Dellaero	.10
59	Carlos Lee	.10
60	Magglio Ordonez	.25
61	Jesus Pena	.10
62	Liu Rodriguez	.10
63	Frank Thomas	.75
64	Checklist (Magglio Ordonez)	.15
65	Aaron Boone	.10
66	Mike Cameron	.10
67	Sean Casey	.20
68	Juan Guzman	.10
69	Barry Larkin	.10
70	Pokey Reese	.10
71	Eddie Taubensee	.10
72	Greg Vaughn	.10
73	Checklist (Sean Casey)	.15
74	Roberto Alomar	.25
75	Sandy Alomar Jr.	.10
76	Bartolo Colon	.10
77	Jacob Cruz	.10
78	Einar Diaz	.10
79	David Justice	.10
80	Kenny Lofton	.10
81	Manny Ramirez	.75
82	Richie Sexson	.10
83	Jim Thome	.75
84	Omar Vizquel	.10
85	Enrique Wilson	.10
86	Checklist (Manny Ramirez)	.40
87	Pedro Astacio	.10
88	Henry Blanco	.10
89	Vinny Castilla	.10
90	Edgard Clemente	.10
91	Todd Helton	.75
92	Neifi Perez	.10
93	Terry Shumpert	.10
94	Juan Sosa RC	.20
95	Larry Walker	.75
96	Checklist (Vinny Castilla)	.10
97	Tony Clark	.10
98	Deivi Cruz	.10
99	Damion Easley	.10
100	Juan Encarnacion	.10
101	Karim Garcia	.10
102	Luis Garcia	.10
103	Juan Gonzalez	.75
104	Jose Macias	.10
105	Dean Palmer	.10
106	Checklist (Juan Encarnacion)	.10
107	Antonio Alfonseca	.10
108	Armando Almanza	.10
109	Bruce Aven	.10
110	Luis Castillo	.10
111	Ramon Castro	.10
112	Alex Fernandez	.10
113	Cliff Floyd	.10
114	Alex Gonzalez	.10
115	Michael Tejera RC	.10
116	Preston Wilson	.10
117	Checklist (Luis Castillo)	.10
118	Jeff Bagwell	.75
119	Craig Biggio	.10
120	Jose Cabrera	.10
121	Tony Eusebio	.10
122	Carl Everett	.10
123	Ricky Gutierrez	.10
124	Mike Hampton	.10
125	Richard Hidalgo	.10
126	Jose Lima	.10
127	Billy Wagner	.10
128	Checklist (Jeff Bagwell)	.10
129	Carlos Beltran	.50
130	Johnny Damon	.25
131	Jermaine Dye	.10
132	Carlos Febles	.10
133	Jeremy Giambi	.10
134	Jose Rosado	.10
135	Rey Sanchez	.10
136	Jose Santiago	.10
137	Checklist (Carlos Beltran)	.10
138	Kevin Brown	.10
139	Craig Counsell	.10
140	Shawn Green	.40
141	Eric Karros	.10
142	Angel Pena	.10
143	Gary Sheffield	.25
144	Ismael Valdes	.10
145	Jose Vizcaino	.10
146	Devon White	.10
147	Checklist (Eric Karros)	.10
148	Ron Belliard	.10
149	Jeromy Burnitz	.10
150	Jeff Cirillo	.10
151	Marquis Grissom	.10
152	Geoff Jenkins	.10
153	Dave Nilsson	.10
154	Rafael Roque	.10
155	Jose Valentin	.10
156	Fernando Vina	.10
157	Jeromy Burnitz	.10
158	Chad Allen	.10
159	Ron Coomer	.10
160	Eddie Guardado	.10
161	Cristian Guzman	.10
162	Jacque Jones	.10
163	Javier Valentin	.10
164	Todd Walker	.10
165	Checklist (Ron Coomer)	.10
166	Michael Barrett	.10
167	Miguel Batista	.10
168	Vladimir Guerrero	.75
169	Wilton Guerrero	.10
170	Fernando Seguignol	.10
171	Ugueth Urbina	.10
172	Javier Vazquez	.10
173	Jose Vidro	.10
174	Rondell White	.10
175	Checklist (Vladimir Guerrero)	.25
176	Edgardo Alfonzo	.10
177	Armando Benitez	.10
178	Roger Cedeno	.10
179	Octavio Dotel	.10
180	Melvin Mora	.10
181	Rey Ordonez	.10
182	Mike Piazza	1.50
183	Jorge Toca	.10
184	Robin Ventura	.10
185	Checklist (Edgardo Alfonzo)	.10
186	Roger Clemens	1.25
187	David Cone	.10
188	Orlando Hernandez	.10
189	Derek Jeter	2.50
190	Ricky Ledee	.10
191	Tino Martinez	.10
192	Ramiro Mendoza	.10
193	Jorge Posada	.10
194	Mariano Rivera	.15
195	Alfonso Soriano	.75
196	Bernie Williams	.30
197	Checklist (Derek Jeter)	1.00
198	Eric Chavez	.15
199	Jason Giambi	.60
200	Ben Grieve	.10
201	Ramon Hernandez	.10
202	Tim Hudson	.25
203	John Jaha	.10
204	Omar Olivares	.10
205	Olmedo Saenz	.10
206	Matt Stairs	.10
207	Miguel Tejada	.20
208	Checklist (Tim Hudson)	.20
209	Rico Brogna	.10
210	Bobby Abreu	.10
211	Marlon Anderson	.10
212	Alex Arias	.10
213	Doug Glanville	.10
214	Robert Person	.10
215	Scott Rolen	.60
216	Curt Schilling	.35
217	Checklist (Scott Rolen)	.25
218	Francisco Cordova	.10
219	Brian Giles	.10
220	Jason Kendall	.10
221	Warren Morris	.10
222	Abraham Nunez	.10
223	Aramis Ramirez	.10
224	Jose Silva	.10
225	Kevin Young	.10
226	Checklist (Brian Giles)	.10
227	Rick Ankiel	.15
228	Ricky Bottalico	.10
229	J.D. Drew	.25
230	Ray Lankford	.10
231	Mark McGwire	2.00
232	Eduardo Perez	.10
233	Placido Polanco	.10
234	Edgar Renteria	.10
235	Fernando Tatis	.10
236	Checklist (Mark McGwire)	.85
237	Carlos Almanzar	.10
238	Wiki Gonzalez	.10
239	Tony Gwynn	1.00
240	Trevor Hoffman	.10
241	Damian Jackson	.10
242	Wally Joyner	.10
243	Ruben Rivera	.10
244	Reggie Sanders	.10
245	Quilvio Veras	.10
246	Checklist (Tony Gwynn)	.50
247	Rich Aurilia	.10
248	Marvin Benard	.10
249	Barry Bonds	2.50
250	Ellis Burks	.10
251	Miguel Del Toro	.10
252	Edwards Guzman	.10
253	Livan Hernandez	.10
254	Jeff Kent	.10
255	Russ Ortiz	.10
256	Armando Rios	.10
257	Checklist (Barry Bonds)	1.00
258	Rafael Bournigal	.10
259	Freddy Garcia	.10
260	Ken Griffey Jr.	15.00
261	Carlos Guillen	.10
262	Raul Ibanez	.10
263	Edgar Martinez	.10
264	Jose Mesa	.10
265	Jamie Moyer	.10
266	John Olerud	.10
267	Jose Paniagua	.10
268	Alex Rodriguez	2.00
269	Checklist (Alex Rodriguez)	1.00
270	Wilson Alvarez	.10
271	Rolando Arrojo	.10
272	Wade Boggs	1.00
273	Miguel Cairo	.10
274	Jose Canseco	.40
275	Jose Guillen	.10
276	Roberto Hernandez	.10
277	Albie Lopez	.10
278	Fred McGriff	.10

279	Esteban Yan	.10
280	Checklist	
	(Jose Canseco)	.20
281	Rusty Greer	.10
282	Roberto Kelly	.10
283	Esteban Loaiza	.10
284	Ruben Mateo	.10
285	Rafael Palmeiro	.65
286	Ivan Rodriguez	.65
287	Aaron Sele	.10
288	John Wetteland	.10
289	Checklist	
	(Ivan Rodriguez)	.25
290	Tony Batista	.10
291	Jose Cruz Jr.	.10
292	Carlos Delgado	.50
293	Kelvim Escobar	.10
294	Tony Fernandez	.10
295	Billy Koch	.10
296	Raul Mondesi	.10
297	Willis Otanez	.10
298	David Segui	.10
299	David Wells	.10
300	Checklist	
	(Carlos Delgado)	.20

Holographic Purple

A parallel to the 300-card base set, holographic purple stamping replaces the gold foil to differentiate these from the base cards. These are limited to 199 numbered sets.

Stars: 4-8X
Production 199 Sets

Platinum Blue

A parallel to the 300-card base set, these have blue foil stamping in place of gold foil and are limited to 67 serial numbered sets.

Stars: 8-15X
Production 67 Sets

In The Cage

These inserts have a die-cut design around an image of a batting cage, with net-fusion technology used to mimic the netting in a batting cage. These were inserted 1:145 packs.

		NM/M
Complete Set (20):		250.00
Common Player:		5.00
Inserted 1:145		
1	Mo Vaughn	5.00
2	Chipper Jones	15.00
3	Cal Ripken Jr.	30.00
4	Nomar Garciaparra	20.00
5	Sammy Sosa	15.00
6	Frank Thomas	10.00
7	Roberto Alomar	6.00
8	Manny Ramirez	10.00
9	Larry Walker	5.00
10	Jeff Bagwell	10.00
11	Vladimir Guerrero	10.00
12	Mike Piazza	20.00
13	Derek Jeter	30.00
14	Bernie Williams	5.00
15	Mark McGwire	25.00
16	Tony Gwynn	15.00
17	Ken Griffey Jr.	20.00
18	Alex Rodriguez	25.00
19	Rafael Palmeiro	8.00
20	Ivan Rodriguez	8.00

Latinos of the Major Leagues

ORLANDO HERNANDEZ

This set salutes major league's who have a latino heritage. These were seeded 2:37 packs and have a horizontal format with two images of the featured player on the card front.

		NM/M
Complete Set (36):		20.00
Common Player:		.25
Inserted 2:37		
Parallel:		2-4X
Production 99 Sets		
1	Erubiel Durazo	.25
2	Luis Gonzalez	.25
3	Andruw Jones	1.00
4	Nomar Garciaparra	2.00
5	Pedro Martinez	1.00
6	Sammy Sosa	2.00
7	Carlos Lee	.25
8	Magglio Ordonez	.25
9	Roberto Alomar	.65
10	Manny Ramirez	1.00
11	Omar Vizquel	.25
12	Vinny Castilla	.25
13	Juan Gonzalez	1.00
14	Luis Castillo	.25
15	Jose Lima	.25
16	Carlos Beltran	.75
17	Vladimir Guerrero	1.00
18	Edgardo Alfonzo	.25
19	Roger Cedeno	.25
20	Rey Ordonez	.25
21	Orlando Hernandez	.25
22	Tino Martinez	.25
23	Mariano Rivera	.35
24	Bernie Williams	.50
25	Miguel Tejada	.50
26	Bobby Abreu	.25
27	Fernando Tatis	.25
28	Freddy Garcia	.25
29	Edgar Martinez	.25
30	Alex Rodriguez	3.00
31	Jose Canseco	.65
32	Ruben Mateo	.25
33	Rafael Palmeiro	.75
34	Ivan Rodriguez	.75
35	Carlos Delgado	.65
36	Raul Mondesi	.25

Moment of Truth

These inserts feature gold foil stamping and a shadow image of the player in the background of the player photo. These were inserted 1:37 packs.

		NM/M
Complete Set (30):		50.00
Common Player:		.50
Inserted 1:37		
1	Mo Vaughn	3.00
2	Chipper Jones	3.00
3	Greg Maddux	3.00
4	Albert Belle	.50
5	Cal Ripken Jr.	6.00
6	Nomar Garciaparra	4.00
7	Pedro Martinez	4.00
8	Sammy Sosa	4.00
9	Frank Thomas	4.00
10	Barry Larkin	.50
11	Kenny Lofton	.50
12	Manny Ramirez	2.00
13	Larry Walker	.50
14	Juan Gonzalez	2.00
15	Jeff Bagwell	2.00
16	Craig Biggio	2.00
17	Carlos Beltran	1.00
18	Vladimir Guerrero	2.00
19	Mike Piazza	4.00
20	Roger Clemens	3.50
21	Derek Jeter	6.00
22	Bernie Williams	.75
23	Mark McGwire	5.00
24	Tony Gwynn	6.00
25	Barry Bonds	6.00
26	Ken Griffey Jr.	4.00
27	Alex Rodriguez	5.00
28	Rafael Palmeiro	1.50
29	Ivan Rodriguez	1.50
30	Carlos Delgado	1.50

Pacific Cup

Pacific Cup's have a horizontal format with gold foil stamping and an image of a

trophy cup beside the player photo. These were inserted 1:721 packs.

		NM/M
Complete Set (10):		220.00
Inserted 1:721		
1	Cal Ripken Jr.	40.00
2	Nomar Garciaparra	25.00
3	Pedro Martinez	15.00
4	Sammy Sosa	25.00
5	Vladimir Guerrero	15.00
6	Derek Jeter	40.00
7	Mark McGwire	35.00
8	Tony Gwynn	20.00
9	Ken Griffey Jr.	25.00
10	Alex Rodriguez	35.00

Timber 2000

These 1:73 pack inserts have a horizontal format highlighted by gold foil stamping. A black bat is in the background of the player image with 2000 written in the bat head.

		NM/M
Complete Set (20):		100.00
Common Player:		2.00
Inserted 1:73		
1	Chipper Jones	8.00
2	Nomar Garciaparra	10.00
3	Sammy Sosa	10.00
4	Magglio Ordonez	2.00
5	Manny Ramirez	6.00
6	Vinny Castilla	2.00
7	Juan Gonzalez	6.00
8	Jeff Bagwell	6.00
9	Shawn Green	3.00
10	Vladimir Guerrero	6.00
11	Mike Piazza	10.00
12	Derek Jeter	15.00
13	Bernie Williams	2.00
14	Mark McGwire	12.00
15	Ken Griffey Jr.	10.00
16	Alex Rodriguez	12.00
17	Jose Canseco	3.00
18	Rafael Palmeiro	5.00
19	Ivan Rodriguez	5.00
20	Carlos Delgado	4.00

2000 Pacific Crown Royale

The Crown Royale 144-card base set has a horizontal format die-cut around a crown design at the top. The cards are double foiled with gold and silver foil etching.

		NM/M
Complete Set (144):		40.00
Common Player:		.25
Common SP:		1.00
Pack (6):		2.50
Box (24):		45.00
1	Darin Erstad	.40
2	Troy Glaus	1.00
3	Adam Kennedy/SP	1.00
4	Derrick Turnbow/SP RC	1.00
5	Mo Vaughn	.25
6	Erubiel Durazo	.25
7	Steve Finley	.25
8	Randy Johnson	1.00
9	Travis Lee	.25
10	Matt Williams	.25
11	Rafael Furcal/SP	1.00
12	Andres Galarraga	.25
13	Andruw Jones	1.00
14	Chipper Jones	1.50
15	Javy Lopez	.25
16	Greg Maddux	1.50
17	Albert Belle	.25
18	Will Clark	.35
19	Mike Mussina	.40
20	Cal Ripken Jr.	3.00
21	Carl Everett	.25
22	Nomar Garciaparra	2.00
23	Pedro Martinez	1.00
24	Jason Varitek	.25
25	Scott Downs/SP RC	.25
26	Mark Grace	.35
27	Sammy Sosa	2.00
28	Kerry Wood	.65
29	Ray Durham	.25
30	Paul Konerko	.25
31	Carlos Lee	.25
32	Magglio Ordonez	.40
33	Frank Thomas	1.00
34	Rob Bell SP	1.00
35	Sean Casey	.25
36	Ken Griffey Jr.	2.00
37	Barry Larkin	.25
38	Pokey Reese	.25
39	Roberto Alomar	.40
40	David Justice	.25
41	Kenny Lofton	.25
42	Manny Ramirez	1.00
43	Richie Sexson	.25
44	Jim Thome	.75
45	Rolando Arrojo	.25
46	Jeff Cirillo	.25
47	Tom Goodwin	.25
48	Todd Helton	1.00
49	Larry Walker	.25
50	Tony Clark	.25
51	Juan Encarnacion	.25
52	Juan Gonzalez	1.00
53	Hideo Nomo	1.00
54	Dean Palmer	.25
55	Cliff Floyd	.25
56	Alex Gonzalez	.25
57	Mike Lowell	.25
58	Brad Penny SP	1.00
59	Preston Wilson	.25
60	Moises Alou	.25
61	Jeff Bagwell	1.00
62	Craig Biggio	.25
63	Roger Cedeno	.25
64	Julio Lugo/SP	1.00
65	Carlos Beltran	.60
66	Johnny Damon	.40
67	Jermaine Dye	.25
68	Carlos Febles	.25
69	Mark Quinn/SP	1.00
70	Kevin Brown	.25
71	Shawn Green	.50
72	Eric Karros	.25
73	Gary Sheffield	.50
74	Kevin Barker/SP	1.00
75	Ron Belliard	.25
76	Jeromy Burnitz	.25
77	Geoff Jenkins	.25
78	Jacque Jones	.25
79	Corey Koskie	.25
80	Matt LeCroy/SP	1.00
81	Brad Radke	.25
82	Peter Bergeron/SP	1.00
83	Matt Blank/SP	1.00
84	Vladimir Guerrero	1.00
85	Hideki Irabu	.25
86	Rondell White	.25
87	Edgardo Alfonzo	.25
88	Mike Hampton	.25
89	Rickey Henderson	1.00
90	Rey Ordonez	.25
91	Jay Payton/SP	1.00
92	Mike Piazza	2.00
93	Roger Clemens	1.75
94	Orlando Hernandez	.25
95	Derek Jeter	3.00
96	Tino Martinez	.25
97	Alfonso Soriano/SP	2.50
98	Bernie Williams	.40
99	Eric Chavez	.40
100	Jason Giambi	.75
101	Ben Grieve	.25
102	Tim Hudson	.50
103	Terrence Long/SP	1.00
104	Mark Mulder/SP	1.00
105	Adam Piatt/SP	1.00
106	Bobby Abreu	.25
107	Doug Glanville	.25
108	Mike Lieberthal	.25
109	Scott Rolen	.75
110	Brian Giles	.25
111	Chad Hermansen/SP	1.00
112	Jason Kendall	.25
113	Warren Morris	.25
114	Rick Ankiel SP	1.00
115	Justin Brunette/SP RC	1.00
116	J.D. Drew	.40
117	Mark McGwire	2.50
118	Fernando Tatis	.25
119	Wiki Gonzalez/SP	1.00
120	Tony Gwynn	1.50
121	Trevor Hoffman	.25
122	Ryan Klesko	.25
123	Barry Bonds	3.00
124	Ellis Burks	.25
125	Jeff Kent	.25
126	Calvin Murray/SP	1.00
127	J.T. Snow	.25
128	Freddy Garcia	.25
129	John Olerud	.25
130	Alex Rodriguez	2.50
131	Kazuhiro Sasaki/SP RC	3.00
132	Jose Canseco	.50
133	Vinny Castilla	.25
134	Fred McGriff	.25
135	Greg Vaughn	.25
136	Gabe Kapler	.25
137	Mike Lamb/SP RC	1.00
138	Ruben Mateo/SP	1.00
139	Rafael Palmeiro	.75
140	Ivan Rodriguez	.75
141	Tony Batista	.25
142	Carlos Delgado	.75
143	Raul Mondesi	.25
144	Shannon Stewart	.25

Limited Series

A parallel to the 144-card base set, silver foil replaces gold foil to differentiate these from regular cards. They are also limited to 144 serial numbered sets.

Stars: 2-4X
Production 144 Sets

Red

Identical in design to the base set, these have red foil instead of gold and are the base cards in retail packaging.

All singles: 1X
Base cards in retail packs.

Platinum Blue

A parallel to the 144-card base set these have blue foil in place of gold foil to differentiate them from regular cards. They are limited to 75 serial numbered sets.

Stars: 3-6X
Production 75 Sets

Premiere Date

A parallel to the 144-card base set these are found exclusively in hobby packs and are limited to 121 serial numbered sets.

Stars: 2-4X
Production 121 Sets

Card-Supials

These inserts feature a superstar's regular sized card paired with a top prospect teammate's smaller card. The standard sized card has a horizontal format with gold foil stamping, the small prospect card has gold foil stamping on a vertical format. These were seeded 2:25 packs.

		NM/M
Complete Set (20):		40.00
Common Card:		1.00
Inserted 2:25		
1	Randy Johnson, Erubiel Durazo	2.00
2	Chipper Jones, Andruw Jones	3.00
3	Cal Ripken Jr., Matt Riley	6.00
4	Nomar Garciaparra, Jason Varitek	4.00
5	Sammy Sosa, Kerry Wood	4.00
6	Frank Thomas, Magglio Ordonez	4.00
7	Ken Griffey Jr., Sean Casey	2.00
8	Manny Ramirez, Richie Sexson	2.00
9	Larry Walker, Ben Petrick	2.00
10	Juan Gonzalez, Juan Encarnacion	2.00
11	Jeff Bagwell, Lance Berkman	2.00
12	Shawn Green, Eric Gagne	1.00
13	Vladimir Guerrero, Peter Bergeron	2.00
14	Mike Piazza, Edgardo Alfonzo	4.00
15	Derek Jeter, Alfonso Soriano	5.00
16	Scott Rolen, Bobby Abreu	1.50
17	Mark McGwire, Rick Ankiel	5.00
18	Tony Gwynn, Ben Davis	3.00
19	Alex Rodriguez, Freddy Garcia	5.00
20	Ivan Rodriguez, Ruben Mateo	1.50

Cramer's Choice Jumbo

This enlarged 10-card set is die-cut into a trophy shape. The jumbo cards are enhanced with a silver holo-foiled front with gold foil stamping and etching across the bottom portion. These were found one per box exclusively in hobby boxes. Six parallels also were randomly inserted with each individual color replacing the gold foil stamping. Aqua's are limited to 20 numbered sets, Blue's 35 sets, Gold's 10 sets, Green's 30 sets, Purple's one set and Red's 25 sets.

		NM/M
Complete Set (10):		35.00
Common Player:		1.00
Inserted 1:box H		
Aqua:		5-10X
Production 20 Sets		
Blue:		2-5X
Production 35 Sets		
Gold:		10-20X
Production 10 Sets		
Green:		3-6X
Production 30 Sets		
Red:		4-8X
Production 25 Sets		
1	Cal Ripken Jr.	6.00
2	Nomar Garciaparra	4.00
3	Ken Griffey Jr.	4.00
4	Sammy Sosa	4.00
5	Mike Piazza	4.00
6	Derek Jeter	6.00
7	Rick Ankiel	1.00
8	Mark McGwire	5.00
9	Tony Gwynn	2.00
10	Alex Rodriguez	5.00

Feature Attractions

This 25-card set has a horizontal format with the featured players achievements on a billboard in the background. These were seeded 1 per hobby pack and one per two retail packs. An Exclusive Showing parallel is also randomly inserted and is limited to 20 serial numbered sets.

		NM/M
Complete Set (25):		10.00
Common Player:		.25
Inserted 1:1		
Exclusive Showing:		30-50X
Production 20 Sets		
1	Erubiel Durazo	.25
2	Chipper Jones	1.00
3	Greg Maddux	1.00
4	Cal Ripken Jr.	2.50
5	Nomar Garciaparra	1.50
6	Pedro Martinez	.75
7	Sammy Sosa	1.50

ABBREVIATIONS

SP - Short Print

8	Frank Thomas	.75
9	Ken Griffey Jr.	1.50
10	Manny Ramirez	.75
11	Larry Walker	.25
12	Juan Gonzalez	.75
13	Jeff Bagwell	.75
14	Carlos Beltran	.50
15	Shawn Green	.50
16	Vladimir Guerrero	.75
17	Mike Piazza	1.50
18	Roger Clemens	1.25
19	Derek Jeter	2.50
20	Ben Grieve	.25
21	Rick Ankiel	.35
22	Mark McGwire	2.00
23	Tony Gwynn	1.00
24	Alex Rodriguez	2.00
25	Ivan Rodriguez	.65

Final Numbers

These inserts are found one per hobby pack and one per two retail packs. The logo, player name and team are stamped in silver foil and has "Final Numbers" written down the right hand portion of the front. A holographic parallel limited to 10 serial numbered sets is also randomly inserted.

		NM/M
Complete Set (25):		10.00
Common Player:		.25
Inserted 1:1		
1	Randy Johnson	.75
2	Andruw Jones	.75
3	Chipper Jones	1.00
4	Cal Ripken Jr.	2.50
5	Nomar Garciaparra	1.50
6	Pedro Martinez	.75
7	Sammy Sosa	1.50
8	Ken Griffey Jr.	1.50
9	Sean Casey	.35
10	Manny Ramirez	.75
11	Larry Walker	.75
12	Jeff Bagwell	.75
13	Craig Biggio	.25
14	Shawn Green	.50
15	Vladimir Guerrero	.75
16	Mike Piazza	1.50
17	Derek Jeter	2.50
18	Bernie Williams	.35
19	Scott Rolen	.65
20	Mark McGwire	2.00
21	Tony Gwynn	1.00
22	Barry Bonds	2.50
23	Alex Rodriguez	2.00
24	Jose Canseco	.40
25	Ivan Rodriguez	.65

Jumbo

These jumbo cards are identical in design to the base cards besides their enlarged size. These were found exclusively in hobby boxes and were found as a box topper in 6:10 boxes.

		NM/M
Complete Set (6):		25.00
Inserted 6:10 Boxes H		
1	Cal Ripken Jr.	6.00
2	Nomar Garciaparra	4.00
3	Ken Griffey Jr.	4.00
4	Derek Jeter	6.00
5	Mark McGwire	5.00
6	Alex Rodriguez	5.00

Proofs

Proofs are the actual printer's proofs used to produce this set. The inserts are transparent and have a coal black tint. These were inserted 1:25 packs. A parallel is also randomly inserted and is limited to 50 serial numbered sets.

		NM/M
Complete Set (36):		90.00
Common Player:		1.00
Inserted 1:25		
Proofs:		2-3X
1	Erubiel Durazo	1.50
2	Randy Johnson	3.00
3	Chipper Jones	5.00
4	Greg Maddux	5.00
5	Cal Ripken Jr.	8.00
6	Nomar Garciaparra	8.00
7	Pedro Martinez	3.00
8	Sammy Sosa	5.00
9	Frank Thomas	2.50
10	Sean Casey	1.50
11	Ken Griffey Jr.	5.00
12	Manny Ramirez	2.50
13	Jim Thome	2.50
14	Larry Walker	1.50
15	Juan Gonzalez	2.50
16	Jeff Bagwell	2.50
17	Craig Biggio	1.50
18	Carlos Beltran	2.00
19	Shawn Green	2.00
20	Vladimir Guerrero	2.50
21	Edgardo Alfonzo	1.00
22	Mike Piazza	5.00
23	Roger Clemens	6.00
24	Derek Jeter	10.00
25	Alfonso Soriano	4.00
26	Bernie Williams	2.00
27	Ben Grieve	1.00
28	Rick Ankiel	1.00
29	Mark McGwire	8.00
30	Tony Gwynn	3.00
31	Barry Bonds	8.00
32	Alex Rodriguez	8.00
33	Jose Canseco	2.00
34	Vinny Castilla	1.00
35	Ivan Rodriguez	2.00
36	Rafael Palmeiro	2.00

Sweet Spot Signatures

These die-cut autographed cards are done on a horizontal format with an image of a baseball beside the player photo. The signature is on the "sweet spot" of the baseball image. Red foil stamping is used on the seams of the baseball and the player name. No insertion ratio was announced.

		NM/M
Common Player:		5.00
1	Adam Kennedy	5.00
2	Trot Nixon	8.00
3	Magglio Ordonez	10.00
4	Sean Casey	8.00
5	Travis Dawkins	5.00
6	Todd Helton	25.00
7	Ben Petrick	5.00
8	Jeff Weaver	6.00
9	Preston Wilson	5.00
10	Lance Berkman	10.00
11	Roger Cedeno	5.00
12	Eric Gagne	10.00
13	Kevin Barker	5.00
14	Kyle Peterson	5.00
15	Tony Armas Jr.	5.00
16	Peter Bergeron	5.00
17	Alfonso Soriano	40.00
18	Ben Grieve	5.00
19	Ramon Hernandez	5.00
20	Brian Giles	8.00
21	Chad Hermansen	5.00
22	Warren Morris	5.00
23	Ben Davis	5.00
24	Rick Ankiel	5.00
25	Chad Hutchinson	5.00
26	Freddy Garcia	10.00
27	Gabe Kapler	5.00
28	Ruben Mateo	5.00
29	Billy Koch	5.00
30	Vernon Wells	5.00

2000 Pacific Invincible

The base set consists of 150 cards. The player image is on an acetate stock with a blue

sky background. The rest of the card is on standard UV coated stock and has the player name stamped in gold foil.

		NM/M
Complete Set (150):		75.00
Common Player:		.25
Pack (3):		2.00
Box (36):		50.00
1	Darin Erstad	.50
2	Troy Glaus	1.50
3	Ramon Ortiz	.25
4	Tim Salmon	.35
5	Mo Vaughn	.25
6	Erubiel Durazo	.25
7	Luis Gonzalez	.35
8	Randy Johnson	1.50
9	Matt Williams	.25
10	Rafael Furcal	.25
11	Andres Galarraga	.25
12	Tom Glavine	.40
13	Andruw Jones	1.50
14	Chipper Jones	2.00
15	Greg Maddux	2.00
16	Kevin Millwood	.25
17	Albert Belle	.35
18	Will Clark	.35
19	Mike Mussina	.40
20	Matt Riley	.25
21	Cal Ripken Jr.	4.00
22	Carl Everett	.25
23	Nomar Garciaparra	2.50
24	Steve Lomasney	.25
25	Pedro Martinez	1.50
26	Tomo Ohka RC	.75
27	Wilton Veras	.25
28	Mark Grace	.35
29	Sammy Sosa	2.50
30	Kerry Wood	.75
31	Eric Young	.25
32	Julio Zuleta RC	.25
33	Paul Konerko	.25
34	Carlos Lee	.25
35	Magglio Ordonez	.35
36	Josh Paul	.25
37	Frank Thomas	1.50
38	Rob Bell	.25
39	Dante Bichette	.25
40	Sean Casey	.35
41	Ken Griffey Jr.	2.50
42	Barry Larkin	.25
43	Pokey Reese	.25
44	Roberto Alomar	.35
45	Manny Ramirez	1.50
46	Richie Sexson	.25
47	Jim Thome	1.50
48	Omar Vizquel	.25
49	Jeff Cirillo	.25
50	Todd Helton	1.50
51	Neifi Perez	.25
52	Larry Walker	.25
53	Tony Clark	.25
54	Juan Encarnacion	.25
55	Juan Gonzalez	1.50
56	Hideo Nomo	1.00
57	Luis Castillo	.25
58	Alex Gonzalez	.25
59	Brad Penny	.25
60	Preston Wilson	.25
61	Moises Alou	.25
62	Jeff Bagwell	1.50
63	Lance Berkman	.25
64	Craig Biggio	.25
65	Roger Cedeno	.25
66	Jose Lima	.25
67	Carlos Beltran	.50
68	Johnny Damon	.35
69	Chad Durbin RC	.50
70	Jermaine Dye	.25
71	Carlos Febles	.25
72	Mark Quinn	.25
73	Kevin Brown	.25
74	Eric Gagne	.25
75	Shawn Green	.50
76	Eric Karros	.25
77	Gary Sheffield	.40
78	Kevin Barker	.25
79	Ron Belliard	.25
80	Jeromy Burnitz	.25
81	Geoff Jenkins	.25
82	Jacque Jones	.25
83	Corey Koskie	.25
84	Matt LeCroy	.25
85	David Ortiz	.25
86	Johan Santana RC	20.00
87	Todd Walker	.25
88	Peter Bergeron	.25
89	Vladimir Guerrero	1.50
90	Jose Vidro	.25
91	Rondell White	.25
92	Edgardo Alfonzo	.25
93	Derek Bell	.25
94	Mike Hampton	.25
95	Rey Ordonez	.25
96	Mike Piazza	2.50
97	Robin Ventura	.25
98	Roger Clemens	2.25
99	Orlando Hernandez	.25
100	Derek Jeter	4.00
101	Alfonso Soriano	.75
102	Bernie Williams	.35
103	Eric Chavez	.40
104	Jason Giambi	.75
105	Ben Grieve	.25
106	Tim Hudson	.40
107	Miguel Tejada	.40
108	Bobby Abreu	.25
109	Doug Glanville	.25
110	Mike Lieberthal	.25
111	Scott Rolen	.75
112	Brian Giles	.25
113	Chad Hermansen	.25
114	Jason Kendall	.25
115	Warren Morris	.25
116	Aramis Ramirez	.25
117	Rick Ankiel	.25
118	J.D. Drew	.40
119	Mark McGwire	3.00
120	Fernando Tatis	.25
121	Fernando Vina	.25
122	Bret Boone	.25
123	Ben Davis	.25
124	Tony Gwynn	2.00
125	Trevor Hoffman	.25
126	Ryan Klesko	.25
127	Rich Aurilia	.25
128	Barry Bonds	4.00
129	Ellis Burks	.25
130	Jeff Kent	.25
131	Freddy Garcia	.25
132	Carlos Guillen	.25
133	Edgar Martinez	.25
134	John Olerud	.25
135	Robert Ramsay	.25
136	Alex Rodriguez	3.00
137	Kazuhiro Sasaki RC	3.00
138	Jose Canseco	.50
139	Vinny Castilla	.25
140	Fred McGriff	.25
141	Greg Vaughn (Front photo is Mo Vaughn.)	.25
142	Dan Wheeler	.25
143	Gabe Kapler	.25
144	Ruben Mateo	.25
145	Rafael Palmeiro	.75
146	Ivan Rodriguez	.75
147	Tony Batista	.25
148	Carlos Delgado	.65
149	Raul Mondesi	.25
150	Vernon Wells	.25

Holographic Purple

A parallel to the 150-card set, holographic purple stamping replaces the gold foil from the base cards. These are limited to 299 serial numbered sets.

Stars:	2-3X
Production 299 Sets	

Platinum Blue

A parallel to the 150-card base set these differ only from the regular cards in that blue foil stamping replaces gold. Each card is also serially numbered on the card front in an edition of 67 sets.

Stars:	4-8X
Production 67 Sets	

Diamond Aces

This insert set highlights the top pitchers in the game. Silver-foil stamping is used on the card fronts, which are designed to duplicate the look of an Ace in a deck of of play-

ing cards. These were seeded 1 per pack. A parallel limited to 399 serial numbered sets is also randomly seeded.

		NM/M
Complete Set (20):		5.00
Common Player:		.25
Inserted 1:1		
Edition of 399 Parallel:		2-3X
1	Randy Johnson	.75
2	Greg Maddux	1.00
3	Tom Glavine	.40
4	John Smoltz	.25
5	Mike Mussina	.50
6	Pedro Martinez	.75
7	Kerry Wood	.60
8	Bartolo Colon	.25
9	Brad Penny	.25
10	Billy Wagner	.25
11	Kevin Brown	.25
12	Mike Hampton	.25
13	Roger Clemens	1.50
14	David Cone	.25
15	Orlando Hernandez	.25
16	Mariano Rivera	.40
17	Tim Hudson	.40
18	Trevor Hoffman	.25
19	Rick Ankiel	.25
20	Freddy Garcia	.25

Eyes of the World

This 20-card set has a horizontal format with gold foil stamping. The background of the player photo has a partial globe with a star and the country the featured player is from stamped in gold foil. These were inserted 1:25 packs.

		NM/M
Complete Set (20):		30.00
Common Player:		.75
Inserted 1:25		
1	Erubiel Durazo	.75
2	Andruw Jones	2.00
3	Cal Ripken Jr.	6.00
4	Nomar Garciaparra	4.00
5	Pedro Martinez	2.00
6	Sammy Sosa	4.00
7	Ken Griffey Jr.	4.00
8	Manny Ramirez	2.00
9	Larry Walker	.75
10	Juan Gonzalez	2.00
11	Carlos Beltran	1.25
12	Vladimir Guerrero	2.00
13	Orlando Hernandez	.75
14	Derek Jeter	6.00
15	Mark McGwire	5.00
16	Tony Gwynn	3.00
17	Freddy Garcia	.75
18	Alex Rodriguez	5.00
19	Jose Canseco	1.25
20	Ivan Rodriguez	1.50

Game Gear

		NM/M
Common Card:		4.00
1	Jeff Bagwell/Jsy/1000	8.00
2	Tom Glavine/Jsy/1000	6.00
3	Mark Grace/Jsy/1000	8.00
4	Eric Karros/Jsy/1000	4.00
5	Edgar Martinez/ Jsy/800	6.00
6	Manny Ramirez/ Jsy/975	8.00
7	Cal Ripken Jr./ Jsy/1000	25.00
8	Alex Rodriguez/ Jsy/900	15.00
9	Ivan Rodriguez/ Jsy/675	6.00
10	Mo Vaughn/Jsy/1000	4.00
11	Edgar Martinez/ Bat-Jsy/200	8.00
12	Manny Ramirez/ Jsy/145	15.00
13	Alex Rodriguez/ Bat-Jsy/200	25.00
14	Ivan Rodriguez/ Bat-Jsy/200	10.00
15	Edgar Martinez/ Bat/200	10.00
16	Manny Ramirez/ Bat/200	15.00
17	Ivan Rodriguez/ Bat/200	8.00
18	Alex Rodriguez/ Bat/200	20.00
19	Jeff Bagwell Patch/125	30.00
20	Tom Glavine Patch/110	25.00
21	Mark Grace Patch/125	25.00
22	Tony Gwynn Patch/65	40.00
23	Chipper Jones Patch/80	40.00
24	Eric Karros Patch/125	15.00
25	Greg Maddux Patch/80	50.00
26	Edgar Martinez Patch/125	20.00
27	Manny Ramirez Patch/125	30.00
28	Cal Ripken Jr. Patch/125	65.00
29	Alex Rodriguez Patch/125	50.00
30	Ivan Rodriguez Patch/125	25.00
31	Frank Thomas Patch/125	25.00
32	Mo Vaughn Patch/125	15.00

Kings of the Diamond

Twenty of the top hitters in the game are featured on a design intended to duplicate the look of a King card in a playing deck of cards. These were seeded 1 per pack. A parallel version limited to 299 serial numbered sets is also randomly seeded.

		NM/M
Complete Set (30):		10.00
Common Player:		.20
Inserted 1:1		
1	Mo Vaughn	.20
2	Erubiel Durazo	.20
3	Andruw Jones	.65
4	Chipper Jones	.75
5	Cal Ripken Jr.	1.50
6	Nomar Garciaparra	1.00
7	Sammy Sosa	1.00
8	Frank Thomas	.65
9	Sean Casey	.25
10	Ken Griffey Jr.	1.00
11	Manny Ramirez	.65
12	Larry Walker	.20
13	Juan Gonzalez	.65
14	Jeff Bagwell	.65
15	Craig Biggio	.20
16	Carlos Beltran	.50
17	Shawn Green	.35
18	Vladimir Guerrero	.65
19	Mike Piazza	1.00
20	Derek Jeter	1.50
21	Bernie Williams	.40
22	Ben Grieve	.20
23	Scott Rolen	.40
24	Mark McGwire	1.25
25	Tony Gwynn	.75
26	Barry Bonds	1.50
27	Alex Rodriguez	1.25

28 Jose Canseco .25
29 Rafael Palmeiro .50
30 Ivan Rodriguez .50

Lighting The Fire

These full foiled inserts are die-cut in the shape of a flame, with an image of a baseball at the core of the fiery image. These were inserted 1:49 packs.

		NM/M
Complete Set (20):		120.00
Common Player:		3.00
Inserted 1:49		
1	Chipper Jones	8.00
2	Greg Maddux	8.00
3	Cal Ripken Jr.	15.00
4	Nomar Garciaparra	10.00
5	Pedro Martinez	6.00
6	Ken Griffey Jr.	10.00
7	Sammy Sosa	10.00
8	Manny Ramirez	6.00
9	Juan Gonzalez	6.00
10	Jeff Bagwell	6.00
11	Shawn Green	3.00
12	Vladimir Guerrero	6.00
13	Mike Piazza	10.00
14	Roger Clemens	9.00
15	Derek Jeter	15.00
16	Mark McGwire	12.00
17	Tony Gwynn	8.00
18	Alex Rodriguez	12.00
19	Jose Canseco	3.00
20	Ivan Rodriguez	5.00

Ticket To Stardom

These unique cards have a design intended to replicate a ticket stub. Two images of the featured player are on the front, the bigger primary photo is vertical, while the smaller photo is horizontal. Silver foil stamping is used throughout. These are found 1:121 packs.

		NM/M
Complete Set (20):		250.00
Common Player:		5.00
Inserted 1:121		
1	Andruw Jones	10.00
2	Chipper Jones	15.00
3	Cal Ripken Jr.	30.00
4	Nomar Garciaparra	20.00
5	Pedro Martinez	10.00
6	Ken Griffey Jr.	20.00
7	Sammy Sosa	20.00
8	Manny Ramirez	10.00
9	Jeff Bagwell	10.00
10	Shawn Green	5.00
11	Vladimir Guerrero	10.00
12	Mike Piazza	20.00
13	Derek Jeter	30.00
14	Alfonso Soriano	8.00
15	Scott Rolen	6.00
16	Rick Ankiel	5.00
17	Mark McGwire	25.00
18	Tony Gwynn	15.00
19	Alex Rodriguez	25.00
20	Ivan Rodriguez	8.00

Wild Vinyl

This scarce 10-card insert set is serial numbered on the card front, limited to only 10 sets.

Complete Set (10):
Common Player:
Production 10 Sets

2000 Pacific Omega

		NM/M
Complete Set (255):		300.00
Common Player:		.10
Common (151-255):		4.00
Production 999 Sets		
1	Garret Anderson	.10
2	Darin Erstad	.25
3	Troy Glaus	.75
4	Tim Salmon	.20
5	Mo Vaughn	.20
6	Jay Bell	.10
7	Steve Finley	.10
8	Luis Gonzalez	.20
9	Randy Johnson	.75
10	Matt Williams	.10
11	Andres Galarraga	.10
12	Andruw Jones	.75
13	Chipper Jones	1.00
14	Brian Jordan	.10
15	Greg Maddux	1.00
16	B.J. Surhoff	.10
17	Brady Anderson	.10
18	Albert Belle	.10
19	Mike Mussina	.40
20	Cal Ripken Jr.	2.50
21	Carl Everett	.10
22	Nomar Garciaparra	1.50
23	Pedro Martinez	.75
24	Jason Varitek	.10
25	Mark Grace	.10
26	Sammy Sosa	1.50
27	Rondell White	.10
28	Kerry Wood	.35
29	Eric Young	.10
30	Ray Durham	.10
31	Carlos Lee	.10
32	Magglio Ordonez	.25
33	Frank Thomas	.75
34	Sean Casey	.10
35	Ken Griffey Jr.	1.50
36	Barry Larkin	.10
37	Pokey Reese	.10
38	Roberto Alomar	.40
39	Kenny Lofton	.10
40	Manny Ramirez	.75
41	David Segui	.10
42	Jim Thome	.60
43	Omar Vizquel	.10
44	Jeff Cirillo	.10
45	Jeffrey Hammonds	.10
46	Todd Helton	.75
47	Todd Hollandsworth	.10
48	Larry Walker	.10
49	Tony Clark	.10
50	Juan Encarnacion	.10
51	Juan Gonzalez	.75
52	Bobby Higginson	.10
53	Hideo Nomo	.75
54	Dean Palmer	.10
55	Luis Castillo	.10
56	Cliff Floyd	.10
57	Derek Lee	.10
58	Mike Lowell	.10
59	Henry Rodriguez	.10
60	Preston Wilson	.10
61	Moises Alou	.10
62	Jeff Bagwell	.75
63	Craig Biggio	.10
64	Ken Caminiti	.10
65	Richard Hidalgo	.10
66	Carlos Beltran	.40
67	Johnny Damon	.25
68	Jermaine Dye	.10
69	Joe Randa	.10
70	Mike Sweeney	.10
71	Adrian Beltre	.20
72	Kevin Brown	.10
73	Shawn Green	.35
74	Eric Karros	.10
75	Chan Ho Park	.10
76	Gary Sheffield	.30
77	Ron Belliard	.10
78	Jeromy Burnitz	.10
79	Geoff Jenkins	.10
80	Richie Sexson	.10
81	Ron Coomer	.10
82	Jacque Jones	.10
83	Corey Koskie	.10
84	Matt Lawton	.10
85	Vladimir Guerrero	.75
86	Lee Stevens	.10
87	Jose Vidro	.10
88	Edgardo Alfonzo	.10
89	Derek Bell	.10
90	Mike Bordick	.10
91	Mike Piazza	1.50
92	Robin Ventura	.10
93	Jose Canseco	.40
94	Roger Clemens	1.25
95	Orlando Hernandez	.10
96	Derek Jeter	2.50
97	David Justice	.10
98	Tino Martinez	.10
99	Jorge Posada	.10
100	Bernie Williams	.40
101	Eric Chavez	.20
102	Jason Giambi	.50
103	Ben Grieve	.10
104	Miguel Tejada	.25
105	Bobby Abreu	.10
106	Doug Glanville	.10
107	Travis Lee	.10
108	Mike Lieberthal	.10
109	Scott Rolen	.65
110	Brian S. Giles	.10
111	Jason Kendall	.10
112	Warren Morris	.10
113	Kevin Young	.10
114	Will Clark	.20
115	J.D. Drew	.20
116	Jim Edmonds	.10
117	Mark McGwire	2.00
118	Edgar Renteria	.10
119	Fernando Tatis	.10
120	Fernando Vina	.10
121	Bret Boone	.10
122	Tony Gwynn	1.00
123	Trevor Hoffman	.10
124	Phil Nevin	.10
125	Eric Owens	.10
126	Barry Bonds	2.50
127	Ellis Burks	.10
128	Jeff Kent	.10
129	J.T. Snow	.10
130	Jay Buhner	.10
131	Mike Cameron	.10
132	Rickey Henderson	.75
133	Edgar Martinez	.10
134	John Olerud	.10
135	Alex Rodriguez	2.00
136	Kazuhiro Sasaki RC	1.00
137	Fred McGriff	.10
138	Greg Vaughn	.10
139	Gerald Williams	.10
140	Rusty Greer	.10
141	Gabe Kapler	.10
142	Ricky Ledee	.10
143	Rafael Palmeiro	.65
144	Ivan Rodriguez	.65
145	Tony/ Batista	.10
146	Jose Cruz Jr.	.10
147	Carlos Delgado	.50
148	Brad Fullmer	.10
149	Shannon Stewart	.10
150	David Wells	.10
151	Juan Alvarez, Jeff DaVanon	6.00
152	Seth Etherton, Adam Kennedy	4.00
153	Ramon Ortiz, Lou Pote	4.00
154	Derrick Turnbow RC, Eric Weaver	4.00
155	Rod Barajas, Jason Conti	4.00
156	Byung-Hyun Kim, Rob Ryan	4.00
157	David Cortes, George Lombard	4.00
158	Ivanon Coffie, Melvin Mora	4.00
159	Ryan Kohlmeier RC, Luis Matos RC	6.00
160	Willie Morales, John Parrish RC	4.00
161	Chris Richard RC, Jay Spurgeon RC	5.00
162	Israel Alcantara, Tomokazu Ohka RC	5.00
163	Paxton Crawford RC, Sang-Hoon Lee RC	4.00
164	Mike Mahoney RC, Wilton Veras	4.00
165	Daniel Garibay RC, Ross Gload RC	4.00
166	Gary Matthews Jr., Phil Norton	4.00
167	Roosevelt Brown, Ruben Quevedo	4.00
168	Lorenzo Barcelo RC, Rocky Biddle RC	4.00
169	Mark Buehrle RC, John Garland	8.00
170	Aaron Myette, Josh Paul	4.00
171	Kip Wells, Kelly Wunsch	4.00
172	Rob Bell, Travis Dawkins	4.00
173	Hector Mercado RC, John Riedling RC	4.00
174	Russell Branyan, Sean DePaula	4.00
175	Tim Drew, Mark Watson	4.00
176	Craig House RC, Ben Petrick	5.00
177	Robert Fick, Jose Macias	4.00
178	Javier Cardona RC, Brandon Villafuerte	4.00
179	Armando Almanza, A.J. Burnett	4.00
180	Ramon Castro, Pablo Ozuna	4.00
181	Lance Berkman, Jason Green	4.00
182	Julio Lugo, Tony McKnight	4.00
183	Mitch Meluskey, Wade Miller	4.00
184	Chad Durbin RC, Hector Ortiz RC	5.00
185	Dermal Brown, Mark Quinn	4.00
186	Eric Gagne, Mike Judd	4.00
187	Kane Davis RC, Valerio de los Santos	4.00
188	Santiago Perez, Paul Rigdon RC	4.00
189	Matt Kinney, Matt LeCroy	4.00
190	Jason Maxwell, A.J. Pierzynski	4.00
191	J.C. Romero RC, Johan Santana	50.00
192	Tony Armas Jr., Peter Bergeron	4.00
193	Matt Blank, Milton Bradley	4.00
194	Tomas De La Rossa, Scott Forster	4.00
195	Yovanny Lara RC, Talmadge Nunnari RC	4.00
196	Brian Schneider, Andy Tracy	4.00
197	Scott Strickland, T.J. Tucker	4.00
198	Eric Cammack, Jim Mann RC	4.00
199	Grant Roberts, Jorge Toca	4.00
200	Alfonso Soriano, Jay Tessmer	8.00
201	Terrence Long, Mark Mulder	4.00
202	Pat Burrell, Cliff Politte	4.00
203	Jimmy Anderson, Bronson Arroyo	4.00
204	Mike Darr, Kory DeHaan	4.00
205	Adam Eaton, Wiki Gonzalez	4.00
206	Brandon Kolb RC, Kevin Walker	4.00
207	Damon Minor, Calvin Murray	4.00
208	Kevin Hodges, Joel Pineiro RC	40.00
209	Rob Ramsay RC, Kazuhiro Sasaki RC	8.00
210	Rick Ankiel, Mike Matthews	4.00
211	Steve Cox, Travis Harper	4.00
212	Kenny Kelly RC, Damian Rolls RC	4.00
213	Doug Davis, Scott Sheldon	4.00
214	Brian Sikorski, Pedro Valdes	4.00
215	Francisco Cordero, B.J. Waszgis	4.00
216	Matt DeWitt, Josh Phelps RC	8.00
217	Vernon Wells, Dewayne Wise	4.00
218	Geraldo Guzman RC, Jason Marquis	4.00
219	Rafael Furcal, Steve Sisco RC	4.00
220	B.J. Ryan, Kevin Beirne	4.00
221	Matt Ginter RC, Brad Penny	4.00
222	Julio Zuleta RC, Eric Munson	5.00
223	Dan Reichert, Jeff Williams	4.00
224	Jason LaRue, Danny Ardoin	4.00
225	Ray King, Mark Redman	4.00
226	Joe Crede, Mike Bell	4.00
227	Juan Pierre RC, Jay Payton	6.00
228	Wayne Franklin, Randy Choate RC	4.00
229	Chris Truby, Adam Piatt	4.00
230	Kevin Nicholson, Chris Woodward	4.00
231	Barry Zito RC, Jason Boyd	15.00
232	Brian O'Connor RC, Miguel Del Toro	4.00
233	Carlos Guillen, Aubrey Huff	4.00
234	Chad Hermansen, Jason Tyner	4.00
235	Aaron Fultz, Ryan Vogelsong	4.00
236	Shawn Wooten, Vance Wilson	4.00
237	Danny Klassen, Mike Lamb RC	4.00
238	Chad Bradford, Gene Stechschulte RC	4.00
239	Ismael Villegas, Hector Ramirez, Matt T. Williams, Luis Vizcaino	4.00
240	Mike Garcia, Domingo Guzman, Justin Brunette RC, Pasqual Coco RC	4.00
241	Frank Charles, Keith McDonald RC	4.00
242	Carlos Casimiro RC, Morgan Burkhart RC	4.00
243	Raul Gonzalez RC, Shawn Gilbert	4.00
244	Darrell Einertson, Jeff Sparks RC	4.00
245	Augie Ojeda RC, Brady Clark, Todd Belitz, Eric Byrnes RC	6.00
246	Leo Estrella RC, Charlie Greene	4.00
247	Trace Coquillette, Pedro Feliz RC	6.00
248	Tike Redman RC, David Newhan	4.00
249	Rodrigo Lopez RC, John Bales	6.00
250	Corey Patterson, Jose Ortiz RC	6.00
251	Britt Reames RC, Oswaldo Mairena RC	4.00
252	Xavier Nady RC, Timoniel Perez RC	4.00
253	Tom Jacquez, Vicente Padilla	4.00
254	Elvis Pena RC, Adam Melhuse RC	4.00
255	Ben Weber, Alex Cabrera RC	6.00

Copper

Stars (1-150): 8-15X
Production 45 Sets

Gold

Stars (1-150): 4-8X
Production 120 Sets

Platinum Blue

Stars (1-150): 6-10X

Production 55 Sets

Premiere Date

Stars (1-150): 4-8X
Production 77 Sets

AL Contenders

		NM/M
Complete Set (18):		20.00
Common Player:		.50
Inserted 2:37		
1	Darin Erstad	.75
2	Troy Glaus	1.50
3	Mo Vaughn	.50
4	Albert Belle	.50
5	Cal Ripken Jr.	4.00
6	Nomar Garciaparra	3.00
7	Pedro Martinez	1.50
8	Frank Thomas	1.50
9	Manny Ramirez	1.50
10	Jim Thome	1.25
11	Juan Gonzalez	1.50
12	Roger Clemens	2.50
13	Derek Jeter	4.00
14	Bernie Williams	.75
15	Jason Giambi	1.00
16	Alex Rodriguez	3.50
17	Edgar Martinez	.50
18	Carlos Delgado	1.00

EO Portraits

		NM/M
Complete Set (20):		125.00
Common Player:		3.00
Inserted 1:73		
1-of-1 Die-Cut Parallels Exist		
1	Chipper Jones	8.00
2	Greg Maddux	8.00
3	Cal Ripken Jr.	15.00
4	Pedro Martinez	6.00
5	Nomar Garciaparra	10.00
6	Sammy Sosa	10.00
7	Frank Thomas	6.00
8	Ken Griffey Jr.	10.00
9	Gary Sheffield	4.00
10	Vladimir Guerrero	6.00
11	Mike Piazza	10.00
12	Roger Clemens	9.00
13	Derek Jeter	15.00
14	Pat Burrell	4.00
15	Tony Gwynn	8.00
16	Barry Bonds	15.00
17	Alex Rodriguez	12.00
18	Rick Ankiel	3.00
19	Mark McGwire	12.00
20	Ivan Rodriguez	5.00

Full Court

		NM/M
Complete Set (36):		30.00
Common Player:		.50
Inserted 4:37 H		
1	Magglio Ordonez	.50
2	Manny Ramirez	1.50
3	Todd Helton	1.50
4	David Justice	.50
5	Bernie Williams	1.00
6	Jason Giambi	1.00
7	Scott Rolen	1.00
8	Jeff Kent	.50
9	Edgar Martinez	.50
10	Randy Johnson	1.50
11	Greg Maddux	2.00
12	Mike Mussina	.60
13	Pedro Martinez	1.50
14	Chuck Finley	.50
15	Kevin Brown	.50
16	Roger Clemens	2.25
17	Tim Hudson	.50
18	Rick Ankiel	.50
19	Troy Glaus	1.50
20	Chipper Jones	2.00
21	Nomar Garciaparra	2.50
22	Jeff Bagwell	1.50
23	Shawn Green	.60
24	Vladimir Guerrero	1.50

25	Mike Piazza	2.50
26	Jim Edmonds	.50
27	Rafael Palmeiro	.75
28	Cal Ripken Jr.	4.00
29	Sammy Sosa	2.50
30	Frank Thomas	1.50
31	Ken Griffey Jr.	2.50
32	Gary Sheffield	.50
33	Barry Bonds	4.00
34	Alex Rodriguez	3.00
35	Mark McGwire	3.00
36	Carlos Delgado	1.00

MLB Generations

		NM/M
Complete Set (20):		100.00
Common Card:		3.00
Inserted 1:145		
1	Mark McGwire, Pat Burrell	12.00
2	Cal Ripken Jr., Alex Rodriguez	15.00
3	Randy Johnson, Rick Ankiel	6.00
4	Tony Gwynn, Darin Erstad	8.00
5	Barry Bonds, Magglio Ordonez	15.00
6	Frank Thomas, Jason Giambi	6.00
7	Roger Clemens, Kerry Wood	10.00
8	Mike Piazza, Mitch Meluskey	10.00
9	Ken Griffey Jr., Andruw Jones	10.00
10	Bernie Williams, J.D. Drew	4.00
11	Chipper Jones, Troy Glaus	8.00
12	Andres Galarraga, Todd Helton	6.00
13	Juan Gonzalez, Vladimir Guerrero	6.00
14	Craig Biggio, Rafael Furcal	3.00
15	Sammy Sosa, Jermaine Dye	10.00
16	Larry Walker, Richard Hidalgo	3.00
17	Greg Maddux, Adam Eaton	8.00
18	Barry Larkin, Derek Jeter	15.00
19	Roberto Alomar, Jose Vidro	4.00
20	Jeff Kent, Edgardo Alfonzo	3.00

NL Contenders

		NM/M
Complete Set (18):		20.00
Common Player:		.50
Inserted 2:37		
1	Randy Johnson	1.50
2	Chipper Jones	2.00
3	Greg Maddux	2.00
4	Sammy Sosa	2.50
5	Sean Casey	.50
6	Ken Griffey Jr.	2.50
7	Todd Helton	1.50
8	Jeff Bagwell	1.50
9	Shawn Green	.50
10	Gary Sheffield	.75
11	Vladimir Guerrero	1.50
12	Mike Piazza	2.50
13	Scott Rolen	1.50
14	Barry Bonds	4.00
15	Rick Ankiel	.50
16	J.D. Drew	.50
17	Jim Edmonds	.50
18	Mark McGwire	3.00

Signatures

		NM/M
Common Player:		5.00

1	Darin Erstad	10.00
2	Nomar Garciaparra	125.00
3	Cal Eldred	5.00
4	Magglio Ordonez	5.00
5	Frank Thomas	30.00
6	Brady Clark	5.00
7	Richard Hidalgo	5.00
8	Gary Sheffield	10.00
9	Pat Burrell	15.00
10	Jim Edmonds	5.00

Stellar Performers

		NM/M
Complete Set (20):		50.00
Common Player:		1.00
Inserted 1:37		
1	Darin Erstad	1.00
2	Chipper Jones	3.00
3	Greg Maddux	3.00
4	Cal Ripken Jr.	6.00
5	Pedro Martinez	2.00
6	Nomar Garciaparra	4.00
7	Sammy Sosa	4.00
8	Frank Thomas	2.00
9	Ken Griffey Jr.	4.00
10	Todd Helton	2.00
11	Jeff Bagwell	2.00
12	Vladimir Guerrero	2.00
13	Mike Piazza	4.00
14	Derek Jeter	6.00
15	Roger Clemens	3.50
16	Tony Gwynn	3.00
17	Barry Bonds	6.00
18	Alex Rodriguez	5.00
19	Mark McGwire	5.00
20	Ivan Rodriguez	1.50

Opening Day 2K

As part of a multi-manufacturer promotion, Pacific issued eight cards of an "Opening Day 2K" set. Packages containing some of the 32 cards in the issue were distributed by MLB teams early in the season. The cards were also available exclusively as inserts in Pacific Crown Collection and Pacific Aurora packs sold at K-Mart stores early in the season. The Pacific OD2K cards have gold-foil graphic highlights on front. Backs have a portrait photo and are numbered with an "OD" prefix.

		NM/M
Complete Set (8):		4.00
Common Player:		.50
25	Mo Vaughn	.50
26	Chipper Jones	1.00
27	Nomar Garciaparra	1.00
28	Larry Walker	.65

29	Corey Koskie	.50
30	Scott Rolen	.75
31	Tony Gwynn	1.00
32	Jose Canseco	.65

2000 Pacific Paramount Sample

Nearly identical to the issued version of spokesman Tony Gwynn's card, this features a large white diagonal "SAMPLE" overprint on back and in the space where a card number usually appears.

	NM/M
Tony Gwynn	3.00

2000 Pacific Paramount

		NM/M
Complete Set (250):		25.00
Common Player:		.10
Pack (6):		1.50
Wax Box (36):		40.00
1	Garret Anderson	.10
2	Jim Edmonds	.10
3	Darin Erstad	.25
4	Chuck Finley	.10
5	Troy Glaus	.75
6	Troy Percival	.10
7	Tim Salmon	.20
8	Mo Vaughn	.10
9	Jay Bell	.10
10	Erubiel Durazo	.10
11	Steve Finley	.10
12	Luis Gonzalez	.20
13	Randy Johnson	.75
14	Travis Lee	.10
15	Matt Mantei	.10
16	Matt Williams	.10
17	Tony Womack	.10
18	Bret Boone	.10
19	Tom Glavine	.35
20	Andruw Jones	.75
21	Chipper Jones	1.00
22	Brian Jordan	.10
23	Javy Lopez	.10
24	Greg Maddux	1.00
25	Kevin Millwood	.10
26	John Rocker	.10
27	John Smoltz	.10
28	Brady Anderson	.10
29	Albert Belle	.10
30	Will Clark	.20
31	Charles Johnson	.10
32	Mike Mussina	.35
33	Cal Ripken Jr.	2.00
34	B.J. Surhoff	.10
35	Nomar Garciaparra	1.25
36	Derek Lowe	.10
37	Pedro Martinez	.75
38	Trot Nixon	.10
39	Troy O'Leary	.10
40	Jose Offerman	.10
41	John Valentin	.10
42	Jason Varitek	.10
43	Mark Grace	.20
44	Glenallen Hill	.10
45	Jon Lieber	.10
46	Cole Liniak	.10
47	Jose Nieves	.10
48	Henry Rodriguez	.10

49	Sammy Sosa	1.25
50	Kerry Wood	.65
51	Jason Dellaero	.10
52	Ray Durham	.10
53	Paul Konerko	.10
54	Carlos Lee	.10
55	Greg Norton	.10
56	Magglio Ordonez	.10
57	Chris Singleton	.10
58	Frank Thomas	.75
59	Aaron Boone	.10
60	Mike Cameron	.10
61	Sean Casey	.20
62	Pete Harnisch	.10
63	Barry Larkin	.10
64	Pokey Reese	.10
65	Greg Vaughn	.10
66	Scott Williamson	.10
67	Roberto Alomar	.35
68	Sean DePaula RC	.20
69	Travis Fryman	.10
70	David Justice	.10
71	Kenny Lofton	.10
72	Manny Ramirez	.75
73	Richie Sexson	.10
74	Jim Thome	.65
75	Omar Vizquel	.10
76	Pedro Astacio	.10
77	Vinny Castilla	.10
78	Derrick Gibson	.10
79	Todd Helton	.75
80	Neifi Perez	.10
81	Ben Petrick	.10
82	Larry Walker	.10
83	Brad Ausmus	.10
84	Tony Clark	.10
85	Deivi Cruz	.10
86	Damion Easley	.10
87	Juan Encarnacion	.10
88	Juan Gonzalez	.75
89	Bobby Higginson	.10
90	Dave Mlicki	.10
91	Dean Palmer	.10
92	Bruce Aven	.10
93	Luis Castillo	.10
94	Ramon Castro	.10
95	Cliff Floyd	.10
96	Alex Gonzalez	.10
97	Mike Lowell	.10
98	Preston Wilson	.10
99	Jeff Bagwell	.75
100	Derek Bell	.10
101	Craig Biggio	.35
102	Ken Caminiti	.10
103	Carl Everett	.10
104	Mike Hampton	.10
105	Jose Lima	.10
106	Billy Wagner	.10
107	Daryle Ward	.10
108	Carlos Beltran	.40
109	Johnny Damon	.25
110	Jermaine Dye	.10
111	Carlos Febles	.10
112	Mark Quinn	.10
113	Joe Randa	.10
114	Jose Rosado	.10
115	Mike Sweeney	.10
116	Kevin Brown	.10
117	Shawn Green	.35
118	Mark Grudzielanek	.10
119	Todd Hollandsworth	.10
120	Eric Karros	.10
121	Chan Ho Park	.10
122	Gary Sheffield	.35
123	Devon White	.10
124	Eric Young	.10
125	Kevin Barker	.10
126	Ron Belliard	.10
127	Jeromy Burnitz	.10
128	Jeff Cirillo	.10
129	Marquis Grissom	.10
130	Geoff Jenkins	.10
131	David Nilsson	.10
132	Chad Allen	.10
133	Ron Coomer	.10
134	Jacque Jones	.10
135	Corey Koskie	.10
136	Matt Lawton	.10
137	Brad Radke	.10
138	Todd Walker	.10
139	Michael Barrett	.10
140	Peter Bergeron	.10
141	Brad Fullmer	.10
142	Vladimir Guerrero	.75
143	Ugueth Urbina	.10
144	Jose Vidro	.10
145	Rondell White	.10
146	Edgardo Alfonzo	.10
147	Armando Benitez	.10
148	Roger Cedeno	.10
149	Rickey Henderson	.75
150	Melvin Mora	.10
151	John Olerud	.10
152	Rey Ordonez	.10
153	Mike Piazza	1.25
154	Jorge Toca	.10
155	Robin Ventura	.10
156	Roger Clemens	1.00
157	David Cone	.10
158	Orlando Hernandez	.10
159	Derek Jeter	2.00
160	Chuck Knoblauch	.10
161	Ricky Ledee	.10
162	Tino Martinez	.10
163	Paul O'Neill	.10
164	Mariano Rivera	.20
165	Alfonso Soriano	.75
166	Bernie Williams	.25

167	Eric Chavez	.25
168	Jason Giambi	.50
169	Ben Grieve	.10
170	Tim Hudson	.25
171	John Jaha	.10
172	Matt Stairs	.10
173	Miguel Tejada	.25
174	Randy Velarde	.10
175	Bobby Abreu	.10
176	Marlon Anderson	.10
177	Rico Brogna	.10
178	Ron Gant	.10
179	Doug Glanville	.10
180	Mike Lieberthal	.10
181	Scott Rolen	.65
182	Curt Schilling	.35
183	Brian Giles	.10
184	Chad Hermansen	.10
185	Jason Kendall	.10
186	Al Martin	.10
187	Pat Meares	.10
188	Warren Morris	.10
189	Ed Sprague	.10
190	Kevin Young	.10
191	Rick Ankiel	.20
192	Kent Bottenfield	.10
193	Eric Davis	.10
194	J.D. Drew	.25
195	Adam Kennedy	.10
196	Ray Lankford	.10
197	Joe McEwing	.10
198	Mark McGwire	1.50
199	Edgar Renteria	.10
200	Fernando Tatis	.10
201	Mike Darr	.10
202	Ben Davis	.10
203	Tony Gwynn	1.00
204	Trevor Hoffman	.10
205	Damian Jackson	.10
206	Phil Nevin	.10
207	Reggie Sanders	.10
208	Quilvio Veras	.10
209	Rich Aurilia	.10
210	Marvin Benard	.10
211	Barry Bonds	2.00
212	Ellis Burks	.10
213	Livan Hernandez	.10
214	Jeff Kent	.10
215	Russ Ortiz	.10
216	J.T. Snow	.10
217	Paul Abbott	.10
218	David Bell	.10
219	Freddy Garcia	.10
220	Ken Griffey Jr.	1.50
221	Carlos Guillen	.10
222	Brian Hunter	.10
223	Edgar Martinez	.10
224	Jamie Moyer	.10
225	Alex Rodriguez	1.50
226	Wade Boggs	1.00
227	Miguel Cairo	.10
228	Jose Canseco	.40
229	Roberto Hernandez	.10
230	Dave Martinez	.10
231	Quinton McCracken	.10
232	Fred McGriff	.10
233	Kevin Stocker	.10
234	Royce Clayton	.10
235	Rusty Greer	.10
236	Ruben Mateo	.10
237	Rafael Palmeiro	.65
238	Ivan Rodriguez	.65
239	Aaron Sele	.10
240	John Wetteland	.10
241	Todd Zeile	.10
242	Tony Batista	.10
243	Homer Bush	.10
244	Carlos Delgado	.50
245	Tony Fernandez	.10
246	Billy Koch	.10
247	Raul Mondesi	.10
248	Shannon Stewart	.10
249	David Wells	.10
250	Vernon Wells	.10

Copper

Stars:		2X
Inserted 1:1 H		

Emerald

Stars:		1-2X
Yng Stars & RC's:		1X
Inserted 1:1 7-11 Pack		

Gold

Inserted 1:1 R		
Stars:		1-2X
Yng Stars & RC's:		1X

Holographic Gold

Stars:		3-6X
Production 199 Sets		

Holographic Green

Stars:		6-10X
Production 99 Sets, 7-11 insert		

Holographic Silver

Stars:		5-10X
Production 99 Sets		

Platinum Blue

Stars:		6-12X
Production 67 Sets		

Premiere Date

Stars:		8-15X
Production 50 Sets		

Ruby Red

Stars:		1-2X
RC's:		1X
Inserted 9 per 7-11 pack.		

Cooperstown Bound

		NM/M
Complete Set (10):		220.00
Common Player:		20.00
Inserted 1:361		
Proofs:		2X
Production 20 Sets, hobby only.		
Canvas Proofs: Values Undetermined		
Production One Set		
1	Greg Maddux	20.00
2	Cal Ripken Jr.	40.00
3	Nomar Garciaparra	25.00
4	Sammy Sosa	25.00
5	Roger Clemens	30.00
6	Derek Jeter	40.00
7	Mark McGwire	30.00
8	Tony Gwynn	20.00
9	Ken Griffey Jr.	25.00
10	Alex Rodriguez	30.00

Double Vision

		NM/M
Complete Set (36):		220.00
Common Player:		3.00
Inserted 1:37		
1	Chipper Jones	8.00
2	Cal Ripken Jr.	15.00
3	Nomar Garciaparra	10.00
4	Pedro Martinez	6.00
5	Sammy Sosa	10.00
6	Manny Ramirez	6.00
7	Jeff Bagwell	6.00
8	Craig Biggio	3.00
9	Vladimir Guerrero	6.00
10	Mike Piazza	10.00
11	Roger Clemens	9.00
12	Derek Jeter	15.00

13	Mark McGwire	12.00
14	Tony Gwynn	8.00
15	Ken Griffey Jr.	10.00
16	Alex Rodriguez	12.00
17	Rafael Palmeiro	5.00
18	Ivan Rodriguez	5.00
19	Chipper Jones	8.00
20	Cal Ripken Jr.	15.00
21	Nomar Garciaparra	6.00
22	Pedro Martinez	6.00
23	Sammy Sosa	10.00
24	Manny Ramirez	6.00
25	Jeff Bagwell	6.00
26	Craig Biggio	3.00
27	Vladimir Guerrero	6.00
28	Mike Piazza	10.00
29	Roger Clemens	9.00
30	Derek Jeter	15.00
31	Mark McGwire	12.00
32	Tony Gwynn	8.00
33	Ken Griffey Jr.	10.00
34	Alex Rodriguez	12.00
35	Rafael Palmeiro	5.00
36	Ivan Rodriguez	5.00

Fielder's Choice

		NM/M
Complete Set (20):		150.00
Common Player:		3.00
Inserted 1:73		
Gold Parallel		
(10 Sets issued.):		6-8X
1	Andruw Jones	5.00
2	Chipper Jones	8.00
3	Greg Maddux	8.00
4	Cal Ripken Jr.	20.00
5	Nomar Garciaparra	10.00
6	Sammy Sosa	10.00
7	Sean Casey	3.00
8	Manny Ramirez	5.00
9	Larry Walker	3.00
10	Jeff Bagwell	5.00
11	Mike Piazza	10.00
12	Derek Jeter	20.00
13	Bernie Williams	3.00
14	Scott Rolen	4.00
15	Mark McGwire	15.00
16	Tony Gwynn	8.00
17	Barry Bonds	20.00
18	Ken Griffey Jr.	10.00
19	Alex Rodriguez	15.00
20	Ivan Rodriguez	4.00

Maximum Impact

		NM/M
Complete Set (20):		25.00
Common Player:		.50
Inserted 2:25 7-11 packs.		
1	Chipper Jones	2.00
2	Cal Ripken Jr.	4.00
3	Nomar Garciaparra	2.50
4	Pedro Martinez	2.50
5	Sammy Sosa	2.50
6	Manny Ramirez	1.50
7	Larry Walker	.50
8	Jeff Bagwell	1.50
9	Carlos Beltran	.75
10	Vladimir Guerrero	1.50
11	Mike Piazza	4.00
12	Derek Jeter	4.00
13	Roger Clemens	2.25
14	Mark McGwire	3.00
15	Tony Gwynn	1.50
16	Barry Bonds	4.00
17	Ken Griffey Jr.	2.50
18	Alex Rodriguez	3.00
19	Ivan Rodriguez	1.00
20	Carlos Delgado	.75

Season in Review

		NM/M
Complete Set (30):		25.00
Common Player:		.50
Inserted 2:37		
1	Randy Johnson	1.50
2	Matt Williams	.50
3	Chipper Jones	2.00
4	Greg Maddux	2.00
5	Cal Ripken Jr.	4.00
6	Nomar Garciaparra	2.50
7	Pedro Martinez	1.50
8	Sammy Sosa	2.50
9	Manny Ramirez	1.50
10	Larry Walker	.50
11	Jeff Bagwell	1.50
12	Craig Biggio	.50
13	Carlos Beltran	.75
14	Mark Quinn	.50
15	Vladimir Guerrero	1.50
16	Mike Piazza	2.50
17	Robin Ventura	.50
18	Roger Clemens	2.25
19	David Cone	.50
20	Derek Jeter	4.00
21	Mark McGwire	3.00
22	Fernando Tatis	.50
23	Tony Gwynn	2.00
24	Barry Bonds	4.00
25	Ken Griffey Jr.	2.50
26	Alex Rodriguez	3.00
27	Wade Boggs	2.00
28	Jose Canseco	.65
29	Rafael Palmeiro	1.00
30	Ivan Rodriguez	1.00

Update

		NM/M
Complete Set (100):		10.00
Common Player:		.10
Production 12,500 Sets; retail exclusive		
1-U	Adam Kennedy	.10
2-U	Bengie Molina	.10
3-U	Derrick Turnbow	.10
4-U	Randy Johnson	.75
5-U	Danny Klassen	.10
6-U	Vicente Padilla	.10
7-U	Rafael Furcal	.10
8-U	Andres Galarraga	.10
9-U	Chipper Jones	1.00
10-U	Fernando Lunar	.10
11-U	Willie Morales	.10
12-U	Cal Ripken Jr.	2.00
13-U	B.J. Ryan	.10
14-U	Carl Everett	.10
15-U	Nomar Garciaparra	1.25
16-U	Pedro Martinez	.75
17-U	Wilton Veras	.10
18-U	Scott Downs	.10
19-U	Daniel Garibay	.10
20-U	Sammy Sosa	1.25
21-U	Julio Zuleta	.10
22-U	Josh Paul	.10
23-U	Frank Thomas	.75
24-U	Rob Bell	.10
25-U	Dante Bichette	.10
26-U	Travis Dawkins	.10
27-U	Ken Griffey Jr.	1.25
28-U	Chuck Finley	.10
29-U	Manny Ramirez	.75
30-U	Paul Rigdon	.10
31-U	Jeff Cirillo	.10
32-U	Larry Walker	.10
33-U	Masato Yoshii	.10
34-U	Robert Fick	.10
35-U	Jose Macias	.10
36-U	Juan Gonzalez	.75
37-U	Hideo Nomo	.75
38-U	Jason Grilli	.10
39-U	Pablo Ozuna	.10
40-U	Brad Penny	.10
41-U	Jeff Bagwell	.75
42-U	Lance Berkman	.10
43-U	Roger Cedeno	.10
44-U	Octavio Dotel	.10
45-U	Chad Durbin	.10
46-U	Eric Gagne	.10
47-U	Shawn Green	.35
48-U	Jose Hernandez	.10
49-U	Matt LeCroy	.10
50-U	Johan Santana	.10
51-U	Vladimir Guerrero	.75
52-U	Hideki Irabu	.10
53-U	Andrew Tracy	.10
54-U	Derek Bell	.10
55-U	Eric Cammack	.10
56-U	Mike Hampton	.10
57-U	Jay Payton	.10
58-U	Mike Piazza	1.25
59-U	Todd Zeile	.10
60-U	Roger Clemens	1.00
61-U	Darrell Einertson	.10
62-U	Derek Jeter	2.00
63-U	Jason Giambi	.60
64-U	Terrence Long	.10
65-U	Mark Mulder	.50
66-U	Adam Piatt	.10
67-U	Luis Vizcaino	.10
68-U	Pat Burrell	.35
69-U	Scott Rolen	.65
70-U	Chad Hermansen	.10
71-U	Rick Ankiel	.15
72-U	Jim Edmonds	.10
73-U	Mark McGwire	1.50
74-U	Gene Stechschulte	.10
75-U	Fernando Vina	.10
76-U	Bret Boone	.10
77-U	Tony Gwynn	1.00
78-U	Ryan Klesko	.10
79-U	David Newhan	.10
80-U	Kevin Walker	.10
81-U	Barry Bonds	2.00
82-U	Aaron Fultz	.10
83-U	Ben Weber	.10
84-U	Rickey Henderson	.75
85-U	Kevin Hodges	.10
86-U	John Olerud	.10
87-U	Robert Ramsay	.10
88-U	Alex Rodriguez	1.50
89-U	Kazuhiro Sasaki	.15
90-U	Vinny Castilla	.10
91-U	Jeff Sparks	.10
92-U	Greg Vaughn	.10
93-U	Francisco Cordero	.10
94-U	Gabe Kapler	.10
95-U	Mike Lamb	.10
96-U	Ivan Rodriguez	.65
97-U	Clayton Andrews	.10
98-U	Brad Fullmer	.10
99-U	Raul Mondesi	.10
100-U	Dewayne Wise	.10

2000 Pacific Prism

		NM/M
Complete Set (150):		10.00
Common Player:		.10
Pack (5):		1.50
Wax Box (24):		15.00
1	Jeff DaVanon RC	.10
2	Troy Glaus	.50
3	Tim Salmon	.15
4	Mo Vaughn	.10
5	Jay Bell	.10
6	Erubiel Durazo	.10
7	Luis Gonzalez	.20
8	Randy Johnson	.50
9	Matt Williams	.10
10	Andres Galarraga	.10
11	Andruw Jones	.50
12	Chipper Jones	.65
13	Brian Jordan	.10
14	Greg Maddux	.65
15	Kevin Millwood	.10
16	John Smoltz	.10
17	Albert Belle	.15
18	Mike Mussina	.25
19	Calvin Pickering	.10
20	Cal Ripken Jr.	1.50
21	B.J. Surhoff	.10
22	Nomar Garciaparra	1.00
23	Pedro Martinez	.50
24	Troy O'Leary	.10
25	John Valentin	.10
26	Jason Varitek	.10
27	Mark Grace	.15
28	Henry Rodriguez	.10
29	Sammy Sosa	1.00
30	Kerry Wood	.25
31	Ray Durham	.10
32	Carlos Lee	.10
33	Magglio Ordonez	.10
34	Chris Singleton	.10
35	Frank Thomas	.50
36	Sean Casey	.15
37	Travis Dawkins	.10
38	Barry Larkin	.10
39	Pokey Reese	.10
40	Scott Williamson	.10
41	Roberto Alomar	.20
42	Bartolo Colon	.10
43	David Justice	.10
44	Manny Ramirez	.50
45	Richie Sexson	.10
46	Jim Thome	.50
47	Omar Vizquel	.10
48	Pedro Astacio	.10
49	Todd Helton	.50
50	Neifi Perez	.10
51	Ben Petrick	.10
52	Larry Walker	.10
53	Tony Clark	.10
54	Damion Easley	.10
55	Juan Gonzalez	.50
56	Dean Palmer	.10
57	A.J. Burnett	.10
58	Luis Castillo	.10
59	Cliff Floyd	.10
60	Alex Gonzalez	.10
61	Preston Wilson	.10
62	Jeff Bagwell	.50
63	Craig Biggio	.10
64	Ken Caminiti	.10
65	Jose Lima	.10
66	Billy Wagner	.10
67	Carlos Beltran	.30
68	Johnny Damon	.25
69	Jermaine Dye	.10
70	Carlos Febles	.10
71	Mike Sweeney	.10
72	Kevin Brown	.10
73	Shawn Green	.25
74	Eric Karros	.10
75	Chan Ho Park	.10
76	Gary Sheffield	.30
77	Ron Belliard	.10
78	Jeromy Burnitz	.10
79	Marquis Grissom	.10
80	Geoff Jenkins	.10
81	Mark Loretta	.10
82	Ron Coomer	.10
83	Jacque Jones	.10
84	Corey Koskie	.10
85	Brad Radke	.10
86	Todd Walker	.10
87	Michael Barrett	.10
88	Peter Bergeron	.10
89	Vladimir Guerrero	.50
90	Jose Vidro	.10
91	Rondell White	.10
92	Edgardo Alfonzo	.10
93	Rickey Henderson	.50
94	Rey Ordonez	.10
95	Mike Piazza	1.00
96	Robin Ventura	.10
97	Roger Clemens	.75
98	Orlando Hernandez	.10
99	Derek Jeter	1.50
100	Tino Martinez	.10
101	Mariano Rivera	.15
102	Alfonso Soriano	.50
103	Bernie Williams	.20
104	Eric Chavez	.15
105	Jason Giambi	.30
106	Ben Grieve	.10
107	Tim Hudson	.20
108	John Jaha	.10
109	Bobby Abreu	.10
110	Doug Glanville	.10
111	Mike Liebethal	.10
112	Scott Rolen	.40
113	Curt Schilling	.25
114	Brian Giles	.10
115	Jason Kendall	.10
116	Warren Morris	.10
117	Kevin Young	.10
118	Rick Ankiel	.10
119	J.D. Drew	.15
120	Chad Hutchinson	.10
121	Ray Lankford	.10
122	Mark McGwire	1.25
123	Fernando Tatis	.10
124	Bret Boone	.10
125	Ben Davis	.10
126	Tony Gwynn	.65
127	Trevor Hoffman	.10
128	Barry Bonds	1.50
129	Ellis Burks	.10
130	Jeff Kent	.10
131	J.T. Snow	.10
132	Freddy Garcia	.10
133	Ken Griffey Jr.	1.00
134	Edgar Martinez	.10
135	John Olerud	.10
136	Alex Rodriguez	1.25
137	Jose Canseco	.20
138	Vinny Castilla	.10
139	Roberto Hernandez	.10
140	Fred McGriff	.10
141	Rusty Greer	.10
142	Ruben Mateo	.10
143	Rafael Palmeiro	.40
144	Ivan Rodriguez	.40
145	Lee Stevens	.10
146	Tony Batista	.10
147	Carlos Delgado	.35
148	Shannon Stewart	.10
149	David Wells	.10
150	Vernon Wells	.10

Drops Silver

One of eight silver-foil parallels to Prism, this version features a raindrop-like patterned background. Inserted into both hobby and retail packaging, production was reported as 799 of 100 of the cards, and 916 of the other 50 cards (indicated with a (*) in the checklist. The cards are not serially numbered.

		NM/M
Common Player:		.50
Stars:		2-4X
1	Jeff DaVanon RC	.50
2	Troy Glaus	1.00
3	Tim Salmon	.60
4	Mo Vaughn (*)	.50
5	Jay Bell	.50
6	Erubiel Durazo	.50
7	Luis Gonzalez	.50
8	Randy Johnson (*)	1.00
9	Matt Williams (*)	.50
10	Andres Galarraga	.50
11	Andruw Jones (*)	1.00
12	Chipper Jones (*)	1.50
13	Brian Jordan	.50
14	Greg Maddux (*)	1.50
15	Kevin Millwood	.50
16	John Smoltz	.50
17	Albert Belle	.50
18	Mike Mussina (*)	.60
19	Calvin Pickering	.50
20	Cal Ripken Jr. (*)	3.00
22	Nomar Garciaparra (*)	2.00
23	Pedro Martinez (*)	1.00
24	Troy O'Leary	.50
25	John Valentin	.50
26	Jason Varitek	.50
27	Mark Grace	.60
29	Sammy Sosa (*)	2.00
30	Kerry Wood (*)	.65
31	Ray Durham	.50
32	Carlos Lee	.50
33	Magglio Ordonez (*)	.50
34	Chris Singleton	.50
35	Frank Thomas (*)	1.00
36	Sean Casey (*)	.50
37	Travis Dawkins	.50
38	Barry Larkin	.50
39	Pokey Reese	.50
40	Scott Williamson	.50
41	Roberto Alomar (*)	.60
42	Bartolo Colon	.50
43	David Justice	.50
44	Manny Ramirez (*)	1.00
45	Richie Sexson	.50
46	Jim Thome (*)	1.00
47	Omar Vizquel	.50
48	Pedro Astacio	.50
49	Todd Helton (*)	1.00
50	Neifi Perez	.50
51	Ben Petrick	.50
52	Larry Walker (*)	.50
53	Tony Clark	.50
54	Damion Easley	.50
55	Juan Gonzalez (*)	1.00
56	Dean Palmer	.50
57	A.J. Burnett	.50
58	Luis Castillo	.50
59	Cliff Floyd	.50
60	Alex Gonzalez	.50
61	Preston Wilson (*)	.50
62	Jeff Bagwell (*)	1.00
63	Craig Biggio	.50
64	Ken Caminiti	.50
65	Jose Lima	.50
66	Billy Wagner	.50
67	Carlos Beltran (*)	.65
68	Johnny Damon	.65
69	Jermaine Dye	.50
70	Carlos Febles	.50
71	Mike Sweeney	.50
72	Kevin Brown (*)	.50
73	Shawn Green (*)	.75
74	Eric Karros	.50
75	Chan Ho Park	.50
76	Gary Sheffield (*)	.60
77	Ron Belliard	.50
x8	Jeromy Burnitz (*)	.50
79	Marquis Grissom	.50
80	Geoff Jenkins	.50
81	Mark Loretta	.50
82	Ron Coomer	.50
83	Jacque Jones	.50
84	Corey Koskie	.50
85	Brad Radke	.50
86	Todd Walker	.50
87	Michael Barrett	.50
88	Peter Bergeron	.50
89	Vladimir Guerrero (*)	1.00
90	Jose Vidro	.50
91	Rondell White	.50
92	Edgardo Alfonzo (*)	.50
93	Rickey Henderson	1.00
94	Rey Ordonez	.50
95	Mike Piazza (*)	2.00
96	Robin Ventura	.50
97	Roger Clemens (*)	1.75
98	Orlando Hernandez	.50
99	Derek Jeter (*)	3.00
100	Tino Martinez	.50
101	Mariano Rivera	.50
102	Alfonso Soriano	.75
103	Bernie Williams (*)	.60
104	Eric Chavez	.50
105	Jason Giambi	.50
106	Ben Grieve	.50
107	Tim Hudson	.75
108	John Jaha	.50
109	Bobby Abreu	.50
110	Doug Glanville	.50
111	Mike Lieberthal	.50
112	Scott Rolen (*)	.75
113	Curt Schilling	.60
114	Brian Giles (*)	.50
115	Jason Kendall	.50
116	Warren Morris	.50
117	Kevin Young	.50
118	Rick Ankiel (*)	.50
119	J.D. Drew (*)	.60
120	Chad Hutchinson	.50
121	Ray Lankford	.50
122	Mark McGwire (*)	2.50
123	Fernando Tatis	.50
124	Bret Boone	.60
125	Ben Davis	.50
126	Tony Gwynn (*)	1.50
127	Trevor Hoffman	.50
128	Barry Bonds (*)	3.00
129	Ellis Burks	.50
130	Jeff Kent	.50
131	J.T. Snow	.50
132	Freddy Garcia (*)	.50
133	Ken Griffey Jr. (*)	2.00
134	Edgar Martinez	.50
135	John Olerud	.50
136	Alex Rodriguez (*)	2.50
137	Jose Canseco (*)	.50
138	Vinny Castilla	.50
139	Roberto Hernandez	.50
140	Fred McGriff	.50
141	Rusty Greer	.50
142	Ruben Mateo (*)	.50
143	Rafael Palmeiro (*)	.75
144	Ivan Rodriguez (*)	.75
145	Lee Stevens	.50
146	Tony Batista	.50
147	Carlos Delgado (*)	.60
148	Shannon Stewart	.50
149	David Wells	.50
150	Vernon Wells	.50

Holographic Blue

	NM/M
Common Player:	1.00
Stars:	4-6X
Production 80 Sets	

Holographic Gold

	NM/M
Common Player:	.50
Stars:	2-4X
Production 480 Sets	

Holographic Mirror

	NM/M
Common Player:	1.50
Stars:	4-6X
Production 160 Sets	

Holographic Purple

	NM/M
Common Player:	1.00
Stars:	6-8X
Production 99 Sets	

Pebbly Dots

One of eight silver-foil versions of Prism, there is virtually no way to describe the silver metallic foil background of this parallel set dubbed "Pebbly Dots" by the maker to allow its differentiation from the set labeled "Texture Silver," other than perhaps the vaguely vertical orientation of the texture. Production of 100 of the cards was 691 apiece, with the other 50 cards produced in an edition of 448 each indicated with an (*) in the checklist. They were inserted into both hobby and retail packaging. The cards are not serially numbered.

	NM/M
Complete Set (150):	50.00
Common Player:	.50
1 Jeff DaVanon RC	.50
2 Troy Glaus	.75
3 Tim Salmon	.60
4 Mo Vaughn (*)	.50
5 Jay Bell	.50
6 Erubiel Durazo	.50
7 Luis Gonzalez	.60
8 Randy Johnson (*)	.75
9 Matt Williams (*)	.50
10 Andres Galarraga	.50
11 Andruw Jones (*)	.75
12 Chipper Jones (*)	1.00
13 Brian Jordan	.50
14 Greg Maddux (*)	1.00
15 Kevin Millwood	.50
16 John Smoltz	.50
17 Albert Belle	.50
18 Mike Mussina (*)	.60
19 Calvin Pickering	.50
20 Cal Ripken Jr. (*)	3.00
21 B.J. Surhoff	.50
22 Nomar Garciaparra (*)	2.00
23 Pedro Martinez (*)	.75
24 Troy O'Leary	.50
25 John Valentin	.50
26 Jason Varitek	.50
27 Mark Grace	.50
28 Henry Rodriguez	.50
29 Sammy Sosa (*)	2.00
30 Kerry Wood (*)	.65
31 Ray Durham	.50
32 Carlos Lee	.50
33 Magglio Ordonez (*)	.50
34 Chris Singleton	.50
35 Frank Thomas (*)	.75
36 Sean Casey (*)	.60
37 Travis Dawkins	.50
38 Barry Larkin	.50
39 Pokey Reese	.50
40 Scott Williamson	.50
41 Roberto Alomar (*)	.60
42 Bartolo Colon	.50
43 David Justice	.50
44 Manny Ramirez (*)	.75
45 Richie Sexson	.50
46 Jim Thome (*)	.75
47 Omar Vizquel	.50
48 Pedro Astacio	.50
49 Todd Helton (*)	.75
50 Neifi Perez	.50
51 Ben Petrick	.50
52 Larry Walker (*)	.50
53 Tony Clark	.50
54 Damion Easley	.50
55 Juan Gonzalez (*)	.75
56 Dean Palmer	.50
57 A.J. Burnett	.50
58 Luis Castillo	.50
59 Cliff Floyd	.50
60 Alex Gonzalez	.50
61 Preston Wilson (*)	.50

62 Jeff Bagwell (*)	.75
63 Craig Biggio (*)	.50
64 Ken Caminiti	.50
65 Jose Lima	.50
66 Billy Wagner	.50
67 Carlos Beltran (*)	.65
68 Johnny Damon	.60
69 Jermaine Dye	.50
70 Carlos Febles	.50
71 Mike Sweeney	.50
72 Kevin Brown (*)	.50
73 Shawn Green (*)	.65
74 Eric Karros	.50
75 Chan Ho Park	.50
76 Gary Sheffield (*)	.60
77 Ron Belliard	.50
78 Jeromy Burnitz (*)	.50
79 Marquis Grissom	.50
80 Geoff Jenkins	.50
81 Mark Loretta	.50
82 Ron Coomer	.50
83 Jacque Jones	.50
84 Corey Koskie	.50
85 Brad Radke	.50
86 Todd Walker	.50
87 Michael Barrett	.50
88 Peter Bergeron	.50
89 Vladimir Guerrero (*)	.75
90 Jose Vidro	.50
91 Rondell White	.50
92 Edgardo Alfonzo (*)	.50
93 Rickey Henderson	.75
94 Rey Ordonez	.50
95 Mike Piazza (*)	2.00
96 Robin Ventura	.50
97 Roger Clemens (*)	1.50
98 Orlando Hernandez	.50
99 Derek Jeter (*)	3.00
100 Tino Martinez	.50
101 Mariano Rivera	.50
102 Alfonso Soriano	.65
103 Bernie Williams (*)	.50
104 Eric Chavez	.50
105 Jason Giambi	.60
106 Ben Grieve	.50
107 Tim Hudson	.60
108 John Jaha	.50
109 Bobby Abreu	.50
110 Doug Glanville	.50
111 Mike Lieberthal	.50
112 Scott Rolen (*)	.60
113 Curt Schilling	.60
114 Brian Giles (*)	.50
115 Jason Kendall	.50
116 Warren Morris	.50
117 Kevin Young	.50
118 Rick Ankiel (*)	.50
119 J.D. Drew (*)	.60
120 Chad Hutchinson	.50
121 Ray Lankford	.50
122 Mark McGwire (*)	2.50
123 Fernando Tatis	.50
124 Bret Boone	.50
125 Ben Davis	.50
126 Tony Gwynn (*)	1.00
127 Trevor Hoffman	.50
128 Barry Bonds (*)	3.00
129 Ellis Burks	.50
130 Jeff Kent	.50
131 J.T. Snow	.50
132 Freddy Garcia	.50
133 Ken Griffey Jr. (*)	2.00
134 Edgar Martinez	.50
135 John Olerud	.50
136 Alex Rodriguez (*)	2.50
137 Jose Canseco (*)	.60
138 Vinny Castilla	.50
139 Roberto Hernandez	.50
140 Fred McGriff	.50
141 Rusty Greer	.50
142 Ruben Mateo (*)	.50
143 Rafael Palmeiro (*)	.65
144 Ivan Rodriguez (*)	.65
145 Lee Stevens	.50
146 Tony Batista	.50
147 Carlos Delgado	.50
148 Shannon Stewart	.50
149 David Wells	.50
150 Vernon Wells	.50

Premiere Date

Sixty-one of each card in '00 Prism were embossed with a round seal at center: "PREMIERE DATE / PRISM / 2000 / APRIL 12, 2000" and have a dot-matrix serial number at bottom-right on front.

	NM/M
Common Player:	1.50
Stars:	8-10X
Production 61 Sets	

Rapture Gold

This complete-set parallel to Prism, features a diagonally striped metallic gold-foil background. A retail-only insert, 565 sets were produced. The cards are not serially numbered.

	NM/M
Complete Set (150):	50.00
Common Player:	.50
Stars:	2-3X

Rapture Silver

One of eight silver-foil parallels to Prism, this version features a diagonally striped background. A hobby-only insert, 916 sets were produced. The cards are not serially numbered.

	NM/M
Complete Set (150):	50.00
Common Player:	.50
Stars:	2-3X

Sheen Silver

One of eight silver-foil versions of Prism, there is virtually no way to describe the silver metallic foil background of this partial-parallel set dubbed "Sheen Silver" by the maker, other than perhaps the diagonal orientation of the jagged-edged forms. Production was reported as 565 each of the cards in the numerical range of #1-40 and #80-110, and 448 each for cards skip-numbered between #42-79 and #111-150. They were inserted into both hobby and retail packaging. The cards are not serially numbered. The 100-card partial-parallel does not include most of the top stars.

	NM/M
Complete Set (100):	40.00
Common Player:	.50
1 Jeff DaVanon RC	.50
2 Troy Glaus	1.50
3 Tim Salmon	.50
5 Jay Bell	.50
6 Erubiel Durazo	.50
7 Luis Gonzalez	.50
10 Andres Galarraga	.50
13 Brian Jordan	.50
15 Kevin Millwood	.50
16 John Smoltz	.50
17 Albert Belle	.50
19 Calvin Pickering	.50
21 B.J. Surhoff	.50
24 Troy O'Leary	.50
25 John Valentin	.50
26 Jason Varitek	.50
27 Mark Grace	.50
28 Henry Rodriguez	.50
31 Ray Durham	.50
32 Carlos Lee	.50
34 Chris Singleton	.50
37 Travis Dawkins	.50
39 Barry Larkin	.50
39 Pokey Reese	.50
40 Scott Williamson	.50
42 Bartolo Colon	.50
43 David Justice	.50
47 Richie Sexson	.50
47 Omar Vizquel	.50
48 Pedro Astacio	.50
50 Neifi Perez	.50
51 Ben Petrick	.50
53 Tony Clark	.50
54 Damion Easley	.50
56 Dean Palmer	.50
57 A.J. Burnett	.50
58 Luis Castillo	.50
59 Cliff Floyd	.50
60 Alex Gonzalez	.50
64 Ken Caminiti	.50
65 Jose Lima	.50
66 Billy Wagner	.50
68 Johnny Damon	.50
69 Jermaine Dye	.50
70 Carlos Febles	.50
71 Mike Sweeney	.50
74 Eric Karros	.50
75 Chan Ho Park	.50
77 Ron Belliard	.50
79 Marquis Grissom	.50
80 Geoff Jenkins	.50
81 Mark Loretta	.50
82 Ron Coomer	.50
83 Jacque Jones	.50
84 Corey Koskie	.50
85 Brad Radke	.50
86 Todd Walker	.50
87 Michael Barrett	.50
88 Peter Bergeron	.50
90 Jose Vidro	.50
93 Rondell White	.50
93 Rickey Henderson	1.50
95 Rey Ordonez	.50
96 Robin Ventura	.50
98 Orlando Hernandez	.50
100 Tino Martinez	.50
101 Mariano Rivera	.50
103 Alfonso Soriano	1.00
104 Eric Chavez	.50
105 Jason Giambi	1.00
106 Ben Grieve	.50
107 Tim Hudson	.50
108 John Jaha	.50
109 Bobby Abreu	.50
110 Doug Glanville	.50
111 Mike Lieberthal	.50
113 Curt Schilling	.50
115 Jason Kendall	.50
116 Warren Morris	.50
117 Kevin Young	.50
120 Chad Hutchinson	.50
121 Ray Lankford	.50
123 Fernando Tatis	.50
124 Bret Boone	.50
125 Ben Davis	.50
127 Trevor Hoffman	.50
129 Ellis Burks	.50
130 Jeff Kent	.50
131 J.T. Snow	.50
134 Edgar Martinez	.50
135 John Olerud	.50
138 Vinny Castilla	.50
139 Roberto Hernandez	.50
140 Fred McGriff	.50
141 Rusty Greer	.50
145 Lee Stevens	.50
146 Tony Batista	.50
148 Shannon Stewart	.50
149 David Wells	.50
150 Vernon Wells	.50

Slider Silver

One of eight silver-foil versions of Prism, there is virtually no way to describe the silver metallic foil background of this parallel set dubbed "Slider Silver" by the

maker, other than perhaps noting the horizontally oriented arrowhead-shaped forms in the background. Production was reported as either 334 each, 448, or 565, depending on press sheet. The number of each card produced is noted parenthetically in this checklist. They were inserted into both hobby and retail packaging. The cards are not serially numbered.

	NM/M
Complete Set (150):	50.00
Common Player:	.50
1 Jeff DaVanon/334 RC	.50
2 Troy Glaus/334	.50
3 Tim Salmon/334	.60
4 Mo Vaughn/565	.50
5 Jay Bell/334	.50
6 Erubiel Durazo/334	.50
7 Luis Gonzalez/334	.50
8 Randy Johnson/565	.75
9 Matt Williams/565	.50
10 Andres Galarraga/334	.50
11 Andruw Jones/565	.75
12 Chipper Jones/565	1.00
13 Brian Jordan/334	.50
14 Greg Maddux/565	1.00
15 Kevin Millwood/334	.50
16 John Smoltz/334	.50
17 Albert Belle/334	.50
18 Mike Mussina/565	.45
19 Calvin Pickering/334	.50
20 Cal Ripken Jr./565	3.00
21 B.J. Surhoff/334	.50
22 Nomar Garciaparra/565	
23 Pedro Martinez/565	.75
24 Troy O'Leary/334	.50
25 John Valentin/334	.50
26 Jason Varitek/334	.50
27 Mark Grace/334	.50
28 Henry Rodriguez/334	.50
29 Sammy Sosa/565	2.00
30 Kerry Wood/565	.60
31 Ray Durham/334	.50
32 Carlos Lee/334	.50
33 Magglio Ordonez/565	.60
34 Chris Singleton/334	.50
35 Frank Thomas/565	.75
36 Sean Casey/565	.60
37 Travis Dawkins/334	.50
38 Barry Larkin/334	.50
39 Pokey Reese/334	.50
40 Scott Williamson/334	.50
41 Roberto Alomar/565	.60
42 Bartolo Colon/448	.50
43 David Justice/448	.50
44 Manny Ramirez/565	.75
45 Richie Sexson/448	.50
46 Jim Thome/565	.65
47 Omar Vizquel/448	.50
48 Pedro Astacio/448	.50
49 Todd Helton/565	.75
50 Neifi Perez/448	.50
51 Ben Petrick/448	.50
52 Larry Walker/565	.50
53 Tony Clark/448	.50
54 Damion Easley/448	.50
55 Juan Gonzalez/565	.75
56 Dean Palmer/448	.50
57 A.J. Burnett/448	.50
58 Luis Castillo/448	.50
59 Cliff Floyd/448	.50
60 Alex Gonzalez/448	.50
61 Preston Wilson/565	.50
62 Jeff Bagwell/565	.75
63 Craig Biggio/565	.50
64 Ken Caminiti/448	.50
65 Jose Lima/448	.50
66 Billy Wagner/448	.50
67 Carlos Beltran/565	.65
68 Johnny Damon/448	.50
69 Jermaine Dye/448	.50
70 Carlos Febles/448	.50
71 Mike Sweeney/448	.50
72 Kevin Brown/565	.50
73 Shawn Green/565	.50
74 Eric Karros/448	.50
75 Chan Ho Park/448	.50
76 Gary Sheffield/565	.50
77 Ron Belliard/448	.50
78 Jeromy Burnitz/565	.50

79 Marquis Grissom/448	.50
80 Geoff Jenkins/334	.50
81 Mark Loretta/334	.50
82 Ron Coomer/334	.50
83 Jacque Jones/334	.50
84 Corey Koskie/334	.50
85 Brad Radke/334	.50
86 Todd Walker/334	.50
87 Michael Barrett/334	.50
88 Peter Bergeron/334	.50
89 Vladimir Guerrero/565	.75
90 Jose Vidro/334	.50
91 Rondell White/334	.50
92 Edgardo Alfonzo/334	.50
93 Rickey Henderson/334	.75
94 Rey Ordonez/334	.50
95 Mike Piazza/565	2.00
96 Robin Ventura/334	.50
97 Roger Clemens/565	1.50
98 Orlando Hernandez/334	.50
99 Derek Jeter/565	3.00
100 Tino Martinez/334	.50
101 Mariano Rivera/334	.50
102 Alfonso Soriano/334	2.00
103 Bernie Williams/334	.60
104 Eric Chavez/334	.50
105 Jason Giambi/334	.50
106 Ben Grieve/334	.50
107 Tim Hudson/334	.60
108 John Jaha/334	.50
109 Bobby Abreu/334	.50
110 Doug Glanville/334	.50
111 Mike Lieberthal/448	.50
112 Scott Rolen/565	.65
113 Curt Schilling/448	.60
114 Brian Giles/565	.60
115 Jason Kendall/448	.50
116 Warren Morris/448	.50
117 Kevin Young/448	.50
118 Rick Ankiel/565	.60
119 J.D. Drew/565	.60
120 Chad Hutchinson/448	.50
121 Ray Lankford/448	.50
122 Mark McGwire/565	2.50
123 Fernando Tatis/448	.50
124 Bret Boone/448	.50
125 Ben Davis/448	.50
126 Tony Gwynn/565	1.00
127 Trevor Hoffman/448	.50
128 Barry Bonds/565	3.00
129 Ellis Burks/448	.50
130 Jeff Kent/448	.50
131 J.T. Snow/448	.50
132 Freddy Garcia/565	.50
133 Ken Griffey Jr./565	2.00
134 Edgar Martinez/448	.50
135 John Olerud/448	.50
136 Alex Rodriguez/565	2.50
137 Jose Canseco/565	.60
138 Vinny Castilla/448	.50
139 Roberto Hernandez/448	.50
140 Fred McGriff/448	.50
141 Rusty Greer/448	.50
142 Ruben Mateo/565	.50
143 Rafael Palmeiro/565	.65
144 Ivan Rodriguez/565	.65
145 Lee Stevens/448	.50
146 Tony Batista/448	.50
147 Carlos Delgado/565	.60
148 Shannon Stewart/448	.50
149 David Wells/448	.50
150 Vernon Wells/448	.50

Texture Silver

One of eight silver-foil versions of Prism, there is virtually no way to describe the silver metallic foil background of this parallel set dubbed "Texture Silver" by the maker to allow its differentiation from the set labeled "Silver Pebbly Drops," other than perhaps the vaguely diagonal orientation of the texture. Production was reported as 448 sets inserted only into retail packaging. The cards are not serially numbered.

	NM/M
Complete Set (150):	50.00
Common Player:	
Stars:	2-3X

Tinsel Silver

One of eight silver-foil parallels to Prism, this version features a horizontally striped

		NM/M
Complete Set (20):		40.00
Common Player:		1.00
Inserted 1:25		
1	Chipper Jones	3.00
2	Cal Ripken Jr.	6.00
3	Nomar Garciaparra	4.00
4	Pedro Martinez	2.00
5	Sammy Sosa	4.00
6	Sean Casey	1.00
7	Manny Ramirez	2.00
8	Jim Thome	1.50
9	Jeff Bagwell	2.00
10	Carlos Beltran	1.50
11	Vladimir Guerrero	2.00
12	Mike Piazza	4.00
13	Derek Jeter	6.00
14	Bernie Williams	1.00
15	Scott Rolen	1.50
16	Mark McGwire	5.00
17	Tony Gwynn	3.00
18	Ken Griffey Jr.	4.00
19	Alex Rodriguez	5.00
20	Ivan Rodriguez	1.50

background that the makers labeled "Tinsel Silver." Inserted only into hobby packaging, production was reported as 331 sets. The cards are not serially numbered.

	NM/M
Complete Set (150):	50.00
Common Player:	.50
Stars:	2-3X

Woodgrain Silver

One of eight silver-foil parallels to Prism, this version features a mottled patterned background which the makers insist resembles woodgrain. Inserted only into retail packaging, production was reported as 331 sets. The cards are not serially numbered.

	NM/M
Complete Set (150):	50.00
Common Player:	.50
Stars:	2-3X

A.L. Legends

		NM/M
Complete Set (10):		15.00
Common Player:		.50
Inserted 1:25		
1	Chipper Jones	2.00
2	Greg Maddux	2.00
3	Sammy Sosa	2.50
4	Larry Walker	.50
5	Jeff Bagwell	1.00
6	Vladimir Guerrero	2.00
7	Mike Piazza	2.50
8	Mark McGwire	3.00
9	Tony Gwynn	2.00
10	Barry Bonds	4.00

		NM/M
Complete Set (10):		15.00
Common Player:		.50
Inserted 1:25		
1	Mo Vaughn	.50
2	Cal Ripken Jr.	4.00
3	Nomar Garciaparra	2.50
4	Manny Ramirez	1.50
5	Roger Clemens	2.00
6	Derek Jeter	4.00
7	Ken Griffey Jr.	2.50
8	Alex Rodriguez	3.00
9	Jose Canseco	.75
10	Rafael Palmeiro	1.00

Center Stage

2000 Pacific Private Stock

This base set consists of 150-cards, each card image uses an artist's computer generated brush strokes. Short-printed prospects are seeded 1:4 packs. The logo, player name and team are stamped in gold foil.

		NM/M
Complete Set (150):		50.00
Common Player:		.15
Common SP Prospect:		1.00
Inserted 1:4		
Pack (7):		2.00
Wax Box (24):		35.00
1	Darin Erstad	.25
2	Troy Glaus	.75
3	Tim Salmon	.25
4	Mo Vaughn	.15
5	Jay Bell	.15
6	Luis Gonzalez	.25
7	Randy Johnson	.75
8	Matt Williams	.15
9	Andruw Jones	.75
10	Chipper Jones	1.00
11	Brian Jordan	.15
12	Greg Maddux	1.00
13	Kevin Millwood	.15
14	Albert Belle	.20
15	Mike Mussina	.35
16	Cal Ripken Jr.	2.00
17	B.J. Surhoff	.15
18	Nomar Garciaparra	1.25
19	Butch Huskey	.15
20	Pedro Martinez	.75
21	Troy O'Leary	.15
22	Mark Grace	.25
23	Bo Porter/SP	1.00
24	Henry Rodriguez	.15
25	Sammy Sosa	1.25
26	Kerry Wood	.40
27	Jason Dellaero/SP	1.00
28	Ray Durham	.15
29	Paul Konerko	.20
30	Carlos Lee	.15
31	Magglio Ordonez	.25
32	Frank Thomas	.75
33	Mike Cameron	.15
34	Sean Casey	.25
35	Barry Larkin	.15
36	Greg Vaughn	.15
37	Roberto Alomar	.40
38	Russell Branyan/SP	1.00
39	Kenny Lofton	.15
40	Manny Ramirez	.75
41	Richie Sexson	.15
42	Jim Thome	.75
43	Omar Vizquel	.15
44	Dante Bichette	.15
45	Vinny Castilla	.15
46	Todd Helton	.75
47	Ben Petrick/SP	1.00
48	Juan Sosa/SP	1.00
49	Larry Walker	.15
50	Tony Clark	.15
51	Damion Easley	.15
52	Juan Encarnacion	.15
53	Robert Fick/SP	1.00
54	Dean Palmer	.15
55	A.J. Burnett/SP	1.00
56	Luis Castillo	.15
57	Alex Gonzalez	.15
58	Julio Ramirez/SP	1.00
59	Preston Wilson	.15
60	Jeff Bagwell	.75
61	Craig Biggio	.15
62	Ken Caminiti	.15
63	Carl Everett	.15
64	Mike Hampton	.15
65	Billy Wagner	.15
66	Carlos Beltran	.50
67	Dermal Brown/SP	1.00
68	Jermaine Dye	.15
69	Carlos Febles	.15
70	Mark Quinn/SP	1.00
71	Mike Sweeney	.15
72	Kevin Brown	.15

Diamond Dial-A-Stats

		NM/M
Complete Set (10):		90.00
Common Player:		8.00
Inserted 1:193		
1	Chipper Jones	8.00
2	Greg Maddux	8.00
3	Cal Ripken Jr.	20.00
4	Sammy Sosa	10.00
5	Mike Piazza	10.00
6	Roger Clemens	9.00
7	Mark McGwire	15.00
8	Tony Gwynn	8.00
9	Ken Griffey Jr.	10.00
10	Alex Rodriguez	15.00

N.L. Legends

Prospects

		NM/M
Complete Set (10):		12.00
Common Player:		1.00
Inserted 1:97		
1	Erubiel Durazo	1.00
2	Wilton Veras	1.00
3	Ben Petrick	1.00
4	Mark Quinn	1.00
5	Peter Bergeron	1.00
6	Alfonso Soriano	5.00
7	Tim Hudson	2.00
8	Chad Hermansen	1.00
9	Rick Ankiel	1.50
10	Ruben Mateo	1.00

ABBREVIATIONS
SP - Short Print

73	Eric Gagne/SP	1.50
74	Eric Karros	.15
75	Raul Mondesi	.15
76	Gary Sheffield	.40
77	Jeromy Burnitz	.15
78	Jeff Cirillo	.15
79	Geoff Jenkins	.15
80	David Nilsson	.15
81	Ron Coomer	.15
82	Jacque Jones	.15
83	Corey Koskie	.15
84	Brad Radke	.15
85	Tony Armas Jr./SP	1.50
86	Peter Bergeron/SP	1.00
87	Vladimir Guerrero	.75
88	Jose Vidro	.15
89	Rondell White	.15
90	Edgardo Alfonzo	.15
91	Roger Cedeno	.15
92	Rickey Henderson	.75
93	Jay Payton/SP	1.00
94	Mike Piazza	1.25
95	Jorge Toca/SP	1.00
96	Robin Ventura	.15
97	Roger Clemens	1.00
98	David Cone	.15
99	Derek Jeter	2.00
100	D'Angelo Jimenez/SP	1.00
101	Tino Martinez	.15
102	Alfonso Soriano/SP	3.00
103	Bernie Williams	.25
104	Jason Giambi	.50
105	Ben Grieve	.15
106	Tim Hudson	.25
107	Matt Stairs	.15
108	Bobby Abreu	.15
109	Doug Glanville	.15
110	Scott Rolen	.65
111	Curt Schilling	.40
112	Brian Giles	.15
113	Chad Hermansen/SP	1.00
114	Jason Kendall	.15
115	Warren Morris	.15
116	Rick Ankiel/SP	1.00
117	J.D. Drew	.25
118	Adam Kennedy/SP	1.00
119	Ray Lankford	.15
120	Mark McGwire	1.50
121	Fernando Tatis	.15
122	Mike Darr/SP	1.00
123	Ben Davis	.15
124	Tony Gwynn	1.00
125	Trevor Hoffman	.15
126	Reggie Sanders	.15
127	Barry Bonds	2.00
128	Ellis Burks	.15
129	Jeff Kent	.15
130	J.T. Snow	.15
131	Freddy Garcia	.15
132	Ken Griffey Jr.	1.25
133	Carlos Guillen/SP	1.00
134	Edgar Martinez	.15
135	Alex Rodriguez	1.50
136	Miguel Cairo	.15
137	Jose Canseco	.40
138	Steve Cox/SP	1.00
139	Roberto Hernandez	.15
140	Fred McGriff	.15
141	Juan Gonzalez	.75
142	Rusty Greer	.15
143	Ruben Mateo/SP	1.00
144	Rafael Palmeiro	.65
145	Ivan Rodriguez	.65
146	Carlos Delgado	.50
147	Tony Fernandez	.15
148	Shawn Green	.35
149	Shannon Stewart	.15
150	Vernon Wells/SP	1.00

Gold Portraits

A parallel to the 150-card base set these have a gold foiled border. These are found exclusively in hobby packs and are limited to 99 serial numbered sets.

Stars:	5-10X
Prospects:	1-2X
Production 99 Sets	

Silver Portraits

A parallel to the 150-card base set. These have a silver foiled border. Found exclusively in retail packs, these are limited to 199 serial numbered sets.

Stars:	3-6X
Prospects:	1-2X
Production 199 Sets	

Premiere Date

A parallel to the 150-card base set these are limited to 34 serial numbered sets.

Stars:	5-10X
Prospects:	1-2X
Inserted 1:24	

Canvas

This 20-card set is printed on real artist's canvas and has the look of a miniature piece of art.

		NM/M
Complete Set (20):		120.00
Common Player:		2.00
Inserted 1:49		
1	Chipper Jones	8.00
2	Greg Maddux	8.00
3	Cal Ripken Jr.	15.00
4	Nomar Garciaparra	10.00
5	Sammy Sosa	10.00
6	Frank Thomas	6.00
7	Manny Ramirez	6.00
8	Larry Walker	2.00
9	Jeff Bagwell	6.00
10	Vladimir Guerrero	6.00
11	Mike Piazza	10.00
12	Roger Clemens	9.00
13	Derek Jeter	15.00
14	Mark McGwire	12.00
15	Tony Gwynn	8.00
16	Barry Bonds	15.00
17	Ken Griffey Jr.	10.00
18	Alex Rodriguez	12.00
19	Juan Gonzalez	6.00
20	Ivan Rodriguez	5.00

Extreme Action

The focus of this 20-card set is the action photography, hence the name Extreme Action. They are seeded 2:25 packs.

		NM/M
Complete Set (20):		25.00
Common Player:		.50
Inserted 2:25		
1	Andruw Jones	1.50
2	Chipper Jones	2.00
3	Cal Ripken Jr.	4.00
4	Nomar Garciaparra	2.50
5	Sammy Sosa	2.50
6	Frank Thomas	1.50
7	Roberto Alomar	.60
8	Manny Ramirez	1.50
9	Larry Walker	.50
10	Jeff Bagwell	1.50
11	Vladimir Guerrero	1.50
12	Mike Piazza	2.50
13	Derek Jeter	4.00
14	Bernie Williams	.50
15	Scott Rolen	1.00
16	Mark McGwire	3.00
17	Tony Gwynn	2.00
18	Ken Griffey Jr.	2.50
19	Alex Rodriguez	3.00
20	Ivan Rodriguez	1.00

Reserve

Found exclusively in hobby packs these have a paper thin stock, enhanced with gold foil stamping. These are seeded 1:25 packs.

		NM/M
Complete Set (20):		50.00
Common Player:		1.00
Inserted 1:25		
1	Chipper Jones	3.00
2	Greg Maddux	3.00
3	Cal Ripken Jr.	6.00
4	Nomar Garciaparra	4.00
5	Sammy Sosa	4.00
6	Frank Thomas	2.00
7	Manny Ramirez	2.00
8	Larry Walker	1.00
9	Jeff Bagwell	2.00
10	Vladimir Guerrero	2.00
11	Mike Piazza	4.00
12	Roger Clemens	3.50
13	Derek Jeter	6.00
14	Mark McGwire	5.00
15	Tony Gwynn	3.00
16	Barry Bonds	6.00
17	Ken Griffey Jr.	4.00
18	Alex Rodriguez	5.00
19	Ivan Rodriguez	1.50
20	Shawn Green	1.25

PS-2000

This miniature 60-card set has a white border with gold foil stamping and are seeded 2 per pack.

		NM/M
Complete Set (60):		15.00
Common Player:		.15
Inserted 2:Pack		
1	Mo Vaughn	.15
2	Greg Maddux	1.00
3	Andruw Jones	.75
4	Chipper Jones	1.00
5	Cal Ripken Jr.	2.50
6	Nomar Garciaparra	1.50
7	Pedro Martinez	.75
8	Sammy Sosa	1.50
9	Jason Dellaero	.15
10	Magglio Ordonez	.15
11	Frank Thomas	.75
12	Sean Casey	.25
13	Russell Branyan	.15
14	Manny Ramirez	.75
15	Richie Sexson	.15
16	Ben Petrick	.15
17	Juan Sosa	.15
18	Larry Walker	.15
19	Robert Fick	.15
20	Craig Biggio	.15
21	Jeff Bagwell	.75
22	Carlos Beltran	.50
23	Dermal Brown	.15
24	Mark Quinn	.15

25	Eric Gagne	.15
26	Jeromy Burnitz	.15
27	Tony Armas Jr.	.15
28	Peter Bergeron	.15
29	Vladimir Guerrero	.75
30	Edgardo Alfonzo	.15
31	Mike Piazza	1.50
32	Jorge Toca	.15
33	Roger Clemens	1.25
34	Alfonso Soriano	.65
35	Bernie Williams	.25
36	Derek Jeter	1.50
37	Tim Hudson	.25
38	Bobby Abreu	.15
39	Scott Rolen	.65
40	Brian Giles	.15
41	Chad Hermansen	.15
42	Warren Morris	.15
43	Rick Ankiel	.25
44	J.D. Drew	.15
45	Adam Kennedy	.15
46	Mark McGwire	2.00
47	Mike Darr	.15
48	Tony Gwynn	1.00
49	Barry Bonds	2.50
50	Ken Griffey Jr.	1.50
51	Carlos Guillen	.15
52	Alex Rodriguez	1.50
53	Juan Gonzalez	.75
54	Ruben Mateo	.15
55	Ivan Rodriguez	.65
56	Rafael Palmeiro	.65
57	Jose Canseco	.40
58	Steve Cox	.15
59	Shawn Green	.30
60	Vernon Wells	.15

PS-2000 New Wave

This miniature 20-card set has copper foil stamping and is limited to 199 serial numbered sets.

		NM/M
Complete Set (20):		40.00
Common Player:		1.00
Production 199 Sets		
1	Andruw Jones	3.50
2	Chipper Jones	5.00
3	Nomar Garciaparra	6.00
4	Magglio Ordonez	1.00
5	Sean Casey	1.00
6	Manny Ramirez	3.50
7	Richie Sexson	1.00
8	Carlos Beltran	2.00
9	Jeromy Burnitz	1.00
10	Vladimir Guerrero	3.50
11	Edgardo Alfonzo	1.00
12	Derek Jeter	10.00
13	Tim Hudson	1.00
14	Bobby Abreu	1.00
15	Scott Rolen	2.50
16	Brian Giles	1.00
17	Warren Morris	1.00
18	J.D. Drew	1.25
19	Alex Rodriguez	8.00
20	Shawn Green	1.25

PS-2000 Rookies

This miniature 20-card set has holographic silver foil stamping and is limited to 99 serial numbered sets.

		NM/M
Complete Set (20):		20.00
Common Player:		1.00
Inserted 99 Sets		
1	Jason Dellaero	1.00
2	Russell Branyan	1.00
3	Ben Petrick	1.00
4	Juan Sosa	1.00
5	Robert Fick	1.00
6	Dermal Brown	1.00
7	Mark Quinn	1.00
8	Eric Gagne	1.50
9	Tony Armas Jr.	1.00
10	Peter Bergeron	1.00
11	Jorge Toca	1.00
12	Alfonso Soriano	6.00
13	Chad Hermansen	1.00
14	Rick Ankiel	1.00

15	Adam Kennedy	1.50
16	Mike Darr	1.00
17	Carlos Guillen	1.00
18	Steve Cox	1.00
19	Ruben Mateo	1.50
20	Vernon Wells	1.50

PS-2000 Stars

This miniature 20-card set is limited to 299 serial numbered sets.

		NM/M
Complete Set (20):		40.00
Common Player:		1.00
Production 299 Sets		
1	Mo Vaughn	1.00
2	Greg Maddux	4.00
3	Cal Ripken Jr.	8.00
4	Pedro Martinez	3.00
5	Sammy Sosa	5.00
6	Frank Thomas	4.00
7	Larry Walker	1.00
8	Craig Biggio	1.00
9	Jeff Bagwell	3.00
10	Mike Piazza	5.00
11	Roger Clemens	4.50
12	Bernie Williams	1.00
13	Mark McGwire	6.00
14	Tony Gwynn	3.00
15	Barry Bonds	8.00
16	Ken Griffey Jr.	5.00
17	Juan Gonzalez	3.00
18	Ivan Rodriguez	2.00
19	Rafael Palmeiro	2.00
20	Jose Canseco	1.00

2000 Pacific Revolution

The base set consists of 150 cards with silver holofoil throughout the card front. "Revolution" is embossed on the left portion and the logo is stamped in gold foil. Twenty-five short-printed prospects are seeded 1:4 packs.

		NM/M
Complete Set (150):		60.00
Common Player:		.25
Common SP:		.50
Pack (3):		2.00
Box:		35.00
1	Darin Erstad	.50
2	Troy Glaus	1.00
3	Adam Kennedy/SP	1.50
4	Mo Vaughn	.25
5	Erubiel Durazo	.25
6	Steve Finley	.25
7	Luis Gonzalez	.35
8	Randy Johnson	.75
9	Travis Lee	.25
10	Vicente Padilla/SP	1.00
11	Matt Williams	.25
12	Rafael Furcal/SP	1.00
13	Andres Galarraga	.25
14	Andruw Jones	.75
15	Chipper Jones	1.50
16	Greg Maddux	1.50
17	Luis Rivera/SP	1.00
18	Albert Belle	.25
19	Mike Bordick	.25
20	Will Clark	.35
21	Mike Mussina	.40
22	Cal Ripken Jr.	.25
23	B.J. Surhoff	.25
24	Carl Everett	.25
25	Nomar Garciaparra	2.00
26	Pedro Martinez	1.00
27	Jason Varitek	.25
28	Wilton Veras/SP	1.00
29	Shane Andrews	.25
30	Scott Downs/SP RC	1.00
31	Mark Grace	.35
32	Sammy Sosa	1.50
33	Kerry Wood	.50
34	Ray Durham	.25
35	Paul Konerko	.35
36	Carlos Lee	.25
37	Magglio Ordonez	.25
38	Frank Thomas	1.00
39	Rob Bell/SP	1.00
40	Sean Casey	.25
41	Ken Griffey Jr.	2.00
42	Barry Larkin	.25

43	Pokey Reese	.25
44	Roberto Alomar	.40
45	David Justice	.25
46	Kenny Lofton	.25
47	Manny Ramirez	1.00
48	Richie Sexson	.25
49	Jim Thome	1.00
50	Jeff Cirillo	.25
51	Jeffrey Hammonds	.25
52	Todd Helton	1.00
53	Larry Walker	.25
54	Tony Clark	.25
55	Juan Gonzalez	1.00
56	Hideo Nomo	1.00
57	Dean Palmer	.25
58	Alex Gonzalez	.25
59	Mike Lowell	.25
60	Pablo Ozuna/SP	1.00
61	Brad Penny/SP	.25
62	Preston Wilson	.25
63	Moises Alou	.25
64	Jeff Bagwell	1.00
65	Craig Biggio	.25
66	Ken Caminiti	.25
67	Julio Lugo/SP	1.00
68	Carlos Beltran	.60
69	Johnny Damon	.40
70	Jermaine Dye	.25
71	Carlos Febles	.25
72	Mark Quinn/SP	1.00
73	Kevin Brown	.25
74	Shawn Green	.65
75	Chan Ho Park	.25
76	Gary Sheffield	.50
77	Kevin Barker/SP	1.00
78	Ron Belliard	.25
79	Jeromy Burnitz	.25
80	Geoff Jenkins	.25
81	Cristian Guzman	.25
82	Jacque Jones	.25
83	Corey Koskie	.25
84	Matt Lawton	.25
85	Peter Bergeron/SP	1.00
86	Vladimir Guerrero	1.00
87	Andy Tracy/SP	1.00
88	Jose Vidro	.25
89	Rondell White	.25
90	Edgardo Alfonzo	.25
91	Derek Bell	.25
92	Eric Cammack/SP	1.00
93	Mike Piazza	2.00
94	Robin Ventura	.25
95	Roger Clemens	1.75
96	Orlando Hernandez	.25
97	Derek Jeter	3.00
98	Tino Martinez	.25
99	Alfonso Soriano/SP	3.00
100	Bernie Williams	.35
101	Eric Chavez	.35
102	Jason Giambi	.75
103	Ben Grieve	.25
104	Terrence Long/SP	1.00
105	Mark Mulder/SP	1.00
106	Adam Piatt/SP	1.00
107	Bobby Abreu	.25
108	Rico Brogna	.25
109	Doug Glanville	.25
110	Mike Lieberthal	.25
111	Scott Rolen	.75
112	Brian Giles	.25
113	Chad Hermansen/SP	1.00
114	Jason Kendall	.25
115	Warren Morris	.25
116	Rick Ankiel/SP	1.00
117	J.D. Drew	.40
118	Jim Edmonds	.25
119	Mark McGwire	2.50
120	Fernando Tatis	.25
121	Fernando Vina	.25
122	Tony Gwynn	1.50
123	Trevor Hoffman	.25
124	Ryan Klesko	.25
125	Eric Owens	.25
126	Barry Bonds	3.00
127	Ellis Burks	.25
128	Bobby Estalella	.25
129	Jeff Kent	.25
130	Scott Linebrink/SP RC	1.00
131	Jay Buhner	.25
132	Stan Javier	.25
133	Edgar Martinez	.25
134	John Olerud	.25
135	Alex Rodriguez/SP	2.50
136	Kazuhiro Sasaki/SP RC	2.00
137	Jose Canseco	.40
138	Vinny Castilla	.25
139	Fred McGriff	.25
140	Greg Vaughn	.25
141	Gabe Kapler	.25
142	Mike Lamb/SP RC	1.00
143	Ruben Mateo	.25
144	Rafael Palmeiro	.75
145	Ivan Rodriguez	.75
146	Tony Batista	.25
147	Jose Cruz Jr.	.25
148	Carlos Delgado	.75
149	Brad Fullmer	.25
150	Raul Mondesi	.25

Revolution Red

A parallel to the 150-card base set these insert have red

ABBREVIATIONS

SP - Short Print

foil in place of the gold from the base version. These are also serial numbered on the card front, limited to 299 sets.

Stars:	1-2X
SP's:	1X
Production 299 Sets	

Shadow

This parallel to the 150-card base set replaces the gold foil on front with blue foil and has an embossed box at center which reads "SHADOW SERIES." Backs have a serial number ink-jetted from within an edition of 99 each.

Stars:	3-6X
SP's:	1-2X
Production 99 Sets	

Foul Pole Net-Fusions

These inserts utilize net-fusion technology, with netting infused in the left and right portion. The player name and logo are stamped in gold foil. These are found on the average of 1:49 packs.

		NM/M
Complete Set (20):		110.00
Common Player:		2.00
Inserted 1:49		
1	Chipper Jones	8.00
2	Cal Ripken Jr.	15.00
3	Nomar Garciaparra	10.00
4	Pedro Martinez	10.00
5	Sammy Sosa	10.00
6	Frank Thomas	6.00
7	Ken Griffey Jr.	10.00
8	Manny Ramirez	6.00
9	Jeff Bagwell	6.00
10	Shawn Green	3.00
11	Vladimir Guerrero	6.00
12	Mike Piazza	10.00
13	Derek Jeter	15.00
14	Bernie Williams	2.00
15	Rick Ankiel	2.00
16	Mark McGwire	12.00
17	Tony Gwynn	8.00
18	Barry Bonds	15.00
19	Alex Rodriguez	12.00
20	Ivan Rodriguez	8.00

Game-Ball Signatures

These inserts have a die-cut rounded bottom and feature the player in a simulated on-deck circle enhanced by green foil stamping. These are seeded 1:25 packs.

This 25-card autographed set has a piece of baseball leather embedded into the front on which the player penned his signature.

		NM/M
Common Player:		5.00
1	Randy Johnson	40.00
2	Greg Maddux	90.00
3	Rafael Furcal	7.50
4	Shane Andrews	5.00
5	Sean Casey	10.00
6	Travis Dawkins	5.00
7	Alex Gonzalez	5.00
8	Shane Reynolds	5.00
9	Eric Gagne	10.00
10	Kevin Barker	5.00
11	Eric Milton	5.00
12	Mark Quinn	5.00
13	Alfonso Soriano	40.00
14	Brian Giles	6.00
15	Mark Mulder	10.00
16	Adam Piatt	5.00
17	Warren Morris	6.00
18	Rick Ankiel	6.00
19	Adam Kennedy	6.00
20	Fernando Tatis	5.00
21	Barry Bonds	100.00
22	Alex Rodriguez	75.00
23	Ruben Mateo	5.00
24	Billy Koch	5.00
25	Brad Penny	5.00

Icons

These die-cut cards feature silver foil stamping and the player's team logo in the background. These are found on the average of 1:121 packs.

		NM/M
Complete Set (20):		250.00
Common Player:		8.00
Inserted 1:121		
1	Randy Johnson	10.00
2	Chipper Jones	15.00
3	Greg Maddux	15.00
4	Cal Ripken Jr.	30.00
5	Nomar Garciaparra	20.00
6	Pedro Martinez	10.00
7	Sammy Sosa	10.00
8	Frank Thomas	10.00
9	Ken Griffey Jr.	20.00
10	Juan Gonzalez	10.00
11	Jeff Bagwell	10.00
12	Vladimir Guerrero	10.00
13	Mike Piazza	20.00
14	Roger Clemens	17.50
15	Derek Jeter	30.00
16	Mark McGwire	25.00
17	Tony Gwynn	15.00
18	Barry Bonds	30.00
19	Alex Rodriguez	25.00
20	Ivan Rodriguez	8.00

On Deck

These inserts have a die-cut rounded bottom and feature the player in a simulated on-deck circle enhanced by green foil stamping. These are seeded 1:25 packs.

		NM/M
Complete Set (20):		40.00
Common Player:		1.00
Inserted 1:25		
1	Chipper Jones	3.00
2	Cal Ripken Jr.	6.00
3	Nomar Garciaparra	4.00
4	Sammy Sosa	4.00
5	Frank Thomas	2.00
6	Ken Griffey Jr.	4.00
7	Manny Ramirez	2.00
8	Larry Walker	1.00
9	Juan Gonzalez	2.00
10	Jeff Bagwell	2.00
11	Shawn Green	1.50
12	Vladimir Guerrero	2.00
13	Mike Piazza	4.00
14	Derek Jeter	6.00
15	Scott Rolen	1.50
16	Mark McGwire	5.00
17	Tony Gwynn	3.00
18	Alex Rodriguez	5.00
19	Jose Canseco	1.50
20	Ivan Rodriguez	1.75

Season Opener

This 36-card set has a horizontal format with the set name, team logo, player name and Revolution logo stamped in gold foil. These are seeded 2:25 packs.

		NM/M
Complete Set (36):		35.00
Common Player:		.50
Inserted 2:25		
1	Erubiel Durazo	.50
2	Randy Johnson	1.50
3	Andruw Jones	1.50
4	Chipper Jones	2.00
5	Greg Maddux	2.00
6	Cal Ripken Jr.	4.00
7	Nomar Garciaparra	3.00
8	Pedro Martinez	1.50
9	Sammy Sosa	1.50
10	Frank Thomas	1.50
11	Magglio Ordonez	.50
12	Ken Griffey Jr.	2.50
13	Barry Larkin	.50
14	Kenny Lofton	.50
15	Manny Ramirez	1.50
16	Jim Thome	1.50
17	Larry Walker	.50
18	Juan Gonzalez	1.50
19	Jeff Bagwell	1.50
20	Craig Biggio	.50
21	Carlos Beltran	.75
22	Shawn Green	.75
23	Vladimir Guerrero	1.50
24	Mike Piazza	2.50
25	Orlando Hernandez	.50
26	Derek Jeter	4.00
27	Bernie Williams	.50
28	Eric Chavez	.50
29	Scott Rolen	1.00
30	Jim Edmonds	.50
31	Tony Gwynn	2.00
32	Barry Bonds	4.00
33	Alex Rodriguez	3.00
34	Jose Canseco	.65
35	Ivan Rodriguez	1.00
36	Rafael Palmeiro	1.00

Triple Header

This 30-card set is broken down into three tiers with cards 1-10 spotlighting batting average leaders, 11-20 home run leaders and 21-30 strikeout leaders. The base versions are seeded 4:25 packs. A parallel version for each of the three groups is also inserted. Cards 1-20 are limited to 99 serial numbered sets while cards 21-30 are limited to 599 serial numbered sets.

	NM/M
Complete Set (30):	25.00

Common Player:		.25
Inserted 4:25		
Parallel (1-10):		3-6X
99 Sets Produced		
Parallel (11-20):		3-6X
99 Sets Produced		
Parallel (21-30):		1-2X
599 Sets Produced		
1	Chipper Jones	1.50
2	Cal Ripken Jr.	3.00
3	Nomar Garciaparra	2.00
4	Frank Thomas	1.00
5	Larry Walker	.25
6	Vladimir Guerrero	1.00
7	Mike Piazza	2.00
8	Derek Jeter	3.00
9	Tony Gwynn	1.50
10	Ivan Rodriguez	.75
11	Sammy Sosa	2.00
12	Ken Griffey Jr.	2.00
13	Manny Ramirez	1.00
14	Jeff Bagwell	1.00
15	Shawn Green	.40
16	Mark McGwire	2.50
17	Barry Bonds	3.00
18	Alex Rodriguez	2.50
19	Jose Canseco	.50
20	Rafael Palmeiro	.75
21	Randy Johnson	1.00
22	Tom Glavine	.40
23	Greg Maddux	1.50
24	Mike Mussina	.40
25	Pedro Martinez	1.00
26	Kerry Wood	.60
27	Chuck Finley	.25
28	Kevin Brown	.25
29	Roger Clemens	1.75
30	Rick Ankiel	.25

2000 Pacific Vanguard Sample

To introduce the hobby to its new Vanguard brand, Pacific issued this card of principal spokesman Tony Gwynn. Using the same "Vision-Glow" technology as the regular-issue cards, the sample has a large white diagonal overprint on back and "SAMPLE" instead of a card number.

NM/M
Tony Gwynn 3.00

2000 Pacific Vanguard

		NM/M
Complete Set (100):		30.00
Common Player:		.15
Pack (4):		2.00
Wax Box (24):		35.00
1	Troy Glaus	1.00
2	Tim Salmon	.25
3	Mo Vaughn	.15
4	Albert Belle	.15
5	Mike Mussina	.35
6	Cal Ripken Jr.	3.00
7	Nomar Garciaparra	2.00
8	Pedro Martinez	1.00
9	Troy O'Leary	.15
10	Wilton Veras	.15
11	Magglio Ordonez	.15
12	Chris Singleton	.15
13	Frank Thomas	1.00
14	Roberto Alomar	.40
15	Russell Branyan	.15

16	Manny Ramirez	1.00
17	Jim Thome	.75
18	Omar Vizquel	.15
19	Tony Clark	.15
20	Juan Gonzalez	1.00
21	Dean Palmer	.15
22	Carlos Beltran	.50
23	Johnny Damon	.30
24	Jermaine Dye	.15
25	Mark Quinn	.15
26	Jacque Jones	.15
27	Corey Koskie	.15
28	Brad Radke	.15
29	Roger Clemens	1.75
30	Derek Jeter	3.00
31	Alfonso Soriano	.75
32	Bernie Williams	.30
33	Eric Chavez	.30
34	Jason Giambi	.75
35	Ben Grieve	.15
36	Tim Hudson	.30
37	Mike Cameron	.15
38	Freddy Garcia	.15
39	Edgar Martinez	.15
40	Alex Rodriguez	2.50
41	Jose Canseco	.50
42	Vinny Castilla	.15
43	Fred McGriff	.15
44	Rusty Greer	.15
45	Ruben Mateo	.15
46	Rafael Palmeiro	.75
47	Ivan Rodriguez	.65
48	Carlos Delgado	.75
49	Shannon Stewart	.15
50	Vernon Wells	.15
51	Erubiel Durazo	.15
52	Randy Johnson	1.00
53	Matt Williams	.15
54	Andruw Jones	1.00
55	Chipper Jones	1.50
56	Greg Maddux	1.50
57	Mark Grace	.25
58	Sammy Sosa	2.00
59	Kerry Wood	.50
60	Sean Casey	.25
61	Ken Griffey Jr.	2.00
62	Barry Larkin	.15
63	Todd Helton	1.00
64	Ben Petrick	.15
65	Larry Walker	.15
66	Luis Castillo	.15
67	Alex Gonzalez	.15
68	Preston Wilson	.15
69	Jeff Bagwell	1.00
70	Craig Biggio	.15
71	Billy Wagner	.15
72	Kevin Brown	.15
73	Shawn Green	.40
74	Gary Sheffield	.40
75	Kevin Barker	.15
76	Ron Belliard	.15
77	Jeromy Burnitz	.15
78	Michael Barrett	.15
79	Peter Bergeron	.15
80	Vladimir Guerrero	1.00
81	Edgardo Alfonzo	.15
82	Rey Ordonez	.15
83	Mike Piazza	2.00
84	Robin Ventura	.15
85	Bobby Abreu	.15
86	Mike Lieberthal	.15
87	Scott Rolen	.75
88	Brian Giles	.15
89	Chad Hermansen	.15
90	Jason Kendall	.15
91	Rick Ankiel	.15
92	J.D. Drew	.25
93	Mark McGwire	2.50
94	Fernando Tatis	.15
95	Ben Davis	.15
96	Tony Gwynn	1.50
97	Trevor Hoffman	.15
98	Barry Bonds	3.00
99	Ellis Burks	.15
100	Jeff Kent	.15

Gold

A.L. (1-50):	2-4X
Production 199 Sets R	
N.L. (51-100):	3-6X
Production 99 Sets R	

Green

A.L. (1-50):	3-6X
Production 99 Sets	
N.L. (51-100):	2-4X
Production 199 Sets	

Vanguard Purple

ROBERTO ALOMAR
CLEVELAND INDIANS
04/10

Production 10 Sets
Values Undetermined

Premiere Date

Stars:	3-5X
Production 135 Sets H	

A.L. Vanguard Press

		NM/M
Complete Set (10):		10.00
Common Player:		.65
Inserted 2:25		
1	Cal Ripken Jr.	3.00
2	Nomar Garciaparra	2.00
3	Pedro Martinez	1.00
4	Manny Ramirez	1.00
5	Carlos Beltran	.65
6	Roger Clemens	1.50
7	Derek Jeter	3.00
8	Alex Rodriguez	2.50
9	Rafael Palmeiro	.75
10	Ivan Rodriguez	.75

Cosmic Force

		NM/M
Complete Set (10):		30.00
Common Player:		3.00
Inserted 1:73		
1	Chipper Jones	2.00
2	Cal Ripken Jr.	6.00
3	Nomar Garciaparra	4.00
4	Sammy Sosa	4.00
5	Ken Griffey Jr.	4.00
6	Mike Piazza	4.00
7	Derek Jeter	6.00
8	Mark McGwire	5.00
9	Tony Gwynn	5.00
10	Alex Rodriguez	5.00

Diamond Architects

SCOTT ROLEN
Philadelphia Phillies

		NM/M
Complete Set (20):		25.00
Common Player:		.50
Inserted 1:25		
1	Chipper Jones	2.00
2	Greg Maddux	2.00
3	Cal Ripken Jr.	4.00
4	Nomar Garciaparra	2.50
5	Sammy Sosa	2.50
6	Ken Griffey Jr.	2.50
7	Manny Ramirez	1.50
8	Larry Walker	.50
9	Jeff Bagwell	1.50
10	Vladimir Guerrero	1.50
11	Mike Piazza	2.50
12	Roger Clemens	2.25
13	Derek Jeter	4.00
14	Bernie Williams	.50
15	Scott Rolen	1.00
16	Mark McGwire	3.00
17	Tony Gwynn	2.00
18	Alex Rodriguez	3.00
19	Rafael Palmeiro	.75
20	Ivan Rodriguez	.75

Game Worn Jersey

		NM/M
Inserted 1:120		
1	Greg Maddux	10.00
2	Tony Gwynn	10.00
3	Alex Rodriguez	20.00
4	Frank Thomas	8.00
5	Chipper Jones	10.00

High Voltage

		NM/M
Complete Set (36):		10.00
Common Player:		.15
Inserted 1:1		

ROGER CLEMENS

1	Mo Vaughn	.15
2	Erubiel Durazo	.15
3	Randy Johnson	.60
4	Andruw Jones	.60
5	Chipper Jones	.75
6	Greg Maddux	.75
7	Cal Ripken Jr.	2.00
8	Nomar Garciaparra	1.25
9	Pedro Martinez	.60
10	Sammy Sosa	1.25
11	Frank Thomas	.60
12	Sean Casey	.25
13	Ken Griffey Jr.	1.25
14	Barry Larkin	.15
15	Manny Ramirez	.60
16	Jim Thome	.50
17	Larry Walker	.15
18	Jeff Bagwell	.60
19	Craig Biggio	.15
20	Carlos Beltran	.40
21	Shawn Green	.25
22	Vladimir Guerrero	.60
23	Edgardo Alfonzo	.15
24	Mike Piazza	1.50
25	Roger Clemens	1.00
26	Derek Jeter	2.00
27	Bernie Williams	.25
28	Scott Rolen	.60
29	Brian Giles	.15
30	Rick Ankiel	.15
31	Mark McGwire	1.50
32	Tony Gwynn	.75
33	Barry Bonds	2.00
34	Alex Rodriguez	1.50
35	Rafael Palmeiro	.60
36	Ivan Rodriguez	.60

N.L. Vanguard Press

Guerrero sets Expos' homer record

		NM/M
Complete Set (10):		10.00
Common Player:		.50
Inserted 2:37		
1	Chipper Jones	1.50
2	Greg Maddux	1.50
3	Sammy Sosa	2.00
4	Ken Griffey Jr.	2.00
5	Larry Walker	.50
6	Jeff Bagwell	1.00
7	Vladimir Guerrero	1.00
8	Mike Piazza	2.00
9	Mark McGwire	2.50
10	Tony Gwynn	1.50

2001 Pacific

		NM/M
Complete Set (500):		40.00
Common Player:		.10
Pack (12):		1.00
Box (36):		25.00
1	Garret Anderson	.10
2	Gary DiSarcina	.10
3	Darin Erstad	.25
4	Seth Etherton	.10
5	Ron Gant	.10
6	Troy Glaus	.75
7	Shigetosi Hasegawa	.10
8	Adam Kennedy	.10
9	Ben Molina	.10
10	Ramon Ortiz	.10
11	Troy Percival	.10
12	Tim Salmon	.20
13	Scott Schoeneweis	.10
14	Mo Vaughn	.10
15	Jarrod Washburn	.10
16	Brian Anderson	.10
17	Danny Bautista	.10
18	Jay Bell	.10
19	Greg Colbrunn	.10
20	Erubiel Durazo	.10
21	Steve Finley	.10
22	Luis Gonzalez	.20
23	Randy Johnson	.75
24	Byung-Hyun Kim	.10
25	Matt Mantei	.10
26	Armando Reynoso	.10
27	Todd Stottlemyre	.10
28	Matt Williams	.10
29	Tony Womack	.10
30	Andy Ashby	.10
31	Bobby Bonilla	.10
32	Rafael Furcal	.10
33	Andres Galarraga	.10
34	Tom Glavine	.35
35	Andruw Jones	.75
36	Chipper Jones	1.00
37	Brian Jordan	.10
38	Wally Joyner	.10
39	Keith Lockhart	.10
40	Javy Lopez	.10
41	Greg Maddux	1.00
42	Kevin Millwood	.10
43	John Rocker	.10
44	Reggie Sanders	.10
45	John Smoltz	.10
46	B.J. Surhoff	.10
47	Quilvio Veras	.10
48	Walt Weiss	.10
49	Brady Anderson	.10
50	Albert Belle	.15
51	Jeff Conine	.10
52	Delino DeShields	.10
53	Brook Fordyce	.10
54	Jerry Hairston Jr.	.10
55	Mark Lewis	.10
56	Luis Matos	.10
57	Melvin Mora	.10
58	Mike Mussina	.35
59	Chris Richard	.10
60	Cal Ripken Jr.	2.00
61	Manny Alexander	.10
62	Rolando Arrojo	.10
63	Midre Cummings	.10
64	Carl Everett	.10
65	Nomar Garciaparra	1.25
66	Mike Lansing	.10
67	Darren Lewis	.10
68	Derek Lowe	.10
69	Pedro Martinez	.75
70	Ramon Martinez	.10
71	Trot Nixon	.10
72	Troy O'Leary	.10
73	Jose Offerman	.10
74	Tomo Ohka	.10
75	Jason Varitek	.10
76	Rick Aguilera	.10
77	Shane Andrews	.10
78	Brant Brown	.10
79	Damon Buford	.10
80	Joe Girardi	.10
81	Mark Grace	.20
82	Willie Greene	.10
83	Ricky Gutierrez	.10
84	Jon Lieber	.10
85	Sammy Sosa	1.25
86	Kevin Tapani	.10
87	Rondell White	.10
88	Kerry Wood	.50
89	Eric Young	.10
90	Harold Baines	.10
91	James Baldwin	.10
92	Ray Durham	.10
93	Cal Eldred	.10
94	Keith Foulke	.10
95	Charles Johnson	.10
96	Paul Konerko	.20
97	Carlos Lee	.10
98	Magglio Ordonez	.10
99	Jim Parque	.10
100	Herbert Perry	.10
101	Chris Singleton	.10
102	Mike Sirotka	.10
103	Frank Thomas	.75
104	Jose Valentin	.10
105	Rob Bell	.10
106	Aaron Boone	.10
107	Sean Casey	.20
108	Danny Graves	.10
109	Ken Griffey Jr.	1.25
110	Pete Harnisch	.10
111	Brian L. Hunter	.10
112	Barry Larkin	.10
113	Pokey Reese	.10
114	Benito Santiago	.10
115	Chris Stynes	.10

116	Michael Tucker	.10
117	Ron Villone	.10
118	Scott Williamson	.10
119	Dmitri Young	.10
120	Roberto Alomar	.35
121	Sandy Alomar Jr.	.10
122	Russell Branyan	.10
123	Dave Burba	.10
124	Bartolo Colon	.10
125	Wil Cordero	.10
126	Einar Diaz	.10
127	Chuck Finley	.10
128	Travis Fryman	.10
129	Kenny Lofton	.10
130	Charles Nagy	.10
131	Manny Ramirez	.75
132	David Segui	.10
133	Jim Thome	.65
134	Omar Vizquel	.10
135	Brian Bohanon	.10
136	Jeff Cirillo	.10
137	Jeff Frye	.10
138	Jeffrey Hammonds	.10
139	Todd Helton	.75
140	Todd Hollandsworth	.10
141	Jose Jimenez	.10
142	Brent Mayne	.10
143	Neifi Perez	.10
144	Ben Petrick	.10
145	Juan Pierre	.10
146	Larry Walker	.10
147	Todd Walker	.10
148	Masato Yoshii	.10
149	Brad Ausmus	.10
150	Rich Becker	.10
151	Tony Clark	.10
152	Deivi Cruz	.10
153	Damion Easley	.10
154	Juan Encarnacion	.10
155	Robert Fick	.10
156	Juan Gonzalez	.75
157	Bobby Higginson	.10
158	Todd Jones	.10
159	Wendell Magee Jr.	.10
160	Brian Moehler	.10
161	Hideo Nomo	.75
162	Dean Palmer	.10
163	Jeff Weaver	.10
164	Antonio Alfonseca	.10
165	David Berg	.10
166	A.J. Burnett	.10
167	Luis Castillo	.10
168	Ryan Dempster	.10
169	Cliff Floyd	.10
170	Alex Gonzalez	.10
171	Mark Kotsay	.10
172	Derrek Lee	.10
173	Mike Lowell	.10
174	Mike Redmond	.10
175	Henry Rodriguez	.10
176	Jesus Sanchez	.10
177	Preston Wilson	.10
178	Moises Alou	.10
179	Jeff Bagwell	.75
180	Glen Barker	.10
181	Lance Berkman	.10
182	Craig Biggio	.10
183	Tim Bogar	.10
184	Ken Caminiti	.10
185	Roger Cedeno	.10
186	Scott Elarton	.10
187	Tony Eusebio	.10
188	Richard Hidalgo	.10
189	Jose Lima	.10
190	Mitch Meluskey	.10
191	Shane Reynolds	.10
192	Bill Spiers	.10
193	Billy Wagner	.10
194	Daryle Ward	.10
195	Carlos Beltran	.40
196	Ricky Bottalico	.10
197	Johnny Damon	.25
198	Jermaine Dye	.10
199	Jorge Fabregas	.10
200	David McCarty	.10
201	Mark Quinn	.10
202	Joe Randa	.10
203	Jeff Reboulet	.10
204	Rey Sanchez	.10
205	Blake Stein	.10
206	Jeff Suppan	.10
207	Mac Suzuki	.10
208	Mike Sweeney	.10
209	Gregg Zaun	.10
210	Adrian Beltre	.25
211	Kevin Brown	.10
212	Alex Cora	.10
213	Darren Dreifort	.10
214	Tom Goodwin	.10
215	Shawn Green	.30
216	Mark Grudzielanek	.10
217	Todd Hundley	.10
218	Eric Karros	.10
219	Chad Kreuter	.10
220	Jim Leyritz	.10
221	Chan Ho Park	.10
222	Jeff Shaw	.10
223	Gary Sheffield	.25
224	Devon White	.10
225	Ron Belliard	.10
226	Henry Blanco	.10
227	Jeromy Burnitz	.10
228	Jeff D'Amico	.10
229	Marquis Grissom	.10
230	Charlie Hayes	.10
231	Jimmy Haynes	.10
232	Tyler Houston	.10
233	Geoff Jenkins	.10

No.	Player	Price
234	Mark Loretta	.10
235	James Mouton	.10
236	Richie Sexson	.10
237	Jamey Wright	.10
238	Jay Canizaro	.10
239	Ron Coomer	.10
240	Cristian Guzman	.10
241	Denny Hocking	.10
242	Torii Hunter	.10
243	Jacque Jones	.10
244	Corey Koskie	.10
245	Matt Lawton	.10
246	Matt LeCroy	.10
247	Eric Milton	.10
248	David Ortiz	.25
249	Brad Radke	.10
250	Mark Redman	.10
251	Michael Barrett	.10
252	Peter Bergeron	.10
253	Milton Bradley	.10
254	Orlando Cabrera	.10
255	Vladimir Guerrero	.75
256	Wilton Guerrero	.10
257	Dustin Hermanson	.10
258	Hideki Irabu	.10
259	Fernando Seguignol	.10
260	Lee Stevens	.10
261	Andy Tracy	.10
262	Javier Vazquez	.10
263	Jose Vidro	.10
264	Edgardo Alfonzo	.10
265	Derek Bell	.10
266	Armando Benitez	.10
267	Mike Bordick	.10
268	John Franco	.10
269	Darryl Hamilton	.10
270	Mike Hampton	.10
271	Lenny Harris	.10
272	Al Leiter	.10
273	Joe McEwing	.10
274	Rey Ordonez	.10
275	Jay Payton	.10
276	Mike Piazza	1.25
277	Glendon Rusch	.10
278	Bubba Trammell	.10
279	Robin Ventura	.10
280	Todd Zeile	.10
281	Scott Brosius	.10
282	Jose Canseco	.25
283	Roger Clemens	1.00
284	David Cone	.10
285	Dwight Gooden	.10
286	Orlando Hernandez	.10
287	Glenallen Hill	.10
288	Derek Jeter	2.00
289	David Justice	.10
290	Chuck Knoblauch	.10
291	Tino Martinez	.10
292	Denny Neagle	.10
293	Paul O'Neill	.10
294	Andy Pettitte	.20
295	Jorge Posada	.10
296	Mariano Rivera	.20
297	Luis Sojo	.10
298	Jose Vizcaino	.10
299	Bernie Williams	.25
300	Kevin Appier	.10
301	Eric Chavez	.20
302	Ryan Christenson	.10
303	Jason Giambi	.50
304	Jeremy Giambi	.10
305	Ben Grieve	.10
306	Gil Heredia	.10
307	Ramon Hernandez	.10
308	Tim Hudson	.20
309	Jason Isringhausen	.10
310	Terrence Long	.10
311	Mark Mulder	.10
312	Adam Piatt	.10
313	Matt Stairs	.10
314	Miguel Tejada	.25
315	Randy Velarde	.10
316	Alex Arias	.10
317	Pat Burrell	.25
318	Omar Daal	.10
319	Travis Lee	.10
320	Mike Lieberthal	.10
321	Randy Wolf	.10
322	Bobby Abreu	.10
323	Jeff Brantley	.10
324	Bruce Chen	.10
325	Doug Glanville	.10
326	Kevin Jordan	.10
327	Robert Person	.10
328	Scott Rolen	.65
329	Jimmy Anderson	.10
330	Mike Benjamin	.10
331	Kris Benson	.10
332	Adam Brown	.10
333	Brian Giles	.10
334	Jason Kendall	.10
335	Pat Meares	.10
336	Warren Morris	.10
337	Aramis Ramirez	.10
338	Todd Ritchie	.10
339	Jason Schmidt	.10
340	John Vander Wal	.10
341	Mike Williams	.10
342	Enrique Wilson	.10
343	Kevin Young	.10
344	Rick Ankiel	.10
345	Andy Benes	.10
346	Will Clark	.15
347	Eric Davis	.10
348	J.D. Drew	.20
349	Shawon Dunston	.10
350	Jim Edmonds	.10
351	Pat Hentgen	.10
352	Darryl Kile	.10
353	Ray Lankford	.10
354	Mike Matheny	.10
355	Mark McGwire	1.50
356	Craig Paquette	.10
357	Edgar Renteria	.10
358	Garrett Stephenson	.10
359	Fernando Tatis	.10
360	Dave Veres	.10
361	Fernando Vina	.10
362	Bret Boone	.10
363	Matt Clement	.10
364	Ben Davis	.10
365	Adam Eaton	.10
366	Wiki Gonzalez	.10
367	Tony Gwynn	1.00
368	Damian Jackson	.10
369	Ryan Klesko	.10
370	John Mabry	.10
371	Dave Magadan	.10
372	Phil Nevin	.10
373	Eric Owens	.10
374	Desi Relaford	.10
375	Ruben Rivera	.10
376	Woody Williams	.10
377	Rich Aurilia	.10
378	Marvin Bernard	.10
379	Barry Bonds	2.00
380	Ellis Burks	.10
381	Bobby Estalella	.10
382	Shawn Estes	.10
383	Mark Gardner	.10
384	Livan Hernandez	.10
385	Jeff Kent	.10
386	Bill Mueller	.10
387	Robb Nen	.10
388	Russ Ortiz	.10
389	Armando Rios	.10
390	Kirk Rueter	.10
391	J.T. Snow	.10
392	David Bell	.10
393	Jay Buhner	.10
394	Mike Cameron	.10
395	Freddy Garcia	.10
396	Carlos Guillen	.10
397	John Halama	.10
398	Rickey Henderson	.75
399	Al Martin	.10
400	Edgar Martinez	.10
401	Mark McLemore	.10
402	Jamie Moyer	.10
403	John Olerud	.10
404	Joe Oliver	.10
405	Alex Rodriguez	1.50
406	Kazuhiro Sasaki	.15
407	Aaron Sele	.10
408	Dan Wilson	.10
409	Miguel Cairo	.10
410	Vinny Castilla	.10
411	Steve Cox	.10
412	John Flaherty	.10
413	Jose Guillen	.10
414	Roberto Hernandez	.10
415	Russ Johnson	.10
416	Felix Martinez	.10
417	Fred McGriff	.10
418	Greg Vaughn	.10
419	Gerald Williams	.10
420	Luis Alicea	.10
421	Frank Catalanotto	.10
422	Royce Clayton	.10
423	Chad Curtis	.10
424	Rusty Greer	.10
425	Bill Haselman	.10
426	Rick Helling	.10
427	Gabe Kapler	.10
428	Mike Lamb	.10
429	Ricky Ledee	.10
430	Ruben Mateo	.10
431	Rafael Palmeiro	.65
432	Ivan Rodriguez	.65
433	Kenny Rogers	.10
434	John Wetteland	.10
435	Jeff Zimmerman	.10
436	Tony Batista	.10
437	Homer Bush	.10
438	Chris Carpenter	.10
439	Marty Cordova	.10
440	Jose Cruz Jr.	.40
441	Carlos Delgado	.40
442	Darrin Fletcher	.10
443	Brad Fullmer	.10
444	Alex S. Gonzalez	.10
445	Billy Koch	.10
446	Raul Mondesi	.10
447	Mickey Morandini	.10
448	Shannon Stewart	.10
449	Steve Trachsel	.10
450	David Wells	.10
451	Juan Alvarez	.10
452	Shawn Wooten	.10
453	Ismael Villegas	.10
454	Carlos Casimiro	.10
455	Morgan Burkhart	.10
456	Paxton Crawford	.10
457	Dernell Stenson	.10
458	Ross Gload	.10
459	Raul Gonzalez	.10
460	Corey Patterson	.10
461	Julio Zuleta	.10
462	Rocky Biddle	.10
463	Joe Crede	.10
464	Matt Ginter	.10
465	Aaron Myette	.10
466	Mike Bell	.10
467	Travis Dawkins	.10
468	Mark Watson	.10
469	Elvis Pena	.10
470	Eric Munson	.10
471	Pablo Ozuna	.10
472	Frank Charles	.10
473	Mike Judd	.10
474	Hector Ramirez	.10
475	Jack Cressend	.10
476	Talmadge Nunnari	.10
477	Jorge Toca	.10
478	Alfonso Soriano	.65
479	Jay Tessmer	.10
480	Jake Westbrook	.10
481	Todd Belitz	.10
482	Eric Byrnes	.10
483	Jose Ortiz	.10
484	Tike Redman	.10
485	Domingo Guzman	.10
486	Rodrigo Lopez	.10
487	Pedro Feliz	.10
488	Damon Minor	.10
489	Ryan Vogelsong	.10
490	Joel Pineiro	.10
491	Justin Brunette	.10
492	Keith McDonald	.10
493	Aubrey Huff	.10
494	Kenny Kelly	.10
495	Damian Rolls	.10
496	John Bale	.10
497	Pasqual Coco	.10
498	Matt DeWitt	.10
499	Leo Estrella	.10
500	Josh Phelps	.10

Hobby Limited

Stars: 8-15X
Production 70 Sets

Retail Limited

Stars: 4-8X
Production 85 Sets

Premiere Date

Stars: 20-30X
Production 35 Sets

Extreme

Stars: 15-25X
Production 45 Sets

AL Decade's Best

Complete Set (18): 20.00
Common Player: .50
Inserted 2:37

No.	Player	Price
1	Rickey Henderson	1.50
2	Rafael Palmeiro	1.00
3	Cal Ripken Jr.	4.00
4	Jose Canseco	.75
5	Juan Gonzalez	1.50
6	Frank Thomas	1.50
7	Albert Belle	.50
8	Edgar Martinez	.50
9	Mo Vaughn	.50
10	Derek Jeter	4.00
11	Mark McGwire	3.00
12	Alex Rodriguez	3.00
13	Ken Griffey Jr.	2.50
14	Nomar Garciaparra	2.50
15	Roger Clemens	2.00
16	Bernie Williams	.50
17	Ivan Rodriguez	1.00
18	Pedro Martinez	1.50

Cramer's Choice Awards

Gold Crown Die-Cuts

Complete Set (36): 100.00
Common Player: 1.50
Inserted 1:73

No.	Player	Price
1	Darin Erstad	1.50
2	Troy Glaus	4.00
3	Randy Johnson	4.00
4	Rafael Furcal	1.50
5	Andruw Jones	4.00
6	Chipper Jones	5.00
7	Greg Maddux	5.00
8	Cal Ripken Jr.	10.00
9	Nomar Garciaparra	8.00
10	Pedro Martinez	4.00
11	Sammy Sosa	8.00
12	Kerry Wood	2.50
13	Frank Thomas	8.00
14	Ken Griffey Jr.	8.00
15	Manny Ramirez	4.00
16	Todd Helton	4.00
17	Jeff Bagwell	4.00
18	Shawn Green	1.50
19	Gary Sheffield	1.50
20	Vladimir Guerrero	4.00
21	Mike Piazza	8.00
22	Jose Canseco	2.00
23	Roger Clemens	6.00
24	Derek Jeter	10.00
25	Jason Giambi	2.50
26	Pat Burrell	2.00
27	Rick Ankiel	1.50
28	Jim Edmonds	1.50
29	Mark McGwire	9.00
30	Tony Gwynn	5.00
31	Barry Bonds	10.00
32	Rickey Henderson	1.50
33	Edgar Martinez	1.50
34	Alex Rodriguez	9.00
35	Ivan Rodriguez	2.00
36	Carlos Delgado	2.00

NL Decade's Best

Complete Set (18): 15.00
Common Player: .50
Inserted 2:37

No.	Player	Price
1	Barry Bonds	4.00
2	Jeff Bagwell	1.00
3	Tom Glavine	.65
4	Gary Sheffield	.65
5	Fred McGriff	.50
6	Greg Maddux	1.50
7	Mike Piazza	2.00
8	Tony Gwynn	1.50
9	Hideo Nomo	1.00
10	Andres Galarraga	.50
11	Larry Walker	.50
12	Scott Rolen	.75
13	Pedro Martinez	1.00
14	Sammy Sosa	2.00
15	Mark McGwire	3.00
16	Kerry Wood	.75
17	Chipper Jones	1.50
18	Mark Grace	.75

On The Horizon

Complete Set (10): 20.00
Common Player: 2.00
Inserted 1:145

No.	Player	Price
1	Rafael Furcal	2.00
2	Corey Patterson	2.50
3	Russell Branyan	2.00
4	Juan Pierre	2.50
5	Mark Quinn	2.00
6	Alfonso Soriano	6.00
7	Adam Piatt	2.00
8	Pat Burrell	4.50
9	Kazuhiro Sasaki	2.50
10	Aubrey Huff	2.00

Ornaments

Complete Set (24): 25.00
Common Player: .50
Inserted 2:37

No.	Player	Price
1	Rafael Furcal	.50
2	Chipper Jones	2.00
3	Greg Maddux	2.00
4	Cal Ripken Jr.	4.00
5	Nomar Garciaparra	2.50
6	Pedro Martinez	1.50
7	Sammy Sosa	2.50
8	Frank Thomas	1.50
9	Ken Griffey Jr.	2.50
10	Manny Ramirez	1.50
11	Todd Helton	1.50
12	Vladimir Guerrero	1.50
13	Mike Piazza	2.50
14	Roger Clemens	2.25
15	Derek Jeter	4.00
16	Pat Burrell	1.00
17	Rick Ankiel	.50
18	Mark McGwire	3.00
19	Barry Bonds	4.00
20	Alex Rodriguez	3.00
21	Troy Glaus	1.50
22	Tom Glavine	.50
23	Jim Edmonds	.50
24	Ivan Rodriguez	1.00

Paramount Samples

While the Paramount brand was never produced due to Pacific's loss of its licensing early in 2001, a trio of base-set sample cards were created and distributed to media and dealers. Fronts have vignetted photos and silver-foil highlights. Backs have portrait photos and the usual data and stats. Cards have "SAMPLE" in place of the card number on back.

Complete Set (3): 7.50
Common Player: 3.00

No.	Player	Price
(1)	Barry Bonds	3.00
(2)	Vladimir Guerrero	3.00
(3)	Greg Maddux	3.00

2001 Pacific Private Stock

MARK McGWIRE

Complete Set (150): 50.00
Common Player: .25
Common (126-150): 1.00
Inserted 1:4
Hobby Pack (7): 10.00
Hobby Box (10): 75.00

No.	Player	Price
1	Darin Erstad	.50
2	Troy Glaus	1.00
3	Tim Salmon	.35
4	Mo Vaughn	.25
5	Steve Finley	.25
6	Luis Gonzalez	.35
7	Randy Johnson	1.00
8	Matt Williams	.25
9	Rafael Furcal	.25
10	Andres Galarraga	.25
11	Tom Glavine	.45
12	Andruw Jones	1.00
13	Chipper Jones	1.50
14	Greg Maddux	1.50
15	B.J. Surhoff	.25
16	Brady Anderson	.25
17	Albert Belle	.25
18	Mike Mussina	.45
19	Cal Ripken Jr.	3.00
20	Carl Everett	.25
21	Nomar Garciaparra	2.00
22	Pedro Martinez	1.00
23	Mark Grace	.35
24	Sammy Sosa	2.00
25	Kerry Wood	.50
26	Carlos Lee	.25
27	Magglio Ordonez	.25
28	Frank Thomas	1.00
29	Sean Casey	.35
30	Ken Griffey Jr.	2.00
31	Barry Larkin	.25
32	Pokey Reese	.25
33	Roberto Alomar	.40
34	Kenny Lofton	.25
35	Manny Ramirez	1.00
36	Jim Thome	.75
37	Omar Vizquel	.25
38	Jeff Cirillo	.25
39	Jeffrey Hammonds	.25
40	Todd Helton	1.00
41	Larry Walker	.25
42	Tony Clark	.25
43	Juan Encarnacion	.25
44	Juan Gonzalez	1.00
45	Hideo Nomo	1.00
46	Cliff Floyd	.25
47	Derrek Lee	.25
48	Henry Rodriguez	.25
49	Preston Wilson	.25
50	Jeff Bagwell	1.00
51	Craig Biggio	.25
52	Richard Hidalgo	.25
53	Moises Alou	.25
54	Carlos Beltran	.50
55	Johnny Damon	.40
56	Jermaine Dye	.25
57	Mac Suzuki	.25
58	Mike Sweeney	.25
59	Adrian Beltre	.40
60	Kevin Brown	.25
61	Shawn Green	.50
62	Eric Karros	.25
63	Chan Ho Park	.25
64	Gary Sheffield	.40
65	Jeromy Burnitz	.25
66	Geoff Jenkins	.25
67	Richie Sexson	.25
68	Jacque Jones	.25

69	Matt Lawton	.25
70	Eric Milton	.25
71	Vladimir Guerrero	1.00
72	Jose Vidro	.25
73	Edgardo Alfonzo	.25
74	Mike Hampton	.25
75	Mike Piazza	2.00
76	Robin Ventura	.25
77	Jose Canseco	.50
78	Roger Clemens	1.75
79	Derek Jeter	3.00
80	David Justice	.25
81	Jorge Posada	.25
82	Bernie Williams	.35
83	Jason Giambi	.65
84	Ben Grieve	.25
85	Tim Hudson	.35
86	Terrence Long	.35
87	Miguel Tejada	.35
88	Bobby Abreu	.25
89	Pat Burrell	.50
90	Mike Lieberthal	.25
91	Scott Rolen	.75
92	Kris Benson	.25
93	Brian Giles	.25
94	Jason Kendall	.25
95	Aramis Ramirez	.25
96	Rick Ankiel	.25
97	Will Clark	.35
98	J.D. Drew	.25
99	Jim Edmonds	.25
100	Mark McGwire	2.50
101	Fernando Tatis	.25
102	Adam Eaton	.25
103	Tony Gwynn	1.50
104	Phil Nevin	.25
105	Eric Owens	.25
106	Barry Bonds	3.00
107	Jeff Kent	.25
108	J.T. Snow	.25
109	Rickey Henderson	1.00
110	Edgar Martinez	.25
111	John Olerud	.25
112	Alex Rodriguez	2.50
113	Kazuhiro Sasaki	.25
114	Vinny Castilla	.25
115	Fred McGriff	.25
116	Greg Vaughn	.25
117	Gabe Kapler	.25
118	Ruben Mateo	.25
119	Rafael Palmeiro	.75
120	Ivan Rodriguez	.75
121	Tony Batista	.25
122	Jose Cruz Jr.	.25
123	Carlos Delgado	.75
124	Shannon Stewart	.25
125	David Wells	.25
126	Shawn Wooten	1.00
127	George Lombard	1.00
128	Morgan Burkhart	1.00
129	Ross Gload	1.00
130	Corey Patterson	1.00
131	Julio Zuleta	1.00
132	Joe Crede	1.00
133	Matt Ginter	1.00
134	Travis Dawkins	1.00
135	Eric Munson	1.00
136	Dee Brown	1.00
137	Luke Prokopec	1.00
138	Timoniel Perez	1.00
139	Alfonso Soriano	2.00
140	Jake Westbrook	1.00
141	Eric Byrnes	1.00
142	Adam Hyzdu	1.00
143	Jimmy Rollins	1.50
144	Xavier Nady	1.00
145	Ryan Vogelsong	1.00
146	Joel Pineiro	2.00
147	Aubrey Huff	1.00
148	Kenny Kelly	1.00
149	Josh Phelps	1.00
150	Vernon Wells	1.00

Silver
Stars: .5-1.5X
SP's: .5-1X
Base cards in retail.

Gold Portraits
Stars: 6-10X
SP's (126-150): 1-2X
Production 75 Sets H

Silver Portraits

237/290

Stars: 2-5X
SP's: 1X
Production 290 Sets R

Premiere Date
Stars: 4-8X
SP's: 1-2X
Production 90 Sets

Artist's Canvas

CAL RIPKEN JR.

NM/M
Complete Set (20): 50.00
Common Player: 1.00
Inserted 1:21

1	Randy Johnson	2.50
2	Chipper Jones	4.00
3	Greg Maddux	4.00
4	Cal Ripken Jr.	8.00
5	Nomar Garciaparra	5.00
6	Pedro Martinez	2.50
7	Sammy Sosa	5.00
8	Frank Thomas	2.50
9	Ken Griffey Jr.	5.00
10	Manny Ramirez	2.50
11	Vladimir Guerrero	2.50
12	Mike Piazza	5.00
13	Roger Clemens	4.50
14	Derek Jeter	6.00
15	Jason Giambi	2.50
16	Rick Ankiel	4.00
17	Mark McGwire	6.00
18	Barry Bonds	8.00
19	Alex Rodriguez	6.00
20	Ivan Rodriguez	2.00

Extreme Action

NM/M
Complete Set (20): 20.00
Common Player: 2.00
Inserted 1:11

1	Troy Glaus	1.00
2	Rafael Furcal	.50
3	Chipper Jones	1.50
4	Cal Ripken Jr.	3.00
5	Nomar Garciaparra	2.00
6	Sammy Sosa	2.00
7	Ken Griffey Jr.	2.00
8	Manny Ramirez	1.00
9	Todd Helton	1.00
10	Jeff Bagwell	1.00
11	Vladimir Guerrero	1.00
12	Derek Jeter	3.00
13	Mike Piazza	2.00
14	Pat Burrell	.75
15	Jim Edmonds	.50
16	Mark McGwire	2.50
17	Barry Bonds	3.00
18	Alex Rodriguez	2.50
19	Ivan Rodriguez	.75
20	Carlos Delgado	.75

Game Gear

NM/M
Common Player: 4.00
Inserted 1:1 H

1	Garret Anderson/Jsy	4.00
2	Darin Erstad/Jsy	5.00
3	Ron Gant/Bat	4.00
4	Troy Glaus/Jsy	8.00
5	Tim Salmon/Bat	5.00
6	Mo Vaughn/Jsy Grey	4.00
7	Mo Vaughn/Jsy White	4.00
8	Mo Vaughn/Jsy	4.00
9	Jay Bell/Jsy	4.00
10	Jay Bell/Bat	4.00
11	Erubiel Durazo/Jsy Black	4.00
12	Erubiel Durazo/Jsy White	4.00
13	Erubiel Durazo/Bat	4.00
14	Steve Finley/Bat	4.00
15	Randy Johnson/Jsy	10.00
16	Byung-Hyun Kim/Jsy White	4.00
17	Byung-Hyun Kim/Jsy Grey	4.00
18	Matt Williams/Jsy Grey	4.00
19	Matt Williams/Jsy White	4.00
20	Matt Williams/Jsy Purple	4.00
21	Bobby Bonilla/Jsy	4.00
22	Rafael Furcal	8.00
23	Andruw Jones/Bat	4.00
24	Chipper Jones	10.00
25	Chipper Jones/Bat	10.00
26	Brian Jordan/Jsy	4.00
27	Javier Lopez/Bat	4.00
28	Greg Maddux/Jsy	15.00
29	Greg Maddux/Bat	15.00
30	Brady Anderson/Bat	4.00
31	Albert Belle/Bat	4.00
32	Nomar Garciaparra/Bat	8.00
33	Pedro Martinez/Bat	10.00
34	Jose Offerman/Bat	4.00
35	Damon Buford/Jsy	4.00
36	Jose Nieves/Bat	4.00
37	Kerry Wood/Bat	8.00
38	James Baldwin/Jsy	4.00
39	Ray Durham/Jsy	4.00
40	Ray Durham/Bat	4.00
41	Carlos Lee/Bat	4.00
42	Maggio Ordonez/Jsy	6.00
43	Maggio Ordonez/Bat	6.00
44	Chris Singleton/Jsy	4.00
45	Aaron Boone/Bat	4.00
46	Sean Casey/Bat	4.00
47	Barry Larkin/Jsy	6.00
48	Pokey Reese/Jsy	4.00
49	Pokey Reese/Bat	4.00
50	Dmitri Young/Bat	4.00
51	Roberto Alomar/Bat	8.00
52	Einar Diaz/Bat	4.00
53	Kenny Lofton/Jsy	4.00
54	David Segui/Bat	4.00
55	Omar Vizquel/Jsy	5.00
56	Luis Castillo/Jsy	4.00
57	Jeff Cirillo/Jsy	4.00
58	Jeff Frye/Bat	4.00
59	Todd Helton/Jsy	8.00
60	Todd Helton/Bat	8.00
61	Neifi Perez/Bat	4.00
62	Larry Walker/Jsy	4.00
63	Larry Walker/Bat	4.00
64	Masato Yoshii/Jsy	4.00
65	Brad Ausmus/Bat	4.00
66	Rich Becker/Bat	4.00
67	Tony Clark/Bat	4.00
68	Deivi Cruz/Bat	4.00
69	Juan Gonzalez/Bat	6.00
70	Dean Palmer/Bat	4.00
71	Cliff Floyd/Jsy White	4.00
72	Cliff Floyd/Jsy Teal	4.00
73	Cliff Floyd/Bat	4.00
74	Alex Gonzalez/Jsy	4.00
75	Alex Gonzalez Marlins/Bat	4.00
76	Mark Kotsay/Bat	4.00
77	Derrek Lee/Bat	4.00
78	Pablo Ozuna/Bat	4.00
79	Craig Biggio/Bat	4.00
80	Ken Caminiti/Bat	4.00
81	Roger Cedeno/Bat	4.00
82	Ricky Bottalico/Bat	4.00
83	Dee Brown/Bat	4.00
84	Jermaine Dye/Bat	4.00
85	David McCarty/Bat	4.00
86	Hector Ortiz/Bat	4.00
87	Joe Randa/Bat	4.00
88	Adrian Beltre/Jsy	4.00
89	Kevin Brown/	6.00
90	Alex Cora/Bat	4.00
91	Darren Dreifort/Bat	4.00
92	Shawn Green/Jsy White	6.00
93	Shawn Green/Jsy Grey	6.00
94	Shawn Green/Bat	6.00
95	Todd Hundley/Jsy	4.00
96	Eric Karros/Bat	4.00
97	Chan Ho Park/Jsy	4.00
98	Chan Ho Park/Bat	4.00
99	Gary Sheffield/Bat	6.00
100	Ismael Valdes/Bat	4.00
101	Jeromy Burnitz/Bat	4.00
102	Marquis Grissom/Bat	4.00
103	Matt Lawton/Bat	4.00
104	Fernando Seguignol/Bat	4.00
105	Edgardo Alfonzo/White Swing	4.00
106	Edgardo Alfonzo/Jsy White Drop	4.00
107	Edgardo Alfonzo/Jsy Black	4.00
110	Derek Bell/Jsy White	4.00
111	Derek Bell/Jsy Black	4.00
112	Armando Benitez/Bat	4.00
113	Al Leiter/Bat	4.00
114	Rey Ordonez/Jsy Grey Field	4.00
115	Rey Ordonez/Jsy White	4.00
116	Rey Ordonez/Jsy Grey Bunt	4.00
117	Rey Ordonez/Bat	4.00
118	Jay Payton/Bat	4.00
119	Mike Piazza/Jsy	10.00
120	Robin Ventura/Jsy Black Hit	4.00
121	Robin Ventura/Jsy Black Field	4.00
122	Robin Ventura/Jsy White	4.00
123	Luis Polonia/Bat	4.00
124	Bernie Williams/Bat	6.00
125	Eric Chavez/Bat	4.00
126	Jason Giambi/Jsy	8.00
127	Jason Giambi/Bat	8.00
128	Ben Grieve/Jsy	4.00
129	Ben Grieve/Bat	4.00
130	Ramon Hernandez/Bat	4.00
131	Tim Hudson/Jsy	6.00
132	Terrence Long/Bat	4.00
133	Mark Mulder/Jsy	6.00
134	Adam Piatt/Jsy	4.00
135	Olmedo Saenz/Bat	4.00
136	Matt Stairs/Bat	4.00
137	Mike Stanley/Bat	4.00
138	Miguel Tejada/Bat	6.00
139	Travis Lee/Bat	4.00
140	Brian Giles/Bat	5.00
141	Jason Kendall/Jsy	4.00
142	Will Clark/Bat	6.00
143	J.D. Drew/Bat	4.00
144	Jim Edmonds/Bat	6.00
145	Mark McGwire/Bat	50.00
146	Edgar Renteria/Bat	4.00
147	Garrett Stephenson/Jsy	4.00
148	Tony Gwynn/Jsy	10.00
149	Ruben Rivera/Bat	4.00
150	Barry Bonds/Jsy	40.00
151	Barry Bonds/Bat	40.00
152	Ellis Burks/Jsy	4.00
153	J.T. Snow/Bat	4.00
154	Jay Buhner/Jsy	4.00
155	Jay Buhner/Bat	4.00
156	Carlos Guillen/Jsy	4.00
157	Carlos Guillen/Bat	4.00
158	Rickey Henderson/Bat	15.00
159	Edgar Martinez/Bat	6.00
160	Gil Meche/Jsy	4.00
161	John Olerud/Bat	5.00
162	Joe Oliver/Bat	4.00
163	Alex Rodriguez/Bat	30.00
164	Kazuhiro Sasaki/Jsy	4.00
165	Dan Wilson/Jsy	4.00
166	Dan Wilson/Bat	4.00
167	Vinny Castilla/Bat	4.00
168	Jose Guillen/Bat	4.00
169	Fred McGriff/Jsy	5.00
170	Rusty Greer/Bat	4.00
171	Mike Lamb/Bat	4.00
172	Ruben Mateo/Jsy	4.00
173	Ruben Mateo/Bat	4.00
174	Rafael Palmeiro/Jsy	8.00
175	Rafael Palmeiro/Bat	8.00
178	Tony Batista/Bat	4.00
179	Marty Cordova/Bat	4.00
180	Jose Cruz Jr./Bat	4.00
181	Alex Gonzalez Blue Jays/Bat	4.00
182	Raul Mondesi/Bat	4.00

Game Jersey Patch

NM/M
Common Player: 8.00

2	Darin Erstad	8.00
4	Troy Glaus	15.00
5	Mo Vaughn/Grey	8.00
6	Mo Vaughn/White	8.00
7	Jay Bell	8.00
9	Shawn Green/Jsy White	6.00
11	Erubiel Durazo/Black	8.00
12	Erubiel Durazo/White	8.00
15	Randy Johnson	40.00
16	Byung-Hyun Kim/White	8.00
17	Byung-Hyun Kim/Grey	8.00
18	Matt Williams/Grey	8.00
19	Matt Williams/White	8.00
20	Matt Williams/Purple	8.00
21	Bobby Bonilla	8.00
24	Chipper Jones	25.00
26	Brian Jordan	8.00
28	Greg Maddux	80.00
35	Damon Buford	8.00
39	James Baldwin	8.00
40	Ray Durham	8.00
43	Maggio Ordonez	20.00
45	Chris Singleton	8.00
48	Barry Larkin	15.00
49	Pokey Reese	8.00
54	Kenny Lofton	10.00
56	Omar Vizquel	10.00
57	Luis Castillo	8.00
58	Jeff Cirillo	8.00
60	Todd Helton	20.00
63	Larry Walker	10.00
65	Masato Yoshii	8.00
66	Brad Ausmus	8.00
72	Cliff Floyd White	8.00
73	Cliff Floyd Teal	8.00
75	Alex Gonzalez	8.00
79	Pablo Ozuna	8.00
89	Adrian Beltre	8.00
90	Kevin Brown	15.00
93	Shawn Green/White	15.00
94	Shawn Green/Grey	15.00
96	Todd Hundley	8.00
98	Chan Ho Park	8.00
107	Edgardo Alfonzo/White Swing	8.00
108	Edgardo Alfonzo/White Drop	8.00
109	Edgardo Alfonzo/Black	8.00
110	Derek Bell/White	8.00
111	Derek Bell/Black	8.00
114	Rey Ordonez/Grey Field	8.00
115	Rey Ordonez/White	8.00
116	Rey Ordonez/Grey Bunt	8.00
119	Mike Piazza	75.00
120	Robin Ventura/Black Hit	10.00
121	Robin Ventura/Black Field	10.00
122	Robin Ventura/White	10.00
125	Eric Chavez	8.00
126	Jason Giambi	15.00
128	Ben Grieve	8.00
131	Tim Hudson	8.00
133	Mark Mulder	15.00
134	Adam Piatt	8.00
141	Jason Kendall	10.00
147	Garrett Stephenson	8.00
148	Tony Gwynn	40.00
150	Barry Bonds	90.00
152	Ellis Burks	8.00
154	Jay Buhner	8.00
156	Carlos Guillen	8.00
160	Gil Meche	8.00
164	Kazuhiro Sasaki	15.00
165	Dan Wilson	8.00
169	Fred McGriff	10.00
172	Ruben Mateo	8.00
174	Rafael Palmeiro	25.00

Reserve
NM/M
Complete Set (20): 25.00
Common Player: .50
Inserted 1:21 H

1	Randy Johnson	1.50
2	Chipper Jones	2.00
3	Greg Maddux	4.00
4	Cal Ripken Jr.	4.00
5	Nomar Garciaparra	2.50
6	Pedro Martinez	1.50
7	Sammy Sosa	1.50
8	Frank Thomas	1.50
9	Ken Griffey Jr.	2.50
10	Todd Helton	1.50
11	Vladimir Guerrero	1.50
12	Mike Piazza	2.50
13	Roger Clemens	2.25
14	Derek Jeter	4.00
15	Rick Ankiel	.50
16	Mark McGwire	3.00
17	Tony Gwynn	3.00
18	Barry Bonds	4.00
19	Alex Rodriguez	3.00
20	Ivan Rodriguez	1.00

PS-206 Action
NM/M
Complete Set (60): 20.00
Common Player: .15
Inserted 2:Pack

1	Darin Erstad	.25
2	Troy Glaus	.65
3	Randy Johnson	.65
4	Rafael Furcal	.15
5	Tom Glavine	.40
6	Andruw Jones	.65
7	Chipper Jones	.75
8	Greg Maddux	.75
9	Albert Belle	.15
10	Mike Mussina	.40
11	Cal Ripken Jr.	1.50
12	Nomar Garciaparra	1.00
13	Pedro Martinez	.65
14	Mark Grace	.25
15	Sammy Sosa	.65
16	Kerry Wood	.35
17	Magglio Ordonez	.15
18	Frank Thomas	.65
19	Ken Griffey Jr.	1.00
20	Barry Larkin	.15
21	Roberto Alomar	.35
22	Manny Ramirez	.65
23	Jim Thome	.60
24	Jeff Cirillo	.15
25	Todd Helton	.65
26	Larry Walker	.15
27	Juan Gonzalez	.65
28	Hideo Nomo	.65
29	Preston Wilson	.15
30	Jeff Bagwell	.65
31	Craig Biggio	.15
32	Johnny Damon	.25
33	Jermaine Dye	.15
34	Shawn Green	.30
35	Gary Sheffield	.25
36	Vladimir Guerrero	.65
37	Mike Piazza	1.00
38	Jose Canseco	.40
39	Roger Clemens	.85
40	Derek Jeter	1.50
41	Bernie Williams	.30
42	Jason Giambi	.50
43	Ben Grieve	.15
44	Pat Burrell	.40
45	Scott Rolen	.50
46	Rick Ankiel	.15
47	J.D. Drew	.25
48	Jim Edmonds	.15
49	Mark McGwire	1.25
50	Tony Gwynn	.75
51	Barry Bonds	1.50
52	Jeff Kent	.15
53	Edgar Martinez	.15
54	Alex Rodriguez	1.25
55	Kazuhiro Sasaki	.15
56	Fred McGriff	.15
57	Rafael Palmeiro	.50
58	Ivan Rodriguez	.50
59	Tony Batista	.15
60	Carlos Delgado	.45

PS-206 New Wave
NM/M
Complete Set (20): 30.00
Common Player: 1.00
Inserted 2:Hobby Case

1	Darin Erstad	1.50
2	Troy Glaus	5.00
3	Rafael Furcal	1.00
4	Andruw Jones	1.50
5	Magglio Ordonez	1.00
6	Carlos Lee	1.00
7	Todd Helton	2.00
8	Johnny Damon	1.50
9	Jermaine Dye	1.00
10	Vladimir Guerrero	5.00
11	Jason Giambi	4.00
12	Ben Grieve	1.00
13	Pat Burrell	3.00
14	Rick Ankiel	1.00
15	J.D. Drew	1.50
16	Adam Eaton	1.00
17	Kazuhiro Sasaki	1.00
18	Ruben Mateo	1.00
19	Tony Batista	1.00
20	Carlos Delgado	3.00

PS-206 Rookies
NM/M
Complete Set (20): 50.00
Common Player: 3.00
Inserted 1:Case

1	George Lombard	3.00
2	Morgan Burkhart	3.00
3	Corey Patterson	5.00
4	Julio Zuleta	3.00
5	Joe Crede	3.00
6	Matt Ginter	3.00
7	Aaron Myette	3.00
8	Travis Dawkins	3.00
9	Eric Munson	3.00
10	Dee Brown	3.00
11	Luke Prokopec	3.00
12	Jorge Toca	3.00
13	Alfonso Soriano	7.50
14	Eric Byrnes	3.00
15	Adam Hyzdu	3.00
16	Jimmy Rollins	4.00
17	Joel Pineiro	5.00
18	Aubrey Huff	4.00
19	Kenny Kelly	3.00
20	Vernon Wells	3.00

PS-206 Stars
NM/M
Complete Set (20): 50.00
Common Player: 1.00
Inserted 3:Hobby Case

1	Chipper Jones	3.00
2	Greg Maddux	3.00
3	Cal Ripken Jr.	6.00
4	Nomar Garciaparra	4.00
5	Pedro Martinez	2.00
6	Sammy Sosa	2.00
7	Frank Thomas	2.00
8	Ken Griffey Jr.	4.00
9	Manny Ramirez	2.00
10	Jeff Bagwell	2.00
11	Gary Sheffield	1.00
12	Mike Piazza	2.00
13	Roger Clemens	3.50
14	Derek Jeter	6.00
15	Rick Ankiel	1.00
16	Mark McGwire	5.00
17	Tony Gwynn	3.00
18	Barry Bonds	6.00
19	Alex Rodriguez	5.00
20	Ivan Rodriguez	1.50

1991 Pacific Gas & Electric S.F. Giants

Perforated panels of six
2-3/4" x 3-3/4" Giants cards

were included in each of five editions of Giants Magazine, the team's official program, for 1991. The set was sponsored by PG&E. Cards have color action photos on front with a graduated gray frame and white borders. At bottom is a team typographical logo, crossed bats and a red ribbon with player identification. A pentagon at top has the date "91." Backs are in black-and-white with a large sponsor's ad, the player's career stats, a few biographical details and uniform and card numbers.

		NM/M
Complete Set (30):		15.00
Common Player:		.50
1	Kevin Mitchell	.50
2	Robby Thompson	.50
3	John Burkett	.50
4	Kelly Downs	.50
5	Terry Kennedy	.50
6	Roger Craig	.50
7	Jeff Brantley	.50
8	Greg Litton	.50
9	Trevor Wilson	.50
10	Kevin Bass	.50
11	Matt Williams	1.00
12	Jose Uribe	.50
13	Steve Decker	.50
14	Will Clark	1.00
15	Dave Righetti	.50
16	Mike Kingery	.50
17	Mike LaCoss	.50
18	Dave Anderson	.50
19	Bud Black	.50
20	Mike Benjamin	.50
21	Don Robinson	.50
22	Mark Leonard	.50
23	Willie McGee	.50
24	Francisco Oliveras	.50
25	Kirt Manwaring	.50
26	Rick Parker	.50
27	Mike Remlinger	.50
28	Mike Felder	.50
29	Scott Garrelts	.50
30	Tony Perezchica	.50

1992 Pacific Gas & Electric S.F. Giants

Perforated panels of six 2-3/4" x 3-3/4" Giants cards were included in each of six editions of Giants Magazine, the team's official program, for 1992. The set was sponsored by PG&E. Cards have color action photos on front with a wood-look frame and white borders. At top is a gold ribbon with player name and position. At bottom is the team logo, crossed bats, uniform number and the year of issue. Horizontal backs are in black-and-white with a large sponsor's ad, the player's career stats, a few biographical details, uniform number and energy conservation tip. Cards are unnumbered and are listed here by panel.

		NM/M
Complete Set, Panels (6):		25.00
Complete Set, Singles (36):		20.00
Common Player:		.50
	PANEL 1	5.00
(1)	Rod Beck	
(2)	Wendell Kim	.50
(3)	Gil Heredia	.50
(4)	Mike Benjamin	.50
(5)	Matt Williams	1.00
(6)	Robby Thompson	.50
	PANEL 2	5.00
(7)	Will Clark/AS	1.00
(8)	Bob Brenly	.50
(9)	Bryan Hickerson	.50
(10)	Bob Lillis	.50

---

(11)	Royce Clayton	.50
(12)	Mark Leonard (Dropping bat.)	.50
	PANEL 3	5.00
(13)	Roger Craig	.50
(14)	Jeff Brantley	.50
(15)	Darren Lewis	.50
(16)	Mark Leonard/Btg	.50
(17)	John Burkett	.50
(18)	Mike Felder	.50
	PANEL 4	5.00
(19)	Kelly Downs	.50
(20)	Jose Uribe	.50
(21)	Bud Black	.50
(22)	Kirt Manwaring	.50
(23)	Trevor Wilson	.50
(24)	Kevin Bass	.50
	PANEL 5	5.00
(25)	Mike Jackson	.50
(26)	Will Clark	1.00
(27)	Jim McNamara	.50
(28)	Dusty Baker	.50
(29)	Scott Garrelts	.50
(30)	Chris James	.50
	PANEL 6	5.00
(31)	Dave Righetti	.50
(32)	Cory Snyder	.50
(33)	Dave Burba	.50
(34)	Carlos Alfonso	.50
(35)	Bill Swift	.50
(36)	Willie McGee	.50

2000 Palm Beach Post Montreal Expos

At each of the spring training games between March 3-April 1 each copy of the newspaper sold at the ballpark contained a random insert of two Expos and two Cardinals cards. The 3-1/8" x 4-3/4" blank-back cards have action color photos on front.

		NM/M
Complete Set (20):		15.00
Common Player:		.50
(1)	Felipe Alou	.65
(2)	Michael Barrett	.50
(3)	Geoff Blum	.50
(4)	Orlando Cabrera	.75
(5)	Brad Fullmer	.65
(6)	Vladimir Guerrero	5.00
(7)	Dustin Hermanson	.75
(8)	Hideki Irabu	.50
(9)	Steve Kline	.50
(10)	Graeme Lloyd	.50
(11)	Trey Moore	.50
(12)	Mickey Morandini	.50
(13)	Mike Mordecai	.50
(14)	Carl Pavano	.75
(15)	Anthony Telford	.50
(16)	Ugueth Urbina	.50
(17)	Jose Vidro	.75
(18)	Rondell White/Btg	1.00
(19)	Rondell White/ Standing	1.00
(20)	Chris Widger	.50

St. Louis Cardinals

During spring training each copy of the newspaper sold at the ballpark contained a random insert of two Expos and two Cardinals cards. The 3-1/8" x 4-3/4" blank-back cards have action color photos on front.

		NM/M
Complete Set (20):		20.00
Common Player:		.50
(1)	Rick Ankiel	.50
(2)	Andy Benes	.50
(3)	Kent Bottenfield	.50
(4)	Eric Davis	.50
(5)	J.D. Drew	2.00
(6)	Pat Hentgen	.50
(7)	Chad Hutchinson	.50
(8)	Darryl Kile	.50
(9)	Ray Lankford	.50
(10)	Tony LaRussa	.50
(11)	Eli Marrero	.50
(12)	Joe McEwing	.50
(13)	Mark McGwire/Btg	5.00
(14)	Mark McGwire/ Standing	5.00
(15)	Matt Morris	.50
(16)	Edgar Renteria	.50
(17)	Heathcliff Slocumb	.50
(18)	Fernando Tatis	.50
(19)	Dave Veres	.50
(20)	Fernando Vina	.50

2001 Palm Beach Post N.Y. Mets

During spring training the local newspaper distributed (in unknown manner) this set of 2-1/2" x 3-1/2" cards printed on thin stock. Fronts have purplish-gray gray borders and

---

game-action photos. Backs are in black-and-white with a portrait photo, career notes, stats and player personal data. The set is checklisted here by uniform number, as printed on front and back.

		NM/M
Complete Set (10):		10.00
Common Player:		.50
4	Robin Ventura	.50
9	Todd Zeile	.50
10	Rey Ordonez	.50
13	Edgardo Alfonzo	.50
22	Al Leiter	.50
31	Mike Piazza	6.00
35	Rick Reed	.50
45	John Franco	.50
49	Armando Benitez	.50
50	Benny Agbayani	.50

2002 Palm Beach Post N.Y. Mets

During spring training the local newspaper distributed (in unknown manner) this set of 2-1/2" x 3-1/2" cards printed on thin stock. Fronts have purple borders and posed or game-action photos. Backs are in black-and-white and have a large team logo and minimal player personal data. The set is checklisted here by uniform number, as printed on front and back.

		NM/M
Complete Set (10):		8.00
Common Player:		.50
2	Bobby Valentine	.50
6	Timo Perez	.50
10	Rey Ordonez	.50
13	Edgardo Alfonzo	.50
22	Al Leiter	.50
31	Mike Piazza	5.00
44	Jay Payton	.50
45	John Franco	.50
47	Joe McEwing	.50
49	Armando Benitez	.50

1988 Panini Stickers

BOSTON RED SOX
ROGER CLEMENS

This set of 480 stickers features 312 major league players, both rookies and superstar veterans. The full-color stickers measure 2-11/16" x 1-7/8" (team emblem and uniform stickers are slightly larger). Individual players, duos and group action shots are included in the set which also contains 14 stickers that depict 1987 season highlights. Panini also produced a 64-page album with Don Mattingly on the cover and two pages devoted to each team with a space marked for each sticker in the set. Individual sticker packets contained a total of six stickers; four players, one team logo and one uniform sticker. Panini offered a collectors' sticker exchange service in which up to 30 stickers could be traded or specific stickers purchased for 10 cents each. The 26 team logo/pennant stickers (numbered A-1 through Z-1) are listed as #455-480 in the following checklist.

		NM/M
Complete Set (480):		15.00
Common Player:		.05
Sticker Album:		1.00
Wax Pack (6):		.25
Wax Box (100):		7.50
1	World Series Trophy	.05
2	Orioles Logo	.05
3	Orioles Uniform	.05
4	Eric Bell	.05
5	Mike Boddicker	.05
6	Dave Schmidt	.05
7	Terry Kennedy	.05
8	Eddie Murray	.45
9	Bill Ripken	.05
10	Orioles Action (Tony Armas, Cal Ripken Jr.)	.25
11	Orioles Action (Tony Armas, Cal Ripken Jr.)	.25
12	Ray Knight	.05
13	Cal Ripken, Jr.	1.00
14	Ken Gerhart	.05
15	Fred Lynn	.05
16	Larry Sheets	.05
17	Mike Young	.05
18	Red Sox Logo	.05
19	Red Sox Uniform	.05
20	Oil Can Boyd	.05
21	Roger Clemens	.65
22	Bruce Hurst	.05
23	Bob Stanley	.05
24	Rich Gedman	.05
25	Dwight Evans	.05
26	Red Sox Action (Marty Barrett, Tim Laudner)	.05
27	Red Sox Action (Marty Barrett, Tim Laudner)	.05
28	Marty Barrett	.05
29	Wade Boggs	.50
30	Spike Owen	.05
31	Ellis Burks	.05
32	Mike Greenwell	.05
33	Jim Rice	.10
34	Angels Logo	.05
35	Angels Uniform	.05
36	Kirk McCaskill	.05
37	Don Sutton	.40
38	Mike Witt	.05
39	Bob Boone	.05
40	Wally Joyner	.05
41	Mark McLemore	.05
42	Angels Action (Juan Bonilla, Devon White)	.05
43	Angels Action (Juan Bonilla, Devon White)	.05
44	Jack Howell	.05
45	Dick Schofield	.05
46	Brian Downing	.05
47	Ruppert Jones	.05
48	Gary Pettis	.05
49	Devon White	.05
50	White Sox Logo	.05
51	White Sox Uniform	.05
52	Floyd Bannister	.05
53	Richard Dotson	.05
54	Bob James	.05
55	Carlton Fisk	.45
56	Greg Walker	.05
57	Fred Manrique	.05
58	White Sox Action (Ozzie Guillen, Donnie Hill, Pat Sheridan)	.05
59	White Sox Action (Ozzie Guillen, Donnie Hill, Pat Sheridan)	.05
60	Steve Lyons	.05
61	Ozzie Guillen	.05

62	Harold Baines	.05
63	Ivan Calderon	.05
64	Gary Redus	.05
65	Ken Williams	.05
66	Indians Logo	.05
67	Indians Uniform	.05
68	Scott Bailes	.05
69	Tom Candiotti	.05
70	Greg Swindell	.05
71	Chris Bando	.05
72	Joe Carter	.05
73	Tommy Hinzo	.05
74	Indians Action (Juan Bonilla, Joe Carter)	.05
75	Indians Action (Juan Bonilla, Joe Carter)	.05
76	Brook Jacoby	.05
77	Julio Franco	.05
78	Brett Butler	.05
79	Mel Hall	.05
80	Cory Snyder	.05
81	Pat Tabler	.05
82	Tigers Logo	.05
83	Tigers Uniform	.05
84	Willie Hernandez	.05
85	Jack Morris	.05
86	Frank Tanana	.05
87	Walt Terrell	.05
88	Matt Nokes	.05
89	Darrell Evans	.05
90	Tigers Action (Darrell Evans, Carlton Fisk)	.05
91	Tigers Action (Darrell Evans, Carlton Fisk)	.05
92	Lou Whitaker	.05
93	Tom Brookens	.05
94	Alan Trammell	.05
95	Kirk Gibson	.05
96	Chet Lemon	.05
97	Pat Sheridan	.05
98	Royals Logo	.05
99	Royals Uniform	.05
100	Charlie Leibrandt	.05
101	Dan Quisenberry	.05
102	Bret Saberhagen	.05
103	Jamie Quirk	.05
104	George Brett	.60
105	Frank White	.05
106	Royals Action (Bret Saberhagen)	.05
107	Royals Action (Bret Saberhagen)	.05
108	Kevin Seitzer	.05
109	Angel Salazar	.05
110	Bo Jackson	.10
111	Lonnie Smith	.05
112	Danny Tartabull	.05
113	Willie Wilson	.05
114	Brewers Logo	.05
115	Brewers Uniform	.05
116	Ted Higuera	.05
117	Juan Nieves	.05
118	Dan Plesac	.05
119	Bill Wegman	.05
120	B.J. Surhoff	.05
121	Greg Brock	.05
122	Brewers Action (Jim Gantner, Lou Whitaker)	.05
123	Brewers Action (Jim Gantner, Lou Whitaker)	.05
124	Jim Gantner	.05
125	Paul Molitor	.45
126	Dale Sveum	.05
127	Glenn Braggs	.05
128	Rob Deer	.05
129	Robin Yount	.45
130	Twins Logo	.05
131	Twins Uniform	.05
132	Bert Blyleven	.05
133	Jeff Reardon	.05
134	Frank Viola	.05
135	Tim Laudner	.05
136	Kent Hrbek	.05
137	Steve Lombardozzi	.05
138	Twins Action (Steve Lombardozzi, Frank White)	.05
139	Twins Action (Steve Lombardozzi, Frank White)	.05
140	Gary Gaetti	.05
141	Greg Gagne	.05
142	Tom Brunansky	.05
143	Dan Gladden	.05
144	Kirby Puckett	.50
145	Gene Larkin	.05
146	Yankees Logo	.05
147	Yankees Uniform	.05
148	Tommy John	.05
149	Rick Rhoden	.05
150	Dave Righetti	.05
151	Rick Cerone	.05
152	Don Mattingly	.60
153	Willie Randolph	.05
154	Yankees Action (Scott Fletcher, Don Mattingly)	.25
155	Yankees Action (Scott Fletcher, Don Mattingly)	.20
156	Mike Pagliarulo	.05
157	Wayne Tolleson	.05

158	Rickey Henderson	.45
159	Dan Pasqua	.05
160	Gary Ward	.05
161	Dave Winfield	.45
162	Athletics Logo	.05
163	Athletics Uniform	.05
164	Dave Stewart	.05
165	Curt Young	.05
166	Terry Steinbach	.05
167	Mark McGwire	.75
168	Tony Phillips	.05
169	Carney Lansford	.05
170	Athletics Action (Mike Gallego, Tony Phillips)	.05
171	Athletics Action (Mike Gallego, Tony Phillips)	
172	Alfredo Griffin	.05
173	Jose Canseco	.30
174	Mike Davis	.05
175	Reggie Jackson	.60
176	Dwayne Murphy	.05
177	Luis Polonia	.05
178	Mariners Logo	.05
179	Mariners Uniform	.05
180	Scott Bankhead	.05
181	Mark Langston	.05
182	Edwin Nunez	.05
183	Scott Bradley	.05
184	Dave Valle	.05
185	Alvin Davis	.05
186	Mariners Action (Jack Howell, Rey Quinones)	.05
187	Mariners Action (Jack Howell, Rey Quinones)	.05
188	Harold Reynolds	.05
189	Jim Presley	.05
190	Rey Quinones	.05
191	Phil Bradley	.05
192	Mickey Brantley	.05
193	Mike Kingery	.05
194	Rangers Logo	.05
195	Rangers Uniform	.05
196	Edwin Correa	.05
197	Charlie Hough	.05
198	Bobby Witt	.05
199	Mike Stanley	.05
200	Pete O'Brien	.05
201	Jerry Browne	.05
202	Rangers Action (Steve Buechele, Eddie Murray)	.05
203	Rangers Action (Steve Buechele, Eddie Murray)	.05
204	Steve Buechele	.05
205	Larry Parrish	.05
206	Scott Fletcher	.05
207	Pete Incaviglia	.05
208	Oddibe McDowell	.05
209	Ruben Sierra	.05
210	Blue Jays Logo	.05
211	Blue Jays Uniform	.05
212	Mark Eichhorn	.05
213	Tom Henke	.05
214	Jimmy Key	.05
215	Dave Stieb	.05
216	Ernie Whitt	.05
217	Willie Upshaw	.05
218	Blue Jays Action (Harold Reynolds, Willie Upshaw)	.05
219	Blue Jays Action (Harold Reynolds, Willie Upshaw)	.05
220	Garth Iorg	.05
221	Kelly Gruber	.05
222	Tony Fernandez	.05
223	Jesse Barfield	.05
224	George Bell	.05
225	Lloyd Moseby	.05
226	National League Logo	.05
227	Terry Kennedy, Don Mattingly	.20
228	Wade Boggs, Willie Randolph	.05
229	Bret Saberhagen	.05
230	George Bell, Cal Ripken Jr.	.45
231	Rickey Henderson, Dave Winfield	.10
232	Gary Carter, Jack Clark	.05
233	Mike Scott	.05
234	Ryne Sandberg, Mike Schmidt	.25
235	Ozzie Smith, Eric Davis	.10
236	Andre Dawson, Darryl Strawberry	.05
237	Braves Logo	.05
238	Braves Uniform	.05
239	Rick Mahler	.05
240	Zane Smith	.05
241	Ozzie Virgil	.05
242	Gerald Perry	.05
243	Glenn Hubbard	.05
244	Ken Oberkfell	.05
245	Braves Action (Glenn Hubbard, Jeffrey Leonard)	.05
246	Braves Action (Glenn Hubbard, Jeffrey Leonard)	.05
247	Rafael Ramirez	.05
248	Ken Griffey	.05
249	Albert Hall	.05

No.	Player	Price
250	Dion James	.05
251	Dale Murphy	.20
252	Gary Roenicke	.05
253	Cubs Logo	.05
254	Cubs Uniform	.05
255	Jamie Moyer	.05
256	Lee Smith	.05
257	Rick Sutcliffe	.05
258	Jody Davis	.05
259	Leon Durham	.05
260	Ryne Sandberg	.50
261	Cubs Action (Jody Davis)	.05
262	Cubs Action (Jody Davis)	.05
263	Keith Moreland	.05
264	Shawon Dunston	.05
265	Andre Dawson	.25
266	Dave Martinez	.05
267	Jerry Mumphrey	.05
268	Rafael Palmeiro	.45
269	Reds Logo	.05
270	Reds Uniform	.05
271	John Franco	.05
272	Ted Power	.05
273	Bo Diaz	.05
274	Nick Esasky	.05
275	Dave Concepcion	.05
276	Kurt Stillwell	.05
277	Reds Action (Bob Melvin, Dave Parker)	.05
278	Reds Action (Bob Melvin, Dave Parker)	.05
279	Buddy Bell	.05
280	Barry Larkin	.05
281	Kal Daniels	.05
282	Eric Davis	.05
283	Tracy Jones	.05
284	Dave Parker	.05
285	Astros Logo	.05
286	Astros Uniform	.05
287	Jim Deshaies	.05
288	Nolan Ryan	1.00
289	Mike Scott	.05
290	Dave Smith	.05
291	Alan Ashby	.05
292	Glenn Davis	.05
293	Astros Action (Alan Ashby, Gary Carter)	.05
294	Astros Action (Alan Ashby, Gary Carter)	.05
295	Bill Doran	.05
296	Denny Walling	.05
297	Craig Reynolds	.05
298	Kevin Bass	.05
299	Jose Cruz	.05
300	Billy Hatcher	.05
301	Dodgers Logo	.05
302	Dodgers Uniform	.05
303	Orel Hershiser	.05
304	Fernando Valenzuela	.05
305	Bob Welch	.05
306	Matt Young	.05
307	Mike Scioscia	.05
308	Franklin Stubbs	.05
309	Dodgers Action (Mariano Duncan, Junior Ortiz)	.05
310	Dodgers Action (Mariano Duncan, Junior Ortiz)	.05
311	Steve Sax	.05
312	Jeff Hamilton	.05
313	Dave Anderson	.05
314	Pedro Guerrero	.05
315	Mike Marshall	.05
316	John Shelby	.05
317	Expos Logo	.05
318	Expos Uniform	.05
319	Neal Heaton	.05
320	Bryn Smith	.05
321	Floyd Youmans	.05
322	Mike Fitzgerald	.05
323	Andres Galarraga	.05
324	Vance Law	.05
325	Expos Action (John Kruk, Tim Raines)	.05
326	Expos Action (John Kruk, Tim Raines)	.05
327	Tim Wallach	.05
328	Hubie Brooks	.05
329	Casey Candaele	.05
330	Tim Raines	.05
331	Mitch Webster	.05
332	Herm Winningham	.05
333	Mets Logo	.05
334	Mets Uniform	.05
335	Ron Darling	.05
336	Sid Fernandez	.05
337	Dwight Gooden	.05
338	Gary Carter	.45
339	Keith Hernandez	.05
340	Wally Backman	.05
341	Mets Action (Mike Diaz, Darryl Strawberry, Tim Teufel, Mookie Wilson)	.05
342	Mets Action (Mike Diaz, Darryl Strawberry, Tim Teufel, Mookie Wilson)	.05
343	Howard Johnson	.05
344	Rafael Santana	.05
345	Lenny Dykstra	.05
346	Kevin McReynolds	.05
347	Darryl Strawberry	.05
348	Mookie Wilson	.05
349	Phillies Logo	.05
350	Phillies Uniform	.05
351	Steve Bedrosian	.05
352	Shane Rawley	.05
353	Bruce Ruffin	.05
354	Kent Tekulve	.05
355	Lance Parrish	.05
356	Von Hayes	.05
357	Phillies Action (Tony Pena, Glenn Wilson)	.05
358	Phillies Action (Tony Pena, Glenn Wilson)	.05
359	Juan Samuel	.05
360	Mike Schmidt	.60
361	Steve Jeltz	.05
362	Chris James	.05
363	Milt Thompson	.05
364	Glenn Wilson	.05
365	Pirates Logo	.05
366	Pirates Uniform	.05
367	Mike Dunne	.05
368	Brian Fisher	.05
369	Mike LaValliere	.05
370	Sid Bream	.05
371	Jose Lind	.05
372	Bobby Bonilla	.05
373	Pirates Action (Bobby Bonilla)	.05
374	Pirates Action (Bobby Bonilla)	.05
375	Al Pedrique	.05
376	Barry Bonds	1.00
377	John Cangelosi	.05
378	Mike Diaz	.05
379	R.J. Reynolds	.05
380	Andy Van Slyke	.05
381	Cardinals Logo	.05
382	Cardinals Uniform	.05
383	Danny Cox	.05
384	Bob Forsch	.05
385	Joe Magrane	.05
386	Todd Worrell	.05
387	Tony Pena	.05
388	Jack Clark	.05
389	Cardinals Action (Jody Davis, Tom Herr)	.05
390	Cardinals Action (Jody Davis, Tom Herr)	.05
391	Tom Herr	.05
392	Terry Pendleton	.05
393	Ozzie Smith	.50
394	Vince Coleman	.05
395	Curt Ford	.05
396	Willie McGee	.05
397	Padres Logo	.05
398	Padres Uniform	.05
399	Lance McCullers	.05
400	Eric Show	.05
401	Ed Whitson	.05
402	Benito Santiago	.05
403	John Kruk	.05
404	Tim Flannery	.05
405	Padres Action (Randy Ready, Benito Santiago)	.05
406	Padres Action (Randy Ready, Benito Santiago)	.05
407	Randy Ready	.05
408	Chris Brown	.05
409	Garry Templeton	.05
410	Tony Gwynn	.50
411	Stan Jefferson	.05
412	Carmelo Martinez	.05
413	Giants Logo	.05
414	Giants Uniform	.05
415	Kelly Downs	.05
416	Scott Garrelts	.05
417	Mike Krukow	.05
418	Mike LaCoss	.05
419	Bob Brenly	.05
420	Will Clark	.05
421	Giants Action (Will Clark, Mike Fitzgerald)	.05
422	Giants Action (Will Clark, Mike Fitzgerald)	.05
423	Robby Thompson	.05
424	Kevin Mitchell	.05
425	Jose Uribe	.05
426	Mike Aldrete	.05
427	Jeffrey Leonard	.05
428	Candy Maldonado	.05
429	Mike Schmidt	.40
430	Don Mattingly	.40
431	Juan Nieves	.05
432	Paul Molitor	.25
433	Benito Santiago	.05
434	Rickey Henderson	.25
435	Nolan Ryan	.65
436	Kevin Seitzer	.05
437	Tony Gwynn	.35
438	Mark McGwire	.55
439	Howard Johnson	.05
440	Steve Bedrosian	.05
441	Darrell Evans	.05
442	Eddie Murray	.05
443	1987 A.L. Championship Series (Kirby Puckett, Alan Trammell, Lou Whitaker)	.05
444	1987 A.L. Championship Series (Kirby Puckett, Alan Trammell, Lou Whitaker)	.05
445	American League Championship Series MVP (Gary Gaetti)	.05
446	National League Championship Series MVP (Jeffrey Leonard)	.05
447	1987 N.L. Championship Series (Kevin Mitchell, Tony Pena)	.05
448	1987 N.L. Championship Series (Kevin Mitchell, Tony Pena)	.05
449	1987 World Series (Tom Brunansky, Tony Pena)	.05
450	1987 World Series (Tom Brunansky, Tony Pena)	.05
451	World Series Celebration	.05
452	World Series Celebration	.05
453	World Series Celebration	.05
454	World Series Celebration	.05
(455)	Orioles Logo/Pennant	.05
(456)	Red Sox Logo/Pennant	.05
(457)	Angels Logo/Pennant	.05
(458)	White Sox Logo/Pennant	.05
(459)	Indians Logo/Pennant	.05
(460)	Tigers Logo/Pennant	.05
(461)	Royals Logo/Pennant	.05
(462)	Brewers Logo/Pennant	.05
(463)	Twins Logo/Pennant	.05
(464)	Yankees Logo/Pennant	.05
(465)	Athletics Logo/Pennant	.05
(466)	Mariners Logo/Pennant	.05
(467)	Rangers Logo/Pennant	.05
(468)	Blue Jays Logo/Pennant	.05
(469)	Braves Logo/Pennant	.05
(470)	Cubs Logo/Pennant	.05
(471)	Reds Logo/Pennant	.05
(472)	Astros Logo/Pennant	.05
(473)	Dodgers Logo/Pennant	.05
(474)	Expos Logo/Pennant	.05
(475)	Mets Logo/Pennant	.05
(476)	Phillies Logo/Pennant	.05
(477)	Pirates Logo/Pennant	.05
(478)	Cardinals Logo/Pennant	.05
(479)	Padres Logo/Pennant	.05
(480)	Giants Logo/Pennant	.05

1989 Panini Stickers

CUBS
MARK GRACE

For a second straight year, the Italian sticker manufacturer produced a 480-piece set for the American market. The 1-7/8" x 2-11/16" stickers were sold in packs of six for 30 cents. Packs contain five player stickers and a foil depicting team logos, lettering or ballparks. A 64-page album depicting Jose Canseco on the cover was offered for 69 cents. The 1989 Panini stickers used more action photos than the previous year. Color photos had banners at the bottom with team and player name. Backs had appropriate logos, sticker number and ads for Panini's sticker book.

	NM/M
Complete Set (480):	12.50
Common Player:	.05
Sticker Album:	1.00
Wax Pack (6):	.25
Wax Box (100):	7.50

No.	Player	Price
1	World Series Trophy	.05
2	World Series Trophy	.05
3	Mike Schmidt	.40
4	Tom Browning	.05
5	Doug Jones	.05
6	Wrigley Field	.05
7	Wade Boggs	.30
8	Jose Canseco	.20
9	Orel Hershiser	.05
10	Oakland A's Win ALCS	.05
11	Oakland A's Win ALCS	.05
12	Dennis Eckersley (ALCS MVP)	.20
13	Orel Hershiser (NLCS MVP)	.05
14	Dodgers Win NLCS	.05
15	Dodgers Win NLCS	.05
16	Kirk Gibson	.05
17	Kirk Gibson	.05
18	Orel Hershiser	.05
19	Orel Hershiser	.05
20	Mark McGwire	.50
21	Tim Belcher	.05
22	Jay Howell	.05
23	Mickey Hatcher	.05
24	Mike Davis	.05
25	Orel Hershiser (World Series MVP)	.05
26	Dodgers Win World Series	.05
27	Dodgers Win World Series	.05
28	Dodgers Win World Series	.05
29	Dodgers Win World Series	.05
30	Braves Logo	.05
31	Jose Alvarez	.05
32	Tommy Gregg	.05
33	Paul Assenmacher	.05
34	Tom Glavine	.25
35	Rick Mahler	.05
36	Pete Smith	.05
37	Atlanta Stadium	.05
38	Braves Script	.05
39	Bruce Sutter	.20
40	Gerald Perry	.05
41	Jeff Blauser	.05
42	Ron Gant	.05
43	Andres Thomas	.05
44	Dion James	.05
45	Dale Murphy	.20
46	Cubs Logo	.05
47	Doug Dascenzo	.05
48	Mike Harkey	.05
49	Greg Maddux	.50
50	Jeff Pico	.05
51	Rick Sutcliffe	.05
52	Damon Berryhill	.05
53	Wrigley Field	.05
54	Cubs Script	.05
55	Mark Grace	.15
56	Ryne Sandberg	.50
57	Vance Law	.05
58	Shawon Dunston	.05
59	Andre Dawson	.25
60	Rafael Palmeiro	.40
61	Mitch Webster	.05
62	Reds Logo	.05
63	Jack Armstrong	.05
64	Chris Sabo	.05
65	Tom Browning	.05
66	John Franco	.05
67	Danny Jackson	.05
68	Jose Rijo	.05
69	Riverfront Stadium	.05
70	Reds Script	.05
71	Bo Diaz	.05
72	Nick Esasky	.05
73	Jeff Treadway	.05
74	Barry Larkin	.05
75	Kal Daniels	.05
76	Eric Davis	.05
77	Paul O'Neill	.05
78	Astros Logo	.05
79	Craig Biggio	.05
80	John Fishel	.05
81	Juan Agosto	.05
82	Bob Knepper	.05
83	Nolan Ryan	1.00
84	Mike Scott	.05
85	The Astrodome	.05
86	Astros Script	.05
87	Dave Smith	.05
88	Glenn Davis	.05
89	Bill Doran	.05
90	Rafael Ramirez	.05
91	Kevin Bass	.05
92	Billy Hatcher	.05
93	Gerald Young	.05
94	Dodgers Logo	.05
95	Tim Belcher	.05
96	Tim Crews	.05
97	Orel Hershiser	.05
98	Jay Howell	.05
99	Tim Leary	.05
100	John Tudor	.05
101	Dodgers Stadium	.05
102	Dodgers Script	.05
103	Fernando Valenzuela	.05
104	Mike Scioscia	.05
105	Mickey Hatcher	.05
106	Steve Sax	.05
107	Kirk Gibson	.05
108	Mike Marshall	.05
109	John Shelby	.05
110	Expos Logo	.05
111	Randy Johnson	.40
112	Nelson Santovenia	.05
113	Tim Burke	.05
114	Dennis Martinez	.05
115	Pascual Perez	.05
116	Bryn Smith	.05
117	Olympic Stadium	.05
118	Expos Script	.05
119	Andres Galarraga	.05
120	Wallace Johnson	.05
121	Tom Foley	.05
122	Tim Wallach	.05
123	Hubie Brooks	.05
124	Tracy Jones	.05
125	Tim Raines	.05
126	Mets Logo	.05
127	Kevin Elster	.05
128	Gregg Jefferies	.05
129	David Cone	.05
130	Ron Darling	.05
131	Dwight Gooden	.05
132	Roger McDowell	.05
133	Shea Stadium	.05
134	Mets Script	.05
135	Randy Myers	.05
136	Gary Carter	.40
137	Keith Hernandez	.05
138	Lenny Dykstra	.05
139	Kevin McReynolds	.05
140	Darryl Strawberry	.05
141	Mookie Wilson	.05
142	Phillies Logo	.05
143	Ron Jones	.05
144	Ricky Jordan	.05
145	Steve Bedrosian	.05
146	Don Carman	.05
147	Kevin Gross	.05
148	Bruce Ruffin	.05
149	Veterans Stadium	.05
150	Phillies Script	.05
151	Von Hayes	.05
152	Juan Samuel	.05
153	Mike Schmidt	.55
154	Phil Bradley	.05
155	Bob Dernier	.05
156	Chris James	.05
157	Milt Thompson	.05
158	Pirates Logo	.05
159	Randy Kramer	.05
160	Scott Medvin	.05
161	Doug Drabek	.05
162	Mike Dunne	.05
163	Jim Gott	.05
164	Jeff Robinson	.05
165	Three Rivers Stadium	.05
166	Pirates Script	.05
167	John Smiley	.05
168	Mike LaValliere	.05
169	Sid Bream	.05
170	Jose Lind	.05
171	Bobby Bonilla	.05
172	Barry Bonds	1.00
173	Andy Van Slyke	.05
174	Cardinals Logo	.05
175	Luis Alicea	.05
176	John Costello	.05
177	Jose DeLeon	.05
178	Joe Magrane	.05
179	Todd Worrell	.05
180	Tony Pena	.05
181	Busch Stadium	.05
182	Cardinals Script	.05
183	Pedro Guerrero	.05
184	Jose Oquendo	.05
185	Terry Pendleton	.05
186	Ozzie Smith	.50
187	Tom Brunansky	.05
188	Vince Coleman	.05
189	Willie McGee	.05
190	Padres Logo	.05
191	Roberto Alomar	.15
192	Sandy Alomar, Jr.	.05
193	Mark Davis	.05
194	Andy Hawkins	.05
195	Dennis Rasmussen	.05
196	Eric Show	.05
197	Jack Murphy Stadium	.05
198	Padres Script	.05
199	Benito Santiago	.05
200	John Kruk	.05
201	Randy Ready	.05
202	Garry Templeton	.05
203	Tony Gwynn	.50
204	Carmelo Martinez	.05
205	Marvell Wynne	.05
206	Giants Logo	.05
207	Dennis Cook	.05
208	Kirt Manwaring	.05
209	Kelly Downs	.05
210	Rick Reuschel	.05
211	Don Robinson	.05
212	Will Clark	.05
213	Candlestick Park	.05
214	Giants Script	.05
215	Robby Thompson	.05
216	Kevin Mitchell	.05
217	Jose Uribe	.05
218	Matt Williams	.05
219	Mike Aldrete	.05
220	Brett Butler	.05
221	Candy Maldonado	.05
222	Tony Gwynn	.30
223	Darryl Strawberry	.05
224	Andres Galarraga	.05
225	Orel Hershiser, Danny Jackson	.05
226	Nolan Ryan	.50
227	Dwight Gooden/AS	.05
228	Gary Carter/AS	.05
229	Vince Coleman/AS	.05
230	Andre Dawson/AS	.05
231	Darryl Strawberry/AS	.05
232	Will Clark/AS	.05
233	Ryne Sandberg/AS	.25
234	Bobby Bonilla/AS	.05
235	Ozzie Smith/AS	.30
236	Terry Steinbach/AS	.05
237	Frank Viola/AS	.05
238	Jose Canseco/AS	.10
239	Rickey Henderson/AS	.20
240	Dave Winfield/AS	.05
241	Cal Ripken, Jr./AS	.50
242	Wade Boggs/AS	.25
243	Paul Molitor/AS	.20
244	Mark McGwire/AS	.40
245	Wade Boggs	.05
246	Jose Canseco	.10
247	Kirby Puckett	.30
248	Frank Viola	.05
249	Roger Clemens	.35
250	Orioles Logo	.05
251	Bob Milacki	.05
252	Craig Worthington	.05
253	Jeff Ballard	.05
254	Tom Niedenfeur	.05
255	Dave Schmidt	.05
256	Terry Kennedy	.05
257	Memorial Stadium	.05
258	Orioles Script	.05
259	Mickey Tettleton	.05
260	Eddie Murray	.40
261	Billy Ripken	.05
262	Cal Ripken, Jr.	1.00
263	Joe Orsulak	.05
264	Larry Sheets	.05
265	Pete Stanicek	.05
266	Red Sox Logo	.05
267	Steve Curry	.05
268	Jody Reed	.05
269	"Oil Can" Boyd	.05
270	Roger Clemens	.55
271	Bruce Hurst	.05
272	Lee Smith	.05
273	Fenway Park	.05
274	Red Sox Script	.05
275	Todd Benzinger	.05
276	Marty Barrett	.05
277	Wade Boggs	.50
278	Ellis Burks	.05
279	Dwight Evans	.05
280	Mike Greenwell	.05
281	Jim Rice	.10
282	Angels Logo	.05
283	Dante Bichette	.05
284	Bryan Harvey	.05
285	Kirk McCaskill	.05
286	Mike Witt	.05
287	Bob Boone	.05
288	Brian Downing	.05
289	Anaheim Stadium	.05
290	Angels Script	.05
291	Wally Joyner	.05
292	Johnny Ray	.05
293	Jack Howell	.05
294	Dick Schofield	.05
295	Tony Armas	.05
296	Chili Davis	.05
297	Devon White	.05
298	White Sox Logo	.05
299	Dave Gallagher	.05
300	Melido Perez	.05
301	Shawn Hillegas	.05
302	Jack McDowell	.05
303	Bobby Thigpen	.05
304	Carlton Fisk	.40
305	Comiskey Park	.05
306	White Sox Script	.05
307	Greg Walker	.05
308	Steve Lyons	.05
309	Ozzie Guillen	.05
310	Harold Baines	.05
311	Daryl Boston	.05
312	Lance Johnson	.05
313	Dan Pasqua	.05
314	Indians Logo	.05
315	Luis Medina	.05
316	Ron Tingley	.05
317	Tom Candiotti	.05
318	John Farrell	.05
319	Doug Jones	.05
320	Greg Swindell	.05
321	Cleveland Stadium	.05
322	Indians Script	.05
323	Andy Allanson	.05
324	Willie Upshaw	.05
325	Julio Franco	.05
326	Brook Jacoby	.05
327	Joe Carter	.05
328	Mel Hall	.05
329	Cory Snyder	.05
330	Tigers Logo	.05
331	Paul Gibson	.05
332	Torey Lovullo	.05
333	Mike Henneman	.05
334	Jack Morris	.05
335	Jeff Robinson	.05
336	Frank Tanana	.05
337	Tiger Stadium	.05
338	Tigers Script	.05
339	Matt Nokes	.05
340	Tom Brookens	.05
341	Lou Whitaker	.05
342	Luis Salazar	.05
343	Alan Trammell	.05
344	Chet Lemon	.05
345	Gary Pettis	.05
346	Royals Logo	.05
347	Luis de los Santos	.05
348	Gary Thurman	.05
349	Steve Farr	.05
350	Mark Gubicza	.05
351	Charlie Leibrandt	.05
352	Bret Saberhagen	.05

ABBREVIATIONS
AS - All-Star

353	Royals Stadium	.05
354	Royals Script	.05
355	George Brett	.05
356	Frank White	.05
357	Kevin Seitzer	.05
358	Bo Jackson	.10
359	Pat Tabler	.05
360	Danny Tartabull	.05
361	Willie Wilson	.05
362	Brewers Logo	.05
363	Joey Meyer	.05
364	Gary Sheffield	.25
365	Don August	.05
366	Ted Higuera	.05
367	Dan Plesac	.05
368	B.J. Surhoff	.05
369	County Stadium	.05
370	Brewers Script	.05
371	Greg Brock	.05
372	Jim Gantner	.05
373	Paul Molitor	.40
374	Dale Sveum	.05
375	Glenn Braggs	.05
376	Rob Deer	.05
377	Robin Yount	.40
378	Twins Logo	.05
379	German Gonzalez	.05
380	Kelvin Torve	.05
381	Allan Anderson	.05
382	Jeff Reardon	.05
383	Frank Viola	.05
384	Tim Laudner	.05
385	HHH Metrodome	.05
386	Twins Script	.05
387	Kent Hrbek	.05
388	Gene Larkin	.05
389	Gary Gaetti	.05
390	Greg Gagne	.05
391	Randy Bush	.05
392	Dan Gladden	.05
393	Kirby Puckett	.50
394	Yankees Logo	.05
395	Roberto Kelly	.05
396	Al Leiter	.05
397	John Candelaria	.05
398	Rich Dotson	.05
399	Rick Rhoden	.05
400	Dave Righetti	.05
401	Yankees Stadium	.05
402	Yankees Script	.05
403	Don Slaught	.05
404	Don Mattingly	.55
405	Willie Randolph	.05
406	Mike Pagliarulo	.05
407	Rafael Santana	.05
408	Rickey Henderson	.40
409	Dave Winfield	.40
410	A's Logo	.05
411	Todd Burns	.05
412	Walt Weiss	.05
413	Storm Davis	.05
414	Dennis Eckersley	.35
415	Dave Stewart	.05
416	Bob Welch	.05
417	Oakland Coliseum	.05
418	A's Script	.05
419	Terry Steinbach	.05
420	Mark McGwire	.75
421	Carney Lansford	.05
422	Jose Canseco	.35
423	Dave Henderson	.05
424	Dave Parker	.05
425	Luis Polonia	.05
426	Mariners Logo	.05
427	Mario Diaz	.05
428	Edgar Martinez	.05
429	Scott Bankhead	.05
430	Mark Langston	.05
431	Mike Moore	.05
432	Scott Bradley	.05
433	The Kingdome	.05
434	Mariners Script	.05
435	Alvin Davis	.05
436	Harold Reynolds	.05
437	Jim Presley	.05
438	Rey Quinonez	.05
439	Mickey Brantley	.05
440	Jay Buhner	.05
441	Henry Cotto	.05
442	Rangers Logo	.05
443	Cecil Espy	.05
444	Chad Kreuter	.05
445	Jose Guzman	.05
446	Charlie Hough	.05
447	Jeff Russell	.05
448	Bobby Witt	.05
449	Arlington Stadium	.05
450	Rangers Script	.05
451	Geno Petralli	.05
452	Pete O'Brien	.05
453	Steve Buechele	.05
454	Scott Fletcher	.05
455	Pete Incaviglia	.05
456	Oddibe McDowell	.05
457	Ruben Sierra	.05
458	Blue Jays Logo	.05
459	Rob Ducey	.05
460	Todd Stottlemyre	.05
461	Tom Henke	.05
462	Jimmy Key	.05
463	Dave Steib	.05
464	Pat Borders	.05
465	Exhibition Stadium	.05
466	Blue Jays Script	.05
467	Fred McGriff	.05
468	Manny Lee	.05
469	Kelly Gruber	.05
470	Tony Fernandez	.05
471	Jesse Barfield	.05
472	George Bell	.05
473	Lloyd Moseby	.05
474	Orel Hershiser	.05
475	Frank Viola	.05
476	Chris Sabo	.05
477	Jose Canseco	.10
478	Walt Weiss	.05
479	Kirk Gibson	.05
480	Jose Canseco	.10

1990 Panini Stickers

BRAVES
JOHN SMOLTZ

Nearly 400 individual player and specialty stickers comprise the 1990 issue from this Italian company. Sold in packs of five regular and one foil sticker, the set includes 388 2-1/8" x 3" stickers. Fronts feature color action photos. Backs are printed in black-and-white and include a sticker number and appropriate logos. A 68-page album with Nolan Ryan on the cover was sold as an adjunct to the stickers. Among the foil stickers in the set are those featuring the team logo and batting helmet of each team.

		NM/M
Complete Set (388):		9.00
Common Player:		.05
English Album:		1.00
French Album:		3.00
Wax Pack (5+1):		.25
Wax Box (100):		7.50
1	Randy Milligan	.05
2	Gregg Olson	.05
3	Bill Ripken	.05
4	Phil Bradley	.05
5	Joe Orsulak	.05
6	Bob Milacki	.05
7	Cal Ripken, Jr.	1.00
8	Mickey Tettleton	.05
9	Orioles Logo/Foil	.05
10	Orioles Helmet/Foil	.05
11	Craig Worthington	.05
12	Mike Devereaux	.05
13	Jeff Ballard	.05
14	Lee Smith	.05
15	Marty Barrett	.05
16	Mike Greenwell	.05
17	Dwight Evans	.05
18	John Dopson	.05
19	Wade Boggs	.50
20	Mike Boddicker	.05
21	Ellis Burks	.05
22	Red Sox Logo/Foil	.05
23	Red Sox Helmet/Foil	.05
24	Roger Clemens	.55
25	Jody Reed	.05
26	Nick Esasky	.05
27	Brian Downing	.05
28	Bert Blyleven	.05
29	Devon White	.05
30	Claudell Washington	.05
31	Wally Joyner	.05
32	Chuck Finley	.05
33	Johnny Ray	.05
34	Jim Abbott	.05
35	Angels Logo/Foil	.05
36	Angels Helmet/Foil	.05
37	Kirk McCaskill	.05
38	Lance Parrish	.05
39	Chili Davis	.05
40	Steve Lyons	.05
41	Ozzie Guillen	.05
42	Melido Perez	.05
43	Scott Fletcher	.05
44	Carlton Fisk	.40
45	Greg Walker	.05
46	Dave Gallagher	.05
47	Ivan Calderon	.05
48	White Sox Logo/Foil	.05
49	White Sox Helmet/Foil	.05
50	Bobby Thigpen	.05
51	Ron Kittle	.05
52	Daryl Boston	.05
53	John Farrell	.05
54	Jerry Browne	.05
55	Pete O'Brien	.05
56	Cory Snyder	.05
57	Tom Candiotti	.05
58	Brook Jacoby	.05
59	Greg Swindell	.05
60	Felix Fermin	.05
61	Indians Logo/Foil	.05
62	Indians Helmet/Foil	.05
63	Doug Jones	.05
64	Dion James	.05
65	Joe Carter	.05
66	Mike Heath	.05
67	Dave Bergman	.05
68	Gary Ward	.05
69	Mike Henneman	.05
70	Alan Trammell	.05
71	Lou Whitaker	.05
72	Frank Tanana	.05
73	Fred Lynn	.05
74	Tigers Logo/Foil	.05
75	Tigers Helmet/Foil	.05
76	Jack Morris	.05
77	Chet Lemon	.05
78	Gary Pettis	.05
79	Kurt Stillwell	.05
80	Jim Eisenreich	.05
81	Bret Saberhagen	.05
82	Mark Gubicza	.05
83	Frank White	.05
84	Bo Jackson	.10
85	Jeff Montgomery	.05
86	Kevin Seitzer	.05
87	Royals Logo/Foil	.05
88	Royals Helmet/Foil	.05
89	Tom Gordon	.05
90	Danny Tartabull	.05
91	George Brett	.55
92	Robin Yount	.40
93	B.J. Surhoff	.05
94	Jim Gantner	.05
95	Dan Plesac	.05
96	Ted Higuera	.05
97	Glenn Braggs	.05
98	Paul Molitor	.40
99	Chris Bosio	.05
100	Brewers Logo/Foil	.05
101	Brewers Helmet/Foil	.05
102	Rob Deer	.05
103	Chuck Crim	.05
104	Greg Brock	.05
105	Kirby Puckett	.50
106	Gary Gaetti	.05
107	Roy Smith	.05
108	Jeff Reardon	.05
109	Randy Bush	.05
110	Al Newman	.05
111	Dan Gladden	.05
112	Kent Hrbek	.05
113	Twins Logo/Foil	.05
114	Twins Helmet/Foil	.05
115	Greg Gagne	.05
116	Brian Harper	.05
117	Allan Anderson	.05
118	Lee Guetterman	.05
119	Roberto Kelly	.05
120	Jesse Barfield	.05
121	Alvaro Espinoza	.05
122	Mel Hall	.05
123	Chuck Cary	.05
124	Dave Righetti	.05
125	Don Mattingly	.55
126	Yankees Logo/Foil	.05
127	Yankees Helmet/Foil	.05
128	Bob Geren	.05
129	Steve Sax	.05
130	Andy Hawkins	.05
131	Bob Welch	.05
132	Mark McGwire	.75
133	Dave Henderson	.05
134	Carney Lansford	.05
135	Walt Weiss	.05
136	Mike Moore	.05
137	Dennis Eckersley	.35
138	Rickey Henderson	.40
139	A's Logo/Foil	.05
140	A's Helmet/Foil	.05
141	Dave Stewart	.05
142	Jose Canseco	.30
143	Terry Steinbach	.05
144	Harold Reynolds	.05
145	Darnell Coles	.05
146	Brian Holman	.05
147	Scott Bankhead	.05
148	Greg Briley	.05
149	Alvin Davis	.05
150	Jeffrey Leonard	.05
151	Mike Schooler	.05
152	Mariners Logo/Foil	.05
153	Mariners Helmet/Foil	.05
154	Randy Johnson	.40
155	Ken Griffey Jr.	.65
156	Dave Valle	.05
157	Pete Incaviglia	.05
158	Fred Manrique	.05
159	Jeff Russell	.05
160	Nolan Ryan	1.00
161	Geno Petralli	.05
162	Ruben Sierra	.05
163	Julio Franco	.05
164	Rafael Palmeiro	.35
165	Rangers Logo/Foil	.05
166	Rangers Helmet/Foil	.05
167	Harold Baines	.05
168	Kevin Brown	.05
169	Steve Buechele	.05
170	Fred McGriff	.05
171	Kelly Gruber	.05
172	Todd Stottlemyre	.05
173	Dave Steib	.05
174	Mookie Wilson	.05
175	Pat Borders	.05
176	Tony Fernandez	.05
177	John Cerutti	.05
178	Blue Jays Logo/Foil	.05
179	Blue Jays Helmet/Foil	.05
180	George Bell	.05
181	Jimmy Key	.05
182	Nelson Liriano	.05
183	Kirby Puckett (BA leader)	.30
184	Carney Lansford (Stats leader.)	.05
185	Nolan Ryan (K leader)	.50
186	American League Logo/Foil	.05
187	National League Logo/Foil	.05
188	World's Championship Trophy/Foil	.05
189	1988 L.A. Dodgers World Series Ring/Foil	.05
190	1987 Minnesota Twins World Series Ring/Foil	.05
191	1986 N.Y. Mets World Series Ring/Foil	.05
192	1985 K.C. Royals World Series Ring/Foil	.05
193	1984 Detroit Tigers World Series Ring/Foil	.05
194	1983 Baltimore Orioles World Series Ring/Foil	.05
195	1982 Cardinals World Series Ring/Foil	.05
196	1981 L.A. Dodgers World Series Ring/Foil	.05
197	1980 Phillies World Series Ring/Foil	.05
198	Dave Stewart, Bo Jackson/AS	.05
199	Wade Boggs, Kirby Puckett/AS	.15
200	Harold Baines/AS	.05
201	Julio Franco/AS	.05
202	Cal Ripken, Jr./AS	.50
203	Ruben Sierra/AS	.05
204	Mark McGwire/AS	.40
205	Terry Steinbach/AS	.05
206	Rick Reuschel, Ozzie Smith/AS	.05
207	Tony Gwynn, Will Clark/AS	.05
208	Kevin Mitchell/AS	.05
209	Eric Davis/AS	.05
210	Howard Johnson/AS	.05
211	Pedro Guerrero/AS	.05
212	Ryne Sandberg/AS	.25
213	Benito Santiago/AS	.05
214	Kevin Mitchell (HR leaders)	.05
215	Mark Davis (Saves leader.)	.05
216	Vince Coleman (SB leader.)	.05
217	Jeff Blauser	.05
218	Jeff Treadway	.05
219	Tom Glavine	.20
220	Joe Boever	.05
221	Oddibe McDowell	.05
222	Dale Murphy	.20
223	Derek Lilliquist	.05
224	Tommy Gregg	.05
225	Braves Logo/Foil	.05
226	Braves Helmet/Foil	.05
227	Lonnie Smith	.05
228	John Smoltz	.05
229	Andres Thomas	.05
230	Jerome Walton	.05
231	Ryne Sandberg	.50
232	Mitch Williams	.05
233	Rick Sutcliffe	.05
234	Damon Berryhill	.05
235	Dwight Smith	.05
236	Shawon Dunston	.05
237	Greg Maddux	.50
238	Cubs Logo/Foil	.05
239	Cubs Helmet/Foil	.05
240	Andre Dawson	.25
241	Mark Grace	.05
242	Mike Bielecki	.05
243	Jose Rijo	.05
244	John Franco	.05
245	Paul O'Neill	.05
246	Eric Davis	.05
247	Tom Browning	.05
248	Chris Sabo	.05
249	Rob Dibble	.05
250	Todd Benzinger	.05
251	Reds Logo/Foil	.05
252	Reds Helmet/Foil	.05
253	Barry Larkin	.05
254	Rolando Roomes	.05
255	Danny Jackson	.05
256	Terry Puhl	.05
257	Dave Smith	.05
258	Glenn Davis	.05
259	Craig Biggio	.05
260	Ken Caminiti	.05
261	Kevin Bass	.05
262	Mike Scott	.05
263	Gerald Young	.05
264	Astros Logo/Foil	.05
265	Astros Helmet/Foil	.05
266	Rafael Ramirez	.05
267	Jim Deshaies	.05
268	Bill Doran	.05
269	Fernando Valenzuela	.05
270	Alfredo Griffin	.05
271	Kirk Gibson	.05
272	Mike Marshall	.05
273	Eddie Murray	.40
274	Jay Howell	.05
275	Orel Hershiser	.05
276	Mike Scioscia	.05
277	Dodgers Logo/Foil	.05
278	Dodgers Helmet/Foil	.05
279	Willie Randolph	.05
280	Kal Daniels	.05
281	Tim Belcher	.05
282	Pascual Perez	.05
283	Tim Raines	.05
284	Andres Galarraga	.05
285	Spike Owen	.05
286	Tim Wallach	.05
287	Mark Langston	.05
288	Dennis Martinez	.05
289	Nelson Santovenia	.05
290	Expos Logo/Foil	.05
291	Expos Helmet/Foil	.05
292	Tom Foley	.05
293	Dave Martinez	.05
294	Tim Burke	.05
295	Ron Darling	.05
296	Kevin Elster	.05
297	Dwight Gooden	.05
298	Gregg Jefferies	.05
299	Sid Fernandez	.05
300	Dave Magadan	.05
301	David Cone	.05
302	Darryl Strawberry	.05
303	Mets Logo/Foil	.05
304	Mets Helmet/Foil	.05
305	Kevin McReynolds	.05
306	Howard Johnson	.05
307	Randy Myers	.05
308	Roger McDowell	.05
309	Tom Herr	.05
310	John Kruk	.05
311	Randy Ready	.05
312	Jeff Parrett	.05
313	Lenny Dykstra	.05
314	Ken Howell	.05
315	Ricky Jordan	.05
316	Phillies Logo/Foil	.05
317	Phillies Helmet/Foil	.05
318	Dickie Thon	.05
319	Von Hayes	.05
320	Dennis Cook	.05
321	Jay Bell	.05
322	Barry Bonds	1.00
323	John Smiley	.05
324	Andy Van Slyke	.05
325	Bobby Bonilla	.05
326	Bill Landrum	.05
327	Randy Kramer	.05
328	Jose Lind	.05
329	Pirates Logo/Foil	.05
330	Pirates Helmet/Foil	.05
331	Gary Redus	.05
332	Doug Drabek	.05
333	Mike LaValliere	.05
334	Jose DeLeon	.05
335	Pedro Guerrero	.05
336	Vince Coleman	.05
337	Terry Pendleton	.05
338	Ozzie Smith	.50
339	Willie McGee	.05
340	Todd Worrell	.05
341	Jose Oquendo	.05
342	Cardinals Logo/Foil	.05
343	Cardinals Helmet/Foil	.05
344	Tom Brunansky	.05
345	Milt Thompson	.05
346	Joe Magrane	.05
347	Ed Whitson	.05
348	Jack Clark	.05
349	Roberto Alomar	.10
350	Chris James	.05
351	Tony Gwynn	.50
352	Mark Davis	.05
353	Greg W. Harris	.05
354	Garry Templeton	.05
355	Padres Logo/Foil	.05
356	Padres Helmet/Foil	.05
357	Bruce Hurst	.05
358	Benito Santiago	.05
359	Bip Roberts	.05
360	Dave Dravecky	.05
361	Kevin Mitchell	.05
362	Craig Lefferts	.05
363	Will Clark	.05
364	Steve Bedrosian	.05
365	Brett Butler	.05
366	Matt Williams	.05
367	Scott Garrelts	.05
368	Giants Logo/Foil	.05
369	Giants Helmet/Foil	.05
370	Rick Reuschel	.05
371	Robby Thompson	.05
372	Jose Uribe	.05
373	Ben McDonald (Headliner)	.05
374	Carlos Martinez (Headliner)	.05
375	Steve Olin (Headliner)	.05
376	Bill Spiers (Headliner)	.05
377	Junior Felix (Headliner)	.05
378	Joe Oliver (Headliner)	.05
379	Eric Anthony (Headliner)	.05
380	Ramon Martinez (Headliner)	.05
381	Todd Zeile (Headliner)	.05
382	Andy Benes (Headliner)	.05
383	Vince Coleman (Highlight)	.05
384	Bo Jackson (Highlight)	.05
385	Howard Johnson (Highlight)	.05
386	Dave Dravecky (Highlight)	.05
387	Nolan Ryan (Highlight)	.50
388	Cal Ripken, Jr. (Highlight)	.50

1991 Panini Stickers

JIM PRESLEY, 3B

For 1991 the Panini stickers were considerably downsized in both the number of pieces in the set (271) and in the size of each sticker (1-1/2" x 2-9/16"). Player stickers have a color action photo at center with a few stats at bottom. There are foil pennant and team logo stickers for each team as well as 1990 season highlights kicking off the set. Backs are printed in black-and-white and have MLB and Players Association logos, along with Panini advertising. A colorful album was available to house the stickers, featuring on its cover Ken Griffey, Jr., Ryne Sandberg and Rickey Henderson.

		NM/M
Complete Set (271):		12.50
Common Player:		.05
Album:		1.00
Wax Pack (5+1):		.25
Wax Box (100):		9.00
1	Mark Langston, Mike Witt (No-hitter.)	.05
2	Randy Johnson (No-hitter.)	.20
3	Nolan Ryan (No-hitter.)	.50
4	Dave Stewart (No-hitter.)	.05
5	Fernando Valenzuela (No-hitter.)	.05
6	Andy Hawkins (No-hitter.)	.05
7	Melido Perez (No-hitter.)	.05
8	Terry Mullholland (no-hitter)	.05
9	Dave Steib (No-hitter.)	.05
10	Craig Biggio	.05
11	Jim Deshaies	.05
12	Dave Smith	.05
13	Eric Yelding	.05
14	Astros pennant	.05
15	Astros logo	.05
16	Mike Scott	.05
17	Ken Caminiti	.05
18	Danny Darwin	.05
19	Glenn Davis	.05
20	Braves pennant	.05
21	Braves logo	.05
22	Lonnie Smith	.05
23	Charlie Leibrandt	.05
24	Jim Presley	.05
25	Greg Olson	.05
26	John Smoltz	.05
27	Ron Gant	.05
28	Jeff Treadway	.05
29	Dave Justice	.05
30	Jose Oquendo	.05
31	Joe Magrane	.05
32	Cardinals pennant	.05
33	Cardinals logo	.05
34	Todd Zeile	.05
35	Vince Coleman	.05
36	Bob Tewksbury	.05
37	Pedro Guerrero	.05
38	Lee Smith	.05
39	Ozzie Smith	.50
40	Ryne Sandberg	.50
41	Andre Dawson	.25
42	Cubs pennant	.05
43	Greg Maddux	.50
44	Jerome Walton	.05
45	Cubs logo	.05
46	Mike Harkey	.05

No.	Player	NM/M
47	Shawon Dunston	.05
48	Mark Grace	.05
49	Joe Girardi	.05
50	Ramon Martinez	.05
51	Lenny Harris	.05
52	Mike Morgan	.05
53	Eddie Murray	.40
54	Dodgers pennant	.05
55	Dodgers logo	.05
56	Hubie Brooks	.05
57	Mike Scioscia	.05
58	Kal Daniels	.05
59	Fernando Valenzuela	.05
60	Expos pennant	.05
61	Expos logo	.05
62	Spike Owen	.05
63	Tim Raines	.05
64	Tim Wallach	.05
65	Larry Walker	.05
66	Dave Martinez	.05
67	Mark Gardner	.05
68	Dennis Martinez	.05
69	Delino DeShields	.05
70	Jeff Brantley	.05
71	Kevin Mitchell	.05
72	Giants pennant	.05
73	Giants logo	.05
74	Don Robinson	.05
75	Brett Butler	.05
76	Matt Williams	.05
77	Robby Thompson	.05
78	John Burkett	.05
79	Will Clark	.05
80	David Cone	.05
81	Dave Magadan	.05
82	Mets pennant	.05
83	Gregg Jefferies	.05
84	Frank Viola	.05
85	Mets logo	.05
86	Howard Johnson	.05
87	John Franco	.05
88	Darryl Strawberry	.05
89	Dwight Gooden	.05
90	Joe Carter	.05
91	Ed Whitson	.05
92	Andy Benes	.05
93	Benito Santiago	.05
94	Padres pennant	.05
95	Padres logo	.05
96	Roberto Alomar	.10
97	Bip Roberts	.05
98	Jack Clark	.05
99	Tony Gwynn	.50
100	Phillies pennant	.05
101	Phillies logo	.05
102	Charlie Hayes	.05
103	Lenny Dykstra	.05
104	Dale Murphy	.20
105	Von Hayes	.05
106	Dickie Thon	.05
107	John Kruk	.05
108	Ken Howell	.05
109	Darren Daulton	.05
110	Jay Bell	.05
111	Bobby Bonilla	.05
112	Pirates pennant	.05
113	Pirates logo	.05
114	Barry Bonds	1.00
115	Neal Heaton	.05
116	Doug Drabek	.05
117	Jose Lind	.05
118	Andy Van Slyke	.05
119	Sid Bream	.05
120	Paul O'Neill	.05
121	Randy Myers	.05
122	Reds pennant	.05
123	Mariano Duncan	.05
124	Eric Davis	.05
125	Red logo	.05
126	Jack Armstrong	.05
127	Chris Sabo	.05
128	Rob Dibble	.05
129	Barry Larkin	.05
130	National League logo	.05
131	American League logo	.05
132	Dave Winfield	.40
133	Lance Parrish	.05
134	Chili Davis	.05
135	Chuck Finley	.05
136	Angels pennant	.05
137	Angels logo	.05
138	Johnny Ray	.05
139	Dante Bichette	.05
140	Jim Abbott	.05
141	Wally Joyner	.05
142	A's pennant	.05
143	A's logo	.05
144	Dave Stewart	.05
145	Mark McGwire	.75
146	Rickey Henderson	.40
147	Walt Weiss	.05
148	Dennis Eckersley	.35
149	Jose Canseco	.30
150	Dave Henderson	.05
151	Bob Welch	.05
152	Tony Fernandez	.05
153	David Wells	.05
154	Blue Jays pennant	.05
155	Blue Jays logo	.05
156	Pat Borders	.05
157	Fred McGriff	.05
158	George Bell	.05
159	John Olerud	.05
160	Dave Steib	.05
161	Kelly Gruber	.05
162	Billy Spiers	.05
163	Dan Plesac	.05
164	Brewers pennant	.05
165	Mark Knudson	.05
166	Robin Yount	.40
167	Brewers logo	.05
168	Paul Molitor	.40
169	B.J. Surhoff	.05
170	Gary Sheffield	.30
171	Dave Parker	.05
172	Sandy Alomar	.05
173	Doug Jones	.05
174	Tom Candiotti	.05
175	Mitch Webster	.05
176	Indians pennant	.05
177	Indians logo	.05
178	Brook Jacoby	.05
179	Candy Maldonado	.05
180	Carlos Baerga	.05
181	Chris James	.05
182	Mariners pennant	.05
183	Mariners logo	.05
184	Mike Schooler	.05
185	Alvin Davis	.05
186	Erik Hanson	.05
187	Edgar Martinez	.05
188	Randy Johnson	.40
189	Ken Griffey Jr.	.60
190	Jay Buhner	.05
191	Harold Reynolds	.05
192	Cal Ripken Jr.	1.00
193	Gregg Olson	.05
194	Orioles pennant	.05
195	Orioles logo	.05
196	Mike Devereaux	.05
197	Ben McDonald	.05
198	Craig Worthington	.05
199	Dave Johnson	.05
200	Joe Orsulak	.05
201	Randy Milligan	.05
202	Ruben Sierra	.05
203	Bobby Witt	.05
204	Rangers pennant	.05
205	Nolan Ryan	1.00
206	Jeff Huson	.05
207	Rangers logo	.05
208	Kevin Brown	.05
209	Steve Buechele	.05
210	Julio Franco	.05
211	Rafael Palmeiro	.05
212	Ellis Burks	.05
213	Dwight Evans	.05
214	Wade Boggs	.50
215	Roger Clemens	.55
216	Red Sox pennant	.05
217	Red Sox logo	.05
218	Jeff Reardon	.05
219	Tony Pena	.05
220	Jody Reed	.05
221	Carlos Quintana	.05
222	Royals pennant	.05
223	Royals logo	.05
224	George Brett	.55
225	Bret Saberhagen	.05
226	Bo Jackson	.10
227	Kevin Seitzer	.05
228	Mark Gubicza	.05
229	Jim Eisenreich	.05
230	Gerald Perry	.05
231	Tom Gordon	.05
232	Cecil Fielder	.05
233	Lou Whitaker	.05
234	Tigers pennant	.05
235	Tigers logo	.05
236	Mike Henneman	.05
237	Mike Heath	.05
238	Alan Trammell	.05
239	Lloyd Moseby	.05
240	Dan Petry	.05
241	Dave Bergman	.05
242	Brian Harper	.05
243	Rick Aguilera	.05
244	Twins pennant	.05
245	Greg Gagne	.05
246	Gene Larkin	.05
247	Twins logo	.05
248	Kirby Puckett	.50
249	Kevin Tapani	.05
250	Gary Gaetti	.05
251	Kent Hrbek	.05
252	Bobby Thigpen	.05
253	Lance Johnson	.05
254	Greg Hibbard	.05
255	Carlton Fisk	.40
256	White Sox pennant	.05
257	White Sox logo	.05
258	Ivan Calderon	.05
259	Barry Jones	.05
260	Robin Ventura	.05
261	Ozzie Guillen	.05
262	Yankees pennant	.05
263	Yankees logo	.05
264	Kevin Maas	.05
265	Bob Geren	.05
266	Dave Righetti	.05
267	Don Mattingly	.55
268	Roberto Kelly	.05
269	Alvaro Espinoza	.05
270	Oscar Azocar	.05
271	Steve Sax	.05

1991 Panini Stickers - Canadian

CHET LEMON
DETROIT TIGERS

While the U.S. sticker set from Panini was downsized both in physical format and number of stickers in the set, a special issue for the Canadian market was produced in the 2-1/8" x 3" size to a total of 360 pieces. The relatively simple design has a color game-action photo with a wide white border. The black player name and team at bottom are highlighted by a red (American League) or blue (National League) splash of color at lower-left. Black-and-white backs have a sticker number and a few words about the collection in English and French. Besides player stickers there are foil specialty stickers for the teams and a subset of All-Star stickers.

	NM/M
Complete Set (360):	20.00
Common Player:	.05
Album:	3.00

No.	Player	NM/M
1	Major League Baseball logo/Foil	.05
2	MLB Players Association Logo/Foil	.05
3	Panini logo/Foil	.05
4	Houston Astros Pennant/Foil	.05
5	Houston Astros Logo/Foil	.05
6	Craig Biggio	.05
7	Glenn Davis	.05
8	Casey Candaele	.05
9	Ken Caminiti	.05
10	Rafael Ramirez	.05
11	Glenn Wilson	.05
12	Eric Yelding	.05
13	Franklin Stubbs	.05
14	Mike Scott	.05
15	Danny Darwin	.05
16	Atlanta Braves Pennant/Foil	.05
17	Atlanta Braves Logo/Foil	.05
18	Greg Olson	.05
19	Tommy Gregg	.05
20	Jeff Treadway	.05
21	Jim Presley	.05
22	Jeff Blauser	.05
23	Ron Gant	.05
24	Lonnie Smith	.05
25	Dave Justice	.05
26	John Smoltz	.05
27	Charlie Leibrandt	.05
28	St. Louis Cardinals pennant/Foil	.05
29	St. Louis Cardinals Logo/Foil	.05
30	Tom Pagnozzi	.05
31	Pedro Guerrero	.05
32	Jose Oquendo	.05
33	Todd Zeile	.05
34	Ozzie Smith	.50
35	Vince Coleman	.05
36	Milt Thompson	.05
37	Rex Hudler	.05
38	Joe Magrane	.05
39	Lee Smith	.05
40	Chicago Cubs Pennant/Foil	.05
41	Chicago Cubs Logo/Foil	.05
42	Joe Girardi	.05
43	Mark Grace	.05
44	Ryne Sandberg	.50
45	Luis Salazar	.05
46	Shawon Dunston	.05
47	Dwight Smith	.05
48	Jerome Walton	.05
49	Andre Dawson	.25
50	Greg Maddux	.50
51	Mike Harkey	.05
52	Los Angeles Dodgers Pennant/Foil	.05
53	Los Angeles Dodgers Logo/Foil	.05
54	Mike Scioscia	.05
55	Eddie Murray	.40
56	Juan Samuel	.05
57	Lenny Harris	.05
58	Alfredo Griffin	.05
59	Hubie Brooks	.05
60	Kal Daniels	.05
61	Stan Javier	.05
62	Ramon Martinez	.05
63	Mike Morgan	.05
64	San Francisco Giants Pennant/Foil	.05
65	San Francisco Giants Logo/Foil	.05
66	Terry Kennedy	.05
67	Will Clark	.05
68	Robby Thompson	.05
69	Matt Williams	.05
70	Jose Uribe	.05
71	Kevin Mitchell	.05
72	Brett Butler	.05
73	Don Robinson	.05
74	John Burkett	.05
75	Jeff Brantley	.05
76	New York Mets Pennant/Foil	.05
77	New York Mets Logo/Foil	.05
78	Mackey Sasser	.05
79	Dave Magadan	.05
80	Gregg Jefferies	.05
81	Howard Johnson	.05
82	Kevin Elster	.05
83	Kevin McReynolds	.05
84	Daryl Boston	.05
85	Darryl Strawberry	.05
86	Dwight Gooden	.05
87	Frank Viola	.05
88	San Diego Padres Pennant/Foil	.05
89	San Diego Padres Logo/Foil	.05
90	Benito Santiago	.05
91	Jack Clark	.05
92	Roberto Alomar	.10
93	Mike Pagliarulo	.05
94	Garry Templeton	.05
95	Joe Carter	.05
96	Bip Roberts	.05
97	Tony Gwynn	.50
98	Ed Whitson	.05
99	Andy Benes	.05
100	Philadelphia Phillies Pennant/Foil	.05
101	Philadelphia Phillies Logo/Foil	.05
102	Darren Daulton	.05
103	Ricky Jordan	.05
104	Randy Ready	.05
105	Charlie Hayes	.05
106	Dickie Thon	.05
107	Von Hayes	.05
108	Lenny Dykstra	.05
109	Dale Murphy	.20
110	Ken Howell	.05
111	Roger McDowell	.05
112	Pittsburgh Pirates pennant/Foil	.05
113	Pittsburgh Pirates Logo/Foil	.05
114	Mike LaValliere	.05
115	Sid Bream	.05
116	Jose Lind	.05
117	Jeff King	.05
118	Jay Bell	.05
119	Barry Bonds	1.00
120	Bobby Bonilla	.05
121	Andy Van Slyke	.05
121	Doug Drabek	.05
123	Neal Heaton	.05
124	Cincinnati Reds pennant/Foil	.05
125	Cincinnati Reds Logo/Foil	.05
126	Joe Oliver	.05
127	Todd Benzinger	.05
128	Mariano Duncan	.05
129	Chris Sabo	.05
130	Barry Larkin	.05
131	Eric Davis	.05
132	Billy Hatcher	.05
133	Paul O'Neill	.05
134	Jose Rijo	.05
135	Randy Myers	.05
136	Montreal Expos Pennant/Foil	.05
137	Montreal Expos Logo/Foil	.05
138	Mike Fitzgerald	.05
139	Andres Galarraga	.05
140	Delino DeShields	.05
141	Tim Wallach	.05
142	Spike Owen	.05
143	Tim Raines	.05
144	Dave Martinez	.05
145	Larry Walker	.05
146	Expos Batting Helmet/Foil	.05
147	Dennis Boyd	.05
148	Tim Burke	.05
149	Bill Sampen	.05
150	Dennis Martinez	.05
151	Marquis Grissom	.05
152	Otis Nixon	.05
153	Jerry Goff	.05
154	Steve Frey	.05
155	National League Logo/Foil	.05
156	American League Logo/Foil	.05
157	Benito Santiago/AS	.05
158	Will Clark/AS	.05
159	Ryne Sandberg/AS	.25
160	Chris Sabo/AS	.05
161	Ozzie Smith/AS	.25
162	Kevin Mitchell/AS	.05
163	Lenny Dykstra/AS	.05
164	Darryl Strawberry/AS	.05
165	Jack Armstrong/AS	.05
166	Sandy Alomar, Jr./AS	.05
167	Mark Griffey Jr./AS	.45
168	Steve Sax/AS	.05
169	Wade Boggs/AS	.25
170	Cal Ripken, Jr./AS	.50
171	Rickey Henderson/AS	.20
172	Ken Griffey Jr./AS	.40
173	Jose Canseco/AS	.15
174	Bob Welch/AS	.05
175	All-Star Game - Wrigley Field	.05
176	World's Championship Trophy/Foil	.05
177	California Angels Pennant/Foil	.05
178	California Angels Logo/Foil	.05
179	Lance Parrish	.05
180	Wally Joyner	.05
181	Johnny Ray	.05
182	Jack Howell	.05
183	Dick Schofield	.05
184	Dave Winfield	.40
185	Devon White	.05
186	Dante Bichette	.05
187	Chuck Finley	.05
188	Jim Abbott	.05
189	Oakland A's Pennant/Foil	.05
190	Oakland A's Logo/Foil	.05
191	Terry Steinbach	.05
192	Mark McGwire	.85
193	Willie Randolph	.05
194	Carney Lansford	.05
195	Walt Weiss	.05
196	Rickey Henderson	.40
197	Dave Henderson	.05
198	Jose Canseco	.30
199	Dave Stewart	.05
200	Dennis Eckersley	.35
201	Milwaukee Brewers Pennant/Foil	.05
202	Milwaukee Brewers Logo/Foil	.05
203	B.J. Surhoff	.05
204	Greg Brock	.05
205	Paul Molitor	.40
206	Gary Sheffield	.20
207	Billy Spiers	.05
208	Robin Yount	.40
209	Rob Deer	.05
210	Dave Parker	.05
211	Mark Knudson	.05
212	Dan Plesac	.05
213	Cleveland Indians Pennant/Foil	.05
214	Cleveland Indians Logo/Foil	.05
215	Sandy Alomar, Jr.	.05
216	Brook Jacoby	.05
217	Jerry Browne	.05
218	Carlos Baerga	.05
219	Felix Fermin	.05
220	Candy Maldonado	.05
221	Cory Snyder	.05
222	Alex Cole, Jr.	.05
223	Tom Candiotti	.05
224	Doug Jones	.05
225	Seattle Mariners Pennant/Foil	.05
226	Seattle Mariners Logo/Foil	.05
227	Dave Valle	.05
228	Pete O'Brien	.05
229	Harold Reynolds	.05
230	Edgar Martinez	.05
231	Omar Vizquel	.05
232	Henry Cotto	.05
233	Ken Griffey Jr.	.75
234	Jay Buhner	.05
235	Eric Hanson (Erik)	.05
236	Mike Schooler	.05
237	Baltimore Orioles Pennant/Foil	.05
238	Baltimore Orioles Logo/Foil	.05
239	Mickey Tettleton	.05
240	Randy Milligan	.05
241	Billy Ripken	.05
242	Craig Worthington	.05
243	Cal Ripken, Jr.	1.00
244	Steve Finley	.05
245	Mike Devereaux	.05
246	Joe Orsulak	.05
247	Ben McDonald	.05
248	Gregg Olson	.05
249	Texas Rangers Pennant/Foil	.05
250	Texas Rangers Logo/Foil	.05
251	Geno Petralli	.05
252	Rafael Palmeiro	.40
253	Julio Franco	.05
254	Steve Buechele	.05
255	Jeff Huson	.05
256	Gary Pettis	.05
257	Ruben Sierra	.05
258	Pete Incaviglia	.05
259	Nolan Ryan	1.00
260	Bobby Witt	.05
261	Boston Red Sox Pennant/Foil	.05
262	Boston Red Sox Logo/Foil	.05
263	Tony Pena	.05
264	Carlos Quintana	.05
265	Jody Reed	.05
266	Wade Boggs	.50
267	Luis Rivera	.05
268	Mike Greenwell	.05
269	Ellis Burks	.05
270	Tom Brunansky	.05
271	Roger Clemens	.60
272	Jeff Reardon	.05
273	Kansas City Royals Pennant/Foil	.05
274	Kansas City Royals Logo/Foil	.05
275	Mike Macfarlane	.05
276	George Brett	.60
277	Bill Pecota	.05
278	Kevin Seitzer	.05
279	Kurt Stillwell	.05
280	Jim Eisenreich	.05
281	Bo Jackson	.10
282	Danny Tartabull	.05
283	Bret Saberhagen	.05
284	Tom Gordon	.05
285	Detroit Tigers Pennant/Foil	.05
286	Detroit Tigers Logo/Foil	.05
287	Mike Heath	.05
288	Cecil Fielder	.05
289	Lou Whitaker	.05
290	Tony Phillips	.05
291	Alan Trammell	.05
292	Chet Lemon	.05
293	Lloyd Moseby	.05
294	Gary Ward	.05
295	Dan Petry	.05
296	Jack Morris	.05
297	Minnesota Twins Pennant/Foil	.05
298	Minnesota Twins Logo/Foil	.05
299	Brian Harper	.05
300	Kent Hrbek	.05
301	Al Newman	.05
302	Gary Gaetti	.05
303	Greg Gagne	.05
304	Dan Gladden	.05
305	Kirby Puckett	.50
306	Gene Larkin	.05
307	Kevin Tapani	.05
308	Rick Aguilera	.05
309	Chicago White Sox Pennant/Foil	.05
310	Chicago White Sox Logo/Foil	.05
311	Carlton Fisk	.40
312	Carlos Martinez	.05
313	Scott Fletcher	.05
314	Robin Ventura	.05
315	Ozzie Guillen	.05
316	Sammy Sosa	.65
317	Lance Johnson	.05
318	Ivan Calderon	.05
319	Greg Hibbard	.05
320	Bobby Thigpen	.05
321	New York Yankees Pennant/Foil	.05
322	New York Yankees Logo/Foil	.05
323	Bob Geren	.05
324	Don Mattingly	.60
325	Steve Sax	.05
326	Jim Leyritz	.05
327	Alvaro Espinoza	.05
328	Roberto Kelly	.05
329	Oscar Azocar	.05
330	Jesse Barfield	.05
331	Chuck Cary	.05
332	Dave Righetti	.05
333	Toronto Blue Jays Pennant/Foil	.05
334	Toronto Blue Jays Logo/Foil	.05
335	Pat Borders	.05
336	Fred McGriff	.05
337	Manny Lee	.05
338	Kelly Gruber	.05
339	Tony Fernandez	.05
340	George Bell	.05
341	Mookie Wilson	.05
342	Junior Felix	.05
343	Blue Jays Batting Helmet/Foil	.05
344	Dave Steib	.05
345	Tom Henke	.05
346	Greg Myers	.05
347	Glenallen Hill	.05
348	John Olerud	.05
349	Todd Stottlemyre	.05
350	David Wells	.05
351	Jimmy Key	.05
352	Mark Langston (No-hitter.)	.05
353	Randy Johnson (No-hitter.)	.20
354	Nolan Ryan (No-hitter.)	.50
355	Dave Stewart (No-hitter.)	.05
356	Fernando Valenzuela (No-hitter.)	.05
357	Andy Hawkins (No-hitter.)	.05

ABBREVIATIONS

AS - All-Star

358	Melido Perez (No-hitter.)	.05
359	Terry Mulholland (No-hitter.)	.05
360	Dave Stieb (No-hitter.)	.05

1991 Panini Top 15 Stickers (Canadian)

WILLIE McGEE
ST. LOUIS CARDINALS
BATTING AVERAGE
MOYENNE AU BÂTON
.335

The four leaders from each league in major statistical categories from the 1990 season are featured in this set of stickers marketed in Canada. The 2-1/2" x 3-1/2" stickers feature a large color photo at top. In the white border at bottom is the player's name and team, the stat in which he excelled (printed in both English and French), the number achieved, and, at lower-left, his rank among the top four. A series of team logo metallic stickers honors the teams which led in various stats. Backs are printed in black with appropriate logos and sticker number. A colorful album could be purchased to the house the sticker collection.

		NM/M
Complete Set (136):		10.00
Common Player:		.10
1	Willie McGee	.10
2	Eddie Murray	.30
3	Dave Magadan	.10
4	Lenny Dykstra	.10
5	George Brett	.45
6	Rickey Henderson	.30
7	Rafael Palmeiro	.30
8	Alan Trammell	.10
9	Ryne Sandberg	.40
10	Darryl Strawberry	.10
11	Kevin Mitchell	.10
12	Barry Bonds	.75
13	Cecil Fielder	.10
14	Mark McGwire	.65
15	Jose Canseco	.15
16	Fred McGriff	.10
17	Matt Williams	.10
18	Bobby Bonilla	.10
19	Joe Carter	.10
20	Barry Bonds	.75
21	Cecil Fielder	.10
22	Kelly Gruber	.10
23	Mark McGwire	.65
24	Jose Canseco	.15
25	Brett Butler	.10
26	Lenny Dykstra	.10
27	Ryne Sandberg	.40
28	Barry Larkin	.10
29	Rafael Palmeiro	.30
30	Wade Boggs	.40
31	Roberto Kelly	.10
32	Mike Greenwell	.10
33	Barry Bonds	.75
34	Ryne Sandberg	.40
35	Kevin Mitchell	.10
36	Ron Gant	.10
37	Cecil Fielder	.10
38	Rickey Henderson	.30
39	Jose Canseco	.15
40	Fred McGriff	.10
41	Vince Coleman	.10
42	Eric Yelding	.10
43	Barry Bonds	.75
44	Brett Butler	.10
45	Rickey Henderson	.30
46	Steve Sax	.10
47	Roberto Kelly	.10
48	Alex Cole, Jr.	.10
49	Ryne Sandberg	.40
50	Bobby Bonilla	.10
51	Brett Butler	.10
52	Ron Gant	.10
53	Rickey Henderson	.30
54	Cecil Fielder	.10
55	Harold Reynolds	.10
56	Robin Yount	.10
57	Doug Drabek	.10
58	Ramon Martinez	.10
59	Frank Viola	.10
60	Dwight Gooden	.10
61	Bob Welch	.10

62	Dave Stewart	.10
63	Roger Clemens	.45
64	Dave Stieb	.10
65	Danny Darwin	.10
66	Zane Smith	.10
67	Ed Whitson	.10
68	Frank Viola	.10
69	Roger Clemens	.45
70	Chuck Finley	.10
71	Dave Stewart	.10
72	Kevin Appier	.10
73	David Cone	.10
74	Dwight Gooden	.10
75	Ramon Martinez	.10
76	Frank Viola	.10
77	Nolan Ryan	.75
78	Bobby Witt	.10
79	Erik Hanson	.10
80	Roger Clemens	.45
81	John Franco	.10
82	Randy Myers	.10
83	Lee Smith	.10
84	Craig Lefferts	.10
85	Bobby Thigpen	.10
86	Dennis Eckersley	.25
87	Doug Jones	.10
88	Gregg Olson	.10
89	Mike Morgan	.10
90	Bruce Hurst	.10
91	Mark Gardner	.10
92	Doug Drabek	.10
93	Dave Stewart	.10
94	Roger Clemens	.45
95	Kevin Appier	.10
96	Melido Perez	.10
97	National Logo	.10
98	Greg Maddux	.40
99	Benito Santiago	.10
100	Andres Galarraga	.10
101	Ryne Sandberg	.40
102	Tim Wallach	.10
103	Ozzie Smith	.40
104	Tony Gwynn	.40
105	Barry Bonds	.75
106	Andy Van Slyke	.10
107	American League Logo	.10
108	Mike Boddicker	.10
109	Sandy Alomar Jr.	.10
110	Mark McGwire	.65
111	Harold Reynolds	.10
112	Kelly Gruber	.10
113	Ozzie Guillen	.10
114	Ellis Burks	.10
115	Gary Pettis	.10
116	Ken Griffey Jr.	.50
117	Cincinnati Reds Logo	.10
118	New York Mets Logo	.10
119	New York Mets Script	.10
120	Chicago Cubs Logo	.10
121	Montreal Expos Logo	.10
122	Boston Red Sox Logo	.10
123	Detroit Tigers Logo	.10
124	Toronto Blue Jays Logo	.10
125	Boston Red Sox script	.10
126	Milwaukee Brewers Logo	.10
127	Philadelphia Phillies Logo	.10
128	Cincinnati Reds Logo	.10
129	Montreal Expos Logo	.10
130	New York Mets Logo	.10
131	Cincinnati Reds Logo	.10
132	California Angels Logo	.10
133	Toronto Blue Jays Logo	.10
134	Oakland A's logo	.10
135	Oakland A's script	.10
136	Chicago White Sox Logo	.10

1992 Panini Stickers

TIM WALLACH
THIRD BASE
204

A 288-piece set comprised Panini's annual baseball issue in 1992. Stickers were sold in packs of six for 39 cents. A colorful album for housing the stickers was also available, picturing members of the World Champion Twins. Individual stickers measured 2-1/8" x 3". Player stickers feature a color action photo at center, with a shark's tooth border at right. A colored diamond is overprinted on the first letters of the name,

while a rule of the same color is printed around the photo. On American League stickers the color highlights are in magenta; teal for N.L. Stickers are numbered by position within team, and each team set includes a foil-glitter team logo stickers. Similar special stickers honor the 1991 All-Star Game starters and a few other special themes. Backs of the foils are printed in blue and promote sticker collecting. Backs of the player stickers are special themes. Backs of the foils are printed in blue and in full color and include trivia questions, "Play Ball" game situations and score cards for the game.

		NM/M
Complete Set (288):		10.00
Common Player:		.05
Album:		1.00
Wax Pack (5+1):		.25
Wax Box (50):		5.00
1	Panini logo/Foil	.05
2	Major League Baseball Logo/Foil	.05
3	Players Association logo/Foil	.05
4	Lance Parrish	.05
5	Wally Joyner	.05
6	Luis Sojo	.05
7	Gary Gaetti	.05
8	Dick Schofield	.05
9	Junior Felix	.05
10	Luis Polonia	.05
11	Mark Langston	.05
12	Jim Abbott	.05
13	California Angels Logo/Foil	.05
14	Terry Steinbach	.05
15	Mark Whiten	.75
16	Mike Gallego	.05
17	Carney Lansford	.05
18	Walt Weiss	.05
19	Jose Canseco	.30
20	Dave Henderson	.05
21	Rickey Henderson	.40
22	Dennis Eckersley	.35
23	Oakland A's Logo/Foil	.05
24	Pat Borders	.05
25	John Olerud	.05
26	Roberto Alomar	.20
27	Kelly Gruber	.05
28	Manuel Lee	.05
29	Joe Carter	.05
30	Devon White	.05
31	Candy Maldonado	.05
32	Jimmy Key	.05
33	Toronto Blue Jays Logo/Foil	.05
34	B.J. Surhoff	.05
35	Franklin Stubbs	.05
36	Willie Randolph	.05
37	Jim Gantner	.05
38	Bill Spiers	.05
39	Dante Bichette	.05
40	Robin Yount	.40
41	Greg Vaughn	.05
42	Jaime Navarro	.05
43	Milwaukee Brewers Logo/Foil	.05
44	Sandy Alomar Jr.	.05
45	Mike Aldrete	.05
46	Mark Lewis	.05
47	Carlos Baerga	.05
48	Felix Fermin	.05
49	Mark Whiten	.05
50	Alex Cole	.05
51	Albert Belle	.10
52	Greg Swindell	.05
53	Cleveland Indians Logo/Foil	.05
54	Dave Valle	.05
55	Pete O'Brien	.05
56	Harold Reynolds	.05
57	Edgar Martinez	.05
58	Omar Vizquel	.05
59	Jay Buhner	.05
60	Ken Griffey Jr.	.60
61	Greg Briley	.05
62	Randy Johnson	.40
63	Seattle Mariners Logo/Foil	.05
64	Chris Hoiles	.05
65	Randy Milligan	.05
66	Billy Ripken	.05
67	Leo Gomez	.05
68	Cal Ripken Jr.	1.00
69	Dwight Evans	.05
70	Mike Devereaux	.05
71	Joe Orsulak	.05
72	Gregg Olson	.05
73	Baltimore Orioles Logo/Foil	.05
74	Ivan Rodriguez	.40
75	Rafael Palmeiro	.40
76	Julio Franco	.05
77	Dean Palmer	.05
78	Jeff Huson	.05
79	Ruben Sierra	.05
80	Gary Pettis	.05

81	Juan Gonzalez	.40
82	Nolan Ryan	1.00
83	Texas Rangers Logo/Foil	.05
84	Tony Pena	.05
85	Carlos Quintana	.05
86	Jody Reed	.05
87	Wade Boggs	.50
88	Luis Rivera	.05
89	Tom Brunansky	.05
90	Ellis Burks	.05
91	Mike Greenwell	.05
92	Roger Clemens	.55
93	Boston Red Sox Logo/Foil	.05
94	Todd Benzinger	.05
95	Terry Shumpert	.05
96	Bill Pecota	.05
97	Kurt Stillwell	.05
98	Danny Tartabull	.05
99	Brian McRae	.05
100	Kirk Gibson	.05
101	Bret Saberhagen	.05
102	George Brett	.55
103	Kansas City Royals Logo/Foil	.05
104	Mickey Tettleton	.05
105	Cecil Fielder	.05
106	Lou Whitaker	.05
107	Travis Fryman	.05
108	Alan Trammell	.05
109	Rob Deer	.05
110	Milt Cuyler	.05
111	Lloyd Moseby	.05
112	Bill Gullickson	.05
113	Detroit Tigers Logo/Foil	.05
114	Brian Harper	.05
115	Kent Hrbek	.05
116	Chuck Knoblauch	.05
117	Mike Pagliarulo	.05
118	Greg Gagne	.05
119	Shane Mack	.05
120	Kirby Puckett	.50
121	Dan Gladden	.05
122	Jack Morris	.05
123	Minnesota Twins Logo/Foil	.05
124	Carlton Fisk	.40
125	Frank Thomas	.40
126	Joey Cora	.05
127	Robin Ventura	.05
128	Ozzie Guillen	.05
129	Sammy Sosa	.60
130	Lance Johnson	.05
131	Tim Raines	.05
132	Bobby Thigpen	.05
133	Chicago White Sox Logo/Foil	.05
134	Matt Nokes	.05
135	Don Mattingly	.55
136	Steve Sax	.05
137	Pat Kelly	.05
138	Alvaro Espinoza	.05
139	Jesse Barfield	.05
140	Roberto Kelly	.05
141	Mel Hall	.05
142	Scott Sanderson	.05
143	New York Yankees Logo/Foil	.05
144	A.L. HR Leaders (Cecil Fielder, Jose Canseco)	.05
145	A.L. BA Leader (Julio Franco)	.05
146	A.L. ERA Leader (Roger Clemens)	.25
147	N.L. HR Leader (Howard Johnson)	.05
148	N.L. BA Leader (Terry Pendleton)	.05
149	N.L. ERA Leader (Dennis Martinez)	.05
150	Houston Astros Logo/Foil	.05
151	Craig Biggio	.05
152	Jeff Bagwell	.40
153	Casey Candaele	.05
154	Ken Caminiti	.05
155	Andujar Cedeno	.05
156	Mike Simms	.05
157	Steve Finley	.05
158	Luis Gonzalez	.05
159	Pete Harnisch	.05
160	Atlanta Braves Logo/Foil	.05
161	Greg Olson	.05
162	Sid Bream	.05
163	Mark Lemke	.05
164	Terry Pendleton	.05
165	Rafael Belliard	.05
166	Dave Justice	.05
167	Ron Gant	.05
168	Lonnie Smith	.05
169	Steve Avery	.05
170	St. Louis Cardinals Logo/Foil	.05
171	Tom Pagnozzi	.05
172	Pedro Guerrero	.05
173	Jose Oquendo	.05
174	Todd Zeile	.05
175	Ozzie Smith	.50
176	Felix Jose	.05
177	Ray Lankford	.05
178	Jose DeLeon	.05
179	Lee Smith	.05
180	Chicago Cubs Logo/Foil	.05
181	Hector Villanueva	.05
182	Mark Grace	.10
183	Ryne Sandberg	.50

184	Luis Salazar	.05
185	Shawon Dunston	.05
186	Andre Dawson	.20
187	Jerome Walton	.05
188	George Bell	.05
189	Greg Maddux	.50
190	Los Angeles Dodgers Logo/Foil	.05
191	Mike Scioscia	.05
192	Eddie Murray	.40
193	Juan Samuel	.05
194	Lenny Harris	.05
195	Alfredo Griffin	.05
196	Darryl Strawberry	.05
197	Brett Butler	.05
198	Kal Daniels	.05
199	Orel Hershiser	.05
200	Montreal Expos Logo/Foil	.05
201	Gilberto Reyes	.05
202	Andres Galarraga	.05
203	Delino DeShields	.05
204	Tim Wallach	.05
205	Spike Owen	.05
206	Larry Walker	.05
207	Marquis Grissom	.05
208	Ivan Calderon	.05
209	Dennis Martinez	.05
210	San Francisco Giants Logo/Foil	.05
211	Steve Decker	.05
212	Will Clark	.10
213	Robby Thompson	.05
214	Matt Williams	.05
215	Jose Uribe	.05
216	Kevin Bass	.05
217	Willie McGee	.05
218	Kevin Mitchell	.05
219	Dave Righetti	.05
220	New York Mets Logo/Foil	.05
221	Rick Cerone	.05
222	Dave Magadan	.05
223	Gregg Jefferies	.05
224	Howard Johnson	.05
225	Kevin Elster	.05
226	Hubie Brooks	.05
227	Vince Coleman	.05
228	Kevin McReynolds	.05
229	Frank Viola	.05
230	San Diego Padres Logo/Foil	.05
231	Benito Santiago	.05
232	Fred McGriff	.05
233	Bip Roberts	.05
234	Jack Howell	.05
235	Tony Fernandez	.05
236	Tony Gwynn	.50
237	Darrin Jackson	.05
238	Bruce Hurst	.05
239	Craig Lefferts	.05
240	Philadelphia Phillies Logo/Foil	.05
241	Darren Daulton	.05
242	John Kruk	.05
243	Mickey Morandini	.05
244	Charlie Hayes	.05
245	Dickie Thon	.05
246	Dale Murphy	.25
247	Lenny Dykstra	.05
248	Von Hayes	.05
249	Terry Mulholland	.05
250	Pittsburgh Pirates Logo/Foil	.05
251	Mike LaValliere	.05
252	Orlando Merced	.05
253	Jose Lind	.05
254	Steve Buechele	.05
255	Jay Bell	.05
256	Bobby Bonilla	.05
257	Andy Van Slyke	.05
258	Barry Bonds	1.00
259	Doug Drabek	.05
260	Cincinnati Reds Logo/Foil	.05
261	Joe Oliver	.05
262	Hal Morris	.05
263	Bill Doran	.05
264	Chris Sabo	.05
265	Barry Larkin	.05
266	Paul O'Neill	.05
267	Eric Davis	.05
268	Glenn Braggs	.05
269	Jose Rijo	.05
270	Toronto Sky Dome/Foil	.05
271	Sandy Alomar Jr. (All-Star foil)	.05
272	Cecil Fielder (All-Star foil)	.05
273	Roberto Alomar (All-Star foil)	.10
274	Wade Boggs (All-Star foil)	.25
275	Cal Ripken Jr. (All-Star foil)	.50
276	Dave Henderson (All-Star foil)	.05
277	Ken Griffey Jr. (All-Star foil)	.40
278	Rickey Henderson (All-Star foil)	.20
279	Jack Morris (All-Star foil)	.05
280	Benito Santiago (All-Star foil)	.05
281	Will Clark (All-Star foil)	.05
282	Ryne Sandberg (All-Star foil)	.25

283	Chris Sabo (All-Star foil)	.05
284	Ozzie Smith (All-Star foil)	.25
285	Andre Dawson (All-Star foil)	.05
286	Tony Gwynn (All-Star foil)	.25
287	Ivan Calderon (All-Star foil)	.05
288	Tom Glavine (All-Star foil)	.05

1992 Panini Stickers - Canadian

ROBIN VENTURA
THIRD BASE/TROISIÈME BUT
127

The Canadian version of the 1992 Panini stickers mirrors the U.S. set's checklist (and price guide). In the same size (2-1/8" x 3") and format, the Canadian stickers differ from the U.S. version in the addition of French position on front and bilingual back.

		NM/M
Complete Set (288):		10.00
Common Player:		.05
Album:		1.00

1993 Panini Stickers

BASEBALL
ATLANTA BRAVES
DAVE JUSTICE

The 1993 issue is complete at 300 stickers. Besides 10 player stickers for each major league team, there are stickers for league leaders and major 1992-season award winners. There is a gold-foil team logo sticker for each team and one of the player stickers on each team is produced in a glitter technology. Stickers measure 2-3/8" x 3-3/8". Fronts have an action photo at center with team logo in the lower-left corner. Backs are printed in green and include the sticker number and appropriate Panini and baseball logos. A 58-page album was available to house the stickers.

		NM/M
Complete Set (300):		10.00
Common Player:		.05
Sticker Album:		1.00
1	California Angels Logo	.05
2	Mark Langston	.05
3	Ron Tingley	.05
4	Gary Gaetti	.05
5	Kelly Gruber	.05
6	Gary Disarcina	.05
7	Damion Easley (Glitter)	.05
8	Luis Polonia	.05
9	Lee Stevens	.05
10	Chad Curtis	.05
11	Rene Gonzales	.05
12	Oakland A's Logo	.05
13	Dennis Eckersley	.35
14	Terry Steinbach	.05
15	Mark McGwire	.75
16	Mike Bordick (Glitter)	.05

No.	Player	Price
17	Carney Lansford	.05
18	Jerry Browne	.05
19	Rickey Henderson	.40
20	Dave Henderson	.05
21	Ruben Sierra	.05
22	Ron Darling	.05
23	Toronto Blue Jays Logo	.05
24	Jack Morris	.05
25	Pat Borders	.05
26	John Olerud	.05
27	Roberto Alomar	.10
28	Luis Sojo	.05
29	Dave Stewart	.05
30	Devon White	.05
31	Joe Carter	.05
32	Derek Bell	.05
33	Juan Guzman (Glitter)	.05
34	Milwaukee Brewers Logo	.05
35	Jaime Navarro	.05
36	B.J. Surhoff	.05
37	Franklin Stubbs	.05
38	Billy Spiers	.05
39	Pat Listach (Glitter)	.05
40	Kevin Seitzer	.05
41	Darryl Hamilton	.05
42	Robin Yount	.40
43	Kevin Reimer	.05
44	Greg Vaughn	.05
45	Cleveland Indians Logo	.05
46	Charles Nagy	.05
47	Sandy Alomar Jr.	.05
48	Reggie Jefferson	.05
49	Mark Lewis	.05
50	Felix Fermin	.05
51	Carlos Baerga	.05
52	Albert Belle	.05
53	Kenny Lofton (Glitter)	.05
54	Mark Whiten	.05
55	Paul Sorrento	.05
56	Seattle Mariners Logo	.05
57	Dave Fleming	.05
58	Dave Valle	.05
59	Pete O'Brien	.05
60	Randy Johnson	.40
61	Omar Vizquel	.05
62	Edgar Martinez	.06
63	Ken Griffey Jr. (Glitter)	.75
64	Henry Cotto	.05
65	Jay Buhner	.05
66	Tino Martinez	.05
67	Baltimore Orioles Logo	.05
68	Ben McDonald	.05
69	Mike Mussina (Glitter)	.35
70	Chris Hoiles	.05
71	Randy Milligan	.05
72	Billy Ripken	.05
73	Cal Ripken Jr.	1.00
74	Leo Gomez	.05
75	Mike Devereaux	.05
76	Brady Anderson	.05
77	Joe Orsulak	.05
78	Texas Rangers Logo	.05
79	Kevin Brown	.05
80	Ivan Rodriguez (Glitter)	.40
81	Rafael Palmeiro	.40
82	Julio Franco	.05
83	Jeff Huson	.05
84	Dean Palmer	.05
85	Jose Canseco	.30
86	Juan Gonzalez	.40
87	Nolan Ryan	1.00
88	Brian Downing	.05
89	Boston Red Sox Logo	.05
90	Roger Clemens	.55
91	Tony Pena	.05
92	Mo Vaughn	.05
93	Scott Cooper	.05
94	Luis Rivera	.05
95	Ellis Burks	.05
96	Mike Greenwell	.05
97	Andre Dawson	.20
98	Ivan Calderon	.05
99	Phil Plantier (Glitter)	.05
100	Kansas City Royals Logo	.05
101	Kevin Appier	.05
102	Mike MacFarlane	.05
103	Wally Joyner	.05
104	Jim Eisenreich	.05
105	Greg Gagne	.05
106	Gregg Jefferies	.05
107	Kevin McReynolds	.05
108	Brian McRae (Glitter)	.05
109	Keith Miller	.05
110	George Brett	.55
111	Detroit Tigers Logo	.05
112	Bill Gullickson	.05
113	Mickey Tettleton	.05
114	Cecil Fielder	.05
115	Tony Phillips	.05
116	Scott Livingstone	.05
117	Travis Fryman (Glitter)	.05
118	Dan Gladden	.05
119	Rob Deer	.05
120	Frank Tanana	.05
121	Skeeter Barnes	.05
122	Minnesota Twins Logo	.05
123	Scott Erickson	.05
124	Brian Harper	.05
125	Kent Hrbek	.05
126	Chuck Knoblauch (Glitter)	.05
127	Willie Banks	.05
128	Scott Leius	.05
129	Shane Mack	.05
130	Kirby Puckett	.50
131	Chili Davis	.05
132	Pedro Munoz	.05
133	Chicago White Sox Logo	.05
134	Jack McDowell	.05
135	Carlton Fisk	.40
136	Frank Thomas (Glitter)	.45
137	Steve Sax	.05
138	Ozzie Guillen	.05
139	Robin Ventura	.05
140	Tim Raines	.05
141	Lance Johnson	.05
142	Ron Karkovice	.05
143	George Bell	.05
144	New York Yankees Logo	.05
145	Scott Sanderson	.05
146	Matt Nokes	.05
147	Kevin Maas (Glitter)	.05
148	Randy Velarde	.05
149	Andy Stankiewicz	.05
150	Pat Kelly	.05
151	Paul O'Neill	.05
152	Wade Boggs	.50
153	Danny Tartabull	.05
154	Don Mattingly	.55
155	Edgar Martinez (B.A. leader)	.05
156	Kevin Brown (W-L leader)	.05
157	Dennis Eckersley (Saves leader)	.15
158	Gary Sheffield (B.A. leader)	.05
159	Tom Glavine, Greg Maddux (W-L leaders)	.05
160	Lee Smith (Saves leader)	.05
161	Dennis Eckersley (Cy Young)	.15
162	Dennis Eckersley/MVP	.15
163	Pat Listach (Rookie/year)	.05
164	Greg Maddux (Cy Young)	.50
165	Barry Bonds/MVP	.50
166	Eric Karros (Rookie/year)	.05
167	Houston Astros Logo	.05
168	Pete Harnisch	.05
169	Eddie Taubensee	.05
170	Jeff Bagwell (Glitter)	.45
171	Craig Biggio	.05
172	Andujar Cedeno	.05
173	Ken Caminiti	.05
174	Steve Finley	.05
175	Luis Gonzalez	.05
176	Eric Anthony	.05
177	Casey Candaele	.05
178	Atlanta Braves logo	.05
179	Tom Glavine	.25
180	Greg Olson	.05
181	Sid Bream	.05
182	Mark Lemke	.05
183	Jeff Blauser	.05
184	Terry Pendleton	.05
185	Ron Gant	.05
186	Otis Nixon	.05
187	Dave Justice	.05
188	Deion Sanders (Glitter)	.20
189	St. Louis Cardinals Logo	.05
190	Bob Tewksbury	.05
191	Tom Pagnozzi	.05
192	Lee Smith	.05
193	Geronimo Pena	.05
194	Ozzie Smith	.50
195	Todd Zeile	.05
196	Ray Lankford	.05
197	Bernard Gilkey	.05
198	Felix Jose	.05
199	Donovan Osborne (Glitter)	.05
200	Chicago Cubs Logo	.05
201	Mike Morgan	.05
202	Rick Wilkins	.05
203	Mark Grace (Glitter)	.05
204	Ryne Sandberg	.50
205	Shawon Dunston	.05
206	Steve Buechele	.05
207	Kal Daniels	.05
208	Sammy Sosa	.50
209	Derrick May	.05
210	Doug Dascenzo	.05
211	Los Angeles Dodgers Logo	.05
212	Ramon Martinez	.05
213	Mike Scioscia	.05
214	Eric Karros (Glitter)	.05
215	Tim Wallach	.05
216	Jose Offerman	.05
217	Mike Sharperson	.05
218	Brett Butler	.05
219	Darryl Strawberry	.05
220	Lenny Harris	.05
221	Eric Davis	.05
222	Montreal Expos Logo	.05
223	Ken Hill	.05
224	Darrin Fletcher	.05
225	Greg Colbrunn (Glitter)	.05
226	Delino DeShields	.05
227	Wil Cordero	.05
228	Dennis Martinez	.05
229	John Vander Wal	.05
230	Marquis Grissom	.05
231	Larry Walker	.05
232	Moises Alou	.05
233	San Francisco Giants Logo	.05
234	Billy Swift	.05
235	Kirt Manwaring	.05
236	Will Clark	.05
237	Robby Thompson	.05
238	Royce Clayton (Glitter)	.05
239	Matt Williams	.05
240	Willie McGee	.05
241	Mark Leonard	.05
242	Cory Snyder	.05
243	Barry Bonds	1.00
244	New York Mets Logo	.05
245	Dwight Gooden	.05
246	Todd Hundley (Glitter)	.05
247	Eddie Murray	.40
248	Sid Fernandez	.05
249	Tony Fernandez	.05
250	Dave Magadan	.05
251	Howard Johnson	.05
252	Vince Coleman	.05
253	Bobby Bonilla	.05
254	Daryl Boston	.05
255	San Diego Padres Logo	.05
256	Bruce Hurst	.05
257	Dan Walters	.05
258	Fred McGriff	.05
259	Kurt Stillwell	.05
260	Craig Shipley	.05
261	Gary Sheffield (Glitter)	.35
262	Tony Gwynn	.50
263	Oscar Azocar	.05
264	Darrin Jackson	.05
265	Andy Benes	.05
266	Philadelphia Phillies Logo	.05
267	Terry Mulholland	.05
268	Curt Schilling	.25
269	Darren Daulton	.05
270	John Kruk	.05
271	Mickey Morandini (Glitter)	.05
272	Mariano Duncan	.05
273	Dave Hollins	.05
274	Lenny Dykstra	.05
275	Wes Chamberlain	.05
276	Stan Javier	.05
277	Pittsburgh Pirates Logo	.05
278	Zane Smith	.05
279	Tim Wakefield (Glitter)	.05
280	Mike LaValliere	.05
281	Orlando Merced	.05
282	Stan Belinda	.05
283	Jay Bell	.05
284	Jeff King	.05
285	Andy Van Slyke	.05
286	Bob Walk	.05
287	Gary Varsho	.05
288	Cincinnati Reds Logo	.05
289	Jose Rijo	.05
290	Joe Oliver	.05
291	Hal Morris	.05
292	Bip Roberts	.05
293	Barry Larkin	.05
294	Chris Sabo	.05
295	Roberto Kelly	.05
296	Kevin Mitchell	.05
297	Rob Dibble	.05
298	Reggie Sanders (Glitter)	.05
299	Florida Marlins Logo	.05
300	Colorado Rockies Logo	.05

1994 Panini Stickers

With set size at the reduced count of 268, Panini retained the larger format 2-3/8" x 3-3/8" sticker size. Stickers featured green borders surrounding a color action photo on front. Below the player photo is a pennant with the team logo and player name. Backs have a sticker number at center, with appropriate licensor logos and Panini advertising in black-and-white. The set includes 16 foil stickers honoring major 1993 season award winners in the A.L. and N.L. and four World Series action stickers. The set is arranged alphabetically within team and league. Stickers were sold in packs of six for 49 cents. A colorful album to house the stickers was also available.

No.	Player	NM/M
	Complete Set (268):	5.00
	Common Player:	.05
1	World Series Action/Foil	
2	World Series Action/Foil	
3	World Series Action/Foil	
4	World Series Action/Foil	
5	BA Leader (John Olerud/Foil)	.05
6	HR Leader (Juan Gonzalez/Foil)	.20
7	RBI Leader (Albert Belle/Foil)	.05
8	Wins Leader (Jack McDowell/Foil)	.05
9	K Leader (Randy Johnson/Foil)	.20
10	Saves Leader (Jeff Montgomery/Foil)	.05
11	BA Leader (Andres Galarraga/Foil)	.05
12	HR Leader (Barry Bonds/Foil)	.50
13	RBI Leader (Barry Bonds/Foil)	.50
14	Wins Leader (Tom Glavine, John Burkett/Foil)	.05
15	K Leader (Jose Rijo/Foil)	.05
16	Saves Leader (Randy Myers/Foil)	.05
17	Brady Anderson	.05
18	Harold Baines	.05
19	Mike Devereaux	.05
20	Chris Hoiles	.05
21	Mike Mussina	.30
22	Harold Reynolds	.05
23	Cal Ripken Jr.	1.00
24	David Segui	.05
25	Fernando Valenzuela	.05
26	Roger Clemens	.60
27	Scott Cooper	.05
28	Andre Dawson	.20
29	Scott Fletcher	.05
30	Mike Greenwell	.05
31	Billy Hatcher	.05
32	Tony Pena	.05
33	John Valentin	.05
34	Mo Vaughn	.50
35	Chad Curtis	.05
36	Gary DiSarcina	.05
37	Damion Easley	.05
38	Mark Langston	.05
39	Torey Lovullo	.05
40	Greg Myers	.05
41	Luis Polonia	.05
42	Tim Salmon	.05
43	J.T. Snow	.05
44	George Bell	.05
45	Ellis Burks	.05
46	Joey Cora	.05
47	Ozzie Guillen	.05
48	Roberto Hernandez	.05
49	Bo Jackson	.10
50	Jack McDowell	.05
51	Frank Thomas	.40
52	Robin Ventura	.05
53	Sandy Alomar Jr.	.05
54	Carlos Baerga	.05
55	Albert Belle	.05
56	Felix Fermin	.05
57	Wayne Kirby	.05
58	Kenny Lofton	.05
59	Charles Nagy	.05
60	Paul Sorrento	.05
61	Jeff Treadway	.05
62	Eric Davis	.05
63	Cecil Fielder	.05
64	Travis Fryman	.05
65	Bill Gullickson	.05
66	Mike Moore	.05
67	Tony Phillips	.05
68	Mickey Tettleton	.05
69	Alan Trammell	.05
70	Lou Whitaker	.05
71	Kevin Appier	.05
72	Greg Gagne	.05
73	Tom Gordon	.05
74	Felix Jose	.05
75	Wally Joyner	.05
76	Jose Lind	.05
77	Mike Macfarlane	.05
78	Brian McRae	.05
79	Kevin McReynolds	.05
80	Darryl Hamilton	.05
81	Teddy Higuera	.05
82	John Jaha	.05
83	Pat Listach	.05
84	Dave Nilsson	.05
85	Kevin Reimer	.05
86	Kevin Seitzer	.05
87	B. J. Surhoff	.05
88	Greg Vaughn	.05
89	Willie Banks	.05
90	Brian Harper	.05
91	Kent Hrbek	.05
92	Chuck Knoblauch	.05
93	Shane Mack	.05
94	Pat Meares	.05
95	Pedro Munoz	.05
96	Kirby Puckett	.50
97	Dave Winfield	.40
98	Jim Abbott	.05
99	Wade Boggs	.50
100	Mike Gallego	.05
101	Pat Kelly	.05
102	Don Mattingly	.60
103	Paul O'Neill	.05
104	Mike Stanley	.05
105	Danny Tartabull	.05
106	Bernie Williams	.05
107	Mike Bordick	.05
108	Dennis Eckersley	.35
109	Dave Henderson	.05
110	Mark McGwire	.75
111	Troy Neel	.05
112	Ruben Sierra	.05
113	Terry Steinbach	.05
114	Todd Van Poppel	.05
115	Bob Welch	.05
116	Bret Boone	.05
117	Jay Buhner	.05
118	Ken Griffey Jr.	.65
119	Randy Johnson	.50
120	Rich Amaral	.05
121	Edgar Martinez	.05
122	Tino Martinez	.05
123	Dave Valle	.05
124	Omar Vizquel	.05
125	Jose Canseco	.25
126	Julio Franco	.05
127	Juan Gonzalez	.20
128	Tom Henke	.05
129	Manuel Lee	.05
130	Rafael Palmeiro	.35
131	Dean Palmer	.05
132	Ivan Rodriguez	.35
133	Doug Strange	.05
134	Roberto Alomar	.10
135	Pat Borders	.05
136	Joe Carter	.05
137	Tony Fernandez	.05
138	Juan Guzman	.05
139	Rickey Henderson	.40
140	Paul Molitor	.05
141	John Olerud	.05
142	Devon White	.05
143	Jeff Blauser	.05
144	Ron Gant	.05
145	Tom Glavine	.05
146	Dave Justice	.05
147	Greg Maddux	.50
148	Fred McGriff	.05
149	Terry Pendleton	.05
150	Deion Sanders	.05
151	John Smoltz	.05
152	Shawon Dunston	.05
153	Mark Grace	.05
154	Derrick May	.05
155	Randy Myers	.05
156	Ryne Sandberg	.50
157	Dwight Smith	.05
158	Sammy Sosa	.50
159	Jose Vizcaino	.05
160	Rick Wilkins	.05
161	Tom Browning	.05
162	Roberto Kelly	.05
163	Barry Larkin	.05
164	Kevin Mitchell	.05
165	Hal Morris	.05
166	Joe Oliver	.05
167	Jose Rijo	.05
168	Chris Sabo	.05
169	Reggie Sanders	.05
170	Freddie Benavides	.05
171	Dante Bichette	.05
172	Vinny Castilla	.05
173	Jerald Clark	.05
174	Andres Galarraga	.05
175	Charlie Hayes	.05
176	Chris Jones	.05
177	Roberto Mejia	.05
178	Eric Young	.05
179	Bret Barberie	.05
180	Chuck Carr	.05
181	Jeff Conine	.05
182	Orestes Destrade	.05
183	Bryan Harvey	.05
184	Rich Renteria	.05
185	Benito Santiago	.05
186	Gary Sheffield	.20
187	Walt Weiss	.05
188	Eric Anthony	.05
189	Jeff Bagwell	.40
190	Craig Biggio	.05
191	Ken Caminiti	.05
192	Andujar Cedeno	.05
193	Doug Drabek	.05
194	Steve Finley	.05
195	Doug Jones	.05
196	Darryl Kile	.05
197	Brett Butler	.05
198	Tom Candiotti	.05
199	Dave Hansen	.05
200	Orel Hershiser	.05
201	Eric Karros	.05
202	Jose Offerman	.05
203	Mike Piazza	.60
204	Cory Snyder	.05
205	Darryl Strawberry	.05
206	Moises Alou	.05
207	Sean Berry	.05
208	Wil Cordero	.05
209	Delino DeShields	.05
210	Marquis Grissom	.05
211	Ken Hill	.05
212	Mike Lansing	.05
213	Larry Walker	.05
214	John Wetteland	.05
215	Bobby Bonilla	.05
216	Jeromy Burnitz	.05
217	Dwight Gooden	.05
218	Todd Hundley	.05
219	Howard Johnson	.05
220	Jeff Kent	.05
221	Eddie Murray	.40
222	Bret Saberhagen	.05
223	Ryan Thompson	.05
224	Darren Daulton	.05
225	Mariano Duncan	.05
226	Lenny Dykstra	.05
227	Jim Eisenreich	.05
228	Dave Hollins	.05
229	John Kruk	.05
230	Curt Schilling	.20
231	Kevin Stocker	.05
232	Mitch Williams	.05
233	Jay Bell	.05
234	Steve Cooke	.05
235	Carlos Garcia	.05
236	Jeff King	.05
237	Orlando Merced	.05
238	Don Slaught	.05
239	Zane Smith	.05
240	Andy Van Slyke	.05
241	Kevin Young	.05
242	Bernard Gilkey	.05
243	Gregg Jefferies	.05
244	Brian Jordan	.05
245	Ray Lankford	.05
246	Tom Pagnozzi	.05
247	Geronimo Pena	.05
248	Ozzie Smith	.50
249	Bob Tewksbury	.05
250	Mark Whiten	.05
251	Brad Ausmus	.05
252	Derek Bell	.05
253	Andy Benes	.05
254	Phil Clark	.05
255	Jeff Gardner	.05
256	Tony Gwynn	.50
257	Trevor Hoffman	.05
258	Phil Plantier	.05
259	Craig Shipley	.05
260	Rod Beck	.05
261	Barry Bonds	1.00
262	John Burkett	.05
263	Will Clark	.05
264	Royce Clayton	.05
265	Willie McGee	.05
266	Bill Swift	.05
267	Robby Thompson	.05
268	Matt Williams	.05
	Album:	1.00
	Wax Pack (5+1):	.25
	Wax Box (50):	5.00

2005 Parody Productions Boston Baseball Heroes

This deck of poker-format (2-1/2" x 3-1/2", round-cornered, linen finish) playing cards features color caricatures of past and contemporary Red Sox stars. Player name, sometimes a nickname, and his dates of service with the team are included. Backs have a baseball on a red background with white borders. The issue is apparently not licensed by MLB or the players.

		NM/M
	Complete Set (55):	10.00
	Common Player:	.25
AS	Curt Schilling	.35
2S	Jason Varitek	.25
3S	Mo Vaughn	.25
4S	Bill Mueller	.25
5S	Wade Boggs	1.00
6S	Nomar Garciaparra	1.00
7S	Manny Ramirez	1.00
8S	Johnny Damon	.40
9S	Trot Nixon	.35
10S	Tim Wakefield	.25
JS	Pedro Martinez	.35
QS	Roger Clemens	1.50

		NM/M
KS	David Ortiz	.50
AD	Mel Parnell	.25
2D	Sammy White	.25
3D	Billy Goodman	.25
4D	Bobby Doerr	.25
5D	Frank Malzone	.25
6D	Johnny Pesky	.25
7D	Jimmy Piersall	.35
8D	Dominic DiMaggio	.35
9D	Jackie Jensen	.35
10D	Vern Stephens	.25
JD	Dave Ferriss	.25
QD	Tex Hughson	.25
KD	Ted Williams	2.00
AC	Cy Young	.50
2C	Wally Schang	.25
3C	Jimmy Foxx	.50
4C	Jack Berry (Barry)	.25
5C	Jimmy Collins	.25
6C	Joe Cronin	.25
7C	Duffy Lewis	.25
8C	Doc Cramer	.25
9C	Harry Hooper	.25
10C	Bill Carrigan	.25
JC	Lefty Grove	.35
QC	Joe Wood	.25
KC	Tris Speaker	.40
AH	Luis Tiant	.35
2H	Carlton Fisk	.40
3H	George Scott	.25
4H	Tony Conigliaro	.35
5H	Rico Petrocelli	.25
6H	Rick Burleson	.25
7H	Reggie Smith	.25
8H	Fred Lynn	.35
9H	Dwight Evans	.35
10H	Jim Rice	.35
JH	Dick Radatz	.25
QH	Bill Lee	.25
KH	Carl Yastrzemski	1.50
---	Ken Coleman/ Broadcaster	.25
---	Ned Martin/Broadcaster	.25
---	Tom Yawkey/Owner	.25

Chicago (Cubs) Baseball Heroes

This deck of poker-format (2-1/2" x 3-1/2", round-cornered, linen finish) playing cards features color caricatures of past and contemporary Cubs stars. Player name, sometimes a nickname, and his dates of service with the team are included. Backs have a baseball on a blue background with white borders. The issue is apparently not licensed by MLB or the players.

		NM/M
	Complete Set (55):	10.00
	Common Player:	.25
AS	Mark Prior	1.00
2S	Joe Girardi	.25
3S	Mark Grace	.35
4S	Ryne Sandberg	2.00
5S	Aramis Ramirez	.25
6S	Shawon Dunston	.25
7S	Moises Alou	.25
8S	Corey Patterson	.25
9S	Andre Dawson	.50
10S	Carlos Zambrano	.25
JS	Kerry Wood	.35
QS	Lee Smith	.35
KS	Sammy Sosa	1.50
AD	Fergie Jenkins	.50
2D	Randy Hundley	.25
3D	Phil Cavarretta	.35
4D	Glenn Beckert	.35
5D	Ron Santo	.50
6D	Don Kessinger	.25
7D	Billy Williams	.75
8D	Hank Sauer	.25
9D	Jose Cardenal	.25
10D	Billy Herman	.35
JD	Bill Hands	.25
QD	Ken Holtzman	.25
KD	Ernie Banks	2.00
AC	Mordecai Brown	.25
2C	Gabby Hartnett	.25
3C	Frank Chance	.35
4C	Johnny Evers	.25
5C	Stan Hack	.25
6C	Joe Tinker	.35
7C	Bill Nicholson	.25
8C	Andy Pafko	.25
9C	Lewis Wilson	.35
10C	Kiki Cuyler	.25
JC	Charley Root	.25
QC	Grover Cleveland Alexander	.35
KC	Cap Anson	.25
AH	Greg Maddux	1.50
2H	Jody Davis	.25
3H	Bill Buckner	.25
4H	Manny Trillo	.25
5H	Bill Madlock	.25
6H	Ivan DeJesus	.25
7H	Gary Matthews	.25
8H	Leon Durham	.25
9H	Keith Moreland	.25
10H	Rick Reuschel	.25
JH	Rick Sutcliffe	.25
QH	Bruce Sutter	.50
KH	Dave Kingman	.25
---	Jack Brickhouse/ Broadcaster	.25
---	Harry Carey (Caray)/ Broadcaster	.50
---	Charlie Grimm	.25

Cincinnati Baseball Heroes

This deck of poker-format (2-1/2" x 3-1/2", round-nered, linen finish) playing cards features color caricatures of past and contemporary Reds stars. Player name, sometimes a nickname, and his dates of service with the team are included. Backs have a baseball on a red background with white borders. The issue is apparently not licensed by MLB or the players.

		NM/M
	Complete Set (55):	10.00
	Common Player:	.25
AS	Don Gullett	.25
2S	Johnny Bench	1.50
3S	Tony Perez	1.50
4S	Joe Morgan	1.50
5S	Pete Rose	2.00
6S	Dave Concepcion	.50
7S	George Foster	.50
8S	Cesar Geronimo	.25
9S	Ken Griffey	.50
10S	Sparky Anderson	1.00
JS	Rawly Eastwick	.25
QS	Pedro Borbon	.25
KS	Fred Norman	.25
AD	Johnny Vander Meer	.25
2D	Ernie Lombardi	.25
3D	Ted Kluszewski	1.00
4D	Johnny Temple	.25
5D	Ray Knight	.25
6D	Roy McMillan	.25
7D	Gus Bell	.25
8D	Eric Davis	.25
9D	Vada Pinson	.50
10D	Fred Hutchinson	.25
JD	Joe Nuxhall	.35
QD	Bucky Walters	.25
KD	Frank Robinson	1.50
AC	Eppa Rixey	.25
2C	Bubbles Hargrave	.25
3C	Frank McCormick	.25
4C	Hughie Critz	.25
5C	Heinie Groh	.25
6C	Billy Myers	.25
7C	Wally Post	.25
8C	Edd Roush	.25
9C	Red Lucas	.25
10C	Bill McKechnie	.25
JC	Dolf Luque	.25
QC	Paul Derringer	.25
KC	Noodles Hahn	.25
AH	Jose Rijo	.25
2H	Jason LaRue	.35
3H	Sean Casey	.50
4H	Tommy Helms	.25
5H	Chris Sabo	.25
6H	Barry Larkin	.25
7H	Adam Dunn	.25
8H	Ken Griffey Jr.	2.00
9H	Paul O'Neill	.25
10H	Lou Piniella	.25
JH	Mario Soto	.25
QH	Rob Dibble	.25
KH	Tom Browning	.25
---	Marty Brennaman/ Announcer	.25
---	Powel Crosley/Owner	.25
---	Marge Schott/Owner	.25

L.A. & Brooklyn Baseball Heroes

This deck of poker-format (2-1/2" x 3-1/2", round-cornered, linen finish) playing cards features color caricatures of past and contemporary Dodgers stars. Player name, sometimes a nickname, and his dates of service with the team are included. Backs have a baseball on a blue background with white borders. The issue is apparently not licensed by MLB or the players.

		NM/M
	Complete Set (55):	10.00
	Common Player:	.25
AS	Eric Gagne	.25
2S	Mike Scioscia	.25
3S	Eric Karros	.25
4S	Steve Sax	.25
5S	Adrian Beltre	.25
6S	Cesar Izturis	.25
7S	Gary Sheffield	.25
8S	Milton Bradley	.25
9S	Shawn Green	.35
10S	Ramon Martinez	.25
JS	Hideo Nomo	.50
QS	Kevin Brown	.25
KS	Mike Piazza	1.00
AD	Sandy Koufax	2.00
2D	John Roseboro	.25
3D	Wes Parker	.25
4D	Jim Gilliam	.25
5D	Bill Buckner	.25
6D	Maury Wills	.35
7D	Tommy Davis	.25
8D	Willie Davis	.25
9D	Ron Fairly	.25
10D	Ron Perranoski	.25
JD	Johnny Podres	.25
QD	Don Drysdale	.50
KD	Frank Howard	.40
AC	Don Newcombe	.25
2C	Roy Campanella	.50
3C	Gil Hodges	.50
4C	Jackie Robinson	1.50
5C	Billy Cox	.25
6C	Pee Wee Reese	.50
7C	Zach Wheat	.25
8C	Duke Snider	.50
9C	Carl Furillo	.25
10C	Dazzy Vance	.25
JC	Clem Labine	.25
QC	Carl Erskine	.25
KC	Jake Daubert	.25
AH	Orel Hershiser	.25
2H	Steve Yeager	.25
3H	Steve Garvey	.35
4H	Davey Lopes	.25
5H	Ron Cey	.25
6H	Bill Russell	.25
7H	Dusty Baker	.25
8H	Claude Osteen	.25
9H	Reggie Smith	.25
10H	Burt Hooten (Hooton)	.25
JH	Fernando Valenzuela	.35
QH	Don Sutton	.25
KH	Kirk Gibson	.25
---	Walter Alston	.25
---	Tommy Lasorda	.25
---	Vin Scully/Announcer	.25

N.Y. (Yankees) Baseball Heroes

This deck of poker-format (2-1/2" x 3-1/2", round-cornered, linen finish) playing cards features color caricatures of past and contemporary Yankees stars. Player name, sometimes a nickname, and his dates of service with the team are included.

Backs have a baseball on a white pinstriped background. The issue is apparently not licensed by MLB or the players.

		NM/M
	Complete Set (55):	10.00
	Common Player:	.25
AS	Roger Clemens	1.50
2S	Jorge Posada	.25
3S	Tino Martinez	.25
4S	Alfonso Soriano	.25
5S	Alex Rodriguez	1.50
6S	Derek Jeter	1.50
7S	Hideki Matsui	.50
8S	Bernie Williams	.25
9S	Paul O'Neill	.25
10S	Mike Mussina	.25
JS	Andy Petitte	.25
QS	Mariano Rivera	.25
KS	Don Mattingly	1.00
AD	Whitey Ford	.50
2D	Yogi Berra	.25
3D	Joe Pepitone	.35
4D	Bobby Richardson	.25
5D	Clete Boyer	.25
6D	Phil Rizzuto	.35
7D	Roy White	.25
8D	Roger Maris	.50
9D	Hank Bauer	.25
10D	Allie Reynolds	.25
JD	Ed Lopat	.25
QD	Mel Stottlemyre	.25
KD	Mickey Mantle	2.00
AC	Charles Ruffing	.25
2C	Bill Dickey	.25
3C	Lou Gehrig	2.00
4C	Tony Lazzeri	.25
5C	Red Rolfe	.25
6C	Frank Crosetti	.25
7C	Earle Combs	.25
8C	Joe DiMaggio	2.00
9C	Charlie Keller	.25
10C	Waite Hoyt	.25
JC	Herb Pennock	.25
QC	Lefty Gomez	.25
KC	George Herman Ruth	2.00
AH	Ron Guidry	.25
2H	Thurman Munson	.50
3H	Chris Chambliss	.25
4H	Willie Randolph	.25
5H	Graig Nettles	.25
6H	Bucky Dent	.25
7H	Dave Winfield	.50
8H	Mickey Rivers	.25
9H	Bobby Murcer	.25
10H	Jim Hunter	.35
JH	Dave Righetti	.25
QH	Rich Gossage	.25
KH	Reggie Jackson	.40
---	Billy Martin	.40
---	Casey Stengel	.40
---	Joe Torre	.40

1988 Pepsi-Cola/ Kroger Tigers

Approximately 38,000 sets of cards were given to fans at Tiger Stadium on July 30th, 1988. The set, sponsored by Pepsi-Cola and Kroger, includes 25 oversized (2-7/8" x 4-1/4") cards printed on glossy white stock with blue and orange borders. The card backs include small black and white close-up photos, the players' professional records and sponsor logos. The numbers in the following checklist refer to the players' uniform.

		NM/M
	Complete Set (25):	4.00
	Common Player:	.25
1	Lou Whitaker	.50
2	Alan Trammell	1.00
8	Mike Heath	.25
11	Sparky Anderson	.50
12	Luis Salazar	.25
14	Dave Bergman	.25
15	Pat Sheridan	.25
16	Tom Brookens	.25
19	Doyle Alexander	.25
21	Guillermo Hernandez	.25
22	Ray Knight	.25
24	Gary Pettis	.25
25	Eric King	.25
26	Frank Tanana	.25
31	Larry Herndon	.25
32	Jim Walewander	.25
33	Matt Nokes	.25
34	Chet Lemon	.25
35	Walt Terrell	.25
39	Mike Henneman	.25
41	Darrell Evans	.50
44	Jeff Robinson	.25
47	Jack Morris	.25
48	Paul Gibson	.25
---	Coaches (Billy Consolo, Alex Grammas, Billy Muffett, Vada Pinson, Dick Tracewski)	.25

1989 Pepsi-Cola Mark McGwire

During the summer of 1989, selected Pepsi products in the Northern California area carried these special McGwire cards. Photos were posed with McGwire wearing a generic white uniform trimmed in A's colors and bearing his number 25 and a Pepsi logo patch. Backs have the same biographical details, recent stats and career highlights. A card number is printed at lower-right.

		NM/M
	Complete Set (12):	10.00
	Common Card:	1.50
1	Mark McGwire/Btg (Left foot raised.)	1.50
2	Mark McGwire/ Fielding	1.50
3	Mark McGwire (Reaching for ball with glove.)	1.50
4	Mark McGwire/Btg (Foot down.)	1.50
5	Mark McGwire (Kneeling with bat.)	1.50
6	Mark McGwire (Stretching for throw at first.)	1.50
7	Mark McGwire (Bat on shoulder.)	1.50
8	Mark McGwire (Holding bat.)	1.50
9	Mark McGwire (Bat on shoulder.)	1.50
10	Mark McGwire (Holding bat.)	1.50
11	Mark McGwire (Holding bat.)	1.50
12	Mark McGwire/Btg (Follow-through.)	1.50

1990 Pepsi-Cola Boston Red Sox

Pepsi combined with Score to produce this special 20-card Boston Red Sox team set. Cards were inserted regionally in 12-packs of Pepsi and Diet Pepsi. The card fronts feature full-color action photos with the team name across the top border and the player's name along the bottom border. The Pepsi and Diet Pepsi logos also appear on the bottom border. The card backs represent standard Score card backs, but are not numbered and also once again feature the Pepsi and Diet Pepsi logos.

		NM/M
	Complete Set (20):	5.00
	Common Player:	.25
(1)	Marty Barrett	.25
(2)	Mike Boddicker	.25
(3)	Wade Boggs	1.50
(4)	Bill Buckner	.35
(5)	Ellis Burks	.25
(6)	Roger Clemens	3.00
(7)	John Dopson	.25
(8)	Dwight Evans	.35
(9)	Wes Gardner	.25
(10)	Rich Gedman	.25
(11)	Mike Greenwell	.25
(12)	Dennis Lamp	.25
(13)	Rob Murphy	.25
(14)	Tony Pena	.25
(15)	Carlos Quintana	.25
(16)	Jeff Reardon	.25
(17)	Jody Reed	.25
(18)	Luis Rivera	.25
(19)	Kevin Romine	.25
(20)	Lee Smith	.25

Jose Canseco

Single cards from this issue were distributed in packs of Pepsi products in the San Francisco Bay area. Each card has a photo of Canseco in a generic red, white and blue uniform. Fronts have a blue border with a Pepsi logo. Backs have biographical data, recent stats and career highlights. The cards are numbered in the lower-right corner.

		NM/M
	Complete Set (10):	5.00
	Common Card:	.75
1	Jose Canseco/Btg (Follow-through.)	.75
2	Jose Canseco/Btg (Follow-through.)	.75
3	Jose Canseco/Fielding	.75
4	Jose Canseco/Btg	.75
5	Jose Canseco (Holding glove.)	.75
6	Jose Canseco/Btg (Follow-through.)	.75
7	Jose Canseco (On dugout steps.)	.75
8	Jose Canseco/Btg	.75
9	Jose Canseco/Portrait	.75
10	Jose Canseco/Portrait	.75

1991 Pepsi-Cola Superstars

This Florida regional issue was distributed by gluing cards

inside of specially marked Pepsi products. Both front and back feature a "Flavor of Baseball" headline and logo of a glove catching a flying Pepsi can. Fronts have an action photo with colored strips at top and bottom. Player photos have uniform logos deleted. Backs have career stats, a few biographical details and a card number. The cards are slightly larger than current standards, measuring 2-5/8" x 3-1/2".

		NM/M
Complete Set (17):		18.50
Common Player:		.35
1	Dwight Gooden	.35
2	Andre Dawson	.65
3	Ryne Sandberg	2.00
4	Dave Steib	.35
5	Jose Rijo	.35
6	Roger Clemens	2.50
7	Barry Bonds	4.00
8	Cal Ripken, Jr.	4.00
9	Dave Justice	.35
10	Cecil Fielder	.35
11	Don Mattingly	2.50
12	Ozzie Smith	2.00
13	Kirby Puckett	2.00
14	Rafael Palmeiro	1.50
15	Bobby Bonilla	.35
16	Len Dykstra	.35
17	Jose Canseco	1.00

Cincinnati Reds

This team set was produced for inclusion in packages of Pepsi products in the Ohio area by Michael Schecheter Assoc. Like most MSA issues, the cards have had cap and uniform logos airbrushed away because they are licensed only by the players' union, and not MLB. Fronts have red borders with Pepsi, Diet Pepsi and MLBPA logos. Backs are in red, white and blue with the soda logos at top a few biographical notes, complete major and minor league stats and a facsimile autograph. The unnumbered cards are checklisted here alphabetically.

		NM/M
Complete Set (20):		8.00
Common Player:		.50
(1)	Jack Armstrong	.50
(2)	Todd Benzinger	.50
(3)	Glenn Braggs	.50
(4)	Tom Browning	.50
(5)	Norm Charlton	.50
(6)	Eric Davis	.75
(7)	Rob Dibble	.50
(8)	Bill Doran	.50
(9)	Mariano Duncan	.50
(10)	Billy Hatcher	.50
(11)	Barry Larkin	.75
(12)	Hal Morris	.50
(13)	Randy Myers	.50
(14)	Joe Oliver	.50

(15)	Paul O'Neill	.75
(16)	Lou Piniella	.50
(17)	Jeff Reed	.50
(18)	Jose Rijo	.50
(19)	Chris Sabo	.50
(20)	Herm Winningham	.50

Red Sox

For the second consecutive year, Pepsi/Diet Pepsi sponsored Boston Red Sox trading cards. The cards were inserted in specially marked packs of Pepsi and Diet Pepsi and were made available from July 1 through August 10. A consumer sweepstakes was also included with this promotion. Player jersey numbers are featured on the backs of the cards. Danny Darwin's jersey is incorrectly listed as #46. He actually wears #44 for the BoSox. Wade Boggs is not featured on a 1991 Pepsi-Cola Red Sox card.

		NM/M
Complete Set (20):		6.00
Common Player:		.25
2	Luis Rivera	.25
3	Jody Reed	.25
6	Tony Pena	.25
11	Tim Naehring	.25
12	Ellis Burks	.25
15	Dennis Lamp	.25
18	Carlos Quintana	.25
19	Dana Kiecker	.25
20	John Marzano	.25
21	Roger Clemens	5.00
23	Tom Brunansky	.25
25	Jack Clark	.25
27	Greg Harris	.25
29	Phil Plantier	.25
30	Matt Young	.25
38	Jeff Gray	.25
39	Mike Greenwell	.25
41	Jeff Reardon	.25
46	Danny Darwin	.25
50	Tom Bolton	.25

Griffeys

This regionally released set features Ken Griffey, Sr. and Jr. and was distributed in Pepsi products. In the photos the players are shown in generic white uniforms with Pepsi logo patches. Backs are printed in black-and-white and include biographical, personal, recent stats and career highlights. Card numbers are in the lower-right.

		NM/M
Complete Set (8):		7.50
Common Card:		.40
1	Ken Griffey Jr. (Swinging bat.)	2.00
2	Ken Griffey Jr./ Throwing	2.00
3	Ken Griffey Jr./ Catching	2.00

4	Ken Griffey Jr. (Bat on shoulder.)	2.00
5	Ken Griffey Jr. (Leaning on father.)	.75
6	Ken Griffey Jr. (Standing with father.)	.75
7	Ken Griffey Sr./Btg	.25
8	Ken Griffey Sr./Fielding	.25

Rickey Henderson

A third annual issue distributed with Pepsi products in the San Francisco Bay area this set features photos of the all-time base stealing king in airbrushed uniforms. Borders are red, white and blue pinstripes. A line-art figure of a base runner appears in the lower-right. Backs have a few bits of biographical data, career stats and a career highlight. Card numbers are printed in the lower-right.

		NM/M
Complete Set (10):		9.00
Common Card:		1.00
Uncut Prize Sheet:		25.00
1	Rickey Henderson/Btg (Follow-through.)	1.00
2	Rickey Henderson (Base running.)	1.00
3	Rickey Henderson (Warm-up stretches.)	1.00
4	Rickey Henderson (Taking lead-off.)	1.00
5	Rickey Henderson (Bat on shoulder.)	1.00
6	Rickey Henderson/Btg (Follow-through.)	1.00
7	Rickey Henderson (Squatting with bat.)	1.00
8	Rickey Henderson (Throwing follow-through.)	1.00
9	Rickey Henderson (Leading off.)	1.00
10	Rickey Henderson (Warm-up swings.)	1.00

Rickey Henderson Discs

Intended as a giveaway with Pepsi fountain drinks, this four-piece set of "3-D" discs pictures Rickey Henderson in a generic Pepsi-logo uniform. Each 2-1/4" diameter disc has two pictures of Henderson which change when the disc is moved. There is a purple border around the color photos, with "Pepsi," decorative stars and Henderson's name in white. Backs are printed in red and blue on white and are identical and unnumbered. The date and Pepsi logo are at top with 1990 season and career stats beneath.

		NM/M
Complete Set (4):		2.50
Common Disc:		1.00
(1)	Rickey Henderson (Bat on shoulder/ follow-through.)	1.00

(2)	Rickey Henderson (Warm-up swing/Btg follow-through.)	1.00
(3)	Rickey Henderson (Lead-off/running for 2nd.)	1.00
(4)	Rickey Henderson (Lead-off/headfirst slide.)	1.00

1996 Pepsi-Cola Cubs Convention

In conjunction with the Chicago Cubs 11th annual winter fan convention, Pepsi issued this boxed set featuring past and current Cubs with an emphasis on those appearing as convention guests. Individual cards are 4" x 5-1/2" and feature black-and-white or color photos inside a black border with white piping. The team and convention logos are printed in red, white and blue. Backs are printed in black on white and feature stats and biographical data plus the team and sponsor logos. The unnumbered cards are checklisted here in alphabetical order.

		NM/M
Complete Set (24):		8.00
Common Player:		.25
(1)	Ernie Banks	3.00
(2)	Glenn Beckert	.25
(3)	Larry Bowa	.25
(4)	Harry Caray	.25
(5)	Frank Castillo	.25
(6)	Jody Davis	.25
(7)	Dynamic Duo (Scott Bullett, Ozzie Timmons)	.25
(8)	Flashback Favorites (Milt Pappas, Tim Stoddard)	.25
(9)	Golden Voices (Jack Brickhouse, Vince Lloyd)	.25
(10)	Randy Hundley	.25
(11)	Fergie Jenkins	.50
(12)	Don Kessinger	.35
(13)	Gary Matthews	.25
(14)	Brian McRae	.25
(15)	Jim Riggleman	.25
(16)	Ron Santo	.50
(17)	Sensational 70's (Jose Cardenal, Rick Monday)	.25
(18)	Scott Servais	.25
(19)	Rick Sutcliffe	.25
(20)	Steve Trachsel	.75
(21)	Billy Williams	.25
(22)	Wrigleyville Sluggers (Keith Moreland, Richie Hebner)	.25
(23)	Young Guns (Turk Wendell, Terry Adams)	.25
(24)	Vine Line subscription offer (Ernie Banks)	.25

1998 Pepsi-Cola Arizona Diamondbacks

JAY BELL

Pepsi-Cola and Circle K stores ran a baseball-season promotion to distribute 15 cards of Arizona Diamondback players on a regional basis. By use of a punchcard to record the purchase of five 20-oz. or 1-liter Pepsi products a customer could receive a series of three players cards each month. Produced by Pinnacle, the D'back cards have action photos on front against a stylized semi-circular background. Team, Pinnacle and Pepsi logos are in three of the corners with the player name at lower-right. Backs have a red, white and blue Pepsi-style whirlpool background, another player photo, major league stats, a career highlight and licensor logos. Final production of the cards differs considerably from the player checklist provided on the punchcard and ads.

		NM/M
Complete Set (15):		6.00
Common Player:		.50
1	Andy Benes	.50
2	Willie Blair	.50
3	Jorge Fabregas	.50
4	Jay Bell	.50
5	Travis Lee	1.00
6	Matt Williams	.50
7	Devon White	.50
8	Karim Garcia	.65
9	Yamil Benitez	.50
10	Brian Anderson	.50
11	Scott Brow	.50
12	Felix Rodriguez	.50
13	Jeff Suppan	.50
14	Andy Fox	.50
15	Andy Stankiewicz	.50

Cubs Convention

In conjunction with the Chicago Cubs 13th annual winter fan convention, Pepsi issued this boxed set featuring past and current Cubs with an emphasis on those appearing as convention guests. Individual cards are 3-1/2" x 4" and feature black-and-white or color photos bordered in blue and sand. The team and convention logos are printed in red, white and blue. Backs are printed in black on white and feature stats and biographical data plus the team and sponsor logos. The unnumbered cards are checklisted here in alphabetical order.

		NM/M
Complete Set (30):		7.00
Common Card:		.25
(1)	Terry Adams	.25
(2)	Alumni Club (Carmen Fanzone, Paul Reuschel)	.25
(3)	Alumni Club (Oscar Gamble, Larry Bowa)	.25
(4)	Ernie Banks	2.00
(5)	Behind the Plate (Randy Hundley, Jody Davis)	.25
(6)	Booth Banter (Pat Hughes, Josh Lewin)	.25
(7)	Jack Brickhouse	.25
(8)	Harry Caray	.25
(9)	Catching Corps (Mike Hubbard, Tyler Houston)	.25
(10)	Andre Dawson	.50
(11)	Flame-Throwers (Kevin Foster, Marc Pisciotta)	.25
(12)	Future Stars (Kerry Wood, Pat Cline)	.50
(13)	Mark Grace	.50

(14)	Hot Prospects (Robin Jennings, Rodney Myers)	.25
(15)	Mound Mates (Mark Clark, Jeremi Gonzalez)	.25
(16)	New Cubs (Jeff Blauser, Mickey Morandini)	.25
(17)	No-Hit Hurlers (Milt Pappas, Don Cardwell)	.25
(18)	Kevin Orie	.25
(19)	Outfield Greats (Andy Pafko, Gary Matthews)	.35
(20)	Jim Riggleman	.25
(21)	Ron Santo	1.00
(22)	Scott Servais	.25
(23)	Sammy Sosa	2.00
(24)	Rick Sutcliffe	.25
(25)	Steve Trachsel	.25
(26)	Veteran Hurlers (Bob Patterson, Kevin Tapani)	.25
(27)	Billy Williams	1.00
(28)	1969 Cubs (Dick Selma, Willie Smith)	.25
(29)	1969 Infield (Glenn Beckert, Don Kessinger)	.50
(30)	89er's (Mike Bielecki, Vance Law)	.25

1999 Pepsi-Cola Arizona Diamondbacks

Sponsored by Pepsi and produced by Fleer, this team-set promotion features action photos on front on a metallic-foil background which approximates the colors and design of the soft drink logo, which also appears at lower-left. The player's uniform is at top-left. On back is a portrait photo on a repeat of the red, white and blue background. Full Major League stats are provided, along with career highlights and biographical data. At bottom is a row of licensor and sponsor logos.

		NM/M
Complete Set (15):		9.00
Common Player:		.50
1	Jay Bell	.50
2	Andy Benes	.50
3	Randy Johnson	3.00
4	Matt Williams	.50
5	Steve Finley	.50
6	Todd Stottlemyre	.50
7	Omar Daal	.50
8	Travis Lee	.50
9	Armando Reynoso	.50
10	Gregg Olson	.50
11	Tony Batista	.50
12	Greg Swindell	.50
13	Greg Colbrunn	.50
14	Damian Miller	.50
15	Kelly Stinnett	.50
---	Checklist 1	.10
---	Checklist 2	.10
---	Checklist 3	.10
---	Checklist 4	.10

2000 Pepsi-Cola Arizona Diamondbacks

JOHNSON

Pepsi-Cola and Circle K stores ran a baseball-season promotion to distribute 15 cards of Arizona Diamondback players on a regional basis. Produced by Upper Deck, the D'back cards have large portrait and smaller action photos in a horizontal format on a red, white and blue wave background. Team, UD and Pepsi logos appear in the corners with the player name at right. Backs have the same background, another player photo, major league stats, a career highlight and licensor logos. Cards were distributed in three five-card series, with a checklist card in each pack.

		NM/M
Complete Set (18):		9.00
Common Player:		.50
1	Jay Bell	.50
2	Matt Mantei	.50
3	Greg Swindell	.50
4	Matt Williams	.50
5	Erubiel Durazo	.50
6	Todd Stottlemyre	.50
7	Randy Johnson	3.00
8	Tony Womack	.50
9	Greg Colbrunn	.50
10	Brian Anderson	.50
11	Omar Daal	.50
12	Travis Lee	.50
13	Steve Finley	.50
14	Luis Gonzalez	.50
15	Kelly Stinnett	.50
	Checklist 1	.10
	Checklist 2	.10
	Checklist 3	.10

Detroit Tigers

Pepsi-Cola ran a late-season promotion to distribute 15 cards of Detroit Tigers players on a regional basis. Produced by Upper Deck, the cards have large portrait and smaller action photos in a horizontal format on a red, white and blue wave background. Team, UD and Pepsi logos appear in the corners with the player name at right. Backs have the same background, another action photo, major league stats, a career highlight and licensor logos. Cards were distributed in one per 12-pack of Pepsi products.

		NM/M
Complete Set (15):		5.00
Common Player:		.50
1	Damion Easley	.50
2	Dave Mlicki	.50
3	Jeff Weaver	.50
4	Deivi Cruz	.50
5	Juan Encarnacion	.50
6	Brian Moehler	.50
7	Robert Fick	.50
8	Juan Gonzalez	1.50
9	Phil Garner	.50
10	Brad Ausmus	.50
11	Todd Jones	.50
12	Bobby Higginson	.50
13	Tony Clark	.50
14	Dean Palmer	.50
15	Doug Brocail	.50

2001 Pepsi-Cola Arizona Diamondbacks

Pepsi-Cola ran a baseball-season promotion to distribute 15 cards of Arizona Diamondback players on a regional basis. Produced by Upper Deck, the D'back cards have a circular action photo in a horizontal format on a red,

white and blue wave background. At right is a rattlesnake skin design. Team, UD and Pepsi logos appear at right, with the player name at left. Backs have the same background, another player photo, recent major league stats, a career highlight and licensor logos. Cards were distributed in five three-card series. They are checklisted here by uniform number which appears on front.

		NM/M
Complete Set (15):		10.00
Common Player:		.25
5	Tony Womack	.25
9	Matt Williams	.25
12	Steve Finley	.25
16	Reggie Sanders	.25
17	Mark Grace	.50
20	Luis Gonzalez	.25
22	Greg Swindell	.25
27	Armando Reynoso	.25
28	Greg Colbrunn	.25
30	Todd Stottlemyre	.25
31	Matt Mantei	.25
33	Jay Bell	.25
34	Brian Anderson	.25
38	Curt Schilling	2.00
51	Randy Johnson	3.00

2002 Pepsi-Cola Seattle Mariners

Pepsi-Cola and the Mariners teamed up for this 25th Anniversary promotion distributing eight cards on a regional basis. Produced by Upper Deck, the M's cards have a game-action photo at left. At right is the team name along with Pepsi and anniversary logos. Backs have player stats and career highlights, a few sentences of team history and licensor logos. Cards were distributed in two-card cello packs.

		NM/M
Complete Set (8):		10.00
Common Player:		.50
1	John Olerud	.50
2	Mike Cameron	.50
3	Edgar Martinez	.75
4	Ichiro	6.00
5	Bret Boone	.75
6	Jeff Nelson	.50
7	Freddy Garcia	.50
8	Jamie Moyer	.50

2003 Pepsi-Cola

Unusual for modern promotional cards, Pepsi chose a smaller, 2" x 2-3/4" format for its Fleer-produced issue. Specially marked 24-can "Value Cubes" of Pepsi products included one of the cards. A total of 9.75 million

(about 325,000 sets) were reportedly produced. Fronts have action photos in a format similar to the soda logo, with red border at top and blue at bottom. Fleer, Pepsi and MLB logos appear. Backs have a team logo, player data, recent stats and career highlights, along with appropriate logos and copyright information. There is one player from each team in the issue.

		NM/M
Complete Set (30):		6.00
Common Player:		.15
1	Troy Glaus	.30
2	Chipper Jones	.35
3	Randy Johnson	.30
4	Tony Batista	.15
5	Magglio Ordonez	.25
6	Ken Griffey Jr.	.40
7	Omar Vizquel	.15
8	Todd Helton	.30
9	Bobby Higginson	.15
10	Luis Castillo	.15
11	Jeff Bagwell	.30
12	Mike Sweeney	.15
13	Shawn Green	.25
14	Richie Sexson	.15
15	Torii Hunter	.15
16	Vladimir Guerrero	.30
17	Mike Piazza	.35
18	Jason Giambi	.25
19	Barry Zito	.15
20	Pat Burrell	.25
21	Brian Giles	.15
22	Trevor Hoffman	.15
23	Barry Bonds	.75
24	Ichiro	.50
25	Albert Pujols	.60
26	Ben Grieve	.15
27	Alex Rodriguez	.60
28	Carlos Delgado	.25
29	Kerry Wood	.20
30	Pedro Martinez	.30

2004 Pepsi-Cola Arizona Diamondbacks

Pepsi-Cola offered this team set of Arizona Diamondback players as a stadium giveaway. Produced by Upper Deck, the cards have a game-action photo on a blue background. Backs have the same background, two more player photos, recent major league stats, a career highlight and licensor logos.

		NM/M
Complete Set (15):		7.00
Common Player:		.25
1	Randy Johnson	5.00
2	Richie Sexson	.35
3	Roberto Alomar	.35
4	Shea Hillenbrand	.35
5	Alex Cintron	.25
6	Matt Kata	.25
7	Robby Hammock	.25
8	Luis Gonzalez	.25
9	Steve Finley	.25
10	Danny Bautista	.25
11	Matt Mantei	.25
12	Brandon Webb	.35
13	Elmer Dessens	.25
14	Oscar Villarreal	.25
15	Jose Valverde	.25

1980-2001 Perez-Steele Hall of Fame Postcards

In 1980, Perez-Steele Galleries of Ft. Washington, Pa., produced the first in an ongoing series of limited-edition (10,000 each) postcards devot-

ed to members of the Hall of Fame. The company updated its series regularly through 2001 to add new inductees. The 3-1/2" x 5-1/2" cards feature color portrait and smaller sepia action watercolor paintings by Dick Perez. Decorative postcard backs have a few words about the player, card and series number and individual set number from within the edition of 10,000. Cards were sold by series only, in a color-coded box which includes a checklist. To a great degree, value of unsigned Perez-Steele cards depends on whether the player is still alive to autograph them.

		NM/M
Complete Set (270):		750.00
Common Player:		2.00
	First Series, 1980	75.00
1	Ty Cobb	20.00
2	Walter Johnson	6.00
3	Christy Mathewson	7.50
4	Babe Ruth	25.00
5	Honus Wagner	7.50
6	Morgan Bulkeley	2.00
7	Ban Johnson	2.00
8	Nap Lajoie	4.00
9	Connie Mack	4.00
10	John McGraw	2.00
11	Tris Speaker	4.00
12	George Wright	2.00
13	Cy Young	7.50
14	Grover Alexander	4.00
15	Alexander Cartwright	2.00
16	Henry Chadwick	2.00
17	Cap Anson	2.00
18	Eddie Collins	2.00
19	Candy Cummings	2.00
20	Charles Comiskey	2.00
21	Buck Ewing	2.00
22	Lou Gehrig	20.00
23	Willie Keeler	2.00
24	Hoss Radbourne	2.00
25	George Sisler	2.00
26	A.G. Spalding	2.00
27	Rogers Hornsby	4.00
28	Kenesaw Landis	2.00
29	Roger Breshnahan	2.00
30	Dan Brouthers	2.00
---	First Series Checklist	1.00
	Second Series, 1980	50.00
31	Fred Clarke	2.00
32	Jimmy Collins	2.00
33	Ed Delahanty	2.00
34	Hugh Duffy	2.00
35	Hughie Jennings	2.00
36	King Kelly	2.00
37	Jim O'Rourke	2.00
38	Wilbert Robinson	2.00
39	Jesse Burkett	2.00
40	Frank Chance	2.00
41	Jack Chesbro	2.00
42	Johnny Evers	2.00
43	Clark Griffith	2.00
44	Thomas McCarthy	2.00
45	Joe McGinnity	2.00
46	Eddie Plank	2.00
47	Joe Tinker	2.00
48	Rube Waddell	2.00
49	Ed Walsh	2.00
50	Mickey Cochrane	2.00
51	Frankie Frisch	2.00
52	Lefty Grove	2.00
53	Carl Hubbell	2.00
54	Herb Pennock	2.00
55	Pie Traynor	2.00
56	Mordecai Brown	2.00
57	Charlie Gehringer	2.00
58	Kid Nichols	2.00
59	Jimmie Foxx	4.00
60	Mel Ott	2.00
---	Second Series Checklist	1.00
	Third Series, 1980	75.00
61	Harry Heilmann	2.00
62	Paul Waner	2.00
63	Ed Barrow	2.00
64	Chief Bender	2.00
65	Tom Connolly	2.00
66	Dizzy Dean	7.50
67	Bill Klem	2.00
68	Al Simmons	2.00
69	Bobby Wallace	2.00
70	Harry Wright	2.00
71	Bill Dickey	2.00
72	Rabbit Maranville	2.00
73	Bill Terry	2.00
74	Frank Baker	2.00
75	Joe DiMaggio	20.00
76	Gabby Hartnett	2.00
77	Ted Lyons	2.00
78	Ray Schalk	2.00
79	Dazzy Vance	2.00
80	Joe Cronin	2.00
81	Hank Greenberg	7.50
82	Sam Crawford	2.00
83	Joe McCarthy	2.00
84	Zack Wheat	2.00
85	Max Carey	2.00
86	Billy Hamilton	2.00
87	Bob Feller	6.00
88	Bill McKechnie	2.00
89	Jackie Robinson	10.00
90	Edd Roush	2.00
---	Third Series Checklist	2.00
	Fourth Series, 1981	65.00
91	John Clarkson	2.00
92	Elmer Flick	2.00
93	Sam Rice	2.00
94	Eppa Rixey	2.00
95	Luke Appling	2.00
96	Red Faber	2.00
97	Burleigh Grimes	2.00
98	Miller Huggins	2.00
99	Tim Keefe	2.00
100	Heinie Manush	2.00
101	John Ward	2.00
102	Pud Galvin	2.00
103	Casey Stengel	3.00
104	Ted Williams	20.00
105	Branch Rickey	2.00
106	Red Ruffing	2.00
107	Lloyd Waner	2.00
108	Kiki Cuyler	2.00
109	Goose Goslin	2.00
110	Joe Medwick	2.00
111	Roy Campanella	7.50
112	Stan Coveleski	2.00
113	Waite Hoyt	2.00
114	Stan Musial	10.00
115	Lou Boudreau	2.00
116	Earle Combs	2.00
117	Ford Frick	2.00
118	Jesse Haines	2.00
119	David Bancroft	2.00
120	Jake Beckley	2.00
---	Fourth Series Checklist	1.00
	Fifth Series, 1981	85.00
121	Chick Hafey	2.00
122	Harry Hooper	2.00
123	Joe Kelley	2.00
124	Rube Marquard	2.00
125	Satchel Paige	10.00
126	George Weiss	2.00
127	Yogi Berra	6.00
128	Josh Gibson	4.00
129	Lefty Gomez	2.00
130	William Harridge	2.00
131	Sandy Koufax	15.00
132	Buck Leonard	2.00
133	Early Wynn	2.00
134	Ross Youngs	2.00
135	Roberto Clemente	20.00
136	Billy Evans	2.00
137	Monte Irvin	4.00
138	George Kelly	2.00
139	Warren Spahn	4.00
140	Mickey Welch	2.00
141	Cool Papa Bell	2.00
142	Jim Bottomley	2.00
143	Jocko Conlan	2.00
144	Whitey Ford	5.00
145	Mickey Mantle	25.00
146	Sam Thompson	2.00
147	Earl Averill	2.00
148	Bucky Harris	2.00
149	Billy Herman	2.00
150	Judy Johnson	2.00
---	Fifth Series Checklist	1.00
	Sixth Series, 1981	85.00
151	Ralph Kiner	2.00
152	Oscar Charleston	2.00
153	Roger Connor	2.00
154	Cal Hubbard	2.00
155	Bob Lemon	2.00
156	Freddie Lindstrom	2.00
157	Robin Roberts	4.00
158	Ernie Banks	6.00
159	Martin DiHigo	2.00
160	John Lloyd	2.00
161	Al Lopez	2.00
162	Amos Rusie	2.00
163	Joe Sewell	2.00
164	Addie Joss	2.00
165	Larry MacPhail	2.00
166	Eddie Mathews	2.00
167	Warren Giles	2.00
168	Willie Mays	15.00
169	Hack Wilson	2.00
170	Al Kaline	5.00
171	Chuck Klein	2.00
172	Duke Snider	5.00
173	Tom Yawkey	2.00
174	Rube Foster	2.00
175	Bob Gibson	4.00
176	Johnny Mize	2.00
A	Abner Doubleday	2.00
B	Stephen Clark	2.00
C	Paul Kerr	2.00
D	Edward W. Stack	2.00
---	Sixth Series Checklist	1.00
	Seventh Series, 1983	55.00
177	Hank Aaron	20.00
178	Happy Chandler	2.00
179	Travis Jackson	3.00
180	Frank Robinson	10.00
181	Walter Alston	3.00
182	George Kell	6.00
183	Juan Marichal	7.50
184	Brooks Robinson	10.00
	Eighth Series, 1985	55.00
185	Luis Aparicio	7.50
186	Don Drysdale	3.00
187	Rick Ferrell	3.00
188	Harmon Killebrew	3.00
189	Pee Wee Reese	3.00
190	Lou Brock	6.00
191	Enos Slaughter	3.00
192	Arky Vaughn	3.00
193	Hoyt Wilhelm	3.00
	Ninth Series, 1987	15.00
194	Bobby Doerr	2.00
195	Ernie Lombardi	2.00
196	Willie McCovey	2.00
197	Ray Dandridge	2.00
198	Catfish Hunter	2.00
199	Billy Williams	4.00
E	Frank Steele, Peggy Steele, Dick Perez	2.00
	Tenth Series, 1989	20.00
200	Willie Stargell	2.00
201	Al Barlick	2.00
202	Johnny Bench	4.00
203	Red Schoendienst	4.00
204	Carl Yastrzemski	4.00
F	George Bush, Edward Stack	4.00
	Eleventh Series, 1991	30.00
205	Joe Morgan	4.00
206	Jim Palmer	4.00
207	Rod Carew	4.00
208	Ferguson Jenkins	4.00
209	Tony Lazzeri	2.00
210	Gaylord Perry	4.00
211	Bill Veeck	2.00
	Twelfth Series, 1993	35.00
212	Rollie Fingers	4.00
213	Bill McGowan	3.00
214	Hal Newhouser	3.00
215	Tom Seaver	6.00
216	Reggie Jackson	7.50
217	Steve Carlton	6.00
218	Leo Durocher	3.00
219	Phil Rizzuto	6.00
	Thirteenth Series, 1995	40.00
220	Richie Ashburn	4.00
221	Leon Day	3.00
222	William Hulbert	3.00
223	Mike Schmidt	10.00
224	Vic Willis	3.00
225	Jim Bunning	4.00
226	Andrew "Rube" Foster	3.00
227	Ned Hanlon	3.00
228	Earl Weaver	6.00
	Fourteenth Series, 1997	85.00
229	Nellie Fox	6.00
230	Tommy Lasorda	6.00
231	Phil Niekro	4.00
232	Willie Wells	3.00
233	George Davis	3.00
234	Larry Doby	4.00
235	Lee MacPhail	3.00
236	Joe Rogan	3.00
237	Don Sutton	4.00
238	George Brett	15.00
239	Orlando Cepeda	6.00
240	Nestor Chylak	3.00
241	Nolan Ryan	20.00
242	Frank Selee	3.00
243	Joe Williams	3.00
244	Robin Yount	7.50
	Fifteenth Series, 2001	50.00
245	Sparky Anderson	6.00
246	Carlton Fisk	7.50
247	Bid McPhee	6.00
248	Tony Perez	6.00
249	Turkey Stearnes	3.00
250	Bill Mazeroski	7.50
251	Kirby Puckett	7.50
252	Hilton Smith	7.50
253	Dave Winfield	7.50
G	Franklin A. Steele	

1980-2001 Perez-Steele Hall of Fame Postcards - Autographed

Because the cards are so popular with autograph collectors, a listing of Perez-Steele Hall of Fame postcards which are possible to acquire in authentically autographed form is provided here, along with current retail values. Only those players who were alive at the

Satchel Paige

time of their cards' issue are included in this listings; no cards from Series 1 and very few from Series 2 are available in autographed form.

		NM/M
Common Player:		17.50
53	Carl Hubbell	80.00
57	Charlie Gehringer	80.00
71	Bill Dickey	65.00
73	Bill Terry	90.00
75	Joe DiMaggio	325.00
77	Ted Lyons	235.00
80	Joe Cronin	750.00
81	Hank Greenberg	300.00
87	Bob Feller	25.00
90	Edd Roush	75.00
95	Luke Appling	50.00
97	Burleigh Grimes	190.00
104	Ted Williams	300.00
106	Red Ruffing	450.00
107	Lloyd Waner	2,250
111	Roy Campanella	300.00
112	Stan Coveleski	300.00
113	Waite Hoyt	495.00
114	Stan Musial	75.00
115	Lou Boudreau	25.00
125	Satchel Paige	2,500
127	Yogi Berra	40.00
129	Lefty Gomez	60.00
131	Sandy Koufax	90.00
132a	Buck Leonard (pre-stroke)	45.00
132b	Buck Leonard (post-stroke)	25.00
133	Early Wynn	40.00
137	Monte Irvin	20.00
138	George Kelly	350.00
139	Warren Spahn	30.00
141	Cool Papa Bell	75.00
143	Jocko Conlan	60.00
144	Whitey Ford	40.00
145	Mickey Mantle	300.00
147	Earl Averill	450.00
149	Billy Herman	35.00
150	Judy Johnson	50.00
151	Ralph Kiner	30.00
155	Bob Lemon	30.00
157	Robin Roberts	25.00
158	Ernie Banks	30.00
161	Al Lopez	75.00
163	Joe Sewell	45.00
166	Eddie Mathews	40.00
168	Willie Mays	75.00
170	Al Kaline	25.00
172	Duke Snider	30.00
175	Bob Gibson	25.00
176	Johnny Mize	35.00
D	Edward W. Stack	15.00
177	Hank Aaron	45.00
178	Happy Chandler	50.00
179	Travis Jackson	80.00
180	Frank Robinson	35.00
181	Walter Alston	675.00
182	George Kell	20.00
183	Juan Marichal	20.00
184	Brooks Robinson	22.50
185	Luis Aparicio	22.50
186	Don Drysdale	40.00
187	Rick Ferrell	25.00
188	Harmon Killebrew	30.00
189	Pee Wee Reese	55.00
190	Lou Brock	25.00
191	Enos Slaughter	20.00
193	Hoyt Wilhelm	20.00
194	Bobby Doerr	17.50
196	Willie McCovey	35.00
197	Ray Dandridge	30.00
198	Catfish Hunter	40.00
199	Billy Williams	22.50
E	Frank Steele, Peggy Steele, Dick Perez	15.00
200	Willie Stargell	35.00
201	Al Barlick	20.00
202	Johnny Bench	45.00
203	Red Schoendienst	25.00
204	Carl Yastrzemski	65.00
F	George Bush, Edward Stack	60.00
205	Joe Morgan	35.00
206	Jim Palmer	25.00
207	Rod Carew	45.00
208	Ferguson Jenkins	30.00
210	Gaylord Perry	17.50

212	Rollie Fingers	35.00
214	Hal Newhouser	60.00
215	Tom Seaver	60.00
216	Reggie Jackson	75.00
217	Steve Carlton	45.00
219	Phil Rizzuto	40.00
220	Richie Ashburn	30.00
223	Mike Schmidt	75.00
225	Jim Bunning	35.00
228	Earl Weaver	35.00
230	Tommy Lasorda	35.00
231	Phil Niekro	35.00
234	Larry Doby	90.00
235	Lee MacPhail	35.00
237	Don Sutton	35.00
238	George Brett	100.00
239	Orlando Cepeda	40.00
241	Nolan Ryan	100.00
244	Robin Yount	100.00
245	Sparky Anderson	45.00
246	Carlton Fisk	60.00
248	Tony Perez	45.00
250	Bill Mazeroski	45.00
251	Kirby Puckett	85.00
253	Dave Winfield	85.00

1981 Perez-Steele Yankee Greats Promotional Postcard

To advertise the availability of a "Yankee Greats" lithograph by Dick Perez, the Perez-Steele Galleries issued this promotional postcard. The 3-1/2" x 5-1/2" card is printed on thin cardboard with a reproduction of the lithograph on front. Printed in blue, the postcard-style back has information on the lithograph, which was issued in a size of 19" x 24-1/2" in an edition of 1,000 signed pieces.

	NM/M
Yankee Greats (Babe Ruth, Lou Gehrig, Earle Combs)	4.00

1985-95 Perez-Steele Great Moments Postcards

Yet another collectors issue devoted solely to Hall of Fame players, the Great Moments series borrows the format of the 1911 Turkey Red cabinet cards. The 5-3/4" x 8" cards are printed on textured cardboard (which was noticeably downgraded beginning with the 1993 series). Fronts have Dick Perez paintings surrounded by a greenish-brown border; backs are in black-and-white. Each card carries a series checklist on back and an indi-

vidual set serial number from within an edition of 5,000. Cards were issued in series of 12.

		NM/M
Complete Set (108):		400.00
Common Player:		3.00
1	Babe Ruth	20.00
2	Al Kaline	6.00
3	Jackie Robinson	10.00
4	Lou Gehrig	15.00
5	Whitey Ford	6.00
6	Christy Mathewson	5.00
7	Roy Campanella	7.50
8	Walter Johnson	6.00
9	Hank Aaron	12.50
10	Cy Young	5.00
11	Stan Musial	12.50
12	Ty Cobb	15.00
13	Ted Williams	15.00
14	Warren Spahn	3.00
15	Lloyd Waner, Paul Waner	3.00
16	Sandy Koufax	12.50
17	Robin Roberts	3.00
18	Dizzy Dean	4.00
19	Mickey Mantle	25.00
20	Satchel Paige	10.00
21	Ernie Banks	6.00
22	Willie McCovey	3.00
23	Johnny Mize	3.00
24	Honus Wagner	7.50
25	Willie Keeler	3.00
26	Pee Wee Reese	3.00
27	Monte Irvin	3.00
28	Eddie Mathews	3.00
29	Enos Slaughter	3.00
30	Rube Marquard	3.00
31	Charlie Gehringer	3.00
32	Roberto Clemente	15.00
33	Duke Snider	4.50
34	Ray Dandridge	3.00
35	Carl Hubbell	3.00
36	Bobby Doerr	3.00
37	Bill Dickey	3.00
38	Willie Stargell	3.00
39	Brooks Robinson	3.00
40	Joe Tinker, Johnny Evers, Frank Chance	5.00
41	Billy Herman	3.00
42	Grover Alexander	4.00
43	Luis Aparicio	3.00
44	Lefty Gomez	3.00
45	Eddie Collins	3.00
46	Judy Johnson	3.00
47	Harry Heilmann	3.00
48	Harmon Killebrew	3.00
49	Johnny Bench	4.50
51	Max Carey	3.00
52	Cool Papa Bell	3.00
53	Rube Waddell	3.00
54	Yogi Berra	6.00
55	Herb Pennock	3.00
56	Red Schoendienst	3.00
57	Juan Marichal	3.00
58	Frankie Frisch	3.00
59	Buck Leonard	3.00
60	George Kell	3.00
61	Chuck Klein	3.00
62	King Kelly	3.00
63	Jim Hunter	3.00
64	Lou Boudreau	3.00
65	Al Lopez	3.00
66	Willie Mays	12.50
67	Lou Brock	3.00
68	Bob Lemon	3.00
69	Joe Sewell	3.00
70	Billy Williams	3.00
71	Rick Ferrell	3.00
72	Arky Vaughn	3.00
73	Carl Yastrzemski	4.50
74	Tom Seaver	6.00
75	Rollie Fingers	3.00
76	Ralph Kiner	3.00
77	Frank Baker	3.00
78	Rod Carew	3.00
79	Goose Goslin	3.00
80	Gaylord Perry	3.00
81	Hack Wilson	3.00
82	Hal Newhouser	3.00
83	Early Wynn	3.00
84	Bob Feller	4.00
85	Branch Rickey (w/ Jackie Robinson)	3.00
86	Jim Palmer	3.00
87	Al Barlick	3.00
88	Willie Mays, Mickey Mantle, Duke Snider	20.00
89	Hank Greenberg	6.00
90	Joe Morgan	3.00
91	Chief Bender	3.00
92	Pee Wee Reese, Jackie Robinson	5.00
93	Jim Bottomley	3.00
94	Ferguson Jenkins	3.00
95	Frank Robinson	3.00
96	Hoyt Wilhelm	3.00
97	Cap Anson	3.00
98	Jim Bunning	3.00
99	Richie Ashburn	4.00
100	Steve Carlton	3.00
101	Mike Schmidt	6.00
102	Nellie Fox	3.00
103	Tommy Lasorda	3.00
104	Leo Durocher	3.00
104	Reggie Jackson	6.00

105	Phil Rizzuto	4.50
106	Phil Niekro	3.00
107	Willie Wells	3.00
108	Earl Weaver	3.00

1985-95 Perez-Steele Great Moments Postcards - Autographed

Because the Perez-Steele postcards are so popular with autograph collectors, separate listings for authentically autographed examples of the cards are provided here. Those cards not listed cannot possibly have been signed because the player was deceased prior to issue.

		NM/M
Complete Set (70):		1,800
Common Player:		17.50
2	Al Kaline	30.00
5	Whitey Ford	35.00
7	Roy Campanella	400.00
9	Hank Aaron	60.00
11	Stan Musial	60.00
13	Ted Williams	300.00
14	Warren Spahn	30.00
16	Sandy Koufax	95.00
17	Robin Roberts	25.00
19	Mickey Mantle	300.00
21	Ernie Banks	55.00
22	Willie McCovey	40.00
23	Johnny Mize	40.00
26	Pee Wee Reese	60.00
27	Monte Irvin	20.00
28	Eddie Mathews	50.00
29	Enos Slaughter	27.50
31	Charlie Gehringer	65.00
33	Duke Snider	40.00
34	Ray Dandridge	45.00
35	Carl Hubbell	65.00
36	Bobby Doerr	17.50
37	Bill Dickey	65.00
38	Willie Stargell	35.00
39	Brooks Robinson	30.00
41	Billy Herman	40.00
43	Luis Aparicio	25.00
44	Lefty Gomez	55.00
48	Harmon Killebrew	35.00
49	Johnny Bench	40.00
51	Cool Papa Bell	90.00
54	Yogi Berra	25.00
55	Red Schoendienst	25.00
57	Juan Marichal	40.00
58	Buck Leonard	40.00
59	George Kell	20.00
62	Jim Hunter	25.00
63	Lou Boudreau	30.00
64	Al Lopez	40.00
65	Willie Mays	80.00
66	Lou Brock	30.00
67	Bob Lemon	35.00
68	Joe Sewell	50.00
69	Billy Williams	25.00
70	Rick Ferrell	35.00
72	Carl Yastrzemski	60.00
73	Tom Seaver	50.00
74	Rollie Fingers	32.50
75	Ralph Kiner	27.50
77	Rod Carew	35.00
79	Gaylord Perry	25.00
81	Hal Newhouser	30.00
82	Early Wynn	40.00
83	Bob Feller	30.00
85	Jim Palmer	32.50
86	Al Barlick	25.00
87	Willie Mays, Mickey Mantle, Duke Snider	325.00
89	Joe Morgan	30.00
93	Ferguson Jenkins	25.00
94	Frank Robinson	40.00
95	Hoyt Wilhelm	30.00
97	Jim Bunning	30.00
98	Richie Ashburn	25.00
99	Steve Carlton	45.00
100	Mike Schmidt	75.00
102	Tommy Lasorda	50.00
104	Reggie Jackson	50.00
105	Phil Rizzuto	35.00
106	Phil Niekro	30.00
108	Earl Weaver	30.00

1989 Perez-Steele Celebration Postcards

The Celebrations postcard issue from Perez-Steele was an attempt to offer collectors an original medium on which to obtain autgraphs of Hall of Famers. All 44 of the players included in the issue were alive when the set was conceived and most were still around when it was actually issued. The 3-1/2" x 5-1/2" cards have color portrait and action paintings by Dick Perez on front, which features a linen texture. Backs have postcard indicia, Perez-Steele and Hall of Fame logos, card number and individual serial number from within the edition limit of 10,000. Cards were originally sold only as complete sets.

		NM/M
Complete Set (45):		100.00
Common Player:		2.50
1	Hank Aaron	10.00
2	Luis Aparicio	2.50
3	Ernie Banks	6.00
4	Cool Papa Bell	2.50
5	Johnny Bench	6.00
6	Yogi Berra	6.00
7	Lou Boudreau	2.50
8	Roy Campanella	7.50
9	Happy Chandler	2.50
10	Jocko Conlan	2.50
11	Ray Dandridge	2.50
12	Bill Dickey	3.00
13	Bobby Doerr	2.50
14	Rick Ferrell	2.50
15	Charlie Gehringer	3.00
16	Lefty Gomez	3.00
17	Billy Herman	2.50
18	Catfish Hunter	2.50
19	Monte Irvin	2.50
20	Judy Johnson	2.50
21	Al Kaline	6.00
22	George Kell	2.50
23	Harmon Killebrew	2.50
24	Ralph Kiner	2.50
25	Bob Lemon	2.50
26	Buck Leonard	2.50
27	Al Lopez	2.50
28	Mickey Mantle	20.00
29	Juan Marichal	2.50
30	Eddie Mathews	2.50
31	Willie McCovey	2.50
32	Johnny Mize	2.50
33	Stan Musial	7.50
34	Pee Wee Reese	2.50
35	Brooks Robinson	2.50
36	Joe Sewell	2.50
37	Enos Slaughter	2.50
38	Duke Snider	6.00
39	Warren Spahn	2.50
40	Willie Stargell	2.50
41	Bill Terry	2.50
42	Billy Williams	2.50
43	Ted Williams	15.00
44	Carl Yastrzemski	2.50
---	Checklist	1.00

1989 Perez-Steele Celebration Postcards - Autographed

Because of their popularity as an autograph vehicle, values for authentically signed examples of the Perez-Steele Celebrations postcards are presented here. Cards of Lefty Gomez (#16), Judy Johnson (#20) and Bill Terry (#41) cannot exist

with genuine autographs because those players were deceased by the time the cards were issued.

		NM/M
Common Player:		15.00
1	Hank Aaron	40.00
2	Luis Aparicio	15.00
3	Ernie Banks	30.00
4	Cool Papa Bell	60.00
5	Johnny Bench	35.00
6	Yogi Berra	25.00
7	Lou Boudreau	20.00
8	Roy Campanella	400.00
9	Happy Chandler	35.00
10	Jocko Conlan	450.00
11	Ray Dandridge	30.00
12	Bill Dickey	65.00
13	Bobby Doerr	15.00
14	Rick Ferrell	40.00
15	Charlie Gehringer	45.00
17	Billy Herman	30.00
18	Catfish Hunter	40.00
19	Monte Irvin	22.50
21	Al Kaline	30.00
22	George Kell	20.00
23	Harmon Killebrew	20.00
24	Ralph Kiner	25.00
25	Bob Lemon	30.00
26	Buck Leonard	30.00
27	Al Lopez	75.00
28	Mickey Mantle	300.00
29	Juan Marichal	30.00
30	Eddie Mathews	40.00
31	Willie McCovey	30.00
32	Johnny Mize	30.00
33	Stan Musial	50.00
34	Pee Wee Reese	55.00
35	Brooks Robinson	40.00
36	Joe Sewell	40.00
37	Enos Slaughter	25.00
38	Duke Snider	30.00
39	Warren Spahn	25.00
40	Willie Stargell	30.00
42	Billy Williams	20.00
43	Ted Williams	250.00
44	Carl Yastrzemski	60.00

1990-92 Perez-Steele Master Works Postcards

A blending of the designs of classic early baseball cards with the artwork of one of today's most recognized baseball artists produced the Perez-Steele Master Works postcard series. Each of the players in the collection (living players selected for inclusion on the basis of autograph possibilities) is shown on five different cards, one of original design and four adapting the formats of the 1909 Ramly (T204), 1911 "Gold Borders" (T205) and 1908 Rose Co. postcards (PC760) and 1888 Goodwin Champions (N162). The Ramly and Rose takeoffs feature gold-foil embossing. Postcard backs are printed in brown (#1-25) or dark green (#26-50). Information on back includes a description of the card set on which the design is based, card and series number and the individual set serial number from within the edition of 10,000. Series 1 (#1-25) was issued in 1990; Series 2 (#26-50) in 1992. Each was available only as a complete boxed set.

	NM/M
Complete Set (52):	150.00
Common Player:	3.00

1	Charlie Gehringer (Ramly)	3.00
2	Charlie Gehringer (Goodwin)	3.00
3	Charlie Gehringer (Rose)	3.00
4	Charlie Gehringer (Gold Border)	3.00
5	Charlie Gehringer (Perez-Steele)	3.00
6	Mickey Mantle (Ramly)	15.00
7	Mickey Mantle (Goodwin)	15.00
8	Mickey Mantle (Rose)	15.00
9	Mickey Mantle (Gold Border)	15.00
10	Mickey Mantle (Perez-Steele)	15.00
11	Willie Mays (Ramly)	9.00
12	Willie Mays (Goodwin)	9.00
13	Willie Mays (Rose)	9.00
14	Willie Mays (Gold Border)	9.00
15	Willie Mays (Perez-Steele)	9.00
16	Duke Snider (Ramly)	6.00
17	Duke Snider (Goodwin)	6.00
18	Duke Snider (Rose)	6.00
19	Duke Snider (Gold Border)	6.00
20	Duke Snider (Perez-Steele)	6.00
21	Warren Spahn (Ramly)	3.00
22	Warren Spahn (Goodwin)	3.00
23	Warren Spahn (Rose)	3.00
24	Warren Spahn (Gold Border)	3.00
25	Warren Spahn (Perez-Steele)	3.00
---	Checklist 1-25	1.00
26	Yogi Berra (Ramly)	5.00
27	Yogi Berra (Goodwin)	5.00
28	Yogi Berra (Rose)	5.00
29	Yogi Berra (Gold Border)	5.00
30	Yogi Berra (Perez-Steele)	5.00
31	Johnny Mize (Ramly)	3.00
32	Johnny Mize (Goodwin)	3.00
33	Johnny Mize (Rose)	3.00
34	Johnny Mize (Gold Border)	3.00
35	Johnny Mize (Perez-Steele)	3.00
36	Willie Stargell (Ramly)	3.00
37	Willie Stargell (Goodwin)	3.00
38	Willie Stargell (Rose)	3.00
39	Willie Stargell (Gold Border)	3.00
40	Willie Stargell (Perez-Steele)	3.00
41	Ted Williams (Ramly)	12.00
42	Ted Williams (Goodwin)	12.00
43	Ted Williams (Rose)	12.00
44	Ted Williams (Gold Border)	12.00
45	Ted Williams (Perez-Steele)	12.00
46	Carl Yastrzemski (Ramly)	4.00
47	Carl Yastrzemski (Goodwin)	4.00
48	Carl Yastrzemski (Rose)	4.00
49	Carl Yastrzemski (Gold Border)	4.00
50	Carl Yastrzemski (Perez-Steele)	4.00
	Checklist 26-50	1.00

1985 Performance Printing Texas Rangers

A local printing company sponsored this 28-card set of the Texas Rangers. The 2-3/8" x 3-1/2" cards are in full color and are numbered on the back by uniform number. Card fronts feature full-color, game-action photos. The 25 players on the Rangers' active roster at press time are included, along with manager Bobby Valentine and unnumbered coaches and trainer cards. The black and white card backs have a smaller portrait photo of each player, as well as biographical information and career statistics.

		NM/M
	Complete Set (28):	9.00
	Common Player:	.50
0	Oddibe McDowell	.50
1	Bill Stein	.50
2	Bobby Valentine	.50
3	Wayne Tolleson	.50
4	Don Slaught	.50
5	Alan Bannister	.50
6	Bobby Jones	.50
7	Glenn Brummer	.50
8	Luis Pujols	.50
9	Pete O'Brien	.50
11	Toby Harrah	.50
13	Tommy Dunbar	.50
15	Larry Parrish	.50
16	Mike Mason	.50
17	Curtis Wilkerson	.50
24	Dave Schmidt	.50
25	Buddy Bell	.50
27	Greg Harris	.50
30	Dave Rozema	.50
32	Gary Ward	.50
36	Dickie Noles	.50
41	Chris Welsh	.50
44	Cliff Johnson	.50
46	Burt Hooton	.50
48	Dave Stewart	.50
49	Charlie Hough	.50
---	Trainers (Danny Wheat, Bill Ziegler)	.50
---	Rangers Coaches (Rich Donnelly, Glenn Ezell, Tom House, Art Howe, Wayne Terwilliger)	.50

1986 Performance Printing Texas Rangers

For the second time, the Texas Rangers issued a full-color card set in conjunction with this local printing company. Fronts of the 28-card set include player name, position and team logo beneath the color photo. Backs of the 2-3/8" x 3-1/2" cards are in black and white, with a small portrait photo of each player along with personal and professional statistics. Cards were distributed at the August 23 Rangers home game, and the set includes all of the Rangers' fine rookies such as Bobby Witt, Pete Incaviglia and Edwin Correa and Ruben Sierra.

		NM/M
	Complete Set (28):	5.00
	Common Player:	.25
0	Oddibe McDowell	.25
1	Scott Fletcher	.25
2	Bobby Valentine	.25
3	Ruben Sierra	.35
4	Don Slaught	.25
9	Pete O'Brien	.25
11	Toby Harrah	.25
12	Geno Petralli	.25
15	Larry Parrish	.25
16	Mike Mason	.25
17	Darrell Porter	.25
18	Edwin Correa	.25
19	Curtis Wilkerson	.25
22	Steve Buechele	.25
23	Jose Guzman	.25
24	Ricky Wright	.25
27	Greg Harris	.25
28	Mitch Williams	.25
29	Pete Incaviglia	.50
32	Gary Ward	.25
34	Dale Mohorcic	.25
42	Jeff Russell	.25
44	Tom Paciorek	.25
46	Mike Loynd	.25
48	Bobby Witt	.25
49	Charlie Hough	.25
---	Coaching Staff (Joe Ferguson, Tim Foli, Tom House, Art Howe, Tom Robson)	.25
---	Trainers (Danny Wheat, Bill Ziegler)	.25

1981 Perma-Graphics All-Star Credit Cards

Using the same "credit card" style of its previous 1981 issue, Perma-Graphics issued an 18-card set in the fall of 1981 featuring the starting players from the 1981 All-Star Game. The front of the card contains a full-color photo, plus the player's name, position and team. The back includes personal data, career records, highlights and an "autograph panel."

		NM/M
	Complete Set (18):	15.00
	Common Player:	1.00
1	Gary Carter	1.50
2	Dave Concepcion	1.00
3	Andre Dawson	1.25
4	George Foster	1.00
5	Davey Lopes	1.00
6	Dave Parker	1.00
7	Pete Rose	5.00
8	Mike Schmidt	4.00
9	Fernando Valenzuela	1.00
10	George Brett	4.00
11a	Rod Carew/Outfield	2.50
11b	Rod Carew/First base	2.50
11c	Rod Carew/First base (#20 on back.)	2.50
11d	Rod Carew/First base (#29 on back.)	2.50
12	Bucky Dent	1.00
13	Carlton Fisk	1.50
14	Reggie Jackson	3.00
15	Jack Morris	1.00
16	Willie Randolph	1.00
17	Ken Singleton	1.00
18	Dave Winfield	1.50

Super Star Credit Cards

Issued in 1981 by Perma-Graphics of Maryland Heights, Mo., this innovative 32-card set was printed on high-impact, permanently laminated vinyl to give the appearance of a real credit card. The front of the wallet-sized cards includes career statistics and highlights, along with an "autograph panel" for obtaining the player's signature.

		NM/M
	Complete Set (32):	25.00
	Common Player:	1.00
1	Johnny Bench	2.00

2	Mike Schmidt	4.00
3	George Brett	4.00
4	Carl Yastrzemski	2.00
5	Pete Rose	5.00
6	Bob Horner	1.00
7	Reggie Jackson	3.00
8	Keith Hernandez	1.00
9	George Foster	1.00
10	Garry Templeton	1.00
11	Tom Seaver	1.25
12	Steve Garvey	1.25
13	Dave Parker	1.00
14	Willie Stargell	1.50
15	Cecil Cooper	1.00
16	Steve Carlton	1.50
17	Ted Simmons	1.00
18	Dave Kingman	1.00
19	Rickey Henderson	1.50
20	Fred Lynn	1.00
21	Dave Winfield	1.50
22a	Rod Carew (Uniform #20 on back.)	2.00
22b	Rod Carew (Uniform #29 on back.)	2.00
23	Jim Rice	1.25
24	Bruce Sutter	1.50
25	Cesar Cedeno	1.00
26	Nolan Ryan	6.00
27	Dusty Baker	1.00
28	Jim Palmer	1.50
29	Gorman Thomas	1.00
30	Ben Oglivie	1.00
31	Willie Wilson	1.00
32	Gary Carter	1.50

1982 Perma-Graphics All-Star Credit Cards

Perma-Graphics issued its second "All-Star Credit Card" set in the fall of 1982. Consisting of 18 cards, the set pictured the starters from both leagues in the 1982 All-Star Game. The set was also available in a more limited "gold" version.

		NM/M
	Complete Set (18):	15.00
	Common Player:	1.00
	Gold:	3X
1	Dennis Eckersley	1.50
2	Cecil Cooper	1.00
3	Carlton Fisk	2.00
4	Robin Yount	2.00
5	Bobby Grich	1.00
6	Rickey Henderson	2.00
7	Reggie Jackson	3.00
8	Fred Lynn	1.00
9	George Brett	4.00
10	Gary Carter	2.00
11	Dave Concepcion	1.00
12	Andre Dawson	1.25
13	Tim Raines	1.00
14	Dale Murphy	1.25
15	Steve Rogers	1.00
16	Pete Rose	5.00
17	Mike Schmidt	4.00
18	Manny Trillo	1.00

1982 Perma-Graphics Super Star Credit Cards

Perma-Graphics reduced its "Superstar Credit Card Set" to 24 players in 1982, maintaining the same basic credit card appearance. The player photos on the front of the cards are surrounded by a wood-tone border and the backs include the usual personal data, career statistics, highlights and autograph panel. The set was also issued in a limited-edition "gold" version.

		NM/M
	Complete Set (24):	25.00
	Common Player:	1.00
	Gold:	3X

1	Johnny Bench	2.00
2	Tom Seaver	2.00
3	Mike Schmidt	4.00
4	Gary Carter	1.50
5	Willie Stargell	1.50
6	Tim Raines	1.00
7	Bill Madlock	1.00
8	Keith Hernandez	1.00
9	Pete Rose	5.00
10	Steve Carlton	1.00
11	Steve Garvey	1.25
12	Fernando Valenzuela	1.00
13	Carl Yastrzemski	2.00
14	Dave Winfield	1.00
15	Carney Lansford	1.00
16	Rollie Fingers	1.00
17	Tony Armas	1.00
18	Cecil Cooper	1.00
19	George Brett	4.00
20	Reggie Jackson	3.00
21	Rod Carew	1.50
22	Eddie Murray	1.50
23	Rickey Henderson	1.50
24	Kirk Gibson	1.00

1983 Perma-Graphics All-Star Credit Cards

The final issue from Perma-Graphics, this 18-card set was produced in the fall of 1983 and features the 18 starting players from the 1983 All-Star Game. Similar to other Perma-Graphics sets, the cards were printed on wallet-size vinyl to give the appearance of a real credit card. The set was also available in a limited-edition "gold" version.

		NM/M
	Complete Set (18):	17.50
	Common Player:	1.00
	Gold:	3X
1	George Brett	4.00
2	Rod Carew	2.00
3	Fred Lynn	1.00
4	Jim Rice	1.50
5	Ted Simmons	1.00
6	Dave Stieb	1.00
7	Manny Trillo	1.00
8	Dave Winfield	2.00
9	Robin Yount	2.00
10	Gary Carter	2.00
11	Andre Dawson	1.50
12	Dale Murphy	1.50
13	Al Oliver	1.00
14	Tim Raines	1.00
15	Steve Sax	1.00
16	Mike Schmidt	4.00
17	Ozzie Smith	3.00
18	Mario Soto	1.00

Super Star Credit Cards

Similar in design to its previous sets, Perma-Graphics increased the number of cards in

1	Johnny Bench	2.00
2	Tom Seaver	2.00
3	Mike Schmidt	4.00
4	Gary Carter	1.50
5	Willie Stargell	1.50
6	Tim Raines	1.00
7	Bill Madlock	1.00
8	Keith Hernandez	1.00
9	Pete Rose	5.00
10	Steve Carlton	1.00
11	Steve Garvey	1.25
12	Fernando Valenzuela	1.00
13	Carl Yastrzemski	2.00
14	Dave Winfield	1.00
15	Carney Lansford	1.00
16	Rollie Fingers	1.00
17	Tony Armas	1.00
18	Cecil Cooper	1.00
19	George Brett	4.00
20	Reggie Jackson	3.00
21	Rod Carew	1.50
22	Eddie Murray	1.50
23	Rickey Henderson	1.50
24	Kirk Gibson	1.00

its 1983 "Superstar" set to 36, including 18 players from each league. The front of the vinyl card has a full-color photo with the player's name, team, league and position below. The backs contain career records, highlights and autograph panel. The cards were also issued in a special "gold" version, more limited than the regular edition.

		NM/M
	Complete Set (36):	25.00
	Common Player:	1.00
	Gold:	3X
1	Bill Buckner	1.00
2	Steve Carlton	2.00
3	Gary Carter	2.00
4	Andre Dawson	1.25
5	Pedro Guerrero	1.00
6	George Hendrick	1.00
7	Keith Hernandez	1.00
8	Bill Madlock	1.00
9	Dale Murphy	1.25
10	Al Oliver	1.00
11	Dave Parker	1.00
12	Darrell Porter	1.00
13	Pete Rose	5.00
14	Mike Schmidt	4.00
15	Lonnie Smith	1.00
16	Ozzie Smith	2.50
17	Bruce Sutter	1.50
18	Fernando Valenzuela	1.00
19	George Brett	4.00
20	Rod Carew	2.00
21	Cecil Cooper	1.00
22	Doug DeCinces	1.00
23	Rollie Fingers	1.50
24	Damaso Garcia	1.00
25	Toby Harrah	1.00
26	Rickey Henderson	2.00
27	Reggie Jackson	3.00
28	Hal McRae	1.00
29	Eddie Murray	2.00
30	Lance Parrish	1.00
31	Jim Rice	1.25
32	Gorman Thomas	1.00
33	Willie Wilson	1.00
34	Dave Winfield	2.00
35	Carl Yastrzemski	2.50
36	Robin Yount	2.00

1983 Gaylord Perry Career Highlights

Although their name does not appear anywhere on the six cards in this set, Topps was the manufacturer of this career highlights issue which was distributed by Perry's own memorabilia company. In standard 2-1/2" x 3-1/2" format, card fronts feature a color photo with various colored borders and name plates. The year of the career highlight printed on back is presented in the lower-right. Backs have a card number in a peanut and a write-up of the career accomplishment, printed in brown and orange.

	NM/M
Complete Set (6):	8.00
Common Card:	1.50
1 Gaylord Perry (First win.)	1.50
2 Gaylord Perry (No-hitter.)	1.50
3 Gaylord Perry (Cy Young Award)	1.50
4 Gaylord Perry (2,500th K)	1.50
5 Gaylord Perry (Cy Young/3,000th K)	1.50
6 Gaylord Perry (300th win)	1.50

1981 Peter Pan Bakery Discs

(See 1981 MSA/Peter Pan - Sunbeam Bakery Discs.)

1991 Petro Canada All-Star FanFest Standups

Petro-Canada Standups are vaguely reminiscent of the 1964 Topps Standups. The set was distributed at Fanfest in Toronto in conjunction with the All-Star Game. The folded card as issued measures 2-7/8" x 3-9/16". The card can be unfolded to reveal a die-cut action figure of the player superimposed in front of a photo of stadium surroundings. The base which the player stands on has major league and All-Star Game statistics, with career highlights on the back and a player quiz.

	NM/M
Complete Set (26):	12.50
Common Player:	.25
1 Cal Ripken, Jr.	3.00
2 Greg Olson	.25
3 Roger Clemens	2.00
4 Ryne Sandberg	1.50
5 Dave Winfield	1.00
6 Eric Davis	.25
7 Carlton Fisk	1.00
8 Mike Scott	.25
9 Sandy Alomar, Jr.	.25
10 Tim Wallach	.25
11 Cecil Fielder	.25
12 Dwight Gooden	.25
13 George Brett	2.00
14 Dale Murphy	.50
15 Paul Molitor	1.00
16 Barry Bonds	3.00
17 Kirby Puckett	1.50
18 Ozzie Smith	1.50
19 Don Mattingly	2.00
20 Will Clark	.25
21 Rickey Henderson	1.00
22 Orel Hershiser	.25
23 Ken Griffey Jr.	2.50
24 Tony Gwynn	1.50
25 Nolan Ryan	3.00
26 Kelly Gruber	.25

1998-99 Philadelphia A's Historical Society

A major undertaking by the Philadelphia A's Historical Society was the creation

of this collectors card set in conjunction with the group's fourth reunion in 1998. Card designs are strongly reminiscent of the classic Topps and Bowman cards of the early 1950s. Fronts have a painting of each player by Ron Joyner, noted sports artist. Backs have a cartoon, career stats with the A's and lifetime, biographical data and career highlights. Backs are printed in blue and black on white. A card of 1908-09 A's Joe Jackson has been printed in a limited edition of 500 numbered cards and is available only in those sets sold directly through the Society at its original $18.50 price. Seventy-five sets of the cards, which included a sample Joe Jackson card and a pair of large-format cards of Jimmie Foxx and Roger Cramer, were sold as uncut sheets.

	NM/M
Complete Set, w/Jackson (42):	24.00
Complete Set, no/Jackson (41):	18.50
Complete Set, uncut sheet:	60.00
Common Player:	.50
1 Connie Mack	.75
2 Sam Chapman	.50
3 Bobby Shantz	.60
4 Al Brancato	.50
5 Bob Dillinger	.50
6 Irv Hall	.50
7 Joe Hauser	.50
8 Taffy Wright	.50
9 Gus Zernial	.60
10 Ray Murray	.50
11 Skeeter Kell	.50
12 Morrie Martin	.50
13 Pete Suder	.50
14 Pinky Higgins	.50
15 Allie Clark	.50
16 Hank Wyse	.50
17 George Kell	.75
18 Hank Majeski	.50
19 Jimmie Foxx	1.00
20 Crash Davis	.50
21 Elmer Valo	.50
22 Ray Coleman	.50
23 Carl Scheib	.50
24 Billy Hitchcock	.50
25 Earle Brucker Jr.	.50
26 Dave Philley	.50
27 Joe DeMaestri	.50
28 Eddie Collins Jr.	.50
29 Eddie Joost	.50
30 Spook Jacobs	.50
31 Ferris Fain	.60
32 Eddie Robinson	.50
33 Vic Power	.60
34 Lou Brissie	.50
35 Bill Renna	.50
36 Nellie Fox	1.00
37 Lou Limmer	.50
38 Eddie Collins Sr.	1.00
39 Roger Cramer	.50
40 Joe Astroth	.50
--- Joe Jackson (# of 500)	8.00
--- Joe Jackson (sample overprint)	4.00
--- Roger Cramer (3-1/2" x 6")	2.00
--- Jimmie Foxx (3-1/2" x 8-1/2")	4.00
41 Bill Werber (Issued 1999)	.50

2001 Philadelphia A's Historical Society Update

Selected by the Society's members as "Fan Favorites" of each decade from the 1900s

through the 1930s, this collectors' issue updates the group's original 1998-99 card issue. Cards are in 2-5/8" x 3-3/4" format with painted portraits on front. Black, blue and white backs have a cartoon highlight, personal data, career summary and lifetime A's and major league stats. The cards were also pictured on a 10-3/4" x 12-3/4" "Decades of Greatness" uncut sheet.

	NM/M
Complete Set (4):	6.00
Common Player:	2.00
Uncut Sheet:	10.00
42 Rube Oldring	2.00
43 Stuffy McInnis	2.00
44 Bing Miller	2.00
45 Bob Johnson	2.00

1985 Philadelphia Phillies Police

This is a brilliantly colored 2-5/8" x 4-1/8" set, co-sponsored by the Phillies and Cigna Corp.. Card fronts include the player name, number, position and team logo. The 16 cards are numbered on the back and include biographical information and a safety tip. The cards were distributed by several Philadelphia area police departments.

	NM/M
Complete Set (16):	4.00
Common Player:	.15
1 Juan Samuel	.15
2 Von Hayes	.15
3 Ozzie Virgil	.15
4 Mike Schmidt	3.50
5 Greg Gross	.15
6 Tim Corcoran	.15
7 Jerry Koosman	.15
8 Jeff Stone	.15
9 Glenn Wilson	.15
10 Steve Jeltz	.15
11 Garry Maddox	.15
12 Steve Carlton	1.50
13 John Denny	.15
14 Kevin Gross	.15
15 Shane Rawley	.15
16 Charlie Hudson	.15

1986 Philadelphia Phillies Fire Safety

For the second straight year, the Philadelphia Phillies issued a 16-card safety set. However, in 1986 the set was issued in conjunction with the Philadelphia Fire Department rather than the police. Cigna Corp. remained a sponsor. The cards,

which measure 2-5/8" x 4-1/8" in size, feature full color photos. Along with other pertinent information, the card backs contain a short player biography and a "Tips From The Dugout" fire safety hint.

	NM/M
Complete Set (16):	3.00
Common Player:	.15
1 Juan Samuel	.15
2 Don Carman	.15
3 Von Hayes	.15
4 Kent Tekulve	.15
5 Greg Gross	.15
6 Shane Rawley	.15
7 Darren Daulton	.25
8 Kevin Gross	.15
9 Steve Jeltz	.15
10 Mike Schmidt	3.00
11 Steve Bedrosian	.15
12 Gary Redus	.15
13 Charles Hudson	.15
14 John Russell	.15
15 Fred Toliver	.15
16 Glenn Wilson	.15

2005 Philadelphia Phillies Medallion Collection

A set of 21 commemorative medallions was sponsored by the Philadelphia Daily News and The Inquirer in this early-season promotion. Coupons found in the newspapers between April 18 and May 18 could be redeemed at newsstands (along with $2.99) for that day's medallion. Larger and thicker than a quarter, the 1-3/16" diameter medals are struck in nickel and have on their fronts an enameled portrait photo. A team logo dominates the back. A colorful, photo-filled 7-3/4" x 13" album was available to house the pieces. The medals are listed here in order of their issue.

	NM/M
Complete Set (21):	65.00
Common Player:	3.00
Album:	8.00
(1) Jim Thome	5.00
(2) Placido Polanco	3.00
(3) Randy Wolf	3.00
(4) Mike Lieberthal	3.00
(5) Jon Lieber	3.00
(6) Jimmy Rollins	4.50
(7) Kenny Lofton	3.00
(8) Brett Myers	3.00
(9) Tomas Perez	3.00
(10) Rheal Cormier	3.00
(11) Vicente Padilla	3.00
(12) David Bell	3.00
(13) Bobby Abreu	4.50
(14) Tim Worrell	3.00
(15) Ryan Madson	3.00
(16) Chase Utley	4.50
(17) Charlie Manuel	3.00
(18) Jason Michaels	3.00
(19) Pat Burrell	5.00
(20) Billy Wagner	3.00
(21) Phillie Phanatic/ Mascot	3.00

1992 Pinnacle

Score entered the high-end card market with the release of this 620-card set. The cards feature black borders surrounding a white frame with a full-color action photo inside. The player extends beyond the natural background. The backs are horizontal and feature a closeup photo, statistics, team logo, biographical information and career notes. Several subsets can be found within the set including "Idols, Sidelines, Grips, Shades" and "Technicians." The set was released in two 310-card series.

	NM/M
Complete Set (620):	15.00
Common Player:	.05
Foil Pack (16):	.75
Foil Box (36):	17.50
Jumbo Pack (24+3):	1.50
Jumbo Box (12):	22.50
1 Frank Thomas	.75
2 Benito Santiago	.05
3 Carlos Baerga	.05
4 Cecil Fielder	.05
5 Barry Larkin	.05
6 Ozzie Smith	1.00
7 Willie McGee	.05
8 Paul Molitor	.75
9 Andy Van Slyke	.05
10 Ryne Sandberg	1.00
11 Kevin Seitzer	.05
12 Len Dykstra	.05
13 Edgar Martinez	.05
14 Ruben Sierra	.05
15 Howard Johnson	.05
16 Dave Henderson	.05
17 Devon White	.05
18 Terry Pendleton	.05
19 Steve Finley	.05
20 Kirby Puckett	1.00
21 Orel Hershiser	.05
22 Hal Morris	.05
23 Don Mattingly	1.25
24 Delino DeShields	.05
25 Dennis Eckersley	.60
26 Ellis Burks	.05
27 Jay Buhner	.05
28 Matt Williams	.05
29 Lou Whitaker	.05
30 Alex Fernandez	.05
31 Albert Belle	.05
32 Todd Zeile	.05
33 Tony Pena	.05
34 Jay Bell	.05
35 Rafael Palmeiro	.65
36 Wes Chamberlain	.05
37 George Bell	.05
38 Robin Yount	.75
39 Vince Coleman	.05
40 Bruce Hurst	.05
41 Harold Baines	.05
42 Chuck Finley	.05
43 Ken Caminiti	.05
44 Ben McDonald	.05
45 Roberto Alomar	.15
46 Chili Davis	.05
47 Bill Doran	.05
48 Jerald Clark	.05
49 Jose Lind	.05
50 Nolan Ryan	2.00
51 Phil Plantier	.05
52 Gary DiSarcina	.05
53 Kevin Bass	.05
54 Pat Kelly	.05
55 Mark Wohlers	.05
56 Walt Weiss	.05
57 Lenny Harris	.05
58 Ivan Calderon	.05
59 Harold Reynolds	.05
60 George Brett	1.25
61 Gregg Olson	.05
62 Orlando Merced	.05
63 Steve Decker	.05
64 John Franco	.05
65 Greg Maddux	1.00
66 Alex Cole	.05
67 Dave Hollins	.05
68 Kent Hrbek	.05
69 Tom Pagnozzi	.05
70 Jeff Bagwell	.75
71 Jim Gantner	.05
72 Matt Nokes	.05
73 Brian Harper	.05
74 Andy Benes	.05
75 Tom Glavine	.35
76 Terry Steinbach	.05
77 Dennis Martinez	.05
78 John Olerud	.05
79 Ozzie Guillen	.05
80 Darryl Strawberry	.05
81 Gary Gaetti	.05
82 Dave Righetti	.05
83 Chris Hoiles	.05
84 Andujar Cedeno	.05
85 Jack Clark	.05
86 David Howard	.05
87 Bill Gullickson	.05
88 Bernard Gilkey	.05
89 Kevin Elster	.05
90 Kevin Maas	.05
91 Mark Lewis	.05
92 Greg Vaughn	.05
93 Bret Barberie	.05
94 Dave Smith	.05
95 Roger Clemens	1.25
96 Doug Drabek	.05
97 Omar Vizquel	.05
98 Jose Guzman	.05
99 Juan Samuel	.05
100 Dave Justice	.05
101 Tom Browning	.05
102 Mark Gubicza	.05
103 Mickey Morandini	.05
104 Ed Whitson	.05
105 Lance Parrish	.05
106 Scott Erickson	.05
107 Jack McDowell	.05
108 Dave Stieb	.05
109 Mike Moore	.05
110 Travis Fryman	.05
111 Dwight Gooden	.05
112 Fred McGriff	.05
113 Alan Trammell	.05
114 Roberto Kelly	.05
115 Andre Dawson	.25
116 Bill Landrum	.05
117 Brian McRae	.05
118 B.J. Surhoff	.05
119 Chuck Knoblauch	.05
120 Steve Olin	.05
121 Robin Ventura	.05
122 Will Clark	.05
123 Tino Martinez	.05
124 Dale Murphy	.25
125 Pete O'Brien	.05
126 Ray Lankford	.05
127 Juan Gonzalez	.40
128 Ron Gant	.05
129 Marquis Grissom	.05
130 Jose Canseco	.50
131 Mike Greenwell	.05
132 Mark Langston	.05
133 Brett Butler	.05
134 Kelly Gruber	.05
135 Chris Sabo	.05
136 Mark Grace	.05
137 Tony Fernandez	.05
138 Glenn Davis	.05
139 Pedro Munoz	.05
140 Craig Biggio	.05
141 Pete Schourek	.05
142 Mike Boddicker	.05
143 Robby Thompson	.05
144 Mel Hall	.05
145 Bryan Harvey	.05
146 Mike LaValliere	.05
147 John Kruk	.05
148 Joe Carter	.05
149 Greg Olson	.05
150 Julio Franco	.05
151 Darryl Hamilton	.05
152 Felix Fermin	.05
153 Jose Offerman	.05
154 Paul O'Neill	.05
155 Tommy Greene	.05
156 Ivan Rodriguez	.65
157 Dave Stewart	.05
158 Jeff Reardon	.05
159 Felix Jose	.05
160 Doug Dascenzo	.05
161 Tim Wallach	.05
162 Dan Plesac	.05
163 Luis Gonzalez	.05
164 Mike Henneman	.05
165 Mike Devereaux	.05
166 Luis Polonia	.05
167 Mike Sharperson	.05
168 Chris Donnels	.05
169 Greg Harris	.05
170 Deion Sanders	.05
171 Mike Schooler	.05
172 Jose DeJesus	.05
173 Jeff Montgomery	.05
174 Milt Cuyler	.05
175 Wade Boggs	1.00
176 Kevin Tapani	.05
177 Bill Spiers	.05
178 Tim Raines	.05
179 Randy Milligan	.05
180 Rob Dibble	.05
181 Kirt Manwaring	.05

182	Pascual Perez	.05
183	Juan Guzman	.05
184	John Smiley	.05
185	David Segui	.05
186	Omar Olivares	.05
187	Joe Slusarski	.05
188	Erik Hanson	.05
189	Mark Portugal	.05
190	Walt Terrell	.05
191	John Smoltz	.05
192	Wilson Alvarez	.05
193	Jimmy Key	.05
194	Larry Walker	.05
195	Lee Smith	.05
196	Pete Harnisch	.05
197	Mike Harkey	.05
198	Frank Tanana	.05
199	Terry Mulholland	.05
200	Cal Ripken, Jr.	2.00
201	Dave Magadan	.05
202	Bud Black	.05
203	Terry Shumpert	.05
204	Mike Mussina	.40
205	Mo Vaughn	.05
206	Steve Farr	.05
207	Darrin Jackson	.05
208	Jerry Browne	.05
209	Jeff Russell	.05
210	Mike Scioscia	.05
211	Rick Aguilera	.05
212	Jaime Navarro	.05
213	Randy Tomlin	.05
214	Bobby Thigpen	.05
215	Mark Gardner	.05
216	Norm Charlton	.05
217	Mark McGwire	1.75
218	Skeeter Barnes	.05
219	Bob Tewksbury	.05
220	Junior Felix	.05
221	Sam Horn	.05
222	Jody Reed	.05
223	Luis Sojo	.05
224	Jerome Walton	.05
225	Darryl Kile	.05
226	Mickey Tettleton	.05
227	Dan Pasqua	.05
228	Jim Gott	.05
229	Bernie Williams	.05
230	Shane Mack	.05
231	Steve Avery	.05
232	Dave Valle	.05
233	Mark Leonard	.05
234	Spike Owen	.05
235	Gary Sheffield	.20
236	Steve Chitren	.05
237	Zane Smith	.05
238	Tom Gordon	.05
239	Jose Oquendo	.05
240	Todd Stottlemyre	.05
241	Darren Daulton	.05
242	Tim Naehring	.05
243	Tony Phillips	.05
244	Shawon Dunston	.05
245	Manuel Lee	.05
246	Mike Pagliarulo	.05
247	Jim Thome (Rookie Prospect)	.65
248	Luis Mercedes (Rookie Prospect)	.05
249	Cal Eldred (Rookie Prospect)	.05
250	Derek Bell (Rookie Prospect)	.05
251	Arthur Rhodes (Rookie Prospect)	.05
252	Scott Cooper (Rookie Prospect)	.05
253	Roberto Hernandez (Rookie Prospect)	.05
254	Mo Sanford (Rookie Prospect)	.05
255	Scott Servais (Rookie Prospect)	.05
256	Eric Karros (Rookie Prospect)	.05
257	Andy Mota	.05
258	Keith Mitchell	.05
259	Joel Johnston (Rookie Prospect)	.05
260	John Wehner (Rookie Prospect)	.05
261	Gino Minutelli (Rookie Prospect)	.05
262	Greg Gagne	.05
263	Stan Royer (Rookie Prospect)	.05
264	Carlos Garcia (Rookie Prospect)	.05
265	Andy Ashby (Rookie Prospect)	.05
266	Kim Batiste (Rookie Prospect)	.05
267	Julio Valera (Rookie Prospect)	.05
268	Royce Clayton (Rookie Prospect)	.05
269	Gary Scott (Rookie Prospect)	.05
270	Kirk Dressendorfer (Rookie Prospect)	.05
271	Sean Berry (Rookie Prospect)	.05
272	Lance Dickson (Rookie Prospect)	.05
273	Rob Maurer (Rookie Prospect)	.05
274	Scott Brosius (Rookie Prospect)	.05
275	Dave Fleming (Rookie Prospect)	.05
276	Lenny Webster (Rookie Prospect)	.05
277	Mike Humphreys	.05
278	Freddie Benavides (Rookie Prospect)	.05
279	Harvey Pulliam (Rookie Prospect)	.05
280	Jeff Carter (Rookie Prospect)	.05
281	Jim Abbott, Nolan Ryan (Idols)	.25
282	Wade Boggs, George Brett (Idols)	.25
283	Ken Griffey Jr., Rickey Henderson (Idols)	.50
284	Dale Murphy, Wally Joyner (Idols)	.10
285	Chuck Knoblauch, Ozzie Smith (Idols)	.20
286	Robin Ventura, Lou Gehrig (Idols)	.20
287	Robin Yount(Sidelines - Motocross)	.30
288	Bob Tewksbury (Sidelines - Cartoonist)	.05
289	Kirby Puckett (Sidelines - Pool Player)	.50
290	Kenny Lofton (Sidelines - Basketball Player)	.05
291	Jack McDowell (Sidelines - Guitarist)	.05
292	John Burkett (Sidelines - Bowler)	.05
293	Dwight Smith (Sidelines - Singer)	.05
294	Nolan Ryan (Sidelines - Cattle Rancher)	1.00
295	Manny Ramirez RC (1st Round Draft Pick)	2.50
296	Cliff Floyd RC (1st Round Draft Pick)	.50
297	Al Shirley RC (1st Round Draft Pick)	.05
298	Brian Barber RC (1st Round Draft Pick)	.05
299	Jon Farrell RC (1st Round Draft Pick)	.05
300	Scott Ruffcorn RC (1st Round Draft Pick)	.05
301	Tyrone Hill RC (1st Round Draft Pick)	.05
302	Benji Gil RC (1st Round Draft Pick)	.05
303	Tyler Green RC (1st Round Draft Pick)	.05
304	Allen Watson (Shades)	.05
305	Jay Buhner (Shades)	.05
306	Roberto Alomar (Shades)	.05
307	Chuck Knoblauch (Shades)	.05
308	Darryl Strawberry (Shades)	.05
309	Danny Tartabull (Shades)	.05
310	Bobby Bonilla (Shades)	.05
311	Mike Felder	.05
312	Storm Davis	.05
313	Tim Teufel	.05
314	Tom Brunansky	.05
315	Rex Hudler	.05
316	Dave Otto	.05
317	Jeff King	.05
318	Dan Gladden	.05
319	Bill Pecota	.05
320	Franklin Stubbs	.05
321	Gary Carter	.75
322	Melido Perez	.05
323	Eric Davis	.05
324	Greg Myers	.05
325	Pete Incaviglia	.05
326	Von Hayes	.05
327	Greg Swindell	.05
328	Steve Sax	.05
329	Chuck McElroy	.05
330	Gregg Jefferies	.05
331	Joe Oliver	.05
332	Paul Faries	.05
333	David West	.05
334	Craig Grebeck	.05
335	Chris Hammond	.05
336	Billy Ripken	.05
337	Scott Sanderson	.05
338	Dick Schofield	.05
339	Bob Milacki	.05
340	Kevin Reimer	.05
341	Jose DeLeon	.05
342	Henry Cotto	.05
343	Daryl Boston	.05
344	Kevin Gross	.05
345	Milt Thompson	.05
346	Luis Rivera	.05
347	Al Osuna	.05
348	Rob Deer	.05
349	Tim Leary	.05
350	Mike Stanton	.05
351	Dean Palmer	.05
352	Trevor Wilson	.05
353	Mark Eichhorn	.05
354	Scott Aldred	.05
355	Mark Whiten	.05
356	Leo Gomez	.05
357	Rafael Belliard	.05
358	Carlos Quintana	.05
359	Mark Davis	.05
360	Chris Nabholz	.05
361	Carlton Fisk	.75
362	Joe Orsulak	.05
363	Eric Anthony	.05
364	Greg Hibbard	.05
365	Scott Leius	.05
366	Hensley Meulens	.05
367	Chris Bosio	.05
368	Brian Downing	.05
369	Sammy Sosa	1.00
370	Stan Belinda	.05
371	Joe Grahe	.05
372	Luis Salazar	.05
373	Lance Johnson	.05
374	Kal Daniels	.05
375	Dave Winfield	.75
376	Brook Jacoby	.05
377	Mariano Duncan	.05
378	Ron Darling	.05
379	Randy Johnson	.75
380	Chito Martinez	.05
381	Andres Galarraga	.05
382	Willie Randolph	.05
383	Charles Nagy	.05
384	Tim Belcher	.05
385	Duane Ward	.05
386	Vicente Palacios	.05
387	Mike Gallego	.05
388	Rich DeLucia	.05
389	Scott Radinsky	.05
390	Damon Berryhill	.05
391	Kirk McCaskill	.05
392	Pedro Guerrero	.05
393	Kevin Mitchell	.05
394	Dickie Thon	.05
395	Bobby Bonilla	.05
396	Bill Wegman	.05
397	Dave Martinez	.05
398	Rick Sutcliffe	.05
399	Larry Andersen	.05
400	Tony Gwynn	1.00
401	Rickey Henderson	.75
402	Greg Cadaret	.05
403	Keith Miller	.05
404	Bip Roberts	.05
405	Kevin Brown	.05
406	Mitch Williams	.05
407	Frank Viola	.05
408	Darren Lewis	.05
409	Bob Walk	.05
410	Bob Walk	.05
411	Todd Frohwirth	.05
412	Brian Hunter	.05
413	Ron Karkovice	.05
414	Mike Morgan	.05
415	Joe Hesketh	.05
416	Don Slaught	.05
417	Tom Henke	.05
418	Kurt Stillwell	.05
419	Hector Villanueva	.05
420	Glenallen Hill	.05
421	Pat Borders	.05
422	Charlie Hough	.05
423	Charlie Leibrandt	.05
424	Eddie Murray	.75
425	Jesse Barfield	.05
426	Mark Lemke	.05
427	Kevin McReynolds	.05
428	Gilberto Reyes	.05
429	Ramon Martinez	.05
430	Steve Buechele	.05
431	David Wells	.05
432	Kyle Abbott (Rookie Prospect)	.05
433	John Habyan	.05
434	Kevin Appier	.05
435	Gene Larkin	.05
436	Sandy Alomar, Jr.	.05
437	Mike Jackson	.05
438	Todd Benzinger	.05
439	Teddy Higuera	.05
440	Reggie Sanders (Rookie Prospect)	.05
441	Mark Carreon	.05
442	Bret Saberhagen	.05
443	Gene Nelson	.05
444	Jay Howell	.05
445	Roger McDowell	.05
446	Sid Bream	.05
447	Mackey Sasser	.05
448	Bill Swift	.05
449	Hubie Brooks	.05
450	David Cone	.05
451	Bobby Witt	.05
452	Brady Anderson	.05
453	Lee Stevens	.05
454	Luis Aquino	.05
455	Carney Lansford	.05
456	Carlos Hernandez (Rookie Prospect)	.05
457	Danny Jackson	.05
458	Gerald Young	.05
459	Tom Candiotti	.05
460	Billy Hatcher	.05
461	John Wetteland	.05
462	Mike Bordick	.05
463	Don Robinson	.05
464	Jeff Johnson	.05
465	Lonnie Smith	.05
466	Paul Assenmacher	.05
467	Alvin Davis	.05
468	Jim Eisenreich	.05
469	Brent Mayne	.05
470	Jeff Brantley	.05
471	Tim Burke	.05
472	Pat Mahomes RC (Rookie Prospect)	.05
473	Ryan Bowen	.05
474	Bryn Smith	.05
475	Mike Flanagan	.05
476	Reggie Jefferson (Rookie Prospect)	.05
477	Jeff Blauser	.05
478	Craig Lefferts	.05
479	Todd Worrell	.05
480	Scott Scudder	.05
481	Kirk Gibson	.05
482	Kenny Rogers	.05
483	Jack Morris	.05
484	Russ Swan	.05
485	Mike Huff	.05
486	Ken Hill	.05
487	Geronimo Pena	.05
488	Charlie O'Brien	.05
489	Mike Maddux	.05
490	Scott Livingstone (Rookie Prospect)	.05
491	Carl Willis	.05
492	Kelly Downs	.05
493	Dennis Cook	.05
494	Joe Magrane	.05
495	Bob Kipper	.05
496	Jose Mesa	.05
497	Charlie Hayes	.05
498	Joe Girardi	.05
499	Doug Jones	.05
500	Barry Bonds	2.00
501	Bill Krueger	.05
502	Glenn Braggs	.05
503	Eric King	.05
504	Frank Castillo	.05
505	Mike Gardiner	.05
506	Cory Snyder	.05
507	Steve Howe	.05
508	Jose Rijo	.05
509	Sid Fernandez	.05
510	Archi Cianfrocco RC (Rookie Prospect)	.05
511	Mark Guthrie	.05
512	Bob Ojeda	.05
513	John Doherty (Rookie Prospect)	.05
514	Dante Bichette	.05
515	Juan Berenguer	.05
516	Jeff Robinson	.05
517	Mike MacFarlane	.05
518	Matt Young	.05
519	Otis Nixon	.05
520	Brian Holman	.05
521	Chris Haney	.05
522	Jeff Kent RC (Rookie Prospect)	.75
523	Chad Curtis RC (Rookie Prospect)	.25
524	Vince Horsman	.05
525	Rod Nichols	.05
526	Peter Hoy RC (Rookie Prospect)	.05
527	Shawn Boskie	.05
528	Alejandro Pena	.05
529	Dave Burba (Rookie Prospect)	.05
530	Ricky Jordan	.05
531	David Silvestri (Rookie Prospect)	.05
532	John Patterson (Rookie Prospect)	.05
533	Jeff Branson (Rookie Prospect)	.05
534	Derrick May (Rookie Prospect)	.05
535	Esteban Beltre (Rookie Prospect)	.05
536	Jose Melendez	.05
537	Wally Joyner	.05
538	Eddie Taubensee (Rookie Prospect)	.05
539	Jim Abbott	.05
540	Brian Williams RC (Rookie Prospect)	.05
541	Donovan Osborne (Rookie Prospect)	.05
542	Patrick Lennon (Rookie Prospect)	.05
543	Mike Groppuso RC (Rookie Prospect)	.05
544	Jarvis Brown RC (Rookie Prospect)	.05
545	Shawn Livesy RC (1st Round Draft Pick)	.05
546	Jeff Ware (1st Round Draft Pick)	.05
547	Danny Tartabull	.05
548	Bobby Jones RC (1st Round Draft Pick)	.05
549	Ken Griffey Jr.	1.50
550	Rey Sanchez RC (Rookie Prospect)	.05
551	Pedro Astacio RC (Rookie Prospect)	.10
552	Juan Guerrero RC (Rookie Prospect)	.05
553	Jacob Brumfield RC (Rookie Prospect)	.05
554	Ben Rivera RC (Rookie Prospect)	.05
555	Brian Jordan RC (Rookie Prospect)	.40
556	Denny Neagle (Rookie Prospect)	.05
557	Cliff Brantley (Rookie Prospect)	.05
558	Anthony Young (Rookie Prospect)	.05
559	John VanderWal RC (Rookie Prospect)	.05
560	Monty Fariss RC (Rookie Prospect)	.05
561	Russ Springer RC (Rookie Prospect)	.05
562	Pat Listach RC (Rookie Prospect)	.05
563	Pat Hentgen (Rookie Prospect)	.05
564	Andy Stankiewicz (Rookie Prospect)	.05
565	Mike Perez (Rookie Prospect)	.05
566	Mike Bielecki	.05
567	Butch Henry (Rookie Prospect)	.05
568	Dave Nilsson RC	.05
569	Scott Hatteberg RC (Rookie Prospect)	.05
570	Ruben Amaro Jr. (Rookie Prospect)	.05
571	Todd Hundley (Rookie Prospect)	.05
572	Moises Alou (Rookie Prospect)	.05
573	Hector Fajardo (Rookie Prospect)	.05
574	Todd Van Poppel (Rookie Prospect)	.05
575	Willie Banks (Rookie Prospect)	.05
576	Bob Zupcic (Rookie Prospect)	.05
577	J.J. Johnson RC (1st Round Draft Pick)	.05
578	John Burkett	.05
579	Trever Miller (1st Round Draft Pick)	.05
580	Scott Bankhead	.05
581	Rich Amaral (Rookie Prospect)	.05
582	Kenny Lofton (Rookie Prospect)	.05
583	Matt Stairs (Rookie Prospect)	.05
584	Don Mattingly, Rod Carew (Idols)	.25
585	Jack Morris, Steve Avery (Idols)	.05
586	Roberto Alomar, Sandy Alomar (Idols)	.10
587	Scott Sanderson, Catfish Hunter (Idols)	.05
588	Dave Justice, Willie Stargell (Idols)	.05
589	Rex Hudler, Roger Staubach (Idols)	.05
590	David Cone, Jackie Gleason (Idols)	.05
591	Willie Davis, Tony Gwynn (Idols)	.15
592	Orel Hershiser (Sidelines)	.05
593	John Wetteland (Sidelines)	.05
594	Tom Glavine (Sidelines)	.05
595	Randy Johnson (Sidelines)	.25
596	Jim Gott (Sidelines)	.05
597	Donald Harris	.05
598	Shawn Hare RC	.05
599	Chris Gardner	.05
600	Rusty Meacham	.05
601	Benito Santiago (Shades)	.05
602	Eric Davis (Shades)	.05
603	Jose Lind (Shades)	.05
604	Dave Justice (Shades)	.05
605	Tim Raines (Shades)	.05
606	Randy Tomlin (Grips)	.05
607	Jack McDowell (Grips)	.05
608	Greg Maddux (Grips)	.30
609	Charles Nagy (Grips)	.05
610	Tom Candiotti (Grips)	.05
611	David Cone (Grips)	.05
612	Steve Avery (Grips)	.05
613	Rod Beck RC	.10
614	Rickey Henderson (Technician)	.25
615	Benito Santiago (Technician)	.05
616	Ruben Sierra (Technician)	.05
617	Ryne Sandberg (Technician)	.50
618	Nolan Ryan (Technician)	1.00
619	Brett Butler (Technician)	.05
620	Dave Justice (Technician)	.05

Carrying on with the Idols subset theme in the regular issue, these Series 2 foil-pack inserts feature 18 young prospects sharing cards with their baseball heroes. Both front and back are horizontal in format and include photos of both the rookie and his idol.

		NM/M
Complete Set (18):		20.00
Common Player:		.50
1	Reggie Sanders, Eric Davis	.50
2	Hector Fajardo, Jim Abbott	.50
3	Gary Cooper, George Brett	3.50
4	Mark Wohlers, Roger Clemens	3.50
5	Luis Mercedes, Julio Franco	.50
6	Willie Banks, Dwight Gooden	.50
7	Kenny Lofton, Rickey Henderson	1.50
8	Keith Mitchell, Dave Henderson	.50
9	Kim Batiste, Barry Larkin	.50
10	Thurman Munson, Todd Hundley	1.00
11	Eddie Zosky, Cal Ripken Jr.	4.50
12	Todd Van Poppel, Nolan Ryan	4.50
13	Ryne Sandberg, Jim Thome	2.50
14	Dave Fleming, Bobby Murcer	.50
15	Royce Clayton, Ozzie Smith	2.50
16	Don Harris, Darryl Strawberry	.50
17	Alan Trammell, Chad Curtis	.50
18	Derek Bell, Dave Winfield	1.50

Rookies

Styled after the regular 1992 Pinnacle cards, this 30-card boxed set features the year's top rookies. The cards have a game-action photo which is borderless on the top and sides. Beneath the photo a team color-coded strip carries the player's name in gold foil, with a gold-bordered team logo at left. A black strip at bottom has the notation "1992 Rookie." Horizontal backs follow a similar design and include a bit of player information. Pinnacle's anti-counterfeiting strip and some gold-foil enhancements.

		NM/M
Complete Set (30):		2.00
Common Player:		.05
1	Luis Mercedes	.05
2	Scott Cooper	.05
3	Kenny Lofton	.25
4	John Doherty	.05
5	Pat Listach	.05
6	Andy Stankiewicz	.05
7	Derek Bell	.05
8	Gary DiSarcina	.05
9	Roberto Hernandez	.15
10	Joel Johnston	.05
11	Pat Mahomes	.05
12	Todd Van Poppel	.05
13	Dave Fleming	.05
14	Monty Fariss	.05
15	Gary Scott	.05
16	Moises Alou	.25
17	Todd Hundley	.05
18	Kim Batiste	.05
19	Denny Neagle	.05
20	Donovan Osborne	.05
21	Mark Wohlers	.05

Rookie Idols

22	Reggie Sanders	.10
23	Brian Williams	.05
24	Eric Karros	.25
25	Frank Seminara	.05
26	Royce Clayton	.05
27	Dave Nilsson	.05
28	Matt Stairs	.25
29	Chad Curtis	.25
30	Carlos Hernandez	.25

Slugfest

Each specially marked Slugfest jumbo pack of '92 Pinnacle contained one of these horizontal-format cards of the game's top hitters. The player's name is printed in gold foil at the bottom of the card, along with a red and white Slugfest logo. Backs, which are vertical, have a color player photo, a career summary and a few lifetime stats.

		NM/M
Complete Set (15):		15.00
Common Player:		.30
1	Cecil Fielder	.30
2	Mark McGwire	2.50
3	Jose Canseco	.65
4	Barry Bonds	3.00
5	Dave Justice	.30
6	Bobby Bonilla	.30
7	Ken Griffey Jr.	2.00
8	Ron Gant	.30
9	Ryne Sandberg	1.50
10	Ruben Sierra	.30
11	Frank Thomas	3.00
12	Will Clark	.30
13	Kirby Puckett	1.50
14	Cal Ripken, Jr.	3.00
15	Jeff Bagwell	1.00

Team Pinnacle

The most sought-after of the 1992 Pinnacle inserts is this 12-piece set of "two-headed" cards. An American and a National League superstar at each position are featured on each card, with two cards each for starting and relief pitchers. The ultra-realistic artwork of Chris Greco is featured on the cards, which were inserted into Series 1 foil packs.

		NM/M
Complete Set (12):		40.00
Common Player:		1.50
1	Roger Clemens, Ramon Martinez	8.00
2	Jim Abbott, Steve Avery	1.50
3	Benito Santiago, Ivan Rodriguez	3.00
4	Frank Thomas, Will Clark	3.00
5	Roberto Alomar, Ryne Sandberg	6.00
6	Robin Ventura, Matt Williams	1.50
7	Cal Ripken, Jr., Barry Larkin	10.00
8	Danny Tartabull, Barry Bonds	8.00
9	Brett Butler, Ken Griffey Jr.	8.00
10	Ruben Sierra, Dave Justice	1.50
11	Dennis Eckersley, Rob Dibble	1.50
12	Scott Radinsky, John Franco	1.50

Team 2000

KENNY LOFTON

Young stars projected to be the superstars of the 2000 season were chosen for this insert set found three at a time in jumbo packs. Cards #1-40 were included in Series 1 packaging, while cards #41-80 were inserted with Series 2 Pinnacle. Cards feature gold foil highlights on both front and back.

		NM/M
Complete Set (80):		3.00
Common Player:		.05
1	Mike Mussina	.30
2	Phil Plantier	.05
3	Frank Thomas	.50
4	Travis Fryman	.05
5	Kevin Appier	.05
6	Chuck Knoblauch	.05
7	Pat Kelly	.05
8	Ivan Rodriguez	.40
9	Dave Justice	.50
10	Jeff Bagwell	.50
11	Marquis Grissom	.05
12	Andy Benes	.05
13	Gregg Olson	.05
14	Kevin Morton	.05
15	Tim Naehring	.05
16	Dave Hollins	.05
17	Sandy Alomar Jr.	.05
18	Albert Belle	.05
19	Charles Nagy	.05
20	Brian McRae	.05
21	Larry Walker	.05
22	Delino DeShields	.05
23	Jeff Johnson	.05
24	Bernie Williams	.05
25	Jose Offerman	.05
26	Juan Gonzalez	.25
27	Juan Guzman	.05
28	Eric Anthony	.05
29	Brian Hunter	.05
30	John Smoltz	.05
31	Deion Sanders	.05
32	Greg Maddux	.75
33	Andujar Cedeno	.05
34	Royce Clayton	.05
35	Kenny Lofton	.05
36	Cal Eldred	.05
37	Jim Thome	.50
38	Gary DiSarcina	.05
39	Brian Jordan	.05
40	Chad Curtis	.05
41	Ben McDonald	.05
42	Jim Abbott	.05
43	Robin Ventura	.05
44	Milt Cuyler	.05
45	Gregg Jefferies	.05
46	Scott Radinsky	.05
47	Ken Griffey Jr.	1.00
48	Roberto Alomar	.15
49	Ramon Martinez	.05
50	Bret Barberie	.05
51	Ray Lankford	.05
52	Leo Gomez	.05
53	Tommy Greene	.05
54	Mo Vaughn	.05
55	Sammy Sosa	.75
56	Carlos Baerga	.05
57	Mark Lewis	.05
58	Tom Gordon	.05
59	Gary Sheffield	.25
60	Scott Erickson	.05
61	Pedro Munoz	.05
62	Tino Martinez	.05
63	Darren Lewis	.05
64	Dean Palmer	.05
65	John Olerud	.05
66	Steve Avery	.05
67	Pete Harnisch	.05
68	Luis Gonzalez	.05
69	Kim Batiste	.05
70	Reggie Sanders	.05
71	Luis Mercedes	.05
72	Todd Van Poppel	.05
73	Gary Scott	.05
74	Monty Fariss	.05
75	Kyle Abbott	.05
76	Eric Karros	.05
77	Mo Sanford	.05
78	Todd Hundley	.05
79	Reggie Jefferson	.05
80	Pat Mahomes	.05

Mickey Mantle

MICKEY MANTLE

This boxed set highlighting the career of Mickey Mantle was issued in a reported edition of 180,000 sets. Fronts and backs feature an assortment of black-and-white, color and colorized photos. Fronts have gold-foil stamped highlights. Card backs have a few sentences about Mantle's life or career.

		NM/M
Complete Set (30):		20.00
Common Card:		1.00
1	Father and Son	1.00
2	High School	1.00
3	Commerce Comet	1.00
4	Spring Training	1.00
5	The Beginning	1.00
6	No. 6	1.00
7	The Rookie	1.00
8	Tape-Measure Shots	1.00
9	Shortstop	1.00
10	Outfield	1.00
11	Speed, Speed, Speed	1.00
12	Contracts	1.00
13	Three-time MVP	1.00
14	Triple Crown	1.00
15	Series Slam	1.00
16	Series Star	1.00
17	Switch Hitter	1.00
18	Fan Favorite	1.00
19	Milestones	1.00
20	Enthusiasm	1.00
21	Hitting	1.00
22	First Base	1.00
23	Courage	1.00
24	Mick & Stan (Musial)	1.00
25	Whitey & Yogi (Ford, Berra)	1.00
26	Mick & Billy (Martin)	1.00
27	Mick & Casey (Stengel)	1.00
28	Awards	1.00
29	Retirement	1.00
30	Cooperstown	1.00

1993 Pinnacle Promos

Dave Fleming

On six of the eight cards issued to premiere Pinnacle's '93 set, the difference between the promo version and the issued version is so slight it can easily go unnoticed. The "TM" in the upper-right corner on front is larger on the promo than on the regular card. Promo cards #3 and 5 are easier to spot because the team logos on back of the promos are the old Expos and Mariners logos, rather than the new versions found on issued cards.

		NM/M
Complete Set (8):		10.00
Common Player:		1.25
1	Gary Sheffield	3.00
2	Cal Eldred	1.25
3	Larry Walker	1.25

4	Deion Sanders	1.50
5	Dave Fleming	1.25
6	Carlos Baerga	1.25
7	Bernie Williams	1.25
8	John Kruk	1.25

1993 Pinnacle

Ruben Sierra

This set offers many of the same features which made the debut Pinnacle set so popular in 1992. Subsets are titled Rookies, Now & Then (which shows the player as he looked as a rookie and in 1993), Idols (active players and their heroes on the same card), Hometown Heroes (players who are playing with their hometown team), Draft Picks and Rookies. More than 100 rookies and 10 draft picks are featured. All regular cards have an action photo, a black border and the Pinnacle name in gold foil. Series 1 cards feature portraits of players on the two new expansion teams; Series 2 cards feature action shots of them. Team Pinnacle insert cards returned, while Rookie Team Pinnacle cards made their debut. Other insert sets are titled Team 2001, Slugfest and Tribute, which features five cards each of Nolan Ryan and George Brett.

		NM/M
Complete Set (620):		17.50
Common Player:		.05
Series 1 Pack (15):		.35
Series 1 Box (36):		8.00
Series 2 Pack (15):		.75
Series 2 Box (36):		20.00
1	Gary Sheffield	.30
2	Cal Eldred	.05
3	Larry Walker	.05
4	Deion Sanders	.05
5	Dave Fleming	.05
6	Carlos Baerga	.05
7	Bernie Williams	.05
8	John Kruk	.05
9	Jimmy Key	.05
10	Jeff Bagwell	.60
11	Jim Abbott	.05
12	Terry Steinbach	.05
13	Bob Tewksbury	.05
14	Eric Karros	.05
15	Ryne Sandberg	.75
16	Will Clark	.05
17	Edgar Martinez	.05
18	Eddie Murray	.60
19	Andy Van Slyke	.05
20	Cal Ripken, Jr.	2.00
21	Ivan Rodriguez	.50
22	Barry Larkin	.05
23	Don Mattingly	.85
24	Gregg Jefferies	.05
25	Roger Clemens	.85
26	Cecil Fielder	.05
27	Kent Hrbek	.05
28	Robin Ventura	.05
29	Rickey Henderson	.60
30	Roberto Alomar	.15
31	Luis Polonia	.05
32	Andujar Cedeno	.05
33	Pat Listach	.05
34	Mark Grace	.05
35	Otis Nixon	.05
36	Felix Jose	.05
37	Mike Sharperson	.05
38	Dennis Martinez	.05
39	Willie McGee	.05
40	Kenny Lofton	.05
41	Randy Johnson	.60
42	Andy Benes	.05
43	Bobby Bonilla	.05
44	Mike Mussina	.50
45	Len Dykstra	.05
46	Ellis Burks	.05
47	Chris Sabo	.05
48	Jay Bell	.05
49	Jose Canseco	.40
50	Craig Biggio	.05

51	Wally Joyner	.05
52	Mickey Tettleton	.05
53	Tim Raines	.05
54	Brian Harper	.05
55	Rene Gonzales	.05
56	Mark Langston	.05
57	Jack Morris	.05
58	Mark McGwire	1.50
59	Ken Caminiti	.05
60	Terry Pendleton	.05
61	Dave Nilsson	.05
62	Tom Pagnozzi	.05
63	Mike Morgan	.05
64	Darryl Strawberry	.05
65	Charles Nagy	.05
66	Ken Hill	.05
67	Matt Williams	.05
68	Jay Buhner	.05
69	Vince Coleman	.05
70	Brady Anderson	.05
71	Fred McGriff	.05
72	Ben McDonald	.05
73	Terry Mulholland	.05
74	Randy Tomlin	.05
75	Nolan Ryan	2.00
76	Frank Viola	.05
77	Jose Rijo	.05
78	Shane Mack	.05
79	Travis Fryman	.05
80	Jack McDowell	.05
81	Mark Gubicza	.05
82	Matt Nokes	.05
83	Bert Blyleven	.05
84	Eric Anthony	.05
85	Mike Bordick	.05
86	John Olerud	.05
87	B.J. Surhoff	.05
88	Bernard Gilkey	.05
89	Shawon Dunston	.05
90	Tom Glavine	.30
91	Brett Butler	.05
92	Moises Alou	.05
93	Albert Belle	.05
94	Darren Lewis	.05
95	Omar Vizquel	.05
96	Dwight Gooden	.05
97	Gregg Olson	.05
98	Tony Gwynn	.75
99	Darren Daulton	.05
100	Dennis Eckersley	.50
101	Rob Dibble	.05
102	Mike Greenwell	.05
103	Jose Lind	.05
104	Julio Franco	.05
105	Tom Gordon	.05
106	Scott Livingstone	.05
107	Chuck Knoblauch	.05
108	Frank Thomas	.60
109	Melido Perez	.05
110	Ken Griffey Jr.	1.00
111	Harold Baines	.05
112	Gary Gaetti	.05
113	Pete Harnisch	.05
114	David Wells	.05
115	Charlie Leibrandt	.05
116	Ray Lankford	.05
117	Kevin Seitzer	.05
118	Robin Yount	.60
119	Lenny Harris	.05
120	Chris James	.05
121	Delino DeShields	.05
122	Kirt Manwaring	.05
123	Glenallen Hill	.05
124	Hensley Meulens	.05
125	Darrin Jackson	.05
126	Todd Hundley	.05
127	Dave Hollins	.05
128	Sam Horn	.05
129	Roberto Hernandez	.05
130	Vicente Palacios	.05
131	George Brett	.85
132	Dave Martinez	.05
133	Kevin Appier	.05
134	Pat Kelly	.05
135	Pedro Munoz	.05
136	Mark Carreon	.05
137	Lance Johnson	.05
138	Devon White	.05
139	Julio Valera	.05
140	Eddie Taubensee	.05
141	Willie Wilson	.05
142	Stan Belinda	.05
143	John Smoltz	.05
144	Darryl Hamilton	.05
145	Sammy Sosa	.75
146	Carlos Hernandez	.05
147	Tom Candiotti	.05
148	Mike Felder	.05
149	Rusty Meacham	.05
150	Ivan Calderon	.05
151	Pete O'Brien	.05
152	Erik Hanson	.05
153	Billy Ripken	.05
154	Kurt Stilwell	.05
155	Jeff Kent	.05
156	Mickey Morandini	.05
157	Randy Milligan	.05
158	Reggie Sanders	.05
159	Luis Rivera	.05
160	Orlando Merced	.05
161	Dean Palmer	.05
162	Mike Perez	.05
163	Scott Erickson	.05
164	Kevin McReynolds	.05
165	Kevin Maas	.05
166	Ozzie Guillen	.05
167	Rob Deer	.05
168	Danny Tartabull	.05

169	Lee Stevens	.05
170	Dave Henderson	.05
171	Derek Bell	.05
172	Steve Finley	.05
173	Greg Olson	.05
174	Geronimo Pena	.05
175	Paul Quantrill	.05
176	Steve Buechele	.05
177	Kevin Gross	.05
178	Tim Wallach	.05
179	Dave Valle	.05
180	Dave Silvestri	.05
181	Bud Black	.05
182	Henry Rodriguez	.05
183	Tim Teufel	.05
184	Mark McLemore	.05
185	Bret Saberhagen	.05
186	Chris Hoiles	.05
187	Ricky Jordan	.05
188	Don Slaught	.05
189	Mo Vaughn	.05
190	Joe Oliver	.05
191	Juan Gonzalez	.30
192	Scott Leius	.05
193	Milt Cuyler	.05
194	Chris Haney	.05
195	Ron Karkovice	.05
196	Steve Farr	.05
197	John Orton	.05
198	Kelly Gruber	.05
199	Ron Darling	.05
200	Ruben Sierra	.05
201	Chuck Finley	.05
202	Mike Moore	.05
203	Pat Borders	.05
204	Sid Bream	.05
205	Todd Zeile	.05
206	Rick Wilkins	.05
207	Jim Gantner	.05
208	Frank Castillo	.05
209	Dave Hansen	.05
210	Trevor Wilson	.05
211	Sandy Alomar, Jr.	.05
212	Sean Berry	.05
213	Tino Martinez	.05
214	Chito Martinez	.05
215	Dan Walters	.05
216	John Franco	.05
217	Glenn Davis	.05
218	Mariano Duncan	.05
219	Mike LaValliere	.05
220	Rafael Palmeiro	.50
221	Jack Clark	.05
222	Hal Morris	.05
223	Ed Sprague	.05
224	John Valentin	.05
225	Sam Militello	.05
226	Bob Wickman	.05
227	Damion Easley	.05
228	John Jaha	.05
229	Bob Ayrault	.05
230	Mo Sanford/ED	.05
231	Walt Weiss/ED	.05
232	Dante Bichette/ED	.05
233	Steve Decker/ED	.05
234	Jerald Clark/ED	.05
235	Bryan Harvey/ED	.05
236	Joe Girardi/ED	.05
237	Dave Magadan/ED	.05
238	David Nied (Rookie Prospect)	.05
239	Eric Wedge **RC** (Rookie Prospect)	.05
240	Rico Brogna (Rookie Prospect)	.05
241	J.T. Bruett (Rookie Prospect)	.05
242	Jonathan Hurst (Rookie Prospect)	.05
243	Bret Boone (Rookie Prospect)	.05
244	Manny Alexander (Rookie Prospect)	.05
245	Scooter Tucker (Rookie Prospect)	.05
246	Troy Neel (Rookie Prospect)	.05
247	Eddie Zosky (Rookie Prospect)	.05
248	Melvin Nieves (Rookie Prospect)	.05
249	Ryan Thompson (Rookie Prospect)	.05
250	Shawn Barton (Rookie Prospect)	.05
251	Ryan Klesko (Rookie Prospect)	.05
252	Mike Piazza (Rookie Prospect)	1.00
253	Steve Hosey (Rookie Prospect)	.05
254	Shane Reynolds (Rookie Prospect)	.05
255	Dan Wilson (Rookie Prospect)	.05
256	Tom Marsh (Rookie Prospect)	.05
257	Barry Manuel (Rookie Prospect)	.05
258	Paul Miller (Rookie Prospect)	.05

ABBREVIATIONS

ED - Expansion Draft

No.	Player	Price
259	Pedro Martinez (Rookie Prospect)	.60
260	Steve Cooke (Rookie Prospect)	.05
261	Johnny Guzman (Rookie Prospect)	.05
262	Mike Butcher (Rookie Prospect)	.05
263	Bien Figueroa (Rookie Prospect)	.05
264	Rich Rowland (Rookie Prospect)	.05
265	Shawn Jeter (Rookie Prospect)	.05
266	Gerald Williams (Rookie Prospect)	.05
267	Derek Parks (Rookie Prospect)	.05
268	Henry Mercedes (Rookie Prospect)	.05
269	David Hulse RC (Rookie Prospect)	.05
270	Tim Pugh RC (Rookie Prospect)	.05
271	William Suero (Rookie Prospect)	.05
272	Ozzie Canseco (Rookie Prospect)	.05
273	Fernando Ramsey (Rookie Prospect)	.05
274	Bernardo Brito (Rookie Prospect)	.05
275	Dave Mlicki (Rookie Prospect)	.05
276	Tim Salmon (Rookie Prospect)	.05
277	Mike Raczka (Rookie Prospect)	.05
278	Ken Ryan RC (Rookie Prospect)	.05
279	Rafael Bournigal (Rookie Prospect)	.05
280	Wil Cordero (Rookie Prospect)	.05
281	Billy Ashley (Rookie Prospect)	.05
282	Paul Wagner (Rookie Prospect)	.05
283	Blas Minor (Rookie Prospect)	.05
284	Rick Trlicek (Rookie Prospect)	.05
285	Willie Greene (Rookie Prospect)	.05
286	Ted Wood (Rookie Prospect)	.05
287	Phil Clark (Rookie Prospect)	.05
288	Jesse Levis (Rookie Prospect)	.05
289	Tony Gwynn (Now & Then)	.40
290	Nolan Ryan (Now & Then)	1.00
291	Dennis Martinez (Now & Then)	.05
292	Eddie Murray (Now & Then)	.30
293	Robin Yount (Now & Then)	.30
294	George Brett (Now & Then)	.45
295	Dave Winfield (Now & Then)	.30
296	Bert Blyleven (Now & Then)	.05
297	Jeff Bagwell (Idols - Carl Yastrzemski)	.30
298	John Smoltz (Idols - Jack Morris)	.05
299	Larry Walker (Idols - Mike Bossy)	.05
300	Gary Sheffield (Idols - Barry Larkin)	.15
301	Ivan Rodriguez (Idols - Carlton Fisk)	.30
302	Delino DeShields (Idols - Malcolm X)	.05
303	Tim Salmon (Idols - Dwight Evans)	.05
304	Bernard Gilkey (Hometown Heroes)	.05
305	Cal Ripken, Jr. (Hometown Heroes)	1.00
306	Barry Larkin (Hometown Heroes)	.05
307	Kent Hrbek (Hometown Heroes)	.05
308	Rickey Henderson (Hometown Heroes)	.30
309	Darryl Strawberry (Hometown Heroes)	.05
310	John Franco (Hometown Heroes)	.05
311	Todd Stottlemyre	.05
312	Luis Gonzalez	.05
313	Tommy Greene	.05
314	Randy Velarde	.05
315	Steve Avery	.05
316	Jose Oquendo	.05
317	Rey Sanchez	.05
318	Greg Vaughn	.05
319	Orel Hershiser	.05
320	Paul Sorrento	.05
321	Royce Clayton	.05
322	John Vander Wal	.05
323	Henry Cotto	.05
324	Pete Schourek	.05
325	David Segui	.05
326	Arthur Rhodes	.05
327	Bruce Hurst	.05
328	Wes Chamberlain	.05
329	Ozzie Smith	.75
330	Scott Cooper	.05
331	Felix Fermin	.05
332	Mike Macfarlane	.05
333	Dan Gladden	.05
334	Kevin Tapani	.05
335	Steve Sax	.05
336	Jeff Montgomery	.05
337	Gary DiSarcina	.05
338	Lance Blankenship	.05
339	Brian Williams	.05
340	Duane Ward	.05
341	Chuck McElroy	.05
342	Joe Magrane	.05
343	Jaime Navarro	.05
344	Dave Justice	.05
345	Jose Offerman	.05
346	Marquis Grissom	.05
347	Bill Swift	.05
348	Jim Thome	.50
349	Archi Cianfrocco	.05
350	Anthony Young	.05
351	Leo Gomez	.05
352	Bill Gullickson	.05
353	Alan Trammell	.05
354	Dan Pasqua	.05
355	Jeff King	.05
356	Kevin Brown	.05
357	Tim Belcher	.05
358	Bip Roberts	.05
359	Brent Mayne	.05
360	Rheal Cormier	.05
361	Mark Guthrie	.05
362	Craig Grebeck	.05
363	Andy Stankiewicz	.05
364	Juan Guzman	.05
365	Bobby Witt	.05
366	Mark Portugal	.05
367	Brian McRae	.05
368	Mark Lemke	.05
369	Bill Wegman	.05
370	Donovan Osborne	.05
371	Derrick May	.05
372	Carl Willis	.05
373	Chris Nabholz	.05
374	Mark Lewis	.05
375	John Burkett	.05
376	Luis Mercedes	.05
377	Ramon Martinez	.05
378	Kyle Abbott	.05
379	Mark Wohlers	.05
380	Bob Walk	.05
381	Kenny Rogers	.05
382	Tim Naehring	.05
383	Alex Fernandez	.05
384	Keith Miller	.05
385	Mike Henneman	.05
386	Rick Aguilera	.05
387	George Bell	.05
388	Mike Gallego	.05
389	Howard Johnson	.05
390	Kim Batiste	.05
391	Jerry Browne	.05
392	Damon Berryhill	.05
393	Ricky Bones	.05
394	Omar Olivares	.05
395	Mike Harkey	.05
396	Pedro Astacio	.05
397	John Wetteland	.05
398	Rod Beck	.05
399	Thomas Howard	.05
400	Mike Devereaux	.05
401	Tim Wakefield	.05
402	Curt Schilling	.30
403	Zane Smith	.05
404	Bob Zupcic	.05
405	Tom Browning	.05
406	Tony Phillips	.05
407	John Doherty	.05
408	Pat Mahomes	.05
409	John Habyan	.05
410	Steve Olin	.05
411	Chad Curtis	.05
412	Joe Grahe	.05
413	John Patterson	.05
414	Brian Hunter	.05
415	Doug Henry	.05
416	Lee Smith	.05
417	Bob Scanlan	.05
418	Kent Mercker	.05
419	Mel Rojas	.05
420	Mark Whiten	.05
421	Carlton Fisk	.60
422	Candy Maldonado	.05
423	Doug Drabek	.05
424	Wade Boggs	.75
425	Mark Davis	.05
426	Kirby Puckett	.75
427	Joe Carter	.05
428	Paul Molitor	.60
429	Eric Davis	.05
430	Darryl Kile	.05
431	Jeff Parrett/ED	.05
432	Jeff Blauser	.05
433	Dan Plesac	.05
434	Andres Galarraga/ED	.05
435	Jim Gott	.05
436	Jose Mesa	.05
437	Ben Rivera	.05
438	Dave Winfield	.60
439	Norm Charlton	.05
440	Chris Bosio	.05
441	Wilson Alvarez	.05
442	Dave Stewart	.05
443	Doug Jones	.05
444	Jeff Russell	.05
445	Ron Gant	.05
446	Paul O'Neill	.05
447	Charlie Hayes/ED	.05
448	Joe Hesketh	.05
449	Chris Hammond	.05
450	Hipolito Pichardo	.05
451	Scott Radinsky	.05
452	Bobby Thigpen	.05
453	Xavier Hernandez	.05
454	Lonnie Smith	.05
455	Jamie Arnold RC (1st Draft Pick)	.05
456	B.J. Wallace (1st Draft Pick)	.05
457	Derek Jeter RC (Rookie Prospect)	10.00
458	Jason Kendall RC (Rookie Prospect)	.75
459	Rick Helling (Rookie Prospect)	.05
460	Derek Wallace RC (Rookie Prospect)	.05
461	Sean Lowe RC (Rookie Prospect)	.05
462	Shannon Stewart RC (Rookie Prospect)	.60
463	Benji Grigsby RC (Rookie Prospect)	.05
464	Todd Steverson RC (Rookie Prospect)	.05
465	Dan Serafini RC (Rookie Prospect)	.05
466	Michael Tucker (Rookie Prospect)	.05
467	Chris Roberts (Rookie Prospect)	.05
468	Pete Janicki RC (1st Draft Pick)	.05
469	Jeff Schmidt RC (1st Draft Pick)	.05
470	Don Mattingly (Now & Then)	.45
471	Cal Ripken, Jr. (Now & Then)	1.00
472	Jack Morris (Now & Then)	.05
473	Terry Pendleton (Now & Then)	.05
474	Dennis Eckersley (Now & Then)	.25
475	Carlton Fisk (Now & Then)	.30
476	Wade Boggs (Now & Then)	.35
477	Len Dykstra (Idols - Ken Stabler)	.05
478	Danny Tartabull (Idols - Jose Tartabull)	.05
479	Jeff Conine (Idols - Dale Murphy)	.10
480	Gregg Jefferies (Idols - Ron Cey)	.05
481	Paul Molitor (Idols - Harmon Killebrew)	.30
482	John Valentin (Idols - Dave Concepcion)	.05
483	Alex Arias (Idols - Dave Winfield)	.10
484	Barry Bonds (Hometown Heroes)	1.00
485	Doug Drabek (Hometown Heroes)	.05
486	Dave Winfield (Hometown Heroes)	.30
487	Brett Butler (Hometown Heroes)	.05
488	Harold Baines (Hometown Heroes)	.05
489	David Cone (Hometown Heroes)	.05
490	Willie McGee (Hometown Heroes)	.05
491	Robby Thompson	.05
492	Pete Incaviglia	.05
493	Manuel Lee	.05
494	Rafael Belliard	.05
495	Scott Fletcher	.05
496	Jeff Frye	.05
497	Andre Dawson	.25
498	Mike Scioscia	.05
499	Spike Owen	.05
500	Sid Fernandez	.05
501	Joe Orsulak	.05
502	Benito Santiago/ED	.05
503	Dale Murphy	.25
504	Barry Bonds	2.00
505	Jose Guzman	.05
506	Tony Pena	.05
507	Greg Swindell	.05
508	Mike Pagliarulo	.05
509	Lou Whitaker	.05
510	Greg Gagne	.05
511	Butch Henry/ED	.05
512	Jeff Brantley	.05
513	Jack Armstrong (Expansion Draft)	.05
514	Danny Jackson	.05
515	Junior Felix/ED	.05
516	Milt Thompson	.05
517	Greg Maddux	.75
518	Eric Young/ED	.05
519	Jody Reed	.05
520	Roberto Kelly	.05
521	Darren Holmes/ED	.05
522	Craig Lefferts	.05
523	Charlie Hough/ED	.05
524	Bo Jackson	.10
525	Bill Spiers	.05
526	Orestes Destrade/ED	.05
527	Greg Hibbard	.05
528	Roger McDowell	.05
529	Cory Snyder	.05
530	Harold Reynolds	.05
531	Kevin Reimer	.05
532	Rick Sutcliffe	.05
533	Tony Fernandez	.05
534	Tom Brunansky	.05
535	Jeff Reardon	.05
536	Chili Davis	.05
537	Bob Ojeda	.05
538	Greg Colbrunn	.05
539	Phil Plantier	.05
540	Brian Jordan	.05
541	Pete Smith	.05
542	Frank Tanana	.05
543	John Smiley	.05
544	David Cone	.05
545	Daryl Boston/ED	.05
546	Tom Henke	.05
547	Bill Krueger	.05
548	Freddie Benavides/ED	.05
549	Randy Myers	.05
550	Reggie Jefferson	.05
551	Kevin Mitchell	.05
552	Dave Stieb	.05
553	Bret Barberie/ED	.05
554	Tim Crews	.05
555	Doug Dascenzo	.05
556	Alex Cole/ED	.05
557	Jeff Innis	.05
558	Carlos Garcia	.05
559	Steve Howe	.05
560	Kirk McCaskill	.05
561	Frank Seminara	.05
562	Cris Carpenter/ED	.05
563	Mike Stanley	.05
564	Carlos Quintana	.05
565	Mitch Williams	.05
566	Juan Bell	.05
567	Eric Fox	.05
568	Al Leiter	.05
569	Mike Stanton	.05
570	Scott Kamieniecki	.05
571	Ryan Bowen/ED	.05
572	Andy Ashby/ED	.05
573	Bob Welch	.05
574	Scott Sanderson	.05
575	Joe Kmak (Rookie Prospect)	.05
576	Scott Pose/ED (Rookie Prospect)	.05
577	Ricky Gutierrez (Rookie Prospect)	.05
578	Mike Trombley (Rookie Prospect)	.05
579	Sterling Hitchcock RC (Rookie Prospect)	.10
580	Rodney Bolton (Rookie Prospect)	.05
581	Tyler Green (Rookie Prospect)	.05
582	Tim Costo (Rookie Prospect)	.05
583	Tim Laker RC (Rookie Prospect)	.05
584	Steve Reed/ED RC (Rookie Prospect)	.05
585	Tom Kramer RC (Rookie Prospect)	.05
586	Robb Nen (Rookie Prospect)	.05
587	Jim Tatum RC (Rookie Prospect)	.05
588	Frank Bolick (Rookie Prospect)	.05
589	Kevin Young (Rookie Prospect)	.05
590	Matt Whiteside RC (Rookie Prospect)	.05
591	Cesar Hernandez (Rookie Prospect)	.05
592	Mike Mohler RC (Rookie Prospect)	.05
593	Alan Embree (Rookie Prospect)	.05
594	Terry Jorgensen (Rookie Prospect)	.05
595	John Cummings RC (Rookie Prospect)	.05
596	Domingo Martinez (Rookie Prospect)	.05
597	Benji Gil (Rookie Prospect)	.05
598	Todd Pratt RC (Rookie Prospect)	.05
599	Rene Arocha RC (Rookie Prospect)	.05
600	Dennis Moeller (Rookie Prospect)	.05
601	Jeff Conine (Rookie Prospect)	.05
602	Trevor Hoffman/ED (Rookie Prospect)	.05
603	Daniel Smith (Rookie Prospect)	.05
604	Lee Tinsley (Rookie Prospect)	.05
605	Dan Peltier (Rookie Prospect)	.05
606	Billy Brewer (Rookie Prospect)	.05
607	Matt Walbeck RC (Rookie Prospect)	.05
608	Richie Lewis/ED (Rookie Prospect)	.05
609	J.T. Snow RC (Rookie Prospect)	.40
610	Pat Gomez RC (Rookie Prospect)	.05
611	Phil Hiatt (Rookie Prospect)	.05
612	Alex Arias/ED (Rookie Prospect)	.05
613	Kevin Rogers (Rookie Prospect)	.05
614	Al Martin (Rookie Prospect)	.05
615	Greg Gohr (Rookie Prospect)	.05
616	Grame Lloyd RC (Rookie Prospect)	.05
617	Kent Bottenfield (Rookie Prospect)	.05
618	Chuck Carr/ED (Rookie Prospect)	.05
619	Darrell Sherman RC (Rookie Prospect)	.05
620	Mike Lansing RC (Rookie Prospect)	.15

ABBREVIATIONS

SP - Short Print

Expansion Opening Day

JERALD CLARK - LF
OPENING DAY, APRIL 5th, 1993
PINNACLE 7 of 9

This nine-card set features 18 players for the two N.L. expansion teams: Florida Marlins and Colorado Rockies. Each "two-headed" card shows a projected Opening Day starter for each team. Cards were available one per Series 2 hobby box. Complete sets were available through a special mail-in offer.

		NM/M
Complete Set (9):		2.50
Common Player:		.25
1	Charlie Hough, David Nied	.25
2	Benito Santiago, Joe Girardi	.40
3	Orestes Destrade, Andres Galarraga	.75
4	Bret Barberie, Eric Young	.25
5	Dave Magadan, Charlie Hayes	.25
6	Walt Weiss, Freddie Benavides	.25
7	Jeff Conine, Jerald Clark	.50
8	Scott Pose, Alex Cole	.25
9	Junior Felix, Dante Bichette	.40

Rookie Team Pinnacle

ROOKIE TEAM PINNACLE
PINNACLE 3 of 10

These 10 cards were randomly inserted into Series 2 packs. Rookie Team Pinnacle is printed in gold foil on both sides of the card. Cards are numbered 1 of 10, etc., and use the special Dufex process. Each card shows two players painted by artist Christopher Greco. Stated odds of finding a Rookie Team Pinnacle insert were one in 90 packs.

		NM/M
Complete Set (10):		20.00
Common Player:		1.50
1	Pedro Martinez, Mike Trombley	6.00
2	Kevin Rogers, Sterling Hitchcock	1.50
3	Mike Piazza, Jesse Levis	10.00
4	Ryan Klesko, J.T. Snow	1.50
5	John Patterson, Bret Boone	1.50
6	Domingo Martinez, Kevin Young	1.50
7	Wil Cordero, Manny Alexander	1.50
8	Steve Hosey, Tim Salmon	1.50
9	Ryan Thompson, Gerald Williams	1.50
10	Melvin Nieves, David Hulse	1.50

Slugfest

RUBEN SIERRA
SLUGFEST

Baseball's top sluggers are featured in this 30-card insert set. Cards were available one per Series 2 jumbo pack. Slugfest is printed in gold foil on the card front.

		NM/M
Complete Set (30):		12.50
Common Player:		.25
1	Juan Gonzalez	.50
2	Mark McGwire	2.00
3	Cecil Fielder	.25
4	Joe Carter	.25
5	Fred McGriff	.25
6	Barry Bonds	2.50
7	Gary Sheffield	.50
8	Dave Hollins	.25
9	Frank Thomas	1.00
10	Danny Tartabull	.25
11	Albert Belle	.25
12	Ruben Sierra	.25
13	Larry Walker	.25
14	Jeff Bagwell	1.00
15	Dave Justice	.25
16	Kirby Puckett	1.25
17	John Kruk	.25
18	Howard Johnson	.25
19	Darryl Strawberry	.25
20	Will Clark	.25
21	Kevin Mitchell	.25
22	Mickey Tettleton	.25
23	Don Mattingly	1.50
24	Jose Canseco	.75
25	Sam Militello	.25
26	Andre Dawson	.50
27	Ryne Sandberg	1.25
28	Ken Griffey Jr.	1.75
29	Carlos Baerga	.25
30	Travis Fryman	.25

Team Pinnacle

TEAM PINNACLE
GARY SHEFFIELD • 3B National League
PINNACLE 6 of 10

These cards were randomly inserted in Series 1 at a rate of about one in every 24 packs. Each card features two players painted by artist Christopher Greco. An eleventh card, featuring relief pitchers, was available only via a mail-in offer.

		NM/M
Complete Set (11):		40.00
Common Player:		1.50
1	Greg Maddux, Mike Mussina	10.00
2	Tom Glavine, John Smiley	2.00
3	Darren Daulton, Ivan Rodriguez	3.00
4	Fred McGriff, Frank Thomas	4.00
5	Delino DeShields, Carlos Baerga	1.50
6	Gary Sheffield, Edgar Martinez	2.00
7	Ozzie Smith, Pat Listach	8.00
8	Barry Bonds, Juan Gonzalez	15.00
9	Kirby Puckett, Andy Van Slyke	8.00
10	Larry Walker, Joe Carter	1.50
11	Rick Aguilera, Rob Dibble	1.50

Team 2001

This insert set features 30 players who are expected to be stars in the year 2001. Cards were randomly inserted into 27-card jumbo packs from Series 1.

		NM/M
Complete Set (30):		5.00
Common Player:		.05
1	Wil Cordero	.05
2	Cal Eldred	.05
3	Mike Mussina	.60
4	Chuck Knoblauch	.05
5	Melvin Nieves	.05
6	Tim Wakefield	.05
7	Carlos Baerga	.05
8	Bret Boone	.05
9	Jeff Bagwell	1.00
10	Travis Fryman	.05
11	Royce Clayton	.05
12	Delino DeShields	.05
13	Juan Gonzalez	.50
14	Pedro Martinez	1.00
15	Bernie Williams	.05
16	Billy Ashley	.05
17	Marquis Grissom	.05
18	Kenny Lofton	.05
19	Ray Lankford	.05
20	Tim Salmon	.05
21	Steve Hosey	.05
22	Charles Nagy	.05
23	Dave Fleming	.05
24	Reggie Sanders	.05
25	Sam Militello	.05
26	Eric Karros	.05
27	Ryan Klesko	.05
28	Dean Palmer	.05
29	Ivan Rodriguez	.75
30	Sterling Hitchcock	.05

Tribute

These Hall of Famers each have five-card sets devoted to their career achievements. Each card commemorates a career milestone. Cards were random inserts in Series 2, about one every 24 packs. Fronts have a gold-foil stamped "Tribute" vertically at right.

	NM/M
Complete Set (10):	10.00
George Brett Card (1-5):	1.00
Nolan Ryan Card (6-10):	1.50
1 Kansas City Royalty (George Brett)	1.00

2	The Chase for .400 (George Brett)	1.00
3	Pine Tar Pandemonium - "The Bat"	1.00
4	MVP and a World Series, Too (George Brett)	1.00
5	3,000 or Bust (George Brett)	1.00
6	The Rookie (Nolan Ryan)	1.50
7	Angel of No Mercy (Nolan Ryan)	1.50
8	Astronomical Success (Nolan Ryan)	1.50
9	5,000 Ks (Nolan Ryan)	1.50
10	No-Hitter No. 7 (Nolan Ryan)	1.50

Cooperstown

This boxed set features "today's superstar players bound to become Cooperstown inductees." In standard 2-1/2" x 3-1/2" format, the cards feature on both front and back an action photo which is borderless at the top and sides. At bottom-center of each photo is a half-moon green and gold-foil "Cooperstown Card" logo. On front, the player's name is gold-foil stamped in a black bar at bottom. On back is a black box, again with the player's name in gold-foil, plus a few stats justifying the player's Hall of Fame potential. Pinnacle's trademark optical-variable anti-counterfeiting device is at the bottom. Cards are UV coated on both sides. A special edition of 1,000 of the Cooperstown sets was produced in Pinnacle's "Dufex" technology and distributed at the 1993 SCAI trade show. Other than being printed on foil, the cards are identical to the regular-issue Cooperstown cards. Each of the Pinnacle Cooperstown cards can also be found in a sample version which differs from the issued cards principally in the appearance on back of a large "PROMO" overprint.

		NM/M
Complete Set (30):		7.50
Common Player:		.25
Dufex:		25X
Promo:		30X
1	Nolan Ryan	2.00
2	George Brett	.85
3	Robin Yount	.65
4	Carlton Fisk	.65
5	Dale Murphy	.35
6	Dennis Eckersley	.50
7	Rickey Henderson	.65
8	Ryne Sandberg	.75
9	Ozzie Smith	.75
10	Dave Winfield	.65
11	Andre Dawson	.35
12	Kirby Puckett	.75
13	Wade Boggs	.75
14	Don Mattingly	.85
15	Barry Bonds	2.00
16	Will Clark	.25
17	Cal Ripken, Jr.	2.00
18	Roger Clemens	.85
19	Dwight Gooden	.75
20	Tony Gwynn	.75
21	Joe Carter	.25
22	Ken Griffey Jr.	1.00
23	Paul Molitor	.60
24	Frank Thomas	.60
25	Juan Gonzalez	.35
26	Barry Larkin	.25
27	Eddie Murray	.60
28	Cecil Fielder	.25
29	Roberto Alomar	.25
30	Mark McGwire	1.50

Joe DiMaggio

Sold in a special tin box in a limited edition of 200,000 sets, this set highlights the career of "The Yankee Clipper." Fronts feature black-and-white or colorized photos with a black border and gold-foil highlights. Backs feature a woodgrain center panel with a portion of DiMaggio's career recounted. The boxed set includes an "Authenticator" lens through which the name "DiMaggio" can be seen when placed over the optical-variable printing on back. Genuine DiMaggio autographed cards were randomly inserted into 9,000 sets.

		NM/M
Complete Set (30):		7.50
Common Card:		.35
1	An American Hero	.50
2	San Francisco Seals	.35
3	Seals Farewell	.35
4	First Game	.35
5	The Rookie	.35
6	Rookie All-Star (With Dizzy Dean.)	.45
7	Fan Favorite	.35
8	Teammates' Awe	.35
9	Classic Swing	.35
10	Joltin' Power	.35
11	Rapid Robert vs. Joltin' Joe (With Bob Feller.)	.45
12	The Complete Hitter	.35
13	Makin' It Look Easy	.35
14	Extra Swings	.35
15	The Run Producer	.35
16	Quiet Confidence	.35
17	Sticks 'N' Bones	.35
18	A Link to the Past (With Lou Gehrig.)	.50
19	The Center of Attention	.35
20	The DiMaggio Mystique	.35
21	Joe McCarthy (With Joe McCarthy.)	.35
22	World War II	.35
23	Fearless Baserunner	.35
24	The Summer of '41	.35
25	Career Statistics	.50
26	No. 45	.35
27	Chasing Ruth	.35
28	The Final Season	.35
29	Retirement	.35
30	Baseball's Greatest Living Player	.50

Joe DiMaggio Autographs

Eighteen hundred of each of five different insert cards were personally autographed by the Yankee Clipper and randomly inserted into the Joe DiMaggio box set tins at a rate of about one autograph per 22 sets. Fronts of the 2-1/8" x 3-1/2" cards have sepia artwork of DiMaggio at a particular stage of his career. In the wide white border at bottom is the autograph. Backs have a photo, part of a narrative about DiMaggio's career, and a serial number. A certificate of authenticity accompanies each signed card.

		NM/M
Complete Set (5):		850.00
1-5	Joe DiMaggio	175.00

Home Run Club

Pinnacle released this boxed set produced in a special metallic-foil printing process called "Dufex." Limited to 200,000 numbered sets, the cards are UV-coated and gold-foil stamped. The checklist includes 28 American League and 20 National League sluggers.

		NM/M
Complete Set (30):		6.00
Common Player:		.10
1	Juan Gonzalez	.40
2	Fred McGriff	.10
3	Cecil Fielder	.10
4	Barry Bonds	1.50
5	Albert Belle	.10
6	Gary Sheffield	.25
7	Joe Carter	.10
8	Mark McGwire	1.25
9	Darren Daulton	.10
10	Jose Canseco	.50
11	Dave Hollins	.10
12	Ryne Sandberg	.85
13	Ken Griffey Jr.	1.00
14	Larry Walker	.10
15	Rob Deer	.10
16	Andre Dawson	.25
17	Frank Thomas	.75
18	Mickey Tettleton	.10
19	Charlie Hayes	.10
20	Ron Gant	.10
21	Rickey Henderson	.75
22	Matt Williams	.10
23	Kevin Mitchell	.10
24	Robin Ventura	.10
25	Dean Palmer	.10
26	Mike Piazza	1.00
27	J.T. Snow	.10
28	Jeff Bagwell	.75
29	John Olerud	.10
30	Greg Vaughn	.10
31	Dave Justice	.10
32	Dave Winfield	.75
33	Danny Tartabull	.10
34	Eric Anthony	.10
35	Eddie Murray	.75
36	Jay Buhner	.10
37	Derek Bell	.10
38	Will Clark	.10
39	Carlos Baerga	.10
40	Mo Vaughn	.10
41	Bobby Bonilla	.10
42	Tim Salmon	.10
43	Bo Jackson	.10
44	Howard Johnson	.10
45	Kent Hrbek	.10
46	Ruben Sierra	.10
47	Cal Ripken, Jr.	1.50
48	Travis Fryman	.10

1994 Pinnacle Samples

Basically the same as the issued versions, these promo cards differ in the presence of a diagonal "SAMPLE" overprint on front and back. Cello-wrapped packs of hobby and retail versions were produced, with appropriate header cards.

		NM/M
Complete Set (12):		10.00
Common Player:		.50
2	Carlos Baerga	.50
3	Sammy Sosa	2.00
5	John Olerud	.75
7	Moises Alou	.50
8	Steve Avery	.50
10	Cecil Fielder	.50
11	Greg Maddux	2.00
269	Jeff Granger	.50
---	Jeff Granger (Museum) (Blank-back.)	1.00
---	Jeff Granger (Museum) (Black print on back.)	1.00
TR1	Paul Molitor (Tribute)	1.50
---	Hobby version header card	.05
---	Retail version header card	.05

1994 Pinnacle

Pinnacle's 1994 mid-priced brand features full bleed photos, gold-foil graphics and UV coating. On front, player and team names appear in a shield-and-bar motif in the lower-left corner. On horizontal backs, the front photo is reproduced as a subdued background photo, over which are printed recent stats and a few biographical details. A different player photo is featured at left, while the brand's optical-variable anti-counterfeiting device is at bottom center. Subsets include major award winners, Rookie Prospects and Draft Picks which are appropriately noted with gold-foil lettering on front. The issue was produced in two series of 270 cards each.

		NM/M
Complete Set (540):		15.00
Common Player:		.05
Artist's Proofs:		20X
Museums:		6X
Series 1 or 2 Pack (14):		.50
Series 1 or 2 Box (24):		12.50
1	Frank Thomas	.65
2	Carlos Baerga	.05
3	Sammy Sosa	.75
4	Tony Gwynn	.75
5	John Olerud	.05
6	Ryne Sandberg	.75
7	Moises Alou	.05
8	Steve Avery	.05
9	Tim Salmon	.05
10	Cecil Fielder	.05
11	Greg Maddux	.75
12	Barry Larkin	.05
13	Mike Devereaux	.05
14	Charlie Hayes	.05
15	Albert Belle	.05
16	Andy Van Slyke	.05
17	Mo Vaughn	.05
18	Brian McRae	.05
19	Cal Eldred	.05
20	Craig Biggio	.05
21	Kirby Puckett	.75
22	Derek Bell	.05
23	Don Mattingly	.85
24	John Burkett	.05
25	Roger Clemens	.85
26	Barry Bonds	2.00
27	Paul Molitor	.65
28	Mike Piazza	1.00
29	Robin Ventura	.05
30	Jeff Conine	.05
31	Wade Boggs	.75
32	Dennis Eckersley	.50
33	Bobby Bonilla	.05
34	Len Dykstra	.05
35	Manny Alexander	.05
36	Ray Lankford	.05
37	Greg Vaughn	.05
38	Chuck Finley	.05
39	Todd Benzinger	.05
40	Dave Justice	.05
41	Rob Dibble	.05
42	Tom Henke	.05
43	David Nied	.05
44	Sandy Alomar Jr.	.05
45	Pete Harnisch	.05
46	Jeff Russell	.05
47	Terry Mulholland	.05
48	Kevin Appier	.05
49	Randy Tomlin	.05
50	Cal Ripken, Jr.	2.00
51	Andy Benes	.05
52	Jimmy Key	.05
53	Kirt Manwaring	.05
54	Kevin Tapani	.05
55	Jose Guzman	.05
56	Todd Stottlemyre	.05
57	Jack McDowell	.05
58	Orel Hershiser	.05
59	Chris Hammond	.05
60	Chris Nabholz	.05
61	Ruben Sierra	.05
62	Dwight Gooden	.05
63	John Kruk	.05
64	Omar Vizquel	.05
65	Tim Naehring	.05
66	Dwight Smith	.05
67	Mickey Tettleton	.05
68	J.T. Snow	.05
69	Greg McMichael	.05
70	Kevin Mitchell	.05
71	Kevin Brown	.05
72	Scott Cooper	.05
73	Jim Thome	.60
74	Joe Girardi	.05
75	Eric Anthony	.05
76	Orlando Merced	.05
77	Felix Jose	.05
78	Tommy Greene	.05
79	Bernard Gilkey	.05
80	Phil Plantier	.05
81	Danny Tartabull	.05
82	Trevor Wilson	.05
83	Chuck Knoblauch	.05
84	Rick Wilkins	.05
85	Devon White	.05
86	Lance Johnson	.05
87	Eric Karros	.05
88	Gary Sheffield	.35
89	Wil Cordero	.05
90	Ron Darling	.05
91	Darren Daulton	.05
92	Joe Orsulak	.05
93	Steve Cooke	.05
94	Darryl Hamilton	.05
95	Aaron Sele	.05
96	John Doherty	.05
97	Gary DiSarcina	.05
98	Jeff Blauser	.05
99	John Smiley	.05
100	Ken Griffey Jr.	1.00
101	Dean Palmer	.05
102	Felix Fermin	.05
103	Jerald Clark	.05
104	Doug Drabek	.05
105	Curt Schilling	.30
106	Jeff Montgomery	.05
107	Rene Arocha	.05
108	Carlos Garcia	.05
109	Wally Whitehurst	.05
110	Jim Abbott	.05
111	Royce Clayton	.05
112	Chris Hoiles	.05
113	Mike Morgan	.05
114	Joe Magrane	.05
115	Tom Candiotti	.05
116	Ron Karkovice	.05
117	Ryan Bowen	.05
118	Rod Beck	.05
119	John Wetteland	.05
120	Terry Steinbach	.05
121	Dave Hollins	.05
122	Jeff Kent	.05
123	Ricky Bones	.05
124	Brian Jordan	.05
125	Chad Kreuter	.05
126	John Valentin	.05
127	Billy Hathaway	.05
128	Wilson Alvarez	.05
129	Tino Martinez	.05
130	Rodney Bolton	.05
131	David Segui	.05
132	Wayne Kirby	.05
133	Eric Young	.05
134	Scott Servais	.05

#	Player	Price		#	Player	Price		#	Player	Price		#	Player	Price
135	Scott Radinsky	.05		253	John O'Donoghue	.05		371	Terry Pendleton	.05		489	Jerry Browne	.05
136	Bret Barberie	.05		254	Turk Wendell	.05		372	Chris Bosio	.05		490	Chris Sabo	.05
137	John Roper	.05		255	Scott Ruffcorn	.05		373	Orestes Destrade	.05		491	Tim Belcher	.05
138	Ricky Gutierrez	.05		256	Tony Tarasco	.05		374	Dave Stewart	.05		492	Spike Owen	.05
139	Bernie Williams	.05		257	Andy Cook	.05		375	Darren Holmes	.05		493	Rafael Palmeiro	.60
140	Bud Black	.05		258	Matt Mieske	.05		376	Doug Strange	.05		494	Brian Harper	.05
141	Jose Vizcaino	.05		259	Luis Lopez	.05		377	Brian Turang	.05		495	Eddie Murray	.65
142	Gerald Williams	.05		260	Ramon Caraballo	.05		378	Carl Willis	.05		496	Ellis Burks	.05
143	Duane Ward	.05		261	Salomon Torres	.05		379	Mark McLemore	.05		497	Karl Rhodes	.05
144	Danny Jackson	.05		262	Brooks Kieschnick RC	.05		380	Bobby Jones	.05		498	Otis Nixon	.05
145	Allen Watson	.05		263	Daron Kirkreit RC	.05		381	Scott Sanders	.05		499	Lee Smith	.05
146	Scott Fletcher	.05		264	Bill Wagner RC	.10		382	Kirk Rueter	.05		500	Bip Roberts	.05
147	Delino DeShields	.05		265	Matt Drews RC	.05		383	Randy Velarde	.05		501	Pedro Martinez	.65
148	Shane Mack	.05		266	Scott Christman	.05		384	Fred McGriff	.05		502	Brian L. Hunter	.05
149	Jim Eisenreich	.05		267	Torii Hunter RC	1.00		385	Charles Nagy	.05		503	Tyler Green	.05
150	Troy Neel	.05		268	Jamey Wright RC	.05		386	Rich Amaral	.05		504	Bruce Hurst	.05
151	Jay Bell	.05		269	Jeff Granger	.05		387	Geronimo Berroa	.05		505	Alex Gonzalez	.05
152	B.J. Surhoff	.05		270	Trot Nixon RC	1.00		388	Eric Davis	.05		506	Mark Portugal	.05
153	Mark Whiten	.05		271	Randy Myers	.05		389	Ozzie Smith	.75		507	Bob Ojeda	.05
154	Mike Henneman	.05		272	Trevor Hoffman	.05		390	Alex Arias	.05		508	Dave Henderson	.05
155	Todd Hundley	.05		273	Bob Wickman	.05		391	Brad Ausmus	.05		509	Bo Jackson	.10
156	Greg Myers	.05		274	Willie McGee	.05		392	Cliff Floyd	.05		510	Bret Boone	.05
157	Ryan Klesko	.25		275	Hipolito Pichardo	.05		393	Roger Salkeld	.05		511	Mark Eichhorn	.05
158	Dave Fleming	.05		276	Bobby Witt	.05		394	Jim Edmonds	.05		512	Luis Polonia	.05
159	Mickey Morandini	.05		277	Gregg Olson	.05		395	Jeromy Burnitz	.05		513	Will Clark	.05
160	Blas Minor	.05		278	Randy Johnson	.65		396	Dave Staton	.05		514	Dave Valle	.05
161	Reggie Jefferson	.05		279	Robb Nen	.05		397	Rob Butler	.05		515	Dan Wilson	.05
162	David Hulse	.05		280	Paul O'Neill	.05		398	Marcos Armas	.05		516	Dennis Martinez	.05
163	Greg Swindell	.05		281	Lou Whitaker	.05		399	Darrell Whitmore	.05		517	Jim Leyritz	.05
164	Roberto Hernandez	.05		282	Chad Curtis	.05		400	Ryan Thompson	.05		518	Howard Johnson	.05
165	Brady Anderson	.05		283	Doug Henry	.05		401	Ross Powell RC	.05		519	Jody Reed	.05
166	Jack Armstrong	.05		284	Tom Glavine	.30		402	Joe Oliver	.05		520	Julio Franco	.05
167	Phil Clark	.05		285	Mike Greenwell	.05		403	Paul Carey	.05		521	Jeff Reardon	.05
168	Melido Perez	.05		286	Roberto Kelly	.05		404	Bob Hamelin	.05		522	Willie Greene	.05
169	Darren Lewis	.05		287	Roberto Alomar	.15		405	Chris Turner	.05		523	Shawon Dunston	.05
170	Sam Horn	.05		288	Charlie Hough	.05		406	Nate Minchey	.05		524	Keith Mitchell	.05
171	Mike Harkey	.05		289	Alex Fernandez	.05		407	Lonnie Maclin RC	.05		525	Rick Helling	.05
172	Juan Guzman	.05		290	Jeff Bagwell	.65		408	Harold Baines	.05		526	Mark Kiefer	.05
173	Bob Natal	.05		291	Wally Joyner	.05		409	Brian Williams	.05		527	Chan Ho Park RC	.75
174	Deion Sanders	.25		292	Andujar Cedeno	.05		410	Johnny Ruffin	.05		528	Tony Longmire	.05
175	Carlos Quintana	.05		293	Rick Aguilera	.05		411	Julian Tavarez RC	.05		529	Rich Becker	.05
176	Mel Rojas	.05		294	Darryl Strawberry	.05		412	Mark Hutton	.05		530	Tim Hyers	.05
177	Willie Banks	.05		295	Mike Mussina	.35		413	Carlos Delgado	.50		531	Darrin Jackson	.05
178	Ben Rivera	.05		296	Jeff Gardner	.05		414	Chris Gomez	.05		532	Jack Morris	.05
179	Kenny Lofton	.05		297	Chris Gwynn	.05		415	Mike Hampton	.05		533	Rick White	.05
180	Leo Gomez	.05		298	Matt Williams	.05		416	Alex Diaz	.05		534	Mike Kelly	.05
181	Roberto Mejia	.05		299	Brent Gates	.05		417	Jeffrey Hammonds	.05		535	James Mouton	.05
182	Mike Perez	.05		300	Mark McGwire	1.50		418	Jayhawk Owens	.05		536	Steve Trachsel	.05
183	Travis Fryman	.05		301	Jim Deshaies	.05		419	J.R. Phillips	.05		537	Tony Eusebio	.05
184	Ben McDonald	.05		302	Edgar Martinez	.05		420	Cory Bailey RC	.05		538	Kelly Stinnett	.05
185	Steve Frey	.05		303	Danny Darwin	.05		421	Denny Hocking	.05		539	Paul Spoljaric	.05
186	Kevin Young	.05		304	Pat Meares	.05		422	Jon Shave	.05		540	Darren Dreifort	.05
187	Dave Magadan	.05		305	Benito Santiago	.05		423	Damon Buford	.05				
188	Bobby Munoz	.05		306	Jose Canseco	.40		424	Troy O'Leary	.05				
189	Pat Rapp	.05		307	Jim Gott	.05		425	Tripp Cromer	.05				
190	Jose Offerman	.05		308	Paul Sorrento	.05		426	Albie Lopez	.05				
191	Vinny Castilla	.05		309	Scott Kamieniecki	.05		427	Tony Fernandez	.05				
192	Ivan Calderon	.05		310	Larry Walker	.05		428	Ozzie Guillen	.05				
193	Ken Caminiti	.05		311	Mark Langston	.05		429	Alan Trammell	.05				
194	Benji Gil	.05		312	John Jaha	.05		430	John Wasdin RC	.05				
195	Chuck Carr	.05		313	Stan Javier	.05		431	Marc Valdes	.05				
196	Derrick May	.05		314	Hal Morris	.05		432	Brian Anderson RC	.20				
197	Pat Kelly	.05		315	Robby Thompson	.05		433	Matt Brunson RC	.05				
198	Jeff Brantley	.05		316	Pat Hentgen	.05		434	Wayne Gomes RC	.05				
199	Jose Lind	.05		317	Tom Gordon	.05		435	Jay Powell RC	.05				
200	Steve Buechele	.05		318	Joey Cora	.05		436	Kirk Presley RC	.05				
201	Wes Chamberlain	.05		319	Luis Alicea	.05		437	Jon Ratliff RC	.05				
202	Eduardo Perez	.05		320	Andre Dawson	.25		438	Derrek Lee RC	2.00				
203	Bret Saberhagen	.05		321	Darryl Kile	.05		439	Tom Pagnozzi	.05				
204	Gregg Jefferies	.05		322	Jose Rijo	.05		440	Kent Mercker	.05				
205	Darrin Fletcher	.05		323	Luis Gonzalez	.05		441	Phil Leftwich RC	.05				
206	Kent Hrbek	.05		324	Billy Ashley	.05		442	Jamie Moyer	.05				
207	Kim Batiste	.05		325	David Cone	.05		443	John Flaherty	.05				
208	Jeff King	.05		326	Bill Swift	.05		444	Mark Wohlers	.05				
209	Donovan Osborne	.05		327	Phil Hiatt	.05		445	Jose Bautista	.05				
210	Dave Nilsson	.05		328	Craig Paquette	.05		446	Andres Galarraga	.05				
211	Al Martin	.05		329	Bob Welch	.05		447	Mark Lemke	.05				
212	Mike Moore	.05		330	Tony Phillips	.05		448	Tim Wakefield	.05				
213	Sterling Hitchcock	.05		331	Archi Cianfrocco	.05		449	Pat Listach	.05				
214	Geronimo Pena	.05		332	Dave Winfield	.65		450	Rickey Henderson	.65				
215	Kevin Higgins	.05		333	David McCarty	.05		451	Mike Gallego	.05				
216	Norm Charlton	.05		334	Al Leiter	.05		452	Bob Tewksbury	.05				
217	Don Slaught	.05		335	Tom Browning	.05		453	Kirk Gibson	.05				
218	Mitch Williams	.05		336	Mark Grace	.05		454	Pedro Astacio	.05				
219	Derek Lilliquist	.05		337	Jose Mesa	.05		455	Mike Lansing	.05				
220	Armando Reynoso	.05		338	Mike Stanley	.05		456	Sean Berry	.05				
221	Kenny Rogers	.05		339	Roger McDowell	.05		457	Bob Walk	.05				
222	Doug Jones	.05		340	Damion Easley	.05		458	Chili Davis	.05				
223	Luis Aquino	.05		341	Angel Miranda	.05		459	Ed Sprague	.05				
224	Mike Oquist	.05		342	John Smoltz	.05		460	Kevin Stocker	.05				
225	Darryl Scott	.05		343	Jay Buhner	.05		461	Mike Stanton	.05				
226	Kurt Abbott	.05		344	Bryan Harvey	.05		462	Tim Raines	.05				
227	Andy Tomberlin	.05		345	Joe Carter	.05		463	Mike Bordick	.05				
228	Norberto Martin	.05		346	Dante Bichette	.05		464	David Wells	.05				
229	Pedro Castellano	.05		347	Jason Bere	.05		465	Tim Laker	.05				
230	Curtis Pride RC	.05		348	Frank Viola	.05		466	Cory Snyder	.05				
231	Jeff McNeely	.05		349	Ivan Rodriguez	.60		467	Alex Cole	.05				
232	Scott Lydy	.05		350	Juan Gonzalez	.35		468	Pete Incaviglia	.05				
233	Darren Oliver	.05		351	Steve Finley	.05		469	Roger Pavlik	.05				
234	Danny Bautista	.05		352	Mike Felder	.05		470	Greg W. Harris	.05				
235	Butch Huskey	.05		353	Ramon Martinez	.05		471	Xavier Hernandez	.05				
236	Chipper Jones	.75		354	Greg Gagne	.05		472	Erik Hanson	.05				
237	Eddie Zambrano	.05		355	Ken Hill	.05		473	Jesse Orosco	.05				
238	Jean Domingo	.05		356	Pedro Munoz	.05		474	Greg Colbrunn	.05				
239	Javier Lopez	.05		357	Todd Van Poppel	.05		475	Harold Reynolds	.05				
240	Nigel Wilson	.05		358	Marquis Grissom	.05		476	Greg Harris	.05				
241	Drew Denson RC	.05		359	Milt Cuyler	.05		477	Pat Borders	.05				
242	Raul Mondesi	.05		360	Reggie Sanders	.05		478	Melvin Nieves	.05				
243	Luis Ortiz	.05		361	Scott Erickson	.05		479	Mariano Duncan	.05				
244	Manny Ramirez	.65		362	Billy Hatcher	.05		480	Greg Hibbard	.05				
245	Greg Blosser	.05		363	Gene Harris	.05		481	Tim Pugh	.05				
246	Rondell White	.05		364	Rene Gonzales	.05		482	Bobby Ayala	.05				
247	Steve Karsay	.05		365	Kevin Rogers	.05		483	Sid Fernandez	.05				
248	Scott Stahoviak	.05		366	Eric Plunk	.05		484	Tim Wallach	.05				
249	Jose Valentin	.05		367	Todd Zeile	.05		485	Randy Milligan	.05				
250	Marc Newfield	.05		368	John Franco	.05		486	Walt Weiss	.05				
251	Keith Kessinger	.05		369	Brett Butler	.05		487	Matt Walbeck	.05				
252	Carl Everett	.05		370	Bill Spiers	.05		488	Mike Macfarlane	.05				

Each card in the 1994 Pinnacle set was produced in a parallel "Museum Collection" version. The inserts were produced utilizing the company's Dufex foil-printing technology on front, with rays emanating from the Pinnacle logo. Backs are identical to the regular-issue version except for the substitution of a "1994 Museum Collection" logo for the optical-variable anti-counterfeiting bar at bottom-center. Museums were random package inserts, appearing at the rate of about once per four packs.

	NM/M
Complete Set (540):	225.00
Common Player:	1.00
Stars/Rookies:	6X

Artist's Proof

A specially designated version of the regular Pinnacle set, described as the first day's production of the first 1,000 of each card, was issued as a random pack insert. Cards feature a small gold-foil "Artist's Proof" rectangle embossed above the player/team name shield on front. In all other respects the cards are identical to the regular-issue versions.

	NM/M
Complete Set (540):	250.00
Common Player:	1.50
Stars/Rookies:	20X

Museum Collection

Rookie Team Pinnacle

The popular Rookie Team Pinnacle insert card tradition continued in 1994 with a series of nine "two-headed" cards featuring the top prospect from each league at each position. The cards again feature the ultra-realistic artwork of Chris Greco. Each side is enhanced with gold-foil presentations of the player's name, the Pinnacle logo and the Rookie Team Pinnacle logo. The inserts were packaged, on average, one per 90 packs of hobby foil only.

		NM/M
Complete Set (9):		12.00
Common Player:		.75
1	Carlos Delgado, Javier Lopez	2.50
2	Bob Hamelin, J.R. Phillips	.75
3	Jon Shave, Keith Kessinger	.75
4	Butch Huskey, Luis Ortiz	.75
5	Chipper Jones, Kurt Abbott	5.00
6	Rondell White, Manny Ramirez	3.00
7	Cliff Floyd, Jeffrey Hammonds	.75
8	Marc Newfield, Nigel Wilson	.75
9	Salomon Torres, Mark Hutton	.75

Run Creators

This insert set, exclusive to Pinnacle jumbo packaging, features the top 44 performers of the previous season in the arcane statistic of "runs created." Fronts have an action photo on which the stadium background has been muted in soft-focus red or blue. The player's last name appears at right in gold foil; the logo, "The Run Creators" is in one of the lower corners. Backs are printed in teal with a color team logo at center, beneath the stats that earned the player's inclusion in the series. The player's runs created are in gold foil above the write-up. Cards are numbered with an "RC" prefix.

		NM/M
Complete Set (44):		17.50
Common Player:		.25
1	John Olerud	.25
2	Frank Thomas	1.00
3	Ken Griffey Jr.	3.00
4	Paul Molitor	1.00
5	Rafael Palmeiro	.75
6	Roberto Alomar	.35
7	Juan Gonzalez	.50
8	Albert Belle	.25
9	Travis Fryman	.25
10	Rickey Henderson	1.00
11	Tony Phillips	.25
12	Mo Vaughn	.25
13	Tim Salmon	.25
14	Kenny Lofton	.25
15	Carlos Baerga	.25
16	Greg Vaughn	.25
17	Jay Buhner	.25
18	Chris Hoiles	.25
19	Mickey Tettleton	.25
20	Kirby Puckett	1.50
21	Danny Tartabull	.25
22	Devon White	.25
23	Barry Bonds	4.00
24	Lenny Dykstra	.25
25	John Kruk	.25
26	Fred McGriff	.25
27	Gregg Jefferies	.25
28	Mike Piazza	3.00
29	Jeff Blauser	.25
30	Andres Galarraga	.25
31	Darren Daulton	.25
32	Dave Justice	.25
33	Craig Biggio	.25
34	Mark Grace	.25
35	Tony Gwynn	1.50
36	Jeff Bagwell	1.00
37	Jay Bell	.25
38	Marquis Grissom	.25
39	Matt Williams	.25
40	Charlie Hayes	.25
41	Dante Bichette	.25
42	Bernard Gilkey	.25
43	Brett Butler	.25
44	Rick Wilkins	.25

Team Pinnacle

The double-sided Team Pinnacle insert set features 18 of the top players in the game. They were inserted into Series 2 at a rate of one every 90 packs.

		NM/M
Complete Set (9):		35.00
Common Player:		1.50
1	Jeff Bagwell, Frank Thomas	4.00
2	Carlos Baerga, Robby Thompson	1.50
3	Matt Williams, Dean Palmer	1.50
4	Cal Ripken, Jr., Jay Bell	12.00
5	Ivan Rodriguez, Mike Piazza	6.00
6	Len Dykstra, Ken Griffey Jr.	8.00
7	Juan Gonzalez, Barry Bonds	10.00
8	Tim Salmon, Dave Justice	1.50
9	Greg Maddux, Jack McDowell	

Tribute

A hobby-only insert set, found approximately one per 18

foil packs, this nine-card series honors players who reached significant season or career milestones or otherwise had special achievements in 1993. Fronts feature full-bleed action photos. At left is a black strip with "TRIBUTE" in gold foil. A colored strip at bottom has the player name in gold foil and a short description of why he is being feted beneath. The Pinnacle logo is in gold foil at top. The same gold-foil enhancements are found on back, along with a portrait photo. In a black box at bottom are details of the tribute. The Pinnacle optical-variable anti-counterfeiting device is at bottom center. Card numbers are prefixed with "TR."

		NM/M
Complete Set (18):		15.00
Common Player:		.25
1	Paul Molitor	1.00
2	Jim Abbott	.25
3	Dave Winfield	1.00
4	Bo Jackson	.35
5	Dave Justice	.25
6	Len Dykstra	.25
7	Mike Piazza	2.50
8	Barry Bonds	4.50
9	Randy Johnson	1.00
10	Ozzie Smith	1.50
11	Mark Whiten	.25
12	Greg Maddux	1.50
13	Cal Ripken, Jr.	4.50
14	Frank Thomas	1.00
15	Juan Gonzalez	.45
16	Roberto Alomar	.25
17	Ken Griffey Jr.	3.00
18	Lee Smith	.25

New Generation

Baseball's hottest rookies and second-year players were featured in this boxed set. Cards are typical Pinnacle quality with full-bleed action photos, UV coating and gold-foil stamping on front and back. A total of 100,000 sets was produced, with a suggested retail price of $9.95.

		NM/M
Complete Set (25):		5.00
Common Player:		.25
1	Tim Salmon	.25
2	Mike Piazza	2.00
3	Jason Bere	.25
4	Jeffrey Hammonds	.25
5	Aaron Sele	.25
6	Salomon Torres	.25
7	Wil Cordero	.25
8	Allen Watson	.25
9	J.T. Snow	.25
10	Cliff Floyd	.25
10a	Cliff Floyd/OPS	.50
11	Jeff McNeely	.25
12	Butch Huskey	.25
13	J.R. Phillips	.25
14	Bobby Jones	.25

15	Javier Lopez	.25
16	Scott Ruffcorn	.25
17	Manny Ramirez	1.25
18	Carlos Delgado	1.00
19	Rondell White	.25
20	Chipper Jones	1.50
21	Billy Ashley	.25
22	Nigel Wilson	.25
23	Jeromy Burnitz	.25
24	Danny Bautista	.25
25	Darrell Whitmore	.25

Power Surge

The major leagues' heaviest hitters are featured in this boxed set. Cards are typical Pinnacle quality with gold-foil stamping, on front, UV coating on both sides and high-tech graphics. Fronts feature game-action photos while backs have smaller portrait and action photos on a marbled background, along with 1993 and career stats and a description of the player's power potential. Cards are numbered with a "PS" prefix. A total of 100,000 sets was produced.

		NM/M
Complete Set (25):		4.00
Common Player:		.25
1	Dave Justice	.25
2	Chris Hoiles	.25
3	Mo Vaughn	.25
4	Tim Salmon	.25
5	J.T. Snow	.25
6	Frank Thomas	.65
7	Sammy Sosa	.75
8	Rick Wilkins	.25
9	Robin Ventura	.25
10	Reggie Sanders	.25
11	Albert Belle	.25
12	Carlos Baerga	.35
12a	Carlos Baerga/OPS	.50
13	Manny Ramirez	.65
14	Travis Fryman	.25
15	Gary Sheffield	.35
16	Jeff Bagwell	.65
17	Mike Piazza	1.00
18	Eric Karros	.25
19	Cliff Floyd	.25
20	Mark Whiten	.25
21	Phil Plantier	.25
22	Derek Bell	.25
23	Ken Griffey Jr.	1.00
24	Juan Gonzalez	.35
25	Dean Palmer	.25

The Naturals

The Naturals boxed set puts a game-action photo against a textured-foil background. Backs picture the player on a background of nature photography, including lightning, blue skies and clouds. Pinnacle produced 100,000 sets, which come in a numbered, sealed box with a certificate of authenticity.

		NM/M
Complete Set (25):		6.00

Common Player:		.15
1	Frank Thomas	.50
2	Barry Bonds	1.50
3	Ken Griffey Jr.	1.00
4	Juan Gonzalez	.25
5	Dave Justice	.15
6	Albert Belle	.15
7	Kenny Lofton	.15
8	Roberto Alomar	.35
9	Tim Salmon	.15
10	Randy Johnson	.50
11	Kirby Puckett	.65
12	Tony Gwynn	.65
13	Fred McGriff	.15
14	Ryne Sandberg	.65
15	Greg Maddux	.65
16	Matt Williams	.15
17	Lenny Dykstra	.15
18	Gary Sheffield	.35
18a	Gary Sheffield/OPS	.50
19	Mike Piazza	1.00
20	Dean Palmer	.15
21	Travis Fryman	.15
22	Carlos Baerga	.15
23	Cal Ripken, Jr.	1.50
24	John Olerud	.15
25	Roger Clemens	.75

1995 Pinnacle Series 1 Samples

This eight-card cello-wrapped sample set was sent to dealers to preview the 1995 Pinnacle Series 1 cards. The cards are identical to regular-issue Pinnacle cards except they carry a white diagonal "SAMPLE" notation on front and back.

		NM/M
Complete Set (9):		6.00
Common Player:		.50
16	Mickey Morandini	.50
22US	Wil Cordero (Upstart)	
	(Card not included in most	
	packs.)	2.00
119	Gary Sheffield	1.00
122	Ivan Rodriguez	1.50
132	Alex Rodriguez	
	(Rookie)	3.00
208	Bo Jackson	.75
223	Jose Rijo	.50
224	Ryan Klesko	.50
----	Header Card	.05

1995 Pinnacle

The 1995 Pinnacle set was produced in two series of 225 base cards each, plus inserts. Fronts feature borderless photos with a large embossed gold foil "wave" at bottom containing the player's last name and team logo. Horizontal backs have a portrait photo at left, an action photo at right and a few sentences about the player at center. Stats at the bottom offer previous year, career and career-best numbers. Subsets with the base cards include rookie specials in both Series 1 and 2 have a design featuring a green stripe at

one side or bottom with the player's name in gold and a special round gold-foil logo. A similar design, with red stripes, is used for Series 1 cards featuring Draft Picks. In Series 2, a 30-card Swing Men subset has a blue vortex background design and special gold-foil identifier. Basic pack configurations offered 12-card ($2.49) and 15-card ($2.99) counts in both retail and hobby versions, each with some unique inserts.

		NM/M
Complete Set (450):		15.00
Artist's Proofs:		10X
Museum Collection:		4X
Hobby Pack (12):		.15
Hobby Wax Box (24):		15.00
Retail Pack (12):		1.00
Retail Wax Box (36):		20.00
1	Jeff Bagwell	.75
2	Roger Clemens	1.25
3	Mark Whiten	.10
4	Shawon Dunston	.10
5	Bobby Bonilla	.10
6	Kevin Tapani	.10
7	Eric Karros	.10
8	Cliff Floyd	.10
9	Pat Kelly	.10
10	Jeffrey Hammonds	.10
11	Jeff Conine	.10
12	Fred McGriff	.10
13	Chris Bosio	.10
14	Mike Mussina	.40
15	Danny Bautista	.10
16	Mickey Morandini	.10
17	Chuck Finley	.10
18	Jim Thome	.65
19	Luis Ortiz	.10
20	Walt Weiss	.10
21	Don Mattingly	1.25
22	Bob Hamelin	.10
23	Melido Perez	.10
24	Kevin Mitchell	.10
25	John Smoltz	.10
26	Hector Carrasco	.10
27	Pat Hentgen	.10
28	Derrick May	.10
29	Mike Kingery	.10
30	Chuck Carr	.10
31	Billy Ashley	.10
32	Todd Hundley	.10
33	Luis Gonzalez	.10
34	Marquis Grissom	.10
35	Jeff King	.10
36	Eddie Williams	.10
37	Tom Pagnozzi	.10
38	Chris Hoiles	.10
39	Sandy Alomar	.10
40	Mike Greenwell	.10
41	Lance Johnson	.10
42	Junior Felix	.10
43	Felix Jose	.10
44	Scott Leius	.10
45	Ruben Sierra	.10
46	Kevin Seitzer	.10
47	Wade Boggs	1.00
48	Reggie Jefferson	.10
49	Jose Canseco	.40
50	Dave Justice	.10
51	John Smiley	.10
52	Joe Carter	.10
53	Rick Wilkins	.10
54	Ellis Burks	.10
55	Dave Weathers	.10
56	Pedro Astacio	.10
57	Ryan Thompson	.10
58	James Mouton	.10
59	Mel Rojas	.10
60	Orlando Merced	.10
61	Matt Williams	.10
62	Bernard Gilkey	.10
63	J.R. Phillips	.10
64	Lee Smith	.10
65	Jim Edmonds	.10
66	Darrin Jackson	.10
67	Scott Cooper	.10
68	Ron Karkovice	.10
69	Chris Gomez	.10
70	Kevin Appier	.10
71	Bobby Jones	.10
72	Doug Drabek	.10
73	Matt Mieske	.10
74	Sterling Hitchcock	.10
75	John Valentin	.10
76	Reggie Sanders	.10
77	Wally Joyner	.10
78	Turk Wendell	.10
79	Wendell Hayes	.10
80	Bret Barberie	.10
81	Troy Neel	.10
82	Ken Caminiti	.10
83	Milt Thompson	.10
84	Paul Sorrento	.10
85	Trevor Hoffman	.10
86	Jay Bell	.10
87	Mark Portugal	.10
88	Sid Fernandez	.10
89	Charles Nagy	.10
90	Jeff Montgomery	.10
91	Chuck Knoblauch	.10
92	Jeff Frye	.10

93	Tony Gwynn	1.00
94	John Olerud	.10
95	David Nied	.10
96	Chris Hammond	.10
97	Edgar Martinez	.10
98	Kevin Stocker	.10
99	Jeff Fassero	.10
100	Curt Schilling	.30
101	Dave Clark	.10
102	Delino DeShields	.10
103	Leo Gomez	.10
104	Dave Hollins	.10
105	Tim Naehring	.10
106	Otis Nixon	.10
107	Ozzie Guillen	.10
108	Jose Lind	.10
109	Stan Javier	.10
110	Greg Vaughn	.10
111	Chipper Jones	1.00
112	Ed Sprague	.10
113	Mike Macfarlane	.10
114	Steve Finley	.10
115	Ken Hill	.10
116	Carlos Garcia	.10
117	Lou Whitaker	.10
118	Todd Zeile	.10
119	Gary Sheffield	.40
120	Ben McDonald	.10
121	Pete Harnisch	.10
122	Ivan Rodriguez	.65
123	Wilson Alvarez	.10
124	Travis Fryman	.10
125	Pedro Munoz	.10
126	Mark Lemke	.10
127	Jose Valentin	.10
128	Ken Griffey Jr.	1.50
129	Omar Vizquel	.10
130	Milt Cuyler	.10
131	Steve Traschel	.10
132	Alex Rodriguez	2.00
133	Garret Anderson	.10
134	Armando Benitez	.10
135	Shawn Green	.35
136	Jorge Fabregas	.10
137	Orlando Miller	.10
138	Rikkert Faneyte	.10
139	Ismael Valdes	.10
140	Jose Oliva	.10
141	Aaron Small	.10
142	Tim Davis	.10
143	Ricky Bottalacio	.10
144	Mike Matheny	.10
145	Roberto Petagine	.10
146	Fausto Cruz	.10
147	Bryce Florie	.10
148	Jose Lima	.10
149	John Hudek	.10
150	Duane Singleton	.10
151	John Mabry	.10
152	Robert Eenhoorn	.10
153	Jon Lieber	.10
154	Garey Ingram	.10
155	Paul Shuey	.10
156	Mike Lieberthal	.10
157	Steve Dunn	.10
158	Charles Johnson	.10
159	Ernie Young	.10
160	Jose Martinez	.10
161	Kurt Miller	.10
162	Joey Eischen	.10
163	Dave Stevens	.10
164	Brian Hunter	.10
165	Jeff Cirillo	.10
166	Mark Smith	.10
167	McKay Christensen RC	.10
168	C.J. Nitkowski	.10
169	Antone Williamson RC	.10
170	Paul Konerko	.15
171	Scott Elarton RC	.15
172	Jacob Shumate	.10
173	Terrence Long	.10
174	Mark Johnson RC	.10
175	Ben Grieve	.10
176	Jayson Peterson RC	.10
177	Checklist	.10
178	Checklist	.10
179	Checklist	.10
180	Checklist	.10
181	Brian Anderson	.10
182	Steve Buechele	.10
183	Mark Clark	.10
184	Cecil Fielder	.10
185	Steve Avery	.10
186	Devon White	.10
187	Craig Shipley	.10
188	Brady Anderson	.10
189	Kenny Lofton	.10
190	Alex Cole	.10
191	Brent Gates	.10
192	Dean Palmer	.10
193	Alex Gonzalez	.10
194	Steve Cooke	.10
195	Ray Lankford	.10
196	Mark McGwire	2.00
197	Marc Newfield	.10
198	Pat Rapp	.10
199	Darren Lewis	.10
200	Carlos Baerga	.10
201	Rickey Henderson	.75
202	Kurt Abbott	.10
203	Kirt Manwaring	.10
204	Cal Ripken Jr.	2.50
205	Darren Daulton	.10
206	Greg Colbrunn	.10
207	Darryl Hamilton	.10
208	Bo Jackson	.15
209	Tony Phillips	.10
210	Geronimo Berroa	.10

211	Rich Becker	.10
212	Tony Tarasco	.10
213	Karl Rhodes	.10
214	Phil Plantier	.10
215	J.T. Snow	.10
216	Mo Vaughn	.10
217	Greg Gagne	.10
218	Rickey Bones	.10
219	Mike Bordick	.10
220	Chad Curtis	.10
221	Royce Clayton	.10
222	Roberto Alomar	.15
223	Jose Rijo	.10
224	Ryan Klesko	.10
225	Mark Langston	.10
226	Frank Thomas	.75
227	Juan Gonzalez	.40
228	Ron Gant	.10
229	Javier Lopez	.10
230	Sammy Sosa	1.00
231	Kevin Brown	.10
232	Gary DiSarcina	.10
233	Albert Belle	.10
234	Jay Buhner	.10
235	Pedro Martinez	.75
236	Bob Tewksbury	.10
237	Mike Piazza	1.50
238	Darryl Kile	.10
239	Bryan Harvey	.10
240	Andres Galarraga	.10
241	Jeff Blauser	.10
242	Jeff Kent	.10
243	Bobby Munoz	.10
244	Greg Maddux	1.00
245	Paul O'Neill	.10
246	Lenny Dykstra	.10
247	Todd Van Poppel	.10
248	Bernie Williams	.05
249	Glenallen Hill	.10
250	Duane Ward	.10
251	Dennis Eckersley	.60
252	Pat Mahomes	.10
253	Rusty Greer (Photo actually	
	Jeff Frye.)	.10
254	Roberto Kelly	.10
255	Randy Myers	.10
256	Scott Ruffcorn	.10
257	Robin Ventura	.10
258	Eduardo Perez	.10
259	Aaron Sele	.10
260	Paul Molitor	.75
261	Juan Guzman	.10
262	Darren Oliver	.10
263	Mike Stanley	.10
264	Tom Glavine	.30
265	Rico Brogna	.10
266	Craig Biggio	.10
267	Darrell Whitmore	.10
268	Jimmy Key	.10
269	Will Clark	.10
270	David Cone	.10
271	Brian Jordan	.10
272	Barry Bonds	2.50
273	Danny Tartabull	.10
274	Ramon Martinez	.10
275	Al Martin	.10
276	Fred McGriff	
	(Swing Men)	.10
277	Carlos Delgado	
	(Swing Men)	.25
278	Juan Gonzalez	
	(Swing Men)	.20
279	Shawn Green	
	(Swing Men)	.20
280	Carlos Baerga	
	(Swing Men)	.10
281	Cliff Floyd (Swing Men)	.10
282	Ozzie Smith	
	(Swing Men)	.50
283	Alex Rodriguez	
	(Swing Men)	1.00
284	Kenny Lofton	
	(Swing Men)	.10
285	Dave Justice	
	(Swing Men)	.10
286	Tim Salmon	
	(Swing Men)	.10
287	Manny Ramirez	
	(Swing Men)	.40
288	Will Clark (Swing Men)	.10
289	Garret Anderson	
	(Swing Men)	.10
290	Billy Ashley	
	(Swing Men)	.10
291	Tony Gwynn	
	(Swing Men)	.50
292	Raul Mondesi	
	(Swing Men)	.10
293	Rafael Palmeiro	
	(Swing Men)	.30
294	Matt Williams	
	(Swing Men)	.10
295	Don Mattingly	
	(Swing Men)	.60
296	Kirby Puckett	
	(Swing Men)	.50
297	Paul Molitor	
	(Swing Men)	.40
298	Albert Belle	
	(Swing Men)	.10
299	Barry Bonds	
	(Swing Men)	1.25
300	Mike Piazza	
	(Swing Men)	.85
301	Jeff Bagwell	
	(Swing Men)	.40
302	Frank Thomas	
	(Swing Men)	.40

303	Chipper Jones	
	(Swing Men)	.50
304	Ken Griffey Jr.	
	(Swing Men)	.75
305	Cal Ripken Jr.	
	(Swing Men)	1.25
306	Eric Anthony	.10
307	Todd Benzinger	.10
308	Jacob Brumfield	.10
309	Wes Chamberlain	.10
310	Tino Martinez	.10
311	Roberto Mejia	.10
312	Jose Offerman	.10
313	David Segui	.10
314	Eric Young	.10
315	Rey Sanchez	.10
316	Raul Mondesi	.10
317	Bret Boone	.10
318	Andre Dawson	.30
319	Brian McRae	.10
320	Dave Nilsson	.10
321	Moises Alou	.10
322	Don Slaught	.10
323	Dave McCarty	.10
324	Mike Huff	.10
325	Rick Aguilera	.10
326	Rod Beck	.10
327	Kenny Rogers	.10
328	Andy Benes	.10
329	Allen Watson	.10
330	Randy Johnson	.75
331	Willie Greene	.10
332	Hal Morris	.10
333	Ozzie Smith	1.00
334	Jason Bere	.10
335	Scott Erickson	.10
336	Dante Bichette	.10
337	Willie Banks	.10
338	Eric Davis	.10
339	Rondell White	.10
340	Kirby Puckett	1.00
341	Deion Sanders	.10
342	Eddie Murray	.75
343	Mike Harkey	.10
344	Joey Hamilton	.10
345	Roger Salkeld	.10
346	Wil Cordero	.10
347	John Wetteland	.10
348	Geronimo Pena	.10
349	Kirk Gibson	.10
350	Manny Ramirez	.75
351	William	
	Van Landingham	.10
352	B.J. Surhoff	.10
353	Ken Ryan	.10
354	Terry Steinbach	.10
355	Bret Saberhagen	.10
356	John Jaha	.10
357	Joe Girardi	.10
358	Steve Karsay	.10
359	Alex Fernandez	.10
360	Salomon Torres	.10
361	John Burkett	.10
362	Derek Bell	.10
363	Tom Henke	.10
364	Gregg Jefferies	.10
365	Jack McDowell	.10
366	Andujar Cedeno	.10
367	Dave Winfield	.75
368	Carl Everett	.10
369	Danny Jackson	.10
370	Jeromy Burnitz	.10
371	Mark Grace	.10
372	Larry Walker	.10
373	Bill Swift	.10
374	Dennis Martinez	.10
375	Mickey Tettleton	.10
376	Mel Nieves	.10
377	Cal Eldred	.10
378	Orel Hershiser	.10
379	David Wells	.10
380	Gary Gaetti	.10
381	Tim Raines	.10
382	Barry Larkin	.10
383	Jason Jacome	.10
384	Tim Wallach	.10
385	Robby Thompson	.10
386	Frank Viola	.10
387	Dave Stewart	.10
388	Bip Roberts	.10
389	Ron Darling	.10
390	Carlos Delgado	.45
391	Tim Salmon	.10
392	Alan Trammell	.10
393	Kevin Foster	.10
394	Jim Abbott	.10
395	John Kruk	.10
396	Andy Van Slyke	.10
397	Dave Magadan	.10
398	Rafael Palmeiro	.65
399	Mike Devereaux	.10
400	Benito Santiago	.10
401	Brett Butler	.10
402	John Franco	.10
403	Matt Walbeck	.10
404	Terry Pendleton	.10
405	Chris Sabo	.10
406	Andrew Lorraine	.10
407	Dan Wilson	.10
408	Mike Lansing	.10
409	Ray McDavid	.10
410	Shane Andrews	.10
411	Tom Gordon	.10
412	Chad Ogea	.10
413	James Baldwin	.10
414	Russ Davis	.10
415	Ray Holbert	.10
416	Ray Durham	.10

417	Matt Nokes	.10
418	Rodney Henderson	.10
419	Gabe White	.10
420	Todd Hollandsworth	.10
421	Midre Cummings	.10
422	Harold Baines	.10
423	Troy Percival	.10
424	Joe Vitiello	.10
425	Andy Ashby	.10
426	Michael Tucker	.10
427	Mark Gubicza	.10
428	Jim Bullinger	.10
429	Jose Malave	.10
430	Pete Schourek	.10
431	Bobby Ayala	.10
432	Marvin Freeman	.10
433	Pat Listach	.10
434	Eddie Taubensee	.10
435	Steve Howe	.10
436	Kent Mercker	.10
437	Hector Fajardo	.10
438	Scott Kamieniecki	.10
439	Robb Nen	.10
440	Mike Kelly	.10
441	Tom Candiotti	.10
442	Albie Lopez	.10
443	Jeff Granger	.10
444	Rich Aude	.10
445	Luis Polonia	.10
446	A.L. Checklist	
	(Frank Thomas)	.65
447	A.L. Checklist	
	(Ken Griffey Jr.)	.65
448	N.L. Checklist	
	(Mike Piazza)	.75
449	N.L. Checklist	
	(Jeff Bagwell)	.40
450	Insert Checklist	
	(Frank Thomas,	
	Ken Griffey Jr.,	
	Mike Piazza,	
	Jeff Bagwell)	.40

Artist's Proof

Said to represent the first 1,000 of each card printed, the Artist's Proof chase set is a parallel issue with a counterpart for each of the regular-issue cards. The proofs differ in the use of silver, rather than gold foil for front graphic highlights, and the inclusion of a rectangular silver-foil "ARTIST'S PROOF" logo on front. The AP inserts were reported seeded at an average rate of one per 26 packs.

	NM/M
Complete Set (450):	300.00
Common Player:	1.00
Stars/Rookies:	10X

Museum Collection

Pinnacle's Dufex foil-printing technology on the card fronts differentiates this parallel insert from the corresponding cards in the regular issue. Backs have a rectangular "1995 Museum Collection" logo at lower-left. Museum inserts are found at an average rate of one per four packs. Because of production difficulties, trade cards had to be issued in place of seven of the rookie cards in Series 2. Those redemption cards were valid only through Dec. 31, 1995.

	NM/M
Complete Set (450):	200.00
Common Player:	.50
Stars/Rookies:	4X
Redemption card	.25

E.T.A. '95

This hobby-only chase set identifies six players picked to arrive in the major leagues for a 1995 debut. Both sides have borderless action photos on which the background has been subdued and posterized. Gold-foil headlines on each side of the card give the player's credentials. These inserts are found on average of once per 24 packs.

	NM/M
Complete Set (6):	5.00
Common Player:	.70
1	Ben Grieve	.75
2	Alex Ochoa	.75
3	Joe Vitiello	.75
4	Johnny Damon	3.00
5	Trey Beamon	.75
6	Brooks Kieschnick	.75

Gate Attraction

Series 2 jumbo packs are the exclusive source for this chase set. Printed on metallic foil, the cards have a color photo at top and a second photo at bottom that is shown in gold tones only. A "Gate Attraction" seal is in the lower-left corner. Backs have a large portrait photo on a color-streaked background, plus a few words about the player.

	NM/M
Complete Set (18):	25.00
Common Player:	.50
1	Ken Griffey Jr	3.50
2	Frank Thomas	1.50
3	Cal Ripken Jr.	5.00
4	Jeff Bagwell	1.50
5	Mike Piazza	3.50
6	Barry Bonds	5.00
7	Kirby Puckett	2.00
8	Albert Belle	.50
9	Tony Gwynn	2.00
10	Raul Mondesi	.50
11	Will Clark	.50
12	Don Mattingly	2.75
13	Roger Clemens	2.75
14	Paul Molitor	1.50
15	Matt Williams	.50
16	Greg Maddux	2.00
17	Kenny Lofton	.50
18	Cliff Floyd	.50

New Blood

Both hobby and retail packs of Series 2 hide this insert set of young stars, at an average rate of one card per 90 packs. A player photo appears in the red and silver foil-

printed background, and there is a color action photo in the foreground. Conventionally printed backs feature the same photos, but with their prominence reversed. A few words of text describe the player's star potential.

	NM/M
Complete Set (9):	10.00
Common Player:	.70
1	Alex Rodriguez	5.00
2	Shawn Green	1.50
3	Brian Hunter	.75
4	Garret Anderson	.75
5	Charles Johnson	.75
6	Chipper Jones	3.00
7	Carlos Delgado	1.50
8	Billy Ashley	.75
9	J.R. Phillips	.75

Performers

Series 1 jumbos were the only place to find this chase set. Fronts have a deep red background with a golden pyramid at center and a silver apex, all in foil printing. A color player action photo is in the center foreground. The reverse repeats the front photo in the background, in one color, and has a second color photo, along with a few words about the player.

	NM/M
Complete Set (18):	15.00
Common Player:	.35
1	Frank Thomas	2.00
2	Albert Belle	.35
3	Barry Bonds	3.50
4	Juan Gonzalez	1.00
5	Andres Galarraga	.35
6	Raul Mondesi	.35
7	Paul Molitor	2.00
8	Tim Salmon	.35
9	Mike Piazza	2.50
10	Gregg Jefferies	.35
11	Will Clark	.35
12	Greg Maddux	2.25
13	Manny Ramirez	2.00
14	Kirby Puckett	2.25
15	Shawn Green	1.25
16	Rafael Palmeiro	1.75
17	Paul O'Neill	.35
18	Jason Bere	.35

Red Hot

These Series 2 inserts are found at an average rate of one per 16 packs and feature top veteran stars. Fronts have a large action photo on right, over a background of foil-printed red and yellow flames. A vertical strip at left of graduated red tones has a player portrait photo and the "RED HOT" flame logo, again printed on foil. Backs are con-

ventionally printed and have a black background with large flaming "RED HOT" letters and a color player photo.

	NM/M
Complete Set (25):	35.00
Common Player:	.75
1	Cal Ripken Jr.	5.50
2	Ken Griffey Jr.	4.00
3	Frank Thomas	1.50
4	Jeff Bagwell	1.50
5	Mike Piazza	4.00
6	Barry Bonds	5.50
7	Albert Belle	.75
8	Tony Gwynn	2.00
9	Kirby Puckett	2.00
10	Don Mattingly	2.50
11	Matt Williams	.75
12	Greg Maddux	2.00
13	Raul Mondesi	.75
14	Paul Molitor	1.50
15	Manny Ramirez	1.50
16	Joe Carter	.75
17	Will Clark	.75
18	Roger Clemens	2.50
19	Tim Salmon	.75
20	Dave Justice	.75
21	Kenny Lofton	.75
22	Deion Sanders	.75
23	Roberto Alomar	1.00
24	Cliff Floyd	.75
25	Carlos Baerga	.75

White Hot

Similar in format to the Red Hot inserts, and featuring the same players, the hobby-only White Hot cards are a chase set of a chase set. Seeded once per 36 packs on average (more than twice as scarce as the Red Hots), the White Hot cards have fronts totally printed in the Dufex process, with predominantly blue and white background colors, while the backs are highlighted by blue foil printing in the "WHITE HOT" background lettering on black background.

	NM/M
Complete Set (25):	140.00
Common Player:	2.50
1	Cal Ripken Jr.	16.00
2	Ken Griffey Jr.	13.50
3	Frank Thomas	8.00
4	Jeff Bagwell	8.00
5	Mike Piazza	13.50
6	Barry Bonds	16.00
7	Albert Belle	2.50
8	Tony Gwynn	10.00
9	Kirby Puckett	10.00
10	Don Mattingly	12.00
11	Matt Williams	2.50
12	Greg Maddux	10.00
13	Raul Mondesi	2.50
14	Paul Molitor	8.00
15	Manny Ramirez	8.00
16	Joe Carter	2.50
17	Will Clark	2.50
18	Roger Clemens	12.00
19	Tim Salmon	2.50
20	Dave Justice	2.50
21	Kenny Lofton	2.50
22	Deion Sanders	2.50
23	Roberto Alomar	3.50
24	Cliff Floyd	2.50
25	Carlos Baerga	2.50

Team Pinnacle

This nine-card Series 1 insert set becomes an 18-card challenge if the collector decides to hunt for both versions of each card. As in the past the Team Pinnacle cards picture National and American League counterparts at each position on different sides of the same card. In 1995 each card is printed with one side in Pinnacle's Dufex foil technology, and the other side conventionally printed. Thus card #1 can be found with Mike Mussina in Dufex and Greg Maddux conventionally printed, or with Maddux in Dufex and Mussina conventional. Team Pinnacle cards are found inserted at an average rate of only one per 90 packs. Card numbers have a "TP" prefix.

	NM/M
Complete Set (9):	35.00
Common Player:	1.50
1	Mike Mussina,	
	Greg Maddux	8.00
2	Carlos Delgado,	
	Mike Piazza	6.00
3	Frank Thomas,	
	Jeff Bagwell	4.00
4	Roberto Alomar,	
	Craig Biggio	3.00
5	Cal Ripken Jr.,	
	Ozzie Smith	12.00
6	Travis Fryman,	
	Matt Williams	1.50
7	Ken Griffey Jr.,	
	Barry Bonds	10.00
8	Albert Belle,	
	Dave Justice	1.50
9	Kirby Puckett,	
	Tony Gwynn	8.00

Team Pinnacle Pin Trade Cards

In one of the hobby's first major attempts to cross-promote pin- and card-collecting, Series 2 Pinnacle packs offered a special insert set of cards which could be redeemed for a collector's pin of the same player. Seeded at the rate of one per 48 regular packs and one per 36 jumbo packs, the pin redemption cards were valid until Nov. 15, 1995. Payment of $2 handling fee was required for redemption.

	NM/M
Complete Set (18):	40.00
Common Player:	.70
1	Greg Maddux	4.00
2	Mike Mussina	1.50
3	Mike Piazza	5.00
4	Carlos Delgado	1.50
5	Jeff Bagwell	3.00
6	Frank Thomas	3.00

22	Deion Sanders	2.50
23	Roberto Alomar	3.50
24	Cliff Floyd	2.50
25	Carlos Baerga	2.50

7 Craig Biggio .75
8 Roberto Alomar 1.00
9 Ozzie Smith 4.00
10 Cal Ripken Jr. 6.00
11 Matt Williams .75
12 Travis Fryman .75
13 Barry Bonds 6.00
14 Ken Griffey Jr. 5.00
15 Dave Justice .75
16 Albert Belle .75
17 Tony Gwynn 4.00
18 Kirby Puckett 4.00

Team Pinnacle Collector Pins

Redemption cards in Series 2 packs could be traded in (until Nov. 15, 1995) for an enameled pin of the player pictured on the trade card. Pins are about 1-3/8" x 1-1/4". A raised relief portrait of the player is at center with his name in pennants above and his team logo at bottom, along with the Pinnacle logo. Backs are gold-tone with a post-and-button style of pin-back. The unnumbered pins are listed here in the same sequence as the redemption cards.

	NM/M
Complete Set (18):	135.00
Common Player:	5.00
(1) Greg Maddux	10.00
(2) Mike Mussina	6.00
(3) Mike Piazza	15.00
(4) Carlos Delgado	6.00
(5) Jeff Bagwell	8.00
(6) Frank Thomas	8.00
(7) Craig Biggio	5.00
(8) Roberto Alomar	6.00
(9) Ozzie Smith	10.00
(10) Cal Ripken Jr.	20.00
(11) Matt Williams	5.00
(12) Travis Fryman	5.00
(13) Barry Bonds	20.00
(14) Ken Griffey Jr.	15.00
(15) Dave Justice	5.00
(16) Albert Belle	5.00
(17) Tony Gwynn	10.00
(18) Kirby Puckett	10.00

Pin-Cards

Virtually nothing is known of this issue except that it is connected in some way to the Series 2 Pinnacle player pin issue. The front features portrait and action photos on a red background with gold-foil graphics. Backs have career highlights, a large color photo and a card number with "PPC" prefix. To date only a single card is known.

Upstarts

The most dominant young players in the game were featured in this insert series. Cards are printed with most of the photo's background covered by the legs of

a large blue-and-gold star device, which includes the team logo at its red center. A blue circular "'95 UPSTARTS" logo at bottom-left has the player name in gold. These cards are exclusive to Series 1, found at an average rate of one per eight packs.

	NM/M
Complete Set (30):	10.00
Common Player:	.15
1 Frank Thomas	1.50
2 Roberto Alomar	.30
3 Mike Piazza	2.50
4 Javier Lopez	.15
5 Albert Belle	.15
6 Carlos Delgado	.75
7 Rusty Greer	.15
8 Tim Salmon	.15
9 Raul Mondesi	.15
10 Juan Gonzalez	.75
11 Manny Ramirez	1.50
12 Sammy Sosa	2.00
13 Jeff Kent	.15
14 Melvin Nieves	.15
15 Rondell White	.15
16 Shawn Green	.75
17 Bernie Williams	.15
18 Aaron Sele	.15
19 Jason Bere	.15
20 Joey Hamilton	.15
21 Mike Kelly	.15
22 Wil Cordero	.15
23 Moises Alou	.15
24 Roberto Kelly	.15
25 Deion Sanders	.15
26 Steve Karsay	.15
27 Bret Boone	.15
28 Willie Greene	.15
29 Billy Ashley	.15
30 Brian Anderson	.15

FanFest

Pinnacle's sponsorship of the July 7-11 All-Star FanFest was marked with the issue of this set. Cards were distributed in two-card packs at various venues around the All-Star celebration in Arlington, Texas. Each card features the FanFest logo at lower-left on front, with the player's name and team logo in a stylized gold-foil baseball diamond diagram at lower-right. A full-bleed action photo comprises the rest of the front. Horizontal backs show a portrait photo of the player before a photo of The Ballpark at Arlington. The FanFast logo is repeated at bottom-center.

	NM/M
Complete Set (30):	7.50
Common Player:	.15
1 Cal Ripken Jr.	1.50
2 Roger Clemens	.75
3 Don Mattingly	.75
4 Albert Belle	.15
5 Kirby Puckett	.65
6 Cecil Fielder	.15
7 Kevin Appier	.15
8 Will Clark	.15
9 Juan Gonzalez	.25
10 Ivan Rodriguez	.45
11 Ken Griffey Jr.	1.00
12 Tim Salmon	.15
13 Frank Thomas	.50
14 Roberto Alomar	.20
15 Rickey Henderson	.50
16 Raul Mondesi	.15
17 Matt Williams	.15
18 Ozzie Smith	.65
19 Deion Sanders	.15
20 Tony Gwynn	.65
21 Greg Maddux	.65
22 Sammy Sosa	.65
23 Mike Piazza	1.00
24 Barry Bonds	1.50
25 Jeff Bagwell	.50
26 Len Dykstra	.15
27 Rico Brogna	.15
28 Larry Walker	.15
29 Gary Sheffield	.35
30 Wil Cordero	.15

1996 Pinnacle Samples

Pinnacle's 1996 issue was premiered with this nine-card sample set. The cards are virtually identical in format to the regular-issue cards, but feature a large white "SAMPLE" printed diagonally on front and back. The cards were sent to dealers and hobby media in a cello pack.

	NM/M
Complete Set (9):	5.00
Common Player:	.75
1 Greg Maddux	1.50
2 Bill Pulsipher	.75
3 Dante Bichette	.75
4 Mike Piazza	2.00
5 Garret Anderson	.75
165 Ruben Rivera	.75
168 Tony Clark	.75
2 Mo Vaughn (Pinnacle Power)	1.00
--- Header Card	

1996 Pinnacle

Pinnacle's 400-card regular-issue set has borderless front photos highlighted by prismatic gold-foil graphics in a triangle at bottom. Backs have another photo along with stats and data. Parallel Starburst and Starburst Artist's Proof sets contain only 200 of the cards in the base issue. Series 1 inserts include a Cal Ripken Jr. "Tribute" card, numbered "1 of 1," along with Team Pinnacle, Pinnacle Power, Team Tomorrow, Essence of the Game and First Rate. Series 2 inserts are Christie Brinkley Collection, Project Stardom, Skylines, Slugfest and Team Spirit. Pinnacle was sold in 10-card hobby and retail foil packs, and 18-card jumbo packs.

	NM/M
Complete Set (400):	15.00
Common Player:	.10
Series 1 or 2 Pack (10):	.75
Series 1 or 2 Box (24):	15.00
1 Greg Maddux	1.00
2 Bill Pulsipher	.10
3 Dante Bichette	.10
4 Mike Piazza	1.50
5 Garret Anderson	.10
6 Steve Finley	.10
7 Andy Benes	.10
8 Chuck Knoblauch	.10
9 Tom Gordon	.10
10 Jeff Bagwell	.75
11 Wil Cordero	.10
12 John Mabry	.10
13 Jeff Frye	.10
14 Travis Fryman	.10
15 John Wetteland	.10
16 Jason Bates	.10
17 Danny Tartabull	.10
18 Charles Nagy	.10
19 Robin Ventura	.10
20 Reggie Sanders	.10
21 Dave Clark	.10
22 Jaime Navarro	.10
23 Joey Hamilton	.10
24 Al Leiter	.10
25 Deion Sanders	.10
26 Tim Salmon	.10
27 Tino Martinez	.10
28 Mike Greenwell	.10
29 Phil Plantier	.10
30 Bobby Bonilla	.10
31 Kenny Rogers	.10
32 Chili Davis	.10
33 Joe Carter	.10
34 Mike Mussina	.40
35 Matt Mieske	.10
36 Jose Canseco	.40
37 Brad Radke	.10
38 Juan Gonzalez	.40
39 David Segui	.10
40 Alex Fernandez	.10
41 Jeff Kent	.10
42 Todd Zeile	.10
43 Darryl Strawberry	.10
44 Jose Rijo	.10
45 Ramon Martinez	.10
46 Manny Ramirez	.75
47 Gregg Jefferies	.10
48 Bryan Rekar	.10
49 Jeff King	.10
50 John Olerud	.10
51 Marc Newfield	.10
52 Charles Johnson	.10
53 Robby Thompson	.10
54 Brian Hunter	.10
55 Mike Blowers	.10
56 Keith Lockhart	.10
57 Ray Lankford	.10
58 Tim Wallach	.10
59 Ivan Rodriguez	.65
60 Ed Sprague	.10
61 Paul Molitor	.75
62 Eric Karros	.10
63 Glenallen Hill	.10
64 Jay Bell	.10
65 Tom Pagnozzi	.10
66 Greg Colbrunn	.10
67 Edgar Martinez	.10
68 Paul Sorrento	.10
69 Kirt Manwaring	.10
70 Pete Schourek	.10
71 Orlando Merced	.10
72 Shawon Dunston	.10
73 Ricky Bottalico	.10
74 Brady Anderson	.10
75 Steve Ontiveros	.10
76 Jim Abbott	.10
77 Carl Everett	.10
78 Mo Vaughn	.75
79 Pedro Martinez	.10
80 Harold Baines	.10
81 Alan Trammell	.10
82 Steve Avery	.10
83 Jeff Cirillo	.10
84 John Valentin	.10
85 Bernie Williams	.10
86 Andre Dawson	.30
87 Dave Winfield	.75
88 B.J. Surhoff	.10
89 Jeff Blauser	.10
90 Barry Larkin	.10
91 Cliff Floyd	.10
92 Sammy Sosa	1.00
93 Andres Galarraga	.10
94 Dave Nilsson	.10
95 James Mouton	.10
96 Marquis Grissom	.10
97 Matt Williams	.10
98 John Jaha	.10
99 Don Mattingly	1.25
100 Tim Naehring	.10
101 Kevin Appier	.10
102 Bobby Higginson	.10
103 Andy Pettitte	.25
104 Ozzie Smith	1.00
105 Kenny Lofton	.10
106 Ken Caminiti	.10
107 Walt Weiss	.10
108 Jack McDowell	.10
109 Brian McRae	.10
110 Gary Gaetti	.10
111 Curtis Goodwin	.10
112 Dennis Martinez	.10
113 Omar Vizquel	.10
114 Chipper Jones	1.00
115 Mark Gubicza	.10
116 Ruben Sierra	.10
117 Eddie Murray	.75
118 Chad Curtis	.10
119 Hal Morris	.10
120 Ben McDonald	.10
121 Marty Cordova	.10
122 Ken Griffey Jr.	1.50
123 Gary Sheffield	.40
124 Charlie Hayes	.10
125 Shawn Green	.40
126 Jason Giambi	.50
127 Mark Langston	.10
128 Mark Whiten	.10
129 Greg Vaughn	.10
130 Mark McGwire	1.75
131 Hideo Nomo	.40
132 Eric Karros, Raul Mondesi, Hideo Nomo, Mike Piazza	.50
133 Jason Bere	.10
134 Ken Griffey Jr. (The Naturals)	.65
135 Frank Thomas (The Naturals)	.40
136 Cal Ripken Jr. (The Naturals)	1.00
137 Albert Belle (The Naturals)	.65
138 Mike Piazza (The Naturals)	.65
139 Dante Bichette (The Naturals)	.10
140 Sammy Sosa (The Naturals)	.50
141 Mo Vaughn (The Naturals)	.10
142 Tim Salmon (The Naturals)	.10
143 Reggie Sanders (The Naturals)	.10
144 Cecil Fielder (The Naturals)	.10
145 Jim Edmonds (The Naturals)	.10
146 Rafael Palmeiro (The Naturals)	.10
147 Edgar Martinez (The Naturals)	.10
148 Barry Bonds (The Naturals)	1.00
149 Manny Ramirez (The Naturals)	.35
150 Larry Walker (The Naturals)	.10
151 Jeff Bagwell (The Naturals)	.35
152 Ron Gant (The Naturals)	.10
153 Andres Galarraga (The Naturals)	.10
154 Eddie Murray (The Naturals)	.35
155 Kirby Puckett (The Naturals)	.50
156 Will Clark (The Naturals)	.10
157 Don Mattingly (The Naturals)	.60
158 Mark McGwire (The Naturals)	.75
159 Dean Palmer (The Naturals)	.10
160 Matt Williams (The Naturals)	.10
161 Fred McGriff (The Naturals)	.10
162 Joe Carter (The Naturals)	.10
163 Juan Gonzalez (The Naturals)	.15
164 Alex Ochoa	.10
165 Ruben Rivera	.10
166 Tony Clark	.10
167 Brian Barber	.10
168 Matt Lawton	.10
169 Terrell Wade	.10
170 Johnny Damon	.30
171 Derek Jeter	2.00
172 Phil Nevin	.10
173 Robert Perez	.10
174 C.J. Nitkowski	.10
175 Joe Vitiello	.10
176 Roger Cedeno	.10
177 Ron Coomer	.10
178 Chris Widger	.10
179 Jimmy Haynes	.10
180 Mike Sweeney RC	.50
181 Howard Battle	.10
182 John Wasdin	.10
183 Jim Pittsley	.10
184 Bob Wolcott	.10
185 LaTroy Hawkins	.10
186 Nigel Wilson	.10
187 Dustin Hermanson	.10
188 Chris Snopek	.10
189 Mariano Rivera	.15
190 Jose Herrera	.10
191 Chris Stynes	.10
192 Larry Thomas	.10
193 David Bell	.10
194 Frank Thomas (Checklist)	.40
195 Ken Griffey Jr. (Checklist)	.65
196 Cal Ripken Jr. (Checklist)	.75
197 Jeff Bagwell (Checklist)	.35
198 Mike Piazza (Checklist)	.60
199 Barry Bonds (Checklist)	.75
200 Garret Anderson, Chipper Jones (checklist)	.25
201 Frank Thomas	.75
202 Michael Tucker	.10
203 Kirby Puckett	1.00
204 Alex Gonzalez	.10
205 Tony Gwynn	1.00
206 Moises Alou	.10
207 Albert Belle	.10
208 Barry Bonds	2.00
209 Fred McGriff	.10
210 Dennis Eckersley	.65
211 Craig Biggio	.10
212 David Cone	.10
213 Will Clark	.10
214 Cal Ripken Jr.	2.00
215 Wade Boggs	1.00
216 Pete Schourek	.10
217 Darren Daulton	.10
218 Carlos Baerga	.10
219 Larry Walker	.10
220 Denny Neagle	.10
221 Jim Edmonds	.10
222 Lee Smith	.10
223 Jason Isringhausen	.10
224 Jay Buhner	.10
225 John Olerud	.10
226 Jeff Conine	.10
227 Dean Palmer	.10
228 Jim Abbott	.10
229 Raul Mondesi	.10
230 Tom Glavine	.35
231 Kevin Seitzer	.10
232 Lenny Dykstra	.10
233 Brian Jordan	.10
234 Rondell White	.10
235 Bret Boone	.10
236 Randy Johnson	.75
237 Paul O'Neill	.10
238 Jim Thome	.65
239 Edgardo Alfonzo	.10
240 Terry Pendleton	.10
241 Harold Baines	.10
242 Roberto Alomar	.20
243 Mark Grace	.10
244 Derek Bell	.10
245 Vinny Castilla	.10
246 Cecil Fielder	.10
247 Roger Clemens	1.25
248 Orel Hershiser	.10
249 J.T. Snow	.10
250 Rafael Palmeiro	.65
251 Bret Saberhagen	.10
252 Todd Hollandsworth	.10
253 Ryan Klesko	.10
254 Greg Maddux (Hardball Heroes)	.50
255 Ken Griffey Jr. (Hardball Heroes)	.65
256 Hideo Nomo (Hardball Heroes)	.15
257 Frank Thomas (Hardball Heroes)	.40
258 Cal Ripken Jr. (Hardball Heroes)	1.00
259 Jeff Bagwell (Hardball Heroes)	.35
260 Barry Bonds (Hardball Heroes)	1.00
261 Mo Vaughn (Hardball Heroes)	.10
262 Albert Belle (Hardball Heroes)	.10
263 Sammy Sosa (Hardball Heroes)	.50
264 Reggie Sanders (Hardball Heroes)	.10
265 Mike Piazza (Hardball Heroes)	.65
266 Chipper Jones (Hardball Heroes)	.50
267 Tony Gwynn (Hardball Heroes)	.50
268 Kirby Puckett (Hardball Heroes)	.10
269 Wade Boggs (Hardball Heroes)	.45
270 Will Clark (Hardball Heroes)	.10
271 Gary Sheffield (Hardball Heroes)	.10
272 Dante Bichette (Hardball Heroes)	.10
273 Randy Johnson (Hardball Heroes)	.35
274 Matt Williams (Hardball Heroes)	.10
275 Alex Rodriguez (Hardball Heroes)	.75
276 Tim Salmon (Hardball Heroes)	.10
277 Johnny Damon (Hardball Heroes)	.10
278 Manny Ramirez (Hardball Heroes)	.35
279 Derek Jeter (Hardball Heroes)	1.00

280	Eddie Murray (Hardball Heroes)	.35
281	Ozzie Smith (Hardball Heroes)	.50
282	Garret Anderson (Hardball Heroes)	.10
283	Raul Mondesi (Hardball Heroes)	.10
284	Terry Steinbach	.10
285	Carlos Garcia	.10
286	Dave Justice	.10
287	Eric Anthony	.10
288	Benji Gil	.10
289	Bob Hamelin	.10
290	Dwayne Hosey	.10
291	Andy Pettitte	.25
292	Rod Beck	.10
293	Shane Andrews	.10
294	Julian Tavarez	.10
295	Willie Greene	.10
296	Ismael Valdes	.10
297	Glenallen Hill	.10
298	Troy Percival	.10
299	Ray Durham	.10
300	Jeff Conine (.300 Series)	.10
301.8	Ken Griffey Jr. (.300 Series)	.75
302	Will Clark (.300 Series)	.10
303	Mike Greenwell (.300 Series)	.10
304.9	Carlos Baerga (.300 Series)	.10
305.3	Paul Molitor (.300 Series)	.35
305.6	Jeff Bagwell (.300 Series)	.35
306	Mark Grace (.300 Series)	.10
307	Don Mattingly (.300 Series)	.60
308	Hal Morris (.300 Series)	.10
309	Butch Huskey	.10
310	Ozzie Guillen	.10
311	Erik Hanson	.10
312	Kenny Lofton (.300 Series)	.10
313	Edgar Martinez (.300 Series)	.10
314	Kurt Abbott	.10
315	John Smoltz	.10
316	Ariel Prieto	.10
317	Mark Carreon	.10
318	Kirby Puckett (.300 Series)	.50
319	Carlos Perez	.10
320	Gary DiSarcina	.10
321	Trevor Hoffman	.10
322	Mike Piazza (.300 Series)	.65
323	Frank Thomas (.300 Series)	.40
324	Juan Acevedo	.10
325	Bip Roberts	.10
326	Javier Lopez	.10
327	Benito Santiago	.10
328	Mark Lewis	.10
329	Royce Clayton	.10
330	Tom Gordon	.10
331	Ben McDonald	.10
332	Dan Wilson	.10
333	Ron Gant	.10
334	Wade Boggs (.300 Series)	.45
335	Paul Molitor	.75
336	Tony Gwynn (.300 Series)	.50
337	Sean Berry	.10
338	Rickey Henderson	.75
339	Wil Cordero	.10
340	Kent Mercker	.10
341	Kenny Rogers	.10
342	Ryne Sandberg	1.00
343	Charlie Hayes	.10
344	Andy Benes	.10
345	Sterling Hitchcock	.10
346	Bernard Gilkey	.10
347	Julio Franco	.10
348	Ken Hill	.10
349	Russ Davis	.10
350	Mike Blowers	.10
351	B.J. Surhoff	.10
352	Lance Johnson	.10
353	Darryl Hamilton	.10
354	Shawon Dunston	.10
355	Rick Aguilera	.10
356	Danny Tartabull	.10
357	Todd Stottlemyre	.10
358	Mike Bordick	.10
359	Jack McDowell	.10
360	Todd Zeile	.10
361	Tino Martinez	.10
362	Greg Gagne	.10
363	Mike Kelly	.10
364	Tim Raines	.10
365	Ernie Young	.10
366	Mike Stanley	.10
367	Wally Joyner	.10
368	Karim Garcia	.10
369	Paul Wilson	.10
370	Sal Fasano	.10
371	Jason Schmidt	.10
372	Livan Hernandez RC	.25
373	George Arias	.10
374	Steve Gibralter	.10
375	Jermaine Dye	.10
376	Jason Kendall	.10
377	Brooks Kieschnick	.10
378	Jeff Ware	.10
379	Alan Benes	.10
380	Rey Ordonez	.10
381	Jay Powell	.10
382	Osvaldo Fernandez RC	.15
383	Wilton Guerrero RC	.10
384	Eric Owens	.10
385	George Williams	.10
386	Chan Ho Park	.10
387	Jeff Suppan	.10
388	F.P. Santangelo RC	.10
389	Terry Adams	.10
390	Bob Abreu	.10
391	Quinton McCracken RC	.10
392	Mike Busby RC	.10
393	Cal Ripken Jr. (Checklist)	.75
394	Ken Griffey Jr. (Checklist)	.60
395	Frank Thomas (Checklist)	.40
396	Chipper Jones (Checklist)	.50
397	Greg Maddux (Checklist)	.50
398	Mike Piazza (Checklist)	.65
399	Ken Griffey Jr., Frank Thomas, Cal Ripken Jr., Greg Maddux, Chipper Jones, Mike Piazza (Checklist)	.50

Artist's Proof

AP is a parallel to the Starburst partial parallel of '96 Pinnacle. Like Starburst, the Artist's Proof cards are printed in Dufex technology on front, with the AP cards having the words "ARTIST'S PROOF" repeated throughout the background. AP backs are identical to Starburst. Stated insertion rate for the Artist's Proofs was one per 47 packs in hobby and one per 67 retail packs.

	NM/M
Common Artist's Proof:	2.00
Stars:	3X

Starburst

For 1996 Pinnacle abbreviated its parallel insert set to just half of the cards from the base issue. Only 200 select players are included in the Starburst Dufex-printed parallel set found on average of once per seven hobby packs and once per 10 retail packs.

	NM/M
Complete Set (200):	150.00
Common Player:	.40
Common Artist's Proof:	.75
Artist's Proofs:	2X
1 Greg Maddux	3.00
2 Bill Pulsipher	.40
3 Dante Bichette	.40
4 Mike Piazza	4.00
5 Garret Anderson	.40
6 Chuck Knoblauch	.40
7 Jeff Bagwell	2.25
8 Wil Cordero	.40
9 Travis Fryman	.40
10 Reggie Sanders	.40
11 Deion Sanders	.40
12 Tim Salmon	.40
13 Tino Martinez	.40
14 Bobby Bonilla	.40
15 Joe Carter	.40
16 Mike Mussina	1.25
17 Jose Canseco	1.25
18 Manny Ramirez	2.25
19 Gregg Jefferies	.40
20 Charles Johnson	.40
21 Brian Hunter	.40
22 Ray Lankford	.40
23 Ivan Rodriguez	2.00
24 Paul Molitor	2.25
25 Eric Karros	.40
26 Edgar Martinez	.40
27 Shawon Dunston	.40
28 Mo Vaughn	.40
29 Pedro Martinez	2.25
30 Marty Cordova	.40
31 Ken Caminiti	.40
32 Gary Sheffield	.75
33 Shawn Green	.75
34 Cliff Floyd	.40
35 Andres Galarraga	.40
36 Matt Williams	.40
37 Don Mattingly	3.50
38 Kevin Appier	.40
39 Ozzie Smith	3.00
40 Kenny Lofton	.40
41 Ken Griffey Jr.	4.00
42 Jack McDowell	.40
43 Gary Gaetti	.40
44 Dennis Martinez	.40
45 Chipper Jones	3.00
46 Eddie Murray	2.25
47 Bernie Williams	.40
48 Andre Dawson	.60
49 Dave Winfield	2.25
50 B.J. Surhoff	.40
51 Barry Larkin	.40
52 Alan Trammell	.40
53 Sammy Sosa	3.00
54 Hideo Nomo	1.00
55 Mark McGwire	4.50
56 Jay Bell	.40
57 Juan Gonzalez	1.00
58 Chili Davis	.40
59 Robin Ventura	.40
60 John Mabry	.40
61 Ken Griffey Jr. (Naturals)	2.00
62 Frank Thomas (Naturals)	1.25
63 Cal Ripken Jr. (Naturals)	3.00
64 Albert Belle (Naturals)	.40
65 Mike Piazza (Naturals)	2.00
66 Dante Bichette (Naturals)	.40
67 Sammy Sosa (Naturals)	1.50
68 Mo Vaughn (Naturals)	.40
69 Tim Salmon (Naturals)	.40
70 Reggie Sanders (Naturals)	.40
71 Cecil Fielder (Naturals)	.40
72 Jim Edmonds (Naturals)	.40
73 Rafael Palmeiro (Naturals)	.75
74 Edgar Martinez (Naturals)	.40
75 Barry Bonds (Naturals)	3.00
76 Manny Ramirez (Naturals)	1.25
77 Larry Walker (Naturals)	.40
78 Jeff Bagwell (Naturals)	1.25
79 Ron Gant (Naturals)	.40
80 Andres Galarraga (Naturals)	.40
81 Eddie Murray (Naturals)	1.25
82 Kirby Puckett (Naturals)	1.50
83 Will Clark (Naturals)	.40
84 Don Mattingly (Naturals)	1.75
85 Mark McGwire (Naturals)	2.25
86 Dean Palmer (Naturals)	.40
87 Matt Williams (Naturals)	.40
88 Fred McGriff (Naturals)	.40
89 Joe Carter (Naturals)	.40
90 Juan Gonzalez (Naturals)	.65
91 Alex Ochoa	.40
92 Ruben Rivera	.40
93 Tony Clark	.40
94 Pete Schourek	.40
95 Terrell Wade	.40
96 Johnny Damon	.65
97 Derek Jeter	6.00
98 Phil Nevin	.40
99 Robert Perez	.40
100 Dustin Hermanson	.40
101 Frank Thomas	2.25
102 Michael Tucker	.40
103 Kirby Puckett	3.00
104 Alex Gonzalez	.40
105 Tony Gwynn	3.00
106 Moises Alou	.40
107 Albert Belle	2.00
108 Barry Bonds	6.00
109 Fred McGriff	.40
110 Dennis Eckersley	1.50
111 Craig Biggio	.40
112 David Cone	.40
113 Will Clark	.40
114 Cal Ripken Jr.	6.00
115 Wade Boggs	3.00
116 Pete Schourek	.40
117 Darren Daulton	.40
118 Carlos Baerga	.40
119 Larry Walker	.40
120 Denny Neagle	.40
121 Jim Edmonds	.40
122 Lee Smith	.40
123 Jason Isringhausen	.40
124 Jay Buhner	.40
125 John Olerud	.40
126 Jeff Conine	.40
127 Dean Palmer	.40
128 Jim Abbott	.40
129 Raul Mondesi	.40
130 Tom Glavine	.60
131 Kevin Seitzer	.40
132 Lenny Dykstra	.40
133 Brian Jordan	.40
134 Rondell White	.40
135 Bret Boone	.40
136 Randy Johnson	2.25
137 Paul O'Neill	.40
138 Jim Thome	.75
139 Edgardo Alfonzo	.40
140 Terry Pendleton	.40
141 Harold Baines	.40
142 Roberto Alomar	.45
143 Mark Grace	.40
144 Derek Bell	.40
145 Vinny Castilla	.40
146 Cecil Fielder	.40
147 Roger Clemens	3.50
148 Orel Hershiser	.40
149 J.T. Snow	.40
150 Rafael Palmeiro	1.75
151 Bret Saberhagen	.40
152 Todd Hollandsworth	.40
153 Ryan Klesko	.40
154 Greg Maddux (Hardball Heroes)	1.50
155 Ken Griffey Jr. (Hardball Heroes)	2.00
156 Hideo Nomo (Hardball Heroes)	.65
157 Frank Thomas (Hardball Heroes)	1.25
158 Cal Ripken Jr. (Hardball Heroes)	3.00
159 Jeff Bagwell (Hardball Heroes)	1.25
160 Barry Bonds (Hardball Heroes)	3.00
161 Mo Vaughn (Hardball Heroes)	.40
162 Albert Belle (Hardball Heroes)	.40
163 Sammy Sosa (Hardball Heroes)	1.50
164 Reggie Sanders (Hardball Heroes)	.40
165 Mike Piazza (Hardball Heroes)	2.00
166 Chipper Jones (Hardball Heroes)	1.50
167 Tony Gwynn (Hardball Heroes)	1.50
168 Kirby Puckett (Hardball Heroes)	1.50
169 Wade Boggs (Hardball Heroes)	1.25
170 Will Clark (Hardball Heroes)	.40
171 Gary Sheffield (Hardball Heroes)	.45
172 Dante Bichette (Hardball Heroes)	.40
173 Randy Johnson (Hardball Heroes)	1.25
174 Matt Williams (Hardball Heroes)	.40
175 Alex Rodriguez (Hardball Heroes)	4.50
176 Tim Salmon (Hardball Heroes)	.40
177 Johnny Damon (Hardball Heroes)	.40
178 Manny Ramirez (Hardball Heroes)	1.25
179 Derek Jeter (Hardball Heroes)	3.00
180 Eddie Murray (Hardball Heroes)	1.25
181 Ozzie Smith (Hardball Heroes)	1.50
182 Garret Anderson (Hardball Heroes)	.40
183 Raul Mondesi (Hardball Heroes)	.40
184 Jeff Conine (.300 Series)	.40
185 Ken Griffey Jr. (.300 Series)	2.00
186 Will Clark (.300 Series)	.40
187 Mike Greenwell (.300 Series)	.40
188 Carlos Baerga (.300 Series)	.40
189 Paul Molitor (.300 Series)	1.25
190 Jeff Bagwell (.300 Series)	1.25
191 Mark Grace (.300 Series)	.40
192 Don Mattingly (.300 Series)	1.75
193 Hal Morris (.300 Series)	.40
194 Kenny Lofton (.300 Series)	.40
195 Edgar Martinez (.300 Series)	.40
196 Kirby Puckett (.300 Series)	1.50
197 Mike Piazza (.300 Series)	2.00
198 Frank Thomas (.300 Series)	1.25
199 Wade Boggs (.300 Series)	1.25
200 Tony Gwynn (.300 Series)	1.50

Foil Series 2

The 200 cards from Series 2 were paralleled in a special foil edition which was sold at retail outlets only in five-card $2.99 packs. Fronts have a metallic foil background to differentiate them from the regular-issue Series 2 version.

	NM/M
Complete Set (200):	15.00
Common Player:	.20
Stars:	1.5X

Christie Brinkley Collection Promo

To promote its Brinkley-photographed insert cards in Series 2 Pinnacle, the company issued a card of the celebrity photographer. In the same format as the player inserts, the promo card has a gold-foil enhanced borderless glamor photo on front. The back repeats a detail of the front photo and has details of the insert series.

	NM/M
Christie Brinkley	5.00

Christie Brinkley Collection

Supermodel Christie Brinkley took the photos for these 1996 Pinnacle Series 2 inserts. The cards capture players from the 1995 World Series participants during a spring training photo session. Cards were seeded one per every 23 hobby packs or 32 retail packs.

	NM/M
Complete Set (16):	15.00
Common Player:	.80
1 Greg Maddux	3.50
2 Ryan Klesko	.75
3 Dave Justice	.75
4 Tom Glavine	1.50
5 Chipper Jones	3.50
6 Fred McGriff	.75
7 Javier Lopez	.75
8 Marquis Grissom	.75
9 Jason Schmidt	.75
10 Albert Belle	.75
11 Manny Ramirez	2.25
12 Carlos Baerga	.75
13 Sandy Alomar	.75
14 Jim Thome	2.25
15 Julio Franco	.75
16 Kenny Lofton	.75

Essence of the Game

Essence of the Game is an 18-card insert set found only in hobby packs at a one per 23 packs rate in Series 1. Cards are printed on clear plastic with the front photo also appearing in an inverted fashion on back. Micro-etched Dufex printing technology is utilized on the front.

	NM/M
Complete Set (18):	35.00
Common Player:	.70
1 Cal Ripken Jr.	6.00
2 Greg Maddux	3.00
3 Frank Thomas	2.50
4 Matt Williams	.75
5 Chipper Jones	3.00
6 Reggie Sanders	.75
7 Ken Griffey Jr.	4.00
8 Kirby Puckett	3.00
9 Hideo Nomo	1.50
10 Mike Piazza	4.00
11 Jeff Bagwell	2.50
12 Mo Vaughn	.75
13 Albert Belle	.75
14 Tim Salmon	.75
15 Don Mattingly	3.50
16 Will Clark	.75
17 Eddie Murray	2.50
18 Barry Bonds	6.00

First Rate

Retail-exclusive First Rate showcases former first round draft picks playing in the majors. Printed in Dufex foil throughout, a red swirl pattern covers the left 2/3 of the front. Backs show the player again, within a large numeral "1." These inserts are found at an average rate of one per 23 packs in Series 1.

	NM/M
Complete Set (18):	40.00
Common Player:	1.25
1 Ken Griffey Jr.	5.00
2 Frank Thomas	2.50
3 Mo Vaughn	1.25
4 Chipper Jones	3.50
5 Alex Rodriguez	6.50
6 Kirby Puckett	3.50
7 Gary Sheffield	1.25

8	Matt Williams	1.25
9	Barry Bonds	7.50
10	Craig Biggio	1.25
11	Robin Ventura	1.25
12	Michael Tucker	1.25
13	Derek Jeter	7.50
14	Manny Ramirez	2.50
15	Barry Larkin	1.25
16	Shawn Green	1.75
17	Will Clark	1.25
18	Mark McGwire	6.50

Pinnacle Power

Pinnacle Power inserts are seeded at the rate of one per 47 packs in both hobby and retail Series 1. The sluggers are featured on a two-layered front. The bottom layer is silver Dufex foil with solid black on top; a color action photo of the player is at center, giving the card a die-cut appearance.

NM/M
Complete Set (20):		40.00
Common Player:		1.25
1	Frank Thomas	2.50
2	Mo Vaughn	1.25
2p	Mo Vaughn/Promo	1.50
3	Ken Griffey Jr.	4.50
4	Matt Williams	1.25
5	Barry Bonds	6.00
6	Reggie Sanders	1.25
7	Mike Piazza	4.50
8	Jim Edmonds	1.25
9	Dante Bichette	1.25
10	Sammy Sosa	3.50
11	Jeff Bagwell	2.50
12	Fred McGriff	1.25
13	Albert Belle	1.25
14	Tim Salmon	1.25
15	Joe Carter	1.25
16	Manny Ramirez	2.50
17	Eddie Murray	2.50
18	Cecil Fielder	1.25
19	Larry Walker	1.25
20	Juan Gonzalez	1.75

Project Stardom

These inserts feature young players on their way to stardom. The cards, which use Dufex technology, are seeded one per every 35 packs of Series 2 hobby packs.

NM/M
Complete Set (18):		35.00
Common Player:		1.00
1	Paul Wilson	1.00
2	Derek Jeter	8.50
3	Karim Garcia	1.00
4	Johnny Damon	2.75
5	Alex Rodriguez	7.50
6	Chipper Jones	6.50
7	Charles Johnson	1.00
8	Bob Abreu	1.25
9	Alan Benes	1.00
10	Richard Hidalgo	1.00
11	Brooks Kieschnick	1.00
12	Garret Anderson	1.00
13	Livan Hernandez	1.00
14	Manny Ramirez	5.00
15	Jermaine Dye	1.00
16	Todd Hollandsworth	1.00
17	Raul Mondesi	1.00
18	Ryan Klesko	1.00

Cal Ripken Tribute

A special Cal Ripken Tribute card was issued in Series 1 Pinnacle packs at a rate of

1:150. Front features an etched metallic foil background, a gold-foil facsimile autograph and a "2,131+ Consecutive Games Played" starburst. Back has a photo of the scoreboard on that historic occasion, and a photo of Ripken being driven around Camden Yards in a red Corvette. The card is numbered "1 of 1," but it is not unique.

NM/M
1 of 1	Cal Ripken Jr.	5.00

Skylines

These inserts feature player portraits looming over the city skyline where they play their home games. Printed on a clear plastic stock, the cards were seeded one per every 29 Series 2 magazine packs, and one per 50 retail packs.

NM/M
Complete Set (18):		375.00
Common Player:		10.00
1	Ken Griffey Jr.	50.00
2	Frank Thomas	30.00
3	Greg Maddux	40.00
4	Cal Ripken Jr.	65.00
5	Albert Belle	10.00
6	Mo Vaughn	10.00
7	Mike Piazza	50.00
8	Wade Boggs	40.00
9	Will Clark	10.00
10	Barry Bonds	65.00
11	Gary Sheffield	10.00
12	Hideo Nomo	25.00
13	Tony Gwynn	40.00
14	Kirby Puckett	40.00
15	Chipper Jones	40.00
16	Jeff Bagwell	30.00
17	Manny Ramirez	30.00
18	Raul Mondesi	10.00

Slugfest

These Series 2 inserts feature the game's heaviest hitters on all-foil Dufex cards. The cards were seeded one per every 35 retail packs.

NM/M
Complete Set (18):		40.00
Common Player:		1.25
1	Frank Thomas	2.75
2	Ken Griffey Jr.	4.00
3	Jeff Bagwell	2.75
4	Barry Bonds	5.00
5	Mo Vaughn	1.25
6	Albert Belle	1.25

7	Mike Piazza	4.00
8	Matt Williams	1.25
9	Dante Bichette	1.25
10	Sammy Sosa	3.00
11	Gary Sheffield	2.00
12	Reggie Sanders	1.25
13	Manny Ramirez	2.75
14	Eddie Murray	2.75
15	Juan Gonzalez	2.25
16	Dean Palmer	1.25
17	Rafael Palmeiro	2.75
18	Cecil Fielder	1.25

Team Pinnacle

Team Pinnacle inserts offer 18 players in a double-sided nine-card set. Each card can be found with Dufex printing on one side and regular gold-foil printing on the other. Inserted one per 72 packs of Series 1, Team Pinnacle pairs up an American League player and a National Leaguer at the same position on each card.

NM/M
Complete Set (9):		35.00
Common Player:		1.50
1	Frank Thomas,	
	Jeff Bagwell	4.00
2	Chuck Knoblauch,	
	Craig Biggio	1.50
3	Jim Thome,	
	Matt Williams	3.00
4	Barry Larkin,	
	Cal Ripken Jr.	12.00
5	Barry Bonds,	
	Tim Salmon	10.00
6	Ken Griffey Jr.,	
	Reggie Sanders	8.00
7	Albert Belle,	
	Sammy Sosa	6.00
8	Ivan Rodriguez,	
	Mike Piazza	6.00
9	Greg Maddux,	
	Randy Johnson	8.00

Team Spirit

One in every 72 Series 2 hobby packs or every 103 retail packs has one of these die-cut insert cards. Each card has a holographic baseball design behind an embossed glossy action photo of the player on a flat black background. Backs are conventionally printed.

NM/M
Complete Set (12):		45.00
Common Player:		1.25
1	Greg Maddux	4.00
2	Ken Griffey Jr.	8.00
3	Derek Jeter	8.00
4	Mike Piazza	5.00
5	Cal Ripken Jr.	8.00
6	Frank Thomas	2.75
7	Jeff Bagwell	2.75
8	Mo Vaughn	1.25
9	Albert Belle	1.25
10	Chipper Jones	4.00
11	Johnny Damon	1.50
12	Barry Bonds	8.00

Team Tomorrow

Team Tomorrow showcases young superstars on a horizontal Dufex design. While the player appears twice on the card front, the left side is merely a close-up of the same shot appearing on the right. These inserts are exclusive to Series 1 jumbo packs, found on average at the rate of one per 19 packs.

NM/M
Complete Set (10):		20.00
Common Player:		.50
1	Ruben Rivera	.50
2	Johnny Damon	1.00
3	Raul Mondesi	.50
4	Manny Ramirez	3.00
5	Hideo Nomo	1.50
6	Chipper Jones	4.00
7	Garret Anderson	.50
8	Alex Rodriguez	5.00
9	Derek Jeter	6.00
10	Karim Garcia	.50

1996 Pinnacle/Aficionado

Pinnacle's 1996 Aficionado set gives every card the look of maple woodgrain. The 200 regular issue cards include 160 cards in an antique-look sepiatone finish. The horizontal front also has a rainbow holographic foil image of the player. The back has comparison statistics that show how the player compares with the league average at that position and the league average at that position in different eras. There are also 60 four-color cards, which include 25 rookie cards, and a 10-card Global Reach subset. This subset, which honors baseball's international flavor, features Aficionado's new heliogram printing process. Artist's Proof parallel cards, seeded about one per 35 packs, were also created. These cards mirror the regular issue and use a unique gold foil stamp. There were three insert sets: Slick Picks, Rivals and Magic Numbers.

NM/M
Complete Set (200):		20.00
Common Player:		.10
Common Artist's Proof:		.40
Artist's Proof Stars:		8X
Pack (5):		1.50
Wax Box (16):		30.00
1	Jack McDowell	.10
2	Jay Bell	.10
3	Rafael Palmeiro	1.25
4	Wally Joyner	.10
5	Ozzie Smith	2.00
6	Mark McGwire	3.00
7	Kevin Seitzer	.10
8	Fred McGriff	.10
9	Roger Clemens	2.25
9s	Roger Clemens	
	(Marked "SAMPLE")	4.00
10	Randy Johnson	1.50
11	Cecil Fielder	.10
12	David Cone	.10
13	Chili Davis	.10
14	Andres Galarraga	.10
15	Joe Carter	.10
16	Ryne Sandberg	2.00
17	Paul O'Neill	.10
18	Cal Ripken Jr.	4.00
19	Wade Boggs	2.00
20	Greg Gagne	.10
21	Edgar Martinez	.10
22	Greg Maddux	2.00

23	Ken Caminiti	.10
24	Kirby Puckett	2.00
25	Craig Biggio	.10
26	Will Clark	.10
27	Ron Gant	.10
28	Eddie Murray	1.50
29	Lance Johnson	.10
30	Tony Gwynn	2.00
31	Dante Bichette	.10
32	Darren Daulton	.10
33	Danny Tartabull	.10
34	Jeff King	.10
35	Tom Glavine	.40
36	Rickey Henderson	1.50
37	Jose Canseco	1.00
38	Barry Larkin	.10
39	Dennis Martinez	.10
40	Ruben Sierra	.10
41	Bobby Bonilla	.10
42	Jeff Conine	.10
43	Lee Smith	.10
44	Charlie Hayes	.10
45	Walt Weiss	.10
46	Jay Buhner	.10
47	Kenny Rogers	.10
48	Paul Molitor	1.50
49	Hal Morris	.10
50	Todd Stottlemyre	.10
51	Mike Stanley	.10
52	Mark Grace	.10
53	Lenny Dykstra	.10
54	Andre Dawson	.25
55	Dennis Eckersley	1.25
56	Ben McDonald	.10
57	Ray Lankford	.10
58	Mo Vaughn	.10
59	Frank Thomas	1.50
60	Julio Franco	.10
61	Jim Abbott	.10
62	Greg Vaughn	.10
63	Marquis Grissom	.10
64	Tino Martinez	.10
65	Kevin Appier	.10
66	Matt Williams	.10
67	Sammy Sosa	2.00
68	Larry Walker	.10
69	Ivan Rodriguez	1.25
70	Eric Karros	.10
71	Bernie Williams	.10
72	Carlos Baerga	.10
73	Jeff Bagwell	1.50
74	Pete Schourek	.10
75	Ken Griffey Jr.	2.50
76	Bernard Gilkey	.10
77	Albert Belle	.10
78	Chuck Knoblauch	.10
79	John Smoltz	.10
80	Barry Bonds	4.00
81	Vinny Castilla	.10
82	John Olerud	.10
83	Mike Mussina	1.00
84	Alex Fernandez	.10
85	Shawon Dunston	.10
86	Travis Fryman	.10
87	Moises Alou	.10
88	Dean Palmer	.10
89	Gregg Jefferies	.10
90	Jim Thome	1.25
91	Dave Justice	.10
92	B.J. Surhoff	.10
93	Ramon Martinez	.10
94	Gary Sheffield	.40
95	Andy Benes	.10
96	Reggie Sanders	.10
97	Roberto Alomar	.35
98	Omar Vizquel	.10
99	Juan Gonzalez	.75
100	Robin Ventura	.10
101	Jason Isringhausen	.10
102	Greg Colbrunn	.10
103	Brian Jordan	.10
104	Shawn Green	.40
105	Brian Hunter	.10
106	Rondell White	.10
107	Ryan Klesko	.10
107s	Ryan Klesko	
	(Marked "SAMPLE")	1.00
108	Sterling Hitchcock	.10
109	Manny Ramirez	1.50
110	Bret Boone	.10
111	Michael Tucker	.10
112	Julian Tavarez	.10
113	Benji Gil	.10
114	Kenny Lofton	.10
115	Mike Kelly	.10
116	Ray Durham	.10
117	Trevor Hoffman	.10
118	Butch Huskey	.10
119	Phil Nevin	.10
120	Pedro Martinez	1.50
121	Wil Cordero	.10
122	Tim Salmon	.10
123	Jim Edmonds	.10
124	Mike Piazza	2.50
125	Rico Brogna	.10
126	John Mabry	.10
127	Chipper Jones	2.00
128	Johnny Damon	.35
129	Raul Mondesi	.10
130	Denny Neagle	.10
131	Marc Newfield	.10
132	Hideo Nomo	.75
133	Joe Vitiello	.10
134	Garret Anderson	.10
135	Dave Nilsson	.10
136	Alex Rodriguez	3.00
137	Russ Davis	.10
138	Frank Rodriguez	.10

139	Royce Clayton	.10
140	John Valentin	.10
141	Marty Cordova	.10
142	Alex Gonzalez	.10
143	Carlos Delgado	.75
144	Willie Greene	.10
145	Cliff Floyd	.10
146	Bobby Higginson	.10
147	J.T. Snow	.10
148	Derek Bell	.10
149	Edgardo Alfonzo	.10
150	Charles Johnson	.10
151	Hideo Nomo	
	(Global Reach)	.60
152	Larry Walker	
	(Global Reach)	.10
153	Bob Abreu	
	(Global Reach)	.10
154	Karim Garcia	
	(Global Reach)	.10
155	Dave Nilsson	
	(Global Reach)	.10
156	Chan Ho Park	
	(Global Reach)	.10
157	Dennis Martinez	
	(Global Reach)	.10
158	Sammy Sosa	
	(Global Reach)	1.25
159	Rey Ordonez	
	(Global Reach)	.10
160	Roberto Alomar	
	(Global Reach)	.10
161	George Arias	.10
162	Jason Schmidt	.10
163	Derek Jeter	4.00
164	Chris Snopek	.10
165	Todd Hollandsworth	.10
166	Sal Fasano	.10
167	Jay Powell	.10
168	Paul Wilson	.10
169	Jim Pittsley	.10
170	LaTroy Hawkins	.10
171	Bob Abreu	.10
172	Mike Grace RC	.10
173	Karim Garcia	.10
174	Richard Hidalgo	.10
175	Felipe Crespo	.10
176	Terrell Wade	.10
177	Steve Gibralter	.10
178	Jermaine Dye	.10
179	Alan Benes	.10
180	Wilton Guerrero RC	.10
181	Brooks Kieschnick	.10
182	Roger Cedeno	.10
183	Osvaldo Fernandez RC	.10
184	Matt Lawton RC	.50
185	George Williams	.10
186	Jimmy Haynes	.10
187	Mike Busby RC	.10
188	Chan Ho Park	.10
189	Marc Barcelo	.10
190	Jason Kendall	.10
191	Rey Ordonez	.10
192	Tyler Houston	.10
193	John Wasdin	.10
194	Jeff Suppan	.10
195	Jeff Ware	.10
196	Checklist	.10
197	Checklist	.10
198	Checklist	.10
199	Checklist	.10
200	Checklist	.10

First Pitch Previews

This parallel set differs from the regularly issued version in that there is a "FIRST PITCH / PREVIEW" label printed on the front on the end opposite the heliogram player portrait. Also, whereas on the regular cards, the player portrait is in silver metallic composition, the First Pitch Preview cards have the portrait in gold. These cards were most often obtained by visiting Pinnacle's site on the Internet and answering a trivia question.

NM/M
Complete Set (200):		250.00
Common Player:		2.00

Magic Numbers

This insert set focuses on 10 of the game's best players, printing them on a wooden stock which carries the distinct grain and color of natural wood. The cards, seeded one every 72 packs, compares current players with others who have worn the same uniform number. Each card can also be found with a large black "SAMPLE" printed on back.

		NM/M
Complete Set (10):		15.50
Common Player:		.75
Samples:		1X
1	Ken Griffey Jr.	3.25
2	Greg Maddux	2.50
3	Frank Thomas	1.50
4	Mo Vaughn	.75
5	Jeff Bagwell	1.50
6	Chipper Jones	2.50
7	Albert Belle	.75
8	Cal Ripken Jr.	4.50
9	Matt Williams	.75
10	Sammy Sosa	2.50

Rivals

These inserts concentrate on the many matchups and rivalries that make baseball fun. Each card uses spot embossing. The cards are seeded one per every 24 packs.

		NM/M
Complete Set (24):		65.00
Common Player:		2.00
1	Ken Griffey Jr., Frank Thomas	4.00
2	Frank Thomas, Cal Ripken Jr.	4.50
3	Cal Ripken Jr., Mo Vaughn	4.00
4	Mo Vaughn, Ken Griffey Jr.	2.50
5	Ken Griffey Jr., Cal Ripken Jr.	5.00
6	Frank Thomas, Mo Vaughn	2.00
7	Cal Ripken Jr., Ken Griffey Jr.	5.00
8	Mo Vaughn, Frank Thomas	2.00
9	Ken Griffey Jr., Mo Vaughn	2.50
10	Frank Thomas, Ken Griffey Jr.	4.00
11	Cal Ripken Jr., Frank Thomas	4.50
12	Mo Vaughn, Cal Ripken Jr.	4.00
13	Mike Piazza, Jeff Bagwell	2.50
14	Jeff Bagwell, Barry Bonds	4.50
15	Jeff Bagwell, Mike Piazza	2.50
16	Tony Gwynn, Mike Piazza	3.00
17	Mike Piazza, Barry Bonds	5.00
18	Jeff Bagwell, Tony Gwynn	2.00
19	Barry Bonds, Mike Piazza	5.00
20	Tony Gwynn, Jeff Bagwell	2.00
21	Mike Piazza, Tony Gwynn	3.00
22	Barry Bonds, Jeff Bagwell	
23	Tony Gwynn, Barry Bonds	4.50

24	Barry Bonds, Tony Gwynn	4.50

Slick Picks

This insert set pictures 32 of the best players in baseball on cards which use Spectroetch printing. Each card notes where that player was selected in the annual draft, emphasizing that there are numerous bargains available throughout the amateur draft. The cards were seeded one per 10 packs, making them the easiest to obtain of the set's insert cards.

		NM/M
Complete Set (32):		40.00
Common Player:		.50
1	Mike Piazza	2.50
2	Cal Ripken Jr.	4.00
3	Ken Griffey Jr.	2.50
4	Paul Wilson	.50
5	Frank Thomas	1.50
6	Mo Vaughn	.50
7	Barry Bonds	4.00
8	Albert Belle	.50
9	Jeff Bagwell	1.50
10	Dante Bichette	.50
11	Hideo Nomo	.75
12	Raul Mondesi	.50
13	Manny Ramirez	1.50
14	Greg Maddux	2.00
15	Tony Gwynn	2.00
16	Ryne Sandberg	2.00
17	Reggie Sanders	.50
18	Derek Jeter	4.00
19	Johnny Damon	.75
20	Alex Rodriguez	3.00
21	Ryan Klesko	.50
22	Jim Thome	1.50
23	Kenny Lofton	.50
24	Tino Martinez	.50
25	Randy Johnson	1.50
26	Wade Boggs	2.00
27	Juan Gonzalez	.75
28	Kirby Puckett	2.00
29	Tim Salmon	.50
30	Chipper Jones	2.00
31	Garret Anderson	.50
32	Eddie Murray	1.50

FanFest

In conjunction with its title sponsorship of baseball's All-Star FanFest, July 5-9 in Philadelphia, the company distributed two-card foil packs prior to and at the show. Fronts have a negative posterized image of Independence Hall as a backdrop for a player action photo. Textured gold-foil bottom corners hold a team logo and a Liberty Bell silhouette with the player's position. The player name appears in gold foil above the Fan-Fest logo at bottom center. Backs repeat the negative background and have another player photo, a few words about him and all the appropriate logos. The Darren Daulton card is in Sportflix technology as a tribute to the recently retired Phillies fan favorite. Card #31, Steve Carlton, was not distributed in packs. Cards of the Phillie Phanatic team mascot, the city's

---

mayor and several other local dignitaries were produced and given to those persons.

		NM/M
Complete Set (30, no Carlton):		25.00
Common Player:		.50
1	Cal Ripken Jr.	4.00
2	Greg Maddux	2.00
3	Ken Griffey Jr.	2.50
4	Frank Thomas	1.50
5	Jeff Bagwell	1.50
6	Hideo Nomo	.75
7	Tony Gwynn	2.00
8	Albert Belle	.50
9	Mo Vaughn	.50
10	Mike Piazza	2.50
11	Dante Bichette	.50
12	Ryne Sandberg	2.00
13	Wade Boggs	2.00
14	Kirby Puckett	2.00
15	Ozzie Smith	2.00
16	Barry Bonds	4.00
17	Gary Sheffield	.75
18	Barry Larkin	.50
19	Kevin Seitzer	.50
20	Jay Bell	.50
21	Chipper Jones	2.00
22	Ivan Rodriguez	1.25
23	Cecil Fielder	.50
24	Manny Ramirez	1.50
25	Randy Johnson	1.50
26	Moises Alou	.50
27	Mark McGwire	3.00
28	Jason Isringhausen	.50
29	Joe Carter	.50
30	Darren Daulton (Sportflix)	1.50
31	Steve Carlton	10.00
---	Benjamin Franklin	5.00
---	Phillie Phanatic/Mascot	5.00
---	Edward G. Rendell (Mayor)	3.00

FanFest Playing Cards

A special version of Pinnacle's FanFest cards was produced for construction of a large "house of cards" at the FanFest site. Following the event, some of the cards made their way into the hobby. Similar in format to the regular cards, the special issue was produced on textured playing-card stock in a 2-1/4" x 3-1/2" format with rounded corners. The playing cards lack the gold-foil found on regular cards and thus the player's name is nowhere to be found. Backs have a large gold-and-white Pinnacle logo on a black background. Cards are listed here using the numbering found on the regular version; the playing cards are unnumbered.

		NM/M
Complete Set (29):		300.00
Common Player:		10.00
(1)	Cal Ripken Jr.	30.00
(2)	Greg Maddux	17.50
(3)	Ken Griffey Jr.	20.00
(4)	Frank Thomas	15.00
(5)	Jeff Bagwell	15.00
(6)	Hideo Nomo	12.50
(7)	Tony Gwynn	17.50
(8)	Albert Belle	10.00
(9)	Mo Vaughn	10.00
(10)	Mike Piazza	20.00
(11)	Dante Bichette	10.00
(12)	Ryne Sandberg	17.50
(13)	Wade Boggs	17.50
(14)	Kirby Puckett	17.50
(15)	Ozzie Smith	17.50
(16)	Barry Bonds	30.00
(17)	Gary Sheffield	12.50
(18)	Barry Larkin	10.00

---

(19)	Kevin Seitzer	10.00
(20)	Jay Bell	10.00
(21)	Chipper Jones	17.50
(22)	Ivan Rodriguez	12.50
(23)	Cecil Fielder	10.00
(24)	Manny Ramirez	15.00
(25)	Randy Johnson	15.00
(26)	Moises Alou	10.00
(27)	Mark McGwire	25.00
(28)	Jason Isringhausen	10.00
(29)	Joe Carter	10.00

1997 Pinnacle

MARIANO RIVERA

Pinnacle baseball consists of 200 base cards. Fronts have the player's name stamped within a foil baseball-diamond shape at the bottom of each card. Backs contain summaries of the players' 1996 and lifetime statistics. Included within the base set is a 30-card Rookies subset, a 12-card Clout subset and three checklists. Inserts include two parallel sets (Artist's Proof and Museum Collection), Passport to the Majors, Shades, Team Pinnacle, Cardfrontations, and Home/Away. Cards were sold in 10-card packs for $2.49 each.

		NM/M
Complete Set (200):		10.00
Common Player:		.05
Pack (10):		1.00
Wax Box (24):		12.50
Wax Retail Box (16):		10.00
1	Cecil Fielder	.05
2	Garret Anderson	.05
3	Charles Nagy	.05
4	Darryl Hamilton	.05
5	Greg Myers	.05
6	Eric Davis	.05
7	Jeff Frye	.05
8	Marquis Grissom	.05
9	Curt Schilling	.35
10	Jeff Fassero	.05
11	Alan Benes	.05
12	Orlando Miller	.05
13	Alex Fernandez	.05
14	Andy Pettitte	.25
15	Andre Dawson	.25
16	Mark Grudzielanek	.05
17	Joe Vitiello	.05
18	Juan Gonzalez	.40
19	Mark Whiten	.05
20	Lance Johnson	.05
21	Trevor Hoffman	.05
22	Marc Newfield	.05
23	Jim Eisenreich	.05
24	Joe Carter	.05
25	Jose Canseco	.30
26	Bill Swift	.05
27	Ellis Burks	.05
28	Ben McDonald	.05
29	Edgar Martinez	.05
30	Jamie Moyer	.05
31	Chan Ho Park	.05
32	Carlos Delgado	.50
33	Kevin Mitchell	.05
34	Carlos Garcia	.05
35	Darryl Strawberry	.05
36	Jim Thome	.60
37	Jose Offerman	.05
38	Ryan Klesko	.05
39	Ruben Sierra	.05
40	Devon White	.05
41	Brian Jordan	.05
42	Tony Gwynn	.75
43	Rafael Palmeiro	.50
44	Dante Bichette	.05
45	Scott Stahoviak	.05
46	Roger Cedeno	.05
47	Ivan Rodriguez	.50
48	Bob Abreu	.05
49	Darryl Kile	.05
50	Darren Dreifort	.05
51	Shawon Dunston	.05
52	Mark McGwire	1.50
53	Tim Salmon	.05
54	Gene Schall	.05
55	Roger Clemens	.85
56	Rondell White	.05
57	Ed Sprague	.05

58	Craig Paquette	.05
59	David Segui	.05
60	Jaime Navarro	.05
61	Tom Glavine	.35
62	Jeff Brantley	.05
63	Kimera Bartee	.05
64	Fernando Vina	.05
65	Eddie Murray	.65
66	Lenny Dykstra	.05
67	Kevin Elster	.05
68	Vinny Castilla	.05
69	Todd Greene	.05
70	Brett Butler	.05
71	Robby Thompson	.05
72	Reggie Jefferson	.05
73	Todd Hundley	.05
74	Jeff King	.05
75	Ernie Young	.05
76	Jeff Bagwell	.65
77	Dan Wilson	.05
78	Paul Molitor	.65
79	Kevin Seitzer	.05
80	Kevin Brown	.05
81	Ron Gant	.05
82	Dwight Gooden	.05
83	Todd Stottlemyre	.05
84	Ken Caminiti	.05
85	James Baldwin	.05
86	Jermaine Dye	.05
87	Harold Baines	.05
88	Pat Hentgen	.05
89	Frank Rodriguez	.05
90	Mark Johnson	.05
91	Jason Kendall	.05
92	Alex Rodriguez	1.50
93	Alan Trammell	.05
94	Scott Brosius	.05
95	Delino DeShields	.05
96	Chipper Jones	.75
97	Barry Bonds	2.00
98	Brady Anderson	.05
99	Ryne Sandberg	.05
100	Albert Belle	.05
101	Jeff Cirillo	.05
102	Frank Thomas	.65
103	Mike Piazza	1.00
104	Rickey Henderson	.05
105	Rey Ordonez	.05
106	Mark Grace	.05
107	Terry Steinbach	.05
108	Ray Durham	.05
109	Barry Larkin	.05
110	Tony Clark	.05
111	Bernie Williams	.05
112	John Smoltz	.05
113	Moises Alou	.05
114	Alex Gonzalez	.05
115	Rico Brogna	.05
116	Eric Karros	.05
117	Jeff Conine	.05
118	Todd Hollandsworth	.05
119	Troy Percival	.05
120	Paul Wilson	.05
121	Orel Hershiser	.05
122	Ozzie Smith	.75
123	Dave Hollins	.05
124	Ken Hill	.05
125	Rick Wilkins	.05
126	Scott Servais	.05
127	Fernando Valenzuela	.05
128	Mariano Rivera	.15
129	Mark Loretta	.05
130	Shane Reynolds	.05
131	Darren Oliver	.05
132	Steve Trachsel	.05
133	Darren Bragg	.05
134	Jason Dickson	.05
135	Darren Fletcher	.05
136	Gary Gaetti	.05
137	Joey Cora	.05
138	Terry Pendleton	.05
139	Derek Jeter	2.00
140	Danny Tartabull	.05
141	John Flaherty	.05
142	B.J. Surhoff	.05
143	Mark Sweeney	.05
144	Chad Mottola	.05
145	Andujar Cedeno	.05
146	Tim Belcher	.05
147	Mark Thompson	.05
148	Rafael Bournigal	.05
149	Marty Cordova	.05
150	Osvaldo Fernandez	.05
151	Mike Stanley	.05
152	Ricky Bottalico	.05
153	Donnie Wall	.05
154	Omar Vizquel	.05
155	Mike Mussina	.30
156	Brant Brown	.05
157	F.P. Santangelo	.05
158	Ryan Hancock	.05
159	Jeff D'Amico	.05
160	Luis Castillo	.05
161	Darin Erstad	.10
162	Ugueth Urbina	.05
163	Andruw Jones	.65
164	Steve Gibralter	.05
165	Robin Jennings	.05
166	Mike Cameron	.05
167	George Arias	.05
168	Chris Stynes	.05
169	Justin Thompson	.05
170	Jamey Wright	.05
171	Todd Walker	.05
172	Nomar Garciaparra	.75
173	Jose Paniagua	.05
174	Marvin Benard	.05
175	Rocky Coppinger	.05

176	Quinton McCracken	.05
177	Amaury Telemaco	.05
178	Neifi Perez	.05
179	Todd Greene	.05
180	Jason Thompson	.05
181	Wilton Guerrero	.05
182	Edgar Renteria	.05
183	Billy Wagner	.05
184	Alex Ochoa	.05
185	Billy McMillon	.05
186	Kenny Lofton	.05
187	Andres Galarraga (Clout)	.05
188	Chuck Knoblauch (Clout)	.05
189	Greg Maddux (Clout)	.75
190	Mo Vaughn (Clout)	.05
191	Cal Ripken Jr. (Clout)	2.00
192	Hideo Nomo (Clout)	.40
193	Ken Griffey Jr. (Clout)	1.00
194	Sammy Sosa (Clout)	.75
195	Jay Buhner (Clout)	.05
196	Manny Ramirez (Clout)	.65
197	Matt Williams (Clout)	.05
198	Andruw Jones (Checklist)	.30
199	Darin Erstad (Checklist)	.05
200	Trey Beamon (Checklist)	.05

Artist's Proofs

Artist's Proofs parallels for 1997 Pinnacle were issued in a "fractured" set form. That is, three levels of scarcity were created, with each card available in only one of those levels. For 125 of the players, bronze is the scarcity level; 50 of the players have a silver-level scarcity and 25 players are found in the top-shelf gold level, with a reported production of 300 each. Stated odds of finding an AP parallel were 1:47 in hobby and retail packs, and 1:55 in magazine packs.

	NM/M
Common Bronze (125):	1.00
Bronze Stars:	30X
Common Silver (50):	2.50
Silver Stars:	12X
Common Gold (25):	4.00
Gold Stars:	10X

Museum Collection

DARIN ERSTAD

Each of the 200 cards in 1997 Pinnacle Series 1 was also issued in a graphically enhanced Museum Collection parallel set. The Museum cards utilize basically the same design as the regular-issue Pinnacle cards, but the front is printed in the company's Dufex gold-foil technology. On back, a small rectangular logo verifies the card's special status.

	NM/M
Complete Set (200):	100.00

Common Player: 1.00
Stars/Rookies: 6X

Cardfrontations

This hobby-only set was inserted every 23 packs of 1997 Pinnacle baseball. Fronts depict a player portrait imaged over a foil rainbow background. The same player is then pictured in action shots with the "Cardfrontation" logo in gold foil in the lower right half. The player's name appears in gold foil below the gold-foil team logo. Backs depict another player's portrait with text describing interaction between the two players. The cards are numbered as "x of 20."

		NM/M
Complete Set (20):		35.00
Common Player:		.50
1	Greg Maddux, Mike Piazza	3.00
2	Tom Glavine, Ken Caminiti	.75
3	Randy Johnson, Cal Ripken Jr.	5.00
4	Kevin Appier, Mark McGwire	4.00
5	Andy Pettitte, Juan Gonzalez	1.00
6	Pat Hentgen, Albert Belle	.50
7	Hideo Nomo, Chipper Jones	2.00
8	Ismael Valdes, Sammy Sosa	2.50
9	Mike Mussina, Manny Ramirez	1.50
10	David Cone, Jay Buhner	.50
11	Mark Wohlers, Gary Sheffield	.75
12	Alan Benes, Barry Bonds	5.00
13	Roger Clemens, Ivan Rodriguez	2.50
14	Mariano Rivera, Ken Griffey Jr.	3.00
15	Dwight Gooden, Frank Thomas	1.50
16	John Wetteland, Darin Erstad	.50
17	John Smoltz, Brian Jordan	.50
18	Kevin Brown, Jeff Bagwell	1.50
19	Jack McDowell, Alex Rodriguez	4.00
20	Charles Nagy, Bernie Williams	.50

Home/Away

The 24-card, shirt-shaped, die-cut set was inserted every 33 retail packs. The background on front and back is a facsimile of the player's home or road jersey. A color action photo is on front with gold-foil graphics. Backs have a few words about the player.

		NM/M
Complete Set (24):		65.00
Common Player:		2.00
1	Chipper Jones	5.00
2	Ken Griffey Jr.	6.00
3	Mike Piazza	6.00
4	Frank Thomas	4.00
5	Jeff Bagwell	4.00
6	Alex Rodriguez	8.00
7	Barry Bonds	10.00
8	Mo Vaughn	2.00
9	Derek Jeter	10.00
10	Mark McGwire	8.00
11	Cal Ripken Jr.	10.00
12	Albert Belle	2.00

Passport to the Majors

The 25-card, regular-sized set was inserted every 36 packs of 1997 Pinnacle baseball. The cards fold out and resemble a mini passport.

		NM/M
Complete Set (25):		55.00
Common Player:		1.00
1	Greg Maddux	4.00
1s	Greg Maddux ("SAMPLE" overprint.)	4.00
2	Ken Griffey Jr.	6.00
3	Frank Thomas	3.00
4	Cal Ripken Jr.	10.00
5	Mike Piazza	6.00
6	Alex Rodriguez	7.50
7	Mo Vaughn	1.00
8	Chipper Jones	4.00
9	Roberto Alomar	1.00
10	Edgar Martinez	1.00
11	Javier Lopez	1.00
12	Ivan Rodriguez	2.50
13	Juan Gonzalez	1.50
14	Carlos Baerga	1.00
15	Sammy Sosa	4.00
16	Manny Ramirez	3.00
17	Raul Mondesi	1.00
18	Henry Rodriguez	1.00
19	Rafael Palmeiro	2.50
20	Rey Ordonez	1.00
21	Hideo Nomo	1.50
22	Makoto Suzuki	1.00
23	Chan Ho Park	1.00
24	Larry Walker	1.00
25	Ruben Rivera	1.00

Shades

This set was inserted every 23 retail packs of Pinnacle baseball. The horizontal cards are die-cut at the top of a pair of sunglasses whose lenses contain color portrait and action pictures of the player. The player face beneath the shades is printed on silver foil stock. Backs have a mirror-image of the front photos in the lenses and a baseball diamond in the background.

		NM/M
Complete Set (10):		15.00
Common Player:		.75
1	Ken Griffey Jr.	3.00
2	Juan Gonzalez	1.50
3	John Smoltz	.75
4	Gary Sheffield	1.00
5	Cal Ripken Jr.	5.00
6	Mo Vaughn	.75
7	Brian Jordan	.75
8	Mike Piazza	3.00
9	Frank Thomas	2.25
10	Alex Rodriguez	4.00

Team Pinnacle

This insert features top National League players from a position on one side with the best American League players on the other. One side of the card is in Dufex printing and there is actually two versions of each card, as either side can feature the Dufex foil. Team Pinnacle is inserted every 90 packs.

		NM/M
Complete Set (10):		30.00
Common Player:		1.50
1	Frank Thomas, Jeff Bagwell	4.00
2	Chuck Knoblauch, Eric Young	1.50
3	Ken Caminiti, Jim Thome	3.00
4	Alex Rodriguez, Chipper Jones	6.00
5	Mike Piazza, Ivan Rodriguez	5.00
6	Albert Belle, Barry Bonds	8.00
7	Ken Griffey Jr., Ellis Burks	6.00
8	Juan Gonzalez, Gary Sheffield	3.00
9	John Smoltz, Andy Pettitte	2.00
10	All Players	2.00

1997 New Pinnacle Samples

This group of sample cards was sent to dealers to introduce the New Pinnacle brand which took the place of a second series of Pinnacle Baseball in 1997. Cards are virtually identical to the issued versions except for the large diagonal black-and-white "SAMPLE" overprint on front and back.

		NM/M
Complete Set (6):		7.50
Common Player:		1.25
2	Sammy Sosa	2.00
45	Mike Piazza	3.00
57	Jeff Bagwell	1.25
81	Alex Rodriguez	2.50
127	Ryan Klesko	.50
175	Andruw Jones	1.25

1997 New Pinnacle

In lieu of a second series of Pinnacle Baseball, the company offered collectors New Pinnacle, a 200-card set sold in 10-card packs for $2.99. Two parallel versions of the 200-card set exist in Museum Collection and Artist's Proofs. Other inserts include Press Plates, Spellbound, Keeping the Pace and Interleague Encounter. Collectors who obtained four Press Plates of the same player's card back or front were eligible to win cash prizes.

	NM/M
Complete Set (200):	12.50
Common Player:	.05
Common Museum:	1.00
Museum Stars:	8X
Common Red Artist's Proof:	1.00
Red AP Stars:	10X
Common Blue Artist's Proof:	3.00
Blue AP Stars:	25X
Common Green Artist's Proof:	6.00
Green AP Stars:	35X
Pack (10):	1.50
Wax Box (18):	15.00

1	Ken Griffey Jr.	1.00
2	Sammy Sosa	.75
3	Greg Maddux	.75
4	Matt Williams	.05
5	Jason Isringhausen	.05
6	Gregg Jefferies	.05
7	Chili Davis	.05
8	Paul O'Neill	.05
9	Larry Walker	.05
10	Ellis Burks	.05
11	Cliff Floyd	.05
12	Albert Belle	.05
13	Javier Lopez	.05
14	David Cone	.05
15	Jose Canseco	.40
16	Todd Zeile	.05
17	Bernard Gilkey	.05
18	Andres Galarraga	.05
19	Chris Snopek	.05
20	Tim Salmon	.05
21	Roger Clemens	.85
22	Reggie Sanders	.05
23	John Jaha	.05
24	Andy Pettitte	.25
25	Kenny Lofton	.05
26	Robb Nen	.05
27	John Wetteland	.05
28	Bobby Bonilla	.05
29	Hideo Nomo	.40
30	Cecil Fielder	.05
31	Garret Anderson	.05
32	Pat Hentgen	.05
33	David Justice	.05
34	Billy Wagner	.05
35	Al Leiter	.05
36	Mark Wohlers	.05
37	Rondell White	.05
38	Charles Johnson	.05
39	Mark Grace	.05
40	Pedro Martinez	.65
41	Tom Goodwin	.05
42	Manny Ramirez	.65
43	Greg Vaughn	.05
44	Brian Jordan	.05
45	Mike Piazza	1.00
46	Roberto Hernandez	.05
47	Wade Boggs	.75
48	Scott Sanders	.05
49	Alex Gonzalez	.05
50	Kevin Brown	.05
51	Bob Higginson	.05
52	Ken Caminiti	.05
53	Derek Jeter	2.00
54	Carlos Baerga	.05
55	Jay Buhner	.05
56	Tim Naehring	.05
57	Jeff Bagwell	.65
58	Steve Finley	.05
59	Kevin Appier	.05
60	Jay Bell	.05
61	Ivan Rodriguez	.60
62	Terrell Wade	.05
63	Rusty Greer	.05
64	Juan Guzman	.05
65	Fred McGriff	.05
66	Tino Martinez	.05
67	Ray Lankford	.05
68	Juan Gonzalez	.40
69	Ron Gant	.05
70	Jack McDowell	.05
71	Tony Gwynn	.75
72	Joe Carter	.05
73	Wilson Alvarez	.05
74	Jason Giambi	.60
75	Brian Hunter	.05
76	Michael Tucker	.05
77	Andy Benes	.05
78	Brady Anderson	.05
79	Ramon Martinez	.05
80	Troy Percival	.05
81	Alex Rodriguez	1.50
82	Jim Thome	.60
83	Denny Neagle	.05
84	Rafael Palmeiro	.60
85	Jose Valentin	.05
86	Marc Newfield	.05
87	Mariano Rivera	.15
88	Alan Benes	.05
89	Jimmy Key	.05
90	Joe Randa	.05
91	Cal Ripken Jr.	2.00
92	Craig Biggio	.05
93	Dean Palmer	.05
94	Gary Sheffield	.45
95	Ismael Valdez	.05
96	John Valentin	.05
97	Johnny Damon	.35
98	Mo Vaughn	.05
99	Paul Sorrento	.05
100	Randy Johnson	.65
101	Raul Mondesi	.05
102	Roberto Alomar	.20
103	Royce Clayton	.05
104	Mark Grudzielanek	.05
105	Wally Joyner	.05
106	Wil Cordero	.05
107	Will Clark	.05
108	Chuck Knoblauch	.05
109	Derek Bell	.05
110	Henry Rodriguez	.05
111	Edgar Renteria	.05
112	Travis Fryman	.05
113	Eric Young	.05
114	Sandy Alomar Jr.	.05
115	Darin Erstad	.25
116	Barry Larkin	.05
117	Barry Bonds	2.00
118	Frank Thomas	.65
119	Carlos Delgado	.50
120	Jason Kendall	.05
121	Todd Hollandsworth	.05
122	Jim Edmonds	.05
123	Chipper Jones	.75
124	Jeff Fassero	.05
125	Deion Sanders	.05
126	Matt Lawton	.05
127	Ryan Klesko	.05
128	Mike Mussina	.40
129	Paul Molitor	.65
130	Dante Bichette	.05
131	Bill Pulsipher	.05
132	Todd Hundley	.05
133	J.T. Snow	.05
134	Chuck Finley	.05
135	Shawn Green	.30
136	Charles Nagy	.05
137	Willie Greene	.05
138	Marty Cordova	.05
139	Eddie Murray	.65
140	Ryne Sandberg	.75
141	Alex Fernandez	.05
142	Mark McGwire	1.50
143	Eric Davis	.05
144	Jermaine Dye	.05
145	Ruben Sierra	.05
146	Damon Buford	.05
147	John Smoltz	.05
148	Alex Ochoa	.05
149	Moises Alou	.05
150	Rico Brogna	.05
151	Terry Steinbach	.05
152	Jeff King	.05
153	Carlos Garcia	.05
154	Tom Glavine	.35
155	Edgar Martinez	.05
156	Kevin Elster	.05
157	Darryl Hamilton	.05
158	Jason Dickson	.05
159	Kevin Orie	.05
160	Bubba Trammell RC	.25
161	Jose Guillen	.05
162	Brant Brown	.05
163	Wendell Magee	.05
164	Scott Spiezio	.05
165	Todd Walker	.05
166	Rod Myers RC	.05
167	Damon Mashore	.05
168	Wilton Guerrero	.05
169	Vladimir Guerrero	.65
170	Nomar Garciaparra	.75
171	Shannon Stewart	.05
172	Scott Rolen	.60
173	Bob Abreu	.05
174	Danny Patterson RC	.05
175	Andruw Jones	.65
176	Brian Giles RC	.50
177	Dmitri Young	.05
178	Cal Ripken Jr. (East Meets West)	1.00
179	Chuck Knoblauch (East Meets West)	.05
180	Alex Rodriguez (East Meets West)	.75
181	Andres Galarraga (East Meets West)	.05
182	Pedro Martinez (East Meets West)	.35
183	Brady Anderson (East Meets West)	.05
184	Barry Bonds (East Meets West)	1.00
185	Ivan Rodriguez (East Meets West)	.30
186	Gary Sheffield (East Meets West)	.05
187	Denny Neagle (East Meets West)	.05
188	Mark McGwire (Aura)	.75
189	Ellis Burks (Aura)	.05
190	Alex Rodriguez (Aura)	.75
191	Mike Piazza (Aura)	.65
192	Barry Bonds (Aura)	1.00
193	Albert Belle (Aura)	.05
194	Chipper Jones (Aura)	.40
195	Juan Gonzalez (Aura)	.20
196	Brady Anderson (Aura)	.05
197	Frank Thomas (Aura)	.35
198	Checklist (Vladimir Guerrero)	.35
199	Checklist (Todd Walker)	.05
200	Checklist (Scott Rolen)	.30

Artist's Proof

This 200-card parallel set features a special AP seal and foil treatment and is fractured into three levels of scarcity - Red (125 cards), Blue (50 cards) and Green (25 cards). Cards were inserted at a rate of 1:39 packs. "Artist's Proof" is stamped along the lower edge.

	NM/M
Common Red Artist's Proof:	1.00
Red Artist's Proofs:	10X
Common Blue Artist's Proof:	3.00
Blue Artist's Proofs:	25X
Common Green Artist's Proof:	6.00
Green Artist's Proofs:	35X

Museum Collection

Dufex printing on gold-foil backgrounds differentiates the Museum Collection parallel of New Pinnacle from the regular-issue cards. Museums were inserted at an average rate of one per nine packs.

	NM/M
Complete Set (200):	200.00
Common Player:	1.00
Stars/Rookies:	8X

Interleague Encounter

Inserted 1:240 packs, this 10-card sets showcases 20 American League and National League rivals with the date of their first interleague match-up on double-sided mirror mylar cards.

		NM/M
Complete Set (10):		60.00
Common Player:		2.50
1	Albert Belle, Brian Jordan	2.50

2	Andruw Jones,	
	Brady Anderson	4.50
3	Ken Griffey Jr.,	
	Tony Gwynn	7.50
4	Cal Ripken Jr.,	
	Chipper Jones	12.00
5	Mike Piazza,	
	Ivan Rodriguez	7.50
6	Derek Jeter,	
	Vladimir Guerrero	12.00
7	Greg Maddux,	
	Mo Vaughn	6.00
8	Alex Rodriguez,	
	Hideo Nomo	10.00
9	Juan Gonzalez,	
	Barry Bonds	12.00
10	Frank Thomas,	
	Jeff Bagwell	4.50

Keeping the Pace

Top sluggers who were considered candidates to break Roger Maris' single-season record of 61 home runs were featured in this insert set. Cards feature Dot Matrix holographic borders and backgrounds on front. Backs present career stats of an all-time great and project future numbers for the current player. The cards were inserted 1:89 packs.

		NM/M
Complete Set (18):		100.00
Common Player:		1.00
1	Juan Gonzalez	3.00
2	Greg Maddux	7.50
3	Ivan Rodriguez	4.50
4	Ken Griffey Jr.	12.00
5	Alex Rodriguez	13.50
6	Barry Bonds	15.00
7	Frank Thomas	6.00
8	Chuck Knoblauch	1.00
9	Derek Jeter	15.00
10	Roger Clemens	9.00
11	Kenny Lofton	1.00
12	Tony Gwynn	7.50
13	Troy Percival	1.00
14	Cal Ripken Jr.	15.00
15	Andy Pettitte	1.50
16	Hideo Nomo	3.00
17	Randy Johnson	6.00
18	Mike Piazza	12.00

Press Plates

Just when collectors thought they had seen every type of insert card imaginable, New Pinnacle proved them wrong by cutting up and inserting into packs (about one per 1,250) the metal plates used to print the set. There are black, blue, red and yellow plates for the front and back of each card. Rather than touting the collector value of the plates, Pinnacle created a treasure hunt by offering $20,000-35,000 to anybody assembling a complete set of four plates for either the front or back of any card. The $35,000, which would have been awarded for completion prior to August 22, was unclaimed. The amount decreased to $20,000 for any set redeemed by the end of 1997.

Spellbound

Each of the 50 cards in this insert features a letter of the alphabet as the basic card design. The letters can be used to spell out the names of nine players featured in the set. Cards feature micro-etched foil and are inserted 1:19 packs. Cards of Griffey, Ripken and the Jones were inserted only in hobby packs; retail packs have cards of Belle, Thomas, Piazza and the Rodriguezes. Values shown are per card; multiply by number of cards to determine a player's set value.

		NM/M
Complete Set (50):		110.00
1-5AB	Albert Belle	1.00
1-6AJ	Andruw Jones	2.00
1-4AR	Alex Rodriguez	4.50
1-7CJ	Chipper Jones	2.50
1-6CR	Cal Ripken Jr.	6.00
1-5FT	Frank Thomas	2.00
1-5IR	Ivan Rodriguez	1.50
1-6KG	Ken Griffey Jr.	3.50
1-6MP	Mike Piazza	3.50

1997 Pinnacle Certified

This 150-card base features a mirror-like mylar finish and a peel-off protector on each card front. Backs feature the player's 1996 statistics against each opponent. There are four different parallel sets, each with varying degrees of scarcity: Certified Red (1:5), Mirror Red (1:99), Mirror Blue (1:199) and Mirror Gold (1:299). Other inserts include Lasting Impressions, Certified Team, and Certified Gold Team. Cards were sold in six-card packs for a suggested price of $4.99.

		NM/M
Complete Set (150):		30.00
Common Player:		.15
Common Certified Red:		1.00
Certified Red Stars:		5X
Common Mirror Red:		3.00
Mirror Red Stars:		12X
Common Mirror Blue:		4.00
Mirror Blue Stars:		15X
Common Mirror Gold:		7.50
Mirror Gold Stars:		35X
Jose Cruz Jr. Redemption:		2.00
Pack (6):		2.00
Wax Box (20):		35.00

1	Barry Bonds	3.00
2	Mo Vaughn	.15
3	Matt Williams	.15
4	Ryne Sandberg	1.25
5	Jeff Bagwell	1.00
6	Alan Benes	.15
7	John Wetteland	.15
8	Fred McGriff	.15
9	Craig Biggio	.15
10	Bernie Williams	.15
11	Brian L. Hunter	.15
12	Sandy Alomar Jr.	.15
13	Ray Lankford	.15
14	Ryan Klesko	.15
15	Jermaine Dye	.15
16	Andy Benes	.15
17	Albert Belle	.15
18	Tony Clark	.15
19	Dean Palmer	.15
20	Bernard Gilkey	.15
21	Ken Caminiti	.15
22	Alex Rodriguez	2.25
23	Tim Salmon	.15
24	Larry Walker	.15
25	Barry Larkin	.15
26	Mike Piazza	1.50
27	Brady Anderson	.15
28	Cal Ripken Jr.	3.00
29	Charles Nagy	.15
30	Paul Molitor	1.00
31	Darin Erstad	.25
32	Rey Ordonez	.15
33	Wally Joyner	.15
34	David Cone	.15
35	Sammy Sosa	1.25
36	Dante Bichette	.15
37	Eric Karros	.15
38	Omar Vizquel	.15
39	Roger Clemens	1.25
40	Joe Carter	.15
41	Frank Thomas	1.00
42	Javier Lopez	.15
43	Mike Mussina	.45
44	Gary Sheffield	.60
45	Tony Gwynn	1.25
46	Jason Kendall	.15
47	Jim Thome	.75
48	Andres Galarraga	.15
49	Mark McGwire	2.25
50	Troy Percival	.15
51	Derek Jeter	3.00
52	Todd Hollandsworth	.15
53	Ken Griffey Jr.	1.50
54	Randy Johnson	1.00
55	Pat Hentgen	.15
56	Rusty Greer	.15
57	John Jaha	.15
58	Kenny Lofton	.15
59	Chipper Jones	1.25
60	Robb Nen	.15
61	Rafael Palmeiro	.75
62	Mariano Rivera	.30
63	Hideo Nomo	.50
64	Greg Vaughn	.15
65	Ron Gant	.15
66	Eddie Murray	1.00
67	John Smoltz	.15
68	Manny Ramirez	1.00
69	Juan Gonzalez	.50
70	F.P. Santangelo	.15
71	Moises Alou	.15
72	Alex Ochoa	.15
73	Chuck Knoblauch	.15
74	Raul Mondesi	.15
75	J.T. Snow	.15
76	Rickey Henderson	1.00
77	Bobby Bonilla	.15
78	Wade Boggs	1.25
79	Ivan Rodriguez	.75
80	Brian Jordan	.15
81	Al Leiter	.15
82	Jay Buhner	.15
83	Greg Maddux	1.25
84	Edgar Martinez	.15
85	Kevin Brown	.15
86	Eric Young	.15
87	Todd Hundley	.15
88	Ellis Burks	.15
89	Marquis Grissom	.15
90	Jose Canseco	.60
91	Henry Rodriguez	.15
92	Andy Pettitte	.45
93	Mark Grudzielanek	.15
94	Dwight Gooden	.15
95	Roberto Alomar	.50
96	Paul Wilson	.15
97	Will Clark	.15
98	Rondell White	.15
99	Charles Johnson	.15
100	Jim Edmonds	.15
101	Jason Giambi	.60
102	Billy Wagner	.15
103	Edgar Renteria	.15
104	Johnny Damon	.45
105	Jason Isringhausen	.15
106	Andruw Jones	1.00
107	Jose Guillen	.15
108	Kevin Orie	.15
109	Brian Giles RC	1.25
110	Danny Patterson	.15
111	Vladimir Guerrero	1.00
112	Scott Rolen	.75
113	Damon Mashore	.15
114	Nomar Garciaparra	1.25
115	Todd Walker	.15
116	Wilton Guerrero	.15
117	Bob Abreu	.25
118	Brooks Kieschnick	.15
119	Pokey Reese	.15
120	Todd Greene	.15
121	Dmitri Young	.15
122	Raul Casanova	.15
123	Glendon Rusch	.15
124	Jason Dickson	.15
125	Jorge Posada	.15
126	Rod Myers RC	.15
127	Bubba Trammell RC	.40
128	Scott Spiezio	.15
129	Hideki Irabu RC	.40
130	Wendell Magee	.15
131	Bartolo Colon	.15
132	Chris Holt	.15
133	Calvin Maduro	.15
134	Ray Montgomery	.15
135	Shannon Stewart	.15
136	Ken Griffey Jr. (Certified Stars)	1.00
137	Vladimir Guerrero (Certified Stars)	.50
138	Roger Clemens (Certified Stars)	.75
139	Mark McGwire (Certified Stars)	1.25
140	Albert Belle (Certified Stars)	.15
141	Derek Jeter (Certified Stars)	1.50
142	Juan Gonzalez (Certified Stars)	.25
143	Greg Maddux (Certified Stars)	.60
144	Alex Rodriguez (Certified Stars)	1.25
145	Jeff Bagwell (Certified Stars)	.50
146	Cal Ripken Jr. (Certified Stars)	1.50
147	Tony Gwynn (Certified Stars)	.60
148	Frank Thomas (Certified Stars)	.50
149	Hideo Nomo (Certified Stars)	.25
150	Andruw Jones (Certified Stars)	.50

Red

This parallel set features a red tint to the triangular mylar background left and right of the photo on front. "CERTIFIED RED" is printed vertically on both edges. Backs are identical to regular Certified cards. A peel-off protection coating is on the front of the card. Cards were inserted 1:5 packs.

		NM/M
Common Certified Red:		1.00
Certified Red Stars:		5X

Mirror Red

This parallel set features a red design element on the front of each card. Cards were inserted 1:99 packs.

		NM/M
Common Mirror Red:		3.00
Mirror Red Stars:		12X

Mirror Blue

This parallel set features a blue design element on the front of each card. Cards were inserted 1:199 packs.

		NM/M
Common Mirror Blue:		4.00
Mirror Blue Stars:		15X

Mirror Gold

This parallel set features a holographic gold design on the front of each card. Cards were inserted 1:299 packs.

		NM/M
Common Mirror Gold:		7.50
Mirror Gold Stars:		35X

Mirror Black

The exact nature of these cards is undetermined. They may have been intentionally created and "secretly" seeded in packs as an insert or they may have been test cards which were mistakenly inserted. They are not marked in any fashion. The cards are said to reflect in bright green under direct light. It is commonly believed that each "Mirror Black" card exists in only a single piece, but that has not been verified. Neither is it confirmed that a Mirror Black parallel exists for each of the 151 cards in the base set. Even the most undistinguished player's card can sell for $100 or more due to the scarcity of the type.

		NM/M
Common Player:		100.00

Lasting Impression

This insert features an hour-glass die-cut design and a mirror mylar finish and pictures some of baseball's top veteran stars. Backs are conventionally printed and include a color portrait photo and a few words about the player. Cards were inserted 1:19 packs.

		NM/M
Complete Set (20):		40.00
Common Player:		1.00
1	Cal Ripken Jr.	7.50
2	Ken Griffey Jr.	5.00
3	Mo Vaughn	1.00
4	Brian Jordan	1.00
5	Mark McGwire	6.00
6	Chuck Knoblauch	1.00
7	Sammy Sosa	1.00
8	Brady Anderson	1.00
9	Frank Thomas	2.00
10	Tony Gwynn	3.00
11	Roger Clemens	4.00

Team

The top 20 players in the game are honored on cards with frosted silver mylar printing. Cards were inserted 1:19 packs. A parallel version of this set, Certified Gold Team, has a gold mylar design with each card numbered to 500; while a super-premium parallel, Mirror Gold, is numbered to 25. Each card can also be found in a promo version overprinted "SAMPLE."

		NM/M
Complete Set (20):		30.00
Common Player:		.50
Gold:		3X
Mirror Gold:		15X
Sample:		1X
1	Frank Thomas	1.50
2	Jeff Bagwell	1.50
3	Derek Jeter	4.00
4	Chipper Jones	2.00
5	Alex Rodriguez	3.00
6	Ken Caminiti	.50
7	Cal Ripken Jr.	4.00
8	Mo Vaughn	.50
9	Ivan Rodriguez	1.00
10	Mike Piazza	2.50
11	Juan Gonzalez	.75
12	Barry Bonds	4.00
13	Ken Griffey Jr.	2.50
14	Andruw Jones	1.50
15	Albert Belle	.50
16	Gary Sheffield	.75
17	Andy Pettitte	.65
18	Hideo Nomo	.75
19	Greg Maddux	2.00
20	John Smoltz	.50

1997 Totally Certified Samples

This trio of promo cards previews the high-tech, all-numbered Totally Certified issue. The samples are similar in format to the issued versions except they carry a large, black "SAMPLE" overprint diagonally on front and back. Also, backs have a gold-foil "PROMO" instead of the individual serial number.

		NM/M
Complete Set (3):		5.00
Common Player:		1.00
18	Tony Clark (Platinum Red)	1.00
39	Roger Clemens (Platinum Blue)	3.00
41	Frank Thomas (Platinum Gold)	2.00

12	Alex Rodriguez	6.00
13	Paul Molitor	2.00
14	Kenny Lofton	1.00
15	John Smoltz	1.00
16	Roberto Alomar	1.50
17	Randy Johnson	2.00
18	Ryne Sandberg	3.00
19	Manny Ramirez	2.00
20	Mike Mussina	1.50

Platinum Red

Totally Certified doesn't have a true base set. Instead, the product consists of three different 150-card parallel sets. Packs consisted of three cards for $6.99 each. The first of three parallels is the Platinum Red set, inserted two per pack, and featuring micro-etched holographic mylar stock with red accents and foil stamping. Each card in the Red set is sequentially-numbered to 3,999.

		NM/M
Complete Set (150):		75.00
Common Player:		.25
Pack (3):		3.00
Wax Box (20):		45.00
1	Barry Bonds	4.00
2	Mo Vaughn	.25
3	Matt Williams	.25
4	Ryne Sandberg	2.00
5	Jeff Bagwell	1.25
6	Alan Benes	.25
7	John Wetteland	.25
8	Fred McGriff	.25
9	Craig Biggio	.25
10	Bernie Williams	.25
11	Brian Hunter	.25
12	Sandy Alomar Jr.	.25
13	Ray Lankford	.25
14	Ryan Klesko	.25
15	Jermaine Dye	.25
16	Andy Benes	.25
17	Albert Belle	.25
18	Tony Clark	.25
19	Dean Palmer	.25
20	Bernard Gilkey	.25
21	Ken Caminiti	.25
22	Alex Rodriguez	3.00
23	Tim Salmon	.25
24	Larry Walker	.25
25	Barry Larkin	.25
26	Mike Piazza	2.50
27	Brady Anderson	.25
28	Cal Ripken Jr.	4.00
29	Charles Nagy	.25
30	Paul Molitor	1.25
31	Darin Erstad	.35
32	Rey Ordonez	.25
33	Wally Joyner	.25
34	David Cone	.25
35	Sammy Sosa	2.00
36	Dante Bichette	.25
37	Eric Karros	.25
38	Omar Vizquel	.25
39	Roger Clemens	2.25
40	Joe Carter	.25
41	Frank Thomas	1.25
42	Javier Lopez	.25
43	Mike Mussina	.75
44	Gary Sheffield	.60
45	Tony Gwynn	2.00
46	Jason Kendall	.25
47	Jim Thome	1.00
48	Andres Galarraga	.25
49	Mark McGwire	3.00
50	Troy Percival	.25
51	Derek Jeter	4.00
52	Todd Hollandsworth	.25
53	Ken Griffey Jr.	2.50
54	Randy Johnson	1.25
55	Pat Hentgen	.25
56	Rusty Greer	.25
57	John Jaha	.25
58	Kenny Lofton	.25
59	Chipper Jones	2.00
60	Robb Nen	.25
61	Rafael Palmeiro	1.00
62	Mariano Rivera	.35
63	Hideo Nomo	.65
64	Greg Vaughn	.25
65	Ron Gant	.25
66	Eddie Murray	1.25
67	John Smoltz	.25
68	Manny Ramirez	.25
69	Juan Gonzalez	.65
70	F.P. Santangelo	.25
71	Moises Alou	.25
72	Alex Ochoa	.25
73	Chuck Knoblauch	.25
74	Raul Mondesi	.25
75	J.T. Snow	.25

76	Rickey Henderson	1.25
77	Bobby Bonilla	.25
78	Wade Boggs	2.00
79	Ivan Rodriguez	1.00
80	Brian Jordan	.25
81	Al Leiter	.25
82	Jay Buhner	.25
83	Greg Maddux	2.00
84	Edgar Martinez	.25
85	Kevin Brown	.25
86	Eric Young	.25
87	Todd Hundley	.25
88	Ellis Burks	.25
89	Marquis Grissom	.25
90	Jose Canseco	.60
91	Henry Rodriguez	.25
92	Andy Pettitte	.50
93	Mark Grudzielanek	.25
94	Dwight Gooden	.25
95	Roberto Alomar	.35
96	Paul Wilson	.25
97	Will Clark	.25
98	Rondell White	.25
99	Charles Johnson	.25
100	Jim Edmonds	.25
101	Jason Giambi	.75
102	Billy Wagner	.25
103	Edgar Renteria	.25
104	Johnny Damon	.45
105	Jason Isringhausen	.25
106	Andruw Jones	1.25
107	Jose Guillen	.25
108	Kevin Orie	.25
109	Brian Giles RC	2.00
110	Danny Patterson	.25
111	Vladimir Guerrero	1.00
112	Scott Rolen	1.00
113	Damon Mashore	.25
114	Nomar Garciaparra	2.00
115	Todd Walker	.25
116	Wilton Guerrero	.25
117	Bob Abreu	.35
118	Brooks Kieschnick	.25
119	Pokey Reese	.25
120	Todd Greene	.25
121	Dmitri Young	.25
122	Raul Casanova	.25
123	Glendon Rusch	.25
124	Jason Dickson	.25
125	Jorge Posada	.25
126	Rod Myers	.25
127	Bubba Trammell	.25
128	Scott Spiezio	.25
129	Hideki Irabu	.25
130	Wendell Magee	.25
131	Bartolo Colon	.25
132	Chris Holt	.25
133	Calvin Maduro	.25
134	Ray Montgomery	.25
135	Shannon Stewart	.25
136	Ken Griffey Jr. (Certified Stars)	1.50
137	Vladimir Guerrero (Certified Stars)	.60
138	Roger Clemens (Certified Stars)	1.25
139	Mark McGwire (Certified Stars)	1.50
140	Albert Belle (Certified Stars)	.25
141	Derek Jeter (Certified Stars)	2.00
142	Juan Gonzalez (Certified Stars)	.30
143	Greg Maddux (Certified Stars)	1.00
144	Alex Rodriguez (Certified Stars)	1.50
145	Jeff Bagwell (Certified Stars)	.60
146	Cal Ripken Jr. (Certified Stars)	2.00
147	Tony Gwynn (Certified Stars)	1.00
148	Frank Thomas (Certified Stars)	.60
149	Hideo Nomo (Certified Stars)	.30
150	Andruw Jones (Certified Stars)	.60

Platinum Blue

Featuring blue accents and foil stamping, the Platinum Blue cards are sequentially numbered on back in gold foil to 1,999 and inserted per pack.

	NM/M
Complete Set (150):	200.00
Common Player:	1.00
Platinum Blue Stars:	1.5X

Platinum Gold

The most difficult to find of the Totally Certified cards, the Platinum Gold versions are sequentially-numbered to 30 per card and inserted 1:79 packs.

	NM/M
Common Player:	25.00
Platinum Gold Stars:	30X

FanFest

As title sponsor for baseball's All-Star FanFest in Cleveland, July 4-8, Pinnacle issued a number of special cards including this set which was distributed in three-card cello packs both prior to and during the event. To help promote the event, six of the cards were issued with a schedule back, as well as the regular back design. Fronts have action photos highlighted at bottom by a stadium facade in gold foil. The FanFest logo is at bottom center. Backs feature a player portrait photo within a large star. Also on back are a few stats and personal data, a few words about the player and appropriate logos. Cards are numbered with an "FF" prefix and "of 21" following the number. Card #21 of the host team's Sandy Alomar, Jr., was not issued in packs. A redemption card, which could be traded in at area card shops for the Alomar card, was substituted.

		NM/M
Complete Set (21):		12.50
Common Player:		.25
FF1	Frank Thomas	.65
FF2	Jeff Bagwell	.65
FF3	Chuck Knoblauch	.25
FF4	Craig Biggio	.25
FF5	Alex Rodriguez	1.50
FF6	Chipper Jones	.75
FF7	Cal Ripken Jr.	1.50
FF8	Ken Caminiti	.25
FF9	Juan Gonzalez	.45
FF10	Barry Bonds	2.00
FF11	Ken Griffey Jr.	.65
FF12	Andruw Jones	.65
FF13	Manny Ramirez	.65
FF14	Tony Gwynn	.75
FF15a	Ivan Rodriguez (Schedule back.)	2.50
FF15b	Ivan Rodriguez (Regular back.)	.50
FF16a	Mike Piazza (Schedule back.)	4.50
FF16b	Mike Piazza (Regular back.)	1.00
FF17a	Andy Pettitte (Schedule back.)	2.00
FF17b	Andy Pettitte (Regular back.)	.40
FF18a	Hideo Nomo (Schedule back.)	1.50
FF18b	Hideo Nomo (Regular back.)	.45
FF19a	Roger Clemens (Schedule back.)	4.00
FF19b	Roger Clemens (Regular back.)	.85
FF20a	Greg Maddux (Schedule back.)	3.50
FF20b	Greg Maddux (Regular back.)	.75
FF21	Sandy Alomar Jr.	2.50
----	Sandy Alomar Jr. (Trade-in card.)	.25

FanFest Larry Doby

Marking the 50th anniversary of the American League's integration, Pinnacle, title sponsor of baseball's All-Star FanFest, issued a special card of black A.L. pioneer Larry Doby, who debuted in 1947 with the Indians. FanFest and the All-Star Game were held in Cleveland in 1997, with Doby attending many of the functions. In the same format as its FanFest set of current players, the special Doby card has a black-and-white action photo on front, with gold-foil highlights at bottom. Back repeats the front photo within a star and offers some career notes and stats. The Doby card was given away to FanFest volunteer workers and laminated into identification badges for FanFest dealers.

	NM/M
Larry Doby	4.00

FanFest Personal Cards

Continuing a tradition begun a year earlier, Pinnacle, the title sponsor for baseball's FanFest, produced a series of cards for various local and media celebrities. The cards are in the same format as the FanFest player cards, with color photos on front and gold-foil highlights. Backs have a photo detail within a star design and a few words about the personality, along with stats such as Indians' games attended, pop-corn consumed, etc. Cards are numbered with a PC prefix and are difficult to find because their distribution was controlled by the person pictured. Rick Manning was an Indians outfielder from 1975-83. Mike Hegan played in the American League from 1964-77; his father, Jim, was a staple behind the plate for the Indians between 1941-57. Six of the cards feature members of the Fox network which televised the 1997 All-Star Game.

		NM/M
Complete Set (12):		30.00
Common Player:		2.00
PC1	Macie McInnis (Fox)	2.00
PC2	Bill Martin (Fox)	2.00
PC3	Dick Gaddard (Fox)	2.00
PC4	Jack Corrigan (WUAB-TV)	2.00
PC5	Mike Hegan (WUAB-TV)	6.00
PC6	Rick Manning (Sports Channel)	5.00
PC7	John Sanders (Sports Channel)	2.00
PC8	Mayor Michael R. White	4.50
PC9	Wilma Smith (Fox)	2.00
PC10	Tim Taylor (Fox)	2.00
PC11	Robin Swoboda (Fox)	2.00
PC12	Slider (mascot)	3.00

1997 Pinnacle Inside

The first baseball card set to be sold within a sealed tin can, Inside Baseball consists of a 150-card base set featuring both a color and black-and-white photo of the player on front. Included in the base set are 20 Rookies cards and three checklists. Inserts include the Club Edition and Diamond Edition parallel sets, Dueling Dugouts and Fortysomething. In addition, 24 different cans, each featuring a different player, were available. Cans containing one pack of 10 cards were sold for $2.99 each.

	NM/M
Complete Set (150):	15.00
Common Player:	.05
Common Club Edition:	.75
Club Edition Stars:	5X
Common Diamond Edition:	5.00
Diamond Edition Stars:	25X
Unopened Can (10):	2.00
Case Cans (48):	60.00

1	David Cone	.05
2	Sammy Sosa	1.00
3	Joe Carter	.05
4	Juan Gonzalez	.40
5	Hideo Nomo	.40
6	Moises Alou	.05
7	Marc Newfield	.05
8	Alex Rodriguez	2.00
9	Kimera Bartee	.05
10	Chuck Knoblauch	.05
11	Jason Isringhausen	.05
12	Jermaine Allensworth	.05
13	Frank Thomas	.75
14	Paul Molitor	.75
15	John Mabry	.05
16	Greg Maddux	1.00
17	Rafael Palmeiro	.65
18	Brian Jordan	.05
19	Ken Griffey Jr.	1.50
20	Brady Anderson	.05
21	Ruben Sierra	.05
22	Travis Fryman	.05
23	Cal Ripken Jr.	2.50
24	Will Clark	.05
25	Todd Hollandsworth	.05
26	Kevin Brown	.05
27	Mike Piazza	1.50
28	Craig Biggio	.05
29	Paul Wilson	.05
30	Andres Galarraga	.05
31	Chipper Jones	1.00

32	Jason Giambi	.65
33	Ernie Young	.05
34	Marty Cordova	.05
35	Albert Belle	.05
36	Roger Clemens	1.25
37	Ryne Sandberg	1.00
38	Henry Rodriguez	.05
39	Jay Buhner	.05
40	Raul Mondesi	.05
41	Jeff Fassero	.05
42	Edgar Martinez	.05
43	Trey Beamon	.05
44	Mo Vaughn	.05
45	Gary Sheffield	.40
46	Ray Durham	.05
47	Brett Butler	.05
48	Ivan Rodriguez	.65
49	Fred McGriff	.05
50	Dean Palmer	.05
51	Rickey Henderson	.75
52	Andy Pettitte	.30
53	Bobby Bonilla	.05
54	Shawn Green	.50
55	Tino Martinez	.05
56	Tony Gwynn	1.00
57	Tom Glavine	.35
58	Eric Young	.05
59	Kevin Appier	.05
60	Barry Bonds	2.50
61	Wade Boggs	1.00
62	Jason Kendall	.05
63	Jeff Bagwell	.75
64	Jeff Conine	.05
65	Greg Vaughn	.05
66	Eric Karros	.05
67	Manny Ramirez	.75
68	John Smoltz	.05
69	Terrell Wade	.05
70	John Wetteland	.05
71	Kenny Lofton	.05
72	Jim Thome	.65
73	Bill Pulsipher	.05
74	Darryl Strawberry	.05
75	Roberto Alomar	.25
76	Bobby Higginson	.05
77	James Baldwin	.05
78	Mark McGwire	2.00
79	Jose Canseco	.40
80	Mark Grudzielanek	.05
81	Ryan Klesko	.05
82	Javier Lopez	.05
83	Ken Caminiti	.05
84	Dave Nilsson	.05
85	Tim Salmon	.05
86	Cecil Fielder	.05
87	Derek Jeter	2.50
88	Garret Anderson	.05
89	Dwight Gooden	.05
90	Carlos Delgado	.50
91	Ugueth Urbina	.05
92	Chan Ho Park	.05
93	Eddie Murray	.75
94	Alex Ochoa	.05
95	Rusty Greer	.05
96	Mark Grace	.05
97	Pat Hentgen	.05
98	John Jaha	.05
99	Charles Johnson	.05
100	Jermaine Dye	.05
101	Quinton McCracken	.05
102	Troy Percival	.05
103	Shane Reynolds	.05
104	Rondell White	.05
105	Charles Nagy	.05
106	Alan Benes	.05
107	Tom Goodwin	.05
108	Ron Gant	.05
109	Dan Wilson	.05
110	Darin Erstad	.10
111	Matt Williams	.05
112	Barry Larkin	.05
113	Mariano Rivera	.15
114	Larry Walker	.05
115	Jim Edmonds	.05
116	Michael Tucker	.05
117	Todd Hundley	.05
118	Alex Fernandez	.05
119	J.T. Snow	.05
120	Ellis Burks	.05
121	Steve Finley	.05
122	Mike Mussina	.40
123	Curtis Pride	.05
124	Derek Bell	.05
125	Dante Bichette	.05
126	Terry Steinbach	.05
127	Randy Johnson	.75
128	Andruw Jones	.75
129	Vladimir Guerrero	.75
130	Ruben Rivera	.05
131	Billy Wagner	.05
132	Scott Rolen	.65
133	Rey Ordonez	.05
134	Karim Garcia	.05
135	George Arias	.05
136	Todd Greene	.05
137	Robin Jennings	.05
138	Raul Casanova	.05
139	Josh Booty	.05
140	Edgar Renteria	.05
141	Chad Mottola	.05
142	Dmitri Young	.05
143	Tony Clark	.05
144	Todd Walker	.05
145	Kevin Brown	.05
146	Nomar Garciaparra	1.00
147	Neifi Perez	.05
148	Derek Jeter, Todd Hollandsworth	.50

149	Pat Hentgen, John Smoltz	.05
150	Juan Gonzalez, Ken Caminiti	.05

Club Edition

A 150-card parallel set featuring a special silver foil design and "CLUB EDITION" notation on back, these cards were inserted 1:7 can of Inside.

	NM/M
Complete Club Edition Set (150):	300.00
Common Club Edition:	.75
Stars:	5X

Diamond Edition

A second parallel set, this time featuring a special die-cut design and gold holographic stamping. Cards were inserted 1:63 packs.

	NM/M
Common Diamond Edition:	5.00
Stars:	25X

Cans

In addition to the cards, collectors had the option of collecting the 24 different player cans which are the "packs" in which the cards were sold. About the size of a can of peas (3" diameter, 4-1/2" tall), the cans feature several color and black-and-white reproductions of the player's Inside card. The package had to be opened with a can opener to access the cards. Values shown are for empty cans which have been opened from the bottom; top-opened cans have little collectible value.

	NM/M
Complete Set (24):	10.00
Common Can:	.25

	Sealed Cans:	2X
1	Ken Griffey Jr.	.75
2	Juan Gonzalez	.30
3	Frank Thomas	.40
4	Cal Ripken Jr.	1.50
5	Derek Jeter	1.50
6	Andruw Jones	.40
7	Alex Rodriguez	1.00
8	Mike Piazza	.75
9	Mo Vaughn	.25
10	Jeff Bagwell	.40
11	Ken Caminiti	.25
12	Andy Pettitte	.30
13	Barry Bonds	1.50
14	Mark McGwire	1.00
15	Ryan Klesko	.25
16	Manny Ramirez	.40
17	Ivan Rodriguez	.35
18	Chipper Jones	.50
19	Albert Belle	.25
20	Tony Gwynn	.50
21	Kenny Lofton	.25
22	Greg Maddux	.50
23	Hideo Nomo	.40
24	John Smoltz	.25

Dueling Dugouts

This 20-card insert set features a veteran player on one side, a rising star on the other, and a spinning wheel that reveals their respective achievements in various statistical categories. Cards were inserted 1:23 packs.

		NM/M
Complete Set (20):		65.00
Common Player:		1.25
1	Alex Rodriguez, Cal Ripken Jr.	10.00
2	Jeff Bagwell, Ken Caminiti	3.00
3	Barry Bonds, Albert Belle	10.00
4	Mike Piazza, Ivan Rodriguez	6.00
5	Chuck Knoblauch, Roberto Alomar	1.25
6	Ken Griffey Jr., Andruw Jones	6.00
7	Chipper Jones, Jim Thome	4.00
8	Frank Thomas, Mo Vaughn	3.00
9	Fred McGriff, Mark McGwire	7.50
10	Brian Jordan, Tony Gwynn	4.00
11	Barry Larkin, Derek Jeter	10.00
12	Kenny Lofton, Bernie Williams	1.25
13	Juan Gonzalez, Manny Ramirez	3.00
14	Will Clark, Rafael Palmeiro	2.50
15	Greg Maddux, Roger Clemens	4.50
16	John Smoltz, Andy Pettitte	1.25
17	Mariano Rivera, John Wetteland	1.25
18	Hideo Nomo, Mike Mussina	2.00
19	Todd Hollandsworth, Darin Erstad	1.25
20	Vladimir Guerrero, Karim Garcia	3.00

Fortysomething

The top home run hitters in the game are pictured in this 16-card set. Cards were inserted 1:47 packs.

		NM/M
Complete Set (16):		50.00
Common Player:		1.00
1	Juan Gonzalez	3.00
2	Barry Bonds	12.00
3	Ken Caminiti	1.00
4	Mark McGwire	10.00
5	Todd Hundley	1.00
6	Albert Belle	1.00
7	Ellis Burks	1.00
8	Jay Buhner	1.00
9	Brady Anderson	1.00

10	Vinny Castilla	1.00
11	Mo Vaughn	1.00
12	Ken Griffey Jr.	7.50
13	Sammy Sosa	6.50
14	Andres Galarraga	1.00
15	Gary Sheffield	2.00
16	Frank Thomas	5.00

Mint Collection

The 30-card Mint Collection set came in three-card packs that also contained two coins. Cards come in two versions: die-cut and foil. Three foil versions appear with Bronze as the "common." Silver (1:15) and Gold (1:48) parallels also appear. The coins that come with each pack arrive in brass, silver and gold and can be matched up with the corresponding player's die-cut card. Fronts feature a player action shot on the left side with a shadowed portrait at right. On the die-cut versions, the coin-size hole is in the lower-right; the foil team stamp for the common cards is in the same location. Backs are numbered as "x of 30" and deliver a short text.

		NM/M
Complete Set (30):		25.00
Common Player:		.25
Silver Cards:		4X
Gold Cards:		6X
Die-Cut: 50%		
Wax Box (24):		25.00
1	Ken Griffey Jr.	2.00
2	Frank Thomas	1.25
3	Alex Rodriguez	2.50
4	Cal Ripken Jr.	3.00
5	Mo Vaughn	.25
6	Juan Gonzalez	.60
7	Mike Piazza	2.00
8	Albert Belle	.25
9	Chipper Jones	1.50
10	Andruw Jones	1.25
11	Greg Maddux	1.50
12	Hideo Nomo	.60
13	Jeff Bagwell	1.25
14	Manny Ramirez	1.25
15	Mark McGwire	2.50
16	Derek Jeter	3.00
17	Sammy Sosa	1.50
18	Barry Bonds	3.00
19	Chuck Knoblauch	.25
20	Dante Bichette	.25
21	Tony Gwynn	1.50
22	Ken Caminiti	.25
23	Gary Sheffield	.60
24	Tim Salmon	.25
25	Ivan Rodriguez	1.00
26	Henry Rodriguez	.25
27	Barry Larkin	.25
28	Ryan Klesko	.25
29	Brian Jordan	.25
30	Jay Buhner	.25

Mint Collection Coins

Two coins from the 30-coin set were included in each

three-card pack of 1997 Pinnacle Mint Collection. Brass coins are common while nickel-silver coins were inserted every 20 packs and gold-plated coins were inserted every 48 packs. Redemption cards for solid silver coins were found every 2,300 packs and a redemption card for a solid gold coin was inserted one per 47,200 packs. Only one of each 24K gold coin was produced. The front of the coins feature the player's portrait while the backs have a baseball diamond and "Limited Edition, Pinnacle Mint Collection 1997" printed.

		NM/M
Complete Set (30):		35.00
Common Brass Coin:		.25
Nickel Coins:		2X
Gold Plated Coins:		6X
Silver Coins:		20X
24K Gold Coins: Value Undetermined		
1	Ken Griffey Jr.	2.50
2	Frank Thomas	1.50
3	Alex Rodriguez	3.00
4	Cal Ripken Jr.	4.00
5	Mo Vaughn	.25
6	Juan Gonzalez	.75
7	Mike Piazza	2.50
8	Albert Belle	.25
9	Chipper Jones	2.00
10	Andruw Jones	1.50
11	Greg Maddux	2.00
12	Hideo Nomo	.75
13	Jeff Bagwell	1.50
14	Manny Ramirez	1.50
15	Mark McGwire	3.00
16	Derek Jeter	4.00
17	Sammy Sosa	2.00
18	Barry Bonds	4.00
19	Chuck Knoblauch	.25
20	Dante Bichette	.25
21	Tony Gwynn	2.00
22	Ken Caminiti	.25
23	Gary Sheffield	.65
24	Tim Salmon	.25
25	Ivan Rodriguez	1.00
26	Henry Rodriguez	.25
27	Barry Larkin	.25
28	Ryan Klesko	.25
29	Brian Jordan	.25
30	Jay Buhner	.25

1997 Pinnacle X-Press

The 150-card set features 115 base cards, a 22-card Rookies subset, 10 Peak Performers and three checklist cards. Each of the regular cards features a horizontal design with two photos of each player on front. Inserts include Swing for the Fences (regular player cards as well as base and booster cards that can be used to accumulate points for a sweepstakes), Men of Summer, Far & Away, Melting Pot, and Metal Works Silver and Gold redemptions. Cards were sold in eight-card packs for $1.99. X-Press Metal Works boxes were also available for $14.99 and contained a regular pack, one metal card and a master deck used to play the Swing for the Fences game.

		NM/M
Complete Set (150):		7.50
Common Player:		.05
Men of Summer:		4X
Pack (8):		.75
Wax Box (24):		10.00
1	Larry Walker	.05
2	Andy Pettitte	.30
3	Matt Williams	.05
4	Juan Gonzalez	.40
5	Frank Thomas	.75
6	Kenny Lofton	.05
7	Ken Griffey Jr.	1.25
8	Andres Galarraga	.05
9	Greg Maddux	1.00
10	Hideo Nomo	.40
11	Cecil Fielder	.05
12	Jose Canseco	.40
13	Tony Gwynn	1.00
14	Eddie Murray	.75
15	Alex Rodriguez	1.50
16	Mike Piazza	1.25
17	Ken Hill	.05
18	Chuck Knoblauch	.05
19	Ellis Burks	.05
20	Rafael Palmeiro	.65
21	Vinny Castilla	.05
22	Rusty Greer	.05
23	Chipper Jones	1.00
24	Rey Ordonez	.05
25	Mariano Rivera	.15
26	Garret Anderson	.05
27	Edgar Martinez	.05
28	Dante Bichette	.05
29	Todd Hundley	.05
30	Barry Bonds	2.00
31	Barry Larkin	.05
32	Derek Jeter	2.00
33	Marquis Grissom	.05
34	David Justice	.05
35	Ivan Rodriguez	.65
36	Jay Buhner	.05
37	Fred McGriff	.05
38	Brady Anderson	.05
39	Tony Clark	.05
40	Eric Young	.05
41	Charles Nagy	.05
42	Mark McGwire	1.50
43	Paul O'Neill	.05
44	Tino Martinez	.05
45	Ryne Sandberg	1.00
46	Bernie Williams	.05
47	Albert Belle	.05
48	Jeff Cirillo	.05
49	Tim Salmon	.05
50	Steve Finley	.05
51	Lance Johnson	.05
52	John Smoltz	.05
53	Javier Lopez	.05
54	Roger Clemens	1.00
55	Kevin Appier	.05
56	Ken Caminiti	.05
57	Cal Ripken Jr.	2.00
58	Moises Alou	.05
59	Marty Cordova	.05
60	David Cone	.05
61	Manny Ramirez	.75
62	Ray Durham	.05
63	Jermaine Dye	.05
64	Craig Biggio	.05
65	Will Clark	.05
66	Omar Vizquel	.05
67	Bernard Gilkey	.05
68	Greg Vaughn	.05
69	Wade Boggs	1.00
70	Dave Nilsson	.05
71	Mark Grace	.05
72	Dean Palmer	.05
73	Sammy Sosa	1.00
74	Mike Mussina	.30
75	Alex Fernandez	.05
76	Henry Rodriguez	.05
77	Travis Fryman	.05
78	Jeff Bagwell	.75
79	Pat Hentgen	.05
80	Gary Sheffield	.40
81	Jim Edmonds	.10
82	Darin Erstad	.05
83	Mark Grudzielanek	.05
84	Jim Thome	.65
85	Bobby Higginson	.05
86	Al Martin	.05
87	Jason Giambi	.50
88	Mo Vaughn	.05
89	Jeff Conine	.05
90	Edgar Renteria	.05
91	Andy Ashby	.05
92	Ryan Klesko	.05
93	John Jaha	.05
94	Paul Molitor	.75
95	Brian Hunter	.05
96	Randy Johnson	.75
97	Joey Hamilton	.05
98	Billy Wagner	.05
99	John Wetteland	.05
100	Jeff Fassero	.05
101	Rondell White	.05
102	Kevin Brown	.05
103	Andy Benes	.05
104	Raul Mondesi	.05
105	Todd Hollandsworth	.05
106	Alex Ochoa	.05
107	Bobby Bonilla	.05
108	Brian Jordan	.05
109	Tom Glavine	.35
110	Ron Gant	.05
111	Jason Kendall	.05
112	Roberto Alomar	.30
113	Troy Percival	.05
114	Michael Tucker	.05
115	Joe Carter	.05
116	Andruw Jones	.05
117	Nomar Garciaparra	1.00
118	Todd Walker	.05
119	Jose Guillen	.05
120	Bubba Trammell RC	.20
121	Wilton Guerrero	.05
122	Bob Abreu	.15
123	Vladimir Guerrero	.75
124	Dmitri Young	.05
125	Kevin Orie	.05
126	Glendon Rusch	.05
127	Brooks Kieschnick	.05
128	Scott Spiezio	.05
129	Brian Giles RC	.75
130	Jason Dickson	.05
131	Damon Mashore	.05
132	Wendell Magee	.05
133	Matt Morris	.05
134	Scott Rolen	.65
135	Shannon Stewart	.05
136	Deivi Cruz RC	.15
137	Hideki Irabu RC	.15
138	Larry Walker (Peak Performers)	.05
139	Ken Griffey Jr. (Peak Performers)	.65
140	Frank Thomas (Peak Performers)	.40
141	Ivan Rodriguez (Peak Performers)	.30
142	Randy Johnson (Peak Performers)	.40
143	Mark McGwire (Peak Performers)	.75
144	Tino Martinez (Peak Performers)	.05
145	Tony Clark (Peak Performers)	.05
146	Mike Piazza (Peak Performers)	.50
147	Alex Rodriguez (Peak Performers)	.75
148	Checklist (Roger Clemens)	.50
149	Checklist (Greg Maddux)	.45
150	Checklist (Hideo Nomo)	.20

Men of Summer

This parallel set of the 150 cards in the base X-Press issue differs in that the fronts are printed on foil backgrounds and the backs have a notation "MEN OF SUMMER" printed in gold vertically at top.

	NM/M
Complete Set (150):	50.00
Common Player:	.25
Stars:	3X

Far & Away

This 18-card insert highlights the top home run hitters in baseball and is printed with Dufex technology. Cards were inserted 1:19 packs.

		NM/M
Complete Set (18):		25.00
Common Player:		.50
1	Albert Belle	.50
2	Mark McGwire	4.50
3	Frank Thomas	1.75
4	Mo Vaughn	.50
5	Jeff Bagwell	1.75
6	Juan Gonzalez	1.00
7	Mike Piazza	3.50
8	Andruw Jones	1.75
9	Chipper Jones	2.50

10	Gary Sheffield	1.00
11	Sammy Sosa	2.50
12	Darin Erstad	.75
13	Jay Buhner	.50
14	Ken Griffey Jr.	3.50
15	Ken Caminiti	.50
16	Brady Anderson	.50
17	Manny Ramirez	1.75
18	Alex Rodriguez	4.50

Melting Pot

This insert showcases the talents of major leaguers from various countries. Fronts have color player photos on a background which combines shiny silver foil and textured foil in the design of the player's native flag. Backs have another photo and are ink-jet numbered in a white stripe at bottom in an edition of 500 each. Stated insertion rate was one per 288 packs. Each card can also be found in a promo card version overprinted "SAMPLE."

		NM/M
Complete Set (20):		110.00
Common Player:		1.50
Samples:		1X
1	Jose Guillen	1.50
2	Vladimir Guerrero	8.00
3	Andruw Jones	8.00
4	Larry Walker	1.50
5	Manny Ramirez	8.00
6	Ken Griffey Jr.	10.00
7	Alex Rodriguez	12.00
8	Frank Thomas	8.00
9	Juan Gonzalez	4.00
10	Ivan Rodriguez	6.00
11	Hideo Nomo	4.00
12	Rafael Palmeiro	6.00
13	Dave Nilsson	1.50
14	Nomar Garciaparra	9.00
15	Wilton Guerrero	1.50
16	Sammy Sosa	9.00
17	Edgar Renteria	1.50
18	Cal Ripken Jr.	16.00
19	Derek Jeter	16.00
20	Rey Ordonez	1.50

Metal Works

Each Home Plate Box of X-Press contains one heavy bronze Metal Works "card." The 2-3/8" x 3-1/2" slabs have a player portrait on front. Backs have a few words about the player. Redemption cards for silver-plated parallels were inserted 1:470 packs, while a silver slab was found 1:54 Home Plate Boxes. Silver Metal Works are serially numbered to 400 each. Gold-plated Metal Works were produced in an edition of 200 each, with redemption cards inserted 1:950 packs or one per 108 Home Plate Boxes.

	NM/M
Complete Set (20):	25.00

Common Player:		.50
Silver:		3X
Gold:		6X
1	Ken Griffey Jr.	2.00
2	Frank Thomas	1.00
3	Andruw Jones	1.00
4	Alex Rodriguez	2.50
5	Derek Jeter	3.00
6	Cal Ripken Jr.	3.00
7	Mike Piazza	2.00
8	Chipper Jones	1.50
9	Juan Gonzalez	.65
10	Greg Maddux	1.50
11	Tony Gwynn	1.50
12	Jeff Bagwell	1.00
13	Albert Belle	.50
14	Mark McGwire	2.50
15	Nomar Garciaparra	1.50
16	Mo Vaughn	.50
17	Andy Pettitte	.65
18	Manny Ramirez	1.00
19	Kenny Lofton	.50
20	Roger Clemens	1.75

Swing for the Fences

These inserts allowed collectors to play an interactive game based on the number of home runs hit by the home run champion of each league. Cards feature 60 different players and were inserted 1:2 packs. Base cards feature a number between 20-42 printed on them and are found one in every master deck. Booster cards feature a plus-or-minus point total (i.e. +7, -2) that can be used to add or subtract points to get to the winning home run total. Booster cards are found 1:2 packs. Collectors who accumulated the winning home run totals were eligible to win prizes ranging from autographs to a trip to the 1998 All-Star Game. The unnumbered cards are checklisted here in alphabetical order.

		NM/M
Complete Set (60):		20.00
Common Player:		.15
(1)	Sandy Alomar Jr.	.15
(2)	Moises Alou	.15
(3)	Brady Anderson	.15
(4)	Jeff Bagwell	1.00
(5)	Derek Bell	.15
(6)	Jay Bell	.15
(7)	Albert Belle	.15
(8)	Geronimo Berroa	.15
(9)	Dante Bichette	.15
(10)	Barry Bonds	2.50
(11)	Bobby Bonilla	.15
(12)	Jay Buhner	.15
(13)	Ellis Burks	.15
(14)	Ken Caminiti	.15
(15)	Jose Canseco	.40
(16)	Joe Carter	.15
(17)	Vinny Castilla	.15
(18)	Tony Clark	.15
(19)	Carlos Delgado	.50
(20)	Jim Edmonds	.15
(21)	Cecil Fielder	.15
(22)	Andres Galarraga	.15
(23)	Ron Gant	.15
(24)	Bernard Gilkey	.15
(25)	Juan Gonzalez	.50
(26)	Ken Griffey Jr. (AL WINNER)	4.00
(27)	Vladimir Guerrero	1.00
(28)	Todd Hundley	.15
(29)	John Jaha	.15
(30)	Andruw Jones	1.00
(31)	Chipper Jones	1.25
(32)	David Justice	.15
(33)	Jeff Kent	.15
(34)	Ryan Klesko	.15
(35)	Barry Larkin	.15
(36)	Mike Lieberthal	.15
(37)	Javy Lopez	.15
(38)	Edgar Martinez	.15
(39)	Tino Martinez	.15
(40)	Fred McGriff	.15
(41)	Mark McGwire (AL/NL WINNER)	4.00
(42)	Raul Mondesi	.15
(43)	Tim Naehring	.15
(44)	Dave Nillson	.15
(45)	Rafael Palmeiro	.75
(46)	Dean Palmer	.15
(47)	Mike Piazza	1.50
(48)	Cal Ripken Jr.	2.50
(49)	Henry Rodriguez	.15
(50)	Tim Salmon	.15
(51)	Gary Sheffield	.40
(52)	Sammy Sosa	1.25
(53)	Terry Steinbach	.15
(54)	Frank Thomas	1.00
(55)	Jim Thome	.75
(56)	Mo Vaughn	.15
(57)	Larry Walker (NL Winner)	1.25
(58)	Rondell White	.15
(59)	Matt Williams	.15
(60)	Todd Zeile	.15

Swing/Fences Gold

Collectors who correctly matched Swing for the Fences insert game cards of the final 1997 season American and National home run champions with proper point cards equal to the number of home runs each hit could exchange them for a random assortment of 10 upgraded cards featuring gold-foil highlights and a premium card stock. The first 1,000 redemptions received an autographed Andruw Jones gold card. The redemption period ended March 1, 1998.

	NM/M
Complete Set (60):	125.00
Common Player:	1.00
Stars:	4X
Andruw Jones Autograph:	25.00

1998 Pinnacle Samples

Six stars from its 1998 issue were issued in a promo card version with "SAMPLE" printed in large black letters diagonally on back. They were distributed in two-card cello packs.

		NM/M
Complete Set (6):		6.00
Common Player:		1.00
8	Nomar Garciaparra	2.00
9	Ken Griffey Jr.	2.00
24	Frank Thomas	1.25
33	Mike Piazza	2.00
56	Chipper Jones	1.00
72	Larry Walker	1.00

1998 Pinnacle

Pinnacle's 200-card base set features full-bleed photos on front. Three different backs were produced for each card #1-157: home stats, away stats and seasonal stats. The set also includes cards, 24 Rookies, six Field of Vision, 10 Goin' Jake cards and three checklists. Parallel sets include Artist's Proofs, Press Plates and Museum Collection. Inserts include Epix, Hit it Here, Spellbound and Uncut.

		NM/M
Complete Set (200):		12.50
Common Player:		.05
Pack (10):		1.00
Wax Box (18):		12.00
1	Tony Gwynn/AS	1.00
2	Pedro Martinez/AS	.75
3	Kenny Lofton/AS	.05
4	Curt Schilling/AS	.35
5	Shawn Estes/AS	.05
6	Tom Glavine/AS	.35
7	Mike Piazza/AS	1.50
8	Ray Lankford/AS	.05
9	Barry Larkin/AS	.05
10	Tony Womack/AS	.05
11	Jeff Blauser/AS	.05
12	Rod Beck/AS	.05
13	Larry Walker/AS	.05
14	Greg Maddux/AS	1.00
15	Mark Grace/AS	.05
16	Ken Caminiti/AS	.05
17	Bobby Jones/AS	.05
18	Chipper Jones/AS	1.00
19	Javier Lopez/AS	.05
20	Moises Alou/AS	.05
21	Royce Clayton/AS	.05
22	Darryl Kile/AS	.05
23	Barry Bonds/AS	2.50
24	Steve Finley/AS	.05
25	Andres Galarraga/AS	.05
26	Denny Neagle/AS	.05
27	Todd Hundley/AS	.05
28	Jeff Bagwell	.75
29	Andy Pettitte	.25
30	Darin Erstad	.15
31	Carlos Delgado	.50
32	Matt Williams	.05
33	Will Clark	.05
34	Vinny Castilla	.05
35	Brad Radke	.05
36	John Olerud	.05
37	Andruw Jones	.75
38	Jason Giambi	.50
39	Scott Rolen	.65
40	Gary Sheffield	.40
41	Jimmy Key	.05
42	Kevin Appier	.05
43	Wade Boggs	1.00
44	Hideo Nomo	.40
45	Manny Ramirez	.75
46	Wilton Guerrero	.05
47	Travis Fryman	.05
48	Chili Davis	.05
49	Jeromy Burnitz	.05
50	Craig Biggio	.25
51	Tim Salmon	.25
52	Jose Cruz Jr.	.65
53	Sammy Sosa	1.00
54	Hideki Irabu	.05
55	Chan Ho Park	.05
56	Robin Ventura	.05
57	Jose Guillen	.05
58	Deion Sanders	.15
59	Jose Canseco	.40
60	Jay Buhner	.05
61	Rafael Palmeiro	.65
62	Vladimir Guerrero	.75
63	Mark McGwire	2.00
64	Derek Jeter	2.50
65	Bobby Bonilla	.05
66	Raul Mondesi	.05
67	Paul Molitor	.75
68	Joe Carter	.05
69	Marquis Grissom	.05
70	Juan Gonzalez	.40
71	Kevin Orie	.05
72	Rusty Greer	.05
73	Henry Rodriguez	.05
74	Fernando Tatis	.05
75	John Valentin	.05
76	Matt Morris	.05
77	Ray Durham	.05
78	Geronimo Berroa	.05
79	Scott Brosius	.05
80	Willie Greene	.05
81	Rondell White	.05
82	Doug Drabek	.05
83	Derek Bell	.05
84	Butch Huskey	.05
85	Doug Jones	.05
86	Jeff Kent	.05
87	Jim Edmonds	.05
88	Mark McLemore	.05
89	Todd Zeile	.05
90	Edgardo Alfonzo	.05
91	Carlos Baerga	.05
92	Jorge Fabregas	.05
93	Alan Benes	.05
94	Troy Percival	.05
95	Edgar Renteria	.05
96	Jeff Fassero	.05
97	Reggie Sanders	.05
98	Dean Palmer	.05
99	J.T. Snow	.05
100	Dave Nilsson	.05
101	Dan Wilson	.05
102	Robb Nen	.05
103	Damion Easley	.05
104	Kevin Foster	.05
105	Jose Offerman	.05
106	Steve Cooke	.05
107	Matt Stairs	.05
108	Darryl Hamilton	.05
109	Steve Karsay	.05
110	Gary DiSarcina	.05
111	Dante Bichette	.05
112	Billy Wagner	.05
113	David Segui	.05
114	Bobby Higginson	.05
115	Jeffrey Hammonds	.05
116	Kevin Brown	.05
117	Paul Sorrento	.05
118	Mark Leiter	.05
119	Charles Nagy	.05
120	Danny Patterson	.05
121	Brian McRae	.05
122	Jay Bell	.05
123	Jamie Moyer	.05
124	Carl Everett	.05
125	Greg Colbrunn	.05
126	Jason Kendall	.05
127	Luis Sojo	.05
128	Mike Lieberthal	.05
129	Reggie Jefferson	.05
130	Cal Eldred	.05
131	Orel Hershiser	.05
132	Doug Glanville	.05
133	Willie Blair	.05
134	Neifi Perez	.05
135	Sean Berry	.05
136	Chuck Finley	.05
137	Alex Gonzalez	.05
138	Dennis Eckersley	.65
139	Kenny Rogers	.05
140	Troy O'Leary	.05
141	Roger Bailey	.05
142	Yamil Benitez	.05
143	Wally Joyner	.05
144	Bobby Witt	.05
145	Pete Schourek	.05
146	Terry Steinbach	.05
147	B.J. Surhoff	.05
148	Esteban Loaiza	.05
149	Heathcliff Slocumb	.05
150	Ed Sprague	.05
151	Gregg Jefferies	.05
152	Scott Erickson	.05
153	Jaime Navarro	.05
154	David Wells	.05
155	Alex Fernandez	.05
156	Tim Belcher	.05
157	Mark Grudzielanek	.05
158	Scott Hatteberg	.05
159	Paul Konerko	.15
160	Ben Grieve	.05
161	Abraham Nunez	.05
162	Shannon Stewart	.05
163	Jaret Wright	.05
164	Derrek Lee	.50
165	Todd Dunwoody	.05
166	Steve Woodard RC	.10
167	Ryan McGuire	.05
168	Jeremi Gonzalez	.05
169	Mark Kotsay	.05
170	Brett Tomko	.05
171	Bobby Estalella	.05
172	Livan Hernandez	.05
173	Todd Helton	.75
174	Garrett Stephenson	.05
175	Pokey Reese	.05
176	Tony Saunders	.05
177	Antone Williamson	.05
178	Bartolo Colon	.05
179	Karim Garcia	.05
180	Juan Encarnacion	.05
181	Jacob Cruz	.05
182	Alex Rodriguez (Field of Vision)	2.00
183	Cal Ripken Jr., Roberto Alomar (Field of Vision)	1.00
184	Roger Clemens (Field of Vision)	1.25
185	Derek Jeter (Field of Vision)	2.00
186	Frank Thomas (Field of Vision)	.75
187	Ken Griffey Jr. (Field of Vision)	1.50
188	Mark McGwire (Goin' Jake)	1.00
189	Tino Martinez (Goin' Jake)	.05
190	Larry Walker (Goin' Jake)	.05
191	Brady Anderson (Goin' Jake)	.05
192	Jeff Bagwell (Goin' Jake)	.75
193	Ken Griffey Jr. (Goin' Jake)	1.50
194	Chipper Jones (Goin' Jake)	1.00
195	Ray Lankford (Goin' Jake)	.05
196	Jim Thome (Goin' Jake)	.65
197	Nomar Garciaparra (Goin' Jake)	1.00
198	Checklist (1997 HR Contest)	.05
199	Checklist (1997 HR Contest Winner)	.05
200	Checklist (Overall View of the Park)	.05
9	Ken Griffey Jr./AS (Overprinted "SAMPLE" on back.)	2.00
24	Frank Thomas/AS (Overprinted "SAMPLE" on back.)	1.50

Artist's Proofs

Artist's Proofs is a 100-card partial parallel of the Pinnacle base set. The gold-foil Dufex cards were renumbered with a "PP" prefix and inserted one per 39 packs. A red AP seal appears on front.

		NM/M
Complete Set (100):		375.00
Common Artist's Proof:		1.50
1	Tony Gwynn/AS	12.50
2	Pedro Martinez/AS	10.00
3	Kenny Lofton/AS	1.50
4	Curt Schilling/AS	3.00
5	Shawn Estes/AS	1.50
6	Tom Glavine/AS	3.00
7	Mike Piazza/AS	16.00
8	Ray Lankford/AS	1.50
9	Barry Larkin/AS	1.50
10	Tony Womack/AS	1.50
11	Jeff Blauser/AS	1.50
12	Rod Beck/AS	1.50
13	Larry Walker/AS	1.50
14	Greg Maddux/AS	12.50
15	Mark Grace/AS	1.50
16	Ken Caminiti/AS	1.50
17	Bobby Jones/AS	1.50
18	Chipper Jones/AS	12.50
19	Javier Lopez/AS	1.50
20	Moises Alou/AS	1.50
21	Royce Clayton/AS	1.50
22	Darryl Kile/AS	1.50
23	Barry Bonds/AS	25.00
24	Steve Finley/AS	1.50
25	Andres Galarraga/AS	1.50
26	Denny Neagle/AS	1.50
27	Todd Hundley/AS	1.50
28	Jeff Bagwell	10.00
29	Andy Pettitte	2.50
30	Darin Erstad	2.00
31	Carlos Delgado	4.00
32	Matt Williams	1.50
33	Will Clark	1.50
34	Brad Radke	1.50
35	John Olerud	1.50
36	Andruw Jones	10.00
37	Scott Rolen	7.50
38	Gary Sheffield	3.00
39	Jimmy Key	1.50
40	Wade Boggs	12.50
41	Hideo Nomo	5.00
42	Manny Ramirez	10.00
43	Wilton Guerrero	1.50
44	Travis Fryman	1.50

ABBREVIATIONS

AS - All-Star

45	Craig Biggio	1.50
46	Tim Salmon	1.50
47	Jose Cruz Jr.	1.50
48	Sammy Sosa	12.50
49	Hideki Irabu	1.50
50	Jose Guillen	1.50
51	Deion Sanders	1.50
52	Jose Canseco	4.00
53	Jay Buhner	1.50
54	Rafael Palmeiro	7.50
55	Vladimir Guerrero	10.00
56	Mark McGwire	20.00
57	Derek Jeter	25.00
58	Bobby Bonilla	1.50
59	Raul Mondesi	1.50
60	Paul Molitor	10.00
61	Joe Carter	1.50
62	Marquis Grissom	1.50
63	Juan Gonzalez	5.00
64	Dante Bichette	1.50
65	Shannon Stewart (Rookie)	1.50
66	Jaret Wright (Rookie)	1.50
67	Derrek Lee (Rookie)	6.00
68	Todd Dunwoody (Rookie)	1.50
69	Steve Woodard (Rookie)	1.50
70	Ryan McGuire (Rookie)	1.50
71	Jeremi Gonzalez (Rookie)	1.50
72	Mark Kotsay (Rookie)	1.50
73	Brett Tomko (Rookie)	1.50
74	Bobby Estalella (Rookie)	1.50
75	Livan Hernandez (Rookie)	1.50
76	Todd Helton (Rookie)	10.00
77	Garrett Stephenson (Rookie)	1.50
78	Pokey Reese (Rookie)	1.50
79	Tony Saunders (Rookie)	1.50
80	Antone Williamson (Rookie)	1.50
81	Bartolo Colon (Rookie)	1.50
82	Karim Garcia (Rookie)	1.50
83	Juan Encarnacion (Rookie)	1.50
84	Jacob Cruz (Rookie)	1.50
85	Alex Rodriguez (Field of Vision)	20.00
86	Cal Ripken Jr., Roberto Alomar (Field of Vision)	15.00
87	Roger Clemens (Field of Vision)	13.50
88	Derek Jeter (Field of Vision)	25.00
89	Frank Thomas (Field of Vision)	10.00
90	Ken Griffey Jr. (Field of Vision)	16.00
91	Mark McGwire (Goin' Jake)	20.00
92	Tino Martinez (Goin' Jake)	1.50
93	Larry Walker (Goin' Jake)	1.50
94	Brady Anderson (Goin' Jake)	1.50
95	Jeff Bagwell (Goin' Jake)	10.00
96	Ken Griffey Jr. (Goin' Jake)	16.00
97	Chipper Jones (Goin' Jake)	12.50
98	Ray Lankford (Goin' Jake)	1.50
99	Jim Thome (Goin' Jake)	7.50
100	Nomar Garciaparra (Goin' Jake)	12.50

Museum Collection

Museum Collection is a 100-card partial parallel of the Pinnacle base set. The silver-foil Dufex cards were renumbered with a "PP" prefix. Backs have a small "Museum Collection" logo at bottom-center. The cards were inserted one per nine packs.

Complete Museum Set (100):		110.00
Common Museum:		.50
1	Tony Gwynn/AS	3.00
2	Pedro Martinez/AS	2.50
3	Kenny Lofton/AS	.50
4	Curt Schilling/AS	1.50
5	Shawn Estes/AS	.50
6	Tom Glavine/AS	1.50
7	Mike Piazza/AS	4.00
8	Ray Lankford/AS	.50
9	Barry Larkin/AS	.50
10	Tony Womack/AS	.50
11	Jeff Blauser/AS	.50
12	Rod Beck/AS	.50
13	Larry Walker/AS	.50
14	Greg Maddux/AS	3.00
15	Mark Grace/AS	.50
16	Ken Caminiti/AS	.50
17	Bobby Jones/AS	.50
18	Chipper Jones/AS	3.00
19	Javier Lopez/AS	.50
20	Moises Alou/AS	.50
21	Royce Clayton/AS	.50
22	Darryl Kile/AS	.50
23	Barry Bonds/AS	6.00
24	Steve Finley/AS	.50
25	Andres Galarraga/AS	.50
26	Denny Neagle/AS	.50
27	Todd Hundley/AS	.50
28	Jeff Bagwell	2.50
29	Andy Pettitte	1.00
30	Darin Erstad	1.00
31	Carlos Delgado	1.50
32	Matt Williams	.50
33	Will Clark	.50
34	Brad Radke	.50
35	John Olerud	.50
36	Andruw Jones	2.50
37	Scott Rolen	2.00
38	Gary Sheffield	1.50
39	Jimmy Key	.50
40	Wade Boggs	3.00
41	Hideo Nomo	1.25
42	Manny Ramirez	2.50
43	Wilton Guerrero	.50
44	Travis Fryman	.50
45	Craig Biggio	.50
46	Tim Salmon	.50
47	Jose Cruz Jr.	.50
48	Sammy Sosa	3.00
49	Hideki Irabu	.50
50	Jose Guillen	.50
51	Deion Sanders	.50
52	Jose Canseco	1.50
53	Jay Buhner	.50
54	Rafael Palmeiro	2.00
55	Vladimir Guerrero	2.50
56	Mark McGwire	6.00
57	Derek Jeter	6.00
58	Bobby Bonilla	.50
59	Raul Mondesi	.50
60	Paul Molitor	2.50
61	Joe Carter	.50
62	Marquis Grissom	.50
63	Juan Gonzalez	1.25
64	Dante Bichette	.50
65	Shannon Stewart (Rookie)	.50
66	Jaret Wright (Rookie)	.50
67	Derrek Lee (Rookie)	2.00
68	Todd Dunwoody (Rookie)	.50
69	Steve Woodard (Rookie)	.50
70	Ryan McGuire (Rookie)	.50
71	Jeremi Gonzalez (Rookie)	.50
72	Mark Kotsay (Rookie)	.50
73	Brett Tomko (Rookie)	.50
74	Bobby Estalella (Rookie)	.50
75	Livan Hernandez (Rookie)	.50
76	Todd Helton (Rookie)	2.50
77	Garrett Stephenson (Rookie)	.50
78	Pokey Reese (Rookie)	.50
79	Tony Saunders (Rookie)	.50
80	Antone Williamson (Rookie)	.50
81	Bartolo Colon (Rookie)	.50
82	Karim Garcia (Rookie)	.50
83	Juan Encarnacion (Rookie)	.50
84	Jacob Cruz (Rookie)	.50
85	Alex Rodriguez (Field of Vision)	5.00
86	Cal Ripken Jr., Roberto Alomar (Field of Vision)	3.50
87	Roger Clemens (Field of Vision)	2.50
88	Derek Jeter (Field of Vision)	6.00
89	Frank Thomas (Field of Vision)	2.50
90	Ken Griffey Jr. (Field of Vision)	4.00
91	Mark McGwire (Goin' Jake)	5.00
92	Tino Martinez (Goin' Jake)	.50
93	Larry Walker (Goin' Jake)	.50
94	Brady Anderson (Goin' Jake)	.50
95	Jeff Bagwell (Goin' Jake)	2.50
96	Ken Griffey Jr. (Goin' Jake)	4.00
97	Chipper Jones (Goin' Jake)	3.00
98	Ray Lankford (Goin' Jake)	.50
99	Jim Thome (Goin' Jake)	2.00
100	Nomar Garciaparra (Goin' Jake)	3.00

Power Packs Supers

FRANK THOMAS

Two dozen regular and subset (Goin' Jake, Field of Vision) cards from Pinnacle are paralleled in this super-size (3-1/2" x 5") version which was included along with 21 regular cards in a $5.99 "Power Pack." Other than being four times the size of the regular card, these supers differ only in their numbering which specifies "x of 24" on back. Each card can also be found in a promo version with a large black "SAMPLE" overprinted on back.

		NM/M
Complete Set (24):		30.00
Common Player:		.50
Samples:		1.5X
1	Alex Rodriguez (Field of Vision)	3.00
2	Cal Ripken Jr., Roberto Alomar (Field of Vision)	2.00
3	Roger Clemens (Field of Vision)	2.25
4	Derek Jeter (Field of Vision)	3.50
5	Frank Thomas (Field of Vision)	1.50
6	Ken Griffey Jr. (Field of Vision)	2.50
7	Mark McGwire (Goin' Jake)	3.00
8	Tino Martinez (Goin' Jake)	.50
9	Larry Walker (Goin' Jake)	.50
10	Brady Anderson (Goin' Jake)	.50
11	Jeff Bagwell (Goin' Jake)	1.50
12	Ken Griffey Jr. (Goin' Jake)	2.50
13	Chipper Jones (Goin' Jake)	2.00
14	Ray Lankford (Goin' Jake)	.50
15	Jim Thome (Goin' Jake)	1.00
16	Nomar Garciaparra (Goin' Jake)	2.00
17	Mike Piazza	2.50
18	Andruw Jones	1.50
19	Greg Maddux	2.00
20	Tony Gwynn	2.00
21	Larry Walker	.50
22	Jeff Bagwell	1.50
23	Chipper Jones	2.00
24	Scott Rolen	1.50

Epix

This cross-brand insert was included in Pinnacle, Score, Pinnacle Certified and Zenith. Twenty-four cards were seeded in Pinnacle packs (1:21). The four-tiered set high-lights a memorable Game, Season, Moment and Play in a player's career. The holographic foil cards came in three colors: orange, purple and emerald.

		NM/M
Complete Set (24):		45.00
Common Player:		1.00
Purples:		2X
Emeralds:		4X
1	Ken Griffey Jr./G	3.00
2	Juan Gonzalez/G	1.25
3	Jeff Bagwell/G	2.00
4	Ivan Rodriguez/G	1.50
5	Nomar Garciaparra/G	2.50
6	Ryne Sandberg/G	2.50
7	Frank Thomas/S	2.00
8	Derek Jeter/S	5.00
9	Tony Gwynn/S	2.50
10	Albert Belle/S	1.00
11	Scott Rolen/S	1.50
12	Barry Larkin/S	1.00
13	Alex Rodriguez/M	4.00
14	Cal Ripken Jr./M	5.00
15	Chipper Jones/M	2.50
16	Roger Clemens/M	2.75
17	Mo Vaughn/M	1.00
18	Mark McGwire/M	4.00
19	Mike Piazza/P	3.00
20	Andruw Jones/P	2.00
21	Greg Maddux/P	2.50
22	Barry Bonds/P	5.00
23	Paul Molitor/P	2.00
24	Eddie Murray/P	2.00

Hit It Here

Hit it Here is seeded one per 17 packs. The micro-etched silver foil cards feature a color player photo with a red "Hit it Here" target at left. Each card has a serial number. If the pictured player hit for the cycle on Opening Day 1998, the collector with the correct serially numbered card would have won $1 million. Each card was also produced in a promo version without serial number and with a large black "SAMPLE" overprint on back.

		NM/M
Complete Set (10):		12.00
Common Player:		.50
Inserted 1:17		
Samples:		1X
1	Larry Walker	.50
2	Ken Griffey Jr.	2.00
3	Mike Piazza	2.00
4	Frank Thomas	1.50
5	Barry Bonds	3.00
6	Albert Belle	.50
7	Tino Martinez	.50
8	Mark McGwire	2.50
9	Juan Gonzalez	.75
10	Jeff Bagwell	1.00

Press Plates

Pinnacle cut up and inserted into packs (about one per 1,250) the metal plates used to print the regular and insert cards in the set. There are black, blue, magenta and yellow plates for the front and back of each card. Because of their unique nature, establishment of catalog values isn't feasible.

	NM/M
Common Player:	50.00

Spellbound

Spellbound is a 50-card insert seeded one per 17 packs. Nine players are featured in the set. The cards feature a photo of the player with a letter from his first or last name in the background. Each player has enough cards to spell his first or last name or a nickname. Values shown are per card and should be multiplied by the number of cards in a player name to arrive at a value for a complete-player set.

		NM/M
Complete Set (50):		90.00
Common Card:		.75
Inserted 1:17		
1	Mark McGwire/M	3.50
2	Mark McGwire/C	3.50
3	Mark McGwire/W	3.50
4	Mark McGwire/I	3.50
5	Mark McGwire/R	3.50
6	Mark McGwire/E	3.50
7	Roger Clemens/R	2.50
8	Roger Clemens/O	2.50
9	Roger Clemens/C	2.50
10	Roger Clemens/K	2.50
11	Roger Clemens/E	2.50
12	Roger Clemens/E	2.50
13	Roger Clemens/T	2.50
14	Frank Thomas/B	1.50
15	Frank Thomas/I	1.50
16	Frank Thomas/H	1.50
17	Frank Thomas/U	1.50
18	Frank Thomas/R	1.50
19	Frank Thomas/T	1.50
20	Frank Thomas/T	1.50
21	Scott Rolen/R	1.25
22	Scott Rolen/O	1.25
23	Scott Rolen/L	1.25
24	Scott Rolen/E	1.25
25	Scott Rolen/N	1.25
26	Ken Griffey Jr./G	3.00
27	Ken Griffey Jr./R	3.00
28	Ken Griffey Jr./I	3.00
29	Ken Griffey Jr./F	3.00
30	Ken Griffey Jr./F	3.00
31	Ken Griffey Jr./E	3.00
32	Ken Griffey Jr./Y	3.00
33	Larry Walker/W	.75
34	Larry Walker/A	.75
35	Larry Walker/L	.75
36	Larry Walker/K	.75
37	Larry Walker/E	.75
38	Larry Walker/R	.75
39	Nomar Garciaparra/N	2.25
40	Nomar Garciaparra/O	2.25
41	Nomar Garciaparra/M	2.25
42	Nomar Garciaparra/A	2.25
43	Nomar Garciaparra/R	2.25
44	Cal Ripken Jr./C	4.50
45	Cal Ripken Jr./A	4.50
46	Cal Ripken Jr./L	4.50
47	Tony Gwynn/T	2.25
48	Tony Gwynn/O	2.25
49	Tony Gwynn/N	2.25
50	Tony Gwynn/Y	2.25

All-Star FanFest John Elway

The quarterback of the World's Champion Denver Broncos was featured on a card harkening back to his minor league baseball playing days. During the July 1998 All-Star FanFest in Denver, Pinnacle sold a special card of Elway, with proceeds benefiting the city's schools. Initial cost was $2 per card. Front has a black-and-white posed action photo with blue and white pinstriped backgrounds. Back has a ghosted photo of Elway in his Broncos uniform and provides details of his baseball career.

	NM/M
John Elway	3.00

Certified Mirrors

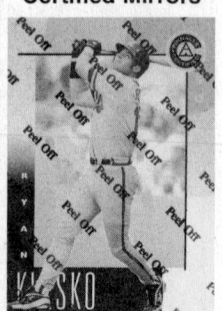

Among several card issues that were aborted by Pinnacle's bankruptcy in mid-1998, but that have leaked into the hobby market in dribs and drabs, are specimens of some of the intended mirror parallels for a Pinnacle Certified set. The majority of cards seen have been Mirror Reds, with a few Mirror Gold issues and even fewer Mirror Blues. Many cards are known in only a single example, and some commons have not yet been verified, though it is presumed that all cards among the first 99 numbers on the unissued Certified base set checklist will be found eventually.

		NM/M
Common Player:		15.00
1	Vladimir Guerrero	25.00
2	Andruw Jones	25.00
3	Paul Molitor	25.00
4	Jose Cruz Jr.	15.00
5	Edgar Martinez	15.00
6	Andy Pettitte	15.00
7	Darin Erstad	15.00
8	Barry Larkin	15.00
9	Derek Jeter	60.00
10	Rusty Greer	15.00
11	Brady Anderson	15.00
12	Tony Clark	15.00
13	Manny Ramirez	25.00
14	Jim Thome	20.00
15	Matt Williams	15.00
16	Ivan Rodriguez	20.00
17	Scott Rolen	20.00
18	Gary Sheffield	15.00

ABBREVIATIONS

AS - All-Star

19	David Justice	15.00
20	Roberto Alomar	15.00
21	Ken Caminiti	15.00
22	Sammy Sosa	40.00
23	Albert Belle	15.00
24	Chuck Knoblauch	15.00
25	Mo Vaughn	15.00
26	Raul Mondesi	15.00
27	Tim Salmon	15.00
28	Bernie Williams	15.00
29	Tony Gwynn	25.00
30	Pedro Martinez	25.00
31	Roger Clemens	40.00
32	Craig Biggio	15.00
33	Randy Johnson	25.00
34	Tino Martinez	15.00
35	Chipper Jones	25.00
36	Kenny Lofton	15.00
37	Greg Maddux	25.00
38	Hideo Nomo	15.00
39	Andres Galarraga	15.00
40	Nomar Garciaparra	30.00
41	Juan Gonzalez	20.00
42	Mark McGwire	50.00
43	Mike Piazza	30.00
44	Jeff Bagwell	25.00
45	Barry Bonds	60.00
46	Larry Walker	15.00
47	Alex Rodriguez	60.00
48	Frank Thomas	30.00
49	Cal Ripken Jr.	75.00
50	Ken Griffey Jr.	50.00
51	Todd Walker	15.00
52	Jose Guillen	15.00
53	Vinny Castilla	15.00
54	Shannon Stewart	15.00
55	Jim Edmonds	15.00
56	Bobby Higginson	15.00
57	Jay Buhner	15.00
58	Mike Mussina	15.00
59	Todd Greene	15.00
60	Chan Ho Park	15.00
61	Livan Hernandez	15.00
62	Sandy Alomar Jr.	15.00
63	Fred McGriff	15.00
64	Travis Fryman	15.00
65	Jaret Wright	15.00
66	Bobby Bonilla	15.00
67	Moises Alou	15.00
68	Rafael Palmeiro	25.00
69	Charles Johnson	15.00
70	Ray Lankford	15.00
71	Kevin Brown	15.00
72	Neifi Perez	15.00
73	Rondell White	15.00
74	Bartolo Colon	15.00
75	Bob Abreu	15.00
76	Eric Young	15.00
77	Jason Giambi	20.00
78	Edgardo Alfonzo	15.00
79	Dante Bichette	15.00
80	Eric Karros	15.00
81	Matt Morris	15.00
82	Tom Glavine	15.00
83	Randy Hundley	15.00
84	Jason Dickson	15.00
85	Ryan Klesko	15.00
86	Mark Grace	15.00
87	Brett Tomko	15.00
88	Kevin Orie	15.00
89	Robin Ventura	15.00
90	Jose Canseco	15.00
91	Brian Jordan	15.00
92	Jason Kendall	15.00
93	Mike Cameron	15.00
94	Curt Schilling	20.00
95	Carlos Delgado	15.00
96	Garret Anderson	15.00
97	John Smoltz	15.00
98	Wade Boggs	25.00
99	Javy Lopez	15.00

1998 Pinnacle Inside

Pinnacle Inside features cards in a can. The 150 base cards have full-bleed photos on front with stats on the right and the player's name and position at bottom. The Club Edition parallel (1:7) is printed on silver foil board and the Diamond Edition parallel (1:67) is printed on prismatic foil board. Each pack of cards was packaged inside a collectible can. Inserts include Behind the Numbers and Stand Up Guys.

		NM/M
Complete Set (150):		12.00
Common Player:		.05
Club Edition (1:7):		4X
Diamond Edition (1:67):		10X
Can (10):		.05
Box (48):		45.00
1	Darin Erstad	.15
2	Derek Jeter	2.50
3	Alex Rodriguez	2.00
4	Bobby Higginson	.05
5	Nomar Garciaparra	1.00
6	Kenny Lofton	.05
7	Ivan Rodriguez	.65
8	Cal Ripken Jr.	2.50
9	Todd Hundley	.05
10	Chipper Jones	1.00
11	Barry Larkin	.05
12	Roberto Alomar	.15
13	Mo Vaughn	1.00
14	Sammy Sosa	1.00
15	Sandy Alomar Jr.	.05
16	Albert Belle	.05
17	Scott Rolen	.65
18	Pokey Reese	.05
19	Ryan Klesko	.05
20	Andres Galarraga	.05
21	Justin Thompson	.05
22	Gary Sheffield	.40
23	David Justice	.05
24	Ken Griffey Jr.	1.50
25	Andruw Jones	.75
26	Jeff Bagwell	.75
27	Vladimir Guerrero	.75
28	Mike Piazza	1.50
29	Chuck Knoblauch	.05
30	Rondell White	.05
31	Greg Maddux	1.00
32	Andy Pettitte	.20
33	Larry Walker	.05
34	Bobby Estalella	.05
35	Frank Thomas	.75
36	Tony Womack	.05
37	Tony Gwynn	1.00
38	Barry Bonds	2.50
39	Randy Johnson	.75
40	Mark McGwire	2.00
41	Juan Gonzalez	.40
42	Tim Salmon	.05
43	John Smoltz	.05
44	Rafael Palmeiro	.05
45	Mark Grace	.05
46	Mike Cameron	.05
47	Jim Thome	.65
48	Neifi Perez	.05
49	Kevin Brown	.05
50	Craig Biggio	.05
51	Bernie Williams	.05
52	Hideo Nomo	.40
53	Bob Abreu	.15
54	Edgardo Alfonzo	.05
55	Wade Boggs	1.00
56	Jose Guillen	.05
57	Ken Caminiti	.05
58	Paul Molitor	.75
59	Shawn Estes	.05
60	Edgar Martinez	.05
61	Livan Hernandez	.05
62	Ray Lankford	.05
63	Rusty Greer	.05
64	Jim Edmonds	.05
65	Tom Glavine	.35
66	Alan Benes	.05
67	Will Clark	.05
68	Garret Anderson	.05
69	Javier Lopez	.05
70	Mike Mussina	.35
71	Kevin Orie	.05
72	Matt Williams	.05
73	Bobby Bonilla	.05
74	Ruben Rivera	.05
75	Jason Giambi	.60
76	Todd Walker	.05
77	Tino Martinez	.05
78	Matt Morris	.05
79	Fernando Tatis	.05
80	Todd Greene	.05
81	Fred McGriff	.05
82	Brady Anderson	.05
83	Mark Kotsay	.05
84	Raul Mondesi	.05
85	Moises Alou	.05
86	Roger Clemens	1.25
87	Wilton Guerrero	.05
88	Shannon Stewart	.05
89	Chan Ho Park	.05
90	Carlos Delgado	.60
91	Jose Cruz Jr.	.05
92	Shawn Green	.35
93	Robin Ventura	.05
94	Reggie Sanders	.05
95	Orel Hershiser	.05
96	Dante Bichette	.05
97	Charles Johnson	.05
98	Pedro Martinez	.05
99	Mariano Rivera	.15
100	Joe Randa	.05
101	Jeff Kent	.05
102	Jay Buhner	.05
103	Brian Jordan	.05
104	Jason Kendall	.05
105	Scott Spiezio	.05
106	Desi Relaford	.05
107	Bernard Gilkey	.05
108	Manny Ramirez	.75
109	Tony Clark	.05
110	Eric Young	.05
111	Johnny Damon	.30
112	Glendon Rusch	.05
113	Ben Grieve	.05
114	Homer Bush	.05
115	Miguel Tejada	.25
116	Lou Collier	.05
117	Derrek Lee	.60
118	Jacob Cruz	.05
119	Raul Ibanez	.05
120	Ryan McGuire	.05
121	Antone Williamson	.05
122	Abraham Nunez	.05
123	Jeff Abbott	.05
124	Brett Tomko	.05
125	Richie Sexson	.05
126	Todd Helton	.75
127	Juan Encarnacion	.05
128	Richard Hidalgo	.05
129	Paul Konerko	.10
130	Brad Fullmer	.05
131	Jeremi Gonzalez	.05
132	Jaret Wright	.05
133	Derek Jeter (Inside Tips)	1.25
134	Frank Thomas (Inside Tips)	.40
135	Nomar Garciaparra (Inside Tips)	.50
136	Kenny Lofton (Inside Tips)	.05
137	Jeff Bagwell (Inside Tips)	.40
138	Todd Hundley (Inside Tips)	.05
139	Alex Rodriguez (Inside Tips)	1.00
140	Ken Griffey Jr. (Inside Tips)	.75
141	Sammy Sosa (Inside Tips)	.50
142	Greg Maddux (Inside Tips)	.50
143	Albert Belle (Inside Tips)	.05
144	Cal Ripken Jr. (Inside Tips)	1.25
145	Mark McGwire (Inside Tips)	1.00
146	Chipper Jones (Inside Tips)	.50
147	Charles Johnson (Inside Tips)	.05
148	Checklist (Ken Griffey Jr.)	.75
149	Checklist (Jose Cruz Jr.)	.05
150	Checklist (Larry Walker)	.05

Club Edition

This parallel set is virtually identical to the regular Inside cards, except for the addition of a "CLUB EDITION" notice to the right of the player's first name, and the use of gold foil highlights instead of silver on front.

	NM/M
Complete Set (150):	50.00
Common Player:	2.00
Stars:	4X
Inserted 1:7	

Diamond Edition

Diamond Edition cards parallel all 150 cards in Pinnacle Inside. The fronts have the insert name. These are printed on prismatic foil board and inserted one per 67 cans.

	NM/M
Common Card:	6.00

	NM/M
Stars:	10X
Inserted 1:67	

Behind the Numbers

Behind the Numbers is seeded one per 23 cans. Fronts feature an action photo printed in front of the player's number. The card is die-cut around the large metallic foil numerals. The back has a portrait photo and text explaining why the player wears that number.

		NM/M
Complete Set (20):		85.00
Common Player:		1.50
Inserted 1:23		
1	Ken Griffey Jr.	7.50
2	Cal Ripken Jr.	12.00
3	Alex Rodriguez	10.00
4	Jose Cruz Jr.	1.50
5	Mike Piazza	7.50
6	Nomar Garciaparra	5.50
7	Scott Rolen	2.50
8	Andruw Jones	4.00
9	Frank Thomas	4.00
10	Mark McGwire	10.00
11	Ivan Rodriguez	3.00
12	Greg Maddux	5.50
13	Roger Clemens	6.50
14	Derek Jeter	12.00
15	Tony Gwynn	5.50
16	Ben Grieve	1.50
17	Jeff Bagwell	4.00
18	Chipper Jones	5.50
19	Hideo Nomo	2.00
20	Sandy Alomar Jr.	1.50

Stand Up Guys

This 50-card insert was seeded one per can. Each card has a match; the two cards join together in the center to form a stand-up collectible featuring four Major League players. Each card can also be found in a promo edition with a large "SAMPLE" overprint.

	NM/M
Complete Set (50):	35.00
Common Card:	.25
Sample:	3X

1-A/B	Ken Griffey Jr., Cal Ripken Jr.	2.00
1-C/D	Tony Gwynn, Mike Piazza	1.25
2-A/B	Andruw Jones, Alex Rodriguez	1.50
2-C/D	Scott Rolen, Nomar Garciaparra	1.00
3-A/B	Andruw Jones, Greg Maddux	1.00
3-C/D	Javy Lopez, Chipper Jones	1.00
4-A/B	Jay Buhner, Randy Johnson	.75
4-C/D	Ken Griffey Jr., Alex Rodriguez	1.50
5-A/B	Frank Thomas, Jeff Bagwell	.75
5-C/D	Mark McGwire, Mo Vaughn	1.50
6-A/B	Nomar Garciaparra, Derek Jeter	2.00
6-C/D	Alex Rodriguez, Barry Larkin	1.50
7-A/B	Mike Piazza, Ivan Rodriguez	1.25
7-C/D	Charles Johnson, Javy Lopez	.25
8-A/B	Cal Ripken Jr., Chipper Jones	2.00
8-C/D	Ken Caminiti, Scott Rolen	.65
9-A/B	Jose Cruz Jr., Vladimir Guerrero	.75
9-C/D	Andruw Jones, Jose Guillen	.75
10-A/B	Larry Walker, Dante Bichette	.25
10-C/D	Ellis Burks, Neifi Perez	.25
11-A/B	Juan Gonzalez, Sammy Sosa	1.00
11-C/D	Vladimir Guerrero, Manny Ramirez	.75
12-A/B	Greg Maddux, Roger Clemens	1.00
12-C/D	Hideo Nomo, Randy Johnson	.75
13-A/B	Ben Grieve, Paul Konerko	.40
13-C/D	Jose Cruz Jr., Fernando Tatis	.25
14-A/B	Ryne Sandberg, Chuck Knoblauch	1.00
14-C/D	Roberto Alomar, Craig Biggio	.35
15-A/B	Cal Ripken Jr., Brady Anderson	2.00
15-C/D	Rafael Palmeiro, Roberto Alomar	.65
16-A/B	Darin Erstad, Jim Edmonds	.35
16-C/D	Tim Salmon, Garret Anderson	.25
17-A/B	Mike Piazza, Hideo Nomo	1.25
17-C/D	Raul Mondesi, Eric Karros	.25
18-A/B	Ivan Rodriguez, Juan Gonzalez	.65
18-C/D	Will Clark, Rusty Greer	.25
19-A/B	Derek Jeter, Bernie Williams	2.00
19-C/D	Tino Martinez, Andy Pettitte	.25
20-A/B	Kenny Lofton, Ken Griffey Jr.	1.50
20-C/D	Brady Anderson, Bernie Williams	.25
21-A/B	Paul Molitor, Eddie Murray	.75
21-C/D	Ryne Sandberg, Rickey Henderson	1.00
22-A/B	Tony Clark, Frank Thomas	.75
22-C/D	Jeff Bagwell, Mark McGwire	1.50
23-A/B	Manny Ramirez, Jim Thome	.75
23-C/D	David Justice, Sandy Alomar Jr.	.25
24-A/B	Barry Bonds, Albert Belle	2.00
24-C/D	Jeff Bagwell, Dante Bichette	.60
25-A/B	Ken Griffey Jr., Frank Thomas	1.25
25-C/D	Alex Rodriguez, Andruw Jones	1.50

Cans

Ten-card packs of Pinnacle Inside were packaged in collectible cans. The 24 cans featured a player photo or team logo. Cans were created to honor the Florida Marlins' world championship and the expansion Arizona and Tampa Bay teams. Gold parallel versions of the cans were found one every 47 cans. Values shown are for bot-

tom-opened cans; cans opened from the top have little collectible value.

		NM/M
Complete Set (23):		15.00
Common Can:		.40
Gold Cans:		2X
1	Ken Griffey Jr.	1.25
2	Frank Thomas	.65
3	Alex Rodriguez	1.50
4	Andruw Jones	.65
5	Mike Piazza	1.25
6	Ben Grieve	.40
7	Hideo Nomo	.50
8	Vladimir Guerrero	.65
9	Roger Clemens	1.00
10	Tony Gwynn	.75
11	Mark McGwire	1.50
12	Cal Ripken Jr.	2.00
13	Jose Cruz Jr.	.40
14	Greg Maddux	.75
15	Chipper Jones	.75
16	Derek Jeter	2.00
17	Juan Gonzalez	.50
18	Nomar Garciaparra (AL ROY)	1.00
19	Scott Rolen (NL ROY)	.65
20	Florida Marlins World Series Winner	.40
21	Larry Walker (NL MVP)	.40
22	Tampa Bay Devil Rays	.40
23	Arizona Diamondbacks	.40

Mint Collection

Mint Collection consists of 30 cards and 30 matching coins with numerous parallels of each. The cards come in four different versions. The base card features a player photo at left with a circular bronze foil team logo at right. The base cards were inserted one per hobby pack and two per retail pack. Die-cut versions removed the team logo and were inserted two per hobby and one per retail packs. Silver Mint Team (1:15 hobby, 1:23 retail) and Gold Mint Team (1:47 hobby, 1:71 retail) parallels were printed on silver foil and gold foil board, respectively.

	NM/M
Complete Set (30):	10.00
Common Die-Cut:	.25
Bronze (1:1H):	2X
Silver (1:15H):	5X
Gold (1:47):	12X
Pack (3+2):	1.00
Wax Box (24):	12.00

1	Jeff Bagwell	.65
2	Albert Belle	.25
3	Barry Bonds	2.00
4	Tony Clark	.25
5	Roger Clemens	1.00
6	Juan Gonzalez	.35
7	Ken Griffey Jr.	1.25
8	Tony Gwynn	.75
9	Derek Jeter	2.00
10	Randy Johnson	.65
11	Chipper Jones	.75
12	Greg Maddux	.75
13	Tino Martinez	.25
14	Mark McGwire	1.50
15	Hideo Nomo	.35
16	Andy Pettitte	.25
17	Mike Piazza	1.25
18	Cal Ripken Jr.	2.00

19	Alex Rodriguez	1.50
20	Ivan Rodriguez	.50
21	Sammy Sosa	.75
22	Frank Thomas	.65
23	Mo Vaughn	.25
24	Larry Walker	.25
25	Jose Cruz Jr.	.25
26	Nomar Garciaparra	.75
27	Vladimir Guerrero	.65
28	Livan Hernandez	.25
29	Andruw Jones	.65
30	Scott Rolen	.50

Mint Collection Coins

Two base coins were included in each pack of Mint Collection. The coins feature the player's image, name and number on the front along with his team's name and logo. The back has the Mint Collection logo. Seven parallels were included: Nickel-Silver (1:41), Brass Proof (numbered to 500), Nickel Proof (numbered to 250), Gold Proof (numbered to 100), Gold-Plated (1:199), Solid Silver (1:288 hobby, 1:960 retail) and Solid Gold by redemption (1-of-1).

		NM/M
Complete Set (30)		20.00
Common Brass Coin:		.25
Brass Proof (500):		5X
Nickel (1:41):		3X
Nickel Proof (250):		12X
Silver:		12X
Inserted 1:288 H, 1:960 R		
Gold Plated (1:199):		15X
Gold Proof (100):		20X
1	Jeff Bagwell	.75
2	Albert Belle	.25
3	Barry Bonds	2.00
4	Tony Clark	.25
5	Roger Clemens	1.00
6	Juan Gonzalez	.45
7	Ken Griffey Jr.	1.25
8	Tony Gwynn	1.00
9	Derek Jeter	2.00
10	Randy Johnson	.75
11	Chipper Jones	1.00
12	Greg Maddux	1.00
13	Tino Martinez	.25
14	Mark McGwire	1.50
15	Hideo Nomo	.45
16	Andy Pettitte	.35
17	Mike Piazza	1.25
18	Cal Ripken Jr.	2.00
19	Alex Rodriguez	1.50
20	Ivan Rodriguez	.50
21	Sammy Sosa	1.00
22	Frank Thomas	.75
23	Mo Vaughn	.25
24	Larry Walker	.25
25	Jose Cruz Jr.	.25
26	Nomar Garciaparra	1.00
27	Vladimir Guerrero	.75
28	Livan Hernandez	.25
29	Andruw Jones	.75
30	Scott Rolen	.65

Mint Collection Mint Gems

Scott Rolen

Mint Gems is a six-card insert printed on silver foil board. The cards were inserted 1:31 hobby packs and 1:47 retail. The oversized Mint Gems coins are twice the size of the regular coins. The six coins were inserted 1:31 hobby packs.

		NM/M
Complete Set (6)		20.00
Common Player:		2.00
Coins:		1X
1	Ken Griffey Jr.	6.00
2	Larry Walker	2.00
3	Roger Clemens	5.00
4	Pedro Martinez	4.00
5	Nomar Garciaparra	4.50
6	Scott Rolen	3.00

1998 Pinnacle Performers

Pinnacle Performers consists of a 150-card base set. The Peak Performers parallel adds silver foil to the base cards and was inserted 1:7. Inserts in the home run-themed product include Big Bang, Launching Pad, Player's Card and Power Trip.

		NM/M
Complete Set (150):		12.00
Common Player:		.05
Peak Performers (1:7):		2X
Pack (10):		1.00
Wax Box (24):		15.00
1	Ken Griffey Jr.	1.00
2	Frank Thomas	.65
3	Cal Ripken Jr.	.75
4	Alex Rodriguez	1.25
5	Greg Maddux	.75
6	Mike Piazza	1.00
7	Chipper Jones	.75
8	Tony Gwynn	.75
9	Derek Jeter	1.50
10	Jeff Bagwell	.65
11	Juan Gonzalez	.35
12	Nomar Garciaparra	.75
13	Andruw Jones	.65
14	Hideo Nomo	.35
15	Roger Clemens	.85
16	Mark McGwire	1.25
17	Scott Rolen	.60
18	Vladimir Guerrero	.65
19	Barry Bonds	1.50
20	Darin Erstad	.15
21	Albert Belle	.05
22	Kenny Lofton	.05
23	Mo Vaughn	.05
24	Tony Clark	.05
25	Ivan Rodriguez	.60
26	Jose Cruz Jr.	.05
27	Larry Walker	.05
28	Jaret Wright	.05
29	Andy Pettitte	.25
30	Roberto Alomar	.20
31	Randy Johnson	.65
32	Manny Ramirez	.65
33	Paul Molitor	.35
34	Mike Mussina	.35
35	Jim Thome	.60
36	Tino Martinez	.05
37	Gary Sheffield	.45
38	Chuck Knoblauch	.05
39	Bernie Williams	.05
40	Tim Salmon	.05
41	Sammy Sosa	.75
42	Wade Boggs	.75
43	Will Clark	.05
44	Andres Galarraga	.05
45	Raul Mondesi	.05
46	Rickey Henderson	.65
47	Jose Canseco	.45
48	Pedro Martinez	.65
49	Jay Buhner	.05
50	Ryan Klesko	.05
51	Barry Larkin	.05
52	Charles Johnson	.05
53	Tom Glavine	.35
54	Edgar Martinez	.05
55	Fred McGriff	.05
56	Moises Alou	.05
57	Dante Bichette	.05
58	Jim Edmonds	.05
59	Mark Grace	.05
60	Chan Ho Park	.05
61	Justin Thompson	.05
62	John Smoltz	.05
63	Craig Biggio	.05
64	Ken Caminiti	.05
65	Richard Hidalgo	.05
66	Carlos Delgado	.50
67	David Justice	.05
68	J.T. Snow	.05
69	Jason Giambi	.50
70	Garret Anderson	.05
71	Rondell White	.05
72	Matt Williams	.05
73	Brady Anderson	.05
74	Eric Karros	.05
75	Javier Lopez	.05
76	Pat Hentgen	.05
77	Todd Hundley	.05
78	Ray Lankford	.05
79	Denny Neagle	.05
80	Sandy Alomar Jr.	.05
81	Jason Kendall	.05
82	Omar Vizquel	.05
83	Kevin Brown	.05
84	Kevin Appier	.05
85	Al Martin	.05
86	Rusty Greer	.05
87	Bobby Bonilla	.05
88	Shawn Estes	.05
89	Rafael Palmeiro	.60
90	Edgar Renteria	.05
91	Alan Benes	.05
92	Bobby Higginson	.05
93	Mark Grudzielanek	.05
94	Jose Guillen	.05
95	Neifi Perez	.05
96	Jeff Abbott	.05
97	Todd Walker	.05
98	Eric Young	.05
99	Brett Tomko	.05
100	Mike Cameron	.05
101	Karim Garcia	.05
102	Brian Jordan	.05
103	Jeff Suppan	.05
104	Robin Ventura	.05
105	Henry Rodriguez	.05
106	Shannon Stewart	.05
107	Kevin Orie	.05
108	Bartolo Colon	.05
109	Bob Abreu	.15
110	Vinny Castilla	.05
111	Livan Hernandez	.05
112	Derek Lee	.50
113	Mark Kotsay	.05
114	Todd Greene	.05
115	Edgardo Alfonzo	.05
116	A.J. Hinch	.05
117	Paul Konerko	.15
118	Todd Helton	.65
119	Miguel Tejada	.20
120	Fernando Tatis	.05
121	Ben Grieve	.05
122	Travis Lee	.05
123	Kerry Wood	.25
124	Eli Marrero	.05
125	David Ortiz	.50
126	Juan Encarnacion	.05
127	Brad Fullmer	.05
128	Richie Sexson	.05
129	Aaron Boone	.05
130	Enrique Wilson	.05
131	Javier Valentin	.05
132	Abraham Nunez	.05
133	Ricky Ledee	.05
134	Carl Pavano	.05
135	Bobby Estalella	.05
136	Homer Bush	.05
137	Brian Rose	.05
138	Ken Griffey Jr. (Far and Away)	.50
139	Frank Thomas (Far and Away)	.35
140	Cal Ripken Jr. (Far and Away)	.75
141	Alex Rodriguez (Far and Away)	.65
142	Greg Maddux (Far and Away)	.40
143	Chipper Jones (Far and Away)	.40
144	Mike Piazza (Far and Away)	.50
145	Tony Gwynn (Far and Away)	.40
146	Derek Jeter (Far and Away)	.75
147	Jeff Bagwell (Far and Away)	.35
148	Checklist (Hideo Nomo)	.20
149	Checklist (Roger Clemens)	.45
150	Checklist (Greg Maddux)	.35

Peak Performers

This 150-card parallel set is printed on silver foil vs. the white cardboard stock used on regular-issue cards. The parallel set name is printed down the right side in gold letters. They were seeded one per seven packs.

	NM/M
Complete Set (150):	100.00
Common Player:	2.00

Stars:		6X
Inserted 1:7		

Big Bang

This 20-card insert features top power hitters. The micro-etched cards are sequentially numbered to 2,500. Each player has a Seasonal Outburst parallel, with a red overlay and numbered to that player's best seasonal home run total. Each card is also found in a promo edition with a large black "SAMPLE" overprinted on back.

		NM/M
Complete Set (20):		27.50
Common Player:		.50
Production 2,500 Sets		
Sample:		1X
1	Ken Griffey Jr.	2.50
2	Frank Thomas	1.50
3	Mike Piazza	2.50
4	Chipper Jones	2.00
5	Alex Rodriguez	3.00
6	Nomar Garciaparra	2.00
7	Jeff Bagwell	1.50
8	Cal Ripken Jr.	3.50
9	Albert Belle	.50
10	Mark McGwire	3.00
11	Juan Gonzalez	.75
12	Larry Walker	.50
13	Tino Martinez	.50
14	Jim Thome	1.00
15	Manny Ramirez	.50
16	Barry Bonds	3.50
17	Mo Vaughn	.50
18	Jose Cruz Jr.	.50
19	Tony Clark	.50
20	Andruw Jones	1.50

Big Bang Seasonal Outburst

Season Outburst parallels the Big Bang insert. The cards have a red overlay and are sequentially numbered to each player's season-high home run total. Unnumbered versions of the cards, likely leaked into the market after Pinnacle went bankrupt in mid-1998, have been seen; their value is much lower than the issued version.

		NM/M
Complete Set (20):		500.00
Common Player:		10.00
#'d to player's 1997 HR total		
Unnumbered: 25%		
1	Ken Griffey Jr./56	40.00
2	Frank Thomas/35	20.00
3	Mike Piazza/40	40.00
4	Chipper Jones/21	65.00
5	Alex Rodriguez/23	75.00
6	Nomar Garciaparra/30	40.00
7	Jeff Bagwell/43	40.00
8	Cal Ripken Jr./17	80.00
9	Albert Belle/30	40.00
10	Mark McGwire/58	65.00
11	Juan Gonzalez/42	12.50
12	Larry Walker/49	10.00

13	Tino Martinez/44	10.00
14	Jim Thome/40	15.00
15	Manny Ramirez/26	25.00
16	Barry Bonds/40	75.00
17	Mo Vaughn/35	10.00
18	Jose Cruz Jr./26	10.00
19	Tony Clark/32	10.00
20	Andruw Jones/18	25.00

Launching Pad

Launching Pad is a 20-card insert seeded one per nine packs. It features top sluggers on foil-on-foil cards with an outer space background.

		NM/M
Complete Set (20):		25.00
Common Player:		.50
Inserted 1:9		
1	Ben Grieve	.50
2	Ken Griffey Jr.	2.50
3	Derek Jeter	3.50
4	Frank Thomas	1.00
5	Travis Lee	.50
6	Vladimir Guerrero	1.00
7	Tony Gwynn	2.00
8	Jose Cruz Jr.	.50
9	Cal Ripken Jr.	3.50
10	Chipper Jones	2.00
11	Scott Rolen	.75
12	Andruw Jones	1.00
13	Ivan Rodriguez	.75
14	Todd Helton	1.00
15	Nomar Garciaparra	2.00
16	Mark McGwire	3.00
17	Gary Sheffield	.60
18	Bernie Williams	.50
19	Alex Rodriguez	3.00
20	Mike Piazza	2.50

Power Trip

This 10-card insert was seeded 1:21. Printed on silver foil, each card is sequentially-numbered to 10,000. Cards backs have details about one of the player's power-hitting highlights of the previous season.

		NM/M
Complete Set (10):		16.00
Common Player:		1.00
Production 10,000 Sets		
1	Frank Thomas	1.00
2	Alex Rodriguez	3.00
3	Nomar Garciaparra	1.50
4	Jeff Bagwell	1.00
5	Cal Ripken Jr.	4.00
6	Mike Piazza	2.00
7	Chipper Jones	1.50
8	Ken Griffey Jr.	2.00
9	Mark McGwire	3.00
10	Juan Gonzalez	1.50

Swing for the Fences

Pinnacle Performers included the "Swing for the Fences" sweepstakes. Fifty players were featured on cards with numbers on an all-red background. Fifty Home Run Points cards were also

inserted, with each card featuring a point total on the front. Collectors who found the player cards of the AL and NL home run leaders, as well as enough point cards to match each of their season totals, were eligible to win prizes. A player or point card was inserted in each pack.

		NM/M
Complete Set (50):		24.00
Common Player:		.25
Inserted 1:1		
1	Brady Anderson	.25
2	Albert Belle	.25
3	Jay Buhner	.25
4	Jose Canseco	.50
5	Tony Clark	.25
6	Jose Cruz Jr.	.25
7	Jim Edmonds	.25
8	Cecil Fielder	.25
9	Travis Fryman	.25
10	Nomar Garciaparra	1.00
11	Juan Gonzalez	.40
12	Ken Griffey Jr.	1.50
13	David Justice	.25
14	Travis Lee	.25
15	Edgar Martinez	.25
16	Tino Martinez	.25
17	Rafael Palmeiro	.65
18	Manny Ramirez	.75
19	Cal Ripken Jr.	2.50
20	Alex Rodriguez	2.00
21	Tim Salmon	.25
22	Frank Thomas	.75
23	Jim Thome	.65
24	Mo Vaughn	.25
25	Bernie Williams	.25
26	Fred McGriff	.25
27	Jeff Bagwell	.75
28	Dante Bichette	.25
29	Barry Bonds	2.50
30	Ellis Burks	.25
31	Ken Caminiti	.25
32	Vinny Castilla	.25
33	Andres Galarraga	.25
34	Vladimir Guerrero	.75
35	Todd Helton	.75
36	Todd Hundley	.25
37	Andruw Jones	.75
38	Chipper Jones	1.00
39	Eric Karros	.25
40	Ryan Klesko	.25
41	Ray Lankford	.25
42	Mark McGwire	2.00
43	Raul Mondesi	.25
44	Mike Piazza	1.50
45	Scott Rolen	.65
46	Gary Sheffield	.50
47	Sammy Sosa	.75
48	Larry Walker	.25
49	Matt Williams	.25
50	WILDCARD	.25

Swing/Fences Prize Cards

This set was evidently intended to be one of the prizes in Pinnacle's Swing for the Fences sweepstakes, but the cards were never officially distributed due to the company's midyear bankruptcy.

Making their way out the back into hobby channels in later years, the cards feature action photos on a silver prismatic foil background. Unnumbered backs have the player's career home run totals versus each team.

		NM/M
Complete Set (10):		10.00
Common Player:		.50
(1)	Jeff Bagwell	1.00
(2)	Barry Bonds	3.00
(3)	Nomar Garciaparra	1.50
(4)	Juan Gonzalez	.50
(5)	Ken Griffey Jr.	2.00
(6)	Chipper Jones	1.50
(7)	Mark McGwire	2.50
(8)	Mike Piazza	1.50
(9)	Alex Rodriguez	2.50
(10)	Frank Thomas	1.00

1998 Pinnacle Plus

Pinnacle Plus consists of a 200-card base set. Five subsets are included: Field of Vision, Naturals, All-Stars, Devil Rays and Diamondbacks. Artist's Proof is a 60-card partial parallel of the base set, inserted 1:35 packs. Gold Artist's Proof cards are numbered to 100 and Mirror Artist's Proofs are 1-of-1 inserts. Inserts include Lasting Memories, Yardwork, A Piece of the Game, All-Star Epix, Team Pinnacle, Gold Team Pinnacle, Pinnabilia and Certified Souvenir.

		NM/M
Complete Set (200):		12.00
Common Player:		.05
Pack (10):		1.00
Wax Box (20):		12.00
1	Roberto Alomar/AS	.20
2	Sandy Alomar Jr./AS	.05
3	Brady Anderson/AS	.05
4	Albert Belle/AS	.05
5	Jeff Cirillo/AS	.05
6	Roger Clemens/AS	1.25
7	David Cone/AS	.05
8	Nomar Garciaparra/AS	1.00
9	Ken Griffey Jr./AS	1.50
10	Jason Dickson/AS	.05
11	Edgar Martinez/AS	.05
12	Tino Martinez/AS	.05
13	Randy Johnson/AS	.25
14	Mark McGwire/AS	2.00
15	David Justice/AS	.05
16	Mike Mussina/AS	.40
17	Chuck Knoblauch/AS	.05
18	Joey Cora/AS	.05
19	Pat Hentgen/AS	.05
20	Randy Myers/AS	.05
21	Cal Ripken Jr./AS	2.50
22	Mariano Rivera/AS	.15
23	Jose Rosado/AS	.05
24	Frank Thomas/AS	.75
25	Alex Rodriguez/AS	2.00
26	Justin Thompson/AS	.05
27	Ivan Rodriguez/AS	.65
28	Bernie Williams/AS	.05
29	Pedro Martinez/AS	.75
30	Tony Clark/AS	.05
31	Garret Anderson/AS	.05
32	Travis Fryman/AS	.05
33	Mike Piazza	1.50
34	Carl Pavano	.05
35	Kevin Millwood RC	1.00
36	Miguel Tejada	.20
37	Willie Blair	.05
38	Devon White	.05
39	Andres Galarraga	.05
40	Barry Larkin	.05
41	Al Leiter	.05
42	Moises Alou	.05
43	Eric Young	.05
44	John Jaha	.05
45	Bernard Gilkey	.05
46	Freddy Garcia	.05
47	Ruben Rivera	.05
48	Robb Nen	.05

49	Ray Lankford	.05
50	Kenny Lofton	.05
51	Joe Carter	.05
52	Jason McDonald	.05
53	Quinton McCracken	.05
54	Kerry Wood	.50
55	Mike Lansing	.05
56	Chipper Jones	1.00
57	Barry Bonds	2.50
58	Brad Fullmer	.05
59	Jeff Bagwell	.75
60	Rondell White	.05
61	Geronimo Berroa	.05
62	Magglio Ordonez RC	1.50
63	Dwight Gooden	.05
64	Brian Hunter	.05
65	Todd Walker	.05
66	Frank Catalanotto RC	.05
67	Tony Saunders	.05
68	Travis Lee	.05
69	Michael Tucker	.05
70	Reggie Sanders	.05
71	Derrek Lee	.50
72	Larry Walker	.05
73	Marquis Grissom	.05
74	Craig Biggio	.05
75	Kevin Brown	.05
76	J.T. Snow	.05
77	Eric Davis	.05
78	Jeff Abbott	.05
79	Jermaine Dye	.05
80	Otis Nixon	.05
81	Curt Schilling	.35
82	Enrique Wilson	.05
83	Tony Gwynn	1.00
84	Orlando Cabrera	.05
85	Ramon Martinez	.05
86	Greg Vaughn	.05
87	Alan Benes	.05
88	Dennis Eckersley	.65
89	Jim Thome	.65
90	Juan Encarnacion	.05
91	Jeff King	.05
92	Shannon Stewart	.05
93	Roberto Hernandez	.05
94	Raul Ibanez	.05
95	Darryl Kile	.05
96	Charles Johnson	.05
97	Rich Becker	.05
98	Hal Morris	.05
99	Ismael Valdes	.05
100	Orel Hershiser	.05
101	Mo Vaughn	.05
102	Aaron Boone	.05
103	Jeff Conine	.05
104	Paul O'Neill	.05
105	Tom Candiotti	.05
106	Wilson Alvarez	.05
107	Mike Stanley	.05
108	Carlos Delgado	.50
109	Tony Batista	.05
110	Dante Bichette	.05
111	Henry Rodriguez	.05
112	Karim Garcia	.05
113	Shane Reynolds	.05
114	Ken Caminiti	.05
115	Jose Silva	.05
116	Juan Gonzalez	.40
117	Brian Jordan	.05
118	Jim Leyritz	.05
119	Manny Ramirez	.75
120	Fred McGriff	.05
121	Brooks Kieschnick	.05
122	Sean Casey	.15
123	John Smoltz	.05
124	Rusty Greer	.05
125	Cecil Fielder	.05
126	Mike Cameron	.05
127	Reggie Jefferson	.05
128	Bobby Higginson	.05
129	Kevin Appier	.05
130	Robin Ventura	.05
131	Ben Grieve	.05
132	Wade Boggs	1.00
133	Jose Cruz Jr.	.05
134	Jeff Suppan	.05
135	Vinny Castilla	.05
136	Sammy Sosa	1.00
137	Mark Wohlers	.05
138	Jay Bell	.05
139	Brett Tomko	.05
140	Gary Sheffield	.40
141	Tim Salmon	.05
142	Jaret Wright	.05
143	Kenny Rogers	.05
144	Brian Anderson	.05
145	Darrin Fletcher	.05
146	John Flaherty	.05
147	Dmitri Young	.05
148	Andruw Jones	.75
149	Matt Williams	.05
150	Bobby Bonilla	.05
151	Mike Hampton	.05
152	Al Martin	.05
153	Mark Grudzielanek	.05
154	Dave Nilsson	.05
155	Roger Cedeno	.05
156	Greg Maddux	1.00
157	Mark Kotsay	.05
158	Steve Finley	.05
159	Wilson Delgado	.05
160	Ron Gant	.05
161	Jim Edmonds	.05
162	Jeff Blauser	.05
163	Dave Burba	.05
164	Pedro Astacio	.05
165	Livan Hernandez	.05
166	Neifi Perez	.05

167	Ryan Klesko	.05
168	Fernando Tatis	.05
169	Richard Hidalgo	.05
170	Carlos Perez	.05
171	Bob Abreu	.15
172	Francisco Cordova	.05
173	Todd Helton	.75
174	Doug Glanville	.05
175	Brian Rose	.05
176	Yamil Benitez	.05
177	Darin Erstad	.15
178	Scott Rolen	.60
179	John Wetteland	.05
180	Paul Sorrento	.05
181	Walt Weiss	.05
182	Vladimir Guerrero	.75
183	Ken Griffey Jr. (The Naturals)	.75
184	Alex Rodriguez (The Naturals)	1.00
185	Cal Ripken Jr. (The Naturals)	1.25
186	Frank Thomas (The Naturals)	.40
187	Chipper Jones (The Naturals)	.50
188	Hideo Nomo (The Naturals)	.20
189	Nomar Garciaparra (The Naturals)	.60
190	Mike Piazza (The Naturals)	1.00
191	Greg Maddux (The Naturals)	.50
192	Tony Gwynn (The Naturals)	.50
193	Mark McGwire (The Naturals)	1.00
194	Roger Clemens (The Naturals)	.65
195	Mike Piazza (Field of Vision)	.75
196	Mark McGwire (Field of Vision)	1.00
197	Chipper Jones (Field of Vision)	.50
198	Larry Walker (Field of Vision)	.05
199	Hideo Nomo (Field of Vision)	.20
200	Barry Bonds (Field of Vision)	1.25

Artist's Proofs

Artist's Proofs is a 60-card partial parallel of the Pinnacle Plus base set. The dot matrix hologram cards were inserted 1:35. Gold Artist's Proofs added a gold finish and are sequentially numbered to 100. Mirror Artist's Proofs are a "1-of-1" insert. Card numbers have an "AP" prefix.

		NM/M
Complete Set (60):		150.00
Common Player:		.75
Inserted 1:35		
Golds:		10X
Production 100 Sets		
1	Roberto Alomar/AS	1.50
2	Albert Belle/AS	.75
3	Roger Clemens/AS	8.00
4	Nomar Garciaparra/AS	7.50
5	Ken Griffey Jr./AS	10.00
6	Tino Martinez/AS	.75
7	Randy Johnson/AS	6.00
8	Mark McGwire/AS	12.50
9	David Justice/AS	.75
10	Chuck Knoblauch/AS	.75
11	Cal Ripken Jr./AS	15.00
12	Frank Thomas/AS	6.00
13	Alex Rodriguez/AS	12.50
14	Ivan Rodriguez/AS	5.00
15	Bernie Williams/AS	.75
16	Pedro Martinez	6.00
17	Tony Clark	.75
18	Mike Piazza	10.00
19	Miguel Tejada	1.00
20	Andres Galarraga	.75

ABBREVIATIONS

AS - All-Star

21	Barry Larkin	.75
22	Kenny Lofton	.75
23	Chipper Jones	7.50
24	Barry Bonds	15.00
25	Brad Fullmer	.75
26	Jeff Bagwell	6.00
27	Todd Walker	.75
28	Travis Lee	.75
29	Larry Walker	.75
30	Craig Biggio	.75
31	Tony Gwynn	7.50
32	Jim Thome	5.00
33	Juan Encarnacion	.75
34	Mo Vaughn	.75
35	Karim Garcia	.75
36	Ken Caminiti	.75
37	Juan Gonzalez	3.00
38	Manny Ramirez	6.00
39	Fred McGriff	.75
40	Rusty Greer	.75
41	Bobby Higginson	.75
42	Ben Grieve	.75
43	Wade Boggs	7.50
44	Jose Cruz Jr.	.75
45	Sammy Sosa	7.50
46	Gary Sheffield	2.00
47	Tim Salmon	.75
48	Jaret Wright	.75
49	Andruw Jones	6.00
50	Matt Williams	.75
51	Greg Maddux	7.50
52	Jim Edmonds	.75
53	Livan Hernandez	.75
54	Neifi Perez	.75
55	Fernando Tatis	.75
56	Richard Hidalgo	.75
57	Todd Helton	6.00
58	Darin Erstad	1.50
59	Scott Rolen	5.00
60	Vladimir Guerrero	6.00

A Piece of the Game

Inserted 1:17 hobby packs (1:19 retail), this 10-card insert features baseball's top players on micro-etched foil cards.

		NM/M
Complete Set (10):		8.00
Common Player:		.50
Inserted 1:19		
1	Ken Griffey Jr.	1.00
2	Frank Thomas	.65
3	Alex Rodriguez	1.50
4	Chipper Jones	.75
5	Cal Ripken Jr.	1.00
6	Mike Piazza	1.00
7	Greg Maddux	.50
8	Juan Gonzalez	.50
9	Nomar Garciaparra	.75
10	Larry Walker	.50

Epix All-Star Moment

The All-Star Epix insert is part of the cross-brand Epix set. The cards honor the All-Star Game achievements of baseball's stars on cards with dot matrix holograms. All-Star Epix was seeded 1:21. Cards #1-12 were distributed in Score Rookie/Traded.

		NM/M
Complete Set (12):		25.00
Common Player:		1.00
Purples:		1.5X
Emeralds:		2.5X
Inserted 1:21		
13	Alex Rodriguez	3.50
14	Cal Ripken Jr.	5.00
15	Chipper Jones	2.50
16	Roger Clemens	2.75
17	Mo Vaughn	1.00
18	Mark McGwire	3.50
19	Mike Piazza	3.00
20	Andruw Jones	2.00
21	Greg Maddux	2.50
22	Barry Bonds	5.00
23	Paul Molitor	2.00
24	Hideo Nomo	1.50

Lasting Memories

Lasting Memories is a 30-card insert seeded 1:5. Printed on foil board, the cards feature a player photo with a sky background.

		NM/M
Complete Set (30):		16.00
Common Player:		.25
Inserted 1:5		
1	Nomar Garciaparra	.75
2	Ken Griffey Jr.	1.00
3	Livan Hernandez	.25
4	Hideo Nomo	.40
5	Ben Grieve	.25
6	Scott Rolen	.50
7	Roger Clemens	.85
8	Cal Ripken Jr.	2.00
9	Mo Vaughn	.25
10	Frank Thomas	.65
11	Mark McGwire	1.50
12	Barry Larkin	.25
13	Matt Williams	.25
14	Jose Cruz Jr.	.25
15	Andruw Jones	.65
16	Mike Piazza	1.00
17	Jeff Bagwell	.65
18	Chipper Jones	.75
19	Juan Gonzalez	.40
20	Kenny Lofton	.25
21	Greg Maddux	.75
22	Ivan Rodriguez	.50
23	Alex Rodriguez	1.50
24	Derek Jeter	2.00
25	Albert Belle	.25
26	Barry Bonds	2.00
27	Larry Walker	.25
28	Sammy Sosa	1.00
29	Tony Gwynn	.75
30	Randy Johnson	.65

Team Pinnacle

Team Pinnacle is a 15-card, double-sided insert. Printed on mirror-mylar, the cards were inserted 1:71. The hobby-only Gold Team Pinnacle parallel was inserted 1:199 packs.

		NM/M
Complete Set (15):		50.00
Common Player:		1.50
Inserted 1:71		
Golds:		2X
Inserted 1:199		

1	Mike Piazza, Ivan Rodriguez	6.00
2	Mark McGwire, Mo Vaughn	5.00
3	Roberto Alomar, Craig Biggio	2.00
4	Alex Rodriguez, Barry Larkin	8.00
5	Cal Ripken Jr., Chipper Jones	10.00
6	Ken Griffey Jr., Larry Walker	6.00
7	Juan Gonzalez, Tony Gwynn	4.00
8	Albert Belle, Barry Bonds	8.00
9	Kenny Lofton, Andruw Jones	3.00
10	Tino Martinez, Jeff Bagwell	3.00
11	Frank Thomas, Andres Galarraga	3.00
12	Roger Clemens, Greg Maddux	8.00
13	Pedro Martinez, Hideo Nomo	4.00
14	Nomar Garciaparra, Scott Rolen	5.00
15	Ben Grieve, Paul Konerko	1.50

Yardwork

Yardwork is a 15-card insert seeded one per 19 packs. It features the top home run hitters in Major League Baseball.

		NM/M
Complete Set (15):		12.50
Common Player:		.35
Inserted 1:9		
1	Mo Vaughn	.35
2	Frank Thomas	.75
3	Albert Belle	.35
4	Nomar Garciaparra	1.00
5	Tony Gwynn	.35
6	Tino Martinez	.35
7	Ken Griffey Jr.	1.50
8	Juan Gonzalez	.60
9	Sammy Sosa	1.00
10	Jose Cruz Jr.	.35
11	Jeff Bagwell	.75
12	Mike Piazza	1.50
13	Larry Walker	.35
14	Mark McGwire	2.00
15	Barry Bonds	2.50

1998 Pinnacle Snapshots

One of Pinnacle's last issues was a team-oriented presentation of large-format (4" x 6") cards called Snapshots. Like their namesake, the focus on this issue is on candid photos rather than posed portraits or game-action pictures. The cards are printed on thin high-gloss cardboard stock resembling photo paper. Fronts, many of them horizontally formatted, are borderless and have no graphic enhancement. Backs are lightly printed with Pinnacle and licensor logos and a card number expressed "x of 18." The player's name is nowhere to be found. Snapshots were sold regionally in single-team boxes of 25 packs with eight cards each.

Angels

		NM/M
	Complete Set (18):	7.50
	Common Player:	.50
1	Jason Dickson	.50
2	Gary DiSarcina	.50
3	Garret Anderson	.50
4	Shigetosi Hasegawa	.50
5	Ken Hill	.50
6	Todd Greene	.50
7	Tim Salmon	.75
8	Jim Edmonds	.60
9	Garret Anderson	.50
10	Dave Hollins	.50
11	Todd Greene	.50
12	Troy Percival	.50
13	Gary DiSarcina	.50
14	Cecil Fielder	.50
15	Darin Erstad	.75
16	Chuck Finley	.50
17	Jim Edmonds	.50
18	Jason Dickson	.50

Braves

		NM/M
	Complete Set (18):	11.00
	Common Player:	.50
1	Ryan Klesko	.50
2	Walt Weiss	.50
3	Tom Glavine	.75
4	Randall Simon	.50
5	John Smoltz	.50
6	Chipper Jones	1.50
7	Javier Lopez	.50
8	Greg Maddux	1.50
9	Andruw Jones	1.00
10	Michael Tucker	.50
11	Andres Galarraga	.50
12	Andres Galarraga	.50
13	Greg Maddux	1.50
14	Wes Helms	.50
15	Bruce Chen	.50
16	Denny Neagle	.50
17	Mark Wohlers	.50
18	Kevin Millwood	.60

Cardinals

		NM/M
	Complete Set (18):	10.00
	Common Player:	.50
1	Alan Benes	.50
2	Ron Gant	.50
3	Donovan Osborne	.50

Cubs

		NM/M
	Complete Set (18):	9.00
	Common Player:	.50
1	Mark Grace	.60
2	Manny Alexander	.50
3	Jeremi Gonzalez	.50
4	Brant Brown	.50
5	Mark Grace	.60
6	Lance Johnson	.50
7	Mark Clark	.50
8	Kevin Foster	.50
9	Brant Brown	.50
10	Kevin Foster	.50
11	Kevin Tapani	.50
12	Sammy Sosa	1.50
13	Sammy Sosa	1.50
14	Pat Cline	.50
15	Kevin Orie	.50
16	Steve Trachsel	.50
17	Lance Johnson	.50
18	Robin Jennings	.50

1998 Pinnacle Snapshots Devil Rays

		NM/M
	Complete Set (18):	7.50
	Common Player:	.50
1	Kevin Stocker	.50
2	Paul Sorrento	.50
3	John Flaherty	.50
4	Wade Boggs	1.50
5	Rich Butler	.50
6	Wilson Alvarez	.50
7	Bubba Trammell	.50
8	David Martinez	.50
9	Brooks Kieschnick	.50
10	Tony Saunders	.50
11	Esteban Yan	.50
12	Quinton McCracken	.50
13	Albie Lopez	.50
14	Roberto Hernandez	.50
15	Fred McGriff	.50
16	Bubba Trammell	.50
17	Brooks Kieschnick	.50
18	Fred McGriff	.50

Diamondbacks

		NM/M
	Complete Set (18):	7.50
	Common Player:	.50
1	Travis Lee	1.00
2	Matt Williams	.50
3	Jay Bell	.50
4	Devon White	.50
5	Andy Benes	.50
6	Tony Batista	.50
7	Jay Bell	.50
8	Edwin Diaz	.50
9	Devon White	.50
10	Bob Wolcott	.50
11	Karim Garcia	1.00
12	Yamil Benitez	.50
13	Jorge Fabregas	.50
14	Jeff Suppan	.50
15	Ben Ford	.50
16	Brian Anderson	.50
17	Travis Lee	1.00
18	Matt Williams	.50

Dodgers

		NM/M
	Complete Set (18):	12.00
	Common Player:	.50
1	Mike Piazza	2.50
2	Eric Karros	.50

4	Eli Marrero	.50
5	Mark McGwire	2.50
6	Delino DeShields	.50
7	Tom Pagnozzi	.50
8	Delino DeShields	.50
9	Mark McGwire	2.50
10	Royce Clayton	.50
11	Brian Jordan	.50
12	Ray Lankford	.50
13	Brian Jordan	.50
14	Matt Morris	.50
15	John Mabry	.50
16	Luis Ordaz	.50
17	Ron Gant	.50
18	Todd Stottlemyre	.50

Indians

		NM/M
	Complete Set (18):	7.50
	Common Player:	.50
1	Manny Ramirez	1.50
2	Travis Fryman	.50
3	Jaret Wright	.50
4	Brian Giles	.50
5	Bartolo Colon	.50
6	Kenny Lofton	.50
7	David Justice	.50
8	Brian Giles	.50
9	Sandy Alomar Jr.	.50
10	Jose Mesa	.50
11	Jim Thome	1.00
12	Sandy Alomar Jr.	.50
13	Omar Vizquel	.50
14	Geronimo Berroa	.50
15	John Smiley	.50
16	Chad Ogea	.50
17	Charles Nagy	.50
18	Enrique Wilson	.50

Mariners

		NM/M
	Complete Set (18):	12.00
	Common Player:	.50
1	Alex Rodriguez	2.50
2	Jay Buhner	.50
3	Russ Davis	.50
4	Joey Cora	.50
5	Joey Cora	.50
6	Jay Buhner	.50
7	Ken Griffey Jr.	2.00
8	Raul Ibanez	.50
9	Rich Amaral	.50
10	Shane Monahan	.50
11	Alex Rodriguez	2.50
12	Dan Wilson	.50
13	Bob Wells	.50
14	Randy Johnson	1.00
15	Randy Johnson	1.00
16	Jeff Fassero	.50
17	Ken Cloude	.50
18	Edgar Martinez	.50

Mets

		NM/M
	Complete Set (18):	7.50
	Common Player:	.50
1	Rey Ordonez	.50
2	Todd Hundley	.50
3	Preston Wilson	.50
4	Rich Becker	.50
5	Bernard Gilkey	.50
6	Rey Ordonez	.50
7	Butch Huskey	.50
8	Carlos Baerga	.50
9	Edgardo Alfonzo	.50
10	Bill Pulsipher	.50
11	John Franco	.50
12	Todd Pratt	.50
13	Brian McRae	.50
14	Bobby Jones	.50
15	John Olerud	.50
16	Todd Hundley	.50
17	Jay Payton	.50
18	Paul Wilson	.50

Orioles

		NM/M
	Complete Set (18):	12.50
	Common Player:	.50
1	Cal Ripken Jr.	3.00
2	Rocky Coppinger	.50
3	Eric Davis	.50
4	Chris Hoiles	.50

3	Raul Mondesi	.50
4	Wilton Guerrero	.50
5	Darren Dreifort	.50
6	Roger Cedeno	.50
7	Todd Zeile	.50
8	Paul Konerko	.75
9	Todd Hollandsworth	.50
10	Ismael Valdes	.50
11	Hideo Nomo	1.00
12	Ramon Martinez	.50
13	Chan Ho Park	.75
14	Eric Young	.50
15	Dennis Reyes	.50
16	Eric Karros	.50
17	Mike Piazza	2.50
18	Raul Mondesi	.50

Rangers

		NM/M
	Complete Set (18):	9.00
	Common Player:	.50
1	Ivan Rodriguez	1.00
2	Fernando Tatis	.50
3	Danny Patterson	.50
4	Will Clark	.66
5	Kevin Elster	.50
6	Rusty Greer	.50
7	Darren Oliver	.50
8	John Burkett	.50
9	Tom Goodwin	.50
10	Roberto Kelly	.50
11	Aaron Sele	.50
12	Rick Helling	.50
13	Mark McLemore	.50
14	Lee Stevens	.50
15	John Wetteland	.50
16	Will Clark	.65
17	Juan Gonzalez	.75
18	Roger Pavlik	.50

Red Sox

		NM/M
	Complete Set (18):	9.00
	Common Player:	.50
1	Tim Naehring	.50
2	Brian Rose	.50
3	Darren Bragg	.50
4	Pedro Martinez	1.00
5	Mo Vaughn	.50
6	Jim Leyritz	.50
7	Troy O'Leary	.50
8	Mo Vaughn	.50
9	Nomar Garciaparra	1.50
10	Michael Coleman	.50
11	Tom Gordon	.50
12	Tim Naehring	.50
13	Nomar Garciaparra	1.50
14	John Valentin	.50
15	Steve Avery	.50
16	Damon Buford	.50
17	Troy O'Leary	.50
18	Bret Saberhagen	.50

Rockies

		NM/M
	Complete Set (18):	7.50
	Common Player:	.50
1	Larry Walker	.50
2	Pedro Astacio	.50
3	Jamey Wright	.50
4	Darryl Kile	.50
5	Kirt Manwaring	.50
6	Todd Helton	1.50
7	Mike Lansing	.50
8	Neifi Perez	.50
9	Dante Bichette	.50

10	Derrick Gibson	.50
11	Neifi Perez	.50
12	Darryl Kile	.50
13	Larry Walker	.50
14	Roger Bailey	.50
15	Ellis Burks	.50
16	Dante Bichette	.50
17	Derrick Gibson	.50
18	Ellis Burks	.50

Yankees

		NM/M
	Complete Set (18):	12.50
	Common Player:	.75
1	Andy Pettitte	.75
2	Darryl Strawberry	.50
3	Joe Girardi	.50
4	Derek Jeter	3.00
5	Andy Pettitte	.75
6	Tim Raines	.50
7	Mariano Rivera	.75
8	Tino Martinez	.50
9	Derek Jeter	3.00
10	Hideki Irabu	.50
11	Tino Martinez	.50
12	David Cone	.50
13	Bernie Williams	.65
14	David Cone	.50
15	Bernie Williams	.65
16	Chuck Knoblauch	.50
17	Paul O'Neill	.50
18	David Wells	.50

Sport Block

By manipulating the eight cubes of which this novelty is comprised, pictures of eight popular players and the team logo can be displayed. The cube measures 2-3/4" x 2-3/4" x 2-3/4".

		NM/M
	Complete Set (10):	20.00
	Common Team:	3.00
(1)	Anaheim Angels (Garret Anderson, Jason Dickson, Jim Edmonds, Darin Erstad, Chuck Finley, Todd Greene, Troy Percival, Tim Salmon, Angels logo)	3.00
(2)	Arizona Diamondbacks	3.00
(3)	Atlanta Braves (Andres Galarraga, Tom Glavine, Andruw Jones, Chipper Jones, Ryan Klesko, Javier Lopez, Greg Maddux, John Smoltz, Braves logo)	3.00
(4)	Baltimore Orioles	3.00
(5)	Boston Red Sox (Darren Bragg, Nomar Garciaparra, Reggie Jefferson, Jim Leyritz, Pedro Martinez, Troy O'Leary, John Valentin, Mo Vaughn, Red Sox logo)	3.00
(6)	Cleveland Indians	3.00
(7)	Los Angeles Dodgers (Eric Karros, Paul Konerko, Ramon Martinez, Raul Mondesi, Hideo Nomo, Chan Ho Park, Mike Piazza, Ismael Valdes, Dodgers logo)	3.00
(8)	New York Yankees	3.00
(9)	Seattle Mariners (Jay Buhner, Russ Davis, Jeff Fassero, Ken Griffey Jr., Randy Johnson, Edgar Martinez, Alex Rodriguez, Dan Wilson, Mariners logo)	3.00
(10)	Tampa Bay Devil Rays (Wilson Alvarez, Wade Boggs, Dave Martinez, Quinton McCracken, Fred McGriff, Tony Saunders,	

Paul Sorrento, Bubba Trammell, Devil Rays logo) 3.00

Totally Certified Platinum Gold

Among several card issues that were aborted by Pinnacle's bankruptcy in mid-1998, but which have leaked into the hobby market in dribs and drabs, are 10 Totally Certified Platinum Gold cards that were intended to be random pack inserts in 1998 Certified. Each of the cards was produced in an edition of 30 serially numbered pieces. To date, confirmation of back-door release of the Platinum Red and Platinum Blue versions has not been made.

		NM/M
	Complete Set (10):	125.00
	Common Player:	7.50
1	Vladimir Guerrero	15.00
2	Andruw Jones	12.00
3	Paul Molitor	15.00
4	Jose Cruz Jr.	7.50
5	Edgar Martinez	7.50
6	Andy Pettitte	9.00
7	Darin Erstad	9.00
8	Barry Larkin	7.50
9	Derek Jeter	40.00
10	Rusty Greer	7.50

1998 Team Pinnacle Baseball

With each $30 membership in Pinnacle's collectors' club, "Team Pinnacle," the member received a litho tin box with 10 each special baseball, football and hockey cards, and a pack of unnumbered promo cards. In standard 2-1/2" x 3-1/2", cards have game-action photos on front, bordered in a dominant team color and enhanced with a gold-foil Team Pinnacle logo at bottom. Backs have portrait photos, a few personal details, career highlights and the player's uniform number ghosted in the background.

		NM/M
	Complete Set (10):	16.00
	Common Player:	1.00
B1	Ken Griffey Jr.	2.00
B2	Frank Thomas	1.25
B3	Cal Ripken Jr.	3.00
B4	Alex Rodriguez	2.50
B5	Mike Piazza	2.00
B6	Derek Jeter	3.00
B7	Greg Maddux	1.50
B8	Chipper Jones	1.50
B9	Mark McGwire	2.50
B10	Juan Gonzalez	1.00
---	Cal Ripken Jr. (Unmarked sample.)	2.50

Team Pinnacle (Unissued)

This four-card set was reportedly created for distribution to members of the card company's "Team Pinnacle" but was never officially issued due to the manufacturer's bankruptcy. The 2-1/2" x 3-1/2" cards have game-action photos on front with a wide diagonal color stripe at top and a gold-foil "98 TEAM PINNACLE" logo at bottom. Backs have a color portrait photo along with some stats and highlights. The cards are unnumbered.

	NM/M
Complete Set (4):	7.50
Common Player:	3.00
(1) John Elway/Football	2.00
(2) Ken Griffey Jr.	2.00
(3) Derek Jeter	3.00
(4) Eric Lindros/Hockey	2.00

Uncut

Advertised as the "BIGGEST CARD EVER!" these 13-3/8 x 18-5/8" cards are approximately 30 times larger than standard cards. Sold in individual cello bags with a suggested retail price of around $10, the cards are super-size replicas of the same players' cards found in the Field of Vision subset in regular 1998 Pinnacle. The giant cards have an etched metallic foil front not found on the regular cards. They are packaged with a die-cut cardboard backing which tends to bruise the edges or chip off small patches of ink.

	NM/M
Complete Set (6):	20.00
Common Card:	3.00
182 Alex Rodriguez	6.00
183 Cal Ripken Jr., Roberto Alomar	4.50
184 Roger Clemens	3.50
185 Derek Jeter	7.50
186 Frank Thomas	3.00
186p Frank Thomas ("SAMPLE" on back.)	4.50
187 Ken Griffey Jr.	4.50

2004 Pitt Ohio Express 1979 Pirates

The purpose for which the Pennsylvania trucking company produced this card set, and the manner of their distribution, is unclear. The set commemorates the World Champion Pittsburgh Pirates

of 1979. Fronts of the approximately 4-3/4" x 3-5/8" cards have large black-and-white portrait photos. Highlighted by gold graphics, the fronts also include a team logo, player name, position and uniform number. Backs have an ad for the trucking company.

	NM/M
Complete Set (19):	20.00
Common Player:	2.00
(1) Matt Alexander	2.00
(2) Tony Bartirome	2.00
(3) Jim Bibby	2.00
(4) Mike Easler	2.00
(5) Grant Jackson	2.00
(6) Bruce Kison	2.00
(7) Lee Lacy	2.00
(8) Bill Madlock	3.00
(9) Omar Moreno	2.00
(10) Steve Nicosia	2.00
(11) Ed Ott	2.00
(12) Dave Parker	4.00
(13) Dave Roberts	2.00
(14) Don Robinson	2.00
(15) Jim Rooker	2.00
(16) Manny Sanguillen	3.00
(17) Chuck Tanner	2.00
(18) Kent Tekulve	2.00

1992 Pittsburgh Brewing Co. Roberto Clemente Tribute

The first 15,000 fans at Three Rivers Stadium on September 6 at a special promotional Clemente tribute night received this perforated pair of cards honoring the Pirates superstar. The 7" square panel has a pair of two-part cards. Each side has a 3-1/2" x 5-1/2" picture portion at top and a 1-1/2" tab at bottom, perforated for easy separation. The left side has a portrait of the Pirate great with his first name; at right is his last name and an action picture. Back of the portrait card has career stats; back of the action card has career highlights. Artwork on each card is by Tom Mosser. The sponsor logo is on back of each tab along with a quotation and copyright information.

	NM/M
Complete Panel:	18.00
Complete Set (2):	15.00
#21 Roberto/Portrait	7.50
#21 Clemente/Action	7.50

1985 Pittsburgh Pirates Yearbook Cards

This 18-card set was issued on two nine-card perforated panels inserted into the Bucs' 1985 yearbook. Individual cards measure 2-1/2" x 3-1/2" and feature color photos surrounded by black and gold bor-

ders. The player's name, position and uniform number are printed in a white panel at bottom. Backs are in black-and-white and offer complete major and minor league stats, along with the logos of sponsor Cameron/Coca-Cola.

	NM/M
Complete Set (18):	7.50
Common Player:	.50
2 Jim Morrison	.50
5 Johnny Ray	.50
6 Bill Madlock	.60
7 Tony Pena	.50
7 Chuck Tanner	.50
10 Tim Foli	.50
13 Steve Kemp	.50
15 George Hendrick	.50
25 Jose DeLeon	.50
27 Kent Tekulve	.50
28 Sixto Lezcano	.50
29 Rick Rhoden	.50
30 Jason Thompson	.50
36 Marvell Wynne	.50
43 Don Robinson	.50
45 John Candelaria	.50
49 Larry McWilliams	.50
51 Doug Frobel	.50

1996 Pizza Hut

In conjunction with a foam bat/ball promotion, Pizza Hut issued a small set of small cards (2-1/2" x 2-1/4") featuring players involved in the endorsement. The player portrait photos on the cards are devoid of cap logos and surrounded by a rainbow border. Player names are in yellow with a nickname in red. A choking hazard warning is in black-and-white on bottom. Backs are printed in red and black and have career summaries, logos and copyright notice. The unnumbered cards are checklisted here alphabetically.

	NM/M
Complete Set (4):	8.00
Common Card:	1.50
(1) Jeff Bagwell/Thumper, Orel Hershiser/ Bulldawg	1.50
(2) David Cone/Controller, Mike Piazza/Crusher	3.00
(3) Ken Griffey Jr./Junior, Greg Maddux/ Surgeon	3.00
(4) Randy Johnson/Big unit, Mo Vaughn/Hit dog	1.50

2001 Playoff Absolute Memorabilia

	NM/M
Complete Set (200):	
Common Player:	.25
Common SP (151-200):	5.00
Production 700	
Pack (6):	8.00
Box (18) w/Baseball:	150.00
1 Alex Rodriguez	2.50
2 Barry Bonds	3.00
3 Cal Ripken Jr.	3.00
4 Chipper Jones	1.50
5 Derek Jeter	3.00
6 Troy Glaus	1.00
7 Frank Thomas	1.00
8 Greg Maddux	1.50
9 Ivan Rodriguez	.75
10 Jeff Bagwell	1.00
11 Ryan Dempster	.25
12 Todd Helton	1.00
13 Ken Griffey Jr.	2.00
14 Manny Ramirez	1.00
15 Mark McGwire	2.50
16 Mike Piazza	2.00
17 Nomar Garciaparra	1.00
18 Pedro Martinez	1.00
19 Randy Johnson	1.00
20 Rick Ankiel	.25
21 Rickey Henderson	1.00
22 Roger Clemens	1.75
23 Sammy Sosa	2.00
24 Tony Gwynn	1.00
25 Vladimir Guerrero	1.00
26 Kazuhiro Sasaki	.25
27 Roberto Alomar	.50
28 Barry Zito	.35
29 Pat Burrell	.50
30 Harold Baines	.25
31 Carlos Delgado	.65
32 J.D. Drew	.50
33 Jim Edmonds	.25
34 Darin Erstad	.50
35 Jason Giambi	.75
36 Tom Glavine	.50
37 Juan Gonzalez	.50
38 Mark Grace	.35
39 Shawn Green	.50
40 Tim Hudson	.50
41 Andruw Jones	1.00
42 David Justice	.25
43 Jeff Kent	.25
44 Barry Larkin	.25
45 Rafael Furcal	.50
46 Mike Mussina	.50
47 Hideo Nomo	1.00
48 Rafael Palmeiro	.75
49 Adam Piatt	.25
50 Scott Rolen	.75
51 Gary Sheffield	.50
52 Bernie Williams	.35
53 Bob Abreu	.25
54 Edgardo Alfonzo	.25
55 Edgar Renteria	.25
56 Phil Nevin	.25
57 Craig Biggio	.25
58 Andres Galarraga	.25
59 Edgar Martinez	.25
60 Fred McGriff	.25
61 Magglio Ordonez	.25
62 Jim Thome	.75
63 Matt Williams	.25
64 Kerry Wood	.65
65 Moises Alou	.25
66 Brady Anderson	.25
67 Garret Anderson	.25
68 Russell Branyan	.25
69 Tony Batista	.25
70 Vernon Wells	.25
71 Carlos Beltran	.60
72 Adrian Beltre	.25
73 Kris Benson	.25
74 Lance Berkman	.50
75 Kevin Brown	.25
76 Dee Brown	.25
77 Jeromy Burnitz	.25
78 Timoniel Perez	.25
79 Sean Casey	.40
80 Luis Castillo	.25
81 Eric Chavez	.35
82 Jeff Cirillo	.25
83 Bartolo Colon	.25
84 David Cone	.25
85 Freddy Garcia	.25
86 Johnny Damon	.40
87 Ray Durham	.25
88 Jermaine Dye	.25
89 Juan Encarnacion	.25
90 Terrence Long	.25
91 Carl Everett	.25
92 Steve Finley	.25
93 Cliff Floyd	.25
94 Brad Fullmer	.25
95 Brian Giles	.25
96 Luis Gonzalez	.25
97 Rusty Greer	.25
98 Jeffrey Hammonds	.25
99 Mike Hampton	.25
100 Orlando Hernandez	.25
101 Richard Hidalgo	.25
102 Geoff Jenkins	.25
103 Jacque Jones	.25

104	Brian Jordan	.25
105	Gabe Kapler	.25
106	Eric Karros	.25
107	Jason Kendall	.25
108	Adam Kennedy	.25
109	Deion Sanders	.25
110	Ryan Klesko	.25
111	Chuck Knoblauch	.25
112	Paul Konerko	.25
113	Carlos Lee	.25
114	Kenny Lofton	.25
115	Javy Lopez	.25
116	Tino Martinez	.25
117	Ruben Mateo	.25
118	Kevin Millwood	.25
119	Jimmy Rollins	.25
120	Raul Mondesi	.25
121	Trot Nixon	.25
122	John Olerud	.25
123	Paul O'Neill	.25
124	Chan Ho Park	.25
125	Andy Pettitte	.35
126	Jorge Posada	.25
127	Mark Quinn	.25
128	Aramis Ramirez	.25
129	Mariano Rivera	.25
130	Tim Salmon	.35
131	Curt Schilling	.50
132	Richie Sexson	.25
133	John Smoltz	.25
134	J.T. Snow	.25
135	Jay Payton	.25
136	Shannon Stewart	.25
137	B.J. Surhoff	.25
138	Mike Sweeney	.25
139	Fernando Tatis	.25
140	Miguel Tejada	.35
141	Jason Varitek	.25
142	Greg Vaughn	.25
143	Mo Vaughn	.25
144	Robin Ventura	.25
145	Jose Vidro	.25
146	Omar Vizquel	.25
147	Larry Walker	.25
148	David Wells	.25
149	Rondell White	.25
150	Preston Wilson	.25
151	Bud Smith **RC**	5.00
152	Cory Aldridge **RC**	5.00
153	Wilmy Caceres **RC**	5.00
154	Josh Beckett **RC**	5.00
155	Wilson Betemit **RC**	10.00
156	Jason Michaels **RC**	5.00
157	Albert Pujols **RC**	125.00
158	Andres Torres **RC**	5.00
159	Jack Wilson **RC**	5.00
160	Alex Escobar	5.00
161	Ben Sheets	5.00
162	Rafael Soriano **RC**	10.00
163	Nate Frese **RC**	5.00
164	Carlos Garcia **RC**	5.00
165	Brandon Larson **RC**	5.00
166	Alexis Gomez **RC**	8.00
167	Jason Hart	5.00
168	Nick Johnson	5.00
169	Donaldo Mendez **RC**	5.00
170	Christian Parker **RC**	5.00
171	Jackson Melian **RC**	5.00
172	Jack Cust	5.00
173	Adrian Hernandez **RC**	5.00
174	Joe Crede	5.00
175	Jose Mieses **RC**	5.00
176	Roy Oswalt	5.00
177	Eric Munson	5.00
178	Xavier Nady	5.00
179	Horacio Ramirez **RC**	8.00
180	Abraham Nunez	5.00
181	Jose Ortiz	5.00
182	Jeremy Owens **RC**	5.00
183	Claudio Vargas **RC**	5.00
184	Marcus Giles	5.00
185	Aubrey Huff	5.00
186	C.C. Sabathia	5.00
187	Adam Dunn	5.00
188	Adam Pettyjohn **RC**	5.00
189	Elpidio Guzman **RC**	5.00
190	Jay Gibbons **RC**	10.00
191	Wilkin Ruan **RC**	5.00
192	Tsuyoshi Shinjo **RC**	5.00
193	Alfonso Soriano	5.00
194	Corey Patterson	5.00
195	Ichiro Suzuki **RC**	75.00
196	Billy Sylvester **RC**	5.00
197	Juan Uribe **RC**	5.00
198	Johnny Estrada **RC**	8.00
199	Carlos Valderrama **RC**	5.00
200	Matt White **RC**	5.00

Ball Hoggs

		NM/M
Common Player:		8.00
Production 75 unless noted.		
1	Vladimir Guerrero	15.00
2	Troy Glaus	10.00
3	Tony Gwynn	20.00
4	Cal Ripken/125	50.00
5	Todd Helton	15.00
6	Jacque Jones/125	8.00
7	Shawn Green/100	8.00
8	Ichiro Suzuki	85.00
9	Scott Rolen	15.00
10	Roger Clemens	30.00
13	Ken Griffey/25	50.00
14	Sammy Sosa	25.00
15	J.D. Drew	10.00
16	Barry Bonds/100	40.00
17	Pat Burrell	15.00
18	Mark McGwire/100	65.00
19	Mike Piazza	20.00
20	Magglio Ordonez/ 150	10.00
21	Miguel Tejada	8.00
22	Albert Pujols/100	150.00
23	Derek Jeter	40.00
24	Johnny Damon	15.00
25	Mike Sweeney	8.00
26	Ben Grieve	8.00
27	Jeff Kent	8.00
28	Andres Galarraga	8.00
29	Richie Sexson	10.00
30	Juan Encarnacion	8.00
31	Ruben Mateo	8.00
33	Manny Ramirez	15.00
34	Ivan Rodriguez	15.00
36	Darin Erstad	8.00
37	Carlos Delgado	10.00
38	Jeff Bagwell	15.00
39	Jermaine Dye	8.00
40	Jose Ortiz	8.00
41	Gary Sheffield	10.00
42	Eric Chavez	8.00
43	Mark Grace	15.00
44	Rafael Palmeiro	15.00
45	Tsuyoshi Shinjo/100	15.00
46	Terrence Long	8.00
47	Carlos Delgado/25	20.00
48	Frank Thomas	15.00
49	Chipper Jones/25	40.00
50	Jason Giambi	15.00

Ballpark Souvenirs

		NM/M
Common Player:		4.00
Production 400 Sets		
Doubles:		1-1.5X
Production 200 Sets		
Triples:		1.5-2X
Production 75 Sets		
Home Runs:		2-4X
Production 25 Sets		
1	Barry Bonds	20.00
2	Cal Ripken Jr.	25.00
3	Pedro Martinez	10.00
4	Troy Glaus	6.00
5	Frank Thomas	8.00
6	Alex Rodriguez	10.00
7	Ivan Rodriguez	8.00
8	Jeff Bagwell	8.00
9	Mark McGwire	30.00
10	Todd Helton	8.00
11	Gary Sheffield	5.00
12	Manny Ramirez	8.00
13	Mike Piazza	10.00
14	Sammy Sosa	15.00
15	Preston Wilson	4.00
16	Tony Gwynn	8.00
17	Vladimir Guerrero	8.00
18	Carlos Delgado	6.00
19	Roberto Alomar	6.00
20	Todd Helton	8.00
21	Albert Pujols	50.00
22	Jason Giambi	8.00
23	Sammy Sosa	15.00
24	Ken Griffey Jr.	8.00
25	Darin Erstad	4.00
26	Mark McGwire	30.00
27	Carlos Delgado	8.00
28	Juan Gonzalez	8.00
29	Mike Sweeney	4.00
30	Alex Rodriguez	10.00
31	Roger Clemens	15.00
32	Tsuyoshi Shinjo	4.00
33	Ben Grieve	4.00
34	Jeff Kent	4.00
35	Vladimir Guerrero	8.00

36	Shawn Green	6.00
37	Rafael Palmeiro	6.00
38	Tony Gwynn	8.00
39	Scott Rolen	8.00
40	Ken Griffey Jr.	10.00
41	Albert Pujols	50.00
42	Barry Bonds	20.00
43	Mark Grace	6.00
44	Bernie Williams	6.00
45	Frank Thomas	8.00
46	Jermaine Dye	4.00
47	Mike Piazza	10.00
48	Chipper Jones	10.00
49	Richie Sexson	6.00
50	Magglio Ordonez	4.00

Boss Hoggs

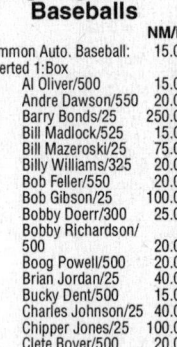

JOSE ORTIZ

NM/M

Production 25 Sets

4	Cal Ripken	80.00
6	Jacque Jones	15.00
7	Shawn Green	15.00
8	Ichiro Suzuki	100.00
9	Scott Rolen	20.00
11	Ken Griffey	50.00
14	Sammy Sosa	50.00
15	J.D. Drew	15.00
16	Barry Bonds	80.00
17	Pat Burrell	20.00
18	Mark McGwire	100.00
19	Mike Piazza	75.00
20	Magglio Ordonez	20.00
21	Miguel Tejada	20.00
23	Derek Jeter	85.00
24	Johnny Damon	15.00
25	Mike Sweeney	15.00
26	Ben Grieve	15.00
27	Jeff Kent	15.00
28	Andres Galarraga	20.00
29	Richie Sexson	15.00
30	Juan Encarnacion	15.00
31	Ruben Mateo	15.00
33	Manny Ramirez	20.00
35	Ivan Rodriguez	20.00
36	Darin Erstad	15.00
37	Carlos Delgado	20.00
38	Jeff Bagwell	20.00
39	Jermaine Dye	15.00
40	Jose Ortiz	15.00
42	Eric Chavez	15.00
43	Mark Grace	30.00
44	Rafael Palmeiro	30.00
45	Tsuyoshi Shinjo	20.00
46	Terrence Long	15.00
47	Carlos Delgado	15.00
48	Frank Thomas	25.00
50	Jason Giambi	25.00

Rookie Premiere Autographs

ANDRES TORRES

NM/M

Production 25 Sets

151	Bud Smith	15.00
152	Cory Aldridge	15.00
154	Josh Beckett	40.00
155	Wilson Betemit	15.00
157	Albert Pujols	500.00
158	Andres Torres	15.00
160	Alex Escobar	15.00
161	Ben Sheets	30.00
162	Rafael Soriano	15.00
164	Carlos Garcia	15.00
165	Brandon Larson	15.00
167	Jason Hart	15.00
168	Nick Johnson	25.00
169	Donaldo Mendez	15.00
170	Christian Parker	15.00
171	Jackson Melian	15.00
173	Adrian Hernandez	15.00
174	Joe Crede	15.00
175	Jose Mieses	15.00
176	Roy Oswalt	30.00
178	Xavier Nady	15.00
179	Horacio Ramirez	20.00
180	Abraham Nunez	15.00
181	Jose Ortiz	15.00

182	Jeremy Owens	15.00
183	Claudio Vargas	15.00
184	Marcus Giles	20.00
186	C.C. Sabathia	25.00
187	Adam Dunn	50.00
188	Adam Pettyjohn	15.00
190	Jay Gibbons	25.00
191	Wilkin Ruan	15.00
193	Alfonso Soriano	85.00
194	Corey Patterson	20.00
196	Billy Sylvester	15.00
197	Juan Uribe	15.00
198	Johnny Estrada	15.00
199	Carlos Valderrama	15.00
200	Matt White	15.00

Signing Bonus Baseballs

NM/M

Common Auto. Baseball: 15.00
Inserted 1:Box

Al Oliver/500	15.00
Andre Dawson/550	20.00
Barry Bonds/25	250.00
Bill Madlock/525	15.00
Bill Mazeroski/25	75.00
Billy Williams/325	20.00
Bob Feller/550	20.00
Bob Gibson/25	100.00
Bobby Doerr/300	25.00
Bobby Richardson/500	20.00
Boog Powell/500	15.00
Brian Jordan/25	40.00
Bucky Dent/500	15.00
Charles Johnson/25	40.00
Chipper Jones/25	100.00
Clete Boyer/500	20.00
Dale Murphy/25	80.00
Dave Concepcion/500	15.00
Dave Kingman/500	15.00
Don Larsen/200	40.00
Don Newcombe/500	15.00
Don Zimmer/500	15.00
Duke Snider/25	100.00
Earl Weaver/300	20.00
Enos Slaughter/525	20.00
Fergie Jenkins/1000	20.00
Frank Howard/500	15.00
Frank Robinson/25	100.00
Frank Thomas/25	85.00
Gary Carter/200	30.00
Gaylord Perry/1000	15.00
George Foster/500	15.00
George Kell/300	20.00
Goose Gossage/500	15.00
Greg Maddux/25	100.00
Hank Aaron/25	150.00
Hank Bauer/500	20.00
Harmon Killebrew/200	60.00
Henry Rodriguez/400	15.00
Herb Score/500	15.00
Hoyt Wilhelm/500	15.00
J.D. Drew/75	20.00
Javy Lopez/25	40.00
Jim Edmonds/25	50.00
Jim Palmer/500	15.00
Joe Pepitone/500	15.00
Johnny Bench/25	120.00
Johnny Podres/500	25.00
Juan Marichal/485	20.00
Kirby Puckett/25	100.00
Larry Doby/300	30.00
Lou Brock/25	75.00
Luis Tiant/500	15.00
Magglio Ordonez/200	15.00
Manny Ramirez/25	60.00
Maury Wills/500	20.00
Mike Schmidt/25	150.00
Minnie Minoso/1000	15.00
Monte Irvin/500	20.00
Moose Skowron/500	20.00
Nolan Ryan/25	250.00
Ozzie Smith/25	100.00
Phil Rizzuto/25	75.00
Ralph Kiner/100	40.00
Randy Johnson/25	100.00
Red Schoendienst/500	20.00
Reggie Jackson/25	80.00
Rickey Henderson/25	100.00
Robin Roberts/500	25.00
Roger Clemens/25	125.00
Rollie Fingers/575	20.00
Ryne Sandberg/25	100.00
Sean Casey/25	15.00
Stan Musial/25	100.00
Steve Carlton/25	75.00
Steve Garvey/1000	15.00
Todd Helton/25	50.00
Tom Glavine/25	50.00
Tom Seaver/25	75.00
Tommy John/1000	15.00
Tony Gwynn/25	75.00
Tony Perez/400	15.00
Wade Boggs/25	75.00
Warren Spahn/500	60.00
Whitey Ford/25	75.00
Willie Mays/25	150.00
Willie McCovey/25	60.00
Willie Stargell/25	75.00
Yogi Berra/25	75.00

Spectrum

SPECTRUM
ALEX RODRIGUEZ•SS

NM/M

Stars (1-150):	No Pricing
Production 10	
RK's (151-200):	2-4X
Production 25	

Tools Of The Trade

NM/M

Common Player: 5.00
Jerseys (1-20):
Production 300
Bats (21-40):
Production 125
Batting Glove (41-45):
Production 50
Hat (46-50):
Production 100
Autographs: No Pricing
Production 25 Sets

1	Vladimir Guerrero	10.00
2	Troy Glaus	6.00
3	Tony Gwynn	10.00
4	Todd Helton	8.00
5	Scott Rolen	8.00
6	Roger Clemens	20.00
7	Pedro Martinez	10.00
8	Richie Sexson	6.00
9	Magglio Ordonez	5.00
10	Ben Grieve	5.00
11	Jeff Bagwell	8.00
12	Edgar Martinez	5.00
13	Greg Maddux	22.00
15	Frank Thomas	10.00
16	Edgardo Alfonzo	5.00
17	Cal Ripken Jr.	40.00
18	Jose Vidro	5.00
19	Andruw Jones	8.00
21	Barry Bonds	50.00
22	Juan Gonzalez	8.00
23	Andruw Jones	8.00
24	Cal Ripken Jr.	60.00
25	Greg Maddux	30.00
26	Manny Ramirez	20.00
27	Roberto Alomar	8.00
28	Shawn Green	6.00
29	Edgardo Alfonzo	5.00
30	Rafael Palmeiro	10.00
31	Hideo Nomo	100.00
32	Andres Galarraga	6.00
33	Todd Helton	15.00
34	Darin Erstad	15.00
35	Ivan Rodriguez	15.00
36	Sean Casey	6.00
37	Vladimir Guerrero	20.00
39	Troy Glaus	8.00
40	Jeff Bagwell	10.00
41	Barry Bonds	100.00
42	Cal Ripken Jr.	125.00
43	Roberto Alomar	30.00
44	Sean Casey	20.00
45	Tony Gwynn	40.00
46	Bernie Williams	25.00
47	Barry Zito	20.00
49	Tom Glavine	25.00

2002 Playoff Absolute Memorabilia Samples

Selected issues of the September 2002 Beckett Baseball Card Monthly included a sample 2002 Playoff Absolute Memorabilia card rubber-cemented inside. The cards differ from the issued version only in the appearance on back of a (usually) silver-foil "SAMPLE" notation. Some cards were produced with the overprint in gold-foil, in much more limited quantities. The number of different players' cards involved in the promotion is unknown.

NM/M

Common Player:	.10
Stars:	1.5-2X
Gold:	20X

2002 Playoff Absolute Memorabilia

NM/M

Complete Set (200):
Common Player: .50
Common RK/Prospect (151-200): 3.00
Production 1,000
Pack (6): 3.00
Box + 8X10: 140.00

1	David Eckstein	.50
2	Darin Erstad	.75
3	Troy Glaus	1.50
4	Garret Anderson	.50
5	Tim Salmon	.50
6	Curt Schilling	1.00
7	Randy Johnson	1.50
8	Luis Gonzalez	.50
9	Mark Grace	.60
10	Tom Glavine	.75
11	Greg Maddux	2.00
12	Chipper Jones	2.00
13	Gary Sheffield	.75
14	John Smoltz	.50
15	Andruw Jones	1.50
16	Wilson Betemit	.50
17	Tony Batista	.50
18	Javier Vazquez	.50
19	Scott Erickson	.50
20	Josh Towers	.50
21	Pedro J. Martinez	1.50
22	Johnny Damon	.60
23	Manny Ramirez	1.50
24	Rickey Henderson	1.50
25	Trot Nixon	.50
26	Nomar Garciaparra	2.50
27	Juan Cruz	.50
28	Kerry Wood	1.25
29	Fred McGriff	.50
30	Moises Alou	.50
31	Sammy Sosa	2.50
32	Corey Patterson	.50
33	Mark Buehrle	.50
34	Keith Foulke	.50
35	Frank Thomas	1.50
36	Kenny Lofton	.50
37	Magglio Ordonez	.50
38	Barry Larkin	.50
39	Ken Griffey Jr.	2.50
40	Adam Dunn	.75
41	Juan Encarnacion	.50
42	Sean Casey	.60
43	Bartolo Colon	.50
44	C.C. Sabathia	.50
45	Travis Fryman	.50
46	Jim Thome	1.50
47	Omar Vizquel	.50
48	Ellis Burks	.50
49	Russell Branyan	.50
50	Mike Hampton	.50
51	Todd Helton	1.50
52	Jose Ortiz	.50
53	Juan Uribe	.50
54	Juan Pierre	.50
55	Larry Walker	.50
56	Mike Rivera	.50
57	Robert Fick	.50
58	Bobby Higginson	.50
59	Josh Beckett	.50
60	Richard Hidalgo	.50
61	Cliff Floyd	.50
62	Mike Lowell	.50
63	Roy Oswalt	.50
64	Morgan Ensberg	.50
65	Jeff Bagwell	1.50
66	Craig Biggio	.50
67	Lance Berkman	.50
68	Carlos Beltran	.75
69	Mike Sweeney	.50
70	Neifi Perez	.50
71	Kevin Brown	.50
72	Hideo Nomo	1.50
73	Paul LoDuca	.50
74	Adrian Beltre	.50
75	Shawn Green	.75
76	Eric Karros	.50
77	Brad Radke	.50
78	Corey Koskie	.50
79	Doug Mientkiewicz	.50
80	Torii Hunter	.50
81	Jacque Jones	.50
82	Ben Sheets	.50
83	Richie Sexson	.50
84	Geoff Jenkins	.50
85	Tony Armas	.50

86	Michael Barrett	.50
87	Jose Vidro	.50
88	Vladimir Guerrero	1.50
89	Roger Clemens	2.25
90	Derek Jeter	4.00
91	Bernie Williams	.60
92	Jason Giambi	1.25
93	Jorge Posada	.50
94	Mike Mussina	.65
95	Andy Pettitte	.65
96	Nick Johnson	.50
97	Alfonso Soriano	1.25
98	Shawn Estes	.50
99	Al Leiter	.50
100	Mike Piazza	2.50
101	Roberto Alomar	.75
102	Mo Vaughn	.50
103	Jeromy Burnitz	.50
104	Tim Hudson	.65
105	Barry Zito	.50
106	Mark Mulder	.50
107	Eric Chavez	.65
108	Miguel Tejada	.65
109	Jeremy Giambi	.50
110	Jermaine Dye	.50
111	Mike Lieberthal	.50
112	Scott Rolen	1.25
113	Pat Burrell	.75
114	Brandon Duckworth	.50
115	Bobby Abreu	.50
116	Jason Kendall	.50
117	Aramis Ramirez	.50
118	Brian Giles	.50
119	Pokey Reese	.50
120	Phil Nevin	.50
121	Ryan Klesko	.50
122	Carlos Pena	.50
123	Trevor Hoffman	.50
124	Barry Bonds	4.00
125	Rich Aurilia	.50
126	Jeff Kent	.50
127	Tsuyoshi Shinjo	.50
128	Ichiro Suzuki	2.00
129	Edgar Martinez	.50
130	Freddy Garcia	.50
131	Bret Boone	.50
132	Matt Morris	.50
133	Tino Martinez	.50
134	Albert Pujols	3.00
135	J.D. Drew	.75
136	Jim Edmonds	.50
137	Gabe Kapler	.50
138	Paul Wilson	.50
139	Ben Grieve	.50
140	Wade Miller	.50
141	Chan Ho Park	.50
142	Alex Rodriguez	3.00
143	Rafael Palmeiro	1.25
144	Juan Gonzalez	1.50
145	Ivan Rodriguez	1.25
146	Carlos Delgado	.75
147	Jose Cruz Jr.	.50
148	Shannon Stewart	.50
149	Raul Mondesi	.50
150	Vernon Wells	.50
151	So Taguchi RC	8.00
152	Kazuhisa Ishii RC	8.00
153	Hank Blalock	6.00
154	Sean Burroughs	3.00
155	Geronimo Gil	3.00
156	Jon Rauch	3.00
157	Fernando Rodney	3.00
158	Miguel Asencio RC	3.00
159	Franklyn German RC	3.00
160	Luis Ugueto RC	3.00
161	Jorge Sosa RC	3.00
162	Felix Escalona RC	3.00
163	Colby Lewis	3.00
164	Mark Teixeira	15.00
165	Mark Prior	6.00
166	Francis Beltran RC	3.00
167	Joe Thurston	3.00
168	Earl Snyder RC	3.00
169	Takahito Nomura RC	3.00
170	Bill Hall	3.00
171	Marlon Byrd	3.00
172	Dave Williams	3.00
173	Yorvit Torrealba	3.00
174	Brandon Backe RC	3.00
175	Jorge de la Rosa RC	3.00
176	Brian Mallette RC	3.00
177	Rodrigo Rosario RC	3.00
178	Anderson Machado RC	3.00
179	Jorge Padilla RC	3.00
180	Allan Simpson RC	3.00
181	Doug DeVore RC	3.00
182	Steve Bechler RC	3.00
183	Raul Chavez	3.00
184	Tom Shearn RC	3.00
185	Ben Howard RC	3.00
186	Chris Baker RC	3.00
187	Travis Hughes RC	3.00
188	Kevin Mench	3.00
189	Drew Henson	3.00
190	Mike Moriarty RC	3.00
191	Corey Thurman RC	3.00
192	Bobby Hill	3.00
193	Steve Kent RC	3.00
194	Satoru Komiyama RC	3.00
195	Jason Lane	3.00
196	Angel Berroa	3.00
197	Brandon Puffer RC	3.00
198	Brian Fitzgerald RC	3.00
199	Rene Reyes RC	3.00
200	Hee Seop Choi	5.00

Spectrum

Stars (1-150):	3-5X
Production 100	
SP's:	1-1.5X
Production 50	

Absolutely Ink

NM/M

Common Autograph: 5.00
Inserted 1:27
Gold Parallel #'d to 25 not priced.
Jsy Parallel #'d to Jsy # not priced.

Adrian Beltre	20.00
Alex Rodriguez/50	100.00
Ben Sheets	20.00
Bobby Doerr	15.00
Blaine Neal	5.00
Carlos Beltran	25.00
Carlos Pena	5.00
Corey Patterson/150	5.00
Dave Parker	10.00
David Justice/65	25.00
Don Mattingly/75	65.00
Duaner Sanchez	5.00
Eric Chavez/100	15.00
Freddy Garcia	10.00
Gary Carter	15.00
Ivan Rodriguez/50	40.00
J.D. Drew/100	20.00
Jack Cust	5.00
Jason Michaels	5.00
Jermaine Dye/125	5.00
Jose Vidro	8.00
Josh Towers	5.00
Kerry Wood/50	40.00
Kirby Puckett/50	75.00
Luis Gonzalez/75	25.00
Luis Rivera	5.00
Manny Ramirez/40	15.00
Marcus Giles	10.00
Mark Prior/100	30.00
Mark Teixeira/100	25.00
Marlon Byrd/250	15.00
Matt Ginter	5.00
Moises Alou/150	15.00
Nate Frese	5.00
Nick Johnson	5.00
Pablo Ozuna	5.00
Paul LoDuca/200	20.00
Richie Sexson	15.00
Roberto Alomar/100	40.00
Roy Oswalt/300	15.00
Ryan Klesko/75	25.00
Sean Casey/125	10.00
Shannon Stewart	8.00
So Taguchi	15.00
Terrence Long	8.00
Timoniel Perez	5.00
Tony Gwynn/50	60.00
Troy Glaus/300	15.00
Vladimir Guerrero/225	40.00
Wade Miller	15.00
Wilson Betemit	5.00

Signing Bonus

NM/M

Common Player:

Bobby Abreu/53	40.00
Roberto Alomar/100	30.00
Moises Alou/250	30.00
Carlos Beltran/50	50.00
Adrian Beltre/29	40.00
Adrian Beltre/150	30.00
Angel Berroa/50	30.00
Angel Berroa/100	20.00
Wilson Betemit/250	25.00
Hank Blalock/50	50.00
Hank Blalock/40	40.00
Lou Brock/100	60.00
Lou Brock/200	50.00
Kevin Brown/27	40.00
Kevin Brown/100	25.00
Kevin Brown/150	25.00
Mark Buehrle/56	60.00
Mark Buehrle/200	40.00
Marlon Byrd/61	25.00
Steve Carlton/100	50.00
Steve Carlton/150	50.00
Sean Casey/100	30.00
Eric Chavez/28	50.00
Juan Cruz/51	25.00
J.D. Drew/100	30.00

Brandon Duckworth/56 25.00
Brandon Duckworth/150 15.00
Adam Dunn/44 60.00
Jermaine Dye/100 40.00
Jermaine Dye/250 30.00
Morgan Ensberg/100 25.00
Cliff Floyd/200 25.00
Freddy Garcia/34 50.00
Freddy Garcia/125 25.00
Troy Glaus/50 65.00
Troy Glaus/100 40.00
Tom Glavine/200 60.00
Luis Gonzalez/125 30.00
Vladimir Guerrero/27 120.00
Vladimir Guerrero/150 80.00
Richard Hidalgo/100 20.00
Richard Hidalgo/135 20.00
Richard Hidalgo/150 20.00
Tim Hudson/50 60.00
Tim Hudson/100 40.00
Reggie Jackson/44 75.00
Nick Johnson/200 30.00
Andruw Jones/75 40.00
Al Kaline/250 60.00
Gabe Kapler/125 25.00
Gabe Kapler/175 25.00
Ryan Klesko/30 40.00
Jason Lane/100 30.00
Barry Larkin/50 60.00
Barry Larkin/100 40.00
Paul LoDuca/50 40.00
Fred Lynn/150 30.00
Fred Lynn/250 30.00
Greg Maddux/31 200.00
Edgar Martinez/150 50.00
Pedro J. Martinez/45 125.00
Don Mattingly/100 140.00
Willie McCovey/190 40.00
Willie McCovey/250 40.00
Wade Miller/52 25.00
Wade Miller/150 25.00
Wade Miller/250 20.00
Paul Molitor/75 50.00
Paul Molitor/100 40.00
Paul Molitor/125 40.00
Mark Mulder/40 35.00
Jose Ortiz/125 15.00
Roy Oswalt/44 40.00
Roy Oswalt/100 40.00
Jim Palmer/150 30.00
Jim Palmer/250 30.00
Dave Parker/150 25.00
Corey Patterson/250 25.00
Carlos Pena/150 15.00
Carlos Pena/150 15.00
Tony Perez/24 40.00
Tony Perez/250 25.00
Juan Pierre/75 25.00
Mark Prior/50 50.00
Mark Prior/75 40.00
Mark Prior/125 40.00
Kirby Puckett/34 125.00
Albert Pujols/100 250.00
Aramis Ramirez/50 50.00
Aramis Ramirez/125 40.00
Phil Rizzuto/10 265.00
Phil Rizzuto/250 70.00
Brooks Robinson/150 70.00
Brooks Robinson/250 60.00
Nolan Ryan/30 200.00
Nolan Ryan/34 200.00
Ryne Sandberg/50 150.00
Mike Schmidt/100 100.00
Richie Sexson/100 30.00
Ben Sheets/100 30.00
Ben Sheets/150 30.00
Alfonso Soriano/100 50.00
Shannon Stewart/100 25.00
Shannon Stewart/150 25.00
Mike Sweeney/100 30.00
So Taguchi/99 15.00
Mark Teixeira/23 65.00
Mark Teixeira/100 60.00
Miguel Tejada/40 60.00
Miguel Tejada/50 60.00
Frank Thomas/35 120.00
Javier Vazquez/125 25.00
Jose Vidro/150 20.00
Kerry Wood/34 75.00
Barry Zito/50 60.00

Team Tandems

NM/M
Complete Set (40): 80.00
Common Card: 1.00
Inserted 1:12
Golds: 2-3X
Inserted 1:72
1 Troy Glaus, Darin Erstad 1.50
2 Curt Schilling, Randy Johnson 3.00
3 Chipper Jones, Andruw Jones 3.00
4 Greg Maddux, Tom Glavine 4.00
5 Nomar Garciaparra, Manny Ramirez 6.00

6 Pedro J. Martinez, Trot Nixon 3.00
7 Kerry Wood, Sammy Sosa 5.00
8 Frank Thomas, Magglio Ordonez 2.00
9 Ken Griffey Jr., Barry Larkin 5.00
10 C.C. Sabathia, Jim Thome 2.50
11 Todd Helton, Larry Walker 2.00
12 Bobby Higginson, Shane Halter 1.00
13 Cliff Floyd, Brad Penny 1.00
14 Jeff Bagwell, Craig Biggio 2.00
15 Shawn Green, Adrian Beltre 1.50
16 Ben Sheets, Richie Sexson 1.50
17 Vladimir Guerrero, Jose Vidro 3.00
18 Mike Piazza, Roberto Alomar 5.00
19 Roger Clemens, Mike Mussina 6.00
20 Derek Jeter, Jason Giambi 8.00
21 Barry Zito, Tim Hudson 1.50
22 Eric Chavez, Miguel Tejada 1.50
23 Pat Burrell, Scott Rolen 3.00
24 Brian Giles, Aramis Ramirez 1.50
25 Ryan Klesko, Phil Nevin 1.50
26 Barry Bonds, Rich Aurilia 8.00
27 Ichiro Suzuki, Kazuhiro Sasaki 5.00
28 Albert Pujols, J.D. Drew 6.00
29 Alex Rodriguez, Ivan Rodriguez 6.00
30 Carlos Delgado, Shannon Stewart 1.50
31 Mo Vaughn, Roger Cedeno 1.00
32 Carlos Beltran, Mike Sweeney 1.50
33 Edgar Martinez, Bret Boone 1.50
34 Juan Gonzalez, Rafael Palmeiro 2.00
35 Johnny Damon, Rickey Henderson 1.50
36 Sean Casey, Adam Dunn 2.00
37 Jeff Kent, Tsuyoshi Shinjo 1.50
38 Lance Berkman, Richard Hidalgo 1.50
39 So Taguchi, Tino Martinez 1.50
40 Hideo Nomo, Kazuhisa Ishii 1.50

Team Tandems G-U

NM/M
Common Card: 5.00
Inserted 1:33
Golds: 2-3X

Production 50

1 Troy Glaus, Darin Erstad 8.00
2 Curt Schilling, Randy Johnson 10.00
3 Chipper Jones, Andruw Jones 10.00
4 Greg Maddux, Tom Glavine 20.00
5 Nomar Garciaparra, Manny Ramirez 25.00
6 Pedro J. Martinez, Trot Nixon 15.00
7 Kerry Wood, Sammy Sosa 15.00
8 Frank Thomas, Magglio Ordonez 10.00
9 Ken Griffey Jr., Barry Larkin 15.00
10 C.C. Sabathia, Jim Thome 15.00
11 Todd Helton, Larry Walker 8.00
12 Bobby Higginson, Shane Halter 8.00
13 Cliff Floyd, Brad Penny 8.00
14 Jeff Bagwell, Craig Biggio 15.00
15 Shawn Green, Adrian Beltre 8.00
16 Ben Sheets, Richie Sexson 8.00
17 Vladimir Guerrero, Jose Vidro 12.00
18 Mike Piazza, Roberto Alomar 15.00
19 Roger Clemens, Mike Mussina 50.00
20 Derek Jeter, Jason Giambi 30.00
21 Barry Zito, Tim Hudson 15.00
22 Eric Chavez, Miguel Tejada 10.00
23 Pat Burrell, Scott Rolen 15.00
24 Brian Giles, Aramis Ramirez 10.00
25 Ryan Klesko, Phil Nevin 8.00
26 Barry Bonds, Rich Aurilia 15.00
27 Ichiro Suzuki, Kazuhiro Sasaki 5.00
28 Albert Pujols, J.D. Drew 15.00
29 Alex Rodriguez, Ivan Rodriguez 15.00
30 Carlos Delgado, Shannon Stewart 8.00
31 Mo Vaughn, Roger Cedeno 5.00
32 Carlos Beltran, Mike Sweeney 8.00
33 Edgar Martinez, Bret Boone 8.00
34 Juan Gonzalez, Rafael Palmeiro 12.00
35 Johnny Damon, Rickey Henderson 10.00
36 Sean Casey, Adam Dunn 15.00
37 Jeff Kent, Tsuyoshi Shinjo 10.00
38 Lance Berkman, Richard Hidalgo 8.00
39 So Taguchi, Tino Martinez 15.00
40 Hideo Nomo, Kazuhisa Ishii 35.00

Team Quads

NM/M
Complete Set (20): 75.00
Common Card: 2.00
Inserted 1:18
Golds: 2X
Inserted 1:72
1 Troy Glaus, Darin Erstad, Garret Anderson, Troy Percival 2.00
2 Curt Schilling, Randy Johnson, Luis Gonzalez, Mark Grace 4.00
3 Chipper Jones, Andruw Jones, Greg Maddux, Tom Glavine 5.00
4 Nomar Garciaparra, Manny Ramirez, Trot Nixon, Pedro J. Martinez 6.00
5 Kerry Wood, Sammy Sosa, Fred McGriff, Moises Alou 6.00
6 Frank Thomas, Magglio Ordonez, Mark Buehrle, Kenny Lofton 3.00
7 Ken Griffey Jr., Barry Larkin, Juan Encarnacion, Sean Casey 6.00
8 C.C. Sabathia, Jim Thome, Bartolo Colon, Russell Branyan 4.00
9 Todd Helton, Larry Walker, Juan Pierre, Mike Hampton 2.50
10 Jeff Bagwell, Craig Biggio, Lance Berkman, Richard Hidalgo 3.00
11 Shawn Green, Adrian Beltre, Hideo Nomo, Paul LoDuca 2.00
12 Mike Piazza, Roberto Alomar, Mo Vaughn, Roger Cedeno 6.00
13 Roger Clemens, Derek Jeter, Jason Giambi, Mike Mussina 10.00
14 Barry Zito, Tim Hudson, Eric Chavez, Miguel Tejada 2.50
15 Pat Burrell, Scott Rolen, Bobby Abreu, Marlon Byrd 4.00
16 Bernie Williams, Jorge Posada, Alfonso Soriano, Andy Pettitte 3.00
17 Barry Bonds, Rich Aurilia, Tsuyoshi Shinjo, Jeff Kent 4.00
18 Ichiro Suzuki, Kazuhiro Sasaki, Bret Boone, Edgar Martinez 6.00
19 Albert Pujols, J.D. Drew, Jim Edmonds, Tino Martinez 8.00
20 Alex Rodriguez, Ivan Rodriguez, Juan Gonzalez, Rafael Palmeiro 8.00

Team Quads Game-Used

NM/M
Numbered to 100
Prime: No Pricing
Production 25
1 Troy Glaus, Darin Erstad, Garret Anderson, Troy Percival 25.00
2 Curt Schilling, Randy Johnson, Luis Gonzalez, Mark Grace 30.00
3 Chipper Jones, Andruw Jones, Greg Maddux, Tom Glavine 40.00
4 Nomar Garciaparra, Manny Ramirez, Trot Nixon, Pedro J. Martinez 50.00
5 Kerry Wood, Sammy Sosa, Fred McGriff, Moises Alou 35.00
6 Frank Thomas, Magglio Ordonez, Mark Buehrle, Kenny Lofton 25.00
8 C.C. Sabathia, Jim Thome, Bartolo Colon, Russell Branyan 40.00
9 Todd Helton, Larry Walker, Juan Pierre, Mike Hampton 30.00
10 Jeff Bagwell, Craig Biggio, Lance Berkman, Richard Hidalgo 30.00
11 Shawn Green, Adrian Beltre, Hideo Nomo, Paul LoDuca 40.00
12 Mike Piazza, Roberto Alomar, Mo Vaughn, Roger Cedeno 40.00
13 Roger Clemens, Derek Jeter, Jason Giambi, Mike Mussina 75.00
14 Barry Zito, Tim Hudson, Eric Chavez, Miguel Tejada 20.00
15 Pat Burrell, Scott Rolen, Bobby Abreu, Marlon Byrd 35.00
16 Bernie Williams, Jorge Posada, Alfonso Soriano, Andy Pettitte 30.00
17 Barry Bonds, Rich Aurilia, Tsuyoshi Shinjo, Jeff Kent 40.00
18 Ichiro Suzuki, Kazuhiro Sasaki, Bret Boone, Edgar Martinez 50.00
19 Albert Pujols, J.D. Drew, Jim Edmonds, Tino Martinez 40.00
20 Alex Rodriguez, Ivan Rodriguez, Juan Gonzalez, Rafael Palmeiro 40.00

Tools of the Trade

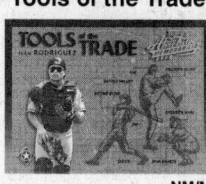

NM/M
Complete Set (95): 120.00
Common Player: 1.00
Inserted 1:9
Golds: 2-3X
Inserted 1:45
1 Mike Mussina 2.00
2 Rickey Henderson 2.00
3 Raul Mondesi 1.00
4 Nomar Garciaparra 6.00
5 Randy Johnson 3.00
6 Roger Clemens 6.00
7 Shawn Green 1.00
8 Todd Helton 2.00
9 Aramis Ramirez 1.50
10 Barry Larkin 1.50
11 Byung-Hyun Kim 1.00
12 C.C. Sabathia 1.00
13 Curt Schilling 2.50
14 Darin Erstad 1.50
15 Eric Karros 1.00
16 Freddy Garcia 1.00
17 Greg Maddux 4.00
18 Jason Kendall 1.00
19 Jim Thome 3.00
20 Juan Gonzalez 2.00
21 Kazuhiro Sasaki 1.00
22 Kerry Wood 3.00
23 Luis Gonzalez 1.50
24 Mark Mulder 1.00
25 Rich Aurilia 1.00
26 Ray Durham 1.00
27 Ben Grieve 1.00
28 Bret Boone 1.00
29 Edgar Martinez 1.00
30 Ivan Rodriguez 2.00
31 Jorge Posada 2.00
32 Mike Piazza 6.00
33 Pat Burrell 1.50
34 Robin Ventura 1.00
35 Trot Nixon 1.00
36 Adrian Beltre 1.50
37 Bernie Williams 1.50
38 Bobby Abreu 1.50
39 Carlos Delgado 1.50
40 Craig Biggio 1.50
41 Garret Anderson 1.50
42 Jermaine Dye 1.00
43 Johnny Damon 1.00
44 Tim Salmon 1.00
45 Tino Martinez 1.00
46 Fred McGriff 1.50
47 Gary Sheffield 1.00
48 Adam Dunn 2.00
49 Joe Mays 1.00
50 Kenny Lofton 1.00
51 Josh Beckett 1.50
52 Bud Smith 1.00
53 Johnny Estrada 1.00
54 Charles Johnson 1.00
55 Craig Wilson 1.00
56 Terrence Long 1.00
57 Andy Pettitte 1.50
58 Brian Giles 1.50
59 Juan Pierre 1.00
60 Cliff Floyd 1.00
61 Ivan Rodriguez 2.00
62 Andruw Jones 1.50
63 Lance Berkman 1.50
64 Mark Buehrle 1.00
65 Miguel Tejada 1.50
66 Wade Miller 1.00
67 Johnny Estrada 1.00
68 Tsuyoshi Shinjo 1.00
69 Scott Rolen 2.50
70 Roberto Alomar 2.00
71 Mark Grace 1.50
72 Larry Walker 1.50
73 Jim Edmonds 1.50
74 Jeff Kent 1.50
75 Frank Thomas 2.50
76 Carlos Beltran 1.50
77 Barry Zito 1.50
78 Alex Rodriguez 8.00
79 Troy Glaus 1.50
80 Ryan Klesko 1.00
81 Tom Glavine 1.50
82 Ben Sheets 1.50
83 Manny Ramirez 2.50
84 Shannon Stewart 1.00
85 Vladimir Guerrero 4.00
86 Chipper Jones 3.00
87 Jeff Bagwell 2.50
88 Richie Sexson 1.50
89 Sean Casey 1.50
90 Tim Hudson 1.50
91 J.D. Drew 1.50
92 Ivan Rodriguez 2.00
93 Magglio Ordonez 1.50
94 John Buck 1.00
95 Paul LoDuca 1.00

Tools of Trade G-U

NM/M
Common Player: 5.00
Jerseys #'d to 300.
Bats #'d to 250.
Shoes #'d to 150.
Shin Guard #'d to 150.
Glove #'d to 125.
Mask #'d to 100.
Hat #'d to 50.
Doubles #'d to 200.
Triples #'d to 75.
Quads #'d to 50.
1 Mike Mussina/Jsy 10.00
2 Rickey Henderson/Jsy 10.00
3 Raul Mondesi/Jsy 8.00
4 Nomar Garciaparra/Jsy 15.00
5 Randy Johnson/Jsy 10.00
6 Roger Clemens/Jsy 15.00
7 Shawn Green/Jsy 8.00
8 Todd Helton/Jsy 8.00
9 Aramis Ramirez/Jsy 8.00
10 Barry Larkin/Jsy 10.00
11 Byung-Hyun Kim/Jsy 5.00
12 C.C. Sabathia/Jsy 5.00
13 Curt Schilling/Jsy 10.00
14 Darin Erstad/Jsy 5.00
15 Eric Karros/Jsy 5.00
16 Freddy Garcia/Jsy 5.00
17 Greg Maddux/Jsy 15.00
18 Jason Kendall/Jsy 5.00
19 Jim Thome/Jsy 10.00
20 Juan Gonzalez/Jsy 8.00
21 Kazuhiro Sasaki/Jsy 5.00
22 Kerry Wood/Jsy 10.00
23 Luis Gonzalez/Jsy 8.00
24 Mark Mulder/Jsy 8.00
25 Rich Aurilia/Jsy 5.00
26 Ray Durham/Jsy 5.00
27 Ben Grieve/Jsy 5.00
28 Bret Boone/Jsy 5.00
29 Edgar Martinez/Jsy 8.00
30 Ivan Rodriguez/Jsy 10.00
31 Jorge Posada/Jsy 10.00
32 Mike Piazza/Jsy 15.00
33 Pat Burrell/Bat 8.00
34 Robin Ventura/Bat 5.00
35 Trot Nixon/Bat 5.00
36 Adrian Beltre/Bat 5.00
37 Bernie Williams/Bat 10.00
38 Bobby Abreu/Bat 8.00
39 Carlos Delgado/Bat 8.00
40 Craig Biggio/Bat 8.00
41 Garret Anderson/Bat 8.00
42 Jermaine Dye/Bat 5.00
43 Johnny Damon/Bat 8.00
44 Tim Salmon/Bat 8.00
45 Tino Martinez/Bat 10.00
46 Fred McGriff/Bat 8.00
47 Gary Sheffield/Bat 8.00
48 Adam Dunn/Shoe 15.00
49 Joe Mays/Shoe 8.00
50 Kenny Lofton/Shoe 10.00
51 Josh Beckett/Shoe 10.00
52 Bud Smith/Shoe 5.00
53 Johnny Estrada/Shin 10.00
54 Charles Johnson/Shin 8.00
55 Craig Wilson/Shin 15.00
56 Terrence Long/Glv 8.00
57 Andy Pettitte/Glv 15.00
58 Brian Giles/Glv 10.00
59 Juan Pierre/Glv 10.00
60 Cliff Floyd/Glv 10.00
61 Ivan Rodriguez/Glv 15.00
62 Andruw Jones/Hat 15.00
63 Lance Berkman/Hat 15.00
64 Mark Buehrle/Hat 15.00
65 Miguel Tejada/Hat 15.00
66 Wade Miller/Hat 10.00
67 Johnny Estrada/Shin 15.00
68 T. Shinjo/Bat/Shoe 15.00
69 S. Nolen/Bat/Jsy 20.00
70 R. Alomar/Bat/Shoe 20.00
71 M. Grace/Jsy/Glv 15.00
72 L. Walker/Jsy/Bat 15.00
73 J. Edmonds/Jsy/Bat 15.00
74 J. Kent/Jsy/Bat 15.00
75 F. Thomas/Jsy/Bat 15.00
76 C. Beltran/Jsy/Bat 10.00

77	B. Zito/Shoe/Jsy	15.00
78	A. Rodriguez/Jsy/Bat	25.00
79	T. Glaus/Dualjsy	15.00
80	R. Klesko/Bat/Glv	10.00
81	T. Glavine/Jsy/Shoe	20.00
82	B. Sheets/Bat/Jsy	10.00
83	M. Ramirez/Shoe/ Glv/Jsy	25.00
84	S. Stewart/Hat/ Jsy/Bat	15.00
85	V. Guerrero/Glv/ Bat/Jsy	45.00
86	C. Jones/Glv/Bat/Jsy	40.00
87	J. Bagwell/Jsy/ Hat/Bat	40.00
88	R. Sexson/Bat/Jsy/ Glv/Shoe	40.00
89	S. Casey/Jsy/Hat/ Shoe/Bat	30.00
90	T Hudson/Shoe/Hat/ Glv/Jsy	30.00
91	JD Drew/Shoe/Jsy/ Hat/Bat	40.00
92	I Rodriguez/Jsy/ Mask/Chst/Glv	60.00
93	M Ordonez/Hat/ Glv/Jsy/Shoe	40.00
94	J Buck/Glv/Chst/ Shin/Msk	20.00
95	P LoDuca/Jsy/ Chst/Shin/Msk	30.00

2002 Playoff Piece of the Game

NM/M

Complete Set (100):
Common Player: .50
Common SP (51-100): 5.00
Production 500
Pack (5): 15.00
Box (6): 75.00

1	Vladimir Guerrero	1.50
2	Troy Glaus	1.50
3	Ichiro Suzuki	2.50
4	Chipper Jones	2.00
5	Roberto Alomar	.75
6	Scott Rolen	1.25
7	Randy Johnson	1.50
8	Roger Clemens	2.25
9	Nomar Garciaparra	2.50
10	Greg Maddux	2.50
11	Barry Bonds	4.00
12	Derek Jeter	4.00
13	Albert Pujols	3.00
14	Kerry Wood	1.25
15	Jim Thome	1.50
16	Manny Ramirez	1.50
17	Carlos Delgado	.75
18	Magglio Ordonez	.50
19	Torii Hunter	.50
20	Garret Anderson	.50
21	Eric Chavez	.60
22	Rafael Palmeiro	1.25
23	Andruw Jones	1.50
24	Cliff Floyd	.50
25	Sammy Sosa	2.50
26	Mike Mussina	1.50
27	Jeff Bagwell	1.50
28	Miguel Tejada	.60
29	Curt Schilling	1.00
30	Tom Glavine	.75
31	Frank Thomas	1.50
32	Jim Edmonds	.50
33	Juan Gonzalez	1.50
34	Todd Helton	1.50
35	Shawn Green	.75
36	Alfonso Soriano	1.25
37	Lance Berkman	.50
38	Barry Zito	.60
39	Ryan Klesko	.50
40	Larry Walker	.50
41	Craig Biggio	.50
42	Luis Gonzalez	.50
43	Ivan Rodriguez	1.25
44	J.D. Drew	.75
45	Roy Oswalt	.50
46	Jason Giambi	1.25
47	Brian Giles	.50
48	Richie Sexson	.50
49	Pat Burrell	.75
50	Alex Rodriguez	3.00
51	So Taguchi RC	8.00
52	Allan Simpson RC	5.00
53	Oliver Perez RC	10.00
54	Ben Howard RC	5.00
55	Kirk Saarloos RC	5.00
56	Francis Beltran RC	5.00
57	Jorge Padilla RC	5.00
58	Brandon Puffer RC	5.00
59	Brian Mallette RC	5.00
60	Kyle Kane RC	5.00
61	Travis Driskill RC	5.00
62	Jeremy Lambert RC	5.00
63	Steve Kent RC	5.00
64	Julius Matos RC	5.00
65	Julio Mateo RC	5.00
66	Kazuhisa Ishii RC	8.00
67	Franklyn German RC	5.00
68	John Foster RC	5.00
69	Luis Ugueto RC	5.00
70	Shawn Sedlacek RC	5.00
71	Earl Snyder RC	5.00
72	Alex Pelaez RC	5.00
73	Victor Alvarez RC	5.00
74	Tom Shearn RC	5.00
75	Corey Thurman RC	5.00
76	Eric Junge RC	5.00
77	Hansel Izquierdo RC	5.00
78	Elio Serrano RC	5.00
79	J.J. Trujillo RC	5.00
80	Chris Snelling RC	6.00
81	Satoru Komiyama RC	5.00
82	Brandon Backe RC	5.00
83	Anderson Machado RC	5.00
84	Doug DeVore RC	5.00
85	Steve Bechler RC	5.00
86	John Ennis RC	5.00
87	Rodrigo Rosario RC	5.00
88	Jorge Sosa RC	5.00
89	Ken Huckaby RC	5.00
90	Mike Moriarty RC	5.00
91	Michael Crudale RC	5.00
92	Kevin Frederick RC	5.00
93	Aaron Guiel RC	5.00
94	Jose Rodriguez RC	5.00
95	Andy Shibilo RC	5.00
96	Deivis Santos RC	5.00
97	Felix Escalona RC	5.00
98	Miguel Asencio RC	5.00
99	Takahito Nomura RC	5.00
100	Cam Esslinger RC	5.00

Piece of the Game Materials

NM/M

Common Materials (1-90): 4.00
Team Connections (91-95):
Superstar Combos (96-100):
Production 500
Bronze Materials (1-90): 1-2X
Production 250
Bronze Team Connect.
(91-95): 1.5-2X
Production 100
Bronze Combos (96-100): 2-3X
Production 50
Silver Materials (1-90): 1.5-2.5X
Production 150
Silver Tm. Connect.
(91-95): 1.5-3X
Production 50
Silver Combos (96-100): No Pricing
Production 25
Gold Materials (1-90): 2-5X
Production 50
Gold Tm. Connect.
(91-95): No Pricing
Production 25
Gold Combos (96-100):No Pricing
Production 10
Platinum Materials
(1-90): No Pricing
Production 25
Platinum Tm Connect.
(91-95): No Pricing
Production 10
Platinum Combos
(96-100): No Pricing
Production 5

1	Adam Dunn/Bat	8.00
2	Adrian Beltre/Bat	4.00
3	Albert Pujols/Base	10.00
4	Alex Rodriguez/Jsy	12.00
5	Alex Rodriguez/Jsy	12.00
6	Andruw Jones/Jsy	5.00
7	Andruw Jones/Bat	5.00
8	Barry Bonds/Base	15.00
9	Barry Larkin/Bat	5.00
10	Juan Gonzalez/Jsy	5.00
11	Bernie Williams/Bat	5.00
12	Carlos Delgado/Jsy	5.00
13	Chipper Jones/Jsy	10.00
14	Chipper Jones/Bat	10.00
15	Craig Biggio/Jsy	5.00
16	Craig Biggio/Bat	5.00
17	Cristian Guzman/Jsy	5.00
18	Curt Schilling/Jsy	5.00
19	Derek Jeter/Base	15.00
20	Edgar Martinez/Jsy	4.00
21	Edgardo Alfonzo/Jsy	4.00
22	Ellis Burks/Jsy	4.00
23	Frank Thomas/Bat	6.00
24	Freddy Garcia/Jsy	4.00
25	Greg Maddux/Jsy	10.00
26	Harmon Killebrew/ Pants	15.00
27	Hideo Nomo/Jsy	12.00
28	Ichiro Suzuki/Base	15.00
29	Ivan Rodriguez/Jsy	8.00
30	Ivan Rodriguez/Bat	8.00
31	J.D. Drew/Bat	6.00
32	J.D. Drew/Jsy	6.00
33	Javy Lopez/Jsy	6.00
34	Jeff Bagwell/Jsy	6.00
35	Jim Edmonds/Jsy	6.00
36	Jim Edmonds/Bat	6.00
37	John Olerud/Bat	4.00
38	John Smoltz/Jsy	6.00
39	Jose Cruz Jr/Jsy	4.00
40	Jose Vidro/Jsy	4.00
41	Juan Gonzalez/Bat	6.00
42	Juan Pierre/Jsy	6.00
43	Ken Griffey Jr./Base	10.00
44	Kenny Lofton/Bat	4.00
45	Kerry Wood/Bat	5.00
46	Kevin Brown/Jsy	4.00
47	Lance Berkman/Jsy	6.00
48	Lance Berkman/Bat	6.00
49	Larry Walker/Jsy	5.00
50	Luis Gonzalez/Jsy	5.00
51	Magglio Ordonez/Jsy	5.00
52	Magglio Ordonez/Bat	5.00
53	Manny Ramirez/Jsy	8.00
54	Manny Ramirez/Bat	8.00
55	Vladimir Guerrero/Jsy	8.00
56	Mark Grace/Bat	5.00
57	Michael Barrett/Jsy	4.00
58	Miguel Tejada/Jsy	8.00
59	Mike Piazza/Jsy	12.00
60	Mike Piazza/Bat	12.00
61	Mike Schmidt/Bat	15.00
62	Mike Sweeney/Jsy	4.00
63	Nolan Ryan/Jsy	30.00
64	Nomar Garciaparra/ Jsy	15.00
65	Paul LoDuca/Jsy	4.00
66	Rafael Palmeiro/Jsy	8.00
67	Rafael Palmeiro/Jsy	8.00
68	Jose Canseco/Bat	8.00
69	Raul Mondesi/Jsy	4.00
70	Reggie Jackson/Bat	8.00
71	Rickey Henderson/Bat	8.00
72	Roberto Alomar/Bat	6.00
73	Robin Ventura/Jsy	4.00
74	Rod Carew/Bat	10.00
75	Roger Clemens/Jsy	15.00
76	Sammy Sosa/Base	10.00
77	Sean Casey/Jsy	4.00
78	Shannon Stewart/Jsy	4.00
79	Shawn Green/Jsy	6.00
80	Shawn Green/Bat	6.00
81	Tim Hudson/Jsy	6.00
82	Todd Helton/Bat	6.00
83	Tom Glavine/Jsy	6.00
84	Tony Gwynn/Jsy	10.00
85	Tony Gwynn/Jsy	10.00
86	Tony Gwynn/Bat	10.00
87	Troy Glaus/Bat	6.00
88	Tsuyoshi Shinjo/Bat	4.00
89	Vladimir Guerrero/Jsy	8.00
90	Vladimir Guerrero/Bat	8.00
91	Nomar Garciaparra, Pedro J. Martinez	30.00
92	Randy Johnson, Curt Schilling	15.00
93	Andruw Jones, Chipper Jones	15.00
94	Todd Helton, Larry Walker	15.00
95	Jeff Bagwell, Craig Biggio	15.00
96	Alex Rodriguez	25.00
97	Greg Maddux	25.00
98	Mike Piazza	25.00
99	Lance Berkman	15.00
100	Vladimir Guerrero	20.00

LCS Programs

A perforated sheet of Piece of the Game cards was inserted into some of the programs sold for the American and National League Championship Series. The 8-1/2" x 11" sheet features eight player cards and a header card advertising the brand. Each 3-1/2" x 2-1/2" card is perforated on all sides and differs from the regularly issued version only in the card number on back. Sheet cards have either an "ALCS-" or "NLCS-" prefix to the number. Other programs could be found with similar sheets of Donruss Originals, Donruss Studio or Donruss Diamond Kings cards.

NM/M

Complete Sheet Set (2): 14.00
Common Player:

	ALCS SHEET	7.00
17	Jim Thome	1.00
18	Garret Anderson	.50
19	Alfonso Soriano	1.00
20	Nomar Garciaparra	2.50
21	Eric Chavez	.60
22	Magglio Ordonez	.50
23	Roger Clemens	2.25
24	Torii Hunter	.50
---	Header Card	.10
	NLCS SHEET	7.00
9	Jeff Bagwell	1.50
10	Shawn Green	.75
11	Vladimir Guerrero	1.50
12	Greg Maddux	2.00
13	Luis Gonzalez	.50
14	Todd Helton	1.50
15	Richie Sexson	.50
16	Chipper Jones	2.00
---	Header Card	.10

2003 Playoff Absolute Memorabilia

NM/M

Complete Set (200):
Common Player: .50
Common SP (151-200): 3.00
Production 1,500
Pack (6): 3.00
Box (18 + Glass Plaque): 85.00

1	Nomar Garciaparra	2.50
2	Barry Bonds	4.00
3	Greg Maddux	2.00
4	Roger Clemens	3.00
5	Derek Jeter	4.00
6	Alex Rodriguez	3.00
7	Chipper Jones	2.00
8	Sammy Sosa	2.50
9	Alfonso Soriano	1.00
10	Albert Pujols	3.00
11	Adam Dunn	1.00
12	Tom Glavine	.75
13	Pedro J. Martinez	1.50
14	Jim Thome	1.00
15	Hideo Nomo	1.50
16	Roberto Alomar	.75
17	Barry Zito	.65
18	Troy Glaus	1.50
19	Kerry Wood	1.00
20	Magglio Ordonez	.50
21	Todd Helton	1.50
22	Craig Biggio	.75
23	Roy Oswalt	.50
24	Torii Hunter	.50
25	Miguel Tejada	.65
26	Tsuyoshi Shinjo	.50
27	Scott Rolen	1.00
28	Rafael Palmeiro	1.00
29	Victor Martinez	.75
30	Hank Blalock	.75
31	Jason Lane	.50
32	Junior Spivey	.50
33	Gary Sheffield	.75
34	Corey Patterson	.50
35	Corky Miller	.50
36	Brian Tallet	.50
37	Cliff Lee	.50
38	Jason Jennings	.50
39	Kirk Saarloos	.50
40	Wade Miller	.50
41	Angel Berroa	.50
42	Mike Sweeney	.50
43	Paul LoDuca	.50
44	A.J. Pierzynski	.50
45	Drew Henson	.50
46	Eric Chavez	.65
47	Tim Hudson	.75
48	Aramis Ramirez	.50
49	Jack Wilson	.50
50	Ryan Klesko	.50
51	Antonio Perez	.50
52	Dewon Brazelton	.50
53	Mark Teixeira	.50
54	Eric Hinske	.50
55	Freddy Sanchez	.50
56	Mike Rivera	.50
57	Alfredo Amezaga	.50
58	Cliff Floyd	.50
59	Brandon Larson	.50
60	Richard Hidalgo	.50
61	Cesar Izturis	.50
62	Richie Sexson	.50
63	Michael Cuddyer	.50
64	Javier Vazquez	.50
65	Brandon Claussen	.50
66	Carlos Rivera	.50
67	Vernon Wells	.50
68	Kenny Lofton	.50
69	Aubrey Huff	.50
70	Adam LaRoche	.50
71	Jeff Baker	.50
72	Jose Castillo	.50
73	Joe Borchard	.50
74	Walter Young	.50
75	Jose Morban	.50
76	Vinnie Chulk	.50
77	Christian Parker	.50
78	Mike Piazza	2.50
79	Ichiro Suzuki	2.50
80	Kazuhisa Ishii	.50
81	Rickey Henderson	1.50
82	Ken Griffey Jr.	2.50
83	Jason Giambi	.75
84	Randy Johnson	1.50
85	Curt Schilling	.75
86	Manny Ramirez	1.50
87	Barry Larkin	.50
88	Jeff Bagwell	1.50
89	Vladimir Guerrero	1.50
90	Mike Mussina	.65
91	Juan Gonzalez	1.50
92	Andruw Jones	1.50
93	Frank Thomas	1.50
94	Sean Casey	.50
95	Josh Beckett	.50
96	Lance Berkman	.50
97	Shawn Green	.75
98	Bernie Williams	.65
99	Pat Burrell	.75
100	Edgar Martinez	.50
101	Ivan Rodriguez	1.00
102	Jeremy Guthrie	.50
103	Alexis Rios	.50
104	Nic Jackson	.50
105	Jason Anderson	.50
106	Travis Chapman	.50
107	Mac Suzuki	.50
108	Toby Hall	.50
109	Mark Prior	1.50
110	So Taguchi	.50
111	Marlon Byrd	.50
112	Garret Anderson	.50
113	Luis Gonzalez	.50
114	Jay Gibbons	.50
115	Mark Buehrle	.50
116	Wily Mo Pena	.50
117	C.C. Sabathia	.50
118	Ricardo Rodriguez	.50
119	Robert Fick	.50
120	Rodrigo Rosario	.50
121	Alexis Gomez	.50
122	Carlos Beltran	1.00
123	Joe Thurston	.50
124	Ben Sheets	.50
125	Jose Vidro	.50
126	Nick Johnson	.50
127	Mark Mulder	.50
128	Bobby Abreu	.50
129	Brian Giles	.50
130	Brian Lawrence	.50
131	Jeff Kent	.50
132	Chris Snelling	.50
133	Kevin Mench	.50
134	Carlos Delgado	.75
135	Orlando Hudson	.50
136	Juan Cruz	.50
137	Jim Edmonds	.50
138	Geronimo Gil	.50
139	Joe Crede	.50
140	Wilson Valdez	.50
141	Runelvys Hernandez	.50
142	Nick Neugebauer	.50
143	Takahito Nomura	.50
144	Andres Galarraga	.50
145	Mark Grace	.65
146	Brandon Duckworth	.50
147	Oliver Perez	.50
148	Xavier Nady	.50
149	Rafael Soriano	.50
150	Ben Kozlowski	.50
151	Prentice Redman RC	3.00
152	Craig Brazell RC	5.00
153	Nook Logan RC	4.00
154	Greg Aquino RC	5.00
155	Matt Kata RC	5.00
156	Ian Ferguson RC	3.00
157	Chien-Ming Wang RC	30.00
158	Beau Kemp RC	3.00
159	Alejandro Machado RC	3.00
160	Michael Hessman RC	3.00
161	Francisco Rosario RC	4.00
162	Pedro Liriano RC	3.00
163	Richard Fischer RC	3.00
164	Franklin Perez RC	3.00
165	Oscar Villarreal RC	3.00
166	Arnie Munoz RC	3.00
167	Tim Olson RC	3.00
168	Jose Contreras RC	5.00
169	Francisco Cruceta RC	3.00
170	Jeremy Bonderman RC	10.00
171	Jeremy Griffiths RC	3.00
172	John Webb RC	3.00
173	Phil Seibel RC	3.00
174	Aaron Looper RC	3.00
175	Brian Stokes RC	3.00
176	Guillermo Quiroz RC	4.00
177	Fernando Cabrera RC	3.00
178	Josh Hall RC	3.00
179	Diegomar Markwell RC	3.00
180	Andrew Brown RC	4.00
181	Doug Waechter RC	4.00
182	Felix Sanchez RC	3.00
183	Gerardo Garcia RC	3.00
184	Matt Bruback RC	3.00
185	Michel Hernandez RC	3.00
186	Rett Johnson RC	3.00
187	Ryan Cameron RC	3.00
188	Rob Hammock RC	4.00
189	Clint Barmes RC	10.00
190	Brandon Webb RC	10.00
191	Jon Leicester RC	3.00
192	Shane Bazzell RC	3.00
193	Joe Valentine RC	3.00
194	Josh Stewart RC	3.00
195	Pete LaForest RC	3.00
196	Shane Victorino RC	4.00
197	Terrmel Sledge RC	3.00
198	Lew Ford RC	5.00
199	Todd Wellemeyer RC	4.00
200	Hideki Matsui RC	10.00

Spectrum

Stars (1-150): 3-5X
Rookies (151-200): .75-2X
Production 100 Sets

Absolutely Ink

NM/M

Inserted 1:552
Blues: No Pricing
Production 10-25
Golds: No Pricing
Production 5-10

1	Vladimir Guerrero	50.00
6	Eric Hinske	15.00
8	Jose Vidro	8.00
16	Rodrigo Rosario	8.00
17	Brandon Claussen	20.00
18	Jermaine Dye	8.00
22	Mark Prior	50.00
24	Brian Lawrence	8.00
29	Barry Larkin	50.00
30	Drew Henson	40.00
36	Mark Teixeira	30.00
38	Roberto Alomar	30.00
39	Barry Zito	35.00

Glass Plaques

NM/M

One Per Box:

Roberto Alomar/ Bat/Jsy/100	40.00
Roberto Alomar/ Jsy/100	30.00
Jeff Bagwell/Bat/ Jsy/100	40.00
Jeff Bagwell/Jsy/150	30.00
Ernie Banks/Jsy/150	40.00
Lance Berkman/ Bat/Jsy/100	35.00
Lance Berkman/ Jsy/150	25.00
Barry Bonds/Ball/ Base/50	85.00
Barry Bonds/Ball/ Base/100	75.00
Barry Bonds/ Base/200	50.00
George Brett/Bat/ Jsy/50	125.00
George Brett/Jsy/200	50.00
Pat Burrell/Bat/ Jsy/100	35.00
Pat Burrell/Jsy/150	30.00
Steve Carlton/ Auto./50	60.00
Steve Carlton/ Bat/Jsy/100	40.00
Steve Carlton/ Jsy/150	30.00
Roger Clemens/ Glv/Jsy/50	150.00
Roger Clemens/ Jsy/150	60.00
Roger Clemens/ Glv/Jsy/60	150.00
Roger Clemens/ Jsy/200	60.00
Roberto Clemente/ Bat/Jsy/150	80.00
Roberto Clemente/ Jsy/200	60.00
Jose Contreras/ Jsy/Jsy/100	30.00
Jose Contreras/ Jsy/150	25.00
Adam Dunn/Bat/ Jsy/100	40.00
Adam Dunn/Jsy/150	30.00
Bob Feller/Auto./50	65.00
Bob Feller/Jsy/ Jsy/100	50.00
Bob Feller/Jsy/100	30.00
Nomar Garciaparra/ Bat/Jsy/100	65.00
Nomar Garciaparra/ Jsy/200	55.00
Jason Giambi/Bat/ Jsy/100	50.00
Jason Giambi/ Jsy/150	40.00

Troy Glaus/Bat/Jsy/100	40.00	
Troy Glaus/Jsy/150	35.00	
Juan Gonzalez/Bat/Jsy/100	40.00	
Juan Gonzalez/Jsy/150	30.00	
Luis Gonzalez/Bat/Jsy/100	30.00	
Luis Gonzalez/Jsy/150	25.00	
Mark Grace/Auto./50	100.00	
Mark Grace/Bat/Jsy/100	45.00	
Mark Grace/Jsy/150	35.00	
Shawn Green/Bat/Jsy/100	30.00	
Shawn Green/Jsy/150	25.00	
Ken Griffey Jr./Ball/Base/100	50.00	
Ken Griffey Jr./Base/200	40.00	
Vladimir Guerrero/Bat/Jsy/100	40.00	
Vladimir Guerrero/Jsy/150	35.00	
Tony Gwynn/Bat/Jsy/150	50.00	
Tony Gwynn/Jsy/200	40.00	
Todd Helton/Bat/Jsy/150	40.00	
Todd Helton/Jsy/150	30.00	
Rickey Henderson/Bat/Jsy/100	50.00	
Rickey Henderson/Jsy/200	40.00	
Tim Hudson/Auto./50	65.00	
Tim Hudson/Hat/Jsy/100	30.00	
Tim Hudson/Jsy/150	25.00	
Torii Hunter/Auto./50	65.00	
Torii Hunter/Hat/Jsy/100	40.00	
Torii Hunter/Jsy/150	30.00	
Kazuhisa Ishii/Bat/Jsy/100	30.00	
Kazuhisa Ishii/Jsy/200	25.00	
Derek Jeter/Ball/Base/150	60.00	
Derek Jeter/Base/200	50.00	
Randy Johnson/Bat/Jsy/100	50.00	
Randy Johnson/Jsy/150	40.00	
Andruw Jones/Bat/Jsy/100	35.00	
Andruw Jones/Jsy/150	30.00	
Chipper Jones/Bat/Jsy/100	40.00	
Chipper Jones/Jsy/150	30.00	
Al Kaline/Bat/Jsy/100	40.00	
Al Kaline/Jsy/150	35.00	
Barry Larkin/Auto./50	60.00	
Barry Larkin/Bat/Jsy/100	40.00	
Barry Larkin/Jsy/150	30.00	
Greg Maddux/Bat/Jsy/100	50.00	
Greg Maddux/Jsy/200	40.00	
Pedro Martinez/Bat/Jsy/100	40.00	
Pedro Martinez/Jsy/150	35.00	
Hideki Matsui/Ball/Base/50	110.00	
Hideki Matsui/Base/150	75.00	
Hideki Matsui/Base/200	55.00	
Don Mattingly/Bat/Jsy/100	65.00	
Don Mattingly/Jsy/200	50.00	
Mark Mulder/Auto./50	60.00	
Mark Mulder/Jsy/150	25.00	
Mark Mulder/Jsy/150	30.00	
Stan Musial/Bat/Jsy/150	65.00	
Stan Musial/Jsy/200	60.00	
Hideo Nomo/Bat/Jsy/50	60.00	
Hideo Nomo/Bat/Jsy/100	40.00	
Hideo Nomo/Jsy/200	30.00	
Magglio Ordonez/Auto./50	50.00	
Magglio Ordonez/Bat/Jsy/100	30.00	
Magglio Ordonez/Jsy/150	25.00	
Roy Oswalt/Auto./50	50.00	
Roy Oswalt/Bat/Jsy/100	30.00	
Roy Oswalt/Jsy/150	25.00	
Rafael Palmeiro/Bat/Jsy/100	40.00	

Rafael Palmeiro/Jsy/100	30.00	
Mike Piazza/Bat/Jsy/50	75.00	
Mike Piazza/Bat/Jsy/100	50.00	
Mike Piazza/Jsy/200	40.00	
Mark Prior/Bat/Jsy/100	60.00	
Mark Prior/Jsy/150	40.00	
Albert Pujols/Bat/Jsy/150	75.00	
Albert Pujols/Jsy/150	60.00	
Manny Ramirez/Bat/Jsy/100	40.00	
Manny Ramirez/Jsy/150	30.00	
Cal Ripken Jr./Bat/Jsy/150	90.00	
Cal Ripken Jr/Jsy/200	70.00	
Frank Robinson/Auto./50	65.00	
Frank Robinson/Bat/Jsy/100	40.00	
Frank Robinson/Jsy/150	30.00	
Alex Rodriguez/Bat/Jsy/100	50.00	
Alex Rodriguez/Jsy/200	40.00	
Nolan Ryan/Jkt/Jsy/150	90.00	
Nolan Ryan/Jsy/200	75.00	
Nolan Ryan/Jsy/Jsy/100	100.00	
Ryne Sandberg/Bat/Jsy/50	100.00	
Ryne Sandberg/Jsy/200	65.00	
Curt Schilling/Glv/Jsy/50	50.00	
Curt Schilling/Jsy/150	30.00	
Mike Schmidt/Bat/Jsy/100	70.00	
Mike Schmidt/Jsy/200	50.00	
Ozzie Smith/Bat/Jsy/150	65.00	
Ozzie Smith/Jsy/150	50.00	
Alfonso Soriano/Bat/Jsy/150	60.00	
Alfonso Soriano/Jsy/150	50.00	
Sammy Sosa/Bat/Jsy/150	50.00	
Sammy Sosa/Jsy/200	40.00	
Junior Spivey/Auto./50	50.00	
Junior Spivey/Bat/Jsy/100	30.00	
Junior Spivey/Jsy/150	25.00	
Ichiro Suzuki/Ball/Base/50	80.00	
Ichiro Suzuki/Ball/Base/150	60.00	
Ichiro Suzuki/Base/200	40.00	
Mark Teixeira/Bat/Jsy/100	40.00	
Mark Teixeira/Jsy/150	30.00	
Miguel Tejada/Auto./50	60.00	
Miguel Tejada/Bat/Jsy/100	40.00	
Miguel Tejada/Jsy/150	30.00	
Frank Thomas/Bat/Jsy/100	40.00	
Frank Thomas/Jsy/150	30.00	
Bernie Williams/Bat/Jsy/100	40.00	
Bernie Williams/Jsy/150	35.00	
Kerry Wood/Auto./50	80.00	
Kerry Wood/Bat/Jsy/100	45.00	
Kerry Wood/Jsy/150	35.00	
Barry Zito/Auto./50	75.00	
Barry Zito/Hat/Jsy/100		
Barry Zito/Jsy/100	45.00	
Barry Zito/Jsy/150	30.00	

Player's Collection - Bat

		NM/M
Common Player:		4.00
Production 75 Sets		
81	Alex Rodriguez	15.00
82	Alfonso Soriano	12.00
83	Barry Larkin	8.00
84	Roberto Alomar	8.00
85	Ivan Rodriguez	8.00
86	Jason Giambi	8.00
87	Jeff Bagwell	8.00
88	Juan Gonzalez	8.00
89	Larry Walker	4.00
90	Luis Gonzalez	4.00
91	Magglio Ordonez	4.00
92	Manny Ramirez	8.00
93	Marlon Byrd	4.00

94	Mike Piazza	12.00
95	Pat Burrell	8.00
96	Todd Helton	8.00
97	Rickey Henderson	8.00
98	Andruw Jones	8.00
99	Craig Biggio	4.00
100	Mark Prior	10.00

Player's Collection - Jersey

		NM/M
Common Player:		4.00
Production 75 Sets		
1	Adam Dunn	6.00
2	Adrian Beltre	4.00
3	Alex Rodriguez	15.00
4	Alfonso Soriano	12.00
5	Andruw Jones	8.00
6	Andy Pettitte	4.00
7	Barry Larkin	6.00
8	Barry Zito	6.00
9	Ben Grieve	4.00
10	Bernie Williams	6.00
11	Cal Ripken Jr.	40.00
12	Carlos Delgado	6.00
13	C.C. Sabathia	4.00
14	Chipper Jones	10.00
15	Craig Biggio	4.00
16	Curt Schilling	6.00
17	Alex Rodriguez	15.00
18	Frank Thomas	8.00
19	Freddy Garcia	4.00
20	Jay Bell	4.00
21	Roger Clemens	15.00
22	Tony Gwynn	10.00
23	Ivan Rodriguez	8.00
24	Jason Giambi	8.00
25	Jason Jennings	4.00
26	Jay Payton	4.00
27	J.D. Drew	5.00
28	Jeff Bagwell	8.00
29	Jeromy Burnitz	4.00
30	Jim Edmonds	6.00
31	Jim Thome	8.00
32	Joe Borchard	4.00
33	Joe Mays	4.00
34	John Olerud	5.00
35	David Wells	4.00
36	Juan Gonzalez	8.00
37	Kazuhiro Sasaki	4.00
38	Chan Ho Park	4.00
39	Kerry Wood	10.00
40	Kevin Brown	4.00
41	Lance Berkman	6.00
42	Larry Walker	4.00
43	Bret Boone	6.00
44	Magglio Ordonez	6.00
45	Manny Ramirez	8.00
46	Mark Mulder	6.00
47	Mark Prior	10.00
48	Matt Williams	6.00
49	Miguel Tejada	5.00
50	Mike Piazza	12.00
51	Nomar Garciaparra	15.00
52	Doug Davis	4.00
53	Paul Konerko	4.00
54	Paul LoDuca	4.00
55	Pedro J. Martinez	10.00
56	Preston Wilson	4.00
57		4.00
58	Marlon Byrd	4.00
59	Reggie Sanders	4.00
60	Richie Sexson	6.00
61		4.00
62	Rickey Henderson	8.00
63	Robert Person	4.00
64		4.00
65	Roger Clemens	15.00
66	Roy Oswalt	4.00
67	Ryan Klesko	4.00
68	Sammy Sosa	15.00
69	Shawn Green	6.00
70	Steve Finley	4.00
71	Terrence Long	4.00
72	Tim Hudson	6.00
73	Toby Hall	4.00
74	Todd Helton	8.00
75	Travis Lee	4.00
76	Troy Glaus	8.00
77	Tsuyoshi Shinjo	4.00
78	Vernon Wells	6.00
79	Vladimir Guerrero	8.00
80	Wes Helms	4.00

Rookie Materials Jersey Number

		NM/M
Many not priced due to scarcity.		
2	Yogi Berra/35	40.00
3	Vladimir Guerrero/27	15.00
4	Randy Johnson/51	25.00
8	Andruw Jones/25	10.00
10	Alfonso Soriano/33	35.00
13	Rafael Palmeiro/25	20.00

Rookie Materials Season

		NM/M
Common Player:		5.00
Quantity produced listed		
1	Stan Musial/42	75.00
2	Yogi Berra/47	40.00
3	Vladimir Guerrero/97	15.00
4	Randy Johnson/89	25.00
5	Andruw Jones/96	10.00
6	Jeff Kent/92	5.00
8	Hideo Nomo/95	20.00
9	Ivan Rodriguez/91	10.00
10	Alfonso Soriano/101	20.00
11	Scott Rolen/96	5.00
12	Juan Gonzalez/89	15.00
13	Rafael Palmeiro/86	15.00
14	Mike Schmidt/73	60.00
15	Cal Ripken Jr./82	75.00

Signing Bonus

Production 15 Sets
No Pricing

Spectrum Signatures

		NM/M
Common Autograph:		6.00
Varying quantities produced		
10	Albert Pujols/10	275.00
16	Roberto Alomar/15	100.00
17	Barry Zito/25	
20	Magglio Ordonez/25	50.00
23	Roy Oswalt/25	30.00
24	Torii Hunter/25	40.00
29	Victor Martinez/100	30.00
30	Hank Blalock/50	15.00
32	Junior Spivey/50	15.00
34	Corey Patterson/50	20.00
35	Corky Miller/100	6.00
36	Brian Tallet/100	6.00
37	Cliff Lee/100	8.00
38	Jason Jennings/100	8.00
39	Kirk Saarloos/100	6.00
40	Wade Miller/50	15.00
41	Angel Berroa/100	8.00
42	Mike Sweeney/50	15.00
43	Paul LoDuca/50	15.00
44	A.J. Pierzynski/100	15.00
45	Drew Henson/50	25.00
47	Tim Hudson/50	15.00
51	Antonio Perez/25	15.00
52	Dewon Brazelton/50	15.00
53	Mark Teixeira/50	40.00
54	Eric Hinske/100	15.00
55	Freddy Sanchez/100	15.00
57	Alfredo Amezaga/100	10.00
59	Brandon Larson/100	8.00
60	Richard Hidalgo/100	8.00
62	Richie Sexson/25	30.00
63	Michael Cuddyer/100	15.00
68	Kenny Lofton/100	15.00
69	Aubrey Huff/100	15.00
70	Adam LaRoche/100	15.00
71	Jeff Baker/100	10.00
72	Jose Castillo/100	10.00
73	Joe Borchard/100	10.00
74	Walter Young/100	8.00
76	Vinnie Chulk/100	8.00
80	Kazuhisa Ishii/25	60.00
87	Barry Larkin/50	50.00
89	Vladimir Guerrero/50	50.00
92	Andruw Jones/25	60.00

95	Josh Beckett/100	25.00
100	Edgar Martinez/100	15.00
102	Jeremy Guthrie/100	15.00
103	Alexis Rios/100	20.00
104	Nic Jackson/100	8.00
105	Jason Anderson/100	8.00
106	Travis Chapman/100	8.00
107	Mac Suzuki/304	15.00
109	Mark Prior/50	30.00
111	Marlon Byrd/100	10.00
114	Jay Gibbons/100	10.00
118	Ricardo Rodriguez/100	10.00
119	Robert Fick/100	10.00
120	Rodrigo Rosario/250	8.00
121	Alexis Gomez/100	10.00
124	Ben Sheets/50	20.00
126	Nick Johnson/50	10.00
127	Mark Mulder/50	40.00
132	Chris Snelling/100	8.00
133	Kevin Mench/100	8.00
135	Orlando Hudson/50	15.00
139	Joe Crede/100	10.00
140	Wilson Valdez/25	10.00
141	Runelvys Hernandez/100	10.00
143	Takahito Nomura/47	15.00
147	Oliver Perez/50	15.00
148	Xavier Nady/100	12.00
150	Ben Kozlowski/100	8.00
151	Prentice Redman/250	8.00
152	Craig Brazell/250	10.00
153	Nook Logan/250	6.00
154	Greg Aquino/250	8.00
155	Matt Kata/250	15.00
156	Ian Ferguson/250	6.00
157	Chien-Ming Wang/250	200.00
158	Beau Kemp/250	6.00
159	Alejandro Machado/250	6.00
160	Michael Hessman/160	6.00
161	Francisco Rosario/250	6.00
162	Pedro Liriano/250	6.00
163	Richard Fischer/250	6.00
164	Franklin Perez/250	6.00
165	Oscar Villarreal/250	10.00
166	Arnie Munoz/250	6.00
167	Tim Olson/250	6.00
168	Jose Contreras/250	25.00
169	Francisco Cruceta/250	8.00
170	Jeremy Bonderman/250	40.00
171	Jeremy Griffiths/250	8.00
172	John Webb/250	6.00
173	Phil Seibel/250	6.00
174	Aaron Looper/250	6.00
175	Brian Stokes/250	6.00
176	Guillermo Quiroz/250	8.00
177	Fernando Cabrera/250	10.00
178	Josh Hall/250	10.00
179	Diegomar Markwell/250	6.00
180	Andrew Brown/250	8.00
181	Doug Waechter/250	8.00
182	Felix Sanchez/250	6.00
183	Gerardo Garcia/250	6.00
184	Matt Bruback/250	6.00
185	Michel Hernandez/250	6.00
186	Rett Johnson/250	10.00
187	Ryan Cameron/250	8.00
188	Rob Hammock/250	15.00
189	Clint Barmes/250	15.00
190	Brandon Webb/250	25.00
191	Jon Leicester/250	6.00
192	Shane Bazzell/250	10.00
193	Joe Valentine/250	6.00
194	Josh Stewart/250	15.00
195	Pete LaForest/250	8.00
196	Shane Victorino/250	6.00
197	Terrmel Sledge/250	6.00
198	Lew Ford/250	15.00
199	Todd Wellemeyer/250	10.00

Team Tandems

		NM/M
Common Duo:		2.00
Inserted 1:48		
Spectrums:		1-2X
Production 100 Sets		
1	Mark Prior, Sammy Sosa	5.00
2	Vladimir Guerrero, Jose Vidro	3.00
3	Bernie Williams, Alfonso Soriano	6.00
4	Mike Sweeney, Carlos Beltran	2.00
5	Magglio Ordonez, Paul Konerko	2.00
6	Adam Dunn, Austin Kearns	3.00
7	Randy Johnson, Curt Schilling	4.00
8	Hideo Nomo, Kazuhisa Ishii	2.00
9	Pat Burrell, Bobby Abreu	3.00
10	Todd Helton, Larry Walker	2.00

Team Tandems Material

		NM/M
Common Duo:		
Quantity produced listed		
Spectrums:		No Pricing
Production 25 or 10		
1	Mark Prior, Sammy Sosa/100	30.00
2	Vladimir Guerrero, Jose Vidro/100	10.00
3	Bernie Williams, Alfonso Soriano/100	20.00
4	Mike Sweeney, Carlos Beltran/100	6.00
5	Magglio Ordonez, Paul Konerko/100	6.00
6	Adam Dunn, Austin Kearns/100	15.00
7	Randy Johnson, Curt Schilling/100	15.00
8	Hideo Nomo, Kazuhisa Ishii/40	50.00
9	Pat Burrell, Bobby Abreu/40	20.00
10	Todd Helton, Larry Walker/100	8.00

Team Trios

		NM/M
Common Trio:		5.00
Inserted 1:88		
Spectrums:		1-2X
Production 50 Sets		
1	Greg Maddux, Chipper Jones, Andruw Jones	8.00
2	Sammy Sosa, Mark Prior, Kerry Wood	8.00
3	Pedro Martinez, Nomar Garciaparra, Manny Ramirez	8.00
4	Jason Giambi, Roger Clemens, Alfonso Soriano	8.00
5	Alex Rodriguez, Rafael Palmeiro, Mark Teixeira	8.00
6	Mike Piazza, Roberto Alomar, Tsuyoshi Shinjo	6.00
7	Jeff Bagwell, Craig Biggio, Lance Berkman	5.00
8	Troy Glaus, Garret Anderson, Troy Percival	5.00
9	Miguel Tejada, Eric Chavez, Barry Zito	5.00
10	Luis Gonzalez, Randy Johnson, Curt Schilling	6.00

Team Trios Materials

		NM/M
Quantity produced listed		5.00
Spectrums:		No Pricing
Production 10 or 25		
1	Greg Maddux, Chipper Jones, Andruw Jones/100	30.00
2	Sammy Sosa, Mark Prior, Kerry Wood/100	30.00
3	Pedro Martinez, Nomar Garciaparra, Manny Ramirez/50	50.00
4	Jason Giambi, Roger Clemens, Alfonso Soriano/100	40.00
5	Alex Rodriguez, Rafael Palmeiro, Mark Teixeira/100	25.00
6	Mike Piazza, Roberto Alomar, Tsuyoshi Shinjo/40	40.00
7	Jeff Bagwell, Craig Biggio, Lance Berkman/100	20.00
8	Troy Glaus, Garret Anderson, Troy Percival/40	25.00
9	Miguel Tejada, Eric Chavez, Barry Zito/100	20.00
10	Luis Gonzalez, Randy Johnson, Curt Schilling/100	25.00

Tools of the Trade

	NM/M
Complete Set (110):	125.00

TOOLS OF THE TRADE

Common Player:		1.00
Inserted 1:5		
1	Sammy Sosa	4.00
2	Nomar Garciaparra	5.00
3	Andruw Jones	1.50
4	Troy Glaus	1.00
5	Greg Maddux	4.00
6	Rickey Henderson	1.00
7	Alex Rodriguez	6.00
8	Manny Ramirez	1.50
9	Lance Berkman	1.00
10	Roger Clemens	5.00
11	Ivan Rodriguez	1.00
12	Kazuhisa Ishii	1.00
13	Alfonso Soriano	3.00
14	Austin Kearns	1.00
15	Mike Piazza	3.00
16	Curt Schilling	1.00
17	Jeff Bagwell	1.50
18	Todd Helton	1.50
19	Randy Johnson	2.00
20	Vladimir Guerrero	1.50
21	Kerry Wood	1.00
22	Rafael Palmeiro	1.00
23	Roy Oswalt	1.00
24	Chipper Jones	3.00
25	Pat Burrell	1.00
26	Jason Giambi	2.00
27	Pedro J. Martinez	1.00
28	Roberto Alomar	1.00
29	Shawn Green	1.00
30	Adam Dunn	1.00
31	Juan Gonzalez	1.50
32	Mark Prior	5.00
33	Hideo Nomo	1.00
34	Torii Hunter	1.00
35	Mark Teixeira	1.00
36	Craig Biggio	1.00
37	Rafael Palmeiro	1.00
38	Jeff Bagwell	1.50
39	Albert Pujols	6.00
40	Richie Sexson	1.00
41	Alex Rodriguez	6.00
42	Carlos Delgado	1.50
43	Frank Thomas	1.50
44	Sammy Sosa	4.00
45	Marlon Byrd	1.00
46	Mark Prior	5.00
47	Adrian Beltre	1.00
48	Tom Glavine	1.00
49	So Taguchi	1.00
50	Jeff Bagwell	1.00
51	Mike Sweeney	1.00
52	Luis Gonzalez	1.00
53	Chipper Jones	3.00
54	Jason Giambi	2.00
55	Miguel Tejada	1.50
56	Todd Helton	1.50
57	Andruw Jones	1.50
58	Mike Piazza	3.00
59	Manny Ramirez	1.50
60	Randy Johnson	1.00
61	Carlos Beltran	1.00
62	Victor Martinez	1.00
63	Orlando Hudson	1.00
64	Jeff Kent	1.00
65	Greg Maddux	4.00
66	Garret Anderson	1.00
67	Joe Thurston	1.00
68	Mark Teixeira	1.00
69	Kazuhisa Ishii	1.00
70	Austin Kearns	1.00
71	Pat Burrell	1.00
72	Joe Borchard	1.00
73	Josh Phelps	1.00
74	Travis Hafner	1.00
75	So Taguchi	1.00
76	Victor Martinez	1.00
77	Paul LoDuca	1.00
78	Bernie Williams	1.00
79	Josh Phelps	1.00
80	Marlon Byrd	1.00
81	Manny Ramirez	1.00
82	Jason Giambi	2.00
83	Jeff Bagwell	1.50
84	Sammy Sosa	4.00
85	Josh Phelps	1.00
86	Tim Hudson	1.00
87	Randy Johnson	2.00
88	Troy Glaus	1.00
89	Joe Thurston	1.00
90	Miguel Tejada	1.00
91	Adam Dunn	1.00
92	Magglio Ordonez	1.00
93	Mike Sweeney	1.00
94	Andruw Jones	1.50
95	Carlos Beltran	1.00
96	Joe Borchard	1.00
97	Austin Kearns	1.00
98	Richie Sexson	1.00
99	Mark Prior	5.00
100	Mark Teixeira	1.00
101	Ryan Klesko	1.00
102	Jason Jennings	1.00
103	Travis Hafner	1.00
104	Mark Buehrle	1.00
105	Eric Hinske	1.00
106	Rafael Palmeiro	1.00
107	Roy Oswalt	1.00
108	Kerry Wood	1.00
109	Brian Giles	1.00
110	Ivan Rodriguez	1.00

Tools of the Trade Materials

		NM/M
Common Player:		3.00
Quantity produced listed		
Spectrums:		1-2.5X
Production 10 to 50		
1	Sammy Sosa/250	10.00
2	Nomar Garciaparra/250	10.00
3	Andruw Jones/250	5.00
4	Troy Glaus/250	5.00
5	Greg Maddux/250	10.00
6	Rickey Henderson/40	25.00
7	Alex Rodriguez/250	10.00
8	Manny Ramirez/250	6.00
9	Lance Berkman/250	4.00
10	Roger Clemens/250	10.00
11	Ivan Rodriguez/250	6.00
12	Kazuhisa Ishii/40	25.00
13	Alfonso Soriano/250	10.00
14	Austin Kearns/250	5.00
15	Mike Piazza/250	10.00
16	Curt Schilling/250	5.00
17	Jeff Bagwell/250	6.00
18	Todd Helton/250	6.00
19	Randy Johnson/250	6.00
20	Vladimir Guerrero/250	6.00
21	Kerry Wood/250	6.00
22	Rafael Palmeiro/250	5.00
23	Roy Oswalt/250	3.00
24	Chipper Jones/250	8.00
25	Pat Burrell/40	15.00
26	Jason Giambi/250	5.00
27	Pedro J. Martinez/250	8.00
28	Roberto Alomar/40	15.00
29	Shawn Green/250	3.00
30	Adam Dunn/250	5.00
31	Juan Gonzalez/40	15.00
32	Mark Prior/250	8.00
33	Hideo Nomo/250	8.00
34	Torii Hunter/250	5.00
35	Mark Teixeira/250	5.00
36	Craig Biggio/250	4.00
37	Rafael Palmeiro/250	5.00
38	Jeff Bagwell/250	5.00
39	Albert Pujols/200	12.00
40	Richie Sexson/250	3.00
41	Alex Rodriguez/250	10.00
42	Carlos Delgado/250	3.00
43	Frank Thomas/75	8.00
44	Sammy Sosa/250	10.00
45	Marlon Byrd/250	3.00
46	Mark Prior/250	8.00
47	Adrian Beltre/250	3.00
48	Tom Glavine/250	3.00
49	So Taguchi/250	3.00
50	Jeff Bagwell/250	3.00
51	Mike Sweeney/250	3.00
52	Luis Gonzalez/250	3.00
53	Chipper Jones/100	8.00
54	Jason Giambi/250	6.00
55	Miguel Tejada/250	3.00
56	Todd Helton/250	5.00
57	Andruw Jones/250	5.00
58	Mike Piazza/250	8.00
59	Manny Ramirez/250	6.00
60	Randy Johnson/250	5.00
61	Carlos Beltran/250	3.00
62	Victor Martinez/250	3.00
63	Orlando Hudson/250	3.00
64	Jeff Kent/250	3.00
65	Greg Maddux/250	8.00
66	Garret Anderson/150	4.00
67	Joe Thurston/250	3.00
68	Mark Teixeira/250	3.00
69	Kazuhisa Ishii/250	3.00
70	Austin Kearns/250	4.00
71	Pat Burrell/100	8.00
72	Joe Borchard/250	3.00
73	Josh Phelps/250	3.00
74	Travis Hafner/250	3.00
75	So Taguchi/125	3.00
76	Victor Martinez/125	3.00
77	Paul LoDuca/125	3.00
78	Bernie Williams/125	3.00
79	Josh Phelps/125	5.00
80	Marlon Byrd/125	5.00
81	Manny Ramirez/100	10.00
82	Jason Giambi/125	5.00
83	Jeff Bagwell/50	15.00
84	Sammy Sosa/125	20.00
85	Josh Phelps/125	5.00
86	Tim Hudson/125	5.00
87	Randy Johnson/125	10.00
88	Troy Glaus/125	5.00
89	Joe Thurston/125	4.00
90	Miguel Tejada/125	5.00
91	Adam Dunn/100	15.00
92	Magglio Ordonez/100	10.00
93	Mike Sweeney/100	10.00
94	Andruw Jones/100	15.00
95	Carlos Beltran/100	8.00
96	Joe Borchard/100	8.00
97	Austin Kearns/100	15.00
98	Richie Sexson/100	15.00
99	Mark Prior/50	50.00
100	Mark Teixeira/50	20.00
101	Ryan Klesko/50	10.00
102	Jason Jennings/50	10.00
103	Travis Hafner/50	10.00
104	Mark Buehrle/50	15.00
105	Eric Hinske/50	20.00
106	Rafael Palmeiro/50	40.00
107	Roy Oswalt/50	20.00
108	Kerry Wood/50	40.00
109	Brian Giles/50	15.00
110	Ivan Rodriguez/50	25.00

Total Bases

		NM/M
Complete Set (30):		60.00
Common Player:		1.00
Inserted 1:16		
1	Albert Pujols	6.00
2	Nomar Garciaparra	6.00
3	Jason Giambi	3.00
4	Miguel Tejada	1.00
5	Rafael Palmeiro	1.50
6	Sammy Sosa	5.00
7	Pat Burrell	1.50
8	Lance Berkman	1.00
9	Bernie Williams	1.50
10	Jim Thome	2.00
11	Carlos Beltran	1.00
12	Eric Chavez	1.00
13	Alex Rodriguez	6.00
14	Magglio Ordonez	1.00
15	Brian Giles	1.00
16	Alfonso Soriano	3.00
17	Shawn Green	1.00
18	Vladimir Guerrero	2.00
19	Garret Anderson	1.00
20	Todd Helton	2.00
21	Barry Bonds	8.00
22	Jeff Kent	1.00
23	Torii Hunter	1.00
24	Ichiro Suzuki	4.00
25	Derek Jeter	8.00
26	Chipper Jones	4.00
27	Jeff Bagwell	2.00
28	Mike Piazza	4.00
29	Rickey Henderson	1.50
30	Ken Griffey Jr.	4.00

Total Bases Materials 1B

		NM/M
Common Player:		4.00
Quantity produced listed		
1	Albert Pujols/109	12.00
2	Nomar Garciaparra/112	12.00
3	Jason Giambi/100	8.00
4	Miguel Tejada/140	4.00
5	Rafael Palmeiro/58	5.00
6	Sammy Sosa/90	15.00
7	Pat Burrell/87	8.00
8	Lance Berkman/90	4.00
9	Bernie Williams/146	6.00
10	Jim Thome/73	8.00
11	Carlos Beltran/94	4.00
12	Eric Chavez/93	4.00
13	Alex Rodriguez/101	15.00
14	Magglio Ordonez/103	4.00
15	Brian Giles/68	4.00
16	Alfonso Soriano/117	10.00
17	Shawn Green/92	4.00
18	Vladimir Guerrero/128	6.00
19	Garret Anderson/107	4.00
20	Todd Helton/109	6.00
21	Barry Bonds/70	20.00
22	Jeff Kent/114	4.00
23	Torii Hunter/92	4.00
24	Ichiro Suzuki/165	25.00
25	Derek Jeter/147	25.00
26	Chipper Jones/117	8.00
27	Jeff Bagwell/100	8.00
28	Mike Piazza/76	10.00
29	Rickey Henderson/28	40.00
30	Ken Griffey Jr./36	40.00

Total Bases Materials 2B

		NM/M
Quantity produced listed		
1	Albert Pujols/40	40.00
2	Nomar Garciaparra/56	25.00
3	Jason Giambi/34	15.00
4	Miguel Tejada/30	8.00
5	Rafael Palmeiro/34	15.00
6	Pat Burrell/39	8.00
7	Lance Berkman/35	8.00
9	Bernie Williams/37	15.00
12	Carlos Beltran/44	8.00
13	Eric Chavez/31	10.00
14	Alex Rodriguez/27	50.00
14	Magglio Ordonez/47	8.00
15	Brian Giles/37	8.00
16	Alfonso Soriano/51	25.00
17	Shawn Green/31	10.00
18	Vladimir Guerrero/37	15.00
19	Garret Anderson/56	9.00
20	Todd Helton/39	15.00
21	Barry Bonds/31	50.00
22	Jeff Kent/42	7.00
23	Torii Hunter/37	15.00
25	Derek Jeter/26	50.00
26	Chipper Jones/35	25.00
27	Jeff Bagwell/33	25.00
28	Mike Piazza/23	35.00

Total Bases Materials 3B

No pricing due to scarcity.

Total Bases Materials HR

		NM/M
Quantity produced listed		
1	Albert Pujols/34	40.00
3	Jason Giambi/41	20.00
4	Miguel Tejada/41	10.00
5	Rafael Palmeiro/43	15.00
6	Sammy Sosa/49	30.00
7	Pat Burrell/37	15.00
8	Lance Berkman/42	10.00
10	Jim Thome/52	15.00
11	Carlos Beltran/29	10.00
12	Eric Chavez/34	12.00
13	Alex Rodriguez/57	25.00
14	Magglio Ordonez/58	8.00
15	Brian Giles/38	8.00
16	Alfonso Soriano/39	30.00
17	Shawn Green/42	8.00
18	Vladimir Guerrero/39	15.00
19	Garret Anderson/29	10.00
20	Todd Helton/30	15.00
21	Barry Bonds/46	40.00
22	Jeff Kent/37	8.00
23	Torii Hunter/29	25.00
26	Chipper Jones/35	35.00
27	Jeff Bagwell/31	20.00
28	Mike Piazza/33	30.00

2003 Playoff Piece of the Game

		NM/M
Common Player:		4.00
Pack (1):		12.00
Box (6):		60.00
1	Adam Dunn/Bat	8.00
2	Adam Dunn/Jsy	8.00
3	Adrian Beltre/Bat	6.00
4	Albert Pujols/Jsy	15.00
5	Albert Pujols/Bat	15.00
6	Alex Rodriguez/Bat	10.00
7	Alex Rodriguez/Blue/Jsy	10.00
8	Alex Rodriguez/White/Jsy	10.00
9	Alfonso Soriano/Bat	8.00
10	Alfonso Soriano/Gray/Jsy	8.00
11	Alfonso Soriano/White/Jsy	8.00
12	Brett Myers/Jsy	4.00
13	Andruw Jones/Jsy	6.00
14	Austin Kearns/Jsy	6.00
15	Barry Larkin/Jsy	6.00
16	Barry Zito/Jsy	4.00
17	Bernie Williams/Jsy	6.00
18	Brian Giles/Bat	4.00
19	Zach Day/Jsy	4.00
20	Carlos Beltran/Bat	4.00
21	Brandon Phillips/Bat	4.00
22	Carlos Lee/Bat	4.00
23	Casey Fossum/Jsy	4.00
24	Chipper Jones/Jsy	8.00
25	Marcus Giles/Jsy	4.00
26	Craig Biggio/Jsy	6.00
27	Curt Schilling/Jsy	8.00
28	Derek Jeter/Base	15.00
29	Edgar Martinez/Jsy	6.00
30	Eric Chavez/Jsy	6.00
31	Eric Hinske/Bat	4.00
32	Frank Thomas/190/Bat	8.00
33	Aubrey Huff/Jsy	4.00
34	Gary Carter/Jkt	8.00
35	Greg Maddux/Gray/Jsy	8.00
36	Greg Maddux/White/Jsy	8.00
37	Hideki Matsui/Base RC	15.00
38	Hideo Nomo/White/Jsy	8.00
39	Rod Carew/Jkt	8.00
40	Ichiro Suzuki/Base	8.00
41	Ivan Rodriguez/Bat	8.00
42	Jason Giambi/Bat	6.00
43	Jason Giambi/Bat	6.00
44	J.C. Romero/Jsy	4.00
45	Jason Giambi/White/Jsy	6.00
46	Jeff Bagwell/Jsy	6.00
47	Josh Bard/Jsy	4.00
48	Jim Thome/Jsy	8.00
49	Jay Gibbons/Jsy	4.00
50	Jorge Posada/Jsy	6.00
51	Juan Gonzalez/Jsy	6.00
52	Kazuhisa Ishii/Bat	4.00
53	George Brett/Bat	15.00
54	Kenny Lofton/Bat	4.00
55	Kerry Wood/Jsy	8.00
56	Kevin Brown/Jsy	4.00
57	Kirk Saarloos/Jsy	4.00
58	Lance Berkman/Jsy	5.00
59	Larry Walker/Jsy	4.00
60	Magglio Ordonez/Jsy	4.00
61	Manny Ramirez/Jsy	8.00
62	Mark Mulder/Jsy	8.00
63	Mark Prior/Jsy	8.00
64	Matt Williams/Jsy	4.00
65	Miguel Tejada/Jsy	4.00
66	Mike Mussina/Jsy	6.00
67	Mike Piazza/Bat	10.00
68	Mike Piazza/Black/Jsy	10.00
69	Mike Piazza/White/Jsy	10.00
70	Nomar Garciaparra/Bat	10.00
71	Nomar Garciaparra/Gray/Jsy	10.00
72	Nomar Garciaparra/White/Jsy	10.00
73	Paul LoDuca/Jsy	4.00
74	Pedro Martinez/Jsy	8.00
75	Rafael Palmeiro/Jsy	8.00
76	Randy Johnson/Gray/Jsy	8.00
77	Randy Johnson/White/Jsy	8.00
78	Rickey Henderson/Jsy	8.00
79	Roberto Alomar/Jsy	6.00
80	Rod Carew/Jkt	8.00
81	Roger Clemens/Gray/Jsy	15.00
82	Roger Clemens/White/Jsy	15.00
83	Cal Ripken Jr./Jsy	25.00
84	Roy Oswalt/Jsy	4.00
85	Jeremy Bonderman/Jsy	4.00
86	Ryne Sandberg/Bat	15.00
87	Sammy Sosa/Bat	12.00
88	Sammy Sosa/Grey/Jsy	15.00
89	Sammy Sosa/White/Jsy	15.00
90	Scott Rolen/Jsy	8.00
91	Frank Catalanotto/Jsy	4.00
92	Shawn Green/Jsy	5.00
93	Tim Hudson/Jsy	4.00
94	Todd Helton/Jsy	8.00
95	Tony Gwynn/Jsy	8.00
96	Torii Hunter/Jsy	6.00
97	Troy Glaus/Jsy	6.00
98	Runelvys Hernandez/Jsy	4.00
99	Vernon Wells/Jsy	4.00
100	Vladimir Guerrero/Jsy	8.00

Autographs

		NM/M
Common Player:		
Varying quantities produced		
Prime Autos:		No Pricing
Production 4-20		
12	Brett Myers	10.00
18	Brian Giles/30	30.00
19	Zach Day	8.00
21	Brandon Phillips	10.00
22	Carlos Lee	12.00
23	Casey Fossum	10.00
25	Marcus Giles	15.00
29	Edgar Martinez/100	40.00
30	Eric Chavez/75	25.00
31	Eric Hinske	10.00
33	Aubrey Huff	10.00
41	Ivan Rodriguez/50	50.00
42	Ivan Rodriguez/75	40.00
44	J.C. Romero	8.00
47	Josh Bard	8.00
49	Jay Gibbons	10.00
51	Juan Gonzalez/50	50.00
57	Kirk Saarloos	8.00
62	Mark Mulder/100	25.00
63	Mark Prior/25	75.00
64	Matt Williams	15.00
73	Paul LoDuca	15.00
84	Roy Oswalt/50	25.00
85	Jeremy Bonderman	50.00
86	Ryne Sandberg/40	100.00
90	Scott Rolen/50	40.00
91	Frank Catalanotto	8.00
96	Torii Hunter/140	20.00
98	Runelvys Hernandez	10.00
100	Vladimir Guerrero/150	40.00

Prime Materials

No Pricing
Production 25 Sets

Bronze Materials

Cards (1-100): 1-1.5X
Production 150 Sets

Silver Materials

Cards (1-100): 1-2X
Production 75 Sets

Gold Materials

Cards (1-100): 1.5-2.5X
Production 50 Sets

Platinum Materials

No pricing due to scarcity.
Production 25 Sets

2003 Playoff Portraits Promos

To introduce its textured artwork issue, Playoff produced several types of promo cards. Two styles of white-bordered samples were issued; one has a blank-back and was distributed to dealers with ordering information, the other has a sample-marked back and was found one per box of Playoff Absolute. Otherwise unmarked promos with green top and bottom borders were distributed at All-Star FanFest, while similar promos with red top and bottom borders were handed out the Atlantic City National convention. Checklists for each of these styles are undetermined.

Common Player:

2003 Playoff Portraits Samples

Each issue of the October 2003 Beckett Baseball Card Monthly included a sample 2003 Playoff Portraits card rubber-cemented inside. The cards differ from the issued version only in the appearance on back of a (usually) black dot-matrix printed "SAMPLE" notation. Some cards were produced with the overprint in silver, in much more limited quantities.

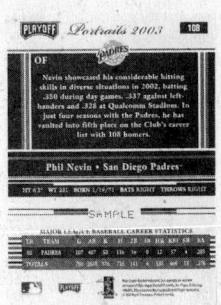

The number of different players' cards involved in the promotion is unknown.

	NM/M
Common Player:	.10
Stars:	1.5-2X
Silvers:	10X

2003 Playoff Portraits

Greg Maddux • Atlanta Braves

	NM/M
Complete Set (144):	40.00
Common Player:	.25
Pack (7):	4.00
Box (20):	60.00
1 Vladimir Guerrero	1.50
2 Luis Gonzalez	.35
3 Andruw Jones	1.50
4 Manny Ramirez	1.50
5 Derek Jeter	4.00
6 Eric Hinske	.45
7 Curt Schilling	.45
8 Adam Dunn	1.00
9 Jason Jennings	.25
10 Mike Piazza	2.50
11 Jason Giambi	.75
12 Jeff Bagwell	1.50
13 Rickey Henderson	1.50
14 Randy Johnson	1.50
15 Roger Clemens	3.00
16 Troy Glaus	1.50
17 Hideo Nomo	1.50
18 Joe Borchard	.25
19 Torii Hunter	.25
20 Lance Berkman	.25
21 Todd Helton	1.50
22 Mike Mussina	.40
23 Vernon Wells	.25
24 Pat Burrell	.50
25 Ichiro Suzuki	2.50
26 Shawn Green	.50
27 Frank Thomas	1.50
28 Barry Zito	.40
29 Barry Bonds	4.00
30 Ken Griffey Jr.	2.50
31 Albert Pujols	3.00
32 Roberto Alomar	.50
33 Barry Larkin	.25
34 Tony Gwynn	2.00
35 Chipper Jones	2.00
36 Pedro J. Martinez	1.50
37 Juan Gonzalez	1.50
38 Greg Maddux	2.00
39 Tim Hudson	.35
40 Sammy Sosa	2.50
41 Victor Martinez	.25
42 Mark Buehrle	.25
43 Austin Kearns	.25
44 Kerry Wood	1.00
45 Nomar Garciaparra	2.50
46 Alfonso Soriano	1.00
47 Mark Prior	1.50
48 Richie Sexson	.25
49 Mark Teixeira	.75
50 Craig Biggio	.25
51 Rafael Palmeiro	1.00
52 Carlos Beltran	.75
53 Bernie Williams	.35
54 Eric Chavez	.35
55 Paul Konerko	.35
56 Nolan Ryan	4.00
57 Mark Mulder	.25
58 Miguel Tejada	.35
59 Roy Oswalt	.25
60 Jim Edmonds	.25
61 Ryan Klesko	.25

62 Cal Ripken Jr.	4.00
63 Josh Beckett	.25
64 Kazuhisa Ishii	.25
65 Alex Rodriguez	3.00
66 Mike Sweeney	.25
67 C.C. Sabathia	.25
68 Jose Vidro	.25
69 Magglio Ordonez	.25
70 Carlos Delgado	.75
71 Jorge Posada	.25
72 Bobby Abreu	.25
73 Brian Giles	.25
74 Kirby Puckett	2.00
75 Yogi Berra	2.00
76 Ryne Sandberg	2.00
77 Tom Glavine	.45
78 Jim Thome	1.00
79 Chris Snelling	.25
80 Drew Henson	.25
81 Junior Spivey	.25
82 Mike Schmidt	3.00
83 Jeff Kent	.25
84 Stan Musial	2.00
85 Garret Anderson	.25
86 Jose Contreras RC	3.00
87 Ivan Rodriguez	1.00
88 Hideki Matsui RC	6.00
89 Don Mattingly	2.00
90 Angel Berroa	.25
91 George Brett	3.00
92 Jermaine Dye	.25
93 John Olerud	.25
94 Josh Phelps	.25
95 Sean Casey	.35
96 Larry Walker	.25
97 Jason Lane	.25
98 Travis Hafner	.25
99 Terrence Long	.25
100 Shannon Stewart	.25
101 Richard Hidalgo	.25
102 Joe Thurston	.25
103 Ben Sheets	.25
104 Orlando Cabrera	.25
105 Aramis Ramirez	.25
106 So Taguchi	.25
107 Frank Robinson	.75
108 Phil Nevin	.25
109 Dennis Tankersley	.25
110 J.D. Drew	.50
111 Paul LoDuca	.25
112 Ozzie Smith	2.00
113 Carlos Lee	.25
114 Nick Johnson	.25
115 Edgar Martinez	.25
116 Hank Blalock	.75
117 Orlando Hudson	.25
118 Corey Patterson	.25
119 Steve Carlton	.50
120 Wade Miller	.25
121 Adrian Beltre	.75
122 Scott Rolen	1.00
123 Brian Lawrence	.25
124 Rich Aurilia	.25
125 Tsuyoshi Shinjo	.25
126 John Buck	.25
127 Marlon Byrd	.25
128 Michael Cuddyer	.25
129 Marshall McDougall	.25
130 Travis Chapman	.25
131 Jose Morban	.25
132 Adam LaRoche	.25
133 Jose Castillo	.25
134 Walter Young	.25
135 Jeff Baker	.25
136 Jeremy Guthrie	.25
137 Pedro J. Martinez	.75
138 Randy Johnson	.75
139 Alex Rodriguez	1.50
140 Hideo Nomo	.75
141 Roger Clemens	1.00
142 Rickey Henderson	.50
143 Jason Giambi	.40
144 Mike Piazza	1.00

Artifacts Bronze

	NM/M
Common Player:	4.00
Production 100 or less.	
Silvers:	1-1.5X
Production 50 or less.	
Golds:	No Pricing
Production 25 or less.	
Bronze Combos:	1-1.5X
Production 50 or less.	
Silver Combos:	No Pricing
Production 25 or less.	
Gold Combos:	No Pricing
Production 10 or less.	
1 Vladimir Guerrero/100	8.00
2 Luis Gonzalez/100	5.00
3 Andruw Jones/100	8.00
4 Manny Ramirez/50	10.00
5 Derek Jeter/100	20.00
6 Eric Hinske/100	4.00
7 Curt Schilling/100	6.00
8 Adam Dunn/100	8.00
9 Jason Jennings/100	4.00
10 Mike Piazza/100	12.00
11 Jason Giambi/100	6.00
12 Jeff Bagwell/100	15.00
13 Rickey Henderson/50	20.00
14 Randy Johnson/100	15.00
15 Roger Clemens/100	20.00
16 Troy Glaus/100	6.00
17 Hideo Nomo/100	20.00
19 Torii Hunter/100	6.00
20 Lance Berkman/100	6.00

21 Todd Helton/50	15.00
22 Mike Mussina/100	8.00
23 Vernon Wells/100	4.00
24 Pat Burrell/100	6.00
25 Ichiro Suzuki/100	25.00
26 Shawn Green/100	6.00
27 Frank Thomas/100	10.00
28 Barry Zito/100	6.00
29 Barry Bonds/100	20.00
30 Ken Griffey Jr./100	15.00
31 Albert Pujols/100	20.00
32 Roberto Alomar/50	10.00
33 Barry Larkin/100	10.00
34 Tony Gwynn/100	10.00
35 Chipper Jones/100	10.00
36 Pedro Martinez/100	10.00
37 Juan Gonzalez/50	10.00
38 Greg Maddux/100	15.00
39 Tim Hudson/100	6.00
40 Sammy Sosa/100	20.00
41 Victor Martinez/100	6.00
42 Mark Buehrle/50	6.00
43 Austin Kearns/100	6.00
44 Kerry Wood/100	15.00
45 Nomar Garciaparra/100	15.00
46 Alfonso Soriano/100	10.00
47 Mark Prior/100	10.00
48 Richie Sexson/100	6.00
49 Mark Teixeira/100	8.00
50 Craig Biggio/50	10.00
51 Rafael Palmeiro/100	10.00
52 Carlos Beltran/50	6.00
53 Bernie Williams/50	10.00
54 Eric Chavez/100	6.00
55 Paul Konerko/100	4.00
56 Nolan Ryan/100	35.00
57 Mark Mulder/100	6.00
58 Miguel Tejada/100	6.00
59 Roy Oswalt/50	8.00
60 Jim Edmonds/50	8.00
61 Ryan Klesko/50	8.00
62 Cal Ripken Jr/100	40.00
63 Josh Beckett/100	6.00
64 Kazuhisa Ishii/50	6.00
65 Alex Rodriguez/100	15.00
66 Mike Sweeney/100	4.00
67 C.C. Sabathia/100	6.00
68 Jose Vidro/100	6.00
69 Magglio Ordonez/50	6.00
70 Carlos Delgado/50	8.00
71 Jorge Posada/100	6.00
72 Bobby Abreu/100	6.00
73 Brian Giles/100	6.00
74 Kirby Puckett/50	30.00
75 Yogi Berra/50	25.00
76 Ryne Sandberg/50	40.00
77 Tom Glavine/50	8.00
78 Jim Thome/100	10.00
79 Chris Snelling/50	4.00
80 Drew Henson/50	10.00
81 Junior Spivey/50	4.00
82 Mike Schmidt/50	50.00
83 Jeff Kent/50	6.00
84 Stan Musial/100	30.00
85 Garret Anderson/50	8.00
87 Ivan Rodriguez/50	12.00
88 Hideki Matsui/100	25.00
89 Don Mattingly/100	30.00
90 Angel Berroa/100	4.00
91 George Brett/50	50.00
92 Jermaine Dye/50	4.00
93 John Olerud/100	4.00
94 Josh Phelps/50	4.00
95 Sean Casey/50	4.00
96 Larry Walker/50	8.00
97 Jason Lane/50	4.00
98 Travis Hafner/100	6.00
99 Terrence Long/100	4.00
100 Shannon Stewart/50	4.00
101 Richard Hidalgo/50	4.00
102 Joe Thurston/100	4.00
103 Ben Sheets/50	6.00
104 Orlando Cabrera/50	6.00
105 Aramis Ramirez/100	4.00
106 So Taguchi/100	5.00
107 Frank Robinson/50	12.00
108 Dennis Tankersley/100	4.00
110 J.D. Drew/50	6.00
111 Paul LoDuca/50	6.00
112 Ozzie Smith/50	40.00
113 Carlos Lee/50	6.00
114 Nick Johnson/100	4.00
115 Edgar Martinez/100	8.00
116 Hank Blalock/50	15.00
117 Orlando Hudson/50	4.00
118 Corey Patterson/100	6.00
119 Steve Carlton/100	10.00
120 Wade Miller/50	6.00
121 Adrian Beltre/50	8.00
122 Scott Rolen/50	8.00
123 Brian Lawrence/50	4.00
124 Rich Aurilia/50	4.00
125 Tsuyoshi Shinjo/50	8.00
126 John Buck/50	4.00
127 Marlon Byrd/100	4.00
128 Michael Cuddyer/50	4.00
130 Travis Chapman/100	4.00
131 Jose Morban/100	4.00
132 Adam LaRoche/50	4.00
133 Jose Castillo/100	4.00
134 Walter Young/100	4.00

Beige

Beige:	1-3X
Production 250 Sets	

Bronze

Bronze:	2-4X
Production 100 Sets	

Bronze Autographs

	NM/M
Common Bronze Auto.:	
Production 100 or less.	
Silvers:	1-1.5X
Production 50 or less.	
No Pricing for production 25 or less.	
Golds:	No Pricing
Production 25 or less.	
1 Vladimir Guerrero/100	35.00
3 Andruw Jones/25	50.00
6 Eric Hinske/100	10.00
8 Adam Dunn/50	35.00
9 Jason Jennings/100	8.00
16 Troy Glaus/60	25.00
18 Joe Borchard/100	6.00
19 Torii Hunter/40	40.00
31 Albert Pujols/25	150.00
32 Roberto Alomar/100	35.00
33 Barry Larkin/95	25.00
34 Tony Gwynn/60	75.00
37 Juan Gonzalez/50	50.00
41 Victor Martinez/20	20.00
44 Mark Buehrle/100	10.00
44 Kerry Wood/40	20.00
47 Mark Prior/20	60.00
48 Richie Sexson/100	20.00
49 Mark Teixeira/25	45.00
50 Craig Biggio/25	45.00
56 Nolan Ryan/25	150.00
57 Mark Mulder/100	20.00
59 Roy Oswalt/40	25.00
61 Ryan Klesko/40	20.00
62 Cal Ripken Jr./25	150.00
67 C.C. Sabathia/50	15.00
72 Bobby Abreu/100	15.00
73 Brian Giles/50	15.00
74 Kirby Puckett/60	60.00
77 Tom Glavine/100	35.00
79 Chris Snelling/100	8.00
80 Drew Henson/25	40.00
81 Junior Spivey/100	10.00
82 Mike Schmidt/75	75.00
83 Jeff Kent/50	25.00
84 Stan Musial/50	65.00
85 Garret Anderson/25	30.00
86 Jose Contreras/50	40.00
90 Angel Berroa/100	10.00
92 Jermaine Dye/100	10.00
94 Josh Phelps/100	10.00
97 Jason Lane/100	8.00
98 Travis Hafner/100	12.00
99 Terrence Long/100	6.00
100 Shannon Stewart/100	8.00
101 Richard Hidalgo/25	20.00
102 Joe Thurston/100	8.00
103 Ben Sheets/100	15.00
105 Aramis Ramirez/40	15.00
106 So Taguchi/29	30.00
108 Phil Nevin/100	12.00
109 Dennis Tankersley/100	8.00
110 J.D. Drew/25	30.00
111 Paul LoDuca/100	15.00
113 Carlos Lee/100	15.00
114 Nick Johnson/100	10.00
115 Edgar Martinez/100	35.00
117 Orlando Hudson/100	8.00
119 Steve Carlton/25	40.00
120 Wade Miller/50	6.00
121 Adrian Beltre/25	30.00
122 Scott Rolen/100	30.00
123 Brian Lawrence/50	4.00
126 John Buck/100	6.00
127 Marlon Byrd/100	8.00
128 Michael Cuddyer/100	8.00
129 Marshall McDougall/100	6.00
130 Travis Chapman/100	6.00
131 Jose Morban/100	6.00
132 Adam LaRoche/100	12.00
133 Jose Castillo/100	6.00
134 Walter Young/100	6.00
135 Jeff Baker/100	6.00
136 Jeremy Guthrie/100	10.00

Silver Autographs

Production 50 or less.	
Production 50 or less.	

2003 Playoff Prestige Samples

Each issue of the July 2003 Beckett Baseball Card Monthly included a sample 2003 Playoff Prestige card rubber-cemented inside. The cards differ from the issued version in the appearance on back of a (usually) silver-foil "SAMPLE" notation. Some cards were produced with the overprint in gold-foil, in much more limited quantities. The number of different players' cards involved in the promotion is unknown.

	NM/M
Common Player:	.10
Stars:	1.5-2X
Gold:	10X

2003 Playoff Prestige

	NM/M
Complete Set (200):	35.00
Common Player:	.15
Pack (6):	2.00
Box (24):	45.00
1 Darin Erstad	.25
2 David Eckstein	.15
3 Garret Anderson	.15
4 Jarrod Washburn	.15
5 Tim Salmon	.25
6 Troy Glaus	.75
7 Jay Gibbons	.15
8 Marty Cordova	.15
9 Melvin Mora	.15
10 Rodrigo Lopez	.15
11 Tony Batista	.15
12 Cliff Floyd	.15
13 Derek Lowe	.15
14 Johnny Damon	.30
15 Manny Ramirez	.75
16 Nomar Garciaparra	1.50
17 Pedro J. Martinez	.75
18 Rickey Henderson	.75
19 Shea Hillenbrand	.15
20 Carlos Lee	.15
21 Frank Thomas	.75
22 Magglio Ordonez	.15
23 Mark Buehrle	.15
24 Paul Konerko	.15
25 C.C. Sabathia	.15
26 Danys Baez	.15
27 Ellis Burks	.15
28 Travis Hafner	.15
29 Omar Vizquel	.15
30 Bobby Higginson	.15
31 Carlos Pena	.15
32 Mark Redman	.15
33 Robert Fick	.15
34 Steve Sparks	.15
35 Carlos Beltran	.50
36 Joe Randa	.15
37 Mike Sweeney	.15
38 Paul Byrd	.15
39 Raul Ibanez	.15
40 Runelvys Hernandez	.15
41 Brad Radke	.15

42 Corey Koskie	.15
43 Cristian Guzman	.15
44 David Ortiz	.35
45 Doug Mientkiewicz	.15
46 Dustan Mohr	.15
47 Jacque Jones	.15
48 Torii Hunter	.75
49 Alfonso Soriano	.75
50 Andy Pettitte	.30
51 Bernie Williams	.15
52 David Wells	.15
53 Derek Jeter	2.00
54 Jason Giambi	.50
55 Jeff Weaver	.15
56 Jorge Posada	.15
57 Mike Mussina	.35
58 Roger Clemens	1.25
59 Barry Zito	.25
60 David Justice	.15
61 Eric Chavez	.30
62 Jermaine Dye	.15
63 Mark Mulder	.15
64 Miguel Tejada	.30
65 Ray Durham	.15
66 Tim Hudson	.30
67 Bret Boone	.15
68 Chris Snelling	.15
69 Edgar Martinez	.15
70 Freddy Garcia	.15
71 Ichiro Suzuki	1.50
72 Jamie Moyer	.15
73 John Olerud	.15
74 Kazuhiro Sasaki	.15
75 Aubrey Huff	.15
76 Joe Kennedy	.15
77 Paul Wilson	.15
78 Alex Rodriguez	1.75
79 Chan Ho Park	.15
80 Hank Blalock	.50
81 Ivan Rodriguez	.65
82 Juan Gonzalez	.75
83 Kevin Mench	.15
84 Rafael Palmeiro	.40
85 Carlos Delgado	.40
86 Eric Hinske	.15
87 Jose Cruz	.15
88 Josh Phelps	.15
89 Roy Halladay	.15
90 Shannon Stewart	.15
91 Vernon Wells	.15
92 Curt Schilling	.40
93 Junior Spivey	.15
94 Luis Gonzalez	.25
95 Mark Grace	.25
96 Randy Johnson	.75
97 Andruw Jones	.75
98 Chipper Jones	1.00
99 Gary Sheffield	.40
100 Greg Maddux	1.00
101 John Smoltz	.15
102 Kevin Millwood	.15
103 Mike Hampton	.15
104 Corey Patterson	.15
105 Fred McGriff	.15
106 Kerry Wood	.65
107 Mark Prior	.75
108 Moises Alou	.15
109 Sammy Sosa	1.50
110 Adam Dunn	.50
111 Austin Kearns	.15
112 Barry Larkin	.15
113 Ken Griffey Jr.	1.50
114 Sean Casey	.30
115 Jason Jennings	.15
116 Jay Payton	.15
117 Larry Walker	.15
118 Todd Helton	.75
119 A.J. Burnett	.15
120 Josh Beckett	.15
121 Juan Encarnacion	.15
122 Mike Lowell	.15
123 Craig Biggio	.30
124 Daryle Ward	.15
125 Jeff Bagwell	.75
126 Lance Berkman	.15
127 Roy Oswalt	.15
128 Adrian Beltre	.35
129 Hideo Nomo	.75
130 Kazuhisa Ishii	.15
131 Kevin Brown	.15
132 Odalis Perez	.15
133 Paul LoDuca	.15
134 Shawn Green	.35
135 Jeff Kent	.15
136 Ben Sheets	.15
137 Jeffrey Hammonds	.15
138 Jose Hernandez	.15
139 Richie Sexson	.15
140 Bartolo Colon	.15
141 Brad Wilkerson	.15
142 Javier Vazquez	.15
143 Jose Vidro	.15
144 Michael Barrett	.15
145 Vladimir Guerrero	.15
146 Al Leiter	.15
147 Mike Piazza	1.25
148 Mo Vaughn	.15
149 Pedro Astacio	.15
150 Roberto Alomar	.40
151 Roger Cedeno	.15
152 Tom Glavine	.40
153 Bobby Abreu	.15
154 Jimmy Rollins	.15
155 Mike Lieberthal	.15
156 Pat Burrell	.15
157 Vicente Padilla	.15
158 Jim Thome	.65
159 Aramis Ramirez	.15

160	Brian Giles	.15
161	Jason Kendall	.15
162	Josh Fogg	.15
163	Kip Wells	.15
164	Mark Kotsay	.15
165	Oliver Perez	.15
166	Phil Nevin	.15
167	Ryan Klesko	.15
168	Sean Burroughs	.15
169	Trevor Hoffman	.15
170	Barry Bonds	2.00
171	Benito Santiago	.15
172	Reggie Sanders	.15
173	Rich Aurilia	.15
174	Russ Ortiz	.15
175	Albert Pujols	1.75
176	J.D. Drew	.25
177	Jim Edmonds	.15
178	Matt Morris	.15
179	Tino Martinez	.15
180	Scott Rolen	.65
181	Joe Borchard	.15
182	Freddy Sanchez	.15
183	Jose Contreras RC	3.00
184	Jeff Baker	.15
185	Ryan Church	.15
186	Mario Ramos	.15
187	Corwin Malone	.15
188	Jimmy Gobble	.15
189	Jon Adkins	.15
190	Tim Kalita	.15
191	Nelson Castro	.15
192	Colin Young	.15
193	Luis Martinez	.15
194	Todd Donovan	.15
195	Jeremy Ward	.15
196	Wilson Valdez	.15
197	Hideki Matsui RC	6.00
198	Mitch Wylie	.15
199	Adam Walker	.15
200	Clifford Bartosh	.15

X-tra Points

Stars (1-180): 4-8X
Production 150
Prospects (181-200): 4-8X
Production 50

Award Winners

Complete Set (15): 25.00
Common Player: 1.00
#'d to year of award

1	Barry Zito	1.00
2	Barry Bonds	5.00
3	Randy Johnson	1.50
4	Roger Clemens	2.50
5	Ichiro Suzuki	3.00
6	Chipper Jones	2.00
7	Ken Griffey Jr.	3.00
8	Miguel Tejada	1.00
9	Greg Maddux	2.00
10	Jeff Bagwell	1.50
11	Rickey Henderson	1.00
12	Tom Glavine	1.00
13	Albert Pujols	4.00
14	Nomar Garciaparra	3.00
15	Derek Jeter	5.00

Connections

Complete Set (70): 90.00
Common Duo: 1.00
Inserted 1:8
Century Connections: 3-6X
Production 100 Sets

1	Troy Glaus, Garret Anderson	1.50
2	Troy Glaus, Tim Salmon	1.50
3	Randy Johnson, Curt Schilling	1.50
4	Matt Williams, Luis Gonzalez	1.00
5	Greg Maddux, John Smoltz	2.00
6	Andruw Jones, Chipper Jones	2.00
7	Greg Maddux, Kevin Millwood	2.00
8	Tony Batista, Geronimo Gil	1.00
9	Pedro J. Martinez, Nomar Garciaparra	3.00
10	Manny Ramirez, Nomar Garciaparra	3.00
11	Nomar Garciaparra, Rickey Henderson	3.00
12	Trot Nixon, Manny Ramirez	1.50
13	Kerry Wood, Mark Prior	1.00
14	Sammy Sosa, Fred McGriff	3.00
15	Sammy Sosa, Corey Patterson	3.00
16	Frank Thomas, Magglio Ordonez	1.50
17	Joe Borchard, Magglio Ordonez	1.00
18	Adam Dunn, Austin Kearns	1.00
19	Barry Larkin, Ken Griffey Jr.	3.00
20	Adam Dunn, Barry Larkin	1.00
21	Adam Dunn, Ken Griffey Jr.	3.00
22	Victor Martinez, Omar Vizquel	1.00
23	C.C. Sabathia, Victor Martinez	1.00
24	Larry Walker, Todd Helton	1.00
25	Carlos Pena, Robert Fick	1.00
26	Josh Beckett, Juan Encarnacion	1.00
27	Jeff Bagwell, Craig Biggio	1.50
28	Lance Berkman, Roy Oswalt	1.00
29	Lance Berkman, Jeff Bagwell	1.50
30	Mike Sweeney, Carlos Beltran	1.00
31	Mike Sweeney, Angel Berroa	1.00
32	Kazuhisa Ishii, Shawn Green	1.00
33	Adrian Beltre, Shawn Green	1.00
34	Kazuhisa Ishii, Hideo Nomo	1.50
35	Richie Sexson, Ben Sheets	1.00
36	Jacque Jones, Torii Hunter	1.00
37	Doug Mientkiewicz, David Ortiz	1.00
38	Vladimir Guerrero, Jose Vidro	1.50
39	Derek Jeter, Jason Giambi	5.00
40	Derek Jeter, Bernie Williams	5.00
41	Roger Clemens, Mike Mussina	2.50
42	Alfonso Soriano, Jorge Posada	1.50
43	Derek Jeter, Alfonso Soriano	5.00
44	Mike Piazza, Roberto Alomar	3.00
45	Mike Piazza, Mo Vaughn	3.00
46	Eric Chavez, Miguel Tejada	1.00
47	Mark Mulder, Barry Zito	1.00
48	Tim Hudson, Barry Zito	1.00
49	Pat Burrell, Bobby Abreu	1.00
50	Jim Thome, Pat Burrell	1.00
51	Jim Thome, Marlon Byrd	1.00
52	Brian Giles, Aramis Ramirez	1.00
53	Ryan Klesko, Phil Nevin	1.00
54	Barry Bonds, Benito Santiago	5.00
55	Jeff Kent, Rich Aurilia	1.00
56	Barry Bonds, Jeff Kent	5.00
57	Ichiro Suzuki, Kazuhiro Sasaki	3.00
58	Edgar Martinez, John Olerud	1.00
59	Albert Pujols, Scott Rolen	4.00
60	Jim Edmonds, J.D. Drew	1.00
61	Albert Pujols, Jim Edmonds	4.00
62	Dewon Brazelton, Joe Kennedy	1.00
63	Alex Rodriguez, Ivan Rodriguez	4.00
64	Juan Gonzalez, Rafael Palmeiro	1.50
65	Mark Teixeira, Hank Blalock	1.00
66	Alex Rodriguez, Juan Gonzalez	4.00
67	Alex Rodriguez, Juan Gonzalez	4.00
68	Shannon Stewart, Carlos Delgado	1.00
69	Josh Phelps, Eric Hinske	1.00
70	Vernon Wells, Roy Halladay	1.00

Material Connections

Common Duo: 4.00
Production 400 Sets

1	Troy Glaus, Garret Anderson	8.00
2	Troy Glaus, Tim Salmon	8.00
4	Matt Williams, Luis Gonzalez	6.00
5	Greg Maddux, John Smoltz	12.00
6	Andruw Jones, Chipper Jones	12.00
7	Greg Maddux, Kevin Millwood	12.00
8	Tony Batista, Geronimo Gil	4.00
9	Pedro J. Martinez, Nomar Garciaparra	15.00
10	Manny Ramirez, Nomar Garciaparra	15.00
11	Nomar Garciaparra, Rickey Henderson	15.00
12	Trot Nixon, Manny Ramirez	10.00
13	Kerry Wood, Mark Prior	10.00
14	Sammy Sosa, Fred McGriff	10.00
15	Sammy Sosa, Corey Patterson	10.00
16	Frank Thomas, Magglio Ordonez	8.00
17	Joe Borchard, Magglio Ordonez	6.00
18	Adam Dunn, Austin Kearns	20.00
20	Adam Dunn, Barry Larkin	15.00
22	Victor Martinez, Omar Vizquel	4.00
23	C.C. Sabathia, Victor Martinez	6.00
24	Larry Walker, Todd Helton	8.00
26	Josh Beckett, Juan Encarnacion	8.00
27	Jeff Bagwell, Craig Biggio	10.00
28	Lance Berkman, Roy Oswalt	8.00
29	Lance Berkman, Jeff Bagwell	10.00
30	Mike Sweeney, Carlos Beltran	8.00
31	Mike Sweeney, Angel Berroa	4.00
32	Kazuhisa Ishii, Shawn Green	10.00
33	Adrian Beltre, Shawn Green	6.00
34	Kazuhisa Ishii, Hideo Nomo	25.00
35	Richie Sexson, Ben Sheets	8.00
36	Jacque Jones, Torii Hunter	10.00
37	Doug Mientkiewicz, David Ortiz	6.00
38	Vladimir Guerrero, Jose Vidro	10.00
39	Derek Jeter, Jason Giambi	15.00
40	Derek Jeter, Bernie Williams	15.00
41	Roger Clemens, Mike Mussina	20.00
42	Alfonso Soriano, Jorge Posada	10.00
43	Derek Jeter, Alfonso Soriano	20.00
44	Mike Piazza, Roberto Alomar	15.00
45	Mike Piazza, Mo Vaughn	10.00
46	Eric Chavez, Miguel Tejada	8.00
47	Mark Mulder, Barry Zito	10.00
48	Tim Hudson, Barry Zito	10.00
49	Pat Burrell, Bobby Abreu	8.00
50	Jim Thome, Pat Burrell	10.00
51	Jim Thome, Marlon Byrd	10.00
52	Brian Giles, Aramis Ramirez	6.00
53	Ryan Klesko, Phil Nevin	6.00
54	Barry Bonds, Benito Santiago	12.00
55	Jeff Kent, Rich Aurilia	5.00
56	Barry Bonds, Jeff Kent	12.00
57	Ichiro Suzuki, Kazuhiro Sasaki	25.00
58	Edgar Martinez, John Olerud	8.00
59	Albert Pujols, Scott Rolen	15.00
60	Jim Edmonds, J.D. Drew	8.00
61	Albert Pujols, Jim Edmonds	12.00
62	Dewon Brazelton, Joe Kennedy	8.00
63	Alex Rodriguez, Ivan Rodriguez	12.00
64	Juan Gonzalez, Rafael Palmeiro	8.00
65	Mark Teixeira, Hank Blalock	10.00
66	Alex Rodriguez, Juan Gonzalez	15.00
67	Alex Rodriguez, Juan Gonzalez	12.00
68	Shannon Stewart, Carlos Delgado	6.00
69	Josh Phelps, Eric Hinske	4.00
70	Vernon Wells, Roy Halladay	4.00

Diamond Heritage

Complete Set (30): 35.00
Common Player: 1.00
Inserted 1:21
Golds: 5-10X
Production 50 Sets

1	Larry Walker	1.00
2	Troy Glaus	1.50
3	Magglio Ordonez	1.00
4	Roy Oswalt	1.00
5	Barry Zito	1.00
6	Nomar Garciaparra	3.00
7	Kerry Wood	1.25
8	Roger Clemens	2.50
9	Pedro J. Martinez	1.50
10	Mark Prior	1.50
11	Sammy Sosa	3.00
12	Randy Johnson	1.50
13	Greg Maddux	2.00
14	Manny Ramirez	1.50
15	Torii Hunter	1.00
16	Alex Rodriguez	4.00
17	Mike Piazza	3.00
18	Vladimir Guerrero	1.50
19	Ivan Rodriguez	1.25
20	Lance Berkman	1.00
21	Miguel Tejada	1.00
22	Chipper Jones	2.00
23	Todd Helton	1.50
24	Shawn Green	1.00
25	Scott Rolen	1.25
26	Adam Dunn	1.25
27	Jim Thome	1.25
28	Rafael Palmeiro	1.25
29	Eric Chavez	1.00
30	Andruw Jones	1.50

Diamond Heritage Materials

Common Player: 5.00
Production 200 unless noted.
Autographs: Not Priced
Production 15 to 25

1	Larry Walker	6.00
2	Troy Glaus	6.00
3	Magglio Ordonez	5.00
4	Roy Oswalt	5.00
5	Barry Zito	8.00
6	Nomar Garciaparra	15.00
7	Kerry Wood	8.00
8	Roger Clemens	15.00
9	Pedro J. Martinez	10.00
10	Mark Prior	6.00
11	Sammy Sosa	15.00
12	Randy Johnson	10.00
13	Greg Maddux	10.00
14	Manny Ramirez	8.00
15	Torii Hunter	10.00
16	Alex Rodriguez	10.00
17	Mike Piazza	15.00
18	Vladimir Guerrero	15.00
19	Ivan Rodriguez	15.00
20	Lance Berkman	8.00
21	Miguel Tejada	8.00
22	Chipper Jones	15.00
23	Todd Helton	10.00
24	Shawn Green	15.00
25	Scott Rolen	15.00
26	Adam Dunn	12.00
27	Jim Thome	10.00
28	Rafael Palmeiro	10.00
29	Eric Chavez	8.00
30	Andruw Jones	8.00

Diamond Heritage Material Autograph

Quantity produced listed

Draft Class Reunion

Complete Set (10): 20.00
Common Player: 1.00
Inserted 1:24

1	Mike Piazza, John Olerud	3.00
2	Derek Jeter, Shannon Stewart	5.00
3	Alex Rodriguez, Torii Hunter	4.00
4	Nomar Garciaparra, Paul Konerko	3.00
5	Kerry Wood, Todd Helton	1.50
6	Eric Chavez, Billy Koch	1.50
7	Lance Berkman, Troy Glaus	1.50
8	Pat Burrell, Mark Mulder	1.50
9	Barry Zito, Jason Jennings	1.00
10	Mark Prior, Mark Teixeira	1.50

Infield/Outfield Tandems Material

Common Duo: 8.00
Production 100 Sets

1	Troy Glaus, Garret Anderson	10.00
2	Mark Grace, Luis Gonzalez	10.00
3	Nomar Garciaparra, Manny Ramirez	20.00
4	Alfonso Soriano, Bernie Williams	15.00
5	Jeff Bagwell, Lance Berkman	15.00
6	Alex Rodriguez, Juan Gonzalez	15.00
7	Barry Larkin, Adam Dunn	15.00
8	Scott Rolen, Jim Edmonds	20.00
9	Todd Helton, Larry Walker	10.00
10	Adrian Beltre, Shawn Green	10.00
11	Jose Vidro, Vladimir Guerrero	12.00
12	Mike Sweeney, Carlos Beltran	10.00
13	Josh Phelps, Vernon Wells	8.00
14	Paul Konerko, Magglio Ordonez	10.00
15	Phil Nevin, Ryan Klesko	10.00

Inside The Numbers

Complete Set (25): 35.00
Common Player: 1.00
Production 2,002 Sets
Die-Cut: 10-25X
#'d to jersey number

1	Roger Clemens	2.50
2	Greg Maddux	2.00
3	Miguel Tejada	1.00
4	Alex Rodriguez	4.00
5	Ichiro Suzuki	2.50
6	Sammy Sosa	3.00
7	Jim Thome	1.50
8	Derek Jeter	5.00
9	Randy Johnson	1.50
10	Barry Zito	1.50
11	Jason Giambi	1.50
12	Shawn Green	1.00
13	Curt Schilling	1.00
14	Albert Pujols	4.00
15	Vladimir Guerrero	1.50
16	Pedro J. Martinez	1.50
17	Alfonso Soriano	1.50
18	Barry Bonds	5.00
19	Magglio Ordonez	1.00
20	Chipper Jones	2.00
21	Pat Burrell	1.00
22	Luis Gonzalez	1.00
23	Jeff Bagwell	1.50
24	Garret Anderson	1.00
25	Larry Walker	1.00

League Leaders

Complete Set (15): 25.00
Common Player: 1.00
Production 2,002 Sets

1	Manny Ramirez	2.00
2	Sammy Sosa	3.00
3	Alex Rodriguez	4.00
4	Alfonso Soriano	2.00
5	Vladimir Guerrero	2.00
6	Nomar Garciaparra	3.00
7	Johnny Damon	1.00
8	Alfonso Soriano	2.00
9	Barry Bonds	5.00
10	Barry Zito	1.00
11	Pedro J. Martinez	2.00
12	John Smoltz	1.00
13	Randy Johnson	2.00
14	Lance Berkman	1.00
15	Randy Johnson	2.00

League Leaders Materials

Common Player: 4.00
Production 250 Sets

1	Manny Ramirez/Jsy	8.00
2	Sammy Sosa/Base	8.00
3	Alex Rodriguez/Jsy	10.00
4	Alfonso Soriano/Jsy	8.00
5	Vladimir Guerrero/Jsy	8.00
6	Nomar Garciaparra /Jsy	10.00
7	Johnny Damon/Bat	4.00
8	Alfonso Soriano/Jsy	10.00
9	Barry Bonds/Base	12.00
10	Barry Zito/Jsy	6.00
11	Pedro J. Martinez/Jsy	10.00
12	John Smoltz	6.00
13	Randy Johnson/Jsy	10.00
14	Lance Berkman/Jsy	6.00
15	Randy Johnson/Jsy	10.00

Player Collection

Common Player: 4.00
Production 325 Sets

1	Adam Dunn	8.00
2	Adrian Beltre	6.00
3	Alex Rodriguez	20.00
4	Alfonso Soriano	10.00
5	Andruw Jones	8.00
6	Andy Pettitte	6.00
7	Barry Larkin	4.00
8	Barry Zito	4.00
9	Ben Grieve	4.00
10	Bernie Williams	4.00
11	Cal Ripken Jr.	25.00
12	Carlos Delgado	5.00
13	C.C. Sabathia	4.00
14	Chipper Jones	12.00
15	Craig Biggio	4.00
16	Curt Schilling	5.00
17	Alex Rodriguez	20.00

#	Player	NM/M
18	Frank Thomas	8.00
19	Freddy Garcia	4.00
20	Jay Bell	4.00
21	Roger Clemens	15.00
22	Tony Gwynn	12.00
23	Ivan Rodriguez	8.00
24	Jason Giambi	8.00
25	Jason Jennings	4.00
26	Jay Payton	4.00
27	J.D. Drew	6.00
28	Jeff Bagwell	8.00
29	Jeromy Burnitz	4.00
30	Jim Edmonds	4.00
31	Jim Thome	8.00
32	Joe Borchard	4.00
33	Joe Mays	4.00
34	John Olerud	4.00
35	David Wells	4.00
36	Juan Gonzalez	8.00
37	Kazuhiro Sasaki	4.00
38	Chan Ho Park	4.00
39	Kerry Wood	4.00
40	Kevin Brown	4.00
41	Lance Berkman	4.00
42	Larry Walker	4.00
43	Bret Boone	4.00
44	Magglio Ordonez	4.00
45	Manny Ramirez	8.00
46	Mark Mulder	4.00
47	Mark Prior	6.00
48	Matt Williams	4.00
49	Miguel Tejada	4.00
50	Mike Piazza	15.00
51	Nomar Garciaparra	15.00
52	Doug Davis	4.00
53	Paul Konerko	4.00
54	Paul LoDuca	4.00
55	Pedro J. Martinez	8.00
56	Preston Wilson	4.00
57	Rafael Palmeiro	8.00
58	Marlon Byrd	4.00
59	Reggie Sanders	4.00
60	Richie Sexson	4.00
61	Rickey Henderson	10.00
62	Rickey Henderson	10.00
63	Robert Person	4.00
64	Jeff Bagwell	8.00
65	Roger Clemens	15.00
66	Roy Oswalt	4.00
67	Ryan Klesko	4.00
68	Sammy Sosa	15.00
69	Shawn Green	5.00
70	Steve Finley	4.00
71	Terrence Long	4.00
72	Tim Hudson	4.00
73	Toby Hall	4.00
74	Todd Helton	8.00
75	Travis Lee	4.00
76	Troy Glaus	8.00
77	Tsuyoshi Shinjo	4.00
78	Vernon Wells	4.00
79	Vladimir Guerrero	8.00
80	Wes Helms	4.00
81	Alex Rodriguez	20.00
82	Alfonso Soriano	10.00
83	Barry Larkin	4.00
84	Roberto Alomar	5.00
85	Ivan Rodriguez	8.00
86	Jason Giambi	8.00
87	Jeff Bagwell	8.00
88	Juan Gonzalez	8.00
89	Larry Walker	4.00
90	Luis Gonzalez	4.00
91	Magglio Ordonez	4.00
92	Manny Ramirez	8.00
93	Marlon Byrd	4.00
94	Mike Piazza	15.00
95	Pat Burrell	6.00
96	Todd Helton	8.00
97	Rickey Henderson	10.00
98	Andruw Jones	4.00
99	Craig Biggio	4.00
100	Mark Prior	6.00

Signature Impressions

NM/M
Varying quantities produced

#	Player	NM/M
1	A.J. Pierzynski/50	20.00
2	Adam Dunn/25	60.00
3	Barry Zito/25	50.00
4	Bobby Abreu/20	20.00
5	Brandon Phillips/25	25.00
7	Don Mattingly/15	250.00
9	Eric Hinske/25	25.00
12	John Candelaria/50	15.00
16	Lance Berkman/30	30.00
18	Miguel Tejada/25	40.00
22	Roy Oswalt/30	30.00
27	Yogi Berra/15	100.00
28	Joe Kennedy/50	10.00
30	Lenny Dykstra/50	25.00
39	Toby Hall/50	15.00
40	Victor Martinez/25	45.00
46	Brian Giles/15	40.00
50	Jeremy Bonderman/100	35.00

Stars of MLB

NM/M
Common Player: 5.00
Production 150 Sets
Patches: 4-8X
Production 25 Sets
Autographs: No Pricing
Production 25

Patch Autographs: No Pricing
Production 5 to 10

#	Player	NM/M
1	Roger Clemens	12.00
2	Randy Johnson	8.00
3	Sammy Sosa	12.00
4	Vladimir Guerrero	8.00
5	Lance Berkman	5.00
6	Alfonso Soriano	8.00
7	Alex Rodriguez	15.00
8	Roberto Alomar	6.00
9	Miguel Tejada	4.00
10	Pedro J. Martinez	8.00
11	Greg Maddux	10.00
12	Barry Zito	5.00
13	Magglio Ordonez	5.00
14	Chipper Jones	10.00
15	Manny Ramirez	8.00
16	Troy Glaus	4.00
17	Pat Burrell	6.00
18	Roy Oswalt	5.00
19	Mike Piazza	12.00
20	Nomar Garciaparra	12.00

2004 Playoff Absolute Memorabilia

NM/M
Complete Set (250):
Common Player (1-200): 1.50
Production 1,349
Common Non-Auto. (201-250): 2.00
Production 1,000
Common Auto. (201-250): 8.00
Production 500-700
Pack (4): 40.00
Box (6): 185.00

#	Player	NM/M
1	Troy Glaus	2.00
2	Garret Anderson	2.00
3	Tim Salmon	2.00
4	Bartolo Colon	1.50
5	Troy Percival	1.50
6	Nolan Ryan Angels	10.00
7	Vladimir Guerrero	2.00
8	Richie Sexson	2.00
9	Shea Hillenbrand	1.50
10	Luis Gonzalez	1.50
11	Brandon Webb	2.00
12	Randy Johnson	4.00
13	Robby Hammock	1.50
14	Edgar Gonzalez	1.50
15	Roberto Alomar	3.00
16	Andruw Jones	3.00
17	Chipper Jones	4.00
18	Dale Murphy	2.00
19	Rafael Furcal	1.50
20	J.D. Drew	2.00
21	Bubba Nelson	1.50
22	Julio Franco	1.50
23	Adam LaRoche	1.50
24	Michael Hessman	1.50
25	Warren Spahn	3.00
26	Jay Gibbons	1.50
27	Cal Ripken Jr.	10.00
28	Miguel Tejada	2.50
29	Adam Loewen	1.50
30	Rafael Palmeiro	3.00
31	Javy Lopez	1.50
32	Luis Matos	1.50
33	Jason Varitek	2.00
34	Carl Yastrzemski	3.00
35	Manny Ramirez	2.00
36	Trot Nixon	1.50
37	Curt Schilling	3.00
38	Pedro J. Martinez	3.00
39	Nomar Garciaparra	5.00
40	Luis Tiant	1.50
41	Kevin Youkilis	1.50
42	Michel Hernandez	1.50
43	Sammy Sosa	5.00
44	Greg Maddux	4.00
45	Kerry Wood	4.00
46	Mark Prior	4.00
47	Ernie Banks	4.00
48	Aramis Ramirez	2.00
49	Brendan Harris	1.50
50	Todd Wellemeyer	1.50
51	Frank Thomas	3.00
52	Magglio Ordonez	2.00
53	Carlos Lee	1.50
54	Joe Crede	1.50
55	Joe Borchard	1.50
56	Mark Buehrle	1.50
57	Sean Casey	2.00
58	Adam Dunn	2.50
59	Austin Kearns	1.50
60	Ken Griffey Jr.	5.00
61	Barry Larkin	1.50
62	Ryan Wagner	1.50
63	Jody Gerut	1.50
64	Jeremy Guthrie	1.50
65	Travis Hafner	2.00
66	Brian Tallet	1.50
67	Todd Helton	3.00
68	Preston Wilson	1.50
69	Jeff Baker	1.50
70	Clint Barmes	1.50
71	Joe Kennedy	1.50
72	Jack Morris	1.50
73	George Kell	1.50
74	Preston Larrison	1.50
75	Dmitri Young	1.50
76	Ivan Rodriguez	3.00
77	Dontrelle Willis	2.00
78	Josh Beckett	2.50
79	Miguel Cabrera	4.00
80	Mike Lowell	2.00
81	Luis Castillo	1.50
82	Juan Pierre	1.50
83	Jeff Bagwell	3.00
84	Jeff Kent	2.00
85	Craig Biggio	2.00
86	Lance Berkman	2.00
87	Andy Pettitte	2.00
88	Roy Oswalt	2.00
89	Chris Burke	1.50
90	Jason Lane	1.50
91	Roger Clemens	6.00
92	Mike Sweeney	1.50
93	Carlos Beltran	2.00
94	Angel Berroa	1.50
95	Juan Gonzalez	2.50
96	Ken Harvey	1.50
97	Byron Gettis	1.50
98	Alexis Gomez	1.50
99	Ian Ferguson	1.50
100	Duke Snider	3.00
101	Shawn Green	2.00
102	Hideo Nomo	2.00
103	Kazuhisa Ishii	1.50
104	Edwin Jackson	1.50
105	Fred McGriff	2.00
106	Hong-Chih Kou	1.50
107	Don Sutton RC	2.00
108	Rickey Henderson	2.00
109	Cesar Izturis	1.50
110	Robin Ventura	1.50
111	Paul LoDuca	1.50
112	Rickie Weeks	2.00
113	Scott Podsednik	2.00
114	Junior Spivey	1.50
115	Lyle Overbay	2.00
116	Tony Oliva	1.50
117	Jacque Jones	1.50
118	Shannon Stewart	1.50
119	Torii Hunter	2.00
120	Johan Santana	1.50
121	J.D. Durbin	1.50
122	Jason Kubel	1.50
123	Michael Cuddyer	1.50
124	Nick Johnson	1.50
125	Jose Vidro	1.50
126	Orlando Cabrera	1.50
127	Zach Day	1.50
128	Mike Piazza	5.00
129	Tom Glavine	2.00
130	Jae Weong Seo	1.50
131	Gary Carter	2.00
132	Phil Seibel	1.50
133	Edwin Almonte	1.50
134	Aaron Boone	1.50
135	Kenny Lofton	2.00
136	Don Mattingly	6.00
137	Jason Giambi	3.00
138	Alex Rodriguez/Yanks	8.00
139	Jorge Posada	2.00
140	Bernie Williams	2.00
141	Hideki Matsui	5.00
142	Mike Mussina	2.00
143	Mariano Rivera	2.00
144	Gary Sheffield	2.00
145	Derek Jeter	8.00
146	Chien-Ming Wang	1.50
147	Javier Vazquez	1.50
148	Jose Contreras	1.50
149	Whitey Ford	2.00
150	Kevin Brown	2.00
151	Eric Chavez	2.00
152	Barry Zito	2.00
153	Mark Mulder	2.00
154	Tim Hudson	2.00
155	Rich Harden	1.50
156	Eric Byrnes	1.50
157	Jim Thome	4.00
158	Bobby Abreu	2.00
159	Marlon Byrd	1.50
160	Lenny Dykstra	1.50
161	Steve Carlton	2.00
162	Ryan Howard	2.00
163	Bobby Hill	1.50
164	Jose Castillo	1.50
165	Jay Payton	1.50
166	Ryan Klesko	1.50
167	Brian Giles	1.50
168	Henri Stanley	1.50
169	Jason Schmidt	2.00
170	Jerome Williams	1.50
171	J.T. Snow	1.50
172	Bret Boone	2.00
173	Edgar Martinez	2.00
174	Ichiro Suzuki	5.00
175	Jamie Moyer	1.50
176	Rich Aurilia	1.50
177	Chris Snelling	1.50
178	Scott Rolen	4.00
179	Albert Pujols	6.00
180	Jim Edmonds	2.00
181	Stan Musial	4.00
182	Dan Haren	1.50
183	Red Schoendienst	1.50
184	Aubrey Huff	1.50
185	Delmon Young	1.50
186	Rocco Baldelli	2.00
187	Dewon Brazelton	1.50
188	Mark Teixeira	2.50
189	Hank Blalock	3.00
190	Nolan Ryan Ranger	10.00
191	Alfonso Soriano	4.00
192	Michael Young	1.50
193	Vernon Wells	1.50
194	Roy Halladay	2.00
195	Carlos Delgado	2.50
196	Dustin McGowan	1.50
197	Josh Phelps	1.50
198	Alexis Rios	1.50
199	Eric Hinske	1.50
200	Josh Towers	1.50
201	Kazuo Matsui/1000 RC	5.00
202	Fernando Nieve AU/500 RC	8.00
203	Mike Rouse/1000	3.00
204	Dennis Sarfate AU/500 RC	8.00
205	Josh Labandeira AU/500 RC	8.00
206	Chris Oxspring AU/500 RC	8.00
207	Alfredo Simon/1000 RC	2.00
208	Cory Sullivan AU/500 RC	8.00
209	Ruddy Yan AU/500 RC	8.00
210	Jason Bartlett AU/500 RC	8.00
211	Akinori Otsuka/1000 RC	2.00
212	Lincoln Holdzkom/1000 RC	2.00
213	Justin Leone/1000 RC	4.00
214	Jorge Sequea AU/500 RC	8.00
215	John Gall/1000 RC RC	3.00
216	Jerome Gamble/1000 RC RC	2.00
217	Tim Bittner AU/500 RC	8.00
218	Ronny Cedeno AU/500 RC RC	12.00
219	Justin Hampson/1000 RC RC	2.00
220	Ryan Wing AU/500	8.00
221	Mariano Gomez AU/500 RC	8.00
222	Carlos Vasquez/1000 RC	2.00
223	Casey Daigle AU/500 RC RC	8.00
224	Renyel Pinto AU/500 RC	8.00
225	Chris Shelton AU/500 RC	25.00
226	Mike Gosling AU/700	8.00
227	Aarom Baldiris AU/500 RC	8.00
228	Ramon Ramirez AU/700 RC	8.00
229	Roberto Novoa AU/500 RC	8.00
230	Sean Henn AU/500	10.00
231	Jamie Brown AU/500 RC	8.00
232	Nick Regilio AU/500 RC	8.00
233	David Crouthers AU/700	8.00
234	Greg Dobbs AU/500 RC	8.00
235	Angel Chavez AU/500 RC	8.00
236	Willy Taveras AU/500 RC	20.00
237	Justin Knoedler AU/500 RC	8.00
238	Ian Snell AU/700 RC	20.00
239	Jason Frasor AU/500 RC	8.00
240	Jerry Gil AU/500 RC	8.00
241	Carlos Hines AU/500 RC	8.00
242	Ivan Ochoa AU/500 RC	8.00
243	Jose Capellan AU/700 RC	10.00
244	Onil Joseph AU/700 RC	8.00
245	Hector Gimenez AU/700 RC	8.00
246	Shawn Hill AU/700 RC RC	8.00
247	Freddy Guzman AU/700 RC	8.00
248	Graham Koonce AU/500	8.00
249	Ronald Belisario AU/500 RC	8.00
250	Merkin Valdez AU/700 RC	8.00

Retail
Cards (1-200): .15X
1-200 are not serial numbered

Spectrum Silver
Stars (1-200): 1-2X
Gold Auto. (201-250): .25-.4X
Non-Auto. (201-250): 1X
Production 100 Sets

Spectrum Gold
Stars (1-200): 2-4X
Gold Auto. (201-250): .5X
Non-Auto. (201-250): 1-2X
Production 50 Sets

Spectrum Platinum
No Pricing
Production One Set

Absolutely Ink

NM/M
Quantity produced listed
Spectrum: .75-1.5X
Production 1-25
No pricing 15 or less.

#	Player	NM/M
1	Adam Dunn/100	25.00
2	Al Kaline/100	25.00
3	Alan Trammell/100	15.00
6	Andre Dawson/Cubs/100	15.00
7	Andre Dawson/Expos/100	15.00
9	Angel Berroa/50	10.00
11	Aubrey Huff/100	12.00
12	Austin Kearns/100	15.00
16	Barry Larkin/50	30.00
17	Billy Williams/100	15.00
19	Bob Feller/100	20.00
20	Bob Gibson/25	35.00
22	Brandon Webb/100	10.00
23	Brett Myers/50	8.00
24	Brooks Robinson/100	40.00
27	Carlos Beltran/100	30.00
28	Carlos Lee/100	10.00
31	Craig Biggio/50	25.00
33	Dale Murphy/100	25.00
34	Darryl Strawberry/100	15.00
35	Dave Concepcion/50	20.00
36	Dave Parker/50	15.00
38	Don Mattingly/100	60.00
39	Dontrelle Willis/100	20.00
40	Duke Snider/100	30.00
41	Dwight Gooden/100	15.00
42	Edgar Martinez/50	30.00
43	Eric Chavez/50	25.00
44	Ernie Banks/100	50.00
45	Fergie Jenkins/100	15.00
46	Frank Robinson/100	20.00
47	Frank Thomas/25	50.00
48	Fred Lynn/100	15.00
49	Fred McGriff/25	50.00
50	Garret Anderson/100	15.00
52	Gary Carter/Expos/100	15.00
53	Gary Carter/Mets/100	15.00
54	Gaylord Perry/100	15.00
57	Hank Blalock/50	25.00
58	Harold Baines/50	25.00
63	Jae Weong Seo/100	15.00
65	Jamie Moyer/25	25.00
66	Jason Varitek/50	35.00
67	Jay Gibbons/50	15.00
68	Jim Edmonds/25	35.00
69	Jim Palmer/50	20.00
70	Jim Rice/50	20.00
71	Johan Santana/50	20.00
72	Jorge Posada/50	40.00
73	Josh Beckett/25	40.00
74	Juan Gonzalez/25	40.00
75	Keith Hernandez/100	15.00
76	Kirby Puckett/25	60.00
77	Luis Tiant/100	15.00
78	Magglio Ordonez/100	15.00
81	Mark Grace/25	50.00
82	Mark Mulder/100	20.00
83	Mark Prior/100	40.00
84	Mark Teixeira/100	25.00
85	Marty Marion/100	15.00
86	Mike Lowell/75	15.00
90	Nolan Ryan/25	125.00
92	Orel Hershiser/100	30.00
97	Phil Niekro/100	15.00
98	Ralph Kiner/100	20.00
101	Red Schoendienst/100	15.00
103	Robin Roberts/50	25.00
104	Robin Ventura/50	15.00
106	Rocco Baldelli/25	30.00
109	Sammy Sosa/21	150.00
111	Sean Casey/25	25.00
111	Shannon Stewart/50	15.00
114	Stan Musial/100	60.00
114	Steve Carlton/50	40.00
115	Steve Garvey/50	15.00
117	Tommy John/100	15.00
118	Tony Gwynn/25	60.00
119	Tony Oliva/100	15.00
120	Torii Hunter/100	15.00
121	Trot Nixon/50	30.00
122	Troy Glaus/50	20.00
123	Vernon Wells/25	20.00
124	Vladimir Guerrero/100	35.00
125	Will Clark/100	35.00

Absolutely Ink Material

NM/M
Quantity produced listed
Prime: .5-1X
Production 1-25
No pricing 10 or less.

#	Player	NM/M
1	Adam Dunn/100	30.00
2	Al Kaline/Pants/50	50.00
3	Alan Trammell/Jsy/100	20.00
6	Andre Dawson/Cubs/Jsy/100	20.00
7	Andre Dawson/Expos/Jsy/100	20.00
9	Angel Berroa/Jsy/100	10.00
11	Aubrey Huff/Jsy/100	15.00
12	Austin Kearns/Jsy/100	
16	Bert Blyleven/Jsy/100	15.00
17	Billy Williams/Jsy/100	25.00
19	Bob Feller/Jsy/100	25.00
21	Bobby Doerr/Jsy/100	25.00
22	Brandon Webb/Jsy/100	15.00
23	Brett Myers/Jsy/100	15.00
24	Brooks Robinson/Jsy/100	40.00
27	Carlos Beltran/Jsy/100	40.00
28	Carlos Lee/Jsy/100	15.00
33	Dale Murphy/Jsy/100	30.00
34	Darryl Strawberry/Jsy/100	20.00
35	Dave Concepcion/Jsy/100	20.00
36	Dave Parker/Jsy/100	15.00
38	Don Mattingly/Jsy/100	75.00
39	Dontrelle Willis/Jsy/20	25.00
41	Dwight Gooden/Jsy/60	15.00
44	Ernie Banks/Jsy/50	50.00
45	Fergie Jenkins/Pants/100	15.00
46	Frank Robinson/Jsy/100	40.00
48	Fred Lynn/Jsy/100	15.00
49	Fred McGriff/Jsy/20	60.00
50	Garret Anderson/Jsy/100	15.00
51	Gary Carter/Expos/Jsy/100	20.00
52	Gary Carter/Mets/Jkt/100	20.00
53	Gary Sheffield/Jsy/100	20.00
54	Gaylord Perry/Jsy/100	15.00
57	Hank Blalock/Jsy/100	30.00
58	Harold Baines/Jsy/100	15.00
63	Jae Weong Seo/Jsy/100	15.00
64	Jamie Moyer/Jsy/100	20.00
65	Jason Varitek/Jsy/100	30.00
67	Jay Gibbons/Jsy/Jsy/100	15.00
68	Jim Palmer/Jsy/100	25.00
69	Jim Rice/Jsy/100	20.00
70	Joe Carter/Jsy/50	20.00
71	Johan Santana/Jsy/100	40.00
72	Jorge Posada/Jsy/15	75.00
75	Keith Hernandez/Jsy/100	15.00
77	Luis Tiant/Jsy/100	20.00
85	Mark Mulder/Jsy/20	40.00
85	Marty Marion/Jsy/100	15.00
86	Mike Lowell/Jsy/60	20.00
92	Orlando Cepeda/Bat/65	20.00
97	Phil Niekro/Jsy/25	25.00
101	Ralph Kiner/Bat/100	25.00
103	Robin Roberts/Hat/100	
104	Robin Ventura/Jsy/65	20.00
110	Sean Casey/Jsy/75	20.00
111	Shannon Stewart/Jsy/100	15.00
114	Steve Carlton/Jsy/50	40.00
115	Steve Garvey/Bat/100	
117	Tommy John/Jsy/100	15.00
119	Tony Oliva/Jsy/100	20.00
120	Torii Hunter/Jsy/50	20.00

121 Trot Nixon/Jsy/100 30.00
124 Vladimir Guerrero/ Jsy/55 50.00
125 Will Clark/Jsy/100 40.00

Absolutely Ink Triple
No Pricing
Production 1-10
Prime: No Pricing
Production 1-5

Marks of Fame
NM/M
Production 100 Sets
Spectrum: 1-2X
Production 25 Sets
1 Nolan Ryan 15.00
2 Ernie Banks 6.00
3 Bob Feller 5.00
4 Duke Snider 5.00
5 Sammy Sosa 10.00
6 Whitey Ford 6.00
7 Steve Carlton 4.00
8 Tony Gwynn 8.00
9 Jim Bunning 4.00
10 Stan Musial 8.00
11 Cal Ripken Jr. 20.00
12 George Brett 15.00
13 Gary Carter 4.00
14 Jim Palmer 4.00
15 Gaylord Perry 4.00

Marks of Fame Signature
NM/M
Quantity produced listed
Spectrum: .75-1.5X
Production 1-25
No pricing 15 or less.
1 Nolan Ryan/50 120.00
2 Ernie Banks/50 50.00
3 Bob Feller/100 25.00
4 Duke Snider/100 25.00
5 Sammy Sosa/21 125.00
6 Whitey Ford/25 50.00
7 Steve Carlton 25.00
8 Tony Gwynn/25 75.00
9 Jim Bunning/100 20.00
10 Stan Musial/50 60.00
12 George Brett/25 100.00
13 Gary Carter/100 15.00
14 Jim Palmer/50 25.00
15 Gaylord Perry/100 15.00

Signature Club
NM/M
Quantity produced listed
2 Gary Sheffield/ Bat/50 20.00
4 Will Clark/Bat/50 40.00
5 Ernie Banks/Bat/50 40.00

Signature Material
NM/M
Quantity produced listed
Prime: No Pricing
Production 5 Sets
Combo: 1X
Production 25-50
Combo Prime: No Pricing
Production 5 Sets
2 Gary Carter/Jsy/50 25.00
3 Dale Murphy/Jsy/50 35.00
4 Don Mattingly/ Jsy/25 100.00
5 Stan Musial/Jsy/25 100.00

Signature Spectrum Silver
NM/M
Quantity produced listed
1 Troy Glaus/34 25.00
2 Garret Anderson/100 15.00
6 Nolan Ryan/ Angels/25 150.00
7 Vladimir Guerrero/ 100 40.00
8 Richie Sexson/34 20.00
9 Shea Hillenbrand/100 10.00
11 Brandon Webb/100 10.00
13 Robby Hammock/ 250 10.00
14 Edgar Gabrera/104 10.00
15 Roberto Alomar/32 50.00
16 Andruw Jones/50 10.00
18 Dale Murphy/100 25.00
19 Rafael Furcal/100 12.00
21 Bubba Nelson/250 10.00
22 Julio Franco/100 15.00
23 Adam LaRoche/100 10.00
24 Michael Hessman/ 250 10.00
26 Jay Gibbons/100 10.00
29 Adam Loewen/100 10.00
32 Luis Matos/100 10.00
33 Jason Varitek/50 35.00
36 Trot Nixon/100 20.00
40 Luis Tiant/100 15.00
41 Kevin Youkilis/25 40.00
42 Michel Hernandez/ 190 10.00
43 Sammy Sosa/21 150.00

45 Kerry Wood/50 40.00
46 Mark Prior/100 40.00
47 Ernie Banks/50 40.00
48 Aramis Ramirez/50 30.00
49 Brendan Harris/250 10.00
50 Todd Wellemeyer/ 250 10.00
51 Frank Thomas/50 40.00
52 Magglio Ordonez/ 100 20.00
53 Carlos Lee/100 15.00
54 Joe Crede/100 10.00
55 Joe Borchard/250 10.00
57 Sean Casey/50 20.00
58 Adam Dunn/100 25.00
59 Austin Kearns/100 10.00
61 Barry Larkin/50 30.00
62 Ryan Wagner/100 10.00
63 Jody Gerut/100 10.00
64 Jeremy Guthrie/50 10.00
65 Travis Hafner/50 20.00
66 Brian Tallet/50 10.00
68 Preston Wilson/100 10.00
69 Jeff Baker/50 10.00
70 Clint Barmes/250 10.00
71 Joe Kennedy/250 10.00
73 George Kell/100 10.00
74 Preston Larrison/250 10.00
77 Dontrelle Willis/25 35.00
78 Josh Beckett/25 35.00
79 Miguel Cabrera/100 35.00
80 Mike Lowell/25 25.00
81 Luis Castillo/50 10.00
83 Jeff Bagwell/50 10.00
85 Craig Biggio/50 30.00
86 Lance Berkman/25 20.00
87 Andy Pettitte/25 50.00
88 Roy Oswalt/25 25.00
89 Chris Burke/50 10.00
90 Jason Lane/231 10.00
93 Carlos Beltran/100 25.00
94 Angel Berroa/100 10.00
95 Juan Gonzalez/25 10.00
96 Ken Harvey/100 15.00
97 Byron Gettis/250 10.00
98 Alexis Gomez/250 10.00
99 Ian Ferguson/104 10.00
100 Duke Snider/100 25.00
103 Kazuhisa Ishii/25 40.00
104 Edwin Jackson/100 15.00
105 Fred McGriff/50 15.00
106 Hong-Chih Kou/50 15.00
107 Don Sutton/50 15.00
108 Cesar Izturis/101 10.00
110 Robin Ventura/25 20.00
111 Paul LoDuca/50 15.00
112 Rickie Weeks/21 40.00
113 Scott Podsednik/100 10.00
114 Junior Spivey/89 10.00
115 Lyle Overbay/89 10.00
116 Tony Oliva/72 15.00
117 Jacque Jones/89 10.00
118 Shannon Stewart/100 10.00
119 Torii Hunter/100 15.00
120 Johan Santana/50 30.00
121 J.D. Durbin/250 10.00
122 Jason Kubel/250 20.00
123 Michael Cuddyer/225 10.00
124 Nick Johnson/25 15.00
125 Jose Vidro/25 15.00
126 Orlando Cabrera/25 20.00
127 Zach Day/100 15.00
130 Jae Weong Seo/100 10.00
131 Gary Carter/100 15.00
132 Phil Seibel/177 10.00
133 Edwin Almonte/250 10.00
136 Don Mattingly/100 50.00
139 Jorge Posada/50 40.00
144 Gary Sheffield/100 15.00
146 Chien-Ming Wang/ 50 150.00
147 Javier Vazquez/25 40.00
148 Jose Contreras/25 35.00
149 Whitey Ford/50 30.00
152 Eric Chavez/50 25.00
153 Mark Mulder/100 25.00
154 Tim Hudson/50 25.00
155 Rich Harden/100 15.00
156 Eric Byrnes/250 10.00
159 Marlon Byrd/100 15.00
160 Lenny Dykstra/100 15.00
161 Steve Carlton/100 15.00
162 Ryan Howard/250 75.00
163 Bobby Hill/250 10.00
164 Jose Castillo/100 10.00
165 Jay Payton/100 10.00
168 Henri Stanley/112 10.00
170 Jerome Williams/100 15.00
171 J.T. Snow/89 15.00
173 Edgar Renteria/50 30.00
175 Jamie Moyer/19 25.00
176 Rich Aurilia/25 15.00
177 Chris Snelling/177 10.00
178 Scott Rolen/100 30.00
180 Jim Edmonds/50 30.00
181 Stan Musial/100 60.00
182 Dan Haren/200 10.00
183 Red Schoendienst/ 100 15.00
184 Aubrey Huff/100 10.00
185 Delmon Young/100 10.00
186 Rocco Baldelli/50 20.00
187 Dewon Brazelton/25 15.00
188 Mark Teixeira/100 20.00
189 Hank Blalock/25 30.00
190 Nolan Ryan Rgr/25 125.00
192 Michael Young/100 25.00
194 Roy Halladay/50 20.00

196 Dustin McGowan/ 250 10.00
197 Josh Phelps/25 15.00
198 Alexis Rios/100 15.00
200 Josh Towers/158 10.00
202 Fernando Nieve/25 15.00
203 Mike Rouse/100 10.00
204 Dennis Sarfate/100 10.00
205 Josh Labandeira/250 10.00
206 Chris Oxspring/250 10.00
207 Alfredo Simon/100 10.00
208 Cory Sullivan/250 10.00
209 Ruddy Yan/250 10.00
210 Jason Bartlett/250 10.00
211 Akinori Otsuka/100 50.00
212 Lincoln Holdzkom/ 250 10.00
213 Justin Leone/250 10.00
214 Jorge Sequea/250 10.00
215 John Gall/50 25.00
217 Tim Bittner/100 10.00
219 Justin Hampson/250 10.00
220 Ryan Wing/100 10.00
221 Mariano Gomez/250 10.00
222 Carlos Vasquez/250 10.00
223 Casey Daigle/150 10.00
224 Renyel Pinto/250 10.00
225 Chris Shelton/250 35.00
229 Roberto Novoa/225 10.00
230 Sean Henn/250 10.00
231 Jamie Brown/200 10.00
232 Nick Regilio/250 10.00
234 Greg Dobbs/250 10.00
235 Angel Chavez/250 10.00
236 Willy Taveras/225 10.00
237 Justin Knoedler/225 10.00
239 Jason Frasor/225 10.00
240 Jerry Gil/225 10.00
241 Carlos Hines/225 10.00
242 Ivan Ochoa/250 10.00
248 Graham Koonce/250 10.00
249 Ronald Belisario/225 10.00

Signature Spectrum Gold
NM/M
Quantity produced listed
1 Troy Glaus/15 35.00
2 Garret Anderson/15 15.00
7 Vladimir Guerrero/25 60.00
8 Richie Sexson/15 25.00
9 Shea Hillenbrand/ 100 10.00
11 Brandon Webb/10 10.00
15 Roberto Alomar/25 50.00
18 Dale Murphy/100 25.00
19 Rafael Furcal/100 12.00
22 Julio Franco/25 20.00
23 Adam LaRoche/100 10.00
26 Jay Gibbons/100 10.00
29 Adam Loewen/100 10.00
32 Luis Matos/15 15.00
33 Jason Varitek/25 40.00
36 Trot Nixon/100 15.00
40 Luis Tiant/50 20.00
41 Kevin Youkilis/25 15.00
45 Kerry Wood/25 50.00
46 Mark Prior/100 40.00
47 Ernie Banks/100 40.00
52 Magglio Ordonez/100 15.00
53 Carlos Lee/100 10.00
54 Joe Crede/50 10.00
59 Austin Kearns/100 10.00
61 Barry Larkin/25 40.00
62 Ryan Wagner/50 10.00
63 Jody Gerut/50 10.00
64 Jeremy Guthrie/25 10.00
65 Travis Hafner/25 25.00
68 Preston Wilson/100 10.00
69 Jeff Baker/25 10.00
73 George Kell/100 15.00
79 Miguel Cabrera/100 35.00
81 Luis Castillo/25 10.00
83 Jeff Bagwell/25 10.00
87 Andy Pettitte/25 50.00
93 Carlos Beltran/100 25.00
94 Angel Berroa/100 10.00
100 Duke Snider/100 25.00
104 Edwin Jackson/50 15.00
106 Hong-Chih Kou/25 15.00
107 Don Sutton/25 15.00
112 Rickie Weeks/24 40.00
113 Scott Podsednik/100 15.00
116 Tony Oliva/75 15.00
117 Jacque Jones/100 15.00
119 Torii Hunter/100 15.00
130 Jae Weong Seo/100 15.00
131 Gary Carter/100 15.00
136 Don Mattingly/100 50.00
139 Jorge Posada/25 50.00
144 Gary Sheffield/25 15.00
146 Chien-Ming Wang/ 25 180.00
153 Mark Mulder/100 25.00
155 Rich Harden/100 15.00
159 Marlon Byrd/100 10.00
160 Lenny Dykstra/100 15.00
161 Steve Carlton/100 40.00
164 Jose Castillo/50 15.00
165 Jay Payton/100 10.00
170 Jerome Williams/50 25.00
178 Scott Rolen/100 40.00
181 Stan Musial/100 60.00
182 Dan Haren/25 15.00
183 Red Schoendienst/ 100 15.00
184 Aubrey Huff/100 10.00

185 Delmon Young/100 20.00
187 Dewon Brazelton/25 15.00
188 Mark Teixeira/50 30.00
189 Hank Blalock/25 40.00
192 Michael Young/100 25.00
194 Roy Halladay/25 25.00
198 Alexis Rios/50 25.00
202 Fernando Nieve/100 10.00
205 Josh Labandeira/100 10.00
206 Chris Oxspring/100 15.00
208 Cory Sullivan/100 10.00
209 Ruddy Yan/100 10.00
210 Jason Bartlett/100 15.00
212 Lincoln Holdzkom/ 100 10.00
213 Justin Leone/100 20.00
214 Jorge Sequea/100 10.00
217 Tim Bittner/100 10.00
219 Justin Hampson/100 10.00
220 Ryan Wing/100 10.00
221 Mariano Gomez/100 10.00
222 Carlos Vasquez/100 10.00
225 Renyel Pinto/100 15.00
225 Chris Shelton/100 35.00
230 Sean Henn/100 10.00
232 Nick Regilio/100 10.00
234 Greg Dobbs/50 15.00
235 Angel Chavez/100 10.00
242 Ivan Ochoa/100 10.00
248 Graham Koonce/100 10.00

Team Tandem
NM/M
Production 250 Sets
Spectrum: 2-4X
Production 25 Sets
1 Vladimir Guerrero, Reggie Jackson 3.00
2 Dale Murphy, Chipper Jones 3.00
3 Gary Carter, Mike Piazza 4.00
4 Miguel Tejada, Cal Ripken Jr. 8.00
5 Gary Sheffield, Derek Jeter 6.00
6 Curt Schilling, Pedro J. Martinez 3.00
7 Roger Clemens, Andy Pettitte 5.00
8 Mike Sweeney, George Brett 6.00
9 Kazuhisa Ishii, Hideo Nomo 3.00
10 Austin Kearns, Adam Dunn 3.00
11 Miguel Cabrera, Dontrelle Willis 3.00
12 Don Mattingly, Derek Jeter 8.00
13 Barry Zito, Eric Chavez 2.00
14 Jim Thome, Mike Schmidt 4.00
15 Albert Pujols, Stan Musial 4.00
16 Nolan Ryan, Alex Rodriguez 8.00
17 Kerry Wood, Mark Prior 4.00
18 Rafael Palmeiro, Jay Gibbons 3.00
19 Nomar Garciaparra, Manny Ramirez 4.00
20 Ivan Rodriguez, Mike Piazza 4.00

Team Tandem Material
NM/M
Production 250 Sets
Prime: No Pricing
Production 5 Sets
1 Reggie Jackson/Bat, Vladimir Guerrero/ Bat 10.00
2 Chipper Jones/Jsy, Dale Murphy/Jsy 10.00
3 Gary Carter/Jsy, Mike Piazza/Jsy 10.00
4 Miguel Tejada/Bat, Cal Ripken Jr./Bat 25.00
5 Derek Jeter/Bat, Gary Sheffield/Bat 25.00
6 Curt Schilling/Bat, Pedro J. Martinez/Bat 25.00
7 Roger Clemens/Bat, Andy Pettitte/Bat 15.00
8 Mike Sweeney/Jsy, George Brett/Jsy 15.00
9 Kazuhisa Ishii/Jsy, Hideo Nomo/Jsy 15.00
10 Austin Kearns/Jsy, Adam Dunn/Jsy 10.00
11 Dontrelle Willis/Jsy, Miguel Cabrera/Jsy 10.00
12 Don Mattingly/Jsy, Derek Jeter/Jsy 35.00
13 Barry Zito/Jsy, Eric Chavez/Jsy 8.00
14 Jim Thome/Jsy, Mike Schmidt/Jsy 20.00
15 Albert Pujols/Jsy, Stan Musial/Jsy 40.00
16 Nolan Ryan/Jsy, Alex Rodriguez/Jsy 25.00

17 Mark Prior/Jsy, Kerry Wood/Jsy 15.00
18 Rafael Palmeiro/Jsy, Jay Gibbons/Jsy 10.00
19 Nomar Garciaparra/Jsy, Manny Ramirez/Jsy 15.00
20 Ivan Rodriguez/Jsy, Mike Piazza/Jsy 10.00

Team Trio
NM/M
Production 100 Sets
Spectrum: 1.5-2X
Production 25 Sets
1 Sammy Sosa, Kerry Wood, Mark Prior 10.00
2 Hank Blalock, Mark Teixeira, Alex Rodriguez 10.00
3 Vernon Wells, Roy Halladay, Carlos Delgado 4.00
4 Mike Mussina, Jorge Posada, Mariano Rivera 6.00
5 Shannon Stewart, Torii Hunter, Jacque Jones 4.00
6 Carlos Beltran, Mike Sweeney, Angel Berroa 4.00
7 Dontrelle Willis, Miguel Cabrera, Josh Beckett 6.00
8 Jeff Bagwell, Craig Biggio, Lance Berkman 6.00
9 Nomar Garciaparra, Pedro J. Martinez, Manny Ramirez 10.00
10 Shawn Green, Kazuhisa Ishii, Hideo Nomo 4.00
11 Mark Mulder, Barry Zito, Tim Hudson 8.00
12 Jim Edmonds, Scott Rolen, Albert Pujols 15.00
13 Cal Ripken Jr., Jay Gibbons, Rafael Palmeiro 20.00
14 Sammy Sosa, Mark Grace, Ryne Sandberg 10.00
15 Nolan Ryan, Roger Clemens, Randy Johnson 20.00

Team Trio Material
NM/M
Production 100 Sets
Prime: No Pricing
Production 5 Sets
1 Sammy Sosa, Kerry Wood, Mark Prior 25.00
2 Hank Blalock, Mark Teixeira, Alex Rodriguez 15.00
3 Vernon Wells, Roy Halladay, Carlos Delgado 8.00
4 Mike Mussina, Jorge Posada, Mariano Rivera 25.00
5 Shannon Stewart, Torii Hunter, Jacque Jones 8.00
6 Carlos Beltran, Mike Sweeney, Angel Berroa 8.00
7 Dontrelle Willis, Miguel Cabrera, Josh Beckett 15.00
8 Jeff Bagwell, Craig Biggio, Lance Berkman 10.00
9 Nomar Garciaparra, Pedro J. Martinez, Manny Ramirez 20.00
10 Shawn Green, Kazuhisa Ishii, Hideo Nomo 10.00
11 Mark Mulder, Barry Zito, Tim Hudson 8.00
12 Jim Edmonds, Scott Rolen, Albert Pujols 25.00
13 Cal Ripken Jr., Jay Gibbons, Rafael Palmeiro 40.00
14 Sammy Sosa, Mark Grace, Ryne Sandberg 35.00
15 Nolan Ryan, Roger Clemens, Randy Johnson/25 80.00

Team Quad
NM/M
Production 100 Sets
Spectrum: 1.5-2X
Production 25 Sets
1 Jeff Kent, Lance Berkman, Craig Biggio, Jeff Bagwell 6.00
2 Nomar Garciaparra, Manny Ramirez, Pedro Martinez, Trot Nixon 10.00
3 Paul Konerko, Carlos Lee, Magglio Ordonez, Frank Thomas 6.00

4 John Smoltz, Chipper Jones, Andruw Jones, Rafael Furcal 6.00
5 Garret Anderson, Troy Percival, Troy Glaus, Darin Erstad 4.00
6 Steve Finley, Brandon Webb, Randy Johnson, Luis Gonzalez 6.00
7 Paul LoDuca, Hideo Nomo, Shawn Green, Kazuhisa Ishii 6.00
8 Larry Walker, Todd Helton, Jason Jennings, Preston Wilson 6.00
9 Dontrelle Willis, Brad Penny, Josh Beckett 4.00
10 Jose Reyes, Jae Weong Seo, Tom Glavine, Mike Piazza 10.00
11 Bernie Williams, Derek Jeter, Jason Giambi, Alfonso Soriano 6.00
12 Rich Harden, Tim Hudson, Barry Zito, Mark Mulder 4.00
13 Kevin Millwood, Marlon Byrd, Jim Thome, Bobby Abreu 8.00
14 Edgar Renteria, Jim Edmonds, Albert Pujols, Scott Rolen 10.00
15 Roger Clemens, Andy Pettitte, Wade Miller, Roy Oswalt 10.00

Team Quad Material
NM/M
Production 100 Sets
Prime: No Pricing
Production 5 Sets
1 Jeff Kent, Lance Berkman, Craig Biggio, Jeff Bagwell 20.00
2 Nomar Garciaparra, Manny Ramirez, Pedro Martinez, Trot Nixon 35.00
3 Paul Konerko, Carlos Lee, Magglio Ordonez, Frank Thomas 20.00
4 John Smoltz, Chipper Jones, Andruw Jones, Rafael Furcal 20.00
5 Garret Anderson, Troy Percival, Troy Glaus, Darin Erstad 10.00
6 Steve Finley, Brandon Webb, Randy Johnson, Luis Gonzalez 20.00
7 Paul LoDuca, Hideo Nomo, Shawn Green, Kazuhisa Ishii 20.00
8 Larry Walker, Todd Helton, Jason Jennings, Preston Wilson 10.00
9 Dontrelle Willis, Brad Penny, Josh Beckett 20.00
10 Jose Reyes, Jae Weong Seo, Tom Glavine, Mike Piazza 20.00
11 Bernie Williams, Derek Jeter, Jason Giambi, Alfonso Soriano 40.00
12 Rich Harden, Tim Hudson, Barry Zito, Mark Mulder 10.00
13 Kevin Millwood, Marlon Byrd, Jim Thome, Bobby Abreu 20.00
14 Edgar Renteria, Jim Edmonds, Albert Pujols, Scott Rolen 40.00
15 Roger Clemens, Andy Pettitte, Wade Miller, Roy Oswalt 30.00

Tools of Trade Blue
NM/M
Common Player: 1.50
Production 250 Sets
Black: No Pricing
Production One Set
Blue Spectrum: 1-1.5X
Production 125 Sets
Green: 1-1.5X
Production 150 Sets
Green Spectrum: 2-3X
Production 50 Sets
Red: 1X
Production 200 Sets
Red Spectrum: 1-2X
Production 100 Sets
1 Adam Dunn/H 2.50

#	Player	Price
2	Adam Dunn/A	2.50
3	Alan Trammell	2.00
4	Albert Pujols/H	6.00
5	Albert Pujols/A	6.00
6	Alex Rodriguez	6.00
7	Alex Rodriguez	6.00
8	Alex Rodriguez	6.00
9	Alfonso Soriano	4.00
10	Andre Dawson	2.00
11	Andruw Jones/H	2.00
12	Andruw Jones/A	2.00
13	Andy Pettitte/H	2.00
14	Andy Pettitte/A	2.00
15	Angel Berroa	1.50
16	Aubrey Huff	1.50
17	Austin Kearns	2.00
18	Barry Zito	2.00
19	Barry Zito/A	2.00
20	Bernie Williams	2.00
21	Bobby Abreu	2.00
22	Brandon Webb	1.50
23	Cal Ripken Jr./H	8.00
24	Cal Ripken Jr./A	8.00
25	Cal Ripken Jr.	8.00
26	Carlos Beltran	2.00
27	Carlos Delgado/H	6.00
28	Carlos Delgado/A	6.00
29	Carlos Lee	1.50
30	Chipper Jones/H	3.00
31	Chipper Jones/A	3.00
32	Craig Biggio/H	2.00
33	Craig Biggio/A	2.00
34	Curt Schilling	2.00
35	Curt Schilling	2.00
36	Dale Murphy/H	2.00
37	Dale Murphy/A	2.00
38	Darryl Strawberry	1.50
39	Derek Jeter/H	8.00
40	Derek Jeter/A	8.00
41	Don Mattingly/H	8.00
42	Don Mattingly/A	8.00
43	Dontrelle Willis/H	2.00
44	Dontrelle Willis/A	2.00
45	Dwight Gooden	1.50
46	Edgar Martinez	1.50
47	Eric Chavez	1.50
48	Frank Thomas/A	2.00
49	Frank Thomas	2.00
50	Garret Anderson	2.00
51	Gary Carter	2.00
52	Gary Sheffield	2.00
53	George Brett/H	6.00
54	George Brett/A	6.00
55	Greg Maddux	4.00
56	Hank Blalock	2.00
57	Hideo Nomo	2.00
58	Ivan Rodriguez	2.00
59	Ivan Rodriguez	2.00
60	Jacque Jones	1.50
61	Jae Weong Seo	1.50
62	Jason Giambi	2.00
63	Jason Giambi	2.00
64	Javy Lopez	2.00
65	Jay Gibbons	1.50
66	Jeff Bagwell	2.00
67	Jeff Bagwell	2.00
68	Jeff Kent	1.50
69	Jim Edmonds	2.00
70	Jim Thome	3.00
71	Jorge Posada	2.00
72	Jose Canseco	2.00
73	Jose Reyes	2.00
74	Josh Beckett	2.00
75	Juan Gonzalez	2.00
76	Kazuhisa Ishii	1.50
77	Kerry Wood	3.00
78	Kerry Wood	3.00
79	Kirby Puckett	3.00
80	Lance Berkman	2.00
81	Lou Brock	2.00
82	Luis Castillo	1.50
83	Luis Gonzalez	1.50
84	Magglio Ordonez	1.50
85	Manny Ramirez	2.00
86	Manny Ramirez	2.00
87	Marcus Giles	1.50
88	Mark Grace	2.00
89	Mark Mulder	2.00
90	Mark Prior	4.00
91	Mark Prior	4.00
92	Mark Teixeira	2.00
93	Marlon Byrd	1.50
94	Miguel Cabrera	3.00
95	Miguel Tejada	2.00
96	Mike Lowell	2.00
97	Mike Mussina	2.00
98	Mike Mussina	2.00
99	Mike Piazza	4.00
100	Mike Piazza	4.00
101	Mike Piazza	4.00
102	Mike Schmidt	5.00
103	Mike Schmidt	5.00
104	Mike Sweeney	1.50
105	Nick Johnson	1.50
106	Nolan Ryan	8.00
107	Nolan Ryan	8.00
108	Nolan Ryan	8.00
109	Nomar Garciaparra	5.00
110	Nomar Garciaparra	5.00
111	Pat Burrell	2.00
112	Paul LoDuca	1.50
113	Pedro Martinez	3.00
114	Pedro Martinez	3.00
115	Preston Wilson	1.50
116	Rafael Palmeiro	2.00
117	Rafael Palmeiro	2.00
118	Randy Johnson	4.00
119	Randy Johnson	4.00
120	Richie Sexson	2.00
121	Rickey Henderson	2.00
122	Rickey Henderson	2.00
123	Rickey Henderson	2.00
124	Roberto Alomar	2.00
125	Rocco Baldelli	2.00
126	Rod Carew	2.00
127	Roger Clemens	6.00
128	Roger Clemens	6.00
129	Roy Halladay	2.00
130	Roy Oswalt	1.50
131	Ryne Sandberg	5.00
132	Sammy Sosa	5.00
133	Sammy Sosa	5.00
134	Sammy Sosa	5.00
135	Scott Rolen	4.00
136	Shawn Green	2.00
137	Steve Carlton	2.00
138	Tim Hudson	2.00
139	Todd Helton	2.00
140	Todd Helton	2.00
141	Tom Glavine	2.00
142	Tom Glavine	2.00
143	Tony Gwynn	4.00
144	Tony Gwynn	4.00
145	Torii Hunter	2.00
146	Trot Nixon	2.00
147	Troy Glaus	2.00
148	Vernon Wells	2.00
149	Vladimir Guerrero	4.00
150	Will Clark	3.00

Tools of Trade Sig Blue Spectrum
NM/M

Black: No Pricing
Production One Set
Green: No Pricing
Production 1-10
Red: .75-1.5X
Production 1-50
No pricing 15 or less.

#	Player	Price
3	Alan Trammell/100	15.00
10	Andre Dawson/100	15.00
15	Angel Berroa/100	8.00
16	Aubrey Huff/100	10.00
17	Austin Kearns/100	8.00
22	Brandon Webb/100	8.00
26	Carlos Beltran/100	20.00
29	Carlos Lee/100	15.00
36	Dale Murphy/H/50	30.00
37	Dale Murphy/A/50	30.00
38	Darryl Strawberry/50	20.00
41	Don Mattingly/H/50	75.00
42	Don Mattingly/A/50	75.00
43	Dontrelle Willis/H/25	30.00
44	Dontrelle Willis/A/25	30.00
45	Dwight Gooden/50	25.00
46	Edgar Martinez/25	30.00
48	Frank Thomas/A/25	50.00
49	Frank Thomas/25	50.00
50	Garret Anderson/100	15.00
51	Gary Carter/25	15.00
60	Jacque Jones/50	15.00
61	Jae Weong Seo/25	25.00
65	Jay Gibbons/25	15.00
69	Jim Edmonds/25	35.00
71	Jorge Posada/25	40.00
73	Jose Reyes/25	25.00
75	Juan Gonzalez/20	40.00
77	Kerry Wood/H/25	50.00
78	Kerry Wood/25	50.00
81	Lou Brock/100	25.00
84	Magglio Ordonez/50	20.00
87	Marcus Giles/50	20.00
89	Mark Mulder/25	40.00
90	Mark Prior/H/50	60.00
91	Mark Prior/A/50	60.00
92	Mark Teixeira/50	30.00
93	Marlon Byrd/50	15.00
94	Miguel Cabrera/100	35.00
102	Mike Schmidt/H/25	75.00
103	Mike Schmidt/A/25	75.00
106	Nolan Ryan/25	125.00
107	Nolan Ryan/25	125.00
108	Nolan Ryan/25	125.00
112	Paul LoDuca/50	25.00
129	Roy Halladay/25	30.00
130	Roy Oswalt/25	25.00
135	Scott Rolen/50	40.00
137	Steve Carlton/50	30.00
143	Tony Gwynn/A/25	60.00
144	Tony Gwynn/25	60.00
145	Torii Hunter/25	25.00
146	Trot Nixon/25	30.00
149	Vladimir Guerrero/25	65.00
150	Will Clark/50	50.00

Tools of Trade Material Signature Sing
NM/M

Quantity produced listed
Combo: 1-2X
Production 1-25
Combo Prime: No Pricing
Production 1-5
Trio: No Pricing
Production 1-10
Quad: No Pricing
Production 1-10

#	Player	Price
1	Adam Dunn H/Jsy/25	50.00
2	Adam Dunn A/Jsy/25	50.00
3	Alan Trammell/Jsy/25	50.00
10	Andre Dawson/Jsy/25	25.00
15	Angel Berroa/Jsy/50	15.00
17	Austin Kearns/Jsy/28	25.00
21	Bobby Abreu/Jsy/25	25.00
22	Brandon Webb/Jsy/25	20.00
26	Carlos Beltran/Jsy/15	50.00
29	Carlos Lee/Jsy/25	20.00
36	Dale Murphy/25	40.00
37	Dale Murphy/25	40.00
38	Darryl Strawberry/Jsy/39	20.00
43	Dontrelle Willis/Jsy/25	30.00
44	Dontrelle Willis/Jsy/25	30.00
45	Dwight Gooden/Jsy/16	35.00
50	Garret Anderson/Jsy/16	30.00
61	Jae Weong Seo/Jsy/25	20.00
71	Jorge Posada/Jsy/20	60.00
74	Josh Beckett/Jsy/21	40.00
82	Luis Castillo/Jsy/25	20.00
89	Mark Mulder/Jsy/20	40.00
93	Marlon Byrd/Jsy/29	20.00
94	Miguel Cabrera/Jsy/20	50.00
96	Mike Lowell/Jsy/19	30.00
112	Paul LoDuca/Jsy/50	25.00
115	Preston Wilson/Jsy/44	20.00
125	Rocco Baldelli/Jsy/25	30.00
129	Roy Halladay/Jsy/32	25.00
137	Steve Carlton/Jsy/25	50.00
145	Torii Hunter/Jsy/25	50.00
146	Trot Nixon Jsy/25	50.00

Tools of Trade Material Combo
NM/M

Production 25-250
Single: No Pricing
Production 1-5
Combo Price Single: 2-4X
Production 1-25
Trio: 1-3X
Production 5-100
No pricing 15 or less.
Quad: 2-4X
Production 1-50
No pricing 15 or less.
Five: 3-5X
Production 10-25
Six: 3-6X
Production 5-25

#	Player	Price
1	Adam Dunn Bat-Jsy/250	6.00
2	Adam Dunn Bat-Jsy/250	6.00
3	Alan Trammell Bat-Jsy/250	4.00
4	Albert Pujols/Bat-Jsy/250	20.00
5	Albert Pujols/Bat-Jsy/250	20.00
6	Alex Rodriguez/Bat-Jsy/250	10.00
7	Alex Rodriguez/Bat-Jsy/250	10.00
8	Alex Rodriguez/Bat-Jsy/250	10.00
9	Alfonso Soriano/Bat-Jsy/250	10.00
10	Andre Dawson/Bat-Jsy/250	5.00
11	Andruw Jones/Bat-Jsy/250	8.00
12	Andruw Jones/Bat-Jsy/250	8.00
13	Andy Pettitte/Bat-Jsy/250	10.00
14	Andy Pettitte/Bat-Jsy/250	10.00
15	Angel Berroa/Bat-Jsy/250	4.00
16	Aubrey Huff/Bat-Jsy/250	4.00
17	Austin Kearns/Bat-Jsy/250	6.00
18	Barry Zito/Bat-Jsy/250	6.00
19	Barry Zito/Bat-Jsy/250	6.00
20	Bernie Williams/Bat-Jsy/250	8.00
21	Bobby Abreu/Bat-Jsy/250	6.00
22	Brandon Webb/Bat-Jsy/250	6.00
23	Cal Ripken Jr./Bat-Jsy/250	30.00
24	Cal Ripken Jr./Bat-Jsy/250	30.00
25	Cal Ripken Jr./Bat-Jsy/250	30.00
26	Carlos Beltran/Bat-Jsy/250	6.00
27	Carlos Delgado/Bat-Jsy/250	6.00
28	Carlos Delgado/Bat-Jsy/250	6.00
29	Carlos Lee/Bat-Jsy/250	4.00
30	Chipper Jones/Bat-Jsy/250	10.00
31	Chipper Jones/Bat-Jsy/250	10.00
32	Craig Biggio/Bat-Jsy/250	6.00
33	Craig Biggio/Bat-Jsy/100	6.00
34	Curt Schilling/Bat-Jsy/250	8.00
35	Curt Schilling/Bat-Jsy/250	8.00
36	Dale Murphy/Bat-Jsy/250	8.00
37	Dale Murphy/Bat-Jsy/250	8.00
38	Darryl Strawberry/Bat-Jsy/250	4.00
39	Derek Jeter/Bat-Jsy/100	30.00
40	Derek Jeter/Bat-Jsy/100	30.00
41	Don Mattingly/Bat-Jsy/100	30.00
42	Don Mattingly/Bat-Jsy/100	30.00
43	Dontrelle Willis/Bat-Jsy/250	6.00
44	Dontrelle Willis/Bat-Jsy/250	6.00
45	Dwight Gooden/Bat-Jsy/250	6.00
46	Edgar Martinez/Bat-Jsy/250	6.00
47	Eric Chavez/Bat-Jsy/250	6.00
48	Frank Thomas/Bat-Jsy/250	10.00
49	Frank Thomas/Bat-Jsy/250	10.00
50	Garret Anderson/Bat-Jsy/250	6.00
51	Gary Carter/Bat-Jsy/250	6.00
52	Gary Sheffield/Bat-Jsy/250	6.00
53	George Brett/Bat-Jsy/250	20.00
54	George Brett/Bat-Jsy/250	20.00
55	Greg Maddux/Bat-Jsy/250	10.00
56	Hank Blalock/Bat-Jsy/250	8.00
57	Hideo Nomo/Bat-Jsy/250	10.00
58	Ivan Rodriguez/Bat-Jsy/250	8.00
59	Ivan Rodriguez/Bat-Jsy/250	8.00
60	Jacque Jones/Bat-Jsy/250	4.00
61	Jason Giambi/Bat-Jsy/250	8.00
62	Jason Giambi/Bat-Jsy/250	8.00
63	Jason Giambi/Bat-Jsy/250	8.00
64	Javy Lopez/Bat-Jsy/250	6.00
65	Jay Gibbons/Bat-Jsy/250	4.00
66	Jeff Bagwell/Bat-Jsy/250	8.00
67	Jeff Bagwell/Bat-Jsy/250	8.00
68	Jeff Kent Bat-Jsy/250	5.00
69	Jim Edmonds/Bat-Jsy/250	8.00
70	Jim Thome/Bat-Jsy/250	12.00
71	Jorge Posada/Bat-Jsy/250	8.00
72	Jose Canseco/Bat-Jsy/250	8.00
73	Jose Reyes/Bat-Jsy/250	8.00
74	Josh Beckett/Bat-Jsy/250	8.00
75	Juan Gonzalez/Bat-Jsy/250	8.00
76	Kazuhisa Ishii/Bat-Jsy/250	4.00
77	Kerry Wood/Bat-Jsy/250	10.00
78	Kerry Wood/Bat-Jsy/250	10.00
79	Kirby Puckett/Bat-Jsy/250	10.00
80	Lance Berkman/Bat-Jsy/250	8.00
81	Lou Brock/Bat-Jsy/250	8.00
82	Luis Castillo/Bat-Jsy/250	4.00
83	Luis Gonzalez/Bat-Jsy/250	4.00
84	Magglio Ordonez/Bat-Jsy/250	6.00
85	Manny Ramirez/Bat-Jsy/250	8.00
86	Manny Ramirez/Bat-Jsy/250	8.00
87	Marcus Giles/Bat-Jsy/250	4.00
88	Mark Grace/Bat-Jsy/250	8.00
89	Mark Mulder/Bat-Jsy/250	8.00
90	Mark Prior/Bat-Jsy/250	10.00
91	Mark Prior/Bat-Jsy/250	10.00
92	Mark Teixeira/Bat-Jsy/250	6.00
93	Marlon Byrd/Bat-Jsy/250	4.00
94	Miguel Cabrera/Bat-Jsy/250	10.00
95	Miguel Tejada/Bat-Jsy/250	6.00
96	Mike Lowell/Bat-Jsy/250	6.00
97	Mike Mussina/Jsy-Jsy/250	8.00
98	Mike Mussina/Jsy-Jsy/250	8.00
99	Mike Piazza/Bat-Jsy/250	12.00
100	Mike Piazza/Bat-Jsy/250	12.00
101	Mike Piazza/Bat-Jsy/250	12.00
102	Mike Schmidt/Bat-Jsy/100	20.00
103	Mike Schmidt/Bat-Jsy/100	20.00
104	Mike Sweeney/Bat-Jsy/250	4.00
105	Nick Johnson/Bat-Jsy/250	4.00
106	Nolan Ryan/Jkt-Jsy/250	30.00
107	Nolan Ryan/Jkt-Jsy/250	30.00
108	Nolan Ryan/Jsy-Pants/250	30.00
109	Nomar Garciaparra/Bat-Jsy/250	15.00
110	Nomar Garciaparra/Bat-Jsy/250	15.00
111	Pat Burrell/Bat-Jsy/250	8.00
112	Paul LoDuca/Bat-Jsy/250	6.00
113	Pedro J. Martinez/Bat-Jsy/250	10.00
114	Pedro Martinez/Bat-Jsy/250	10.00
115	Preston Wilson/Bat-Jsy/250	4.00
116	Rafael Palmeiro/Bat-Jsy/250	8.00
117	Rafael Palmeiro/Bat-Jsy/250	8.00
118	Randy Johnson/Bat-Jsy/250	10.00
119	Randy Johnson/Bat-Jsy/250	10.00
120	Richie Sexson/Jsy-Pants/250	6.00
121	Rickey Henderson/Bat-Jsy/250	8.00
122	Rickey Henderson/Bat-Jsy/250	8.00
123	Rickey Henderson/Bat-Jsy/250	8.00
124	Roberto Alomar/Bat-Jsy/250	8.00
125	Rocco Baldelli/Bat-Jsy/250	6.00
126	Rod Carew/Bat-Jsy/250	8.00
127	Roger Clemens/Bat-Jsy/250	15.00
128	Roger Clemens/Bat-Jsy/250	15.00
129	Roy Halladay/Jsy-Jsy/250	4.00
130	Roy Oswalt/Bat-Jsy/250	6.00
131	Ryne Sandberg/Bat-Jsy/250	15.00
132	Sammy Sosa/Bat-Jsy/250	15.00
133	Sammy Sosa/Bat-Jsy/250	15.00
134	Sammy Sosa/Bat-Jsy/250	15.00
135	Scott Rolen/Bat-Jsy/250	10.00
136	Shawn Green/Bat-Jsy/250	6.00
137	Steve Carlton/Bat-Jsy/250	6.00
138	Tim Hudson/Bat-Jsy/250	6.00
139	Todd Helton/Bat-Jsy/250	8.00
140	Todd Helton/Bat-Jsy/250	8.00
141	Tom Glavine/Bat-Jsy/250	8.00
142	Tom Glavine/Bat-Jsy/250	8.00
143	Tony Gwynn/Bat-Jsy/250	12.00
144	Tony Gwynn/Bat-Jsy/250	12.00
145	Torii Hunter/Bat-Jsy/250	6.00
146	Trot Nixon/Bat-Jsy/250	6.00
147	Troy Glaus/Bat-Jsy/250	6.00
148	Vernon Wells/Bat-Jsy/250	4.00
149	Vladimir Guerrero/Bat-Jsy/250	10.00
150	Will Clark/Bat-Jsy/250	10.00

2004 Playoff Honors
NM/M

Complete Set (250):
Common Player (1-200): .15
Common SP (201-250): 3.00
Production 1,999
Common SP Auto.
(226-250): 8.00
Pack (6): 5.00
Box (12): 55.00

#	Player	Price
1	Bartolo Colon	.15
2	Garret Anderson	.40
3	Tim Salmon	.25
4	Troy Glaus	.25
5	Vladimir Guerrero	.75
6	Brandon Webb	.15
7	Brian Bruney	.15
8	Luis Gonzalez	.25
9	Randy Johnson	.75
10	Richie Sexson	.40
11	Robby Hammock	.15
12	Roberto Alomar	.40
13	Shea Hillenbrand	.15
14	Steve Finley	.15
15	Adam LaRoche	.15
16	Andruw Jones	.50
17	Bubba Nelson	.15
18	Chipper Jones	.75
19	Dale Murphy	.50
20	J.D. Drew	.25
21	John Smoltz	.25
22	Marcus Giles	.15
23	Rafael Furcal	.25
24	Warren Spahn	.75
25	Greg Maddux	1.00
26	Adam Loewen	.15
27	Cal Ripken Jr.	3.00
28	Javy Lopez	.25
29	Jay Gibbons	.15
30	Luis Matos	.15
31	Miguel Tejada	.40
32	Rafael Palmeiro	.25
33	Bobby Doerr	.15
34	Curt Schilling	.50
35	Edwin Almonte	.15
36	Jason Varitek	.25
37	Kevin Youkilis	.15
38	Manny Ramirez	.50
39	Nomar Garciaparra	1.00
40	Pedro J. Martinez	.75
41	Trot Nixon	.25
42	Andre Dawson	.25
43	Aramis Ramirez	.40
44	Brendan Harris	.15
45	Derek Lee	.25
46	Ernie Banks	.75
47	Kerry Wood	.75
48	Mark Prior	1.00
49	Ryne Sandberg	1.00
50	Sammy Sosa	1.50
51	Carlos Lee	.15
52	Frank Thomas	.75
53	Joe Borchard	.15
54	Joe Crede	.15
55	Magglio Ordonez	.50
56	Adam Dunn	.50
57	Austin Kearns	.25
58	Barry Larkin	.40
59	Brandon Larson	.15
60	Ken Griffey Jr.	1.00
61	Ryan Wagner	.15
62	Sean Casey	.25
63	Bob Feller	.25
64	Brian Tallet	.15
65	C.C. Sabathia	.15
66	Jeremy Guthrie	.15
67	Jody Gerut	.15
68	Clint Barmes	.15
69	Jeff Baker	.15
70	Joe Kennedy	.15
71	Larry Walker	.25
72	Preston Wilson	.15
73	Todd Helton	.50
74	Alan Trammell	.15
75	Dmitri Young	.15
76	Ivan Rodriguez	.50
77	Jeremy Bonderman	.15
78	Preston Larrison	.15
79	Dontrelle Willis	.25
80	Josh Beckett	.50
81	Juan Pierre	.15
82	Luis Castillo	.15
83	Miguel Cabrera	.75
84	Mike Lowell	.25
85	Andy Pettitte	.25
86	Chris Burke	.15
87	Craig Biggio	.25
88	Jeff Bagwell	.50
89	Jeff Kent	.25
90	Lance Berkman	.25
91	Morgan Ensberg	.15
92	Richard Hidalgo	.15
93	Roger Clemens	1.50
94	Roy Oswalt	.25
95	Angel Berroa	.15
96	Byron Gettis	.15
97	Carlos Beltran	.40
98	George Brett	2.00
99	Juan Gonzalez	.50

100	Mike Sweeney	.15
101	Duke Snider	.50
102	Edwin Jackson	.15
103	Eric Gagne	.50
104	Hideo Nomo	.40
105	Hong-Chih Kuo	.15
106	Kazuhisa Ishii	.15
107	Paul LoDuca	.15
108	Robin Ventura	.15
109	Shawn Green	.25
110	Junior Spivey	.15
111	Rickie Weeks	.25
112	Scott Podsednik	.25
113	J.D. Durbin	.15
114	Jacque Jones	.15
115	Jason Kubel	.25
116	Johan Santana	.15
117	Shannon Stewart	.15
118	Torii Hunter	.25
119	Brad Wilkerson	.15
120	Jose Vidro	.15
121	Nick Johnson	.15
122	Orlando Cabrera	.15
123	Gary Carter	.25
124	Jae Weong Seo	.15
125	Lenny Dykstra	.15
126	Mike Piazza	1.00
127	Tom Glavine	.25
128	Alex Rodriguez	1.50
129	Bernie Williams	.40
130	Chien-Ming Wang	1.00
131	Derek Jeter	2.00
132	Don Mattingly	1.50
133	Gary Sheffield	.40
134	Hideki Matsui	1.50
135	Jason Giambi	.50
136	Javier Vazquez	.25
137	Jorge Posada	.40
138	Jose Contreras	.15
139	Kevin Brown	.25
140	Mariano Rivera	.40
141	Mike Mussina	.40
142	Whitey Ford	.50
143	Barry Zito	.40
144	Eric Chavez	.25
145	Mark Mulder	.40
146	Rich Harden	.15
147	Tim Hudson	.25
148	Reggie Jackson	.50
149	Rickey Henderson	.50
150	Brett Myers	.15
151	Bobby Abreu	.25
152	Jim Thome	.75
153	Kevin Millwood	.25
154	Marlon Byrd	.15
155	Mike Schmidt	1.50
156	Ryan Howard	3.00
157	Jack Wilson	.15
158	Jason Kendall	.15
159	Brian Giles	.25
160	David Wells	.15
161	Jay Payton	.15
162	Phil Nevin	.15
163	Ryan Klesko	.15
164	Sean Burroughs	.15
165	A.J. Pierzynski	.15
166	J.T. Snow	.15
167	Jason Schmidt	.50
168	Jerome Williams	.15
169	Will Clark	.50
170	Bret Boone	.15
171	Chris Snelling	.15
172	Edgar Martinez	.25
173	Ichiro Suzuki	1.50
174	Randy Winn	.15
175	Rich Aurilia	.15
176	Shigetoshi Hasegawa	.15
177	Albert Pujols	.15
178	Dan Haren	.15
179	Edgar Renteria	.25
180	Jim Edmonds	.40
181	Matt Morris	.15
182	Scott Rolen	.75
183	Stan Musial	1.00
184	Aubrey Huff	.15
185	Chad Gaudin	.15
186	Delmon Young	.25
187	Fred McGriff	.15
188	Rocco Baldelli	.15
189	Alfonso Soriano	.75
190	Hank Blalock	.50
191	Mark Teixeira	.40
192	Nolan Ryan	2.00
193	Alexis Rios	.15
194	Carlos Delgado	.40
195	Dustin McGowan	.15
196	Guillermo Quiroz	.15
197	Josh Phelps	.15
198	Roy Halladay	.25
199	Vernon Wells	.15
200	Vinnie Chulk	.15
201	Jose Capellan/ 1999 RC	5.00
202	Kazuo Matsui/ 1999 RC	5.00
203	David Crouthers/1999	3.00
204	Akinori Otsuka/ 1999 RC	5.00
205	Nick Regilio/1999 RC	3.00
206	Justin Hampson/ 1999 RC	3.00
207	Lincoln Holdzkom/ 1999 RC	5.00
208	Jorge Sequea/ 1999 RC	3.00
209	Justin Leone/1999 RC	5.00
210	Renyel Pinto/1999 RC	3.00

211	Mariano Gomez/ 1999 RC	3.00
212	Onil Joseph/ Auto./1000 RC	8.00
213	Josh Labandeira/ AU/1000 RC	10.00
214	Cory Sullivan/ 1999 RC	3.00
215	Carlos Vasquez/ Auto./675 RC	8.00
216	Chris Shelton/ 1999 RC	8.00
217	Willy Taveras/1999 RC	6.00
218	John Gall/1999 RC	5.00
219	Jerry Gil/1999 RC	5.00
220	Jason Frasor/1999 RC	3.00
221	Justin Knoedler/ 1999 RC	3.00
222	Ronald Belisario/ 1999 RC	3.00
223	Mike Rouse/1999 RC	3.00
224	Dennis Sarfate/ 1999 RC	3.00
225	Casey Daigle/1999 RC	3.00
226	Shingo Takatsu/ Auto./800 RC	10.00
227	Jason Bartlett/ Auto./800 RC	8.00
228	Alfredo Simon/ Auto./1000 RC	8.00
229	Chris Oxspring/ 1999 RC	3.00
230	Fernando Nieve/ Auto./1000 RC	8.00
231	Ruddy Yan/ Auto./800 RC	8.00
232	Ryan Wing/1999 RC	3.00
233	Tim Bittner/ Auto./1000 RC	8.00
234	Ramon Ramirez/ Auto./1000 RC	8.00
235	Sean Henn/Auto./1000 RC	8.00
236	Roberto Novoa RC	4.00
237	Jerome Gamble/ Auto./800 RC	8.00
238	Jamie Brown/ Auto./800 RC	8.00
239	Ian Snell/ Auto./800 RC	30.00
240	Freddy Guzman/ Auto./800 RC	8.00
241	Aarom Baldiris/ Auto./1000 RC	8.00
242	Greg Dobbs/1999 RC	3.00
243	Ivan Ochoa/1999 RC	3.00
244	Angel Chavez/ Auto./800 RC	8.00
245	Merkin Valdez/ Auto./800 RC	10.00
246	Mike Gosling/ Auto./800	8.00
247	Carlos Hines/ Auto./800 RC	8.00
248	Graham Koonce/ Auto./1000	10.00
249	William Bergolla/ Auto./1000 RC	8.00
250	Hector Gimenez/ Auto./1000 RC	8.00

Credits Bronze

Bronze (1-200):	3-6X
Bronze (201-250):	.5-1X
Production 100 Sets	

Credits Silver

Silver (1-200):	4-8X
Silver (201-250):	No Pricing
Production 50 Sets	

Credits Gold

Gold (1-200):	8-15X
Gold (201-250):	No Pricing
Production 25 Sets	

Credits Platinum

No Pricing
Production One Set

Awards

		NM/M
Common Player:		2.00
Quantity produced listed		
1	Phil Rizzuto/1950	3.00
2	Fred Lynn/1975	2.00
3	George Brett/1980	8.00
4	Cal Ripken Jr./1983	10.00
5	Don Mattingly/1985	8.00
6	Rickey Henderson/ 1990	
7	Stan Musial/1943	5.00
8	Marty Marion/1944	3.00
9	Ernie Banks/1958	5.00
10	Sammy Sosa/1998	3.00
11	Terry Pendleton/1991	2.00
12	Ryne Sandberg/1984	3.00
13	Andre Dawson/1987	3.00
14	George Foster/1977	2.00
15	Dave Parker/1978	2.00
16	Keith Hernandez/1979	3.00
17	Mike Schmidt/1980	6.00
18	Dale Murphy/1982	3.00
19	Whitey Ford/1961	3.00
20	Roy Halladay/2003	2.00
21	Orel Hershiser/1988	2.00
22	Bob Feller/1940	3.00

23	Dwight Gooden/1985	2.00
24	Steve Carlton/1972	3.00
25	Randy Johnson/2002	4.00

Awards Signature

		NM/M
Quantity produced listed		
1	Phil Rizzuto/50	25.00
3	Fred Lynn/100	15.00
7	Stan Musial/50	50.00
8	Marty Marion/50	10.00
10	Sammy Sosa/21	125.00
11	Terry Pendleton/100	10.00
13	Andre Dawson/100	15.00
14	George Foster/100	15.00
15	Dave Parker/88	15.00
16	Keith Hernandez/100	20.00
19	Whitey Ford/50	25.00
20	Roy Halladay/25	25.00
21	Orel Hershiser/25	40.00
22	Bob Feller/100	15.00
23	Dwight Gooden/100	15.00

Champions

		NM/M
Common Player:		2.00
Quantity produced listed		
1	Stan Musial/1951	5.00
2	Warren Spahn/1958	3.00
3	Bob Gibson/1968	3.00
4	Mike Schmidt/1980	6.00
5	Dale Murphy/1982	4.00
6	Steve Carlton/1983	4.00
7	Will Clark/1988	4.00
8	Nolan Ryan/1990	10.00
9	Ryne Sandberg/1990	6.00
10	Roger Clemens/1990	8.00
11	George Brett/1990	8.00
12	Tony Gwynn/1997	5.00
13	Todd Helton/2000	4.00
14	Troy Glaus/2000	2.00
15	Sammy Sosa/2000	6.00
16	Pedro J. Martinez/ 2000	4.00
17	Mark Mulder/2001	3.00
18	Manny Ramirez/2002	3.00
19	Lance Berkman/2002	2.00
20	Alex Rodriguez/ Rgr/2002	6.00

Champions Jersey

		NM/M
Common Jersey:		5.00
Quantity produced listed		
1	Stan Musial/100	30.00
2	Warren Spahn/100	10.00
3	Bob Gibson/100	10.00
4	Mike Schmidt/100	20.00
5	Dale Murphy/82	8.00
6	Steve Carlton/100	8.00
7	Will Clark/100	8.00
8	Nolan Ryan/100	25.00
9	Ryne Sandberg/100	8.00
10	Roger Clemens/100	15.00
11	George Brett/100	25.00
12	Tony Gwynn/250	10.00
13	Todd Helton/250	8.00
14	Troy Glaus/250	5.00
15	Sammy Sosa/250	15.00
16	Pedro J. Martinez/250	8.00
17	Mark Mulder/250	5.00
18	Manny Ramirez/250	8.00
19	Lance Berkman/250	5.00
20	Alex Rodriguez/250	10.00

Champions Signature

		NM/M
Quantity produced listed		
1	Stan Musial/50	50.00
3	Bob Gibson/50	25.00
7	Will Clark/50	40.00
8	Nolan Ryan/34	100.00

Champions Jersey Signature

No Pricing
Production Five Sets

Class Reunion

		NM/M
Quantity produced listed		
1	Eddie Murray, Gary Carter/2003	3.00

2	Carlton Fisk, Tony Perez/2000	3.00
3	Nolan Ryan, George Brett/1999	10.00
4	Rod Carew, Fergie Jenkins/1991	3.00
5	Joe Morgan, Jim Palmer/1990	3.00
6	Carl Yastrzemski, Johnny Bench/1989	5.00
	Harmon Killebrew, Luis Aparicio/1984	3.00
8	Brooks Robinson, Juan Marichal/1983	3.00
9	Al Kaline, Duke Snider/1980	3.00
10	Roberto Clemente, Warren Spahn/1973	8.00
11	Mark Prior, Mark Teixeira/2001	3.00
12	Josh Beckett, Barry Zito/1999	3.00
13	Mark Mulder, Adam Dunn/1998	3.00
14	Vernon Wells, Lance Berkman/1997	3.00
15	Eric Chavez, Nick Johnson/1996	3.00
16	Kerry Wood, Roy Halladay/1995	4.00
17	Todd Helton, Carlos Beltran/1995	4.00
18	Derek Jeter, Jason Giambi/1992	8.00
19	Manny Ramirez, Shawn Green/1991	4.00
20	Chipper Jones, Mike Mussina/1990	4.00

Class Reunion Material

		NM/M
Quantity produced listed		
1	Eddie Murray/Jsy, Gary Carter/Jsy/100	15.00
2	Carlton Fisk/Jsy, Tony Perez/Bat/250	20.00
3	Nolan Ryan/Jsy, George Brett/Jsy/100	50.00
4	Rod Carew/Jsy, Fergie Jenkins, Pants/250	15.00
5	Joe Morgan/Jsy, Jim Palmer/Jsy/100	10.00
6	Carl Yastrzemski/Jsy, Johnny Bench/ Jsy/250	30.00
7	Harmon Killebrew/Jsy, Luis Aparicio/Jsy/250	15.00
8	Brooks Robinson/Jsy, Juan Marichal/ Jsy/100	15.00
9	Al Kaline/Jsy, Duke Snider/Jsy/25	35.00
10	Roger Clemens/Jsy, Warren Spahn/ Jsy/100	80.00
11	Mark Prior/Jsy, Mark Teixeira/Jsy/250	10.00
12	Josh Beckett/Jsy, Barry Zito/Jsy/250	8.00
13	Mark Mulder/Jsy, Adam Dunn/Jsy/250	10.00
14	Vernon Wells/Jsy, Lance Berkman/Jsy/250	8.00
15	Eric Chavez/Jsy, Nick Johnson/Jsy/250	8.00
16	Kerry Wood/Jsy, Roy Halladay/Jsy/250	12.00
17	Todd Helton/Jsy, Carlos Beltran/Jsy/250	
18	Derek Jeter/Jsy, Jason Giambi/Jsy/250	20.00
19	Manny Ramirez/Jsy, Shawn Green/Jsy/50	10.00
20	Chipper Jones/Jsy, Mike Mussina/Jsy/250	10.00

Game Day Souvenir

		NM/M
2	Bob Gibson/Jsy/75	15.00
3	Frank Robinson/ Bat/61	10.00

4	Tony Gwynn/ Pants/99	20.00
5	Warren Spahn/ Jsy/53	20.00
6	George Brett/Bat/77	25.00
7	Cal Ripken Jr./ Hat/19	100.00
8	Frank Thomas/Bat/93	10.00
9	Sammy Sosa/ Jsy/100	15.00
10	Harmon Killebrew/ Bat/75	15.00

Game Day Souvenir Signature

No Pricing
Production 5 Sets

Piece of the Game Bat

		NM/M
1	Albert Pujols/250	15.00
2	Angel Berroa/250	4.00
3	Aubrey Huff/250	4.00
4	Barry Zito/250	6.00
5	Bobby Abreu/250	4.00
6	Carlos Beltran/250	4.00
7	Chipper Jones/250	8.00
8	Derek Jeter/250	20.00
9	Eric Chavez/150	6.00
10	Eric Hinske/250	6.00
11	Gary Sheffield/250	6.00
12	George Brett/250	15.00
13	Jay Gibbons/250	4.00
14	Jim Edmonds/250	6.00
15	Josh Beckett/250	6.00
16	Manny Ramirez/250	8.00
17	Mark Mulder/250	6.00
18	Marlon Byrd/250	4.00
19	Mike Lowell/250	4.00
20	Mike Schmidt/250	20.00
21	Nolan Ryan/250	20.00
22	Rafael Furcal/250	4.00
23	Randy Johnson/100	10.00
24	Rod Carew/250	8.00
25	Torii Hunter/250	4.00

Piece of the Game Bat Signature

No Pricing
Production 1-10

Piece of the Game Jersey

		NM/M
Quantity produced listed		
1	Albert Pujols/250	15.00
2	Angel Berroa/250	4.00
3	Aubrey Huff/250	4.00
4	Barry Zito/250	6.00
5	Bobby Abreu/250	4.00
6	Carlos Beltran/250	4.00
7	Chipper Jones/250	8.00
8	Derek Jeter/250	40.00
9	Eric Chavez/250	5.00
10	Eric Hinske/250	4.00
12	George Brett/250	15.00
13	Jay Gibbons/250	4.00
14	Jim Edmonds/250	6.00
15	Josh Beckett/250	4.00
16	Manny Ramirez/250	6.00
17	Mark Mulder/100	6.00
18	Marlon Byrd/250	4.00
19	Mike Lowell/250	4.00
20	Mike Schmidt/250	35.00
21	Nolan Ryan/100	25.00
22	Rafael Furcal/250	4.00
23	Randy Johnson/250	8.00
24	Rod Carew/250	8.00
25	Torii Hunter/250	4.00

Piece of the Game Jersey Signature

Quantity produced listed

Piece of the Game Combo

		NM/M
1	Albert Pujols/ Bat-Jsy/100	25.00
2	Angel Berroa/ Bat-Pants/100	6.00
3	Aubrey Huff/ Bat-Jsy/100	6.00
4	Barry Zito/Bat-Jsy/100	6.00
5	Bobby Abreu/ Bat-Jsy/100	6.00
6	Carlos Beltran/ Bat-Jsy/100	6.00

7	Chipper Jones/ Bat-Jsy/100	10.00
8	Derek Jeter/ Bat-Jsy/100	40.00
9	Eric Chavez/ Bat-Jsy/50	8.00
10	Eric Hinske/Bat-Jsy/25	8.00
12	George Brett/ Bat-Jsy/100	6.00
13	Jay Gibbons/ Bat-Jsy/100	6.00
14	Jim Edmonds/ Bat-Jsy/100	8.00
15	Josh Beckett/ Bat-Jsy/100	6.00
16	Manny Ramirez/ Bat-Jsy/100	10.00
17	Mark Mulder/ Bat-Jsy/25	15.00
18	Marlon Byrd/ Bat-Jsy/100	6.00
19	Mike Lowell/ Bat-Jsy/100	6.00
20	Mike Schmidt/ Bat-Jsy/50	50.00
21	Nolan Ryan/ Bat-Jsy/100	35.00
22	Rafael Furcal/ Bat-Jsy/100	6.00
23	Randy Johnson/ Bat-Jsy/100	15.00
24	Rod Carew/ Bat-Jsy/100	15.00
25	Torii Hunter/ Bat-Jsy/100	8.00

Piece of the Game Combo Signature

No Pricing
Production 1-10

Prime Signature Autograph

		NM/M
1	Garret Anderson/100	15.00
2	Rafael Palmeiro/50	40.00
3	Vladimir Guerrero/50	50.00
5	Dontrelle Willis/50	30.00
6	Miguel Cabrera/50	35.00
7	Shannon Stewart/100	15.00
9	Gary Sheffield/50	25.00
12	Tom Glavine/25	40.00
13	Brandon Webb/100	10.00
14	Carlos Lee/100	10.00
17	Magglio Ordonez/100	15.00
19	Andruw Jones/50	20.00
21	Sammy Sosa/50	100.00
22	Juan Gonzalez/50	25.00
23	Jeff Bagwell/25	50.00
24	Rickey Henderson/25	75.00
25	Mike Schmidt/50	60.00
26	Jim Rice/100	15.00
27	Billy Williams/100	15.00
28	Lou Brock/100	20.00
29	Robin Yount/25	75.00
30	Nolan Ryan/50	85.00
31	Darryl Strawberry/ 100	15.00
32	Cal Ripken Jr./25	200.00
33	Andre Dawson/100	15.00
34	Don Mattingly/50	75.00
35	Paul Molitor/25	50.00
36	Bo Jackson/50	75.00
37	Ernie Banks/50	50.00
38	Orel Hershiser/100	20.00
39	Mark Grace/50	40.00
40	Carlton Fisk/50	25.00

Prime Signature Autograph Bat

Quantity produced listed

Prime Signature Autograph Jersey

		NM/M
Quantity produced listed		
2	Rafael Palmeiro/25	75.00
6	Miguel Cabrera/20	75.00
7	Shannon Stewart/23	15.00
29	Robin Yount/19	75.00
31	Darryl Strawberry/25	25.00
34	Don Mattingly/23	100.00
39	Mark Grace/17	65.00

Prime Signature Insert

		NM/M
Production 2,500 Sets		
1	Garret Anderson	2.00
2	Rafael Palmeiro	3.00
3	Vladimir Guerrero	3.00
4	Alex Rodriguez	5.00
5	Dontrelle Willis	2.00
6	Miguel Cabrera	3.00
7	Shannon Stewart	2.00
8	Mike Piazza	4.00
9	Gary Sheffield	2.00
10	Ivan Rodriguez	3.00
11	Randy Johnson	3.00
12	Tom Glavine	2.00
13	Brandon Webb	2.00
14	Carlos Lee	2.00
15	Hideo Nomo	2.00

16 Mike Mussina 3.00
17 Magglio Ordonez 2.00
18 Austin Kearns 2.00
19 Andruw Jones 3.00
20 Mariano Rivera 3.00
21 Sammy Sosa 4.00
22 Juan Gonzalez 3.00
23 Jeff Bagwell 3.00
24 Rickey Henderson 3.00
25 Mike Schmidt 5.00
26 Jim Rice 2.00
27 Billy Williams 2.00
28 Lou Brock 2.00
29 Robin Yount 4.00
30 Nolan Ryan 4.00
31 Darryl Strawberry 2.00
32 Cal Ripken Jr. 10.00
33 Andre Dawson 2.00
34 Don Mattingly 8.00
35 Paul Molitor 3.00
36 Bo Jackson 3.00
37 Ernie Banks 4.00
38 Orel Hershiser 2.00
39 Mark Grace 3.00
40 Carlton Fisk 3.00

Quad Material
NM/M
Quantity produced listed
1 Matt Williams, Mark Grace, Will Clark, Keith Hernandez/100 60.00
2 Jason Giambi, Jim Thome, Carlos Delgado, Rafael Palmeiro/100 20.00
3 Albert Pujols, Ernie Banks, Jeff Bagwell, Jim Thome/100 50.00
4 Paul Molitor, Joe Morgan, Ryne Sandberg, Alfonso Soriano/50 50.00
5 Cal Ripken Jr., Derek Jeter, Alex Rodriguez, Nomar Garciaparra/100 75.00
6 Ozzie Smith, Robin Yount, Alan Trammell, Dave Concepcion/50 50.00
8 Johnny Bench, Carlton Fisk, Gary Carter, Mike Piazza/100 40.00
9 Todd Helton, Brian Giles, Edgar Renteria, Scott Rolen/25 40.00
10 Carlos Delgado, Alfonso Soriano, Alex Rodriguez, Troy Glaus/20 20.00
11 Harmon Killebrew, Reggie Jackson, Mike Schmidt, Sammy Sosa/100 65.00
12 Stan Musial, Rickey Henderson, Tony Gwynn, Lou Brock/25 80.00
13 Cal Ripken Jr., George Brett, Paul Molitor, Rod Carew/100 75.00
14 Sammy Sosa, Vladimir Guerrero, Manny Ramirez, Magglio Ordonez/100 40.00
15 Andruw Jones, Jim Edmonds, Torii Hunter, Vernon Wells/100 20.00
16 Chipper Jones, Shawn Green, Andruw Jones, Lance Berkman/100 20.00
17 Tony Gwynn, Dale Murphy, Kirby Puckett, Andre Dawson/100 40.00
19 Nolan Ryan, Roger Clemens, Kerry Wood, Josh Beckett/100 75.00
21 Dennis Eckersley, John Smoltz, Mariano Rivera, Lee Smith/100 40.00
22 Mike Mussina, Greg Maddux, Jack Morris, Bert Blyleven/100 40.00
23 Steve Carlton, Tom Glavine, Barry Zito, Andy Pettitte/100 20.00
24 Whitey Ford, Warren Spahn, Bob Feller, Juan Marichal/25 80.00
25 Nolan Ryan, Roger Clemens, Steve Carlton, Randy Johnson/100 80.00

Rookie Year Jersey Number
NM/M
1 Gary Carter/50 50.00
2 Robin Yount/50 30.00
3 Roger Clemens/25 40.00
4 Gary Sheffield/50 30.00
5 Mike Piazza/25 30.00
6 Hideo Nomo/25 30.00
7 Alex Rodriguez/50 20.00
8 Mark Prior/25 15.00

9 Dontrelle Willis/100 10.00
10 Angel Berroa/100 8.00

Rookie Year Jersey Signature
No Pricing
Production 1-10

Signature Bronze
NM/M
Quantity produced listed
2 Garret Anderson/100 15.00
5 Vladimir Guerrero/50 50.00
6 Brandon Webb/100 8.00
7 Brian Bruney/96 8.00
11 Robby Hammock/100 8.00
13 Shea Hillenbrand/100 8.00
15 Adam LaRoche/100 10.00
16 Andruw Jones/100 25.00
17 Bubba Nelson/100 8.00
22 Marcus Giles/100 15.00
23 Rafael Furcal/100 15.00
26 Adam Loewen/100 8.00
27 Cal Ripken Jr./25 150.00
29 Jay Gibbons/100 8.00
30 Luis Matos/100 8.00
33 Bobby Doerr/100 15.00
35 Edwin Almonte/99 8.00
36 Jason Varitek/50 30.00
37 Kevin Youkilis/100 15.00
42 Andre Dawson/100 15.00
43 Aramis Ramirez/25 25.00
44 Brendan Harris/100 8.00
45 Derek Lee/100 20.00
46 Ernie Banks/25 60.00
47 Kerry Wood/25 50.00
48 Mark Prior/50 40.00
50 Sammy Sosa/50 125.00
51 Carlos Lee/100 8.00
52 Frank Thomas/25 50.00
53 Joe Borchard/100 8.00
54 Joe Crede/50 10.00
55 Magglio Ordonez/50 15.00
58 Barry Larkin/25 40.00
59 Brandon Larson/100 8.00
61 Ryan Wagner/100 8.00
63 Bob Feller/100 20.00
64 Brian Tallet/100 8.00
66 Jeremy Guthrie/100 8.00
67 Jody Gerut/100 10.00
68 Clint Barmes/100 8.00
69 Jeff Baker/25 15.00
72 Preston Wilson/100 15.00
74 Alan Trammell/100 15.00
78 Preston Larrison/100 8.00
79 Dontrelle Willis/25 30.00
83 Miguel Cabrera/100 40.00
85 Andy Pettitte/25 50.00
86 Chris Burke/100 8.00
88 Jeff Bagwell/25 50.00
91 Morgan Ensberg/100 10.00
96 Byron Gettis/100 8.00
97 Carlos Beltran/100 30.00
98 George Brett/25 100.00
101 Duke Snider/100 25.00
102 Edwin Jackson/100 8.00
105 Hong-Chih Kuo/100 25.00
106 Kazuhisa Ishii/25 40.00
107 Paul LoDuca/100 15.00
108 Robin Ventura/50 15.00
110 Junior Spivey/50 10.00
112 Scott Podsednik/100 15.00
113 J.D. Durbin/100 8.00
114 Jacque Jones/100 15.00
116 Johan Santana/100 25.00
117 Shannon Stewart/50 10.00
123 Gary Carter/100 15.00
125 Lenny Dykstra/100 15.00
130 Chien-Ming Wang/100 100.00
132 Don Mattingly/25 80.00
133 Gary Sheffield/50 25.00
137 Jorge Posada/50 25.00
142 Whitey Ford/25 25.00
145 Mark Mulder/100 15.00
146 Rich Harden/100 15.00
147 Tim Hudson/25 15.00
148 Reggie Jackson/25 50.00
149 Rickey Henderson/25 80.00
150 Brett Myers/100 8.00
154 Marlon Byrd/100 8.00
155 Mike Schmidt/50 60.00
156 Ryan Howard/100 8.00
161 Jay Payton/100 10.00
168 Jerome Williams/50 10.00
169 Will Clark/50 50.00
171 Chris Snelling/100 8.00
176 Shigetoshi Hasegawa/100 50.00
178 Dan Haren/100 8.00
180 Jim Edmonds/25 30.00
182 Scott Rolen/25 30.00
183 Stan Musial/50 60.00
184 Aubrey Huff/100 15.00
185 Chad Gaudin/100 8.00
190 Delmon Young/50 30.00
191 Mark Teixeira/50 25.00
192 Nolan Ryan/50 100.00
193 Alexis Rios/100 15.00
195 Dustin McGowan/100 10.00
196 Guillermo Quiroz/50 15.00
197 Josh Phelps/25 15.00
198 Roy Halladay/25 15.00
200 Vinnie Chulk/25 15.00
201 Jose Capellan/100 35.00
203 David Crouthers/100 8.00

204 Akinori Otsuka/100 35.00
205 Nick Regilio/100 8.00
206 Justin Hampson/100 8.00
207 Lincoln Holdzkom/100 8.00
208 Jorge Sequea/100 8.00
209 Justin Leone/100 15.00
210 Renyel Pinto/100 8.00
211 Mariano Gomez/100 8.00
214 Cory Sullivan/100 8.00
216 Chris Shelton/100 40.00
217 Willy Taveras/25 8.00
218 John Gall/100 15.00
222 Ronald Belisario/100 8.00
223 Mike Rouse/100 8.00
224 Dennis Sarfate/100 8.00

2004 Playoff Honors Signature Silver
Silver: .75-1.5X Bronze
Production 1-100
No pricing 25 or less.

Signature Gold
Gold: .75-1.5X Bronze
Production 1-50
No pricing 25 or less.

Signature Platinum
No Pricing
Production One Set

Signs of Greatness
NM/M
Quantity produced listed
1 Mark Prior/25 50.00
2 Scott Podsednik/25 25.00
3 Dontrelle Willis/25 30.00
4 Rocco Baldelli/20 40.00
5 Brandon Webb/25 20.00
6 Rich Harden/25 25.00
7 Miguel Cabrera/25 50.00
8 Josh Beckett/25 25.00
9 Mark Teixeira/25 40.00

Tandem Material
NM/M
Common Duo: 10.00
Quantity produced listed
1 Bo Jackson, Deion Sanders/100 30.00
2 Eddie Murray, Rafael Palmeiro/250 15.00
3 Alex Rodriguez, Dale Murphy/250 15.00
4 Carlton Fisk, Ivan Rodriguez/250 15.00
5 Rickey Henderson, Lou Brock/50 30.00
6 Sammy Sosa, Ernie Banks/250 25.00
7 Warren Spahn, Steve Carlton/100 15.00
8 Carl Yastrzemski, Darrell Evans/250 25.00
9 Keith Hernandez, Lenny Dykstra/250 10.00
10 Pee Wee Reese, Marty Marion/100 15.00
11 Hideo Nomo, Chipper Jones/250 15.00
12 Willie McCovey, Reggie Jackson/100 20.00
13 Mark Prior, Barry Zito/250 10.00
14 Cal Ripken Jr., Miguel Tejada/Bat/100 50.00
15 Roberto Clemente, Vladimir Guerrero/Bat/100 75.00
16 Gary Carter, Mike Piazza/250 15.00
17 Jim Rice, Fred Lynn/50 20.00
18 Willie Stargell, Keith Hernandez/250 15.00
19 Nomar Garciaparra, Mark Teixeira/100 20.00
20 Derek Jeter, Phil Rizzuto/50 50.00
21 Eric Chavez, Hank Blalock/100 15.00
22 Eric Davis, Darryl Strawberry/100 15.00
23 Rickey Henderson, Deion Sanders/100 30.00
24 Dave Parker, Austin Kearns/250 10.00

25 Luis Aparicio, Dave Concepcion/100 15.00
26 Rafael Palmeiro, Will Clark/100 25.00
27 Ryne Sandberg, Ozzie Smith/250 50.00
28 Alex Rodriguez M's, Jose Canseco/250 15.00
29 Sammy Sosa, Juan Gonzalez/250 15.00
30 Pedro J. Martinez, Juan Marichal/50 20.00
32 Dwight Gooden, Gary Sheffield/250 10.00
33 Lou Boudreau, Omar Vizquel/100 15.00
34 Mark Prior, Ron Santo Bat/100 30.00
35 Albert Pujols, Ken Boyer/250 25.00
36 Tom Seaver, Curt Schilling/250 15.00
37 Joe Morgan, Jeff Kent/250 10.00
38 Steve Garvey, Ozzie Smith/250 25.00
39 Mike Piazza, Ivan Rodriguez/250 15.00
40 Mike Schmidt, Jim Thome/100 25.00

2004 Playoff Prestige
NM/M
Complete Set (200): 35.00
Common Player: .15
Pack (6): 3.50
Box (24): 75.00
1 Bengie Molina .15
2 Garret Anderson .25
3 Jarrod Washburn .15
4 Scott Spiezio .15
5 Tim Salmon .25
6 Troy Glaus .40
7 Alex Cintron .15
8 Brandon Webb .25
9 Curt Schilling .50
10 Edgar Gonzalez .50
11 Luis Gonzalez .25
12 Randy Johnson .75
13 Steve Finley .15
14 Andruw Jones .50
15 Bubba Nelson .50
16 Chipper Jones 1.00
17 Gary Sheffield .40
18 Greg Maddux 1.00
19 Javy Lopez .40
20 John Smoltz .25
21 Marcus Giles .25
22 Rafael Furcal .25
23 Brian Roberts .15
24 Jason Johnson .15
25 Jay Gibbons .25
26 Luis Matos .15
27 Melvin Mora .15
28 Tony Batista .15
29 Bill Mueller .25
30 David Ortiz .40
31 Johnny Damon .25
32 Kevin Youkilis 1.00
33 Manny Ramirez .50
34 Nomar Garciaparra 1.50
35 Pedro Martinez .75
36 Trot Nixon .25
37 Aramis Ramirez .25
38 Brendan Harris .50
39 Carlos Zambrano .15
40 Corey Patterson .25
41 Kenny Lofton .25
42 Kerry Wood .75
43 Mark Prior 1.50
44 Sammy Sosa 1.50
45 Bartolo Colon .25
46 Carlos Lee .25
47 Esteban Loaiza .15
48 Frank Thomas .50
49 Joe Crede .15
50 Magglio Ordonez .25
51 Roberto Alomar .25
52 Adam Dunn .40
53 Austin Kearns .40
54 Josh Hall .15
55 Ken Griffey Jr. 1.00
56 Sean Casey .15
57 Micheal Nakamura .15
58 C.C. Sabathia .15

59 Casey Blake .15
60 Jody Gerut .15
61 Matt Lawton .15
62 Milton Bradley .25
63 Omar Vizquel .25
64 Jason Jennings .15
65 Jay Payton .25
66 Larry Walker .25
67 Preston Wilson .25
68 Todd Helton .50
69 Bobby Higginson .15
70 Carlos Pena .15
71 Dmitri Young .15
72 Jeremy Bonderman .15
73 Preston Larrison .50
74 Derrek Lee .25
75 Dontrelle Willis .50
76 Ivan Rodriguez .50
77 Josh Beckett .50
78 Juan Pierre .15
79 Miguel Cabrera .75
80 Mike Lowell .25
81 Chris Burke .15
82 Craig Biggio .25
83 Jeff Bagwell .50
84 Jeff Kent .25
85 Lance Berkman .40
86 Richard Hidalgo .25
87 Roy Oswalt .25
88 Aaron Guiel .15
89 Angel Berroa .40
90 Carlos Beltran .40
91 Jeremy Affeldt .15
92 Michael Sweeney .15
93 Runelvys Hernandez .15
94 Dave Roberts .15
95 Eric Gagne .40
96 Hideo Nomo .40
97 Kevin Brown .25
98 Paul Lo Duca .15
99 Shawn Green .40
100 Ben Sheets .25
101 Geoff Jenkins .40
102 Richie Sexson .40
103 Rickie Weeks 1.00
104 Scott Podsednik .50
105 J.D. Durbin .50
106 Jacque Jones .15
107 Jason Kubel .50
108 Shannon Stewart .15
109 Torii Hunter .40
110 Chad Cordero .50
111 Javier Vazquez .25
112 Jose Vidro .15
113 Livan Hernandez .15
114 Orlando Cabrera .15
115 Tony Armas Jr. .15
116 Vladimir Guerrero .75
117 Al Leiter .15
118 Cliff Floyd .15
119 Jae Weong So .15
120 Jose Reyes .25
121 Mike Piazza 1.00
122 Tom Glavine .25
123 Aaron Boone .15
124 Alfonso Soriano .75
125 Andy Pettitte .15
126 Derek Jeter .75
127 Hideki Matsui .15
128 Jason Giambi .15
129 Jorge Posada .50
130 Jose Contreras .25
131 Mike Mussina .50
132 Barry Zito .40
133 Eric Byrnes .15
134 Eric Chavez .40
135 Jose Guillen .15
136 Mark Mulder .40
137 Miguel Tejada .40
138 Ramon Hernandez .15
139 Rich Harden .15
140 Tim Hudson .40
141 Bobby Abreu .25
142 Brett Myers .15
143 Jim Thome .75
144 Kevin Millwood .40
145 Mike Lieberthal .15
146 Ryan Howard 1.50
147 Craig Wilson .15
148 Jack Wilson .15
149 Jason Kendall .15
150 Kip Wells .15
151 Reggie Sanders .15
152 Albert Pujols 1.50
153 Edgar Renteria .25
154 Jim Edmonds .25
155 Matt Morris .15
156 Scott Rolen .75
157 Tino Martinez .15
158 Woody Williams .15
159 Brian Giles .25
160 Freddy Guzman RC .50
161 Jake Peavy .15
162 Khalil Greene .50
163 Phil Nevin .15
164 Ryan Klesko .25
165 Ray Durham .15
166 Jason Schmidt .25
167 Jerome Williams .50
168 Jesse Foppert .15
169 Jose Cruz .15
170 Marquis Grissom .15
171 Merkin Valdez RC 1.50
172 Rich Aurilia .15
173 Bret Boone .25
174 Freddy Garcia .15
175 Ichiro Suzuki 1.50
176 Jamie Moyer .15

177 John Olerud .25
178 Mike Cameron .15
179 Randy Winn .15
180 Aubrey Huff .25
181 Carl Crawford .25
182 Chad Gaudin .50
183 Rocco Baldelli .50
184 Toby Hall .15
185 Travis Lee .15
186 Alex Rodriguez 1.50
187 Hank Blalock .40
188 John Thomson .15
189 Juan Gonzalez .50
190 Mark Teixeira .40
191 Michael Young .15
192 Rafael Palmeiro .50
193 Ramon Nivar .15
194 Carlos Delgado .50
195 Dustin McGowan .50
196 Frank Catalanotto .15
197 Vinnie Chulk .15
198 Orlando Hudson .15
199 Roy Halladay .40
200 Vernon Wells .25

Xtra Bases Black
Black (1-200): 4-8X
Production 75 Sets

Xtra Bases Black Autographs
No Pricing
Production 25 Sets

Xtra Bases Purple
Purple (1-200): 2-5X
Production 150 Sets

Xtra Bases Purple Autographs
NM/M
Production 100 Sets
10 Edgar Gonzalez 6.00
15 Bubba Nelson 8.00
32 Kevin Youkilis 15.00
38 Brendan Harris 8.00
57 Micheal Nakamura 6.00
73 Preston Larrison 8.00
79 Miguel Cabrera 35.00
81 Chris Burke 15.00
105 J.D. Durbin 10.00
107 Jason Kubel 8.00
146 Ryan Howard 75.00
193 Ramon Nivar 8.00
195 Dustin McGowan 10.00
197 Orlando Hudson 8.00

Xtra Bases Red Autographs
Complete Set:
Common Player:

Achievements
NM/M
1 Hideo Nomo 95 ROY 1.50
2 Don Mattingly 85/MVP 6.00
3 Roger Clemens 86 CY/MVP 6.00
4 Greg Maddux 95 CY 4.00
5 Stan Musial 43/MVP 4.00
6 Roberto Clemente 66/MVP 6.00
7 Derek Jeter 96 ROY 6.00

8 Albert Pujols 01 ROY 6.00
9 Cal Ripken Jr. 91/MVP 8.00
10 George Brett 80/MVP 8.00
11 Carl Yastrzemski 67/MVP 4.00
12 Rickey Henderson 90/MVP 2.00
13 Sammy Sosa 98/MVP 5.00
14 Randy Johnson 02 CY 3.00
15 Bob Gibson 68 CY/MVP 3.00

Autographs

NM/M

Quantity produced listed

8 Brandon Webb/100 20.00
10 Edgar Gonzalez PROS/150 8.00
15 Bubba Nelson PROS/250 10.00
25 Jay Gibbons/50 20.00
32 Kevin Youkilis PROS/100 20.00
36 Trot Nixon/25 40.00
37 Aramis Ramirez/25 25.00
38 Brendan Harris PROS/400 8.00
49 Joe Crede/25 15.00
54 Josh Hall/25 15.00
57 Mike Nakamura/250 8.00
60 Jody Gerut/50 15.00
73 Preston Larrison PROS/250 8.00
75 Dontrelle Willis/25 40.00
79 Miguel Cabrera/100 30.00
81 Chris Burke PROS/250 10.00
93 Runelvys Hernandez/50 10.00
98 Paul Lo Duca/25 15.00
102 Richie Sexson/25 25.00
105 J.D. Durbin PROS/500 10.00
106 Jacque Jones/50 12.00
107 Jason Kubel PROS/400 8.00
108 Shannon Stewart/50 15.00
112 Jose Vidro/25 15.00
114 Orlando Cabrera/25 20.00
119 Jae Weong Seo/25 15.00
133 Eric Byrnes/50 15.00
136 Mark Mulder/25 20.00
139 Rich Harden/50 25.00
146 Ryan Howard PROS/400 75.00
193 Ramon Nivar PROS/100 8.00
195 Dustin McGowan PROS/100 10.00
197 Vinnie Chulk/112 8.00
198 Orlando Hudson/100 10.00

Changing Stripes

NM/M
Inserted 1:11
Foil: 1-2X
Production 150 Sets
Holofoil: 2-3X
Production 50 Sets

1 Rickey Henderson/ A's-Yanks 4.00
2 Mike Mussina/ O's-Yanks 2.00
3 Jim Thome/ Indians-Phils 3.00
4 Hideo Nomo/ Sox-Dodgers 1.50
5 Scott Rolen/ Phils-Cards 3.00
6 Jason Giambi/ A's-Yanks 3.00
7 Randy Johnson/ Astros-D'backs 1.50
8 Shawn Green/ Jays-Dodgers 1.50
9 Curt Schilling/ Phils-D'backs 2.00
10 Alex Rodriguez/ M's-Rangers 5.00
11 Greg Maddux/ Cubs-Braves 4.00
12 Randy Johnson/ M's-Astros 3.00
13 Hideo Nomo/ Dodgers-Mets 1.50
14 Juan Rodriguez/ Rgr-Marlins 2.00
15 Juan Gonzalez/ Indians-Rangers 2.00
16 Manny Ramirez/ Indians-Sox 2.00
17 Mike Piazza/ Dodgers-Mets 4.00
18 Nolan Ryan/ Angels-Astros 8.00
19 Nolan Ryan/ Astros-Rangers 8.00
20 Pedro Martinez/ Expos-Sox 3.00
21 Reggie Jackson/ Yanks-Angels 2.00
22 Roberto Alomar/ Mets-Sox 1.50
23 Rod Carew/ Twins-Angels 2.00
24 Roger Clemens/ Sox-Yanks 6.00
25 Sammy Sosa/ Sox-Cubs 5.00

Changing Stripes Dual Jersey

NM/M
Prodcution 150 Sets
Primes: No Pricing
Production 25 Sets

1 Rickey Henderson/ A's-Yanks 10.00
2 Mike Mussina/ O's-Yanks 8.00
3 Jim Thome/ Indians-Phils 10.00
4 Hideo Nomo/ Sox-Dodgers 15.00
5 Scott Rolen/ Phils-Cards 10.00
6 Jason Giambi/ A's-Yanks 12.00
7 Randy Johnson/ Astros-D'backs 10.00
8 Shawn Green/ Jays-Dodgers 6.00
9 Curt Schilling/ Phils-D'backs 8.00
10 Alex Rodriguez/ M's-Rangers 15.00
11 Randy Johnson/ M's-Astros 10.00
12 Randy Johnson/ M's-Astros 10.00
13 Hideo Nomo/ Dodgers-Mets 15.00
14 Ivan Rodriguez/ Rgr-Marlins 10.00
15 Juan Gonzalez/ Indians-Rangers 8.00
16 Manny Ramirez/ Indians-Sox 8.00
17 Mike Piazza/ Dodgers-Mets 10.00
18 Nolan Ryan/ Angels-Astros 30.00
19 Nolan Ryan/ Astros-Rangers 30.00
20 Pedro Martinez/ Expos-Sox 10.00
22 Roberto Alomar/ Mets-Sox 8.00
23 Rod Carew/ Twins-Angels 12.00
24 Roger Clemens/ Sox-Yanks 15.00
25 Sammy Sosa/ Sox-Cubs 15.00

Connections

NM/M
Inserted 1:9
Foil: 1.5-2X
Production 100 Sets
Holofoil: No Pricing
Production 21 Sets

1 Derek Jeter, Alfonso Soriano 4.00
2 Greg Maddux, Chipper Jones 2.00
3 Albert Pujols, Scott Rolen 3.00
4 Randy Johnson, Curt Schilling 1.50
5 Nomar Garciaparra, Manny Ramirez 3.00
6 Alex Rodriguez, Mark Teixeira 3.00
7 Barry Zito, Tim Hudson .75
8 Sammy Sosa, Mark Prior 2.00
9 Derek Jeter, Jason Giambi 4.00
10 Roger Clemens, Mike Mussina 3.00
11 Mark Prior, Kerry Wood 2.00
12 Alex Rodriguez, Hank Blalock 3.00
13 Frank Thomas, Magglio Ordonez 1.00
14 Nomar Garciaparra, Pedro Martinez 3.00
15 Carlos Delgado, Vernon Wells 1.00
16 Miguel Tejada, Eric Chavez .75
17 Jeff Bagwell, Lance Berkman 1.00
18 Jim Thome, Bobby Abreu 1.50
19 Todd Helton, Preston Wilson 1.00
20 Vladimir Guerrero, Javier Vazquez 1.50

Connections Material

NM/M
Production 250 Sets

1 Derek Jeter/Bat, Alfonso Soriano/Bat 20.00
2 Greg Maddux/Bat, Chipper Jones/Bat 12.00
3 Albert Pujols/Bat, Scott Rolen/Bat 15.00
4 Randy Johnson/Bat, Curt Schilling/Bat 10.00
5 Nomar Garciaparra/Bat, Manny Ramirez/Bat 10.00
6 Alex Rodriguez/Bat, Mark Teixeira/Bat 10.00
7 Barry Zito/Bat, Tim Hudson/Bat 10.00
8 Sammy Sosa/Bat, Mark Prior/Bat 15.00
9 Derek Jeter/Bat, Jason Giambi/Bat 20.00
10 Roger Clemens/Jsy, Mike Mussina/Bat 15.00
11 Mark Prior/Bat, Kerry Wood/Bat 10.00
12 Alex Rodriguez/Bat, Hank Blalock/Bat 10.00
13 Frank Thomas/Bat, Magglio Ordonez/Bat 8.00
14 Nomar Garciaparra/Bat, Pedro Martinez/Bat 15.00
15 Carlos Delgado/Bat, Vernon Wells/Bat 8.00
16 Miguel Tejada/Bat, Eric Chavez/Bat 8.00
17 Jeff Bagwell/Bat, Lance Berkman/Bat 10.00
18 Jim Thome/Jsy, Bobby Abreu/Bat 10.00
19 Todd Helton/Bat, Preston Wilson 8.00
20 Vladimir Guerrero/Bat, Javier Vazquez/Jsy

Diamond Heritage

NM/M
Inserted 1:13

1 Mike Piazza 3.00
2 Greg Maddux 2.50
3 Nomar Garciaparra 3.00
4 Chipper Jones 2.00
5 Albert Pujols 4.00
6 Derek Jeter 5.00
7 Shawn Green .75
8 Alex Rodriguez 4.00
9 Jim Thome 2.00
10 Jason Giambi 1.50
11 Sammy Sosa 3.00
12 Hank Blalock 1.50
13 Garret Anderson .75
14 Manny Ramirez 1.50
15 Scott Rolen 1.50
16 Jeff Bagwell 1.50
17 Randy Johnson 2.00
18 Ichiro Suzuki 3.00
19 Ivan Rodriguez 1.50
20 Alfonso Soriano 1.50

Diamond Heritage Material

NM/M
Inserted 1:92

1 Mike Piazza/Bat 10.00
2 Greg Maddux/Bat 8.00
3 Nomar Garciaparra/ Bat 10.00
4 Chipper Jones/Bat 8.00
5 Albert Pujols/Bat 15.00
6 Derek Jeter/Jsy 15.00
7 Shawn Green/Bat 5.00
8 Alex Rodriguez/Bat 10.00
9 Jim Thome/Bat 8.00
10 Jason Giambi/Bat 8.00
11 Sammy Sosa/Bat 12.00
12 Hank Blalock/Bat 6.00
13 Garret Anderson/Bat 5.00
14 Manny Ramirez/Bat 6.00
15 Scott Rolen/Bat 6.00
16 Jeff Bagwell/Bat 6.00
17 Randy Johnson/Bat 8.00
18 Ivan Rodriguez/Bat 6.00
20 Alfonso Soriano/Bat 6.00

League Leaders Single

NM/M
Foil: 2-3X
Production 100 Sets
Holofoil: No Pricing
Production 25 Sets

1 Alex Rodriguez AL HR 3.00
2 Albert Pujols NL Hit 3.00
3 Albert Pujols NL Avg 3.00
4 Nomar Garciaparra AL Hit 2.00
5 Mark Prior NL ERA 2.00
6 Pedro Martinez AL ERA 1.00
7 Kerry Wood NL SO 1.00
8 Derek Jeter AL Avg 3.00
9 Jason Giambi AL BB 1.00
10 Roger Clemens AL SO 2.00

League Leaders Single Material

NM/M
Production 250 Sets

1 Alex Rodriguez/Bat 10.00
2 Albert Pujols/Bat 15.00
3 Albert Pujols/Bat 15.00
4 Nomar Garciaparra/ Bat 10.00
5 Mark Prior/Jsy 10.00
6 Pedro Martinez/Jsy 8.00
7 Kerry Wood/Jsy 8.00
8 Derek Jeter/Jsy 15.00
9 Jason Giambi/Jsy 6.00
10 Roger Clemens/Jsy 12.00

League Leaders Double

NM/M
Production 500 Sets
Foil: 1-2X
Production 75 Sets
Holofoil: No Pricing
Production 10 Sets

1 Alex Rodriguez, Jim Thome HR 5.00
2 Mark Prior, Pedro Martinez ERA 4.00
3 Roger Clemens, Kerry Wood SO 5.00
4 Nomar Garciaparra, Albert Pujols Hit 5.00
5 Derek Jeter, Albert Pujols Avg 5.00

League Leaders Double Material

NM/M
Production 100 Sets

1 Alex Rodriguez/Bat, Jim Thome/Bat 20.00
2 Mark Prior/Jsy, Pedro Martinez/Jsy 15.00
3 Roger Clemens/Jsy, Kerry Wood/Jsy 20.00
4 Nomar Garciaparra/Bat, Albert Pujols/Bat 25.00
5 Derek Jeter/Jsy, Albert Pujols/Bat 25.00

League Leaders Quad

NM/M
Production 250 Sets
Foil: 1-2X
Production 50 Sets
Holofoil: No Pricing
Production 5 Sets

1 Albert Pujols, Todd Helton, Edgar Renteria, Gary Sheffield 10.00
2 Derek Jeter, Manny Ramirez, Nomar Garciaparra, Ichiro Suzuki 10.00
3 Mark Prior, Curt Schilling, Nomar Garciaparra, Kevin Brown 8.00
4 Richie Sexson, Sammy Sosa, Albert Pujols, Jim Thome 10.00
5 Alex Rodriguez, Frank Thomas, Jason Giambi, Carlos Delgado 8.00

League Leaders Quad Material

NM/M
Production 50 Sets

1 Albert Pujols, Todd Helton, Edgar Renteria, Gary Sheffield 30.00
3 Mark Prior, Curt Schilling, Hideo Nomo, Kevin Brown 30.00
4 Richie Sexson, Sammy Sosa, Albert Pujols, Jim Thome 40.00
5 Alex Rodriguez, Frank Thomas, Jason Giambi, Carlos Delgado 35.00

Players Collection Jersey

NM/M
Inserted 1:79
Platinum: 1-2X
Production 50

1 Adam Dunn 5.00
2 Adam Dunn 5.00
3 Adam Dunn 5.00
4 Alex Rodriguez 10.00
5 Alex Rodriguez 10.00
6 Alex Rodriguez 10.00
7 Alex Rodriguez 10.00
8 Andruw Jones 6.00
9 Andruw Jones 6.00
10 Austin Kearns 6.00
11 Brandon Webb 4.00
12 C.C. Sabathia 4.00
13 Cal Ripken Jr. 25.00
14 Carlos Beltran 5.00
15 Carlos Delgado 6.00
16 Carlos Lee 4.00
17 Chipper Jones 8.00
18 Chipper Jones 8.00
19 Craig Biggio 6.00
20 Curt Schilling 6.00
21 David Wells 4.00
22 Don Mattingly 15.00
23 Dontrelle Willis 6.00
24 Frank Thomas 8.00
25 Frank Thomas 8.00
26 Fred McGriff 6.00
27 Garret Anderson 6.00
28 Gary Sheffield 8.00
29 Gary Sheffield 8.00
30 Greg Maddux 10.00
31 Hank Blalock 6.00
32 Hank Blalock 6.00
33 Hee Seop Choi 4.00
34 Hideo Nomo 8.00
35 Hideo Nomo 8.00
36 Hideo Nomo 8.00
37 Ivan Rodriguez 6.00
38 Ivan Rodriguez 6.00
39 Jason Giambi 6.00
40 Jim Edmonds 6.00
41 Jim Thome 8.00
42 John Olerud 4.00
43 John Smoltz 6.00
44 Josh Beckett 6.00
45 Josh Phelps 6.00
46 Juan Gonzalez 6.00
47 Juan Gonzalez 6.00
48 Kazuhisa Ishii 4.00
49 Lance Berkman 5.00
50 Larry Walker 5.00
51 Larry Walker 5.00
52 Luis Gonzalez 5.00
53 Magglio Ordonez 6.00
54 Magglio Ordonez 6.00
55 Manny Ramirez 6.00
56 Manny Ramirez 6.00
57 Mark Prior 8.00
58 Mark Prior 8.00
59 Mark Teixeira 6.00
60 Mike Mussina 6.00
61 Mike Piazza 8.00
62 Mike Piazza 8.00
63 Mike Piazza 8.00
64 Nomar Garciaparra 8.00
65 Nomar Garciaparra 8.00
66 Pat Burrell 6.00
67 Paul Konerko 5.00
68 Paul Lo Duca 5.00
69 Pedro Martinez 8.00
70 Rafael Furcal 5.00
71 Rafael Palmeiro 8.00
72 Rafael Palmeiro 8.00
73 Ramon Hernandez 4.00
74 Rickey Henderson 8.00
75 Rickey Henderson 8.00
76 Rickey Henderson 8.00
77 Roberto Alomar 6.00
78 Roberto Alomar 6.00
79 Robin Ventura 5.00
80 Roger Clemens 10.00
81 Roger Clemens 10.00
82 Roy Halladay 6.00
83 Sammy Sosa 12.00
84 Sammy Sosa 12.00
85 Sammy Sosa 12.00
86 Scott Rolen 8.00
87 Shannon Stewart 4.00
88 Shawn Green 5.00
89 Shawn Green 5.00
90 Shawn Green 5.00
91 Terrence Long 4.00
92 Tim Hudson 5.00
93 Todd Helton 8.00
94 Todd Helton 8.00
95 Tom Glavine 6.00
96 Tom Glavine 6.00
97 Torii Hunter 6.00
98 Vernon Wells 4.00
99 Vladimir Guerrero 8.00
100 Vladimir Guerrero 8.00

Prestigious Pros

NM/M
Inserted 1:23

1 Mark Prior 3.00
2 Derek Jeter 5.00
3 Mike Mussina 1.50
4 Nomar Garciaparra 3.00
5 Roger Clemens 4.00
6 Jason Giambi 1.50
7 Randy Johnson 2.00
8 Rafael Palmeiro 1.50
9 Barry Zito 1.00
10 Pat Burrell 1.00

Stars of MLB

NM/M
Foil: 1-2X
Production 100 Sets
Holofoil: No Pricing
Prod. 25 Sets

1 Albert Pujols 6.00

2	Derek Jeter	8.00
3	Mike Piazza	4.00
4	Greg Maddux	4.00
5	Ichiro Suzuki	5.00
6	Nomar Garciaparra	5.00
7	Ivan Rodriguez	2.00
8	Randy Johnson	3.00
9	Alex Rodriguez	6.00
10	Sammy Sosa	5.00
11	Alfonso Soriano	3.00
12	Vladimir Guerrero	3.00
13	Jason Giambi	3.00
14	Mark Prior	4.00
15	Chipper Jones	3.00

Stars of MLB Jersey

NM/M

Production 250 Sets
Prime: 1-2X
Production 50

1	Albert Pujols	15.00
2	Derek Jeter	15.00
3	Mike Piazza	8.00
4	Greg Maddux	10.00
6	Nomar Garciaparra	6.00
7	Ivan Rodriguez	6.00
8	Randy Johnson	8.00
9	Alex Rodriguez	10.00
10	Sammy Sosa	12.00
11	Alfonso Soriano	8.00
12	Vladimir Guerrero	8.00
13	Jason Giambi	6.00
14	Mark Prior	10.00
15	Chipper Jones	8.00

Stars of MLB Jersey Autographs

NM/M
Quantity produced listed

14	Mark Prior/50	75.00

2004 Playoff Prime Cuts

NM/M
Complete Set (50): 150.00
Common Player: 1.50
Production 949 Sets
Box (1): 185.00

1	Roger Clemens	6.00
2	Nomar Garciaparra	6.00
3	Albert Pujols	6.00
4	Sammy Sosa	6.00
5	Greg Maddux	4.00
6	Jason Giambi	3.00
7	Hideo Nomo	1.50
8	Mike Piazza	5.00
9	Ichiro Suzuki	5.00
10	Jeff Bagwell	2.00
11	Derek Jeter	8.00
12	Manny Ramirez	3.00
13	Rickey Henderson	1.50
14	Alex Rodriguez	1.50
15	Troy Glaus	1.50
16	Mike Mussina	1.50
17	Kerry Wood	2.00
18	Kazuhisa Ishii	1.00
19	Hideki Matsui	8.00
20	Frank Thomas	2.00
21	Barry Bonds	8.00
22	Adam Dunn	2.00
23	Randy Johnson	3.00
24	Alfonso Soriano	3.00
25	Pedro J. Martinez	3.00
26	Andruw Jones	2.00
27	Mark Prior	4.00
28	Vladimir Guerrero	3.00
29	Chipper Jones	4.00
30	Todd Helton	2.00
31	Rafael Palmeiro	2.00
32	Mark Grace	2.00
33	Pedro J. Martinez	3.00
34	Randy Johnson	3.00
35	Randy Johnson	3.00
36	Roger Clemens	6.00
37	Roger Clemens	6.00
38	Alex Rodriguez	6.00
39	Greg Maddux	4.00
40	Mike Piazza	4.00
41	Mike Piazza	4.00
42	Hideo Nomo	1.50
43	Rickey Henderson	1.50
44	Rickey Henderson	1.50
45	Barry Bonds	8.00
46	Ivan Rodriguez	2.00
47	George Brett	8.00
48	Cal Ripken Jr.	8.00
49	Nolan Ryan	10.00
50	Don Mattingly	6.00

Century

Cards (1-50): 1-2X
Production 100 Sets
Century Gold: No Pricing
Production 10 Sets
Century Proof: No Pricing
Production One Set

Icons Material

NM/M
Varying quantities produced

4	Johnny Bench/50	35.00
5	Lefty Grove/25	75.00
6	Carlton Fisk/50	25.00
7	Mel Ott/25	75.00
8	Bob Feller/25	35.00
9	Jackie Robinson/25	75.00
10	Ted Williams/50	135.00
11	Roy Campanella/50	40.00
12	Stan Musial/50	40.00
13	Yogi Berra/50	40.00
14	Babe Ruth/25	750.00
15	Roberto Clemente/50	100.00
16	Warren Spahn/50	40.00
17	Ernie Banks/50	40.00
18	Eddie Mathews/50	35.00
19	Ryne Sandberg/50	40.00
20	Rod Carew/50	25.00
21	Duke Snider/50	25.00
22	Jim Palmer/50	20.00
24	Frank Robinson/50	20.00
25	Brooks Robinson/50	25.00
26	Harmon Killebrew/50	40.00
27	Carl Yastrzemski/50	40.00
28	Reggie Jackson/50	25.00
29	Mike Schmidt/50	30.00
30	Robin Yount/50	30.00
31	George Brett/50	40.00
32	Nolan Ryan/50	40.00
33	Kirby Puckett/50	40.00
34	Cal Ripken Jr./50	60.00
35	Don Mattingly/50	35.00
36	Tony Gwynn/50	65.00
37	Deion Sanders/19	40.00
39	Eddie Murray/19	60.00
40	Tom Seaver/19	40.00
41	Willie Stargell/19	40.00
42	Wade Boggs/19	50.00
43	Ozzie Smith/19	60.00
44	Willie McCovey/19	40.00
45	Reggie Jackson/19	40.00
46	Whitey Ford/19	40.00
47	Lou Brock/19	40.00
48	Lou Boudreau/19	40.00
49	Steve Carlton/19	45.00
50	Rod Carew/19	40.00
51	Bob Gibson/19	35.00
52	Thurman Munson/19	60.00
53	Roger Maris/19	80.00
54	Nolan Ryan/50	40.00
55	Nolan Ryan/50	40.00
56	Bo Jackson/19	50.00
57	Joe Morgan/19	30.00
58	Phil Rizzuto/19	35.00
59	Gary Carter/19	40.00
60	Paul Molitor/19	40.00
61	Don Drysdale/19	50.00
62	Jim "Catfish" Hunter/19	30.00
63	Fergie Jenkins/19	30.00
64	Pee Wee Reese/19	40.00
65	Dave Winfield/19	40.00
66	Wade Boggs/19	40.00
67	Lefty Grove/19	80.00
68	Rickey Henderson/19	45.00
69	Roger Clemens/19	50.00
70	Roger Clemens/19	50.00

Icons Material Signature

NM/M
Varying quantities produced

4	Johnny Bench/18	75.00
8	Bob Feller/45	50.00
12	Stan Musial/30	100.00
13	Yogi Berra/42	65.00
21	Duke Snider/35	50.00
26	Harmon Killebrew/30	100.00
33	Kirby Puckett/16	80.00
69	Roger Clemens/25	150.00

Icons Material Signature Prime

NM/M
Many not priced due to scarcity.

6	Carlton Fisk/50	
11	Roy Campanella/1 (8/05 auction)	2,020
15	Stan Musial/20	120.00
16	Warren Spahn/25	90.00
17	Ernie Banks/50	70.00
19	Ryne Sandberg/50	100.00
20	Rod Carew/50	100.00
22	Jim Palmer/50	40.00
24	Frank Robinson/50	40.00
25	Brooks Robinson/50	60.00
26	Harmon Killebrew/20	100.00
27	Carl Yastrzemski/50	90.00
28	Reggie Jackson/50	60.00
29	Mike Schmidt/20	125.00
30	Robin Yount/50	65.00
31	George Brett/50	100.00
32	Nolan Ryan/50	120.00
33	Kirby Puckett/34	40.00
34	Cal Ripken Jr./50	100.00
35	Don Mattingly/50	35.00
36	Tony Gwynn/50	70.00
37	Deion Sanders/50	40.00
38	Dave Winfield/50	45.00
39	Eddie Murray/50	75.00
42	Wade Boggs/50	40.00
43	Ozzie Smith/50	75.00
44	Willie McCovey/50	50.00
45	Reggie Jackson/50	50.00
46	Whitey Ford/50	50.00
47	Lou Brock/25	50.00
48	Lou Boudreau/50	75.00
49	Steve Carlton/50	40.00
50	Rod Carew/50	40.00
51	Bob Gibson/50	70.00
54	Nolan Ryan/50	125.00
55	Nolan Ryan/50	125.00
56	Bo Jackson/50	60.00
57	Joe Morgan/50	35.00
58	Phil Rizzuto/50	40.00
59	Gary Carter/50	40.00
60	Paul Molitor/50	55.00
63	Fergie Jenkins/50	40.00
65	Dave Winfield/50	40.00
66	Wade Boggs/50	60.00
68	Rickey Henderson/50	85.00
69	Roger Clemens/25	150.00
70	Roger Clemens/50	120.00

Icons Material Combo Prime

NM/M
Varying quantities produced

6	Carlton Fisk/25	50.00
7	Mel Ott/25	85.00
11	Roy Campanella/25	70.00
15	Roberto Clemente/25	200.00
17	Ernie Banks/25	85.00
18	Eddie Mathews/25	50.00
19	Ryne Sandberg/25	80.00
20	Rod Carew/25	40.00
25	Frank Robinson/25	40.00
26	Brooks Robinson/25	50.00
27	Carl Yastrzemski/25	80.00
28	Reggie Jackson/25	50.00
29	Mike Schmidt/25	75.00
30	Robin Yount/25	50.00
31	George Brett/25	75.00
32	Nolan Ryan/25	75.00
33	Kirby Puckett/25	60.00
34	Cal Ripken Jr./25	120.00
35	Don Mattingly/25	70.00
36	Tony Gwynn/25	80.00
37	Deion Sanders/19	40.00
38	Dave Winfield/19	50.00
39	Eddie Murray/19	70.00
41	Willie Stargell/19	40.00
42	Wade Boggs/19	60.00
43	Ozzie Smith/19	70.00
44	Willie McCovey/19	50.00
45	Reggie Jackson/19	50.00
46	Whitey Ford/19	50.00
47	Lou Brock/19	50.00
48	Lou Boudreau/19	50.00
49	Steve Carlton/19	60.00
50	Rod Carew/19	60.00
52	Thurman Munson/19	70.00
53	Roger Maris/19	110.00
54	Nolan Ryan/19	75.00
55	Nolan Ryan/19	75.00
56	Bo Jackson/19	60.00
57	Joe Morgan/19	40.00
58	Phil Rizzuto/19	45.00
59	Gary Carter/19	50.00
60	Paul Molitor/19	50.00
63	Fergie Jenkins/19	40.00
64	Pee Wee Reese/19	50.00
65	Dave Winfield/19	50.00
66	Wade Boggs/19	50.00
69	Roger Clemens/19	60.00
70	Roger Clemens/19	60.00

Icons Signature

NM/M
Varying quantities produced

4	Johnny Bench/50	60.00
6	Carlton Fisk/50	40.00
8	Bob Feller/50	40.00
12	Stan Musial/50	65.00
16	Yogi Berra/50	40.00
16	Warren Spahn/25	100.00
17	Ernie Banks/50	60.00
19	Ryne Sandberg/50	70.00
21	Duke Snider/25	50.00
22	Jim Palmer/50	40.00
24	Frank Robinson/50	40.00
26	Brooks Robinson/50	40.00
27	Harmon Killebrew/25	75.00
28	Carl Yastrzemski/50	60.00
29	Reggie Jackson/50	50.00
29	Mike Schmidt/20	75.00
30	Robin Yount/25	65.00
31	George Brett/25	120.00
32	Nolan Ryan/50	110.00
33	Kirby Puckett/25	60.00
34	Cal Ripken Jr./25	200.00
35	Don Mattingly/50	85.00
36	Tony Gwynn/50	70.00
38	Dave Winfield/50	50.00
39	Eddie Murray/25	75.00
42	Wade Boggs/25	60.00
43	Ozzie Smith/25	75.00
44	Willie McCovey/25	50.00
47	Reggie Jackson/25	50.00
48	Lou Brock/25	50.00
51	Lou Boudreau/25	90.00
57	Bob Gibson/25	65.00
57	Bo Jackson/25	65.00
59	Joe Morgan/25	35.00
59	Gary Carter/25	45.00
65	Paul Molitor/25	55.00
66	Dave Winfield/25	50.00
66	Wade Boggs/25	60.00

Prime Cut Materials

NM/M
Varying quantities produced

1	Roger Clemens/150	40.00
2	Nomar Garciaparra/150	45.00
3	Albert Pujols/150	40.00
4	Sammy Sosa/150	40.00
5	Greg Maddux/150	40.00
6	Jason Giambi/125	40.00
7	Hideo Nomo/150	30.00
8	Mike Piazza/150	40.00
9	Ichiro Suzuki/25	60.00
10	Jeff Bagwell/25	35.00
11	Derek Jeter/25	50.00
12	Manny Ramirez/25	50.00
13	Rickey Henderson/50	30.00
14	Alex Rodriguez/25	60.00
15	Troy Glaus/25	40.00
16	Kerry Wood/25	40.00
17	Kazuhisa Ishii/25	40.00
18	Hideki Matsui/25	65.00
19	Frank Thomas/25	40.00
20	Barry Bonds/25	40.00
21	Adam Dunn/25	30.00
22	Randy Johnson/25	30.00
23	Alfonso Soriano/35	40.00
24	Pedro J. Martinez/25	40.00
25	Andruw Jones/25	30.00
26	Mark Prior/25	30.00
27	Vladimir Guerrero/25	40.00
28	Chipper Jones/25	40.00
29	Todd Helton/25	35.00
30	Rafael Palmeiro/25	40.00
31	Mark Grace/25	35.00
32	Pedro J. Martinez/25	40.00
33	Randy Johnson/25	40.00
34	Randy Johnson/25	40.00
35	Roger Clemens/25	45.00
36	Alex Rodriguez/25	60.00
37	Mike Piazza/50	30.00
38	Hideo Nomo/50	25.00
43	Rickey Henderson/50	30.00
46	Rickey Henderson/50	30.00
44	Ivan Rodriguez/25	30.00
47	George Brett/50	50.00
48	Cal Ripken Jr./50	65.00
49	Nolan Ryan/50	50.00
50	Don Mattingly/50	40.00

Signature

NM/M
Varying quantities produced

1	Roger Clemens/25	150.00
3	Albert Pujols/25	150.00
10	Jeff Bagwell/25	50.00
13	Rickey Henderson/25	80.00
14	Alex Rodriguez/25	150.00
15	Troy Glaus/25	35.00
16	Mike Mussina/25	60.00
17	Kerry Wood/25	80.00
18	Kazuhisa Ishii/25	40.00
22	Frank Thomas/25	70.00
24	Alfonso Soriano/25	75.00
26	Andruw Jones/25	60.00
27	Mark Prior/25	80.00
28	Vladimir Guerrero/25	60.00
29	Chipper Jones/25	75.00
31	Rafael Palmeiro/25	65.00
32	Mark Grace/25	60.00
36	Roger Clemens/25	150.00
37	Roger Clemens/25	150.00
38	Alex Rodriguez/25	150.00
43	Rickey Henderson/25	80.00
44	Rickey Henderson/25	80.00
46	Ivan Rodriguez/25	50.00
47	George Brett/25	120.00
48	Cal Ripken Jr./25	200.00
49	Nolan Ryan/25	125.00
50	Don Mattingly/25	100.00

Prime Cut Material Signature

NM/M
Varying quantities produced

1	Roger Clemens/25	185.00
3	Albert Pujols/25	180.00
5	Greg Maddux/25	175.00
10	Jeff Bagwell/25	70.00
12	Manny Ramirez/25	60.00
13	Rickey Henderson/25	100.00
14	Alex Rodriguez/25	180.00
15	Troy Glaus/25	40.00
16	Mike Mussina/25	70.00
17	Kerry Wood/25	90.00
18	Kazuhisa Ishii/50	50.00
20	Frank Thomas/25	60.00
24	Adam Dunn/50	60.00
26	Alfonso Soriano/25	85.00
26	Andruw Jones/25	60.00
28	Mark Prior/50	75.00
28	Vladimir Guerrero/50	75.00
29	Chipper Jones/25	85.00
30	Todd Helton/50	60.00
31	Rafael Palmeiro/25	75.00
32	Mark Grace/25	70.00
36	Roger Clemens/25	185.00
38	Alex Rodriguez/25	180.00
44	Rickey Henderson/25	100.00
46	Ivan Rodriguez/25	60.00
47	George Brett/50	120.00
48	Cal Ripken Jr./50	200.00
49	Nolan Ryan/25	140.00
50	Don Mattingly/50	120.00

Material Combos

NM/M
Production 25 Sets

1	Roger Clemens	60.00
2	Nomar Garciaparra	50.00
3	Albert Pujols	80.00
4	Sammy Sosa	50.00
5	Greg Maddux	50.00
6	Jason Giambi	40.00
7	Hideo Nomo	30.00
8	Mike Piazza	40.00
9	Ichiro Suzuki	70.00
10	Jeff Bagwell	40.00
11	Derek Jeter	60.00
12	Manny Ramirez	30.00
13	Rickey Henderson	40.00
14	Alex Rodriguez	70.00
15	Troy Glaus	35.00
16	Mike Mussina	40.00
17	Kerry Wood	50.00
18	Kazuhisa Ishii	35.00
19	Hideki Matsui	75.00
20	Frank Thomas	45.00
21	Barry Bonds	60.00
22	Adam Dunn	35.00
23	Randy Johnson	50.00
24	Alfonso Soriano	40.00
25	Pedro J. Martinez	45.00
26	Andruw Jones	35.00
27	Mark Prior	40.00
28	Vladimir Guerrero	45.00
29	Chipper Jones	45.00
30	Todd Helton	40.00
31	Rafael Palmeiro	40.00
32	Mark Grace	45.00
33	Pedro J. Martinez	45.00
34	Randy Johnson	50.00
35	Randy Johnson	50.00
36	Roger Clemens	60.00
38	Alex Rodriguez	70.00
42	Mike Piazza	40.00
43	Hideo Nomo	25.00
44	Rickey Henderson	40.00
46	Ivan Rodriguez	35.00
47	George Brett	85.00
48	Cal Ripken Jr.	140.00
49	Nolan Ryan	75.00
50	Don Mattingly	75.00

Timeline Dual Achievement Material

NM/M
Varying quantities produced

3	Stan Musial, Ted Williams/19	175.00
4	George Brett, Mike Schmidt/19	75.00
5	Cal Ripken Jr., Dale Murphy/19	90.00
6	Mike Schmidt, Roger Clemens/19	65.00
10	George Brett, Nolan Ryan/19	100.00
12	Al Kaline, Duke Snider/19	50.00

Timeline Dual Achievement Material Signature

NM/M
Varying quantities produced

4	George Brett, Mike Schmidt/24	150.00
5	Cal Ripken Jr., Dale Murphy/25	200.00
6	Mike Schmidt, Roger Clemens/24	220.00
7	Babe Ruth, Ty Cobb/1 (4/04 auction)	18,000
10	George Brett, Nolan Ryan/25	220.00

Timeline Dual Achievement Material Prime

NM/M
Varying quantities produced

4	George Brett, Mike Schmidt/19	120.00
5	Cal Ripken Jr., Dale Murphy/19	120.00
6	Mike Schmidt, Roger Clemens/19	90.00
10	George Brett, Nolan Ryan/19	140.00

Timeline Dual Achieve Material Combo

No Pricing

Timeline Dual Achievement Signature

NM/M
Production 24 or 25

4	George Brett, Mike Schmidt/24	160.00
5	Cal Ripken Jr., Dale Murphy/25	180.00
6	Mike Schmidt, Roger Clemens/24	220.00
10	George Brett, Nolan Ryan/25	220.00
12	Al Kaline, Duke Snider/25	100.00

Timeline Dual League Leader Material

NM/M
Production 9 or 19

4	Jim Palmer, Steve Carlton/19	40.00
7	Nolan Ryan, Steve Carlton/19	70.00
8	Don Mattingly, Tony Gwynn/19	70.00
9	Nolan Ryan, Roger Clemens/19	80.00

Timeline Dual League Leader Material Prime

NM/M
Production 9 or 19

7	Nolan Ryan, Steve Carlton/19	80.00
8	Don Mattingly, Tony Gwynn/19	80.00
9	Nolan Ryan, Roger Clemens/19	100.00

Timeline Dual League Leader Material Signature

NM/M
Varying quantities produced

4	Jim Palmer, Steve Carlton/50	60.00
7	Nolan Ryan, Steve Carlton/25	200.00
8	Don Mattingly, Tony Gwynn/	150.00

9 Nolan Ryan, Roger Clemens/25 350.00

Timeline Dual League Leader Signature
NM/M
Production 25 or 50
4 Jim Palmer, Steve Carlton/25 60.00
7 Nolan Ryan, Steve Carlton/25 180.00
8 Don Mattingly, Tony Gwynn/25 140.00
9 Nolan Ryan, Roger Clemens/25 300.00

Timeline Dual League Leader Material Combo
NM/M
Production 9 or 19
7 Nolan Ryan, Steve Carlton/19 80.00
8 Don Mattingly, Tony Gwynn/19 80.00
9 Nolan Ryan, Roger Clemens/19 100.00

Timeline - Material
NM/M
Varying quantities produced
4 Ted Williams/50 140.00
5 Roy Campanella/50 30.00
6 Stan Musial/50 35.00
7 Yogi Berra/50 25.00
9 Roberto Clemente/50 85.00
12 Carl Yastrzemski/50 35.00
13 Mike Schmidt/50 30.00
14 George Brett/50 30.00
15 Nolan Ryan/50 35.00
16 Stan Musial/50 35.00
17 Ted Williams/50 140.00
18 Roberto Clemente/50 90.00
19 Greg Maddux/50 25.00
21 Robin Yount/50 20.00
22 Nolan Ryan/50 35.00
23 Ted Williams/50 140.00
24 George Brett/50 30.00
25 Yogi Berra/50 25.00
26 Rod Carew/50 20.00
27 Dale Murphy/25 40.00

Timeline Material Signature
NM/M
Varying quantities produced
6 Stan Musial/33 100.00
7 Yogi Berra/42 75.00
16 Stan Musial/38 100.00
25 Yogi Berra/42 75.00

Timeline Material Prime
NM/M
Varying quantities produced
5 Roy Campanella/25 40.00
10 Will Clark/25 50.00
12 Carl Yastrzemski/25 75.00
13 Mike Schmidt/25 50.00
15 Nolan Ryan/25 50.00
19 Greg Maddux/25 40.00
21 Robin Yount/25 50.00
22 Nolan Ryan/25 50.00
24 George Brett/25 50.00
26 Rod Carew/25 50.00
27 Dale Murphy/25 40.00

Timeline Material Combo
NM/M
Varying quantities produced
10 Will Clark/19 60.00
12 Carl Yastrzemski/19 80.00
13 Mike Schmidt/19 60.00
14 George Brett/19 65.00
15 Nolan Ryan/19 100.00
19 Greg Maddux/19 50.00
21 Robin Yount/19 50.00
22 Nolan Ryan/19 100.00
24 George Brett/19 65.00
26 Rod Carew/19 40.00
27 Dale Murphy/19 50.00

Timeline Signature
NM/M
Varying quantities produced
6 Stan Musial/50 70.00
7 Yogi Berra/50 50.00
10 Will Clark/25 100.00
12 Carl Yastrzemski/50 80.00
13 Mike Schmidt/20 85.00
14 George Brett/50 90.00
15 Nolan Ryan/50 110.00
16 Stan Musial/50 70.00
19 Greg Maddux/31 120.00
21 Robin Yount/25 75.00
22 Nolan Ryan/50 110.00

24 George Brett/25 90.00
25 Yogi Berra/50 50.00
27 Dale Murphy/25 50.00

Timeline Material Signature Prime
NM/M
Varying quantities produced
10 Will Clark/50 75.00
12 Carl Yastrzemski/50 80.00
13 Mike Schmidt/20 120.00
14 George Brett/50 100.00
15 Nolan Ryan/50 125.00
19 Greg Maddux/50 75.00
21 Robin Yount/50 75.00
22 Nolan Ryan/50 125.00
27 George Brett/50 100.00

2004 Playoff Prime Cuts II

NM/M
Complete Set (100):
Common (1-91): 1.50
Common (92-100): 3.00
Production 699
Wood Box (1 Pack): 150.00
1 Mark Prior 2.00
2 Derek Jeter 8.00
3 Eric Chavez 1.50
4 Carlos Delgado 1.50
5 Albert Pujols 8.00
6 Miguel Cabrera 2.00
7 Ivan Rodriguez 2.00
8 Javy Lopez 1.50
9 Hank Blalock 1.50
10 Chipper Jones 3.00
11 Gary Sheffield 2.00
12 Alfonso Soriano 3.00
13 Alex Rodriguez/Yanks 6.00
14 Edgar Renteria 1.50
15 Jim Edmonds 1.50
16 Garret Anderson 1.50
17 Lance Berkman 1.50
18 Brandon Webb 1.50
19 Mike Lowell 1.50
20 Mark Mulder 1.50
21 Sammy Sosa 5.00
22 Roger Clemens/Astros 8.00
23 Mark Teixeira 1.50
24 Manny Ramirez 3.00
25 Rafael Palmeiro 2.00
26 Ichiro Suzuki 6.00
27 Vladimir Guerrero 3.00
28 Austin Kearns 1.50
29 Troy Glaus 1.50
30 Ken Griffey Jr. 4.00
31 Greg Maddux 4.00
32 Roy Halladay 1.50
33 Roy Oswalt 1.50
34 Kerry Wood 3.00
35 Mike Mussina/Yanks 2.00
36 Michael Young 1.50
37 Juan Gonzalez 1.50
38 Curt Schilling 2.00
39 Shannon Stewart 1.50
40 Todd Helton 2.00
41 Larry Walker Cards 1.50
42 Mariano Rivera 1.50
43 Nomar Garciaparra 4.00
44 Adam Dunn 2.00
45 Pedro J. Martinez/Sox 3.00
46 Bernie Williams 1.50
47 Tom Glavine 1.50
48 Torii Hunter 1.50
49 David Ortiz 3.00
50 Frank Thomas 2.00
51 Randy Johnson/D'backs 3.00
52 Jason Giambi 1.50
53 Carlos Lee 1.50
54 Mike Sweeney 1.50
55 Hideki Matsui 6.00
56 Dontrelle Willis 1.50
57 Tim Hudson 1.50
58 Jose Vidro 1.50
59 Jeff Bagwell 2.00
60 Rocco Baldelli 1.50
61 Craig Biggio 1.50
62 Mike Piazza Mets 4.00
63 Magglio Ordonez 1.50
64 Hideo Nomo 1.50
65 Miguel Tejada 1.50
66 Vernon Wells 1.50
67 Barry Larkin 1.50
68 Jacque Jones 1.50
69 Scott Rolen 3.00
70 Jeff Kent 1.50
71 Steve Finley 1.50
72 Kazuo Matsui 6.00
73 Carlos Beltran 2.00
74 Shawn Green 1.50
75 Barry Zito 1.50
76 Aramis Ramirez 1.50
77 Paul LoDuca 1.50
78 Kazuhisa Ishii 1.50

79 Aubrey Huff 1.50
80 Jim Thome 3.00
81 Andy Pettitte/Astros 1.50
82 Andruw Jones 1.50
83 Josh Beckett 1.50
84 Sean Casey 1.50
85 Alex Rodriguez/M's 6.00
86 Roger Clemens/Yanks 4.00
87 Mike Mussina/O's 2.00
88 Pedro Martinez/Dgr 3.00
89 Randy Johnson/Astros 3.00
90 Mike Piazza/Dgr 4.00
91 Andy Pettitte/Yanks 1.50
92 Cal Ripken Jr. 15.00
93 Dale Murphy 3.00
94 Don Mattingly 8.00
95 Gary Carter 3.00
96 George Brett 8.00
97 Nolan Ryan 10.00
98 Ozzie Smith 8.00
99 Steve Carlton 3.00
100 Tony Gwynn 6.00

Silver
Silver (1-91): 1-2X
Silver (92-100): 1-1.5X
Production 50 Sets

Gold
Gold (1-91): 2-4X
Gold (92-100): 1.5-2X
Production 25 Sets

Platinum
No Pricing
Production One Set

Icons
NM/M
Common Player: 4.00
Production 50 Sets
Gold: No Pricing
Production 10 Sets
Platinum: No Pricing
Production One Set
Silver: 1-1.5X
Production 25 Sets
1 Dale Murphy 6.00
2 Eddie Mathews 8.00
3 Brooks Robinson 8.00
4 Cal Ripken Jr. 25.00
5 Cal Ripken Jr. 25.00
6 Eddie Murray 8.00
7 Frank Robinson 4.00
8 Jim Palmer 4.00
9 Bobby Doerr 4.00
10 Carl Yastrzemski 10.00
11 Carlton Fisk 6.00
12 Dennis Eckersley 6.00
13 Luis Aparicio 4.00
14 Luis Tiant 4.00
15 Ted Williams 12.00
16 Wade Boggs 4.00
17 Duke Snider 6.00
18 Jackie Robinson 8.00
19 Pee Wee Reese 6.00
20 Burleigh Grimes 4.00
21 Nolan Ryan 20.00
22 Reggie Jackson 6.00
23 Rod Carew 6.00
24 Rod Carew 6.00
25 Billy Williams 6.00
26 Ernie Banks 8.00
27 Mark Grace 4.00
28 Ron Santo 4.00
29 Paul Molitor 6.00
30 Bo Jackson 6.00
31 Carlton Fisk 6.00
32 Johnny Bench 8.00
33 Tom Seaver 6.00
34 Tony Perez 4.00
35 Bob Feller 4.00
36 Lou Boudreau 4.00
37 Al Kaline 8.00
38 Alan Trammell 4.00
39 Ty Cobb 8.00
40 Don Sutton 4.00
41 Nolan Ryan 20.00
42 Roger Maris 8.00
43 Bo Jackson 6.00
44 George Brett 12.00
45 George Brett 12.00
46 Maury Wills 4.00
47 Warren Spahn 6.00
48 Robin Yount 10.00
49 Harmon Killebrew 4.00
50 Kirby Puckett 8.00
51 Paul Molitor 6.00
52 Andre Dawson 4.00
53 Mel Ott 6.00
54 Mel Ott 6.00
55 Duke Snider 6.00
56 Rickey Henderson 8.00
57 Tom Seaver 6.00
58 Babe Ruth 15.00
59 Babe Ruth 15.00
60 Jim "Catfish" Hunter 4.00
61 Dave Righetti 4.00
62 Dave Winfield 6.00
63 Don Mattingly 15.00
64 Don Mattingly 15.00
65 Lou Gehrig 10.00
66 Lou Gehrig 10.00
67 Phil Niekro 4.00
68 Phil Rizzuto 6.00
69 Reggie Jackson 6.00

70 Rickey Henderson 6.00
71 Roger Maris 8.00
72 Thurman Munson 8.00
73 Thurman Munson 8.00
74 Wade Boggs 6.00
75 Whitey Ford 6.00
76 Yogi Berra 8.00
77 Lefty Grove 4.00
78 Mike Schmidt 10.00
79 Mike Schmidt 10.00
80 Steve Carlton 4.00
81 Ralph Kiner 4.00
82 Roberto Clemente 15.00
83 Roberto Clemente 15.00
84 Dave Winfield 4.00
85 Rickey Henderson 6.00
86 Steve Garvey 4.00
87 Tony Gwynn 8.00
88 Tony Gwynn 8.00
89 Juan Marichal 4.00
90 Joe Morgan 4.00
91 Juan Marichal 4.00
92 Steve Carlton 4.00
93 Will Clark 6.00
94 Willie McCovey 4.00
95 Bob Gibson 6.00
96 Lou Brock 6.00
97 Stan Musial 10.00
98 Fergie Jenkins 4.00
99 Nolan Ryan 20.00
100 Harmon Killebrew 8.00

Icons Material Combo
NM/M
Many not priced.
Prime: No Pricing
Production 1-10
4 Cal Ripken Jr./Bat-Jsy/25 75.00
5 Cal Ripken Jr./Jkt-Pants/25 75.00
6 Eddie Murray/Bat-Jsy/25 30.00
7 Frank Robinson/Bat-Jsy/20 20.00
10 Carl Yastrzemski/Bat-Jsy/25 40.00
11 Carlton Fisk/Bat-Jsy/25 25.00
15 Ted Williams/Bat-Jsy/25 100.00
17 Duke Snider/Jsy-Pants/25 80.00
18 Jackie Robinson/Jkt-Jsy/25 80.00
21 Nolan Ryan/Jkt-Jsy/25 50.00
22 Reggie Jackson/Hat-Jsy/25 25.00
23 Rod Carew/Bat-Jsy/25 25.00
24 Rod Carew/Jkt-Jsy/25 25.00
29 Paul Molitor/Jsy-Pants/25 25.00
31 Carlton Fisk/Bat-Jsy/25 25.00
33 Tom Seaver/Bat-Jsy/25 25.00
39 Ty Cobb/Bat-Pants/25 150.00
41 Nolan Ryan/Bat-Jsy/25 50.00
42 Roger Maris/Jsy-Pants/25 75.00
44 George Brett/Bat-Jsy/25 50.00
45 George Brett/Hat-Jsy/25 50.00
47 Warren Spahn/Jsy-Pants/25 30.00
48 Robin Yount/Bat-Jsy/19 50.00
49 Harmon Killebrew/Jsy-Jsy/25 40.00
53 Mel Ott/Bat-Jsy/25 50.00
54 Mel Ott/Bat-Pants/25 50.00
55 Duke Snider/Jsy/25 25.00
58 Babe Ruth/Bat-Jsy/25 300.00
59 Babe Ruth/Bat-Pants/25 300.00
65 Lou Gehrig/Bat-Jsy/25 200.00
66 Lou Gehrig/Bat-Pants/25 200.00
69 Reggie Jackson/Bat-Jsy/25 25.00
71 Roger Maris/Bat-Pants/25 60.00
72 Thurman Munson/Jsy/50 50.00
73 Thurman Munson/Bat-Pants/25 50.00
75 Whitey Ford/Jsy-Jsy/16 40.00
78 Mike Schmidt/Bat-Jsy/50 50.00
79 Mike Schmidt/Hat-Jsy/50 50.00
82 Roberto Clemente/Bat-Jsy/25 150.00
83 Roberto Clemente/Bat-Hat/21 150.00
93 Will Clark/Bat-Jsy/22 30.00

94 Willie McCovey/Jsy-Jsy/25 25.00
99 Nolan Ryan/Jsy-Pants/25 50.00
100 Harmon Killebrew/Bat-Jsy/25 40.00

Icons Material Number
NM/M
Many not priced.
1 Dale Murphy/Jsy/25 20.00
2 Brooks Robinson/Jsy/25 20.00
4 Cal Ripken Jr./Jsy/25 60.00
5 Cal Ripken Jr./Jkt/25 60.00
6 Eddie Murray/Jsy/25 30.00
7 Frank Robinson/Jsy/25 10.00
8 Jim Palmer/Jsy/25 15.00
9 Bobby Doerr/Jsy/25 10.00
10 Carl Yastrzemski/Jsy/25 40.00
11 Carlton Fisk/Jsy/25 20.00
15 Ted Williams/Jsy/50 100.00
17 Duke Snider/Jsy/25 20.00
18 Jackie Robinson/Jkt/50 65.00
19 Pee Wee Reese/Jsy/25 20.00
20 Burleigh Grimes/Pants/25 50.00
21 Nolan Ryan/Jsy/25 40.00
22 Reggie Jackson/Jsy/25 2.00
23 Rod Carew/Jsy/25 20.00
24 Rod Carew/Jkt/25 20.00
25 Billy Williams/Jsy/25 10.00
26 Ernie Banks/Jsy/25 25.00
29 Paul Molitor/Pants/25 25.00
31 Carlton Fisk/Jsy/25 20.00
32 Johnny Bench/Jsy/25 30.00
35 Tom Seaver/Jsy/25 30.00
36 Bob Feller/Jsy/25 15.00
37 Lou Boudreau/Jsy/25 20.00
39 Ty Cobb/Pants/50 100.00
41 Nolan Ryan/Jsy/25 40.00
42 Roger Maris/Jsy/25 50.00
44 George Brett/Jsy/25 40.00
45 George Brett/Jsy/25 40.00
47 Warren Spahn/Jsy/25 25.00
48 Robin Yount/Jsy/25 30.00
49 Harmon Killebrew/Jsy/25 30.00
50 Kirby Puckett/Jsy/25 25.00
51 Paul Molitor/Jsy/25 20.00
53 Mel Ott/Pants/25 40.00
54 Mel Ott/Pants/25 40.00
55 Duke Snider/Jsy/25 40.00
58 Babe Ruth/Jsy/25 300.00
59 Babe Ruth/Pants/25 180.00
60 Jim "Catfish" Hunter/Jsy/25 20.00
63 Don Mattingly/Jsy/25 40.00
64 Don Mattingly/Jkt/25 40.00
65 Lou Boudreau/Jsy/25 150.00
66 Lou Gehrig/Pants/25 100.00
68 Phil Rizzuto/Pants/25 20.00
69 Reggie Jackson/Jsy/25 20.00
71 Roger Maris/Pants/25 40.00
72 Thurman Munson/Jsy/50 35.00
73 Thurman Munson/Pants/50 35.00
77 Lefty Grove/Hat/25 120.00
78 Mike Schmidt/Jsy/20 40.00
79 Mike Schmidt/Jkt/20 40.00
82 Roberto Clemente/Jsy/21 100.00
83 Roberto Clemente/Hat/21 100.00
91 Juan Marichal/Jsy/25 15.00
93 Will Clark/Jsy/22 25.00
94 Willie McCovey/Jsy/25 20.00
95 Bob Gibson/Jsy/25 25.00
96 Lou Brock/Jkt/20 20.00
99 Nolan Ryan/Pants/25 40.00
100 Harmon Killebrew/Jsy/25 35.00

Icons Material Prime
No Pricing
Production 1-10

Icons Signature Century Silver
NM/M
1 Dale Murphy/25 40.00
2 Brooks Robinson/50 30.00
4 Cal Ripken Jr./25 180.00
5 Cal Ripken Jr./25 180.00
6 Eddie Murray/50 50.00
7 Frank Robinson/50 30.00
8 Jim Palmer/50 30.00
9 Bobby Doerr/25 30.00
10 Carl Yastrzemski/25 75.00

11 Carlton Fisk/27 40.00
12 Dennis Eckersley/43 30.00
13 Luis Aparicio/25 25.00
16 Wade Boggs/25 40.00
18 Duke Snider/50 30.00
21 Nolan Ryan/30 100.00
22 Reggie Jackson/25 50.00
23 Rod Carew/29 35.00
24 Rod Carew/29 35.00
25 Billy Williams/26 20.00
29 Paul Molitor/25 35.00
30 Bo Jackson/25 50.00
31 Carlton Fisk/25 40.00
32 Johnny Bench/50 30.00
33 Tom Seaver/25 40.00
34 Tony Perez/25 40.00
35 Bob Feller/25 30.00
37 Al Kaline/50 40.00
40 Don Sutton/20 20.00
41 Nolan Ryan/34 100.00
43 Bo Jackson/25 50.00
44 George Brett/25 100.00
45 George Brett/25 100.00
48 Robin Yount/19 65.00
49 Harmon Killebrew/50 40.00
51 Paul Molitor/50 30.00
55 Duke Snider/50 30.00
56 Rickey Henderson/24 60.00
57 Tom Seaver/25 40.00
62 Dave Winfield/31 35.00
63 Don Mattingly/50 60.00
64 Don Mattingly/50 60.00
67 Phil Niekro/35 20.00
68 Phil Rizzuto/25 50.00
69 Reggie Jackson/25 50.00
70 Rickey Henderson/24 60.00
72 Whitey Ford/25 50.00
76 Yogi Berra/25 50.00
78 Mike Schmidt/20 80.00
79 Mike Schmidt/20 80.00
80 Steve Carlton/32 30.00
81 Ralph Kiner/25 45.00
84 Dave Winfield/31 35.00
85 Rickey Henderson/24 60.00
87 Tony Gwynn/50 40.00
88 Tony Gwynn/50 40.00
89 Gaylord Perry/25 50.00
90 Joe Morgan/24 25.00
91 Juan Marichal/27 25.00
92 Steve Carlton/32 30.00
93 Will Clark/22 50.00
94 Willie McCovey/25 50.00
96 Bob Gibson/45 30.00
96 Lou Brock/50 30.00
97 Stan Musial/50 65.00
98 Fergie Jenkins/31 25.00
99 Nolan Ryan/34 100.00
100 Harmon Killebrew/50 40.00

Icons Signature Century Gold
NM/M
Many not priced.
1 Dale Murphy/25 40.00
7 Brooks Robinson/25 40.00
8 Frank Robinson/20 35.00
9 Jim Palmer/22 35.00
9 Bobby Doerr/25 30.00
17 Duke Snider/25 35.00
32 Johnny Bench/25 50.00
34 Tony Perez/24 40.00
35 Bob Feller/19 40.00
37 Al Kaline/25 50.00
43 Bo Jackson/16 75.00
49 Harmon Killebrew/25 40.00
51 Paul Molitor/25 35.00
55 Duke Snider/25 40.00
63 Don Mattingly/23 75.00
64 Don Mattingly/23 75.00
80 Steve Carlton/25 35.00
81 Ralph Kiner/25 45.00
87 Tony Gwynn/19 50.00
88 Tony Gwynn/19 50.00
92 Steve Carlton/25 35.00
95 Bob Gibson/25 30.00
96 Lou Brock/25 40.00
97 Stan Musial/25 90.00
100 Harmon Killebrew/25 50.00

Icons Signature Century Platinum
No Pricing
Production One Set

Icons Signature Material Combo
NM/M
Many not priced.
Prime: No Pricing
Production 1-10
1 Dale Murphy/Bat-Jsy/25 50.00
7 Frank Robinson/Bat-Jsy/20 45.00
8 Jim Palmer/Hat-Jsy/22 50.00
9 Bobby Doerr/Bat-Jsy/25 40.00
17 Duke Snider/Jsy-Pants/25 50.00
25 Billy Williams/Bat-Jsy/26 30.00
29 Paul Molitor/Jsy-Pants/25 50.00

34	Tony Perez/Bat-Fld Glv/24	50.00
48	Robin Yount/Bat-Jsy/19	100.00
49	Harmon Killebrew/Jsy/25	80.00
51	Paul Molitor/Bat-Jsy/25	50.00
63	Don Mattingly/Bat-Jsy/23	100.00
64	Don Mattingly/Hat-Jkt/23	100.00
78	Mike Schmidt/Bat-Jsy/20	100.00
79	Mike Schmidt/Hat-Jkt/20	100.00
80	Steve Carlton/Fld Glv-Pants/32	50.00
87	Tony Gwynn/Fld Glv-Jsy/19	80.00
88	Tony Gwynn/Jsy-Pants/19	80.00
92	Steve Carlton/Bat-Jsy/32	50.00
93	Will Clark/Bat-Jsy/22	75.00
98	Fergie Jenkins/Fld Glv-Hat/31	40.00

Icons Signature Material Number
NM/M
Many not priced.
Prime: No Pricing
Production 1-10

7	Frank Robinson/Jsy/20	40.00
8	Jim Palmer/Jsy/22	40.00
9	Bobby Doerr/Jsy/25	30.00
11	Carlton Fisk/Jsy/27	40.00
12	Dennis Eckersley/Jsy/43	30.00
16	Wade Boggs/Jsy/26	40.00
21	Nolan Ryan/Jsy/30	100.00
22	Reggie Jackson/Jsy/44	50.00
25	Billy Williams/Jsy/26	25.00
27	Mark Grace/Jsy/17	45.00
35	Bob Feller/Jsy/19	40.00
40	Don Sutton/Jsy/20	25.00
41	Nolan Ryan/Jsy/34	100.00
43	Bo Jackson/Jsy/16	75.00
48	Robin Yount/Jsy/19	65.00
62	Dave Winfield/Pants/31	40.00
63	Don Mattingly/Jsy/23	80.00
64	Don Mattingly/Jkt/23	80.00
69	Reggie Jackson/Jsy/44	65.00
78	Mike Schmidt/Jsy/20	80.00
79	Mike Schmidt/Jkt/20	80.00
80	Steve Carlton/Pants/32	40.00
84	Dave Winfield/Jsy/31	40.00
87	Tony Gwynn/Jsy/19	75.00
88	Tony Gwynn/Jsy/19	75.00
91	Gaylord Perry/Jsy/36	20.00
92	Juan Marichal/Jsy/27	25.00
93	Steve Carlton/Jsy/32	40.00
93	Will Clark/Jsy/22	65.00
96	Bob Gibson/Jsy/45	35.00
96	Lou Brock/Jkt/20	40.00
98	Fergie Jenkins/Hat/31	25.00
99	Nolan Ryan/Pants/34	65.00

Material Combo
NM/M
Many not priced due to scarcity.
Prime: No Pricing
Production 1-9

1	Mark Prior/Hat-Jsy/22	20.00
12	Alfonso Soriano/Jsy/25	25.00
15	Jim Edmonds/Bat-Jsy/15	20.00
16	Garret Anderson/Bat-Jsy/16	15.00
21	Sammy Sosa/Bat-Jsy/21	40.00
22	Roger Clemens/Bat-Jsy/22	50.00
24	Manny Ramirez/Bat-Jsy/24	25.00
25	Rafael Palmeiro/Bat-Jsy/25	20.00
27	Vladimir Guerrero/Bat-Jsy/27	25.00
31	Greg Maddux/Bat-Jsy/31	40.00
35	Mike Mussina/Bat-Jsy/35	25.00
40	Todd Helton/Bat-Jsy/17	25.00
86	Roger Clemens/Fld Glv-Jsy/22	50.00
92	Cal Ripken Jr./Bat-Jsy/25	75.00
93	Dale Murphy/Bat-Jsy/25	20.00
94	Don Mattingly/Bat-Jsy/25	50.00
96	George Brett/Bat-Jsy/25	50.00
97	Nolan Ryan/Bat-Jkt/25	60.00
98	Ozzie Smith/Bat-Jsy/25	40.00

Material Number
NM/M
Most not priced.
Prime: No Pricing
Production 1-10

86	Roger Clemens/Jsy/25	40.00
92	Cal Ripken Jr./Jsy/25	60.00
93	Dale Murphy/Jsy/25	20.00
94	Don Mattingly/Jsy/25	40.00
96	George Brett/Jsy/25	40.00
97	Nolan Ryan/Jkt/25	50.00
98	Ozzie Smith/Jsy/25	30.00

Signature Century Silver
NM/M
Many not priced.

1	Mark Prior/22	30.00
6	Miguel Cabrera/24	40.00
9	Hank Blalock/25	40.00
11	Gary Sheffield/25	40.00
15	Jim Edmonds/25	40.00
16	Garret Anderson/25	25.00
17	Lance Berkman/25	40.00
20	Mark Mulder/20	25.00
21	Sammy Sosa/25	125.00
23	Mark Teixeira/40	40.00
24	Manny Ramirez/24	75.00
25	Rafael Palmeiro/25	50.00
31	Greg Maddux/31	100.00
34	Kerry Wood/34	50.00
35	Mike Mussina/35	40.00
37	Juan Gonzalez/22	40.00
44	Adam Dunn/44	30.00
49	David Ortiz/34	50.00
50	Frank Thomas/35	40.00
61	Craig Biggio/25	35.00
63	Magglio Ordonez/30	25.00
66	Vernon Wells/25	20.00
69	Scott Rolen/27	50.00
82	Andruw Jones/25	35.00
83	Josh Beckett/21	25.00
87	Mike Mussina/35	40.00
92	Cal Ripken Jr./25	175.00
93	Dale Murphy/25	40.00
94	Don Mattingly/23	75.00
95	Gary Carter/25	25.00
97	Nolan Ryan/34	100.00
99	Steve Carlton/32	30.00
100	Tony Gwynn/25	50.00

Signature Century Gold

No Pricing
Production 1-17

Signature Century Platinum
No Pricing
Production One Set

Signature Material Combo
NM/M
Most not priced.
Prime: No Pricing
Production 1-9

1	Mark Prior/Hat-Jsy/22	50.00
20	Mark Mulder/Jsy-Jsy/20	35.00
40	Todd Helton/Bat-Jsy/17	75.00
83	Josh Beckett/Bat-Jsy/21	35.00
93	Dale Murphy/Bat-Jsy/25	50.00
94	Don Mattingly/Bat-Jsy/25	100.00

Signature Material Number
NM/M
Most not priced.
Prime: No Pricing
Production 1-9

1	Mark Prior/Jsy/22	40.00
17	Lance Berkman/Jsy/17	50.00
20	Mark Mulder/Jsy/20	25.00
40	Todd Helton/Jsy/17	60.00
57	Tim Hudson/Jsy/15	35.00
83	Josh Beckett/Jsy/21	25.00
94	Don Mattingly/Jsy/23	75.00
97	Nolan Ryan/Jkt/34	125.00
99	Steve Carlton/Jsy/32	40.00
100	Tony Gwynn/Jsy/19	80.00

Timeline

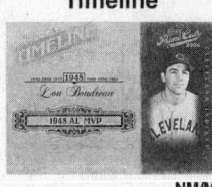

NM/M
Common Player: 4.00
Production 50 Sets
Century Gold: No Pricing
Production 10 Sets
Century Platinum: No Pricing
Production One Set
Century Silver: 1-1.5X
Production 25 Sets

1	Al Kaline	8.00
2	Alex Rodriguez	10.00
3	Andre Dawson	4.00
4	Babe Ruth	15.00
5	Barry Zito	4.00
6	Bob Feller	4.00
7	Bob Gibson	6.00
8	Bobby Doerr	4.00
9	Brooks Robinson	6.00
10	Cal Ripken Jr.	25.00
11	Carl Hubbell	4.00
12	Carl Yastrzemski	10.00
13	Carlton Fisk	6.00
14	Jim "Catfish" Hunter	6.00
15	Chipper Jones	8.00
16	Cy Young	6.00
17	Dale Murphy	4.00
18	Dave Parker	4.00
19	Dennis Eckersley	4.00
20	Don Drysdale	4.00
21	Don Mattingly	15.00
22	Duke Snider	6.00
23	Dwight Gooden	4.00
24	Early Wynn	8.00
25	Eddie Mathews	8.00
26	Eddie Murray	6.00
27	Enos Slaughter	4.00
28	Ernie Banks	8.00
29	Fergie Jenkins	6.00
30	Frank Robinson	6.00
31	Frank Thomas	8.00
32	Frankie Frisch	4.00
33	Fred Lynn	4.00
34	Gary Carter	4.00
35	Gaylord Perry	4.00
36	George Brett	15.00
37	Greg Maddux	10.00
38	Hal Newhouser	4.00
39	Harmon Killebrew	8.00
40	Honus Wagner	8.00
41	Hoyt Wilhelm	4.00
42	Ivan Rodriguez	8.00
43	Jackie Robinson	8.00
44	Jason Giambi	4.00
45	Jeff Bagwell	4.00
46	Jim Palmer	4.00
47	Jimmie Foxx	4.00
48	Joe Morgan	4.00
49	Johnny Bench	8.00
50	Johnny Mize	4.00
51	Jose Canseco	6.00
52	Juan Gonzalez	6.00
53	Juan Marichal	4.00
54	Keith Hernandez	4.00
55	Kirby Puckett	8.00
56	Lefty Grove	4.00
57	Lou Boudreau	4.00
58	Lou Brock	6.00
59	Lou Gehrig	10.00
60	Luis Aparicio	4.00
61	Marty Marion	4.00
62	Mel Ott	6.00
63	Miguel Tejada	4.00
64	Mike Schmidt	10.00
65	Nellie Fox	6.00
66	Nolan Ryan	15.00
67	Orel Hershiser	4.00
68	Orlando Cepeda	4.00
69	Paul Molitor	8.00
70	Pedro Martinez	8.00
71	Pee Wee Reese	4.00
72	Phil Niekro	4.00
73	Phil Rizzuto	6.00
74	Ralph Kiner	4.00
75	Randy Johnson	8.00
76	Red Schoendienst	4.00
77	Reggie Jackson	6.00
78	Rickey Henderson	6.00
79	Roberto Clemente	15.00
80	Robin Yount	6.00
81	Rod Carew	6.00
82	Roger Clemens	10.00
83	Roger Maris	10.00
84	Rogers Hornsby	6.00
85	Roy Campanella	6.00
86	Ozzie Smith	10.00
87	Sammy Sosa	6.00
88	Satchel Paige	6.00
89	Stan Musial	10.00
90	Steve Carlton	6.00
91	Ted Williams	10.00
92	Thurman Munson	6.00
93	Tom Seaver	6.00
94	Ty Cobb	10.00
95	Walter Johnson	6.00
96	Warren Spahn	8.00
97	Whitey Ford	6.00
98	Willie McCovey	6.00
99	Willie Stargell	6.00
100	Yogi Berra	8.00

Timeline Material Combo
NM/M
Quantity produced listed

4	Babe Ruth/Jsy/25	350.00
7	Bob Gibson/Hat-Jsy/25	35.00
10	Cal Ripken Jr./Jkt/25	75.00
13	Carlton Fisk/Jsy/25	25.00
14	Jim "Catfish" Hunter/Jsy/27	25.00
17	Dale Murphy/Bat-Jsy/25	25.00
21	Don Mattingly/Btg Glv-Pants/25	50.00
25	Eddie Mathews/Bat/41	40.00
26	Eddie Murray/Bat/33	40.00
36	George Brett/Hat-Jsy/25	60.00
39	Harmon Killebrew/Jsy/25	50.00
43	Jackie Robinson/Jkt/42	100.00
46	Jim Palmer/Hat-Jsy/22	20.00
47	Jimmie Foxx/Bat-Fld Glv/25	125.00
49	Johnny Bench/Bat-Jsy/25	40.00
58	Lou Brock/Bat-Jsy/20	25.00
59	Lou Gehrig/Jsy-Pants/25	250.00
62	Mel Ott/Jsy-Pants/25	50.00
64	Mike Schmidt/Bat-Jsy/20	60.00
66	Nolan Ryan/Jsy/25	60.00
68	Orlando Cepeda/Bat-Pants/25	20.00
71	Pee Wee Reese/Bat-Jsy/25	30.00
77	Reggie Jackson/Jsy-Jsy/25	30.00
79	Roberto Clemente/Hat-Jsy/21	150.00
80	Robin Yount/Bat-Jsy/19	50.00
81	Rod Carew/Bat-Jsy/29	30.00
82	Roger Clemens/Jsy-Jsy/21	40.00
83	Roger Maris/Jsy-Pants/25	75.00
85	Roy Campanella/Bat-Pants/39	35.00
86	Ozzie Smith/Bat-Jsy/21	40.00
87	Sammy Sosa/Bat-Jsy/21	40.00
90	Steve Carlton/Hat-Jsy/32	20.00
91	Ted Williams/Jsy/25	140.00
92	Thurman Munson/Jsy-Pants/10	50.00
94	Ty Cobb/Bat-Pants/25	160.00
96	Warren Spahn/Jsy-Jsy/21	40.00
98	Willie McCovey/Bat-Jsy/25	25.00

Timeline Material Combo CY
Quantity produced listed

Timeline Material Number
NM/M
Quantity produced listed

4	Babe Ruth/Jsy/25	350.00
6	Bob Feller/Pants/19	25.00
7	Bob Gibson/Jsy/25	30.00
10	Cal Ripken Jr./Jsy/25	60.00
12	Carl Yastrzemski/Jsy/25	40.00
13	Carlton Fisk/Jsy/27	25.00
14	Jim "Catfish" Hunter/Jsy/27	20.00
22	Don Drysdale/Jsy/25	40.00
22	Duke Snider/Pants/25	25.00
24	Early Wynn/Jsy/24	15.00
25	Eddie Mathews/Jsy/25	30.00
26	Eddie Murray/Jsy/25	25.00
28	Ernie Banks/Jsy/25	35.00
32	Frankie Frisch/Jkt/25	40.00
36	George Brett/Jsy/25	40.00
39	Harmon Killebrew/Jsy/25	35.00
43	Jackie Robinson/Jkt/42	60.00
46	Jim Palmer/Jsy/22	15.00

Timeline Material Position
NM/M
Quantity produced listed

4	Babe Ruth/Jsy/25	350.00
6	Bob Feller/Pants/19	25.00
7	Bob Gibson/Jsy/25	30.00
10	Cal Ripken Jr./Jsy/25	60.00
12	Carl Yastrzemski/Jsy/25	40.00
13	Carlton Fisk/Jsy/27	25.00
14	Jim "Catfish" Hunter/Jsy/27	20.00
22	Don Drysdale/Jsy/25	40.00
22	Duke Snider/Pants/25	25.00
24	Early Wynn/Jsy/24	15.00
25	Eddie Mathews/Jsy/25	30.00
26	Eddie Murray/Jsy/25	25.00
28	Ernie Banks/Jsy/25	35.00
32	Frankie Frisch/Jkt/25	40.00
36	George Brett/Jsy/25	40.00
39	Harmon Killebrew/Jsy/25	35.00
43	Jackie Robinson/Jkt/42	60.00
46	Jim Palmer/Jsy/22	15.00
47	Jimmie Foxx/Fld Glv/25	85.00
49	Johnny Bench/Jsy/25	25.00
53	Juan Marichal/Jsy/27	15.00
55	Kirby Puckett/Jsy/25	30.00
58	Lou Brock/Jsy/20	25.00
59	Lou Gehrig/Jsy/25	180.00
62	Mel Ott/Pants/25	40.00
64	Mike Schmidt/Jsy/25	50.00
66	Nolan Ryan/Jsy/25	50.00
68	Orlando Cepeda/Pants/25	15.00
71	Pee Wee Reese/Jsy/25	25.00
74	Ralph Kiner/Bat/25	25.00
77	Reggie Jackson/Jsy/25	25.00
80	Robin Yount/Jsy/19	40.00
81	Rod Carew/Jsy/25	25.00
82	Roger Clemens/Jsy/21	30.00
84	Rogers Hornsby/Bat/75	75.00
86	Ozzie Smith/Jsy/25	35.00
87	Sammy Sosa/Jsy/21	30.00
88	Satchel Paige CO/Jsy/25	75.00
90	Steve Carlton/Jsy/25	15.00
92	Thurman Munson/Jsy/25	40.00
93	Tom Seaver/Pants/25	25.00
96	Warren Spahn/Jsy/21	35.00
98	Willie McCovey/Jsy/25	25.00

Timeline Material Prime
No Pricing
Production 1-10

Timeline Material Quad
No Pricing
Production 1-25

47	Jimmie Foxx/Fld Glv/25	85.00
49	Johnny Bench/Jsy/25	25.00
53	Juan Marichal/Jsy/25	35.00
55	Kirby Puckett/Jsy/25	30.00
58	Lou Brock/Jsy/25	25.00
59	Lou Gehrig/Jsy/25	180.00
62	Mel Ott/Pants/25	40.00
64	Mike Schmidt/Jsy/20	50.00
66	Nolan Ryan/Jsy/25	50.00
68	Orlando Cepeda/Pants/25	15.00
71	Pee Wee Reese/Jsy/25	25.00
74	Ralph Kiner/Bat/25	25.00
77	Reggie Jackson/Jsy/25	25.00
80	Robin Yount/Jsy/19	40.00
81	Rod Carew/Jsy/25	25.00
82	Roger Clemens/Jsy/21	30.00
83	Roger Maris/Jsy/25	60.00
84	Rogers Hornsby/Bat/75	75.00
85	Roy Campanella/Pants/25	30.00
86	Ozzie Smith/Jsy/25	35.00
87	Sammy Sosa/Jsy/21	30.00
88	Satchel Paige/Jsy/25	75.00
90	Steve Carlton/Jsy/25	15.00
91	Ted Williams/Jsy/25	100.00
92	Thurman Munson/Jsy/25	40.00
93	Tom Seaver/Pants/25	25.00
94	Ty Cobb/Pants/25	140.00
96	Warren Spahn/Jsy/21	35.00
98	Willie McCovey/Jsy/8	25.00

Timeline Material Trio
NM/M
Most not priced.
Trio HOF: No Pricing
Production 1-9
Trio MVP: No Pricing
Production 1-10
Trio Stats: No Pricing
Production 1-15

10	Cal Ripken Jr./Jkt-Jsy-Pants/25	100.00
17	Dale Murphy/Bat-Jsy-Jsy/25	40.00
21	Don Mattingly/Bat-Jkt-Pants/25	75.00
26	Eddie Murray/Bat-Jsy-Shoe/25	85.00
80	Robin Yount/Bat-Jsy/19	70.00
82	Roger Clemens/Bat-Jsy-Jsy/21	50.00

Timeline Signature Material Combo
NM/M
Most not priced.

7	Bob Gibson/Hat-Jsy/25	50.00
8	Bobby Doerr/Bat-Jsy/25	50.00
58	Lou Brock/Bat-Jsy/20	50.00

Timeline Signature Material Combo CY
NM/M
Most not priced.

7	Bob Gibson/Hat-Jsy/25	50.00
46	Jim Palmer/Hat-Jsy/22	50.00
90	Steve Carlton/Hat-Jsy/32	50.00

Timeline Signature Material Number
NM/M
Most not priced.

6	Bob Feller/Pants/19	40.00
7	Bob Gibson/Jsy/25	50.00
8	Bobby Doerr/Jsy/25	40.00
21	Don Mattingly/Pants/23	80.00
46	Jim Palmer/Jsy/22	40.00
53	Juan Marichal/Jsy/27	40.00
58	Lou Brock/Jsy/20	50.00
66	Nolan Ryan/Jsy/34	150.00
90	Steve Carlton/Jsy/32	50.00

Timeline Signature Material Position
NM/M
Most not priced.

6	Bob Feller/Pants/19	40.00
8	Bobby Doerr/Jsy/25	40.00
21	Don Mattingly/Pants/23	80.00
46	Jim Palmer/Jsy/22	40.00
53	Juan Marichal/Jsy/27	40.00
58	Lou Brock/Jsy/20	50.00
66	Nolan Ryan/Jsy/34	150.00
67	Orel Hershiser/Jsy/25	30.00

Timeline Signature Material Prime
No Pricing
Production 1-9

Timeline Signature Material Quad
NM/M
Most not priced.

21	Don Mattingly/25	180.00

Timeline Signature Material Trio

NM/M
No Pricing
Production 1-9
Trio HOF: No Pricing
Production 1-9
Trio MVP: No Pricing
Production 1-8
Trio Stats: No Pricing
Production 1-9

91	Ted Williams/Bat-Jkt-Jsy/1 (2/06 auction)	1,483

2005 Playoff Absolute Memorabilia

NM/M
Common Player: .50
Retail: .3X
Retail doesn't have foil front.
Pack (4): 50.00
Box (4): 185.00

1 Andruw Jones .75
2 B.J. Upton .75
3 Jim Edmonds .75
4 Johan Santana 1.00
5 Jeff Bagwell .75
6 Derek Jeter 3.00
7 Eric Chavez .75
8 Albert Pujols 3.00
9 Craig Biggio .75
10 Hank Blalock .75
11 Chipper Jones 1.00
12 Jacque Jones .50
13 Alfonso Soriano 1.00
14 Carl Crawford .50
15 Ben Sheets .50
16 Garret Anderson .75
17 Luis Gonzalez .50
18 Andy Pettitte .75
19 Miguel Tejada .75
20 Carlos Delgado .75
21 Austin Kearns .50
22 Adrian Beltre .50
23 Rafael Palmeiro .75
24 Greg Maddux 2.00
25 Jason Bay .75
26 Jason Varitek .75
27 David Ortiz 1.00
28 Dontrelle Willis 1.00
29 Adam Dunn 1.00
30 Carlos Lee .50
31 Manny Ramirez 1.00
32 Rocco Baldelli .50
33 Jeff Kent .50
34 Jake Peavy .75
35 Vernon Wells .50
36 Ichiro Suzuki 2.00
37 C.C. Sabathia .50
38 Hideki Matsui 2.00
39 Gary Sheffield .75
40 Paul LoDuca .50
41 Vladimir Guerrero 1.00
42 Omar Vizquel .50
43 Lance Berkman .50
44 Shawn Green .50
45 Josh Beckett .50
46 Barry Zito .50
47 Roger Clemens 3.00
48 Sean Casey .50
49 Edgar Renteria .50
50 Mark Teixeira .75
51 Frank Thomas .50
52 Khalil Greene .50
53 Bobby Abreu .75
54 Rafael Furcal .50
55 Jose Vidro .50
56 Nomar Garciaparra 1.00
57 Melvin Mora .50
58 Trot Nixon .50
59 Magglio Ordonez .50
60 Michael Young .50
61 Richie Sexson .50
62 Alex Rodriguez 3.00
63 Tim Hudson .75
64 Todd Helton .75
65 Mike Lowell .50
66 Mark Mulder .50
67 Sammy Sosa 1.50
68 Mark Prior .50
69 Shannon Stewart .50
70 Miguel Cabrera 1.00
71 Troy Glaus .50
72 Scott Rolen 1.00
73 Ken Griffey Jr. 2.00
74 Mike Piazza 1.00
75 Roy Halladay .50
76 Larry Walker .75
77 Kerry Wood .75
78 Mike Mussina .75
79 Curt Schilling 1.00
80 Rich Harden .50
81 Victor Martinez .50
82 Roy Oswalt .50
83 Pedro Martinez 1.00
84 Tom Glavine .50
85 Randy Johnson 1.00
86 Ivan Rodriguez 1.00
87 Carlos Beltran .75
88 Torii Hunter .50
89 Hideo Nomo .50
90 Jim Thome 1.00
91 Aramis Ramirez .50
92 J.D. Drew .50
93 Javy Lopez .50
94 David Wright 2.00
95 Bobby Crosby .50
96 Jeff Niemann RC 3.00
97 Yuniesky Betancourt RC 3.00
98 Tadahito Iguchi RC 5.00
99 Philip Humber RC 3.00
100 Justin Verlander RC 5.00

Black
Black: 2-4X
Inserted 1:18 Retail

Blue
Blue: 1-2X
Inserted 1:3 Retail

Red
Red: 2-3X
Inserted 1:8 Retail

Spectrum Gold
No Pricing
Production 10 Sets

Spectrum Platinum
No Pricing
Production One Set

Spectrum Silver
Silver: 2-3X
Production 100 Sets

Absolutely Ink Swatch Single
NM/M
Production 5-50
1 Rafael Furcal/Jsy 15.00
3 Dale Murphy/Jsy/50 25.00
4 Duke Snider/Pants/25 40.00
5 Bill Madlock/Bat/50 25.00
7 Bobby Crosby/Jsy 15.00
8 Cal Ripken Jr./Jsy/25 140.00
9 Hank Blalock/Jsy/25 25.00
10 Vernon Wells/Jsy/50 15.00
11 Lyle Overbay/Jsy/50 15.00
13 Omar Vizquel/Jsy/25 15.00
15 Ben Sheets/Jsy/25 20.00
16 Aramis Ramirez/Jsy/25 30.00
18 Travis Hafner/Jsy 20.00
19 Mike Lowell/Jsy/25 15.00
20 Frank Robinson/Bat/50 30.00
22 Juan Gonzalez/Jsy/50 25.00
27 Darryl Strawberry/Jsy/50 15.00
28 Alexis Rios/Bat/50 15.00
30 Magglio Ordonez/Jsy/50 15.00
31 Jay Gibbons/Jsy/50 15.00
32 Steve Carlton/Jsy/25 35.00
34 Kerry Wood/Jsy/50 15.00
36 Eric Chavez/Jsy/25 25.00
37 Keith Hernandez/Jsy/50 15.00
38 Carlos Zambrano/Jsy/50 25.00
39 Brett Myers/Jsy/50 15.00
40 Rich Harden/Jsy/25 15.00
41 Danny Kolb/Jsy/25 15.00
42 Mark Prior/Jsy/25 40.00
43 Joey Gathright/Jsy/50 15.00
44 David Cone/Jsy/50 15.00
45 Carlos Lee/Jsy/50 20.00
47 Jack Morris/Jsy/50 20.00
48 Torii Hunter/Jsy/50 20.00
49 Garret Anderson/Jsy/50 25.00
51 Dave Parker/Bat/50 20.00
52 C.C. Sabathia/Jsy/50 15.00
53 Dennis Eckersley/Jsy/50 20.00
54 Barry Larkin/Jsy/25 40.00
55 Brandon Webb/Pants/50 15.00
56 Sean Casey/Jsy/50 20.00
57 Johan Santana/Jsy/50 40.00
58 Miguel Cabrera/Jsy/50 40.00
59 Bert Blyleven/Jsy/50 15.00
60 Casey Kotchman/Jsy/50 15.00
61 Dwight Gooden/Jsy/50 20.00
62 Milton Bradley/Jsy/50 20.00
63 John Kruk/Jsy/50 25.00
64 Michael Young/Jsy/50 20.00
66 Robin Ventura/Jsy/50 20.00
67 Tim Hudson/Jsy/25 30.00
68 Will Clark/Bat/50 40.00
69 Lew Ford/Jsy/50 15.00
70 Jody Gerut/Jsy/50 15.00
71 Don Sutton/Jsy/50 15.00
72 B.J. Upton/Bat/25 20.00
73 Austin Kearns/Jsy/50 20.00
77 Ryan Wagner/Jsy/50 15.00
78 Jermaine Dye/Jsy/50 15.00
80 Al Oliver/Jsy/50 15.00
81 Angel Berroa/Pants/50 15.00
82 Edgar Renteria/Jsy/50 20.00
83 Dennis Eckersley/Jsy/25 25.00
84 Roy Oswalt/Jsy/50 20.00
86 Dave Righetti/Jsy/25 20.00
87 Aubrey Huff/Jsy/25 20.00
89 Jose Vidro/Jsy/50 15.00
90 Harold Baines/Jsy/50 15.00
93 Ken Harvey/Jsy 15.00
95 Jason Bay/Jsy 20.00
96 Dwight Evans/Jsy/50 30.00
97 Luis Tiant/Pants/50 15.00
98 Ron Santo/Bat/50 30.00
99 Brian Roberts/Jsy/50 40.00
100 Marty Marion/Jsy 15.00

Absolutley Ink Swatch Single Spectrum
NM/M
Production 1-25
Prime: No Pricing
Production One Set
2 Rafael Furcal/Jsy 20.00
3 Dale Murphy/Jsy/25 35.00
5 Bill Madlock/Bat/25 25.00
7 Bobby Crosby/Jsy 20.00
11 Lyle Overbay/Jsy/25 15.00
18 Travis Hafner/Jsy 25.00
23 Mark Teixeira/Jsy 50.00
27 Darryl Strawberry/Jsy/50 15.00
28 Alexis Rios/Bat/25 15.00
30 Magglio Ordonez/Jsy/25 15.00
31 Jay Gibbons/Jsy/25 15.00
37 Keith Hernandez/Jsy/50 20.00
38 Carlos Zambrano/Jsy/25 30.00
39 Brett Myers/Jsy/25 15.00
40 Rich Harden/Jsy/25 15.00
41 Danny Kolb/Jsy/25 15.00
45 Carlos Lee/Jsy/25 20.00
47 Jack Morris/Jsy/25 20.00
51 Dave Parker/Bat/25 20.00
52 C.C. Sabathia/Jsy/25 15.00
53 Dennis Eckersley/Jsy/50 20.00
54 Barry Larkin/Jsy/25 40.00
55 Brandon Webb/Pants/50 15.00
56 Sean Casey/Jsy/25 20.00
57 Johan Santana/Jsy/50 40.00
58 Miguel Cabrera/Jsy/50 40.00
59 Bert Blyleven/Jsy/50 15.00
60 Casey Kotchman/Jsy/50 15.00
61 Dwight Gooden/Jsy/50 20.00
62 Milton Bradley/Jsy/50 20.00
63 John Kruk/Jsy/50 25.00
64 Michael Young/Jsy/50 20.00
69 Lew Ford/Jsy/25 15.00
70 Jody Gerut/Jsy/25 15.00
71 Don Sutton/Jsy/25 20.00
73 Austin Kearns/Jsy/25 20.00
77 Ryan Wagner/Jsy/25 15.00
78 Jermaine Dye/Jsy/25 15.00
80 Al Oliver/Jsy/25 15.00
81 Angel Berroa/Pants/25 15.00
89 Jose Vidro/Jsy/25 15.00
90 Harold Baines/Jsy/25 15.00
92 Mark Mulder/Jsy/25 25.00
93 Ken Harvey/Jsy/25 15.00
95 Jason Bay/Jsy/25 25.00
96 Dwight Evans/Jsy/25 40.00
97 Luis Tiant/Pants/25 15.00
98 Ron Santo/Bat/25 30.00
99 Brian Roberts/Jsy/25 40.00
100 Marty Marion/Jsy/25 25.00

Absolutely Ink Swatch Double
NM/M
Production 1-50
1 Rafael Furcal B-J/25 20.00
3 Dale Murphy B-J/25 30.00
7 Bobby Crosby J-J/50 20.00
8 Cal Ripken Jr. J-P/25 150.00
10 Vernon Wells J-J/25 20.00
11 Lyle Overbay J-J/50 15.00
13 Omar Vizquel J-J/50 20.00
16 Aramis Ramirez J-J/25 30.00
18 Travis Hafner BG-J/25 30.00
22 Juan Gonzalez B-J/25 25.00
23 Mark Teixeira FG-J/25 35.00
27 Darryl Strawberry J-J/25 20.00
30 Magglio Ordonez B-J/25 20.00
31 Jay Gibbons B-J/50 15.00
37 Steve Carlton FG-J/25 40.00
37 Keith Hernandez J-J/25 20.00
38 Carlos Zambrano J-J/25 25.00
39 Brett Myers J-J/50 15.00
41 Danny Kolb J-J/50 15.00
42 Mark Prior FG-J/50 40.00
43 Joey Gathright B-J/25 15.00
44 David Cone J-J/50 15.00
45 Carlos Lee FG-J/50 20.00
49 Garret Anderson J-J/25 25.00
51 Dave Parker B-J/25 25.00
52 C.C. Sabathia J-J/50 20.00
53 Dennis Eckersley A's J-P/25 20.00
55 Brandon Webb B-P/25 15.00
56 Sean Casey B-J/25 20.00
57 Johan Santana J-J/25 60.00
58 Miguel Cabrera J-J/50 40.00
59 Bert Blyleven J-J/50 15.00
60 Casey Kotchman B-J/50 20.00
62 Milton Bradley J-J/50 15.00
63 John Kruk J-J/50 25.00
64 Michael Young B-J/50 20.00
69 Lew Ford B-J/50 15.00
70 Jody Gerut B-J/50 15.00
71 Don Sutton J-J/50 15.00
73 Austin Kearns B-J/50 15.00
77 Ryan Wagner J-J/50 15.00
78 Jermaine Dye J-J/25 15.00
80 Al Oliver B-J/50 15.00
81 Angel Berroa B-P/50 15.00
82 Edgar Renteria J-J/50 20.00
84 Roy Oswalt FG-J/25 25.00
86 Dave Righetti J-J/25 20.00
87 Aubrey Huff H-J/25 20.00
89 Jose Vidro B-J/50 15.00
90 Harold Baines J-J/25 15.00
93 Ken Harvey J-J/50 15.00
95 Jason Bay J-J/50 25.00
96 Dwight Evans B-J/50 40.00
99 Brian Roberts J-J/50 40.00

Absolutely Ink Swatch Triple
NM/M
Production 1-75
1 Rafael Furcal/50 20.00
3 Dale Murphy/50 30.00
8 Cal Ripken Jr./25 160.00
9 Hank Blalock/25 20.00
13 Omar Vizquel/25 30.00
16 Aramis Ramirez/25 35.00
18 Travis Hafner/50 25.00
22 Juan Gonzalez/25 30.00
23 Mark Teixeira/75 40.00
27 Darryl Strawberry/25 20.00
31 Jay Gibbons/25 20.00
37 Keith Hernandez/25 25.00
45 Carlos Lee/50 20.00
49 Garret Anderson/25 30.00
52 C.C. Sabathia/25 20.00
53 Dennis Eckersley/25 25.00
56 Sean Casey/25 20.00
58 Miguel Cabrera/50 50.00
60 Casey Kotchman/25 25.00
64 Michael Young/75 25.00
69 Lew Ford/50 15.00
70 Jody Gerut/50 15.00
73 Austin Kearns/50 20.00

Absolutely Ink Swatch Double Spectrum
NM/M
Production 1-25
Prime: No Pricing
Production One Set
1 Rafael Furcal B-J/25 20.00
3 Dale Murphy B-J/25 40.00
7 Bobby Crosby J-J/25 20.00
10 Vernon Wells J-J/25 20.00
11 Lyle Overbay J-J/25 15.00
18 Travis Hafner BG-J/25 30.00
27 Darryl Strawberry J-J/25 25.00
31 Jay Gibbons B-J/25 20.00
37 Keith Hernandez B-J/25 25.00
38 Carlos Zambrano J-J/25 30.00
39 Brett Myers J-J/25 15.00
41 Danny Kolb J-J/25 15.00
45 Carlos Lee FG-J/25 20.00
55 Brandon Webb B-P/25 25.00
59 Bert Blyleven J-J/25 20.00
60 Casey Kotchman B-J/25 25.00
62 Milton Bradley J-J/25 20.00
63 John Kruk J-J/25 25.00
64 Michael Young B-J/25 25.00
69 Lew Ford B-J/25 15.00
70 Jody Gerut B-J/25 15.00
71 Don Sutton J-J/25 20.00
73 Austin Kearns B-J/25 20.00
77 Ryan Wagner J-J/25 15.00
78 Jermaine Dye J-J/25 15.00
81 Angel Berroa B-P/25 15.00
89 Jose Vidro B-J/25 15.00
90 Harold Baines J-J/25 20.00
93 Ken Harvey J-J/25 15.00
95 Jason Bay J-J/25 25.00
96 Dwight Evans B-J/25 40.00
99 Brian Roberts J-J/25 40.00

Absolutely Ink Swatch Triple Spectrum
NM/M
Production 1-25
Prime: No Pricing
Production One Set
1 Rafael Furcal/25 20.00
3 Dale Murphy/25 40.00
18 Travis Hafner/25 25.00
23 Mark Teixeira/25 50.00
27 Darryl Strawberry/25 20.00
60 Casey Kotchman/25 25.00
64 Michael Young/25 30.00
69 Lew Ford/25 15.00
70 Jody Gerut/25 15.00
73 Austin Kearns/25 20.00
77 Ryan Wagner/25 15.00
78 Jermaine Dye/25 15.00
81 Angel Berroa/25 15.00
89 Jose Vidro/25 15.00
90 Harold Baines/25 20.00

Absolute Memorabilia Heroes

NM/M
Common Player: 1.50
Production 250 Sets
Spectrum: 1-2X
Production 50 Sets
Reverse Spectrum: 2-4X
Production 25 Sets
1 Billy Martin 3.00
2 Rickey Henderson 2.00
3 Alan Trammell 2.00
4 Lenny Dykstra 1.50
5 Jeff Bagwell 2.00
6 Steve Garvey 1.50
7 Jim "Catfish" Hunter 2.00
8 Cal Ripken Jr. 10.00
9 Reggie Jackson 3.00
10 Gary Sheffield 2.00
11 Edgar Martinez 1.50
12 Roberto Alomar 2.00
13 Luis Tiant 1.50
14 Jim Rice 2.00
15 Carlos Beltran 2.00
16 Hideo Nomo 2.00
17 Mark Grace 2.00
18 Joe Cronin 2.00
19 Tony Gwynn 3.00
20 Bo Jackson 3.00
21 Roger Clemens 5.00
22 Roger Clemens 5.00
23 Don Mattingly 3.00
24 Willie Mays 5.00
25 Andruw Jones 2.00
26 Andre Dawson 2.00
27 Carlton Fisk 2.00
28 Robin Yount 3.00
29 Joe Carter 1.50
30 Dale Murphy 2.00
31 Greg Maddux 5.00
32 Ichiro Suzuki 4.00
33 Jose Canseco 2.00
34 Nolan Ryan 8.00
35 Frank Thomas 2.00
36 Fred Lynn 1.50
37 Curt Schilling 2.00
38 Curt Schilling 2.00
39 Dave Parker 1.50
40 Randy Johnson 2.50
41 Randy Johnson 2.50
42 Vladimir Guerrero 2.50
43 Bernie Williams 1.50
44 Wade Boggs 2.00
45 Pedro Martinez 2.00
46 Andy Pettitte 1.50
47 Fergie Jenkins 2.00
48 Darryl Strawberry 1.50
49 Rafael Palmeiro 2.00
50 Albert Pujols 5.00

Heroes Swatch Double
NM/M
Production 25-50
Spectrum Prime: No Pricing
Production 1-15
1 Billy Martin J-P/50 25.00
2 Rickey Henderson B-J/50 10.00
3 Alan Trammell B-J/50 10.00
4 Lenny Dykstra B-J/50 8.00
5 Jeff Bagwell B-J/50 8.00
6 Steve Garvey B-J/50 8.00
7 Jim "Catfish" Hunter J-J/25 10.00
8 Cal Ripken Jr. J-P/50 40.00
9 Reggie Jackson JK-J/50 10.00
10 Gary Sheffield FG-J/50 8.00
11 Edgar Martinez J-J/50 8.00
12 Roberto Alomar J-J/50 8.00
13 Luis Tiant H-J/25 8.00
14 Jim Rice J-P/50 8.00
15 Carlos Beltran B-J/50 10.00
16 Hideo Nomo B-J/50 10.00
17 Mark Grace FG-J/50 10.00
18 Joe Cronin B-J/50 30.00
19 Tony Gwynn B-J/50 15.00
20 Bo Jackson B-J/50 10.00
21 Roger Clemens J-J/50 25.00
22 Roger Clemens J-J/50 25.00
23 Don Mattingly B-J/50 20.00
24 Willie Mays B-J/50 50.00
25 Andruw Jones B-J/50 8.00
26 Andre Dawson J-P/50 8.00
27 Robin Yount H-J/50 15.00
28 Joe Carter B-J/50 8.00
29 Dale Murphy B-J/50 8.00
31 Greg Maddux J-J/50 15.00
33 Jose Canseco H-J/50 10.00
34 Nolan Ryan J-J/50 30.00
35 Frank Thomas J-P/50 10.00
36 Fred Lynn J-P/50 8.00
37 Curt Schilling J-J/50 10.00
38 Curt Schilling J-J/50 10.00
39 Dave Parker B-J/50 8.00
40 Randy Johnson J-J/50 10.00
41 Randy Johnson B-J/25 10.00
42 Vladimir Guerrero J-J/50 10.00
43 Bernie Williams J-J/50 8.00
44 Wade Boggs B-J/50 10.00
45 Pedro Martinez J-J/50 10.00
46 Andy Pettitte J-J/50 8.00
47 Fergie Jenkins H-J/50 8.00
48 Darryl Strawberry J-P/50 8.00
49 Rafael Palmeiro B-J/50 8.00
50 Albert Pujols J-J/50 30.00

Heroes Autograph Swatch Double Spec Prime
No Pricing
Production 1-15
Triple: No Pricing
Production One Set

Heroes Swatch Triple
NM/M
Production 1-50
Spectrum Prime: No Pricing
Production 1-15
1 Billy Martin/25 35.00
2 Rickey Henderson/25 15.00
3 Alan Trammell/25 10.00
4 Lenny Dykstra/25 10.00
5 Jeff Bagwell/50 10.00
6 Steve Garvey/25 10.00
7 Jim "Catfish" Hunter 10.00
8 Cal Ripken Jr./25 50.00
9 Reggie Jackson/25 15.00
10 Gary Sheffield/50 10.00
11 Edgar Martinez/50 10.00
12 Roberto Alomar/50 10.00
14 Jim Rice/25 15.00
15 Carlos Beltran/25 15.00
16 Hideo Nomo/25 20.00
17 Mark Grace/25 15.00
18 Joe Cronin/25 40.00
19 Tony Gwynn/25 25.00
20 Bo Jackson/25 20.00
21 Roger Clemens/25 25.00
22 Roger Clemens/50 25.00
23 Don Mattingly/25 30.00
24 Andruw Jones/50 10.00
26 Andre Dawson/25 10.00
28 Robin Yount/50 60.00
31 Greg Maddux/50 15.00
34 Nolan Ryan/50 40.00
35 Frank Thomas/50 15.00
36 Fred Lynn/25 10.00
37 Curt Schilling/50 15.00
38 Curt Schilling/50 15.00
39 Dave Parker/25 10.00
42 Vladimir Guerrero/50 15.00
43 Bernie Williams/25 10.00
44 Wade Boggs/25 15.00
45 Pedro Martinez/25 15.00
46 Andy Pettitte/50 10.00
47 Fergie Jenkins/25 10.00
48 Darryl Strawberry/25 15.00
49 Rafael Palmeiro/25 15.00
50 Albert Pujols/50 40.00

Marks of Fame

		NM/M
Common Player:		2.00
Production 150 Sets		
Spectrum:		2-3X
Production 25 Sets		
1	Bobby Doerr	2.00
2	Reggie Jackson	3.00
3	Harmon Killebrew	4.00
4	Duke Snider	3.00
5	Brooks Robinson	3.00
6	Al Kaline	4.00
7	Carlton Fisk	3.00
8	Willie Stargell	3.00
9	Enos Slaughter	2.00
10	Nolan Ryan	10.00
11	Luis Aparicio	2.00
12	Hoyt Wilhelm	2.00
13	Orlando Cepeda	2.00
14	Mike Schmidt	6.00
15	Frank Robinson	3.00
16	Whitey Ford	3.00
17	Don Sutton	2.00
18	Joe Morgan	2.00
19	Bob Feller	3.00
20	Lou Brock	3.00
21	Warren Spahn	4.00
22	Jim Palmer	2.00
23	Reggie Jackson	3.00
24	Willie Mays	8.00
25	George Brett	8.00
26	Billy Williams	2.00
27	Juan Marichal	2.00
28	Early Wynn	2.00
29	Rod Carew	3.00
30	Maury Wills	2.00
31	Fergie Jenkins	2.00
32	Steve Carlton	3.00
33	Eddie Murray	3.00
34	Kirby Puckett	3.00
35	Johnny Bench	4.00
36	Gaylord Perry	2.00
37	Gary Carter	2.00
38	Tony Perez	2.00
39	Tony Oliva	2.00
40	Luis Aparicio	2.00
41	Tom Seaver	3.00
42	Paul Molitor	3.00
43	Dennis Eckersley	2.00
44	Willie McCovey	3.00
45	Bob Gibson	3.00
46	Robin Roberts	2.00
47	Carl Yastrzemski	4.00
48	Ozzie Smith	4.00
49	Nolan Ryan	10.00
50	Stan Musial	6.00

Marks of Fame Autograph Swatch Single

		NM/M
Production 5-125		
1	Bobby Doerr/Pants/125	20.00
3	Harmon Killebrew/Jsy/50	40.00
4	Duke Snider/Jsy/25	40.00
5	Brooks Robinson/Jsy/50	
6	Al Kaline/Bat/125	35.00
7	Carlton Fisk/Jkt/50	40.00
9	Nolan Ryan/Pants/50	80.00
11	Luis Aparicio/Jsy/125	20.00
13	Orlando Cepeda/Pants/50	
14	Mike Schmidt/Jsy/50	60.00
15	Frank Robinson/Bat/125	30.00
16	Whitey Ford/Jsy/50	50.00
17	Don Sutton/Jsy/125	20.00
19	Bob Feller/Pants/125	30.00
20	Lou Brock/Jkt/125	30.00
22	Jim Palmer/Pants/50	25.00
26	Billy Williams/Jsy/50	25.00
27	Juan Marichal/Pants/125	25.00
29	Rod Carew/Jsy/50	35.00
31	Fergie Jenkins/Pants/125	20.00
32	Steve Carlton/Pants/125	25.00
35	Johnny Bench/Pants/50	50.00
36	Gaylord Perry/Jsy/125	15.00
37	Gary Carter/Pants/50	20.00
38	Tony Perez/Jsy/50	20.00
39	Tony Oliva/Jsy/125	25.00
40	Luis Aparicio/Bat/125	20.00
41	Tom Seaver/Pants/50	35.00
42	Paul Molitor/Pants/50	35.00
43	Dennis Eckersley/Jsy/125	20.00
44	Willie McCovey/Pants/50	35.00
46	Robin Roberts/Hat/125	35.00
48	Ozzie Smith/Pants/50	50.00
49	Nolan Ryan/Jkt/50	80.00
50	Stan Musial/Pants/50	60.00

Marks of Fame Swatch Double

		NM/M
Production 1-50		
Spectrum Prime:		No Pricing
Production 1-25		
1	Bobby Doerr/50	10.00
2	Reggie Jackson B-P/50	10.00
3	Harmon Killebrew B-J/50	15.00
4	Duke Snider J-P/50 B-J/50	15.00
5	Brooks Robinson B-J/50	15.00
7	Carlton Fisk B-JK/50	10.00
8	Willie Stargell B-J/50	10.00
9	Enos Slaughter J-J/50	10.00
10	Nolan Ryan J-P/50	25.00
11	Luis Aparicio B-J/50	8.00
12	Hoyt Wilhelm J-J/50	8.00
13	Orlando Cepeda B-P/50	8.00
15	Mike Schmidt B-J/50	20.00
	B-S/50	15.00
16	Whitey Ford J-J/25	15.00
17	Don Sutton J-J/50	8.00
18	Joe Morgan B-J/50	8.00
20	Lou Brock B-JK/50	10.00
21	Warren Spahn J-P/50	12.00
22	Jim Palmer H-P/50	8.00
23	Reggie Jackson B-J/50	10.00
24	Willie Mays B-J/25	50.00
26	Billy Williams J-J/50	8.00
27	Juan Marichal J-P/50	8.00
28	Early Wynn J-J/50	8.00
29	Rod Carew B-J/50	10.00
31	Fergie Jenkins FG-P/50	8.00
32	Steve Carlton B-P/50	8.00
33	Eddie Murray B-J/50	15.00
34	Kirby Puckett B-J/50	15.00
35	Johnny Bench B-J/50	15.00
36	Gaylord Perry J-J/50	8.00
37	Gary Carter B-J/50	8.00
39	Tony Oliva B-J/50	8.00
41	Tom Seaver J-P/50	15.00
42	Paul Molitor B-J/50	15.00
43	Dennis Eckersley J-J/50	10.00
44	Willie McCovey J-P/50	10.00
47	Carl Yastrzemski B-J/50	25.00
48	Ozzie Smith H-P/50	25.00
49	Nolan Ryan JK-J/50	25.00
50	Stan Musial B-P/50	30.00

Marks of Fame Autograph Swatch Double

		NM/M
Production 1-75		
Prime:		No Pricing
Production 1-10		
1	Bobby Doerr B-P/50	25.00
3	Harmon Killebrew B-J/50	40.00
4	Duke Snider J-P/25	40.00
5	Brooks Robinson B-J/25	40.00
7	Carlton Fisk B-JK/25	40.00
10	Nolan Ryan J-P/25	100.00
11	Luis Aparicio B-J/75	20.00
12	Hoyt Wilhelm J-J/25	25.00
13	Orlando Cepeda B-S/25	25.00
14	Mike Schmidt B-J/75	75.00
15	Frank Robinson B-S/25	50.00
16	Whitey Ford J-J/25	50.00
17	Don Sutton J-J/25	20.00
20	Lou Brock B-JK/25	50.00
22	Jim Palmer H-P/25	30.00
27	Juan Marichal J-P/25	25.00
29	Rod Carew B-J/25	40.00
31	Fergie Jenkins FG-P/25	20.00
32	Steve Carlton B-P/25	40.00
35	Johnny Bench B-J/25	50.00
36	Gaylord Perry J-J/25	20.00
37	Gary Carter B-J/25	25.00
38	Tony Perez FG-J/25	25.00
39	Tony Oliva B-J/25	25.00
41	Tom Seaver J-P/25	40.00
42	Paul Molitor B-J/25	35.00
43	Dennis Eckersley J-J/25	25.00
44	Willie McCovey J-P/25	40.00
48	Ozzie Smith H-P/25	50.00
49	Nolan Ryan JK-J/25	100.00
50	Stan Musial B-P/25	80.00

Marks of Fame Swatch Triple

		NM/M
Production 1-25		
Spectrum Prime:		No Pricing
Production 1-15		
1	Bobby Doerr/25	15.00
7	Carlton Fisk/25	15.00
8	Willie Stargell/25	15.00
10	Nolan Ryan/25	40.00
11	Luis Aparicio/25	12.00
12	Hoyt Wilhelm/25	10.00
14	Mike Schmidt/25	30.00
18	Joe Morgan/25	12.00
20	Lou Brock/25	15.00
21	Warren Spahn/25	50.00
23	Reggie Jackson/25	15.00
24	Willie Mays/25	60.00
27	Juan Marichal/25	12.00
29	Rod Carew/25	15.00
32	Steve Carlton/25	12.00
33	Eddie Murray/25	20.00
34	Kirby Puckett/25	20.00
35	Johnny Bench/25	20.00
37	Gary Carter/25	12.00
39	Tony Oliva/25	12.00
41	Tom Seaver/25	15.00
42	Paul Molitor/25	15.00
43	Dennis Eckersley/25	12.00
44	Willie McCovey/25	15.00
47	Carl Yastrzemski/25	35.00
48	Ozzie Smith/25	25.00
49	Nolan Ryan/25	40.00
50	Stan Musial/25	40.00

Marks of Fame Autograph Swatch Triple

		NM/M
No Pricing		
Production 1-10		
Prime:		No Pricing
Production One Set		

Team Tandems

		NM/M
Common Card:		1.50
Production 250 Sets		
Spectrum:		.75-1.5X
Production 150 Sets		
1	Mark Prior, Kerry Wood	2.00
2	Barry Zito, Tim Hudson	1.50
3	Curt Schilling, Pedro Martinez	2.50
4	Will Clark, Matt Williams	2.00
5	Bernie Williams, Jason Giambi	2.00
6	Vernon Wells, Roy Halladay	1.50
7	Josh Beckett, A.J. Burnett	1.50
8	Dale Murphy, Phil Niekro	2.00
9	Mike Schmidt, Steve Carlton	5.00
10	Tony Oliva, Harmon Killebrew	2.00
11	Robin Yount, Paul Molitor	2.50
12	Francisco Rodriguez, Troy Percival	1.50
13	Ben Sheets, Danny Kolb	1.50
14	Andruw Jones, Rafael Furcal	1.50
15	Todd Helton, Preston Wilson	1.50
16	Wade Boggs, Fred McGriff	2.00
17	Manny Ramirez, David Ortiz	2.50
18	Miguel Cabrera, Dontrelle Willis	2.00
19	Edgar Renteria, Scott Rolen	2.00
20	Carlos Beltran, Jeff Kent	2.00
21	Eric Davis, Deion Sanders	2.00
22	Frank Thomas, Paul Konerko	2.00
23	Mike Piazza, Al Leiter	3.00
24	Sean Burroughs, Ryan Klesko	1.50
25	Ken Harvey, Mike Sweeney	1.50
26	David Sanders, Hideki Matsui	4.00
27	Steve Carlton, Mark Buehrle	2.00
28	Gaylord Perry, Randy Johnson	2.00
29	Joe Morgan, Steve Carlton	2.00
30	Vladimir Guerrero, Orlando Cabrera	
31	Scott Rolen, John Kruk	2.00
32	Aaron Boone, Dmitri Young	1.50
33	Rickey Henderson, Vladimir Guerrero	
34	Charles Johnson, Cliff Floyd	
35	Cal Ripken Jr., Rafael Palmeiro	8.00

Team Tandems Swatch Single

		NM/M
Production 10-125		
1	Mark Prior, Kerry Wood/125	6.00
2	Barry Zito, Tim Hudson/125	5.00
3	Curt Schilling, Pedro Martinez/125	8.00
4	Will Clark, Matt Williams/125	8.00
5	Bernie Williams, Jason Giambi/125	5.00
6	Vernon Wells, Roy Halladay/125	5.00
7	Josh Beckett, A.J. Burnett/125	5.00
8	Dale Murphy, Phil Niekro/125	15.00
9	Mike Schmidt, Steve Carlton/125	15.00
10	Tony Oliva, Harmon Killebrew/50	15.00
11	Robin Yount, Paul Molitor/125	15.00
12	Felix Rodriguez, Troy Percival/25	10.00
13	Ben Sheets, Danny Kolb/125	5.00
14	Andruw Jones, Rafael Furcal/125	5.00
15	Todd Helton, Preston Wilson/125	5.00
16	Wade Boggs, Fred McGriff/50	10.00
17	Manny Ramirez, David Ortiz/125	15.00
18	Miguel Cabrera, Dontrelle Willis/125	12.00
19	Edgar Renteria, Scott Rolen/125	10.00
20	Carlos Beltran, Jeff Kent/50	12.00
21	Eric Davis, Deion Sanders/125	8.00
22	Frank Thomas, Paul Konerko/50	10.00
23	Mike Piazza, Al Leiter/125	20.00
24	Sean Burroughs, Ryan Klesko/50	10.00
25	Ken Harvey, Mike Sweeney/125	5.00
26	Deion Sanders, Hideki Matsui/125	25.00
27	Steve Carlton, Mark Buehrle/50	8.00
28	Gaylord Perry, Randy Johnson/125	10.00
29	Joe Morgan, Steve Carlton/25	10.00
31	Scott Rolen, John Kruk/125	10.00
32	Aaron Boone, Dmitri Young/125	5.00
33	Rickey Henderson, Vladimir Guerrero/25	15.00
34	Charles Johnson, Cliff Floyd/125	5.00
35	Cal Ripken Jr., Rafael Palmeiro/125	25.00

Team Tandems Swatch Double

		NM/M
Production 1-125		
Spectrum:		1-2X
Production 1-50		
No pricing 20 or less.		
1	Mark Prior, Kerry Wood/125	8.00
2	Barry Zito, Tim Hudson/125	5.00
3	Curt Schilling, Pedro Martinez/125	15.00
5	Bernie Williams, Jason Giambi/125	10.00
7	Josh Beckett, A.J. Burnett/125	8.00
8	Dale Murphy, Phil Niekro/125	20.00
10	Tony Oliva, Harmon Killebrew/50	30.00
11	Robin Yount, Paul Molitor/125	20.00
14	Andruw Jones, Rafael Furcal/125	8.00
15	Todd Helton, Preston Wilson/125	10.00
16	Wade Boggs, Fred McGriff/125	15.00
17	Manny Ramirez, David Ortiz/125	15.00
18	Miguel Cabrera, Dontrelle Willis/125	12.00
20	Carlos Beltran, Jeff Kent/50	12.00
21	Eric Davis, Deion Sanders/25	15.00
22	Frank Thomas, Paul Konerko/50	15.00
23	Mike Piazza, Al Leiter/125	20.00
24	Sean Burroughs, Ryan Klesko/50	10.00
27	Steve Carlton, Mark Buehrle/50	12.00
29	Joe Morgan, Steve Carlton/25	15.00
33	Rickey Henderson, Vladimir Guerrero/50	15.00
34	Charles Johnson, Cliff Floyd/125	8.00
35	Cal Ripken Jr., Rafael Palmeiro/125	40.00

Team Tandems Swatch Single Spectrum

		NM/M
Production 1-75		
1	Mark Prior, Kerry Wood/75	6.00
2	Barry Zito, Tim Hudson/75	5.00
3	Curt Schilling, Pedro Martinez/75	10.00
4	Will Clark, M. Williams/75	8.00
5	Bernie Williams, Jason Giambi/75	5.00
6	Vernon Wells, Roy Halladay/75	5.00
7	Josh Beckett, A.J. Burnett/75	5.00
8	Dale Murphy, Phil Niekro/75	10.00
11	Robin Yount, Paul Molitor/75	15.00
13	Ben Sheets, Danny Kolb/75	5.00
14	Andruw Jones, Rafael Furcal/75	5.00
15	Todd Helton, Preston Wilson/75	5.00
17	Manny Ramirez, David Ortiz/75	10.00
18	Miguel Cabrera, Dontrelle Willis/75	8.00
19	Edgar Renteria, Scott Rolen/75	5.00
20	Carlos Beltran, Jeff Kent/75	5.00
21	Eric Davis Bat, Deion Sanders/75	5.00
23	Mike Piazza, Al Leiter/75	10.00
24	Sean Burroughs, Ryan Klesko/75	5.00
25	Ken Harvey, Mike Sweeney/75	5.00
26	Deion Sanders, Hideki Matsui/75	25.00

Team Tandems Swatch Double

		NM/M
28	Gaylord Perry, Randy Johnson/75	8.00
31	Scott Rolen, John Kruk/75	8.00
32	Aaron Boone, D. Young/75	5.00
34	Charles Johnson, Cliff Floyd/75	5.00
35	Cal Ripken Jr., Rafael Palmeiro/75	25.00

Team Tandems Swatch Double

		NM/M
Production 1-125		
Spectrum:		1-2X
Production 1-50		
No pricing 20 or less.		
1	Mark Prior, Kerry Wood/125	8.00
2	Barry Zito, Tim Hudson/125	5.00
3	Curt Schilling, Pedro Martinez/125	15.00
5	Bernie Williams, Jason Giambi/125	10.00
7	Josh Beckett, A.J. Burnett/125	8.00
8	Dale Murphy, Phil Niekro/125	20.00
10	Tony Oliva, Harmon Killebrew/50	30.00
11	Robin Yount, Paul Molitor/125	20.00
14	Andruw Jones, Rafael Furcal/125	8.00
15	Todd Helton, Preston Wilson/125	10.00
16	Wade Boggs, Fred McGriff/125	15.00
17	Manny Ramirez, David Ortiz/125	15.00
18	Miguel Cabrera, Dontrelle Willis/125	12.00
20	Carlos Beltran, Jeff Kent/50	12.00
21	Eric Davis, Deion Sanders/25	15.00
22	Frank Thomas, Paul Konerko/50	15.00
23	Mike Piazza, Al Leiter/125	20.00
24	Sean Burroughs, Ryan Klesko/50	10.00
27	Steve Carlton, Mark Buehrle/50	12.00
29	Joe Morgan, Steve Carlton/25	15.00
33	Rickey Henderson, Vladimir Guerrero/50	15.00
34	Charles Johnson, Cliff Floyd/125	8.00
35	Cal Ripken Jr., Rafael Palmeiro/125	40.00

Team Trios

		NM/M
Common Card:		
Production 200 Sets		
Spectrum:		1X
Production 125 Sets		
1	Cal Ripken Jr., Jim Palmer, Eddie Murray	10.00
2	Roger Clemens, Wade Boggs, Evans	5.00
3	Rafael Palmeiro, Miguel Tejada, Javy Lopez	2.00
4	Carl Crawford, Rocco Baldelli, B.J. Upton	1.50
5	Mark Buehrle, Magglio Ordonez, Carlos Lee	1.50
6	Victor Martinez, Travis Hafner, Jody Gerut	1.50
7	Bobby Abreu, Brett Myers, Kevin Millwood	1.50
8	Sammy Sosa, Aramis Ramirez, Carlos Zambrano	3.00
9	Bo, George Brett, Carlos Beltran	5.00
10	Hideo Nomo, Adrian Beltre, Shawn Green	2.00
11	Wilson, Wilson, Jason Bay	1.50
12	Tom Seaver, Nolan Ryan, Dwight Gooden	8.00
13	David Dellucci, Laynce Nix, Kevin Mench	1.50
14	Alan Trammell, Morris, Gibson	
15	M. Will, Grace, Randy Johnson	
16	Dawson, Gary Carter, Tony Perez	2.00
17	Dale Murphy, John Kruk, Lenny Dykstra	2.00
18	B. Roberts, Ian Gibb, Larry Bigbie	1.50

Team Trios Swatch Single

		NM/M
Production 50 unless noted.		
1	Cal Ripken Jr., Jim Palmer, Murray	40.00
2	Roger Clemens, Wade Boggs, Evans	25.00
3	Rafael Palmeiro, Miguel Tejada, Javy Lopez	12.00
4	Carl Crawford, Rocco Baldelli, B.J. Upton	10.00
5	Mark Buehrle, Magglio Ordonez, Carlos Lee	10.00
6	Victor Martinez, Travis Hafner, Jody Gerut	10.00
7	Bobby Abreu, Brett Myers, Kevin Millwood	10.00
8	Sammy Sosa, Aramis Ramirez, Carlos Zambrano	15.00
9	Bo, George Brett, Carlos Beltran	30.00
10	Hideo Nomo, Adrian Beltre, Shawn Green	15.00
11	Wilson, Wilson, Jason Bay	10.00
12	Tom Seaver, Nolan Ryan, Dwight Gooden	35.00
13	David Dellucci, Laynce Nix, Kevin Mench	8.00
14	Alan Trammell, Morris, Gibson	15.00
15	M. Will, Grace, Randy Johnson	15.00
16	Dawson, Gary Carter, Tony Perez	10.00
17	Dale Murphy, Tomas Kurka, Lenny Dykstra	20.00
18	Roberts, Ian Gibb, Larry Bigbie	15.00
19	Mike Lowell, Ivan Rodriguez, Brad Penny	2.00
20	Murray, Darryl Strawberry, Oliver	2.00
21	Darryl Strawberry, Rickey Henderson, Gary Sheffield	2.00
22	Roberto Alomar, Joe Crede, Durham	2.00
23	Jason Kendall, Giles, Aramis Ramirez	1.50
24	Delmon, Aubrey Huff, Tino	2.00
25	Jeff Bagwell, Cruz, Joe Morgan	2.00
26	Snow, Rich Aurilia, Jeff Kent	1.50
27	Jenkins, Nolan Ryan, Cordero	8.00
28	Lofton, Jim Thome, Roberto Alomar	2.00
29	Atkins, Todd Helton, Jennings	2.00
30	Gary Carter, Pedro, Randy Johnson	2.50

Team Trios Swatch Single

		NM/M
Production 50 unless noted.		
1	Cal Ripken Jr., Jim Palmer, Murray	40.00
2	Roger Clemens, Wade Boggs, Evans	25.00
3	Rafael Palmeiro, Miguel Tejada, Javy Lopez	12.00
4	Carl Crawford, Rocco Baldelli, B.J. Upton	10.00
5	Mark Buehrle, Magglio Ordonez, Carlos Lee	10.00
6	Victor Martinez, Travis Hafner, Jody Gerut	10.00
7	Bobby Abreu, Brett Myers, Kevin Millwood	10.00
8	Sammy Sosa, Aramis Ramirez, Carlos Zambrano	15.00
9	Bo, George Brett, Carlos Beltran	30.00
10	Hideo Nomo, Adrian Beltre, Shawn Green	15.00
11	Wilson, Wilson, Jason Bay	10.00
12	Tom Seaver, Nolan Ryan, Dwight Gooden	35.00
13	David Dellucci, Laynce Nix, Kevin Mench	8.00
14	Alan Trammell, Morris, Gibson	15.00
15	M. Will, Grace, Randy Johnson	15.00
16	Dawson, Gary Carter, Tony Perez	10.00
17	Dale Murphy, Tomas Kurka, Lenny Dykstra	20.00
18	Roberts, Ian Gibb, Larry Bigbie	15.00
19	Mike Lowell, Ivan Rodriguez, Brad Penny	15.00
20	Murray, Darryl Strawberry, Oliver	20.00
21	Darryl Strawberry, Rickey Henderson, Gary Sheffield	15.00
22	Roberto Alomar, Joe Crede, Durham	10.00
23	Jason Kendall, Giles, Aramis Ramirez	10.00
24	Delmon, Aubrey Huff, Tino	10.00
25	Jeff Bagwell, Cruz, Joe Morgan	12.00
26	Snow, Rich Aurilia, Jeff Kent	8.00
27	Jenkins, Nolan Ryan, Cordero	25.00
28	Lofton, Jim Thome, Roberto Alomar	20.00
29	Atkins, Todd Helton, Jennings	15.00
30	Gary Carter, Pedro, Randy Johnson	15.00

Team Trios Swatch Single Spectrum

		NM/M
Production 10-50		
Prime Black:		No Pricing
Production 10 Sets		
1	Cal Ripken Jr., Jim Palmer, Murray/50	40.00
2	Roger Clemens, Wade Boggs, Evans/50	30.00
4	Carl Crawford, Rocco Baldelli, B.J. Upton/50	10.00

5	Mark Buehrle, Magglio Ordonez, Carlos Lee/50	
7	Bobby Abreu, Brett Myers, Kevin Millwood/50	10.00
8	Sammy Sosa, Aramis Ramirez, Carlos Zambrano/50	15.00
9	Bo, George Brett, Carlos Beltran/50	25.00
10	Hideo Nomo, Adrian Beltre, Shawn Green/50	15.00
11	Wilson, Wilson, Jason Bay/50	8.00
12	Tom Seaver, Nolan Ryan, Dwight Gooden/50	30.00
13	David Dellucci, Laynce Nix, Kevin Mench/50	10.00
14	Alan Trammell, Morris, Gibson/50	15.00
16	Dawson, Gary Carter, Tony Perez/50	15.00
17	Dale Murphy, Tomas Kurka, Lenny Dykstra/50	15.00
18	Roberts, Ian Gibb, Larry Bigbie/50	10.00
19	Mike Lowell, Ivan Rodriguez, Brad Penny/25	10.00
20	Murray, Darryl Strawberry, Oliver/50	20.00
21	Darryl Strawberry, Rickey Henderson, Gary Sheffield/50	15.00
22	Roberto Alomar, Joe Crede, Durham/50	10.00
24	Delmon, Aubrey Huff, Tino/50	10.00
25	Jeff Bagwell, Cruz, Joe Morgan/50	10.00
26	Snow, Rich Aurilia, Jeff Kent/50	8.00
27	Jenkins, Nolan Ryan, Cordero/50	25.00
28	Lofton, Jim Thome, Roberto Alomar/50	10.00
29	Atkins, Todd Helton, Jennings/50	10.00
30	Gary Carter, Pedro, Randy Johnson/50	15.00

Team Trios Swatch Double

NM/M
Production 25-100
Spectrum: .75-1.5X
Production 5-35
No pricing production 20 or less.
Prime Black: No Pricing
Production 5-10

1	Cal Ripken Jr., Jim Palmer, Murray/100	75.00
2	Roger Clemens, Wade Boggs, Evans/100	50.00
3	Rafael Palmeiro, Miguel Tejada, Javy Lopez/50	25.00
5	Mark Buehrle, Magglio Ordonez, Carlos Lee/100	15.00
6	Victor Martinez, Travis Hafner, Jody Gerut/50	20.00
9	Bo, George Brett, Carlos Beltran/100	40.00
10	Hideo Nomo, Adrian Beltre, Shawn Green/100	25.00
11	Wilson, Wilson, Jason Bay/100	
12	Tom Seaver, Nolan Ryan, Dwight Gooden/100	50.00
14	Alan Trammell, Morris, Gibson/50	30.00
15	M. Will, Mark Grace, Randy Johnson/50	30.00
16	Dawson, Gary Carter, Tony Perez/100	20.00
19	Mike Lowell, Ivan Rodriguez, Brad Penny/50	25.00
20	Murray, Darryl Strawberry, Oliver/100	30.00
21	Darryl Strawberry, Rickey Henderson, Gary Sheffield/100	25.00
22	Roberto Alomar, Joe Crede, Durham/100	20.00
28	Lofton, Jim Thome, Roberto Alomar/100	40.00
29	Atkins, Todd Helton, Jennings/100	20.00
30	Gary Carter, Pedro, Randy Johnson/50	30.00

Team Quads

NM/M
Common Quad:
Production 150 Sets
Spectrum: 1X
Production 100 Sets

1	St. Louis Card Active	6.00
2	Cleveland Indians	2.00
3	California Angels	2.00
4	Boston Red Sox	5.00
5	New York Yanks Active	6.00
6	Atlanta Braves	3.00
7	Oakland A's	3.00
8	Anaheim Angels	3.00
10	Texas Rangers Active	2.00
	Minnesota Twins Active	3.00
11	New York Mets	4.00
12	Houston Astros	5.00
14	San Diego Padres	4.00
14	Cincinnati Reds	2.00
16	Texas Rangers Retro	8.00
16	New York Yankees Retro	8.00
17	St. Louis Cards Retro	6.00
18	Pittsburgh Pirates	2.00
19	Chicago Cubs	4.00
20	Minnesota Twins Retro	3.00

Team Quads Swatch Single

Production 25-100

1	St. Louis Card Active/	25.00
2	Cleveland Indians/100	30.00
3	California Angels/100	15.00
4	Boston Red Sox/100	20.00
5	New York Yanks Active/100	30.00
6	Atlanta Braves/100	25.00
7	Oakland A's/100	6.00
8	Anaheim Angels/100	15.00
9	Texas Rangers Active/100	10.00
10	Minnesota Twins Active/25	25.00
11	New York Mets/100	20.00
12	Houston Astros/100	8.00
13	San Diego Padres/100	25.00
14	Cincinnati Reds/100	10.00
15	Texas Rangers Retro/100	30.00
16	New York Yanks Retro/100	50.00
17	St. Louis Cards Retro/25	50.00
18	Pittsburgh Pirates/100	15.00
19	Chicago Cubs/100	25.00
20	Minnesota Twins Retro/100	20.00

Team Quads Swatch Single Spectrum

NM/M
Production 10-35
Prime Black: No Pricing
Production 10 Sets

1	St. Louis Card Active/35	40.00
2	Cleveland Indians/35	50.00
3	California Angels/35	25.00
4	Boston Red Sox/35	30.00
5	New York Yanks Active/35	40.00
6	Atlanta Braves/35	20.00
7	Oakland A's/35	20.00
8	Anaheim Angels/35	25.00
9	Texas Rangers Active/35	30.00
11	New York Mets/35	30.00
12	Houston Astros/35	50.00
13	San Diego Padres/35	40.00
14	Cincinnati Reds/35	20.00
15	Texas Rangers Retro/35	40.00
16	New York Yanks Retro/35	75.00
18	Pittsburgh Pirates/35	20.00
19	Chicago Cubs/35	15.00
20	Minnesota Twins Retro/35	30.00

Team Quads Swatch Double

NM/M
Production 25-75

1	St. Louis Card Active/75	25.00
3	California Angels/75	30.00
4	Boston Red Sox/75	30.00
5	New York Yanks Active/25	75.00
6	Atlanta Braves/25	60.00
7	Oakland A's/75	25.00
8	Anaheim Angels/25	40.00
9	Texas Rangers Active/75	20.00
10	Minnesota Twins Active/25	40.00
11	New York Mets/75	30.00
12	Houston Astros/75	45.00
13	San Diego Padres/75	40.00
14	Cincinnati Reds/75	20.00
15	Texas Rangers Retro/75	50.00
18	Pittsburgh Pirates/75	20.00
20	Minnesota Twins Retro/75	30.00

Team Quads Swatch Double Spectrum

NM/M
Production 1-25
Prime Black: No Pricing
Production 1-5

1	St. Louis Card Active/5	40.00
3	California Angels/25	50.00
4	Boston Red Sox/25	60.00
5	Texas Rangers Active/25	30.00
11	New York Mets/25	50.00
13	San Diego Padres/25	60.00
14	Cincinnati Reds/25	30.00
15	Texas Rangers Retro/25	70.00

Team Six

NM/M
Common Card: 1.50
Production 100 Sets
Spectrum: 1-1.5X
Production 50 Sets

1	San Francisco Giants	8.00
2	Houston Astros	6.00
3	Cincinnati Reds	5.00
4	St. Louis Cardinals	8.00
5	New York Yankees	10.00
6	Chicago Cubs	6.00
7	Arizona Diamondbacks	1.50
8	Los Angeles Dodgers	6.00
9	Anaheim Angels	4.00
10	Boston Red Sox	8.00
11	Seattle Mariners	8.00
12	Chicago White Sox	4.00
13	Philadelphia Phillies	10.00
14	New York Mets	10.00
15	Atlanta Braves	4.00

Team Six Swatch Single

NM/M
Production 15-50

1	San Francisco Giants/50	80.00
2	Houston Astros/50	40.00
5	New York Yankees/50	60.00
6	Chicago Cubs/50	40.00
7	Arizona Diamondbacks/50	20.00
8	Los Angeles Dodgers/50	40.00
9	Anaheim Angeles/50	30.00
10	Boston Red Sox/50	50.00
12	Chicago White Sox/50	30.00
13	Philadelphia Phillies/50	40.00
14	New York Mets/50	40.00
15	Atlanta Braves/50	50.00

Team Six Swatch Single Spectrum

NM/M
Production 5-25
Prime Black: No Pricing
Production 5 Sets

1	San Francisco Giants/25	100.00
2	Houston Astros/25	50.00
5	New York Yankees/25	75.00
6	Chicago Cubs/25	50.00
7	Arizona Diamondbacks/25	25.00
8	Los Angeles Dodgers/25	50.00
10	Boston Red Sox/25	65.00
12	Chicago White Sox/25	40.00
13	Philadelphia Phillies/25	50.00
14	New York Mets/25	50.00
15	Atlanta Braves/25	50.00

Tools of the Trade Red

NM/M
Common Player:
Production 250 Sets
Black: 1-1.5X
Production 100 Sets
Blue: 1-1.5X
Production 150 Sets
Rev. Spectrum Red: 1-2X
Production 50 Sets
Rev. Spectrum Blue: No Pricing
Production 10 Sets

1	Ozzie Smith	5.00
2	Carlos Beltran	2.00
3	Dale Murphy	2.00
4	Paul Molitor	2.00
6	George Brett	6.00
7	Stan Musial	5.00
7	Ivan Rodriguez	2.00
8	Carl Yastrzemski	4.00
	Reggie Jackson	2.00
10	Hideo Nomo	2.00
11	Gary Sheffield	2.00
12	Roberto Alomar	2.00
13	Pedro Martinez	3.00
14	Ernie Banks	3.00
15	Tim Hudson	1.50
16	Dwight Gooden	1.50
17	Lance Berkman	1.50
18	Darryl Strawberry	1.50
19	Larry Walker	1.50
20	Lou Brock	2.00
21	Roger Clemens	6.00
22	Paul LoDuca	1.50
23	Don Mattingly	6.00
24	Willie Mays	6.00
25	Rafael Palmeiro	2.00
26	Roy Oswalt	1.50
27	Vladimir Guerrero	3.00
28	Austin Kearns	1.50
29	Rod Carew	2.00
30	Nolan Ryan	8.00
31	Richie Sexson	2.00
32	Steve Carlton	2.00
33	Eddie Murray	2.00
34	Nolan Ryan	8.00
35	Mike Mussina	2.00
36	Sean Casey	1.50
37	Juan Gonzalez	1.50
38	Curt Schilling	2.00
39	Darryl Strawberry	1.50
40	Alfonso Soriano	3.00
41	Tom Seaver	3.00
42	Mike Schmidt	5.00
43	Todd Helton	2.00
44	Reggie Jackson	6.00
45	Shawn Green	1.50
46	Mike Mussina	2.00
47	Tom Glavine	2.00
48	Torii Hunter	1.50
49	Kerry Wood	2.00
50	Carlos Delgado	2.00
51	Randy Johnson	3.00
52	David Ortiz	2.00
53	Troy Glaus	2.00
54	Rickey Henderson	2.00
55	Craig Biggio	2.00
56	Brad Penny	1.50
57	Gary Carter	2.00
58	Andy Pettitte	1.50
59	Mark Prior	2.00
60	Kirby Puckett	2.00
61	Willie McCovey	3.00
62	Andre Dawson	2.00
63	Greg Maddux	4.00
64	Adrian Beltre	1.50
65	Andruw Jones	2.00
66	Juan Gonzalez	1.50
67	Frank Thomas	2.00
68	Victor Martinez	1.50
69	Randy Johnson	3.00
70	Andre Dawson	2.00
71	Adam Dunn	2.00
72	Carlton Fisk	2.00
73	Cal Ripken Jr.	8.00
74	Kenny Lofton	1.50
75	Barry Zito	1.50
76	Sammy Sosa	4.00
77	Deion Sanders	2.00
78	Tony Gwynn	3.00
79	Mike Piazza	4.00
80	Jeff Bagwell	2.00
81	Manny Ramirez	3.00
82	Carlos Beltran	2.00
83	Mark Grace	2.00
84	Robin Yount	4.00
85	Albert Pujols	6.00
86	Dontrelle Willis	2.00
87	Jim Thome	2.00
88	Magglio Ordonez	1.50
89	Miguel Tejada	2.00
90	Mark Teixeira	2.00
91	Gary Carter	2.00
92	Ivan Rodriguez	2.00
93	Jason Giambi	1.50
94	Rickey Henderson	2.00
95	Curt Schilling	2.00
96	Bobby Doerr	2.00
97	Chipper Jones	3.00
98	Eric Chavez	1.50
99	Johnny Bench	4.00
100	Harmon Killebrew	3.00

Tools of Trade Laundry Tag Prime Red

No Pricing
Production One Set

Tools of Trade Swatch Single Jumbo

NM/M
Production 1-100
Prime Red: No Pricing
Production 1-25
Reverse: 1-2X
Production 1-50
Prime Black: No Pricing
Production One Set

1	Ozzie Smith/25	30.00
2	Carlos Beltran/Jsy/50	10.00
3	Dale Murphy/Jsy/25	20.00
4	Paul Molitor/Jsy/25	25.00
6	Stan Musial/Pants/25	50.00
7	Ivan Rodriguez/Jsy/100	10.00
10	Hideo Nomo/Jsy/100	10.00
11	Gary Sheffield/Jsy/25	15.00
12	Roberto Alomar/Jsy/100	10.00
13	Pedro Martinez/Jsy/50	12.00
15	Tim Hudson/Jsy/100	10.00
17	Lance Berkman/Jsy/75	8.00
19	Larry Walker/Jsy/100	10.00
21	Lou Brock Jkt/50	20.00
21	Roger Clemens/Jsy/50	30.00
23	Don Mattingly/Jsy/25	40.00
25	Rafael Palmeiro/Jsy/100	25.00
27	Vladimir Guerrero/Jsy/15	15.00
29	Rod Carew/Jsy/50	15.00
30	Nolan Ryan/Jsy/50	50.00
31	Richie Sexson/Jsy/100	10.00
33	Eddie Murray/Jsy/50	20.00
35	Mike Mussina/Jsy/50	12.00
36	Sean Casey/Jsy/50	10.00
37	Juan Gonzalez/Jsy/25	15.00
39	Darryl Strawberry/Jsy/50	15.00
41	Tom Seaver/Jsy/75	10.00
42	Mike Schmidt/Jsy/25	40.00
43	Todd Helton/Jsy/50	10.00
45	Shawn Green/Jsy/100	8.00
47	Tom Glavine/Jsy/100	15.00
49	Kerry Wood/Jsy/50	10.00
51	R. John Jsy/25	20.00
52	David Ortiz/Jsy/75	15.00
53	Troy Glaus/Jsy/50	10.00
54	Rickey Henderson/Jsy/25	15.00
55	Craig Biggio/Jsy/75	10.00
56	Brad Penny/Jsy/100	8.00
57	Gary Carter/Jsy/50	15.00
58	Andy Pettitte/Jsy/50	10.00
60	Mark Prior/Jsy/50	10.00
60	Kirby Puckett/Jsy/50	20.00
61	Willie McCovey/Jsy/50	15.00
63	Greg Maddux/Jsy/50	20.00
65	Andruw Jones/Jsy/50	10.00
68	Victor Martinez/Jsy/50	8.00
70	Andre Dawson/Jsy/50	10.00
72	Carlton Fisk/Jsy/100	10.00
73	Cal Ripken Jr./Jsy/50	35.00
74	Kenny Lofton/Hat/25	10.00
75	Barry Zito/Jsy/100	8.00
76	Sammy Sosa/Jsy/50	15.00
77	Deion Sanders/Jsy/25	20.00
78	Tony Gwynn/Jsy/100	20.00
79	Mike Piazza/Jsy/100	20.00
83	Jeff Bagwell/Jsy/100	10.00
83	Mark Grace/Jsy/50	15.00
84	Robin Yount/Jsy/50	10.00
86	Albert Pujols/Jsy/100	30.00
86	Dontrelle Willis/Jsy/50	10.00
89	Miguel Tejada/Jsy/100	12.00
90	Mark Teixeira/Jsy/25	15.00
92	Ivan Rodriguez/Jsy/100	10.00
93	Jason Giambi/Jsy/25	10.00
94	Rickey Henderson/Jsy/25	15.00
95	Curt Schilling/Jsy/50	10.00
96	Bobby Doerr/Pants/25	20.00
97	Chipper Jones/Jsy/25	25.00
98	Eric Chavez/Jsy/100	8.00
99	Johnny Bench/Jsy/25	25.00
100	Harmon Killebrew/Jsy/25	40.00

Tools of the Trade Swatch Double

NM/M
Production 1-150
Prime Red: No Pricing
Production 1-25
Prime Black: No Pricing
Production 1-25

1	Ozzie Smith B-P/50	15.00
2	Carlos Beltran J-S/50	8.00
3	Dale Murphy J-J/50	8.00
4	Paul Molitor J-P/50	8.00
5	George Brett B-H/25	25.00
6	Stan Musial B-P/25	30.00
7	Ivan Rodriguez J-J/150	8.00
8	Carl Yastrzemski B-J/25	30.00
9	Reggie Jackson J-J/50	10.00
10	Hideo Nomo J-P/150	10.00
11	Gary Sheffield H-J/25	8.00
12	Roberto Alomar B-J/150	8.00
13	Pedro Martinez J-P/150	8.00
15	Tim Hudson H-J/100	5.00
17	Lance Berkman B-J/150	5.00
19	Larry Walker J-J/150	5.00
21	Lou Brock B-JK/150	10.00
21	Roger Clemens B-J/150	15.00
22	Paul LoDuca B-J/50	5.00
23	Don Mattingly BG-P/50	20.00
24	Willie Mays B-P/25	50.00
25	Rafael Palmeiro B-J/150	8.00
27	Vladimir Guerrero B-J/150	8.00
29	Rod Carew JK-JK/150	8.00
30	Nolan Ryan B-JK/150	25.00
31	Richie Sexson H-J/150	8.00
32	Steve Carlton B-H/150	10.00
33	Eddie Murray B-J/150	10.00
34	Nolan Ryan B-J/150	25.00
35	Mike Mussina B-P/125	8.00
36	Sean Casey J-P/150	8.00
38	Curt Schilling J-J/150	8.00
39	Darryl Strawberry B-J/150	5.00
41	Tom Seaver J-P/150	10.00
42	Mike Schmidt B-J/150	15.00
43	Todd Helton B-J/150	8.00
45	Shawn Green B-J/150	8.00
47	Tom Glavine B-J/150	8.00
49	Kerry Wood FG-J/150	8.00
50	Carlos Delgado B-J/100	5.00
51	R. John J-P/150	8.00
52	David Ortiz B-J/150	8.00
53	Troy Glaus J-J/150	5.00
54	Rickey Henderson B-J/150	8.00
55	Craig Biggio B-J/150	8.00
56	Brad Penny FG-J/150	5.00
57	Gary Carter J-P/150	8.00
58	Andy Pettitte J-J/150	8.00
59	Mark Prior FG-J/150	5.00
60	Kirby Puckett B-FG/100	10.00
61	Willie McCovey J-P/150	10.00
63	Greg Maddux B-J/150	15.00
64	Adrian Beltre B-J/150	5.00
65	Andruw Jones B-J/150	8.00
67	Frank Thomas J-J/150	8.00
68	Victor Martinez CP-J/150	5.00
69	R. John J-P/150	8.00
71	Adam Dunn B-J/95	5.00
72	Carlton Fisk B-J/150	8.00
73	Cal Ripken Jr. J-P/150	25.00
74	Kenny Lofton B-H/150	5.00
75	Barry Zito J-J/150	5.00
76	Sammy Sosa B-J/150	10.00
77	Deion Sanders J-P/150	10.00
79	Tony Gwynn J-P/150	10.00
79	Mike Piazza J-P/150	10.00
80	Jeff Bagwell J-P/150	8.00
81	Manny Ramirez B-J/150	8.00
83	Mark Grace B-J/50	8.00
84	Robin Yount B-J/150	12.00
86	Albert Pujols B-J/150	20.00
86	Dontrelle Willis B-J/150	8.00
88	Magglio Ordonez B-S/150	5.00
89	Miguel Tejada H-J/150	8.00
90	Mark Teixeira FG-J/150	8.00
91	Gary Carter B-J/25	10.00
92	Ivan Rodriguez CP-J/150	8.00
93	Jason Giambi H-J/50	5.00
94	Rickey Henderson B-P/150	8.00
95	Curt Schilling J-J/150	8.00
96	Bobby Doerr B-P/150	8.00
97	Chipper Jones B-J/150	8.00
99	Johnny Bench B-P/150	10.00
100	Harmon Killebrew H-J/50	10.00

Tools of Trade Autograph Swatch Double

NM/M
Production 1-75
Prime Red: .75-1.5X
Production 1-50
No pricing production 20 or less.
Prime Black: No Pricing
Production One Set

1	Ozzie Smith B-P/25	50.00
3	Dale Murphy J-J/50	30.00
4	Paul Molitor J-P/25	40.00

#		$
20	Lou Brock B-JK/50	40.00
22	Paul LoDuca B-J/25	25.00
36	Sean Casey J-P/50	25.00
37	Juan Gonzalez J-P/25	30.00
39	Darryl Strawberry B-J/50	25.00
41	Tom Seaver J-P/25	40.00
48	Torii Hunter B-J/40	25.00
56	Brad Penny FG-J/75	10.00
57	Gary Carter J-P/25	30.00
62	Andre Dawson B-J/50	25.00
64	Adrian Beltre B-J/50	25.00
66	Juan Gonzalez B-J/25	30.00
70	Andre Dawson J-P/50	25.00
73	Cal Ripken Jr. J-P/25	160.00
88	Magglio Ordonez B-S/25	20.00
91	Gary Carter B-J/25	25.00
96	Bobby Doerr B-P/50	25.00
98	Eric Chavez B-J/25	25.00
100	Harmon Killebrew H-J/25	50.00

Tools/Trade Autograph Swatch Double Reverse

NM/M
Production 1-75

20	Lou Brock B-JK/50	40.00
36	Sean Casey J-P/50	25.00
39	Darryl Strawberry B-J/75	20.00
48	Torii Hunter B-J/50	25.00
56	Brad Penny FG-J/50	12.00
62	Andre Dawson B-J/50	25.00
64	Adrian Beltre B-J/50	20.00
66	Juan Gonzalez B-J/25	30.00
70	Andre Dawson J-P/25	30.00

Tools of the Trade Swatch Triple

NM/M
Production 1-25
Prime Red: No Pricing
Production 1-25
Prime Black: No Pricing
Production 1-15

2	Carlos Beltran/25	15.00
3	Dale Murphy/25	15.00
4	Paul Molitor/25	20.00
5	George Brett/25	35.00
6	Stan Musial/25	40.00
7	Ivan Rodriguez/25	15.00
9	Reggie Jackson/25	15.00
10	Hideo Nomo/25	20.00
12	Roberto Alomar/25	15.00
13	Pedro Martinez/25	15.00
15	Tim Hudson/25	10.00
17	Lance Berkman/25	10.00
19	Larry Walker/25	10.00
21	Roger Clemens/25	30.00
22	Paul LoDuca/25	10.00
23	Don Mattingly/25	30.00
25	Rafael Palmeiro/25	15.00
27	Vladimir Guerrero/25	15.00
29	Rod Carew/25	15.00
30	Nolan Ryan/25	40.00
31	Richie Sexson/25	10.00
33	Eddie Murray/25	20.00
36	Nolan Ryan/25	40.00
36	Sean Casey/25	10.00
37	Juan Gonzalez/25	10.00
38	Curt Schilling/25	15.00
42	Mike Schmidt/25	30.00
43	Todd Helton/25	12.00
45	Shawn Green/25	10.00
47	Tom Glavine/25	10.00
49	Kerry Wood/25	15.00
50	Carlos Delgado/25	10.00
51	R. John/25	15.00
52	David Ortiz/25	10.00
53	Troy Glaus/25	10.00
54	Rickey Henderson/25	15.00
55	Craig Biggio/25	12.00
56	Brad Penny/25	10.00
57	Gary Carter/25	15.00
58	Andy Pettitte/25	10.00
59	Mark Prior/25	10.00
62	Kirby Puckett/25	20.00
63	Greg Maddux/25	25.00
65	Adrian Beltre/25	12.00
65	Andruw Jones/25	12.00
67	Frank Thomas/25	25.00
68	Victor Martinez/25	10.00
70	Andre Dawson/25	15.00
72	Carlton Fisk/25	15.00
73	Cal Ripken Jr./25	40.00
74	Kenny Lofton/25	10.00
75	Barry Zito/25	10.00
76	Sammy Sosa/25	15.00
77	Deion Sanders/25	20.00
78	Tony Gwynn/25	20.00
79	Mike Piazza/25	20.00
80	Jeff Bagwell/25	15.00
81	Manny Ramirez/25	15.00
83	Mark Grace/25	15.00
84	Robin Yount/25	40.00
85	Albert Pujols/25	40.00
86	Dontrelle Willis/25	15.00
88	Magglio Ordonez/25	10.00
89	Miguel Tejada/25	15.00
90	Mark Teixeira/25	12.00
91	Gary Carter/25	15.00
92	Ivan Rodriguez/25	15.00
93	Jason Giambi/25	10.00
94	Rickey Henderson/25	15.00
96	Curt Schilling/25	15.00
96	Bobby Doerr/25	15.00
97	Chipper Jones/25	15.00
98	Eric Chavez/25	15.00
99	Johnny Bench/25	20.00
100	Harmon Killebrew/25	30.00

Tools of Trade Autograph Swatch Triple

NM/M
Production 1-75
Prime Red: No Pricing
Production 1-25
Prime Black: No Pricing
Production One Set

2	Carlos Beltran/25	40.00
3	Dale Murphy/25	50.00
18	Darryl Strawberry/75	20.00
20	Lou Brock/50	40.00
36	Sean Casey/25	20.00
37	Juan Gonzalez/75	25.00
39	Darryl Strawberry/75	20.00
56	Brad Penny/25	20.00
57	Gary Carter/25	30.00
64	Adrian Beltre/25	25.00
66	Juan Gonzalez/50	25.00
70	Andre Dawson/75	25.00
73	Cal Ripken Jr./25	200.00
82	Carlos Beltran/25	40.00
91	Gary Carter/25	30.00
96	Bobby Doerr/25	25.00
100	Harmon Killebrew/25	60.00

Tools/Trade Autograph Swatch Triple Reverse

NM/M
Production 1-50

18	Darryl Strawberry/50	25.00
20	Lou Brock/50	50.00
36	Sean Casey/25	25.00
37	Juan Gonzalez/25	30.00
39	Darryl Strawberry/25	25.00
70	Andre Dawson/50	25.00

Tools of the Trade Swatch Quad

NM/M
Production 1-100
Prime Red: No Pricing
Production 1-10
Prime Black: No Pricing
Production One Set

3	Dale Murphy/50	20.00
4	Paul Molitor/25	30.00
7	Ivan Rodriguez/25	15.00
8	Carl Yastrzemski/25	50.00
9	Reggie Jackson/100	25.00
10	Hideo Nomo/75	15.00
11	Gary Sheffield/30	15.00
12	Roberto Alomar/50	15.00
13	Pedro Martinez/50	15.00
14	Ernie Banks/25	40.00
15	Tim Hudson/25	10.00
17	Lance Berkman/65	15.00
19	Larry Walker/100	10.00
20	Lou Brock/50	25.00
21	Roger Clemens/25	40.00
22	Paul LoDuca/50	15.00
23	Don Mattingly/50	40.00
24	Willie Mays/25	80.00
25	Rafael Palmeiro/100	15.00
26	Roy Oswalt/30	15.00
27	Vladimir Guerrero/50	20.00
29	Rod Carew/75	15.00
31	Richie Sexson/100	15.00
33	Eddie Murray/25	15.00
36	Sean Casey/75	10.00
39	Darryl Strawberry/50	15.00
41	Tom Seaver/35	25.00
42	Mike Schmidt/50	40.00
43	Todd Helton/100	12.00
45	Shawn Green/100	10.00
46	Mike Mussina/25	20.00
50	Carlos Delgado/50	10.00
52	David Ortiz/50	30.00
53	Troy Glaus/50	12.00
54	Rickey Henderson/100	25.00
55	Craig Biggio/100	15.00
56	Brad Penny/50	15.00
57	Gary Carter/50	15.00
58	Andy Pettitte/25	15.00
59	Mark Prior/50	15.00
60	Kirby Puckett/25	15.00
63	Adrian Beltre/25	10.00
65	Andruw Jones/50	10.00
66	Juan Gonzalez/30	20.00
67	Frank Thomas/50	25.00
68	Victor Martinez/50	15.00
70	Andre Dawson/25	15.00
72	Carlton Fisk/25	15.00
73	Cal Ripken Jr./100	50.00
74	Kenny Lofton/100	10.00
75	Barry Zito/25	10.00
76	Sammy Sosa/100	15.00
78	Tony Gwynn/100	20.00
79	Mike Piazza/100	20.00
80	Jeff Bagwell/100	10.00
83	Mark Grace/50	10.00
85	Albert Pujols/50	60.00
86	Dontrelle Willis/50	15.00
88	Magglio Ordonez/50	15.00
89	Miguel Tejada/100	15.00
90	Mark Teixeira/100	15.00
91	Gary Carter/90	15.00
92	Ivan Rodriguez/50	15.00
93	Jason Giambi/25	15.00
94	Rickey Henderson/100	15.00
95	Curt Schilling/100	15.00
100	Harmon Killebrew/25	40.00

Tools of Trade Autograph Swatch Quad

NM/M
Production 1-25
Prime Red: No Pricing
Production 1-5

3	Dale Murphy/25	60.00
20	Lou Brock/25	80.00
23	Don Mattingly/25	120.00
36	Sean Casey/25	20.00
39	Darryl Strawberry/25	40.00
41	Tom Seaver/25	75.00
42	Mike Schmidt/25	100.00
56	Brad Penny/25	20.00
57	Gary Carter/25	40.00
73	Cal Ripken Jr./25	200.00
78	Tony Gwynn/25	75.00
88	Magglio Ordonez/25	30.00
91	Gary Carter/25	30.00
100	Harmon Killebrew/25	80.00

Tools/Trade Autograph Swatch Quad Reverse

No Pricing
Production 1-15

Tools of the Trade Swatch Five

NM/M
Production 1-50
Prime Red: No Pricing
Production 1-10
Prime Black: No Pricing
Production One Set
Reverse: No Pricing
Production 1-15

4	Paul Molitor/25	35.00
7	Ivan Rodriguez/25	25.00
12	Roberto Alomar/25	30.00
13	Pedro Martinez/25	20.00
15	Tim Hudson/25	25.00
17	Lance Berkman/25	25.00
22	Paul LoDuca/50	15.00
23	Don Mattingly/25	65.00
25	Rafael Palmeiro/25	20.00
26	Roy Oswalt/25	20.00
28	Austin Kearns/25	15.00
29	Rod Carew/25	40.00
31	Richie Sexson/50	15.00
33	Eddie Murray/25	50.00
36	Sean Casey/25	20.00
42	Mike Schmidt/25	70.00
43	Todd Helton/25	20.00
52	David Ortiz/25	35.00
53	Troy Glaus/25	20.00
54	Rickey Henderson/50	25.00
55	Craig Biggio/25	25.00
56	Brad Penny/45	15.00
57	Gary Carter/40	25.00
58	Andy Pettitte/25	25.00
59	Mark Prior/25	25.00
60	Kirby Puckett/25	50.00
64	Adrian Beltre/25	20.00
65	Andruw Jones/25	15.00
67	Frank Thomas/25	25.00
68	Victor Martinez/25	15.00
73	Cal Ripken Jr./50	75.00
76	Sammy Sosa/25	35.00
78	Tony Gwynn/50	40.00
79	Mike Piazza/25	50.00
80	Jeff Bagwell/50	25.00
82	Carlos Beltran/20	25.00
84	Robin Yount/50	40.00
88	Magglio Ordonez/25	20.00
89	Miguel Tejada/50	20.00
90	Mark Teixeira/50	20.00
91	Gary Carter/25	25.00
92	Ivan Rodriguez/25	25.00
94	Rickey Henderson/50	25.00
95	Curt Schilling/25	25.00

Tools of the Trade Swatch Six

NM/M
Production 1-50
Reverse: No Pricing
Production 1-10
Prime Red: No Pricing
Production 1-5
Prime Black: No Pricing
Production One Set

22	Paul LoDuca/50	20.00
31	Richie Sexson/25	20.00
52	David Ortiz/50	40.00
53	Troy Glaus/50	25.00
57	Gary Carter/25	35.00
59	Mark Prior/50	25.00
73	Cal Ripken Jr./50	85.00
76	Sammy Sosa/25	15.00
78	Tony Gwynn/50	40.00
79	Mike Piazza/50	25.00
80	Jeff Bagwell/50	25.00
90	Mark Teixeira/100	15.00
92	Ivan Rodriguez/25	30.00
94	Rickey Henderson/50	30.00

2005 Playoff Prestige

		NM/M
Complete Set (200):		35.00
Common Player:		.25
Hobby Pack (8):		3.00
Hobby Box (24):		65.00
1	Rafael Furcal	.25
2	Derek Jeter	2.00
3	Edgar Renteria	.40
4	Jeff Bagwell	.50
5	Nomar Garciaparra	1.25
6	Melvin Mora	.25
7	Craig Biggio	.40
8	Brad Penny	.25
9	Hank Blalock	.50
10	Vernon Wells	.25
11	Gary Sheffield	.50
12	Jeff Kent	.25
13	Carl Crawford	.25
14	Paul Konerko	.25
15	Carlos Beltran	.50
16	Garret Anderson	.40
17	Todd Helton	.50
18	Javy Lopez	.40
19	Mike Lowell	.25
20	Robb Quinlan	.25
21	Andy Pettitte	.40
22	Roger Clemens	2.00
23	Mark Teixeira	.50
24	Miguel Cabrera	.75
25	Andruw Jones	.40
26	Josh Beckett	.40
27	Scott Rolen	.75
28	J.J. Putz	.25
29	Adrian Beltre	.50
30	Magglio Ordonez	.25
31	Mike Piazza	1.00
32	Danny Graves	.25
33	Larry Walker	.40
34	Kerry Wood	.75
35	Mike Mussina	.50
36	Joe Nathan	.25
37	Chone Figgins	.25
38	Curt Schilling	.75
39	Brett Myers	.25
40	Jae Weong Seo	.25
41	Danny Kolb	.25
42	Mariano Rivera	.50
43	Francisco Cordero	.25
44	Adam Dunn	.50
45	Pedro Martinez	.75
46	Frank Thomas	.50
47	Tom Glavine	.40
48	Torii Hunter	.40
49	Ben Sheets	.40
50	Shawn Green	.25
51	Randy Johnson	.75
52	C.C. Sabathia	.25
53	Bobby Abreu	.25
54	Octavio Dotel	.25
55	Hideki Matsui	1.50
56	Mark Buehrle	.25
57	Johan Santana	.50
58	Brandon Inge	.25
59	Dewon Brazelton	.25
60	Ryan Wagner	.25
61	Kevin Brown	.25
62	Laynce Nix	.25
63	Jason Bay	.40
64	J.D. Drew	.40
65	Jacque Jones	.25
66	Jason Schmidt	.40
67	Joe Kennedy	.25
68	Miguel Tejada	.50
69	Hideo Nomo	.40
70	Michael Young	.25
71	Lyle Overbay	.25
72	Omar Vizquel	.25
73	Johnny Estrada	.25
74	Khalil Greene	.40
75	Barry Zito	.25
76	Wilson Valdez	.25
77	Nick Green	.25
78	Bucky Jacobsen	.25
79	Keith Foulke	.25
80	Sean Burroughs	.25
81	Carlos Zambrano	.40
82	Orlando Cabrera	.25
83	Shigetoshi Hasegawa	.25
84	Troy Glaus	.40
85	Mike Sweeney	.25
86	Jason Giambi	.40
87	Derek Lee	.40
88	Carlos Delgado	.40
89	Kazuo Matsui	.25
90	Lew Ford	.25
91	Akinori Otsuka	.25
92	Bobby Crosby	.25
93	Jose Reyes	.40
94	Jose Vidro	.25
95	Shingo Takatsu	.25
96	Sean Casey	.25
97	Tim Olson	.25
98	Jeff Suppan	.25
99	Rafael Palmeiro	.50
100	Esteban Loaiza	.25
101	Brian Roberts	.25
102	Jack Wilson	.25
103	Eric Chavez	.40
104	Eric Milton	.25
105	Albert Pujols	2.00
106	Jake Peavy	.25
107	Ivan Rodriguez	.50
108	Chad Cordero	.25
109	Jody Gerut	.25
110	Chipper Jones	.75
111	Barry Larkin	.40
112	Alfonso Soriano	.75
113	Alex Rodriguez	1.50
114	Paul LoDuca	.25
115	Jim Edmonds	.40
116	Aramis Ramirez	.40
117	Lance Berkman	.40
118	Johnny Damon	.75
119	Aubrey Huff	.25
120	Mark Mulder	.40
121	Sammy Sosa	1.50
122	Mark Prior	.75
123	Shannon Stewart	.25
124	Manny Ramirez	.75
125	Jim Thome	.75
126	Doug DeVore	.25
127	Vladimir Guerrero	.75
128	Ken Harvey	.25
129	Jacob Cruz	.25
130	Ken Griffey Jr.	1.00
131	Greg Maddux	1.00
132	Derek Lowe	.25
133	Craig Monroe	.25
134	David Ortiz	.75
135	Dontrelle Willis	.40
136	Tom Gordon	.25
137	David Dellucci	.25
138	Vance Wilson	.25
139	Milton Bradley	.25
140	Ichiro Suzuki	1.50
141	Victor Martinez	.40
142	Wade Miller	.25
143	Francisco Rodriguez	.25
144	Roy Oswalt	.40
145	Carlos Lee	.25
146	Kazuhisa Ishii	.25
147	Tim Hudson	.25
148	Travis Hafner	.25
149	Jermaine Dye	.25
150	Steve Finley	.25
151	Justin Verlander RC	1.50
152	Yadier Molina	.25
153	Andy Green	.25
154	Nick Swisher	.25
155	Clint Nageotte	.25
156	Grady Sizemore	.50
157	Gavin Floyd	.25
158	Josh Kroeger	.25
159	Russ Adams	.25
160	Jeff Baker	.25
161	Dioner Navarro	.25
162	Shawn Hill	.25
163	Ryan Howard	1.00
164	Scott Proctor	.25
165	Jason Kubel	.25
166	Jose Lopez	.25
167	Ryan Church	.25
168	Yhency Brazoban	.25
169	Jeff Francis	.25
170	Angel Guzman	.25
171	John Van Benschoten	.25
172	Adrian Gonzalez	.25
173	Casey Kotchman	.25
174	David Wright	.75
175	B.J. Upton	.50
176	Dallas McPherson	.50
177	Rene Rivera	.25
178	Denny Bautista	.25
179	Logan Kensing	.25
180	Matt Peterson	.25
181	Jeremy Reed	.25
182	Jairo Garcia	.25
183	Val Majewski	.25
184	Victor Diaz	.25
185	David Krynzel	.25
186	Ron Cey	.25
187	Bill Madlock	.25
188	Dave Stewart	.25
189	Billy Ripken	.25
190	Gary Carter	.50
191	Darryl Strawberry	.25
192	Dave Parker	.25
193	Ron Guidry	.25
194	Gaylord Perry	.25
195	Fred Lynn	.25
196	Jack Morris	.25
197	Steve Garvey	.25
198	Andre Dawson	.50
199	Nolan Ryan	2.50
200	Paul Molitor	.75

Red Foil

Red Foil: 8-15X
Production 25 Sets

Xtra Bases Black

Black: 8-15X
Production 25 Sets

Xtra Bases Green

Green: 5-10X
Production 50 Sets

Xtra Bases Purple

Purple: 4-8X
Production 100 Sets

Xtra Bases Red

Red: 3-6X
Production 150 Sets

Autographs

		NM/M
	Common Autograph:	8.00
20	Robb Quinlan	8.00
28	J.J. Putz	8.00
58	Brandon Inge/SP	15.00
67	Joe Kennedy	8.00
77	Wilson Valdez	8.00
77	Nick Green	8.00
78	Bucky Jacobsen	10.00
97	Tim Olson	8.00
98	Jeff Suppan/SP	15.00
128	Doug DeVore	8.00
129	Jacob Cruz	8.00
133	Craig Monroe	10.00
138	Vance Wilson	8.00
153	Andy Green	8.00
164	Scott Proctor	8.00

Changing Stripes

		NM/M
Complete Set (25):		25.00
Common Player:		.75

Inserted 1:8
Foil: 2-3X
Production 100 Sets
Holo-Foil: 3-6X
Production 25 Sets

1	Ivan Rodriguez	1.00
2	Roger Clemens	4.00
3	Curt Schilling	1.50
4	Alex Rodriguez	4.00
5	Greg Maddux	2.00
6	Juan Gonzalez	.75
7	Pedro Martinez	1.50
8	Roberto Alomar	.75
9	Randy Johnson	1.50
10	Ken Griffey Jr.	2.00
11	Carlos Beltran	1.00
12	Andy Pettitte	1.00
13	Tom Glavine	.75
14	Miguel Tejada	1.50
15	Alfonso Soriano	1.50
16	Shannon Stewart	.75
17	Nomar Garciaparra	2.00
18	Jeff Kent	.75
19	David Ortiz	1.50
20	Sean Casey	.75
21	Rickey Henderson	1.00
22	Carlton Fisk	.75
23	Phil Niekro	.75
24	Dale Murphy	1.00
25	Reggie Jackson	1.50

Changing Stripes Material Dual Jersey

NM/M
Production 12-250

1	Ivan Rodriguez/250	10.00
2	Roger Clemens/50	20.00

ABBREVIATIONS

SP - Short Print

Connections

		NM/M
Complete Set (25):		40.00
Common Duo:		1.50
Inserted 1:8		
Foil:		2-3X
Production 100 Sets		
Holo-Foil:		3-6X
Production 25 Sets		
1	Josh Beckett, Dontrelle Willis	1.50
2	Andruw Jones, Chipper Jones	2.00
3	Kazuo Matsui, Jose Reyes	1.50
4	Bobby Abreu, Jim Thome	2.00
5	Jeff Bagwell, Lance Berkman	
6	Roger Clemens, Roy Oswalt	4.00
7	Scott Rolen, Larry Walker	2.00
8	Albert Pujols, Jim Edmonds	4.00
9	Greg Maddux, Sammy Sosa	2.50
10	Mark Prior, Nomar Garciaparra	2.00
11	Barry Larkin, Sean Casey	1.50
12	Adrian Beltre, Shawn Green	1.50
13	Alex Rodriguez, Derek Jeter	6.00
14	Manny Ramirez, Jason Varitek	3.00
15	Miguel Tejada, Javy Lopez	2.00
16	B.J. Upton, Carl Crawford	1.50
17	Frank Thomas, Paul Konerko	2.00
18	Joe Mauer, Justin Morneau	2.00
19	Victor Martinez, Jody Gerut	1.50
20	Bobby Crosby, Barry Zito	1.50
21	Mark Teixeira, Hank Blalock	
22	Reggie Jackson, Rod Carew	2.00
23	Rickey Henderson, Tony Gwynn	2.50
24	Tom Seaver, Johnny Bench	3.00
25	Don Mattingly, Dave Righetti	4.00

Connections Material Dual Bat

		NM/M
Production 25-250		
2	Andruw Jones, Chipper Jones/250	10.00
3	Kazuo Matsui, Jose Reyes/100	10.00
4	Bobby Abreu, Jim Thome/100	12.00
5	Jeff Bagwell, Lance Berkman/250	10.00
6	Roger Clemens, Roy Oswalt/250	15.00
10	Mark Prior, Nomar Garciaparra/100	
11	Barry Larkin, Sean Casey/100	10.00
12	Shawn Green, Adrian Beltre/250	5.00
14	Jason Varitek, Manny Ramirez/100	15.00
15	Miguel Tejada, Javy Lopez/100	10.00
17	Frank Thomas, Paul Konerko/100	10.00
19	Victor Martinez, Jody Gerut/25	12.00
21	Mark Teixeira, Hank Blalock/100	10.00
22	Reggie Jackson, Rod Carew/250	10.00
23	Tony Gwynn, Rickey Henderson/250	15.00
24	Tom Seaver, Johnny Bench/250	15.00

Connections Material Dual Jersey

		NM/M
Production 10-250		
Prime:		1-2X
Production 10-25		
No pricing 20 or less.		
1	Josh Beckett, Dontrelle Willis/250	8.00
2	Andruw Jones, Chipper Jones/250	10.00
3	Kazuo Matsui, Jose Reyes/100	10.00
4	Bobby Abreu, Jim Thome/250	10.00
6	Jeff Bagwell, Lance Berkman/250	10.00
6	Roger Clemens, Roy Oswalt/250	15.00
8	Albert Pujols, Jim Edmonds/250	25.00
11	Barry Larkin, Sean Casey/50	15.00
12	Shawn Green, Adrian Beltre/250	8.00
14	Jason Varitek, Manny Ramirez/50	20.00
15	Miguel Tejada, Javy Lopez/50	12.00
17	Frank Thomas/Pants, Paul Konerko/250	10.00
20	Bobby Crosby, Barry Zito/250	10.00
21	Mark Teixeira, Hank Blalock/100	10.00
22	Reggie Jackson, Rod Carew/Jkt/250	12.00
23	Rickey Henderson, Tony Gwynn/250	15.00
24	Tom Seaver, Johnny Bench/Pants/100	15.00
25	Don Mattingly, Dave Righetti/250	20.00

Diamond Heritage

		NM/M
Complete Set (15):		20.00
Common Player:		.75
Inserted 1:12		
1	Pedro Martinez	1.50
2	Mark Teixeira	1.00
3	Lance Berkman	.75
4	Vladimir Guerrero	1.50
5	Albert Pujols	4.00
6	Roger Clemens	1.50
7	Manny Ramirez	1.50
8	Mike Piazza	2.00
9	Jim Thome	1.50
10	Mark Prior	1.00
11	Gary Sheffield	.75
12	Sammy Sosa	2.50
13	Tim Hudson	.75
14	Hideki Matsui	3.00
15	Jim Edmonds	.75

Diamond Heritage Matierial Bat

		NM/M
Production 100 Sets		
1	Pedro Martinez	10.00
2	Mark Teixeira	10.00
3	Lance Berkman	5.00
4	Vladimir Guerrero	10.00
6	Roger Clemens	15.00
7	Manny Ramirez	10.00
8	Mike Piazza	10.00
9	Jim Thome	10.00
10	Mark Prior	8.00
11	Gary Sheffield	8.00
12	Sammy Sosa	10.00
13	Tim Hudson	5.00
14	Hideki Matsui	25.00
15	Jim Edmonds	8.00

Diamond Heritage Material Jersey

		NM/M
Production 100 Sets		
1	Pedro Martinez	10.00
2	Mark Teixeira	10.00
3	Lance Berkman	5.00
4	Vladimir Guerrero	10.00
5	Albert Pujols	25.00
6	Roger Clemens	15.00
7	Manny Ramirez	10.00
8	Mike Piazza	10.00
9	Jim Thome	10.00
10	Mark Prior	8.00
11	Gary Sheffield	8.00
12	Sammy Sosa	10.00
13	Tim Hudson	5.00
14	Hideki Matsui/Pants	25.00
15	Jim Edmonds	8.00

League Leaders Single

		NM/M
Complete Set (10):		25.00
Inserted 1:21		
Foil:		2-4X
Production 100 Sets		
Holo-Foil:		4-8X
Production 25 Sets		
1	Gary Sheffield	2.00
2	Ben Sheets	2.00
3	Adrian Beltre	2.00
4	Scott Rolen	3.00
5	George Brett	4.00
6	Johan Santana	3.00
7	Manny Ramirez	3.00
8	Cal Ripken Jr.	8.00
9	Carlos Zambrano	2.00
10	Tony Gwynn	4.00

League Leader Single Material Bat

		NM/M
Production 250 Sets		
1	Gary Sheffield	8.00
2	Ben Sheets	5.00
3	Adrian Beltre	5.00
5	George Brett	12.00
7	Manny Ramirez	8.00
8	Cal Ripken Jr.	25.00
10	Tony Gwynn	8.00

League Leaders Single Material Jersey

		NM/M
Production 25-250		
1	Gary Sheffield/250	8.00
2	Ben Sheets/250	5.00
3	Adrian Beltre/50	8.00
4	Scott Rolen/250	8.00
5	George Brett/250	15.00
6	Johan Santana/25	20.00
7	Manny Ramirez/250	8.00
8	Cal Ripken Jr./250	25.00
9	Carlos Zambrano/250	5.00
10	Tony Gwynn/250	8.00

League Leaders Double

		NM/M
Complete Set (5):		15.00
Inserted 1:39		
Foil:		2-3X
Production 100 Sets		
Holo-Foil:		3-6X
Production 25 Sets		
1	Tim Hudson, Roy Oswalt	2.00
2	Ivan Rodriguez, Todd Helton	3.00

		NM/M
3	Mark Teixeira, Jim Edmonds	2.00
4	Nolan Ryan, Roger Clemens	8.00
5	Sammy Sosa, Troy Glaus	3.00

League Leader Double Material Bat

		NM/M
Production 250 Sets		
1	Tim Hudson, Roy Oswalt	8.00
2	Ivan Rodriguez, Todd Helton	15.00
3	Mark Teixeira, Jim Edmonds	10.00
4	Nolan Ryan, Roger Clemens	25.00
5	Sammy Sosa, Troy Glaus	15.00

League Leaders Double Material Jersey

		NM/M
Production 50-250		
1	Tim Hudson, Roy Oswalt/100	10.00
2	Ivan Rodriguez, Todd Helton/50	15.00
3	Mark Teixeira, Jim Edmonds/250	15.00
4	Nolan Ryan, Roger Clemens/250	25.00
5	Sammy Sosa, Troy Glaus/250	15.00

League Leaders Quad

		NM/M
Inserted 1:39		
Foil:		1-2X
Production 100 Sets		
Holo-Foil:		3-5X
Production 25 Sets		
1	Wade Boggs, Paul Molitor, Alan Trammell, Kirby Puckett	4.00
2	Dale Murphy, Mike Schmidt, Gary Carter, Darryl Strawberry	6.00
3	Jose Canseco, Kirby Puckett, Will Clark, Darryl Strawberry	4.00
4	Pedro Martinez, Kevin Brown, Randy Johnson, Roger Clemens	6.00
5	Don Mattingly, Dave Parker, Eddie Murray, Dale Murphy	4.00

League Leaders Quad Material Bat

		NM/M
Production 100 Sets		
2	Dale Murphy, Mike Schmidt, Gary Carter, Darryl Strawberry	40.00
4	Pedro Martinez, Kevin Brown, Randy Johnson, Roger Clemens	50.00
5	Don Mattingly, Dave Parker, Eddie Murray, Dale Murphy	50.00

League Leaders Quad Material Jersey

		NM/M
Production 100 Sets		
1	Wade Boggs, Paul Molitor, Alan Trammell, Kirby Puckett	40.00
2	Dale Murphy, Mike Schmidt, Gary Carter, Darryl Strawberry	40.00
3	Jose Canseco, Kirby Puckett, Will Clark, Darryl Strawberry	40.00
4	Pedro Martinez, Kevin Brown, Randy Johnson, Roger Clemens	50.00
5	Don Mattingly, Dave Parker, Eddie Murray, Dale Murphy	50.00

Playoff Champions Combo Wild Card

		NM/M
Inserted 1:391		
Division Combo:		.75-1X
League Combo:		.75-1X
World Series Combo:		.75-1X
Redemption Deadline 4-15-06.		

		NM/M
Production 350 Sets		
Orange:		1-1.5X
Production 500 Sets		
Platinum:		3-5X
Production 25 Sets		
Purple:		1-2X
Production 200 Sets		
Red:		1X
Production 70 Sets		
Silver:		2-3X
Production 75 Sets		
1	Andruw Jones, Johnny Estrada, Chipper Jones	10.00
2	Miguel Cabrera, Josh Beckett, Dontrelle Willis	10.00
3	Chad Cordero, Nick Johnson, Brad Wilkerson	5.00
4	Jim Thome, Bobby Abreu, Chase Utley	10.00
5	Mike Piazza, Kazuo Matsui, David Wright	10.00
6	Albert Pujols, Scott Rolen, Jim Edmonds	8.00
7	Kerry Wood, Mark Prior, Carlos Zambrano	8.00
8	Ben Sheets, Geoff Jenkins, Lyle Overbay	5.00
9	Kip Wells, Jack Wilson, Jason Bay	5.00
10	Austin Kearns, Adam Dunn, Ken Griffey Jr.	10.00
11	Roy Oswalt, Lance Berkman, Jeff Bagwell	10.00
12	Jason Jennings, Matt Holliday, Todd Helton	8.00
13	Eric Gagne, Jayson Werth, Milton Bradley	8.00
14	Alex Cintron, Brandon Webb, Luis Gonzalez	5.00
15	Jason Schmidt, Edgardo Alfonzo, Kirk Rueter	5.00
16	Khalil Greene, Jake Peavy, Trevor Hoffman	10.00
17	Manny Ramirez, Curt Schilling, David Ortiz	15.00
18	Miguel Tejada, Melvin Mora, Javy Lopez	8.00
19	Roy Halladay, Alexis Rios, Gabe Gross	5.00
20	Alex Rodriguez, Derek Jeter, Hideki Matsui	20.00
21	B.J. Upton, Scott Kazmir, Carl Crawford	10.00
22	Frank Thomas, Shingo Takatsu, Aaron Rowand	8.00
23	Victor Martinez, C.C. Sabathia, Travis Hafner	5.00
24	Torii Hunter, Johan Santana, Justin Morneau	10.00
25	Zack Greinke, Mike Sweeney, Ken Harvey	8.00
26	Ivan Rodriguez, Jeremy Bonderman, Carlos Guillen	8.00
27	Rich Harden, Bobby Crosby, Barry Zito	5.00
28	Bret Boone, Ichiro Suzuki, Jeremy Reed	12.00
29	Michael Young, Mark Teixeira, Hank Blalock	10.00
30	Vladimir Guerrero, Darin Erstad, Garret Anderson	10.00

Playoff Game Jersey Collection

Inserted 1:8 Retail

Prestigious Pros Blue

		NM/M
Common Player:		1.00
Production 900 Sets		
Black:		No Pricing
Production 10 Sets		
Bronze:		2-3X
Production 100 Sets		
Gold:		2-4X
Production 50 Sets		
Green:		1-2X

		NM/M
1	Ozzie Smith	3.00
2	Derek Jeter	6.00
3	Eric Chavez	1.00
4	Paul Molitor	2.00
5	Jeff Bagwell	1.50
6	Melvin Mora	1.00
7	Craig Biggio	1.00
8	Cal Ripken Jr.	8.00
9	Hank Blalock	1.50
10	Miguel Tejada	2.00
11	Jacque Jones	1.00
12	Alfonso Soriano	1.00
13	Omar Vizquel	1.00
14	Paul Konerko	1.00
15	Tim Hudson	1.00
16	Garret Anderson	1.00
17	Lance Berkman	1.00
18	Randy Johnson	2.00
19	Robin Yount	3.00
20	Mark Mulder	1.00
21	Sean Casey	1.00
22	Jim Palmer	2.00
23	Don Mattingly	5.00
24	Manny Ramirez	2.00
25	Rafael Palmeiro	1.50
26	Vernon Wells	1.00
27	Vladimir Guerrero	2.00
28	Ken Harvey	1.00
29	Rod Carew	1.50
30	Nolan Ryan	8.00
31	Mike Piazza	3.00
32	Steve Carlton	1.50
33	Miguel Cabrera	2.00
34	Kerry Wood	2.00
35	Mike Mussina	1.00
36	Gaylord Perry	1.00
37	Gary Sheffield	1.50
38	Curt Schilling	2.00
39	Don Sutton	1.00
40	Roger Clemens	6.00
41	Victor Martinez	1.00
42	Jason Giambi	2.00
43	Dennis Eckersley	1.00
44	Adam Dunn	1.50
45	Pedro Martinez	2.00
46	Tony Perez	1.00
47	Tom Glavine	1.00
48	Torii Hunter	1.00
49	Hideo Nomo	1.00
50	Scott Rolen	2.00
51	Ichiro Suzuki	5.00
52	C.C. Sabathia	1.00
53	George Brett	5.00
54	David Ortiz	2.00
55	Hideki Matsui	4.00
56	Nomar Garciaparra	4.00
57	Johan Santana	2.00
58	Phil Niekro	1.00
59	Dontrelle Willis	1.00
60	Magglio Ordonez	1.00
61	Livan Hernandez	1.00
62	Edgar Renteria	1.00
63	Todd Helton	1.50
64	Carlos Beltran	1.50
65	Sammy Sosa	4.00
66	Albert Pujols	6.00
67	Mike Lowell	1.00
68	Mark Prior	1.50
69	Ivan Rodriguez	1.50
70	Jake Peavy	1.00
71	Jim Thome	1.50
72	Mark Teixeira	1.50
73	Shawn Green	1.00
74	Rollie Fingers	1.00
75	Barry Zito	1.00
76	Jose Vidro	1.00
77	Ben Sheets	1.00
78	Roy Halladay	1.00
79	Frank Thomas	1.50
80	Chipper Jones	2.00
81	Jason Bay	1.00
82	Tony Gwynn	2.00
83	Shannon Stewart	1.00
84	Carl Crawford	1.00
85	Andruw Jones	1.00
86	Greg Maddux	3.00
87	Barry Larkin	1.00
88	Alex Rodriguez	5.00
89	Rickey Henderson	1.50
90	Troy Glaus	1.00
91	Roy Oswalt	1.00
92	Michael Young	1.00
93	Carlos Lee	1.00
94	Jim Edmonds	1.00
95	Fergie Jenkins	1.00
96	Paul LoDuca	1.00
97	Aubrey Huff	1.00
98	Ken Griffey Jr.	3.00
99	Carlos Delgado	1.50
100	Mike Schmidt	5.00

Prestigious Pros Material Bat Silver

	NM/M
Production 5-50	
No pricing 20 or less.	

1 Ozzie Smith/50 25.00
3 Eric Chavez/25 10.00
4 Paul Molitor/50 12.00
5 Jeff Bagwell/50 10.00
7 Craig Biggio/25 15.00
8 Cal Ripken Jr./50 40.00
9 Hank Blalock/25 12.00
10 Miguel Tejada/25 12.00
12 Paul Konerko/25 8.00
15 Tim Hudson/25 10.00
16 Garret Anderson/25 10.00
17 Lance Berkman/50 8.00
18 Randy Johnson/25 20.00
19 Robin Yount/50 15.00
21 Sean Casey/25 10.00
22 Don Mattingly/50 25.00
25 Rafael Palmeiro/25 15.00
27 Vladimir Guerrero/25 8.00
28 Ken Harvey/25 8.00
29 Rod Carew/50 10.00
30 Nolan Ryan/50 35.00
31 Mike Piazza/25 20.00
34 Steve Carlton/50 8.00
35 Kerry Wood/25 15.00
37 Mike Mussina/25 15.00
38 Gary Sheffield/25 10.00
39 Curt Schilling/25 15.00
40 Roger Clemens/25 25.00
41 Victor Martinez/25 10.00
43 Jason Giambi/25 10.00
44 Adam Dunn/25 12.00
45 Pedro Martinez/25 15.00
46 Tony Perez/50 8.00
47 Tom Glavine/25 12.00
48 Torii Hunter/50 8.00
49 Hideo Nomo/25 25.00
53 Scott Rolen/25 20.00
53 George Brett/50 25.00
53 David Ortiz/50 10.00
55 Hideki Matsui/50 40.00
56 Nomar Garciaparra/25 20.00
58 Phil Niekro/50 8.00
60 Magglio Ordonez/50 8.00
62 Edgar Renteria/25 10.00
63 Todd Helton/25 15.00
64 Carlos Beltran/25 15.00
65 Sammy Sosa/25 10.00
66 Mike Lowell/25 10.00
68 Mark Prior/25 15.00
69 Ivan Rodriguez/50 10.00
71 Jim Thome/50 10.00
72 Mark Teixeira/50 10.00
73 Shawn Green/50 10.00
76 Jose Vidro/25 8.00
77 Ben Sheets/25 10.00
79 Frank Thomas/25 15.00
81 Jason Bay/25 10.00
82 Tony Gwynn/50 15.00
83 Shannon Stewart/25 8.00
85 Andruw Jones/25 10.00
87 Barry Larkin/25 10.00
89 Rickey Henderson/50 15.00
90 Troy Glaus/25 10.00
91 Roy Oswalt/25 10.00
92 Michael Young/25 10.00
93 Carlos Lee/25 10.00
95 Jim Edmonds/25 10.00
96 Paul LoDuca/25 10.00
99 Carlos Delgado/25 10.00
100 Mike Schmidt/50 25.00

Prestigious Pros Material Jersey Gold

NM/M
Production 5-50
No pricing 20 or less.
Platinum Patch: No Pricing
Production 5-10

1 Ozzie Smith/50 25.00
3 Eric Chavez/25 10.00
4 Paul Molitor/50 12.00
5 Jeff Bagwell/50 10.00
6 Melvin Mora/25 10.00
7 Craig Biggio/50 15.00
8 Cal Ripken Jr./50 40.00
10 Miguel Tejada/50 12.00
12 Omar Vizquel/50 15.00
14 Paul Konerko/25 8.00
15 Tim Hudson/50 10.00
17 Lance Berkman/50 8.00
18 Randy Johnson/50 20.00
19 Robin Yount/50 15.00
20 Mark Mulder/20 10.00
21 Sean Casey/50 10.00
22 Jim Palmer/50 8.00
23 Don Mattingly/50 25.00
26 Vernon Wells/25 8.00
27 Vladimir Guerrero/25 8.00
28 Ken Harvey/25 8.00
29 Rod Carew/50 10.00
30 Nolan Ryan/50 35.00
31 Mike Piazza/50 20.00
32 Steve Carlton/50 8.00
34 Kerry Wood/50 15.00
35 Mike Mussina/25 15.00
36 Gaylord Perry/50 8.00
37 Gary Sheffield/25 10.00
38 Curt Schilling/25 15.00
39 Don Sutton/50 8.00
40 Roger Clemens/25 25.00
41 Victor Martinez/25 10.00
42 Jason Giambi/25 10.00
43 Dennis Eckersley/50 10.00
45 Pedro Martinez/25 15.00

46 Tony Perez/50 8.00
49 Hideo Nomo/25 25.00
50 Scott Rolen/25 20.00
52 C.C. Sabathia/25 10.00
53 George Brett/50 25.00
55 Hideki Matsui/50 40.00
58 Phil Niekro/50 10.00
59 Dontrelle Willis/25 10.00
61 Magglio Ordonez/25 10.00
61 Livan Hernandez/25 8.00
62 Edgar Renteria/25 10.00
63 Todd Helton/25 15.00
65 Sammy Sosa/25 10.00
66 Albert Pujols/25 35.00
68 Mark Prior/25 10.00
71 Jim Thome/25 15.00
72 Mark Teixeira/25 12.00
73 Shawn Green/25 10.00
74 Rollie Fingers/50 8.00
77 Ben Sheets/25 10.00
78 Roy Halladay/25 10.00
79 Frank Thomas/25 15.00
80 Chipper Jones/25 15.00
81 Jason Bay/25 10.00
82 Tony Gwynn/25 15.00
84 Carl Crawford/25 10.00
85 Andruw Jones/25 10.00
86 Greg Maddux/25 20.00
87 Barry Larkin/25 12.00
89 Rickey Henderson/50 15.00
90 Troy Glaus/25 10.00
92 Michael Young/25 10.00
93 Carlos Lee/25 10.00
94 Jim Edmonds/25 12.00
95 Fergie Jenkins/50 10.00
97 Aubrey Huff/25 10.00
99 Carlos Delgado/25 10.00
100 Mike Schmidt/50 25.00

Prestigious Pros Signature Black

No Pricing
Production 5 Sets

Signature Xtra Bases Black

No Pricing
Production 3-10

Signature Xtra Bases Purple

NM/M
Production 5-50
6 Melvin Mora/25 25.00
8 Brad Penny/50 10.00
13 Carl Crawford/25 25.00
20 Robb Quinlan/50 8.00
28 J.J. Putz/50 8.00
32 Danny Graves/50 10.00
36 Joe Nathan/50 25.00
37 Chone Figgins/50 10.00
39 Brett Myers/50 10.00
41 Danny Kolb/50 10.00
43 Francisco Cordero/50 10.00
52 C.C. Sabathia/25 25.00
54 Octavio Dotel/50 10.00
56 Mark Buehrle/25 20.00
58 Brandon Inge/50 10.00
59 Dewon Brazelton/50 10.00
60 Ryan Wagner/50 10.00
62 Laynce Nix/50 15.00
63 Jason Bay/50 15.00
66 Jacque Jones/25 20.00
67 Joe Kennedy/50 8.00
71 Lyle Overbay/25 10.00
73 Johnny Estrada/50 15.00
76 Wilson Valdez/50 8.00
77 Nick Green/50 10.00
78 Bucky Jacobsen/50 10.00
79 Keith Foulke/50 15.00
81 Carlos Zambrano/25 35.00
82 Orlando Cabrera/25 15.00
90 Lew Ford/50 15.00
92 Bobby Crosby/50 20.00
97 Tim Olson/50 10.00
98 Jeff Suppan/50 10.00
100 Esteban Loaiza/50 10.00
101 Brian Roberts/50 35.00
102 Jack Wilson/50 10.00
106 Jake Peavy/50 30.00
108 Chad Cordero/50 10.00
109 Jody Gerut/50 10.00
126 Doug DeVore/50 8.00
128 Ken Harvey/50 8.00
129 Jacob Cruz/50 8.00
133 Craig Monroe/50 10.00
136 Tom Gordon/50 15.00
137 David Dellucci/50 20.00
138 Vance Wilson/50 15.00
139 Milton Bradley/50 15.00
141 Victor Martinez/25 30.00
142 Wade Miller/50 15.00
145 Carlos Lee/25 20.00
148 Travis Hafner/50 15.00
149 Jermaine Dye/25 15.00
152 Yadier Molina/25 20.00
153 Andy Green/50 8.00
161 Dioner Navarro/50 15.00
162 Shawn Hill/50 10.00
164 Scott Proctor/50 10.00
165 Jason Kubel/50 15.00
168 Yhency Brazoban/50 10.00
170 Angel Guzman/50 8.00
172 Adrian Gonzalez/50 12.00
173 Casey Kotchman/50 15.00

187 Bill Madlock/25 20.00
189 Billy Ripken/25 10.00
190 Gary Carter/25 25.00
191 Darryl Strawberry/25 20.00
192 Dave Parker/25 25.00
195 Fred Lynn/25 25.00
196 Jack Morris/25 25.00
198 Andre Dawson/25 25.00

Stars of MLB

NM/M
Complete Set (15): 20.00
Common Player: 1.00
Inserted 1:12
Foil: 2-4X
Production 100 Sets
Holo-Foil: 4-8X
Production 25 Sets
1 Randy Johnson 3.00
2 Adrian Beltre 1.00
3 Eric Chavez 1.00
4 Mike Mussina 1.50
5 Todd Helton 2.00
6 Curt Schilling 2.00
7 Miguel Cabrera 3.00
8 Kerry Wood 2.50
9 David Ortiz 3.00
10 Michael Young 2.00
11 Mark Mulder 1.00
12 Victor Martinez 1.00
13 Johan Santana 2.00
14 Scott Rolen 3.00
15 Carlos Beltran 2.00

Stars of MLB Material Bat

NM/M
Production 50-100
1 Randy Johnson/100 10.00
2 Adrian Beltre/100 5.00
3 Eric Chavez/100 5.00
4 Mike Mussina/100 8.00
5 Todd Helton/100 8.00
6 Curt Schilling/100 10.00
7 Miguel Cabrera/100 8.00
8 Kerry Wood/100 10.00
9 David Ortiz/100 10.00
10 Michael Young/100 8.00
11 Mark Mulder/100 8.00
14 Scott Rolen/100 8.00
15 Carlos Beltran/100 8.00

Stars of MLB Signature Material Bat

NM/M
Production 10-50
2 Adrian Beltre/50 25.00
3 Eric Chavez/50 50.00
8 Kerry Wood/25 50.00
9 David Ortiz/50 40.00
10 Michael Young/50 50.00
15 Carlos Beltran/25 50.00

Stars of MLB Material Jersey

NM/M
Production 100 Sets
Prime: 1-2X
Production 25 Sets
1 Randy Johnson/Pants 10.00
2 Adrian Beltre 5.00
3 Eric Chavez 5.00
4 Mike Mussina 8.00
5 Todd Helton 10.00
6 Curt Schilling 10.00
7 Miguel Cabrera 8.00
8 Kerry Wood 10.00
9 David Ortiz 12.00
10 Michael Young 5.00
11 Mark Mulder 5.00
12 Victor Martinez 10.00
13 Johan Santana 10.00
14 Scott Rolen 5.00
15 Carlos Beltran 8.00

Stars of MLB Signature Material Jersey

NM/M
Production 10-50

Prime: No Pricing
Production 5 Sets
2 Adrian Beltre/50 25.00
4 Eric Chavez/50 20.00
8 Kerry Wood/25 50.00
9 David Ortiz/50 40.00
10 Michael Young/50 25.00
12 Victor Martinez/50 20.00
13 Johan Santana/50 50.00
15 Carlos Beltran/25 50.00

2002 Poland Spring Boston Red Sox

This cello-wrapped stadium give-away set was sponsored by the team's bottled water concessionaire. Fronts have poses or action photos with team and sponsor logos in opposite corners. Backs have a U.S. flag ghost image in the background with a close-up repeat of the front photo. Personal data, '01 stats and career highlights appear along with the logos. The set is listed here by uniform number.

NM/M
Complete Set (24): 7.50
Common Player: .25
3 Grady Little .25
5 Nomar Garciaparra 2.00
7 Trot Nixon .50
10 Carlos Baerga .25
19 Johnny Damon .75
19 John Burkett .25
22 Tony Clark .25
23 Brian Daubach .25
24 Manny Ramirez 1.50
26 Lou Merloni .25
28 Doug Mirabelli .25
29 Shea Hillenbrand .25
30 Jose Offerman .25
32 Derek Lowe .25
33 Jason Varitek .25
34 Rich Garces .25
35 Rickey Henderson 1.50
37 Frank Castillo .25
41 Ugueth Urbina .25
44 Rolando Arrojo .25
45 Pedro Martinez 1.50
49 Tim Wakefield .25
--- Wally the Green Monster .25
--- Sponsor's Card .05

1985 Polaroid/J.C. Penney Indians

While the Cleveland Indians continued its four-year

tradition of baseball promotional game issues in 1985, the sponsor changed from Wheaties to Polaroid/J.C. Penney. The set features 30 player cards, a manager card and a group card of the coaching staff. Though produced in the "safety set" format - slightly oversize (2-13/16" by 4-1/8") with wide white borders - the Indians cards carry no safety message. Backs, once again numbered by uniform number, contain major and minor league stats.

NM/M
Complete Set (32): 9.00
Common Player: .50
2 Brett Butler .50
4 Tony Bernazard .50
8 Carmen Castillo .50
10 Pat Tabler .50
12 Benny Ayala .50
13 Ernie Camacho .50
14 Julio Franco .50
16 Jerry Willard .50
18 Pat Corrales .50
20 Otis Nixon .35
21 Mike Hargrove .50
22 Mike Fischlin .50
24 Chris Bando .50
24 George Vukovich .50
26 Brook Jacoby .50
27 Mel Hall .50
28 Bert Blyleven 1.00
29 Andre Thornton .30
30 Joe Carter .50
32 Rick Behenna .50
33 Roy Smith .50
35 Jerry Reed .50
36 Jamie Easterly .50
38 Dave Von Ohlen .50
41 Rich Thompson .50
43 Bryan Clark .50
44 Neal Heaton .50
48 Vern Ruhle .50
49 Jeff Barkley .50
50 Ramon Romero .50
54 Tom Waddell .50
--- Coaches (Bobby Bonds, Johnny Goryl, Don McMahon, Ed Napolean, Dennis Sommers) .50

1999 Pop Secret Detroit Tigers

This team set was sponsored by the snack food company and distributed at a promotional game at Tiger Stadium. The 2-1/2 x 3-1/2 cards have color photos which are borderless at top, bottom and right. At left are black and blue vertical stripes with player identification. Backs have a color portrait photo, career stats and team and sponsor logos. The unnumbered cards are checklisted here alphabetically.

NM/M
Complete Set (26): 9.00
Common Player: .50
(1) Matt Anderson .50
(2) Brad Ausmus .50
(3) Willie Blair .50
(4) Doug Brocail .50
(5) Frank Catalanotto .50
(6) Tony Clark .50
(7) Deivi Cruz .50
(8) Damion Easley .50
(9) Juan Encarnacion .50
(10) Karim Garcia .50
(11) Seth Greisinger .50
(12) Bill Haselman .50
(13) Bobby Higginson .50
(14) Gregg Jefferies .50
(15) Todd Jones .50
(16) Gabe Kapler 1.00

(17) Masao Kida .50
(18) Dave Mlicki .50
(19) Brian Moehler .50
(20) C.J. Nitkowski .50
(21) Dean Palmer .50
(22) Larry Parrish .50
(23) Luis Polonia .50
(24) Justin Thompson .50
(25) Jeff Weaver .50
(26) The Corner (Tiger Stadium) .50

1990 Post Cereal

Post Cereal returned in 1990 with a 30-card set. Card fronts feature borders in white, red and blue, with the Post logo at top-left and the Major League Baseball logo at top-right. Backs show complete major league statistics; underneath is a facsimile autograph. The player photos do not display team logos. Cards were included three per box, inside Alpha-Bits cereal. An uncut sheet version of the set was also offered in a run of 5,000 serially numbered pieces.

NM/M
Complete Set (30): 4.00
Common Player: .10
Uncut Sheet: 15.00
1 Don Mattingly .75
2 Roger Clemens .75
3 Kirby Puckett .60
4 George Brett .75
5 Tony Gwynn .60
6 Ozzie Smith .60
7 Will Clark .10
8 Orel Hershiser .10
9 Ryne Sandberg .60
10 Darryl Strawberry .10
11 Nolan Ryan 1.50
12 Mark McGwire 1.00
13 Jim Abbott .20
14 Bo Jackson .20
15 Kevin Mitchell .10
16 Jose Canseco .35
17 Wade Boggs .60
18 Dale Murphy .20
19 Mark Grace .10
20 Mike Scott .10
21 Cal Ripken, Jr. 1.50
22 Pedro Guerrero .10
23 Ken Griffey Jr. .85
24 Eric Davis .10
25 Rickey Henderson .45
26 Robin Yount .45
27 Von Hayes .10
28 Alan Trammell .10
29 Dwight Gooden .10
30 Joe Carter .10

1991 Post Cereal

These superstar trading cards were inserted in several brands of Post's children's cereals. The cards were produced by Mike Schechter Associates, Inc. and are authorized by the Players Association, but not MLB, so team logos have been removed from the photos. Card backs feature statistics and a facsimile autograph.

		NM/M
	Complete Set (30):	4.00
	Common Player:	.10
1	Dave Justice	.10
2	Mark McGwire	.75
3	Will Clark	.10
4	Jose Canseco	.30
5	Vince Coleman	.10
6	Sandy Alomar, Jr.	.10
7	Darryl Strawberry	.10
8	Len Dykstra	.10
9	Gregg Jefferies	.10
10	Tony Gwynn	.50
11	Ken Griffey Jr.	.75
12	Roger Clemens	.65
13	Chris Sabo	.10
14	Bobby Bonilla	.10
15	Gary Sheffield	.30
16	Ryne Sandberg	.50
17	Nolan Ryan	1.00
18	Barry Larkin	.10
19	Cal Ripken, Jr.	1.00
20	Jim Abbott	.10
21	Barry Bonds	1.00
22	Mark Grace	.10
23	Cecil Fielder	.10
24	Kevin Mitchell	.10
25	Todd Zeile	.10
26	George Brett	.65
27	Rickey Henderson	.45
28	Kirby Puckett	.50
29	Don Mattingly	.65
30	Kevin Maas	.10

1991 Post Cereal - Canadian

Specially-marked Post cereal boxes sold in Canada included one of 30 cards from a 1991 Super Star series. Cards are bilingual, and include player statistics and biographical information on the backs. The major league logos are airbrushed from the players caps and uniforms. American Leaguers. cards have blue stripes above and below the photo on front and as a back border color; National Leaguers are in red.

		NM/M
	Complete Set (30):	10.00
	Set in Album:	12.50
	Common Player:	.25
1	Delino DeShields	.25
2	Tim Wallach	.25
3	Andres Galarraga	.25
4	Dave Magadan	.25
5	Barry Bonds	2.00
6	Len Dykstra	.25
7	Andre Dawson	.35
8	Ozzie Smith	.65
9	Will Clark	.25
10	Chris Sabo	.25
11	Eddie Murray	.60
12	Dave Justice	.25
13	Benito Santiago	.25
14	Glenn Davis	.25
15	Kelly Gruber	.25
16	Dave Stieb	.25
17	John Olerud	.25
18	Roger Clemens	.85
19	Cecil Fielder	.25
20	Kevin Maas	.25
21	Robin Yount	.60
22	Cal Ripken, Jr.	2.00
23	Sandy Alomar	.25
24	Rickey Henderson	.60
25	Bobby Thigpen	.25
26	Ken Griffey Jr.	1.00
27	Nolan Ryan	2.00
28	Dave Winfield	.60
29	George Brett	.75
30	Kirby Puckett	.65

1992 Post Cereal

The addition of a back photo is notable on Post's 1992 set. Again packaged at

the rate of three cards in specially marked boxes, a complete set was available via a mail-in offer. Front photos have a blue strip at top with the Post logo at upper-left. A red stripe at bottom has the player's name and the logo of the Major League Baseball Players Association. The absence of a Major League Baseball logo, and the airbrushing of uniform logos on all photos identifies this set as the work of Mike Schechter Associates. Backs have a small photo at left, bordered in red. At right are biographical details, career stats and a facsimile autograph. The cards of 1991 Rookies of the Year Jeff Bagwell and Chuck Knoblauch are designated with a "Rookie Star" banner over the front photo.

		NM/M
	Complete Set (30):	3.00
	Common Player:	.10
1	Jeff Bagwell	.35
2	Ryne Sandberg	.45
3	Don Mattingly	.50
4	Wally Joyner	.10
5	Dwight Gooden	.10
6	Chuck Knoblauch	.10
7	Kirby Puckett	.45
8	Ozzie Smith	.45
9	Cal Ripken, Jr.	.75
10	Darryl Strawberry	.10
11	George Brett	.50
12	Joe Carter	.10
13	Cecil Fielder	.10
14	Will Clark	.10
15	Barry Bonds	.75
16	Roger Clemens	.50
17	Paul Molitor	.35
18	Scott Erickson	.10
19	Wade Boggs	.45
20	Ken Griffey Jr.	.60
21	Bobby Bonilla	.10
22	Terry Pendleton	.10
23	Barry Larkin	.10
24	Frank Thomas	.35
25	Jose Canseco	.25
26	Tony Gwynn	.45
27	Nolan Ryan	.75
28	Howard Johnson	.10
29	Dave Justice	.10
30	Danny Tartabull	.10

1992 Post Cereal - Canadian

For the second year in a row Post Cereal of Canada issued a set of cards inserted in cereal boxes. The 1992 cards have a player photo on front (with airbrushed cap) and information on the reverse in both English and French. The back of the card also contains an action

photo, which has a pop-up tab which when opened stands up, revealing a statistical base.

		NM/M
	Complete Set (18):	9.00
	Common Player:	.25
1	Dennis Martinez	.25
2	Benito Santiago	.25
3	Will Clark	.25
4	Ryne Sandberg	1.00
5	Tim Wallach	.25
6	Ozzie Smith	1.00
7	Darryl Strawberry	.25
8	Brett Butler	.25
9	Barry Bonds	2.00
10	Roger Clemens	1.25
11	Sandy Alomar	.25
12	Cecil Fielder	.25
13	Roberto Alomar	.35
14	Kelly Gruber	.25
15	Cal Ripken, Jr.	2.00
16	Jose Canseco	.50
17	Kirby Puckett	1.00
18	Rickey Henderson	.75

1993 Post Cereal

Post Cereal's 1993 Collectors Series cards feature a black border on the bottom and the right side, with the Post logo located at top right and the player's name, team and position along the bottom. Team logos have been air-brushed from the uniforms. Backs have a black background, a color player portrait photo, personal data, a career summary, 1992 and career stats, and a red strip with a white facsimile autograph. A special edition of 5,000 numbered uncut sheets was also produced.

		NM/M
	Complete Set (30):	3.00
	Common Player:	.10
	Uncut Sheet:	10.00
1	Dave Fleming	.10
2	Will Clark	.10
3	Kirby Puckett	.60
4	Roger Clemens	.65
5	Fred McGriff	.10
6	Eric Karros	.10
7	Ken Griffey Jr.	.75
8	Tony Gwynn	.60
9	Cal Ripken, Jr.	1.25
10	Cecil Fielder	.10
11	Gary Sheffield	.25
12	Don Mattingly	.65
13	Ryne Sandberg	.60
14	Frank Thomas	.50
15	Barry Bonds	1.25
16	Paul Molitor	.50
17	Terry Pendleton	.10
18	Darren Daulton	.10
19	Mark McGwire	1.00
20	Nolan Ryan	1.25
21	Tom Glavine	.30
22	Roberto Alomar	.20
23	Juan Gonzalez	.20
24	Bobby Bonilla	.10
25	George Brett	.60
26	Ozzie Smith	.60
27	Andy Van Slyke	.10
28	Barry Larkin	.10
29	John Kruk	.10
30	Robin Yount	.50

1993 Post Cereal - Canadian

For the third consecutive year, Post Canada produced a set of cards. The 1993 set features a two-sided card with one side containing a special pop-up feature, much the same as their 1992 offering. There are 18 black-bordered and gold-lettered cards in the set. The cards were available in specially-marked boxes of cereal.

		NM/M
	Complete Set (18):	10.00
	Common Player:	.25
1	Pat Borders	.25
2	Juan Guzman	.25
3	Roger Clemens	1.25
4	Joe Carter	.25
5	Roberto Alomar	.35
6	Robin Yount	.75
7	Cal Ripken, Jr.	3.00
8	Kirby Puckett	1.00
9	Ken Griffey Jr.	2.00
10	Darren Daulton	.25
11	Andy Van Slyke	.25
12	Bobby Bonilla	.25
13	Larry Walker	.25
14	Ryne Sandberg	1.00
15	Barry Larkin	.25
16	Gary Sheffield	.40
17	Ozzie Smith	1.00
18	Terry Pendleton	.25

1994 Post Cereal

Post cereals' 1994 set was issued three cards at a time in cellophane packages in cereal boxes. A special edition of 5,000 numbered 15-1/2" x 20-1/2" uncut sheets was also produced.

		NM/M
	Complete Set (30):	3.00
	Common Player:	.10
	Uncut Sheet:	15.00
1	Mike Piazza	.75
2	Don Mattingly	.65
3	Juan Gonzalez	.35
4	Kirby Puckett	.60
5	Gary Sheffield	.25
6	David Justice	.10
7	Jack McDowell	.10
8	Mo Vaughn	.10
9	Darren Daulton	.10
10	Bobby Bonilla	.10
11	Barry Bonds	1.00
12	Barry Larkin	.10
13	Tony Gwynn	.60
14	Mark Grace	.10
15	Ken Griffey Jr.	.75
16	Tom Glavine	.35
17	Cecil Fielder	.10
18	Roberto Alomar	.25
19	Mark Whiten	.10
20	Lenny Dykstra	.10
21	Frank Thomas	.45
22	Will Clark	.10
23	Andres Galarraga	.10
24	John Olerud	.10
25	Cal Ripken, Jr.	1.00
26	Tim Salmon	.10
27	Albert Belle	.10
28	Gregg Jefferies	.10
29	Jeff Bagwell	.45
30	Orlando Merced	.10

1994 Post Cereal - Canadian

The emphasis was on Expos and Blue Jays players in the 1994 Post cereal cards issued in Canada. Several of the cards featured gold-foil stamping on the fronts. Like all contemporary Post cards, the uniform logos were air-

brushed from the photos due to lack of licensing from Major League Baseball.

		NM/M
	Complete Set (18):	12.00
	Common Player:	.25
1	Joe Carter	1.00
2	Paul Molitor	.75
3	Roberto Alomar	.40
4	John Olerud	.25
5	Dave Stewart	.25
6	Juan Guzman	.25
7	Pat Borders	.25
8	Larry Walker	.25
9	Moises Alou	.25
10	Ken Griffey Jr.	1.50
11	Barry Bonds	2.50
12	Frank Thomas	.75
13	Cal Ripken, Jr.	2.50
14	Mike Piazza	1.50
15	Juan Gonzalez	.40
16	Lenny Dykstra	.25
17	David Justice	.25
18	Kirby Puckett	1.25

1995 Post Cereal

The 1995 Post Collector Series differs dramatically in format from the company's recent cereal-box insert issues. Each card measures 5" x 3-1/2" and is vertically scored at center to allow it to be folded. When folded, the front has a player action photo against a blue marbled background. On back is another photo, with career stats and highlights and a yellow facsimile autograph. In the center of the folded piece is a large game-action photo. All pictures have had the team logos removed for lack of a license by MLB. The cards are licensed by the Players Association. Complete sets of the '95 Post cards were available in a special cardboard display folder. Large quantities of the set made their way into dealer hands by 1998, and the value plummeted.

		NM/M
	Complete Set (18):	2.50
	Common Player:	.10
1	Wade Boggs	.60
2	Jeff Bagwell	.45
3	Greg Maddux	.60
4	Ken Griffey Jr.	.65
5	Roberto Alomar	.20
6	Kirby Puckett	.60
7	Tony Gwynn	.60
8	Cal Ripken Jr.	1.00
9	Matt Williams	.10
10	Dave Justice	.10
11	Barry Bonds	1.00
12	Mike Piazza	.65
13	Albert Belle	.10
14	Frank Thomas	.45
15	Len Dykstra	.10
16	Will Clark	.10

1995 Post Cereal - Canadian

Post cereals celebrated its fifth anniversary of baseball card production for the Canadian market by switching providers to Upper Deck, and issuing a high-quality album to house the 18-card set. Cards feature color action photos that are borderless at top, bottom and right.

At left is a vertical black marbled panel with the player's name, team and position. An Upper Deck logo is at top-right; a Post anniversary logo at lower-left. Because the cards are licensed by the Major League Players Association, but not Major League Baseball, team logos have been airbrushed from photos. Backs have another player photo plus bilingual biographical data, career highlights and stats for the previous five seasons and lifetime. A ghost image of the front photo appears under the typography. As might be expected, the set's roster is especially rich in Expos and Blue Jays players.

		NM/M
	Complete Set (18):	12.00
	Common Player:	.50
	Album:	6.00
1	Ken Griffey Jr.	2.00
2	Roberto Alomar	.35
3	Paul Molitor	.75
4	Devon White	.25
5	Moises Alou	.25
6	Ken Hill	.25
7	Paul O'Neill	.25
8	Joe Carter	.25
9	Kirby Puckett	1.50
10	Jimmy Key	.25
11	Frank Thomas	.75
12	David Cone	.25
13	Tony Gwynn	1.50
14	Matt Williams	.25
15	Jeff Bagwell	.75
16	Greg Maddux	1.50
17	Barry Bonds	3.00
18	Cal Ripken Jr.	3.00

2001 Post Collector's Series

JERMAINE DYE

(See 2001 Topps/Post Collector's Series.)

2001 Post 500 Home Run Club

FRANK ROBINSON
INDUCTED IN 1982
586 CAREER HOME RUNS

(See 2001 Topps/Post 500 Hom Run Club for checklist and values.)

2002 Post Collector's Series

(See 2002 Topps/Post Collector's Series.)

2003 Post MVP Action

(See 2003 Upper Deck/Post MVP Action.)

1985 P.R.E. Pete Rose Set

This 120-card set traces the career of Pete Rose through the 1985 season. Many cards feature photos used on earlier Topps cards. Each card, and the box in which they were sold, says the set was "Designed by Topps Chewing Gum Inc." The set was distributed within the hobby by Renata Galasso and the copyright-holder is identified as "P.R.E." (Pete Rose Enterprises?). Besides the Topps photos, the cards include a number of original paintings by Ron Lewis, a few family-album type photos and some game-action shots of career highlights. Backs of the first three cards offer complete minor and major league stats through 1985. Cards #4-90 have a question and answer format on back and the final 30 cards in the set have a puzzle-back depicting Rose's Topps cards in full color. Single cards from the set are seldom offered in the market. A borderless version of card #1 was issued in an edition of 1,000, all cards being autographed.

	NM/M
Complete Set (120):	15.00
Single Card:	.25
Autographed #1:	35.00
1-120 Pete Rose	.25

1986 Provigo Expos

11 DANN BILARDELLO provigo

This 28-card set was issued in three-card panels of 7-1/2" x 3-3/8". Each card measures 2-1/2" x 3-3/8", and each panel includes two players and an advertising card. Panels are perforated to allow for separation, if desired. Card fronts have high quality game-action color photos with the player's name, uniform number and Expos and Provigo logos. Card backs include biographical information in both French and English and list the card's number within the set. There are 24 player, one manager and two coaches cards, along with a card of the Expos mascot, Youppi.

	NM/M
Complete Panel Set:	3.00
Complete Singles Set:	2.50
Common Panel:	.15
Common Single Player:	.10
Album:	5.00

Panel 1		.15
1	Hubie Brooks	.10
2	Dann Bilardello	.10
----	Checklist	.02
Panel 2		.15
3	Buck Rodgers	.10
4	Andy McGaffigan	.10
----	Album Offer	.02
Panel 3		.15
5	Mitch Webster	.10
6	Jim Wohlford	.10
----	Album Offer	.02
Panel 4		1.00
7	Tim Raines	.35
8	Jay Tibbs	.10
----	Album Offer	.02
Panel 5		.75
9	Andre Dawson	.50
10	Andres Galarraga	.35
----	Album Offer	.02
Panel 6		.30
11	Tim Wallach	.10
12	Dan Schatzeder	.10
----	Checklist	.02
Panel 7		.15
13	Jeff Reardon	.10
14	Expos' Coaching Staff (Larry Bearnarth, Joe Kerrigan, Bobby Winkles)	.10
----	Album Offer	.02
Panel 8		.15
15	Jason Thompson	.10
16	Bert Roberge	.10
----	$1 Expos Ticket Coupon	.02
Panel 9		.15
17	Al Newman	.10
18	Tim Burke	.10
----	Album Offer	.02
Panel 10		.15
19	Bryn Smith	.10
20	Wayne Krenchicki	.10
----	Album Offer	.02
Panel 11		.15
21	Joe Hesketh	.10
22	Herman Winningham	.10
----	Album Offer	.02
Panel 12		.15
23	Vance Law	.10
24	Floyd Youmans	.10
----	Album Offer	.02
Panel 13		.15
25	Jeff Parrett	.10
26	Mike Fitzgerald	.10
----	Album Offer	.02
Panel 14		.15
27	Youppi/Mascot	.10
28	Expos' Coaching Staff (Ron Hansen, Ken Macha, Rick Renick)	.10
----	Album Offer	.02

1986 Provigo Expos Posters

This Provigo issue is much scarcer than the smaller card panels issued the same year. These posters measure about 9" x 14-7/8". A large (9" x 12-1/2") player portrait is separated from a bottom coupon panel. Backs are blank and can be found in red, white or blue. The player pictures have facsimile autographs and a white strip at bottom with identification, uniform number, team and sponsor logos and card number. Values shown are for complete poster/coupon combinations.

	NM/M
Complete Set (12):	20.00
Common Player:	2.00
1 Tim Raines	4.00
2 Bryn Smith	2.00
3 Hubie Brooks	2.00
4 Buck Rodgers	2.00
5 Mitch Webster	2.00
6 Joe Hesketh	2.00
7 Mike Fitzgerald	2.00
8 Andy McGaffigan	2.00
9 Andre Dawson	7.50
10 Tim Wallach	2.00
11 Jeff Reardon	2.00
12 Vance Law	2.00

1994 PruCare N.Y. Mets

Bobby Bonilla   #25 Infield

Top names on the 1994 Mets are featured in this issue sponsored by PruCare, a division of Prudential Insurance, whose logo appears on front and back. Cards were issued in a nine-card panel, perforated for easy separation. Individual cards are 2-1/2" x 3-1/2". Fronts have color action photos surrounded by team-color frames and white borders. Backs are printed in orange and blue with personal data, 1993 stats and highlights and career major league stats. The unnumbered cards are checklisted here in alphabetical order.

	NM/M
Complete Sheet:	3.50
Complete Set (9):	3.00
Common Player:	.50
(1)	Bobby Bonilla	.50
(2)	Jeromy Burnitz	.50
(3)	John Franco	.50
(4)	Dwight Gooden	.50
(5)	Bud Harrelson	.50
(6)	Jeff Kent	.50
(7)	Kevin McReynolds	.50
(8)	Ryan Thompson	.50
(9)	Mookie Wilson	.50

1990 Publications International Stickers

Nolan Ryan

This large set was issued in the form of an album with pages of bound-in stickers which were to be removed and placed in the appropriately numbered spots. Arranged by team, the album's spaces have a trivia question about the player whose sticker belongs there. The 1-3/8" x 1-3/4" stickers are unnumbered and are listed here according to the number of their album space.

		NM/M
Complete Album:		20.00
Complete Sticker Set (648):		15.00
Common Player:		.05
(1)	Dave Anderson	.05
(2)	Tim Belcher	.05
(3)	Mike Davis	.05
(4)	Rick Dempsey	.05
(5)	Kirk Gibson	.05
(6)	Alfredo Griffin	.05
(7)	Jeff Hamilton	.05
(8)	Mickey Hatcher	.05
(9)	Orel Hershiser	.05
(10)	Ricky Horton	.05
(11)	Jay Howell	.05
(12)	Tim Leary	.05
(13)	Mike Marshall	.05
(14)	Eddie Murray	.60
(15)	Alejandro Pena	.05
(16)	Willie Randolph	.05
(17)	Mike Scoscia	.05
(18)	John Shelby	.05
(19)	Franklin Stubbs	.05
(20)	John Tudor	.05
(21)	Fernando Valenzuela	.05
(22)	Todd Benzinger	.05
(23)	Tom Browning	.05
(24)	Norm Charlton	.05
(25)	Kal Daniels	.05
(26)	Eric Davis	.05
(27)	Bo Diaz	.05
(28)	Rob Dibble	.05
(29)	John Franco	.05
(30)	Ken Griffey Sr.	.05
(31)	Lenny Harris	.05
(32)	Danny Jackson	.05
(33)	Barry Larkin	.05
(34)	Rick Mahler	.05
(35)	Ron Oester	.05
(36)	Paul O'Neill	.05
(37)	Jeff Reed	.05
(38)	Jose Rijo	.05
(39)	Chris Sabo	.05
(40)	Kent Tekulve	.05
(41)	Manny Trillo	.05
(42)	Joel Youngblood	.05
(43)	Roberto Alomar	.15
(44)	Greg Booker	.05
(45)	Jack Clark	.05
(46)	Jerald Clark	.05
(47)	Mark Davis	.05
(48)	Tim Flannery	.05
(49)	Mark Grant	.05
(50)	Tony Gwynn	.75
(51)	Bruce Hurst	.05
(52)	John Kruk	.05
(53)	Dave Leiper	.05
(54)	Carmelo Martinez	.05
(55)	Mark Parent	.05
(56)	Dennis Rasmussen	.05
(57)	Randy Ready	.05
(58)	Benito Santiago	.05
(59)	Eric Show	.05
(60)	Garry Templeton	.05
(61)	Walt Terrell	.05
(62)	Ed Whitson	.05
(63)	Marvell Wynne	.05
(64)	Brett Butler	.05
(65)	Will Clark	.05
(66)	Kelly Downs	.05
(67)	Scott Garrelts	.05
(68)	Rich "Goose" Gossage	.05
(69)	Atlee Hammaker	.05
(70)	Tracy Jones	.05
(71)	Terry Kennedy	.05
(72)	Mike Krukow	.05
(73)	Mike LaCoss	.05
(74)	Craig Lefferts	.05
(75)	Candy Maldonado	.05
(76)	Kirt Manwaring	.05
(77)	Kevin Mitchell	.05
(78)	Donell Nixon	.05
(79)	Rick Reuschel	.05
(80)	Ernest Riles	.05
(81)	Don Robinson	.05
(82)	Chris Speier	.05
(83)	Robby Thompson	.05
(84)	Jose Uribe	.05
(85)	Juan Agosto	.05
(86)	Larry Andersen	.05
(87)	Kevin Bass	.05
(88)	Craig Biggio	.05
(89)	Ken Caminiti	.05
(90)	Jim Clancy	.05
(91)	Danny Darwin	.05
(92)	Glenn Davis	.05
(93)	Jim Deshaies	.05
(94)	Bill Doran	.05
(95)	Bob Forsch	.05
(96)	Billy Hatcher	.05
(97)	Bob Knepper	.05
(98)	Terry Puhl	.05
(99)	Rafael Ramirez	.05
(100)	Craig Reynolds	.05
(101)	Rick Rhoden	.05
(102)	Mike Scott	.05
(103)	Dave Smith	.05
(104)	Alex Trevino	.05
(105)	Gerald Young	.05
(106)	Jose Alvarez	.05
(107)	Paul Assenmacher	.05
(108)	Bruce Benedict	.05
(109)	Jeff Blauser	.05
(110)	Joe Boever	.05
(111)	Jody Davis	.05
(112)	Darrell Evans	.05
(113)	Ron Gant	.05
(114)	Tommy Gregg	.05
(115)	Dion James	.05
(116)	Derek Lilliquist	.05
(117)	Dale Murphy	.20
(118)	Gerald Perry	.05
(119)	Charlie Puleo	.05
(120)	John Russell	.05
(121)	Lonnie Smith	.05
(122)	Pete Smith	.05
(123)	Zane Smith	.05
(124)	John Smoltz	.05
(125)	Bruce Sutter	.20
(126)	Andres Thomas	.05
(127)	Rick Aguilera	.05
(128)	Gary Carter	.60
(129)	David Cone	.05
(130)	Ron Darling	.05
(131)	Lenny Dykstra	.05
(132)	Kevin Elster	.05
(133)	Sid Fernandez	.05
(134)	Dwight Gooden	.05
(135)	Keith Hernandez	.05
(136)	Gregg Jeffries	.05
(137)	Howard Johnson	.05
(138)	Dave Magadan	.05
(139)	Lee Mazzilli	.05
(140)	Roger McDowell	.05
(141)	Kevin McReynolds	.05
(142)	Randy Myers	.05
(143)	Bob Ojeda	.05
(144)	Mackey Sasser	.05
(145)	Darryl Strawberry	.05
(146)	Tim Teufel	.05
(147)	Mookie Wilson	.05
(148)	Rafael Belliard	.05
(149)	Barry Bonds	1.50
(150)	Bobby Bonilla	.05
(151)	Sid Bream	.05
(152)	Benny Distefano	.05
(153)	Doug Drabek	.05
(154)	Brian Fisher	.05
(155)	Jim Gott	.05
(156)	Neal Heaton	.05
(157)	Bill Landrum	.05
(158)	Mike LaValliere	.05
(159)	Jose Lind	.05
(160)	Junior Ortiz	.05
(161)	Tom Prince	.05
(162)	Gary Redus	.05
(163)	R.J. Reynolds	.05
(164)	Jeff Robinson	.05
(165)	John Smiley	.05
(166)	Andy Van Slyke	.05
(167)	Bob Walk	.05
(168)	Glenn Wilson	.05
(169)	Hubie Brooks	.05
(170)	Tim Burke	.05
(171)	Mike Fitzgerald	.05
(172)	Tom Foley	.05
(173)	Andres Galarraga	.05
(174)	Kevin Gross	.05
(175)	Joe Hesketh	.05
(176)	Brian Holman	.05
(177)	Rex Hudler	.05
(178)	Wallace Johnson	.05
(179)	Mark Langston	.05
(180)	Dave Martinez	.05
(181)	Dennis Martinez	.05
(182)	Andy McGaffigan	.05
(183)	Otis Nixon	.05
(184)	Spike Owen	.05
(185)	Pascual Perez	.05
(186)	Tim Raines	.05
(187)	Nelson Santovenia	.05
(188)	Bryn Smith	.05
(189)	Tim Wallach	.05
(190)	Damon Berryhill	.05
(191)	Mike Bielecki	.05
(192)	Andre Dawson	.20
(193)	Shawon Dunston	.05
(194)	Mark Grace	.05
(195)	Darrin Jackson	.05
(196)	Paul Kilgus	.05
(197)	Vance Law	.05
(198)	Greg Maddux	.75
(199)	Pat Perry	.05
(200)	Jeff Pico	.05
(201)	Ryne Sandberg	.75
(202)	Scott Sanderson	.05
(203)	Calvin Schiraldi	.05
(204)	Dwight Smith	.05
(205)	Rick Sutcliffe	.05
(206)	Gary Varsho	.05
(207)	Jerome Walton	.05
(208)	Mitch Webster	.05
(209)	Curtis Wilkerson	.05
(210)	Mitch Williams	.05
(211)	Tom Brunansky	.05
(212)	Cris Carpenter	.05
(213)	Vince Coleman	.05
(214)	John Costello	.05
(215)	Danny Cox	.05
(216)	Ken Dayley	.05
(217)	Jose DeLeon	.05
(218)	Frank DiPino	.05
(219)	Pedro Guerrero	.05
(220)	Joe Magrane	.05
(221)	Greg Mathews	.05
(222)	Willie McGee	.05
(223)	Jose Oquendo	.05
(224)	Tom Pagnozzi	.05
(225)	Tony Pena	.05
(226)	Terry Pendleton	.05
(227)	Dan Quisenberry	.05
(228)	Ozzie Smith	.75
(229)	Scott Terry	.05
(230)	Milt Thompson	.05
(231)	Todd Worrell	.05
(232)	Steve Bedrosian	.05
(233)	Don Carman	.05
(234)	Darren Daulton	.05
(235)	Bob Dernier	.05
(236)	Marvin Freeman	.05
(237)	Greg Harris	.05
(238)	Von Hayes	.05
(239)	Tommy Herr	.05
(240)	Ken Howell	.05
(241)	Chris James	.05
(242)	Steve Jeltz	.05
(243)	Ron Jones	.05
(244)	Ricky Jordan	.05
(245)	Steve Lake	.05
(246)	Mike Maddux	.05
(247)	Larry McWilliams	.05
(248)	Jeff Parrett	.05
(249)	Juan Samuel	.05
(250)	Mike Schmidt	.85
(251)	Dickie Thon	.05
(252)	Floyd Youmans	.05
(253)	Bobby Bonilla/AS	.05
(254)	Will Clark/AS	.05
(255)	Eric Davis/AS	.05
(256)	Andre Dawson/AS	.05
(257)	Bill Doran/AS	.05
(258)	John Franco/AS	.05
(259)	Kirk Gibson/AS	.05
(260)	Dwight Gooden/AS	.05
(261)	Tony Gwynn/AS	.35
(262)	Keith Hernandez/AS	.05
(263)	Orel Hershiser/AS	.05
(264)	Danny Jackson/AS	.05
(265)	Howard Johnson/AS	.05
(266)	Barry Larkin/AS	.05
(267)	Joe Magrane/AS	.05
(268)	Kevin McReynolds/AS	.05
(269)	Tony Pena/AS	.05
(270)	Ryne Sandberg/AS	.35
(271)	Benito Santiago/AS	.05
(272)	Ozzie Smith/AS	.35
(273)	Darryl Strawberry/AS	.05
(274)	Todd Worrell/AS	.05
(275)	Harold Baines/AS	.05
(276)	George Bell/AS	.05
(277)	Wade Boggs/AS	.35
(278)	Bob Boone/AS	.05
(279)	Jose Canseco/AS	.20
(280)	Joe Carter/AS	.05
(281)	Roger Clemens/AS	.40
(282)	Dennis Eckersley/AS	.25
(283)	Tony Fernandez/AS	.05
(284)	Carlton Fisk/AS	.30
(285)	Julio Franco/AS	.05
(286)	Gary Gaetti/AS	.05
(287)	Mike Greenwell/AS	.05
(288)	Rickey Henderson/AS	.30
(289)	Teddy Higuera/AS	.05
(290)	Kent Hrbek/AS	.05
(291)	Don Mattingly/AS	.40
(292)	Kirby Puckett/AS	.35
(293)	Jeff Reardon/AS	.05
(294)	Harold Reynolds/AS	.05
(295)	Dave Stewart/AS	.05
(296)	Alan Trammell/AS	.05
(297)	Frank Viola/AS	.05
(298)	Dave Winfield/AS	.30
(299)	Todd Burns	.05
(300)	Greg Cadaret	.05
(301)	Jose Canseco	.30
(302)	Storm Davis	.05
(303)	Dennis Eckersley	.45
(304)	Mike Gallego	.05
(305)	Ron Hassey	.05
(306)	Dave Henderson	.05
(307)	Rick Honeycutt	.05
(308)	Stan Javier	.05
(309)	Carney Lansford	.05
(310)	Mark McGwire	1.25
(311)	Mike Moore	.05
(312)	Dave Parker	.05
(313)	Eric Plunk	.05
(314)	Luis Polonia	.05
(315)	Terry Steinbach	.05
(316)	Dave Stewart	.05
(317)	Walt Weiss	.05
(318)	Bob Welch	.05
(319)	Curt Young	.05
(320)	Allan Anderson	.05
(321)	Wally Backman	.05
(322)	Doug Baker	.05
(323)	Juan Berenguer	.05
(324)	Randy Bush	.05
(325)	Jim Dwyer	.05
(326)	Gary Gaetti	.05
(327)	Greg Gagne	.05

ABBREVIATIONS

AS - All-Star

(328)	Dan Gladden	.05
(329)	Brian Harper	.05
(330)	Kent Hrbek	.05
(331)	Gene Larkin	.05
(332)	Tim Laudner	.05
(333)	John Moses	.05
(334)	Al Newman	.05
(335)	Kirby Puckett	.75
(336)	Shane Rawley	.05
(337)	Jeff Reardon	.05
(338)	Steve Shields	.05
(339)	Frank Viola	.05
(340)	Gary Wayne	.05
(341)	Luis Aquino	.05
(342)	Floyd Bannister	.05
(343)	Bob Boone	.05
(344)	George Brett	.85
(345)	Bill Buckner	.10
(346)	Jim Eisenreich	.05
(347)	Steve Farr	.05
(348)	Tom Gordon	.05
(349)	Mark Gubicza	.05
(350)	Bo Jackson	.10
(351)	Charlie Leibrandt	.05
(352)	Mike Macfarlane	.05
(353)	Jeff Montgomery	.05
(354)	Bret Saberhagen	.05
(355)	Kevin Seitzer	.05
(356)	Kurt Stillwell	.05
(357)	Pat Tabler	.05
(358)	Danny Tartabull	.05
(359)	Gary Thurman	.05
(360)	Frank White	.05
(361)	Willie Wilson	.05
(362)	Jim Abbott	.05
(363)	Kent Anderson	.05
(364)	Tony Armas	.05
(365)	Dante Bichette	.05
(366)	Bert Blyleven	.05
(367)	Chili Davis	.05
(368)	Brian Downing	.05
(369)	Chuck Finley	.05
(370)	Willie Fraser	.05
(371)	Jack Howell	.05
(372)	Wally Joyner	.05
(373)	Kirk McCaskill	.05
(374)	Bob McClure	.05
(375)	Greg Minton	.05
(376)	Lance Parrish	.05
(377)	Dan Petry	.05
(378)	Johnny Ray	.05
(379)	Dick Schofield	.05
(380)	Claudell Washington	.05
(381)	Devon White	.05
(382)	Mike Witt	.05
(383)	Harold Baines	.05
(384)	Daryl Boston	.05
(385)	Ivan Calderon	.05
(386)	Carlton Fisk	.60
(387)	Dave Gallagher	.05
(388)	Ozzie Guillen	.05
(389)	Shawn Hillegas	.05
(390)	Barry Jones	.05
(391)	Ron Karkovice	.05
(392)	Eric King	.05
(393)	Ron Kittle	.05
(394)	Bill Long	.05
(395)	Steve Lyons	.05
(396)	Fred Manrique	.05
(397)	Donn Pall	.05
(398)	Dan Pasqua	.05
(399)	Melido Perez	.05
(400)	Jerry Reuss	.05
(401)	Bobby Thigpen	.05
(402)	Greg Walker	.05
(403)	Eddie Williams	.05
(404)	Buddy Bell	.05
(405)	Kevin Brown	.05
(406)	Steve Buechele	.05
(407)	Cecil Espy	.05
(408)	Scott Fletcher	.05
(409)	Julio Franco	.05
(410)	Cecilio Guante	.05
(411)	Jose Guzman	.05
(412)	Charlie Hough	.05
(413)	Pete Incaviglia	.05
(414)	Chad Kreuter	.05
(415)	Jeff Kunkel	.05
(416)	Rick Leach	.05
(417)	Jamie Moyer	.05
(418)	Rafael Palmeiro	.50
(419)	Geno Petralli	.05
(420)	Jeff Russell	.05
(421)	Nolan Ryan	1.50
(422)	Ruben Sierra	.05
(423)	Jim Sundberg	.05
(424)	Bobby Witt	.05
(425)	Steve Balboni	.05
(426)	Scott Bankhead	.05
(427)	Scott Bradley	.05
(428)	Mickey Brantley	.05
(429)	Darnell Coles	.05
(430)	Henry Cotto	.05
(431)	Alvin Davis	.05
(432)	Mario Diaz	.05
(433)	Ken Griffey Jr.	1.00
(434)	Erik Hanson	.05
(435)	Mike Jackson	.05
(436)	Jeffrey Leonard	.05
(437)	Edgar Martinez	.05
(438)	Tom Niedenfuer	.05
(439)	Jim Presley	.05
(440)	Jerry Reed	.05
(441)	Harold Reynolds	.05
(442)	Bill Swift	.05
(443)	Steve Trout	.05
(444)	Dave Valle	.05
(445)	Omar Vizquel	.05

(446)	Marty Barrett	.05
(447)	Mike Boddicker	.05
(448)	Wade Boggs	.75
(449)	Dennis "Oil Can" Boyd	.05
(450)	Ellis Burks	.05
(451)	Rick Cerone	.05
(452)	Roger Clemens	.85
(453)	Nick Esasky	.05
(454)	Dwight Evans	.05
(455)	Wes Gardner	.05
(456)	Rich Gedman	.05
(457)	Mike Greenwell	.05
(458)	Sam Horn	.05
(459)	Randy Kutcher	.05
(460)	Dennis Lamp	.05
(461)	Rob Murphy	.05
(462)	Jody Reed	.05
(463)	Jim Rice	.10
(464)	Lee Smith	.05
(465)	Mike Smithson	.05
(466)	Bob Stanley	.05
(467)	Doyle Alexander	.05
(468)	Dave Bergman	.05
(469)	Chris Brown	.05
(470)	Paul Gibson	.05
(471)	Mike Heath	.05
(472)	Mike Henneman	.05
(473)	Guillermo Hernandez	.05
(474)	Charles Hudson	.05
(475)	Chet Lemon	.05
(476)	Fred Lynn	.05
(477)	Keith Moreland	.05
(478)	Jack Morris	.05
(479)	Matt Nokes	.05
(480)	Gary Pettis	.05
(481)	Jeff Robinson	.05
(482)	Pat Sheridan	.05
(483)	Frank Tanana	.05
(484)	Alan Trammell	.05
(485)	Lou Whitaker	.05
(486)	Frank Williams	.05
(487)	Kenny Williams	.05
(488)	Don August	.05
(489)	Mike Birkbeck	.05
(490)	Chris Bosio	.05
(491)	Glenn Braggs	.05
(492)	Greg Brock	.05
(493)	Chuck Crim	.05
(494)	Rob Deer	.05
(495)	Mike Felder	.05
(496)	Jim Gantner	.05
(497)	Ted Higuera	.05
(498)	Joey Meyer	.05
(499)	Paul Mirabella	.05
(500)	Paul Molitor	.60
(501)	Juan Nieves	.05
(502)	Charlie O'Brien	.05
(503)	Dan Plesac	.05
(504)	Gary Sheffield	.30
(505)	B.J. Surhoff	.05
(506)	Dale Sveum	.05
(507)	Bill Wegman	.05
(508)	Robin Yount	.60
(509)	George Bell	.05
(510)	Pat Borders	.05
(511)	John Cerutti	.05
(512)	Rob Ducey	.05
(513)	Tony Fernandez	.05
(514)	Mike Flanagan	.05
(515)	Kelly Gruber	.05
(516)	Tom Henke	.05
(517)	Alexis Infante	.05
(518)	Jimmy Key	.05
(519)	Tom Lawless	.05
(520)	Manny Lee	.05
(521)	Al Leiter	.05
(522)	Nelson Liriano	.05
(523)	Fred McGriff	.05
(524)	Lloyd Moseby	.05
(525)	Rance Mulliniks	.05
(526)	Dave Steib	.05
(527)	Todd Stottlemyre	.05
(528)	Duane Ward	.05
(529)	Ernie Whitt	.05
(530)	Jesse Barfield	.05
(531)	Bob Brower	.05
(532)	John Candelaria	.05
(533)	Richard Dotson	.05
(534)	Lee Guetterman	.05
(535)	Mel Hall	.05
(536)	Andy Hawkins	.05
(537)	Rickey Henderson	.60
(538)	Roberto Kelly	.05
(539)	Dave LaPoint	.05
(540)	Don Mattingly	.85
(541)	Lance McCullers	.05
(542)	Mike Pagliarulo	.05
(543)	Clay Parker	.05
(544)	Ken Phelps	.05
(545)	Dave Righetti	.05
(546)	Rafael Santana	.05
(547)	Steve Sax	.05
(548)	Don Slaught	.05
(549)	Wayne Tolleson	.05
(550)	Dave Winfield	.60
(551)	Andy Allanson	.05
(552)	Keith Atherton	.05
(553)	Scott Bailes	.05
(554)	Bud Black	.05
(555)	Jerry Browne	.05
(556)	Tom Candiotti	.05
(557)	Joe Carter	.05
(558)	David Clark	.05
(559)	John Farrell	.05
(560)	Felix Fermin	.05
(561)	Brook Jacoby	.05
(562)	Doug Jones	.05
(563)	Oddibe McDowell	.05

(564)	Luis Medina	.05
(565)	Pete O'Brien	.05
(566)	Jesse Orosco	.05
(567)	Joel Skinner	.05
(568)	Cory Snyder	.05
(569)	Greg Swindell	.05
(570)	Rich Yett	.05
(571)	Mike Young	.05
(572)	Brady Anderson	.05
(573)	Jeff Ballard	.05
(574)	Jose Bautista	.05
(575)	Phil Bradley	.05
(576)	Mike Devereaux	.05
(577)	Kevin Hickey	.05
(578)	Brian Holton	.05
(579)	Bob Melvin	.05
(580)	Bob Milacki	.05
(581)	Gregg Olson	.05
(582)	Joe Orsulak	.05
(583)	Bill Ripken	.05
(584)	Cal Ripken Jr.	1.50
(585)	Dave Schmidt	.05
(586)	Larry Sheets	.05
(587)	Mickey Tettleton	.05
(588)	Mark Thurmond	.05
(589)	Jay Tibbs	.05
(590)	Jim Traber	.05
(591)	Mark Williamson	.05
(592)	Craig Worthington	.05
(593)	Allan Anderson	.05
(594)	Ellis Burks	.05
(595)	Ken Griffey Jr.	1.00
(596)	Bo Jackson	.05
(597)	Roberto Kelly	.05
(598)	Kirk McCaskill	.05
(599)	Fred McGriff	.05
(600)	Mark McGwire	1.25
(601)	Bob Milacki	.05
(602)	Melido Perez	.05
(603)	Jeff Robinson	.05
(604)	Gary Sheffield	.05
(605)	Ruben Sierra	.05
(606)	Greg Swindell	.05
(607)	Roberto Alomar	.15
(608)	Tim Belcher	.05
(609)	Vince Coleman	.05
(610)	Kal Daniels	.05
(611)	Andres Galarraga	.05
(612)	Ron Gant	.05
(613)	Mark Grace	.05
(614)	Gregg Jeffries	.05
(615)	Ricky Jordan	.05
(616)	Jose Lind	.05
(617)	Kevin Mitchell	.05
(618)	Gerald Young	.05
(619)	Base	.05
(620)	Batting Helmets	.05
(621)	Bats	.05
(622)	Batting Gloves	.05
(623)	Los Angeles Dodgers	.05
(624)	Cincinnati Reds	.05
(625)	San Diego Padres	.05
(626)	San Francisco Giants	.05
(627)	Houston Astros	.05
(628)	Atlanta Braves	.05
(629)	New York Mets	.05
(630)	Pittsburgh Pirates	.05
(631)	Montreal Expos	.05
(632)	Chicago Cubs	.05
(633)	St. Louis Cardinals	.05
(634)	Philadelphia Phillies	.05
(635)	Oakland A's	.05
(636)	Minnesota Twins	.05
(637)	Kansas City Royals	.05
(638)	California Angels	.05
(639)	Chicago White Sox	.05
(640)	Texas Rangers	.05
(641)	Seattle Mariners	.05
(642)	Boston Red Sox	.05
(643)	Detroit Tigers	.05
(644)	Milwaukee Brewers	.05
(645)	Toronto Blue Jays	.05
(646)	New York Yankees	.05
(647)	Cleveland Indians	.05
(648)	Baltimore Orioles	.05

Stickers have color action photos with a white frame at center. There is a red stripe at top of the frame and a blue stripe at bottom, which contains the player name. The unnumbered stickers are checklisted here in alphabetical order.

		NM/M
Complete Set, W/Album (56):		4.00
Common Player:		.05
(1)	George Bell	.05
(2)	Wade Boggs	.50
(3)	Bobby Bonilla	.05
(4)	Jose Canseco	.25
(5)	Joe Carter	.05
(6)	Will Clark	.05
(7)	Roger Clemens	.60
(8)	Alvin Davis	.05
(9)	Eric Davis	.05
(10)	Glenn Davis	.05
(11)	Mark Davis	.05
(12)	Carlton Fisk	.35
(13)	John Franco	.05
(14)	Gary Gaetti	.05
(15)	Andres Galarraga	.05
(16)	Dwight Gooden	.05
(17)	Mark Grace	.05
(18)	Pedro Guerrero	.05
(19)	Tony Gwynn	.50
(20)	Rickey Henderson	.35
(21)	Orel Hershiser	.05
(22)	Bo Jackson	.05
(23)	Ricky Jordan	.05
(24)	Wally Joyner	.05
(25)	Don Mattingly	.60
(26)	Fred McGriff	.05
(27)	Kevin Mitchell	.05
(28)	Paul Molitor	.35
(29)	Dale Murphy	.05
(30)	Eddie Murray	.35
(31)	Kirby Puckett	.50
(32)	Tim Raines	.05
(33)	Harold Reynolds	.05
(34)	Cal Ripken Jr.	1.00
(35)	Nolan Ryan	1.00
(36)	Bret Saberhagen	.05
(37)	Ryne Sandberg	.50
(38)	Steve Sax	.05
(39)	Mike Scott	.05
(40)	Ruben Sierra	.05
(41)	Ozzie Smith	.50
(42)	John Smoltz	.05
(43)	Darryl Strawberry	.05
(44)	Greg Swindell	.05
(45)	Mickey Tettleton	.05
(46)	Alan Trammell	.05
(47)	Andy Van Slyke	.05
(48)	Lou Whitaker	.05
(49)	Devon White	.05
(50)	Robin Yount	.35
(51)	Dodger Stadium	.05
(52)	Jack Murphy Stadium	.05
(53)	Shea Stadium	.05
(54)	Three Rivers Stadium	.05
(55)	Tiger Stadium	.05
(56)	Yankee Stadium	.05

Hottest Rookies Stickers

This set of large-format (4-1/8" x 5-7/16") stickers features the rookie crop of 1990 along with other young players who were not technically rookies in 1990. The stickers were sold four per sheet in complete sets which included a 36-page color album to mount the stamps. The album pages have personal data, career stats and highlights about each player. On the stickers, each action photo has a central frame in white with a blue stripe at top and a red stripe at bottom bearing the player name. Backs are, of course, blank. The set is checklisted here alphabetically.

	NM/M
Complete Set, W/Album (56):	4.00
Common Player:	.05

Hottest Players Stickers

RYNE SANDBERG

Established major league stars are featured in this set of large format (4-1/8" x 5-7/16") blank-back stickers. The stickers are printed four per sheet and were sold with a 36-page album for mounting. The album has player data, stats and highlights for each of the stars.

(1)	Jim Abbott	.05
(2)	Sandy Alomar	.05
(3)	Kent Anderson	.05
(4)	Eric Anthony	.05
(5)	Jeff Ballard	.05
(6)	Joey Belle	.15
(7)	Andy Benes	.05
(8)	Lance Blankenship	.05
(9)	Jeff Brantley	.05
(10)	Cris Carpenter	.05
(11)	Mark Carreon	.05
(12)	Dennis Cook	.05
(13)	Scott Coolbaugh	.05
(14)	Luis de los Santos	.05
(15)	Junior Felix	.05
(16)	Mark Gardner	.05
(17)	German Gonzalez	.05
(18)	Tom Gordon	.05
(19)	Ken Griffey Jr.	2.00
(20)	Marquis Grissom	.05
(21)	Charlie Hayes	.05
(22)	Gregg Jefferies	.05
(23)	Randy Johnson	1.00
(24)	Felix Jose	.05
(25)	Jeff King	.05
(26)	Randy Kramer	.05
(27)	Derek Lilliquist	.05
(28)	Greg Litton	.05
(29)	Kelly Mann	.05
(30)	Ramon Martinez	.05
(31)	Luis Medina	.05
(32)	Hal Morris	.05
(33)	Joe Oliver	.05
(34)	Gregg Olson	.05
(35)	Dean Palmer	.05
(36)	Carlos Quintana	.05
(37)	Kevin Ritz	.05
(38)	Deion Sanders	.05
(39)	Scott Scudder	.05
(40)	Steve Searcy	.05
(41)	Gary Sheffield	.25
(42)	Dwight Smith	.05
(43)	Sam Sosa	1.50
(44)	Greg Vaughn	.05
(45)	Robin Ventura	.05
(46)	Jerome Walton	.05
(47)	Dave West	.05
(48)	John Wetteland	.05
(49)	Eric Yelding	.05
(50)	Todd Zeile	.05
(51)	Dodger Stadium	.05
(52)	Jack Murphy Stadium	.05
(53)	Shea Stadium	.05
(54)	Three Rivers Stadium	.05
(55)	Tiger Stadium	.05
(56)	Yankee Stadium	.05

1993 Publix Florida Marlins

BRYAN HARVEY

		NM/M
Complete Set (29):		10.00
Common Player:		.50
6	Rich Renteria	.50
8	Bret Barbarie	.50
09	Benito Santiago	.50
10	Gary Sheffield	1.50
13	Chris Hammond	.50
13	Bob Natal	.50
15	Rene Lachemann	.50
17	Darrell Whitmore	.50
19	Jeff Conine	.50
20	Greg Briley	.50
21	Chuck Carr	.50
22	Walt Weiss	.50
24	Richie Lewis	.50
26	Alex Arias	.50
27	Luis Aquino	.50
29	Henry Cotto	.50
30	Nigel Wilson	.50
31	Robb Nen	.50
34	Bryan Harvey	.50
42	Orestes Destrade	.50
43	Rich Rodriguez	.50
46	Ryan Bowen	.50
48	Pat Rapp	.50
49	Charlie Hough	.50
54	Matt Turner	.50
58	Joe Klink	.50
77	Jack Armstrong	.50
---	Marlins Coaches	
	(Marcel Lachemann, Doug Rader, Vada Pinson, Frank Reberger, Cookie Rojas)	.50
---	Billy/Mascot	.50
---	$1 Coke-Publix Coupon	.50

Q

DON MATTINGLY
NEW YORK YANKEES

1986 Quaker Oats

The Quaker Co., in conjunction with Topps, produced this 33-card set of current baseball stars for packaging in groups of three in Chewy Granola Bars packages. The cards are noted as the "1st Annual Collectors Edition." They are numbered and measure 2-1/2" x 3-1/2". Card fronts feature full-color player photos with the product name at the top and the player name, team and position below the photo. The complete set was offered via mail order by the Quaker Company.

		NM/M
Complete Set (33):		4.00
Common Player:		.05
1	Willie McGee	.05
2	Dwight Gooden	.05
3	Vince Coleman	.05
4	Gary Carter	.50
5	Jack Clark	.05
6	Steve Garvey	.15
7	Tony Gwynn	.65
8	Dale Murphy	.25
9	Dave Parker	.05
10	Tim Raines	.05
11	Pete Rose	1.00
12	Nolan Ryan	1.50
13	Ryne Sandberg	.65
14	Mike Schmidt	.75
15	Ozzie Smith	.65
16	Darryl Strawberry	.65
17	Fernando Valenzuela	.05
18	Don Mattingly	.75
19	Bret Saberhagen	.05
20	Ozzie Guillen	.05
21	Bert Blyleven	.05
22	Wade Boggs	.65
23	George Brett	.75
24	Darrell Evans	.05
25	Rickey Henderson	.50
26	Reggie Jackson	.50
27	Eddie Murray	.50
28	Phil Niekro	.25
29	Dan Quisenberry	.05
30	Jim Rice	.15
31	Cal Ripken, Jr.	1.50
32	Tom Seaver	.65
33	Dave Winfield	.50
----	Offer Card	.03

R

1993 Rainbow Foods Dave Winfield

Dave Winfield's return to Minnesota where he excelled in college sports was marked by the "Homecoming Collection," tracing the future Hall of Famer's career. The 2-1/2" x 3-1/2" cards have black-and-white or color photos on front and back. Each side also sports a special logo identifying the issue. Rainbow's logo appears on front, while that of a major food brand such as Kraft or Oscar Mayer appear on back, along with information about Winfield's career. Cards were sold in five-card packs with four blue-bordered cards and one gold-bordered parallel card.

	NM/M
Complete Set, Blue (10):	7.50
Common Player, Blue:	1.00
Gold:	2-3X
1 Dave Winfield (University of Minnesota Outfielder)	1.00
2 Dave Winfield (University of Minnesota Pitcher)	1.00
3 Dave Winfield (University of Minnesota Basketball Star)	1.00
4 Dave Winfield (San Diego Padres 1973-1980)	1.00
5 Dave Winfield (N.Y. Yankees 1981-1990)	1.00
6 Dave Winfield (California Angels 1990-1991)	1.00
7 Dave Winfield (Toronto Blue Jays 1992)	1.00
8 Dave Winfield (Minnesota Twins 1993-)	1.00
9 Dave Winfield (7-time Gold Glove Winner)	1.00
10 Dave Winfield (Pride of Minnesota)	1.00

2001 Rainbow Foods Minnesota Twins 10th Anniversary

As part of a three-game celebration of the 10th annivsary of the Twins 1991 World's Championship, Rainbow Foods sponsored a team-set card giveaway on June 29, distributing 10,000 sets. Fronts of the 2-1/2" x 3-1/2" cards have borderless game-action photos with an anniversary logo. Backs have team and sponsor logos and player career highlights on a baseball diamond design in color. The unnumbered cards are checklisted here in alphabetical order.

	NM/M
Complete Set (26):	9.00
Common Player:	.25
(1) Rick Aguilera	.25
(2) Steve Bedrosian	.25
(3) Jarvis Brown	.25
(4) Randy Bush	.25
(5) Chili Davis	.25
(6) Scott Erickson	.25
(7) Greg Gagne	.25
(8) Dan Gladden	.25
(9) Mark Guthrie	.25
(10) Brian Harper	.25
(11) Kent Hrbek	.50
(12) Tom Kelly	.25
(13) Chuck Knoblauch	.25
(14) Gene Larkin	.25
(15) Terry Leach	.25
(16) Scott Leius	.25

(17) Shane Mack	.25
(18) Jack Morris	.25
(19) Al Newman	.25
(20) Junior Ortiz	.25
(21) Mike Pagliarulo	.25
(22) Kirby Puckett	5.00
(23) Paul Sorrento	.25
(24) Kevin Tapani	.25
(25) David West	.25
(26) Carl Willis	.25

1989 Rainier Farms Super Stars Discs

This set is one of the scarcer late-1980s disc issues produced by Michael Schechter Associates for various local businesses. The bakery began distribution of the discs by placing them directly in the cello wrapper with a loaf of bread. This resulted in those cards being severely grease stained and often creased. It also resulted in problems with public health officials who halted the distribution. Since the bakery could not economically and sanitarily package the cards they dropped the promotion and sold the remainder cards into the hobby. Discs measure 2-3/4" in diameter and have a color player photo (with team logos airbrushed away) at center with a white border. A Rainier Farms Homestyle logo is at top in red and black. Backs are printed in dark blue and feature a few stats, biographical details and a card number.

	NM/M
Complete Set (20):	15.00
Common Player:	.60
1 Wally Joyner	.60
2 Wade Boggs	2.25
3 Ozzie Smith	2.25
4 Don Mattingly	2.50
5 Jose Canseco	1.25
6 Tony Gwynn	2.25
7 Eric Davis	.60
8 Kirby Puckett	2.25
9 Kevin Seitzer	.60
10 Darryl Strawberry	.60
11 Gregg Jefferies	.60
12 Mark Grace	.60
13 Matt Nokes	.60
14 Mark McGwire	3.50
15 Bobby Bonilla	.60
16 Roger Clemens	2.50
17 Frank Viola	.60
18 Orel Hershiser	.60
19 Dave Cone	.60
20 Kirk Gibson	.60

1984 Ralston Purina

This set, produced by Topps, features the game's top players. Photos on the 2-1/2" x 3-1/2" cards are all close-up poses. Topps' logo appears only on the card fronts, and the backs are completely different

from Topps' regular issue of 1984, featuring a checkerboard look, coinciding with the well-known Ralston Purina logo. Cards are numbered with odd numbers for American Leaguers and even numbered cards for National Leaguers. Four cards were packed in boxes of Cookie Crisp and Donkey Kong Junior brand cereals, and the complete set was available via a mail-in offer in panel form.

	NM/M
Complete Set, Singles (33):	4.00
Complete Set, Panel	4.00
Common Player:	.05
1 Eddie Murray	.25
2 Ozzie Smith	.35
3 Ted Simmons	.05
4 Pete Rose	.75
5 Greg Luzinski	.05
6 Andre Dawson	.15
7 Dave Winfield	.25
8 Tom Seaver	.25
9 Jim Rice	.15
10 Fernando Valenzuela	.05
11 Wade Boggs	.35
12 Dale Murphy	.15
13 George Brett	.50
14 Nolan Ryan	1.00
15 Rickey Henderson	.25
16 Steve Carlton	.25
17 Rod Carew	.25
18 Steve Garvey	.15
19 Reggie Jackson	.50
20 Dave Concepcion	.05
21 Robin Yount	.25
22 Mike Schmidt	.50
23 Jim Palmer	.25
24 Bruce Sutter	.20
25 Dan Quisenberry	.05
26 Bill Madlock	.05
27 Cecil Cooper	.05
28 Gary Carter	.25
29 Fred Lynn	.05
30 Pedro Guerrero	.05
31 Ron Guidry	.05
32 Keith Hernandez	.05
33 Carlton Fisk	.25

1987 Ralston Purina

Ralston Purina, in conjunction with Mike Schechter Associates, issued this set in specially marked boxes of Cookie Crisp and Honey Graham Chex. Three cards, wrapped in cellophane, were inserted in each box. Fronts contain a full-color photo with the team insignia airbrushed away. Above the photo are two yellow crossed bats and a star, with the player's uniform number inside the star. Backs are grey with red printing and contain personal information and career major league statistics. As part of the promotion, the company advertised an uncut sheet of cards which was available by finding an "instant-winner" game card or sending $1 plus two non-winning cards. Cards on the uncut sheet are identical in design to the single cards, save the omission of the words "1987 Collectors Edition" in the upper-right corner.

	NM/M
Complete Set (15):	7.50
Common Player:	.25
1 Nolan Ryan	1.50
2 Steve Garvey	.35
3 Wade Boggs	.65
4 Dave Winfield	.50
5 Don Mattingly	.75
6 Don Sutton	.35
7 Dave Parker	.25

8 Eddie Murray	.50
9 Gary Carter	.50
10 Roger Clemens	.75
11 Fernando Valenzuela	.25
12 Cal Ripken Jr.	1.50
13 Ozzie Smith	.65
14 Mike Schmidt	.75
15 Ryne Sandberg	.65

1987 Ralston Purina Collectors' Sheet

Cards obtained from the mail-in redemption uncut sheet offer are identical to the cereal-box insert versions except that they lack the "1987 / COLLECTORS'/EDITION" legend at top-right.

	NM/M
Complete Panel:	8.00
Complete Singles Set (15):	5.00
Common Single Player:	.15
1 Nolan Ryan	1.00
2 Steve Garvey	.25
3 Wade Boggs	.50
4 Dave Winfield	.40
5 Don Mattingly	.65
6 Don Sutton	.30
7 Dave Parker	.15
8 Eddie Murray	.40
9 Gary Carter	.40
10 Roger Clemens	.65
11 Fernando Valenzuela	.15
12 Cal Ripken Jr.	1.00
13 Ozzie Smith	.50
14 Mike Schmidt	.65
15 Ryne Sandberg	.50

1989 Ralston Purina

Ralston Purina, in conjunction with Mike Schechter Associates, issued this "Superstars" set in 1989. As part of a late-spring and early-summer promotion, the standard-size cards were inserted, two per box, in specially-marked boxes of Crisp Crunch, Honey Nut O's, Fruit Rings and Frosted Flakes in most parts of the country. Ads on cereal boxes also offered complete sets through a mail-in offer. Fronts feature player portraits flanked by stars in all four corners. Backs include stats and player data. Team logos have been removed from the photos.

	NM/M
Complete Set (12):	3.00
Common Player:	.10
1 Ozzie Smith	.75
2 Andre Dawson	.20
3 Darryl Strawberry	.10
4 Mike Schmidt	1.00
5 Orel Hershiser	.10
6 Tim Raines	.10
7 Roger Clemens	1.00
8 Kirby Puckett	.75
9 George Brett	1.00
10 Alan Trammell	.10

1990 Real Milk Mike Henneman

"Get in the Game" urges the headline on each of the cards in this collection featuring then-star Tiger relief pitcher Mike Henneman. The 2-1/2" x 3-1/2" cards have red, white and blue borders with a color photo at center. Backs are in red, black and white with Henneman's stats or career highlights. The set was available as a mail-in premium.

	NM/M
Complete Set (8):	6.00
Common Card:	.25
1 Mike Henneman/ Drinking milk	2.00
2 Mike Henneman/ Pitching	2.00
3 Mike Henneman/ In jacket	2.00
4 Mike Henneman/ Rubbing up ball	2.00
5 Milk carton	.25
-- Hand holding carton	.25
-- Title card	.25
-- Tiger Clubhouse membership card	.25

1990 Red Apple Mariners Pin/Cards

It is unknown whether the checklist presented here is complete. This combination promotional issue features a 2-1/2" x 3-13/16" baseball card separated by perforations from a 2-1/2" x 1-7/16" tab. The card portion has a color player photo with a large M's logo. The front of the tab is a coupon for a food product. On back the card has a black-and-white portrait photo along with player data and career highlights. The back of the tab has a Red Apple Markets logo. Attached to the tab is a color enameled pin of the player in action.

	NM/M
Common Player:	5.00
(1) Alvin Davis	6.00
(2) Ken Griffey Jr.	12.00

(3) Harold Reynolds	6.00
(4) David Valle	5.00

1982 Red Lobster Cubs

This 28-card set was co-sponsored by the team and a seafood restaurant chain for distribution at a 1982 Cubs promotional game. Card fronts are unbordered color photos, with player name, number, position and a superimposed facsimile autograph. The set includes 25 players on the 2-1/4" x 3-1/2" cards, along with a card for manager Lee Elia, an unnumbered card for the coaching staff and a team picture. Card backs have complete player statistics and a Red Lobster ad. Production was reported to be 15,000 sets.

	NM/M
Complete Set (28):	60.00
Common Player:	.50
1 Larry Bowa	.50
4 Lee Elia	.50
6 Keith Moreland	.50
7 Jody Davis	.50
10 Leon Durham	.50
15 Junior Kennedy	.50
17 Bump Wills	.50
18 Scot Thompson	.50
21 Jay Johnstone	.50
22 Bill Buckner	.50
23 Ryne Sandberg	50.00
24 Jerry Morales	.50
25 Gary Woods	.50
28 Steve Henderson	.50
29 Bob Molinaro	.50
31 Fergie Jenkins	2.00
33 Al Ripley	.50
34 Randy Martz	.50
36 Mike Proly	.50
37 Ken Kravec	.50
38 Willie Hernandez	.50
39 Bill Campbell	.50
41 Dick Tidrow	.50
46 Lee Smith	1.00
47 Doug Bird	.50
48 Dickie Noles	.50
--- Team Photo	.50
--- Coaching Staff (Billy Connors, Tom Harmon, Gordy MacKenzie, John Vukovich, Billy Williams)	.50

1991 Retort Negro League Legends, Series 1

One of the most extensive collectors' issues featuring former Negro League players was issued over a two-year period by Robert Retort Enterprises. Sold only in a boxed set with accompanying history book, the premiere issue featured 65 individual players, plus game-action and team photos. Fronts of the 3-1/2" x 5-1/2" cards feature sepia photos with a sepia border. Player identification is in the bottom border. Postcard style backs specify the teams on which the player appeared, have a card number and a serial number from within the edition of 10,000 sets.

		NM/M
Complete Set (100):		35.00
Common Player:		.50
1	Otha Bailey	.50
2	Harry Barnes	.50
3	Gene Benson	.50
4	Bill Beverly	.50
5	Charlie Biot	.50
6	Bob Boyd	.65
7	Allen Bryant	.50
8	Marlin Carter	.50
9	Bill Cash	.50
10	Jim Cohen	.50
11	Elliott Coleman	.50
12	Johnnie Cowan	.50
13	Jimmie Crutchfield	.65
14	Saul Davis	.50
15	Piper Davis	.65
16	Leon Day	2.00
17	Lou Dials	.75
18	Mahlon Duckett	.50
19	Felix Evans	.50
20	Rudy Fernandez	.50
21	Joe Fillmore	.50
22	George Giles	.50
23	Louis Gillis	.50
24	Stanley Glenn	.50
25	Willie Grace	.50
26	Wiley Griggs	.50
27	Albert Haywood	.50
28	Jimmy Hill	.50
29	Cowan Hyde	.50
30	Monte Irvin	1.50
31	Sam Jethroe	1.00
32	Connie Johnson	.65
33	Josh Johnson	.50
34	Clinton Jones	.50
35	Larry Kimbrough	.50
36	Clarence King	.50
37	Jim LaMarque	.50
38	Buck Leonard	2.00
39	Max Manning	.50
40	Verdell Mathis	.50
41	Nath McClinic	.50
42	Clinton McCord	.50
43	Clyde McNeal	.50
44	John Miles	.50
45	Buck O'Neil	2.00
46	Frank Pearson	.50
47	Art Pennington	.75
48	Nathan Peoples	.50
49	Andy Porter	.50
50	Ted Radcliffe	.50
51	Chico Renfroe	.50
52	Bobby Robinson	.50
53	Tommy Sampson	.50
54	Joe Scott	.50
55	Joe Burt Scott	.50
56	Herb Simpson	.50
57	Lonnie Summers	.50
58	Alfred Surratt	.50
59	Bob Thurman	.50
60	Harold Tinker	.50
61	Quincy Trouppe	.75
62	Edsall Walker	.50
63	Al Wilmore	.50
64	Artie Wilson	.75
65	Jim Zapp	.50
66	Grays vs. Stars 1937	.50
67	Grays vs. Eagles 1943	.50
68	Homestead Grays 1944	.50
69	Grays vs. Cuban Stars 1944	.50
70	Grays vs. Cubans 1944	.50
71	Grays vs. Eagles 1945	.50
72	Eagles Pitching Staff 1941	.50
73	Buckeyes Infield 1945	.50
74	Homestead Grays 1948	.50
75	Chicago Murderers Row 1943	.50
76	Indianapolis Clowns 1945	.50
77	East All-Stars 1937	.50
78	East All-Stars 1938	.50
79	East All-Stars 1939	.50
80	East All-Stars 1948	.50
81	West All-Stars 1948	.50
82	Homestead Grays 1931	.50
83	Homestead Grays 1938	.50
84	Pittsburgh Crawfords 1936	.50
85	Kansas City Monarchs 1934	.50
86	Kansas City Monarchs 1949	.50
87	Chicago American Giants 1941	.50
88	Chicago American Giants 1947	.50
89	Memphis Red Sox 1940	.50

90	Memphis Red Sox 1946	.50
91	Birmingham Black Barons 1946	.50
92	Birmingham Black Barons 1948	.50
93	Birmingham Black Barons 1950	.50
94	Harlem Globetrotters 1948	.50
95	Cleveland Buckeyes 1947	.50
96	Philadelphia Stars 1944	.50
97	Newark Eagles 1939	.50
98	Baltimore Elite Giants 1949	.50
99	Indianapolis Clowns 1943	.50
100	Cincinnati Tigers 1937	.50

1993 Retort Negro League Legends, Series 2

One of the most extensive collectors' issues featuring former Negro League players was issued over a two-year period by Robert Retort Enterprises. Sold only in a boxed set, the Series 2 issue features 41 individual players, plus game-action and team photos. Fronts of the 3-1/2" x 5-1/2" cards feature sepia photos with a white border. Player identification is in the bottom border, which also has space for autographing. Postcard style backs specify the teams on which the player appeared, have a card number and a serial number from within the edition of 10,000 sets.

		NM/M
Complete Set (100):		30.00
Common Player:		.50
1	Frank Barnes	.50
2	John Bissant	.50
3	Garnett Blair	.50
4	Jim "Fireball" Bolden	.50
5	Luther Branham	.50
6	Sherwood Brewer	.50
7	Jimmy Dean	.50
8	Frank Duncan, Jr.	.50
9	Wilmer Fields	.50
10	Harold Gordon	.50
11	Bill Greason	.50
12	Acie Griggs	.50
13	Napoleon Gulley	.75
14	Ray Haggins	.50
15	Wilmer Harris	.50
16	Bob Harvey	.50
17	Jehosie Heard	.65
18	Gordon Hopkins	.50
19	Herman Horn	.50
20	James Ivory	.50
21	Henry Kimbro	.75
22	Milford Laurent	.50
23	Ernest Long	.50
24	Frank Marsh	.50
25	Francis Matthews	.50
26	Jim McCurine	.50
27	John Mitchell	.50
28	Lee Moody	.50
29	Rogers Pierre	.50
30	Nathaniel Pollard	.50
31	Merle Porter	.50
32	William Powell	.50
33	Ulysses Redd	.50
34	Harry Rhodes	.50
35	DeWitt Smallwood	.50
36	Joseph Spencer	.50
37	Riley Stewart	.50
38	Earl Taborn	.50
39	Ron Teasley	.50
40	Joe Wiley	.50
41	Buck Leonard	2.00
42	Grays vs. Giants 1945	.50
43	Grays vs. Monarchs 1945	.50
44	Homestead Grays 1948	.50
45	Pittsburgh Crawfords 1928	.50
46	Pittsburgh Crawfords 1935	.50
47	Kansas City Monarchs 1942	.50
48	Buck O'Neil, William Dismukes	.50
49	Chicago American Giants 1942	.50
50	Nashville Elite Giants 1935	.50
51	Baltimore Elite Giants 1941	.50
52	Birmingham Black Barons 1948	.50
53	Birmingham Black Barons 1959	.50
54	Memphis Red Sox 1954	.50
55	Indianapolis ABCs 1923	.50
56	Harlem Globetrotters 1948	.50
57	Harlem Globetrotters 1948	.50
58	Bismarck Barons 1955	.50
59	Culican 1952	.50
60	Santurce 1947	.50
61	Pittsburgh Crawfords 1928	.50
62	Pittsburgh Crawfords 1932	.50
63	Pittsburgh Crawfords 1935	.50
64	Homestead Grays 1937	.50
65	Homestead Grays 1938	.50
66	Homestead Grays 1940	.50
67	Homestead Grays 1945	.50
68	Homestead Grays 1945	.50
69	Kansas City Monarchs 1932	.50
70	Kansas City Monarchs 1934	.50
71	Kansas City Monarchs 1941	.50
72	Kansas City Monarchs 1946	.50
73	Chicago American Giants 1950	.50
74	Memphis Red Sox 1949	.50
75	Birmingham Black Barons 1946	.50
76	Birmingham Black Barons 1948	.50
77	Birmingham Black Barons 1951	.50
78	Birmingham Black Barons 1954	.50
79	St. Louis Stars 1931	.50
80	Newark Dodgers 1935	.50
81	Brooklyn Eagles 1935	.50
82	Newark Eagles 1946	.50
83	Philadelphia Stars 1939	.50
84	Philadelphia Stars 1946	.50
85	Philadelphia Stars 1949	.50
86	Nashville Elite Giants 1935	.50
87	Baltimore Elite Giants 1939	.50
88	Baltimore Elite Giants 1949	.50
89	Cleveland Buckeyes 1947	.50
90	Cincinnati Tigers 1936	.50
91	Miami Ethiopian Clowns 1940	.50
92	Indianapolis Clowns 1944	.50
93	Indianapolis Clowns 1948	.50
94	New York Cubans 1943	.50
95	Harlem Globetrotters 1948	.50
96	House of David 1938	.50
97	E.T. Community 1926	.50
98	Bismarck Giants 1935	.50
99	American All-Stars 1945	.50
100	New York Stars 1949	.50

1988 Revco

This super-glossy boxed set of 33 standard-size cards was produced by Topps for exclusive distribution by Revco stores east of the Mississippi River. Card fronts feature a large blue Revco logo in the upper-left corner opposite a yellow and black boxed "Topps League Leader" label. Player photos are framed in black and orange with a diagonal player identification banner in the lower-right corner. Backs are horizontal, printed in red and black on white stock and include the player name, biographical data, batting/pitching stats and a brief career summary.

		NM/M
Complete Set (33):		4.00
Common Player:		.05
1	Tony Gwynn	.65
2	Andre Dawson	.25
3	Vince Coleman	.05
4	Jack Clark	.05
5	Tim Raines	.05
6	Tim Raines	.05
7	Juan Samuel	.05
8	Nolan Ryan	1.50
9	Rick Sutcliffe	.05
10	Kent Tekulve	.05
11	Steve Bedrosian	.05
12	Orel Hershiser	.05
13	Rick Rueschel	.05
14	Fernando Valenzuela	.05
15	Bob Welch	.05
16	Wade Boggs	.50
17	Mark McGwire	1.00
18	George Bell	.05
19	Harold Reynolds	.05
20	Paul Molitor	.05
21	Kirby Puckett	.65
22	Kevin Seitzer	.05
23	Brian Downing	.05
24	Dwight Evans	.05
25	Willie Wilson	.05
26	Danny Tartabull	.05
27	Jimmy Key	.05
28	Roger Clemens	.75
29	Dave Stewart	.05
30	Mark Eichhorn	.05
31	Tom Henke	.05
32	Charlie Hough	.05
33	Mark Langston	.05

1996 Revco Cleveland Indians

This set is identified by a logo on front as the "1995 Award Winner Series," but its manner of distribution is unknown. Fronts of the 2-1/2" x 3-1/2" cards have action photos with mottled border. Backs have logos of the 1995 Indians A.L. Championship and of the sponsor, Revco drug stores. Listed on back are the awards earned by the player for the 1995 season. A uniform number also appears, where applicable.

		NM/M
Complete Set (12):		12.00
Common Player:		.50
(1)	Carlos Baerga	.50
(2)	Albert Belle	1.25
(3)	Mike Hargrove	.50
(4)	John Hart (GM)	.50
(5)	Orel Hershiser	1.00
(6)	Kenny Lofton	1.00
(7)	Jose Mesa	.50
(8)	Manny Ramirez	5.00
(9)	Julian Tavares	.50
(10)	Jim Thome	2.50
(11)	Omar Vizquel	1.00
(12)	Cleveland Indians (On-field celebration.)	.50

1985-86 RGI

Renata Galasso Inc.

(See listings under Renata Galasso.)

1988 Rite Aid

This premiere edition was produced by Topps for distribution by Rite Aid discount drug stores in the Eastern U.S. The boxed set includes 33 standard-size full-color cards with at least one card for each major league team. Four cards in the set highlight MVPs from the 1987 season. Card fronts have white borders and carry a yellow "Team MVP's" header above the player photo which is bordered in red and blue. A large Rite Aid logo appears upper-left; the player's name appears bottom center. The numbered card backs are black on blue and white card stock in a horizontal layout containing the player name, biography and statistics.

		NM/M
Complete Set (33):		4.00
Common Player:		.05
1	Dale Murphy	.15
2	Andre Dawson	.15
3	Eric Davis	.05
4	Mike Scott	.05
5	Pedro Guerrero	.05
6	Tim Raines	.05
7	Darryl Strawberry	.05
8	Mike Schmidt	.65
9	Mike Dunne	.05
10	Jack Clark	.05
11	Tony Gwynn	.60
12	Will Clark	.50
13	Cal Ripken, Jr.	1.00
14	Wade Boggs	.60
15	Wally Joyner	.50
16	Harold Baines	.05
17	Joe Carter	.05
18	Alan Trammell	.05
19	Kevin Seitzer	.05
20	Paul Molitor	.50
21	Kirby Puckett	.60
22	Don Mattingly	.65
23	Mark McGwire	.75
24	Alvin Davis	.05
25	Ruben Sierra	.05
26	George Bell	.05
27	Jack Morris	.05
28	Jeff Reardon	.05
29	John Tudor	.05
30	Rick Rueschel	.05
31	Gary Gaetti	.05
32	Jeffrey Leonard	.05
33	Frank Viola	.05

1982 Roy Rogers N.Y. Yankees Lids

Members of the N.Y. Yankees (although in uniform which have the logos removed) are featured on these soft drink lids given away at Roy Rogers restaurants in the metropolitan area. Lids are 3-9/16" in diameter with a red plastic ring around a cardboard disc. At the center of the disc is a black-and-white player portrait photo. Player data appears in colored panels at the sides and in the white center section at bottom. The unnumbered lids are checklisted here in alphabetical order.

		NM/M
Complete Set (12):		35.00
Common Player:		2.50
(1)	Rick Cerone	2.50
(2)	Goose Gossage	3.50
(3)	Ken Griffey	2.50
(4)	Ron Guidry	3.00
(5)	Steve Kemp	2.50
(6)	Jerry Mumphrey	2.50
(7)	Graig Nettles	3.00
(8)	Lou Piniella	3.00
(9)	Willie Randolph	3.00
(10)	Andre Robertson	2.50
(11)	Roy Smalley	2.50
(12)	Dave Winfield	7.50

1993 Rolaids Cubs Relief Pitchers

The Chicago Cubs issued a four-card All-Time Cubs Relief Pitchers set as a giveaway at the September 4, 1993 game at Wrigley Field The four were selected by Cubs fans in a ballot conducted by Rolaids. The standard-sized cards have white borders with a color photo at center. Backs include the player's name, years he pitched for the Cubs, the Rolaids logo and an explanation of the card set's purpose.

		NM/M
Complete Set (4):		4.50
Common Player:		1.00
(1)	Randy Myers	1.00
(2)	Lee Smith	1.50
(3)	Bruce Sutter	2.50
(4)	Mitch Williams	1.00

1993 Nolan Ryan Topps Stickers

Twenty-seven of Nolan Ryan's Topps cards from 1968 through 1992 were reproduced, probably without authorization from Topps or Ryan, in a sticker format for regional distribution in Texas area grocery stores. Printed just slightly smaller than the 2-1/2" x 3-1/2" cards, the stickers were issued in strips of three. When the front picture was peeled away, the back of the sticker could be used as a coupon for specific purchases. Stores known to have participated in the program include: Brookshire Bros., Budget Chopper, Minyards and Super S. Strips of three were generally offered on a weekly basis.

	NM/M
Complete Set, Strips (9):	30.00
Common Sticker:	2.00

S

1986 Safeway Houston Astros

Though not marked, these 6" x 9" color player photo were given away over the course of several weeks by area Safeway food stores. The pictures are player portraits in uniform, but witthott caps because they were licensed by the Players Union, but not MLB. The white-bordered pictures have a facsimile autograph and are blank-backed. Unnumbered, the pictures are checklisted here in alphabetical order.

		NM/M
Complete Set (16):		25.00
Common Player:		1.00
(1)	Alan Ashby	1.00
(2)	Kevin Bass	1.00
(3)	Jose Cruz	1.00
(4)	Glenn Davis	1.00
(5)	Bill Doran	1.00
(6)	Phil Garner	1.00
(7)	Billy Hatcher	1.00
(8)	Charlie Kerfeld	1.00
(9)	Bob Knepper	1.00
(10)	Aurelio Lopez	1.00
(11)	Terry Puhl	1.00
(12)	Craig Reynolds	1.00
(13)	Nolan Ryan	15.00
(14)	Mike Scott	1.00
(15)	Dickie Thon	1.00
(16)	Denny Walling	1.00

2005 Ryne Sandberg Jersey Retirement Day

Stadium giveaway August 28.

	NM/M
Ryne Sandberg	6.00

1984 San Diego Padres Fire Safety

This set of 28 full-color 2-1/2" x 3-1/2" cards pictures Padres players, coaches, broadcasters and the Famous Chicken each posing with Smokey the

Bear. Smokey's portrait and logo of the California and U.S. Forest Services are printed in the bottom border. Backs offer brief player information and a fire prevention tip. The cards were given away at a home game.

		NM/M
Complete Set (28):		7.00
Common Player:		.25
1	Garry Templeton	.25
2	Alan Wiggins	.25
4	Luis Salazar	.25
6	Steve Garvey	1.00
7	Kurt Bevacqua	.25
10	Doug Gwosdz	.25
11	Tim Flannery	.25
16	Terry Kennedy	.25
18	Kevin McReynolds	.25
19	Tony Gwynn	5.00
20	Bobby Brown	.25
30	Eric Show	.25
31	Ed Whitson	.25
35	Luis DeLeon	.25
38	Mark Thurmond	.25
42	Sid Monge	.25
43	Dave Dravecky	.25
48	Tim Lollar	.25
---	Smokey Logo Card	
---	The Chicken/Mascot	.25
---	Dave Campbell/ Broadcaster	.25
---	Jerry Coleman/ Broadcaster	.25
---	Harry Dunlop	.25
---	Harold (Doug) Harvey/ Umpire	.25
---	Jack Krol/Coach	.25
---	Jack McKeon/ Vice President	.25
---	Norm Sherry/Coach	.25
---	Ozzie Virgil/Coach	.25
---	Dick Williams/Manager	.25

1986-87 San Diego Padres Fire Safety Flip Books

Differing from the contemporary fire safety issues of its time, the 1986-87 Padres promotional effort took the form of 24-page flip books, rather than cards. About 3-1/2" x 2-1/2", the multi-page black-and-white books offered photographic playing tips when the pictures were rapidly thumbed. When turned over, the books showed Smokey in action preventing forest fires. The 1987 books, McCullers and Santiago, are slightly larger, at about 4-1/2" x 2-3/4".

		NM/M
Complete Set (5):		25.00
Common Player:		4.00
(1)	Dave Dravecky	4.00
(2)	Tim Flannery	4.00
(3)	Tony Gwynn	15.00
(4)	Lance McCullers	4.00
(5)	Benito Santiago	4.00

1988 San Diego Padres Fire Safety

This oversized (3" x 5") set was produced in conjunction with the U.S. Forest Service as a fire prevention campaign promotion. A full-color player pho-

to, framed by a thin white line, fills the card face. The player number, position and Smokey Bear logo appear at lower-right. Backs are printed in horizontal postcard format, with player info and a Smokey Bear cartoon on the left half of the card back. The set was available for purchase at the Padres Gift Shop. Cards of Candy Sierra and Larry Bowa were not officially released and are quite rare.

		NM/M
Complete Set (33):		45.00
Common Player:		.50
(1)	Shawn Abner	.50
(2)	Roberto Alomar	8.00
(3)	Sandy Alomar	3.00
(4)	Greg Booker	.50
(5)	Larry Bowa	15.00
(6)	Chris Brown	.50
(7)	Mark Davis	.50
(8)	Pat Dobson	.50
(9)	Tim Flannery	.50
(10)	Mark Grant	.50
(11)	Tony Gwynn	15.00
(12)	Andy Hawkins	.50
(13)	Stan Jefferson	.50
(14)	Jimmy Jones	.50
(15)	John Kruk	.50
(16)	Dave Leiper	.50
(17)	Shane Mack	.50
(18)	Carmelo Martinez	.50
(19)	Lance McCullers	.50
(20)	Keith Moreland	.50
(21)	Eric Nolte	.50
(22)	Amos Otis	.50
(23)	Mark Parent	.50
(24)	Randy Ready	.50
(25)	Greg Riddoch	.50
(26)	Benito Santiago	1.00
(27)	Eric Show	.50
(28)	Candy Sierra	10.00
(29)	Denny Sommers	.50
(30)	Garry Templeton	.50
(31)	Dickie Thon	.50
(32)	Ed Whitson	.50
(33)	Marvell Wynne	.50

1989 San Diego Padres Magazine/ S.D. Sports inserts

During the course of the 1989 season, a 24-card set sponsored by a local baseball card dealer was offered to collectors as an insert to the team's official game program, "Padres Magazine." The cards were offered in six panels of four cards. Each panel included a former Padres star and a career highlight. To complete the set, at least six copies of the $1.50 program had to be purchased. The 2-1/2" x 3-1/2" cards have color portrait photos on front. Backs have player identification and a career stats line, along with trivia about the player.

		NM/M
Complete Set (24):		15.00
Common Player:		.50
1	Jack McKeon	.50
2	Sandy Alomar Jr.	.50
3	Tony Gwynn	6.00
4	Willie McCovey	2.00
5	John Kruk	.50
6	Jack Clark	.50
7	Eric Show	.50
8	Rollie Fingers	1.50
9	The Alomars (Sandy Alomar, Roberto Alomar, Sandy Alomar Jr.)	.65
10	Carmelo Martinez	.50
11	Benito Santiago	.50

12	Nate Colbert	.50
13	Mark Davis	.50
14	Roberto Alomar	1.50
15	Tim Flannery	.50
16	Randy Jones	.50
17	Dennis Rasmussen	.50
18	Greg Harris	.50
19	Garry Templeton	.50
20	Steve Garvey	1.50
21	Bruce Hurst	.50
22	Ed Whitson	.50
23	Chris James	.50
24	Gaylord Perry	1.50

1990 San Diego Padres Magazine/ Unocal inserts

Ed Whitson
Pitcher (76)

The first 24 cards in this set, sponsored by area Unocal service stations, were found in four-card panels bound into various issues of Padres Magazine, the team's official program. Sheets measure about 5" x 9" and the individual perforated cards are about 2-1/2" x 3-1/2". A coupon attached to the sheets could be redeemed at participating gas stations for cards #25-27. Fronts have color action photos with team logo at top and sponsor logo at lower-right. Black-and-white backs have player data, a line of career stats and highlights of his time with the Padres.

		NM/M
Complete Set (27):		15.00
Common Player:		.50
1	Tony Gwynn	5.00
2	Benito Santiago	.50
3	Mike Pagliarulo	.50
4	Dennis Rasmussen	.50
5	Eric Show	.50
6	Darrin Jackson	.50
7	Mark Parent	.50
8	Jerry Coleman, Rick Monday/ Announcers	.50
9	Andy Benes	.50
10	Roberto Alomar	2.50
11	Craig Lefferts	.50
12	Ed Whitson	.50
13	Calvin Schiraldi	.50
14	Garry Templeton	.50
15	Tony Gwynn	1.50
16	Bob Chandler, Ted Leitner/ Announcers	.50
17	Fred Lynn	.50
18	Jack Clark	.50
19	Mike Dunne	.50
20	Mark Grant	.50
21	Benito Santiago	.50
22	Sandy Alomar Sr., Pat Dobson, Amos Otis, Greg Riddoch, Denny Sommers	.50
23	Bruce Hurst	.50
24	Greg Harris	.50
25	Jack McKeon	1.00
26	Bip Roberts	1.00
27	Joe Carter	4.00

1991 San Diego Padres Magazine/ Rally's inserts

The first 24 cards of this set were issued as 5" x 8" perforated panels stapled into issues of "Padres Magazine." Due to substitutions dictated by player moves during the season (which also created Short-Printed cards) it would have been necessary to purchase six of the $2 programs to get the 27-card basic set.

Cards #25-27 were only available at Rally's restaurants with a coupon attached to the magazine panels. Single cards measure about 2-1/2" x 3-1/2". Fronts have color portrait photos on a diamond background. Player name and position are in an orange banner at bottom. Team and sponsor logos appear in the upper corners on a dark blue background. Backs are in black-and-white with player identification, a line of career stats and highlights of his tenure in San Diego.

		NM/M
Complete Set (30):		27.50
Common Player:		.50
1	Greg Riddoch	.50
2	Dennis Rasmussen	.50
3	Thomas Howard	.50
4	Tom Lampkin	.50
5	Bruce Hurst	.50
6	Darrin Jackson	.50
7	Jerald Clark	.50
8	Shawn Abner	.50
9	Bip Roberts	.50
10	Marty Barrett	.50
11	Jim Vatcher	.50
12	Greg Gross	.50
13	Greg Harris	.50
14	Ed Whitson	.50
15a	Calvin Schiraldi/SP	1.50
15b	Jerald Clark	.50
16	Rich Rodriguez	.50
17	Larry Andersen	.50
18	Andy Benes	.50
19a	Wes Gardner/SP	1.50
19b	Bruce Hurst	.50
20	Paul Faries	.50
21	Craig Lefferts	.50
22	Tony Gwynn	8.00
23a	Jim Presley/SP	1.50
23b	Bip Roberts	.50
24	Fred McGriff	1.00
25	Gaylord Perry	2.00
26	Benito Santiago	1.50
27	Tony Fernandez	1.50

1992 San Diego Padres Fire Safety

The Padres issued a Smokey the Bear postcard set, sponsored by the U.S. Forest Service. Backs contain the usual fire safety messages, but they are also translated into Spanish. Fronts have full-bleed color photos with the player's name and position in orange in a dark blue box at bottom-center. A color Smokey logo appears in one of the upper corners. The unnumbered cards are checklisted here alphabetically.

		NM/M
Complete Set (36):		15.00
Common Player:		.25
(1)	Larry Andersen	.25
(2)	Oscar Azocar	.25
(3)	Andy Benes	.25
(4)	Dan Bilardello	.25
(5)	Jerald Clark	.25
(6)	Pat Clements	.25
(7)	Dave Eiland	.25
(8)	Tony Fernandez	.25
(9)	Tony Gwynn	6.00
(10)	Gene Harris	.25
(11)	Greg Harris	.25
(12)	Jeremy Hernandez	.25
(13)	Bruce Hurst	.25
(14)	Darrin Jackson	.25
(15)	Tom Lampkin	.25
(16)	Bruce Kimm	.25
(17)	Craig Lefferts	.25
(18)	Mike Maddux	.25
(19)	Fred McGriff	.25
(20)	Jose Melendez	.25

(21)	Randy Myers, Craig Shipley,	.25
(22)	Gary Pettis	.25
(23)	Rob Picciolo	.25
(24)	Merv Rettenmund	.25
(25)	Greg Riddoch	.25
(26)	Mike Roarke	.25
(27)	Rich Rodriguez	.25
(28)	Benito Santiago	.25
(29)	Frank Seminara	.25
(30)	Gary Sheffield	2.00
(32)	Jim Snyder	.25
(33)	Dave Staton	.25
(34)	Kurt Stillwell	.25
(35)	Tim Teufel	.25
(36)	Kevin Ward	.25

1992 San Diego Padres Police

TONY FERNANDEZ   INF

Anti-drug messages are featured on this safety set. The 2-1/2" x 3-1/2" cards have color action photos on front with wide white borders. Backs are horizontally formatted and feature a few player biographical notes, the D.A.R.E. logo and safety message. Unnumbered cards are checklisted here in alphabetical order. Cards #28-30 in this checklist were not distributed with the rest of the set and are scarcer.

		NM/M
Complete Set (30):		12.00
Common Player:		.25
(1)	Oscar Azocar	.25
(2)	Andy Benes	.25
(3)	Jerald Clark	.25
(4)	Jim Deshaies	.25
(5)	Dave Eiland	.25
(6)	Tony Fernandez	.25
(7)	Tony Gwynn	6.00
(8)	Greg W. Harris	.25
(9)	Bruce Hurst	.25
(10)	Darrin Jackson	.25
(11)	Tom Lampkin	.25
(12)	Fred McGriff	.25
(13)	Merv Rettenmund	.25
(14)	Greg Riddoch	.25
(15)	Benito Santiago	.25
(16)	Frank Seminara	.25
(17)	Gary Sheffield	1.00
(18)	Craig Shipley	.25
(19)	Phil Stephenson	.25
(20)	Kurt Stillwell	.25
(21)	Tim Teufel	.25
(22)	Dan Walters	.25
(23)	Kevin Ward	.25
(24)	Padres relievers (Larry Andersen, Mike Maddux, Jose Melendez, Rich Rodriguez, Tim Scott)	.25
(25)	Coaches (Bruce Kimm, Rob Picciolo, Merv Rettenmund, Mike Roarke, Jim Snyder)	.25
(26)	Bluepper/Mascot	.25
(27)	Jack Murphy Stadium	.25
(28)	Craig Lefferts	1.00
(29)	Rob Picciolo	1.00
(30)	Fred McGriff, Tony Fernandez, Gary Sheffield, Tony Gwynn	2.00

1991 San Francisco Examiner A's

Evidently issued over the course of the season by the Bay Area daily newspaper, these large-format (8-3/8" x 10-7/8") cards are printed on light cardboard pre-punched for a three-ring binder. Color photos on the fronts are surrounded by team colors of green and yellow. The newspaper's logo appears in black at the top. Backs are in black-and-white with a portrait photo of the player, biographical data, major league stats and career highlights. The unnumbered cards are checklisted here alphabetically.

		NM/M
Complete Set (15):		45.00
Common Player:		2.00
(1)	Harold Baines	2.00
(2)	Jose Canseco	5.00
(3)	Dennis Eckersley	5.00
(4)	Mike Gallego	2.00
(5)	Dave Henderson	2.00
(6)	Rickey Henderson	6.00
(7)	Rick Honeycutt	2.00
(8)	Mark McGwire	10.00
(9)	Mike Moore	2.00
(10)	Gene Nelson	2.00
(11)	Eric Show	2.00
(12)	Terry Steinbach	2.00
(13)	Dave Stewart	2.00
(14)	Walt Weiss	2.00
(15)	Bob Welch	2.00

1991 San Francisco Examiner Giants

Evidently issued over the course of the season by the Bay Area daily newspaper, these large-format (8-3/8" x 10-7/8") cards are printed on light cardboard pre-punched for a three-ring binder. Color photos on the fronts are surrounded by team-color borders of orange and black on a gray background. The newspaper's logo appears in black at the top. Backs are in black-and-white with a portrait photo of the player, biographical data, major league stats and career highlights. The unnumbered cards are checklisted here alphabetically.

		NM/M
Complete Set (16):		35.00
Common Player:		2.00
(1)	Kevin Bass	2.00
(2)	Mike Benjamin	2.00
(3)	Bud Black	2.00
(4)	Jeff Brantley	2.00
(5)	John Burkett	2.00
(6)	Will Clark	4.00
(7)	Steve Decker	2.00
(8)	Scott Garrelts	2.00
(9)	Mike LaCoss	2.00
(10)	Willie McGee	2.00
(11)	Kevin Mitchell	2.00
(12)	Dave Righetti	2.00
(13)	Don Robinson	2.00
(14)	Robby Thompson	2.00
(15)	Jose Uribe	2.00
(16)	Matt Williams	4.00

2003 Ron Santo Jersey Retirement Card

This high-gloss, 2-1/2" x 3-1/2" card was a Wrigley Field

giveaway on Sept. 23, 2003, on the occasion of the Cubs' retirement of the star third baseman's uniform number. The back has Santo's complete Major League stats.

	NM/M
Ron Santo	6.00

1989 SCD Baseball Card Price Guide Pocket Price Guides

Between its premiere issue of April, 1988, and the September 1989 issue, SCD's monthly price guide magazine issued a gatefold player poster in each issue. Beginning with the October 1989 issue, panels of five (later six) repli-cards were stapled into the magazine in place of the posters. The 1989 repli-card series depicts contemporary players in the design of the 1964 Topps cards. Backs are in black-and-white with a photo of the player's rookie card and market advice pertaining to the player.

		NM/M
Complete Set (15):		6.00
Common Player:		.25
1	Mark McGwire	1.50
2	Bo Jackson	.35
3	Ken Griffey	1.50
4	Kevin Mitchell	.25
5	Ryne Sandberg	1.00
6	Will Clark	.25
7	Gregg Jefferies	.25
8	Gary Sheffield	.50
9	Fred McGriff	.25
10	Don Mattingly	1.00
11	Jim Abbott	.25
12	Mitch Williams	.25
13	Glenn Davis	.25
14	Ruben Sierra	.25
15	Robin Yount	.75

1990 SCD Baseball Card Price Guide Pocket Price Guides

For its first full year of inserting repli-cards in each issue, SCD Baseball Card Price Guide Monthly magazine rendered the game's stars and hot rookies in the style of 1957 Topps cards. Black, white and red backs have a photo of one of the player's other cards, personal data, current values of selected cards and market advice. Cards were printed on panels of five stapled into each month's issue.

	NM/M
Complete Set (60):	20.00

Common Player:		.25
1	Darryl Strawberry	.25
2	Wade Boggs	.75
3	Roger Clemens	1.00
4	Paul Molitor	.60
5	Craig Biggio	.25
6	Ruben Sierra	.25
7	Sandy Alomar Jr.	.25
8	Rickey Henderson	.60
9	Mark Langston	.25
10	Dwight Evans	.25
11	Ben McDonald	.25
12	Bo Jackson	.35
13	Don Mattingly	1.00
14	Todd Zeile	.25
15	Mike Greenwell	.25
16	Eric Anthony	.25
17	Dennis Eckersley	.50
18	Greg Vaughn	.25
19	Kevin Mitchell	.25
20	Ryne Sandberg	.75
21	Will Clark	.25
22	Robin Yount	.60
23	Kirby Puckett	.75
24	Andy Benes	.25
25	Wally Joyner	.25
26	Ozzie Smith	.75
27	John Olerud	.25
28	Devon White	.25
29	Alan Trammell	.25
30	Bobby Bonilla	.25
31	Jose Canseco	.40
32	Fred McGriff	.25
33	Mark Grace	.25
34	Ricky Jordan	.25
35	George Brett	1.00
36	Eric Davis	.25
37	Tony Gwynn	.75
38	Cal Ripken Jr.	2.00
39	Bret Saberhagen	.25
40	Howard Johnson	.25
41	Jerome Walton	.25
42	Mark McGwire	1.50
43	A.L. East Power Hitters (Mike Greenwell, Don Mattingly)	.50
44	Ken Griffey Jr.	1.25
45	Texas' Top Twirlers (Nolan Ryan, Mike Scott)	1.00
46	Barry Larkin	.25
47	Delino DeShields	.25
48	Roberto Alomar	.35
49	Frank Viola	.25
50	Kelly Gruber	.25
51	Michael Jordan	7.50
52	Glenn Davis	.25
53	Marquis Grissom	.25
54	Joe Carter	.25
55	Gregg Jefferies	.25
56	Gary Sheffield	.45
57	Cecil Fielder	.25
58	Matt Williams	.25
59	Ramon Martinez	.25
60	Len Dykstra	.25

1991 SCD Baseball Card Price Guide Pocket Price Guides

In its third year of including insert cards with each issue, the Price Guide chose the classic 1971 Topps design to showcase the game's top stars and hot rookies. The first five cards

have red backgrounds on their backs, the rest are deep green. Backs have a black-and-white photo of one of the player's other cards, along with selected card value data. Also presented are some personal data and the editors' thoughts on each player's future market value.

		NM/M
Complete Set (60):		15.00
Common Player:		.25
1	Ryne Sandberg	.75
2	Bobby Thigpen	.25
3	Rickey Henderson	.65
4	Dwight Gooden	.25
5	Kevin Maas	.25
6	Ron Gant	.25
7	Frank Thomas	.65
8	Doug Drabek	.25
9	Bobby Bonilla	.25
10	Sandy Alomar Jr.	.25
11	Bob Welch	.25
12	Joe Carter	.25
13	Cecil Fielder	.25
14	Dave Justice	.25
15	Barry Bonds	2.00
16	Barry Larkin	.25
17	Ramon Martinez	.25
18	Ben McDonald	.25
19	Roger Clemens	1.00
20	Jose Canseco	.40
21	Will Clark	.25
22	Jeff Conine	.25
23	Chris Sabo	.25
24	Alan Trammell	.25
25	Howard Johnson	.25
26	Dale Murphy	.30
27	Gregg Jefferies	.25
28	Bo Jackson	.30
29	Craig Biggio	.25
30	Delino DeShields	.25
31	Rafael Palmeiro	.50
32	Robin Yount	.65
33	Mark McGwire	1.50
34	Kevin Mitchell	.25
35	George Brett	1.00
36	Tim Wallach	.25
37	Andre Dawson	.30
38	Kirby Puckett	.75
39	Matt Williams	.25
40	Wade Boggs	.75
41	Dave Winfield	.65
42	Don Mattingly	1.00
43	Carlton Fisk	.65
44	Dave Stewart	.25
45	Ken Griffey Jr.	1.25
46	Ruben Sierra	.25
47	George Bell	.25
48	Cal Ripken	2.00
49	Ellis Burks	.25
50	Roberto Alomar	.30
51	Tim Raines	.25
52	Mike Greenwell	.25
53	Benito Santiago	.25
54	Tom Glavine	.35
55	Scott Erickson	.25
56	Chuck Finley	.25
57	Julio Franco	.25
58	Paul Molitor	.65
59	Todd Van Poppel	.25
60	Mo Vaughn	.25

1992 BB Card Price Guide/Sports Card Price Guide

New collector focus on other team sports resulted in SCD's Baseball Card Price Guide Monthly changing its name to Sports Card Price Guide Monthly with its May 1992 issue. The title change was also reflected in the annual series of repli-cards stapled into each issue. For the first time football, basketball and hockey players joined the baseball stars. That change was effective with card #19. The '92 series utilized the design of Topps' 1974 baseball cards. Backs are printed in black, white and green

and, as in previous years, include a photo of one of the player's cards along with selective current values and a market forecast. Only the set's baseball players are listed here.

		NM/M
Complete (Baseball) Set (56):		20.00
Common Player:		.25
1	Will Clark	.25
2	Albert Belle	.25
3	Luis Gonzalez	.25
4	Ramon Martinez	.25
5	Frank Thomas	.65
6	Travis Fryman	.25
7	Carlton Fisk	.65
8	Bo Jackson	.35
9	Chuck Knoblauch	.25
10	Ron Gant	.25
11	Jose Canseco	.45
12	Roger Clemens	1.00
13	Darren Lewis	.25
14	Kirby Puckett	.75
15	Tom Glavine	.35
16	Royce Clayton	.25
17	Ozzie Smith	.75
18	Robin Ventura	.25
21	Derek Bell	.25
23	Ryne Sandberg	.75
24	Andy Van Slyke	.25
26	Jim Abbott	.25
27	Ken Griffey Jr.	1.25
30	Jeff Bagwell	.65
32	Dwight Gooden	.25
33	Ruben Sierra	.25
35	David Justice	.25
36	Wade Boggs	.75
38	Barry Larkin	.25
39	Felix Jose	.25
40	Howard Johnson	.25
44	Fred McGriff	.25
45	Todd Van Poppel	.25
47	Brien Taylor	.25
48	Cal Ripken Jr.	2.00
50	Dave Winfield	.65
52	Juan Gonzalez	.40
53	Reggie Sanders	.25
57	Gary Sheffield	.45
58	Roberto Alomar	.40
59	Barry Bonds	2.00
60	Tom Glavine	.35
62	Kenny Lofton	.25
63	Joe Carter	.25
66	Paul Molitor	.65
67	Phil Plantier	.25
69	Mark McGwire	1.50
70	Nolan Ryan	2.00
72	Darryl Strawberry	.25
73	Pat Listach	.25
74	Dennis Eckersley	.50
75	Bobby Bonilla	.25
78	Delino DeShields	.25
80	Doug Drabek	.25
81	Deion Sanders	.25
84	Darren Daulton	.25

1993 Sports Card Pocket Price Guide

The final year of production of an annual repli-card insert set for the SCD price guide magazine combined stars and hot rookies from all four major team sports. Cards were produced in the style of Topps' 1973 football issue, with varying colored striped pennants down the left side of the front. Backs are printed in black, white and green (#1-8) and black, white and red (#9-104), and include a cartoon trivia question along with price guide and player data. The repli-cards were printed on sheets of eight stapled into the magazine's monthly issues. Only the baseball players are listed here.

	NM/M
Complete (Baseball) Set (54)	20.00

Common Player:		.25
1	Tyler Green	.25
3	Ozzie Smith	.75
5	Fred McGriff	.25
7	Marquis Grissom	.25
13	John Smoltz	.25
16	Ruben Sierra	.25
19	Roberto Alomar	.40
20	Gary Sheffield	.40
23	Carlos Baerga	.25
24	Robin Ventura	.25
26	Nigel Wilson	.25
27	David Nied	.25
28	Cal Ripken Jr.	2.00
31	Albert Belle	.25
34	Larry Walker	.25
37	Eric Karros	.25
38	Dwight Gooden	.25
39	Nolan Ryan	2.00
40	Juan Gonzalez	.45
41	Robin Yount	.25
44	Darryl Strawberry	.25
45	George Brett	1.00
46	Ray Lankford	.25
47	Kirby Puckett	.75
48	David Justice	.25
49	Travis Fryman	.25
50	Eddie Murray	.65
51	Tony Gwynn	.75
52	Jack McDowell	.25
57	Ryne Sandberg	.75
58	Deion Sanders	.25
61	Frank Thomas	.65
62	Carlton Fisk	.65
65	Tim Salmon	.25
66	Jeff Conine	.25
67	Benito Santiago	.25
68	Mike Piazza	1.50
72	Andres Galarraga	.25
71	Gregg Jefferies	.25
76	Joe Carter	.25
77	Rickey Henderson	.65
80	Barry Larkin	.25
81	Juan Gonzalez	.45
83	Gary Sheffield	.40
84	Will Clark	.25
89	Mark Grace	.25
90	Cliff Floyd	.25
91	Bobby Bonds Jr.	.25
92	Barry Bonds	2.00
94	Matt Williams	.25
97	Paul Molitor	.65
99	Ken Griffey Jr.	1.50
99	Steve Avery	.25
100	Kirby Puckett	.65

1989 Schafer's Bakery Super Stars Discs

(See 1989 Holsum for checklist and vlue information. Distributed in Michigan.)

1987 Schnucks St. Louis Cardinals

Sponsored by Schnucks food stores, and distributed at more than 50 locations around St. Louis, the company is not mentioned anywhere on these photos. The set of 6" x 9" photocards depicts the players without caps or other visible uniform logos in color photos against a plain blue backdrop. A facsimile autograph appears in the lower-left corner, with a Players' Association logo at upper-left. Backs are blank. The unnumbered cards are checklisted here alphabetically. A Schnucks spokesman said about 50,000 of each picture was produced.

		NM/M
Complete Set (16):		14.00
Common Player:		.50
(1)	Jack Clark	.50
(2)	Vince Coleman	.75
(3)	Danny Cox	.50
(4)	Curt Ford	.50
(5)	Bob Forsch	.50
(6)	Tom Herr	.50
(7)	Whitey Herzog	.50
(8)	Ricky Horton	.50
(9)	Greg Mathews	.50
(10)	Willie McGee	.75
(11)	Jose Oquendo	.50
(12)	Tony Pena	.50
(13)	Terry Pendleton	.75
(14)	Ozzie Smith	6.00
(15)	John Tudor	.50
(16)	Todd Worrell	.50

1996 Schwebel's Stars Discs

Distributed in loaves of bread in the Youngstown, Ohio, area, the players in this disc set lean heavily towards Cleveland Indians. The 2-3/4" diameter discs were inserted into a special pocket in the bread wrapper to keep them from contact with the bread. Fronts have a purple-to-red graduated color scheme around the border, with a player photo at center. Uniform logos have been removed from the photos because the discs are licensed only by the players' union; they are a product of Mike Schechter Assoc. Backs are printed in purple with 1995 and career stats along with appropriate logos. A die-cut poster into which the discs could be inserted for display was also available.

		NM/M
Complete Set (20):		20.00
Common Player:		1.00
1	Jim Thome	1.50
2	Orel Hershiser	1.00
3	Greg Maddux	2.50
4	Charles Nagy	1.00
5	Omar Vizquel	1.00
6	Manny Ramirez	2.00
7	Dennis Martinez	1.00
8	Eddie Murray	2.00
9	Albert Belle	1.00
10	Fred McGriff	1.00
11	Jack McDowell	1.00
12	Kenny Lofton	1.00
13	Cal Ripken Jr.	4.00
14	Jose Mesa	1.00
15	Randy Johnson	2.00
16	Ken Griffey Jr.	3.00
17	Carlos Baerga	1.00
18	Frank Thomas	2.00
19	Sandy Alomar Jr.	1.00
20	Barry Bonds	4.00

1988 Score Promo Cards

While these Score promotional sample cards carry a 1988 copyright date on back, they were actually released to hobby dealers late in 1987. They can be easily differentiated from regular-issue 1988 cards by the use of zeros in the stats lines on back for 1987 and career figures. Most of the promos are otherwise identical to the issued versions of the same players. These were among the first promo cards to be widely distributed within the hobby.

		NM/M
Complete Set (6):		20.00
Common Player:		4.00
30	Mark Langston	4.00
48	Tony Pena	4.00
71	Keith Moreland	4.00
72	Barry Larkin	4.00
121	Dennis Boyd	4.00
149	Denny Walling	4.00

1988 Score Proofs

The first six cards in the eventual 1988 Score debut issue can also be found in proof versions intended to test various inks, finishes, etc. These cards are differentiated from regular issues (and promo cards) by the use of zeros in place of actual stats for 1987 and career on the backs.

		NM/M
Complete Set (6):		150.00
Common Player:		15.00
1	Don Mattingly	45.00
2	Wade Boggs	35.00
3	Tim Raines	15.00
4	Andre Dawson	25.00
5	Mark McGwire	60.00
6	Kevin Seitzer	15.00

1988 Score

A fifth member joined the group of nationally distributed baseball cards in 1988. Titled "Score," the cards are characterized by extremely sharp color photography and printing. Card backs are full-color also and carry a player portrait along with a brief biography, player data and statistics. The 660 cards in the set are standard 2-1/2" x 3-1/2" format. The fronts come with one of six different border colors which are equally divided at 110 cards per color. The Score set was produced by Major League Marketing, the same company that marketed the "triple-action" Sportflics card sets.

	NM/M
Unopened Fact. Set (660):	9.00
Complete Set (660):	6.00
Common Player:	.05

Pack:		.35
Wax Box:		9.00
Rack Pack (54):		.75
Rack Box (24):		12.00
1	Don Mattingly	.65
2	Wade Boggs	.50
3	Tim Raines	.05
4	Andre Dawson	.25
5	Mark McGwire	.75
6	Kevin Seitzer	.05
7	Wally Joyner	.05
8	Jesse Barfield	.05
9	Pedro Guerrero	.05
10	Eric Davis	.05
11	George Brett	.65
12	Ozzie Smith	.50
13	Rickey Henderson	.40
14	Jim Rice	.15
15	Matt Nokes RC	.05
16	Mike Schmidt	.65
17	Dave Parker	.05
18	Eddie Murray	.40
19	Andres Galarraga	.05
20	Tony Fernandez	.05
21	Kevin McReynolds	.05
22	B.J. Surhoff	.05
23	Pat Tabler	.05
24	Kirby Puckett	.50
25	Benny Santiago	.05
26	Ryne Sandberg	.50
27	Kelly Downs	.05
28	Jose Cruz	.05
29	Pete O'Brien	.05
30	Mark Langston	.05
31	Lee Smith	.05
32	Juan Samuel	.05
33	Kevin Bass	.05
34	R.J. Reynolds	.05
35	Steve Sax	.05
36	John Kruk	.05
37	Alan Trammell	.05
38	Chris Bosio	.05
39	Brook Jacoby	.05
40	Willie McGee	.05
41	Dave Magadan	.05
42	Fred Lynn	.05
43	Kent Hrbek	.05
44	Brian Downing	.05
45	Jose Canseco	.30
46	Jim Presley	.05
47	Mike Stanley	.05
48	Tony Pena	.05
49	David Cone	.05
50	Rick Sutcliffe	.05
51	Doug Drabek	.05
52	Bill Doran	.05
53	Mike Scioscia	.05
54	Candy Maldonado	.05
55	Dave Winfield	.40
56	Lou Whitaker	.05
57	Tom Henke	.05
58	Ken Gerhart	.05
59	Glenn Braggs	.05
60	Julio Franco	.05
61	Charlie Leibrandt	.05
62	Gary Gaetti	.05
63	Bob Boone	.05
64	Luis Polonia RC	.05
65	Dwight Evans	.05
66	Phil Bradley	.05
67	Mike Boddicker	.05
68	Vince Coleman	.05
69	Howard Johnson	.05
70	Tim Wallach	.05
71	Keith Moreland	.05
72	Barry Larkin	.05
73	Alan Ashby	.05
74	Rick Rhoden	.05
75	Darrell Evans	.05
76	Dave Stieb	.05
77	Dan Plesac	.05
78	Will Clark	.05
79	Frank White	.05
80	Joe Carter	.05
81	Mike Witt	.05
82	Terry Steinbach	.05
83	Alvin Davis	.05
84	Tom Herr	.05
85	Vance Law	.05
86	Kal Daniels	.05
87	Rick Honeycutt	.05
88	Alfredo Griffin	.05
89	Bret Saberhagen	.05
90	Bert Blyleven	.05
91	Jeff Reardon	.05
92	Cory Snyder	.05
93	Greg Walker	.05
94	Joe Magrane RC	.10
95	Rob Deer	.05
96	Ray Knight	.05
97	Casey Candaele	.05
98	John Cerutti	.05
99	Buddy Bell	.05
100	Jack Clark	.05
101	Eric Bell	.05
102	Willie Wilson	.05
103	Dave Schmidt	.05
104	Dennis Eckersley	.35
105	Don Sutton	.35
106	Danny Tartabull	.05
107	Fred McGriff	.05
108	Les Straker RC	.05
109	Lloyd Moseby	.05
110	Roger Clemens	.65
111	Glenn Hubbard	.05
112	Ken Williams RC	.05
113	Ruben Sierra	.05
114	Stan Jefferson	.05
115	Milt Thompson	.05
116	Bobby Bonilla	.05
117	Wayne Tolleson	.05
118	Matt Williams	.05
119	Chet Lemon	.05
120	Dale Sveum	.05
121	Dennis Boyd	.05
122	Brett Butler	.05
123	Terry Kennedy	.05
124	Jack Howell	.05
125	Curt Young	.05
126a	Dale Valle (First name incorrect.)	.25
126b	Dave Valle (Correct spelling.)	.05
127	Curt Wilkerson	.05
128	Tim Teufel	.05
129	Ozzie Virgil	.05
130	Brian Fisher	.05
131	Lance Parrish	.05
132	Tom Browning	.05
133a	Larry Anderson (Incorrect spelling.)	.25
133b	Larry Andersen (Correct spelling.)	.05
134a	Bob Brenley (Incorrect spelling.)	.25
134b	Bob Brenly (Correct spelling.)	.05
135	Mike Marshall	.05
136	Gerald Perry	.05
137	Bobby Meacham	.05
138	Larry Herndon	.05
139	Fred Manrique RC	.05
140	Charlie Hough	.05
141	Ron Darling	.05
142	Herm Winningham	.05
143	Mike Diaz	.05
144	Mike Jackson RC	.05
145	Denny Walling	.05
146	Rob Thompson	.05
147	Franklin Stubbs	.05
148	Albert Hall	.05
149	Bobby Witt	.05
150	Lance McCullers	.05
151	Scott Bradley	.05
152	Mark McLemore	.05
153	Tim Laudner	.05
154	Greg Swindell	.05
155	Marty Barrett	.05
156	Mike Heath	.05
157	Gary Ward	.05
158a	Lee Mazilli (Incorrect spelling.)	.25
158b	Lee Mazzilli (Correct spelling.)	.05
159	Tom Foley	.05
160	Robin Yount	.40
161	Steve Bedrosian	.05
162	Bob Walk	.05
163	Nick Esasky	.05
164	Ken Caminiti RC	.15
165	Jose Uribe	.05
166	Dave Anderson	.05
167	Ed Whitson	.05
168	Ernie Whitt	.05
169	Cecil Cooper	.05
170	Mike Pagliarulo	.05
171	Pat Sheridan	.05
172	Chris Bando	.05
173	Lee Lacy	.05
174	Steve Lombardozzi	.05
175	Mike Greenwell	.05
176	Greg Minton	.05
177	Moose Haas	.05
178	Mike Kingery	.05
179	Greg Harris	.05
180	Bo Jackson	.10
181	Carmelo Martinez	.05
182	Alex Trevino	.05
183	Ron Oester	.05
184	Danny Darwin	.05
185	Mike Krukow	.05
186	Rafael Palmeiro	.40
187	Tim Burke	.05
188	Roger McDowell	.05
189	Garry Templeton	.05
190	Terry Pendleton	.05
191	Larry Parrish	.05
192	Rey Quinones	.05
193	Joaquin Andujar	.05
194	Tom Brunansky	.05
195	Donnie Moore	.05
196	Dan Pasqua	.05
197	Jim Gantner	.05
198	Mark Eichhorn	.05
199	John Grubb	.05
200	Bill Ripken RC	.05
201	Sam Horn RC	.05
202	Todd Worrell	.05
203	Terry Leach	.05
204	Garth Iorg	.05
205	Brian Dayett	.05
206	Bo Diaz	.05
207	Craig Reynolds	.05
208	Brian Holton	.05
209	Marvelle Wynne (Marvell)	.05
210	Dave Concepcion	.05
211	Mike Davis	.05
212	Devon White	.05
213	Mickey Brantley	.05
214	Greg Gagne	.05
215	Oddibe McDowell	.05
216	Jimmy Key	.05
217	Dave Bergman	.05
218	Calvin Schiraldi	.05
219	Larry Sheets	.05
220	Mike Easler	.05
221	Kurt Stillwell	.05
222	Chuck Jackson RC	.05
223	Dave Martinez	.05
224	Tim Leary	.05
225	Steve Garvey	.20
226	Greg Mathews	.05
227	Doug Sisk	.05
228	Dave Henderson	.05
229	Jimmy Dwyer	.05
230	Larry Owen	.05
231	Andre Thornton	.05
232	Mark Salas	.05
233	Tom Brookens	.05
234	Greg Brock	.05
235	Rance Mulliniks	.05
236	Bob Brower	.05
237	Joe Niekro	.05
238	Scott Bankhead	.05
239	Doug DeCinces	.05
240	Tommy John	.05
241	Rich Gedman	.05
242	Ted Power	.05
243	Dave Meads RC	.05
244	Jim Sundberg	.05
245	Ken Oberkfell	.05
246	Jimmy Jones	.05
247	Ken Landreaux	.05
248	Jose Oquendo	.05
249	John Mitchell RC	.05
250	Don Baylor	.05
251	Scott Fletcher	.05
252	Al Newman	.05
253	Carney Lansford	.05
254	Johnny Ray	.05
255	Gary Pettis	.05
256	Ken Phelps	.05
257	Rick Leach	.05
258	Tim Stoddard	.05
259	Ed Romero	.05
260	Sid Bream	.05
261a	Tom Neidenfuer (Incorrect spelling.)	.25
261b	Tom Niedenfuer (Correct spelling.)	.05
262	Rick Dempsey	.05
263	Lonnie Smith	.05
264	Bob Forsch	.05
265	Barry Bonds	1.00
266	Willie Randolph	.05
267	Mike Ramsey	.05
268	Don Slaught	.05
269	Mickey Tettleton	.05
270	Jerry Reuss	.05
271	Marc Sullivan	.05
272	Jim Morrison	.05
273	Steve Balboni	.05
274	Dick Schofield	.05
275	John Tudor	.05
276	Gene Larkin RC	.05
277	Harold Reynolds	.05
278	Jerry Browne	.05
279	Willie Upshaw	.05
280	Ted Higuera	.05
281	Terry McGriff	.05
282	Terry Puhl	.05
283	Mark Wasinger RC	.05
284	Luis Salazar	.05
285	Ted Simmons	.05
286	John Shelby	.05
287	John Smiley RC	.05
288	Curt Ford	.05
289	Steve Crawford	.05
290	Dan Quisenberry	.05
291	Alan Wiggins	.05
292	Randy Bush	.05
293	John Candelaria	.05
294	Tony Phillips	.05
295	Mike Morgan	.05
296	Bill Wegman	.05
297a	Terry Franconia (Incorrect spelling.)	.25
297b	Terry Francona (Correct spelling.)	.05
298	Mickey Hatcher	.05
299	Andres Thomas	.05
300	Bob Stanley	.05
301	Alfredo Pedrique RC	.05
302	Jim Lindeman	.05
303	Wally Backman	.05
304	Paul O'Neill	.05
305	Hubie Brooks	.05
306	Steve Buechele	.05
307	Bobby Thigpen	.05
308	George Hendrick	.05
309	John Moses	.05
310	Ron Guidry	.05
311	Bill Schroeder	.05
312	Jose Nunez RC	.05
313	Bud Black	.05
314	Joe Sambito	.05
315	Scott McGregor	.05
316	Rafael Santana	.05
317	Frank Williams	.05
318	Mike Fitzgerald	.05
319	Rick Mahler	.05
320	Jim Gott	.05
321	Mariano Duncan	.05
322	Jose Guzman	.05
323	Lee Guetterman	.05
324	Dan Gladden	.05
325	Gary Carter	.40
326	Tracy Jones	.05
327	Floyd Youmans	.05
328	Bill Dawley	.05
329	Paul Noce RC	.05
330	Angel Salazar	.05
331	Goose Gossage	.10
332	George Frazier	.05
333	Ruppert Jones	.05
334	Billy Jo Robidoux	.05
335	Mike Scott	.05
336	Randy Myers	.05
337	Bob Sebra	.05
338	Eric Show	.05
339	Mitch Williams	.05
340	Paul Molitor	.40
341	Gus Polidor	.05
342	Steve Trout	.05
343	Jerry Don Gleaton	.05
344	Bob Knepper	.05
345	Mitch Webster	.05
346	John Morris	.05
347	Andy Hawkins	.05
348	Dave Leiper	.05
349	Ernest Riles	.05
350	Dwight Gooden	.05
351	Dave Righetti	.05
352	Pat Dodson	.05
353	John Habyan	.05
354	Jim Deshaies	.05
355	Butch Wynegar	.05
356	Bryn Smith	.05
357	Matt Young	.05
358	Tom Pagnozzi RC	.05
359	Floyd Rayford	.05
360	Darryl Strawberry	.05
361	Sal Butera	.05
362	Domingo Ramos	.05
363	Chris Brown	.05
364	Jose Gonzalez	.05
365	Dave Smith	.05
366	Andy McGaffigan	.05
367	Stan Javier	.05
368	Henry Cotto	.05
369	Mike Birkbeck	.05
370	Len Dykstra	.05
371	Dave Collins	.05
372	Spike Owen	.05
373	Geno Petralli	.05
374	Ron Karkovice	.05
375	Shane Rawley	.05
376	DeWayne Buice RC	.05
377	Bill Pecota RC	.05
378	Leon Durham	.05
379	Ed Olwine	.05
380	Bruce Hurst	.05
381	Bob McClure	.05
382	Mark Thurmond	.05
383	Buddy Biancalana	.05
384	Tim Conroy	.05
385	Tony Gwynn	.50
386	Greg Gross	.05
387	Barry Lyons RC	.05
388	Mike Felder	.05
389	Pat Clements	.05
390	Ken Griffey	.05
391	Mark Davis	.05
392	Jose Rijo	.05
393	Mike Young	.05
394	Willie Fraser	.05
395	Dion James	.05
396	Steve Shields RC	.05
397	Randy St. Claire	.05
398	Danny Jackson	.05
399	Cecil Fielder	.05
400	Keith Hernandez	.05
401	Don Carman	.05
402	Chuck Crim RC	.05
403	Rob Woodward	.05
404	Junior Ortiz	.05
405	Glenn Wilson	.05
406	Ken Howell	.05
407	Jeff Kunkel	.05
408	Jeff Reed	.05
409	Chris James	.05
410	Zane Smith	.05
411	Ken Dixon	.05
412	Ricky Horton	.05
413	Frank DiPino	.05
414	Shane Mack RC	.05
415	Danny Cox	.05
416	Andy Van Slyke	.05
417	Danny Heep	.05
418	John Cangelosi	.05
419a	John Christiansen (Incorrect spelling.)	.25
419b	John Christensen (Correct spelling.)	.05
420	Joey Cora RC	.05
421	Mike LaValliere	.05
422	Kelly Gruber	.05
423	Bruce Benedict	.05
424	Len Matuszek	.05
425	Kent Tekulve	.05
426	Rafael Ramirez	.05
427	Mike Flanagan	.05
428	Mike Gallego	.05
429	Juan Castillo	.05
430	Neal Heaton	.05
431	Phil Garner	.05
432	Mike Dunne RC	.05
433	Wallace Johnson	.05
434	Jack O'Connor	.05
435	Steve Jeltz	.05
436	Donnell Nixon RC	.05
437	Jack Lazorko	.05
438	Keith Comstock RC	.05
439	Jeff Robinson	.05
440	Graig Nettles	.05
441	Mel Hall	.05
442	Gerald Young RC	.05
443	Gary Redus	.05
444	Charlie Moore	.05
445	Bill Madlock	.05
446	Mark Clear	.05

447	Greg Booker	.05
448	Rick Schu	.05
449	Ron Kittle	.05
450	Dale Murphy	.25
451	Bob Dernier	.05
452	Dale Mohorcic	.05
453	Rafael Belliard	.05
454	Charlie Puleo	.05
455	Dwayne Murphy	.05
456	Jim Eisenreich	.05
457	David Palmer	.05
458	Dave Stewart	.05
459	Pascual Perez	.05
460	Glenn Davis	.05
461	Dan Petry	.05
462	Jim Winn	.05
463	Darrell Miller	.05
464	Mike Moore	.05
465	Mike LaCoss	.05
466	Steve Farr	.05
467	Jerry Mumphrey	.05
468	Kevin Gross	.05
469	Bruce Bochy	.05
470	Orel Hershiser	.05
471	Eric King	.05
472	Ellis Burks **RC**	.25
473	Darren Daulton	.05
474	Mookie Wilson	.05
475	Frank Viola	.05
476	Ron Robinson	.05
477	Bob Melvin	.05
478	Jeff Musselman	.05
479	Charlie Kerfeld	.05
480	Richard Dotson	.05
481	Kevin Mitchell	.05
482	Gary Roenicke	.05
483	Tim Flannery	.05
484	Rich Yett	.05
485	Pete Incaviglia	.05
486	Rick Cerone	.05
487	Tony Armas	.05
488	Jerry Reed	.05
489	Davey Lopes	.05
490	Frank Tanana	.05
491	Mike Loynd	.05
492	Bruce Ruffin	.05
493	Chris Speier	.05
494	Tom Hume	.05
495	Jesse Orosco	.05
496	Robby Wine, Jr. **RC**	.05
497	Jeff Montgomery **RC**	.15
498	Jeff Dedmon	.05
499	Luis Aguayo	.05
500	Reggie Jackson (1968-75)	.15
501	Reggie Jackson/1976	.15
502	Reggie Jackson (1977-81)	.15
503	Reggie Jackson (1982-86)	.15
504	Reggie Jackson/1987	.15
505	Billy Hatcher	.05
506	Ed Lynch	.05
507	Willie Hernandez	.05
508	Jose DeLeon	.05
509	Joel Youngblood	.05
510	Bob Welch	.05
511	Steve Ontiveros	.05
512	Randy Ready	.05
513	Juan Nieves	.05
514	Jeff Russell	.05
515	Von Hayes	.05
516	Mark Gubicza	.05
517	Ken Dayley	.05
518	Don Aase	.05
519	Rick Reuschel	.05
520	Mike Henneman **RC**	.10
521	Rick Aguilera	.05
522	Jay Howell	.05
523	Ed Correa	.05
524	Manny Trillo	.05
525	Kirk Gibson	.05
526	Wally Ritchie **RC**	.05
527	Al Nipper	.05
528	Atlee Hammaker	.05
529	Shawon Dunston	.05
530	Jim Clancy	.05
531	Tom Paciorek	.05
532	Joel Skinner	.05
533	Scott Garrelts	.05
534	Tom O'Malley	.05
535	John Franco	.05
536	Paul Kilgus **RC**	.05
537	Darrell Porter	.05
538	Walt Terrell	.05
539	Bill Long **RC**	.05
540	George Bell	.05
541	Jeff Sellers	.05
542	Joe Boever **RC**	.05
543	Steve Howe	.05
544	Scott Sanderson	.05
545	Jack Morris	.05
546	Todd Benzinger **RC**	.05
547	Steve Henderson	.05
548	Eddie Milner	.05
549	Jeff Robinson **RC**	.05
550	Cal Ripken, Jr.	1.00
551	Jody Davis	.05
552	Kirk McCaskill	.05
553	Craig Lefferts	.05
554	Darnell Coles	.05
555	Phil Niekro	.35
556	Mike Aldrete	.05
557	Pat Perry	.05
558	Juan Agosto	.05
559	Rob Murphy	.05
560	Dennis Rasmussen	.05
561	Manny Lee	.05

562	Jeff Blauser **RC**	.10
563	Bob Ojeda	.05
564	Dave Dravecky	.05
565	Gene Garber	.05
566	Ron Roenicke	.05
567	Tommy Hinzo **RC**	.05
568	Eric Nolte **RC**	.05
569	Ed Hearn	.05
570	Mark Davidson **RC**	.05
571	Jim Walewander **RC**	.05
572	Donnie Hill	.05
573	Jamie Moyer	.05
574	Ken Schrom	.05
575	Nolan Ryan	1.00
576	Jim Acker	.05
577	Jamie Quirk	.05
578	Jay Aldrich **RC**	.05
579	Claudell Washington	.05
580	Jeff Leonard	.05
581	Carmen Castillo	.05
582	Daryl Boston	.05
583	Jeff DeWillis **RC**	.05
584	John Marzano **RC**	.05
585	Bill Gullickson	.05
586	Andy Allanson	.05
587	Lee Tunnell	.05
588	Gene Nelson	.05
589	Dave LaPoint	.05
590	Harold Baines	.05
591	Bill Buckner	.05
592	Carlton Fisk	.40
593	Rick Manning	.05
594	Doug Jones **RC**	.10
595	Tom Candiotti	.05
596	Steve Lake	.05
597	Jose Lind **RC**	.05
598	Ross Jones **RC**	.05
599	Gary Matthews	.05
600	Fernando Valenzuela	.05
601	Dennis Martinez	.05
602	Les Lancaster **RC**	.05
603	Ozzie Guillen	.05
604	Tony Bernazard	.05
605	Chili Davis	.05
606	Roy Smalley	.05
607	Ivan Calderon	.05
608	Jay Tibbs	.05
609	Guy Hoffman	.05
610	Doyle Alexander	.05
611	Mike Bielecki	.05
612	Shawn Hillegas **RC**	.05
613	Keith Atherton	.05
614	Eric Plunk	.05
615	Sid Fernandez	.05
616	Dennis Lamp	.05
617	Dave Engle	.05
618	Harry Spilman	.05
619	Don Robinson	.05
620	John Farrell **RC**	.05
621	Nelson Liriano **RC**	.05
622	Floyd Bannister	.05
623	Randy Milligan **RC**	.05
624	Kevin Elster **RC**	.10
625	Jody Reed **RC**	.05
626	Shawn Abner **RC**	.05
627	Kirt Manwaring **RC**	.10
628	Pete Stanicek **RC**	.05
629	Rob Ducey **RC**	.05
630	Steve Kiefer	.05
631	Gary Thurman **RC**	.05
632	Darrel Akerfelds **RC**	.05
633	Dave Clark	.05
634	Roberto Kelly **RC**	.05
635	Keith Hughes **RC**	.05
636	John Davis **RC**	.05
637	Mike Devereaux **RC**	.10
638	Tom Glavine **RC**	1.00
639	Keith Miller **RC**	.05
640	Chris Gwynn **RC**	.05
641	Tim Crews **RC**	.05
642	Mackey Sasser **RC**	.05
643	Vicente Palacios **RC**	.05
644	Kevin Romine	.05
645	Gregg Jefferies **RC**	.25
646	Jeff Treadway **RC**	.05
647	Ron Gant **RC**	.25
648	Rookie Sluggers (Mark McGwire, Matt Nokes)	.35
649	Speed and Power (Tim Raines, Eric Davis)	.05
650	Game Breakers (Jack Clark, Don Mattingly)	.25
651	Super Shortstops (Tony Fernandez, Cal Ripken, Jr., Alan Trammell)	.25
652	Vince Coleman/ Highlight	.05
653	Kirby Puckett/ Highlight	.25
654	Benito Santiago/ Highlight	.05
655	Juan Nieves/ Highlight	.05
656	Steve Bedrosian/ Highlight	.05
657	Mike Schmidt/ Highlight	.30
658	Don Mattingly/ Highlight	.30
659	Mark McGwire/ Highlight	.35
660	Paul Molitor/ Highlight	.20

Glossy

With production of a reported 5,000 sets, there is a significant premium attached to the glossy version of Score's debut baseball card issue. The specially packaged collector's edition features cards with a high-gloss front finish and was sold only as a complete set.

	NM/M
Complete Set (660):	65.00
Common Player:	.25
Stars:	15X

Box Panels

1987 ALL-STAR — ERIC DAVIS

This 18-card set, produced by Major League Marketing and manufactured by Optigraphics, is the premiere box-bottom set issued under the Score trademark. The set features 1987 major league All-star players in full-color action poses, framed by a white border. A "1987 All-Star" banner (red or purple) curves above an orange player name block beneath the player photo. Card backs are printed in red, blue, gold and black and carry the card number, player name and position and league logo. Six colorful "Great Moments in Baseball" trivia cards are also included in this set.

	NM/M
Complete Panel Set:	7.50
Complete Singles Set (18):	7.50
Common Panel:	.50
Common Single Player:	.15

Panel 1		1.00
1	Terry Kennedy	.15
3	Willie Randolph	.15
15	Eric Davis	.15
Panel 2		4.50
1	Don Mattingly	1.00
5	Cal Ripken, Jr.	2.00
11	Jack Clark	.15
Panel 3		3.00
4	Wade Boggs	.75
9	Bret Saberhagen	.25
12	Ryne Sandberg	.75
Panel 4		2.50
6	George Bell	.15
18	Mike Schmidt	1.00
18	Mike Scott	.15
Panel 5		2.00
7	Rickey Henderson	.65
16	Andre Dawson	.25
17	Darryl Strawberry	.25
Panel 6		3.50
8	Dave Winfield	.65
10	Gary Carter	.65
14	Ozzie Smith	.75

Traded/Rookie

JACK CLARK

This 110-card set featuring rookies and traded veterans is similar in design to the 1988 Score set, except for a change in border color. Individual standard-size player cards (2-1/2" x 3-1/2") feature a bright orange border framing an action photos highlighted by a thin white outline. The player name (in white) is centered in the bottom margin, flanked by three yellow stars lower left and a yellow Score logo lower right. The backs carry full-color player portraits on a cream-colored background, plus team name and logo, personal information and a purple stats chart that lists year-by-year and major league totals. A brief player profile follows the stats chart and, on some cards, information is included about the player's trade or acquisition. The boxed update set also includes 10 Magic Motion 3-D trivia cards. The cards are numbered with a "T" suffix.

		NM/M
Complete Set (110):		12.00
Common Player:		.05
1	Jack Clark	.05
2	Danny Jackson	.05
3	Brett Butler	.05
4	Kurt Stillwell	.05
5	Tom Brunansky	.05
6	Dennis Lamp	.05
7	Jose DeLeon	.05
8	Tom Herr	.05
9	Keith Moreland	.05
10	Kirk Gibson	.05
11	Bud Black	.05
12	Rafael Ramirez	.05
13	Luis Salazar	.05
14	Goose Gossage	.05
15	Bob Welch	.05
16	Vance Law	.05
17	Ray Knight	.05
18	Dan Quisenberry	.05
19	Don Slaught	.05
20	Lee Smith	.05
21	Rick Cerone	.05
22	Pat Tabler	.05
23	Larry McWilliams	.05
24	Rick Horton	.05
25	Graig Nettles	.05
26	Dan Petry	.05
27	Jose Rijo	.05
28	Chili Davis	.05
29	Dickie Thon	.05
30	Mackey Sasser	.05
31	Mickey Tettleton	.05
32	Rick Dempsey	.05
33	Ron Hassey	.05
34	Phil Bradley	.05
35	Jay Howell	.05
36	Bill Buckner	.05
37	Alfredo Griffin	.05
38	Gary Pettis	.05
39	Calvin Schiraldi	.05
40	John Candelaria	.05
41	Joe Orsulak	.05
42	Willie Upshaw	.05
43	Herm Winningham	.05
44	Ron Kittle	.05
45	Bob Dernier	.05
46	Steve Balboni	.05
47	Steve Shields	.05
48	Henry Cotto	.05
49	Dave Henderson	.05
50	Dave Parker	.05
51	Mike Young	.05
52	Mark Salas	.05
53	Mike Davis	.05
54	Rafael Santana	.05
55	Don Baylor	.05
56	Dan Pasqua	.05
57	Ernest Riles	.05
58	Glenn Hubbard	.05
59	Mike Smithson	.05
60	Richard Dotson	.05
61	Jerry Reuss	.05
62	Mike Jackson	.05
63	Floyd Bannister	.05
64	Jesse Orosco	.05
65	Larry Parrish	.05
66	Jeff Bittiger **RC**	.05
67	Ray Hayward **RC**	.05
68	Ricky Jordan **RC**	.05
69	Tommy Gregg **RC**	.05
70	Brady Anderson **RC**	.50
71	Jeff Montgomery	.05
72	Darryl Hamilton **RC**	.25
73	Cecil Espy **RC**	.05
74	Greg Briley **RC**	.05
75	Joey Meyer **RC**	.05
76	Mike Macfarlane **RC**	.05
77	Oswald Peraza **RC**	.05
78	Jack Armstrong **RC**	.05
79	Don Heinkel **RC**	.05
80	Mark Grace **RC**	1.50
81	Steve Curry **RC**	.05
82	Damon Berryhill **RC**	.05
83	Steve Ellsworth **RC**	.05
84	Pete Smith **RC**	.05
85	Jack McDowell **RC**	.25
86	Rob Dibble **RC**	.05
87	Bryan Harvey **RC**	.05
88	John Dopson **RC**	.05
89	Dave Gallagher **RC**	.05
90	Todd Stottlemyre **RC**	.25
91	Mike Schooler **RC**	.05
92	Don Gordon **RC**	.05
93	Sil Campusano **RC**	.05
94	Jeff Pico **RC**	.05
95	Jay Buhner **RC**	.75
96	Nelson Santovenia **RC**	.05
97	Al Leiter **RC**	.05
98	Luis Alicea **RC**	.05
99	Pat Borders **RC**	.05
100	Chris Sabo **RC**	.25
101	Tim Belcher **RC**	.05
102	Walt Weiss **RC**	.05
103	Craig Biggio **RC**	6.00
104	Don August **RC**	.05
105	Roberto Alomar **RC**	4.00
106	Todd Burns **RC**	.05
107	John Costello **RC**	.05
108	Melido Perez **RC**	.05
109	Darrin Jackson **RC**	.05
110	Orestes Destrade **RC**	.05

Traded/ Rookie Glossy

Among the scarcest of the major card companies' high-gloss collector's editions of the late 1980s is the 1988 Score Rookie/Traded issue. Production of the regular-finish set was limited in itself and the glossy version is more so, adding a significant premium value.

	NM/M
Complete Set (110):	60.00
Common Player:	.25
Stars:	3X

Young Superstar Series 1

MATT WILLIAMS — THIRD BASE 10

This 40-card set of 2-1/2" x 3-1/2" cards is divided into five separate 8-card subsets. Similar to the company's regular issue, these cards are distinguished by excellent full-color photography on both front and back. The glossy player photos are centered on a white background and framed by a vivid blue and green border. A player name banner beneath the photo includes the name, position and uniform number. The card backs feature color player portraits beneath a hot pink player name/Score logo banner. Hot pink also frames the personal stats (in green), career stats (in black) and career biography (in blue). The backs also include quotes from well-known baseball authorities discussing player performance. This set was distributed via a write-in offer printed on 1988 Score 17-card package wrappers.

		NM/M
Complete Set (40):		3.00
Common Player:		.10
1	Mark McGwire	2.50
2	Benito Santiago	.10
3	Sam Horn	.10
4	Chris Bosio	.10
5	Matt Nokes	.10
6	Ken Williams	.10
7	Dion James	.10
8	B.J. Surhoff	.10
9	Joe Magrane	.10
10	Kevin Seitzer	.10
11	Stanley Jefferson	.10
12	Devon White	.10
13	Nelson Liriano	.10
14	Chris James	.10
15	Mike Henneman	.10
16	Terry Steinbach	.10
17	John Kruk	.10
18	Matt Williams	.10
19	Kelly Downs	.10
20	Bill Ripken	.10
21	Ozzie Guillen	.10
22	Luis Polonia	.10
23	Dave Magadan	.10
24	Mike Greenwell	.10
25	Will Clark	.10
26	Mike Dunne	.10
27	Wally Joyner	.10
28	Robby Thompson	.10
29	Ken Caminiti	.10
30	Jose Canseco	.50
31	Todd Benzinger	.10
32	Pete Incaviglia	.10
33	John Farrell	.10
34	Casey Candaele	.10
35	Mike Aldrete	.10
36	Ruben Sierra	.10
37	Ellis Burks	.10
38	Tracy Jones	.10
39	Kal Daniels	.10
40	Cory Snyder	.10

Young Superstar Series 2

DON MATTINGLY — FIRST BASE 23

This set of 40 standard-size cards and five Magic trivia cards is part of a double series issued by Score. Each series is divided into five smaller sets of eight baseball cards and one trivia card. The design on both series is similar, except for border color. Series I has blue and green borders. Series II has red and blue borders framing full-color player photos. Backs carry color portrait photos and stats in a variety of colors. Young Superstar series were offered via a write-in offer on '88 Score wrappers. For each 8-card subset, collectors were instructed to send two Score wrappers and $1. Complete sets were offered by a number of hobby dealers nationwide.

		NM/M
Complete Set (40):		4.00
Common Player:		.10
1	Don Mattingly	1.00
2	Glenn Braggs	.10
3	Dwight Gooden	.10
4	Jose Lind	.10
5	Danny Tartabull	.10
6	Tony Fernandez	.10
7	Julio Franco	.10
8	Andres Galarraga	.10
9	Bobby Bonilla	.10
10	Eric Davis	.10
11	Gerald Young	.10
12	Barry Bonds	2.00
13	Jerry Browne	.10
14	Jeff Blauser	.10
15	Mickey Brantley	.10
16	Floyd Youmans	.10
17	Bret Saberhagen	.10
18	Shawon Dunston	.10
19	Len Dykstra	.10
20	Darryl Strawberry	.10
21	Rick Aguilera	.10
22	Ivan Calderon	.10
23	Roger Clemens	1.00
24	Vince Coleman	.10
25	Gary Thurman	.10
26	Jeff Treadway	.10
27	Oddibe McDowell	.10
28	Fred McGriff	.10
29	Mark McLemore	.10
30	Jeff Musselman	.10
31	Mitch Williams	.10
32	Dan Plesac	.10
33	Juan Nieves	.10
34	Barry Larkin	.10
35	Greg Mathews	.10
36	Shane Mack	.10
37	Scott Bankhead	.10

#	Player	Price
38	Eric Bell	.10
39	Greg Swindell	.10
40	Kevin Elster	.10

1989 Score

This set of 660 cards plus 56 Magic Motion trivia cards is the second annual basic issue from Score. Full-color player photos highlight 651 individual players and 9 season highlights, including the first Wrigley Field night game. Action photos are framed by thin brightly colored borders (green, cyan blue, purple, orange, red, royal blue) with a baseball diamond logo/player name beneath the photo. Full-color player close-ups (1-5/16" x 1-5/8") are printed on the pastel-colored backs, along with personal information, stats and career highlights. The cards measure 2-1/2" x 3-1/2".

	NM/M
Unopened Fact. Set (660):	12.00
Complete Set (660):	9.00
Common Player:	.05
Pack (16):	.50
Wax Box (36):	10.00

#	Player	Price
1	Jose Canseco	.25
2	Andre Dawson	.25
3	Mark McGwire	.65
4	Benny Santiago	.05
5	Rick Reuschel	.05
6	Fred McGriff	.05
7	Kal Daniels	.05
8	Gary Gaetti	.05
9	Ellis Burks	.05
10	Darryl Strawberry	.05
11	Julio Franco	.05
12	Lloyd Moseby	.05
13	Jeff Pico RC	.05
14	Johnny Ray	.05
15	Cal Ripken, Jr.	.75
16	Dick Schofield	.05
17	Mel Hall	.05
18	Bill Ripken	.05
19	Brook Jacoby	.05
20	Kirby Puckett	.50
21	Bill Doran	.05
22	Pete O'Brien	.05
23	Matt Nokes	.05
24	Brian Fisher	.05
25	Jack Clark	.05
26	Gary Pettis	.05
27	Dave Valle	.05
28	Willie Wilson	.05
29	Curt Young	.05
30	Dale Murphy	.20
31	Barry Larkin	.05
32	Dave Stewart	.05
33	Mike LaValliere	.05
34	Glenn Hubbard	.05
35	Ryne Sandberg	.50
36	Tony Pena	.05
37	Greg Walker	.05
38	Von Hayes	.05
39	Kevin Mitchell	.05
40	Tim Raines	.05
41	Keith Hernandez	.05
42	Keith Moreland	.05
43	Ruben Sierra	.05
44	Chet Lemon	.05
45	Willie Randolph	.05
46	Andy Allanson	.05
47	Candy Maldonado	.05
48	Sid Bream	.05
49	Denny Walling	.05
50	Dave Winfield	.40
51	Alvin Davis	.05
52	Cory Snyder	.05
53	Hubie Brooks	.05
54	Chili Davis	.05
55	Kevin Seitzer	.05
56	Jose Uribe	.05
57	Tony Fernandez	.05
58	Tim Teufel	.05
59	Oddibe McDowell	.05
60	Les Lancaster	.05
61	Billy Hatcher	.05
62	Dan Gladden	.05
63	Marty Barrett	.05
64	Nick Esasky	.05
65	Wally Joyner	.05
66	Mike Greenwell	.05
67	Ken Williams	.05
68	Bob Horner	.05
69	Steve Sax	.05
70	Rickey Henderson	.40
71	Mitch Webster	.05
72	Rob Deer	.05
73	Jim Presley	.05
74	Albert Hall	.05
75a	George Brett ("At age 33 ...")	1.00
75b	George Brett ("At age 35 ...")	.50
76	Brian Downing	.05
77	Dave Martinez	.05
78	Scott Fletcher	.05
79	Phil Bradley	.05
80	Ozzie Smith	.50
81	Larry Sheets	.05
82	Mike Aldrete	.05
83	Darnell Coles	.05
84	Len Dykstra	.05
85	Jim Rice	.15
86	Jeff Treadway	.05
87	Jose Lind	.05
88	Willie McGee	.05
89	Mickey Brantley	.05
90	Tony Gwynn	.50
91	R.J. Reynolds	.05
92	Milt Thompson	.05
93	Kevin McReynolds	.05
94	Eddie Murray	.40
95	Lance Parrish	.05
96	Ron Kittle	.05
97	Gerald Young	.05
98	Ernie Whitt	.05
99	Jeff Reed	.05
100	Don Mattingly	.60
101	Gerald Perry	.05
102	Vance Law	.05
103	John Shelby	.05
104	Chris Sabo	.05
105	Danny Tartabull	.05
106	Glenn Wilson	.05
107	Mark Davidson	.05
108	Dave Parker	.05
109	Eric Davis	.05
110	Alan Trammell	.05
111	Ozzie Virgil	.05
112	Frank Tanana	.05
113	Rafael Ramirez	.05
114	Dennis Martinez	.05
115	Jose DeLeon	.05
116	Bob Ojeda	.05
117	Doug Drabek	.05
118	Andy Hawkins	.05
119	Greg Maddux	.50
120	Cecil Fielder (Reversed negative.)	.05
121	Mike Scioscia	.05
122	Dan Petry	.05
123	Terry Kennedy	.05
124	Kelly Downs	.05
125	Greg Gross	.05
126	Fred Lynn	.05
127	Barry Bonds	.75
128	Harold Baines	.05
129	Doyle Alexander	.05
130	Kevin Elster	.05
131	Mike Heath	.05
132	Teddy Higuera	.05
133	Charlie Leibrandt	.05
134	Tim Laudner	.05
135a	Ray Knight (Photo reversed.)	.40
135b	Ray Knight (Correct photo.)	.05
136	Howard Johnson	.05
137	Terry Pendleton	.05
138	Andy McGaffigan	.05
139	Ken Oberkfell	.05
140	Butch Wynegar	.05
141	Rob Murphy	.05
142	Rich Renteria RC	.05
143	Jose Guzman	.05
144	Andres Galarraga	.05
145	Rick Horton	.05
146	Frank DiPino	.05
147	Glenn Braggs	.05
148	John Kruk	.05
149	Mike Schmidt	.60
150	Lee Smith	.05
151	Robin Yount	.40
152	Mark Eichhorn	.05
153	DeWayne Buice	.05
154	B.J. Surhoff	.05
155	Vince Coleman	.05
156	Tony Phillips	.05
157	Willie Fraser	.05
158	Lance McCullers	.05
159	Greg Gagne	.05
160	Jesse Barfield	.05
161	Mark Langston	.05
162	Kurt Stillwell	.05
163	Dion James	.05
164	Glenn Davis	.05
165	Walt Weiss	.05
166	Dave Concepcion	.05
167	Alfredo Griffin	.05
168	Don Heinkel RC	.05
169	Luis Rivera RC	.05
170	Shane Rawley	.05
171	Darrell Evans	.05
172	Robby Thompson	.05
173	Jody Davis	.05
174	Andy Van Slyke	.05
175	Wade Boggs	.50
176	Garry Templeton	.05
177	Gary Redus	.05
178	Craig Lefferts	.05
179	Carney Lansford	.05
180	Ron Darling	.05
181	Kirk McCaskill	.05
182	Tony Armas	.05
183	Steve Farr	.05
184	Tom Brunansky	.05
185	Bryan Harvey RC	.05
186	Mike Marshall	.05
187	Bo Diaz	.05
188	Willie Upshaw	.05
189	Mike Pagliarulo	.05
190	Mike Krukow	.05
191	Tommy Herr	.05
192	Jim Pankovits	.05
193	Dwight Evans	.05
194	Kelly Gruber	.05
195	Bobby Bonilla	.05
196	Wallace Johnson	.05
197	Dave Stieb	.05
198	Pat Borders RC	.05
199	Rafael Palmeiro	.35
200	Dwight Gooden	.05
201	Pete Incaviglia	.05
202	Chris James	.05
203	Marvell Wynne	.05
204	Pat Sheridan	.05
205	Don Baylor	.05
206	Paul O'Neill	.05
207	Pete Smith	.05
208	Mark McLemore	.05
209	Henry Cotto	.05
210	Kirk Gibson	.05
211	Claudell Washington	.05
212	Randy Bush	.05
213	Joe Carter	.05
214	Bill Buckner	.05
215	Bert Blyleven	.05
216	Brett Butler	.05
217	Lee Mazzilli	.05
218	Spike Owen	.05
219	Bill Swift	.05
220	Tim Wallach	.05
221	David Cone	.05
222	Don Carman	.05
223	Rich Gossage	.05
224	Bob Walk	.05
225	Dave Righetti	.05
226	Kevin Bass	.05
227	Kevin Gross	.05
228	Tim Burke	.05
229	Rick Mahler	.05
230	Lou Whitaker	.05
231	Luis Alicea RC	.05
232	Roberto Alomar	.25
233	Bob Boone	.05
234	Dickie Thon	.05
235	Shawon Dunston	.05
236	Pete Stanicek	.05
237	Craig Biggio	.05
238	Dennis Boyd	.05
239	Tom Candiotti	.05
240	Gary Carter	.40
241	Mike Stanley	.05
242	Ken Phelps	.05
243	Chris Bosio	.05
244	Les Straker	.05
245	Dave Smith	.05
246	John Candelaria	.05
247	Joe Orsulak	.05
248	Storm Davis	.05
249	Floyd Bannister	.05
250	Jack Morris	.05
251	Bret Saberhagen	.05
252	Tom Niedenfuer	.05
253	Neal Heaton	.05
254	Eric Show	.05
255	Juan Samuel	.05
256	Dale Sveum	.05
257	Jim Gott	.05
258	Scott Garrelts	.05
259	Larry McWilliams	.05
260	Steve Bedrosian	.05
261	Jack Howell	.05
262	Jay Tibbs	.05
263	Jamie Moyer	.05
264	Doug Sisk	.05
265	Todd Worrell	.05
266	John Farrell	.05
267	Dave Collins	.05
268	Sid Fernandez	.05
269	Tom Brookens	.05
270	Shane Mack	.05
271	Paul Kilgus	.05
272	Chuck Crim	.05
273	Bob Knepper	.05
274	Mike Moore	.05
275	Guillermo Hernandez	.05
276	Dennis Eckersley	.35
277	Graig Nettles	.05
278	Rich Dotson	.05
279	Larry Herndon	.05
280	Gene Larkin	.05
281	Roger McDowell	.05
282	Greg Swindell	.05
283	Juan Agosto	.05
284	Jeff Robinson	.05
285	Mike Dunne	.05
286	Greg Mathews	.05
287	Kent Tekulve	.05
288	Jerry Mumphrey	.05
289	Jack McDowell	.05
290	Frank Viola	.05
291	Mark Gubicza	.05
292	Dave Schmidt	.05
293	Mike Henneman	.05
294	Jimmy Jones	.05
295	Charlie Hough	.05
296	Rafael Santana	.05
297	Chris Speier	.05
298	Mike Witt	.05
299	Pascual Perez	.05
300	Nolan Ryan	.75
301	Mitch Williams	.05
302	Mookie Wilson	.05
303	Mackey Sasser	.05
304	John Cerutti	.05
305	Jeff Reardon	.05
306	Randy Myers	.05
307	Greg Brock	.05
308	Bob Welch	.05
309	Jeff Robinson	.05
310	Harold Reynolds	.05
311	Jim Walewander	.05
312	Dave Magadan	.05
313	Jim Gantner	.05
314	Walt Terrell	.05
315	Wally Backman	.05
316	Luis Salazar	.05
317	Rick Rhoden	.05
318	Tom Henke	.05
319	Mike Macfarlane	.05
320	Dan Plesac	.05
321	Calvin Schiraldi	.05
322	Stan Javier	.05
323	Devon White	.05
324	Scott Bradley	.05
325	Bruce Hurst	.05
326	Manny Lee	.05
327	Rick Aguilera	.05
328	Bruce Ruffin	.05
329	Ed Whitson	.05
330	Bo Jackson	.10
331	Ivan Calderon	.05
332	Mickey Hatcher	.05
333	Barry Jones RC	.05
334	Ron Hassey	.05
335	Bill Wegman	.05
336	Damon Berryhill	.05
337	Steve Ontiveros	.05
338	Dan Pasqua	.05
339	Bill Pecota	.05
340	Greg Cadaret	.05
341	Scott Bankhead	.05
342	Ron Guidry	.10
343	Danny Heep	.05
344	Bob Brower	.05
345	Rich Gedman	.05
346	Nelson Santovenia RC	.05
347	George Bell	.05
348	Ted Power	.05
349	Mark Grant	.05
350a	Roger Clemens (778 wins)	2.00
350b	Roger Clemens (78 wins)	.60
351	Bill Long	.05
352	Jay Bell RC	.05
353	Steve Balboni	.05
354	Bob Kipper	.05
355	Steve Jeltz	.05
356	Jesse Orosco	.05
357	Bob Dernier	.05
358	Mickey Tettleton	.05
359	Duane Ward RC	.05
360	Darrin Jackson	.05
361	Rey Quinones	.05
362	Mark Grace	.05
363	Steve Lake	.05
364	Pat Perry	.05
365	Terry Steinbach	.05
366	Alan Ashby	.05
367	Jeff Montgomery	.05
368	Steve Buechele	.05
369	Chris Brown	.05
370	Orel Hershiser	.05
371	Todd Benzinger	.05
372	Ron Gant	.05
373	Paul Assenmacher RC	.05
374	Joey Meyer	.05
375	Neil Allen	.05
376	Mike Davis	.05
377	Jeff Parrett RC	.05
378	Jay Howell	.05
379	Rafael Belliard	.05
380	Luis Polonia	.05
381	Keith Atherton	.05
382	Kent Hrbek	.05
383	Bob Stanley	.05
384	Dave LaPoint	.05
385	Rance Mulliniks	.05
386	Melido Perez	.05
387	Doug Jones	.05
388	Steve Lyons	.05
389	Alejandro Pena	.05
390	Frank White	.05
391	Pat Tabler	.05
392	Eric Plunk RC	.05
393	Mike Maddux RC	.05
394	Allan Anderson RC	.05
395	Bob Brenly	.05
396	Rick Cerone	.05
397	Scott Terry RC	.05
398	Mike Jackson	.05
399	Bobby Thigpen	.05
400	Don Sutton	.35
401	Cecil Espy	.05
402	Junior Ortiz	.05
403	Mike Smithson	.05
404	Bud Black	.05
405	Tom Foley	.05
406	Andres Thomas	.05
407	Rick Sutcliffe	.05
408	Brian Harper	.05
409	John Smiley	.05
410	Juan Nieves	.05
411	Shawn Abner RC	.05
412	Wes Gardner RC	.05
413	Darren Daulton	.05
414	Juan Berenguer	.05
415	Charles Hudson	.05
416	Rick Honeycutt	.05
417	Greg Booker	.05
418	Tim Belcher	.05
419	Don August	.05
420	Dale Mohorcic	.05
421	Steve Lombardozzi	.05
422	Atlee Hammaker	.05
423	Jerry Don Gleaton	.05
424	Scott Bailes RC	.05
425	Bruce Sutter	.40
426	Randy Ready	.05
427	Jerry Reed	.05
428	Bryn Smith	.05
429	Tim Leary	.05
430	Mark Clear	.05
431	Terry Leach	.05
432	John Moses	.05
433	Ozzie Guillen	.05
434	Gene Nelson	.05
435	Gary Ward	.05
436	Luis Aguayo	.05
437	Fernando Valenzuela	.05
438	Jeff Russell	.05
439	Cecilio Guante	.05
440	Don Robinson	.05
441	Rick Anderson RC	.05
442	Tom Glavine	.35
443	Daryl Boston	.05
444	Joe Price	.05
445	Stewart Cliburn	.05
446	Manny Trillo	.05
447	Joel Skinner	.05
448	Charlie Puleo	.05
449	Carlton Fisk	.40
450	Will Clark	.05
451	Otis Nixon	.05
452	Rick Schu	.05
453	Todd Stottlemyre	.05
454	Tim Birtsas	.05
455	Dave Gallagher RC	.05
456	Barry Lyons	.05
457	Fred Manrique	.05
458	Ernest Riles	.05
459	Doug Jennings RC	.05
460	Joe Magrane	.05
461	Jamie Quirk	.05
462	Jack Armstrong RC	.05
463	Bobby Witt	.05
464	Keith Miller	.05
465	Todd Burns RC	.05
466	John Dopson RC	.05
467	Rich Yett	.05
468	Craig Reynolds	.05
469	Dave Bergman	.05
470	Rex Hudler	.05
471	Eric King	.05
472	Joaquin Andujar	.05
473	Sil Campusano RC	.05
474	Terry Mulholland RC	.05
475	Mike Flanagan	.05
476	Greg Harris	.05
477	Tommy John	.10
478	Dave Anderson	.05
479	Fred Toliver	.05
480	Jimmy Key	.05
481	Donell Nixon	.05
482	Mark Portugal RC	.05
483	Tom Pagnozzi	.05
484	Jeff Kunkel	.05
485	Frank Williams	.05
486	Jody Reed	.05
487	Roberto Kelly	.05
488	Shawn Hillegas	.05
489	Jerry Reuss	.05
490	Mark Grant	.05
491	Jeff Sellers	.05
492	Zane Smith	.05
493	Al Newman RC	.05
494	Mike Young	.05
495	Larry Parrish	.05
496	Herm Winningham	.05
497	Carmen Castillo	.05
498	Joe Hesketh	.05
499	Darrell Miller	.05
500	Mike LaCoss	.05
501	Charlie Lea	.05
502	Bruce Benedict	.05
503	Chuck Finley RC	.05
504	Brad Wellman RC	.05
505	Tim Crews	.05
506	Ken Gerhart	.05
507a	Brian Holton (Born: 1/25/65, Denver.)	.15
507b	Brian Holton (Born: 11/29/59, McKeesport.)	.05
508	Dennis Lamp	.05
509	Bobby Meacham	.05
510	Tracy Jones	.05
511	Mike Fitzgerald	.05
512	Jeff Bittiger RC	.05
513	Tim Flannery	.05
514	Ray Hayward RC	.05
515	Dave Leiper	.05
516	Rod Scurry	.05
517	Carmelo Martinez	.05
518	Curtis Wilkerson	.05
519	Stan Jefferson	.05
520	Dan Quisenberry	.05
521	Lloyd McClendon RC	.05
522	Steve Trout	.05
523	Larry Andersen	.05
524	Don Aase	.05
525	Bob Forsch	.05
526	Geno Petralli	.05
527	Angel Salazar	.05
528	Mike Schooler RC	.05
529	Jose Oquendo	.05
530	Jay Buhner	.05
531	Tom Bolton RC	.05
532	Al Nipper	.05
533	Dave Henderson	.05
534	John Costello RC	.05
535	Donnie Moore	.05
536	Mike Laga	.05
537	Mike Gallego	.05
538	Jim Clancy	.05
539	Joel Youngblood	.05
540	Rick Leach	.05
541	Kevin Romine	.05
542	Mark Salas	.05
543	Greg Minton	.05
544	Dave Palmer	.05
545	Dwayne Murphy	.05
546	Jim Deshaies	.05
547	Don Gordon RC	.05
548	Ricky Jordan	.05
549	Mike Boddicker	.05
550	Mike Scott	.05
551	Jeff Ballard RC	.05
552a	Jose Rijo (Uniform number #24 on card back.)	.15
552b	Jose Rijo (Uniform number #27 on card back.)	.10
553	Danny Darwin	.05
554	Tom Browning	.05
555	Danny Jackson	.05
556	Rick Dempsey	.05
557	Jeffrey Leonard	.05
558	Jeff Musselman	.05
559	Ron Robinson	.05
560	John Tudor	.05
561	Don Slaught	.05
562	Dennis Rasmussen	.05
563	Brady Anderson	.05
564	Pedro Guerrero	.05
565	Paul Molitor	.40
566	Terry Clark RC	.05
567	Terry Puhl	.05
568	Mike Campbell RC	.05
569	Paul Mirabella	.05
570	Jeff Hamilton RC	.05
571	Oswald Peraza RC	.05
572	Bob McClure	.05
573	Jose Bautista RC	.05
574	Alex Trevino	.05
575	John Franco	.05
576	Mark Parent RC	.05
577	Nelson Liriano	.05
578	Steve Shields	.05
579	Odell Jones	.05
580	Al Leiter	.05
581	Dave Stapleton RC	.05
582	1988 World Series (Jose Canseco, Kirk Gibson, Orel Hershiser, Dave Stewart)	.10
583	Donnie Hill	.05
584	Chuck Jackson	.05
585	Rene Gonzales RC	.05
586	Tracy Woodson RC	.05
587	Jim Adduci RC	.05
588	Mario Soto	.05
589	Jeff Blauser	.05
590	Jim Traber	.05
591	Jon Perlman RC	.05
592	Mark Williamson RC	.05
593	Dave Meads	.05
594	Jim Eisenreich	.05
595a	Paul Gibson RC (Player in background adjusting cup.)	.25
595b	Paul Gibson RC (Hand airbrushed away.)	.05
596	Mike Birkbeck	.05
597	Terry Francona	.05
598	Paul Zuvella	.05
599	Franklin Stubbs	.05
600	Gregg Jefferies	.05
601	John Cangelosi	.05
602	Mike Sharperson RC	.05
603	Mike Diaz	.05
604	Gary Varsho RC	.05
605	Terry Blocker RC	.05
606	Charlie O'Brien RC	.05
607	Jim Eppard RC	.05
608	John Davis	.05
609	Ken Griffey Sr.	.05
610	Buddy Bell	.05
611	Ted Simmons	.05
612	Matt Williams	.05
613	Danny Cox	.05
614	Al Pedrique	.05
615	Ron Oester	.05
616	John Smoltz	.05
617	Bob Melvin	.05
618	Rob Dibble RC	.10
619	Kirt Manwaring	.05
620	Felix Fermin RC	.05
621	Doug Dascenzo RC	.05
622	Bill Brennan RC	.05
623	Carlos Quintana RC	.05
624	Mike Harkey RC	.05
625	Gary Sheffield RC	1.25
626	Tom Prince RC	.05
627	Steve Searcy RC	.05
628	Charlie Hayes RC	.05

629	Felix Jose RC	.05
630	Sandy Alomar RC	.50
631	Derek Lilliquist RC	.05
632	Geronimo Berroa	.05
633	Luis Medina RC	.05
634	Tom Gordon RC	.10
635	Ramon Martinez RC	.25
636	Craig Worthington RC	.05
637	Edgar Martinez RC	.05
638	Chad Krueter RC	.05
639	Ron Jones RC	.05
640	Van Snider RC	.05
641	Lance Blankenship RC	.05
642	Dwight Smith RC	.05
643	Cameron Drew RC	.05
644	Jerald Clark RC	.05
645	Randy Johnson RC	2.00
646	Norm Charlton RC	.05
647	Todd Frohwirth RC	.05
648	Luis de los Santos RC	.05
649	Tim Jones RC	.05
650	Dave West RC	.05
651	Bob Milacki RC	.05
652	1988 Highlight (Wrigley Field)	.05
653	1988 Highlight (Orel Hershiser)	.05
654a	1988 Highlight Wade Boggs ("...sixth consecutive seeason..." on back)	2.00
654b	1988 Highlight Wade Boggs ("Season" corrected.)	.10
655	1988 Highlight (Jose Canseco)	.15
656	1988 Highlight (Doug Jones)	.05
657	1988 Highlight (Rickey Henderson)	.10
658	1988 Highlight (Tom Browning)	.05
659	1988 Highlight (Mike Greenwell)	.05
660	1988 Highlight Joe Morgan (A.L. Win Streak)	.05

Rookie/Traded

Score issued its second consecutive traded set in 1989 to supplement and update its regular set. The 110-card traded set features the same basic card design as the regular 1989 Score set. The set consists of rookies and traded players pictured with correct teams. The set was sold by hobby dealers in a special box that included an assortment of "Magic Motion" trivia cards. Cards are numbered with a "T" suffix.

		NM/M
	Complete Set (110):	10.00
	Common Player:	.05
1	Rafael Palmeiro	.35
2	Nolan Ryan	1.00
3	Jack Clark	.05
4	Dave LaPoint	.05
5	Mike Moore	.05
6	Pete O'Brien	.05
7	Jeffrey Leonard	.05
8	Rob Murphy	.05
9	Tom Herr	.05
10	Claudell Washington	.05
11	Mike Pagliarulo	.05
12	Steve Lake	.05
13	Spike Owen	.05
14	Andy Hawkins	.05
15	Todd Benzinger	.05
16	Mookie Wilson	.05
17	Bert Blyleven	.05
18	Jeff Treadway	.05
19	Bruce Hurst	.05
20	Steve Sax	.05
21	Juan Samuel	.05
22	Jesse Barfield	.05
23	Carmelo Castillo	.05
24	Terry Leach	.05
25	Mark Langston	.05
26	Eric King	.05
27	Steve Balboni	.05
28	Len Dykstra	.05
29	Keith Moreland	.05
30	Terry Kennedy	.05
31	Eddie Murray	.45
32	Mitch Williams	.05
33	Jeff Parrett	.05
34	Wally Backman	.05
35	Julio Franco	.05
36	Lance Parrish	.05
37	Nick Esasky	.05
38	Luis Polonia	.05
39	Kevin Gross	.05
40	John Dopson	.05
41	Willie Randolph	.05
42	Jim Clancy	.05
43	Tracy Jones	.05
44	Phil Bradley	.05
45	Milt Thompson	.05
46	Chris James	.05
47	Scott Fletcher	.05
48	Kal Daniels	.05
49	Steve Bedrosian	.05
50	Rickey Henderson	.45
51	Dion James	.05
52	Tim Leary	.05
53	Roger McDowell	.05
54	Mel Hall	.05
55	Dickie Thon	.05
56	Zane Smith	.05
57	Danny Heep	.05
58	Bob McClure	.05
59	Brian Holton	.05
60	Randy Ready	.05
61	Bob Melvin	.05
62	Harold Baines	.05
63	Lance McCullers	.05
64	Jody Davis	.05
65	Darrell Evans	.05
66	Joel Youngblood	.05
67	Frank Viola	.05
68	Mike Aldrete	.05
69	Greg Cadaret	.05
70	John Kruk	.05
71	Pat Sheridan	.05
72	Oddibe McDowell	.05
73	Tom Brookens	.05
74	Bob Boone	.05
75	Walt Terrell	.05
76	Joel Skinner	.05
77	Randy Johnson	1.50
78	Felix Fermin	.05
79	Rick Mahler	.05
80	Rich Dotson	.05
81	Cris Carpenter RC	.05
82	Bill Spiers RC	.05
83	Junior Felix RC	.05
84	Joe Girardi RC	.05
85	Jerome Walton RC	.05
86	Greg Litton RC	.05
87	Greg Harris RC	.05
88	Jim Abbott RC	.05
89	Kevin Brown RC	.05
90	John Wetteland RC	.10
91	Gary Wayne RC	.05
92	Rich Monteleone RC	.05
93	Bob Geren RC	.05
94	Clay Parker RC	.05
95	Steve Finley RC	.05
96	Gregg Olson RC	.05
97	Ken Patterson RC	.05
98	Ken Hill RC	.05
99	Scott Scudder RC	.05
100	Ken Griffey Jr. RC	6.00
101	Jeff Brantley RC	.05
102	Donn Pall RC	.05
103	Carlos Martinez RC	.05
104	Joe Oliver RC	.05
105	Omar Vizquel RC	.25
106	Albert Belle RC	1.00
107	Kenny Rogers RC	.10
108	Mark Carreon RC	.05
109	Rolando Roomes RC	.05
110	Pete Harnisch RC	.05

Rising Stars

Similar in design to the Score Superstar set, this 100-card set showcased a host of rookies. Full-color action photos are surrounded by a bright blue border with a green inner highlight line. Backs display a full-color player portrait above his name and career highlights. The card number and player's rookie year are featured to the right. A "Rising Star" headline highlights the top border. The Score "Rising Star" set was marketed as a combination with a related magazine: "1988-89 Baseball's 100 Hottest Rookies." The set also includes six Magic Motion baseball trivia cards featuring "Rookies to Remember." The magazine/card sets were available at a select group of retailers.

		NM/M
	Complete Set (100):	5.00
	Common Player:	.10
1	Gregg Jefferies	.10
2	Vicente Palacios	.10
3	Cameron Drew	.10
4	Doug Dascenzo	.10
5	Luis Medina	.10
6	Craig Worthington	.10
7	Rob Ducey	.10
8	Hal Morris	.10
9	Bill Brennan	.10
10	Gary Sheffield	.25
11	Mike Devereaux	.10
12	Hensley Meulens	.10
13	Carlos Quintana	.10
14	Todd Frohwirth	.10
15	Scott Lusader	.10
16	Mark Carreon	.10
17	Torey Lovullo	.10
18	Randy Velarde	.10
19	Billy Bean	.10
20	Lance Blankenship	.10
21	Chris Gwynn	.10
22	Felix Jose	.10
23	Derek Lilliquist	.10
24	Gary Thurman	.10
25	Ron Jones	.10
26	Dave Justice	.10
27	Johnny Paredes	.10
28	Tim Jones	.10
29	Jose Gonzalez	.10
30	Geronimo Berroa	.10
31	Trevor Wilson	.10
32	Morris Madden	.10
33	Lance Johnson	.10
34	Marvin Freeman	.10
35	Jose Cecena	.10
36	Jim Corsi	.10
37	Rolando Roomes	.10
38	Scott Medvin	.10
39	Charlie Hayes	.10
40	Edgar Martinez	.10
41	Van Snider	.10
42	John Fishel	.10
43	Bruce Fields	.10
44	Darryl Hamilton	.10
45	Tom Prince	.10
46	Kirt Manwaring	.10
47	Steve Searcy	.10
48	Mike Harkey	.10
49	German Gonzalez	.10
50	Tony Perezchica	.10
51	Chad Kreuter	.10
52	Luis de los Santos	.10
53	Steve Curry	.10
54	Greg Bailey	.10
55	Ramon Martinez	.10
56	Ron Tingley	.10
57	Randy Kramer	.10
58	Alex Madrid	.10
59	Kevin Reimer	.10
60	Dave Otto	.10
61	Ken Patterson	.10
62	Keith Miller	.10
63	Randy Johnson	2.50
64	Dwight Smith	.10
65	Eric Yelding	.10
66	Bob Geren	.10
67	Shane Turner	.10
68	Tom Gordon	.10
69	Jeff Huson	.10
70	Marty Brown	.10
71	Nelson Santovenia	.10
72	Roberto Alomar	1.00
73	Mike Schooler	.10
74	Pete Smith	.10
75	John Costello	.10
76	Chris Sabo	.10
77	Damon Berryhill	.10
78	Mark Grace	.20
79	Melido Perez	.10
80	Al Leiter	.10
81	Todd Stottlemyre	.10
82	Mackey Sasser	.10
83	Don August	.10
84	Jeff Treadway	.10
85	Jody Reed	.10
86	Mike Campbell	.10
87	Ron Gant	.10
88	Ricky Jordan	.10
89	Terry Clark	.10
90	Roberto Kelly	.10
91	Pat Borders	.10
92	Bryan Harvey	.10
93	Joey Meyer	.10
94	Tim Belcher	.10
95	Walt Weiss	.10
96	Dave Gallagher	.10
97	Mike Macfarlane	.10
98	Craig Biggio	.10
99	Jack Armstrong	.10
100	Todd Burns	.10

Superstars

This 100-card set features full-color action photos of baseball's superstars, and six Magic Motion "Rookies to Remember" baseball trivia cards. Card fronts have a bright red border with a blue line inside highlighting the photo. The player ID is displayed in overlapping triangles of white, green, and yellow. The flip side features a full-color player close-up directly beneath a bright red "Superstar" headline. The set was marketed along with the magazine "1989 Baseball's 100 Hottest Players," at select retailers.

		NM/M
	Complete Set (100):	6.00
	Common Player:	.05
1	Jose Canseco	.35
2	David Cone	.05
3	Dave Winfield	.50
4	George Brett	.75
5	Frank Viola	.05
6	Cory Snyder	.05
7	Alan Trammell	.05
8	Dwight Evans	.05
9	Tim Leary	.05
10	Don Mattingly	.75
11	Kirby Puckett	.65
12	Carney Lansford	.05
13	Dennis Martinez	.05
14	Kent Hrbek	.05
15	Doc Gooden	.05
16	Dennis Eckersley	.40
17	Kevin Seitzer	.05
18	Lee Smith	.05
19	Danny Tartabull	.05
20	Gerald Perry	.05
21	Gary Gaetti	.05
22	Rick Reuschel	.05
23	Keith Hernandez	.05
24	Jeff Reardon	.05
25	Mark McGwire	.85
26	Juan Samuel	.05
27	Jack Clark	.05
28	Robin Yount	.50
29	Steve Bedrosian	.05
30	Kirk Gibson	.05
31	Barry Bonds	1.00
32	Dan Plesac	.05
33	Steve Sax	.05
34	Jeff Robinson	.05
35	Orel Hershiser	.05
36	Julio Franco	.05
37	Dave Righetti	.05
38	Bob Knepper	.05
39	Carlton Fisk	.50
40	Tony Gwynn	.65
41	Doug Jones	.05
42	Bobby Bonilla	.05
43	Ellis Burks	.05
44	Pedro Guerrero	.05
45	Rickey Henderson	.50
46	Glenn Davis	.05
47	Benny Santiago	.05
48	Greg Maddux	.65
49	Teddy Higuera	.05
50	Darryl Strawberry	.05
51	Ozzie Guillen	.05
52	Barry Larkin	.05
53	Tony Fernandez	.05
54	Ryne Sandberg	.65
55	Joe Carter	.05
56	Rafael Palmeiro	.40
57	Paul Molitor	.50
58	Eric Davis	.05
59	Mike Henneman	.05
60	Mike Scott	.05
61	Tom Browning	.05
62	Mark Davis	.05
63	Tom Henke	.05
64	Nolan Ryan	1.00
65	Fred McGriff	.05
66	Dale Murphy	.05
67	Mark Langston	.05
68	Bobby Thigpen	.05
69	Mark Gubicza	.05
70	Mike Greenwell	.05
71	Ron Darling	.05
72	Gerald Young	.05
73	Wally Joyner	.05
74	Andres Galarraga	.05
75	Danny Jackson	.05
76	Mike Schmidt	.75
77	Cal Ripken, Jr.	1.00
78	Alvin Davis	.05
79	Bruce Hurst	.05
80	Andre Dawson	.25
81	Bob Boone	.05
82	Harold Reynolds	.05
83	Eddie Murray	.50
84	Robby Thompson	.05
85	Will Clark	.05
86	Vince Coleman	.05
87	Doug Drabek	.05
88	Ozzie Smith	.65
89	Bob Welch	.05
90	Roger Clemens	.75
91	George Bell	.05
92	Andy Van Slyke	.05
93	Willie McGee	.05
94	Todd Worrell	.05
95	Tim Raines	.05
96	Kevin McReynolds	.05
97	John Franco	.05
98	Jim Gott	.05
99	Johnny Ray	.05
100	Wade Boggs	.65

Yankees

This team set was sponsored by National Westminster Bank and produced by Score as an in-stadium promotion in 1989; distributed to fans attending the July 29 game at Yankee Stadium. The standard-size cards include a full-color player photo with a line drawing of the famous Yankee Stadium facade running along the top of the card. The player's name, "New York Yankees" and position appear below the photo. A second full-color photo is included on the back of the card, along with stats, data and a brief player profile. The set includes a special Thurman Munson commemorative card.

		NM/M
	Complete Set (33):	4.00
	Common Player:	.15
1	Don Mattingly	2.00
2	Steve Sax	.15
3	Alvaro Espinoza	.15
4	Luis Polonia	.15
5	Jesse Barfield	.15
6	Dave Righetti	.15
7	Dave Winfield	1.00
8	John Candelaria	.15
9	Wayne Tolleson	.15
10	Ken Phelps	.15
11	Rafael Santana	.15
12	Don Slaught	.15
13	Mike Pagliarulo	.15
14	Lance McCullers	.15
15	Dave LaPoint	.15
16	Dale Mohorcic	.15
17	Steve Balboni	.15
18	Roberto Kelly	.15
19	Andy Hawkins	.15
20	Mel Hall	.15
21	Tom Brookens	.15
22	Deion Sanders	.50
23	Richard Dotson	.15
24	Lee Guetterman	.15
25	Bob Geren	.15
26	Jimmy Jones	.15
27	Chuck Cary	.15
28	Ron Guidry	.15
29	Hal Morris	.15
30	Clay Parker	.15
31	Dallas Green	.15
32	Thurman Munson	1.00
33	Sponsor card	.05

Young Superstars Series 1

These standard-size cards (2-1/2" x 3-1/2") display color action photos with a high-gloss finish. Fronts feature a red and blue border surrounding the photo with the team logo in the lower right. A red band beneath the photo provides the setting for the player ID including name, position, and uniform number. Backs feature a red "Young Superstar" headline above a portrait photo. Above the headline appears the player's personal information and statistics in orange and black. To the right photo a condensed scouting report and career highlights are revealed. The card number and related logos appear on the bottom portion. Five trivia cards featuring "A Year to Remember" accompanied the series. Each trivia card relates to a highlight from the past 56 years. This set was distributed via a write-in offer with Score card wrappers.

		NM/M
	Complete Set (42):	3.00
	Common Player:	.10
1	Gregg Jefferies	.10
2	Jody Reed	.10
3	Mark Grace	.10
4	Dave Gallagher	.10
5	Bo Jackson	.15
6	Jay Buhner	.10
7	Melido Perez	.10
8	Bobby Witt	.10
9	David Cone	.10
10	Chris Sabo	.10
11	Pat Borders	.10
12	Mark Grant	.10
13	Mike Macfarlane	.10
14	Mike Jackson	.10
15	Ricky Jordan	.10
16	Ron Gant	.10
17	Al Leiter	.10
18	Jeff Parrett	.10
19	Pete Smith	.10
20	Walt Weiss	.10
21	Doug Drabek	.10
22	Kirt Manwaring	.10
23	Keith Miller	.10
24	Damon Berryhill	.10
25	Gary Sheffield	.25
26	Brady Anderson	.10
27	Mitch Williams	.10
28	Roberto Alomar	.25
29	Bobby Thigpen	.10
30	Bryan Harvey	.10
31	Jose Rijo	.10
32	Dave West	.10
33	Joey Meyer	.10
34	Allan Anderson	.10
35	Rafael Palmeiro	.75
36	Tim Belcher	.10
37	John Smiley	.10
38	Mackey Sasser	.10
39	Greg Maddux	1.00
40	Ramon Martinez	.10
41	Randy Myers	.10
42	Scott Bankhead	.10

Young Superstars Series 2

Score followed up with a second series of Young Superstars in 1989. The second series also included 42 cards and featured the same design as the first series. The set was also distributed via a write-in offer with Score card wrappers.

		NM/M
Complete Set (42):		10.00
Common Player:		.10
1	Sandy Alomar	.10
2	Tom Gordon	.10
3	Ron Jones	.10
4	Todd Burns	.10
5	Paul O'Neill	.10
6	Gene Larkin	.10
7	Eric King	.10
8	Jeff Robinson	.10
9	Bill Wegman	.10
10	Cecil Espy	.10
11	Jose Guzman	.10
12	Kelly Gruber	.10
13	Duane Ward	.10
14	Mark Gubicza	.10
15	Norm Charlton	.10
16	Jose Oquendo	.10
17	Geronimo Berroa	.10
18	Ken Griffey Jr.	9.00
19	Lance McCullers	.10
20	Todd Stottlemyre	.10
21	Craig Worthington	.10
22	Mike Devereaux	.10
23	Tom Glavine	.50
24	Dale Sveum	.10
25	Roberto Kelly	.10
26	Luis Medina	.10
27	Steve Searcy	.10
28	Don August	.10
29	Shawn Hillegas	.10
30	Mike Campbell	.10
31	Mike Harkey	.10
32	Randy Johnson	1.00
33	Craig Biggio	.10
34	Mike Schooler	.10
35	Andres Thomas	.10
36	Jerome Walton	.10
37	Cris Carpenter	.10
38	Kevin Mitchell	.10
39	Eddie Williams	.10
40	Chad Kreuter	.10
41	Danny Jackson	.10
42	Kurt Stillwell	.10

Scoremasters

This unique 42-card boxed set from Score was reproduced from original artwork done by New York artist Jeffrey Rubin. The paintings are reproduced on a standard-size, white, glossy stock, and the set includes the top stars of the game, plus selected rookies.

		NM/M
Complete Set (42):		8.00
Common Player:		.10
1	Bo Jackson	.20
2	Jerome Walton	.10
3	Cal Ripken, Jr.	2.00
4	Mike Scott	.10
5	Nolan Ryan	2.00
6	Don Mattingly	1.00
7	Tom Gordon	.10
8	Jack Morris	.10
9	Carlton Fisk	.75
10	Will Clark	.10
11	George Brett	1.00
12	Kevin Mitchell	.10
13	Mark Langston	.10
14	Dave Stewart	.10
15	Dale Murphy	.30
16	Gary Gaetti	.10
17	Wade Boggs	.85
18	Eric Davis	.85
19	Kirby Puckett	.85
20	Roger Clemens	1.00
21	Orel Hershiser	.10
22	Mark Grace	.10
23	Ryne Sandberg	.85
24	Barry Larkin	.10
25	Ellis Burks	.10
26	Dwight Gooden	.10
27	Ozzie Smith	.85
28	Andre Dawson	.30
29	Julio Franco	.10
30	Ken Griffey Jr.	1.25
31	Ruben Sierra	.10
32	Mark McGwire	1.50
33	Andres Galarraga	.10
34	Joe Carter	.10
35	Vince Coleman	.10
36	Mike Greenwell	.10
37	Tony Gwynn	.85
38	Andy Van Slyke	.10
39	Gregg Jefferies	.10
40	Jose Canseco	.50
41	Dave Winfield	.75
42	Darryl Strawberry	.10

1990 Score Promos

To preview its 1990 baseball cards, Score pre-released the first 110 cards (#221-330) from its red-bordered series as samples. Subtle differences exist on most cards between the samples and the issued version; most easily spotted is that the samples have no statistics on the 1989 season or career lines. Many cards have different versions of the career highlight write-ups on the back, as well. A handful of the sample cards were widely distributed to dealers and the hobby press, while others from the sheet were released more sparingly, creating inequities in the number of each card available. As few as two examples are known of some of the superstar cards, making them extremely expensive among the single-player specialists.

		NM/M
Common Player:		5.00
221	Steve Buechele	5.00
222	Jesse Barfield	5.00
223	Juan Berenguer	5.00
224	Andy McGaffigan	5.00
225	Pete Smith	5.00
226	Mike Witt	5.00
227	Jay Howell	5.00
228	Scott Bradley	5.00
229	Jerome Walton	5.00
230	Greg Swindell	5.00
231	Atlee Hammaker	5.00
232	Mike Devereaux	5.00
233	Ken Hill	5.00
234	Craig Worthington	5.00
235	Scott Terry	5.00
236	Brett Butler	5.00
237	Doyle Alexander	5.00
238	Dave Anderson	5.00
239	Bob Milacki	5.00
240	Dwight Smith	5.00
241	Otis Nixon	5.00
242	Pat Tabler	5.00
243	Derek Lilliquist	5.00
244	Danny Tartabull	5.00
245	Wade Boggs	65.00
246	Scott Garrelts	5.00
247	Spike Owen	5.00
248	Norm Charlton	5.00
249	Gerald Perry	5.00
250	Nolan Ryan	150.00
251	Kevin Gross	5.00
252	Randy Milligan	5.00
253	Mike LaCoss	5.00
254	Dave Bergman	5.00
255	Tony Gwynn	65.00
256	Felix Fermin	5.00
257	Greg W. Harris	5.00
258	Junior Felix	5.00
259	Mark Davis	5.00
260	Vince Coleman	5.00
261	Paul Gibson	5.00
262	Mitch Williams	5.00
263	Jeff Russell	5.00
264	Omar Vizquel	5.00
265	Andre Dawson	20.00
266	Storm Davis	5.00
267	Guillermo Hernandez	5.00
268	Mike Felder	5.00
269	Tom Candiotti	5.00
270	Bruce Hurst	5.00
271	Fred McGriff	5.00
272	Glenn Davis	5.00
273	John Franco	5.00
274	Rich Yett	5.00
275	Craig Biggio	5.00
276	Gene Larkin	5.00
277	Rob Dibble	5.00
278	Randy Bush	5.00
279	Kevin Bass	5.00
280	Bo Jackson	12.50
281	Wally Backman	5.00
282	Larry Andersen	5.00
283	Chris Bosio	5.00
284	Juan Agosto	5.00
285	Ozzie Smith	65.00
286	George Bell	5.00
287	Rex Hudler	5.00
288	Pat Borders	5.00
289	Danny Jackson	5.00
290	Carlton Fisk	30.00
291	Tracy Jones	-5.00
292	Allan Anderson	5.00
293	Johnny Ray	5.00
294	Lee Guetterman	5.00
295	Paul O'Neill	5.00
296	Carney Lansford	5.00
297	Tom Brookens	5.00
298	Claudell Washington	5.00
299	Hubie Brooks	5.00
300	Will Clark	5.00
301	Kenny Rogers	5.00
302	Darrell Evans	5.00
303	Greg Briley	5.00
304	Donn Pall	5.00
305	Teddy Higuera	5.00
306	Dan Pasqua	5.00
307	Dave Winfield	30.00
308	Dennis Powell	5.00
309	Jose DeLeon	5.00
310	Roger Clemens	90.00
311	Melido Perez	5.00
312	Devon White	5.00
313	Dwight Gooden	5.00
314	Carlos Martinez	5.00
315	Dennis Eckersley	25.00
316	Clay Parker	5.00
317	Rick Honeycutt	5.00
318	Tim Laudner	5.00
319	Joe Carter	5.00
320	Robin Yount	30.00
321	Felix Jose	5.00
322	Mickey Tettleton	5.00
323	Mike Gallego	5.00
324	Edgar Martinez	5.00
325	Dave Henderson	5.00
326	Chili Davis	5.00
327	Steve Balboni	5.00
328	Jody Davis	5.00
329	Shawn Hillegas	5.00
330	Jim Abbott	5.00

1990 Score

The regular Score set increased to 704 cards in 1990. Included were a series of cards picturing first-round draft picks, an expanded subset of rookie cards, four World Series specials, five Highlight cards, and a 13-card "Dream Team" series featuring the game's top players pictured on old tobacco-style cards. For the first time in a Score set, team logos are displayed on the card fronts Card backs include a full-color portrait photo with player data. A one-paragraph write-up of each player was again provided by former Sports Illustrated editor Les Woodcock. The Score set was again distributed with "Magic Motion" trivia cards, this year using "Baseball's Most Valuable Players" as its theme.

		NM/M
Hobby Factory Set (714):		8.00
Retail Factory Set (704):		7.00
Complete Set (704):		6.00
Common Player:		.05
Plastic Pack (16):		.40
Plastic Wax Box (36):		9.00
1	Don Mattingly	.50
2	Cal Ripken, Jr.	1.00
3	Dwight Evans	.05
4	Barry Bonds	1.00
5	Kevin McReynolds	.05
6	Ozzie Guillen	.05
7	Terry Kennedy	.05
8	Bryan Harvey	.05
9	Alan Trammell	.05
10	Cory Snyder	.05
11	Jody Reed	.05
12	Roberto Alomar	.20
13	Pedro Guerrero	.05
14	Gary Redus	.05
15	Marty Barrett	.05
16	Ricky Jordan	.05
17	Joe Magrane	.05
18	Sid Fernandez	.05
19	Rich Dotson	.05
20	Jack Clark	.05
21	Bob Walk	.05
22	Ron Karkovice	.05
23	Lenny Harris RC	.05
24	Phil Bradley	.05
25	Andres Galarraga	.05
26	Brian Downing	.05
27	Dave Martinez	.05
28	Eric King	.05
29	Barry Lyons	.05
30	Dave Schmidt	.05
31	Mike Boddicker	.05
32	Tom Foley	.05
33	Brady Anderson	.05
34	Jim Presley	.05
35	Lance Parrish	.05
36	Von Hayes	.05
37	Lee Smith	.05
38	Herm Winningham	.05
39	Alejandro Pena	.05
40	Mike Scott	.05
41	Joe Orsulak	.05
42	Rafael Ramirez	.05
43	Gerald Young	.05
44	Dick Schofield	.05
45	Dave Smith	.05
46	Dave Magadan	.05
47	Dennis Martinez	.05
48	Greg Minton	.05
49	Milt Thompson	.05
50	Orel Hershiser	.05
51	Bip Roberts	.05
52	Jerry Browne	.05
53	Bob Ojeda	.05
54	Fernando Valenzuela	.05
55	Matt Nokes	.05
56	Brook Jacoby	.05
57	Frank Tanana	.05
58	Scott Fletcher	.05
59	Ron Oester	.05
60	Bob Boone	.05
61	Dan Gladden	.05
62	Darnell Coles	.05
63	Gregg Olson	.05
64	Todd Burns	.05
65	Todd Benzinger	.05
66	Dale Murphy	.25
67	Mike Flanagan	.05
68	Jose Oquendo	.05
69	Cecil Espy	.05
70	Chris Sabo	.05
71	Shane Rawley	.05
72	Tom Brunansky	.05
73	Vance Law	.05
74	B.J. Surhoff	.05
75	Lou Whitaker	.05
76	Ken Caminiti	.05
77	Nelson Liriano	.05
78	Tommy Gregg	.05
79	Don Slaught	.05
80	Eddie Murray	.40
81	Joe Boever	.05
82	Charlie Leibrandt	.05
83	Jose Lind	.05
84	Tony Phillips	.05
85	Mitch Webster	.05
86	Dan Plesac	.05
87	Rick Mahler	.05
88	Steve Lyons	.05
89	Tony Fernandez	.05
90	Ryne Sandberg	.45
91	Nick Esasky	.05
92	Luis Salazar	.05
93	Pete Incaviglia	.05
94	Ivan Calderon	.05
95	Jeff Treadway	.05
96	Kurt Stillwell	.05
97	Gary Sheffield	.30
98	Jeffrey Leonard	.05
99	Andres Thomas	.05
100	Roberto Kelly	.05
101	Alvaro Espinoza RC	.05
102	Greg Gagne	.05
103	John Farrell	.05
104	Willie Wilson	.05
105	Glenn Braggs	.05
106	Chet Lemon	.05
107	Jamie Moyer	.05
108	Chuck Crim	.05
109	Dave Valle	.05
110	Walt Weiss	.05
111	Larry Sheets	.05
112	Don Robinson	.05
113	Danny Heep	.05
114	Carmelo Martinez	.05
115	Dave Gallagher	.05
116	Mike LaValliere	.05
117	Bob McClure	.05
118	Rene Gonzales	.05
119	Mark Parent	.05
120	Wally Joyner	.05
121	Mark Gubicza	.05
122	Tony Pena	.05
123	Carmen Castillo	.05
124	Howard Johnson	.05
125	Steve Sax	.05
126	Tim Belcher	.05
127	Tim Burke	.05
128	Al Newman	.05
129	Dennis Rasmussen	.05
130	Doug Jones	.05
131	Fred Lynn	.05
132	Jeff Hamilton	.05
133	German Gonzalez	.05
134	John Morris	.05
135	Dave Parker	.05
136	Gary Pettis	.05
137	Dennis Boyd	.05
138	Candy Maldonado	.05
139	Rick Cerone	.05
140	George Brett	.50
141	Dave Clark	.05
142	Dickie Thon	.05
143	Junior Ortiz	.05
144	Don August	.05
145	Gary Gaetti	.05
146	Kirt Manwaring	.05
147	Jeff Reed	.05
148	Jose Alvarez RC	.05
149	Mike Schooler	.05
150	Mark Grace	.05
151	Geronimo Berroa	.05
152	Barry Jones	.05
153	Geno Petralli	.05
154	Jim Deshaies	.05
155	Barry Larkin	.05
156	Alfredo Griffin	.05
157	Tom Henke	.05
158	Mike Jeffcoat RC	.05
159	Bob Welch	.05
160	Julio Franco	.05
161	Henry Cotto	.05
162	Terry Steinbach	.05
163	Damon Berryhill	.05
164	Tim Crews	.05
165	Tom Browning	.05
166	Frd Manrique	.05
167	Harold Reynolds	.05
168a	Ron Hassey (Uniform #27 on back.)	.05
168b	Ron Hassey (Uniform #24 on back.)	.50
169	Shawon Dunston	.05
170	Bobby Bonilla	.05
171	Tom Herr	.05
172	Mike Heath	.05
173	Rich Gedman	.05
174	Bill Ripken	.05
175	Pete O'Brien	.05
176a	Lloyd McClendon (Uniform number 1 on back.)	.50
176b	Lloyd McClendon (Uniform number 10 on back.)	.05
177	Brian Holton	.05
178	Jeff Blauser	.05
179	Jim Eisenreich	.05
180	Bert Blyleven	.05
181	Rob Murphy	.05
182	Bill Doran	.05
183	Curt Ford	.05
184	Mike Henneman	.05
185	Eric Davis	.05
186	Lance McCullers	.05
187	Steve Davis RC	.05
188	Bill Wegman	.05
189	Brian Harper	.05
190	Mike Moore	.05
191	Dale Mohorcic	.05
192	Tim Wallach	.05
193	Keith Hernandez	.05
194	Dave Righetti	.05
195a	Bret Saberhagen ("Joke" on card back.)	.10
195b	Bret Saberhagen ("Joker" on card back.)	.30
196	Paul Kilgus	.05
197	Bud Black	.05
198	Juan Samuel	.05
199	Kevin Seitzer	.05
200	Darryl Strawberry	.05
201	Dave Steib	.05
202	Charlie Hough	.05
203	Jack Morris	.05
204	Rance Mulliniks	.05
205	Alvin Davis	.05
206	Jack Howell	.05
207	Ken Patterson RC	.05
208	Terry Pendleton	.05
209	Craig Lefferts	.05
210	Kevin Brown RC	.05
211	Dan Petry	.05
212	Dave Leiper	.05
213	Daryl Boston	.05
214	Kevin Hickey RC	.05
215	Mike Krukow	.05
216	Terry Francona	.05
217	Kirk McCaskill	.05
218	Scott Bailes	.05
219	Bob Forsch	.05
220	Mike Aldrete	.05
221	Steve Buechele	.05
222	Jesse Barfield	.05
223	Juan Berenguer	.05
224	Andy McGaffigan	.05
225	Pete Smith	.05
226	Mike Witt	.05
227	Jay Howell	.05
228	Scott Bradley	.05
229	Jerome Walton RC	.05
230	Greg Swindell	.05
231	Atlee Hammaker	.05
232a	Mike Devereaux/RF	.05
232b	Mike Devereaux/CF	2.00
233	Ken Hill	.05
234	Craig Worthington	.05
235	Scott Terry	.05
236	Brett Butler	.05
237	Doyle Alexander	.05
238	Dave Anderson	.05
239	Bob Milacki	.05
240	Dwight Smith	.05
241	Otis Nixon	.05
242	Pat Tabler	.05
243	Derek Lilliquist	.05
244	Danny Tartabull	.05
245	Wade Boggs	.45
246	Scott Garrelts	.05
247	Spike Owen	.05
248	Norm Charlton	.05
249	Gerald Perry	.05
250	Nolan Ryan	1.00
251	Kevin Gross	.05
252	Randy Milligan	.05
253	Mike LaCoss	.05
254	Dave Bergman	.05
255	Tony Gwynn	.45
256	Felix Fermin	.05
257	Greg Harris	.05
258	Junior Felix RC	.05
259	Mark Davis	.05
260	Vince Coleman	.05
261	Paul Gibson	.05
262	Mitch Williams	.05
263	Jeff Russell	.05
264	Omar Vizquel	.25
265	Andre Dawson	.05
266	Storm Davis	.05
267	Guillermo Hernandez	.05
268	Mike Felder	.05
269	Tom Candiotti	.05
270	Bruce Hurst	.05
271	Fred McGriff	.05
272	Glenn Davis	.05
273	John Franco	.05
274	Rich Yett	.05
275	Craig Biggio	.05
276	Gene Larkin	.05
277	Rob Dibble	.05
278	Randy Bush	.05
279	Kevin Bass	.05
280a	Bo Jackson ("Watham" on back.)	.15
280b	Bo Jackson ("Wathan" on back.)	.50
281	Wally Backman	.05
282	Larry Andersen	.05
283	Chris Bosio	.05
284	Juan Agosto	.05
285	Ozzie Smith	.45
286	George Bell	.05
287	Rex Hudler	.05
288	Pat Borders	.05
289	Danny Jackson	.05
290	Carlton Fisk	.40
291	Tracy Jones	.05
292	Allan Anderson	.05
293	Johnny Ray	.05
294	Lee Guetterman	.05
295	Paul O'Neill	.05
296	Carney Lansford	.05
297	Tom Brookens	.05
298	Claudell Washington	.05
299	Hubie Brooks	.05
300	Will Clark	.05
301	Kenny Rogers	.05
302	Darrell Evans	.05
303	Greg Briley	.05
304	Donn Pall	.05
305	Teddy Higuera	.05
306	Dan Pasqua	.05
307	Dave Winfield	.40
308	Dennis Powell	.05
309	Jose DeLeon	.05
310	Roger Clemens	.50
311	Melido Perez	.05
312	Devon White	.05
313	Dwight Gooden	.05
314	Carlos Martinez RC	.05
315	Dennis Eckersley	.35
316	Clay Parker	.05
317	Rick Honeycutt	.05
318	Tim Laudner	.05
319	Joe Carter	.05
320	Robin Yount	.40
321	Felix Jose	.05
322	Mickey Tettleton	.05
323	Mike Gallego	.05
324	Edgar Martinez	.05
325	Dave Henderson	.05
326	Chili Davis	.05
327	Steve Balboni	.05
328	Jody Davis	.05
329	Shawn Hillegas	.05
330	Jim Abbott	.05
331	John Dopson	.05
332	Mark Williamson	.05
333	Jeff Robinson	.05
334	John Smiley	.05
335	Bobby Thigpen	.05
336	Garry Templeton	.05
337	Marvell Wynne	.05
338a	Ken Griffey Sr. (Uniform #25 on card back.)	.05
338b	Ken Griffey Sr. (Uniform #30 on card back.)	1.00
339	Steve Finley	.05

#	Player	Price
340	Ellis Burks	.05
341	Frank Williams	.05
342	Mike Morgan	.05
343	Kevin Mitchell	.05
344	Joel Youngblood	.05
345	Mike Greenwell	.05
346	Glenn Wilson	.05
347	John Costello	.05
348	Wes Gardner	.05
349	Jeff Ballard	.05
350	Mark Thurmond	.05
351	Randy Myers	.05
352	Shawn Abner	.05
353	Jesse Orosco	.05
354	Greg Walker	.05
355	Pete Harnisch	.05
356	Steve Farr	.05
357	Dave LaPoint	.05
358	Willie Fraser	.05
359	Mickey Hatcher	.05
360	Rickey Henderson	.40
361	Mike Fitzgerald	.05
362	Bill Schroeder	.05
363	Mark Carreon	.05
364	Ron Jones	.05
365	Jeff Montgomery	.05
366	Bill Krueger RC	.05
367	John Cangelosi	.05
368	Jose Gonzalez	.05
369	Greg Hibbard RC	.05
370	John Smoltz	.35
371	Jeff Brantley RC	.05
372	Frank White	.05
373	Ed Whitson	.05
374	Willie McGee	.05
375	Jose Canseco	.30
376	Randy Ready	.05
377	Don Aase	.05
378	Tony Armas	.05
379	Steve Bedrosian	.05
380	Chuck Finley	.05
381	Kent Hrbek	.05
382	Jim Gantner	.05
383	Mel Hall	.05
384	Mike Marshall	.05
385	Mark McGwire	.75
386	Wayne Tolleson	.05
387	Brian Holton	.05
388	John Wetteland	.05
389	Darren Daulton	.05
390	Rob Deer	.05
391	John Moses	.05
392	Todd Worrell	.05
393	Chuck Cary RC	.05
394	Stan Javier	.05
395	Willie Randolph	.05
396	Bill Buckner	.05
397	Robby Thompson	.05
398	Mike Scioscia	.05
399	Lonnie Smith	.05
400	Kirby Puckett	.45
401	Mark Langston	.05
402	Danny Darwin	.05
403	Greg Maddux	.45
404	Lloyd Moseby	.05
405	Rafael Palmeiro	.35
406	Chad Kreuter	.05
407	Jimmy Key	.05
408	Tim Birtsas	.05
409	Tim Raines	.05
410	Dave Stewart	.05
411	Eric Yelding RC	.05
412	Kent Anderson RC	.05
413	Les Lancaster	.05
414	Rick Dempsey	.05
415	Randy Johnson	.40
416	Gary Carter	.40
417	Rolando Roomes	.05
418	Dan Schatzeder	.05
419	Bryn Smith	.05
420	Ruben Sierra	.05
421	Steve Jeltz	.05
422	Ken Oberkfell	.05
423	Sid Bream	.05
424	Jim Clancy	.05
425	Kelly Gruber	.05
426	Rick Leach	.05
427	Len Dykstra	.05
428	Jeff Pico	.05
429	John Cerutti	.05
430	David Cone	.05
431	Jeff Kunkel	.05
432	Luis Aquino	.05
433	Ernie Whitt	.05
434	Bo Diaz	.05
435	Steve Lake	.05
436	Pat Perry	.05
437	Mike Davis	.05
438	Cecilio Guante	.05
439	Duane Ward	.05
440	Andy Van Slyke	.05
441	Gene Nelson	.05
442	Luis Polonia	.05
443	Kevin Elster	.05
444	Keith Moreland	.05
445	Roger McDowell	.05
446	Ron Darling	.05
447	Ernest Riles	.05
448	Mookie Wilson	.05
449a	Bill Spiers RC (66 missing for year of birth)	.50
449b	Bill Spiers RC (1966 for birth year)	.05
450	Rick Sutcliffe	.05
451	Nelson Santovenia	.05
452	Andy Allanson	.05
453	Bob Melvin	.05
454	Benny Santiago	.05

#	Player	Price
455	Jose Uribe	.05
456	Bill Landrum RC	.05
457	Bobby Witt	.05
458	Kevin Romine	.05
459	Lee Mazzilli	.05
460	Paul Molitor	.40
461	Ramon Martinez	.05
462	Frank DiPino	.05
463	Walt Terrell	.05
464	Bob Geren RC	.05
465	Rick Reuchel	.05
466	Mark Grant	.05
467	John Kruk	.05
468	Gregg Jefferies	.05
469	R.J. Reynolds	.05
470	Harold Baines	.05
471	Dennis Lamp	.05
472	Tom Gordon	.05
473	Terry Puhl	.05
474	Curtis Wilkerson	.05
475	Dan Quisenberry	.05
476	Oddibe McDowell	.05
477a	Zane Smith (Career ERA 3.93.)	.50
477b	Zane Smith	.05
478	Franklin Stubbs	.05
479	Wallace Johnson	.05
480	Jay Tibbs	.05
481	Tom Glavine	.35
482	Manny Lee	.05
483	Joe Hesketh	.05
484	Mike Bielecki	.05
485	Greg Brock	.05
486	Pascual Perez	.05
487	Kirk Gibson	.05
488	Scott Sanderson	.05
489	Domingo Ramos	.05
490	Kal Daniels	.05
491a	David Wells (Reversed negative on back photo.)	1.50
491b	David Wells (Corrected)	.05
492	Jerry Reed	.05
493	Eric Show	.05
494	Mike Pagliarulo	.05
495	Ron Robinson	.05
496	Brad Komminsk	.05
497	Greg Litton RC	.05
498	Chris James	.05
499	Luis Quinones RC	.05
500	Frank Viola	.05
501	Tim Teufel	.05
502	Terry Leach	.05
503	Matt Williams	.05
504	Tim Leary	.05
505	Doug Drabek	.05
506	Mariano Duncan	.05
507	Charlie Hayes	.05
508	Albert Belle	.05
509	Pat Sheridan	.05
510	Mackey Sasser	.05
511	Jose Rijo	.05
512	Mike Smithson	.05
513	Gary Ward	.05
514	Dion James	.05
515	Jim Gott	.05
516	Drew Hall RC	.05
517	Doug Bair	.05
518	Scott Scudder RC	.05
519	Rick Aguilera	.05
520	Rafael Belliard	.05
521	Jay Buhner	.05
522	Jeff Reardon	.05
523	Steve Rosenberg RC	.05
524	Randy Velarde RC	.05
525	Jeff Musselman	.05
526	Bill Long	.05
527	Gary Wayne RC	.05
528	Dave Johnson RC	.05
529	Ron Kittle	.05
530	Erik Hanson RC	.05
531	Steve Wilson RC	.05
532	Joey Meyer	.05
533	Curt Young	.05
534	Kelly Downs	.05
535	Joe Girardi	.05
536	Lance Blankenship	.05
537	Greg Mathews	.05
538	Donell Nixon	.05
539	Mark Knudson RC	.05
540	Jeff Wetherby RC	.05
541	Darrin Jackson	.05
542	Terry Mulholland	.05
543	Eric Hetzel RC	.05
544	Rick Reed RC	.05
545	Dennis Cook RC	.05
546	Mike Jackson	.05
547	Brian Fisher	.05
548	Gene Harris RC	.05
549	Jeff King RC	.05
550	Dave Dravecky (Salute)	.05
551	Randy Kutcher RC	.05
552	Mark Portugal	.05
553	Jim Corsi RC	.05
554	Todd Stottlemyre	.05
555	Scott Bankhead	.05
556	Ken Dayley	.05
557	Rick Wrona RC	.10
558	Sammy Sosa RC	3.00
559	Keith Miller	.05
560	Ken Griffey Jr.	.65
561a	Ryne Sandberg (Highlight, 3B on front.)	2.00
561b	Ryne Sandberg (Highlight, no position.)	.25
562	Billy Hatcher	.05
563	Jay Bell	.05
564	Jack Daugherty RC	.05

#	Player	Price
565	Rich Monteleone RC	.05
566	Bo Jackson (All-Star MVP)	.10
567	Tony Fossas RC	.05
568	Roy Smith RC	.05
569	Jaime Navarro RC	.05
570	Lance Johnson	.05
571	Mike Dyer RC	.05
572	Kevin Ritz RC	.05
573	Dave West	.05
574	Gary Mielke RC	.05
575	Scott Lusader RC	.05
576	Joe Oliver	.05
577	Sandy Alomar, Jr.	.05
578	Andy Benes	.05
579	Tim Jones	.05
580	Randy McCament RC	.05
581	Curt Schilling RC	.35
582	John Orton RC	.05
583a	Milt Cuyler RC (998 games)	1.00
583b	Milt Cuyler RC (98 games)	.05
584	Eric Anthony RC	.05
585	Greg Vaughn RC	.15
586	Deion Sanders	.05
587	Jose DeJesus RC	.05
588	Chip Hale RC	.05
589	John Olerud RC	.50
590	Steve Olin RC	.05
591	Marquis Grissom RC	.40
592	Moises Alou RC	.40
593	Mark Lemke RC	.05
594	Dean Palmer RC	.15
595	Robin Ventura RC	.05
596	Tino Martinez RC	.05
597	Mike Huff RC	.05
598	Scott Hemond RC	.05
599	Wally Whitehurst RC	.05
600	Todd Zeile RC	.15
601	Glenallen Hill RC	.05
602	Hal Morris RC	.05
603	Juan Bell RC	.05
604	Bobby Rose RC	.05
605	Matt Merullo RC	.05
606	Kevin Maas RC	.05
607	Randy Nosek RC	.05
608a	Billy Bates RC ("12 triples" mentioned in second-last line.)	.05
608b	Billy Bates (Triples not mentioned.)	.75
609	Mike Stanton RC	.05
610	Goose Gozzo RC	.05
611	Charles Nagy RC	.40
612	Scott Coolbaugh RC	.05
613	Jose Vizcaino RC	.10
614	Greg Smith RC	.05
615	Jeff Huson RC	.05
616	Mickey Weston RC	.05
617	John Pawlowski RC	.05
618a	Joe Skalski (Uniform #27 on card back.)	.15
618b	Joe Skalski (Uniform #67 on card back.)	1.00
619	Bernie Williams RC	1.00
620	Shawn Holman RC	.05
621	Gary Eave RC	.05
622	Darrin Fletcher RC	.10
623	Pat Combs RC	.05
624	Mike Blowers RC	.05
625	Kevin Appier RC	.05
626	Pat Austin RC	.05
627	Kelly Mann RC	.05
628	Matt Kinzer RC	.05
629	Chris Hammond RC	.10
630	Dean Wilkins RC	.05
631	Larry Walker RC	.50
632	Blaine Beatty RC	.05
633a	Tom Barrett RC (Uniform #29 on card back.)	.05
633b	Tom Barrett RC (Uniform #14 on card back.)	1.00
634	Stan Belinda RC	.05
635	Tex Smith RC	.05
636	Hensley Meulens RC	.10
637	Juan Gonzalez RC	1.50
638	Lenny Webster RC	.10
639	Mark Gardner RC	.05
640	Tommy Greene RC	.05
641	Mike Hartley RC	.05
642	Phil Stephenson RC	.05
643	Kevin Mmahat RC	.05
644	Ed Whited RC	.05
645	Delino DeShields RC	.15
646	Kevin Blankenship RC	.05
647	Paul Sorrento RC	.05
648	Mike Roesler RC	.05
649	Jason Grimsley RC	.05
650	Dave Justice RC	1.00
651	Scott Cooper RC	.05
652	Dave Eiland RC	.05
653	Mike Munoz RC	.05
654	Jeff Fischer RC	.05
655	Terry Jorgenson RC	.05
656	George Canale RC	.05
657	Brian DuBois RC	.05
658	Carlos Quintana	.05
659	Luis de los Santos	.05
660	Jerald Clark	.05
661	Donald Harris RC (1st Round Pick)	.05
662	Paul Coleman RC (1st Round Pick)	.05
663	Frank Thomas RC (1st Round Pick)	2.00
664	Brent Mayne RC (1st Round Pick)	.10

#	Player	Price
665	Eddie Zosky RC (1st Round Pick)	.05
666	Steve Hosey RC (1st Round Pick)	.05
667	Scott Bryant RC (1st Round Pick)	.05
668	Tom Goodwin RC (1st Round Pick)	.10
669	Cal Eldred RC (1st Round Pick)	.10
670	Earl Cunningham RC (1st Round Pick)	.05
671	Alan Zinter RC (1st Round Pick)	.05
672	Chuck Knoblauch RC (1st Round Pick)	.40
672(a)	Chuck Knoblauch (3,000 autographed cards with a special hologram on back were inserted into 1992 rack packs)	10.00
673	Kyle Abbott RC (1st Round Pick)	.10
674	Roger Salkeld RC (1st Round Pick)	.05
675	Mo Vaughn RC (1st Round Pick)	.50
676	Kiki Jones RC (1st Round Pick)	.05
677	Tyler Houston RC (1st Round Pick)	.10
678	Jeff Jackson RC (1st Round Pick)	.05
679	Greg Gohr RC (1st Round Pick)	.05
680	Ben McDonald RC (1st Round Pick)	.15
681	Greg Blosser RC (1st Round Pick)	.05
682	Willie Green RC (Greene) (1st Round Pick)	.05
683	Wade Boggs (Dream Team)	.25
684	Will Clark (Dream Team)	.25
685	Tony Gwynn (Dream Team)	.25
686	Rickey Henderson (Dream Team)	.20
687	Bo Jackson (Dream Team)	.15
688	Mark Langston (Dream Team)	.05
689	Barry Larkin (Dream Team)	.05
690	Kirby Puckett (Dream Team)	.25
691	Ryne Sandberg (Dream Team)	.25
692	Mike Scott (Dream Team)	.05
693	Terry Steinbach (Dream Team)	.05
694	Bobby Thigpen (Dream Team)	.05
695	Mitch Williams (Dream Team)	.05
696	Nolan Ryan/HL	.40
697	Bo Jackson (FB/BB)	.25
698	Rickey Henderson (ALCS MVP)	.20
699	Will Clark (NLCS MVP)	.05
700	World Series Games 1-2	.05
701	Lights Out: Candlestick	.15
702	World Series Game 3	.05
703	World Series Wrap-up	.05
704	Wade Boggs/HL	.25

Rookie Dream Team

MARK LEMKE   BRAVES•2B

This 10-card "Rookie Dream Team" set, in the same format as those found in the regular-issue 1990 Score, was available only in factory sets for the hobby trade. Factory sets for general retail outlets did not include these cards, nor were they available in Score packs. Cards carry a "B" prefix to their numbers.

		NM/M
Complete Set (10):		1.00
Common Player:		.10

#	Player	Price
1	A. Bartlett Giamatti	.10
2	Pat Combs	.10
3	Todd Zeile	.10
4	Luis de los Santos	.10
5	Mark Lemke	.10
6	Robin Ventura	.10
7	Jeff Huson	.10
8	Greg Vaughn	.10
9	Marquis Grissom	.10
10	Eric Anthony	.10

Traded

This 110-card set features players with new teams as well as 1990 Major League rookies. The cards feature full-color action photos framed in yellow with an orange border. The player's ID appears in green below the photo. The team logo is displayed next to the player's name. The card backs feature posed player photos and follow the style of the regular 1990 Score issue. The cards are numbered 1T-110T. Young hockey phenom Eric Lindros is featured trying out for the Toronto Blue Jays.

		NM/M
Complete Set (110):		4.00
Common Player:		.05

#	Player	Price
1	Dave Winfield	.75
2	Kevin Bass	.05
3	Nick Esasky	.05
4	Mitch Webster	.05
5	Pascual Perez	.05
6	Gary Pettis	.05
7	Tony Pena	.05
8	Candy Maldonado	.05
9	Cecil Fielder	.05
10	Carmelo Martinez	.05
11	Mark Langston	.05
12	Dave Parker	.05
13	Don Slaught	.05
14	Tony Phillips	.05
15	John Franco	.05
16	Randy Myers	.05
17	Jeff Reardon	.05
18	Sandy Alomar, Jr.	.05
19	Joe Carter	.05
20	Fred Lynn	.05
21	Storm Davis	.05
22	Craig Lefferts	.05
23	Pete O'Brien	.05
24	Dennis Boyd	.05
25	Lloyd Moseby	.05
26	Mark Davis	.05
27	Tim Leary	.05
28	Gerald Perry	.05
29	Don Aase	.05
30	Ernie Whitt	.05
31	Dale Murphy	.35
32	Alejandro Pena	.05
33	Juan Samuel	.05
34	Hubie Brooks	.05
35	Gary Carter	.75
36	Jim Presley	.05
37	Wally Backman	.05
38	Matt Nokes	.05
39	Dan Petry	.05
40	Franklin Stubbs	.05
41	Jeff Huson	.05
42	Billy Hatcher	.05
43	Terry Leach	.05
44	Phil Bradley	.05
45	Claudell Washington	.05
46	Luis Polonia	.05
47	Daryl Boston	.05
48	Lee Smith	.05
49	Tom Brunansky	.05
50	Mike Witt	.05
51	Willie Randolph	.05
52	Stan Javier	.05
53	Brad Komminsk	.05
54	John Candelaria	.05
55	Bryn Smith	.05
56	Glenn Braggs	.05
57	Keith Hernandez	.05
58	Ken Oberkfell	.05
59	Steve Jeltz	.05
60	Chris James	.05
61	Scott Sanderson	.05
62	Bill Long	.05

Rising Stars

TODD ZEILE   Cardinals

For the second consecutive year Score produced a 100-card "Rising Stars" set. The 1990 issue was made available as a boxed set and also marketed with a related magazine like the 1989 issue. Magic Motion trivia cards featuring past MVP's accompany the card set. The cards feature full-color action photos on the front and portrait photos on the back.

		NM/M
Complete Set (100):		5.00
Common Player:		.05

#	Player	Price
1	Tom Gordon	.05
2	Jerome Walton	.05
3	Ken Griffey Jr.	1.25
4	Dwight Smith	.05
5	Jim Abbott	.05
6	Todd Zeile	.05
7	Donn Pall	.05
8	Rick Reed	.05
9	Joey Belle	.05
10	Gregg Jefferies	.05
11	Kevin Ritz	.05
12	Charlie Hayes	.05
13	Kevin Appier	.05
14	Jeff Huson	.05
15	Gary Wayne	.05
16	Eric Yelding	.05
17	Clay Parker	.05
18	Junior Felix	.05
19	Derek Lilliquist	.05
20	Gary Sheffield	.25
21	Craig Worthington	.05
22	Jeff Brantley	.05
23	Eric Hetzel	.05
24	Greg Harris	.05
25	John Wetteland	.05
26	Joe Oliver	.05
27	Kevin Maas	.05
28	Kevin Brown	.05
29	Mike Stanton	.05
30	Greg Vaughn	.05

#	Player	Price
63	Rick Cerone	.05
64	Scott Bailes	.05
65	Larry Sheets	.05
66	Junior Ortiz	.05
67	Francisco Cabrera RC	.05
68	Gary DiSarcina RC	.05
69	Greg Olson RC	.05
70	Beau Allred RC	.05
71	Oscar Azocar RC	.05
72	Kent Mercker RC	.05
73	John Burkett RC	.05
74	Carlos Baerga RC	.05
75	Dave Hollins RC	.05
76	Todd Hundley RC	.25
77	Rick Parker RC	.05
78	Steve Cummings RC	.05
79	Bill Sampen RC	.05
80	Jerry Kutzler RC	.05
81	Derek Bell RC	.05
82	Kevin Tapani RC	.05
83	Jim Leyritz RC	.25
84	Ray Lankford RC	.25
85	Wayne Edwards RC	.05
86	Frank Thomas	2.00
87	Tim Naehring RC	.05
88	Willie Blair RC	.05
89	Alan Mills RC	.05
90	Scott Radinsky RC	.05
91	Howard Farmer RC	.05
92	Julio Machado RC	.05
93	Rafael Valdez RC	.05
94	Shawn Boskie RC	.05
95	David Segui RC	.05
96	Chris Hoiles RC	.05
97	D.J. Dozier RC	.05
98	Hector Villanueva RC	.05
99	Eric Gunderson RC	.05
100	Eric Lindros RC	1.00
101	Dave Otto RC	.05
102	Dana Kiecker RC	.05
103	Tim Drummond RC	.05
104	Mickey Pina RC	.05
105	Craig Grebeck RC	.05
106	Bernard Gilkey RC	.25
107	Tim Layana RC	.05
108	Scott Chiamparino RC	.05
109	Steve Avery RC	.05
110	Terry Shumpert RC	.05

31	Ron Jones	.05
32	Gregg Olson	.05
33	Joe Girardi	.05
34	Ken Hill	.05
35	Sammy Sosa	3.00
36	Geronimo Berroa	.05
37	Omar Vizquel	.05
38	Dean Palmer	.05
39	John Olerud	.05
40	Deion Sanders	.05
41	Randy Kramer	.05
42	Scott Lusader	.05
43	Dave Johnson	.05
44	Jeff Wetherby	.05
45	Eric Anthony	.05
46	Kenny Rogers	.05
47	Matt Winters	.05
48	Goose Gozzo	.05
49	Carlos Quintana	.05
50	Bob Geren	.05
51	Chad Kreuter	.05
52	Randy Johnson	.75
53	Hensley Meulens	.05
54	Gene Harris	.05
55	Bill Spiers	.05
56	Kelly Mann	.05
57	Tom McCarthy	.05
58	Steve Finley	.05
59	Ramon Martinez	.05
60	Greg Briley	.05
61	Jack Daugherty	.05
62	Tim Jones	.05
63	Doug Strange	.05
64	John Orton	.05
65	Scott Scudder	.05
66	Mark Gardner (Photo on back actually Steve Frey.)	.05
67	Mark Carreon	.05
68	Bob Milacki	.05
69	Andy Benes	.05
70	Carlos Martinez	.05
71	Jeff King	.05
72	Brad Arnsberg	.05
73	Rick Wrona	.05
74	Cris Carpenter	.05
75	Dennis Cook	.05
76	Pete Harnisch	.05
77	Greg Hibbard	.05
78	Ed Whited	.05
79	Scott Coolbaugh	.05
80	Billy Bates	.05
81	German Gonzalez	.05
82	Lance Blankenship	.05
83	Lenny Harris	.05
84	Milt Cuyler	.05
85	Erik Hanson	.05
86	Kent Anderson	.05
87	Hal Morris	.05
88	Mike Brumley	.05
89	Ken Patterson	.05
90	Mike Devereaux	.05
91	Greg Litton	.05
92	Rolando Roomes	.05
93	Ben McDonald	.05
94	Curt Schilling	.35
95	Jose DeJesus	.05
96	Robin Ventura	.05
97	Steve Searcy	.05
98	Chip Hale	.05
99	Marquis Grissom	.05
100	Luis de los Santos	.05

Superstars

The game's top 100 players are featured in this set. The card fronts feature full-color action photos and are similar in style to the past Score Superstar set. The set was marketed as a boxed set and with a special magazine devoted to baseball's 100 hottest players. Each set includes a series of Magic Motion cards honoring past MVP winners. The player cards measure 2-1/2" x 3-1/2".

		NM/M
Complete Set (100):		3.00
Common Player:		.05
1	Kirby Puckett	.50
2	Steve Sax	.05
3	Tony Gwynn	.50
4	Willie Randolph	.05
5	Jose Canseco	.25

6	Ozzie Smith	.50
7	Rick Reuschel	.05
8	Bill Doran	.05
9	Mickey Tettleton	.05
10	Don Mattingly	.60
11	Greg Swindell	.05
12	Bert Blyleven	.05
13	Dave Stewart	.05
14	Andres Galarraga	.05
15	Darryl Strawberry	.05
16	Ellis Burks	.05
17	Paul O'Neill	.05
18	Bruce Hurst	.05
19	Dave Smith	.05
20	Carney Lansford	.05
21	Robby Thompson	.05
22	Gary Gaetti	.05
23	Jeff Russell	.05
24	Chuck Finley	.05
25	Mark McGwire	.65
26	Alvin Davis	.05
27	George Bell	.05
28	Cory Snyder	.05
29	Keith Hernandez	.05
30	Will Clark	.05
31	Steve Bedrosian	.05
32	Ryne Sandberg	.50
33	Tom Browning	.05
34	Tim Burke	.05
35	John Smoltz	.05
36	Phil Bradley	.05
37	Bobby Bonilla	.05
38	Kirk McCaskill	.05
39	Dave Righetti	.05
40	Bo Jackson	.10
41	Alan Trammell	.05
42	Mike Moore	.05
43	Harold Reynolds	.05
44	Nolan Ryan	.75
45	Fred McGriff	.05
46	Brian Downing	.05
47	Brett Butler	.05
48	Mike Scioscia	.05
49	John Franco	.05
50	Kevin Mitchell	.05
51	Mark Davis	.05
52	Glenn Davis	.05
53	Barry Bonds	.75
54	Dwight Evans	.05
55	Terry Steinbach	.05
56	Dave Gallagher	.05
57	Roberto Kelly	.05
58	Rafael Palmeiro	.35
59	Joe Carter	.05
60	Mark Grace	.05
61	Pedro Guerrero	.05
62	Von Hayes	.05
63	Benny Santiago	.05
64	Dale Murphy	.25
65	John Smiley	.05
66	Cal Ripken, Jr.	.75
67	Mike Greenwell	.05
68	Devon White	.05
69	Ed Whitson	.05
70	Carlton Fisk	.40
71	Lou Whitaker	.05
72	Danny Tartabull	.05
73	Vince Coleman	.05
74	Andre Dawson	.25
75	Tim Raines	.05
76	George Brett	.60
77	Tom Herr	.05
78	Andy Van Slyke	.05
79	Roger Clemens	.60
80	Wade Boggs	.50
81	Wally Joyner	.05
82	Lonnie Smith	.05
83	Howard Johnson	.05
84	Julio Franco	.05
85	Ruben Sierra	.05
86	Dan Plesac	.05
87	Bobby Thigpen	.05
88	Kevin Seitzer	.05
89	Dave Steib	.05
90	Rickey Henderson	.40
91	Jeffrey Leonard	.05
92	Robin Yount	.40
93	Mitch Williams	.05
94	Orel Hershiser	.05
95	Eric Davis	.05
96	Mark Langston	.05
97	Mike Scott	.05
98	Paul Molitor	.40
99	Dwight Gooden	.05
100	Kevin Bass	.05

Yankees

For a second year, National Westminster Bank sponsored a Score-produced team set as a stadium promotion. The set features color player photos on front and back and is graphically enhanced by the team's traditional pinstripe motif. A tribute card to former Yankees infielder and manager Billy Martin, who was killed the previous Christmas, is included in the set. The set was given to fans attending the August 18 game.

		NM/M
Complete Set (32):		4.00
Common Player:		.15
1	Stump Merrill	.15
2	Don Mattingly	2.50
3	Steve Sax	.15
4	Alvaro Espinoza	.15
5	Jesse Barfield	.15
6	Roberto Kelly	.15
7	Mel Hall	.15
8	Claudell Washington	.15
9	Bob Geren	.15
10	Jim Leyritz	.15
11	Pascual Perez	.15
12	Dave LaPoint	.15
13	Tim Leary	.15
14	Mike Witt	.15
15	Chuck Cary	.15
16	Dave Righetti	.15
17	Lee Guetterman	.15
18	Andy Hawkins	.15
19	Greg Cadaret	.15
20	Eric Plunk	.15
21	Jimmy Jones	.15
22	Deion Sanders	.75
23	Jeff Robinson	.15
24	Matt Nokes	.15
25	Steve Balboni	.15
26	Wayne Tolleson	.15
27	Randy Velarde	.15
28	Rick Cerone	.15
29	Alan Mills	.15
30	Billy Martin	.30
31	Yankee Stadium	.15
32	All-Time Yankee Records	.15

Young Superstars Set 1

For the third consecutive year, Score produced Young Superstars boxed sets. The 1990 versions contain 42 player cards plus five Magic-Motion trivia cards. The cards are similar to previous Young Superstar sets, with action photography on the front and a glossy finish. Card backs have a color portrait, major league statistics and scouting reports. Besides the boxed set, cards from Set I were inserted into rack packs.

		NM/M
Complete Set (42):		2.00
Common Player:		.10
1	Bo Jackson	.25
2	Dwight Smith	.10
3	Joey Belle	.25
4	Gregg Olson	.10
5	Jim Abbott	.10
6	Felix Fermin	.10
7	Brian Holman	.10
8	Clay Parker	.10
9	Junior Felix	.10
10	Joe Oliver	.10
11	Steve Finley	.10
12	Greg Briley	.10
13	Greg Vaughn	.10
14	Bill Spiers	.10
15	Eric Yelding	.10
16	Jose Gonzalez	.10
17	Mark Carreon	.10
18	Greg Harris	.10
19	Felix Jose	.10
20	Bob Milacki	.10
21	Kenny Rogers	.10

22	Rolando Roomes	.10
23	Bip Roberts	.10
24	Jeff Brantley	.10
25	Jeff Ballard	.10
26	John Dopson	.10
27	Ken Patterson	.10
28	Omar Vizquel	.10
29	Kevin Brown	.10
30	Derek Lilliquist	.10
31	David Wells	.10
32	Ken Hill	.10
33	Greg Litton	.10
34	Rob Ducey	.10
35	Carlos Martinez	.10
36	John Smoltz	.10
37	Lenny Harris	.10
38	Charlie Hayes	.10
39	Tommy Gregg	.10
40	John Wetteland	.10
41	Jeff Huson	.10
42	Eric Anthony	.10

Young Superstars Set 2

Available only as a boxed set via a mail-order offer, Set II of 1990 Score Young Superstars is identical in format to Set I, with the exception that the graphic elements on the front of Set II cards are in red and green, while in Set I they are in blue and magenta.

		NM/M
Complete Set (42):		5.00
Common Player:		.10
1	Todd Zeile	.10
2	Ben McDonald	.10
3	Delino DeShields	.10
4	Pat Combs	.10
5	John Olerud	.10
6	Marquis Grissom	.10
7	Mike Stanton	.10
8	Robin Ventura	.10
9	Larry Walker	.10
10	Dante Bichette	.10
11	Jack Armstrong	.10
12	Jay Bell	.10
13	Andy Benes	.10
14	Joey Cora	.10
15	Rob Dibble	.10
16	Jeff King	.10
17	Jeff Hamilton	.10
18	Erik Hanson	.10
19	Pete Harnisch	.10
20	Greg Hibbard	.10
21	Stan Javier	.10
22	Mark Lemke	.10
23	Steve Olin	.10
24	Tommy Greene	.10
25	Sammy Sosa	4.00
26	Gary Wayne	.10
27	Deion Sanders	.10
28	Steve Wilson	.10
29	Joe Girardi	.10
30	John Orton	.10
31	Kevin Tapani	.10
32	Carlos Baerga	.10
33	Glenallen Hill	.10
34	Mike Blowers	.10
35	Dave Hollins	.10
36	Lance Blankenship	.10
37	Hal Morris	.10
38	Lance Johnson	.10
39	Chris Gwynn	.10
40	Doug Dascenzo	.10
41	Jerald Clark	.10
42	Carlos Quintana	.10

Sportflics 11th National Nolan Ryan

This two-fronted card is a unique souvenir given to those who participated in a special 1990 convention tour of the Optigraphics card manufacturing plant in Dallas. The card features Nolan Ryan on two of the company's best-known products, Score on one side, Sportflics on

the other. Each side is similar to Ryan's regularly issued card in those sets, but carries logos or typography related to the 11th Annual National Sports Collectors Convention, held in nearby Arlington. Only 600 of the cards were reported produced.

	NM/M
Nolan Ryan	100.00

1991 Score Promos

To preview its 1991 baseball cards Score pre-released the 110 cards from its teal-bordered series (cards #111-220) as samples. The main difference on most cards between the samples and the issued version is that the samples have no statistics on the 1990 season or career lines. Many cards have different career highlight write-ups on back, as well. A handful of the sample cards were widely distributed to dealers and the hobby press, while others from the sheet were released more sparingly. As few as two specimens are known of some superstar cards, driving up their prices among single-player specialty collectors.

		NM/M
Common Player:		5.00
111	Juan Berenguer	5.00
112	Mike Heath	5.00
113	Scott Bradley	5.00
114	Jack Morris	5.00
115	Barry Jones	5.00
116	Kevin Romine	5.00
117	Garry Templeton	5.00
118	Scott Sanderson	5.00
119	Roberto Kelly	5.00
120	George Brett	60.00
121	Oddibe McDowell	5.00
122	Jim Acker	5.00
123	Bill Swift	5.00
124	Eric King	5.00
125	Jay Buhner	5.00
126	Matt Young	5.00
127	Alvaro Espinoza	5.00
128	Greg Hibbard	5.00
129	Jeff M. Robinson	5.00
130	Mike Greenwell	5.00
131	Dion James	5.00
132	Donn Pall	5.00
133	Lloyd Moseby	5.00
134	Randy Velarde	5.00
135	Allan Anderson	5.00
136	Mark Davis	5.00
137	Eric Davis	5.00
138	Phil Stephenson	5.00
139	Felix Fermin	5.00
140	Pedro Guerrero	5.00
141	Charlie Hough	5.00
142	Mike Henneman	5.00
143	Jeff Montgomery	5.00
144	Lenny Harris	5.00
145	Bruce Hurst	5.00
146	Eric Anthony	5.00

147	Paul Assenmacher	5.00
148	Jesse Barfield	5.00
149	Carlos Quintana	5.00
150	Dave Stewart	5.00
151	Roy Smith	5.00
152	Paul Gibson	5.00
153	Mickey Hatcher	5.00
154	Jim Eisenreich	5.00
155	Kenny Rogers	5.00
156	Dave Schmidt	5.00
157	Lance Johnson	5.00
158	Dave West	5.00
159	Steve Balboni	5.00
160	Jeff Brantley	5.00
161	Craig Biggio	5.00
162	Brook Jacoby	5.00
163	Dan Gladden	5.00
164	Jeff Reardon	5.00
165	Mark Carreon	5.00
166	Mel Hall	5.00
167	Gary Mielke	5.00
168	Cecil Fielder	5.00
169	Darrin Jackson	5.00
170	Rick Aguilera	5.00
171	Walt Weiss	5.00
172	Steve Farr	5.00
173	Jody Reed	5.00
174	Mike Jeffcoat	5.00
175	Mark Grace	5.00
176	Larry Sheets	5.00
177	Bill Gullickson	5.00
178	Chris Gwynn	5.00
179	Melido Perez	5.00
180	Sid Fernandez	5.00
181	Tim Burke	5.00
182	Gary Pettis	5.00
183	Rob Murphy	5.00
184	Craig Lefferts	5.00
185	Howard Johnson	5.00
186	Ken Caminiti	5.00
187	Tim Belcher	5.00
188	Greg Cadaret	5.00
189	Matt Williams	5.00
190	Dave Magadan	5.00
191	Geno Petralli	5.00
192	Jeff D. Robinson	5.00
193	Jim Deshaies	5.00
194	Willie Randolph	5.00
195	George Bell	5.00
196	Hubie Brooks	5.00
197	Tom Gordon	5.00
198	Mike Fitzgerald	5.00
199	Mike Pagliarulo	5.00
200	Kirby Puckett	40.00
201	Shawon Dunston	5.00
202	Dennis Boyd	5.00
203	Junior Felix	5.00
204	Alejandro Pena	5.00
205	Pete Smith	5.00
206	Tom Glavine	20.00
207	Luis Salazar	5.00
208	John Smoltz	5.00
209	Doug Dascenzo	5.00
210	Tim Wallach	5.00
211	Greg Gagne	5.00
212	Mark Gubicza	5.00
213	Mark Parent	5.00
214	Ken Oberkfell	5.00
215	Gary Carter	30.00
216	Rafael Palmeiro	25.00
217	Tom Niedenfuer	5.00
218	Dave LaPoint	5.00
219	Jeff Treadway	5.00
220	Mitch Williams	5.00

1991 Score

Score introduced a two-series format in 1991. The first series includes cards 1-441. Score cards once again feature multiple border colors within the set, several subsets (Master Blaster, K-Man, Highlights and Riflemen), full-color action photos on the front and portraits on the flip side. Score eliminated display of the player's uniform number on the 1991 cards. Black-and-white Dream Team cards, plus Prospects and #1 Draft Picks highlight the 1991 set. The second series was released in February of 1991.

	NM/M
Unopened Fact. Set (900):	10.00
Complete Set (893):	6.00
Common Player:	.05
Series 1 or 2 Pack (16):	.25
Series 1 or 2 Box (36):	6.00

#	Player	Price
1	Jose Canseco	.25
2	Ken Griffey Jr.	.60
3	Ryne Sandberg	.50
4	Nolan Ryan	.75
5	Bo Jackson	.10
6	Bret Saberhagen	.05
7	Will Clark	.05
8	Ellis Burks	.05
9	Joe Carter	.05
10	Rickey Henderson	.40
11	Ozzie Guillen	.05
12	Wade Boggs	.50
13	Jerome Walton	.05
14	John Franco	.05
15	Ricky Jordan	.05
16	Wally Backman	.05
17	Rob Dibble	.05
18	Glenn Braggs	.05
19	Cory Snyder	.05
20	Kal Daniels	.05
21	Mark Langston	.05
22	Kevin Gross	.05
23	Don Mattingly	.55
24	Dave Righetti	.05
25	Roberto Alomar	.15
26	Robby Thompson	.05
27	Jack McDowell	.05
28	Bip Roberts	.05
29	Jay Howell	.05
30	Dave Steib	.05
31	Johnny Ray	.05
32	Steve Sax	.05
33	Terry Mulholland	.05
34	Lee Guetterman	.05
35	Tim Raines	.05
36	Scott Fletcher	.05
37	Lance Parrish	.05
38	Tony Phillips	.05
39	Todd Stottlemyre	.05
40	Alan Trammell	.05
41	Todd Burns	.05
42	Mookie Wilson	.05
43	Chris Bosio	.05
44	Jeffrey Leonard	.05
45	Doug Jones	.05
46	Mike Scott	.05
47	Andy Hawkins	.05
48	Harold Reynolds	.05
49	Paul Molitor	.40
50	John Farrell	.05
51	Danny Darwin	.05
52	Jeff Blauser	.05
53	John Tudor	.05
54	Milt Thompson	.05
55	Dave Justice	.05
56	Greg Olson RC	.05
57	Willie Blair RC	.05
58	Rick Parker RC	.05
59	Shawn Boskie	.05
60	Kevin Tapani	.05
61	Dave Hollins	.05
62	Scott Radinsky RC	.05
63	Francisco Cabrera	.05
64	Tim Layana RC	.05
65	Jim Leyritz	.05
66	Wayne Edwards	.05
67	Lee Stevens RC	.05
68	Bill Sampen RC	.05
69	Craig Grebeck RC	.05
70	John Burkett	.05
71	Hector Villanueva RC	.05
72	Oscar Azocar RC	.05
73	Alan Mills	.05
74	Carlos Baerga	.05
75	Charles Nagy	.05
76	Tim Drummond	.05
77	Dana Kiecker RC	.05
78	Tom Edens RC	.05
79	Kent Mercker	.05
80	Steve Avery	.05
81	Lee Smith	.05
82	Dave Martinez	.05
83	Dave Winfield	.40
84	Bill Spiers	.05
85	Dan Pasqua	.05
86	Randy Milligan	.05
87	Tracy Jones	.05
88	Greg Myers RC	.05
89	Keith Hernandez	.05
90	Todd Benzinger	.05
91	Mike Jackson	.05
92	Mike Stanley	.05
93	Candy Maldonado	.05
94	John Kruk	.05
95	Cal Ripken, Jr.	.75
96	Willie Fraser	.05
97	Mike Felder	.05
98	Bill Landrum	.05
99	Chuck Crim	.05
100	Chuck Finley	.05
101	Kirt Manwaring	.05
102	Jaime Navarro	.05
103	Dickie Thon	.05
104	Brian Downing	.05
105	Jim Abbott	.05
106	Tom Brookens	.05
107	Darryl Hamilton	.05
108	Bryan Harvey	.05
109	Greg Harris	.05
110	Greg Swindell	.05
111	Juan Berenguer	.05
112	Mike Heath	.05
113	Scott Bradley	.05
114	Jack Morris	.05
115	Barry Jones	.05
116	Kevin Romine	.05
117	Garry Templeton	.05
118	Scott Sanderson	.05
119	Roberto Kelly	.05
120	George Brett	.50
121	Oddibe McDowell	.05
122	Jim Acker	.05
123	Bill Swift	.05
124	Eric King	.05
125	Jay Buhner	.05
126	Matt Young	.05
127	Alvaro Espinoza	.05
128	Greg Hibbard	.05
129	Jeff Robinson	.05
130	Mike Greenwell	.05
131	Dion James	.05
132	Donn Pall	.05
133	Lloyd Moseby	.05
134	Randy Velarde	.05
135	Allan Anderson	.05
136	Mark Davis	.05
137	Eric Davis	.05
138	Phil Stephenson	.05
139	Felix Fermin	.05
140	Pedro Guerrero	.05
141	Charlie Hough	.05
142	Mike Henneman	.05
143	Jeff Montgomery	.05
144	Lenny Harris	.05
145	Bruce Hurst	.05
146	Eric Anthony	.05
147	Paul Assenmacher	.05
148	Jesse Barfield	.05
149	Carlos Quintana	.05
150	Dave Stewart	.05
151	Roy Smith	.05
152	Paul Gibson	.05
153	Mickey Hatcher	.05
154	Jim Eisenreich	.05
155	Kenny Rogers	.05
156	Dave Schmidt	.05
157	Lance Johnson	.05
158	Dave West	.05
159	Steve Balboni	.05
160	Jeff Brantley	.05
161	Craig Biggio	.05
162	Brook Jacoby	.05
163	Dan Gladden	.05
164	Jeff Reardon	.05
165	Mark Carreon	.05
166	Mel Hall	.05
167	Gary Mielke	.05
168	Cecil Fielder	.05
169	Darrin Jackson	.05
170	Rick Aguilera	.05
171	Walt Weiss	.05
172	Steve Farr	.05
173	Jody Reed	.05
174	Mike Jeffcoat	.05
175	Mark Grace	.05
176	Larry Sheets	.05
177	Bill Gullickson	.05
178	Chris Gwynn	.05
179	Melido Perez	.05
180	Sid Fernandez	.05
181	Tim Burke	.05
182	Gary Pettis	.05
183	Rob Murphy	.05
184	Craig Lefferts	.05
185	Howard Johnson	.05
186	Ken Caminiti	.05
187	Tim Belcher	.05
188	Greg Cadaret	.05
189	Matt Williams	.05
190	Dave Magadan	.05
191	Geno Petralli	.05
192	Jeff Robinson	.05
193	Jim Deshaies	.05
194	Willie Randolph	.05
195	George Bell	.05
196	Hubie Brooks	.05
197	Tom Gordon	.05
198	Mike Fitzgerald	.05
199	Mike Pagliarulo	.05
200	Kirby Puckett	.50
201	Shawon Dunston	.05
202	Dennis Boyd	.05
203	Junior Felix	.05
204	Alejandro Pena	.05
205	Pete Smith	.05
206	Tom Glavine	.35
207	Luis Salazar	.05
208	John Smoltz	.05
209	Doug Dascenzo	.05
210	Tim Wallach	.05
211	Greg Gagne	.05
212	Mark Gubicza	.05
213	Mark Parent	.05
214	Ken Oberkfell	.05
215	Gary Carter	.40
216	Rafael Palmeiro	.35
217	Tom Niedenfuer	.05
218	Dave LaPoint	.05
219	Jeff Treadway	.05
220	Mitch Williams	.05
221	Jose DeLeon	.05
222	Mike LaValliere	.05
223	Darrel Akerfelds	.05
224a	Kent Anderson ("Flachy" in first line.)	.05
224b	Kent Anderson ("Flashy" in first line.)	.05
225	Dwight Evans	.05
226	Gary Redus	.05
227	Paul O'Neill	.05
228	Marty Barrett	.05
229	Tom Browning	.05
230	Terry Pendleton	.05
231	Jack Armstrong	.05
232	Mike Boddicker	.05
233	Neal Heaton	.05
234	Marquis Grissom	.05
235	Bert Blyleven	.05
236	Curt Young	.05
237	Don Carman	.05
238	Charlie Hayes	.05
239	Mark Knudson	.05
240	Todd Zeile	.05
241	Larry Walker	.05
242	Jerald Clark	.05
243	Jeff Ballard	.05
244	Jeff King	.05
245	Tom Brunansky	.05
246	Darren Daulton	.05
247	Scott Terry	.05
248	Rob Deer	.05
249	Brady Anderson	.05
250	Len Dykstra	.05
251	Greg Harris	.05
252	Mike Hartley	.05
253	Joey Cora	.05
254	Ivan Calderon	.05
255	Ted Power	.05
256	Sammy Sosa	.50
257	Steve Buechele	.05
258	Mike Devereaux	.05
259	Brad Komminsk	.05
260	Teddy Higuera	.05
261	Shawn Abner	.05
262	Dave Valle	.05
263	Jeff Huson	.05
264	Edgar Martinez	.05
265	Carlton Fisk	.40
266	Steve Finley	.05
267	John Wetteland	.05
268	Kevin Appier	.05
269	Steve Lyons	.05
270	Mickey Tettleton	.05
271	Luis Rivera	.05
272	Steve Jeltz	.05
273	R.J. Reynolds	.05
274	Carlos Martinez	.05
275	Dan Plesac	.05
276	Mike Morgan	.05
277	Jeff Russell	.05
278	Pete Incaviglia	.05
279	Kevin Seitzer	.05
280	Bobby Thigpen	.05
281	Stan Javier	.05
282	Henry Cotto	.05
283	Gary Wayne	.05
284	Shane Mack	.05
285	Brian Holman	.05
286	Gerald Perry	.05
287	Steve Crawford	.05
288	Nelson Liriano	.05
289	Don Aase	.05
290	Randy Johnson	.40
291	Harold Baines	.05
292	Kent Hrbek	.05
293a	Les Lancaster ("Dallas Texas")	.05
293b	Les Lancaster ("Dallas, Texas")	
294	Jeff Musselman	.05
295	Kurt Stillwell	.05
296	Stan Belinda	.05
297	Lou Whitaker	.05
298	Glenn Wilson	.05
299	Omar Vizquel	.05
300	Ramon Martinez	.05
301	Dwight Smith	.05
302	Tim Crews	.05
303	Lance Blankenship	.05
304	Sid Bream	.05
305	Rafael Ramirez	.05
306	Steve Wilson	.05
307	Mackey Sasser	.05
308	Franklin Stubbs	.05
309	Jack Daugherty	.05
310	Eddie Murray	.40
311	Bob Welch	.05
312	Brian Harper	.05
313	Lance McCullers	.05
314	Dave Smith	.05
315	Bobby Bonilla	.05
316	Jerry Don Gleaton	.05
317	Greg Maddux	.50
318	Keith Miller	.05
319	Mark Portugal	.05
320	Robin Ventura	.05
321	Bob Ojeda	.05
322	Mike Harkey	.05
323	Jay Bell	.05
324	Mark McGwire	.65
325	Gary Gaetti	.05
326	Jeff Pico	.05
327	Kevin McReynolds	.05
328	Frank Tanana	.05
329	Eric Yelding	.05
330	Barry Bonds	.75
331	Brian McRae RC	.05
332	Pedro Munoz RC	.05
333	Daryl Irvine RC	.05
334	Chris Hoiles	.05
335	Thomas Howard RC	.05
336	Jeff Schulz RC	.05
337	Jeff Manto RC	.05
338	Beau Allred	.05
339	Mike Bordick RC	.10
340	Todd Hundley	.05
341	Jim Vatcher RC	.05
342	Luis Sojo RC	.05
343	Jose Offerman RC	.05
344	Pete Coachman RC	.05
345	Mike Benjamin RC	.05
346	Ozzie Canseco RC	.05
347	Tim McIntosh RC	.05
348	Phil Plantier RC	.05
349	Terry Shumpert RC	.05
350	Darren Lewis RC	.05
351	David Walsh RC	.05
352a	Scott Chiamparino RC (Bats: Left)	.05
352b	Scott Chiamparino RC (Bats: Right)	
353	Julio Valera RC	.05
354	Anthony Telford RC	.05
355	Kevin Wickander RC	.05
356	Tim Naehring RC	.05
357	Jim Poole RC	.05
358	Mark Whiten RC	.05
359	Terry Wells RC	.05
360	Rafael Valdez RC	.05
361	Mel Stottlemyre RC	.05
362	David Segui RC	.10
363	Paul Abbott RC	.05
364	Steve Howard RC	.05
365	Karl Rhodes RC	.10
366	Rafael Novoa RC	.05
367	Joe Grahe RC	.05
368	Darren Reed RC	.05
369	Jeff McKnight RC	.05
370	Scott Leius RC	.05
371	Mark Dewey RC	.05
372	Mark Lee RC	.05
373	Rosario Rodriguez RC	.05
374	Chuck McElroy RC	.05
375	Mike Bell RC	.05
376	Mickey Morandini RC	.05
377	Bill Haselman RC	.05
378	Dave Pavlas RC	.05
379	Derrick May	.05
380	Jeromy Burnitz RC (1st Draft Pick)	.25
381	Donald Peters (1st Draft Pick)	.05
382	Alex Fernandez RC (1st Draft Pick)	.05
383	Mike Mussina RC (1st Draft Pick)	1.00
384	Daniel Smith RC (1st Draft Pick)	.05
385	Lance Dickson RC (1st Draft Pick)	.10
386	Carl Everett RC (1st Draft Pick)	.40
387	Thomas Nevers RC (1st Draft Pick)	.05
388	Adam Hyzdu RC (1st Draft Pick)	.05
389	Todd Van Poppel RC (1st Draft Pick)	.10
390	Rondell White RC (1st Draft Pick)	.30
391	Marc Newfield RC (1st Draft Pick)	.05
392	Julio Franco/AS	.05
393	Wade Boggs/AS	.25
394	Ozzie Guillen/AS	.05
395	Cecil Fielder/AS	.05
396	Ken Griffey Jr./AS	.30
397	Rickey Henderson/AS	.15
398	Jose Canseco/AS	.15
399	Roger Clemens/AS	.30
400	Sandy Alomar,Jr./AS	.05
401	Bobby Thigpen/AS	.05
402	Bobby Bonilla (Master Blaster)	.05
403	Eric Davis (Master Blaster)	.05
404	Fred McGriff (Master Blaster)	.05
405	Glenn Davis (Master Blaster)	.05
406	Kevin Mitchell (Master Blaster)	.05
407	Rob Dibble (K-Man)	.05
408	Ramon Martinez (K-Man)	.05
409	David Cone (K-Man)	.05
410	Bobby Witt (K-Man)	.05
411	Mark Langston (K-Man)	.05
412	Bo Jackson (Rifleman)	.10
413	Shawon Dunston (Rifleman)	.05
414	Jesse Barfield (Rifleman)	.05
415	Ken Caminiti (Rifleman)	.05
416	Benito Santiago (Rifleman)	.05
417	Nolan Ryan/HL	.40
418	Bobby Thigpen/HL	.05
419	Ramon Martinez/HL	.05
420	Bo Jackson/HL	.10
421	Carlton Fisk/HL	.20
422	Jimmy Key	.05
423	Junior Noboa RC	.05
424	Al Newman	.05
425	Pat Borders	.05
426	Von Hayes	.05
427	Tim Teufel	.05
428	Eric Plunk	.05
429	John Moses	.05
430	Mike Witt	.05
431	Otis Nixon	.05
432	Tony Fernandez	.05
433	Rance Mulliniks	.05
434	Dan Petry	.05
435	Bob Geren	.05
436	Steve Frey RC	.05
437	Jamie Moyer	.05
438	Junior Ortiz	.05
439	Tom O'Malley	.05
440	Pat Combs	.05
441	Jose Canseco (Dream Team)	.15
442	Alfredo Griffin	.05
443	Andres Galarraga	.05
444	Bryn Smith	.05
445	Andre Dawson	.25
446	Juan Samuel	.05
447	Mike Aldrete	.05
448	Ron Gant	.05
449	Fernando Valenzuela	.05
450	Vince Coleman	.05
451	Kevin Mitchell	.05
452	Spike Owen	.05
453	Mike Bielecki	.05
454	Dennis Martinez	.05
455	Brett Butler	.05
456	Ron Darling	.05
457	Dennis Rasmussen	.05
458	Ken Howell	.05
459	Steve Bedrosian	.05
460	Frank Viola	.05
461	Jose Lind	.05
462	Chris Sabo	.05
463	Dante Bichette	.05
464	Rick Mahler	.05
465	John Smiley	.05
466	Devon White	.05
467	John Orton	.05
468	Mike Stanton	.05
469	Billy Hatcher	.05
470	Wally Joyner	.05
471	Gene Larkin	.05
472	Doug Drabek	.05
473	Gary Sheffield	.30
474	David Wells	.05
475	Andy Van Slyke	.05
476	Mike Gallego	.05
477	B.J. Surhoff	.05
478	Gene Nelson	.05
479	Mariano Duncan	.05
480	Fred McGriff	.05
481	Jerry Browne	.05
482	Andy Davis	.05
483	Bill Wegman	.05
484	Dave Parker	.05
485	Dennis Eckersley	.35
486	Erik Hanson	.05
487	Bill Ripken	.05
488	Tom Candiotti	.05
489	Mike Schooler	.05
490	Gregg Olson	.05
491	Chris James	.05
492	Pete Harnisch	.05
493	Julio Franco	.05
494	Greg Briley	.05
495	Ruben Sierra	.05
496	Steve Olin	.05
497	Mike Fetters	.05
498	Mark Williamson	.05
499	Bob Tewksbury	.05
500	Tony Gwynn	.50
501	Randy Myers	.05
502	Keith Comstock	.05
503	Craig Worthington	.05
504	Mark Eichhorn	.05
505	Barry Larkin	.05
506	Dave Johnson	.05
507	Bobby Witt	.05
508	Joe Orsulak	.05
509	Pete O'Brien	.05
510	Brad Arnsberg	.05
511	Storm Davis	.05
512	Bob Milacki	.05
513	Bill Pecota	.05
514	Glenallen Hill	.05
515	Danny Tartabull	.05
516	Mike Moore	.05
517	Ron Robinson	.05
518	Mark Gardner	.05
519	Rick Wrona	.05
520	Mike Scioscia	.05
521	Frank Wills	.05
522	Greg Brock	.05
523	Jack Clark	.05
524	Bruce Ruffin	.05
525	Robin Yount	.40
526	Tom Foley	.05
527	Pat Perry	.05
528	Greg Vaughn	.05
529	Wally Whitehurst	.05
530	Norm Charlton	.05
531	Marvell Wynne	.05
532	Jim Gantner	.05
533	Greg Litton	.05
534	Manny Lee	.05
535	Scott Bailes	.05
536	Charlie Leibrandt	.05
537	Roger McDowell	.05
538	Andy Benes	.05
539	Rick Honeycutt	.05
540	Dwight Gooden	.05
541	Scott Garrelts	.05
542	Dave Clark	.05
543	Lonnie Smith	.05
544	Rick Rueschel	.05
545	Delino DeShields	.05
546	Mike Sharperson	.05
547	Mike Kingery	.05
548	Terry Kennedy	.05
549	David Cone	.05
550	Orel Hershiser	.05
551	Matt Nokes	.05
552	Eddie Williams	.05
553	Frank DiPino	.05
554	Fred Lynn	.05
555	Alex Cole RC	.05
556	Terry Leach	.05
557	Chet Lemon	.05
558	Paul Mirabella	.05
559	Bill Long	.05
560	Phil Bradley	.05
561	Duane Ward	.05
562	Dave Bergman	.05
563	Eric Show	.05
564	Xavier Hernandez RC	.05
565	Jeff Parrett	.05
566	Chuck Cary	.05
567	Ken Hill	.05
568	Bob Welch	.05
569	John Mitchell	.05
570	Travis Fryman	.05
571	Derek Lilliquist	.05
572	Steve Lake	.05
573	John Barfield RC	.05
574	Randy Bush	.05
575	Joe Magrane	.05
576	Edgar Diaz	.05
577	Casy Candaele	.05
578	Jesse Orosco	.05
579	Tom Henke	.05
580	Rick Cerone	.05
581	Drew Hall	.05
582	Tony Castillo	.05
583	Jimmy Jones	.05
584	Rick Reed	.05
585	Joe Girardi	.05
586	Jeff Gray RC	.05
587	Luis Polonia	.05
588	Joe Klink RC	.05
589	Rex Hudler	.05
590	Kirk McCaskill	.05
591	Juan Agosto	.05
592	Wes Gardner	.05
593	Rich Rodriguez RC	.05
594	Mitch Webster	.05
595	Kelly Gruber	.05
596	Dale Mohorcic	.05
597	Willie McGee	.05
598	Bill Krueger	.05
599	Bob Walk	.05
600	Kevin Maas	.05
601	Danny Jackson	.05
602	Craig McMurtry	.05
603	Curtis Wilkerson	.05
604	Adam Peterson	.05
605	Sam Horn	.05
606	Tommy Gregg	.05
607	Ken Dayley	.05
608	Carmelo Castillo	.05
609	John Shelby	.05
610	Don Slaught	.05
611	Calvin Schiraldi	.05
612	Dennis Lamp	.05
613	Andres Thomas	.05
614	Jose Gonzales	.05
615	Randy Ready	.05
616	Kevin Bass	.05
617	Mike Marshall	.05
618	Daryl Boston	.05
619	Andy McGaffigan	.05
620	Joe Oliver	.05
621	Jim Gott	.05
622	Jose Oquendo	.05
623	Jose DeJesus	.05
624	John Olerud	.05
625	John Brumley	.05
626	Ernest Riles	.05
627	Gene Harris	.05
628	Jose Uribe	.05
629	Darnell Coles	.05
630	Carney Lansford	.05
631	Tim Leary	.05
632	Tim Hulett	.05
633	Kevin Elster	.05
634	Tony Fossas	.05
635	Francisco Oliveras	.05
636	Bob Patterson	.05
637	Gary Ward	.05
638	Rene Gonzales	.05
639	Don Robinson	.05
640	Darryl Strawberry	.05
641	Dave Anderson	.05
642	Scott Scudder	.05
643	Reggie Harris RC	.05
644	Dave Henderson	.05
645	Ben McDonald	.05
646	Bob Kipper	.05
647	Hal Morris	.05
648	Tim Birtsas	.05
649	Steve Searcy	.05
650	Dale Murphy	.20
651	Ron Oester	.05
652	Mike LaCoss	.05
653	Ron Jones	.05
654	Kelly Downs	.05
655	Roger Clemens	.55
656	Herm Winningham	.05
657	Trevor Wilson	.05
658	Jose Rijo	.05
659	Dann Bilardello	.05
660	Gregg Jefferies	.05
661	Doug Drabek/AS	.05
662	Randy Myers/AS	.05
663	Benito Santiago/AS	.05

ABBREVIATIONS

AS - All-Star

#	Player	Price
664	Will Clark/AS	.05
665	Ryne Sandberg/AS	.25
666	Barry Larkin/AS	.05
667	Matt Williams/AS	.05
668	Barry Bonds/AS	.35
669	Eric Davis/AS	.05
670	Bobby Bonilla/AS	.05
671	Chipper Jones (1st Draft Pick)	1.50
672	Eric Christopherson RC (1st Draft Pick)	.05
673	Robbie Beckett RC (1st Draft Pick)	.05
674	Shane Andrews RC (1st Draft Pick)	.15
675	Steve Karsay RC (1st Draft Pick)	.10
676	Aaron Holbert RC (1st Draft Pick)	.05
677	Donovan Osborne RC (1st Draft Pick)	.05
678	Todd Ritchie RC (1st Draft Pick)	.05
679	Ron Walden RC (1st Draft Pick)	.05
680	Tim Costo RC (1st Draft Pick)	.10
681	Dan Wilson RC (1st Draft Pick)	.05
682	Kurt Miller RC (1st Draft Pick)	.05
683	Mike Lieberthal RC (1st Draft Pick)	.25
684	Roger Clemens (K-Man)	.25
685	Dwight Gooden (K-Man)	.05
686	Nolan Ryan (K-Man)	.35
687	Frank Viola (K-Man)	.05
688	Erik Hanson (K-Man)	.05
689	Matt Williams (Master Blaster)	.05
690	Jose Canseco (Master Blaster)	.10
691	Darryl Strawberry (Master Blaster)	.05
692	Bo Jackson (Master Blaster)	.10
693	Cecil Fielder (Master Blaster)	.05
694	Sandy Alomar, Jr. (Rifleman)	.05
695	Cory Snyder (Rifleman)	.05
696	Eric Davis (Rifleman)	.05
697	Ken Griffey Jr. (Rifleman)	.30
698	Andy Van Slyke (Rifleman)	.05
699	Mark Langston, Mike Witt (No-hitter)	.05
700	Randy Johnson (No-hitter)	.20
701a	Nolan Ryan (No-hitter) (White background on stat box.)	2.00
701b	Nolan Ryan (No-hitter) (Blue background on stat box.)	.35
702	Dave Stewart (No-hitter)	.05
703	Fernando Valenzuela (No-hitter)	.05
704	Andy Hawkins (No-hitter)	.05
705	Melido Perez (No-hitter)	.05
706	Terry Mulholland (No-hitter)	.05
707	Dave Stieb (No-hitter)	.05
708	Brian Barnes RC	.05
709	Bernard Gilkey RC	.05
710	Steve Decker RC	.05
711	Paul Faries RC	.05
712	Paul Marak RC	.05
713	Wes Chamberlain RC	.05
714	Kevin Belcher RC	.05
715	Dan Boone RC	.05
716	Steve Adkins RC	.05
717	Geronimo Pena RC	.05
718	Howard Farmer RC	.05
719	Mark Leonard RC	.05
720	Tom Lampkin RC	.05
721	Mike Gardiner RC	.05
722	Jeff Conine RC	.25
723	Efrain Valdez RC	.05
724	Chuck Malone RC	.05
725	Leo Gomez RC	.05
726	Paul McClellan RC	.05
727	Mark Leiter RC	.05
728	Rich DeLucia RC	.05
729	Mel Rojas RC	.05
730	Hector Wagner RC	.05
731	Ray Lankford RC	.05
732	Turner Ward RC	.05
733	Gerald Alexander RC	.05
734	Scott Anderson RC	.05
735	Tony Perezchica RC	.05
736	Jimmy Kremers RC	.05
737a	American Flag (SCORE 1991 copyright, unmarked promo.)	.25
737b	American Flag (1991 SCORE in copyright)	.25
738	Mike York RC	.05
739	Mike Rochford RC	.05
740	Scott Aldred RC	.05
741	Rico Brogna RC	.05
742	Dave Burba RC	.05
743	Ray Stephens RC	.05
744	Eric Gunderson RC	.05
745	Troy Afenir RC	.05
746	Jeff Shaw RC	.05
747	Orlando Merced RC	.10
748	Omar Oliveras RC	.05
749	Jerry Kutzler RC	.05
750	Mo Vaughn	.05
751	Matt Stark RC	.05
752	Randy Hennis RC	.05
753	Andujar Cedeno RC	.05
754	Kelvin Torve RC	.05
755	Joe Kraemer RC	.05
756	Phil Clark RC	.05
757	Ed Vosberg RC	.05
758	Mike Perez RC	.05
759	Scott Lewis RC	.05
760	Steve Chitren RC	.05
761	Ray Young RC	.05
762	Andres Santana RC	.05
763	Rodney McCray RC	.05
764	Sean Berry RC	.05
765	Brent Mayne RC	.05
766	Mike Simms RC	.05
767	Glenn Sutko RC	.05
768	Gary Disarcina RC	.05
769	George Brett/HL	.25
770	Cecil Fielder/HL	.05
771	Jim Presley	.05
772	John Dopson	.05
773	Bo Jackson (Breaker)	.10
774	Brent Knackert RC	.05
775	Bill Doran	.05
776	Dick Schofield	.05
777	Nelson Santovenia	.05
778	Mark Guthrie RC	.05
779	Mark Lemke	.05
780	Terry Steinbach	.05
781	Tom Bolton	.05
782	Randy Tomlin RC	.05
783	Jeff Kunkel	.05
784	Felix Jose	.05
785	Rick Sutcliffe	.05
786	John Cerutti	.05
787	Jose Vizcaino	.05
788	Curt Schilling	.35
789	Ed Whitson	.05
790	Tony Pena	.05
791	John Candelaria	.05
792	Carmelo Martinez	.05
793	Sandy Alomar, Jr.	.05
794	Jim Neidlinger RC	.05
795	Red's October (Barry Larkin, Chris Sabo)	.10
796	Paul Sorrento	.05
797	Tom Pagnozzi	.05
798	Tino Martinez	.05
799	Scott Ruskin RC	.05
800	Kirk Gibson	.05
801	Walt Terrell	.05
802	John Russell	.05
803	Chili Davis	.05
804	Chris Nabholz RC	.05
805	Juan Gonzalez	.20
806	Ron Hassey	.05
807	Todd Worrell	.05
808	Tommy Greene	.05
809	Joel Skinner	.05
810	Benito Santiago	.05
811	Pat Tabler	.05
812	Scott Erickson RC	.05
813	Moises Alou	.05
814	Dale Sveum	.05
815	Ryne Sandberg (Man of the Year)	.25
816	Rick Dempsey	.05
817	Scott Bankhead	.05
818	Jason Grimsley	.05
819	Doug Jennings	.05
820	Tom Herr	.05
821	Rob Ducey	.05
822	Luis Quinones	.05
823	Greg Minton	.05
824	Mark Grant	.05
825	Ozzie Smith	.50
826	Dave Eiland	.05
827	Danny Heep	.05
828	Hensley Meulens	.05
829	Charlie O'Brien	.05
830	Glenn Davis	.05
831	John Marzano	.05
832	Steve Ontiveros	.05
833	Ron Karkovice	.05
834	Jerry Goff RC	.05
835	Ken Griffey Sr.	.05
836	Kevin Reimer RC	.05
837	Randy Kutcher	.05
838	Mike Blowers	.05
839	Mike Macfarlane	.05
840	Frank Thomas	.40
841	Ken Griffey Sr., Ken Griffey Jr.	.20
842	Jack Howell	.05
843	Mauro Gozzo RC	.05
844	Gerald Young	.05
845	Zane Smith	.05
846	Kevin Brown	.05
847	Sil Campusano	.05
848	Larry Andersen	.05
849	Cal Ripken, Jr.	.35
850	Roger Clemens (Franchise)	.30
851	Sandy Alomar, Jr. (Franchise)	.05
852	Alan Trammell (Franchise)	.05
853	George Brett (Franchise)	.25
854	Robin Yount (Franchise)	.25
855	Kirby Puckett (Franchise)	.25
856	Don Mattingly (Franchise)	.30
857	Rickey Henderson (Franchise)	.20
858	Ken Griffey Jr. (Franchise)	.30
859	Ruben Sierra (Franchise)	.05
860	John Olerud (Franchise)	.05
861	Dave Justice (Franchise)	.05
862	Ryne Sandberg (Franchise)	.25
863	Eric Davis (Franchise)	.05
864	Darryl Strawberry (Franchise)	.05
865	Tim Wallach (Franchise)	.05
866	Dwight Gooden (Franchise)	.05
867	Len Dykstra (Franchise)	.05
868	Barry Bonds (Franchise)	.35
869	Todd Zeile (Franchise)	.05
870	Benito Santiago (Franchise)	.05
871	Will Clark (Franchise)	.05
872	Craig Biggio (Franchise)	.05
873	Wally Joyner (Franchise)	.05
874	Frank Thomas (Franchise)	.20
875	Rickey Henderson/MVP	.20
876	Barry Bonds/MVP	.35
877	Bob Welch (Cy Young)	.05
878	Doug Drabek (Cy Young)	.05
879	Sandy Alomar, Jr. (ROY)	.05
880	Dave Justice (ROY)	.05
881	Damon Berryhill	.05
882	Frank Viola (Dream Team)	.05
883	Dave Stewart (Dream Team)	.05
884	Doug Jones (Dream Team)	.05
885	Randy Myers (Dream Team)	.05
886	Will Clark (Dream Team)	.05
887	Roberto Alomar (Dream Team)	.10
888	Barry Larkin (Dream Team)	.05
889	Wade Boggs (Dream Team)	.25
890	Rickey Henderson (Dream Team)	.20
891	Kirby Puckett (Dream Team)	.20
892	Ken Griffey Jr. (Dream Team)	.30
893	Benito Santiago (Dream Team)	.05

Cooperstown

This seven-card set was included as an insert in every factory set. The card fronts are white, with an oval-vignetted player portrait. The backs have green borders surrounding a yellow background which contains a summary of the player's career.

		NM/M
Complete Set (7):		3.50
Common Player:		
B1	Wade Boggs	.50
B2	Barry Larkin	.25
B3	Ken Griffey Jr.	1.00
B4	Rickey Henderson	.35
B5	George Brett	.75
B6	Will Clark	.25
B7	Nolan Ryan	1.50

Hot Rookies

These standard-size cards were inserted one per every 100-card 1991 Score blister pack.

This 110-card set features players with new teams as well as 1991 Major League rookies. The cards are designed in the same style as the regular 1991 Score issue. The cards once again feature a "T" designation along with the card number. The complete set was sold at hobby shops in a special box.

		NM/M
Complete Set (110):		4.00
Common Player:		.10
1	Bo Jackson	.10
2	Mike Flanagan	.05
3	Pete Incaviglia	.05
4	Jack Clark	.05
5	Hubie Brooks	.05
6	Ivan Calderon	.05
7	Glenn Davis	.05
8	Wally Backman	.05
9	Dave Smith	.05
10	Tim Raines	.05
11	Joe Carter	.05
12	Sid Bream	.05
13	George Bell	.05
14	Steve Bedrosian	.05
15	Willie Wilson	.05
16	Darryl Strawberry	.05
17	Danny Jackson	.05
18	Kirk Gibson	.05
19	Willie McGee	.05
20	Junior Felix	.05
21	Steve Farr	.05
22	Pat Tabler	.05
23	Brett Butler	.05
24	Danny Darwin	.05
25	Mickey Tettleton	.05
26	Gary Carter	.50
27	Mitch Williams	.05
28	Candy Maldonado	.05
29	Otis Nixon	.05
30	Brian Downing	.05
31	Tom Candiotti	.05
32	John Candelaria	.05
33	Rob Murphy	.05
34	Deion Sanders	.05
35	Willie Randolph	.05
36	Pete Harnisch	.05
37	Dante Bichette	.05
38	Garry Templeton	.05
39	Gary Gaetti	.05
40	John Cerutti	.05
41	Rick Cerone	.05
42	Mike Pagliarulo	.05
43	Ron Hassey	.05
44	Roberto Alomar	.20
45	Mike Boddicker	.05
46	Bud Black	.05
47	Rob Deer	.05
48	Devon White	.05
49	Luis Sojo	.05
50	Terry Pendleton	.05
51	Kevin Gross	.05
52	Mike Huff	.05
53	Dave Righetti	.05
54	Matt Young	.05
55	Ernest Riles	.05
56	Bill Gullickson	.05
57	Vince Coleman	.05
58	Fred McGriff	.05
59	Franklin Stubbs	.05
60	Eric King	.05
61	Cory Snyder	.05
62	Dwight Evans	.05
63	Gerald Perry	.05
64	Eric Show	.05
65	Shawn Hillegas	.05
66	Tony Fernandez	.05
67	Tim Teufel	.05
68	Mitch Webster	.05
69	Mike Heath	.05
70	Chili Davis	.05
71	Larry Andersen	.05
72	Gary Varsho	.05
73	Juan Berenguer	.05
74	Jack Morris	.05
75	Barry Jones	.05
76	Rafael Belliard	.05
77	Steve Buechele	.05
78	Scott Sanderson	.05
79	Bob Ojeda	.05
80	Curt Schilling	.05
81	Brian Drahman RC	.05
82	Ivan Rodriguez RC	1.00
83	David Howard RC	.05
84	Heath Slocumb RC	.05
85	Mike Timlin RC	.05
86	Darryl Kile RC	.05
87	Pete Schourek RC	.05
88	Bruce Walton RC	.05
89	Al Osuna RC	.05
90	Gary Scott RC	.05
91	Doug Simons RC	.05
92	Chris Jones RC	.05
93	Chuck Knoblauch RC	.05
94	Dana Allison RC	.05
95	Erik Pappas RC	.05
96	Jeff Bagwell RC	2.50

		NM/M
Complete Set (10):		2.50
Common Player:		.10
1	Dave Justice	.25
2	Kevin Maas	.10
3	Hal Morris	.10
4	Frank Thomas	1.50
5	Jeff Conine	.10
6	Sandy Alomar Jr.	.10
7	Ray Lankford	.10
8	Steve Decker	.10
9	Juan Gonzalez	.50
10	Jose Offerman	.10

Mickey Mantle

This special set recalls Mickey Mantle's career as a Yankee. Card fronts are glossy and have red and white borders. The card's caption appears at the bottom in a blue stripe. The backs have a photo and a summary of the caption, plus the card number and serial number. Dealers and media members received the sets, which were limited to 5,000, in a fin-fold plastic wrapper. A total of 2,500 of the cards were numbered and autographed.

		NM/M
Complete Set (7):		35.00
Common Card:		6.00
Autographed Card:		575.00
1	The Rookie	9.00
2	Triple Crown	7.50
3	World Series	7.50
4	Going, Going, Gone	7.50
5	Speed and Grace	7.50
6	A True Yankee	7.50
7	Twilight	7.50

Traded

ABBREVIATIONS

AS - All-Star

#	Player	Price
97	Kirk Dressendorfer RC	.05
98	Freddie Benavides RC	.05
99	Luis Lopez RC	.50
100	Wade Taylor RC	.05
101	Ed Sprague RC	.05
102	Bob Scanlan RC	.05
103	Rick Wilkins RC	.05
104	Chris Donnels RC	.05
105	Joe Slusarski RC	.05
106	Mark Lewis RC	.05
107	Pat Kelly RC	.05
108	John Briscoe RC	.05
109	Luis Lopez RC	.05
110	Jeff Johnson RC	.05

Blue Jays

Sold as a special boxed issue including 40 player cards and five trivia cards, this set features the 1991 Blue Jays and their hosting of the 1991 All-Star Game. Cards carry a super-glossy front finish that features a player action photo in a home plate-shaped frame at center. Around the photo are blue and white border designs with the player's name and position at top, and Score and Blue Jays logos at bottom. Backs repeat the blue and white motif with a color player portrait, biographical notes, stats and career summary.

		NM/M
Complete Set (40):		7.00
Common Player:		.25
1	Joe Carter	.35
2	Tom Henke	.25
3	Jimmy Key	.25
4	Al Leiter	.25
5	Dave Stieb	.25
6	Todd Stottlemyre	.35
7	Mike Timlin	.25
8	Duane Ward	.25
9	David Wells	.50
10	Frank Wills	.25
11	Pat Borders	.25
12	Greg Myers	.25
13	Roberto Alomar	2.50
14	Rene Gonzalez	.25
15	Kelly Gruber	.25
16	Manny Lee	.25
17	Rance Mulliniks	.25
18	John Olerud	1.00
19	Pat Tabler	.25
20	Derek Bell	.25
21	Jim Acker	.25
22	Rob Ducey	.25
23	Devon White	.35
24	Mookie Wilson	.25
25	Juan Guzman	.25
26	Ed Sprague	.25
27	Ken Dayley	.25
28	Tom Candiotti	.25
29	Candy Maldonado	.25
30	Eddie Zosky	.25
31	Steve Karsay	.25
32	Bob MacDonald	.25
33	Ray Giannelli	.25
34	Jerry Schunk	.25
35	Dave Weathers	.25
36	Cito Gaston	.25
37	Joe Carter/AS	.25
38	Jimmy Key/AS	.25
39	Roberto Alomar/AS	1.50
40	1991 All-Star Game	.25

FanFest/National

Two versions of this 10-card set were produced for distribution at the All-Star FanFest and the National Sports Collectors Convention. The appropriate venue is listed in a red stripe on back under the player career summary. Fronts have a color action photo against a background of pale green with blue ballplayer silhouettes and yellow base-balls. Backs repeat the player figure and baseball motif on a white background. A trapezoid at center has a player portrait photo, color team logo, bio-graphical details and career highlights. At present neither version of these cards carries a premium over the other.

		NM/M
Complete Set (10):		2.00
Common Player:		.25
1	Ray Lankford	.25
2	Steve Decker	.25
3	Gary Scott	.25
4	Hensley Meulens	.25
5	Tim Naehring	.25
6	Mark Whiten	.25
7	Ed Sprague	.25
8	Charles Nagy	.25
9	Terry Shumpert	.25
10	Chuck Knoblauch	.25

"Life and Times of Nolan Ryan"

This four-card career high-lights set was distributed with a series of four collector maga-zines. Cards feature color pho-tos with Score and Texas Rang-ers logos in separate corners. A red stripe above the photo, or to its left, names the highlight; a blue stripe above or to the left of that has his name and position. Horizontally formatted backs have another color photo and a paragraph about the milestone.

		NM/M
Complete Set (4):		6.00
Common Player:		1.50
1	5,000th Career Strikeout (Nolan Ryan)	1.50
2	6th Career No-Hitter (Nolan Ryan)	1.50
3	300th Career Victory (Nolan Ryan)	1.50
4	7th Career No-Hitter (Nolan Ryan)	1.50

Rising Stars

Marketed along with 1990-91 "Baseball's Hottest Rookies" magazine, this 100-card set features top rookies and young players. The cards are similar in design to the

Score Superstar set. The mag-azine/card sets were available to a select group of retailers.

		NM/M
Complete Set (100):		2.50
Common Player:		.05
1	Sandy Alomar, Jr.	.05
2	Tom Edens	.05
3	Terry Shumpert	.05
4	Shawn Boskie	.05
5	Steve Avery	.05
6	Deion Sanders	.05
7	John Burkett	.05
8	Stan Belinda	.05
9	Thomas Howard	.05
10	Wayne Edwards	.05
11	Rick Parker	.05
12	Randy Veres	.05
13	Alex Cole	.05
14	Scott Chaimparino	.05
15	Greg Olson	.05
16	Jose DeJesus	.05
17	Mike Blowers	.05
18	Jeff Huson	.05
19	Willie Blair	.05
20	Howard Farmer	.05
21	Larry Walker	.05
22	Scott Hemond	.05
23	Mel Stottlemyre	.05
24	Mark Whiten	.05
25	Jeff Schulz	.05
26	Gary Disarcina	.05
27	George Canale	.05
28	Dean Palmer	.05
29	Jim Leyritz	.05
30	Carlos Baerga	.05
31	Rafael Valdez	.05
32	Derek Bell	.05
33	Francisco Cabrera	.05
34	Chris Hoiles	.05
35	Craig Grebeck	.05
36	Scott Coolbaugh	.05
37	Kevin Wickander	.05
38	Marquis Grissom	.05
39	Chip Hale	.05
40	Kevin Maas	.50
41	Juan Gonzalez	.50
42	Eric Anthony	.05
43	Luis Sojo	.05
44	Paul Sorrento	.05
45	Dave Justice	.05
46	Oscar Azocar	.05
47	Charles Nagy	.05
48	Robin Ventura	.05
49	Reggie Harris	.05
50	Ben McDonald	.05
51	Hector Villanueva	.05
52	Kevin Tapani	.05
53	Brian Bohanon	.05
54	Tim Layana	.05
55	Delino DeShields	.05
56	Beau Allred	.05
57	Eric Gunderson	.05
58	Kent Mercker	.05
59	Juan Bell	.05
60	Glenallen Hill	.05
61	David Segui	.05
62	Alan Mills	.05
63	Mike Harkey	.05
64	Bill Sampen	.05
65	Greg Vaughn	.05
66	Alex Fernandez	.05
67	Mike Hartley	.05
68	Travis Fryman	.05
69	Dave Rohde	.05
70	Tom Lampkin	.05
71	Mark Gardner	.05
72	Pat Combs	.05
73	Kevin Appier	.05
74	Mike Fetters	.05
75	Greg Myers	.05
76	Steve Searcy	.05
77	Tim Naehring	.05
78	Frank Thomas	1.50
79	Todd Hundley	.05
80	Ed Vosberg	.05
81	Todd Zeile	.05
82	Lee Stevens	.05
83	Scott Radinsky	.05
84	Hensley Meulens	.05
85	Brian DuBois	.05
86	Steve Olin	.05
87	Julio Machado	.05
88	Jose Vizcaino	.05
89	Mark Lemke	.05
90	Felix Jose	.05
91	Wally Whitehurst	.05
92	Dana Kiecker	.05
93	Mike Munoz	.05
94	Adam Peterson	.05
95	Tim Drummond	.05
96	Dave Hollins	.05
97	Craig Wilson	.05
98	Hal Morris	.05
99	Jose Offerman	.05
100	John Olerud	.05

Rookies

This 40-card boxed set did not receive much attention in the hobby world, but features some of the top young players of 1991. The card fronts feature full-color action photos with a

"Rookies" banner along the side border. The backs feature sta-tistics and a player profile. This set was available through hobby dealers and is Score's first re-lease of its kind.

		NM/M
Complete Set (40):		1.00
Common Player:		.05
1	Mel Rojas	.05
2	Ray Lankford	.05
3	Scott Aldred	.05
4	Turner Ward	.05
5	Omar Olivares	.05
6	Mo Vaughn	.05
7	Phil Clark	.05
8	Brent Mayne	.05
9	Scott Lewis	.05
10	Brian Barnes	.05
11	Bernard Gilkey	.05
12	Steve Decker	.05
13	Paul Marak	.05
14	Wes Chamberlain	.05
15	Kevin Belcher	.05
16	Steve Adkins	.05
17	Geronimo Pena	.05
18	Mark Leonard	.05
19	Jeff Conine	.05
20	Leo Gomez	.05
21	Chuck Malone	.05
22	Beau Allred	.05
23	Todd Hundley	.05
24	Lance Dickson	.05
25	Mike Benjamin	.05
26	Jose Offerman	.05
27	Terry Shumpert	.05
28	Darren Lewis	.05
29	Scott Chiamparino	.05
30	Tim Naehring	.05
31	David Segui	.05
32	Karl Rhodes	.05
33	Mickey Morandini	.05
34	Chuck McElroy	.05
35	Tim McIntosh	.05
36	Derrick May	.05
37	Rich DeLucia	.05
38	Tino Martinez	.05
39	Hensley Meulens	.05
40	Andujar Cedeno	.05

Superstars

This 100-card set fea-tures full-color action photos on the card fronts and posed shots on the flip sides. The set was marketed along with the magazine "1991 Baseball's Hottest Players." The cards feature red, white, and blue borders. The backs contain brief career highlights. The magazine/card set combo was available to select retailers.

		NM/M
Complete Set (100):		5.00
Common Player:		.05
1	Jose Canseco	.25
2	Bo Jackson	.10
3	Wade Boggs	.50
4	Will Clark	.05
5	Ken Griffey Jr.	.65
6	Doug Drabek	.05
7	Kirby Puckett	.50

8	Joe Orsulak	.05
9	Eric Davis	.05
10	Rickey Henderson	.40
11	Lenny Dykstra	.05
12	Ruben Sierra	.05
13	Paul Molitor	.40
14	Ron Gant	.05
15	Ozzie Guillen	.05
16	Ramon Martinez	.05
17	Edgar Martinez	.05
18	Ozzie Smith	.50
19	Charlie Hayes	.05
20	Barry Larkin	.05
21	Cal Ripken, Jr.	1.00
22	Andy Van Slyke	.05
23	Don Mattingly	.60
24	Dave Stewart	.05
25	Nolan Ryan	1.00
26	Barry Bonds	1.00
27	Gregg Olson	.05
28	Chris Sabo	.05
29	John Franco	.05
30	Gary Sheffield	.25
31	Jeff Treadway	.05
32	Tom Browning	.05
33	Jose Lind	.05
34	Dave Magadan	.05
35	Dale Murphy	.20
36	Tom Candiotti	.05
37	Willie McGee	.05
38	Robin Yount	.40
39	Mark McGwire	.75
40	George Bell	.05
41	Carlton Fisk	.40
42	Bobby Bonilla	.05
43	Randy Milligan	.05
44	Dave Parker	.05
45	Shawon Dunston	.05
46	Brian Harper	.05
47	John Tudor	.05
48	Ellis Burks	.05
49	Bob Welch	.05
50	Roger Clemens	.60
51	Mike Henneman	.05
52	Eddie Murray	.40
53	Kal Daniels	.05
54	Doug Jones	.05
55	Craig Biggio	.05
56	Rafael Palmeiro	.35
57	Wally Joyner	.05
58	Tim Wallach	.05
59	Bret Saberhagen	.05
60	Ryne Sandberg	.50
61	Benito Santiago	.05
62	Darryl Strawberry	.05
63	Alan Trammell	.05
64	Kelly Gruber	.05
65	Dwight Gooden	.05
66	Dave Winfield	.40
67	Rick Aguilera	.05
68	Dave Righetti	.05
69	Jim Abbott	.05
70	Frank Viola	.05
71	Fred McGriff	.05
72	Steve Sax	.05
73	Dennis Eckersley	.35
74	Cory Snyder	.05
75	Mackey Sasser	.05
76	Candy Maldonado	.05
77	Matt Williams	.05
78	Kent Hrbek	.05
79	Randy Myers	.05
80	Gregg Jefferies	.05
81	Joe Carter	.05
82	Mike Greenwell	.05
83	Jack Armstrong	.05
84	Julio Franco	.05
85	George Brett	.60
86	Howard Johnson	.05
87	Andre Dawson	.25
88	Cecil Fielder	.05
89	Tim Raines	.05
90	Chuck Finley	.05
91	Mark Grace	.05
92	Brook Jacoby	.05
93	Dave Steib	.05
94	Tony Gwynn	.50
95	Bobby Thigpen	.05
96	Roberto Kelly	.05
97	Kevin Seitzer	.05
98	Kevin Mitchell	.05
99	Dwight Evans	.05
100	Roberto Alomar	.20

1992 Score Promos

The six known Score promo cards differ from the is-sued versions in 1992 only in the lack of 1991 and career stats on the back and changes in the career summaries on some of the cards. The pro-mos of Sandberg and Mack were distributed at a St. Louis baseball card show in Novem-ber 1991, and are somewhat scarcer than the others.

		NM/M
Complete Set (6):		15.00
Common Player:		2.00
1	Ken Griffey Jr.	6.00
2	Dave Justice	2.00
122	Robin Ventura	2.00
200	Ryne Sandberg	5.00
241	Steve Avery	2.00
284	Shane Mack	2.00

1992 Score/Pinnacle Promo Panels

Score debuted both its base-brand (Score) and premi-um-brand (Pinnacle) sets at one time in 1992 with this issue of four-card panels. Each panel measures 1/16" short each way of 5" x 7" and features Score cards in the upper-left and lower-right, with Pinnacle sam-ples at upper-right and lower-left. Backs have a very light gray overprint, "FOR PROMOTION-AL PURPOSES ONLY NOT FOR RESALE." Cards cut from the panels would be otherwise in-distinguishable from the issued versions. Panels are checklisted here alphabetically according to the lowest-numbered Score player. S prefix to the card num-ber indicates Score, P is for Pin-nacle. The prefixes do not ap-pear on the cards.

		NM/M
Complete Set (25):		100.00
Common Panel:		3.00
(1)	S2 Nolan Ryan, S13 Lonnie Smith, P7 Willie McGee, P18 Terry Pendleton	15.00
(2)	S3 Will Clark, S12 Mark Langston, P8 Paul Molitor, P17 Devon White	4.50
(3)	S4 Dave Justice, S19 Mark Carreon, P1 Frank Thomas, P16 Dave Henderson	4.50
(4)	S5 Dave Henderson, S15 Roberto Alomar, P10 Ryne Sandberg, P20 Kirby Puckett	7.50
(5)	S9 Darryl Strawberry, S14 Jeff Montgomery, P6 Ozzie Smith, P11 Kevin Seitzer	5.00
(6)	S22 Chuck Crim, S33 Jimmy Jones, P27 Jay Buhner, P38 Robin Yount	4.50
(7)	S23 Don Mattingly, S32 Dave Winfield, P28 Matt Williams, P37 George Bell	10.00
(8)	S24 Dickie Thon, S39 Gary Gaetti, P21 Orel Hershiser, P36 Wes Chamberlain	3.00
(9)	S25 Ron Gant, S35 Andres Galarraga, P30 Alex Fernandez, P40 Bruce Hurst	3.00
(10)	S29 Melido Perez, S34 Kevin Gross, P26 Ellis Burks, P31 Albert Belle	3.00
(11)	S42 Rick Aguilera, S53 Doug Jones, P47 Bill Doran, P58 Ivan Calderon	3.00
(12)	S43 Mike Gallego, S52 Todd Zeile, P48 Jerald Clark, P57 Lenny Harris	3.00
(13)	S44 Eric Davis, S59 Randy Ready, P41 Harold Baines, P56 Walt Weiss	3.00
(14)	S45 George Bell, S55 Rafael Palmeiro, P50 Nolan Ryan, P60 George Brett	20.00
(15)	S49 David Wells, S54 Bob Walk, P46 Chili Davis, P51 Phil Plantier	3.00
(16)	S62 Jack McDowell, S73 Juan Samuel, P67 Dave Hollins, P78 John Olerud	3.00
(17)	S63 Jim Acker, S72 Carlton Fisk, P68 Kent Hrbek, P77 Dennis Martinez	3.00
(18)	S64 Jay Buhner, S79 Kirk McCaskill, P61 Gregg Olson, P76 Terry Steinbach	3.00
(19)	S65 Travis Fryman, S75 Andre Dawson, P70 Jeff Bagwell, P80 Darryl Strawberry	4.50
(20)	S69 Ken Caminiti, S74 Todd Stottlemyre, P66 Alex Cole, P71 Jim Gantner	3.00
(21)	S82 Alex Fernandez, S93 Shawn Hillegas, P87 Bill Gullickson, P98 Jose Guzman	3.00
(22)	S83 Ivan Calderon, S92 Ozzie Guillen, P88 Bernard Gilkey, P97 Omar Vizquel	3.00
(23)	S84 Brent Mayne, S99 Tom Bolton, P81 Gary Gaetti, P96 Doug Drabek	3.00
(24)	S85 Jody Reed, S95 Vince Coleman, P90 Kevin Maas, P100 Dave Justice	3.00
(25)	S89 Hensley Meulens, S94 Chili Davis, P86 David Howard, P91 Mark Lewis	3.00

1992 Score

Score used a two series format for the second consecu-tive year in 1992. Cards 1-442 are featured in the first series. Fronts feature full-color game action photos. Backs feature color head shots of the players, team logo and career stats. Sev-eral subsets are included in 1992, including a five-card Joe DiMaggio subset. DiMaggio auto-graphed cards were also insert-ed into random packs. Cards 736-772 can be found with or without a "Rookie Prospects" banner on the card front. Rack packs could be found with ran-dom inserts of 1991 Rookie of the Year Chuck Knoblauch's 1990 Score #1 Draft Pick card in a special autographed editon of 3,000. Factory sets contain 17 bonus cards not found in any other packaging.

	NM/M
Unopened Fact. Set (910):	7.50
Complete Set (893):	5.00

	Player	Price
	Common Player:	.05
	Wax Pack (16):	.40
	Wax Box (36):	7.50
1	Ken Griffey Jr.	.65
2	Nolan Ryan	1.00
3	Will Clark	.05
4	Dave Justice	.05
5	Dave Henderson	.05
6	Bret Saberhagen	.05
7	Fred McGriff	.05
8	Erik Hanson	.05
9	Darryl Strawberry	.05
10	Dwight Gooden	.05
11	Juan Gonzalez	.20
12	Mark Langston	.05
13	Lonnie Smith	.05
14	Jeff Montgomery	.05
15	Roberto Alomar	.20
16	Delino DeShields	.05
17	Steve Bedrosian	.05
18	Terry Pendleton	.05
19	Mark Carreon	.05
20	Mark McGwire	.75
21	Roger Clemens	.60
22	Chuck Crim	.05
23	Don Mattingly	.60
24	Dickie Thon	.05
25	Ron Gant	.05
26	Milt Cuyler	.05
27	Mike Macfarlane	.05
28	Dan Gladden	.05
29	Melido Perez	.05
30	Willie Randolph	.05
31	Albert Belle	.05
32	Dave Winfield	.40
33	Jimmy Jones	.05
34	Kevin Gross	.05
35	Andres Galarraga	.05
36	Mike Devereaux	.05
37	Chris Bosio	.05
38	Mike LaValliere	.05
39	Gary Gaetti	.05
40	Felix Jose	.05
41	Alvaro Espinoza	.05
42	Rick Aguilera	.05
43	Mike Gallego	.05
44	Eric Davis	.05
45	George Bell	.05
46	Tom Brunansky	.05
47	Steve Farr	.05
48	Duane Ward	.05
49	David Wells	.05
50	Cecil Fielder	.05
51	Walt Weiss	.05
52	Todd Zeile	.05
53	Doug Jones	.05
54	Bob Walk	.05
55	Rafael Palmeiro	.35
56	Rob Deer	.05
57	Paul O'Neill	.05
58	Jeff Reardon	.05
59	Randy Ready	.05
60	Scott Erickson	.05
61	Paul Molitor	.40
62	Jack McDowell	.05
63	Jim Acker	.05
64	Jay Buhner	.05
65	Travis Fryman	.05
66	Marquis Grissom	.05
67	Mike Harkey	.05
68	Luis Polonia	.05
69	Ken Caminiti	.05
70	Chris Sabo	.05
71	Gregg Olson	.05
72	Carlton Fisk	.40
73	Juan Samuel	.05
74	Todd Stottlemyre	.05
75	Andre Dawson	.25
76	Alvin Davis	.05
77	Bill Doran	.05
78	B.J. Surhoff	.05
79	Kirk McCaskill	.05
80	Dale Murphy	.25
81	Jose DeLeon	.05
82	Alex Fernandez	.05
83	Ivan Calderon	.05
84	Brent Mayne	.05
85	Jody Reed	.05
86	Randy Tomlin	.05
87	Randy Milligan	.05
88	Pascual Perez	.05
89	Hensley Meulens	.05
90	Joe Carter	.05
91	Mike Moore	.05
92	Ozzie Guillen	.05
93	Shawn Hillegas	.05
94	Chili Davis	.05
95	Vince Coleman	.05
96	Jimmy Key	.05
97	Billy Ripken	.05
98	Dave Smith	.05
99	Tom Bolton	.05
100	Barry Larkin	.05
101	Kenny Rogers	.05
102	Mike Boddicker	.05
103	Kevin Elster	.05
104	Ken Hill	.05
105	Charlie Leibrandt	.05
106	Pat Combs	.05
107	Hubie Brooks	.05
108	Julio Franco	.05
109	Vicente Palacios	.05
110	Kal Daniels	.05
111	Bruce Hurst	.05
112	Willie McGee	.05
113	Ted Power	.05
114	Milt Thompson	.05
115	Doug Drabek	.05
116	Rafael Belliard	.05
117	Scott Garrelts	.05
118	Terry Mulholland	.05
119	Jay Howell	.05
120	Danny Jackson	.05
121	Scott Ruskin	.05
122	Robin Ventura	.05
123	Bip Roberts	.05
124	Jeff Russell	.05
125	Hal Morris	.05
126	Teddy Higuera	.05
127	Luis Sojo	.05
128	Carlos Baerga	.05
129	Jeff Ballard	.05
130	Tom Gordon	.05
131	Sid Bream	.05
132	Rance Mulliniks	.05
133	Andy Benes	.05
134	Mickey Tettleton	.05
135	Rich DeLucia	.05
136	Tom Pagnozzi	.05
137	Harold Baines	.05
138	Danny Darwin	.05
139	Kevin Bass	.05
140	Chris Nabholz	.05
141	Pete O'Brien	.05
142	Jeff Treadway	.05
143	Mickey Morandini	.05
144	Eric King	.05
145	Danny Tartabull	.05
146	Lance Johnson	.05
147	Casey Candaele	.05
148	Felix Fermin	.05
149	Rich Rodriguez	.05
150	Dwight Evans	.05
151	Joe Klink	.05
152	Kevin Reimer	.05
153	Orlando Merced	.05
154	Mel Hall	.05
155	Randy Myers	.05
156	Greg Harris	.05
157	Jeff Brantley	.05
158	Jim Eisenreich	.05
159	Luis Rivera	.05
160	Cris Carpenter	.05
161	Bruce Ruffin	.05
162	Omar Vizquel	.05
163	Gerald Alexander	.05
164	Mark Guthrie	.05
165	Scott Lewis	.05
166	Bill Sampen	.05
167	Dave Anderson	.05
168	Kevin McReynolds	.05
169	Jose Vizcaino	.05
170	Bob Geren	.05
171	Mike Morgan	.05
172	Jim Gott	.05
173	Mike Pagliarulo	.05
174	Mike Jeffcoat	.05
175	Craig Lefferts	.05
176	Steve Finley	.05
177	Wally Backman	.05
178	Kent Mercker	.05
179	John Cerutti	.05
180	Jay Bell	.05
181	Dale Sveum	.05
182	Greg Gagne	.05
183	Donnie Hill	.05
184	Rex Hudler	.05
185	Pat Kelly	.05
186	Jeff Robinson	.05
187	Jeff Gray	.05
188	Jerry Willard	.05
189	Carlos Quintana	.05
190	Dennis Eckersley	.35
191	Kelly Downs	.05
192	Gregg Jefferies	.05
193	Darrin Fletcher	.05
194	Mike Jackson	.05
195	Eddie Murray	.40
196	Billy Landrum	.05
197	Eric Yelding	.05
198	Devon White	.05
199	Larry Walker	.05
200	Ryne Sandberg	.50
201	Dave Magadan	.05
202	Steve Chitren	.05
203	Scott Fletcher	.05
204	Dwayne Henry	.05
205	Scott Coolbaugh	.05
206	Tracy Jones	.05
207	Von Hayes	.05
208	Bob Melvin	.05
209	Scott Scudder	.05
210	Luis Gonzalez	.25
211	Scott Sanderson	.05
212	Chris Donnels	.05
213	Heath Slocumb	.05
214	Mike Timlin	.05
215	Brian Harper	.05
216	Juan Berenguer	.05
217	Mike Henneman	.05
218	Bill Spiers	.05
219	Scott Terry	.05
220	Frank Viola	.05
221	Mark Eichhorn	.05
222	Ernest Riles	.05
223	Ray Lankford	.05
224	Pete Harnisch	.05
225	Bobby Bonilla	.05
226	Mike Scioscia	.05
227	Joel Skinner	.05
228	Brian Holman	.05
229	Gilberto Reyes RC	.05
230	Matt Williams	.05
231	Jaime Navarro	.05
232	Jose Rijo	.05
233	Atlee Hammaker	.05
234	Tim Teufel	.05
235	John Kruk	.05
236	Kurt Stillwell	.05
237	Dan Pasqua	.05
238	Tim Crews	.05
239	Dave Gallagher	.05
240	Leo Gomez	.05
241	Steve Avery	.05
242	Bill Gullickson	.05
243	Mark Portugal	.05
244	Lee Guetterman	.05
245	Benny Santiago	.05
246	Jim Gantner	.05
247	Robby Thompson	.05
248	Terry Shumpert	.05
249	Mike Bell RC	.05
250	Harold Reynolds	.05
251	Mike Felder	.05
252	Bill Pecota	.05
253	Bill Krueger	.05
254	Alfredo Griffin	.05
255	Lou Whitaker	.05
256	Roy Smith	.05
257	Jerald Clark	.05
258	Sammy Sosa	.50
259	Tim Naehring	.05
260	Dave Righetti	.05
261	Paul Gibson	.05
262	Chris James	.05
263	Larry Andersen	.05
264	Storm Davis	.05
265	Jose Lind	.05
266	Greg Hibbard	.05
267	Norm Charlton	.05
268	Paul Kilgus	.05
269	Greg Maddux	.50
270	Ellis Burks	.05
271	Frank Tanana	.05
272	Gene Larkin	.05
273	Ron Hassey	.05
274	Jeff Robinson	.05
275	Steve Howe	.05
276	Daryl Boston	.05
277	Mark Lee	.05
278	Jose Segura RC	.05
279	Lance Blankenship	.05
280	Don Slaught	.05
281	Russ Swan	.05
282	Bob Tewksbury	.05
283	Geno Petralli	.05
284	Shane Mack	.05
285	Bob Scanlan	.05
286	Tim Leary	.05
287	John Smoltz	.05
288	Pat Borders	.05
289	Mark Davidson	.05
290	Sam Horn	.05
291	Lenny Harris	.05
292	Franklin Stubbs	.05
293	Thomas Howard	.05
294	Steve Lyons	.05
295	Francisco Oliveras	.05
296	Terry Leach	.05
297	Barry Jones	.05
298	Lance Parrish	.05
299	Wally Whitehurst	.05
300	Bob Welch	.05
301	Charlie Hayes	.05
302	Charlie Hough	.05
303	Gary Redus	.05
304	Scott Bradley	.05
305	Jose Oquendo	.05
306	Pete Incaviglia	.05
307	Marvin Freeman	.05
308	Gary Pettis	.05
309	Joe Slusarski	.05
310	Kevin Seitzer	.05
311	Jeff Reed	.05
312	Pat Tabler	.05
313	Mike Maddux	.05
314	Bob Milacki	.05
315	Eric Anthony	.05
316	Dante Bichette	.05
317	Steve Decker	.05
318	Jack Clark	.05
319	Doug Dascenzo	.05
320	Scott Leius	.05
321	Jim Lindeman	.05
322	Bryan Harvey	.05
323	Spike Owen	.05
324	Roberto Kelly	.05
325	Stan Belinda	.05
326	Joey Cora	.05
327	Jeff Innis	.05
328	Willie Wilson	.05
329	Juan Agosto	.05
330	Charles Nagy	.05
331	Scott Bailes	.05
332	Pete Schourek	.05
333	Mike Flanagan	.05
334	Omar Olivares	.05
335	Dennis Lamp	.05
336	Tommy Greene	.05
337	Randy Velarde	.05
338	Tom Lampkin	.05
339	John Russell	.05
340	Bob Kipper	.05
341	Todd Burns	.05
342	Ron Jones	.05
343	Dave Valle	.05
344	Mike Heath	.05
345	John Olerud	.05
346	Gerald Young	.05
347	Ken Patterson	.05
348	Les Lancaster	.05
349	Steve Crawford	.05
350	John Candelaria	.05
351	Mike Aldrete	.05
352	Mariano Duncan	.05
353	Julio Machado	.05
354	Ken Williams	.05
355	Walt Terrell	.05
356	Mitch Williams	.05
357	Al Newman	.05
358	Bud Black	.05
359	Joe Hesketh	.05
360	Paul Assenmacher	.05
361	Bo Jackson	.05
362	Jeff Blauser	.05
363	Mike Brumley	.05
364	Jim Deshaies	.05
365	Brady Anderson	.05
366	Chuck McElroy	.05
367	Matt Merullo	.05
368	Tim Belcher	.05
369	Luis Aquino	.05
370	Joe Oliver	.05
371	Greg Swindell	.05
372	Lee Stevens	.05
373	Mark Knudson	.05
374	Bill Wegman	.05
375	Jerry Don Gleaton	.05
376	Pedro Guerrero	.05
377	Randy Bush	.05
378	Greg Harris	.05
379	Eric Plunk	.05
380	Jose DeJesus	.05
381	Bobby Witt	.05
382	Curtis Wilkerson	.05
383	Gene Nelson	.05
384	Wes Chamberlain	.05
385	Tom Henke	.05
386	Mark Lemke	.05
387	Greg Briley	.05
388	Rafael Ramirez	.05
389	Tony Fossas	.05
390	Henry Cotto	.05
391	Tim Hulett	.05
392	Dean Palmer	.05
393	Glenn Braggs	.05
394	Mark Salas	.05
395	Rusty Meacham RC	.05
396	Andy Ashby RC	.10
397	Jose Melendez RC	.05
398	Warren Newson RC	.05
399	Frank Castillo RC	.05
400	Chito Martinez RC	.05
401	Bernie Williams	.05
402	Derek Bell	.05
403	Javier Ortiz RC	.05
404	Tim Sherrill RC	.05
405	Rob MacDonald RC	.05
406	Phil Plantier	.05
407	Troy Afenir RC	.05
408	Gino Minutelli RC	.05
409	Reggie Jefferson RC	.05
410	Mike Remlinger RC	.05
411	Carlos Rodriguez RC	.05
412	Joe Redfield RC	.05
413	Alonzo Powell RC	.05
414	Scott Livingstone RC	.05
415	Scott Kamieniecki RC	.05
416	Tim Spehr RC	.05
417	Brian Hunter RC	.05
418	Ced Landrum RC	.05
419	Bret Barberie RC	.05
420	Kevin Morton RC	.05
421	Doug Henry RC	.05
422	Doug Piatt RC	.05
423	Pat Rice RC	.05
424	Juan Guzman	.05
425	Nolan Ryan (No-Hit)	.50
426	Tommy Greene (No-Hit)	.05
427	Bob Milacki, Mike Flanagan, Mark Williamson, Gregg Olson (No-Hit)	.05
428	Wilson Alvarez (No-Hit)	.05
429	Otis Nixon/HL	.05
430	Rickey Henderson/HL	.20
431	Cecil Fielder/AS	.05
432	Julio Franco/AS	.05
433	Cal Ripken, Jr./AS	.50
434	Wade Boggs/AS	.25
435	Joe Carter/AS	.05
436	Ken Griffey Jr./AS	.35
437	Ruben Sierra/AS	.05
438	Scott Erickson/AS	.05
439	Tom Henke/AS	.05
440	Terry Steinbach/AS	.05
441	Rickey Henderson (Dream Team)	.20
442	Ryne Sandberg (Dream Team)	.30
443	Otis Nixon	.05
444	Scott Radinsky	.05
445	Mark Grace	.05
446	Tony Pena	.05
447	Billy Hatcher	.05
448	Glenallen Hill	.05
449	Chris Gwynn	.05
450	Tom Glavine	.35
451	John Habyan	.05
452	Al Osuna	.05
453	Tony Phillips	.05
454	Greg Cadaret	.05
455	Rob Dibble	.05
456	Rick Honeycutt	.05
457	Jerome Walton	.05
458	Mookie Wilson	.05
459	Mark Gubicza	.05
460	Craig Biggio	.05
461	Dave Cochrane	.05
462	Keith Miller	.05
463	Alex Cole	.05
464	Pete Smith	.05
465	Brett Butler	.05
466	Jeff Huson	.05
467	Steve Lake	.05
468	Lloyd Moseby	.05
469	Tim McIntosh	.05
470	Dennis Martinez	.05
471	Greg Myers	.05
472	Mackey Sasser	.05
473	Junior Ortiz	.05
474	Greg Olson	.05
475	Steve Sax	.05
476	Ricky Jordan	.05
477	Max Venable	.05
478	Brian McRae	.05
479	Doug Simons	.05
480	Rickey Henderson	.40
481	Gary Varsho	.05
482	Carl Willis	.05
483	Rick Wilkins	.05
484	Donn Pall	.05
485	Edgar Martinez	.05
486	Tom Foley	.05
487	Mark Williamson	.05
488	Jack Armstrong	.05
489	Gary Carter	.40
490	Ruben Sierra	.05
491	Gerald Perry	.05
492	Rob Murphy	.05
493	Zane Smith	.05
494	Darryl Kile	.05
495	Kelly Gruber	.05
496	Jerry Browne	.05
497	Darryl Hamilton	.05
498	Mike Stanton	.05
499	Mark Leonard	.05
500	Jose Canseco	.30
501	Dave Martinez	.05
502	Jose Guzman	.05
503	Terry Kennedy	.05
504	Ed Sprague	.05
505	Frank Thomas	.40
506	Darren Daulton	.05
507	Kevin Tapani	.05
508	Luis Salazar	.05
509	Paul Faries	.05
510	Sandy Alomar, Jr.	.05
511	Jeff King	.05
512	Gary Thurman	.05
513	Chris Hammond	.05
514	Pedro Munoz RC	.05
515	Alan Trammell	.05
516	Geronimo Pena	.05
517	Rodney McCray	.05
518	Manny Lee	.05
519	Junior Felix	.05
520	Kirk Gibson	.05
521	Darrin Jackson	.05
522	John Burkett	.05
523	Jeff Johnson	.05
524	Jim Corsi	.05
525	Robin Yount	.40
526	Jamie Quirk	.05
527	Bob Ojeda	.05
528	Mark Lewis	.05
529	Bryn Smith	.05
530	Kent Hrbek	.05
531	Dennis Boyd	.05
532	Ron Karkovice	.05
533	Don August	.05
534	Todd Frohwirth	.05
535	Wally Joyner	.05
536	Dennis Rasmussen	.05
537	Andy Allanson	.05
538	Rich Gossage	.05
539	John Marzano	.05
540	Cal Ripken, Jr.	1.00
541	Bill Swift	.05
542	Kevin Appier	.05
543	Dave Bergman	.05
544	Bernard Gilkey	.05
545	Mike Greenwell	.05
546	Jose Uribe	.05
547	Jesse Orosco	.05
548	Bob Patterson	.05
549	Mike Stanley	.05
550	Howard Johnson	.05
551	Joe Orsulak	.05
552	Dick Schofield	.05
553	Dave Hollins	.05
554	David Segui	.05
555	Barry Bonds	1.00
556	Mo Vaughn	.05
557	Craig Wilson	.05
558	Bobby Rose	.05
559	Rod Nichols	.05
560	Len Dykstra	.05
561	Craig Grebeck	.05
562	Darren Lewis	.05
563	Todd Benzinger	.05
564	Ed Whitson	.05
565	Jesse Barfield	.05
566	Lloyd McClendon	.05
567	Dan Plesac	.05
568	Danny Cox	.05
569	Skeeter Barnes	.05
570	Bobby Thigpen	.05
571	Deion Sanders	.05
572	Chuck Knoblauch	.05
573	Matt Nokes	.05
574	Herm Winningham	.05
575	Tom Candiotti	.05
576	Jeff Bagwell	.40
577	Brook Jacoby	.05
578	Chico Walker	.05
579	Brian Downing	.05
580	Dave Stewart	.05
581	Francisco Cabrera	.05
582	Rene Gonzales	.05
583	Stan Javier	.05
584	Randy Johnson	.40
585	Chuck Finley	.05
586	Mark Gardner	.05
587	Mark Whiten	.05
588	Garry Templeton	.05
589	Gary Sheffield	.30
590	Ozzie Smith	.50
591	Candy Maldonado	.05
592	Mike Sharperson	.05
593	Carlos Martinez	.05
594	Scott Bankhead	.05
595	Tim Wallach	.05
596	Tino Martinez	.05
597	Roger McDowell	.05
598	Cory Snyder	.05
599	Andujar Cedeno	.05
600	Kirby Puckett	.50
601	Rick Parker	.05
602	Todd Hundley	.05
603	Greg Litton	.05
604	Dave Johnson	.05
605	John Franco	.05
606	Mike Fetters	.05
607	Luis Alicea	.05
608	Trevor Wilson	.05
609	Rob Ducey	.05
610	Ramon Martinez	.05
611	Dave Burba	.05
612	Dwight Smith	.05
613	Kevin Maas	.05
614	John Costello	.05
615	Glenn Davis	.05
616	Shawn Abner	.05
617	Scott Hemond	.05
618	Tom Prince	.05
619	Wally Ritchie	.05
620	Jim Abbott	.05
621	Charlie O'Brien	.05
622	Jack Daugherty	.05
623	Tommy Gregg	.05
624	Jeff Shaw	.05
625	Tony Gwynn	.50
626	Mark Leiter	.05
627	Jim Clancy	.05
628	Tim Layana	.05
629	Jeff Schaefer	.05
630	Lee Smith	.05
631	Wade Taylor	.05
632	Mike Simms	.05
633	Terry Steinbach	.05
634	Shawon Dunston	.05
635	Tim Raines	.05
636	Kirt Manwaring	.05
637	Warren Cromartie	.05
638	Luis Quinones	.05
639	Greg Vaughn	.05
640	Kevin Mitchell	.05
641	Chris Hoiles	.05
642	Tom Browning	.05
643	Mitch Webster	.05
644	Steve Olin	.05
645	Tony Fernandez	.05
646	Juan Bell	.05
647	Joe Boever	.05
648	Carney Lansford	.05
649	Mike Benjamin	.05
650	George Brett	.60
651	Tim Burke	.05
652	Jack Morris	.05
653	Orel Hershiser	.05
654	Mike Schooler	.05
655	Andy Van Slyke	.05
656	Dave Stieb	.05
657	Dave Clark	.05
658	Ben McDonald	.05
659	John Smiley	.05
660	Wade Boggs	.50
661	Eric Bullock	.05
662	Eric Show	.05
663	Lenny Webster	.05
664	Mike Huff	.05
665	Rick Sutcliffe	.05
666	Jeff Manto	.05
667	Mike Fitzgerald	.05
668	Matt Young	.05
669	Dave West	.05
670	Mike Hartley	.05
671	Curt Schilling	.35
672	Brian Bohanon	.05
673	Cecil Espy	.05
674	Joe Grahe	.05
675	Sid Fernandez	.05
676	Edwin Nunez	.05
677	Hector Villanueva	.05
678	Sean Berry	.05
679	Dave Eiland	.05
680	David Cone	.05
681	Mike Bordick	.05
682	Tony Castillo	.05
683	John Barfield	.05
684	Jeff Hamilton	.05
685	Ken Dayley	.05
686	Carmelo Martinez	.05
687	Mike Capel	.05
688	Scott Chiamparino	.05
689	Rich Gedman	.05
690	Rich Monteleone	.05
691	Alejandro Pena	.05
692	Oscar Azocar	.05
693	Jim Poole	.05
694	Mike Gardiner	.05
695	Steve Buechele	.05
696	Rudy Seanez	.05
697	Paul Abbott	.05
698	Steve Searcy	.05
699	Jose Offerman	.05
700	Ivan Rodriguez	.35

701	Joe Girardi	.05
702	Tony Perezchica	.05
703	Paul McClellan	.05
704	David Howard RC	.05
705	Dan Petry	.05
706	Jack Howell	.05
707	Jose Mesa	.05
708	Randy St. Claire	.05
709	Kevin Brown	.05
710	Ron Darling	.05
711	Jason Grimsley	.05
712	John Orton	.05
713	Shawn Boskie	.05
714	Pat Clements	.05
715	Brian Barnes	.05
716	Luis Lopez RC	.05
717	Bob McClure	.05
718	Mark Davis	.05
719	Dann Bilardello	.05
720	Tom Edens	.05
721	Willie Fraser	.05
722	Curt Young	.05
723	Neal Heaton	.05
724	Craig Worthington	.05
725	Mel Rojas	.05
726	Daryl Irvine	.05
727	Roger Mason	.05
728	Kirk Dressendorfer	.05
729	Scott Aldred	.05
730	Willie Blair	.05
731	Allan Anderson	.05
732	Dana Kiecker	.05
733	Jose Gonzalez	.05
734	Brian Drahman	.05
735	Brad Komminsk	.05
736	Arthur Rhodes RC	.10
737	Terry Mathews RC	.05
738	Jeff Fassero RC	.05
739	Mike Magnante RC	.05
740	Kip Gross RC	.05
741	Jim Hunter RC	.05
742	Jose Mota RC	.05
743	Joe Bitker	.05
744	Tim Mauser RC	.05
745	Ramon Garcia RC	.05
746	Rod Beck RC	.10
747	Jim Austin RC	.05
748	Keith Mitchell RC	.05
749	Wayne Rosenthal RC	.05
750	Bryan Hickerson RC	.05
751	Bruce Egloff RC	.05
752	John Wehner RC	.05
753	Darren Holmes RC	.05
754	Dave Hansen	.05
755	Mike Mussina	.30
756	Anthony Young RC	.05
757	Ron Tingley	.05
758	Ricky Bones RC	.05
759	Mark Wohlers RC	.05
760	Wilson Alvarez RC	.05
761	Harvey Pulliam RC	.05
762	Ryan Bowen RC	.05
763	Terry Bross RC	.05
764	Joel Johnston RC	.05
765	Terry McDaniel RC	.05
766	Esteban Beltre RC	.05
767	Rob Maurer RC	.05
768	Ted Wood	.05
769	Mo Sanford RC	.05
770	Jeff Carter RC	.05
771	Gil Heredia RC	.05
772	Monty Fariss RC	.05
773	Will Clark/AS	.05
774	Ryne Sandberg/AS	.25
775	Barry Larkin/AS	.05
776	Howard Johnson/AS	.05
777	Barry Bonds/AS	.50
778	Brett Butler/AS	.05
779	Tony Gwynn/AS	.25
780	Ramon Martinez/AS	.05
781	Lee Smith/AS	.05
782	Mike Scioscia/AS	.05
783	Dennis Martinez/HL	.05
784	Dennis Martinez (No-Hit)	.05
785	Mark Gardner (No-Hit)	.05
786	Bret Saberhagen (No-Hit)	.05
787	Kent Mercker, Mark Wohlers, Alejandro Pena (No-Hit)	.05
788	Cal Ripken/MVP	.05
789	Terry Pendleton/MVP	.06
790	Roger Clemens (CY)	.35
791	Tom Glavine (CY)	.05
792	Chuck Knoblauch (ROY)	.05
793	Jeff Bagwell (ROY)	.20
794	Cal Ripken, Jr. (Man of the Year)	.50
795	David Cone/HL	.05
796	Kirby Puckett/HL	.05
797	Steve Averyv	.05
798	Jack Morris/HL	.05
799	Allen Watson/HL	.05
800	Manny Ramirez RC	2.00
801	Cliff Floyd RC	.50
802	Al Shirley RC	.05
803	Brian Barber RC	.05
804	Jon Farrell RC	.05
805	Brent Gates RC	.05
806	Scott Ruffcorn RC	.05
807	Tyrone Hill RC	.05
808	Benji Gil RC	.05
809	Aaron Sele RC	.25
810	Tyler Green RC	.05
811	Chris Jones	.05
812	Steve Wilson	.05
813	Cliff Young RC	.05

814	Don Wakamatsu RC	.05
815	Mike Humphreys RC	.05
816	Scott Servais RC	.05
817	Rico Rossy RC	.05
818	John Ramos RC	.05
819	Rob Mallicoat RC	.05
820	Milt Hill RC	.05
821	Carlos Garcia RC	.05
822	Stan Royer	.05
823	Jeff Plympton RC	.05
824	Braulio Castillo RC	.05
825	David Haas RC	.05
826	Luis Mercedes RC	.05
827	Eric Karros	.05
828	Shawn Hare RC	.05
829	Reggie Sanders	.05
830	Tom Goodwin	.05
831	Dan Gakeler RC	.05
832	Stacy Jones RC	.05
833	Kim Batiste RC	.05
834	Cal Eldred	.05
835	Chris George RC	.05
836	Wayne Housie RC	.05
837	Mike Ignasiak RC	.05
838	Josias Manzanillo RC	.05
839	Jim Olander RC	.05
840	Gary Cooper RC	.05
841	Royce Clayton	.05
842	Hector Fajardo	.05
843	Blaine Beatty	.05
844	Jorge Pedre RC	.05
845	Kenny Lofton	.05
846	Scott Brosius	.05
847	Chris Cron RC	.05
848	Denis Boucher	.05
849	Kyle Abbott	.05
850	Bob Zupcic	.05
851	Rheal Cormier RC	.05
852	Jim Lewis RC	.05
853	Anthony Telford	.05
854	Cliff Brantley RC	.05
855	Kevin Campbell RC	.05
856	Craig Shipley RC	.05
857	Chuck Carr	.05
858	Tony Eusebio RC	.10
859	Jim Thome	.35
860	Vinny Castilla RC	.30
861	Dann Howitt	.05
862	Kevin Ward RC	.05
863	Steve Wapnick RC	.05
864	Rod Brewer	.05
865	Todd Van Poppel	.05
866	Jose Hernandez RC	.05
867	Amalio Carreno RC	.05
868	Calvin Jones RC	.05
869	Jeff Gardner RC	.05
870	Jarvis Brown RC	.05
871	Eddie Taubensee RC	.10
872	Andy Mota RC	.05
873	Chris Haney (Front photo actually Scott Ruskin.)	.05
874	Roberto Hernandez	.05
875	Laddie Renfroe RC	.05
876	Scott Cooper	.05
877	Armando Reynoso RC	.05
878	Ty Cobb (Memorabilia)	.30
879	Babe Ruth (Memorabilia)	.40
880	Honus Wagner (Memorabilia)	.30
881	Lou Gehrig (Memorabilia)	.30
882	Satchel Paige (Memorabilia)	.35
883	Will Clark (Dream Team)	.05
884	Cal Ripken, Jr. (Dream Team)	.50
885	Wade Boggs (Dream Team)	.25
886	Kirby Puckett (Dream Team)	.30
887	Tony Gwynn (Dream Team)	.30
888	Craig Biggio (Dream Team)	.05
889	Scott Erickson (Dream Team)	.05
890	Tom Glavine (Dream Team)	.10
891	Rob Dibble (Dream Team)	.05
892	Mitch Williams (Dream Team)	.05
893	Frank Thomas (Dream Team)	.25

Joe DiMaggio

Colorized vintage photos are featured on the front and back of each of five Joe DiMaggio tribute cards which were issued as random inserts in 1992 Score Series 1 packs. It was reported at the time that 30,000 of each card were produced. A limited number (from an edition of 2,500) of each card were autographed.

	NM/M
Complete Set (5):	25.00
Common Card:	8.00
Autographed Card:	365.00
1 Joe DiMaggio (The Minors)	8.00
2 Joe DiMaggio (The Rookie)	8.00
3 Joe DiMaggio (The MVP)	8.00
4 Joe DiMaggio (The Streak)	8.00
5 Joe DiMaggio (The Legend)	8.00

Factory Set Inserts - Cooperstown

Available exclusively in factory sets, these bonus cards have posterized color portraits vignetted on a white background. Blue-bordered backs have a yellow "tombstone" at center with career highlights and a quote or two about the player.

	NM/M
Complete Set (4):	1.50
Common Player:	.50
B8 Carlton Fisk	.50
B9 Ozzie Smith	.75
B10 Dave Winfield	.50
B11 Robin Yount	.50

Factory Set Inserts - DiMaggio

Available exclusively in factory sets, these bonus cards honor Joe DiMaggio career. Fronts have black-and-white photos with silver borders. Color backs have quotes from the Clipper or other ballplayers, plus detailed career highlights.

	NM/M
Complete Set (3):	4.00
Common Card:	1.25
B12 Joe DiMaggio (The Hard Hitter)	1.50
B13 Joe DiMaggio (The Stylish Fielder)	1.50
B14 Joe DiMaggio (The Championship Player)	1.50

Factory Set Inserts - World Series

Available exclusively in factory sets 17 bonus cards are divided into four subsets commemorating the 1991 World Series, potential Hall of Famers, the career of Joe DiMaggio and Carl Yastrzemski's 1967 Triple Crown season. Cards carry a "B" prefix to the card number.

	NM/M
Complete Set (7):	1.00
Common Card:	.15
1 World Series Game 1 (Greg Gagne)	.15
2 World Series Game 2 (Scott Leius)	.15
3 World Series Game 3 (David Justice, Brian Harper)	.15
4 World Series Game 4 (Lonnie Smith, Brian Harper)	.15
5 World Series Game 5 (David Justice)	.15
6 World Series Game 6 (Kirby Puckett)	1.00
7 World Series Game 7 (Gene Larkin)	.15

Factory Set Inserts - Yastrzemski

Available exclusively in factory sets, these bonus cards honor Carl Yastrzemski's 1967 Triple Crown season. Fronts have game-action photos with silver borders and a silver 25 Years logo. Color backs have quotes from Yaz or teammates, plus details of the season's highlights.

	NM/M
Complete Set (3):	2.00
Common Card:	1.00
B15 Carl Yastrzemski (The Impossible Dream)	1.00
B16 Carl Yastrzemski (The Triple Crown)	1.00
B17 Carl Yastrzemski (The World Series)	1.00

Hot Rookies

This 10-card rookie issue was produced as an insert in special blister packs of 1992 Score cards sold at retail outlets. Action photos on front and portraits on back are set against white backgrounds with orange highlights. Cards are standard 2-1/2" x 3-1/2".

	NM/M
Complete Set (10):	4.00
Common Player:	.50
1 Cal Eldred	.50
2 Royce Clayton	.50
3 Kenny Lofton	.75
4 Todd Van Poppel	.50
5 Scott Cooper	.50
6 Todd Hundley	.50
7 Tino Martinez	.75
8 Anthony Telford	.50
9 Derek Bell	.50
10 Reggie Jefferson	.50

Impact Players

Jumbo packs of 1992 Score Series 1 and 2 contained five of these special inserts labeled "90's Impact Players." Front action photos contrast with portrait photos on the backs, which are color-coded by team. Cards #1-45 were packaged with Series 1, cards #46-90 were included in Series 2 packs.

	NM/M
Complete Set (90):	3.00
Common Player:	.05
1 Chuck Knoblauch	.05
2 Jeff Bagwell	.50
3 Juan Guzman	.05
4 Milt Cuyler	.05
5 Ivan Rodriguez	.45
6 Rich DeLucia	.05
7 Orlando Merced	.05
8 Ray Lankford	.05
9 Brian Hunter	.05
10 Roberto Alomar	.25
11 Wes Chamberlain	.05
12 Steve Avery	.05
13 Scott Erickson	.05
14 Jim Abbott	.05
15 Mark Whiten	.05
16 Leo Gomez	.05
17 Doug Henry	.05
18 Brent Mayne	.05
19 Charles Nagy	.05
20 Phil Plantier	.05
21 Mo Vaughn	.05
22 Craig Biggio	.05
23 Derek Bell	.05
24 Royce Clayton	.05
25 Gary Cooper	.05
26 Scott Cooper	.05
27 Juan Gonzalez	.25
28 Ken Griffey Jr.	.75
29 Larry Walker	.05
30 John Smoltz	.05
31 Todd Hundley	.05
32 Kenny Lofton	.05
33 Andy Mota	.05
34 Todd Zeile	.05
35 Arthur Rhodes	.05
36 Jim Thome	.45
37 Todd Van Poppel	.05
38 Mark Wohlers	.05
39 Anthony Young	.05
40 Sandy Alomar Jr.	.05
41 John Olerud	.05
42 Robin Ventura	.05
43 Frank Thomas	.50
44 Dave Justice	.05
45 Hal Morris	.05
46 Ruben Sierra	.05
47 Travis Fryman	.05
48 Mike Mussina	.25
49 Tom Glavine	.35
50 Barry Larkin	.05
51 Will Clark	.05
52 Jose Canseco	.30
53 Bo Jackson	.10
54 Dwight Gooden	.05
55 Barry Bonds	1.00
56 Fred McGriff	.05
57 Roger Clemens	.65
58 Benito Santiago	.05
59 Darryl Strawberry	.05

60	Cecil Fielder	.05
61	John Franco	.05
62	Matt Williams	.05
63	Marquis Grissom	.05
64	Danny Tartabull	.05
65	Ron Gant	.05
66	Paul O'Neill	.05
67	Devon White	.05
68	Rafael Palmeiro	.45
69	Tom Gordon	.05
70	Shawon Dunston	.05
71	Rob Dibble	.05
72	Eddie Zosky	.05
73	Jack McDowell	.05
74	Len Dykstra	.05
75	Ramon Martinez	.05
76	Reggie Sanders	.05
77	Greg Maddux	.60
78	Ellis Burks	.05
79	John Smiley	.05
80	Roberto Kelly	.05
81	Ben McDonald	.05
82	Mark Lewis	.05
83	Jose Rijo	.05
84	Ozzie Guillen	.05
85	Lance Dickson	.05
86	Kim Batiste	.05
87	Gregg Olson	.05
88	Andy Benes	.05
89	Cal Eldred	.05
90	David Cone	.05

The Franchise

This four-card set, in both autographed and unautographed form, was a random insert in various premium packaging of Score's 1992 Series II cards. Each of the four cards was produced in an edition of 150,000, with 2,000 of each player's card being autographed and 500 of the triple-player card carrying the autographs of all three superstars.

	NM/M
Complete Set (4):	5.00
Common Player:	1.25
Musial Autograph:	80.00
Mantle Autograph:	450.00
Yastrzemski Autograph:	80.00
Triple Autograph:	1,100
1 Stan Musial	1.50
2 Mickey Mantle	2.50
3 Carl Yastrzemski	1.25
4 Stan Musial, Mickey Mantle, Carl Yastrzemski	1.50

Rookie & Traded

This 110-card set features traded players, free agents and top rookies from 1992. The cards are styled after the regular 1992 Score cards. Cards 80-110 feature the rookies. The set was released as a boxed set and was available only through hobby dealers.

	NM/M
Complete Set (110):	5.00
Common Player:	

1	Gary Sheffield	.20
2	Kevin Seitzer	.05
3	Danny Tartabull	.05
4	Steve Sax	.05
5	Bobby Bonilla	.05
6	Frank Viola	.05
7	Dave Winfield	.60
8	Rick Sutcliffe	.05
9	Jose Canseco	.45
10	Greg Swindell	.05
11	Eddie Murray	.60
12	Randy Myers	.05
13	Wally Joyner	.05
14	Kenny Lofton	.05
15	Jack Morris	.05
16	Charlie Hayes	.05
17	Pete Incaviglia	.05
18	Kevin Mitchell	.05
19	Kurt Stillwell	.05
20	Bret Saberhagen	.05
21	Steve Buechele	.05
22	John Smiley	.05
23	Sammy Sosa	3.00
24	George Bell	.05
25	Curt Schilling	.30
26	Dick Schofield	.05
27	David Cone	.05
28	Dan Gladden	.05
29	Kirk McCaskill	.05
30	Mike Gallego	.05
31	Kevin McReynolds	.05
32	Bill Swift	.05
33	Dave Martinez	.05
34	Storm Davis	.05
35	Willie Randolph	.05
36	Melido Perez	.05
37	Mark Carreon	.05
38	Doug Jones	.05
39	Gregg Jefferies	.05
40	Mike Jackson	.05
41	Dickie Thon	.05
42	Eric King	.05
43	Herm Winningham	.05
44	Derek Lilliquist	.05
45	Dave Anderson	.05
46	Jeff Reardon	.05
47	Scott Bankhead	.05
48	Cory Snyder	.05
49	Al Newman	.05
50	Keith Miller	.05
51	Dave Burba	.05
52	Bill Pecota	.05
53	Chuck Crim	.05
54	Mariano Duncan	.05
55	Dave Gallagher	.05
56	Chris Gwynn	.05
57	Scott Ruskin	.05
58	Jack Armstrong	.05
59	Gary Carter	.60
60	Andres Galarraga	.05
61	Ken Hill	.05
62	Eric Davis	.05
63	Ruben Sierra	.05
64	Darrin Fletcher	.05
65	Tim Belcher	.05
66	Mike Morgan	.05
67	Scott Scudder	.05
68	Tom Candiotti	.05
69	Hubie Brooks	.05
70	Kal Daniels	.05
71	Bruce Ruffin	.05
72	Billy Hatcher	.05
73	Bob Melvin	.05
74	Lee Guetterman	.05
75	Rene Gonzales	.05
76	Kevin Bass	.05
77	Tom Bolton	.05
78	John Wetteland	.05
79	Bip Roberts	.05
80	Pat Listach RC	.05
81	John Doherty RC	.05
82	Sam Militello RC	.05
83	Brian Jordan RC	.05
84	Jeff Kent RC	.10
85	Dave Fleming RC	.05
86	Jeff Tackett RC	.05
87	Chad Curtis RC	.05
88	Eric Fox	.05
89	Denny Neagle RC	.05
90	Donovan Osborne RC	.05
91	Carlos Hernandez RC	.05
92	Tim Wakefield RC	.05
93	Tim Salmon RC	.05
94	Dave Nilsson RC	.05
95	Mike Perez RC	.05
96	Pat Hentgen RC	.05
97	Frank Seminara RC	.05
98	Ruben Amaro Jr. RC	.05
99	Archi Cianfrocco RC	.05
100	Andy Stankiewicz RC	.05
101	Jim Bullinger RC	.05
102	Pat Mahomes RC	.05
103	Hipolito Pichardo RC	.05
104	Bret Boone RC	.05
105	John Vander Wal RC	.05
106	Vince Horsman RC	.05
107	James Austin RC	.05
108	Brian Williams RC	.05
109	Dan Walters RC	.05
110	Wil Cordero RC	.05

Procter & Gamble

In 1992 Score and Procter & Gamble combined to produce an 18-card All-Star set, reportedly two million cards mak-

MARK McGWIRE 18

ing 101,000 sets offered to collectors originally for $1.49 along with proof of purchase from P & G products. Card fronts feature a color player action photo set against a background of blue star and pink-to-purple diagonal stripes (American Leaguers) or red star and green stripes (National Leaguers). Back designs include a color player portrait photo at upper-right, with personal data, career stats and highlights. Appropriate logos and card number complete the design, which is bordered in color striping similar to the front background.

		NM/M
Complete Set (18):		3.00
Common Player:		.10
1	Sandy Alomar Jr.	.10
2	Mark McGwire	.75
3	Roberto Alomar	.20
4	Wade Boggs	.50
5	Cal Ripken, Jr.	1.00
6	Kirby Puckett	.50
7	Ken Griffey Jr.	.65
8	Jose Canseco	.25
9	Kevin Brown	.10
10	Benito Santiago	.10
11	Fred McGriff	.10
12	Ryne Sandberg	.50
13	Terry Pendleton	.10
14	Ozzie Smith	.50
15	Barry Bonds	1.00
16	Tony Gwynn	.50
17	Andy Van Slyke	.10
18	Tom Glavine	.35

Rising Stars

RISING STAR
CHARLES NAGY
P • CLEVELAND INDIANS

Sold in a blister pack with a book and a handful of "Magic Motion" trivia cards this 100-card set features baseball's top young players. Backs have a player portrait, a career summary and team, league and card company logos.

		NM/M
Complete Set (100):		3.00
Common Player:		.10
1	Milt Cuyler	.10
2	David Howard	.10
3	Brian Hunter	.10
4	Darryl Kile	.10
5	Pat Kelly	.10
6	Luis Gonzalez	.10
7	Mike Benjamin	.10
8	Eric Anthony	.10
9	Moises Alou	.10
10	Darren Lewis	.10
11	Chuck Knoblauch	.10
12	Geronimo Pena	.10
13	Jeff Plympton	.10
14	Bret Barberie	.10
15	Chris Haney	.10
16	Rick Wilkins	.10
17	Julio Valera	.10
18	Joe Slusarski	.10
19	Jose Melendez	.10
20	Pete Schourek	.10
21	Jeff Conine	.10
22	Paul Faries	.10
23	Scott Kamieniecki	.10
24	Bernard Gilkey	.10
25	Wes Chamberlain	.10
26	Charles Nagy	.10
27	Juan Guzman	.10
28	Heath Slocumb	.10
29	Eddie Taubensee	.10
30	Cedric Landrum	.10
31	Jose Offerman	.10
32	Andres Santana	.10
33	David Segui	.10
34	Bernie Williams	.10
35	Jeff Bagwell	1.50
36	Kevin Morton	.10
37	Kirk Dressendorfer	.10
38	Mike Fetters	.10
39	Darren Holmes	.10
40	Jeff Johnson	.10
41	Scott Aldred	.10
42	Kevin Ward	.10
43	Ray Lankford	.10
44	Terry Shumpert	.10
45	Wade Taylor	.10
46	Rob MacDonald	.10
47	Jose Mota	.10
48	Reggie Harris	.10
49	Mike Remlinger	.10
50	Mark Lewis	.10
51	Tino Martinez	.10
52	Ed Sprague	.10
53	Freddie Benavides	.10
54	Rich DeLucia	.10
55	Brian Drahman	.10
56	Steve Decker	.10
57	Scott Livingstone	.10
58	Mike Timlin	.10
59	Bob Scanlan	.10
60	Dean Palmer	.10
61	Frank Castillo	.10
62	Mark Leonard	.10
63	Chuck McElroy	.10
64	Derek Bell	.10
65	Andujar Cedeno	.10
66	Leo Gomez	.10
67	Rusty Meacham	.10
68	Dann Howitt	.10
69	Chris Jones	.10
70	Dave Cochrane	.10
71	Carlos Martinez	.10
72	Hensley Meulens	.10
73	Rich Reed	.10
74	Pedro Munoz	.10
75	Orlando Merced	.10
76	Chito Martinez	.10
77	Ivan Rodriguez	.75
78	Brian Barnes	.10
79	Chris Donnels	.10
80	Todd Hundley	.10
81	Gary Scott	.10
82	John Wehner	.10
83	Al Osuna	.10
84	Luis Lopez	.10
85	Brent Mayne	.10
86	Phil Plantier	.10
87	Joe Bitker	.10
88	Scott Cooper	.10
89	Chris Hammond	.10
90	Tim Sherrill	.10
91	Doug Simons	.10
92	Kip Gross	.10
93	Tim McIntosh	.10
94	Larry Casian	.10
95	Mike Dalton	.10
96	Lance Dickson	.10
97	Joe Grahe	.10
98	Glenn Sutko	.10
99	Gerald Alexander	.10
100	Mo Vaughn	.10

Rookies

1992 ROOKIE

A selection of 40 1992 rookie players is featured in this boxed set. Fronts have green borders with a red and white "1992 ROOKIE" notation printed vertically to the left of a game-action photo. Backs repeat the notation on a graduated blue background with a player portrait photo at top, biographical details and a career summary at center and appropriate logos at bottom.

		NM/M
Complete Set (40):		1.50
Common Player:		.05
1	Todd Van Poppel	.05
2	Kyle Abbott	.05
3	Derek Bell	.05
4	Jim Thome	.50
5	Mark Wohlers	.05
6	Todd Hundley	.05
7	Arthur Rhodes	.05
8	John Ramos	.05
9	Chris George	.05
10	Kenny Lofton	.05
11	Ted Wood	.05
12	Royce Clayton	.05
13	Scott Cooper	.05
14	Anthony Young	.05
15	Joel Johnston	.05
16	Andy Mota	.05
17	Lenny Webster	.05
18	Andy Ashby	.05
19	Jose Mota	.05
20	Tim McIntosh	.05
21	Terry Bross	.05
22	Harvey Pulliam	.05
23	Hector Fajardo	.05
24	Esteban Beltre	.05
25	Gary DiSarcina	.05
26	Mike Humphreys	.05
27	Jarvis Brown	.05
28	Gary Cooper	.05
29	Chris Donnels	.05
30	Monty Fariss	.05
31	Eric Karros	.05
32	Braulio Castillo	.05
33	Cal Eldred	.05
34	Tom Goodwin	.05
35	Reggie Sanders	.05
36	Scott Servais	.05
37	Kim Batiste	.05
38	Eric Wedge	.05
39	Willie Banks	.05
40	Mo Sanford	.05

Superstars

SUPERSTAR
SCOTT ERICKSON
P • MINNESOTA TWINS

Available in a blister pack with a book and six "Magic Motion" trivia cards, this 100-card set spotlights the games top veteran stars.

		NM/M
Complete Set (100):		4.00
Common Player:		.05
1	Ken Griffey Jr.	.75
2	Scott Erickson	.05
3	John Smiley	.05
4	Rick Aguilera	.05
5	Jeff Reardon	.05
6	Chuck Finley	.05
7	Kirby Puckett	.50
8	Paul Molitor	.40
9	Dave Winfield	.40
10	Mike Greenwell	.05
11	Bret Saberhagen	.05
12	Pete Harnisch	.05
13	Ozzie Guillen	.05
14	Hal Morris	.05
15	Tom Glavine	.30
16	David Cone	.05
17	Edgar Martinez	.05
18	Willie McGee	.05
19	Jim Abbott	.05
20	Mark Grace	.05
21	George Brett	.65
22	Jack McDowell	.05
23	Don Mattingly	.05
24	Will Clark	.05
25	Dwight Gooden	.05
26	Barry Bonds	1.00
27	Rafael Palmeiro	.35
28	Lee Smith	.05
29	Wally Joyner	.05
30	Wade Boggs	.50
31	Tom Henke	.05
32	Mark Langston	.05
33	Robin Ventura	.05
34	Steve Avery	.05
35	Joe Carter	.05
36	Benito Santiago	.05
37	Dave Stieb	.05
38	Julio Franco	.05
39	Albert Belle	.05
40	Dale Murphy	.05
41	Rob Dibble	.05
42	Dave Justice	.05
43	Jose Rijo	.05
44	Eric Davis	.05
45	Terry Pendleton	.05
46	Kevin Maas	.05
47	Ozzie Smith	.50
48	Andre Dawson	.25
49	Sandy Alomar, Jr.	.05
50	Nolan Ryan	1.00
51	Frank Thomas	.40
52	Craig Biggio	.05
53	Doug Drabek	.05
54	Bobby Thigpen	.05
55	Darryl Strawberry	.05
56	Dennis Eckersley	.35
57	John Franco	.05
58	Paul O'Neill	.05
59	Scott Sanderson	.05
60	Dave Stewart	.05
61	Ivan Calderon	.05
62	Frank Viola	.05
63	Mark McGwire	.75
64	Kelly Gruber	.05
65	Fred McGriff	.05
66	Cecil Fielder	.05
67	Jose Canseco	.30
68	Howard Johnson	.05
69	Juan Gonzalez	.20
70	Tim Wallach	.05
71	John Olerud	.05
72	Carlton Fisk	.40
73	Otis Nixon	.05
74	Roger Clemens	.05
75	Ramon Martinez	.05
76	Ron Gant	.05
77	Barry Larkin	.05
78	Eddie Murray	.40
79	Vince Coleman	.05
80	Bobby Bonilla	.05
81	Tony Gwynn	.50
82	Roberto Alomar	.20
83	Ellis Burks	.05
84	Robin Yount	.40
85	Ryne Sandberg	.50
86	Len Dykstra	.05
87	Ruben Sierra	.05
88	George Bell	.05
89	Cal Ripken, Jr.	1.00
90	Danny Tartabull	.05
91	Gregg Olson	.05
92	Dave Henderson	.05
93	Kevin Mitchell	.05
94	Ben McDonald	.05
95	Matt Williams	.05
96	Roberto Kelly	.05
97	Dennis Martinez	.05
98	Kent Hrbek	.05
99	Felix Jose	.05
100	Rickey Henderson	.40

1993 Score Promos

DARREN DAULTON

Only close comparison with regularly issued versions can detect these unmarked promos. The promos feature slightly different croppings of the pictures, situated higher than the normal version.

		NM/M
Complete Set (8):		15.00
Common Player:		1.00
1	Ken Griffey Jr.	4.00
3	Frank Thomas	2.00
5	Ryne Sandberg	3.00
6	Cal Ripken, Jr.	5.00
7	Roger Clemens	2.50
8	Bobby Bonilla	1.00
10	Darren Daulton	1.00
11	Travis Fryman	1.00

1993 Score

Score's 1993 cards have white borders surrounding color action photographs. The player's name is at the bottom of the card, while his team's name and position appears on the left side in a color band. Backs have color portraits, statistics and text. Subsets feature rookies, award winners, draft picks, highlights, World Series highlights, all-star caricatures, dream team players, and the Man of the Year (Kirby Puckett). Insert sets include: Boys of Summer, the Franchise and Stat Leaders, which feature Select's card design.

DARREN DAULTON

		NM/M
Complete Set (660):		15.00
Common Player:		.05
Pack (16):		.75
Wax Box (36):		17.50
1	Ken Griffey Jr.	.65
2	Gary Sheffield	.30
3	Frank Thomas	.40
4	Ryne Sandberg	.45
5	Larry Walker	.05
6	Cal Ripken, Jr.	1.00
7	Roger Clemens	.50
8	Bobby Bonilla	.05
9	Carlos Baerga	.05
10	Darren Daulton	.05
11	Travis Fryman	.05
12	Andy Van Slyke	.05
13	Jose Canseco	.30
14	Roberto Alomar	.15
15	Tom Glavine	.30
16	Barry Larkin	.05
17	Gregg Jefferies	.05
18	Craig Biggio	.05
19	Shane Mack	.05
20	Brett Butler	.05
21	Dennis Eckersley	.35
22	Will Clark	.05
23	Don Mattingly	.50
24	Tony Gwynn	.45
25	Ivan Rodriguez	.35
26	Shawon Dunston	.05
27	Mike Mussina	.30
28	Marquis Grissom	.05
29	Charles Nagy	.05
30	Len Dykstra	.05
31	Cecil Fielder	.05
32	Jay Bell	.05
33	B.J. Surhoff	.05
34	Bob Tewksbury	.05
35	Danny Tartabull	.05
36	Terry Pendleton	.05
37	Jack Morris	.05
38	Hal Morris	.05
39	Luis Polonia	.05
40	Ken Caminiti	.05
41	Robin Ventura	.05
42	Darryl Strawberry	.05
43	Wally Joyner	.05
44	Fred McGriff	.05
45	Kevin Tapani	.05
46	Matt Williams	.05
47	Robin Yount	.40
48	Ken Hill	.05
49	Edgar Martinez	.05
50	Mark Grace	.05
51	Juan Gonzalez	.20
52	Curt Schilling	.30
53	Dwight Gooden	.05
54	Chris Hoiles	.05
55	Frank Viola	.05
56	Ray Lankford	.05
57	George Brett	.50
58	Kenny Lofton	.05
59	Nolan Ryan	1.00
60	Mickey Tettleton	.05
61	John Smoltz	.05
62	Howard Johnson	.05
63	Eric Karros	.05
64	Rick Aguilera	.05
65	Steve Finley	.05
66	Mark Langston	.05
67	Bill Swift	.05
68	John Olerud	.05
69	Kevin McReynolds	.05
70	Jack McDowell	.05
71	Rickey Henderson	.40
72	Brian Harper	.05
73	Mike Morgan	.05
74	Rafael Palmeiro	.40
75	Dennis Martinez	.05
76	Tino Martinez	.05
77	Eddie Murray	.40
78	Ellis Burks	.05
79	John Kruk	.05
80	Gregg Olson	.05
81	Bernard Gilkey	.05
82	Milt Cuyler	.05
83	Mike LaValliere	.05
84	Albert Belle	.05
85	Bip Roberts	.05

No.	Player	Price
86	Melido Perez	.05
87	Otis Nixon	.05
88	Bill Spiers	.05
89	Jeff Bagwell	.40
90	Orel Hershiser	.05
91	Andy Benes	.05
92	Devon White	.05
93	Willie McGee	.05
94	Ozzie Guillen	.05
95	Ivan Calderon	.05
96	Keith Miller	.05
97	Steve Buechele	.05
98	Kent Hrbek	.05
99	Dave Hollins	.05
100	Mike Bordick	.05
101	Randy Tomlin	.05
102	Omar Vizquel	.05
103	Lee Smith	.05
104	Leo Gomez	.05
105	Jose Rijo	.05
106	Mark Whiten	.05
107	Dave Justice	.05
108	Eddie Taubensee	.05
109	Lance Johnson	.05
110	Felix Jose	.05
111	Mike Harkey	.05
112	Randy Milligan	.05
113	Anthony Young	.05
114	Rico Brogna	.05
115	Bret Saberhagen	.05
116	Sandy Alomar, Jr.	.05
117	Terry Mulholland	.05
118	Darryl Hamilton	.05
119	Todd Zeile	.05
120	Bernie Williams	.05
121	Zane Smith	.05
122	Derek Bell	.05
123	Deion Sanders	.05
124	Luis Sojo	.05
125	Joe Oliver	.05
126	Craig Grebeck	.05
127	Andujar Cedeno	.05
128	Brian McRae	.05
129	Jose Offerman	.05
130	Pedro Munoz	.05
131	Bud Black	.05
132	Mo Vaughn	.05
133	Bruce Hurst	.05
134	Dave Henderson	.05
135	Tom Pagnozzi	.05
136	Erik Hanson	.05
137	Orlando Merced	.05
138	Dean Palmer	.05
139	John Franco	.05
140	Brady Anderson	.05
141	Ricky Jordan	.05
142	Jeff Blauser	.05
143	Sammy Sosa	.45
144	Bob Walk	.05
145	Delino DeShields	.05
146	Kevin Brown	.05
147	Mark Lemke	.05
148	Chuck Knoblauch	.05
149	Chris Sabo	.05
150	Bobby Witt	.05
151	Luis Gonzalez	.05
152	Ron Karkovice	.05
153	Jeff Brantley	.05
154	Kevin Appier	.05
155	Darrin Jackson	.05
156	Kelly Gruber	.05
157	Royce Clayton	.05
158	Chuck Finley	.05
159	Jeff King	.05
160	Greg Vaughn	.05
161	Geronimo Pena	.05
162	Steve Farr	.05
163	Jose Oquendo	.05
164	Mark Lewis	.05
165	John Wetteland	.05
166	Mike Henneman	.05
167	Todd Hundley	.05
168	Wes Chamberlain	.05
169	Steve Avery	.05
170	Mike Devereaux	.05
171	Reggie Sanders	.05
172	Jay Buhner	.05
173	Eric Anthony	.05
174	John Burkett	.05
175	Tom Candiotti	.05
176	Phil Plantier	.05
177	Doug Henry	.05
178	Scott Leius	.05
179	Kirt Manwaring	.05
180	Jeff Parrett	.05
181	Don Slaught	.05
182	Scott Radinsky	.05
183	Luis Alicea	.05
184	Tom Gordon	.05
185	Rick Wilkins	.05
186	Todd Stottlemyre	.05
187	Moises Alou	.05
188	Joe Grahe	.05
189	Jeff Kent	.05
190	Bill Wegman	.05
191	Kim Batiste	.05
192	Matt Nokes	.05
193	Mark Wohlers	.05
194	Paul Sorrento	.05
195	Chris Hammond	.05
196	Scott Livingstone	.05
197	Doug Jones	.05
198	Scott Cooper	.05
199	Ramon Martinez	.05
200	Dave Valle	.05
201	Mariano Duncan	.05
202	Ben McDonald	.05
203	Darren Lewis	.05

No.	Player	Price
204	Kenny Rogers	.05
205	Manuel Lee	.05
206	Scott Erickson	.05
207	Dan Gladden	.05
208	Bob Welch	.05
209	Greg Olson	.05
210	Dan Pasqua	.05
211	Tim Wallach	.05
212	Jeff Montgomery	.05
213	Derrick May	.05
214	Ed Sprague	.05
215	David Haas	.05
216	Darrin Fletcher	.05
217	Brian Jordan	.05
218	Jaime Navarro	.05
219	Randy Velarde	.05
220	Ron Gant	.05
221	Paul Quantrill	.05
222	Damion Easley	.05
223	Charlie Hough	.05
224	Brad Brink RC	.05
225	Barry Manual RC	.05
226	Kevin Koslofski RC	.05
227	Ryan Thompson RC	.05
228	Mike Munoz RC	.05
229	Dan Wilson RC	.10
230	Peter Hoy RC	.05
231	Pedro Astacio RC	.10
232	Matt Stairs RC	.10
233	Jeff Reboulet RC	.05
234	Manny Alexander RC	.05
235	Willie Banks RC	.05
236	John Jaha RC	.05
237	Scooter Tucker RC	.05
238	Russ Springer RC	.05
239	Paul Miller RC	.05
240	Dan Peltier RC	.05
241	Ozzie Canseco RC	.05
242	Ben Rivera RC	.05
243	John Valentin RC	.05
244	Henry Rodriguez RC	.05
245	Derek Parks RC	.05
246	Carlos Garcia RC	.10
247	Tim Pugh RC	.05
248	Melvin Nieves RC	.05
249	Rich Amaral RC	.05
250	Willie Greene RC	.05
251	Tim Scott RC	.05
252	Dave Silvestri RC	.05
253	Rob Mallicoat RC	.05
254	Donald Harris RC	.05
255	Craig Colbert RC	.05
256	Jose Guzman	.05
257	Domingo Martinez RC	.05
258	William Suero RC	.05
259	Juan Guerrero RC	.05
260	J.T. Snow RC	.45
261	Tony Pena	.05
262	Tim Fortugno RC	.05
263	Tom Marsh RC	.05
264	Kurt Knudsen RC	.05
265	Tim Costo RC	.05
266	Steve Shifflett RC	.05
267	Billy Ashley RC	.05
268	Jerry Nielsen RC	.05
269	Pete Young RC	.05
270	Johnny Guzman RC	.05
271	Greg Colbrunn RC	.05
272	Jeff Nelson RC	.05
273	Kevin Young RC	.05
274	Jeff Frye RC	.05
275	J.T. Bruett RC	.05
276	Todd Pratt RC	.05
277	Mike Butcher RC	.05
278	John Flaherty RC	.05
279	John Patterson RC	.05
280	Eric Hillman RC	.05
281	Bien Figueros RC	.05
282	Shane Reynolds RC	.05
283	Rich Rowland RC	.05
284	Steve Foster RC	.05
285	Dave Mlicki RC	.05
286	Mike Piazza RC	.65
287	Mike Trombley RC	.05
288	Jim Pena RC	.05
289	Bob Ayrault RC	.05
290	Henry Mercedes RC	.05
291	Bob Wickman	.05
292	Jacob Brumfield RC	.05
293	David Hulse RC	.05
294	Ryan Klesko	.05
295	Doug Linton	.05
296	Steve Cooke	.05
297	Eddie Zosky	.05
298	Gerald Williams RC	.05
299	Jonathan Hurst RC	.05
300	Larry Carter RC	.05
301	William Pennyfeather RC	.05
302	Cesar Hernandez RC	.05
303	Steve Hosey RC	.05
304	Blas Minor RC	.05
305	Jeff Grotewold RC	.05
306	Bernardo Brito RC	.05
307	Rafael Bournigal RC	.05
308	Jeff Branson RC	.05
309	Tom Quinlan RC	.05
310	Pat Gomez RC	.05
311	Sterling Hitchcock RC	.10
312	Kent Bottenfield RC	.05
313	Alan Trammell	.05
314	Cris Colon RC	.05
315	Paul Wagner RC	.05
316	Matt Maysey RC	.05
317	Mike Stanton	.05
318	Rick Trlicek RC	.05
319	Kevin Rogers RC	.05
320	Mark Clark RC	.05

No.	Player	Price
321	Pedro Martinez	.40
322	Al Martin RC	.05
323	Mike Macfarlane	.05
324	Rey Sanchez RC	.10
325	Roger Pavlik RC	.05
326	Troy Neel	.05
327	Kerry Woodson RC	.05
328	Wayne Kirby RC	.05
329	Ken Ryan RC	.05
330	Jesse Levis RC	.05
331	James Austin	.05
332	Dan Walters	.05
333	Brian Williams	.05
334	Wil Cordero	.05
335	Bret Boone	.05
336	Hipolito Pichardo	.05
337	Pat Mahomes	.05
338	Andy Stankiewicz	.05
339	Jim Bullinger	.05
340	Archi Cianfrocco	.05
341	Ruben Amaro Jr.	.05
342	Frank Seminara	.05
343	Pat Hentgen	.05
344	Dave Nilsson	.05
345	Mike Perez	.05
346	Tim Salmon	.05
347	Tim Wakefield RC	.10
348	Carlos Hernandez	.05
349	Donovan Osborne	.05
350	Denny Naegle	.05
351	Sam Militello	.05
352	Eric Fox	.05
353	John Doherty	.05
354	Chad Curtis	.05
355	Jeff Tackett	.05
356	Dave Fleming	.05
357	Pat Listach	.05
358	Kevin Wickander	.05
359	John VanderWal	.05
360	Arthur Rhodes	.05
361	Bob Scanlan	.05
362	Bob Zupcic	.05
363	Mel Rojas	.05
364	Jim Thome	.35
365	Bill Pecota	.05
366	Mark Carreon	.05
367	Mitch Williams	.05
368	Cal Eldred	.05
369	Stan Belinda	.05
370	Pat Kelly	.05
371	Pheal Cormier	.05
372	Juan Guzman	.05
373	Damon Berryhill	.05
374	Gary DiSarcina	.05
375	Norm Charlton	.05
376	Roberto Hernandez	.05
377	Scott Kamieniecki	.05
378	Rusty Meacham	.05
379	Kurt Stillwell	.05
380	Lloyd McClendon	.05
381	Mark Leonard	.05
382	Jerry Browne	.05
383	Glenn Davis	.05
384	Randy Johnson	.40
385	Mike Greenwell	.05
386	Scott Chiamparino	.05
387	George Bell	.05
388	Steve Olin	.05
389	Chuck McElroy	.05
390	Mark Gardner	.05
391	Rod Beck	.05
392	Dennis Rasmussen	.05
393	Charlie Leibrandt	.05
394	Julio Franco	.05
395	Pete Harnisch	.05
396	Sid Bream	.05
397	Milt Thompson	.05
398	Glenallen Hill	.05
399	Chico Walker	.05
400	Alex Cole	.05
401	Trevor Wilson	.05
402	Jeff Conine	.05
403	Kyle Abbott	.05
404	Tom Browning	.05
405	Jerald Clark	.05
406	Vince Horsman	.05
407	Kevin Mitchell	.05
408	Pete Smith	.05
409	Jeff Innis	.05
410	Mike Timlin	.05
411	Charlie Hayes	.05
412	Alex Fernandez	.05
413	Jeff Russell	.05
414	Jody Reed	.05
415	Mickey Morandini	.05
416	Darnell Coles	.05
417	Xavier Hernandez	.05
418	Steve Sax	.05
419	Joe Girardi	.05
420	Mike Fetters	.05
421	Danny Jackson	.05
422	Jim Gott	.05
423	Tim Belcher	.05
424	Jose Mesa	.05
425	Junior Felix	.05
426	Thomas Howard	.05
427	Julio Valera	.05
428	Dante Bichette	.05
429	Mike Sharperson	.05
430	Darryl Kile	.05
431	Lonnie Smith	.05
432	Monty Fariss	.05
433	Reggie Jefferson	.05
434	Bob McClure	.05
435	Craig Lefferts	.05
436	Duane Ward	.05
437	Shawn Abner	.05
438	Roberto Kelly	.05

No.	Player	Price
439	Paul O'Neill	.05
440	Alan Mills RC	.05
441	Roger Mason	.05
442	Gary Pettis	.05
443	Steve Lake	.05
444	Gene Larkin	.05
445	Larry Anderson	.05
446	Doug Dascenzo	.05
447	Daryl Boston	.05
448	John Candelaria	.05
449	Storm Davis	.05
450	Tom Edens	.05
451	Mike Maddux	.05
452	Tim Naehring	.05
453	John Orton	.05
454	Joey Cora	.05
455	Chuck Crim	.05
456	Dan Plesac	.05
457	Mike Bielecki	.05
458	Terry Jorgensen RC	.05
459	John Habyan	.05
460	Pete O'Brien	.05
461	Jeff Treadway	.05
462	Frank Castillo	.05
463	Jimmy Jones	.05
464	Tommy Greene	.05
465	Tracy Woodson	.05
466	Rich Rodriguez	.05
467	Joe Hesketh	.05
468	Greg Myers	.05
469	Kirk McCaskill	.05
470	Ricky Bones	.05
471	Lenny Webster	.05
472	Francisco Cabrera	.05
473	Turner Ward	.05
474	Dwayne Henry	.05
475	Al Osuna	.05
476	Craig Wilson	.05
477	Chris Nabholz	.05
478	Rafael Belliard	.05
479	Terry Leach	.05
480	Tim Teufel	.05
481	Dennis Eckersley (Award Winner)	.15
482	Barry Bonds (Award Winner)	.50
483	Dennis Eckersley (Award Winner)	.15
484	Greg Maddux (Award Winner)	.25
485	Pat Listach (ROY)	.05
486	Eric Karros (ROY)	.05
487	Jamie Arnold RC	.05
488	B.J. Wallace	.05
489	Derek Jeter RC	8.00
490	Jason Kendall	.45
491	Rick Helling	.05
492	Derek Wallace RC	.05
493	Sean Lowe RC	.05
494	Shannon Stewart RC	.65
495	Benji Grigsby RC	.05
496	Todd Steverson RC	.05
497	Dan Serafini RC	.05
498	Michael Tucker	.05
499	Chris Roberts (Draft Pick)	.05
500	Pete Janicki (Draft Pick)	.05
501	Jeff Schmidt RC	.05
502	Edgar Martinez/AS	.05
503	Omar Vizquel/AS	.05
504	Ken Griffey Jr./AS	.35
505	Kirby Puckett/AS	.25
506	Joe Carter/AS	.05
507	Ivan Rodriguez/AS	.15
508	Jack Morris/AS	.05
509	Dennis Eckersley/AS	.15
510	Frank Thomas/AS	.20
511	Roberto Alomar/AS	.10
512	Mickey Morandini/ Highlight	.05
513	Dennis Eckersley/ Highlight	.15
514	Jeff Reardon/Highlight	.05
515	Danny Tartabull/ Highlight	.05
516	Bip Roberts/Highlight	.05
517	George Brett/Highlight	.30
518	Robin Yount/Highlight	.20
519	Kevin Gross/Highlight	.05
520	Ed Sprague (World Series Highlight)	.05
521	Dave Winfield (World Series Highlight)	.20
522	Ozzie Smith/AS	.25
523	Barry Bonds/AS	.50
524	Andy Van Slyke/AS	.25
525	Tony Gwynn/AS	.25
526	Darren Daulton/AS	.05
527	Greg Maddux/AS	.25
528	Fred McGriff/AS	.05
529	Lee Smith/AS	.05
530	Ryne Sandberg/AS	.25
531	Gary Sheffield/AS	.10
532	Ozzie Smith (Dream Team)	.25
533	Kirby Puckett (Dream Team)	.25
534	Gary Sheffield (Dream Team)	.10

No.	Player	Price
535	Andy Van Slyke (Dream Team)	.05
536	Ken Griffey Jr. (Dream Team)	.35
537	Ivan Rodriguez (Dream Team)	.15
538	Charles Nagy (Dream Team)	.05
539	Tom Glavine (Dream Team)	.10
540	Dennis Eckersley (Dream Team)	.15
541	Frank Thomas (Dream Team)	.20
542	Roberto Alomar (Dream Team)	.10
543	Sean Barry	.05
544	Mike Schooler	.05
545	Chuck Carr	.05
546	Lenny Harris	.05
547	Gary Scott	.05
548	Derek Lilliquist	.05
549	Brian Hunter	.05
550	Kirby Puckett (MOY)	.25
551	Jim Eisenreich	.05
552	Andre Dawson	.25
553	David Nied	.05
554	Spike Owen	.05
555	Greg Gagne	.05
556	Sid Fernandez	.05
557	Mark McGwire	.75
558	Bryan Harvey	.05
559	Harold Reynolds	.05
560	Barry Bonds	1.00
561	Eric Wedge RC	.05
562	Ozzie Smith	.45
563	Rick Sutcliffe	.05
564	Alex Arias RC	.05
565	Greg Swindell	.05
566	Brook Jacoby	.05
567	Pete Incaviglia	.05
568	Butch Henry RC	.05
569	Kevin Seitzer	.05
570	Eric Davis	.05
571	Kevin Seitzer	.05
572	Tony Fernandez	.05
573	Steve Reed RC	.05
574	Cory Snyder	.05
575	Joe Carter	.05
576	Greg Maddux	.45
577	Bert Blyleven	.05
578	Kevin Bass	.05
579	Carlton Fisk	.40
580	Doug Drabek	.05
581	Mark Gubicza	.05
582	Bobby Thigpen	.05
583	Chili Davis	.05
584	Scott Bankhead	.05
585	Harold Baines	.05
586	Eric Young RC	.15
587	Lance Parrish	.05
588	Juan Bell	.05
589	Bob Ojeda	.05
590	Joe Orsulak	.05
591	Benito Santiago	.05
592	Wade Boggs	.45
593	Robby Thompson	.05
594	Erik Plunk	.05
595	Hensley Meulens	.05
596	Lou Whitaker	.05
597	Dale Murphy	.25
598	Paul Molitor	.40
599	Greg W. Harris	.05
600	Darren Holmes	.05
601	Dave Martinez	.05
602	Tom Henke	.05
603	Mike Benjamin	.05
604	Rene Gonzales	.05
605	Roger McDowell	.05
606	Kirby Puckett	.45
607	Randy Myers	.05
608	Ruben Sierra	.05
609	Wilson Alvarez	.05
610	Dave Segui	.05
611	Juan Samuel	.05
612	Tom Brunansky	.05
613	Willie Randolph	.05
614	Tony Phillips	.05
615	Candy Maldonado	.05
616	Chris Bosio	.05
617	Bret Barberie	.05
618	Scott Sanderson	.05
619	Ron Darling	.05
620	Dave Winfield	.40
621	Mike Felder	.05
622	Greg Hibbard	.05
623	Mike Scioscia	.05
624	John Smiley	.05
625	Alejandro Pena	.05
626	Terry Steinbach	.05
627	Freddie Benavides	.05
628	Kevin Reimer	.05
629	Braulio Castillo	.05
630	Dave Stieb	.05
631	Dave Magadan	.05
632	Scott Fletcher	.05
633	Cris Carpenter	.05
634	Kevin Maas	.05
635	Todd Worrell	.05
636	Rob Deer	.05
637	Dwight Smith	.05
638	Chito Martinez	.05
639	Jimmy Key	.05
640	Greg Harris	.05
641	Mike Moore	.05
642	Pat Borders	.05
643	Bill Gullickson	.05
644	Gary Gaetti	.05

No.	Player	Price
645	David Howard	.05
646	Jim Abbott	.05
647	Willie Wilson	.05
648	David Wells	.05
649	Andres Galarraga	.05
650	Vince Coleman	.05
651	Rob Dibble	.05
652	Frank Tanana	.05
653	Steve Decker	.05
654	David Cone	.05
655	Jack Armstrong	.05
656	Dave Stewart	.05
657	Billy Hatcher	.05
658	Tim Raines	.05
659	Walt Weiss	.05
660	Jose Lind	.05

Boys of Summer

These cards were available as inserts only in Score 35-card Super Packs, about one in every four packs. Borderless fronts have a color action photo of the player superimposed over the sun. The player's name is in black script in a green strip at bottom, along with a subset logo. On back is a player portrait, again with the sun as a background. Subset, company, team and major league logos are in color on the right, and there is a short career summary on the green background at bottom.

		NM/M
Complete Set (30):		12.50
Common Player:		.25
1	Billy Ashley	.25
2	Tim Salmon	.50
3	Pedro Martinez	4.00
4	Luis Mercedes	.25
5	Mike Piazza	8.00
6	Troy Neel	.25
7	Melvin Nieves	.25
8	Ryan Klesko	.25
9	Ryan Thompson	.25
10	Kevin Young	.25
11	Gerald Williams	.25
12	Willie Greene	.25
13	John Patterson	.25
14	Carlos Garcia	.25
15	Eddie Zosky	.25
16	Sean Berry	.25
17	Rico Brogna	.25
18	Larry Carter	.25
19	Bobby Ayala	.25
20	Alan Embree	.25
21	Donald Harris	.25
22	Sterling Hitchcock	.25
23	David Nied	.25
24	Henry Mercedes	.25
25	Ozzie Canseco	.25
26	David Hulse	.25
27	Al Martin	.25
28	Dan Wilson	.25
29	Paul Miller	.25
30	Rich Rowland	.25

Dream Team

OZZIE SMITH

This set which features most of the players in street clothes in sepia-toned photos

---

ABBREVIATIONS

AS - All-Star

on a white background, has gold-foil graphics and was available only via a mail-in offer.

		NM/M
Complete Set (12):		5.00
Common Player:		.25
1	Ozzie Smith	1.00
2	Kirby Puckett	1.00
3	Gary Sheffield	.35
4	Andy Van Slyke	.25
5	Ken Griffey Jr.	2.00
6	Ivan Rodriguez	.60
7	Charles Nagy	.25
8	Tom Glavine	.35
9	Dennis Eckersley	.60
10	Frank Thomas	.75
11	Roberto Alomar	.30
---	Header Card	

The Franchise

These glossy inserts have full-bleed color action photos against a darkened background so that the player stands out. Cards could be found in 16-card packs only; odds of finding one are 1 in every 24 packs. The fronts have gold-foil highlights.

		NM/M
Complete Set (28):		50.00
Common Player:		.60
1	Cal Ripken, Jr.	12.00
2	Roger Clemens	6.00
3	Mark Langston	.60
4	Frank Thomas	3.50
5	Carlos Baerga	.60
6	Cecil Fielder	.60
7	Gregg Jefferies	.60
8	Robin Yount	3.50
9	Kirby Puckett	5.00
10	Don Mattingly	6.00
11	Dennis Eckersley	3.00
12	Ken Griffey Jr.	9.00
13	Juan Gonzalez	3.50
14	Roberto Alomar	1.50
15	Terry Pendleton	.60
16	Ryne Sandberg	5.00
17	Barry Larkin	.60
18	Jeff Bagwell	3.50
19	Brett Butler	.60
20	Larry Walker	.60
21	Bobby Bonilla	.60
22	Darren Daulton	.60
23	Andy Van Slyke	.60
24	Ray Lankford	.60
25	Gary Sheffield	1.50
26	Will Clark	.60
27	Bryan Harvey	.60
28	David Nied	.60

Procter & Gamble Rookies

This set was available via a mail-in offer in the summer of 1993. Ten proofs of purchase were required along with a small amount of cash for postage. Fronts feature a player action photo in a diamond at center with the name, position and team logo in a home plate device at the bottom of the pho-to. At bottom center is a color photo of the player's home stadium, flanked by silver-foil stripes on a dark green background. Above the player photo are gold-foil Score and P&G logos on a dark green background. A center bar in gold foil has the word "ROOKIE" in green. Backs have a small player portrait photo at top against a dark green background. His name and position are in white at left and personal data at right. At center is a large color photo of the player's hometeam skyline, with the city name in gold type in a green stripe below. At bottom are complete major and minor league stats, MLB and MLBPA logos and the card number.

		NM/M
Complete Set (10):		3.00
Common Player:		.25
1	Wil Cordero	.25
2	Pedro Martinez	2.00
3	Bret Boone	.25
4	Melvin Nieves	.25
5	Ryan Klesko	.25
6	Ryan Thompson	.25
7	Kevin Young	.25
8	Willie Greene	.25
9	Eric Wedge	.25
10	David Nied	.25

1994 Score Samples

Regular and Gold Rush versions of the first eight cards in the 1994 Score set were produced in a special promo version to familiarize buyers with the new issue. Cards have all zeroes in place of the 1993 stats and are overprinted on front and back with a diagonal black "SAMPLE." The samples were distributed in 11-card cello packs containing eight regular sample cards, one of the Gold Rush samples, a Barry Larkin Dream Team promo card and a header.

		NM/M
Complete Set (18):		20.00
Common Player:		.40
1	Barry Bonds	2.00
1	Barry Bonds (Gold Rush)	6.00
2	John Olerud	.40
2	John Olerud (Gold Rush)	1.00
3	Ken Griffey Jr.	1.50
3	Ken Griffey Jr. (Gold Rush)	4.50
4	Jeff Bagwell	1.00
4	Jeff Bagwell (Gold Rush)	3.00
5	John Burkett	.40
5	John Burkett (Gold Rush)	1.00
6	Jack McDowell	.40
6	Jack McDowell (Gold Rush)	1.00
7	Albert Belle	.50
7	Albert Belle (Gold Rush)	1.50
8	Andres Galarraga	.40
8	Andres Galarraga (Gold Rush)	1.00
5	Barry Larkin (Dream Team)	.50
---	Hobby Header Card	.05
---	Retail Header Card	.05

1994 Score

Score's 1994 set, with a new design and UV coating,

was issued in two series of 330 cards each. The cards, which use more action photos than before, have dark blue borders with the player's name in a team color-coded strip at the bottom. A special Gold Rush card, done for each card in the set, is included in every pack. Series 1 includes American League checklists, which are printed on the backs of cards depicting panoramic views of each team's ballpark. Series 2 has the National League team checklists. Insert sets include Dream Team players, and National (Series 1 packs) and American League Gold Stars (Series 2 packs), which use the Gold Rush process and appear once every 18 packs.

		NM/M
Complete Set (660):		15.00
Common Player:		.05
Gold Rush:		2X
Pack (14):		.75
Wax Box (36):		15.00
1	Barry Bonds	1.00
2	John Olerud	.05
3	Ken Griffey Jr.	.65
4	Jeff Bagwell	.40
5	John Burkett	.05
6	Jack McDowell	.05
7	Albert Belle	.05
8	Andres Galarraga	.05
9	Mike Mussina	.30
10	Will Clark	.05
11	Travis Fryman	.05
12	Tony Gwynn	.50
13	Robin Yount	.40
14	Dave Magadan	.05
15	Paul O'Neill	.05
16	Ray Lankford	.05
17	Damion Easley	.05
18	Andy Van Slyke	.05
19	Brian McRae	.05
20	Ryne Sandberg	.50
21	Kirby Puckett	.50
22	Dwight Gooden	.05
23	Don Mattingly	.60
24	Kevin Mitchell	.05
25	Roger Clemens	.60
26	Eric Karros	.05
27	Juan Gonzalez	.20
28	John Kruk	.05
29	Gregg Jefferies	.05
30	Tom Glavine	.30
31	Ivan Rodriguez	.35
32	Jay Bell	.05
33	Randy Johnson	.40
34	Darren Daulton	.05
35	Rickey Henderson	.40
36	Eddie Murray	.40
37	Brian Harper	.05
38	Delino DeShields	.05
39	Jose Lind	.05
40	Benito Santiago	.05
41	Frank Thomas	.40
42	Mark Grace	.05
43	Roberto Alomar	.20
44	Andy Benes	.05
45	Luis Polonia	.05
46	Brett Butler	.05
47	Terry Steinbach	.05
48	Craig Biggio	.05
49	Greg Vaughn	.05
50	Charlie Hayes	.05
51	Mickey Tettleton	.05
52	Jose Rijo	.05
53	Carlos Baerga	.05
54	Jeff Blauser	.05
55	Leo Gomez	.05
56	Bob Tewksbury	.05
57	Mo Vaughn	.05
58	Orlando Merced	.05
59	Tino Martinez	.05
60	Len Dykstra	.05
61	Jose Canseco	.25
62	Tony Fernandez	.05
63	Donovan Osborne	.05
64	Ken Hill	.05
65	Kent Hrbek	.05
66	Bryan Harvey	.05
67	Wally Joyner	.05
68	Derrick May	.05
69	Lance Johnson	.05
70	Willie McGee	.05
71	Mark Langston	.05
72	Terry Pendleton	.05
73	Joe Carter	.05
74	Barry Larkin	.05
75	Jimmy Key	.05
76	Joe Girardi	.05
77	B.J. Surhoff	.05
78	Pete Harnisch	.05
79	Lou Whitaker	.05
80	Cory Snyder	.05
81	Kenny Lofton	.05
82	Fred McGriff	.05
83	Mike Greenwell	.05
84	Mike Perez	.05
85	Cal Ripken, Jr.	1.00
86	Don Slaught	.05
87	Omar Vizquel	.05
88	Curt Schilling	.30
89	Chuck Knoblauch	.05
90	Moises Alou	.05
91	Greg Gagne	.05
92	Bret Saberhagen	.05
93	Ozzie Guillen	.05
94	Matt Williams	.05
95	Chad Curtis	.05
96	Mike Harkey	.05
97	Devon White	.05
98	Walt Weiss	.05
99	Kevin Brown	.05
100	Gary Sheffield	.25
101	Wade Boggs	.50
102	Orel Hershiser	.05
103	Tony Phillips	.05
104	Andujar Cedeno	.05
105	Bill Spiers	.05
106	Otis Nixon	.05
107	Felix Fermin	.05
108	Bip Roberts	.05
109	Dennis Eckersley	.35
110	Dante Bichette	.05
111	Ben McDonald	.05
112	Jim Poole	.05
113	John Dopson	.05
114	Rob Dibble	.05
115	Jeff Treadway	.05
116	Ricky Jordan	.05
117	Mike Henneman	.05
118	Willie Blair	.05
119	Doug Henry	.05
120	Gerald Perry	.05
121	Greg Myers	.05
122	John Franco	.05
123	Roger Mason	.05
124	Chris Hammond	.05
125	Hubie Brooks	.05
126	Kent Mercker	.05
127	Jim Abbott	.05
128	Kevin Bass	.05
129	Rick Aguilera	.05
130	Mitch Webster	.05
131	Eric Plunk	.05
132	Mark Carreon	.05
133	Dave Stewart	.05
134	Willie Wilson	.05
135	Dave Fleming	.05
136	Jeff Tackett	.05
137	Geno Petralli	.05
138	Gene Harris	.05
139	Scott Bankhead	.05
140	Trevor Wilson	.05
141	Alvaro Espinoza	.05
142	Ryan Bowen	.05
143	Mike Moore	.05
144	Bill Pecota	.05
145	Jaime Navarro	.05
146	Jack Daugherty	.05
147	Bob Wickman	.05
148	Chris Jones	.05
149	Todd Stottlemyre	.05
150	Brian Williams	.05
151	Chuck Finley	.05
152	Lenny Harris	.05
153	Alex Fernandez	.05
154	Candy Maldonado	.05
155	Jeff Montgomery	.05
156	David West	.05
157	Mark Williamson	.05
158	Milt Thompson	.05
159	Ron Darling	.05
160	Stan Belinda	.05
161	Henry Cotto	.05
162	Mel Rojas	.05
163	Doug Strange	.05
164	Rene Arocha (1993 Rookie)	.05
165	Tim Hulett	.05
166	Steve Avery	.05
167	Jim Thome	.35
168	Tom Browning	.05
169	Mario Diaz	.05
170	Steve Reed (1993 Rookie)	.05
171	Scott Livingstone	.05
172	Chris Donnels	.05
173	John Jaha	.05
174	Carlos Hernandez	.05
175	Dion James	.05
176	Bud Black	.05
177	Tony Castillo	.05
178	Jose Guzman	.05
179	Torey Lovullo	.05
180	John Vander Wal	.05
181	Mike LaValliere	.05
182	Sid Fernandez	.05
183	Brent Mayne	.05
184	Terry Mulholland	.05
185	Willie Banks	.05
186	Steve Cooke (1993 Rookie)	.05
187	Brent Gates (1993 Rookie)	.05
188	Erik Pappas (1993 Rookie)	.05
189	Bill Haselman (1993 Rookie)	.05
190	Fernando Valenzuela	.05
191	Gary Redus	.05
192	Danny Darwin	.05
193	Mark Portugal	.05
194	Derek Lilliquist	.05
195	Charlie O'Brien	.05
196	Matt Nokes	.05
197	Danny Sheaffer	.05
198	Bill Gullickson	.05
199	Alex Arias (1993 Rookie)	.05
200	Mike Fetters	.05
201	Brian Jordan	.05
202	Joe Grahe	.05
203	Tom Candiotti	.05
204	Jeremy Stanton	.05
205	Mike Stanton	.05
206	David Howard	.05
207	Darren Holmes	.05
208	Rick Honeycutt	.05
209	Danny Jackson	.05
210	Rich Amaral (1993 Rookie)	.05
211	Blas Minor (1993 Rookie)	.05
212	Kenny Rogers	.05
213	Jim Leyritz	.05
214	Mike Morgan	.05
215	Dan Gladden	.05
216	Randy Velarde	.05
217	Mitch Williams	.05
218	Hipolito Pichardo	.05
219	Dave Burba	.05
220	Wilson Alvarez	.05
221	Bob Zupcic	.05
222	Francisco Cabrera	.05
223	Julio Valera	.05
224	Paul Assenmacher	.05
225	Jeff Branson	.05
226	Todd Frohwirth	.05
227	Armando Reynoso	.05
228	Rich Rowland (1993 Rookie)	.05
229	Freddie Benavides	.05
230	Wayne Kirby (1993 Rookie)	.05
231	Darryl Kile	.05
232	Skeeter Barnes	.05
233	Ramon Martinez	.05
234	Tom Gordon	.05
235	Dave Gallagher	.05
236	Ricky Bones	.05
237	Larry Andersen	.05
238	Pat Meares (1993 Rookie)	.05
239	Zane Smith	.05
240	Tim Leary	.05
241	Phil Clark	.05
242	Danny Cox	.05
243	Mike Jackson	.05
244	Mike Gallego	.05
245	Lee Smith	.05
246	Todd Jones (1993 Rookie)	.05
247	Steve Bedrosian	.05
248	Troy Neel	.05
249	Jose Bautista	.05
250	Steve Frey	.05
251	Jeff Reardon	.05
252	Stan Javier	.05
253	Mo Sanford (1993 Rookie)	.05
254	Steve Sax	.05
255	Luis Aquino	.05
256	Domingo Jean (1993 Rookie)	.05
257	Scott Servais	.05
258	Brad Pennington (1993 Rookie)	.05
259	Dave Hansen	.05
260	Goose Gossage	.05
261	Jeff Fassero	.05
262	Junior Ortiz	.05
263	Anthony Young	.05
264	Chris Bosio	.05
265	Ruben Amaro Jr.	.05
266	Mark Eichhorn	.05
267	Dave Clark	.05
268	Gary Thurman	.05
269	Les Lancaster	.05
270	Jamie Moyer	.05
271	Ricky Gutierrez (1993 Rookie)	.05
272	Greg Harris	.05
273	Mike Benjamin	.05
274	Gene Nelson	.05
275	Damon Berryhill	.05
276	Scott Radinsky	.05
277	Mike Aldrete	.05
278	Jerry DiPoto (1993 Rookie)	.05
279	Chris Haney	.05
280	Richie Lewis (1993 Rookie)	.05
281	Jarvis Brown	.05
282	Juan Bell	.05
283	Joe Klink	.05
284	Graeme Lloyd (1993 Rookie)	.05
285	Casey Candaele	.05
286	Bob MacDonald	.05
287	Mike Sharperson	.05
288	Gene Larkin	.05
289	Brian Barnes	.05
290	David McCarty (1993 Rookie)	.05
291	Jeff Innis	.05
292	Bob Patterson	.05
293	Ben Rivera	.05
294	John Habyan	.05
295	Rich Rodriguez	.05
296	Edwin Nunez	.05
297	Rod Brewer	.05
298	Mike Timlin	.05
299	Jesse Orosco	.05
300	Gary Gaetti	.05
301	Todd Benzinger	.05
302	Jeff Nelson	.05
303	Rafael Belliard	.05
304	Matt Whiteside	.05
305	Vinny Castilla	.05
306	Matt Turner	.05
307	Eduardo Perez	.05
308	Joel Johnston	.05
309	Chris Gomez	.05
310	Pat Rapp	.05
311	Jim Tatum	.05
312	Kirk Rueter	.05
313	John Flaherty	.05
314	Tom Kramer	.05
315	Mark Whiten (Highlights)	.05
316	Chris Bosio (Highlights)	.05
317	Orioles Checklist	.05
318	Red Sox Checklist	.05
319	Angels Checklist	.05
320	White Sox Checklist	.05
321	Indians Checklist	.05
322	Tigers Checklist	.05
323	Royals Checklist	.05
324	Brewers Checklist	.05
325	Twins Checklist	.05
326	Yankees Checklist	.05
327	Athletics Checklist	.05
328	Mariners Checklist	.05
329	Rangers Checklist	.05
330	Blue Jays Checklist	.05
331	Frank Viola	.05
332	Ron Gant	.05
333	Charles Nagy	.05
334	Roberto Kelly	.05
335	Brady Anderson	.05
336	Alex Cole	.05
337	Alan Trammell	.05
338	Derek Bell	.05
339	Bernie Williams	.05
340	Jose Offerman	.05
341	Bill Wegman	.05
342	Ken Caminiti	.05
343	Pat Borders	.05
344	Kirt Manwaring	.05
345	Chili Davis	.05
346	Steve Buechele	.05
347	Robin Ventura	.05
348	Teddy Higuera	.05
349	Jerry Browne	.05
350	Scott Kamieniecki	.05
351	Kevin Tapani	.05
352	Marquis Grissom	.05
353	Jay Buhner	.05
354	Dave Hollins	.05
355	Dan Wilson	.05
356	Bob Walk	.05
357	Chris Hoiles	.05
358	Todd Zeile	.05
359	Kevin Appier	.05
360	Chris Sabo	.05
361	David Segui	.05
362	Jerald Clark	.05
363	Tony Pena	.05
364	Steve Finley	.05
365	Roger Pavlik	.05
366	John Smoltz	.05
367	Scott Fletcher	.05
368	Jody Reed	.05
369	David Wells	.05
370	Jose Vizcaino	.05
371	Pat Listach	.05
372	Orestes Destrade	.05
373	Danny Tartabull	.05
374	Greg W. Harris	.05
375	Juan Guzman	.05
376	Larry Walker	.05
377	Gary DiSarcina	.05
378	Bobby Bonilla	.05
379	Tim Raines	.05
380	Tommy Greene	.05
381	Chris Gwynn	.05
382	Jeff King	.05
383	Shane Mack	.05
384	Ozzie Smith	.50
385	Eddie Zambrano **RC**	.05
386	Mike Devereaux	.05
387	Erik Hanson	.05
388	Scott Cooper	.05
389	Dean Palmer	.05
390	John Wetteland	.05
391	Reggie Jefferson	.05
392	Mark Lemke	.05
393	Cecil Fielder	.05
394	Reggie Sanders	.05
395	Darryl Hamilton	.05
396	Daryl Boston	.05
397	Pat Kelly	.05

No.	Player	Price
398	Joe Orsulak	.05
399	Ed Sprague	.05
400	Eric Anthony	.05
401	Scott Sanderson	.05
402	Jim Gott	.05
403	Ron Karkovice	.05
404	Phil Plantier	.05
405	David Cone	.05
406	Robby Thompson	.05
407	Dave Winfield	.40
408	Dwight Smith	.05
409	Ruben Sierra	.05
410	Jack Armstrong	.05
411	Mike Felder	.05
412	Wil Cordero	.05
413	Julio Franco	.05
414	Howard Johnson	.05
415	Mark McLemore	.05
416	Pete Incaviglia	.05
417	John Valentin	.05
418	Tim Wakefield	.05
419	Jose Mesa	.05
420	Bernard Gilkey	.05
421	Kirk Gibson	.05
422	Dave Justice	.05
423	Tom Brunansky	.05
424	John Smiley	.05
425	Kevin Maas	.05
426	Doug Drabek	.05
427	Paul Molitor	.40
428	Darryl Strawberry	.05
429	Tim Naehring	.05
430	Bill Swift	.05
431	Ellis Burks	.05
432	Greg Hibbard	.05
433	Felix Jose	.05
434	Bret Barberie	.05
435	Pedro Munoz	.05
436	Darrin Fletcher	.05
437	Bobby Witt	.05
438	Wes Chamberlain	.05
439	Mackey Sasser	.05
440	Mark Whiten	.05
441	Harold Reynolds	.05
442	Greg Olson	.05
443	Billy Hatcher	.05
444	Joe Oliver	.05
445	Sandy Alomar Jr.	.05
446	Tim Wallach	.05
447	Karl Rhodes	.05
448	Royce Clayton	.05
449	Cal Eldred	.05
450	Rick Wilkins	.05
451	Mike Stanley	.05
452	Charlie Hough	.05
453	Jack Morris	.05
454	Jon Ratliff RC	.05
455	Rene Gonzales	.05
456	Eddie Taubensee	.05
457	Roberto Hernandez	.05
458	Todd Hundley	.05
459	Mike MacFarlane	.05
460	Mickey Morandini	.05
461	Scott Erickson	.05
462	Lonnie Smith	.05
463	Dave Henderson	.05
464	Ryan Klesko	.05
465	Edgar Martinez	.05
466	Tom Pagnozzi	.05
467	Charlie Leibrandt	.05
468	Brian Anderson RC	.10
469	Harold Baines	.05
470	Tim Belcher	.05
471	Andre Dawson	.05
472	Eric Young	.05
473	Paul Sorrento	.05
474	Luis Gonzalez	.05
475	Rob Deer	.05
476	Mike Piazza	.65
477	Kevin Reimer	.05
478	Jeff Gardner	.05
479	Melido Perez	.05
480	Darren Lewis	.05
481	Duane Ward	.05
482	Rey Sanchez	.05
483	Mark Lewis	.05
484	Jeff Conine	.05
485	Joey Cora	.05
486	Trot Nixon RC	.50
487	Kevin McReynolds	.05
488	Mike Lansing	.05
489	Mike Pagliarulo	.05
490	Mariano Duncan	.05
491	Mike Bordick	.05
492	Kevin Young	.05
493	Dave Valle	.05
494	Wayne Gomes RC	.05
495	Rafael Palmeiro	.05
496	Deion Sanders	.05
497	Rick Sutcliffe	.05
498	Randy Milligan	.05
499	Carlos Quintana	.05
500	Chris Turner	.05
501	Thomas Howard	.05
502	Greg Swindell	.05
503	Chad Kreuter	.05
504	Eric Davis	.05
505	Dickie Thon	.05
506	Matt Drews RC	.05
507	Spike Owen	.05
508	Rod Beck	.05
509	Pat Hentgen	.05
510	Sammy Sosa	.50
511	J.T. Snow	.05
512	Chuck Carr	.05
513	Bo Jackson	.10
514	Dennis Martinez	.05
515	Phil Hiatt	.05
516	Jeff Kent	.05
517	Brooks Kieschnick RC	.05
518	Kirk Presley RC	.05
519	Kevin Seitzer	.05
520	Carlos Garcia	.05
521	Mike Blowers	.05
522	Luis Alicea	.05
523	David Hulse	.05
524	Greg Maddux	.50
525	Gregg Olson	.05
526	Hal Morris	.05
527	Daron Kirkreit	.05
528	David Nied	.05
529	Jeff Russell	.05
530	Kevin Gross	.05
531	John Doherty	.05
532	Matt Brunson RC	.05
533	Dave Nilsson	.05
534	Randy Myers	.05
535	Steve Farr	.05
536	Billy Wagner RC	.10
537	Darnell Coles	.05
538	Frank Tanana	.05
539	Tim Salmon	.05
540	Kim Batiste	.05
541	George Bell	.05
542	Tom Henke	.05
543	Sam Horn	.05
544	Doug Jones	.05
545	Scott Leius	.05
546	Al Martin	.05
547	Bob Welch	.05
548	Scott Christman RC	.05
549	Norm Charlton	.05
550	Mark McGwire	.75
551	Greg McMichael	.05
552	Tim Costo	.05
553	Rodney Bolton	.05
554	Pedro Martinez	.40
555	Marc Valdes	.05
556	Darrell Whitmore	.05
557	Tim Bogar	.05
558	Steve Karsay	.05
559	Danny Bautista	.05
560	Jeffrey Hammonds	.05
561	Aaron Sele	.05
562	Russ Springer	.05
563	Jason Bere	.05
564	Billy Brewer	.05
565	Sterling Hitchcock	.05
566	Bobby Munoz	.05
567	Craig Paquette	.05
568	Bret Boone	.05
569	Dan Peltier	.05
570	Jeromy Burnitz	.05
571	John Wasdin RC	.05
572	Chipper Jones	.50
573	Jamey Wright RC	.05
574	Jeff Granger	.05
575	Jay Powell RC	.05
576	Ryan Thompson	.05
577	Lou Frazier	.05
578	Paul Wagner	.05
579	Brad Ausmus	.05
580	Jack Voigt	.05
581	Kevin Rogers	.05
582	Damon Buford	.05
583	Paul Quantrill	.05
584	Marc Newfield	.05
585	Derrek Lee RC	1.00
586	Shane Reynolds	.05
587	Cliff Floyd	.05
588	Jeff Schwarz	.05
589	Ross Powell RC	.05
590	Gerald Williams	.05
591	Mike Trombley	.05
592	Ken Ryan	.05
593	John O'Donoghue	.05
594	Rod Correia	.05
595	Darrell Sherman	.05
596	Steve Scarsone	.05
597	Sherman Obando	.05
598	Kurt Abbott	.05
599	Dave Telgheder	.05
600	Rick Trlicek	.05
601	Carl Everett	.05
602	Luis Ortiz	.05
603	Larry Luebbers RC	.05
604	Kevin Roberson	.05
605	Butch Huskey	.05
606	Benji Gil	.05
607	Todd Van Poppel	.05
608	Mark Hutton	.05
609	Chip Hale	.05
610	Matt Maysey	.05
611	Scott Ruffcorn	.05
612	Hilly Hathaway	.05
613	Allen Watson	.05
614	Carlos Delgado	.30
615	Roberto Mejia	.05
616	Turk Wendell	.05
617	Tony Tarasco	.05
618	Raul Mondesi	.05
619	Kevin Stocker	.05
620	Javier Lopez	.05
621	Keith Kessinger RC	.05
622	Bob Hamelin	.05
623	John Roper	.05
624	Len Dykstra (World Series)	.05
625	Joe Carter (World Series)	.05
626	Jim Abbott/Highlight	.05
627	Lee Smith/Highlight	.05
628	Ken Griffey Jr./Highlight	.35
629	Dave Winfield/Highlight	.05
630	Darryl Kile/Highlight	.05
631	Frank Thomas/MVP	.25
632	Barry Bonds/MVP	.50
633	Jack McDowell (Cy Young)	.05
634	Greg Maddux (Cy Young)	.25
635	Tim Salmon (ROY)	.05
636	Mike Piazza (ROY)	.40
637	Brian Turang RC	.05
638	Rondell White	.05
639	Nigel Wilson	.05
640	Torii Hunter RC	.75
641	Salomon Torres	.05
642	Kevin Higgins	.05
643	Eric Wedge	.05
644	Roger Salkeld	.05
645	Manny Ramirez	.40
646	Jeff McNeely	.05
647	Braves Checklist	.05
648	Cubs Checklist	.05
649	Reds Checklist	.05
650	Rockies Checklist	.05
651	Marlins Checklist	.05
652	Astros Checklist	.05
653	Dodgers Checklist	.05
654	Expos Checklist	.05
655	Mets Checklist	.05
656	Phillies Checklist	.05
657	Pirates Checklist	.05
658	Cardinals Checklist	.05
659	Padres Checklist	.05
660	Giants Checklist	.05

Gold Rush

Opting to include one insert card in each pack of its 1994 product, Score created a "Gold Rush" version of each card in its regular set. Gold Rush cards are basically the same as their counterparts with a few enhancements. Card fronts are printed on foil with a gold border and a Score Gold Rush logo in one of the upper corners. The background of the photo has been metalized, allowing the color player portion to stand out in sharp contrast. Backs are identical to the regular cards except for the appearance of a large Gold Rush logo under the typography.

	NM/M
Complete Set (660):	40.00
Common Player:	.15
Stars:	2X

Boys of Summer

A heavy emphasis on rookies and recent rookies is noted in this insert set. Released in two series, cards #1-30 are found in Series 1, with #31-60 packaged with Series 2. Fronts feature a color action photo on which the background has been rendered in a blurred watercolor effect. A hot-color aura separates the player from the background. The player's name appears vertically in gold foil. Backs have the background in reds and orange with a portrait-style player photo on one side and a large "Boys of Summer" logo on the other. A short description of the player's talents appears at center.

	NM/M
Complete Set (60):	25.00
Common Player:	.25

No.	Player	Price
1	Jeff Conine	.25
2	Aaron Sele	.25
3	Kevin Stocker	.25
4	Pat Meares	.25
5	Jeromy Burnitz	.25
6	Mike Piazza	6.00
7	Allen Watson	.25
8	Jeffrey Hammonds	.25
9	Kevin Roberson	.25
10	Hilly Hathaway	.25
11	Kirk Reuter	.25
12	Eduardo Perez	.25
13	Ricky Gutierrez	.25
14	Domingo Jean	.25
15	David Nied	.25
16	Wayne Kirby	.25
17	Mike Lansing	.25
18	Jason Bere	.25
19	Brent Gates	.25
20	Javier Lopez	.25
21	Greg McMichael	.25
22	David Hulse	.25
23	Roberto Mejia	.25
24	Tim Salmon	.50
25	Rene Arocha	.25
26	Bret Boone	.25
27	David McCarty	.25
28	Todd Van Poppel	.25
29	Lance Painter	.25
30	Erik Pappas	.25
31	Chuck Carr	.25
32	Mark Hutton	.25
33	Jeff McNeely	.25
34	Willie Greene	.25
35	Nigel Wilson	.25
36	Rondell White	.25
37	Brian Turang	.25
38	Manny Ramirez	3.00
39	Salomon Torres	.25
40	Melvin Nieves	.25
41	Ryan Klesko	.25
42	Keith Kessinger	.25
43	Eric Wedge	.25
44	Bob Hamelin	.25
45	Carlos Delgado	2.50
46	Marc Newfield	.25
47	Raul Mondesi	.25
48	Tim Costo	.25
49	Pedro Martinez	3.00
50	Steve Karsay	.25
51	Danny Bautista	.25
52	Butch Huskey	.25
53	Kurt Abbott	.25
54	Darrell Sherman	.25
55	Damon Buford	.25
56	Ross Powell	.25
57	Darrell Whitmore	.25
58	Chipper Jones	5.00
59	Jeff Granger	.25
60	Cliff Floyd	.25

Dream Team

Score's 1994 "Dream Team," one top player at each position, was featured in a 10-card insert set. The stars were decked out in vintage uniforms and equipment for the photos. Green and black bars at top and bottom frame the photo, and all printing on the front is in gold foil. Backs have a white background with green highlights. A color player portrait photo is featured, along with a brief justification for the player's selection to the squad. Cards are UV coated on both sides. Stated odds of finding a Dream Team insert were given as one per 72 packs.

	NM/M
Complete Set (10):	15.00
Common Player:	1.00
1 Mike Mussina	2.00
2 Tom Glavine	2.00
3 Don Mattingly	10.00
4 Carlos Baerga	1.00
5 Barry Larkin	1.00
6 Matt Williams	1.00
7 Juan Gonzalez	4.00
8 Andy Van Slyke	1.00
9 Larry Walker	1.00
10 Mike Stanley	1.00

Gold Stars

Limited to inclusion in hobby packs, Score's 60-card "Gold Stars" insert set features 30 National League players, found in Series I packs, and 30 American Leaguers inserted with Series II. Stated odds of finding a Gold Stars card were listed on the wrapper as one in 18 packs. A notation on the cards' back indicates that no more than 6,500 sets of Gold Stars were produced. The high-tech cards feature a color player action photo, the full-bleed background of which has been converted to metallic tones. Backs have a graduated gold background with a portrait-style color player photo.

	NM/M
Complete Set (60):	40.00
Common Player:	.25

No.	Player	Price
1	Barry Bonds	6.00
2	Orlando Merced	.25
3	Mark Grace	.25
4	Darren Daulton	.25
5	Jeff Blauser	.25
6	Deion Sanders	.25
7	John Kruk	.25
8	Jeff Bagwell	2.50
9	Gregg Jefferies	.25
10	Matt Williams	.25
11	Andres Galarraga	.25
12	Jay Bell	.25
13	Mike Piazza	4.50
14	Ron Gant	.25
15	Barry Larkin	.25
16	Tom Glavine	.50
17	Len Dykstra	.25
18	Fred McGriff	.25
19	Andy Van Slyke	.25
20	Gary Sheffield	.75
21	John Burkett	.25
22	Dante Bichette	.25
23	Tony Gwynn	3.50
24	Dave Justice	.25
25	Marquis Grissom	.25
26	Bobby Bonilla	.25
27	Larry Walker	.25
28	Brett Butler	.25
29	Robby Thompson	.25
30	Jeff Conine	.25
31	Joe Carter	.25
32	Ken Griffey Jr.	4.50
33	Juan Gonzalez	1.25
34	Rickey Henderson	2.50
35	Bo Jackson	.35
36	Cal Ripken, Jr.	6.00
37	John Olerud	.25
38	Carlos Baerga	.25
39	Jack McDowell	.25
40	Cecil Fielder	.25
41	Kenny Lofton	.25
42	Roberto Alomar	1.00
43	Randy Johnson	2.50
44	Tim Salmon	.25
45	Frank Thomas	2.50
46	Albert Belle	.25
47	Greg Vaughn	.25
48	Travis Fryman	.25
49	Don Mattingly	4.00
50	Wade Boggs	3.50
51	Mo Vaughn	.25
52	Kirby Puckett	3.50
53	Devon White	.25
54	Tony Phillips	.25
55	Brian Harper	.25
56	Chad Curtis	.25
57	Paul Molitor	2.50
58	Ivan Rodriguez	2.00
59	Rafael Palmeiro	2.00
60	Brian McRae	.25

The Cycle

Leaders in the previous season's production of singles, doubles, triples and home runs are featured in this insert set which was packaged with Series II Score. Player action photos pop out of a circle at center and are surrounded by dark blue borders. "The Cycle" in printed in green at top. The player's name is in gold foil at bottom, printed over an infield diagram in a green strip. The stat which earned the player inclusion in the set is in gold foil at bottom right. On back are the rankings for the statistical category. Cards are numbered with a "TC" prefix.

	NM/M
Complete Set (20):	12.00
Common Player:	.50
1 Brett Butler	.50
2 Kenny Lofton	.50
3 Paul Molitor	2.00
4 Carlos Baerga	.50
5 Gregg Jefferies, Tony Phillips	.50
6 John Olerud	.50
7 Charlie Hayes	.50
8 Len Dykstra	.50
9 Dante Bichette	.50
10 Devon White	.50
11 Lance Johnson	.50
12 Joey Cora, Steve Finley	.50
13 Tony Fernandez	.50
14 David Hulse, Brett Butler	.50
15 Jay Bell, Brian McRae, Mickey Morandini	.50
16 Juan Gonzalez, Barry Bonds	4.00
17 Ken Griffey Jr.	4.00
18 Frank Thomas	2.50
19 Dave Justice	.50
20 Matt Williams, Albert Belle	.50

Cal Ripken, Jr.

Although the cards themselves do not indicate it, this issue was co-sponsored by Burger King and Coke, and distributed in BK restaurants in the Baltimore-Washington area. Cards were available in three-card packs for 25 cents with the purchase of a Coke product. Each pack contains two regular cards and a gold card. Each of the nine cards could be found in a regular and gold version. Cards feature color photos with a semi-circular black border at top or left. "Score '94" appears in orange in one of the upper corners, along with an Orioles logo. Cal Ripken, Jr.'s name appears at the bottom. On the gold premium version, there is a gold-foil circle around the Orioles logo and Ripken's name appears in gold, rather than white. Backs have a smaller color photo, again meeting at a semi-circular edge with the black border at left and bottom. In the black are another Score logo, a card number, an Orioles logo, a headline and a few career details and/or stats. Cards are UV coated on each side. Several hundred of the cards were personally autographed by Ripken and distributed in a drawing.

		NM/M
Complete Set (9):		3.00
Complete Set, Gold (9):		6.00
Common Player:		.50
Common Card, Gold:		1.00
Autographed Card:		200.00
1	Double Honors	.50
1a	Double Honors/Gold	1.00
2	Perennial All-Star	.50
2a	Perennial All-Star/Gold	1.00
3	Peerless Power	.50
3a	Peerless Power/Gold	1.00
4	Fitness Fan	.50
4a	Fitness Fan/Gold	1.00
5	Prime Concerns	.50
5a	Prime Concerns/Gold	1.00
6	Home Run Club	.50
6a	Home Run Club/Gold	1.00
7	The Iron Man	.50
7a	The Iron Man/Gold	1.00
8	Heavy Hitter	.50
8a	Heavy Hitter/Gold	1.00
9	Gold Glover	.50
9a	Gold Glover/Gold	1.00

1994 Score Rookie/Traded Samples

To introduce the various types of card which would be included in the 1994 Score Rookie/Traded set, the company produced this sample set. Cards are virtually identical to the issued versions except for the overprint "SAMPLE" running diagonally on front and back. The Rafael Palmeiro "Changing Places" sample card does not feature the red foil logo found on issued cards.

		NM/M
Complete Set (11):		7.50
Common Player:		.50
1RT	Lee Smith	.50
2CP	Rafael Palmeiro (Changing Places)	2.00
2RT	Will Clark	.50
2SU	Manny Ramirez (Super Rookie)	2.50
3RT	Bo Jackson (Gold Rush)	1.00
4RT	Ellis Burks	.50
5RT	Eddie Murray	2.00
6RT	Delino DeShields	.50
102RT	Carlos Delgado	1.50
---	September Call-Up Winner Card	.10
---	Hobby header card	.10
---	Retail header card	.10

1994 Score Rookie/Traded

Score Rookie & Traded completed the 1994 baseball season with a 165-card update set. These were available in both retail and hobby packs.

Score issued Super Rookies and Changing Places insert sets, as well as a Traded Redemption card and a parallel Gold Rush set. Basic cards features red front borders. Team logos are in a bottom corner in a gold polygon. One of the upper corners contains a green polygon with a gold Score logo. Most cards #71-163 feature a square multi-colored "Rookie '94" logo in a lower corner. Backs of all cards have a purple background. Traded players' card backs are vertical and contain two additional photos. Backs of the rookie cards are horizontal and feature a portrait photo at left. The "Rookie '94" logo is repeated in the upper-right corner. This is in reverse of the fronts, on which traded players have a single photo and rookie cards have both portrait and action photos. Card numbers have an "RT" prefix.

		NM/M
Complete Set (165):		5.00
Common Player:		.05
Gold Rush:		2X
Pack (10):		.40
Wax Box (36):		9.00
1	Will Clark	.05
2	Lee Smith	.05
3	Bo Jackson	.10
4	Ellis Burks	.05
5	Eddie Murray	1.00
6	Delino DeShields	.05
7	Erik Hanson	.05
8	Rafael Palmeiro	.75
9	Luis Polonia	.05
10	Omar Vizquel	.05
11	Kurt Abbott	.05
12	Vince Coleman	.05
13	Rickey Henderson	1.00
14	Terry Mulholland	.05
15	Greg Hibbard	.05
16	Walt Weiss	.05
17	Chris Sabo	.05
18	Dave Henderson	.05
19	Rick Sutcliffe	.05
20	Harold Reynolds	.05
21	Jack Morris	.05
22	Dan Wilson	.05
23	Dave Magadan	.05
24	Dennis Martinez	.05
25	Wes Chamberlain	.05
26	Otis Nixon	.05
27	Eric Anthony	.05
28	Randy Milligan	.05
29	Julio Franco	.05
30	Kevin McReynolds	.05
31	Anthony Young	.05
32	Brian Harper	.05
33	Lenny Harris	.05
34	Eddie Taubensee	.05
35	David Segui	.05
36	Stan Javier	.05
37	Felix Fermin	.05
38	Darrin Jackson	.05
39	Tony Fernandez	.05
40	Jose Vizcaino	.05
41	Willie Banks	.05
42	Brian Hunter	.05
43	Reggie Jefferson	.05
44	Junior Felix	.05
45	Jack Armstrong	.05
46	Bip Roberts	.05
47	Jerry Browne	.05
48	Marvin Freeman	.05
49	Jody Reed	.05
50	Alex Cole	.05
51	Sid Fernandez	.05
52	Pete Smith	.05
53	Xavier Hernandez	.05
54	Scott Sanderson	.05
55	Turner Ward	.05
56	Rex Hudler	.05
57	Deion Sanders	.05
58	Sid Bream	.05
59	Tony Pena	.05

		NM/M
60	Bret Boone	.05
61	Bobby Ayala	.05
62	Pedro Martinez	1.00
63	Howard Johnson	.05
64	Mark Portugal	.05
65	Roberto Kelly	.05
66	Spike Owen	.05
67	Jeff Treadway	.05
68	Mike Harkey	.05
69	Doug Jones	.05
70	Steve Farr	.05
71	Billy Taylor	.05
72	Manny Ramirez	1.00
73	Bob Hamelin	.05
74	Steve Karsay	.05
75	Ryan Klesko	.05
76	Cliff Floyd	.05
77	Jeffrey Hammonds	.05
78	Javier Lopez	.05
79	Roger Salkeld	.05
80	Hector Carrasco	.05
81	Gerald Williams	.05
82	Raul Mondesi	.05
83	Sterling Hitchcock	.05
84	Danny Bautista	.05
85	Chris Turner	.05
86	Shane Reynolds	.05
87	Rondell White	.05
88	Salomon Torres	.05
89	Turk Wendell	.05
90	Tony Tarasco	.05
91	Shawn Green	.65
92	Greg Colbrunn	.05
93	Eddie Zambrano	.05
94	Rich Becker	.05
95	Chris Gomez	.05
96	John Patterson	.05
97	Derek Parks	.05
98	Rich Rowland	.05
99	James Mouton	.05
100	Tim Hyers	.05
101	Jose Valentin	.05
102	Carlos Delgado	.65
103	Robert Esenhoorn	.05
104	John Hudek	.05
105	Domingo Cedeno	.05
106	Denny Hocking	.05
107	Greg Pirkl	.05
108	Mark Smith	.05
109	Paul Shuey	.05
110	Jorge Fabregas	.05
111	Rikkert Faneyte	.05
112	Rob Butler	.05
113	Darren Oliver	.05
114	Troy O'Leary	.05
115	Scott Brow	.05
116	Tony Eusebio	.05
117	Carlos Reyes	.05
118	J.R. Phillips	.05
119	Alex Diaz	.05
120	Charles Johnson	.05
121	Nate Minchey	.05
122	Scott Sanders	.05
123	Daryl Boston	.05
124	Joey Hamilton	.05
125	Brian Anderson	.05
126	Dan Miceli	.05
127	Tom Brunansky	.05
128	Dave Staton	.05
129	Mike Oquist	.05
130	John Mabry	.05
131	Norberto Martin	.05
132	Hector Fajardo	.05
133	Mark Hutton	.05
134	Fernando Vina	.05
135	Lee Tinsley	.05
136	Chan Ho Park RC	1.50
137	Paul Spoljaric	.05
138	Matias Carrillo	.05
139	Mark Kiefer	.05
140	Stan Royer	.05
141	Bryan Eversgerd	.05
143	Joe Hall	.05
144	Johnny Ruffin	.05
145	Alex Gonzalez	.05
146	Keith Lockhart	.05
147	Tom Marsh	.05
148	Tony Longmire	.05
149	Keith Mitchell	.05
150	Melvin Nieves	.05
151	Kelly Stinnett	.05
152	Miguel Jimenez	.05
153	Jeff Juden	.05
154	Matt Walbeck	.05
155	Marc Newfield	.05
156	Matt Mieske	.05
157	Marcus Moore	.05
158	Jose Lima RC	.25
159	Mike Kelly	.05
160	Jim Edmonds	.05
161	Steve Trachsel	.05
162	Greg Blosser	.05
163	Mark Acre	.05
164	AL Checklist	.05
165	NL Checklist	.05

Gold Rush

Each pack of Score Rookie and Traded cards included one Gold Rush parallel version of one of the set's cards. The insert cards feature fronts that are printed directly on gold foil and include a Gold Rush logo in an upper corner.

		NM/M
Complete Set (165):		15.00
Common Player:		.15
Stars:		2X

Changing Places

Changing Places documents the relocation of 10 veteran stars. Cards were inserted into one of every 36 retail or hobby packs. Fronts have a color photo of the player in his new uniform and are enhanced with red foil. Backs have a montage of color and black-and-white photos and a few words about the trade. Card numbers have a "CP" prefix.

		NM/M
Complete Set (10):		15.00
Common Player:		1.00
1	Will Clark	1.00
2	Rafael Palmeiro	4.00
3	Roberto Kelly	1.00
4	Bo Jackson	1.25
5	Otis Nixon	1.00
6	Rickey Henderson	5.00
7	Ellis Burks	1.00
8	Lee Smith	1.00
9	Delino DeShields	1.00
10	Deion Sanders	1.00

Super Rookies

Super Rookies is an 18-card set honoring baseball's brightest young stars. They appear only in hobby packs at a rate of one every 36 packs. Fronts are printed on foil, with a multi-colored border. Backs feature another photo, most of which is rendered in single-color blocks, along with a few words about the player and a large Super Rookie logo. Cards are numbered with an "SU" prefix.

		NM/M
Complete Set (18):		15.00
Common Player:		1.00
1	Carlos Delgado	5.00
2	Manny Ramirez	5.00
3	Ryan Klesko	1.00

		NM/M
4	Raul Mondesi	1.00
5	Bob Hamelin	1.00
6	Steve Karsay	1.00
7	Jeffrey Hammonds	1.00
8	Cliff Floyd	1.00
9	Kurt Abbott	1.00
10	Marc Newfield	1.00
11	Javier Lopez	1.00
12	Rich Becker	1.00
13	Greg Pirkl	1.00
14	Rondell White	1.00
15	James Mouton	1.00
16	Tony Tarasco	1.00
17	Brian Anderson	1.00
18	Jim Edmonds	1.00

Redemption Card

The Score Rookie and Traded Redemption card was inserted at a rate of one every 240 packs. It gave collectors a chance to mail in for the best rookie in the annual September call-up: Alex Rodriguez.

		NM/M
September Call-Up redemption card (Expired)		2.00
Alex Rodriguez		400.00

1995 Score Samples

This cello-wrapped 10-card sample set of 1995 Score cards was sent to dealers to preview the issue. Cards are identical to the regular-issue versions except they have a diagonal white "SAMPLE" printed on front and back.

		NM/M
Complete Set (10):		6.00
Common Player:		.50
2	Roberto Alomar	.75
4	Jose Canseco	1.00
5	Matt Williams	.50
5HG	Cal Ripken, Jr. (Hall of Gold)	2.50
8DP	McKay Christensen ('94 Draft Pick)	.50
221	Jeff Bagwell	1.25
223	Albert Belle	.50
224	Chuck Carr	.50
288	Jorge Fabregas (Rookie)	.50
	Header Card	.05

1995 Score

Score 1995 Baseball is composed of 605 cards, issued in two series; the first comprising 330 cards, the second, 275. Basic cards have photos placed on a dirt-like background with a green strip running up each side. The player's name, position, and team logo is given in white letters on a blue strip across the bottom. Backs resemble the fronts, except with a

smaller, portrait photo of the player, which leaves room for statistics and biographical information. Score had a parallel set of Gold Rush cards, along with several other series of inserts. Eleven players in Series 2 can be found in two team variations as the result of a redemption program for updated cards.

		NM/M
Complete Set (605):		13.50
Common Player:		.05
Gold Rush:		2X
Platinums:		3X
Series 1 or 2 Pack (12):		.75
Series 1 or 2 Box (36):		12.50
1	Frank Thomas	.50
2	Roberto Alomar	.15
3	Cal Ripken, Jr.	1.50
4	Jose Canseco	.30
5	Matt Williams	.05
6	Esteban Beltre	.05
7	Domingo Cedeno	.05
8	John Valentin	.05
9	Glenallen Hill	.05
10	Rafael Belliard	.05
11	Randy Myers	.05
12	Mo Vaughn	.05
13	Hector Carrasco	.05
14	Chili Davis	.05
15	Dante Bichette	.05
16	Darren Jackson	.05
17	Mike Piazza	.75
18	Junior Felix	.05
19	Moises Alou	.05
20	Mark Gubicza	.05
21	Bret Saberhagen	.05
22	Len Dykstra	.05
23	Steve Howe	.05
24	Mark Dewey	.05
25	Brian Harper	.05
26	Ozzie Smith	.60
27	Scott Erickson	.05
28	Tony Gwynn	.60
29	Bob Welch	.05
30	Barry Bonds	1.50
31	Leo Gomez	.05
32	Greg Maddux	.60
33	Mike Greenwell	.05
34	Sammy Sosa	.60
35	Darnell Coles	.05
36	Tommy Greene	.05
37	Will Clark	.05
38	Steve Ontiveros	.05
39	Stan Javier	.05
40	Bip Roberts	.05
41	Paul O'Neill	.05
42	Bill Haselman	.05
43	Shane Mack	.05
44	Orlando Merced	.05
45	Kevin Seitzer	.05
46	Trevor Hoffman	.05
47	Greg Gagne	.05
48	Jeff Kent	.05
49	Tony Phillips	.05
50	Ken Hill	.05
51	Carlos Baerga	.05
52	Henry Rodriguez	.05
53	Scott Sanderson	.05
54	Jeff Conine	.05
55	Chris Turner	.05
56	Ken Caminiti	.05
57	Harold Baines	.05
58	Charlie Hayes	.05
59	Roberto Kelly	.05
60	John Olerud	.05
61	Tim Davis	.05
62	Rich Rowland	.05
63	Rey Sanchez	.05
64	Junior Ortiz	.05
65	Ricky Gutierrez	.05
66	Rex Hudler	.05
67	Johnny Ruffin	.05
68	Jay Buhner	.05
69	Tom Pagnozzi	.05
70	Julio Franco	.05
71	Eric Young	.05
72	Mike Bordick	.05
73	Don Slaught	.05
74	Goose Gossage	.05
75	Lonnie Smith	.05
76	Jimmy Key	.05
77	Dave Hollins	.05
78	Mickey Tettleton	.05

79 Luis Gonzalez .05
80 Dave Winfield .50
81 Ryan Thompson .05
82 Felix Jose .05
83 Rusty Meacham .05
84 Darryl Hamilton .05
85 John Wetteland .05
86 Tom Brunansky .05
87 Mark Lemke .05
88 Spike Owen .05
89 Shawon Dunston .05
90 Wilson Alvarez .05
91 Lee Smith .05
92 Scott Kamieniecki .05
93 Jacob Brumfield .05
94 Kirk Gibson .05
95 Joe Girardi .05
96 Mike Macfarlane .05
97 Greg Colbrunn .05
98 Ricky Bones .05
99 Delino DeShields .05
100 Pat Meares .05
101 Jeff Fassero .05
102 Jim Leyritz .05
103 Gary Redus .05
104 Terry Steinbach .05
105 Kevin McReynolds .05
106 Felix Fermin .05
107 Danny Jackson .05
108 Chris James .05
109 Jeff King .05
110 Pat Hentgen .05
111 Gerald Perry .05
112 Tim Raines .05
113 Eddie Williams .05
114 Jamie Moyer .05
115 Bud Black .05
116 Chris Gomez .05
117 Luis Lopez .05
118 Roger Clemens .65
119 Javier Lopez .10
120 Dave Nilsson .05
121 Karl Rhodes .05
122 Rick Aguilera .05
123 Tony Fernandez .05
124 Bernie Williams .05
125 James Mouton .05
126 Mark Langston .05
127 Mike Lansing .05
128 Tino Martinez .05
129 Joe Orsulak .05
130 David Hulse .05
131 Pete Incaviglia .05
132 Mark Clark .05
133 Tony Eusebio .05
134 Chuck Finley .05
135 Lou Frazier .05
136 Craig Grebeck .05
137 Kelly Stinnett .05
138 Paul Shuey .05
139 David Nied .05
140 Billy Brewer .05
141 Dave Weathers .05
142 Scott Leius .05
143 Brian Jordan .05
144 Melido Perez .05
145 Tony Tarasco .05
146 Dan Wilson .05
147 Rondell White .05
148 Mike Henneman .05
149 Brian Johnson .05
150 Tom Henke .05
151 John Patterson .05
152 Bobby Witt .05
153 Eddie Taubensee .05
154 Pat Borders .05
155 Ramon Martinez .05
156 Mike Kingery .05
157 Zane Smith .05
158 Benito Santiago .05
159 Matias Carrillo .05
160 Scott Brosius .05
161 Dave Clark .05
162 Mark McLemore .05
163 Curt Schilling .30
164 J.T. Snow .05
165 Rod Beck .05
166 Scott Fletcher .05
167 Bob Tewksbury .05
168 Mike LaValliere .05
169 Dave Hansen .05
170 Pedro Martinez .50
171 Kirk Rueter .05
172 Jose Lind .05
173 Luis Alicea .05
174 Mike Moore .05
175 Andy Ashby .05
176 Jody Reed .05
177 Darryl Kile .05
178 Carl Willis .05
179 Jeromy Burnitz .05
180 Mike Gallego .05
181 W. Van Landingham RC .05
182 Sid Fernandez .05
183 Kim Batiste .05
184 Greg Myers .05
185 Steve Avery .05
186 Steve Farr .05
187 Robb Nen .05
188 Dan Pasqua .05
189 Bruce Ruffin .05
190 Jose Valentin .05
191 Willie Banks .05
192 Mike Aldrete .05
193 Randy Milligan .05
194 Steve Karsay .05
195 Mike Stanley .05
196 Jose Mesa .05

197 Tom Browning .05
198 John Vander Wal .05
199 Kevin Brown .05
200 Mike Oquist .05
201 Greg Swindell .05
202 Eddie Zambrano .05
203 Joe Boever .05
204 Gary Varsho .05
205 Chris Gwynn .05
206 David Howard .05
207 Jerome Walton .05
208 Danny Darwin .05
209 Darryl Strawberry .05
210 Todd Van Poppel .05
211 Scott Livingstone .05
212 Dave Fleming .05
213 Todd Worrell .05
214 Carlos Delgado .40
215 Bill Pecota .05
216 Jim Lindeman .05
217 Rick White .05
218 Jose Oquendo .05
219 Tony Castillo .05
220 Fernando Vina .05
221 Jeff Bagwell .50
222 Randy Johnson .50
223 Albert Belle .05
224 Chuck Carr .05
225 Mark Leiter .05
226 Hal Morris .05
227 Robin Ventura .05
228 Mike Munoz .05
229 Jim Thome .40
230 Mario Diaz .05
231 John Doherty .05
232 Bobby Jones .05
233 Raul Mondesi .05
234 Ricky Jordan .05
235 John Jaha .05
236 Carlos Garcia .05
237 Kirby Puckett .60
238 Orel Hershiser .05
239 Don Mattingly .65
240 Sid Bream .05
241 Brent Gates .05
242 Tony Longmire .05
243 Robby Thompson .05
244 Rick Sutcliffe .05
245 Dean Palmer .05
246 Marquis Grissom .05
247 Paul Molitor .50
248 Mark Carreon .05
249 Jack Voight .05
250 Greg McMichael (Photo on front is Mike Stanton.) .05
251 Damon Berryhill .05
252 Brian Dorsett .05
253 Jim Edmonds .05
254 Barry Larkin .05
255 Jack McDowell .05
256 Wally Joyner .05
257 Eddie Murray .50
258 Lenny Webster .05
259 Milt Cuyler .05
260 Todd Benzinger .05
261 Vince Coleman .05
262 Todd Stottlemyre .05
263 Turner Ward .05
264 Ray Lankford .05
265 Matt Walbeck .05
266 Deion Sanders .05
267 Gerald Williams .05
268 Jim Gott .05
269 Jeff Frye .05
270 Jose Rijo .05
271 Dave Justice .05
272 Ismael Valdes .05
273 Ben McDonald .05
274 Darren Lewis .05
275 Graeme Lloyd .05
276 Luis Ortiz .05
277 Julian Tavarez .05
278 Mark Dalesandro .05
279 Brett Merriman .05
280 Ricky Bottalico .05
281 Robert Eenhoorn .05
282 Rikkert Faneyte .05
283 Mike Kelly .05
284 Mark Smith .05
285 Turk Wendell .05
286 Greg Blosser .05
287 Garey Ingram .05
288 Jorge Fabregas .05
289 Blaise Ilsley .05
290 Joe Hall .05
291 Orlando Miller .05
292 Jose Lima .05
293 Greg O'Halloran .05
294 Mark Kiefer .05
295 Jose Oliva .05
296 Rich Becker .05
297 Brian Hunter .05
298 Dave Silvestri .05
299 Armando Benitez RC .10
300 Darren Dreifort .05
301 John Mabry .05
302 Greg Pirkl .05
303 J.R. Phillips .05
304 Shawn Green .30
305 Roberto Petagine .05
306 Keith Lockhart .05
307 Jonathon Hurst .05
308 Paul Spoljaric .05
309 Mike Lieberthal .05
310 Garret Anderson .05
311 John Johnston .05
312 Alex Rodriguez 1.50
313 Kent Mercker .05

314 John Valentin .05
315 Kenny Rogers .05
316 Fred McGriff .05
317 Atlanta Braves, Baltimore Orioles .05
318 Chicago Cubs, Boston Red Sox .05
319 Cincinnati Reds, California Angels .05
320 Colorado Rockies, Chicago White Sox .05
321 Cleveland Indians, Florida Marlins .05
322 Houston Astros, Detroit Tigers .05
323 Los Angels Dodgers, Kansas City Royals .05
324 Montreal Expos, Milwaukee Brewers .05
325 New York Mets, Minnesota Twins .05
326 Philadelphia Phillies, New York Yankees .05
327 Pittsburgh Pirates, Oakland Athletics .05
328 San Diego Padres, Seattle Mariners .05
329 San Francisco Giants, Texas Rangers .05
330 St. Louis Cardinals, Toronto Blue Jays .05
331 Pedro Munoz .05
332 Ryan Klesko .05
333a Andre Dawson/Red Sox .25
333b Andre Dawson/Marlins .35
334 Derrick May .05
335 Aaron Sele .05
336 Kevin Mitchell .05
337 Steve Traschel .05
338 Andres Galarraga .05
339a Terry Pendleton/Braves .05
339b Terry Pendleton/Marlins .10
340 Gary Sheffield .30
341 Travis Fryman .05
342 Bo Jackson .10
343 Gary Gaetti .05
344a Brett Butler/Dodgers .05
344b Brett Butler/Mets .10
345 B.J. Surhoff .05
346a Larry Walker/Expos .05
346b Larry Walker/Rockies .10
347 Kevin Tapani .05
348 Rick Wilkins .05
349 Wade Boggs .60
350 Mariano Duncan .05
351 Ruben Sierra .05
352a Andy Van Slyke/Pirates .05
352b Andy Van Slyke/Orioles .10
353 Reggie Jefferson .05
354 Gregg Jefferies .05
355 Tim Naehring .05
356 John Roper .05
357 Joe Carter .05
358 Kurt Abbott .05
359 Lenny Harris .05
360 Lance Johnson .05
361 Brian Anderson .05
362 Jim Eisenreich .05
363 Jerry Browne .05
364 Mark Grace .05
365 Devon White .05
366 Reggie Sanders .05
367 Ivan Rodriguez .40
368 Kirt Manwaring .05
369 Pat Kelly .05
370 Ellis Burks .05
371 Charles Nagy .05
372 Kevin Bass .05
373. Lou Whitaker .05
374 Rene Arocha .05
375 Derrick Parks .05
376 Mark Whiten .05
377 Mark McGwire 1.00
378 Doug Drabek .05
379 Greg Vaughn .05
380 Al Martin .05
381 Ron Darling .05
382 Tim Wallach .05
383 Alan Trammell .05
384 Randy Velarde .05
385 Chris Sabo .05
386 Wil Cordero .05
387 Darrin Fletcher .05
388 David Segui .05
389 Steve Buechele .05
390 Otis Nixon .05
391 Jeff Brantley .05
392a Chad Curtis/Angels .05
392b Chad Curtis/Tigers .10
393 Cal Eldred .05
394 Jason Bere .05
395 Bret Barberie .05
396 Paul Sorrento .05
397 Steve Finley .05
398 Cecil Fielder .05
399 Eric Karros .05
400 Jeff Montgomery .05
401 Cliff Floyd .05
402 Matt Mieske .05
403 Brian Hunter .05
404 Alex Cole .05
405 Kevin Stocker .05
406 Eric Davis .05
407 Marvin Freeman .05
408 Dennis Eckersley .40
409 Todd Zeile .05
410 Keith Mitchell .05

411 Andy Benes .05
412 Juan Bell .05
413 Royce Clayton .05
414 Ed Sprague .05
415 Mike Mussina .30
416 Todd Hundley .05
417 Pat Listach .05
418 Joe Oliver .05
419 Rafael Palmeiro .40
420 Tim Salmon .05
421 Brady Anderson .05
422 Kenny Lofton .05
423 Craig Biggio .05
424 Bobby Bonilla .05
425 Kenny Rogers .05
426 Derek Bell .05
427a Scott Cooper/Red Sox .05
427b Scott Cooper/Cardinals .10
428 Ozzie Guillen .05
429 Omar Vizquel .05
430 Phil Plantier .05
431 Chuck Knoblauch .05
432 Darren Daulton .05
433 Bob Hamelin .05
434 Tom Glavine .30
435 Walt Weiss .05
436 Jose Vizcaino .05
437 Ken Griffey Jr. .75
438 Jay Bell .05
439 Juan Gonzalez .25
440 Jeff Blauser .05
441 Rickey Henderson .50
442 Bobby Ayala .05
443a David Cone/Royals .05
443b David Cone/Blue Jays .10
444 Pedro Martinez .05
445 Manny Ramirez .50
446 Mark Portugal .05
447 Damion Easley .05
448 Gary DiSarcina .05
449 Roberto Hernandez .05
450 Jeffrey Hammonds .05
451 Jeff Treadway .05
452a Jim Abbott/Yanks .05
452b Jim Abbott/White Sox .10
453 Carlos Rodriguez .05
454 Joey Cora .05
455 Bret Boone .05
456 Danny Tartabull .05
457 John Franco .05
458 Roger Salkeld .05
459 Fred McGriff .05
460 Pedro Astacio .05
461 Jon Lieber .05
462 Luis Polonia .05
463 Geronimo Pena .05
464 Tom Gordon .05
465 Brad Ausmus .05
466 Willie McGee .05
467 Doug Jones .05
468 John Smoltz .05
469 Troy Neel .05
470 Luis Sojo .05
471 John Smiley .05
472 Rafael Bournigal .05
473 Billy Taylor .05
474 Juan Guzman .05
475 Dave Magadan .05
476 Mike Devereaux .05
477 Andujar Cedeno .05
478 Edgar Martinez .05
479 Troy Neel .05
480 Allen Watson .05
481 Ron Karkovice .05
482 Joey Hamilton .05
483 Vinny Castilla .05
484 Kevin Gross .05
485 Bernard Gilkey .05
486 John Burkett .05
487 Matt Nokes .05
488 Mel Rojas .05
489 Craig Shipley .05
490 Chip Hale .05
491 Bill Swift .05
492 Pat Rapp .05
493a Brian McRae/Royals .05
493b Brian McRae/Cubs .10
494 Mickey Morandini .05
495 Tony Pena .05
496 Danny Bautista .05
497 Armando Reynoso .05
498 Ken Ryan .05
499 Billy Ripken .05
500 Pat Mahomes .05
501 Mark Acre .05
502 Geronimo Berroa .05
503 Norberto Martin .05
504 Chad Kreuter .05
505 Howard Johnson .05
506 Eric Anthony .05
507 Mark Wohlers .05
508 Scott Sanders .05
509 Pete Harnisch .05
510 Wes Chamberlain .05
511 Tom Candiotti .05
512 Albie Lopez .05
513 Denny Neagle .05
514 Sean Berry .05
515 Billy Hatcher .05
516 Todd Jones .05
517 Wayne Kirby .05
518 Butch Henry .05
519 Sandy Alomar Jr. .05
520 Kevin Appier .05
521 Robert Mejia .05
522 Steve Cooke .05
523 Terry Shumpert .05
524 Mike Jackson .05

525 Kent Mercker .05
526 David Wells .05
527 Juan Samuel .05
528 Salomon Torres .05
529 Duane Ward .05
530a Rob Dibble/Reds .05
530b Rob Dibble/White Sox .10
531 Mike Blowers .05
532 Mark Eichhorn .05
533 Alex Diaz .05
534 Dan Miceli .05
535 Jeff Branson .05
536 Dave Stevens .05
537 Charlie O'Brien .05
538 Shane Reynolds .05
539 Rich Amaral .05
540 Rusty Greer .05
541 Alex Arias .05
542 Eric Plunk .05
543 John Hudek .05
544 Kirk McCaskill .05
545 Jeff Reboulet .05
546 Sterling Hitchcock .05
547 Warren Newson .05
548 Bryan Harvey .05
549 Mike Huff .05
550 Lance Parrish .05
551 Ken Griffey Jr. (Hitters Inc.) .65
552 Matt Williams (Hitters Inc.) .05
553 Roberto Alomar (Hitters Inc.) .10
554 Jeff Bagwell (Hitters Inc.) .25
555 Dave Justice (Hitters Inc.) .05
556 Cal Ripken Jr. (Hitters Inc.) .75
557 Albert Belle (Hitters Inc.) .05
558 Mike Piazza (Hitters Inc.) .45
559 Kirby Puckett (Hitters Inc.) .35
560 Wade Boggs (Hitters Inc.) .30
561 Tony Gwynn (Hitters Inc.) .35
562 Barry Bonds (Hitters Inc.) .75
563 Mo Vaughn (Hitters Inc.) .05
564 Don Mattingly (Hitters Inc.) .40
565 Carlos Baerga (Hitters Inc.) .05
566 Paul Molitor (Hitters Inc.) .25
567 Raul Mondesi (Hitters Inc.) .05
568 Manny Ramirez (Hitters Inc.) .25
569 Alex Rodriguez (Hitters Inc.) .75
570 Will Clark (Hitters Inc.) .05
571 Frank Thomas (Hitters Inc.) .30
572 Moises Alou (Hitters Inc.) .05
573 Jeff Conine (Hitters Inc.) .05
574 Joe Ausanio .05
575 Charles Johnson .05
576 Ernie Young .05
577 Jeff Granger .05
578 Robert Perez .05
579 Melvin Nieves .05
580 Gar Finnvold .05
581 Duane Singleton .05
582 Chan Ho Park .05
583 Fausto Cruz .05
584 Dave Staton .05
585 Denny Hocking .05
586 Nate Minchey .05
587 Marc Newfield .05
588 Jayhawk Owens .05
589 Darren Bragg .05
590 Kevin King .05
591 Kurt Miller .05
592 Aaron Small .05
593 Troy O'Leary .05
594 Phil Stidham .05
595 Steve Dunn .05
596 Cory Bailey .05
597 Alex Gonzalez .05
598 Jim Bowie .05
599 Jeff Cirillo .05
600 Mark Hutton .05
601 Russ Davis .05
602 Checklist #331-400 .05
603 Checklist #401-469 .05
604 Checklist #470-537 .05
605 Checklist #538-605 .05
---- "You Trade 'em" redemption card (Expired Dec. 31, 1995.) .10

sions. The deadline for redemption of Series I was July 1, 1995; Oct. 1, 1995, for Series II. Gold Rush cards were found either one or two per pack, depending on pack card count. Gold Rush versions exist for each card in the Score set and have fronts that are identical to the regular cards except they are printed on foil and have gold borders. Backs of the Gold Rush cards have a small rectangular "GOLD RUSH" logo overprinted.

	NM/M
Complete Set (605):	35.00
Common Player:	.10
Gold Rush Stars:	2X

Platinum Redemption Team Sets

This top of the line parallel set was only available by exchanging a complete Series 1 or Series 2 Gold Rush team set, along with a redemption card. Production of the Platinum sets was limited to 4,950 of each team in each series. Using the same photos and format as the regular issue and Gold Rush cards, the Platinum parallels have card fronts printed on silver prismatic foil. Backs are identical to the regular versions. Platinum series team sets were sent to collectors in specially printed plastic cases with a certificate of authenticity.

	NM/M
Complete Set (587):	100.00
Complete Series 1 (316):	60.00
Complete Series 2 (271):	40.00
Common Player:	.25
Platinum Stars:	3X

Airmail

Gold Rush

Besides being collectible in their own right, the gold-foil printed parallel versions of the Score regular-issue cards could be collected into team sets and exchanged with a trade card for platinum ver-

Young ballplayers with a propensity for hitting the long ball are featured in this insert set found only in Series II jumbo packs. Cards have a player batting action photo set in sky-and-clouds background. A gold-foil stamp in the upper-left corner identifies the series. Backs have a background photo of sunset and dark clouds, with a player portrait photo in the foreground. A few stats and sentences describe the player's power hitting potential. Cards have an AM prefix to the number. Stated odds for insertion rate are an average of one Airmail chase card per 24 packs.

		NM/M
Complete Set (18):		8.00
Common Player:		.25
1	Bob Hamelin	.25
2	John Mabry	.25
3	Marc Newfield	.25
4	Jose Oliva	.25
5	Charles Johnson	.25
6	Russ Davis	.25
7	Ernie Young	.25
8	Billy Ashley	.25
9	Ryan Klesko	.25
10	J.R. Phillips	.25
11	Cliff Floyd	.25
12	Carlos Delgado	1.50
13	Melvin Nieves	.25
14	Raul Mondesi	.25
15	Manny Ramirez	2.00
16	Mike Kelly	.25
17	Alex Rodriguez	5.00
18	Rusty Greer	.25

Double Gold Champions

A dozen veteran players, who have won at least two of the game's top awards, are designated as "Double Gold Champs," in this Series II hobby insert set. Fronts have horizontal action photos at top, with a speckled red border at bottom. Vertical backs have a portrait photo and a list of the major awards won by the player. Cards have a GC prefix to the number. These chase cards were reportedly inserted at an average rate of one per 36.

		NM/M
Complete Set (12):		25.00
Common Player:		.40
1	Frank Thomas	2.00
2	Ken Griffey Jr.	3.50
3	Barry Bonds	5.00
4	Tony Gwynn	2.50
5	Don Mattingly	3.00
6	Greg Maddux	2.50
7	Roger Clemens	3.00
8	Kenny Lofton	.40
9	Jeff Bagwell	2.00
10	Matt Williams	.40
11	Kirby Puckett	2.50
12	Cal Ripken Jr.	5.00

Draft Picks

These cards were randomly included in 1995 Score hobby packs at a rate of one per every 36 packs. The cards showcase 18 of baseball's potential superstars and document their professional beginnings. The card front has the player's team logo and name in the lower-right corner. "'94 Draft Pick" appears in the upper-right corner. The front also has a mug shot and an action shot of the player. The card back has a portrait and career summary and is numbered with a DP prefix.

		NM/M
Complete Set (18):		4.00
Common Player:		.50
1	McKay Christensen	.50
2	Brett Wagner	.50
3	Paul Wilson	.50
4	C.J. Nitkowski	.50
5	Josh Booty	.50
6	Antone Williamson	.50
7	Paul Konerko	1.50
8	Scott Elarton	.50
9	Jacob Shumate	.50
10	Terrence Long	.50
11	Mark Johnson	.50
12	Ben Grieve	.50
13	Doug Million	.50
14	Jayson Peterson	.50
15	Dustin Hermanson	.50
16	Matt Smith	.50
17	Kevin Witt	.50
18	Brian Buchanan	.50

Dream Team Gold

The Major Leagues' top players at each position are featured in this Series I insert set. Fronts are printed entirely on rainbow holographic foil and feature a large and a small player action photo. Backs have a single-color version of one of the front photos as well as a color portrait photo in a circle at center, all in conventional printing technology. Card numbers have a DG prefix.

		NM/M
Complete Set (12):		12.00
Common Player:		.30
1	Frank Thomas	1.25
2	Roberto Alomar	.50
3	Cal Ripken Jr.	4.00
4	Matt Williams	.30
5	Mike Piazza	2.50
6	Albert Belle	.30
7	Ken Griffey Jr.	2.50
8	Tony Gwynn	1.50
9	Paul Molitor	1.25
10	Jimmy Key	.30
11	Greg Maddux	1.50
12	Lee Smith	.30

Hall of Gold

Hall of Gold inserts picture 110 of the top players on gold foil cards. Each card front has the Hall of Gold logo in an upper corner, plus a color action photo of the player, and his name and team logo at the bottom. The card back is numbered using an "HG" prefix and includes another color photo of the player, his team's name, his position, and a career summary. Cards were inserted one per every six regular 1995 Score packs and one per every two jumbo packs. Updated versions of five traded players were issued in Series II, available only via mail-in offer with a trade card found randomly inserted in packs.

		NM/M
Complete Set (110):		25.00
Common Player:		.10
1	Ken Griffey Jr.	1.25
2	Matt Williams	.10
3	Roberto Alomar	.25
4	Jeff Bagwell	.75
5	Dave Justice	.10
6	Cal Ripken Jr.	2.00
7	Randy Johnson	.75
8	Barry Larkin	.10
9	Albert Belle	.10
10	Mike Piazza	1.25
11	Kirby Puckett	1.00
12	Moises Alou	.10
13	Jose Canseco	.45
14	Tony Gwynn	1.00
15	Roger Clemens	1.00
16	Barry Bonds	2.00
17	Mo Vaughn	.10
18	Greg Maddux	1.00
19	Dante Bichette	.10
20	Will Clark	.10
21	Len Dykstra	.10
22	Don Mattingly	1.00
23	Carlos Baerga	.10
24	Ozzie Smith	1.00
25	Paul Molitor	.75
26	Paul O'Neill	.10
27	Deion Sanders	.10
28	Jeff Conine	.10
29	John Olerud	.10
30	Jose Rijo	.10
31	Sammy Sosa	1.00
32	Robin Ventura	.10
33	Raul Mondesi	.10
34	Eddie Murray	.75
35	Marquis Grissom	.10
36	Darryl Strawberry	.10
37	Dave Nilsson	.10
38	Manny Ramirez	.75
39	Delino DeShields	.10
40	Lee Smith	.10
41	Alex Rodriguez	1.50
42	Julio Franco	.10
43	Bret Saberhagen	.10
44	Ken Hill	.10
45	Roberto Kelly	.10
46	Hal Morris	.10
47	Jimmy Key	.10
48	Terry Steinbach	.10
49	Mickey Tettleton	.10
50	Tony Phillips	.10
51	Carlos Garcia	.10
52	Jim Edmonds	.10
53	Rod Beck	.10
54	Shane Mack	.10
55	Ken Caminiti	.10
56	Frank Thomas	.75
57	Kenny Lofton	.10
58	Jack McDowell	.10
59	Jason Bere	.10
60	Joe Carter	.10
61	Gary Sheffield	.10
62	Andres Galarraga	.10
63	Gregg Jefferies	.10
64	Bobby Bonilla	.10
65	Tom Glavine	.35
66	John Smoltz	.10
67	Fred McGriff	.10
68	Craig Biggio	.10
69	Reggie Sanders	.10
70	Kevin Mitchell	.10
71a	Larry Walker/Expos	.10
71b	Larry Walker/Rockies	.10
72	Carlos Delgado	.50
73	Andujar Cedeno	.10
74	Ivan Rodriguez	.65
75	Ryan Klesko	.10
76a	John Kruk/Phillies	.10
76b	John Kruk/White Sox	.10
77a	Brian McRae/Royal	.10
77b	Brian McRae/Cubs	.10
78	Tim Salmon	.10
79	Travis Fryman	.10
80	Chuck Knoblauch	.10
81	Jay Bell	.10
82	Cecil Fielder	.10
83	Cliff Floyd	.10
84	Ruben Sierra	.10
85	Mike Mussina	.45
86	Mark Grace	.10
87	Dennis Eckersley	.65
88	Dennis Martinez	.10
89	Rafael Palmeiro	.65
90	Ben McDonald	.10
91	Dave Hollins	.10
92	Steve Avery	.10
93a	David Cone/Royals	.10
93b	David Cone/Blue Jays	.10
94	Darren Daulton	.10
95	Bret Boone	.10
96	Wade Boggs	1.00
97	Doug Drabek	.10
98	Derek Bell	.10
99	Jim Thome	.65
100	Chili Davis	.10
101	Jeffrey Hammonds	.10
102	Rickey Henderson	.75
103	Brett Butler	.10
104	Tim Wallach	.10
105	Wil Cordero	.10
106	Mark Whiten	.10
107	Bob Hamelin	.10
108	Rondell White	.10
109	Devon White	.10
110a	Tony Tarasco/Braves	.10
110b	Tony Tarasco/Expos	.10
----	Redemption trade card (Expired Dec. 31, 1995.)	.10

Rookie Dream Team

These Series 2 inserts feature a dozen of 1995's best rookie prospects. Fronts are printed on a silver-foil background. The words "ROOKIE DREAM TEAM" are formed of sky-and-cloud images within the letters. Horizontal backs repeat the motif and include another player photo in a vignette at center. Card numbers have an RDT prefix.

		NM/M
Complete Set (12):		9.00
Common Player:		.50
1	J.R. Phillips	.50
2	Alex Gonzalez	.50
3	Alex Rodriguez	6.00
4	Jose Oliva	.50
5	Charles Johnson	.50
6	Shawn Green	1.50
7	Brian Hunter	.50
8	Garret Anderson	.50
9	Julian Tavarez	.50
10	Jose Lima	.50
11	Armando Benitez	.50
12	Ricky Bottalico	.50

Rookie Greatness

This single-card insert set is the toughest pull among the 1995 Score chase cards. Honoring slugging Braves star Ryan Klesko, the card is inserted at the rate of one per 720 retail packs. An even scarcer autographed version of the card in an edition of just over 6,000 was also created for insertion into hobby packs.

		NM/M
RG1	Ryan Klesko	1.00
SG1	Ryan Klesko/Auto.	7.50

Score Rules

Series I jumbo packs were the only sources for "Score Rules" insert set of rookie and veteran stars. A color player photo at left has a team logo toward the bottom, beneath which is a gold-foil "tie tack" device with the league initials and position. At top-right is a baseball which appears to be dripping orange and green goop down the card. The player's last name is presented vertically with a sepia photo of the player within the letters. Backs repeat the green baseball and ooze motif, with three progressive color proof versions of the sepia front photo and a few sentences about the star. Cards are numbered with an "SR" prefix.

		NM/M
Complete Set (30):		30.00
Common Player:		.30
1	Ken Griffey Jr.	3.50
2	Frank Thomas	1.50
3	Mike Piazza	3.50
4	Jeff Bagwell	1.50
5	Alex Rodriguez	4.50
6	Albert Belle	.30
7	Matt Williams	.30
8	Roberto Alomar	.45
9	Barry Bonds	5.00
10	Raul Mondesi	.30
11	Jose Canseco	.60
12	Kirby Puckett	2.50
13	Fred McGriff	.30
14	Kenny Lofton	.30
15	Greg Maddux	2.50
16	Juan Gonzalez	.75
17	Cliff Floyd	.30
18	Cal Ripken, Jr.	5.00
19	Will Clark	.30
20	Tim Salmon	.30
21	Paul O'Neill	.30
22	Jason Bere	.30
23	Tony Gwynn	2.50
24	Manny Ramirez	1.50
25	Don Mattingly	3.00
26	Dave Justice	.30
27	Javier Lopez	.30
28	Ryan Klesko	.30
29	Carlos Delgado	.90
30	Mike Mussina	.60

Score Rules Supers

While colorful in the standard size, the Score Rules super-size cards found in special collectors kits are positively garish. The 7-1/2" x 10-1/2" cards are virtually identical to the Series 1 inserts, except that on back is a box with a serial number identifying the card from among an edition of 3,000. The Score Rules supers were available only in a collectors kit sold at large retail chains and came packaged with 26 Series 1 and 2 foil packs, a three-ring binder and 10 plastic sheets with a suggested retail price of around $25.

		NM/M
Complete Set (30):		60.00
Common Player:		.90
1	Ken Griffey Jr.	5.00
2	Frank Thomas	3.50
3	Mike Piazza	5.00
4	Jeff Bagwell	3.50
5	Alex Rodriguez	6.00
6	Albert Belle	.90
7	Matt Williams	.90
8	Roberto Alomar	1.25
9	Barry Bonds	7.50
10	Raul Mondesi	.90
11	Jose Canseco	2.50
12	Kirby Puckett	4.50
13	Fred McGriff	.90
14	Kenny Lofton	.90
15	Greg Maddux	4.50
16	Juan Gonzalez	2.00
17	Cliff Floyd	.90
18	Cal Ripken, Jr.	7.50
19	Will Clark	.90
20	Tim Salmon	.90
21	Paul O'Neill	.90
22	Jason Bere	.90
23	Tony Gwynn	4.50
24	Manny Ramirez	3.75
25	Don Mattingly	4.50
26	Dave Justice	.90
27	Javier Lopez	.90
28	Ryan Klesko	.90
29	Carlos Delgado	2.00
30	Mike Mussina	1.50

Ad Prize Cards

In a series of ads in hobby and public media, Score offered a pair of special cards as prizes in a mail-in offer. Cards feature the same basic design as 1995 Score, but are printed on platinum foil on front. Backs are conventionally printed with a portrait photo and a few words about the player.

		NM/M
Complete Set (2):		10.00
AD1	Alex Rodriguez	6.50
AD2	Ivan Rodriguez	3.50

1996 Score Samples

Score premiered its 1996 base brand offering with a cello pack of nine cards, including one of its new Dugout Collection inserts. The samples are virtually identical to the issued versions except that all 1995 and career stats are stated as zeros and the word "SAMPLE" is printed in white letters diagonally across front and back. Each of the cards can be found as a Dugout Collection version, making them eight times scarcer than the other samples.

		NM/M
Complete Set (16):		12.00
Common Player:		.50
3	Ryan Klesko	.50
3	Ryan Klesko (Dugout Collection)	1.00
4	Jim Edmonds	.50

4	Jim Edmonds (Dugout Collection)	1.00
5	Barry Larkin	.50
5	Barry Larkin (Dugout Collection)	1.00
6	Jim Thome	1.00
6	Jim Thome (Dugout Collection)	1.50
7	Raul Mondesi	.50
7	Raul Mondesi (Dugout Collection)	1.00
110	Derek Bell	.50
110	Derek Bell (Dugout Collection)	1.00
240	Derek Jeter	2.00
240	Derek Jeter (Dugout Collection)	4.50
241	Michael Tucker	.50
241	Michael Tucker (Dugout Collection)	1.00

1996 Score

Large, irregularly shaped action photos are featured on the fronts of the basic cards in the 1996 Score issue. Backs feature a portrait photo (in most cases) at left and a full slate of major and minor league stats at right, along with a few words about the player. Slightly different design details and a "ROOK-IE" headline identify that subset within the regular series. A wide variety of insert cards was produced, most of them exclusive to one type of packaging.

	NM/M
Complete Set (510):	15.00
Common Player:	.05
Wax Pack (10):	.45
Wax Box (36):	10.00

1	Will Clark	.05
2	Rich Becker	.05
3	Ryan Klesko	.05
4	Jim Edmonds	.05
5	Barry Larkin	.05
6	Jim Thome	.40
7	Raul Mondesi	.05
8	Don Mattingly	.65
9	Jeff Conine	.05
10	Rickey Henderson	.50
11	Chad Curtis	.05
12	Darren Daulton	.05
13	Larry Walker	.05
14	Carlos Garcia	.05
15	Carlos Baerga	.05
16	Tony Gwynn	.60
17	Jon Nunally	.05
18	Deion Sanders	.05
19	Mark Grace	.05
20	Alex Rodriguez	1.00
21	Frank Thomas	.50
22	Brian Jordan	.05
23	J.T. Snow	.05
24	Shawn Green	.30
25	Tim Wakefield	.05
26	Curtis Goodwin	.05
27	John Smoltz	.05
28	Devon White	.05
29	Brian Hunter	.05
30	Rusty Greer	.05
31	Rafael Palmeiro	.40
32	Bernard Gilkey	.05
33	John Valentin	.05
34	Randy Johnson	.50
35	Garret Anderson	.05
36	Rikkert Faneyte	.05
37	Ray Durham	.05
38	Bip Roberts	.05
39	Jaime Navarro	.05
40	Mark Johnson	.05
41	Darren Lewis	.05
42	Tyler Green	.05
43	Bill Pulsipher	.05
44	Jason Giambi	.40
45	Kevin Ritz	.05
46	Jack McDowell	.05
47	Felipe Lira	.05
48	Rico Brogna	.05
49	Terry Pendleton	.05
50	Rondell White	.05
51	Andre Dawson	.25
52	Kirby Puckett	.60
53	Wally Joyner	.05
54	B.J. Surhoff	.05
55	Chan Ho Park	.05
56	Greg Vaughn	.05
57	Roberto Alomar	.20
58	Dave Justice	.05
59	Kevin Seitzer	.05
60	Cal Ripken Jr.	1.50
61	Ozzie Smith	.60
62	Mo Vaughn	.05
63	Ricky Bones	.05
64	Gary DiSarcina	.05
65	Matt Williams	.05
66	Wilson Alvarez	.05
67	Lenny Dykstra	.05
68	Brian McRae	.05
69	Todd Stottlemyre	.05
70	Bret Boone	.05
71	Sterling Hitchcock	.05
72	Albert Belle	.05
73	Todd Hundley	.05
74	Vinny Castilla	.05
75	Moises Alou	.05
76	Cecil Fielder	.05
77	Brad Radke	.05
78	Quivio Veras	.05
79	Eddie Murray	.50
80	James Mouton	.05
81	Pat Listach	.05
82	Mark Gubicza	.05
83	Dave Winfield	.50
84	Fred McGriff	.05
85	Darryl Hamilton	.05
86	Jeffrey Hammonds	.05
87	Pedro Munoz	.05
88	Craig Biggio	.05
89	Cliff Floyd	.05
90	Tim Naehring	.05
91	Brett Butler	.05
92	Kevin Foster	.05
93	Patrick Kelly	.05
94	John Smiley	.05
95	Terry Steinbach	.05
96	Orel Hershiser	.05
97	Darrin Fletcher	.05
98	Walt Weiss	.05
99	John Wetteland	.05
100	Alan Trammell	.05
101	Steve Avery	.05
102	Tony Eusebio	.05
103	Sandy Alomar	.05
104	Joe Girardi	.05
105	Rick Aguilera	.05
106	Tony Tarasco	.05
107	Chris Hammond	.05
108	Mike McFarlane	.05
109	Doug Drabek	.05
110	Derek Bell	.05
111	Ed Sprague	.05
112	Todd Hollandsworth	.05
113	Otis Nixon	.05
114	Keith Lockhart	.05
115	Donovan Osborne	.05
116	Dave Magadan	.05
117	Edgar Martinez	.05
118	Chuck Carr	.05
119	J.R. Phillips	.05
120	Sean Bergman	.05
121	Andujar Cedeno	.05
122	Eric Young	.05
123	Al Martin	.05
124	Ken Hill	.05
125	Jim Eisenreich	.05
126	Benito Santiago	.05
127	Ariel Prieto	.05
128	Jim Bullinger	.05
129	Russ Davis	.05
130	Jim Abbott	.05
131	Jason Isringhausen	.05
132	Carlos Perez	.05
133	David Segui	.05
134	Troy O'Leary	.05
135	Pat Meares	.05
136	Chris Hoiles	.05
137	Ismael Valdes	.05
138	Jose Oliva	.05
139	Carlos Delgado	.35
140	Tom Goodwin	.05
141	Bob Tewksbury	.05
142	Chris Gomez	.05
143	Jose Oquendo	.05
144	Mark Lewis	.05
145	Salomon Torres	.05
146	Luis Gonzalez	.05
147	Mark Carreon	.05
148	Lance Johnson	.05
149	Melvin Nieves	.05
150	Lee Smith	.05
151	Jacob Brumfield	.05
152	Armando Benitez	.05
153	Curt Schilling	.30
154	Javier Lopez	.05
155	Frank Rodriguez	.05
156	Alex Gonzalez	.05
157	Todd Worrell	.05
158	Benji Gil	.05
159	Greg Gagne	.05
160	Tom Henke	.05
161	Randy Myers	.05
162	Joey Cora	.05
163	Scott Ruffcorn	.05
164	William Van Landingham	.05
165	Tony Phillips	.05
166	Eddie Williams	.05
167	Bobby Bonilla	.05
168	Denny Neagle	.05
169	Troy Percival	.05
170	Billy Ashley	.05
171	Andy Van Slyke	.05
172	Jose Offerman	.05
173	Mark Parent	.05
174	Edgardo Alfonzo	.05
175	Trevor Hoffman	.05
176	David Cone	.05
177	Dan Wilson	.05
178	Steve Ontiveros	.05
179	Dean Palmer	.05
180	Mike Kelly	.05
181	Jim Leyritz	.05
182	Ron Karkovice	.05
183	Kevin Brown	.05
184	Jose Valentin RC	.05
185	Jorge Fabregas	.05
186	Jose Mesa	.05
187	Brent Mayne	.05
188	Carl Everett	.05
189	Paul Sorrento	.05
190	Pete Shourek	.05
191	Scott Kamieniecki	.05
192	Roberto Hernandez	.05
193	Randy Johnson (Radar Rating)	.25
194	Greg Maddux (Radar Rating)	.35
195	Hideo Nomo (Radar Rating)	.15
196	David Cone (Radar Rating)	.05
197	Mike Mussina (Radar Rating)	.15
198	Andy Benes (Radar Rating)	.05
199	Kevin Appier (Radar Rating)	.05
200	John Smoltz (Radar Rating)	.05
201	John Wetteland (Radar Rating)	.05
202	Mark Wohlers (Radar Rating)	.05
203	Stan Belinda	.05
204	Brian Anderson	.05
205	Mike Devereaux	.05
206	Mark Wohlers	.05
207	Omar Vizquel	.05
208	Jose Rijo	.05
209	Willie Blair	.05
210	Jamie Moyer	.05
211	Craig Shipley	.05
212	Shane Reynolds	.05
213	Chad Fonville	.05
214	Jose Vizcaino	.05
215	Sid Fernandez	.05
216	Andy Ashby	.05
217	Frank Castillo	.05
218	Kevin Tapani	.05
219	Kent Mercker	.05
220	Karim Garcia	.05
221	Chris Snopek	.05
222	Tim Unroe	.05
223	Johnny Damon	.25
224	LaTroy Hawkins	.05
225	Mariano Rivera	.10
226	Jose Alberro	.05
227	Angel Martinez	.05
228	Jason Schmidt	.05
229	Tony Clark	.05
230	Kevin Jordan	.05
231	Mark Thompson	.05
232	Jim Dougherty	.05
233	Roger Cedeno	.05
234	Ugueth Urbina	.05
235	Ricky Otero	.05
236	Mark Smith	.05
237	Brian Barber	.05
238	Marc Kroon	.05
239	Joe Rosselli	.05
240	Derek Jeter	1.50
241	Michael Tucker	.05
242	Joe Borowski RC	.05
243	Joe Vitiello	.05
244	Orlando Palmeiro	.05
245	James Baldwin	.05
246	Alan Embree	.05
247	Shannon Penn	.05
248	Chris Stynes	.05
249	Oscar Munoz	.05
250	Jose Herrera	.05
251	Scott Sullivan	.05
252	Reggie Williams	.05
253	Mark Grudzielanek	.05
254	Kevin Jordan	.20
255	Terry Bradshaw	.05
256	F.P. Santangelo RC	.05
257	Doug Johns	.05
258	George Williams	.10
259	Larry Thomas	.05
260	Rudy Pemberton	.05
261	Jim Pittsley	.05
262	Les Norman	.05
263	Ruben Rivera	.05
264	Cesar Devarez RC	.05
265	Gregg Zaun	.05
266	Eric Owens	.05
267	John Frascatore	.05
268	Shannon Stewart	.05
269	Checklist	.05
270	Checklist	.05
271	Checklist	.05
272	Checklist	.05
273	Checklist	.05
274	Checklist	.05
275	Checklist	.05
276	Greg Maddux	.60
277	Pedro Martinez	.50
278	Bobby Higginson	.05
279	Ray Lankford	.05
280	Shawon Dunston	.05
281	Gary Sheffield	.35
282	Ken Griffey Jr.	.75
283	Paul Molitor	.50
284	Kevin Appier	.05
285	Chuck Knoblauch	.05
286	Alex Fernandez	.05
287	Steve Finley	.05
288	Jeff Blauser	.05
289	Charles Johnson	.05
290	John Franco	.05
291	Mark Langston	.05
292	Bret Saberhagen	.05
293	John Mabry	.05
294	Ramon Martinez	.05
295	Mike Blowers	.05
296	Paul O'Neill	.05
297	Dave Nilsson	.05
298	Dante Bichette	.05
299	Marty Cordova	.05
300	Jay Bell	.05
301	Mike Mussina	.30
302	Ivan Rodriguez	.30
303	Jose Canseco	.30
304	Jeff Bagwell	.50
305	Manny Ramirez	.05
306	Dennis Martinez	.05
307	Charlie Hayes	.05
308	Joe Carter	.05
309	Travis Fryman	.05
310	Mark McGwire	1.00
311	Reggie Sanders	.05
312	Julian Tavarez	.05
313	Jeff Montgomery	.05
314	Andy Benes	.05
315	John Jaha	.05
316	Jeff Kent	.05
317	Mike Piazza	.75
318	Erik Hanson	.05
319	Kenny Rogers	.05
320	Hideo Nomo	.25
321	Gregg Jefferies	.05
322	Chipper Jones	.60
323	Jay Buhner	.05
324	Dennis Eckersley	.40
325	Kenny Lofton	.05
326	Robin Ventura	.05
327	Tom Glavine	.35
328	Tim Salmon	.05
329	Andres Galarraga	.05
330	Hal Morris	.05
331	Brady Anderson	.05
332	Chili Davis	.05
333	Roger Clemens	.65
334	Marquis Grissom	.05
335	Jeff (Mike) Greenwell	.05
336	Sammy Sosa	.60
337	Ron Gant	.05
338	Ken Caminiti	.05
339	Danny Tartabull	.05
340	Barry Bonds	1.50
341	Ben McDonald	.05
342	Ruben Sierra	.05
343	Bernie Williams	.05
344	Wil Cordero	.05
345	Wade Boggs	.60
346	Gary Gaetti	.05
347	Greg Colbrunn	.05
348	Juan Gonzalez	.25
349	Marc Newfield	.05
350	Charles Nagy	.05
351	Robby Thompson	.05
352	Roberto Petagine	.05
353	Darryl Strawberry	.05
354	Tino Martinez	.05
355	Eric Karros	.05
356	Cal Ripken Jr. (Star Struck)	.75
357	Cecil Fielder (Star Struck)	.05
358	Kirby Puckett (Star Struck)	.35
359	Jim Edmonds (Star Struck)	.05
360	Matt Williams (Star Struck)	.05
361	Alex Rodriguez (Star Struck)	.50
362	Barry Larkin (Star Struck)	.05
363	Rafael Palmeiro (Star Struck)	.20
364	David Cone (Star Struck)	.05
365	Roberto Alomar (Star Struck)	.10
366	Eddie Murray (Star Struck)	.25
367	Randy Johnson (Star Struck)	.20
368	Ryan Klesko (Star Struck)	.05
369	Raul Mondesi (Star Struck)	.05
370	Mo Vaughn (Star Struck)	.05
371	Will Clark (Star Struck)	.05
372	Carlos Baerga (Star Struck)	.05
373	Frank Thomas (Star Struck)	.30
374	Larry Walker (Star Struck)	.05
375	Garret Anderson (Star Struck)	.05
376	Edgar Martinez (Star Struck)	.05
377	Don Mattingly (Star Struck)	.40
378	Tony Gwynn (Star Struck)	.35
379	Albert Belle (Star Struck)	.05
380	Jason Isringhausen (Star Struck)	.05
381	Ruben Rivera (Star Struck)	.05
382	Johnny Damon (Star Struck)	.05
383	Karim Garcia (Star Struck)	.05
384	Derek Jeter (Star Struck)	.75
385	David Justice (Star Struck)	.05
386	Royce Clayton	.05
387	Mark Whiten	.05
388	Mickey Tettleton	.05
389	Steve Trachsel	.05
390	Danny Bautista	.05
391	Midre Cummings	.05
392	Scott Leius	.05
393	Manny Alexander	.05
394	Brent Gates	.05
395	Rey Sanchez	.05
396	Andy Pettitte	.20
397	Jeff Cirillo	.05
398	Kurt Abbott	.05
399	Lee Tinsley	.05
400	Paul Assenmacher	.05
401	Scott Erickson	.05
402	Todd Zeile	.05
403	Tom Pagnozzi	.05
404	Ozzie Guillen	.05
405	Jeff Frye	.05
406	Kirt Manwaring	.05
407	Chad Ogea	.05
408	Harold Baines	.05
409	Jason Bere	.05
410	Chuck Finley	.05
411	Jeff Fassero	.05
412	Joey Hamilton	.05
413	John Olerud	.05
414	Kevin Stocker	.05
415	Eric Anthony	.05
416	Aaron Sele	.05
417	Chris Bosio	.05
418	Michael Mimbs	.05
419	Orlando Miller	.05
420	Stan Javier	.05
421	Matt Mieske	.05
422	Jason Bates	.05
423	Orlando Merced	.05
424	John Flaherty	.05
425	Reggie Jefferson	.05
426	Scott Stahoviak	.05
427	John Burkett	.05
428	Rod Beck	.05
429	Bill Swift	.05
430	Scott Cooper	.05
431	Mel Rojas	.05
432	Todd Van Poppel	.05
433	Bobby Jones	.05
434	Mike Harkey	.05
435	Sean Berry	.05
436	Glenallen Hill	.05
437	Ryan Thompson	.05
438	Luis Alicea	.05
439	Esteban Loaiza	.05
440	Jeff Reboulet	.05
441	Vince Coleman	.05
442	Ellis Burks	.05
443	Allen Battle	.05
444	Jimmy Key	.05
445	Ricky Bottalico	.05
446	Delino DeShields	.05
447	Albie Lopez	.05
448	Mark Petkovsek	.05
449	Tim Raines	.05
450	Bryan Harvey	.05
451	Pat Hentgen	.05
452	Tim Laker	.05
453	Tom Gordon	.05
454	Phil Plantier	.05
455	Ernie Young	.05
456	Pete Harnisch	.05
457	Roberto Kelly	.05
458	Mark Portugal	.05
459	Mark Leiter	.05
460	Tony Pena	.05
461	Roger Pavlik	.05
462	Jeff King	.05
463	Bryan Rekar	.05
464	Al Leiter	.05
465	Phil Nevin	.05
466	Jose Lima	.05
467	Mike Stanley	.05
468	David McCarty	.05
469	Herb Perry	.05
470	Geronimo Berroa	.05
471	David Wells	.05
472	Vaughn Eshelman	.05
473	Greg Swindell	.05
474	Steve Sparks	.05
475	Luis Sojo	.05
476	Derrick May	.05
477	Joe Oliver	.05
478	Alex Arias	.05
479	Brad Ausmus	.05
480	Gabe White	.05
481	Pat Rapp	.05
482	Damon Buford	.05
483	Turk Wendell	.05
484	Jeff Brantley	.05
485	Curtis Leskanic	.05
486	Robb Nen	.05
487	Lou Whitaker	.05
488	Melido Perez	.05
489	Luis Polonia	.05
490	Scott Brosius	.05
491	Robert Perez	.05
492	Mike Sweeney RC	.50
493	Mark Loretta	.05
494	Alex Ochoa	.05
495	Matt Lawton RC	.10
496	Shawn Estes	.05
497	John Wasdin	.05
498	Marc Kroon	.05
499	Chris Snopek	.05
500	Jeff Suppan	.05
501	Terrell Wade	.05
502	Marvin Benard RC	.10
503	Chris Widger	.05
504	Quinton McCracken	.05
505	Bob Wolcott	.05
506	C.J. Nitkowski	.05
507	Aaron Ledesma	.05
508	Scott Hatteberg	.05
509	Jimmy Haynes	.05
510	Howard Battle	.05

Dugout Collection

The concept of a partial parallel set, including the stars and rookies, but not the journeymen and bench warmers, was initiated with Score's "Dugout Collection," with fewer than half of the cards from the regular series chosen for inclusion. The white borders of the regular cards are replaced with copper-foil and background printing is also done on foil in this special version. On back is a special "Dugout Collection '96" logo. Advertised insertion rate of the copper-version cards is one per three packs.

	NM/M
Complete Set (220):	60.00
Complete Series 1 (1-110):	30.00
Complete Series 2 (1-110):	30.00
Common Player:	.05
Artist's Proofs:	4X

1	Will Clark	.20
2	Rich Becker	.20
3	Ryan Klesko	.20
4	Jim Edmonds	.20
5	Barry Larkin	.20
6	Jim Thome	.65
7	Raul Mondesi	.20
8	Don Mattingly	1.25
9	Jeff Conine	.20
10	Rickey Henderson	.75
11	Chad Curtis	.20
12	Darren Daulton	.20
13	Larry Walker	.20
14	Carlos Baerga	.20
15	Tony Gwynn	1.00
16	Jon Nunnally	.20
17	Deion Sanders	.20
18	Mark Grace	.20
19	Alex Rodriguez	2.00
20	Frank Thomas	.75
21	Brian Jordan	.20
22	J.T. Snow	.20
23	Shawn Green	.50
24	Tim Wakefield	.20
25	Curtis Goodwin	.20
26	John Smoltz	.20
27	Devon White	.20
28	Brian Hunter	.20
29	Rusty Greer	.20
30	Rafael Palmeiro	.65
31	Bernard Gilkey	.20
32	John Valentin	.20
33	Randy Johnson	.75
34	Garret Anderson	.20
35	Ray Durham	.20
36	Bip Roberts	.20
37	Tyler Green	.20
38	Bill Pulsipher	.20
39	Jason Giambi	.50
40	Jack McDowell	.20
41	Rico Brogna	.20

#	Player		#	Player	
42	Terry Pendleton	.20	50	Kenny Lofton	.20
43	Rondell White	.20	51	Robin Ventura	.20
44	Andre Dawson	.35	52	Tom Glavine	.30
45	Kirby Puckett	1.00	53	Tim Salmon	.20
46	Wally Joyner	.20	54	Andres Galarraga	.20
47	B.J. Surhoff	.20	55	Hal Morris	.20
48	Randy Velarde	.20	56	Brady Anderson	.20
49	Greg Vaughn	.20	57	Chili Davis	.20
50	Roberto Alomar	.30	58	Roger Clemens	1.25
51	David Justice	.20	59	Marquis Grissom	.20
52	Cal Ripken Jr.	3.00	60	Mike Greenwell	.20
53	Ozzie Smith	1.00	61	Sammy Sosa	1.00
54	Mo Vaughn	.20	62	Ron Gant	.20
55	Gary DiSarcina	.20	63	Ken Caminiti	.20
56	Matt Williams	.20	64	Danny Tartabull	.20
57	Lenny Dykstra	.20	65	Barry Bonds	3.00
58	Bret Boone	.20	66	Ben McDonald	.20
59	Albert Belle	.20	67	Ruben Sierra	.20
60	Vinny Castilla	.20	68	Bernie Williams	.20
61	Moises Alou	.20	69	Wil Cordero	.20
62	Cecil Fielder	.20	70	Wade Boggs	1.00
63	Brad Radke	.20	71	Gary Gaetti	.20
64	Quilvio Veras	.20	72	Greg Colbrunn	.20
65	Eddie Murray	.75	73	Juan Gonzalez	.50
66	Dave Winfield	.75	74	Marc Newfield	.20
67	Fred McGriff	.20	75	Charles Nagy	.20
68	Craig Biggio	.20	76	Robby Thompson	.20
69	Cliff Floyd	.20	77	Roberto Petagine	.20
70	Tim Naehring	.20	78	Darryl Strawberry	.20
71	John Wetteland	.20	79	Tino Martinez	.20
72	Alan Trammell	.20	80	Eric Karros	.20
73	Steve Avery	.20	81	Cal Ripken Jr. (Star Struck)	1.50
74	Rick Aguilera	.20	82	Cecil Fielder (Star Struck)	.20
75	Derek Bell	.20	83	Kirby Puckett (Star Struck)	.50
76	Todd Hollandsworth	.20	84	Jim Edmonds (Star Struck)	.20
77	Edgar Martinez	.20	85	Matt Williams (Star Struck)	.20
78	Mark Lemke	.20	86	Alex Rodriguez (Star Struck)	1.00
79	Ariel Prieto	.20	87	Barry Larkin (Star Struck)	.20
80	Russ Davis	.20	88	Rafael Palmeiro (Star Struck)	.40
81	Jim Abbott	.20	89	David Cone (Star Struck)	.20
82	Jason Isringhausen	.20	90	Roberto Alomar (Star Struck)	.25
83	Carlos Perez	.20	91	Eddie Murray (Star Struck)	.40
84	David Segui	.20	92	Randy Johnson (Star Struck)	.40
85	Troy O'Leary	.20	93	Ryan Klesko (Star Struck)	.20
86	Ismael Valdes	.20	94	Raul Mondesi (Star Struck)	.20
87	Carlos Delgado	.50	95	Mo Vaughn (Star Struck)	.20
88	Lee Smith	.20	96	Will Clark (Star Struck)	.20
89	Javy Lopez	.20	97	Carlos Baerga (Star Struck)	.20
90	Frank Rodriguez	.20	98	Frank Thomas (Star Struck)	.45
91	Alex Gonzalez	.20	99	Larry Walker (Star Struck)	.20
92	Benji Gil	.20	100	Garret Anderson (Star Struck)	
93	Greg Gagne	.20	101	Edgar Martinez (Star Struck)	
94	Randy Myers	.20	102	Don Mattingly (Star Struck)	.60
95	Bobby Bonilla	.20	103	Tony Gwynn (Star Struck)	.50
96	Billy Ashley	.20	104	Albert Belle (Star Struck)	
97	Andy Van Slyke	.20	105	Jason Isringhausen (Star Struck)	
98	Edgardo Alfonzo	.20	106	Ruben Rivera (Star Struck)	
99	David Cone	.20	107	Johnny Damon (Star Struck)	.35
100	Dean Palmer	.20	108	Karim Garcia (Star Struck)	.20
101	Jose Mesa	.20	109	Derek Jeter (Star Struck)	1.50
102	Karim Garcia	.20	110	David Justice (Star Struck)	.20
103	Johnny Damon	.40			
104	LaTroy Hawkins	.20			
105	Mark Smith	.20			
106	Derek Jeter	3.00			
107	Michael Tucker	.20			
108	Joe Vitiello	.20			
109	Ruben Rivera	.20			
110	Gregg Zaun	.20			
1	Greg Maddux	1.00			
2	Pedro Martinez	.75			
3	Bobby Higginson	.20			
4	Ray Lankford	.20			
5	Shawon Dunston	.20			
6	Gary Sheffield	.45			
7	Ken Griffey Jr.	1.50			
8	Paul Molitor	.75			
9	Kevin Appier	.20			
10	Chuck Knoblauch	.20			
11	Alex Fernandez	.20			
12	Steve Finley	.20			
13	Jeff Blauser	.20			
14	Charles Johnson	.20			
15	John Franco	.20			
16	Mark Langston	.20			
17	Bret Saberhagen	.20			
18	John Mabry	.20			
19	Ramon Martinez	.20			
20	Mike Blowers	.20			
21	Paul O'Neill	.20			
22	Dave Nilsson	.20			
23	Dante Bichette	.20			
24	Marty Cordova	.20			
25	Jay Bell	.20			
26	Mike Mussina	.20			
27	Ivan Rodriguez	.65			
28	Jose Canseco	.50			
29	Jeff Bagwell	.75			
30	Manny Ramirez	.75			
31	Dennis Martinez	.20			
32	Charlie Hayes	.20			
33	Joe Carter	.20			
34	Travis Fryman	.20			
35	Mark McGwire	2.00			
36	Reggie Sanders	.20			
37	Julian Tavarez	.20			
38	Jeff Montgomery	.20			
39	Andy Benes	.20			
40	John Jaha	.20			
41	Jeff Kent	.20			
42	Mike Piazza	1.50			
43	Erik Hanson	.20			
44	Kenny Rogers	.20			
45	Hideo Nomo	.50			
46	Gregg Jefferies	.20			
47	Chipper Jones	1.00			
48	Jay Buhner	.20			
49	Dennis Eckersley	.65			

Dugout Collection Artist's Proofs

A parallel set within a parallel set, the Artist's Proof logo added to the copper-foil design of the Dugout Collection cards raises the odds of finding one to just once in 36 packs.

		NM/M
Complete Set (220):		300.00
Common Player:		1.00
Artist's Proof Stars:		4X

All-Stars

Chipper Jones All-Stars

An exclusive insert found only in 20-card Series 2 jumbo packs at an average rate of one per nine packs, these inserts feature the game's top stars printed in a rainbow holographic-foil technology.

		NM/M
Complete Set (20):		13.50
Common Player:		.25
1	Frank Thomas	1.25
2	Albert Belle	.25
3	Ken Griffey Jr.	2.00
4	Cal Ripken Jr.	3.00
5	Mo Vaughn	.25
6	Matt Williams	.25
7	Barry Bonds	3.00
8	Dante Bichette	.25
9	Tony Gwynn	1.50
10	Greg Maddux	1.50
11	Randy Johnson	1.25
12	Hideo Nomo	.75
13	Tim Salmon	.25
14	Jeff Bagwell	1.25
15	Edgar Martinez	.25
16	Reggie Sanders	.25
17	Larry Walker	.25
18	Chipper Jones	1.50
19	Manny Ramirez	1.25
20	Eddie Murray	1.25

Big Bats

Big Bats Tony GWYNN Padres

Gold-foil printing highlights cards of 20 of the game's top hitters found in this retail-packaging exclusive insert set. Stated odds of picking a Big Bats card are one in 31 packs.

		NM/M
Complete Set (20):		12.50
Common Player:		.45
1	Cal Ripken Jr.	3.00
2	Ken Griffey Jr.	2.00
3	Frank Thomas	.75
4	Jeff Bagwell	.75
5	Mike Piazza	2.00
6	Barry Bonds	3.00
7	Matt Williams	.45
8	Raul Mondesi	.45
9	Tony Gwynn	1.25
10	Albert Belle	.45
11	Manny Ramirez	.75
12	Carlos Baerga	.45
13	Mo Vaughn	.45
14	Derek Bell	.45
15	Larry Walker	.45
16	Kenny Lofton	.45
17	Edgar Martinez	.45
18	Reggie Sanders	.45
19	Eddie Murray	.75
20	Chipper Jones	1.25

Diamond Aces

MONDESI
RAUL MONDESI
Los Angeles Dodgers

Thirty of the top veterans and young stars are included in this jumbo-only insert set, seeded at a rate of one per eight packs.

		NM/M
Complete Set (30):		25.00
Common Player:		.35
1	Hideo Nomo	.60
2	Brian Hunter	.35
3	Ray Durham	.35
4	Frank Thomas	1.00
5	Cal Ripken Jr.	3.50
6	Barry Bonds	3.50
7	Greg Maddux	1.25
8	Chipper Jones	1.25
9	Raul Mondesi	.35
10	Mike Piazza	2.00
11	Derek Jeter	3.50
12	Bill Pulsipher	.35
13	Larry Walker	.35
14	Ken Griffey Jr.	2.00
15	Alex Rodriguez	3.00
16	Manny Ramirez	1.00
17	Mo Vaughn	.35
18	Reggie Sanders	.35
19	Derek Bell	.35
20	Jim Edmonds	.35
21	Albert Belle	.35
22	Eddie Murray	1.00
23	Tony Gwynn	1.25
24	Jeff Bagwell	1.00
25	Carlos Baerga	.35
26	Matt Williams	.35
27	Garret Anderson	.35
28	Todd Hollandsworth	.35
29	Johnny Damon	.75
30	Tim Salmon	.35

Dream Team

The hottest player at each position is honored in the Dream Team insert set. Once again featured on holographic foil printing technology, the cards are found in all types of Score packaging at a rate of once per 72 packs.

		NM/M
Complete Set (9):		15.00
Common Player:		.75
1	Cal Ripken Jr.	4.00
2	Frank Thomas	1.50
3	Carlos Baerga	.75
4	Matt Williams	.75
5	Mike Piazza	3.00
6	Barry Bonds	4.00
7	Ken Griffey Jr.	3.00
8	Manny Ramirez	1.50
9	Greg Maddux	2.00

Future Franchise

Future Franchise is the most difficult insert to pull from packs of Series 2, at the rate of once per 72 packs, on average. Sixteen young stars are showcased on holographic gold-foil printing in the set.

		NM/M
Complete Set (16):		20.00

Marc Newfield — FUTURE FRANCHISE — J.T. SNOW NUMBERS

		NM/M
Common Player:		.75
1	Jason Isringhausen	.75
2	Chipper Jones	2.50
3	Derek Jeter	5.00
4	Alex Rodriguez	4.00
5	Alex Ochoa	.75
6	Manny Ramirez	1.50
7	Johnny Damon	1.00
8	Ruben Rivera	.75
9	Karim Garcia	.75
10	Garret Anderson	.75
11	Marty Cordova	.75
12	Bill Pulsipher	.75
13	Hideo Nomo	1.00
14	Marc Newfield	.75
15	Charles Johnson	.75
16	Raul Mondesi	.75

Gold Stars

BARRY LARKIN

Appearing once in every 15 packs of Series 2, Gold Stars are labeled with a stamp in the upper-left corner. The set contains 30 top current stars printed on gold-foil and seeded at the average rate of one per 15 packs.

		NM/M
Complete Set (30):		20.00
Common Player:		.20
1	Ken Griffey Jr.	2.00
2	Frank Thomas	1.00
3	Reggie Sanders	.20
4	Tim Salmon	.20
5	Mike Piazza	2.00
6	Tony Gwynn	1.50
7	Gary Sheffield	.45
8	Matt Williams	.20
9	Bernie Williams	.20
10	Jason Isringhausen	.20
11	Albert Belle	.20
12	Chipper Jones	1.50
13	Edgar Martinez	.20
14	Barry Larkin	.20
15	Barry Bonds	3.00
16	Jeff Bagwell	1.00
17	Greg Maddux	1.50
18	Mo Vaughn	.20
19	Ryan Klesko	.20
20	Sammy Sosa	1.50
21	Darren Daulton	.20
22	Ivan Rodriguez	.75
23	Dante Bichette	.20
24	Hideo Nomo	.50
25	Cal Ripken Jr.	3.00
26	Rafael Palmeiro	.75
27	Larry Walker	.20
28	Carlos Baerga	.20
29	Randy Johnson	1.00
30	Manny Ramirez	1.00

Numbers Game

Some of the 1995 season's most impressive statistical accomplishments are featured in this chase set. Cards are enhanced with gold foil and found in all types of Score packs at an average rate of one per 15 packs.

		NM/M
Complete Set (30):		17.50
Common Player:		.15
1	Cal Ripken Jr.	2.50
2	Frank Thomas	.75
3	Ken Griffey Jr.	1.50
4	Mike Piazza	1.50
5	Barry Bonds	2.50
6	Greg Maddux	1.00
7	Jeff Bagwell	.75
8	Derek Bell	.15
9	Tony Gwynn	1.00
10	Hideo Nomo	.50
11	Raul Mondesi	.15
12	Manny Ramirez	.75
13	Albert Belle	.15
14	Matt Williams	.15
15	Jim Edmonds	.15
16	Edgar Martinez	.15
17	Mo Vaughn	.15
18	Reggie Sanders	.15
19	Chipper Jones	1.00
20	Larry Walker	.15
21	Juan Gonzalez	.50
22	Kenny Lofton	.15
23	Don Mattingly	1.25
24	Ivan Rodriguez	.65
25	Randy Johnson	.75
26	Derek Jeter	2.50
27	J.T. Snow	.15
28	Will Clark	.15
29	Rafael Palmeiro	.65
30	Alex Rodriguez	2.00

Power Pace

eric KARROS — POWER PACE

Power Pace is exclusive to retail packs in Series 2, where they are found on average every 31 packs. Eighteen top power hitters are featured in this issue in a gold-foil design.

		NM/M
Complete Set (18):		24.00
Common Player:		.50
1	Mark McGwire	4.00
2	Albert Belle	.50
3	Jay Buhner	.50
4	Frank Thomas	1.50
5	Matt Williams	.50
6	Gary Sheffield	.75
7	Mike Piazza	3.00
8	Larry Walker	.50
9	Mo Vaughn	.50
10	Rafael Palmeiro	1.25
11	Dante Bichette	.50
12	Ken Griffey Jr.	3.00
13	Barry Bonds	5.00
14	Manny Ramirez	1.50
15	Sammy Sosa	2.00
16	Tim Salmon	.50
17	Dave Justice	.50
18	Eric Karros	.50

Reflexions

REFLEXIONS — HIDEO NOMO-P

Appearing only in hobby packs this insert set pairs 20 veteran stars with 20 up-and-coming players in a foil-printed format. Odds of finding a Reflexions insert are stated as one per 31 packs.

		NM/M
Complete Set (20):		35.00
Common Player:		.45
1	Cal Ripken Jr., Chipper Jones	5.00

2	Ken Griffey Jr., Alex Rodriguez	4.50
3	Frank Thomas, Mo Vaughn	2.50
4	Kenny Lofton, Brian Hunter	.45
5	Don Mattingly, J.T. Snow	3.75
6	Manny Ramirez, Raul Mondesi	2.50
7	Tony Gwynn, Garret Anderson	3.75
8	Roberto Alomar, Carlos Baerga	.50
9	Andre Dawson, Larry Walker	.50
10	Barry Larkin, Derek Jeter	5.00
11	Barry Bonds, Reggie Sanders	5.00
12	Mike Piazza, Albert Belle	4.00
13	Wade Boggs, Edgar Martinez	3.75
14	David Cone, John Smoltz	.45
15	Will Clark, Jeff Bagwell	2.50
16	Mark McGwire, Cecil Fielder	4.50
17	Greg Maddux, Mike Mussina	3.75
18	Randy Johnson, Hideo Nomo	2.50
19	Jim Thome, Dean Palmer	2.00
20	Chuck Knoblauch, Craig Biggio	.45

Cal Ripken Tribute

The toughest pick among the 1996 Score inserts is this special card marking Cal Ripken's 2,131st consecutive game. The insertion rate is one per 300 packs hobby and retail, one per 150 jumbo packs.

NM/M

2131	Cal Ripken Jr. (Tribute)	4.00

Titantic Taters

One of the more creative names in the 1996 insert lineup, Titanic Taters are found one in every 31 packs of Series 2 hobby. Gold-foil fronts feature 18 of the game's heaviest hitters.

NM/M

Complete Set (18):		25.00
Common Player:		.60
1	Albert Belle	.60
2	Frank Thomas	2.00
3	Mo Vaughn	.60
4	Ken Griffey Jr.	3.00
5	Matt Williams	.60
6	Mark McGwire	3.50
7	Dante Bichette	.60
8	Tim Salmon	.60
9	Jeff Bagwell	2.00
10	Rafael Palmeiro	1.50
11	Mike Piazza	.60
12	Cecil Fielder	.60
13	Larry Walker	.60
14	Sammy Sosa	2.50
15	Manny Ramirez	2.00
16	Gary Sheffield	.90
17	Barry Bonds	5.00
18	Jay Buhner	.60

1997 Score

A total of 551 cards make up the base set, with 330 cards sold in Series I and 221 making

up Series II. The basic card design features a color action photo surrounded by a white border. The player's name is above the photo, with the team name underneath. Backs feature text and statistics against a white background with the image of the team logo ghosted into the background. Two parallel insert sets - Artist's Proof and Showcase Series - were part of each series. Other inserts in Series I were Pitcher Perfect, The Franchise, The Glowing Franchise, Titanic Taters (retail exclusive), Stellar Season (magazine packs only), and The Highlight Zone (hobby exclusive). Series II inserts were Blastmasters, Heart of the Order and Stand and Deliver. Cards were sold in 10-card packs for 99 cents each.

	NM/M
Complete Set (551):	16.00
Factory Tin-Box Set (551):	17.50
Common Player:	.05
Showcase:	3X
Artist's Proofs:	10X
Premium Stocks:	3X
Wax Pack (10):	.50
Wax Box (36):	12.00

1	Jeff Bagwell	.50
2	Mickey Tettleton	.05
3	Johnny Damon	.25
4	Jeff Conine	.05
5	Bernie Williams	.05
6	Will Clark	.05
7	Ryan Klesko	.05
8	Cecil Fielder	.05
9	Paul Wilson	.05
10	Gregg Jefferies	.05
11	Chili Davis	.05
12	Albert Belle	.05
13	Ken Hill	.05
14	Cliff Floyd	.05
15	Jaime Navarro	.05
16	Ismael Valdes	.05
17	Jeff King	.05
18	Chris Bosio	.05
19	Reggie Sanders	.05
20	Darren Daulton	.05
21	Ken Caminiti	.05
22	Mike Piazza	.75
23	Chad Mottola	.05
24	Darin Erstad	.15
25	Dante Bichette	.05
26	Frank Thomas	.50
27	Ben McDonald	.05
28	Raul Casanova	.05
29	Kevin Ritz	.05
30	Garret Anderson	.05
31	Jason Kendall	.05
32	Billy Wagner	.05
33	David Justice	.05
34	Marty Cordova	.05
35	Derek Jeter	1.50
36	Trevor Hoffman	.05
37	Geronimo Berroa	.05
38	Walt Weiss	.05
39	Kirt Manwaring	.05
40	Alex Gonzalez	.05
41	Sean Berry	.05
42	Kevin Appier	.05
43	Rusty Greer	.05
44	Pete Incaviglia	.05
45	Rafael Palmeiro	.45
46	Eddie Murray	.50
47	Moises Alou	.05
48	Mark Lewis	.05
49	Hal Morris	.05
50	Edgar Renteria	.05
51	Rickey Henderson	.50
52	Pat Listach	.05
53	John Wasdin	.05
54	James Baldwin	.05
55	Brian Jordan	.05
56	Edgar Martinez	.05
57	Wil Cordero	.05
58	Danny Tartabull	.05
59	Keith Lockhart	.05
60	Rico Brogna	.05

61	Ricky Bottalico	.05
62	Terry Pendleton	.05
63	Bret Boone	.05
64	Charlie Hayes	.05
65	Marc Newfield	.05
66	Sterling Hitchcock	.05
67	Roberto Alomar	.15
68	John Jaha	.05
69	Greg Colbrunn	.05
70	Sal Fasano	.05
71	Brooks Kieschnick	.05
72	Pedro Martinez	.50
73	Kevin Elster	.05
74	Ellis Burks	.05
75	Chuck Finley	.05
76	John Olerud	.05
77	Jay Bell	.05
78	Allen Watson	.05
79	Darryl Strawberry	.05
80	Orlando Miller	.05
81	Jose Herrera	.05
82	Andy Pettitte	.20
83	Juan Guzman	.05
84	Alan Benes	.05
85	Jack McDowell	.05
86	Ugueth Urbina	.05
87	Rocky Coppinger	.05
88	Jeff Cirillo	.05
89	Tom Glavine	.35
90	Robby Thompson	.05
91	Barry Bonds	1.50
92	Carlos Delgado	.40
93	Mo Vaughn	.05
94	Ryne Sandberg	.65
95	Alex Rodriguez	1.00
96	Brady Anderson	.05
97	Scott Brosius	.05
98	Dennis Eckersley	.45
99	Brian McRae	.05
100	Rey Ordonez	.05
101	John Valentin	.05
102	Brett Butler	.05
103	Eric Karros	.05
104	Harold Baines	.05
105	Javier Lopez	.05
106	Alan Trammell	.05
107	Jim Thome	.45
108	Frank Rodriguez	.05
109	Bernard Gilkey	.05
110	Reggie Jefferson	.05
111	Scott Stahoviak	.05
112	Steve Gibralter	.05
113	Todd Hollandsworth	.05
114	Ruben Rivera	.05
115	Dennis Martinez	.05
116	Mariano Rivera	.10
117	John Smoltz	.05
118	John Mabry	.05
119	Tom Gordon	.05
120	Alex Ochoa	.05
121	Jamey Wright	.05
122	Dave Nilsson	.05
123	Bobby Bonilla	.05
124	Al Leiter	.05
125	Rick Aguilera	.05
126	Jeff Brantley	.05
127	Kevin Brown	.05
128	George Arias	.05
129	Darren Oliver	.05
130	Bill Pulsipher	.05
131	Roberto Hernandez	.05
132	Delino DeShields	.05
133	Mark Grudzielanek	.05
134	John Wetteland	.05
135	Carlos Baerga	.05
136	Paul Sorrento	.05
137	Leo Gomez	.05
138	Andy Ashby	.05
139	Julio Franco	.05
140	Brian Hunter	.05
141	Jermaine Dye	.05
142	Tony Clark	.15
143	Ruben Sierra	.05
144	Donovan Osborne	.05
145	Mark McLemore	.05
146	Terry Steinbach	.05
147	Bob Wells	.05
148	Chan Ho Park	.05
149	Tim Salmon	.05
150	Paul O'Neill	.05
151	Cal Ripken Jr.	1.50
152	Wally Joyner	.05
153	Omar Vizquel	.05
154	Mike Mussina	.30
155	Andres Galarraga	.05
156	Ken Griffey Jr.	.75
157	Kenny Lofton	.05
158	Ray Durham	.05
159	Hideo Nomo	.25
160	Ozzie Guillen	.05
161	Roger Pavlik	.05
162	Manny Ramirez	.50
163	Mark Lemke	.05
164	Mike Stanley	.05
165	Chuck Knoblauch	.05
166	Kimera Bartee	.05
167	Wade Boggs	.65
168	Jay Buhner	.05
169	Eric Young	.05
170	Jose Canseco	.30
171	Dwight Gooden	.05
172	Fred McGriff	.05
173	Sandy Alomar Jr.	.05
174	Andy Benes	.05
175	Dean Palmer	.05
176	Larry Walker	.05
177	Charles Nagy	.05
178	David Cone	.05

179	Mark Grace	.05
180	Robin Ventura	.05
181	Roger Clemens	.70
182	Bobby Witt	.05
183	Vinny Castilla	.05
184	Gary Sheffield	.35
185	Dan Wilson	.05
186	Roger Cedeno	.05
187	Mark McGwire	1.00
188	Darren Bragg	.05
189	Quinton McCracken	.05
190	Randy Myers	.05
191	Jeromy Burnitz	.05
192	Randy Johnson	.50
193	Chipper Jones	.65
194	Greg Vaughn	.05
195	Travis Fryman	.05
196	Tim Naehring	.05
197	B.J. Surhoff	.05
198	Juan Gonzalez	.25
199	Terrell Wade	.05
200	Jeff Frye	.05
201	Joey Cora	.05
202	Raul Mondesi	.05
203	Ivan Rodriguez	.45
204	Armando Reynoso	.05
205	Jeffrey Hammonds	.05
206	Darren Dreifort	.05
207	Kevin Seitzer	.05
208	Tino Martinez	.05
209	Jim Bruske	.05
210	Jeff Suppan	.05
211	Mark Carreon	.05
212	Wilson Alvarez	.05
213	John Burkett	.05
214	Tony Phillips	.05
215	Greg Maddux	.65
216	Mark Whiten	.05
217	Curtis Pride	.05
218	Lyle Mouton	.05
219	Todd Hundley	.05
220	Greg Gagne	.05
221	Rich Amaral	.05
222	Tom Goodwin	.05
223	Chris Hoiles	.05
224	Jayhawk Owens	.05
225	Kenny Rogers	.05
226	Mike Greenwell	.05
227	Mark Wohlers	.05
228	Henry Rodriguez	.05
229	Robert Perez	.05
230	Jeff Kent	.05
231	Darryl Hamilton	.05
232	Alex Fernandez	.05
233	Ron Karkovice	.05
234	Jimmy Haynes	.05
235	Craig Biggio	.05
236	Ray Lankford	.05
237	Lance Johnson	.05
238	Matt Williams	.05
239	Chad Curtis	.05
240	Mark Thompson	.05
241	Jason Giambi	.40
242	Barry Larkin	.05
243	Paul Molitor	.50
244	Sammy Sosa	.65
245	Kevin Tapani	.05
246	Marquis Grissom	.05
247	Joe Carter	.05
248	Ramon Martinez	.05
249	Tony Gwynn	.65
250	Andy Fox	.05
251	Troy O'Leary	.05
252	Warren Newson	.05
253	Troy Percival	.05
254	Jamie Moyer	.05
255	Danny Graves	.05
256	David Wells	.05
257	Todd Zeile	.05
258	Raul Ibanez	.05
259	Tyler Houston	.05
260	LaTroy Hawkins	.05
261	Joey Hamilton	.05
262	Mike Sweeney	.05
263	Brant Brown	.05
264	Pat Hentgen	.05
265	Mark Johnson	.05
266	Robb Nen	.05
267	Justin Thompson	.05
268	Ron Gant	.05
269	Jeff D'Amico	.05
270	Shawn Estes	.05
271	Derek Bell	.05
272	Fernando Valenzuela	.05
273	Luis Castillo	.05
274	Ray Montgomery	.05
275	Ed Sprague	.05
276	F.P. Santangelo	.05
277	Todd Greene	.05
278	Butch Huskey	.05
279	Steve Finley	.05
280	Eric Davis	.05
281	Shawn Green	.30
282	Al Martin	.05
283	Michael Tucker	.05
284	Shane Reynolds	.05
285	Matt Mieske	.05
286	Jose Rosado	.05
287	Mark Langston	.05
288	Ralph Milliard	.05
289	Mike Lansing	.05
290	Scott Servais	.05
291	Royce Clayton	.05
292	Mike Grace	.05
293	James Mouton	.05
294	Charles Johnson	.05
295	Gary Gaetti	.05
296	Kevin Mitchell	.05

297	Carlos Garcia	.05
298	Desi Relaford	.05
299	Jason Thompson	.05
300	Osvaldo Fernandez	.05
301	Fernando Vina	.05
302	Jose Offerman	.05
303	Yamil Benitez	.05
304	J.T. Snow	.05
305	Rafael Bournigal	.05
306	Jason Isringhausen	.05
307	Bob Higginson	.05
308	Nerio Rodriguez RC	.05
309	Brian Giles RC	.50
310	Andruw Jones	.50
311	Billy McMillon	.05
312	Arquimedez Pozo	.05
313	Jermaine Allensworth	.05
314	Luis Andujar	.05
315	Angel Echevarria	.05
316	Karim Garcia	.05
317	Trey Beamon	.05
318	Makoto Suzuki	.05
319	Robin Jennings	.05
320	Dmitri Young	.05
321	Damon Mashore RC	.05
322	Wendell Magee	.05
323	Dax Jones RC	.05
324	Todd Walker	.05
325	Marvin Benard	.05
326	Brian Raabe RC	.05
327	Marcus Jensen	.05
328	Checklist	.05
329	Checklist	.05
330	Checklist	.05
331	Norm Charlton	.05
332	Bruce Ruffin	.05
333	John Wetteland	.05
334	Marquis Grissom	.05
335	Sterling Hitchcock	.05
336	John Olerud	.05
337	David Wells	.05
338	Chili Davis	.05
339	Mark Lewis	.05
340	Kenny Lofton	.05
341	Alex Fernandez	.05
342	Ruben Sierra	.05
343	Delino DeShields	.05
344	John Wasdin	.05
345	Dennis Martinez	.05
346	Kevin Elster	.05
347	Bobby Bonilla	.05
348	Jaime Navarro	.05
349	Chad Curtis	.05
350	Terry Steinbach	.05
351	Ariel Prieto	.05
352	Jeff Kent	.05
353	Carlos Garcia	.05
354	Mark Whiten	.05
355	Todd Zelle	.05
356	Eric Davis	.05
357	Greg Colbrunn	.05
358	Moises Alou	.05
359	Allen Watson	.05
360	Jose Canseco	.30
361	Matt Williams	.05
362	Jeff King	.05
363	Darryl Hamilton	.05
364	Mark Clark	.05
365	J.T. Snow	.05
366	Kevin Mitchell	.05
367	Orlando Miller	.05
368	Rico Brogna	.05
369	Mike James	.05
370	Brad Ausmus	.05
371	Darryl Kile	.05
372	Edgardo Alfonzo	.05
373	Julian Tavarez	.05
374	Darren Lewis	.05
375	Steve Karsay	.05
376	Lee Stevens	.05
377	Albie Lopez	.05
378	Orel Hershiser	.05
379	Lee Smith	.05
380	Rick Helling	.05
381	Carlos Perez	.05
382	Tony Tarasco	.05
383	Melvin Nieves	.05
384	Benji Gil	.05
385	Devon White	.05
386	Armando Benitez	.05
387	Bill Swift	.05
388	John Smiley	.05
389	Midre Cummings	.05
390	Tim Belcher	.05
391	Tim Raines	.05
392	Todd Worrell	.05
393	Quilvio Veras	.05
394	Matt Lawton	.05
395	Aaron Sele	.05
396	Bip Roberts	.05
397	Denny Neagle	.05
398	Tyler Green	.05
399	Hipolito Pichardo	.05
400	Scott Erickson	.05
401	Bobby Jones	.05
402	Jim Edmonds	.05
403	Chad Ogea	.05
404	Cal Eldred	.05
405	Pat Listach	.05
406	Todd Stottlemyre	.05
407	Phil Nevin	.05
408	Otis Nixon	.05
409	Billy Ashley	.05
410	Jimmy Key	.05
411	Mike Timlin	.05
412	Joe Vitiello	.05
413	Rondell White	.05
414	Jeff Fassero	.05

415	Rex Hudler	.05
416	Curt Schilling	.35
417	Rich Becker	.05
418	William Van Landingham	.05
419	Chris Snopek	.05
420	David Segui	.05
421	Eddie Murray	.50
422	Shane Andrews	.05
423	Gary DiSarcina	.05
424	Brian Hunter	.05
425	Willie Greene	.05
426	Felipe Crespo	.05
427	Jason Bates	.05
428	Albert Belle	.05
429	Rey Sanchez	.05
430	Roger Clemens	.70
431	Deion Sanders	.05
432	Ernie Young	.05
433	Jay Bell	.05
434	Jeff Blauser	.05
435	Lenny Dykstra	.05
436	Chuck Carr	.05
437	Russ Davis	.05
438	Carl Everett	.05
439	Damion Easley	.05
440	Pat Kelly	.05
441	Pat Rapp	.05
442	David Justice	.05
443	Graeme Lloyd	.05
444	Damon Buford	.05
445	Jose Valentin	.05
446	Jason Schmidt	.05
447	Dave Martinez	.05
448	Danny Tartabull	.05
449	Jose Vizcaino	.05
450	Steve Avery	.05
451	Mike Devereaux	.05
452	Jim Eisenreich	.05
453	Mark Leiter	.05
454	Roberto Kelly	.05
455	Benito Santiago	.05
456	Steve Trachsel	.05
457	Gerald Williams	.05
458	Pete Schourek	.05
459	Esteban Loaiza	.05
460	Mel Rojas	.05
461	Tim Wakefield	.05
462	Tony Fernandez	.05
463	Doug Drabek	.05
464	Joe Girardi	.05
465	Mike Bordick	.05
466	Jim Leyritz	.05
467	Erik Hanson	.05
468	Michael Tucker	.05
469	Tony Womack RC	.10
470	Doug Glanville	.05
471	Rudy Pemberton	.05
472	Keith Lockhart	.05
473	Nomar Garciaparra	.65
474	Scott Rolen	.40
475	Jason Dickson	.05
476	Glendon Rusch	.05
477	Todd Walker	.05
478	Dmitri Young	.05
479	Rod Myers RC	.05
480	Wilton Guerrero	.05
481	Jorge Posada	.05
482	Brant Brown	.05
483	Bubba Trammell RC	.10
485	Jose Guillen	.05
485	Scott Spiezio	.05
486	Bob Abreu	.10
487	Chris Holt	.05
488	Deivi Cruz RC	.05
489	Vladimir Guerrero	.50
490	Julio Santana	.05
491	Ray Montgomery	.05
492	Kevin Orie	.05
493	Todd Hundley (Goin' Yard)	.05
494	Tim Salmon (Goin' Yard)	.05
495	Albert Belle (Goin' Yard)	.05
496	Manny Ramirez (Goin' Yard)	.25
497	Rafael Palmeiro (Goin' Yard)	.20
498	Juan Gonzalez (Goin' Yard)	.15
499	Ken Griffey Jr. (Goin' Yard)	.40
500	Andruw Jones (Goin' Yard)	.25
501	Mike Piazza (Goin' Yard)	.40
502	Jeff Bagwell (Goin' Yard)	.25
503	Bernie Williams (Goin' Yard)	.05
504	Barry Bonds (Goin' Yard)	.65
505	Ken Caminiti (Goin' Yard)	.05
506	Darin Erstad (Goin' Yard)	.10
507	Alex Rodriguez (Goin' Yard)	.50
508	Frank Thomas (Goin' Yard)	.30
509	Chipper Jones (Goin' Yard)	.35
510	Mo Vaughn (Goin' Yard)	.05
511	Mark McGwire (Goin' Yard)	.50

512	Fred McGriff (Goin' Yard)	.05
513	Jay Buhner (Goin' Yard)	.05
514	Jim Thome (Goin' Yard)	.20
515	Gary Sheffield (Goin' Yard)	.20
516	Dean Palmer (Goin' Yard)	.05
517	Henry Rodriguez (Goin' Yard)	.05
518	Andy Pettitte (Rock & Fire)	.10
519	Mike Mussina (Rock & Fire)	.10
520	Greg Maddux (Rock & Fire)	.35
521	John Smoltz (Rock & Fire)	.05
522	Hideo Nomo (Rock & Fire)	.15
523	Troy Percival (Rock & Fire)	.05
524	John Wetteland (Rock & Fire)	.05
525	Roger Clemens (Rock & Fire)	.40
526	Charles Nagy (Rock & Fire)	.05
527	Mariano Rivera (Rock & Fire)	.10
528	Tom Glavine (Rock & Fire)	.15
529	Randy Johnson (Rock & Fire)	.25
530	Jason Isringhausen (Rock & Fire)	.05
531	Alex Fernandez (Rock & Fire)	.05
532	Kevin Brown (Rock & Fire)	.05
533	Chuck Knoblauch (True Grit)	.05
534	Rusty Greer (True Grit)	.05
535	Tony Gwynn (True Grit)	.35
536	Ryan Klesko (True Grit)	.05
537	Ryne Sandberg (True Grit)	.35
538	Barry Larkin (True Grit)	.05
539	Will Clark (True Grit)	.05
540	Kenny Lofton (True Grit)	.05
541	Paul Molitor (True Grit)	.30
542	Roberto Alomar (True Grit)	.10
543	Rey Ordonez (True Grit)	.05
544	Jason Giambi (True Grit)	.25
545	Derek Jeter (True Grit)	.75
546	Cal Ripken Jr. (True Grit)	.75
547	Ivan Rodriguez (True Grit)	.25
548	Checklist (Ken Griffey Jr.)	.35
549	Checklist (Frank Thomas)	.25
550	Checklist (Mike Piazza)	.40
551a	Hideki Irabu/SP **RC** (English on back; factory sets/retailpacks.)	.25
551b	Hideki Irabu/SP **RC** (Japanese back; Hobby Reserve packs.)	.35

White Border Artist's Proofs

Specially marked Artist's Proof cards were random inserts in Series 1 retail packs. Like the regular-issue cards, they have white borders, so the gold-foil "ARTIST'S PROOF" logo on front may be overlooked. Only Series 1 (#1-330) are found in this style.

	NM/M
Complete Set (330):	150.00
Common Player:	.50
Artist's Proof Stars:	10X

Hobby Reserve

This is a hobby-only parallel version of Score Series 2,

similar in concept to the Series 1 Premium Stock. Cards are identical to the regular Series 2 cards except for the addition of a gold Hobby Reserve foil seal on front.

	NM/M
Complete Set (221):	35.00
Common Player:	.10
Hobby Reserve Stars:	3X

Premium Stock

This is an upscale version of Score's regular Series 1 1997 issue, designated for hobby sales only. The cards are basically the same as the regular issue, except for the use of gray borders on front and an embossed gold-foil "Premium Stock" logo.

	NM/M
Complete Set (330):	17.50
Common Player:	.10
Premium Stock Stars:	3X

Reserve Collection

This was a hobby-only parallel version of Score Series 2, Cards are similar to regular Series 2 except for the use of a textured ray-like silver-foil background on front and a Reserve Collection underprint on back. Cards are numbered with an "HR" prefix. Average insertion rate was one per 11 packs.

	NM/M
Complete Set (221):	250.00
Common Player:	1.00
Reserve Collection Stars:	8X

Showcase

A silver metallic-foil background distinguishes the cards in this parallel set, inserted at a rate of about one per seven packs of both hobby and retail.

	NM/M
Complete Set (551):	200.00

	NM/M
Common Player:	.50
Showcase Stars:	3X

Showcase Artist's Proofs

This is a parallel of the Showcase parallel set covering all 551 cards of the base '97 Score set. The Artist's Proofs cards carry over the silver foil background of the Showcase cards on front with a rainbow-wave effect, and are marked with a round red "ARTIST'S PROOF" logo.

	NM/M
Common Player:	1.00
Showcase AP Stars:	10X

All-Star Fanfest

Highlighted with red foil and featuring participants in the 1996 All-Star Game, these inserts were a 1:29 seed in special retail boxes of Series 1 Score.

		NM/M
Complete Set (20):		15.00
Common Player:		.30
1	Frank Thomas	1.00
2	Jeff Bagwell	1.00
3	Chuck Knoblauch	.30
4	Ryne Sandberg	1.50
5	Alex Rodriguez	3.00
6	Chipper Jones	1.50
7	Jim Thome	.75
8	Ken Caminiti	.30
9	Albert Belle	.30
10	Tony Gwynn	1.50
11	Ken Griffey Jr.	2.00
12	Andruw Jones	1.00
13	Juan Gonzalez	.50
14	Brian Jordan	.30
15	Ivan Rodriguez	.75
16	Mike Piazza	2.00
17	Andy Pettitte	.30
18	John Smoltz	.30
19	John Wetteland	.30
20	Mark Wohlers	.30

Blast Masters

This set was inserted one per 35 Series 2 retail packs and every 23 hobby packs. The set displays the top power hitters in the game over a prismatic gold foil background. The word "Blast" is printed across the top, while "Master" is printed across

Common Player:		.50
Showcase Stars:		3X

the bottom, both in red. Backs are predominantly black with a color player photo at center.

		NM/M
Complete Set (18):		17.50
Common Player:		.25
1	Mo Vaughn	.25
2	Mark McGwire	2.25
3	Juan Gonzalez	.75
4	Albert Belle	.25
5	Barry Bonds	3.00
6	Ken Griffey Jr.	2.00
7	Andruw Jones	1.25
8	Chipper Jones	1.50
9	Mike Piazza	2.00
10	Jeff Bagwell	1.25
11	Dante Bichette	.25
12	Alex Rodriguez	2.25
13	Gary Sheffield	.60
14	Ken Caminiti	.25
15	Sammy Sosa	1.50
16	Vladimir Guerrero	1.25
17	Brian Jordan	.25
18	Tim Salmon	.25

Heart of the Order

This 36-card set was distributed in Series 2 retail and hobby packs, with cards 1-18 in retail (one per 23 packs) and cards 19-36 in hobby (one per 15). The cards are printed in a horizontal format, with some of the top hitters in the game included in the insert. Fronts are highlighted in red metallic foil. Backs have a color portrait photo and a few words about the player.

		NM/M
Complete Set (36):		35.00
Complete Retail Set (1-18):		20.00
Complete Hobby Set (19-36):		15.00
Common Player:		.50
1	Ivan Rodriguez	1.00
2	Will Clark	.50
3	Juan Gonzalez	.75
4	Frank Thomas	1.25
5	Albert Belle	.50
6	Robin Ventura	.50
7	Alex Rodriguez	3.00
8	Ken Griffey Jr.	2.50
9	Jay Buhner	.50
10	Roberto Alomar	.65
11	Rafael Palmeiro	1.00
12	Cal Ripken Jr.	4.00
13	Manny Ramirez	1.25
14	Matt Williams	.50
15	Jim Thome	.50
16	Derek Jeter	4.00
17	Wade Boggs	2.00
18	Bernie Williams	.50
19	Chipper Jones	2.00
20	Andruw Jones	1.25
21	Ryan Klesko	.50
22	Wilton Guerrero	.50
23	Mike Piazza	2.50
24	Raul Mondesi	.50
25	Tony Gwynn	2.00
26	Ken Caminiti	.50
27	Greg Vaughn	.50
28	Brian Jordan	.50
29	Ron Gant	.50
30	Dmitri Young	.50
31	Darin Erstad	.50
32	Jim Edmonds	.50
33	Tim Salmon	.50
34	Chuck Knoblauch	.50
35	Paul Molitor	1.25
36	Todd Walker	.50

Highlight Zone

Exclusive to 1997 Score Series 1 hobby packs are these Highlight Zone inserts, seeded one per every 35 packs. Within the 18-card set, card numbers 1-9 are in regular hobby packs, while numbers 10-18 are found only in premium stock packs.

		NM/M
Complete Set (18):		30.00
Common Player:		.60
1	Frank Thomas	1.50
2	Ken Griffey Jr.	3.00
3	Mo Vaughn	.60
4	Albert Belle	.60
5	Mike Piazza	3.00
6	Barry Bonds	4.50
7	Greg Maddux	2.25
8	Sammy Sosa	2.25
9	Jeff Bagwell	1.50
10	Alex Rodriguez	3.50
11	Chipper Jones	2.25
12	Brady Anderson	.60
13	Ozzie Smith	2.25
14	Edgar Martinez	.60
15	Cal Ripken Jr.	4.50
16	Ryan Klesko	.60
17	Randy Johnson	1.50
18	Eddie Murray	1.50

Andruw Jones Goin' Yard

This special card was a blister-pack topper on Series 2 jumbo retail packs. Jones' home run swing is featured on front with a background of the distances of his blasts. Back has details on Series 2 inserts and the Stand and Deliver promotion.

	NM/M
Andruw Jones	2.50

Pitcher Perfect

Seattle Mariners' star pitcher and accomplished photographer Randy Johnson makes his picks for the top talent in this 1997 Score Series 1 insert set. Fronts have player photos with a gold-foil filmstrip graphic at bottom featuring player names and a portrait of The Big Unit. Backs have additional color photos in a filmstrip design and a few words about the player.

		NM/M
Complete Set (15):		6.50
Common Player:		.15
1	Cal Ripken Jr.	2.00
2	Alex Rodriguez	1.25
3	Cal Ripken Jr., Alex Rodriguez	1.25
4	Edgar Martinez	.15
5	Ivan Rodriguez	.50
6	Mark McGwire	1.25
7	Tim Salmon	.15
8	Chili Davis	.15
9	Joe Carter	.15
10	Frank Thomas	.60
11	Will Clark	.15
12	Mo Vaughn	.15
13	Wade Boggs	.75
14	Ken Griffey Jr.	1.00
15	Randy Johnson	.60

Stand & Deliver

This 24-card insert was printed on a silver foil background, with the series name and team logo in gold foil across the bottom. Cards were found in Series 2 packs at the rate of one per 71 retail, one per 41 hobby. Card numbers 21-24 (Wild Card) were the winning group in a World Series contest, allowing the first 225 collectors that mailed in those four cards to receive a gold upgrade version of the set framed in glass. The gold cards have a gold foil background and red foil highlights.

		NM/M
Complete Set (24):		50.00
Common Player:		.50
Gold:		4X
1	Andruw Jones	4.00
2	Greg Maddux	4.00
3	Chipper Jones	4.00
4	John Smoltz	.50
5	Ken Griffey Jr.	5.00
6	Alex Rodriguez	6.00
7	Jay Buhner	.50
8	Randy Johnson	3.00
9	Derek Jeter	7.50
10	Andy Pettitte	.75
11	Bernie Williams	.50
12	Mariano Rivera	.50
13	Mike Piazza	5.00
14	Hideo Nomo	1.50
15	Raul Mondesi	.50
16	Todd Hollandsworth	.50
17	Manny Ramirez	3.00
18	Jim Thome	2.00
19	David Justice	.50
20	Matt Williams	.50
21	Juan Gonzalez	1.50
22	Jeff Bagwell	3.00
23	Cal Ripken Jr.	7.50
24	Frank Thomas	3.00

Stellar Season

These 1997 Score Series 1 inserts were seeded one per every 17 magazine packs.

		NM/M
Complete Set (18):		15.00
Common Player:		.50
1	Juan Gonzalez	.75
2	Chuck Knoblauch	.50
3	Jeff Bagwell	1.50
4	John Smoltz	.50
5	Mark McGwire	3.00
6	Ken Griffey Jr.	2.50
7	Frank Thomas	1.50
8	Alex Rodriguez	3.00
9	Mike Piazza	2.50
10	Albert Belle	.50
11	Roberto Alomar	.60
12	Sammy Sosa	2.00
13	Mo Vaughn	.50
14	Brady Anderson	.50
15	Henry Rodriguez	.50
16	Eric Young	.50
17	Gary Sheffield	.75
18	Ryan Klesko	.50

The Franchise

There were two versions made for these 1997 Score Series 1 inserts - regular and The Glowing Franchise, which has glow-in-the-dark highlights. The regular version is seeded one per 72 packs; glow-in-the-dark cards are seeded one per 240 packs. Each regular card can also be found in a promo version with a large, black "SAMPLE" on front and back.

	NM/M
Complete Set (9):	5.00
Common Player:	.15
Glowing:	2.5X
Samples:	2.5X
1 Ken Griffey Jr.	1.00
2 John Smoltz	.15
3 Cal Ripken Jr.	2.00
4 Chipper Jones	.75
5 Mike Piazza	1.00
6 Albert Belle	.15
7 Frank Thomas	.60
8 Sammy Sosa	.75
9 Roberto Alomar	.30

Titanic Taters

Some of the game's most powerful hitters are featured on these Series 1 inserts, found on average of one per 35 retail packs.

	NM/M
Complete Set (18):	25.00
Common Player:	.35
1 Mark McGwire	4.00
2 Mike Piazza	3.50
3 Ken Griffey Jr.	3.50
4 Juan Gonzalez	1.00
5 Frank Thomas	1.50
6 Albert Belle	.35
7 Sammy Sosa	2.50
8 Jeff Bagwell	1.50
9 Todd Hundley	.35
10 Ryan Klesko	.35
11 Brady Anderson	.35
12 Mo Vaughn	.35
13 Jay Buhner	.35
14 Chipper Jones	2.75
15 Barry Bonds	6.00
16 Gary Sheffield	.75
17 Alex Rodriguez	4.00
18 Cecil Fielder	.35

Team Collection

Team sets consisting of 15 players each were produced for 10 different teams. Each card is similar in design to the regular 1997 Score set except for a special foil stamping at the bottom of the card that corresponds with team colors. In a parallel "Platinum" version, seeded one per six packs, the background and team foil on front are replaced with silver prismatic foil. A top of the line parallel set,

"Premier" utilizes gold foil highlights on fronts and is found one per 31 packs. Team Collection was sold in five-card, single-team packs with a suggested retail price of about $1.29. It was reported that 100 cases of each team were issued.

	NM/M
Complete Set (150):	30.00
Common Player:	.10
Platinums:	4X
Premiers:	15X
Braves Wax Box:	7.50
Orioles Wax Box:	6.00
Red Sox Wax Box:	6.00
White Sox Wax Box:	6.00
Indians Wax Box:	6.00
Rockies Wax Box:	5.00
Dodgers Wax Box:	6.00
Yankees Wax Box:	7.50
Mariners Wax Box:	7.50
Rangers Wax Box:	5.00
Atlanta Braves	5.00
1 Ryan Klesko	.10
2 David Justice	.10
3 Terry Pendleton	.10
4 Tom Glavine	.35
5 Javier Lopez	.10
6 John Smoltz	.10
7 Jermaine Dye	.10
8 Mark Lemke	.10
9 Fred McGriff	.10
10 Chipper Jones	1.50
11 Terrell Wade	.10
12 Greg Maddux	1.50
13 Mark Wohlers	.10
14 Marquis Grissom	.10
15 Andruw Jones	1.00
Baltimore Orioles	4.50
1 Rafael Palmeiro	.75
2 Eddie Murray	1.00
3 Roberto Alomar	.40
4 Rocky Coppinger	.10
5 Brady Anderson	.10
6 Bobby Bonilla	.10
7 Cal Ripken Jr.	2.50
8 Mike Mussina	.45
9 Nerio Rodriguez	.10
10 Randy Myers	.10
11 B.J. Surhoff	.10
12 Jeffrey Hammonds	.10
13 Chris Hoiles	.10
14 Jimmy Haynes	.10
15 David Wells	.10
Boston Red Sox	3.00
1 Wil Cordero	.10
2 Mo Vaughn	.10
3 John Valentin	.10
4 Reggie Jefferson	.10
5 Tom Gordon	.10
6 Mike Stanley	.10
7 Jose Canseco	.45
8 Roger Clemens	1.75
9 Darren Bragg	.10
10 Jeff Frye	.10
11 Jeff Suppan	.10
12 Mike Greenwell	.10
13 Arquimedez Pozo	.10
14 Tim Naehring	.10
15 Troy O'Leary	.10
Chicago White Sox	2.25
1 Frank Thomas	1.00
2 James Baldwin	.10
3 Danny Tartabull	.10
4 Jeff Darwin	.10
5 Harold Baines	.10
6 Roberto Hernandez	.10
7 Ray Durham	.10
8 Robin Ventura	.10
9 Wilson Alvarez	.10
10 Lyle Mouton	.10
11 Alex Fernandez	.10
12 Ron Karkovice	.10
13 Kevin Tapani	.10
14 Tony Phillips	.10
15 Mike Cameron	.10
Cleveland Indians	2.25
1 Albert Belle	.10
2 Jack McDowell	.10
3 Jim Thome	.75
4 Dennis Martinez	.10
5 Julio Franco	.10
6 Omar Vizquel	.10
7 Kenny Lofton	.10
8 Manny Ramirez	1.00
9 Sandy Alomar Jr.	.10
10 Charles Nagy	.10
11 Kevin Seitzer	.10
12 Mark Carreon	.10
13 Jeff Kent	.10
14 Danny Graves	.10
15 Brian Giles	.10
Colorado Rockies	1.75
1 Dante Bichette	.10
2 Kevin Ritz	.10
3 Walt Weiss	.10
4 Ellis Burks	.10
5 Jamey Wright	.10
6 Andres Galarraga	.10
7 Eric Young	.10
8 Larry Walker	.10
9 Vinny Castilla	.10
10 Quinton McCracken	.10
11 Armando Reynoso	.10
12 Jayhawk Owens	.10
13 Mark Thompson	.10
14 John Burke	.10
15 Bruce Ruffin	.10
Los Angeles Dodgers	4.00
1 Ismael Valdez	.10
2 Mike Piazza	2.00
3 Todd Hollandsworth	.10
4 Delino DeShields	.10
5 Chan Ho Park	.10
6 Roger Cedeno	.10
7 Raul Mondesi	.10
8 Darren Dreifort	.10
9 Jim Bruske	.10
10 Greg Gagne	.10
11 Chad Curtis	.10
12 Ramon Martinez	.10
13 Brett Butler	.10
14 Eric Karros	.10
15 Hideo Nomo	.50
New York Yankees	4.50
1 Bernie Williams	.10
2 Cecil Fielder	.10
3 Derek Jeter	2.50
4 Darryl Strawberry	.10
5 Andy Pettitte	.20
6 Ruben Rivera	.15
7 Mariano Rivera	.15
8 John Wetteland	.10
9 Paul O'Neill	.10
10 Wade Boggs	1.50
11 Dwight Gooden	.10
12 David Cone	.10
13 Tino Martinez	.10
14 Kenny Rogers	.10
15 Andy Fox	.10
Seattle Mariners	5.00
1 Chris Bosio	.10
2 Edgar Martinez	.10
3 Alex Rodriguez	2.25
4 Paul Sorrento	.10
5 Bob Wells	.10
6 Ken Griffey Jr.	.10
7 Jay Buhner	.10
8 Dan Wilson	.10
9 Randy Johnson	1.00
10 Joey Cora	.10
11 Mark Whiten	.10
12 Rich Amaral	.10
13 Raul Ibanez	.10
14 Jamie Moyer	.10
15 Makoto Suzuki	.10
Texas Rangers	2.25
1 Mickey Tettleton	.10
2 Will Clark	.10
3 Ken Hill	.10
4 Rusty Greer	.10
5 Kevin Elster	.10
6 Darren Oliver	.10
7 Mark McLemore	.10
8 Roger Pavlik	.10
9 Dean Palmer	.10
10 Bobby Witt	.10
11 Juan Gonzalez	.50
12 Ivan Rodriguez	.75
13 Darryl Hamilton	.10
14 John Burkett	.10
15 Warren Newson	.10

Team Collection Platinum Team

Team sets consisting of 15 players each were produced for 10 different teams. Each card is similar in design to the regular 1997 Score set except for a special foil stamping at the bottom of the card that corresponds with team colors. In a parallel "Platinum" version, seeded one per six packs, the background and team foil on front are replaced with silver prismatic foil. Backs are overprinted in gold script, "Platinum Team." Team Collection was sold in five-card, single-team packs with a suggested retail price of about $1.29. It was reported that 100 cases of each team were issued.

	NM/M
Common Player:	2.00
Platinum Stars:	3X

Team Collection Premier Club

Team sets consisting of 15 players each were produced for 10 different teams. Each card is similar in design to the regular 1997 Score set except for a special foil stamping at the bottom of the card that corresponds with team colors. In a top of the line parallel "Premier Club" version, seeded one per 31 packs, the background and team foil on front are replaced with gold prismatic foil, and backs are overprinted "Premier Club" in gold script. Team Collection was sold in five-card, single-team packs with a suggested retail price of about $1.29. It was reported that 100 cases of each team were issued.

	NM/M
Common Player:	5.00
Premier Club Stars:	15X

1998 Score Samples

Half a dozen top stars were picked to introduce 1998 Score in this series of promo cards. Cards are virtually identical to the issued version except for the large black overprinted "SAMPLE" on back and the use of zeroes to replace 1997 stats.

	NM/M
Complete Set (6):	7.50
Common Player:	1.00
10 Alex Rodriguez	1.50
24 Mike Piazza	1.50
34 Ken Griffey Jr.	1.50
43 Cal Ripken Jr.	2.00
51 Chipper Jones	1.25
60 Carlos Delgado	1.00

1998 Score

The cards in the 270-card base set feature a color photo inside a black and white border. The player's name is printed in the left border. The entire base set is paralleled in the silver-foil Showcase Series (1:5). The Artist's Proof partial parallel gives a prismatic foil treatment to 165 base cards and was seeded 1:23. Inserts included All-Stars, Complete Players and Epix.

	NM/M
Complete Set (270):	12.00
Common Player:	.05
Showcases:	3X
Artist's Proofs:	6X
Pack (10):	.75
Wax Box (36):	15.00
All-Star Edition Box (36/10):	10.00
Jumbo Pack (20):	15.00
Jumbo Box (24):	15.00
1 Andruw Jones	.50
2 Dan Wilson	.05
3 Hideo Nomo	.30
4 Chuck Carr	.05
5 Barry Bonds	1.50
6 Jack McDowell	.05
7 Albert Belle	.05
8 Francisco Cordova	.05
9 Greg Maddux	.65
10 Alex Rodriguez	1.00
11 Steve Avery	.05
12 Chuck McElroy	.05
13 Larry Walker	.05
14 Hideki Irabu	.05
15 Roberto Alomar	.20
16 Neifi Perez	.05
17 Jim Thome	.40
18 Rickey Henderson	.05
19 Andres Galarraga	.05
20 Jeff Fassero	.05
21 Kevin Young	.05
22 Derek Jeter	1.50
23 Andy Benes	.05
24 Mike Piazza	.75
25 Todd Stottlemyre	.05
26 Michael Tucker	.05
27 Denny Neagle	.05
28 Javier Lopez	.05
29 Aaron Sele	.05
30 Ryan Klesko	.05
31 Dennis Eckersley	.40
32 Quinton McCracken	.05
33 Brian Anderson	.05
34 Ken Griffey Jr.	.75
35 Shawn Estes	.05
36 Tim Wakefield	.05
37 Jimmy Key	.05
38 Jeff Bagwell	.50
39 Edgardo Alfonzo	.05
40 Mike Cameron	.05
41 Mark McGwire	1.00
42 Tino Martinez	.05
43 Cal Ripken Jr.	1.50
44 Curtis Goodwin	.05
45 Bobby Ayala	.05
46 Sandy Alomar Jr.	.05
47 Bobby Jones	.05
48 Omar Vizquel	.05
49 Roger Clemens	.70
50 Tony Gwynn	.65
51 Chipper Jones	.65
52 Ron Coomer	.05
53 Dmitri Young	.05
54 Brian Giles	.05
55 Steve Finley	.05
56 David Cone	.05
57 Andy Pettitte	.20
58 Wilton Guerrero	.05
59 Deion Sanders	.05
60 Carlos Delgado	.30
61 Jason Giambi	.30
62 Ozzie Guillen	.05
63 Jay Bell	.05
64 Barry Larkin	.05
65 Sammy Sosa	.65
66 Bernie Williams	.05
67 Terry Steinbach	.05
68 Scott Rolen	.40
69 Melvin Nieves	.05
70 Craig Biggio	.05
71 Todd Greene	.05
72 Greg Gagne	.05
73 Shigetosi Hasegawa	.05
74 Mark McLemore	.05
75 Darren Bragg	.05
76 Brett Butler	.05
77 Ron Gant	.05
78 Mike Difelice	.05
79 Charles Nagy	.05
80 Scott Hatteberg	.05
81 Brady Anderson	.05
82 Jay Buhner	.05
83 Todd Hollandsworth	.05
84 Geronimo Berroa	.05
85 Jeff Suppan	.05
86 Pedro Martinez	.50
87 Roger Cedeno	.05
88 Ivan Rodriguez	.40
89 Jaime Navarro	.05
90 Chris Hoiles	.05
91 Nomar Garciaparra	.65
92 Rafael Palmeiro	.40
93 Darin Erstad	.15
94 Kenny Lofton	.05
95 Mike Timlin	.05
96 Chris Clemons	.05
97 Vinny Castilla	.05
98 Charlie Hayes	.05
99 Lyle Mouton	.05
100 Jason Dickson	.05
101 Justin Thompson	.05
102 Pat Kelly	.05
103 Chan Ho Park	.05
104 Ray Lankford	.05
105 Frank Thomas	.50
106 Jermaine Allensworth	.05
107 Doug Drabek	.05
108 Todd Hundley	.05
109 Carl Everett	.05
110 Edgar Martinez	.05
111 Robin Ventura	.05
112 John Wetteland	.05
113 Mariano Rivera	.05
114 Jose Rosado	.05
115 Ken Caminiti	.05
116 Paul O'Neill	.05
117 Tim Salmon	.05
118 Eduardo Perez	.05
119 Mike Jackson	.05
120 John Smoltz	.05
121 Brant Brown	.05
122 John Mabry	.05
123 Chuck Knoblauch	.05
124 Reggie Sanders	.05
125 Ken Hill	.05
126 Mike Mussina	.25
127 Chad Curtis	.05
128 Todd Worrell	.05
129 Chris Widger	.05
130 Damon Mashore	.05
131 Kevin Brown	.05
132 Bip Roberts	.05
133 Tim Naehring	.05
134 Dave Martinez	.05
135 Jeff Blauser	.05
136 David Justice	.05
137 Dave Hollins	.05
138 Pat Hentgen	.05
139 Darren Daulton	.05
140 Ramon Martinez	.05
141 Raul Casanova	.05
142 Tom Glavine	.30
143 J.T. Snow	.05
144 Tony Graffanino	.05
145 Randy Johnson	.50
146 Orlando Merced	.05
147 Jeff Juden	.05
148 Darryl Kile	.05
149 Ray Durham	.05
150 Alex Fernandez	.05
151 Joey Cora	.05
152 Royce Clayton	.05
153 Randy Myers	.05
154 Charles Johnson	.05
155 Alan Benes	.05
156 Mike Bordick	.05
157 Heathcliff Slocumb	.05
158 Roger Bailey	.05
159 Reggie Jefferson	.05
160 Ricky Bottalico	.05
161 Scott Erickson	.05
162 Matt Williams	.05
163 Robb Nen	.05
164 Matt Stairs	.05
165 Ismael Valdes	.05
166 Lee Stevens	.05
167 Gary DiSarcina	.05
168 Brad Radke	.05
169 Mike Lansing	.05
170 Armando Benitez	.05
171 Mike James	.05
172 Russ Davis	.05
173 Lance Johnson	.05
174 Joey Hamilton	.05
175 John Valentin	.05
176 David Segui	.05
177 David Wells	.05
178 Delino DeShields	.05
179 Eric Karros	.05
180 Jim Leyritz	.05
181 Raul Mondesi	.05
182 Travis Fryman	.05
183 Todd Zeile	.05
184 Brian Jordan	.05
185 Rey Ordonez	.05
186 Jim Edmonds	.05
187 Terrell Wade	.05
188 Marquis Grissom	.05
189 Chris Snopek	.05
190 Shane Reynolds	.05
191 Jeff Frye	.05
192 Paul Sorrento	.05
193 James Baldwin	.05
194 Brian McRae	.05
195 Fred McGriff	.05
196 Troy Percival	.05
197 Rich Amaral	.05
198 Juan Guzman	.05
199 Cecil Fielder	.05
200 Willie Blair	.05
201 Chili Davis	.05
202 Gary Gaetti	.05
203 B.J. Surhoff	.05
204 Steve Cooke	.05
205 Chuck Finley	.05
206 Jeff Kent	.05
207 Ben McDonald	.05
208 Jeffrey Hammonds	.05
209 Tom Goodwin	.05
210 Billy Ashley	.05
211 Wil Cordero	.05
212 Shawon Dunston	.05
213 Tony Phillips	.05
214 Jamie Moyer	.05
215 John Jaha	.05
216 Troy O'Leary	.05
217 Brad Ausmus	.05
218 Garret Anderson	.05
219 Wilson Alvarez	.05
220 Kent Mercker	.05
221 Wade Boggs	.65
222 Mark Wohlers	.05
223 Kevin Appier	.05
224 Tony Fernandez	.05
225 Ugueth Urbina	.05
226 Gregg Jefferies	.05
227 Mo Vaughn	.05
228 Arthur Rhodes	.05
229 Jorge Fabregas	.05
230 Mark Gardner	.05
231 Shane Mack	.05
232 Jorge Posada	.05
233 Jose Cruz Jr.	.05

234	Paul Konerko	.15
235	Derek Lee	.30
236	Steve Woodard RC	.15
237	Todd Dunwoody	.05
238	Fernando Tatis	.05
239	Jacob Cruz	.05
240	Pokey Reese RC	.25
241	Mark Kotsay	.05
242	Matt Morris	.05
243	Antone Williamson RC	.05
244	Ben Grieve	.05
245	Ryan McGuire	.05
246	Lou Collier RC	.05
247	Shannon Stewart	.05
248	Brett Tomko RC	.10
249	Bobby Estalella	.05
250	Livan Hernandez RC	.15
251	Todd Helton	.40
252	Jaret Wright	.05
253	Darryl Hamilton (Interleague Moments)	.05
254	Stan Javier (Interleague Moments)	.05
255	Glenallen Hill (Interleague Moments)	.05
256	Mark Gardner (Interleague Moments)	.05
257	Cal Ripken Jr. (Interleague Moments)	.75
258	Mike Mussina (Interleague Moments)	.15
259	Mike Piazza (Interleague Moments)	.45
260	Sammy Sosa (Interleague Moments)	.35
261	Todd Hundley (Interleague Moments)	.05
262	Eric Karros (Interleague Moments)	.05
263	Denny Neagle (Interleague Moments)	.05
264	Jeromy Burnitz (Interleague Moments)	.05
265	Greg Maddux (Interleague Moments)	.35
266	Tony Clark (Interleague Moments)	.05
267	Vladimir Guerrero (Interleague Moments)	.25
268	Checklist	.05
269	Checklist	.05
270	Checklist	.05

Artist's Proofs

This partial parallel reprinted 160 of the 270 cards in Score Baseball on a foil background with an Artist's Proof logo on the front. The cards were renumbered within the 160-card set and inserted one per 35 packs. Cards have a "PP" prefix to the number on back.

		NM/M
Complete Set (160):		125.00
Common Player:		.50
Inserted 1:35		
1	Andruw Jones	1.25
2	Dan Wilson	.50
3	Hideo Nomo	.75
4	Neifi Perez	.50
5	Jim Thome	1.00
6	Jeff Fassero	.50
7	Derek Jeter	4.00
8	Andy Benes	.50
9	Michael Tucker	.50
10	Ryan Klesko	.50
11	Dennis Eckersley	1.00
12	Jimmy Key	.50
13	Edgardo Alfonzo	.50
14	Mike Cameron	.50
15	Omar Vizquel	.50
16	Ron Coomer	.50
17	Dmitri Young	.50
18	Brian Giles	.50
19	Steve Finley	.50
20	Andy Pettitte	.75
21	Wilton Guerrero	.50
22	Deion Sanders	.75
23	Carlos Delgado	.75
24	Jason Giambi	.75
25	David Cone	.50
26	Jay Bell	.50
27	Sammy Sosa	2.00
28	Barry Larkin	.50
29	Scott Rolen	1.00
30	Todd Greene	.50
31	Bernie Williams	.50
32	Brett Butler	.50
33	Ron Gant	.50
34	Brady Anderson	.50
35	Craig Biggio	.50
36	Charles Nagy	.50
37	Jay Buhner	.50
38	Geronimo Berroa	.50
39	Jeff Suppan	.50
40	Rafael Palmeiro	1.00
41	Darin Erstad	.65
42	Mike Timlin	.50
43	Vinny Castilla	.50
44	Carl Everett	.50
45	Robin Ventura	.50
46	John Wetteland	.50
47	Paul O'Neill	.50
48	Tim Salmon	.50
49	Mike Jackson	.50
50	John Smoltz	.50
51	Brant Brown	.50
52	Reggie Sanders	.50
53	Ken Hill	.50
54	Todd Worrell	.50
55	Bip Roberts	.50
56	Tim Naehring	.50
57	Darren Daulton	.50
58	Ramon Martinez	.50
59	Raul Casanova	.50
60	J.T. Snow	.50
61	Jeff Juden	.50
62	Royce Clayton	.50
63	Charles Johnson	.50
64	Alan Benes	.50
65	Reggie Jefferson	.50
66	Ricky Bottalico	.50
67	Scott Erickson	.50
68	Matt Williams	.50
69	Robb Nen	.50
70	Matt Stairs	.50
71	Ismael Valdes	.50
72	Brad Radke	.50
73	Armando Benitez	.50
74	Russ Davis	.50
75	Lance Johnson	.50
76	Joey Hamilton	.50
77	John Valentin	.50
78	David Segui	.50
79	David Wells	.50
80	Eric Karros	.50
81	Raul Mondesi	.50
82	Travis Fryman	.50
83	Todd Zeile	.50
84	Brian Jordan	.50
85	Rey Ordonez	.50
86	Jim Edmonds	.50
87	Marquis Grissom	.50
88	Shane Reynolds	.50
89	Paul Sorrento	.50
90	Brian McRae	.50
91	Fred McGriff	.50
92	Troy Percival	.50
93	Juan Guzman	.50
94	Cecil Fielder	.50
95	Chili Davis	.50
96	B.J. Surhoff	.50
97	Chuck Finley	.50
98	Jeff Kent	.50
99	Ben McDonald	.50
100	Jeffrey Hammonds	.50
101	Tom Goodwin	.50
102	Wil Cordero	.50
103	Tony Phillips	.50
104	John Jaha	.50
105	Garret Anderson	.50
106	Wilson Alvarez	.50
107	Wade Boggs	2.00
108	Mark Wohlers	.50
109	Kevin Appier	.50
110	Mo Vaughn	.50
111	Ray Durham	.50
112	Alex Fernandez	.50
113	Barry Bonds	4.00
114	Albert Belle	2.00
115	Greg Maddux	2.00
116	Alex Rodriguez	3.00
117	Larry Walker	.60
118	Roberto Alomar	.60
119	Andres Galarraga	.50
120	Mike Piazza	2.50
121	Denny Neagle	.50
122	Javier Lopez	.50
123	Ken Griffey Jr.	2.50
124	Shawn Estes	.50
125	Jeff Bagwell	1.25
126	Mark McGwire	.50
127	Tino Martinez	.50
128	Cal Ripken Jr.	4.00
129	Sandy Alomar Jr.	.50
130	Bobby Jones	.50
131	Roger Clemens	2.25
132	Tony Gwynn	2.00
133	Chipper Jones	2.00
134	Orlando Merced	.50
135	Todd Stottlemyre	.50
136	Delino DeShields	.50
137	Pedro Martinez	1.25
138	Ivan Rodriguez	1.00
139	Nomar Garciaparra	2.00
140	Kenny Lofton	.50
141	Jason Dickson	.50
142	Justin Thompson	.50
143	Ray Lankford	.50
144	Frank Thomas	1.25
145	Todd Hundley	.50
146	Edgar Martinez	.50
147	Mariano Rivera	.50
148	Jose Rosado	.50
149	Ken Caminiti	.50
150	Chuck Knoblauch	.50
151	Mike Mussina	.65
152	Kevin Brown	.50
153	Jeff Blauser	.50
154	David Justice	.50
155	Pat Hentgen	.50
156	Tom Glavine	.65
157	Randy Johnson	1.25
158	Darryl Kile	.50
159	Joey Cora	.50
160	Randy Myers	.50

Showcase Series

This partial parallel, reprinted 160 of the 270 cards in Score Baseball on silver foil. They were marked on the back and renumbered within the 160-card set. Showcase parallels were inserted one per seven packs. All Showcase Series cards except #1 have a "PP" prefix to the number.

		NM/M
Complete Set (160):		40.00
Common Player:		.25
Inserted 1:7		
1	Andruw Jones	.75
2	Dan Wilson	.25
3	Hideo Nomo	.40
4	Neifi Perez	.25
5	Jim Thome	.60
6	Jeff Fassero	.25
7	Derek Jeter	2.00
8	Andy Benes	.25
9	Michael Tucker	.25
10	Ryan Klesko	.25
11	Dennis Eckersley	.65
12	Jimmy Key	.25
13	Edgardo Alfonzo	.25
14	Mike Cameron	.25
15	Omar Vizquel	.25
16	Ron Coomer	.25
17	Dmitri Young	.25
18	Brian Giles	.25
19	Steve Finley	.25
20	Andy Pettitte	.40
21	Wilton Guerrero	.25
22	Deion Sanders	.50
23	Carlos Delgado	.25
24	Jason Giambi	.25
25	David Cone	.25
26	Jay Bell	.25
27	Sammy Sosa	1.00
28	Barry Larkin	.50
29	Scott Rolen	.60
30	Todd Greene	.25
31	Bernie Williams	.50
32	Brett Butler	.25
33	Ron Gant	.25
34	Brady Anderson	.25
35	Craig Biggio	.50
36	Charles Nagy	.25
37	Jay Buhner	.25
38	Geronimo Berroa	.25
39	Jeff Suppan	.25
40	Rafael Palmeiro	.65
41	Darin Erstad	.35
42	Mike Timlin	.25
43	Vinny Castilla	.25
44	Carl Everett	.25
45	Robin Ventura	.25
46	John Wetteland	.25
47	Paul O'Neill	.25
48	Tim Salmon	.25
49	Mike Jackson	.25
50	John Smoltz	.25
51	Brant Brown	.25
52	Reggie Sanders	.25
53	Ken Hill	.25
54	Todd Worrell	.25
55	Bip Roberts	.25
56	Tim Naehring	.25
57	Darren Daulton	.25
58	Ramon Martinez	.25
59	Raul Casanova	.25
60	J.T. Snow	.25
61	Jeff Juden	.25
62	Royce Clayton	.25
63	Charles Johnson	.25
64	Alan Benes	.25
65	Reggie Jefferson	.25
66	Ricky Bottalico	.25
67	Scott Erickson	.25
68	Matt Williams	.25
69	Robb Nen	.25
70	Matt Stairs	.25
71	Ismael Valdes	.25
72	Brad Radke	.25
73	Armando Benitez	.25
74	Russ Davis	.25
75	Lance Johnson	.25
76	Joey Hamilton	.25
77	John Valentin	.25
78	David Segui	.25
79	David Wells	.25
80	Eric Karros	.25
81	Raul Mondesi	.25
82	Travis Fryman	.25
83	Todd Zeile	.25
84	Brian Jordan	.25
85	Rey Ordonez	.25
86	Jim Edmonds	.25
87	Marquis Grissom	.25
88	Shane Reynolds	.25
89	Paul Sorrento	.25
90	Brian McRae	.25
91	Fred McGriff	.25
92	Troy Percival	.25
93	Juan Guzman	.25
94	Cecil Fielder	.25
95	Chili Davis	.25
96	B.J. Surhoff	.25
97	Chuck Finley	.25
98	Jeff Kent	.25
99	Ben McDonald	.25
100	Jeffrey Hammonds	.25
101	Tom Goodwin	.25
102	Wil Cordero	.25
103	Tony Phillips	.25
104	John Jaha	.25
105	Garret Anderson	.25
106	Wilson Alvarez	.25
107	Wade Boggs	1.00
108	Mark Wohlers	.25
109	Kevin Appier	.25
110	Mo Vaughn	.25
111	Ray Durham	.25
112	Alex Fernandez	.25
113	Barry Bonds	2.00
114	Albert Belle	.25
115	Greg Maddux	1.00
116	Alex Rodriguez	1.50
117	Larry Walker	.25
118	Roberto Alomar	.35
119	Andres Galarraga	.25
120	Mike Piazza	1.25
121	Denny Neagle	.25
122	Javier Lopez	.25
123	Ken Griffey Jr.	1.25
124	Shawn Estes	.25
125	Jeff Bagwell	.75
126	Mark McGwire	1.50
127	Tino Martinez	.25
128	Cal Ripken Jr.	2.00
129	Sandy Alomar Jr.	.25
130	Bobby Jones	.25
131	Roger Clemens	1.00
132	Tony Gwynn	1.00
133	Chipper Jones	1.00
134	Orlando Merced	.25
135	Todd Stottlemyre	.25
136	Delino DeShields	.25
137	Pedro Martinez	.75
138	Ivan Rodriguez	.65
139	Nomar Garciaparra	1.00
140	Kenny Lofton	.25
141	Jason Dickson	.25
142	Justin Thompson	.25
143	Ray Lankford	.25
144	Frank Thomas	.75
145	Todd Hundley	.25
146	Edgar Martinez	.25
147	Mariano Rivera	.25
148	Jose Rosado	.25
149	Ken Caminiti	.25
150	Chuck Knoblauch	.25
151	Mike Mussina	.40
152	Kevin Brown	.25
153	Jeff Blauser	.25
154	David Justice	.25
155	Pat Hentgen	.40
156	Tom Glavine	.25
157	Randy Johnson	.75
158	Darryl Kile	.25
159	Joey Cora	.25
160	Randy Myers	.25

All Score Team

For its 10th anniversary Score selected an all-star team and issued this insert set. Cards have player action photos on a silver-foil background with an anniversary logo at bottom. Backs have a portrait photo and a career summary. The cards were inserted one per 35 packs.

		NM/M
Complete Set (20):		15.00
Common Player:		.25
Inserted 1:35		
1	Mike Piazza	1.50
2	Ivan Rodriguez	.65
3	Frank Thomas	.75
4	Mark McGwire	2.00
5	Ryne Sandberg	1.00
6	Roberto Alomar	.35
7	Cal Ripken Jr.	2.50
8	Barry Larkin	.25
9	Paul Molitor	.25
10	Travis Fryman	.25
11	Kirby Puckett	1.00
12	Tony Gwynn	1.50
13	Ken Griffey Jr.	1.50
14	Juan Gonzalez	.45
15	Barry Bonds	2.50
16	Andruw Jones	1.00
17	Roger Clemens	1.25
18	Randy Johnson	1.00
19	Greg Maddux	1.00
20	Dennis Eckersley	.65

All Score Team - Gold

The purpose for which this variation of the regular All Score Team insert was created will likely remain unknown. A small number of the Gold version have turned up in the hobby market since early-1998. A small number of the Gold version have turned up in the hobby market since Score's bankruptcy in mid-1998. This apparently premium version differs from the issued silver version only in its use of gold metallic foil background on front.

		NM/M
Complete Set (20):		115.00
Common Player:		2.00
1	Mike Piazza	10.00
2	Ivan Rodriguez	5.00
3	Frank Thomas	6.00
4	Mark McGwire	12.00
5	Ryne Sandberg	7.50
6	Roberto Alomar	2.50
7	Cal Ripken Jr.	15.00
8	Barry Larkin	2.00
9	Paul Molitor	6.00
10	Travis Fryman	2.00
11	Kirby Puckett	7.50
12	Tony Gwynn	7.50
13	Ken Griffey Jr.	10.00
14	Juan Gonzalez	3.00
15	Barry Bonds	15.00
16	Andruw Jones	6.00
17	Roger Clemens	8.00
18	Randy Johnson	6.00
19	Greg Maddux	7.50
20	Dennis Eckersley	5.00

All Score Team Andruw Jones Autograph

This special version of Jones' All Score Team was a prize in a random hobby-shop drawing. Instead of the silver foil seen on regular All Score Team inserts, this version has a gold-foil background and an "AUTHENTIC SIGNATURE" notation at right-center. Only 500 of the cards were produced.

		NM/M
16	Andruw Jones	25.00

Complete Players

Complete Players is a 30-card insert featuring 10 players who can do it all. Each player had three cards displaying their variety of skills. The cards feature holographic foil highlights on fronts. Backs form a three-piece vertical picture of the player. The cards were inserted about one per 23 packs. Cards can be found with either gold or silver holographic foil. The gold version was found in packs of Score Team Collection at a 1:11 pack ratio. Because of these looser odds, the gold cards are valued lower than the silver.

		NM/M
Complete Set (30):		75.00
Common Player:		1.00
Inserted 1:23		
Golds: 75%		
1A	Ken Griffey Jr.	3.25
1B	Ken Griffey Jr.	3.25
1C	Ken Griffey Jr.	3.25
2A	Mark McGwire	3.75
2B	Mark McGwire	3.75
2C	Mark McGwire	3.75
3A	Derek Jeter	5.00
3B	Derek Jeter	5.00
3C	Derek Jeter	5.00
4A	Cal Ripken Jr.	5.00
4B	Cal Ripken Jr.	5.00
4C	Cal Ripken Jr.	5.00
5A	Mike Piazza	3.25
5B	Mike Piazza	3.25
5C	Mike Piazza	3.25
6A	Darin Erstad	1.00
6B	Darin Erstad	1.00
6C	Darin Erstad	1.00
7A	Frank Thomas	2.00
7B	Frank Thomas	2.00
7C	Frank Thomas	2.00
8A	Andruw Jones	3.00
8B	Andruw Jones	3.00
8C	Andruw Jones	3.00
9A	Nomar Garciaparra	3.00
9B	Nomar Garciaparra	3.00
9C	Nomar Garciaparra	3.00
10A	Manny Ramirez	2.00
10B	Manny Ramirez	2.00
10C	Manny Ramirez	2.00

Epix

Epix is a cross-brand insert, with 24 cards appearing in Score. The cards are printed on 20-point stock with holographic foil technology. The cards honor the top Play, Game, Season and Moment in a player's career and come in Orange, Purple and Emerald versions. Game cards were inserted 1:141, Plays 1:171, Seasons 1:437 and Moments 1:757.

	NM/M
Common Card:	.50
Purple:	2X

Emeralds:

	Ken Griffey Jr./P	3X
1	Ken Griffey Jr./P	2.50
2	Juan Gonzalez/P	.75
3	Jeff Bagwell/P	1.25
4	Ivan Rodriguez/P	1.00
5	Nomar Garciaparra/P	2.00
6	Ryne Sandberg/G	1.50
7	Frank Thomas/G	1.25
8	Derek Jeter/G	3.50
9	Tony Gwynn/G	2.00
10	Albert Belle/G	.50
11	Scott Rolen/G	1.00
12	Barry Larkin/G	.50
13	Alex Rodriguez/S	6.00
14	Cal Ripken Jr./S	7.50
15	Chipper Jones/S	4.00
16	Roger Clemens/S	4.50
17	Mo Vaughn/S	3.00
18	Mark McGwire/S	6.00
19	Mike Piazza/M	8.00
20	Andruw Jones/M	4.00
21	Greg Maddux/M	6.00
22	Barry Bonds/M	12.00
23	Paul Molitor/M	4.00
24	Eddie Murray/M	4.00

First Pitch

These inserts were a 1:11 pack find in Score's All-Star edition. Fronts have portrait photos printed in the center of textured foil background of red and silver. The basic design is repeated on back, with career highlights and team logo instead of a photo.

		NM/M
Complete Set (20):		25.00
Common Player:		.50
Inserted 1:11 All-Star Edition.		
1	Ken Griffey Jr.	2.00
2	Frank Thomas	1.25
3	Alex Rodriguez	3.25
4	Cal Ripken Jr.	3.25
5	Chipper Jones	1.50
6	Juan Gonzalez	.75
7	Derek Jeter	3.25
8	Mike Piazza	2.00
9	Andruw Jones	1.25
10	Nomar Garciaparra	1.50
11	Barry Bonds	1.25
12	Jeff Bagwell	1.25
13	Scott Rolen	1.00
14	Hideo Nomo	.75
15	Roger Clemens	1.75
16	Mark McGwire	2.50
17	Greg Maddux	1.50
18	Albert Belle	.50
19	Ivan Rodriguez	1.00
20	Mo Vaughn	.50

Andruw Jones Icon Order Card

This special card was the pack-topper on retail 27-card blister packs of 1998 Score. The front is identical to the regular Jones card in the set, but the back carries an ad for Pinnacle's Icon card display mail-in offer.

	NM/M
Andruw Jones	2.50

Loaded Lineup

This insert series was packaged on average of one card per 45 packs of Score's All-Star edition. Fronts have action photos printed on a copper and silver textured metallic-foil background. Backs have a portrait photo, career highlights, the Loaded Lineup batting order and stats for the player's best season. Cards have an "LL" prefix to their number.

		NM/M
Complete Set (10):		20.00
Common Player:		.50
Inserted 1:45 All-Star Edition.		
LL1	Chuck Knoblauch	.50
LL2	Tony Gwynn	2.25
LL3	Frank Thomas	1.50
LL4	Ken Griffey Jr.	3.00
LL5	Mike Piazza	3.00
LL6	Barry Bonds	4.50
LL7	Cal Ripken Jr.	4.50
LL8	Paul Molitor	1.50
LL9	Nomar Garciaparra	2.25
LL10	Greg Maddux	2.25

New Season

Found only in Score All-Star Edition, at an average rate of one per 23 packs, this insert series mixes veteran stars with hot young players. Fronts have a large portrait photo. Horizontal backs have an action photo.

		NM/M
Complete Set (15):		18.00
Common Player:		.50
Inserted 1:23 All-Star Edition.		
NS1	Kenny Lofton	.50
NS2	Nomar Garciaparra	2.00
NS3	Todd Helton	1.00
NS4	Miguel Tejada	.75
NS5	Jaret Wright	.50
NS6	Alex Rodriguez	3.00
NS7	Vladimir Guerrero	1.25
NS8	Ken Griffey Jr.	2.50
NS9	Ben Grieve	.50
NS10	Travis Lee	.50
NS11	Jose Cruz Jr.	.50
NS12	Paul Konerko	.50
NS13	Frank Thomas	1.25
NS14	Chipper Jones	2.00
NS15	Cal Ripken Jr.	4.00

1998 Score Rookie & Traded

Score Rookie/Traded consists of a 270-card base set. The base cards have a white and gray border with the player's name on the left. Cards are printed on a slightly glossier stock. Cards #1-50 were short-printed and inserted at a rate of one per pack. Ten-card packs carried an SRP of 99 cents. The Showcase Series parallels 110 base cards and was inserted

1:7. Artist's Proofs is a 50-card partial parallel done on prismatic foil and inserted 1:35. Inserts included All-Star Epix, Complete Players and Star Gazing.

		NM/M
Complete Set (270):		10.00
Common SP (1-50):		.10
Common Player (51-270):		.05
Artist's Proofs:		4X
Inserted 1:35		
Paul Konerko Auto. (500):		15.00
Pack (10):		.65
Wax Box (36):		15.00
Jumbo Pack (20):		1.50
Jumbo Box (24):		25.00
1	Tony Clark	.10
2	Juan Gonzalez	.35
3	Frank Thomas	.60
4	Greg Maddux	.75
5	Barry Larkin	.10
6	Derek Jeter	1.50
7	Randy Johnson	.60
8	Roger Clemens	.85
9	Tony Gwynn	.75
10	Barry Bonds	1.50
11	Jim Edmonds	.10
12	Bernie Williams	.10
13	Ken Griffey Jr.	1.00
14	Tim Salmon	.10
15	Mo Vaughn	.10
16	David Justice	.10
17	Jose Cruz Jr.	.10
18	Andruw Jones	.60
19	Sammy Sosa	.75
20	Jeff Bagwell	.60
21	Scott Rolen	.50
22	Darin Erstad	.30
23	Andy Pettitte	.35
24	Mike Mussina	.40
25	Mark McGwire	1.25
26	Hideo Nomo	.35
27	Chipper Jones	.75
28	Cal Ripken Jr.	1.50
29	Chuck Knoblauch	.10
30	Alex Rodriguez	1.25
31	Jim Thome	.50
32	Mike Piazza	1.00
33	Ivan Rodriguez	.50
34	Roberto Alomar	.40
35	Nomar Garciaparra	.75
36	Albert Belle	.10
37	Vladimir Guerrero	.10
38	Raul Mondesi	.10
39	Larry Walker	.10
40	Manny Ramirez	.60
41	Tino Martinez	.10
42	Craig Biggio	.10
43	Jay Buhner	.10
44	Kenny Lofton	.10
45	Pedro Martinez	.60
46	Edgar Martinez	.10
47	Gary Sheffield	.45
48	Jose Guillen	.10
49	Ken Caminiti	.10
50	Bobby Higginson	.05
51	Alan Benes	.05
52	Shawn Green	.15
53	Ron Coomer	.05
54	Charles Nagy	.05
55	Steve Karsay	.05
56	Matt Morris	.05
57	Bobby Jones	.05
58	Jason Kendall	.05
59	Jeff Conine	.05
60	Joe Girardi	.05
61	Mark Kotsay	.05
62	Eric Karros	.05
63	Bartolo Colon	.05
64	Mariano Rivera	.05
65	Alex Gonzalez	.05
66	Scott Spiezio	.05
67	Luis Castillo	.05
68	Joey Cora	.05
69	Mark McLemore	.05
70	Reggie Jefferson	.05
71	Lance Johnson	.05
72	Damian Jackson	.05
73	Jeff D'Amico	.05
74	David Ortiz	.30
75	J.T. Snow	.05
76	Todd Hundley	.05
77	Billy Wagner	.05
78	Vinny Castilla	.05
79	Ismael Valdes	.05
80	Neifi Perez	.05
81	Derek Bell	.05
82	Ryan Klesko	.05
83	Rey Ordonez	.05
84	Carlos Garcia	.05
85	Curt Schilling	.05
86	Robin Ventura	.05
87	Pat Hentgen	.05
88	Glendon Rusch	.05
89	Hideki Irabu	.05
90	Antone Williamson	.05
91	Denny Neagle	.05
92	Kevin Orie	.05
93	Reggie Sanders	.05
94	Brady Anderson	.05
95	Andy Benes	.05
96	John Valentin	.05
97	Bobby Bonilla	.05
98	Walt Weiss	.05
99	Robin Jennings	.05
100	Marty Cordova	.05
101	Brad Ausmus	.05
102	Brian Rose	.05
103	Calvin Maduro	.05
104	Raul Casanova	.05
105	Jeff King	.05
106	Sandy Alomar	.05
107	Tim Naehring	.05
108	Mike Cameron	.05
109	Omar Vizquel	.05
110	Brad Radke	.05
111	Jeff Fassero	.05
112	Deivi Cruz	.05
113	Dave Hollins	.05
114	Dean Palmer	.05
115	Esteban Loaiza	.05
116	Brian Giles	.05
117	Steve Finley	.05
118	Jose Canseco	.30
119	Al Martin	.05
120	Eric Young	.05
121	Curtis Goodwin	.05
122	Ellis Burks	.05
123	Mike Hampton	.05
124	Lou Collier	.05
125	John Olerud	.05
126	Ramon Martinez	.05
127	Todd Dunwoody	.05
128	Jermaine Allensworth	.05
129	Eduardo Perez	.05
130	Dante Bichette	.05
131	Edgar Renteria	.05
132	Bob Abreu	.10
133	Rondell White	.05
134	Michael Coleman	.05
135	Jason Giambi	.30
136	Brant Brown	.05
137	Michael Tucker	.05
138	Dave Nilsson	.05
139	Benito Santiago	.05
140	Ray Durham	.05
141	Jeff Kent	.05
142	Matt Stairs	.05
143	Kevin Young	.05
144	Eric Davis	.05
145	John Wetteland	.05
146	Esteban Yan	.05
147	Wilton Guerrero	.05
148	Moises Alou	.05
149	Edgardo Alfonzo	.05
150	Andy Ashby	.05
151	Todd Walker	.05
152	Jermaine Dye	.05
153	Brian Hunter	.05
154	Shawn Estes	.05
155	Bernard Gilkey	.05
156	Tony Womack	.05
157	John Smoltz	.05
158	Delino DeShields	.05
159	Jacob Cruz	.05
160	Javier Valentin	.05
161	Chris Hoiles	.05
162	Garret Anderson	.05
163	Dan Wilson	.05
164	Paul O'Neill	.05
165	Matt Williams	.05
166	Travis Fryman	.05
167	Javier Lopez	.05
168	Ray Lankford	.05
169	Bobby Estalella	.05
170	Henry Rodriguez	.05
171	Quinton McCracken	.05
172	Jaret Wright	.05
173	Darryl Kile	.05
174	Wade Boggs	.65
175	Orel Hershiser	.05
176	B.J. Surhoff	.05
177	Fernando Tatis	.05
178	Carlos Delgado	.30
179	Jorge Fabregas	.05
180	Tony Saunders	.05
181	Devon White	.05
182	Dmitri Young	.05
183	Ryan McGuire	.05
184	Mark Bellhorn	.05
185	Joe Carter	.05
186	Kevin Stocker	.05
187	Mike Lansing	.05
188	Jason Dickson	.05
189	Charles Johnson	.05
190	Will Clark	.05
191	Shannon Stewart	.05
192	Johnny Damon	.20
193	Todd Greene	.05
194	Carlos Baerga	.05
195	David Cone	.05
196	Pokey Reese	.05
197	Livan Hernandez	.05
198	Tom Glavine	.25
199	Geronimo Berroa	.05
200	Darryl Hamilton	.05
201	Terry Steinbach	.05
202	Robb Nen	.05
203	Ron Gant	.05
204	Rafael Palmeiro	.40
205	Rickey Henderson	.40
206	Justin Thompson	.05
207	Jeff Suppan	.05
208	Kevin Brown	.05
209	Jimmy Key	.05
210	Brian Jordan	.05
211	Aaron Sele	.05
212	Fred McGriff	.05
213	Jay Bell	.05
214	Andres Galarraga	.05
215	Mark Grace	.05
216	Brett Tomko	.05
217	Francisco Cordova	.05
218	Rusty Greer	.05
219	Bubba Trammell	.05
220	Derrek Lee	.35
221	Brian Anderson	.05
222	Mark Grudzielanek	.05
223	Marquis Grissom	.05
224	Gary DiSarcina	.05
225	Jim Leyritz	.05
226	Jeffrey Hammonds	.05
227	Karim Garcia	.05
228	Chan Ho Park	.05
229	Brooks Kieschnick	.05
230	Trey Beamon	.05
231	Kevin Appier	.05
232	Wally Joyner	.05
233	Richie Sexson	.05
234	Frank Catalanotto **RC**	.15
235	Rafael Medina	.05
236	Travis Lee	.05
237	Eli Marrero	.05
238	Carl Pavano	.05
239	Enrique Wilson	.05
240	Richard Hidalgo	.05
241	Todd Helton	.40
242	Ben Grieve	.05
243	Mario Valdez	.05
244	Magglio Ordonez **RC**	.75
245	Juan Encarnacion	.05
246	Russell Branyan	.05
247	Sean Casey	.10
248	Abraham Nunez	.05
249	Brad Fullmer	.05
250	Paul Konerko	.20
251	Miguel Tejada	.15
252	Mike Lowell **RC**	.50
253	Ken Griffey Jr. (Spring Training)	.35
254	Frank Thomas (Spring Training)	.25
255	Alex Rodriguez (Spring Training)	.45
256	Jose Cruz Jr. (Spring Training)	.05
257	Jeff Bagwell (Spring Training)	.20
258	Chipper Jones (Spring Training)	.30
259	Mo Vaughn (Spring Training)	.05
260	Nomar Garciaparra (Spring Training)	.30
261	Jim Thome (Spring Training)	.05
262	Derek Jeter (Spring Training)	.50
263	Mike Piazza (Spring Training)	.45
264	Tony Gwynn (Spring Training)	.30
265	Scott Rolen (Spring Training)	.15
266	Andruw Jones (Spring Training)	.20
267	Cal Ripken Jr. (Spring Training)	.50
268	Checklist (Ken Griffey Jr.)	.30
269	Checklist (Cal Ripken Jr.)	.45
270	Checklist (Jose Cruz Jr.)	.05

Artist's Proofs

This partial parallel reprints 160 (the same cards as the Showcase Series) of the 270 cards in Score Rookie & Traded. The cards are printed on a foil surface and feature an Artist's Proof logo on front. The cards were renumbered within the 160-card set and inserted one per 35 packs.

	NM/M
Common Player:	1.00
AP Stars:	4X

Artist's Proofs 1 of 1

Printed on primatic gold metallic foil background and featuring a gold "001/001 One of One" seal on front, these were random inserts in hobby packs.

More than one "1/1" from this issue are known for some players, probably having been produced for use as replacements for damaged cards pulled from packs, then entering the hobby with the company's demise in mid-1998.

	NM/M
Common Player:	40.00

Showcase Series

The Showcase Series is a partial parallel reprint of 160 of the 270 cards in Rookie & Traded. The cards are printed on a silver-foil surface, marked on the back and re-numbered (with an "RTPP" prefix) within the 160-card set. Showcase parallels were inserted one per seven packs.

		NM/M
Complete Set (160):		10.00
Common Player:		.15
1	Tony Clark	.15
2	Juan Gonzalez	.30
3	Frank Thomas	.60
4	Greg Maddux	.75
5	Barry Larkin	.15
6	Derek Jeter	1.50
7	Randy Johnson	.60
8	Roger Clemens	.85
9	Tony Gwynn	.75
10	Barry Bonds	1.50
11	Jim Edmonds	.15
12	Bernie Williams	.15
13	Ken Griffey Jr.	1.00
14	Tim Salmon	.15
15	Mo Vaughn	.15
16	David Justice	.15
17	Jose Cruz Jr.	.15
18	Andruw Jones	.60
19	Sammy Sosa	.75
20	Jeff Bagwell	.60
21	Scott Rolen	.50
22	Darin Erstad	.25
23	Andy Pettitte	.30
24	Mike Mussina	.30
25	Mark McGwire	1.25
26	Hideo Nomo	.30
27	Chipper Jones	.75
28	Cal Ripken Jr.	1.50
29	Chuck Knoblauch	.15
30	Alex Rodriguez	1.25
31	Jim Thome	.50
32	Mike Piazza	1.00
33	Ivan Rodriguez	.50
34	Roberto Alomar	.25
35	Nomar Garciaparra	1.00
36	Albert Belle	.15
37	Vladimir Guerrero	.60
38	Raul Mondesi	.15
39	Larry Walker	.15
40	Manny Ramirez	.60
41	Tino Martinez	.15
42	Craig Biggio	.15
43	Jay Buhner	.15
44	Kenny Lofton	.15
45	Pedro Martinez	.60
46	Edgar Martinez	.15
47	Gary Sheffield	.40
48	Jose Guillen	.15
49	Ken Caminiti	.15

50	Bobby Higginson	.15
51	Alan Benes	.15
52	Shawn Green	.35
53	Matt Morris	.15
54	Jason Kendall	.15
55	Mark Kotsay	.15
56	Bartolo Colon	.15
57	Damian Jackson	.15
58	David Ortiz	.35
59	J.T. Snow	.15
60	Todd Hundley	.15
61	Neifi Perez	.15
62	Ryan Klesko	.15
63	Robin Ventura	.15
64	Pat Hentgen	.15
65	Antone Williamson	.15
66	Kevin Orie	.15
67	Brady Anderson	.15
68	Bobby Bonilla	.15
69	Brian Rose	.15
70	Sandy Alomar Jr.	.15
71	Mike Cameron	.15
72	Omar Vizquel	.15
73	Steve Finley	.15
74	Jose Canseco	.40
75	Al Martin	.15
76	Eric Young	.15
77	Ellis Burks	.15
78	Todd Dunwoody	.15
79	Dante Bichette	.15
80	Edgar Renteria	.15
81	Bobby Abreu	.15
82	Rondell White	.15
83	Michael Coleman	.15
84	Jason Giambi	.50
85	Wilton Guerrero	.15
86	Moises Alou	.15
87	Todd Walker	.15
88	Shawn Estes	.15
89	John Smoltz	.15
90	Jacob Cruz	.15
91	Javier Valentin	.15
92	Garret Anderson	.15
93	Paul O'Neill	.15
94	Matt Williams	.15
95	Travis Fryman	.15
96	Javier Lopez	.15
97	Ray Lankford	.15
98	Bobby Estalella	.15
99	Jaret Wright	.15
100	Wade Boggs	.75
101	Fernando Tatis	.15
102	Carlos Delgado	.50
103	Joe Carter	.15
104	Jason Dickson	.15
105	Charles Johnson	.15
106	Will Clark	.15
107	Shannon Stewart	.15
108	Todd Greene	.15
109	Pokey Reese	.15
110	Livan Hernandez	.15
111	Tom Glavine	.35
112	Rafael Palmeiro	.50
113	Justin Thompson	.15
114	Jeff Suppan	.15
115	Kevin Brown	.15
116	Brian Jordan	.15
117	Fred McGriff	.15
118	Andres Galarraga	.15
119	Mark Grace	.15
120	Rusty Greer	.15
121	Bubba Trammell	.15
122	Derrek Lee	.40
123	Brian Anderson	.15
124	Karim Garcia	.15
125	Chan Ho Park	.15
126	Richie Sexson	.15
127	Frank Catalanotto	.15
128	Rafael Medina	.15
129	Travis Lee	.15
130	Eli Marrero	.15
131	Carl Pavano	.15
132	Enrique Wilson	.15
133	Richard Hidalgo	.15
134	Todd Helton	.40
135	Ben Grieve	.15
136	Mario Valdez	.15
137	Magglio Ordonez	.15
138	Juan Encarnacion	.15
139	Russell Branyan	.15
140	Sean Casey	.25
141	Abraham Nunez	.15
142	Brad Fullmer	.15
143	Paul Konerko	.25
144	Miguel Tejada	.30
145	Mike Lowell	.15
146	Ken Griffey Jr. (Spring Training)	.50
147	Frank Thomas (Spring Training)	.35
148	Alex Rodriguez (Spring Training)	.65
149	Jose Cruz Jr. (Spring Training)	.15
150	Jeff Bagwell (Spring Training)	.35
151	Chipper Jones (Spring Training)	.40
152	Mo Vaughn (Spring Training)	.15
153	Nomar Garciaparra (Spring Training)	.40
154	Jim Thome (Spring Training)	.30
155	Derek Jeter (Spring Training)	.75
156	Mike Piazza (Spring Training)	.50

157	Tony Gwynn (Spring Training)	.40
158	Scott Rolen (Spring Training)	.25
159	Andruw Jones (Spring Training)	.35
160	Cal Ripken Jr. (Spring Training)	.75

Complete Players

Complete Players is a 30-card insert seeded one per 11 packs. The set highlights 10 players who can do it all on the field. Each player has three cards showcasing one of their talents. The cards feature holographic foil stamping. Each card can also be found in a promo version with a large, black "SAMPLE" overprinted on front and back.

	NM/M
Complete Set (30):	65.00
Common Player:	1.00
Inserted 1:11	
Samples:	1X
1A	Ken Griffey Jr.	3.50
1B	Ken Griffey Jr.	3.50
1C	Ken Griffey Jr.	3.50
2A	Larry Walker	1.00
2B	Larry Walker	1.00
2C	Larry Walker	1.00
3A	Alex Rodriguez	4.00
3B	Alex Rodriguez	4.00
3C	Alex Rodriguez	4.00
4A	Jose Cruz Jr.	1.00
4B	Jose Cruz Jr.	1.00
4C	Jose Cruz Jr.	1.00
5A	Jeff Bagwell	2.00
5B	Jeff Bagwell	2.00
5C	Jeff Bagwell	2.00
6A	Greg Maddux	2.75
6B	Greg Maddux	2.75
6C	Greg Maddux	2.75
7A	Ivan Rodriguez	1.75
7B	Ivan Rodriguez	1.75
7C	Ivan Rodriguez	1.75
8A	Roger Clemens	3.00
8B	Roger Clemens	3.00
8C	Roger Clemens	3.00
9A	Chipper Jones	2.75
9B	Chipper Jones	2.75
9C	Chipper Jones	2.75
10A	Hideo Nomo	1.50
10B	Hideo Nomo	1.50
10C	Hideo Nomo	1.50

Epix All-Star Moment

All-Star Epix is a 1:61 insert. The cards honor the top All-Star Game moments of 12 star players. The dot matrix hologram cards were printed in orange, purple and emerald versions. This series was continued with cards numbered 13-24 in Pinnacle Plus.

	NM/M
Complete Set (12):	25.00
Common Player:	1.00

| Purples: | 1.5X |
Emeralds:	2.5X
1	Ken Griffey Jr.	4.00
2	Juan Gonzalez	1.50
3	Jeff Bagwell	2.50
4	Ivan Rodriguez	2.00
5	Nomar Garciaparra	3.00
6	Ryne Sandberg	3.00
7	Frank Thomas	2.50
8	Derek Jeter	5.00
9	Tony Gwynn	3.00
10	Albert Belle	1.00
11	Scott Rolen	2.00
12	Barry Larkin	1.00

Star Gazing

Printed on micro-etched foil board, Star Gazing features 20 top players and was seeded 1:35.

	NM/M
Complete Set (20):	12.00
Common Player:	.25
Inserted 1:35	
1	Ken Griffey Jr.	1.00
2	Frank Thomas	.60
3	Chipper Jones	.75
4	Mark McGwire	1.25
5	Cal Ripken Jr.	1.50
6	Mike Piazza	1.00
7	Nomar Garciaparra	.75
8	Derek Jeter	1.50
9	Juan Gonzalez	.35
10	Vladimir Guerrero	.60
11	Alex Rodriguez	1.25
12	Tony Gwynn	.75
13	Andruw Jones	.60
14	Scott Rolen	.40
15	Jose Cruz Jr.	.25
16	Mo Vaughn	.25
17	Bernie Williams	.25
18	Greg Maddux	.75
19	Tony Clark	.25
20	Ben Grieve	.25

1998 Score Team Collection

Team sets of 15 players each were produced for 10 different teams. Each card is similar in design to the regular 1998 Score set except for a special silver-foil team logo stamped at the bottom of the card. On back, this version has a "Team Collection" underprinted and each card is numbered "_ of 15." In a parallel, "Platinum" version, seeded one per six packs, the front background is replaced with silver prismatic foil. A gold highlighted version of the three-card Complete Players inserts were found one per 11 packs. Team Collection was sold in five-card, single-team packs (32 per box).

	NM/M
Complete Set (150):	25.00
Common Player:	.10

Anaheim Angels
	Team Set:	2.00
1	Rickey Henderson	.60
2	Todd Greene	.10
3	Shigetoshi Hasegawa	.10
4	Darin Erstad	.20
5	Jason Dickson	.10
6	Tim Salmon	.10
7	Ken Hill	.10
8	Dave Hollins	.10
9	Gary DiSarcina	.10
10	Mike James	.10
11	Jim Edmonds	.10
12	Troy Percival	.10
13	Chuck Finley	.10
14	Tony Phillips	.10
15	Garret Anderson	.10

Atlanta Braves
	Team Set:	2.75
1	Andruw Jones	.60
2	Greg Maddux	.75
3	Michael Tucker	.10
4	Denny Naegle	.10
5	Javier Lopez	.10
6	Ryan Klesko	.10
7	Chipper Jones	.75
8	Kenny Lofton	.10
9	John Smoltz	.10
10	Jeff Blauser	.10
11	Tom Glavine	.30
12	Tony Graffanino	.10
13	Terrell Wade	.10
14	Fred McGriff	.10
15	Mark Wohlers	.10

Baltimore Orioles
	Team Set:	3.25
1	Roberto Alomar	.20
2	Jimmy Key	.10
3	Cal Ripken Jr.	1.75
4	Brady Anderson	.10
5	Geronimo Berroa	.10
6	Chris Hoiles	.10
7	Rafael Palmeiro	.50
8	Mike Mussina	.30
9	Randy Myers	.10
10	Mike Bordick	.10
11	Scott Erickson	.10
12	Armando Benitez	.10
13	B.J. Surhoff	.10
14	Jeffrey Hammonds	.10
15	Arthur Rhodes	.10

Boston Red Sox
	Team Set:	2.25
1	Steve Avery	.10
2	Aaron Sele	.10
3	Tim Wakefield	.10
4	Darren Bragg	.10
5	Scott Hatteberg	.10
6	Jeff Suppan	.10
7	Nomar Garciaparra	.75
8	Tim Naehring	.10
9	Reggie Jefferson	.10
10	John Valentin	.10
11	Jeff Frye	.10
12	Wil Cordero	.10
13	Troy O'Leary	.10
14	Mo Vaughn	.10
15	Shane Mack	.10

Chicago White Sox
	Team Set:	2.00
1	Albert Belle	.10
2	Chuck McElroy	.10
3	Mike Cameron	.10
4	Ozzie Guillen	.10
5	Jaime Navarro	.10
6	Chris Clemons	.10
7	Lyle Mouton	.10
8	Frank Thomas	.60
9	Doug Drabek	.10
10	Robin Ventura	.10
11	Dave Martinez	.10
12	Ray Durham	.10
13	Chris Snopek	.10
14	James Baldwin	.10
15	Jorge Fabregas	.10

Cleveland Indians
	Team Set:	1.25
1	Jack McDowell	.10
2	Jim Thome	.50
3	Brian Anderson	.10
4	Sandy Alomar Jr.	.10
5	Omar Vizquel	.10
6	Brian Giles	.10
7	Charles Nagy	.10
8	Mike Jackson	.10
9	David Justice	.10
10	Jeff Juden	.10
11	Matt Williams	.10
12	Marquis Grissom	.10
13	Tony Fernandez	.10
14	Bartolo Colon	.10
15	Jaret Wright	.10

Los Angeles Dodgers
	Team Set:	2.75
1	Hideo Nomo	.30
2	Mike Piazza	1.00
3	Wilton Guerrero	.10
4	Greg Gagne	.10
5	Brett Butler	.10
6	Todd Hollandsworth	.10
7	Roger Cedeno	.10
8	Chan Ho Park	.10
9	Todd Worrell	.10
10	Ramon Martinez	.10
11	Ismael Valdes	.10
12	Eric Karros	.10
13	Raul Mondesi	.10
14	Todd Zeile	.10

15	Billy Ashley	.10

New York Yankees
	Team Set:	3.25
1	Hideki Irabu	.10
2	Derek Jeter	1.75
3	Tino Martinez	.10
4	David Cone	.10
5	Andy Pettitte	.25
6	Bernie Williams	.10
7	Charlie Hayes	.10
8	Pat Kelly	.10
9	Mariano Rivera	.15
10	Paul O'Neill	.10
11	Chad Curtis	.10
12	David Wells	.10
13	Cecil Fielder	.10
14	Wade Boggs	.75
15	Jorge Posada	.10

Seattle Mariners
	Team Set:	3.25
1	Dan Wilson	.10
2	Alex Rodriguez	1.25
3	Jeff Fassero	.10
4	Ken Griffey Jr.	1.00
5	Bobby Ayala	.10
6	Jay Buhner	.10
7	Mike Timlin	.10
8	Edgar Martinez	.10
9	Randy Johnson	.60
10	Joey Cora	.10
11	Heathcliff Slocumb	.10
12	Russ Davis	.10
13	Paul Sorrento	.10
14	Rich Amaral	.10
15	Jamie Moyer	.10

St. Louis Cardinals
	Team Set:	2.25
1	Andy Benes	.10
2	Todd Stottlemyre	.10
3	Dennis Eckersley	.45
4	Mark McGwire	1.25
5	Dmitri Young	.10
6	Ron Gant	.10
7	Mike Difelice	.10
8	Ray Lankford	.10
9	John Mabry	.10
10	Royce Clayton	.10
11	Alan Benes	.10
12	Delino DeShields	.10
13	Brian Jordan	.10
14	Gary Gaetti	.10
15	Matt Morris	.10

Platinum

Each of the Team Collection cards was also issued in a Platinum Team version, inserted on average of one card per six packs. The front has a background of star-studded refractive silver foil and a "PLATINUM TEAM" designation at the right edge of the photo. That designation is repeated on back as an underprint.

	NM/M
Common Player:	.50
Stars:	4X

Complete Players

1996-97 Score Board All Sport PPF

Stars and prospects, Past, Present and Future (PPF), in the

four major team sports are featured in this two series set whose issue spanned late 1996 and early 1997. Borderless action photos and gold-foil graphic highlights are featured on front. Another photo, stats and personal data can be found on back. Only the baseball players from the 200-card set are listed here. A gold parallel edition was also issued.

	NM/M
Common Player:	.10
Gold:	2X
Wax Pack (6):	.65
Wax Box (18):	7.50
Wax Box (36):	15.00
21	Ryan Minor	.10
60	Rey Ordonez	.10
61	Todd Greene	.10
62	Jermaine Dye	.10
63	Karim Garcia	.10
64	Todd Walker	.10
65	Calvin Reese	.10
66	Roger Cedeno	.10
67	Ben Davis	.10
68	Chad Hermansen	.10
69	Vladimir Guerrero	.50
70	Billy Wagner	.10
94	Barry Bonds	.50
95	Vladimir Guerrero	.50
96	Livan Hernandez	.50
160	Barry Bonds	.50
161	Jay Payton	.10
162	Jose Cruz Jr.	.10
163	Richard Hidalgo	.10
164	Bartolo Colon	.10
165	Matt Drews	.10
166	Kerry Wood	.35
167	Ben Grieve	.10
168	Wes Helms	.10
169	Livan Hernandez	.10
196	Todd Walker	.10
197	Rey Ordonez	.10
198	Todd Greene	.10

Retro

Current and potential stars in the format of classic sports cards are featured in this Series 2 insert found at an announced rate of one per 35 packs. Only a single baseball player is included among the 10 cards in the set.

	NM/M
R10	Rey Ordonez	.50

Revivals

Current and potential stars in the format of classic sports cards are featured in this Series 1 insert found at an announced rate of one per 35 packs. Only a single baseball player is included among the 10 cards in the set.

	NM/M
REV10	Barry Bonds	1.00

1997 Score Board Mickey Mantle Shoe Box Collection

Yet another collectors' issue of Mickey Mantle cards, the Score Board "Shoe Box Collection" offered packs containing two of the 75 Mantle cards or seven-card insert set, along with a genuine - usually a low-grade common - Topps card from 1951-69. Several designs of Mantle cards are featured in the set, including color photos as well as blue-and-white duotones. Five of the cards are printed with gold-foil backgrounds and die-cut. Cards #51-69 are short-printed at a ratio of about 1-to-3 with cards #1-50. Suggested retail price was $6.50 per pack.

		NM/M
Complete Set (75):		60.00
Common Card:		.75
1	Summary Of The Legend (Foil die-cut.)	3.00
1p	Summary of the Legend/PC	3.00
2	Triple Crown 1956	.75
3	MVP 1956	.75
4	MVP 1957	.75
5	MVP 1962	.75
6	Uniform #6 (Foil die-cut.)	3.00
6p	Uniform #6/PC	3.00
7	Uniform #7 (Foil die-cut.)	3.00
7p	Uniform #7/PC	3.00
8	Gold Glove Winner	.75
9	17-time All-Star	.75
10	4-time HR Champion	.75
11	World Series Records	.75
12	The Dirty Dozen (Post-seasons.)	.75
13	World Champion-1951	.75
14	World Champion-1952	.75
15	World Champion-1953	.75
16	World Champion-1956	.75
17	World Champion-1958	.75
18	World Champion-1961	.75
19	World Champion-1962	.75
20	Replacing A Legend	.75
21	Casey On Mantle	.75
22	Mickey & The Media	.75
23	Family Man	.75
24	Fan Favorite	.75
25	Playing Injured	.75
26	Clubhouse Leader	.75
27	Team Leader	.75
28	M & M Boys	.75
29	Legendary Friendships	.75
30	Time Out	.75
31	Mantle Is Born	.75
32	Mutt Mantle	.75
33	Growing Up	.75
34	5-tool player-Arm	.75
35	5-tool player-Defense	.75
36	5-tool player-Average	.75
37	5-tool player-Speed	.75
38	5-tool player-Power	.75
39	First Homer	.75
40	100th Homer	.75
41	200th Homer	.75
42	300th Homer	.75
43	400th Homer	.75
44	500th Homer	.75
45	536 Career Homers	.75
46	Yankee Stadium Blasts	.75
47	Switch-hit Home Runs	.75
48	565-ft. Home Run	.75
49	Signs 1st Pro Contract	.75
50	Mickey In The Minors	.75
51	1951 Trading Card	3.00
52	1952 Trading Card	3.00
53	1953 Trading Card	3.00
54	1954 Trading Card	3.00
55	1955 Trading Card	3.00
56A	1956 Trading Card	3.00
56B	1956 Trading Card	3.00
57	1957 Trading Card	3.00
58	1958 Trading Card	3.00
59	1959 Trading Card	3.00
60	1960 Trading Card	3.00
61	1961 Trading Card	3.00
62	1962 Trading Card	3.00
63	1963 Trading Card	3.00
64	1964 Trading Card	3.00
65	1965 Trading Card	3.00
66	1966 Trading Card	3.00
67	1967 Trading Card	3.00
68	1968 Trading Card	3.00
69	1969 Trading Card	3.00
70	Number Retired By Yankees (Foil die-cut.)	3.00
70p	Number Retired By Yankees/PC	3.00
71	Mickey Mantle Day/ 1965	.75
72	Mickey Mantle Day/ 1969	.75
73	Life After Baseball	.75
74	Hall Of Fame Induction (Foil die-cut.)	3.00
74p	Hall of Fame Induction/PC	3.00

1997 Score Board Mickey Mantle Shoe Box Inserts

A set of seven insert cards, found on average of one per 16 packs, was part of the Mickey Mantle Shoe Box Collection. The inserts have a photo of Mantle on front, with blue metallic foil highlights. Contest rules on the back specify that the first seven persons to redeem a complete set of the seven insert cards will win a $7,000 Mantle phone card. All others redeeming the set of seven prior to July 7, 1998, received a $700 Mantle phone card. The #7 insert card was short-printed to limit the number of phone card winners.

		NM/M
Complete Set (7):		70.00
Common Card:		6.00
$700 Phone Card:		115.00
$7,000 Phone Card:		850.00
1	Mickey Mantle Insert #1	6.00
2	Mickey Mantle Insert #2	6.00
3	Mickey Mantle Insert #3	6.00
4	Mickey Mantle Insert #4	6.00
5	Mickey Mantle Insert #5	25.00
6	Mickey Mantle Insert #6	6.00
7	Mickey Mantle Insert #7 (Short-print.)	40.00

1997 Score Board Players Club

Seven baseball players are among the cards in this multi-sport issue. Card fronts feature borderless action photos from which uniform logos have been removed. The player's name and the city in which he plays are in gold-foil in a baseball strip at bottom. Backs have another photo, biographical data and stats, including projected 1998 figures. Only the baseball players in the set are listed here.

		NM/M
Common Player:		.05
3	Barry Bonds	.50
7	Jose Cruz Jr.	.25
17	Matt Drews	.25
27	Wes Helms	.25
37	Richard Hidalgo	.25
48	Jay Payton	.25
69	Kerry Wood	.35

Die-Cuts

Former #1 draft picks from all four major sports are included in this insert set. Highlighted in gold foil, cards are die-cut into the shape of a numeral 1. Backs have biographical information and stats. Cards are numbered with a "D" prefix. Only the baseball players are listed here. They were a 1:32 pack insert.

		NM/M
D10	Jose Cruz Jr.	1.00
D11	Barry Bonds	5.00

Talk N' Sports

Insert phone cards with talk time worth up to $1,000, along with trivia contests to win memorabilia were among the incentives to purchase this four-sport issue. The base card set features 50 stars and prospects, all of whom are also found, along with a few other superstars, in the inserts. Fronts of the base cards have action photos on which uniform logos have been airbrushed away. Backs have a couple more photos, some player bio and stats. Only the baseball players from the set are listed here.

		NM/M
Common Player:		.10
40	Barry Bonds	.50
41	Jay Payton	.10
42	Todd Walker	.10
43	Jose Cruz Jr.	.10
44	Kerry Wood	.30
45	Wes Helms	.10

Talk N' Sports Essentials

See-through plastic and action photos are combined

on this 1:20 pack insert. Only a single baseball player is included among the four-sport stars and prospects.

		NM/M
E3	Barry Bonds	7.50

Visions Signings

Stars and prospects from all four major team sports are included in this issue. Fronts have borderless action photos with professional logos removed as necessary to meet licensing regulations. Front graphics feature holographic foil highlights. Backs have another photo along with stats, personal data and career notes. Cards were sold in five-card packs, each of which contained either an autographed card or an insert card. Only the seven baseball players from the 50-card set are listed here.

		NM/M
Common Player:		.25
Gold Parallel:		2X
1	Barry Bonds	1.50
5	Jose Cruz Jr.	.25
6	Ben Grieve	.25
7	Kerry Wood	.75
44	Wes Helms	.25
45	Richard Hidalgo	.25
46	Jay Payton	.25

Visions Signings Autographs

Each five-card pack of Score Board Vision Signings contained either an authentically autographed card or an insert card. Only the baseball players from the 63 autographed cards in the multi-sports set of stars and prospects are listed here. Barry Bonds autographs can be found on other companies' cards, with a Score Board authenticity seal.

		NM/M
9	Jose Cruz Jr.	2.00
20	Ben Grieve	2.00
21	Vladimir Guerrero	30.00
26	Wes Helms	2.00
27	Richard Hidalgo	2.00
34	Jason Kendall	2.00
44	Jay Payton	2.00
62	Paul Wilson	2.00
63	Kerry Wood	20.00
	Barry Bonds	45.00

Visions Signings Artistry

These specially printed cards were a one-in-six packs insert (regular version; 1:18 autographed) in five-card Visions Signings packs. Only a single baseball player is represented among the 20 cards in the set.

		NM/M
1	Jose Cruz Jr.	1.00
1	Jose Cruz Jr./Auto.	3.00

1998 Score Board Autographed Collection

A handful of baseball players are among the four-sport stars and prospects in this set. Luring collectors was the presence of autographed cards at the rate of one per 4-1/2 packs, Blue Ribbon serially numbered autographs and memorabilia redemption cards (many of which became worthless when Score Board went bankrupt shortly after the set was issued). Because the cards are licensed only by the players, and not leagues, there are no uniform logos on the photos, nor mention of team names, only cities. Only the baseball players are listed here.

		NM/M
Common Player:		.25
3	J.D. Drew	1.50
11	Matt White	.25
12	Jay Payton	.25
23	Brandon Larson	.25
28	Jose Cruz Jr.	.25
49	Adrian Beltre	.50

Strongbox

As part of a special $125 television offer, a parallel version of Score Board's Autographed Collection was offered featuring special inserts, autographs and memorabilia. The parallel cards are marked with an embossed "Strongbox" logo.

		NM/M
Common Player:		.25
3	J.D. Drew	2.00

		NM/M
11	Matt White	.50
12	Jay Payton	.50
23	Brandon Larson	.50
28	Jose Cruz Jr.	.50
49	Adrian Beltre	1.50

Autographs

Authentically autographed cards were inserted in this issue at the rate of about four per 18-pack box. Cards have a round player photo at center with the signature in a white oval below. Backs have a congratulatory message. Only the baseball players among the four-sport stars and prospects are listed here. Cards are unnumbered.

		NM/M
	Ben Grieve	2.00
	Wes Helms	2.00
	Jay Payton	2.00
	Kerry Wood	20.00

Blue Ribbon

These one-per-box inserts are similar in format to the autographed cards, but have a blue ribbon beneath the player photo on which the signature has been penned. Each card is individually serial numbered from within editions which vary from fewer than 100 to nearly 2,000. Only one baseball player was among the four-sport stars and prospects.

		NM/M
	Jose Cruz Jr./1,600	3.00

Sports City USA

Players whose teams share a common city are featured in this insert series, found on average one per nine packs. A parallel version, embossed "Strongbox" was issued in special $125 television-offer packages of Autographed Collection. The parallels are individually serial numbered to 600. Only cards with baseball players are listed here.

		NM/M
Common Card:		1.00
Embossed:		2X
SC3	Richard Hidalgo (Olajuwon, Drexler)	

		NM/M
SC4	Kerry Wood (Pippen, Autry)	2.50
SC6	Adrian Beltre (Bryant)	1.50
SC7	J.D. Drew (Thomas, Staley)	2.50
SC12	Wes Helms (Hanspard, Gray)	1.00
SC14	Jay Payton (Barber, Van Horn)	1.00
SC15	Matt Drews (Westbrook, Pollard)	1.00

1981 Seattle Mariners Police

These 2-5/8" x 4-1/8" cards were co-sponsored by the Washington State Crime Prevention Association, Coca-Cola, Kiawanis and Ernst Home Centers. Fronts have a color photo, player name and position and a team logo. Card backs are printed in blue and red and offer a "Tip from the Mariners" along with the four sponsor logos.

		NM/M
Complete Set (16):		3.00
Common Player:		.25
1	Jeff Burroughs	.25
2	Floyd Bannister	.25
3	Glenn Abbott	.25
4	Jim Anderson	.25
5	Danny Meyer	.25
6	Dave Edler	.25
7	Julio Cruz	.25
8	Kenny Clay	.25
9	Lenny Randle	.25
10	Mike Parrott	.25
11	Tom Paciorek	.25
12	Jerry Narron	.25
13	Richie Zisk	.25
14	Maury Wills	.50
15	Joe Simpson	.25
16	Shane Rawley	.25

1993 Select Promos

Zeroes in the career stats line on the back of the card distinguish the promo cards for Score's premiere issue of its Select brand name. The promo cards were distributed to introduce dealers and collectors to the new mid-range set.

		NM/M
Complete Set (8):		12.00
Common Player:		1.00
22	Robin Yount	3.00
24	Don Mattingly	5.00
26	Sandy Alomar Jr.	1.00
41	Gary Sheffield	2.00
56	Brady Anderson	1.00
65	Rob Dibble	1.00
75	John Smiley	1.00
79	Mitch Williams	1.00

1993 Select Dufex Proofs

To test the Dufex textured foil printing technology

DAVE FLEMING P

which was used on its Stars, Rookies and Triple Crown insert sets, Select produced a very limited number of blank-back proof cards.

Select Rookies:	15X
Select Stars:	20X
Select Triple Crown:	20X

1993 Select

TIM RAINES

This 400-card set from Score is designed for the mid-priced card market. The card fronts feature green borders on two sides of the card with the photo filling the remaining portion of the card front. The backs feature an additional photo, player information and statistics. Cards numbered 271-360 are devoted to rookies and draft picks.

		NM/M
Complete Set (405):		13.50
Common Player:		.05
Pack (15):		.75
Wax Box (36):		22.50
1	Barry Bonds	1.50
2	Ken Griffey Jr.	1.00
3	Will Clark	.05
4	Kirby Puckett	.75
5	Tony Gwynn	.75
6	Frank Thomas	.65
7	Tom Glavine	.35
8	Roberto Alomar	.25
9	Andre Dawson	.25
10	Ron Darling	.05
11	Bobby Bonilla	.05
12	Danny Tartabull	.05
13	Darren Daulton	.05
14	Roger Clemens	.85
15	Ozzie Smith	.75
16	Mark McGwire	1.25
17	Terry Pendleton	.05
18	Cal Ripken, Jr.	1.50
19	Fred McGriff	.05
20	Cecil Fielder	.05
21	Darryl Strawberry	.05
22	Robin Yount	.85
23	Barry Larkin	.05
24	Don Mattingly	.85
25	Craig Biggio	.05
26	Sandy Alomar Jr.	.05
27	Larry Walker	.05
28	Junior Felix	.05
29	Eddie Murray	.65
30	Robin Ventura	.05
31	Greg Maddux	.75
32	Dave Winfield	.65
33	John Kruk	.05
34	Wally Joyner	.05
35	Andy Van Slyke	.05
36	Chuck Knoblauch	.05
37	Tom Pagnozzi	.05
38	Dennis Eckersley	.60
39	Dave Justice	.65
40	Juan Gonzalez	.35
41	Gary Sheffield	.40
42	Paul Molitor	.65
43	Delino DeShields	.05
44	Travis Fryman	.05
45	Hal Morris	.05
46	Gregg Olson	.05
47	Ken Caminiti	.05
48	Wade Boggs	.75
49	Orel Hershiser	.05
50	Albert Belle	.05
51	Bill Swift	.05
52	Mark Langston	.05
53	Joe Girardi	.05
54	Keith Miller	.05
55	Gary Carter	.65
56	Brady Anderson	.05
57	Dwight Gooden	.05
58	Julio Franco	.05
59	Len Dykstra	.05
60	Mickey Tettleton	.05
61	Randy Tomlin	.05
62	B.J. Surhoff	.05
63	Todd Zeile	.05
64	Roberto Kelly	.05
65	Rob Dibble	.05
66	Leo Gomez	.05
67	Doug Jones	.05
68	Ellis Burks	.05
69	Mike Scioscia	.05
70	Charles Nagy	.05
71	Cory Snyder	.05
72	Devon White	.05
73	Mark Grace	.05
74	Luis Polonia	.05
75	John Smiley	.05
76	Carlton Fisk	.65
77	Luis Sojo	.05
78	George Brett	.85
79	Mitch Williams	.05
80	Kent Hrbek	.05
81	Jay Bell	.05
82	Edgar Martinez	.05
83	Lee Smith	.05
84	Deion Sanders	.05
85	Bill Gullickson	.05
86	Paul O'Neill	.05
87	Kevin Seitzer	.05
88	Steve Finley	.05
89	Mel Hall	.05
90	Nolan Ryan	1.50
91	Eric Davis	.05
92	Mike Mussina	.35
93	Tony Fernandez	.05
94	Frank Viola	.05
95	Matt Williams	.05
96	Joe Carter	.05
97	Ryne Sandberg	.75
98	Jim Abbott	.05
99	Marquis Grissom	.05
100	George Bell	.05
101	Howard Johnson	.05
102	Kevin Appier	.05
103	Dale Murphy	.20
104	Shane Mack	.05
105	Jose Lind	.05
106	Rickey Henderson	.65
107	Bob Tewksbury	.05
108	Kevin Mitchell	.05
109	Steve Avery	.05
110	Candy Maldonado	.05
111	Bip Roberts	.05
112	Lou Whitaker	.05
113	Jeff Bagwell	.65
114	Dante Bichette	.05
115	Brett Butler	.05
116	Melido Perez	.05
117	Andy Benes	.05
118	Randy Johnson	.65
119	Willie McGee	.05
120	Jody Reed	.05
121	Shawon Dunston	.05
122	Carlos Baerga	.05
123	Bret Saberhagen	.05
124	John Olerud	.05
125	Ivan Calderon	.05
126	Bryan Harvey	.05
127	Terry Mulholland	.05
128	Ozzie Guillen	.05
129	Steve Buechele	.05
130	Kevin Tapani	.05
131	Felix Jose	.05
132	Terry Steinbach	.05
133	Ron Gant	.05
134	Harold Reynolds	.05
135	Chris Sabo	.05
136	Ivan Rodriguez	.60
137	Eric Anthony	.05
138	Mike Henneman	.05
139	Robby Thompson	.05
140	Scott Fletcher	.05
141	Bruce Hurst	.05
142	Kevin Maas	.05
143	Tom Candiotti	.05
144	Chris Hoiles	.05
145	Mike Morgan	.05
146	Mark Whiten	.05
147	Dennis Martinez	.05
148	Tony Pena	.05
149	Dave Magadan	.05
150	Mark Lewis	.05
151	Mariano Duncan	.05
152	Gregg Jefferies	.05
153	Doug Drabek	.05
154	Brian Harper	.05
155	Ray Lankford	.05
156	Carney Lansford	.05
157	Mike Sharperson	.05
158	Jack Morris	.05
159	Otis Nixon	.05
160	Steve Sax	.05
161	Mark Lemke	.05
162	Rafael Palmeiro	.60
163	Jose Rijo	.05
164	Omar Vizquel	.05
165	Sammy Sosa	.75
166	Milt Cuyler	.05
167	John Franco	.05
168	Darryl Hamilton	.05
169	Ken Hill	.05
170	Mike Devereaux	.05
171	Don Slaught	.05
172	Steve Farr	.05
173	Bernard Gilkey	.05
174	Mike Fetters	.05
175	Vince Coleman	.05
176	Kevin McReynolds	.05
177	John Smoltz	.05
178	Greg Gagne	.05
179	Greg Swindell	.05
180	Juan Guzman	.05
181	Kal Daniels	.05
182	Rick Sutcliffe	.05
183	Orlando Merced	.05
184	Bill Wegman	.05
185	Mark Gardner	.05
186	Rob Deer	.05
187	Dave Hollins	.05
188	Jack Clark	.05
189	Brian Hunter	.05
190	Tim Wallach	.05
191	Tim Belcher	.05
192	Walt Weiss	.05
193	Kurt Stillwell	.05
194	Charlie Hayes	.05
195	Willie Randolph	.05
196	Jack McDowell	.05
197	Jose Offerman	.05
198	Chuck Finley	.05
199	Darrin Jackson	.05
200	Kelly Gruber	.05
201	John Wetteland	.05
202	Jay Buhner	.05
203	Mike LaValliere	.05
204	Kevin Brown	.05
205	Luis Gonzalez	.05
206	Rick Aguilera	.05
207	Norm Charlton	.05
208	Mike Bordick	.05
209	Charlie Leibrandt	.05
210	Tom Brunansky	.05
211	Tom Henke	.05
212	Randy Milligan	.05
213	Ramon Martinez	.05
214	Mo Vaughn	.05
215	Randy Myers	.05
216	Greg Hibbard	.05
217	Wes Chamberlain	.05
218	Tony Phillips	.05
219	Pete Harnisch	.05
220	Mike Gallego	.05
221	Bud Black	.05
222	Greg Vaughn	.05
223	Milt Thompson	.05
224	Ben McDonald	.05
225	Billy Hatcher	.05
226	Paul Sorrento	.05
227	Mark Gubicza	.05
228	Mike Greenwell	.05
229	Curt Schilling	.35
230	Alan Trammell	.05
231	Zane Smith	.05
232	Bobby Thigpen	.05
233	Greg Olson	.05
234	Joe Orsulak	.05
235	Joe Oliver	.05
236	Tim Raines	.05
237	Juan Samuel	.05
238	Chili Davis	.05
239	Spike Owen	.05
240	Dave Stewart	.05
241	Jim Eisenreich	.05
242	Phil Plantier	.05
243	Sid Fernandez	.05
244	Dan Gladden	.05
245	Mickey Morandini	.05
246	Tino Martinez	.05
247	Kirt Manwaring	.05
248	Dean Palmer	.05
249	Tom Browning	.05
250	Brian McRae	.05
251	Scott Leius	.05
252	Bert Blyleven	.05
253	Scott Erickson	.05
254	Bob Welch	.05
255	Pat Kelly	.05
256	Felix Fermin	.05
257	Harold Baines	.05
258	Duane Ward	.05
259	Bill Spiers	.05
260	Jaime Navarro	.05
261	Scott Sanderson	.05
262	Gary Gaetti	.05
263	Bob Ojeda	.05
264	Jeff Montgomery	.05
265	Scott Bankhead	.05
266	Lance Johnson	.05
267	Rafael Belliard	.05
268	Kevin Reimer	.05
269	Benito Santiago	.05
270	Mike Moore	.05
271	Dave Fleming	.05
272	Moises Alou	.05
273	Pat Listach	.05
274	Reggie Sanders	.05
275	Kenny Lofton	.05
276	Donovan Osborne	.05
277	Rusty Meacham	.05
278	Eric Karros	.05
279	Andy Stankiewicz	.05
280	Brian Jordan	.05
281	Gary DiSarcina	.05
282	Mark Wohlers	.05
283	Dave Nilsson	.05
284	Anthony Young	.05
285	Jim Bullinger	.05
286	Derek Bell	.05
287	Brian Williams	.05
288	Julio Valera	.05
289	Dan Walters	.05
290	Chad Curtis	.05
291	Michael Tucker	.05
292	Bob Zupcic	.05
293	Todd Hundley	.05
294	Jeff Tackett	.05
295	Greg Colbrunn	.05
296	Cal Eldred	.05
297	Chris Roberts	.05
298	John Doherty	.05
299	Denny Neagle	.05
300	Arthur Rhodes	.05
301	Mark Clark	.05
302	Scott Cooper	.05
303	Jamie Arnold RC	.05
304	Jim Thome	.60
305	Frank Seminara	.05
306	Kurt Knudsen	.05
307	Tim Wakefield	.05
308	John Jaha	.05
309	Pat Hentgen	.05
310	B.J. Wallace	.05
311	Roberto Hernandez	.05
312	Hipolito Pichardo	.05
313	Eric Fox	.05
314	Willie Banks	.05
315	Sam Militello	.05
316	Vince Horsman	.05
317	Carlos Hernandez	.05
318	Jeff Kent	.05
319	Mike Perez	.05
320	Scott Livingstone	.05
321	Jeff Conine	.05
322	James Austin	.05
323	John Vander Wal	.05
324	Pat Mahomes	.05
325	Pedro Astacio	.05
326	Bret Boone	.05
327	Matt Stairs	.05
328	Damion Easley	.05
329	Ben Rivera	.05
330	Reggie Jefferson	.05
331	Luis Mercedes	.05
332	Kyle Abbott	.05
333	Eddie Taubensee	.05
334	Tim McIntosh	.05
335	Phil Clark	.05
336	Wil Cordero	.05
337	Russ Springer	.05
338	Craig Colbert	.05
339	Tim Salmon	.05
340	Braulio Castillo	.05
341	Donald Harris	.05
342	Eric Young	.05
343	Bob Wickman	.05
344	John Valentin	.05
345	Dan Wilson	.05
346	Steve Hosey	.05
347	Mike Piazza	1.00
348	Willie Greene	.05
349	Tom Goodwin	.05
350	Eric Hillman	.05
351	Steve Reed RC	.05
352	Dan Serafini RC	.05
353	Todd Steverson RC	.05
354	Benji Grigsby	.05
355	Shannon Stewart RC	1.00
356	Sean Lowe	.05
357	Derek Wallace	.05
358	Rick Helling	.05
359	Jason Kendall RC	.05
360	Derek Jeter RC	10.00
361	David Cone	.05
362	Jeff Reardon	.05
363	Bobby Witt	.05
364	Jose Canseco	.40
365	Jeff Russell	.05
366	Ruben Sierra	.05
367	Alan Mills	.05
368	Matt Nokes	.05
369	Pat Borders	.05
370	Pedro Munoz	.05
371	Danny Jackson	.05
372	Geronimo Pena	.05
373	Craig Lefferts	.05
374	Joe Grahe	.05
375	Roger McDowell	.05
376	Jimmy Key	.05
377	Steve Olin	.05
378	Glenn Davis	.05
379	Rene Gonzales	.05
380	Manuel Lee	.05
381	Ron Karkovice	.05
382	Sid Bream	.05
383	Gerald Williams	.05
384	Lenny Harris	.05
385	J.T. Snow RC	.75
386	Dave Stieb	.05
387	Kirk McCaskill	.05
388	Lance Parrish	.05
389	Craig Grebeck	.05
390	Rick Wilkins	.05
391	Manny Alexander	.05
392	Mike Schooler	.05
393	Bernie Williams	.05
394	Kevin Koslofski	.05
395	Willie Wilson	.05
396	Jeff Parrett	.05
397	Mike Harkey	.05
398	Frank Tanana	.05
399	Doug Henry	.05
400	Royce Clayton	.05
401	Eric Wedge	.05
402	Derrick May	.05
403	Carlos Garcia	.05
404	Henry Rodriguez	.05
405	Ryan Klesko	.05

Aces

Cards from this set feature 24 of the top pitchers from 1992 and were included one per every 27-card Super Pack. The fronts have a picture of the player in action against an Ace card background. Backs have text and a portrait in the middle of a card suit for an Ace.

		NM/M
Complete Set (24):		20.00
Common Player:		1.00
1	Roger Clemens	6.00
2	Tom Glavine	3.00
3	Jack McDowell	1.00
4	Greg Maddux	4.50
5	Jack Morris	1.00
6	Dennis Martinez	1.00
7	Kevin Brown	1.00
8	Dwight Gooden	1.00
9	Kevin Appier	1.00
10	Mike Morgan	1.00
11	Juan Guzman	1.00
12	Charles Nagy	1.00
13	John Smiley	1.00
14	Ken Hill	1.00
15	Bob Tewksbury	1.00
16	Doug Drabek	1.00
17	John Smoltz	1.00
18	Greg Swindell	1.00
19	Bruce Hurst	1.00
20	Mike Mussina	2.00
21	Cal Eldred	1.00
22	Melido Perez	1.00
23	Dave Fleming	1.00
24	Kevin Tapani	1.00

Rookies

Top newcomers in 1992 are featured in this 21-card insert set. Cards were randomly inserted in 15-card hobby packs. The fronts, printed on metallic foil, have a Score Select Rookies logo on the front. The backs have text and a player portrait.

		NM/M
Complete Set (21):		4.00
Common Player:		.50
1	Pat Listach	.50
2	Moises Alou	.50
3	Reggie Sanders	.50
4	Kenny Lofton	.50
5	Eric Karros	.50
6	Brian Williams	.50
7	Donovan Osborne	.50
8	Sam Militello	.50
9	Chad Curtis	.50
10	Bob Zupcic	.50
11	Tim Salmon	1.50
12	Jeff Conine	.50
13	Pedro Astacio	.50
14	Arthur Rhodes	.50
15	Cal Eldred	.50
16	Tim Wakefield	.50
17	Andy Stankiewicz	.50

18	Wil Cordero	.50
19	Todd Hundley	.50
20	Dave Fleming	.50
21	Bret Boone	1.00

Stars

The top 24 players from 1992 are featured in this insert set. Cards were randomly inserted in 15-card retail packs. Fronts are printed on metallic foil.

		NM/M
Complete Set (24):		40.00
Common Player:		.60
1	Fred McGriff	.60
2	Ryne Sandberg	4.00
3	Ozzie Smith	4.00
4	Gary Sheffield	1.25
5	Darren Daulton	.60
6	Andy Van Slyke	.60
7	Barry Bonds	7.50
8	Tony Gwynn	4.00
9	Greg Maddux	4.00
10	Tom Glavine	1.00
11	John Franco	.60
12	Lee Smith	.60
13	Cecil Fielder	.60
14	Roberto Alomar	1.00
15	Cal Ripken, Jr.	7.50
16	Edgar Martinez	.60
17	Ivan Rodriguez	2.50
18	Kirby Puckett	4.00
19	Ken Griffey Jr.	6.00
20	Joe Carter	.60
21	Roger Clemens	4.50
22	Dave Fleming	.60
(22)	Dave Fleming (Blank-back sample card.)	1.00
23	Paul Molitor	3.00
(23)	Paul Molitor (Blank-back sample card.)	2.75
24	Dennis Eckersley	2.50

Stat Leaders

This 90-card set features 1992 American League and National League leaders in various statistical categories. Each card front indicates the league and the category in which the player finished at or near the top. The backs have a list of the leaders; the pictured player's name is in larger type size. Cards were inserted one per foil pack.

		NM/M
Complete Set (90):		8.00
Common Player:		.05
1	Edgar Martinez	.05
2	Kirby Puckett	.30
3	Frank Thomas	.25
4	Gary Sheffield	.15
5	Andy Van Slyke	.05
6	John Kruk	.05
7	Kirby Puckett	.30
8	Carlos Baerga	.05
9	Paul Molitor	.25
10	Andy Van Slyke, Terry Pendleton	.05
11	Ryne Sandberg	.30
12	Mark Grace	.05
13	Frank Thomas	.25
14	Don Mattingly	.35
15	Ken Griffey Jr.	.45
16	Andy Van Slyke	.05
17	Mariano Duncan, Jerald Clark, Ray Lankford	.05
18	Marquis Grissom, Terry Pendleton	.05
19	Lance Johnson	.05
20	Mike Devereaux	.05
21	Brady Anderson	.05
22	Deion Sanders	.05
23	Steve Finley	.05
24	Andy Van Slyke	.05
25	Juan Gonzalez	.15
26	Mark McGwire	.50
27	Cecil Fielder	.05
28	Fred McGriff	.05
29	Barry Bonds	.60
30	Gary Sheffield	.15
31	Cecil Fielder	.05
32	Joe Carter	.05
33	Frank Thomas	.25
34	Darren Daulton	.05
35	Terry Pendleton	.05
36	Fred McGriff	.05
37	Tony Phillips	.05
38	Frank Thomas	.25
39	Roberto Alomar	.15
40	Barry Bonds	.60
41	Dave Hollins	.05
42	Andy Van Slyke	.05
43	Mark McGwire	.50
44	Edgar Martinez	.05
45	Frank Thomas	.25
46	Barry Bonds	.60
47	Gary Sheffield	.15
48	Fred McGriff	.05
49	Frank Thomas	.25
50	Danny Tartabull	.05
51	Roberto Alomar	.15
52	Barry Bonds	.60
53	John Kruk	.05
54	Brett Butler	.05
55	Kenny Lofton	.05
56	Pat Listach	.05
57	Brady Anderson	.05
58	Marquis Grissom	.05
59	Delino DeShields	.05
60	Steve Finley, Bip Roberts	.05
61	Jack McDowell	.05
62	Kevin Brown	.05
63	Melido Perez	.05
64	Terry Mulholland	.05
65	Curt Schilling	.20
66	John Smoltz, Doug Drabek, Greg Maddux	.05
67	Dennis Eckersley	.20
68	Rick Aguilera	.05
69	Jeff Montgomery	.05
70	Lee Smith	.05
71	Randy Myers	.05
72	John Wetteland	.05
73	Randy Johnson	.25
74	Melido Perez	.05
75	Roger Clemens	.35
76	John Smoltz	.05
77	David Cone	.05
78	Greg Maddux	.30
79	Roger Clemens	.35
80	Kevin Appier	.05
81	Mike Mussina	.15
82	Bill Swift	.05
83	Bob Tewksbury	.05
84	Greg Maddux	.30
85	Kevin Brown	.05
86	Jack McDowell	.05
87	Roger Clemens	.35
88	Tom Glavine	.10
89	Ken Hill, Bob Tewksbury	.05
90	Dennis Martinez, Mike Morgan	.05

Triple Crown

This three-card set commemorates the Triple Crown seasons of Hall of Famers Mickey Mantle, Frank Robinson and Carl Yastrzemski. Cards were randomly inserted in 15-card hobby packs. Card fronts have a green metallic-look textured border, with the player's name at top in gold, and "Triple Crown" in gold at bottom. There are other silver and green highlights around the photo, which feature the player set against a metallized background. Dark green backs have a player photo and information on his Triple Crown season.

		NM/M
Complete Set (3):		35.00
Common Player:		10.00
1	Mickey Mantle	22.50
2	Frank Robinson	10.00
3	Carl Yastrzemski	12.50

1993 Select Rookie/Traded

Production of this 150-card set was limited to 1,950 numbered cases. Several future Hall of Famers and six dozen top rookies are featured in the set. Cards were available in packs rather than collated sets and include randomly inserted FX cards, which feature Nolan Ryan (two per 24-box case), Tim Salmon and Mike Piazza (one per 576 packs) and All-Star Rookie Team members (one per 58 packs).

		NM/M
Complete Set (150):		11.00
Common Player:		.05
Pack (12):		1.25
Wax Box (24):		20.00
1	Rickey Henderson	.75
2	Rob Deer	.05
3	Tim Belcher	.05
4	Gary Sheffield	.35
5	Fred McGriff	.05
6	Mark Whiten	.05
7	Jeff Russell	.05
8	Harold Baines	.05
9	Dave Winfield	.75
10	Ellis Burks	.05
11	Andre Dawson	.25
12	Gregg Jefferies	.05
13	Jimmy Key	.05
14	Harold Reynolds	.05
15	Tom Henke	.05
16	Paul Molitor	.75
17	Wade Boggs	1.00
18	David Cone	.05
19	Tony Fernandez	.05
20	Roberto Kelly	.05
21	Paul O'Neill	.05
22	Jose Lind	.05
23	Barry Bonds	2.00
24	Dave Stewart	.05
25	Randy Myers	.05
26	Benito Santiago	.05
27	Tim Wallach	.05
28	Greg Gagne	.05
29	Kevin Mitchell	.05
30	Jim Abbott	.05
31	Lee Smith	.05
32	Bobby Munoz RC	.05
33	Mo Sanford RC	.05
34	John Roper	.05
35	David Hulse RC	.05
36	Pedro Martinez	.75
37	Chuck Carr RC	.05
38	Armando Reynoso RC	.10
39	Ryan Thompson	.05
40	Carlos Garcia RC	.05
41	Matt Whiteside	.05
42	Benji Gil	.05
43	Rodney Bolton RC	.05
44	J.T. Snow	.05
45	David McCarty	.05
46	Paul Quantrill RC	.05
47	Al Martin	.05
48	Lance Painter	.05
49	Lou Frazier RC	.05
50	Eduardo Perez	.05
51	Kevin Young	.05
52	Mike Trombley	.05
53	Sterling Hitchcock RC	.10
54	Tim Bogar RC	.05
55	Hilly Hathaway RC	.05
56	Wayne Kirby RC	.05
57	Craig Paquette RC	.05
58	Bret Boone	.05
59	Greg McMichael RC	.05
60	Mike Lansing RC	.35
61	Brent Gates	.05
62	Rene Arocha	.05
63	Ricky Gutierrez	.05
64	Kevin Rogers RC	.05
65	Ken Ryan RC	.05
66	Phil Hiatt	.05
67	Pat Meares RC	.05
68	Troy Neel	.05
69	Steve Cooke	.05
70	Sherman Obando RC	.05
71	Blas Minor RC	.05
72	Angel Miranda RC	.05
73	Tom Kramer RC	.05
74	Chip Hale RC	.05
75	Brad Pennington RC	.05
76	Graeme Lloyd RC	.05
77	Darrell Whitmore RC	.05
78	David Nied	.05
79	Todd Van Poppel	.05
80	Chris Gomez RC	.10
81	Jason Bere	.05
82	Jeffrey Hammonds	.05
83	Brad Ausmus RC	.10
84	Kevin Stocker	.05
85	Jeromy Burnitz	.05
86	Aaron Sele	.05
87	Roberto Mejia RC	.05
88	Kirk Rueter RC	.10
89	Kevin Roberson RC	.05
90	Allen Watson RC	.05
91	Charlie Leibrandt	.05
92	Eric Davis	.05
93	Jody Reed	.05
94	Danny Jackson	.05
95	Gary Gaetti	.05
96	Norm Charlton	.05
97	Doug Drabek	.05
98	Scott Fletcher	.05
99	Greg Swindell	.05
100	John Smiley	.05
101	Kevin Reimer	.05
102	Andres Galarraga	.05
103	Greg Hibbard	.05
104	Chris Hammond	.05
105	Darnell Coles	.05
106	Mike Felder	.05
107	Jose Guzman	.05
108	Chris Bosio	.05
109	Spike Owen	.05
110	Felix Jose	.05
111	Cory Snyder	.05
112	Craig Lefferts	.05
113	David Wells	.05
114	Pete Incaviglia	.05
115	Mike Pagliarulo	.05
116	Dave Magadan	.05
117	Charlie Hough	.05
118	Ivan Calderon	.05
119	Manuel Lee	.05
120	Bob Patterson	.05
121	Bob Ojeda	.05
122	Scott Bankhead	.05
123	Greg Maddux	1.00
124	Chili Davis	.05
125	Milt Thompson	.05
126	Dave Martinez	.05
127	Frank Tanana	.05
128	Phil Plantier	.05
129	Juan Samuel	.05
130	Eric Young	.05
131	Joe Orsulak	.05
132	Derek Bell	.05
133	Darrin Jackson	.05
134	Tom Brunansky	.05
135	Jeff Reardon	.05
136	Kevin Higgins RC	.05
137	Joel Johnston RC	.05
138	Rick Trlicek RC	.05
139	Richie Lewis RC	.05
140	Jeff Gardner RC	.05
141	Jack Voigt RC	.05
142	Rod Correia RC	.05
143	Billy Brewer RC	.05
144	Terry Jorgensen RC	.05
145	Rich Amaral RC	.05
146	Sean Berry RC	.05
147	Dan Peltier RC	.05
148	Paul Wagner RC	.05
149	Damon Buford RC	.05
150	Wil Cordero	.05

All-Star Rookies

KEVIN STOCKER

'93 ALL-STAR ROOKIE TEAM

These cards were randomly inserted into the Score Select Rookie/Traded packs, making them among the scarcest of the year's many "chase" cards. Card fronts feature metallic foil printing. Backs have a few words about the player. Stated odds of finding an All-Star Rookie Team insert card are one per 58 packs.

		NM/M
Complete Set (10):		30.00
Common Player:		1.00
1	Jeff Conine	1.00
2	Brent Gates	1.00
3	Mike Lansing	1.00
4	Kevin Stocker	1.00
5	Mike Piazza	25.00
6	Jeffrey Hammonds	1.00
7	David Hulse	1.00
8	Tim Salmon	2.00
9	Rene Arocha	1.00
10	Greg McMichael	1.00

Inserts

MIKE PIAZZA

Three cards honoring the 1993 Rookies of the Year and retiring superstar Nolan Ryan were issued as random inserts in the Select Rookie/Traded packs. Cards are printed with metallic foil front backgrounds. Stated odds of finding a Piazza or Salmon card are about one per 24-box case; Ryan cards are found on average two per case.

		NM/M
Complete Set (3):		60.00
Common Player:		6.00
1NR	Nolan Ryan	40.00
1ROY	Tim Salmon	6.00
2ROY	Mike Piazza	20.00

1994 Select Promos

To introduce its 1994 offering to dealers and collectors, Score Select created an eight-card promo set. Cards are identical in format to regular-issue cards with the exception of the word "SAMPLE" overprinted diagonally on front and back. The promos included five of the regular-run cards, a Rookie Prospect card and one each of its Rookie Surge '94 and Crown Contenders insert sets. The promos were cello-packaged with a header card describing the set and chase cards.

		NM/M
Complete Set (8):		7.50
Common Player:		.75
3	Paul Molitor	1.50
17	Kirby Puckett	2.50
19	Randy Johnson	1.50
24	John Kruk	.75
25	Jose Lind	.75
197	Ryan Klesko (Rookie Prospect)	1.00
1CC	Lenny Dykstra (Crown Contenders)	1.00
1RS	Cliff Floyd (Rookie Surge)	1.00
---	Header Card	.05

1994 Select

Both series of this premium brand from the Score/Pinnacle lineup offered 210 regular cards for a combined 420 cards, and seven insert sets. The announced press run for each series was 4,950 20-box cases. Cards have a horizontal format with a color action photo at right and a second photo at left done in a single team color-coded hue. The player's last name is dropped out of a vertical gold-foil strip between the two photos, with his first name in white at top-center. Backs are vertical with yet another color action photo at center. In a vertical bar at right, matching the color-coding on front and printed over the photo are 1993 and career stats, a "Select Stat," and a few sentences about the player. The appropriate logos and Pinnacle's optical-variable anti-counterfeiting device are at bottom-center. Thirty of the final 33 cards in the first series are a "1994 Rookie Prospect" sub-set, so noted in a special gold-foil logo on front.

		NM/M
Complete Set (420):		12.50
Common Player:		.05
Pack (12):		1.25
Wax Box (24):		16.00
1	Ken Griffey Jr.	1.50
2	Greg Maddux	1.00
3	Paul Molitor	.75
4	Mike Piazza	1.50
5	Jay Bell	.05
6	Frank Thomas	.75
7	Barry Larkin	.05
8	Paul O'Neill	.05
9	Darren Daulton	.05
10	Mike Greenwell	.05
11	Chuck Carr	.05
12	Joe Carter	.05
13	Lance Johnson	.05
14	Jeff Blauser	.05
15	Chris Hoiles	.05
16	Rick Wilkins	.05
17	Kirby Puckett	1.00
18	Larry Walker	.05
19	Randy Johnson	.75
20	Bernard Gilkey	.05
21	Devon White	.05
22	Randy Myers	.05
23	Don Mattingly	1.25
24	John Kruk	.05
25	Ozzie Guillen	.05
26	Jeff Conine	.05
27	Mike Macfarlane	.05
28	Dave Hollins	.05
29	Chuck Knoblauch	.05
30	Ozzie Smith	1.00
31	Harold Baines	.05
32	Ryne Sandberg	1.00
33	Ron Karkovice	.05
34	Terry Pendleton	.05
35	Wally Joyner	.05
36	Mike Mussina	.35
37	Felix Jose	.05
38	Derrick May	.05
39	Scott Cooper	.05
40	Jose Rijo	.05
41	Robin Ventura	.05
42	Charlie Hayes	.05
43	Jimmy Key	.05
44	Eric Karros	.05
45	Ruben Sierra	.05
46	Ryan Thompson	.05
47	Brian McRae	.05
48	Pat Hentgen	.05
49	John Valentin	.05
50	Al Martin	.05
51	Jose Lind	.05
52	Kevin Stocker	.05
53	Mike Gallego	.05
54	Dwight Gooden	.05
55	Brady Anderson	.05
56	Jeff King	.05
57	Mark McGwire	1.75
58	Sammy Sosa	1.00
59	Ryan Bowen	.05
60	Mark Lemke	.05
61	Roger Clemens	1.25
62	Brian Jordan	.05
63	Andres Galarraga	.05
64	Kevin Appier	.05
65	Don Slaught	.05
66	Mike Blowers	.05
67	Wes Chamberlain	.05
68	Troy Neel	.05

No	Player	Value
69	John Wetteland	.05
70	Joe Girardi	.05
71	Reggie Sanders	.05
72	Edgar Martinez	.05
73	Todd Hundley	.05
74	Pat Borders	.05
75	Roberto Mejia	.05
76	David Cone	.05
77	Tony Gwynn	1.00
78	Jim Abbott	.05
79	Jay Buhner	.05
80	Mark McLemore	.05
81	Wil Cordero	.05
82	Pedro Astacio	.05
83	Bob Tewksbury	.05
84	Dave Winfield	.75
85	Jeff Kent	.05
86	Todd Van Poppel	.05
87	Steve Avery	.05
88	Mike Lansing	.05
89	Len Dykstra	.05
90	Jose Guzman	.05
91	Brian Hunter	.05
92	Tim Raines	.05
93	Andre Dawson	.25
94	Joe Orsulak	.05
95	Ricky Jordan	.05
96	Billy Hatcher	.05
97	Jack McDowell	.05
98	Tom Pagnozzi	.05
99	Darryl Strawberry	.05
100	Mike Stanley	.05
101	Bret Saberhagen	.05
102	Willie Greene	.05
103	Bryan Harvey	.05
104	Tim Bogar	.05
105	Jack Voight	.05
106	Brad Ausmus	.05
107	Ramon Martinez	.05
108	Mike Perez	.05
109	Jeff Montgomery	.05
110	Danny Darwin	.05
111	Wilson Alvarez	.05
112	Kevin Mitchell	.05
113	David Nied	.05
114	Rich Amaral	.05
115	Stan Javier	.05
116	Mo Vaughn	.75
117	Ben McDonald	.05
118	Tom Gordon	.05
119	Carlos Garcia	.05
120	Phil Plantier	.05
121	Mike Morgan	.05
122	Pat Meares	.05
123	Kevin Young	.05
124	Jeff Fassero	.05
125	Gene Harris	.05
126	Bob Welch	.05
127	Walt Weiss	.05
128	Bobby Witt	.05
129	Andy Van Slyke	.05
130	Steve Cooke	.05
131	Mike Devereaux	.05
132	Joey Cora	.05
133	Bret Barberie	.05
134	Orel Hershiser	.05
135	Ed Sprague	.05
136	Shawon Dunston	.05
137	Alex Arias	.05
138	Archi Cianfrocco	.05
139	Tim Wallach	.05
140	Bernie Williams	.05
141	Karl Rhodes	.05
142	Pat Kelly	.05
143	Dave Magadan	.05
144	Kevin Tapani	.05
145	Eric Young	.05
146	Derek Bell	.05
147	Dante Bichette	.05
148	Geronimo Pena	.05
149	Joe Oliver	.05
150	Orestes Destrade	.05
151	Tim Naehring	.05
152	Ray Lankford	.05
153	Phil Clark	.05
154	David McCarty	.05
155	Tommy Greene	.05
156	Wade Boggs	1.00
157	Kevin Gross	.05
158	Hal Morris	.05
159	Moises Alou	.05
160	Rick Aguilera	.05
161	Curt Schilling	.35
162	Chip Hale	.05
163	Tino Martinez	.05
164	Mark Whiten	.05
165	Dave Stewart	.05
166	Steve Buechele	.05
167	Bobby Jones	.05
168	Darrin Fletcher	.05
169	John Smiley	.05
170	Cory Snyder	.05
171	Scott Erickson	.05
172	Kirk Rueter	.05
173	Dave Fleming	.05
174	John Smoltz	.05
175	Ricky Gutierrez	.05
176	Mike Bordick	.05
177	Chan Ho Park RC	1.00
178	Alex Gonzalez	.05
179	Steve Karsay	.05
180	Jeffrey Hammonds	.05
181	Manny Ramirez	.75
182	Salomon Torres	.05
183	Raul Mondesi	.05
184	James Mouton	.05
185	Cliff Floyd	.05
186	Danny Bautista	.05

No	Player	Value
187	Kurt Abbott RC	.05
188	Javier Lopez	.05
189	John Patterson	.05
190	Greg Blosser	.05
191	Bob Hamelin	.05
192	Tony Eusebio	.05
193	Carlos Delgado	.50
194	Chris Gomez	.05
195	Kelly Stinnett	.05
196	Shane Reynolds	.05
197	Ryan Klesko	.05
198	Jim Edmonds	.05
199	James Hurst	.05
200	Dave Staton	.05
201	Rondell White	.05
202	Keith Mitchell	.05
203	Darren Oliver	.05
204	Mike Matheny	.05
205	Chris Turner	.05
206	Matt Mieske	.05
207	N.L. team checklist	.05
208	N.L. team checklist	.05
209	A.L. team checklist	.05
210	A.L. team checklist	.05
211	Barry Bonds	2.00
212	Juan Gonzalez	.40
213	Jim Eisenreich	.05
214	Ivan Rodriguez	.65
215	Tony Phillips	.05
216	John Jaha	.05
217	Lee Smith	.05
218	Bip Roberts	.05
219	Dave Hansen	.05
220	Pat Listach	.05
221	Willie McGee	.05
222	Damion Easley	.05
223	Dean Palmer	.05
224	Mike Moore	.05
225	Brian Harper	.05
226	Gary DiSarcina	.05
227	Delino DeShields	.05
228	Otis Nixon	.05
229	Roberto Alomar	.30
230	Mark Grace	.05
231	Kenny Lofton	.05
232	Gregg Jefferies	.05
233	Cecil Fielder	.05
234	Jeff Bagwell	.75
235	Albert Belle	.05
236	Dave Justice	.05
237	Tom Henke	.05
238	Bobby Bonilla	.05
239	John Olerud	.05
240	Robby Thompson	.05
241	Dave Valle	.05
242	Marquis Grissom	.05
243	Greg Swindell	.05
244	Todd Zeile	.05
245	Dennis Eckersley	.65
246	Jose Offerman	.05
247	Greg McMichael	.05
248	Tim Belcher	.05
249	Cal Ripken, Jr.	2.00
250	Tom Glavine	.05
251	Luis Polonia	.05
252	Bill Swift	.05
253	Juan Guzman	.05
254	Rickey Henderson	.75
255	Terry Mulholland	.05
256	Gary Sheffield	.40
257	Terry Steinbach	.05
258	Brett Butler	.05
259	Jason Bere	.05
260	Doug Strange	.05
261	Kent Hrbek	.05
262	Graeme Lloyd	.05
263	Lou Frazier	.05
264	Charles Nagy	.05
265	Bret Boone	.05
266	Kirk Gibson	.05
267	Kevin Brown	.05
269	Matt Williams	.05
270	Greg Gagne	.05
271	Mariano Duncan	.05
272	Jeff Russell	.05
273	Eric Davis	.05
274	Shane Mack	.05
275	Jose Vizcaino	.05
276	Jose Canseco	.45
277	Roberto Hernandez	.05
278	Royce Clayton	.05
279	Carlos Baerga	.05
280	Pete Incaviglia	.05
281	Brent Gates	.05
282	Jeromy Burnitz	.05
283	Chili Davis	.05
284	Pete Harnisch	.05
285	Alan Trammell	.05
286	Eric Anthony	.05
287	Ellis Burks	.05
288	Julio Franco	.05
289	Jack Morris	.05
290	Erik Hanson	.05
291	Chuck Finley	.05
292	Reggie Jefferson	.05
293	Kevin McReynolds	.05
294	Greg Hibbard	.05
295	Travis Fryman	.05
296	Craig Biggio	.05
297	Kenny Rogers	.05
298	Dave Henderson	.05
299	Jim Thome	.50
300	Rene Arocha	.05
301	Pedro Munoz	.05
302	David Hulse	.05
303	Greg Vaughn	.05
304	Darren Lewis	.05
305	Deion Sanders	.05

No	Player	Value
306	Danny Tartabull	.05
307	Darryl Hamilton	.05
308	Andujar Cedeno	.05
309	Tim Salmon	.05
310	Tony Fernandez	.05
311	Alex Fernandez	.05
312	Roberto Kelly	.05
313	Harold Reynolds	.05
314	Chris Sabo	.05
315	Howard Johnson	.05
316	Mark Portugal	.05
317	Rafael Palmeiro	.65
318	Pete Smith	.05
319	Will Clark	.05
320	Henry Rodriguez	.05
321	Omar Vizquel	.05
322	David Segui	.05
323	Lou Whitaker	.05
324	Felix Fermin	.05
325	Spike Owen	.05
326	Darryl Kile	.05
327	Chad Kreuter	.05
328	Rod Beck	.05
329	Eddie Murray	.75
330	B.J. Surhoff	.05
331	Mickey Tettleton	.05
332	Pedro Martinez	.75
333	Roger Pavlik	.05
334	Eddie Taubensee	.05
335	John Doherty	.05
336	Jody Reed	.05
337	Aaron Sele	.05
338	Leo Gomez	.05
339	Dave Nilsson	.05
340	Rob Dibble	.05
341	John Burkett	.05
342	Wayne Kirby	.05
343	Dan Wilson	.05
344	Armando Reynoso	.05
345	Chad Curtis	.05
346	Dennis Martinez	.05
347	Cal Eldred	.05
348	Luis Gonzalez	.05
349	Doug Drabek	.05
350	Jim Leyritz	.05
351	Mark Langston	.05
352	Darrin Jackson	.05
353	Sid Fernandez	.05
354	Benito Santiago	.05
355	Kevin Seitzer	.05
356	Bo Jackson	.10
357	David Wells	.05
358	Paul Sorrento	.05
359	Ken Caminiti	.05
360	Eduardo Perez	.05
361	Orlando Merced	.05
362	Steve Finley	.05
363	Andy Benes	.05
364	Manuel Lee	.05
365	Todd Benzinger	.05
366	Sandy Alomar Jr.	.05
367	Rex Hudler	.05
368	Mike Henneman	.05
369	Vince Coleman	.05
370	Kirt Manwaring	.05
371	Ken Hill	.05
372	Glenallen Hill	.05
373	Sean Berry	.05
374	Geronimo Berroa	.05
375	Duane Ward	.05
376	Allen Watson	.05
377	Marc Newfield	.05
378	Dan Miceli	.05
379	Denny Hocking	.05
380	Mark Kiefer	.05
381	Tony Tarasco	.05
382	Tony Longmire	.05
383	Brian Anderson RC	.05
384	Fernando Vina	.05
385	Hector Carrasco	.05
386	Mike Kelly	.05
387	Greg Colbrunn	.05
388	Roger Salkeld	.05
389	Steve Trachsel	.05
390	Rich Becker	.05
391	Billy Taylor RC	.05
392	Rich Rowland	.05
393	Carl Everett	.05
394	Johnny Ruffin	.05
395	Keith Lockhart RC	.05
396	J.R. Phillips	.05
397	Sterling Hitchcock	.05
398	Jorge Fabregas	.05
399	Jeff Granger	.05
400	Eddie Zambrano RC	.05
401	Rikkert Faneyte RC	.05
402	Gerald Williams	.05
403	Joey Hamilton	.05
404	Joe Hall RC	.05
405	John Hudek RC	.05
406	Roberto Petagine	.05
407	Charles Johnson	.05
408	Mark Smith	.05
409	Jeff Juden	.05
410	Carlos Pulido RC	.05
411	Paul Shuey	.05
412	Rob Butler	.05
413	Mark Acre	.05
414	Greg Pirkl	.05
415	Melvin Nieves	.05
416	Tim Hyers RC	.05
417	N.L. checklist	.05
418	N.L. checklist	.05
419	A.L. checklist	.05
420	A.L. checklist	.05

Crown Contenders

Candidates for the major baseball annual awards are

featured in this subset. Horizontal-format cards have a color player photo printed on a holographic foil background. Backs are vertically oriented with a player portrait photo and justification for the player's inclusion in the set. Cards are numbered with a "CC" prefix and feature a special optical-variable anti-counterfeiting device at bottom-center. According to stated odds of one card on average in every 24 packs it has been estimated that fewer than 12,000 of each Crown Contenders card was produced.

		NM/M
Complete Set (10):		12.50
Common Player:		.50
1	Len Dykstra	.50
2	Greg Maddux	1.75
3	Roger Clemens	2.00
4	Randy Johnson	1.50
5	Frank Thomas	1.50
6	Barry Bonds	3.00
7	Juan Gonzalez	1.00
8	John Olerud	.50
9	Mike Piazza	2.50
10	Ken Griffey Jr.	2.50

MVP

Paul Molitor was the 1994 Select MVP and is featured in this one card set. Molitor is pictured in front of three distinct foil designs across the rest of the card.

		NM/M
MVP1	Paul Molitor	5.00

Rookie of the Year

Carlos Delgado was the 1994 Select Rookie of the Year. Delgado is pictured on top of a glowing foil background with his initials in large capital letters in the background and Rookie of the Year printed across the bottom.

		NM/M
RY1	Carlos Delgado	7.50

Rookie Surge

Each series of 1994 Score Select offered a chase card set of nine top rookies. Fronts feature action photos set against

a rainbow-colored metallic foil background. Backs have a portrait photo and a few words about the player. Cards are numbered with an "RS" prefix and were inserted at an average rate of one per 48 packs.

		NM/M
Complete Set (18):		10.00
Common Player:		.75
1	Cliff Floyd	.75
2	Bob Hamelin	.75
3	Ryan Klesko	.75
4	Carlos Delgado	3.00
5	Jeffrey Hammonds	.75
6	Rondell White	.75
7	Salomon Torres	.75
8	Steve Karsay	.75
9	Javier Lopez	.75
10	Manny Ramirez	3.00
11	Tony Tarasco	.75
12	Kurt Abbott	.75
13	Chan Ho Park	.75
14	Rich Becker	.75
15	James Mouton	.75
16	Alex Gonzalez	.75
17	Raul Mondesi	.75
18	Steve Trachsel	.75

Salute

With odds of finding one of these cards stated at one per 360 packs, it is estimated that only about 4,000 of each of this two-card chase set were produced.

		NM/M
Complete Set (2):		15.00
1	Cal Ripken, Jr.	12.50
2	Dave Winfield	5.00

Skills

Select Skills is a 10-card insert that was randomly inserted into every 24 packs. Ten specific skills were designated and matched with the player whom, in the opinion of Select officials, demonstrated that particular skill the best in baseball. Each card is printed on a foil background with the player name vertically on left side of the card and the skill that they are being featured for along the bottom.

		NM/M
Complete Set (10):		15.00
Common Player:		.75
1	Randy Johnson	3.00
2	Barry Larkin	.75
3	Len Dykstra	.75
4	Kenny Lofton	.75
5	Juan Gonzalez	1.50
6	Barry Bonds	6.00
7	Marquis Grissom	.75
8	Ivan Rodriguez	2.50
9	Larry Walker	.75
10	Travis Fryman	.75

1995 Select Samples

Pinnacle's hobby-only Select brand issue for 1995 was previewed with this four-card cello-packed sample set. Three player cards are in the basic format of the regular-issue Select cards, except they have a large white "SAMPLE" printed diagonally across the front and back. The fourth card in the sample pack is a header card advertising the features of the issue.

		NM/M
Complete Set (4):		4.00
Common Player:		.75
34	Roberto Alomar	.50
37	Jeff Bagwell	.75
241	Alex Rodriguez	4.00
--	Header Card	.05

1995 Select

The 250 regular-issue cards in Pinnacle's mid-price brand feature three basic formats. Veteran players' cards are presented horizontally and feature an action photo at left. At right is a portrait in a trapezoidal gold-foil frame set against a team color-coordinated marbled background. The team logo beneath the portrait and the player's name below that are printed in gold foil. Backs feature a black-and-white photo with a few career highlights, 1994 and career stats, and a "Select Stat" printed in red. The colored marble effect is carried over from the front. The Select Rookie cards, which are grouped toward the end of the set, are vertical in format and feature a borderless player photo with a gold-foil band at bottom which includes the player name and team logo, along with waves of gold emanating from the logo. Backs have a small, narrow color photo at left, with a large sepia version of the same photo ghosted at center and overprinted with a career summary. At bottom are 1994 and career stats. Ending the set are a series of "Show Time" cards of top prospects. Cards feature large gold-foil "Show Time" and team logos at bottom, with a facsimile autograph printed above. The player photo is shown as if at a curtain raising, with spotlight effects behind. Backs repeat the curtain and spotlight motif and feature another player photo, with autograph above. Production of this hobby-only product was stated as 4,950 cases, which translates to about 110,000 of each regular-issue card. A special card (#251) of Hideo Nomo was added to the set later. It was not issued in foil packs, but distributed to dealers who had purchased Select cases.

		NM/M
Complete Set (251):		9.00
Common Player:		.05
Artist's Proofs:		10X
Pack (12):		1.50
Wax Box (24):		17.50
1	Cal Ripken Jr.	1.50
2	Robin Ventura	.05
3	Al Martin	.05
4	Jeff Frye	.05
5	Darryl Strawberry	.05
6	Chan Ho Park	.05
7	Steve Avery	.05
8	Bret Boone	.05
9	Danny Tartabull	.05
10	Dante Bichette	.05
11	Rondell White	.05
12	Dave McCarty	.05
13	Bernard Gilkey	.05
14	Mark McGwire	1.25
15	Ruben Sierra	.05
16	Wade Boggs	.75
17	Mike Piazza	1.00
18	Jeffrey Hammonds	.05
19	Mike Mussina	.35
20	Darryl Kile	.05
21	Greg Maddux	.75
22	Frank Thomas	.65
23	Kevin Appier	.05
24	Jay Bell	.05
25	Kirk Gibson	.05
26	Pat Hentgen	.05
27	Joey Hamilton	.05
28	Bernie Williams	.05
29	Aaron Sele	.05
30	Delino DeShields	.05
31	Danny Bautista	.05
32	Jim Thome	.45
33	Rikkert Faneyte	.05
34	Roberto Alomar	.20
35	Paul Molitor	.65
36	Allen Watson	.05
37	Jeff Bagwell	.65
38	Jay Buhner	.05
39	Marquis Grissom	.05
40	Jim Edmonds	.05
41	Ryan Klesko	.05
42	Fred McGriff	.05
43	Tony Tarasco	.05
44	Darren Daulton	.05
45	Marc Newfield	.05
46	Barry Bonds	1.50
47	Bobby Bonilla	.05
48	Greg Pirkl	.05
49	Steve Karsay	.05
50	Bob Hamelin	.05
51	Javier Lopez	.05
52	Barry Larkin	.05
53	Kevin Young	.05
54	Sterling Hitchcock	.05
55	Tom Glavine	.05
56	Carlos Delgado	.40
57	Darren Oliver	.05
58	Cliff Floyd	.05
59	Tim Salmon	.05
60	Albert Belle	.05
61	Salomon Torres	.05
62	Gary Sheffield	.35
63	Ivan Rodriguez	.50
64	Charles Nagy	.05
65	Eduardo Perez	.05
66	Terry Steinbach	.05
67	Dave Justice	.05
68	Jason Bere	.05
69	Dave Nilsson	.05
70	Brian Anderson	.05
71	Billy Ashley	.05
72	Roger Clemens	.85
73	Jimmy Key	.05
74	Wally Joyner	.05
75	Andy Benes	.05
76	Ray Lankford	.05
77	Jeff Kent	.05
78	Moises Alou	.05
79	Kirby Puckett	.75
80	Joe Carter	.05
81	Manny Ramirez	.65
82	J.R. Phillips	.05
83	Matt Mieske	.05
84	John Olerud	.05
85	Andres Galarraga	.05
86	Juan Gonzalez	.35
87	Pedro Martinez	.65
88	Dean Palmer	.05
89	Ken Griffey Jr.	1.00
90	Brian Jordan	.05
91	Hal Morris	.05
92	Lenny Dykstra	.05
93	Wil Cordero	.05
94	Tony Gwynn	.75
95	Alex Gonzalez	.05
96	Cecil Fielder	.05
97	Mo Vaughn	.05

98	John Valentin	.05
99	Will Clark	.05
100	Geronimo Pena	.05
101	Don Mattingly	.85
102	Charles Johnson	.05
103	Raul Mondesi	.05
104	Reggie Sanders	.05
105	Royce Clayton	.05
106	Reggie Jefferson	.05
107	Craig Biggio	.05
108	Jack McDowell	.05
109	James Mouton	.05
110	Mike Greenwell	.05
111	David Cone	.05
112	Matt Williams	.05
113	Garret Anderson	.05
114	Carlos Garcia	.05
115	Alex Fernandez	.05
116	Deion Sanders	.05
117	Chili Davis	.05
118	Mike Kelly	.05
119	Jeff Conine	.05
120	Kenny Lofton	.05
121	Rafael Palmeiro	.50
122	Chuck Knoblauch	.05
123	Ozzie Smith	.75
124	Carlos Baerga	.05
125	Brett Butler	.05
126	Sammy Sosa	.75
127	Ellis Burks	.05
128	Bret Saberhagen	.05
129	Doug Drabek	.05
130	Dennis Martinez	.05
131	Paul O'Neill	.05
132	Travis Fryman	.05
133	Brent Gates	.05
134	Rickey Henderson	.65
135	Randy Johnson	.65
136	Mark Langston	.05
137	Greg Colbrunn	.05
138	Jose Rijo	.05
139	Bryan Harvey	.05
140	Dennis Eckersley	.50
141	Ron Gant	.05
142	Carl Everett	.05
143	Jeff Granger	.05
144	Ben McDonald	.05
145	Kurt Abbott	.05
146	Jim Abbott	.05
147	Jason Jacome	.05
148	Rico Brogna	.05
149	Cal Eldred	.05
150	Rich Becker	.05
151	Pete Harnisch	.05
152	Roberto Petagine	.05
153	Jacob Brumfield	.05
154	Todd Hundley	.05
155	Roger Cedeno	.05
156	Harold Baines	.05
157	Steve Dunn	.05
158	Tim Belk	.05
159	Marty Cordova	.05
160	Russ Davis	.05
161	Jose Malave	.05
162	Brian Hunter	.05
163	Andy Pettitte	.20
164	Brooks Kieschnick	.05
165	Midre Cummings	.05
166	Frank Rodriguez	.05
167	Chad Mottola	.05
168	Brian Barber	.05
169	Tim Unroe	.05
170	Shane Andrews	.05
171	Kevin Flora	.05
172	Ray Durham	.05
173	Chipper Jones	.75
174	Butch Huskey	.05
175	Ray McDavid	.05
176	Jeff Cirillo	.05
177	Terry Pendleton	.05
178	Scott Ruffcorn	.05
179	Ray Holbert	.05
180	Joe Randa	.05
181	Jose Oliva	.05
182	Andy Van Slyke	.05
183	Albie Lopez	.05
184	Chad Curtis	.05
185	Ozzie Guillen	.05
186	Chad Ogea	.05
187	Dan Wilson	.05
188	Tony Fernandez	.05
189	John Smoltz	.05
190	Willie Greene	.05
191	Darren Lewis	.05
192	Orlando Miller	.05
193	Kurt Miller	.05
194	Andrew Lorraine	.05
195	Ernie Young	.05
196	Jimmy Haynes	.05
197	Raul Casanova RC	.05
198	Joe Vitiello	.05
199	Brad Woodall	.05
200	Juan Acevedo	.05
201	Michael Tucker	.05
202	Shawn Green	.35
203	Alex Rodriguez	1.25
204	Julian Tavarez	.05
205	Jose Lima	.05
206	Wilson Alvarez	.05
207	Rich Aude	.05
208	Armando Benitez	.05
209	Dwayne Hosey	.05
210	Gabe White	.05
211	Joey Eischen	.05
212	Bill Pulsipher	.05
213	Robby Thompson	.05
214	Toby Borland	.05
215	Rusty Greer	.05

216	Fausto Cruz	.05
217	Luis Ortiz	.05
218	Duane Singleton	.05
219	Troy Percival	.05
220	Gregg Jefferies	.05
221	Mark Grace	.05
222	Mickey Tettleton	.05
223	Phil Plantier	.05
224	Larry Walker	.05
225	Ken Caminiti	.05
226	Dave Winfield	.65
227	Brady Anderson	.05
228	Kevin Brown	.05
229	Andujar Cedeno	.05
230	Roberto Kelly	.05
231	Jose Canseco	.35
231	Scott Ruffcorn (Showtime)	.05
232	Billy Ashley (Showtime)	.05
234	J.R. Phillips (Showtime)	.05
235	Chipper Jones (Showtime)	.40
236	Charles Johnson (Showtime)	.05
237	Midre Cummings (Showtime)	.05
238	Brian Hunter (Showtime)	.05
239	Garret Anderson (Showtime)	.05
240	Shawn Green (Showtime)	.10
241	Alex Rodriguez (Showtime)	.65
242	Checklist #1 (Frank Thomas)	.35
243	Checklist #2 (Ken Griffey Jr.)	.50
244	Checklist #3 (Albert Belle)	.05
245	Checklist #4 (Cal Ripken Jr.)	.65
246	Checklist #5 (Barry Bonds)	.75
247	Checklist #6 (Raul Mondesi)	.05
248	Checklist #7 (Mike Piazza)	.65
249	Checklist #8 (Jeff Bagwell)	.30
250	Checklist #9 (Jeff Bagwell, Frank Thomas, Ken Griffey Jr., Mike Piazza)	.25
251	Hideo Nomo	.35

Artist's Proofs

Among the scarcest and most valuable of 1995's baseball card inserts are the Select Artist's Proof parallel set. While an AP card is found on average once per 24 packs, the limited print run of the basic Select set means that only about 475 of each of the 250 regular-issue cards in the Select set were made in this edition. The AP inserts have a gold-foil "ARTIST'S PROOF" line at bottom, and other gold-foil highlights are embossed, rather than merely stamped on, as on regular Select cards.

		NM/M
Complete Set (250):		100.00
Common Player:		1.00
AP Stars:		10X

Big Sticks

With fronts printed in what Pinnacle describes as "holographic Gold Rush technology," the Big Sticks chase card

issue offers a dozen of the game's big hitters in action photos superimposed over their team'a logo. Conventionally printed backs have another player photo, along with a summary of career highlights and description of the player's power potential. Stated odds of pulling a Big Sticks chase card are one per 48 packs, on average. Cards are numbered with a "BS" prefix.

		NM/M
Complete Set (12):		40.00
Common Player:		1.50
1	Frank Thomas	4.00
2	Ken Griffey Jr.	7.50
3	Cal Ripken Jr.	10.00
4	Mike Piazza	7.50
5	Don Mattingly	6.00
6	Will Clark	1.50
7	Tony Gwynn	5.00
8	Jeff Bagwell	4.00
9	Barry Bonds	10.00
10	Paul Molitor	4.00
11	Matt Williams	1.50
12	Albert Belle	1.50

Can't Miss

A mix of rookies and sophomore standouts, along with a few players of slightly longer service are presented in this chase set. Cards feature color player action photos printed on a metallic red background, with their last name in gold foil at lower-left. An umpire on the "Can't Miss" logo is at upper-left. Backs repeat the logo, have a tall, narrow player photo, a few biographical details and a paragraph of career summary. Cards are numbered with a "CM" prefix.

		NM/M
Complete Set (12):		10.00
Common Player:		.35
1	Cliff Floyd	.35
2	Ryan Klesko	.35
3	Charles Johnson	.35
4	Raul Mondesi	.35
5	Manny Ramirez	2.00
6	Billy Ashley	.35
7	Alex Gonzalez	.35
8	Carlos Delgado	.75
9	Garret Anderson	.35
10	Alex Rodriguez	5.00
11	Chipper Jones	3.00
12	Shawn Green	.75

Sure Shots

Ten of Select's picks for future stardom are featured in this chase set, the toughest find of any of the 1995 Select inserts, at an average rate of one per 90 packs. Card fronts feature player action photos set against a

gold "Dufex" foil printed background with a Sure Shots logo vertically at left. Backs have a blue background with a few words about the player and a portrait photo at left. Cards are numbered with a "SS" prefix.

		NM/M
Complete Set (10):		10.00
Common Player:		1.00
1	Ben Grieve	1.00
2	Kevin Witt	1.00
3	Mark Farris	1.00
4	Paul Konerko	3.00
5	Dustin Hermanson	1.00
6	Ramon Castro	1.00
7	McKay Christensen	1.00
8	Brian Buchanan	1.00
9	Paul Wilson	1.00
10	Terrence Long	1.00

Certified Samples

Pinnacle's hobby-only Select brand issue for 1995 was previewed with this four-card cello-packed sample set. Three player cards are in the basic format of the regular-issue Select cards, except they have a large "SAMPLE" printed diagonally across the front and back. The fourth card in the sample pack is a header card advertising the features of the issue.

		NM/M
Complete Set (8):		7.50
Common Player:		.50
2	Reggie Sanders	.50
10	Mo Vaughn	.50
39	Mike Piazza	2.00
50	Mark McGwire	2.50
89	Roberto Alomar	.65
110	Larry Walker	.50
3 of 12	Cal Ripken Jr. (Gold Team)	4.00

1995 Select Certified

The concepts of hobby-only distribution and limited production, which were the hallmarks of Pinnacle's Select brand, were carried a step further with the post-season release of Select Certified baseball. Printed on double-thick cardboard stock card fronts feature all metallic-foil printing protected by a double laminated gloss coat. Backs have key player stats against each team in the league. The final 44 cards in the set are distinguished with a special Rookie logo and with gold added to the silver foil in the photo background.

		NM/M
Complete Set (135):		10.00

Common Player:		.05
Mirror Gold Stars:		5X
Pack (6):		2.00
Wax Box (20):		25.00
1	Barry Bonds	2.50
2	Reggie Sanders	.05
3	Terry Steinbach	.05
4	Eduardo Perez	.05
5	Frank Thomas	.05
6	Wil Cordero	.05
7	John Olerud	.05
8	Deion Sanders	.05
9	Mike Mussina	.40
10	Mo Vaughn	.05
11	Will Clark	.05
12	Chili Davis	.05
13	Jimmy Key	.05
14	Eddie Murray	.75
15	Bernard Gilkey	.05
16	David Cone	.05
17	Tim Salmon	.05
18	Steve Ontiveros	.05
19	Andres Galarraga	.05
20	Don Mattingly	1.25
21	Kevin Appier	.05
22	Paul Molitor	.75
24	Edgar Martinez	.05
25	Andy Benes	.05
26	Rafael Palmeiro	.65
27	Barry Larkin	.05
28	Gary Sheffield	.25
29	Wally Joyner	.05
30	Wade Boggs	1.00
31	Rico Brogna	.05
32	Eddie Murray (Murray Tribute)	.40
33	Kirby Puckett	1.00
34	Bobby Bonilla	.05
35	Hal Morris	.05
36	Moises Alou	.05
37	Javier Lopez	.05
38	Chuck Knoblauch	.05
39	Mike Piazza	1.50
40	Travis Fryman	.05
41	Rickey Henderson	.75
42	Jim Thome	.60
43	Carlos Baerga	.05
44	Dean Palmer	.05
45	Kirk Gibson	.05
46	Bret Saberhagen	.05
47	Cecil Fielder	.05
48	Manny Ramirez	.75
49	Derek Bell	.05
50	Mark McGwire	2.00
51	Jim Edmonds	.05
52	Robin Ventura	.05
53	Ryan Klesko	.05
54	Jeff Bagwell	.75
55	Ozzie Smith	1.00
56	Albert Belle	.05
57	Darren Daulton	.05
58	Jeff Conine	.05
59	Greg Maddux	1.00
60	Lenny Dykstra	.05
61	Randy Johnson	.75
62	Fred McGriff	.05
63	Ray Lankford	.05
64	Dave Justice	.05
65	Paul O'Neill	.05
66	Tony Gwynn	1.00
67	Matt Williams	.05
68	Dante Bichette	.05
69	Craig Biggio	.05
70	Ken Griffey Jr.	1.50
71	J.T. Snow	.05
72	Cal Ripken Jr.	2.50
73	Jay Bell	.05
74	Joe Carter	.05
75	Roberto Alomar	.30
76	Benji Gil	.05
77	Ivan Rodriguez	.65
78	Raul Mondesi	.05
79	Cliff Floyd	.05
80	Eric Karros, Mike Piazza, Raul Mondesi (Dodger Dynasty)	.30
81	Royce Clayton	.05
82	Billy Ashley	.05
83	Joey Hamilton	.05
84	Sammy Sosa	1.00
85	Jason Bere	.05
86	Dennis Martinez	.05
87	Greg Vaughn	.05
88	Roger Clemens	1.25
89	Larry Walker	.05
90	Mark Grace	.05
91	Kenny Lofton	.05
92	Carlos Perez RC	.05
93	Roger Cedeno	.05
94	Scott Ruffcorn	.05
95	Jim Pittsley	.05
96	Andy Pettitte	.20
97	James Baldwin	.05
98	Hideo Nomo RC	1.50
99	Ismael Valdes	.05
100	Armando Benitez	.05
101	Jose Malave	.05
102	Bobby Higginson RC	.25
103	LaTroy Hawkins	.05
104	Russ Davis	.05
105	Shawn Green	.40
106	Joe Vitiello	.05
107	Chipper Jones	1.00
108	Shane Andrews	.05
109	Jose Oliva	.05
110	Ray Durham	.05
111	Jon Nunnally	.05
112	Alex Gonzalez	.05

113	Vaughn Eshelman	.05
114	Marty Cordova	.05
115	Mark Grudzielanek RC	.25
116	Brian Hunter	.05
117	Charles Johnson	.05
118	Alex Rodriguez	2.00
119	David Bell	.05
120	Todd Hollandsworth	.05
121	Joe Randa	.05
122	Derek Jeter	2.50
123	Frank Rodriguez	.05
124	Curtis Goodwin	.05
125	Bill Pulsipher	.05
126	John Mabry	.05
127	Julian Tavarez	.05
128	Edgardo Alfonzo	.05
129	Orlando Miller	.05
130	Juan Acevedo	.05
131	Jeff Cirillo	.05
132	Roberto Petagine	.05
133	Antonio Osuna	.05
134	Michael Tucker	.05
135	Garret Anderson	.05
2131	Cal Ripken Jr. (Consecutive Game Record)	1.00

Mirror Gold

Inserted at an average rate of one per nine packs, this parallel set is a gold-foil version of the regular Select Certified set. Backs have a "MIRROR GOLD" notation at bottom.

	NM/M
Complete Set (135):	150.00
Common Player:	1.00
Mirror Gold Stars:	5X

Checklists

The seven checklists issued with Select Certified are not numbered as part of the set. They are found one per foil pack and are printed on much thinner card stock than the regular-issue cards.

		NM/M
Complete Set (7):		2.00
Common Player:		.35
1	Ken Griffey Jr. (A.L., #3-41)	.50
2	Frank Thomas (A.L., #42-95)	.40
3	Cal Ripken Jr. (A.L., #96-135)	.65
4	Jeff Bagwell (N.L., #1-58)	.40
5	Mike Piazza (N.L., #59-92)	.50
6	Barry Bonds (N.L., #93-133)	.65
7	Manny Ramirez, Raul Mondesi (Chase cards)	.40

Future

A striking new all-metal, brushed-foil printing technology was used in the production of this chase set of 10 rookie players with "unlimited

Carlos Delgado

future potential." Stated odds of finding a Certified Future insert card were one in 19 packs.

		NM/M
Complete Set (10):		10.00
Common Player:		.50
1	Chipper Jones	2.00
2	Curtis Goodwin	.50
3	Hideo Nomo	1.00
4	Shawn Green	1.00
5	Ray Durham	.50
6	Todd Hollandsworth	.50
7	Brian Hunter	.50
8	Carlos Delgado	1.00
9	Michael Tucker	.50
10	Alex Rodriguez	4.00

Gold Team

Barry Bonds

A dozen of the top position players in the league were selected for appearance in this insert set. Cards are printed in a special double-sided, all-gold Dufex technology. An action photo is featured on the front, a portrait on back. Odds of picking a Gold Team card were stated as one in 41 packs.

		NM/M
Complete Set (12):		40.00
Common Player:		2.00
1	Ken Griffey Jr.	7.50
2	Frank Thomas	4.00
3	Cal Ripken Jr.	10.00
4	Jeff Bagwell	4.00
5	Mike Piazza	7.50
6	Barry Bonds	10.00
7	Matt Williams	2.00
8	Don Mattingly	6.00
9	Will Clark	2.00
10	Tony Gwynn	5.00
11	Kirby Puckett	5.00
12	Jose Canseco	2.50

Potential Unlimited

RAUL MONDESI

Dufex printing with textured foil highlights and transparent inks is featured in this chase set, produced in an edition of 1,975, as witnessed by the numbering on card backs. Approximate odds of finding a Potential Unlimited card are one per 29 packs. A super-scarce edition of 903 cards each featuring "microetch" foil printing technology was issued at the rate of one per 70 packs.

		NM/M
Complete Set (20):		35.00
Common Player:		1.00
903s:		2.5X
1	Cliff Floyd	1.00
2	Manny Ramirez	4.50
3	Raul Mondesi	1.00
4	Scott Ruffcorn	1.00
5	Billy Ashley	1.00
6	Alex Gonzalez	1.00
7	Midre Cummings	1.00
8	Charles Johnson	1.00
9	Garret Anderson	1.00
10	Hideo Nomo	2.00
11	Chipper Jones	7.00
12	Curtis Goodwin	1.00
13	Frank Rodriguez	1.00
14	Shawn Green	2.00
15	Ray Durham	1.00
16	Todd Hollandsworth	1.00
17	Brian Hunter	1.00
18	Carlos Delgado	2.00
19	Michael Tucker	1.00
20	Alex Rodriguez	9.00

1996 Select

Select's 1996 baseball set has 200 cards in it, including 35 rookies, five checklists and 10 Lineup Leaders subset cards. All 200 cards are also reprinted as part of an Artist's Proof parallel set, using a holographic Artist's Proof logo. Cards were seeded one per every 35 packs; there were approximately 435 sets produced. Three insert sets were also created: Claim to Fame, En Fuego and Team Nucleus.

		NM/M
Complete Set (200):		9.00
Common Player:		.05
Artist's Proofs:		7X
Pack (10):		1.00
Wax Box (24):		16.00
1	Wade Boggs	1.00
2	Shawn Green	.35
3	Andres Galarraga	.05
4	Bill Pulsipher	.05
5	Chuck Knoblauch	.05
6	Ken Griffey Jr.	1.25
7	Greg Maddux	1.00
8	Manny Ramirez	.75
9	Ivan Rodriguez	.65
10	Tim Salmon	.05
11	Frank Thomas	.75
12	Jeff Bagwell	.75
13	Travis Fryman	.05
14	Kenny Lofton	.05
15	Matt Williams	.05
16	Jay Bell	.05
17	Ken Caminiti	.05
18	Ray Lankford	.05
19	Cal Ripken Jr.	2.00
20	Roger Clemens	1.00
21	Carlos Baerga	.05
22	Mike Piazza	1.25
23	Gregg Jefferies	.05
24	Reggie Sanders	.05
25	Rondell White	.05
26	Sammy Sosa	1.00
27	Kevin Appier	.05
28	Kevin Seitzer	.05
29	Gary Sheffield	.40
30	Mike Mussina	.35
31	Mark McGwire	1.50
32	Barry Larkin	.05
33	Marc Newfield	.05
34	Ismael Valdes	.05
35	Marty Cordova	.05
36	Albert Belle	.05
37	Johnny Damon	.35
38	Garret Anderson	.05
39	Cecil Fielder	.05
40	John Mabry	.05
41	Chipper Jones	1.00
42	Omar Vizquel	.05
43	Jose Rijo	.05
44	Charles Johnson	.05
45	Alex Rodriguez	1.50
46	Rico Brogna	.05
47	Joe Carter	.05
48	Mo Vaughn	.05
49	Moises Alou	.05
50	Raul Mondesi	.05
51	Robin Ventura	.05
52	Jim Thome	.60
53	Dave Justice	.05
54	Jeff King	.05
55	Brian Hunter	.05
56	Juan Gonzalez	.40
57	John Olerud	.05
58	Rafael Palmeiro	.05
59	Tony Gwynn	1.00
60	Eddie Murray	.75
61	Jason Isringhausen	.05
62	Dante Bichette	.05
63	Randy Johnson	.75
64	Kirby Puckett	1.00
65	Jim Edmonds	.05
66	David Cone	.05
67	Ozzie Smith	1.00
68	Fred McGriff	.05
69	Darren Daulton	.05
70	Edgar Martinez	.05
71	J.T. Snow	.05
72	Butch Huskey	.05
73	Hideo Nomo	.40
74	Pedro Martinez	.05
75	Bobby Bonilla	.05
76	Jeff Conine	.05
77	Ryan Klesko	.05
78	Bernie Williams	.05
79	Andre Dawson	.25
80	Trevor Hoffman	.05
81	Mark Grace	.05
82	Benji Gil	.05
83	Eric Karros	.05
84	Pete Schourek	.05
85	Edgardo Alfonzo	.05
86	Jay Buhner	.05
87	Vinny Castilla	.05
88	Bret Boone	.05
89	Ray Durham	.05
90	Brian Jordan	.05
91	Jose Canseco	.40
92	Paul O'Neill	.05
93	Chili Davis	.05
94	Tom Glavine	.30
95	Julian Tavarez	.05
96	Derek Bell	.05
97	Will Clark	.05
98	Larry Walker	.05
99	Denny Neagle	.05
100	Alex Fernandez	.05
101	Barry Bonds	2.00
102	Ben McDonald	.05
103	Andy Pettitte	.25
104	Tino Martinez	.05
105	Sterling Hitchcock	.05
106	Royce Clayton	.05
107	Jim Abbott	.05
108	Rickey Henderson	.75
109	Ramon Martinez	.05
110	Paul Molitor	.75
111	Dennis Eckersley	.65
112	Alex Gonzalez	.05
113	Marquis Grissom	.05
114	Greg Vaughn	.05
115	Lance Johnson	.05
116	Todd Stottlemyre	.05
117	Jack McDowell	.05
118	Ruben Sierra	.05
119	Brady Anderson	.05
120	Julio Franco	.05
121	Brooks Kieschnick	.05
122	Roberto Alomar	.20
123	Greg Gagne	.05
124	Wally Joyner	.05
125	John Smoltz	.05
126	John Valentin	.05
127	Russ Davis	.05
128	Joe Vitiello	.05
129	Shawon Dunston	.05
130	Frank Rodriguez	.05
131	Charlie Hayes	.05
132	Andy Benes	.05
133	B.J. Surhoff	.05
134	Dave Nilsson	.05
135	Carlos Delgado	.50
136	Walt Weiss	.05
137	Mike Stanley	.05
138	Greg Colbrunn	.05
139	Mike Kelly	.05
140	Ryne Sandberg	1.00
141	Lee Smith	.05
142	Dennis Martinez	.05
143	Bernard Gilkey	.05
144	Lenny Dykstra	.05
145	Danny Tartabull	.05
146	Dean Palmer	.05
147	Craig Biggio	.05
148	Juan Acevedo	.05
149	Michael Tucker	.05
150	Bobby Higginson	.05
151	Ken Griffey Jr. (Line Up Leaders)	.65
152	Frank Thomas (Line Up Leaders)	.45
153	Cal Ripken Jr. (Line Up Leaders)	1.00
154	Albert Belle (Line Up Leaders)	.05
155	Mike Piazza (Line Up Leaders)	.65
156	Barry Bonds (Line Up Leaders)	1.00
157	Sammy Sosa (Line Up Leaders)	.60
158	Mo Vaughn (Line Up Leaders)	.05
159	Greg Maddux (Line Up Leaders)	.50
160	Jeff Bagwell (Line Up Leaders)	.40
161	Derek Jeter	2.00
162	Paul Wilson	.05
163	Chris Snopek	.05
164	Jason Schmidt	.05
165	Jimmy Haynes	.05
166	George Arias	.05
167	Steve Gibralter	.05
168	Bob Wolcott	.05
169	Jason Kendall	.05
170	Gregg Zaun	.05
171	Quinton McCracken	.05
172	Alan Benes	.05
173	Rey Ordonez	.05
174	Ugueth Urbina	.05
175	Osvaldo Fernandez RC	.10
176	Marc Barcelo	.05
177	Sal Fasano	.05
178	Mike Grace RC	.05
179	Chan Ho Park	.05
180	Robert Perez	.05
181	Todd Hollandsworth	.05
182	Wilton Guerrero RC	.05
183	John Wasdin	.05
184	Jim Pittsley	.05
185	LaTroy Hawkins	.05
186	Jay Powell	.05
187	Felipe Crespo	.05
188	Jermaine Dye	.05
189	Bob Abreu	.05
190	Matt Luke RC	.05
191	Richard Hidalgo	.05
192	Karim Garcia	.05
193	Tavo Alvarez	.05
194	Andy Fox RC	.05
195	Terrell Wade	.05
196	Frank Thomas (Checklist)	.40
197	Ken Griffey Jr. (Checklist)	.65
198	Greg Maddux (Checklist)	.05
199	Mike Piazza (Checklist)	.65
200	Cal Ripken Jr. (Checklist)	.75

Artist's Proofs

Approximately once per 35 packs, a card from this parallel chase set is encountered among 1996 Select. Reported production was 435 sets. The Artist's Proof cards are distinguished by a holographic logo testifying to their status on the front of the card.

	NM/M
Complete Set (200):	200.00
Common Player:	1.00
AP Stars:	7X

Claim to Fame

Twenty different stars are featured on these 1996 Select insert cards. Each card is numbered "1 of 2100" and uses an external die-cut design. The cards were seeded one per every 72 packs.

		NM/M
Complete Set (20):		45.00
Common Player:		.75
1	Cal Ripken Jr.	7.50
2	Greg Maddux	4.50
3	Ken Griffey Jr.	6.00
4	Frank Thomas	3.50
5	Mo Vaughn	.75
6	Albert Belle	.75
7	Jeff Bagwell	3.50
8	Sammy Sosa	4.50
8s	Sammy Sosa/OPS	2.50
9	Reggie Sanders	.75
10	Hideo Nomo	2.00
11	Chipper Jones	4.50
12	Mike Piazza	6.00
13	Matt Williams	.75
14	Tony Gwynn	4.50
15	Johnny Damon	1.50
16	Dante Bichette	.75
17	Kirby Puckett	4.50
18	Barry Bonds	7.50
19	Randy Johnson	3.50
20	Eddie Murray	3.50

En Fuego

ESPN announcer Dan Patrick is featured on his own card in this set, inspired by his Sportscenter catch phrase "en fuego," which means "on fire." Patrick's teammate, Keith Olberman, wrote the card backs. The 25 cards, printed on all-foil Dufex stock, are seeded one per every 48 packs of 1996 Select baseball.

		NM/M
Complete Set (25):		35.00
Common Player:		.75
1	Ken Griffey Jr.	3.50
2	Frank Thomas	2.00
3	Cal Ripken Jr.	5.00
4	Greg Maddux	3.00
5	Jeff Bagwell	2.00
6	Barry Bonds	5.00
7	Mo Vaughn	.75
8	Albert Belle	.75
9	Sammy Sosa	3.00
10	Reggie Sanders	.75
11	Mike Piazza	3.50
12	Chipper Jones	3.00
13	Tony Gwynn	3.00
14	Kirby Puckett	3.00
15	Wade Boggs	3.00
16	Dan Patrick	.75
17	Gary Sheffield	1.25
18	Dante Bichette	.75
19	Randy Johnson	2.00
20	Matt Williams	.75
21	Alex Rodriguez	4.00
22	Tim Salmon	.75
23	Johnny Damon	1.25
24	Manny Ramirez	2.00
25	Hideo Nomo	1.25

Team Nucleus

This 1996 Select insert set pays tribute to the three top players from each Major League Baseball team; each card features the three teammates on it. The cards are printed on a clear plastic, utilizing a holographic micro-etched design. They are seeded one per every 18 packs.

		NM/M
Complete Set (28):		20.00
Common Player:		.50
1	Albert Belle, Manny Ramirez, Carlos Baerga	1.00
2	Ray Lankford, Brian Jordan, Ozzie Smith	1.25
3	Jay Bell, Jeff King, Denny Neagle	.50

ABBREVIATIONS

OPS - Overprinted "Promotional Sample"

4 Dante Bichette, Andres Galarraga, Larry Walker .50
5 Mark McGwire, Mike Bordick, Terry Steinbach 1.75
6 Bernie Williams, Wade Boggs, David Cone 1.25
7 Joe Carter, Alex Gonzalez, Shawn Green .50
8 Roger Clemens, Mo Vaughn, Jose Canseco 1.25
9 Ken Griffey Jr., Edgar Martinez, Randy Johnson 1.50
10 Gregg Jefferies, Darren Daulton, Lenny Dykstra .50
11 Mike Piazza, Raul Mondesi, Hideo Nomo 1.50
12 Greg Maddux, Chipper Jones, Ryan Klesko 1.25
13 Cecil Fielder, Travis Fryman, Phil Nevin .50
14 Ivan Rodriguez, Will Clark, Juan Gonzalez 1.00
15 Ryne Sandberg, Sammy Sosa, Mark Grace 1.50
16 Gary Sheffield, Charles Johnson, Andre Dawson .60
17 Johnny Damon, Michael Tucker, Kevin Appier .65
18 Barry Bonds, Matt Williams, Rod Beck 2.00
19 Kirby Puckett, Chuck Knoblauch, Marty Cordova 1.25
20 Cal Ripken Jr., Bobby Bonilla, Mike Mussina 2.00
21 Jason Isringhausen, Bill Pulsipher, Rico Brogna .50
22 Tony Gwynn, Ken Caminiti, Marc Newfield 1.25
23 Tim Salmon, Garret Anderson, Jim Edmonds .50
24 Moises Alou, Rondell White, Cliff Floyd .50
25 Barry Larkin, Reggie Sanders, Bret Boone .50
26 Jeff Bagwell, Craig Biggio, Derek Bell 1.00
27 Frank Thomas, Robin Ventura, Alex Fernandez 1.00
28 John Jaha, Greg Vaughn, Kevin Seitzer .50

1996 Select Certified

This hobby-exclusive set has 144 cards in its regular issue, plus six parallel versions and two insert sets. The parallel sets are: Certified Red (one per five packs), Certified Blue (one per 50), Artist's Proofs (one per 12), Mirror Red (one per 100), Mirror Blue (one per 200), and Mirror Gold (one per 300). Breaking down the numbers, there are 1,800 Certified Red sets, 180 Certified Blue, 500 Artist's Proofs, 90 Mirror Red 45 Mirror Blue and 30 Mirror Gold sets. The insert sets are Interleague Preview cards and Select Few. Cards #135-144 are a "Pastime Power" subset.

NM/M
Complete Set (144): 20.00

Common Player: .15
Pack (6): 2.50
Wax Box (20): 40.00
1 Frank Thomas 1.25
2 Tino Martinez .15
3 Gary Sheffield .50
4 Kenny Lofton .15
5 Joe Carter .15
6 Alex Rodriguez 2.50
7 Chipper Jones 1.50
8 Roger Clemens 1.75
9 Jay Bell .15
10 Eddie Murray 1.00
11 Will Clark .15
12 Mike Mussina .35
13 Hideo Nomo .50
14 Andres Galarraga .15
15 Jason Isringhausen .15
16 Marc Newfield .15
17 Randy Johnson 1.00
18 Chuck Knoblauch .15
19 J.T. Snow .15
20 Mark McGwire 2.50
21 Tony Gwynn 1.50
22 Albert Belle .15
23 Gregg Jefferies .15
24 Reggie Sanders .15
25 Bernie Williams .15
26 Ray Lankford .15
27 Johnny Damon .40
28 Ryne Sandberg 1.50
29 Rondell White .15
30 Mike Piazza 2.00
31 Barry Bonds 3.00
32 Greg Maddux 1.50
33 Craig Biggio .15
34 John Valentin .15
35 Ivan Rodriguez .75
36 Rico Brogna .15
37 Tim Salmon .15
38 Sterling Hitchcock .15
39 Charles Johnson .15
40 Travis Fryman .15
41 Barry Larkin .15
42 Tom Glavine .35
43 Marty Cordova .15
44 Shawn Green .40
45 Ben McDonald .15
46 Robin Ventura .15
47 Ken Griffey Jr. 2.00
48 Orlando Merced .15
49 Paul O'Neill .15
50 Ozzie Smith 1.50
51 Manny Ramirez 1.00
52 Ismael Valdes .15
53 Cal Ripken Jr. 3.00
54 Jeff Bagwell 1.00
55 Greg Vaughn .15
56 Juan Gonzalez .50
57 Raul Mondesi .15
58 Carlos Baerga .15
59 Sammy Sosa 1.50
60 Mike Kelly .15
61 Edgar Martinez .15
62 Kirby Puckett 1.50
63 Cecil Fielder .15
64 David Cone .15
65 Moises Alou .15
66 Fred McGriff .15
67 Mo Vaughn .15
68 Edgardo Alfonzo .15
69 Jim Thome .75
70 Rickey Henderson 1.00
71 Dante Bichette .15
72 Lenny Dykstra .15
73 Benji Gil .15
74 Wade Boggs 1.50
75 Jim Edmonds .15
76 Michael Tucker .15
77 Carlos Delgado .65
78 Butch Huskey .15
79 Billy Ashley .15
80 Dean Palmer .15
81 Paul Molitor 1.00
82 Ryan Klesko .15
83 Brian Hunter .15
84 Jay Buhner .15
85 Larry Walker .15
86 Mike Bordick .15
87 Matt Williams .15
88 Jack McDowell .15
89 Hal Morris .15
90 Brian Jordan .15
91 Andy Pettitte .35
92 Melvin Nieves .15
93 Pedro Martinez 1.00
94 Mark Grace .15
95 Garret Anderson .15
96 Andre Dawson .30
97 Ray Durham .15
98 Jose Canseco .50
99 Roberto Alomar .30
100 Derek Jeter 3.00
101 Alan Benes .15
102 Karim Garcia .15
103 Robin Jennings RC .15
104 Bob Abreu .15
105 Sal Fasano (Livan Hernandez' name on front.) .15
106 Steve Gibralter .15
107 Jermaine Dye .15
108 Jason Kendall .15
109 Mike Grace RC .15
110 Jason Schmidt .15
111 Paul Wilson .15
112 Rey Ordonez .15
113 Wilton Guerrero RC .15

114 Brooks Kieschnick .15
115 George Arias .15
116 Osvaldo Fernandez RC .15
117 Todd Hollandsworth .15
118 John Wasdin .15
119 Eric Owens .15
120 Chan Ho Park .15
121 Mark Loretta .15
122 Richard Hidalgo .15
123 Jeff Suppan .15
124 Jim Pittsley .15
125 LaTroy Hawkins .15
126 Chris Snopek .15
127 Justin Thompson .15
128 Jay Powell .15
129 Alex Ochoa .15
130 Felipe Crespo .15
131 Matt Lawton RC .15
132 Jimmy Haynes .15
133 Terrell Wade .15
134 Ruben Rivera .15
135 Frank Thomas (Pastime Power) .55
136 Ken Griffey Jr. (Pastime Power) 1.00
137 Greg Maddux (Pastime Power) .65
138 Mike Piazza (Pastime Power) .75
139 Cal Ripken Jr. (Pastime Power) 1.50
140 Albert Belle (Pastime Power) .15
141 Mo Vaughn (Pastime Power) .15
142 Chipper Jones (Pastime Power) .65
143 Hideo Nomo (Pastime Power) .25
144 Ryan Klesko (Pastime Power) .15

Artist's Proofs

Only 500 cards each of this parallel issue were produced, seeded one in every dozen packs. The cards are identical to the regular-issue Select Certified except for the presence on front of a prismatic gold Artist's Proof logo.

NM/M
Complete Set (144): 200.00
Common Player: 1.00
AP Stars: 7X

Red, Blue

These 1996 Select Certified insert cards were the most common of the parallel cards issued; they were seeded one per five packs. There were 1,800 Certified Red sets produced, with the number of Certified Blue sets at 180. Cards are essentially the same as regular-issue Select Certified except for the color of the foil background on front.

NM/M
Common Red: .50
Red Stars: 3X
Common Blue: 2.50
Blue Stars: 10X

Mirror Red, Blue, Gold

These 1996 Select Certified inserts are the scarcest of the set. Only 30 Mirror Gold sets were made, with 60 Mirror Blue sets and 90 Mirror Red. Due to the improbability of completing the collection, no complete set price is given.

NM/M
Common Mirror Red: 6.00
Mirror Red Stars: 20X
Common Mirror Blue: 12.00
Mirror Blue Stars: 30X
Common Mirror Gold: 20.00
Mirror Gold Stars: 100X

Interleague Preview

These 1996 Select Certified insert cards feature 21 prospective matchups from interleague play's beginnings. The cards were seeded one per 42 packs. Each card can also be found in a promo version with a large, black "SAMPLE" overprint on front and back.

NM/M
Complete Set (25): 45.00
Common Card: .75
Promos: 1X
1 Ken Griffey Jr., Hideo Nomo 3.50
2 Greg Maddux, Mo Vaughn 3.00
3 Frank Thomas, Sammy Sosa 3.00
4 Mike Piazza, Jim Edmonds 3.50
5 Ryan Klesko, Roger Clemens 3.25
6 Derek Jeter, Rey Ordonez 4.50
7 Johnny Damon, Ray Lankford 1.00
8 Manny Ramirez, Reggie Sanders 2.50
9 Barry Bonds, Jay Buhner 4.50
10 Jason Isringhausen, Wade Boggs 3.00
11 David Cone, Chipper Jones 3.00
12 Jeff Bagwell, Will Clark 2.50
13 Tony Gwynn, Randy Johnson 3.00
14 Cal Ripken Jr., Tom Glavine 4.50
15 Kirby Puckett, Alan Benes 3.00
16 Gary Sheffield, Mike Mussina 1.00
17 Raul Mondesi, Tim Salmon .75
18 Rondell White, Carlos Delgado 1.00
19 Cecil Fielder, Ryne Sandberg 1.00
20 Kenny Lofton, Brian Hunter .75
21 Paul Wilson, Paul O'Neill .75
22 Ismael Valdes, Edgar Martinez .75
23 Matt Williams, Mark McGwire 4.00
24 Albert Belle, Barry Larkin .75

25 Brady Anderson, Marquis Grissom .75

Select Few

Eighteen top players are featured on these 1996 Select Certified inserts, which utilize holographic technology with a dot matrix hologram. Cards were seeded one per every 60 packs.

NM/M
Complete Set (18): 40.00
Common Player: 1.00
1 Sammy Sosa 3.00
2 Derek Jeter 5.00
3 Ken Griffey Jr. 3.50
4 Albert Belle 1.00
5 Cal Ripken Jr. 5.00
6 Greg Maddux 3.00
7 Frank Thomas 2.50
8 Mo Vaughn 1.00
9 Chipper Jones 3.00
10 Mike Piazza 3.50
11 Ryan Klesko 1.00
12 Hideo Nomo 1.50
13 Alan Benes 1.00
14 Manny Ramirez 2.50
15 Gary Sheffield 2.00
16 Barry Bonds 5.00
17 Matt Williams 1.00
18 Johnny Damon 2.00

1997 Select Samples

The 1997 edition of Select was previewed with the issue of several regular-issue and Select Company cards carrying a large black "SAMPLE" overprint on front and back. The Rodriguez sample, untrimmed and larger than standard size, was not distributed in three-card cello packs like the other cards. This checklist may not be complete.

NM/M
Common Player: 1.00
2 Tony Gwynn 2.00
8 Frank Thomas 1.50
15 Paul Molitor 1.50
23 Greg Maddux 2.00
28 Javy Lopez 1.00
47 Ken Griffey Jr. 3.00
53 Alex Rodriguez 4.00
94 Will Clark 1.00

1997 Select

The Series 1 base set is made up of 150 cards printed on thick 16-point stock. Each card features a distinctive silver-foil treatment and either red (100 cards) or blue (50 cards) foil accent. Blue-foiled cards were short-printed at a ratio of 1:2 compared to the red-foil cards. Blue-foiled cards are indicated with a (B) in the checklist. Subsets in-

clude 40 Rookies, eight Super Stars and two checklists. Inserts include two parallel sets, (Artist's Proof and Registered Gold), Tools of the Trade, Mirror Blue Tools of the Trade, and Rookie Revolution. The cards were sold only at hobby shops in six-card packs for $2.99 each. A high-number series was issued with each card bearing a "Select Company" notation.

NM/M
Complete Set (200): 30.00
Series 1 (#1-150): 20.00
Common Red Player: .10
Common Blue Player: .25
Registered Golds: 2X
Artist's Proofs: 5X
High Series (#151-200): 10.00
Common High Series: .25
Pack (6): 1.50
Wax Box (24): 25.00
1 Juan Gonzalez/B 2.00
2 Mo Vaughn/B .25
3 Tony Gwynn 1.50
4 Manny Ramirez/B .50
5 Jose Canseco .50
6 David Cone .10
7 Chan Ho Park .10
8 Frank Thomas/B 2.50
9 Todd Hollandsworth .10
10 Marty Cordova .10
11 Gary Sheffield/B .75
12 John Smoltz/B .25
13 Mark Grudzielanek .10
14 Sammy Sosa/B 3.00
15 Paul Molitor 1.00
16 Kevin Brown .10
17 Albert Belle/B .25
18 Eric Young .10
19 John Wetteland .10
20 Ryan Klesko/B .25
21 Joe Carter .10
22 Alex Ochoa .10
23 Greg Maddux/B 3.00
24 Roger Clemens/B 3.25
25 Ivan Rodriguez/B 1.50
26 Barry Bonds/B 5.00
27 Kenny Lofton/B .25
28 Javy Lopez .10
29 Hideo Nomo/B 1.00
30 Rusty Greer .10
31 Rafael Palmeiro .75
32 Mike Piazza/B 3.50
33 Ryne Sandberg 1.50
34 Wade Boggs 1.50
35 Jim Thome/B 1.50
36 Ken Caminiti/B .25
37 Mark Grace .25
38 Brian Jordan/B .25
39 Craig Biggio .10
40 Henry Rodriguez .10
41 Dean Palmer .10
42 Jason Kendall .10
43 Bill Pulsipher .10
44 Tim Salmon/B .25
45 Marc Newfield .10
46 Pat Hentgen .10
47 Ken Griffey Jr./B 3.50
48 Paul Wilson .10
49 Jay Buhner/B .10
50 Rickey Henderson 1.00
51 Jeff Bagwell/B 2.00
52 Cecil Fielder .10
53 Alex Rodriguez/B 4.00
54 John Jaha .10
55 Brady Anderson/B .25
56 Andres Galarraga .10
57 Raul Mondesi .10
58 Andy Pettitte .10
59 Roberto Alomar/B 1.00
60 Derek Jeter 5.00
61 Charles Johnson .10
62 Travis Fryman .10
63 Chipper Jones/B 3.00
64 Edgar Martinez .10
65 Bobby Bonilla .10
66 Greg Vaughn .10
67 Bobby Higginson .10
68 Garret Anderson .10
69 Chuck Knoblauch/B .25
70 Jermaine Dye .10
71 Cal Ripken Jr./B 5.00
72 Jason Giambi

73	Trey Beamon	.10
74	Shawn Green	.35
75	Mark McGwire/B	4.00
76	Carlos Delgado	.60
77	Jason Isringhausen	.10
78	Randy Johnson/B	2.00
79	Troy Percival/B	.25
80	Ron Gant	.10
81	Ellis Burks	.10
82	Mike Mussina/B	1.00
83	Todd Hundley	.10
84	Jim Edmonds	.10
85	Charles Nagy	.10
86	Dante Bichette/B	.25
87	Mariano Rivera	.20
88	Matt Williams/B	.25
89	Rondell White	.10
90	Steve Finley	.10
91	Alex Fernandez	.10
92	Barry Larkin	.25
93	Tom Goodwin	.10
94	Will Clark	.10
95	Michael Tucker	.10
96	Derek Bell	.10
97	Larry Walker	.10
98	Alan Benes	.10
99	Tom Glavine	.35
100	Darin Erstad/B	.35
101	Andruw Jones/B	2.00
102	Scott Rolen	.65
103	Todd Walker/B	.25
104	Dmitri Young	.10
105	Vladimir Guerrero/B	2.00
106	Nomar Garciaparra	1.50
107	Danny Patterson RC	.10
108	Karim Garcia	.10
109	Todd Greene	.10
110	Ruben Rivera	.10
111	Raul Casanova	.10
112	Mike Cameron	.10
113	Bartolo Colon	.10
114	Rod Myers	.10
115	Todd Dunn	.10
116	Torii Hunter	.10
117	Jason Dickson	.10
118	Gene Kingsale RC	.10
119	Rafael Medina	.10
120	Raul Ibanez	.10
121	Bobby Henley RC	.10
122	Scott Spiezio	.10
123	Bobby Smith RC	.10
124	J.J. Johnson	.10
125	Bubba Trammell RC	.50
126	Jeff Abbott	.10
127	Neifi Perez	.10
128	Derrek Lee	.65
129	Kevin Brown RC	.10
130	Mendy Lopez	.10
131	Kevin Orie	.10
132	Ryan Jones	.10
133	Juan Encarnacion	.10
134	Jose Guillen/B	.25
135	Greg Norton	.10
136	Richie Sexson	.10
137	Jay Payton	.10
138	Bob Abreu	.15
139	Ronnie Belliard RC	.10
140	Wilton Guerrero/B	.25
141	Alex Rodriguez/B (Select Stars)	2.00
142	Juan Gonzalez/B (Select Stars)	.50
143	Ken Caminiti/B (Select Stars)	.25
144	Frank Thomas/B (Select Stars)	1.25
145	Ken Griffey Jr./B (Select Stars)	1.75
146	John Smoltz/B (Select Stars)	.25
147	Mike Piazza/B (Select Stars)	1.75
148	Derek Jeter/B (Select Stars)	3.00
149	Frank Thomas (Checklist)	.75
150	Ken Griffey Jr. (Checklist)	1.00
151	Jose Cruz Jr. RC	1.00
152	Moises Alou	.25
153	Hideki Irabu RC	.25
154	Glendon Rusch	.25
155	Ron Coomer	.25
156	Jeremi Gonzalez RC	.25
157	Fernando Tatis RC	.40
158	John Olerud	.25
159	Rickey Henderson	1.00
160	Shannon Stewart	.25
161	Kevin Polcovich	.25
162	Jose Rosado	.25
163	Ray Lankford	.25
164	David Justice	.25
165	Mark Kotsay RC	.50
166	Deivi Cruz RC	.50
167	Billy Wagner	.25
168	Jacob Cruz	.25
169	Matt Morris	.25
170	Brian Banks	.25
171	Brett Tomko	.25
172	Todd Helton	.75
173	Eric Young	.25
174	Bernie Williams	.25
175	Jeff Fassero	.25
176	Ryan McGuire	.25
177	Darryl Kile	.25
178	Kelvim Escobar RC	.50
179	Dave Nilsson	.25
180	Geronimo Berroa	.25

181	Livan Hernandez	.25
182	Tony Womack RC	.50
183	Deion Sanders	.25
184	Jeff Kent	.25
185	Brian Hunter	.25
186	Jose Malave	.25
187	Steve Woodard RC	.50
188	Brad Radke	.25
189	Todd Dunwoody	.25
190	Joey Hamilton	.25
191	Denny Naegle	.25
192	Bobby Jones	.25
193	Tony Clark	.25
194	Jaret Wright RC	.50
195	Matt Stairs	.25
196	Francisco Cordova	.25
197	Justin Thompson	.25
198	Pokey Reese	.25
199	Garrett Stephenson	.25
200	Carl Everett	.25

Artist's Proofs

Featuring a holographic foil background and special Artist's Proof logo on front, this parallel of the 150-card Series 1 Select was a random pack insert at an average pull rate of 1:71 for reds and 1:355 for blues.

	NM/M
Complete Set (150):	450.00
Common Red:	1.25
Red Stars:	5X
Common Blue:	2.50
Blue Stars:	1.5X

Company

Select Company was intended to be a one-per-pack parallel found in '97 high series. The cards have the front background photo replaced with textured silver metallic foil and "Select Company" printed vertically at right-center. While all high-number (151-200) cards have the "Select Company" notation erroneously printed on front, only those cards with silver-foil backgrounds are true parallels. All Select Company cards can also be found in a promo version with a large black "SAMPLE" overprinted on back.

	NM/M
Complete Set (200):	150.00
Common Player:	.50
Red Stars:	3X
Blue Stars:	1.5X
High-Series Stars:	1.5X
Samples:	10X

Registered Gold

This parallel insert set, like the regular issue, can be found with 100 red-foil and 50 blue-foil enhanced cards. They differ from the regular issue in the use of gold foil instead of silver on the right side

of the front. Also, the inserts have "Registered Gold" printed vertically on the right side of the photo. Backs are identical to the regular issue. Red-foil Registered Gold cards are found on average of once every 11 packs; blue-foiled cards are a 1-in-47 pick.

	NM/M
Complete Set (150):	300.00
Common Red Gold:	.75
Common Blue Gold:	1.50
Registered Gold Stars:	2X

Autographs

Four top candidates for the 1997 Rookie of the Year Award - Wilton Guerrero, Jose Guillen, Andruw Jones and Todd Walker - each signed a limited number of their Select Rookie cards. Jones signed 2,500 cards while each of the other players signed 3,000 each.

		NM/M
Complete Set (4):		15.00
Common Autograph:		3.00
AU1	Wilton Guerrero	3.00
AU2	Jose Guillen	3.00
AU3	Andruw Jones	10.00
AU4	Todd Walker	3.00

Rookie Revolution

This 20-card insert highlights some of the top young stars in the game. Cards feature a silver micro-etched mylar design on front. Backs are sequentially numbered and contain a few words about the player. Odds of finding a card are 1:56 packs.

		NM/M
Complete Set (20):		21.00
Common Player:		.50
1	Andruw Jones	2.50
2	Derek Jeter	6.00
3	Todd Hollandsworth	.50
4	Edgar Renteria	.50
5	Jason Kendall	.50
6	Rey Ordonez	.50
7	F.P. Santangelo	.50
8	Jermaine Dye	.50
9	Alex Ochoa	.50
10	Vladimir Guerrero	2.50
11	Dmitri Young	.50
12	Todd Walker	.50
13	Scott Rolen	1.50
14	Nomar Garciaparra	3.50
15	Ruben Rivera	.50
16	Darin Erstad	1.00
17	Todd Greene	.50
18	Mariano Rivera	1.00
19	Trey Beamon	.50
20	Karim Garcia	.50

Tools of the Trade

A 25-card insert featuring a double-front design salutes

a top veteran player on one side and a promising youngster on the other. Cards feature a silver-foil card stock with gold-foil stamping. Cards were inserted 1:9 packs. A parallel to this set - Blue Mirror Tools of the Trade - features blue-foil stock with an insert ratio of 1:240 packs.

		NM/M
Complete Set (25):		25.00
Common Player:		.40
Mirror Blues:		2.5X
1	Ken Griffey Jr., Andruw Jones	2.00
2	Greg Maddux, Andy Pettitte	1.50
3	Cal Ripken Jr., Chipper Jones	2.50
4	Mike Piazza, Jason Kendall	2.00
5	Albert Belle, Karim Garcia	.40
6	Mo Vaughn, Dmitri Young	.40
7	Juan Gonzalez, Vladimir Guerrero	1.00
8	Tony Gwynn, Jermaine Dye	1.50
9	Barry Bonds, Alex Ochoa	2.50
10	Jeff Bagwell, Jason Giambi	1.00
11	Kenny Lofton, Darin Erstad	.50
12	Gary Sheffield, Manny Ramirez	1.00
13	Tim Salmon, Todd Hollandsworth	.40
14	Sammy Sosa, Ruben Rivera	1.50
15	Paul Molitor, George Arias	1.00
16	Jim Thome, Todd Walker	.75
17	Wade Boggs, Scott Rolen	1.50
18	Ryne Sandberg, Chuck Knoblauch	1.50
19	Mark McGwire, Frank Thomas	2.25
20	Ivan Rodriguez, Charles Johnson	.75
21	Brian Jordan, Trey Beamon	.40
22	Roger Clemens, Troy Percival	1.75
23	John Smoltz, Mike Mussina	.65
24	Alex Rodriguez, Rey Ordonez	2.25
25	Derek Jeter, Nomar Garciaparra	2.50

1998 Select

Select was intended to be a four-tier, 100-player, 250-card base set based on the "Quasar System." One hundred players were to appear as 1-star cards; 2-star cards comprised a shortened checklist of 75 of those players, and so on

through 3- and 4-star subsets. Besides an increase in player popularity, each level featured enhanced technical bells and whistles on the cards themselves. Each five-card $3.99 pack was to have three 1-star cards and two 2-star cards, unless one or more were replaced with 3- or 4-star cards or one of several insert series. The set was never officially released due to the mid-year collapse and subsequent bankruptcy of Select's parent firm, Pinnacle. Some cards, however, have made their way into the hobby market. Given the possibility that more - perhaps all - of the 2-star cards may some day become available, the complete checklist is provided as originally formulated by Select. Values are shown only for those cards confirmed to exist.

	NM/M
Common Player:	10.00

Numbers

Five players from each of four major statistical categories were selected for inclusion in this all-numbered insert issue. Each player in the chase set was intended to have cards numbered to his 1997 performance in the category for which he was chosen. While distribution of the cards was halted by Pinnacle's bankruptcy, limited quantities of these insert cards have found their way into the hobby. Those cards seen thus far do not bear sequential numbers. The number of cards intended for each player is listed, although it is unknown how many of each player were actually released.

		NM/M
Complete Set (20):		1,150
Common Player:		20.00
1	Mark McGwire/58	225.00
2	Juan Gonzalez/42	40.00
3	Ken Griffey Jr./56	225.00
4	Jeff Bagwell/43	60.00
5	Andres Galarraga/41	40.00
6	Frank Thomas/347	30.00
7	Mike Piazza/362	100.00
8	Tony Gwynn/372	35.00
9	Larry Walker/366	20.00
10	Kenny Lofton/333	20.00
11	Barry Bonds/446	50.00
12	Chuck Knoblauch/390	20.00
13	Derek Jeter/370	150.00
14	Nomar Garciaparra/342	75.00
15	Chipper Jones/371	60.00
16	Pedro Martinez/305	40.00
17	Hideo Nomo/233	40.00
18	Randy Johnson/291	30.00
19	Roger Clemens/292	75.00
20	Greg Maddux/177	75.00

Jersey Numbers

Whatever the intended scope and manner of distribution for this parallel insert may never be known because Pinnacle's bankruptcy interrupted the issue. Only a few specimens have made their way into the hobby. The gold-foil highlighted cards were in-

tended to be serially numbered on back to the extent of the player's uniform number.

		NM/M
116	Ken Griffey Jr./24	65.00

1998 Select Selected Samples

Selected promos were released in two-card cello packs prior to Pinnacle's bankruptcy. Fronts have color action photos on bright metallic-foil backgrounds was a large "S." Backs have a smaller version of the front photo along with career highlights and a large overprinted "SAMPLE."

		NM/M
Complete Set (10):		30.00
Common Player:		2.50
1	Vladimir Guerrero	4.00
2	Nomar Garciaparra	5.00
3	Ben Grieve	2.50
4	Travis Lee	2.50
5	Jose Cruz Jr.	2.50
6	Alex Rodriguez	6.00
7	Todd Helton	3.50
8	Derek Jeter	7.00
9	Scott Rolen	3.50
10	Jaret Wright	2.50

1998 Select Selected

Intended as a 1:23 pack insert for a set which was never released due to Pinnacle's bankruptcy, Selected cards later leaked out into the hobby market. Fronts have color action photos on bright metallic-foil backgrounds with a large "S." Backs have a smaller version of the front photo along with career highlights.

		NM/M
Complete Set (10):		135.00
Common Player:		10.00
1	Vladimir Guerrero	15.00
2	Nomar Garciaparra	20.00
3	Ben Grieve	10.00

		NM/M
4	Travis Lee	10.00
5	Jose Cruz Jr.	10.00
6	Alex Rodriguez	22.50
7	Todd Helton	12.50
8	Derek Jeter	25.00
9	Scott Rolen	12.50
10	Jaret Wright	10.00

2002 Select Rookies & Prospects Autographs

		NM/M
Common Player:		3.00
Retail-exclusive		
1	Abraham Nunez	5.00
2	Adam Bernero	3.00
3	Adam Pettyjohn	3.00
4	Alex Escobar	4.00
5	Allan Simpson	3.00
6	Andres Torres	3.00
7	Andy Pratt	3.00
8	Bert Snow	3.00
9	Bill Ortega	3.00
10	Billy Sylvester	3.00
11	Brad Voyles	3.00
12	Brandon Backe	3.00
13	Brent Abernathy	3.00
14	Brian Mallette	3.00
15	Brian Rogers	3.00
16	Cam Esslinger	3.00
17	Carlos Garcia	3.00
18	Carlos Valderrama	3.00
19	Cesar Izturis	6.00
20	Chad Durbin	3.00
21	Chris Baker	3.00
22	Claudio Vargas	3.00
23	Cory Aldridge	4.00
24	Craig Monroe	5.00
25	David Elder	3.00
26	David Brous	3.00
27	David Espinosa	3.00
28	Derrick Lewis	3.00
29	Elio Serrano	3.00
30	Elpidio Guzman	3.00
31	Eric Cyr	3.00
32	Eric Valent	4.00
33	Erik Bedard	5.00
34	Esix Snead	3.00
35	Francis Beltran	3.00
36	George Perez	3.00
37	Gene Altman	3.00
38	Greg Miller	4.00
39	Horacio Ramirez	3.00
40	Jason Hart	4.50
41	Jason Karnuth	3.00
42	Jason Romano	3.00
43	Jeff Deardorff	3.00
44	Jeremy Affeldt	3.00
45	Jeremy Lambert	3.00
46	John Ennis	3.00
47	John Grabow	3.00
48	Jose Cueto	3.00
49	Jose Mieses	3.00
50	Jose Ortiz	3.00
51	Josh Pearce	3.00
52	Josue Perez	3.00
53	Juan Diaz	3.00
54	Juan Pena	3.00
55	Keith Ginter	3.00
56	Kevin Frederick	3.00
57	Kevin Joseph	3.00
58	Kevin Olsen	3.00
60	Kris Keller	3.00
61	Larry Bigbie	3.00
62	Les Walrond	3.00
63	Luis Pineda	3.00
64	Luis Rivas	3.00
65	Luis Rivera	4.50
66	Luke Hudson	3.00
67	Marcus Giles	8.00
68	Mark Ellis	3.00
69	Martin Vargas	3.00
70	Matt Childers	3.00
71	Matt Guerrier	3.00
72	Matt Thornton	3.00
73	Matt White	3.00
74	Mike Penney	3.00
75	Nate Teut	3.00
76	Nick Maness	3.00
77	Orlando Woodards	3.00
78	Paul Phillips	3.00
79	Pedro Feliz	3.00
80	Ramon Vazquez	3.00
81	Raul Chavez	3.00
82	Reed Johnson	3.00

83	Ryan Freel	4.50
84	Ryan Jamison	3.00
85	Ryan Ludwick	3.00
86	Saul Rivera	3.00
87	Steve Bechler	3.00
88	Steve Green	3.00
89	Steve Smyth	3.00
90	Tike Redman	3.00
91	Tom Shearn	3.00
92	Tomas de la Rosa	3.00
93	Tony Cogan	3.00
94	Travis Hafner	25.00
95	Travis Hughes	3.00
96	Wilkin Ruan	3.00
97	Will Ohman	3.00
98	Wilmy Caceres	3.00
99	Wilson Guzman	3.00
100	Winston Abreu	3.00

1992 Sentry Robin Yount

At the Sept. 25, 1992, Brewers home game, the first 25,000 fans through the turnstile received a four-card set commemorating Robin Yount's 3,000th career hit. The 2-1/2" x 3-1/2" cards feature on a front a gold-foil framed action photo set against a purple marbled border. Backs have a write-up about the career milestone hit and include the grocery store logo at bottom. The cards are unnumbered and were issued in a heavy paper wrapper.

		NM/M
Complete Set (4):		15.00
Common Card:		5.00
(1)	Hit #1, April 12, 1974 (Robin Yount)	5.00
(2)	Hit #1,000, Aug. 16, 1980 (Robin Yount)	5.00
(3)	Hit #2,000, Sept. 6, 1986 (Robin Yount)	5.00
(4)	Hit #3,000, Sept. 9, 1992 (Robin Yount)	5.00

1993 Sentry Brewers Memorable Moments

Fans at a special Brewer home game were given this set of team highlight cards. Fronts have a color photo of the highlight with a brief description and date printed in gold foil. The photo is framed in dark blue, which is also used for the border of the card. The territory between the photo and border is printed in light blue and includes the Brewers logo and "Memorable Moments" headline. Backs have a description of the action shown on front, and the spon-

sor's logo. Cards are numbered according to player uniform number printed on back.

		NM/M
Complete Set (4):		8.00
Common Card:		1.00
4	Paul Molitor	3.50
4	Dale Sveum	1.00
19	Robin Yount	3.50
20	Juan Nieves	1.00

1993 Sentry Milwaukee Brewers

B.J. Surhoff-3B
Collector Series - 3 of 12

This set of a dozen coupon/card combos was distributed at Milwaukee area Sentry grocery stores during the 1993 season. A new card was issued every week or two between April 27 and September 28. Each piece measures 12-1/2" x 7" and has a 5" x 7" Brewer player photo attached to six perforated coupons, each of which has a postage stamp-size Brewer photo at lower-right. Cards #11 and 12 were never officially issued and have blank coupons.

		NM/M
Complete Set (12):		7.00
Common Player:		.60
1	Pat Listach	.50
2	Tom Brunansky	.50
3	B.J. Surhoff	.50
4	Kevin Reimer	.50
5	Darryl Hamilton	.50
6	Greg Vaughn	.50
7	Robin Yount	4.00
8	Phil Garner	.50
9	Bill Spiers	.50
10	Dave Nilsson	.50
11	Bill Wegman	.50
12	Cal Eldred	.50

1994 Sentry Brewer Highlights

This eight-card set featuring highlights from Brewers history was issued in the team's 25th anniversary season. Sponsored by Sentry Foods, the cards were available on a one-per-week basis, attached to an 8-1/2" x 11" sheet of coupons, from May through August. (The last two cards were never officially issued due to the strike.) In standard 2-1/2" x 3-1/2" cards feature wide violet borders highlighted by green and gold geometric shapes. The team's 25th anniversary logo is at top-left, with the featured highlight at upper-right in gold. The player's name appears in white in a black ribbon beneath the color photo. Backs describe the highlight and are printed in blue and black. There is no

sponsor's logo or card number. Cards are checklisted here alphabetically.

		NM/M
Complete Set (8):		14.00
Common Player:		1.00
(1)	Hank Aaron (Final Home Run)	5.00
(2)	Rollie Fingers (Cy Young/MVP Season)	1.50
(3)	Pat Listach (Rookie of the Year)	1.00
(4)	Paul Molitor (39-game Hitting Streak)	3.50
(5)	Juan Nieves (No-hitter)	1.00
(6)	Don Sutton (3,000th Strikeout)	1.00
(7)	Robin Yount (3,000 Hit)	3.50
(8)	Triumphant Trio (Jim Gantner, Paul Molitor, Robin Yount)	2.50

1983 7-11 Slurpee Coins

This first production of player coins by 7-Eleven stores was distributed only in the Los Angeles area. The test promotion, which awarded a coin to every purchaser of a large Slurpee drink, must have proved successful, as it was expanded nationally in subsequent years. Six California Angels and six Los Angeles Dodgers are included in the full-color set, with Angels players in red backgrounds and the Dodgers in blue. The 1-3/4" diameter plastic coins feature both an action and a portrait photo of the player, which can be alternately seen by moving the coin slightly from side to side. The 12 coin backs are numbered and include brief statistics and the company logo.

		NM/M
Complete Set (12):		6.00
Common Player:		.50
1	Rod Carew	2.00
2	Steve Sax	.50
3	Fred Lynn	.50
4	Pedro Guerrero	.50
5	Reggie Jackson	3.00
6	Dusty Baker	.50
7	Doug DeCinces	.50
8	Fernando Valenzuela	.50
9	Tommy John	.50
10	Rick Monday	.50
11	Bobby Grich	.50
12	Greg Brock	.50

1984 7-11 Slurpee Coins Central Region

The 7-Eleven/Slurpee coins were distributed nationally in 1984 with 60 different players in three regional issues of 24 pieces each. Coins of Brett, Dawson, Murphy, Murray, Schmidt and Yount were common to all three regions. The 1-3/4" diameter plastic coins feature an action and a portrait photo on front which change

when the viewing angle is altered. Statistics and coin numbers are found on the backs, along with the 7-Eleven logo.

		NM/M
Complete Set (24):		7.50
Common Player:		.25
1	Andre Dawson	.40
2	Robin Yount	.75
3	Dale Murphy	.50
4	Mike Schmidt	1.25
5	George Brett	1.25
6	Eddie Murray	.75
7	Bruce Sutter	.65
8	Cecil Cooper	.25
9	Willie McGee	.25
10	Mike Hargrove	.25
11	Kent Hrbek	.25
12	Carlton Fisk	.75
13	Mario Soto	.25
14	Lonnie Smith	.25
15	Gary Carter	.75
16	Lou Whitaker	.25
17	Ron Kittle	.25
18	Paul Molitor	.75
19	Ozzie Smith	1.00
20	Fergie Jenkins	.40
21	Ted Simmons	.25
22	Pete Rose	1.50
23	LaMarr Hoyt	.25
24	Dan Quisenberry	.25

Eastern Region

		NM/M
Complete Set (24):		10.00
Common Player:		.25
1	Andre Dawson	.40
2	Robin Yount	.75
3	Dale Murphy	.50
4	Mike Schmidt	1.25
5	George Brett	1.25
6	Eddie Murray	.75
7	Dave Winfield	.75
8	Tom Seaver	.75
9	Mike Boddicker	.25
10	Wade Boggs	1.00
11	Bill Madlock	.25
12	Steve Carlton	.50
13	Dave Stieb	.25
14	Cal Ripken, Jr.	3.00
15	Jim Rice	.40
16	Ron Guidry	.25
17	Darryl Strawberry	.25
18	Tony Pena	.25
19	John Denny	.25
20	Tim Raines	.25
21	Rick Dempsey	.25
22	Rich Gossage	.25
23	Gary Matthews	.25
24	Keith Hernandez	.25

Western Region

		NM/M
Complete Set (24):		9.00
Common Player:		.25
1	Andre Dawson	.40
2	Robin Yount	.75
3	Dale Murphy	.50
4	Mike Schmidt	1.25
5	George Brett	1.25
6	Eddie Murray	.75
7	Steve Garvey	.35
8	Rod Carew	.75
9	Fernando Valenzuela	.25
10	Bob Horner	.25
11	Buddy Bell	.25
12	Reggie Jackson	1.00
13	Nolan Ryan	2.00
14	Pedro Guerrero	.25
15	Atlee Hammaker	.25
16	Fred Lynn	.25
17	Terry Kennedy	.25
18	Dusty Baker	.25
19	Jose Cruz	.25
20	Steve Rogers	.25
21	Rickey Henderson	.75
22	Steve Sax	.25
23	Dickie Thon	.25
24	Matt Young	.25

Jumbo Coin

Dale Murphy, the MVP of the National League in 1983 was featured on a jumbo-format (4-1/2" diameter) "3D" disc distributed by 7-11 stores in conjunction with their Slurpee fountain drink. Like the smaller Slurpee coins, the photos on the disc change as the viewing angle is changed.

	NM/M
Dale Murphy	15.00

1985 7-11 Slurpee Coins Eastern Region

In 1985, the "Slurpee Disc" promotion was further expanded to a total of 94 full-color

coins. The formats were very similar to the previous two years, but there were six different regional sets. Five of these regional series contain 16 coins, with a Detroit series totaling 14. The other five regions are: East, West, Great Lakes, Central and Southeast. The coins are again 1-1/4" in diameter, printed on plastic with double-image photos. All coins are numbered. No player appears in all regions, although several are in two or more.

		NM/M
Complete Set (16):		10.00
Common Player:		.25
1	Eddie Murray	1.00
2	George Brett	2.50
3	Steve Carlton	1.00
4	Jim Rice	.45
5	Dave Winfield	1.00
6	Mike Boddicker	.25
7	Wade Boggs	2.00
8	Dwight Evans	.25
9	Dwight Gooden	.25
10	Keith Hernandez	.25
11	Bill Madlock	.25
12	Don Mattingly	2.50
13	Dave Righetti	.25
14	Cal Ripken, Jr.	4.00
15	Juan Samuel	.25
16	Mike Schmidt	2.50

Great Lakes Region

		NM/M
Complete Set (16):		10.00
Common Player:		.25
1	Willie Hernandez	.25
2	George Brett	2.50
3	Dave Winfield	1.00
4	Eddie Murray	1.00
5	Bruce Sutter	.75
6	Harold Baines	.25
7	Bert Blyleven	.25
8	Leon Durham	.25
9	Chet Lemon	.25
10	Pete Rose	3.00
11	Ryne Sandberg	2.00
12	Tom Seaver	1.00
13	Mario Soto	.25
14	Rick Sutcliffe	.25
15	Alan Trammell	.25
16	Robin Yount	1.00

Southeastern Region

		NM/M
Complete Set (16):		7.50
Common Player:		.25
1	Dale Murphy	.75
2	Steve Carlton	1.00
3	Nolan Ryan	4.00
4	Bruce Sutter	.75
5	Dave Winfield	1.00
6	Steve Bedrosian	.25
7	Andre Dawson	.50
8	Kirk Gibson	.25
9	Fred Lynn	.25
10	Gary Matthews	.25
11	Phil Niekro	1.00
12	Tim Raines	.25
13	Darryl Strawberry	.25
14	Dave Stieb	.25
15	Willie Upshaw	.25
16	Lou Whitaker	.25

Southwest/ Central Region

		NM/M
Complete Set (16):		10.00
Common Player:		.25
1	Nolan Ryan	4.00
2	George Brett	2.50
3	Dave Winfield	1.00
4	Mike Schmidt	2.50
5	Bruce Sutter	.75
6	Joaquin Andujar	.25
7	Willie Hernandez	.25
8	Wade Boggs	1.50
9	Gary Carter	1.00
10	Jose Cruz	.25
11	Kent Hrbek	.25
12	Reggie Jackson	1.50
13	Lance Parrish	.25

14	Terry Puhl	.25
15	Dan Quisenberry	.25
16	Ozzie Smith	1.50

Western Region

NM/M

Complete Set (16):		7.50
Common Player:		.25
1	Mike Schmidt	2.50
2	Jim Rice	.45
3	Dale Murphy	.50
4	Eddie Murray	1.00
5	Dave Winfield	1.00
6	Rod Carew	1.00
7	Alvin Davis	.25
8	Steve Garvey	.35
9	Rich Gossage	.25
10	Pedro Guerrero	.25
11	Tony Gwynn	1.50
12	Rickey Henderson	1.00
13	Reggie Jackson	2.00
14	Jeff Leonard	.25
15	Alejandro Pena	.25
16	Fernando Valenzuela	.25

Tigers

NM/M

Complete Set (14):		7.50
Common Player:		.75
1	Sparky Anderson	1.00
2	Darrell Evans	1.00
3	Kirk Gibson	1.00
4	Willie Hernandez	.75
5	Larry Herndon	.75
6	Chet Lemon	.75
7	Aurelio Lopez	.75
8	Jack Morris	.75
9	Lance Parrish	.75
10	Dan Petry	.75
11	Dave Rozema	.75
12	Alan Trammell	1.00
13	Lou Whitaker	1.00
14	Milt Wilcox	.75

Test Coins

These 3-D "Magic Motion" coins are identical to the regional issues in all aspects except size. These test coins are 2-1/4" diameter, an inch bigger than the issued versions.

NM/M

Complete Set (3):		4.00
Common Player:		.50
4	Mike Schmidt	2.50
5	Bruce Sutter	1.00
6	Dave Winfield	1.50

Jumbo Coins

World Series MVP Alan Trammell and Yankees slugger Dave Winfield were featured on jumbo-format (4-1/2" diameter) "3D" discs distributed by 7-11 stores in conjunction with their Slurpee fountain drink. Like the smaller Slurpee coins, the photos on the disc change as the viewing angle is changed.

NM/M

Complete Set (2):		15.00
(1)	Alan Trammell	5.00
(2)	Dave Winfield	10.00

Twins

The Minnesota Twins, in co-operation with 7-Eleven and the Fire Marshall's Association, issued this set of 13 baseball fire safety cards. The

card fronts feature full-color pictures of Twins players. A fire safety tip and short player history appear on the back. The cards were given out at all 7-Eleven stores in the state and at the Twins June 3 baseball game. Each fan received one baseball card with a poster which told how to collect the other cards in the set. Twelve cards feature players and the 13th card has an artist's rendering of Twins players on the front and a checklist of the set on the back. A group of 50,000 cards was distributed to fifth graders throughout the state by the fire departments.

NM/M

Complete Set (13):		6.00
Common Player:		.35
1	Kirby Puckett	5.00
2	Frank Viola	.35
3	Mickey Hatcher	.35
4	Kent Hrbek	.35
5	John Butcher	.35
6	Roy Smalley	.35
7	Tom Brunansky	.35
8	Ron Davis	.35
9	Gary Gaetti	.35
10	Tim Teufel	.35
11	Mike Smithson	.35
12	Tim Laudner	.35
---	Checklist	.10

1986 7-11 Slurpee Coins Eastern Region

This marked the fourth year of production for these coins, issued with the purchase of a large Slurpee drink at 7-Eleven stores. Once again, there are different regional issues, with 16 coins issued for four different regions in 1986. The 1-3/4" diameter plastic coins each feature three different players' pictures, which can be seen alternately by tilting from side to side. Eight of the coins are the same in every region. Each coin is numbered on the back, along with brief player information.

NM/M

Complete Set (16):		7.50
Common Coin:		.25
1	Dwight Gooden	.25
2	Batting Champs (Wade Boggs, George Brett, Pete Rose)	2.50
3	MVP's (Keith Hernandez, Don Mattingly, Cal Ripken, Jr.)	2.50
4	Slugging Champs (Harold Baines, Pedro Guerrero, Dave Parker)	.25
5	Home Run Champs (Dale Murphy, Jim Rice, Mike Schmidt)	2.00
6	Cy Young Winners (Ron Guidry, Bret Saberhagen, Fernando Valenzuela)	.25
7	Bullpen Aces (Rich Gossage, Dan Quisenberry, Bruce Sutter)	.50
8	Strikeout Kings (Steve Carlton, Nolan Ryan, Tom Seaver)	2.50
9	1985 Rookies (Steve Lyons, Rick Schu, Larry Sheets)	.25
10	Bullpen Aces (Jeff Reardon, Dave Righetti, Bob Stanley)	.25
11	Power Hitters (George Bell, Darryl Strawberry, Dave Winfield)	.75
12	Base Stealers (Rickey Henderson, Tim Raines, Juan Samuel)	.75
13	Home Run Hitters (Andre Dawson, Dwight Evans, Eddie Murray)	.75
14	Ace Pitchers (Mike Boddicker, Ron Darling, Dave Stieb)	.25
15	1985 Bullpen Rookies (Tim Burke, Brian Fisher, Roger McDowell)	.25
16	Sluggers (Jesse Barfield, Gary Carter, Fred Lynn)	.75

Mideastern Region

NM/M

Complete Set (16):		7.50
Common Coin:		.25
1	Dwight Gooden	.25
2	Batting Champs (Wade Boggs, George Brett, Pete Rose)	2.50
3	MVP's (Keith Hernandez, Don Mattingly, Cal Ripken)	2.50
4	Slugging Champs (Harold Baines, Pedro Guerrero, Dave Parker)	.25
5	Home Run Champs (Dale Murphy, Jim Rice, Mike Schmidt)	2.00
6	Cy Young Winners (Ron Guidry, Bret Saberhagen, Fernando Valenzuela)	.25
7	Bullpen Aces (Rich Gossage, Dan Quisenberry, Bruce Sutter)	.50
8	Strikeout Kings (Steve Carlton, Nolan Ryan, Tom Seaver)	2.50
9	MVP's (Willie Hernandez, Ryne Sandberg, Robin Yount)	1.50
10	Ace Pitchers (Bert Blyleven, Jack Morris, Rick Sutcliffe)	.25
11	Bullpen Aces (Rollie Fingers, Bob James, Lee Smith)	.50
12	All-Star Catchers (Carlton Fisk, Lance Parrish, Tony Pena)	.75
13	1985 Rookies (Shawon Dunston, Ozzie Guillen, Ernest Riles)	.25
14	Star Outfielders (Brett Butler, Chet Lemon, Willie Wilson)	.25
15	Home Run Hitters (Tom Brunansky, Cecil Cooper, Darrell Evans)	.25
16	Big Hitters (Kirk Gibson, Paul Molitor, Greg Walker)	.75

Midwestern Region

NM/M

Complete Set (16):		7.50
Common Coin:		.25
1	Dwight Gooden	.25
2	Batting Champs (Wade Boggs, George Brett, Pete Rose)	2.50
3	MVP's (Keith Hernandez, Don Mattingly, Cal Ripken, Jr.)	2.50
4	Slugging Champs (Harold Baines, Pedro Guerrero, Dave Parker)	.25
5	Home Run Champs (Dale Murphy, Jim Rice, Mike Schmidt)	2.00
6	Cy Young Winners (Ron Guidry, Bret Saberhagen, Fernando Valenzuela)	.25
7	Bullpen Aces (Rich Gossage, Dan Quisenberry, Bruce Sutter)	.50
8	Strikeout Kings (Steve Carlton, Nolan Ryan, Tom Seaver)	2.50
9	1985 Rookies (Vince Coleman, Glenn Davis, Oddibe McDowell)	.25
10	Gold Glovers (Buddy Bell, Ozzie Smith, Lou Whitaker)	1.00
11	Ace Pitchers (Mike Scott, Mario Soto, John Tudor)	.25
12	Bullpen Aces (Jeff Lahti, Ted Power, Dave Smith)	.25
13	Big Hitters (Jack Clark, Jose Cruz, Bob Horner)	.25
14	Star Second Basemen (Bill Doran, Tommy Herr, Ron Oester)	.25
15	1985 Rookie Pitchers (Tom Browning, Joe Hesketh, Todd Worrell)	.25
16	Top Switch-Hitters (Willie McGee, Jerry Mumphrey, Pete Rose)	2.00

Western Region

NM/M

Complete Set (16):		7.50
Common Coin:		.25
1	Dwight Gooden	.25
2	Batting Champs (Wade Boggs, George Brett, Pete Rose)	2.50
3	MVP's (Keith Hernandez, Don Mattingly, Cal Ripken, Jr.)	2.50
4	Slugging Champs (Harold Baines, Pedro Guerrero, Dave Parker)	.25
5	Home Run Champs (Dale Murphy, Jim Rice, Mike Schmidt)	2.00
6	Cy Young Winners (Ron Guidry, Bret Saberhagen, Fernando Valenzuela)	.25
7	Bullpen Aces (Rich Gossage, Dan Quisenberry, Bruce Sutter)	.50
8	Strikeout Kings (Steve Carlton, Nolan Ryan, Tom Seaver)	2.50
9	Home Run Champs (Reggie Jackson, Dave Kingman, Gorman Thomas)	1.00
10	Batting Champs (Rod Carew, Tony Gwynn, Carney Lansford)	1.00
11	Sluggers (Phil Bradley, Mike Marshall, Graig Nettles)	.25
12	Ace Pitchers (Andy Hawkins, Orel Hershiser, Mike Witt)	.25
13	1985 Rookies (Chris Brown, Ivan Calderon, Mariano Duncan)	.25
14	Big Hitters (Steve Garvey, Bill Madlock, Jim Presley)	.25
15	Bullpen Aces (Jay Howell, Donnie Moore, Ed Nunez)	.25
16	1985 Bullpen Rookies (Karl Best, Stewart Cliburn, Steve Ontiveros)	.25

Jumbo Coin

Three of the game's top stars were featured on a jumbo-format (4-1/2" diameter) "3D" disc distributed by 7-11 stores in conjunction with their Slurpee fountain drink. Like the smaller Slurpee coins, the photos on the disc change as the viewing angle is changed.

NM/M

Wade Boggs, George Brett, Pete Rose	10.00

1987 7-11 Slurpee Coins Eastern Region

Continuing with a tradition started in 1983, 7-Eleven stores offered a free "Super Star Sports Coin" with the purchase of a Slurpee drink. Five different regional sets of Slurpee coins were issued for 1987, a total of 75 coins. Each coin measures 1-3/4" in diameter and features a multiple image effect which allows three different pictures to be seen, depending on how the coin is tilted. The coin reverses contain career records and personal player information.

NM/M

Complete Set (15):		7.50
Common Player:		.25
1	Gary Carter	1.00
2	Don Baylor	.25
3	Rickey Henderson	1.00
4	Lenny Dykstra	.25
5	Wade Boggs	1.50
6	Mike Pagliarulo	.25
7	Dwight Gooden	.25
8	Roger Clemens	2.00
9	Dave Righetti	.25
10	Keith Hernandez	.25
11	Pat Dodson	.25
12	Don Mattingly	2.00
13	Darryl Strawberry	.25
14	Jim Rice	.45
15	Dave Winfield	1.00

Great Lakes Region

NM/M

Complete Set (16):		6.00
Common Player:		.25
1	Harold Baines	.25
2	Jody Davis	.25
3	John Cangelosi	.25
4	Shawon Dunston	.25
5	Dave Cochrane	.25
6	Leon Durham	.25
7	Carlton Fisk	1.50
8	Dennis Eckersley	1.00
9	Ozzie Guillen	.25
10	Gary Matthews	.25
11	Ron Karkovice	.25
12	Keith Moreland	.25
13	Bobby Thigpen	.25
14	Ryne Sandberg	2.50
15	Greg Walker	.25
16	Lee Smith	.25

Mideastern Region

NM/M

Complete Set (16):		7.50
Common Player:		.25
1	Gary Carter	1.00
2	Marty Barrett	.25
3	Jody Davis	.25
4	Don Aase	.25
5	Lenny Dykstra	.25
6	Wade Boggs	1.50
7	Keith Moreland	.25
8	Mike Boddicker	.25
9	Dwight Gooden	.25
10	Roger Clemens	2.00
11	Ryne Sandberg	1.50
12	Eddie Murray	1.00
13	Keith Hernandez	.25
14	Jim Rice	.45
15	Lee Smith	.25
16	Cal Ripken, Jr.	4.00

Western Region

NM/M

Complete Set (16):		2.00
Common Player:		.25
1	Doug DeCinces	.25
2	Mariano Duncan	.25
3	Wally Joyner	.25
4	Pedro Guerrero	.25
5	Kirk McCaskill	.25
6	Orel Hershiser	.25
7	Gary Pettis	.25
8	Mike Marshall	.25
9	Dick Schofield	.25
10	Steve Sax	.25
11	Don Sutton	1.00
12	Mike Scioscia	.25
13	Devon White	.25
14	Franklin Stubbs	.25
15	Mike Witt	.25
16	Fernando Valenzuela	.25

Tigers Coins

NM/M

Complete Set (12):		6.00
Common Player:		.50
1	Darnell Coles	.50
2	Darrell Evans	.60
3	Kirk Gibson	.60
4	Willie Hernandez	.50
5	Larry Herndon	.50
6	Chet Lemon	.50
7	Dwight Lowry	.50
8	Jack Morris	.60
9	Dan Petry	.50
10	Frank Tanana	.50
11	Alan Trammell	.75
12	Lou Whitaker	.65

1991 7-11 Slurpee Coins Atlantic Region

After a three-year hiatus, "3-D" magic-motion coins returned to 7-11 stores in the form of regional sets produced by Score under the name Superstar Sports Coins and given away with the purchase of Slurpee fountain drinks. In the familiar 1-3/4" diameter, the discs have alternating portrait and action images on the front with the player name at top, the team at bottom, the uniform number at left and position at right. Each regional set has a different border color. Backs have 7-11 and Score logos along with career stats and a short career summary. The 120 coins in the sets feature 81 different major leaguers.

NM/M

Complete Set (15):		7.50
Common Player:		.25
1	Glenn Davis	.25
2	Dwight Evans	.25
3	Leo Gomez	.25
4	Ken Griffey Jr.	1.50
5	Rickey Henderson	.75
6	Jose Canseco	.60
7	Dave Justice	.25
8	Ben McDonald	.25
9	Randy Milligan	.25
10	Gregg Olson	.25
11	Kirby Puckett	1.00
12	Bill Ripken	.25
13	Cal Ripken Jr.	2.50
14	Nolan Ryan	2.50
15	David Segui	.25

Florida Region

NM/M

Complete Set (15):		10.00
Common Player:		.25
1	Barry Bonds	2.50
2	George Brett	1.50
3	Roger Clemens	1.50
4	Glenn Davis	.25
5	Alex Fernandez	.25
6	Cecil Fielder	.25
7	Ken Griffey Jr.	2.00
8	Dwight Gooden	.25
9	Dave Justice	.25
10	Barry Larkin	.25
11	Ramon Martinez	.25
12	Jose Offerman	.25
13	Kirby Puckett	1.00
14	Nolan Ryan	2.50
15	Terry Schumpert	.25

Metro Northeast Region

NM/M

Complete Set (15):		9.00
Common Player:		.25
1	Wade Boggs	1.00
2	Barry Bonds	2.50
3	Roger Clemens	1.50
4	Len Dykstra	.25
5	Dwight Gooden	.25
6	Ken Griffey Jr.	2.00
7	Rickey Henderson	.75
8	Gregg Jefferies	.25
9	Roberto Kelly	.25
10	Kevin Maas	.25
11	Don Mattingly	1.50
12	Mickey Morandini	.25
13	Dale Murphy	.50
14	Darryl Strawberry	.25
15	Frank Viola	.25

Midwest

NM/M

Complete Set (15):		6.00
Common Player:		.25

		NM/M
1	George Brett	1.50
2	Andre Dawson	.40
3	Cecil Fielder	.25
4	Carlton Fisk	.75
5	Travis Fryman	.25
6	Mark Grace	.25
7	Ken Griffey Jr.	2.00
8	Ozzie Guillen	.25
9	Alex Fernandez	.25
10	Ray Lankford	.25
11	Ryne Sandberg	1.00
12	Ozzie Smith	1.00
13	Bobby Thigpen	.25
14	Frank Thomas	.75
15	Alan Trammell	.25

Northern California Region

		NM/M
Complete Set (15):		9.00
Common Player:		.25
1	John Burkett	.25
2	Jose Canseco	.65
3	Will Clark	.25
4	Steve Decker	.25
5	Dennis Eckersley	.25
6	Ken Griffey Jr.	2.00
7	Rickey Henderson	.75
8	Nolan Ryan	3.00
9	Mark McGwire	2.50
10	Kevin Mitchell	.25
11	Terry Steinbach	.25
12	Dave Stewart	.25
13	Todd Van Poppel	.25
14	Bob Welch	.25
15	Matt Williams	.25

Northwest Region

		NM/M
Complete Set (15):		9.00
Common Player:		.25
1	George Brett	1.50
2	Jose Canseco	.60
3	Alvin Davis	.25
4	Ken Griffey Jr.	
5	Ken Griffey Sr.	1.00
5	Ken Griffey Jr.	2.00
6	Erik Hanson	.25
7	Rickey Henderson	.75
8	Ryne Sandberg	1.00
9	Randy Johnson	.75
10	Dave Justice	.25
11	Edgar Martinez	.25
12	Tino Martinez	.25
13	Harold Reynolds	.25
14	Nolan Ryan	3.00
15	Mike Schooler	.25

Southern California Region

		NM/M
Complete Set (15):		7.00
Common Player:		.25
1	Jim Abbott	.25
2	Jose Canseco	.60
3	Ken Griffey Jr.	2.00
4	Tony Gwynn	1.00
5	Orel Hershiser	.25
6	Eric Davis	.25
7	Wally Joyner	.25
8	Ramon Martinez	.25
9	Fred McGriff	.25
10	Eddie Murray	.75
11	Jose Offerman	.25
12	Nolan Ryan	3.00
13	Benito Santiago	.25
14	Darryl Strawberry	.25
15	Fernando Valenzuela	.25

Texas Region

		NM/M
Complete Set (15):		10.00
Common Player:		.25
1	Craig Biggio	.25
2	Barry Bonds	3.00
3	Jose Canseco	.50
4	Roger Clemens	1.50
5	Glenn Davis	.25
6	Julio Franco	.25
7	Juan Gonzalez	.50
8	Ken Griffey Jr.	2.00
9	Mike Scott	.25
10	Rafael Palmeiro	.75
11	Nolan Ryan	3.00
12	Ryne Sandberg	1.00
13	Ruben Sierra	.25
14	Todd Van Poppel	.25
15	Bobby Witt	.25

1992 7-11 Slurpee Superstar Action Coins

Score baseball 3-D coins returned to 7-11 stores on a very limited basis in 1992. A 26-piece set of the plastic coins (one for each major league team) was produced by Score in the familiar 1-3/4" diameter format. The coins feature a maroon border on which is printed in white the player's name, team, position and uniform number. At center is a 1-1/4" circle with "flasher" portrait and action photos of the player. Backs have a black border with the player name in yellow at the top, a few career stats, 7-11 and Score logos and a coin number in a pale yellow center circle. At bottom in green is "Superstar Action Coin."

		NM/M
Complete Set (26):		10.00
Common Player:		.25
1	Dwight Gooden	.25
2	Don Mattingly	1.00
3	Roger Clemens	1.00
4	Ivan Calderon	.25
5	Roberto Alomar	.40
6	Sandy Alomar, Jr.	.25
7	Andy Van Slyke	.25
8	Lenny Dykstra	.25
9	Cal Ripken, Jr.	2.00
10	Dave Justice	.25
11	Nolan Ryan	2.00
12	Craig Biggio	.25
13	Barry Larkin	.25
14	Ozzie Smith	.75
15	Ryne Sandberg	.75
16	Frank Thomas	.60
17	Robin Yount	.60
18	Kirby Puckett	.75
19	Cecil Fielder	.25
20	Will Clark	.25
21	Jose Canseco	.45
22	Jim Abbott	.25
23	Tony Gwynn	.75
24	Darryl Strawberry	.25
25	George Brett	1.00
26	Ken Griffey Jr.	1.50

2000 7-11 Slurpee Coins

Returning after a long hiatus, lenticular-motion player discs were once again affixed to the bottoms of Super Big Gulp and 32-oz. Slurpee cups at 20,000 convenience stores nationwide. A step up in quality from the "flicker image" coins of the 1980s, this generation was produced by Pacific Trading Cards and licensed by MLB and the players' union. The 1-3/4" plastic discs have three photos at center with player identification at top and bottom; uniform numbers and logos are at the sides. On back, conventionally printed, is a color portrait photo, a few stats and vital data and appropriate copyright and licensing notices. There is one player

coin from each major league team. An album was available to house the set.

		NM/M
Complete Set (30):		10.00
Common Player:		.25
Album:		3.00
In-Store Ad Sheet:		6.00
1	Tim Salmon	.25
2	Erubiel Durazo	.25
3	Chipper Jones	.65
4	Cal Ripken Jr.	2.00
5	Nomar Garciaparra	.65
6	Mark Grace	.25
7	Frank Thomas	.50
8	Sean Casey	.25
9	Manny Ramirez	.50
10	Larry Walker	.25
11	Dean Palmer	.25
12	Alex Gonzalez	.25
13	Jeff Bagwell	.50
14	Carlos Beltran	.45
15	Gary Sheffield	.40
16	Jeromy Burnitz	.25
17	Corey Koskie	.25
18	Vladimir Guerrero	.50
19	Mike Piazza	1.00
20	Roger Clemens	.75
21	Ben Grieve	.25
22	Scott Rolen	.45
23	Jason Kendall	.25
24	Mark McGwire	1.50
25	Tony Gwynn	.65
26	Jeff Kent	.25
27	Jay Buhner	.25
28	Jose Canseco	.40
29	Ivan Rodriguez	.45
30	Carlos Delgado	.45

1981 7-Up

These 5-1/2" x 8-1/2" color photocards are part of a multi-sport series. Fronts have a borderless photo, a facsimile autograph and, at lower-right, a 7-Up logo and slogan. Back is printed in black, red and green on white and features a career summary through the 1980 season, and a large version of the soda logo. Posters in 19" x 25" size were also issued.

		NM/M
	Common Player:	3.00
(1)	George Brett	6.00
(3)	Dave Parker	3.00
(5)	Mike Schmidt	6.00

1984 7-Up Cubs

"#40 RICK SUTCLIFFE P"

The Chicago Cubs and 7-Up issued this 28-card set featuring full-color game-action photos on a 2-1/4" x 3-1/2" borderless front. The backs have the player's stats and personal information. This was the third consecutive year the Cubs issued this type of set as a giveaway at a "Baseball Card Day" promotional game.

		NM/M
Complete Set (28):		13.50
Common Player:		.25
1	Larry Bowa	.25
4	Keith Moreland	.25
7	Jody Davis	.25
10	Leon Durham	.25
11	Ron Cey	.25
15	Ron Hassey	.25
18	Richie Hebner	.25
19	Dave Owen	.25
20	Bob Dernier	.25
21	Jay Johnstone	.25
23	Ryne Sandberg	9.00
24	Scott Sanderson	.25
25	Gary Woods	.25
27	Thad Bosley	.25
28	Henry Cotto	.25
34	Steve Trout	.25
36	Gary Matthews	.25
39	George Frazier	.25
40	Rick Sutcliffe	.25
42	Warren Brusstar	.25
42	Rich Bordi	.25
43	Dennis Eckersley	3.00
44	Dick Ruthven	.25
46	Lee Smith	.25
47	Rick Reuschel	.25
49	Tim Stoddard	.25
---	Jim Frey	.25
---	Cubs Coaches (Ruben Amaro, Billy Connors, Johnny Oates, John Vukovich, Don Zimmer)	.25

1985 7-Up Cubs

"(7) JODY DAVIS C"

This was the second year a Chicago Cubs card set was released with 7-Up as the sponsor. The set has 28 un-numbered cards in the standard 2-1/2" x 3-1/2" size. They were distributed to fans attending the Cubs game on August 14 at Wrigley Field. They feature full-color game-action photos of the players. Card backs contain the player's professional stats.

		NM/M
Complete Set (28):		10.00
Common Player:		.25
1	Larry Bowa	.25
6	Keith Moreland	.25
7	Jody Davis	.25
10	Leon Durham	.25
11	Ron Cey	.25
15	Davey Lopes	.25
16	Steve Lake	.25
18	Richie Hebner	.25
20	Bob Dernier	.25
21	Scott Sanderson	.25
22	Billy Hatcher	.25
23	Ryne Sandberg	7.50
24	Brian Dayett	.25
25	Gary Woods	.25
27	Thad Bosley	.25
28	Chris Speier	.25
31	Ray Fontenot	.25
34	Steve Trout	.25
36	Gary Matthews	.25
39	George Frazier	.25
40	Rick Sutcliffe	.25
41	Warren Brusstar	.25
42	Lary Sorensen	.25
43	Dennis Eckersley	2.00
44	Dick Ruthven	.25
46	Lee Smith	.25
---	Jim Frey	.25
---	Coaching Staff (Ruben Amaro, Billy Connors, Johnny Oates, John Vukovich, Don Zimmer)	.25

1995 Skin Bracer

This three-card set was included in several packagings of

"BILL MAZEROSKI"

Mennen skin care products for men. Three sepia-toned 3-1/2" x 2-1/2" cards feature great moments in post-season play. Fronts are trimmed in gold ink and feature the player's name in a green box. Backs are printed in black, green and gold and describe the highlight. Logos of the sponsor and Major League Baseball Players Alumni Association are also included on back. A related offer allowed collectors to purchase autographed 8" x 10" photos of the events for $7.99 each via a coupon.

		NM/M
Complete Set (3):		6.00
Common Player:		2.00
(1)	The Perfect Game (Don Larsen)	2.00
(2)	The Series Ender (Bill Mazeroski)	2.00
(3)	The Shot Heard 'Round the World (Bobby Thomson)	2.00

2001 Skippy Peanut Butter Derek Jeter

Specially marked jars Skippy Peanut Butter had a Derek Jeter "Digital Card" under the cap, enclosed in protective plastic. The 2-1/2" diameter discs are printed on thin cardboard and have portrait and action photos of the spokesman on front (Yankees team logos have been removed) along with a facsimile autograph and logos of Skippy and CyberAction. Backs are in red and blue with information on the company's website and a card title.

		NM/M
Complete Set (4):		6.00
Common Card:		2.00
1	1,000 Hits Club (Derek Jeter/Btg.)	2.00
2	1998 Runs Leader (Derek Jeter/Running)	2.00
3	Three Time All-Star (Derek Jeter/Leaping)	2.00
4	World Champion MVP (Derek Jeter/Throwing)	2.00

1995 SkyBox E-Motion Promo

To introduce its new super-premium baseball card line, SkyBox debuted a Cal Ripken promo card at the

1995 National Sports Collectors Convention. The card is virtually identical to Ripken's card in the regular issue, except for diagonal overprinting on each side which reads, "Promotional Sample."

		NM/M
8	Cal Ripken Jr. (Class)	2.50

1995 SkyBox E-Motion

This is a super-premium debut issue from the newly merged Fleer/SkyBox company. Printed on double-thick cardboard, card fronts have borderless photos marred by the presence of four gold-foil "viewfinder" corner marks. The player's last name and team are printed in gold foil near the bottom. On each card there is a large silver-foil word printed in block letters; either a nickname or an emotion or attribute associated with the player. Backs have two more player photos, 1994 and career stats and a few biographical bits. Eight-cards packs were issued with a suggested retail price of $4.99.

		NM/M
Complete Set (200):		15.00
Common Player:		.05
Pack (8):		1.00
Wax Box (36):		20.00
1	Brady Anderson	.05
2	Kevin Brown	.05
3	Curtis Goodwin	.05
4	Jeffrey Hammonds	.05
5	Ben McDonald	.05
6	Mike Mussina	.35
7	Rafael Palmeiro	.65
8	Cal Ripken Jr.	2.00
9	Jose Canseco	.45
10	Roger Clemens	1.00
11	Vaughn Eshelman	.05
12	Mike Greenwell	.05
13	Erik Hanson	.05
14	Tim Naehring	.05
15	Aaron Sele	.05
16	John Valentin	.05
17	Mo Vaughn	.05
18	Chili Davis	.05
19	Gary DiSarcina	.05
20	Chuck Finley	.05
21	Tim Salmon	.05
22	Lee Smith	.05
23	J.T. Snow	.05
24	Jim Abbott	.05
25	Jason Bere	.05
26	Ray Durham	.05
27	Ozzie Guillen	.05
28	Tim Raines	.05
29	Frank Thomas	.75
30	Robin Ventura	.05
31	Carlos Baerga	.05
32	Albert Belle	.05
33	Orel Hershiser	.05
34	Kenny Lofton	.05
35	Dennis Martinez	.05
36	Eddie Murray	.75
37	Manny Ramirez	.75
38	Julian Tavarez	.05
39	Jim Thome	.60
40	Dave Winfield	.75
41	Chad Curtis	.05
42	Cecil Fielder	.05
43	Travis Fryman	.05
44	Kirk Gibson	.05
45	Bob Higginson **RC**	.05
46	Alan Trammell	.05
47	Lou Whitaker	.05
48	Kevin Appier	.05
49	Gary Gaetti	.05
50	Jeff Montgomery	.05
51	Jon Nunnally	.05
52	Ricky Bones	.05
53	Cal Eldred	.05
54	Joe Oliver	.05

55	Kevin Seitzer	.05
56	Marty Cordova	.05
57	Chuck Knoblauch	.05
58	Kirby Puckett	1.00
59	Wade Boggs	1.00
60	Derek Jeter	2.00
61	Jimmy Key	.05
62	Don Mattingly	1.00
63	Jack McDowell	.05
64	Paul O'Neill	.05
65	Andy Pettitte	.30
66	Ruben Rivera	.05
67	Mike Stanley	.05
68	John Wetteland	.05
69	Geronimo Berroa	.05
70	Dennis Eckersley	.65
71	Rickey Henderson	.75
72	Mark McGwire	1.50
73	Steve Ontiveros	.05
74	Ruben Sierra	.05
75	Terry Steinbach	.05
76	Jay Buhner	.05
77	Ken Griffey Jr.	1.25
78	Randy Johnson	.75
79	Edgar Martinez	.05
80	Tino Martinez	.05
81	Marc Newfield	.05
82	Alex Rodriguez	1.50
83	Will Clark	.05
84	Benji Gil	.05
85	Juan Gonzalez	.40
86	Rusty Greer	.05
87	Dean Palmer	.05
88	Ivan Rodriguez	.65
89	Kenny Rogers	.05
90	Roberto Alomar	.30
91	Joe Carter	.05
92	David Cone	.05
93	Alex Gonzalez	.05
94	Shawn Green	.40
95	Pat Hentgen	.05
96	Paul Molitor	.75
97	John Olerud	.05
98	Devon White	.05
99	Steve Avery	.05
100	Tom Glavine	.35
101	Marquis Grissom	.05
102	Chipper Jones	1.00
103	Dave Justice	.05
104	Ryan Klesko	.05
105	Javier Lopez	.05
106	Greg Maddux	1.00
107	Fred McGriff	.05
108	John Smoltz	.05
109	Shawon Dunston	.05
110	Mark Grace	.05
111	Brian McRae	.05
112	Randy Myers	.05
113	Sammy Sosa	1.00
114	Steve Trachsel	.05
115	Bret Boone	.05
116	Ron Gant	.05
117	Barry Larkin	.05
118	Deion Sanders	.05
119	Reggie Sanders	.05
120	Pete Schourek	.05
121	John Smiley	.05
122	Jason Bates	.05
123	Dante Bichette	.05
124	Vinny Castilla	.05
125	Andres Galarraga	.05
126	Larry Walker	.05
127	Greg Colbrunn	.05
128	Jeff Conine	.05
129	Andre Dawson	.30
130	Chris Hammond	.05
131	Charles Johnson	.05
132	Gary Sheffield	.45
133	Quilvio Veras	.05
134	Jeff Bagwell	.75
135	Derek Bell	.05
136	Craig Biggio	.05
137	Jim Dougherty	.05
138	John Hudek	.05
139	Orlando Miller	.05
140	Phil Plantier	.05
141	Eric Karros	.05
142	Ramon Martinez	.05
143	Raul Mondesi	.05
144	Hideo Nomo RC	2.00
145	Mike Piazza	1.25
146	Ismael Valdes	.05
147	Todd Worrell	.05
148	Moises Alou	.05
149	Yamil Benitez RC	.05
150	Wil Cordero	.05
151	Jeff Fassero	.05
152	Cliff Floyd	.05
153	Pedro Martinez	.75
154	Carlos Perez RC	.05
155	Tony Tarasco	.05
156	Rondell White	.05
157	Edgardo Alfonzo	.05
158	Bobby Bonilla	.05
159	Rico Brogna	.05
160	Bobby Jones	.05
161	Bill Pulsipher	.05
162	Bret Saberhagen	.05
163	Ricky Bottalico	.05
164	Darren Daulton	.05
165	Lenny Dykstra	.05
166	Charlie Hayes	.05
167	Dave Hollins	.05
168	Gregg Jefferies	.05
169	Michael Mimbs RC	.05
170	Curt Schilling	.35
171	Heathcliff Slocumb	.05
172	Jay Bell	.05
173	Micah Franklin RC	.05
174	Mark Johnson RC	.05
175	Jeff King	.05
176	Al Martin	.05
177	Dan Miceli	.05
178	Denny Neagle	.05
179	Bernard Gilkey	.05
180	Ken Hill	.05
181	Brian Jordan	.05
182	Ray Lankford	.05
183	Ozzie Smith	1.00
184	Andy Benes	.05
185	Ken Caminiti	.05
186	Steve Finley	.05
187	Tony Gwynn	1.00
188	Joey Hamilton	.05
189	Melvin Nieves	.05
190	Scott Sanders	.05
191	Rod Beck	.05
192	Barry Bonds	2.00
193	Royce Clayton	.05
194	Glenallen Hill	.05
195	Darren Lewis	.05
196	Mark Portugal	.05
197	Matt Williams	.05
198	Checklist	.05
199	Checklist	.05
200	Checklist	.05

Masters

Ten of the game's top veterans are featured in this chase card set. A large close-up photo in a single team-related color in the background, with a color action photo in the foreground. Backs have a borderless color photo and a top to bottom color bar with some good words about the player. The Masters inserts are found at an average rate of one per eight packs.

		NM/M
	Complete Set (10):	12.00
	Common Player:	.50
1	Barry Bonds	2.50
2	Juan Gonzalez	.65
3	Ken Griffey Jr.	2.00
4	Tony Gwynn	1.50
5	Kenny Lofton	.50
6	Greg Maddux	1.50
7	Raul Mondesi	.50
8	Cal Ripken Jr.	2.50
9	Frank Thomas	1.00
10	Matt Williams	.50

N-Tense

A colored wave-pattern printed on metallic foil is the background for the action photo of one of baseball's top sluggers in this chase card set. A huge rainbow prismatic foil "N" appears in an upper corner. The player's name and team are at lower-right in gold foil. Backs are conventionally printed and repeat the front's patterned background, with another color player photo and a shaded box with a few career highlights.

	NM/M
Complete Set (12):	16.00

	Common Player:	.50
1	Jeff Bagwell	2.00
2	Albert Belle	.50
3	Barry Bonds	4.00
4	Cecil Fielder	.50
5	Ron Gant	.50
6	Ken Griffey Jr.	2.50
7	Mark McGwire	3.00
8	Mike Piazza	2.50
9	Manny Ramirez	2.00
10	Frank Thomas	2.00
11	Mo Vaughn	.50
12	Matt Williams	.50

Cal Ripken Jr. Timeless

A white background with a clockface and gold-foil "TIMELESS" logo are the standard elements of this insert tribute to Cal Ripken, Jr. Fronts also feature a large color photo and a smaller sepia photo contemporary to some phase of his career. The first 10 cards in the set chronicle Ripken's career through 1994. A special mail-in offer provided five more cards featuring highlights of his 1995 season.

		NM/M
	Complete Set (15):	20.00
	Common Card:	1.50
1	High School Pitcher	1.50
2	Role Model	1.50
3	Rookie of the Year	1.50
4	1st MVP Season	1.50
5	95 Consecutive Errorless Games	1.50
6	All-Star MVP	1.50
7	Conditioning	1.50
8	Shortstop HR Record	1.50
9	Literacy Work	1.50
10	2000th Consecutive Game	1.50
11	All-Star Selection	2.25
12	Record-tying Game	2.25
13	Record-breaking Game	2.25
14	2,153 and Counting	2.25
15	Birthday	2.25

Rookies

A bold colored background with outline white letters repeating the word "ROOKIE" is the frame for the central action photo in this insert series. The top of the photo is vignetted with a white circle that has the player's name in gold at left, and his team in white at right. Backs repeat the front background and include a player portrait photo and a few sentences about his potential. Rookie inserts are found at an average rate of one per five packs.

	NM/M
Complete Set (10):	6.50

	Common Player:	.25
1	Edgardo Alfonzo	.25
2	Jason Bates	.25
3	Marty Cordova	.25
4	Ray Durham	.25
5	Alex Gonzalez	.25
6	Shawn Green	.75
7	Charles Johnson	.25
8	Chipper Jones	1.50
9	Hideo Nomo	1.00
10	Alex Rodriguez	3.00

1996 SkyBox E-Motion XL

Each card in SkyBox's 1996 E-Motion XL Baseball arrives on two layers of stock - a die-cut matte frame over a UV-coated card. The frames come in three colors - blue, green and maroon (but each player has only one color version). The 300-card set also includes four insert sets: Legion of Boom, D-Fense, N-Tense and Rare Breed.

		NM/M
	Complete Set (300):	10.00
	Common Player:	.05
	Pack (7):	1.00
	Wax Box (24):	20.00
1	Roberto Alomar	.15
2	Brady Anderson	.05
3	Bobby Bonilla	.05
4	Jeffrey Hammonds	.05
5	Chris Hoiles	.05
6	Mike Mussina	.30
7	Randy Myers	.05
8	Rafael Palmeiro	.05
9	Cal Ripken Jr.	2.00
10	B.J. Surhoff	.05
11	Jose Canseco	.25
12	Roger Clemens	1.00
13	Wil Cordero	.05
14	Mike Greenwell	.05
15	Dwayne Hosey	.05
16	Tim Naehring	.05
17	Troy O'Leary	.05
18	Mike Stanley	.05
19	John Valentin	.05
20	Mo Vaughn	.05
21	Jim Abbott	.05
22	Garret Anderson	.05
23	George Arias	.05
24	Chili Davis	.05
25	Jim Edmonds	.05
26	Chuck Finley	.05
27	Todd Greene	.05
28	Mark Langston	.05
29	Troy Percival	.05
30	Tim Salmon	.05
31	Lee Smith	.05
32	J.T. Snow	.05
33	Harold Baines	.05
34	Jason Bere	.05
35	Ray Durham	.05
36	Alex Fernandez	.05
37	Ozzie Guillen	.05
38	Darren Lewis	.05
39	Lyle Mouton	.05
40	Tony Phillips	.05
41	Danny Tartabull	.05
42	Frank Thomas	.60
43	Robin Ventura	.05
44	Sandy Alomar	.05
45	Carlos Baerga	.05
46	Albert Belle	.05
47	Julio Franco	.05
48	Orel Hershiser	.05
49	Kenny Lofton	.05
50	Dennis Martinez	.05
51	Jack McDowell	.05
52	Jose Mesa	.05
53	Eddie Murray	.60
54	Charles Nagy	.05
55	Manny Ramirez	.05
55p	Manny Ramirez/OPS	.60
56	Jim Thome	.45
57	Omar Vizquel	.05
58	Chad Curtis	.05
59	Cecil Fielder	.05
60	Travis Fryman	.05
61	Chris Gomez	.05
62	Felipe Lira	.05
63	Alan Trammell	.05
64	Kevin Appier	.05
65	Johnny Damon	.35
66	Tom Goodwin	.05
67	Mark Gubicza	.05
68	Jeff Montgomery	.05
69	Jon Nunnally	.05
70	Bip Roberts	.05
71	Ricky Bones	.05
72	Chuck Carr	.05
73	John Jaha	.05
74	Ben McDonald	.05
75	Matt Mieske	.05
76	Dave Nilsson	.05
77	Kevin Seitzer	.05
78	Greg Vaughn	.05
79	Rick Aguilera	.05
80	Marty Cordova	.05
81	Roberto Kelly	.05
82	Chuck Knoblauch	.05
83	Pat Meares	.05
84	Paul Molitor	.60
85	Kirby Puckett	.75
86	Brad Radke	.05
87	Wade Boggs	.05
88	David Cone	.05
89	Dwight Gooden	.05
90	Derek Jeter	2.00
91	Tino Martinez	.05
92	Paul O'Neill	.05
93	Andy Pettitte	.15
94	Tim Raines	.05
95	Ruben Rivera	.05
96	Kenny Rogers	.05
97	Ruben Sierra	.05
98	John Wetteland	.05
99	Bernie Williams	.05
100	Allen Battle	.05
101	Geronimo Berroa	.05
102	Brent Gates	.05
103	Doug Johns	.05
104	Mark McGwire	1.50
105	Pedro Munoz	.05
106	Ariel Prieto	.05
107	Terry Steinbach	.05
108	Todd Van Poppel	.05
109	Chris Bosio	.05
110	Jay Buhner	.05
111	Joey Cora	.05
112	Russ Davis	.05
113	Ken Griffey Jr.	1.25
114	Sterling Hitchcock	.05
115	Randy Johnson	.60
116	Edgar Martinez	.05
117	Alex Rodriguez	1.50
118	Paul Sorrento	.05
119	Dan Wilson	.05
120	Will Clark	.05
121	Juan Gonzalez	.30
122	Rusty Greer	.05
123	Kevin Gross	.05
124	Ken Hill	.05
125	Dean Palmer	.05
126	Roger Pavlik	.05
127	Ivan Rodriguez	.50
128	Mickey Tettleton	.05
129	Joe Carter	.05
130	Carlos Delgado	.40
131	Alex Gonzalez	.05
132	Shawn Green	.25
133	Erik Hanson	.05
134	Pat Hentgen	.05
135	Otis Nixon	.05
136	John Olerud	.05
137	Ed Sprague	.05
138	Steve Avery	.05
139	Jermaine Dye	.05
140	Tom Glavine	.35
141	Marquis Grissom	.05
142	Chipper Jones	.75
143	David Justice	.05
144	Ryan Klesko	.05
145	Javier Lopez	.05
146	Greg Maddux	.75
147	Fred McGriff	.05
148	Jason Schmidt	.05
149	John Smoltz	.05
150	Mark Wohlers	.05
151	Jim Bullinger	.05
152	Frank Castillo	.05
153	Kevin Foster	.05
154	Luis Gonzalez	.05
155	Mark Grace	.05
156	Brian McRae	.05
157	Jaime Navarro	.05
158	Rey Sanchez	.05
159	Ryne Sandberg	.75
160	Sammy Sosa	.75
161	Bret Boone	.05
162	Jeff Brantley	.05
163	Vince Coleman	.05
164	Steve Gibralter	.05
165	Barry Larkin	.05
166	Hal Morris	.05
167	Mark Portugal	.05
168	Reggie Sanders	.05
169	Pete Schourek	.05
170	John Smiley	.05
171	Jason Bates	.05
172	Dante Bichette	.05
173	Ellis Burks	.05
174	Vinny Castilla	.05
175	Andres Galarraga	.05
176	Kevin Ritz	.05
177	Bill Swift	.05
178	Larry Walker	.05
179	Walt Weiss	.05
180	Eric Young	.05
181	Kurt Abbott	.05
182	Kevin Brown	.05
183	John Burkett	.05
184	Greg Colbrunn	.05
185	Jeff Conine	.05
186	Chris Hammond	.05
187	Charles Johnson	.05
188	Terry Pendleton	.05
189	Pat Rapp	.05
190	Gary Sheffield	.25
191	Quilvio Veras	.05
192	Devon White	.05
193	Jeff Bagwell	.60
194	Derek Bell	.05
195	Sean Berry	.05
196	Craig Biggio	.05
197	Doug Drabek	.05
198	Tony Eusebio	.05
199	Mike Hampton	.05
200	Brian Hunter	.05
201	Derrick May	.05
202	Orlando Miller	.05
203	Shane Reynolds	.05
204	Mike Blowers	.05
205	Tom Candiotti	.05
206	Delino DeShields	.05
207	Greg Gagne	.05
208	Karim Garcia	.05
209	Todd Hollandsworth	.05
210	Eric Karros	.05
211	Ramon Martinez	.05
212	Raul Mondesi	.05
213	Hideo Nomo	.30
214	Chan Ho Park	.05
215	Mike Piazza	1.25
216	Ismael Valdes	.05
217	Todd Worrell	.05
218	Moises Alou	.05
219	Yamil Benitez	.05
220	Jeff Fassero	.05
221	Darrin Fletcher	.05
222	Cliff Floyd	.05
223	Pedro Martinez	.60
224	Carlos Perez	.05
225	Mel Rojas	.05
226	David Segui	.05
227	Rondell White	.05
228	Rico Brogna	.05
229	Carl Everett	.05
230	John Franco	.05
231	Bernard Gilkey	.05
232	Todd Hundley	.05
233	Jason Isringhausen	.05
234	Lance Johnson	.05
235	Bobby Jones	.05
236	Jeff Kent	.05
237	Rey Ordonez	.05
238	Bill Pulsipher	.05
239	Jose Vizcaino	.05
240	Paul Wilson	.05
241	Ricky Bottalico	.05
242	Darren Daulton	.05
243	Lenny Dykstra	.05
244	Jim Eisenreich	.05
245	Sid Fernandez	.05
246	Gregg Jefferies	.05
247	Mickey Morandini	.05
248	Benito Santiago	.05
249	Curt Schilling	.35
250	Mark Whiten	.05
251	Todd Zeile	.05
252	Jay Bell	.05
253	Carlos Garcia	.05
254	Charlie Hayes	.05
255	Jason Kendall	.05
256	Jeff King	.05
257	Al Martin	.05
258	Orlando Merced	.05
259	Dan Miceli	.05
260	Denny Neagle	.05
261	Alan Benes	.05
262	Andy Benes	.05
263	Royce Clayton	.05
264	Dennis Eckersley	.50
265	Gary Gaetti	.05
266	Ron Gant	.05
267	Brian Jordan	.05
268	Ray Lankford	.05
269	John Mabry	.05
270	Tom Pagnozzi	.05
271	Ozzie Smith	.75
272	Todd Stottlemyre	.05
273	Andy Ashby	.05
274	Brad Ausmus	.05
275	Ken Caminiti	.05
276	Steve Finley	.05
277	Tony Gwynn	.75
278	Joey Hamilton	.05
279	Rickey Henderson	.60
280	Trevor Hoffman	.05
281	Wally Joyner	.05
282	Jody Reed	.05
283	Bob Tewksbury	.05
284	Fernando Valenzuela	.05
285	Rod Beck	.05
286	Barry Bonds	2.00
287	Mark Carreon	.05
288	Shawon Dunston	.05
289	Osvaldo Fernandez RC	.10
290	Glenallen Hill	.05

Abbreviations

OPS - Overprinted "Promotional Sample"

291	Stan Javier Jr.	.05
292	Mark Leiter	.05
293	Kirt Manwaring	.05
294	Robby Thompson	.05
295	William	.05
	Van Landingham	.05
296	Allen Watson	.05
297	Matt Williams	.05
298	Checklist	.05
299	Checklist	.05
300	Checklist	.05

D-Fense

Ten top defensive players are featured on these 1996 SkyBox E-Motion XL insert cards. The cards were seeded at a rate of one per every four packs.

		NM/M
Complete Set (10):		9.00
Common Player:		.50
1	Roberto Alomar	.65
2	Barry Bonds	3.50
3	Mark Grace	.50
4	Ken Griffey Jr.	2.50
5	Kenny Lofton	.50
6	Greg Maddux	1.50
7	Raul Mondesi	.50
8	Cal Ripken Jr.	3.50
9	Ivan Rodriguez	1.00
10	Matt Williams	.50

Legion of Boom

The top power hitters in baseball are featured on these 1996 SkyBox E-Motion XL insert cards. The cards, exclusive to hobby packs at a ratio of one per every 36 packs, have translucent card backs.

		NM/M
Complete Set (12):		27.50
Common Player:		2.00
1	Albert Belle	2.00
2	Barry Bonds	6.00
3	Juan Gonzalez	2.50
4	Ken Griffey Jr.	4.00
5	Mark McGwire	5.00
6	Mike Piazza	4.00
7	Manny Ramirez	3.00
8	Tim Salmon	2.00
9	Sammy Sosa	3.50
10	Frank Thomas	3.00
11	Mo Vaughn	2.00
12	Matt Williams	2.00

N-Tense

Ten top clutch performers are featured on these 1996 SkyBox E-Motion XL insert cards. The cards, which use an N-shaped die-cut design, were included one per every 12 packs.

		NM/M
Complete Set (10):		17.50
Common Player:		.50
1	Albert Belle	.50
2	Barry Bonds	3.50
3	Jose Canseco	1.00
4	Ken Griffey Jr.	3.00
5	Tony Gwynn	2.50
6	Randy Johnson	2.00

7	Greg Maddux	2.50
8	Cal Ripken Jr.	3.50
9	Frank Thomas	2.00
10	Matt Williams	.50

Rare Breed

These 1996 E-Motion XL inserts are the most difficult to find; they are seeded one per every 100 packs. The cards showcase top young stars on a 3-D lenticular-motion design.

		NM/M
Complete Set (10):		50.00
Common Player:		3.00
1	Garret Anderson	3.00
2	Marty Cordova	3.00
3	Brian Hunter	3.00
4	Jason Isringhausen	3.00
5	Charles Johnson	3.00
6	Chipper Jones	16.00
7	Raul Mondesi	3.00
8	Hideo Nomo	6.00
9	Manny Ramirez	12.00
10	Rondell White	3.00

1997 SkyBox E-X2000 Sample

To introduce its innovative high-tech premium brand, Sky-Box released this promo card. It is identical in format to the issued version, except it carries a "SAMPLE" notation instead of a card number on back.

	NM/M
Alex Rodriguez	4.00

1997 SkyBox E-X2000

The premiere issue of E-X2000 consists of 100 base cards designed with "SkyView" technology, utilizing a die-cut holofoil border and the player silhouetted in front of a transparent "window" featuring a variety of sky patterns. Inserts include two sequentially-numbered parallel sets - Credentials

(1:50 packs) and Essential Credentials (1:200 packs) - as well as Emerald Autograph Exchange Cards, A Cut Above, Hall of Nothing, and Star Date. Cards were sold in two-card packs for $3.99 each.

		NM/M
Complete Set (100):		20.00
Common Player:		.15
Credentials Stars:		6X
Essential Credentials:		10X
Pack (2):		1.25
Wax Box (24):		20.00
1	Jim Edmonds	.15
2	Darin Erstad	.25
3	Eddie Murray	1.00
4	Roberto Alomar	.25
5	Brady Anderson	.15
6	Mike Mussina	.45
7	Rafael Palmeiro	.75
8	Cal Ripken Jr.	3.00
9	Steve Avery	.15
10	Nomar Garciaparra	1.50
11	Mo Vaughn	.15
12	Albert Belle	.15
13	Mike Cameron	.15
14	Ray Durham	.15
15	Frank Thomas	1.00
16	Robin Ventura	.15
17	Manny Ramirez	1.00
18	Jim Thome	.65
19	Matt Williams	.15
20	Tony Clark	.15
21	Travis Fryman	.15
22	Bob Higginson	.15
23	Kevin Appier	.15
24	Johnny Damon	.45
25	Jermaine Dye	.15
26	Jeff Cirillo	.15
27	Ben McDonald	.15
28	Chuck Knoblauch	.15
29	Paul Molitor	1.00
30	Todd Walker	.15
31	Wade Boggs	1.50
32	Cecil Fielder	.15
33	Derek Jeter	3.00
34	Andy Pettitte	.25
35	Ruben Rivera	.15
36	Bernie Williams	.15
37	Jose Canseco	.15
38	Mark McGwire	2.50
39	Jay Buhner	.15
40	Ken Griffey Jr.	2.00
41	Randy Johnson	1.00
42	Edgar Martinez	.15
43	Alex Rodriguez	2.50
44	Dan Wilson	.15
45	Will Clark	.40
46	Juan Gonzalez	.50
47	Ivan Rodriguez	.75
48	Joe Carter	.15
49	Roger Clemens	1.75
50	Juan Guzman	.15
51	Pat Hentgen	.15
52	Tom Glavine	.35
53	Andruw Jones	1.00
54	Chipper Jones	1.50
55	Ryan Klesko	.15
56	Kenny Lofton	.15
57	Greg Maddux	1.50
58	Fred McGriff	.15
59	John Smoltz	.15
60	Mark Wohlers	.15
61	Mark Grace	.15
62	Ryne Sandberg	1.50
63	Sammy Sosa	1.50
64	Barry Larkin	.15
65	Deion Sanders	.15
66	Reggie Sanders	.15
67	Dante Bichette	.15
68	Ellis Burks	.15
69	Andres Galarraga	.15
70	Moises Alou	.15
71	Kevin Brown	.15
72	Cliff Floyd	.15
73	Edgar Renteria	.15
74	Gary Sheffield	.50
75	Bob Abreu	.15
76	Jeff Bagwell	1.00
77	Craig Biggio	.15
78	Todd Hollandsworth	.15
79	Eric Karros	.15
80	Raul Mondesi	.15
81	Hideo Nomo	.50
82	Mike Piazza	2.00

83	Vladimir Guerrero	1.00
84	Henry Rodriguez	.15
85	Todd Hundley	.15
86	Rey Ordonez	.15
87	Alex Ochoa	.15
88	Gregg Jefferies	.15
89	Scott Rolen	.65
90	Jermaine Allensworth	.15
91	Jason Kendall	.15
92	Ken Caminiti	.15
93	Tony Gwynn	1.50
94	Rickey Henderson	1.00
95	Barry Bonds	3.00
96	J.T. Snow	.15
97	Dennis Eckersley	.75
98	Ron Gant	.15
99	Brian Jordan	.15
100	Ray Lankford	.15

Credentials

This parallel set features different colored foils from the base cards, as well as different images on the "window." Cards are sequentially numbered on back within an issue of 299. Cards were inserted 1:50 packs.

	NM/M
Common Player:	1.00
Credentials Stars:	6X

Essential Credentials

A sequentially-numbered parallel set, found one per 200 packs, and limited to 99 total sets.

	NM/M
Common Player:	3.00
Essential Credentials Stars:	10X

A Cut Above

Some of the game's elite players are featured in this 1:288 pack insert that features a die-cut design resembling a saw blade. Printed on silver-foil stock, the player's name and Cut Above logo are embossed on front. On back is another color photo and a few words about the player.

Complete Set (10):		55.00
Common Player:		2.00
1	Frank Thomas	7.50
2	Ken Griffey Jr.	9.00
3	Alex Rodriguez	12.00
4	Albert Belle	2.00
5	Juan Gonzalez	4.00
6	Mark McGwire	10.00
7	Mo Vaughn	2.00
8	Manny Ramirez	7.50
9	Barry Bonds	12.00
10	Fred McGriff	2.00

Emerald Autograph Redemptions

Inserted 1:480 packs, these cards could be exchanged by mail prior to May 1, 1998 for autographed cards or memorabilia from one of six major leaguers.

		NM/M
Complete Set (6):		17.50
Common Player:		1.00
(1)	Darin Erstad	2.50
(2)	Todd Hollandsworth	1.00
(3)	Alex Ochoa	1.00
(4)	Alex Rodriguez	10.00
(5)	Scott Rolen	3.00
(6)	Todd Walker	1.00

Emerald Autographs

These authentically autographed versions of the players' E-X2000 cards were available (until May 1, 1998) by a mail-in exchange of redemption cards. The autographed cards are authenticated by the presence of an embossed SkyBox logo seal.

		NM/M
Complete Set (6):		75.00
Common Player:		3.00
2	Darin Erstad	12.00
30	Todd Walker	5.00
43	Alex Rodriguez	60.00
78	Todd Hollandsworth	3.00
86	Alex Ochoa	3.00
89	Scott Rolen	25.00

Hall or Nothing

This 20-card insert, featuring players who are candidates for the Hall of Fame, utilizes a die-cut design on plastic stock. Stately architectural details and brush bronze highlights frame the player picture on front. The player silhouette on back contains career information. Cards were inserted 1:20 packs.

		NM/M
Complete Set (20):		55.00
Common Player:		1.00
1	Frank Thomas	2.50
2	Ken Griffey Jr.	5.00
3	Eddie Murray	2.50
4	Cal Ripken Jr.	7.00

5	Ryne Sandberg	4.00
6	Wade Boggs	4.00
7	Roger Clemens	4.50
8	Tony Gwynn	4.00
9	Alex Rodriguez	6.00
10	Mark McGwire	6.00
11	Barry Bonds	7.00
12	Greg Maddux	4.00
13	Juan Gonzalez	1.25
14	Albert Belle	1.00
15	Mike Piazza	5.00
16	Jeff Bagwell	2.50
17	Dennis Eckersley	1.50
18	Mo Vaughn	1.00
19	Roberto Alomar	1.00
20	Kenny Lofton	1.00

Alex Rodriguez Jumbo

This 8" x 10" version of A-Rod's SkyBox E-X2000 card was given to dealers who ordered case quantities of the new product. The card is identical in design to the standard-sized issued version, but is numbered on back from within an edition of 3,000.

	NM/M
Alex Rodriguez	12.00

Star Date 2000

A 15-card set highlighting young stars that are likely to be the game's top players in the year 2000. Cards were inserted 1:9 packs.

		NM/M
Complete Set (15):		10.00
Common Player:		.40
1	Alex Rodriguez	2.00
2	Andruw Jones	1.25
3	Andy Pettitte	.60
4	Brooks Kieschnick	.40
5	Chipper Jones	1.50
6	Darin Erstad	.60
7	Derek Jeter	2.50
8	Jason Kendall	.40
9	Jermaine Dye	.40
10	Neifi Perez	.40
11	Scott Rolen	.90
12	Todd Hollandsworth	.40
13	Todd Walker	.40
14	Tony Clark	.40
15	Vladimir Guerrero	1.25

1998 SkyBox E-X2001 Sample

To preview its high-tech E-X2001 brand for 1998, Sky-Box issued this sample card of A-Rod. Similar in format to the issued version, it is numbered "SAMPLE" on back and has a "PROMOTIONAL SAMPLE" overprint on back.

	NM/M
Alex Rodriguez	2.00

1998 SkyBox E-X2001

This super-premium set featured 100 players on a layered, die-cuct design utilizing mirror-image silhouetted photography and etched holofoil treatment over a clear, 20-point plastic card.

		NM/M
Complete Set (100):		25.00
Common Player:		.15
Pack (2):		1.50
Wax Box (24):		25.00
1	Alex Rodriguez	2.50
2	Barry Bonds	3.00
3	Greg Maddux	1.50
4	Roger Clemens	1.75
5	Juan Gonzalez	.50
6	Chipper Jones	1.50
7	Derek Jeter	3.00
8	Frank Thomas	1.00
9	Cal Ripken Jr.	3.00
10	Ken Griffey Jr.	2.00
11	Mark McGwire	2.50
12	Hideo Nomo	.50
13	Tony Gwynn	1.50
14	Ivan Rodriguez	.75
15	Mike Piazza	2.00
16	Roberto Alomar	.30
17	Jeff Bagwell	1.00
18	Andruw Jones	1.00
19	Albert Belle	.15
20	Mo Vaughn	.15
21	Kenny Lofton	.15
22	Gary Sheffield	.15
23	Tony Clark	.15
24	Mike Mussina	.30
25	Barry Larkin	.15
26	Moises Alou	.15
27	Brady Anderson	.15
28	Andy Pettitte	.25
29	Sammy Sosa	1.50
30	Raul Mondesi	.15
31	Andres Galarraga	.15
32	Chuck Knoblauch	.15
33	Jim Thome	.65
34	Craig Biggio	.15
35	Jay Buhner	.15
36	Rafael Palmeiro	.75
37	Curt Schilling	.35
38	Tino Martinez	.15
39	Pedro Martinez	1.00
40	Jose Canseco	.50
41	Jeff Cirillo	.15
42	Dean Palmer	.15
43	Tim Salmon	.15
44	Jason Giambi	.50
45	Bobby Higginson	.15
46	Jim Edmonds	.15
47	David Justice	.15
48	John Olerud	.15
49	Ray Lankford	.15
50	Al Martin	.15
51	Mike Lieberthal	.15
52	Henry Rodriguez	.15
53	Edgar Renteria	.15
54	Eric Karros	.15
55	Marquis Grissom	.15
56	Wilson Alvarez	.15
57	Darryl Kile	.15
58	Jeff King	.15
59	Shawn Estes	.15
60	Tony Womack	.15
61	Willie Greene	.15
62	Ken Caminiti	.15
63	Vinny Castilla	.15
64	Mark Grace	.15
65	Ryan Klesko	.15
66	Robin Ventura	.15
67	Todd Hundley	.15
68	Travis Fryman	.15
69	Edgar Martinez	.15
70	Matt Williams	.15
71	Paul Molitor	1.00
72	Kevin Brown	.15
73	Randy Johnson	1.00
74	Bernie Williams	.10
75	Manny Ramirez	1.00
76	Fred McGriff	.15
77	Tom Glavine	.35
78	Carlos Delgado	.60
79	Larry Walker	.15
80	Hideki Irabu	.15
81	Ryan McGuire	.15
82	Justin Thompson	.15
83	Kevin Orie	.15
84	Jon Nunnally	.15
85	Mark Kotsay	.15
86	Todd Walker	.15
87	Jason Dickson	.15
88	Fernando Tatis	.15
89	Karim Garcia	.15
90	Ricky Ledee	.15
91	Paul Konerko	.25
92	Jaret Wright	.15
93	Darin Erstad	.30
94	Livan Hernandez	.15
95	Nomar Garciaparra	1.50
96	Jose Cruz Jr.	.15
97	Scott Rolen	.65
98	Ben Grieve	.15
99	Vladimir Guerrero	1.00
100	Travis Lee	.15

Essential Credentials Future

Essential Credentials Future, along with Essential Credentials Now, paralleled all 100 cards in the base set. Production varied depending on the card number, with the exact production number of each player determined by subtracting his card number from 101. Number issued for each card is shown in parentheses.

		NM/M
Common Player:		5.00
1	Alex Rodriguez/100	55.00
2	Barry Bonds/99	60.00
3	Greg Maddux/98	40.00
4	Roger Clemens/97	45.00
5	Juan Gonzalez/96	15.00
6	Chipper Jones/95	40.00
7	Derek Jeter/94	55.00
8	Frank Thomas/93	35.00
9	Cal Ripken Jr./92	45.00
10	Ken Griffey Jr./91	45.00
11	Mark McGwire/90	45.00
12	Hideo Nomo/89	15.00
13	Tony Gwynn/88	25.00
14	Ivan Rodriguez/87	40.00
15	Roberto Alomar/85	15.00
16	Jeff Bagwell/84	25.00
17	Andruw Jones/83	25.00
18	Albert Belle/82	5.00
19	Mo Vaughn/81	5.00
20	Kenny Lofton/80	5.00
21	Gary Sheffield/79	12.00
22	Tony Clark/78	5.00
23	Mike Mussina/77	25.00
24	Barry Larkin/76	5.00
25	Moises Alou/75	5.00
26	Brady Anderson/74	5.00
27	Andy Pettitte/73	7.50
28	Sammy Sosa/72	40.00
29	Raul Mondesi/71	5.00
30	Andres Galarraga/70	6.00
31	Chuck Knoblauch/69	6.00
32	Jim Thome/68	20.00
33	Craig Biggio/67	6.00
34	Jay Buhner/66	6.00
35	Rafael Palmeiro/65	30.00
36	Curt Schilling/64	20.00
37	Tino Martinez/63	6.00
38	Pedro Martinez/62	32.50
39	Jose Canseco/61	30.00
40	Jeff Cirillo/60	6.00
41	Dean Palmer/59	6.00
42	Tim Salmon/58	7.50
43	Jason Giambi/57	25.00
44	Bobby Higginson/56	6.00
45	Jim Edmonds/55	6.00
46	David Justice/54	6.00
47	John Olerud/53	6.00
48	Ray Lankford/52	6.00
49	Al Martin/51	6.00
50	Mike Lieberthal/50	6.00
51	Henry Rodriguez/49	6.00
52	Edgar Renteria/48	6.00
53	Eric Karros/47	6.00
54	Marquis Grissom/46	6.00
55	Wilson Alvarez/45	6.00
56	Darryl Kile/44	6.00
57	Jeff King/43	6.00
58	Shawn Estes/42	6.00
59	Tony Womack/41	6.00
60	Willie Greene/40	6.00
61	Ken Caminiti/39	6.00
62	Vinny Castilla/38	6.00
63	Mark Grace/37	6.00
64	Ryan Klesko/36	6.00
65	Robin Ventura/35	6.00
66	Todd Hundley/34	6.00
67	Travis Fryman/33	6.00
68	Edgar Martinez/32	7.50
69	Matt Williams/31	6.00
70	Paul Molitor/30	45.00
71	Kevin Brown/29	7.50
72	Randy Johnson/28	40.00
73	Bernie Williams/27	20.00
74	Manny Ramirez/26	45.00
75	Fred McGriff/25	9.00
76	Tom Glavine/24	15.00
77	Carlos Delgado/23	35.00
78	Larry Walker/22	9.00
79	Hideki Irabu/21	9.00
80	Ryan McGuire/20	9.00
81	Justin Thompson/19	9.00
82	Kevin Orie/18	9.00
83	Jon Nunnally/17	9.00
84	Mark Kotsay/16	9.00

Essential Credentials Now

Essential Credentials Now parallels all 100 cards in the E-X2001 base set. Production for each card was limited to that player's card number, as shown in parentheses.

		NM/M
Common Player:		5.00
1	Alex Rodriguez/1	850.00
2	Barry Bonds/2	650.00
3	Greg Maddux/3	175.00
4	Roger Clemens/4	200.00
5	Juan Gonzalez/5	75.00
6	Chipper Jones/6	160.00
7	Derek Jeter/7	350.00
8	Frank Thomas/8	150.00
9	Cal Ripken Jr./9	350.00
10	Ken Griffey Jr./10	350.00
11	Mark McGwire/11	250.00
12	Hideo Nomo/12	45.00
13	Tony Gwynn/13	75.00
14	Ivan Rodriguez/14	55.00
15	Mike Piazza/15	90.00
16	Roberto Alomar/16	30.00
17	Jeff Bagwell/17	50.00
18	Andruw Jones/18	50.00
19	Albert Belle/19	15.00
20	Mo Vaughn/20	15.00
21	Kenny Lofton/21	10.00
22	Gary Sheffield/22	10.00
23	Tony Clark/23	10.00
24	Mike Mussina/24	30.00
25	Barry Larkin/25	10.00
26	Moises Alou/26	10.00
27	Brady Anderson/27	10.00
28	Andy Pettitte/28	15.00
29	Sammy Sosa/29	140.00
30	Raul Mondesi/30	10.00
31	Andres Galarraga/31	10.00
32	Chuck Knoblauch/32	10.00
33	Jim Thome/33	25.00
34	Craig Biggio/34	10.00
35	Jay Buhner/35	10.00
36	Rafael Palmeiro/36	25.00
37	Curt Schilling/37	20.00
38	Tino Martinez/38	10.00
39	Pedro Martinez/39	35.00
40	Jose Canseco/40	30.00
41	Jeff Cirillo/41	7.50
42	Dean Palmer/42	7.50
43	Tim Salmon/43	7.50
44	Jason Giambi/44	25.00
45	Bobby Higginson/45	7.50
46	Jim Edmonds/46	7.50
47	David Justice/47	7.50
48	John Olerud/48	7.50
49	Ray Lankford/49	5.00
50	Al Martin/50	5.00
51	Mike Lieberthal/51	5.00
52	Henry Rodriguez/52	5.00
53	Edgar Renteria/53	5.00
54	Eric Karros/54	5.00
55	Marquis Grissom/55	5.00
56	Wilson Alvarez/56	5.00
57	Darryl Kile/57	5.00
58	Jeff King/58	5.00
59	Shawn Estes/59	5.00
60	Tony Womack/60	5.00
61	Willie Greene/61	5.00
62	Ken Caminiti/62	5.00
63	Vinny Castilla/63	5.00
64	Mark Grace/64	5.00
65	Ryan Klesko/65	5.00
66	Robin Ventura/66	5.00
67	Todd Hundley/67	5.00
68	Travis Fryman/68	5.00
69	Edgar Martinez/69	5.00
70	Matt Williams/70	5.00
71	Paul Molitor/71	20.00
72	Kevin Brown/72	5.00
73	Randy Johnson/73	20.00
74	Bernie Williams/74	5.00
75	Manny Ramirez/75	20.00
76	Fred McGriff/76	5.00
77	Tom Glavine/77	12.00
78	Carlos Delgado/78	15.00
79	Larry Walker/79	5.00
80	Hideki Irabu/80	5.00
81	Ryan McGuire/81	5.00
82	Justin Thompson/82	5.00
83	Kevin Orie/83	5.00
84	Jon Nunnally/84	5.00
85	Mark Kotsay/85	5.00
86	Todd Walker/86	5.00
87	Jason Dickson/87	5.00
88	Fernando Tatis/88	5.00
89	Karim Garcia/89	5.00
90	Ricky Ledee/90	5.00
91	Paul Konerko/91	7.50
92	Jaret Wright/92	5.00
93	Darin Erstad/93	7.50
94	Livan Hernandez/94	5.00
95	Nomar Garciaparra/95	35.00
96	Jose Cruz Jr./96	5.00
97	Scott Rolen/97	12.00
98	Ben Grieve/98	5.00
99	Vladimir Guerrero/99	17.50
100	Travis Lee/100	5.00

Cheap Seat Treats

This 20-card die-cut insert arrived in the shape of a stadium seat. Inserted at one per 24 packs, Cheap Seat Treats included some of the top home run hitters and were numbered with a "CS" prefix.

		NM/M
Complete Set (20):		30.00
Common Player:		1.00
Inserted 1:24		
1	Frank Thomas	2.00
2	Ken Griffey Jr.	3.00
3	Mark McGwire	4.00
4	Tino Martinez	1.00
5	Larry Walker	1.00
6	Juan Gonzalez	1.50
7	Mike Piazza	1.50
8	Jeff Bagwell	2.00
9	Tony Clark	1.00
10	Albert Belle	1.00
11	Andres Galarraga	1.00
12	Jim Thome	1.50
13	Mo Vaughn	1.00
14	Barry Bonds	1.00
15	Vladimir Guerrero	2.00
16	Scott Rolen	1.25
17	Travis Lee	1.00
18	David Justice	1.00
19	Jose Cruz Jr.	1.00
20	Andruw Jones	2.00

Destination: Cooperstown

Destination: Cooperstown captures a mixture of rising young stars and top veterans on die-cut cards that were inserted one per 720 packs. Cards resemble a luggage tag and have a string through a hole at top. Fronts have an action photo, backs have a portrait. Cards are numbered with a "DC" prefix.

		NM/M
Complete Set (15):		375.00
Common Player:		8.00
Inserted 1:720		

Signature 2001

Seventeen top young and future stars signed cards for Signature 2001 inserts in E-X2001. The cards featured the player over a blue and white, sky-like background, with an embossed SkyBox seal of authenticity. Backs were horizontal and also included a Certificate of Authenticity. These cards were unnumbered and inserted one per 60 packs.

		NM/M
Complete Set (17):		100.00
Common Player:		3.00
Inserted 1:60		
1	Ricky Ledee	3.00
2	Derrick Gibson	3.00
3	Mark Kotsay	3.00
4	Kevin Millwood	10.00
5	Brad Fullmer	3.00
6	Todd Walker	4.00
7	Ben Grieve	3.00
8	Tony Clark	4.00
9	Jaret Wright	3.00
10	Randall Simon	3.00
11	Paul Konerko	15.00
12	Todd Helton	15.00
13	David Ortiz	30.00
14	Alex Gonzalez	4.00
15	Bobby Estalella	3.00
16	Alex Rodriguez	50.00
17	Mike Lowell	7.50

Star Date 2001

Star Date 2001 displays 15 of the top rising stars on an acetate space/planet background with gold-foil printing on front. This insert was seeded one per 12 packs and was numbered with a "SD" prefix.

		NM/M
Complete Set (15):		5.00
Common Player:		.25
Inserted 1:12		
1	Travis Lee	.25
2	Jose Cruz Jr.	.25
3	Paul Konerko	1.00
4	Bobby Estalella	.25
5	Magglio Ordonez	1.00
6	Juan Encarnacion	.25
7	Richard Hidalgo	.25
8	Abraham Nunez	.25
9	Sean Casey	.50
10	Todd Helton	1.50
11	Brad Fullmer	.25
12	Ben Grieve	.25
13	Livan Hernandez	.25
14	Jaret Wright	.25
15	Todd Dunwoody	.25

Kerry Wood

In an effort to get rookie pitching phenom Kerry Wood

into its E-X2001 set, SkyBox created a cardboard, rather than plastic, trade card and inserted it at a rate of one per 50 packs. The trade card could be exchanged by mail for a plastic version.

		NM/M
Complete Set (2):		2.00
---	Kerry Wood (Cardboard trade card.)	1.00
101	Kerry Wood (Plastic redemption card.)	4.00

1998 SkyBox Dugout Axcess Promo

This introduction to Sky-Box's new brand is labeled front and back as a "PROMO-TIONAL SAMPLE."

		NM/M
15	Alex Rodriguez	3.00

1998 SkyBox Dugout Axcess

Dugout Axcess was a 150-card set that attempted to provide collectors with an inside look at baseball. The cards were printed on "playing card" quality stock and used unique information and photography. The product arrived in 12-card packs with an Inside Axcess parallel set that was individually numbered to 50 sets. Six different inserts were available, including Double Header, Frequent Flyers, Dishwashers, Superheroes, Gronks and Autograph Redemptions.

		NM/M
Complete Set (150):		12.00
Common Player:		.05
Inside Axcess Stars:		25X
Production 50 Sets		
Pack (12):		1.00
Wax Box (36):		20.00
1	Travis Lee	.05

2	Matt Williams	.05
3	Andy Benes	.05
4	Chipper Jones	.75
5	Ryan Klesko	.05
6	Greg Maddux	.75
7	Sammy Sosa	.75
8	Henry Rodriguez	.05
9	Mark Grace	.05
10	Barry Larkin	.05
11	Bret Boone	.05
12	Reggie Sanders	.05
13	Vinny Castilla	.05
14	Larry Walker	.05
15	Darryl Kile	.05
16	Charles Johnson	.05
17	Edgar Renteria	.05
18	Gary Sheffield	.40
19	Jeff Bagwell	.65
20	Craig Biggio	.05
21	Moises Alou	.05
22	Mike Piazza	1.00
23	Hideo Nomo	.35
24	Raul Mondesi	.05
25	John Jaha	.05
26	Jeff Cirillo	.05
27	Jeromy Burnitz	.05
28	Mark Grudzielanek	.05
29	Vladimir Guerrero	.65
30	Rondell White	.05
31	Edgardo Alfonzo	.05
32	Rey Ordonez	.05
33	Bernard Gilkey	.05
34	Scott Rolen	.50
35	Curt Schilling	.35
36	Ricky Bottalico	.05
37	Tony Womack	.05
38	Al Martin	.05
39	Jason Kendall	.05
40	Ron Gant	.05
41	Mark McGwire	1.25
42	Ray Lankford	.05
43	Tony Gwynn	.75
44	Ken Caminiti	.05
45	Kevin Brown	.05
46	Barry Bonds	1.50
47	J.T. Snow	.05
48	Shawn Estes	.05
49	Jim Edmonds	.05
50	Tim Salmon	.05
51	Jason Dickson	.05
52	Cal Ripken Jr.	1.50
53	Mike Mussina	.35
54	Roberto Alomar	.20
55	Mo Vaughn	.05
56	Pedro Martinez	.65
57	Nomar Garciaparra	.75
58	Albert Belle	.05
59	Frank Thomas	.65
60	Robin Ventura	.05
61	Jim Thome	.60
62	Sandy Alomar Jr.	.05
63	Jaret Wright	.05
64	Bobby Higginson	.05
65	Tony Clark	.05
66	Justin Thompson	.05
67	Dean Palmer	.05
68	Kevin Appier	.05
69	Johnny Damon	.35
70	Paul Molitor	.65
71	Marty Cordova	.05
72	Brad Radke	.05
73	Derek Jeter	1.50
74	Bernie Williams	.05
75	Andy Pettitte	.25
76	Matt Stairs	.05
77	Ben Grieve	.05
78	Jason Giambi	.50
79	Randy Johnson	.65
80	Ken Griffey Jr.	1.00
81	Alex Rodriguez	1.25
82	Fred McGriff	.05
83	Wade Boggs	.75
84	Wilson Alvarez	.05
85	Juan Gonzalez	.35
86	Ivan Rodriguez	.50
87	Fernando Tatis	.05
88	Roger Clemens	.85
89	Jose Cruz Jr.	.05
90	Shawn Green	.30
91	Jeff Suppan	
	(Little Dawgs)	.05
92	Eli Marrero	
	(Little Dawgs)	.05
93	Mike Lowell RC	
	(Little Dawgs)	.50
94	Ben Grieve	
	(Little Dawgs)	.05
95	Cliff Politte	
	(Little Dawgs)	.05
96	Rolando Arrojo RC	
	(Little Dawgs)	.25
97	Mike Caruso	
	(Little Dawgs)	.05
98	Miguel Tejada	
	(Little Dawgs)	.15
99	Rod Myers	
	(Little Dawgs)	.05
100	Juan Encarnacion	
	(Little Dawgs)	.05
101	Enrique Wilson	
	(Little Dawgs)	.05
102	Brian Giles	
	(Little Dawgs)	.05
103	Magglio Ordonez RC	
	(Little Dawgs)	1.00
104	Brian Rose	
	(Little Dawgs)	.05

105	Ryan Jackson RC	
	(Little Dawgs)	.05
106	Mark Kotsay	
	(Little Dawgs)	.05
107	Desi Relaford	
	(Little Dawgs)	.05
108	A.J. Hinch	
	(Little Dawgs)	.05
109	Eric Milton	
	(Little Dawgs)	.05
110	Ricky Ledee	
	(Little Dawgs)	.05
111	Karim Garcia	
	(Little Dawgs)	.05
112	Derrek Lee	
	(Little Dawgs)	.60
113	Brad Fullmer	
	(Little Dawgs)	.05
114	Travis Lee	
	(Little Dawgs)	.05
115	Greg Norton	
	(Little Dawgs)	.05
116	Rich Butler	
	(Little Dawgs)	.05
117	Masato Yoshii RC	
	(Little Dawgs)	.25
118	Paul Konerko	
	(Little Dawgs)	.20
119	Richard Hidalgo	
	(Little Dawgs)	.05
120	Todd Helton	
	(Little Dawgs)	.60
121	Nomar Garciaparra	
	(7th Inning Sketch)	.40
122	Scott Rolen	
	(7th Inning Sketch)	.25
123	Cal Ripken Jr.	
	(7th Inning Sketch)	.75
124	Derek Jeter	
	(7th Inning Sketch)	.75
125	Mike Piazza	
	(7th Inning Sketch)	.45
126	Tony Gwynn	
	(7th Inning Sketch)	.40
127	Mark McGwire	
	(7th Inning Sketch)	.65
128	Kenny Lofton	
	(7th Inning Sketch)	.05
129	Greg Maddux	
	(7th Inning Sketch)	.40
130	Jeff Bagwell	
	(7th Inning Sketch)	.30
131	Randy Johnson	
	(7th Inning Sketch)	.30
132	Alex Rodriguez	
	(7th Inning Sketch)	.65
133	Mo Vaughn	
	(Name Plates)	.05
134	Chipper Jones	
	(Name Plates)	.40
135	Juan Gonzalez	
	(Name Plates)	.15
136	Tony Clark	
	(Name Plates)	.05
137	Fred McGriff	
	(Name Plates)	.05
138	Roger Clemens	
	(Name Plates)	.45
139	Ken Griffey Jr.	
	(Name Plates)	.65
140	Ivan Rodriguez	
	(Name Plates)	.25
141	Vinny Castilla	
	(Trivia Card)	.05
142	Livan Hernandez	
	(Trivia Card)	.05
143	Jose Cruz Jr.	
	(Trivia Card)	.05
144	Andruw Jones	
	(Trivia Card)	.30
145	Rafael Palmeiro	
	(Trivia Card)	.50
146	Chuck Knoblauch	
	(Trivia Card)	.05
147	Jay Buhner	
	(Trivia Card)	.05
148	Andres Galarraga	
	(Trivia Card)	.05
149	Frank Thomas	
	(Trivia Card)	.35
150	Todd Hundley	
	(Trivia Card)	.05

Inside Axcess

ken griffey jr.

This 150-card parallel set was sequentially numbered to 50 sets, with each card containing a stamped logo on the front and serial numbering on the back.

	NM/M
Common Player:	4.00
Inside Axcess Stars:	25X

Autograph Redemption Cards

These scarce - one per 96 packs - inserts were redeemable (until March 31, 1999) for autographed baseballs or gloves from more than a dozen established stars and promising youngsters. Because the cards do not picture the player involved, having a generic photo of a person's arm signing an autograph, the exchange cards don't have tremendous collector value now that the redemption period has expired. The autographed balls and gloves would be valued according to supply and demand in the memorabilia marketplace.

		NM/M
Complete Set (15):		37.00
Common Card:		1.50
(1)	Jay Buhner/Ball	1.50
(2)	Roger Clemens/Ball	3.00
(3)	Jose Cruz Jr./Ball	2.25
(4)	Darin Erstad/Glv	4.50
(5)	Nomar Garciaparra/Ball	3.00
(6)	Tony Gwynn/Ball	2.75
(7)	Roberto Hernandez/Ball	1.50
(8)	Todd Hollandsworth/Glv	3.00
(9)	Greg Maddux/Ball	3.00
(10)	Alex Ochoa/Glv	3.00
(11)	Alex Rodriguez/Ball	4.00
(12)	Scott Rolen/Glv	4.50
(13)	Scott Rolen/Ball	2.50
(14)	Todd Walker/Glv	3.00
(15)	Tony Womack/Ball	1.50

Dishwashers

DISHWASHERS

This 10-card set was a tribute to the game's best pitchers who "clean the home plate of opposing batters." Cards were inserted one per eight packs.

		NM/M
Complete Set (10):		7.00
Common Player:		.50
Inserted 1:8		
D1	Greg Maddux	2.00
D2	Kevin Brown	.50
D3	Pedro Martinez	1.00
D4	Randy Johnson	1.00
D5	Curt Schilling	.75
D6	John Smoltz	.50
D7	Darryl Kile	.50
D8	Roger Clemens	2.25
D9	Andy Pettitte	.60
D10	Mike Mussina	.65

Double Header

Double Header featured 20 players on cards that doubled as game pieces. The game instructions were on the card and required two dice to play. These were inserted at a rate of two per pack.

		NM/M
Complete Set (20):		2.00
Common Player:		.05
Inserted 2:1		
DH1	Jeff Bagwell	.15
DH2	Albert Belle	.05
DH3	Barry Bonds	.40
DH4	Derek Jeter	.40
DH5	Tony Clark	.05

DH6	Nomar Garciaparra	.20
DH7	Juan Gonzalez	.10
DH8	Ken Griffey Jr.	.25
DH9	Chipper Jones	.20
DH10	Kenny Lofton	.05
DH11	Mark McGwire	.30
DH12	Mo Vaughn	.05
DH13	Mike Piazza	.25
DH14	Cal Ripken Jr.	.40
DH15	Ivan Rodriguez	.10
DH16	Scott Rolen	.05
DH17	Frank Thomas	.15
DH18	Tony Gwynn	.20
DH19	Travis Lee	.05
DH20	Jose Cruz Jr.	.05

Frequent Flyers

The game's top 10 base stealers were included in Frequent Flyers. This insert was designed to look like airline frequent flyer cards and was inserted one per four packs. Fronts have player action photos on a metallic-foil background of a cloudy sky. Backs have a portrait photo and a few words about the player's basestealing ability. Cards are numbered with an "FF" prefix.

		NM/M
Complete Set (10):		2.50
Common Player:		.25
FF1	Brian Hunter	.25
FF2	Kenny Lofton	.25
FF3	Chuck Knoblauch	.25
FF4	Tony Womack	.25
FF5	Marquis Grissom	.25
FF6	Craig Biggio	.25
FF7	Barry Bonds	2.00
FF8	Tom Goodwin	.25
FF9	Delino DeShields	.25
FF10	Eric Young	.25

Gronks

GRONKS

JUAN GONZALEZ Texas Ranger

Gronks featured 10 of the top home run hitters and was a hobby exclusive insert. The name of the insert originated from shortstop Greg Gagne, and the cards were inserted in one per 72 packs.

		NM/M
Complete Set (10):		30.00
Common Player:		1.50
G1	Jeff Bagwell	3.50
G2	Albert Belle	1.50
G3	Juan Gonzalez	2.00
G4	Ken Griffey Jr.	6.00
G5	Mark McGwire	7.50

DOUBLE HEADER
NOMAR GARCIAPARRA

G6	Mike Piazza	6.00
G7	Frank Thomas	3.50
G8	Mo Vaughn	1.50
G9	Ken Caminiti	1.50
G10	Tony Clark	1.50

SuperHeroes

SUPERHEROES

ALEX RODRIGUEZ & NAMOR

SuperHeroes combined 10 top superstars with the Marvel Comics superhero with whom they share a common trait in this 10-card insert set. Cards were inserted at a rate of one per 20 packs.

		NM/M
Complete Set (10):		10.00
Common Player:		.50
Inserted 1:20		
SH1	Barry Bonds	3.00
SH2	Andres Galarraga	.50
SH3	Ken Griffey Jr.	1.50
SH4	Chipper Jones	1.00
SH5	Andruw Jones	.75
SH6	Hideo Nomo	.60
SH7	Cal Ripken Jr.	3.00
SH8	Alex Rodriguez	2.00
SH9	Frank Thomas	.75
SH10	Mo Vaughn	.50

Todd Helton Autograph

Little Dawgs
TODD HELTON

For use in various promotions, Fleer arranged to have Todd Helton autograph 800 of his SkyBox Dugout Axcess Little Dawgs subset cards. Besides the signature, the cards feature an embossed authentication logo.

		NM/M
120	Todd Helton	15.00

SportsFest

As part of its participation at SportsFest in Philadelphia in May 1998, SkyBox issued a special card of hometown hero Scott Rolen. The card was available only as a wrapper redemption at the show and was limited to 5,000. Front has an action photo of Rolen on a colorful background with the team and show logos at bottom. Back has a portrait photo and stats.

		NM/M
SF1	Scott Rolen	3.00

1999 SkyBox E-X Century

The 120-card base set features a clear plastic stock with the player name, logo and position stamped in holographic foil. Card backs have the featured player's vital information along with his '98 statistics and his major league totals. Cards 91-120 are part of a prospects subset and are short-printed seeded 1:2 packs. Three-card packs have a SRP of $5.99.

		NM/M
Complete Set (120):		35.00
Common Player:		.15
Common SP (91-120):		.60
Inserted 1:2		
Pack (3):		3.00
Wax Box (18):		40.00
1	Scott Rolen	.75
2	Nomar Garciaparra	1.50
3	Mike Piazza	2.00
4	Tony Gwynn	1.50
5	Sammy Sosa	1.50
6	Alex Rodriguez	2.50
7	Vladimir Guerrero	1.50
8	Chipper Jones	1.50
9	Derek Jeter	3.00
10	Kerry Wood	.50
11	Juan Gonzalez	.50
12	Frank Thomas	1.00
13	Mo Vaughn	.15
14	Greg Maddux	1.50
15	Jeff Bagwell	1.00
16	Mark McGwire	2.50
17	Ken Griffey Jr.	2.00
18	Roger Clemens	1.75
19	Cal Ripken Jr.	3.00
20	Travis Lee	.15
21	Todd Helton	.75
22	Darin Erstad	.30
23	Pedro Martinez	1.00
24	Barry Bonds	3.00
25	Andruw Jones	1.00
26	Larry Walker	.15
27	Albert Belle	.15
28	Ivan Rodriguez	.75
29	Magglio Ordonez	.25
30	Andres Galarraga	.15
31	Mike Mussina	.35
32	Randy Johnson	1.00
33	Tom Glavine	.35
34	Barry Larkin	.15
35	Jim Thome	.75
36	Gary Sheffield	.45
37	Bernie Williams	.15
38	Carlos Delgado	.60
39	Rafael Palmeiro	.75
40	Edgar Renteria	.15
41	Brad Fullmer	.15
42	David Wells	.15
43	Dante Bichette	.15
44	Jaret Wright	.15
45	Ricky Ledee	.15
46	Ray Lankford	.15
47	Mark Grace	.15
48	Jeff Cirillo	.15
49	Rondell White	.15
50	Jeromy Burnitz	.15
51	Sean Casey	.15
52	Rolando Arrojo	.15
53	Jason Giambi	.65
54	John Olerud	.15
55	Will Clark	.15
56	Raul Mondesi	.15
57	Scott Brosius	.15
58	Bartolo Colon	.15
59	Steve Finley	.15
60	Javy Lopez	.15
61	Tim Salmon	.15
62	Roberto Alomar	.30
63	Vinny Castilla	.15
64	Craig Biggio	.15
65	Jose Guillen	.15

66	Greg Vaughn	.15
67	Jose Canseco	.40
68	Shawn Green	.50
69	Curt Schilling	.35
70	Orlando Hernandez	.15
71	Jose Cruz Jr.	.15
72	Alex Gonzalez	.15
73	Tino Martinez	.15
74	Todd Hundley	.15
75	Brian Giles	.15
76	Cliff Floyd	.15
77	Paul O'Neill	.15
78	Ken Caminiti	.15
79	Ron Gant	.15
80	Juan Encarnacion	.15
81	Ben Grieve	.15
82	Brian Jordan	.15
83	Rickey Henderson	1.00
84	Tony Clark	.15
85	Shannon Stewart	.15
86	Robin Ventura	.15
87	Todd Walker	.15
88	Kevin Brown	.15
89	Moises Alou	.15
90	Manny Ramirez	1.00
91	Gabe Alvarez	.60
92	Jeremy Giambi	.60
93	Adrian Beltre	.75
94	George Lombard	.60
95	Ryan Minor	.60
96	Kevin Witt	.60
97	Scott Hunter RC	.60
98	Carlos Guillen	.60
99	Derrick Gibson	.60
100	Trot Nixon	.75
101	Troy Glaus	3.00
102	Armando Rios	.60
103	Preston Wilson	.60
104	Pat Burrell RC	3.00
105	J.D. Drew	1.50
106	Bruce Chen	.60
107	Matt Clement	.60
108	Carlos Beltran	1.50
109	Carlos Febles	.60
110	Rob Fick	.60
111	Russell Branyan	.60
112	Roosevelt Brown RC	.60
113	Corey Koskie	.60
114	Mario Encarnacion	.60
115	Peter Tucci RC	.60
116	Eric Chavez	.75
117	Gabe Kapler	.60
118	Marlon Anderson	.60
119	A.J. Burnett RC	.75
120	Ryan Bradley	.60
---	Checklist 1-96	.05
---	Checklist 97-120/ Inserts	.05

Essential Credentials Future

A glossy silver design replaces the clear plastic portions seen on the base cards. Production varied depending on the card number, with the exact production number of each player determined by subtracting his card number from 121. Quantity issued is listed in parentheses.

		NM/M
Common Player:		7.50
1	Scott Rolen/120	12.00
2	Nomar Garciaparra/119	20.00
3	Mike Piazza/118	35.00
4	Tony Gwynn/117	20.00
5	Sammy Sosa/116	20.00
6	Alex Rodriguez/115	45.00
7	Vladimir Guerrero/114	16.00
8	Chipper Jones/113	20.00
9	Derek Jeter/112	50.00
10	Kerry Wood/111	20.00
11	Juan Gonzalez/110	12.50
12	Frank Thomas/109	35.00
13	Mo Vaughn/108	7.50
14	Greg Maddux/107	35.00
15	Jeff Bagwell/106	30.00
16	Mark McGwire/105	45.00
17	Ken Griffey Jr./104	35.00
18	Roger Clemens/103	35.00
19	Cal Ripken Jr./102	60.00
20	Travis Lee/101	10.00

21	Todd Helton/100	20.00
22	Darin Erstad/99	10.00
23	Pedro Martinez/98	20.00
24	Barry Bonds/97	50.00
25	Andruw Jones/96	25.00
26	Larry Walker/95	7.50
27	Albert Belle/94	7.50
28	Ivan Rodriguez/93	20.00
29	Magglio Ordonez/92	10.00
30	Andres Galarraga/91	7.50
31	Mike Mussina/90	7.50
32	Randy Johnson/89	30.00
33	Tom Glavine/88	7.50
34	Barry Larkin/87	7.50
35	Jim Thome/86	25.00
36	Gary Sheffield/85	7.50
37	Bernie Williams/84	7.50
38	Carlos Delgado/83	20.00
39	Rafael Palmeiro/82	35.00
40	Edgar Renteria/81	7.50
41	Brad Fullmer/80	7.50
42	David Wells/79	7.50
43	Dante Bichette/78	7.50
44	Jaret Wright/77	7.50
45	Ricky Ledee/76	7.50
46	Ray Lankford/75	7.50
47	Mark Grace/74	7.50
48	Jeff Cirillo/73	7.50
49	Rondell White/72	7.50
50	Jeromy Burnitz/71	7.50
51	Sean Casey/70	12.50
52	Rolando Arrojo/69	7.50
53	Jason Giambi/68	30.00
54	John Olerud/67	7.50
56	Will Clark/66	7.50
56	Raul Mondesi/65	7.50
57	Scott Brosius/64	7.50
58	Bartolo Colon/63	7.50
59	Steve Finley/62	7.50
60	Javy Lopez/61	7.50
61	Tim Salmon/60	7.50
62	Roberto Alomar/59	15.00
63	Vinny Castilla/58	7.50
64	Craig Biggio/57	7.50
65	Jose Guillen/56	7.50
66	Greg Vaughn/55	7.50
67	Jose Canseco/54	35.00
68	Shawn Green/53	12.50
69	Curt Schilling/52	30.00
70	Orlando Hernandez/51	12.50
71	Jose Cruz Jr./50	10.00
72	Alex Gonzalez/49	10.00
73	Tino Martinez/48	10.00
74	Todd Hundley/47	10.00
75	Brian Giles/46	10.00
76	Cliff Floyd/45	10.00
77	Paul O'Neill/44	10.00
78	Ken Caminiti/43	10.00
79	Ron Gant/42	10.00
80	Juan Encarnacion/41	10.00
81	Ben Grieve/40	10.00
82	Brian Jordan/39	10.00
83	Rickey Henderson/38	30.00
84	Tony Clark/37	10.00
85	Shannon Stewart/36	12.50
86	Robin Ventura/35	10.00
87	Todd Walker/34	10.00
88	Kevin Brown/33	10.00
89	Moises Alou/32	10.00
90	Manny Ramirez/31	50.00
91	Gabe Alvarez/30	10.00
92	Jeremy Giambi/29	10.00
93	Adrian Beltre/28	15.00
94	George Lombard/27	10.00
95	Ryan Minor/26	10.00
96	Kevin Witt/25	10.00
97	Scott Hunter/24	10.00
98	Carlos Guillen/23	10.00
99	Derrick Gibson/22	10.00
100	Trot Nixon/21	20.00
101	Troy Glaus/20	50.00
102	Armando Rios/19	10.00
103	Preston Wilson/18	10.00
104	Pat Burrell/17	50.00
105	J.D. Drew/16	50.00
106	Bruce Chen/15	10.00
107	Matt Clement/14	10.00
108	Carlos Beltran/13	60.00
109	Carlos Febles/12	20.00
110	Rob Fick/11	20.00
111	Russell Branyan/10	20.00
112	Roosevelt Brown/9	20.00
113	Corey Koskie/8	20.00
114	Mario Encarnacion/7	20.00
115	Peter Tucci/6	20.00
116	Eric Chavez/5	65.00
117	Gabe Kapler/4	35.00
118	Marlon Anderson/3	75.00
119	A.J. Burnett/2	90.00
120	Ryan Bradley/1	90.00

Essential Credentials Now

Like Future, this is a parallel of the base set, with production of each card limited to that player's card number. These cards have a glossy gold look.

		NM/M
Common Player:		7.50
1	Scott Rolen/1	150.00
2	Nomar Garciaparra/2	150.00
3	Mike Piazza/3	250.00

4	Tony Gwynn/4	125.00
5	Sammy Sosa/5	150.00
6	Alex Rodriguez/6	300.00
7	Vladimir Guerrero/7	125.00
8	Chipper Jones/8	150.00
9	Derek Jeter/9	250.00
10	Kerry Wood/10	75.00
11	Juan Gonzalez/11	60.00
12	Frank Thomas/12	125.00
13	Mo Vaughn/13	25.00
14	Greg Maddux/14	125.00
15	Jeff Bagwell/15	100.00
16	Mark McGwire/16	250.00
17	Ken Griffey Jr./17	200.00
18	Roger Clemens/18	125.00
19	Cal Ripken Jr./19	350.00
20	Travis Lee/20	10.00
21	Todd Helton/21	25.00
22	Darin Erstad/22	15.00
23	Pedro Martinez/23	30.00
24	Barry Bonds/24	175.00
25	Andruw Jones/25	45.00
26	Larry Walker/26	10.00
27	Albert Belle/27	10.00
28	Ivan Rodriguez/28	30.00
29	Magglio Ordonez/29	30.00
30	Andres Galarraga/30	10.00
31	Mike Mussina/31	30.00
32	Randy Johnson/32	50.00
33	Tom Glavine/33	10.00
34	Barry Larkin/34	10.00
35	Jim Thome/35	45.00
36	Gary Sheffield/36	25.00
37	Bernie Williams/37	10.00
38	Carlos Delgado/38	25.00
39	Rafael Palmeiro/39	40.00
40	Edgar Renteria/40	10.00
41	Brad Fullmer/41	10.00
42	David Wells/42	10.00
43	Dante Bichette/43	10.00
44	Jaret Wright/44	10.00
45	Ricky Ledee/45	10.00
46	Ray Lankford/46	7.50
47	Mark Grace/47	7.50
48	Jeff Cirillo/48	7.50
49	Rondell White/49	7.50
50	Jeromy Burnitz/50	7.50
51	Sean Casey/51	10.00
52	Rolando Arrojo/52	7.50
53	Jason Giambi/53	25.00
54	John Olerud/54	7.50
55	Will Clark/55	7.50
56	Raul Mondesi/56	7.50
57	Scott Brosius/57	7.50
58	Bartolo Colon/58	7.50
59	Steve Finley/59	7.50
60	Javy Lopez/60	7.50
61	Tim Salmon/61	7.50
62	Roberto Alomar/62	12.50
63	Vinny Castilla/63	7.50
64	Craig Biggio/64	7.50
65	Jose Guillen/65	7.50
66	Greg Vaughn/66	7.50
67	Jose Canseco/67	30.00
68	Shawn Green/68	12.50
69	Curt Schilling/69	25.00
70	Orlando Hernandez/70	7.50
71	Jose Cruz Jr./71	7.50
72	Alex Gonzalez/72	7.50
73	Tino Martinez/73	7.50
74	Todd Hundley/74	7.50
75	Brian Giles/75	7.50
76	Cliff Floyd/76	7.50
77	Paul O'Neill/77	7.50
78	Ken Caminiti/78	7.50
79	Ron Gant/79	7.50
80	Juan Encarnacion/80	7.50
81	Ben Grieve/81	7.50
82	Brian Jordan/82	7.50
83	Rickey Henderson/83	25.00
84	Tony Clark/84	7.50
85	Shannon Stewart/85	7.50
86	Robin Ventura/86	7.50
87	Todd Walker/87	7.50
88	Kevin Brown/88	7.50
89	Moises Alou/89	7.50
90	Manny Ramirez/90	30.00
91	Gabe Alvarez/91	7.50
92	Jeremy Giambi/92	7.50
93	Adrian Beltre/93	10.00
94	George Lombard/94	7.50
95	Ryan Minor/95	7.50
96	Kevin Witt/96	7.50
97	Scott Hunter/97	7.50
98	Carlos Guillen/98	7.50
99	Derrick Gibson/99	7.50
100	Trot Nixon/100	9.00
101	Troy Glaus/101	20.00

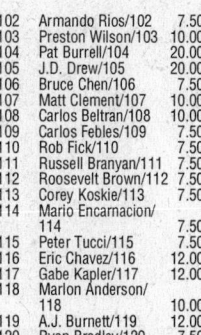

102	Armando Rios/102	7.50
103	Preston Wilson/103	10.00
104	Pat Burrell/104	20.00
105	J.D. Drew/105	7.50
106	Bruce Chen/106	7.50
107	Matt Clement/107	10.00
108	Carlos Beltran/108	7.50
109	Carlos Febles/109	7.50
110	Rob Fick/110	7.50
111	Russell Branyan/111	7.50
112	Roosevelt Brown/112	7.50
113	Corey Koskie/113	7.50
114	Mario Encarnacion/114	7.50
115	Peter Tucci/115	7.50
116	Eric Chavez/116	12.00
117	Gabe Kapler/117	12.00
118	Marlon Anderson/118	10.00
119	A.J. Burnett/119	12.00
120	Ryan Bradley/120	7.50

Authen-Kicks

Authen-Kicks is a game-used insert that embeds game-worn shoe swatches from the featured player. Each is done in a horizontal format and is sequentially hand-numbered. The number of swatch cards differs from player to player, and is indicated here in parentheses. Autographed versions of two colors of J.D. Drew shoes were also produced.

		NM/M
Complete Set (10):		125.00
Common Player:		2.50
(1)	J.D. Drew/160	7.50
(1ab)	J.D. Drew/8 (Autographed black)	75.00
(1ar)	J.D. Drew/8 (Autographed red)	75.00
(2)	Travis Lee/175	5.00
(3)	Kevin Millwood/160	5.00
(4)	Bruce Chen/205	2.50
(5)	Troy Glaus/205	15.00
(6)	Todd Helton/205	15.00
(7)	Ricky Ledee/180	2.50
(8)	Scott Rolen/205	15.00
(9)	Jeremy Giambi/205	2.50

E-X Quisite

15 of baseball's top young players are showcased, with a black background and interior die-cutting around the player image. These are seeded 1:18 packs.

		NM/M
Complete Set (15):		17.50
Common Player:		.50
Inserted 1:18		
1	Troy Glaus	3.50
2	J.D. Drew	2.50
3	Pat Burrell	3.50
4	Russell Branyan	.50
5	Kerry Wood	2.00
6	Eric Chavez	1.00
7	Ben Grieve	.50
8	Gabe Kapler	.50
9	Adrian Beltre	.50
10	Todd Helton	3.00
11	Roosevelt Brown	.50
12	Marlon Anderson	.50
13	Jeremy Giambi	.50
14	Magglio Ordonez	.50
15	Travis Lee	.50

Favorites for Fenway

This 20-card set pays tribute to one of baseball's favorite

ballparks, Fenway Park the venue for the 1999 All-Star Game. These have a photo of the featured player with an image of Fenway Park in the background on a horizontal format. These are seeded 1:36 packs.

		NM/M
Complete Set (20):		45.00
Common Player:		1.00
Inserted 1:36		
1	Mo Vaughn	1.00
2	Nomar Garciaparra	2.25
3	Frank Thomas	2.00
4	Ken Griffey Jr.	3.00
5	Roger Clemens	2.50
6	Alex Rodriguez	4.00
7	Derek Jeter	4.00
8	Juan Gonzalez	1.50
9	Cal Ripken Jr.	5.00
10	Ivan Rodriguez	1.50
11	J.D. Drew	1.50
12	Barry Bonds	5.00
13	Tony Gwynn	2.25
14	Vladimir Guerrero	2.00
15	Chipper Jones	2.25
16	Kerry Wood	1.50
17	Mike Piazza	3.00
18	Sammy Sosa	2.25
19	Scott Rolen	1.50
20	Mark McGwire	4.00

Milestones of the Century

This 10-card set spotlights the top statistical performances from the 1998 season, sequentially numbered to that performance in a multi-layered design.

		NM/M
Complete Set (10):		375.00
Common Player:		10.00
Numbered to featured milestone.		
1	Kerry Wood/20	20.00
2	Mark McGwire/70	60.00
3	Sammy Sosa/66	40.00
4	Ken Griffey Jr./350	17.50
5	Roger Clemens/98	25.00
6	Cal Ripken Jr./17	165.00
7	Alex Rodriguez/40	90.00
8	Barry Bonds/400	25.00
9	N.Y. Yankees/114	150.00
10	Travis Lee/98	10.00

1999 SkyBox Molten Metal

Distributed exclusively to the hobby, this 150-card set consists of three subsets: Metal Smiths, Heavy Metal and Supernatural. Metal Smiths (1-100) show baseball's top players, Heavy Metal (101-130) focus on power hitters and Supernatural (131-150) focus on rookies. Base cards feature silver foil stamping on a 24-point stock with holofoil and wet-laminate overlays. Molten Metal was released in six-card packs with a SRP of $4.99. A special version of the issue was sold only at the 20th Nat'l Sports Collectors Convention in Atlanta, July 19-24. The show version includes autograph redemption cards for show guests and a die-cut series of 30 current and former Braves favorites. Each of the show version cards has a small National Convention logo printed on back; they currently carry no premium.

		NM/M
Complete Set (150):		35.00
Common Metalsmiths (1-100):		.15
Inserted 4:1		
Common Heavy Metal (101-130):		.25
Inserted 1:1		
Common Supernatural (131-150):		.50
Inserted 1:2		
Pack (6):		1.00
Wax Box (24):		20.00
1	Larry Walker	.15
2	Jose Canseco	.50
3	Brian Jordan	.15
4	Rafael Palmeiro	.65
5	Edgar Renteria	.15
6	Dante Bichette	.15
7	Mark Kotsay	.15
8	Denny Neagle	.15
9	Ellis Burks	.15
10	Paul O'Neill	.15
11	Miguel Tejada	.30
12	Ken Caminiti	.15
13	David Cone	.15
14	Jason Kendall	.15
15	Ruben Rivera	.15
16	Todd Walker	.15
17	Bobby Higginson	.15
18	Derek Lee	.60
19	Rondell White	.15
20	Pedro J. Martinez	.75
21	Jeff Kent	.15
22	Randy Johnson	.75
23	Matt Williams	.15
24	Sean Casey	.25
25	Eric Davis	.15
26	Ryan Klesko	.15
27	Curt Schilling	.35
28	Geoff Jenkins	.15
29	Armand Abreu	.15
30	Vinny Castilla	.15
31	Will Clark	.15
32	Ray Durham	.15
33	Ray Lankford	.15
34	Richie Sexson	.15
35	Derrick Gibson	.15
36	Mark Grace	.15
37	Greg Vaughn	.15
38	Bartolo Colon	.15
39	Steve Finley	.15
40	Chuck Knoblauch	.15
41	Ricky Ledee	.15
42	John Smoltz	.15
43	Moises Alou	.15
44	Jim Edmonds	.15
45	Cliff Floyd	.15
46	Javy Lopez	.15
47	Jim Thome	.65
48	J.T. Snow	.15
49	Sandy Alomar Jr.	.15
50	Andy Pettitte	.25
51	Juan Encarnacion	.15
52	Travis Fryman	.15
53	Eli Marrero	.15
54	Jeff Cirillo	.15
55	Brady Anderson	.15
56	Jose Cruz Jr.	.15
57	Edgar Martinez	.15
58	Garret Anderson	.15
59	Paul Konerko	.30
60	Eric Milton	.15
61	Jason Giambi	.45
62	Tom Glavine	.35
63	Justin Thompson	.15
64	Brad Fullmer	.15
65	Marquis Grissom	.15
66	Fernando Tatis	.15
67	Carlos Beltran	.45
68	Charles Johnson	.15
69	Raul Mondesi	.15
70	Richard Hidalgo	.15
71	Barry Larkin	.25
72	David Wells	.15
73	Jay Buhner	.15
74	Matt Clement	.15
75	Eric Karros	.15
76	Carl Pavano	.15
77	Mariano Rivera	.15
78	Livan Hernandez	.15
79	A.J. Hinch	.15
80	Tino Martinez	.15

81	Rusty Greer	.15
82	Jose Guillen	.15
83	Robin Ventura	.15
84	Kevin Brown	.15
85	Chan Ho Park	.15
86	John Olerud	.15
87	Johnny Damon	.35
88	Todd Hundley	.15
89	Fred McGriff	.15
90	Wade Boggs	1.00
91	Mike Cameron	.15
92	Gary Sheffield	.50
93	Rickey Henderson	.75
94	Pat Hentgen	.15
95	Omar Vizquel	.15
96	Craig Biggio	.15
97	Mike Caruso	.15
98	Neifi Perez	.15
99	Mike Mussina	.50
100	Carlos Delgado	.45
101	Andruw Jones (Heavy Metal)	1.00
102	Pat Burrell RC (Heavy Metal)	3.00
103	Orlando Hernandez (Heavy Metal)	.25
104	Darin Erstad (Heavy Metal)	.40
105	Roberto Alomar (Heavy Metal)	.35
106	Tim Salmon (Heavy Metal)	.25
107	Albert Belle (Heavy Metal)	.25
108	Chad Allen RC (Heavy Metal)	.25
109	Travis Lee (Heavy Metal)	.25
110	Jesse Garcia RC (Heavy Metal)	.25
111	Tony Clark (Heavy Metal)	.25
112	Ivan Rodriguez (Heavy Metal)	.75
113	Troy Glaus (Heavy Metal)	1.00
114	A.J. Burnett RC (Heavy Metal)	1.50
115	David Justice (Heavy Metal)	.25
116	Adrian Beltre (Heavy Metal)	.50
117	Eric Chavez (Heavy Metal)	.35
118	Kenny Lofton (Heavy Metal)	.25
119	Michael Barrett (Heavy Metal)	.25
120	Jeff Weaver RC (Heavy Metal)	1.50
121	Manny Ramirez (Heavy Metal)	1.00
122	Barry Bonds (Heavy Metal)	2.00
123	Bernie Williams (Heavy Metal)	.25
124	Freddy Garcia RC (Heavy Metal)	1.50
125	Scott Hunter RC (Heavy Metal)	.25
126	Jeremy Giambi (Heavy Metal)	.25
127	Masao Kida RC (Heavy Metal)	.25
128	Todd Helton (Heavy Metal)	1.00
129	Mike Figga (Heavy Metal)	.25
130	Mo Vaughn (Heavy Metal)	.25
131	J.D. Drew (Supernaturals)	.65
132	Cal Ripken Jr. (Supernaturals)	3.00
133	Ken Griffey Jr. (Supernaturals)	1.50
134	Mark McGwire (Supernaturals)	2.00
135	Nomar Garciaparra (Supernaturals)	1.00
136	Greg Maddux (Supernaturals)	1.00
137	Mike Piazza (Supernaturals)	1.50
138	Alex Rodriguez (Supernaturals)	2.00
139	Frank Thomas (Supernaturals)	.85
140	Juan Gonzalez (Supernaturals)	.65
141	Tony Gwynn (Supernaturals)	1.00
142	Derek Jeter (Supernaturals)	3.00
143	Chipper Jones (Supernaturals)	1.00
144	Scott Rolen (Supernaturals)	.65
145	Sammy Sosa (Supernaturals)	1.00
146	Kerry Wood (Supernaturals)	.50
147	Roger Clemens (Supernaturals)	1.25
148	Jeff Bagwell (Supernaturals)	.75
149	Vladimir Guerrero (Supernaturals)	.75
150	Ben Grieve (Supernaturals)	.50

Fusion

Fusion is a 50-card partial parallel that is paralleled three times: Fusion, Sterling Fusion and Titanium Fusion. The three parallels consist of the two subsets Heavy Metal and Supernatural. Fusion Heavy Metals (1-30) are seeded 1:12 packs and Supernatural Fusions are seeded 1:24 packs. Fusions are laser die-cut with additional silver-foil stamping. Sterling Fusions are limited to 500 numbered sets with each card laser die-cut on a blue background with blue foil stamping. Titanium Fusions are limited to 50 sequentially numbered sets with gold background and enhanced with gold foil highlights.

	NM/M
Complete Set (50):	100.00
Common Heavy Metal (1-30):	1.00
Inserted 1:12	
Common Supernatural (31-50):	2.50
Inserted 1:24	
Sterling (31-50):	1.5X
Production 500 Sets	
Titanium (31-50):	6X
Production 50 Sets	
1	Andruw Jones	4.00
2	Pat Burrell	2.00
3	Orlando Hernandez	1.00
4	Darin Erstad	1.50
5	Roberto Alomar	1.50
6	Tim Salmon	1.00
7	Albert Belle	1.00
8	Chad Allen	1.00
9	Travis Lee	1.00
10	Jesse Garcia	1.00
11	Tony Clark	1.00
12	Ivan Rodriguez	3.00
13	Troy Glaus	3.00
14	A.J. Burnett	1.00
15	David Justice	1.00
16	Adrian Beltre	1.50
17	Eric Chavez	1.50
18	Kenny Lofton	1.00
19	Michael Barrett	1.00
20	Jeff Weaver	1.00
21	Manny Ramirez	4.00
22	Barry Bonds	10.00
23	Bernie Williams	1.00
24	Freddy Garcia	1.00
25	Scott Hunter	1.00
26	Jeremy Giambi	1.00
27	Masao Kida	1.00
28	Todd Helton	3.00
29	Mike Figga	1.00
30	Mo Vaughn	1.00
31	J.D. Drew	2.00
32	Cal Ripken Jr.	10.00
33	Ken Griffey Jr.	6.00
34	Mark McGwire	7.50
35	Nomar Garciaparra	5.00
36	Greg Maddux	5.00
37	Mike Piazza	6.00
38	Alex Rodriguez	7.50
39	Frank Thomas	4.00
40	Juan Gonzalez	1.50
41	Tony Gwynn	5.00
42	Derek Jeter	10.00
43	Chipper Jones	5.00
44	Scott Rolen	3.00
45	Sammy Sosa	5.00
46	Kerry Wood	2.00
47	Roger Clemens	5.50
48	Jeff Bagwell	4.00
49	Vladimir Guerrero	4.00
50	Ben Grieve	1.00

Fusion - Sterling

Sterling Fusions are limited to 500 numbered sets with each card laser die-cut on a blue background with blue foil graphic highlights. A special version of the issue was sold only at the 20th Nat'l

Sports Collectors Convention in Atlanta, July 19-24. Each of the show-version cards has a small National Convention logo printed on back; they currently carry no premium.

	NM/M
Common Player:	1.50
Sterling Stars:	1.5X

Fusion - Titanium

Titanium Fusions are limited to 50 sequentially numbered sets with gold background and enhanced with gold foil highlights. A special version of the issue was sold only at the 20th Nat'l Sports Collectors Convention in Atlanta, July 19-24. Each of the show-version cards has a small National Convention logo printed on back; they currently carry no premium.

	NM/M
Common Player:	4.00
Titanium Stars:	6X

Oh Atlanta!

This 30-card set features players who are either current or former Atlanta Braves like Chipper Jones and Dave Justice. These inserts are seeded one per pack and was produced in conjunction with the 20th annual National Sports Collectors Convention in Atlanta.

	NM/M
Complete Set (30):	30.00
Common Player:	.60
Inserted 1:1	
1	Kenny Lofton	.60
2	Kevin Millwood	.60
3	Bret Boone	.60
4	Otis Nixon	.60
5	Vinny Castilla	.60
6	Brian Jordan	.60
7	Chipper Jones	8.00
8	Dave Justice	.60
9	Micah Bowie	.60
10	Fred McGriff	.60

11	Ron Gant	.60
12	Andruw Jones	4.00
13	Kent Mercker	.60
14*	Greg McMichael	.60
15	Steve Avery	.60
16	Marquis Grissom	.60
17	Jason Schmidt	.60
18	Ryan Klesko	.60
19	Charlie O'Brien	.60
20	Terry Pendleton	.60
21	Denny Neagle	.60
22	Greg Maddux	8.00
23	Tom Glavine	1.50
24	Javy Lopez	.60
25	John Rocker	.60
26	Walt Weiss	.60
27	John Smoltz	.60
28	Michael Tucker	.60
29	Odalis Perez	.60
30	Andres Galarraga	.60

Xplosion Sample

This sample card was issued to preview SkyBox's Xplosion metal inserts. Etched and printed on metal stock, the card is identical in format to the issued versions, except for sample notations on back.

	NM/M
Kerry Wood	3.00

Xplosion

This is a 150-card parallel set, which is seeeded 1:2 packs. These are made of actual metal that have added etching and some foil stamping.

	NM/M
Complete Set (150):	300.00
Common Player:	1.00
Stars:	3X
Inserted 1:2	

1999 SkyBox Premium

The base set consists of 300 cards, base cards feature full bleed fronts with gold-foil stamped player and team names. Card backs have complete year-by-year stats along with a close-up photo. The Rookie subset (223-272) also have a short-printed parallel version as well. Different photos are used but they have the same card number and card back. The short-print versions are seeded 1:8 packs and have an action photo front while the non-seeded cards have a close-up photo.

	NM/M
Complete Set (300):	20.00
Complete Set w/SP's (350):	40.00
Common Player:	.10
Common SP (223-272):	.60
SP's inserted 1:8	
Star Rubies:	50X
Production 50 Sets	
SP Star Rubies:	15X
Production 15 Sets	
Pack (8):	1.50
Wax Box (24):	25.00
1	Alex Rodriguez	2.00
2	Sidney Ponson	.10
3	Shawn Green	.35
4	Dan Wilson	.10
5	Rolando Arrojo	.10
6	Roberto Alomar	.30
7	Matt Anderson	.10
8	David Segui	.10
9	Alex Gonzalez	.10
10	Edgar Renteria	.10
11	Benito Santiago	.10
12	Todd Stottlemyre	.10
13	Rico Brogna	.10
14	Troy Glaus	.65
15	Al Leiter	.10
16	Pedro J. Martinez	.75
17	Paul O'Neill	.10
18	Manny Ramirez	.75
19	Scott Rolen	.65
20	Curt Schilling	.35
21	Bobby Abreu	.10
22	Robb Nen	.10
23	Andy Pettitte	.25
24	John Wetteland	.10
25	Bobby Bonilla	.10
26	Darin Erstad	.20
27	Shawn Estes	.10
28	John Franco	.10
29	Nomar Garciaparra	1.00
30	Rick Helling	.10
31	David Justice	.10
32	Chuck Knoblauch	.10
33	Quinton McCracken	.10
34	Kenny Rogers	.10
35	Brian Giles	.10
36	Armando Benitez	.10
37	Trevor Hoffman	.10
38	Charles Johnson	.10
39	Travis Lee	.10
40	Tom Glavine	.35
41	Rondell White	.10
42	Orlando Hernandez	.10
43	Mickey Morandini	.10
44	Darryl Kile	.10
45	Greg Vaughn	.10
46	Gregg Jefferies	.10
47	Mark McGwire	2.00
48	Kerry Wood	.40
49	Jeromy Burnitz	.10
50	Ron Gant	.10
51	Vinny Castilla	.10
52	Doug Glanville	.10
53	Juan Guzman	.10
54	Dustin Hermanson	.10
55	Jose Hernandez	.10
56	Bob Higginson	.10
57	A.J. Hinch	.10
58	Randy Johnson	.75
59	Eli Marrero	.10
60	Rafael Palmeiro	.65
61	Carl Pavano	.10
62	Brett Tomko	.10
63	Jose Guillen	.10
64	Mike Lieberthal	.10
65	Jim Abbott	.10
66	Dante Bichette	.10
67	Jeff Cirillo	.10
68	Eric Davis	.10
69	Delino DeShields	.10
70	Steve Finley	.10
71	Mark Grace	.10
72	Jason Kendall	.10
73	Jeff Kent	.10
74	Desi Relaford	.10
75	Ivan Rodriguez	.65
76	Shannon Stewart	.10
77	Geoff Jenkins	.10
78	Ben Grieve	.10
79	Cliff Floyd	.10
80	Jason Giambi	.50
81	Rod Beck	.10
82	Derek Bell	.10
83	Will Clark	.10
84	David Dellucci	.10
85	Joey Hamilton	.10
86	Livan Hernandez	.10
87	Barry Larkin	.10
88	Matt Mantei	.10
89	Dean Palmer	.10
90	Chan Ho Park	.10
91	Jim Thome	.65
92	Miguel Tejada	.20
93	Justin Thompson	.10
94	David Wells	.10
95	Bernie Williams	.10
96	Jeff Bagwell	.75
97	Derrek Lee	.50
98	Devon White	.10
99	Jeff Shaw	.10
100	Brad Radke	.10
101	Mark Grudzielanek	.10
102	Javy Lopez	.10
103	Mike Sirotka	.10
104	Robin Ventura	.10
105	Andy Ashby	.10
106	Juan Gonzalez	.40
107	Albert Belle	.10
108	Andy Benes	.10
109	Jay Buhner	.10
110	Ken Caminiti	.10
111	Roger Clemens	1.25
112	Mike Hampton	.10
113	Pete Harnisch	.10
114	Mike Piazza	1.50
115	J.T. Snow	.10
116	John Olerud	.10
117	Tony Womack	.10
118	Todd Zeile	.10
119	Tony Gwynn	1.00
120	Brady Anderson	.10
121	Sean Casey	.20
122	Jose Cruz Jr.	.10
123	Carlos Delgado	.50
124	Edgar Martinez	.10
125	Jose Mesa	.10
126	Shane Reynolds	.10
127	John Valentin	.10
128	Mo Vaughn	.10
129	Kevin Young	.10
130	Jay Bell	.10
131	Aaron Boone	.10
132	John Smoltz	.10
133	Mike Stanley	.10
134	Bret Saberhagen	.10
135	Tim Salmon	.10
136	Mariano Rivera	.15
137	Ken Griffey Jr.	1.50
138	Jose Offerman	.10
139	Troy Percival	.10
140	Greg Maddux	1.00
141	Frank Thomas	.75
142	Steve Avery	.10
143	Kevin Millwood	.10
144	Sammy Sosa	1.00
145	Larry Walker	.10
146	Matt Williams	.10
147	Mike Caruso	.10
148	Todd Helton	.65
149	Andruw Jones	.75
150	Ray Lankford	.10
151	Craig Biggio	.10
152	Ugueth Urbina	.10
153	Wade Boggs	1.00
154	Derek Jeter	2.50
155	Wally Joyner	.10
156	Mike Mussina	.30
157	Gregg Olson	.10
158	Henry Rodriguez	.10
159	Reggie Sanders	.10
160	Fernando Tatis	.10
161	Dmitri Young	.10
162	Rick Aguilera	.10
163	Marty Cordova	.10
164	Johnny Damon	.30
165	Ray Durham	.10
166	Brad Fullmer	.10
167	Chipper Jones	1.00
168	Bobby Smith	.10
169	Omar Vizquel	.10
170	Todd Hundley	.10
171	David Cone	.10
172	Royce Clayton	.10
173	Ryan Klesko	.10
174	Jeff Montgomery	.10
175	Magglio Ordonez	.10
176	Billy Wagner	.10
177	Masato Yoshii	.10
178	Jason Christiansen	.10
179	Chuck Finley	.10
180	Tom Gordon	.10
181	Wilton Guerrero	.10
182	Rickey Henderson	.75
183	Sterling Hitchcock	.10
184	Kenny Lofton	.10
185	Tino Martinez	.10
186	Fred McGriff	.10
187	Matt Stairs	.10
188	Neifi Perez	.10
189	Bob Wickman	.10
190	Barry Bonds	2.50
191	Jose Canseco	.40
192	Damion Easley	.10
193	Jim Edmonds	.10
194	Juan Encarnacion	.10
195	Travis Fryman	.10
196	Tom Goodwin	.10
197	Rusty Greer	.10
198	Roberto Hernandez	.10
199	B.J. Surhoff	.10
200	Scott Brosius	.10
201	Brian Jordan	.10
202	Paul Konerko	.20
203	Ismael Valdes	.10
204	Eric Milton	.10
205	Adrian Beltre	.10
206	Tony Clark	.10
207	Bartolo Colon	.10
208	Cal Ripken Jr.	2.50
209	Moises Alou	.10
210	Wilson Alvarez	.10
211	Kevin Brown	.10
212	Orlando Cabrera	.10

213 Vladimir Guerrero .75
214 Jose Rosado .10
215 Raul Mondesi .10
216 Dave Nilsson .10
217 Carlos Perez .10
218 Jason Schmidt .10
219 Richie Sexson .10
220 Gary Sheffield .40
221 Fernando Vina .10
222 Todd Walker .10
223 Scott Sauerbeck RC .10
223 Scott Sauerbeck/SP RC .60
224 Pascual Matos RC .10
224 Pascual Matos/SP RC .60
225 Kyle Farnsworth RC .15
225 Kyle Farnsworth/SP RC .60
226 Freddy Garcia RC .75
226 Freddy Garcia/SP RC 1.50
227 David Lundquist RC .10
227 David Lundquist/SP RC .60
228 Jolbert Cabrera RC .10
228 Jolbert Cabrera/SP RC .60
229 Dan Perkins RC .10
229 Dan Perkins/SP RC .60
230 Warren Morris RC .10
230 Warren Morris/SP .60
231 Carlos Febles .10
231 Carlos Febles/SP .60
232 Brett Hinchliffe RC .10
232 Brett Hinchliffe/SP RC .60
233 Jason Phillips RC .10
233 Jason Phillips/SP RC .60
234 Glen Barker RC .10
234 Glen Barker/SP RC .60
235 Jose Macias RC .25
235 Jose Macias/SP RC 1.00
236 Joe Mays RC .10
236 Joe Mays/SP RC .60
237 Chad Allen RC .10
237 Chad Allen/SP RC .60
238 Miguel Del Toro RC .10
238 Miguel Del Toro/SP RC .60
239 Chris Singleton .10
239 Chris Singleton/SP .60
240 Jesse Garcia RC .10
240 Jesse Garcia/SP RC .60
241 Kris Benson .10
241 Kris Benson/SP .60
242 Clay Bellinger RC .10
242 Clay Bellinger/SP RC .60
243 Scott Williamson .10
243 Scott Williamson/SP .60
244 Masao Kida RC .10
244 Masao Kida/SP RC .60
245 Guillermo Garcia RC .10
245 Guillermo Garcia/SP RC .60
246 A.J. Burnett RC .25
246 A.J. Burnett/SP RC 1.50
247 Bo Porter RC .10
247 Bo Porter/SP RC .60
248 Pat Burrell RC .75
248 Pat Burrell/SP RC 4.00
249 Carlos Lee .50
249 Carlos Lee/SP 1.50
250 Jeff Weaver RC .50
250 Jeff Weaver/SP RC 1.50
251 Ruben Mateo .10
251 Ruben Mateo/SP .40
252 J.D. Drew .40
252 J.D. Drew/SP 2.00
253 Jeremy Giambi .10
253 Jeremy Giambi/SP .60
254 Gary Bennett RC .10
254 Gary Bennett/SP RC .60
255 Edwards Guzman RC .10
255 Edwards Guzman/SP RC .60
256 Ramon Martinez .10
256 Ramon Martinez/SP .60
257 Giomar Guevara RC .10
257 Giomar Guevara/SP RC .60
258 Joe McEwing RC .10
258 Joe McEwing/SP RC .60
259 Tom Davey RC .10
259 Tom Davey/SP RC .60
260 Gabe Kapler .10
260 Gabe Kapler/SP .60
261 Ryan Rupe RC .10
261 Ryan Rupe/SP RC .60
262 Kelly Dransfeldt RC .10
262 Kelly Dransfeldt/SP RC .60
263 Michael Barrett .10
263 Michael Barrett/SP .60
264 Eric Chavez .25
264 Eric Chavez/SP 1.00
265 Orber Moreno RC .10
265 Orber Moreno/SP RC .60
266 Marlon Anderson .10
266 Marlon Anderson/SP .60
267 Carlos Beltran .50
267 Carlos Beltran/SP 1.50
268 Doug Mientkiewicz .10
268 Doug Mientkiewicz/SP .60
269 Roy Halladay .10
269 Roy Halladay/SP .60
270 Torii Hunter .10
270 Torii Hunter/SP .60
271 Stan Spencer .10
271 Stan Spencer/SP .60
272 Alex Gonzalez .10
272 Alex Gonzalez/SP .60

ABBREVIATIONS

SP - Short Print

273 Mark McGwire (Spring Fling) 1.00
274 Scott Rolen (Spring Fling) .30
275 Jeff Bagwell (Spring Fling) .40
276 Derek Jeter (Spring Fling) 1.50
277 Tony Gwynn (Spring Fling) .50
278 Frank Thomas (Spring Fling) .40
279 Sammy Sosa (Spring Fling) .50
280 Nomar Garciaparra (Spring Fling) .50
281 Cal Ripken Jr. (Spring Fling) 1.50
282 Albert Belle (Spring Fling) .10
283 Kerry Wood (Spring Fling) .20
284 Greg Maddux (Spring Fling) .50
285 Barry Bonds (Spring Fling) 1.50
286 Juan Gonzalez (Spring Fling) .25
287 Ken Griffey Jr. (Spring Fling) .75
288 Alex Rodriguez (Spring Fling) 1.00
289 Ben Grieve (Spring Fling) .10
290 Travis Lee (Spring Fling) .10
291 Mo Vaughn (Spring Fling) .10
292 Mike Piazza (Spring Fling) .85
293 Roger Clemens (Spring Fling) .60
294 J.D. Drew (Spring Fling) .20
295 Randy Johnson (Spring Fling) .40
296 Chipper Jones (Spring Fling) .50
297 Vladimir Guerrero (Spring Fling) .40
298 Checklist (Nomar Garciaparra) .40
299 Checklist (Ken Griffey Jr.) .50
300 Checklist (Mark McGwire) .60

Star Rubies

Star Rubies are a parallel of the base set and are limited to 50 sequentially numbered sets. SP Rookie parallels are limited to 15 numbered sets. Rubies feature a complete prism foil front with red-foil stamping.

Star Rubies: 50X
Production 50 Sets
SP Star Rubies: 15X
Production 15 Sets

Autographics

This 54-card autographed set feature an embossed Sky-Box Seal of Authenticity stamp and are seeded 1:68 packs.

Cards are commonly found signed in black ink. Blue-ink versions, serially numbered to 50 each, were also produced.

	NM/M
Common Player:	3.00
Inserted 1:68	
Blue Ink:	1.5X
Production 50 Sets	
Roberto Alomar	15.00
Paul Bako	3.00
Michael Barrett	8.00
Kris Benson	8.00
Micah Bowie	3.00
Roosevelt Brown	3.00
A.J. Burnett	8.00
Pat Burrell	15.00
Ken Caminiti	15.00
Royce Clayton	3.00
Edgard Clemente	3.00
Bartolo Colon	10.00
J.D. Drew	15.00
Damion Easley	5.00
Derrin Ebert	3.00
Mario Encarnacion	3.00
Juan Encarnacion	5.00
Troy Glaus	15.00
Tom Glavine	20.00
Juan Gonzalez/SP	50.00
Shawn Green	10.00
Wilton Guerrero	3.00
Jose Guillen	8.00
Tony Gwynn	30.00
Mark Harriger	3.00
Bobby Higginson	3.00
Todd Hollandsworth	3.00
Scott Hunter	3.00
Gabe Kapler	3.00
Scott Karl	3.00
Mike Kinkade	3.00
Ray Lankford	3.00
Barry Larkin	15.00
Matt Lawton	5.00
Ricky Ledee	3.00
Travis Lee	5.00
Eli Marrero	5.00
Ruben Mateo	3.00
Joe McEwing	3.00
Doug Mientkiewicz	4.00
Russ Ortiz	3.00
Jim Parque	3.00
Robert Person	3.00
Alex Rodriguez	80.00
Scott Rolen	20.00
Benj Sampson	3.00
Luis Saturria	3.00
Curt Schilling	35.00
David Segui	3.00
Fernando Tatis	3.00
Peter Tucci	3.00
Javier Vasquez	6.00
Robin Ventura	10.00
	3.00
Checklist	.05

Diamond Debuts

This 15-card set features the best rookies of 1999 on a silver rainbow holo-foil card stock. These are seeded 1:49 packs. Card backs are numbered with a "DD" suffix.

		NM/M
Complete Set (15):		17.50
Common Player:		2.00
Inserted 1:49		
1	Eric Chavez	3.00
2	Kyle Farnsworth	2.00
3	Ryan Rupe	2.00
4	Jeremy Giambi	2.00
5	Marlon Anderson	2.00
6	J.D. Drew	4.00
7	Carlos Febles	2.00
8	Joe McEwing	2.00
9	Jeff Weaver	2.00
10	Alex Gonzalez	2.00
11	Chad Allen	2.00
12	Michael Barrett	2.00
13	Gabe Kapler	2.00
14	Carlos Lee	2.00
15	Edwards Guzman	2.00

Intimidation Nation

This 15-card set highlights the top performers in baseball and features gold rainbow holo-foil stamping. These are limited to 99 sequentially numbered sets. Card backs are numbered with a "IN" suffix.

		NM/M
Complete Set (15):		280.00
Common Player:		12.00
Production 99 Sets		
1	Cal Ripken Jr.	40.00
2	Tony Gwynn	20.00
3	Nomar Garciaparra	20.00
4	Frank Thomas	15.00
5	Mike Piazza	25.00
6	Mark McGwire	30.00
7	Scott Rolen	12.00
8	Chipper Jones	20.00
9	Greg Maddux	20.00
10	Ken Griffey Jr.	25.00
11	Juan Gonzalez	12.00
12	Derek Jeter	40.00
13	J.D. Drew	12.00
14	Roger Clemens	22.50
15	Alex Rodriguez	30.00

Live Bats

This 15-card set spotlights baseball's top hitters and feature red foil stamping. Card backs are numbered with a "LB" suffix and are seeded 1:7 packs.

		NM/M
Complete Set (15):		10.00
Common Player:		.25
Inserted 1:7		
1	Juan Gonzalez	.35
2	Mark McGwire	1.50
3	Jeff Bagwell	.50
4	Frank Thomas	.50
5	Mike Piazza	1.00
6	Nomar Garciaparra	.75
7	Alex Rodriguez	1.50
8	Scott Rolen	.40
9	Travis Lee	.25
10	Tony Gwynn	.75
11	Derek Jeter	2.00
12	Ben Grieve	.25
13	Chipper Jones	.75
14	Ken Griffey Jr.	1.00
15	Cal Ripken Jr.	2.00

Show Business

This 15-card set features some of the best players in the "show" on double foil-stamped card fronts. Card backs are numbered with a "SB" suffix and are seeded 1:70 packs.

		NM/M
Complete Set (15):		60.00
Common Player:		2.00
Inserted 1:70		
1	Mark McGwire	7.50
2	Tony Gwynn	5.00
3	Nomar Garciaparra	5.00
4	Juan Gonzalez	2.50
5	Roger Clemens	5.00
6	Chipper Jones	5.00
7	Cal Ripken Jr.	10.00
8	Alex Rodriguez	7.50
9	Orlando Hernandez	2.00
10	Greg Maddux	5.00
11	Mike Piazza	6.00
12	Frank Thomas	4.00
13	Ken Griffey Jr.	6.00
14	Scott Rolen	3.00
15	Derek Jeter	10.00

Soul of The Game

This 15-card set features rainbow foil stamping and the name Soul of the Game prominently stamped, covering the entire card behind the player photo. Card backs are numbered with a "SG" suffix and are seeded 1:14 packs.

		NM/M
Complete Set (15):		15.00
Common Player:		.60
Inserted 1:14		
1	Alex Rodriguez	2.00
2	Vladimir Guerrero	.90
3	Chipper Jones	1.25
4	Derek Jeter	2.50
5	Tony Gwynn	1.25
6	Scott Rolen	.60
7	Juan Gonzalez	.60
8	Mark McGwire	2.00
9	Ken Griffey Jr.	1.50
10	Jeff Bagwell	.90
11	Cal Ripken Jr.	2.50
12	Frank Thomas	.90
13	Mike Piazza	1.50
14	Nomar Garciaparra	1.25
15	Sammy Sosa	1.25

1999 SkyBox Thunder

Skybox Thunder consists of a 300-card base set with three parallels and six inserts. The base set is inserted at varying odds. In hobby packs, regular-player cards #1-140 come 4-5 per pack, veteran stars on cards #141-240 come two per pack, and superstars on cards #241-300 are seeded one per pack. For retail packs the odds were: #1-141 (3-4 per pack), #141-240 (two per pack), and #241-300 (one per pack). Parallels include Rave (numbered to 150 sets) and Super Rave (25 sets), which are both hobby exclusive. The Rant parallel set is retail exclusive (1:2).

	NM/M
Complete Set (300):	15.00
Common Player (1-240):	.05
Common Player (241-300):	.05
Raves:	15X
Production 150 Sets	
SuperRaves:	45X
Production 25 Sets	
Rants:	8X
Inserted 1:2 R	
Pack (8):	1.50
Wax Box (36):	25.00

1 John Smoltz .05
2 Garret Anderson .05
3 Matt Williams .05
4 Daryle Ward .05
5 Andy Ashby .05
6 Miguel Tejada .15
7 Dmitri Young .05
8 Roberto Alomar .25
9 Kevin Brown .05
10 Eric Young .05
11 Odalis Perez .05
12 Preston Wilson .05
13 Jeff Abbott .05
14 Bret Boone .05
15 Mendy Lopez .05
16 B.J. Surhoff .05
17 Steve Woodard .05
18 Ron Coomer .05
19 Rondell White .05
20 Edgardo Alfonzo .05
21 Kevin Millwood .05
22 Jose Canseco .45
23 Blake Stein .05
24 Quivio Veras .05
25 Chuck Knoblauch .05
26 David Segui .05
27 Eric Davis .05
28 Francisco Cordova .05
29 Randy Winn .05
30 Will Clark .05
31 Billy Wagner .05
32 Kevin Witt .05
33 Jim Edmonds .05
34 Todd Stottlemyre .05
35 Shane Andrews .05
36 Michael Tucker .05
37 Sandy Alomar Jr. .05
38 Neifi Perez .05
39 Jaret Wright .05
40 Devon White .05
41 Edgar Renteria .05
42 Shane Reynolds .05
43 Jeff King .05
44 Darren Dreifort .05
45 Fernando Vina .05
46 Marty Cordova .05
47 Ugueth Urbina .05
48 Bobby Bonilla .05
49 Omar Vizquel .05
50 Tom Gordon .05
51 Ryan Christenson .05
52 Aaron Boone .05
53 Jamie Moyer .05
54 Brian Giles .05
55 Kevin Tapani .05
56 Scott Brosius .05
57 Ellis Burks .05
58 Al Leiter .05
59 Royce Clayton .05
60 Chris Carpenter .05
61 Bubba Trammell .05
62 Tom Glavine .35
63 Shannon Stewart .05
64 Todd Zeile .05
65 J.T. Snow .05
66 Matt Clement .05
67 Matt Stairs .05
68 Ismael Valdes .05
69 Todd Walker .05
70 Jose Lima .05
71 Mike Caruso .05
72 Brett Tomko .05
73 Mike Lansing .05
74 Justin Thompson .05
75 Damion Easley .05
76 Derrek Lee .50
77 Derek Bell .05
78 Brady Anderson .05
79 Charles Johnson .05
80 Rafael Roque RC .05
81 Corey Koskie .05
82 Fernando Seguignol .05
83 Jay Tessmer .05
84 Jason Giambi .50
85 Mike Lieberthal .05
86 Jose Guillen .05
87 Jim Leyritz .05
88 Shawn Estes .05
89 Ray Lankford .05
90 Paul Sorrento .05
91 Javy Lopez .05
92 John Wetteland .05
93 Sean Casey .15
94 Chuck Finley .05
95 Trot Nixon .05
96 Ray Durham .05
97 Reggie Sanders .05
98 Bartolo Colon .05
99 Henry Rodriguez .05
100 Rolando Arrojo .05
101 Geoff Jenkins .05
102 Darryl Kile .05
103 Mark Kotsay .05
104 Craig Biggio .15
105 Omar Daal .05
106 Carlos Febles .05
107 Eric Karros .05
108 Matt Lawton .05
109 Carl Pavano .05
110 Brian McRae .05
111 Mariano Rivera .15
112 Jay Buhner .05
113 Doug Glanville .05
114 Jason Kendall .05
115 Wally Joyner .05
116 Jeff Kent .05
117 Shane Monahan .05
118 Eli Marrero .05

#	Player	Price
119	Bobby Smith	.05
120	Shawn Green	.20
121	Kirk Rueter	.05
122	Tom Goodwin	.05
123	Andy Benes	.05
124	Ed Sprague	.05
125	Mike Mussina	.25
126	Jose Offerman	.05
127	Mickey Morandini	.05
128	Paul Konerko	.20
129	Denny Neagle	.05
130	Travis Fryman	.05
131	John Rocker	.05
132	Rob Fick RC	.05
133	Livan Hernandez	.05
134	Ken Caminiti	.05
135	Johnny Damon	.30
136	Jeff Kubenka	.05
137	Marquis Grissom	.05
138	Doug Mientkiewicz	.05
139	Dustin Hermanson	.05
140	Carl Everett	.05
141	Hideo Nomo	.40
142	Jorge Posada	.05
143	Rickey Henderson	.75
144	Robb Nen	.05
145	Ron Gant	.05
146	Aramis Ramirez	.05
147	Trevor Hoffman	.05
148	Bill Mueller	.05
149	Edgar Martinez	.05
150	Fred McGriff	.05
151	Rusty Greer	.05
152	Tom Evans	.05
153	Todd Greene	.05
154	Jay Bell	.05
155	Mike Lowell	.05
156	Orlando Cabrera	.05
157	Troy O'Leary	.05
158	Jose Hernandez	.05
159	Magglio Ordonez	.05
160	Barry Larkin	.05
161	David Justice	.05
162	Derrick Gibson	.05
163	Luis Gonzalez	.05
164	Alex Gonzalez	.05
165	Scott Elarton	.05
166	Dermal Brown	.05
167	Eric Milton	.05
168	Raul Mondesi	.05
169	Jeff Cirillo	.05
170	Benj Sampson	.05
171	John Olerud	.05
172	Andy Pettitte	.20
173	A.J. Hinch	.05
174	Rico Brogna	.05
175	Jason Schmidt	.05
176	Dean Palmer	.05
177	Matt Morris	.05
178	Quinton McCracken	.05
179	Rick Helling	.05
180	Walt Weiss	.05
181	Troy Percival	.05
182	Tony Batista	.05
183	Brian Jordan	.05
184	Jerry Hairston Jr.	.05
185	Bret Saberhagen	.05
186	Mark Grace	.05
187	Brian Simmons	.05
188	Pete Harnisch	.05
189	Kenny Lofton	.05
190	Vinny Castilla	.05
191	Bobby Higginson	.05
192	Joey Hamilton	.05
193	Cliff Floyd	.05
194	Andres Galarraga	.05
195	Chan Ho Park	.05
196	Jeromy Burnitz	.05
197	David Ortiz	.35
198	Wilton Guerrero	.05
199	Rey Ordonez	.05
200	Paul O'Neill	.05
201	Kenny Rogers	.05
202	Marlon Anderson	.05
203	Tony Womack	.05
204	Robin Ventura	.05
205	Russ Ortiz	.05
206	Mike Frank	.05
207	Fernando Tatis	.05
208	Miguel Cairo	.05
209	Ivan Rodriguez	.65
210	Carlos Delgado	.50
211	Tim Salmon	.15
212	Brian Anderson	.05
213	Ryan Klesko	.05
214	Scott Erickson	.05
215	Mike Stanley	.05
216	Brant Brown	.05
217	Rod Beck	.05
218	Guillermo Garcia RC	.05
219	David Wells	.05
220	Dante Bichette	.05
221	Armando Benitez	.05
222	Todd Dunwoody	.05
223	Kelvim Escobar	.05
224	Richard Hidalgo	.05
225	Angel Pena	.05
226	Ronnie Belliard	.05
227	Brad Radke	.05
228	Brad Fullmer	.05
229	Jay Payton	.05
230	Tino Martinez	.05
231	Scott Spiezio	.05
232	Bobby Abreu	.05
233	John Valentin	.05
234	Kevin Young	.05
235	Steve Finley	.05
236	David Cone	.05

#	Player	Price
237	Armando Rios	.05
238	Russ Davis	.05
239	Wade Boggs	1.00
240	Aaron Sele	.05
241	Jose Cruz Jr.	.15
242	George Lombard	.15
243	Todd Helton	.65
244	Andruw Jones	.75
245	Troy Glaus	.65
246	Manny Ramirez	.75
247	Ben Grieve	.15
247p	Ben Grieve/OPS	.15
248	Richie Sexson	.15
249	Juan Encarnacion	.15
250	Randy Johnson	.75
251	Gary Sheffield	.45
252	Rafael Palmeiro	.65
253	Roy Halladay	.15
254	Mike Piazza	1.50
255	Tony Gwynn	1.00
256	Juan Gonzalez	.40
257	Jeremy Giambi	.15
258	Ben Davis	.15
259	Russ Branyan	.15
260	Pedro Martinez	.75
261	Frank Thomas	.75
262	Calvin Pickering	.15
263	Chipper Jones	1.00
264	Ryan Minor	.15
265	Roger Clemens	1.25
266	Sammy Sosa	1.00
267	Mo Vaughn	.15
268	Carlos Beltran	.50
269	Jim Thome	.65
270	Mark McGwire	2.00
271	Travis Lee	.15
272	Darin Erstad	.30
273	Derek Jeter	2.50
274	Greg Maddux	1.00
275	Ricky Ledee	.15
276	Alex Rodriguez	2.00
277	Vladimir Guerrero	.75
278	Greg Vaughn	.15
279	Scott Rolen	.60
280	Carlos Guillen	.15
281	Jeff Bagwell	.75
282	Bruce Chen	.15
283	Tony Clark	.15
284	Albert Belle	.05
285	Cal Ripken Jr.	2.50
286	Barry Bonds	2.50
287	Curt Schilling	.35
288	Eric Chavez	.30
289	Larry Walker	.15
290	Orlando Hernandez	.15
291	Moises Alou	.15
292	Ken Griffey Jr.	1.50
293	Kerry Wood	.50
294	Nomar Garciaparra	1.00
295	Gabe Kapler	.15
296	Bernie Williams	.05
297	Matt Anderson	.15
298	Adrian Beltre	.35
299	J.D. Drew	.40
300	Ryan Bradley	.15
---	Checklist 1-230	.05
---	Checklist 231-300 and inserts	.05
---	Video Game Sweepstakes form (Derek Jeter)	.05

Dial 1

Designed to look like a mobile phone, this insert set features 10 cards of long distance hitters. The format consists of black plastic cards with rounded corners.

		NM/M
Complete Set (10):		70.00
Common Player:		2.50
Inserted 1:300		
1D	Nomar Garciaparra	7.50
2D	Juan Gonzalez	3.40
3D	Ken Griffey Jr.	10.00
4D	Chipper Jones	7.50
5D	Mark McGwire	12.50
6D	Mike Piazza	10.00

ABBREVIATIONS

OPS - Overprinted "Promotional Sample"

	Player	Price
7D	Manny Ramirez	6.00
8D	Alex Rodriguez	12.50
9D	Sammy Sosa	7.50
10D	Mo Vaughn	2.50

Rant

A retail-only parallel of the 300-card base set, Rant substitutes purple metallic foil highlights for the regular-issue's silver on front, and a has a "RANT" notation at upper-right on back, also in purple. The stated insertion rate for the parallel is one per two retail packs.

	NM/M
Common Player:	.50
Rant Stars:	8X

Todd Helton Autograph

An unknown number of Helton's regular card (#243) were autographed and received an embossed seal of authenticity for use in various promotional endeavors.

		NM/M
243	Todd Helton	15.00

Hip-No-Tized

This insert set consisted of 15 cards, featuring both hitters and pitchers. The cards were seeded one card in every 36 packs, and consist of mesmerizing patterned holo-foil stamping.

		NM/M
Complete Set (15):		20.00
Common Player:		1.25
Inserted 1:36		
1H	J.D. Drew	1.25
2H	Nomar Garciaparra	2.00
3H	Juan Gonzalez	1.25
4H	Ken Griffey Jr.	2.50
5H	Derek Jeter	4.00
6H	Randy Johnson	1.50
7H	Chipper Jones	2.00
8H	Mark McGwire	3.00
9H	Mike Piazza	2.50

	Player	Price
10H	Cal Ripken Jr.	4.00
11H	Alex Rodriguez	3.00
12H	Sammy Sosa	2.00
13H	Frank Thomas	1.50
14H	Jim Thome	1.25
15H	Kerry Wood	1.25

In Depth

This insert set consists of 10 cards, featuring baseball's elite players. The cards are highlighted with gold rainbow holofoil and gold metallic ink. The insertion rate for this insert was one card in every 24 packs.

		NM/M
Complete Set (10):		17.50
Common Player:		1.00
Inserted 1:24		
1ID	Albert Belle	1.00
2ID	Barry Bonds	5.00
3ID	Roger Clemens	1.50
4ID	Juan Gonzalez	1.25
5ID	Ken Griffey Jr.	4.00
6ID	Mark McGwire	4.00
7ID	Mike Piazza	3.00
8ID	Sammy Sosa	2.50
9ID	Mo Vaughn	1.00
10ID	Kerry Wood	1.25

Turbo Charged

This 10-card insert set consisted of the top home run hitters. The players were featured on plastic see-through cards with rainbow holofoil.

		NM/M
Complete Set (10):		35.00
Common Player:		2.00
Inserted 1:72		
1TC	Jose Canseco	2.50
2TC	Juan Gonzalez	2.00
3TC	Ken Griffey Jr.	5.00
4TC	Vladimir Guerrero	3.00
5TC	Mark McGwire	6.00
6TC	Mike Piazza	5.00
7TC	Manny Ramirez	3.00
8TC	Alex Rodriguez	6.00
9TC	Sammy Sosa	4.00
10TC	Mo Vaughn	2.00

Unleashed

Six-card cello packs of specially marked (printed logo in top corner) cards were distributed at the 2000 National Sports Collectors Convention in Anaheim, Calif., to promote Fleer's SkyBox brand. Cards are numbered "X of 6" on back.

This insert set contained 15 cards designed to resemble a cereal box. The players featured included the best young talent in baseball. The cards were silver-foil stamped, and offered facsimile signatures of each player. One card was included with every six packs.

		NM/M
Complete Set (15):		10.00
Common Player:		.50
Inserted 1:6		
1U	Carlos Beltran	1.50
2U	Adrian Beltre	1.00
3U	Eric Chavez	.75
4U	J.D. Drew	1.00
5U	Juan Encarnacion	.50
6U	Jeremy Giambi	.50
7U	Troy Glaus	2.00
8U	Ben Grieve	.50
9U	Todd Helton	2.00
10U	Orlando Hernandez	.50
11U	Gabe Kapler	.50
12U	Travis Lee	.50
13U	Calvin Pickering	.50
14U	Richie Sexson	.50
15U	Kerry Wood	1.00

www.Batterz.com

www.batterz.com is a 10-card insert set that was seeded one card per every 18 packs. The game's best hitters are in their own home site in this computer-inspired set.

		NM/M
Complete Set (10):		12.00
Common Player:		.50
Inserted 1:18		
1WB	J.D. Drew	.60
2WB	Nomar Garciaparra	1.00
3WB	Ken Griffey Jr.	1.50
4WB	Tony Gwynn	1.00
5WB	Derek Jeter	3.00
6WB	Mark McGwire	2.00
7WB	Alex Rodriguez	2.00
8WB	Scott Rolen	.65
9WB	Sammy Sosa	1.00
10WB	Bernie Williams	.50

2000 SkyBox National Covention Promos

		NM/M
Complete Set (6):		8.00
Common Player:		1.25
1	Cal Ripken Jr.	2.00
2	Ken Griffey Jr.	1.25
3	Derek Jeter	2.00
4	Alex Rodriguez	1.50
5	Mark McGwire	1.50
6	Mike Piazza	1.25

2000 SkyBox

		NM/M
Complete Set (250):		25.00
Comp. Set w/SPs (300):		85.00
Common Player:		.10
Common SP (201-240):		1.00
Inserted 1:8		
Common SP (241-250):		.50
Inserted 1:12		
Pack (10):		1.50
Wax Box (24):		30.00
1	Cal Ripken Jr.	2.00
2	Ivan Rodriguez	.65
3	Chipper Jones	1.00
4	Dean Palmer	.10
5	Devon White	.10
6	Ugueth Urbina	.10
7	Doug Glanville	.10
8	Damian Jackson	.10
9	Jose Canseco	.40
10	Billy Koch	.10
11	Brady Anderson	.10
12	Vladimir Guerrero	.75
13	Dan Wilson	.10
14	Kevin Brown	.10
15	Eddie Taubensee	.10
16	Jose Lima	.10
17	Greg Maddux	1.00
18	Manny Ramirez	.75
19	Brad Fullmer	.10
20	Ron Gant	.10
21	Edgar Martinez	.10
22	Pokey Reese	.10
23	Jason Varitek	.10
24	Neifi Perez	.10
25	Shane Reynolds	.10
26	Robin Ventura	.10
27	Scott Rolen	.65
28	Trevor Hoffman	.10
29	John Valentin	.10
30	Shannon Stewart	.10
31	Troy Glaus	.75
32	Kerry Wood	.65
33	Jim Thome	.65
34	Rafael Roque	.10
35	Tino Martinez	.10
36	Jeffrey Hammonds	.10
37	Orlando Hernandez	.10
38	Kris Benson	.10
39	Fred McGriff	.10
40	Brian Jordan	.10
41	Trot Nixon	.10
42	Matt Clement	.10
43	Ray Durham	.10
44	Johnny Damon	.30
45	Todd Hollandsworth	.10
46	Edgardo Alfonzo	.10
47	Tim Hudson	.25
48	Tony Gwynn	1.00
49	Barry Bonds	2.00
50	Andruw Jones	.75
51	Pedro Martinez	.75
52	Mike Hampton	.10
53	Miguel Tejada	.25
54	Kevin Young	.10
55	J.T. Snow	.10
56	Carlos Delgado	.50
57	Bobby Howry	.10
58	Andres Galarraga	.10
59	Paul Konerko	.20
60	Mike Cameron	.10
61	Jeremy Giambi	.10
62	Todd Hundley	.10
63	Al Leiter	.10
64	Matt Stairs	.10
65	Edgar Renteria	.10
66	Jeff Kent	.10
67	John Wetteland	.10
68	Nomar Garciaparra	1.25
69	Jeff Weaver	.10
70	Matt Williams	.10
71	Kyle Farnsworth	.10
72	Brad Radke	.10
73	Eric Chavez	.25
74	J.D. Drew	.25
75	Steve Finley	.10
76	Pete Harnisch	.10
77	Chad Kreuter	.10
78	Todd Pratt	.10
79	John Jaha	.10
80	Armando Rios	.10
81	Luis Gonzalez	.10
82	Ryan Minor	.10
83	Juan Gonzalez	.75
84	Rickey Henderson	.25
85	Jason Giambi	.50
86	Shawn Estes	.10

#	Player	Price
87	Chad Curtis	.10
88	Jeff Cirillo	.10
89	Juan Encarnacion	.10
90	Tony Womack	.10
91	Mike Mussina	.35
92	Jeff Bagwell	.75
93	Rey Ordonez	.10
94	Joe McEwing	.10
95	Robb Nen	.10
96	Will Clark	.10
97	Chris Singleton	.10
98	Jason Kendall	.10
99	Ken Griffey Jr.	1.25
100	Rusty Greer	.10
101	Charles Johnson	.10
102	Carlos Lee	.10
103	Brad Ausmus	.10
104	Preston Wilson	.10
105	Ronnie Belliard	.10
106	Mike Lieberthal	.10
107	Alex Rodriguez	1.50
108	Jay Bell	.10
109	Frank Thomas	.75
110	Adrian Beltre	.30
111	Ron Coomer	.10
112	Ben Grieve	.10
113	Darryl Kile	.10
114	Erubiel Durazo	.10
115	Magglio Ordonez	.10
116	Gary Sheffield	.40
117	Joe Mays	.10
118	Fernando Tatis	.10
119	David Wells	.10
120	Tim Salmon	.20
121	Troy O'Leary	.10
122	Roberto Alomar	.40
123	Damion Easley	.10
124	Brant Brown	.10
125	Carlos Beltran	.45
126	Eric Karros	.10
127	Geoff Jenkins	.10
128	Roger Clemens	1.00
129	Warren Morris	.10
130	Eric Owens	.10
131	Jose Cruz Jr.	.10
132	Mo Vaughn	.10
133	Eric Young	.10
134	Kenny Lofton	.10
135	Marquis Grissom	.10
136	A.J. Burnett	.10
137	Bernie Williams	.25
138	Javy Lopez	.10
139	Jose Offerman	.10
140	Sean Casey	.25
141	Alex Gonzalez	.10
142	Carlos Febles	.10
143	Mike Piazza	1.25
144	Curt Schilling	.35
145	Ben Davis	.10
146	Rafael Palmeiro	.65
147	Scott Williamson	.10
148	Darin Erstad	.25
149	Joe Girardi	.10
150	Gerald Williams	.10
151	Richie Sexson	.10
152	Corey Koskie	.10
153	Paul O'Neill	.10
154	Chad Hermansen	.10
155	Randy Johnson	.75
156	Henry Rodriguez	.10
157	Bartolo Colon	.10
158	Tony Clark	.10
159	Mike Lowell	.10
160	Moises Alou	.10
161	Todd Walker	.10
162	Mariano Rivera	.20
163	Mark McGwire	1.50
164	Roberto Hernandez	.10
165	Larry Walker	.10
166	Albert Belle	.15
167	Barry Larkin	.10
168	Rolando Arrojo	.10
169	Mark Kotsay	.10
170	Ken Caminiti	.10
171	Dermal Brown	.10
172	Michael Barrett	.10
173	Jay Buhner	.10
174	Ruben Mateo	.10
175	Jim Edmonds	.10
176	Sammy Sosa	1.25
177	Omar Vizquel	.10
178	Todd Helton	.75
179	Kevin Barker	.10
180	Derek Jeter	2.00
181	Brian Giles	.10
182	Greg Vaughn	.10
183	Roy Halladay	.10
184	Tom Glavine	.35
185	Craig Biggio	.10
186	Jose Vidro	.10
187	Andy Ashby	.10
188	Freddy Garcia	.10
189	Garret Anderson	.10
190	Mark Grace	.20
191	Travis Fryman	.10
192	Jeromy Burnitz	.10
193	Jacque Jones	.10
194	David Cone	.10
195	Ryan Rupe	.10
196	John Smoltz	.10
197	Daryle Ward	.10
198	Rondell White	.10
199	Bobby Abreu	.10
200	Justin Thompson	.10
201	Norm Hutchins (Prospect)	.10
201	Norm Hutchins/SP	1.00
202	Ramon Ortiz (Prospect)	.10

ABBREVIATIONS

SP - Short Print

#	Player	Price
202	Ramon Ortiz/SP	1.00
203	Dan Wheeler (Prospect)	.10
203	Dan Wheeler/SP	1.00
204	Matt Riley (Prospect)	.10
204	Matt Riley/SP	1.00
205	Steve Lomasney (Prospect)	.10
205	Steve Lomasney/SP	1.00
206	Chad Meyers (Prospect)	.10
206	Chad Meyers/SP	1.00
207	Gary Glover RC (Prospect)	.20
207	Gary Glover/SP	1.00
208	Joe Crede (Prospect)	.10
208	Joe Crede/SP	1.00
209	Kip Wells (Prospect)	.10
209	Kip Wells/SP	1.00
210	Travis Dawkins (Prospect)	.10
210	Travis Dawkins/SP	1.00
211	Denny Stark RC (Prospect)	.20
211	Denny Stark/SP	1.00
212	Ben Petrick (Prospect)	.10
212	Ben Petrick/SP	1.00
213	Eric Munson (Prospect)	.10
213	Eric Munson/SP	1.00
214	Josh Beckett (Prospect)	.25
214	Josh Beckett/SP	1.50
215	Pablo Ozuna (Prospect)	.10
215	Pablo Ozuna/SP	1.00
216	Brad Penny (Prospect)	.10
216	Brad Penny/SP	1.00
217	Julio Ramirez (Prospect)	.10
217	Julio Ramirez/SP	1.00
218	Danny Peoples (Prospect)	.10
218	Danny Peoples/SP	1.00
219	Wilfredo Rodriguez RC (Prospect)	.10
219	Wilfredo Rodriguez/SP RC	1.00
220	Julio Lugo (Prospect)	.10
220	Julio Lugo/SP	1.00
221	Mark Quinn (Prospect)	.10
221	Mark Quinn/SP	1.00
222	Eric Gagne (Prospect)	.10
222	Eric Gagne/SP	1.00
223	Chad Green (Prospect)	.10
223	Chad Green/SP	1.00
224	Tony Armas Jr. (Prospect)	.10
224	Tony Armas Jr./SP	1.00
225	Milton Bradley (Prospect)	.10
225	Milton Bradley/SP	1.00
226	Rob Bell (Prospect)	.10
226	Rob Bell/SP	1.00
227	Alfonso Soriano (Prospect)	1.00
227	Alfonso Soriano/SP	4.00
228	Wily Pena (Prospect)	.10
228	Wily Pena/SP	1.00
229	Nick Johnson (Prospect)	.10
229	Nick Johnson/SP	1.50
230	Ed Yarnall (Prospect)	.10
230	Ed Yarnall/SP	1.00
231	Ryan Bradley (Prospect)	.10
231	Ryan Bradley/SP	1.00
232	Adam Piatt (Prospect)	.10
232	Adam Piatt/SP	1.00
233	Chad Harville (Prospect)	.10
233	Chad Harville/SP	1.00
234	Alex Sanchez (Prospect)	.10
234	Alex Sanchez/SP	1.00
235	Michael Coleman (Prospect)	.10
235	Michael Coleman/SP	1.00
236	Pat Burrell (Prospect)	.25
236	Pat Burrell/SP	1.50
237	Wascar Serrano RC (Prospect)	.10
237	Wascar Serrano/SP RC	1.00
238	Rick Ankiel (Prospect)	.10
238	Rick Ankiel/SP	1.00
239	Mike Lamb RC (Prospect)	.10
239	Mike Lamb/SP RC	1.00
240	Vernon Wells (Prospect)	.10
240	Vernon Wells/SP	1.00
241	Jorge Toca, Goefrey Tomlinson (Premium Pairs)	.10
241	Jorge Toca, Goefrey Tomlinson/SP	.50
242	Shea Hillenbrand, Josh Phelps RC (Premium Pairs)	2.00
242	Shea Hillenbrand, Josh Phelps/SP RC	4.00
243	Aaron Myette, Doug Davis (Premium Pairs)	.10

#	Player	Price
243	Aaron Myette, Doug Davis/SP	.50
244	Brett Laxton, Robert Ramsay (Premium Pairs)	.10
244	Brett Laxton, Robert Ramsay/SP	.50
245	B.J. Ryan, Corey Lee (Premium Pairs)	.10
245	B.J. Ryan, Corey Lee/SP	.50
246	Chris Haas, Wilton Veras (Premium Pairs)	.10
246	Chris Haas, Wilton Veras/SP	.50
247	Jimmy Anderson, Kyle Peterson (Premium Pairs)	.10
247	Jimmy Anderson, Kyle Peterson/SP	.50
248	Jason Dewey, Giuseppe Chiaramonte (Premium Pairs)	.10
248	Jason Dewey, Giuseppe Chiaramonte/SP	.50
249	Guillermo Mota, Orber Moreno (Premium Pairs)	.10
249	Guillermo Mota, Orber Moreno/SP	.50
250	Steve Cox, Julio Zuleta RC (Premium Pairs)	.15
250	Steve Cox, Julio Zuleta/SP RC	.50

Star Rubies

This parallel of the 250-card SkyBox base set shares the same format and photos. On front, however, the player identification and SkyBox logo are in red foil. On back, an SR has been added beneath the card number. Insertion rate was one per 12 packs.

	NM/M
Complete Set (250):	200.00
Common Player (1-200):	.50
Common SP Prospect (201-250):	3.00
Stars:	6X
Star SP's:	3X

Star Rubies Extreme

This parallel of the 250-card SkyBox base set shares the same format and photos. On front, however, the player identification and SkyBox logo are in red foil, and the metallic-foil background has an optical variable layer of stars. On back, an SRE has been added beneath the card number, as well as a strip with a red-foil serial number from within an edition of 50 cards each.

	NM/M
Common Player (1-200):	3.00
Common SP Prospect (201-250):	4.50
Stars:	25X
Star SP's:	15X

Autographics

	NM/M
Common Player	5.00
Rick Ankiel	6.00
Michael Barrett	5.00
Josh Beckett	20.00
Rob Bell	5.00
Adrian Beltre	15.00
Peter Bergeron	5.00
Lance Berkman	15.00
Rico Brogna	5.00
Pat Burrell	20.00
Orlando Cabrera	15.00
Mike Cameron	8.00
Roger Cedeno	5.00
Eric Chavez	15.00

Player	Price
Bruce Chen	5.00
Johnny Damon	20.00
Ben Davis	5.00
Jason Dewey	5.00
Octavio Dotel	6.00
J.D. Drew	15.00
Erubiel Durazo	8.00
Jason Giambi	20.00
Doug Glanville	5.00
Troy Glaus	20.00
Alex Gonzalez	5.00
Shawn Green	15.00
Jason Grilli	5.00
Tony Gwynn	40.00
Mike Hampton	8.00
Tim Hudson	15.00
Norm Hutchins	5.00
John Jaha	5.00
Derek Jeter	100.00
D'Angelo Jimenez	5.00
Randy Johnson	60.00
Andruw Jones	20.00
Gabe Kapler	8.00
Jason Kendall	10.00
Adam Kennedy	8.00
Cesar King	5.00
Paul Konerko	8.00
Mark Kotsay	8.00
Carlos Lee	8.00
Mike Lieberthal	5.00
Steve Lomasney	5.00
Greg Maddux	50.00
Edgar Martinez	15.00
Aaron McNeal	5.00
Kevin Millwood	10.00
Raul Mondesi	8.00
Joe Nathan	5.00
Magglio Ordonez	15.00
Eric Owens	5.00
Rafael Palmeiro	25.00
Angel Pena	5.00
Wily Pena	15.00
Cal Ripken Jr.	85.00
Scott Rolen	20.00
Jimmy Rollins	15.00
B.J. Ryan	5.00
Tim Salmon	10.00
Chris Singleton	5.00
J.T. Snow	6.00
Mike Sweeney	8.00
Jose Vidro	8.00
Rondell White	8.00
Jaret Wright	5.00

E-Ticket

	NM/M
Complete Set (14):	15.00
Common Player:	.50
Inserted 1:4	
Star Ruby:	4-8X
Production 100 Sets	
1	Alex Rodriguez	2.50
2	Derek Jeter	3.00
3	Nomar Garciaparra	1.50
4	Cal Ripken Jr.	3.00
5	Sean Casey	.50
6	Mark McGwire	2.50
7	Sammy Sosa	1.50
8	Ken Griffey Jr.	2.00
9	Tony Gwynn	1.50
10	Pedro Martinez	1.50
11	Chipper Jones	1.50
12	Vladimir Guerrero	1.00
13	Roger Clemens	1.75
14	Mike Piazza	2.00

Genuine Coverage

	NM/M
Common Player:	8.00
Inserted 1:399	
1	Troy Glaus	15.00
2	Cal Ripken Jr.	40.00
3	Alex Rodriguez	25.00
4	Mike Mussina	10.00
5	J.D. Drew	8.00
6	Robin Ventura	8.00
7	Matt Williams	8.00

Genuine Coverage HOBBY

	NM/M
Common Player:	10.00
Inserted 1:144	
1	Ivan Rodriguez	12.00
2	Jose Canseco	10.00
3	Frank Thomas	15.00
4	Manny Ramirez	15.00

Higher Level

	NM/M
Complete Set (10):	20.00
Common Player:	1.00
Inserted 1:24	
Star Ruby:	5-10X
Production 50 Sets	
1	Cal Ripken Jr.	4.00
2	Derek Jeter	4.00
3	Nomar Garciaparra	2.00
4	Chipper Jones	2.00
5	Mike Piazza	2.50
6	Ivan Rodriguez	1.00
7	Ken Griffey Jr.	2.50
8	Sammy Sosa	2.00
9	Alex Rodriguez	3.00
10	Mark McGwire	3.00

Preeminence

	NM/M
Complete Set (10):	15.00
Common Player:	.50
Inserted 1:24	
Star Ruby:	5-10X
Production 50 Sets	
1	Pedro Martinez	1.25
2	Derek Jeter	4.00
3	Nomar Garciaparra	1.50
4	Alex Rodriguez	3.00
5	Mark McGwire	3.00
6	Sammy Sosa	1.50
7	Sean Casey	.50
8	Mike Piazza	2.00
9	Chipper Jones	1.50
10	Ivan Rodriguez	1.00

SkyLines

	NM/M
Complete Set (10):	10.00
Common Player:	.50
Inserted 1:11	
Star Ruby:	10-20X
Production 50 Sets	

	NM/M
1	Cal Ripken Jr.	2.00
2	Mark McGwire	1.50
3	Alex Rodriguez	1.50
4	Sammy Sosa	.75
5	Derek Jeter	2.00
6	Mike Piazza	1.00
7	Nomar Garciaparra	.75
8	Chipper Jones	.75
9	Ken Griffey Jr.	1.00
10	Manny Ramirez	.50

Speed Merchants

	NM/M
Common Player:	10.00
Inserted 1:8	
1	Ivan Rodriguez	12.00
2	Jose Canseco	10.00
3	Frank Thomas	15.00
4	Manny Ramirez	15.00

	NM/M
Complete Set (10):	12.00
Common Player:	.50
Inserted 1:8	
Star Ruby:	3-6X
Production 100 Sets	
1	Derek Jeter	3.00
2	Sammy Sosa	1.25
3	Nomar Garciaparra	1.25
4	Alex Rodriguez	2.50
5	Randy Johnson	1.00
6	Ken Griffey Jr.	1.50
7	Pedro Martinez	1.00
8	Pat Burrell	.50
9	Barry Bonds	3.00
10	Mark McGwire	2.50

The Technique

	NM/M
Complete Set (15):	20.00
Common Player:	
Inserted 1:11	
Star Ruby:	3-6X
Production 50 Sets	
1	Alex Rodriguez	3.00
2	Tony Gwynn	1.50
3	Sean Casey	.50
4	Mark McGwire	3.00
5	Sammy Sosa	1.50
6	Ken Griffey Jr.	2.00
7	Mike Piazza	2.00
8	Nomar Garciaparra	1.50
9	Derek Jeter	4.00
10	Vladimir Guerrero	1.00
11	Cal Ripken Jr.	4.00
12	Chipper Jones	1.50
13	Frank Thomas	1.00
14	Manny Ramirez	1.00
15	Jeff Bagwell	1.00

2000 SkyBox Dominion

	NM/M
Complete Set (300):	20.00

Common Player:		.10
Pack (10):		1.50
Wax Box (36):		30.00
1	Mark McGwire, Ken Griffey Jr. (League Leaders)	.40
2	Mark McGwire, Manny Ramirez (League Leaders)	.40
3	Larry Walker, Nomar Garciaparra (League Leaders)	.25
4	Tony Womack, Brian Hunter (League Leaders)	.10
5	Mike Hampton, Pedro Martinez (League Leaders)	.20
6	Randy Johnson, Pedro Martinez (League Leaders)	.20
7	Randy Johnson, Pedro Martinez (League Leaders)	.20
8	Ugueth Urbina, Mariano Rivera (League Leaders)	.10
9	Vinny Castilla (Highlights)	.10
10	Orioles host Cuban National Team (Highlights)	.10
11	Jose Canseco (Highlights)	.10
12	Fernando Tatis (Highlights)	.10
13	Robin Ventura (Highlights)	.10
14	Roger Clemens (Highlights)	.50
15	Jose Jimenez (Highlights)	.10
16	David Cone (Highlights)	.10
17	Mark McGwire (Highlights)	.65
18	Cal Ripken Jr. (Highlights)	.75
19	Tony Gwynn (Highlights)	.30
20	Wade Boggs (Highlights)	.25
21	Ivan Rodriguez (Highlights)	.10
22	Chuck Finley (Highlights)	.10
23	Eric Milton (Highlights)	.10
24	Adrian Beltre (Highlights)	.10
25	Brad Radke	.10
26	Derek Bell	.10
27	Garret Anderson	.10
28	Ivan Rodriguez	.40
29	Jeff Kent	.10
30	Jeremy Giambi	.10
31	John Franco	.10
32	Jose Hernandez	.10
33	Jose Offerman	.10
34	Jose Rosado	.10
35	Kevin Appier	.10
36	Kris Benson	.10
37	Mark McGwire	1.00
38	Matt Williams	.10
39	Paul O'Neill	.10
40	Rickey Henderson	.50
41	Todd Greene	.10
42	Russ Ortiz	.10
43	Sean Casey	.20
44	Tony Womack	.10
45	Troy O'Leary	.10
46	Ugueth Urbina	.10
47	Tom Glavine	.25
48	Mike Mussina	.30
49	Carlos Febles	.10
50	Jon Lieber	.10
51	Juan Gonzalez	.30
52	Matt Clement	.10
53	Moises Alou	.10
54	Ray Durham	.10
55	Robb Nen	.10
56	Tino Martinez	.10
57	Troy Glaus	.40
58	Curt Schilling	.30
59	Mike Sweeney	.10
60	Steve Finley	.10
61	Roger Cedeno	.10
62	Bobby Jones	.10
63	John Smoltz	.10
64	Darin Erstad	.20
65	Carlos Delgado	.35
66	Ray Lankford	.10
67	Todd Stottlemyre	.10
68	Andy Ashby	.10
69	Bobby Abreu	.15
70	Chuck Finley	.10
71	Damion Easley	.10
72	Dustin Hermanson	.10
73	Frank Thomas	.50
74	Kevin Brown	.10
75	Kevin Millwood	.10
76	Mark Grace	.10
77	Matt Stairs	.10
78	Mike Hampton	.10
79	Omar Vizquel	.10
80	Preston Wilson	.10
81	Robin Ventura	.10
82	Todd Helton	.40
83	Tony Clark	.10
84	Al Leiter	.10
85	Alex Fernandez	.10

86	Bernie Williams	.10
87	Edgar Martinez	.10
88	Edgar Renteria	.10
89	Fred McGriff	.10
90	Jermaine Dye	.10
91	Joe McEwing	.10
92	John Halama	.10
93	Lee Stevens	.10
94	Matt Lawton	.10
95	Mike Piazza	.75
96	Pete Harnisch	.10
97	Scott Karl	.10
98	Tony Fernandez	.10
99	Sammy Sosa	.60
100	Bobby Higginson	.10
101	Tony Gwynn	.60
102	J.D. Drew	.20
103	Roberto Hernandez	.10
104	Rondell White	.10
105	David Nilsson	.10
106	Shane Reynolds	.10
107	Jaret Wright	.10
108	Jeff Bagwell	.50
109	Jay Bell	.10
110	Kevin Tapani	.10
111	Michael Barrett	.10
112	Neifi Perez	.10
113	Pat Hentgen	.10
114	Roger Clemens	.65
115	Travis Fryman	.10
116	Aaron Sele	.10
117	Eric Davis	.10
118	Trevor Hoffman	.10
119	Chris Singleton	.10
120	Ryan Klesko	.10
121	Scott Rolen	.40
122	Jorge Posada	.10
123	Abraham Nunez	.10
124	Alex Gonzalez	.10
125	B.J. Surhoff	.10
126	Barry Bonds	1.50
127	Billy Koch	.10
128	Billy Wagner	.10
129	Brad Ausmus	.10
130	Bret Boone	.10
131	Cal Ripken Jr.	1.50
132	Chad Allen	.10
133	Chris Carpenter	.10
134	Craig Biggio	.10
135	Dante Bichette	.10
136	Dean Palmer	.10
137	Derek Jeter	1.50
138	Ellis Burks	.10
139	Freddy Garcia	.10
140	Gabe Kapler	.10
141	Greg Maddux	.60
142	Greg Vaughn	.10
143	Jason Kendall	.10
144	Jim Parque	.10
145	John Valentin	.10
146	Jose Vidro	.10
147	Ken Griffey Jr.	.75
148	Kenny Lofton	.10
149	Kenny Rogers	.10
150	Kent Bottenfield	.10
151	Chuck Knoblauch	.10
152	Larry Walker	.10
153	Manny Ramirez	.50
154	Mickey Morandini	.10
155	Mike Cameron	.10
156	Mike Lieberthal	.10
157	Mo Vaughn	.10
158	Randy Johnson	.50
159	Rey Ordonez	.10
160	Roberto Alomar	.20
161	Scott Williamson	.10
162	Shawn Estes	.10
163	Tim Wakefield	.10
164	Tony Batista	.10
165	Will Clark	.10
166	Wade Boggs	.60
167	David Cone	.10
168	Doug Glanville	.10
169	Jeff Cirillo	.10
170	John Jaha	.10
171	Mariano Rivera	.20
172	Tom Gordon	.10
173	Wally Joyner	.10
174	Alex Gonzalez	.10
175	Andruw Jones	.50
176	Barry Larkin	.10
177	Bartolo Colon	.10
178	Brian Giles	.10
179	Carlos Lee	.10
180	Darren Dreifort	.10
181	Eric Chavez	.20
182	Henry Rodriguez	.10
183	Ismael Valdes	.10
184	Jason Giambi	.40
185	John Wetteland	.10
186	Juan Encarnacion	.10
187	Luis Gonzalez	.10
188	Reggie Sanders	.10
189	Richard Hidalgo	.10
190	Ryan Rupe	.10
191	Sean Berry	.10
192	Rick Helling	.10
193	Randy Wolf	.10
194	Cliff Floyd	.10
195	Jose Lima	.10
196	Chipper Jones	.60
197	Charles Johnson	.10
198	Nomar Garciaparra	.60
199	Magglio Ordonez	.10
200	Shawn Green	.25
201	Travis Lee	.10
202	Jose Canseco	.35
203	Fernando Tatis	.10

204	Bruce Aven	.10
205	Johnny Damon	.35
206	Gary Sheffield	.25
207	Ken Caminiti	.10
208	Ben Grieve	.10
209	Sidney Ponson	.10
210	Vinny Castilla	.10
211	Alex Rodriguez	1.00
212	Chris Widger	.10
213	Carl Pavano	.10
214	J.T. Snow	.10
215	Jim Thome	.40
216	Kevin Young	.10
217	Mike Sirotka	.10
218	Rafael Palmeiro	.40
219	Rico Brogna	.10
220	Todd Walker	.10
221	Todd Zelle	.10
222	Brian Rose	.10
223	Chris Fussell	.10
224	Corey Koskie	.10
225	Rich Aurilia	.10
226	Geoff Jenkins	.10
227	Pedro Martinez	.50
228	Todd Hundley	.10
229	Brian Jordan	.10
230	Cristian Guzman	.10
231	Raul Mondesi	.10
232	Tim Hudson	.20
233	Albert Belle	.10
234	Andy Pettitte	.25
235	Brady Anderson	.10
236	Brian Bohannon	.10
237	Carlos Beltran	.35
238	Doug Mientkiewicz	.10
239	Jason Schmidt	.10
240	Jeff Zimmerman	.10
241	John Olerud	.10
242	Paul Byrd	.10
243	Vladimir Guerrero	.50
244	Warren Morris	.10
245	Eric Karros	.10
246	Jeff Weaver	.10
247	Jeromy Burnitz	.10
248	David Bell	.10
249	Rusty Greer	.10
250	Kevin Stocker	.10
251	Shea Hillenbrand (Prospect)	.15
252	Alfonso Soriano (Prospect)	.50
253	Micah Bowie (Prospect)	.10
254	Gary Matthews Jr. (Prospect)	.10
255	Lance Berkman (Prospect)	.10
256	Pat Burrell (Prospect)	.25
257	Ruben Mateo (Prospect)	.10
258	Kip Wells (Prospect)	.10
259	Wilton Veras (Prospect)	.10
260	Ben Davis (Prospect)	.10
261	Eric Munson (Prospect)	.10
262	Ramon Hernandez (Prospect)	.10
263	Tony Armas Jr. (Prospect)	.10
264	Erubiel Durazo (Prospect)	.10
265	Chad Meyers (Prospect)	.10
266	Rick Ankiel (Prospect)	.10
267	Ramon Ortiz (Prospect)	.10
268	Adam Kennedy (Prospect)	.10
269	Vernon Wells (Prospect)	.10
270	Chad Hermansen (Prospect)	.10
271	Norm Hutchins, Trent Durrington (Prospects)	.10
272	Gabe Molina, B.J. Ryan (Prospects)	.10
273	Juan Pena, Tomokazu Ohka RC (Prospects)	.25
274	Pat Daneker, Aaron Myette (Prospects)	.15
275	Jason Rakers, Russell Branyan (Prospects)	.10
276	Beiker Graterol, Dave Borkowski (Prospects)	.10
277	Mark Quinn, Dan Reichert (Prospects)	.10
278	Mark Redman, Jacque Jones (Prospects)	.15
279	Ed Yarnall, Wily Pena (Prospects)	.10
280	Chad Harville, Brett Laxton (Prospects)	.10
281	Aaron Scheffer, Gil Meche (Prospects)	.10
282	Jim Morris, Dan Wheeler (Prospects)	.10
283	Danny Kolb, Kelly Dransfeldt (Prospects)	.10
284	Peter Munro, Casey Blake (Prospects)	.10
285	Rob Ryan, Byung-Hyun Kim (Prospects)	.10
286	Derrin Ebert, Pascual Matos (Prospects)	.10

287	Richard Barker, Kyle Farnsworth (Prospects)	.10
288	Jason LaRue, Travis Dawkins (Prospects)	.10
289	Chris Sexton, Edgard Clemente (Prospects)	.10
290	Amaury Garcia, A.J. Burnett (Prospects)	.10
291	Carlos Hernandez, Daryle Ward (Prospects)	.10
292	Eric Gagne, Jeff Williams (Prospects)	.10
293	Kyle Peterson, Kevin Barker (Prospects)	.10
294	Fernando Seguignol, Guillermo Mota (Prospects)	.10
295	Melvin Mora, Octavio Dotel (Prospects)	.10
296	Anthony Shumaker, Cliff Politte (Prospects)	.10
297	Yamid Haad, Jimmy Anderson (Prospects)	.10
298	Rick Heiserman, Chad Hutchinson (Prospects)	.10
299	Mike Darr, Wiki Gonzalez (Prospects)	.10
300	Joe Nathan, Calvin Murray (Prospects)	.10

Autographics

		NM/M
Common Player:		5.00
Inserted 1:144		
1	Rick Ankiel	6.00
2	Peter Bergeron	5.00
3	Wade Boggs	25.00
4	Barry Bonds	200.00
5	Pat Burrell	20.00
6	Miguel Cairo	5.00
7	Mike Cameron	8.00
8	Ben Davis	5.00
9	Russ Davis	5.00
10	Einar Diaz	5.00
11	Scott Elarton	5.00
12	Jeremy Giambi	5.00
13	Todd Greene	5.00
14	Vladimir Guerrero	25.00
15	Tony Gwynn	30.00
16	Bobby Howry	5.00
17	Tim Hudson	15.00
18	Randy Johnson	50.00
19	Andruw Jones	20.00
20	Jacque Jones	8.00
21	Jason LaRue	5.00
22	Matt Lawton	6.00
23	Greg Maddux	50.00
24	Pedro Martinez	50.00
25	Pokey Reese	5.00
26	Alex Rodriguez	75.00
27	Ryan Rupe	5.00
28	J.T. Snow	6.00
29	Jose Vidro	6.00
30	Tony Womack	6.00
31	Ed Yarnall	5.00
32	Kevin Young	5.00

Double Play

		NM/M
Complete Set (10):		10.00
Common Player:		1.00
Inserted 1:9		
Plus:		2-4X
Inserted 1:90		
WarpTek:		10-20X
Inserted 1:900		
1	Nomar Garciaparra	1.50
2	Pedro Martinez	1.25
3	Chipper Jones	1.50
4	Mark McGwire	2.50
5	Cal Ripken Jr.	3.00
6	Roger Clemens	1.75
7	Juan Gonzalez	1.00
8	Tony Gwynn	1.50
9	Sammy Sosa	1.50
10	Mike Piazza	2.00

Eye on October

	NM/M
Complete Set (15):	25.00

Common Player:		.50
Inserted 1:24		
Plus:		2-4X
Inserted 1:240		
1	Ken Griffey Jr.	2.50
2	Mark McGwire	3.00
3	Derek Jeter	4.00
4	Juan Gonzalez	1.00
5	Chipper Jones	2.00
6	Sammy Sosa	2.00
7	Greg Maddux	2.00
8	Frank Thomas	1.50
9	Nomar Garciaparra	2.00
10	Shawn Green	1.00
11	Cal Ripken Jr.	4.00
12	Manny Ramirez	1.50
13	Scott Rolen	1.25
14	Mike Piazza	2.50
15	Alex Rodriguez	3.00

Hats Off

		NM/M
Common Player:		15.00
Inserted 1:468 H		
1	Wade Boggs	25.00
2	Barry Bonds	75.00
3	J.D. Drew	15.00
4	Shawn Green	15.00
5	Vladimir Guerrero	25.00
6	Randy Johnson	30.00
7	Andruw Jones	20.00
8	Greg Maddux	40.00
9	Pedro Martinez	25.00
10	Mike Mussina	15.00
11	Rafael Palmeiro	20.00
12	Alex Rodriguez	50.00
13	Scott Rolen	15.00
14	Tim Salmon	15.00
15	Robin Ventura	15.00

Milestones

		NM/M
Common Player:		15.00
Inserted 1:1,999		
1	Mark McGwire	60.00
2	Roger Clemens	40.00
3	Tony Gwynn	25.00
4	Wade Boggs	25.00
5	Cal Ripken Jr.	75.00
6	Jose Canseco	15.00

New Era

		NM/M
Complete Set (20):		5.00
Common Player:		.25
Inserted 1:3		
Plus:		2-4X
Inserted 1:30		
WarpTek:		5-10X
Inserted 1:300		
1	Pat Burrell	.75
2	Ruben Mateo	.25
3	Wilton Veras	.25
4	Eric Munson	.25
5	Jeff Weaver	.25
6	Tim Hudson	.50
7	Carlos Beltran	1.00
8	Chris Singleton	.25
9	Lance Berkman	.25
10	Freddy Garcia	.25
11	Erubiel Durazo	.25
12	Randy Wolf	.25
13	Shea Hillenbrand	.25
14	Kip Wells	.25
15	Alfonso Soriano	.25
16	Rick Ankiel	.25
17	Ramon Ortiz	.25
18	Adam Kennedy	.25
19	Vernon Wells	.25
20	Chad Hermansen	.25

2000 E-X

Released as a 90-card set the card fronts have a holo-foil card front, with the E-X logo and player name stamped in silver foil. Card backs have a player image, 1999 stats and the featured player's career totals.

		NM/M
Complete Set (90):		80.00
Common Player:		.25
Common Prospect (61-90):		3.00
Production 3,499 Sets		
Pack:		2.75
Box:		50.00
1	Alex Rodriguez	2.50
2	Jeff Bagwell	1.00
3	Mike Piazza	2.00
4	Tony Gwynn	1.50
5	Ken Griffey Jr.	2.00
6	Juan Gonzalez	.40
7	Vladimir Guerrero	1.00
8	Cal Ripken Jr.	3.00
9	Mo Vaughn	.25
10	Chipper Jones	1.50
11	Derek Jeter	3.00
12	Nomar Garciaparra	1.50
13	Mark McGwire	2.50
14	Sammy Sosa	1.50
15	Pedro Martinez	1.50
16	Greg Maddux	1.50
17	Frank Thomas	.75
18	Shawn Green	.50
19	Carlos Beltran	.50
20	Roger Clemens	1.75
21	Randy Johnson	1.00
22	Bernie Williams	.25
23	Carlos Delgado	.50
24	Manny Ramirez	.75
25	Freddy Garcia	.25
26	Barry Bonds	3.00
27	Tim Hudson	.40
28	Larry Walker	.25
29	Raul Mondesi	.25
30	Ivan Rodriguez	.65
31	Magglio Ordonez	.25
32	Scott Rolen	.65
33	Mike Mussina	.40
34	J.D. Drew	.50
35	Tom Glavine	.50
36	Barry Larkin	.25
37	Jim Thome	.65
38	Erubiel Durazo	.50
39	Curt Schilling	.50
40	Orlando Hernandez	.25
41	Rafael Palmeiro	.65
42	Gabe Kapler	.25
43	Mark Grace	.25
44	Jeff Cirillo	.25
45	Jeromy Burnitz	.25
46	Sean Casey	.35
47	Kevin Millwood	.25
48	Vinny Castilla	.25
49	Jose Canseco	.50
50	Roberto Alomar	.30
51	Craig Biggio	.25
52	Preston Wilson	.25
53	Jeff Weaver	.25
54	Robin Ventura	.25
55	Ben Grieve	.25
56	Troy Glaus	.65
57	Jacque Jones	.25
58	Brian Giles	.25
59	Kevin Brown	.25
60	Todd Helton	.65
61	Ben Petrick (Prospects)	3.00
62	Chad Hermansen (Prospects)	3.00
63	Kevin Barker (Prospects)	3.00
64	Matt LeCroy (Prospects)	3.00
65	Brad Penny (Prospects)	4.00
66	D.T. Cromer (Prospects)	3.00
67	Steve Lomasney (Prospects)	3.00
68	Cole Liniak (Prospects)	3.00
69	B.J. Ryan (Prospects)	3.00
70	Wilton Veras (Prospects)	3.00
71	Aaron McNeal RC (Prospects)	4.00
72	Nick Johnson (Prospects)	4.00
73	Adam Piatt (Prospects)	3.00

74 Adam Kennedy (Prospects) 3.00
75 Cesar King (Prospects) 3.00
76 Peter Bergeron (Prospects) 3.00
77 Rob Bell (Prospects) 3.00
78 Wily Pena (Prospects) 4.00
79 Ruben Mateo (Prospects) 3.00
80 Kip Wells (Prospects) 3.00
81 Alex Escobar (Prospects) 3.00
82 Danys Baez RC (Prospects) 5.00
83 Travis Dawkins (Prospects) 3.00
84 Mark Quinn (Prospects) 3.00
85 Jimmy Anderson (Prospects) 3.00
86 Rick Ankiel (Prospects) 4.00
87 Alfonso Soriano (Prospects) 5.00
88 Pat Burrell (Prospects) 4.00
89 Eric Munson (Prospects) 3.00
90 Josh Beckett (Prospects) 4.00

Autographics

	NM/M
Common Player:	5.00
Inserted 1:24	
Bob Abreu	15.00
Moises Alou	15.00
Rick Ankiel	6.00
Michael Barrett	5.00
Josh Beckett	20.00
Rob Bell	5.00
Adrian Beltre	15.00
Carlos Beltran	15.00
Wade Boggs	25.00
Barry Bonds	150.00
Kent Bottenfield	5.00
Milton Bradley	10.00
Pat Burrell	20.00
Chris Carpenter	20.00
Sean Casey	10.00
Eric Chavez	15.00
Will Clark	25.00
Johnny Damon	20.00
Mike Darr	5.00
Ben Davis	5.00
Russ Davis	5.00
Carlos Delgado	20.00
Jason Dewey	5.00
Octavio Dotel	5.00
J.D. Drew	15.00
Ray Durham	8.00
Damion Easley	5.00
Kelvim Escobar	6.00
Carlos Febles	5.00
Freddy Garcia	10.00
Jeremy Giambi	10.00
Todd Greene	5.00
Jason Grilli	5.00
Vladimir Guerrero	30.00
Tony Gwynn	40.00
Jerry Hairston Jr.	10.00
Mike Hampton	8.00
Todd Helton	20.00
Trevor Hoffman	10.00
Tim Hudson	15.00
John Jaha	8.00
Derek Jeter	100.00
D'Angelo Jimenez	5.00
Randy Johnson	60.00
Jason Kendall	10.00
Adam Kennedy	8.00
Cesar King	5.00
Paul Konerko	15.00
Mark Kotsay	6.00
Ray Lankford	6.00
Jason LaRue	6.00
Matt Lawton	10.00
Carlos Lee	8.00
Mike Lieberthal	8.00
Cole Liniak	5.00
Steve Lomasney	5.00
Jose Macias	5.00
Greg Maddux	60.00
Edgar Martinez	15.00
Pedro Martinez	75.00
Ruben Mateo	8.00
Gary Matthews Jr.	8.00
Aaron McNeal	5.00
Raul Mondesi	8.00
Orber Moreno	5.00
Warren Morris	5.00
Eric Munson	5.00
Heath Murray	5.00
Mike Mussina	30.00
Joe Nathan	5.00
Rafael Palmeiro	25.00
Jim Parque	6.00
Angel Pena	5.00
Wily Pena	10.00
Pokey Reese	6.00
Matt Riley	5.00
Cal Ripken Jr.	85.00
Alex Rodriguez	75.00
Scott Rolen	20.00
Jimmy Rollins	20.00
B.J. Ryan	8.00
Randall Simon	8.00
Chris Singleton	5.00
Alfonso Soriano	30.00
Shannon Stewart	10.00
Mike Sweeney	8.00
Miguel Tejada	20.00
Frank Thomas	25.00
Wilton Veras	5.00
Billy Wagner	12.00
Jeff Weaver	8.00
Rondell White	8.00
Scott Williamson	8.00
Randy Wolf	8.00
Jaret Wright	8.00
Ed Yarnall	5.00
Kevin Young	10.00

Essential Credentials Future

Production varied for these parallel inserts depending on the card number, with the exact production number for cards 1-60 determined by subtracting the card number from 61. Cards 61-90 are determined by subtracting the card number from 91. Quantity issued is listed in parantheses.

	NM/M
Common Player:	10.00
1 Alex Rodriguez/60	75.00
2 Jeff Bagwell/59	30.00
3 Mike Piazza/58	50.00
4 Tony Gwynn/57	50.00
5 Ken Griffey Jr./56	50.00
6 Juan Gonzalez/55	15.00
7 Vladimir Guerrero/54	20.00
8 Cal Ripken Jr./53	85.00
9 Mo Vaughn/52	15.00
10 Chipper Jones/51	50.00
11 Derek Jeter/50	85.00
12 Nomar Garciaparra/49	45.00
13 Mark McGwire/48	75.00
14 Sammy Sosa/47	50.00
15 Pedro Martinez/46	30.00
16 Greg Maddux/45	50.00
17 Frank Thomas/44	20.00
18 Shawn Green/43	10.00
19 Carlos Beltran/42	10.00
20 Roger Clemens/41	60.00
21 Randy Johnson/40	30.00
22 Bernie Williams/39	10.00
23 Carlos Delgado/38	15.00
24 Manny Ramirez/37	20.00
25 Freddy Garcia/36	10.00
26 Barry Bonds/35	90.00
27 Tim Hudson/34	20.00
28 Larry Walker/33	10.00
29 Raul Mondesi/32	10.00
30 Ivan Rodriguez/31	15.00
31 Magglio Ordonez/30	10.00
32 Scott Rolen/29	20.00
33 Mike Mussina/28	20.00
34 J.D. Drew/27	20.00
35 Tom Glavine/26	15.00
36 Barry Larkin/25	15.00
37 Jim Thome/24	30.00
38 Erubiel Durazo/23	15.00
39 Curt Schilling/22	25.00
40 Orlando Hernandez/21	15.00
41 Rafael Palmeiro/20	40.00
42 Gabe Kapler/19	15.00
43 Mark Grace/18	15.00
44 Jeff Cirillo/17	15.00
45 Jeromy Burnitz/16	15.00
46 Sean Casey/15	20.00
47 Kevin Millwood/14	20.00
48 Vinny Castilla/13	15.00
49 Jose Canseco/12	40.00
50 Roberto Alomar/11	50.00
51 Craig Biggio/10	50.00
52 Ben Petrick/30 (Prospects)	10.00
62 Chad Hermansen/29 (Prospects)	10.00
63 Kevin Barker/28 (Prospects)	10.00
64 Matt LeCroy/27 (Prospects)	10.00
65 Brad Penny/26 (Prospects)	10.00
66 D.T. Cromer/25 (Prospects)	10.00
67 Steve Lomasney/24 (Prospects)	10.00
68 Cole Liniak/23 (Prospects)	10.00
69 B.J. Ryan/22 (Prospects)	10.00
70 Wilton Veras/21 (Prospects)	10.00
71 Aaron McNeal/20 (Prospects)	15.00
72 Nick Johnson/19 (Prospects)	25.00
73 Adam Piatt/18 (Prospects)	15.00
74 Adam Kennedy/17 (Prospects)	15.00
75 Cesar King/16 (Prospects)	15.00
76 Peter Bergeron/15 (Prospects)	15.00
77 Rob Bell/14 (Prospects)	15.00
78 Wily Pena/13 (Prospects)	15.00
79 Ruben Mateo/12 (Prospects)	15.00
80 Kip Wells/11 (Prospects)	15.00
81 Alex Escobar/10 (Prospects)	20.00

Essential Credentials Now

Like Future, this is a parallel of the base set, with the production of cards 1-60 limited to that player's card number. Production for cards 61-90 can be determined by subtracting 60 from the card number. Quantity issued is listed in parantheses.

	NM/M
Common Player:	8.00
20 Roger Clemens/20	50.00
21 Randy Johnson/21	30.00
22 Bernie Williams/22	15.00
23 Carlos Delgado/23	25.00
24 Manny Ramirez/24	30.00
25 Freddy Garcia/25	10.00
26 Barry Bonds/26	75.00
27 Tim Hudson/27	15.00
28 Larry Walker/28	10.00
29 Raul Mondesi/29	10.00
30 Ivan Rodriguez/30	15.00
31 Magglio Ordonez/31	10.00
32 Scott Rolen/32	20.00
33 Mike Mussina/33	15.00
34 J.D. Drew/34	20.00
35 Tom Glavine/35	20.00
36 Barry Larkin/36	15.00
37 Jim Thome/37	25.00
38 Erubiel Durazo/38	8.00
39 Curt Schilling/39	20.00
40 Orlando Hernandez/40	8.00
41 Rafael Palmeiro/41	15.00
42 Gabe Kapler/42	8.00
43 Mark Grace/43	8.00
44 Jeff Cirillo/44	8.00
45 Jeromy Burnitz/45	8.00
46 Sean Casey/46	8.00
47 Kevin Millwood/47	8.00
48 Vinny Castilla/48	8.00
49 Jose Canseco/49	15.00
50 Roberto Alomar/50	12.00
51 Craig Biggio/51	15.00
52 Preston Wilson/52	8.00
53 Jeff Weaver/53	8.00
54 Robin Ventura/54	8.00
55 Ben Grieve/55	8.00
56 Troy Glaus/56	15.00
57 Jacque Jones/57	12.00
58 Brian Giles/58	8.00
59 Kevin Brown/59	8.00
60 Todd Helton/60	20.00
74 Adam Kennedy/14 (Prospects)	15.00
75 Cesar King/15 (Prospects)	15.00
76 Peter Bergeron/16 (Prospects)	15.00
77 Rob Bell/17 (Prospects)	15.00
78 Wily Pena/18 (Prospects)	15.00
79 Ruben Mateo/19 (Prospects)	15.00
80 Kip Wells/20 (Prospects)	15.00
81 Alex Escobar/21 (Prospects)	15.00
82 Danys Baez/22 (Prospects)	15.00
83 Travis Dawkins/23 (Prospects)	15.00
84 Mark Quinn/24 (Prospects)	15.00
85 Jimmy Anderson/25 (Prospects)	15.00
86 Rick Ankiel/26 (Prospects)	15.00
87 Alfonso Soriano/27 (Prospects)	60.00
88 Pat Burrell/28 (Prospects)	30.00
89 Eric Munson/29 (Prospects)	15.00
90 Josh Beckett/30 (Prospects)	20.00

E-Xceptional Red

Die-cut in a shape similar to an oval, these inserts have a cloth like feel with silver foil stamping with a red background. Card backs are numbered consecutively "1 Of 15XC" and so on. These are seeded 1:14 packs. Two parallels are also inserted: Blues are seeded 1:288 packs and Greens are limited to 999 serial numbered sets.

	NM/M
Complete Set (15):	100.00
Common Player:	3.00
Inserted 1:14	
Blue:	2-3X
Inserted 1:288	
Green:	1-1.5X
Production 999 Sets	
1 Ken Griffey Jr.	8.00
2 Derek Jeter	15.00
3 Nomar Garciaparra	6.00
4 Mark McGwire	10.00
5 Sammy Sosa	6.00
6 Mike Piazza	8.00
7 Alex Rodriguez	8.00
8 Cal Ripken Jr.	15.00
9 Chipper Jones	6.00
10 Pedro Martinez	4.00
11 Jeff Bagwell	4.00
12 Greg Maddux	6.00
13 Roger Clemens	7.00
14 Tony Gwynn	5.00
15 Frank Thomas	4.00

E-Xciting

Die-cut in the shape of a jersey card fronts have a holographic appearance with silver foil stamping. These were seeded 1:24 packs. Card backs are numbered with an "XT" suffix.

	NM/M
Complete Set (10):	25.00
Common Player:	1.00
Inserted 1:24	
1 Mark McGwire	6.00
2 Ken Griffey Jr.	4.00
3 Randy Johnson	2.00
4 Sammy Sosa	3.00
5 Manny Ramirez	2.00
6 Jose Canseco	1.00
7 Derek Jeter	6.00
8 Scott Rolen	1.50
9 Juan Gonzalez	1.25
10 Barry Bonds	6.00

E-Xplosive

These inserts have a traditional format, with a holographic star like image in the background and "explosive" running down the top left side. Card backs are numbered with an "XP" suffix and are serial numbered on the bottom portion in an edition of 2,499 sets.

	NM/M
Complete Set (20):	90.00
Common Player:	2.00
Production 2,499 Sets	
1 Tony Gwynn	6.00
2 Alex Rodriguez	10.00
3 Pedro Martinez	5.00
4 Sammy Sosa	6.00
5 Cal Ripken Jr.	15.00
6 Adam Piatt	2.00
7 Pat Burrell	2.50
8 J.D. Drew	2.50
9 Mike Piazza	8.00
10 Shawn Green	2.50
11 Troy Glaus	4.00
12 Randy Johnson	5.00
13 Juan Gonzalez	2.50
14 Chipper Jones	6.00
15 Ivan Rodriguez	4.00
16 Nomar Garciaparra	6.00
17 Ken Griffey Jr.	8.00
18 Nick Johnson	2.50
19 Mark McGwire	10.00
20 Frank Thomas	5.00

Generation E-X

This 15-card set spotlights the top young players in the game and were seeded 1:8 packs. Card fronts have silver foil stamping over a background resembling a sky. These were seeded 1:8 packs. Card backs are numbered with a "GX" suffix.

	NM/M
Complete Set (15):	20.00
Common Player:	1.00
Inserted 1:8	
1 Rick Ankiel	1.00
2 Josh Beckett	1.50
3 Carlos Beltran	2.00
4 Pat Burrell	2.00
5 Freddy Garcia	1.00
6 Alex Rodriguez	5.00
7 Derek Jeter	6.00
8 Tim Hudson	1.50
9 Shawn Green	1.50
10 Eric Munson	1.00
11 Adam Piatt	1.00
12 Adam Kennedy	1.00
13 Nick Johnson	1.00
14 Alfonso Soriano	2.00
15 Nomar Garciaparra	4.00

Genuine Coverage

	NM/M
Common Player:	5.00
Inserted 1:144	
1 Alex Rodriguez	40.00
2 Tom Glavine	10.00
3 Cal Ripken Jr.	50.00
4 Edgar Martinez	5.00
5 Raul Mondesi	5.00
6 Carlos Beltran	5.00
7 Chipper Jones	25.00
8 Barry Bonds	50.00
9 Heath Murray	5.00
10 Tim Hudson	10.00
11 Mike Mussina	10.00
12 Derek Jeter	50.00

2004 SkyBox Autographics

	NM/M
Complete Set (100):	.40
Common Player:	.40
Hobby Box (4):	75.00
1 Albert Pujols	2.50
2 Richie Sexson	.75
3 Scott Rolen	1.00
4 Rafael Palmeiro	.75
5 Ichiro Suzuki	2.00
6 Craig Biggio	.50
7 Todd Helton	.75
8 Miguel Cabrera	.75
9 Ken Griffey Jr.	1.50
10 Pat Burrell	.50
11 Jose Reyes	.50
12 Hideki Matsui	2.50
13 Geoff Jenkins	.50
14 Mark Prior	2.00
15 Gary Sheffield	.50
16 Nomar Garciaparra	2.00
17 Luis Gonzalez	.50
18 Troy Glaus	.50
19 Rocco Baldelli	.75
20 Hank Blalock	.50
21 Bret Boone	.50
22 Mike Sweeney	.40
23 Dmitri Young	.40
24 Dontrelle Willis	.50
25 Austin Kearns	.50
26 Jason Kendall	.40
27 Derek Jeter	3.00
28 Miguel Tejada	.50
29 Torii Hunter	.50
30 Sammy Sosa	2.00
31 Chipper Jones	1.50
32 Pedro J. Martinez	1.00
33 Curt Schilling	.75
34 Roy Halladay	.50
35 Jim Edmonds	.50
36 Alex Rodriguez	2.50
37 Jason Schmidt	.50
38 Jeff Bagwell	.75
39 Omar Vizquel	.40
40 Ivan Rodriguez	.75
41 Magglio Ordonez	.50
42 Jim Thome	1.00
43 Mike Piazza	2.00
44 Alfonso Soriano	1.00
45 Hideo Nomo	.50
46 Kerry Wood	1.00
47 Greg Maddux	1.50
48 Tony Batista	.40
49 Randy Johnson	1.00
50 Garret Anderson	.50
51 Mark Teixeira	.50
52 Carlos Delgado	.75
53 Darin Erstad	.50
54 Shawn Green	.50
55 Josh Beckett	.75
56 Lance Berkman	.50
57 Adam Dunn	.50
58 Brian Giles	.50
59 Jason Giambi	1.00
60 Barry Zito	.50
61 Vladimir Guerrero	1.00
62 Frank Thomas	.75
63 Jay Gibbons	.40

64	Manny Ramirez	.75
65	Andruw Jones	.75
66	Rickie Weeks	5.00
67	Chad Bentz RC	4.00
68	Bobby Crosby	4.00
69	Greg Dobbs RC	5.00
70	John Gall RC	3.00
71	Kazuo Matsui RC	20.00
72	Dallas McPherson	3.00
73	Brandon Watson	3.00
74	Jerry Gil RC	3.00
75	Garrett Atkins	3.00
76	Cory Sullivan RC	3.00
77	Khalil Greene	5.00
78	Shawn Hill RC	3.00
79	Graham Koonce	3.00
80	Chien-Ming Wang	3.00
81	Josh Labandeira RC	3.00
82	Jonny Gomes	3.00
83	Edwin Jackson	3.00
84	Alfredo Simon RC	4.00
85	Delmon Young	6.00
86	Jason Bartlett RC	5.00
87	Angel Chavez RC	3.00
88	Angel Guzman	3.00
89	Ryan Howard	3.00
90	Scott Hairston	3.00
91	Ronny Cedeno RC	3.00
92	Donald Kelly RC	3.00
93	Ivan Ochoa RC	3.00
94	Edwin Encarnacion	3.00
95	Byron Gettis	3.00
96	Kevin Youkilis	4.00
97	Grady Sizemore	3.00
98	Mariano Gomez RC	3.00
99	Hector Gimenez RC	3.00
100	Ruddy Yan RC	3.00

Insignia

Cards (1-65): 3-5X
Rookies (66-100): 1-2X
Production 150 Sets

Royal Insignia

No Pricing
Production 25 Sets

Autoclassics

NM/M
Complete Set (15):
Common Player:

Johnny Bench	4.00
Wade Boggs	2.00
Steve Carlton	2.00
Albert Chandler	1.50
Ty Cobb	4.00
Carlton Fisk	1.50
George Kelly	1.50
Sal Maglie	2.00
Bill Mazeroski	1.50
Jim Palmer	2.00
Nolan Ryan	6.00
Mike Schmidt	3.00
Joe Sewell	2.00
Duke Snider	3.00
Warren Spahn	2.00

Autographics Blue

NM/M
Common Player: 5.00
Silver: .75-1.5X
Production 100 Sets
Gold: 1.5-2X
Production 25 Sets
Purple: No Pricing
Production One Set

Garrett Atkins/175	5.00
Rocco Baldelli/255	15.00
Josh Beckett/100	20.00
Angel Berroa/182	10.00
Hank Blalock/205	15.00
A.J. Burnett/485	10.00
Marlon Byrd/240	8.00
Edwin Encarnacion/188	10.00
Eric Gagne/225	25.00
Jonny Gomes/265	15.00
Khalil Greene/190	25.00
Rich Harden/185	10.00
Dan Haren/176	10.00
Koyie Hill/240	20.00
Shea Hillenbrand/213	10.00
Ryan Howard/170	75.00
Tim Hudson/169	15.00
Aubrey Huff/296	10.00
Torii Hunter/215	10.00
Edwin Jackson/224	10.00
Bobby Jenks/307	10.00
Matt Kata/197	10.00
Austin Kearns/275	8.00
Graham Koonce/190	10.00
Barry Larkin/195	25.00
Dallas McPherson/179	8.00
Aaron Miles/140	10.00
Mark Mulder/186	15.00
Laynce Nix/185	8.00
Trot Nixon/210	15.00
Corey Patterson/220	12.00
Juan Pierre/220	15.00
Scott Podsednik/210	25.00
Albert Pujols/103	160.00
Jose Reyes/195	30.00
Juan Richardson/345	5.00
Gary Sheffield/210	20.00
Chris Snelling/200	5.00
Shannon Stewart/340	10.00
Cory Sullivan/170	5.00
Javier Vazquez/210	15.00
Billy Wagner/180	25.00
Chien-Ming Wang/195	100.00
Brandon Webb/310	12.00
Rickie Weeks/187	8.00
Dontrelle Willis/225	25.00
Kerry Wood/191	25.00
Delmon Young/205	25.00

Jerseygraphics Blue

NM/M
Common Player:
Silver: 1-2X
Production 100 Sets
Gold: No Pricing
Production 25 Sets

Bobby Abreu	5.00
Rocco Baldelli	5.00
Josh Beckett	10.00
Lance Berkman	5.00
Craig Biggio	5.00
Hank Blalock	8.00
Pat Burrell	5.00
Miguel Cabrera	10.00
Carlos Delgado	5.00
Adam Dunn	8.00
Jim Edmonds	5.00
Darin Erstad	5.00
Nomar Garciaparra	8.00
Jason Giambi	8.00
Jay Gibbons	8.00
Troy Glaus	8.00
Shawn Green	5.00
Vladimir Guerrero	8.00
Roy Halladay	8.00
Todd Helton	5.00
Torii Hunter	5.00
Derek Jeter	15.00
Andruw Jones	5.00
Chipper Jones	10.00
Austin Kearns	5.00
Greg Maddux	15.00
Pedro J. Martinez	10.00
Kevin Millwood	5.00
Hideo Nomo	5.00
David Ortiz	10.00
Rafael Palmeiro	5.00
Mike Piazza	10.00
Mark Prior	10.00
Albert Pujols	15.00
Manny Ramirez	15.00
Jose Reyes	5.00
Alex Rodriguez	15.00
Ivan Rodriguez	10.00
Scott Rolen	10.00
Curt Schilling	5.00
Alfonso Soriano	10.00
Sammy Sosa	15.00
Mark Teixeira	8.00
Miguel Tejada	10.00
Frank Thomas	10.00
Jim Thome	10.00
Dontrelle Willis	5.00
Kerry Wood	12.00
Barry Zito	5.00

Prospects Endorsed

NM/M
Complete Set (15): 10.00
Common Duo: .50

1	Albert Pujols, Delmon Young	3.00
2	Eric Gagne, Bobby Jenks	.50
3	Barry Larkin, Kazuo Matsui	2.00
4	Andruw Jones, Jonny Gomes	1.00
5	Hideo Nomo, Chien-Ming Wang	.50
6	Gary Sheffield, Cory Sullivan	.75
7	Billy Wagner, Ryan Howard	1.00
8	Jorge Posada, Koyie Hill	.75
9	Curt Schilling, Ryan Wagner	.75
10	Jose Reyes, Rickie Weeks	1.50
11	Alfonso Soriano, Matt Kata	1.50
12	Barry Zito, Rich Harden	.75
13	Randy Johnson, Brandon Webb	1.50
14	Alex Rodriguez, Angel Berroa	3.00
15	Dontrelle Willis, Edwin Jackson	.50

2004 SkyBox LE

NM/M
Complete Set (160):
Common Player (1-110): .25
Common SP (111-160): 4.00
Production 299 unless noted.
Pack (3): 5.00
Box (18): 80.00

1	Juan Pierre	.25
2	Derek Jeter	3.00
3	Brandon Webb	.25
4	Jeff Bagwell	.75
5	Jason Schmidt	.40
6	Marlon Byrd	.25
7	Garret Anderson	.50
8	Miguel Cabrera	.75
9	Jose Reyes	.50
10	Rocco Baldelli	.50
11	Tony Batista	.25
12	Carlos Beltran	.50
13	Nomar Garciaparra	2.00
14	Shawn Green	.50
15	Albert Pujols	2.50
16	Magglio Ordonez	.50
17	Kip Wells	.25
18	Andruw Jones	.75
19	Ryan Wagner	.25
20	Alex Rodriguez	3.00
21	Vernon Wells	.50
22	Todd Helton	.75
23	David Ortiz	.50
24	Troy Glaus	.50
25	Jim Thome	1.00
26	Greg Maddux	1.50
27	Roberto Alomar	.50
28	Edgardo Alfonzo	.25
29	Hee Seop Choi	.25
30	Ken Griffey Jr.	1.50
31	Tim Hudson	.50
32	Shannon Stewart	.25
33	Ichiro Suzuki	2.00
34	Luis Gonzalez	.50
35	Darin Erstad	.25
36	Dmitri Young	.25
37	Ivan Rodriguez	.75
38	Scott Podsednik	.50
39	Jose Vidro	.25
40	Mark Prior	2.00
41	Mike Mussina	.75
42	Gary Sheffield	.50
43	Manny Ramirez	.75
44	C.C. Sabathia	.40
45	Curt Schilling	.75
46	Scott Rolen	1.00
47	Hideo Nomo	.50
48	Torii Hunter	.50
49	Aubrey Huff	.25
50	Javy Lopez	.50
51	Austin Kearns	.50
52	Mike Piazza	1.50
53	Sean Burroughs	.25
54	Kerry Wood	.75
55	Marquis Grissom	.25
56	Preston Wilson	.25
57	Angel Berroa	.25
58	Jason Kendall	.25
59	Rafael Palmeiro	.25
60	Mike Lowell	.40
61	Eric Chavez	.50
62	Bartolo Colon	.25
63	Adam Dunn	.50
64	Pedro J. Martinez	1.00
65	Lance Berkman	.50
66	Bret Boone	.40
67	Eric Gagne	.40
68	Vladimir Guerrero	1.00
69	Jay Gibbons	.40
70	Larry Walker	.40
71	Orlando Cabrera	.40
72	Jorge Posada	.50
73	Jamie Moyer	.25
74	Carl Crawford	.25
75	Hank Blalock	.50
76	Josh Beckett	.75
77	Jody Gerut	.25
78	Kevin Brown	.25
79	Sammy Sosa	2.00
80	Chipper Jones	1.00
81	Tom Glavine	.50
82	Barry Zito	.50
83	Edgar Renteria	.25
84	Esteban Loaiza	.25
85	Jason Giambi	1.00
86	Miguel Tejada	.50
87	Randy Johnson	1.00
88	A.J. Burnett	.25
89	Richie Sexson	.25
90	Reggie Sanders	.25
91	Carlos Delgado	.75
92	Pat Burrell	.50
93	Jacque Jones	.25
94	Roy Oswalt	.50
95	Frank Thomas	.50
96	Melvin Mora	.25
97	Jeremy Bonderman	.25
98	Mike Sweeney	.25
99	Brian Giles	.25
100	Edgar Martinez	.40
101	Mark Teixeira	.50
102	Sean Casey	.25
103	Javier Vazquez	.50
104	Hideki Matsui	2.50
105	Jim Edmonds	.40
106	Roy Halladay	.50
107	Craig Biggio	.50
108	Geoff Jenkins	.50
109	Alfonso Soriano	1.00
110	Barry Larkin	.50
111	Chris Bootcheck	.50
112	Dallas McPherson/99	6.00
113	Matt Kata/99	6.00
114	Scott Hairston	4.00
115	Bobby Crosby	8.00
116	Adam Wainwright/99	6.00
117	Daniel Cabrera	4.00
118	Kevin Youkilis	6.00
119	Ronny Cedeno RC	8.00
120	Ruddy Yan RC	4.00
121	Ryan Wing	4.00
122	William Bergolla RC	5.00
123	Edwin Encarnacion	6.00
124	Jonny Gomes	4.00
125	Garrett Atkins	4.00
126	Clint Barmes	4.00
127	Wilfredo Ledezma	4.00
128	Cody Ross	6.00
129	Josh Willingham/99	6.00
130	Chin-Hui Tsao	6.00
131	Hector Gimenez RC	6.00
132	David DeJesus	4.00
133	Jimmy Gobble	4.00
134	Edwin Jackson/99	6.00
135	Koyie Hill	4.00
136	Rickie Weeks/99	8.00
137	Graham Koonce	4.00
138	Rob Bowen	6.00
139	Shawn Hill RC	4.00
140	Craig Brazell	4.00
141	Mike Hessman	4.00
142	Jorge DePaula	4.00
143	Chien-Ming Wang/99	6.00
144	Rich Harden	4.00
145	Ryan Howard/99	6.00
146	Alfredo Simon RC	6.00
147	Ian Snell RC	6.00
148	Ryan Doumit	4.00
149	Khalil Greene/99	6.00
150	Angel Chavez RC	4.00
151	Dan Haren	6.00
152	Chris Snelling	4.00
153	Aaron Miles	4.00
154	John Gall RC	8.00
155	Chris Narveson	4.00
156	Delmon Young/99	8.00
157	Chad Gaudin	4.00
158	Gerald Laird	4.00
159	Alexis Rios	8.00
160	Jason Arnold	4.00

Artist's Proof

Cards (1-110): 3-6X
SP's (110-160): 1-1.5X
Production 50 Sets

Executive Proof

No Pricing
Production One Set

Gold Proof

Cards (1-110): 3-5X
SP's (111-160): 1X
Production 150 Sets

Photographer Proof

Cards (1-110): 6-12X
SP's (110-160): 2-3X
Production 25 Sets

History of the Draft Autographs

NM/M
Common Autograph: 10.00
Production 199 Sets
Draft Year: 1-1.25X
#'d to last 2 digits of draft year
Silver Proof: 1-1.5X
Production 50 Sets
Gold Proof: No Pricing
Production 10 Sets

Hank Blalock	20.00
A.J. Burnett	10.00
Marlon Byrd	10.00
Roy Halladay	20.00
Tim Hudson	10.00
Aubrey Huff	15.00
Torii Hunter	15.00
Austin Kearns	20.00
Mike Lowell	10.00
Corey Patterson	20.00
Juan Pierre	15.00
Scott Podsednik	20.00
Albert Pujols	120.00
Scott Rolen	30.00
Shannon Stewart	10.00
Javier Vazquez	10.00
Vernon Wells	15.00

History of the Draft Game-Used

NM/M
Common Player: 5.00
Numbered to last 2 digits of draft yr.
Silver Proof: 1-1.5X
Production 50 Sets
Gold Proof: No Pricing
Production 10 Sets

Garret Anderson	6.00
Josh Beckett	10.00
Carlos Beltran	5.00
Lance Berkman	5.00
Hank Blalock	10.00
Bret Boone	8.00
A.J. Burnett	5.00
Pat Burrell	8.00
Marlon Byrd	5.00
Eric Chavez	6.00
Adam Dunn	8.00
Darin Erstad	5.00
Nomar Garciaparra	10.00
Jason Giambi	8.00
Shawn Green	5.00
Roy Halladay	8.00
Todd Helton	10.00
Tim Hudson	6.00
Aubrey Huff	8.00
Torii Hunter	8.00
Derek Jeter	15.00
Chipper Jones	10.00
Austin Kearns	8.00
Mike Lowell	5.00
Mike Mussina	10.00
Corey Patterson	5.00
Juan Pierre	5.00
Scott Podsednik	8.00
Jorge Posada	10.00
Albert Pujols	20.00
Manny Ramirez	8.00
Alex Rodriguez	10.00
Scott Rolen	8.00
Jason Schmidt	6.00
Richie Sexson	6.00
Shannon Stewart	5.00
Javier Vazquez	8.00
Vernon Wells	8.00
Kerry Wood	8.00
Barry Zito	8.00

Jersey Proof

NM/M
Common Player: 5.00
Production 299 Sets
Silver Proof: 1.5-2X
Production 50 Sets
Gold Proof: No Pricing
Production 10 Sets

1	Troy Glaus	5.00
2	Curt Schilling	6.00
3	Randy Johnson	8.00
4	Brandon Webb	5.00
5	Gary Sheffield	8.00
6	Greg Maddux	15.00
7	Chipper Jones	10.00
8	David Ortiz	10.00
9	Nomar Garciaparra	15.00
10	Pedro J. Martinez	8.00
11	Manny Ramirez	8.00
12	Kerry Wood	8.00
13	Mark Prior	10.00
14	Sammy Sosa	12.00
15	Frank Thomas	8.00
16	Austin Kearns	8.00
17	Todd Helton	8.00
18	Preston Wilson	5.00
19	Juan Pierre	6.00
20	Josh Beckett	6.00
21	Ivan Rodriguez	8.00
22	Miguel Cabrera	8.00
23	Mike Lowell	6.00
24	Lance Berkman	8.00
25	Jeff Bagwell	8.00
26	Angel Berroa	5.00
27	Hideo Nomo	10.00
28	Eric Gagne	8.00
29	Scott Podsednik	10.00
30	Richie Sexson	6.00
31	Torii Hunter	6.00
32	Mike Piazza	10.00
33	Jose Reyes	8.00
34	Tom Glavine	6.00
35	Derek Jeter	30.00
36	Jorge Posada	8.00
37	Jason Giambi	8.00
38	Alfonso Soriano	8.00
39	Eric Chavez	6.00
40	Miguel Tejada	5.00
41	Jim Thome	10.00
42	Albert Pujols	15.00
43	Scott Rolen	6.00
44	Rocco Baldelli	10.00
45	Alex Rodriguez	10.00
46	Hank Blalock	8.00
47	Mark Teixeira	6.00
48	Rafael Palmeiro	10.00
49	Carlos Delgado	8.00
50	Roy Halladay	6.00

L.E.ague L.E.aders

NM/M
Complete Set (10): 10.00
Common Player: .50
Inserted 1:18

1LL	Alex Rodriguez	3.00
2LL	Jim Thome	1.50
3LL	Albert Pujols	3.00
4LL	Pedro J. Martinez	1.50
5LL	Roy Halladay	.75
6LL	Jason Schmidt	.50
7LL	Kerry Wood	1.00
8LL	Juan Pierre	.50
9LL	Preston Wilson	.50
10LL	Carlos Delgado	1.00

L.E.ague L.E.aders Game-Used

NM/M
Common Player: 6.00
Production 75 Sets
Silver Proof: 1-1.5X
Production 50 Sets
Gold Proof: No Pricing
Production 10 Sets

Alex Rodriguez	12.00
Jim Thome	10.00
Albert Pujols	20.00
Pedro J. Martinez	10.00
Roy Halladay	8.00
Jason Schmidt	8.00
Kerry Wood	8.00
Juan Pierre	6.00
Preston Wilson	6.00
Carlos Delgado	8.00

Rare Form

		NM/M
Common Player:		5.00
Inserted 1:288		
1	Albert Pujols	20.00
2	Miguel Cabrera	5.00
3	Jim Thome	10.00
4	Derek Jeter	30.00
5	Nomar Garciaparra	15.00
6	Mike Piazza	15.00
7	Alex Rodriguez	20.00
8	Delmon Young	15.00
9	Chipper Jones	12.00
10	Rickie Weeks	10.00

Rare Form Autographs

		NM/M
Common Autograph:		10.00
Production 299 Sets		
Level 2:		1-1.5X
Production 99 Sets		
Silver Proof:		1.5X
Production 50 Sets		
Gold Proof:		No Pricing
Production 10 Sets		
	Rocco Baldelli	25.00
	Angel Berroa	15.00
	Rich Harden	20.00
	Edwin Jackson	20.00
	Matt Kata	10.00
	Dallas McPherson	15.00
	Brandon Webb	15.00
	Rickie Weeks	30.00
	Delmon Young	30.00

Rare Form Game-Used Silver Proof

		NM/M
Common Player:		8.00
Production 50 Sets		
Gold Proof:		No Pricing
Production 10 Sets		
	Rocco Baldelli	15.00
	Miguel Cabrera	8.00
	Nomar Garciaparra	15.00
	Derek Jeter	30.00
	Chipper Jones	12.00
	Mike Piazza	25.00
	Albert Pujols	25.00
	Alex Rodriguez	15.00
	Jim Thome	12.00

Rare Form Memorabilia Jersey Number

	NM/M
Numbered to jersey number.	
Most not priced due to scarcity.	
Mike Piazza/31	30.00
Jim Thome/25	25.00

Sky's the Limit

		NM/M
Complete Set (20):		20.00
Common Player:		.50
Inserted 1:6		
1SL	Dontrelle Willis	1.00
2SL	Rocco Baldelli	1.00
3SL	Miguel Cabrera	1.00
4SL	Mark Prior	3.00
5SL	Hideki Matsui	4.00
6SL	Kerry Wood	1.50
7SL	Alfonso Soriano	1.50
8SL	Ichiro Suzuki	2.50
9SL	Brandon Webb	.50
10SL	Alex Rodriguez	3.00
11SL	Barry Zito	1.00
12SL	Hank Blalock	1.00
13SL	Jose Reyes	.75
14SL	Torii Hunter	.75
15SL	Josh Beckett	1.00
16SL	Manny Ramirez	1.00
17SL	Andruw Jones	1.00
18SL	Vladimir Guerrero	1.00
19SL	Miguel Tejada	.75
20SL	Carlos Delgado	1.00

Sky's the Limit Game-Used

	NM/M
Common Player:	5.00

45	Khalil Greene	.25
46	Jake Peavy	.25
47	Jason Schmidt	.25
48	Ichiro Suzuki	1.50
49	Adrian Beltre	.25
50	Albert Pujols	2.00
51	Scott Rolen	.50
52	Carl Crawford	.15
53	Rocco Baldelli	.15
54	Alfonso Soriano	.50
55	Hank Blalock	.25
56	Vernon Wells	.15
57	Jose Vidro	.15
58	David Ortiz	.75
59	Bobby Abreu	.25
60	Gary Sheffield	.40
61	Nolan Ryan	15.00
62	Mike Schmidt	10.00
63	Johnny Bench	8.00
64	Lou Brock	3.00
65	Dennis Eckersley	2.00
66	Carlton Fisk	3.00
67	Bob Gibson	4.00
68	Reggie Jackson	4.00
69	Al Kaline	3.00
70	Bill Mazeroski	2.00
71	Willie McCovey	3.00
72	Jim Palmer	3.00
73	Phil Rizzuto	2.00
74	Warren Spahn	4.00
75	Brooks Robinson	3.00
76	Willie Stargell	2.00
77	Jim "Catfish" Hunter	2.00
78	Tony Perez	2.00
79	George Kell	2.00
80	Robin Yount	4.00
81	Fergie Jenkins	3.00
82	Tom Seaver	3.00
83	Eddie Mathews	2.00
84	Enos Slaughter	2.00
85	Pee Wee Reese	2.00
86	Harmon Killebrew	3.00
87	Eddie Murray	3.00
88	Orlando Cepeda	2.00
89	Billy Williams	2.00
90	Ralph Kiner	2.00
91	Ryan Raburn	1.50
92	Justin Morneau	2.00
93	Zack Greinke	1.50
94	David Aardsma	1.50
95	B.J. Upton	1.50
96	Gavin Floyd	1.50
97	David Wright	8.00
98	Russ Adams	1.50
99	Jose Lopez	2.00
100	Scott Kazmir	1.50
101	Mike Gosling	1.50
102	Jeff Keppinger	1.50
103	David Krynzel	1.50
104	Jeff Niemann RC	6.00
105	Ruben Gotay	1.50
106	Dioner Navarro	1.50
107	Nick Swisher	1.50
108	Yadier Molina	1.50
109	Joey Gathright	1.50
110	Jon Knott	1.50
111	J.D. Durbin	1.50
112	Andres Blanco	1.50
113	Charlton Jimerson	1.50
114	Sean Burnett	1.50
115	Justin Verlander RC	6.00

Insignia

Insignia (1-60):	2-3X
Insignia (61-115):	1X
Production 150 Sets	

Royal Insignia

Royal Insignia (1-60):	4-6X
Royal Insignia (61-115):	1.5-2X
Production 25 Sets	

1992 Snyder's Bread Washington Sports Heroes

This set was sponsored by Snyder's, a Northwest baker, and produced by Little Sun, which had earlier done a number of amateur baseball card sets. Two baseball players are included in the set: Ryne Sandberg (in a high school football jersey) and John Olerud (pitch-

---

ing for WSU). Cards picture the athletes against a pine tree border photo. Backs are printed in blue and yellow on white and feature a summary of the athlete's days in Washington.

		NM/M
Complete Set (8):		15.00
1	Ryne Sandberg	12.00
6	John Olerud	3.00

1995 Sonic/Coke Heroes of Baseball

In a promotion with the Sonic chain of Southern drive-in restaurants, Upper Deck issued a 20-card set of baseball greats. Cards featured vintage sepia photos on the front, with player biographies and stats on the back. The Coca-Cola and Sonic logos also appear on back.

		NM/M
Common Player:		.25
1	Whitey Ford	.25
2	Cy Young	.25
3	Babe Ruth	1.50
4	Lou Gehrig	1.00
5	Mike Schmidt	.35
6	Nolan Ryan	1.00
7	Robin Yount	.25
8	Gary Carter	.25
9	Tom Seaver	.25
10	Reggie Jackson	.25
11	Bob Gibson	.25
12	Gil Hodges	.25
13	Monte Irvin	.25
14	Minnie Minoso	.25
15	Willie Stargell	.25
16	Al Kaline	.25
17	Joe Jackson	1.50
18	Walter Johnson	.25
19	Ty Cobb	.50
20	Satchel Paige	.25

1995 Sonic/Pepsi Baseball Greats

While some Sonic drive-in restaurants (basically a Southern chain) featured a baseball card promotion using Upper Deck cards with a Coca-Cola logo on back, other drive-ins in the chain featured a 12-card set sponsored by Pepsi. Cards have a red border on front and a color photo of a player on which team logos have been airbrushed away. Backs have career data and the Pepsi logo, along with that of the Major League Baseball Players Alumni, and are printed in red and blue. The cards were issued in three-card cello packs with a meal purchase. The unnumbered cards are checklisted here in alphabetical order.

		NM/M
Complete Set (12):		4.00
Common Player:		.25
(1)	Bert Campaneris	.25
(2)	George Foster	.25
(3)	Steve Garvey	.25
(4)	Fergie Jenkins	.25
(5)	Tommy John	.25
(6)	Harmon Killebrew	.75
(7)	Sparky Lyle	.25
(8)	Fred Lynn	.25
(9)	Joe Morgan	.60
(10)	Graig Nettles	.25
(11)	Warren Spahn	.75
(12)	Maury Wills	.25

1987 Sonshine Industries 19th Century Baseball

A. C. Anson

There is no indication of the origins of this collectors' issue on the cards themselves. Fronts feature black-and-white reproductions of vintage woodcuts of the players with an ornate orange framework. Backs of the 2-1/2" x 3-1/2" cards are printed in black on blue-gray with lengthy biographical information. The unnumbered cards are checklisted here in alphabetical order.

		NM/M
Complete Set (20):		20.00
Common Player:		1.00
(1)	A.C. Anson	2.00
(2)	Cap Anson	2.00
(3)	D. Brouthers	1.00
(4)	Alexander Cartwright	1.50
(5)	Alexander Cartwright	1.50
(6)	L.N. David	1.00
(7)	Wes Fisler	1.00
(8)	F.E. Goldsmith	1.00
(9)	T.J. Keefe	1.00
(10)	M.J. Kelly	2.00
(11)	Robert T. Mathews	1.00
(12)	Wm. McLean	1.00
(13)	C.A. McVey	1.00
(14)	James Mutrie	1.00
(15)	Lipman Pike	1.50
(16)	John J. Smith	1.00
(17)	A.G. Spalding	1.50
(18)	M. Welch	1.50
(19)	N.E. Young	1.00
(20)	Going to the game	1.00

1995 South Carolina Athletic Hall of Fame

Sports stars from around the state were honored in this 108-card issue. Fronts feature borderless color or sepia photos with the S.C. Athletic Hall of Fame logo in an upper corner and a gold-foil seal at bottom-right. A colored stripe has the athlete's name in gold foil. On back are a few personal and career stats and highlights.

Only the baseball players are listed here. Issue price of the set was $40.

		NM/M
Complete Set (108):		40.00
Common (Baseball) Player:		.50
5	Frank Howard	.75
6	Bobby Richardson	1.00
13	Shoeless Joe Jackson	4.00
27	Van Lingle Mungo	.50
35	Earl Wooten	.50
54	Marty Marion	.50
55	Frank Howard	.75
72	Jim Rice	.75
74	Danny Ford	.50
83	Lou Brissie	.50
84	Billy O'Dell	.50
97	Bobby Richardson	1.00
100	Frank Howard	.75

1993 SP

Tom Glavine

Upper Deck's first super-premium baseball card issue features 290 cards in the single-series set; 252 are individual player cards, while the remainder includes a Premier Prospects subset featuring top prospects (20 cards), 18 All-Stars and a Platinum Power insert set of 20 top home run hitters. Cards, which were available in 12-card foil packs, feature borderless color photos and UV coating on the front, plus a special logo using lenticular printing. Foil is also used intricately in the design. Backs have a large color photo and statistics. Cards are numbered and color-coded by team.

		NM/M
Complete Set (290):		75.00
Common Player:		.10
Pack (12):		10.00
Wax Box (24):		220.00
1	Roberto Alomar	.30
2	Wade Boggs	2.00
3	Joe Carter	.10
4	Ken Griffey Jr.	2.50
5	Mark Langston	.10
6	John Olerud	.10
7	Kirby Puckett	2.00
8	Cal Ripken, Jr.	4.00
9	Ivan Rodriguez	1.25
10	Barry Bonds	4.00
11	Darren Daulton	.10
12	Marquis Grissom	.10
13	Dave Justice	.10
14	John Kruk	.10
15	Barry Larkin	.10
16	Terry Mulholland	.10
17	Ryne Sandberg	2.00
18	Gary Sheffield	.10
19	Chad Curtis	.10
20	Chili Davis	.10
21	Gary DiSarcina	.10
22	Damion Easley	.10
23	Chuck Finley	.10
24	Luis Polonia	.10
25	Tim Salmon	.10
26	J.T. Snow RC	1.00
27	Russ Springer	.10
28	Jeff Bagwell	1.50
29	Craig Biggio	.10
30	Ken Caminiti	.10
31	Andujar Cedeno	.10
32	Doug Drabek	.10
33	Steve Finley	.10
34	Luis Gonzalez	.10
35	Pete Harnisch	.10
36	Darryl Kile	.10
37	Mike Bordick	.10
38	Dennis Eckersley	1.25
39	Brent Gates	.10
40	Rickey Henderson	1.50
41	Mark McGwire	3.00
42	Craig Paquette	.10
43	Ruben Sierra	.10
44	Terry Steinbach	.10
45	Todd Van Poppel	.10
46	Pat Borders	.10

Production 99 Sets

Silver Proof:		1X
Production 50 Sets		
Gold Proof:		No Pricing
Production 10 Sets		
	Rocco Baldelli	15.00
	Josh Beckett	8.00
	Hank Blalock	6.00
	Miguel Cabrera	8.00
	Carlos Delgado	8.00
	Vladimir Guerrero	8.00
	Torii Hunter	8.00
	Andruw Jones	6.00
	Mark Prior	10.00
	Manny Ramirez	8.00
	Jose Reyes	6.00
	Alex Rodriguez	10.00
	Alfonso Soriano	8.00
	Miguel Tejada	6.00
	Brandon Webb	5.00
	Dontrelle Willis	5.00
	Kerry Wood	5.00
	Barry Zito	6.00

2005 SkyBox Autographics

		NM/M
Complete Set (115):		
Common Player (1-60):		.15
Common (61-115):		1.50
Production 750		
Pack (5):		8.00
Box (12):		85.00
1	Vladimir Guerrero	.75
2	Garret Anderson	.25
3	Troy Glaus	.25
4	Shawn Green	.25
5	Chipper Jones	.75
6	Andruw Jones	.40
7	Miguel Tejada	.25
8	Melvin Mora	.15
9	Manny Ramirez	.75
10	Curt Schilling	.75
11	Nomar Garciaparra	.50
12	Mark Prior	.50
13	Sammy Sosa	1.00
14	Frank Thomas	.40
15	Paul Konerko	.25
16	Adam Dunn	.50
17	Ken Griffey Jr.	1.50
18	Victor Martinez	.25
19	Travis Hafner	.25
20	Todd Helton	.50
21	Ivan Rodriguez	.50
22	Carlos Guillen	.15
23	Miguel Cabrera	.75
24	Juan Pierre	.15
25	Roger Clemens	2.00
26	Jeff Bagwell	.50
27	Lance Berkman	.25
28	Mike Sweeney	.15
29	Eric Gagne	.15
30	J.D. Drew	.15
31	Ben Sheets	.25
32	Lyle Overbay	.15
33	Johan Santana	.50
34	Torii Hunter	.15
35	Mike Piazza	1.00
36	Pedro Martinez	.75
37	Carlos Beltran	.25
38	Derek Jeter	2.00
39	Alex Rodriguez	1.50
40	Hideki Matsui	1.50
41	Randy Johnson	.75
42	Eric Chavez	.25
43	Jim Thome	.50
44	Craig Wilson	.15

#	Player	Price
47	Tony Fernandez	.10
48	Juan Guzman	.10
49	Pat Hentgen	.10
50	Paul Molitor	1.50
51	Jack Morris	.10
52	Ed Sprague	.10
53	Duane Ward	.10
54	Devon White	.10
55	Steve Avery	.10
56	Jeff Blauser	.10
57	Ron Gant	.10
58	Tom Glavine	.40
59	Greg Maddux	2.00
60	Fred McGriff	.10
61	Terry Pendleton	.10
62	Deion Sanders	.10
63	John Smoltz	.10
64	Cal Eldred	.10
65	Darryl Hamilton	.10
66	John Jaha	.10
67	Pat Listach	.10
68	Jaime Navarro	.10
69	Kevin Reimer	.10
70	B.J. Surhoff	.10
71	Greg Vaughn	.10
72	Robin Yount	1.50
73	Rene Arocha RC	.10
74	Bernard Gilkey	.10
75	Gregg Jefferies	.10
76	Ray Lankford	.10
77	Tom Pagnozzi	.10
78	Lee Smith	.10
79	Ozzie Smith	2.00
80	Bob Tewksbury	.10
81	Mark Whiten	.10
82	Steve Buechele	.10
83	Mark Grace	.10
84	Jose Guzman	.10
85	Derrick May	.10
86	Mike Morgan	.10
87	Randy Myers	.10
88	Kevin Roberson RC	.10
89	Sammy Sosa	2.00
90	Rick Wilkins	.10
91	Brett Butler	.10
92	Eric Davis	.10
93	Orel Hershiser	.10
94	Eric Karros	.10
95	Ramon Martinez	.10
96	Raul Mondesi	.10
97	Jose Offerman	.10
98	Mike Piazza	2.50
99	Darryl Strawberry	.10
100	Moises Alou	.10
101	Wil Cordero	.10
102	Delino DeShields	.10
103	Darrin Fletcher	.10
104	Ken Hill	.10
105	Mike Lansing RC	.40
106	Dennis Martinez	.10
107	Larry Walker	.10
108	John Wetteland	.10
109	Rod Beck	.10
110	John Burkett	.10
111	Will Clark	.10
112	Royce Clayton	.10
113	Darren Lewis	.10
114	Willie McGee	.10
115	Bill Swift	.10
116	Robby Thompson	.10
117	Matt Williams	.10
118	Sandy Alomar Jr.	.10
119	Carlos Baerga	.10
120	Albert Belle	.10
121	Reggie Jefferson	.10
122	Kenny Lofton	.10
123	Wayne Kirby	.10
124	Carlos Martinez	.10
125	Charles Nagy	.10
126	Paul Sorrento	.10
127	Rich Amaral	.10
128	Jay Buhner	.10
129	Norm Charlton	.10
130	Dave Fleming	.10
131	Erik Hanson	.10
132	Randy Johnson	1.50
133	Edgar Martinez	.10
134	Tino Martinez	.10
135	Omar Vizquel	.10
136	Bret Barberie	.10
137	Chuck Carr	.10
138	Jeff Conine	.10
139	Orestes Destrade	.10
140	Chris Hammond	.10
141	Bryan Harvey	.10
142	Benito Santiago	.10
143	Walt Weiss	.10
144	Darrell Whitmore RC	.10
145	Tim Bolger RC	.10
146	Bobby Bonilla	.10
147	Jeromy Burnitz	.10
148	Vince Coleman	.10
149	Dwight Gooden	.10
150	Todd Hundley	.10
151	Howard Johnson	.10
152	Eddie Murray	1.50
153	Bret Saberhagen	.10
154	Brady Anderson	.10
155	Mike Devereaux	.10
156	Jeffrey Hammonds	.10
157	Chris Hoiles	.10
158	Ben McDonald	.10
159	Mark McLemore	.10
160	Mike Mussina	.50
161	Gregg Olson	.10
162	David Segui	.10
163	Derek Bell	.10
164	Andy Benes	.10

#	Player	Price
165	Archi Cianfrocco	.10
166	Ricky Gutierrez	.10
167	Tony Gwynn	2.00
168	Gene Harris	.10
169	Trevor Hoffman	.10
170	Ray McDavid RC	.10
171	Phil Plantier	.10
172	Mariano Duncan	.10
173	Len Dykstra	.10
174	Tommy Greene	.10
175	Dave Hollins	.10
176	Pete Incaviglia	.10
177	Mickey Morandini	.10
178	Curt Schilling	.40
179	Kevin Stocker	.10
180	Mitch Williams	.10
181	Stan Belinda	.10
182	Jay Bell	.10
183	Steve Cooke	.10
184	Carlos Garcia	.10
185	Jeff King	.10
186	Orlando Merced	.10
187	Don Slaught	.10
188	Andy Van Slyke	.10
189	Kevin Young	.10
190	Kevin Brown	.10
191	Jose Canseco	.60
192	Julio Franco	.10
193	Benji Gil	.10
194	Juan Gonzalez	.75
195	Tom Henke	.10
196	Rafael Palmeiro	1.25
197	Dean Palmer	.10
198	Nolan Ryan	4.00
199	Roger Clemens	2.25
200	Scott Cooper	.10
201	Andre Dawson	.35
202	Mike Greenwell	.10
203	Carlos Quintana	.10
204	Jeff Russell	.10
205	Aaron Sele	.10
206	Mo Vaughn	.10
207	Frank Viola	.10
208	Rob Dibble	.10
209	Roberto Kelly	.10
210	Kevin Mitchell	.10
211	Hal Morris	.10
212	Joe Oliver	.10
213	Jose Rijo	.10
214	Bip Roberts	.10
215	Chris Sabo	.10
216	Reggie Sanders	.10
217	Dante Bichette	.10
218	Jerald Clark	.10
219	Alex Cole	.10
220	Andres Galarraga	.10
221	Joe Girardi	.10
222	Charlie Hayes	.10
223	Robert Mejia RC	.10
224	Armando Reynoso	.10
225	Eric Young	.10
226	Kevin Appier	.10
227	George Brett	2.25
228	David Cone	.10
229	Phil Hiatt	.10
230	Felix Jose	.10
231	Wally Joyner	.10
232	Mike Macfarlane	.10
233	Brian McRae	.10
234	Jeff Montgomery	.10
235	Rob Deer	.10
236	Cecil Fielder	.10
237	Travis Fryman	.10
238	Mike Henneman	.10
239	Tony Phillips	.10
240	Mickey Tettleton	.10
241	Alan Trammell	.10
242	David Wells	.10
243	Lou Whitaker	.10
244	Rick Aguilera	.10
245	Scott Erickson	.10
246	Brian Harper	.10
247	Kent Hrbek	.10
248	Chuck Knoblauch	.10
249	Shane Mack	.10
250	David McCarty	.10
251	Pedro Munoz	.10
252	Dave Winfield	1.50
253	Alex Fernandez	.10
254	Ozzie Guillen	.10
255	Bo Jackson	.20
256	Lance Johnson	.10
257	Ron Karkovice	.10
258	Jack McDowell	.10
259	Tim Raines	.10
260	Frank Thomas	1.50
261	Robin Ventura	.10
262	Jim Abbott	.10
263	Steve Farr	.10
264	Jimmy Key	.10
265	Don Mattingly	2.25
266	Paul O'Neill	.10
267	Mike Stanley	.10
268	Danny Tartabull	.10
269	Bob Wickman	.10
270	Bernie Williams	.10
271	Jason Bere	.10
272	Roger Cedeno RC	.50
273	Johnny Damon RC	12.00
274	Russ Davis RC	.25
275	Carlos Delgado	.75
276	Carl Everett	.10
277	Cliff Floyd	.10
278	Alex Gonzalez	.10
279	Derek Jeter RC	75.00
280	Chipper Jones	2.00
281	Javier Lopez	.10
282	Chad Mottola RC	.10

#	Player	Price
283	Marc Newfield	.10
284	Eduardo Perez	.10
285	Manny Ramirez	1.50
286	Todd Steverson RC	.10
287	Michael Tucker	.10
288	Allen Watson	.10
289	Rondell White	.10
290	Dmitri Young	.10

Platinum Power

This 20-card insert set features 20 of the game's top home run hitters. The top of each insert card features a special die cut treatment. Backs are numbered with a PP prefix.

		NM/M
Complete Set (20):		27.50
Common Player:		.50
1	Albert Belle	.50
2	Barry Bonds	5.00
3	Joe Carter	.50
4	Will Clark	.50
5	Darren Daulton	.50
6	Cecil Fielder	.50
7	Ron Gant	.50
8	Juan Gonzalez	1.00
9	Ken Griffey Jr.	3.00
10	Dave Hollins	.50
11	Dave Justice	.50
12	Fred McGriff	.50
13	Mark McGwire	5.00
14	Dean Palmer	.50
15	Mike Piazza	3.00
16	Tim Salmon	.50
17	Ryne Sandberg	2.50
18	Gary Sheffield	.75
19	Frank Thomas	2.00
20	Matt Williams	.50

Jumbos

These jumbo-size (8-1/2" x 11") versions of the players' 1993 SP cards were sold through Upper Deck Authenticated. Each player's jumbo card was produced in a limited edition of 1,000, except for Frank Thomas, whose jumbo card was an edition of 1,993. The jumbos were sold in heavy plastic screwdown holders.

		NM/M
Complete Set (5):		35.00
Common Player:		5.00
10	Barry Bonds	12.50
58	Tom Glavine	6.00
173	Lenny Dykstra	5.00
199	Roger Clemens	10.00
260	Frank Thomas	7.50

1994 SP Promo

Virtually identical to the issued version of Ken Griffey, Jr.'s card in the regular SP set (#105) this differs in the card number on the back (#24) and the inclusion on front and back of the notice, "For Promotional Use Only."

		NM/M
24	Ken Griffey Jr.	3.00

1994 SP

The second edition of Upper Deck's top-shelf SP brand features each card with a front background printed on metallic foil; the first 20 cards in the set, a series of "Prospects," have front backgrounds of textured metallic foil. Backs are printed with standard processes and include a color player photo a few stats and typical copyright notice and logos. Each foil pack contains one card featuring a special die-cut treatment at top.

		NM/M
Complete Set (200):		100.00
Common Player:		.10
Die-Cut:		1-2X
Pack (8):		15.00
Wax Box (32):		450.00
1	Mike Bell RC	.10
2	D.J. Boston	.10
3	Johnny Damon	.45
4	Brad Fullmer RC	.75
5	Joey Hamilton	.10
6	Todd Hollandsworth	.10
7	Brian Hunter	.10
8	LaTroy Hawkins RC	.25
9	Brooks Kieschnick RC	.10
10	Derrek Lee RC	15.00
11	Trot Nixon RC	3.00
12	Alex Ochoa	.10
13	Chan Ho Park RC	1.50
14	Kirk Presley RC	.10
15	Alex Rodriguez RC	100.00
16	Jose Silva RC	.10
17	Terrell Wade RC	.10
18	Billy Wagner RC	1.00
19	Glenn Williams RC	.10
20	Preston Wilson	.10
21	Brian Anderson	.10
22	Chad Curtis	.10
23	Chili Davis	.10
24	Bo Jackson	.25
25	Mark Langston	.10
26	Tim Salmon	.10
27	Jeff Bagwell	1.00
28	Craig Biggio	.10
29	Ken Caminiti	.10
30	Doug Drabek	.10
31	John Hudek	.10
32	Greg Swindell	.10
33	Brent Gates	.10
34	Rickey Henderson	1.00
35	Steve Karsay	.10
36	Mark McGwire	2.50
37	Ruben Sierra	.10
38	Terry Steinbach	.10
39	Roberto Alomar	.30
40	Joe Carter	.10
41	Carlos Delgado	.50
42	Alex Gonzalez	.10
43	Juan Guzman	.10
44	Paul Molitor	1.00
45	John Olerud	.10
46	Devon White	.10
47	Steve Avery	.10
48	Jeff Blauser	.10
49	Tom Glavine	.35
50	Dave Justice	.10
51	Roberto Kelly	.10
52	Ryan Klesko	.10
53	Javier Lopez	.10
54	Greg Maddux	1.25
55	Fred McGriff	.10
56	Ricky Bones	.10
57	Cal Eldred	.10
58	Brian Harper	.10
59	Pat Listach	.10
60	B.J. Surhoff	.10
61	Greg Vaughn	.10
62	Bernard Gilkey	.10
63	Gregg Jefferies	.10
64	Ray Lankford	.10
65	Ozzie Smith	1.25
66	Bob Tewksbury	.10
67	Mark Whiten	.10
68	Todd Zeile	.10
69	Mark Grace	.10
70	Randy Myers	.10
71	Ryne Sandberg	1.25
72	Sammy Sosa	1.25

#	Player	Price
73	Steve Trachsel	.10
74	Rick Wilkins	.10
75	Brett Butler	.10
76	Delino DeShields	.10
77	Orel Hershiser	.10
78	Eric Karros	.10
79	Raul Mondesi	.10
80	Mike Piazza	2.00
81	Tim Wallach	.10
82	Moises Alou	.10
83	Cliff Floyd	.10
84	Marquis Grissom	.10
85	Pedro Martinez	1.00
86	Larry Walker	.10
87	John Wetteland	.10
88	Rondell White	.10
89	Rod Beck	.10
90	Barry Bonds	3.00
91	John Burkett	.10
92	Royce Clayton	.10
93	Billy Swift	.10
94	Robby Thompson	.10
95	Matt Williams	.10
96	Carlos Baerga	.10
97	Albert Belle	.10
98	Kenny Lofton	.10
99	Dennis Martinez	.10
100	Eddie Murray	1.00
101	Manny Ramirez	1.00
102	Eric Anthony	.10
103	Chris Bosio	.10
104	Jay Buhner	.10
105	Ken Griffey Jr.	2.00
106	Randy Johnson	1.00
107	Edgar Martinez	.10
108	Chuck Carr	.10
109	Jeff Conine	.10
110	Carl Everett	.10
111	Chris Hammond	.10
112	Bryan Harvey	.10
113	Charles Johnson	.10
114	Gary Sheffield	.45
115	Bobby Bonilla	.10
116	Dwight Gooden	.10
117	Todd Hundley	.10
118	Bobby Jones	.10
119	Jeff Kent	.10
120	Bret Saberhagen	.10
121	Jeffrey Hammonds	.10
122	Chris Hoiles	.10
123	Ben McDonald	.10
124	Mike Mussina	.40
125	Rafael Palmeiro	.75
126	Cal Ripken, Jr.	3.00
127	Lee Smith	.10
128	Derek Bell	.10
129	Andy Benes	.10
130	Tony Gwynn	1.25
131	Trevor Hoffman	.10
132	Phil Plantier	.10
133	Bip Roberts	.10
134	Darren Daulton	.10
135	Len Dykstra	.10
136	Dave Hollins	.10
137	Danny Jackson	.10
138	John Kruk	.10
139	Kevin Stocker	.10
140	Jay Bell	.10
141	Carlos Garcia	.10
142	Jeff King	.10
143	Orlando Merced	.10
144	Andy Van Slyke	.10
145	Paul Wagner	.10
146	Jose Canseco	.50
147	Will Clark	.10
148	Juan Gonzalez	.50
149	Rick Helling	.10
150	Dean Palmer	.10
151	Ivan Rodriguez	.75
152	Roger Clemens	1.50
153	Scott Cooper	.10
154	Andre Dawson	.30
155	Mike Greenwell	.10
156	Aaron Sele	.10
157	Mo Vaughn	.10
158	Bret Boone	.10
159	Barry Larkin	.10
160	Kevin Mitchell	.10
161	Jose Rijo	.10
162	Deion Sanders	.10
163	Reggie Sanders	.10
164	Dante Bichette	.10
165	Ellis Burks	.10
166	Andres Galarraga	.10
167	Charlie Hayes	.10
168	David Nied	.10
169	Walt Weiss	.10
170	Kevin Appier	.10
171	David Cone	.10
172	Jeff Granger	.10
173	Felix Jose	.10
174	Wally Joyner	.10
175	Brian McRae	.10
176	Cecil Fielder	.10
177	Travis Fryman	.10
178	Mike Henneman	.10
179	Tony Phillips	.10
180	Mickey Tettleton	.10
181	Alan Trammell	.10
182	Rick Aguilera	.10
183	Rich Becker	.10
184	Scott Erickson	.10
185	Chuck Knoblauch	.10
186	Kirby Puckett	1.25
187	Dave Winfield	1.00
188	Wilson Alvarez	.10
189	Jason Bere	.10
190	Alex Fernandez	.10

#	Player	Price
191	Julio Franco	.10
192	Jack McDowell	.10
193	Frank Thomas	1.00
194	Robin Ventura	.10
195	Jim Abbott	.10
196	Wade Boggs	1.25
197	Jimmy Key	.10
198	Don Mattingly	1.50
199	Paul O'Neill	.10
200	Danny Tartabull	.10

Die-Cut

Upper Deck SP Die-cuts are a 200-card parallel set inserted at the rate of one per foil pack. Each card has a die-cut top instead of the flat-top found on regular SP cards. Die-cuts also have a silver-foil Upper Deck hologram logo on back, in contrast to the gold-tone hologram found on regular SP; this is an effort to prevent fraudulent replication by any crook with a pair of scissors.

Holoview Blue

Holoview F/X Blue is a 38-card set utilizing Holoview printing technology, which uses 200 frames of video to produce a three-dimensional image on the bottom third of each card. The hologram is bordered in blue and there is a blue stripe running down the right side of the card. Backs are done with a blue background and feature a player photo over top of bold letters reading "Holoview FX." This insert could be found in one per five packs of SP baseball.

		NM/M
Complete Set (38):		85.00
Common Player:		.90
1	Roberto Alomar	1.50
2	Kevin Appier	1.00
3	Jeff Bagwell	3.00
4	Jose Canseco	3.00
5	Roger Clemens	6.00
6	Carlos Delgado	2.00
7	Cecil Fielder	1.00
8	Cliff Floyd	1.00
9	Travis Fryman	1.00
10	Andres Galarraga	1.00
11	Juan Gonzalez	1.50
12	Ken Griffey Jr.	6.00
13	Tony Gwynn	4.00
14	Jeffrey Hammonds	1.00
15	Bo Jackson	3.00
16	Michael Jordan	15.00
17	Dave Justice	1.00
18	Steve Karsay	1.00
19	Jeff Kent	1.00
20	Brooks Kieschnick	1.00
21	Ryan Klesko	1.00
22	John Kruk	1.00
23	Barry Larkin	1.50
24	Pat Listach	1.00
25	Don Mattingly	5.00
26	Mark McGwire	8.00
27	Raul Mondesi	1.00

28	Trot Nixon	1.50
29	Mike Piazza	6.00
30	Kirby Puckett	4.00
31	Manny Ramirez	3.00
32	Cal Ripken, Jr.	10.00
33	Alex Rodriguez	60.00
34	Tim Salmon	1.00
35	Gary Sheffield	2.00
36	Ozzie Smith	4.00
37	Sammy Sosa	4.00
38	Andy Van Slyke	1.00

Holoview Blue Mismatches

Some Holoview Blue inserts are known on which the player photograph and data do not match the player shown in the horizontal hologram at bottom front.

Holoview Red

Holoview F/X Red is a parallel set to the Blue insert. Once again, this 38-card set utilizes Holoview printing technology. However, these cards have a red border surrounding the hologram and along the right side, as well as a red background on the back and a large "SPECIAL FX" under the player photo. Holoview red cards also have die-cut tops. Red cards are much scarcer than blue; the red being inserted once per 75 packs of SP baseball.

		NM/M
Complete Set (38):		1,175
Common Player:		12.00
1	Roberto Alomar	15.00
2	Kevin Appier	12.00
3	Jeff Bagwell	30.00
4	Jose Canseco	20.00
5	Roger Clemens	50.00
6	Carlos Delgado	20.00
7	Cecil Fielder	12.00
8	Cliff Floyd	12.00
9	Travis Fryman	12.00
10	Andres Galarraga	12.00
11	Juan Gonzalez	20.00
12	Ken Griffey Jr.	50.00
13	Tony Gwynn	40.00
14	Jeffrey Hammonds	12.00
15	Bo Jackson	20.00
16	Michael Jordan	120.00
17	Dave Justice	12.00
18	Steve Karsay	12.00
19	Jeff Kent	12.00
20	Brooks Kieschnick	12.00
21	Ryan Klesko	12.00
22	John Kruk	12.00
23	Barry Larkin	12.00
24	Pat Listach	12.00
25	Don Mattingly	45.00
26	Mark McGwire	60.00
27	Raul Mondesi	12.00
28	Trot Nixon	20.00
29	Mike Piazza	50.00
30	Kirby Puckett	40.00
31	Manny Ramirez	30.00
32	Cal Ripken, Jr.	80.00
33	Alex Rodriguez	625.00
34	Tim Salmon	12.00
35	Gary Sheffield	15.00
36	Ozzie Smith	40.00
37	Sammy Sosa	40.00
38	Andy Van Slyke	12.00

Alex Rodriguez Autographed Jumbo

This 3-1/2" x 5" version of A-Rod's SP rookie card was produced in an authentically autographed edition of 500. The card has serial numbers on front and back and a numbered UD Authenticated hologram sticker on front. The card was sold sealed in a heavy plastic holder and velour drawstring bag.

		NM/M
15	Alex Rodriguez	200.00

1995 SP

Foil highlights and die-cut specialty cards are once again featured in Upper Deck's premium-brand SP baseball issue. The 207-card set opens with four die-cut tribute cards, followed by 20 Premier Prospect die-cuts printed on metallic foil backgrounds with copper-foil highlights. Three checklists follow, also die-cut. The regular player cards in the set are arranged in team-alphabetical order within league. Card fronts feature photos which are borderless at top, bottom and right. On the left is a gold-highlighted metallic foil border of blue for N.L., red for A.L. Backs have a large photo at top, with a few stats and career highlights at bottom, along with a gold infield-shaped hologram. The SP insert program consists of a "SuperbaFoil" parallel set, in which each card's normal foil highlights are replaced with silver foil; a 48-card Special F/X set utilizing holographic portraits, and, a 20-card Platinum Power set. The hobby-only SP was issued in eight-card foil packs with a $3.99 suggested retail price.

		NM/M
Complete Set (207):		12.50
Common Player:		.05
Pack (8):		1.25
Wax Box (32):		25.00
1	Cal Ripken Jr. (Salute)	2.00
2	Nolan Ryan (Salute)	2.00
3	George Brett (Salute)	1.25
4	Mike Schmidt (Salute)	1.25
5	Dustin Hermanson (Premier Prospects)	.05
6	Antonio Osuna (Premier Prospects)	.05
7	Mark Grudzielanek RC (Premier Prospects)	.35
8	Ray Durham (Premier Prospects)	.05
9	Ugueth Urbina (Premier Prospects)	.05
10	Ruben Rivera (Premier Prospects)	.05
11	Curtis Goodwin (Premier Prospects)	.05
12	Jimmy Hurst (Premier Prospects)	.05
13	Jose Malave (Premier Prospects)	.05
14	Hideo Nomo RC (Premier Prospects)	1.50
15	Juan Acevedo (Premier Prospects)	.05
16	Tony Clark (Premier Prospects)	.05
17	Jim Pittsley (Premier Prospects)	.05
18	Freddy Garcia RC (Premier Prospects)	.50
19	Carlos Perez RC (Premier Prospects)	.05
20	Raul Casanova RC (Premier Prospects)	.05
21	Quilvio Veras (Premier Prospects)	.05
22	Edgardo Alfonzo (Premier Prospects)	.05
23	Marty Cordova (Premier Prospects)	.05
24	C.J. Nitkowski (Premier Prospects)	.05
25	Checklist 1-69 (Wade Boggs)	.30
26	Checklist 70-138 (Dave Winfield)	.25
27	Checklist 139-207 (Eddie Murray)	.25
28	Dave Justice	.05
29	Marquis Grissom	.05
30	Fred McGriff	.05
31	Greg Maddux	1.00
32	Tom Glavine	.35
33	Steve Avery	.05
34	Chipper Jones	1.00
35	Sammy Sosa	1.00
36	Jaime Navarro	.05
37	Randy Myers	.05
38	Mark Grace	.05
39	Todd Zeile	.05
40	Brian McRae	.05
41	Reggie Sanders	.05
42	Ron Gant	.05
43	Deion Sanders	.05
44	Barry Larkin	.05
45	Bret Boone	.05
46	Jose Rijo	.05
47	Jason Bates	.05
48	Andres Galarraga	.05
49	Bill Swift	.05
50	Larry Walker	.05
51	Vinny Castilla	.05
52	Dante Bichette	.05
53	Jeff Conine	.05
54	John Burkett	.05
55	Gary Sheffield	.40
56	Andre Dawson	.30
57	Terry Pendleton	.05
58	Charles Johnson	.05
59	Brian L. Hunter	.05
60	Jeff Bagwell	.75
61	Craig Biggio	.05
62	Phil Nevin	.05
63	Doug Drabek	.05
64	Derek Bell	.05
65	Raul Mondesi	.05
66	Eric Karros	.05
67	Roger Cedeno	.05
68	Delino DeShields	.05
69	Ramon Martinez	.05
70	Mike Piazza	1.50
71	Billy Ashley	.05
72	Jeff Fassero	.05
73	Shane Andrews	.05
74	Wil Cordero	.05
75	Tony Tarasco	.05
76	Rondell White	.05
77	Pedro Martinez	.75
78	Moises Alou	.05
79	Rico Brogna	.05
80	Bobby Bonilla	.05
81	Jeff Kent	.05
82	Brett Butler	.05
83	Bobby Jones	.05
84	Bill Pulsipher	.05
85	Bret Saberhagen	.05
86	Gregg Jefferies	.05
87	Lenny Dykstra	.05
88	Dave Hollins	.05
89	Charlie Hayes	.05
90	Darren Daulton	.05
91	Curt Schilling	.35
92	Heathcliff Slocumb	.05
93	Carlos Garcia	.05
94	Denny Neagle	.05
95	Jay Bell	.05
96	Orlando Merced	.05
97	Dave Clark	.05
98	Bernard Gilkey	.05
99	Scott Cooper	.05
100	Ozzie Smith	1.00
100	Ken Griffey Jr./PC	2.00
101	Tom Henke	.05
102	Ken Hill	.05
103	Brian Jordan	.05
104	Ray Lankford	.05
105	Tony Gwynn	1.00
106	Andy Benes	.05
107	Ken Caminiti	.05
108	Steve Finley	.05
109	Joey Hamilton	.05
110	Bip Roberts	.05
111	Eddie Williams	.05
112	Rod Beck	.05
113	Matt Williams	.05
114	Glenallen Hill	.05
115	Barry Bonds	2.50
116	Robby Thompson	.05
117	Mark Portugal	.05
118	Brady Anderson	.05
119	Mike Mussina	.35
120	Rafael Palmeiro	.65
121	Chris Hoiles	.05
122	Harold Baines	.05
123	Jeffrey Hammonds	.05
124	Tim Naehring	.05
125	Mo Vaughn	.05
126	Mike Macfarlane	.05
127	Roger Clemens	1.25
128	John Valentin	.05
129	Aaron Sele	.05
130	Jose Canseco	.50
131	J.T. Snow	.05
132	Mark Langston	.05
133	Chili Davis	.05
134	Chuck Finley	.05
135	Tim Salmon	.05
136	Tony Phillips	.05
137	Jason Bere	.05
138	Robin Ventura	.05
139	Tim Raines	.05
140a	Frank Thomas (5-yr. BA .326)	.75
140b	Frank Thomas (5-yr. BA .303)	.75
141	Alex Fernandez	.05
142	Jim Abbott	.05
143	Wilson Alvarez	.05
144	Carlos Baerga	.05
145	Albert Belle	.05
146	Jim Thome	.65
147	Dennis Martinez	.05
148	Eddie Murray	.75
149	Dave Winfield	.75
150	Kenny Lofton	.05
151	Manny Ramirez	.75
152	Chad Curtis	.05
153	Lou Whitaker	.05
154	Alan Trammell	.05
155	Cecil Fielder	.05
156	Kirk Gibson	.05
157	Michael Tucker	.05
158	Jon Nunnally	.05
159	Wally Joyner	.05
160	Kevin Appier	.05
161	Jeff Montgomery	.05
162	Greg Gagne	.05
163	Ricky Bones	.05
164	Cal Eldred	.05
165	Greg Vaughn	.05
166	Kevin Seitzer	.05
167	Jose Valentin	.05
168	Joe Oliver	.05
169	Rick Aguilera	.05
170	Kirby Puckett	1.00
171	Scott Stahoviak	.05
172	Kevin Tapani	.05
173	Chuck Knoblauch	.05
174	Rich Becker	.05
175	Don Mattingly	1.25
176	Jack McDowell	.05
177	Jimmy Key	.05
178	Paul O'Neill	.05
179	John Wetteland	.05
180	Wade Boggs	.05
181	Derek Jeter	2.50
182	Rickey Henderson	.75
183	Terry Steinbach	.05
184	Ruben Sierra	.05
185	Mark McGwire	2.00
186	Todd Stottlemyre	.05
187	Dennis Eckersley	.05
188	Alex Rodriguez	2.00
189	Randy Johnson	.75
190	Ken Griffey Jr.	1.50
191	Tino Martinez	.05
192	Jay Buhner	.05
193	Edgar Martinez	.05
194	Mickey Tettleton	.05
195	Juan Gonzalez	.40
196	Benji Gil	.05
197	Dean Palmer	.05
198	Ivan Rodriguez	.65
199	Kenny Rogers	.05
200	Will Clark	.05
201	Roberto Alomar	.20
202	David Cone	.05
203	Paul Molitor	.75
204	Shawn Green	.40
205	Joe Carter	.05
206	Alex Gonzalez	.05
207	Pat Hentgen	.05

SuperbaFoil

This chase set parallels the 207 regular cards in the SP issue. Cards were found at the rate of one per eight-card foil pack. SuperbaFoil cards feature a silver-rainbow metallic foil in place of the gold, copper, red or blue foil highlights on regular-issue SP cards. On back, the SuperbaFoil inserts have a silver hologram instead of the gold version found on standard cards.

	NM/M
Complete Set (207):	30.00
Common Player:	.10
SuperbaFoil Stars:	1.5X

Platinum Power

This die-cut insert set features the game's top power hitters in color action photos set against a background of two-toned gold rays emanating from the SP logo at lower-right. Player name, team and position are printed in white in a black band at bottom. Backs repeat the golden ray effect in the background and have a color photo at center. Career and 1994 stats are presented. An infield-shaped gold foil hologram is at lower-right. Cards have a "PP" prefix. Stated odds of finding one of the 20 Platinum Power inserts are one per five packs.

		NM/M
Complete Set (20):		10.00
Common Player:		.20
1	Jeff Bagwell	.75
2	Barry Bonds	2.00
3	Ron Gant	.20
4	Fred McGriff	.20
5	Raul Mondesi	.20
6	Mike Piazza	1.25
7	Larry Walker	.20
8	Matt Williams	.20
9	Albert Belle	.20
10	Cecil Fielder	.20
11	Juan Gonzalez	.40
12	Ken Griffey Jr.	.20
13	Mark McGwire	1.50
14	Eddie Murray	.75
15	Manny Ramirez	.75
16	Cal Ripken Jr.	2.00
17	Tim Salmon	.20
18	Frank Thomas	.75
19	Jim Thome	.65
20	Mo Vaughn	.20

Special F/X

By far the preferred pick of the '95 SP insert program is the Special F/X set of 48. The cards have a color action photo on front, printed on a metallic foil background. A 3/4" square holographic portrait is printed on

the front. Backs are printed in standard technology and include another photo and a few stats and career highlights. Stated odds of finding a Special F/X card are 1 per 75 packs, or about one per two boxes.

		NM/M
Complete Set (48):		200.00
Common Player:		2.00
1	Jose Canseco	6.00
2	Roger Clemens	20.00
3	Mo Vaughn	2.00
4	Tim Salmon	2.00
5	Chuck Finley	2.00
6	Robin Ventura	2.00
7	Jason Bere	2.00
8	Carlos Baerga	2.00
9	Albert Belle	2.00
10	Kenny Lofton	3.00
11	Manny Ramirez	8.00
12	Jeff Montgomery	2.00
13	Kirby Puckett	15.00
14	Wade Boggs	5.00
15	Don Mattingly	15.00
16	Cal Ripken Jr.	25.00
17	Ruben Sierra	2.00
18	Ken Griffey Jr.	20.00
19	Randy Johnson	8.00
20	Alex Rodriguez	25.00
21	Will Clark	5.00
22	Juan Gonzalez	4.00
23	Roberto Alomar	4.00
24	Joe Carter	3.00
25	Alex Gonzalez	2.00
26	Paul Molitor	6.00
27	Ryan Klesko	2.00
28	Fred McGriff	3.00
29	Greg Maddux	15.00
30	Sammy Sosa	10.00
31	Bret Boone	2.00
32	Barry Larkin	5.00
33	Reggie Sanders	2.00
34	Dante Bichette	2.00
35	Andres Galarraga	2.00
36	Charles Johnson	2.00
37	Gary Sheffield	5.00
38	Jeff Bagwell	6.00
39	Craig Biggio	2.00
40	Eric Karros	2.00
41	Billy Ashley	2.00
42	Raul Mondesi	2.00
43	Mike Piazza	10.00
44	Rondell White	2.00
45	Bret Saberhagen	2.00
46	Tony Gwynn	8.00
47	Melvin Nieves	2.00
48	Matt Williams	2.00

Griffey Gold Signature

A specially autographed version of Griffey's card from 1995 SP was made available from Upper Deck Authenticated. These cards are signed and numbered in gold ink from within an edition of 1,000.

		NM/M
190	Ken Griffey Jr.	65.00

ABBREVIATIONS

PC - Promo Card

1995 SP/Championship

Championship was a version of Upper Deck's popular SP line designed for sale in retail outlets. The first 20 cards in the set are a "Diamond in the Rough" subset featuring hot rookies printed on textured metallic foil background. Regular player cards are arranged by team within league, alphabetically by city name. Each team set is led off with a "Pro Files" card of a star player; those card backs feature team season and post-season results. Each of the regular player cards has a borderless action photo on front, highlighted with a gold-foil SP Championship logo. The team name is in a blue-foil oval on National Leaguers' cards; red on American Leaguers. Backs have a portrait photo, a few stats and career highlights. Situated between the N.L. and A.L. cards in the checklist are a subset of 15 October Legends. A parallel set of cards with die-cut tops was inserted into the six-card foil packs at the rate of one per pack. A special card honoring Cal Ripken's consecutive-game record was issued as a super-scarce insert.

		NM/M
Complete Set (200):		25.00
Common Player:		.05
Die-Cuts:		1.5X
Wax Pack (6):		1.00
Wax Box (44):		30.00
1	Hideo Nomo RC (Diamonds in the Rough)	1.50
2	Roger Cedeno (Diamonds in the Rough)	.05
3	Curtis Goodwin (Diamonds in the Rough)	.05
4	Jon Nunnally (Diamonds in the Rough)	.05
5	Bill Pulsipher (Diamonds in the Rough)	.05
6	C.J. Nitkowski (Diamonds in the Rough)	.05
7	Dustin Hermanson (Diamonds in the Rough)	.05
8	Marty Cordova (Diamonds in the Rough)	.05
9	Ruben Rivera (Diamonds in the Rough)	.05
10	Ariel Prieto RC (Diamonds in the Rough)	.05
11	Edgardo Alfonzo (Diamonds in the Rough)	.05
12	Ray Durham (Diamonds in the Rough)	.05
13	Quilvio Veras (Diamonds in the Rough)	.05
14	Ugueth Urbina (Diamonds in the Rough)	.05
15	Carlos Perez RC (Diamonds in the Rough)	.05
16	Glenn Dishman RC (Diamonds in the Rough)	.05
17	Jeff Suppan (Diamonds in the Rough)	.05
18	Jason Bates (Diamonds in the Rough)	.05
19	Jason Isringhausen (Diamonds in the Rough)	.05
20	Derek Jeter (Diamonds in the Rough)	2.00
21	Fred McGriff (Major League ProFiles)	.05
22	Marquis Grissom	.05
23	Fred McGriff	.05
24	Tom Glavine	.35
25	Greg Maddux	1.00
26	Chipper Jones	1.00
27	Sammy Sosa (Major League ProFiles)	.50
28	Randy Myers	.05
29	Mark Grace	.05
30	Sammy Sosa	1.00
31	Todd Zeile	.05
32	Brian McRae	.05
33	Ron Gant (Major League ProFiles)	.05
34	Reggie Sanders	.05
35	Ron Gant	.05
36	Barry Larkin	.05
37	Bret Boone	.05
38	John Smiley	.05
39	Larry Walker (Major League ProFiles)	.05
40	Andres Galarraga	.05
41	Bill Swift	.05
42	Larry Walker	.05
43	Vinny Castilla	.05
44	Dante Bichette	.05
45	Jeff Conine (Major League ProFiles)	.05
46	Charles Johnson	.05
47	Gary Sheffield	.45
48	Andre Dawson	.25
49	Jeff Conine	.05
50	Jeff Bagwell (Major League ProFiles)	.40
51	Phil Nevin	.05
52	Craig Biggio	.05
53	Brian L. Hunter	.05
54	Doug Drabek	.05
55	Jeff Bagwell	.75
56	Derek Bell	.05
57	Mike Piazza (Major League ProFiles)	.65
58	Raul Mondesi	.05
59	Eric Karros	.05
60	Mike Piazza	1.25
61	Ramon Martinez	.05
62	Billy Ashley	.05
63	Rondell White (Major League ProFiles)	.05
64	Jeff Fassero	.05
65	Moises Alou	.05
66	Tony Tarasco	.05
67	Rondell White	.05
68	Pedro Martinez	.75
69	Bobby Jones (Major League ProFiles)	.05
70	Bobby Bonilla	.05
71	Bobby Jones	.05
72	Bret Saberhagen	.05
73	Darren Daulton (Major League ProFiles)	.05
74	Darren Daulton	.05
75	Gregg Jefferies	.05
76	Tyler Green	.05
77	Heathcliff Slocumb	.05
78	Lenny Dykstra	.05
79	Jay Bell (Major League ProFiles)	.05
80	Denny Neagle	.05
81	Orlando Merced	.05
82	Jay Bell	.05
83	Ozzie Smith (Major League ProFiles)	.50
84	Ken Hill	.05
85	Ozzie Smith	1.00
86	Bernard Gilkey	.05
87	Ray Lankford	.05
88	Tony Gwynn (Major League ProFiles)	.50
89	Ken Caminiti	.05
90	Tony Gwynn	1.00
91	Joey Hamilton	.05
92	Bip Roberts	.05
93	Deion Sanders (Major League ProFiles)	.05
94	Glenallen Hill	.05
95	Matt Williams	.05
96	Barry Bonds	2.00
97	Rod Beck	.05
98	Eddie Murray (Checklist)	.35
99	Cal Ripken Jr. (Checklist)	1.00
100	Roberto Alomar (October Legends)	.10
101	George Brett (October Legends)	.60
102	Joe Carter (October Legends)	.05
103	Will Clark (October Legends)	.05
104	Dennis Eckersley (October Legends)	.40
105	Whitey Ford (October Legends)	.40
106	Steve Garvey (October Legends)	.05
107	Kirk Gibson (October Legends)	.05
108	Orel Hershiser (October Legends)	.05
109	Reggie Jackson (October Legends)	.50
110	Paul Molitor (October Legends)	.40
111	Kirby Puckett (October Legends)	.50
112	Mike Schmidt (October Legends)	.60
113	Dave Stewart (October Legends)	.05
114	Alan Trammell (October Legends)	.05
115	Cal Ripken Jr. (Major League ProFiles)	1.00
116	Brady Anderson	.05
117	Mike Mussina	.30
118	Rafael Palmeiro	.65
119	Chris Hoiles	.05
120	Cal Ripken Jr.	2.00
121	Mo Vaughn (Major League ProFiles)	.05
122	Roger Clemens	1.25
123	Tim Naehring	.05
124	John Valentin	.05
125	Mo Vaughn	.05
126	Tim Wakefield	.05
127	Jose Canseco	.40
128	Rick Aguilera	.05
129	Chili Davis (Major League ProFiles)	.05
130	Lee Smith	.05
131	Jim Edmonds	.05
132	Chuck Finley	.05
133	Chili Davis	.05
134	J.T. Snow	.05
135	Tim Salmon	.05
136	Frank Thomas (Major League ProFiles)	.45
137	Jason Bere	.05
138	Robin Ventura	.05
139	Tim Raines	.05
140	Frank Thomas	.75
141	Alex Fernandez	.05
142	Eddie Murray (Major League ProFiles)	.40
143	Carlos Baerga	.05
144	Eddie Murray	.75
145	Albert Belle	.65
146	Jim Thome	.65
147	Dennis Martinez	.05
148	Dave Winfield	.75
149	Kenny Lofton	.75
150	Manny Ramirez	.75
151	Cecil Fielder (Major League ProFiles)	.05
152	Lou Whitaker	.05
153	Alan Trammell	.05
154	Kirk Gibson	.05
155	Cecil Fielder	.05
156	Bobby Higginson RC	.25
157	Kevin Appier (Major League ProFiles)	.05
158	Wally Joyner	.05
159	Jeff Montgomery	.05
160	Kevin Appier	.05
161	Gary Gaetti	.05
162	Greg Gagne	.05
163	Ricky Bones (Major League ProFiles)	.05
164	Greg Vaughn	.05
165	Kevin Seitzer	.05
166	Ricky Bones	.05
167	Kirby Puckett (Major League ProFiles)	.50
168	Pedro Munoz	.05
169	Chuck Knoblauch	.05
170	Kirby Puckett	1.00
171	Don Mattingly (Major League ProFiles)	.60
172	Wade Boggs	1.00
173	Paul O'Neill	.05
174	John Wetteland	.05
175	Don Mattingly	1.25
176	Jack McDowell	.05
177	Mark McGwire (Major League ProFiles)	.75
178	Rickey Henderson	.75
179	Terry Steinbach	.05
180	Ruben Sierra	.05
181	Mark McGwire	1.50
182	Dennis Eckersley	.05
183	Ken Griffey Jr. (Major League ProFiles)	.65
184	Alex Rodriguez	1.50
185	Ken Griffey Jr.	1.25
186	Randy Johnson	.75
187	Jay Buhner	.05
188	Edgar Martinez	.05
189	Will Clark (Major League ProFiles)	.05
190	Juan Gonzalez	.40
191	Benji Gil	.05
192	Ivan Rodriguez	.65
193	Kenny Rogers	.05
194	Will Clark	.05
195	Paul Molitor (Major League ProFiles)	.40
196	Roberto Alomar	.20
197	David Cone	.05
198	Paul Molitor	.75
199	Shawn Green	.30
200	Joe Carter	.05
CR1	Cal Ripken Jr. (2,131 games tribute)	5.00
CR1	Cal Ripken Jr./Die-Cut	7.50

Die-Cuts

Each of the 200 cards in the regular SP championship issue, plus the 20 insert cards, can also be found in a parallel chase card set with die-cut tops. One die-cut card was found in each six-card foil pack, making them five times scarcer than the regular cards. To prevent regular cards from being fraudulently cut, factory-issue die-cuts have the Upper Deck hologram on back in silver tone, rather than the gold holograms found on regular cards.

	NM/M
Complete Set (200):	50.00
Common Player:	.25
Die-Cut Stars:	1.5X

Classic Performances

Vintage action photos are featured in this chase set marking great post-season performances of modern times. The cards have a wide red strip at top with "CLASSIC PERFORMANCES" in gold-foil; the player's name, team and the SP Championship embossed logo at bottom are also in gold. Backs have a portrait photo and description of the highlight along with stats from that series. Regular Classic Performances cards are found at a stated rate of one per 15 foil packs, with die-cut versions in every 75 packs, on average. The die-cuts have silver UD holograms on back as opposed to the gold hologram found on regular versions of the chase cards.

		NM/M
Complete Set (10):		8.00
Common Player:		.50
Complete Die-Cut Set (10):		16.00
Common Die-Cuts:		1.00
CP1	Reggie Jackson (Game 6 of '77 WS)	.60
CP1	Reggie Jackson/Die-Cut	2.00
CP2	Nolan Ryan (Game 3 of '69 WS)	4.00
CP2	Nolan Ryan/Die-Cut	8.00
CP3	Kirk Gibson (Game 1 of '88 WS)	.50
CP3	Kirk Gibson/Die-Cut	1.00
CP4	Joe Carter (Game 6 of '93 WS)	.50
CP4	Joe Carter/Die-Cut	1.00
CP5	George Brett (Game 3 of '80 ALCS)	1.25
CP5	George Brett/Die-Cut	2.50
CP6	Roberto Alomar (Game 4 of '92 ALCS)	.50
CP6	Roberto Alomar/Die-Cut	1.00
CP7	Ozzie Smith (Game 5 of '85 NLCS)	.75
CP7	Ozzie Smith/Die-Cut	2.00
CP8	Kirby Puckett (Game 6 of '91 WS)	1.25
CP8	Kirby Puckett/Die-Cut	2.00
CP9	Bret Saberhagen (Game 7 of '85 WS)	.50
CP9	Bret Saberhagen/Die-Cut	1.00
CP10	Steve Garvey (Game 4 of '84 NLCS)	.50
CP10	Steve Garvey/Die-Cut	1.00

Destination: Fall Classic

Colored foil background printing and copper-foil graphic highlights are featured on this insert set picturing players who, for the most part, had yet to make a post-season appearance prior to 1995's expanded playoffs. Found at a stated average rate of one per 40 foil packs, the cards have short career summaries and another photo on back. A die-cut version of the cards was also issued, with a silver UD hologram on back rather than the gold found on the standard chase cards. The die-cut Fall Classic cards were inserted at a rate of one per 75 packs.

	NM/M
Complete Set (9):	18.00
Common Player:	1.00
Complete Die-Cut Set (9):	36.00
Common Die-Cut:	2.00
1	Ken Griffey Jr.	3.00
1	Ken Griffey Jr./Die-Cut	6.00
2	Frank Thomas	2.00
2	Frank Thomas/Die-Cut	4.00
3	Albert Belle	1.00
3	Albert Belle/Die-Cut	2.00
4	Mike Piazza	3.00
4	Mike Piazza/Die-Cut	6.00
5	Don Mattingly	2.75
5	Don Mattingly/Die-Cut	5.50
6	Hideo Nomo	1.50
6	Hideo Nomo/Die-Cut	3.00
7	Greg Maddux	2.50
7	Greg Maddux/Die-Cut	5.00
8	Fred McGriff	1.00
8	Fred McGriff/Die-Cut	2.00
9	Barry Bonds	4.00
9	Barry Bonds/Die-Cut	8.00

Ripken Tribute Jumbo

A special super-size (3" x 5") version of the SP/Championship edition Cal Ripken Jr. 2,131 Games tribute card insert was created for sale by Upper Deck Authentic on home shopping programs.

The card is die-cut and serially numbered on back from within an edition of 2,131 pieces.

	NM/M
CR1	Cal Ripken Jr.	12.00

1996 SP FanFest Promos

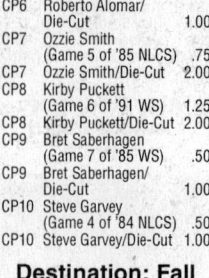

To introduce its SP product, Upper Deck prepared an eight-card promo set for distribution at the All-Star FanFest in Philadelphia. The promos are identical in format to the issued versions except for the presence of a bright silver-foil FanFest logo in the lower-left corner of each card's front. The cards lack the overprint which has become standard on promo cards in the recent years.

	NM/M
Complete Set (8):	8.00
Common Player:	.60
1	Ken Griffey Jr.	1.50
2	Frank Thomas	1.00
3	Albert Belle	.60
4	Mo Vaughn	.60
5	Barry Bonds	2.50
6	Mike Piazza	1.50
7	Matt Williams	.60
8	Sammy Sosa	1.25

1996 SP

This 188-card set, distributed through hobby-only channels, features tremendous photography, including two photos on the front, and six insert sets. The inserts sets are Heroes, Marquee Matchups Blue and Die-Cut Marquee Matchups Red, Hologram Special F/X Blue, Holoview Special F/X Red, and the continuation of the Cal Ripken Collection.

		NM/M
Complete Set (188):		12.50
Common Player:		.05
Pack (8):		1.25
Wax Box (30):		25.00
1	Rey Ordonez (Premier Prospects)	.05
2	George Arias (Premier Prospects)	.05
3	Osvaldo Fernandez RC (Premier Prospects)	.25
4	Darin Erstad RC (Premier Prospects)	2.00
5	Paul Wilson (Premier Prospects)	.05
6	Richard Hidalgo (Premier Prospects)	.05
7	Bob Wolcott (Premier Prospects)	.05
8	Jimmy Haynes (Premier Prospects)	.05
9	Edgar Renteria (Premier Prospects)	.05

10 Alan Benes (Premier Prospects) .05
11 Chris Snopek (Premier Prospects) .05
12 Billy Wagner (Premier Prospects) .05
13 Mike Grace RC (Premier Prospects) .05
14 Todd Greene (Premier Prospects) .05
15 Karim Garcia (Premier Prospects) .05
16 John Wasdin (Premier Prospects) .05
17 Jason Kendall (Premier Prospects) .05
18 Bob Abreu (Premier Prospects) .15
19 Jermaine Dye (Premier Prospects) .05
20 Jason Schmidt (Premier Prospects) .05
21 Javy Lopez .05
22 Ryan Klesko .05
23 Tom Glavine .35
24 John Smoltz .05
25 Greg Maddux 1.00
26 Chipper Jones 1.00
27 Fred McGriff .05
28 David Justice .05
29 Roberto Alomar .20
30 Cal Ripken Jr. 2.00
31 Jeffrey Hammonds .05
32 Bobby Bonilla .05
33 Mike Mussina .30
34 Randy Myers .05
35 Rafael Palmeiro .65
36 Brady Anderson .05
37 Tim Naehring .05
38 Jose Canseco .40
39 Roger Clemens 1.00
40 Mo Vaughn .05
41 Jose Valentin RC .05
42 Kevin Mitchell .05
43 Chili Davis .05
44 Garret Anderson .05
45 Tim Salmon .05
46 Chuck Finley .05
47 Mark Langston .05
48 Jim Abbott .05
49 J.T. Snow .05
50 Jim Edmonds .05
51 Sammy Sosa 1.00
52 Brian McRae .05
53 Ryne Sandberg 1.00
54 Mark Grace .05
55 Jaime Navarro .05
56 Harold Baines .05
57 Robin Ventura .05
58 Tony Phillips .05
59 Alex Fernandez .05
60 Frank Thomas .75
61 Ray Durham .05
62 Bret Boone .05
63 Barry Larkin .05
64 Pete Schourek .05
65 Reggie Sanders .05
66 John Smiley .05
67 Carlos Baerga .05
68 Jim Thome .65
69 Eddie Murray .75
70 Albert Belle .25
71 Dennis Martinez .05
72 Jack McDowell .05
73 Kenny Lofton .05
74 Manny Ramirez .75
75 Dante Bichette .05
76 Vinny Castilla .05
77 Andres Galarraga .05
78 Walt Weiss .05
79 Ellis Burks .05
80 Larry Walker .05
81 Cecil Fielder .05
82 Melvin Nieves .05
83 Travis Fryman .05
84 Chad Curtis .05
85 Alan Trammell .05
86 Gary Sheffield .45
87 Charles Johnson .05
88 Andre Dawson .30
89 Jeff Conine .05
90 Greg Colbrunn .05
91 Derek Bell .05
92 Brian Hunter .05
93 Doug Drabek .05
94 Craig Biggio .05
95 Jeff Bagwell .75
96 Kevin Appier .05
97 Jeff Montgomery .05
98 Michael Tucker .05
99 Bip Roberts .05
100 Johnny Damon .35
101 Eric Karros .05
102 Raul Mondesi .05
103 Ramon Martinez .05
104 Ismael Valdes .05
105 Mike Piazza 1.25
106 Hideo Nomo .40
107 Chan Ho Park .05
108 Ben McDonald .05
109 Kevin Seitzer .05
110 Greg Vaughn .05
111 Jose Valentin .05
112 Rick Aguilera .05
113 Marty Cordova .05
114 Brad Radke .05
115 Kirby Puckett 1.00
116 Chuck Knoblauch .05
117 Paul Molitor .75
118 Pedro Martinez .75
119 Mike Lansing .05
120 Rondell White .05
121 Moises Alou .05
122 Mark Grudzielanek .05
123 Jeff Fassero .05
124 Rico Brogna .05
125 Jason Isringhausen .05
126 Jeff Kent .05
127 Bernard Gilkey .05
128 Todd Hundley .05
129 David Cone .05
130 Andy Pettitte .25
131 Wade Boggs 1.00
132 Paul O'Neill .05
133 Ruben Sierra .05
134 John Wetteland .05
135 Derek Jeter 2.00
136 Geronimo Pena .05
137 Terry Steinbach .05
138 Ariel Prieto .05
139 Scott Brosius .05
140 Mark McGwire 1.50
141 Lenny Dykstra .05
142 Todd Zeile .05
143 Benito Santiago .05
144 Mickey Morandini .05
145 Gregg Jefferies .05
146 Denny Neagle .05
147 Orlando Merced .05
148 Charlie Hayes .05
149 Carlos Garcia .05
150 Jay Bell .05
151 Ray Lankford .05
152 Alan Benes .05
153 Dennis Eckersley .65
154 Gary Gaetti .05
155 Ozzie Smith 1.00
156 Ron Gant .05
157 Brian Jordan .05
158 Ken Caminiti .05
159 Rickey Henderson .75
160 Tony Gwynn 1.00
161 Wally Joyner .05
162 Andy Ashby .05
163 Steve Finley .05
164 Glenallen Hill .05
165 Matt Williams .05
166 Barry Bonds 2.00
167 William Van Landingham .05
168 Rod Beck .05
169 Randy Johnson .75
170 Ken Griffey Jr. 1.25
170p Ken Griffey Jr. (Unmarked promo; bio on back says, "...against Cleveland" as opposed to "...against the Indians.") 4.00
171 Alex Rodriguez 1.50
172 Edgar Martinez .05
173 Jay Buhner .05
174 Russ Davis .05
175 Juan Gonzalez .40
176 Mickey Tettleton .05
177 Will Clark .05
178 Ken Hill .05
179 Dean Palmer .05
180 Ivan Rodriguez .05
181 Carlos Delgado .50
182 Alex Gonzalez .05
183 Shawn Green .30
184 Erik Hanson .05
185 Joe Carter .05
186 Checklist (Hideo Nomo) .20
187 Checklist (Cal Ripken Jr.) 1.00
188 Checklist (Ken Griffey Jr.) .65

Baseball Heroes

This 1996 insert set is a continuation of the series which began in 1990. These cards, numbered 81-90, feature nine of today's top stars, plus a Ken Griffey Jr. header card (#81). The cards were seeded one per every 96 packs.

NM/M
Complete Set (10): 65.00
Common Player: 4.00
81 Ken Griffey Jr. Header 8.00
82 Frank Thomas 6.50
83 Albert Belle 4.00
84 Barry Bonds 12.00
85 Chipper Jones 8.00
86 Hideo Nomo 5.00
87 Mike Piazza 10.00
88 Manny Ramirez 6.50
89 Greg Maddux 8.00
90 Ken Griffey Jr. 10.00

Marquee Matchups Blue

This 20-card Upper Deck SP insert set contains cards that allow collectors to match up the game's top players against each other, such as Greg Maddux against Cal Ripken Jr. The design and stadiums in the background match together when the two cards are next to each other. Blue versions are seeded one per five packs. Cards are numbered with a "MM" prefix.

NM/M
Complete Set (20): 15.00
Common Player: .35
1 Ken Griffey Jr. 1.50
2 Hideo Nomo .60
3 Derek Jeter 2.00
4 Rey Ordonez .50
5 Tim Salmon .50
6 Mike Piazza 1.75
7 Mark McGwire 1.75
8 Barry Bonds 2.00
9 Cal Ripken Jr. 2.00
10 Greg Maddux 1.00
11 Albert Belle .50
12 Barry Larkin .50
13 Jeff Bagwell .75
14 Juan Gonzalez .60
15 Frank Thomas .75
16 Sammy Sosa .50
17 Mike Mussina .50
18 Chipper Jones 1.00
19 Roger Clemens 1.25
20 Fred McGriff .50

Marquee Matchups Red

A parallel set to the blue Marquee Matchups, the red cards are found on average of one per 61 packs. Besides the red background printing, this version is distinguished from the more common blue version by the die-cutting around the top. Cards are numbered with a "MM" prefix.

NM/M
Complete Set (20): 70.00
Common Player: 1.25
1 Ken Griffey Jr. 6.00
2 Hideo Nomo 2.00
3 Derek Jeter 9.00
4 Rey Ordonez 1.25
5 Tim Salmon 1.25
6 Mike Piazza 6.00
7 Mark McGwire 7.50
8 Barry Bonds 9.00
9 Cal Ripken Jr. 9.00
10 Greg Maddux 4.50
11 Albert Belle 1.25
12 Barry Larkin 1.25
13 Jeff Bagwell 3.50
14 Juan Gonzalez 2.00
15 Frank Thomas 3.50
16 Sammy Sosa 4.50
17 Mike Mussina 1.25
18 Chipper Jones 4.50
19 Roger Clemens 5.00
20 Fred McGriff 1.25

Ripken Collection

The last five cards of the Cal Ripken Jr. Collection, which began in Collector's Choice Series I, are featured in this Upper Deck SP product. These five cards, numbered 18-22, cover Ripken's early days, including his 1982 Rookie of the Year Award, his Major League debut, and photos of him playing third base. Ripken Collection inserts are found one per every 45 packs.

NM/M
Complete Set (5): 25.00
Common Card: 5.00
18-22 Cal Ripken Jr. 5.00

1996 SP SpecialFX

These 48 cards capture Upper Deck Holoview technology. Blue versions were seeded one per every five packs of 1996 Upper Deck SP baseball.

NM/M
Complete Set (48): 50.00
Common Player: .60
1 Greg Maddux 2.50
2 Eric Karros .60
3 Mike Piazza 3.00
4 Raul Mondesi .60
5 Hideo Nomo 1.00
6 Jim Edmonds .60
7 Jason Isringhausen .60
8 Jay Buhner .60
9 Barry Larkin .60
10 Ken Griffey Jr. 3.00
11 Gary Sheffield 1.25
12 Craig Biggio .60
13 Paul Wilson .60
14 Rondell White .60
15 Chipper Jones 2.50
16 Kirby Puckett 2.50
17 Ron Gant .60
18 Wade Boggs 2.50
19 Fred McGriff .60
20 Cal Ripken Jr. 5.00
21 Jason Kendall .60
22 Johnny Damon .90
23 Kenny Lofton .60
24 Roberto Alomar 1.00
25 Barry Bonds 4.00
26 Dante Bichette .60
27 Mark McGwire 4.00
28 Rafael Palmeiro 1.00
29 Juan Gonzalez 1.00
30 Albert Belle .60
31 Randy Johnson 1.75
32 Jose Canseco 1.25
33 Sammy Sosa 2.50
34 Eddie Murray 1.75
35 Frank Thomas 1.75
36 Tom Glavine .90
37 Matt Williams 1.50
38 Roger Clemens 2.75
39 Paul Molitor 1.75
40 Tony Gwynn 2.50
41 Mo Vaughn .60
42 Tim Salmon .60
43 Manny Ramirez 1.75
44 Jeff Bagwell 1.75
45 Edgar Martinez .60
46 Rey Ordonez .60
47 Osvaldo Fernandez .60
48 Derek Jeter 5.00

Special FX Red

These 1996 Upper Deck SP red die-cut cards use Upper Deck's Holoview technology. They are scarcer than the blue versions; these being seeded one per every 75 packs.

NM/M
Complete Set (48): 135.00
Common Player: 1.50
1 Greg Maddux 6.00
2 Eric Karros 1.50
3 Mike Piazza 8.00
4 Raul Mondesi 1.50
5 Hideo Nomo 2.25
6 Jim Edmonds 1.50
7 Jason Isringhausen 1.50
8 Jay Buhner 1.50
9 Barry Larkin 1.50
10 Ken Griffey Jr. 8.00
11 Gary Sheffield 2.50
12 Craig Biggio 1.50
13 Paul Wilson 1.50
14 Rondell White 1.50
15 Chipper Jones 6.00
16 Kirby Puckett 6.00
17 Ron Gant 1.50
18 Wade Boggs 6.00
19 Fred McGriff 1.50
20 Cal Ripken Jr. 12.50
21 Jason Kendall 1.50
22 Johnny Damon 2.50
23 Kenny Lofton 1.50
24 Roberto Alomar 2.25
25 Barry Bonds 12.50
26 Dante Bichette 1.50
27 Mark McGwire 10.00
28 Rafael Palmeiro 3.50
29 Juan Gonzalez 2.25
30 Albert Belle 1.50
31 Randy Johnson 4.50
32 Jose Canseco 2.50
33 Sammy Sosa 6.00
34 Eddie Murray 4.50
35 Frank Thomas 2.00
36 Tom Glavine 2.00
37 Matt Williams 1.50
38 Roger Clemens 7.00
39 Paul Molitor 4.50
40 Tony Gwynn 6.00
41 Mo Vaughn 1.50
42 Tim Salmon 1.50
43 Manny Ramirez 4.50
44 Jeff Bagwell 4.50
45 Edgar Martinez 1.50
46 Rey Ordonez 1.50
47 Osvaldo Fernandez 1.50
48 Derek Jeter 12.50

1996 SPx

Upper Deck's 1996 SPx set has 60 players in it, which are each paralleled as a Gold version (one per every seven packs). Base cards feature a new look with a different perimeter die-cut design from those used in the past for basketball and football sets. A 10-card insert set, Bound for Glory, was also produced. Tribute cards were also made for Ken Griffey Jr. and Mike Piazza, with scarcer autographed versions also produced for each player.

NM/M
Complete Set (60): 17.50
Common Player: .15
Golds: 1.5X
Pack (1): 1.25
Wax Box (36): 25.00
1 Greg Maddux 1.50
2 Chipper Jones 1.50
3 Fred McGriff .15
4 Tom Glavine .50
5 Cal Ripken Jr. 3.00
6 Roberto Alomar .50
7 Rafael Palmeiro 1.00
8 Jose Canseco .65
9 Roger Clemens 1.75
10 Mo Vaughn .15
11 Jim Edmonds .15
12 Tim Salmon .15
13 Sammy Sosa 1.50
14 Ryne Sandberg 1.50
15 Mark Grace .15
16 Frank Thomas 1.25
17 Barry Larkin .15
18 Kenny Lofton .15
19 Albert Belle 1.25
20 Eddie Murray 1.25
21 Manny Ramirez 1.25
22 Dante Bichette .15
23 Larry Walker .15
24 Vinny Castilla .15
25 Andres Galarraga .15
26 Cecil Fielder .15
27 Gary Sheffield .75
28 Craig Biggio .15
29 Jeff Bagwell 1.25
30 Derek Bell .15
31 Johnny Damon .60
32 Eric Karros .15
33 Mike Piazza 2.00
34 Raul Mondesi .15
35 Hideo Nomo .65
36 Kirby Puckett 1.50
37 Paul Molitor 1.25
38 Marty Cordova .15
39 Rondell White .15
40 Jason Isringhausen .15
41 Paul Wilson .15
42 Rey Ordonez .15
43 Derek Jeter 3.00
44 Wade Boggs 1.50
45 Mark McGwire 2.50
46 Jason Kendall .15
47 Ron Gant .15
48 Ozzie Smith 1.50
49 Tony Gwynn 1.50
50 Ken Caminiti .15
51 Barry Bonds 3.00
52 Matt Williams .15
53 Osvaldo Fernandez RC .15
54 Jay Buhner .15
55 Ken Griffey Jr. 2.00
55p Ken Griffey Jr./OPS 2.00
56 Randy Johnson 1.25
57 Alex Rodriguez 2.50
58 Juan Gonzalez .65
59 Joe Carter .15
60 Carlos Delgado .75

Bound for Glory

Some of baseball's best players are highlighted on these 1996 Upper Deck SPx insert cards. The cards were seeded one per every 24 packs. Fronts of the die-cut cards feature a color photograph on a background of silver-foil holographic portrait and action photos. Backs have another portrait photo, stats, career highlights and logos.

NM/M
Complete Set (10): 18.00
Common Player: 1.00
1 Ken Griffey Jr. 3.00
2 Frank Thomas 1.50
3 Barry Bonds 4.00

ABBREVIATIONS

OPS - Overprinted "Promotional Sample"

4	Cal Ripken Jr.	4.00
5	Greg Maddux	2.00
6	Chipper Jones	2.00
7	Roberto Alomar	1.00
8	Manny Ramirez	1.50
9	Tony Gwynn	2.00
10	Mike Piazza	3.00

Ken Griffey Jr. Commemorative

Seattle Mariners' star Ken Griffey Jr. has this tribute card in Upper Deck's 1996 SPx set. The card was seeded one per every 75 packs. Autographed versions were also produced; these cards were seeded one per every 2,000 packs.

		NM/M
KG1	Ken Griffey Jr.	2.50
KGA1	Ken Griffey Jr./Auto.	100.00

Mike Piazza Tribute

Los Angeles Dodgers' star catcher Mike Piazza is featured on this 1996 Upper Deck SPx insert card. Normal versions of the card are found one per every 95 packs, making it scarcer than the Ken Griffey Jr. inserts. Autographed Piazza cards are seeded one per every 2,000 packs.

		NM/M
MP1	Mike Piazza	2.00
MP1	Mike Piazza/Auto.	125.00

1997 SP Sample

To preview its SP brand for 1997, Upper Deck issued a sample card of Ken Griffey Jr. Similar in format to the issued cards, the promo bears card number 1 and is overprinted "SAMPLE" on back.

		NM/M
1	Ken Griffey Jr.	3.00

1997 SP

The fifth anniversary edition of SP Baseball features 184 regular cards sold in eight-card packs for $4.39. Card fronts feature the player's name in gold foil-stamping at bottom. Team name and position are vertically at one edge. Backs have two more photos along with "Best Year" and career stats. Inserts include Marquee Matchups, Special FX, Inside Info, Baseball Heroes, Game Film, SPx Force, and Autographed Vintage SP cards.

		NM/M
Complete Set (184):		12.00
Common Player:		.05
Pack (8):		2.00
Wax Box (30):		45.00
1	Andruw Jones (Great Futures)	.75
2	Kevin Orie (Great Futures)	.05
3	Nomar Garciaparra (Great Futures)	1.00
4	Jose Guillen (Great Futures)	.05
5	Todd Walker (Great Futures)	.05
6	Derrick Gibson (Great Futures)	.05
7	Aaron Boone (Great Futures)	.05
8	Bartolo Colon (Great Futures)	.05
9	Derrek Lee (Great Futures)	.50
10	Vladimir Guerrero (Great Futures)	.75
11	Wilton Guerrero (Great Futures)	.05
12	Luis Castillo (Great Futures)	.05
13	Jason Dickson (Great Futures)	.05
14	Bubba Trammell RC (Great Futures)	.25
15	Jose Cruz Jr. RC (Great Futures)	.50
16	Eddie Murray	.75
17	Darin Erstad	.20
18	Garret Anderson	.05
19	Jim Edmonds	.05
20	Tim Salmon	.05
21	Chuck Finley	.05
22	John Smoltz	.05
23	Greg Maddux	1.00
24	Kenny Lofton	.05
25	Chipper Jones	1.00
26	Ryan Klesko	.05
27	Javier Lopez	.05
28	Fred McGriff	.05
29	Roberto Alomar	.20
30	Rafael Palmeiro	.65
31	Mike Mussina	.30
32	Brady Anderson	.05
33	Rocky Coppinger	.05
34	Cal Ripken Jr.	2.00
35	Mo Vaughn	.05
36	Steve Avery	.05
37	Tom Gordon	.05
38	Tim Naehring	.05
39	Troy O'Leary	.05
40	Sammy Sosa	1.00
41	Brian McRae	.05
42	Mel Rojas	.05
43	Ryne Sandberg	1.00
44	Mark Grace	.05
45	Albert Belle	.05
46	Robin Ventura	.05
47	Roberto Hernandez	.05
48	Ray Durham	.05
49	Harold Baines	.05
50	Frank Thomas	.75
51	Bret Boone	.05
52	Reggie Sanders	.05
53	Deion Sanders	.05
54	Hal Morris	.05
55	Barry Larkin	.65
56	Jim Thome	.65
57	Marquis Grissom	.05
58	David Justice	.05
59	Charles Nagy	.05
60	Manny Ramirez	.75
61	Matt Williams	.05
62	Jack McDowell	.05
63	Vinny Castilla	.05
64	Dante Bichette	.05
65	Andres Galarraga	.05
66	Ellis Burks	.05
67	Larry Walker	.05
68	Eric Young	.05
69	Brian L. Hunter	.05
70	Travis Fryman	.05
71	Tony Clark	.05
72	Bobby Higginson	.05
73	Melvin Nieves	.05
74	Jeff Conine	.05
75	Gary Sheffield	.40
76	Moises Alou	.05
77	Edgar Renteria	.05
78	Alex Fernandez	.05
79	Charles Johnson	.05
80	Bobby Bonilla	.05
81	Darryl Kile	.05
82	Derek Bell	.05
83	Shane Reynolds	.05
84	Craig Biggio	.05
85	Jeff Bagwell	.75
86	Billy Wagner	.05
87	Chili Davis	.05
88	Kevin Appier	.05
89	Jay Bell	.05
90	Johnny Damon	.35
91	Jeff King	.05
92	Hideo Nomo	.40
93	Todd Hollandsworth	.05
94	Eric Karros	.05
95	Mike Piazza	1.25
96	Ramon Martinez	.05
97	Todd Worrell	.05
98	Raul Mondesi	.05
99	Dave Nilsson	.05
100	John Jaha	.05
101	Jose Valentin	.05
102	Jeff Cirillo	.05
103	Jeff D'Amico	.05
104	Ben McDonald	.05
105	Paul Molitor	.75
106	Rich Becker	.05
107	Frank Rodriguez	.05
108	Marty Cordova	.05
109	Terry Steinbach	.05
110	Chuck Knoblauch	.05
111	Mark Grudzielanek	.05
112	Mike Lansing	.05
113	Pedro Martinez	.75
114	Henry Rodriguez	.05
115	Rondell White	.05
116	Rey Ordonez	.05
117	Carlos Baerga	.05
118	Lance Johnson	.05
119	Bernard Gilkey	.05
120	Todd Hundley	.05
121	John Franco	.05
122	Bernie Williams	.05
123	David Cone	.05
124	Cecil Fielder	.05
125	Derek Jeter	2.00
126	Tino Martinez	.05
127	Mariano Rivera	.15
128	Andy Pettitte	.15
129	Wade Boggs	1.00
130	Mark McGwire	1.50
131	Jose Canseco	.50
132	Geronimo Berroa	.05
133	Jason Giambi	.45
134	Ernie Young	.05
135	Scott Rolen	.65
136	Ricky Bottalico	.05
137	Curt Schilling	.35
138	Gregg Jefferies	.05
139	Mickey Morandini	.05
140	Jason Kendall	.05
141	Kevin Elster	.05
142	Al Martin	.05
143	Joe Randa	.05
144	Jason Schmidt	.05
145	Ray Lankford	.05
146	Brian Jordan	.05
147	Andy Benes	.05
148	Alan Benes	.05
149	Gary Gaetti	.05
150	Ron Gant	.05
151	Dennis Eckersley	.65
152	Rickey Henderson	.75
153	Joey Hamilton	.05
154	Ken Caminiti	.05
155	Tony Gwynn	1.00
156	Steve Finley	.05
157	Trevor Hoffman	.05
158	Greg Vaughn	.05
159	J.T. Snow	.05
160	Barry Bonds	2.00
161	Glenallen Hill	.05
162	William Van Landingham	.05
163	Jeff Kent	.05
164	Jay Buhner	.05
165	Ken Griffey Jr.	1.25
166	Alex Rodriguez	1.50
167	Randy Johnson	.05
168	Edgar Martinez	.05
169	Dan Wilson	.05
170	Ivan Rodriguez	.65
171	Roger Pavlik	.05
172	Will Clark	.05
173	Dean Palmer	.05
174	Rusty Greer	.05
175	Juan Gonzalez	.40
176	John Wetteland	.05
177	Joe Carter	.05
178	Ed Sprague	.05
179	Carlos Delgado	.45
180	Roger Clemens	1.00
181	Juan Guzman	.05
182	Pat Hentgen	.05
183	Ken Griffey Jr. (Checklist)	.65
184	Hideki Irabu RC	.25

Buy-Back Autographed Inserts

To celebrate the fifth anniversary of its premium SP brand, Upper Deck went into the hobby market to buy nearly 3,000 previous years' cards for a special insert program in 1997 SP packs. Various SP cards from 1993-96 issues and inserts were autographed by star players and a numbered holographic seal added on back. The number of each particular card signed ranged widely from fewer than 10 to more than 100. Numbers in parentheses in the checklist are the quantity reported signed for that card. All cards were inserted into foil packs except those of Mo Vaughn, which were a mail-in redemption.

		NM/M
Common Autograph:		7.50
4	Ken Griffey Jr./16	600.00
28	Jeff Bagwell/7	100.00
167	Tony Gwynn/17	250.00
280	Chipper Jones/34	110.00
PP9	Ken Griffey Jr./5	800.00
6	Todd Hollandsworth/167	7.50
15	Alex Rodriguez/94	1,200
105	Ken Griffey Jr./103	125.00
114	Gary Sheffield/130	25.00
130	Tony Gwynn/367	25.00
13	Tony Gwynn/31	150.00
35	Gary Sheffield/4	60.00
34	Chipper Jones/60	125.00
60	Jeff Bagwell/173	40.00
75	Gary Sheffield/221	25.00
105	Tony Gwynn/64	60.00
188	Alex Rodriguez/63	200.00
190	Ken Griffey Jr./38	200.00
195	Jay Buhner/57	15.00
1	Rey Ordonez/111	7.50
18	Gary Sheffield/58	30.00
26	Chipper Jones/102	50.00
40	Mo Vaughn/250	15.00
95	Jeff Bagwell/292	20.00
160	Tony Gwynn/20	200.00
170	Ken Griffey Jr./312	65.00
171	Alex Rodriguez/73	125.00
173	Jay Buhner/79	30.00
MM13	Jeff Bagwell/23	65.00
MM4	Rey Ordonez/40	15.00
8	Jay Buhner/27	30.00

Game Film

A 10-card insert utilizing pieces of actual game footage to highlight the top stars in the game. Only 500 of each card were available. Cards are numbered with a "GF" prefix.

		NM/M
Complete Set (10):		175.00
Common Player:		12.00
1	Alex Rodriguez	22.50
2	Frank Thomas	12.00
3	Andruw Jones	12.00
4	Cal Ripken Jr.	30.00
5	Mike Piazza	17.50
6	Derek Jeter	30.00
7	Mark McGwire	22.50
8	Chipper Jones	15.00
9	Barry Bonds	30.00
10	Ken Griffey Jr.	17.50

Griffey Baseball Heroes

First started in 1990, this single-player insert continues with a salute to Ken Griffey Jr.

Each card in the set is numbered to 2,000.

		NM/M
Complete Set (10):		75.00
Common Griffey Jr.:		10.00
91-100	Ken Griffey Jr.	10.00

Inside Info

Each of the 25 cards in this insert feature a pull-out panel describing the player's major accomplishments. Both front and back are printed on metallic-foil stock. Cards were inserted one per box.

		NM/M
Complete Set (25):		75.00
Common Player:		1.00
1	Ken Griffey Jr.	5.00
2	Mark McGwire	6.00
3	Kenny Lofton	1.00
4	Paul Molitor	3.00
5	Frank Thomas	3.00
6	Greg Maddux	3.50
7	Mo Vaughn	1.00
8	Cal Ripken Jr.	7.50
9	Jeff Bagwell	3.00
10	Alex Rodriguez	6.00
11	John Smoltz	1.00
12	Manny Ramirez	3.00
13	Sammy Sosa	3.50
14	Vladimir Guerrero	3.00
15	Albert Belle	1.00
16	Mike Piazza	5.00
17	Derek Jeter	7.50
18	Scott Rolen	2.00
19	Tony Gwynn	3.50
20	Barry Bonds	7.50
21	Ken Caminiti	1.00
22	Chipper Jones	3.50
23	Juan Gonzalez	1.50
24	Roger Clemens	4.00
25	Andruw Jones	3.00

Marquee Matchups

A 20-card die-cut set designed to highlight top interleague matchups, when the matching cards are put together, a third player is highlighted in the background. Cards were inserted 1:5 packs and have an "MM" card-number prefix.

	NM/M
Complete Set (20):	20.00
Common Player:	.25
1 Ken Griffey Jr.	1.50
2 Andres Galarraga	.25
3 Barry Bonds	3.00
4 Mark McGwire	2.00
5 Mike Piazza	1.50
6 Tim Salmon	.25
7 Tony Gwynn	1.00
8 Alex Rodriguez	2.00
9 Chipper Jones	1.00
10 Derek Jeter	3.00
11 Manny Ramirez	.75
12 Jeff Bagwell	.75
13 Greg Maddux	1.00
14 Cal Ripken Jr.	3.00
15 Mo Vaughn	.25
16 Gary Sheffield	.45
17 Jim Thome	.65
18 Barry Larkin	.25
19 Frank Thomas	.75
20 Sammy Sosa	1.00

1997 SP Special FX

Color 3-D motion portraits are front and center on these cards that also feature a die-cut design. The rest of the front includes color action photos printed on silver-foil stock. Backs have another color photo. One of the Alex Rodriguez cards (#49) features the 1996 die-cut design. Special FX were inserted 1:9 packs.

		NM/M
Complete Set (48):		60.00
Common Player:		.60
1	Ken Griffey Jr.	3.50
2	Frank Thomas	2.00
3	Barry Bonds	5.00
4	Albert Belle	.60
5	Mike Piazza	3.50
6	Greg Maddux	2.50
7	Chipper Jones	2.50
8	Cal Ripken Jr.	5.00
9	Jeff Bagwell	2.00
10	Alex Rodriguez	4.00
11	Mark McGwire	4.00
12	Kenny Lofton	.60
13	Juan Gonzalez	1.00
14	Mo Vaughn	.60
15	John Smoltz	.60
16	Derek Jeter	5.00
17	Tony Gwynn	2.50
18	Ivan Rodriguez	1.50
19	Barry Larkin	.60
20	Sammy Sosa	2.50
21	Mike Mussina	.75
22	Gary Sheffield	1.00
23	Brady Anderson	.60
24	Roger Clemens	3.00
25	Ken Caminiti	.60
26	Roberto Alomar	1.00
27	Hideo Nomo	1.00
28	Bernie Williams	.60
29	Todd Hundley	.60
30	Manny Ramirez	2.00
31	Eric Karros	.60
32	Tim Salmon	.60
33	Jay Buhner	.60
34	Andy Pettitte	.60
35	Jim Thome	1.50
36	Ryne Sandberg	2.50
37	Matt Williams	.60
38	Ryan Klesko	.60
39	Jose Canseco	1.25
40	Paul Molitor	2.00
41	Eddie Murray	2.00
42	Darin Erstad	.75
43	Todd Walker	.60
44	Wade Boggs	2.50
45	Andruw Jones	2.00
46	Scott Rolen	1.50
47	Vladimir Guerrero	2.00
48	Alex Rodriguez (1996 design)	4.00

SPx Force

Each of the 10 cards in this set feature four different players. Cards are individually numbered to 500. In addition,

a number of players signed 100 versions of their SPx Force cards that are also randomly inserted into packs.

		NM/M
Complete Set (10):		60.00
Common Player:		6.00
1	Ken Griffey Jr., Jay Buhner, Andres Galarraga, Dante Bichette	7.50
2	Albert Belle, Brady Anderson, Mark McGwire, Cecil Fielder	9.00
3	Mo Vaughn, Ken Caminiti, Frank Thomas, Jeff Bagwell	6.00
4	Gary Sheffield, Sammy Sosa, Barry Bonds, Jose Canseco	12.00
5	Greg Maddux, Roger Clemens, John Smoltz, Randy Johnson	6.00
6	Alex Rodriguez, Derek Jeter, Chipper Jones, Rey Ordonez	12.00
7	Todd Hollandsworth, Mike Piazza, Raul Mondesi, Hideo Nomo	7.50
8	Juan Gonzalez, Manny Ramirez, Roberto Alomar, Ivan Rodriguez	6.00
9	Tony Gwynn, Wade Boggs, Eddie Murray, Paul Molitor	6.00
10	Andruw Jones, Vladimir Guerrero, Todd Walker, Scott Rolen	6.00

SPx Force Autographs

Ten players signed cards for this insert, which was serially numbered to 100. The cards were randomly seeded in packs except the Mo Vaughn card which was available by redemption.

		NM/M
Common Player:		20.00
1	Ken Griffey Jr.	125.00
2	Albert Belle	25.00
3	Mo Vaughn	20.00
4	Gary Sheffield	25.00
5	Greg Maddux	100.00
6	Alex Rodriguez	160.00
7	Todd Hollandsworth	20.00
8	Roberto Alomar	30.00
9	Tony Gwynn	75.00
10	Andruw Jones	40.00

1997 SPx

Fifty cards, each featuring a perimeter die-cut design and a 3-D holoview photo, make up the SPx base set. Five different parallel sets - Steel (1:1 pack), Bronze (1:1), Silver (1:1), Gold (1:17) and Grand Finale (50 per

ABBREVIATIONS

OPS - Overprinted "Promotional Sample"
SP - Short Print

card) - are found as inserts, as are Cornerstones of the Game, Bound for Glory and Bound for Glory Signature cards. Packs contain three cards and carried a suggested retail price of $5.99.

		NM/M
Complete Set (50):		17.50
Common Player:		.15
Steel:		1.5X
Bronze:		1.5X
Silver:		1.5X
Gold:		3X
Grand Finale:		4X
Pack (3):		2.00
Wax Box (18):		30.00
1	Eddie Murray	1.00
2	Darin Erstad	.35
3	Tim Salmon	.15
4	Andruw Jones	1.00
5	Chipper Jones	1.50
6	John Smoltz	.15
7	Greg Maddux	1.50
8	Kenny Lofton	.15
9	Roberto Alomar	.30
10	Rafael Palmeiro	.75
11	Brady Anderson	.15
12	Cal Ripken Jr.	3.00
13	Nomar Garciaparra	1.50
14	Mo Vaughn	.15
15	Ryne Sandberg	1.50
16	Sammy Sosa	1.50
17	Frank Thomas	1.00
18	Albert Belle	.15
19	Barry Larkin	.15
20	Deion Sanders	.15
21	Manny Ramirez	1.00
22	Jim Thome	.65
23	Dante Bichette	.15
24	Andres Galarraga	.15
25	Larry Walker	.15
26	Gary Sheffield	.50
27	Jeff Bagwell	1.00
28	Raul Mondesi	.15
29	Hideo Nomo	.50
30	Mike Piazza	2.00
31	Paul Molitor	1.00
32	Todd Walker	.15
33	Vladimir Guerrero	1.00
34	Todd Hundley	.15
35	Andy Pettitte	.25
36	Derek Jeter	3.00
37	Jose Canseco	.50
38	Mark McGwire	2.50
39	Scott Rolen	.65
40	Ron Gant	.15
41	Ken Caminiti	.15
42	Tony Gwynn	1.50
43	Barry Bonds	3.00
44	Jay Buhner	.15
45	Ken Griffey Jr.	2.00
45s	Ken Griffey Jr./OPS	2.00
46	Alex Rodriguez	2.50
47	Jose Cruz Jr. RC	1.00
48	Juan Gonzalez	.50
49	Ivan Rodriguez	.75
50	Roger Clemens	1.75

Bound for Glory

This 20-card insert utilizes holoview technology and is sequentially numbered to 1,500 per card.

		NM/M
Complete Set (20):		60.00
Common Player:		1.00
1	Andruw Jones	3.00
2	Chipper Jones	4.00
3	Greg Maddux	4.00
4	Kenny Lofton	1.50
5	Cal Ripken Jr.	7.50
6	Mo Vaughn	1.00
7	Frank Thomas	3.00
8	Albert Belle	1.00
9	Manny Ramirez	3.00
10	Gary Sheffield	1.50
11	Jeff Bagwell	3.00
12	Mike Piazza	5.00
13	Derek Jeter	7.50
14	Mark McGwire	6.00
15	Tony Gwynn	4.00
16	Ken Caminiti	1.00
17	Barry Bonds	7.50
18	Alex Rodriguez	6.00
19	Ken Griffey Jr.	5.00
20	Juan Gonzalez	1.50

Bound for Glory Supreme Signatures

This five-card set featured autographs from the players

and was sequentially numbered to 250.

		NM/M
Complete Set (5):		250.00
Common Player:		25.00
1	Jeff Bagwell	40.00
2	Ken Griffey Jr.	120.00
3	Andruw Jones	40.00
4	Alex Rodriguez	160.00
5	Gary Sheffield	30.00

Cornerstones of the Game

A 20-card insert utilizing a double-front design highlighting 40 of the top players in the game. Each card is sequentially numbered to 500.

		NM/M
Complete Set (10):		150.00
Common Player:		12.00
1	Ken Griffey Jr., Barry Bonds	25.00
2	Frank Thomas, Albert Belle	12.00
3	Chipper Jones, Greg Maddux	15.00
4	Tony Gwynn, Paul Molitor	15.00
5	Andruw Jones, Vladimir Guerrero	12.00
6	Jeff Bagwell, Ryne Sandberg	15.00
7	Mike Piazza, Ivan Rodriguez	20.00
8	Cal Ripken Jr., Eddie Murray	25.00
9	Mo Vaughn, Mark McGwire	20.00
10	Alex Rodriguez, Derek Jeter	25.00

1998 SP Authentic Sample

This card of Upper Deck spokesman Ken Griffey, Jr., was issued to preview the new SP Authentic line. Design is similar to the issued version but the sample displays different photos, a different the card number and the word "SAMPLE" printed in large letters on back.

	NM/M
Ken Griffey Jr.	3.00

1998 SP Authentic

The SP Authentic base set consists of 198 cards, including the 30-card Future Watch subset and one checklist card. The base cards have a color photo inside a thick white border. Inserts include Chirography, Sheer Dominance and SP Authentics.

		NM/M
Complete Set (198):		15.00
Common Player:		.05

		NM/M
Pack (5):		2.00
Wax Box (24):		35.00
1	Travis Lee (Future Watch)	.10
2	Mike Caruso (Future Watch)	.05
3	Kerry Wood (Future Watch)	.65
4	Mark Kotsay (Future Watch)	.05
5	Magglio Ordonez RC (Future Watch)	2.00
6	Scott Elarton (Future Watch)	.05
7	Carl Pavano (Future Watch)	.10
8	A.J. Hinch (Future Watch)	.05
9	Rolando Arrojo RC (Future Watch)	.40
10	Ben Grieve (Future Watch)	.05
11	Gabe Alvarez (Future Watch)	.05
12	Mike Kinkade RC (Future Watch)	.40
13	Bruce Chen (Future Watch)	.05
14	Juan Encarnacion (Future Watch)	.05
15	Todd Helton (Future Watch)	.75
16	Aaron Boone (Future Watch)	.05
17	Sean Casey (Future Watch)	.15
18	Ramon Hernandez (Future Watch)	.05
19	Daryle Ward (Future Watch)	.05
20	Paul Konerko (Future Watch)	.15
21	David Ortiz (Future Watch)	.50
22	Derek Lee (Future Watch)	.05
23	Brad Fullmer (Future Watch)	.05
24	Javier Vazquez (Future Watch)	.05
25	Miguel Tejada (Future Watch)	.15
26	David Dellucci (Future Watch)	.05
27	Alex Gonzalez (Future Watch)	.05
28	Matt Clement (Future Watch)	.05
29	Eric Milton (Future Watch)	.05
30	Russell Branyan (Future Watch)	.05
31	Chuck Finley	.05
32	Jim Edmonds	.05
33	Darin Erstad	.20
34	Jason Dickson	.05
35	Tim Salmon	.05
36	Cecil Fielder	.05
37	Todd Greene	.05
38	Andy Benes	.05
39	Jay Bell	.05
40	Matt Williams	.05
41	Brian Anderson	.05
42	Karim Garcia	.05
43	Javy Lopez	.05
44	Tom Glavine	.35
45	Greg Maddux	1.50
46	Andruw Jones	1.00
47	Chipper Jones	1.50
48	Ryan Klesko	.05
49	John Smoltz	.05
50	Andres Galarraga	.05
51	Rafael Palmeiro	.75
52	Mike Mussina	.30
53	Roberto Alomar	.20
54	Joe Carter	.05
55	Cal Ripken Jr.	3.00
56	Brady Anderson	.05
57	Mo Vaughn	.05
58	John Valentin	.05
59	Dennis Eckersley	.75
60	Nomar Garciaparra	1.50
61	Pedro J. Martinez	1.00
62	Jeff Blauser	.05
63	Kevin Orie	.05
64	Henry Rodriguez	.05
65	Mark Grace	.05
66	Albert Belle	.05
67	Mike Cameron	.05
68	Robin Ventura	.05
69	Frank Thomas	1.00
70	Barry Larkin	.05
71	Brett Tomko	.05
72	Willie Greene	.05
73	Reggie Sanders	.05
74	Sandy Alomar Jr.	.05
75	Kenny Lofton	.05
76	Jaret Wright	.05
77	David Justice	.05
78	Omar Vizquel	.05
79	Manny Ramirez	1.00
80	Jim Thome	.75
81	Travis Fryman	.05
82	Neifi Perez	.05
83	Mike Lansing	.05
84	Vinny Castilla	.05
85	Larry Walker	.05
86	Dante Bichette	.05
87	Darryl Kile	.05
88	Justin Thompson	.05
89	Damion Easley	.05
90	Tony Clark	.05
91	Bobby Higginson	.05
92	Brian L. Hunter	.05
93	Edgar Renteria	.05
94	Craig Counsell	.05
95	Mike Piazza	2.00
96	Livan Hernandez	.05
97	Todd Zeile	.05
98	Richard Hidalgo	.05
99	Moises Alou	.05
100	Jeff Bagwell	1.00
101	Mike Hampton	.05
102	Craig Biggio	.05
103	Dean Palmer	.05
104	Tim Belcher	.05
105	Jeff King	.05
106	Jeff Conine	.05
107	Johnny Damon	.30
108	Hideo Nomo	.50
109	Raul Mondesi	.05
110	Gary Sheffield	.45
111	Ramon Martinez	.05
112	Chan Ho Park	.05
113	Eric Young	.05
114	Charles Johnson	.05
115	Eric Karros	.05
116	Bobby Bonilla	.05
117	Jeromy Burnitz	.05
118	Carl Eldred	.05
119	Jeff D'Amico	.05
120	Marquis Grissom	.05
121	Dave Nilsson	.05
122	Brad Radke	.05
123	Marty Cordova	.05
124	Ron Coomer	.05
125	Paul Molitor	1.00
126	Todd Walker	.05
127	Rondell White	.05
128	Mark Grudzielanek	.05
129	Carlos Perez	.05
130	Vladimir Guerrero	1.00
131	Dustin Hermanson	.05
132	Butch Huskey	.05
133	John Franco	.05
134	Rey Ordonez	.05
135	Todd Hundley	.05
136	Edgardo Alfonzo	.05
137	Bobby Jones	.05
138	John Olerud	.05
139	Chili Davis	.05
140	Tino Martinez	.05
141	Andy Pettitte	.15
142	Chuck Knoblauch	.05
143	Bernie Williams	.05
144	David Cone	.05
145	Derek Jeter	3.00
146	Paul O'Neill	.05
147	Rickey Henderson	1.00
148	Jason Giambi	.50
149	Kenny Rogers	.05
150	Scott Rolen	.75
151	Curt Schilling	.35
152	Ricky Bottalico	.05
153	Mike Lieberthal	.05
154	Francisco Cordova	.05
155	Jose Guillen	.05
156	Jason Schmidt	.05
157	Jason Kendall	.05
158	Kevin Young	.05
159	Delino DeShields	.05
160	Mark McGwire	2.50
161	Ray Lankford	.05
162	Brian Jordan	.05
163	Ron Gant	.05
164	Todd Stottlemyre	.05
165	Ken Caminiti	.05
166	Kevin Brown	.05
167	Trevor Hoffman	.05
168	Steve Finley	.05
169	Wally Joyner	.05
170	Tony Gwynn	1.50
171	Shawn Estes	.05
172	J.T. Snow	.05
173	Jeff Kent	.05
174	Robb Nen	.05
175	Barry Bonds	3.00
176	Randy Johnson	1.00
177	Edgar Martinez	.05
178	Jay Buhner	.05
179	Alex Rodriguez	2.50
180	Ken Griffey Jr.	2.00
181	Ken Cloude	.05
182	Wade Boggs	1.50
183	Tony Saunders	.05
184	Wilson Alvarez	.05
185	Fred McGriff	.05
186	Roberto Hernandez	.05
187	Kevin Stocker	.05
188	Fernando Tatis	.05
189	Will Clark	.05
190	Juan Gonzalez	.50
191	Rusty Greer	.05
192	Ivan Rodriguez	.75
193	Jose Canseco	.45
194	Carlos Delgado	.50
195	Roger Clemens	1.75
196	Pat Hentgen	.05
197	Randy Myers	.05
198	Checklist (Ken Griffey Jr.)	.85

Chirography

Chirography insert are seeded one per 25 packs. The featured player signed his cards in the white border at the bottom.

		NM/M
Common Card:		4.00
Inserted 1:25		
RA	Roberto Alomar	15.00
RB	Russell Branyan	4.00
SC	Sean Casey	10.00
TC	Tony Clark	4.00
RC	Roger Clemens/SP/400	80.00
JC	Jose Cruz Jr.	4.00
DE	Darin Erstad	7.50
NG	Nomar Garciaparra/SP/400	60.00
BG	Ben Grieve	4.00
KG	Ken Griffey Jr./SP/400	60.00
VG	Vladimir Guerrero	30.00
TG	Tony Gwynn/SP/850	30.00
TH	Todd Helton	15.00
LH	Livan Hernandez	6.00
CJ	Charles Johnson	6.00
AJ	Andruw Jones	17.50
CHIP	Chipper Jones/SP/800	30.00
PK	Paul Konerko	15.00
MK	Mark Kotsay	6.00
RL	Ray Lankford	6.00
TL	Travis Lee	6.00
PM	Paul Molitor/SP/800	20.00
MM	Mike Mussina	20.00
AR	Alex Rodriguez/SP/800	80.00
IR	Ivan Rodriguez	30.00
SR	Scott Rolen	20.00
GS	Gary Sheffield	15.00
MT	Miguel Tejada	20.00
JW	Jaret Wright	6.00
MV	Mo Vaughn/SP/800	12.50

Ken Griffey Jr. 300th HR Redemption

This 5" x 7" version of Ken Griffey Jr.'s SP Authentic card was issued as a redemption for one of the 1000 Trade Cards which were foil-pack inserts.

		NM/M
KG300	Ken Griffey Jr.	30.00

Jersey Swatch

These 5" x 7" redemption cards were issued in exchange for Trade Cards found as random foil-packs inserts. Fronts have a player action photo on a white background. Backs have a congratulatory message of authenticity. Sandwiched between is a swatch of that player's uniform jersey. The large-format jersey cards were available in limited editions which are listed in parentheses, though all might not have been redeemed prior to the Aug. 1, 1999, cut-off date.

		NM/M
Complete Set (6):		130.00
Common Player:		7.50
(1)	Jay Buhner/125	7.50
(2)	Ken Griffey Jr./125	50.00
(3)	Tony Gwynn/415	10.00
(4)	Greg Maddux/125	30.00
(5)	Alex Rodriguez/125	60.00
(6)	Gary Sheffield/125	12.00

Trade Cards

Cards which could be traded (prior to the Aug. 1, 1999 cut-off) for special cards and autographed memorabilia were inserted into SP Authentic foil packs at an announced rate of one per 291 packs. Trade cards have a white background on front with a color player action photo and the name of the redemption item. Backs gives details for redemption. In some cases, because of their insertion-rate rarity, the cards are worth more than the redemption items. The unnumbered cards are listed here alphabetically.

		NM/M
Common Card:		5.00
(1)	Roberto Alomar/Auto. Ball/100	15.00
(2)	Albert Belle/Auto. Ball/100	7.50
(3)	Jay Buhner/Jersey card 125	5.00
(4)	Ken Griffey Jr./Auto. Glv/30	200.00
(5)	Ken Griffey Jr./Auto. Jsy/30	200.00
(6)	Ken Griffey Jr./Jersey card 125	25.00
(7)	Ken Griffey Jr./Standee/200	15.00
(8)	Ken Griffey Jr./300th HR Card 1000	5.00
(9)	Tony Gwynn/Jersey card 415	15.00
(10)	Brian Jordan/Auto. Ball/50	10.00
(11)	Greg Maddux/Jersey card/125	20.00
(12)	Raul Mondesi/Auto. Ball/100	5.00
(13)	Alex Rodriguez/Jersey card/125	40.00
(14)	Gary Sheffield/Jersey card/125	5.00
(15)	Robin Ventura/Auto. Ball/50	10.00

Sheer Dominance

Sheer Dominance is a 42-card insert. The base set is inserted one per three packs. The Sheer Dominance Gold parallel is sequentially numbered to 2,000 and the Titanium parallel is numbered to 100. The cards feature a player photo inside a white border. The background color corresponds to the level of the insert.

	NM/M
Complete Set (42):	32.50
Common Player:	.25
Inserted 1:3	
Gold (2,000 Sets):	2X
Titanium (100 Sets):	12X
SD1 Ken Griffey Jr.	1.75
SD2 Rickey Henderson	1.00
SD3 Jaret Wright	.25
SD4 Craig Biggio	.25
SD5 Travis Lee	.25
SD6 Kenny Lofton	.25
SD7 Raul Mondesi	.25
SD8 Cal Ripken Jr.	2.50
SD9 Matt Williams	.25
SD10 Mark McGwire	2.00
SD11 Alex Rodriguez	2.00
SD12 Fred McGriff	.25
SD13 Scott Rolen	.75
SD14 Paul Molitor	1.00
SD15 Nomar Garciaparra	1.50
SD16 Vladimir Guerrero	1.00
SD17 Andruw Jones	1.00
SD18 Manny Ramirez	1.00
SD19 Tony Gwynn	1.50
SD20 Barry Bonds	2.50
SD21 Ben Grieve	.75
SD22 Ivan Rodriguez	.75
SD23 Jose Cruz Jr.	.25
SD24 Pedro J. Martinez	1.00
SD25 Chipper Jones	1.50
SD26 Albert Belle	.25
SD27 Todd Helton	.75
SD28 Paul Konerko	.35
SD29 Sammy Sosa	1.50
SD30 Frank Thomas	1.00
SD31 Greg Maddux	1.50
SD32 Randy Johnson	1.00
SD33 Larry Walker	.25
SD34 Roberto Alomar	.45
SD35 Roger Clemens	1.50
SD36 Mo Vaughn	.25
SD37 Jim Thome	.75
SD38 Jeff Bagwell	1.00
SD39 Tino Martinez	.25
SD40 Mike Piazza	1.75
SD41 Derek Jeter	2.50
SD42 Juan Gonzalez	.50

Sheer Dominance Gold

CHIPPER JONES

Identical in format and using the same photos as the Silver version, the scarcer Sheer Dominance Gold card differs on front in its use of a gold-metallic foil background within the white border. Backs of the gold version are individually serial numbered within an edition of 2,000 each.

	NM/M
Common Player:	.50
Gold Stars:	2X

Sheer Dominance Titanium

Sheer Dominance Titanium is a parallel of the 42-card Sheer Dominance insert. The cards are numbered to 100 and have a gray background with "Titanium" printed across it.

	NM/M
Common Player:	4.00
Titanium Stars:	12X

1998 SPx Finite Sample

This card was issued to promote SPx's all-numbered Finite issue. The serial number on the card's back is "0000/0000." The card is overprinted "SAMPLE" on back.

	NM/M
1 Ken Griffey Jr.	3.00

1998 SPx Finite

SPx Finite is an all-sequentially numbered set issued in two 180-card series. The Series 1 base set consists of five subsets: 90 regular cards (numbered to 9,000), 30 Star Focus (7,000), 30 Youth Movement (5,000), 20 Power Explosion (4,000) and 10 Heroes of the Game (2,000). The set is paralleled in the Radiance and Spectrum sets. Radiance regular cards are numbered to 4,500, Star Focus to 3,500, Youth Movement to 2,500, Power Explosion to 1,000 and Heroes of the Game to 100. Spectrum regular cards are numbered to 2,250, Star Focus to 1,750, Youth Movement to 1,250, Power Explosion to 50 and Heroes of the Game to 1. The Series 2 base set has 90 regular cards (numbered to 9,000), 30 Power Passion (7,000), 30 Youth Movement (5,000), 20 Tradewinds (4,000) and 10 Cornerstones of the Game (2,000). Series 2 also has Radiance and Spectrum parallels. Radiance regular cards are numbered to 4,500, Power Passion to 3,500, Youth Movement to 2,500, Tradewinds to 1,000 and Cornerstones of the Game to 100. Spectrum regular cards are numbered to 2,250, Power Passion to 1,750, Youth Movement to 1,250, Tradewinds to 50 and Cornerstones of the Game to 1. The 1-of-1 cards are not valued due to scarcity and fluctuating demand. The only insert is Home Run Hysteria.

	NM/M
Complete Set (360):	200.00
Common Youth Movement:	
(#1-30, 181-210):	.50
Radiance YM (2,500):	1.5X
Spectrum YM (1,250):	2X
Common Power Explosion:	
(#31-50):	.50
Radiance PE (1,000):	2X
Spectrum PE (50): 25X	
Common Base Card	
(#51-140, 241-330):	.15
Radiance Base Card (4,500):	1X
Spectrum Base Card (2,250):	2X
Common Star Focus:	
(#141-170):	.35
Radiance SF (3,500):	1X
Spectrum SF (1,750):	2X
Common Heroes of the Game:	
(#171-180):	2.50
Radiance HG (100): 15X	
Common Power Passion:	
(#211-240):	.50
Radiance PP (3,500):	1X
Spectrum PP (1,750):	2X
Common Tradewinds:	
(#331-350):	.75
Radiance TW (1,000):	2X
Spectrum TW (50):	25X
Common Cornerstones/Game:	
(#351-360):	2.50
Radiance CG (100):	15X
Pack (3):	2.00
Wax Box:	25.00

		NM/M
1	Nomar Garciaparra (Youth Movement)	3.00
2	Miguel Tejada (Youth Movement)	.75
3	Mike Cameron (Youth Movement)	.50
4	Ken Cloude (Youth Movement)	.50
5	Jaret Wright (Youth Movement)	.50
6	Mark Kotsay (Youth Movement)	.50
7	Craig Counsell (Youth Movement)	.50
8	Jose Guillen (Youth Movement)	.50
9	Neifi Perez (Youth Movement)	.50
10	Jose Cruz Jr. (Youth Movement)	.50
11	Brett Tomko (Youth Movement)	.50
12	Matt Morris (Youth Movement)	.50
13	Justin Thompson (Youth Movement)	.50
14	Jeremi Gonzalez (Youth Movement)	.50
15	Scott Rolen (Youth Movement)	1.50
16	Vladimir Guerrero (Youth Movement)	2.00
17	Brad Fullmer (Youth Movement)	.50
18	Brian Giles (Youth Movement)	.50
19	Todd Dunwoody (Youth Movement)	.50
20	Ben Grieve (Youth Movement)	.50
21	Juan Encarnacion (Youth Movement)	.50
22	Aaron Boone (Youth Movement)	.50
23	Richie Sexson (Youth Movement)	.50
24	Richard Hidalgo (Youth Movement)	.50
25	Andruw Jones (Youth Movement)	2.00
26	Todd Helton (Youth Movement)	1.50
27	Paul Konerko (Youth Movement)	.75
28	Dante Powell (Youth Movement)	.50
29	Elieser Marrero (Youth Movement)	.50
30	Derek Jeter (Youth Movement)	5.00
31	Mike Piazza (Power Explosion)	3.00
32	Tony Clark (Power Explosion)	.50
33	Larry Walker (Power Explosion)	.50
34	Jim Thome (Power Explosion)	1.50
35	Juan Gonzalez (Power Explosion)	1.00
36	Jeff Bagwell (Power Explosion)	2.00
37	Jay Buhner (Power Explosion)	.50
38	Tim Salmon (Power Explosion)	.50
39	Albert Belle (Power Explosion)	.50
40	Mark McGwire (Power Explosion)	4.00
41	Sammy Sosa (Power Explosion)	2.50
42	Mo Vaughn (Power Explosion)	.50
43	Manny Ramirez (Power Explosion)	2.00
44	Tino Martinez (Power Explosion)	.50
45	Frank Thomas (Power Explosion)	2.00
46	Nomar Garciaparra (Power Explosion)	2.50
47	Alex Rodriguez (Power Explosion)	4.00
48	Chipper Jones (Power Explosion)	2.50
49	Barry Bonds (Power Explosion)	5.00
50	Ken Griffey Jr. (Power Explosion)	3.00
51	Jason Dickson	.15
52	Jim Edmonds	.15
53	Darin Erstad	.35
54	Tim Salmon	.15
55	Chipper Jones	2.00
56	Ryan Klesko	.15
57	Tom Glavine	.35
58	Denny Neagle	.15
59	John Smoltz	.15
60	Javy Lopez	.15
61	Roberto Alomar	.30
62	Rafael Palmeiro	1.25
63	Mike Mussina	.35
64	Cal Ripken Jr.	4.00
65	Mo Vaughn	.15
66	Tim Naehring	.15
67	John Valentin	.15
68	Mark Grace	.15
69	Kevin Orie	.15
70	Sammy Sosa	2.50
71	Albert Belle	.15
72	Frank Thomas	1.50
73	Robin Ventura	.15
74	David Justice	.15
75	Kenny Lofton	.15
76	Omar Vizquel	.15
77	Manny Ramirez	1.50
78	Jim Thome	.65
79	Dante Bichette	.15
80	Larry Walker	.15
81	Vinny Castilla	.15
82	Ellis Burks	.15
83	Bobby Higginson	.15
84	Brian L. Hunter	.15
85	Tony Clark	.15
86	Mike Hampton	.15
87	Jeff Bagwell	1.50
88	Craig Biggio	.15

		NM/M
89	Derek Bell	.15
90	Mike Piazza	3.00
91	Ramon Martinez	.15
92	Raul Mondesi	.15
93	Hideo Nomo	.75
94	Eric Karros	.15
95	Paul Molitor	1.50
96	Marty Cordova	.15
97	Brad Radke	.15
98	Mark Grudzielanek	.15
99	Carlos Perez	.15
100	Rondell White	.15
101	Todd Hundley	.15
102	Edgardo Alfonzo	.15
103	John Franco	.15
104	John Olerud	.15
105	Tino Martinez	.15
106	David Cone	.15
107	Paul O'Neill	.15
108	Andy Pettitte	.25
109	Bernie Williams	.15
110	Rickey Henderson	1.50
111	Jason Giambi	.75
112	Matt Stairs	.15
113	Gregg Jefferies	.15
114	Rico Brogna	.15
115	Curt Schilling	.35
116	Jason Schmidt	.15
117	Jose Guillen	.15
118	Kevin Young	.15
119	Ray Lankford	.15
120	Mark McGwire	3.00
121	Delino DeShields	.15
122	Ken Caminiti	.15
123	Tony Gwynn	2.00
124	Trevor Hoffman	.15
125	Barry Bonds	4.00
126	Jeff Kent	.15
127	Shawn Estes	.15
128	J.T. Snow	.15
129	Jay Buhner	.15
130	Ken Griffey Jr.	2.50
131	Dan Wilson	.15
132	Edgar Martinez	.15
133	Alex Rodriguez	3.00
134	Rusty Greer	.15
135	Juan Gonzalez	.75
136	Fernando Tatis	.15
137	Ivan Rodriguez	1.00
138	Carlos Delgado	.75
139	Pat Hentgen	.15
140	Roger Clemens	2.25
141	Chipper Jones (Star Focus)	2.00
142	Greg Maddux (Star Focus)	2.00
143	Rafael Palmeiro (Star Focus)	1.25
144	Mike Mussina (Star Focus)	.65
145	Cal Ripken Jr. (Star Focus)	4.00
146	Nomar Garciaparra (Star Focus)	2.00
147	Mo Vaughn (Star Focus)	.35
148	Sammy Sosa (Star Focus)	2.00
149	Albert Belle (Star Focus)	.35
150	Frank Thomas (Star Focus)	1.50
151	Jim Thome (Star Focus)	1.25
152	Kenny Lofton (Star Focus)	.35
153	Manny Ramirez (Star Focus)	1.50
154	Larry Walker (Star Focus)	.35
155	Jeff Bagwell (Star Focus)	1.50
156	Craig Biggio (Star Focus)	.35
157	Mike Piazza (Star Focus)	2.50
158	Paul Molitor (Star Focus)	1.50
159	Derek Jeter (Star Focus)	4.00
160	Tino Martinez (Star Focus)	.35
161	Curt Schilling (Star Focus)	.50
162	Mark McGwire (Star Focus)	3.00
163	Tony Gwynn (Star Focus)	2.00
164	Barry Bonds (Star Focus)	4.00
165	Ken Griffey Jr. (Star Focus)	2.50
166	Randy Johnson (Star Focus)	1.50
167	Alex Rodriguez (Star Focus)	3.00
168	Juan Gonzalez (Star Focus)	.75
169	Ivan Rodriguez (Star Focus)	1.25
170	Roger Clemens (Star Focus)	2.25
171	Greg Maddux (Heroes of the Game)	3.00
172	Cal Ripken Jr. (Heroes of the Game)	6.50
173	Frank Thomas (Heroes of the Game)	2.00

		NM/M
174	Jeff Bagwell (Heroes of the Game)	2.00
175	Mike Piazza (Heroes of the Game)	4.00
176	Mark McGwire (Heroes of the Game)	5.00
177	Barry Bonds (Heroes of the Game)	6.50
178	Ken Griffey Jr. (Heroes of the Game)	4.00
179	Alex Rodriguez (Heroes of the Game)	5.00
180	Roger Clemens (Heroes of the Game)	3.25
181	Mike Caruso (Youth Movement)	.50
182	David Ortiz (Youth Movement)	1.00
183	Gabe Alvarez (Youth Movement)	.50
184	Gary Matthews Jr. (Youth Movement)	.50
185	Kerry Wood (Youth Movement)	1.25
186	Carl Pavano (Youth Movement)	.50
187	Alex Gonzalez (Youth Movement)	.50
188	Masato Yoshii (Youth Movement)	.50
189	Larry Sutton (Youth Movement)	.50
190	Russell Branyan (Youth Movement)	.50
191	Bruce Chen (Youth Movement)	.50
192	Rolando Arrojo (Youth Movement)	.50
193	Ryan Christenson (Youth Movement)	.50
194	Cliff Politte (Youth Movement)	.50
195	A.J. Hinch (Youth Movement)	.50
196	Kevin Witt (Youth Movement)	.50
197	Daryle Ward (Youth Movement)	.50
198	Corey Koskie (Youth Movement)	.50
199	Mike Lowell (Youth Movement)	.50
200	Travis Lee (Youth Movement)	.50
201	Kevin Millwood RC (Youth Movement)	1.00
202	Robert Smith (Youth Movement)	.50
203	Magglio Ordonez RC (Youth Movement)	4.00
204	Eric Milton (Youth Movement)	.50
205	Geoff Jenkins (Youth Movement)	.50
206	Rich Butler (Youth Movement)	.50
207	Mike Kinkade RC (Youth Movement)	.75
208	Braden Looper (Youth Movement)	.50
209	Matt Clement (Youth Movement)	.50
210	Derrek Lee (Youth Movement)	1.50
211	Randy Johnson (Power Passion)	1.50
212	John Smoltz (Power Passion)	.50
213	Roger Clemens (Power Passion)	2.25
214	Curt Schilling (Power Passion)	.75
215	Pedro J. Martinez (Power Passion)	1.50
216	Vinny Castilla (Power Passion)	.50
217	Jose Cruz Jr. (Power Passion)	.50
218	Jim Thome (Power Passion)	1.20
219	Alex Rodriguez (Power Passion)	3.00
220	Frank Thomas (Power Passion)	1.50
221	Tim Salmon (Power Passion)	.50
222	Larry Walker (Power Passion)	.50
223	Albert Belle (Power Passion)	.50
224	Manny Ramirez (Power Passion)	1.50
225	Mark McGwire (Power Passion)	3.00
226	Mo Vaughn (Power Passion)	.50
227	Andres Galarraga (Power Passion)	.50
228	Scott Rolen (Power Passion)	1.25
229	Travis Lee (Power Passion)	.50
230	Mike Piazza (Power Passion)	2.50
231	Nomar Garciaparra (Power Passion)	2.00
232	Andruw Jones (Power Passion)	1.50

233	Barry Bonds (Power Passion)	4.00
234	Jeff Bagwell (Power Passion)	1.50
235	Juan Gonzalez (Power Passion)	.75
236	Tino Martinez (Power Passion)	.50
237	Vladimir Guerrero (Power Passion)	1.50
238	Rafael Palmeiro (Power Passion)	1.25
239	Russell Branyan (Power Passion)	.50
240	Ken Griffey Jr. (Power Passion)	2.50
241	Cecil Fielder	.15
242	Chuck Finley	.15
243	Jay Bell	.15
244	Andy Benes	.15
245	Matt Williams	.15
246	Brian Anderson	.15
247	David Dellucci	.15
248	Andres Galarraga	1.50
249	Andruw Jones	1.50
250	Greg Maddux	2.00
251	Brady Anderson	.15
252	Joe Carter	.15
253	Eric Davis	.15
254	Pedro J. Martinez	1.50
255	Nomar Garciaparra	2.00
256	Dennis Eckersley	1.25
257	Henry Rodriguez	.15
258	Jeff Blauser	.15
259	Jaime Navarro	.15
260	Ray Durham	.15
261	Chris Stynes	.15
262	Willie Greene	.15
263	Reggie Sanders	.15
264	Bret Boone	.15
265	Barry Larkin	.15
266	Travis Fryman	.15
267	Charles Nagy	.15
268	Sandy Alomar Jr.	.15
269	Darryl Kile	.15
270	Mike Lansing	.15
271	Pedro Astacio	.15
272	Damion Easley	.15
273	Joe Randa	.15
274	Luis Gonzalez	.15
275	Mike Piazza	2.50
276	Todd Zeile	.15
277	Edgar Renteria	.15
278	Livan Hernandez	.15
279	Cliff Floyd	.15
280	Moises Alou	.15
281	Billy Wagner	.15
282	Jeff King	.15
283	Hal Morris	.15
284	Johnny Damon	.35
285	Dean Palmer	.15
286	Tim Belcher	.15
287	Eric Young	.15
288	Bobby Bonilla	.15
289	Gary Sheffield	.60
290	Chan Ho Park	.15
291	Charles Johnson	.15
292	Jeff Cirillo	.15
293	Jeromy Burnitz	.15
294	Jose Valentin	.15
295	Marquis Grissom	.15
296	Todd Walker	.15
297	Terry Steinbach	.15
298	Rick Aguilera	.15
299	Vladimir Guerrero	1.50
300	Rey Ordonez	.15
301	Butch Huskey	.15
302	Bernard Gilkey	.15
303	Mariano Rivera	.25
304	Chuck Knoblauch	.15
305	Derek Jeter	4.00
306	Ricky Bottalico	.15
307	Bob Abreu	.15
308	Scott Rolen	1.25
309	Al Martin	.15
310	Jason Kendall	.15
311	Brian Jordan	.15
312	Ron Gant	.15
313	Todd Stottlemyre	.15
314	Greg Maddux	.15
315	J. Kevin Brown	.15
316	Wally Joyner	.15
317	Robb Nen	.15
318	Orel Hershiser	.15
319	Russ Davis	.15
320	Randy Johnson	1.50
321	Quinton McCracken	.15
322	Tony Saunders	.15
323	Wilson Alvarez	.15
324	Wade Boggs	2.00
325	Fred McGriff	.15
326	Lee Stevens	.15
327	John Wetteland	.15
328	Jose Canseco	.60
329	Randy Myers	.15
330	Jose Cruz Jr.	.15
331	Matt Williams (Tradewinds)	.50
332	Andres Galarraga (Tradewinds)	.50
333	Walt Weiss (Tradewinds)	.50
334	Joe Carter (Tradewinds)	.50
335	Pedro J. Martinez (Tradewinds)	2.00
336	Henry Rodriguez (Tradewinds)	.50
337	Travis Fryman (Tradewinds)	.50
338	Darryl Kile (Tradewinds)	.50
339	Mike Lansing (Tradewinds)	.50
340	Mike Piazza (Tradewinds)	4.00
341	Moises Alou (Tradewinds)	.50
342	Charles Johnson (Tradewinds)	.50
343	Chuck Knoblauch (Tradewinds)	.50
344	Rickey Henderson (Tradewinds)	2.00
345	J. Kevin Brown (Tradewinds)	.50
346	Orel Hershiser (Tradewinds)	.50
347	Wade Boggs (Tradewinds)	3.00
348	Fred McGriff (Tradewinds)	.50
349	Jose Canseco (Tradewinds)	1.00
350	Gary Sheffield (Tradewinds)	1.00
351	Travis Lee (Cornerstones)	2.50
352	Nomar Garciaparra (Cornerstones)	5.00
353	Frank Thomas (Cornerstones)	4.00
354	Cal Ripken Jr. (Cornerstones)	10.00
355	Mark McGwire (Cornerstones)	8.00
356	Mike Piazza (Cornerstones)	6.00
357	Alex Rodriguez (Cornerstones)	8.00
358	Barry Bonds (Cornerstones)	10.00
359	Tony Gwynn (Cornerstones)	5.00
360	Ken Griffey Jr. (Cornerstones)	6.00

Home Run Hysteria

Home Run Hysteria is a 10-card insert in SPx Finite Series Two. The cards are sequentially numbered to 62.

		NM/M
Complete Set (10):		400.00
Common Player:		15.00
Production 62 Sets		
HR1	Ken Griffey Jr.	75.00
HR2	Mark McGwire	100.00
HR3	Sammy Sosa	60.00
HR4	Albert Belle	15.00
HR5	Alex Rodriguez	100.00
HR6	Greg Vaughn	15.00
HR7	Andres Galarraga	15.00
HR8	Vinny Castilla	15.00
HR9	Juan Gonzalez	25.00
HR10	Chipper Jones	60.00

1999 SP Authentic Sample

UD spokesman Ken Griffey Jr. is featured on the promo card for '99 SP Authentic. In the same format as the issued version, the sample card has different photos on front and back, a different season summary on back and a large, black "SAMPLE" overprint on back.

		NM/M
1	Ken Griffey Jr.	3.00

1999 SP Authentic

SP Authentic was a 135-card set that sold in packs of five cards for $4.99. The set includes a 30-card Future Watch subset and a 15-card Season to Remember subset. Both subsets were shorted-printed, with each card sequentially numbered to 2,700. The insert lineup included Ernie Banks 500 Club "Piece of History" bat cards. Other insert sets included SP Chirography, The Home Run Chronicles, Epic Figures, Reflections, and SP Authentics.

	NM/M
Complete Set (135):	100.00
Common Player (1-90):	.10
Common Future Watch (91-120):	2.00
Production: (2,700)	
Common Season to Remember (121-135):	2.00
Production: (2,700)	
Pack (5):	3.50
Wax Box (24):	75.00

1	Mo Vaughn	.10
2	Jim Edmonds	.10
3	Darin Erstad	.25
4	Travis Lee	.10
5	Matt Williams	.10
6	Randy Johnson	1.50
7	Chipper Jones	1.75
8	Greg Maddux	1.75
9	Andruw Jones	1.50
10	Andres Galarraga	.10
11	Tom Glavine	.35
12	Cal Ripken Jr.	3.00
13	Brady Anderson	.10
14	Albert Belle	.10
15	Nomar Garciaparra	1.75
16	Donnie Sadler	.10
17	Pedro Martinez	1.50
18	Sammy Sosa	1.75
19	Kerry Wood	.60
20	Mark Grace	.10
21	Mike Caruso	.10
22	Frank Thomas	1.50
23	Paul Konerko	.20
24	Sean Casey	.20
25	Barry Larkin	.10
26	Kenny Lofton	.10
27	Manny Ramirez	1.50
28	Jim Thome	1.25
29	Bartolo Colon	.10
30	Jaret Wright	.10
31	Larry Walker	.10
32	Todd Helton	1.25
33	Tony Clark	.10
34	Dean Palmer	.10
35	Mark Kotsay	.10
36	Cliff Floyd	.10
37	Ken Caminiti	.10
38	Craig Biggio	.10
39	Jeff Bagwell	1.50
40	Moises Alou	.10
41	Johnny Damon	.35
42	Larry Sutton	.10
43	Kevin Brown	.10
44	Gary Sheffield	.40
45	Raul Mondesi	.10
46	Jeromy Burnitz	.10
47	Jeff Cirillo	.10
48	Todd Walker	.10
49	David Ortiz	.50
50	Brad Radtke	.10
51	Vladimir Guerrero	1.50
52	Rondell White	.10
53	Brad Fullmer	.10
54	Mike Piazza	2.00
55	Robin Ventura	.10
56	John Olerud	.10
57	Derek Jeter	3.00
58	Tino Martinez	.10
59	Bernie Williams	1.00
60	Roger Clemens	1.75
61	Ben Grieve	.10
62	Miguel Tejada	.20
63	A.J. Hinch	.10
64	Scott Rolen	1.00
65	Curt Schilling	.35
66	Doug Glanville	.10
67	Aramis Ramirez	.10
68	Tony Womack	.10
69	Jason Kendall	.10
70	Tony Gwynn	1.75
71	Wally Joyner	.10
72	Greg Vaughn	.10
73	Barry Bonds	3.00
74	Ellis Burks	.10
75	Jeff Kent	.10
76	Ken Griffey Jr.	2.00
77	Alex Rodriguez	2.50
78	Edgar Martinez	.10
79	Mark McGwire	2.50
80	Eli Marrero	.10
81	Matt Morris	.10
82	Rolando Arrojo	.10
83	Quinton McCracken	.10
84	Jose Canseco	.50
85	Ivan Rodriguez	1.25
86	Juan Gonzalez	.75
87	Royce Clayton	.10
88	Shawn Green	.30
89	Jose Cruz Jr.	.10
90	Carlos Delgado	.60
91	Troy Glaus (Future Watch)	6.00
92	George Lombard (Future Watch)	2.00
93	Ryan Minor (Future Watch)	2.00
94	Calvin Pickering (Future Watch)	2.00
95	Jin Ho Cho (Future Watch)	2.00
96	Russ Branyon (Future Watch)	2.00
97	Derrick Gibson (Future Watch)	2.00
98	Gabe Kapler (Future Watch)	2.00
99	Matt Anderson (Future Watch)	2.00
100	Preston Wilson (Future Watch)	2.00
101	Alex Gonzalez (Future Watch)	2.00
102	Carlos Beltran (Future Watch)	6.00
103	Dee Brown (Future Watch)	2.00
104	Jeremy Giambi (Future Watch)	2.00
105	Angel Pena (Future Watch)	2.00
106	Geoff Jenkins (Future Watch)	2.00
107	Corey Koskie (Future Watch)	2.00
108	A.J. Pierzynski (Future Watch)	2.00
109	Michael Barrett (Future Watch)	2.00
110	Fernando Seguignol (Future Watch)	2.00
111	Mike Kinkade (Future Watch)	2.00
112	Ricky Ledee (Future Watch)	2.00
113	Mike Lowell (Future Watch)	2.00
114	Eric Chavez (Future Watch)	2.50
115	Matt Clement (Future Watch)	2.00
116	Shane Monahan (Future Watch)	2.00
117	J.D. Drew (Future Watch)	4.00
118	Bubba Trammell (Future Watch)	2.00
119	Kevin Witt (Future Watch)	2.00
120	Roy Halladay (Future Watch)	2.50
121	Mark McGwire (Season to Remember)	5.00
122	Mark McGwire, Sammy Sosa (Season to Remember)	4.00
123	Sammy Sosa (Season to Remember)	2.50
124	Ken Griffey Jr. (Season to Remember)	3.00
125	Cal Ripken Jr. (Season to Remember)	6.00
126	Juan Gonzalez (Season to Remember)	2.50
127	Kerry Wood (Season to Remember)	2.50
128	Trevor Hoffman (Season to Remember)	2.00
129	Barry Bonds (Season to Remember)	5.00
130	Alex Rodriguez (Season to Remember)	4.00
131	Ben Grieve (Season to Remember)	2.00
132	Tom Glavine (Season to Remember)	2.00
133	David Wells (Season to Remember)	2.00
134	Mike Piazza (Season to Remember)	3.00
135	Scott Brosius (Season to Remember)	2.00

Chirography

Baseball's top players and future stars are included in this 39-card autograph insert set. The set was split into Level 1 and Level 2 versions. Level 1 cards are not numbered and were inserted one card per 24 packs. Level 2 (gold) cards are sequentially numbered to the featured player's jersey number.

		NM/M
Common Player:		4.00
Inserted 1:24		
EC	Eric Chavez	8.00
GK	Gabe Kapler	4.00
GMj	Gary Matthews Jr.	4.00
CP	Calvin Pickering	4.00
CK	Corey Koskie	6.00
SM	Shane Monahan	4.00
RH	Richard Hidalgo	4.00
MK	Mike Kinkade	4.00
CB	Carlos Beltran	35.00
AG	Alex Gonzalez	4.00
BC	Bruce Chen	4.00
MA	Matt Anderson	4.00
RM	Ryan Minor	4.00
RL	Ricky Ledee	4.00
RR	Ruben Rivera	4.00
BF	Brad Fullmer	4.00
RB	Russ Branyan	4.00
ML	Mike Lowell	6.00
JG	Jeremy Giambi	4.00
GL	George Lombard	4.00
KW	Kevin Witt	4.00
TW	Todd Walker	4.00
SR	Scott Rolen	20.00
KW	Kerry Wood	25.00
BG	Ben Grieve	4.00
JR	Ken Griffey Jr.	75.00
CJ	Chipper Jones	30.00
IR	Ivan Rodriguez	25.00
TGI	Troy Glaus	15.00
TL	Travis Lee	4.00
VG	Vladimir Guerrero	30.00
GV	Greg Vaughn	4.00
JT	Jim Thome	25.00
JD	J.D. Drew	15.00
TH	Todd Helton	15.00
GM	Greg Maddux	75.00
NG	Nomar Garciaparra	75.00
TG	Tony Gwynn	30.00
CR	Cal Ripken Jr.	125.00

Chirography Gold

These Chirography parallels can be identified by the gold tint on the card front and their sequential numbering; each featured player signed to his jersey number.

		NM/M
Common Player:		5.00
Inserted 1:24		
EC	Eric Chavez/30	40.00
GK	Gabe Kapler/51	10.00
GMj	Gary Matthews Jr./68	5.00
CP	Calvin Pickering/6	40.00
CK	Corey Koskie/47	15.00
SM	Shane Monahan/12	20.00
RH	Richard Hidalgo/15	30.00
MK	Mike Kinkade/33	10.00
CB	Carlos Beltran/36	75.00
AG	Alex Gonzalez/22	20.00
BC	Bruce Chen/48	10.00
MA	Matt Anderson/14	20.00
RM	Ryan Minor/10	35.00
RL	Ricky Ledee/38	10.00
RR	Ruben Rivera/28	10.00
BF	Brad Fullmer/20	10.00
RB	Russ Branyon/66	10.00
ML	Mike Lowell/60	15.00
JG	Jeremy Giambi/15	20.00
GL	George Lombard/26	10.00
KW	Kevin Witt/6	20.00
TW	Todd Walker/12	40.00
SR	Scott Rolen/17	75.00
KW	Kerry Wood/34	60.00
BG	Ben Grieve/14	35.00
JR	Ken Griffey Jr./24	250.00
CJ	Chipper Jones/10	200.00
IR	Ivan Rodriguez/7	125.00
TGI	Troy Glaus/14	90.00
TL	Travis Lee/16	35.00
VG	Vladimir Guerrero/27	75.00
GV	Greg Vaughn/23	10.00
JT	Jim Thome/25	40.00
JD	J.D. Drew/8	125.00
TH	Todd Helton/17	75.00
GM	Greg Maddux/31	150.00
NG	Nomar Garciaparra/5	375.00
TG	Tony Gwynn/19	125.00
CR	Cal Ripken Jr./8	650.00

Epic Figures

This 30-card set highlights baseball's biggest talents, including Mark McGwire and Derek Jeter. The card fronts have two photos, with the larger photo done with a shadow look in the background. Fronts also feature a holographic look, while the card backs feature the player's career highlights. These are seeded one per seven packs.

		NM/M
Complete Set (30):		30.00
Common Player:		.50
Inserted 1:7		
E01	Mo Vaughn	.50
E02	Travis Lee	.50
E03	Andres Galarraga	.50
E04	Andruw Jones	1.00
E05	Chipper Jones	1.25
E06	Greg Maddux	1.25
E07	Cal Ripken Jr.	3.00
E08	Nomar Garciaparra	1.25
E09	Sammy Sosa	1.25
E10	Frank Thomas	1.00
E11	Kerry Wood	.60
E12	Kenny Lofton	.50
E13	Manny Ramirez	1.00
E14	Larry Walker	.50
E15	Jeff Bagwell	1.00
E16	Paul Molitor	.50
E17	Vladimir Guerrero	1.00
E18	Derek Jeter	3.00
E19	Tino Martinez	.50
E20	Mike Piazza	1.50
E21	Ben Grieve	.50
E22	Scott Rolen	.75
E23	Mark McGwire	2.00
E24	Tony Gwynn	1.25
E25	Barry Bonds	3.00
E26	Ken Griffey Jr.	1.50
E27	Alex Rodriguez	2.00
E28	J.D. Drew	.65
E29	Juan Gonzalez	.60
E30	Kevin Brown	.50

Home Run Chronicles

This two-tiered 70-card set focuses on the amazing seasons of McGwire and Sammy Sosa. Other players help round out the 70-card set, but special emphasis has been placed on the duo. These are seeded one per pack. A die-cut version also exists, with each card serially numbered to 70.

	NM/M
Complete Set (70):	50.00
Common Player:	.15
Inserted 1:1	
Die-Cuts:	10X
Production 70 Sets	
HR01 Mark McGwire	1.50
HR02 Sammy Sosa	1.25
HR03 Ken Griffey Jr.	1.00
HR04 Mark McGwire	1.50
HR05 Mark McGwire	1.50
HR06 Albert Belle	.15
HR07 Jose Canseco	.30
HR08 Juan Gonzalez	.45
HR09 Manny Ramirez	.65
HR10 Rafael Palmeiro	.50
HR11 Mo Vaughn	.15
HR12 Carlos Delgado	.45
HR13 Nomar Garciaparra	.75
HR14 Barry Bonds	1.50
HR15 Alex Rodriguez	1.25
HR16 Tony Clark	.15
HR17 Jim Thome	.50
HR18 Edgar Martinez	.15
HR19 Frank Thomas	.65
HR20 Greg Vaughn	.15
HR21 Vinny Castilla	.15
HR22 Andres Galarraga	.15
HR23 Moises Alou	.15
HR24 Jeromy Burnitz	.15
HR25 Vladimir Guerrero	.65
HR26 Jeff Bagwell	.65
HR27 Chipper Jones	.75
HR28 Javier Lopez	.15
HR29 Mike Piazza	1.00
HR30 Andruw Jones	.65
HR31 Henry Rodriguez	.15
HR32 Jeff Kent	.15
HR33 Ray Lankford	.15
HR34 Scott Rolen	.50
HR35 Raul Mondesi	.15
HR36 Ken Caminiti	.15
HR37 J.D. Drew	.40
HR38 Troy Glaus	.50
HR39 Gabe Kapler	.15
HR40 Alex Rodriguez	1.25
HR41 Ken Griffey Jr.	1.00
HR42 Sammy Sosa	1.25
HR43 Mark McGwire	1.50
HR44 Sammy Sosa	1.25
HR45 Mark McGwire	1.50
HR46 Vinny Castilla	.15
HR47 Sammy Sosa	1.25
HR48 Mark McGwire	1.50
HR49 Sammy Sosa	1.25
HR50 Greg Vaughn	.15
HR51 Sammy Sosa	1.25
HR52 Mark McGwire	1.50
HR53 Sammy Sosa	1.25
HR54 Mark McGwire	1.50
HR55 Sammy Sosa	1.25
HR56 Ken Griffey Jr.	1.00
HR57 Sammy Sosa	1.25
HR58 Mark McGwire	1.50
HR59 Sammy Sosa	1.25
HR60 Mark McGwire	1.50
HR61 Mark McGwire	2.50
HR62 Mark McGwire	2.50
HR63 Mark McGwire	1.50
HR64 Mark McGwire	1.50
HR65 Mark McGwire	1.50
HR66 Sammy Sosa	2.50
HR67 Mark McGwire	1.50
HR68 Mark McGwire	1.50
HR69 Mark McGwire	1.50
HR70 Mark McGwire	4.00

Home Run Chronicles Die-Cuts

Each of the 70 cards in the Home Run Chronicles insert set was also issued in a die-cut version. The die-cuts share the basic front and back design of the regular HR Chronicle cards but have portions of the upper-left and lower-right cut away. On back, each of the die-cuts features an ink-jetted serial number from within an edition of 70.

HR Chronicle Die-Cuts:	10X

Reflections

Dot Matrix technology is utilized to provide a unique look at 30 of the best players in the game. Card fronts are horizontal with two small and one large photo. These are seeded 1:23 packs.

	NM/M
Complete Set (30):	60.00
Common Player:	.75
Inserted 1:23	
R01 Mo Vaughn	.75
R02 Travis Lee	.75
R03 Andres Galarraga	.75
R04 Andruw Jones	2.50
R05 Chipper Jones	3.00
R06 Greg Maddux	3.00
R07 Cal Ripken Jr.	6.00
R08 Nomar Garciaparra	3.00
R09 Sammy Sosa	3.00
R10 Frank Thomas	2.50
R11 Kerry Wood	1.50
R12 Kenny Lofton	.75
R13 Manny Ramirez	2.50
R14 Larry Walker	.75
R15 Jeff Bagwell	2.50
R16 Paul Molitor	2.50
R17 Vladimir Guerrero	2.50
R18 Derek Jeter	6.00
R19 Tino Martinez	.75
R20 Mike Piazza	3.50
R21 Ben Grieve	.75
R22 Scott Rolen	2.00
R23 Mark McGwire	4.50
R24 Tony Gwynn	3.00
R25 Barry Bonds	6.00
R26 Ken Griffey Jr.	3.50
R27 Alex Rodriguez	4.50
R28 J.D. Drew	1.25
R29 Juan Gonzalez	1.25
R30 Roger Clemens	3.25

SP Authentics

These 1:864 pack inserts are redemption cards that could be redeemed for special pieces of memorabilia from either Ken Griffey Jr. or Mark McGwire. The redemption period ended March 1, 2000. Because of rarity any surviving unredeemed McGwire home run-game autographed tickets cannot be valued.

	NM/M
Common Card:	10.00
(1) K.Griffey Jr./ Auto. Ball/75	60.00
(2) Ken Griffey Jr./ Glv/200	20.00
(3) K. Griffey Jr./ HR Cel card/346	10.00
(4) Ken Griffey Jr./ Auto. Jsy/25	125.00
(5) K. Griffey Jr./Auto. Mini Helmet/75	80.00
(6) Ken Griffey Jr./ SI Cover/200	15.00
(7) K. Griffey Jr./ SI Cover/Auto./75	75.00
(8) Ken Griffey Jr./ Standee/300	10.00

500 Club Piece of History

These cards feature a piece of game-used bat once swung by Ernie Banks. Approximately 350 cards exist. An autographed version of this card also exists, only 14 were produced.

		NM/M
EB	Ernie Banks	120.00
EB	Ernie Banks/ Auto./14	325.00

1999 SP Signature Edition

Even with one autograph per three-card pack, this single-series issue's price of $19.99 per pack shocked the hobby when it was introduced. Horizontal cards have a color or black-and-white photo at the left end with foil highlights and airbrushed geometric designs on a white background. Backs repeat the portrait portion of the front photo and add player data and some stats.

	NM/M
Complete Set (180):	60.00
Common Player:	.15
Pack (3):	20.00
Wax Box (12):	250.00
1 Nomar Garciaparra	2.00
2 Ken Griffey Jr.	2.50
3 J.D. Drew	.50
4 Alex Rodriguez	3.00
5 Juan Gonzalez	.60
6 Mo Vaughn	.15
7 Greg Maddux	2.00
8 Chipper Jones	2.00
9 Frank Thomas	1.50
10 Vladimir Guerrero	1.50
11 Mike Piazza	2.50
12 Eric Chavez	.25
13 Tony Gwynn	2.00
14 Orlando Hernandez	.15
15 Pat Burrell RC	6.00
16 Darin Erstad	.30
17 Greg Vaughn	.15
18 Russ Branyan	.15
19 Gabe Kapler	.15
20 Craig Biggio	.15
21 Troy Glaus	1.25
22 Pedro J. Martinez	1.50
23 Carlos Beltran	.50
24 Derek Lee	.50
25 Manny Ramirez	1.50
26 Shea Hillenbrand RC	1.00
27 Carlos Lee	.25
28 Angel Pena	.15
29 Rafael Roque	.15
30 Octavio Dotel	.15
31 Jeromy Burnitz	.15
32 Jeremy Giambi	.15
33 Andruw Jones	1.50
34 Todd Helton	1.25
35 Scott Rolen	1.25
36 Jason Kendall	.15
37 Trevor Hoffman	.15
38 Barry Bonds	4.00
39 Ivan Rodriguez	1.25
40 Roy Halladay	.15
41 Rickey Henderson	1.50
42 Ryan Minor	.15
43 Brian Jordan	.15
44 Alex Gonzalez	.15
45 Raul Mondesi	.15
46 Corey Koskie	.15
47 Paul O'Neill	.15
48 Todd Walker	.15
49 Carlos Febles	.15
50 Travis Fryman	.15
51 Albert Belle	.15
52 Travis Lee	.15
53 Bruce Chen	.15
54 Reggie Taylor	.15
55 Jerry Hairston Jr.	.15
56 Carlos Guillen	.15
57 Michael Barrett	.15
58 Jason Conti	.15
59 Joe Lawrence	.15
60 Jeff Cirillo	.15
61 Juan Melo	.15
62 Chad Hermansen	.15
63 Ruben Mateo	.15
64 Ben Davis	.15
65 Mike Caruso	.15
66 Jason Giambi	.50
67 Jose Canseco	.50
68 Chad Hutchinson RC	.15
69 Mitch Meluskey	.15
70 Adrian Beltre	.25
71 Mark Kotsay	.15
72 Juan Encarnacion	.15
73 Dermal Brown	.15
74 Kevin Witt	.15
75 Vinny Castilla	.15
76 Aramis Ramirez	.15
77 Marlon Anderson	.15
78 Mike Kinkade	.15
79 Kevin Barker	.15
80 Ron Belliard	.15
81 Chris Haas	.15
82 Bob Henley	.15
83 Fernando Seguignol	.15
84 Damon Minor	.15
85 A.J. Burnett RC	1.00
86 Calvin Pickering	.15
87 Mike Darr	.15
88 Cesar King	.15
89 Rob Bell	.15
90 Derrick Gibson	.15
91 Ober Moreno RC	.15
92 Robert Fick	.15
93 Doug Mientkiewicz RC	.75
94 A.J. Pierzynski	.15
95 Orlando Palmeiro	.15
96 Sidney Ponson	.15
97 Ivanon Coffie RC	.15
98 Juan Pena RC	1.00
99 Mark Karchner	.15
100 Carlos Castillo	.15
101 Bryan Ward	.15
102 Mario Valdez	.15
103 Billy Wagner	.15
104 Miguel Tejada	.25
105 Jose Cruz Jr.	.15
106 George Lombard	.15
107 Geoff Jenkins	.15
108 Ray Lankford	.15
109 Todd Stottlemyre	.15
110 Mike Lowell	.15
111 Matt Clement	.15
112 Scott Brosius	.15
113 Preston Wilson	.15
114 Bartolo Colon	.15
115 Rolando Arrojo	.15
116 Jose Guillen	.15
117 Ron Gant	.15
118 Ricky Ledee	.15
119 Carlos Delgado	.50
120 Abraham Nunez	.15
121 John Olerud	.15
122 Chan Ho Park	.15
123 Brad Radke	.15
124 Al Leiter	.15
125 Gary Matthews Jr.	.15
126 F.P. Santangelo	.15
127 Brad Fullmer	.15
128 Matt Anderson	.15
129 A.J. Hinch	.15
130 Sterling Hitchcock	.15
131 Edgar Martinez	.15
132 Fernando Tatis	.15
133 Bobby Smith	.15
134 Paul Konerko	.25
135 Sean Casey	.25
136 Donnie Sadler	.15
137 Denny Neagle	.15
138 Sandy Alomar	.15
139 Mariano Rivera	.25
140 Emil Brown	.15
141 J.T. Snow	.15
142 Eli Marrero	.15
143 Rusty Greer	.15
144 Johnny Damon	.35
145 Damion Easley	.15
146 Eric Milton	.15
147 Rico Brogna	.15
148 Ray Durham	.15
149 Wally Joyner	.15
150 Royce Clayton	.15
151 David Ortiz	.50
152 Wade Boggs	2.00
153 Ugueth Urbina	.15
154 Richard Hidalgo	.15
155 Bobby Abreu	.15
156 Robb Nen	.15
157 David Segui	.15
158 Sean Berry	.15
159 Kevin Tapani	.15
160 Jason Varitek	.15
161 Fernando Vina	.15
162 Jim Leyritz	.15
163 Enrique Wilson	.15
164 Jim Parque	.15
165 Doug Glanville	.15
166 Jesus Sanchez	.15
167 Nolan Ryan	4.00
168 Robin Yount	.50
169 Stan Musial	1.00
170 Tom Seaver	.50
171 Mike Schmidt	.75
172 Willie Stargell	.50
173 Rollie Fingers	.45
174 Willie McCovey	.50
175 Harmon Killebrew	.50
176 Eddie Mathews	.50
177 Reggie Jackson	1.00
178 Frank Robinson	.50
179 Ken Griffey Sr.	.15
180 Eddie Murray	1.50

Autographs

Authentically autographed cards of nearly 100 current stars, top prospects and Hall of Famers were featured as one-per-pack inserts in SP Signature Edition. Some players did not return their signed cards in time for pack inclusion and had to be obtained by returning an exchange card prior to the May 12, 2000, deadline.

		NM/M
Common Player:		3.00
Inserted 1:1		
BA	Bobby Abreu	10.00
SA	Sandy Alomar	5.00
MA	Marlon Anderson	4.00
KB	Kevin Barker	3.00
MB	Michael Barrett	4.00
RoB	Rob Bell	3.00
AB	Albert Belle	15.00
RBe	Ron Belliard	3.00
CBe	Carlos Beltran	50.00
ABe	Adrian Beltre	25.00
BB	Barry Bonds	180.00
RB	Russ Branyan	3.00
SB	Scott Brosius/SP	30.00
DB	Dermal Brown	3.00
EB	Emil Brown	3.00
AJB	A.J. Burnett (Exchange Card)	3.00
AJB	A.J. Burnett/Auto.	15.00
PB	Pat Burrell	12.50
JoC	Jose Canseco	30.00
MC	Mike Caruso	3.00
SC	Sean Casey (Exchange Card)	3.00
SC	Sean Casey/Auto.	15.00
VC	Vinny Castilla (Exchange Card)	3.00
VC	Vinny Castilla/Auto.	8.00
CC	Carlos Castillo	3.00
EC	Eric Chavez	10.00
BC	Bruce Chen	3.00
JCi	Jeff Cirillo	3.00
RC	Royce Clayton	3.00
MCl	Matt Clement	6.00
IC	Ivanon Coffie	3.00
BCo	Bartolo Colon (Exchange Card)	3.00
BCo	Bartolo Colon/Auto.	6.00
JC	Jason Conti	3.00
JDa	Johnny Damon	25.00
BD	Ben Davis	3.00
CD	Carlos Delgado	15.00
OD	Octavio Dotel	3.00
JD	J.D. Drew	15.00
RD	Ray Durham	3.00
DEa	Damion Easley	3.00
JE	Juan Encarnacion	3.00
DE	Darin Erstad	8.00
CF	Carlos Febles	3.00
Rob	Robert Fick	3.00
Rol	Rollie Fingers	8.00
BF	Brad Fullmer	3.00
RGa	Ron Gant	8.00
NG	Nomar Garciaparra	75.00
JaG	Jason Giambi	20.00
DG	Derrick Gibson	3.00
DGI	Doug Glanville	3.00
TGl	Troy Glaus	15.00
AG	Alex Gonzalez	5.00
RGr	Rusty Greer	3.00
Jr.	Ken Griffey Jr.	80.00
1	Ken Griffey Jr. (Facsimile autographed "SAMPLE.")	15.00
Sr.	Ken Griffey Sr.	8.00
VG	Vladimir Guerrero	30.00
JG	Jose Guillen	8.00
TG	Tony Gwynn	35.00
CHa	Chris Haas	3.00
JHj	Jerry Hairston Jr.	4.00
RH	Roy Halladay	10.00
THe	Todd Helton	20.00
BH	Bob Henley	3.00
ED	Orlando Hernandez	40.00
CH	Chad Hermansen	3.00
ShH	Shea Hillenbrand	8.00
StH	Sterling Hitchcock	3.00
THo	Trevor Hoffman	3.00
CHu	Chad Hutchinson	3.00
RJ	Reggie Jackson/SP	40.00
GJ	Geoff Jenkins	3.00
AJ	Andruw Jones	20.00
CJ	Chipper Jones	40.00
WJ	Wally Joyner	8.00
GK	Gabe Kapler	3.00
MKa	Mark Karchner	3.00
JK	Jason Kendall	3.00
HK	Harmon Killebrew	40.00
CKi	Cesar King	3.00
MKi	Mike Kinkade	3.00
PK	Paul Konerko	10.00
CK	Corey Koskie	6.00
MK	Mark Kotsay	4.00
RL	Ray Lankford	5.00
JLa	Joe Lawrence	3.00
CL	Carlos Lee	10.00
DL	Derrek Lee	25.00
AL	Al Leiter	6.00
JLe	Jim Leyritz	6.00
GL	George Lombard	3.00
GM	Greg Maddux	80.00
Eli	Eli Marrero	3.00
EM	Edgar Martinez	20.00
PM	Pedro J. Martinez (Exchange Card)	5.00
PM	Pedro J. Martinez/ Auto.	100.00
RMa	Ruben Mateo (Exchange Card)	3.00
RMa	Ruben Mateo/Auto.	8.00
EMa	Eddie Mathews	60.00
GMj	Gary Matthews Jr.	3.00
WMc	Willie McCovey	35.00
JM	Juan Melo	3.00
MMe	Mitch Meluskey	3.00
DoM	Doug Mientkiewicz	6.00
EMi	Eric Milton	3.00
DaM	Damon Minor	3.00
RM	Ryan Minor	3.00
EMu	Eddie Murray	20.00
SM	Stan Musial	50.00
RN	Robb Nen	3.00
AN	Abraham Nunez	3.00
JO	John Olerud	10.00
PO	Paul O'Neill	17.50
DO	David Ortiz	35.00
OP	Orlando Palmeiro	3.00
JP	Jim Parque	3.00
AP	Angel Pena	3.00
MP	Mike Piazza (Exchange Card)	6.00
MP	Mike Piazza/Auto.	175.00
CP	Calvin Pickering	3.00
AJP	A.J. Pierzynski	5.00
SP	Sidney Ponson	8.00
BR	Brad Radke	4.00
ARa	Aramis Ramirez	3.00
MR	Manny Ramirez	50.00
MRi	Mariano Rivera	25.00
FR	Frank Robinson	25.00
AR	Alex Rodriguez	120.00
PG	Ivan Rodriguez	25.00
SR	Scott Rolen (Exchange Card)	3.00
SR	Scott Rolen/Auto.	25.00
RR	Rafael Roque	3.00
NR	Nolan Ryan	120.00
DS	Donnie Sadler	3.00
JS	Jesus Sanchez	3.00
MS	Mike Schmidt	60.00
TSe	Tom Seaver	35.00
DSe	David Segui	3.00
FS	Fernando Seguignol	3.00
BS	Bobby Smith	3.00
JT	J.T. Snow (Exchange Card)	3.00
JT	J.T. Snow/Auto.	6.00
POP	Willie Stargell (Exchange Card)	3.00
POP	Willie Stargell/Auto.	40.00
TSt	Todd Stottlemyre	3.00
FTa	Fernando Tatis	3.00
RT	Reggie Taylor	3.00
MT	Miguel Tejada	20.00
FT	Frank Thomas	50.00
MV	Mario Valdez	3.00
JV	Jason Varitek	30.00
GV	Greg Vaughn	3.00
MO	Mo Vaughn	8.00
FV	Fernando Vina	3.00
BWa	Billy Wagner	10.00
TW	Todd Walker	3.00
BW	Bryan Ward	3.00
EW	Enrique Wilson	3.00
KW	Kevin Witt	3.00
RY	Robin Yount	40.00

Autographs Gold

This parallel edition of the Signature Series Autographs features special gold graphic highlights on front and back serially numbered within an edition of 50 each (except A.J. Burnett). Cards of 11 players were never signed, while cards of several others had to be obtained by sending in an exchange card, valid through May 12, 2000.

		NM/M
	Common Player:	12.00
	Production 50 Sets	
MA	Marlon Anderson	12.00
KB	Kevin Barker	12.00
MB	Michael Barrett	12.00
RoB	Rob Bell	12.00
AB	Albert Belle	20.00
RBe	Ron Belliard	12.00
CBe	Carlos Beltran	75.00
ABe	Adrian Beltre	40.00
CB	Craig Biggio	
	(Unsigned)	3.00
BB	Barry Bonds	250.00
RB	Russ Branyan	12.00
DB	Dermal Brown	12.00
AJB	A.J. Burnett	
	(Exchange Card)	4.00
AJB	A.J. Burnett (Autographed edition of 20.)	40.00
JB	Jeromy Burnitz	
	(Unsigned)	3.00
PB	Pat Burrell	40.00
JoC	Jose Canseco	50.00
MC	Mike Caruso	12.00
VC	Vinny Castilla	
	(Exchange Card)	3.00
VC	Vinny Castilla/Auto.	20.00
CC	Carlos Castillo	20.00
EC	Eric Chavez	20.00
BC	Bruce Chen	12.00
JCi	Jeff Cirillo	12.00
JC	Jason Conti	12.00
MD	Mike Darr (Unsigned)	3.00
BD	Ben Davis	12.00
OD	Octavio Dotel	12.00
JD	J.D. Drew	30.00
JE	Juan Encarnacion	12.00
DE	Darin Erstad	20.00
CF	Carlos Febles	12.00
TF	Travis Fryman	
	(Unsigned)	3.00
BF	Brad Fullmer	12.00
NG	Nomar Garciaparra	100.00
JaG	Jason Giambi	40.00
JeG	Jeremy Giambi	
	(Unsigned)	3.00
DG	Derrick Gibson	12.00
DGI	Doug Glanville	12.00
TGI	Troy Glaus	30.00
AG	Alex Gonzalez	12.00
JG	Juan Gonzalez	
	(Unsigned)	6.00
Jr.	Ken Griffey Jr.	150.00
Sr.	Ken Griffey Sr.	12.00
VG	Vladimir Guerrero	75.00
JG	Jose Guillen	
	(Unsigned)	3.00
TG	Tony Gwynn	60.00
CHa	Chris Haas	12.00
JHj	Jerry Hairston Jr.	12.00
RH	Roy Halladay	25.00
THe	Todd Helton	30.00
RH	Rickey Henderson	
	(Unsigned)	6.00
BH	Bob Henley	12.00
ED	Orlando Hernandez	25.00
CH	Chad Hermansen	12.00
ShH	Shea Hillenbrand	20.00
StH	Sterling Hitchcock	12.00
THo	Trevor Hoffman	30.00
CHu	Chad Hutchinson	12.00
GJ	Geoff Jenkins	12.00
AJ	Andruw Jones	40.00
CJ	Chipper Jones	80.00
BJ	Brian Jordan	
	(Unsigned)	3.00
WJ	Wally Joyner	25.00
GK	Gabe Kapler	12.00
MKa	Mark Karchner	12.00
JK	Jason Kendall	20.00
CKi	Cesar King	12.00
MKi	Mike Kinkade	12.00
PK	Paul Konerko	15.00
CK	Corey Koskie	20.00
MK	Mark Kotsay	12.00
RL	Ray Lankford	12.00
JLa	Joe Lawrence	12.00
CL	Carlos Lee	25.00
DL	Derrek Lee	50.00
TL	Travis Lee (Unsigned)	4.00
AL	Al Leiter	12.00
JLe	Jim Leyritz	12.00
GL	George Lombard	12.00
GM	Greg Maddux	150.00
PM	Pedro Martinez	
	(Exchange Card)	6.00
PM	Pedro Martinez/ Auto.	200.00
RMa	Ruben Mateo	
	(Exchange Card)	6.00
RMa	Ruben Mateo/Auto.	15.00
GMj	Gary Matthews Jr.	12.00
JM	Juan Melo	12.00
MMe	Mitch Meluskey	12.00
DoM	Doug Mientkiewicz	12.00
EMi	Eric Milton	12.00
DaM	Damon Minor	12.00
RM	Ryan Minor	12.00
PO	Paul O'Neill	30.00
DO	David Ortiz	75.00
OP	Orlando Palmeiro	12.00
AP	Angel Pena	12.00

MP	Mike Piazza	
	(Exchange Card)	10.00
MP	Mike Piazza/Auto.	250.00
CP	Calvin Pickering	12.00
ARa	Aramis Ramirez	30.00
MR	Manny Ramirez	80.00
AR	Alex Rodriguez	185.00
PG	Ivan Rodriguez	45.00
SR	Scott Rolen	
	(Exchange Card)	4.00
SR	Scott Rolen/Auto.	75.00
RR	Rafael Roque	12.00
DSe	David Segui	12.00
FS	Fernando Seguignol	12.00
BS	Bobby Smith	12.00
RT	Reggie Taylor	12.00
FT	Frank Thomas	70.00
MV	Mario Valdez	12.00
GV	Greg Vaughn	12.00
MO	Mo Vaughn	20.00
TW	Todd Walker	12.00
KW	Kevin Witt	12.00

Legendary Cuts

Each of the cards in this one-of-one insert series is unique, thus catalog values are impossible to assign.

No Pricing
Production One Set

500 Club Piece of History

		NM/M
MO	Mel Ott/350	100.00

1999 SPx

Formerly SPx Finite, this super-premium product showcases 80 of baseball's veteran players on regular cards and a 40-card rookie subset, which are serially numbered to 1,999. Two top rookies, J.D. Drew and Gabe Kapler autographed all 1,999 of their rookie subset cards. There are two parallels, SPx Radiance and SPx Spectrum. Radiance are serially numbered to 100 with Drew and Kapler signing all 100 of their cards. They are exclusive to Finite Radiance Hot Packs. Spectrums are limited to only one set and available only in Finite Spectrum Hot Packs. Packs consist of three cards with a S.R.P. of $5.99.

	NM/M
Complete Set (120):	100.00
Common Player:	.50
Common SPx Rookie (81-120):	2.00
Production 1,999 Sets	
Radiance (1-80):	7X
Radiance SP (81-120):	1.5X
Spectrum (1-of-1):	
Values Undetermined	
Pack (3):	3.00
Wax Box (18):	40.00

		NM/M
1	Mark McGwire #61	2.50
2	Mark McGwire #62	1.00
3	Mark McGwire #63	1.00
4	Mark McGwire #64	1.00
5	Mark McGwire #65	1.00
6	Mark McGwire #66	1.00
7	Mark McGwire #67	1.00
8	Mark McGwire #68	1.00
9	Mark McGwire #69	1.00
10	Mark McGwire #70	2.50

11	Mo Vaughn	.50
12	Darin Erstad	.75
13	Travis Lee	.50
14	Randy Johnson	1.50
15	Matt Williams	.50
16	Chipper Jones	2.00
17	Greg Maddux	2.00
18	Andruw Jones	1.50
19	Andres Galarraga	.50
20	Cal Ripken Jr.	4.00
21	Albert Belle	.50
22	Mike Mussina	.75
23	Nomar Garciaparra	2.00
24	Pedro Martinez	1.50
25	John Valentin	.50
26	Kerry Wood	1.00
27	Sammy Sosa	2.00
28	Mark Grace	1.00
29	Frank Thomas	1.50
30	Mike Caruso	.50
31	Barry Larkin	.50
32	Sean Casey	.50
33	Jim Thome	1.25
34	Kenny Lofton	.50
35	Manny Ramirez	1.50
36	Larry Walker	.50
37	Todd Helton	1.25
38	Vinny Castilla	.50
39	Tony Clark	.50
40	Derrek Lee	1.00
41	Mark Kotsay	.50
42	Jeff Bagwell	1.50
43	Craig Biggio	.50
44	Moises Alou	.50
45	Larry Sutton	.50
46	Johnny Damon	1.00
47	Gary Sheffield	1.00
48	Raul Mondesi	.50
49	Jeromy Burnitz	.50
50	Todd Walker	.50
51	David Ortiz	1.00
52	Vladimir Guerrero	1.50
53	Rondell White	.50
54	Mike Piazza	2.50
55	Derek Jeter	4.00
56	Tino Martinez	.50
57	David Wells	.50
58	Ben Grieve	.50
59	A.J. Hinch	.50
60	Scott Rolen	1.25
61	Doug Glanville	.50
62	Aramis Ramirez	.50
63	Jose Guillen	.50
64	Tony Gwynn	2.00
65	Greg Vaughn	.50
66	Ruben Rivera	.50
67	Barry Bonds	4.00
68	J.T. Snow	.50
69	Alex Rodriguez	3.00
70	Ken Griffey Jr.	2.50
71	Jay Buhner	.50
72	Mark McGwire	3.00
73	Fernando Tatis	.50
74	Quinton McCracken	.50
75	Wade Boggs	2.00
76	Ivan Rodriguez	1.25
77	Juan Gonzalez	1.00
78	Rafael Palmeiro	1.25
79	Jose Cruz Jr.	.50
80	Carlos Delgado	1.00
81	Troy Glaus	5.00
82	Vladimir Nunez	2.00
83	George Lombard	2.00
84	Bruce Chen	2.00
85	Ryan Minor	2.00
86	Calvin Pickering	2.00
87	Jin Ho Cho	2.00
88	Russ Branyan	2.00
89	Derrick Gibson	2.00
90	Gabe Kapler/Auto	6.00
91	Matt Anderson	2.00
92	Robert Fick	2.00
93	Juan Encarnacion	2.00
94	Preston Wilson	2.00
95	Alex Gonzalez	2.00
96	Carlos Beltran	5.00
97	Jeremy Giambi	2.00
98	Dee Brown	2.00
99	Adrian Beltre	4.00
100	Alex Cora	2.00
101	Angel Pena	2.00
102	Geoff Jenkins	2.00
103	Ronnie Belliard	2.00
104	Corey Koskie	2.00
105	A.J. Pierzynski	2.00
106	Michael Barrett	2.00
107	Fernando Seguignol	2.00
108	Mike Kinkade	2.00
109	Mike Lowell	2.00
110	Ricky Ledee	2.00
111	Eric Chavez	3.00
112	Abraham Nunez	2.00
113	Matt Clement	2.00
114	Ben Davis	2.00
115	Mike Darr	2.00
116	Ramon Martinez	2.00
117	Carlos Guillen	2.00
118	Shane Monahan	2.00
119	J.D. Drew/Auto	15.00
120	Kevin Witt	2.00

Dominance

This 20-card set showcases the most dominant MLB superstars, including Derek Jeter

and Alex Rodriguez. These are seeded 1:17 packs and numbered with a FB prefix.

		NM/M
	Complete Set (20):	35.00
	Common Player:	1.00
	Inserted 1:17	
1	Chipper Jones	2.00
2	Greg Maddux	2.00
3	Cal Ripken Jr.	4.00
4	Nomar Garciaparra	2.00
5	Mo Vaughn	1.00
6	Sammy Sosa	2.00
7	Albert Belle	1.00
8	Frank Thomas	1.50
9	Jim Thome	1.25
10	Jeff Bagwell	1.50
11	Vladimir Guerrero	1.50
12	Mike Piazza	2.50
13	Derek Jeter	4.00
14	Tony Gwynn	2.00
15	Barry Bonds	3.00
16	Ken Griffey Jr.	2.50
17	Alex Rodriguez	3.00
18	Mark McGwire	3.00
19	J.D. Drew	1.25
20	Juan Gonzalez	1.25

Power Explosion

This 30-card set salutes the top power hitters in the game today, including Mark McGwire and Sammy Sosa. These are numbered with a PE prefix.

		NM/M
	Complete Set (30):	15.00
	Common Player:	.20
	Inserted 1:3	
1	Troy Glaus	.65
2	Mo Vaughn	.20
3	Travis Lee	.20
4	Chipper Jones	1.00
5	Andres Galarraga	.20
6	Brady Anderson	.20
7	Albert Belle	.20
8	Nomar Garciaparra	1.00
9	Sammy Sosa	1.00
10	Frank Thomas	.75
11	Jim Thome	.65
12	Manny Ramirez	.75
13	Larry Walker	.20
14	Tony Clark	.20
15	Jeff Bagwell	.75
16	Moises Alou	.20
17	Ken Caminiti	.20
18	Vladimir Guerrero	.75
19	Mike Piazza	1.25
20	Tino Martinez	.20
21	Ben Grieve	.20
22	Scott Rolen	.60
23	Greg Vaughn	.20
24	Barry Bonds	2.00
25	Ken Griffey Jr.	1.25
26	Alex Rodriguez	1.50
27	Mark McGwire	1.50
28	J.D. Drew	.35
29	Juan Gonzalez	.45
30	Ivan Rodriguez	.60

Premier Stars

This 30-card set captures baseball's most dominant players, including Randy Johnson

and Ken Griffey Jr. Featured on a rainbow-foil design, these are numbered with a PS prefix.

		NM/M
	Complete Set (30):	45.00
	Common Player:	1.00
	Inserted 1:17	
1	Mark McGwire	3.00
2	Sammy Sosa	2.00
3	Frank Thomas	1.50
4	J.D. Drew	1.25
5	Kerry Wood	1.25
6	Moises Alou	1.00
7	Kenny Lofton	1.00
8	Jeff Bagwell	1.50
9	Tony Clark	1.00
10	Roberto Alomar	1.00
11	Cal Ripken Jr.	4.00
12	Derek Jeter	4.00
13	Mike Piazza	2.50
14	Jose Cruz Jr.	1.00
15	Chipper Jones	2.00
16	Nomar Garciaparra	2.00
17	Greg Maddux	2.00
18	Scott Rolen	1.25
19	Vladimir Guerrero	1.50
20	Albert Belle	1.50
21	Ken Griffey Jr.	2.50
22	Alex Rodriguez	3.00
23	Ben Grieve	1.00
24	Juan Gonzalez	1.25
25	Barry Bonds	4.00
26	Larry Walker	1.00
27	Tony Gwynn	2.00
28	Randy Johnson	1.50
29	Travis Lee	1.00
30	Mo Vaughn	1.00

Star Focus

This 30-card set focuses on the 30 brightest stars in the game. These are numbered with a SF prefix.

		NM/M
	Complete Set (30):	50.00
	Common Player:	.75
	Inserted 1:8	
1	Chipper Jones	2.25
2	Greg Maddux	2.25
3	Cal Ripken Jr.	4.50
4	Nomar Garciaparra	2.25
5	Mo Vaughn	.75
6	Sammy Sosa	2.25
7	Albert Belle	.75
8	Frank Thomas	1.50
9	Jim Thome	1.25
10	Kenny Lofton	.75
11	Manny Ramirez	1.50
12	Larry Walker	.75
13	Jeff Bagwell	1.50
14	Craig Biggio	.75
15	Randy Johnson	1.50
16	Vladimir Guerrero	1.50
17	Mike Piazza	3.00
18	Derek Jeter	4.50
19	Tino Martinez	.75
20	Bernie Williams	.75
21	Curt Schilling	1.00
22	Tony Gwynn	2.25
23	Barry Bonds	4.50
24	Ken Griffey Jr.	3.00
25	Alex Rodriguez	4.00
26	Mark McGwire	4.00
27	J.D. Drew	1.00
28	Juan Gonzalez	1.25
29	Ivan Rodriguez	1.25
30	Ben Grieve	.75

Winning Materials

This eight-card set includes a piece of the featured player's game-worn jersey and game-used bat on each card. These are seeded 1:251 packs.

		NM/M
	Complete Set (8):	90.00
	Common Player:	5.00
	Inserted 1:251	
VC	Vinny Castilla	5.00
JD	J.D. Drew	7.50
JR	Ken Griffey Jr.	
VG	Vladimir Guerrero	12.00
TG	Tony Gwynn	15.00
TH	Todd Helton	10.00
TL	Travis Lee	5.00
IR	Ivan Rodriguez	10.00

500 Club Piece of History

Each of these approximately 350 cards include a piece of game-used Louisville Slugger once swung by Willie Mays. Mays also signed 24 of his Piece of History cards.

		NM/M
WM	Willie Mays/350	275.00
WM	Willie Mays/Auto./24	1,700

2000 SP Authentic

The 135-card base set is composed of 90 regular cards, 30 Future Watch subset cards (serial numbered to 2,500) and 15 SP Superstars (serial numbered to 2,500). The regular cards have a gold foiled stamped line around the player image with a matte finished white border around the player image. The player name is stamped in gold foil in the top portion and the SP Authentic logo is stamped in silver foil. Card backs have a small photo, to a brief career note and to the past five seasons of complete statistics. Five-card packs carried a $4.99 SRP.

	NM/M
Complete Set (135):	150.00
Common Player:	.15
Common (91-105):	2.00
Production 2,500 Sets	
Common (106-135):	2.00
Production 2,500 Sets	
Pack (5):	3.00
Box (24):	60.00

1	Mo Vaughn	.15
2	Troy Glaus	.50
3	Jason Giambi	.75
4	Tim Hudson	.40
5	Eric Chavez	.25
6	Shannon Stewart	.15
7	Raul Mondesi	.15
8	Carlos Delgado	.50
9	Jose Canseco	.50
10	Vinny Castilla	.15
11	Greg Vaughn	.15
12	Manny Ramirez	1.00
13	Roberto Alomar	.40
14	Jim Thome	.75
15	Richie Sexson	.40
16	Alex Rodriguez	2.50
17	Fred Garcia	.15
18	John Olerud	.15
19	Albert Belle	.25
20	Cal Ripken Jr.	3.00

21	Mike Mussina	.50
22	Ivan Rodriguez	.75
23	Gabe Kapler	.15
24	Rafael Palmeiro	.75
25	Nomar Garciaparra	1.00
26	Pedro Martinez	1.00
27	Carl Everett	.15
28	Carlos Beltran	.50
29	Jermaine Dye	.15
30	Juan Gonzalez	.50
31	Dean Palmer	.15
32	Corey Koskie	.15
33	Jacque Jones	.15
34	Frank Thomas	.75
35	Paul Konerko	.40
36	Magglio Ordonez	.25
37	Bernie Williams	.40
38	Derek Jeter	2.50
39	Roger Clemens	2.00
40	Mariano Rivera	.40
41	Jeff Bagwell	.50
42	Craig Biggio	.40
43	Jose Lima	.15
44	Moises Alou	.25
45	Chipper Jones	1.00
46	Greg Maddux	1.50
47	Andruw Jones	1.00
48	Kevin Millwood	.15
49	Jeromy Burnitz	.15
50	Geoff Jenkins	.15
51	Mark McGwire	1.50
52	Fernando Tatis	.15
53	J.D. Drew	.25
54	Sammy Sosa	1.00
55	Kerry Wood	.50
56	Mark Grace	.25
57	Matt Williams	.15
58	Randy Johnson	1.00
59	Erubiel Durazo	.15
60	Gary Sheffield	.50
61	Kevin Brown	.15
62	Shawn Green	.40
63	Vladimir Guerrero	1.00
64	Michael Barrett	.15
65	Barry Bonds	2.50
66	Jeff Kent	.25
67	Russ Ortiz	.15
68	Preston Wilson	.15
69	Mike Lowell	.15
70	Mike Piazza	.15
71	Mike Hampton	.15
72	Robin Ventura	.15
73	Edgardo Alfonzo	.15
74	Tony Gwynn	1.50
75	Ryan Klesko	.15
76	Trevor Hoffman	.15
77	Scott Rolen	1.00
78	Bob Abreu	.40
79	Mike Lieberthal	.15
80	Curt Schilling	.75
81	Jason Kendall	.15
82	Brian Giles	.15
83	Kris Benson	.15
84	Ken Griffey Jr.	2.00
85	Sean Casey	.25
86	Pokey Reese	.15
87	Barry Larkin	.40
88	Larry Walker	.25
89	Todd Helton	.75
90	Jeff Cirillo	.15
91	Ken Griffey Jr. (SP Superstars)	4.00
92	Mark McGwire (SP Superstars)	4.00
93	Chipper Jones (SP Superstars)	3.00
94	Derek Jeter (SP Superstars)	6.00
95	Shawn Green (SP Superstars)	2.00
96	Pedro Martinez (SP Superstars)	4.00
97	Mike Piazza (SP Superstars)	4.00
98	Alex Rodriguez (SP Superstars)	5.00
99	Jeff Bagwell (SP Superstars)	2.50
100	Cal Ripken Jr. (SP Superstars)	6.00
101	Sammy Sosa (SP Superstars)	3.00
102	Barry Bonds (SP Superstars)	5.00
103	Jose Canseco (SP Superstars)	2.00
104	Nomar Garciaparra (SP Superstars)	4.00
105	Ivan Rodriguez (SP Superstars)	2.50
106	Rick Ankiel (Future Watch)	2.00
107	Pat Burrell (Future Watch)	2.50
108	Vernon Wells (Future Watch)	2.50
109	Nick Johnson (Future Watch)	2.00
110	Kip Wells (Future Watch)	2.00
111	Matt Riley (Future Watch)	2.00
112	Alfonso Soriano (Future Watch)	8.00
113	Josh Beckett (Future Watch)	4.00
114	Danys Baez RC (Future Watch)	6.00
115	Travis Dawkins (Future Watch)	2.50
116	Eric Gagne (Future Watch)	4.00
117	Mike Lamb RC (Future Watch)	4.00
118	Eric Munson (Future Watch)	2.50
119	Wilfredo Rodriguez RC (Future Watch)	2.00
120	Kazuhiro Sasaki RC (Future Watch)	3.00
121	Chad Hutchinson (Future Watch)	2.00
122	Peter Bergeron (Future Watch)	2.00
123	Wascar Serrano RC (Future Watch)	2.00
124	Tony Armas Jr. (Future Watch)	2.00
125	Ramon Ortiz (Future Watch)	2.00
126	Adam Kennedy (Future Watch)	2.00
127	Joe Crede (Future Watch)	5.00
128	Roosevelt Brown (Future Watch)	2.00
129	Mark Mulder (Future Watch)	2.50
130	Brad Penny (Future Watch)	2.00
131	Terrence Long (Future Watch)	2.00
132	Ruben Mateo (Future Watch)	2.00
133	Wily Mo Pena (Future Watch)	2.00
134	Rafael Furcal (Future Watch)	2.00
135	Mario Encarnacion (Future Watch)	2.00

Limited

A parallel to the 135-card base set these have "SP Limited" printed down the right side of the front and are serial numbered on the card front in an edition of 100 sets.

Cards (1-90):	4-8X
Cards (91-105):	2-3X
Cards (106-135):	1-2X
Production 100 Sets	

Chirography

This autographed insert set has a horizontal format with two player images on the card front. The player signature appears in the top right portion over a silver, checkered background. The insert name and logo have a silver tint. Card backs are numbered with the featured players first and last initial. Chirographies are seeded 1:23 packs.

NM/M
Common Player:		5.00
Inserted 1:23		
RA	Rick Ankiel	8.00
CBe	Carlos Beltran	30.00
BB	Barry Bonds	200.00
PB	Pat Burrell	15.00
JC	Jose Canseco	25.00
SC	Sean Casey	8.00
RC	Roger Clemens	100.00
ED	Erubiel Durazo	10.00
TGl	Troy Glaus	20.00
VG	Vladimir Guerrero	30.00
TG	Tony Gwynn	40.00
DJ	Derek Jeter	120.00
NJ	Nick Johnson	10.00
CJ	Chipper Jones	35.00
AJ	Andruw Jones	25.00
SK	Sandy Koufax	250.00
BP	Ben Petrick	5.00
MQ	Mark Quinn	5.00
MR	Manny Ramirez	40.00
CR	Cal Ripken Jr.	100.00
AR	Alex Rodriguez	85.00
IR	Ivan Rodriguez	30.00
SR	Scott Rolen	30.00
AS	Alfonso Soriano	30.00
MV	Mo Vaughn	8.00
EY	Ed Yarnall	5.00

Chirography Gold

Golds use the same photos as the regular Chirography inserts and can be differentiated by the gold checkered background of the player signature in the upper right portion as well as the gold tint in the insert name and logo. Golds are also hand-numbered to the player's jersey number on the card front and are numbered with a "G" prefix on the card back before the players initials.

NM/M
Common Player:		
RA	Rick Ankiel/66 Exch	50.00
CBe	Carlos Beltran/15	65.00
BB	Barry Bonds/25	300.00
PB	Pat Burrell/33 Exch	50.00
JC	Jose Canseco/33	75.00
SC	Sean Casey/21	65.00
RC	Roger Clemens/22	300.00
ED	Erubiel Durazo/44	25.00
VG	Vladimir Guerrero/27	100.00
TG	Tony Gwynn/19	200.00
NJ	Nick Johnson/63	15.00
BP	Ben Petrick/15	30.00
MR	Manny Ramirez/24 Exch	100.00
AS	Alfonso Soriano/53	60.00
MV	Mo Vaughn/42	25.00
EY	Ed Yarnall/41	15.00

Joe DiMaggio Game Jersey

This is DiMaggio's first Game Jersey insert and has three different versions. The first is limited to 500 total cards, the second version is Gold and numbered to 56. The rarest version has a DiMaggio cut signature along with a piece of his game-used jersey and is limited to only five total cards.

NM/M
DiMaggio Jersey Card		
JD	Joe DiMaggio/Jsy/500	120.00
JD	Joe DiMaggio/Jsy Gold/56	200.00

Midsummer Classics

This 10-card set spotlights perennial All-Stars and has a silver holo-foiled front with gold foil etching and stamping. These are found 1:12 packs and are numbered on the card back with an "MC" prefix.

NM/M
Complete Set (10):		10.00
Common Player:		.50
Inserted 1:12		
1	Cal Ripken Jr.	3.00
2	Roger Clemens	1.75
3	Jeff Bagwell	.75
4	Barry Bonds	3.00
5	Jose Canseco	.50

6	Frank Thomas	.75
7	Mike Piazza	2.00
8	Tony Gwynn	1.50
9	Juan Gonzalez	.75
10	Greg Maddux	1.50

Premier Performers

This 10-card set spotlights baseball's best on a silver holofoiled card front with the player name, insert name and logo stamped in gold foil. Card backs are numbered with a "PP" prefix and are found 1:12 packs.

NM/M
Complete Set (10):		10.00
Common Player:		.75
Inserted 1:12		
1	Mark McGwire	2.00
2	Alex Rodriguez	2.50
3	Cal Ripken Jr.	3.00
4	Nomar Garciaparra	1.50
5	Ken Griffey Jr.	2.00
6	Chipper Jones	1.50
7	Derek Jeter	3.00
8	Ivan Rodriguez	.75
9	Vladimir Guerrero	.75
10	Sammy Sosa	1.50

SP Buyback

This autographed set features previously issued SP cards that were re-purchased by Upper Deck. The cards are autographed by the featured player and hand-numbered on the card front. The number autographed and released by Upper Deck is listed after the player name. Buybacks are found 1:95 packs.

NM/M
Common Player:		
1	Jeff Bagwell Exch.	50.00
2	Craig Biggio '93/59	50.00
3	Craig Biggio '94/69	50.00
4	Craig Biggio '95/171	40.00
5	Craig Biggio '96/71	50.00
6	Craig Biggio '97/46	50.00
7	Craig Biggio '98/40	50.00
8	Craig Biggio '99/125	40.00
15	Barry Bonds '99/520	150.00
16	Jose Canseco '93/29	60.00
17	Jose Canseco '94/20	60.00
19	Jose Canseco '96/23	60.00
20	Jose Canseco '97/23	60.00
21	Jose Canseco '98/24	60.00
22	Jose Canseco '99/502	30.00
25	Sean Casey '99/139	20.00
26	Roger Clemens '93/68	85.00
27	Roger Clemens '94/60	85.00
28	Roger Clemens '95/68	85.00
30	Roger Clemens '96/68	85.00
31	Roger Clemens '98/25	200.00
	Roger Clemens '99/134	75.00
32	Jason Giambi '97/34	50.00
33	Jason Giambi '98/25	50.00
34	Tom Glavine '93/99	40.00
35	Tom Glavine '94/107	40.00
36	Tom Glavine '95/97	40.00
37	Tom Glavine '96/42	50.00
38	Tom Glavine '98/40	50.00
39	Tom Glavine '99/138	40.00
40	Shawn Green '96/55	30.00
41	Shawn Green '99/530	20.00
42	Ken Griffey Jr. '96/12	275.00
47	Tony Gwynn '97/24	150.00
48	Tony Gwynn '99/129	50.00
50	Tony Gwynn '99/369	40.00
56	Derek Jeter '99/119	200.00
57	Randy Johnson '93/60	75.00
58	Randy Johnson '94/45	80.00
59	Randy Johnson '95/70	75.00
60	Randy Johnson '96/60	75.00
63	Randy Johnson '99/113	75.00
64	Andruw Jones Exch.	40.00
65	Chipper Jones Exch.	75.00
66	Kenny Lofton '94/100	25.00
67	Kenny Lofton '95/84	25.00
68	Kenny Lofton '96/34	40.00
69	Kenny Lofton '97/82	25.00
70	Kenny Lofton '98/21	40.00
71	Kenny Lofton '99/99	20.00
72	Javy Lopez '93/106	15.00
73	Javy Lopez '94/160	15.00
74	Javy Lopez '96/99	15.00
77	Javy Lopez '97/61	15.00
	Greg Maddux '93/22	275.00
78	Greg Maddux '94/19	275.00
83	Greg Maddux '99/504	75.00
84	Paul O'Neill '93/110	25.00
85	Paul O'Neill '94/97	30.00
86	Paul O'Neill '95/142	25.00
87	Paul O'Neill '96/70	30.00
88	Paul O'Neill '98/23	40.00
89	Manny Ramirez/Redemp	50.00
91	Cal Ripken Jr. '94/22	300.00
96	Cal Ripken Jr. '99/510	125.00
97	Alex Rodriguez/Exch.	150.00
98	Ivan Rodriguez '93/29	100.00
100	Ivan Rodriguez '95/18	125.00
101	Ivan Rodriguez '96/22	125.00
103	Ivan Rodriguez '98/27	125.00
109	Frank Thomas '97/20	75.00
111	Frank Thomas '99/100	50.00
112	Greg Vaughn '93/79	20.00
113	Greg Vaughn '94/75	20.00
114	Greg Vaughn '95/155	15.00
115	Greg Vaughn '96/113	15.00
117	Greg Vaughn '99/527	10.00
118	Mo Vaughn '93/119	20.00
120	Mo Vaughn '94/96	20.00
121	Mo Vaughn '95/121	20.00
122	Mo Vaughn '96/114	20.00
124	Mo Vaughn '97/61	25.00
126	Mo Vaughn '99/537	15.00
126	Robin Ventura '93/59	25.00
127	Robin Ventura '94/49	25.00
	Robin Ventura '95/125	25.00
128	Robin Ventura '96/55	25.00
129	Robin Ventura '97/44	30.00
130	Robin Ventura '98/28	35.00
131	Robin Ventura '99/370	25.00
133	Matt Williams '94/50	40.00
134	Matt Williams '95/137	40.00
135	Matt Williams '96/77	40.00
136	Matt Williams '97/54	40.00
137	Matt Williams '98/29	60.00
138	Matt Williams '99/529	15.00
139	Preston Wilson '94/249	15.00
140	Preston Wilson '99/195	15.00

SP Cornerstones

Printed on a silver holo-foiled card front a close-up image of the player appears in a baseball diamond shaped enclosed by gold foil etching. Another shadow image of the featured player appears in the background. The player name, insert name and logo are stamped in gold foil. These are seeded 1:23 packs and are numbered with a "C" prefix on the card back.

NM/M
Complete Set (7):		15.00
Common Player:		2.00
Inserted 1:23		
1	Ken Griffey Jr.	2.00
2	Cal Ripken Jr.	4.00
3	Mike Piazza	2.00
4	Derek Jeter	4.00
5	Mark McGwire	3.00
6	Nomar Garciaparra	2.00
7	Sammy Sosa	2.00

SP Supremacy

This seven-card set has a silver foiled card front with the insert name and logo stamped in gold foil. The inserts are found on the average of 1:23 packs and are numbered with a "S" prefix.

NM/M
Complete Set (7):		8.00
Common Player:		.75
Inserted 1:23		
1	Alex Rodriguez	3.00
2	Shawn Green	.75
3	Pedro Martinez	1.00
4	Chipper Jones	2.00
5	Tony Gwynn	2.00
6	Ivan Rodriguez	1.00
7	Jeff Bagwell	1.00

United Nations

Done on a horizontal format this 10-card set salutes the top international stars of the game. The featured player's country of origin flag is in the background of the player image. The card design features silver holofoil and silver foil etching and stamping. These are seeded 1:4 packs and are numbered with an "UN" prefix on the card back.

NM/M
Complete Set (10):		5.00
Common Player:		.50

Inserted 1:4

1	Sammy Sosa (Dominican Rep.)	1.50
2	Ken Griffey Jr. (USA)	2.00
3	Orlando Hernandez (Cuba)	.50
4	Andres Galarraga (Venezuela)	.50
5	Kazuhiro Sasaki (Japan)	.50
6	Larry Walker (Canada)	.50
7	Vinny Castilla (Mexico)	.50
8	Andruw Jones (Neth. Antilles)	.75
9	Ivan Rodriguez (Puerto Rico)	.75
10	Chan Ho Park (So. Korea)	.50

3,000 Hit Club

A continuation of Upper Deck's cross brand salute to players who have reached the magical 3,000 hit milestone. 350 game- used bat cards and five bat/cut signature combos were issued for each player.

		NM/M
PW	Paul Waner/Bat/350	50.00
TS	Tris Speaker/ Bat/350	100.00

2000 SPx

The base set consists of 120-cards including 30 Rookie/ Young Star subset cards which has three tiers. The first five are numbered to 1,000, the next 22 autographed and numbered to 1,500 and the final three are autographed and numbered to 500. Each base card has a holofoiled front with the SPx logo, player name, team name stamped in gold foil.

		NM/M
Complete Set (120):		400.00
Common Player:		.15
Common Rookie (91-120):		10.00
Pack (4):		6.00
Box (18):		80.00
1	Troy Glaus	.50
2	Mo Vaughn	.15
3	Ramon Ortiz	.15
4	Jeff Bagwell	.75
5	Moises Alou	.25
6	Craig Biggio	.40
7	Jose Lima	.15
8	Jason Giambi	.75
9	John Jaha	.15
10	Matt Stairs	.15
11	Chipper Jones	1.00
12	Greg Maddux	1.50
13	Andres Galarraga	.15
14	Andruw Jones	1.00
15	Jeromy Burnitz	.15
16	Ron Belliard	.15
17	Carlos Delgado	.75
18	David Wells	.15
19	Tony Batista	.15
20	Shannon Stewart	.15
21	Sammy Sosa	1.00
22	Mark Grace	.50
23	Henry Rodriguez	.15
24	Mark McGwire	2.00
25	J.D. Drew	.25
26	Luis Gonzalez	.25
27	Randy Johnson	1.00
28	Matt Williams	.15
29	Steve Finley	.15
30	Shawn Green	.25
31	Kevin Brown	.15
32	Gary Sheffield	.50

33	Jose Canseco	.50
34	Greg Vaughn	.15
35	Vladimir Guerrero	1.00
36	Michael Barrett	.15
37	Russ Ortiz	.15
38	Barry Bonds	3.00
39	Jeff Kent	.25
40	Richie Sexson	.40
41	Manny Ramirez	1.00
42	Jim Thome	1.00
43	Roberto Alomar	.50
44	Edgar Martinez	.15
45	Alex Rodriguez	2.50
46	John Olerud	.15
47	Alex Gonzalez	.15
48	Cliff Floyd	.15
49	Mike Piazza	1.50
50	Al Leiter	.15
51	Robin Ventura	.15
52	Edgardo Alfonzo	.15
53	Albert Belle	.15
54	Cal Ripken Jr.	3.00
55	B.J. Surhoff	.15
56	Tony Gwynn	1.50
57	Trevor Hoffman	.15
58	Brian Giles	.15
59	Jason Kendall	.15
60	Kris Benson	.15
61	Bob Abreu	.50
62	Scott Rolen	1.00
63	Curt Schilling	.75
64	Mike Lieberthal	.15
65	Sean Casey	.25
66	Dante Bichette	.15
67	Ken Griffey Jr.	2.00
68	Pokey Reese	.15
69	Mike Sweeney	.15
70	Carlos Febles	.15
71	Ivan Rodriguez	1.00
72	Ruben Mateo	.15
73	Rafael Palmeiro	1.00
74	Larry Walker	.40
75	Todd Helton	.75
76	Nomar Garciaparra	1.00
77	Pedro Martinez	1.00
78	Troy O'Leary	.15
79	Jacque Jones	.15
80	Corey Koskie	.15
81	Juan Gonzalez	.50
82	Dean Palmer	.15
83	Juan Encarnacion	.15
84	Frank Thomas	1.00
85	Magglio Ordonez	.25
86	Paul Konerko	.50
87	Bernie Williams	.50
88	Derek Jeter	3.00
89	Roger Clemens	2.50
90	Orlando Hernandez	.15
91	Vernon Wells AU-1,000	25.00
92	Rick Ankiel AU-1,000	10.00
93	Eric Chavez AU-1,000	20.00
94	Alfonso Soriano AU-1,000	50.00
95	Eric Gagne AU-1,000	50.00
96	Rob Bell AU-1,500	10.00
97	Matt Riley AU-1,500	10.00
98	Josh Beckett AU-1,500	50.00
99	Ben Petrick AU-1,500	10.00
100	Rob Ramsay AU-1,500 **RC**	10.00
101	Scott Williamson AU-1,500	10.00
102	Doug Davis AU-1,500	10.00
103	Eric Munson AU-1,500	10.00
104	Pat Burrell AU-500	40.00
105	Jim Morris AU-1,500	20.00
106	Gabe Kapler AU-500	15.00
107	Lance Berkman 1,500	20.00
108	Erubiel Durazo AU-1,500	15.00
109	Tim Hudson AU-1,500	35.00
110	Ben Davis AU-1,500	10.00
111	Nick Johnson AU-1,500	20.00
112	Octavio Dotel AU-1,500	10.00
113	Jerry Hairston Jr. 1,500	10.00
114	Ruben Mateo 1,500	10.00
115	Chris Singleton 1,500	10.00
116	Bruce Chen AU-1,500	10.00
117	Derrick Gibson AU-1,500	10.00
118	Carlos Beltran AU-500	125.00
119	Fred Garcia AU-500	10.00
120	Preston Wilson AU-500	15.00

Radiance

A parallel to the 120-card base set these are serially numbered to 100. A one-of-one Spectrum parallel of each base card is also randomly seeded.

	NM/M
Stars (1-90):	4-8X

Common Young Star (91-120): 10.00
Production 100 Sets

Foundations

Manny Ramirez / of

This 10-card set features a holo-foiled front with gold foil stamping. Three miniature action shots appear to the right of a close-up shot of the featured player. Card backs are numbered with an "F" prefix and inserted 1:32 packs.

		NM/M
Complete Set (10):		15.00
Common Player:		.50
Inserted 1:32		
1	Ken Griffey Jr.	3.00
2	Nomar Garciaparra	3.00
3	Cal Ripken Jr.	4.00
4	Chipper Jones	2.00
5	Mike Piazza	3.00
6	Derek Jeter	4.00
7	Manny Ramirez	1.00
8	Jeff Bagwell	1.00
9	Tony Gwynn	2.00
10	Larry Walker	.50

Heart of the Order

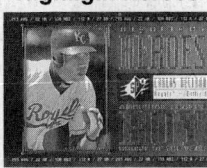

This 20-card set features a top hitter with his teams batting order to the left of his photo. The SPx logo and insert name are stamped in gold foil. Card backs are numbered with an "H" prefix and seeded 1:8 packs.

		NM/M
Complete Set (20):		10.00
Common Player:		.40
Inserted 1:8		
1	Bernie Williams	.50
2	Mike Piazza	2.00
3	Ivan Rodriguez	.75
4	Mark McGwire	2.50
5	Manny Ramirez	1.00
6	Ken Griffey Jr.	2.00
7	Matt Williams	.40
8	Sammy Sosa	2.00
9	Mo Vaughn	.40
10	Carlos Delgado	.40
11	Brian Giles	.40
12	Chipper Jones	1.50
13	Sean Casey	.40
14	Tony Gwynn	1.50
15	Barry Bonds	3.00

16	Carlos Beltran	.65
17	Scott Rolen	.75
18	Juan Gonzalez	1.00
19	Larry Walker	.40
20	Vladimir Guerrero	1.00

Highlight Heroes

This 10-card set has a horizontal format on a holofoiled front with gold foil stamping. Card backs are numbered with an "HH" prefix and inserted 1:16 packs.

		NM/M
Complete Set (10):		10.00
Common Player:		.50
Inserted 1:16		
1	Pedro Martinez	1.00
2	Ivan Rodriguez	.75
3	Carlos Beltran	.65
4	Nomar Garciaparra	2.00
5	Ken Griffey Jr.	2.00
6	Randy Johnson	1.00
7	Chipper Jones	1.50
8	Scott Williamson	.50
9	Larry Walker	.50
10	Mark McGwire	2.50

Power Brokers

This 20-card set has a horizontal format with the background of the player photo having a kaleidoscope effect. The SPx logo is stamped in gold foil. Card backs are numbered with an "PB" prefix and are inserted 1:8 packs.

		NM/M
Complete Set (20):		10.00
Common Player:		.25
Inserted 1:8		
1	Rafael Palmeiro	.75
2	Carlos Delgado	.65
3	Ken Griffey Jr.	2.00
4	Matt Stairs	.25
5	Mike Piazza	2.00
6	Vladimir Guerrero	1.00
7	Chipper Jones	1.50
8	Mark McGwire	2.50
9	Matt Williams	.25
10	Juan Gonzalez	1.00
11	Shawn Green	.50
12	Sammy Sosa	2.00
13	Brian Giles	.25
14	Jeff Bagwell	1.00
15	Alex Rodriguez	2.50
16	Frank Thomas	1.00
17	Larry Walker	.25
18	Albert Belle	.25
19	Dean Palmer	.25
20	Mo Vaughn	.25

SPxcitement

This 20-card set features a holo-foiled front with gold foil stamping. Card backs are numbered with an "XC" prefix and are inserted 1:4 packs.

	NM/M
Complete Set (20):	15.00
Common Player:	.25

SPx Signatures

These autographed inserts are seeded 1:112 packs.

		NM/M
Common Player:		10.00
Inserted 1:179		
JB	Jeff Bagwell	30.00
BB	Barry Bonds	150.00
JC	Jose Canseco	25.00
SC	Sean Casey	15.00
RC	Roger Clemens	125.00
KG	Ken Griffey Jr.	100.00
VG	Vladimir Guerrero	35.00
TG	Tony Gwynn	40.00
OH	Orlando Hernandez	40.00
DJ	Derek Jeter	125.00
CJ	Chipper Jones	40.00
MR	Manny Ramirez	40.00
CR	Cal Ripken Jr.	125.00
IR	Ivan Rodriguez	30.00
SR	Scott Rolen	30.00

Untouchable Talents

These inserts have a holofoiled front and are numbered with an "UT" prefix. They are found on the average of 1:96 packs.

		NM/M
Complete Set (10):		30.00
Common Player:		1.50
Inserted 1:96		
1	Mark McGwire	8.00
2	Ken Griffey Jr.	6.00
3	Shawn Green	2.00
4	Ivan Rodriguez	2.50
5	Sammy Sosa	6.00
6	Derek Jeter	10.00
7	Sean Casey	1.50
8	Chipper Jones	4.50
9	Pedro Martinez	3.00
10	Vladimir Guerrero	3.00

Winning Materials

Five different tiers make up this memorabilia insert set with players having varying levels of their inserts in the set. Each insert has two pieces of memorabilia, combinations

include Jersey/Bat, Jersey/Bat numbered to player's jersey number, Jersey/Cap, Jersey/Ball and Ball/Bat.

		NM/M
Common Bat/Jsy		6.00
AR	Alex Rodriguez/ Bat/Jsy	25.00
AR	Alex Rodriguez/ Cap/Jsy/100	40.00
AR	Alex Rodriguez/ Ball/Jsy/50	50.00
DJ	Derek Jeter/Bat/Jsy	40.00
DJ	Derek Jeter/Ball/ Jsy/50	75.00
BB	Barry Bonds/Bat/Jsy	30.00
BB	Barry Bonds/Cap/ Jsy/100	50.00
BB	Barry Bonds/Ball/ Jsy/Auto./25	350.00
JB	Jeff Bagwell/Bat/Jsy	8.00
JB	Jeff Bagwell/Cap/ Jsy/100	15.00
JB	Jeff Bagwell/ Ball/Jsy/50	25.00
KG	Ken Griffey Jr./ Bat/Jsy	20.00
KG	Ken Griffey Jr./ Cap/Jsy/100	50.00
KG	Ken Griffey Jr./Jsy/ Bat/Auto./24	225.00
TG	Tony Gwynn/Bat/Jsy	10.00
TG	Tony Gwynn/ Ball/Jsy/50	40.00
TG	Tony Gwynn/ Cap/Jsy/100	30.00
BW	Bernie Williams/ Bat/Jsy	8.00
EC	Eric Chavez/Bat/Jsy	8.00
EC	Eric Chavez/Cap/ Jsy/100	15.00
GM	Greg Maddux/Bat/Jsy	25.00
IR	Ivan Rodriguez/ Bat/Jsy	8.00
JC	Jose Canseco/Bat/Jsy	8.00
JL	Javy Lopez/Bat/Jsy	6.00
JL	Javy Lopez/Cap/ Jsy/100	8.00
MM	Mark McGwire/ Base/Ball/500	50.00
MR	Manny Ramirez/ Bat/Jsy	10.00
MW	Matt Williams/Bat/Jsy	6.00
PM	Pedro Martinez/ Cap/Jsy/100	25.00
PO	Paul O'Neill/Bat/Jsy	6.00
VG	Vladimir Guerrero/ Bat/Jsy	10.00
VG	Vladimir Guerrero/ Cap/Jsy/100	20.00
VG	Vladimir Guerrero/ Ball/Jsy/50	30.00
TG	Troy Glaus/Bat/Jsy	8.00

3,000 Hit Club

A continuation of Upper Deck's cross-brand insert program, this set pays tribute to Ty Cobb with three variations. The collection includes 350 bat cards, three cut signatures and one bat/cut signature card.

		NM/M
TC-B	Ty Cobb/Bat/350	130.00

2001 SP Authentic Sample

Base cards in the forthcoming SP Authentic issue were previewed with this card. In a format identical to the regularly issued version, the promo card has a large black "SAMPLE" overprinted diagonally on back.

Ken Griffey Jr.

		NM/M
90	Ken Griffey Jr.	3.00

2001 SP Authentic

Jeff Bagwell

		NM/M
Common Player:		.25
Common SP (91-135):		4.00
Production 1,250		
Common SP (136-180):		2.00
Production 1,250		
Pack (5):		15.00
Box (24):		340.00
1	Troy Glaus	.50
2	Darin Erstad	.40
3	Jason Giambi	.75
4	Tim Hudson	.50
5	Eric Chavez	.40
6	Miguel Tejada	.50
7	Jose Ortiz	.25
8	Carlos Delgado	.75
9	Tony Batista	.25
10	Raul Mondesi	.25
11	Aubrey Huff	.25
12	Greg Vaughn	.25
13	Roberto Alomar	.50
14	Juan Gonzalez	.50
15	Jim Thome	.75
16	Omar Vizquel	.25
17	Edgar Martinez	.50
18	Fred Garcia	.25
19	Cal Ripken Jr.	3.00
20	Ivan Rodriguez	.75
21	Rafael Palmeiro	.75
22	Alex Rodriguez	2.00
23	Manny Ramirez	1.00
24	Pedro Martinez	1.00
25	Nomar Garciaparra	1.00
26	Mike Sweeney	.25
27	Jermaine Dye	.25
28	Bobby Higginson	.25
29	Dean Palmer	.25
30	Matt Lawton	.25
31	Eric Milton	.25
32	Frank Thomas	1.00
33	Magglio Ordonez	.25
34	David Wells	.25
35	Paul Konerko	.50
36	Derek Jeter	3.00
37	Bernie Williams	.50
38	Roger Clemens	2.00
39	Mike Mussina	.50
40	Jorge Posada	.50
41	Jeff Bagwell	.75
42	Richard Hidalgo	.25
43	Craig Biggio	.50
44	Greg Maddux	2.00
45	Chipper Jones	1.00
46	Andruw Jones	1.00
47	Rafael Furcal	.40
48	Tom Glavine	.50
49	Jeromy Burnitz	.25
50	Jeffrey Hammonds	.25
51	Mark McGwire	2.00
52	Jim Edmonds	.50
53	Rick Ankiel	.25
54	J.D. Drew	.40
55	Sammy Sosa	1.50
56	Corey Patterson	.25
57	Kerry Wood	.50
58	Randy Johnson	1.00
59	Luis Gonzalez	.40
60	Curt Schilling	.75
61	Gary Sheffield	.50
62	Shawn Green	.50
63	Kevin Brown	.25
64	Vladimir Guerrero	1.00
65	Jose Vidro	.25
66	Barry Bonds	3.00
67	Jeff Kent	.50
68	Livan Hernandez	.25
69	Preston Wilson	.25
70	Charles Johnson	.25
71	Ryan Dempster	.25
72	Mike Piazza	1.50
73	Al Leiter	.25
74	Edgardo Alfonzo	.25
75	Robin Ventura	.25
76	Tony Gwynn	1.50
77	Phil Nevin	.25
78	Trevor Hoffman	.25
79	Scott Rolen	1.00
80	Pat Burrell	.50
81	Bob Abreu	.40
82	Jason Kendall	.25
83	Brian Giles	.25
84	Kris Benson	.25
85	Ken Griffey Jr.	2.00
86	Barry Larkin	.50
87	Sean Casey	.40
88	Todd Helton	.75
89	Mike Hampton	.25
90	Larry Walker	.25
91	Ichiro Suzuki RC	
	(Future Watch)	180.00
92	Wilson Betemit RC	
	(Future Watch)	4.00
93	Adrian Hernandez RC	
	(Future Watch)	4.00
94	Juan Uribe RC	
	(Future Watch)	6.00
95	Travis Hafner RC	
	(Future Watch)	60.00
96	Morgan Ensberg RC	
	(Future Watch)	15.00
97	Sean Douglass RC	
	(Future Watch)	4.00
98	Juan Diaz RC	
	(Future Watch)	4.00
99	Erick Almonte RC	
	(Future Watch)	4.00
100	Ryan Freel RC	
	(Future Watch)	8.00
101	Elpidio Guzman RC	
	(Future Watch)	4.00
102	Christian Parker RC	
	(Future Watch)	4.00
103	Josh Fogg RC	
	(Future Watch)	6.00
104	Bert Snow RC	
	(Future Watch)	4.00
105	Horacio Ramirez RC	
	(Future Watch)	8.00
106	Ricardo Rodriguez RC	
	(Future Watch)	4.00
107	Tyler Walker RC	
	(Future Watch)	4.00
108	Jose Mieses RC	
	(Future Watch)	6.00
109	Billy Sylvester RC	
	(Future Watch)	4.00
110	Martin Vargas RC	
	(Future Watch)	4.00
111	Andres Torres RC	
	(Future Watch)	4.00
112	Greg Miller RC	
	(Future Watch)	4.00
113	Alexis Gomez RC	
	(Future Watch)	4.00
114	Grant Balfour RC	
	(Future Watch)	4.00
115	Henry Mateo RC	
	(Future Watch)	4.00
116	Esix Snead RC	
	(Future Watch)	4.00
117	Jackson Melian RC	
	(Future Watch)	4.00
118	Nate Teut RC	
	(Future Watch)	4.00
119	Tsuyoshi Shinjo RC	
	(Future Watch)	4.00
120	Carlos Valderrama RC	
	(Future Watch)	6.00
121	Johnny Estrada RC	
	(Future Watch)	10.00
122	Jason Michaels RC	
	(Future Watch)	
123	William Ortega RC	
	(Future Watch)	4.00
124	Jason Smith RC	
	(Future Watch)	4.00
125	Brian Lawrence RC	
	(Future Watch)	4.00
126	Albert Pujols RC	
	(Future Watch)	450.00
127	Wilken Ruan RC	
	(Future Watch)	4.00
128	Josh Towers RC	
	(Future Watch)	6.00
129	Kris Keller RC	
	(Future Watch)	
130	Nick Maness RC	
	(Future Watch)	4.00
131	Jack Wilson RC	
	(Future Watch)	10.00
132	Brandon Duckworth RC	
	(Future Watch)	4.00
133	Mike Penney RC	
	(Future Watch)	4.00
134	Jay Gibbons RC	
	(Future Watch)	10.00
135	Cesar Crespo RC	
	(Future Watch)	4.00
136	Ken Griffey Jr.	
	(SP Superstars)	8.00
137	Barry Bonds	
	(SP Superstars)	8.00
138	Derek Jeter	
	(SP Superstars)	10.00
139	Alex Rodriguez	
	(SP Superstars)	10.00
140	Sammy Sosa	
	(SP Superstars)	4.00
141	Carlos Delgado	
	(SP Superstars)	3.00
142	Cal Ripken Jr.	
	(SP Superstars)	12.00
143	Pedro Martinez	
	(SP Superstars)	5.00
144	Frank Thomas	
	(SP Superstars)	5.00
145	Juan Gonzalez	
	(SP Superstars)	3.00
146	Troy Glaus	
	(SP Superstars)	2.00
147	Jason Giambi	
	(SP Superstars)	4.00
148	Ivan Rodriguez	
	(SP Superstars)	4.00
149	Chipper Jones	
	(SP Superstars)	5.00
150	Vladimir Guerrero	
	(SP Superstars)	5.00
151	Mike Piazza	
	(SP Superstars)	5.00
152	Jeff Bagwell	
	(SP Superstars)	4.00
153	Randy Johnson	
	(SP Superstars)	5.00
154	Todd Helton	
	(SP Superstars)	4.00
155	Gary Sheffield	
	(SP Superstars)	3.00
156	Tony Gwynn	
	(SP Superstars)	5.00
157	Barry Bonds	
	(SP Superstars)	10.00
158	Nomar Garciaparra	
	(SP Superstars)	5.00
159	Bernie Williams	
	(SP Superstars)	3.00
160	Greg Vaughn	
	(SP Superstars)	2.00
161	David Wells	
	(SP Superstars)	2.00
162	Roberto Alomar	
	(SP Superstars)	3.00
163	Jermaine Dye	
	(SP Superstars)	2.00
164	Rafael Palmeiro	
	(SP Superstars)	4.00
165	Andruw Jones	
	(SP Superstars)	4.00
166	Preston Wilson	
	(SP Superstars)	2.00
167	Edgardo Alfonzo	
	(SP Superstars)	2.00
168	Pat Burrell	
	(SP Superstars)	3.00
169	Jim Edmonds	
	(SP Superstars)	3.00
170	Mike Hampton	
	(SP Superstars)	2.00
171	Jeff Kent	
	(SP Superstars)	2.00
172	Kevin Brown	
	(SP Superstars)	2.00
173	Manny Ramirez	
	(SP Superstars)	5.00
174	Magglio Ordonez	
	(SP Superstars)	2.00
175	Roger Clemens	
	(SP Superstars)	8.00
176	Jim Thome	
	(SP Superstars)	4.00
177	Barry Zito	
	(SP Superstars)	2.00
178	Brian Giles	
	(SP Superstars)	2.00
179	Rick Ankiel	
	(SP Superstars)	2.00
180	Corey Patterson	
	(SP Superstars)	2.00

Limited

Stars (1-90):		8-15X
SP (91-135):		1-2X
SP (136-180):		1-3X
Production 50 Sets		

Buyback Autographs

Chirography

		NM/M
Common Player:		5.00
Inserted 1:72		

		NM/M
Inserted 1:144		
Some not priced due to scarcity.		
4	Ken Griffey	
	'93 SP/34	125.00
105	Ken Griffey	
	'94 SP/182	80.00
190'	Ken Griffey	
	'95 SP/116	80.00
170	Ken Griffey	
	'96 SP/53	100.00
84	Ken Griffey	
	'00 SP/333	70.00
188	Alex Rodriguez	
	'95 SP Red/117	z80.00
171	Alex Rodriguez	
	'96 SP/72	100.00
16	Alex Rodriguez	
	'00 SP/332	75.00
260	Frank Thomas	
	'93 SP/79	40.00
193	Frank Thomas	
	'94 SP/165	35.00
50	Frank Thomas	
	'97 SP/34	75.00
34	Frank Thomas	
	'00 SP/302	35.00
34	Chipper Jones	
	'95 SP/118	40.00
26	Chipper Jones	
	'96 SP/72	45.00
45	Chipper Jones	
	'00 SP/303	30.00
132	Randy Johnson	
	'93 SP/97	60.00
106	Randy Johnson	
	'94 SP/146	40.00
189	Randy Johnson	
	'95 SP/121	40.00
169	Randy Johnson	
	'96 SP/78	50.00
58	Randy Johnson	
	'00 SP/213	40.00
41	Carlos Delgado	
	'94 SP/279	15.00
181	Carlos Delgado	
	'96 SP/83	20.00
8	Carlos Delgado	
	'00 SP/174	15.00
50	Jim Edmonds	
	'96 SP/74	20.00
167	Tony Gwynn	
	'93 SP/101	40.00
130	Tony Gwynn	
	'94 SP/88	40.00
105	Tony Gwynn	
	'95 SP/179	30.00
160	Tony Gwynn	
	'96 SP/92	40.00
74	Tony Gwynn	
	'00 SP/95	40.00
3	Jason Giambi	
	'00 SP/290	30.00
9	Ivan Rodriguez	
	'93 SP/89	40.00
180	Ivan Rodriguez	
	'96 SP/64	40.00
22	Ivan Rodriguez	
	'00 SP/163	30.00
47	Andruw Jones	
	'00 SP/336	25.00
10	Barry Bonds	
	'93 SP/75	180.00
90	Barry Bonds	
	'94 SP/103	180.00
166	Barry Bonds	
	'96 SP/49	180.00
65	Barry Bonds	
	'00 SP/146	180.00
18	Gary Sheffield	
	'93 SP/83	20.00
114	Gary Sheffield	
	'94 SP/70	20.00
86	Gary Sheffield	
	'96 SP/69	20.00
60	Gary Sheffield	
	'00 SP/133	15.00
89	Sammy Sosa	
	'93 SP/73	100.00
126	Cal Ripken	
	'94 SP/99	100.00
1	Cal Ripken	
	'95 SP/37	150.00
20	Cal Ripken	
	'00 SP/266	100.00
89	Todd Helton	
	'00 SP/194	25.00
4	Tim Hudson	
	'00 SP/291	20.00
62	Shawn Green	
	'00 SP/340	20.00
52	Fernando Tatis	
	'00 SP/267	8.00
57	Matt Williams	
	'00 SP/340	10.00
72	Robin Ventura	
	'00 SP/340	10.00
2	Troy Glaus	
	'00 SP/340	15.00
39	Roger Clemens	
	'00 SP/145	100.00

Chirography Gold

		NM/M
Common Player:		
G-AB	Albert Belle/88	15.00
G-CD	Carlos Delgado/25	50.00
G-DD	Darren Dreifort/37	25.00
G-DES	David Espinosa/79	15.00
G-KG	Ken Griffey Jr./30	150.00
G-RH	Rick Helling/32	15.00
G-RJ	Randy Johnson/51	65.00
G-DJ	David Justice/28	30.00
G-DS	Dane Sardinha/50	15.00
G-MS	Mike Sweeney/25	25.00
G-MV	Mo Vaughn/42	15.00
G-DW	David Wells/33	20.00

Cooperstown Calling Game Jersey

		NM/M
Common Player:		5.00
Overall jersey odds 1:24.		
JB	Jeff Bagwell	8.00
WB	Wade Boggs	8.00
GC	Gary Carter	5.00
RC	Roger Clemens	30.00
AD	Andre Dawson	5.00
SG	Steve Garvey	5.00
GG	Goose Gossage	5.00
TG	Tony Gwynn	10.00
RM	Roger Maris/243	25.00
PM	Pedro Martinez/SP	15.00
DM	Don Mattingly	30.00
BM	Bill Mazeroski	5.00
PM	Paul Molitor	8.00
EM	Eddie Murray	5.00
MP	Mike Piazza/SP	25.00
KP	Kirby Puckett	15.00
MR	Manny Ramirez/SP	15.00
CR	Cal Ripken Jr.	30.00
RS	Ryne Sandberg	20.00
OS	Ozzie Smith	10.00
DW	Dave Winfield	5.00

		NM/M
EA	Edgardo Alfonzo	5.00
AB	Albert Belle	15.00
CB	Carlos Beltran	35.00
MB	Milton Bradley	12.00
PB	Pat Burrell	10.00
JC	Jose Canseco	30.00
CD	Carlos Delgado	12.00
DD	Darren Dreifort/206	15.00
JD	J.D. Drew	15.00
JE	Jim Edmonds	20.00
DEr	Darin Erstad	10.00
DEs	David Espinosa	10.00
CF	Cliff Floyd	10.00
RF	Rafael Furcal/222	10.00
JG	Jason Giambi	15.00
TrG	Troy Glaus	15.00
LG	Luis Gonzalez/271	15.00
SG	Shawn Green/82	25.00
KG	Ken Griffey Jr./126	80.00
ToG	Tony Gwynn/76	40.00
RH	Rick Helling/211	5.00
ToH	Todd Helton/152	30.00
TiH	Tim Hudson	15.00
RJ	Randy Johnson/143	50.00
AJ	Andruw Jones	20.00
CJ	Chipper Jones/184	40.00
DJ	David Justice	8.00
MK	Mark Kotsay/228	5.00
TL	Travis Lee/226	5.00
AlP	Albert Pujols	550.00
CR	Cal Ripken/109	125.00
AR	Alex Rodriguez/229	90.00
DS	Dane Sardinha	5.00
BS	Ben Sheets	20.00
SS	Sammy Sosa/76	100.00
MS	Mike Sweeney	8.00
MV	Mo Vaughn/103	8.00
RV	Robin Ventura/92	10.00
DW	David Wells	8.00
RW	Rondell White	8.00
MW	Matt Williams	8.00

Game Jersey

		NM/M
Common Player:		5.00
Overall jersey odds 1:24.		
JD	Joe DiMaggio/243	100.00
KG	Ken Griffey Jr.	15.00
MM	Mickey Mantle/243	150.00
AR	Alex Rodriguez	15.00
GS	Gary Sheffield	5.00
SS	Sammy Sosa	10.00

Combo Game Jersey

		NM/M
Overall jersey odds 1:24.		
SD	Sammy Sosa, Andre Dawson	25.00
RS	Alex Rodriguez, Ozzie Smith	35.00
GD	Ken Griffey Jr., Joe DiMaggio/98	120.00
SW	Gary Sheffield, Dave Winfield	15.00
MD	Mickey Mantle, Joe DiMaggio/98	300.00
MG	Mickey Mantle, Ken Griffey /98	160.00

Stars of Japan

Tsuyoshi Shinjo

		NM/M
Complete Set (30):		50.00
Common Player:		1.00
One pack/hobby box.		
RS1	Ichiro Suzuki, Tsuyoshi Shinjo	5.00
RS2	Shigetosi Hasegawa, Hideki Irabu	1.00
RS3	Tomokazu Ohka, Mac Suzuki	1.00
RS4	Tsuyoshi Shinjo, Hideki Irabu	1.00
RS5	Ichiro Suzuki, Hideo Nomo	5.00
RS6	Tsuyoshi Shinjo, Mac Suzuki	1.00
RS7	Tsuyoshi Shinjo, Kazuhiro Sasaki	1.00
RS8	Hideo Nomo, Tomokazu Ohka	1.50
RS9	Ichiro Suzuki, Mac Suzuki	5.00
RS10	Hideo Nomo, Shigetosi Hasegawa	1.50
RS11	Hideo Nomo, Masato Yoshii	1.50
RS12	Hideo Nomo, Hideki Irabu	1.50
RS13	Shigetosi Hasegawa, Kazuhiro Sasaki	1.00
RS14	Shigetosi Hasegawa, Mac Suzuki	1.00
RS15	Tsuyoshi Shinjo, Hideo Nomo	1.50
RS16	Tsuyoshi Shinjo, Tomokazu Ohka	1.00
RS17	Ichiro Suzuki, Kazuhiro Sasaki	5.00
RS18	Masato Yoshii, Hideki Irabu	1.00
RS19	Ichiro Suzuki, Tomokazu Ohka	5.00
RS20	Hideki Irabu, Kazuhiro Sasaki	1.00
RS21	Tsuyoshi Shinjo, Kazuhiro Sasaki	1.00
RS22	Ichiro Suzuki, Shigetosi Hasegawa	5.00
RS23	Mac Suzuki, Kazuhiro Sasaki	1.00
RS24	Ichiro Suzuki, Hideki Irabu	5.00
RS25	Tomokazu Ohka, Kazuhiro Sasaki	1.00
RS26	Tsuyoshi Shinjo, Shigetosi Hasegawa	1.00

RS27 Masato Yoshii, Kazuhiro Sasaki 1.00
RS28 Hideo Nomo, Kazuhiro Sasaki 1.50
RS29 Ichiro Suzuki, Masato Yoshii 5.00
RS30 Hideo Nomo, Ichiro Suzuki 5.00

Stars of Japan Game Ball
NM/M
Common Player: 8.00
BB-SH Shigetosi Hasegawa/SP/30 15.00
BB-HI Hideki Irabu 8.00
BB-KS Kazuhiro Sasaki 10.00
BB-TS Tsuyoshi Shinjo SP/50 20.00
BB-IS Ichiro Suzuki 75.00
BB-MY Masato Yoshii 10.00

Stars of Japan Game Ball Gold

NM/M
Production 25 Sets
BB-SH Shigetosi Hasegawa 40.00
BB-HI Hideki Irabu 20.00
BB-KS Kazuhiro Sasaki 40.00

Stars of Japan Game Ball-Base Combos

NM/M
Inserted 1:576
HI-KS Hideki Irabu, Kazuhiro Sasaki/SP/30 25.00
HN-KS Hideo Nomo, Kazuhiro Sasaki/SP/50 75.00
HN-SH Hideo Nomo, Shigetosi Hasegawa 20.00
IS-KS Ichiro Suzuki, Kazuhiro Sasaki/SP/30 120.00
IS-MY Ichiro Suzuki, Masato Yoshii 50.00
IS-SH Ichiro Suzuki, Shigetosi Hasegawa/SP/72 75.00
IS-TS Ichiro Suzuki, Tsuyoshi Shinjo/SP/40 125.00
MS-KS Mac Suzuki, Kazuhiro Sasaki/SP/30 20.00
MY-KS Masato Yoshii, Kazuhiro Sasaki/SP/30 25.00
SH-KS Shigetosi Hasegawa, Kazuhiro Sasaki SP/30 25.00
TO-KS Tomokazu Ohka, Kazuhiro Sasaki 20.00
TS-HI Tsuyoshi Shinjo, Hideki Irabu/SP/30 25.00
TS-KS Tsuyoshi Shinjo, Kazuhiro Sasaki/SP/30 25.00
TS-SH Tsuyoshi Shinjo, Shigetosi Hasegawa/SP/30 25.00

Stars of Japan Game Ball-Base Combos Gold

NM/M
Common Card: 20.00
Production 25 Sets
HI-KS Hideki Irabu, Kazuhiro Sasaki 25.00
HN-KS Hideo Nomo, Kazuhiro Sasaki 65.00
HN-SH Hideo Nomo, Shigetosi Hasegawa 65.00
IS-KS Ichiro Suzuki, Kazuhiro Sasaki 150.00
IS-MY Ichiro Suzuki, Masato Yoshii 150.00
IS-SH Ichiro Suzuki, Shigetosi Hasegawa 150.00
IS-TS Ichiro Suzuki, Tsuyoshi Shinjo 150.00
MS-KS Mac Suzuki, Kazuhiro Sasaki 20.00
MY-KS Masato Yoshii, Kazuhiro Sasaki 20.00
SH-KS Shigetosi Hasegawa, Kazuhiro Sasaki 20.00
TO-KS Tomokazu Ohka, Kazuhiro Sasaki 20.00
TS-HI Tsuyoshi Shinjo, Hideki Irabu 25.00
TS-KS Tsuyoshi Shinjo, Kazuhiro Sasaki 25.00
TS-SH Tsuyoshi Shinjo, Shigetosi Hasegawa 25.00

Stars of Japan Game Ball-Base Trio
NM/M
Complete Set (1):
BBB-RS Kazuhiro Sasaki, Ichiro Suzuki, Hideo Nomo 175.00

Stars of Japan Game Ball-Base Trio Gold
NM/M
Production 25

Stars of Japan Game Base
NM/M
Common Player: 15.00
SH Shigetosi Hasegawa/SP/33 15.00
HI Hideki Irabu/SP/33 15.00
TO Tomokazu Ohka/SP/33 15.00
KS Kazuhiro Sasaki/SP/33 25.00
TS Tsuyoshi Shinjo/SP/33 25.00
MS Mac Suzuki/SP/23 25.00
MY Masato Yoshii/SP/33 20.00

Stars of Japan Game Base Gold
NM/M
Common Player: 25.00
Production 25 Sets
SH Shigetosi Hasegawa 25.00
HI Hideki Irabu 25.00
TO Tomokazu Ohka 25.00
KS Kazuhiro Sasaki 30.00
TS Tsuyoshi Shinjo 35.00
MS Mac Suzuki 25.00
MY Masato Yoshii 25.00

Stars of Japan Game Bat Gold
NM/M
Common Player: 10.00
Production 25 Sets
B-HN Hideo Nomo 80.00
B-TS Tsuyoshi Shinjo 30.00
B-MY Masato Yoshii 10.00

2001 SP Authentic Stars of Japan Game Jersey

NM/M
Common Player: 5.00
Inserted 1:12
J-SH Shigetosi Hasegawa 5.00
J-HN Hideo Nomo 40.00
J-KS Kazuhiro Sasaki 8.00
J-TS Tsuyoshi Shinjo 8.00
J-IS Ichiro Suzuki/SP/260 Exch 100.00
J-MY Masato Yoshii 5.00

2001 SP Authentic Stars of Japan Game Jersey Gold
NM/M
Common Player: 10.00
Production 25 Sets
J-SH Shigetosi Hasegawa 10.00

J-HN Hideo Nomo 60.00
J-KS Kazuhiro Sasaki 15.00
J-TS Tsuyoshi Shinjo 15.00
J-MY Masato Yoshii 10.00

Stars of Japan Game Jersey-Bat Combos

NM/M
Common Player: 15.00
BB-HS Shigetosi Hasegawa, Tsuyoshi Shinjo 15.00
JB-NN Hideo Nomo 60.00
JB-SN Kazuhiro Sasaki, Hideo Nomo 40.00
JJ-SH Kazuhiro Sasaki, Shigetosi Hasegawa 15.00

Stars of Japan Game Bat-Jersey Combo Gold
NM/M
Production 25 Sets
BB-HS Shigetosi Hasegawa, Tsuyoshi Shinjo 40.00

Stars of Japan Game Bat
NM/M
Inserted 1:12
B-HN Hideo Nomo/SP/30 60.00
B-TS Tsuyoshi Shinjo/SP/30 20.00
B-MY Masato Yoshii 5.00

Sultan of Swatch Jersey or Pants

NM/M
Quantity produced listed
SOS2 Babe Ruth/29 350.00
SOS3 Babe Ruth/94 300.00
SOS4 Babe Ruth/54 350.00
SOS5 Babe Ruth/59 350.00
SOS6 Babe Ruth/26 350.00
SOS7 Babe Ruth/27 350.00
SOS8 Babe Ruth/32 350.00
SOS9 Babe Ruth/20 350.00
SOS10 Babe Ruth/21 350.00
SOS11 Babe Ruth/23 350.00
SOS12 Babe Ruth/24 350.00
SOS13 Babe Ruth/26 350.00
SOS14 Babe Ruth/27 350.00
SOS15 Babe Ruth/28 350.00
SOS16 Babe Ruth/29 350.00
SOS17 Babe Ruth/31 350.00
SOS18 Babe Ruth/31 350.00
SOS19 Babe Ruth/33 350.00
SOS20 Babe Ruth/36 350.00
SOS21 Babe Ruth/48 350.00

ABBREVIATIONS
SP - Short Print

Sultan of Swatch Jersey/Cut

No Pricing
Production One Set

2001 SP Game Bat

NM/M
Complete Set (90): 40.00
Common Player: .25
Pack (4): 10.00
Box (16): 150.00
1 Troy Glaus .50
2 Darin Erstad .50
3 Mo Vaughn .25
4 Jason Giambi .75
5 Ben Grieve .25
6 Eric Chavez .50
7 Carlos Delgado .75
8 Tony Batista .25
9 Shannon Stewart .25
10 Jose Cruz Jr. .25
11 Fred McGriff .25
12 Greg Vaughn .25
13 Roberto Alomar .50
14 Manny Ramirez 1.00
15 Jim Thome .75
16 Russ Branyan .25
17 Alex Rodriguez 2.00
18 John Olerud .25
19 Edgar Martinez .25
20 Cal Ripken Jr. 3.00
21 Albert Belle .25
22 Ivan Rodriguez .75
23 Rafael Palmeiro .25
24 Nomar Garciaparra 1.00
25 Carl Everett .25
26 Dante Bichette .25
27 Mike Sweeney .25
28 Jermaine Dye .25
29 Carlos Beltran .75
30 Juan Gonzalez .50
31 Dean Palmer .25
32 Bobby Higginson .25
33 Matt Lawton .25
34 Jacque Jones .25
35 Frank Thomas 1.00
36 Magglio Ordonez .25
37 Paul Konerko .50
38 Carlos Lee .40
39 Bernie Williams .50
40 Derek Jeter 3.00
41 Paul O'Neill .40
42 Jose Canseco .50
43 Ken Caminiti .25
44 Jeff Bagwell .75
45 Craig Biggio .40
46 Richard Hidalgo .25
47 Andruw Jones 1.00
48 Chipper Jones 1.00
49 Andres Galarraga .25
50 B.J. Surhoff .25
51 Jeromy Burnitz .25
52 Geoff Jenkins .25
53 Richie Sexson .40
54 Mark McGwire 2.50
55 Jim Edmonds .50
56 J.D. Drew .40
57 Fernando Tatis .25
58 Sammy Sosa 1.50
59 Mark Grace .50
60 Eric Young .25
61 Matt Williams .25
62 Luis Gonzalez .25
63 Steve Finley .25
64 Shawn Green .40
65 Gary Sheffield .50
66 Eric Karros .25
67 Vladimir Guerrero 1.00
68 Jose Vidro .25
69 Barry Bonds 3.00
70 Jeff Kent .40
71 Preston Wilson .25
72 Mike Lowell .25
73 Luis Castillo .25
74 Mike Piazza 1.50
75 Robin Ventura .25
76 Edgardo Alfonzo .25
77 Tony Gwynn 1.00
78 Eric Owens .25
79 Ryan Klesko .25
80 Scott Rolen .75
81 Bobby Abreu .50
82 Pat Burrell .25
83 Brian Giles .25
84 Jason Kendall .25
85 Aaron Boone .25
86 Ken Griffey Jr. 2.00
87 Barry Larkin .25
88 Todd Helton 1.00
89 Larry Walker .25
90 Jeffrey Hammonds .25

Big League Hit Parade
NM/M
Complete Set (6): 15.00
Common Player: 1.50
Inserted 1:15
1 Nomar Garciaparra 1.50
2 Ken Griffey Jr. 3.00
3 Sammy Sosa 2.00
4 Alex Rodriguez 4.00
5 Mark McGwire 4.00
6 Ivan Rodriguez 1.50

In the Swing
NM/M
Complete Set (15): 25.00
Common Player: 1.00
Inserted 1:7
1 Ken Griffey Jr. 2.50
2 Jim Edmonds 1.00
3 Carlos Delgado 1.00
4 Frank Thomas 1.50
5 Barry Bonds 4.00
6 Nomar Garciaparra 1.50
7 Gary Sheffield 1.00
8 Vladimir Guerrero 1.50
9 Alex Rodriguez 3.00
10 Todd Helton 1.00
11 Darin Erstad 1.00
12 Derek Jeter 4.00
13 Sammy Sosa 2.50
14 Mark McGwire 3.00
15 Jason Giambi 1.00

Lineup Time
NM/M
Complete Set (11): 20.00
Common Player: 1.00
Inserted 1:8
1 Mark McGwire 3.00
2 Roberto Alomar 1.00
3 Alex Rodriguez 2.00
4 Chipper Jones 1.00
5 Ivan Rodriguez 1.00
6 Ken Griffey Jr. 3.00
7 Sammy Sosa 2.50
8 Barry Bonds 4.00
9 Frank Thomas 1.50
10 Pedro Martinez 1.50
11 Derek Jeter 4.00

Piece of the Game

NM/M
Common Player: 4.00
Inserted 1:1
SP production 1,500 or fewer
Golds: 2-5X
Production 25 Sets
EA Edgardo Alfonzo/SP 10.00
RA Roberto Alomar 8.00
SA Sandy Alomar 4.00
RA Rick Ankiel 5.00
JB Jeff Bagwell/SP 15.00
TB Tony Batista 5.00
CB Carlos Beltran 5.00
JB Johnny Bench/SP 25.00
BB Barry Bonds 25.00
KB Kevin Brown/SP 10.00
PB Pat Burrell 8.00
JC Jose Canseco 6.00
WC Will Clark 6.00
CD Carlos Delgado 6.00
JoD Joe DiMaggio/SP 100.00
JD J.D. Drew 6.00
JE Jim Edmonds 6.00
DE Darin Erstad/SP 10.00
RF Rafael Furcal 4.00
BG Bob Gibson/SP 20.00
TGl Tom Glavine/SP 15.00
MG Mark Grace 8.00
SG Shawn Green 6.00
KG Ken Griffey Jr. 20.00
TGw Tony Gwynn 10.00
TH Todd Helton 8.00
TH Todd Hundley/SP 4.00
RJ Reggie Jackson/SP 20.00
RJ Randy Johnson 10.00
AJ Andruw Jones 8.00
CJ Chipper Jones 10.00
DJ David Justice 5.00
KL Kenny Lofton 4.00
GM Greg Maddux 15.00
EM Edgar Martinez 6.00
TM Tino Martinez 6.00
FM Fred McGriff/SP 10.00
PN Phil Nevin/SP 5.00
JO John Olerud 6.00
PO Paul O'Neill 6.00
MO Magglio Ordonez/SP 10.00
MQ Mark Quinn/SP 10.00
MR Manny Ramirez 8.00
CR Cal Ripken Jr./SP 40.00
AR Alex Rodriguez 6.00
IR Ivan Rodriguez 8.00
SR Scott Rolen 8.00
NR Nolan Ryan/SP 35.00
TS Tim Salmon/SP 10.00
GS Gary Sheffield 5.00
SS Sammy Sosa/SP 25.00
SS Shannon Stewart 4.00
FT Frank Thomas 8.00
GV Greg Vaughn 4.00
MV Mo Vaughn 4.00
RV Robin Ventura 4.00
BW Bernie Williams 4.00
MW Matt Williams 4.00
PW Preston Wilson 4.00

Piece of the Game Autograph

NM/M
Common Autograph: 30.00
Inserted 1:96
BB Barry Bonds 180.00
JC Jose Canseco 40.00
KG Ken Griffey Jr. 100.00
TGw Tony Gwynn 50.00
AJ Andruw Jones 30.00
AR Alex Rodriguez 120.00
NR Nolan Ryan 125.00
FT Frank Thomas 50.00

The Lumber Yard
NM/M
Complete Set (10): 15.00
Common Player: .50
Inserted 1:10
1 Jason Giambi 1.00
2 Chipper Jones 1.50
3 Carl Everett .50
4 Alex Rodriguez 3.00
5 Frank Thomas 1.50
6 Barry Bonds 4.00
7 Jeff Bagwell 1.50
8 Sammy Sosa 2.50
9 Carlos Delgado 1.00
10 Mike Piazza 2.50

Milestone

NM/M
Complete Set (96):
Common Player: .40
Common Rookie (91-96): 5.00
Production 500
Pack (4): 16.00
Box (10): 140.00
1 Troy Glaus .50
2 Darin Erstad .50
3 Jason Giambi .75
4 Jermaine Dye .40
5 Eric Chavez .50
6 Carlos Delgado .40
7 Raul Mondesi .40
8 Shannon Stewart .40
9 Greg Vaughn .40
10 Aubrey Huff .40
11 Juan Gonzalez .50
12 Roberto Alomar .50
13 Jim Thome .40
14 Omar Vizquel .40
15 Mike Cameron .40
16 Edgar Martinez .40
17 John Olerud .40
18 Bret Boone .40

19	Cal Ripken Jr.	3.00
20	Tony Batista	.40
21	Alex Rodriguez	2.50
22	Ivan Rodriguez	.75
23	Rafael Palmeiro	.75
24	Manny Ramirez	1.00
25	Pedro Martinez	1.00
26	Nomar Garciaparra	1.00
27	Carl Everett	.40
28	Mike Sweeney	.40
29	Neifi Perez	.40
30	Mark Quinn	.40
31	Bobby Higginson	.40
32	Tony Clark	.40
33	Doug Mientkiewicz	.40
34	Cristian Guzman	.40
35	Joe Mays	.40
36	David Ortiz	1.00
37	Frank Thomas	1.00
38	Magglio Ordonez	.40
39	Carlos Lee	.50
40	Alfonso Soriano	1.00
41	Bernie Williams	.50
42	Derek Jeter	3.00
43	Roger Clemens	2.50
44	Jeff Bagwell	1.00
45	Richard Hidalgo	.40
46	Moises Alou	.40
47	Chipper Jones	1.00
48	Greg Maddux	2.00
49	Rafael Furcal	.50
50	Andruw Jones	1.00
51	Jeromy Burnitz	.40
52	Geoff Jenkins	.40
53	Richie Sexson	.50
54	Edgar Renteria	.40
55	Mark McGwire	2.50
56	Jim Edmonds	.50
57	J.D. Drew	.50
58	Sammy Sosa	1.50
59	Bill Mueller	.40
60	Luis Gonzalez	.50
61	Randy Johnson	1.00
62	Gary Sheffield	.50
63	Shawn Green	.40
64	Kevin Brown	.40
65	Vladimir Guerrero	1.00
66	Jose Vidro	.40
67	Fernando Tatis	.40
68	Barry Bonds	3.00
69	Jeff Kent	.50
70	Rich Aurilia	.40
71	Preston Wilson	.40
72	Charles Johnson	.40
73	Cliff Floyd	.40
74	Mike Piazza	1.00
75	Matt Lawton	.40
76	Edgardo Alfonzo	.40
77	Tony Gwynn	1.50
78	Phil Nevin	.40
79	Scott Rolen	1.00
80	Pat Burrell	.50
81	Bobby Abreu	.50
82	Brian Giles	.40
83	Jason Kendall	.40
84	Aramis Ramirez	.50
85	Sean Casey	.50
86	Ken Griffey Jr.	2.50
87	Barry Larkin	.50
88	Todd Helton	.75
89	Mike Hampton	.40
90	Larry Walker	.50
91	Ichiro Suzuki RC	70.00
92	Albert Pujols RC	180.00
93	Tsuyoshi Shinjo RC	5.00
94	Jack Wilson RC	8.00
95	Donaldo Mendez RC	5.00
96	Junior Spivey RC	8.00

Milestone Slugging Sensations

		NM/M
Complete Set (12):		12.00
Common Player:		.50
Inserted 1:5		
SS1	Troy Glaus	.50
SS2	Mark McGwire	2.50
SS3	Sammy Sosa	1.50
SS4	Juan Gonzalez	.50
SS5	Barry Bonds	3.00
SS6	Jeff Bagwell	.75
SS7	Jason Giambi	.75
SS8	Ivan Rodriguez	.75
SS9	Mike Piazza	1.50
SS10	Chipper Jones	1.00
SS11	Ken Griffey Jr.	2.00
SS12	Gary Sheffield	.50

Milestone The Art of Hitting

		NM/M
Complete Set (12):		10.00
Common Player:		.50
Inserted 1:5		
AH1	Tony Gwynn	1.50
AH2	Manny Ramirez	1.00
AH3	Todd Helton	1.00
AH4	Nomar Garciaparra	1.00
AH5	Vladimir Guerrero	1.00
AH6	Ichiro Suzuki	1.50
AH7	Darin Erstad	.50
AH8	Alex Rodriguez	2.50
AH9	Carlos Delgado	.75
AH10	Edgar Martinez	.50
AH11	Luis Gonzalez	.50
AH12	Barry Bonds	3.00

Milestone The Trophy Room

		NM/M
Complete Set (6):		8.00
Common Player:		1.00
Inserted 1:10		
TR1	Sammy Sosa	1.50
TR2	Jason Giambi	1.00
TR3	Todd Helton	1.00
TR4	Alex Rodriguez	2.50
TR5	Mark McGwire	2.50
TR6	Ken Griffey Jr.	2.00

Milestone P.O.A. Milestone Bat

		NM/M
Common Player:		5.00
Golds:		3-5X
Production 35 Sets		
JB	Jeff Bagwell	8.00
BB	Barry Bonds	20.00
RB	Russell Branyan	5.00
RC	Jeromy Burnitz	5.00
RC	Roger Clemens	20.00
DE	Darin Erstad	5.00
LG	Luis Gonzalez	5.00
KG	Ken Griffey Jr.	12.00
TH	Todd Helton	8.00
Chj	Chipper Jones	10.00
MP	Mike Piazza	10.00
CR	Cal Ripken Jr.	30.00
AR	Alex Rodriguez	15.00
GS	Gary Sheffield	5.00
SS	Sammy Sosa	10.00
IS	Ichiro Suzuki/203	80.00
FT	Frank Thomas	8.00
JT	Jim Thome	8.00

Milestone P.O.A. Autograph Bat

Gonzalez tied a Major League record with 13 HR in April 2001.

		NM/M
Common Autograph:		15.00
Inserted 1:100		
RB	Russell Branyan	15.00
CD	Carlos Delgado/97	35.00
JDr	J.D. Drew	20.00
JDy	Jermaine Dye	15.00
LG	Luis Gonzalez	20.00
JK	Jason Kendall	15.00
JK	Jeff Kent/194	35.00
AR	Alex Rodriguez/97	120.00
GS	Gary Sheffield/194	40.00
IS	Ichiro Suzuki/53	800.00
MT	Miguel Tejada	40.00
JV	Jose Vidro	15.00
PW	Preston Wilson	15.00

Milestone P.O.A. BFH Bat

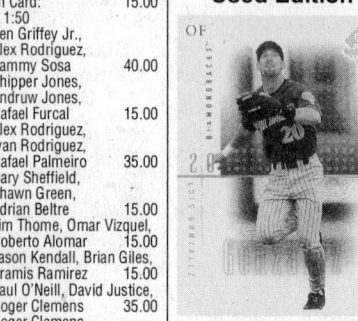

		NM/M
Common Player:		5.00
Golds:		2-3X
Production 35 Sets		
BB	Barry Bonds	20.00
RC	Roger Clemens/203	25.00
CD	Carlos Delgado	5.00
JG	Jason Giambi	5.00
KG	Ken Griffey Jr.	15.00
TGw	Tony Gwynn	15.00
GM	Greg Maddux	12.00
EM	Edgar Martinez	6.00
FM	Fred McGriff	6.00
RP	Rafael Palmeiro	8.00
MP	Mike Piazza	10.00
CR	Cal Ripken Jr.	30.00
AR	Alex Rodriguez	15.00
IR	Ivan Rodriguez	8.00
SS	Sammy Sosa	10.00

Milestone P.O.A. Int. Conn. Bat

Roberto Alomar • Indians

		NM/M
Common Player:		5.00
Golds:		3-5X
Production 35 Sets		
RA	Roberto Alomar	6.00
AB	Adrian Beltre	5.00
RF	Rafael Furcal	5.00
JG	Juan Gonzalez	6.00
AJ	Andruw Jones	8.00
PM	Pedro Martinez	10.00
HN	Hideo Nomo/203	40.00
MO	Magglio Ordonez	5.00

CP	Chan Ho Park	5.00
JP	Jorge Posada	10.00
AP	Albert Pujols	70.00
MR	Manny Ramirez	8.00
TS	Tsuyoshi Shinjo	8.00
IS	Ichiro Suzuki/273	80.00
MT	Miguel Tejada	6.00
OV	Omar Vizquel	5.00

Milestone P.O.A. Triple Bat

		NM/M
Common Card:		15.00
Inserted 1:50		
GRS	Ken Griffey Jr., Alex Rodriguez, Sammy Sosa	40.00
JJF	Chipper Jones, Andruw Jones, Rafael Furcal	15.00
RRP	Alex Rodriguez, Ivan Rodriguez, Rafael Palmeiro	35.00
SGB	Gary Sheffield, Shawn Green, Adrian Beltre	15.00
TVA	Jim Thome, Omar Vizquel, Roberto Alomar	15.00
KGR	Jason Kendall, Brian Giles, Aramis Ramirez	15.00
OJC	Paul O'Neill, David Justice, Roger Clemens	35.00
CMG	Roger Clemens, Greg Maddux, Tom Glavine	40.00
VSA	Robin Ventura, Tsuyoshi Shinjo, Edgardo Alfonzo	15.00
OTA	Magglio Ordonez, Frank Thomas, Sandy Alomar	15.00
PWS	Kirby Puckett, Dave Winfield, Ozzie Smith	25.00
GRB	Tony Gwynn, Cal Ripken Jr., Barry Bonds	60.00
GBM	Ken Griffey Jr., Barry Bonds, Fred McGriff	35.00
SFR	Alfonso Soriano, Rafael Furcal, Alex Ramirez	25.00

Milestone P.O.A. Quad Bat

		NM/M
Common Card:		15.00
Inserted 1:50		
TVAL	Jim Thome, Omar Vizquel, Roberto Alomar, Kenny Lofton	25.00
RRPM	Alex Rodriguez, Ivan Rodriguez, Rafael Palmeiro, Ruben Mateo	50.00
OJCP	Paul O'Neill, David Justice, Roger Clemens, Jorge Posada	60.00
JJFM	Chipper Jones, Andruw Jones, Rafael Furcal, Greg Maddux	40.00
PWSG	Kirby Puckett, Dave Winfield, Ozzie Smith, Steve Garvey	30.00
GRSB	Ken Griffey Jr., Alex Rodriguez, Sammy Sosa, Barry Bonds	80.00
SGBP	Gary Sheffield, Shawn Green, Adrian Beltre, Chan Ho Park	15.00
GGRR	Ken Griffey Jr., Ken Griffey Jr., Alex Rodriguez, Alex Rodriguez	65.00
GRBM	Tony Gwynn, Cal Ripken Jr., Barry Bonds, Fred McGriff	70.00
TDTA	Frank Thomas, Jermaine Dye, Jim Thome, Roberto Alomar	25.00
GHSK	Luis Gonzalez, Todd Helton, Gary Sheffield, Jeff Kent	20.00
GDBS	Ken Griffey Jr., J.D. Drew, Jeromy Burnitz, Sammy Sosa	50.00

JVBW	Chipper Jones, Robin Ventura, Pat Burrell, Preston Wilson	30.00
RGGM	Alex Rodriguez, Troy Glaus, Jason Giambi, Edgar Martinez	40.00
ONRD	Paul O'Neill, Hideo Nomo, Cal Ripken Jr., Carlos Delgado	80.00

2001 SP Game-Used Edition

		NM/M
Common Player:		.50
Common SP (61-90):		5.00
Production 500		
Pack (3):		30.00
Box (6):		150.00
1	Garret Anderson	.50
2	Troy Glaus	1.00
3	Darin Erstad	.75
4	Jason Giambi	1.50
5	Tim Hudson	.75
6	Johnny Damon	.50
7	Carlos Delgado	1.00
8	Greg Vaughn	.50
9	Juan Gonzalez	.75
10	Roberto Alomar	1.00
11	Jim Thome	1.50
12	Edgar Martinez	.50
13	Cal Ripken Jr.	5.00
14	Andres Galarraga	.50
15	Alex Rodriguez	4.00
16	Rafael Palmeiro	1.25
17	Ivan Rodriguez	1.50
18	Manny Ramirez	1.50
19	Nomar Garciaparra	1.50
20	Pedro Martinez	2.00
21	Jermaine Dye	.50
22	Dean Palmer	.50
23	Matt Lawton	.50
24	Frank Thomas	1.50
25	David Wells	.50
26	Magglio Ordonez	.50
27	Derek Jeter	5.00
28	Bernie Williams	.50
29	Roger Clemens	4.00
30	Jeff Bagwell	1.50
31	Richard Hidalgo	.50
32	Chipper Jones	2.00
33	Andruw Jones	1.50
34	Greg Maddux	3.00
35	Jeffrey Hammonds	.50
36	Mark McGwire	4.00
37	Jim Edmonds	.75
38	Sammy Sosa	2.00
39	Corey Patterson	.50
40	Randy Johnson	1.50
41	Luis Gonzalez	.50
42	Gary Sheffield	.75
43	Shawn Green	.50
44	Kevin Brown	.50
45	Vladimir Guerrero	1.50
46	Barry Bonds	5.00
47	Jeff Kent	.75
48	Preston Wilson	.50
49	Charles Johnson	.50
50	Mike Piazza	2.00
51	Edgardo Alfonzo	.50
52	Tony Gwynn	2.00
53	Scott Rolen	1.50
54	Pat Burrell	1.00
55	Brian Giles	.50
56	Jason Kendall	.50
57	Ken Griffey Jr.	3.00
58	Mike Hampton	.50
59	Todd Helton	1.50
60	Larry Walker	.75
61	Wilson Betemit RC	10.00
62	Travis Hafner RC	20.00
63	Ichiro Suzuki RC	60.00
64	Juan Diaz RC	5.00
65	Morgan Ensberg RC	15.00
66	Horacio Ramirez RC	10.00
67	Ricardo Rodriguez RC	5.00
68	Sean Douglass RC	5.00
69	Brandon Duckworth RC	5.00
70	Jackson Melian RC	5.00
71	Adrian Hernandez RC	5.00
72	Kyle Kessel RC	5.00
73	Jason Michaels RC	5.00
74	Esix Snead RC	5.00
75	Jason Smith RC	5.00
76	Tyler Walker RC	5.00
77	Juan Uribe RC	8.00

78	Adam Pettyjohn RC	5.00
79	Tsuyoshi Shinjo RC	5.00
80	Mike Penney RC	5.00
81	Josh Towers RC	5.00
82	Erick Almonte RC	5.00
83	Ryan Freel RC	5.00
84	Juan Pena	5.00
85	Albert Pujols RC	220.00
86	Henry Mateo RC	5.00
87	Greg Miller RC	5.00
88	Jose Mieses RC	5.00
89	Jack Wilson RC	10.00
90	Carlos Valderrama RC	5.00

Authentic Fabric Jersey

		NM/M
Common Player:		4.00
Inserted 1:1		
EA	Edgardo Alfonzo	4.00
RA	Roberto Alomar	6.00
RA	Rick Ankiel	4.00
TB	Tony Batista/SP	8.00
BB	Barry Bonds	25.00
KB	Kevin Brown	6.00
JB	Jeromy Burnitz	4.00
PB	Pat Burrell	4.00
JC(B)	Jose Canseco/BLC	8.00
JC(H)	Jose Canseco/Yanks	8.00
EC	Eric Chavez	4.00
JCi	Jeff Cirillo	4.00
RC	Roger Clemens	20.00
CD	Carlos Delgado/SP	10.00
JDi	Joe DiMaggio/SP/50	160.00
JDr	J.D. Drew	5.00
JDy	Jermaine Dye/SP	6.00
JE	Jim Edmonds	6.00
DE	Darin Erstad	5.00
JG	Jason Giambi	8.00
BG	Brian Giles/SP	8.00
TGI	Troy Glaus	6.00
ToG	Tom Glavine	6.00
LG	Luis Gonzalez	6.00
MG	Mark Grace	8.00
SG	Shawn Green	6.00
KG(H)	Ken Griffey/Reds	12.00
KG(M)	Ken Griffey/M's	12.00
KG(R)	Ken Griffey/Reds	12.00
TGw	Tony Gwynn	10.00
MH	Mike Hampton	4.00
THe	Todd Helton	8.00
TrH	Trevor Hoffman	4.00
TH	Tim Hudson	4.00
AH	Aubrey Huff	4.00
JI	J. Isringhausen/SP	8.00
CJo	Charles Johnson	4.00
RJ	Randy Johnson	10.00
AJ	Andruw Jones	8.00
CJ	Chipper Jones	10.00
JK	Jason Kendall	4.00
JK	Jeff Kent	5.00
BL	Barry Larkin	6.00
AL	Al Leiter	4.00
KL	Kenny Lofton	4.00
TL	Terrence Long	4.00
GM	Greg Maddux	10.00
MM	Mickey Mantle/SP/50	250.00
RM	Roger Maris/SP	75.00
EM	Edgar Martinez	6.00
TM	Tino Martinez	6.00
FM	Fred McGriff	5.00
KM	Kevin Millwood	5.00
PN	Phil Nevin	4.00
JO	John Olerud	5.00
MO	Magglio Ordonez	6.00
AP	Adam Piatt	4.00
CR	Cal Ripken Jr.	25.00
MR	Mariano Rivera	6.00
AR(H)	Alex Rodriguez/Rangers	10.00
AR(M)	Alex Rodriguez/M's	10.00
IR	Ivan Rodriguez	10.00
SR	Scott Rolen	5.00
NR	Nolan Ryan/SP/50	50.00
TS	Tom Seaver/SP/50	30.00
GS	Gary Sheffield	6.00
SS(H)	Sammy Sosa	15.00
SS(M)	Sammy Sosa	15.00
FTa	Fernando Tatis	4.00
MT	Miguel Tejada	4.00
FTh	Frank Thomas	8.00
JT	Jim Thome	8.00
GV	Greg Vaughn	4.00
RV	Robin Ventura	4.00
JV	Jose Vidro	4.00

DW	David Wells/SP	8.00
MW	Matt Williams	5.00
PW	Preston Wilson	4.00
DY	Dmitri Young	4.00
TZ	Todd Zeile	4.00

2-Player Authentic Fabric Jersey

		NM/M
Common Card:		25.00
Production 50 Sets		
R-R	Alex Rodriguez, Ivan Rodriguez	50.00
M-D	Mickey Mantle, Joe DiMaggio	400.00
M-M	Mickey Mantle, Roger Maris	400.00
R-S	Nolan Ryan, Tom Seaver	100.00
B-C	Barry Bonds, Jose Canseco	70.00
S-G	Gary Sheffield, Shawn Green	25.00
J-J	Chipper Jones, Andruw Jones	40.00
C-W	Roger Clemens, Bernie Williams	40.00
J-R	Randy Johnson, Nolan Ryan	75.00
S-T	Sammy Sosa, Frank Thomas	35.00
G-S	Ken Griffey Jr., Sammy Sosa	50.00
G-R	Ken Griffey Jr., Alex Rodriguez	50.00
S-R	Sammy Sosa, Alex Rodriguez	40.00
H-G	Tim Hudson, Jason Giambi	30.00

3-Player Authentic Fabric Jersey

		NM/M
Production 25 Sets		
G-R-S	Ken Griffey Jr., Alex Rodriguez, Sammy Sosa	100.00
M-J-J	Greg Maddux, Chipper Jones, Andruw Jones	80.00
J-B-S	Andruw Jones, Barry Bonds, Sammy Sosa	120.00
J-S-M	Randy Johnson, Tom Seaver, Greg Maddux	80.00

Authentic Fabric Jersey Autograph

		NM/M
Production 50 Sets		
EA	Edgardo Alfonzo	25.00
RA	Rick Ankiel	15.00
BB	Barry Bonds/50	200.00
JC	Jose Canseco	40.00
CD	Carlos Delgado/50	40.00
JDr	J.D. Drew/50	40.00
JG	Jason Giambi/50	40.00
TGl	Troy Glaus/50	50.00
KG	Ken Griffey Jr.	150.00
TH	Tim Hudson/50	50.00
RJ	Randy Johnson	100.00
AJ	Andruw Jones	50.00
CJ	Chipper Jones	80.00
CR	Cal Ripken/50	200.00
AR	Alex Rodriguez	150.00
IR	Ivan Rodriguez	75.00
NR	Nolan Ryan/50	200.00
TS	Tom Seaver/50	80.00
SS	Sammy Sosa/50	120.00
FTh	Frank Thomas	75.00
DW	David Wells/50	25.00

2001 SP Legendary Cuts

		NM/M
Complete Set (90):		25.00
Common Player:		.40
Pack (4):		16.00
Box (18):		250.00
1	Al Simmons	.40
2	Jimmie Foxx (Height, weight and birthplace incorrect.)	1.00

TOM SEAVER
1967 1986

3	Mickey Cochrane	.40
4	Phil Niekro	.40
5	Eddie Mathews	1.00
6	Gary Matthews	.40
7	Hank Aaron	2.50
8	Joe Adcock	.40
9	Warren Spahn	.75
10	George Sisler	.40
11	Stan Musial	1.00
12	Dizzy Dean	.75
13	Frankie Frisch	.40
14	Harvey Haddix	.40
15	Johnny Mize	.75
16	Ken Boyer	.40
17	Rogers Hornsby	.75
18	Cap Anson	.40
19	Andre Dawson	.40
20	Billy Williams	.40
21	Billy Herman	.40
22	Hack Wilson	.40
23	Ron Santo	.40
24	Ryne Sandberg	1.50
25	Ernie Banks	1.50
26	Burleigh Grimes	.40
27	Don Drysdale	.75
28	Gil Hodges	.40
29	Jackie Robinson	2.00
30	Tommy Lasorda	.40
31	Pee Wee Reese	.40
32	Roy Campanella	.75
33	Tommy Davis	.40
34	Branch Rickey	.40
35	Leo Durocher	.75
36	Walt Alston	.40
37	Bill Terry	.40
38	Carl Hubbell	.40
39	Eddie Stanky	.40
40	George Kelly	.40
41	Mel Ott	.75
42	Juan Marichal	.40
43	Rube Marquard	.40
44	Travis Jackson	.40
45	Bob Feller	.40
46	Earl Averill	.40
47	Elmer Flick	.40
48	Ken Keltner	.40
49	Lou Boudreau	.40
50	Early Wynn	.40
51	Satchel Paige	1.50
52	Ron Hunt	.40
53	Tom Seaver	1.00
54	Richie Ashburn	.40
55	Mike Schmidt	1.00
56	Honus Wagner	1.00
57	Lloyd Waner	.40
58	Max Carey	.40
59	Paul Waner	.40
60	Roberto Clemente	2.50
61	Nolan Ryan	3.00
62	Bobby Doerr	.40
63	Carlton Fisk	.75
64	Joe Cronin	.40
65	Smokey Joe Wood	.40
66	Tony Conigliaro	.40
67	Edd Roush	.40
68	Johnny Vander Meer	.40
69	Walter Johnson	.75
70	Charlie Gehringer	.40
71	Al Kaline	1.00
72	Ty Cobb	2.00
73	Tony Oliva	.40
74	Luke Appling	.40
75	Minnie Minoso	.40
76	Nellie Fox	.40
77	Shoeless Joe Jackson	2.00
78	Babe Ruth	3.00
79	Bill Dickey	.40
80	Elston Howard	.40
81	Joe DiMaggio	2.50
82	Lefty Gomez	.40
83	Lou Gehrig	2.50
84	Mickey Mantle	3.00
85	Reggie Jackson	1.00
86	Roger Maris	1.00
87	Whitey Ford	.40
88	Waite Hoyt	.40
89	Yogi Berra	1.00
90	Casey Stengel	.40

Bat

		NM/M
Common Player:		4.00
Inserted 1:18		
HA	Hank Aaron/SP	40.00
YB	Yogi Berra	10.00
WB	Wade Boggs	8.00
GB	George Brett	15.00

RCa	Roy Campanella/SP	40.00
RC	Rico Carty	4.00
RCl	Roberto Clemente	60.00
TC	Ty Cobb/SP	125.00
KC	Kiki Cuyler	8.00
TD	Tommy Davis/SP	40.00
AD	Andre Dawson	8.00
JD	Joe DiMaggio/SP	100.00
DD	Don Drysdale/SP	25.00
CF	Carlton Fisk	10.00
NF	Nellie Fox	10.00
JF	Jimmie Foxx	40.00
GH	Gil Hodges/SP	40.00
THo	Tommy Holmes (Photo on front is Eddie Mathews.)	8.00
RJ	Reggie Jackson	15.00
DJ	Davey Johnson	.75
MM	Mickey Mantle/SP	120.00
RM	Roger Maris/SP	60.00
EM	Eddie Mathews	25.00
WMc	Willie McCovey	75.00
PM	Paul Molitor	15.00
MM	Manny Mota	4.00
MO	Mel Ott/SP	50.00
VP	Vada Pinson	4.00
JR	Jackie Robinson/SP	75.00
BR	Babe Ruth/SP	165.00
NR	Nolan Ryan/SP	40.00
RS	Ryne Sandberg	20.00
AS	Al Simmons/SP	25.00
BT	Bill Terry/SP	25.00
MW	Maury Wills	8.00
RY	Robin Yount	15.00

Combo Bat

23/25

No pricing due to scarcity.
Production 25 Sets

Debut Bat

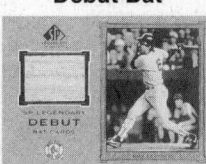

		NM/M
Common Player:		5.00
Inserted 1:18		
JA	Joe Adcock/SP	15.00
LA	Luke Appling/SP	25.00
RA	Richie Ashburn/SP	25.00
BB	Bobby Bonds	5.00
LB	Lou Boudreau	10.00
KB	Ken Boyer/SP	15.00
BB	Bill Buckner	5.00
MC	Mickey Cochrane	60.00
TC	Tony Conigliaro/SP	15.00
JC	Joe Cronin	10.00
BD	Bobby Doerr/SP	15.00
BF	Bob Feller/SP	15.00
BF	Bill Freehan	5.00
FF	Frankie Frisch/SP	15.00
CG	Charlie Gehringer	15.00
BH	Billy Herman/SP	15.00
WH	Willie Horton	6.00
EH	Elston Howard/SP	15.00
RH	Ron Hunt	5.00
JJ	Joe Jackson	300.00
GL	Greg Luzinski	5.00
GM	Gary Matthews	5.00
MM	Minnie Minoso/SP	15.00
TO	Tony Oliva	8.00
WP	Wes Parker	5.00
BR	Bobby Richardson/SP	15.00
SS	Steve Sax	5.00
GS	George Sisler	20.00
ES	Eddie Stanky	5.00
AT	Alan Trammell	5.00
PW	Paul Waner/SP	60.00
HW	Hack Wilson/SP	70.00
SY	Steve Yeager	5.00

Game Jersey

		NM/M
Common Player:		5.00

ABBREVIATIONS

SP - Short Print

Inserted 1:18		
YB	Yogi Berra	15.00
WB	Wade Boggs	5.00
RC	Roberto Clemente	80.00
TC	Tony Conigliaro	5.00
BD	Bill Dickey	25.00
JD	Joe DiMaggio/SP	350.00
LD	Leo Durocher	8.00
WF	Whitey Ford	15.00
NF	Nellie Fox	8.00
JF	Jim Fregosi	5.00
GH	Gil Hodges	10.00
THo	Tommy Holmes	5.00
RJ	Reggie Jackson	15.00
TK	Ted Kluszewski	5.00
BL	Bob Lemon	5.00
VL	Vic Lombardi	5.00
MM	Mickey Mantle/SP	275.00
JM	Juan Marichal	10.00
RM	Roger Maris/SP	150.00
WM	Willie McCovey	10.00
JN	Joe Nuxhall	8.00
GP	Gaylord Perry	5.00
BR	Bobby Richardson	5.00
BRo	Brooks Robinson	5.00
BR	Babe Ruth/SP	600.00
NR	Nolan Ryan	100.00
TS	Tom Seaver/SP	40.00
CS	Casey Stengel	15.00
BT	Bobby Thomson	5.00
HW	Honus Wagner/SP	750.00
BW	Billy Williams	6.00
MW	Maury Wills	5.00
RY	Robin Yount	15.00

Signatures

267/73

		NM/M
Inserted 1:252		
WA	Walt Alston/34	175.00
CA	Cap Anson/2 (11/01 auction)	10,000
LA	Luke Appling/45	205.00
EA	Earl Averill/189	100.00
EB	E.G. Barrow/16	600.00
MC	Max Carey/73	145.00
TC	Ty Cobb/24	2,500
JC	Jocko Conlan/12	1,200
SC	Stanley Coveleski/42	315.00
JC	Joe Cronin/12	1,200
KC	Kiki Cuyler/6	4,000
DDe	Dizzy Dean/56	410.00
BD	Bill Dickey/28	275.00
JD	Joe DiMaggio/25	650.00
JD	Joe DiMaggio/395	395.00
JD	Joe DiMaggio/150	400.00
JD	Joe DiMaggio/275	285.00
DDr	Don Drysdale/12	1,500
LD	Leo Durocher/45	260.00
RF	Rick Ferrell/8	750.00
EF	Elmer Flick/22	400.00
NF	Nellie Fox/9	750.00
JF	Jimmie Foxx/16	2,500
FF	Ford Frick/21	750.00
FF	Frankie Frisch/3	3,500
LGe	Lou Gehrig/7	6,000
WG	Warren Giles/10	800.00
LGo	Lefty Gomez/85	195.00
BG	Burleigh Grimes/18	500.00
LG	Lefty Grove/34	600.00
HH	Harvey Haddix/4	3,000
BH	Bucky Harris/10	750.00
GH	Gabby Hartnett/32	380.00
BH	Billy Herman/88	140.00
GH	Gil Hodges/6	1,050
HH	Harry Hooper/14	800.00
WH	Waite Hoyt/38	245.00
CH	Carl Hubbell/30	375.00
TJ	Travis Jackson/35	225.00
JJ	Judy Johnson/9	650.00
WJ	Walter Johnson/113	510.00
CK	Charlie Keller/16	365.00
GK	George Kelly/4	140.00
KK	Ken Keltner/11	500.00
MK	Mark Koenig/30	275.00
BL	Bob Lemon/23	225.00
EL	Eddie Lopat/22	275.00
TL	Ted Lyons/59	185.00
SM	Sal Maglie/19	400.00
MM	Mickey Mantle/8	5,000
HM	Heinie Manush/50	185.00
RoM	Roger Maris/73	1,675
RuM	Rube Marquard/23	375.00
JMc	Joe McCarthy/40	340.00
JM	Joe Medwick/15	750.00
BM	Bob Meusel/23	400.00
JMi	Johnny Mize/84	160.00

MO	Mel Ott/8	4,000
SP	Satchel Paige/36	900.00
RP	Roger Peckinpaugh/45	200.00
VR	Vic Raschi/26	175.00
BRi	Branch Rickey/16	1,350
JR	Jackie Robinson/147	530.00
ER	Edd Roush/83	170.00
RR	Red Ruffing/5	2,250
BRu	Babe Ruth/7	9,000
GS	George Selkirk/15	450.00
JS	Joe Sewell/55	130.00
RS	Rip Sewell/39	155.00
BS	Bob Shawkey/39	165.00
CS	Casey Stengel/10	1,500
BT	Bill Terry/184	125.00
VM	Johnny Vander Meer/65	125.00
HW	Honus Wagner/24	2,200
BW	Bucky Walters/13	400.00
LW	Lloyd Waner/217	105.00
PW	Paul Waner/4	2,250
HW	Hack Wilson/4	6,000
JW	Smokey Joe Wood/43	215.00

2001 SPx Sample

GRIFFEY JR

To introduce the annual SPx brand, Upper Deck issued this sample card of spokesman Ken Griffey Jr. The card is in the same format as the later-issued version, but has a large red "SAMPLE" overprinted diagonally on back.

		NM/M
001	Ken Griffey Jr.	5.00

2001 SPx

RIPKEN

		NM/M
Complete Set (150):		
Common Player:		.25
Common Young Star (91-120):		4.00
Production 2,000		
Common Prospect Jersey (121-135):		6.00
Common Prosp. Auto. Jersey (136-150):		10.00
Pack (4):		18.00
Box (18):		280.00
1	Darin Erstad	.50
2	Troy Glaus	.50
3	Mo Vaughn	.25
4	Johnny Damon	1.00
5	Jason Giambi	.75
6	Tim Hudson	.50
7	Miguel Tejada	.50
8	Carlos Delgado	.75
9	Raul Mondesi	.25
10	Tony Batista	.25
11	Ben Grieve	.25
12	Greg Vaughn	.25
13	Juan Gonzalez	.75
14	Jim Thome	.75
15	Roberto Alomar	.50
16	John Olerud	.25
17	Edgar Martinez	.25
18	Albert Belle	.25
19	Cal Ripken Jr.	3.00
20	Ivan Rodriguez	.75
21	Rafael Palmeiro	.75
22	Alex Rodriguez	2.50
23	Nomar Garciaparra	1.50

24	Pedro J. Martinez	1.00
25	Manny Ramirez	1.00
26	Jermaine Dye	.25
27	Mark Quinn	.25
28	Carlos Beltran	.75
29	Tony Clark	.25
30	Bobby Higginson	.25
31	Eric Milton	.25
32	Matt Lawton	.25
33	Frank Thomas	1.00
34	Magglio Ordonez	.25
35	Ray Durham	.25
36	David Wells	.25
37	Derek Jeter	3.00
38	Bernie Williams	.50
39	Roger Clemens	1.00
40	David Justice	.25
41	Jeff Bagwell	.75
42	Richard Hidalgo	.25
43	Moises Alou	.40
44	Chipper Jones	1.00
45	Andruw Jones	1.00
46	Greg Maddux	2.00
47	Rafael Furcal	.50
48	Jeromy Burnitz	.25
49	Geoff Jenkins	.25
50	Mark McGwire	2.00
51	Jim Edmonds	.50
52	Rick Ankiel	.25
53	Edgar Renteria	.25
54	Sammy Sosa	1.50
55	Kerry Wood	.50
56	Rondell White	.25
57	Randy Johnson	1.00
58	Steve Finley	.25
59	Matt Williams	.25
60	Luis Gonzalez	.25
61	Kevin Brown	.25
62	Gary Sheffield	.50
63	Shawn Green	.50
64	Vladimir Guerrero	1.00
65	Jose Vidro	.25
66	Barry Bonds	3.00
67	Jeff Kent	.40
68	Livan Hernandez	.25
69	Preston Wilson	.25
70	Charles Johnson	.25
71	Cliff Floyd	.25
72	Mike Piazza	1.50
73	Edgardo Alfonzo	.25
74	Jay Payton	.25
75	Robin Ventura	.25
76	Tony Gwynn	1.50
77	Phil Nevin	.25
78	Ryan Klesko	.25
79	Scott Rolen	.75
80	Pat Burrell	.50
81	Bob Abreu	.50
82	Brian Giles	.25
83	Kris Benson	.25
84	Jason Kendall	.25
85	Ken Griffey Jr.	2.00
86	Barry Larkin	.50
87	Sean Casey	.40
88	Todd Helton	.75
89	Larry Walker	.25
90	Mike Hampton	.25
91	Billy Sylvester RC	4.00
92	Josh Towers RC	8.00
93	Zach Day RC	6.00
94	Martin Vargas RC	4.00
95	Adam Pettyjohn RC	4.00
96	Andres Torres RC	4.00
97	Kris Keller RC	4.00
98	Blaine Neal RC	4.00
99	Kyle Kessel RC	4.00
100	Greg Miller RC	4.00
101	Shawn Sonnier RC	4.00
102	Alexis Gomez RC	4.00
103	Grant Balfour RC	4.00
104	Henry Mateo RC	4.00
105	Wilkin Ruan RC	4.00
106	Nick Maness RC	4.00
107	Jason Michaels RC	4.00
108	Esix Snead RC	4.00
109	William Ortega RC	4.00
110	David Elder RC	4.00
111	Jackson Melian RC	4.00
112	Nate Teut RC	4.00
113	Jason Smith RC	4.00
114	Mike Penney RC	4.00
115	Jose Mieses RC	4.00
116	Juan Pena	4.00
117	Brian Lawrence RC	6.00
118	Jeremy Owens RC	6.00
119	Carlos Valderrama RC	4.00
120	Rafael Soriano RC	6.00
121	Horacio Ramirez RC	10.00
122	Ricardo Rodriguez RC	6.00
123	Juan Diaz RC	6.00
124	Donnie Bridges RC	6.00
125	Tyler Walker RC	6.00
126	Erick Almonte RC	6.00
127	Jesus Colome RC	6.00
128	Ryan Freel RC	6.00
129	Elpidio Guzman RC	6.00
130	Jack Cust	6.00
131	Eric Hinske RC	10.00
132	Josh Fogg RC	6.00
133	Juan Uribe RC	10.00
134	Bert Snow RC	6.00
135	Pedro Feliz	6.00
136	Wilson Betemit RC	30.00
137	Sean Douglass RC	10.00
138	Dernell Stenson	10.00
139	Brandon Inge RC	10.00
140	Morgan Ensberg RC	35.00
141	Brian Cole	10.00

142	Adrian Hernandez RC	10.00
143	Brandon Duckworth RC	10.00
144	Jack Wilson RC	15.00
145	Travis Hafner RC	125.00
146	Carlos Pena	10.00
147	Corey Patterson	15.00
148	Xavier Nady	10.00
149	Jason Hart	10.00
150	Ichiro Suzuki RC	750.00

Spectrum

Stars (1-90): 10-20X
SP's (91-120): 1-1.5X
Production 50 Sets

Foundations

	NM/M
Complete Set (12):	15.00
Common Player:	1.00

Inserted 1:8

F1	Mark McGwire	3.00
F2	Jeff Bagwell	1.00
F3	Alex Rodriguez	3.00
F4	Ken Griffey Jr.	2.00
F5	Andruw Jones	1.00
F6	Cal Ripken Jr.	4.00
F7	Barry Bonds	4.00
F8	Derek Jeter	4.00
F9	Frank Thomas	1.00
F10	Sammy Sosa	2.00
F11	Tony Gwynn	1.50
F12	Vladimir Guerrero	1.50

SPXcitement

	NM/M
Complete Set (12):	15.00
Common Player:	.75

Inserted 1:8

X1	Alex Rodriguez	3.00
X2	Jason Giambi	.75
X3	Ken Griffey Jr.	2.00
X4	Sammy Sosa	1.50
X5	Frank Thomas	1.00
X6	Todd Helton	1.00
X7	Mark McGwire	2.00
X8	Mike Piazza	1.50
X9	Derek Jeter	1.50
X10	Vladimir Guerrero	1.50
X11	Carlos Delgado	.75
X12	Chipper Jones	1.50

Untouchable Talents

	NM/M
Complete Set (6):	10.00

Inserted 1:15

UT1	Ken Griffey Jr.	2.00
UT2	Mike Piazza	2.00
UT3	Mark McGwire	2.50
UT4	Alex Rodriguez	2.50
UT5	Sammy Sosa	1.50
UT6	Derek Jeter	3.00

Winning Materials Base

	NM/M
Common Duo:	40.00

Production 50
Trios: No Pricing
Production 25

MG	Mark McGwire, Ken Griffey Jr.	40.00
MS	Mark McGwire, Sammy Sosa	50.00
MR	Mark McGwire, Alex Rodriguez	40.00
GJ	Nomar Garciaparra, Derek Jeter	50.00
TR	Frank Thomas, Alex Rodriguez	40.00
JG	Derek Jeter, Jason Giambi	40.00
PB	Mike Piazza, Barry Bonds	40.00
RJ	Alex Rodriguez, Derek Jeter	50.00
PM	Mike Piazza, Mark McGwire	40.00
JP	Derek Jeter, Mike Piazza	40.00
MGS	Mark McGwire, Ken Griffey Jr., Sammy Sosa	80.00
JRG	Derek Jeter, Alex Rodriguez, Nomar Garciaparra	100.00
PJW	Mike Piazza, Derek Jeter, Bernie Williams	80.00
BMS	Barry Bonds, Mark McGwire, Sammy Sosa	100.00
GJR	Ken Griffey Jr., Derek Jeter, Alex Rodriguez	100.00

Winning Materials Base/Ball

	NM/M
Common Player:	10.00

Production 250 Sets

BB	Barry Bonds	50.00
NG	Nomar Garciaparra	20.00
KG	Ken Griffey Jr.	30.00
VG	Vladimir Guerrero	15.00
DJ	Derek Jeter	50.00
AJ	Andruw Jones	10.00
CJ	Chipper Jones	15.00
PM	Pedro Martinez	15.00
MM	Mark McGwire	75.00
MP	Mike Piazza	20.00
AR	Alex Rodriguez	20.00
SS	Sammy Sosa	15.00
FT	Frank Thomas	15.00

Winning Materials Jersey Combo

	NM/M
Common Duo:	25.00

Production 50
Common Trio:
Production 25

KG-AR	Ken Griffey Jr., Alex Rodriguez	50.00
KG-BB	Ken Griffey Jr., Barry Bonds	50.00
KG-RJ	Ken Griffey Jr., Randy Johnson	50.00
CJ-DW	Chipper Jones, David Wells	25.00
BB-SS	Barry Bonds, Sammy Sosa	50.00
KG-JD	Ken Griffey Jr., Joe DiMaggio	180.00
KG-SS	Ken Griffey Jr., Sammy Sosa	50.00
SS-CD	Sammy Sosa, Carlos Delgado	25.00
SS-FT	Sammy Sosa, Frank Thomas	25.00
IR-AR	Ivan Rodriguez, Alex Rodriguez	40.00
AR-CR	Alex Rodriguez, Cal Ripken Jr.	60.00
AJ-CJ	Andruw Jones, Chipper Jones	25.00
KG-KG	Ken Griffey Jr., Ken Griffey Jr.	40.00
G-R-B	Ken Griffey Jr., Alex Rodriguez, Barry Bonds	100.00
S-G-C	Sammy Sosa, Ken Griffey Jr., Chipper Jones	60.00
B-G-J	Barry Bonds, Ken Griffey Jr., Andruw Jones	100.00
R-R-D	Alex Rodriguez, Ivan Rodriguez, Carlos Delgado	60.00
D-B-S	Carlos Delgado, Barry Bonds, Sammy Sosa	60.00
R-J-D	Cal Ripken Jr., Chipper Jones, Carlos Delgado	100.00

Winning Materials Jersey/Bat

	NM/M
Common Player:	8.00

Inserted 1:18

RA	Rick Ankiel	8.00
BB1	Barry Bonds	25.00
BB2	Barry Bonds	25.00
CD	Carlos Delgado	10.00
JD	Joe DiMaggio	150.00
JE	Jim Edmonds	8.00
KG1	Ken Griffey Jr.	15.00
KG2	Ken Griffey Jr.	15.00
RJ1	Randy Johnson	15.00
RJ2	Randy Johnson	15.00
AJ1	Andruw Jones	10.00
AJ2	Andruw Jones	10.00
CJ1	Chipper Jones	15.00
CJ2	Chipper Jones	15.00
CR	Cal Ripken Jr.	40.00
AR1	Alex Rodriguez	15.00
AR2	Alex Rodriguez	15.00
IR1	Ivan Rodriguez	10.00
IR2	Ivan Rodriguez	10.00
SS	Sammy Sosa	15.00
FT	Frank Thomas	10.00

2002 SP Authentic

	NM/M
Complete Set (170):	
Common Player:	.25
Common SP (91-135):	4.00

Production 1,999
Common SP Auto. (136-170): 10.00
Production 999

Pack (5):	3.50
Box (24):	75.00

1	Troy Glaus	.50
2	Darin Erstad	.40
3	Barry Zito	.40
4	Eric Chavez	.40
5	Tim Hudson	.50
6	Miguel Tejada	.50
7	Carlos Delgado	.60
8	Shannon Stewart	.25
9	Ben Grieve	.25
10	Jim Thome	.75
11	C.C. Sabathia	.25
12	Ichiro Suzuki	2.00
13	Freddy Garcia	.25
14	Edgar Martinez	.25
15	Bret Boone	.25
16	Jeff Conine	.25
17	Alex Rodriguez	2.00
18	Juan Gonzalez	.50
19	Ivan Rodriguez	.75
20	Rafael Palmeiro	.75
21	Hank Blalock	.50
22	Pedro J. Martinez	1.00
23	Manny Ramirez	1.00
24	Nomar Garciaparra	1.00
25	Carlos Beltran	.75
26	Mike Sweeney	.25
27	Randall Simon	.25
28	Dmitri Young	.25
29	Bobby Higginson	.25
30	Corey Koskie	.25
31	Eric Milton	.25
32	Torii Hunter	.50
33	Joe Mays	.25
34	Frank Thomas	.75
35	Mark Buehrle	.40
36	Magglio Ordonez	.25
37	Kenny Lofton	.25
38	Roger Clemens	2.00
39	Derek Jeter	2.50
40	Jason Giambi	.75
41	Bernie Williams	.50
42	Alfonso Soriano	.75
43	Lance Berkman	.50
44	Roy Oswalt	.50
45	Jeff Bagwell	.75
46	Craig Biggio	.50
47	Chipper Jones	1.00
48	Greg Maddux	1.50
49	Gary Sheffield	.50
50	Andruw Jones	.75
51	Ben Sheets	.40
52	Richie Sexson	.50
53	Albert Pujols	2.50
54	Matt Morris	.25
55	J.D. Drew	.40
56	Sammy Sosa	1.00
57	Kerry Wood	.50
58	Corey Patterson	.25
59	Mark Prior	.75
60	Randy Johnson	.75
61	Luis Gonzalez	.40
62	Curt Schilling	.75
63	Shawn Green	.50
64	Kevin Brown	.25
65	Hideo Nomo	.75
66	Vladimir Guerrero	.75
67	Jose Vidro	.25
68	Barry Bonds	2.50
69	Jeff Kent	.40
70	Rich Aurilia	.25
71	Preston Wilson	.25
72	Josh Beckett	.40
73	Mike Lowell	.25
74	Roberto Alomar	.40
75	Mo Vaughn	.25
76	Jeromy Burnitz	.25
77	Mike Piazza	1.50
78	Sean Burroughs	.25
79	Phil Nevin	.25
80	Bobby Abreu	.50
81	Pat Burrell	.40
82	Scott Rolen	.75
83	Jason Kendall	.25
84	Brian Giles	.25
85	Ken Griffey Jr.	1.50
86	Adam Dunn	.75
87	Sean Casey	.40
88	Todd Helton	.75
89	Larry Walker	.25
90	Mike Hampton	.25
91	Brandon Puffer RC	4.00
92	Tom Shearn RC	4.00
93	Chris Baker RC	4.00
94	Gustavo Chacin RC	10.00
95	Joe Orloski RC	4.00
96	Mike Smith RC	4.00
97	John Ennis RC	4.00
98	John Foster RC	4.00
99	Kevin Gryboski RC	4.00
100	Brian Mallette RC	4.00
101	Takahito Nomura RC	4.00
102	So Taguchi RC	10.00
103	Jeremy Lambert RC	4.00
104	Jason Simontacchi RC	4.00
105	Jorge Sosa RC	4.00
106	Brandon Backe RC	8.00
107	P.J. Bevis RC	4.00
108	Jeremy Ward RC	4.00
109	Doug DeVore RC	4.00
110	Ron Chiavacci RC	4.00
111	Ron Calloway RC	4.00
112	Nelson Castro RC	4.00
113	Deivis Santos RC	4.00
114	Earl Snyder RC	4.00
115	Julio Mateo RC	4.00
116	J.J. Putz RC	4.00
117	Allan Simpson RC	4.00
118	Satoru Komiyama RC	4.00
119	Adam Walker RC	4.00
120	Oliver Perez RC	10.00
121	Clifford Bartosh RC	4.00
122	Todd Donovan RC	4.00
123	Elio Serrano RC	4.00
124	Peter Zamora RC	4.00
125	Mike Gonzalez RC	4.00
126	Travis Hughes RC	4.00
127	Jorge de la Rosa RC	4.00
128	Anastacio Martinez RC	4.00
129	Colin Young RC	4.00
130	Nate Field RC	4.00
131	Tim Kalita RC	4.00
132	Julius Matos RC	4.00
133	Terry Pearson RC	4.00
134	Kyle Kane RC	4.00
135	Mitch Wylie RC	4.00
136	Rodrigo Rosario RC	10.00
137	Franklyn German RC	10.00
138	Reed Johnson RC	15.00
139	Luis Martinez RC	10.00
140	Michael Crudale RC	10.00
141	Francis Beltran RC	10.00
142	Steve Kent RC	10.00
143	Felix Escalona RC	10.00
144	Jose Valverde RC	15.00
145	Victor Alvarez RC	10.00
146	Kazuhisa Ishii/249 RC	40.00
147	Jorge Nunez RC	10.00
148	Eric Good RC	10.00
149	Luis Ugueto RC	10.00
150	Matt Thornton RC	10.00
151	Wilson Valdez RC	10.00
152	Hansel Izquierdo/249 RC	25.00
153	Jaime Cerda RC	10.00
154	Mark Corey RC	10.00
155	Tyler Yates RC	10.00
156	Steve Bechler RC	10.00
157	Ben Howard/249 RC	20.00
158	Anderson Machado RC	15.00
159	Jorge Padilla RC	10.00
160	Eric Junge RC	10.00
161	Adrian Burnside RC	10.00
162	Josh Hancock RC	10.00
163	Chris Booker RC	10.00
164	Cam Esslinger RC	10.00
165	Rene Reyes RC	10.00
166	Aaron Cook RC	10.00
167	Juan Brito RC	10.00
168	Miguel Ascencio RC	10.00
169	Kevin Frederick RC	10.00
170	Edwin Almonte RC	10.00

Limited

Stars (1-90): 5-10X
Cards (91-135): .5-1X
Cards (136-170): .5-1X
Production 125 Sets
Golds (1-90): 10-20X
Golds (91-135): .75-1.5X
Golds (136-170): .75-1.5X
Production 50 Sets

Chirography

	NM/M
Common Autograph:	10.00

Inserted 1:72

HB	Hank Blalock/282	25.00
BB	Barry Bonds/112	180.00
BBo	Bret Boone/500	15.00
MB	Milton Bradley/470	15.00
JB	John Buck/427	10.00
MB	Mark Buehrle/438	15.00
SB	Sean Burroughs/275	15.00
AD	Adam Dunn/348	30.00
DE	Darin Erstad/80	15.00
CF	Cliff Floyd/313	15.00
FG	Freddy Garcia/456	15.00
JG	Jason Giambi/244	25.00
TG	Tom Glavine/376	25.00
AG	Alex Graman/418	10.00
KG	Ken Griffey Jr/238	100.00
TG	Tony Gwynn/75	40.00
JL	Jon Lieber/462	15.00
JM	Joe Mays/469	15.00
MM	Mark McGwire/50	300.00
DM	Doug Mientkiewicz/478	15.00
AR	Alex Rodriguez/391	90.00
CS	C.C. Sabathia/442	15.00
RS	Richie Sexson/483	15.00
SS	Sammy Sosa/247	100.00
IS	Ichiro Suzuki/78	350.00
MS	Mike Sweeney/265	15.00
BZ	Barry Zito/419	20.00

Chirography Gold

	NM/M

Quantity produced listed

MB	Mark Buehrle/56	25.00
AD	Adam Dunn/44	40.00
CF	Cliff Floyd/30	20.00
FG	Freddy Garcia/34	35.00
TG	Tom Glavine/47	50.00
AG	Alex Graman/76	15.00
KG	Ken Griffey Jr./30	200.00
JL	Jon Lieber/32	20.00
CS	C.C. Sabathia/52	20.00
MS	Mike Sweeney/29	40.00
BZ	Barry Zito/75	25.00

Excellence

	NM/M

Production 25

AE-1	Ken Griffey Jr., Sammy Sosa, Cal Ripken Jr., Jason Giambi, Mark McGwire, Ichiro Suzuki	1,500

Future USA Watch

	NM/M
Common Player:	4.00

Production 1,999 Sets

USA1	Chad Cordero	5.00
USA2	Philip Humber	10.00
USA3	Grant Johnson	5.00
USA4	Wes Littleton	5.00
USA5	Kyle Sleeth	10.00
USA6	Huston Street	15.00
USA7	Brad Sullivan	5.00
USA8	Bob Zimmermann	5.00
USA9	Abe Alvarez	5.00
USA10	Kyle Bakker	5.00
USA11	Landon Powell	5.00
USA12	Clint Sammons	5.00
USA13	Michael Aubrey	10.00
USA14	Aaron Hill	5.00
USA15	Conor Jackson	20.00
USA16	Eric Patterson	5.00
USA17	Dustin Pedroia	10.00
USA18	Rickie Weeks	25.00
USA19	Shane Costa	5.00
USA20	Mark Jurich	5.00
USA21	Sam Fuld	5.00
USA22	Carlos Quentin	20.00

Game Jerseys

	NM/M
Common Player:	5.00

Inserted 1:24

RA	Roberto Alomar	8.00
JB	Jeff Bagwell	10.00
JB	Jeromy Burnitz/SP	8.00
RC	Roger Clemens	15.00
CD	Carlos Delgado	6.00
JE	Jim Edmonds	8.00
DE	Darin Erstad	8.00
JGi	Jason Giambi	8.00
JGo	Juan Gonzalez	8.00
SG	Shawn Green	6.00
KG	Ken Griffey Jr./95	40.00
TH	Todd Helton	8.00
KI	Kazuhisa Ishii	10.00
RJ	Randy Johnson	10.00
AJ	Andruw Jones	8.00
CJ	Chipper Jones	10.00
JK	Jason Kendall	5.00
GM	Greg Maddux	10.00
MM	Mark McGwire/SP	100.00
MO	Magglio Ordonez	8.00
AP	Andy Pettitte	10.00
MP	Mike Piazza	15.00
MR	Manny Ramirez	10.00
AR	Alex Rodriguez	15.00
IR	Ivan Rodriguez	8.00
SR	Scott Rolen	10.00
CC	C.C. Sabathia	5.00
CS	Curt Schilling	10.00
GS	Gary Sheffield	6.00
TS	Tsuyoshi Shinjo	5.00
SS	Sammy Sosa	15.00
IS	Ichiro Suzuki/SP	50.00
JT	Jim Thome	10.00
RV	Robin Ventura	5.00
OV	Omar Vizquel	5.00
BW	Bernie Williams	8.00
PW	Preston Wilson	5.00
BZ	Barry Zito	6.00

Game Jersey Gold

	NM/M

Quantity produced listed

KG Ken Griffey Jr./30 65.00
RJ Randy Johnson/51 25.00
GM Greg Maddux/31 50.00
MO Magglio Ordonez/30 15.00
AP Andy Pettitte/46 20.00
MP Mike Piazza/31 50.00
CC C.C. Sabathia/52 10.00
CS Curt Schilling/38 30.00
IS Ichiro Suzuki/51 85.00
BW Bernie Williams/51 20.00
PW Preston Wilson/44
BZ Barry Zito/75 10.00

Prospect Signatures

NM/M
Common Autograph: 5.00
Inserted 1:36
JC Jose Cueto 5.00
JDe Jeff Deardorff 5.00
JDi Jose Diaz 8.00
AG Alex Graman 8.00
MG Matt Guerrier 5.00
BH Bill Hall 15.00
KH Ken Huckaby 5.00
DM Dustan Mohr 5.00
XN Xavier Nady 8.00
MS Marco Scutaro 8.00
ST Steve Torrealba 6.00
DW Danny Wright 5.00

Big Mac Missing Link

Production 25 Sets

Signed SP Big Mac

NM/M
Quantity signed listed
MM6 Mark McGwire/70 250.00

Signs of Greatness

Only one example of this card exists. The card is actually a 3-1/2" x 2-1/2" folder. On front are pictures of the players and a 1/1 designation. On back is a certification of authenticity. Inside are cut signatures of each of the players.

NM/M
Babe Ruth, Joe DiMaggio, Mickey Mantle, Ken Griffey Jr., Sammy Sosa (2/03 auction) 30,000

2002 SP Legendary Cuts

NM/M
Complete Set (90): 30.00
Common Player: .40
Pack (4): 10.00
Box (12): 100.00
1 Al Kaline .75

2 Alvin Dark .40
3 Andre Dawson .75
4 Babe Ruth 3.00
5 Ernie Banks 1.00
6 Bob Lemon .40
7 Bobby Bonds .40
8 Carl Erskine .40
9 Carl Hubbell .40
10 Casey Stengel .40
11 Charlie Gehringer .40
12 Christy Mathewson .75
13 Dale Murphy .40
14 Dave Concepcion .40
15 Dave Parker .40
16 Dazzy Vance .40
17 Dizzy Dean .40
18 Don Baylor .40
19 Don Drysdale .75
20 Duke Snider 1.00
21 Earl Averill .40
22 Early Wynn .40
23 Edd Roush .40
24 Elston Howard .40
25 Ferguson Jenkins .75
26 Frank Crosetti .40
27 Frankie Frisch .40
28 Gaylord Perry .40
29 George Foster .40
30 George Kell .40
31 Gil Hodges .40
32 Hank Greenberg .75
33 Phil Niekro .40
34 Harvey Haddix .40
35 Harvey Kuenn .40
36 Honus Wagner 1.50
37 Jackie Robinson 2.00
38 Orlando Cepeda .40
39 Joe Adcock .40
40 Joe Cronin .40
41 Joe DiMaggio 2.50
42 Joe Morgan .75
43 Johnny Mize .40
44 Lefty Gomez .75
45 Lefty Grove .40
46 Jim Palmer .75
47 Lou Boudreau .40
48 Lou Gehrig 2.50
49 Luke Appling .40
50 Mark McGwire 2.00
51 Mel Ott .75
52 Mickey Cochrane .40
53 Mickey Mantle 3.00
54 Minnie Minoso .40
55 Brooks Robinson 1.00
56 Nellie Fox .40
57 Nolan Ryan 3.00
58 Rollie Fingers .40
59 Pee Wee Reese .40
60 Phil Rizzuto .75
61 Ralph Kiner .40
62 Ray Dandridge .40
63 Richie Ashburn .40
64 Robin Yount .40
65 Rocky Colavito .40
66 Roger Maris 2.00
67 Rogers Hornsby .75
68 Ron Santo .40
69 Ryne Sandberg 1.50
70 Stan Musial 1.50
71 Sam McDowell .40
72 Satchel Paige 1.00
73 Willie McCovey .40
74 Steve Garvey .40
75 Ted Kluszewski .40
76 Catfish Hunter .40
77 Terry Moore .40
78 Thurman Munson 1.00
79 Tom Seaver 1.00
80 Tommy John .40
81 Tony Gwynn 1.00
82 Tony Kubek .40
83 Tony Lazzeri .40
84 Ty Cobb 2.00
85 Wade Boggs .40
86 Waite Hoyt .40
87 Walter Johnson 1.00
88 Willie Stargell .75
89 Yogi Berra 1.00
90 Zack Wheat .40

Bat

NM/M
Common Player: 6.00
Inserted 1:8
DBa Don Baylor .40
YBe Yogi Berra/SP 20.00
BBo Bobby Bonds 6.00
RCo Rocky Colavito 12.00

ADa Alvin Dark 6.00
AnD Andre Dawson 8.00
GFo George Foster 6.00
NFo Nellie Fox 15.00
SGa Steve Garvey 8.00
HGr Hank Greenberg/SP 40.00
LGr Lefty Grove 15.00
TGw Tony Gwynn 12.00
EHo Elston Howard/SP 15.00
GKe George Kell 8.00
RKi Ralph Kiner 10.00
TKu Tonk (Tony) Kubek 8.00
TLa Tony Lazzeri 10.00
MMa Mickey Mantle/SP 120.00
RMa Roger Maris/SP 60.00
MMc Mark McGwire 60.00
JMi Johnny Mize 12.00
TMu Thurman Munson 25.00
DMu Dale Murphy 12.00
DPa Dave Parker 6.00
GPe Gaylord Perry 8.00
PWe Pee Wee Reese 10.00
CRi Cal Ripken Jr. 25.00
JaR Jackie Robinson/SP 50.00
BRu Babe Ruth/SP 150.00
NRy Nolan Ryan 30.00
RSa Ryne Sandberg 12.00
TSe Tom Seaver/SP 20.00
DSn Duke Snider 12.00
WSt Willie Stargell 8.00
RYo Robin Yount 10.00
EWy Early Wynn 8.00

Bat Barrel

NM/M
Many not priced due to scarcity.
BB-ADa Alvin Dark/4 800.00
BB-AnD Andre Dawson/4 750.00
BB-GFo George Foster/5 250.00
BB-LGr Lefty Grove/1 (8/03 auction) 10,000
BB-TGw Tony Gwynn/11 650.00
BB-MMa Mickey Mantle/7 (8/04 auction) 3,000
BB-MMc Mark McGwire/4 2,000
BB-JMi Johnny Mize/2 1,275
BB-DMu Dale Murphy/3 600.00
BB-PWe Pee Wee Reese/4 1,500
BB-BRu Babe Ruth/3 (8/05 auction) 9,500
BB-NRy Nolan Ryan/9 1,500
BB-RSa Ryne Sandberg/4 2,250
BB-DSn Duke Snider/2 1,500
BB-RYo Robin Yount/8 750.00

Jersey

NM/M
Common Player: 6.00
Inserted 1:24
DBa Don Baylor 6.00
YBe Yogi Berra 20.00
BBo Bobby Bonds 6.00
FCr Frank Crosetti 10.00
AnD Andre Dawson 8.00
GFo George Foster 6.00
SGa Steve Garvey 8.00
MMa Mickey Mantle/SP 100.00
RMa Roger Maris 40.00
DPa Dave Parker 6.00
PWe Pee Wee Reese 12.00
JRo Jackie Robinson/SP 45.00
NRy Nolan Ryan 30.00
RSa Ryne Sandberg 25.00
TSe Tom Seaver 10.00

Signatures

NM/M
Quantity signed listed
JAd Joe Adcock/48 145.00
LAp Luke Appling/53 150.00
RAs Richie Ashburn/10 550.00
EAv Earl Averill/22 275.00
JBe Johnny Berardino/12 450.00
LBo Lou Boudreau/85 120.00
GBu Guy Bush/38 125.00
GCa George Case/36 180.00
HCh Happy Chandler/96 95.00
SCh Spud Chandler/17 350.00
TyC Ty Cobb/2 5,500
MCo Mickey Cochrane/2 5,000
JCo Johnny Cooney/64 75.00
SCo Stan Coveleski/85 150.00
JCr Joe Cronin/185 120.00
BDa Babe Dahlgren/51 180.00
RDa Ray Dandridge/179 85.00
DDe Dizzy Dean/4 2,000
JDi Joe DiMaggio/103 175.00
DDo Dick Donovan/23 200.00
TDo Taylor Douthit/60 165.00
DDr Don Drysdale/14 650.00
JDu Joe Dugan/39 150.00
BFa Bibb Falk/44 150.00
RFe Rick Ferrell/19 225.00
NFo Nellie Fox/1 (12/02 auction) 3,100
FoF Ford Frick/1 (10/03 auction) 4,000
LGe Lou Gehrig/3 (6/04 auction) 7,500
CGe Charlie Gehringer/3 700.00
LGo Lefty Gomez/3 750.00
BGo Billy Goodman/53 140.00
HGr Hank Greenberg/94 425.00
LGr Lefty Grove/190 240.00
SHa Stan Hack/36 200.00

HHa Harvey Haddix/37 250.00
BHa Buddy Hassett/56 200.00
WHo Waite Hoyt/62 250.00
CHu Carl Hubbell/17 475.00
LJa Larry Jackson/37 125.00
NJa Newton "Bucky" Jacobs/44 150.00
EJo Earl Johnson/31 200.00
JJo Judy Johnson/86 150.00
WJo Walter Johnson/20 2,000
BKa Bob Kahle/53 150.00
WKa Willie Kamm/57 110.00
CKe Charlie Keller/29 280.00
KKe Ken Keltner/11 415.00
TKl Ted Kluszewski/33 300.00
MKo Mark Koenig/22 260.00
HKu Harvey Kuenn/23 230.00
CLa Cookie Lavagetto/22 200.00
BiL Billy Lee/40 150.00
BoL Bob Lemon/91 110.00
ELo Ed Lopat/58 150.00
SMa Sal Maglie/29 200.00
HMa Hank Majeski/21 300.00
MMa Mickey Mantle/2 (10/04 auction) 6,000
ChrM Christy Mathewson/2 (5/03 auction) 2,000
RMc Roy McMillan/18 250.00
JMi Johnny Mize/3 2,500
JMo Johnny Moore/22 250.00
TMo Terry Moore/86 95.00
ChM Chet Morgan/21 185.00
HNe Hal Newhouser/81 135.00
VRa Vic Raschi/19 110.00
PRe Pete Reiser/73 140.00
RRe Rip Repulski/19 275.00
ORo Oscar Roettger/5 700.00
ERo Edd Roush/101 100.00
ERo2 Edd Roush/99 100.00
BRu Babe Ruth/2 (6/04 auction) 12,500
BSc Bob Scheffing/19 200.00
WSc Willard Schmidt/10 350.00
HSc Hal Schumacher/17 300.00
BSe Bill Serena/16 275.00
JSe Joe Sewell/136 125.00
BSh Bob Shawkey/11 120.00
BSh Bill Sherdel/10 450.00
BSz Bill Shantz/7 300.00
WSt Willie Stargell/153 95.00
CSt Casey Stengel/8 750.00
BVe Bill Veeck/11 500.00
HWa Honus Wagner/6 (2/05 auction) 5,000
BWa Bucky Walters/31 165.00
VWe Vic Wertz/31 300.00
ZWh Zack Wheat/127 150.00
PWi Pete Whisenant/13 300.00
EWy Early Wynn/4 1,650

Swatches

NM/M
Common Player: 6.00
DBa Don Baylor 6.00
WBo Wade Boggs 8.00
FCr Frank Crosetti 8.00
DDr Don Drysdale 20.00
CEr Carl Erskine 8.00
TGw Tony Gwynn 10.00
FJe Ferguson Jenkins 8.00
TJo Tommy John 6.00
SMc Sam McDowell 6.00
MMi Minnie Minoso 8.00
JMo Joe Morgan 8.00
MOt Mel Ott 25.00
DPa Dave Parker 6.00
CRj Cal Ripken Jr. 25.00
RSa Ron Santo 10.00

2002 SPx

NM/M
Common Player: .25
Common SP (91-120): 4.00

Production 1,800
Common SP Auto. (121-150): 10.00
Common Star Swatch (151-190): 5.00
Production 800
Pack (4): 4.00
Box (18): 60.00
1 Troy Glaus .50
2 Darin Erstad .40
3 David Justice .25
4 Tim Hudson .50
5 Miguel Tejada .75
6 Barry Zito .40
7 Carlos Delgado .50
8 Shannon Stewart .25
9 Greg Vaughn .25
10 Toby Hall .25
11 Jim Thome .75
12 C.C. Sabathia .25
13 Ichiro Suzuki 2.00
14 Edgar Martinez .25
15 Freddy Garcia .25
16 Mike Cameron .25
17 Jeff Conine .25
18 Tony Batista .25
19 Alex Rodriguez 2.00
20 Rafael Palmeiro .75
21 Ivan Rodriguez .25
22 Carl Everett .25
23 Pedro J. Martinez 1.00
24 Manny Ramirez 1.00
25 Nomar Garciaparra 1.00
26 Johnny Damon 1.00
27 Mike Sweeney .25
28 Carlos Beltran .75
29 Dmitri Young .25
30 Joe Mays .25
31 Doug Mientkiewicz .25
32 Cristian Guzman .25
33 Corey Koskie .25
34 Frank Thomas .75
35 Magglio Ordonez .25
36 Mark Buehrle .25
37 Bernie Williams .50
38 Roger Clemens 2.00
39 Derek Jeter 2.50
40 Jason Giambi .50
41 Mike Mussina .50
42 Lance Berkman .25
43 Jeff Bagwell .75
44 Roy Oswalt .50
45 Greg Maddux 2.00
46 Chipper Jones 1.00
47 Andruw Jones .75
48 Gary Sheffield .50
49 Geoff Jenkins .25
50 Richie Sexson .50
51 Ben Sheets .40
52 Albert Pujols 2.50
53 J.D. Drew .40
54 Jim Edmonds .50
55 Sammy Sosa 1.50
56 Moises Alou .25
57 Kerry Wood .50
58 Jon Lieber .25
59 Fred McGriff .40
60 Randy Johnson .75
61 Luis Gonzalez .35
62 Curt Schilling .75
63 Kevin Brown .25
64 Hideo Nomo .50
65 Shawn Green .40
66 Vladimir Guerrero 1.00
67 Jose Vidro .25
68 Barry Bonds 2.50
69 Jeff Kent .40
70 Rich Aurilia .25
71 Cliff Floyd .25
72 Josh Beckett .25
73 Preston Wilson .25
74 Mike Piazza 1.00
75 Mo Vaughn .25
76 Jeromy Burnitz .25
77 Roberto Alomar .50
78 Phil Nevin .25
79 Ryan Klesko .25
80 Scott Rolen .75
81 Bobby Abreu .50
82 Jimmy Rollins .50
83 Brian Giles .25
84 Aramis Ramirez .25
85 Ken Griffey Jr. 1.50
86 Sean Casey .25
87 Barry Larkin .50
88 Mike Hampton .25
89 Larry Walker .40
90 Todd Helton .75
91 Ron Calloway RC 4.00
92 Joe Orloski RC 4.00
93 Anderson Machado RC 6.00
94 Eric Good RC 4.00
95 Reed Johnson RC 8.00
96 Brendan Donnelly RC 4.00
97 Chris Baker RC 4.00
98 Wilson Valdez RC 4.00
99 Scotty Layfield RC 4.00
100 P.J. Bevis RC 4.00
101 Edwin Almonte RC 4.00
102 Francis Beltran RC 4.00
103 Valentino Pasucci RC 4.00
104 Nelson Castro RC 4.00
105 Michael Crudale RC 4.00
106 Colin Young RC 4.00
107 Todd Donovan RC 4.00
108 Felix Escalona RC 4.00
109 Brandon Backe RC 8.00
110 Corey Thurman RC 4.00

111 Kyle Kane RC 4.00
112 Allan Simpson RC 4.00
113 Jose Valverde RC 4.00
114 Chris Booker RC 4.00
115 Brandon Puffer RC 4.00
116 John Foster RC 4.00
117 Clifford Bartosh RC 4.00
118 Gustavo Chacin RC 8.00
119 Steve Kent RC 4.00
120 Nate Field RC 4.00
121 Victor Alvarez RC 10.00
122 Steve Bechler RC 10.00
123 Adrian Burnside RC 10.00
124 Marlon Byrd RC 15.00
125 Jaime Cerda RC 10.00
126 Brandon Claussen RC 10.00
127 Mark Corey RC 10.00
128 Doug DeVore RC 10.00
129 Kazuhisa Ishii RC 60.00
130 John Ennis RC 10.00
131 Kevin Frederick RC 10.00
132 Josh Hancock RC 10.00
133 Ben Howard RC 10.00
134 Orlando Hudson RC 20.00
135 Hansel Izquierdo RC 10.00
136 Eric Junge RC 10.00
137 Austin Kearns RC 15.00
138 Victor Martinez RC 25.00
139 Luis Martinez RC 10.00
140 Danny Mota RC 10.00
141 Jorge Padilla RC 10.00
142 Andy Pratt RC 10.00
143 Rene Reyes RC 10.00
144 Rodrigo Rosario RC 10.00
145 Tom Shearn RC 10.00
146 So Taguchi RC 30.00
147 Dennis Tankersley RC 15.00
148 Matt Thornton RC 10.00
149 Jeremy Ward RC 10.00
150 Mitch Wylie RC 10.00
151 Pedro Martinez 8.00
152 Cal Ripken Jr. 25.00
153 Roger Clemens 15.00
154 Bernie Williams 6.00
155 Jason Giambi 8.00
156 Robin Ventura 5.00
157 Carlos Delgado 6.00
158 Frank Thomas 8.00
159 Magglio Ordonez 5.00
160 Jim Thome 10.00
161 Darin Erstad 5.00
162 Tim Salmon 5.00
163 Tim Hudson 5.00
164 Barry Zito 5.00
165 Ichiro Suzuki 30.00
166 Edgar Martinez 8.00
167 Alex Rodriguez 15.00
168 Ivan Rodriguez 8.00
169 Juan Gonzalez 6.00
170 Greg Maddux 12.00
171 Chipper Jones 10.00
172 Andruw Jones 8.00
173 Tom Glavine 6.00
174 Mike Piazza 15.00
175 Roberto Alomar 8.00
176 Scott Rolen 12.00
177 Sammy Sosa 15.00
178 Moises Alou 5.00
179 Ken Griffey Jr. 15.00
180 Jeff Bagwell 8.00
181 Jim Edmonds 6.00
182 J.D. Drew 5.00
183 Brian Giles 5.00
184 Randy Johnson 10.00
185 Curt Schilling 10.00
186 Luis Gonzalez 5.00
187 Todd Helton 8.00
188 Shawn Green 5.00
189 David Wells 5.00
190 Jeff Kent 5.00

SuperStar Swatch Silver

Jersey (151-190): .5-1X
Production 400

SuperStar Swatch Gold

Jersey (151-190): .75-1.5X
Production 150

Sweet Spot Bat Barrel

No Pricing

Winning Materials Ball/ Patch Combo

No Pricing
Production 25 Sets

Winning Materials Base Combo

NM/M
Common Card: 15.00

Production 200

PE Mike Piazza,
Jim Edmonds 20.00
RJ Alex Rodriguez,
Derek Jeter 40.00
BG Barry Bonds,
Shawn Green 20.00
IM Ichiro Suzuki,
Edgar Martinez 50.00
SG Sammy Sosa,
Luis Gonzalez 25.00
GR Troy Glaus,
Alex Rodriguez 20.00
WJ Bernie Williams,
Derek Jeter 30.00
GS Ken Griffey Jr.,
Sammy Sosa 30.00
PI Albert Pujols,
Ichiro Suzuki 60.00
SR Kazuhiro Sasaki,
Mariano Rivera 20.00

Winning Materials Base/Patch Combo
No Pricing
Production 25 Sets

Winning Materials Jersey Combo

NM/M
Common Card: 8.00
Inserted 1:18
AR Alex Rodriguez,
Ivan Rodriguez 20.00
GC Ken Griffey Jr.,
Sean Casey/SP 20.00
BR Jeff Bagwell,
Alex Rodriguez 15.00
WG Bernie Williams,
Jason Giambi 10.00
JS Randy Johnson,
Curt Schilling 15.00
MJ Greg Maddux,
Chipper Jones 20.00
MC Edgar Martinez,
Mike Cameron 10.00
SP Sammy Sosa,
Corey Patterson 20.00
ED Jim Edmonds,
J.D. Drew 10.00
PA Mike Piazza,
Roberto Alomar 15.00
DH Jermaine Dye,
Tim Hudson 8.00
RA Scott Rolen,
Bobby Abreu 15.00
TO Frank Thomas,
Magglio Ordonez 15.00
HW Mike Hampton,
Larry Walker 8.00
TS Jim Thome,
C.C. Sabathia 8.00
GK Shawn Green,
Eric Karros 10.00
KG Jason Kendall,
Brian Giles 8.00
WP David Wells,
Jorge Posada 10.00
NM Hideo Nomo,
Pedro Martinez/SP 20.00
RP Ivan Rodriguez,
Chan Ho Park 10.00
LH Al Leiter,
Mike Hampton 8.00

BA Jeromy Burnitz,
Edgardo Alfonzo 8.00
DS Carlos Delgado,
Shannon Stewart 10.00
BG Jeff Bagwell,
Juan Gonzalez 10.00
GR Juan Gonzalez,
Ivan Rodriguez 10.00
VR Omar Vizquel,
Alex Rodriguez 15.00
SE Aaron Sele,
Darin Erstad 8.00
JJ Chipper Jones,
Andruw Jones 15.00
SH Kazuhiro Sasaki,
Shigetoshi Hasegawa 8.00

Winning Materials USA Jersey Combo
NM/M
Common Card: 10.00
Production 150
AH Brent Abernathy,
Orlando Hudson 8.00
BT Sean Burroughs,
Mark Teixeira 25.00
GB Jason Giambi,
Sean Burroughs 15.00
HD Orlando Hudson,
Jeff Deardorff 10.00
GT Jason Giambi,
Mark Teixeira 20.00
HOU Roy Oswalt,
Adam Everett 10.00
HP Dustin Hermanson,
Mark Prior 15.00
JC Jacque Jones,
Michael Cuddyer 10.00
KB Austin Kearns,
Sean Burroughs 15.00
KC Austin Kearns,
Michael Cuddyer 10.00
MG Doug Mientkiewicz,
Jason Giambi 15.00
MIN Doug Mientkiewicz,
Michael Cuddyer 10.00
MO Matt Morris,
Roy Oswalt 15.00
MP Matt Morris,
Mark Prior 15.00
AW Matt Anderson,
Jeff Weaver 10.00
MW Matt Morris,
Jeff Weaver 10.00
PB Mark Prior,
Dewon Brazelton 15.00
RE Brian Roberts,
Adam Everett 10.00
SD Mark Kotsay,
Sean Burroughs 10.00
TB Brent Abernathy,
Dewon Brazelton 10.00
TP Mark Teixeira,
Mark Prior 25.00
WB Jeff Weaver,
Dewon Brazelton 10.00
WH Jeff Weaver,
Dustin Hermanson 10.00

2003 SP Authentic

NM/M
Complete Set (189):
Common Player: .25
Common RK Archives
(91-123): 1.00
Production 2,500
Common Back to '93
(124-150): 1.50
Production 1,993
Common Future Watch
(150-180): 4.00
Production 2,003
Pack (5): 3.50
Box (24): 70.00
1 Darin Erstad .40
2 Garret Anderson .40
3 Troy Glaus .50
4 Eric Chavez .40
5 Barry Zito .50
6 Miguel Tejada .50
7 Eric Hinske .25
8 Carlos Delgado .50
9 Josh Phelps .25
10 Ben Grieve .25
11 Carl Crawford .25

12 Omar Vizquel .40
13 Matt Lawton .25
14 C.C. Sabathia .25
15 Ichiro Suzuki 1.50
16 John Olerud .40
17 Freddy Garcia .25
18 Jay Gibbons .25
19 Tony Batista .25
20 Melvin Mora .25
21 Alex Rodriguez 2.00
22 Rafael Palmeiro .50
23 Hank Blalock .50
24 Nomar Garciaparra 1.00
25 Pedro J. Martinez .75
26 Johnny Damon .75
27 Mike Sweeney .25
28 Carlos Febles .25
29 Carlos Beltran .50
30 Carlos Pena .25
31 Eric Munson .25
32 Bobby Higginson .25
33 Torii Hunter .25
34 Doug Mientkiewicz .25
35 Jacque Jones .25
36 Paul Konerko .50
37 Bartolo Colon .25
38 Magglio Ordonez .50
39 Derek Jeter 2.00
40 Bernie Williams .50
41 Jason Giambi .50
42 Alfonso Soriano .75
43 Roger Clemens 1.50
44 Jeff Bagwell .50
45 Jeff Kent .40
46 Lance Berkman .50
47 Chipper Jones .75
48 Andruw Jones .50
49 Gary Sheffield .50
50 Ben Sheets .40
51 Richie Sexson .25
52 Geoff Jenkins .25
53 Jim Edmonds .40
54 Albert Pujols 2.00
55 Scott Rolen .75
56 Sammy Sosa 1.00
57 Kerry Wood .75
58 Eric Karros .25
59 Luis Gonzalez .40
60 Randy Johnson .75
61 Curt Schilling .75
62 Fred McGriff .40
63 Shawn Green .25
64 Paul LoDuca .25
65 Vladimir Guerrero .75
66 Jose Vidro .25
67 Barry Bonds 2.00
68 Rich Aurilia .25
69 Edgardo Alfonzo .25
70 Ivan Rodriguez .50
71 Mike Lowell .40
72 Derrek Lee .50
73 Tom Glavine .50
74 Mike Piazza 1.00
75 Roberto Alomar .50
76 Ryan Klesko .25
77 Phil Nevin .25
78 Mark Kotsay .25
79 Jim Thome .75
80 Pat Burrell .40
81 Bobby Abreu .40
82 Jason Kendall .40
83 Brian Giles .40
84 Aramis Ramirez .40
85 Austin Kearns .40
86 Ken Griffey Jr. 1.00
87 Adam Dunn .50
88 Larry Walker .40
89 Todd Helton .40
90 Preston Wilson .40
91 Derek Jeter 6.00
92 Johnny Damon 3.00
93 Chipper Jones 3.00
94 Manny Ramirez 3.00
95 Trot Nixon 1.00
96 Alex Rodriguez 5.00
97 Chan Ho Park 1.00
98 Brad Fullmer 1.00
99 Billy Wagner 1.00
100 Hideo Nomo 1.00
101 Freddy Garcia 1.00
102 Darin Erstad 1.00
103 Jose Cruz Jr. 1.00
104 Nomar Garciaparra 4.00
105 Magglio Ordonez 1.50
106 Kerry Wood 2.00
107 Troy Glaus 1.50
108 J.D. Drew 1.50
109 Alfonso Soriano 3.00
110 Danys Baez 1.00
111 Kazuhiro Sasaki 1.50
112 Barry Zito 2.00
113 Brent Abernathy 1.00
114 Ben Diggins 1.00
115 Ben Sheets 2.00
116 Brad Wilkerson 1.00
117 Juan Pierre 1.00
118 Jon Rauch 1.00
119 Ichiro Suzuki 5.00
120 Albert Pujols 6.00
121 Mark Prior 2.00
122 Mark Teixeira 2.00
123 Kazuhisa Ishii 1.50
124 Troy Glaus 1.50
125 Randy Johnson 3.00
126 Curt Schilling 3.00
127 Chipper Jones 3.00
128 Greg Maddux 4.00
129 Nomar Garciaparra 3.00

130 Pedro J. Martinez 3.00
131 Sammy Sosa 3.00
132 Mark Prior 2.00
133 Ken Griffey Jr. 4.00
134 Adam Dunn 2.00
135 Jeff Bagwell 2.00
136 Vladimir Guerrero 3.00
137 Mike Piazza 4.00
138 Tom Glavine 1.50
139 Derek Jeter 8.00
140 Roger Clemens 6.00
141 Jason Giambi 2.00
142 Alfonso Soriano 3.00
143 Miguel Tejada 2.00
144 Barry Zito 1.50
145 Jim Thome 3.00
146 Barry Bonds 5.00
147 Ichiro Suzuki 5.00
148 Albert Pujols 6.00
149 Alex Rodriguez 6.00
150 Carlos Delgado 2.00
151 Richard Fischer RC 4.00
152 Brandon Webb RC 10.00
153 Rob Hammock RC 4.00
154 Matt Kata RC 4.00
155 Tim Olson RC 4.00
156 Oscar Villarreal RC 4.00
157 Michael Hessman RC 4.00
158 Daniel Cabrera RC 6.00
159 Jon Leicester RC 4.00
160 Todd Wellemeyer RC 4.00
161 Felix Sanchez RC 4.00
162 David Sanders RC 4.00
163 Josh Stewart RC 4.00
164 Arnie Munoz RC 4.00
165 Ryan Cameron RC 4.00
166 Clint Barmes RC 10.00
167 Josh Willingham RC 10.00
168 .25
169 Willie Eyre RC 4.00
170 Brent Hoard RC 4.00
171 Terrmel Sledge RC 4.00
172 Phil Seibel RC 4.00
173 Craig Brazell RC 4.00
174 Jeff Duncan RC 6.00
175 .25
176 Bernie Castro RC 4.00
177 Mike Nicolas RC 4.00
178 Rett Johnson RC 4.00
179 Bobby Madritsch RC 6.00
180 Chris Capuano RC 20.00
181 Hideki Matsui/ 240.00
181 H. Matsui/Bronze/
Auto./75 275.00
182 Jose Contreras/
Auto./500 35.00
183 Lew Ford/Auto./
500 RC 15.00
184 Jeremy Griffiths/
Auto./500 15.00
185 Guillermo Quiroz/
Auto./500 RC 15.00
186 Alejandro Machado/
Auto./500 RC 15.00
187 Francisco Cruceta/
Auto./500 RC 15.00
188 Prentice Redman/
Auto./500 RC 15.00
189 Shane Bazzell/
Auto./500 RC 15.00

Simply Splendid

NM/M
Complete Set (30): 200.00
Common Williams: 8.00
Production 406 sets
TW1-30 Ted Williams 8.00

Chirography

NM/M
Common Autograph: 10.00
Varying quantities produced
Bronze Autos.: 1X
Production 100
Silver Autos.: 1-1.5X
Production 50

Gold Autos.: No Pricing
Production 10
GA1 Garret Anderson/245 15.00
JD Johnny Damon/245 35.00
AD Adam Dunn/170 25.00
JE2 Jim Edmonds/350 20.00
FL Cliff Floyd/125 12.00
FC Rafael Furcal/150 15.00
FG Freddy Garcia/345 15.00
GI Jason Giambi/250 15.00
GL Brian Giles/225 15.00
LG1 Luis Gonzalez/195 15.00
GJ Ken Griffey Jr./350 85.00
JR Ken Griffey Jr./350 85.00
TO Torii Hunter/245 15.00
KE Jason Kendall/145 10.00
MM Mark McGwire/275 275.00
MP Mark Prior/150 40.00
CR Cal Ripken Jr./250 100.00
RO Scott Rolen/345 35.00
TS Tim Salmon/350 20.00
RS Richie Sexson/215 15.00
SA Sammy Sosa/335 75.00
SO Sammy Sosa/335 75.00
IC Ichiro Suzuki/85 350.00
IS Ichiro Suzuki/350 350.00
SW Mike Sweeney/125 15.00
JT1 Jim Thome/250 35.00

Chirography Dodger Stars
NM/M
Common Autograph: 8.00
Bronze Auto.: 1X
Production 100
Silver Autos.: 1-1.5X
Production 50
Gold Autos.: No Pricing
Production 10
BB Bill Buckner/245 10.00
CE Ron Cey/345 15.00
SG Steve Garvey/320 20.00
JN Tommy John/170 15.00
DL Davey Lopes/245 9.00
DN Don Newcombe/345 15.00
BI Bill Russell/245 9.00
BS Duke Snider/345 30.00
SU Don Sutton/245 15.00
MW Maury Wills/320 9.00
SY Steve Yeager/345 15.00

Chirography Double

NM/M
Common Duo Auto.: 40.00
FB Yogi Berra,
Whitey Ford/75 150.00
FE Carlton Fisk,
Dwight Evans/75 65.00
FM Carlton Fisk,
Bill Mazeroski/75 40.00
GG Jason Giambi,
Ken Griffey Jr. 125.00
GR Steve Garvey,
Ron Cey/75 50.00
JI Ken Griffey Jr.,
Ichiro Suzuki 350.00
KR Tony Kubek, Bobby
Richardson/75 80.00
KT Tom Seaver,
Jerry Koosman/75 80.00
MG Don Mattingly,
Jason Giambi/25 150.00
MS Mark McGwire,
Sammy Sosa/15 500.00
SJ Sammy Sosa,
Jason Giambi/25 125.00
WB Bill Buckner,
Mookie Wilson/150 40.00

Chirography Flash Backs

NM/M
Common Autograph: 8.00
Bronze Autos.: 1X
Production 100
Silver Autos.: 1-1.5X
Production 50
Gold Auto.: No Pricing
No Pricing
JE1 Jim Edmonds/350 15.00
CF1 Cliff Floyd/350 8.00
JA Jason Giambi/350 15.00

BN Brian Giles/245 10.00
LA Luis Gonzalez/200 15.00
GM Ken Griffey Jr./350 80.00
MA Mark McGwire/55 280.00
SR Sammy Sosa/245 100.00

Chirography Hall of Famers
NM/M
Common Autograph: 15.00
Bronze Autos.: 1X
Production 100
Silver Autos.: 1-1.5X
Production 50
Gold Autos.: No Pricing
Production 10
JB1 Johnny Bench/350 40.00
GC1 Gary Carter/350 20.00
OC Orlando Cepeda/245 20.00
RF Rollie Fingers/170 15.00
CF Carlton Fisk/240 35.00
WF Whitey Ford/170 40.00
BG Bob Gibson/245 35.00
TP Tony Perez/320 20.00
RR Robin Roberts/170 30.00
NR Nolan Ryan/170 140.00
TS Tom Seaver/170 40.00
DS Duke Snider/250 30.00
DW2 Dave Winfield/350 25.00

Chirography Triple

NM/M
Quantity produced listed
BKR Bobby Richardson,
Yogi Berra,
Tony Kubek/75 120.00
FCG Carlton Fisk, Gary Carter,
Kirk Gibson/75 75.00
GIS Sammy Sosa,
Ichiro Suzuki,
Ken Griffey Jr./75 400.00
GLC Davey Lopes, Ron Cey,
Steve Garvey/75 65.00
GRC Steve Garvey, Ron Cey,
Bill Russell/75 60.00
GSG Sammy Sosa,
Jason Giambi,
Ken Griffey Jr./75 250.00
GSJ Ken Griffey Jr.,
Jason Giambi,
Sammy Sosa/75 250.00
ISG Sammy Sosa,
Jason Giambi,
Ichiro Suzuki/75 300.00
SEA Tim Salmon,
Garret Anderson,
Darin Erstad/75 100.00
SKM Tom Seaver, Tug McGraw,
Jerry Koosman/75 125.00

Chirography World Series Heroes

NM/M
Common Autograph: 10.00
Bronze Autos.: 1X
Production 100
Silver Autos.: 1-1.5X
Production 50
Gold Autos.: No Pricing
Production 10
GA Garret Anderson/245 15.00
GC Gary Carter/345 20.00
DE Darin Erstad/345 15.00
CF Carlton Fisk/200 40.00
KG Kirk Gibson/145 15.00
GO Luis Gonzalez/225 15.00
GS Ken Griffey Sr./295 10.00
AJ1 Andruw Jones/350 20.00
DJ David Justice/170 20.00
JK Jerry Koosman/170 15.00
BM Bill Mazeroski/245 30.00
TM Tug McGraw/75 25.00
JP Jorge Posada/350 35.00
ER Edgar Renteria/220 15.00
CR Cal Ripken Jr./295 100.00

TI	Tim Salmon/245	15.00
CS	Curt Schilling/345	30.00

Chirography Yankee Stars

NM/M
Common Autograph: 8.00
Bronze Autos.: 1X
Production 100
Silver Autos.: 1-1.5X
Production 50
Gold Autos.: No Pricing
Production 10

YB	Yogi Berra/320	35.00
JB	Jim Bouton/345	10.00
RC	Roger Clemens/210	100.00
JG	Jason Giambi/275	15.00
KS	Ken Griffey Sr./350	10.00
TH	Tommy Henrich/345	15.00
HK	Ralph Houk/245	12.00
TJ	Tommy John/245	15.00
TK	Tony Kubek/345	10.00
SL	Sparky Lyle/345	10.00
DM	Don Mattingly/295	60.00
BR	Bobby Richardson/320	20.00
ST	Mel Stottlemyre/345	15.00
DW1	Dave Winfield/350	25.00

Chirography Young Stars

NM/M
Common Autograph: 6.00
Bronze Autos.: 1X
Production 100
Silver Autos.: 1-1.5X
Production 50
Gold Autos.: No Pricing
Production 10

HB	Hank Blalock/245	25.00
BO	Joe Borchard/245	8.00
SB	Sean Burroughs/245	8.00
MB	Marlon Byrd/245	8.00
HC	Hee Seop Choi/245	20.00
DI1	Ben Diggins/350	8.00
DH	Drew Henson/245	15.00
EH	Eric Hinske/245	10.00
OH	Orlando Hudson/245	15.00
JJ	Jacque Jones/245	15.00
JJ1	Jimmy Journell/350	10.00
JL	Jason Lane/245	15.00
JO	Joe Mays/245	6.00
MI	Doug Mientkiewicz/245	15.00
MY	Brett Myers/245	10.00
CP	Corey Patterson/245	15.00
PE	Carlos Pena/245	8.00
OP	Oliver Perez/245	10.00
JP	Josh Phelps/245	8.00
BP1	Brandon Phillips/350	8.00
AP	A.J. Pierzynski/245	15.00
FS1	Freddy Sanchez/350	15.00
TX	Mark Teixeira/245	25.00
BZ	Barry Zito/350	20.00

Splendid Jerseys

NM/M
Production 406 Sets

TW	Mickey Mantle, Ted Williams	180.00
SJ-TW	Ted Williams	100.00
TW-IS	Ted Williams, Ichiro Suzuki	100.00
TW-JG	Ted Williams, Jason Giambi	60.00
TW-KG	Ted Williams, Ken Griffey Jr.	75.00
TW-MM	Mark McGwire, Ted Williams	110.00
TW-SS	Ted Williams, Sammy Sosa	80.00
TW-NM1	Ted Williams, Nomar Garciaparra	80.00
TW-NM2	Nomar Garciaparra, Ted Williams	80.00

Splendid Signatures

NM/M
Hand Numbered to 5 or 3

GA	Nomar Garciaparra/406	100.00

TW-NM3 Ted Williams, Nomar Garciaparra/3 (10/03 auction) 2,400

Spotlight "Godzilla"

Complete Set (15):
Common Matsui:
Production 500 Sets

Superstar Flashback

NM/M
Complete Set (60): 65.00
Common Player: 1.00
Production 2,003 Sets

SF1	Tim Salmon	1.00
SF2	Darin Erstad	1.00
SF3	Troy Glaus	1.50
SF4	Randy Johnson	2.00
SF5	Curt Schilling	1.50
SF6	Steve Finley	1.00
SF7	Greg Maddux	3.00
SF8	Chipper Jones	3.00
SF9	Andruw Jones	1.50
SF10	Gary Sheffield	1.00
SF11	Manny Ramirez	2.00
SF12	Pedro J. Martinez	1.50
SF13	Nomar Garciaparra	2.50
SF14	Sammy Sosa	3.00
SF15	Frank Thomas	1.50
SF16	Kerry Wood	1.50
SF17	Paul Konerko	1.00
SF18	Corey Patterson	1.00
SF19	Mark Prior	2.00
SF20	Ken Griffey Jr.	3.00
SF21	Adam Dunn	1.50
SF22	Larry Walker	1.00
SF23	Preston Wilson	1.00
SF24	Todd Helton	1.50
SF25	Ivan Rodriguez	1.50
SF26	Josh Beckett	1.00
SF27	Jeff Bagwell	1.00
SF28	Jeff Kent	1.00
SF29	Lance Berkman	1.00
SF30	Carlos Beltran	1.50
SF31	Shawn Green	1.00
SF32	Richie Sexson	1.00
SF33	Vladimir Guerrero	1.50
SF34	Mike Piazza	4.00
SF35	Roberto Alomar	1.50
SF36	Roger Clemens	4.00
SF37	Derek Jeter	4.00
SF38	Jason Giambi	1.50
SF39	Bernie Williams	1.50
SF40	Nick Johnson	1.00
SF41	Alfonso Soriano	3.00
SF42	Miguel Tejada	1.50
SF43	Eric Chavez	1.50
SF44	Barry Zito	1.50
SF45	Jim Thome	1.50
SF46	Pat Burrell	1.00
SF47	Marlon Byrd	1.00
SF48	Jason Kendall	1.00
SF49	Aramis Ramirez	1.50
SF50	Brian Giles	1.00
SF51	Phil Nevin	1.00
SF52	Barry Bonds	6.00
SF53	Ichiro Suzuki	4.00
SF54	Scott Rolen	2.00
SF55	J.D. Drew	1.00
SF56	Albert Pujols	6.00
SF57	Mark Teixeira	1.50
SF58	Hank Blalock	2.00
SF59	Carlos Delgado	1.50
SF60	Roy Halladay	1.00

500 Home Run Club

NM/M
Production 25

500HR Ted Williams, Barry Bonds, Mark McGwire, Sammy Sosa, Mickey Mantle 325.00

2003 SP Legendary Cuts

NM/M
Complete Set (130):
Common Player: .25
Common SP: 3.00
Production 1,299
Pack (4): 8.00
Box (12): 85.00

1	Luis Aparicio	.25
2	Al Barlick	.25
3	Al Lopez	.25
4	Ernie Banks	1.00
5	Alexander Cartwright	.25
6	Lou Brock	.50
7	Babe Ruth/SP	10.00
8	Bill Dickey	.50
9	Bill Mazeroski	.50
10	Bob Feller	.50
11	Billy Herman	.25
12	Billy Williams	.25
13	Bob Gibson/SP	4.00
14	Bob Lemon	.25
15	Bobby Doerr	.25
16	Branch Rickey	.25
17	Gary Carter	.50
18	Burleigh Grimes	.25
19	Cap Anson	.25
20	Carl Hubbell	.25
21	Carlton Fisk	.50
22	Casey Stengel	.50
23	Charlie Gehringer	.25
24	Chief Bender	.25
25	Christy Mathewson/SP	5.00
26	Cy Young	1.00
27	Dave Winfield	.50
28	Dazzy Vance	.25
29	Dizzy Dean/SP	4.00
30	Don Drysdale/SP	4.00
31	Duke Snider/SP	4.00
32	Earl Averill	.25
33	Earle Combs	.25
34	Edd Roush	.25
35	Earl Weaver	.25
36	Eddie Collins	.25
37	Eddie Plank	.25
38	Elmer Flick	.25
39	Enos Slaughter	.25
40	Ernie Lombardi	.25
41	Ford Frick	.25
42	Jim "Catfish" Hunter	.25
43	Frankie Frisch	.25
44	Gabby Hartnett	.25
45	George Kell	.25
46	Early Wynn	.25
47	Ferguson Jenkins	.25
48	Al Kaline	1.00
49	Harmon Killebrew	1.00
50	Hal Newhouser	.25
51	Hank Greenberg/SP	5.00
52	Harry Caray	.25
53	Tommy Lasorda	.25
54	Honus Wagner/SP	6.00
55	Hoyt Wilhelm/SP	.25
56	Jackie Robinson/SP	6.00
57	Jim Bottomley	.25
58	Jim Bunning/SP	3.00
59	Jimmie Foxx/SP	.25
60	Eddie Mathews	1.00
61	Joe Cronin	.25
62	Joe DiMaggio/SP	8.00
63	Joe McCarthy/SP	3.00
64	Joe Morgan/SP	3.00
65	Willie McCovey	.50
66	Joe Tinker	.25
67	Johnny Bench/SP	6.00
68	Johnny Evers/SP	3.00
69	Johnny Mize/SP	3.00
70	Josh Gibson/SP	5.00
71	Juan Marichal	.50
72	Judy Johnson	.25
73	Stan Musial	1.50
74	Kiki Cuyler	.25
75	Larry Doby	.75
76	Nap Lajoie	.25
77	Larry MacPhail	.25
78	Phil Niekro	.25
79	Lefty Gomez/SP	3.00
80	Lefty Grove/SP	3.00
81	Leo Durocher/SP	3.00
82	Leon Day	.25
83	Gaylord Perry/SP	3.00
84	Lou Boudreau	.25
85	Lou Gehrig	3.00
86	Luke Appling	.25
87	Max Carey	.25
88	Mel Allen/SP	3.00
89	Mel Ott/SP	5.00
90	Mickey Cochrane	.50
91	Mickey Mantle	4.00
92	Brooks Robinson	3.00
93	Monte Irvin	.50
94	Nellie Fox	.50
95	Nolan Ryan/SP	10.00
96	Ozzie Smith/SP	6.00
97	Mike Schmidt	2.00
98	Pee Wee Reese/SP	3.00
99	Phil Rizzuto	.75
100	Ralph Kiner	.50
101	Ray Dandridge	.25
102	Richie Ashburn	.25
103	Rick Ferrell	.25
104	Roberto Clemente	2.00
105	Robin Roberts	.25
106	Robin Yount	1.00
107	Rogers Hornsby	.50
108	Rollie Fingers	.25
109	Roy Campanella	.50
110	Rube Marquard	.25
111	Sam Crawford	.25
112	Steve Carlton	.50
113	Satchel Paige/SP	5.00
114	Sparky Anderson	.25
115	Stan Coveleski	.25
116	Red Schoendienst	.25
117	Ted Williams	3.00
118	Tom Seaver	1.00
119	Tom Yawkey	.25
120	Tony Lazzeri	.25
121	Tony Perez	.25
122	Tris Speaker	.25
123	Ty Cobb	2.00
124	Waite Hoyt/SP	3.00
125	Walter Alston	.25
126	Walter Johnson	.75
127	Warren Spahn	1.00
128	Whitey Ford	.75
129	Willie Stargell	.50
130	Yogi Berra	.75

Blue

Non SP's (1-130): 2-4X
SP's: 1-2X
Production 275 Sets

Green

No pricing due to scarcity.
Production 25 Sets

Autographs

NM/M
Common Player:
Inserted 1:196
Many not priced due to scarcity.

AL	Alexander Cartwright/1 (6/05 auction)	7,800
BG	Burleigh Grimes/34	150.00
BI	Billy Herman/30	150.00
BL	Bob Lemon/34	150.00
BL1	Bob Lemon/41	150.00
CH	Carl Hubbell/47	300.00
CH1	Carl Hubbell/63	300.00
EA	Earl Averill/96	125.00
EC	Earle Combs/45	150.00
ES	Enos Slaughter/30	200.00
HC	Harry Caray/29	225.00
HC1	Harry Caray/35	225.00
HG	Hank Greenberg/33	375.00
JD	Joe DiMaggio/50	375.00
JD1	Joe DiMaggio/28	400.00
LB	Lou Boudreau/82	110.00
LB1	Lou Boudreau/49	120.00
LU	Luke Appling/52	150.00
RM	Rube Marquard/40	200.00

Autographs Blue

NM/M
Many not priced due to scarcity.

EA	Earl Averill/50	125.00
HC1	Harry Caray/35	240.00
HN1	Hal Newhouser B2B/29	125.00
JD1	Joe DiMaggio/40	375.00

Combo Cuts

No Pricing
Production One Set

Etched in Time

NM/M
Common Player: 3.00
Production 400 Sets
Etched 300: .5-1X
Production 300
Etched 175: .75-1.5X
Production 175

ME	Mel Allen	3.00
RA	Richie Ashburn	4.00
AB	Al Barlick	3.00
LB	Lou Boudreau	3.00
RO	Roy Campanella	4.00
AC	Alexander Cartwright	3.00
HC	Harry Caray	3.00
RC	Roberto Clemente	10.00
TC	Ty Cobb	6.00
EC	Eddie Collins	3.00
DD	Dizzy Dean	3.00
JD	Joe DiMaggio	5.00
DO	Don Drysdale	3.00
LD	Leo Durocher	3.00
JF	Jimmie Foxx	3.00
LO	Lou Gehrig	8.00
CG	Charlie Gehringer	3.00
JG	Josh Gibson	5.00
TL	Lefty Gomez	3.00
HG	Hank Greenberg	5.00
LE	Lefty Grove	3.00
GH	Gabby Hartnett	3.00
RH	Rogers Hornsby	4.00
CH	Carl Hubbell	3.00
TL	Tony Lazzeri	3.00
EL	Ernie Lombardi	3.00
MM	Mickey Mantle	15.00
CM	Christy Mathewson	8.00
JM	Joe McCarthy	3.00
JO	Johnny Mize	4.00
MO	Mel Ott	3.00
SP	Satchel Paige	5.00
PR	Pee Wee Reese	5.00
JR	Jackie Robinson	5.00
BR	Babe Ruth	10.00
TS	Tris Speaker	3.00
CS	Casey Stengel	3.00
HW	Honus Wagner	5.00
TW	Ted Williams	8.00
CY	Cy Young	5.00

Hall Marks Autographs

NM/M
Inserted 1:196
Many not priced due to scarcity.
Greens: No Pricing
Production 10

BD1	Bobby Doerr/Black/50	40.00
BM1	Bill Mazeroski/Black/50	40.00
CF1	Carlton Fisk/Black/50	50.00
CY1	Carl Yastrzemski/Black/50	75.00
DS1	Duke Snider/Black/50	50.00
GC1	Gary Carter/Black/50	30.00
GK1	George Kell/Black/50	30.00
JM1	Juan Marichal/Black/50	35.00
JO1	Joe Morgan/Black/75	30.00
LA1	Luis Aparicio/Black/45	30.00
MI1	Monte Irvin/Black/45	30.00
OS1	Ozzie Smith/Black/45	75.00
PR1	Phil Rizzuto/Black/50	40.00
RF1	Rollie Fingers/Black/99	20.00
RK1	Ralph Kiner/Black/50	30.00
RR1	Robin Roberts/Black/55	40.00
RY1	Robin Yount/Black/45	75.00
TP1	Tony Perez/Black/50	30.00
WS1	Warren Spahn/Black/35	70.00
YB1	Yogi Berra/Black/50	60.00

Historic Impressions

NM/M
Common Player: 3.00
Production 350 Sets
Golds: 1X
Production 200 Sets
Golds 75: 1.5-2X
Production 75
Silvers: 1X
Production 250 Sets

MA	Mel Allen	3.00
RA	Richie Ashburn	5.00
LB	Lou Boudreau	5.00
RO	Roy Campanella	5.00
AC	Alexander Cartwright	3.00
HC	Harry Caray	4.00
RC	Roberto Clemente	15.00
TY	Ty Cobb	8.00
MC	Mickey Cochrane	5.00
EC	Eddie Collins	3.00
DD	Dizzy Dean	5.00
JD	Joe DiMaggio	5.00
DO	Don Drysdale	3.00
LD	Leo Durocher	3.00
JF	Jimmie Foxx	5.00
LO	Lou Gehrig	10.00
CG	Charlie Gehringer	3.00
LG	Lefty Gomez	3.00
HG	Hank Greenberg	5.00
LE	Lefty Grove	6.00
GH	Gabby Hartnett	3.00
RH	Rogers Hornsby	5.00
CH	Carl Hubbell	6.00
TL	Tony Lazzeri	3.00
MM	Mickey Mantle	25.00
CM	Christy Mathewson	6.00
JO	Joe McCarthy	3.00
JM	Johnny Mize	3.00
MO	Mel Ott	3.00
SP	Satchel Paige	6.00
PR	Pee Wee Reese	5.00
JR	Jackie Robinson	5.00
BR	Babe Ruth	15.00
ES	Enos Slaughter	3.00
TS	Tris Speaker	5.00
CS	Casey Stengel	4.00
HW	Honus Wagner	8.00
HO	Hoyt Wilhelm	3.00
TW	Ted Williams	15.00
CY	Cy Young	5.00

Historic Lumber

NM/M
Common Player: 6.00
Inserted 1:12

BR	Babe Ruth/Away/150	125.00
BR1	Babe Ruth/Home/100	125.00
CF	Carlton Fisk/R.Sox/50	15.00
CF1	Carlton Fisk/W.Sox/50	15.00
CY	Carl Yastrzemski/w/Bat/300	20.00
CY1	Carl Yastrzemski/w/Cap/350	20.00
CY2	Carl Yastrzemski/w/Helmet/350	20.00
DW	Dave Winfield/Padres/350	10.00
DW1	Dave Winfield/Yanks/350	10.00
FR	Frank Robinson/O's/300	10.00
FR1	Frank Robinson/Reds/350	10.00
FR2	Frank Robinson/Angels/350	10.00
GC	Gary Carter/Mets/300	6.00
GC1	Gary Carter/Helmet Expos/100	6.00
GC2	Gary Carter/Cap Expos/100	6.00
HK	Harmon Killebrew/350	10.00

JB	Johnny Bench/w/Bat/350	10.00
JB1	Johnny Bench/Swing/350	10.00
JM	Joe Morgan/Reds/350	6.00
JM1	Joe Morgan/Astros/350	6.00
MM	Mickey Mantle/300	100.00
NR	Nolan Ryan/Rgr./225	25.00
OS	Ozzie Smith/Cards/300	15.00
OS1	Ozzie Smith/Padres/350	15.00
RS	Red Schoendienst/Look Right/165	6.00
RS1	Red Schoendienst/Look Left/165	6.00
SC	Steve Carlton/350	8.00
TP	Tony Perez Swing/350	6.00
TP1	Tony Perez/Portrait/350	6.00
TS	Tom Seaver/100	10.00
TW	Ted Williams/w/3 Bats/150	75.00
TW1	Ted Williams/Portrait/150	75.00
WS	Willie Stargell/Arms Down/150	8.00
WS1	Willie Stargell/Arms Up/150	8.00
YB	Yogi Berra/Shout/350	10.00
YB1	Yogi Berra/w/Bat/350	10.00

Historic Lumber Green

Common Player: **NM/M**

BR	Babe Ruth/Away/75	140.00
BR1	Babe Ruth/Home/75	140.00
CY	Carl Yastrzemski/w/Bat/125	25.00
CY1	Carl Yastrzemski/w/Cap/125	25.00
CY2	Carl Yastrzemski/w/Helmet/125	25.00
DW	Dave Winfield/Padres/125	10.00
DW1	Dave Winfield/Yanks/125	10.00
FR	Frank Robinson/O's/125	10.00
FR1	Frank Robinson/Reds/125	10.00
FR2	Frank Robinson/Angels/125	10.00
GC	Gary Carter/Mets/125	6.00
GC1	Gary Carter/Helmet Expos/125	6.00
GC2	Gary Carter/Cap Expos/125	6.00
HK	Harmon Killebrew/125	10.00
JB	Johnny Bench/w/Bat/125	10.00
JB1	Johnny Bench/Swing/125	10.00
JM	Joe Morgan/Reds/125	6.00
JM1	Joe Morgan/Astros/125	6.00
MM	Mickey Mantle/75	120.00
NR	Nolan Ryan/Astros/50	50.00
OS	Ozzie Smith/Cards/125	20.00
OS1	Ozzie Smith/Padres/125	20.00
RS	Red Schoendienst/Look Right/125	8.00
RS1	Red Schoendienst/Look Left/125	8.00
SC	Steve Carlton/125	10.00
TP	Tony Perez/Swing/125	6.00
TP1	Tony Perez/Portrait/125	6.00
TS	Tom Seaver/50	15.00
TW	Ted Williams/w/3 Bats/75	75.00
TW1	Ted Williams/Portrait/75	75.00
WS	Willie Stargell/Arms Down/125	10.00
WS1	Willie Stargell/Arms Up/125	10.00
YB	Yogi Berra/Shout/125	10.00
YB1	Yogi Berra/w/Bat/125	10.00

Historic Swatches

NM/M
Common Player: 5.00
Inserted 1:12
Blues: .75-1.5X
Production 50 Sets
Greens: .75-1X
Production 160 to 250
Purples: .75-1.5X
Production 75 to 150

BG	Bob Gibson/CO Jsy/350	10.00
BM	Bill Mazeroski/Pants/50	15.00
BW	Billy Williams/Jsy/190	5.00
CF	Carlton Fisk/Pants/350	8.00
CM	Christy Mathewson/Pants/300	100.00
CS	Casey Stengel/Jsy/275	10.00
CY	Carl Yastrzemski/Jsy/350	20.00
CY1	Carl Yastrzemski/Pants/350	20.00
DS	Duke Snider/Jsy/350	10.00
DW1	Dave Winfield/Twins/Jsy/300	8.00
FR	Frank Robinson/O's Jsy/350	10.00
FR1	Frank Robinson/Angels Jsy/350	10.00
GC	Gary Carter/Mets Jsy/350	5.00
GC1	Gary Carter/Expos Jsy/350	5.00
HW	Honus Wagner/Pants/275	120.00
JB	Johnny Bench/Jsy/350	10.00
JM	Joe Morgan/Jsy/350	5.00
JN	Juan Marichal/Pants/225	5.00
JN1	Juan Marichal/Jsy/48	5.00
LA	Luis Aparicio/Jsy/230	5.00
LB	Lou Boudreau/Jsy/265	5.00
MM	Mickey Mantle/Pants/350	100.00
NR	Nolan Ryan/Rgr. Pants/350	25.00
NR1	Nolan Ryan/Astro Pants/350	25.00
OS	Ozzie Smith/Jsy/85	25.00
RF	Rollie Fingers/Jsy/105	5.00
RY	Robin Yount/Portrait Jsy/350	5.00
RY1	Robin Yount/Swing Jsy/350	10.00
SA	Sparky Anderson/Jsy/350	5.00
SC	Steve Carlton/Jsy/350	10.00
SM	Stan Musial/Jsy/350	25.00
TC	Ty Cobb/Pants/350	90.00
TP	Tony Perez/Jsy/350	5.00
TS	Tom Seaver/Jsy/350	10.00
TS1	Tom Seaver/Pants/350	10.00
TW	Ted Williams/Jsy/250	85.00
WA	Walter Alston/Look Left/Jsy/350	5.00
WA1	Walter Alston/Ahead/Jsy/350	5.00
WI	Willie Stargell/Jsy/55	15.00
WS	Warren Spahn/CO Jsy/350	15.00
YB	Yogi Berra Jsy/300	10.00

2003 SPx

NM/M
Complete Set (178):
Common Player: .25
Common SP (126-160): 4.00
Production 999
Common Jsy Auto. (161-178): 10.00
Production 1,224 unless noted.
Pack (4): 6.00
Box (18): 90.00

1	Darin Erstad	.50
2	Garret Anderson	.50
3	Tim Salmon	.50
4	Troy Glaus/SP	2.00
5	Luis Gonzalez	.50
6	Randy Johnson	1.50
7	Curt Schilling	1.00
8	Lyle Overbay	.25
9	Andruw Jones/SP	3.00
10	Gary Sheffield	.75
11	Rafael Furcal	.40
12	Greg Maddux	2.00
13	Chipper Jones/SP	3.00
14	Tony Batista	.25
15	Rodrigo Lopez	.25
16	Jay Gibbons	.25
17	Byung-Hyun Kim	1.00
18	Johnny Damon	1.00
19	Derek Lowe	.25
20	Nomar Garciaparra/SP	4.00
21	Pedro J. Martinez	1.50
22	Manny Ramirez/SP	4.00
23	Mark Prior	1.00
24	Kerry Wood	.50
25	Corey Patterson	.50
26	Sammy Sosa/SP	4.00
27	Moises Alou	.50
28	Magglio Ordonez	.50
29	Frank Thomas	1.00
30	Paul Konerko	.50
31	Bartolo Colon	.25
32	Adam Dunn	1.00
33	Austin Kearns	.50
34	Aaron Boone	.25
35	Ken Griffey Jr./SP	5.00
36	Omar Vizquel	.50
37	C.C. Sabathia	.25
38	Jason Davis	.25
39	Travis Hafner	.75
40	Brandon Phillips	.25
41	Larry Walker	.50
42	Preston Wilson	.50
43	Jay Payton	.25
44	Todd Helton	.75
45	Carlos Pena	.25
46	Eric Munson	.25
47	Ivan Rodriguez	1.00
48	Josh Beckett	.25
49	Alex Gonzalez	.25
50	Roy Oswalt	.50
51	Craig Biggio	.50
52	Jeff Bagwell	.75
53	Dontrelle Willis/SP	2.00
54	Mike Sweeney	.25
55	Carlos Beltran	1.00
56	Brent Mayne	.25
57	Hideo Nomo	.75
58	Rickey Henderson	.75
59	Adrian Beltre	.25
60	Miguel Cabrera/SP	4.00
61	Kazuhisa Ishii	.25
62	Ben Sheets	.50
63	Richie Sexson	.50
64	Torii Hunter/SP	2.00
65	Jacque Jones	.25
66	Joe Mays	.25
67	Corey Koskie	.25
68	A.J. Pierzynski	.25
69	Jose Vidro	.25
70	Vladimir Guerrero/SP	4.00
71	Tom Glavine	.50
72	Jose Reyes/SP	4.00
73	Aaron Heilman	.25
74	Mike Piazza	2.00
75	Jorge Posada	.75
76	Mike Mussina	.75
77	Robin Ventura	.25
78	Mariano Rivera	.75
79	Roger Clemens/SP	6.00
80	Jason Giambi	.75
81	Bernie Williams	.75
82	Alfonso Soriano/SP	4.00
83	Derek Jeter	3.00
84	Miguel Tejada/SP	3.00
85	Eric Chavez	.50
86	Tim Hudson	.50
87	Barry Zito	.50
88	Mark Mulder	.50
89	Erubiel Durazo	.25
90	Pat Burrell	.50
91	Jim Thome/SP	3.00
92	Bobby Abreu	.50
93	Brian Giles	.50
94	Reggie Sanders/SP	2.00
95	Kenny Lofton	.50
96	Ryan Klesko	.25
97	Sean Burroughs	.25
98	Edgardo Alfonzo	.25
99	Rich Aurilia	.25
100	Jose Cruz Jr.	.25
101	Barry Bonds/SP	8.00
102	Mike Cameron	.25
103	Kazuhiro Sasaki	.25
104	Bret Boone	.25
105	Ichiro Suzuki/SP	5.00
106	J.D. Drew	.50
107	Jim Edmonds	.50
108	Scott Rolen/SP	3.00
109	Matt Morris	.25
110	Tino Martinez	.50
111	Albert Pujols/SP	8.00
112	Damian Rolls	.25
113	Carl Crawford	.50
114	Rocco Baldelli/SP	2.00
115	Hank Blalock	.50
116	Alex Rodriguez/SP	5.00
117	Kevin Mench	.25
118	Rafael Palmeiro	.75
119	Mark Teixeira	.75
120	Shannon Stewart	.25
121	Vernon Wells	.50
122	Josh Phelps	.25
123	Eric Hinske	.25
124	Orlando Hudson	.25
125	Carlos Delgado	.50
126	Jason Roach RC	4.00
127	Dan Haren	8.00
128	Luis Ayala RC	4.00
129	Bo Hart RC	4.00
130	Wilfredo Ledezma RC	4.00
131	Rick Roberts RC	4.00
132	Miguel Ojeda RC	4.00
133	Aquilino Lopez RC	4.00
134	Roger Deago RC	4.00
135	Arnie Munoz RC	4.00
136	Brent Hoard RC	4.00
137	Terrmel Sledge RC	4.00
138	Ryan Cameron RC	4.00
139	Prentice Redman RC	4.00
140	Clint Barmes RC	6.00
141	Jeremy Griffiths	4.00
142	Jon Leicester RC	4.00
143	Brandon Webb RC	15.00
144	Todd Wellemeyer RC	4.00
145	Felix Sanchez RC	4.00
146	Anthony Ferrari RC	4.00
147	Ian Ferguson RC	4.00
148	Micheal Nakamura RC	4.00
149	Lew Ford RC	8.00
150	Nate Bland RC	4.00
151	Dave Matranga RC	4.00
152	Edgar Gonzalez RC	4.00
153	Carlos Mendez RC	4.00
154	Jason Gilfillan RC	4.00
155	Mike Neu RC	4.00
156	Jason Shiell RC	4.00
157	Jeff Duncan RC	4.00
158	Oscar Villarreal RC	4.00
159	Diegomar Markwell RC	4.00
160	Joe Valentine RC	4.00
161	Hideki Matsui/864 RC	300.00
162	Jose Contreras/800 RC	30.00
163	Willie Eyre RC	10.00
164	Matt Bruback RC	10.00
165	Rett Johnson RC	15.00
166	Jeremy Griffiths RC	15.00
167	Francisco Cruceta RC	10.00
168	Fernando Cabrera RC	10.00
169	Jhonny Peralta RC	30.00
170	Shane Bazzell RC	10.00
171	Bobby Madritsch RC	20.00
172	Phil Seibel RC	10.00
173	Josh Willingham RC	40.00
174	Robby Hammock RC	10.00
175	Alejandro Machado RC	10.00
176	David Sanders RC	10.00
177	Matt Kata RC	15.00
178	Heath Bell RC	4.00

Spectrum

Stars (1-125) print run 51-99: 3-6X
Stars (1-125) p/r 26-50: 6-12X
Print run 25 or less not priced.
Numbered to jersey number.
SP's (126-160): .75-1.5X
Production 125

SPX Combos

NM/M
Common Duo: 20.00
Quantity produced listed

MJ	Hideki Matsui, Derek Jeter/90	100.00
RC	Nolan Ryan, Roger Clemens/90	120.00
SJ	Curt Schilling, Randy Johnson/90	30.00
EG	Darin Erstad, Troy Glaus/90	20.00
GC	Greg Maddux, Chipper Jones/90	50.00
GS	Jason Giambi, Alfonso Soriano/90	30.00
BK	Jeff Bagwell, Jeff Kent/90	25.00
GD	Ken Griffey Jr., Adam Dunn/90	50.00
GR	Ken Griffey Jr., Sammy Sosa/90	50.00
SP	Sammy Sosa, Rafael Palmeiro/90	40.00
MG	Pedro Martinez, Nomar Garciaparra/90	40.00
RG	Alex Rodriguez, Nomar Garciaparra/90	40.00
CM	Jose Contreras, Pedro Martinez/90	40.00
FC	Carlton Fisk, Gary Carter/90	15.00
RR	Cal Ripken Jr., Scott Rolen/90	80.00
JJ	Chipper Jones, Andruw Jones/90	30.00
PM	Rafael Palmeiro, Fred McGriff/90	30.00
RT	Alex Rodriguez, Miguel Tejada/90	30.00
SB	Sammy Sosa, Barry Bonds/90	50.00
SN	Ichiro Suzuki, Hideo Nomo/90	175.00
MS	Hideki Matsui, Ichiro Suzuki/50	350.00
MW	Mickey Mantle, Ted Williams/50	300.00
CC	Jose Contreras, Roger Clemens/50	40.00
CL	Cal Ripken Jr., Lou Gehrig/90	300.00
HJ	Hideki Matsui, Jason Giambi/50	75.00
CA	Cal Ripken Jr., Alex Rodriguez/50	150.00
IA	Ichiro Suzuki, Albert Pujols/50	250.00
NI	Hideo Nomo, Kazuhisa Ishii/50	50.00
MD	Mickey Mantle, Derek Jeter/50	180.00
BT	Barry Bonds, Ted Williams/50	180.00
BM	Barry Bonds, Roger Maris/50	80.00
MB	Mickey Mantle, Barry Bonds/50	150.00
PS	Rafael Palmeiro, Sammy Sosa/90	40.00
RS	Nolan Ryan, Tom Seaver/90	110.00

Stars

NM/M
Common Player: 20.00
Quantity produced listed

LB	Lance Berkman/590	30.00
PB	Pat Burrell/590	25.00
NM	Nomar Garciaparra/195	80.00
JG	Jason Giambi/315	30.00
TG	Troy Glaus/490	25.00
LG	Luis Gonzalez/790	20.00
KG	Ken Griffey Jr./690	80.00
VG	Vladimir Guerrero/390	50.00
CJ	Chipper Jones/195	50.00
MP	Mark Prior/490	40.00
CS	Curt Schilling/490	40.00

Winning Materials

NM/M
Common Player: 5.00
Version 1 Production 375
Golds: 1X
Production 250
Version 2 Production 175
Golds: 1-2X
Production 125

RA1	Roberto Alomar	8.00
RA2	Roberto Alomar	10.00
JB1	Jeff Bagwell	6.00
JB2	Jeff Bagwell	8.00
LB1	Lance Berkman	5.00
LB2	Lance Berkman	5.00
PB1	Pat Burrell	5.00
PB2	Pat Burrell	8.00
RC1	Roger Clemens	15.00
RC2	Roger Clemens	15.00
CD1	Carlos Delgado	6.00
CD2	Carlos Delgado	8.00
RF1	Rafael Furcal	8.00
RF2	Rafael Furcal	8.00
JG1	Jason Giambi	8.00
JG2	Jason Giambi	8.00
TR1	Troy Glaus	6.00
TG2	Troy Glaus	8.00
TG1	Tom Glavine	5.00
TG2	Tom Glavine	5.00
LG1	Luis Gonzalez	5.00
LG2	Luis Gonzalez	5.00
SG1	Shawn Green	5.00
SG2	Shawn Green	5.00
KG1	Ken Griffey Jr.	15.00
KG2	Ken Griffey Jr.	15.00
VG1	Vladimir Guerrero	10.00
VG2	Vladimir Guerrero	12.00
T01	Todd Helton	8.00
TH2	Todd Helton	10.00
TH1	Torii Hunter	8.00
RJ1	Randy Johnson	10.00
RJ2	Randy Johnson	12.00
AJ1	Andruw Jones	8.00
AJ2	Andruw Jones	8.00
CJ1	Chipper Jones	10.00
CJ2	Chipper Jones	15.00
JK1	Jeff Kent	5.00
JK2	Jeff Kent	5.00
GM1	Greg Maddux	15.00
GM2	Greg Maddux	15.00
MM2	Mickey Mantle	120.00
PM1	Pedro Martinez	10.00
PM2	Pedro Martinez	15.00
HM1	Hideki Matsui	30.00
HM2	Hideki Matsui	30.00
HN1	Hideo Nomo	15.00
HN2	Hideo Nomo	20.00
MP1	Mike Piazza	10.00
MP2	Mike Piazza	15.00
MA1	Mark Prior	10.00
MA2	Mark Prior	10.00
AP1	Albert Pujols	20.00
AP2	Albert Pujols	20.00
MR1	Manny Ramirez	10.00
MR2	Manny Ramirez	15.00
AR1	Alex Rodriguez	10.00
AR2	Alex Rodriguez	12.00
IR1	Ivan Rodriguez	8.00
IR2	Ivan Rodriguez	10.00
CS1	Curt Schilling	8.00
CS2	Curt Schilling	10.00
GS1	Gary Sheffield	6.00
GS2	Gary Sheffield	8.00
AS1	Alfonso Soriano	10.00
AS2	Alfonso Soriano	12.00
SS1	Sammy Sosa	10.00
SS2	Sammy Sosa	15.00
IS1	Ichiro Suzuki	25.00
IS2	Ichiro Suzuki	35.00
MT1	Miguel Tejada	6.00
MT2	Miguel Tejada	8.00
FT1	Frank Thomas	6.00
FT2	Frank Thomas	10.00
JT1	Jim Thome	8.00
JT2	Jim Thome	10.00
BW1	Bernie Williams	10.00
BW2	Bernie Williams	10.00
TW2	Ted Williams	80.00
TW2	Ted Williams Gold/50	200.00
BZ1	Barry Zito	6.00
BZ2	Barry Zito	8.00

Young Stars

NM/M
Common Player: 8.00
Production 1,295 unless noted.

KA	Kurt Ainsworth/1,460	8.00
RB	Rocco Baldelli	20.00
JBa	Josh Bard	8.00
HB	Hank Blalock	20.00
SB	Sean Burroughs	8.00
MD	Michael Cuddyer/1,156	10.00
AD	Adam Dunn	20.00
CG	Chris George/1,260	8.00
EH	Eric Hinske	8.00
JA	Jason Jennings	8.00
NJ	Nick Johnson	8.00
JJ	Jacque Jones/1,260	12.00
AK	Austin Kearns/964	15.00
MK	Mike Kinkade	8.00
BM	Brett Myers	8.00
RO	Roy Oswalt	15.00
JP	Josh Phelps	10.00
BP	Brandon Phillips	10.00
KS	Kirk Saarloos	8.00
MT	Mark Teixeira	25.00

2004 SP Authentic

NM/M
Complete Set (191):
Common (1-90): .25
Common RC (91-132, 178-191): 4.00
Production 999
Common SP (133-177): 2.00
Production 999
Pack (5): 5.00
Box (24): 100.00

1	Bret Boone	.25
2	Gary Sheffield	.50
3	Rafael Palmeiro	.75
4	Jorge Posada	.50
5	Derek Jeter	.30
6	Garret Anderson	.50
7	Bartolo Colon	.40
8	Kevin Brown	.40
9	Shea Hillenbrand	.25
10	Ryan Klesko	.25
11	Bobby Abreu	.25
12	Scott Rolen	1.00
13	Alfonso Soriano	.75
14	Jason Giambi	1.00
15	Tom Glavine	.50
16	Hideo Nomo	.50
17	Johan Santana	.75
18	Sammy Sosa	.50
19	Rickie Weeks	.50
20	Barry Zito	.50
21	Kerry Wood	.50
22	Austin Kearns	.40
23	Shawn Green	.40
24	Miguel Cabrera	.75
25	Richard Hidalgo	.25
26	Andruw Jones	.75
27	Randy Wolf	.25
28	David Ortiz	1.00
29	Roy Oswalt	.50
30	Vernon Wells	.50
31	Ben Sheets	.50

32 Mike Lowell .25
33 Todd Helton .75
34 Jacque Jones .25
35 Mike Sweeney .25
36 Hank Blalock .50
37 Jason Schmidt .50
38 Jeff Kent .40
39 Josh Beckett .50
40 Manny Ramirez 1.00
41 Torii Hunter .50
42 Brian Giles .40
43 Javier Vazquez .25
44 Jim Edmonds .50
45 Dmitri Young .25
46 Preston Wilson .25
47 Jeff Bagwell .75
48 Pedro J. Martinez 1.00
49 Eric Chavez .40
50 Ken Griffey Jr. 2.00
51 Shannon Stewart .25
52 Rafael Furcal .40
53 Brandon Webb .25
54 Juan Pierre .25
55 Roger Clemens 2.00
56 Geoff Jenkins .25
57 Lance Berkman .50
58 Albert Pujols 3.00
59 Frank Thomas .75
60 Edgar Martinez .40
61 Tim Hudson .50
62 Eric Gagne .50
63 Richie Sexson .50
64 Corey Patterson .25
65 Nomar Garciaparra 1.00
66 Hideki Matsui 2.00
67 Mark Teixeira .75
68 Troy Glaus .50
69 Carlos Lee .40
70 Mike Mussina .75
71 Magglio Ordonez .50
72 Roy Halladay .50
73 Ichiro Suzuki 2.00
74 Randy Johnson 1.00
75 Luis Gonzalez .40
76 Mark Prior .75
77 Carlos Beltran .50
78 Ivan Rodriguez .75
79 Alex Rodriguez 2.50
80 Dontrelle Willis .50
81 Mike Piazza 1.00
82 Curt Schilling .75
83 Vladimir Guerrero 1.00
84 Greg Maddux 1.50
85 Jim Thome 1.00
86 Miguel Tejada .50
87 Carlos Delgado .50
88 Jose Reyes .75
89 Matt Morris .25
90 Mark Mulder .40
91 Angel Chavez RC 4.00
92 Brandon Medders RC 4.00
93 Carlos Vasquez RC 4.00
94 Chris Aguila RC 4.00
95 Colby Miller RC 4.00
96 David Crouthers 4.00
97 Dennis Sarfate RC 4.00
98 Donnie Kelly RC 4.00
99 Merkin Valdez RC 6.00
100 Eddy Rodriguez RC 4.00
101 Edwin Moreno RC 4.00
102 Enemencio Pacheco RC 4.00
103 Roberto Novoa RC 4.00
104 Greg Dobbs RC 4.00
105 Hector Gimenez RC 4.00
106 Ian Snell RC 10.00
107 Jake Woods 4.00
108 Jamie Brown RC 4.00
109 Jason Frasor RC 4.00
110 Jerome Gamble RC 4.00
111 Jerry Gil RC 6.00
112 Jesse Harper RC 4.00
113 Jorge Vasquez RC 4.00
114 Jose Capellan RC 6.00
115 Josh Labandeira RC 4.00
116 Justin Hampson RC 4.00
117 Justin Huismán RC 4.00
118 Justin Leone RC 6.00
119 Lincoln Holdzkom RC 4.00
120 Lino Urdaneta RC 4.00
121 Mike Gosling 4.00
122 Mike Johnston RC 4.00
123 Mike Rouse 4.00
124 Scott Proctor RC 4.00
125 Roman Colon RC 4.00
126 Ronny Cedeno RC 10.00
127 Ryan Meaux RC 4.00
128 Scott Dohmann RC 4.00
129 Sean Henn 6.00
130 Tim Bausher RC 4.00
131 Tim Bittner RC 4.00
132 William Bergolla RC 6.00
133 Rick Ferrell 2.00
134 Joe DiMaggio 6.00
135 Bob Feller 2.00
136 Ted Williams 6.00
137 Stan Musial 5.00
138 Larry Doby 2.00
139 Red Schoendienst 2.00
140 Enos Slaughter 2.00
141 Stan Musial 5.00
142 Mickey Mantle 8.00
143 Ted Williams 6.00
144 Mickey Mantle 8.00
145 Stan Musial 5.00
146 Tom Seaver 3.00
147 Willie McCovey 2.00
148 Bob Gibson 3.00

149 Frank Robinson 3.00
150 Joe Morgan 2.00
151 Billy Williams 2.00
152 Catfish Hunter 2.00
153 Joe Morgan 2.00
154 Joe Morgan 2.00
155 Mike Schmidt 5.00
156 Tommy Lasorda 2.00
157 Robin Yount 4.00
158 Nolan Ryan 8.00
159 John Franco 2.00
160 Nolan Ryan 8.00
161 Ken Griffey Jr. 8.00
162 Cal Ripken Jr. 8.00
163 Ken Griffey Jr. 5.00
164 Gary Sheffield 2.00
165 Fred McGriff 2.00
166 Hideo Nomo 2.00
167 Mike Piazza 4.00
168 Sandy Alomar Jr. 2.00
169 Roberto Alomar 4.00
170 Ted Williams 6.00
171 Pedro J. Martinez 4.00
172 Derek Jeter 8.00
173 Cal Ripken Jr. 8.00
174 Torii Hunter 2.00
175 Alfonso Soriano 3.00
176 Hank Blalock 2.00
177 Ichiro Suzuki 4.00
178 Orlando Rodriguez RC 4.00
179 Ramon Ramirez RC 4.00
180 Kazuo Matsui RC 6.00
181 Kevin Cave RC 4.00
182 John Gall RC 4.00
183 Freddy Guzman RC 4.00
184 Chris Oxspring RC 4.00
185 Rusty Tucker RC 4.00
186 Jorge Sequea RC 4.00
187 Carlos Hines RC 4.00
188 Luis Gonzalez 4.00
189 Ryan Wing 4.00
190 Jeff Bennett RC 4.00
191 Luis Gonzalez 4.00

Silver

Stars (1-90): 2-4X
Production 499
SP (91-132, 178-191): 1X
Production 249

Gold

Stars (1-90): 4-8X
Gold SP (91-132, 178-191): 2X
Production 99
Gold (133-177): 1-1.5X
Production 499

Chirography

NM/M

Bronze: 1X
Production 65
Bronze Duo Tone: 1X
Production 60
Gold: 1-1.5X
Production 40
Gold Duo Tone: No Pricing
Production 20
Silver: 1X
Production 60
Silver Duo Tone: 1.5-2X
Production 30
Duo Tone: 1X
Production 75
AB Bobby Abreu 15.00
GA Garret Anderson 15.00
RB Rocco Baldelli 20.00
JB Josh Beckett 20.00
CB Carlos Beltran 30.00
HB Hank Blalock 20.00
BB Bret Boone 20.00
MC Miguel Cabrera 40.00
EC Eric Chavez 20.00
DE Dennis Eckersley 30.00
WE Willie Eyre 8.00
EG Eric Gagne 30.00
JG Juan Gonzalez 20.00

KG Ken Griffey Jr. 120.00
TH Travis Hafner 15.00
HY Roy Halladay 20.00
HA Robby Hammock 10.00
BH Bo Hart 8.00
HE Runelvys Hernandez 8.00
HI Bobby Hill 8.00
DJ Derek Jeter 150.00
JJ Jacque Jones 15.00
AK Austin Kearns 15.00
CL Cliff Lee 15.00
AL Al Leiter 15.00
PL Paul LoDuca 15.00
JL Javy Lopez 15.00
ML Mike Lowell 15.00
EM Edgar Martinez 25.00
RO Roy Oswalt 20.00
PA Corey Patterson 15.00
PI Mike Piazza 125.00
CP Colin Porter 10.00
JP Jorge Posada 25.00
MP Mark Prior 30.00
HR Horacio Ramirez 15.00
JR Jose Reyes 35.00
CR Cal Ripken Jr. 100.00
JS Jae Weong Seo 15.00
BS Ben Sheets 20.00
SM John Smoltz 60.00
MT Mark Teixeira 25.00
JV Javier Vazquez 20.00
CW Chien-Ming Wang 125.00
RW Rickie Weeks 15.00
BW Brandon Webb 25.00
VW Vernon Wells 15.00
JW Jerome Williams 10.00
DW Dontrelle Willis 30.00
KW Kerry Wood 25.00
DY Delmon Young 25.00
BZ Barry Zito 20.00

Chirography Dual

NM/M

Common Duo: 40.00
Production 50 Sets
BC Bret Boone, Eric Chavez 50.00
BL Mike Lowell, Josh Beckett 50.00
BP Corey Patterson, Carlos Beltran 50.00
BT Hank Blalock, Mark Teixeira 50.00
EG Dennis Eckersley, Eric Gagne 50.00
HW Vernon Wells, Roy Halladay 40.00
JM Johnny Bench, Mike Piazza 200.00
KG Ken Griffey Jr., Austin Kearns 100.00
PB Yogi Berra, Jorge Posada 100.00
RR Alex Rodriguez, Cal Ripken Jr. 400.00
SG Ken Griffey Jr., Ichiro Suzuki 375.00
SM Stan Musial, Ozzie Smith 175.00
WC Miguel Cabrera, Dontrelle Willis 70.00
WJ Chien-Ming Wang, Derek Jeter 350.00
WR Nolan Ryan, Kerry Wood 225.00
WW Dontrelle Willis, Brandon Webb 50.00
YW Delmon Young, Rickie Weeks 50.00
ZC Eric Chavez, Barry Zito 50.00

Chirography Triple

NM/M

Production 25 Sets
BWR Kerry Wood, Nolan Ryan, Josh Beckett 250.00
FBB Johnny Bench, Carlton Fisk, Yogi Berra 300.00
GSM Bob Gibson, Stan Musial, Ozzie Smith 220.00
JVB Derek Jeter, Yogi Berra, Javier Vazquez 250.00
PRC Jose Reyes, Miguel Cabrera, Colin Porter 100.00
RBT Hank Blalock, Mark Teixeira, Alex Rodriguez 250.00
RRR Alex Rodriguez, Cal Ripken Jr., Phil Rizzuto 400.00
SJB Rocco Baldelli, Jacque Jones, Ichiro Suzuki 275.00
WLE Chien-Ming Wang, Willie Eyre, Cliff Lee 275.00
WPB Mark Prior, Josh Beckett, Brandon Webb 250.00
YYM Robin Yount, Carl Yastrzemski, Stan Musial 300.00
ZHO Barry Zito, Roy Oswalt, Roy Halladay 200.00

Chirography Quad

No Pricing
Production 10 Sets

Chirography Hall of Famers

NM/M

Production 40 Sets
Duo Tone: No Pricing
Production 25
LA Luis Aparicio 20.00
JB Johnny Bench 60.00
YB Yogi Berra 50.00
BD Bobby Doerr 30.00
DE Dennis Eckersley 30.00
CF Carlton Fisk 30.00
BG Bob Gibson 40.00
MI Monte Irvin 40.00
AK Al Kaline 50.00
HK Harmon Killebrew 65.00
RK Ralph Kiner 25.00
PM Paul Molitor 30.00
SM Stan Musial 100.00
TP Tony Perez 30.00
KP Kirby Puckett 100.00
PR Phil Rizzuto 40.00
RR Robin Roberts 40.00
BR Brooks Robinson 40.00
NR Nolan Ryan 120.00
MS Mike Schmidt 120.00
TS Tom Seaver 50.00
OS Ozzie Smith 65.00
DS Duke Snider 30.00
CY Carl Yastrzemski 75.00
RY Robin Yount 75.00

Future Watch Autograph

LINCOLN HOLDZKOM pitcher

NM/M

Production 295 8.00
91 Angel Chavez 8.00
92 Brandon Medders 8.00
93 Carlos Vasquez 10.00
94 Chris Aguila 10.00
95 Colby Miller 10.00
96 David Crouthers 8.00
97 Dennis Sarfate 8.00
98 Donnie Kelly 10.00
99 Merkin Valdez 15.00
100 Eddy Rodriguez 15.00
101 Edwin Moreno 8.00
102 Enemencio Pacheco 10.00
103 Roberto Novoa 8.00
104 Greg Dobbs 8.00
105 Hector Gimenez 10.00
106 Ian Snell 30.00
107 Jake Woods 10.00
108 Jamie Brown 10.00
109 Jason Frasor 10.00
110 Jerome Gamble 8.00
111 Jerry Gil 12.00
112 Jesse Harper 8.00
113 Jorge Vasquez 12.00
114 Jose Capellan 10.00
115 Josh Labandeira 10.00
116 Justin Hampson 8.00
117 Justin Huisman 10.00
118 Justin Leone 15.00
119 Lincoln Holdzkom 8.00
120 Lino Urdaneta 10.00
121 Mike Gosling 10.00
122 Mike Johnston 10.00
123 Mike Rouse 10.00
124 Scott Proctor 15.00
125 Roman Colon 10.00
126 Ronny Cedeno 15.00
127 Ryan Meaux 10.00
128 Scott Dohmann 10.00
129 Sean Henn 15.00
130 Tim Bausher 10.00
131 Tim Bittner 8.00
132 William Bergolla 10.00
178 Orlando Rodriguez 10.00
179 Ramon Ramirez 10.00
181 Kevin Cave 10.00
182 John Gall 15.00
183 Freddy Guzman 10.00
184 Chris Oxspring 10.00
185 Rusty Tucker 10.00
186 Jorge Sequea 10.00
187 Carlos Hines 8.00
188 Luis Gonzalez 10.00
189 Ryan Wing 10.00
190 Jeff Bennett 10.00
191 Luis Gonzalez 10.00

2004 SP Authentic USA Signature

NM/M

Production 445 Sets
Reds: 1.5X
Production 50
USA-1 Ernie Young 6.00
USA-2 Chris Burke 12.00
USA-3 Jesse Crain 15.00
USA-4 Justin Duchscherer 15.00
USA-5 J.D. Durbin 10.00
USA-6 Gerald Laird 10.00
USA-7 John Grabow 8.00
USA-8 Gabe Gross 15.00
USA-9 J.J. Hardy 15.00
USA-10 Jeremy Reed 15.00
USA-11 Graham Koonce 15.00
USA-12 Mike Lamb 15.00
USA-13 Justin Leone 15.00
USA-14 Ryan Madson 12.00
USA-15 Joe Mauer 40.00
USA-16 Todd Williams 15.00
USA-17 Horacio Ramirez 15.00
USA-18 Mike Rouse 15.00
USA-19 Jason Stanford 10.00
USA-20 John Van Benschoten 10.00
USA-21 Grady Sizemore 40.00

2004 SP Game-Used Patch

Rafael Furcal shortstop

NM/M

Complete Set (119):
Common (1-60): 2.00
Common (61-90): 2.00
Quantity produced listed
Common (91-119): 6.00
Production 375
Box (1:Pack): 140.00
1 Miguel Cabrera
2 Alex Rodriguez 10.00
3 Edgar Renteria 2.50
4 Juan Gonzalez 2.50
5 Mike Lowell 2.50
6 Andruw Jones 3.00
7 Eric Chavez 2.00
8 Jim Edmonds 2.00
9 Mike Piazza 5.00
10 Angel Berroa 2.00
11 Eric Gagne 3.00
12 Jody Gerut 2.00
13 Orlando Cabrera 2.00
14 Austin Kearns 2.00
15 Frank Thomas 3.00
16 Johan Santana 2.00
17 Randy Johnson 4.00
18 Preston Wilson 2.00
19 Garret Anderson 2.50
20 Jorge Posada 2.50
21 Rich Harden 2.00
22 Barry Zito 2.00
23 Gary Sheffield 3.00
24 Jose Reyes 3.00
25 Roy Halladay 2.50
26 Ben Sheets 2.00
27 Geoff Jenkins 2.00
28 Josh Beckett 3.00
29 Roy Oswalt 2.50
30 Bobby Abreu 2.50
31 Hank Blalock 2.50
32 Kerry Wood 2.50
33 Ryan Klesko 2.00
34 Rafael Furcal 2.00
35 Tom Glavine 2.50
36 Kevin Brown 2.50
37 Scott Rolen 3.00
38 Bret Boone 2.50
39 Ichiro Suzuki 8.00
40 Lance Berkman 3.00
41 Tim Hudson 2.50
42 Carlos Delgado 3.00
43 Ivan Rodriguez 3.00
44 Luis Gonzalez 2.00
45 Torii Hunter 2.00
46 Carlos Lee 2.00
47 Jacque Jones 2.00
48 Manny Ramirez 3.00
49 Troy Glaus 2.50
50 Corey Patterson 2.00
51 Jason Schmidt 2.50
52 Mark Mulder 2.00
53 Vernon Wells 2.50
54 Curt Schilling 4.00
55 Javy Lopez 2.50

56 Mark Prior 3.00
57 Dontrelle Willis 2.50
58 Derek Jeter 10.00
59 Jeff Bagwell 3.00
60 Marlon Byrd 2.00
61 Rafael Palmeiro/500 5.00
62 Kevin Millwood/165 2.00
63 Greg Maddux/273 3.00
64 Adam Dunn/400 3.00
65 Richie Sexson/469 3.00
66 Magglio Ordonez/567 2.00
67 Hideo Nomo/236 3.00
68 Albert Pujols/194 10.00
69 Rocco Baldelli/368 3.00
70 Mark Teixeira/86 4.00
71 Jason Giambi/660 3.00
72 Alfonso Soriano/230 4.00
73 Roger Clemens/300 8.00
74 Miguel Tejada/359 2.00
75 Jeff Kent/684 2.00
76 Bernie Williams/342 3.00
77 Sammy Sosa/470 3.00
78 Mike Mussina/641 3.00
79 Jim Thome/334 4.00
80 Brian Giles/506 2.00
81 Shawn Green/234 2.00
82 Mike Sweeney/340 2.00
83 John Smoltz/262 3.00
84 Carlos Beltran/319 3.00
85 Todd Helton/384 3.00
86 Nomar Garciaparra/372 4.00
87 Ken Griffey Jr./481 8.00
88 Chipper Jones/633 4.00
89 Vladimir Guerrero/226 4.00
90 Pedro Martinez/313 5.00
91 Brandon Medders RC 6.00
92 Colby Miller RC 6.00
93 David Crouthers 6.00
94 Dennis Sarfate RC 8.00
95 Donald Kelly RC 6.00
96 Alec Zumwalt RC 6.00
97 Chris Aguila RC 6.00
98 Greg Dobbs RC 6.00
99 Ian Snell RC 10.00
100 Jake Woods 6.00
101 Jamie Brown RC 6.00
102 Jason Frasor RC 6.00
103 Jerome Gamble RC 6.00
104 Jesse Harper RC 6.00
105 Josh Labandeira RC 6.00
106 Justin Hampson RC 6.00
107 Justin Huisman RC 6.00
108 Justin Leone RC 6.00
109 Lincoln Holdzkom RC 6.00
110 Mike Bumatay RC 6.00
111 Mike Gosling 6.00
112 Mike Johnston RC 6.00
113 Mike Rouse 6.00
114 Nick Regilio RC 6.00
115 Ryan Meaux RC 6.00
116 Scott Dohmann RC 8.00
117 Sean Henn 6.00
118 Tim Bausher RC 6.00
119 Tim Bittner RC 6.00

Logo Threads

No Pricing
Production One Set

Logo Threads Autograph

ALEX RODRIGUEZ / LOGO THREADS

No Pricing
Production One Set

All-Star Patch Autograph

Production 10 Sets

All-Star Patch Auto-Dual

Production 10 Sets

All-Star Patch Gold

NM/M

Production 50 Sets
AP Albert Pujols 75.00
AR Alex Rodriguez 50.00
AS Alfonso Soriano 25.00
BZ Barry Zito 25.00
CD Carlos Delgado 30.00
CJ Chipper Jones 30.00
CS Curt Schilling 35.00

DJ	Derek Jeter	85.00
EC	Eric Chavez	20.00
FT	Frank Thomas	30.00
GS	Gary Sheffield	20.00
HE	Todd Helton	25.00
HN	Hideo Nomo	50.00
IS	Ichiro Suzuki	80.00
JG	Juan Gonzalez	20.00
JT	Jim Thome	30.00
KG	Ken Griffey Jr.	50.00
MP	Mark Prior	30.00
SS	Sammy Sosa	40.00
TH	Tim Hudson	25.00
VW	Vernon Wells	20.00

All-Star Patch Number

Quantity produced listed | | NM/M
AJ	Andruw Jones/25	30.00
AP	Andy Pettitte/46	25.00
BZ	Barry Zito/50	30.00
CD	Carlos Delgado/25	25.00
CS	Curt Schilling/38	30.00
FT	Frank Thomas/35	40.00
GM	Greg Maddux/31	50.00
IS	Ichiro Suzuki/50	65.00
JG	Juan Gonzalez/19	25.00
JP	Jorge Posada/20	30.00
JT	Jim Thome/25	30.00
KG	Ken Griffey Jr./30	60.00
MM	Mike Mussina/35	30.00
MO	Magglio Ordonez/30	25.00
PM	Pedro Martinez/45	35.00
RC	Roger Clemens/22	50.00
RH	Roy Halladay/32	25.00
RP	Rafael Palmeiro/25	30.00
SG	Shawn Green/15	30.00
SR	Scott Rolen/27	35.00
SS	Sammy Sosa/21	80.00

Famous Nicknames

		NM/M

Quantity produced listed
BR	Brooks Robinson/23	25.00
CR	Cal Ripken Jr./21	140.00
CY	Carl Yastrzemski/20	70.00
DM	Don Mattingly/14	25.00
DS	Darryl Strawberry/17	25.00
ES	Duke Snider/18	45.00
FT	Frank Thomas/14	40.00
GA	Sparky Anderson/27	25.00
GC	Gary Carter/19	30.00
HK	Harmon Killebrew/22	50.00
JF	Nellie Fox/19	120.00
JG	Juan Gonzalez/15	35.00
JH	"Catfish" Hunter/15	80.00
KG	Ken Griffey Jr./15	80.00
LB	Yogi Berra/19	100.00
MM	Mike Mussina/13	35.00
NR	Nolan Ryan/27	60.00
OC	Orlando Cepeda/17	25.00
OS	Ozzie Smith/19	50.00
PN	Phil Niekro/24	25.00
RC	Roger Clemens/20	60.00
RI	Phil Rizzuto/13	50.00
RJ	Randy Johnson/16	40.00
RY	Robin Yount/20	40.00
TS	Tom Seaver/20	60.00
SM	Stan Musial/22	85.00
SS	Sammy Sosa/15	50.00
WS	Willie Stargell/21	40.00

Famous Nicknames Autograph

		NM/M

Production 50 Sets
AD	Andre Dawson	45.00
AR	Alex Rodriguez	150.00
BM	Bill Mazeroski	65.00
BR	Brooks Robinson	60.00
DM	Don Mattingly	120.00
FT	Frank Thomas	70.00
HK	Harmon Killebrew	70.00
HM	Hideki Matsui	350.00
JB	Jeff Bagwell	80.00
JG	Juan Gonzalez	50.00
KG	Ken Griffey Jr.	160.00
LJ	Chipper Jones	80.00
MM	Mike Mussina	60.00
NR	Nolan Ryan	125.00
OS	Ozzie Smith	90.00
PN	Phil Niekro	45.00
RC	Roger Clemens	150.00
RY	Robin Yount	80.00

TS	Tom Seaver	65.00
WI	Dontrelle Willis	60.00

Hall of Fame Numbers

Quantity produced listed
AJ	Andruw Jones/25	30.00
BG	Bob Gibson/45	35.00
BW	Billy Williams/26	20.00
CD	Carlos Delgado/25	25.00
CH	Jim "Catfish" Hunter/41	40.00
CL	Roger Clemens/22	50.00
CS	Curt Schilling/38	25.00
DD	Don Drysdale/50	35.00
DS	Don Sutton/20	25.00
EG	Eric Gagne/38	25.00
EM	Eddie Mathews/41	50.00
FR	Frank Robinson/20	25.00
FT	Frank Thomas/35	40.00
GL	Tom Glavine/47	25.00
GM	Greg Maddux/31	45.00
GO	Juan Gonzalez/35	35.00
GP	Gaylord Perry/36	25.00
HE	Todd Helton/17	35.00
IS	Ichiro Suzuki/50	65.00
JC	Jose Canseco/33	25.00
JG	Jason Giambi/25	30.00
JI	Jim Thome/25	30.00
JP	Jim Palmer/22	25.00
KG	Ken Griffey Jr./30	60.00
MA	Juan Marichal/27	25.00
MP	Mike Piazza/31	40.00
MR	Manny Ramirez/24	30.00
MS	Mike Schmidt/20	60.00
MZ	Pedro Martinez/45	25.00
NR	Nolan Ryan/34	70.00
OC	Orlando Cepeda/30	25.00
PI	Mark Prior/22	40.00
RC	Roberto Clemente/21	200.00
RF	Rollie Fingers/34	25.00
RH	Rickey Henderson/25	40.00
RP	Rafael Palmeiro/45	30.00
RY	Robin Yount/19	45.00
SC	Steve Carlton/32	30.00
SG	Shawn Green/15	25.00
SR	Scott Rolen/27	30.00
SS	Sammy Sosa/21	50.00
TG	Tony Gwynn/19	45.00
TH	Tim Hudson/15	25.00
TS	Tom Seaver/41	25.00
WB	Wade Boggs/26	30.00
WS	Warren Spahn/21	65.00

Hall of Fame Numbers Autograph

Production 10 Sets

Hall of Fame Numbers Autograph Dual

Production 10 Sets

Historic Cut Signatures

Production One Set

Legendary Fabrics

		NM/M

Production 50 unless noted. 20.00
BE	Johnny Bench	25.00
BG	Bob Gibson	30.00
BW	Billy Williams	25.00
CH	"Catfish" Hunter	25.00
CR	Cal Ripken Jr.	60.00
CY	Carl Yastrzemski/31	45.00
EM	Eddie Mathews	35.00
FR	Frank Robinson	20.00
GP	Gaylord Perry	20.00
HK	Harmon Killebrew	40.00
JC	Jose Canseco	40.00
JM	Joe Morgan	20.00
JT	Joe Torre	60.00
LA	Luis Aparicio	25.00
LD	Leo Durocher	30.00
MS	Mike Schmidt	40.00
NR	Nolan Ryan	60.00
OC	Orlando Cepeda	20.00
OS	Ozzie Smith	35.00
PO	Paul O'Neill	20.00
RF	Rollie Fingers	20.00
RY	Robin Yount	35.00
SC	Steve Carlton	25.00
TS	Tom Seaver	50.00
WS	Warren Spahn	40.00

Legendary Fabrics Autograph Dual

		NM/M

Production 25 unless noted.
AD	Andre Dawson	60.00
BE	Johnny Bench	90.00
BR	Brooks Robinson	90.00
BW	Billy Williams	65.00
CR	Cal Ripken Jr.	275.00
CY	Carl Yastrzemski/17	125.00
DE	Dwight Evans	60.00
DM	Don Mattingly	150.00
DS	Don Sutton	65.00

FL	Fred Lynn	70.00
FR	Frank Robinson	75.00
GP	Gaylord Perry	40.00
HK	Harmon Killebrew	100.00
JC	Jose Canseco	100.00
JM	Joe Morgan	50.00
JP	Jim Palmer	60.00
JT	Joe Torre	70.00
KP	Kirby Puckett	100.00
LA	Luis Aparicio	70.00
LB	Lou Brock/13	125.00
NR	Nolan Ryan	200.00
OC	Orlando Cepeda	50.00
OS	Ozzie Smith	100.00
PM	Paul Molitor	75.00
PO	Paul O'Neill	70.00
RC	Roger Clemens	150.00
RF	Rollie Fingers	65.00
RY	Robin Yount	120.00
SG	Steve Garvey	60.00
ST	Darryl Strawberry	65.00
TG	Tony Gwynn	120.00
TS	Tom Seaver	85.00
WB	Wade Boggs	100.00
WI	Maury Wills	50.00

Legendary Combo Cuts

Production One Set

Masters

		NM/M

Quantity produced listed
AJ	Andruw Jones/25	25.00
BE	Josh Beckett/25	40.00
CD	Carlos Delgado/25	25.00
CS	Curt Schilling/38	25.00
FT	Frank Thomas/35	30.00
GM	Greg Maddux/31	45.00
GO	Juan Gonzalez/19	30.00
HE	Todd Helton/17	65.00
IS	Ichiro Suzuki/50	45.00
JG	Jason Giambi/25	30.00
JP	Jorge Posada/20	30.00
JT	Jim Thome/25	30.00
KG	Ken Griffey Jr./30	60.00
MO	Magglio Ordonez/30	20.00
MP	Mark Prior/22	40.00
MR	Manny Ramirez/24	30.00
PI	Mike Piazza/31	40.00
PM	Pedro Martinez/45	25.00
RC	Roger Clemens/22	25.00
RH	Roy Halladay/32	25.00
SG	Shawn Green/15	30.00
SR	Scott Rolen/27	30.00
SS	Sammy Sosa/21	30.00
TH	Tim Hudson/15	25.00

MVP Patch

		NM/M

Production 25 Sets
AR	Alex Rodriguez	60.00
BR	Brooks Robinson	60.00
BW	Bernie Williams	35.00
CJ	Chipper Jones	40.00
CR	Cal Ripken Jr.	90.00
CS	Curt Schilling	35.00
DJ	Derek Jeter	75.00
FT	Frank Thomas	40.00
GA	Garret Anderson	30.00
IS	Ichiro Suzuki	75.00
IV	Ivan Rodriguez	40.00
JB	Josh Beckett	30.00
JG	Jason Giambi	30.00
KG	Ken Griffey Jr.	50.00
MP	Mike Piazza	50.00
MT	Miguel Tejada	40.00
PM	Pedro Martinez	45.00
RC	Roger Clemens	60.00
RJ	Randy Johnson	60.00
SS	Sammy Sosa	40.00
TG	Troy Glaus	25.00

Premium Patch

		NM/M

Production 50 unless noted.
AD	Adam Dunn	30.00
AP	Albert Pujols	50.00
AR	Alex Rodriguez	50.00
AR1	Alex Rodriguez/Yanks	65.00
AS	Alfonso Soriano/34	35.00
BE	Josh Beckett	25.00
BW	Bernie Williams	25.00
BZ	Barry Zito	25.00

CD	Carlos Delgado	25.00
CJ	Chipper Jones	35.00
CS	Curt Schilling	25.00
DJ	Derek Jeter	60.00
DW	Dontrelle Willis	20.00
EC	Eric Chavez	20.00
FT	Frank Thomas	25.00
GM	Greg Maddux	40.00
GO	Juan Gonzalez	25.00
HM	Hideki Matsui	120.00
IR	Ivan Rodriguez	30.00
IS	Ichiro Suzuki	65.00
JB	Jeff Bagwell	30.00
JG	Jason Giambi	25.00
JP	Jorge Posada	30.00
JT	Jim Thome	30.00
KB	Kevin Brown	20.00
KG	Ken Griffey Jr.	50.00
MO	Magglio Ordonez	20.00
MP	Mark Prior	30.00
MR	Manny Ramirez	30.00
MT	Miguel Tejada	20.00
PI	Mike Piazza	35.00
NR	Nolan Ryan	30.00
PM	Pedro Martinez	30.00
RC	Roger Clemens	25.00
RH	Roy Halladay	20.00
RI	Mariano Rivera	30.00
RJ	Randy Johnson	30.00
RP	Rafael Palmeiro	30.00
SG	Shawn Green	20.00
SR	Scott Rolen	30.00
SS	Sammy Sosa	35.00
TE	Mark Teixeira	25.00
TG	Tom Glavine	25.00
TH	Tim Hudson	25.00

Premium Patch Autograph

		NM/M

Production 50 unless noted.
AK	Austin Kearns	45.00
AR	Alex Rodriguez	150.00
BZ	Barry Zito	60.00
CD	Carlos Delgado	50.00
DW	Dontrelle Willis	50.00
EC	Eric Chavez	40.00
EG	Eric Gagne	60.00
HM	Hideki Matsui	350.00
IR	Ivan Rodriguez	80.00
IS	Ichiro Suzuki	300.00
KB	Kevin Brown	45.00
KG	Ken Griffey Jr.	160.00
MP	Mark Prior	50.00
MT	Miguel Tejada	50.00
NG	Nomar Garciaparra/33	140.00
RC	Roger Clemens	150.00
SG	Shawn Green	50.00
TH	Tim Hudson	50.00
TG	Troy Glaus	50.00
VG	Vladimir Guerrero	75.00

Significant Numbers

		NM/M

Quantity produced listed
CR	Cal Ripken Jr./21	120.00
CS	Curt Schilling/16	40.00
CY	Carl Yastrzemski/23	65.00
DS	Darryl Strawberry/17	25.00
EM	Eddie Mathews/17	25.00
FT	Frank Thomas/14	50.00
GM	Greg Maddux/18	25.00
GO	Juan Gonzalez/15	40.00
GS	Gary Sheffield/16	25.00
JB	Jeff Bagwell/13	50.00
KG	Ken Griffey Jr./15	75.00
NR	Nolan Ryan/27	60.00
PO	Paul O'Neill/17	25.00
RC	Roger Clemens/20	60.00
RF	Rollie Fingers/17	25.00
RJ	Randy Johnson/16	35.00
RP	Rafael Palmeiro/18	40.00
SN	Duke Snider/18	45.00
SS	Sammy Sosa/15	50.00
TG	Tom Glavine/17	25.00
TS	Tom Seaver/20	40.00

Significant Numbers Autograph

		NM/M

Production 50 unless noted.

CD	Carlos Delgado	25.00
CJ	Chipper Jones	35.00
CS	Curt Schilling	25.00
DJ	Derek Jeter	60.00
DW	Dontrelle Willis	20.00
EC	Eric Chavez	20.00
FT	Frank Thomas	20.00
GM	Greg Maddux	40.00
GO	Juan Gonzalez	25.00
HM	Hideki Matsui	120.00
IR	Ivan Rodriguez	30.00
IS	Ichiro Suzuki	65.00
JB	Jeff Bagwell	30.00
JG	Jason Giambi	30.00
JP	Jorge Posada	30.00
JT	Jim Thome	30.00
KB	Kevin Brown	20.00
KG	Ken Griffey Jr.	50.00
MO	Magglio Ordonez	20.00
MP	Mark Prior	30.00
MS	Mike Schmidt	90.00
MR	Manny Ramirez	30.00
MT	Miguel Tejada	50.00
PI	Mike Piazza	35.00
NR	Nolan Ryan	140.00
PB	Pat Burrell	40.00
PO	Paul O'Neill	65.00
PR	Mark Prior	60.00
RA	Roberto Alomar	25.00
RB	Rocco Baldelli	55.00
RF	Rollie Fingers	40.00
RO	Roy Oswalt	25.00
RP	Rafael Palmeiro	70.00
RS	Ryne Sandberg	90.00
SG	Shawn Green	50.00
TG	Tom Glavine	50.00
TH	Tim Hudson	50.00
VG	Vladimir Guerrero	75.00

Significant Numbers Autograph Dual

		NM/M

Production 25 unless noted.
AR	Alex Rodriguez	200.00
BA	Bobby Abreu	50.00
BG	Brian Giles	50.00
BW	Bernie Williams	120.00
BZ	Barry Zito	80.00
CD	Carlos Delgado	70.00
CJ	Chipper Jones	100.00
DW	Dontrelle Willis	60.00
EC	Eric Chavez	65.00
EG	Eric Gagne	80.00
GI	Bob Gibson	100.00
GL	Troy Glaus	70.00
GM	Greg Maddux	140.00
HE	Todd Helton	85.00
HM	Hideki Matsui	500.00
KB	Kevin Brown	65.00
KG	Ken Griffey Jr.	200.00
KP	Kirby Puckett	100.00
LB	Lou Brock/14	85.00
LG	Luis Gonzalez	50.00
MM	Mike Mussina	80.00
MP	Mike Piazza	200.00
MS	Mike Schmidt	160.00
MT	Miguel Tejada	100.00
NR	Nolan Ryan	200.00
PB	Pat Burrell	50.00
PO	Paul O'Neill	80.00
RA	Roberto Alomar	60.00
RF	Rollie Fingers	65.00
RP	Rafael Palmeiro	100.00
RS	Ryne Sandberg	150.00
SG	Shawn Green	60.00
TG	Tom Glavine	80.00
TH	Tim Hudson	75.00
VG	Vladimir Guerrero	100.00
TO	Tony Gwynn	120.00
TS	Tom Seaver	85.00

Star Potential Patch

		NM/M

Quantity produced listed
BW	Brandon Webb/50	25.00
CP	Corey Patterson/20	25.00
DW	Dontrelle Willis/35	30.00
HA	Roy Halladay/32	25.00
IS	Ichiro Suzuki/50	65.00
HB	Josh Beckett/21	30.00
LB	Lance Berkman/17	25.00
MM	Mark Mulder/20	30.00
MP	Mark Prior/22	30.00
MT	Mark Teixeira/23	25.00
RH	Rich Harden/40	25.00
RO	Roy Oswalt/44	25.00
RW	Rickie Weeks/23	25.00
TG	Troy Glaus/25	30.00
TH	Tim Hudson/15	30.00

Stellar Combos

		NM/M

Production 25 unless noted.
AD	Derek Jeter, Alfonso Soriano	75.00

AR	Alex Rodriguez	150.00
BA	Bobby Abreu	40.00
BG	Brian Giles	40.00
BW	Bernie Williams	100.00
BZ	Barry Zito	60.00
CD	Carlos Delgado	50.00
CJ	Chipper Jones	90.00
EC	Eric Chavez	60.00
EG	Eric Gagne	60.00
GM	Greg Maddux	110.00
HE	Todd Helton	60.00
GO	Juan Gonzalez	50.00
HM	Hideki Matsui	350.00
KB	Kevin Brown	45.00
KG	Ken Griffey Jr.	160.00
LB	Lou Brock/16	60.00
LG	Luis Gonzalez	50.00
MM	Mike Mussina	60.00
MP	Mike Piazza	185.00
MS	Mike Schmidt	90.00
MT	Miguel Tejada	50.00
NR	Nolan Ryan	140.00
PB	Pat Burrell	40.00
PO	Paul O'Neill	65.00
PR	Mark Prior	60.00
RA	Roberto Alomar	45.00
RB	Rocco Baldelli	55.00
RF	Rollie Fingers	40.00
RO	Roy Oswalt	60.00
RP	Rafael Palmeiro	70.00
RS	Ryne Sandberg	90.00
SG	Shawn Green	50.00
TG	Tom Glavine	60.00
TH	Tim Hudson	50.00
VG	Vladimir Guerrero	75.00

Significant Numbers Autograph Dual

		NM/M

Production 25 unless noted.

AJ	Alex Rodriguez, Juan Gonzalez	50.00
AT	Jim Thome, Bobby Abreu	40.00
BK	Jeff Bagwell, Jeff Kent	30.00
BT	Mark Teixeira, Hank Blalock	40.00
CA	Roberto Alomar, Joe Carter	60.00
CO	Roger Clemens, Roy Oswalt	60.00
CR	Randy Johnson, Curt Schilling	40.00
DG	Jason Giambi, Carlos Delgado	40.00
DK	Austin Kearns, Adam Dunn	40.00
GH	Eric Gagne, Trevor Hoffman	40.00
GT	Greg Maddux, Tom Glavine	65.00
JJ	Andruw Jones, Chipper Jones	50.00
KR	Nolan Ryan, Jerry Koosman	100.00
LP	Mike Piazza, Al Leiter	50.00
LS	Fred Lynn, Ichiro Suzuki	75.00
MG	Don Mattingly, Jason Giambi	80.00
MT	Frank Thomas, Edgar Martinez	50.00
MY	Paul Molitor, Robin Yount	60.00
NB	Hideo Nomo, Kevin Brown	40.00
NY	Alfonso Soriano, Jose Reyes	40.00
PC	Mark Prior, Roger Clemens	60.00
PE	Albert Pujols, Jim Edmonds	80.00
PM	Mike Mussina, Andy Pettitte	50.00
PP	Mike Piazza, Jorge Posada	60.00
PS	Sammy Sosa, Rafael Palmeiro	50.00
RB	Ivan Rodriguez, Josh Beckett	50.00
RJ	Alex Rodriguez, Derek Jeter	100.00
RR	Alex Rodriguez, Cal Ripken Jr.	180.00
RS	Mike Schmidt, Brooks Robinson	85.00
SG	Shawn Green, Duke Snider	40.00
SJ	Randy Johnson, Gary Sheffield	
SM	Pedro Martinez, Curt Schilling	50.00
SR	Nolan Ryan, Curt Schilling	75.00
TO	Frank Thomas, Magglio Ordonez	60.00
WC	Roger Clemens, David Wells	50.00
WH	Larry Walker, Todd Helton	45.00
WS	Sammy Sosa, Billy Williams	60.00
ZH	Barry Zito, Tim Hudson	50.00
RJ	Alex Rodriguez, Derek Jeter	100.00
RG	Cal Ripken Jr., Lou Gehrig	350.00
SC	Ty Cobb, Ichiro Suzuki	180.00

Team Threads

Production 10 unless noted.

Triple Authentic

Production 10

World Series Stars

		NM/M

Production 50 unless noted.
AJ	Andruw Jones	25.00
AP	Andy Pettitte/15	40.00
AS	Alfonso Soriano/15	35.00
BL	Barry Larkin	25.00
BW	Bernie Williams	25.00
CA	Jose Canseco	30.00
CJ	Chipper Jones	30.00
CS	Curt Schilling	25.00
CY	Carl Yastrzemski/31	50.00
DW	Dontrelle Willis	20.00
GA	Garret Anderson	25.00
GL	Troy Glaus	30.00
GM	Greg Maddux	40.00
HM	Hideki Matsui/17	140.00
IR	Ivan Rodriguez	30.00
JB	Josh Beckett	25.00
JE	Derek Jeter	60.00
JM	Joe Morgan	25.00
JP	Jorge Posada	30.00
JT	Jim Thome	25.00
KB	Kevin Brown	20.00
MM	Mike Mussina/43	25.00
MP	Mike Piazza	35.00
MR	Mariano Rivera	30.00
MS	Mike Schmidt	40.00

PM	Paul Molitor	30.00
PO	Paul O'Neill	20.00
RC	Roger Clemens	40.00
RF	Rollie Fingers	25.00
RJ	Randy Johnson	30.00
TG	Tom Glavine	25.00

World Series Stars Autograph
No Pricing
Production One Set

300 Win Club
Production 10 Sets

Autographed 300 Win Club
Production 10 Sets

500 HR Club
Production 10 Sets

Autographed 500 HR Club
Production 10 Sets

500 HR Club Triple Patches
Production 10 Sets

3000 Hit Club
Production 10 Sets

3000 Hit Club Autograph
Production 10 Sets

2004 SP Legendary Cuts

		NM/M
Complete Set (126):		.40
Common Player:		.40
Pack (4):		12.00
Box (12):		120.00
1	Al Kaline	1.00
2	Al Lopez	.40
3	Alan Trammell	.40
4	Andre Dawson	.40
5	Babe Ruth	3.00
6	Bert Campaneris	.40
7	Bill Mazeroski	.40
8	Bill Russell	.40
9	Billy Williams	.40
10	Bob Feller	.50
11	Bob Gibson	.75
12	Bob Lemon	.40
13	Bobby Doerr	.40
14	Brooks Robinson	1.00
15	Cal Ripken Jr.	3.00
16	Carl Yastrzemski	1.00
17	Carlton Fisk	.40
18	Jim "Catfish" Hunter	.40
19	Dale Murphy	.40
20	Darryl Strawberry	.40
21	Dave Concepcion	.40
22	Dave Winfield	.50
23	Dennis Eckersley	.40
24	Denny McLain	.40
25	Don Drysdale	.50
26	Don Larsen	.50
27	Don Mattingly	2.00
28	Don Sutton	.40
29	Duke Snider	1.00
30	Dusty Baker	.40
31	Dwight Gooden	.40
32	Earl Weaver	.40
33	Early Wynn	.40
34	Eddie Mathews	1.00
35	Eddie Murray	.75
36	Enos Slaughter	.40
37	Ernie Banks	1.50
38	Fergie Jenkins	.40
39	Frank Robinson	.75
40	Fred Lynn	.40
41	Gary Carter	.50
42	Gaylord Perry	.40
43	George Brett	2.00
44	George Foster	.40
45	George Kell	.40
46	Greg Luzinski	.40
47	Hal Newhouser	.40
48	Hank Greenberg	1.00

49	Harmon Killebrew	1.00
50	Honus Wagner	1.00
51	Hoyt Wilhelm	.40
52	Jackie Robinson	1.50
53	Jim Bunning	.40
54	Jim Palmer	.75
55	Jimmie Foxx	1.00
56	Joe Carter	.40
57	Joe DiMaggio	2.00
58	Joe Morgan	.40
59	Joe Torre	.40
60	Johnny Bench	1.00
61	Johnny Podres	.40
62	John Roseboro	.40
63	Johnny Sain	.40
64	Juan Marichal	.50
65	Keith Hernandez	.40
66	Kirby Puckett	.75
67	Kirk Gibson	.40
68	Will Clark	.50
69	Jim Rice	.40
70	Larry Doby	.40
71	Lou Boudreau	.40
72	Lou Brock	.50
73	Lou Gehrig	2.50
74	Lou Piniella	.40
75	Luis Aparicio	.40
76	Mark Grace	.50
77	Mel Ott	.40
78	Mickey Lolich	.40
79	Mickey Mantle	3.00
80	Mike Greenwell	.40
81	Mike Schmidt	2.00
82	Monte Irvin	.40
83	Nellie Fox	.50
84	Nolan Ryan	3.00
85	Orlando Cepeda	.40
86	Ozzie Smith	1.00
87	Paul Molitor	.75
88	Pee Wee Reese	.40
89	Phil Niekro	.40
90	Phil Rizzuto	.75
91	Ralph Kiner	.40
92	Red Rolfe	.40
93	Red Schoendienst	.40
94	Reggie Smith	.40
95	Rich "Goose" Gossage	.40
96	Richie Ashburn	.40
97	Rick Ferrell	.40
98	Elston Howard	.40
99	Roberto Clemente	2.00
100	Robin Roberts	.40
101	Robin Yount	1.00
102	Roger Maris	2.00
103	Rollie Fingers	.40
104	Ron Santo	.40
105	Roy Campanella	.40
106	Ryne Sandberg	1.50
107	Sparky Anderson	.40
108	Sparky Lyle	.40
109	Stan Musial	2.00
110	Steve Carlton	.50
111	Steve Garvey	.40
112	Ted Williams	2.50
113	Thurman Munson	1.00
114	Tom Seaver	1.00
115	Tommy Henrich	.40
116	Tommy Lasorda	.40
117	Tony Gwynn	1.00
118	Tony Perez	.40
119	Ty Cobb	1.50
120	Wade Boggs	.50
121	Warren Spahn	.75
122	Whitey Ford	.75
123	Willie McCovey	.40
124	Willie Randolph	.40
125	Willie Stargell	.50
126	Yogi Berra	.75

All-Time Autographs

		NM/M
	Production 50 Sets	
LA	Luis Aparicio	20.00
YB	Yogi Berra	65.00
WB	Wade Boggs	40.00
SC	Steve Carlton	20.00
GC	Gary Carter	25.00
JC	Joe Carter	20.00
OC	Orlando Cepeda	25.00
WC	Will Clark	40.00
BD	Bobby Doerr	20.00
DE	Dennis Eckersley	20.00
RF	Rollie Fingers	20.00
CF	Carlton Fisk	30.00
WF	Whitey Ford	40.00
TG	Tony Gwynn	50.00
MI	Monte Irvin	25.00
FJ	Fergie Jenkins	20.00
AK	Al Kaline	40.00
GK	George Kell	25.00
HK	Harmon Killebrew	40.00
FL	Fred Lynn	15.00
MA	Don Mattingly	60.00
BM	Bill Mazeroski	50.00
WM	Willie McCovey	40.00
MC	Denny McLain	30.00
DM	Dale Murphy	80.00
SM	Stan Musial	80.00
DN	Don Newcombe	25.00
PN	Phil Niekro	20.00
TP	Tony Perez	25.00
GP	Gaylord Perry	20.00
JP	Johnny Podres	20.00
CR	Cal Ripken Jr.	125.00
RR	Robin Roberts	30.00
NR	Nolan Ryan	125.00

SA	Ryne Sandberg	75.00
RS	Red Schoendienst	25.00
TS	Tom Seaver	50.00
DS	Don Sutton	15.00
BW	Billy Williams	20.00
MW	Maury Wills	20.00
RY	Robin Yount	75.00

Game Graphs

		NM/M
	Production 25 Sets	
Gold:		No Pricing
	Production 10 Sets	
LA	Luis Aparicio	25.00
EB	Ernie Banks	75.00
JB	Johnny Bench	80.00
YB	Yogi Berra	80.00
WB	Wade Boggs	50.00
GB	George Brett	100.00
LB	Lou Brock	40.00
SC	Steve Carlton	30.00
GC	Gary Carter	35.00
JC	Joe Carter	30.00
RF	Rollie Fingers	25.00
CF	Carlton Fisk	50.00
BG	Bob Gibson	40.00
TG	Tony Gwynn	65.00
AK	Al Kaline	50.00
HK	Harmon Killebrew	50.00
JM	Juan Marichal	35.00
MA	Don Mattingly	80.00
BM	Bill Mazeroski	50.00
WM	Willie McCovey	50.00
PM	Paul Molitor	40.00
MO	Joe Morgan	40.00
DM	Dale Murphy	40.00
EM	Eddie Murray	85.00
SM	Stan Musial	100.00
PN	Phil Niekro	30.00
KP	Kirby Puckett	75.00
CR	Cal Ripken Jr.	180.00
PR	Phil Rizzuto	40.00
BR	Brooks Robinson	50.00
FR	Frank Robinson	40.00
NR	Nolan Ryan	175.00
RS	Ryne Sandberg	85.00
MS	Mike Schmidt	80.00
TS	Tom Seaver	60.00
OS	Ozzie Smith	75.00
SN	Duke Snider	50.00
DS	Don Sutton	20.00
BW	Billy Williams	25.00
DW	Dave Winfield	30.00
CY	Carl Yastrzemski	85.00
RY	Robin Yount	85.00

Historic Patches

		NM/M
	Production 25 Sets	
EB	Ernie Banks	50.00
GB	George Brett	60.00
DD	Don Drysdale	40.00
BG	Bob Gibson	25.00
TG	Tony Gwynn	50.00
EM	Eddie Mathews	30.00
SM	Stan Musial	60.00
CR	Cal Ripken Jr.	100.00
NR	Nolan Ryan	75.00
TS	Tom Seaver	50.00
DS	Duke Snider	30.00
CY	Carl Yastrzemski	60.00
RY	Robin Yount	50.00

Historic Quads
No Pricing
Production 10 Sets

Historic Swatches

		NM/M
Common Swatch:		4.00
Golds:		2X-3X
	Production 25 Sets	
AN	Sparky Anderson	4.00
JB	Johnny Bench/SP	10.00
GB	George Brett	12.00
LB	Lou Brock	6.00
GC	Gary Carter	6.00
JC	Joe Carter	6.00
DC	Dave Concepcion	4.00
DD	Don Drysdale	6.00
RF	Rollie Fingers	8.00
CF	Carlton Fisk	8.00
GF	George Foster	4.00
SG	Steve Garvey	4.00
CH	Jim "Catfish" Hunter	6.00
FJ	Fergie Jenkins	8.00
HK	Harmon Killebrew	6.00
DL	Don Larsen/SP	10.00
ML	Mickey Lolich	4.00
SL	Sparky Lyle	4.00
MA	Eddie Mathews	10.00
DM	Don Mattingly	15.00
PM	Paul Molitor	6.00
JM	Joe Morgan	6.00
TM	Thurman Munson	12.00

MU	Dale Murphy	8.00
EM	Eddie Murray/SP	10.00
SM	Stan Musial	20.00
PN	Phil Niekro	6.00
GP	Gaylord Perry	6.00
JP	Johnny Podres	6.00
KP	Kirby Puckett	10.00
JR	Jim Rice	8.00
CR	Cal Ripken Jr.	20.00
BR	Brooks Robinson	8.00
NR	Nolan Ryan	20.00
TS	Tom Seaver	8.00
OS	Ozzie Smith	10.00
DS	Don Sutton	4.00
HW	Hoyt Wilhelm	4.00
DW	Dave Winfield	6.00
RY	Robin Yount	8.00

Legendary Cuts

		NM/M
	Quantity produced listed	
WA	Walter Alston/74	200.00
LU	Luke Appling/108	150.00
RA	Richie Ashburn/31	350.00
LB	Lou Boudreau/199	125.00
EC	Earle Combs/27	350.00
ST	Stan Coveleski/102	150.00
RD	Ray Dandridge/199	125.00
DD	Dizzy Dean/33	650.00
BD	Bill Dickey/82	250.00
JD	Joe DiMaggio/111	500.00
DO	Larry Doby/14	400.00
DR	Don Drysdale/66	450.00
LD	Leo Durocher/75	400.00
RF	Rick Ferrell/44	160.00
WF	Wes Ferrell/36	200.00
FF	Frankie Frisch/57	450.00
CG	Charlie Gehringer/171	200.00
LG	Lefty Gomez/98	325.00
HG	Hank Greenberg/37	500.00
BU	Burleigh Grimes/83	200.00
GR	Lefty Grove/75	375.00
GH	Gabby Hartnett/19	475.00
BH	Billy Herman/134	125.00
WH	Waite Hoyt/106	200.00
CH	Carl Hubbell/199	180.00
JH	Jim "Catfish" Hunter/25	220.00
BJ	"Indian" Bob Johnson/32	200.00
HK	Harvey Kuenn/49	150.00
BL	Bob Lemon/199	100.00
EL	Ernie Lombardi/39	475.00
TL	Ted Lyons/199	150.00
RU	Rube Marquard/59	220.00
JM	Joe Medwick/32	450.00
MI	Johnny Mize/118	140.00
HN	Hal Newhouser/51	140.00
KN	Kid Nichols/4	2,500
SP	Satchel Paige/28	1,325
GP	George Pipgras/46	200.00
PR	Pee Wee Reese/35	350.00
SR	Sam Rice/28	500.00
ER	Edd Roush/129	125.00
RR	Red Ruffing/30	500.00
JS	Joe Sewell/199	140.00
GS	George Sisler/32	850.00
ES	Enos Slaughter/147	125.00
WS	Willie Stargell/39	220.00
WM	Hoyt Wilhelm/115	100.00
SW	"Smokey" Joe Wood/79	400.00
EW	Early Wynn/54	200.00

Legendary Duels

		NM/M
	Production 25 Sets	
BG	George Brett, Rich "Goose" Gossage	40.00
DW	Joe DiMaggio, Ted Williams	150.00
EG	Dennis Eckersley, Kirk Gibson	25.00
FM	Joe Morgan, Carlton Fisk	30.00
GL	Bob Gibson, Mickey Lolich	30.00
MW	Mickey Mantle, Ted Williams	200.00
PL	Johnny Podres, Don Larsen	30.00
RM	Juan Marichal, John Roseboro	25.00
RR	Pee Wee Reese, Phil Rizzuto	35.00
SM	Duke Snider, Mickey Mantle	125.00
SS	Ryne Sandberg, Ozzie Smith	80.00
WB	Ernie Banks, Honus Wagner	125.00

Legendary Duels Patch
No Pricing
Production 15 Sets

Legendary Duos

		NM/M
	Production 25 Sets	
CM	Joe Morgan, Dave Concepcion	20.00

DM	Joe DiMaggio, Mickey Mantle	200.00
LB	Yogi Berra, Don Larsen	60.00
MB	Yogi Berra, Mickey Mantle	200.00
MM	Mickey Mantle, Roger Maris	200.00
MY	Paul Molitor, Robin Yount	30.00
PJ	Jackie Robinson, Pee Wee Reese	75.00
RR	Cal Ripken Jr., Brooks Robinson	65.00
RS	Tom Seaver, Nolan Ryan	75.00
SC	Roy Campanella, Duke Snider	40.00
SS	Johnny Sain, Warren Spahn	40.00
WB	Ernie Banks, Billy Williams	40.00

Legendary Duos Patch
No Pricing
Production 15 Sets

Legendary Sigs

		NM/M
	Production 50 Sets	
LA	Luis Aparicio	20.00
EB	Ernie Banks	60.00
JB	Johnny Bench	60.00
WB	Wade Boggs	40.00
GC	Gary Carter	25.00
JC	Joe Carter	20.00
WC	Will Clark	40.00
BD	Bobby Doerr	20.00
DE	Dennis Eckersley	30.00
BF	Bob Feller	30.00
RF	Rollie Fingers	20.00
BG	Bob Gibson	35.00
TG	Tony Gwynn	50.00
MI	Monte Irvin	25.00
AK	Al Kaline	40.00
GK	George Kell	25.00
HK	Harmon Killebrew	40.00
RK	Ralph Kiner	30.00
FL	Fred Lynn	15.00
JM	Juan Marichal	30.00
MA	Don Mattingly	60.00
WM	Willie McCovey	40.00
MC	Denny McLain	30.00
DM	Dale Murphy	30.00
EM	Eddie Murray	80.00
DN	Don Newcombe	25.00
PA	Jim Palmer	30.00
GP	Gaylord Perry	20.00
JP	Johnny Podres	20.00
CR	Cal Ripken Jr.	125.00
PR	Phil Rizzuto	25.00
RR	Robin Roberts	30.00
BR	Brooks Robinson	40.00
SA	Ryne Sandberg	75.00
MS	Mike Schmidt	60.00
RS	Red Schoendienst	25.00
OS	Ozzie Smith	65.00
SN	Duke Snider	40.00
DS	Don Sutton	15.00
MW	Maury Wills	20.00
CY	Carl Yastrzemski	75.00

Legendary Swatches

		NM/M
Common Swatch:		4.00
Golds:		No Pricing
	Production 15 Sets	
EB	Ernie Banks/SP	15.00
JB	Johnny Bench	10.00
YB	Yogi Berra	12.00
WB	Wade Boggs	8.00
GB	George Brett	12.00
RC	Roy Campanella	8.00
SC	Steve Carlton	6.00
OC	Orlando Cepeda	6.00
BD	Bobby Doerr	8.00
DD	Don Drysdale	6.00
CF	Carlton Fisk	8.00
NF	Nellie Fox	10.00
BG	Bob Gibson	8.00
TG	Tony Gwynn	10.00
EH	Elston Howard	8.00
CH	Jim "Catfish" Hunter	8.00

AK	Al Kaline	10.00
HK	Harmon Killebrew	10.00
MA	Juan Marichal	8.00
EM	Eddie Mathews	10.00
DM	Don Mattingly	15.00
WM	Willie McCovey	8.00
TM	Thurman Munson	12.00
SM	Stan Musial	15.00
TP	Tony Perez	8.00
PO	Johnny Podres	6.00
PR	Pee Wee Reese	8.00
JR	Jim Rice	8.00
CR	Cal Ripken Jr.	20.00
RI	Phil Rizzuto	10.00
FR	Frank Robinson	6.00
NR	Nolan Ryan	20.00
MS	Mike Schmidt	15.00
TS	Tom Seaver	10.00
DS	Duke Snider	10.00
WS	Warren Spahn	10.00
ST	Willie Stargell	8.00
BW	Billy Williams	4.00
DW	Dave Winfield	8.00
CY	Carl Yastrzemski	10.00
RY	Robin Yount	8.00

Marked for the Hall

		NM/M
	Production 50 Sets	
LA	Luis Aparicio	20.00
EB	Ernie Banks	60.00
JB	Johnny Bench	60.00
YB	Yogi Berra	65.00
GB	George Brett	75.00
LB	Lou Brock	30.00
SC	Steve Carlton	20.00
GC	Gary Carter	20.00
OC	Orlando Cepeda	25.00
BD	Bobby Doerr	20.00
BF	Bob Feller	30.00
CF	Carlton Fisk	35.00
WF	Whitey Ford	40.00
BG	Bob Gibson	35.00
AK	Al Kaline	40.00
HK	Harmon Killebrew	40.00
RK	Ralph Kiner	30.00
MA	Juan Marichal	30.00
BM	Bill Mazeroski	50.00
WM	Willie McCovey	40.00
PM	Paul Molitor	40.00
JM	Joe Morgan	35.00
EM	Eddie Murray	80.00
SM	Stan Musial	80.00
PN	Phil Niekro	20.00
JP	Jim Palmer	20.00
TP	Tony Perez	25.00
GP	Gaylord Perry	20.00
KP	Kirby Puckett	20.00
PR	Phil Rizzuto	25.00
RR	Robin Roberts	40.00
BR	Brooks Robinson	40.00
FR	Frank Robinson	40.00
NR	Nolan Ryan	125.00
MS	Mike Schmidt	60.00
TS	Tom Seaver	60.00
OS	Ozzie Smith	65.00
DS	Duke Snider	40.00
BW	Billy Williams	20.00
DW	Dave Winfield	40.00
CY	Carl Yastrzemski	75.00
RY	Robin Yount	75.00

Marks of Greatness

		NM/M
	Production 50 Sets	
EB	Ernie Banks	60.00
JB	Johnny Bench	60.00
YB	Yogi Berra	65.00
WB	Wade Boggs	40.00
GB	George Brett	75.00
LB	Lou Brock	30.00
SC	Steve Carlton	20.00
JC	Joe Carter	20.00
OC	Orlando Cepeda	25.00
WC	Will Clark	40.00
RF	Rollie Fingers	20.00
CF	Carlton Fisk	35.00
WF	Whitey Ford	40.00
BG	Bob Gibson	35.00
TG	Tony Gwynn	50.00
FJ	Fergie Jenkins	20.00
AK	Al Kaline	40.00
HK	Harmon Killebrew	40.00
FL	Fred Lynn	15.00
MA	Don Mattingly	60.00
MC	Denny McLain	30.00
PM	Paul Molitor	40.00
JM	Joe Morgan	35.00
DM	Dale Murphy	30.00
SM	Stan Musial	80.00
DN	Don Newcombe	20.00
PN	Phil Niekro	20.00
JP	Jim Palmer	20.00
TP	Tony Perez	25.00
KP	Kirby Puckett	40.00
CR	Cal Ripken Jr.	125.00
BR	Brooks Robinson	30.00
FR	Frank Robinson	40.00
NR	Nolan Ryan	125.00
RS	Ryne Sandberg	75.00
MS	Mike Schmidt	60.00
TS	Tom Seaver	60.00
OZ	Ozzie Smith	65.00
DS	Duke Snider	40.00
BW	Billy Williams	20.00
DW	Dave Winfield	30.00
RY	Robin Yount	75.00

Significant Swatches

NM/M
Common Swatch: 4.00
Golds: 2-3X
Production 25 Sets

SA	Sparky Anderson	4.00
EB	Ernie Banks	10.00
LB	Lou Brock/SP	8.00
GC	Gary Carter	4.00
JC	Joe Carter	4.00
OC	Orlando Cepeda	6.00
DC	Dave Concepcion	4.00
BD	Bobby Doerr	8.00
DD	Don Drysdale	8.00
RF	Rollie Fingers	6.00
CF	Carlton Fisk	8.00
GF	George Foster	4.00
SG	Steve Garvey	6.00
CH	Jim "Catfish" Hunter	8.00
FJ	Fergie Jenkins	4.00
SL	Sparky Lyle	4.00
RM	Roger Maris	30.00
ED	Eddie Mathews	10.00
MA	Don Mattingly	15.00
BM	Bill Mazeroski	8.00
WM	Willie McCovey	6.00
PM	Paul Molitor	6.00
TM	Thurman Munson	12.00
DM	Dale Murphy	8.00
EM	Eddie Murray/SP	8.00
PN	Phil Niekro	4.00
TP	Tony Perez	4.00
GP	Gaylord Perry	6.00
JP	Johnny Podres	6.00
CR	Cal Ripken Jr.	20.00
FR	Frank Robinson	6.00
NR	Nolan Ryan	20.00
MS	Mike Schmidt	15.00
TS	Tom Seaver	8.00
SN	Duke Snider	10.00
WS	Warren Spahn	10.00
ST	Willie Stargell	8.00
DS	Don Sutton	4.00
HW	Hoyt Wilhelm	4.00
DW	Dave Winfield	8.00
CY	Carl Yastrzemski	10.00
RY	Robin Yount	8.00

Significant Trips
No Pricing
Production 15 Sets

Trips Patch
No Pricing
Production 10 Sets

Ultimate Autographs

NM/M
Production 25 Sets

EB	Ernie Banks	60.00
JB	Johnny Bench	60.00
YB	Yogi Berra	60.00
GB	George Brett	90.00
LB	Lou Brock	35.00
SC	Steve Carlton	25.00
DE	Dennis Eckersley	25.00
BF	Bob Feller	35.00
WF	Whitey Ford	40.00
BG	Bob Gibson	40.00
MI	Monte Irvin	30.00
FJ	Fergie Jenkins	25.00
AK	Al Kaline	50.00
GK	George Kell	25.00
HK	Harmon Killebrew	50.00
RK	Ralph Kiner	40.00
MA	Juan Marichal	30.00
DM	Don Mattingly	75.00
BM	Bill Mazeroski	40.00
PM	Paul Molitor	40.00
JM	Joe Morgan	35.00
EM	Eddie Murray	80.00
SM	Stan Musial	80.00
PA	Jim Palmer	40.00
JP	Johnny Podres	25.00
KP	Kirby Puckett	70.00
PR	Phil Rizzuto	35.00
BR	Brooks Robinson	40.00
FR	Frank Robinson	40.00
NR	Nolan Ryan	120.00
SA	Ryne Sandberg	80.00
MS	Mike Schmidt	75.00
RS	Red Schoendienst	25.00
TS	Tom Seaver	50.00
OS	Ozzie Smith	60.00
SN	Duke Snider	50.00
DS	Don Sutton	20.00
MW	Maury Willis	25.00
DW	Dave Winfield	30.00
CY	Carl Yastrzemski	80.00
RY	Robin Yount	60.00

Ultimate Swatches

NM/M
Common Swatch: 6.00
Golds: No Pricing
Production 10 Sets

EB	Ernie Banks	12.00
JB	Johnny Bench	10.00
YB	Yogi Berra	12.00
WB	Wade Boggs	6.00
GB	George Brett	12.00
RC	Roy Campanella	10.00
SC	Steve Carlton	6.00
JD	Joe DiMaggio/SP	75.00
DD	Don Drysdale	6.00
NF	Nellie Fox	12.00
BG	Bob Gibson	8.00
HG	Hank Greenberg	20.00
TG	Tony Gwynn	10.00
CH	Jim "Catfish" Hunter	6.00
HK	Harmon Killebrew	10.00
MM	Mickey Mantle/SP	125.00
MA	Juan Marichal	8.00
RM	Roger Maris	30.00
EM	Eddie Mathews	6.00
DM	Don Mattingly	15.00
WM	Willie McCovey	6.00
TM	Thurman Munson	6.00
SM	Stan Musial	10.00
KP	Kirby Puckett	10.00
PR	Pee Wee Reese	8.00
CR	Cal Ripken Jr.	20.00
BR	Brooks Robinson	8.00
FR	Frank Robinson	6.00
JR	Jackie Robinson	40.00
NR	Nolan Ryan	20.00
MS	Mike Schmidt	15.00
TS	Tom Seaver	10.00
OS	Ozzie Smith	10.00
DS	Duke Snider/SP	10.00
WS	Warren Spahn	10.00
HW	Honus Wagner/SP	140.00
BW	Billy Williams	6.00
TW	Ted Williams	60.00
DW	Dave Winfield	10.00
CY	Carl Yastrzemski	10.00
RY	Robin Yount	8.00

2004 SP Prospects

NM/M
Complete Set (447):

Common SP (1-90): .50
1:Pack
Common Rookie (91-290): 1.00
Common Rookie Auto.
(291-447): 8.00
Production 400 unless noted.
Overall Autos. 1:5
Pack (5): 6.00
Box (24): 125.00

#	Player	Price
1	Roger Clemens	3.00
2	Melvin Mora	.50
3	Dontrelle Willis	.50
4	Jose Vidro	.50
5	Oliver Perez	.50
6	Carlos Zambrano	.50
7	Chipper Jones	1.00
8	Greg Maddux	1.50
9	Curt Schilling	1.00
10	Jose Reyes	.75
11	David Ortiz	1.00
12	Mike Piazza	2.00
13	Jason Schmidt	.50
14	Randy Johnson	1.00
15	Magglio Ordonez	.50
16	Mike Mussina	1.00
17	Jake Peavy	.50
18	Jim Edmonds	.75
19	Ken Griffey Jr.	1.50
20	Jason Giambi	.75
21	Mike Sweeney	.50
22	Carlos Lee	.50
23	Craig Wilson	.50
24	Pedro Martinez	1.00
25	Bobby Abreu	.50
26	Mike Lowell	.50
27	Miguel Cabrera	1.00
28	Hank Blalock	.50
29	Frank Thomas	.75
30	Manny Ramirez	1.00
31	Mark Mulder	.50
32	Scott Podsednik	.50
33	Albert Pujols	3.00
34	Preston Wilson	.50
35	Todd Helton	.75
36	Victor Martinez	.50
37	Kerry Wood	.50
38	Carlos Beltran	1.00
39	Vernon Wells	.50
40	Sammy Sosa	1.00
41	Pat Burrell	.50
42	Tim Hudson	.50
43	Eric Gagne	.75
44	Jim Thome	1.00
45	Vladimir Guerrero	1.00
46	Travis Hafner	.75
47	Rickie Weeks	.50
48	Miguel Tejada	.75
49	Ivan Rodriguez	.75
50	J.D. Drew	.50
51	Ben Sheets	.50
52	Garret Anderson	.50
53	Aubrey Huff	.50
54	Nomar Garciaparra	1.00
55	Luis Gonzalez	.50
56	Lance Berkman	.50
57	Ichiro Suzuki	2.00
58	Torii Hunter	.50
59	Adam Dunn	.75
60	Mark Teixeira	.75
61	Bret Boone	.50
62	Roy Oswalt	.50
63	Joe Mauer	.75
64	Scott Rolen	1.00
65	Hideki Matsui	2.00
66	Richie Sexson	.50
67	Jeff Kent	.50
68	Barry Zito	.50
69	C.C. Sabathia	.50
70	Carlos Delgado	.50
71	Gary Sheffield	.75
72	Shawn Green	.50
73	Jason Bay	.50
74	Andruw Jones	.75
75	Jeff Bagwell	.75
76	Rafael Palmeiro	.75
77	Alex Rodriguez	3.00
78	Adrian Beltre	.50
79	Troy Glaus	.50
80	Tom Glavine	.50
81	Paul Konerko	.50
82	Alfonso Soriano	1.00
83	Roy Halladay	.50
84	Derek Jeter	3.00
85	Josh Beckett	.50
86	Delmon Young	.50
87	Brian Giles	.50
88	Eric Chavez	.50
89	Lyle Overbay	.50
90	Mark Prior	.75
91	Shawn Camp RC	1.00
92	Travis Smith	1.00
93	Juan Padilla RC	1.00
94	Brad Halsey RC	1.00
95	Scott Kazmir	6.00
96	Sam Narron RC	1.00
97	Frank Francisco RC	1.00
98	Mike Johnston RC	1.00
99	Sam McConnell RC	1.00
100	Josh Labandeira RC	1.00
101	Kazuhito Tadano RC	1.00
102	Hector Gimenez RC	1.00
103	David Aardsma RC	1.00
104	Charles Thomas RC	2.00
105	Ian Snell RC	2.00
106	Jeff Keppinger RC	1.00
107	Michael Vento RC	1.00
108	Jerry Gil RC	1.00
109	Marty McLeary RC	1.00
110	Donnie Kelly RC	1.00
111	Roman Colon RC	1.00
112	Travis Blackley RC	1.00
113	Edwardo Sierra RC	1.00
114	Chris Shelton RC	2.00
115	Bartolome Fortunato RC	1.00
116	Brandon Medders RC	1.00-
117	Merkin Valdez RC	1.00
118	Carlos Vasquez RC	1.00
119	Shingo Takatsu RC	1.50
120	Aarom Baldiris RC	1.00
121	Chris Aguila RC	1.00
122	Jimmy Serrano RC	1.00
123	Mike Gosling RC	1.00
124	Brian Dallimore RC	1.00
125	Ronald Belisario RC	1.00
126	George Sherrill RC	1.00
127	Fernando Nieve RC	1.00
128	Abe Alvarez RC	1.50
129	Jeff Bennett RC	1.00
130	Ryan Meaux RC	1.00
131	Edwin Moreno RC	1.00
132	Jesse Crain RC	2.00
133	Scott Dohmann RC	1.00
134	Ronny Cedeno RC	2.00
135	Orlando Rodriguez RC	1.00
136	Mike Wuertz RC	1.00
137	Justin Hampson RC	1.00
138	Matt Treanor RC	1.00
139	Andy Green RC	1.00
140	Yadier Molina RC	2.50
141	Joe Nelson RC	1.00
142	Justin Lehr RC	1.00
143	Ryan Wing RC	1.00
144	Kevin Cave RC	1.50
145	Evan Rust RC	1.00
146	Mike Rouse RC	1.00
147	Lance Cormier RC	1.00
148	Eduardo Villacis RC	1.00
149	Justin Knoedler RC	1.00
150	Freddy Guzman RC	1.00
151	Casey Daigle RC	1.00
152	Joey Gathright RC	2.00
153	Tim Bittner RC	1.00
154	Scott Atchison RC	1.00
155	Ivan Ochoa RC	1.50
156	Lincoln Holdzkom RC	1.00
157	Onil Joseph RC	1.00
158	Jason Bartlett RC	1.50
159	Jon Knott RC	1.00
160	Jake Woods RC	1.00
161	Jerome Gamble RC	1.00
162	Sean Henn RC	1.50
163	Kazuo Matsui RC	1.00
164	Roberto Novoa RC	1.00
165	Eddy Rodriguez RC	1.00
166	Ramon Ramirez RC	1.00
167	Enemencio Pacheco RC	1.00
168	Chad Bentz RC	1.00
169	Chris Oxspring RC	1.00
170	Justin Leone RC	1.00
171	Joe Horgan RC	1.00
172	Jose Capellan RC	1.50
173	Greg Dobbs RC	1.00
174	Jason Frasor RC	1.50
175	Shawn Hill RC	1.00
176	Carlos Hines RC	1.00
177	John Gall RC	1.00
178	Steve Andrade RC	1.00
179	Scott Proctor RC	1.00
180	Rusty Tucker RC	1.00
181	David Crouthers RC	1.00
182	Franklyn Gracesqui RC	1.00
183	Justin Germano RC	1.00
184	Alfredo Simon RC	1.50
185	Jorge Sequea RC	1.00
186	Nick Regilio RC	1.00
187	Justin Huisman RC	1.00
188	Akinori Otsuka RC	1.50
189	Luis Gonzalez RC	1.00
190	Renyel Pinto RC	1.00
191	Josh LeBlanc RC	1.50
192	Devin Ivany RC	1.00
193	Chad Blackwell RC	1.50
194	Brandon Burgess RC	1.50
195	Cory Patton RC	1.50
196	Daniel Batz RC	1.50
197	Adam Russell RC	1.00
198	Jarrett Hoffpauir RC	1.50
199	Patrick Bryant RC	1.00
200	Sean Gamble RC	1.50
201	Jermaine Brock RC	1.50
202	Benjamin Zobrist RC	1.50
203	Cla Meredith RC	1.50
204	Derek Tharpe RC	1.00
205	Brad McCann RC	2.00
206	Justin Hedrick RC	1.00
207	Clint Sammons RC	2.50
208	Richard Steik RC	1.00
209	Fernando Perez RC	1.00
210	Mark Jecmen RC	1.00
211	Benjamin Harrison RC	1.00
212	Jason Quarles RC	1.00
213	William Layman RC	1.00
214	Koley Kolberg RC	1.00
215	Randy Dicken RC	1.00
216	Barry Richmond RC	1.00
217	Timothy Murphey RC	1.50
218	John Hardy RC	1.50
219	Sebastien Boucher RC	1.00
220	Andrew Alvarado RC	1.00
221	Patrick Perry RC	1.00
222	Jarod McAuliff RC	1.00
223	Jared Gaston RC	1.00
224	William Thompson RC	1.50
225	Lucas French RC	1.00
226	Brandon Parillo RC	1.00
227	Greg Goetz RC	1.00
228	David Haehnel RC	1.50
229	James Miller RC	1.00
230	Mark Roberts RC	1.00
231	Eric Ridener RC	1.00
232	Freddy Sandoval RC	1.00
234	Carlos Medero-Stullz RC	1.00
235	Matt Shepherd RC	1.00
236	Thomas Hubbard RC	1.00
237	Kyle Bono RC	1.50
238	Craig Moldrem RC	1.00
239	Brandon Timm RC	1.00
241	Mike Carp RC	2.50
242	Joseph Muro RC	1.00
243	Derek Decarlo RC	1.50
244	Chris Niesel RC	1.00
245	Trevor Lawhorn RC	1.50
246	Joey Howell RC	1.00
247	Dustin Hahn RC	1.00
248	Jim Fasano RC	2.00
249	Hainley Statia RC	1.00
250	Brandon Conway RC	1.00
251	Christopher McConnell RC	2.00
252	Austin Shappi RC	1.50
253	Joey Metropoulos RC	1.50
254	David Nicholson RC	1.50
255	Ryan McCarthy RC	1.00
256	Michael Parisi RC	1.00
257	Andrew Macfarlane RC	1.00
258	Jeffery Dominguez RC	1.50
259	Troy Patton RC	4.00
260	Ryan Norwood RC	1.50
261	Chad Boyd RC	1.00
262	Grant Plumley RC	1.00
263	Jeffrey Katz RC	2.00
264	Cory Middleton RC	1.00
265	Andrew Moffitt RC	1.00
266	Jarrett Grube RC	1.00
267	Derek Hankins RC	1.00
268	Douglas Reinhardt RC	1.00
269	Duron Legrande RC	1.00
270	Steven Jackson RC	1.00
271	Brian Hall RC	2.00
272	Cory Wade RC	1.50
273	John Grogan RC	1.00
274	Robert Asanovich RC	1.50
275	Kevin Hart RC	1.50
276	Matt Guillory RC	1.00
277	Cliff Remole RC	1.00
278	David Trahan RC	1.00
279	Kristian Bell RC	1.00
280	Chris Westervelt RC	1.00
281	Garry Bakker RC	1.00
282	Jonny Ash RC	1.50
283	Ryan Phillips RC	1.00
284	Wes Letson RC	1.00
285	Jeff Landing RC	1.00
286	Mark Worrell RC	1.00
287	Sean Gallagher RC	5.00
288	Nick Blasi RC	1.00
289	Kevin Frandsen RC	2.00
290	Richard Mercado RC	1.00
291	Matt Bush RC	30.00
292	Mark Rogers RC	30.00
293	Homer Bailey RC	150.00
294	Chris Nelson RC	40.00
295	Thomas Diamond RC	30.00
296	Neil Walker RC	65.00
297	Bill Bray RC	15.00
298	David Purcey RC	20.00
299	Scott Elbert RC	75.00
300	Josh Fields RC	75.00
301	Chris Lambert RC	20.00
302	Trevor Plouffe RC	35.00
303	Greg Golson RC	25.00
304	Phillip Hughes RC	250.00
305	Kyle Waldrop RC	30.00
306	Richie Robnett RC/350 RC	30.00
307	Taylor Tankersley RC	20.00
308	Blake Dewitt RC	40.00
309	Eric Hurley RC	60.00
310	James Howell RC	20.00
311	Zachary Jackson RC	15.00
312	Justin Orenduff RC	20.00
313	Tyler Lumsden RC	25.00
314	Matt Fox/600 RC	10.00
315	Dan Putnam/450 RC	15.00
316	Jon Poterson RC	20.00
317	Gio Gonzalez RC	70.00
318	Jay Rainville/475 RC	25.00
319	Huston Street RC	40.00
320	Jeff Marquez RC	15.00
321	Eric Beattie/500 RC	20.00
322	Reid Brignac/325 RC	150.00
323	Yovani Gallardo RC	125.00
324	Justin Hoyman RC	15.00
325	Brandon Szymanski RC	25.00
326	Seth Smith/600 RC	25.00
327	Karl Herren/600 RC	20.00
328	Brian Bixler/600 RC	10.00
329	Wes Whisler/600 RC	15.00
330	Erick San Pedro RC	10.00
331	Billy Buckner RC	20.00
332	Jon Zeringue RC	25.00
333	Curtis Thigpen RC	20.00
334	Blake Johnson RC	15.00
335	Donny Lucy RC	10.00
336	Mike Ferris/600 RC	20.00
337	Anthony Swarzak/600 RC	30.00
338	Jason Jaramillo RC	15.00
339	Hunter Pence/600 RC	200.00
340	Dustin Pedroia RC	60.00
341	Grant Johnson RC	15.00
342	Kurt Suzuki RC	30.00
343	Jason Vargas/600 RC	30.00
344	Ray Liotta RC	30.00
346	Eric Campbell RC	75.00
347	Jeff Frazier RC	15.00
348	Gaby Hernandez RC	40.00
349	Wade Davis/600 RC	40.00
350	Josh Wahpepah RC	15.00
351	Scott Lewis RC	10.00
352	Jeff Fiorentino RC	25.00
353	Steven Register/600 RC	10.00
354	Michael Schlact RC	15.00
355	Eddie Prasch RC	15.00
356	Adam Lind RC	140.00
357	Ian Desmond RC	30.00
358	Josh Johnson/575 RC	15.00
359	Garrett Mock/600 RC	15.00
360	Danny Hill/600 RC	10.00
361	Cory Dunlap/600 RC	25.00
362	Daniel Hansen/600 RC	12.00
363	Eric Haberer RC	15.00
364	Eduardo Morlan RC	20.00
365	James Happ/600 RC	15.00
366	Matt Tuiasosopo/600 RC	40.00
367	Jordan Parraz RC	20.00
368	Andrew Dobies RC	15.00
369	Mark Reed RC	40.00
370	Jason Windsor RC	20.00
371	Gregory Burns/600 RC	20.00
372	Christian Garcia/600 RC	15.00
373	John Bowker/575 RC	15.00
374	John Holt/550 RC	15.00
375	Daryl Jones RC	25.00
376	Colin Mahoney RC	15.00
377	Aaron Hathaway RC	15.00
378	Matt Spring RC	10.00
379	Josh Baker RC	10.00
380	Charles Lofgren RC	15.00
381	Rafael Gonzalez RC	15.00
382	Bradley Bergesen/575 RC	10.00
383	Brandon Boggs RC	15.00
384	Joseph Bauserman RC	15.00
385	Collin Balester/500 RC	40.00
386	James Moore RC	10.00
387	Robert Janssen RC	15.00
388	Luis Garcia RC	12.00
389	Lucas Harrell/550 RC	15.00
390	Donnie Smith/500 RC	15.00
391	Mark Robinson/525 RC	15.00
392	Louis Marson/550 RC	20.00
393	Robert Johnson/600 RC	10.00
394	Lou Santangelo/600 RC	12.00
395	Tommy Hottovy RC	10.00
396	Ryan Webb RC	15.00
397	Jamar Walton RC	20.00
398	Jason Jones RC	20.00
399	Clay Timpner/600 RC	15.00
400	James Parr RC	20.00
401	Sean Kazmar RC	15.00
402	Andrew Kown RC	15.00
403	Jacob McGee/600 RC	50.00
404	Mike Butia/600 RC	15.00
405	Paul Janish/500 RC	15.00
406	Matt Macri RC	25.00
407	Mike Nickeas/500 RC	15.00
408	Kyle Bloom/550 RC	10.00
409	Luis Rivera/500 RC	10.00
410	William Bunn/600 RC	20.00
411	Enrique Barrera RC	20.00
412	Ryan Klosterman RC	15.00
413	John Raglani/515 RC	15.00
414	Brandon Allen/500 RC	25.00
415	Andy Baldwin/600 RC	15.00
416	Mark Lowe RC	35.00
417	Mitch Einertson RC	20.00
418	Ryan Schroyer/600 RC	10.00
419	Brad Davis RC	15.00
420	Jesse Hoover/500 RC	12.00
421	Garrett Broshuis RC	15.00
422	Peter Pope RC	15.00
423	Brent Dlugach RC	15.00
424	Ryan Coultas RC	15.00
425	Ryan Royster RC	20.00
426	Stephen Chapman RC	15.00
427	Bryce Chamberlin RC	20.00
428	Joe Koshansky/550 RC	60.00
429	William Susdorf RC	15.00
430	A.J. Johnson RC	20.00
431	Jeremy Sowers RC	50.00
432	Justin Pekarek RC	15.00
433	Brett Smith RC	15.00
434	Matt Durkin RC	15.00

ABBREVIATIONS
SP - Short Print

435	Daniel Barone RC	15.00
436	Scott Hyde RC	15.00
437	Thomas Everidge RC	25.00
444	Mark Trumbo RC	30.00
446	Eric Patterson RC	25.00
447	Mike Rozier RC	15.00

Gold
Gold (291-447): No Pricing
Production 10 Sets

Platinum
No Pricing
Production One Set

Draft Class
No Pricing
Production 10 Sets

Draft Duos

NM/M
Common Dual Autograph: 15.00
Production 175 Sets

LK	Adam Lind, Ryan Klosterman	40.00
BB	Bill Bray, Collin Balester	25.00
BI	Bill Bray, Ian Desmond	15.00
BM	William Buckner, James Moore	15.00
JH	James Howell, Josh Johnson	15.00
DB	Blake Dewitt, Daniel Batz	25.00
SJ	Brandon Szymanski, Paul Janish	25.00
SH	Brett Smith, Phillip Hughes	50.00
LS	Chris Lambert, Donnie Smith	15.00
LF	Chris Lambert, Mike Ferris	15.00
NS	Chris Nelson, Seth Smith	25.00
NM	Chris Nelson, Matt Macri	30.00
DG	Cory Dunlap, Luis Guerra	30.00
BN	Matt Bush, Chris Nelson	30.00
TH	Curtis Thigpen, Danny Hill	15.00
PT	Dan Putnam, Derek Tharpe	15.00
PJ	David Purcey, Robert Janssen	15.00
DZ	David Purcey, Zachary Jackson	20.00
LH	Donny Lucy, Grant Hansen	15.00
PD	Dustin Pedroia, Andrew Dobies	25.00
MR	Eduardo Morlan, Mark Robinson	15.00
PB	Eddie Prasch, Joseph Bauserman	20.00
EA	Eric Beattie, Andrew Kown	20.00
EJ	Eric Campbell, John Holt	30.00
EM	Eric Hurley, Mike Nickeas	25.00
PI	Erick San Pedro, Devin Ivany	15.00
HH	Gaby Hernandez, Aaron Hathaway	25.00
SK	Seth Smith, Joe Koshansky	30.00
GM	Gio Gonzalez, Timothy Murphey	25.00
BH	Matt Bush, Phillip Hughes	60.00
JR	Grant Johnson, Mark Reed	25.00
GH	Greg Golson, James Happ	20.00
GG	Greg Golson, Sean Gamble	15.00
BS	Homer Bailey, Brandon Szymanski	40.00
BG	Homer Bailey, Rafael Gonzalez	40.00
HJ	Hunter Pence, Jordan Parraz	75.00
SS	Huston Street, Kurt Suzuki	40.00
SW	Huston Street, Ryan Webb	30.00
HB	James Howell, Chad Blackwell	25.00
JM	Jason Jaramillo, Louis Marson	15.00
RS	Jay Rainville, Anthony Swarzak	20.00
JP	Jay Rainville, Patrick Bryant	20.00
FM	Jeff Frazier, Colin Mahoney	15.00
MS	Jeff Marquez, Brett Smith	20.00
MH	Jeff Marquez, Jesse Hoover	25.00
SL	Jeremy Sowers, Charles Lofgren	35.00
JS	Jeremy Sowers, Scott Lewis	25.00
JJ	Jon Poterson, Jason Jones	25.00
ZM	Jon Zeringue, Garrett Mock	20.00
FH	Josh Fields, Lucas Harrell	30.00
FW	Josh Fields, Wes Whisler	40.00
WB	Josh Wahpepah, Josh Baker	15.00
CL	Justin Hoyman, Jeremy Sowers	25.00
OJ	Justin Orenduff, Blake Johnson	25.00
OG	Justin Orenduff, Luis Guerra	20.00
HS	Karl Herren, Michael Schlact	20.00
WF	Kyle Waldrop, Matt Fox	20.00
KB	Kyle Waldrop, Patrick Bryant	25.00
RW	Richie Robnett, Jason Windsor	25.00
SR	Richie Robnett, Kurt Suzuki	25.00
RB	Mark Rogers, Josh Baker	30.00
RG	Mark Rogers, Yovani Gallardo	50.00
BK	Matt Bush, Sean Kazmar	25.00
WE	William Buckner, Enrique Barrera	15.00
WJ	William Buckner, James Howell	20.00
KH	Matt Durkin, Aaron Hathaway	20.00
NB	Neil Walker, Brian Bixler	25.00
NK	Neil Walker, Kyle Bloom	25.00
HG	Phillip Hughes, Christian Garcia	50.00
HP	Phillip Hughes, Jon Poterson	60.00
LA	Ray Liotta, Brandon Allen	25.00
BR	Reid Brignac, Ryan Royster	30.00
RP	Richie Robnett, Dan Putnam	25.00
RH	Richie Robnett, Huston Street	30.00
CO	Steven Register, Seth Smith	25.00
TD	Taylor Tankersley, Brad Davis	15.00
TV	Taylor Tankersley, Jason Vargas	20.00
BT	Thomas Diamond, Brandon Boggs	30.00
DH	Thomas Diamond, Eric Hurley	30.00
ED	Scott Elbert, Blake Dewitt	35.00
ER	Scott Elbert, John Raglani	25.00
PW	Trevor Plouffe, Kyle Waldrop	30.00
PR	Trevor Plouffe, Mark Robinson	25.00
LR	Tyler Lumsden, Adam Russell	15.00
LG	Tyler Lumsden, Gio Gonzalez	25.00
JB	William Buckner, Josh Johnson	20.00
BJ	Matt Bush, Daryl Jones	30.00
GW	Yovani Gallardo, Josh Wahpepah	35.00
JK	Zachary Jackson, Ryan Klosterman	15.00
DR	Blake Dewitt, John Raglani	25.00
GB	Homer Bailey, Greg Goetz	50.00
WR	Reid Brignac, Wade Davis	40.00
HM	Jeff Marquez, Phillip Hughes	50.00
PZ	Jordan Parraz, Benjamin Zobrist	25.00
RL	Luis Rivera, William Layman	15.00
EC	Eric Beattie, Collin Mahoney	15.00
JE	Jeff Frazier, Eric Beattie	15.00
BP	Matt Bush, Trevor Plouffe	30.00
CH	Ryan Coultas, Aaron Hathaway	15.00
SB	Jeremy Sowers, Homer Bailey	75.00
FB	Jeff Fiorentino, Bradley Bergesen	25.00
CF	Bryce Chamberlin, Jeff Fiorentino	20.00
RD	Cory Dunlap, John Raglani	20.00
ZP	Hunter Pence, Benjamin Zobrist	75.00

Draft Generations Triple Autograph
No Pricing
Production 25 Sets
No Pricing
Production 25 Sets

Draft Picks Autographs

NM/M
Common Autograph: 8.00
Golds: No Pricing
Production 10 Sets
Platinum: No Pricing
Production One Set

AA	Andrew Alvarado/400	8.00
RA	Robert Asanovich/400	15.00
JA	Jonny Ash/400	15.00
GB	Garry Bakker/400	10.00
DB	Daniel Batz/400	10.00
KB	Kristian Bell/400	15.00
BL	Chad Blackwell/400	15.00
NB	Nick Blasi/400	15.00
BO	Kyle Bono/400	10.00
SB	Sebastien Boucher/325	15.00
CB	Chad Boyd/475	8.00
JB	Jermaine Brock/400	15.00
PB	Patrick Bryant/400	10.00
BB	Brandon Burgess/400	10.00
CA	Mike Carp/400	25.00
BC	Brandon Conway/400	8.00
DD	Derek Decarlo/400	10.00
RD	Randy Dicken/475	8.00
JD	Jeffery Dominguez/400	15.00
JF	Jim Fasano/400	15.00
KF	Kevin Frandsen/400	25.00
LF	Lucas French/400	15.00
SE	Sean Gallagher/400	50.00
SG	Sean Gamble/400	10.00
GA	Jared Gaston/400	10.00
GG	Greg Goetz/400	10.00
GR	John Grogan/475	10.00
JG	Jarrett Grube/400	8.00
MG	Matt Guillory/400	10.00
DA	David Haehnel/475	12.00
HA	Dustin Hahn/400	8.00
BH	Brian Hall/400	15.00
DH	Derek Hankins/400	8.00
JO	John Hardy/475	15.00
BE	Benjamin Harrison/387	20.00
KH	Kevin Hart/400	10.00
HE	Justin Hedrick/400	15.00
JH	Jarrett Hoffpauir/400	15.00
HO	Joey Howell/400	15.00
TH	Thomas Hubbard/400	10.00
DI	Devin Ivany/550	10.00
SJ	Steven Jackson/400	15.00
MJ	Mark Jecmen/600	10.00
JK	Jeffrey Katz/400	10.00
KK	Koley Kolberg/400	10.00
LA	Jeff Landing/400	10.00
TL	Trevor Lawhorn/475	10.00
WL	William Layman/400	10.00
JL	Josh LeBlanc/400	10.00
DL	Duron Legrande/400	10.00
LE	Wes Letson/400	10.00
MA	Andrew Macfarlane/400	8.00
MC	Jarod McAuliff/400	15.00
BM	Brad McCann/400	25.00
RM	Ryan McCarthy/400	15.00
CH	Christopher McConnell/400	25.00
ME	Carlos Medero-Stullz/400	8.00
RI	Richard Mercado/475	12.00
CL	Cla Meredith/400	15.00
JM	Joey Metropoulos/400	15.00
CM	Cory Middleton/400	20.00
MI	James Miller/475	12.00
AM	Andrew Moffitt/400	10.00
MO	Craig Molldrem/400	12.00
MU	Joseph Muro/400	8.00
TM	Timothy Murphey/400	10.00
DN	David Nicholson/475	10.00
CN	Chris Niesel/475	15.00
RN	Ryan Norwood/400	25.00
BP	Brandon Parillo/475	15.00
MP	Michael Parisi/475	15.00
CP	Cory Patton/400	15.00
TP	Troy Patton/400	75.00
FP	Fernando Perez/400	10.00
PP	Patrick Perry/475	15.00
RP	Ryan Phillips/400	15.00
GP	Grant Plumley/475	10.00
JQ	Jason Quarles/400	8.00
DR	Douglas Reinhardt/400	15.00
CR	Cliff Remole/400	10.00
BR	Barry Richmond/400	20.00
ER	Eric Ridener/475	10.00
MR	Mark Roberts/400	8.00
AR	Adam Russell/550	8.00
CS	Clint Sammons/400	10.00
FS	Freddy Sandoval/400	10.00
AS	Austin Shappi/475	15.00
MS	Matt Shepherd/400	15.00
HS	Hainley Statia/400	20.00
RS	Richard Steik/400	8.00
DT	Derek Tharpe/400	8.00
WT	William Thompson/475	10.00
BT	Brandon Timm/475	15.00
TR	David Trahan/400	10.00
CW	Cory Wade/400	15.00
WE	Chris Westervelt/400	15.00
MW	Mark Worrell/400	15.00
BZ	Benjamin Zobrist/600	25.00

Link to the Future Dual Autograph

NM/M
Common Dual Auto. 10.00
Production 100 Sets

BD	Adrian Beltre, Blake Dewitt	40.00
RF	Scott Rolen, Mike Ferris	40.00
JR	Andruw Jones, Richie Robnett	30.00
KB	Scott Kazmir, Reid Brignac	50.00
JB	Jason Kendall, Brian Bixler	20.00
SR	Ben Sheets, Mark Rogers	40.00
GP	Brian Giles, Dan Putnam	20.00
BG	Carlos Beltran, Greg Golson	30.00
SJ	Johan Santana, Jay Rainville	40.00
WT	Dontrelle Willis, Taylor Tankersley	15.00
JJ	Edwin Jackson, Blake Johnson	15.00
EJ	Eric Chavez, Josh Fields	40.00
QT	Guillermo Quiroz, Curtis Thigpen	10.00
KW	Jason Kendall, Neil Walker	40.00
VM	Javier Vazquez, Jeff Marquez	20.00
MP	Joe Mauer, Trevor Plouffe	50.00
SW	Johan Santana, Kyle Waldrop	40.00
VP	Javier Vazquez, Jon Poterson	20.00
GS	Ken Griffey Jr., Brandon Szymanski	75.00
WB	Kerry Wood, Homer Bailey	50.00
MS	Mike Mussina, Brett Smith	50.00
HS	Todd Helton, Seth Smith	30.00
GZ	Luis Gonzalez, Jon Zeringue	20.00
OH	Magglio Ordonez, Karl Herren	20.00
MB	Mark Mulder, Bill Bray	20.00
PJ	Mark Prior, Grant Johnson	40.00
CF	Matt Clement, Matt Fox	15.00
TN	Miguel Tejada, Chris Nelson	40.00
MH	Mike Mussina, Phillip Hughes	85.00
GB	Nomar Garciaparra, Matt Bush	80.00
PE	Odalis Perez, Scott Elbert	20.00
LS	Paul LoDuca, Erick San Pedro	20.00
HW	Rich Harden, Kyle Waldrop	25.00
CD	Roger Clemens, Thomas Diamond	100.00
RP	Alexis Rios, David Purcey	25.00
RE	Roy Oswalt, Eric Hurley	25.00
RL	Scott Rolen, Chris Lambert	40.00
TS	Tim Hudson, Huston Street	40.00
TJ	Tom Glavine, Jeremy Sowers	35.00
VD	Victor Martinez, Donny Lucy	25.00
BH	Angel Berroa, James Howell	15.00

Link to the Future Triple Autograph
NM/M
Common Triple Auto.
Production 50 Sets

BHH	Hank Blalock, Eric Hurley, Benjamin Harrison	40.00
KBS	Scott Kazmir, Reid Brignac, Matt Spring	75.00
SRB	Ben Sheets, Mark Rogers, Josh Baker	50.00
JJB	Edwin Jackson, Blake Johnson, Daniel Batz	20.00
SWM	Johan Santana, Kyle Waldrop, Eduardo Morlan	60.00
VBB	Jose Vidro, Bill Bray, Collin Balester	30.00
GSJ	Ken Griffey Jr., Brandon Szymanski, Paul Janish	50.00
MSH	Mike Mussina, Brett Smith, Jesse Hoover	50.00
OFA	Magglio Ordonez, Josh Fields, Brandon Allen	30.00
PJR	Mark Prior, Grant Johnson, Mark Reed	100.00
GHM	Juan Gonzalez, James Howell, James Moore	40.00
HSW	Rich Harden, Huston Street, Jason Windsor	50.00
GMZ	Luis Gonzalez, Garrett Mock, Jon Zeringue	25.00
HRW	Tim Hudson, Richie Robnett, Ryan Webb	60.00
GTR	Vladimir Guerrero, Mark Trumbo, Luis Rivera	75.00

Link to the Past Dual Autograph
NM/M
Common Dual Autograph
Production 50 Sets

MB	Bill Mazeroski, Brian Bixler	35.00
FL	Carlton Fisk, Tyler Lumsden	35.00
WJ	Dave Winfield, Zachary Jackson	35.00
BW	Johnny Bench, Neil Walker	40.00
JD	Jose Canseco, Dan Putnam	50.00
AS	Billy Williams, Richie Robnett	40.00
RB	Nolan Ryan, Homer Bailey	180.00
PD	Gaylord Perry, Thomas Diamond	50.00
WR	Wade Boggs, Reid Brignac	60.00
WB	Whitey Ford, Brett Smith	30.00
WP	Whitey Ford, Phillip Hughes	75.00

National Honors

NM/M
Common Player: 4.00
Inserted 1:12

DB	Daniel Bard	8.00
TB	Travis Buck	8.00
JC	Jeff Clement	8.00
BC	Brent Cox	8.00
TC	Trevor Crowe	8.00
JD	Joey Devine	4.00
AG	Alex Gordon	20.00
BH	Brett Hayes	4.00
LH	Luke Hochevar	8.00
SK	Stephen Kahn	4.00
IK	Ian Kennedy	8.00
JL	Jed Lowrie	4.00
JM	John Mayberry Jr.	8.00
MP	Mike Pelfrey	15.00
CR	Cesar Ramos	8.00
MR	Mark Romanczuk	4.00
RR	Ricky Romero	8.00
DS	Drew Stubbs	8.00
TE	Taylor Teagarden	6.00
TT	Troy Tulowitzki	15.00
CV	Chris Valaika	4.00
RZ	Ryan Zimmerman	15.00

2004 SPx

NM/M
Complete Set (202):
Common Player: .25
Common SP (111-145): 3.00
Production 1,599
Common SP (146-154): 5.00
Production 499
Common SP (155-160): 8.00
Production 299
Common Jersey Auto. (161-202): 8.00
Production 799
Pack (4): 5.00
Box (18): 75.00

1	Alfonso Soriano	1.00
2	Todd Helton	.75
3	Andruw Jones	.75
4	Eric Gagne	.50
5	Craig Wilson	.25
6	Brian Giles	.50
7	Miguel Tejada	.50
8	Kevin Brown	.25
9	Shawn Green	.50
10	Ben Sheets	.50
11	John Smoltz	.50
12	Tim Hudson	.50
13	Jason Schmidt	.50
14	Paul Konerko	.50
15	Randy Johnson	1.00
16	Roy Oswalt	.50
17	Mike Lowell	.25
18	Carlos Lee	.50
19	Sean Burroughs	.50
20	Edgar Renteria	.50
21	Michael Young	.25
22	Jose Vidro	.25
23	Scott Rolen	1.00
24	Rafael Furcal	.50
25	Tom Glavine	.75
26	Scott Podsednik	.25
27	Gary Sheffield	.75
28	Eric Chavez	.50
29	Mark Prior	.75
30	Chipper Jones	1.00
31	Frank Thomas	1.00
32	Victor Martinez	.50
33	Jake Peavy	.50
34	Carlos Beltran	1.00
35	Roy Halladay	.50
36	Mark Teixeira	.75
37	Jacque Jones	.25
38	Mike Sweeney	.25
39	Troy Glaus	.50
40	Pat Burrell	.50
41	Ichiro Suzuki	2.00
42	Vladimir Guerrero	1.00
43	Bobby Abreu	.50
44	Jim Edmonds	.50
45	Garret Anderson	.40
46	J.D. Drew	.50
47	C.C. Sabathia	.25
48	Joe Mauer	.50
49	Phil Nevin	.25

#	Player	Price
50	Hank Blalock	.50
51	Carlos Zambrano	.50
52	Mike Piazza	1.50
53	Manny Ramirez	1.00
54	Lance Berkman	.50
55	Delmon Young	.50
56	Nomar Garciaparra	1.00
57	Alex Rodriguez	2.50
58	Rickie Weeks	.50
59	Adrian Beltre	.50
60	Albert Pujols	2.50
61	Richie Sexson	.50
62	Magglio Ordonez	.50
63	Derrek Lee	.75
64	Sammy Sosa	1.50
65	Jason Giambi	.75
66	Curt Schilling	.50
67	Jorge Posada	.50
68	Rafael Palmeiro	.50
69	Jeff Kent	.50
70	Jose Reyes	.50
71	David Ortiz	1.00
72	Aubrey Huff	.25
73	Jim Thome	1.00
74	Andy Pettitte	.50
75	Barry Zito	.50
76	Carlos Delgado	.50
77	Hideki Matsui	2.00
78	Sean Casey	.25
79	Luis Gonzalez	.25
80	Marcus Giles	.25
81	Preston Wilson	.25
82	Javy Lopez	.25
83	Mark Mulder	.50
84	Derek Jeter	2.50
85	Miguel Cabrera	1.00
86	Vernon Wells	.50
87	Roger Clemens	2.50
88	Lyle Overbay	.25
89	Bret Boone	.25
90	Melvin Mora	.25
91	Greg Maddux	2.00
92	Kerry Wood	.50
93	Ivan Rodriguez	.75
94	Pedro J. Martinez	1.00
95	Jeff Bagwell	.75
96	Torii Hunter	.50
97	Ken Griffey Jr.	2.00
98	Mike Mussina	.75
99	Oliver Perez	.25
100	Josh Beckett	.50
101	Bob Gibson	4.00
102	Cal Ripken Jr.	8.00
103	Ted Williams	8.00
104	Nolan Ryan	8.00
105	Mickey Mantle	10.00
106	Ernie Banks	5.00
107	Joe DiMaggio	6.00
108	Stan Musial	5.00
109	Tom Seaver	4.00
110	Mike Schmidt	6.00
111	Jerry Gil RC	3.00
112	Dioner Navarro RC	3.00
113	Bartolome Fortunato RC	3.00
114	Carlos Hines RC	3.00
115	Franklyn Gracesqui RC	3.00
116	Aarom Baldiris RC	5.00
117	Casey Daigle RC	3.00
118	Joey Gathright RC	5.00
119	William Bergolla RC	3.00
120	Jeff Bennett RC	3.00
121	Lincoln Holdzkom RC	3.00
122	Jorge Vasquez RC	3.00
123	Donnie Kelly RC	3.00
124	Yadier Molina RC	8.00
125	Ryan Wing RC	3.00
126	Justin Germano RC	3.00
127	Freddy Guzman RC	3.00
128	Onil Joseph RC	3.00
129	Roman Colon RC	3.00
130	Roberto Novoa RC	5.00
131	Renyel Pinto RC	3.00
132	Evan Rust RC	3.00
133	Orlando Rodriguez RC	3.00
134	Edwardo Sierra RC	5.00
135	Mike Rose RC	3.00
136	Phil Stockman RC	3.00
137	Greg Dobbs RC	3.00
138	Brad Halsey RC	3.00
139	David Aardsma RC	5.00
140	Joe Hietpas RC	3.00
141	Josh Labandeira RC	3.00
142	Mariano Gomez RC	3.00
143	Jeff Bajenaru RC	3.00
144	Travis Blackley RC	3.00
145	Abe Alvarez RC	
146	Ramon Ramirez RC	5.00
147	Edwin Moreno RC	5.00
148	Ronny Cedeno RC	5.00
149	Hector Gimenez RC	5.00
150	Carlos Vasquez RC	8.00
151	Jesse Crain RC	5.00
152	Logan Kensing RC	5.00
153	Sean Henn RC	5.00
154	Rusty Tucker RC	5.00
155	Justin Lehr RC	5.00
156	Ian Snell RC	15.00
157	Merkin Valdez RC	10.00
158	Scott Proctor RC	8.00
159	Jose Capellan RC	8.00
160	Kazuo Matsui RC	8.00
161	Chris Oxspring RC	8.00
162	Jimmy Serrano RC	10.00
163	Jeff Keppinger RC	12.00
164	Brandon Medders RC	8.00
165	Brian Dallimore RC	10.00
166	Chad Bentz RC	12.00
167	Chris Aguila RC	10.00
168	Chris Saenz RC	10.00
169	Frank Francisco RC	10.00
170	Colby Miller RC	12.00
171	David Crouthers RC	10.00
172	Charles Thomas RC	15.00
173	Dennis Sarfate RC	10.00
174	Lance Cormier RC	10.00
175	Joe Horgan RC	10.00
176	Fernando Nieve RC	10.00
177	Jake Woods RC	10.00
178	Matt Treanor RC	12.00
179	Jerome Gamble RC	15.00
180	John Gall RC	15.00
181	Jorge Sequea RC	10.00
182	Justin Hampson RC	10.00
183	Justin Huisman RC	15.00
184	Justin Knoedler RC	12.00
185	Justin Leone RC	10.00
186	Scott Atchison RC	12.00
187	Jon Knott RC	10.00
188	Kevin Cave RC	10.00
189	Jason Frasor RC	10.00
190	George Sherrill RC	12.00
191	Mike Gosling RC	10.00
192	Mike Johnston RC	10.00
193	Mike Rouse RC	10.00
194	Nick Regilio RC	10.00
195	Ryan Meaux RC	10.00
196	Scott Dohmann RC	15.00
197	Shawn Camp RC	10.00
198	Shawn Hill RC	10.00
199	Shingo Takatsu RC	15.00
200	Tim Bausher RC	10.00
201	Tim Bittner RC	10.00
202	Scott Kazmir	60.00

Master Player Prints
No Pricing
Production One Set

Spectrum
Stars (1-100): 5-10X
SP's (101-202): 2-3X
Production 25 Sets

Superscripts
NM/M
Common Player: 8.00
Inserted 1:18

	Player	Price
JB	Josh Beckett	20.00
MC	Miguel Cabrera	25.00
EC	Eric Chavez	15.00
BC	Bobby Crosby	15.00
BF	Bartolome Fortunato	10.00
NG	Nomar Garciaparra/SP	80.00
MG	Mariano Gomez	10.00
KG	Ken Griffey Jr.	75.00
RH	Rich Harden	15.00
SH	Sean Henn	10.00
CH	Carlos Hines	8.00
LH	Lincoln Holdzkom	10.00
EJ	Edwin Jackson	10.00
DJ	Derek Jeter/SP	200.00
DK	Donnie Kelly	8.00
LA	Josh Labandeira	8.00
JL	Justin Lehr	10.00
JM	Joe Mauer	35.00
IO	Ivan Ochoa	8.00
RO	Roy Oswalt	20.00
MP	Mark Prior	40.00
SP	Scott Proctor	10.00
AP	Albert Pujols/SP	240.00
RR	Ramon Ramirez	12.00
JR	Jose Reyes	35.00
CR	Cal Ripken Jr./SP	125.00
RU	Evan Rust	10.00
ES	Edwardo Sierra	10.00
AS	Alfredo Simon	10.00
IS	Ian Snell	25.00
PS	Phil Stockman	10.00
TE	Miguel Tejada	35.00
MT	Mark Teixeira	30.00
MV	Merkin Valdez	12.00
CV	Carlos Vasquez	10.00
VE	Michael Vento	10.00
BW	Brandon Webb	10.00
RW	Rickie Weeks	15.00
DW	Dontrelle Willis	10.00
DY	Delmon Young	25.00

Swatch Supremecy Cut Signatures
No pricing due to scarcity.

Swatch Supremecy Signatures
NM/M
Common Player: 8.00
Production 999 unless noted.
Spectrum: 1.5-3X
Production 25 Sets

	Player	Price
GA	Garret Anderson/275	20.00
RB	Rocco Baldelli	20.00
JB	Josh Beckett	15.00
AB	Angel Berroa	10.00
HB	Hank Blalock	10.00
SB	Sean Burroughs	10.00
MC	Miguel Cabrera	30.00
EC	Eric Chavez/275	20.00
CC	Chad Cordero	10.00
BC	Bobby Crosby	15.00
AE	Adam Eaton	10.00
NG	Nomar Garciaparra/275	60.00
MG	Marcus Giles	15.00
GR	Khalil Greene	25.00
KG	Ken Griffey Jr./275	85.00
RH	Rich Harden	20.00
DJ	Derek Jeter/275	180.00
CK	Casey Kotchman	10.00
CL	Cliff Lee	10.00
DL	Derrek Lee/275	30.00
JM	Joe Mauer	40.00
RO	Roy Oswalt	20.00
LO	Lyle Overbay	15.00
CP	Corey Patterson	10.00
JP	Jake Peavy	35.00
SP	Scott Podsednik	10.00
MP	Mark Prior/275	40.00
AP	Albert Pujols/275	240.00
HR	Horacio Ramirez	10.00
JR	Jose Reyes	35.00
CR	Cal Ripken Jr./275	140.00
NR	Nolan Ryan/275	120.00
BS	Ben Sheets	20.00
MT	Mark Teixeira	15.00
BW	Brandon Webb	15.00
RW	Rickie Weeks	15.00
DW	Dontrelle Willis	25.00
JW	Jerome Williams	10.00
MY	Michael Young	15.00

Winning Materials

NM/M
Common Player: 8.00
Inserted 1:18
Spectrum: 2-3X
Production 25 Sets

	Player	Price
JB	Jeff Bagwell	10.00
BE	Josh Beckett	10.00
HB	Hank Blalock	10.00
KB	Kevin Brown	8.00
EC	Eric Chavez	10.00
RC	Roger Clemens	20.00
CD	Carlos Delgado	10.00
JG	Jason Giambi	12.00
TG	Troy Glaus	8.00
SG	Shawn Green	10.00
VG	Vladimir Guerrero	12.00
DJ	Derek Jeter	35.00
CJ	Chipper Jones	10.00
GM	Greg Maddux	15.00
HM	Hideki Matsui	30.00
MM	Mike Mussina	10.00
RP	Rafael Palmeiro	15.00
PI	Mike Piazza	15.00
JP	Jorge Posada	10.00
MP	Mark Prior	10.00
AP	Albert Pujols	30.00
MR	Manny Ramirez	15.00
JR	Jose Reyes	15.00
SR	Scott Rolen	10.00
GS	Gary Sheffield	10.00
SS	Sammy Sosa	15.00
IS	Ichiro Suzuki	30.00
TE	Miguel Tejada	10.00
JT	Jim Thome	12.00

2005 SP Collection

NM/M
Complete SPx Set (100): 25.00
Common Player: .25
Pack (5): 6.00
Box (20): 100.00

#	Player	Price
1	Aaron Harang	.25
2	Aaron Rowand	.25
3	Aaron Miles	.25
4	Adrian Gonzalez	.25
5	Alex Rios	.25
6	Angel Berroa	.25
7	B.J. Upton	.25
8	Brandon Claussen	.25
9	Andy Marte	.25
10	Brandon Webb	.25
11	Bronson Arroyo	.25
12	Casey Kotchman	.25
13	Cesar Izturis	.25
14	Chad Cordero	.25
15	Chad Tracy	.25
16	Charles Thomas	.25
17	Chase Utley	.50
18	Chone Figgins	.25
19	Chris Burke	.25
20	Cliff Lee	.25
21	Clint Barmes	.25
22	Coco Crisp	.25
23	Bill Hall	.25
24	Dallas McPherson	.25
25	Brad Halsey	.25
26	Daniel Cabrera	.25
27	Danny Haren	.25
28	David Bush	.25
29	David DeJesus	.25
30	D.J. Houlton	.25
31	Derek Jeter	3.00
32	Dewon Brazelton	.25
33	Edwin Jackson	.25
34	Brad Hawpe	.25
35	Brandon Inge	.25
36	Brett Myers	.25
37	Garrett Atkins	.25
38	Gavin Floyd	.25
39	Grady Sizemore	.50
40	Guillermo Mota	.25
41	Carlos Guillen	.25
42	Gustavo Chacin	.25
43	Huston Street	.25
44	Chris Duffy	.25
45	J.D. Closser	.25
46	J.J. Hardy	.25
47	Jason Bartlett	.25
48	Jason Dubois	.25
49	Chris Shelton	.25
50	Jason Lane	.25
51	Jayson Werth	.25
52	Jeff Baker	.25
53	Jeff Francis	.25
54	Jeremy Bonderman	.25
55	Jeremy Reed	.25
56	Jerome Williams	.25
57	Jesse Crain	.25
58	Chris Young	.25
59	Jhonny Peralta	.25
60	Joe Blanton	.25
61	Joe Crede	.25
62	Joel Pineiro	.25
63	Joey Gathright	.25
64	John Buck	.25
65	Jonny Gomes	.25
66	Jorge Cantu	.25
67	Dan Johnson	.25
68	Jose Valverde	.25
69	Ervin Santana	.25
70	Justin Morneau	.50
71	Keiichi Yabu	.25
72	Ken Griffey Jr.	2.00
73	Jason Repko	.25
74	Kevin Youkilis	.25
75	Koyie Hill	.25
76	Laynce Nix	.25
77	Luke Scott RC	1.00
78	Juan Rivera	.25
79	Justin Duchscherer	.25
80	Mark Teahen	.25
81	Lance Niekro	.25
82	Michael Cuddyer	.25
83	Nick Swisher	.25
84	Noah Lowry	.25
85	Matt Holliday	.25
86	Reed Johnson	.25
87	Rich Harden	.25
88	Robb Quinlan	.25
89	Nick Johnson	.25
90	Ryan Howard	1.00
91	Nook Logan	.25
92	Steve Schmoll	.25
93	Tadahito Iguchi	.25
94	Willy Taveras	.25
95	Wily Mo Pena	.25
96	Xavier Nady	.25
97	Yadier Molina	.25
98	Yhency Brazoban	.25
99	Ryan Freel	.25
100	Zack Greinke	.25

Complete SP Authentic Set (100): 25.00
Common Player: .25

#	Player	Price
1	A.J. Burnett	.25
2	Aaron Rowand	.25
3	Adam Dunn	.75
4	Adrian Beltre	.50
5	Adrian Gonzalez	.25
6	Akinori Otsuka	.25
7	Albert Pujols	3.00
8	Andre Dawson	.50
9	Andruw Jones	.50
10	Aramis Ramirez	.50
11	Barry Larkin	.50
12	Ben Sheets	.50
13	Bo Jackson	.50
14	Bobby Abreu	.50
15	Bobby Crosby	.50
16	Bronson Arroyo	.25
17	Cal Ripken Jr.	4.00
18	Carl Crawford	.25
19	Carlos Zambrano	.50
20	Casey Kotchman	.25
21	Cesar Izturis	.25
22	Chone Figgins	.25
23	Corey Patterson	.25
24	Craig Biggio	.50
25	Dale Murphy	.50
26	Dallas McPherson	.25
27	Danny Haren	.25
28	Darryl Strawberry	.25
29	David Ortiz	1.00
30	David Wright	1.00
31	Derek Jeter	3.00
32	Derrek Lee	.50
33	Don Mattingly	1.50
35	Dwight Gooden	.25
35	Edgar Renteria	.50
36	Eric Chavez	.50
37	Eric Gagne	.25
38	Gary Sheffield	.50
39	Gavin Floyd	.25
40	Pedro Martinez	1.00
41	Greg Maddux	2.00
42	Hank Blalock	.50
43	Huston Street	.25
44	J.D. Drew	.25
45	Jake Peavy	.50
46	Jake Westbrook	.25
47	Jason Bay	.25
48	Austin Kearns	.25
49	Jeremy Reed	.25
50	Jim Rice	.50
51	Jimmy Rollins	.50
52	Joe Blanton	.25
53	Joe Mauer	.50
54	Johan Santana	1.00
55	John Smoltz	.25
56	Johnny Estrada	.25
57	Jose Reyes	.50
58	Ken Griffey Jr.	2.00
59	Kerry Wood	.50
60	Khalil Greene	.50
61	Marcus Giles	.25
62	Melvin Mora	.25
63	Mark Grace	.50
64	Mark Mulder	.50
65	Mark Prior	1.00
66	Mark Teixeira	.50
67	Matt Clement	.25
68	Michael Young	.25
69	Miguel Cabrera	1.00
70	Miguel Tejada	.75
71	Mike Piazza	1.50
72	Mike Schmidt	2.00
73	Nolan Ryan	3.00
74	Oliver Perez	.25
75	Nick Johnson	.25
76	Paul Molitor	.75
77	Rafael Palmeiro	.50
78	Randy Johnson	1.00
79	Reggie Jackson	1.00
80	Rich Harden	.25
81	Rickie Weeks	.50
82	Robin Yount	1.00
83	Roger Clemens	3.00
84	Roy Oswalt	.25
85	Ryan Howard	1.00
86	Ryne Sandberg	2.00
87	Scott Kazmir	.25
88	Scott Rolen	1.00
89	Sean Burroughs	.25
90	Sean Casey	.25
91	Shingo Takatsu	.25
92	Tim Hudson	.50
93	Tony Gwynn	1.00
94	Torii Hunter	.50
95	Travis Hafner	.25
96	Victor Martinez	.25
97	Vladimir Guerrero	1.00
98	Wade Boggs	.50
99	Will Clark	.50
100	Yadier Molina	.25

SP Authentic Chirography
No Pricing
Production 15 Sets

SP Authentic Chirography Triple
No Pricing
Production 5 Sets

SP Authentic Honors
NM/M
Common Player: 1.00
Production 299 Sets

	Player	Price
JB	Jason Bay	1.50
AB	Adrian Beltre	1.50
WB	Wade Boggs	1.50
BO	Jeremy Bonderman	1.00
CA	Miguel Cabrera	2.00
WC	Will Clark	1.50
RC	Roger Clemens	6.00
CC	Carl Crawford	1.00
BC	Bobby Crosby	1.50
MG	Marcus Giles	1.00
DG	Dwight Gooden	1.50
GR	Khalil Greene	2.00
ZG	Zack Greinke	1.00
KG	Ken Griffey Jr.	4.00
TG	Tony Gwynn	2.00
TH	Travis Hafner	1.00
RH	Rich Harden	1.00
BJ	Bo Jackson	2.00
DJ	Derek Jeter	6.00
SK	Scott Kazmir	1.00
BL	Barry Larkin	1.50
VM	Victor Martinez	1.00
JM	Joe Mauer	1.50
MC	Dallas McPherson	1.00
PM	Paul Molitor	2.00
MO	Justin Morneau	1.00
DM	Dale Murphy	1.50
DO	David Ortiz	2.00
CP	Corey Patterson	1.00
JP	Jake Peavy	1.50
OP	Oliver Perez	1.00
AP	Albert Pujols	6.00
AR	Aramis Ramirez	1.50
RE	Jose Reyes	1.00
CR	Cal Ripken Jr.	8.00
JR	Jimmy Rollins	1.50
NR	Nolan Ryan	6.00
RS	Ryne Sandberg	4.00
JS	Johan Santana	2.00
MS	Mike Schmidt	4.00
BS	Ben Sheets	1.50
SM	John Smoltz	1.50
ST	Shingo Takatsu	1.50
MT	Mark Teixeira	1.00
TE	Miguel Tejada	2.00
BU	B.J. Upton	1.00
JW	Jake Westbrook	1.00
DW	David Wright	3.00
MY	Michael Young	1.00
CZ	Carlos Zambrano	1.50

SP Authentic Honors Jersey
NM/M
Common Player: 4.00
Production 130 Sets

	Player	Price
JB	Jason Bay	4.00
AB	Adrian Beltre	6.00
WB	Wade Boggs	8.00
BO	Jeremy Bonderman	8.00
CA	Miguel Cabrera	8.00
WC	Will Clark	4.00
RC	Roger Clemens	10.00
CC	Carl Crawford	4.00
BC	Bobby Crosby	4.00
MG	Marcus Giles	4.00
DG	Dwight Gooden	6.00
GR	Khalil Greene	8.00
ZG	Zack Greinke	4.00
KG	Ken Griffey Jr.	15.00
TG	Tony Gwynn	8.00
TH	Travis Hafner	4.00
RH	Rich Harden	4.00
BJ	Bo Jackson	10.00
DJ	Derek Jeter	15.00
SK	Scott Kazmir	4.00
BL	Barry Larkin	6.00
VM	Victor Martinez	4.00
JM	Joe Mauer	6.00
MC	Dallas McPherson	4.00
PM	Paul Molitor	8.00
MO	Justin Morneau	4.00
DM	Dale Murphy	4.00
DO	David Ortiz	8.00
CP	Corey Patterson	4.00
JP	Jake Peavy	4.00
OP	Oliver Perez	4.00
AP	Albert Pujols	15.00
AR	Aramis Ramirez	6.00
RE	Jose Reyes	6.00
CR	Cal Ripken Jr.	20.00
JR	Jimmy Rollins	6.00
NR	Nolan Ryan	15.00
RS	Ryne Sandberg	10.00
JS	Johan Santana	8.00
MS	Mike Schmidt	8.00
BS	Ben Sheets	4.00
SM	John Smoltz	6.00
ST	Shingo Takatsu	4.00
MT	Mark Teixeira	6.00
TE	Miguel Tejada	6.00
BU	B.J. Upton	6.00
JW	Jake Westbrook	4.00
DW	David Wright	15.00
MY	Michael Young	4.00
CZ	Carlos Zambrano	4.00

SP Authentic Honors Signatures
No Pricing
Production 5 Sets

SP Authentic Materials
NM/M
Common Player:
Production 199 Sets
Gold: 1X
Production 99 Sets

#	Player	Price
1	A.J. Burnett	4.00
2	Aaron Rowand	4.00
3	Adam Dunn	6.00
4	Adrian Beltre	6.00
5	Adrian Gonzalez	4.00
6	Akinori Otsuka	4.00
7	Albert Pujols	15.00
8	Andre Dawson	6.00
9	Andruw Jones	6.00
10	Aramis Ramirez	6.00
11	Barry Larkin	6.00
12	Ben Sheets	4.00
13	Bo Jackson	8.00
14	Bobby Abreu	6.00
15	Bobby Crosby	6.00
16	Bronson Arroyo	6.00
17	Cal Ripken Jr.	20.00
18	Carl Crawford	4.00
19	Carlos Zambrano	4.00
20	Casey Kotchman	4.00

21	Cesar Izturis	4.00
22	Chone Figgins	4.00
23	Corey Patterson	4.00
24	Craig Biggio	6.00
25	Dale Murphy	6.00
26	Dallas McPherson	4.00
27	Danny Haren	4.00
28	Darryl Strawberry	4.00
29	David Ortiz	8.00
30	David Wright	10.00
31	Derek Jeter	15.00
32	Derek Lee	8.00
33	Don Mattingly	10.00
34	Dwight Gooden	4.00
35	Edgar Renteria	6.00
36	Eric Chavez	4.00
37	Eric Gagne	6.00
38	Gary Sheffield	6.00
39	Gavin Floyd	4.00
40	Pedro Martinez	8.00
41	Greg Maddux	10.00
42	Hank Blalock	4.00
43	Huston Street	6.00
44	J.D. Drew	4.00
45	Jake Peavy	4.00
46	Jake Westbrook	4.00
47	Jason Bay	4.00
48	Austin Kearns	4.00
49	Jeremy Reed	4.00
50	Jim Rice	6.00
51	Jimmy Rollins	6.00
52	Joe Blanton	4.00
53	Joe Mauer	6.00
54	Johan Santana	6.00
55	John Smoltz	6.00
56	Johnny Estrada	6.00
57	Jose Reyes	6.00
58	Ken Griffey Jr.	12.00
59	Kerry Wood	6.00
60	Khalil Greene	6.00
61	Marcus Giles	4.00
62	Melvin Mora	4.00
63	Mark Grace	6.00
64	Mark Mulder	4.00
65	Mark Prior	8.00
66	Mark Teixeira	4.00
67	Matt Clement	4.00
68	Michael Young	4.00
69	Miguel Cabrera	6.00
70	Miguel Tejada	6.00
71	Mike Piazza	8.00
72	Mike Schmidt	8.00
73	Nolan Ryan	15.00
74	Oliver Perez	4.00
75	Nick Johnson	4.00
76	Paul Molitor	8.00
77	Rafael Palmeiro	4.00
78	Randy Johnson	8.00
79	Reggie Jackson	8.00
80	Rich Harden	6.00
81	Rickie Weeks	6.00
82	Robin Yount	8.00
83	Roger Clemens	10.00
84	Roy Oswalt	4.00
85	Ryan Howard	15.00
86	Ryne Sandberg	8.00
87	Scott Kazmir	4.00
88	Scott Rolen	6.00
89	Sean Burroughs	4.00
90	Sean Casey	4.00
91	Shingo Takatsu	4.00
92	Tim Hudson	6.00
93	Tony Gwynn	8.00
94	Torii Hunter	4.00
95	Travis Hafner	4.00
96	Victor Martinez	4.00
97	Vladimir Guerrero	8.00
98	Wade Boggs	6.00
99	Will Clark	6.00
100	Yadier Molina	4.00

SP Authentic Signatures

NM/M
Production 25-550
Gold: No Pricing
Production 10 Sets

2	Aaron Rowand/550	20.00
3	Adam Dunn/25	20.00
4	Adrian Beltre/125	15.00
5	Adrian Gonzalez/125	15.00
6	Akinori Otsuka/475	15.00
8	Andre Dawson/125	15.00
10	Aramis Ramirez/475	15.00
11	Barry Larkin/125	20.00
12	Ben Sheets/350	12.00
15	Bobby Crosby/350	10.00
16	Bronson Arroyo/550	15.00
18	Carl Crawford/475	12.00
20	Casey Kotchman/550	8.00
21	Cesar Izturis/550	12.00
22	Chone Figgins/550	10.00
23	Corey Patterson/350	10.00
24	Craig Biggio/125	30.00
25	Dale Murphy/350	20.00
26	Dallas McPherson/550	10.00
27	Danny Haren/550	10.00
28	Darryl Strawberry/125	12.00
30	David Wright/350	60.00
31	Derek Jeter/150	140.00
32	Derek Lee/350	15.00
34	Dwight Gooden/475	15.00
36	Eric Chavez/75	12.00
38	Gavin Floyd/550	8.00
43	Huston Street/550	25.00
45	Jake Peavy/475	15.00
46	Jake Westbrook/550	10.00
47	Jason Bay/475	12.00
48	Austin Kearns/75	10.00
49	Jeremy Reed/550	15.00
50	Jim Rice/350	15.00
52	Joe Blanton/550	10.00
53	Joe Mauer/350	20.00
57	Jose Reyes/475	35.00
60	Khalil Greene/350	20.00
62	Melvin Mora/475	12.00
64	Mark Teixeira/125	25.00
66	Mark Mulder/350	15.00
67	Matt Clement/350	20.00
68	Michael Young/475	15.00
69	Miguel Cabrera/125	25.00
74	Oliver Perez/475	15.00
75	Nick Johnson/550	10.00
84	Roy Oswalt/125	20.00
85	Ryan Howard/550	70.00
86	Ryne Sandberg/25	125.00
87	Scott Kazmir/475	15.00
89	Sean Burroughs/475	10.00
91	Shingo Takatsu/550	10.00

SP Authentic Signature Materials

No Pricing
Production 10 Sets

SP Collection of Stars

NM/M
Common Player: 1.00
Production 299 Sets

BR	Bronson Arroyo	1.00
GA	Garrett Atkins	1.00
JE	Jeff Baker	1.00
BA	Clint Barmes	1.00
JB	Jason Bartlett	1.00
JA	Jason Bay	1.00
BE	Adrian Beltre	1.50
BL	Joe Blanton	1.00
BO	Jeremy Bonderman	1.00
YB	Yhency Brazoban	1.00
CB	Chris Burke	1.50
AB	A.J. Burnett	1.00
DB	David Bush	1.00
DC	Daniel Cabrera	1.00
MC	Miguel Cabrera	2.00
CA	Jorge Cantu	1.00
GC	Gustavo Chacin	1.00
RC	Roger Clemens	6.00
JD	J.D. Closser	1.00
CH	Chad Cordero	1.00
JC	Jesse Crain	1.00
CC	Carl Crawford	1.00
CO	Coco Crisp	1.00
DD	David DeJesus	1.00
DU	Jason Dubois	1.00
CD	Chris Duffy	1.00
CF	Chone Figgins	1.00
GF	Gavin Floyd	1.00
JF	Jeff Francis	1.00
RF	Ryan Freel	1.00
JG	Joey Gathright	1.00
GO	Jonny Gomes	1.00
AG	Adrian Gonzalez	1.00
GR	Khalil Greene	2.00
ZG	Zack Greinke	1.00
KG	Ken Griffey Jr.	4.00
CG	Carlos Guillen	1.00
TR	Travis Hafner	1.00
BH	Bill Hall	1.00
RH	Rich Harden	1.50
DH	Danny Haren	1.00
MH	Matt Holliday	1.00
HO	Ryan Howard	2.00
BI	Brandon Inge	1.00
CI	Cesar Izturis	1.00
EJ	Edwin Jackson	1.00
DJ	Derek Jeter	6.00
NJ	Nick Johnson	1.00
RJ	Reed Johnson	1.00
SK	Scott Kazmir	1.00
CK	Casey Kotchman	1.00
JL	Jason Lane	1.00
LE	Brandon League	1.00
CL	Cliff Lee	1.00
GM	Greg Maddux	4.00
AM	Andy Marte	1.00
JM	Joe Mauer	1.50
DM	Dallas McPherson	1.00
YM	Yadier Molina	1.00
MM	Melvin Mora	1.00
MO	Guillermo Mota	1.00
BM	Brett Myers	1.00
DO	David Ortiz	2.00
CP	Corey Patterson	1.00
JP	Jake Peavy	1.50
WM	Wily Mo Pena	1.00
OP	Oliver Perez	1.00
PI	Joel Pineiro	1.00
MP	Mark Prior	2.00
AP	Albert Pujols	5.00
RQ	Robb Quinlan	1.00
RA	Aramis Ramirez	1.50
JR	Jeremy Reed	1.50
RE	Jose Reyes	1.50
RI	Alex Rios	1.00
CR	Cal Ripken Jr.	8.00
RO	Jimmy Rollins	1.00
AR	Aaron Rowand	1.00
JS	Johan Santana	2.00
MS	Mike Schmidt	4.00
LS	Luke Scott	1.00
CS	Chris Shelton	1.00
GS	Grady Sizemore	1.50
SM	John Smoltz	1.50
HS	Huston Street	1.00
NS	Nick Swisher	1.00
ST	Shingo Takatsu	1.00
WT	Willy Taveras	1.00
MT	Mark Teahen	1.50
MI	Miguel Tejada	1.50
TH	Charles Thomas	1.00
CT	Chad Tracy	1.00
BU	B.J. Upton	1.50
WE	Jayson Werth	1.00
JW	Jake Westbrook	1.00
DW	David Wright	3.00
KY	Kevin Youkilis	1.00
MY	Michael Young	1.00
CZ	Carlos Zambrano	1.50

SP Collection of Stars Jersey

NM/M
Production 130 Sets

BR	Bronson Arroyo	4.00
GA	Garrett Atkins	4.00
JE	Jeff Baker	4.00
BA	Clint Barmes	6.00
JB	Jason Bartlett	4.00
JA	Jason Bay	4.00
BE	Adrian Beltre	6.00
BL	Joe Blanton	4.00
BO	Jeremy Bonderman	4.00
YB	Yhency Brazoban	4.00
CB	Chris Burke	4.00
AB	A.J. Burnett	4.00
DB	David Bush	4.00
DC	Daniel Cabrera	4.00
MC	Miguel Cabrera	8.00
CA	Jorge Cantu	4.00
GC	Gustavo Chacin	4.00
RC	Roger Clemens	10.00
JD	J.D. Closser	4.00
CH	Chad Cordero	4.00
JC	Jesse Crain	4.00
CC	Carl Crawford	4.00
CO	Coco Crisp	4.00
DD	David DeJesus	4.00
DU	Jason Dubois	4.00
CD	Chris Duffy	6.00
CF	Chone Figgins	4.00
GF	Gavin Floyd	4.00
JF	Jeff Francis	4.00
RF	Ryan Freel	4.00
JG	Joey Gathright	4.00
GO	Jonny Gomes	6.00
AG	Adrian Gonzalez	4.00
GR	Khalil Greene	6.00
ZG	Zack Greinke	4.00
KG	Ken Griffey Jr.	15.00
CG	Carlos Guillen	4.00
TR	Travis Hafner	4.00
BH	Bill Hall	4.00
RH	Rich Harden	4.00
DH	Danny Haren	4.00
MH	Matt Holliday	4.00
HO	Ryan Howard	15.00
BI	Brandon Inge	4.00
CI	Cesar Izturis	4.00
EJ	Edwin Jackson	4.00
DJ	Derek Jeter	15.00
NJ	Nick Johnson	4.00
RJ	Reed Johnson	4.00
SK	Scott Kazmir	4.00
CK	Casey Kotchman	4.00
JL	Jason Lane	4.00
LE	Brandon League	4.00
CL	Cliff Lee	4.00
GM	Greg Maddux	10.00
AM	Andy Marte	4.00
JM	Joe Mauer	6.00
DM	Dallas McPherson	4.00
YM	Yadier Molina	4.00
MM	Melvin Mora	4.00
MO	Guillermo Mota	4.00
BM	Brett Myers	4.00
DO	David Ortiz	8.00
CP	Corey Patterson	4.00
JP	Jake Peavy	6.00
WM	Wily Mo Pena	4.00
OP	Oliver Perez	4.00
PI	Joel Pineiro	4.00
MP	Mark Prior	6.00
AP	Albert Pujols	15.00
RQ	Robb Quinlan	4.00
RA	Aramis Ramirez	6.00
JR	Jeremy Reed	4.00
RE	Jose Reyes	6.00
RI	Alex Rios	4.00
CR	Cal Ripken Jr.	20.00
RO	Jimmy Rollins	4.00
AR	Aaron Rowand	6.00
JS	Johan Santana	4.00
MS	Mike Schmidt	10.00
LS	Luke Scott	4.00
CS	Chris Shelton	4.00
GS	Grady Sizemore	6.00
SM	John Smoltz	6.00
HS	Huston Street	4.00
NS	Nick Swisher	4.00
ST	Shingo Takatsu	4.00
WT	Willy Taveras	4.00
MT	Mark Teahen	4.00
TE	Mark Teixeira	6.00
MI	Miguel Tejada	6.00
TH	Charles Thomas	4.00
CT	Chad Tracy	4.00
BU	B.J. Upton	4.00
WE	Jayson Werth	4.00
JW	Jake Westbrook	4.00
DW	David Wright	10.00
KY	Kevin Youkilis	4.00
CZ	Carlos Zambrano	6.00

SP Collection of Stars Signatures

No Pricing
Production 5 Sets

SPx Materials

NM/M
Common Player: 3.00
Production 199 Sets
Spectrum: 1X
Production 99 Sets

1	Aaron Harang	3.00
2	Aaron Rowand	5.00
3	Aaron Miles	3.00
4	Adrian Gonzalez	3.00
5	Alex Rios	3.00
6	Angel Berroa	3.00
7	B.J. Upton	5.00
8	Brandon Claussen	3.00
9	Andy Marte	3.00
10	Brandon Webb	5.00
11	Bronson Arroyo	3.00
12	Casey Kotchman	3.00
13	Cesar Izturis	3.00
14	Chad Cordero	3.00
15	Chad Tracy	3.00
16	Charles Thomas	3.00
17	Chase Utley	8.00
18	Chone Figgins	3.00
19	Chris Burke	5.00
20	Cliff Lee	3.00
21	Clint Barmes	5.00
22	Coco Crisp	3.00
23	Bill Hall	3.00
24	Dallas McPherson	3.00
25	Brad Halsey	3.00
26	Daniel Cabrera	3.00
27	Danny Haren	3.00
28	David Bush	3.00
29	David DeJesus	3.00
30	D.J. Houlton	3.00
31	Derek Jeter	20.00
32	Dewon Brazelton	3.00
33	Edwin Jackson	3.00
34	Brad Hawpe	3.00
35	Brandon Inge	3.00
36	Brett Myers	3.00
37	Garrett Atkins	3.00
38	Gavin Floyd	3.00
39	Grady Sizemore	10.00
40	Guillermo Mota	3.00
41	Carlos Guillen	3.00
42	Gustavo Chacin	3.00
43	Huston Street	5.00
44	Chris Duffy	3.00
45	J.D. Closser	3.00
46	J.J. Hardy	3.00
47	Jason Bartlett	3.00
48	Jason Dubois	3.00
49	Chris Shelton	3.00
50	Jason Lane	3.00
51	Jayson Werth	3.00
52	Jeff Baker	3.00
53	Jeff Francis	3.00
54	Jeremy Bonderman	3.00
55	Jeremy Reed	3.00
56	Jerome Williams	3.00
57	Jesse Crain	3.00
58	Chris Young	3.00
59	Jhonny Peralta	3.00
60	Joe Blanton	3.00
61	Joe Crede	3.00
62	Joel Pineiro	3.00
63	Joey Gathright	3.00
64	John Buck	3.00
65	Jonny Gomes	3.00
66	Jorge Cantu	8.00
67	Dan Johnson	3.00
68	Jose Valverde	3.00
69	Ervin Santana	3.00
70	Justin Morneau	5.00
71	Keiichi Yabu	3.00
72	Ken Griffey Jr.	15.00
73	Jason Repko	5.00
74	Kevin Youkilis	3.00
75	Koyie Hill	3.00
76	Laynce Nix	3.00
77	Luke Scott	3.00
78	Juan Rivera	3.00
79	Justin Duchscherer	3.00
80	Mark Teahen	3.00
81	Lance Niekro	3.00
82	Michael Cuddyer	3.00
83	Nick Swisher	3.00
84	Noah Lowry	3.00
85	Matt Holliday	3.00
86	Reed Johnson	3.00
87	Rich Harden	5.00
88	Robb Quinlan	3.00
89	Nick Johnson	3.00
90	Ryan Howard	20.00
91	Nook Logan	3.00
92	Steve Schmoll	3.00
93	Tadahito Iguchi	20.00
94	Willy Taveras	3.00
95	Wily Mo Pena	3.00
96	Xavier Nady	3.00
97	Yadier Molina	3.00
98	Yhency Brazoban	3.00
99	Ryan Freel	3.00
100	Zack Greinke	3.00

SPx Signatures

NM/M
Production 50-350
Spectrum: No Pricing
Production 10 Sets
Jersey Auto.: No Pricing
Production 10 Sets

1	Aaron Harang/350	8.00
2	Aaron Rowand/150	20.00
3	Adrian Gonzalez/225	15.00
4	Angel Berroa/150	8.00
7	B.J. Upton/50	12.00
8	Brandon Claussen/350	8.00
10	Andy Marte/350	10.00
11	Bronson Arroyo/350	8.00
12	Casey Kotchman/225	8.00
13	Cesar Izturis/150	8.00
14	Chad Cordero/350	8.00
15	Chad Tracy/350	10.00
16	Charles Thomas/350	8.00
17	Chase Utley/50	40.00
18	Chone Figgins/150	8.00
19	Chris Burke/350	15.00
20	Cliff Lee/225	8.00
21	Clint Barmes/350	12.00
22	Coco Crisp/225	15.00
23	Bill Hall/350	8.00
24	Dallas McPherson/150	10.00
25	Brad Halsey/350	8.00
26	Daniel Cabrera/350	15.00
27	Danny Haren/225	8.00
28	David Bush/350	10.00
29	David DeJesus/225	8.00
30	D.J. Houlton/350	8.00
31	Derek Jeter/50	150.00
32	Dewon Brazelton/225	8.00
33	Edwin Jackson/150	8.00
34	Brad Hawpe/350	10.00
35	Brandon Inge/350	10.00
36	Brett Myers/150	8.00
37	Garrett Atkins/350	15.00
38	Gavin Floyd/350	10.00
39	Grady Sizemore/350	40.00
40	Guillermo Mota/225	8.00
41	Carlos Guillen/150	20.00
42	Gustavo Chacin/350	10.00
43	Huston Street/350	25.00
44	Chris Duffy/225	15.00
45	J.D. Closser/350	8.00
46	J.J. Hardy/350	10.00
47	Jason Bartlett/350	8.00
48	Jason Dubois/350	10.00
50	Jason Lane/350	10.00
51	Jayson Werth/350	12.00
52	Jeff Baker/350	8.00
53	Jeff Francis/150	10.00
54	Jeremy Bonderman/50	20.00
55	Jeremy Reed/150	10.00
56	Jerome Williams/50	15.00
57	Jesse Crain/350	10.00
59	Jhonny Peralta/350	15.00
60	Joe Blanton/350	8.00
61	Joe Crede/350	25.00
62	Joel Pineiro/150	12.00
63	Joey Gathright/350	8.00
64	John Buck/350	8.00
65	Jonny Gomes/350	15.00
66	Jorge Cantu/350	15.00
67	Dan Johnson/350	15.00
68	Jose Valverde/350	8.00
69	Ervin Santana/350	15.00
71	Keiichi Yabu/350	25.00
73	Jason Repko/350	25.00
74	Kevin Youkilis/225	15.00
75	Koyie Hill/350	10.00
76	Laynce Nix/150	8.00
77	Luke Scott/350	40.00
78	Juan Rivera/225	8.00
79	Justin Duchscherer/350	10.00
80	Mark Teahen/350	8.00
81	Lance Niekro/350	10.00
84	Michael Cuddyer/350	8.00
85	Matt Holliday/150	15.00
86	Reed Johnson/350	8.00
88	Robb Quinlan/150	5.00
89	Nick Johnson/150	8.00
90	Ryan Howard/225	80.00
91	Nook Logan/350	8.00
92	Steve Schmoll/350	5.00
93	Tadahito Iguchi/50	200.00
95	Wily Mo Pena/150	8.00
96	Xavier Nady/150	10.00
98	Yhency Brazoban/350	8.00

SPx Superscripts Signatures

No Pricing
Production 15 Sets

SPx Superscripts Triple Signature

No Pricing
Production 5 Sets

SPx Winning Materials Dual

No Pricing
Production 20 Sets
Dual Auto.: No Pricing
Production 5 Sets

SPXtreme Stats

NM/M
Common Player: 1.00
Production 299 Sets

BA	Bobby Abreu	1.50
AB	Adrian Beltre	1.50
CB	Craig Biggio	1.50
HB	Hank Blalock	1.50
MC	Miguel Cabrera	2.00
SC	Sean Casey	1.00
EC	Eric Chavez	1.00
RC	Roger Clemens	6.00
CC	Carl Crawford	1.00
BC	Bobby Crosby	1.00
JD	J.D. Drew	1.00
AD	Adam Dunn	1.50
EG	Eric Gagne	1.00
GR	Khalil Greene	1.50
KG	Ken Griffey Jr.	4.00
VG	Vladimir Guerrero	2.00
TH	Tim Hudson	1.50
HU	Torii Hunter	1.00
DJ	Derek Jeter	6.00
RJ	Randy Johnson	2.00
AJ	Andruw Jones	1.50
DL	Derek Lee	1.50
GM	Greg Maddux	4.00
VM	Victor Martinez	1.50
JM	Joe Mauer	1.50
MO	Melvin Mora	1.50
MM	Mark Mulder	1.50
DO	David Ortiz	2.00
RO	Roy Oswalt	1.50
RP	Rafael Palmeiro	1.50
CP	Corey Patterson	1.50
JP	Jake Peavy	1.50
OP	Oliver Perez	1.50
PI	Mike Piazza	3.00
MP	Mark Prior	2.00
AP	Albert Pujols	6.00
AR	Aramis Ramirez	1.50
ER	Edgar Renteria	1.50
JR	Jose Reyes	1.00
SR	Scott Rolen	1.50
SA	Johan Santana	2.00
BS	Ben Sheets	1.50
GS	Gary Sheffield	1.50
SM	John Smoltz	1.50
MT	Mark Teixeira	1.50
TE	Miguel Tejada	1.50
KW	Kerry Wood	1.50
MY	Michael Young	1.50
DW	David Wright	3.00
CZ	Carlos Zambrano	1.50

SPXtreme Stats Jersey

NM/M

BA	Bobby Abreu	6.00
AB	Adrian Beltre	6.00
CB	Craig Biggio	6.00
HB	Hank Blalock	8.00
MC	Miguel Cabrera	8.00
SC	Sean Casey	4.00
EC	Eric Chavez	4.00
RC	Roger Clemens	10.00
CC	Carl Crawford	8.00
BC	Bobby Crosby	8.00
JD	J.D. Drew	8.00
AD	Adam Dunn	8.00
EG	Eric Gagne	6.00
GR	Khalil Greene	6.00
KG	Ken Griffey Jr.	15.00
VG	Vladimir Guerrero	8.00
TH	Tim Hudson	4.00
HU	Torii Hunter	4.00
DJ	Derek Jeter	15.00
RJ	Randy Johnson	8.00
AJ	Andruw Jones	6.00
DL	Derek Lee	8.00

GM	Greg Maddux	10.00
VM	Victor Martinez	4.00
JM	Joe Mauer	6.00
MO	Melvin Mora	4.00
MM	Mark Mulder	4.00
DO	David Ortiz	8.00
RO	Roy Oswalt	4.00
RP	Rafael Palmeiro	6.00
CP	Corey Patterson	4.00
JP	Jake Peavy	6.00
OP	Oliver Perez	4.00
PI	Mike Piazza	8.00
MP	Mark Prior	6.00
AP	Albert Pujols	15.00
AR	Aramis Ramirez	6.00
ER	Edgar Renteria	4.00
JR	Jose Reyes	66.00
SR	Scott Rolen	6.00
SA	Johan Santana	8.00
BS	Ben Sheets	4.00
GS	Gary Sheffield	6.00
SM	John Smoltz	6.00
MT	Mark Teixeira	6.00
TE	Miguel Tejada	6.00
KW	Kerry Wood	4.00
DW	David Wright	8.00
MY	Michael Young	4.00
CZ	Carlos Zambrano	6.00

SPXtreme Stats Signatures

No Pricing
Production 5 Sets

2005 SP Legendary Cuts

NM/M
Complete Set (90): 25.00
Common Player: .25
Pack (4): 14.00
Box (12): 150.00

1	Al Kaline	1.00
2	Babe Ruth	3.00
3	Bill Mazeroski	.25
4	Billy Williams	.25
5	Bob Feller	.50
6	Bob Gibson	1.00
7	Bob Lemon	.25
8	Bobby Doerr	.25
9	Brooks Robinson	1.00
10	Carl Yastrzemski	1.50
11	Carlton Fisk	.75
12	Casey Stengel	.50
13	Jim "Catfish" Hunter	.50
14	Christy Mathewson	1.00
15	Cy Young	.50
16	Dennis Eckersley	.25
17	Dizzy Dean	.50
18	Don Drysdale	.25
19	Don Sutton	.25
20	Duke Snider	.75
21	Early Wynn	.25
22	Eddie Mathews	1.00
23	Eddie Murray	.75
24	Enos Slaughter	.25
25	Ernie Banks	1.00
26	Fergie Jenkins	.25
27	Frank Robinson	1.00
28	Gary Carter	.25
29	Gaylord Perry	.25
30	Reggie Jackson	1.00
31	George Kell	.25
32	George Sisler	.25
33	Hal Newhouser	.25
34	Harmon Killebrew	1.00
35	Honus Wagner	1.00
36	Jackie Robinson	1.00
37	Jim Bunning	.25
38	Jim Palmer	.50
39	Jimmie Foxx	.75
40	Joe DiMaggio	2.00
41	Joe Morgan	.50
42	Johnny Bench	1.00
43	Johnny Mize	.25
44	Juan Marichal	.50
45	Kirby Puckett	.75
46	Larry Doby	.25
47	Lefty Grove	.25
48	Lou Boudreau	.25
49	Lou Brock	.50
50	Lou Gehrig	2.00
51	Luis Aparicio	.25
52	Mel Ott	.25
53	Mickey Cochrane	.25
54	Mickey Mantle	4.00
55	Mike Schmidt	1.50
56	Monte Irvin	.25
57	Nolan Ryan	2.00
58	Orlando Cepeda	.25
59	Ozzie Smith	.50
60	Paul Molitor	.50
61	Pee Wee Reese	.25
62	Phil Niekro	.50
63	Phil Rizzuto	.50
64	Ralph Kiner	.25
65	Red Schoendienst	.25
66	Richie Ashburn	.25
67	Rick Ferrell	.25
68	Robin Roberts	.25
69	Robin Yount	1.00
70	Rod Carew	.50
71	Rogers Hornsby	.25
72	Rollie Fingers	.25
73	Roy Campanella	1.00
74	Ryne Sandberg	1.00
75	Satchel Paige	1.00
76	Stan Musial	1.00
77	Steve Carlton	.25
78	Ted Williams	2.00
79	Thurman Munson	1.00
80	Tom Seaver	1.00
81	Tony Gwynn	1.00
82	Tony Perez	.25
83	Ty Cobb	1.50
84	Wade Boggs	.50
85	Walter Johnson	1.00
86	Warren Spahn	1.00
87	Whitey Ford	1.00
88	Willie McCovey	.50
89	Willie Stargell	.75
90	Yogi Berra	1.00

Holofoil

Holofoil: 3-5X
Production 50 Sets

Classic Careers

NM/M
Common Player: 2.00
Production 399 Sets
Gold: 1-2X
Production 75 Sets
Platinum: No Pricing
Production One Set

LA	Luis Aparicio	2.00
HB	Harold Baines	2.00
JB	Jay Buhner	2.00
CA	Jose Canseco	3.00
GC	Gary Carter	2.00
OC	Orlando Cepeda	2.00
JC	Jack Clark	2.00
WC	Will Clark	3.00
DC	David Cone	2.00
AD	Andre Dawson	2.00
BD	Bobby Doerr	2.00
LD	Lenny Dykstra	2.00
CE	Carl Erskine	2.00
SF	Sid Fernandez	2.00
CF	Carlton Fisk	3.00
GF	George Foster	2.00
BF	Bill Freehan	2.00
DG	Dwight Gooden	2.00
GG	Rich "Goose" Gossage	2.00
MG	Mark Grace	2.00
RG	Ron Guidry	2.00
GU	Don Gullett	2.00
KH	Keith Hernandez	2.00
BH	Bob Horner	2.00
FJ	Fergie Jenkins	2.00
BL	Barry Larkin	3.00
SL	Sparky Lyle	2.00
BM	Bill Madlock	2.00
DE	Dennis Martinez	2.00
GM	Gary Mathews	2.00
MA	Don Mattingly	5.00
JM	Jack Morris	2.00
MU	Bobby Murcer	2.00
DM	Dale Murphy	3.00
GN	Graig Nettles	2.00
PN	Phil Niekro	2.00
TO	Tony Oliva	2.00
GP	Gaylord Perry	2.00
JP	Johnny Podres	2.00
TR	Tim Raines	2.00
JR	Jim Rice	2.00
CR	Cal Ripken Jr.	8.00
AR	Al Rosen	2.00
ST	Dave Stewart	2.00
DS	Darryl Strawberry	2.00
SU	Bruce Sutter	2.00
DO	Don Sutton	2.00
LT	Luis Tiant	2.00
AV	Andy Van Slyke	2.00
CY	Carl Yastrzemski	4.00

Classic Careers Autograph

NM/M
Common Player: 15.00
Production 25 Sets
Gold: No Pricing
Production 10 Sets
Platinum: No Pricing
Production One Set

LA	Luis Aparicio	20.00
HB	Harold Baines	25.00
JB	Jay Buhner	30.00
CA	Jose Canseco	40.00
GC	Gary Carter	20.00
OC	Orlando Cepeda	30.00
JC	Jack Clark	20.00
WC	Will Clark	25.00
DC	David Cone	20.00
AD	Andre Dawson	20.00
BD	Bobby Doerr	20.00
LD	Lenny Dykstra	20.00
CE	Carl Erskine	20.00
SF	Sid Fernandez	15.00
CF	Carlton Fisk	35.00
GF	George Foster	25.00
BF	Bill Freehan	25.00
DG	Dwight Gooden	15.00
GG	Rich "Goose" Gossage	20.00
MG	Mark Grace	30.00
RG	Ron Guidry	35.00
GU	Don Gullett	15.00
KH	Keith Hernandez	20.00
BH	Bob Horner	15.00
FJ	Fergie Jenkins	25.00
BL	Barry Larkin	40.00
SL	Sparky Lyle	20.00

Classic Careers Jersey

NM/M
Common Player: 4.00
Gold: 1X
Production 75 Sets
Platinum: No Pricing
Production One Set

LA	Luis Aparicio	6.00
HB	Harold Baines	6.00
JB	Jay Buhner	6.00
CA	Jose Canseco	8.00
GC	Gary Carter	4.00
OC	Orlando Cepeda	6.00
JC	Jack Clark	6.00
WC	Will Clark	6.00
DC	David Cone	4.00
AD	Andre Dawson	6.00
BD	Bobby Doerr	6.00
LD	Lenny Dykstra	4.00
CE	Carl Erskine	4.00
SF	Sid Fernandez	4.00
CF	Carlton Fisk	6.00
GF	George Foster	4.00
BF	Bill Freehan	6.00
DG	Dwight Gooden	4.00
GG	Rich "Goose" Gossage	6.00
MG	Mark Grace	8.00
RG	Ron Guidry	4.00
GU	Don Gullett	4.00
KH	Keith Hernandez	4.00
BH	Bob Horner	4.00
FJ	Fergie Jenkins	4.00
BL	Barry Larkin	6.00
SL	Sparky Lyle	4.00
BM	Bill Madlock	4.00
DE	Dennis Martinez	4.00
GM	Gary Mathews	4.00
MA	Don Mattingly	12.00
JM	Jack Morris	4.00
MU	Bobby Murcer	4.00
DM	Dale Murphy	8.00
PN	Phil Niekro	4.00
GN	Graig Nettles	4.00
TO	Tony Oliva	4.00
GP	Gaylord Perry	4.00
JP	Johnny Podres	4.00
TR	Tim Raines	4.00
JR	Jim Rice	4.00
CR	Cal Ripken Jr.	40.00
AV	Andy Van Slyke	15.00
ST	Dave Stewart	4.00
DS	Darryl Strawberry	12.00

Classic Careers Patch

NM/M
Production 50 Sets
Gold: No Pricing
Production 10 Sets
Platinum: No Pricing
Production One Set

HB	Harold Baines	10.00
CA	Jose Canseco	15.00
JC	Jack Clark	10.00
WC	Will Clark	20.00
DC	David Cone	15.00
AD	Andre Dawson	15.00
BD	Bobby Doerr	15.00
LD	Lenny Dykstra	10.00
SF	Sid Fernandez	10.00
GF	George Foster	10.00
BF	Bill Freehan	10.00
DG	Dwight Gooden	15.00
GG	Rich "Goose" Gossage	12.00
MG	Mark Grace	12.00
KH	Keith Hernandez	12.00
BL	Barry Larkin	25.00
DE	Dennis Martinez	10.00
GM	Gary Mathews	10.00
JM	Jack Morris	10.00
GN	Graig Nettles	10.00
GP	Gaylord Perry	10.00
TR	Tim Raines	12.00
JR	Jim Rice	15.00
CR	Cal Ripken Jr.	40.00
AV	Andy Van Slyke	15.00
ST	Dave Stewart	10.00
DS	Darryl Strawberry	12.00

Classic Careers Patch Autograph

NM/M
Production 25 Sets
Gold: No Pricing
Production 5 Sets
Platinum: No Pricing
Production One Set

HB	Harold Baines	40.00
JB	Jay Buhner	50.00
JC	Jack Clark	35.00
WC	Will Clark	40.00
DC	David Cone	35.00
AD	Andre Dawson	35.00
BD	Bobby Doerr	35.00
LD	Lenny Dykstra	35.00
SF	Sid Fernandez	25.00
GF	George Foster	40.00
BF	Bill Freehan	40.00
DG	Dwight Gooden	25.00
GG	Rich "Goose" Gossage	35.00
MG	Mark Grace	40.00
GU	Don Gullett	25.00
KH	Keith Hernandez	35.00
BL	Barry Larkin	60.00
DE	Dennis Martinez	25.00
GM	Gary Mathews	25.00
JM	Jack Morris	35.00
GN	Graig Nettles	35.00
TO	Tony Oliva	35.00
GP	Gaylord Perry	30.00
TR	Tim Raines	30.00
JR	Jim Rice	40.00
CR	Cal Ripken Jr.	200.00
ST	Dave Stewart	25.00
DS	Darryl Strawberry	25.00
AV	Andy Van Slyke	40.00

Dual Legendary Cuts

Production 1-10

Glory Days

NM/M
Common Player: 2.00
Production 399 Sets
Gold: 1X-2X
Production 75 Sets
Platinum: No Pricing
Production One Set

HB	Harold Baines	2.00
YB	Yogi Berra	4.00
LB	Lou Brock	2.00
JB	Jay Buhner	2.00
CA	Jose Canseco	3.00
JC	Jack Clark	2.00
WC	Will Clark	3.00
DC	David Cone	2.00
AD	Andre Dawson	2.00
BD	Bobby Doerr	2.00
LD	Lenny Dykstra	2.00
SF	Sid Fernandez	2.00
WF	Whitey Ford	3.00
GF	George Foster	2.00
BF	Bill Freehan	2.00
KG	Kirk Gibson	2.00
DG	Dwight Gooden	2.00
RG	Ron Guidry	3.00
GU	Don Gullett	2.00
TG	Tony Gwynn	4.00
KH	Keith Hernandez	2.00
BH	Bob Horner	2.00
FJ	Fergie Jenkins	2.00
BL	Barry Larkin	3.00
FL	Fred Lynn	2.00
BM	Bill Madlock	2.00
MA	Juan Marichal	3.00
DE	Dennis Martinez	2.00
GM	Gary Mathews	2.00
PM	Paul Molitor	4.00
JM	Jack Morris	2.00
MU	Bobby Murcer	2.00
DM	Dale Murphy	3.00
GN	Graig Nettles	2.00
TO	Tony Oliva	2.00
JP	Jim Palmer	2.00
TR	Tim Raines	2.00
JR	Jim Rice	2.00
CR	Cal Ripken Jr.	8.00
AR	Al Rosen	2.00
NR	Nolan Ryan	8.00
RS	Red Schoendienst	2.00
SN	Duke Snider	3.00
ST	Dave Stewart	2.00
DS	Darryl Strawberry	2.00
BS	Bruce Sutter	2.00
LT	Luis Tiant	2.00
AV	Andy Van Slyke	2.00
RY	Robin Yount	4.00

Glory Days Autograph

NM/M
Common Player: 15.00
Production 25 Sets
Gold: No Pricing
Production 10 Sets
Platinum: No Pricing
Production One Set

HB	Harold Baines	25.00
YB	Yogi Berra	50.00
LB	Lou Brock	30.00
JB	Jay Buhner	30.00
CA	Jose Canseco	40.00
JC	Jack Clark	20.00
WC	Will Clark	25.00
DC	David Cone	20.00
AD	Andre Dawson	20.00
BD	Bobby Doerr	20.00
LD	Lenny Dykstra	20.00
SF	Sid Fernandez	15.00
WF	Whitey Ford	40.00
GF	George Foster	25.00
BF	Bill Freehan	25.00
KG	Kirk Gibson	20.00
DG	Dwight Gooden	15.00
RG	Ron Guidry	35.00
GU	Don Gullett	15.00
TG	Tony Gwynn	40.00
KH	Keith Hernandez	20.00
BH	Bob Horner	15.00
FJ	Fergie Jenkins	25.00
BL	Barry Larkin	40.00
SL	Sparky Lyle	20.00
FL	Fred Lynn	15.00
BM	Bill Madlock	20.00
MA	Juan Marichal	25.00
DE	Dennis Martinez	15.00
GM	Gary Mathews	15.00
PM	Paul Molitor	40.00
JM	Jack Morris	25.00
MU	Bobby Murcer	25.00
DM	Dale Murphy	35.00
GN	Graig Nettles	20.00
TO	Tony Oliva	20.00
JP	Jim Palmer	25.00
TR	Tim Raines	20.00
JR	Jim Rice	20.00
CR	Cal Ripken Jr.	125.00
AR	Al Rosen	20.00
NR	Nolan Ryan	100.00
RS	Red Schoendienst	20.00
SN	Duke Snider	40.00
ST	Dave Stewart	15.00
DS	Darryl Strawberry	20.00
BS	Bruce Sutter	25.00
LT	Luis Tiant	20.00
AV	Andy Van Slyke	30.00
RY	Robin Yount	50.00

Glory Days Jersey

NM/M
Common Player: 4.00
Gold: 1X
Production 75 Sets
Platinum: No Pricing
Production One Set

HB	Harold Baines	6.00
YB	Yogi Berra	10.00
LB	Lou Brock	6.00
JB	Jay Buhner	6.00
JC	Jose Canseco	8.00
JC	Jack Clark	4.00
WC	Will Clark	6.00
DC	David Cone	4.00
AD	Andre Dawson	6.00
BD	Bobby Doerr	4.00
LD	Lenny Dykstra	6.00
SF	Sid Fernandez	4.00
WF	Whitey Ford	10.00
GF	George Foster	4.00
BF	Bill Freehan	4.00
KG	Kirk Gibson	4.00
DG	Dwight Gooden	4.00
RG	Ron Guidry	6.00
GU	Don Gullett	4.00
TG	Tony Gwynn	8.00
KH	Keith Hernandez	4.00
BH	Bob Horner	4.00
FJ	Fergie Jenkins	6.00
BL	Barry Larkin	6.00
SL	Sparky Lyle	4.00
FL	Fred Lynn	4.00
MA	Juan Marichal	6.00
DE	Dennis Martinez	4.00
GM	Gary Mathews	4.00
PM	Paul Molitor	8.00
JM	Jack Morris	4.00
MU	Bobby Murcer	4.00
DM	Dale Murphy	8.00
GN	Graig Nettles	4.00
TO	Tony Oliva	4.00
JP	Jim Palmer	6.00
TR	Tim Raines	4.00
JR	Jim Rice	6.00
CR	Cal Ripken Jr.	20.00
AR	Al Rosen	4.00
NR	Nolan Ryan	15.00
RS	Red Schoendienst	4.00
SN	Duke Snider	8.00
ST	Dave Stewart	4.00
DS	Darryl Strawberry	6.00
LT	Luis Tiant	4.00
BS	Bruce Sutter	6.00
AV	Andy Van Slyke	4.00
RY	Robin Yount	10.00

Glory Days Memorabilia Autograph

NM/M
Production 25 Sets
Gold: No Pricing
Production 10 Sets
Platinum: No Pricing
Production One Set

HB	Harold Baines	25.00
YB	Yogi Berra	50.00
JB	Jay Buhner	30.00
JC	Jack Clark	20.00
WC	Will Clark	25.00
DC	David Cone	20.00
AD	Andre Dawson	20.00
BD	Bobby Doerr	20.00
LD	Lenny Dykstra	20.00
SF	Sid Fernandez	15.00
WF	Whitey Ford	40.00
GF	George Foster	25.00
BF	Bill Freehan	25.00
KG	Kirk Gibson	20.00
DG	Dwight Gooden	15.00
RG	Ron Guidry	35.00
GU	Don Gullett	20.00
TG	Tony Gwynn	40.00
KH	Keith Hernandez	20.00
BH	Bob Horner	15.00
FJ	Fergie Jenkins	20.00
BL	Barry Larkin	40.00
SL	Sparky Lyle	20.00
FL	Fred Lynn	15.00
BM	Bill Madlock	20.00
MA	Juan Marichal	25.00
DE	Dennis Martinez	15.00
GM	Gary Mathews	20.00
PM	Paul Molitor	40.00
JM	Jack Morris	20.00
MU	Bobby Murcer	25.00
DM	Dale Murphy	35.00
GN	Graig Nettles	20.00
TO	Tony Oliva	20.00
JP	Jim Palmer	20.00
TR	Tim Raines	20.00
JR	Jim Rice	20.00
AR	Al Rosen	20.00
NR	Nolan Ryan	100.00
RS	Red Schoendienst	20.00
SN	Duke Snider	40.00
ST	Dave Stewart	15.00
DS	Darryl Strawberry	20.00
BS	Bruce Sutter	20.00
LT	Luis Tiant	20.00
AV	Andy Van Slyke	30.00
RY	Robin Yount	50.00

Glory Days Patch

NM/M
Gold: No Pricing
Production 10 Sets
Platinum: No Pricing
Production One Set

HB	Harold Baines	10.00

JC	Jack Clark	10.00
DC	David Cone	15.00
AD	Andre Dawson	15.00
BD	Bobby Doerr	15.00
LD	Lenny Dykstra	15.00
SF	Sid Fernandez	10.00
GF	George Foster	10.00
DG	Dwight Gooden	15.00
KH	Keith Hernandez	12.00
BH	Bob Horner	10.00
FJ	Fergie Jenkins	15.00
BL	Barry Larkin	25.00
GM	Gary Mathews	10.00
JM	Jack Morris	10.00
DM	Dale Murphy	20.00
GN	Graig Nettles	10.00
JP	Jim Palmer	15.00
TR	Tim Raines	10.00
RS	Red Schoendienst	15.00
DS	Darryl Strawberry	12.00
BS	Bruce Sutter	15.00
LT	Luis Tiant	15.00
AV	Andy Van Slyke	15.00

Glory Days Patch Autograph
NM/M
Production 25 Sets
Gold: No Pricing
Production 5 Sets
Platinum: No Pricing
Production One Set

HB	Harold Baines	40.00
JB	Jay Buhner	50.00
JC	Jack Clark	35.00
DC	David Cone	35.00
AD	Andre Dawson	35.00
BD	Bobby Doerr	35.00
LD	Lenny Dykstra	35.00
SF	Sid Fernandez	25.00
GF	George Foster	40.00
DG	Dwight Gooden	25.00
KH	Keith Hernandez	35.00
BH	Bob Horner	25.00
FJ	Fergie Jenkins	40.00
BL	Barry Larkin	60.00
BM	Bill Madlock	25.00
DE	Dennis Martinez	25.00
GM	Gary Mathews	25.00
JM	Jack Morris	35.00
DM	Dale Murphy	40.00
GN	Graig Nettles	35.00
TO	Tony Oliva	35.00
JP	Jim Palmer	40.00
TR	Tim Raines	30.00
JR	Jim Rice	40.00
RS	Red Schoendienst	30.00
DS	Darryl Strawberry	30.00
BS	Bruce Sutter	25.00
LT	Luis Tiant	25.00
AV	Andy Van Slyke	40.00

Historic Cuts
No Pricing
Production One Set

Historic Quads Autograph
No Pricing
Production 5 Sets

Historic Quads Material
No Pricing
Production 5 Sets
Patch: No Pricing
Production One Set

Lasting Legends
NM/M
Common Player: 2.00
Production 399 Sets
Gold: 1-2X
Production 75 Sets
Platinum: No Pricing
Production One Set

LA	Luis Aparicio	2.00
EB	Ernie Banks	4.00
BE	Johnny Bench	4.00
YB	Yogi Berra	4.00
WB	Wade Boggs	3.00
LB	Lou Brock	3.00
RC	Rod Carew	3.00
SC	Steve Carlton	2.00
GC	Gary Carter	2.00
OC	Orlando Cepeda	2.00
BD	Bobby Doerr	2.00
DE	Dennis Eckersley	2.00
RF	Rollie Fingers	2.00
CF	Carlton Fisk	3.00
WF	Whitey Ford	3.00
BG	Bob Gibson	3.00
DG	Dwight Gooden	2.00
TG	Tony Gwynn	3.00
KH	Keith Hernandez	2.00
FJ	Fergie Jenkins	2.00
AK	Al Kaline	3.00
BL	Barry Larkin	3.00
MA	Juan Marichal	2.00
DM	Don Mattingly	5.00
BM	Bill Mazeroski	2.00
PM	Paul Molitor	3.00
JM	Joe Morgan	3.00
MU	Dale Murphy	2.00
EM	Eddie Murray	3.00
SM	Stan Musial	4.00
PN	Phil Niekro	2.00
GN	Graig Nettles	2.00
JP	Jim Palmer	3.00
TP	Tony Perez	2.00
GP	Gaylord Perry	2.00
KP	Kirby Puckett	3.00
JR	Jim Rice	2.00
CR	Cal Ripken Jr.	8.00
BR	Brooks Robinson	3.00
FR	Frank Robinson	3.00
NR	Nolan Ryan	6.00
SA	Ryne Sandberg	4.00
MS	Mike Schmidt	4.00
RS	Red Schoendienst	3.00
OS	Ozzie Smith	4.00
SN	Duke Snider	3.00
BS	Bruce Sutter	2.00
DS	Don Sutton	2.00
CY	Carl Yastrzemski	4.00
RY	Robin Yount	4.00

Lasting Legends Autograph
NM/M
Common Player:
Production 25 Sets
Gold: No Pricing
Production 10 Sets
Platinum: No Pricing
Production One Set

LA	Luis Aparicio	20.00
EB	Ernie Banks	60.00
BE	Johnny Bench	50.00
YB	Yogi Berra	60.00
WB	Wade Boggs	40.00
LB	Lou Brock	25.00
RC	Rod Carew	35.00
SC	Steve Carlton	25.00
GC	Gary Carter	25.00
OC	Orlando Cepeda	25.00
BD	Bobby Doerr	20.00
DE	Dennis Eckersley	25.00
RF	Rollie Fingers	20.00
CF	Carlton Fisk	35.00
WF	Whitey Ford	40.00
BG	Bob Gibson	40.00
DG	Dwight Gooden	15.00
TG	Tony Gwynn	50.00
KH	Keith Hernandez	20.00
FG	Fergie Jenkins	25.00
AK	Al Kaline	40.00
BL	Barry Larkin	40.00
MA	Juan Marichal	25.00
DM	Don Mattingly	60.00
BM	Bill Mazeroski	35.00
PM	Paul Molitor	40.00
JM	Joe Morgan	25.00
DM	Dale Murphy	40.00
EM	Eddie Murray	50.00
SM	Stan Musial	60.00
GN	Graig Nettles	20.00
PN	Phil Niekro	25.00
JP	Jim Palmer	25.00
TP	Tony Perez	20.00
GP	Gaylord Perry	20.00
KP	Kirby Puckett	50.00
JR	Jerry Rice	25.00
CR	Cal Ripken Jr.	125.00
BR	Brooks Robinson	40.00
FR	Frank Robinson	40.00
NR	Nolan Ryan	100.00
SA	Ryne Sandberg	50.00
MS	Mike Schmidt	50.00
RS	Red Schoendienst	20.00
OS	Ozzie Smith	60.00
SN	Duke Snider	40.00
BS	Bruce Sutter	25.00
DS	Don Sutton	20.00
CY	Carl Yastrzemski	50.00
RY	Robin Yount	50.00

Lasting Legends Material
NM/M
Common Player: 4.00
Gold: 1-1.5X
Production 75 Sets
Platinum: No Pricing
Production One Set

LA	Luis Aparicio	4.00
EB	Ernie Banks	10.00
BE	Johnny Bench	8.00
YB	Yogi Berra	8.00
WB	Wade Boggs	6.00
LB	Lou Brock	6.00
RC	Rod Carew	4.00
SC	Steve Carlton	4.00
GC	Gary Carter	4.00
OC	Orlando Cepeda	4.00
BD	Bobby Doerr	6.00
DE	Dennis Eckersley	4.00
RF	Rollie Fingers	4.00
CF	Carlton Fisk	6.00
WF	Whitey Ford	6.00
BG	Bob Gibson	8.00
DG	Dwight Gooden	4.00
TG	Tony Gwynn	8.00
KH	Keith Hernandez	4.00
FJ	Fergie Jenkins	4.00
AK	Al Kaline	10.00
BL	Barry Larkin	6.00
MA	Juan Marichal	6.00
DM	Don Mattingly	10.00
BM	Bill Mazeroski	6.00
PM	Paul Molitor	6.00
JM	Joe Morgan	4.00
MU	Dale Murphy	6.00
EM	Eddie Murray	6.00
SM	Stan Musial	10.00
GN	Graig Nettles	4.00
PN	Phil Niekro	4.00
JP	Jim Palmer	6.00
TP	Tony Perez	4.00
GP	Gaylord Perry	4.00
KP	Kirby Puckett	8.00
JR	Jim Rice	4.00
CR	Cal Ripken Jr.	20.00
BR	Brooks Robinson	6.00
FR	Frank Robinson	6.00
NR	Nolan Ryan	15.00
SA	Ryne Sandberg	8.00
MS	Mike Schmidt	10.00
RS	Red Schoendienst	4.00
OS	Ozzie Smith	6.00
SN	Duke Snider	6.00
BS	Bruce Sutter	4.00
DS	Don Sutton	4.00
CY	Carl Yastrzemski	15.00
RY	Robin Yount	8.00

Lasting Legends Jersey Autograph
NM/M
Production 25 Sets
Gold: No Pricing
Production 10 Sets
Platinum: No Pricing
Production One Set

LA	Luis Aparicio	20.00
EB	Ernie Banks	60.00
BE	Johnny Bench	50.00
YB	Yogi Berra	60.00
WB	Wade Boggs	40.00
LB	Lou Brock	25.00
RC	Rod Carew	40.00
SC	Steve Carlton	25.00
GC	Gary Carter	25.00
OC	Orlando Cepeda	25.00
BD	Bobby Doerr	20.00
DE	Dennis Eckersley	25.00
RF	Rollie Fingers	20.00
CF	Carlton Fisk	40.00
WF	Whitey Ford	40.00
BG	Bob Gibson	40.00
DG	Dwight Gooden	15.00
TG	Tony Gwynn	50.00
KH	Keith Hernandez	20.00
FG	Fergie Jenkins	25.00
AK	Al Kaline	50.00
BL	Barry Larkin	40.00
MA	Juan Marichal	25.00
DM	Don Mattingly	60.00
PM	Paul Molitor	40.00
JM	Joe Morgan	25.00
MU	Dale Murphy	40.00
SM	Stan Musial	60.00
GN	Graig Nettles	20.00
PN	Phil Niekro	25.00
JP	Jim Palmer	25.00
TP	Tony Perez	20.00
GP	Gaylord Perry	20.00
JR	Jim Rice	25.00
CR	Cal Ripken Jr.	140.00
BR	Brooks Robinson	40.00
FR	Frank Robinson	25.00
NR	Nolan Ryan	100.00
SA	Ryne Sandberg	50.00
MS	Mike Schmidt	50.00
RS	Red Schoendienst	20.00
OS	Ozzie Smith	60.00
SN	Duke Snider	40.00
BS	Bruce Sutter	25.00
CY	Carl Yastrzemski	50.00
RY	Robin Yount	50.00

Lasting Legends Patch
NM/M
Production 50 Sets
Gold: No Pricing
Production 10 Sets
Platinum: No Pricing
Production One Set

WB	Wade Boggs	20.00
LB	Lou Brock	15.00
RC	Rod Carew	15.00
SC	Steve Carlton	15.00
GC	Gary Carter	12.00
OC	Orlando Cepeda	15.00
DE	Dennis Eckersley	15.00
RF	Rollie Fingers	10.00
CF	Carlton Fisk	15.00
DG	Dwight Gooden	10.00
KH	Keith Hernandez	15.00
FJ	Fergie Jenkins	15.00
BL	Barry Larkin	25.00
MA	Juan Marichal	15.00
JM	Joe Morgan	15.00
PN	Phil Niekro	15.00
JP	Jim Palmer	15.00
TP	Tony Perez	15.00
GP	Gaylord Perry	12.00
KP	Kirby Puckett	25.00
JR	Jim Rice	15.00
BR	Brooks Robinson	20.00
FR	Frank Robinson	15.00
SA	Ryne Sandberg	25.00
OS	Ozzie Smith	15.00
BS	Bruce Sutter	15.00
DS	Don Sutton	12.00
RY	Robin Yount	25.00

Lasting Legends Patch Autograph
NM/M
Production 25 Sets
Gold: No Pricing
Production 5 Sets
Platinum: No Pricing
Production One Set

WB	Wade Boggs	50.00
RC	Rod Carew	50.00
SC	Steve Carlton	35.00
GC	Gary Carter	35.00
OC	Orlando Cepeda	35.00
DE	Dennis Eckersley	35.00
RF	Rollie Fingers	35.00
DG	Dwight Gooden	25.00
KH	Keith Hernandez	25.00
FJ	Fergie Jenkins	35.00
BL	Barry Larkin	50.00
MA	Juan Marichal	35.00
PM	Paul Molitor	35.00
JM	Joe Morgan	35.00
PN	Phil Niekro	35.00
JP	Jim Palmer	40.00
TP	Tony Perez	30.00
GP	Gaylord Perry	30.00
JR	Jim Rice	35.00
BR	Brooks Robinson	50.00
NR	Nolan Ryan	140.00
SA	Ryne Sandberg	80.00
OS	Ozzie Smith	75.00
BS	Bruce Sutter	30.00
RY	Robin Yount	65.00

Legendary Cuts
NM/M
Production 1-108

LA	Luke Appling/55	125.00
RI	Richie Ashburn/83	150.00
EA	Earl Averill/91	140.00
JB	Cool Papa Bell/78	300.00
LB	Lou Boudreau/99	140.00
MC	Max Carey/84	140.00
HC	Happy Chandler/39	125.00
JC	Jocko Conlan/40	140.00
ST	Stan Covaleski/71	140.00
CR	Joe Cronin/76	140.00
RD	Ray Dandridge/76	100.00
BD	Bill Dickey/95	150.00
JD	Joe DiMaggio/56	500.00
LD	Larry Doby/32	140.00
DD	Don Drysdale/50	200.00
DU	Leo Durocher/57	150.00
FE	Rick Ferrell/80	125.00
CF	Carl Furillo/25	200.00
CG	Charlie Gehringer/97	120.00
GO	Lefty Gomez/68	150.00
HG	Hank Greenberg/44	280.00
BU	Burleigh Grimes/99	125.00
GR	Lefty Grove/41	200.00
HA	Chick Hafey/52	150.00
JH	Jesse Haines/90	150.00
GH	Gabby Hartnett/50	180.00
BH	Billy Herman/99	90.00
WH	Waite Hoyt/99	140.00
CH	Carl Hubbell/150	150.00
HU	Jim "Catfish" Hunter/65	140.00
JJ	Jackie Jensen/48	180.00
JO	Judy Johnson/39	140.00
CK	Charlie Keller/98	140.00
HK	Harvey Kuenn/33	165.00
BL	Bob Lemon/108	100.00
LE	Buck Leonard/71	140.00
LI	Freddie Lindstrom/19	250.00
LO	Ernie Lombardi/29	200.00
HM	Heinie Manush/75	175.00
RU	Rube Marquard/80	150.00
EM	Eddie Mathews/80	150.00
RO	Roy McMillan/23	140.00
MI	Johnny Mize/90	125.00
HN	Hal Newhouser/96	125.00
PR	Pee Wee Reese/69	180.00
SR	Sam Rice/41	140.00
ER	Edd Roush/99	100.00
JS	Joe Sewell/76	140.00
ES	Enos Slaughter/99	100.00
WA	Warren Spahn/92	140.00
WS	Willie Stargell/63	165.00
CS	Casey Stengel/61	250.00
BW	Bucky Walters/34	150.00
JW	Hoyt Wilhelm/48	100.00
EW	Early Wynn/89	120.00

Legendary Cuts Material
NM/M
Production 75 unless noted.
Gold: No Pricing
Production 15 Sets

CA	Roy Campanella	40.00
RC	Roberto Clemente	80.00
TC	Ty Cobb	140.00
CO	Mickey Cochrane	50.00
CR	Joe Cronin	15.00
DE	Dizzy Dean	60.00
BD	Bill Dickey	35.00
JD	Joe DiMaggio	120.00
DD	Don Drysdale	15.00
JF	Jimmie Foxx	60.00
LG	Lou Gehrig	175.00
HG	Hank Greenberg	35.00
HO	Gil Hodges	40.00
RH	Rogers Hornsby	80.00
HU	Jim "Catfish" Hunter	10.00
TK	Ted Kluszewski	40.00
TL	Tony Lazerri	40.00
BL	Bob Lemon	25.00
MM	Mickey Mantle	150.00
RM	Roger Maris	60.00
EM	Eddie Mathews	40.00
CM	Christy Mathewson	125.00
MI	Johnny Mize	35.00
TM	Thurman Munson	35.00
MO	Mel Ott	50.00
SP	Satchel Paige	75.00
PR	Pee Wee Reese	15.00
JR	Jackie Robinson	65.00
BR	Babe Ruth	180.00
SI	George Sisler	25.00
ES	Enos Slaughter	15.00
WA	Warren Spahn	40.00
CS	Casey Stengel	40.00
HW	Honus Wagner/22	40.00
JW	Hoyt Wilhelm	15.00
TW	Ted Williams	75.00
EW	Early Wynn	10.00

Legendary Cuts Quad
No Pricing
Production One Set

Legendary Battery Cuts
NM/M
Production 6-99

SC	Stan Covelski/25	140.00
BD	Bill Dickey/22	200.00
DD	Don Drysdale/31	200.00
LG	Lefty Gomez/77	160.00
JH	Jesse Haines/28	200.00
WH	Waite Hoyt/91	125.00
CH	Carl Hubbell/99	140.00
HN	Hal Newhouser/32	140.00
WS	Warren Spahn/43	150.00
EW	Early Wynn/32	125.00

Legendary Cornerstone Cuts
NM/M
Production 1-79

DC	Dolph Camilli/79	120.00
RD	Ray Dandridge/27	125.00
EM	Eddie Mathews/50	150.00
JM	Johnny Mize/41	150.00
WS	Willie Stargell/36	150.00

Legendary Duels Material
NM/M
Production 25 Sets
Patch: No Pricing
Production 10 Sets

BM	Ernie Banks, Stan Musial	50.00
CC	Jose Canseco, Will Clark	40.00
DM	Paul Molitor, Lenny Dykstra	25.00
EG	Dennis Eckersley, Kirk Gibson	25.00
FB	Carlton Fisk, Johnny Bench	25.00
FR	George Foster, Jim Rice	15.00
JY	Reggie Jackson, Carl Yastrzemski	40.00
MC	Rod Carew, Paul Molitor	25.00
MH	Don Mattingly, Keith Hernandez	35.00
SF	Duke Snider, Whitey Ford	35.00
SG	Ron Guidry, Don Sutton	15.00
SS	Ozzie Smith, Ryne Sandberg	60.00
YS	Mike Schmidt, Robin Yount	35.00

Legendary Duels Autograph
No Pricing
Production 15 Sets

Legendary Duos Material
NM/M
Production 25 Sets
Patch: No Pricing
Production 10 Sets

CO	Tony Oliva, Rod Carew	20.00
ES	Duke Snider, Carl Erskine	15.00
FB	Yogi Berra, Whitey Ford	40.00
GS	Ryne Sandberg, Mark Grace	50.00
JG	Reggie Jackson, Ron Guidry	25.00
MB	Joe Morgan, Johnny Bench	35.00
MY	Robin Yount, Paul Molitor	40.00
RB	Wade Boggs, Jim Rice	20.00
RC	Will Clark, Cal Ripken Jr.	50.00
RM	Cal Ripken Jr., Eddie Murray	50.00
RR	Brooks Robinson, Frank Robinson	25.00
SC	Mike Schmidt, Steve Carlton	30.00
SG	Darryl Strawberry, Dwight Gooden	15.00

Legendary Duos Autograph
No Pricing
Production 15 Sets

Legendary Glovemen Cuts
NM/M

EA	Earl Averill/39	120.00
CP	Cool Papa Bell/29	350.00
MC	Max Carey/50	140.00
JD	Joe DiMaggio/75	400.00
ES	Enos Slaughter/65	120.00

Middlemen Cuts
NM/M
Production 2-99

LA	Luke Appling/32	150.00
LB	Lou Boudreau/99	100.00
JC	Joe Cronin/30	140.00
CG	Charlie Gehringer/95	140.00
BH	Billy Herman/90	90.00
PW	Pee Wee Reese/39	200.00
JS	Joe Sewell/76	140.00

Legendary Lineage
NM/M
Common Player: 2.00
Production 399 Sets
Gold: 1-2X
Production 75 Sets
Platinum: No Pricing
Production One Set

HB	Harold Baines	2.00
JB	Jay Buhner	2.00
CA	Jose Canseco	3.00
SC	Steve Carlton	2.00
JC	Jack Clark	2.00
WC	Will Clark	2.00
DC	David Cone	2.00
AD	Andre Dawson	2.00
BD	Bobby Doerr	2.00
LD	Lenny Dykstra	2.00
EC	Dennis Eckersley	2.00
SF	Sid Fernandez	2.00
BF	Bill Freehan	2.00
DG	Dwight Gooden	2.00
GG	Rich "Goose" Gossage	2.00
MG	Mark Grace	3.00
RG	Ron Guidry	2.00
GU	Don Gullett	2.00
TG	Tony Gwynn	4.00
KH	Keith Hernandez	2.00
BH	Bob Horner	2.00
RJ	Reggie Jackson	2.00
FJ	Fergie Jenkins	2.00
BL	Barry Larkin	3.00
SL	Sparky Lyle	2.00
BM	Bill Madlock	2.00
DE	Dennis Martinez	2.00
GM	Gary Matthews	2.00
MA	Don Mattingly	5.00
PM	Paul Molitor	2.00
JM	Jack Morris	2.00
MU	Bobby Murcer	2.00
DM	Dale Murphy	3.00
GN	Graig Nettles	2.00
TO	Tony Oliva	3.00
JP	Jim Palmer	2.00
KP	Kirby Puckett	4.00
TR	Tim Raines	2.00
JR	Jim Rice	2.00
CR	Cal Ripken Jr.	8.00
BR	Brooks Robinson	2.00
AR	Al Rosen	2.00
MS	Mike Schmidt	5.00
OS	Ozzie Smith	4.00
SN	Duke Snider	3.00
DS	Dave Stewart	2.00
ST	Darryl Strawberry	2.00
SU	Bruce Sutter	2.00
LT	Luis Tiant	2.00
AV	Andy Van Slyke	2.00

Legendary Lineage Autograph
NM/M
Common Player: 15.00
Production 25 Sets
Gold: No Pricing
Production 10 Sets
Platinum: No Pricing
Production One Set

HB	Harold Baines	25.00
JB	Jay Buhner	30.00
CA	Jose Canseco	40.00

SC	Steve Carlton	25.00
JC	Jack Clark	20.00
WC	Will Clark	25.00
DC	David Cone	20.00
AD	Andre Dawson	20.00
BD	Bobby Doerr	20.00
LD	Lenny Dykstra	20.00
EC	Dennis Eckersley	25.00
SF	Sid Fernandez	15.00
BF	Bill Freehan	25.00
DG	Dwight Gooden	15.00
GG	Rich "Goose" Gossage	20.00
MG	Mark Grace	30.00
RG	Ron Guidry	35.00
GU	Don Gullett	15.00
TG	Tony Gwynn	40.00
KH	Keith Hernandez	20.00
BH	Bob Horner	15.00
RJ	Reggie Jackson	40.00
FJ	Fergie Jenkins	25.00
BL	Barry Larkin	40.00
SL	Sparky Lyle	20.00
BM	Bill Madlock	20.00
DE	Dennis Martinez	15.00
GM	Gary Matthews	15.00
MA	Don Mattingly	60.00
PM	Paul Molitor	40.00
JM	Jack Morris	20.00
MU	Bobby Murcer	25.00
DM	Dale Murphy	35.00
GN	Graig Nettles	20.00
TO	Tony Oliva	25.00
JP	Jim Palmer	20.00
KP	Kirby Puckett	50.00
TR	Tim Raines	20.00
JR	Jim Rice	25.00
CR	Cal Ripken Jr.	125.00
BR	Brooks Robinson	40.00
AR	Al Rosen	20.00
MS	Mike Schmidt	60.00
OS	Ozzie Smith	50.00
SN	Duke Snider	40.00
DS	Dave Stewart	15.00
ST	Darryl Strawberry	20.00
SU	Bruce Sutter	25.00
LT	Luis Tiant	20.00
AV	Andy Van Slyke	30.00

Legendary Lineage Jersey

NM/M
Common Player: 4.00
Gold: 1-1.5X
Production 75 Sets
Platinum: No Pricing
Production One Set

HB	Harold Baines	4.00
JB	Jay Buhner	4.00
CA	Jose Canseco	8.00
SC	Steve Carlton	6.00
JC	Jack Clark	4.00
WC	Will Clark	6.00
DC	David Cone	4.00
AD	Andre Dawson	6.00
BD	Bobby Doerr	6.00
LD	Lenny Dykstra	6.00
EC	Dennis Eckersley	6.00
SF	Sid Fernandez	4.00
BF	Bill Freehan	6.00
DG	Dwight Gooden	4.00
GG	Rich "Goose" Gossage	4.00
MG	Mark Grace	8.00
RG	Ron Guidry	4.00
GU	Don Gullett	4.00
TG	Tony Gwynn	8.00
KH	Keith Hernandez	4.00
BH	Bob Horner	4.00
RJ	Reggie Jackson	8.00
FJ	Fergie Jenkins	6.00
BL	Barry Larkin	6.00
SL	Sparky Lyle	4.00
BM	Bill Madlock	4.00
DE	Dennis Martinez	4.00
GM	Gary Matthews	4.00
MA	Don Mattingly	12.00
PM	Paul Molitor	6.00
JM	Jack Morris	4.00
MU	Bobby Murcer	4.00
DM	Dale Murphy	8.00
GN	Graig Nettles	4.00
TO	Tony Oliva	4.00
JP	Jim Palmer	6.00
KP	Kirby Puckett	8.00
TR	Tim Raines	4.00
JR	Jim Rice	6.00
CR	Cal Ripken Jr.	20.00
BR	Brooks Robinson	6.00
AR	Al Rosen	4.00
MS	Mike Schmidt	10.00
OS	Ozzie Smith	8.00
SN	Duke Snider	8.00
DS	Dave Stewart	4.00
ST	Darryl Strawberry	4.00
SU	Bruce Sutter	4.00
LT	Luis Tiant	4.00
AV	Andy Van Slyke	4.00

Legendary Lineage Jersey Autograph

NM/M
Production 25 Sets
Gold: No Pricing
Production 10 Sets
Platinum: No Pricing
Production One Set

HB	Harold Baines	25.00
JB	Jay Buhner	30.00
CA	Jose Canseco	40.00
SC	Steve Carlton	25.00
JC	Jack Clark	20.00
WC	Will Clark	25.00
DC	David Cone	20.00
AD	Andre Dawson	25.00
BD	Bobby Doerr	25.00
LD	Lenny Dykstra	20.00
EC	Dennis Eckersley	25.00
SF	Sid Fernandez	15.00
BF	Bill Freehan	25.00
DG	Dwight Gooden	15.00
GG	Rich "Goose" Gossage	20.00
MG	Mark Grace	30.00
RG	Ron Guidry	35.00
GU	Don Gullett	15.00
TG	Tony Gwynn	40.00
KH	Keith Hernandez	20.00
BH	Bob Horner	15.00
RJ	Reggie Jackson	40.00
FJ	Fergie Jenkins	25.00
BL	Barry Larkin	40.00
SL	Sparky Lyle	20.00
BM	Bill Madlock	20.00
DE	Dennis Martinez	15.00
GM	Gary Matthews	15.00
MA	Don Mattingly	60.00
PM	Paul Molitor	40.00
JM	Jack Morris	20.00
MU	Bobby Murcer	25.00
DM	Dale Murphy	35.00
GN	Graig Nettles	20.00
TO	Tony Oliva	20.00
JP	Jim Palmer	25.00
KP	Kirby Puckett	50.00
TR	Tim Raines	20.00
JR	Jim Rice	25.00
CR	Cal Ripken Jr.	150.00
BR	Brooks Robinson	40.00
AR	Al Rosen	20.00
MS	Mike Schmidt	60.00
OS	Ozzie Smith	50.00
SN	Duke Snider	40.00
DS	Dave Stewart	20.00
ST	Darryl Strawberry	20.00
SU	Bruce Sutter	25.00
LT	Luis Tiant	20.00
AV	Andy Van Slyke	30.00

Legendary Lineage Patch

NM/M
Production 50 Sets
Gold: No Pricing
Production 10 Sets
Platinum: No Pricing
Production One Set

HB	Harold Baines	10.00
JB	Jay Buhner	15.00
JC	Jack Clark	10.00
WC	Will Clark	20.00
DC	David Cone	15.00
AD	Andre Dawson	15.00
BD	Bobby Doerr	15.00
BF	Bill Freehan	12.00
DG	Dwight Gooden	15.00
GG	Rich "Goose" Gossage	12.00
MG	Mark Grace	20.00
TG	Tony Gwynn	20.00
KH	Keith Hernandez	12.00
BH	Bob Horner	10.00
BL	Barry Larkin	25.00
BM	Bill Madlock	10.00
DE	Dennis Martinez	10.00
JM	Jack Morris	10.00
DM	Dale Murphy	20.00
GN	Graig Nettles	10.00
TR	Tim Raines	10.00
CR	Cal Ripken Jr.	40.00
MS	Mike Schmidt	25.00
DS	Dave Stewart	10.00
ST	Darryl Strawberry	12.00
LT	Luis Tiant	10.00
AV	Andy Van Slyke	15.00

Legendary Lineage Patch Autograph

NM/M
Production 25 Sets
Gold: No Pricing
Production 5 Sets
Platinum: No Pricing
Production One Set

HB	Harold Baines	40.00
JB	Jay Buhner	50.00
JC	Jack Clark	35.00
WC	Will Clark	35.00
DC	David Cone	35.00
AD	Andre Dawson	35.00
BD	Bobby Doerr	35.00
BF	Bill Freehan	40.00
DG	Dwight Gooden	25.00
GG	Rich "Goose" Gossage	35.00
MG	Mark Grace	50.00
TG	Tony Gwynn	70.00
KH	Keith Hernandez	35.00
BH	Bob Horner	25.00
BL	Barry Larkin	60.00
BM	Bill Madlock	25.00
DE	Dennis Martinez	25.00
PM	Paul Molitor	50.00
JM	Jack Morris	35.00
DM	Dale Murphy	40.00
GN	Graig Nettles	35.00
TR	Tim Raines	30.00
JR	Jim Rice	25.00
CR	Cal Ripken Jr.	200.00
MS	Mike Schmidt	90.00
DS	Dave Stewart	25.00
ST	Darryl Strawberry	30.00
LT	Luis Tiant	25.00
AV	Andy Van Slyke	40.00

Significant Tips

No Pricing
Production 10 Sets
Patch: No Pricing
Production 5 Sets

Significant Trips Autograph

No Pricing
Production 10 Sets

2006 SP Authentic

NM/M
Complete Set (300):
Common Player (1-100): .25
Common SP (101-200): 2.00
Production 899
Common Auto. (201-300): 8.00
Production 125-899
Pack (5): 5.00
Box (24): 110.00

1	Erik Bedard	.25
2	Corey Patterson	.25
3	Ramon Hernandez	.25
4	Kris Benson	.25
5	Miguel Batista	.25
6	Orlando Hudson	.25
7	Shawn Green	.25
8	Jeff Francoeur	.40
9	Marcus Giles	.25
10	Edgar Renteria	.25
11	Tim Hudson	.40
12	Tim Wakefield	.25
13	Mark Loretta	.25
14	Kevin Youkilis	.25
15	Mike Lowell	.25
16	Coco Crisp	.25
17	Tadahito Iguchi	.25
18	Scott Podsednik	.25
19	Jermaine Dye	.25
20	Jose Contreras	.25
21	Carlos Zambrano	.40
22	Aramis Ramirez	.25
23	Jacque Jones	.25
24	Austin Kearns	.25
25	Felipe Lopez	.25
26	Brandon Phillips	.25
27	Aaron Harang	.25
28	Cliff Lee	.25
29	Jhonny Peralta	.25
30	Jason Michaels	.25
31	Clint Barmes	.25
32	Brad Hawpe	.25
33	Aaron Cook	.25
34	Kenny Rogers	.25
35	Carlos Guillen	.25
36	Brian Moehler	.25
37	Andy Pettitte	.40
38	Wandy Rodriguez	.25
39	Morgan Ensberg	.25
40	Preston Wilson	.25
41	Mark Grudzielanek	.25
42	Angel Berroa	.25
43	Jeremy Affeldt	.25
44	Zack Greinke	.25
45	Orlando Cabrera	.25
46	Garret Anderson	.25
47	Ervin Santana	.25
48	Derek Lowe	.25
49	Nomar Garciaparra	.75
50	J.D. Drew	.25
51	Rafael Furcal	.40
52	Rickie Weeks	.40
53	Geoff Jenkins	.25
54	Bill Hall	.25
55	Chris Capuano	.25
56	Derrick Turnbow	.25
57	Justin Morneau	.40
58	Michael Cuddyer	.25
59	Luis Castillo	.25
60	Hideki Matsui	1.00
61	Jason Giambi	.25
62	Jorge Posada	.50
63	Mariano Rivera	.50
64	Billy Wagner	.25
65	Carlos Delgado	.50
66	Jose Reyes	.75
67	Nick Swisher	.40
68	Bobby Crosby	.25
69	Frank Thomas	.50
70	Ryan Howard	2.00
71	Pat Burrell	.40
72	Jimmy Rollins	.50
73	Craig Wilson	.25
74	Freddy Sanchez	.25
75	Sean Casey	.25
76	Mike Piazza	1.00
77	Dave Roberts	.25
78	Chris Young	.25
79	Noah Lowry	.25
80	Armando Benitez	.25
81	Pedro Feliz	.25
82	Jose Lopez	.25
83	Adrian Beltre	.25
84	Jamie Moyer	.25
85	Jason Isringhausen	.25
86	Jason Marquis	.25
87	David Eckstein	.25
88	Juan Encarnacion	.25
89	Julio Lugo	.25
90	Ty Wigginton	.25
91	Jorge Cantu	.25
92	Akinori Otsuka	.25
93	Hank Blalock	.40
94	Kevin Mench	.25
95	Lyle Overbay	.25
96	Shea Hillenbrand	.25
97	B.J. Ryan	.25
98	Tony Armas	.25
99	Chad Cordero	.25
100	Jose Guillen	.25
101	Miguel Tejada	3.00
102	Brian Roberts	2.00
103	Melvin Mora	2.00
104	Brandon Webb	2.00
105	Chad Tracy	2.00
106	Luis Gonzalez	2.00
107	Andruw Jones	4.00
108	Chipper Jones	5.00
109	John Smoltz	3.00
110	Curt Schilling	4.00
111	Josh Beckett	3.00
112	David Ortiz	5.00
113	Manny Ramirez	4.00
114	Jason Varitek	4.00
115	Jim Thome	4.00
116	Paul Konerko	4.00
117	Javier Vazquez	2.00
118	Mark Prior	4.00
119	Derek Lee	4.00
120	Greg Maddux	6.00
121	Ken Griffey Jr.	6.00
122	Adam Dunn	3.00
123	Bronson Arroyo	2.00
124	Travis Hafner	3.00
125	Victor Martinez	2.00
126	Grady Sizemore	3.00
127	C.C. Sabathia	2.00
128	Todd Helton	3.00
129	Matt Holliday	3.00
130	Garrett Atkins	2.00
131	Jeff Francis	2.00
132	Jeremy Bonderman	3.00
133	Ivan Rodriguez	3.00
134	Chris Shelton	2.00
135	Magglio Ordonez	3.00
136	Dontrelle Willis	3.00
137	Miguel Cabrera	5.00
138	Roger Clemens	8.00
139	Roy Oswalt	3.00
140	Lance Berkman	3.00
141	Reggie Sanders	2.00
142	Vladimir Guerrero	5.00
143	Bartolo Colon	2.00
144	Chone Figgins	2.00
145	Francisco Rodriguez	2.00
146	Brad Penny	2.00
147	Jeff Kent	3.00
148	Eric Gagne	2.00
149	Carlos Lee	2.00
150	Ben Sheets	2.00
151	Johan Santana	4.00
152	Torii Hunter	2.00
153	Joe Nathan	2.00
154	Alex Rodriguez	6.00
155	Derek Jeter	8.00
156	Randy Johnson	4.00
157	Johnny Damon	4.00
158	Mike Mussina	3.00
159	Pedro Martinez	4.00
160	Tom Glavine	3.00
161	David Wright	5.00
162	Carlos Beltran	4.00
163	Rich Harden	2.00
164	Barry Zito	3.00
165	Eric Chavez	2.00
166	Huston Street	2.00
167	Bobby Abreu	2.00
168	Chase Utley	4.00
169	Brett Myers	2.00
170	Jason Bay	3.00
171	Zachary Duke	2.00
172	Jake Peavy	3.00
173	Brian Giles	2.00
174	Khalil Greene	2.00
175	Trevor Hoffman	2.00
176	Jason Schmidt	2.00
177	Randy Winn	2.00
178	Omar Vizquel	2.00
179	Kenji Johjima	5.00
180	Ichiro Suzuki	6.00
181	Richie Sexson	3.00
182	Felix Hernandez	3.00
183	Albert Pujols	8.00
184	Chris Carpenter	3.00
185	Jim Edmonds	3.00
186	Scott Rolen	4.00
187	Carl Crawford	3.00
188	Scott Kazmir	2.00
189	Jonny Gomes	2.00
190	Mark Teixeira	3.00
191	Michael Young	3.00
192	Kevin Millwood	2.00
193	Vernon Wells	2.00
194	Troy Glaus	3.00
195	Roy Halladay	2.00
196	Alex Rios	2.00
197	Nick Johnson	2.00
198	Livan Hernandez	2.00
199	Alfonso Soriano	4.00
200	Jose Vidro	2.00
201	Aaron Rakers/ 399 (RC)	20.00
202	Angel Pagan/ 399 (RC)	20.00
203	Ben Hendrickson/ 399 (RC)	10.00
204	Bobby Livingston/ 399 (RC)	8.00
205	Darrell Rasner/ 399 (RC)	15.00
206	Brian Bannister/ 399 (RC)	20.00
207	Brian Wilson/899 RC	15.00
208	Bobby Keppel/ 399 (RC)	8.00
209	Choo Freeman/ 399 (RC)	10.00
210	Chris Booker/899 (RC)	8.00
211	Chris Britton/399 RC	15.00
212	Chris Demaria/ 329 RC	12.00
213	Chris Resop/899 (RC)	8.00
214	Tony Gwynn Jr./ 399 (RC)	8.00
215	Eric Reed/399 (RC)	8.00
216	Fabio Castro/899 RC	20.00
217	Fernando Nieve/ 299 (RC)	10.00
218	Freddie Bynum/ 899 (RC)	10.00
219	Guillermo Quiroz/ 399 (RC)	8.00
220	Hong-Chih Kuo/ 899 (RC)	60.00
221	Ryan Theriot/ 399 (RC)	40.00
222	Jack Taschner/ 899 (RC)	8.00
223	Jason Bergmann/ 899 RC	8.00
224	Jason Hammel/ 899 (RC)	8.00
225	Jeff Harris/399 RC	8.00
226	Jeremy Accardo/ 399 RC	15.00
227	Ty Taubenheim/ 399 RC	30.00
228	Joel Zumaya/ 399 (RC)	40.00
229	John Koronka/ 399 (RC)	10.00
230	Erick Aybar/399 (RC)	10.00
231	Jordan Tata/399 RC	20.00
232	Russell Martin/ 399 (RC)	20.00
233	Josh Rupe/399 (RC)	10.00
234	Kevin Frandsen/ 399 (RC)	20.00
235	Martin Prado/ 399 (RC)	25.00
236	Matt Capps/399 (RC)	10.00
237	Agustin Montero/ 199 (RC)	10.00
238	Mike Thompson/ 399 RC	10.00
239	Nate McLouth/ 399 (RC)	15.00
240	Peter Moylan/399 RC	15.00
241	Reggie Abercrombie/ 399 (RC)	15.00
242	Carlos Quentin/ 399 (RC)	20.00
243	Ron Flores/399 RC	10.00
244	Ryan Shealy/ 399 (RC)	20.00
245	Mike Rouse/399 (RC)	10.00
246	Santiago Ramirez/ 399 (RC)	10.00
247	Clay Hensley/ 399 (RC)	15.00
248	Skip Schumaker/ 399 (RC)	15.00
249	Eliezer Alfonzo/ 899 RC	15.00
250	Steve Stemle/399 RC	10.00
251	Tim Hamulack/ 399 (RC)	12.00
252	Tony Pena/299 (RC)	10.00
253	Emiliano Fruto/ 899 RC	10.00
254	Wilbert Nieves/ 399 (RC)	15.00
255	Joey Devine/399 RC	15.00
256	Adam Wainwright/ 399 (RC)	40.00
257	Andre Ethier/ 399 (RC)	30.00
258	Ben Johnson/ 399 (RC)	10.00
259	Boone Logan/399 RC	20.00
260	Chris Denorfia/ 899 (RC)	15.00
261	Alay Soler/299 RC	20.00
262	Cody Ross/899 (RC)	10.00
263	Dave Gassner/ 399 (RC)	15.00
264	Fausto Carmona/ 399 (RC)	10.00
265	Jeremy Sowers/ 299 (RC)	25.00
266	Jason Kubel/ 399 (RC)	15.00
267	John Van Benschoten/ 399 (RC)	10.00
268	Jose Capellan/ 399 (RC)	10.00
269	Josh Wilson/399 (RC)	8.00
270	Kelly Shoppach/ 399 (RC)	10.00
271	Macay McBride/ 399 (RC)	15.00
272	Matt Cain/399 (RC)	30.00
273	Mike Jacobs/ 399 (RC)	15.00
274	Paul Maholm/ 399 (RC)	15.00
275	Chad Billingsley/ 399 (RC)	25.00
276	Ruddy Lugo/ 399 (RC)	15.00
277	Jon Lester/399 (RC)	40.00
278	Sean Marshall/ 383 (RC)	25.00
279	Melky Cabrera/ 399 (RC)	30.00
280	Yusmeiro Petit/ 399 (RC)	15.00
281	Anderson Hernandez/ 299 (RC)	10.00
282	Brian Anderson/ 699 (RC)	15.00
283	Cole Hamels/ 299 (RC)	50.00
284	Boof Bonser/ 299 (RC)	25.00
285	Dan Uggla/199 (RC)	25.00
286	Francisco Liriano/ 299 (RC)	50.00
287	Hanley Ramirez/ 199 (RC)	25.00
288	Ian Kinsler/299 (RC)	30.00
289	Jeremy Hermida/ 299 (RC)	20.00
290	Jonathan Papelbon/ 199 (RC)	60.00
291	Jered Weaver/ 199 (RC)	40.00
292	Josh Johnson/ 299 (RC)	20.00
293	Josh Willingham/ 199 (RC)	20.00
294	Justin Verlander/ 199 (RC)	60.00
295	Stephen Drew/ 299 (RC)	50.00
296	Prince Fielder/ 125 (RC)	50.00
297	Ryan Zimmerman/ 199 (RC)	65.00
298	Takashi Saito/283 RC	50.00
299	Taylor Buchholz/ 299 (RC)	10.00
300	Conor Jackson/ 299 (RC)	15.00

Rookie Signatures Platinum

No Pricing
Production One Set

By The Letter

NM/M
Production 4-200

JB	Jason Bay/110	50.00
JB2	Jason Bay/50	50.00
CB	Craig Biggio/55	125.00
BI	Chad Billingsley/75	40.00
HB	Hank Blalock/50	40.00
AB	A.J. Burnett/50	50.00
MC	Miguel Cabrera/35	85.00
EC	Eric Chavez/75	40.00
AD	Adam Dunn/50	40.00
MG	Marcus Giles/136	30.00
JG	Jonny Gomes/175	30.00
KH	Khalil Greene/75	40.00
KG	Ken Griffey Jr./25	200.00
KG2	Ken Griffey Jr./25	200.00
KG3	Ken Griffey Jr./25	200.00
KG4	Ken Griffey Jr./25	200.00
VG	Vladimir Guerrero/ 25	120.00
AG	Tony Gwynn Jr./150	50.00
CO	Cole Hamels/120	65.00
CH	Craig Hansen/30	

DH	Danny Haren/180	35.00
JH	Jeremy Hermida/125	35.00
FH	Felix Hernandez/40	50.00
FH2	Felix Hernandez/75	50.00
MH	Matt Holliday/37	50.00
HU	Tim Hudson/50	40.00
TI	Tadahito Iguchi/20	120.00
HK	Howie Kendrick/75	40.00
IK	Ian Kinsler/125	50.00
DL	Derrek Lee/200	65.00
FL	Francisco Liriano/100	50.00
GM	Greg Maddux/25	140.00
GM2	Greg Maddux/25	140.00
VM	Victor Martinez/75	40.00
JM	Joe Mauer/25	75.00
MO	Justin Morneau/75	50.00
MM	Mark Mulder/50	40.00
JN	Joe Nathan/100	35.00
RO	Roy Oswalt/50	60.00
JP	Jonathan Papelbon/100	80.00
PE	Jake Peavy/100	40.00
HR	Hanley Ramirez/125	40.00
JR	Jose Reyes/75	65.00
AR	Alex Rios/100	50.00
CS	C.C. Sabathia/40	40.00
BS	Ben Sheets/125	35.00
SM	John Smoltz/75	75.00
JS	Jeremy Sowers/60	60.00
HS	Huston Street/75	40.00
NS	Nick Swisher/170	35.00
TE	Miguel Tejada/25	50.00
JT	Jim Thome/30	100.00
DU	Dan Uggla/100	40.00
BU	B.J. Upton/20	50.00
CU	Chase Utley/25	100.00
JW	Jered Weaver/40	60.00
RW	Rickie Weeks/100	40.00
WI	Josh Willingham/75	40.00
DW	Dontrelle Willis/150	40.00
MY	Michael Young/50	45.00
CZ	Carlos Zambrano/17	100.00
RZ	Ryan Zimmerman/17	120.00
JZ	Joel Zumaya/125	85.00

Chirography Dual Signatures

NM/M
Production 25 Sets

CE	Eric Reed, Cody Ross	25.00
FJ	Conor Jackson, Prince Fielder	40.00
GB	Khalil Greene, Josh Barfield	25.00
HA	Jeremy Hermida, Reggie Abercrombie	25.00
HK	Cole Hamels, Scott Kazmir	50.00
KH	Anderson Hernandez, Ian Kinsler	40.00
KS	Takashi Saito, Hong-Chih Kuo	180.00
LB	Francisco Liriano, Boof Bonser	50.00
MH	Rich Hill, Sean Marshall	60.00
MW	Josh Willingham, Victor Martinez	25.00
PB	Freddie Bynum, Angel Pagan	25.00
PG	Ken Griffey Jr., Albert Pujols	350.00
PO	Jake Peavy, Roy Oswalt	40.00
PP	Tony Pena, Martin Prado	30.00
RC	Hanley Ramirez, Miguel Cabrera	50.00
RR	Jose Reyes, Hanley Ramirez	50.00
SC	Jose Capellan, Ben Sheets	25.00
UH	Cole Hamels, Chase Utley	65.00
WS	Josh Wilson, Ryan Shealy	25.00

Chirography

NM/M
Production 75 unless noted.

AN	Brian Anderson	10.00
GA	Garret Anderson	15.00
BB	Brandon Backe	15.00
BA	Brian Bannister	25.00
DB	Denny Bautista	10.00
CB	Craig Biggio	60.00
BI	Chad Billingsley	25.00
HB	Hank Blalock	15.00
JB	Joe Blanton	15.00
BO	Boof Bonser	25.00
TB	Taylor Buchholz	8.00
MC	Matt Cain	35.00
JC	Jose Capellan	8.00
FC	Fausto Carmona	8.00
SC	Sean Casey	35.00
BC	Bobby Crosby	10.00
DD	David DeJesus	15.00
CD	Chris Denorfia	15.00
JD	Joey Devine	10.00
SD	Stephen Drew	50.00
JE	Johnny Estrada	10.00
AE	Andre Ethier	40.00
KF	Keith Foulke	20.00
JF	Jeff Francis	10.00
CF	Choo Freeman	8.00
DG	Dave Gassner	8.00
KG	Khalil Greene	30.00
GR	Ken Griffey Jr.	80.00
CG	Carlos Guillen	15.00
AG	Tony Gwynn Jr.	40.00
TH	Travis Hafner	20.00
CH	Cole Hamels	50.00
RH	Rich Harden	15.00
HA	Jeff Harris	10.00
JH	Jeremy Hermida	15.00
AH	Anderson Hernandez	10.00
FH	Felix Hernandez/25	40.00
CJ	Conor Jackson	20.00
DJ	Derek Jeter	160.00
JJ	Josh Johnson	20.00
JQ	Jacque Jones	15.00
SK	Scott Kazmir/25	20.00
IK	Ian Kinsler	25.00
CK	Casey Kotchman	15.00
JK	Jason Kubel	15.00
HK	Hong-Chih Kuo	140.00
CL	Cliff Lee	8.00
JL	Jon Lester	35.00
LI	Francisco Liriano	35.00
BL	Boone Logan	20.00
FL	Felipe Lopez	15.00
ML	Mark Loretta	10.00
PM	Paul Maholm	15.00
SM	Sean Marshall	20.00
VM	Victor Martinez	10.00
MM	Macay McBride	15.00
KM	Kevin Mench	15.00
JN	Joe Nathan	15.00
LO	Lyle Overbay/40	15.00
VP	Vicente Padilla	15.00
JP	Jonathan Papelbon	50.00
CP	Corey Patterson	10.00
TP	Tony Pena	8.00
WM	Wily Mo Pena	10.00
OP	Oliver Perez	20.00
YP	Yusmeiro Petit	15.00
MP	Mark Prior/55	20.00
HR	Hanley Ramirez	35.00
RE	Eric Reed	10.00
ER	Edgar Renteria	10.00
AR	Alex Rios	15.00
IR	Ivan Rodriguez	30.00
CR	Cody Ross	15.00
JR	Josh Rupe	10.00
CS	C.C. Sabathia	20.00
TS	Takashi Saito	50.00
BS	Ben Sheets	15.00
SH	Chris Shelton	15.00
KS	Kelly Shoppach	15.00
SO	Alay Soler	20.00
AS	Alfonso Soriano	40.00
JS	Jeremy Sowers	15.00
NS	Nick Swisher	20.00
FT	Frank Thomas	65.00
DU	Dan Uggla	25.00
CU	Chase Utley	25.00
VA	John Van Benschoten	15.00
JV	Jason Varitek	15.00
VE	Justin Verlander	40.00
AW	Adam Wainwright	30.00
WE	Jered Weaver	40.00
JW	Josh Willingham	15.00
DW	Dontrelle Willis	30.00
WI	Josh Wilson	10.00
KY	Kevin Youkilis	15.00
RZ	Ryan Zimmerman	50.00

Chirography Triple Signatures

No Pricing
Production 15 Sets

Sign of the Times

NM/M
Production 75 Sets

RA	Reggie Abercrombie	8.00
BA	Bobby Abreu	40.00
AN	Brian Anderson	10.00
BR	Brian Bannister	25.00
AB	Adrian Beltre	10.00
YB	Yuniesky Betancourt	15.00
BI	Chad Billingsley	25.00
BB	Boof Bonser	25.00
CB	Chris Booker	10.00
TB	Taylor Buchholz	8.00
ME	Melky Cabrera	20.00
MC	Miguel Cabrera	30.00
CA	Matt Cain	35.00
JC	Jose Capellan	8.00
FC	Fausto Carmona	8.00
CC	Carl Crawford	15.00
CD	Chris Demaria	15.00
DE	Chris Denorfia	15.00
JD	J.D. Drew	15.00
SD	Stephen Drew	50.00
AE	Andre Ethier	35.00
FR	Ron Flores	10.00
RF	Rafael Furcal	15.00
EG	Eric Gagne	25.00
DG	Dave Gassner	8.00
ZG	Zack Greinke	10.00
KG	Ken Griffey Jr.	80.00
VG	Vladimir Guerrero	40.00
JG	Jose Guillen	8.00
AG	Tony Gwynn Jr.	35.00
CH	Cole Hamels	50.00
JH	Jason Hammel	10.00
HA	Tim Hamulack	10.00
CY	Clay Hensley	10.00
HE	Jeremy Hermida	15.00
AH	Anderson Hernandez	8.00
RH	Ramon Hernandez	20.00
TH	Tim Hudson	15.00
JA	Conor Jackson	20.00
MJ	Mike Jacobs	15.00
DJ	Derek Jeter	160.00
BJ	Ben Johnson	10.00
JJ	Josh Johnson	20.00
RJ	Randy Johnson	50.00
AJ	Andruw Jones	50.00
JK	Jason Kendall	10.00
IK	Ian Kinsler	25.00
MK	Mark Kotsay	15.00
KU	Jason Kubel	15.00
CL	Carlos Lee	15.00
DL	Derrek Lee	25.00
FL	Francisco Liriano	35.00
BL	Boone Logan	15.00
LO	Derek Lowe	25.00
GM	Greg Maddux	140.00
PM	Paul Maholm	15.00
SM	Sean Marshall	20.00
RM	Russell Martin	20.00
JM	Joe Mauer	40.00
MA	Macay McBride	15.00
MO	Justin Morneau	25.00
MM	Mark Mulder	15.00
PA	Jonathan Papelbon	50.00
JP	Jake Peavy	15.00
TP	Tony Pena	8.00
PE	Joel Peralta	10.00
YP	Yusmeiro Petit	15.00
SP	Scott Podsednik	20.00
AR	Aramis Ramirez	20.00
HR	Hanley Ramirez	35.00
ER	Eric Reed	15.00
JR	Jose Reyes	40.00
SR	Scott Rolen	25.00
CR	Cody Ross	15.00
TS	Takashi Saito	50.00
CS	Curt Schilling	15.00
SS	Skip Schumaker	15.00
RS	Ryan Shealy	20.00
JS	John Smoltz	40.00
AS	Alay Soler	20.00
JY	Jeremy Sowers	20.00
ST	Steve Stemle	10.00
MT	Mark Teixeira	15.00
TE	Miguel Tejada	25.00
MI	Mike Thompson	15.00
DU	Dan Uggla	25.00
JV	John Van Benschoten	10.00
VE	Justin Verlander	40.00
AW	Adam Wainwright	15.00
JE	Jered Weaver	25.00
RW	Rickie Weeks	25.00
VW	Vernon Wells	20.00
JW	Josh Willingham	15.00
WI	Josh Wilson	10.00
RZ	Ryan Zimmerman	50.00

Sign of the Times Dual

NM/M
Production 25 Sets

BM	Nate McLouth, Jason Bay	25.00
CH	Jose Capellan, Ben Hendrickson	20.00
FW	Prince Fielder, Rickie Weeks	75.00
GP	Ken Griffey Jr., Albert Pujols	300.00
HD	Tim Hudson, Joey Devine	30.00
HF	Rich Harden, Ron Flores	20.00
KN	Michael Napoli, Howie Kendrick	60.00
LG	Dave Gassner, Francisco Liriano	30.00
MM	Sean Marshall, Greg Maddux	140.00
OB	Roy Oswalt, Taylor Buchholz	30.00
PB	Angel Pagan, Freddie Bynum	20.00
PT	Jake Peavy, Mike Thompson	20.00
RW	Josh Willingham, Hanley Ramirez	40.00
SC	Fausto Carmona, C.C. Sabathia	30.00
WM	Kendry Morales, Jered Weaver	50.00
ZH	Ryan Zimmerman, Brendan Harris	40.00

Signs of the Times Triple

No Pricing
Production 15 Sets

Heroes

NM/M

Common Player:		.50
1	Albert Pujols	3.00
2	Andruw Jones	1.00
3	Aramis Ramirez	.75
4	Brian Roberts	.50
5	Carl Crawford	.75
6	Carlos Lee	.50
7	Vladimir Guerrero	1.00
8	Chris Carpenter	.75
9	Craig Biggio	.75
10	David Ortiz	1.50
11	David Wright	2.00
12	Derrek Lee	.75
13	Dontrelle Willis	.75
14	Felix Hernandez	.75
15	Garrett Atkins	.50
16	Grady Sizemore	.75
17	Huston Street	.50
18	Jake Peavy	.50
19	Jason Bay	.75
20	Joe Mauer	1.00
21	John Smoltz	.75
22	Jonny Gomes	.50
23	Jorge Cantu	.50
24	Ken Griffey Jr.	2.00
25	Marcus Giles	.50
26	Mark Teixeira	.75
27	Matt Cain	.75
28	Michael Young	.50
29	Miguel Cabrera	1.00
30	Johan Santana	1.00
31	Nick Swisher	.50
32	Prince Fielder	1.00
33	Joe Blanton	.50
34	Roy Oswalt	.75
35	Ryan Howard	3.00
36	Scott Kazmir	.50
37	Tadahito Iguchi	.50
38	Travis Hafner	.75
39	Victor Martinez	.50
40	Jose Reyes	1.00
41	Chris Carpenter, Albert Pujols	3.00
42	Albert Pujols, Miguel Cabrera	3.00
43	Andruw Jones, Ken Griffey Jr.	2.00
44	Derrek Lee, Aramis Ramirez	.75
45	Ryan Howard, Prince Fielder	3.00
46	Jake Peavy, Roy Oswalt	.75
47	Morgan Ensberg, Craig Biggio	.75
48	David Ortiz, Travis Hafner	1.50
49	Derek Jeter, David Wright	3.00
50	Derek Jeter, Ken Griffey Jr.	3.00
51	Derek Jeter, Michael Young	3.00
52	Scott Kazmir, Dontrelle Willis	.50
53	Jason Bay, Grady Sizemore	.75
54	Michael Young, Mark Teixeira	.75
55	Brian Roberts, Tadahito Iguchi	.50
56	Matt Cain, Felix Hernandez, Chien-Ming Wang	2.00
57	Mark Teixeira, Derrek Lee, Albert Pujols	3.00
58	Albert Pujols, Ken Griffey Jr., Miguel Cabrera	3.00
59	Marcus Giles, Andruw Jones, John Smoltz	1.00
60	Derrek Lee, Kerry Wood, Aramis Ramirez	1.00
61	Aramis Ramirez, Morgan Ensberg, David Wright	2.00
62	Carl Crawford, Jorge Cantu, Jonny Gomes	.50
63	Jake Peavy, Chris Carpenter, John Smoltz	1.00
64	Travis Hafner, Grady Sizemore, Victor Martinez	.75
65	Ryan Howard, Prince Fielder, David Ortiz	3.00
66	Chris Carpenter, John Smoltz, Jake Peavy, Dontrelle Willis	1.00
67	Ken Griffey Jr., Derek Jeter, David Ortiz, Albert Pujols	3.00
68	David Ortiz, Andruw Jones, Derrek Lee, Mark Teixeira	1.50
69	Brian Roberts, Marcus Giles, Craig Biggio, Tadahito Iguchi	.50
70	Jason Bay, David Wright, Mark Teixeira, Miguel Cabrera	2.00

WBC Future Watch

NM/M
Common Player: 3.00
Production 999 Sets

1	Adrian Burnside	3.00
2	Gavin Fingleson	3.00
3	Bradley Harman	3.00
4	Brendan Kingman	3.00
5	Brett Roneberg	3.00
6	Paul Rutgers	3.00
7	Phil Stockman	3.00
8	Stubby Clapp	3.00
9	Steve Green	3.00
10	Pete LaForest	5.00
11	Adam Loewen	5.00
12	Ryan Radmanovich	3.00
13	Chenhao Li	3.00
15	Guangbiao Liu	3.00
16	Guogang Yang	3.00
17	Lei Li	3.00
18	Jingchao Wang	3.00
19	Lingfeng Sun	3.00
20	Nan Wang	3.00
21	Shuo Yang	3.00
22	Tao Bu	3.00
23	Wei Wang	3.00
24	Yi Feng	3.00
25	Chien-Ming Chiang	15.00
26	Yung-Chi Chen	20.00
27	Chia-Hsien Hseih	15.00
28	Chin-Lung Hu	15.00
29	En-Yu Lin	20.00
30	Wei-Lun Pan	10.00
31	Ariel Borrero	3.00
32	Yadel Marti	3.00
33	Yulieski Gourriel	20.00
34	Yadier Pedroso	3.00
35	Pedro Luis Lazo	3.00
36	Elier Sanchez	3.00
38	Norberto Gonzalez	3.00
39	Carlos Tabares	3.00
40	Eduardo Paret	3.00
41	Osmany Urrutia	3.00
42	Alexei Ramirez	3.00
43	Yoandy Garlobo	3.00
44	Vicyohandry Odelin	3.00
45	Michel Enriquez	3.00
46	Ormari Romero	3.00
47	Ariel Pestano	3.00
48	Francisco Liriano	5.00
49	Dustin Dellucchi	3.00
50	Tony Giarratano	3.00
51	Tom Gregorio	3.00
52	Mark Saccomanno	3.00
53	Takahiro Arai	8.00
54	Akinori Iwamura	20.00
55	Munenori Kawasaki	15.00
56	Nobuhiko Matsunaka	10.00
57	Daisuke Matsuzaka	100.00
58	Shinya Miyamoto	3.00
59	Tsuyoshi Nishioka	15.00
60	Tomoya Satozaki	8.00
61	Koji Uehara	15.00
62	Shunsuke Watanabe	15.00
63	Sadaharu Oh	20.00
64	Byung Kyu Lee	3.00
65	Ji Man Song	3.00
66	Jin Man Park	3.00
67	Jong Beom Lee	3.00
68	Jong Kook Kim	3.00
69	Min Han Son	3.00
70	Min Jae Kim	3.00
71	Seung-Yeop Lee	10.00
72	Luis A. Garcia	3.00
73	Mario Valenzuela	3.00
74	Sharnol Adriana	3.00
75	Rob Cordemans	3.00
76	Michael Duursma	3.00
77	Percy Isenia	3.00
78	Sidney de Jong	3.00
79	Dirk Klooster	3.00
80	Raylinoe Legito	3.00
81	Shairon Martis	5.00
82	Harvey Monte	3.00
83	Hainley Statia	3.00
84	Roger Deago	3.00
85	Audes De Leon	3.00
86	Freddy Herrera	3.00
87	Yoni Lasso	5.00
88	Orlando Miller	3.00
89	Len Picota	3.00
90	Federico Baez	3.00
91	Dicky Gonzalez	3.00
92	Josue Matos	3.00
93	Orlando Roman	3.00
94	Paul Bell	3.00
95	Kyle Botha	3.00
96	Jason Cook	3.00
97	Nicholas Dempsey	3.00
98	Victor Moreno	3.00
99	Ricardo Palma	3.00
100	Chase Utley	3.00

2006 SP Legendary Cuts

NM/M

Complete Set (200):		
Common Player:		.25
Common SP (101-200):		2.00

Production 550		
Pack (4):		12.00
Box (12):		120.00
1	Juan Marichal	.50
2	Monte Irvin	.75
3	Will Clark	.75
4	Willie McCovey	.75
5	Eddie Gaedel	.25
6	Ken Williams	.25
7	Earl Battey	.25
8	Rick Ferrell	.25
9	Bob Gibson	1.00
10	Elmer Flick	.25
11	Joe Medwick	.25
12	Lou Brock	.75
13	Ozzie Smith	1.00
14	Red Schoendienst	.25
15	Stan Musial	2.00
16	Tony Oliva	.50
17	Phil Niekro	.25
18	Boog Powell	.25
19	Brooks Robinson	1.00
20	Cal Ripken Jr.	3.00
21	Eddie Murray	.75
22	Frank Robinson	.50
23	Jim Palmer	.50
24	Jocko Conlon	.25
25	Carlton Fisk	.50
26	Dwight Evans	.25
27	Fred Lynn	.25
28	Jim Rice	.25
29	Ted Williams	2.00
30	Wade Boggs	.75
31	Hugh Duffy	.25
32	Kid Nichols	.25
33	Johnny Vander Meer	.25
34	Dolph Camilli	.25
35	Carl Yastrzemski	1.00
36	Chick Hafey	.25
37	Kirby Higbe	.25
38	Pee Wee Reese	.50
39	Pete Reiser	.25
40	Don Sutton	.25
41	Rod Carew	.75
42	Andre Dawson	.50
43	Billy Herman	.25
44	Billy Williams	.25
45	Charlie Root	.25
46	Hack Wilson	.25
47	Ernie Banks	1.00
48	Fergie Jenkins	.50
49	Gabby Hartnett	.25
50	Ken Hubbs	.25
51	Kiki Cuyler	.25
52	Mark Grace	.25
53	Ryne Sandberg	1.50
54	Harold Newhouser	.25
55	Charlie Robertson	.25
56	Harold Baines	.25
57	Luis Aparicio	.25
58	Luke Appling	.25
59	Nellie Fox	.25
60	Ray Schalk	.25
61	Red Faber	.25
62	Sloppy Thurston	.25
63	Freddie Lindstrom	.25
64	Vern Kennedy	.25
65	Barry Larkin	.50
66	Bucky Walters	.25
67	Dolf Luque	.25
68	Al Campanis	.25
69	Ernie Lombardi	.25
70	George Foster	.25
71	Joe Morgan	.75
72	Johnny Bench	1.00
73	Ken Griffey Sr.	.25
74	Ted Kluszewski	.25
75	Tony Perez	.50
76	Wally Post	.25
77	Bob Feller	.50
78	Bob Lemon	.25
79	Earl Averill	.25
80	Joe Sewell	.25
81	Johnny Hodapp	.25
82	Larry Doby	.50
83	Lou Boudreau	.25
84	Rocky Colavito	.25
85	Stan Coveleski	.25
86	Nap Lajoie	.50
87	Al Kaline	1.00
88	Alan Trammell	.50
89	Charlie Gehringer	.25
90	Denny McLain	.25
91	Hank Greenberg	.25
92	Jack Morris	.25
93	Mark Fidrych	.25
94	Ray Boone	.25
95	Rudy York	.25
96	Buck Leonard	.25
97	Bo Jackson	1.00
98	Zoilo Versalles	.25
99	John Kruk	.25
100	Don Drysdale	.50
101	Cecil Cooper	2.00
102	Vic Wertz	2.00
103	Kirk Gibson	2.00
104	Maury Wills	2.00
105	Steve Garvey	2.00
106	Warren Spahn	5.00
107	Paul Molitor	4.00
108	Robin Yount	5.00
109	Rollie Fingers	3.00
110	Bob Allison	2.00
111	Kirby Puckett	6.00
112	Tim Raines	2.00
113	George Pipgras	2.00
114	Eddie Grant	2.00
115	Hoyt Wilhelm	2.00

116	Sal Maglie	2.00
117	Ron Santo	3.00
118	Wally Joyner	2.00
119	Tom Seaver	5.00
120	Tommie Agee	2.00
121	Harmon Killebrew	4.00
122	Bill Dickey	2.00
123	Early Wynn	2.00
124	Bobby Murcer	2.00
125	Bucky Dent	2.00
126	Dave Winfield	4.00
127	Don Larsen	4.00
128	Don Mattingly	8.00
129	Earle Combs	2.00
130	Ed Lopat	2.00
131	Elston Howard	2.00
132	Everett Scott	2.00
133	Rich "Goose" Gossage	2.00
134	Graig Nettles	2.00
135	Joe DiMaggio	8.00
136	Lou Piniella	2.00
137	Bill "Moose" Skowron	2.00
138	Phil Rizzuto	3.00
139	Red Ruffing	3.00
140	Reggie Jackson	4.00
141	Roger Maris	6.00
142	Ron Guidry	3.00
143	Tiny Bonham	2.00
144	Bruce Sutter	2.00
145	Tony Lazzeri	2.00
146	Waite Hoyt	2.00
147	Whitey Ford	4.00
148	Steve Sax	2.00
149	Yogi Berra	5.00
150	Enos Slaughter	2.00
151	Jim "Catfish" Hunter	2.00
152	Dennis Eckersley	2.00
153	Jose Canseco	3.00
154	Al Rosen	2.00
155	Al Simmons	2.00
156	Chief Bender	2.00
157	Cy Williams	2.00
158	Mike Schmidt	5.00
159	Richie Ashburn	3.00
160	Robin Roberts	3.00
161	Steve Carlton	3.00
162	Judy Johnson	3.00
163	Al Oliver	2.00
164	Bill Mazeroski	3.00
165	Dave Parker	3.00
166	Max Carey	2.00
167	Pie Traynor	3.00
168	Ralph Kiner	2.00
169	Roberto Clemente	10.00
170	Willie Stargell	3.00
171	Gaylord Perry	2.00
172	Tony Gwynn	5.00
173	Nolan Ryan	8.00
174	Joe Carter	2.00
175	Frank Howard	2.00
176	George Kell	2.00
177	Heinie Manush	2.00
178	Sam Rice	2.00
179	Babe Ruth	10.00
180	Casey Stengel	4.00
181	Christy Mathewson	4.00
182	Cy Young	4.00
183	Dizzy Dean	4.00
184	Eddie Mathews	5.00
185	George Sisler	3.00
186	Honus Wagner	8.00
187	Jackie Robinson	6.00
188	Jimmie Foxx	5.00
189	Johnny Mize	4.00
190	Lefty Gomez	2.00
191	Lou Gehrig	8.00
192	Mel Ott	3.00
193	Mickey Cochrane	4.00
194	Rogers Hornsby	4.00
195	Roy Campanella	5.00
196	Satchel Paige	5.00
197	Thurman Munson	5.00
198	Ty Cobb	8.00
199	Walter Johnson	3.00
200	Lefty Grove	3.00

Gold

Gold (101-200): 2-4X
Production 99 Sets

Legendary Materials

NM/M
Production 225 unless noted.
Tier 1: .75-1.5X
Production 50-199
Tier 2: 1-2X

Production 25-99
Tier 3: No Pricing
Production 5-15

HB	Harold Baines	6.00
EB	Ernie Banks	20.00
JB	Johnny Bench	15.00
YB	Yogi Berra	15.00
WB	Wade Boggs	10.00
LB	Lou Brock	10.00
LB2	Lou Brock	10.00
JC	Jose Canseco	10.00
CW	Rod Carew	10.00
SC	Steve Carlton	8.00
SC2	Steve Carlton	8.00
WC	Will Clark	10.00
WC2	Will Clark	10.00
RC	Rocky Colavito	20.00
DC	Dave Concepcion	6.00
CC	Cecil Cooper	6.00
AD	Andre Dawson	8.00
BD	Bucky Dent	6.00
JD	Joe DiMaggio/99	75.00
DE	Dennis Eckersley	8.00
DE2	Dennis Eckersley	8.00
EV	Dwight Evans	8.00
BF	Bob Feller	8.00
RF	Rollie Fingers	8.00
CF	Carlton Fisk	8.00
GF	George Foster	6.00
SG	Steve Garvey	6.00
BG	Bob Gibson	10.00
KI	Kirk Gibson	8.00
GG	Rich "Goose" Gossage	8.00
MG	Mark Grace	10.00
KG	Ken Griffey Sr.	8.00
GU	Ron Guidry	10.00
TG	Tony Gwynn	15.00
FH	Frank Howard	8.00
BO	Bo Jackson	15.00
RJ	Reggie Jackson	10.00
FJ	Fergie Jenkins	8.00
WJ	Wally Joyner	8.00
AK	Al Kaline	12.00
RK	Ralph Kiner	10.00
JK	John Kruk	8.00
BL	Barry Larkin	8.00
DL	Don Larsen	12.00
FL	Fred Lynn	6.00
JU	Juan Marichal	8.00
MA	Don Mattingly	20.00
BM	Bill Mazeroski	10.00
WM	Willie McCovey	10.00
PM	Paul Molitor	8.00
JO	Joe Morgan	8.00
JM	Jack Morris	6.00
MU	Bobby Murcer	8.00
EM	Eddie Murray	10.00
SM	Stan Musial	20.00
GN	Graig Nettles	10.00
PN	Phil Niekro	8.00
PN2	Phil Niekro	8.00
TO	Tony Oliva	8.00
AO	Al Oliver	8.00
JP	Jim Palmer	10.00
JP2	Jim Palmer	10.00
DP	Dave Parker	8.00
TP	Tony Perez	8.00
GP	Gaylord Perry	8.00
GP2	Gaylord Perry	8.00
LP	Lou Piniella	8.00
BP	Boog Powell	8.00
KP	Kirby Puckett	15.00
JR	Jim Rice	8.00
CR	Cal Ripken Jr.	25.00
PR	Phil Rizzuto/99	
RR	Robin Roberts	10.00
RO	Brooks Robinson/175	10.00
FR	Frank Robinson	10.00
FR2	Frank Robinson	10.00
AR	Al Rosen	8.00
BR	Babe Ruth/99	225.00
NR	Nolan Ryan	20.00
RS	Ryne Sandberg	15.00
RN	Ron Santo/125	12.00
RN2	Ron Santo/125	12.00
SS	Steve Sax	6.00
MS	Mike Schmidt	15.00
RE	Red Schoendienst/99	
TS	Tom Seaver	12.00
SK	Bill "Moose" Skowron	8.00
OS	Ozzie Smith	15.00
BS	Bruce Sutter	8.00
SU	Don Sutton	8.00
JT	Joe Torre	10.00
BW	Billy Williams	8.00
DW	Dave Winfield	8.00
CY.	Carl Yastrzemski	15.00
RY	Robin Yount	10.00
MW	Maury Wills	6.00

Baseball Chronology

NM/M
Production 550 Sets

Platinum: 1.5-2X
Production 99 Sets

EB	Ernie Banks	5.00
EB2	Ernie Banks	4.00
JB	Johnny Bench	4.00
YB	Yogi Berra	5.00
WB	Wade Boggs	4.00
WB2	Wade Boggs	4.00
LB	Lou Boudreau	2.00
LO	Lou Brock	4.00
RC	Roy Campanella	4.00
CA	Rod Carew	3.00
SC	Steve Carlton	3.00
SC2	Steve Carlton	3.00
JC	Joe Carter	2.00
WC	Will Clark	3.00
CL	Roberto Clemente	10.00
TC	Ty Cobb	6.00
TC2	Ty Cobb	6.00
MC	Mickey Cochrane	3.00
CN	Joe Cronin	3.00
AD	Andre Dawson	3.00
DZ	Dizzy Dean	3.00
BD	Bucky Dent	2.00
JD	Joe DiMaggio	8.00
DD	Don Drysdale	3.00
DE	Dennis Eckersley	3.00
BF	Bob Feller	3.00
MF	Mark Fidrych	2.00
RF	Rollie Fingers	3.00
CF	Carlton Fisk	3.00
WF	Whitey Ford	3.00
JF	Jimmie Foxx	5.00
JF2	Jimmie Foxx	5.00
SG	Steve Garvey	3.00
LG	Lou Gehrig	8.00
LG2	Lou Gehrig	8.00
BG	Bob Gibson	3.00
KG	Kirk Gibson	3.00
HG	Hank Greenberg	4.00
TG	Tony Gwynn	4.00
GH	Gil Hodges	3.00
RH	Rogers Hornsby	4.00
CH	Jim "Catfish" Hunter	2.00
BO	Bo Jackson	4.00
RJ	Reggie Jackson	4.00
WJ	Walter Johnson	3.00
AK	Al Kaline	4.00
RK	Ralph Kiner	3.00
NL	Nap Lajoie	3.00
DL	Don Larsen	3.00
BL	Bob Lemon	2.00
FL	Fred Lynn	2.00
RM	Roger Maris	4.00
CM	Christy Mathewson	4.00
DM	Don Mattingly	6.00
BM	Bill Mazeroski	3.00
WM	Willie McCovey	3.00
JM	Johnny Mize	3.00
PM	Paul Molitor	3.00
JO	Joe Morgan	3.00
TM	Thurman Munson	5.00
EM	Eddie Murray	3.00
SM	Stan Musial	6.00
PN	Phil Niekro	2.00
MO	Mel Ott	3.00
SP	Satchel Paige	5.00
GP	Gaylord Perry	3.00
KP	Kirby Puckett	5.00
PW	Pee Wee Reese	3.00
RI	Jim Rice	3.00
CR	Cal Ripken Jr.	8.00
RO	Brooks Robinson	8.00
FR	Frank Robinson	8.00
JR	Jackie Robinson	6.00
BR	Babe Ruth	10.00
BR2	Babe Ruth	10.00
BR3	Babe Ruth	10.00
NR	Nolan Ryan	8.00
NR2	Nolan Ryan	8.00
NR3	Nolan Ryan	8.00
RS	Ryne Sandberg	5.00
MS	Mike Schmidt	5.00
TS	Tom Seaver	5.00
GS	George Sisler	3.00
ES	Enos Slaughter	2.00
OS	Ozzie Smith	3.00
WS	Warren Spahn	3.00
ST	Willie Stargell	3.00
CS	Casey Stengel	3.00
CS2	Casey Stengel	3.00
DS	Don Sutton	2.00
AT	Alan Trammell	3.00
HW	Honus Wagner	5.00
HY	Hoyt Wilhelm	2.00
BW	Billy Williams	2.00
TW	Ted Williams	8.00
TW2	Ted Williams	8.00
MW	Maury Wills	3.00
YZ	Carl Yastrzemski	4.00
CY	Cy Young	3.00
RY	Robin Yount	4.00

Baseball Chronology Materials

NM/M
Production 550 Sets

Common Player: NM/M

EB	Ernie Banks	15.00
EB2	Ernie Banks/SP	20.00
JB	Johnny Bench	15.00
YB	Yogi Berra	20.00
WB	Wade Boggs	10.00
WB2	Wade Boggs	10.00
LB	Lou Boudreau	12.00
LO	Lou Brock	10.00
RC	Roy Campanella	20.00
CA	Rod Carew	10.00
SC	Steve Carlton	8.00
SC2	Steve Carlton	8.00
JC	Joe Carter	6.00
WC	Will Clark	10.00
CL	Roberto Clemente/SP	80.00
TC	Ty Cobb/SP	150.00
TC2	Ty Cobb/SP	150.00
CN	Joe Cronin	15.00
AD	Andre Dawson	8.00
DZ	Dizzy Dean/SP	60.00
BD	Bucky Dent	8.00
JD	Joe DiMaggio/SP	75.00
DD	Don Drysdale/SP	25.00
DE	Dennis Eckersley	10.00
BF	Bob Feller	10.00
MF	Mark Fidrych	2.00
RF	Rollie Fingers	8.00
CF	Carlton Fisk	10.00
JF	Jimmie Foxx/SP	40.00
JF2	Jimmie Foxx/SP	40.00
SG	Steve Garvey	6.00
LG	Lou Gehrig/SP	175.00
LG2	Lou Gehrig/SP	175.00
BG	Bob Gibson	8.00
HG	Hank Greenberg	25.00
TG	Tony Gwynn	12.00
GH	Gil Hodges/SP	
RH	Rogers Hornsby/SP	50.00
CH	Jim "Catfish" Hunter	10.00
BO	Bo Jackson	12.00
RJ	Reggie Jackson	12.00
AK	Al Kaline	15.00
RK	Ralph Kiner	12.00
DL	Don Larsen	12.00
BL	Bob Lemon	8.00
FL	Fred Lynn	8.00
RM	Roger Maris	30.00
CM	Christy Mathewson/SP	240.00
DM	Don Mattingly	15.00
BM	Bill Mazeroski/SP	20.00
WM	Willie McCovey	12.00
JM	Johnny Mize	15.00
PM	Paul Molitor	8.00
JO	Joe Morgan	10.00
TM	Thurman Munson	25.00
EM	Eddie Murray	10.00
SM	Stan Musial	20.00
PN	Phil Niekro	8.00
MO	Mel Ott/SP	35.00
SP	Satchel Paige/SP	75.00
GP	Gaylord Perry	8.00
KP	Kirby Puckett	15.00
PW	Pee Wee Reese	10.00
RI	Jim Rice	8.00
CR	Cal Ripken Jr.	25.00
RO	Brooks Robinson	12.00
FR	Frank Robinson	10.00
JR	Jackie Robinson/SP	60.00
BR	Babe Ruth/SP	250.00
BR2	Babe Ruth/SP	250.00
BR3	Babe Ruth/SP	250.00
NR	Nolan Ryan	20.00
NR2	Nolan Ryan	20.00
NR3	Nolan Ryan	20.00
RS	Ryne Sandberg	15.00
MS	Mike Schmidt	12.00
TS	Tom Seaver	15.00
GS	George Sisler/SP	35.00
ES	Enos Slaughter	15.00
OS	Ozzie Smith	12.00
WS	Warren Spahn	15.00
ST	Willie Stargell	15.00
CS	Casey Stengel	15.00
CS2	Casey Stengel/SP	35.00
DS	Don Sutton	8.00
AT	Alan Trammell	8.00
HW	Honus Wagner/SP	160.00
HY	Hoyt Wilhelm/SP	15.00
BW	Billy Williams	8.00
TW	Ted Williams	40.00
TW2	Ted Williams	40.00
MW	Maury Wills	8.00
YZ	Carl Yastrzemski	15.00
RY	Robin Yount	12.00

When It Was A Game

NM/M
Production 550 Sets
Gold: 1.5-2X
Production 99 Sets

LA	Luis Aparicio	2.00
HB	Harold Baines	2.00
EB	Ernie Banks	5.00
JB	Johnny Bench	4.00
YB	Yogi Berra	4.00
WB	Wade Boggs	4.00
LB	Lou Brock	4.00
CA	Rod Carew	3.00
SC	Steve Carlton	3.00
SC2	Steve Carlton	3.00
WC	Will Clark	4.00
RC	Roberto Clemente	10.00

MC	Mickey Cochrane	3.00
CO	Rocky Colavito	3.00
AD	Andre Dawson	3.00
JD	Joe DiMaggio	8.00
DE	Dennis Eckersley	3.00
EV	Dwight Evans	2.00
BF	Bob Feller	3.00
RF	Rollie Fingers	3.00
CF	Carlton Fisk	3.00
WF	Whitey Ford	4.00
JF	Jimmie Foxx	5.00
SG	Steve Garvey	6.00
LG	Lou Gehrig	8.00
BG	Bob Gibson	4.00
KI	Kirk Gibson	
GG	Rich "Goose" Gossage	2.00
HG	Hank Greenberg	
KG	Ken Griffey Sr.	2.00
GU	Ron Guidry	
TG	Tony Gwynn	
HO	Rogers Hornsby	4.00
RJ	Reggie Jackson	4.00
FJ	Fergie Jenkins	
AK	Al Kaline	4.00
RK	Ralph Kiner	
JK	John Kruk	
DL	Don Larsen	3.00
FL	Fred Lynn	
JU	Juan Marichal	
EM	Eddie Mathews	
MA	Don Mattingly	6.00
BM	Bill Mazeroski	3.00
WM	Willie McCovey	3.00
DY	Denny McLain	
MZ	Johnny Mize	2.00
PM	Paul Molitor	
JO	Joe Morgan	
JM	Jack Morris	
TM	Thurman Munson	5.00
MU	Bobby Murcer	
ED	Eddie Murray	
SM	Stan Musial	6.00
GN	Graig Nettles	
PN	Phil Niekro	
TO	Tony Oliva	3.00
TO2	Tony Oliva	3.00
MO	Mel Ott	
SP	Satchel Paige	5.00
JP	Jim Palmer	3.00
DP	Dave Parker	2.00
TP	Tony Perez	2.00
GP	Gaylord Perry	2.00
LP	Lou Piniella	2.00
PS	Johnny Podres	
KP	Kirby Puckett	5.00
TR	Tim Raines	
RI	Jim Rice	3.00
CR	Cal Ripken Jr.	
PR	Phil Rizzuto	3.00
RR	Robin Roberts	2.00
RO	Brooks Robinson	4.00
RO2	Brooks Robinson	4.00
FR	Frank Robinson	4.00
FR2	Frank Robinson	4.00
JR	Jackie Robinson	6.00
AR	Al Rosen	2.00
BR	Babe Ruth	10.00
NR	Nolan Ryan	8.00
SA	Ryne Sandberg	5.00
RN	Ron Santo	3.00
MS	Mike Schmidt	5.00
RS	Red Schoendienst	2.00
TS	Tom Seaver	4.00
GS	George Sisler	3.00
SK	Bill "Moose" Skowron	2.00
OS	Ozzie Smith	5.00
BS	Bruce Sutter	2.00
SU	Don Sutton	2.00
JT	Joe Torre	3.00
BW	Billy Williams	2.00
MW	Maury Wills	2.00
YZ	Carl Yastrzemski	4.00
CY	Cy Young	3.00
RY	Robin Yount	4.00

When It Was A Game-Used

NM/M
Production 75 unless noted.

LA	Luis Aparicio/25	10.00
HB	Harold Baines/25	10.00
EB	Ernie Banks	20.00
JB	Johnny Bench	15.00

YB	Yogi Berra	20.00
WB	Wade Boggs	10.00
LB	Lou Brock/25	12.00
CA	Rod Carew	12.00
SC	Steve Carlton	10.00
SC2	Steve Carlton	10.00
WC	Will Clark	12.00
RC	Roberto Clemente	80.00
MC	Mickey Cochrane/25	12.00
CO	Rocky Colavito	25.00
AD	Andre Dawson	10.00
JD	Joe DiMaggio	80.00
DD	Don Drysdale	15.00
DE	Dennis Eckersley	10.00
EV	Dwight Evans/25	15.00
BF	Bob Feller	10.00
RF	Rollie Fingers	10.00
CF	Carlton Fisk	12.00
JF	Jimmie Foxx	50.00
SG	Steve Garvey	8.00
LG	Lou Gehrig	140.00
BG	Bob Gibson	12.00
KI	Kirk Gibson	10.00
GG	Rich "Goose" Gossage	10.00
HG	Hank Greenberg	30.00
KG	Ken Griffey Sr.	8.00
GU	Ron Guidry	10.00
TG	Tony Gwynn	15.00
HO	Rogers Hornsby	50.00
HF	Frank Howard/25	20.00
RJ	Reggie Jackson/25	15.00
FJ	Fergie Jenkins	12.00
WJ	Wally Joyner	8.00
RK	Ralph Kiner	12.00
JK	John Kruk	10.00
DL	Don Larsen	15.00
FL	Fred Lynn	8.00
JU	Juan Marichal	10.00
EM	Eddie Mathews	15.00
MA	Don Mattingly	15.00
BM	Bill Mazeroski	25.00
WM	Willie McCovey	10.00
MZ	Johnny Mize	10.00
PM	Paul Molitor	10.00
JO	Joe Morgan	10.00
JM	Jack Morris/25	10.00
TM	Thurman Munson	25.00
MU	Bobby Murcer	12.00
ED	Eddie Murray	12.00
SM	Stan Musial	25.00
GN	Graig Nettles	10.00
PN	Phil Niekro	10.00
TO	Tony Oliva	10.00
TO2	Tony Oliva	10.00
MO	Mel Ott	30.00
JP	Jim Palmer	12.00
DP	Dave Parker	8.00
TP	Tony Perez	10.00
GP	Gaylord Perry	10.00
LP	Lou Piniella	12.00
KP	Kirby Puckett	20.00
TR	Tim Raines	10.00
RI	Jim Rice	10.00
CR	Cal Ripken Jr.	25.00
PR	Phil Rizzuto/25	25.00
RR	Robin Roberts	15.00
RO	Brooks Robinson/25	20.00
RO2	Brooks Robinson/25	20.00
FR	Frank Robinson	15.00
FR2	Frank Robinson	15.00
JR	Jackie Robinson	50.00
AR	Al Rosen	10.00
BR	Babe Ruth/350	350.00
NR	Nolan Ryan/25	30.00
SA	Ryne Sandberg/25	20.00
RN	Ron Santo	15.00
MS	Mike Schmidt	20.00
RS	Red Schoendienst	15.00
TS	Tom Seaver	15.00
GS	George Sisler	30.00
SK	Bill "Moose" Skowron	10.00
OS	Ozzie Smith	15.00
BS	Bruce Sutter	10.00
SU	Don Sutton	8.00
JT	Joe Torre	10.00
BW	Billy Williams	10.00
MW	Maury Wills	10.00
YZ	Carl Yastrzemski	15.00
RY	Robin Yount	12.00

Place In History Signatures

NM/M
Production 99 unless noted.

LA	Luis Aparicio	25.00
LA2	Luis Aparicio	25.00
HB	Harold Baines/35	20.00
EB	Ernie Banks/25	75.00
JB	Johnny Bench/42	50.00
WB	Wade Boggs/50	35.00
LB	Lou Brock	25.00
LB2	Lou Brock	25.00
JC	Jose Canseco	40.00
CA	Rod Carew/50	25.00

SC	Steve Carlton	25.00
SC2	Steve Carlton	25.00
WC	Will Clark	25.00
WC2	Will Clark	25.00
CC	Cecil Cooper	20.00
AD	Andre Dawson	20.00
BD	Bucky Dent	15.00
DE	Dennis Eckersley	25.00
DE2	Dennis Eckersley	25.00
EV	Dwight Evans	20.00
BF	Bob Feller/35	40.00
RF	Rollie Fingers/77	20.00
CF	Carlton Fisk	30.00
WF	Whitey Ford/35	60.00
GF	George Foster/56	15.00
SG	Steve Garvey	25.00
MG	Mark Grace	25.00
KG	Ken Griffey Sr.	15.00
TG	Tony Gwynn/26	60.00
FH	Frank Howard	25.00
BO	Bo Jackson	50.00
RJ	Reggie Jackson/25	60.00
FJ	Fergie Jenkins	20.00
WJ	Wally Joyner	25.00
BL	Barry Larkin/49	40.00
FL	Fred Lynn	15.00
JU	Juan Marichal/29	35.00
MA	Don Mattingly/50	100.00
BM	Bill Mazeroski	35.00
MC	Denny McLain/31	25.00
PM	Paul Molitor	35.00
JO	Joe Morgan/50	30.00
JM	Jack Morris/82	20.00
SM	Stan Musial/45	70.00
GN	Graig Nettles	20.00
PN	Phil Niekro/52	20.00
PN2	Phil Niekro/52	20.00
TO	Tony Oliva	20.00
TO2	Tony Oliva	20.00
JP	Jim Palmer	25.00
GP	Gaylord Perry	20.00
GP2	Gaylord Perry	20.00
LP	Lou Piniella	20.00
JY	Johnny Podres/38	20.00
BP	Boog Powell	20.00
KP	Kirby Puckett	80.00
TR	Tim Raines	25.00
JR	Jim Rice	20.00
CR	Cal Ripken Jr./50	140.00
PR	Phil Rizzuto	40.00
RR	Robin Roberts/55	25.00
BR	Brooks Robinson/50	40.00
BR2	Brooks Robinson/50	40.00
FR	Frank Robinson	40.00
FR2	Frank Robinson	40.00
AR	Al Rosen	20.00
RO	Ron Santo	60.00
RO2	Ron Santo	60.00
SS	Steve Sax	20.00
MS	Mike Schmidt/50	75.00
RD	Red Schoendienst	35.00
TS	Tom Seaver/55	50.00
SK	Bill "Moose" Skowron	25.00
OS	Ozzie Smith	50.00
BS	Bruce Sutter	20.00
JT	Joe Torre	40.00
BW	Billy Williams	20.00
MW	Maury Wills/96	20.00
CY	Carl Yastrzemski	40.00
RY	Robin Yount	40.00

Legendary Cuts

NM/M
Production 1-90

JA	Joe Adcock/47	120.00
MA	Mel Allen/67	175.00
WA	Walter Alston/27	160.00
LA	Luke Appling/84	100.00
RA	Richie Ashburn/22	200.00
EA	Earl Averill/40	100.00
EB	Ed Barrow/35	250.00
RB	Ray Boone/51	120.00
LB	Lou Boudreau/86	100.00
DC	Dolph Camilli/58	100.00
MC	Max Carey/79	140.00
EC	Earle Combs/65	200.00
ST	Stan Covaleski/81	120.00
JO	Joe Cronin/30	125.00
RD	Ray Dandridge/35	100.00
DD	Dizzy Dean/21	600.00
BD	Bill Dickey/34	240.00
DR	Don Drysdale/45	200.00
DU	Joe Dugan/25	160.00
DL	Leo Durocher/22	150.00
CG	Charlie Gehringer/76	100.00
LG	Lefty Gomez/44	125.00
HG	Hank Greenberg/60	250.00
BG	Burleigh Grimes/33	100.00
HE	Billy Herman/87	100.00
WH	Waite Hoyt/49	125.00
CH	Jim "Catfish" Hunter/24	150.00
JJ	Judy Johnson/89	120.00
HK	Harvey Kuenn/89	120.00
BL	Bob Lemon/77	80.00
LO	Ernie Lombardi/25	160.00
EL	Ed Lopat/32	150.00
EM	Eddie Mathews/59	150.00
JM	Joe McCarthy/67	180.00
ME	Joe Medwick/82	180.00
MI	Johnny Mize/90	140.00
WP	Wally Post/66	120.00
PR	Pee Wee Reese/47	160.00
SR	Sam Rice/31	180.00
ER	Edd Roush/90	80.00
RR	Red Ruffing/72	200.00
JS	Joe Sewell/83	120.00
WS	Warren Spahn/52	140.00
CS	Casey Stengel/35	300.00
PT	Pie Traynor/26	500.00
BW	Bucky Walters/52	120.00
WI	Hoyt Wilhelm/47	100.00

Place In History Cut Signatures

NM/M
Production 1-98

BA	Bob Allison/94	140.00
LA	Luke Appling/94	100.00
EA	Earl Averill/75	80.00
LB	Lou Boudreau/88	100.00
HC	Happy Chandler/61	100.00
CO	Chuck Connors/25	450.00
JC	Joe Cronin/30	125.00
RD	Ray Dandridge/43	120.00
BD	Bill Dickey/29	200.00
DL	Leo Durocher/42	140.00
DU	Joe Dugan/25	150.00
FF	Ford Frick/30	150.00
CG	Charlie Gehringer/57	120.00
WG	Warren Giles/45	200.00
LG	Lefty Gomez/30	125.00
HG	Hank Greenberg/31	260.00
BG	Burleigh Grimes/43	120.00
HI	Kirby Higbe/59	140.00
JH	Johnny Hodapp/26	125.00
DH	Dick Howser/28	160.00
JJ	Judy Johnson/20	180.00
VK	Vern Kennedy/61	120.00
BL	Bob Lemon/47	90.00
SM	Sal Maglie/73	120.00
EM	Eddie Mathews/34	150.00
JM	Joe McCarthy/35	200.00
ME	Joe Medwick/60	200.00
PR	Pee Wee Reese/57	180.00
RE	Pete Reiser/75	125.00
RO	Charlie Robertson/42	150.00
ER	Edd Roush/98	100.00
JS	Joe Sewell/87	100.00
GS	George Sisler/42	450.00
WS	Warren Spahn/41	140.00
WI	Hoyt Wilhelm/65	100.00
CW	Cy Williams/29	180.00
EW	Early Wynn/36	100.00

Dual Legendary Cuts

Production One Set

Quadruple Legendary Cuts

Production One Set

Historical Cut Signatures

Production One Set

Memorable Moments Swatch

NM/M
Common Player:
Production 225 Sets

JB	Johnny Bench	15.00
CC	Cesar Cedeno	8.00
RC	Rocky Colavito	20.00
DC	David Cone	8.00
CE	Cecil Cooper	10.00
AD	Andre Dawson	10.00
DE	Dwight Evans	8.00
BF	Bob Feller	12.00
RF	Rollie Fingers	8.00
CF	Carlton Fisk	10.00
GF	George Foster	8.00
SG	Steve Garvey	8.00
KG	Kirk Gibson	8.00
GG	Rich "Goose" Gossage	8.00
RG	Ron Guidry	12.00
TG	Tony Gwynn	12.00
BJ	Bo Jackson	15.00
RJ	Reggie Jackson	10.00
JK	John Kruk	10.00
BL	Barry Larkin	10.00
MA	Juan Marichal	10.00
EM	Eddie Mathews	15.00
DM	Don Mattingly	20.00
JM	Johnny Mize	15.00
MO	Joe Morgan	10.00
BM	Bobby Murcer	8.00
MU	Eddie Murray	10.00
SM	Stan Musial	20.00
PO	Paul O'Neill	10.00
DP	Dave Parker	8.00
GP	Gaylord Perry	8.00
TR	Tim Raines	8.00
PR	Phil Rizzuto	10.00
RS	Ron Santo	10.00
SS	Steve Sax	8.00
MS	Mike Schmidt	15.00
TS	Tom Seaver	12.00
OS	Ozzie Smith	15.00
DS	Don Sutton	8.00
RY	Robin Yount	12.00

Memorable Moments Autograph

NM/M
Production 1-99

CC	Cesar Cedeno/99	20.00
RC	Rocky Colavito/25	80.00
DC	David Cone/99	15.00
CE	Cecil Cooper/99	20.00
AD	Andre Dawson/99	20.00
DE	Dwight Evans/25	20.00
BF	Bob Feller/25	40.00
RF	Rollie Fingers/47	20.00
CF	Carlton Fisk/25	30.00
GF	George Foster/25	20.00
SG	Steve Garvey/25	35.00
KG	Kirk Gibson/25	30.00
TG	Tony Gwynn/25	75.00
BJ	Bo Jackson/25	50.00
JK	John Kruk/25	20.00
BL	Barry Larkin/50	40.00
MA	Juan Marichal/25	40.00
DM	Don Mattingly/50	100.00
MO	Joe Morgan/20	30.00
MU	Eddie Murray/45	30.00
GP	Gaylord Perry/99	20.00
TR	Tim Raines/30	30.00
PR	Phil Rizzuto/99	40.00
RS	Ron Santo/25	65.00
TS	Tom Seaver/44	40.00
OS	Ozzie Smith/25	50.00
RY	Robin Yount/60	60.00

When It Was a Game Cut Signature

NM/M
Production 2-99

JA	Joe Adcock/18	150.00
LA	Luke Appling/83	100.00
EA	Earl Averill/67	80.00
EB	Earl Battey/25	175.00
RB	Ray Boone/68	120.00
LB	Lou Boudreau/50	100.00
AC	Al Campanis/30	250.00
MC	Max Carey/71	140.00
HC	Happy Chandler/64	100.00
SC	Stan Covaleski/91	100.00
JC	Joe Cronin/34	120.00
RD	Ray Dandridge/75	120.00
JD	Joe Dugan/30	150.00
DU	Leo Durocher/25	160.00
RF	Rick Ferrell/25	150.00
EF	Elmer Flick/25	150.00
FF	Ford Frick/30	150.00
CG	Charlie Gehringer/64	120.00
LG	Lefty Gomez/36	125.00
HG	Hank Greenberg/21	260.00
BG	Burleigh Grimes/56	140.00
HE	Billy Herman/99	100.00
WH	Waite Hoyt/70	100.00
CH	Carl Hubbell/80	140.00
HU	Jim "Catfish" Hunter/34	150.00
JJ	Judy Johnson/20	180.00
VK	Vern Kennedy/58	120.00
TK	Ted Kluszewski/50	140.00
BL	Bob Lemon/79	90.00
FL	Freddie Lindstrom/25	150.00
EL	Ernie Lombardi/24	150.00
LO	Ed Lopat/28	140.00
SM	Sal Maglie/68	120.00
EM	Eddie Mathews/33	150.00
JM	Joe McCarthy/51	200.00
ME	Joe Medwick/57	200.00
MI	Johnny Mize/70	120.00
GP	George Pipgras/25	180.00
WP	Wally Post/66	120.00
PR	Pee Wee Reese/52	180.00
SR	Sam Rice/33	175.00
ER	Edd Roush/98	100.00
RR	Red Ruffing/44	180.00
SE	George Selkirk/175	175.00
JS	Joe Sewell/78	100.00
GS	George Sisler/37	450.00
WS	Warren Spahn/78	125.00
ST	Willie Stargell/27	160.00
JV	Johnny Vander Meer/45	150.00
VW	Vic Wertz/30	160.00
HW	Hoyt Wilhelm/56	100.00
EW	Early Wynn/40	100.00

2006 SPx

NM/M

Complete Set (160):	
Common Player (1-100):	.25
Common Auto. (101-160):	10.00
Production 190-999	
Pack (4):	8.00
Box (18):	125.00

#	Player	
1	Luis Gonzalez	.25
2	Chad Tracy	.25
3	Brandon Webb	.25
4	Andruw Jones	1.00
5	Chipper Jones	1.00
6	John Smoltz	.75
7	Tim Hudson	.50
8	Miguel Tejada	.75
9	Brian Roberts	.25
10	Ramon Hernandez	.25
11	Curt Schilling	1.00
12	David Ortiz	1.50
13	Manny Ramirez	1.00
14	Jason Varitek	1.00
15	Josh Beckett	.50
16	Greg Maddux	2.00
17	Derek Lee	.75
18	Mark Prior	.75
19	Aramis Ramirez	.50
20	Jim Thome	.75
21	Paul Konerko	.75
22	Scott Podsednik	.25
23	Jose Contreras	.25
24	Ken Griffey Jr.	2.00
25	Adam Dunn	.75
26	Felipe Lopez	.25
27	Travis Hafner	.75
28	Victor Martinez	.75
29	Grady Sizemore	.75
30	Jhonny Peralta	.50
31	Todd Helton	.75
32	Garrett Atkins	.25
33	Clint Barmes	.25
34	Ivan Rodriguez	.75
35	Chris Shelton	.25
36	Jeremy Bonderman	.50
37	Miguel Cabrera	1.00
38	Dontrelle Willis	.50
39	Lance Berkman	.50
40	Morgan Ensberg	.25
41	Roy Oswalt	.50
42	Reggie Sanders	.25
43	Mike Sweeney	.25
44	Vladimir Guerrero	1.00
45	Bartolo Colon	.25
46	Chone Figgins	.25
47	Nomar Garciaparra	1.00
48	Jeff Kent	.50
49	J.D. Drew	.50
50	Carlos Lee	.50
51	Ben Sheets	.50
52	Rickie Weeks	.50
53	Johan Santana	1.00
54	Torii Hunter	.50
55	Joe Mauer	.50
56	Pedro Martinez	1.00
57	David Wright	2.00
58	Carlos Beltran	.75
59	Carlos Delgado	.75
60	Jose Reyes	.75
61	Derek Jeter	3.00
62	Alex Rodriguez	3.00
63	Randy Johnson	1.00
64	Hideki Matsui	2.00
65	Gary Sheffield	.75
66	Rich Harden	.50
67	Eric Chavez	.50
68	Huston Street	.50
69	Bobby Crosby	.25
70	Bobby Abreu	.50
71	Ryan Howard	2.00
72	Chase Utley	.75
73	Pat Burrell	.50
74	Jason Bay	.50
75	Sean Casey	.25
76	Mike Piazza	1.00
77	Jake Peavy	.25
78	Brian Giles	.25
79	Milton Bradley	.25
80	Omar Vizquel	.25
81	Jason Schmidt	.25
82	Ichiro Suzuki	2.00
83	Felix Hernandez	.50
84	Richie Sexson	.50
85	Albert Pujols	3.00
86	Chris Carpenter	.75
87	Scott Rolen	1.00
88	Jim Edmonds	.50
89	Carl Crawford	.50
90	Jonny Gomes	.25
91	Scott Kazmir	.50
92	Mark Teixeira	.75
93	Michael Young	.50
94	Phil Nevin	.25
95	Vernon Wells	.50
96	Roy Halladay	.50
97	Troy Glaus	.50
98	Alfonso Soriano	.50
99	Nick Johnson	.25
100	Jose Vidro	.25
101	Conor Jackson/999 (RC)	15.00
102	Jered Weaver/299 (RC)	50.00
103	Macay McBride/999 (RC)	10.00
104	Aaron Rakers/499 (RC)	10.00
105	Jonathan Papelbon/499 (RC)	50.00
106	Jason Bergmann/999 RC	10.00
107	Stephen Drew/350 (RC)	60.00
108	Chris Denorfia/999 (RC)	10.00
109	Kelly Shoppach/999 (RC)	15.00
110	Ryan Shealy/999 (RC)	15.00
111	Josh Wilson/999 (RC)	10.00
112	Brian Anderson/999 (RC)	10.00
113	Justin Verlander/749 (RC)	40.00
114	Jeremy Hermida/999 (RC)	15.00
115	Mike Jacobs/999 (RC)	15.00
116	Josh Johnson/999 (RC)	20.00
117	Hanley Ramirez/659 (RC)	20.00
118	Chris Resop/999 (RC)	10.00
119	Josh Willingham/999 (RC)	15.00
120	Cole Hamels/499 (RC)	40.00
121	Matt Cain/999 (RC)	30.00
122	Steve Stemle/999 RC	10.00
123	Tim Hamulack/999 (RC)	10.00
124	Choo Freeman/999 (RC)	10.00
125	Hong-Chih Kuo/999 (RC)	60.00
126	Cody Ross/999 (RC)	15.00
127	Jose Capellan/999 (RC)	10.00
128	Prince Fielder/190 (RC)	50.00
129	David Gassner/999 (RC)	10.00
130	Jason Kubel/999 (RC)	15.00
131	Francisco Liriano/299 (RC)	60.00
132	Anderson Hernandez/999 (RC)	10.00
133	Joey Devine/499 RC	15.00
134	Chris Booker/999 (RC)	10.00
135	Matt Capps/999 (RC)	15.00
136	Paul Maholm/999 (RC)	10.00
137	Nate McLouth/999 (RC)	10.00
138	John Van Benschoten/999 (RC)	10.00
139	Jeff Harris/999 RC	10.00
140	Ben Johnson/999 (RC)	10.00
141	Wilbert Nieves/999 (RC)	15.00
142	Guillermo Quiroz/999 (RC)	10.00
143	Josh Rupe/500 (RC)	15.00
144	Skip Schumaker/999 (RC)	15.00
145	Jack Taschner/999 (RC)	10.00
146	Adam Wainwright/999 (RC)	30.00
147	Alay Soler/499 RC	25.00
148	Kendry Morales/999 (RC)	20.00
149	Ian Kinsler/999 (RC)	30.00
150	Jason Hammel/999 (RC)	15.00
151	Chad Billingsley/499 (RC)	30.00
152	Boof Bonser/999 (RC)	25.00
153	Peter Moylan/999 RC	10.00
154	Chris Britton/999 RC	10.00
155	Takashi Saito/999 RC	40.00
156	Scott Dunn/999 (RC)	10.00
157	Joel Zumaya/299 (RC)	30.00
158	Dan Uggla/999 (RC)	30.00
159	Taylor Buchholz/999 (RC)	10.00
160	Melky Cabrera/499 (RC)	40.00

Rookie Signature Printing Plates

No Pricing
Production one set per color.

Rookie Signature Platinum

No Pricing
Production One Set

Rookie Signature Gold

No Pricing
Production Five Sets

Spectrum

Stars (1-100): 2-3X
Inserted 1:3

Next in Line

NM/M

	Common Player:	1.00
BA	Brian Anderson	1.00
BB	Brian Bannister	1.00
JB	Josh Barfield	1.00
TB	Taylor Buchholz	1.00
MC	Matt Cain	1.50
RC	Ryan Church	1.00
PF	Prince Fielder	3.00
JH	Jeremy Hermida	1.50
FH	Felix Hernandez	1.00
RH	Ryan Howard	3.00
TI	Travis Ishikawa	1.00
CJ	Conor Jackson	1.00
MJ	Mike Jacobs	1.00
BJ	Ben Johnson	1.00
IK	Ian Kinsler	1.00
LE	Jon Lester	1.00
FL	Francisco Liriano	3.00
JL	James Loney	1.00
SO	Scott Olsen	1.00
JP	Jonathan Papelbon	3.00
HR	Hanley Ramirez	1.50
NM	Alay Soler	1.00
JS	Jeremy Sowers	1.00
HS	Huston Street	1.00
DU	Dan Uggla	1.00
JV	Justin Verlander	1.00
AW	Adam Wainwright	1.00
JE	Jered Weaver	3.00
JW	Josh Willingham	1.00
RZ	Ryan Zimmerman	3.00

SPxciting Signatures

NM/M
Production 30 unless noted.

JA	Jeremy Accardo	15.00
BA	Brian Anderson	20.00
BY	Jason Bay	30.00
BI	Craig Biggio	40.00
CH	Chad Billingsley	35.00
HB	Hank Blalock	20.00
BR	Chris Britton	15.00
MI	Miguel Cabrera	40.00
MC	Matt Cain	40.00
CA	Matt Capps	15.00
RC	Roger Clemens	165.00
CW	Carl Crawford	30.00
SD	Scott Dunn	15.00
EG	Eric Gagne	35.00
GR	Khalil Greene	30.00
KG	Ken Griffey Jr.	100.00
HT	Travis Hafner	25.00
HA	Jason Hammel	15.00
TH	Tim Hamulack	20.00
JH	Jeff Harris	12.00
HE	Jeremy Hermida	30.00
TR	Trevor Hoffman	50.00
CJ	Conor Jackson	15.00
KU	Jason Kubel	25.00
HK	Hong-Chih Kuo	180.00
CL	Cliff Lee	15.00
PM	Paul Maholm	15.00
VM	Victor Martinez	20.00
MM	Macay McBride	20.00
NM	Nate McLouth	15.00
MU	Mark Mulder	20.00
WN	Wilbert Nieves	35.00
JP	Jonathan Papelbon	100.00
CP	Corey Patterson	15.00
PE	Jake Peavy	25.00
OP	Oliver Perez	15.00
HR	Hanley Ramirez	40.00
CR	Chris Resop	10.00
RO	Cody Ross	30.00
TS	Takashi Saito	140.00
SS	Skip Schumaker	20.00
RS	Ryan Shealy	20.00
KS	Kelly Shoppach	25.00
DU	Dan Uggla	75.00
JV	John Van Benschoten	15.00
VE	Justin Verlander	50.00
AW	Adam Wainwright	50.00
JW	Josh Willingham	20.00
WI	Josh Wilson	15.00

SPxtra Info

NM/M

	Common Player:	.50
BA	Bobby Abreu	.75

JB	Jason Bay	.75
EC	Eric Chavez	.50
CC	Carl Crawford	.75
BG	Brian Giles	.50
LG	Luis Gonzalez	.50
KG	Ken Griffey Jr.	2.00
VG	Vladimir Guerrero	1.00
TH	Travis Hafner	.75
HE	Todd Helton	.75
DJ	Derek Jeter	3.00
NJ	Nick Johnson	.50
AJ	Andruw Jones	.50
JK	Jeff Kent	.50
CL	Carlos Lee	.75
DL	Derrek Lee	1.00
PM	Pedro Martinez	1.00
DO	David Ortiz	1.50
RO	Roy Oswalt	.75
AP	Albert Pujols	3.00
IR	Ivan Rodriguez	.75
RS	Reggie Sanders	.50
JS	Johan Santana	1.00
SC	Jason Schmidt	.50
IS	Ichiro Suzuki	2.00
TE	Mark Teixeira	.75
MT	Miguel Tejada	.75
JT	Jim Thome	1.00
VW	Vernon Wells	.50
DW	Dontrelle Willis	.75

SPxtreme Team

		NM/M
Common Player:		50
BA	Bobby Abreu	.75
JB	Jason Bay	.75
LB	Lance Berkman	.75
MC	Miguel Cabrera	1.00
CC	Chris Carpenter	.75
CR	Carl Crawford	.75
CD	Carlos Delgado	.75
AD	Adam Dunn	.75
PF	Prince Fielder	3.00
KG	Ken Griffey Jr.	2.00
VG	Vladimir Guerrero	1.00
HA	Travis Hafner	.75
RH	Rich Harden	.50
TH	Todd Helton	.75
HO	Ryan Howard	3.00
DJ	Derek Jeter	3.00
AJ	Andruw Jones	1.00
JK	Jeff Kent	.50
PK	Paul Konerko	.75
CL	Carlos Lee	.75
DL	Derrek Lee	1.00
PM	Pedro Martinez	.50
VM	Victor Martinez	.50
HM	Hideki Matsui	2.00
DO	David Ortiz	1.50
JP	Jake Peavy	.75
AP	Albert Pujols	3.00
MR	Manny Ramirez	1.00
JR	Jose Reyes	.75
AR	Alex Rodriguez	3.00
JS	Johan Santana	1.00
GS	Grady Sizemore	.75
AS	Alfonso Soriano	.75
IS	Ichiro Suzuki	2.00
MT	Mark Teixeira	.75
TE	Miguel Tejada	.75
JT	Jim Thome	1.00
VW	Vernon Wells	.50
DW	David Wright	2.00
MY	Michael Young	.50

WBC All-World Team

		NM/M
Common Player:		.50
1	Brett Willemburg	.50
2	Bradley Harman	.50
3	Adam Stern	1.00
4	Jason Bay	1.00
5	Adam Loewen	.50
6	Wei Wang	2.00
7	Yi Feng	1.00
8	Yung-Chi Chen	6.00
9	Chin-Lung Hu	6.00
10	Wei-Lun Pan	5.00
11	Yoandy Garlobo	.50
12	Frederich Cepeda	.50
13	Osmany Urrutia	1.00
14	Yulieski Gourriel	.50
15	Yadel Marti	.50
16	Pedro Luis Lazo	.50
17	Adrian Beltre	.50
18	David Ortiz	2.00

19	Albert Pujols	4.00
20	Bartolo Colon	.50
21	Miguel Tejada	1.00
22	Mike Piazza	1.50
23	Jason Grilli	1.00
24	Nobuhiko Matsunaka	3.00
25	Tomoya Satozaki	3.00
26	Ichiro Suzuki	3.00
27	Hitoshi Tamura	3.00
28	Daisuke Matsuzaka	8.00
29	Koji Uehara	3.00
30	Jong Beom Lee	.50
31	Seung-Yeop Lee	.50
32	Jae Weong Seo	.50
33	Min Han Son	.50
34	Chan Ho Park	.50
35	Jorge Cantu	.50
36	Miguel Ojeda	.50
37	Andruw Jones	1.00
38	Shairon Martis	.50
39	Carlos Lee	.75
40	Carlos Beltran	1.00
41	Javy Lopez	.50
42	Javier Vazquez	.50
43	Ken Griffey Jr.	3.00
44	Derek Jeter	4.00
45	Alex Rodriguez	4.00
46	Derrek Lee	1.50
47	Roger Clemens	3.00
48	Miguel Cabrera	1.50
49	Victor Martinez	1.50
50	Johan Santana	1.50

Winning Materials

		NM/M
Common Player:		5.00
BA	Bobby Abreu	6.00
JB	Jason Bay	10.00
CB	Carlos Beltran	10.00
MC	Miguel Cabrera	10.00
FC	Frederich Cepeda	5.00
HC	Hee Seop Choi	10.00
RC	Roger Clemens	15.00
JD	Johnny Damon	10.00
CD	Carlos Delgado	6.00
ME	Michel Enriquez	5.00
MF	Maikel Folch	5.00
YG	Yulieski Gourriel	8.00
KG	Ken Griffey Jr.	20.00
AI	Akinori Iwamura	25.00
AJ	Andruw Jones	8.00
MK	Munenori Kawasaki	20.00
PL	Pedro Luis Lazo	8.00
DL	Derrek Lee	8.00
JL	Jong Beom Lee	6.00
VM	Victor Martinez	5.00
NM	Nobuhiko Matsunaka	20.00
YM	Yuneiski Maya	5.00
TN	Tsuyoshi Nishioka	25.00
VO	Vicyohandry Odelin	5.00
MO	Michihiro Ogasawara	5.00
DO	David Ortiz	15.00
EP	Eduardo Paret	5.00
AP	Ariel Pestano	5.00
MP	Mike Piazza	15.00
PU	Albert Pujols	20.00
AR	Alex Rodriguez	20.00
JS	Johan Santana	10.00
NS	Naoyuki Shimizu	20.00
MS	Min Han Son	8.00
AS	Alfonso Soriano	5.00
IS	Ichiro Suzuki	90.00
HT	Hitoshi Tamura	5.00
MT	Miguel Tejada	10.00
KU	Koji Uehara	30.00
OU	Osmany Urrutia	8.00
TW	Tsuyoshi Wada	20.00
SW	Shunsuke Watanabe	20.00

Winning Big Materials

		NM/M
Production 5-55		
BA	Bobby Abreu/40	75.00
MA	Moises Alou/53	50.00
JB	Jason Bay/40	80.00
EB	Erik Bedard/40	50.00
CB	Carlos Beltran/40	75.00
AB	Adrian Beltre/40	50.00
MC	Miguel Cabrera/40	80.00
FC	Frederich Cepeda/30	65.00
HC	Hee Seop Choi/32	50.00
JD	Johnny Damon/40	100.00
CD	Carlos Delgado/40	65.00
ME	Michel Enriquez/30	50.00
MF	Maikel Folch/30	50.00
JF	Jeff Francis/40	50.00
YG	Yulieski Gourriel/30	100.00
AI	Akinori Iwamura/30	275.00
AJ	Andruw Jones/40	80.00
MK	Munenori Kawasaki/30	350.00
PL	Pedro Luis Lazo/30	80.00
CL	Carlos Lee/40	60.00
DL	Derrek Lee/40	50.00
JL	Jong Beom Lee/20	75.00
WL	Wei-Chu Lin/45	350.00
LO	Javy Lopez/40	50.00
VM	Victor Martinez/40	75.00
NM	Nobuhiko Matsunaka/30	300.00
YM	Yuneiski Maya/30	60.00
JM	Justin Morneau/25	60.00
TN	Tsuyoshi Nishioka/30	375.00

VO	Vicyohandry Odelin/30	75.00
MO	Michihiro Ogasawara/30	350.00
DO	David Ortiz/30	150.00
WP	Wei-Lun Pan/38	300.00
EP	Eduardo Paret/30	50.00
PE	Wily Mo Pena/60	50.00
AP	Ariel Pestano/30	60.00
MP	Mike Piazza/40	100.00
AR	Alex Rios/55	50.00
IR	Ivan Rodriguez/40	60.00
JS	Johan Santana/40	75.00
NS	Naoyuki Shimizu/30	250.00
AS	Alfonso Soriano/40	90.00
HT	Hitoshi Tamura/30	300.00
MT	Miguel Tejada/40	60.00
KU	Koji Uehara/30	300.00
OU	Osmany Urrutia/30	65.00
JV	Jason Varitek/40	120.00
TW	Tsuyoshi Wada/30	250.00
SW	Shunsuke Watanabe/30	260.00
BW	Bernie Williams/40	75.00
GY	Guogang Yang/52	50.00
CZ	Carlos Zambrano/40	50.00

1993 Spectrum Diamond Club Promo Set

Ten Hall of Famers are featured in this promo card set. Fronts of the 2-1/2" x 3-1/2" cards have borderless player action or posed photos. The issuer's logo, player's name and striping are printed in gold. Backs have a color ghost-image photo of the player along with personal data and career summary. A box near the bottom indicates the set's serial number from within an edition of 10,000. A "Pure Gold" parallel edition of 5,000 each was also produced.

		NM/M
Complete Set (10):		8.00
Common Player:		1.00
Pure Gold:		2X
1	Carl Yastrzemski	1.50
2	Johnny Bench (Numbered promo.)	1.00
--	Johnny Bench ("For Promotional Use Only" on back.)	1.00
3	Al Kaline	1.00
4	Ernie Banks	2.00
5	Catfish Hunter	1.00
6	Rod Carew	1.00
7	Mike Schmidt	2.00
8	Harmon Killebrew	1.00
9	Frank Robinson	1.50
10	Rollie Fingers	1.00

1993 Spectrum Diamond Club Red Sox

This collectors' issue features five stars of the Boston Red Sox from the 1940s-1970s. Fronts have action pho-

1993 Spectrum Legends of Baseball

Dizzy Dean   P

This collectors' edition of 10 of baseball's greatest players was issued in two versions, with and without a gold facsimile autograph on the cards' fronts. The gold-signature cards were limited to an edition of 5,000 numbered cards of each player. Fronts have black-and-white photos with gold-foil graphic highlights. Backs have another photo subdued in the background with career history and stats and personal data overprinted in black. Copyright information is at bottom. Cards were issued in two series of five each and are checklisted here alphabetically.

		NM/M
Complete Set (10):		7.50
Common Player:		.50
Gold Signature:		2X
(1)	Grover Alexander	.50
(2)	Ty Cobb	.75
(3)	Dizzy Dean	.50
(4)	Lou Gehrig	1.00
(5)	Rogers Hornsby	.50
(6)	Satchel Paige	.75
(7)	Babe Ruth	2.00
(8)	Casey Stengel	.50
(9)	Honus Wagner	.75
(10)	Cy Young	.50

Nolan Ryan

Nolan Ryan   P

Produced in the same format as its Legends of Baseball 10-card set, this issue honors the career of Nolan Ryan. Each set comes with a numbered certificate of authenticity. There were 5,000 regular sets produced and 5,000 with gold-foil facsimile autographs

tos on which uniform logos are eliminated. A pinstripe around the photo, the issuer's logo and player name are printed in gold. Size is standard 2-1/2" x 3-1/2". Horizontal backs have a color Fenway Park photo ghosted in the background. Player career highlights and stats are overprinted.

		NM/M
Complete Set (5):		1.00
Common Player:		.25
1	Carl Yastrzemski	.50
2	Bobby Doerr	.25
3	Dwight Evans	.25
4	Fred Lynn	.25
5	Luis Tiant	.25

on fronts. Each card can also be found in a promotional overprinted version.

	NM/M
Complete Set (10):	3.00
Common Card:	.50
Gold:	2X
Promo:	2X

Nolan Ryan 23K

NOLAN RYAN P

A "pure gold" background on front offsets the color action photo of Ryan in action (team logos have been removed for licensing reasons). Backs of the 2-1/2" x 3-1/2" cards have career highlights and stats. Each set was issued with a certificate of authenticity numbered from an edition of 10,000.

		NM/M
Complete Set (3):		3.00
Common Card:		1.00
1	Nolan Ryan	1.00
2	Nolan Ryan	1.00
3	Nolan Ryan	1.00

1994 Spectrum 1969 Miracle Mets

The Miracle of '69

The 1969 Miracle Mets card set, produced by Spectrum Holdings Group of Birmingham, Mich., was part of what the company called "an integrated memorabilia program, with the 1969 Mets card set as the centerpiece." The 70-card set measures the standard 2-1/2" x 3-1/2", with UV coating on both sides and gold foil on fronts. It was sold complete at $24.95, and limited to 25,000 sets. A reported 1,000 numbered sets were signed by all 25 living players, including Hall of Famer Tom Seaver and future Cooperstown resident Nolan Ryan.

		NM/M
Complete Set (70):		20.00
Common Player:		.25
Autographed Set:		500.00
1	Commemorative Card	.25
2	Team Photo	.25
3	Tom Seaver	4.00
4	Jerry Koosman	.35
5	Tommie Agee	.25
6	Bud Harrelson	.25
7	Nolan Ryan	6.00
8	Jerry Grote	.25
9	Ron Swoboda	.25
10	Donn Clendenon	.25
11	Art Shamsky	.25
12	Tug McGraw	.25
13	Ed Kranepool	.25
14	Cleon Jones	.25
15	Ron Taylor	.25
16	Gary Gentry	.25
17	Ken Boswell	.25
18	Ed Charles	.25

19	J.C. Martin	.25
20	Al Weis	.25
21	Jack DiLauro	.25
22	Duffy Dyer	.25
23	Wayne Garrett	.25
24	Jim McAndrew	.25
25	Rod Gaspar	.25
26	Don Cardwell	.25
27	Bob Pfeil	.25
28	Cal Koonce	.25
29	Gil Hodges	1.50
30	Yogi Berra	2.00
31	Joe Pignatano	.25
32	Rube Walker	.25
33	Eddie Yost	.25
34	First-ever Met Game	.25
35	Opening Day 1969	.25
36	Kranepool Breaks Home Run Record	.25
37	Koosman Sets Club Strikeout Record	.25
38	Mets Trade for Clendenon	.25
39	Koosman's 23 Scoreless Innings	.25
40	Mets Begin 7-Game Winning Streak	.25
41	Mets vs. Division Leading Cubs	.25
42	Seaver's Near Perfect Game	.25
43	Mets Trail by 3-1/2	.25
44	All-Star Break	.25
45	All-Star Game	.25
46	Mets Sweep Atlanta	.25
47	Mets Sweep Padres	.25
48	Mets Defeat Cubs, Koosman Strikes Out 1	.25
49	Mets Defeat Cubs 1/2 Game Back	.25
50	First Place!	.25
51	Mets Continue Nine Game Winning Streak	.25
52	Seaver Earns 22nd Victory	.25
53	Mets Win, Carlton Strikes Out 19	.25
54	Koosman Pitches 15th Complete Game	.25
55	Eastern Division Champs!	.25
56	100th Victory	.25
57	Final Game, Mets Prepare for Braves	.25
58	N.L. Championship Series, Game 1	.25
59	N.L. Championship Series, Game 2	.25
60	N.L. Championship Series, Game 3	.25
61	World Series, Game 1	.25
62	World Series, Game 2	.25
63	World Series, Game 3	.25
64	World Series, Game 4	.25
65	World Series, Game 5	.25
66	World Champions	.25
67	World Champions	.25
68	World Champions	.25
69	World Champions	.25
----	Checklist	.25

1986 Sportflics Prototype Cards

This six-card set was apparently produced as a prototype as part of the licensing process. Similar in format to the 1986 Sportflics issue the cards have stats through the 1984 season. The prototype cards are much rarer than the promo cards. The Schmidt, Sutter and Winfield cards are standard 2-1/2" x 3-1/2" in size while the DiMaggio card is 1-5/16" square and the MLB logo card is 1-3/4" x 2".

		NM/M
Complete Set (7):		175.00
Common Card:		2.00
(1)	Joe DiMaggio (Black-and-white.)	100.00
(2)	Mike Schmidt	20.00
(3)	Bruce Sutter	5.00

(4) Dave Winfield (Biographical back.) 50.00
(5) Dave Winfield (Statistical back..) 37.50
(6) Mike Schmidt, Bruce Sutter, Dave Winfield (Blank-back.) 10.00
(7) Major League Baseball Logo 2.00

1986 Sportflics Promo Cards

Though they carry stats only through 1984, and have a 1986 copyright date, these promo cards were issued late in 1985 to preview the "Triple Action Sportflics" concept. They were the first really widely distributed promo cards. Each of the promo cards differs slightly from the issued version. The RBI Sluggers card in the issued set, for instance, was #126 and pictured Gary Carter, George Foster and Al Oliver. In the regular set, Pete Rose's card was #50 while Tom Seaver was #25. The regular-issue 1986 Sportflics cards, of course, include complete 1985 stats on back. Promo cards were distributed in three-card cello packs.

	NM/M
Complete Set (3):	12.50
Common Player:	3.00
1 RBI Sluggers (Dale Murphy, Jim Rice, Mike Schmidt)	3.00
43 Pete Rose	10.00
45 Tom Seaver	4.00

1986 Sportflics

The premiere issue from Sportflics was distributed nationally by Amurol Division of Wrigley Gum Co. The three-phase "Magic Motion" cards depict three different photos per card, with each visible separately as the card is tilted. The 1986 issue features 200 full-color baseball cards plus 133 trivia cards. The cards are in the standard 2-1/2" x 3-1/2" size with the backs containing player stats and personal information. There are three different types of picture cards: 1) Tri-Star cards - 50 cards feature three players on one card; 2) Big Six cards - 10 cards which have six players in special categories; and 3) the Big Twelve card of 12 World Series players from the Kansas City Royals. The trivia cards are 1-3/4" x 2" and do not have player photos.

	NM/M
Unopened Factory Set (200):	10.00
Complete Set (200):	7.50
Common Player:	.10
Foil Pack (3+2):	.50
Foil Box (36):	9.00
1 George Brett	2.25
2 Don Mattingly	2.25
3 Wade Boggs	2.00
4 Eddie Murray	1.00
5 Dale Murphy	.65
6 Rickey Henderson	1.00
7 Harold Baines	.10
8 Cal Ripken, Jr.	3.00
9 Orel Hershiser	.10
10 Bret Saberhagen	.10
11 Tim Raines	.10
12 Fernando Valenzuela	.10
13 Tony Gwynn	2.00
14 Pedro Guerrero	.10
15 Keith Hernandez	.10
16 Ernest Riles	.10
17 Jim Rice	.20
18 Ron Guidry	.10
19 Willie McGee	.10
20 Ryne Sandberg	2.00
21 Kirk Gibson	.10
22 Ozzie Guillen	.10
23 Dave Parker	.10
24 Vince Coleman	.10
25 Tom Seaver	1.00
26 Brett Butler	.10
27 Steve Carlton	1.00
28 Gary Carter	1.00
29 Cecil Cooper	.10
30 Jose Cruz	.10
31 Alvin Davis	.10
32 Dwight Evans	.10
33 Julio Franco	.10
34 Damaso Garcia	.10
35 Steve Garvey	.60
36 Kent Hrbek	.10
37 Reggie Jackson	2.25
38 Fred Lynn	.10
39 Paul Molitor	1.00
40 Jim Presley	.10
41 Dave Righetti	.10
42a Robin Yount (Yankees logo on back.)	85.00
42b Robin Yount (Brewers logo.)	1.00
43 Nolan Ryan	3.00
44 Mike Schmidt	2.25
45 Lee Smith	.10
46 Rick Sutcliffe	.10
47 Bruce Sutter	.75
48 Lou Whitaker	.10
49 Dave Winfield	1.00
50 Pete Rose	2.50
51 N.L. MVPs (Steve Garvey, Pete Rose, Ryne Sandberg)	1.00
52 Slugging Stars (Harold Baines, George Brett, Jim Rice)	.35
53 No-Hitters (Phil Niekro, Jerry Reuss, Mike Witt)	.25
54 Big Hitters (Don Mattingly, Cal Ripken, Jr., Robin Yount)	2.00
55 Bullpen Aces (Goose Gossage, Dan Quisenberry, Lee Smith)	.10
56 Rookies of the Year (Pete Rose, Steve Sax, Darryl Strawberry)	1.00
57 A.L. MVPs (Don Baylor, Reggie Jackson, Cal Ripken, Jr.)	.50
58 Repeat Batting Champs (Bill Madlock, Dave Parker, Pete Rose)	.45
59 Cy Young Winners (Mike Flanagan, Ron Guidry, LaMarr Hoyt)	.10
60 Double Award Winners (Tom Seaver, Rick Sutcliffe, Fernando Valenzuela)	.20
61 Home Run Champs (Tony Armas, Reggie Jackson, Jim Rice)	.25
62 N.L. MVPs (Keith Hernandez, Dale Murphy, Mike Schmidt)	.40
63 A.L. MVPs (George Brett, Fred Lynn, Robin Yount)	.30
64 Comeback Players (Bert Blyleven, John Denny, Jerry Koosman)	.10
65 Cy Young Relievers (Rollie Fingers, Willie Hernandez, Bruce Sutter)	.10
66 Rookies of the Year (Andre Dawson, Bob Horner, Gary Matthews)	.20
67 Rookies of the Year (Carlton Fisk, Ron Kittle, Tom Seaver)	.25
68 Home Run Champs (George Foster, Dave Kingman, Mike Schmidt)	.25
69 Double Award Winners (Rod Carew, Cal Ripken, Jr., Pete Rose)	2.00
70 Cy Young Winners (Steve Carlton, Tom Seaver, Rick Sutcliffe)	.25
71 Top Sluggers (Reggie Jackson, Fred Lynn, Robin Yount)	.30
72 Rookies of the Year (Dave Righetti, Rick Sutcliffe, Fernando Valenzuela)	.10
73 Rookies of the Year (Fred Lynn, Eddie Murray, Cal Ripken, Jr.)	.50
74 Rookies of the Year (Rod Carew, Alvin Davis, Lou Whitaker)	.20
75 Batting Champs (Wade Boggs, Carney Lansford, Don Mattingly)	1.00
76 Jesse Barfield	.10
77 Phil Bradley	.10
78 Chris Brown	.10
79 Tom Browning	.10
80 Tom Brunansky	.10
81 Bill Buckner	.10
82 Chili Davis	.10
83 Mike Davis	.10
84 Rich Gedman	.10
85 Willie Hernandez	.10
86 Ron Kittle	.10
87 Lee Lacy	.10
88 Bill Madlock	.10
89 Mike Marshall	.10
90 Keith Moreland	.10
91 Graig Nettles	.10
92 Lance Parrish	.10
93 Kirby Puckett	2.00
94 Juan Samuel	.10
95 Steve Sax	.10
96 Dave Stieb	.10
97 Darryl Strawberry	.10
98 Willie Upshaw	.10
99 Frank Viola	.10
100 Dwight Gooden	.10
101 Joaquin Andujar	.10
102 George Bell	.10
103 Bert Blyleven	.10
104 Mike Boddicker	.10
105 Britt Burns	.10
106 Rod Carew	1.00
107 Jack Clark	.10
108 Danny Cox	.10
109 Ron Darling	.10
110 Andre Dawson	.45
111 Leon Durham	.10
112 Tony Fernandez	.10
113 Tom Herr	.10
114 Teddy Higuera	.10
115 Bob Horner	.10
116 Dave Kingman	.10
117 Jack Morris	.10
118 Dan Quisenberry	.10
119 Jeff Reardon	.10
120 Bryn Smith	.10
121 Ozzie Smith	2.00
122 John Tudor	.10
123 Tim Wallach	.10
124 Willie Wilson	.10
125 Carlton Fisk	1.00
126 RBI Sluggers (Gary Carter, George Foster, Al Oliver)	.10
127 Run Scorers (Keith Hernandez, Tim Raines, Ryne Sandberg)	.25
128 Run Scorers (Paul Molitor, Cal Ripken, Jr., Willie Wilson)	.50
129 No-Hitters (John Candelaria, Dennis Eckersley, Bob Forsch)	.25
130 World Series MVPs (Ron Cey, Rollie Fingers, Pete Rose)	.35
131 All-Star Game MVPs (Dave Concepcion, George Foster, Bill Madlock)	.25
132 Cy Young Winners (Vida Blue, John Denny, Fernando Valenzuela)	.25
133 Comeback Players (Doyle Alexander, Joaquin Andujar, Richard Dotson)	.25
134 Big Winners (John Denny, Tom Seaver, Rick Sutcliffe)	.50
135 Veteran Pitchers (Phil Niekro, Tom Seaver, Don Sutton)	.25
136 Rookies of the Year (Vince Coleman, Dwight Gooden, Alfredo Griffin)	.20
137 All-Star Game MVPs (Gary Carter, Steve Garvey, Fred Lynn)	.20
138 Veteran Hitters (Tony Perez, Pete Rose, Rusty Staub)	.50
139 Power Hitters (George Foster, Jim Rice, Mike Schmidt)	.30
140 Batting Champs (Bill Buckner, Tony Gwynn, Al Oliver)	.25
141 No-Hitters (Jack Morris, Dave Righetti, Nolan Ryan)	.50
142 No-Hitters (Vida Blue, Bert Blyleven, Tom Seaver)	.10
143 Strikeout Kings (Dwight Gooden, Nolan Ryan, Fernando Valenzuela)	1.25
144 Base Stealers (Dave Lopes, Tim Raines, Willie Wilson)	.10
145 RBI Sluggers (Tony Armas, Cecil Cooper, Eddie Murray)	.15
146 A.L. MVPs (Rod Carew, Rollie Fingers, Jim Rice)	.15
147 World Series MVPs (Rick Dempsey, Reggie Jackson, Alan Trammell)	.25
148 World Series MVPs (Pedro Guerrero, Darrell Porter, Mike Schmidt)	.20
149 ERA Leaders (Mike Boddicker, Ron Guidry, Rick Sutcliffe)	.10
150 Comeback Players (Reggie Jackson, Dave Kingman, Fred Lynn)	.20
151 Buddy Bell	.10
152 Dennis Boyd	.10
153 Dave Concepcion	.10
154 Brian Downing	.10
155 Shawon Dunston	.10
156 John Franco	.10
157 Scott Garrelts	.10
158 Bob James	.10
159 Charlie Leibrandt	.10
160 Oddibe McDowell	.10
161 Roger McDowell	.10
162 Mike Moore	.10
163 Phil Niekro	.75
164 Al Oliver	.10
165 Tony Pena	.10
166 Ted Power	.10
167 Mike Scioscia	.10
168 Mario Soto	.10
169 Bob Stanley	.10
170 Garry Templeton	.10
171 Andre Thornton	.10
172 Alan Trammell	.10
173 Doug DeCinces	.10
174 Greg Walker	.10
175 Don Sutton	.75
176 1985 Award Winners (Vince Coleman, Dwight Gooden, Ozzie Guillen, Don Mattingly, Willie McGee, Bret Saberhagen)	.50
177 1985 Hot Rookies (Stewart Cliburn, Brian Fisher, Joe Hesketh, Joe Orsulak, Mark Salas, Larry Sheets)	.10
178a Future Stars (Jose Canseco RC, Mark Funderburk, Mike Greenwell, Steve Lombardozzi, Billy Joe Robidoux, Danny Tartabull)	2.00
178b Future Stars (Jose Canseco, Mike Greenwell, Steve Lombardozzi, Billy Jo Robidoux, Danny Tartabull, Jim Wilson)	30.00
179 Gold Glove (George Brett, Ron Guidry, Keith Hernandez, Don Mattingly, Willie McGee, Dale Murphy)	1.00
180 .300 (Wade Boggs, George Brett, Rod Carew, Cecil Cooper, Don Mattingly, Willie Wilson)	1.00
181 .300 (Pedro Guerrero, Tony Gwynn, Keith Hernandez, Bill Madlock, Dave Parker, Pete Rose)	.50
182 1985 Milestones (Rod Carew, Phil Niekro, Pete Rose, Nolan Ryan, Tom Seaver, Matt Tallman)	1.50
183 1985 Triple Crown (Wade Boggs, Darrell Evans, Don Mattingly, Willie McGee, Dale Murphy, Dave Parker)	1.00
184 1985 HL (Wade Boggs, Dwight Gooden, Rickey Henderson, Don Mattingly, Willie McGee, John Tudor)	1.00
185 1985 20-Game Winners (Joaquin Andujar, Tom Browning, Dwight Gooden, Ron Guidry, Bret Saberhagen, John Tudor)	.10
186 World Series Champs (Steve Balboni, George Brett, Dane Iorg, Danny Jackson, Charlie Leibrandt, Darryl Motley, Dan Quisenberry, Bret Saberhagen, Lonnie Smith, Jim Sundberg, Frank White, Willie Wilson)	.40
187 Hubie Brooks	.10
188 Glenn Davis	.10
189 Darrell Evans	.10
190 Rich Gossage	.10
191 Andy Hawkins	.10
192 Jay Howell	.10
193 LaMarr Hoyt	.10
194 Davey Lopes	.10
195 Mike Scott	.10
196 Ted Simmons	.10
197 Gary Ward	.10
198 Bob Welch	.10
199 Mike Young	.10
200 Buddy Biancalana	.10

Decade Greats Sample Cards

To promote its Decade Greats set of current and former cards, Sportflics issued this two-card promo set. Card fronts are identical to the issued versions. Backs are printed in blue on white: "DECADE GREATS / SAMPLE CARD." The players are not identified on the cards.

	NM/M
Complete Set (2):	2.00
(1) Dwight Gooden	1.00
(2) Mel Ott	1.00

Decade Greats

This set, produced by Sportflics, features outstanding players, by position, from the 1930s to the 1980s by decades. The card fronts are printed in sepia-toned photos or full-color with the Sportflics three-phase "Magic Motion" animation. The complete set contains 75 cards with 59 single player cards and 16 multi-player cards. Biographies appear on the card backs which are printed in full-color and color-coded by decade. The set was distributed only through hobby dealers and is in the popular 2-1/2" x 3-1/2" size.

	NM/M
Complete Set (75):	9.00

Common Player:	.10
1 Babe Ruth	2.00
2 Jimmie Foxx	.15
3 Lefty Grove	.10
4 Hank Greenberg	.25
5 Al Simmons	.10
6 Carl Hubbell	.10
7 Joe Cronin	.10
8 Mel Ott	.10
9 Lefty Gomez	.10
10 Lou Gehrig	1.25
11 Pie Traynor	.10
12 Charlie Gehringer	.10
13 Catchers (Mickey Cochrane, Bill Dickey, Gabby Hartnett)	.10
14 Pitchers (Dizzy Dean, Paul Derringer, Red Ruffing)	.10
15 Outfielders (Earl Averill, Joe Medwick, Paul Waner)	.10
16 Bob Feller	.40
17 Lou Boudreau	.10
18 Enos Slaughter	.15
19 Hal Newhouser	.10
20 Joe DiMaggio	1.25
21 Pee Wee Reese	.25
22 Phil Rizzuto	.15
23 Ernie Lombardi	.10
24 Infielders (Joe Cronin, George Kell, Johnny Mize)	.10
25 Ted Williams	1.25
26 Mickey Mantle	3.00
27 Warren Spahn	.15
28 Jackie Robinson	1.00
29 Ernie Banks	.20
30 Stan Musial	.75
31 Yogi Berra	.40
32 Duke Snider	.50
33 Roy Campanella	.50
34 Eddie Mathews	.15
35 Ralph Kiner	.15
36 Early Wynn	.10
37 Double Play Duo (Luis Aparicio, Nellie Fox)	.35
38 First Basemen (Gil Hodges, Ted Kluszewski, Mickey Vernon)	.25
40 Henry Aaron	.75
41 Frank Robinson	.20
42 Bob Gibson	.20
43 Roberto Clemente	1.75
44 Whitey Ford	.25
45 Brooks Robinson	.35
46 Juan Marichal	.15
47 Carl Yastrzemski	.15
48 First Basemen (Orlando Cepeda, Harmon Killebrew, Willie McCovey)	.15
49 Catchers (Bill Freehan, Elston Howard, Joe Torre)	.10
50 Willie Mays	.75
51 Outfielders (Al Kaline, Tony Oliva, Billy Williams)	.15
52 Tom Seaver	.40
53 Reggie Jackson	.50
54 Steve Carlton	.25
55 Mike Schmidt	.50
56 Joe Morgan	.15
57 Jim Rice	.15
58 Jim Palmer	.20
59 Lou Brock	.20
60 Pete Rose	1.00
61 Steve Garvey	.25
62 Catchers (Carlton Fisk, Thurman Munson, Ted Simmons)	.15
63 Pitchers (Vida Blue, Catfish Hunter, Nolan Ryan)	.20
64 George Brett	.50
65 Don Mattingly	1.00
66 Fernando Valenzuela	.10
67 Dale Murphy	.25
68 Wade Boggs	.40
69 Rickey Henderson	.40
70 Eddie Murray	.40
71 Ron Guidry	.10
72 Catchers (Gary Carter, Lance Parrish, Tony Pena)	.15
73 Infielders (Cal Ripken, Jr., Lou Whitaker, Robin Yount)	.35
74 Outfielders (Pedro Guerrero, Tim Raines, Dave Winfield)	.15
75 Dwight Gooden	.10

Rookies

The 1986 Rookies set offers 50 cards and features 47 individual rookie players. In addition, there are two Tri-Star cards; one highlights former Rookies of the Year and the other features three prominent players. There is one "Big Six" card featuring six superstars. The full-color photos on the 2-1/2" x 3-1/2" cards use Sportflics three-phase "Magic Motion" animation. The set was packaged in a collector box which also contained 34 trivia cards that measure 1-3/4" x 2". The set was distributed only by hobby dealers.

		NM/M
Complete Set (50):		17.50
Common Player:		.10
1	John Kruk	.10
2	Edwin Correa	.10
3	Pete Incaviglia	.10
4	Dale Sveum	.10
5	Juan Nieves	.10
6	Will Clark	.25
7	Wally Joyner	.25
8	Lance McCullers	.10
9	Scott Bailes	.10
10	Dan Plesac	.10
11	Jose Canseco	1.50
12	Bobby Witt	.10
13	Barry Bonds	15.00
14	Andres Thomas	.10
15	Jim Deshaies	.10
16	Ruben Sierra	.10
17	Steve Lombardozzi	.10
18	Cory Snyder	.10
19	Reggie Williams	.10
20	Mitch Williams	.10
21	Glenn Braggs	.10
22	Danny Tartabull	.10
23	Charlie Kerfeld	.10
24	Paul Assenmacher	.10
25	Robby Thompson	.10
26	Bobby Bonilla	.10
27	Andres Galarraga	.10
28	Billy Jo Robidoux	.10
29	Bruce Ruffin	.10
30	Greg Swindell	.10
31	John Cangelosi	.10
32	Jim Traber	.10
33	Russ Morman	.10
34	Barry Larkin	.10
35	Todd Worrell	.10
36	John Cerutti	.10
37	Mike Kingery	.10
38	Mark Eichhorn	.10
39	Scott Bankhead	.10
40	Bo Jackson	.25
41	Greg Mathews	.10
42	Eric King	.10
43	Kal Daniels	.10
44	Calvin Schiraldi	.10
45	Mickey Brantley	.10
46	Outstanding Rookie Seasons (Fred Lynn, Willie Mays, Pete Rose)	.60
47	Outstanding Rookie Seasons (Dwight Gooden, Tom Seaver, Fernando Valenzuela)	.25
48	Outstanding Rookie Seasons (Eddie Murray, Dave Righetti, Cal Ripken, Jr., Steve Sax, Darryl Strawberry, Lou Whitaker)	.25
49	Kevin Mitchell	.10
50	Mike Diaz	.10

Dwight Gooden Discs

As the viewing angle changes on these 3-D simulated motion plastic discs, three different pictures of "Dr. K" can be seen, two action and one portrait. The discs are found in two diameters, 2-1/4" and 4-1/2". Fronts have team-color borders of blue with orange lettering. Backs are blank.

		NM/M
Complete Set (2):		3.00
(1)	Dwight Gooden (2-1/4")	1.00
(2)	Dwight Gooden (4-1/2")	2.00

Jumbo Discs

A portrait and two action pictures of the players are featured in these large-format (4-1/2" diameter) "Magic Motion" discs. Fronts have the player's name below the photos, with a title above. Backs are printed in purple, red, black and white. Discs were available for $5 each with a paper coupon found in Sportflics packs.

		NM/M
Complete Set (6):		13.50
Common Player:		1.50
(1)	Wade Boggs	4.00
(2)	Roger Clemens	5.00
(3)	Wally Joyner	1.50
(4)	Mickey Mantle	6.00
(5)	Don Mattingly	5.00
(6)	Dave Winfield	3.00
(1)	Wade Boggs	1.00
(2)	Roger Clemens	1.25
(3)	Wally Joyner	.40
(4)	Mickey Mantle	2.00
(5)	Don Mattingly	1.25
(6)	Dave Winfield	.75

1987 Sportflics

In its second year in the national market, Sportflics' basic issue was again a 200-card set of 2-1/2" x 3-1/2" "Magic Motion" cards, which offer three different photos on the same card, each visible in turn as the card is moved from top to bottom or side to side. Besides single-player cards, the '87 Sportflics set includes several three- and six-player cards, though not as many as in the 1986 set. The card backs feature a small player portrait photo on the single-player cards, an innovation for 1987. The cards were issued with a series of 136 team logo trivia cards. Most cards exist in two variations, carrying 1986 and 1987 copyright dates on back.

		NM/M
Factory Set (200+136):		12.00
Complete Set (200):		7.50
Common Player:		.10
Foil Pack (3+2):		.50
Foil Box (36):		10.00
1	Don Mattingly	1.25
2	Wade Boggs	1.00
3	Dale Murphy	.50
4	Rickey Henderson	.75
5	George Brett	1.25
6	Eddie Murray	.75
7	Kirby Puckett	1.00
8	Ryne Sandberg	1.00
9	Cal Ripken, Jr.	2.00
10	Roger Clemens	1.25
11	Ted Higuera	.10
12	Steve Sax	.10
13	Chris Brown	.10
14	Jesse Barfield	.10
15	Kent Hrbek	.10
16	Robin Yount	.75
17	Glenn Davis	.10
18	Hubie Brooks	.10
19	Mike Scott	.10
20	Darryl Strawberry	.10
21	Alvin Davis	.10
22	Eric Davis	.10
23	Danny Tartabull	.10
24a	Cory Snyder (Pat Tabler photo on back.)	1.50
24b	Cory Snyder (Pat Tabler photo on back.) (Facing front,1/4 swing on front.)	1.50
24c	Cory Snyder (Snyder photo on back.) (Facing to side)	.50
25	Pete Rose	1.50
26	Wally Joyner	.10
27	Pedro Guerrero	.10
28	Tom Seaver	.75
29	Bob Knepper	.10
30	Mike Schmidt	1.25
31	Tony Gwynn	1.00
32	Don Slaught	.10
33	Todd Worrell	.10
34	Tim Raines	.10
35	Dave Parker	.10
36	Bob Ojeda	.10
37	Pete Incaviglia	.10
38	Bruce Hurst	.10
39	Bobby Witt	.10
40	Steve Garvey	.40
41	Dave Winfield	.75
42	Jose Cruz	.10
43	Orel Hershiser	.10
44	Reggie Jackson	.75
45	Chili Davis	.10
46	Robby Thompson	.10
47	Dennis Boyd	.10
48	Kirk Gibson	.10
49	Fred Lynn	.10
50	Gary Carter	.75
51	George Bell	.10
52	Pete O'Brien	.10
53	Ron Darling	.10
54	Paul Molitor	.75
55	Mike Pagliarulo	.10
56	Mike Boddicker	.10
57	Dave Righetti	.10
58	Len Dykstra RC	.10
59	Mike Witt	.10
60	Tony Bernazard	.10
61	John Kruk	.10
62	Mike Krukow	.10
63	Sid Fernandez	.10
64	Gary Gaetti	.10
65	Vince Coleman	.10
66	Pat Tabler	.10
67	Mike Scioscia	.10
68	Scott Garrelts	.10
69	Brett Butler	.10
70	Bill Buckner	.10
71a	Dennis Rasmussen (John Montefusco photo on back; mustache.)	.25
71b	Dennis Rasmussen (correct photo on back, no mustache.)	.10
72	Tim Wallach	.10
73	Bob Horner	.10
74	Willie McGee	.10
75	A.L. First Basemen (Wally Joyner, Don Mattingly, Eddie Murray)	.50
76	Jesse Orosco	.10
77	N.L. Relief Pitchers (Jeff Reardon, Dave Smith, Todd Worrell)	.10
78	Candy Maldonado	.10
79	N.L. Shortstops (Hubie Brooks, Shawon Dunston, Ozzie Smith)	.10
80	A.L. Left Fielders (George Bell, Jose Canseco, Jim Rice)	.25
81	Bert Blyleven	.10
82	Mike Marshall	.10
83	Ron Guidry	.10
84	Julio Franco	.10
85	Willie Wilson	.10
86	Lee Lacy	.10
87	Jack Morris	.10
88	Ray Knight	.10
89	Phil Bradley	.10
90	Jose Canseco	.60
91	Gary Ward	.10
92	Mike Easler	.10
93	Tony Pena	.10
94	Dave Smith	.10
95	Will Clark	.10
96	Lloyd Moseby	.10
97	Jim Rice	.25
98	Shawon Dunston	.10
99	Don Sutton	.50
100	Dwight Gooden	.10
101	Lance Parrish	.10
102	Mark Langston	.10
103	Floyd Youmans	.10
104	Lee Smith	.10
105	Willie Hernandez	.10
106	Doug DeCinces	.10
107	Ken Schrom	.10
108	Don Carman	.10
109	Brook Jacoby	.10
110	Steve Bedrosian	.10
111	A.L. Pitchers (Roger Clemens, Teddy Higuera, Jack Morris)	.10
112	A.L. Second Basemen (Marty Barrett, Tony Bernazard, Lou Whitaker)	.10
113	A.L. Shortstops (Tony Fernandez, Scott Fletcher, Cal Ripken, Jr.)	.25
114	A.L. Third Basemen (Wade Boggs, George Brett, Gary Gaetti)	.25
115	N.L. Third Basemen (Chris Brown, Mike Schmidt, Tim Wallach)	.20
116	N.L. Second Basemen (Bill Doran, Johnny Ray, Ryne Sandberg)	.10
117	N.L. Right Fielders (Kevin Bass, Tony Gwynn, Dave Parker)	.10
118	Hot Rookie Prospects (David Clark, Pat Dodson, Ty Gainey, Phil Lombardi, Benito Santiago, Terry Steinbach RC)	.25
119	1986 Season Highlights (Dave Righetti, Mike Scott, Fernando Valenzuela)	.10
120	N.L. Pitchers (Dwight Gooden, Mike Scott, Fernando Valenzuela)	.10
121	Johnny Ray	.10
122	Keith Moreland	.10
123	Juan Samuel	.10
124	Wally Backman	.10
125	Nolan Ryan	2.00
126	Greg Harris	.10
127	Kirk McCaskill	.10
128	Dwight Evans	.10
129	Rick Rhoden	.10
130	Bill Madlock	.10
131	Oddibe McDowell	.10
132	Darrell Evans	.10
133	Keith Hernandez	.10
134	Tom Brunansky	.10
135	Kevin McReynolds	.10
136	Scott Fletcher	.10
137	Lou Whitaker	.10
138	Carney Lansford	.10
139	Andre Dawson	.45
140	Carlton Fisk	.75
141	Buddy Bell	.10
142	Ozzie Smith	1.00
143	Dan Pasqua	.10
144	Kevin Mitchell	.10
145	Bret Saberhagen	.10
146	Charlie Kerfeld	.10
147	Phil Niekro	.50
148	John Candelaria	.10
149	Rich Gedman	.10
150	Fernando Valenzuela	.10
151	N.L. Catchers (Gary Carter, Tony Pena, Mike Scioscia)	.10
152	N.L. Left Fielders (Vince Coleman, Jose Cruz, Tim Raines)	.10
153	A.L. Right Fielders (Harold Baines, Jesse Barfield, Dave Winfield)	.10
154	A.L. Catchers (Rich Gedman, Lance Parrish, Don Slaught)	.10
155	N.L. Center Fielders (Kevin McReynolds, Dale Murphy, Eric Davis)	.10
156	'86 Highlights (Jim Deshaies, Mike Schmidt, Don Sutton)	.10
157	A.L. Speedburners (John Cangelosi, Rickey Henderson, Gary Pettis)	.10
158	Hot Rookie Prospects (Randy Asadoor, Casey Candaele, Dave Cochrane, Rafael Palmeiro, Tim Pyznarski, Kevin Seitzer)	.75
159	The Best of the Best (Roger Clemens, Dwight Gooden, Rickey Henderson, Don Mattingly, Dale Murphy, Eddie Murray)	.75
160	Roger McDowell	.10
161	Brian Downing	.10
162	Bill Doran	.10
163	Don Baylor	.10
164	Alfredo Griffin	.10
165	Don Aase	.10
166	Glenn Wilson	.10
167	Dan Quisenberry	.10
168	Frank White	.10
169	Cecil Cooper	.10
170	Jody Davis	.10
171	Harold Baines	.10
172	Rob Deer	.10
173	John Tudor	.10
174	Larry Parrish	.10
175	Kevin Bass	.10
176	Joe Carter	.10
177	Mitch Webster	.10
178	Dave Kingman	.10
179	Jim Presley	.10
180	Mel Hall	.10
181	Shane Rawley	.10
182	Marty Barrett	.10
183	Damaso Garcia	.10
184	Bobby Grich	.10
185	Leon Durham	.10
186	Ozzie Guillen	.10
187	Tony Fernandez	.10
188	Alan Trammell	.10
189	Jim Clancy	.10
190	Bo Jackson	.15
191	Bob Forsch	.10
192	John Franco	.10
193	Von Hayes	.10
194	A.L. Relief Pitchers (Don Aase, Mark Eichhorn, Dave Righetti)	.10
195	N.L. First Basemen (Will Clark, Glenn Davis, Keith Hernandez)	.10
196	'86 Highlights (Roger Clemens, Joe Cowley, Bob Horner)	.10
197	The Best of the Best (Wade Boggs, George Brett, Hubie Brooks, Tony Gwynn, Tim Raines, Ryne Sandberg)	.75
198	A.L. Center Fielders (Rickey Henderson, Fred Lynn, Kirby Puckett)	.50
199	N.L. Speedburners (Vince Coleman, Tim Raines, Eric Davis)	.10
200	Steve Carlton	.75

Rookie Discs

The 1987 Sportflics Rookie Discs set consists of seven discs which measure 4" in diameter. The front of the discs offer three "Magic Motion" photos in full color, encompassed by a blue border. The disc backs are printed in color and include the team logo, player statistics, biography and the disc number. The set was issued with Cooperstown Timeless Trivia Cards.

		NM/M
Complete Set (7):		8.00
Common Player:		1.00
1	Casey Candaele	1.00
2	Mark McGwire	6.00
3	Kevin Seitzer	1.00
4	Joe Magrane	1.00
5	Benito Santiago	1.00
6	Dave Magadan	1.00
7	Devon White	1.00

Rookie Prospects

The Rookie Prospects set consists of 10 cards in standard 2-1/2" x 3-1/2" size. The card fronts feature Sportflics' "Magic Motion" process. Card backs contain a player photo plus a short biography and player personal and statistical information. The set was offered in two separately wrapped mylar packs of five cards to hobby dealers purchasing cases of Sportflics' Team Preview set. Twenty-four packs of "Rookie Prospects" cards were included with each case.

		NM/M
Complete Set (10):		4.00
Common Player:		.25
1	Terry Steinbach	.25
2	Rafael Palmeiro	3.00
3	Dave Magadan	.25
4	Marvin Freeman	.25
5	Brick Smith	.25
6	B.J. Surhoff	.25
7	John Smiley	.25
8	Alonzo Powell	.25
9	Benny Santiago	.25
10	Devon White	.25

Rookies

The Rookies set was issued in two boxed series of 25 cards. The first was released in July with the second series following in October. The cards, which are the standard 2-1/2" x 3-1/2", feature Sportflics' special "Magic Motion" process. The card fronts contain a full-color photo and present three different pictures, depending on how the card is held. The backs also contain a full-color photo along with player statistics and a biography.

		NM/M
Complete Set One (1-25):		4.00
Complete Set Two (26-50):		2.00
Common Player:		.10
1	Eric Bell	.10
2	Chris Bosio	.10
3	Bob Brower	.10
4	Jerry Browne	.10
5	Ellis Burks	.10
6	Casey Candaele	.10
7	Ken Gerhart	.10
8	Mike Greenwell	.10
9	Stan Jefferson	.10
10	Dave Magadan	.10
11	Joe Magrane	.10
12	Fred McGriff	.25
13	Mark McGwire	3.00
14	Mark McLemore	.10
15	Jeff Musselman	.10
16	Matt Nokes	.10
17	Paul O'Neill	.10
18	Luis Polonia	.10
19	Benny Santiago	.10
20	Kevin Seitzer	.10
21	John Smiley	.10
22	Terry Steinbach	.10
23	B.J. Surhoff	.10
24	Devon White	.10
25	Matt Williams	.25
26	DeWayne Buice	.10
27	Willie Fraser	.10
28	Bill Ripken	.10
29	Mike Henneman	.10
30	Shawn Hillegas	.10
31	Shane Mack	.10
32	Rafael Palmeiro	1.50
33	Mike Jackson	.10
34	Gene Larkin	.10
35	Jimmy Jones	.10
36	Gerald Young	.10
37	Ken Caminiti	.10
38	Sam Horn	.10
39	David Cone	.10
40	Mike Dunne	.10
41	Ken Williams	.10
42	John Morris	.10
43	Jim Lindeman	.10
44	Mike Stanley	.10
45	Les Straker	.10

46	Jeff Robinson	.10
47	Todd Benzinger	.10
48	Jeff Blauser	.10
49	John Marzano	.10
50	Keith Miller	.10

Superstar Discs

Released in three series of six discs, the Superstar Disc set features the special "Magic Motion" process. Each disc, which measures 4-1/2" in diameter, contains three different player photos, depending which way it is tilted. A red border, containing 11 stars, the player's name and uniform number, surrounds the photo. The backs have a turquoise border which carries the words "Superstar Disc Collector Series." The backs also include the team logo, player statistics, biography and the disc number. The discs were issued with 18 1-3/4" x 2-1/2" Cooperstown Timeless Trivia Cards.

		NM/M
Complete Set (18):		35.00
Common Player:		1.50
1	Jose Canseco	2.50
2	Mike Scott	1.50
3	Ryne Sandberg	3.50
4	Mike Schmidt	4.00
5	Dale Murphy	2.00
6	Fernando Valenzuela	1.50
7	Tony Gwynn	3.50
8	Cal Ripken, Jr.	6.00
9	Gary Carter	3.00
10	Cory Snyder	1.50
11	Kirby Puckett	3.50
12	George Brett	3.50
13	Keith Hernandez	1.50
14	Rickey Henderson	3.00
15	Tim Raines	1.50
16	Bo Jackson	2.00
17	Pete Rose	4.50
18	Eric Davis	1.50

Team Previews

The 1987 Sportflics Team Preview set appeared to be a good idea, but never caught on with collectors. The intent of the set is to provide a pre-season look at each of the 26 major league clubs. The card backs contain three categories of the team preview: Outlook, Newcomers to Watch and Summary. Using the "Magic Motion" process, 12 different players are featured on the card fronts. Four of the different player photos can be made visible at once. The cards, which measure 2-1/2" x 3-1/2", were issued with team logo/trivia cards in a specially designed box.

		NM/M
Complete Set (26):		15.00
Common Team:		.50
1	Texas Rangers (Scott Fletcher, Greg Harris, Charlie Hough,	

2	Pete Incaviglia, Mike Loynd, Oddibe McDowell, Pete O'Brien, Larry Parrish, Ruben Sierra, Don Slaught, Mitch Williams, Bobby Witt)	.50
2	New York Mets (Wally Backman, Gary Carter, Ron Darling, Lenny Dykstra, Sid Fernandez, Dwight Gooden, Keith Hernandez, Dave Magadan, Kevin McReynolds, Randy Myers, Bob Ojeda, Darryl Strawberry)	.75
3	Cleveland Indians (Tony Bernazard, Brett Butler, Tom Candiotti, Joe Carter, Julio Franco, Mel Hall, Brook Jacoby, Phil Niekro, Ken Schrom, Cory Snyder, Greg Swindell, Pat Tabler)	.50
4	Cincinnati Reds (Buddy Bell, Tom Browning, Kal Daniels, John Franco, Bill Gullickson, Tracy Jones, Barry Larkin, Rob Murphy, Paul O'Neill, Dave Parker, Pete Rose, Eric Davis)	1.00
5	Toronto Blue Jays (Jesse Barfield, George Bell, John Cerutti, Mark Eichhorn, Tony Fernandez, Tom Henke, Glenallen Hill, Jimmy Key, Fred McGriff, Lloyd Moseby, Dave Stieb, Willie Upshaw)	.50
6	Philadelphia Phillies (Steve Bedrosian, Don Carman, Marvin Freeman, Kevin Gross, Von Hayes, Shane Rawley, Bruce Ruffin, Juan Samuel, Mike Schmidt, Kent Tekulve, Milt Thompson, Glenn Wilson)	.75
7	New York Yankees (Rickey Henderson, Phil Lombardi, Don Mattingly, Mike Pagliarulo, Dan Pasqua, Willie Randolph, Dennis Rasmussen, Rick Rhoden, Dave Righetti, Joel Skinner, Bob Tewksbury, Dave Winfield)	1.25
8	Houston Astros (Kevin Bass, Jose Cruz, Glenn Davis, Jim Deshaies, Bill Doran, Ty Gainey, Charlie Kerfeld, Bob Knepper, Nolan Ryan, Mike Scott, Dave Smith, Robby Wine)	1.50
9	Boston Red Sox (Marty Barrett, Don Baylor, Wade Boggs, Dennis Boyd, Roger Clemens, Pat Dodson, Dwight Evans, Mike Greenwell, Dave Henderson, Bruce Hurst, Jim Rice, Calvin Schiraldi)	1.00
10	San Francisco Giants (Bob Brenly, Chris Brown, Will Clark, Chili Davis, Kelly Downs, Scott Garrelts, Mark Grant, Mike Krukow, Jeff Leonard, Candy Maldonado, Terry Mulholland, Robby Thompson)	.50
11	California Angels (John Candelaria, Doug DeCinces, Brian Downing, Ruppert Jones, Wally Joyner, Kirk McCaskill, Darrell Miller, Donnie Moore, Gary Pettis, Don Sutton, Devon White, Mike Witt)	.50
12	St. Louis Cardinals (Jack Clark, Vince Coleman, Danny Cox, Bob Forsch, Tom Herr, Joe Magrane, Willie McGee, Terry Pendleton, Ozzie Smith, John Tudor, Andy Van Slyke, Todd Worrell)	.75
13	Kansas City Royals (George Brett, Mark Gubicza, Bo Jackson, Charlie Leibrandt, Hal McRae, Dan Quisenberry, Bret Saberhagen, Kevin Seitzer, Lonnie Smith, Danny Tartabull, Frank White, Willie Wilson)	.75
14	Los Angeles Dodgers (Ralph Bryant, Mariano Duncan, Jose Gonzalez, Pedro Guerrero, Orel Hershiser, Mike Marshall, Steve Sax, Mike Scioscia,	

15	Franklin Stubbs, Fernando Valenzuela, Reggie Williams, Matt Young)	.50
15	Detroit Tigers (Darnell Coles, Darrell Evans, Kirk Gibson, Willie Hernandez, Eric King, Chet Lemon, Dwight Lowry, Jack Morris, Dan Petry, Frank Tanana, Alan Trammell, Lou Whitaker)	.50
16	San Diego Padres (Randy Asadoor, Steve Garvey, Tony Gwynn, Andy Hawkins, Jim Jones, John Kruk, Craig Lefferts, Shane Mack, Lance McCullers, Kevin Mitchell, Benny Santiago, Ed Wojna)	.75
17	Minnesota Twins (Bert Blyleven, Tom Brunansky, Gary Gaetti, Greg Gagne, Kent Hrbek, Joe Klink, Steve Lombardozzi, Kirby Puckett, Jeff Reardon, Mark Salas, Roy Smalley, Frank Viola)	.75
18	Pittsburgh Pirates (Barry Bonds, Bobby Bonilla, Sid Bream, Mike Diaz, Brian Fisher, Jim Morrison, Joe Orsulak, Bob Patterson, Tony Pena, Johnny Ray, R.J. Reynolds, John Smiley)	1.50
19	Milwaukee Brewers (Glenn Braggs, Rob Deer, Teddy Higuera, Paul Molitor, Juan Nieves, Dan Plesac, Tim Pyznarski, Ernest Riles, Billy Jo Robidoux, B.J. Surhoff, Dale Sveum, Robin Yount)	.75
20	Montreal Expos (Hubie Brooks, Tim Burke, Casey Candaele, Dave Collins, Mike Fitzgerald, Andres Galarraga, Billy Moore, Alonzo Powell, Randy St. Claire, Tim Wallach, Mitch Webster, Floyd Youmans)	.50
21	Baltimore Orioles (Don Aase, Eric Bell, Mike Boddicker, Ken Gerhardt, Terry Kennedy, Ray Knight, Lee Lacy, Fred Lynn, Eddie Murray, Cal Ripken, Jr., Larry Sheets, Jim Traber)	1.50
22	Chicago Cubs (Jody Davis, Shawon Dunston, Leon Durham, Dennis Eckersley, Greg Maddux, Dave Martinez, Keith Moreland, Jerry Mumphrey, Rafael Palmeiro, Ryne Sandberg, Scott Sanderson, Lee Smith)	1.00
23	Oakland Athletics (Jose Canseco, Mike Davis, Alfredo Griffin, Reggie Jackson, Carney Lansford, Mark McGwire, Dwayne Murphy, Rob Nelson, Tony Phillips, Jose Rijo, Terry Steinbach, Curt Young)	1.50
24	Atlanta Braves (Paul Assenmacher, Gene Garber, Tom Glavine, Ken Griffey, Glenn Hubbard, Dion James, Rick Mahler, Dale Murphy, Ken Oberkfell, David Palmer, Zane Smith, Andres Thomas)	.50
25	Seattle Mariners (Scott Bankhead, Phil Bradley, Scott Bradley, Mickey Brantley, Alvin Davis, Steve Fireovid, Mark Langston, Mike Moore, Donell Nixon, Ken Phelps, Jim Presley, Dave Valle)	.50
26	Chicago White Sox (Harold Baines, John Cangelosi, Dave Cochrane, Joe Cowley, Carlton Fisk, Ozzie Guillen, Ron Hassey, Bob James, Ron Karkovice, Russ Mormon, Bobby Thigpen, Greg Walker)	.50

4-in-1 Panels

These 4-in-1 player and team logo panels were given to dealers who made quantity purchases of Sportflics products. The player panels measure 4-7/8" x 6-7/8", making each of the four cards slightly smaller than the regular-issue versions. Otherwise the cards are identical to the standard

version, right down to the card numbers. The team-logo panels correspond to the players on the player panels, but they are smaller, at 3-3/8" x 3-7/8". The logo cards have two views of each logo on front and on back display various team stats. Each of the panels carries a 1986 copyright.

		NM/M
Complete Set (8):		15.00
Common Panel:		1.00
(1)	1 Don Mattingly, 10 Roger Clemens, 30 Mike Schmidt, 34 Tim Raines	5.00
(2)	2 Wade Boggs, 6 Eddie Murray, 26 Wally Joyner, 150 Fernando Valenzuela	2.50
(3)	3 Dale Murphy, 31 Tony Gwynn, 97 Jim Rice, 133 Keith Hernandez	2.50
(4)	4 Rickey Henderson, 5 George Brett, 9 Cal Ripken Jr., 100 Dwight Gooden	6.50
(5)	Yankees, Expos, Red Sox, Phillies	1.00
(6)	Red Sox, Dodgers, Angels, Orioles	1.00
(7)	Braves, Mets, Red Sox, Padres	1.00
(8)	Mets, Orioles, Yankees, Royals	1.00

1988 Sportflics

RYNE SANDBERG 23 SECOND BASE

The design of the 1988 Sportflics set differs greatly from the previous two years. Besides increasing the number of cards in the set to 225, Sportflics included the player name, team and uniform number on the card front. The triple-action color photos are surrounded by a red border. The backs are re-designed, also. Full-color action photos, plus extensive statistics and informative biographies are utilized. Three highlights cards and three rookie prospects cards are included in the set. The cards are the standard 2-1/2" x 3-1/2".

		NM/M
Factory Set (225+136):		17.50
Complete Set (225):		10.00
Common Player:		.10
Foil Pack (3+2):		.50
Foil Box (36):		9.00
1	Don Mattingly	1.25
2	Tim Raines	.10
3	Andre Dawson	.25
4	George Bell	.10
5	Joe Carter	.10
6	Matt Nokes	.10
7	Dave Winfield	.75
8	Kirby Puckett	1.00
9	Will Clark	.10
10	Eric Davis	.10
11	Rickey Henderson	.75
12	Ryne Sandberg	1.00
13	Jesse Barfield	.10
14	Ozzie Guillen	.10
15	Bret Saberhagen	.10
16	Tony Gwynn	1.00
17	Kevin Seitzer	.10
18	Jack Clark	.10
19	Danny Tartabull	.10
20	Ted Higuera	.10
21	Charlie Leibrandt, Jr.	.10
22	Benny Santiago	.10
23	Fred Lynn	.10
24	Rob Thompson	.10
25	Alan Trammell	.10
26	Tony Fernandez	.10
27	Rick Sutcliffe	.10
28	Gary Carter	.75

29	Cory Snyder	.10
30	Lou Whitaker	.10
31	Keith Hernandez	.10
32	Mike Witt	.10
33	Harold Baines	.10
34	Robin Yount	.75
35	Mike Schmidt	1.25
36	Dion James	.10
37	Tom Candiotti	.10
38	Tracy Jones	.10
39	Nolan Ryan	2.00
40	Fernando Valenzuela	.10
41	Vance Law	.10
42	Roger McDowell	.10
43	Carlton Fisk	.75
44	Scott Garrelts	.10
45	Lee Guetterman	.10
46	Mark Langston	.10
47	Willie Randolph	.10
48	Bill Doran	.10
49	Larry Parrish	.10
50	Wade Boggs	1.00
51	Shane Rawley	.10
52	Alvin Davis	.10
53	Jeff Reardon	.10
54	Jim Presley	.10
55	Kevin Bass	.10
56	Kevin McReynolds	.10
57	B.J. Surhoff	.10
58	Julio Franco	.10
59	Eddie Murray	.75
60	Jody Davis	.10
61	Todd Worrell	.10
62	Von Hayes	.10
63	Billy Hatcher	.10
64	John Kruk	.10
65	Tom Henke	.10
66	Mike Scott	.10
67	Vince Coleman	.10
68	Ozzie Smith	1.00
69	Ken Williams	.10
70	Steve Bedrosian	.10
71	Luis Polonia	.10
72	Brook Jacoby	.10
73	Ron Darling	.10
74	Lloyd Moseby	.10
75	Wally Joyner	.10
76	Dan Quisenberry	.10
77	Scott Fletcher	.10
78	Kirk McCaskill	.10
79	Paul Molitor	.75
80	Mike Aldrete	.10
81	Neal Heaton	.10
82	Jeffrey Leonard	.10
83	Dave Magadan	.10
84	Danny Cox	.10
85	Lance McCullers	.10
86	Jay Howell	.10
87	Charlie Hough	.10
88	Gene Garber	.10
89	Jesse Orosco	.10
90	Don Robinson	.10
91	Willie McGee	.10
92	Bert Blyleven	.10
93	Phil Bradley	.10
94	Terry Kennedy	.10
95	Kent Hrbek	.10
96	Juan Samuel	.10
97	Pedro Guerrero	.10
98	Sid Bream	.10
99	Devon White	.10
100	Mark McGwire	1.50
101	Dave Parker	.10
102	Glenn Davis	.10
103	Greg Walker	.10
104	Rick Rhoden	.10
105	Mitch Webster	.10
106	Lenny Dykstra	.10
107	Gene Larkin	.10
108	Floyd Youmans	.10
109	Andy Van Slyke	.10
110	Mike Scioscia	.10
111	Kirk Gibson	.10
112	Kal Daniels	.10
113	Ruben Sierra	.10
114	Sam Horn	.10
115	Ray Knight	.10
116	Jimmy Key	.10
117	Bo Diaz	.10
118	Mike Greenwell	.10
119	Barry Bonds	2.00
120	Reggie Jackson	1.25
121	Mike Pagliarulo	.10
122	Tommy John	.10
123	Bill Madlock	.10
124	Ken Caminiti	.10
125	Gary Ward	.10
126	Candy Maldonado	.10
127	Harold Reynolds	.10
128	Joe Magrane	.10
129	Mike Henneman	.10
130	Jim Gantner	.10
131	Bobby Bonilla	.10
132	John Farrell	.10
133	Frank Tanana	.10
134	Zane Smith	.10
135	Dave Righetti	.10
136	Rick Reuschel	.10
137	Dwight Evans	.10
138	Howard Johnson	.10
139	Terry Leach	.10
140	Casey Candaele	.10
141	Tom Herr	.10
142	Tony Pena	.10
143	Lance Parrish	.10
144	Ellis Burks	.10
145	Pete O'Brien	.10
146	Mike Boddicker	.10

147	Buddy Bell	.10
148	Bo Jackson	.15
149	Frank White	.10
150	George Brett	1.25
151	Tim Wallach	.10
152	Cal Ripken, Jr.	2.00
153	Brett Butler	.10
154	Gary Gaetti	.10
155	Darryl Strawberry	.10
156	Alfredo Griffin	.10
157	Marty Barrett	.10
158	Jim Rice	.25
159	Terry Pendleton	.10
160	Orel Hershiser	.10
161	Larry Sheets	.10
162	Dave Stewart	.10
163	Shawon Dunston	.10
164	Keith Moreland	.10
165	Ken Oberkfell	.10
166	Ivan Calderon	.10
167	Bob Welch	.10
168	Fred McGriff	.10
169	Pete Incaviglia	.10
170	Dale Murphy	.25
171	Mike Dunne	.10
172	Chili Davis	.10
173	Milt Thompson	.10
174	Terry Steinbach	.10
175	Oddibe McDowell	.10
176	Jack Morris	.10
177	Sid Fernandez	.10
178	Ken Griffey	.10
179	Lee Smith	.10
180	1987 Highlights (Juan Nieves, Kirby Puckett, Mike Schmidt)	.25
181	Brian Downing	.10
182	Andres Galarraga	.10
183	Rob Deer	.10
184	Greg Brock	.10
185	Doug DeCinces	.10
186	Johnny Ray	.10
187	Hubie Brooks	.10
188	Darrell Evans	.10
189	Mel Hall	.10
190	Jim Deshaies	.10
191	Dan Plesac	.10
192	Willie Wilson	.10
193	Mike LaValliere	.10
194	Tom Brunansky	.10
195	John Franco	.10
196	Frank Viola	.10
197	Bruce Hurst	.10
198	John Tudor	.10
199	Bob Forsch	.10
200	Dwight Gooden	.10
201	Jose Canseco	.65
202	Carney Lansford	.10
203	Kelly Downs	.10
204	Glenn Wilson	.10
205	Pat Tabler	.10
206	Mike Davis	.10
207	Roger Clemens	1.25
208	Dave Smith	.10
209	Curt Young	.10
210	Mark Eichhorn	.10
211	Juan Nieves	.10
212	Bob Boone	.10
213	Don Sutton	.50
214	Willie Upshaw	.10
215	Jim Clancy	.10
216	Bill Ripken	.10
217	Ozzie Virgil	.10
218	Dave Concepcion	.10
219	Alan Ashby	.10
220	Mike Marshall	.10
221	'87 Highlights (Vince Coleman, Mark McGwire, Paul Molitor)	.75
222	'87 Highlights (Steve Bedrosian, Don Mattingly, Benito Santiago)	.40
223	Hot Rookie Prospects (Shawn Abner, Jay Buhner RC, Gary Thurman)	.25
224	Hot Rookie Prospects (Tim Crews, John Davis, Vincente Palacios)	.10
225	Hot Rookie Prospects (Keith Miller, Jody Reed, Jeff Treadway)	.10

Gamewinners

GAMEWINNERS DON MATTINGLY

This set of 25 standard-size cards (2-1/2" x 3-1/2"), featuring star players in the Sportflics patented 3-D Magic Motion design, was issued by Weiser Card Co. of Plainsboro, N.J., for use as a youth organizational fundraiser. (Weiser's president was former Yankees outfielder Bobby Murcer.) A limited number of sets was produced for test marketing in the Northwestern U.S., with plans for a 1989 set to be marketed nationwide. A green-and-yellow Gamewinners logo banner spans the upper border of the cards face, with a matching player name (with uniform number and position) below the full-color triple photo. The card backs carry large full-color player photos along with stats, personal information and career highlights.

		NM/M
Complete Set (25):		7.50
Common Player:		.25
1	Don Mattingly	1.50
2	Mark McGwire	3.50
3	Wade Boggs	1.25
4	Will Clark	.25
5	Eric Davis	.25
6	Willie Randolph	.25
7	Dave Winfield	.75
8	Rickey Henderson	.75
9	Dwight Gooden	.25
10	Benny Santiago	.25
11	Keith Hernandez	.25
12	Juan Samuel	.25
13	Kevin Seitzer	.25
14	Gary Carter	.75
15	Darryl Strawberry	.25
16	Rick Rhoden	.25
17	Howard Johnson	.25
18	Matt Nokes	.25
19	Dave Righetti	.25
20	Roger Clemens	1.50
21	Mike Schmidt	1.50
22	Ken McReynolds	.25
23	Mike Pagliarulo	.25
24	Kevin Elster	.25
25	Jack Clark	.25

1989 Sportflics

GEORGE BRETT
KANSAS CITY ROYALS

This basic issue includes 225 standard-size player cards (2-1/2" x 3-1/2") and 153 trivia cards, all featuring the patented Magic Motion design. A 5-card sub-set of "Tri-Star" cards features a mix of veterans and rookies. The card fronts feature a white outer border and double color inner border in one of six color schemes. The inner border color changes when the card is tilted and the bottom border carries a double stripe of colors. The player name appears in the top border, player postition and uniform number appear, alternately, in the bottom border. The card backs contain crisp 1-7/8" by 1-3/4" player action shots, along with personal information, stats and career highlights. "The Unforgettables" trivia cards in this set salute members of the Hall of Fame.

		NM/M
Factory Set (225+153):		17.50
Complete Set (225):		12.00
Common Player:		.10
Foil Pack (3+2):		.50
Foil Box (36):		10.00
1	Jose Canseco	.60
2	Wally Joyner	.10
3	Roger Clemens	1.25
4	Greg Swindell	.10
5	Jack Morris	.10
6	Mickey Brantley	.10
7	Jim Presley	.10
8	Pete O'Brien	.10
9	Jesse Barfield	.10
10	Frank Viola	.10
11	Kevin Bass	.10
12	Glenn Wilson	.10
13	Chris Sabo	.10
14	Fred McGriff	.10
15	Mark Grace	.20
16	Devon White	.10
17	Juan Samuel	.10
18	Lou Whitaker	.10
19	Greg Walker	.10
20	Roberto Alomar	.20
21	Mike Schmidt	1.25
22	Benny Santiago	.10
23	Dave Stewart	.10
24	Dave Winfield	.75
25	George Bell	.10
26	Jack Clark	.10
27	Doug Drabek	.10
28	Ron Gant	.10
29	Glenn Braggs	.10
30	Rafael Palmeiro	.65
31	Brett Butler	.10
32	Ron Darling	.10
33	Alvin Davis	.10
34	Bob Walk	.10
35	Dave Stieb	.10
36	Orel Hershiser	.10
37	John Farrell	.10
38	Doug Jones	.10
39	Kelly Downs	.10
40	Bob Boone	.10
41	Gary Sheffield	.35
42	Doug Dascenzo	.10
43	Chad Krueter	.10
44	Ricky Jordan	.10
45	Dave West	.10
46	Danny Tartabull	.10
47	Teddy Higuera	.10
48	Gary Gaetti	.10
49	Dave Parker	.10
50	Don Mattingly	1.25
51	David Cone	.10
52	Kal Daniels	.10
53	Carney Lansford	.10
54	Mike Marshall	.10
55	Kevin Seitzer	.10
56	Mike Henneman	.10
57	Bill Doran	.10
58	Steve Sax	.10
59	Lance Parrish	.10
60	Keith Hernandez	.10
61	Jose Uribe	.10
62	Jose Lind	.10
63	Steve Bedrosian	.10
64	George Brett	1.25
65	Kirk Gibson	.10
66	Cal Ripken, Jr.	2.00
67	Mitch Webster	.10
68	Fred Lynn	.10
69	Eric Davis	.10
70	Bo Jackson	.15
71	Kevin Elster	.10
72	Rick Reuschel	.10
73	Tim Burke	.10
74	Mark Davis	.10
75	Claudell Washington	.10
76	Lance McCullers	.10
77	Mike Moore	.10
78	Robby Thompson	.10
79	Roger McDowell	.10
80	Danny Jackson	.10
81	Tim Leary	.10
82	Bobby Witt	.10
83	Jim Gott	.10
84	Andy Hawkins	.10
85	Ozzie Guillen	.10
86	John Tudor	.10
87	Todd Burns	.10
88	Dave Gallagher	.10
89	Jay Buhner	.10
90	Gregg Jefferies	.10
91	Bob Welch	.10
92	Charlie Hough	.10
93	Tony Fernandez	.10
94	Ozzie Virgil	.10
95	Andre Dawson	.25
96	Hubie Brooks	.10
97	Kevin McReynolds	.10
98	Mike LaValliere	.10
99	Terry Pendleton	.10
100	Wade Boggs	1.00
101	Dennis Eckersley	.65
102	Mark Gubicza	.10
103	Frank Tanana	.10
104	Joe Carter	.10
105	Ozzie Smith	1.00
106	Dennis Martinez	.10
107	Jeff Treadway	.10
108	Greg Maddux	1.00
109	Bret Saberhagen	.10
110	Dale Murphy	.10
111	Rob Deer	.10
112	Pete Incaviglia	.10
113	Vince Coleman	.10
114	Tim Wallach	.10
115	Nolan Ryan	2.00
116	Walt Weiss	.10
117	Brian Downing	.10
118	Melido Perez	.10
119	Terry Steinbach	.10
120	Mike Scott	.10
121	Tim Belcher	.10
122	Mike Boddicker	.10
123	Len Dykstra	.10
124	Fernando Valenzuela	.10
125	Gerald Young	.10
126	Tom Henke	.10
127	Dave Henderson	.10
128	Dan Plesac	.10
129	Chili Davis	.10
130	Bryan Harvey	.10
131	Don August	.10
132	Mike Harkey	.10
133	Luis Polonia	.10
134	Craig Worthington	.10
135	Joey Meyer	.10
136	Barry Larkin	.10
137	Glenn Davis	.10
138	Mike Scioscia	.10
139	Andres Galarraga	.10
140	Doc Gooden	.10
141	Keith Moreland	.10
142	Kevin Mitchell	.10
143	Mike Greenwell	.10
144	Mel Hall	.10
145	Rickey Henderson	.75
146	Barry Bonds	2.00
147	Eddie Murray	.75
148	Lee Smith	.10
149	Julio Franco	.10
150	Tim Raines	.10
151	Mitch Williams	.10
152	Tim Laudner	.10
153	Mike Pagliarulo	.10
154	Floyd Bannister	.10
155	Gary Carter	.75
156	Kirby Puckett	1.00
157	Harold Baines	.10
158	Dave Righetti	.10
159	Mark Langston	.10
160	Tony Gwynn	1.00
161	Tom Brunansky	.10
162	Vance Law	.10
163	Kelly Gruber	.10
164	Gerald Perry	.10
165	Harold Reynolds	.10
166	Andy Van Slyke	.10
167	Jimmy Key	.10
168	Jeff Reardon	.10
169	Milt Thompson	.10
170	Will Clark	.10
171	Chet Lemon	.10
172	Pat Tabler	.10
173	Jim Rice	.25
174	Billy Hatcher	.10
175	Bruce Hurst	.10
176	John Franco	.10
177	Van Snider	.10
178	Ron Jones	.10
179	Jerald Clark	.10
180	Tom Browning	.10
181	Von Hayes	.10
182	Bobby Bonilla	.10
183	Todd Worrell	.10
184	John Kruk	.10
185	Scott Fletcher	.10
186	Willie Wilson	.10
187	Jody Davis	.10
188	Kent Hrbek	.10
189	Ruben Sierra	.10
190	Shawon Dunston	.10
191	Ellis Burks	.10
192	Brook Jacoby	.10
193	Jeff Robinson	.10
194	Rich Dotson	.10
195	Johnny Ray	.10
196	Cory Snyder	.10
197	Mike Witt	.10
198	Marty Barrett	.10
199	Robin Yount	.75
200	Mark McGwire	1.50
201	Ryne Sandberg	1.00
202	John Candelaria	.10
203	Matt Nokes	.10
204	Dwight Evans	.10
205	Darryl Strawberry	.10
206	Willie McGee	.10
207	Bobby Thigpen	.10
208	B.J. Surhoff	.10
209	Paul Molitor	.75
210	Jody Reed	.10
211	Doyle Alexander	.10
212	Dennis Rasmussen	.10
213	Kevin Gross	.10
214	Kirk McCaskill	.10
215	Alan Trammell	.10
216	Damon Berryhill	.10
217	Rick Sutcliffe	.10
218	Don Slaught	.10
219	Carlton Fisk	.75
220	Allan Anderson	.10
221	'88 Highlights (Wade Boggs, Jose Canseco, Mike Greenwell)	.15
222	'88 Highlights (Tom Browning, Dennis Eckersley, Orel Hershiser)	.20
223	Hot Rookie Prospects (Sandy Alomar, Gregg Jefferies, Gary Sheffield)	.50
224	Hot Rookie Prospects (Randy Johnson, Ramon Martinez, Bob Milacki)	.75
225	Hot Rookie Prospects (Geronimo Berroa, Cameron Drew, Ron Jones)	.10

1990 Sportflics

ROBIN VENTURA
CHICAGO WHITE SOX

The Sportflics set for 1990 again contains 225 cards. The cards feature the unique "Magic Motion" effect which displays either of two different photos depending on how the card is tilted. (Previous years' sets had used three photos per card.) The two-photo "Magic Motion" sequence is designed to depict sequential game-action, showing a batter following through on his swing, a pitcher completing his motion, etc. Sportflics also added a moving red and yellow "marquee" border on the cards to complement the animation effect. The player's name, which appears below the animation, remains stationary. The set includes 19 special rookie cards. The backs contain a color player photo, team logo, player information and stats. The cards were distributed in non-transparent mylar packs with small MVP trivia cards.

		NM/M
Factory Set (225+153):		15.00
Complete Set (225):		12.00
Common Player:		.10
Foil Pack (3+2):		.75
Foil Box (36):		20.00
1	Kevin Mitchell	.10
2	Wade Boggs	1.00
3	Cory Snyder	.10
4	Paul O'Neill	.10
5	Will Clark	.10
6	Tony Fernandez	.10
7	Ken Griffey Jr.	1.50
8	Nolan Ryan	2.00
9	Rafael Palmeiro	.65
10	Jesse Barfield	.10
11	Kirby Puckett	1.00
12	Steve Sax	.10
13	Fred McGriff	.10
14	Gregg Jefferies	.10
15	Mark Grace	.10
16	Devon White	.10
17	Juan Samuel	.10
18	Robin Yount	.75
19	Glenn Davis	.10
20	Jeffrey Leonard	.10
21	Chili Davis	.10
22	Craig Biggio	.10
23	Jose Canseco	.50
24	Derek Lilliquist	.10
25	Chris Bosio	.10
26	Dave Steib	.10
27	Bobby Thigpen	.10
28	Jack Clark	.10
29	Kevin Ritz	.10
30	Tom Gordon	.10
31	Bryan Harvey	.10
32	Jim Deshaies	.10
33	Terry Steinbach	.10
34	Tom Glavine	.35
35	Bob Welch	.10
36	Charlie Hayes	.10
37	Jeff Reardon	.10
38	Joe Orsulak	.10
39	Scott Garrelts	.10
40	Bob Boone	.10
41	Scott Bankhead	.10
42	Tom Henke	.10
43	Greg Briley	.10
44	Teddy Higuera	.10
45	Pat Borders	.10
46	Kevin Seitzer	.10
47	Bruce Hurst	.10
48	Ozzie Guillen	.10
49	Wally Joyner	.10
50	Mike Greenwell	.10
51	Gary Gaetti	.10
52	Gary Sheffield	.30
53	Dennis Martinez	.10
54	Ryne Sandberg	1.00
55	Mike Scott	.10
56	Todd Benzinger	.10
57	Kelly Gruber	.10
58	Jose Lind	.10
59	Allan Anderson	.10
60	Robby Thompson	.10
61	John Smoltz	.10
62	Mark Davis	.10
63	Tom Herr	.10
64	Randy Johnson	.75
65	Lonnie Smith	.10
66	Pedro Guerrero	.10
67	Jerome Walton	.10
68	Ramon Martinez	.10
69	Tim Raines	.10
70	Matt Williams	.10
71	Joe Oliver	.10
72	Nick Esasky	.10
73	Kevin Brown	.10
74	Walt Weiss	.10
75	Roger McDowell	.10
76	Jose DeLeon	.10
77	Brian Downing	.10
78	Jay Howell	.10
79	Jose Uribe	.10
80	Ellis Burks	.10
81	Sammy Sosa	7.50
82	Johnny Ray	.10
83	Danny Darwin	.10
84	Carney Lansford	.10
85	Jose Oquendo	.10
86	John Cerutti	.10
87	Dave Winfield	.75
88	Dave Righetti	.10
89	Danny Jackson	.10
90	Andy Benes	.10
91	Tom Browning	.10
92	Pete O'Brien	.10
93	Roberto Alomar	.20
94	Bret Saberhagen	.10
95	Phil Bradley	.10
96	Doug Jones	.10
97	Eric Davis	.10
98	Tony Gwynn	1.00
99	Jim Abbott	.10
100	Cal Ripken, Jr.	2.00
101	Andy Van Slyke	.10
102	Dan Plesac	.10
103	Lou Whitaker	.10
104	Steve Bedrosian	.10
105	Dave Gallagher	.10
106	Keith Hernandez	.10
107	Duane Ward	.10
108	Andre Dawson	.35
109	Howard Johnson	.10
110	Mark Langston	.10
111	Jerry Browne	.10
112	Alvin Davis	.10
113	Sid Fernandez	.10
114	Mike Devereaux	.10
115	Benny Santiago	.10
116	Bip Roberts	.10
117	Craig Worthington	.10
118	Kevin Elster	.10
119	Harold Reynolds	.10
120	Joe Carter	.10
121	Brian Harper	.10
122	Frank Viola	.10
123	Jeff Ballard	.10
124	John Kruk	.10
125	Harold Baines	.10
126	Tom Candiotti	.10
127	Kevin McReynolds	.10
128	Mookie Wilson	.10
129	Danny Tartabull	.10
130	Craig Lefferts	.10
131	Jose DeJesus	.10
132	John Orton	.10
133	Curt Schilling	.35
134	Marquis Grissom	.10
135	Greg Vaughn	.10
136	Brett Butler	.10
137	Rob Deer	.10
138	John Franco	.10
139	Keith Moreland	.10
140	Dave Smith	.10
141	Mark McGwire	1.50
142	Vince Coleman	.10
143	Barry Bonds	2.00
144	Mike Henneman	.10
145	Doc Gooden	.10
146	Darryl Strawberry	.10
147	Von Hayes	.10
148	Andres Galarraga	.10
149	Roger Clemens	1.25
150	Don Mattingly	1.25
151	Joe Magrane	.10
152	Dwight Smith	.10
153	Ricky Jordan	.10
154	Alan Trammell	.10
155	Brook Jacoby	.10
156	Lenny Dykstra	.10
157	Mike LaValliere	.10
158	Julio Franco	.10
159	Joey Belle	.25
160	Barry Larkin	.10
161	Rick Reuschel	.10
162	Nelson Santovenia	.10
163	Mike Scioscia	.10
164	Damon Berryhill	.10
165	Todd Worrell	.10
166	Jim Eisenreich	.10
167	Ivan Calderon	.10
168	Goose Gozzo	.10
169	Kirk McCaskill	.10
170	Dennis Eckersley	.65
171	Mickey Tettleton	.10
172	Chuck Finley	.10
173	Dave Magadan	.10
174	Terry Pendleton	.10
175	Willie Randolph	.10
176	Jeff Huson	.10
177	Todd Zeile	.10
178	Steve Olin	.10
179	Eric Anthony	.10
180	Scott Coolbaugh	.10
181	Rick Sutcliffe	.10
182	Tim Wallach	.10
183	Paul Molitor	.75
184	Roberto Kelly	.10
185	Mike Moore	.10
186	Junior Felix	.10
187	Mike Schooler	.10
188	Ruben Sierra	.10
189	Dale Murphy	.30
190	Dan Gladden	.10
191	John Smiley	.10
192	Jeff Russell	.10
193	Bert Blyleven	.10
194	Dave Stewart	.10
195	Bobby Bonilla	.10
196	Mitch Williams	.10
197	Orel Hershiser	.10
198	Kevin Bass	.10
199	Tim Burke	.10
200	Bo Jackson	.15
201	David Cone	.10
202	Gary Pettis	.10
203	Kent Hrbek	.10
204	Carlton Fisk	.75
205	Bob Geren	.10
206	Bill Spiers	.10
207	Oddibe McDowell	.10
208	Rickey Henderson	.75
209	Ken Caminiti	.10
210	Devon White	.10
211	Greg Maddux	1.00
212	Ed Whitson	.10
213	Carlos Martinez	.10
214	George Brett	1.25
215	Gregg Olson	.10
216	Kenny Rogers	.10
217	Dwight Evans	.10
218	Pat Tabler	.10
219	Jeff Treadway	.10
220	Scott Fletcher	.10
221	Deion Sanders	.15
222	Robin Ventura	.10
223	Chip Hale	.10
224	Tommy Greene	.10
225	Dean Palmer	.10

1994 Sportflics 2000 Promos

To reintroduce its "Magic Motion" baseball cards to the hobby (last produced by Score in 1990), Pinnacle Brands produced a three-card promo set which it sent to dealers along with a header card explaining the issue. In the same format as the regular issue, though some different photos were used, the promos feature on front what Sportflics calls "state-of-the-art lenticular technology" to create an action effect when the card is moved. Backs are produced by standard printing techniques and are gold-foil highlighted and UV-coated. Each of the promo cards has a large black "SAMPLE" overprinted diagonally across front and back.

		NM/M
Complete Set (4):		5.00
Common Player:		1.00
1a	Lenny Dykstra ("SAMPLE" front only.)	1.00
1b	Lenny Dykstra ("SAMPLE" back and front.)	1.00
7	Javy Lopez (Shakers)	1.00
193	Greg Maddux (Starflics)	3.00
	Header Card	3.00

1994 Sportflics 2000

The concept of "Magic Motion" baseball cards returned to the hobby in 1994 after a three-year hiatus. Pinnacle refined its "state-of-the-art lenticular technology" to produce cards which show alternating pictures when viewed from different angles on the basic cards, and to create a striking 3-D effect on its "Starflics" A.L. and N.L. All-Star team subset. Backs are conventionally printed, UV-coated and gold-foil highlighted, featuring a player photo and recent stats. Cards were sold in eight-card foil packs with a suggested retail price of $2.49.

	NM/M
Complete Set (193):	15.00
Common Player:	.10
Pack (8):	.50
Wax Box (36):	15.00
1 Len Dykstra	.10
2 Mike Stanley	.10
3 Alex Fernandez	.10
4 Mark McGuire (McGwire)	1.50
5 Eric Karros	.10
6 Dave Justice	.10
7 Jeff Bagwell	.65
8 Darren Lewis	.10
9 David McCarty	.10
10 Albert Belle	.10
11 Ben McDonald	.10
12 Joe Carter	.10
13 Benito Santiago	.10
14 Rob Dibble	.10
15 Roger Clemens	.85
16 Travis Fryman	.10
17 Doug Drabek	.10
18 Jay Buhner	.10
19 Orlando Merced	.10
20 Ryan Klesko	.10
21 Chuck Finley	.10
22 Dante Bichette	.10
23 Wally Joyner	.10
24 Robin Yount	.65
25 Tony Gwynn	.75
26 Allen Watson	.10
27 Rick Wilkins	.10
28 Gary Sheffield	.40
29 John Burkett	.10
30 Randy Johnson	.65
31 Roberto Alomar	.25
32 Fred McGriff	.10
33 Ozzie Guillen	.10
34 Jimmy Key	.10
35 Juan Gonzalez	.35
36 Wil Cordero	.10
37 Aaron Sele	.10
38 Mark Langston	.10
39 David Cone	.10
40 John Jaha	.10
41 Ozzie Smith	.75
42 Kirby Puckett	.75
43 Kenny Lofton	.60
44 Mike Mussina	.40
45 Ryne Sandberg	.75
46 Robby Thompson	.10
47 Bryan Harvey	.10
48 Marquis Grissom	.10
49 Bobby Bonilla	.10
50 Dennis Eckersley	.60
51 Curt Schilling	.35
52 Andy Benes	.10
53 Greg Maddux	.75
54 Bill Swift	.10
55 Andres Galarraga	.10
56 Tony Phillips	.10
57 Darryl Hamilton	.10
58 Duane Ward	.10
59 Bernie Williams	.60
60 Steve Avery	.10
61 Eduardo Perez	.10
62 Jeff Conine	.10
63 Dave Winfield	.65
64 Phil Plantier	.10
65 Ray Lankford	.10
66 Robin Ventura	.10
67 Mike Piazza	1.00
68 Jason Bere	.10
69 Cal Ripken, Jr.	2.00
70 Frank Thomas	.65
71 Carlos Baerga	.10
72 Darryl Kile	.10
73 Ruben Sierra	.10
74 Gregg Jefferies	.10
75 John Olerud	.10
76 Andy Van Slyke	.10
77 Larry Walker	.10
78 Cecil Fielder	.10
79 Andre Dawson	.25
80 Tom Glavine	.35
81 Sammy Sosa	.75
82 Charlie Hayes	.10
83 Chuck Knoblauch	.10
84 Kevin Appier	.10
85 Dean Palmer	.10
86 Royce Clayton	.10
87 Moises Alou	.10
88 Ivan Rodriguez	.60
89 Tim Salmon	.10
90 Ron Gant	.10
91 Barry Bonds	2.00
92 Jack McDowell	.10
93 Alan Trammell	.10
94 Dwight Gooden	.10
95 Jay Bell	.10
96 Devon White	.10
97 Wilson Alvarez	.10
98 Jim Abbott	.60
99 Ramon Martinez	.10
100 Kent Hrbek	.10
101 John Kruk	.10
102 Wade Boggs	.75
103 Greg Vaughn	.10
104 Tom Henke	.10
105 Brian Jordan	.10
106 Paul Molitor	.65
107 Cal Eldred	.10
108 Deion Sanders	.10
109 Barry Larkin	.10
110 Mike Greenwell	.10
111 Jeff Blauser	.10
112 Jose Rijo	.10
113 Pete Harnisch	.10
114 Chris Hoiles	.10
115 Edgar Martinez	.10
116 Juan Guzman	.10
117 Todd Zeile	.10
118 Danny Tartabull	.10
119 Chad Curtis	.10
120 Mark Grace	.10
121 J.T. Snow	.10
122 Mo Vaughn	.10
123 Lance Johnson	.10
124 Eric Davis	.10
125 Orel Hershiser	.10
126 Kevin Mitchell	.10
127 Don Mattingly	.85
128 Darren Daulton	.10
129 Rod Beck	.10
130 Charles Nagy	.10
131 Mickey Tettleton	.10
132 Kevin Brown	.10
133 Pat Hentgen	.10
134 Terry Mulholland	.10
135 Steve Finley	.10
136 John Smoltz	.10
137 Frank Viola	.10
138 Jim Abbott	.10
139 Matt Williams	.10
140 Bernard Gilkey	.10
141 Jose Canseco	.45
142 Mark Whiten	.10
143 Ken Griffey Jr.	1.00
144 Rafael Palmeiro	.60
145 Dave Hollins	.10
146 Will Clark	.10
147 Paul O'Neill	.10
148 Bobby Jones	.10
149 Butch Huskey	.10
150 Jeffrey Hammonds	.10
151 Manny Ramirez	.65
152 Bob Hamelin	.10
153 Kurt Abbott	.10
154 Scott Stahoviak	.10
155 Steve Hosey	.10
156 Salomon Torres	.10
157 Sterling Hitchcock	.10
158 Nigel Wilson	.10
159 Luis Lopez	.10
160 Chipper Jones	.75
161 Norberto Martin	.10
162 Raul Mondesi	.60
163 Steve Karsay	.10
164 J.R. Phillips	.10
165 Marc Newfield	.10
166 Mark Hutton	.10
167 Curtis Pride	.10
168 Carl Everett	.10
169 Scott Ruffcorn	.10
170 Turk Wendell	.10
171 Jeff McNeely	.10
172 Javier Lopez	.10
173 Cliff Floyd	.10
174 Rondell White	.10
175 Scott Lydy	.10
176 Frank Thomas/AS	.35
177 Roberto Alomar/AS	.20
178 Travis Fryman/AS	.10
179 Cal Ripken, Jr./AS	1.00
180 Chris Hoiles/AS	.10
181 Ken Griffey Jr./AS	.60
182 Juan Gonzalez/AS	.20
183 Joe Carter/AS	.10
184 Jack McDowell/AS	.10
185 Fred McGriff/AS	.10
186 Robby Thompson/AS	.10
187 Matt Williams/AS	.10
188 Jay Bell/AS	.10
189 Mike Piazza/AS	.60
190 Barry Bonds/AS	1.00
191 Len Dykstra/AS	.10
192 Dave Justice/AS	.10
193 Greg Maddux/AS	.45

Commemoratives

A pair of extra-rare commemorative chase cards was produced for the Sportflics 2000 set honoring Canada's veteran superstar Paul Molitor and its hottest rookie, Cliff Floyd. Cards, utilizing Magic Motion technology to alternate card-front pictures when the viewing angle changes, were inserted on average once in every 360 packs.

	NM/M
Complete Set (2):	5.00
1 Paul Molitor	4.50
2 Cliff Floyd	1.25

Movers

A dozen top veteran ballplayers were featured in the "Movers" insert set produced for inclusion in retail packaging of Sportflics 2000. The inserts feature the same Magic Motion features as the regular cards, showing different images on the card front when the card is viewed from different angles. The UV-coated, gold-foil highlighted backs are printed conventionally. A special "Movers" logo is found on both front and back. Stated odds of finding a Movers card are one in 24 packs.

	NM/M
Complete Set (12):	12.00
Common Player:	.60
1 Gregg Jefferies	.60
2 Ryne Sandberg	2.00
3 Cecil Fielder	.60
4 Kirby Puckett	2.00
5 Tony Gwynn	2.00
6 Andres Galarraga	.60
7 Sammy Sosa	2.00
8 Rickey Henderson	1.00
9 Don Mattingly	2.50
10 Joe Carter	.60
11 Carlos Baerga	.60
12 Len Dykstra	.60

Shakers

Hobby packs are the exclusive source for this 12-card insert set of top rookies, found on average once every 24 packs. The chase cards utilize the Sportflics Magic Motion technology to create two different images on the card front when the card is viewed from different angles. Backs are printed conventionally but feature UV-coating and gold-foil highlights. The "Shakers" logo appears on both front and back.

	NM/M
Complete Set (12):	12.00
Common Player:	.60
1 Kenny Lofton	.60
2 Tim Salmon	.60
3 Jeff Bagwell	2.50
4 Jason Bere	.60
5 Salomon Torres	.60
6 Rondell White	.60
7 Javier Lopez	.60
8 Dean Palmer	.60
9 Jim Thome	2.00
10 J.T. Snow	.60
11 Mike Piazza	4.00
12 Manny Ramirez	2.50

1994 Sportflics 2000 Rookie/Traded Promos

This nine-card set was issued to promote the Sportflics Rookie/Traded update set which was released as a hobby-only product. Cards are virtually identical to the corresponding cards in the R/T set except for the over-printed "SAMPLE" in white on front and back.

	NM/M
Complete Set (9):	5.00
Common Player:	1.00
1 Will Clark	1.00
14 Bret Boone	1.00
20 Ellis Burks	1.00
25 Deion Sanders	1.00
62 Chris Turner	1.00
82 Tony Tarasco	1.00
102 Rich Becker	1.00
GG1 Gary Sheffield (Going, Going, Gone)	2.00
--- Header Card	.25

1994 Sportflics 2000 Rookie/Traded

Each of the 150 regular cards in the Sportflics 2000 Rookie & Traded issue was also produced in a parallel chase card set designated on front with a black and gold "Artist's Proof" logo. Stated odds of finding an AP cards

were one per 24 packs. Fewer than 1,000 or each AP card were reportedly produced.

	NM/M
Complete Set (150):	20.00
Common Player:	.10
Pack (5):	3.00
Wax Box (24):	60.00
1 Will Clark	.10
2 Sid Fernandez	.10
3 Joe Magrane	.10
4 Pete Smith	.10
5 Roberto Kelly	.10
6 Delino DeShields	.10
7 Brian Harper	.10
8 Darrin Jackson	.10
9 Omar Vizquel	.10
10 Luis Polonia	.10
11 Reggie Jefferson	.10
12 Geronimo Berroa	.10
13 Mike Harkey	.10
14 Bret Boone	.10
15 Dave Henderson	.10
16 Pedro Martinez	.75
17 Jose Vizcaino	.10
18 Xavier Hernandez	.10
19 Eddie Taubensee	.10
20 Ellis Burks	.10
21 Turner Ward	.10
22 Terry Mulholland	.10
23 Howard Johnson	.10
24 Vince Coleman	.10
25 Deion Sanders	.10
26 Rafael Palmeiro	.65
27 Dave Weathers	.10
28 Kent Mercker	.10
29 Gregg Olson	.10
30 Cory Bailey	.10
31 Brian Hunter	.10
32 Garey Ingram	.10
33 Daniel Smith	.10
34 Denny Hocking	.10
35 Charles Johnson	.10
36 Otis Nixon	.10
37 Hector Fajardo	.10
38 Lee Smith	.10
39 Phil Stidham	.10
40 Melvin Nieves	.10
41 Julio Franco	.10
42 Greg Gohr	.10
43 Steve Dunn	.10
44 Tony Fernandez	.10
45 Toby Borland	.10
46 Paul Shuey	.10
47 Shawn Hare	.10
48 Shawn Green	.50
49 Julian Tavarez RC	.10
50 Ernie Young	.10
51 Chris Sabo	.10
52 Greg O'Halloran	.10
53 Donnie Elliott	.10
54 Jim Converse	.10
55 Ray Holbert	.10
56 Keith Lockhart	.10
57 Tony Longmire	.10
58 Jorge Fabregas	.10
59 Ravelo Manzanillo	.10
60 Marcus Moore	.10
61 Carlos Rodriguez	.10
62 Mark Portugal	.10
63 Yorkis Perez	.10
64 Dan Miceli	.10
65 Chris Turner	.10
66 Mike Oquist	.10
67 Tom Quinlan	.10
68 Matt Walbeck	.10
69 Dave Staton	.10
70 Bill Van Landingham RC	.10
71 Dave Stevens	.10
72 Domingo Cedeno	.10
73 Alex Diaz	.10
74 Darren Bragg	.10
75 James Hurst	.10
76 Alex Gonzalez	.10
77 Steve Dreyer	.10
78 Robert Eenhoorn	.10
79 Derek Parks	.10
80 Jose Valentin	.10
81 Wes Chamberlain	.10
82 Tony Tarasco	.10
83 Steve Trachsel	.10
84 Willie Banks	.10
85 Rob Butler	.10
86 Miguel Jimenez	.10
87 Gerald Williams	.10
88 Aaron Small	.10
89 Matt Mieske	.10
90 Tim Hyers	.10
91 Eddie Murray	.75
92 Dennis Martinez	.10
93 Tony Eusebio	.10
94 Brian Anderson RC	.25
95 Blaise Ilsley	.10
96 Johnny Ruffin	.10
97 Carlos Reyes	.10
98 Greg Pirkl	.10
99 Jack Morris	.10
100 John Mabry	.10
101 Mike Kelly	.10
102 Rich Becker	.10
103 Chris Gomez	.10
104 Jim Edmonds	.10
105 Rich Rowland	.10
106 Damon Buford	.10
107 Mark Kiefer	.10
108 Matias Carrillo	.10
109 James Mouton	.10
110 Kelly Stinnett	.10
111 Billy Ashley	.10
112 Fausto Cruz RC	.10
113 Roberto Petagine	.10
114 Joe Hall	.10
115 Brian Johnson RC	.10
116 Kevin Jarvis	.10
117 Tim Davis	.10
118 John Patterson	.10
119 Stan Royer	.10
120 Jeff Juden	.10
121 Bryan Eversgerd	.10
122 Chan Ho Park RC	1.00
123 Shane Reynolds	.10
124 Danny Bautista	.10
125 Rikkert Faneyte	.10
126 Carlos Pulido	.10
127 Mike Matheny	.10
128 Hector Carrasco	.10
129 Eddie Zambrano	.10
130 Lee Tinsley	.10
131 Roger Salkeld	.10
132 Carlos Delgado	1.00
133 Troy O'Leary	.10
134 Keith Mitchell	.10
135 Lance Painter	.10
136 Nate Minchey	.10
137 Eric Anthony	.10
138 Rafael Bournigal	.10
139 Joey Hamilton	.10
140 Bobby Munoz	.10
141 Rex Hudler	.10
142 Alex Cole	.10
143 Stan Javier	.10
144 Jose Oliva	.10
145 Tom Brunansky	.10
146 Greg Colbrunn	.10
147 Luis Lopez	.10
148 Alex Rodriguez RC	10.00
149 Darryl Strawberry	.10
150 Bo Jackson	.15

Artist's Proof

Each of the 150 regular cards in the Sportflics 2000 Rookie & Traded issue was also produced in a parallel chase set designated on front with a black and gold "Artist's Proof" logo. Stated odds of finding an AP card were one per 24 packs. Fewer than 1,000 of each AP card were reportedly produced.

	NM/M
Complete Set (150):	300.00
Common Player:	1.00
Stars:	25X
148 Alex Rodriguez:	

Going, Going, Gone

A dozen of the game's top home run hitters are featured in this insert set. On front, simulated 3-D action photos depict the player's swing for the fences. Backs have a portrait photo and information about the player's home run prowess. A crossed bats and "Going, Going, Gone" logo appear on both front and back. Cards are numbered with a "GG" prefix. Stated odds of finding one of these inserts were once in 18 packs.

	NM/M
Complete Set (12):	10.00
Common Player:	.50
1 Gary Sheffield	.75
2 Matt Williams	.50
3 Juan Gonzalez	.90
4 Ken Griffey Jr.	2.00
5 Mike Piazza	2.00
6 Frank Thomas	1.50
7 Tim Salmon	.50
8 Barry Bonds	3.00
9 Fred McGriff	.50
10 Cecil Fielder	.50
11 Albert Belle	.50
12 Joe Carter	.50

Rookies of the Year

Sportflics' choices for Rookies of the Year were featured on this one-card insert set. Ryan Klesko (National League) and Manny Ramirez (American League) are shown on the card when viewed from different angles. Sportflics batted .000 in their guesses, however, as Raul Mondesi and Bob Hamelin were the actual R.O.Y. selections. This card was inserted at the average rate of once per 360 packs.

	NM/M
Complete Set (1):	
RO1 Ryan Klesko, Manny Ramirez	3.00

3-D Rookies

Eighteen of 1994's premier rookies are featured in this insert set. Combining a 3-D look and Sportflics' "Magic Motion" technology, the horizontal-format Starflics rookie cards present a striking appearance. Backs feature a full-bleed color photo overprinted with gold foil. A notice on back gives the production run of the chase cards as "No more than 5,000 sets." Stated odds of finding a Starflics Rookie card were given as one per 36 packs. Cards are numbered with a "TR" prefix.

	NM/M
Complete Set (18):	65.00
Common Player:	2.00
1 John Hudek	2.00
2 Manny Ramirez	15.00
3 Jeffrey Hammonds	2.00
4 Carlos Delgado	7.50
5 Javier Lopez	2.00
6 Alex Gonzalez	2.00
7 Raul Mondesi	2.00
8 Bob Hamelin	2.00
9 Ryan Klesko	2.00
10 Brian Anderson	2.00
11 Alex Rodriguez	40.00
12 Cliff Floyd	2.00
13 Chan Ho Park	2.00
14 Steve Karsay	2.00
15 Rondell White	2.00
16 Shawn Green	6.00
17 Rich Becker	2.00
18 Charles Johnson	2.00

1994 Sportflics FanFest All-Stars

An American and a National League player at each position share the fronts of these "Magic Motion" cards. Cards were available by redeeming coupons acquired at

various locations around the Pittsburgh All-Star FanFest celebration in July 1994. Action photos of the players alternate on the fronts of the cards when the viewing angle is changed. The N.L. player's name appears at upper-left; the A.L. All-Star at lower-right. Backs have portrait photos of the players and a few stats and comments. The players' names, teams, position and card number are printed in gold foil, along with the notation "1 of 10,000". Cards are numbered with an "AS" prefix.

	NM/M
Complete Set (9):	25.00
Common Card:	2.50
1 Fred McGriff, Frank Thomas	3.00
2 Ryne Sandberg, Roberto Alomar	3.50
3 Matt Williams, Travis Fryman	2.50
4 Ozzie Smith, Cal Ripken Jr.	5.00
5 Mike Piazza, Ivan Rodriguez	4.00
6 Barry Bonds, Juan Gonzalez	5.00
7 Len Dykstra, Ken Griffey Jr.	4.00
8 Gary Sheffield, Kirby Puckett	3.50
9 Greg Maddux, Mike Mussina	3.50

1995 Sportflix Samples

This nine-card promo pack was sent to Pinnacle's dealer network to introduce its revamped (new logo, spelling) magic-motion card set for 1995. The sample cards are identical in format to the regular-issue Sportflix cards except that a large white "SAMPLE" is printed diagonally on front and back of the promos.

	NM/M
Complete Set (9):	20.00
Common Player:	2.00
3 Fred McGriff	2.00
20 Frank Thomas	3.50
105 Manny Ramirez	3.00
122 Cal Ripken Jr.	5.00
128 Roberto Alomar	2.25
152 Russ Davis (Rookie)	2.00
162 Chipper Jones (Rookie)	4.00
DE2 Matt Williams (Detonators)	2.00
---- Advertising Card	.10

1995 Sportflix

With only 170 cards in the set, only the biggest stars and hottest rookies (25 of them in

a specially designed subset) are included in this simulated 3-D issue. Fronts feature two borderless action photos which are alternately visible as the card's viewing angle is changed. Backs are conventionally printed and have a portrait photo, a few career stats and a couple of sentences about the player. The basic packaging options for '95 Sportflix were five- and eight card foils at $1.89 and $2.99, respectively.

	NM/M
Complete Set (170):	13.50
Common Player:	.10
Artist's Proofs:	12X
Pack (5):	1.50
Wax Box (36):	30.00
1 Ken Griffey Jr.	1.25
2 Jeffrey Hammonds	.10
3 Fred McGriff	.10
4 Rickey Henderson	.75
5 Derrick May	.10
6 Robin Ventura	.10
7 Royce Clayton	.10
8 Paul Molitor	.75
9 Charlie Hayes	.10
10 David Nied	.10
11 Ellis Burks	.10
12 Bernard Gilkey	.10
13 Don Mattingly	1.00
14 Albert Belle	.10
15 Doug Drabek	.10
16 Tony Gwynn	1.00
17 Delino DeShields	.10
18 Bobby Bonilla	.10
19 Cliff Floyd	.10
20 Frank Thomas	.75
21 Raul Mondesi	.10
22 Dave Nilsson	.10
23 Todd Zeile	.10
24 Bernie Williams	.10
25 Kirby Puckett	1.00
26 David Cone	.10
27 Darren Daulton	.10
28 Marquis Grissom	.10
29 Randy Johnson	.75
30 Jeff Kent	.10
31 Orlando Merced	.10
32 Dave Justice	.10
33 Ivan Rodriguez	.65
34 Kirk Gibson	.10
35 Alex Fernandez	.10
36 Rick Wilkins	.10
37 Andy Benes	.10
38 Bret Saberhagen	.10
39 Billy Ashley	.10
40 Jose Rijo	.10
41 Matt Williams	.10
42 Lenny Dykstra	.10
43 Jay Bell	.10
44 Reggie Jefferson	.10
45 Greg Maddux	1.00
46 Gary Sheffield	.35
47 Bret Boone	.10
48 Jeff Bagwell	.75
49 Ben McDonald	.10
50 Eric Karros	.10
51 Roger Clemens	1.00
52 Sammy Sosa	1.00
53 Barry Bonds	2.00
54 Joey Hamilton	.10
55 Brian Jordan	.10
56 Wil Cordero	.10
57 Aaron Sele	.10
58 Paul O'Neill	.10
59 Carlos Garcia	.10
60 Mike Mussina	.40
61 John Olerud	.10
62 Kevin Appier	.10
63 Matt Mieske	.10
64 Carlos Baerga	.10
65 Ryan Klesko	.10
66 Jimmy Key	.10
67 James Mouton	.10
68 Tim Salmon	.10
69 Hal Morris	.10
70 Albie Lopez	.10
71 Dave Hollins	.10
72 Greg Colbrunn	.10
73 Juan Gonzalez	.40
74 Wally Joyner	.10

	NM/M
75 Bob Hamelin	.10
76 Brady Anderson	.10
77 Deion Sanders	.10
78 Javier Lopez	.10
79 Brian McRae	.10
80 Craig Biggio	.10
81 Kenny Lofton	.10
82 Cecil Fielder	.10
83 Mike Piazza	1.25
84 Rafael Palmeiro	.65
85 Jim Thome	.65
86 Ruben Sierra	.10
87 Mark Langston	.10
88 John Valentin	.10
89 Shawon Dunston	.10
90 Travis Fryman	.10
91 Chuck Knoblauch	.10
92 Dean Palmer	.10
93 Robby Thompson	.10
94 Barry Larkin	.10
95 Darren Lewis	.10
96 Andres Galarraga	.10
97 Tony Phillips	.10
98 Mo Vaughn	.10
99 Pedro Martinez	.75
100 Chad Curtis	.10
101 Brent Gates	.10
102 Pat Hentgen	.10
103 Rico Brogna	.10
104 Carlos Delgado	.50
105 Manny Ramirez	.75
106 Mike Greenwell	.10
107 Wade Boggs	1.00
108 Ozzie Smith	1.00
109 Rusty Greer	.10
110 Willie Greene	.10
111 Chili Davis	.10
112 Reggie Sanders	.10
113 Roberto Kelly	.10
114 Tom Glavine	.35
115 Moises Alou	.10
116 Dennis Eckersley	.65
117 Danny Tartabull	.10
118 Jeff Conine	.10
119 Will Clark	.10
120 Joe Carter	.10
121 Mark McGwire	1.50
122 Cal Ripken Jr.	2.00
123 Danny Jackson	.10
124 Phil Plantier	.10
125 Dante Bichette	.10
126 Jack McDowell	.10
127 Jose Canseco	.40
128 Roberto Alomar	.20
129 Rondell White	.10
130 Ray Lankford	.10
131 Ryan Thompson	.10
132 Ken Caminiti	.10
133 Gregg Jefferies	.10
134 Omar Vizquel	.10
135 Mark Grace	.10
136 Derek Bell	.10
137 Mickey Tettleton	.10
138 Wilson Alvarez	.10
139 Larry Walker	.10
140 Bo Jackson	.10
141 Alex Rodriguez	1.50
142 Orlando Miller	.10
143 Shawn Green	.35
144 Steve Dunn	.10
145 Midre Cummings	.10
146 Chan Ho Park	.10
147 Jose Oliva	.10
148 Armando Benitez	.10
149 J.R. Phillips	.10
150 Charles Johnson	.10
151 Garret Anderson	.10
152 Russ Davis	.10
153 Brian Hunter	.10
154 Ernie Young	.10
155 Marc Newfield	.10
156 Greg Pirkl	.10
157 Scott Ruffcorn	.10
158 Rikkert Faneyte	.10
159 Duane Singleton	.10
160 Gabe White	.10
161 Alex Gonzalez	.10
162 Chipper Jones	1.00
163 Mike Kelly	.10
164 Kurt Miller	.10
165 Roberto Petagine	.10
166 Checklist (Jeff Bagwell)	.40
167 Checklist (Mike Piazza)	.65
168 Checklist (Ken Griffey Jr.)	.65
169 Checklist (Frank Thomas)	.40
170 Checklist (Barry Bonds, Cal Ripken Jr.)	.75

Artist's Proofs

	NM/M
Complete Set (12):	30.00
Common Player:	1.50
1 Ken Griffey Jr.	4.00
2 Frank Thomas	2.50
3 Cal Ripken Jr.	5.00

Each of the 170 cards in the regular Sportflix set can be found with a special tombstone shaped black-and-gold "Artist's Proof" seal designating it as one of a parallel edition of 700 cards each. Cards are otherwise identical to the regular-issue version. AP cards were inserted at an average rate of one per 36 packs.

	NM/M
Complete Set (170):	200.00
Common Player:	.75
Stars:	12X

Double Take

A see-through plastic background and A.L. and N.L. stars at the same position sharing the card with their shadows marks this chase set as the top of the line for '95 Sportflix. Found at an average rate of one per 48 packs, the Double Take inserts represent a new level in "magic motion" card technology.

	NM/M
Complete Set (12):	25.00
Common Player:	1.00
1 Frank Thomas, Jeff Bagwell	1.50
2 Will Clark, Fred McGriff	1.00
3 Roberto Alomar, Jeff Kent	1.00
4 Wade Boggs, Matt Williams	2.00
5 Cal Ripken Jr., Ozzie Smith	6.00
6 Alex Rodriguez, Wil Cordero	4.00
7 Carlos Delgado, Mike Piazza	3.00
8 Kenny Lofton, Dave Justice	1.00
9 Ken Griffey Jr., Barry Bonds	6.00
10 Albert Belle, Raul Mondesi	1.00
11 Kirby Puckett, Tony Gwynn	2.50
12 Jimmy Key, Greg Maddux	2.00

ProMotion

Twelve of baseball's biggest stars morph into team logos on a bright team-color background in this chase series. Backs have a portrait photo and a few words about the players. The ProMotion inserts are a one per 18 pack pick in jumbo packs only.

	2.50
4 Jeff Bagwell	2.50
5 Mike Piazza	4.00
6 Matt Williams	1.50
7 Albert Belle	1.50
8 Jose Canseco	2.00
9 Don Mattingly	3.50
10 Barry Bonds	5.00
11 Will Clark	1.50
12 Kirby Puckett	3.00

3D Detonators

With the players on a pedestal and fireworks in the background, this chase set lives up to its name, "Detonators." The cards feature a deep 3-D look on front. Backs have a close-up photo of the player in the pedestal's column. Detonator cards are pulled at an average rate of one per 16 packs.

	NM/M
Complete Set (9):	8.00
Common Player:	.40
1 Jeff Bagwell	1.00
2 Matt Williams	.40
3 Ken Griffey Jr.	1.50
4 Frank Thomas	1.25
5 Mike Piazza	1.50
6 Barry Bonds	2.00
7 Albert Belle	.40
8 Cliff Floyd	.40
9 Juan Gonzalez	.60

3D Hammer Team

Sledge hammers flying in formation through a cloud-studded sky are the background for this insert set featuring the game's heavy hitters. Backs have a portrait photo and a few words about the player's power hitting prowess. Hammer Team cards are picked on an average of once per four packs.

	NM/M
Complete Set (18):	7.50
Common Player:	.20
1 Ken Griffey Jr.	1.50
2 Frank Thomas	.65
3 Jeff Bagwell	.65
4 Mike Piazza	1.50
5 Cal Ripken Jr.	2.00
6 Albert Belle	.20
7 Barry Bonds	2.00
8 Don Mattingly	1.00
9 Will Clark	.20
10 Tony Gwynn	.75
11 Matt Williams	.20
12 Kirby Puckett	.65
13 Manny Ramirez	.65
14 Fred McGriff	.20
15 Juan Gonzalez	.35
16 Kenny Lofton	.20
17 Raul Mondesi	.20
18 Tim Salmon	.20

1995 Sportflix/ UC3 Samples

To introduce the new technology it was bringing to the insert cards in the Sportflix UC3 issue, the company sent a sample of the Clear Shots insert, along with a header card describing the entire UC3 issue, to card dealers and the media in June 1995. A large, black, "SAMPLE" is overprinted diagonally on the front. A similarly marked Fred McGriff previewed the set's regular cards.

		NM/M
Complete Set (3):		5.00
3	Fred McGriff	2.00
CS8	Cliff Floyd	2.00
CS10	Alex Gonzalez	2.00
--	Header Card	.05

1995 Sportflix/UC3

Using advanced technology to create a premium 3-D card brand and inserts, UC3 offers three distinctly different card formats in the base 147-card set, plus a parallel set and three insert sets. All cards have borderless fronts and feature a heavy ribbed plastic top layer. The first 95 cards are veteran players in a horizontal format. A central action photo is flanked at left by a large gold glove (National Leaguers) or baseball (A.L.), and at right by a blue and green vista from which flies one (N.L.) or three (A.L.) baseballs. Player identification is in red at upper-left, the UC3 logo at lower-left. Backs have another color photo and a few stats set against a background of the team logo. Cards #96-122 are a vertical-format Rookie subset. Player photos are set against a purple and green vista with a large bat, ball and glove behind the player. His name is at upper-right; team logo at lower-right. Horizontal backs are similar to the other cards. The final 25 cards of the set are a subset titled, "In-Depth." These vertically formatted cards feature eye-popping graphics on front in which the main player photo almost jumps from the background. The only graphics are the player's name at left and the UC3 logo at upper-left. Backs have a portrait photo at top, bathed in golden rays. A team logo is at center and an outer space design at bottom. There is a short paragraph describing the player at right.

		NM/M
Complete Set (147):		12.50
Common Player:		.10
Artist's Proofs: 12X		
Pack (5):		1.00
Wax Box (36):		25.00
1	Frank Thomas	.75
2	Wil Cordero	.10
3	John Olerud	.10
4	Deion Sanders	.10

5	Mike Mussina	.30
6	Mo Vaughn	.10
7	Will Clark	.10
8	Chili Davis	.10
9	Jimmy Key	.10
10	John Valentin	.10
11	Tony Tarasco	.10
12	Alan Trammell	.10
13	David Cone	.10
14	Tim Salmon	.10
15	Danny Tartabull	.10
16	Aaron Sele	.10
17	Alex Fernandez	.10
18	Barry Bonds	2.00
19	Andres Galarraga	.10
20	Don Mattingly	1.00
21	Kevin Appier	.10
22	Paul Molitor	.75
23	Omar Vizquel	.10
24	Andy Benes	.10
25	Rafael Palmeiro	.65
26	Barry Larkin	.10
27	Bernie Williams	.10
28	Gary Sheffield	.40
29	Wally Joyner	.10
30	Wade Boggs	1.00
31	Rico Brogna	.10
32	Ken Caminiti	.10
33	Kirby Puckett	1.00
34	Bobby Bonilla	.10
35	Hal Morris	.10
36	Moises Alou	.10
37	Jim Thome	.65
38	Chuck Knoblauch	.10
39	Mike Piazza	1.25
40	Travis Fryman	.10
41	Rickey Henderson	.75
42	Jack McDowell	.10
43	Carlos Baerga	.10
44	Gregg Jeffries	.10
45	Kirk Gibson	.10
46	Bret Saberhagen	.10
47	Cecil Fielder	.10
48	Manny Ramirez	.75
49	Marquis Grissom	.10
50	Dave Winfield	.75
51	Mark McGwire	1.50
52	Dennis Eckersley	.65
53	Robin Ventura	.10
54	Ryan Klesko	.10
55	Jeff Bagwell	.75
56	Ozzie Smith	1.00
57	Brian McRae	.10
58	Albert Belle	.10
59	Darren Daulton	.10
60	Jose Canseco	.40
61	Greg Maddux	1.00
62	Ben McDonald	.10
63	Lenny Dykstra	.10
64	Randy Johnson	.75
65	Fred McGriff	.10
66	Ray Lankford	.10
67	Dave Justice	.10
68	Paul O'Neill	.10
69	Tony Gwynn	1.00
70	Matt Williams	.10
71	Dante Bichette	.10
72	Craig Biggio	.10
73	Ken Griffey Jr.	1.25
74	Juan Gonzalez	.40
75	Cal Ripken Jr.	2.00
76	Jay Bell	.10
77	Joe Carter	.10
78	Roberto Alomar	.20
79	Mark Langston	.10
80	Dave Hollins	.10
81	Tom Glavine	.35
82	Ivan Rodriguez	.65
83	Mark Whiten	.10
84	Raul Mondesi	.10
85	Kenny Lofton	.10
86	Ruben Sierra	.10
87	Mark Grace	.10
88	Royce Clayton	.10
89	Billy Ashley	.10
90	Larry Walker	.10
91	Sammy Sosa	1.00
92	Jason Bere	.10
93	Bob Hamelin	.10
94	Greg Vaughn	.10
95	Roger Clemens	1.00
96	Scott Ruffcorn	.10
97	Hideo Nomo RC	1.50
98	Michael Tucker	.10
99	J.R. Phillips	.10
100	Roberto Petagine	.10
101	Chipper Jones	1.00
102	Armando Benitez	.10
103	Orlando Miller	.10
104	Carlos Delgado	.50
105	Jeff Cirillo	.10
106	Shawn Green	.30
107	Joe Rando	.10
108	Vaughn Eshelman	.10
109	Frank Rodriguez	.10
110	Russ Davis	.10
111	Todd Hollandsworth	.10
112	Mark Grudzielanek	.10
113	Jose Oliva	.10
114	Ray Durham	.10
115	Alex Rodriguez	1.50
116	Alex Gonzalez	.10
117	Midre Cummings	.10
118	Marty Cordova	.10
119	John Mabry	.10
120	Jason Jacome	.10
121	Joe Vitiello	.10
122	Charles Johnson	.10

123	Cal Ripken Jr. (In Depth)	1.00
124	Ken Griffey Jr. (In Depth)	.65
125	Frank Thomas (In Depth)	.40
126	Mike Piazza (In Depth)	.65
127	Matt Williams (In Depth)	.10
128	Barry Bonds (In Depth)	1.00
129	Greg Maddux (In Depth)	.50
130	Randy Johnson (In Depth)	.40
131	Albert Belle (In Depth)	.10
132	Will Clark (In Depth)	.10
133	Tony Gwynn (In Depth)	.50
134	Manny Ramirez (In Depth)	.40
135	Raul Mondesi (In Depth)	.10
136	Mo Vaughn (In Depth)	.10
137	Mark McGwire (In Depth)	.75
138	Kirby Puckett (In Depth)	.50
139	Don Mattingly (In Depth)	.60
140	Carlos Baerga (In Depth)	.10
141	Roger Clemens (In Depth)	.60
142	Fred McGriff (In Depth)	.10
143	Kenny Lofton (In Depth)	.10
144	Jeff Bagwell (In Depth)	.40
145	Larry Walker (In Depth)	.10
146	Joe Carter (In Depth)	.10
147	Rafael Palmeiro (In Depth)	.30

Artist's Proof

This chase set parallels the 147 regular cards in the UC3 set with a version on which a round, gold "ARTIST'S PROOF" seal is printed on the front of the card. The AP cards are found on the average of one per box (36 packs).

	NM/M
Complete Set (147):	200.00
Common Player:	.75
Stars:	12X

Clear Shots

Seeded at the rate of about one per 24 packs, the 12 cards in this chase set feature top rookies in a technologically advanced format. The left two-thirds of the card are clear plastic, the right third is blue (American League) or red-purple (N.L.). At center is a circle which features the player photos, portrait and action, depending on the viewing angle. Also changing with the viewpoint are the words "CLEAR" and "SHOT" at top-right, and team and UC3 logos at bottom-right. The play-

er's last name is in black at lower-left and appears to change size as the card is moved. Backs have a gray strip vertically at left with the card number, manufacturer and licensor logos and copyright information. Card numbers have a "CS" prefix.

	NM/M
Complete Set (12):	12.00
Common Player:	.25
1 Alex Rodriguez	5.00
2 Shawn Green	.75
3 Hideo Nomo	1.25
4 Charles Johnson	.25
5 Orlando Miller	.25
6 Billy Ashley	.25
7 Carlos Delgado	1.50
8 Cliff Floyd	.25
9 Chipper Jones	4.00
10 Alex Gonzalez	.25
11 J.R. Phillips	.25
12 Michael Tucker	.25

Cyclone Squad

The most commonly encountered (one per four packs, on average) of the UC3 chase cards are the 20-card Cyclone Squad, featuring the game's top batsmen. Cards have a player in a batting pose set against a dark copper background with two golden pinwheels behind him which appear to spin when the card is moved. Horizontal backs have a green toned photo of the player in his follow-through swing, with shock waves radiating from the lower-left corner. Cards have a CS prefix.

	NM/M
Complete Set (20):	10.00
Common Player:	.25
1 Frank Thomas	.65
2 Ken Griffey Jr.	1.00
3 Jeff Bagwell	.65
4 Cal Ripken Jr.	2.00
5 Barry Bonds	2.00
6 Mike Piazza	1.00
7 Matt Williams	.25
8 Kirby Puckett	.75
9 Jose Canseco	.45
10 Will Clark	.25
11 Don Mattingly	.85
12 Albert Belle	.25
13 Tony Gwynn	.75
14 Raul Mondesi	.25
15 Bobby Bonilla	.25
16 Rafael Palmeiro	.60
17 Fred McGriff	.25
18 Tim Salmon	.25
19 Kenny Lofton	.25
20 Joe Carter	.25

In Motion

Found on an average of once per 18 packs, the cards in this chase set feature maximum motion. When the card

is held almost vertically a small eight-piece jigsaw puzzle photo of the player is visible against a light blue background. As the card is moved toward a horizontal position, the pieces appear to become large and move together until the picture fills most of the card. The player's name is in orange at lower-left, with manufacturer's logos at top. Horizontal backs have a green background, two color player photos and a few words of career highlights. The In Motion card numbers are preceded by an "IM" prefix.

	NM/M
Complete Set (10):	7.00
Common Player:	.25
1 Cal Ripken Jr.	1.50
2 Ken Griffey Jr.	1.00
3 Frank Thomas	.50
4 Mike Piazza	1.00
5 Barry Bonds	1.50
6 Matt Williams	.25
7 Kirby Puckett	.75
8 Greg Maddux	.75
9 Don Mattingly	.85
10 Will Clark	.25

1996 Sportflix

Distributed in only retail locations, this 1996 Sportflix set has 144 cards, including 24-card UC3 and 21-card Rookies subsets. The set also has a parallel set, Artist's Proof; these cards are seeded one per every 48 packs. Four insert sets were also produced: Double Take, Hit Parade, Power Surge and ProMotion.

	NM/M
Complete Set (144):	17.50
Common Player:	.10
Common Artist's Proof:	1.00
AP Stars:	12X
Pack (5):	1.00
Wax Box (36):	30.00
1 Wade Boggs	1.00
2 Tim Salmon	.10
3 Will Clark	.10
4 Dante Bichette	.10
5 Barry Bonds	2.00
6 Kirby Puckett	1.00
7 Albert Belle	.10
8 Greg Maddux	1.00
9 Tony Gwynn	1.00
10 Mike Piazza	1.25
11 Ivan Rodriguez	.65
12 Marty Cordova	.10
13 Frank Thomas	.75
14 Raul Mondesi	.10
15 Johnny Damon	.35
16 Mark McGwire	.75
17 Lenny Dykstra	.10
18 Ken Griffey Jr.	1.25
19 Chipper Jones	1.00
20 Alex Rodriguez	1.50
21 Jeff Bagwell	.75
22 Jim Edmonds	.10
23 Edgar Martinez	.10
24 David Cone	.10
25 Tom Glavine	.35
26 Eddie Murray	.75
27 Paul Molitor	.75
28 Ryan Klesko	.10
29 Rafael Palmeiro	.65
30 Manny Ramirez	.75
31 Mo Vaughn	.10
32 Rico Brogna	.10
33 Marc Newfield	.10
34 J.T. Snow	.10
35 Reggie Sanders	.10
36 Fred McGriff	.10
37 Craig Biggio	.10
38 Jeff King	.10
39 Kenny Lofton	.10
40 Gary Gaetti	.10

41	Eric Karros	.10
42	Jason Isringhausen	.10
43	B.J. Surhoff	.10
44	Michael Tucker	.10
45	Gary Sheffield	.45
46	Chili Davis	.10
47	Bobby Bonilla	.10
48	Hideo Nomo	.40
49	Ray Durham	.10
50	Phil Nevin	.10
51	Randy Johnson	.75
52	Bill Pulsipher	.10
53	Ozzie Smith	1.00
54	Cal Ripken Jr.	2.00
55	Cecil Fielder	.10
56	Matt Williams	.10
57	Sammy Sosa	1.00
58	Roger Clemens	1.00
59	Brian Hunter	.10
60	Barry Larkin	.10
61	Charles Johnson	.10
62	Dave Justice	.10
63	Garret Anderson	.10
64	Rondell White	.10
65	Derek Bell	.10
66	Andres Galarraga	.10
67	Moises Alou	.10
68	Travis Fryman	.10
69	Pedro Martinez	.75
70	Carlos Baerga	.10
71	John Valentin	.10
72	Larry Walker	.10
73	Roberto Alomar	.20
74	Mike Mussina	.30
75	Kevin Appier	.10
76	Bernie Williams	.10
77	Ray Lankford	.10
78	Gregg Jefferies	.10
79	Robin Ventura	.10
80	Kenny Rogers	.10
81	Paul O'Neill	.10
82	Mark Grace	.10
83	Deion Sanders	.10
84	Tino Martinez	.10
85	Joe Carter	.10
86	Pete Schourek	.10
87	Jack McDowell	.10
88	John Mabry	.10
89	Darren Daulton	.10
90	Jim Thome	.65
91	Jay Buhner	.10
92	Jay Bell	.10
93	Kevin Seitzer	.10
94	Jose Canseco	.40
95	Juan Gonzalez	.40
96	Jeff Conine	.10
97	Chipper Jones (UC3)	.50
98	Ken Griffey Jr. (UC3)	.65
99	Frank Thomas (UC3)	.40
100	Cal Ripken Jr. (UC3)	1.00
101	Albert Belle (UC3)	.10
102	Mike Piazza (UC3)	.65
103	Dante Bichette (UC3)	.10
104	Sammy Sosa (UC3)	.50
105	Mo Vaughn (UC3)	.10
106	Tim Salmon (UC3)	.10
107	Reggie Sanders (UC3)	.10
108	Gary Sheffield (UC3)	.25
109	Ruben Rivera (UC3)	.10
110	Rafael Palmeiro (UC3)	.35
111	Edgar Martinez (UC3)	.10
112	Barry Bonds (UC3)	1.00
113	Manny Ramirez (UC3)	.40
114	Larry Walker (UC3)	.10
115	Jeff Bagwell (UC3)	.40
116	Matt Williams (UC3)	.10
117	Mark McGwire (UC3)	.75
118	Johnny Damon (UC3)	.30
119	Eddie Murray (UC3)	.40
120	Jay Buhner (UC3)	.10
121	Tim Unroe (Rookie)	.10
122	Todd Hollandsworth (Rookie)	.10
123	Tony Clark (Rookie)	.10
124	Roger Cedeno (Rookie)	.10
125	Jim Pittsley (Rookie)	.10
126	Ruben Rivera (Rookie)	.10
127	Bob Wolcott (Rookie)	.10
128	Chan Ho Park (Rookie)	.10
129	Chris Snopek (Rookie)	.10
130	Alex Ochoa (Rookie)	.10
131	Yamil Benitez (Rookie)	.10
132	Jimmy Haynes (Rookie)	.10
133	Dustin Hermanson (Rookie)	.10
134	Shawn Estes (Rookie)	.10
135	Howard Battle (Rookie)	.10
136	Matt Lawton RC (Rookie)	.25
137	Terrell Wade (Rookie)	.10
138	Jason Schmidt (Rookie)	.10
139	Derek Jeter (Rookie)	2.50
140	Shannon Stewart (Rookie)	.10
141	Chris Stynes (Rookie)	.10
142	Ken Griffey Jr. (Checklist)	.65
143	Greg Maddux (Checklist)	.50
144	Cal Ripken Jr. (Checklist)	1.00

Artist's Proofs

Artist's Proof parallels to 1996 Sportflix are a 1:48 find and are distinctively marked with an AP seal on front.

Complete Set (144): 200.00
Common Player: 1.00
AP Stars: 12X

Double Take

These 1996 Sportflix insert cards each feature two players who are tops at a particular position. Tilting the card to change the angle of view brings each player into focus. The cards were seeded one per 22 packs.

		NM/M
Complete Set (12):		30.00
Common Player:		1.50
1	Barry Larkin, Cal Ripken Jr.	6.00
2	Roberto Alomar, Craig Biggio	1.50
3	Chipper Jones, Matt Williams	2.50
4	Ken Griffey Jr., Ruben Rivera	3.50
5	Greg Maddux, Hideo Nomo	3.00
6	Frank Thomas, Mo Vaughn	2.00
7	Mike Piazza, Ivan Rodriguez	3.50
8	Albert Belle, Barry Bonds	6.00
9	Alex Rodriguez, Derek Jeter	8.00
10	Kirby Puckett, Tony Gwynn	3.00
11	Manny Ramirez, Sammy Sosa	3.00
12	Jeff Bagwell, Rico Brogna	2.00

Hit Parade

Sixteen of baseball's most productive hitters are featured on these inserts. Horizontal fronts have a player portrait at right. In the background is a lenticular-motion scene of a generic player swinging the bat. Backs have an action photo and a few career highlights. The cards were seeded one per every 35 packs.

		NM/M
Complete Set (16):		24.00
Common Player:		.50
1	Ken Griffey Jr.	2.50
2	Cal Ripken Jr.	4.00
3	Frank Thomas	1.50
4	Mike Piazza	2.50
5	Mo Vaughn	.50
6	Albert Belle	.50
7	Jeff Bagwell	1.50
8	Matt Williams	.50
9	Sammy Sosa	.50
9p	Sammy Sosa (Overprinted "SAMPLE")	2.00
10	Kirby Puckett	2.00
11	Dante Bichette	.50
12	Gary Sheffield	1.00
13	Tony Gwynn	2.00
14	Wade Boggs	2.00

| 15 | Chipper Jones | 2.00 |
| 16 | Barry Bonds | 4.00 |

Power Surge

This 1996 Sportflix insert set showcases 24 sluggers on a clear 3-D parallel rendition of the UC3 subset in the main issue. These cards are seeded one per every 35 packs.

		NM/M
Complete Set (24):		30.00
Common Player:		.50
1	Chipper Jones	2.00
2	Ken Griffey Jr.	2.50
3	Frank Thomas	1.50
4	Cal Ripken Jr.	4.00
5	Albert Belle	.50
6	Mike Piazza	2.50
7	Dante Bichette	.50
8	Sammy Sosa	2.00
9	Mo Vaughn	.50
10	Tim Salmon	.50
11	Reggie Sanders	.50
12	Gary Sheffield	1.00
13	Ruben Rivera	.50
14	Rafael Palmeiro	1.25
15	Edgar Martinez	.50
16	Barry Bonds	4.00
17	Manny Ramirez	1.50
18	Larry Walker	.50
19	Jeff Bagwell	1.50
20	Matt Williams	.50
21	Mark McGwire	3.00
22	Johnny Damon	.90
23	Eddie Murray	1.50
24	Jay Buhner	.50

ProMotion

These 1996 Sportflix inserts were seeded one per every 17 packs. The cards' "morphing" technology turns baseball equipment, such as bats, balls and gloves, into 20 of the top veteran superstars using multi-phase animation.

		NM/M
Complete Set (20):		22.50
Common Player:		.50
1	Cal Ripken Jr.	5.00
2	Greg Maddux	2.00
3	Mo Vaughn	.50
4	Albert Belle	.50
5	Mike Piazza	3.00
6	Ken Griffey Jr.	3.00
7	Frank Thomas	1.50
8	Jeff Bagwell	1.50
9	Hideo Nomo	1.00
10	Chipper Jones	2.00
11	Tony Gwynn	2.00
12	Don Mattingly	2.50
13	Dante Bichette	.50
14	Matt Williams	.50
15	Manny Ramirez	1.50
16	Barry Bonds	5.00
17	Reggie Sanders	.50
18	Tim Salmon	.50
19	Ruben Rivera	.50
20	Garret Anderson	.50

Rookie Supers

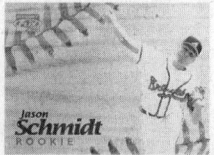

Eight of the young players included in the Sportflix Rookies subset are featured in an enlarged version which was issued one per retail box. The cards measure 3" x 5" and are numbered "X of 8," on back, but are otherwise identical to the smaller version.

		NM/M
Complete Set (8):		12.50
Common player:		1.00
1	Jason Schmidt	1.00
2	Chris Snopek	1.00
3	Tony Clark	1.00
4	Todd Hollandsworth	1.00
5	Alex Ochoa	1.00
6	Derek Jeter	10.00
7	Howard Battle	1.00
8	Bob Wolcott	1.00

1981 Sporting News Conlon Collection

This set of 100 cards was sold directly into the hobby by The Sporting News in a slip-cover case for $50. The blank-backed cards measure 4x5" and feature a sepi-toned photo surrounded by a 1/4" white border. The photos were the first of several uses on baseball cards of TSN's archives of ballplayer photos taken by Charles Martin Conlon between 1915-1935. The paper's logo appears at the top of the card. At bottom are the player's or players' names(s), team at the time the photo was taken, and position or positions played for the season indicated. A card number appears at lower-right.

		NM/M
Complete Set (100):		90.00
Common Player:		1.00
1	Ty Cobb	10.00
2	Hughie Jennings	1.00
3	Miller Huggins	1.00
4	Babe Ruth	12.50
5	Lou Gehrig	10.00
6	John McGraw	1.00
7	Bill Terry	1.00
8	Stan Baumgartner	1.00
9	Christy Mathewson	5.00
10	Grover Alexander	2.00
11	Tony Lazzeri	1.00
12	Frank Chance, Joe Tinker	2.00
13	Johnny Evers	1.00
14	Tris Speaker	2.00
15	Harry Hooper	1.00
16	Duffy Lewis	1.00
17	Joe Wood	1.00
18	Hugh Duffy	1.00
19	Rogers Hornsby	4.00
20	Earl Averill	1.00
21	Dizzy Dean	2.00
22	Daffy Dean	1.00
23	Frankie Frisch	1.00
24	Pepper Martin	1.00
25	Blondie Ryan	1.00
26	Hank Gowdy	1.00
27	Fred Merkle	1.00
28	Ernie Lombardi	1.00
29	Greasy Neale	1.00
30	Morris "Red" Badgro	1.00
31	Jim Thorpe	9.00
32	Roy Johnson	1.00
33	Bob Johnson	1.00
34	Mule Solters	1.00
35	Specs Toporcer	1.00
36	Jackie Hayes	1.00
37	Walter Johnson	5.00
38	Lefty Grove	1.00
39	Eddie Collins	1.00
40	Buck Weaver	7.50
41	Cozy Dolan	1.00
42	Emil Meusel	1.00
43	Bob Meusel	1.00
44	Lefty Gomez	1.00

45	Rube Marquard	1.00
46	Jeff Tesreau	1.00
47	Joe Heving	1.00
48	John Heving	1.00
49	Rick Ferrell	1.00
50	Wes Ferrell	1.00
51	Bill Wambsganss	1.00
52	Ben Chapman	1.00
53	Joe Sewell	1.00
54	Luke Sewell	1.00
55	Odell Hale	1.00
56	Sammy Hale	1.00
57	Earle Mack	1.00
58	Connie Mack	1.00
59	Rube Walberg	1.00
60	Mule Haas	1.00
61	Paul Waner	1.00
62	Lloyd Waner	1.00
63	Pie Traynor	1.00
64	Honus Wagner	2.00
65	Joe Cronin	1.00
66	Joe Harris	1.00
67	Dave Harris	1.00
68	Bucky Harris	1.00
69	Alex Gaston	1.00
70	Milt Gaston	1.00
71	Casey Stengel	1.00
72	Amos Rusie	1.00
73	Mickey Welch	1.00
74	Roger Bresnahan	1.00
75	Jesse Burkett	1.00
76	Harry Heilmann	1.00
77	Heinie Manush	1.00
78	Charlie Gehringer	1.00
79	Hank Greenberg	2.00
80	Jimmie Foxx	4.00
81	Al Simmons	1.00
82	Eddie Plank	1.00
83	George Sisler	1.00
84	Joe Medwick	1.00
85	Mel Ott	1.00
86	Hack Wilson	1.00
87	Jimmy Wilson	1.00
88	Chuck Klein	1.00
89	Gabby Hartnett	1.00
90	Henie Groh	1.00
91	Ping Bodie	1.00
92	Ted Lyons	1.00
93	Jack Quinn	1.00
94	Oscar Roettger	1.00
95	Wally Roettger	1.00
96	Bubbles Hargrave	1.00
97	Pinky Hargrave	1.00
98	Sam Crawford	1.00
99	Gee Walker	1.00
100	Homer Summa	1.00

1983 Sporting News Conlon Collection Prototypes

Unlike the issued cards which were in a large format, these prototypes are in standard 2-1/2" x 3-1/2" size. Fronts are printed in sepia. Black-and-white backs have player data, career summary and stats up to the date the photo was taken. Backs also have the TSN Conlon Collection logo and a Market-com copyright.

		NM/M
Complete Set (5):		7.50
Common Player:		1.00
83-1	Lewis (Hack) Wilson	2.00
83-2	Joe Cronin	2.00
82-3	Walter (Barney) Johnson	3.00
83-4	Paul (Daffy) Dean	2.00
83-5	Connie Mack	2.00

1983 Sporting News Conlon Collection

This set was issued to mark the 50th anniversary of the first All-Star game in 1933. Besides the American and National League players who made up those teams, the set includes a group of all-stars from the Negro Leagues. The oversize (4-1/2" x 6-1/8") cards were sold only as complete sets. The cards feature sepia player photos on front, with a facsimile autograph and appropriate commemorative labeling. Black-and-white backs feature 1933 stats, an anecdote about the player, and the logos of appropriate parties in the set's marketing. The major leaguers' photos were the work of Charles M. Conlon, while the Black ballplayers' pictures were garnered from a variety of sources.

		NM/M
Complete Set (60):		20.00
Common Player:		.25
1	Jimmie Foxx	.50
2	Heinie Manush	.25
3	Lou Gehrig	2.50
4	Al Simmons	.25
5	Charlie Gehringer	.25
6	Luke Appling	.25
7	Mickey Cochrane	.25
8	Joe Kuhel	.25
9	Bill Dickey	.40
10	Pinky Higgins	.25
11	Roy Johnson	.25
12	Ben Chapman	.25
13	Johnny Hodapp	.25
14	Joe Cronin	.25
15	Evar Swanson	.25
16	Earl Averill	.25
17	Babe Ruth	4.00
18	Tony Lazzeri	.40
19	Alvin Crowder	.25
20	Lefty Grove	.25
21	Earl Whitehill	.25
22	Lefty Gomez	.25
23	Mel Harder	.25
24	Tommy Bridges	.25
25	Chuck Klein	.25
26	Spud Davis	.25
27	Riggs Stephenson	.25
28	Tony Piet	.25
29	Bill Terry	.25
30	Wes Schulmerich	.25
31a	Pepper Martin (Teeth don't show.)	.25
31b	Pepper Martin (Teeth show.)	.25
32	Arky Vaughan	.25
33	Wally Berger	.25
34	Rip Collins	.25
35	Fred Lindstrom	.25
36	Chick Fullis	.25
37	Paul Waner	.25
38	Johnny Frederick	.25
39	Joe Medwick	.25
40	Pie Traynor	.25
41	Frank Frisch	.25
42	Chick Hafey	.25
43	Carl Hubbell	.25
44	Guy Bush	.25
45	Dizzy Dean	.40
46	Hal Schumacher	.25
47	Larry French	.25
48	Lon Warneke	.25
49	Cool Papa Bell	.25
50	Oscar Charleston	.25
51	Josh Gibson	.50
52	Satchel Paige	1.00
53	Dave Malarcher	.25
54	Pop Lloyd	.25
55	Rube Foster	.25
56	Buck Leonard	.40
57	Smoky Joe Williams	.25
58	Willie Wells	.40
59	Judy Johnson	.25
60	Martin DiHigo	.25

1984 Sporting News Conlon Collection

This 60-card set, mostly Hall of Famers, was produced in conjunction with the Smithsonian Institution's "Baseball Immortals" photo exhibition

of the work of Charles Martin Conlon. The oversize (4-1/2" x 6-1/8") cards have sepia-toned photos on front; backs are printed in black-and-white. The issue was initially sold only as a complete set.

		NM/M
Complete Set (60):		35.00
Common Player:		.25
1	Grover Cleveland Alexander	.60
2	Chief Bender	.25
3a	Fred Clarke (Jack Coombs front.)	1.50
3b	Fred Clarke (Correct front.)	.40
4	Ty Cobb	1.25
5	Ty Cobb	1.25
6	Ty Cobb	1.25
7	Ty Cobb	1.25
8	Mickey Cochrane	.25
9a	Jack Coombs (Fred Clarke front.)	1.50
9b	Jack Coombs (Correct front.)	.40
10	Charles & Margie Conlon	.25
11	Charles Conlon	.25
12	Joe Cronin	.60
13	Dizzy Dean	.60
14	Leo Durocher	.25
15	Jimmie Foxx	.40
16	The Gashouse Gang (Frank Frisch, Mike Gonzalez, Buzzy Wares)	.25
17	Lou Gehrig	1.75
18	Lou Gehrig	1.75
19	Lou Gehrig	1.75
20	Lou Gehrig	1.75
21	Charlie Gehringer	.25
22	Lefty Gomez	.25
23	Lefty Grove	.25
24	Bucky Harris	.25
25	Harry Heilmann	.25
26	Rogers Hornsby	.40
27	Waite Hoyt	.25
28	Carl Hubbell	.25
29	Miller Huggins	.25
30	Walter Johnson	.60
31	Bill Klem	.25
32	Connie Mack	.25
33	Heinie Manush	.25
34	Rube Marquard	.25
35	Pepper Martin	.25
36	Christy Mathewson	.60
37	Christy Mathewson	.60
38	Christy Mathewson	.60
39	Joe McCarthy	.25
40	John McGraw	.25
41	Fred Merkle	.25
42	Mel Ott	.25
43	Roger Peckinpaugh	.25
44	Herb Pennock	.25
45	Babe Ruth	2.25
46	Babe Ruth	2.25
47	Babe Ruth	2.25
48	Babe Ruth	2.25
49	Babe Ruth	2.25
50	Babe Ruth	2.25
51	Al Simmons	.25
52	Tris Speaker	.40
53	Casey Stengel	.25
54	Bill Terry	.25
55	Pie Traynor	.25
56	Rube Waddell	.25
57	Honus Wagner	1.00
58	Lloyd Waner, Paul Waner	.25
59	Paul Waner	.25
60	Hack Wilson	.25

1981 Sportrait Hall of Fame

This collectors' issue feature portrait art by Stan Sypulski in a blank-back 3-1/2" x 5" format. Portraits have a color frame line and are numbered.

		NM/M
Complete Set (25):		55.00
Common Player:		2.00
1	Honus Wagner	4.00

2	Miller Huggins	2.00
3	Babe Ruth	6.00
4	Connie Mack	2.00
5	Ty Cobb	5.00
6	Lou Gehrig	5.00
7	Eddie Collins	2.00
8	Chuck Klein	2.00
9	Ted Williams	5.00
10	Jimmy Foxx	3.00
11	Frank Baker	2.00
12	Nap Lajoie	2.00
13	Casey Stengel	2.00
14	Joe DiMaggio	5.00
15	Mickey Mantle	6.00
16	Frank Frisch	2.00
17	Bill Terry	2.00
18	Jackie Robinson	5.00
19	Sam Rice	2.00
20	Mickey Cochrane	2.00
21	George Sisler	2.00
22	Bob Feller	3.00
23	Walter Johnson	3.00
24	Tris Speaker	3.00
---	Checklist	2.00

1984 Sports Design Products Doug West

The art of Doug West is featured in portrait and action pictures on each card in this collectors set. The player art is on a blue background. In the white border at bottom a red box displays the player name and position in white. The producer's logo is in black at bottom-right. Backs are printed in red and blue on white with personal data, career summary and stats. Production was reported as 5,000 sets, including 250 uncut sheets. Issue price was about $10.

		NM/M
Complete Set (24):		15.00
Common Player:		.50
1	Jackie Robinson	1.25
2	Luis Aparicio	.50
3	Roberto Clemente	3.00
4	Mickey Mantle	5.00
5	Joe DiMaggio	3.00
6	Willie Stargell	.50
7	Brooks Robinson	.60
8	Ty Cobb	1.50
9	Don Drysdale	.50
10	Bob Feller	.50
11	Stan Musial	1.00
12	Al Kaline	.50
13	Willie Mays	1.75
14	Willie McCovey	.50
15	Thurman Munson	.75
16	Charlie Gehringer	.50
17	Eddie Mathews	.50
18	Carl Yastrzemski	.50
19	Warren Spahn	.50
20	Ted Williams	2.00
21	Ernie Banks	.60
22	Roy Campanella	.75
23	Harmon Killebrew	.50
24	Duke Snider	.75

1985 Sports Design Products Doug West

The art of Doug West is featured in portrait and action pictures on each card in this collectors' set. In the white border at bottom a blue box displays the player name and position in white. The producer's logo is in black at bottom-right. Backs are printed in red and blue on white with personal data, career summary and stats. Cards are numbered sequentially from the previous year's issue. Be-

---

TED KLUSZEWSKI FIRST BASE

sides 5,000 complete sets (issued at $8), 250 uncut sheets were also sold.

		NM/M
Complete Set (24):		7.50
Common Player:		.25
25	Lou Gehrig	1.00
26	Hoyt Wilhelm	.25
27	Enos Slaughter	.25
28	Lou Brock	.25
29	Mickey Cochrane	.25
30	Gil Hodges	.50
31	Yogi Berra	.50
32	Carl Hubbell	.50
33	Hank Greenberg	.50
34	Casey Stengel	.50
35	Pee Wee Reese	.35
36	Ralph Kiner	.25
37	Satchel Paige	.50
38	Richie Ashburn	.35
39	Connie Mack	.25
40	Dick Groat	.25
41	Tony Oliva	.25
42	Honus Wagner	.40
43	Denny McLain	.25
44	Johnny Mize	.25
45	Bob Lemon	.25
46	Fergie Jenkins	.25
47	Babe Ruth	2.00
48	Ted Kluszewski	.35

1997 Sports Illustrated

Fleer teamed up with Sports Illustrated to produce a 180-card World Series Fever set. The regular set is divided into six different subsets: 96 Player Cards, 27 Fresh Faces, 18 Inside Baseball, 18 SIber Vision, 12 covers and 9 Newsmakers. Inserts included the Extra Edition parallel set, Great Shots, Cooperstown Collection and Autographed Mini-Cover Redemption Cards. Cards were sold in six-card packs for $1.99 each.

		NM/M
Complete Set (180):		20.00
Common Player:		.05
Extra Edition Stars:		8X
Pack (6):		1.25
Wax Box (24):		20.00
1	Bob Abreu (Fresh Faces)	.10
2	Jaime Bluma (Fresh Faces)	.05
3	Emil Brown (Fresh Faces)	.05
4	Jose Cruz, Jr. (Fresh Faces)	.05
5	Jason Dickson (Fresh Faces)	.05
6	Nomar Garciaparra (Fresh Faces)	1.00
7	Todd Greene (Fresh Faces)	.05
8	Vladimir Guerrero (Fresh Faces)	.75
9	Wilton Guerrero (Fresh Faces)	.05
10	Jose Guillen (Fresh Faces)	.05

11	Hideki Irabu (Fresh Faces)	.05
12	Russ Johnson (Fresh Faces)	.05
13	Andruw Jones (Fresh Faces)	.75
14	Damon Mashore (Fresh Faces)	.05
15	Jason McDonald (Fresh Faces)	.05
16	Ryan McGuire (Fresh Faces)	.05
17	Matt Morris (Fresh Faces)	.05
18	Kevin Orie (Fresh Faces)	.05
19	Dante Powell (Fresh Faces)	.05
20	Pokey Reese (Fresh Faces)	.05
21	Joe Roa (Fresh Faces)	.05
22	Scott Rolen (Fresh Faces)	.65
23	Glendon Rusch (Fresh Faces)	.05
24	Scott Spiezio (Fresh Faces)	.05
25	Bubba Trammell (Fresh Faces)	.05
26	Todd Walker (Fresh Faces)	.05
27	Jamey Wright (Fresh Faces)	.05
28	Ken Griffey Jr. (Season Highlights)	.75
29	Tino Martinez (Season Highlights)	.05
30	Roger Clemens (Season Highlights)	.65
31	Hideki Irabu (Season Highlights)	.05
32	Kevin Brown (Season Highlights)	.05
33	Chipper Jones, Cal Ripken Jr. (Season Highlights)	.65
34	Sandy Alomar (Season Highlights)	.05
35	Ken Caminiti (Season Highlights)	.05
36	Randy Johnson (Season Highlights)	.40
37	Andy Ashby (Inside Baseball)	.05
38	Jay Buhner (Inside Baseball)	.05
39	Joe Carter (Inside Baseball)	.05
40	Darren Daulton (Inside Baseball)	.05
41	Jeff Fassero (Inside Baseball)	.05
42	Andres Galarraga (Inside Baseball)	.05
43	Rusty Greer (Inside Baseball)	.05
44	Marquis Grissom (Inside Baseball)	.05
45	Joey Hamilton (Inside Baseball)	.05
46	Jimmy Key (Inside Baseball)	.05
47	Ryan Klesko (Inside Baseball)	.05
48	Eddie Murray (Inside Baseball)	.75
49	Charles Nagy (Inside Baseball)	.05
50	Dave Nilsson (Inside Baseball)	.05
51	Ricardo Rincon (Inside Baseball)	.05
52	Billy Wagner (Inside Baseball)	.05
53	Dan Wilson (Inside Baseball)	.05
54	Dmitri Young (Inside Baseball)	.05
55	Roberto Alomar (S.I.BER Vision)	.30
56	Sandy Alomar Jr. (S.I.BER Vision)	.05
57	Scott Brosius (S.I.BER Vision)	.05
58	Tony Clark (S.I.BER Vision)	.05
59	Carlos Delgado (S.I.BER Vision)	.45
60	Jermaine Dye (S.I.BER Vision)	.05
61	Darin Erstad (S.I.BER Vision)	.20
62	Derek Jeter (S.I.BER Vision)	1.00
63	Jason Kendall (S.I.BER Vision)	.05
64	Hideo Nomo (S.I.BER Vision)	.20
65	Rey Ordonez (S.I.BER Vision)	.05
66	Andy Pettitte (S.I.BER Vision)	.10
67	Manny Ramirez (S.I.BER Vision)	.75
68	Edgar Renteria (S.I.BER Vision)	.05
69	Shane Reynolds (S.I.BER Vision)	.05

70	Alex Rodriguez (S.I.BER Vision)	1.00
71	Ivan Rodriguez (S.I.BER Vision)	.65
72	Jose Rosado (S.I.BER Vision)	.05
73	John Smoltz	.05
74	Tom Glavine	.35
75	Greg Maddux	1.00
76	Chipper Jones	1.00
77	Kenny Lofton	.05
78	Fred McGriff	.05
79	Kevin Brown	.05
80	Alex Fernandez	.05
81	Al Leiter	.05
82	Bobby Bonilla	.05
83	Gary Sheffield	.40
84	Moises Alou	.05
85	Henry Rodriguez	.05
86	Mark Grudzielanek	.05
87	Pedro Martinez	.05
88	Todd Hundley	.05
89	Bernard Gilkey	.05
90	Bobby Jones	.05
91	Curt Schilling	.35
92	Ricky Bottalico	.05
93	Mike Lieberthal	.05
94	Sammy Sosa	1.00
95	Ryne Sandberg	1.00
96	Mark Grace	.05
97	Deion Sanders	.05
98	Reggie Sanders	.05
99	Barry Larkin	.05
100	Craig Biggio	.05
101	Jeff Bagwell	.75
102	Derek Bell	.05
103	Brian Jordan	.05
104	Ray Lankford	.05
105	Ron Gant	.05
106	Al Martin	.05
107	Kevin Elster	.05
108	Jermaine Allensworth	.05
109	Vinny Castilla	.05
110	Dante Bichette	.05
111	Larry Walker	.05
112	Mike Piazza	1.25
113	Eric Karros	.05
114	Todd Hollandsworth	.05
115	Raul Mondesi	.05
116	Hideo Nomo	.40
117	Ramon Martinez	.05
118	Ken Caminiti	.05
119	Tony Gwynn	1.00
120	Steve Finley	.05
121	Barry Bonds	2.00
122	J.T. Snow	.05
123	Rod Beck	.05
124	Cal Ripken Jr.	2.00
125	Mike Mussina	.30
126	Brady Anderson	.05
127	Bernie Williams	.05
128	Derek Jeter	2.00
129	Tino Martinez	.05
130	Andy Pettitte	.30
131	David Cone	.05
132	Mariano Rivera	.15
133	Roger Clemens	1.00
134	Pat Hentgen	.05
135	Juan Guzman	.05
136	Bob Higginson	.05
137	Tony Clark	.05
138	Travis Fryman	.05
139	Mo Vaughn	.05
140	Tim Naehring	.05
141	John Valentin	.05
142	Matt Williams	.05
143	David Justice	.05
144	Jim Thome	.65
145	Chuck Knoblauch	.05
146	Paul Molitor	.75
147	Marty Cordova	.05
148	Frank Thomas	.85
149	Albert Belle	.05
150	Robin Ventura	.05
151	John Jaha	.05
152	Jeff Cirillo	.05
153	Jose Valentin	.05
154	Jay Bell	.05
155	Jeff King	.05
156	Kevin Appier	.05
157	Ken Griffey Jr.	1.25
158	Alex Rodriguez	1.50
158p	Alex Rodriguez/OPS	1.50
159	Randy Johnson	.75
160	Juan Gonzalez	.40
161	Will Clark	.05
162	Dean Palmer	.05
163	Tim Salmon	.05
164	Jim Edmonds	.05
165	Jim Leyritz	.05
166	Jose Canseco	.40
167	Jason Giambi	.50
168	Mark McGwire	1.50
169	Barry Bonds (Classic Covers)	1.00
170	Alex Rodriguez (Classic Covers)	.75
171	Roger Clemens (Classic Covers)	.65
172	Ken Griffey Jr. (Classic Covers)	.65
173	Greg Maddux (Classic Covers)	.50
174	Mike Piazza (Classic Covers)	.65
175	Will Clark, Mark McGwire (Classic Covers)	1.00

176	Hideo Nomo (Classic Covers)	.20
177	Cal Ripken Jr. (Classic Covers)	1.00
178	Ken Griffey Jr., Frank Thomas (Classic Covers)	.50
179	Alex Rodriguez, Derek Jeter (Classic Covers)	1.50
180	John Wetteland (Classic Covers)	.05
---	Checklist (Jose Cruz Jr.)	.05

Extra Edition

Each of the regular cards in the premiere Fleer SI issue is also found in a parallel set designated on front in gold holographic foil as "Extra Edition." Backs of the cards carry a serial number from within a production of 500 of each card.

	NM/M
Complete Set (180):	150.00
Common Player:	1.00
Extra Edition Stars:	8X

Autographed Mini-Covers

Six different players autographed 250 magazine mini-covers that were available through randomly seeded redemption cards. The players who autographed cards were Hank Aaron, Willie Mays, Frank Robinson, Kirby Puckett, Cal Ripken Jr., and Alex Rodriguez.

		NM/M
Complete Set (6):		300.00
Common Player:		30.00
	Alex Rodriguez	90.00
	Cal Ripken Jr.	90.00
	Kirby Puckett	45.00
	Willie Mays	45.00
	Frank Robinson	30.00
	Hank Aaron	45.00

Box Topper

This special version of A-Rod's card was packaged one per box of foil packs. It was intended to be inserted into die-cuts on the box to create a sample display for the new issue. The card measures 2-1/2" x 4-1/16". The back is in black-and-white with instructions on how to insert the card into the box.

MAJOR LEAGUE BASEBALL

Alex Rodriguez

	NM/M
Alex Rodriguez	4.50

Cooperstown Collection

715 Braves

This 12-card insert (found 1:12 packs) lets collectors relive classic SI baseball covers with a description of each issue on the back.

		NM/M
Complete Set (12):		27.50
Common Player:		2.00
1	Hank Aaron	6.00
2	Yogi Berra	3.00
3	Lou Brock	2.00
4	Rod Carew	2.00
5	Juan Marichal	2.00
6	Al Kaline	2.50
7	Joe Morgan	2.00
8	Brooks Robinson	3.00
9	Willie Stargell	2.00
10	Kirby Puckett	4.00
11	Willie Mays	6.00
12	Frank Robinson	3.00

Great Shots

Ryan Klesko ATLANTA BRAVES

A 25-card insert, found one per pack, designed to highlight Sports Illustrated's classic photography. Each card in the set folds out to a 5" x 7" format to showcase a larger photo.

		NM/M
Complete Set (25):		10.00
Common Player:		.20
(1)	Roberto Alomar	.30
(2)	Andy Ashby	.20
(3)	Albert Belle	.20
(4)	Barry Bonds	2.00
(5)	Jay Buhner	.20
(6)	Vinny Castilla, Andres Galarraga	.20
(7)	Darren Daulton	.20
(8)	Juan Gonzalez	.40
(9)	Ken Griffey Jr.	1.25
(10)	Derek Jeter	2.00
(11)	Randy Johnson	.75
(12)	Chipper Jones	1.00
(13)	Eric Karros	.20

(14)	Ryan Klesko	.20
(15)	Kenny Lofton	.20
(16)	Greg Maddux	1.00
(17)	Mark McGwire	1.50
(18)	Mike Piazza	1.25
(19)	Cal Ripken Jr.	2.00
(20)	Alex Rodriguez	1.50
(21)	Ryne Sandberg	1.00
(22)	Deion Sanders	.30
(23)	John Smoltz	.20
(24)	Frank Thomas	.75
(25)	Mo Vaughn	.20

1998 Sports Illustrated Promo

This sample card was issued to preview the 1998 Sports Illustrated set presented by Fleer. The card is in the same format as the regular issue, but has a different card number and is overprinted "PROMOTIONAL SAMPLE" on front and back.

		NM/M
8	Cal Ripken Jr.	3.00

1998 Sports Illustrated

The second of three Sports Illustrated releases of 1998 from Fleer contained 200 cards and featured exclusive Sports Illustrated photography and commentary. Cards arrived in six-card packs and carried a Sports Illustrated logo in a top corner. The set included a Travis Lee One to Watch cards (#201) that was inserted just before going to press. Subsets included: Baseball's Best (129-148), One to Watch (149-176), and '97 in Review (177-200). Inserts sets include: Extra Edition and First Edition parallels, Autographs, Covers, Editor's Choice and Opening Day Mini Posters.

		NM/M
Complete Set (201):		20.00
Common Player:		.05
Pack (6):		1.50
Wax Box (24):		25.00
1	Edgardo Alfonzo	.05
2	Roberto Alomar	.20
3	Sandy Alomar	.05
4	Moises Alou	.05
5	Brady Anderson	.05
6	Garret Anderson	.05
7	Kevin Appier	.05
8	Jeff Bagwell	.75
9	Jay Bell	.05
10	Albert Belle	.05
11	Dante Bichette	.05
12	Craig Biggio	.05
13	Barry Bonds	2.00
14	Bobby Bonilla	.05
15	Kevin Brown	.05
16	Jay Buhner	.05
17	Ellis Burks	.05
18	Mike Cameron	.05
19	Ken Caminiti	.05
20	Jose Canseco	.45
21	Joe Carter	.05
22	Vinny Castilla	.05
23	Jeff Cirillo	.05
24	Tony Clark	.05
25	Will Clark	.05
26	Roger Clemens	1.00
27	David Cone	.05
28	Jose Cruz Jr.	.05
29	Carlos Delgado	.50
30	Jason Dickson	.05
31	Dennis Eckersley	.65
32	Jim Edmonds	.05
33	Scott Erickson	.05
34	Darin Erstad	.20
35	Shawn Estes	.05
36	Jeff Fassero	.05
37	Alex Fernandez	.05
38	Chuck Finley	.05
39	Steve Finley	.05
40	Travis Fryman	.05
41	Andres Galarraga	.05
42	Ron Gant	.05
43	Nomar Garciaparra	1.00
44	Jason Giambi	.50
45	Tom Glavine	.35
46	Juan Gonzalez	.40
47	Mark Grace	.05
48	Willie Green	.05
49	Rusty Greer	.05
50	Ben Grieve	.05
51	Ken Griffey Jr.	1.25
52	Mark Grudzielanek	.05
53	Vladimir Guerrero	.75
54	Juan Guzman	.05
55	Tony Gwynn	1.00
56	Joey Hamilton	.05
57	Rickey Henderson	.75
58	Pat Hentgen	.05
59	Livan Hernandez	.05
60	Bobby Higginson	.05
61	Todd Hundley	.05
62	Hideki Irabu	.05
63	John Jaha	.05
64	Derek Jeter	2.00
65	Charles Johnson	.05
66	Randy Johnson	.75
67	Andruw Jones	.75
68	Bobby Jones	.05
69	Chipper Jones	1.00
70	Brian Jordan	.05
71	David Justice	.05
72	Eric Karros	.05
73	Jeff Kent	.05
74	Jimmy Key	.05
75	Darryl Kile	.05
76	Jeff King	.05
77	Ryan Klesko	.05
78	Chuck Knoblauch	.05
79	Ray Lankford	.05
80	Barry Larkin	.05
81	Kenny Lofton	.05
82	Greg Maddux	1.00
83	Al Martin	.05
84	Edgar Martinez	.05
85	Pedro Martinez	.75
86	Tino Martinez	.05
87	Mark McGwire	1.50
88	Paul Molitor	.75
89	Raul Mondesi	.05
90	Jamie Moyer	.05
91	Mike Mussina	.30
92	Tim Naehring	.05
93	Charles Nagy	.05
94	Denny Neagle	.05
95	Dave Nilsson	.05
96	Hideo Nomo	.40
97	Rey Ordonez	.05
98	Dean Palmer	.05
99	Rafael Palmeiro	.65
100	Andy Pettitte	.30
101	Mike Piazza	1.25
102	Brad Radke	.05
103	Manny Ramirez	.75
104	Edgar Renteria	.05
105	Cal Ripken Jr.	2.00
106	Alex Rodriguez	1.50
106p	Alex Rodriguez/OPS	1.50
107	Henry Rodriguez	.05
108	Ivan Rodriguez	.65
109	Scott Rolen	.65
110	Tim Salmon	.05
111	Curt Schilling	.35
112	Gary Sheffield	.45
113	John Smoltz	.05
114	J.T. Snow	.05
115	Sammy Sosa	1.00
116	Matt Stairs	.05
117	Shannon Stewart	.05
118	Frank Thomas	.75
119	Jim Thome	.65
120	Justin Thompson	.05
121	Mo Vaughn	.05
122	Robin Ventura	.05
123	Larry Walker	.05
124	Rondell White	.05
125	Bernie Williams	.05
126	Matt Williams	.05
127	Tony Womack	.05
128	Jaret Wright	.05
129	Edgar Renteria (Baseball's Best)	.05
130	Kenny Lofton (Baseball's Best)	.05
131	Tony Gwynn (Baseball's Best)	.50
132	Mark McGwire (Baseball's Best)	.75
133	Craig Biggio (Baseball's Best)	.05
134	Charles Johnson (Baseball's Best)	.05
135	J.T. Snow (Baseball's Best)	.05
136	Ken Caminiti (Baseball's Best)	.05
137	Vladimir Guerrero (Baseball's Best)	.40
138	Jim Edmonds (Baseball's Best)	.05
139	Randy Johnson (Baseball's Best)	.40
140	Darryl Kile (Baseball's Best)	.05
141	John Smoltz (Baseball's Best)	.05
142	Greg Maddux (Baseball's Best)	.50
143	Andy Pettitte (Baseball's Best)	.05
144	Ken Griffey Jr. (Baseball's Best)	.65
145	Mike Piazza (Baseball's Best)	.65
146	Todd Greene (Baseball's Best)	.05
147	Vinny Castilla (Baseball's Best)	.05
148	Derek Jeter (Baseball's Best)	1.00
149	Robert Machado (One to Watch)	.05
150	Mike Gulan (One to Watch)	.05
151	Randall Simon (One to Watch)	.05
152	Michael Coleman (One to Watch)	.05
153	Brian Rose (One to Watch)	.05
154	Scott Eyre RC (One to Watch)	.05
155	Magglio Ordonez RC (One to Watch)	1.50
156	Todd Helton (One to Watch)	.65
157	Juan Encarnacion (One to Watch)	.05
158	Mark Kotsay (One to Watch)	.05
159	Josh Booty (One to Watch)	.05
160	Melvin Rosario RC (One to Watch)	.05
161	Shane Halter (One to Watch)	.05
162	Paul Konerko (One to Watch)	.25
163	Henry Blanco RC (One to Watch)	.05
164	Antone Williamson (One to Watch)	.05
165	Brad Fullmer (One to Watch)	.05
166	Ricky Ledee (One to Watch)	.05
167	Ben Grieve (One to Watch)	.05
168	Frank Catalanotto RC (One to Watch)	.25
169	Bobby Estalella (One to Watch)	.05
170	Dennis Reyes (One to Watch)	.05
171	Kevin Polcovich (One to Watch)	.05
172	Jacob Cruz (One to Watch)	.05
173	Ken Cloude (One to Watch)	.05
174	Eli Marrero (One to Watch)	.05
175	Fernando Tatis (One to Watch)	.05
176	Tom Evans (One to Watch)	.05
177	Carl Everett, Nomar Garciaparra (97 in Review)	.35
178	Eric Davis (97 in Review)	.05
179	Roger Clemens (97 in Review)	.60
180	Brett Butler, Eddie Murray (97 in Review)	.30
181	Frank Thomas (97 in Review)	.45
182	Curt Schilling (97 in Review)	.15
183	Jeff Bagwell (97 in Review)	.40
184	Mark McGwire, Ken Griffey Jr. (97 in Review)	.75
185	Kevin Brown (97 in Review)	.05
186	Marty Cordova, Ricardo Rincon (97 in Review)	.05
187	Charles Johnson (97 in Review)	.05
188	Hideki Irabu (97 in Review)	.05
189	Tony Gwynn (97 in Review)	.50
190	Sandy Alomar (97 in Review)	.05
191	Ken Griffey Jr. (97 in Review)	.65
192	Larry Walker (97 in Review)	.05
193	Roger Clemens (97 in Review)	.60
194	Pedro Martinez (97 in Review)	.40
195	Nomar Garciaparra (97 in Review)	.60
196	Scott Rolen (97 in Review)	.40
197	Brian Anderson (97 in Review)	.05
198	Tony Saunders (97 in Review)	.05
199	Florida Celebration (97 in Review)	.05
200	Livan Hernandez (97 in Review)	.05
201	Travis Lee/SP (One to Watch)	2.00

Extra Edition

Extra Edition is a 201-card parallel set that includes a holofoil stamp on the front and sequential numbering to 250 on the back. There is also a First Edition version of these that was identical on the front, but contains the text "The Only 1 of 1 First Edition" in purple lettering on the card back.

	NM/M
Common Player:	2.00
Extra Edition Stars:	8X

Autographs

This six-card insert features autographs of players. The Konerko and Grieve cards were available through redemptions until Nov. 1, 1999.

	NM/M
Common Player:	7.50
Lou Brock/500	40.00
Jose Cruz Jr./250	10.00
Rollie Fingers/500	10.00
Ben Grieve/250 (Exchange Card)	3.00
Ben Grieve (Signed Card)	7.50
Paul Konerko/250 (Exchange Card)	3.00
Paul Konerko (Signed Card)	20.00
Brooks Robinson/250	50.00

Covers

This 10-card insert set pictures actual Sports Illustrated covers on trading cards. The cards are numbered with a "C" prefix and inserted one per nine packs.

		NM/M
Complete Set (10):		15.00
Common Player:		1.00
Inserted 1:9		
1	Ken Griffey Jr., Mike Piazza	2.00
2	Derek Jeter	3.00
3	Ken Griffey Jr.	2.50
4	Cal Ripken Jr.	3.00
5	Manny Ramirez	1.50
6	Jay Buhner	1.00
7	Matt Williams	1.00
8	Randy Johnson	1.50
9	Deion Sanders	1.50
10	Jose Canseco	1.50

Editor's Choice

Editor's Choice includes 10 top players in 1998 as profiled by the editors of Sports Illustrated. Cards are numbered with an "EC" prefix and seeded one per 24 packs.

		NM/M
Complete Set (10):		20.00
Common Player:		1.00
Inserted 1:24		
1	Ken Griffey Jr.	3.00
2	Alex Rodriguez	4.00
3	Frank Thomas	1.50
4	Mark McGwire	4.00
5	Greg Maddux	2.00
6	Derek Jeter	5.00
7	Cal Ripken Jr.	5.00
8	Nomar Garciaparra	2.50
9	Jeff Bagwell	1.50
10	Jose Cruz Jr.	1.00

Mini-Posters

Thirty 5" x 7" mini-posters were available at a rate of one per pack. The posters took the top player or two from each team and added their 1998 schedule. Backs were blank so the cards are numbered on the front with an "OD" prefix.

		NM/M
Complete Set (30):		8.00
Common Player:		.10
Inserted 1:1		
1	Tim Salmon	.10
2	Travis Lee	.10
3	John Smoltz, Greg Maddux	.50
4	Cal Ripken Jr.	1.00
5	Nomar Garciaparra	.50
6	Sammy Sosa	.50
7	Frank Thomas	.45
8	Barry Larkin	.10
9	David Justice	.10
10	Larry Walker	.10
11	Tony Clark	.10
12	Livan Hernandez	.10
13	Jeff Bagwell	.45
14	Kevin Appier	.10
15	Mike Piazza	.65
16	Fernando Vina	.10
17	Chuck Knoblauch	.10
18	Vladimir Guerrero	.45
19	Rey Ordonez	.10
20	Bernie Williams	.10
22	Matt Stairs	.10
22	Curt Schilling	.30
23	Tony Womack	.10
24	Mark McGwire	.75
25	Tony Gwynn	.50
26	Barry Bonds	1.00
27	Ken Griffey Jr.	.65
28	Fred McGriff	.10
29	Juan Gonzalez, Alex Rodriguez	.50
30	Roger Clemens	.60

Then & Now

Then and Now was the first of three Sports Illustrated baseball releases in 1998. It contained 150 cards and sold in six-card packs, with five cards and a mini-poster. Fronts carried photos of active and retired players, as well as rookies. There was only one subset - A Place in History (#37-53) - which compares statistics between current players and retired greats. The product arrived with an Extra Edition parallel set, Art of the Game, Autograph Redemptions, Covers and Great Shots inserts. There was also an Alex Rodriguez checklist / mini-poster seeded every 12th pack.

		NM/M
Complete Set (150):		15.00
Common Player:		.05
Extra Edition Stars:		6X
Production 500 Sets		
Pack (5):		1.00
Wax Box (24):		16.00
1	Luis Aparicio (Legends of the Game)	.05
2	Richie Ashburn (Legends of the Game)	.05
3	Ernie Banks (Legends of the Game)	.50
4	Yogi Berra (Legends of the Game)	.50
5	Lou Boudreau (Legends of the Game)	.05
6	Lou Brock (Legends of the Game)	.15
7	Jim Bunning (Legends of the Game)	.05
8	Rod Carew (Legends of the Game)	.15
9	Bob Feller (Legends of the Game)	.25
10	Rollie Fingers (Legends of the Game)	.05
11	Bob Gibson (Legends of the Game)	.15
12	Fergie Jenkins (Legends of the Game)	.05
13	Al Kaline (Legends of the Game)	.25
14	George Kell (Legends of the Game)	.05
15	Harmon Killebrew (Legends of the Game)	.25
16	Ralph Kiner (Legends of the Game)	.05
17	Tommy Lasorda (Legends of the Game)	.05
18	Juan Maricha l (Legends of the Game)	.05
19	Eddie Mathews (Legends of the Game)	.25
20	Willie Mays (Legends of the Game)	1.00
21	Willie McCovey (Legends of the Game)	.05
22	Joe Morgan (Legends of the Game)	.15
23	Gaylord Perry (Legends of the Game)	.05
24	Kirby Puckett (Legends of the Game)	1.00

25	Pee Wee Reese (Legends of the Game)	.25	
26	Phil Rizzuto (Legends of the Game)	.25	
27	Robin Roberts (Legends of the Game)	.05	
28	Brooks Robinson (Legends of the Game)	.35	
29	Frank Robinson (Legends of the Game)	.35	
30	Red Schoendienst (Legends of the Game)	.05	
31	Enos Slaughter (Legends of the Game)	.05	
32	Warren Spahn (Legends of the Game)	.25	
33	Willie Stargell (Legends of the Game)	.15	
34	Earl Weaver (Legends of the Game)	.05	
35	Billy Williams (Legends of the Game)	.15	
36	Early Wynn (Legends of the Game)	.05	
37	Rickey Henderson (A Place in History)	.75	
38	Greg Maddux (A Place in History)	1.00	
39	Mike Mussina (A Place in History)	.40	
40	Cal Ripken Jr. (A Place in History)	2.00	
41	Albert Belle (A Place in History)	.05	
42	Frank Thomas (A Place in History)	.75	
43	Jeff Bagwell (A Place in History)	.75	
44	Paul Molitor (A Place in History)	.75	
45	Chuck Knoblauch (A Place in History)	.05	
46	Todd Hundley (A Place in History)	.05	
47	Bernie Williams (A Place in History)	.05	
48	Tony Gwynn (A Place in History)	1.00	
49	Barry Bonds (A Place in History)	2.00	
50	Ken Griffey Jr. (A Place in History)	1.25	
51	Randy Johnson (A Place in History)	.75	
52	Mark McGwire (A Place in History)	1.50	
53	Roger Clemens (A Place in History)	1.00	
54	Jose Cruz Jr. (A Place in History)	.05	
55	Roberto Alomar (Legends of Today)	.20	
56	Sandy Alomar (Legends of Today)	.05	
57	Brady Anderson (Legends of Today)	.05	
58	Kevin Appier (Legends of Today)	.05	
59	Jeff Bagwell (Legends of Today)	.75	
60	Albert Belle (Legends of Today)	.05	
61	Dante Bichette (Legends of Today)	.05	
62	Craig Biggio (Legends of Today)	.05	
63	Barry Bonds (Legends of Today)	2.00	
64	Kevin Brown (Legends of Today)	.05	
65	Jay Buhner (Legends of Today)	.05	
66	Ellis Burks (Legends of Today)	.05	
67	Ken Caminiti (Legends of Today)	.05	
68	Jose Canseco (Legends of Today)	.50	
69	Joe Carter (Legends of Today)	.05	
70	Vinny Castilla (Legends of Today)	.05	
71	Tony Clark (Legends of Today)	.05	
72	Roger Clemens (Legends of Today)	1.00	
73	David Cone (Legends of Today)	.05	
74	Jose Cruz Jr. (Legends of Today)	.05	
75	Jason Dickson (Legends of Today)	.05	
76	Jim Edmonds (Legends of Today)	.05	
77	Scott Erickson (Legends of Today)	.05	
78	Darin Erstad (Legends of Today)	.20	
79	Alex Fernandez (Legends of Today)	.05	
80	Steve Finley (Legends of Today)	.05	
81	Travis Fryman (Legends of Today)	.05	
82	Andres Galarraga (Legends of Today)	.05	
83	Nomar Garciaparra (Legends of Today)	1.00	
84	Tom Glavine (Legends of Today)	.35	
85	Juan Gonzalez (Legends of Today)	.40	
86	Mark Grace (Legends of Today)	.05	
87	Willie Greene (Legends of Today)	.05	
88	Ken Griffey Jr. (Legends of Today)	1.25	
89	Vladimir Guerrero (Legends of Today)	.75	
90	Tony Gwynn (Legends of Today)	1.00	
91	Livan Hernandez (Legends of Today)	.05	
92	Bobby Higginson (Legends of Today)	.05	
93	Derek Jeter (Legends of Today)	2.00	
94	Charles Johnson (Legends of Today)	.05	
95	Randy Johnson (Legends of Today)	.75	
96	Andruw Jones (Legends of Today)	.75	
97	Chipper Jones (Legends of Today)	1.00	
98	David Justice (Legends of Today)	.05	
99	Eric Karros (Legends of Today)	.05	
100	Jason Kendall (Legends of Today)	.05	
101	Jimmy Key (Legends of Today)	.05	
102	Darryl Kile (Legends of Today)	.05	
103	Chuck Knoblauch (Legends of Today)	.05	
104	Ray Lankford (Legends of Today)	.05	
105	Barry Larkin (Legends of Today)	.05	
106	Kenny Lofton (Legends of Today)	.05	
107	Greg Maddux (Legends of Today)	1.00	
108	Al Martin (Legends of Today)	.05	
109	Edgar Martinez (Legends of Today)	.05	
110	Pedro Martinez (Legends of Today)	.75	
111	Ramon Martinez (Legends of Today)	.05	
112	Tino Martinez (Legends of Today)	.05	
113	Mark McGwire (Legends of Today)	1.50	
114	Raul Mondesi (Legends of Today)	.05	
115	Matt Morris (Legends of Today)	.05	
116	Charles Nagy (Legends of Today)	.05	
117	Denny Neagle (Legends of Today)	.05	
118	Hideo Nomo (Legends of Today)	.40	
119	Dean Palmer (Legends of Today)	.05	
120	Andy Pettitte (Legends of Today)	.25	
121	Mike Piazza (Legends of Today)	1.25	
122	Manny Ramirez (Legends of Today)	.75	
123	Edgar Renteria (Legends of Today)	.05	
124	Cal Ripken Jr. (Legends of Today)	2.00	
125	Alex Rodriguez (Legends of Today)	1.50	
126	Henry Rodriguez (Legends of Today)	.05	
127	Ivan Rodriguez (Legends of Today)	.65	
128	Scott Rolen (Legends of Today)	.65	
129	Tim Salmon (Legends of Today)	.05	
130	Curt Schilling (Legends of Today)	.35	
131	Gary Sheffield (Legends of Today)	.45	
132	John Smoltz (Legends of Today)	.05	
133	Sammy Sosa (Legends of Today)	1.00	
134	Frank Thomas (Legends of Today)	.75	
135	Jim Thome (Legends of Today)	.65	
136	Mo Vaughn (Legends of Today)	.05	
137	Robin Ventura (Legends of Today)	.05	
138	Larry Walker (Legends of Today)	.05	
139	Bernie Williams (Legends of Today)	.05	
140	Matt Williams (Legends of Today)	.05	
141	Jaret Wright (Legends of Today)	.05	
142	Michael Coleman (Legends of the Future)	.05	
143	Juan Encarnacion (Legends of the Future)	.05	
144	Brad Fullmer (Legends of the Future)	.05	
145	Ben Grieve (Legends of the Future)	.05	
146	Todd Helton (Legends of the Future)	.75	
147	Paul Konerko (Legends of the Future)	.20	
148	Derek Lee (Legends of the Future)	.50	
149	Magglio Ordonez **RC** (Legends of the Future)	1.50	
150	Enrique Wilson (Legends of the Future)	.05	
---	Alex Rodriguez (Checklist)	1.00	

Then & Now Extra Edition

Willie Mays

This 150-card set paralleled the base set and was distinguished by an "Extra Edition" foil stamp on the front. There were 500 sets of Extra Edition and the cards were individually numbered on the back.

	NM/M
Common Extra Edition:	1.00
Extra Edition Stars:	6X
Production 500 Sets	

Then & Now Art of the Game

"Brooks"

Art of the Game was an eight-card insert featuring reproductions of original artwork of current and retired baseball stars done by eight popular sports artists. Cards are numbered with a "AG" prefix and inserted one per nine packs.

		NM/M
Complete Set (8):		11.00
Common Player:		1.00
Inserted 1:9		
1	It's Gone (Ken Griffey Jr.)	1.50
2	Alex Rodriguez	2.00
3	Mike Piazza	1.50
4	Brooks Robinson	1.00
5	David Justice/AS	1.00
6	Cal Ripken Jr.	3.00
7	The Prospect and the Prospector	1.00
8	Barry Bonds	3.00

Then & Now Autographs

Six autograph redemption cards were randomly inserted into packs of Then & Now and

ABBREVIATIONS
AS - All-Star
SP - Short Print

Scott Rolen

could be exchanged prior to Nov. 1, 1999. The signed cards were produced in the following quantities: Clemens 250, Gibson 500, Gwynn 250, Killebrew 500, Mays 250 and Rolen 150. Four of the six cards use the same fronts as the Covers insert; Gibson and Rolen cards each feature unique card fronts.

	NM/M
Common Autograph:	15.00
Redemption Cards: 10%	
Bob Gibson/500	15.00
Tony Gwynn/250	35.00
Roger Clemens/250	120.00
Scott Rolen/150	20.00
Willie Mays/250	90.00
Harmon Killebrew/500	25.00

Then & Now Covers

This 12-card insert features color shots of six actual Sports Illustrated covers, including six current players and six retired players. The cards are numbered with a "C" prefix and were seeded one per 18 packs.

		NM/M
Complete Set (12):		22.00
Common Player:		1.00
Inserted 1:18		
1	Lou Brock (10/16/67)	1.00
2	Kirby Puckett (4/6/92)	2.50
3	Harmon Killebrew (4/8/63 - inside)	1.00
4	Eddie Mathews (8/16/54)	1.00
5	Willie Mays (5/22/72)	2.00
6	Frank Robinson (10/6/69)	1.00
7	Cal Ripken Jr. (9/11/95)	5.00
8	Roger Clemens (5/12/86)	2.50
9	Ken Griffey Jr. (10/16/95)	3.00
10	Mark McGwire (6/1/92)	4.00
11	Tony Gwynn (7/28/97)	2.50
12	Ivan Rodriguez (8/11/97)	1.50

Then & Now Great Shots!

This 25-card set featured 5" x 7" fold-out mini-posters using Sports Illustrated photos. Great Shots were inserted one per pack and contained a mix of retired and current players.

		NM/M
Complete Set (25):		7.50
Common Player:		.10
Inserted 1:1		
1	Ken Griffey Jr.	.65
2	Frank Thomas	.45
3	Alex Rodriguez	.75
4	Andruw Jones	.45
5	Chipper Jones	.50

NOMAR GARCIAPARRA BOSTON RED SOX

6	Cal Ripken Jr.	1.00
7	Mark McGwire	.75
8	Derek Jeter	1.00
9	Greg Maddux	.50
10	Jeff Bagwell	.45
11	Mike Piazza	.65
12	Scott Rolen	.35
13	Nomar Garciaparra	.50
14	Jose Cruz Jr.	.10
15	Charles Johnson	.05
16	Fergie Jenkins	.10
17	Lou Brock	.10
18	Bob Gibson	.10
19	Harmon Killebrew	.10
20	Juan Marichal	.10
21	Brooks Robinson	.10
22	Rod Carew	.10
23	Yogi Berra	.25
24	Willie Mays	.10
25	Kirby Puckett	.50

Then & Now Road to Cooperstown

Road to Cooperstown features 10 current players who are having Hall of Fame careers. The insert name is printed across the back in bold, gold letters. Cards are numbered with a "RC" prefix and were inserted one per 24 packs.

		NM/M
Complete Set (10):		10.00
Common Player:		.75
Inserted 1:24		
1	Barry Bonds	2.50
2	Roger Clemens	1.25
3	Ken Griffey Jr.	1.50
4	Tony Gwynn	1.00
5	Rickey Henderson	.75
6	Greg Maddux	1.00
7	Paul Molitor	.75
8	Mike Piazza	1.50
9	Cal Ripken Jr.	2.50
10	Frank Thomas	.75

World Series Fever

ANDRUW JONES OUTFIELD

The third and final Sports Illustrated release of 1998 contained 150 cards and focused on the World Series while recapping memorable moments from the season. The set also included many stars of tomorrow, like Kerry Wood, Orlando Hernandez, Ben Grieve and Travis Lee. Once again, all the photos were taken from Sports Illustrated archives. The set has two subsets - 10 Magnificent Moments and 20 Cover Collection. The set is paralleled twice in Extra and First Edition parallel sets, and has three insert sets - MVP Collection, Reggie Jackson's Picks and Autumn Excellence.

		NM/M
Complete Set (150):		10.00
Common Player:		.05
Pack (6):		1.00
Wax Box (24):		17.50
1	Mickey Mantle (Covers)	1.50
2	1957 World Series Preview (Covers)	.15
3	1958 World Series Preview (Covers)	.15
4	1959 World Series Preview (Covers)	.15
5	1962 World Series (Covers)	.10
6	Lou Brock (Covers)	.10
7	Brooks Robinson (Covers)	.25
8	Frank Robinson (Covers)	.25
9	1974 World Series (Covers)	.10
10	Reggie Jackson (Covers)	.60
11	1985 World Series (Covers)	.10
12	1987 World Series (Covers)	.10
13	Orel Hershiser (Covers)	.05
14	Rickey Henderson (Covers)	.40
15	1991 World Series (Covers)	.10
16	1992 World Series (Covers)	.05
17	Joe Carter (Covers)	.05
18	1995 World Series (Covers)	.10
19	1996 World Series (Covers)	.15
20	Edgar Renteria (Covers)	.05
21	Bill Mazeroski (Magnificent Moments)	.15
22	Joe Carter (Magnificent Moments)	.05
23	Carlton Fisk (Magnificent Moments)	.40
24	Bucky Dent (Magnificent Moments)	.15
25	Mookie Wilson (Magnificent Moments)	.05
26	Enos Slaughter (Magnificent Moments)	.05
27	Mickey Lolich (Magnificent Moments)	.05
28	Bobby Richardson (Magnificent Moments)	.05
29	Kirk Gibson (Magnificent Moments)	.05
30	Edgar Renteria (Magnificent Moments)	.05
31	Albert Belle	.05
32	Kevin Brown	.05
33	Brian Rose	.05
34	Ron Gant	.05
35	Jeromy Burnitz	.05
36	Andres Galarraga	.05
37	Jim Edmonds	.05
38	Jose Cruz Jr.	.05
39	Mark Grudzielanek	.05
40	Shawn Estes	.05
41	Mark Grace	.05
42	Nomar Garciaparra	.50
43	Juan Gonzalez	.20
44	Tom Glavine	.25
45	Brady Anderson	.05
46	Tony Clark	.05
47	Jeff Cirillo	.05
48	Dante Bichette	.05
49	Ben Grieve	.05
50	Ken Griffey Jr.	.65
51	Edgardo Alfonzo	.05
52	Roger Clemens	.60
53	Pat Hentgen	.05
54	Todd Helton	.30
55	Andy Benes	.05
56	Tony Gwynn	.50
57	Andruw Jones	.40
58	Bobby Higginson	.05
59	Bobby Jones	.05
60	Darryl Kile	.05
61	Chan Ho Park	.05
62	Charles Johnson	.05
63	Rusty Greer	.05
64	Travis Fryman	.05
65	Derek Jeter	1.00
66	Jay Buhner	.05
67	Chuck Knoblauch	.05
68	David Justice	.05
69	Brian Hunter	.05
70	Eric Karros	.05
71	Edgar Martinez	.05
72	Chipper Jones	.50

73	Barry Larkin	.05
74	Mike Lansing	.05
75	Craig Biggio	.05
76	Al Martin	.05
77	Barry Bonds	1.00
78	Randy Johnson	.40
79	Ryan Klesko	.05
80	Mark McGwire	.75
81	Fred McGriff	.05
82	Javy Lopez	.05
83	Kenny Lofton	.05
84	Sandy Alomar Jr.	.05
85	Matt Morris	.05
86	Paul Konerko	.10
87	Ray Lankford	.05
88	Kerry Wood	.30
89	Roberto Alomar	.20
90	Greg Maddux	.50
91	Travis Lee	.05
92	Moises Alou	.05
93	Dean Palmer	.05
94	Hideo Nomo	.20
95	Ken Caminiti	.05
96	Pedro Martinez	.40
97	Raul Mondesi	.05
98	Denny Neagle	.05
99	Tino Martinez	.05
100	Mike Mussina	.20
101	Kevin Appier	.05
102	Vinny Castilla	.05
103	Jeff Bagwell	.40
104	Paul O'Neill	.05
105	Rey Ordonez	.05
106	Vladimir Guerrero	.40
107	Rafael Palmeiro	.35
108	Alex Rodriguez	.75
109	Andy Pettitte	.15
110	Carl Pavano	.05
111	Henry Rodriguez	.05
112	Gary Sheffield	.40
113	Curt Schilling	.25
114	John Smoltz	.05
115	Reggie Sanders	.05
116	Scott Rolen	.35
117	Mike Piazza	.65
118	Manny Ramirez	.40
119	Cal Ripken Jr.	1.00
120	Brad Radke	.05
121	Tim Salmon	.05
122	Brett Tomko	.05
123	Robin Ventura	.05
124	Mo Vaughn	.05
125	A.J. Hinch	.05
126	Derrek Lee	.05
127	Orlando Hernandez RC	.40
128	Aramis Ramirez	.05
129	Frank Thomas	.05
130	J.T. Snow	.05
131	Magglio Ordonez RC	1.00
132	Bobby Bonilla	.05
133	Marquis Grissom	.05
134	Jim Thome	.45
135	Justin Thompson	.05
136	Matt Williams	.05
137	Matt Stairs	.05
138	Wade Boggs	.50
139	Chuck Finley	.05
140	Jaret Wright	.05
141	Ivan Rodriguez	.35
142	Brad Fullmer	.05
143	Bernie Williams	.05
144	Jason Giambi	.30
145	Larry Walker	.05
146	Tony Womack	.05
147	Sammy Sosa	.50
148	Rondell White	.05
149	Todd Stottlemyre	.05
150	Shane Reynolds	.05

WS Fever Extra Edition

Extra Edition parallels the entire 150-card base set and is identified by a gold-foil stamp on the card front and sequential numbering to 98 sets on the back. World Series Fever also includes one-of-one parallel versions called First Edition. These have a purple-foil identifier on front, with the legend on back, "THE ONLY 1 OF 1 FIRST EDITION," also in purple foil.

	NM/M
Common EE Player:	2.00

EE Stars: 15X
Production: 98 Sets
Common FE Player: 100.00
FE Stars: Values Undetermined
1 of 1

WS Fever Autumn Excellence

Autumn Excellence honors players with the most select World Series records. The 10-card set was seeded one per 24 packs, while rarer Gold versions were seeded one per 240 packs.

	NM/M
Complete Set (10):	15.00
Common Player:	.50
Inserted 1:24	
Golds:	2X
Inserted 1:240	
AE1 Willie Mays	2.50
AE2 Kirby Puckett	2.00
AE3 Babe Ruth	4.00
AE4 Reggie Jackson	1.50
AE5 Whitey Ford	.50
AE6 Lou Brock	.50
AE7 Mickey Mantle	4.00
AE8 Yogi Berra	.75
AE9 Bob Gibson	.50
AE10 Don Larsen	1.00

WS Fever Reggie Jackson Picks

Reggie Jackson's Picks contains top players that Jackson believes have what it takes to perform on center stage in the World Series. Fronts have a shot of the player with his name in the background, and a head shot of Reggie Jackson in the bottom right corner. These were numbered with a "RP" prefix and inserted one per 12 packs.

		NM/M
Complete Set (15):		12.50
Common Player:		.25
Inserted 1:12		
1	Paul O'Neill	.25
2	Barry Bonds	2.50
3	Ken Griffey Jr.	1.50
4	Juan Gonzalez	.40
5	Greg Maddux	1.00
6	Mike Piazza	1.50
7	Larry Walker	.25
8	Mo Vaughn	.25
9	Roger Clemens	1.25
10	John Smoltz	.25
11	Alex Rodriguez	2.00
12	Frank Thomas	.75
13	Mark McGwire	2.00
14	Jeff Bagwell	.75
15	Randy Johnson	.75

WS Fever MVP Collection

This 10-card insert set features select MVPs from the World Series. Card fronts contain a shot of the player over a

white border with the year in black letters and the insert and player's name in blue foil. MVP Collection inserts were seeded one per four packs and numbered with a "MC" prefix.

		NM/M
Complete Set (10):		1.00
Common Player:		.10
Inserted 1:4		
1	Frank Robinson	.25
2	Brooks Robinson	.25
3	Willie Stargell	.10
4	Bret Saberhagen	.10
5	Rollie Fingers	.10
6	Orel Hershiser	.10
7	Paul Molitor	.50
8	Tom Glavine	.15
9	John Wetteland	.10
10	Livan Hernandez	.10

1999 Sports Illustrated

The Sports Illustrated set from Fleer consists of 180 base cards composed of 107 player cards, and four subsets. They include Team 2000, Postseason Review, Award Winners, and Season Highlights. Cards came in six-card packs with an SRP of $1.99. The set also includes five insert sets, along with hobby exclusive autographed J.D. Drew cards numbered to 250.

		NM/M
Complete Set (180):		15.00
Common Player:		.05
Wax Pack (6):		1.00
Hobby Box (24):		15.00
Retail Box (16):		10.00
1	Yankees (Postseason Review)	.25
2	Scott Brosius (Postseason Review)	.05
3	David Wells (Postseason Review)	.05
4	Sterling Hitchcock (Postseason Review)	.05
5	David Justice (Postseason Review)	.05
6	David Cone (Postseason Review)	.05
7	Greg Maddux (Postseason Review)	.50
8	Jim Leyritz (Postseason Review)	.05
9	Gary Gaetti (Postseason Review)	.05
10	Mark McGwire (Award Winners)	.75
11	Sammy Sosa (Award Winners)	.50
12	Larry Walker (Award Winners)	.05
13	Tony Womack (Award Winners)	.05
14	Tom Glavine (Award Winners)	.10
15	Curt Schilling (Award Winners)	.10
16	Greg Maddux (Award Winners)	.50
17	Trevor Hoffman (Award Winners)	.05
18	Kerry Wood (Award Winners)	.20
19	Tom Glavine (Award Winners)	.10
20	Sammy Sosa (Award Winners)	.50
21	Travis Lee (Season Highlights)	.05
22	Roberto Alomar (Season Highlights)	.05
23	Roger Clemens (Season Highlights)	.60
24	Barry Bonds (Season Highlights)	1.00
25	Paul Molitor (Season Highlights)	.45
26	Todd Stottlemyre (Season Highlights)	.05
27	Chris Hoiles (Season Highlights)	.05
28	Albert Belle (Season Highlights)	.05
29	Tony Clark (Season Highlights)	.05
30	Kerry Wood (Season Highlights)	.20
31	David Wells (Season Highlights)	.05
32	Dennis Eckersley (Season Highlights)	.40
33	Mark McGwire (Season Highlights)	.75
34	Cal Ripken Jr. (Season Highlights)	1.00
35	Ken Griffey Jr. (Season Highlights)	.65
36	Alex Rodriguez (Season Highlights)	.75
37	Craig Biggio (Season Highlights)	.05
38	Sammy Sosa (Season Highlights)	.50
39	Dennis Martinez (Season Highlights)	.05
40	Curt Schilling (Season Highlights)	.10
41	Orlando Hernandez (Season Highlights)	.05
42	Troy Glaus, Ben Molina RC, Todd Greene ("Team" 2000)	.45
43	Mitch Meluskey, Daryle Ward, Mike Grzanich ("Team" 2000)	.05
44	Eric Chavez, Mike Neill, Steve Connelly RC ("Team" 2000)	.05
45	Roy Halladay, Tom Evans, Kevin Witt ("Team" 2000)	.05
46	George Lombard, Adam Butler, Bruce Chen ("Team" 2000)	.05
47	Ronnie Belliard, Valerio de los Santos, Rafael Roque RC ("Team" 2000)	.05
48	J.D. Drew, Placido Polanco, Mark Little RC ("Team" 2000)	.50
49	Jason Maxwell, Jose Nieves RC, Jeremi Gonzalez ("Team" 2000)	.05
50	Scott McClain, Kerry Robinson, Mike Duvall RC ("Team" 2000)	.05
51	Ben Ford, Bryan Corey RC, Danny Klassen ("Team" 2000)	.05
52	Angel Pena, Jeff Kubenka, Paul LoDuca ("Team" 2000)	.05
53	Kirk Bullinger, Fernando Seguignol, Tim Young ("Team" 2000)	.05
54	Ramon Martinez, Wilson Delgado, Armando Rios ("Team" 2000)	.05
55	Russ Branyon, Jolbert Cabrera RC, Jason Rakers ("Team" 2000)	.05
56	Carlos Guillen RC, David Holdridge RC, Giomar Guevara RC ("Team" 2000)	.10
57	Alex Gonzalez, Joe Fontenot, Preston Wilson ("Team" 2000)	.05
58	Mike Kinkade, Jay Payton, Masato Yoshii ("Team" 2000)	.05
59	Willis Otanez, Ryan Minor, Calvin Pickering ("Team" 2000)	.05
60	Ben Davis, Matt Clement, Stan Spencer ("Team" 2000)	.05
61	Marlon Anderson, Mike Welch, Gary Bennett RC ("Team" 2000)	.05
62	Abraham Nunez, Sean Lawrence RC, Aramis Ramirez ("Team" 2000)	.05
63	Jonathan Johnson, Rob Sasser RC, Scott Sheldon RC ("Team" 2000)	.05
64	Keith Glauber RC, Guillermo Garcia RC, Eddie Priest ("Team" 2000)	.05
65	Brian Barkley, Jin Ho Cho, Donnie Sadler ("Team" 2000)	.05
66	Derrick Gibson, Mark Strittmatter, Edgard Clemente RC ("Team" 2000)	.05
67	Jeremy Giambi, Dermal Brown, Chris Hatcher RC ("Team" 2000)	.05
68	Rob Fick RC, Gabe Kapler, Marino Santana ("Team" 2000)	.10
69	Corey Koskie, A.J. Pierzynski, Benj Sampson ("Team" 2000)	.05
70	Brian Simmons, Mark Johnson, Craig Wilson ("Team" 2000)	.05
71	Ryan Bradley, Mike Lowell, Jay Tessmer ("Team" 2000)	.05
72	Ben Grieve	.05
73	Shawn Green	.45
74	Rafael Palmeiro	.65
75	Juan Gonzalez	.65
76	Mike Piazza	1.25
77	Devon White	.05
78	Jim Thome	.65
79	Barry Larkin	.05
80	Scott Rolen	.65
81	Raul Mondesi	.05
82	Jason Giambi	.50
83	Jose Canseco	.45
84	Tony Gwynn	1.00
85	Cal Ripken Jr.	2.00
86	Andy Pettitte	.15
87	Carlos Delgado	.50
88	Jeff Cirillo	.05
89	Bret Saberhagen	.05
90	John Olerud	.05
91	Ron Coomer	.05
92	Todd Helton	.65
93	Ray Lankford	.05
94	Tim Salmon	.05
95	Fred McGriff	.05
96	Matt Stairs	.05
97	Ken Griffey Jr.	1.25
98	Chipper Jones	1.00
99	Mark Grace	.05
100	Ivan Rodriguez	.65
101	Jeromy Burnitz	.05
102	Kenny Rogers	.05
103	Kevin Millwood	.05
104	Vinny Castilla	.05
105	Jim Edmonds	.05
106	Craig Biggio	.05
107	Andres Galarraga	.05
108	Sammy Sosa	1.00
109	Juan Encarnacion	.05
110	Larry Walker	.05
111	John Smoltz	.05
112	Randy Johnson	.75
113	Bobby Higginson	.05
114	Albert Belle	.05
115	Jaret Wright	.05
116	Edgar Renteria	.05
117	Andruw Jones	.75
118	Barry Bonds	2.00
119	Rondell White	.05
120	Jamie Moyer	.05
121	Darin Erstad	.20
122	Al Leiter	.05
123	Mark McGwire	1.50
124	Mo Vaughn	.05
125	Livan Hernandez	.05
126	Jason Kendall	.05
127	Frank Thomas	.75
128	Denny Neagle	.05
129	Johnny Damon	.35
130	Derek Bell	.05
131	Jeff Kent	.05
132	Tony Womack	.05
133	Trevor Hoffman	.05
134	Gary Sheffield	.40
135	Tino Martinez	.05
136	Travis Fryman	.05
137	Rolando Arrojo	.05
138	Dante Bichette	.05
139	Nomar Garciaparra	1.00
140	Moises Alou	.05
141	Chuck Knoblauch	.05
142	Robin Ventura	.05
143	Scott Erickson	.05
144	David Cone	.05
145	Gary Vaughn	.25
146	Wade Boggs	1.00
147	Mike Mussina	.30
148	Tony Clark	.05
149	Alex Rodriguez	1.50
150	Javy Lopez	.05
151	Bartolo Colon	.05
152	Derek Jeter	2.00
153	Greg Maddux	1.00
154	Kevin Brown	.05
155	Curt Schilling	.05
156	Jeff King	.05
157	Bernie Williams	.05
158	Roberto Alomar	.20
159	Travis Lee	.05
160	Kerry Wood	.50
160p	Kerry Wood/OPS	1.00
161	Jeff Bagwell	.75
162	Roger Clemens	1.00
163	Matt Williams	.05
164	Chan Ho Park	.05
165	Damion Easley	.05
166	Manny Ramirez	.75
167	Quinton McCracken	.05
168	Todd Walker	.05
169	Eric Karros	.05
170	Will Clark	.05
171	Edgar Martinez	.05
172	Cliff Floyd	.05
173	Vladimir Guerrero	.75
174	Tom Glavine	.35
175	Pedro Martinez	.75
176	Chuck Finley	.05
177	Dean Palmer	.05
178	Omar Vizquel	.05
179	Checklist	.05
180	Checklist	.05

Diamond Dominators

This 10-card insert set features five hitters and five pitchers on embossed cards. The hitters are seeded 1 in every 180 packs, while the pitchers are seeded 1 in every 90 packs.

		NM/M
Complete Set (10):		30.00
Common Player:		1.50
Pitchers inserted 1:90		
Hitters inserted 1:180		
1DD	Kerry Wood	1.50
2DD	Roger Clemens	3.00
3DD	Randy Johnson	2.00
4DD	Greg Maddux	2.50
5DD	Pedro Martinez	2.50
6DD	Ken Griffey Jr.	5.00
7DD	Sammy Sosa	2.50
8DD	Nomar Garciaparra	2.50
9DD	Mark McGwire	6.00
10DD	Alex Rodriguez	6.00

Fabulous 40s

This 13-card insert set consists of the players that hit 40 or more homers during the 1998 season. The cards are sculpture embossed and foil-stamped, with the player's home run total also on the card. One card comes with every 20 packs.

		NM/M
Complete Set (13):		9.00
Common Player:		.25
Inserted 1:20		
1FF	Mark McGwire	2.00
2FF	Sammy Sosa	1.25

#	Player	Price
3FF	Ken Griffey Jr.	1.50
4FF	Greg Vaughn	.25
5FF	Albert Belle	.25
6FF	Jose Canseco	.50
7FF	Vinny Castilla	.25
8FF	Juan Gonzalez	.50
9FF	Manny Ramirez	1.00
10FF	Andres Galarraga	.25
11FF	Rafael Palmeiro	.75
12FF	Alex Rodriguez	2.00
13FF	Mo Vaughn	.25

Fabulous 40s Extra

The insert set parallels the 13 cards in the Fabulous 40s set. The cards are hobby exclusive, highlighted with silver patterned holofoil. Each player's cards are hand-numbered to the total number of home runs he hit in 1998.

NM/M
Common Player: 12.00
Numbered to amount of HRs

#	Player	Price
1FF	Mark McGwire/70	60.00
2FF	Sammy Sosa/66	40.00
3FF	Ken Griffey Jr./56	35.00
4FF	Greg Vaughn/50	12.00
5FF	Albert Belle/49	12.00
6FF	Jose Canseco/46	25.00
7FF	Vinny Castilla/46	12.00
8FF	Juan Gonzalez/45	20.00
9FF	Manny Ramirez/45	30.00
10FF	Andres Galarraga/44	12.00
11FF	Rafael Palmeiro/43	25.00
12FF	Alex Rodriguez/42	45.00
13FF	Mo Vaughn /40	12.00

Headliners

Headliners is a 25-card insert set that features silver foil stamped, team-color coded cards. One card comes with every four packs.

NM/M
Complete Set (25): 10.00
Common Player: .25
Inserted 1:4

#	Player	Price
1H	Vladimir Guerrero	.40
2H	Randy Johnson	.40
3H	Mo Vaughn	.25
4H	Chipper Jones	.50
5H	Jeff Bagwell	.40
6H	Juan Gonzalez	.30
7H	Mark McGwire	.75
8H	Cal Ripken Jr.	1.00
9H	Frank Thomas	.40
10H	Manny Ramirez	.40
11H	Ken Griffey Jr.	.65
12H	Scott Rolen	.35
13H	Alex Rodriguez	.75
14H	Barry Bonds	1.00
15H	Roger Clemens	.55
16H	Darin Erstad	.30
17H	Nomar Garciaparra	.75
18H	Mike Piazza	.65
19H	Greg Maddux	.50
20H	Ivan Rodriguez	.35
21H	Derek Jeter	1.00
22H	Sammy Sosa	.75
23H	Andruw Jones	.40
24H	Pedro Martinez	.40
25H	Kerry Wood	.35

Ones To Watch

ERIC CHAVEZ-3B

This 15-card insert set features the game's top rookies and young stars. The cards have 100 percent foil background, and are team-color coded. One card was inserted in every 12 packs.

NM/M
Complete Set (15): 5.00
Common Player: .25
Inserted 1:12

#	Player	Price
10W	J.D. Drew	.65
20W	Marlon Anderson	.25
30W	Roy Halladay	.35
40W	Ben Grieve	.40
50W	Todd Helton	.75
60W	Gabe Kapler	.25
70W	Troy Glaus	.75
80W	Ben Davis	.25
90W	Eric Chavez	.35
100W	Richie Sexson	.25
110W	Fernando Seguignol	.25
120W	Kerry Wood	.50
130W	Bobby Smith	.25
140W	Ryan Minor	.25
150W	Jeremy Giambi	.25
	J.D. Drew/250/Auto.	15.00

Greats of the Game

Frank Thomas

The 90-card base set includes many legendary major-leaguers including Babe Ruth and Cy Young. Card fronts feature a full bleed photo with the player name across the bottom and Greats of the Game printed on the bottom left portion of the card. Card backs have the player's vital information, along with career statistics and a few career highlights. Seven-card packs were issued with a SRP of $15.

NM/M
Complete Set (90): 12.00
Common Player: .05
Pack (7): 15.00
Wax Box (12): 150.00

#	Player	Price
1	Jimmie Foxx	.05
2	Red Schoendienst	.05
3	Babe Ruth	3.00
4	Lou Gehrig	2.00
5	Mel Ott	.05
6	Stan Musial	.25
7	Mickey Mantle	3.00
8	Carl Yastrzemski	.15
9	Enos Slaughter	.05
10	Andre Dawson	.05
11	Luis Aparicio	.05
12	Ferguson Jenkins	.05
13	Christy Mathewson	.25
14	Ernie Banks	.15
15	Johnny Podres	.05
16	George Foster	.05
17	Jerry Koosman	.05
18	Curt Simmons	.05
19	Bob Feller	.05
20	Frank Robinson	.05
21	Gary Carter	.05
22	Frank Thomas	.05
23	Bill Lee	.05
24	Willie Mays	1.00
25	Tommie Agee	.05
26	Boog Powell	.05
27	Jimmy Wynn	.05
28	Sparky Lyle	.05
29	Bo Belinsky	.05
30	Maury Wills	.05
31	Bill Buckner	.05
32	Steve Carlton	.05
33	Harmon Killebrew	.05
34	Nolan Ryan	1.00
35	Randy Jones	.05
36	Robin Roberts	.05
37	Al Oliver	.05
38	Rico Petrocelli	.05
39	Dave Parker	.05
40	Eddie Mathews	.05
41	Earl Weaver	.05
42	Jackie Robinson	1.50
43	Lou Brock	.05
44	Reggie Jackson	.15
45	Bob Gibson	.05
46	Jeff Burroughs	.05
47	Jim Bouton	.05
48	Bob Forsch	.05
49	Ron Guidry	.05
50	Ty Cobb	2.00
51	Roy White	.05
52	Joe Rudi	.05
53	Moose Skowron	.05
54	Goose Gossage	.05
55	Ed Kranepool	.05
56	Paul Blair	.05
57	Kent Hrbek	.05
58	Orlando Cepeda	.05
59	Buck O'Neil	.05
60	Al Kaline	.05
61	Vida Blue	.05
62	Sam McDowell	.05
63	Jesse Barfield	.05
64	Dave Kingman	.05
65	Ron Santo	.05
66	Steve Garvey	.05
67	Gaylord Perry	.05
68	Darrell Evans	.05
69	Rollie Fingers	.05
70	Walter Johnson	.25
71	Al Hrabosky	.05
72	Mickey Rivers	.05
73	Mike Torrez	.05
74	Hank Bauer	.05
75	Tug McGraw	.05
76	David Clyde	.05
77	Jim Lonborg	.05
78	Clete Boyer	.05
79	Harry Walker	.05
80	Cy Young	.25
81	Bud Harrelson	.05
82	Paul Splittorff	.05
83	Bert Campaneris	.05
84	Joe Niekro	.05
85	Bob Horner	.05
86	Jerry Royster	.05
87	Tommy John	.05
88	Mark Fidrych	.05
89	Dick Williams	.05
90	Graig Nettles	.05

Greats/Game Autographs

Each Greats of the Game pack has one autograph from the 80 card checklist. Each card is autographed on the white portion on the bottom of the card, and is stamped "seal of authenticity." Card backs certify the autograph is authentic and "has been embossed with the Fleer Mark of Authenticity." The unnumbered cards are checklisted here in alphabetical order.

NM/M
Common Player: 4.00
Inserted 1:1

#	Player	Price
(1)	Tommie Agee	8.00
(2)	Luis Aparicio	12.00
(3)	Ernie Banks	25.00
(4)	Jesse Barfield	6.00
(5)	Hank Bauer	10.00
(6)	Bo Belinsky	6.00
(7)	Paul Blair	6.00
(8)	Vida Blue	10.00
(9)	Jim Bouton	10.00
(10)	Clete Boyer	10.00
(11)	Lou Brock	15.00
(12)	Bill Buckner	10.00
(13)	Jeff Burroughs	5.00
(14)	Bert Campaneris	8.00
(15)	Steve Carlton	.20.00
(16)	Gary Carter	12.00
(17)	Orlando Cepeda	12.00
(18)	David Clyde	5.00
(19)	Andre Dawson	10.00
(20)	Darrell Evans	8.00
(21)	Bob Feller	12.00
(22)	Mark Fidrych	15.00
(23)	Rollie Fingers	10.00
(24)	Bob Forsch	6.00
(25)	George Foster	10.00
(26)	Steve Garvey	10.00
(27)	Bob Gibson	15.00
(28)	Goose Gossage	10.00
(29)	Ron Guidry	20.00
(30)	Bud Harrelson	10.00
(31)	Bob Horner	10.00
(32)	Al Hrabosky	8.00
(33)	Kent Hrbek	10.00
(34a)	Reggie Jackson	150.00
(34b)	Reggie Jackson ("Mr. October")	200.00
(34c)	Reggie Jackson ("HoF 93")	200.00
(35)	Ferguson Jenkins	10.00
(36)	Tommy John	8.00
(37)	Randy Jones	4.00
(38)	Al Kaline	25.00
(39)	Harmon Killebrew	25.00
(40)	Dave Kingman	8.00
(41)	Jerry Koosman	8.00
(42)	Ed Kranepool	8.00
(43)	Bill Lee	10.00
(44)	Jim Lonborg	5.00
(45)	Sparky Lyle	8.00
(46)	Eddie Mathews	60.00
(47)	Willie Mays	125.00
(48)	Sam McDowell	8.00
(49)	Tug McGraw	25.00
(50)	Stan Musial	100.00
(51)	Graig Nettles	10.00
(52)	Joe Niekro	8.00
(53)	Buck O'Neil	20.00
(54)	Al Oliver	10.00
(55)	Dave Parker	10.00
(56)	Gaylord Perry	10.00
(57)	Rico Petrocelli	12.00
(58)	Johnny Podres	20.00
(59)	Boog Powell	12.50
(60)	Mickey Rivers	8.00
(61)	Robin Roberts	20.00
(62)	Frank Robinson	17.50
(63)	Jerry Royster	4.00
(64)	Joe Rudi	8.00
(65)	Nolan Ryan	200.00
(66)	Ron Santo	17.50
(67)	Red Schoendienst	12.00
(68)	Curt Simmons	6.00
(69)	Moose Skowron	15.00
(70)	Enos Slaughter	20.00
(71)	Paul Splittorff	6.00
(72)	Frank Thomas	8.00
(73)	Mike Torrez	4.00
(74)	Harry Walker	4.00
(75)	Earl Weaver	10.00
(76)	Roy White	9.00
(77)	Dick Williams	10.00
(78)	Maury Wills	10.00
(79)	Jimmy Wynn	10.00
(80)	Carl Yastrzemski	45.00

Greats/Game Cover Collection

Each pack features one of the 50 chosen baseball covers from the Sports Illustrated archives. Card fronts are a reprint of the actual cover, while the backs give a brief description of the cover article and date of the magazine cover. Each card is numbered with a "C" suffix.

NM/M
Complete Set (50): 25.00
Common Player: .50
Inserted 1:1

#	Player	Price
1	Johnny Podres	.50
2	Mickey Mantle	5.00
3	Stan Musial	.50
4	Eddie Mathews	.50
5	Frank Thomas	.50
6	Willie Mays	1.00
7	Red Schoendienst	.50
8	Luis Aparicio	.50
9	Mickey Mantle	3.00
10	Al Kaline	.50
11	Maury Wills	.50
12	Sam McDowell	.50
13	Harry Walker	.50
14	Carl Yastrzemski	.50
15	Carl Yastrzemski	.50
16	Lou Brock	.50
17	Ron Santo	.50
18	Reggie Jackson	.50
19	Frank Robinson	.50
20	Jerry Koosman	.50
21	Bud Harrelson	.50
22	Vida Blue	.50
23	Ferguson Jenkins	.50
24	Sparky Lyle	.50
25	Steve Carlton	.50
26	Bert Campaneris	.50
27	Jimmy Wynn	.50
28	Steve Garvey	.50
29	Nolan Ryan	1.00
30	Randy Jones	.50
31	Reggie Jackson	.50
32	Joe Rudi	.50
33	Reggie Jackson	.50
34	Dave Parker	.50
35	Mark Fidrych	.50
36	Earl Weaver	.50
37	Nolan Ryan	1.00
38	Steve Carlton	.50
39	Reggie Jackson	.50
40	Rollie Fingers	.50
41	Gary Carter	.50
42	Graig Nettles	.50
43	Gaylord Perry	.50
44	Kent Hrbek	.50
45	Gary Carter	.50
46	Steve Garvey	.50
47	Steve Carlton	.50
48	Nolan Ryan	1.00
49	Nolan Ryan	1.00
50	Mickey Mantle	3.00

Greats/Game Record Breakers

CHRISTY MATHEWSON

This 10-card set spotlights the top record breakers in the past century from Christy Mathewson to Nolan Ryan. Card fronts are full foiled with an oblong stamp on the bottom portion detailing the player's respective record. Card backs are numbered with a "RB" suffix and gives more detail on the featured player's record. These are seeded 1:12 packs. A Gold parallel is also randomly seeded 1:120 packs and have gold holo-foil.

NM/M
Complete Set (10): 40.00
Common Player: 2.00
Inserted 1:12
Golds: 6X
Inserted 1:120

#	Player	Price
1	Mickey Mantle	8.00
2	Stan Musial	3.50
3	Babe Ruth	8.00
4	Christy Mathewson	2.00
5	Cy Young	2.00
6	Nolan Ryan	7.50
7	Jackie Robinson	6.00
8	Lou Gehrig	7.00
9	Ty Cobb	3.50
10	Walter Johnson	2.00

1989-91 Sports Illustrated For Kids

Beginning with its January 1989 issue and continuing for three years, the magazine "Sports Illustrated For Kids" produced a set of sportscards featuring many professional and amateur stars in more than a dozen sports. Generally issued in a nine-card panel, cards were perforated so they could

CARLTON FISK
CATCHER
Chicago White Sox

be removed from the magazine and separated from each other. A variety of designs and formats were used in that period. Only the pro baseball cards from the series are checklisted here.

NM/M
Complete Set (60): 55.00
Common Player: .50

#	Player	Price
5	Orel Hershiser	.50
11	Jose Canseco	1.00
21	Darryl Strawberry	.50
31	Mike Greenwell	.50
33	Tony Gwynn	2.00
35	Frank Viola	.50
37	Don Mattingly	2.25
43	Ozzie Smith	2.00
46	Rickey Henderson	1.50
48	Chris Sabo	.50
52	Andre Dawson	.75
56	Alan Trammell	.50
63	Roger Clemens	2.25
64	Andres Galarraga	.50
64	John Franco	.50
69	Cal Ripken Jr.	4.00
70	Will Clark	.50
75	Bo Jackson	.75
81	Nolan Ryan	4.00
90	Mike Schmidt	2.25
112	Kevin Mitchell	.50
121	Ryne Sandberg	2.00
127	Robin Yount	1.50
133	Dave Stewart	.50
140	Eric Davis	.50
144	Mike Scott	.50
146	Mark McGwire	3.00
151	Dwight Gooden	.50
158	Ken Griffey Jr.	2.50
165	George Brett	2.25
166	Ruben Sierra	.50
167	Kirby Puckett	2.00
171	Carlton Fisk	1.50
176	Fred McGriff	.50
176	Wade Boggs	2.00
178	Tim Raines	.50
181	Bobby Bonilla	.50
189	Kelly Gruber	.50
197	Dennis Eckersley	1.00
205	Cecil Fielder	.50
212	Jackie Robinson	2.00
216	Babe Ruth	3.00
229	Barry Bonds	4.00
240	Jose Rijo	.50
248	Sandy Alomar Jr.	.50
251	Ron Gant	.50
259	David Justice	.50
261	Bob Welch	.50
266	Doug Drabek	.50
268	Rafael Palmeiro	1.25
271	Paul Molitor	1.50
275	Bobby Thigpen	.50
279	Edgar Martinez	.50
282	Dave Winfield	1.50
283	Mark Grace	.50
288	Dwight Evans	.50
289	Dave Henderson	.50
294	Lee Smith	.50
303	Ramon Martinez	.50
321	Ty Cobb	1.50

1992-2000 Sports Illustrated For Kids

MICHAEL JORDAN

BIRMINGHAM BARONS

A new series, with cards numbered consecutively from #1, of magazine insert cards was begun with SI For Kids' in its January 1992 issue. Like the earlier series, cards are 2-1/2" x 3-1/2" inches and most often found as a nine-card panel, with each card perforated for removal from the magazine and separation from the other cards. As before, the cards feature a number of different designs, formats and back treatments. Backs usually include a few personal details and a trivia question. Only the cards of pro baseball players are checklisted here.

		NM/M
Complete Set (157):		150.00
Common Player:		.25
24	Terry Pendleton	.25
29	Kirby Puckett	2.00
36	Roger Clemens	2.25
40	Tom Glavine	.45
45	Frank Thomas	1.50
50	Jim Abbott	.25
54	Roberto Alomar	.35
64	Matt Williams	.25
68	Bobby Bonilla	.25
72	Chuck Finley	.25
75	Danny Tartabull	.25
81	Jack Morris	.25
86	Will Clark	.25
108	Lou Gehrig	2.50
121	Juan Gonzalez	.75
132	Cal Ripken Jr.	4.00
136	Jack McDowell	.25
144	Marquis Grissom	.25
145	Andy Van Slyke	.25
152	Dennis Eckersley	1.00
157	Barry Bonds	4.00
162	Greg Maddux	2.00
168	Nolan Ryan	1.50
170	Dave Winfield	1.50
173	Ken Griffey Jr.	4.00
178	Wade Boggs	2.00
185	Kirk Gibson	.25
187	Albert Belle	.25
190	John Burkett	.25
196	John Kruk	.25
199	Randy Johnson	1.50
204	Lou Whitaker	.25
212	Yogi Berra	.50
236	Lenny Dykstra	.25
244	Carlos Baerga	.25
254	Joe Carter	.25
266	Chuck Carr	.25
268	Julie Croteau (Colorado Silver Bullets)	.25
270	Michael Jordan	3.00
274	Andres Galarraga	.25
278	Jeff Bagwell	1.50
281	John Olerud	.25
288	Tony Gwynn	2.00
292	Gregg Jefferies	.25
297	Mo Vaughn	.25
298	Moises Alou	.25
305	Jimmy Key	.25
311	Mike Mussina	.40
313	Mike Piazza	2.50
320	Stan Musial	2.00
327	Matt Williams	.25
343	Frank Thomas (Boyhood photo.)	1.00
349	Michael Jordan (Boyhood photo.)	2.00
359	Kenny Lofton	.25
362	Raul Mondesi	.25
381	David Cone	.25
386	Brady Anderson	.25
390	Eric Karros	.25
391	Paul O'Neill	.25
398	Eddie Murray	1.50
402	Barry Larkin	.25
407	Edgar Martinez	.25
412	Mark McGwire	3.00
416	Albert Belle (Cartoon)	.25
430	Mark Grace	.25
433	Chuck Knoblauch	.25
447	Chipper Jones	2.00
451	Tom Glavine (Boyhood photo.)	.25
455	Cal Ripken Jr. (Boyhood photo.)	3.00
462	Jeff Conine	.25
470	Hideo Nomo	.75
475	Bernie Williams	.25
478	Craig Biggio	.25
485	Jose Mesa	.25
497	Roberto Alomar	.35
503	John Smoltz	.25
505	Henry Rodriguez	.25
513	Rey Ordonez	.25
516	Ellis Burks	.25
518	Ivan Rodriguez	1.25
543	Alex Rodriguez	3.00
553	Mo Vaughn	.25
561	Andy Pettitte	.25
562	Barry Bonds	4.00
582	Andruw Jones	.25
570	Randy Johnson (April Fool card as L.A. Laker.)	1.50
572	Ken Griffey Jr. (April Fool card as Orlando Magic.)	2.50
588	Brian Jordan	.25

589	Derek Jeter	4.00
596	Juan Gonzalez	.75
598	Andres Galarraga	.25
608	Mark McGwire	3.00
611	Pat Hentgen	.25
627	Cal Ripken Jr. (Cartoon as Tin Man.)	4.00
634	Sandy Alomar Jr.	.25
641	Brady Anderson	.25
652	Jeff Bagwell	1.50
669	Larry Walker	.25
673	Roger Clemens	2.25
685	Frank Thomas	1.50
693	Denny Neagle	.25
695	Tony Gwynn	2.00
697	Mike Piazza	2.50
703	Kenny Lofton	.25
708	Moises Alou	.25
712	Dante Bichette	.25
720	John Wetteland	.25
721	Curt Schilling	.45
725	Nomar Garciaparra	2.00
734	Ken Griffey Jr. (Cartoon as The Cat in the Hat.)	2.50
737	Greg Maddux (Cartoon as Encyclopedia Brown.)	2.00
743	Sammy Sosa	2.00
749	David Wells	.25
No#	Mark McGwire (The Best of 1998)	2.50
758	Pedro Martinez	1.50
768	Ila Borders	.25
770	David Cone	.25
784	Mike Piazza (April Fool's - hockey player.)	2.50
790	Mark McGwire (April Fool's - Chicago Cub.)	3.00
795	Craig Biggio	.25
796	Tom Glavine	.45
802	Alex Rodriguez	3.00
804	Trevor Hoffman	.25
813	Rickey Henderson	1.50
815	Mo Vaughn	.25
817	Vinny Castilla	.25
820	John Smoltz	.25
825	Jose Canseco	.65
831	Matt Williams	.25
833	Derek Jeter	4.00
840	Ivan Rodriguez (As Darth Vader.)	1.25
841	Roger Clemens (As lion.)	2.25
846	Ken Caminiti (As ghoul.)	.25
849	Roberto Alomar	.35
No#	Greg Maddux (Fall/Winter 1999)	2.00
No#	Ken Griffey Jr. (Fall/Winter 1999)	2.50
856	Randy Johnson	1.50
866	Babe Ruth	5.00
869	Mickey Mantle	5.00
870	Jackie Robinson	.25
882	Mark McGwire (Kid photo.)	3.00
884	Mariano Rivera	.35
892	Billy the Marlin/Mascot	.25
896	The Phillie Phanatic/ Mascot	.25
901	Kevin Millwood	.25
906	Manny Ramirez	1.50
910	Bernie Williams	.25
914	Larry Walker	.25
920	Ken Griffey Jr.	2.50
922	David Wells	.25
929	Chipper Jones	2.00
935	Carlos Beltran	.50
941	Vladimir Guerrero	1.50
945	Andres Galarraga	.25
953	Jason Kendall (As Pokemon's Ash Ketchum.)	.40
955	Pedro Martinez	1.50
962	Todd Helton	1.25

1996-98 Sports Illustrated For Kids Legends

Unlike the nine-card panels which appear in every issue of SI For Kids, the Legends series appeared sporadically as a four-card panel honoring the past greats of many sports. While designs vary from issue to is-

sue, the format of the cards has remained a consistent 2-9/16" x 4". Only the baseball players are listed here.

		NM/M
Complete Set (7):		9.00
Common Player:		.25
45	Sadaharu Oh	1.00
52	Willie Mays	2.00
66	Mike Schmidt	1.50
(1)	Mickey Mantle	3.00
(2)	Bob Feller	.50
(3)	Lou Brock	.50
(4)	Honus Wagner	.50

1999 SI for Kids 10th Anniversary Sheet

Saluting Sports Illustrated for Kids on its 10th anniversary, Major League Baseball, the Players' Association and the four card licensees created a a special eight-card insert sheet which appears in the magazine's July 1999 issue. The sheet consists of nine 2-1/2" x 3-1/2" cards printed on thin cardboard and perforated for easy separation. The Fleer and Upper Deck cards are very similar to those companies' regular 1999 issues, except for the absence of foil printing and UV coating. The Topps and Pacific offerings are new designs. All player cards feature action photos on front along with card company and SI for Kids logos. Backs have another photo plus stats, biographical data and copyright notice.

		NM/M
Complete Sheet:		6.00
Complete Set (9):		5.00
Common Player:		.50
7	J.D. Drew (Fleer Tradition)	.50
49	Cal Ripken Jr. (Upper Deck)	1.00
205	Ken Griffey Jr. (Upper Deck)	.65
266	Sammy Sosa (SkyBox Thunder)	.65
---	Roger Clemens (Topps)	.50
---	Tony Gwynn (Pacific)	.50
---	Mark McGwire (Pacific)	.75
---	Mike Piazza (Topps)	.65
---	Sponsors' Card	.10

2000-2005 Sports Illustrated for Kids

Beginning with its December 2000-dated edition, SI/Kids launched a new series of collectible sportscard inserts. Like earlier series, cards were inserted into the magazine as nine-card perforated sheets. Each

card, if separated from the sheet, measures the standard 2-1/2" x 3-1/2". Fronts feature borderless color action photos with a Sports Illustrated for Kids logo in an upper corner. The athlete is identified in red and blue typography in a silver panel at bottom. Horizontal backs have a blue background. In a black box at right is a portrait photo and trivia question. A black box at bottom has recent and career stats. At top is player personal data; at center are career highlights. Only the baseball players from the multi-sport issue are listed here.

		NM/M
Complete Set (90):		55.00
Common Player:		.25
8	Gary Sheffield	.35
10	Carlos Delgado	.50
24	Jason Giambi	.50
30	Kazuhiro Sasaki	.25
34	Jeff Kent	.25
39	Randy Johnson	.75
40	Rafael Furcal	.25
50	Nomar Garciaparra	1.00
54	Darin Erstad	.35
57	Edgar Martinez	.25
62	Andruw Jones	.75
68	Edgardo Alfonzo	.25
72	Tim Hudson	.25
74	Barry Bonds	2.50
80	Juan Gonzalez	.40
85	Kevin Brown	.25
87	Luis Gonzalez	.25
92	Bret Boone	.25
98	Mike Hampton	.25
101	Mike Piazza	1.50
110	Alex Rodriguez	2.00
122	Sammy Sosa	1.00
131	Ichiro Suzuki	2.00
141	Curt Schilling	.35
148	Albert Pujols	2.00
152	Derek Jeter	2.50
157	Mariano Rivera	.25
162	Juan Pierre	.25
164	Robb Nen	.25
169	Jim Thome	.65
174	Ken Griffey Jr.	1.50
176	Hideo Nomo	.40
182	Pedro Martinez	.75
186	Tino Martinez	.25
191	Lance Berkman	.25
195	Omar Vizquel	.25
199	Tom Glavine	.35
207	Torii Hunter	.25
209	Luis Castillo	.25
221	Jorge Posada	.25
228	Barry Zito	.25
237	Manny Ramirez	.75
246	Troy Glaus	.65
248	Scott Rolen	.65
255	Alex Rodriguez	2.00
257	Eric Hinske	.25
267	John Smoltz	.25
269	Alfonso Soriano	.50
271	Derek Lowe	.25
276	Roy Oswalt	.25
339	Miguel Tejada	.25
347	Barry Bonds	2.50
356	Ivan Rodriguez	.65
361	Eric Gagne	.25
366	Hideki Matsui	2.00
369	Todd Helton	.65
374	Kerry Wood	.50
381	Carlos Delgado	.50
383	Tim Hudson	.25
388	Jim Thome	.65
393	Josh Beckett	.25
398	Andruw Jones	.75
402	Bill Mueller	.25
408	Sean Casey	.25
410	Dontrelle Willis	.25
417	Vladimir Guerrero	.75
422	Randy Johnson	.25
429	Ichiro Suzuki	2.00
430	Ben Sheets	.25
442	Eric Chavez	.25
447	Russ Ortiz	.25
462	Adrian Beltre	.35
466	Curt Schilling	.35
470	Jason Schmidt	.25
472	Adam Dunn	.40
479	Joe Nathan	.25
483	Jason Bay	.25
488	Roger Clemens	1.25
490	Melvin Mora	.25
497	Gary Sheffield	.25
505	C.C. Sabathia	.25
509	Miguel Cabrera	.25
514	Paul Konerko	.25
523	Pedro Martinez	.50
527	Derrek Lee	.50
536	Chris Carpenter	.25
538	Mark Teixeira	.25
	Chad Cordero	.25
	Tim Wakefield	.25
	Carlos Lee	.25

2005 Sports Illustrated for Kids

Beginning with its December 2005-dated edition, SI/Kids launched a new series of collectible sportscard inserts. Like earlier series, cards were inserted into the magazine as nine-card perforated sheets. Each card, if separated from the sheet, measures the standard 2-1/2" x 3-1/2". Fronts feature color action photos, bordered in black, with a Sports Illustrated for Kids logo in in an upper corner. The athlete is identified in white and yellow typography at bottom. Horizontal backs have a blue background. At right is a portrait photo and trivia question. A black box at bottom has recent and career stats. At top is player personal data; at center are career highlights. Only the baseball players from the multi-sport issue are listed here.

		NM/M
Complete Set (12):		4.50
Common Player:		.25
5	Bartolo Colon	.25
7	Andruw Jones	.50
10	Roy Oswalt	.25
15	Alex Rodriguez	1.00
20	Jermaine Dye	.25
25	Jake Peavy	.25
30	David Ortiz	.50
34	Huston Street	.50
39	Chone Figgins	.25
40	Cliff Lee	.25
48	Dontrelle Willis	.25
53	Jim Edmonds	.25

1981 Spot-bilt George Brett

This one-card set was released in both 1981 and 1982 (see stats on back to differentiate) in boxes of turf baseball shoes, for which Brett served on the athletic advisory staff. Cards are standard 2-1/2" x 3-1/2". Despite the card number 5 on the back, there are no other players in the series. Brett wore uniform #5.

		NM/M
5	George Brett	2.50

1981 Squirt

These cards, issued in conjunction with Topps, were issued as two-card panels in

eight-pack cartons of the soft drink. Individual cards measure the standard 2-1/2" x 3-1/2", while the vertical panels measure 2-1/2" x 10-1/2", with a promotional card reading "Free Topps 1981 Baseball Cards" attached. The promotional card is blank-backed, while the player card backs are similar to Topps' regular issue, though re-numbered for inclusion in this 33-card set. Most of the game's top players are included. There are only 22 different two-card panels, as card numbers 1-11 appear in two different bottom panel combinations. Card fronts feature a color player portrait photo within a baseball design, team and position designation, and the Squirt logo.

		NM/M
Complete Panel Set (22):		20.00
Complete Singles Set (33):		20.00
Common Panel:		.50
Common Player:		.15
Panel (1)		2.00
1	George Brett	1.50
12	Garry Templeton	.15
Panel (2)		2.00
1	George Brett	1.50
23	Jerry Mumphrey	.15
Panel (3)		.50
2	George Foster	.25
13	Rick Burleson	.15
Panel (4)		.50
2	George Foster	.25
24	Tony Armas	.15
Panel (5)		.50
3	Ben Oglivie	.15
14	Dave Kingman	.15
Panel (6)		.50
3	Ben Oglivie	.15
25	Fred Lynn	.15
Panel (7)		1.50
4	Steve Garvey	.50
15	Eddie Murray	.75
Panel (8)		.50
4	Steve Garvey	.50
26	Ron LeFlore	.15
Panel (9)		2.00
5	Reggie Jackson	1.50
16	Don Sutton	.15
Panel (10)		2.00
5	Reggie Jackson	1.50
27	Steve Kemp	.15
Panel (11)		.75
6	Bill Buckner	.15
17	Dusty Baker	.15
Panel (12)		1.50
6	Bill Buckner	.15
28	Rickey Henderson	.75
Panel (13)		.50
7	Jim Rice	.25
18	Jack Clark	.15
Panel (14)		.25
7	Jim Rice	.25
29	John Castino	.15
Panel (15)		3.00
8	Mike Schmidt	1.50
19	Dave Winfield	.75
Panel (16)		2.00
8	Mike Schmidt	1.50
30	Cecil Cooper	.15
Panel (17)		2.50
9	Rod Carew	1.00
20	Johnny Bench	1.00
Panel (18)		1.00
9	Rod Carew	1.00
31	Bruce Bochte	.15
Panel (19)		.50
10	Dave Parker	.15
21	Lee Mazzilli	.15
Panel (20)		.65
10	Dave Parker	.15
32	Joe Charboneau	.25
Panel (21)		3.00
11	Pete Rose	2.00
22	Al Oliver	.15
Panel (22)		3.00
11	Pete Rose	2.00
33	Chet Lemon	.15

1982 Squirt

This set was again prepared in conjunction with Topps, but the 1982 Squirt cards are completely different from Topps' regular issue. Only 22 players are included in the full-color set, with the 2-1/2" x 3-1/2" player cards available on one- or two-player panels. Card panels come in four variations, with free grocery contest and scratch-off game cards taking one or two of the positions on the three-card panels. Card backs are numbered and list player statistics.

		NM/M
	Complete Set (22):	12.00
	Common Player:	.15
1	Cecil Cooper	.15
2	Jerry Remy	.15
3	George Brett	2.00
4	Alan Trammell	.15
5	Reggie Jackson	2.00
6	Kirk Gibson	.15
7	Dave Winfield	.75
8	Carlton Fisk	.75
9	Ron Guidry	.15
10	Dennis Leonard	.15
11	Rollie Fingers	.60
12	Pete Rose	2.50
13	Phil Garner	.15
14	Mike Schmidt	2.00
15	Dave Concepcion	.15
16	George Hendrick	.15
17	Andre Dawson	.35
18	George Foster	.15
19	Gary Carter	.75
20	Fernando Valenzuela	.15
21	Tom Seaver	1.00
22	Bruce Sutter	.60

1996 St. Louis Browns Historical Society

This collectors issue honoring the 1944 American League Champion St. Louis Browns was issued in conjunction with a reunion of that team in 1996, sponsored by the St. Louis Browns Historical Society. Every player on the '44 team is included in the set, representing the first-ever baseball card for some of them. Fronts of the 2-5/8" x 3-3/4" cards feature color portraits by artist Ronnie Joyner. Shades of brown form the border. Backs are also printed in brown tones and include a cartoon, 1944 season and World Series stats, lifetime stats, personal data, a career summary and part of a team "Timeline" of the 1944 season. It was reported 2,500 sets were issued at $10 retail.

		NM/M
	Complete Set (36):	10.00
	Common Player:	.50
1	Team logo card	.50
2	Don Gutteridge	.50
3	Milt Byrnes	.50
4	Al Hollingsworth	.50
5	Willis Hudlin	.50
6	Sig Jakucki	.50

7	Nelson Potter	.50
8	Len Schulte	.50
9	Vern Stephens	.50
10	Frank Demaree	.50
11	Al Zarilla	.50
12	Bob Muncrief	.50
13	Steve Sundra	.50
14	Jack Kramer	.50
15	Lefty West	.50
16	Denny Galehouse	.50
17	Luke Sewell	.50
18	Joe Schultz	.50
19	George McQuinn	.50
20	Ellis Clary	.50
21	Babe Martin	.50
22	Red Hayworth	.50
23	Frank Mancuso	.50
24	Tex Shirley	.50
25	Mike Chartak	.50
26	Mark Christman	.50
27	Tom Hafey	.50
28	Tom Turner	.50
29	Floyd Baker	.50
30	Mike Kreevich	.50
31	George Caster	.50
32	Gene Moore	.50
33	Chet Laabs	.50
34	Sam Zoldak	.50
35	Hal Epps	.50
36	Team composite/ checklist card	.50

1987 St. Louis Cardinals Fire Safety

Approximately 25,000 fans in attendance at Busch Stadium on August 24 received this set produced by the U.S. Forestry Service. The cards measure 4" x 6". Fronts feature a full-color photo set inside an oval frame. Only the player's last name appears on front. Backs carry the player's name, position and personal data plus a Smokey Bear cartoon fire prevention message.

		NM/M
	Complete Set (25):	6.00
	Common Player:	.25
1	Ray Soff	.25
2	Todd Worrell	.25
3	John Tudor	.25
4	Pat Perry	.25
5	Rick Horton	.25
6	Dan Cox	.25
7	Bob Forsch	.25
8	Greg Mathews	.25
9	Bill Dawley	.25
10	Steve Lake	.25
11	Tony Pena	.25
12	Tom Pagnozzi	.25
13	Jack Clark	.25
14	Jim Lindeman	.25
15	Mike Laga	.25
16	Terry Pendleton	.25
17	Ozzie Smith	3.50
18	Jose Oquendo	.25
19	Tom Lawless	.25
20	Tom Herr	.25
21	Curt Ford	.25
22	Willie McGee	.25
23	Tito Landrum	.25
24	Vince Coleman	.25
25	Whitey Herzog	.25

1988 St. Louis Cardinals Fire Safety

This set of oversized (3" x 5") cards features full-color action photos that fill the entire front. A thin white line frames the player photo. The player name, team logo and Smokey Bear picture logo are printed in the lower-right corner. Black-and-white backs

contain player information and a Smokey Bear fire prevention cartoon. The sets were distributed to young St. Louis fans as part of a U.S. Forest Service fire prevention campaign. The National Association of State Foresters co-sponsored this set.

		NM/M
	Complete Set (25):	6.00
	Common Player:	.25
1	Whitey Herzog	.25
2	Danny Cox	.25
3	Ken Dayley	.25
4	Jose DeLeon	.25
5	Bob Forsch	.25
6	Joe Magrane	.25
7	Greg Mathews	.25
8	Scott Terry	.25
9	John Tudor	.25
10	Todd Worrell	.25
11	Steve Lake	.25
12	Tom Pagnozzi	.25
13	Tony Pena	.25
14	Bob Horner	.25
15	Tom Lawless	.25
16	Jose Oquendo	.25
17	Terry Pendleton	.25
18	Ozzie Smith	3.50
19	Vince Coleman	.25
20	Curt Ford	.25
21	Willie McGee	.25
22	Larry McWilliams	.25
23	Steve Peters	.25
24	Luis Alicea	.25
25	Tom Brunansky	.25

1989 St. Louis Cardinals Fire Safety

This set featuring action player photos was issued by the U.S. Forest Service to promote fire safety. The cards measure 4" x 6" and include the player's name, team logo and a small picture of Smokey Bear beneath the player photo.

		NM/M
	Complete Set (25):	6.00
	Common Player:	.25
(1)	Tom Brunansky	.25
(2)	Cris Carpenter	.25
(3)	Vince Coleman	.25
(4)	John Costello	.25
(5)	Ken Dayley	.25
(6)	Jose DeLeon	.25
(7)	Frank DiPino	.25
(8)	Whitey Herzog	.25
(9)	Ken Hill	.25
(10)	Pedro Guerrero	.25
(11)	Tim Jones	.25
(12)	Jim Lindeman	.25
(13)	Joe Magrane	.25
(14)	Willie McGee	.25
(15)	John Morris	.25
(16)	Jose Oquendo	.25
(17)	Tom Pagnozzi	.25
(18)	Tony Pena	.25
(19)	Terry Pendleton	.25
(20)	Dan Quisenberry	.25
(21)	Ozzie Smith	3.50
(22)	Scott Terry	.25
(23)	Milt Thompson	.25
(24)	Denny Walling	.25
(25)	Todd Worrell	.25

1990 St. Louis Cardinals Fire Safety

Player photos dominate the fronts of this large-format (3" x 5") set sponsored by the U.S. Forest Service. Backs have a cartoon fire safety tip

plus a few stats and personal data. The unnumbered cards are checklisted here in alphabetical order.

		NM/M
	Complete Set (27):	6.00
	Common Player:	.25
(1)	Vince Coleman	.25
(2)	Dave Collins	.25
(3)	Danny Cox	.25
(4)	Ken Dayley	.25
(5)	Frank DiPino	.25
(6)	Jose DeLeon	.25
(7)	Pedro Guerrero	.25
(8)	Whitey Herzog	.25
(9)	Rick Horton	.25
(10)	Rex Hudler	.25
(11)	Tim Jones	.25
(12)	Joe Magrane	.25
(13)	Greg Mathews	.25
(14)	Willie McGee	.25
(15)	John Morris	.25
(16)	Tom Niedenfuer	.25
(17)	Jose Oquendo	.25
(18)	Tom Pagnozzi	.25
(19)	Terry Pendleton	.25
(20)	Bryn Smith	.25
(21)	Lee Smith	.35
(22)	Ozzie Smith	3.50
(23)	Scott Terry	.25
(24)	Milt Thompson	.25
(25)	John Tudor	.25
(26)	Denny Walling	.25
(27)	Todd Zeile	.25

1991 St. Louis Cardinals Police

Color action photos are featured prominently on these large-format (2-5/8" x 4-1/16") cards. In the white border at bottom, the team name is printed in red, with the player name and uniform number printed in black. Backs feature a large cartoon safety message, career stats, some biographical data and the logos of the set's sponsors, Kansas City Life Insurance and the Greater St. Louis Law Enforcement Agencies. Backs are printed in red on white.

		NM/M
	Complete Set (24):	7.50
	Common Player:	.15
1	Ozzie Smith	5.00
7	Geronimo Pena	.15
9	Joe Torre	.50
10	Rex Hudler	.15
11	Jose Oquendo	.15
12	Craig Wilson	.15
16	Ray Lankford	.25
19	Tom Pagnozzi	.15
21	Gerald Perry	.15
23	Bernard Gilkey	.15
25	Milt Thompson	.15
27	Todd Zeile	.15
28	Pedro Guerrero	.15
29	Rich Gedman	.15
34	Felix Jose	.15
36	Frank DiPino	.15
37	Bryn Smith	.15
38	Scott Terry	.15
39	Bob Tewksbury	.15
43	Ken Hill	.15
47	Lee Smith	.25
48	Jose DeLeon	.15
49	Juan Agosto	.15

1992 St. Louis Cardinals Police

The Cardinals were the subject of this set given out at Busch Stadium on April 25. Sponsored by Kansas City Life Insurance and distributed by Greater St. Louis law enforce-

ment agencies, the cards are 2-1/2" x 4", and contain a special logo on the front which commemorates the team's 100th anniversary.

		NM/M
	Complete Set (27):	7.50
	Common Player:	.25
1	Ozzie Smith	5.00
7	Geronimo Pena	.25
9	Joe Torre	.50
10	Rex Hudler	.25
11	Jose Oquendo	.25
12	Craig Wilson	.25
16	Ray Lankford	.25
19	Tom Pagnozzi	.25
21	Gerald Perry	.25
23	Bernard Gilkey	.25
25	Milt Thompson	.25
26	Omar Olivares	.25
27	Todd Zeile	.25
28	Pedro Guerrero	.25
29	Rich Gedman	.25
32	Joe Magrane	.25
34	Felix Jose	.25
36	Bryn Smith	.25
37	Scott Terry	.25
38	Todd Worrell	.25
39	Bob Tewksbury	.25
41	Andres Galarraga	.25
44	Cris Carpenter	.25
47	Lee Smith	.30
48	Jose DeLeon	.25
49	Juan Agosto	.25
---	Checklist	.25

1993 St. Louis Cardinals Police

This Cardinals/Kansas City Life police set features 2-5/8" x 4" cards with a blue border and "Cardinals" printed in red at top. The team logo appears in the lower-left corner, while the player's name, position and number appear lower-right. Backs are printed in red on a white background with the player's biography and statistics listed above a safety message.

		NM/M
	Complete Set (25):	7.50
	Common Player:	.25
1	Ozzie Smith	5.00
3	Brian Jordan	.25
5	Stan Royer	.50
9	Joe Torre	.50
11	Jose Oquendo	.25
16	Ray Lankford	.25
18	Luis Alicea	.25
19	Tom Pagnozzi	.25
21	Geronimo Pena	.25
23	Bernard Gilkey	.25
25	Gregg Jefferies	.25
26	Rob Murphy	.25
27	Todd Zeile	.25
28	Gerald Perry	.25
29	Hector Villanueva	.25
31	Donovan Osborne	.25

33	Rod Brewer	.25
39	Bob Tewksbury	.25
42	Mike Perez	.25
43	Rene Arocha	.25
46	Ozzie Canseco	.25
47	Lee Smith	.25
52	Rheal Cormier	.25
54	Tracy Woodson	.25
---	Checklist	.25

1994 St. Louis Cardinals Police

An emphasis on border graphics marks the perennial Cardinals safety set for 1994. The 2-5/8" x 4" cards have a cream colored border. Near the left edge is a vertical red stripe with a team logo at top. Above the color photo at center is the team name. The player name and position are at lower-left. A baseball zooms out of the photo at lower-right carrying the uniform number. Backs are printed in red on white and feature a large cartoon safety message at center. Career stats and biographical data are at top. At bottom are sponsors' logos for the Kansas City Life Insurance Co. and Greater St. Louis Law Enforcement Agencies.

		NM/M
	Complete Set (26):	7.50
	Common Player:	.15
1	Ozzie Smith	5.00
3	Brian Jordan	.25
5	Stan Royer	.15
9	Joe Torre	.50
11	Jose Oquendo	.15
12	Erik Pappas	.15
16	Ray Lankford	.15
18	Luis Alicea	.15
19	Tom Pagnozzi	.15
21	Geronimo Pena	.15
22	Mark Whiten	.15
23	Bernard Gilkey	.15
25	Gregg Jefferies	.15
26	Omar Olivares	.15
27	Todd Zeile	.15
28	Gerald Perry	.15
34	Tom Urbani	.15
36	Paul Kilgus	.15
38	Allen Watson	.15
39	Bob Tewksbury	.15
40	Rick Sutcliffe	.15
42	Mike Perez	.15
43	Rene Arocha	.15
46	Rob Murphy	.15
48	Rich Batchelor	.15
52	Rheal Cormier	.15

1995 St. Louis Cardinals Police

In 1995, the Cardinals safety set was sponsored by Kansas City Life Insurance Co., and distributed by law enforcement agencies in the greater St. Louis area. The cards measure about 2-5/8" x 4" and feature action photos on front. The team name is scripted at bottom and the player's last name and "1995" are vertically at right. Backs have a few vital data, a career stats line, a safety message and sponsor's logo. Cards are listed here in alphabetical order.

		NM/M
	Complete Set (12):	7.50
	Common Player:	.50
(1)	Rene Arocha	.50
(2)	Scott Cooper	.50
(3)	Tripp Cromer	.50
(4)	Bernard Gilkey	.50

(5)	Tom Henke	.50
(6)	Ken Hill	.50
(7)	Danny Jackson	.50
(8)	Brian Jordan	.50
(9)	Ray Lankford	.50
(10)	Jose Oquendo	.50
(11)	Tom Pagnozzi	.50
(12)	Ozzie Smith	5.00

1996 St. Louis Cardinals Police

Once again for 1996, the Cardinals safety set was sponsored by Kansas City Life Insurance Co., and distributed by law enforcement agencies in the greater St. Louis area. The cards measure about 2-5/8" x 4" and feature action photos on front. The team name is vertically in a ghosted strip at left. At bottom, beneath a "torn" photo edge are the player's last name, uniform number and the team logo. Backs have a few vital data, a career stats line, a safety message and sponsor's logo.

		NM/M
Complete Set (26):		10.00
Common Player:		.25
1	Ozzie Smith	5.00
3	Brian Jordan	.25
5	Ron Gant	.25
8	Gary Gaetti	.25
10	Tony LaRussa	.25
12	Royce Clayton	.25
16	Ray Lankford	.25
19	Tom Pagnozzi	.25
22	Mike Gallego	.25
23	Mark Sweeney	.25
24	Tom Urbani	.25
29	Danny Jackson	.25
30	Todd Stottlemyre	.25
31	Donovan Osborne	.25
32	Rick Honeycutt	.25
33	T.J. Mathews	.25
36	Mike Morgan	.25
38	Pat Borders	.25
40	Andy Benes	.25
41	Alan Benes	.25
43	Dennis Eckersley	3.00
46	Mark Petkovsek	.25
47	John Mabry	.25
48	Tony Fossas	.25
51	Willie McGee	.25
---	Fredbird/checklist (mascot)	.25

1998 St. Louis Cardinals Police

Similar in format to those used in the preceding years, this safety issue is printed on a 2-1/4" x 4" format. Fronts have color action photos surrounded by busy borders in predominantly yellow and green. A blue strip at bottom has player name and uniform number and team logo. Backs are in red-and-white with a few biographical details and stats, a cartoon baseball figure, safety message and sponsors' credits. Cards are checklisted here by uniform number.

		NM/M
Complete Set (26):		8.00
Common Player:		.25
3	Brian Jordan	.25
5	Ron Gant	.25
7	Delino DeShields	.25
8	Gary Gaetti	.25
10	Tony LaRussa	.25
11	Royce Clayton	.25
13	David Howard	.25
16	Ray Lankford	.25
19	Tom Pagnozzi	.25

25	Mark McGwire	6.00
26	Eli Marrero	.25
28	Lance Painter	.25
30	Todd Stottlemyre	.25
35	Matt Morris	.25
37	Kent Bottenfield	.25
38	Manny Aybar	.25
43	Alan Benes	.25
43	Kent Mercker	.25
46	Jeff Brantley	.25
46	Mark Petkovsek	.25
47	John Mabry	.25
49	Tom Lampkin	.25
50	John Frascatore	.25
51	Willie McGee	.25
57	Curtis King	.25
	Fredbird/Mascot	.25

2000 St. Louis Cardinals Police

The Cardinals issued this safety set to fans 15 and under at the April 22 game in Busch Stadium. The 2-5/8" x 4" cards have game-action color photos bordered in white. Backs are in red on white with a few bits of personal data, a cartoon safety message and the logo of sponsoring Kansas City Life Insurance, which provided the cards for distribution by the Metropolitan Chiefs and Sheriffs Assn. Cards are checklisted here by uniform number. The checklist of actually-issued cards does not correspond with the checklist on the Fredbird card due to the trades which sent away Kent Bottenfield, Joe McEwing, Brian McRae and Paul Spoljaric.

		NM/M
Complete Set (23):		6.00
Common Player:		.25
3	Edgar Renteria	.45
4	Fernando Vina	.25
5	Thomas Howard	.25
7	J.D. Drew	1.50
10	Tony LaRussa	.25
12	Shawon Dunston	.25
16	Ray Lankford	.25
21	Craig Paquette	.25
22	Mike Matheny	.25
23	Fernando Tatis	.25
24	Eric Davis	.25
25	Mark McGwire	3.00
26	Eli Marrero	.25
31	Alan Benes	.25
36	Scott Radinsky	.25
40	Andy Benes	.25
41	Pat Hentgen	.25
43	Dave Veres	.25
55	Garrett Stephenson	.25
57	Darryl Kile	.25
58	Heathcliff Slocumb	.25
66	Rick Ankiel	.25
	Fredbird/Checklist	.25

2001 St. Louis Cardinals Police

The Cardinals issued this safety set to fans attending a promotional game. The 2-5/8" x 4" cards have a game-action color photo on front. The same photo is vertically squeezed rendered in red and run three times as a background. A red arc at left has player identification. Backs have a few bits of personal data, a cartoon safety message and the logo of sponsoring Kansas City Life Insurance, which provided the cards for distribution by St. Louis area law enforcement agencies.

		NM/M
Complete Set (27):		5.00
Common Player:		.25
3	Edgar Renteria	.25
4	Fernando Vina	.25
5	Albert Pujols	3.00
7	J.D. Drew	.50
8	Mike DiFelice	.25
10	Tony LaRussa	.25
13	Kerry Robinson	.25
15	Jim Edmonds	.40
19	Woody Williams	.25
21	Tino Martinez	.25
22	Mike Matheny	.25
26	Eli Marrero	.25
27	Placido Polanco	.25
35	Matt Morris	.25
36	Gene Stechschulte	.25
40	Andy Benes	.25
43	Dave Veres	.25
44	Jason Isringhausen	.25
48	Mike Matthews	.25

The Cardinals issued this safety set to fans attending a promotional game. The 2-5/8" x 4" cards have a game-action color photo on front. The same photo is enlarged, posterized and rendered in red as a background. A yellow stripe at left and top has player identification. Backs have a few bits of personal data, a cartoon safety message and the logo of sponsoring Kansas City Life Insurance, which provided the cards for distribution by the Metropolitan Chiefs and Sheriffs Assn. Cards are checklisted here alphabetically.

		NM/M
Complete Set (27):		5.00
Common Player:		.25
(1)	Rick Ankiel	.25
(2)	Alan Benes	.25
(3)	Andy Benes	.25
(4)	Bobby Bonilla	.25
(5)	Jack Buck/Broadcaster	.25
(6)	Jason Christiansen	.25
(7)	J.D. Drew	.75
(8)	Jim Edmonds	.50
(9)	Dustin Hermanson	.35
(10)	Carlos Hernandez	.25
(11)	Mike James	.25
(12)	Darryl Kile	.25
(13)	Steve Kline	.25
(14)	Ray Lankford	.25
(15)	Tony LaRussa	.25
(16)	Mark McGwire	2.00
(17)	Eli Marrero	.25
(18)	Mike Matheny	.25
(19)	Matt Morris	.25
(20)	Craig Paquette	.25
(21)	Placido Polanco	.25
(22)	Edgar Renteria	.25
(23)	Larry Sutton	.25
(24)	Mike Timlin	.25
(25)	Dave Veres	.25
(26)	Fernando Vina	.25
(27)	Fredbird/Mascot	.25

2002 St. Louis Cardinals Police

The Cardinals issued this safety set to fans attending a promotional game. The 2-5/8" x 4" cards have a game-action color photo on front. The same photo is vertically squeezed rendered in red and run three times as a background. A red arc at left has player identification. Backs have a few bits of personal data, a cartoon safety message and the logo of sponsoring Kansas City Life Insurance, which provided the cards for distribution by St. Louis area law enforcement agencies.

		NM/M
Complete Set (26):		5.00
Common Player:		.25
0	Kerry Robinson	.35
3	Edgar Renteria	.25
4	Fernando Vina	.25
5	Albert Pujols	3.00
7	J.D. Drew	.50
8a	Joe Girardi	.25
8b	Dustin Hermanson (Should be 32.)	.25
10	Tony LaRussa	.25
13	Jeff Fassero	.25
15	Jim Edmonds	.50
16	Orlando Palmeiro	.25
19	Woody Williams	.25
21	Tino Martinez	.25
22	Mike Matheny	.25
26	Eli Marrero	.25
27	Scott Rolen	.50
30	Brett Tomko	.25
33	Eduardo Perez	.25
35	Matt Morris	.25
41	Miguel Cairo	.25
44	Jason Isringhausen	.25
44	Jason Simontacchi	.25
48	Russ Springer	.25
57	Steve Kline	.25
55	Garrett Stephenson	.25
---	Fredbird/Mascot	.25

2004 St. Louis Cardinals Police

The Cardinals issued this safety set to 10,000 fans 15 and under attending the May 15 game. The 2-5/8" x 4" cards have a game-action color photo on front on a red, orange and black benday-dot background. Backs are printed in red, with a few bits of personal data, 2003 stats, a cartoon safety message and the

49	Steve Kline	.25
50	Mike Timlin	.25
52	Bud Smith	.25
55	Garrett Stephenson	.25
57	Darryl Kile	.25
63	Luther Hackman	.25
66	Rick Ankiel	.25
---	Fredbird/Mascot	.25

2003 St. Louis Cardinals Police

The Cardinals issued this safety set to fans 15 and under attending the May 18 game. The 2-5/8" x 4" cards have a game-action color photo on front along with a red and gold geometric lines design and player identification. Backs have a few bits of personal data, a cartoon safety message and the logo of sponsoring Kansas City Life Insurance, which provided the cards for distribution by St. Louis area law enforcement agencies.

		NM/M
Complete Set (26):		5.00
Common Player:		.25
0	Kerry Robinson	.35
3	Edgar Renteria	.25
4	Fernando Vina	.25
5	Albert Pujols	3.00
7	J.D. Drew	.50
8a	Joe Girardi	.25
8b	Dustin Hermanson (Should be 32.)	.25
10	Tony LaRussa	.25
13	Jeff Fassero	.25
15	Jim Edmonds	.50
16	Orlando Palmeiro	.25
19	Woody Williams	.25
21	Tino Martinez	.25
22	Mike Matheny	.25
26	Eli Marrero	.25
27	Scott Rolen	.50
30	Brett Tomko	.25
33	Eduardo Perez	.25
35	Matt Morris	.25
41	Miguel Cairo	.25
44	Jason Isringhausen	.25
44	Jason Simontacchi	.25
48	Russ Springer	.25
57	Steve Kline	.25
55	Garrett Stephenson	.25
---	Fredbird/Mascot	.25

2005 St. Louis Cardinals Police

The Cardinals issued this safety set to fans 15 and under attending the May 29 game. The 2-5/8" x 4" cards have a game-action color photo or portrait on front. Backs are printed in red, with a few bits of personal data, a 2004 stats, a cartoon safety message and the logo of sponsoring Kansas City Life Insurance, which provided the cards for distribution by St. Louis area law enforcement agencies.

		NM/M
Complete Set (27):		8.00
Common Player:		.25
3	Abraham Nunez	.25
5	Albert Pujols	2.00
7	Hector Luna	.25
8	Mark Grudzielanek	.25
10	Tony LaRussa	.25
15	Jim Edmonds	1.00
16	Reggie Sanders	.25
21	Jason Marquis	.25
22	David Eckstein	.25
23	Cal Eldred	.25
27	Scott Rolen	1.00
29	Chris Carpenter	.25
30	Mark Mulder	.50
32	Roger Cedeno	.50
33	Larry Walker	.50
35	Matt Morris	.25
36	Mike Lincoln	.25
37	Jeff Suppan	.25
40	Bill Pulsipher	.25
41	Yadier Molina	.25
44	Jason Isringhausen	.25
47	John Mabry	.25
50	Julian Tavarez	.25
56	Ray King	.25
68	Carmen Cali	.25
99	So Taguchi	.25
---	Fredbird/Mascot	.25

1991 Stadium Club Promos

Topps' response to the upscale Leaf baseball card issue was a new brand labeled Stadium Club. To introduce the pre-

Complete Set (26):		5.00
3	Edgar Renteria	.35
5	Albert Pujols	3.00
8	Marlon Anderson	.35
12	Tony LaRussa	.25
15	Jim Edmonds	.50
16	Reggie Sanders	.25
20	Woody Williams	.25
21	Jason Marquis	.25
23	Mike Matheny	.25
23	Cal Eldred	.25
27	Scott Rolen	.50
29	Chris Carpenter	.25
31	Bo Hart	.35
33	Mike Lincoln	.25
34	Steve Kline	.25
35	Matt Morris	.25
37	Jeff Suppan	.25
40a	Kiko Calero	.25
40b	Fredbird (Mascot)	.25
44	Jason Isringhausen	.25
44	Jason Simontacchi	.25
50a	Danny Haren	.25
50b	Julian Tavarez	.25
56	Ray King	.25
99	So Taguchi	.25
---	Busch Stadium 1966-2005	.25

mium cards, a set of 50 promo cards was produced with single cards distributed to employees and candy companies. Production has been reported in the area of 600 of each card. The promos differ from the issued cards on front in that there are four horizontal gold-foil stripes on the promos, instead of three. The back of each promo card is identical, showing a 1986 Topps Traded Jose Canseco card. The unnumbered cards are checklisted here in alphabetical order.

		NM/M
Complete Set (50):		150.00
Common Player:		2.50
(1)	Allan Anderson	2.50
(2)	Steve Balboni	2.50
(3)	Jeff Ballard	2.50
(4)	Jesse Barfield	2.50
(5)	Andy Benes	2.50
(6)	Bobby Bonilla	2.50
(7)	Chris Bosio	2.50
(8)	Daryl Boston	2.50
(9)	Chuck Cary	2.50
(10)	Pat Combs	2.50
(11)	Delino DeShields	2.50
(12)	Shawon Dunston	2.50
(13)	Alvaro Espinoza	2.50
(14)	Sid Fernandez	2.50
(15)	Bob Geren	2.50
(16)	Brian Holman	2.50
(17)	Jay Howell	2.50
(18)	Stan Javier	2.50
(19)	Dave Johnson	2.50
(20)	Howard Johnson	2.50
(21)	Kevin Maas	2.50
(22)	Shane Mack	2.50
(23)	Joe Magrane	2.50
(24)	Denny Martinez	2.50
(25)	Don Mattingly	30.00
(26)	Ben McDonald	2.50
(27)	Eddie Murray	15.00
(28)	Matt Nokes	2.50
(29)	Greg Olson	2.50
(30)	Gregg Olson	2.50
(31)	Jose Oquendo	2.50
(32)	Tony Phillips	2.50
(33)	Rafael Ramirez	2.50
(34)	Dennis Rasmussen	2.50
(35)	Billy Ripken	2.50
(36)	Nolan Ryan	65.00
(37)	Bill Sampen	2.50
(38)	Steve Sax	2.50
(39)	Mike Scioscia	2.50
(40)	David Segui	2.50
(41)	Zane Smith	2.50
(42)	B.J. Surhoff	2.50
(43)	Bobby Thigpen	2.50
(44)	Alan Trammell	2.50
(45)	Fernando Valenzuela	2.50
(46)	Andy Van Slyke	2.50
(47)	Hector Villanueva	2.50
(48)	Larry Walker	2.50
(49)	Walt Weiss	2.50
(50)	Bob Welch	2.50

1991 Stadium Club

One of the most popular sets of 1991, this 600-card issue was released in two 300-card series. The cards were available in foil packs only. No factory sets were available. The cards feature borderless high gloss photos on the front and a player evaluation and card photo on the back. Each card can be found with two different letters preceding the copyright cymbol on back. A special Stadium Club membership package was made available for $29.95 with 10 proof of purchase seals from wrappers.

	NM/M
Complete Set (600):	20.00
Common Player:	.05
Series 1 or 2 Pack (13):	.60
Series 1 or 2 Box (36):	15.00

#	Player	Price
1	Dave Stewart	.05
2	Wally Joyner	.05
3	Shawon Dunston	.05
4	Darren Daulton	.05
5	Will Clark	.05
6	Sammy Sosa	1.00
7	Dan Plesac	.05
8	Marquis Grissom	.05
9	Erik Hanson	.05
10	Geno Petralli	.05
11	Jose Rijo	.05
12	Carlos Quintana	.05
13	Junior Ortiz	.05
14	Bob Walk	.05
15	Mike Macfarlane	.05
16	Eric Yelding	.05
17	Bryn Smith	.05
18	Bip Roberts	.05
19	Mike Scioscia	.05
20	Mark Williamson	.05
21	Don Mattingly	1.00
22	John Franco	.05
23	Chet Lemon	.05
24	Tom Henke	.05
25	Jerry Browne	.05
26	Dave Justice	.05
27	Mark Langston	.05
28	Damon Berryhill	.05
29	Kevin Bass	.05
30	Scott Fletcher	.05
31	Moises Alou	.05
32	Dave Valle	.05
33	Jody Reed	.05
34	Dave West	.05
35	Kevin McReynolds	.05
36	Pat Combs	.05
37	Eric Davis	.05
38	Bret Saberhagen	.05
39	Stan Javier	.05
40	Chuck Cary	.05
41	Tony Phillips	.05
42	Lee Smith	.05
43	Tim Teufel	.05
44	Lance Dickson	.05
45	Greg Litton	.05
46	Teddy Higuera	.05
47	Edgar Martinez	.05
48	Steve Avery	.05
49	Walt Weiss	.05
50	David Segui	.05
51	Andy Benes	.05
52	Karl Rhodes	.05
53	Neal Heaton	.05
54	Dan Gladden	.05
55	Luis Rivera	.05
56	Kevin Brown	.05
57	Frank Thomas	.75
58	Terry Mulholland	.05
59	Dick Schofield	.05
60	Ron Darling	.05
61	Sandy Alomar, Jr.	.05
62	Dave Stieb	.05
63	Alan Trammell	.05
64	Matt Nokes	.05
65	Lenny Harris	.05
66	Milt Thompson	.05
67	Storm Davis	.05
68	Joe Oliver	.05
69	Andres Galarraga	.05
70	Ozzie Guillen	.05
71	Ken Howell	.05
72	Garry Templeton	.05
73	Derrick May	.05
74	Xavier Hernandez	.05
75	Dave Parker	.05
76	Rick Aguilera	.05
77	Robby Thompson	.05
78	Pete Incaviglia	.05
79	Bob Welch	.05
80	Randy Milligan	.05
81	Chuck Finley	.05
82	Alvin Davis	.05
83	Tim Naehring	.05
84	Jay Bell	.05
85	Joe Magrane	.05
86	Howard Johnson	.05
87	Jack McDowell	.05
88	Kevin Seitzer	.05
89	Bruce Ruffin	.05
90	Fernando Valenzuela	.05
91	Terry Kennedy	.05
92	Barry Larkin	.05
93	Larry Walker	.05
94	Luis Salazar	.05
95	Gary Sheffield	.45
96	Bobby Witt	.05
97	Lonnie Smith	.05
98	Bryan Harvey	.05
99	Mookie Wilson	.05
100	Dwight Gooden	.05
101	Lou Whitaker	.05
102	Ron Karkovice	.05
103	Jesse Barfield	.05
104	Jose DeJesus	.05
105	Benito Santiago	.05
106	Brian Holman	.05
107	Rafael Ramirez	.05
108	Ellis Burks	.05
109	Mike Bielecki	.05
110	Kirby Puckett	1.00
111	Terry Shumpert	.05
112	Chuck Crim	.05
113	Todd Benzinger	.05
114	Brian Barnes	.05
115	Carlos Baerga	.05
116	Kal Daniels	.05
117	Dave Johnson	.05
118	Andy Van Slyke	.05
119	John Burkett	.05
120	Rickey Henderson	.75
121	Tim Jones	.05
122	Daryl Irvine	.05
123	Ruben Sierra	.05
124	Jim Abbott	.05
125	Daryl Boston	.05
126	Greg Maddux	1.00
127	Von Hayes	.05
128	Mike Fitzgerald	.05
129	Wayne Edwards	.05
130	Greg Briley	.05
131	Rob Dibble	.05
132	Gene Larkin	.05
133	David Wells	.05
134	Steve Balboni	.05
135	Greg Vaughn	.05
136	Mark Davis	.05
137	Dave Rohde	.05
138	Eric Show	.05
139	Bobby Bonilla	.05
140	Dana Kiecker	.05
141	Gary Pettis	.05
142	Dennis Boyd	.05
143	Mike Benjamin	.05
144	Luis Polonia	.05
145	Doug Jones	.05
146	Al Newman	.05
147	Alex Fernandez	.05
148	Bill Doran	.05
149	Kevin Elster	.05
150	Len Dykstra	.05
151	Mike Gallego	.05
152	Tim Belcher	.05
153	Jay Buhner	.05
154	Ozzie Smith	1.00
155	Jose Canseco	.50
156	Gregg Olson	.05
157	Charlie O'Brien	.05
158	Frank Tanana	.05
159	George Brett	1.00
160	Jeff Huson	.05
161	Kevin Tapani	.05
162	Jerome Walton	.05
163	Charlie Hayes	.05
164	Chris Bosio	.05
165	Chris Sabo	.05
166	Lance Parrish	.05
167	Don Robinson	.05
168	Manuel Lee	.05
169	Dennis Rasmussen	.05
170	Wade Boggs	1.00
171	Bob Geren	.05
172	Mackey Sasser	.05
173	Julio Franco	.05
174	Otis Nixon	.05
175	Bert Blyleven	.05
176	Craig Biggio	.05
177	Eddie Murray	.75
178	Randy Tomlin	.05
179	Tino Martinez	.05
180	Carlton Fisk	.75
181	Dwight Smith	.05
182	Scott Garrelts	.05
183	Jim Gantner	.05
184	Dickie Thon	.05
185	John Farrell	.05
186	Cecil Fielder	.05
187	Glenn Braggs	.05
188	Allan Anderson	.05
189	Kurt Stillwell	.05
190	Jose Oquendo	.05
191	Joe Orsulak	.05
192	Ricky Jordan	.05
193	Kelly Downs	.05
194	Delino DeShields	.05
195	Omar Vizquel	.05
196	Mark Carreon	.05
197	Mike Harkey	.05
198	Jack Howell	.05
199	Lance Johnson	.05
200	Nolan Ryan	2.00
201	John Marzano	.05
202	Doug Drabek	.05
203	Mark Lemke	.05
204	Steve Sax	.05
205	Greg Harris	.05
206	B.J. Surhoff	.05
207	Todd Burns	.05
208	Jose Gonzalez	.05
209	Mike Scott	.05
210	Dave Magadan	.05
211	Dante Bichette	.05
212	Trevor Wilson	.05
213	Hector Villanueva	.05
214	Dan Pasqua	.05
215	Greg Colbrunn	.05
216	Mike Jeffcoat	.05
217	Harold Reynolds	.05
218	Paul O'Neill	.05
219	Mark Guthrie	.05
220	Barry Bonds	2.00
221	Jimmy Key	.05
222	Billy Ripken	.05
223	Tom Pagnozzi	.05
224	Bo Jackson	.10
225	Sid Fernandez	.05
226	Mike Marshall	.05
227	John Kruk	.05
228	Mike Fetters	.05
229	Eric Anthony	.05
230	Ryne Sandberg	1.00
231	Carney Lansford	.05
232	Melido Perez	.05
233	Jose Lind	.05
234	Darryl Hamilton	.05
235	Tom Browning	.05
236	Spike Owen	.05
237	Juan Gonzalez	.40
238	Felix Fermin	.05
239	Keith Miller	.05
240	Mark Gubicza	.05
241	Kent Anderson	.05
242	Alvaro Espinoza	.05
243	Dale Murphy	.20
244	Orel Hershiser	.05
245	Paul Molitor	.75
246	Eddie Whitson	.05
247	Joe Girardi	.05
248	Ken Hrbek	.05
249	Bill Sampen	.05
250	Kevin Mitchell	.05
251	Mariano Duncan	.05
252	Scott Bradley	.05
253	Mike Greenwell	.05
254	Tom Gordon	.05
255	Todd Zeile	.05
256	Bobby Thigpen	.05
257	Gregg Jefferies	.05
258	Kenny Rogers	.05
259	Shane Mack	.05
260	Zane Smith	.05
261	Mitch Williams	.05
262	Jim DeShaies	.05
263	Dave Winfield	.75
264	Ben McDonald	.05
265	Randy Ready	.05
266	Pat Borders	.05
267	Jose Uribe	.05
268	Derek Lilliquist	.05
269	Greg Brock	.05
270	Ken Griffey Jr.	1.25
271	Jeff Gray	.05
272	Danny Tartabull	.05
273	Dennis Martinez	.05
274	Robin Ventura	.05
275	Randy Myers	.05
276	Jack Daugherty	.05
277	Greg Gagne	.05
278	Jay Howell	.05
279	Mike LaValliere	.05
280	Rex Hudler	.05
281	Mike Simms	.05
282	Kevin Maas	.05
283	Jeff Ballard	.05
284	Dave Henderson	.05
285	Pete O'Brien	.05
286	Brook Jacoby	.05
287	Mike Henneman	.05
288	Greg Olson	.05
289	Greg Myers	.05
290	Mark Grace	.05
291	Shawn Abner	.05
292	Frank Viola	.05
293	Lee Stevens	.05
294	Jason Grimsley	.05
295	Matt Williams	.05
296	Ron Robinson	.05
297	Tom Brunansky	.05
298	Checklist	.05
299	Checklist	.05
300	Checklist	.05
301	Darryl Strawberry	.05
302	Bud Black	.05
303	Harold Baines	.05
304	Roberto Alomar	.20
305	Norm Charlton	.05
306	Gary Thurman	.05
307	Mike Felder	.05
308	Tony Gwynn	1.00
309	Roger Clemens	1.00
310	Andre Dawson	.25
311	Scott Radinsky	.05
312	Bob Melvin	.05
313	Kirk McCaskill	.05
314	Pedro Guerrero	.05
315	Walt Terrell	.05
316	Sam Horn	.05
317	Wes Chamberlain RC	.05
318	Pedro Munoz RC	.05
319	Roberto Kelly	.05
320	Mark Portugal	.05
321	Tim McIntosh	.05
322	Jesse Orosco	.05
323	Gary Green	.05
324	Greg Harris	.05
325	Hubie Brooks	.05
326	Chris Nabholz	.05
327	Terry Pendleton	.05
328	Eric King	.05
329	Chili Davis	.05
330	Antonio Telford	.05
331	Kelly Gruber	.05
332	Dennis Eckersley	.65
333	Mel Hall	.05
334	Bob Kipper	.05
335	Willie McGee	.05
336	Steve Olin	.05
337	Steve Buechele	.05
338	Scott Leius	.05
339	Hal Morris	.05
340	Jose Offerman	.05
341	Kent Mercker	.05
342	Ken Griffey	.05
343	Pete Harnisch	.05
344	Kirk Gibson	.05
345	Dave Smith	.05
346	Dave Martinez	.05
347	Atlee Hammaker	.05
348	Brian Downing	.05
349	Todd Hundley	.05
350	Candy Maldonado	.05
351	Dwight Evans	.05
352	Steve Searcy	.05
353	Gary Gaetti	.05
354	Jeff Reardon	.05
355	Travis Fryman	.05
356	Dave Righetti	.05
357	Fred McGriff	.05
358	Don Slaught	.05
359	Gene Nelson	.05
360	Billy Spiers	.05
361	Lee Guetterman	.05
362	Darren Lewis	.05
363	Duane Ward	.05
364	Lloyd Moseby	.05
365	John Smoltz	.05
366	Felix Jose	.05
367	David Cone	.05
368	Wally Backman	.05
369	Jeff Montgomery	.05
370	Rich Garces	.05
371	Billy Hatcher	.05
372	Bill Swift	.05
373	Jim Eisenreich	.05
374	Rob Ducey	.05
375	Tim Crews	.05
376	Steve Finley	.05
377	Jeff Blauser	.05
378	Willie Wilson	.05
379	Gerald Perry	.05
380	Jose Mesa	.05
381	Pat Kelly	.05
382	Matt Merullo	.05
383	Ivan Calderon	.05
384	Scott Chiamparino	.05
385	Lloyd McClendon	.05
386	Dave Bergman	.05
387	Ed Sprague	.05
388	Jeff Bagwell RC	3.00
389	Brett Butler	.05
390	Larry Andersen	.05
391	Glenn Davis	.05
392	Alex Cole (Photo is Otis Nixon.)	.05
393	Mike Heath	.05
394	Danny Darwin	.05
395	Steve Lake	.05
396	Tim Layana	.05
397	Terry Leach	.05
398	Bill Wegman	.05
399	Mark McGwire	1.50
400	Mike Boddicker	.05
401	Steve Howe	.05
402	Bernard Gilkey	.05
403	Thomas Howard	.05
404	Rafael Belliard	.05
405	Tom Candiotti	.05
406	Rene Gonzales	.05
407	Chuck McElroy	.05
408	Paul Sorrento	.05
409	Randy Johnson	.75
410	Brady Anderson	.05
411	Dennis Cook	.05
412	Mickey Tettleton	.05
413	Mike Stanton	.05
414	Ken Oberkfell	.05
415	Rick Honeycutt	.05
416	Nelson Santovenia	.05
417	Bob Tewksbury	.05
418	Brent Mayne	.05
419	Steve Farr	.05
420	Phil Stephenson	.05
421	Jeff Russell	.05
422	Chris James	.05
423	Tim Leary	.05
424	Gary Carter	.75
425	Glenallen Hill	.05
426	Matt Young	.05
427	Sid Bream	.05
428	Greg Swindell	.05
429	Scott Aldred	.05
430	Cal Ripken, Jr.	2.00
431	Bill Landrum	.05
432	Ernie Riles	.05
433	Danny Jackson	.05
434	Casey Candaele	.05
435	Ken Hill	.05
436	Jaime Navarro	.05
437	Lance Blankenship	.05
438	Randy Velarde	.05
439	Frank DiPino	.05
440	Carl Nichols	.05
441	Jeff Robinson	.05
442	Deion Sanders	.05
443	Vincente Palacios	.05
444	Devon White	.05
445	John Cerutti	.05
446	Tracy Jones	.05
447	Jack Morris	.05
448	Mitch Webster	.05
449	Bob Ojeda	.05
450	Oscar Azocar	.05
451	Luis Aquino	.05
452	Mark Whiten	.05
453	Stan Belinda	.05
454	Ron Gant	.05
455	Jose DeLeon	.05
456	Mark Salas	.05
457	Junior Felix	.05
458	Wally Whitehurst	.05
459	Phil Plantier RC	.05
460	Juan Berenguer	.05
461	Franklin Stubbs	.05
462	Joe Boever	.05
463	Tim Wallach	.05
464	Mike Moore	.05
465	Albert Belle	.05
466	Mike Witt	.05
467	Craig Worthington	.05
468	Jerald Clark	.05
469	Scott Terry	.05
470	Milt Cuyler	.05
471	John Smiley	.05
472	Charles Nagy	.05
473	Alan Mills	.05
474	John Russell	.05
475	Bruce Hurst	.05
476	Andujar Cedeno	.05
477	Dave Eiland	.05
478	Brian McRae RC	.10
479	Mike LaCoss	.05
480	Chris Gwynn	.05
481	Jamie Moyer	.05
482	John Olerud	.05
483	Efrain Valdez	.05
484	Sil Campusano	.05
485	Pascual Perez	.05
486	Gary Redus	.05
487	Andy Hawkins	.05
488	Cory Snyder	.05
489	Chris Hoiles	.05
490	Ron Hassey	.05
491	Gary Wayne	.05
492	Mark Lewis	.05
493	Scott Coolbaugh	.05
494	Gerald Young	.05
495	Juan Samuel	.05
496	Willie Fraser	.05
497	Jeff Treadway	.05
498	Vince Coleman	.05
499	Cris Carpenter	.05
500	Jack Clark	.05
501	Kevin Appier	.05
502	Rafael Palmeiro	.65
503	Hensley Meulens	.05
504	George Bell	.05
505	Tony Pena	.05
506	Roger McDowell	.05
507	Luis Sojo	.05
508	Mike Schooler	.05
509	Robin Yount	.75
510	Jack Armstrong	.05
511	Rick Cerone	.05
512	Curt Wilkerson	.05
513	Joe Carter	.05
514	Tim Burke	.05
515	Tony Fernandez	.05
516	Ramon Martinez	.05
517	Tim Hulett	.05
518	Terry Steinbach	.05
519	Pete Smith	.05
520	Ken Caminiti	.05
521	Shawn Boskie	.05
522	Mike Pagliarulo	.05
523	Tim Raines	.05
524	Alfredo Griffin	.05
525	Henry Cotto	.05
526	Mike Stanley	.05
527	Charlie Leibrandt	.05
528	Jeff King	.05
529	Eric Plunk	.05
530	Tom Lampkin	.05
531	Steve Bedrosian	.05
532	Tom Herr	.05
533	Craig Lefferts	.05
534	Jeff Reed	.05
535	Mickey Morandini	.05
536	Greg Cadaret	.05
537	Ray Lankford	.05
538	John Candelaria	.05
539	Rob Deer	.05
540	Brad Arnsberg	.05
541	Mike Sharperson	.05
542	Jeff Robinson	.05
543	Mo Vaughn	.05
544	Jeff Parrett	.05
545	Willie Randolph	.05
546	Herm Winningham	.05
547	Jeff Innis	.05
548	Chuck Knoblauch	.05
549	Tommy Greene	.05
550	Jeff Hamilton	.05
551	Barry Jones	.05
552	Ken Dayley	.05
553	Rick Dempsey	.05
554	Greg Smith	.05
555	Mike Devereaux	.05
556	Keith Comstock	.05
557	Paul Faries	.05
558	Tom Glavine	.35
559	Craig Grebeck	.05
560	Scott Erickson	.05
561	Joel Skinner	.05
562	Mike Morgan	.05
563	Dave Gallagher	.05
564	Todd Stottlemyre	.05
565	Rich Rodriguez	.05
566	Craig Wilson RC	.05
567	Jeff Brantley	.05
568	Scott Kamieniecki	.05
569	Steve Decker	.05
570	Juan Agosto	.05
571	Tommy Gregg	.05
572	Kevin Wickander	.05
573	Jamie Quirk	.05
574	Jerry Don Gleaton	.05
575	Chris Hammond	.05
576	Luis Gonzalez RC	1.00
577	Russ Swan	.05
578	Jeff Conine RC	.50
579	Charlie Hough	.05
580	Jeff Kunkel	.05
581	Darrel Akerfelds	.05
582	Jeff Manto	.05
583	Alejandro Pena	.05
584	Mark Davidson	.05
585	Bob MacDonald	.05
586	Paul Assenmacher	.05
587	Dan Wilson	.05
588	Tom Bolton	.05
589	Brian Harper	.05
590	John Habyan	.05
591	John Orton	.05
592	Mark Gardner	.05
593	Turner Ward	.05
594	Bob Patterson	.05
595	Edwin Nunez	.05
596	Gary Scott	.05
597	Scott Bankhead	.05
598	Checklist	.05
599	Checklist	.05
600	Checklist	.05

Charter Members

Charter members of Topps Stadium Club received a package which included a 50-card multi-sport set unavailable in any other fashion. Cards are similar in format to S.C. regular issues, with full-bleed photos on front, UV coating and gold-foil highlights. This special edition has a gold foil "Charter Member" notation at the bottom of each card front. Backs have a simulated newspaper page describing a career highlight. The cards are unnumbered and the checklist here includes only the baseball cards from the set.

	NM/M
Complete Set (50):	12.50
Common Player:	.15
(1) Sandy Alomar, Jr.	.15
(2) George Brett	1.00
(3) Barry Bonds	2.50
(4) Ellis Burks	.15
(5) Eric Davis	.15
(6) Delino DeShields	.15
(7) Doug Drabek	.15
(8) Cecil Fielder	.15
(9) Carlton Fisk	.50
(10) Ken Griffey Jr., Ken Griffey Sr.	1.50
(11) Billy Hatcher	.15
(12) Andy Hawkins	.15
(13) Rickey Henderson (A.L. MVP)	.50
(14) Rickey Henderson (A.L. base-stealing leader)	.50
(15) Randy Johnson	.50
(16) Dave Justice	.15
(17) Mark Langston, Mike Witt	.15
(18) Kevin Maas	.15
(19) Ramon Martinez	.15
(20) Willie McGee	.15
(21) Terry Mulholland	.15
(22) Jose Offerman	.15
(23) Melido Perez	.15
(24) Nolan Ryan (No-hitter.)	2.50
(25) Nolan Ryan (300th win)	2.50
(26) Ryne Sandberg	.75
(27) Dave Stewart	.15
(28) Dave Stieb	.15
(29) Bobby Thigpen	.15
(30) Fernando Valenzuela	.15
(31) Frank Viola	.15
(32) Bob Welch	.15

Members Only

Each member of Topps Stadium Club during 1991 received three packages of multi-sport cards bearing a special design and stamped "Members Only" in gold foil on the front. Cards followed the basic Stadium Club format of full-bleed action photos on front. Backs have a facsimile newspaper page - the "Stadium Club Herald" - which gives details of a career highlight. Cards are unnumbered and the baseball-only checklist here is arranged alphabetically.

	NM/M
Complete Set (30):	9.00
Common Player:	.15
(1) A.L. Home Run Leaders (Jose Canseco, Cecil Fielder)	.15
(2) Wilson Alvarez	.15
(3) Andy Ashby	.15
(4) Jeff Bagwell	1.00
(5) Braves no-hitter (Kent Mercker, Mark Wohlers, Alejandro Pena)	.15
(6) Roger Clemens	.75
(7) David Cone	.15
(8) Carlton Fisk	.50
(9) Julio Franco	.15
(10) Tom Glavine	.35
(11) Tommy Greene	.15
(12) Pete Harnisch	.15
(13) Rickey Henderson (All-time theft leader.)	.50
(14) Rickey Henderson (11th time A.L. theft leader.)	.50
(15) Howard Johnson	.15
(16) Chuck Knoblauch	.15
(17) Ray Lankford	.15
(18) Denny Martinez	.15
(19) Paul Molitor	.15
(20) Jack Morris	.15
(21) Orioles No-Hitter (Bob Milacki, Mike Flanagan, Mark Williamson, Gregg Olson, Chris Hoiles)	.15
(22) Terry Pendleton (N.L. leading hitter)	.15
(23) Terry Pendleton/MVP	.15
(24) Jeff Reardon	.15
(25) Cal Ripken, Jr.	2.50
(26) Nolan Ryan (7th no-hitter)	2.50
(27) Nolan Ryan (22nd 100-K season)	2.50
(28) Bret Saberhagen	.15
(29) Robby Thompson	.15
(30) Dave Winfield	.50

Nolan Ryan Bronze

One of the premiums included with charter membership in the Topps Stadium Club was a bronze replica of the Nolan Ryan card from the

Charter Member's card set. The replica measures 2-1/2" x 3-1/2" and reproduces both front and back of the Ryan card on a 10-oz. metal slab.

	NM/M
Nolan Ryan/Bronze	15.00

1992 Stadium Club

This 900-card set was released in three 100-card series. Like the 1991 issue, the cards feature borderless high-gloss photos on the front. The flip sides feature the player's first Topps card and a player evaluation. Topps released updated cards in the third series for traded player and free agents. Several players appear on two cards. Special Members Choice cards are included in the set. Series III features special inserts of the last three number one draft picks: Phil Nevin, Brien Taylor and Chipper Jones.

	NM/M
Complete Set (900):	20.00
Common Player:	.05
Series 1, 2, 3 Pack (15):	.75
Series 1, 2, 3 Box (36):	15.00
1 Cal Ripken, Jr.	1.50
2 Eric Yelding	.05
3 Geno Petralli	.05
4 Wally Backman	.05
5 Milt Cuyler	.05
6 Kevin Bass	.05
7 Dante Bichette	.05
8 Ray Lankford	.05
9 Mel Hall	.05
10 Joe Carter	.05
11 Juan Samuel	.05
12 Jeff Montgomery	.05
13 Glenn Braggs	.05
14 Henry Cotto	.05
15 Deion Sanders	.05
16 Dick Schofield	.05
17 David Cone	.05
18 Chili Davis	.05
19 Tom Foley	.05
20 Ozzie Guillen	.05
21 Luis Salazar	.05
22 Terry Steinbach	.05
23 Chris James	.05
24 Jeff King	.05
25 Carlos Quintana	.05
26 Mike Maddux	.05
27 Tommy Greene	.05
28 Jeff Russell	.05
29 Steve Finley	.05
30 Mike Flanagan	.05
31 Darren Lewis	.05
32 Mark Lee	.05
33 Willie Fraser	.05
34 Mike Henneman	.05
35 Kevin Maas	.05
36 Dave Hansen	.05
37 Erik Hanson	.05
38 Bill Doran	.05
39 Mike Boddicker	.05
40 Vince Coleman	.05
41 Devon White	.08
42 Mark Gardner	.05
43 Scott Lewis	.05
44 Juan Berenguer	.05
45 Carney Lansford	.05
46 Curt Wilkerson	.05
47 Shane Mack	.05
48 Bip Roberts	.05
49 Greg Harris	.05
50 Ryne Sandberg	.75
51 Mark Whiten	.05
52 Jack McDowell	.05
53 Jimmy Jones	.05
54 Steve Lake	.05
55 Bud Black	.05
56 Dave Valle	.05
57 Kevin Reimer	.05
58 Rich Gedman	.05
59 Travis Fryman	.05
60 Steve Avery	.05
61 Francisco de la Rosa	.05

62 Scott Hemond	.05
63 Hal Morris	.05
64 Hensley Meulens	.05
65 Frank Castillo	.05
66 Gene Larkin	.05
67 Jose DeLeon	.05
68 Al Osuna	.05
69 Dave Cochrane	.05
70 Robin Ventura	.05
71 John Cerutti	.05
72 Kevin Gross	.05
73 Ivan Calderon	.05
74 Mike Macfarlane	.05
75 Stan Belinda	.05
76 Shawn Hillegas	.05
77 Pat Borders	.05
78 Jim Vatcher	.05
79 Bobby Rose	.05
80 Roger Clemens	.85
81 Jeff Treadway	.05
82 Jamie Quirk	.05
83 Randy Bush	.05
84 Anthony Young	.05
85 Trevor Wilson	.05
86 Jaime Navarro	.05
87 Les Lancaster	.05
88 Pat Kelly	.05
89 Alvin Davis	.08
90 Larry Andersen	.05
91 Rob Deer	.05
92 Mike Sharperson	.05
93 Lance Parrish	.05
94 Cecil Espy	.05
95 Tim Spehr	.05
96 Dave Stieb	.05
97 Terry Mulholland	.05
98 Dennis Boyd	.05
99 Barry Larkin	.05
100 Ryan Bowen	.05
101 Felix Fermin	.05
102 Luis Alicea	.05
103 Tim Hulett	.05
104 Rafael Belliard	.05
105 Mike Gallego	.05
106 Dave Righetti	.05
107 Jeff Schaefer	.05
108 Ricky Bones	.05
109 Scott Erickson	.05
110 Matt Nokes	.05
111 Bob Scanlan	.05
112 Tom Candiotti	.05
113 Sean Berry	.05
114 Kevin Morton	.05
115 Scott Fletcher	.05
116 B.J. Surhoff	.05
117 Dave Magadan	.05
118 Bill Gullickson	.05
119 Marquis Grissom	.05
120 Lenny Harris	.05
121 Wally Joyner	.05
122 Kevin Brown	.05
123 Braulio Castillo	.05
124 Eric King	.05
125 Mark Portugal	.05
126 Calvin Jones	.05
127 Mike Heath	.05
128 Todd Van Poppel	.05
129 Benny Santiago	.05
130 Gary Thurman	.05
131 Joe Girardi	.05
132 Dave Eiland	.05
133 Orlando Merced	.05
134 Joe Orsulak	.05
135 John Burkett	.05
136 Ken Dayley	.05
137 Ken Hill	.05
138 Walt Terrell	.05
139 Mike Scioscia	.05
140 Junior Felix	.05
141 Ken Caminiti	.05
142 Carlos Baerga	.05
143 Tony Fossas	.05
144 Craig Grebeck	.05
145 Scott Bradley	.05
146 Kent Mercker	.05
147 Derrick May	.05
148 Jerald Clark	.05
149 George Brett	.85
150 Luis Quinones	.05
151 Mike Pagliarulo	.05
152 Jose Guzman	.05
153 Charlie O'Brien	.05
154 Darren Holmes	.05
155 Joe Boever	.05
156 Rich Monteleone	.05
157 Reggie Harris	.05
158 Roberto Alomar	.20
159 Robby Thompson	.05
160 Chris Hoiles	.05
161 Tom Pagnozzi	.05
162 Omar Vizquel	.05
163 John Candelaria	.05
164 Terry Shumpert	.05
165 Andy Mota	.05
166 Scott Bailes	.05
167 Jeff Blauser	.05
168 Steve Olin	.05
169 Doug Drabek	.05
170 Dave Bergman	.05
171 Eddie Whitson	.05
172 Gilberto Reyes	.05
173 Mark Grace	.08
174 Paul O'Neill	.05
175 Greg Cadaret	.05
176 Mark Williamson	.05
177 Casey Candaele	.05
178 Candy Maldonado	.05

180 Lee Smith	.05
181 Harold Reynolds	.05
182 Dave Justice	.05
183 Lenny Webster	.05
184 Donn Pall	.05
185 Gerald Alexander	.05
186 Jack Clark	.05
187 Stan Javier	.05
188 Ricky Jordan	.05
189 Franklin Stubbs	.05
190 Dennis Eckersley	.60
191 Danny Tartabull	.05
192 Pete O'Brien	.05
193 Mark Lewis	.05
194 Mike Felder	.05
195 Mickey Tettleton	.05
196 Dwight Smith	.05
197 Shawn Abner	.05
198 Jim Leyritz	.05
199 Mike Devereaux	.05
200 Craig Biggio	.05
201 Kevin Elster	.05
202 Rance Mulliniks	.05
203 Tony Fernandez	.05
204 Allan Anderson	.05
205 Herm Winningham	.05
206 Tim Jones	.05
207 Ramon Martinez	.05
208 Teddy Higuera	.05
209 John Kruk	.05
210 Jim Abbott	.05
211 Dean Palmer	.05
212 Mark Davis	.05
213 Jay Buhner	.05
214 Jesse Barfield	.05
215 Kevin Mitchell	.05
216 Mike LaValliere	.05
217 Mark Wohlers	.05
218 Dave Henderson	.05
219 Dave Smith	.05
220 Albert Belle	.05
221 Spike Owen	.05
222 Jeff Gray	.05
223 Paul Gibson	.05
224 Bobby Thigpen	.05
225 Mike Mussina	.30
226 Darrin Jackson	.05
227 Luis Gonzalez	.05
228 Greg Briley	.05
229 Brent Mayne	.05
230 Paul Molitor	.05
231 Al Leiter	.05
232 Andy Van Slyke	.05
233 Ron Tingley	.05
234 Bernard Gilkey	.05
235 Kent Hrbek	.05
236 Eric Karros	.05
237 Randy Velarde	.05
238 Andy Allanson	.05
239 Willie McGee	.05
240 Juan Gonzalez	.35
241 Karl Rhodes	.05
242 Luis Mercedes	.05
243 Billy Swift	.05
244 Tommy Gregg	.05
245 David Howard	.05
246 Dave Hollins	.05
247 Kip Gross	.05
248 Walt Weiss	.05
249 Mackey Sasser	.05
250 Cecil Fielder	.05
251 Jerry Browne	.05
252 Doug Dascenzo	.05
253 Darryl Hamilton	.05
254 Dann Bilardello	.05
255 Luis Rivera	.05
256 Larry Walker	.05
257 Ron Karkovice	.05
258 Bob Tewksbury	.05
259 Jimmy Key	.05
260 Bernie Williams	.05
261 Gary Wayne	.05
262 Mike Simms	.05
263 John Orton	.05
264 Marvin Freeman	.05
265 Mike Jeffcoat	.05
266 Roger Mason	.05
267 Edgar Martinez	.05
268 Henry Rodriguez	.05
269 Sam Horn	.05
270 Brian McRae	.05
271 Kirt Manwaring	.05
272 Mike Bordick	.05
273 Chris Sabo	.05
274 Jim Olander	.05
275 Greg Harris	.05
276 Dan Gakeler	.05
277 Bill Sampen	.05
278 Joel Skinner	.05
279 Curt Schilling	.35
280 Dale Murphy	.25
281 Lee Stevens	.05
282 Lonnie Smith	.05
283 Manuel Lee	.05
284 Shawn Boskie	.05
285 Kevin Seitzer	.05
286 Stan Royer	.05
287 John Dopson	.05
288 Scott Bullett	.05
289 Ken Patterson	.05
290 Todd Hundley	.05
291 Tim Leary	.05
292 Brett Butler	.05
293 Gregg Olson	.05
294 Jeff Brantley	.05
295 Brian Holman	.05
296 Brian Harper	.05
297 Brian Bohanon	.05

298 Checklist 1-100	.05
299 Checklist 101-200	.05
300 Checklist 201-300	.05
301 Frank Thomas	.65
302 Lloyd McClendon	.05
303 Brady Anderson	.05
304 Julio Valera	.05
305 Mike Aldrete	.05
306 Joe Oliver	.05
307 Todd Stottlemyre	.05
308 Rey Sanchez	.05
309 Gary Sheffield	.35
310 Andujar Cedeno	.05
311 Kenny Rogers	.05
312 Bruce Hurst	.05
313 Mike Schooler	.05
314 Mike Benjamin	.05
315 Chuck Finley	.05
316 Mark Lemke	.05
317 Scott Livingstone	.05
318 Chris Nabholz	.05
319 Mike Humphreys	.05
320 Pedro Guerrero	.05
321 Willie Banks	.05
322 Tom Goodwin	.05
323 Hector Wagner	.05
324 Wally Ritchie	.05
325 Mo Vaughn	.05
326 Joe Klink	.05
327 Cal Eldred	.05
328 Daryl Boston	.05
329 Mike Huff	.05
330 Jeff Bagwell	.65
331 Bob Milacki	.05
332 Tom Prince	.05
333 Pat Tabler	.05
334 Ced Landrum	.05
335 Reggie Jefferson	.05
336 Mo Sanford	.05
337 Kevin Ritz	.05
338 Gerald Perry	.05
339 Jeff Hamilton	.05
340 Tim Wallach	.05
341 Jeff Huson	.05
342 Jose Melendez	.05
343 Willie Wilson	.05
344 Mike Stanton	.05
345 Joel Johnston	.05
346 Lee Guetterman	.05
347 Francisco Olivares	.05
348 Dave Burba	.05
349 Tim Crews	.05
350 Scott Leius	.05
351 Danny Cox	.05
352 Wayne Housie	.05
353 Chris Donnels	.05
354 Chris George	.05
355 Gerald Young	.05
356 Roberto Hernandez	.05
357 Neal Heaton	.05
358 Todd Frohwirth	.05
359 Jose Vizcaino	.05
360 Jim Thome	.60
361 Craig Wilson	.05
362 Dave Haas	.05
363 Billy Hatcher	.05
364 John Barfield	.05
365 Luis Aquino	.05
366 Charlie Leibrandt	.05
367 Howard Farmer	.05
368 Bryn Smith	.05
369 Mickey Morandini	.05
370 Jose Canseco (Members Choice, should have been #597.)	.35
371 Jose Uribe	.05
372 Bob MacDonald	.05
373 Luis Sojo	.05
374 Craig Shipley	.05
375 Scott Bankhead	.05
376 Greg Gagne	.05
377 Scott Cooper	.05
378 Jose Offerman	.05
379 Billy Spiers	.05
380 John Smiley	.05
381 Jeff Carter	.05
382 Heathcliff Slocumb	.05
383 Jeff Tackett	.05
384 John Kiely	.05
385 John Vander Wal	.05
386 Omar Olivares	.05
387 Ruben Sierra	.05
388 Tom Gordon	.05
389 Charles Nagy	.05
390 Dave Stewart	.05
391 Pete Harnisch	.05
392 Tim Burke	.05
393 Roberto Kelly	.05
394 Freddie Benavides	.05
395 Tom Glavine	.35
396 Wes Chamberlain	.05
397 Eric Gunderson	.05
398 Dave West	.05
399 Ellis Burks	.05
400 Ken Griffey Jr.	1.00
401 Thomas Howard	.05
402 Juan Guzman	.05
403 Mitch Webster	.05
404 Matt Merullo	.05
405 Steve Buechele	.05
406 Danny Jackson	.05
407 Felix Jose	.05
408 Doug Piatt	.05
409 Jim Eisenreich	.05
410 Bryan Harvey	.05
411 Jim Austin	.05
412 Jim Poole	.05
413 Glenallen Hill	.05

414 Gene Nelson	.05
415 Ivan Rodriguez	.60
416 Frank Tanana	.05
417 Steve Decker	.05
418 Jason Grimsley	.05
419 Tim Layana	.05
420 Don Mattingly	.85
421 Jerome Walton	.05
422 Rob Ducey	.05
423 Andy Benes	.05
424 John Marzano	.05
425 Gene Harris	.05
426 Tim Raines	.05
427 Bret Barberie	.05
428 Harvey Pulliam	.05
429 Cris Carpenter	.05
430 Howard Johnson	.05
431 Orel Hershiser	.05
432 Brian Hunter	.05
433 Kevin Tapani	.05
434 Rick Reed	.05
435 Ron Witmeyer	.05
436 Gary Gaetti	.05
437 Alex Cole	.05
438 Chito Martinez	.05
439 Greg Litton	.05
440 Julio Franco	.05
441 Mike Munoz	.05
442 Erik Pappas	.05
443 Pat Combs	.05
444 Lance Johnson	.05
445 Ed Sprague	.05
446 Mike Greenwell	.05
447 Milt Thompson	.05
448 Mike Magnante	.05
449 Chris Haney	.05
450 Robin Yount	.65
451 Rafael Ramirez	.05
452 Gino Minutelli	.05
453 Tom Lampkin	.05
454 Tony Perezchica	.05
455 Dwight Gooden	.05
456 Mark Guthrie	.05
457 Jay Howell	.05
458 Gary DiSarcina	.05
459 John Smoltz	.05
460 Will Clark	.05
461 Dave Otto	.05
462 Rob Maurer	.05
463 Dwight Evans	.05
464 Tom Brunansky	.05
465 Shawn Hare RC	.05
466 Geronimo Pena	.05
467 Alex Fernandez	.05
468 Greg Myers	.05
469 Jeff Fassero	.05
470 Len Dykstra	.05
471 Jeff Johnson	.05
472 Russ Swan	.05
473 Archie Corbin	.05
474 Chuck McElroy	.05
475 Mark McGwire	1.25
476 Wally Whitehurst	.05
477 Tim McIntosh	.05
478 Sid Bream	.05
479 Jeff Juden	.05
480 Carlton Fisk	.65
481 Jeff Plympton	.05
482 Carlos Martinez	.05
483 Jim Gott	.05
484 Bob McClure	.05
485 Tim Teufel	.05
486 Vicente Palacios	.05
487 Jeff Reed	.05
488 Tony Phillips	.05
489 Mel Rojas	.05
490 Ben McDonald	.05
491 Andres Santana	.05
492 Chris Beasley	.05
493 Mike Timlin	.05
494 Brian Downing	.05
495 Kirk Gibson	.05
496 Scott Sanderson	.05
497 Nick Esasky	.05
498 Johnny Guzman RC	.05
499 Mitch Williams	.05
500 Kirby Puckett	.75
501 Mike Harkey	.05
502 Jim Gantner	.05
503 Bruce Egloff	.05
504 Josias Manzanillo	.05
505 Delino DeShields	.05
506 Rheal Cormier	.05
507 Jay Bell	.05
508 Rich Rowland	.05
509 Scott Servais	.05
510 Terry Pendleton	.05
511 Rich DeLucia	.05
512 Warren Newson	.05
513 Paul Faries	.05
514 Kal Daniels	.05
515 Jarvis Brown	.05
516 Rafael Palmeiro	.60
517 Kelly Downs	.05
518 Steve Chitren	.05
519 Moises Alou	.05
520 Wade Boggs	.75
521 Pete Schourek	.05
522 Scott Terry	.05
523 Kevin Appier	.05
524 Gary Redus	.05
525 George Bell	.05
526 Jeff Kaiser	.05
527 Alvaro Espinoza	.05
528 Luis Polonia	.05
529 Darren Daulton	.05
530 Norm Charlton	.05
531 John Olerud	.05

No.	Player	Price
532	Dan Plesac	.05
533	Billy Ripken	.05
534	Rod Nichols	.05
535	Joey Cora	.05
536	Harold Baines	.05
537	Bob Ojeda	.05
538	Mark Leonard	.05
539	Danny Darwin	.05
540	Shawon Dunston	.05
541	Pedro Munoz	.05
542	Mark Gubicza	.05
543	Kevin Baez	.05
544	Todd Zeile	.05
545	Don Slaught	.05
546	Tony Eusebio	.05
547	Alonzo Powell	.05
548	Gary Pettis	.05
549	Brian Barnes	.05
550	Lou Whitaker	.05
551	Keith Mitchell	.05
552	Oscar Azocar	.05
553	Stu Cole	.05
554	Steve Wapnick	.05
555	Derek Bell	.05
556	Luis Lopez	.05
557	Anthony Telford	.05
558	Tim Mauser	.05
559	Glenn Sutko	.05
560	Darryl Strawberry	.05
561	Tom Bolton	.05
562	Cliff Young	.05
563	Bruce Walton	.05
564	Chico Walker	.05
565	John Franco	.05
566	Paul McClellan	.05
567	Paul Abbott	.05
568	Gary Varsho	.05
569	Carlos Maldonado	.05
570	Kelly Gruber	.05
571	Jose Oquendo	.05
572	Steve Frey	.05
573	Tino Martinez	.05
574	Bill Haselman	.05
575	Eric Anthony	.05
576	John Habyan	.05
577	Jeffrey McNeely	.05
578	Chris Bosio	.05
579	Joe Grahe	.05
580	Fred McGriff	.05
581	Rick Honeycutt	.05
582	Matt Williams	.05
583	Cliff Brantley	.05
584	Rob Dibble	.05
585	Skeeter Barnes	.05
586	Greg Hibbard	.05
587	Randy Milligan	.05
588	Checklist 301-400	.05
589	Checklist 401-500	.05
590	Checklist 501-600	.05
591	Frank Thomas (Members Choice)	.35
592	Dave Justice (Members Choice)	.05
593	Roger Clemens (Members Choice)	.45
594	Steve Avery (Members Choice)	.05
595	Cal Ripken (Members Choice)	.75
596	Barry Larkin (Members Choice)	.05
597	Not issued (See #370)	
598	Will Clark (Members Choice)	.05
599	Cecil Fielder (Members Choice)	.05
600	Ryne Sandberg (Members Choice)	.40
601	Chuck Knoblauch (Members Choice)	.05
602	Dwight Gooden (Members Choice)	.05
603	Ken Griffey Jr. (Members Choice)	.65
604	Barry Bonds (Members Choice)	.75
605	Nolan Ryan (Members Choice)	.75
606	Jeff Bagwell (Members Choice)	.35
607	Robin Yount (Members Choice)	.30
608	Bobby Bonilla (Members Choice)	.05
609	George Brett (Members Choice)	.50
610	Howard Johnson (Members Choice)	.05
611	Esteban Beltre	.05
612	Mike Christopher	.05
613	Troy Afenir	.05
614	Mariano Duncan	.05
615	Doug Henry	.05
616	Doug Jones	.05
617	Alvin Davis	.05
618	Craig Lefferts	.05
619	Kevin McReynolds	.05
620	Barry Bonds	1.50
621	Turner Ward	.05
622	Joe Magrane	.05
623	Mark Parent	.05
624	Tom Browning	.05
625	John Smiley	.05
626	Steve Wilson	.05
627	Mike Gallego	.05
628	Sammy Sosa	.75
629	Rico Rossy	.05
630	Royce Clayton	.05
631	Clay Parker	.05
632	Pete Smith	.05
633	Jeff McKnight	.05
634	Jack Daugherty	.05
635	Steve Sax	.05
636	Joe Hesketh	.05
637	Vince Horsman	.05
638	Eric King	.05
639	Joe Boever	.05
640	Jack Morris	.05
641	Arthur Rhodes	.05
642	Bob Melvin	.05
643	Rick Wilkins	.05
644	Scott Scudder	.05
645	Bip Roberts	.05
646	Julio Valera	.05
647	Kevin Campbell	.05
648	Steve Searcy	.05
649	Scott Kamieniecki	.05
650	Kurt Stillwell	.05
651	Bob Welch	.05
652	Andres Galarraga	.05
653	Mike Jackson	.05
654	Bo Jackson	.10
655	Sid Fernandez	.05
656	Mike Bielecki	.05
657	Jeff Reardon	.05
658	Wayne Rosenthal	.05
659	Eric Bullock	.05
660	Eric Davis	.05
661	Randy Tomlin	.05
662	Tom Edens	.05
663	Rob Murphy	.05
664	Leo Gomez	.05
665	Greg Maddux	.75
666	Greg Vaughn	.05
667	Wade Taylor	.05
668	Brad Arnsberg	.05
669	Mike Moore	.05
670	Mark Langston	.05
671	Barry Jones	.05
672	Bill Landrum	.05
673	Greg Swindell	.05
674	Wayne Edwards	.05
675	Greg Olson	.05
676	Bill Pulsipher RC	.05
677	Bobby Witt	.05
678	Mark Carreon	.05
679	Patrick Lennon	.05
680	Ozzie Smith	.75
681	John Briscoe	.05
682	Matt Young	.05
683	Jeff Conine	.05
684	Phil Stephenson	.05
685	Ron Darling	.05
686	Bryan Hickerson	.05
687	Dale Sveum	.05
688	Kirk McCaskill	.05
689	Rich Amaral	
690	Danny Tartabull	
691	Donald Harris	.05
692	Doug Davis	.05
693	John Farrell	.05
694	Paul Gibson	.05
695	Kenny Lofton	.05
696	Mike Fetters	.05
697	Rosario Rodriguez	.05
698	Chris Jones	.05
699	Jeff Manto	.05
700	Rick Sutcliffe	.05
701	Scott Bankhead	.05
702	Donnie Hill	.05
703	Todd Worrell	.05
704	Rene Gonzales	.05
705	Rick Cerone	.05
706	Tony Pena	.05
707	Paul Sorrento	.05
708	Gary Scott	.05
709	Junior Noboa	.05
710	Wally Joyner	.05
711	Charlie Hayes	.05
712	Rich Rodriguez	.05
713	Rudy Seanez	.05
714	Jim Bullinger	.05
715	Jeff Robinson	.05
716	Jeff Branson	.05
717	Andy Ashby	.05
718	Dave Burba	.05
719	Rich Gossage	.05
720	Randy Johnson	.65
721	David Wells	.05
722	Paul Kilgus	.05
723	Dave Martinez	.05
724	Denny Neagle	.05
725	Andy Stankiewicz	.05
726	Rick Aguilera	.05
727	Junior Ortiz	.05
728	Storm Davis	.05
729	Don Robinson	.05
730	Ron Gant	.05
731	Paul Assenmacher	.05
732	Mark Gardiner	.05
733	Milt Hill	.05
734	Jeremy Hernandez	.05
735	Ken Hill	.05
736	Xavier Hernandez	.05
737	Gregg Jefferies	.05
738	Dick Schofield	.05
739	Ron Robinson	.05
740	Sandy Alomar	.05
741	Mike Stanley	.05
742	Butch Henry	.05
743	Floyd Bannister	.05
744	Brian Drahman	.05
745	Dave Winfield	.65
746	Bob Walk	.05
747	Chris James	.05
748	Don Prybylinski	.05
749	Dennis Rasmussen	.05
750	Rickey Henderson	.65
751	Chris Hammond	.05
752	Bob Kipper	.05
753	Dave Rohde	.05
754	Hubie Brooks	.05
755	Bret Saberhagen	.05
756	Jeff Robinson	.05
757	Pat Listach RC	.05
758	Bill Wegman	.05
759	John Wetteland	.05
760	Phil Plantier	.05
761	Wilson Alvarez	.05
762	Scott Aldred	.05
763	Armando Reynoso RC	.05
764	Todd Benzinger	.05
765	Kevin Mitchell	.05
766	Gary Sheffield	.35
767	Allan Anderson	.05
768	Rusty Meacham	.05
769	Rick Parker	.05
770	Nolan Ryan	1.50
771	Jeff Ballard	.05
772	Cory Snyder	.05
773	Denis Boucher	.05
774	Jose Gonzales	.05
775	Juan Guerrero	.05
776	Ed Nunez	.05
777	Scott Ruskin	.05
778	Terry Leach	.05
779	Carl Willis	.05
780	Bobby Bonilla	.05
781	Duane Ward	.05
782	Joe Slusarski	.05
783	David Segui	.05
784	Kirk Gibson	.05
785	Frank Viola	.05
786	Keith Miller	.05
787	Mike Morgan	.05
788	Kim Batiste	.05
789	Sergio Valdez	.05
790	Eddie Taubensee	.05
791	Jack Armstrong	.05
792	Scott Fletcher	.05
793	Steve Farr	.05
794	Dan Pasqua	.05
795	Eddie Murray	.65
796	John Morris	.05
797	Francisco Cabrera	.05
798	Mike Perez	.05
799	Ted Wood	.05
800	Jose Rijo	.05
801	Danny Gladden	.05
802	Arci Cianfrocco	.05
803	Monty Fariss	.05
804	Roger McDowell	.05
805	Randy Myers	.05
806	Kirk Dressendorfer	.05
807	Zane Smith	.05
808	Glenn Davis	.05
809	Torey Lovullo	.05
810	Andre Dawson	.25
811	Bill Pecota	.05
812	Ted Power	.05
813	Willie Blair	.05
814	Dave Fleming	.05
815	Chris Gwynn	.05
816	Jody Reed	.05
817	Mark Dewey	.05
818	Kyle Abbott	.05
819	Tom Henke	.05
820	Kevin Seitzer	.05
821	Al Newman	.05
822	Tim Sherrill	.05
823	Chuck Crim	.05
824	Darren Reed	.05
825	Tony Gwynn	.75
826	Steve Foster	.05
827	Steve Howe	.05
828	Brook Jacoby	.05
829	Rodney McCray	.05
830	Chuck Knoblauch	.05
831	John Wehner	.05
832	Scott Garrelts	.05
833	Alejandro Pena	.05
834	Jeff Parrett	.05
835	Juan Bell	.05
836	Lance Dickson	.05
837	Darryl Kile	.05
838	Efrain Valdez	.05
839	Bob Zupcic RC	.05
840	George Bell	.05
841	Dave Gallagher	.05
842	Tim Belcher	.05
843	Jeff Shaw	.05
844	Mike Fitzgerald	.05
845	Gary Carter	.65
846	John Russell	.05
847	Eric Hillman RC	.05
848	Mike Witt	.05
849	Curt Wilkerson	.05
850	Alan Trammell	.05
851	Rex Hudler	.05
852	Michael Walkden RC	.05
853	Kevin Ward	.05
854	Tim Naehring	.05
855	Bill Swift	.05
856	Damon Berryhill	.05
857	Mark Eichhorn	.05
858	Hector Villanueva	.05
859	Jose Lind	.05
860	Denny Martinez	.05
861	Bill Krueger	.05
862	Mike Kingery	.05
863	Jeff Innis	.05
864	Derek Lilliquist	.05
865	Reggie Sanders	.05
866	Ramon Garcia	.05
867	Bruce Ruffin	.05
868	Dickie Thon	.05
869	Melido Perez	.05
870	Ruben Amaro	.05
871	Alan Mills	.05
872	Matt Sinatro	.05
873	Eddie Zosky	.05
874	Pete Incaviglia	.05
875	Tom Candiotti	.05
876	Bob Patterson	.05
877	Neal Heaton	.05
878	Terrel Hansen RC	.05
879	Dave Eiland	.05
880	Von Hayes	.05
881	Tim Scott	.05
882	Otis Nixon	.05
883	Herm Winningham	.05
884	Dion James	.05
885	Dave Wainhouse	.05
886	Frank DiPino	.05
887	Dennis Cook	.05
888	Jose Mesa	.05
889	Mark Leiter	.05
890	Willie Randolph	.05
891	Craig Colbert	.05
892	Dwayne Henry	.05
893	Jim Lindeman	.05
894	Charlie Hough	.05
895	Gil Heredia	.05
896	Scott Chiamparino	.05
897	Lance Blankenship	.05
898	Checklist 601-700	.05
899	Checklist 701-800	.05
900	Checklist 801-900	.05

First Draft Picks

Issued as inserts with Stadium Club Series 3, this three-card set features the No. 1 draft picks of 1990-92. Fronts have a full-bleed photo with S.C. logo and player name in the lower-right corner. At bottom-left in a red strip is a gold-foil stamping, "#1 Draft Pick of the '90's." An orange circle at upper-right has the year the player was the No. 1 choice. The basic red-and-black back has a color photo, a few biographical and draft details and a gold facsimile autograph among other gold-foil highlights.

		NM/M
Complete Set (3):		4.50
Common Player:		.25
1	Chipper Jones	4.00
2	Brien Taylor	.25
3	Phil Nevin	.25

Master Photos

Uncropped versions of the photos which appear on regular Stadium Club cards are featured on these large-format (5" x 7") cards. The photos are set against a white background and trimmed with holographic foil. Backs are blank and the cards are unnumbered. Members of Topps' Stadium Club received a Master Photo in their members' packs for 1992. The cards were also available as inserts in special boxes of Stadium Club cards sold at Wal-Mart stores.

		NM/M
Complete Set (15):		20.00
Common Player:		.50
(1)	Wade Boggs	2.25
(2)	Barry Bonds	4.00
(3)	Jose Canseco	1.00
(4)	Will Clark	.50
(5)	Cecil Fielder	.50
(6)	Dwight Gooden	.50
(7)	Ken Griffey Jr.	3.00
(8)	Rickey Henderson	2.00
(9)	Lance Johnson	.50
(10)	Cal Ripken, Jr.	4.00
(11)	Nolan Ryan	4.00
(12)	Deion Sanders	.50
(13)	Darryl Strawberry	.50
(14)	Danny Tartabull	.50
(15)	Frank Thomas	2.00

East Coast National

In conjunction with its appearance at the August 1992 East Coast National card show, Topps distributed 22,000 five-card cello packs of its 1992 Stadium Club series bearing a special gold-foil show commemorative overprint. The cards are in all other respects identical to regular issue '92 S.C. Only 100 cards from Series III can be found with the overprint. Production of each card thus totals 1,100.

		NM/M
Complete Set (100):		40.00
Common Player:		.60
601	Chuck Knoblauch (Members Choice)	.60
602	Dwight Gooden (Members Choice)	.60
603	Ken Griffey Jr. (Members Choice)	6.00
604	Barry Bonds (Members Choice)	6.50
605	Nolan Ryan (Members Choice)	7.50
606	Jeff Bagwell (Members Choice)	2.50
607	Robin Yount (Members Choice)	2.50
608	Bobby Bonilla (Members Choice)	.60
609	George Brett (Members Choice)	5.50
610	Howard Johnson (Members Choice)	.60
611	Esteban Beltre	.60
612	Mike Christopher	.60
613	Troy Afenir	.60
619	Kevin McReynolds	.60
620	Barry Bonds	7.50
622	Joe Magrane	.60
623	Mark Parent	.60
626	Steve Wilson	.60
629	Rico Rossy	.60
631	Clay Parker	.60
633	Jeff McKnight	.60
637	Vince Horsman	.60
638	Eric King	.60
639	Joe Boever	.60
641	Arthur Rhodes	.60
647	Kevin Campbell	.60
653	Mike Jackson	.60
661	Randy Tomlin	.60
665	Greg Maddux	3.00
668	Brad Arnsberg	.60
671	Barry Jones	.60
672	Bill Landrum	.60
673	Greg Swindell	.60
676	Bill Pulsipher	.60
679	Patrick Lennon	.60
681	John Briscoe	.60
684	Phil Stephenson	.60
685	Ron Darling	.60
686	Bryan Hickerson	.60
688	Kirk McCaskill	.60
689	Rich Amaral	.60
692	Doug Davis	.60
693	John Farrell	.60
700	Rick Sutcliffe	.60
704	Rene Gonzales	.60
713	Rudy Seanez	.60
714	Jim Bullinger	.60
716	Jeff Branson	.60
717	Andy Ashby	.60
725	Andy Stankiewicz	.60
733	Milt Hill	.60
739	Ron Robinson	.60
747	Chris James	.60
749	Dennis Rasmussen	.60
753	Dave Rohde	.60
757	Pat Listach	.60
758	Bill Wegman	.60
763	Armando Reynoso	.60
766	Gary Sheffield	.90
769	Rick Parker	.60
771	Jeff Ballard	.60
772	Cory Snyder	.60
774	Jose Gonzales	.60
775	Juan Guerrero	.60
776	Edwin Nunez	.60
778	Terry Leach	.60
782	Joe Slusarski	.60
784	Kirk Gibson	.60
788	Kim Batiste	.60
802	Arci Cianfrocco	.60
806	Kirk Dressendorfer	.60
807	Zane Smith	.60
814	Dave Fleming	.60
815	Chris Gwynn	.60
817	Mark Dewey	.60
819	Tom Henke	.60
822	Tim Sherrill	.60
826	Steve Foster	.60
831	John Wehner	.60
832	Scott Garrelts	.60
840	George Bell	.60
841	Dave Gallagher	.60
846	John Russell	.60
847	Eric Hillman	.60
852	Michael Walkden	.60
864	Derek Lilliquist	.60
876	Bob Patterson	.60
878	Terrel Hansen	.60
881	Tim Scott	.60
886	Frank DiPino	.60
891	Craig Colbert	.60
892	Dwayne Henry	.60
893	Jim Lindeman	.60
895	Gil Heredia	.60
898	Checklist 601-700	.05
899	Checklist 701-800	.05
900	Checklist 801-900	.05

National Convention

To promote its Stadium Club baseball card brand to dealers, Topps distributed sample cards during the National Sports Collectors Convention in Atlanta, Ga. The sample cards are regular-issue S.C. cards which have received a gold-foil overprint of the 1992 National logo. Only 100 cards from the third series can be found with the overprint. Only 5,000 4-card packs were distributed, thus only 200 of each card were made.

		NM/M
Complete Set (100):		135.00
Common Player:		1.50
616	Doug Jones	1.50
617	Alvin Davis	1.50
618	Craig Lefferts	1.50
621	Turner Ward	1.50
625	John Smiley	1.50
627	Mike Gallego	1.50
630	Royce Clayton	1.50
634	Jack Daugherty	1.50
635	Steve Sax	1.50
636	Joe Hesketh	1.50
643	Rick Wilkins	1.50
644	Scott Scudder	1.50
645	Bip Roberts	1.50
650	Kurt Stillwell	1.50
652	Andres Galarraga	1.50
657	Jeff Reardon	1.50
662	Tom Edens	1.50
675	Greg Olson	1.50
678	Mark Carreon	1.50
680	Ozzie Smith	15.00
682	Matt Young	1.50
690	Danny Tartabull	1.50

691	Donald Harris	1.50
695	Kenny Lofton	1.50
697	Rosario Rodriguez	1.50
701	Scott Bankhead	1.50
705	Rick Cerone	1.50
706	Tony Pena	1.50
709	Junior Noboa	1.50
710	Wally Joyner	1.50
711	Charlie Hayes	1.50
712	Rich Rodriguez	1.50
721	David Wells	1.50
723	Dave Martinez	1.50
726	Rick Aguilera	1.50
727	Junior Ortiz	1.50
729	Don Robinson	1.50
730	Ron Gant	1.50
731	Paul Assenmacher	1.50
732	Mark Gardiner	1.50
735	Ken Hill	1.50
736	Xavier Hernandez	1.50
737	Gregg Jefferies	1.50
740	Sandy Alomar, Jr.	1.50
741	Mike Stanley	1.50
744	Brian Drahman	1.50
746	Bob Walk	1.50
751	Chris Hammond	1.50
759	John Wetteland	1.50
760	Phil Plantier	1.50
761	Wilson Alvarez	1.50
773	Denis Boucher	1.50
777	Scott Ruskin	1.50
779	Carl Willis	1.50
783	David Segui	1.50
786	Keith Miller	1.50
790	Eddie Taubensee	1.50
791	Jack Armstrong	1.50
792	Scott Fletcher	1.50
793	Steve Farr	1.50
794	Dan Pasqua	1.50
797	Francisco Cabrera	1.50
798	Mike Perez	1.50
801	Danny Gladden	1.50
803	Monty Fariss	1.50
804	Roger McDowell	1.50
805	Randy Myers	1.50
808	Glenn Davis	1.50
809	Torey Lovullo	1.50
816	Jody Reed	1.50
825	Tony Gwynn	15.00
827	Steve Howe	1.50
828	Brook Jacoby	1.50
829	Rodney McCray	1.50
830	Chuck Knoblauch	1.50
835	Juan Bell	1.50
836	Lance Dickson	1.50
837	Darryl Kile	1.50
842	Tim Belcher	1.50
843	Jeff Shaw	1.50
844	Mike Fitzgerald	1.50
845	Gary Carter	6.00
850	Alan Trammell	1.50
851	Rex Hudler	1.50
856	Damon Berryhill	1.50
857	Mark Eichhorn	1.50
858	Hector Villanueva	1.50
860	Denny Martinez	1.50
865	Reggie Sanders	1.50
869	Melido Perez	1.50
874	Pete Incaviglia	1.50
875	Tom Candiotti	1.50
877	Neal Heaton	1.50
879	Dave Eiland	1.50
882	Otis Nixon	1.50
883	Herm Winningham	1.50
884	Dion James	1.50
887	Dennis Cook	1.50
894	Charlie Hough	1.50

Members Only

A multi-sport set of 50 cards was sent in four installments to members of Topps' Stadium Club as part of their 1992 benefits package. Cards are similar in format to regular Stadium Club cards, 2-1/2" x 3-1/2", UV coated on front. Fronts have a special gold foil "Members Only" logo on front. Backs have a stadium scoreboard design with details of a career highlight. The unnumbered cards (baseball only) are checklisted here alphabetically.

		NM/M
Complete Set (36):		18.00
Common Player:		.15
(1)	Carlos Baerga	.15
(2)	Wade Boggs	1.00
(3)	Barry Bonds	2.50
(4)	Bret Boone	.15
(5)	Pat Borders	.15
(6)	George Brett	1.00
(7)	George Brett (3,000 hits)	1.00
(8)	Jim Bullinger	.15
(9)	Gary Carter	.75
(10)	Andujar Cedeno	.15
(11)	Roger Clemens, Matt Young	.45
(12)	Dennis Eckersley (Cy Young Award)	.60
(13)	Dennis Eckersley/MVP	.60
(14)	Dave Eiland	.15
(15)	Dwight Gooden, Gary Sheffield	.25
(16)	Ken Griffey Jr.	1.50
(17)	Kevin Gross	.15
(18)	Bo Jackson	.25
(19)	Eric Karros	.15
(20)	Pat Listach	.15
(21)	Greg Maddux	1.00
(22)	Fred McGriff, Gary Sheffield	.25
(23)	Mickey Morandini	.15
(24)	Jack Morris	.15
(25)	Eddie Murray	.75
(26)	Eddie Murray	.75
(27)	Bip Roberts	.15
(28)	Nolan Ryan (27 seasons)	2.50
(29)	Nolan Ryan (1993 finale)	2.50
(30)	Lee Smith	.15
(31)	Ozzie Smith (2,000 hits)	1.00
(32)	Ozzie Smith (7,000 assists)	1.00
(33)	Ozzie Smith (Stolen base record.)	1.00
(34)	Bobby Thigpen	.15
(35)	Dave Winfield	.75
(36)	Robin Yount	.75

SkyDome

This 200-card special Stadium Club set from Topps was uniquely packaged in a plastic replica of the Toronto Sky-Dome, the home of the 1991 All-Star Game. Featured in the set are members of Team USA, All-Stars, draft picks, top prospects and eight cards from the World Series between the Twins and Braves. The cards are styled much like the regular Stadium Club cards. Some cards have been found with incorrect gold-foil identifiers as well as the correct version.

		NM/M
Unopened Factory Set (200):		15.00
Complete Set (200):		10.00
Common Player:		.05
1	Terry Adams RC	.05
2	Tommy Adams	.05
3	Rick Aguilera	.05
4	Ron Allen	.05
5	Roberto Alomar/AS	.20
6	Sandy Alomar	.05
7	Greg Anthony	.05
8	James Austin	.05
9	Steve Avery	.05
10	Harold Baines	.05
11	Brian Barber RC	.05
12	Jon Barnes	.05
13	George Bell	.05
14	Doug Bennett	.05
15	Sean Bergman	.05
16	Craig Biggio	.05
17	Bill Bliss	.05
18	Wade Boggs/AS	.60
19	Bobby Bonilla/AS	.05
20	Russell Brock	.05
21	Tarrik Brock	.05
22	Tom Browning	.05
23	Brett Butler	.05
24	Ivan Calderon	.05
25	Joe Carter	.05
26	Joe Caruso	.05
27	Dan Cholowsky	.05
28	Will Clark/AS	.05
29	Roger Clemens/AS	.65
30	Shawn Curran	.05
31	Chris Curtis	.05
32	Chili Davis	.05
33	Andre Dawson	.25
34	Joe DeBerry	.05
35	John Dettmer	.05
36	Rob Dibble	.05
37	John Donati RC	.05
38	Dave Doorneweerd	.05
39	Darren Dreifort	.05
40	Mike Durant	.05
41	Chris Durkin	.05
42	Dennis Eckersley	.40
43	Brian Edmondson RC	.05
44	Vaughn Eshelman RC	.05
45	Shawn Estes RC	.50
46	Jorge Fabregas RC	.10
47	Jon Farrell	.05
48	Cecil Fielder/AS	.05
49	Carlton Fisk	.05
50	Tim Flannelly	.05
51	Cliff Floyd RC	.50
52	Julio Franco	.05
53	Greg Gagne	.05
54	Chris Gambs RC	.05
55	Ron Gant	.05
56	Brent Gates	.05
57	Dwayne Gerald	.05
58	Jason Giambi	1.50
59	Benji Gil RC	.05
60	Mark Gipner	.05
61	Danny Gladden	.05
62	Tom Glavine	.35
63	Jimmy Gonzalez	.05
64	Jeff Granger	.05
65	Dan Grapenthien	.05
66	Dennis Gray	.05
67	Shawn Green RC	2.00
68	Tyler Green	.05
69	Todd Greene	.05
70	Ken Griffey Jr./AS	.75
71	Kelly Gruber	.05
72	Ozzie Guillen	.05
73	Tony Gwynn/AS	.60
74	Shane Halter	.05
75	Jeffrey Hammonds	.05
76	Larry Hanlon	.05
77	Pete Harnisch	.05
78	Mike Harrison	.05
79	Bryan Harvey	.05
80	Scott Hatteberg	.05
81	Rick Helling	.05
82	Dave Henderson	.05
83	Rickey Henderson/AS	.50
84	Tyrone Hill	.05
85	Todd Hollandsworth RC	.10
86	Brian Holliday	.05
87	Terry Horn	.05
88	Jeff Hostetler	.05
89	Kent Hrbek	.05
90	Mark Hubbard	.05
91	Charles Johnson	.05
92	Howard Johnson	.05
93	Todd Johnson	.05
94	Bobby Jones RC	.10
95	Dan Jones	.05
96	Felix Jose	.05
97	Dave Justice	.05
98	Jimmy Key	.05
99	Marc Kroom RC	.05
100	John Kruk	.05
101	Mark Langston	.05
102	Barry Larkin	.05
103	Mike LaValliere	.05
104a	Scott Leius (1991 N.L. All-Star - error)	.05
104b	Scott Leius (1991 World Series - correct)	.25
105	Mark Lemke	.05
106	Donnie Leshnock	.05
107	Jimmy Lewis	.05
108	Shawn Livesy	.05
109	Ryan Long	.05
110	Trevor Mallory	.05
111	Denny Martinez	.05
112	Justin Mashore	.05
113	Jason McDonald	.05
114	Jack McDowell	.05
115	Tom McKinnon	.05
116	Billy McKinnon	.05
117	Buck McNabb RC	.05
118	Jim Mecir	.05
119	Dan Melendez	.05
120	Shawn Miller RC	.05
121	Trever Miller	.05
122	Paul Molitor	.50
123	Vincent Moore	.05
124	Mike Morgan	.05
125	Jack Morris (World Series)	.05
126	Jack Morris/AS	.05
127	Sean Mulligan	.05
128	Eddie Murray	.05
129	Mike Neill	.05
130	Phil Nevin	.05
131	Mark O'Brien	.05
132	Alex Ochoa RC	.05
133	Chad Ogea RC	.05
134	Greg Olson	.05
135	Paul O'Neill	.05
136a	Jared Osentowski (1991 World Series - error)	.05
136b	Jared Osentowski (Draft Pick - correct)	.25
137	Mike Pagliarulo	.05
138	Rafael Palmeiro	.40
139	Rodney Pedraza	.05
140	Tony Phillips	.05
141	Scott Pisciotta RC	.05
142	Chris Pritchett	.05
143	Jason Pruitt	.05
144a	Kirby Puckett (1991 N.L. All-Star - error)	.60
144b	Kirby Puckett (1991 World Series - correct)	3.00
145	Kirby Puckett/AS	.60
146	Manny Ramirez RC	5.00
147	Eddie Ramos	.05
148	Mark Ratekin	.05
149	Jeff Reardon	.05
150	Sean Rees	.05
151	Calvin Reese RC	.05
152	Desmond Relaford RC	.10
153	Eric Richardson	.05
154	Cal Ripken, Jr./AS	1.50
155	Chris Roberts	.05
156	Mike Robertson	.05
157	Steve Rodriguez	.05
158	Mike Rossiter	.05
159	Scott Ruffcorn	.05
160a	Chris Sabo (1991 World Series - error)	.05
160b	Chris Sabo (1991 N.L. All-Star - correct)	.25
161	Juan Samuel	.05
162	Ryne Sandberg/AS	.60
163	Scott Sanderson	.05
164	Benito Santiago	.05
165	Gene Schall RC	.05
166	Chad Schoenvogel	.05
167	Chris Seelbach RC	.05
168	Aaron Sele RC	.50
169	Basil Shabazz	.05
170	Al Shirley RC	.05
171	Paul Shuey	.05
172	Ruben Sierra	.05
173	John Smiley	.05
174	Lee Smith	.05
175	Ozzie Smith	.60
176	Tim Smith	.05
177	Zane Smith	.05
178	John Smoltz	.05
179	Scott Stahoviak	.05
180	Kennie Steenstra	.05
181	Kevin Stocker	.05
182	Chris Stynes RC	.05
183	Danny Tartabull	.05
184	Brien Taylor	.05
185	Todd Taylor	.05
186	Larry Thomas	.05
187a	Ozzie Timmons RC	.05
187b	David Tuttle (Should be #188.)	.05
188	Not issued	.05
189	Andy Van Slyke	.05
190a	Frank Viola (1991 World Series - error)	.05
190b	Frank Viola (1991 N.L. All-Star - correct)	.25
191	Michael Walkden	.05
192	Jeff Ware	.05
193	Allen Watson RC	.05
194	Steve Whitaker	.05
195a	Jerry Willard (1991 Draft Pick - error)	.05
195b	Jerry Willard (1991 World Series - correct)	.25
196	Craig Wilson	.05
197	Chris Wimmer	.05
198	Steve Wojciechowski RC	.05
199	Joel Wolfe	.05
200	Ivan Zweig	.05

Abbreviations

AS - All-Star

1993 Stadium Club

Topps' premium set for 1993 was issued in three series, two 300-card series and a final series of 150. Boxes contained 24 packs this year, compared to 36 in the past. Packs had 14 cards and an insert card. Each box had a 5" x 7" Master Photo card.

		NM/M
Complete Set (750):		25.00
Common Player:		.05
First Day:		8X
Pack (15):		.75
Wax Box (24):		10.00
1	Pat Borders	.05
2	Greg Maddux	.85
3	Daryl Boston	.05
4	Bob Ayrault	.05
5	Tony Phillips	.05
6	Damion Easley	.05
7	Kip Gross	.05
8	Jim Thome	.65
9	Tim Belcher	.05
10	Gary Wayne	.05
11	Sam Militello	.05
12	Mike Magnante	.05
13	Tim Wakefield	.05
14	Tim Hulett	.05
15	Rheal Cormier	.05
16	Juan Guerrero	.05
17	Rich Gossage	.05
18	Tim Laker	.05
19	Darrin Jackson	.05
20	Jack Clark	.05
21	Roberto Hernandez	.05
22	Dean Palmer	.05
23	Harold Reynolds	.05
24	Dan Plesac	.05
25	Brent Mayne	.05
26	Pat Hentgen	.05
27	Luis Sojo	.05
28	Ron Gant	.05
29	Paul Gibson	.05
30	Bip Roberts	.05
31	Mickey Tettleton	.05
32	Randy Velarde	.05
33	Brian McRae	.05
34	Wes Chamberlain	.05
35	Wayne Kirby	.05
36	Rey Sanchez	.05
37	Jesse Orosco	.05
38	Mike Stanton	.05
39	Royce Clayton	.05
40	Cal Ripken, Jr.	2.50
41	John Dopson	.05
42	Gene Larkin	.05
43	Tim Raines	.05
44	Randy Myers	.05
45	Clay Parker	.05
46	Mike Scioscia	.05
47	Pete Incaviglia	.05
48	Todd Van Poppel	.05
49	Ray Lankford	.05
50	Eddie Murray	.75
51	Barry Bonds	2.50
52	Gary Thurman	.05
53	Bob Wickman	.05
54	Joey Cora	.05
55	Kenny Rogers	.05
56	Mike Devereaux	.05
57	Kevin Seitzer	.05
58	Rafael Belliard	.05
59	David Wells	.05
60	Mark Clark	.05
61	Carlos Baerga	.05
62	Scott Brosius	.05
63	Jeff Grotewold	.05
64	Rick Wrona	.05
65	Kurt Knudsen	.05
66	Lloyd McClendon	.05
67	Omar Vizquel	.05
68	Jose Vizcaino	.05
69	Rob Ducey	.05
70	Casey Candaele	.05
71	Ramon Martinez	.05
72	Todd Hundley	.05
73	John Marzano	.05
74	Derek Parks	.05
75	Jack McDowell	.05
76	Tim Scott	.05
77	Mike Mussina	.40
78	Delino DeShields	.05
79	Chris Bosio	.05
80	Mike Bordick	.05
81	Rod Beck	.05
82	Ted Power	.05
83	John Kruk	.05
84	Steve Shifflett	.05
85	Danny Tartabull	.05
86	Mike Greenwell	.05
87	Jose Melendez	.05
88	Craig Wilson	.05
89	Melvin Nieves	.05
90	Ed Sprague	.05
91	Willie McGee	.05
92	Joe Orsulak	.05
93	Jeff King	.05
94	Dan Pasqua	.05
95	Brian Harper	.05
96	Joe Oliver	.05
97	Shane Turner	.05
98	Lenny Harris	.05
99	Jeff Parrett	.05
100	Luis Polonia	.05
101	Kent Bottenfield	.05
102	Albert Belle	.05
103	Mike Maddux	.05
104	Randy Tomlin	.05
105	Andy Stankiewicz	.05
106	Rico Rossy	.05
107	Joe Hesketh	.05
108	Dennis Powell	.05
109	Derrick May	.05
110	Pete Harnisch	.05
111	Kent Mercker	.05
112	Scott Fletcher	.05
113	Rex Hudler	.05
114	Chico Walker	.05
115	Rafael Palmeiro	.65
116	Mark Leiter	.05
117	Pedro Munoz	.05
118	Jim Bullinger	.05
119	Ivan Calderon	.05
120	Mike Timlin	.05
121	Rene Gonzales	.05
122	Greg Vaughn	.05
123	Mike Flanagan	.05
124	Mike Hartley	.05
125	Jeff Montgomery	.05
126	Mike Gallego	.05
127	Don Slaught	.05
128	Charlie O'Brien	.05
129a	Jose Offerman (Home: (blank)	2.00
129b	Jose Offerman (Home: S.P. de MACORIS, D.R.)	.05
130	Mark Wohlers	.05
131	Eric Fox	.05
132	Doug Strange	.05
133	Jeff Frye	.05
134	Wade Boggs	.85
135	Lou Whitaker	.05
136	Craig Grebeck	.05
137	Rich Rodriguez	.05
138	Jay Bell	.05
139	Felix Fermin	.05
140	Denny Martinez	.05
141	Eric Anthony	.05
142	Roberto Alomar	.20
143	Darren Lewis	.05
144	Mike Blowers	.05
145	Scott Bankhead	.05
146	Jeff Reboulet	.05
147	Frank Viola	.05
148	Bill Pecota	.05
149	Carlos Hernandez	.05
150	Bobby Witt	.05
151	Sid Bream	.05
152	Todd Zeile	.05
153	Dennis Cook	.05
154	Brian Bohanon	.05
155	Pat Kelly	.05
156	Milt Cuyler	.05
157	Juan Bell	.05
158	Randy Milligan	.05
159	Mark Gardner	.05
160	Pat Tabler	.05
161	Jeff Reardon	.05
162	Ken Patterson	.05
163	Bobby Bonilla	.05
164	Tony Pena	.05
165	Greg Swindell	.05
166	Kirk McCaskill	.05
167	Doug Drabek	.05
168	Franklin Stubbs	.05
169	Ron Tingley	.05
170	Willie Banks	.05
171	Sergio Valdez	.05
172	Mark Lemke	.05
173	Robin Yount	.75
174	Storm Davis	.05
175	Dan Walters	.05
176	Steve Farr	.05
177	Curt Wilkerson	.05
178	Luis Alicea	.05
179	Russ Swan	.05
180	Mitch Williams	.05
181	Wilson Alvarez	.05
182	Carl Willis	.05
183	Craig Biggio	.05
184	Sean Berry	.05
185	Trevor Wilson	.05
186	Jeff Tackett	.05
187	Ellis Burks	.05
188	Jeff Branson	.05
189	Matt Nokes	.05
190	John Smiley	.05
191	Danny Gladden	.05
192	Mike Boddicker	.05
193	Roger Pavlik	.05
194	Paul Sorrento	.05
195	Vince Coleman	.05
196	Gary DiSarcina	.05
197	Rafael Bournigal	.05
198	Mike Schooler	.05
199	Scott Ruskin	.05
200	Frank Thomas	.75
201	Kyle Abbott	.05
202	Mike Perez	.05
203	Andre Dawson	.25
204	Bill Swift	.05
205	Alejandro Pena	.05
206	Dave Winfield	.75
207	Andujar Cedeno	.05
208	Terry Steinbach	.05
209	Chris Hammond	.05
210	Todd Burns	.05
211	Hipolito Pichardo	.05
212	John Kiely	.05
213	Tim Teufel	.05
214	Lee Guetterman	.05
215	Geronimo Pena	.05
216	Brett Butler	.05
217	Bryan Hickerson	.05
218	Rick Trlicek	.05
219	Lee Stevens	.05
220	Roger Clemens	1.25
221	Carlton Fisk	.75
222	Chili Davis	.05

No.	Player	Price
223	Walt Terrell	.05
224	Jim Eisenreich	.05
225	Ricky Bones	.05
226	Henry Rodriguez	.05
227	Ken Hill	.05
228	Rick Wilkins	.05
229	Ricky Jordan	.05
230	Bernard Gilkey	.05
231	Tim Fortugno	.05
232	Geno Petralli	.05
233	Jose Rijo	.05
234	Jim Leyritz	.05
235	Kevin Campbell	.05
236	Al Osuna	.05
237	Pete Smith	.05
238	Pete Schourek	.05
239	Moises Alou	.05
240	Donn Pall	.05
241	Denny Neagle	.05
242	Dan Peltier	.05
243	Scott Scudder	.05
244	Juan Guzman	.05
245	Dave Burba	.05
246	Rick Sutcliffe	.05
247	Tony Fossas	.05
248	Mike Munoz	.05
249	Tim Salmon	.05
250	Rob Murphy	.05
251	Roger McDowell	.05
252	Lance Parrish	.05
253	Cliff Brantley	.05
254	Scott Leius	.05
255	Carlos Martinez	.05
256	Vince Horsman	.05
257	Oscar Azocar	.05
258	Craig Shipley	.05
259	Ben McDonald	.05
260	Jeff Brantley	.05
261	Damon Berryhill	.05
262	Joe Grahe	.05
263	Dave Hansen	.05
264	Rich Amaral	.05
265	Tim Pugh RC	.05
266	Dion James	.05
267	Frank Tanana	.05
268	Stan Belinda	.05
269	Jeff Kent	.05
270	Bruce Ruffin	.05
271	Xavier Hernandez	.05
272	Darrin Fletcher	.05
273	Tino Martinez	.05
274	Benny Santiago	.05
275	Scott Radinsky	.05
276	Mariano Duncan	.05
277	Kenny Lofton	.05
278	Dwight Smith	.05
279	Joe Carter	.05
280	Tim Jones	.05
281	Jeff Huson	.05
282	Phil Plantier	.05
283	Kirby Puckett	.85
284	Johnny Guzman	.05
285	Mike Morgan	.05
286	Chris Sabo	.05
287	Matt Williams	.05
288	Checklist 1-100	.05
289	Checklist 101-200	.05
290	Checklist 201-300	.05
291	Dennis Eckersley (Members Choice)	.30
292	Eric Karros (Members Choice)	.05
293	Pat Listach (Members Choice)	.05
294	Andy Van Slyke (Members Choice)	.05
295	Robin Ventura (Members Choice)	.05
296	Tom Glavine (Members Choice)	.05
297	Juan Gonzalez (Members Choice)	.20
298	Travis Fryman (Members Choice)	.05
299	Larry Walker (Members Choice)	.05
300	Gary Sheffield (Members Choice)	.20
301	Chuck Finley	.05
302	Luis Gonzalez	.05
303	Darryl Hamilton	.05
304	Bien Figueroa	.05
305	Ron Darling	.05
306	Jonathan Hurst	.05
307	Mike Sharperson	.05
308	Mike Christopher	.05
309	Marvin Freeman	.05
310	Jay Buhner	.05
311	Butch Henry	.05
312	Greg Harris	.05
313	Darren Daulton	.05
314	Chuck Knoblauch	.05
315	Greg Harris	.05
316	John Franco	.05
317	John Wehner	.05
318	Donald Harris	.05
319	Benny Santiago	.05
320	Larry Walker	.05
321	Randy Knorr	.05
322	Ramon D. Martinez RC	.05
323	Mike Stanley	.05
324	Bill Wegman	.05
325	Tom Candiotti	.05
326	Glenn Davis	.05
327	Chuck Crim	.05
328	Scott Livingstone	.05
329	Eddie Taubensee	.05
330	George Bell	.05
331	Edgar Martinez	.05
332	Paul Assenmacher	.05
333	Steve Hosey	.05
334	Mo Vaughn	.05
335	Bret Saberhagen	.05
336	Mike Trombley	.05
337	Mark Lewis	.05
338	Terry Pendleton	.05
339	Dave Hollins	.05
340	Jeff Conine	.05
341	Bob Tewksbury	.05
342	Billy Ashley	.05
343	Zane Smith	.05
344	John Wetteland	.05
345	Chris Hoiles	.05
346	Frank Castillo	.05
347	Bruce Hurst	.05
348	Kevin McReynolds	.05
349	Dave Henderson	.05
350	Ryan Bowen	.05
351	Sid Fernandez	.05
352	Mark Whiten	.05
353	Nolan Ryan	2.50
354	Rick Aguilera	.05
355	Mark Langston	.05
356	Jack Morris	.05
357	Rob Deer	.05
358	Dave Fleming	.05
359	Lance Johnson	.05
360	Joe Millette	.05
361	Wil Cordero	.05
362	Chito Martinez	.05
363	Scott Servais	.05
364	Bernie Williams	.05
365	Pedro Martinez	.75
366	Ryne Sandberg	.85
367	Brad Ausmus	.05
368	Scott Cooper	.05
369	Rob Dibble	.05
370	Walt Weiss	.05
371	Mark Davis	.05
372	Orlando Merced	.05
373	Mike Jackson	.05
374	Kevin Appier	.05
375	Esteban Beltre	.05
376	Joe Slusarski	.05
377	William Suero	.05
378	Pete O'Brien	.05
379	Alan Embree	.05
380	Lenny Webster	.05
381	Eric Davis	.05
382	Duane Ward	.05
383	John Habyan	.05
384	Jeff Bagwell	.75
385	Ruben Amaro	.05
386	Julio Valera	.05
387	Robin Ventura	.05
388	Archi Cianfrocco	.05
389	Skeeter Barnes	.05
390	Tim Costo	.05
391	Luis Mercedes	.05
392	Jeremy Hernandez	.05
393	Shawon Dunston	.05
394	Andy Van Slyke	.05
395	Kevin Maas	.05
396	Kevin Brown	.05
397	J.T. Bruett	.05
398	Darryl Strawberry	.05
399	Tom Pagnozzi	.05
400	Sandy Alomar	.05
401	Keith Miller	.05
402	Rich DeLucia	.05
403	Shawn Abner	.05
404	Howard Johnson	.05
405	Mike Benjamin	.05
406	Roberto Mejia RC	.05
407	Mike Butcher	.05
408	Deion Sanders	.05
409	Todd Stottlemyre	.05
410	Scott Kamieniecki	.05
411	Doug Jones	.05
412	John Burkett	.05
413	Lance Blankenship	.05
414	Jeff Parrett	.05
415	Barry Larkin	.05
416	Alan Trammell	.05
417	Mark Kiefer	.05
418	Gregg Olson	.05
419	Mark Grace	.05
420	Shane Mack	.05
421	Bob Walk	.05
422	Curt Schilling	.25
423	Erik Hanson	.05
424	George Brett	1.25
425	Reggie Jefferson	.05
426	Mark Portugal	.05
427	Ron Karkovice	.05
428	Matt Young	.05
429	Troy Neel	.05
430	Hector Fajardo	.05
431	Dave Righetti	.05
432	Pat Listach	.05
433	Jeff Innis	.05
434	Bob MacDonald	.05
435	Brian Jordan	.05
436	Jeff Blauser	.05
437	Mike Myers RC	.05
438	Frank Seminara	.05
439	Rusty Meacham	.05
440	Greg Briley	.05
441	Derek Lilliquist	.05
442	John Vander Wal	.05
443	Scott Erickson	.05
444	Bob Scanlan	.05
445	Todd Frohwirth	.05
446	Tom Goodwin	.05
447	William Pennyfeather	.05
448	Travis Fryman	.05
449	Mickey Morandini	.05
450	Greg Olson	.05
451	Trevor Hoffman	.05
452	Dave Magadan	.05
453	Shawn Jeter	.05
454	Andres Galarraga	.05
455	Ted Wood	.05
456	Freddie Benavides	.05
457	Junior Felix	.05
458	Alex Cole	.05
459	John Orton	.05
460	Eddie Zosky	.05
461	Dennis Eckersley	.65
462	Lee Smith	.05
463	John Smoltz	.05
464	Ken Caminiti	.05
465	Melido Perez	.05
466	Tom Marsh	.05
467	Jeff Nelson	.05
468	Jesse Levis	.05
469	Chris Nabholz	.05
470	Mike Mcfarlane	.05
471	Reggie Sanders	.05
472	Chuck McElroy	.05
473	Kevin Gross	.05
474	Matt Whiteside RC	.05
475	Cal Eldred	.05
476	Dave Gallagher	.05
477	Len Dykstra	.05
478	Mark McGwire	2.00
479	David Segui	.05
480	Mike Henneman	.05
481	Bret Barberie	.05
482	Steve Sax	.05
483	Dave Valle	.05
484	Danny Darwin	.05
485	Devon White	.05
486	Eric Plunk	.05
487	Jim Gott	.05
488	Scooter Tucker	.05
489	Omar Oliveres	.05
490	Greg Myers	.05
491	Brian Hunter	.05
492	Kevin Tapani	.05
493	Rich Monteleone	.05
494	Steve Buechele	.05
495	Bo Jackson	.10
496	Mike LaValliere	.05
497	Mark Leonard	.05
498	Daryl Boston	.05
499	Jose Canseco	.45
500	Brian Barnes	.05
501	Randy Johnson	.75
502	Tim McIntosh	.05
503	Cecil Fielder	.05
504	Derek Bell	.05
505	Kevin Koslofski	.05
506	Darren Holmes	.05
507	Brady Anderson	.05
508	John Valentin	.05
509	Jerry Browne	.05
510	Fred McGriff	.05
511	Pedro Astacio	.05
512	Gary Gaetti	.05
513	John Burke RC	.05
514	Dwight Gooden	.05
515	Thomas Howard	.05
516	Darrell Whitmore RC	.05
517	Ozzie Guillen	.05
518	Darryl Kile	.05
519	Rich Rowland	.05
520	Carlos Delgado	.50
521	Doug Henry	.05
522	Greg Colbrunn	.05
523	Tom Gordon	.05
524	Ivan Rodriguez	.65
525	Kent Hrbek	.05
526	Eric Young	.05
527	Rod Brewer	.05
528	Eric Karros	.05
529	Marquis Grissom	.05
530	Rico Brogna	.05
531	Sammy Sosa	1.00
532	Bret Boone	.05
533	Luis Rivera	.05
534	Hal Morris	.05
535	Monty Fariss	.05
536	Leo Gomez	.05
537	Wally Joyner	.05
538	Tony Gwynn	.85
539	Mike Williams	.05
540	Juan Gonzalez	.40
541	Ryan Klesko	.05
542	Ryan Thompson	.05
543	Chad Curtis	.05
544	Orel Hershiser	.05
545	Carlos Garcia	.05
546	Bob Welch	.05
547	Vinny Castilla	.05
548	Ozzie Smith	.85
549	Luis Salazar	.05
550	Mark Guthrie	.05
551	Charles Nagy	.05
552	Alex Fernandez	.05
553	Mel Rojas	.05
554	Orestes Destrade	.05
555	Mark Gubicza	.05
556	Steve Finley	.05
557	Don Mattingly	1.25
558	Rickey Henderson	.75
559	Tommy Greene	.05
560	Arthur Rhodes	.05
561	Alfredo Griffin	.05
562	Will Clark	.05
563	Bob Zupcic	.05
564	Chuck Carr	.05
565	Henry Cotto	.05
566	Billy Spiers	.05
567	Jack Armstrong	.05
568	Kurt Stillwell	.05
569	David McCarty	.05
570	Joe Vitiello	.05
571	Gerald Williams	.05
572	Dale Murphy	.25
573	Scott Aldred	.05
574	Bill Gullickson	.05
575	Bobby Thigpen	.05
576	Glenallen Hill	.05
577	Dwayne Henry	.05
578	Calvin Jones	.05
579	Al Martin	.05
580	Ruben Sierra	.05
581	Andy Benes	.05
582	Anthony Young	.05
583	Shawn Boskie	.05
584	Scott Pose RC	.05
585	Mike Piazza	1.50
586	Donovan Osborne	.05
587	James Austin	.05
588	Checklist 301-400	.05
589	Checklist 401-500	.05
590	Checklist 501-600	.05
591	Ken Griffey Jr. (Members Choice)	.75
592	Ivan Rodriguez (Members Choice)	.40
593	Carlos Baerga (Members Choice)	.05
594	Fred McGriff (Members Choice)	.05
595	Mark McGwire (Members Choice)	1.00
596	Roberto Alomar (Members Choice)	.10
597	Kirby Puckett (Members Choice)	.45
598	Marquis Grissom (Members Choice)	.05
599	John Smoltz (Members Choice)	.05
600	Ryne Sandberg (Members Choice)	.45
601	Wade Boggs	.85
602	Jeff Reardon	.05
603	Billy Ripken	.05
604	Bryan Harvey	.05
605	Carlos Quintana	.05
606	Greg Hibbard	.05
607	Ellis Burks	.05
608	Greg Swindell	.05
609	Dave Winfield	.75
610	Charlie Hough	.05
611	Chili Davis	.05
612	Jody Reed	.05
613	Mark Williamson	.05
614	Phil Plantier	.05
615	Jim Abbott	.05
616	Dante Bichette	.05
617	Mark Eichhorn	.05
618	Gary Sheffield	.45
619	Richie Lewis RC	.05
620	Joe Girardi	.05
621	Jaime Navarro	.05
622	Willie Wilson	.05
623	Scott Fletcher	.05
624	Bud Black	.05
625	Tom Brunansky	.05
626	Steve Avery	.05
627	Paul Molitor	.75
628	Gregg Jefferies	.05
629	Dave Stewart	.05
630	Javier Lopez	.05
631	Greg Gagne	.05
632	Bobby Kelly	.05
633	Mike Fetters	.05
634	Ozzie Canseco	.05
635	Jeff Russell	.05
636	Pete Incaviglia	.05
637	Tom Henke	.05
638	Chipper Jones	1.00
639	Jimmy Key	.05
640	Dave Martinez	.05
641	Dave Stieb	.05
642	Milt Thompson	.05
643	Alan Mills	.05
644	Tony Fernandez	.05
645	Randy Bush	.05
646	Joe Magrane	.05
647	Ivan Calderon	.05
648	Jose Guzman	.05
649	John Olerud	.05
650	Tom Glavine	.25
651	Julio Franco	.05
652	Armando Reynoso	.05
653	Felix Jose	.05
654	Ben Rivera	.05
655	Andre Dawson	.25
656	Mike Harkey	.05
657	Kevin Seitzer	.05
658	Lonnie Smith	.05
659	Norm Charlton	.05
660	Dave Justice	.05
661	Fernando Valenzuela	.05
662	Dan Wilson	.05
663	Mark Gardner	.05
664	Doug Dascenzo	.05
665	Greg Maddux	.85
666	Harold Baines	.05
667	Randy Myers	.05
668	Harold Reynolds	.05
669	Candy Maldonado	.05
670	Al Leiter	.05
671	Jerald Clark	.05
672	Doug Drabek	.05
673	Kirk Gibson	.05
674	Steve Reed RC	.05
675	Mike Felder	.05
676	Ricky Gutierrez	.05
677	Spike Owen	.05
678	Otis Nixon	.05
679	Scott Sanderson	.05
680	Mark Carreon	.05
681	Troy Percival	.05
682	Kevin Stocker	.05
683	Jim Converse RC	.05
684	Barry Bonds	2.50
685	Greg Gohr	.05
686	Tim Wallach	.05
687	Matt Mieske	.05
688	Robby Thompson	.05
689	Brien Taylor	.05
690	Kirt Manwaring	.05
691	Mike Lansing RC	.25
692	Steve Decker	.05
693	Mike Moore	.05
694	Kevin Mitchell	.05
695	Phil Hiatt	.05
696	Tony Tarasco RC	.05
697	Benji Gil	.05
698	Jeff Juden	.05
699	Kevin Reimer	.05
700	Andy Ashby	.05
701	John Jaha	.05
702	Tim Bogar RC	.05
703	David Cone	.05
704	Willie Greene	.05
705	David Hulse RC	.05
706	Cris Carpenter	.05
707	Ken Griffey Jr.	1.50
708	Steve Bedrosian	.05
709	Dave Nilsson	.05
710	Paul Wagner	.05
711	B.J. Surhoff	.05
712	Rene Arocha RC	.05
713	Manny Lee	.05
714	Brian Williams	.05
715	Sherman Obando RC	.05
716	Terry Mulholland	.05
717	Paul O'Neill	.05
718	David Nied	.05
719	J.T. Snow RC	.50
720	Nigel Wilson	.05
721	Mike Bielecki	.05
722	Kevin Young	.05
723	Charlie Leibrandt	.05
724	Frank Bolick	.05
725	Jon Shave RC	.05
726	Steve Cooke	.05
727	Domingo Martinez RC	.05
728	Todd Worrell	.05
729	Jose Lind	.05
730	Jim Tatum RC	.05
731	Mike Hampton	.05
732	Mike Draper	.05
733	Henry Mercedes	.05
734	John Johnstone RC	.05
735	Mitch Webster	.05
736	Russ Springer	.05
737	Rob Natal	.05
738	Steve Howe	.05
739	Darrell Sherman RC	.05
740	Pat Mahomes	.05
741	Alex Arias	.05
742	Damon Buford	.05
743	Charlie Hayes	.05
744	Guillermo Velasquez	.05
745	Checklist 601-750	.05
746	Frank Thomas (Members Choice)	.40
747	Barry Bonds (Members Choice)	1.50
748	Roger Clemens (Members Choice)	.50
749	Joe Carter (Members Choice)	.05
750	Greg Maddux (Members Choice)	.45

the logo off a common player's card and attaching it to a super-star card.

	NM/M
Common Player:	1.00
1st Day Stars:	8X

Series 1 Inserts

Four bonus cards were produced as special inserts in Series I Stadium Club packs. Two of the full-bleed, gold-foil enhanced cards honor Robin Yount and George Brett for achieving the 3,000-hit mark, while the other two commemorate the first picks in the 1993 expansion draft by the Colorado Rockies (David Nied) and Marlins (Nigel Wilson).

		NM/M
Complete Set (4):		3.00
Common Player:		.25
1	Robin Yount (3,000 hits)	1.00
2	George Brett (3,000 hits)	2.00
3	David Nied (#1 pick)	.25
4	Nigel Wilson (#1 pick)	.25

Series 2 Inserts

Cross-town and regional rivals were featured in this four-card insert set found, on average, one per 24 packs of Series II Stadium Club. Each of the two-faced cards is typical S.C. quality with gold-foil stamping and UV coating front and back.

		NM/M
Complete Set (4):		5.00
Common Card:		1.50
1	Pacific Terrific (Will Clark, Mark McGwire)	2.00
2	Broadway Stars (Dwight Gooden, Don Mattingly)	1.50
3	Second City Sluggers (Ryne Sandberg, Frank Thomas)	1.50
4	Pacific Terrific (Ken Griffey Jr., Darryl Strawberry)	1.50

1st Day Production

Inserted at the rate of about one per box, with an estimated production of 2,000 apiece, 1st Day Production cards are a parallel of 1993 TSC on which an embossed silver holographic foil logo has been added. Because of the considerably higher value of the 1st Day parallels, collectors should be aware that fakes can be created by cutting

Series 3 Inserts

Team "firsts" - first game, first pitch, first batter, etc. - for the 1993 expansion Florida Marlins and Colorado Rockies are featured on this pair of inserts found in Series III Stadium Club packs. Fronts featured game-action photos with the player's name in gold foil. On back is a stadium scene with the team first overprinted in black. At top the team name and Stadium Club logo are in gold foil.

	NM/M
Complete Set (2):	.50
Common Player:	.25
1 David Nied	.25
2 Charlie Hough	.25

Master Photos

Each box of 1993 Stadium Club packs included one Master Photo premium insert. Prize cards good for three Master Photos in a mail-in offer were also included in each of the three series. The 5" x 7" Master Photos feature wide white borders and a large Stadium Club logo at top, highlighted by prismatic foil. The same foil is used as a border for a larger-format version of the player's regular S.C. card at the center of the Master Photo. A "Members Only" version of each of the 1993 Master Photos was available as a premium with the purchase of a Members Only Stadium Club set. the Members Only Master Photos have a gold-foil seal in the upper-right corner.

	NM/M
Complete Set (30):	15.00
Common Player:	.20
Series 1	
(1) Carlos Baerga	.20
(2) Delino DeShields	.20
(3) Brian McRae	.20
(4) Sam Militello	.20
(5) Joe Oliver	.20
(6) Kirby Puckett	1.50
(7) Cal Ripken Jr.	4.00
(8) Bip Roberts	.20
(9) Mike Scioscia	.20
(10) Rick Sutcliffe	.20
(11) Danny Tartabull	.20
(12) Tim Wakefield	.20
Series 2	
(13) George Brett	3.00
(14) Jose Canseco	.50
(15) Will Clark	.20
(16) Travis Fryman	.20
(17) Dwight Gooden	.20
(18) Mark Grace	.30
(19) Rickey Henderson	1.00
(20) Mark McGwire	2.50
(21) Nolan Ryan	4.00
(22) Ruben Sierra	.20
(23) Darryl Strawberry	.20
(24) Larry Walker	.20
Series 3	
(25) Barry Bonds	5.00
(26) Ken Griffey Jr.	2.50
(27) Greg Maddux	2.00
(28) David Nied	.20
(29) J.T. Snow	.20
(30) Brien Taylor	.20
Redemption Card:	3X

Members Only

A special version of the Topps' 1993 Stadium Club set was made available exclusively to members of the company's Stadium Club program. The set is a parallel of the regular-issue SC set (plus insert) on which a gold-foil "Members Only" shield logo has been added to the card front. In all other re-

spects the cards are identical to the regular SC issue. Production was a reported 12,000 sets.

	NM/M
Complete Set (750):	100.00
Common Player:	.50
Members Only Stars:	8X

Members Only Baseball

As a benefit of membership in Topps' Stadium Club, each member received a 59-card set in four separate shipments. The cards featured highlights of the 1993 baseball, hockey, football and basketball seasons. Besides the 28 baseball player cards checklisted here there were nine football cards, six hockey card and 16 basketball cards. Each sport's cards came separately in a heat-sealed cello wrap in a special box. Cards were typical S.C. quality, featuring full-bleed action photos on the front, with the Stadium Club log and player name enhanced with gold-foil stamping and a gold-foil "Members Only" notice beneath the player's name. Backs feature a parti-color background with a colorized, stylized player figure at right. At left is the story of the player's season or career highlight. The cards are unnumbered and are checklisted alphabetically.

	NM/M
Complete Set (28):	9.00
Common Player:	.10
(1) Jim Abbott	.10
(2) Barry Bonds	2.50
(3) Chris Bosio	.10
(4) George Brett	.75
(5) Jay Buhner	.10
(6) Joe Carter (3 HR in game 5th time)	.10
(7) Joe Carter (World Series-winning HR)	.10
(8) Carlton Fisk	.60
(9) Travis Fryman	.10
(10) Mark Grace	.20
(11) Ken Griffey Jr.	1.50
(12) Darryl Kile	.10
(13) Darren Lewis	.10
(14) Greg Maddux	.65
(15) Jack McDowell	.10
(16) Paul Molitor	.60
(17) Eddie Murray	.60
(18) Mike Piazza (Rookie catcher HR record)	1.50
(19) Mike Piazza (N.L. Rookie of the Year)	1.50
(20) Kirby Puckett	.65
(21) Jeff Reardon	.10
(22) Tim Salmon	.20
(23) Curt Schilling	.35
(24) Lee Smith	.10
(25) Dave Stewart	.10
(26) Frank Thomas	.60

(27) Mark Whiten	.10
(28) Dave Winfield	.60

Special

Though the packaging and the cards themselves identify this 200-card set as a 1992 issue, it was not released until 1993 and is thought of by the hobby at large as a 1993 set. The set is sold in a plastic replica of Jack Murphy Stadium in San Diego, venue for the 1993 All-Star Game. Fifty-six of the cards feature players from that contest and are so identified by a line of gold-foil on the card front and an All-Star logo on back. Twenty-five members of the 1992 Team U.S.A. Olympic baseball squad are also included in the set, with appropriate logos and notations front and back. There are 19 cards depicting action and stars of the 1992 League Championships and World Series. The other 100 cards in the set are 1992 draft picks. All cards have the same basic format as the regular-issue 1992 Topps Stadium Club cards, full-bleed photos on front and back, UV coating on both sides and gold-foil highlights on front. Besides the 200 standard-size cards, the Special Edition set included a dozen "Master Photos," 5" x 7" white-bordered premium cards.

	NM/M
Unopened Set (200):	45.00
Complete Set (200):	40.00
Common Player:	.05
1 Dave Winfield	.75
2 Juan Guzman	.05
3 Tony Gwynn	.85
4 Chris Roberts	.05
5 Benny Santiago	.05
6 Sherard Clinkscales	.05
7 Jonathan Nunnally RC	.05
8 Chuck Knoblauch	.05
9 Bob Wolcott RC	.05
10 Steve Rodriguez	.05
11 Mark Williams RC	.05
12 Danny Clyburn RC	.05
13 Darren Dreifort	.05
14 Andy Van Slyke	.05
15 Wade Boggs	.85
16 Scott Patton	.05
17 Gary Sheffield	.45
18 Ron Villone	.05
19 Roberto Alomar	.20
20 Marc Valdes	.05
21 Daron Kirkreit	.05
22 Jeff Granger	.05
23 Levon Largusa	.05
24 Jimmy Key	.05
25 Kevin Pearson	.05
26 Michael Moore	.05
27 Preston Wilson RC	1.00
28 Kirby Puckett	.85
29 Tim Crabtree RC	.05
30 Bip Roberts	.05
31 Kelly Gruber	.05
32 Tony Fernandez	.05
33 Jason Angel	.05
34 Calvin Murray	.05
35 Chad McConnell	.05
36 Jason Moler	.05
37 Mark Lemke	.05
38 Tom Knauss	.05
39 Larry Mitchell	.05
40 Doug Mirabelli	.05
41 Everett Stull II	.05
42 Chris Wimmer	.05
43 Dan Serafini RC	.05
44 Ryne Sandberg	.85
45 Steve Lyons	.05
46 Ryan Freeburg	.05
47 Ruben Sierra	.05
48 David Mysel	.05

49 Joe Hamilton	.05
50 Steve Rodriguez	.05
51 Tim Wakefield	.05
52 Scott Gentile	.05
53 Doug Jones	.05
54 Willie Brown	.05
55 Chad Mottola RC	.05
56 Ken Griffey Jr.	1.50
57 Jon Lieber RC	.50
58 Denny Martinez	.05
59 Joe Petcka	.05
60 Benji Simonton	.05
61 Brett Backlund	.05
62 Damon Berryhill	.05
63 Juan Guzman	.05
64 Doug Hecker	.05
65 Jamie Arnold	.05
66 Bob Tewksbury	.05
67 Tim Leger	.05
68 Todd Etler	.05
69 Lloyd McClendon	.05
70 Kurt Ehmann	.05
71 Rick Magdaleno	.05
72 Tom Pagnozzi	.05
73 Jeffrey Hammonds	.05
74 Joe Carter	.05
75 Chris Holt	.05
76 Charles Johnson	.05
77 Bob Walk	.05
78 Fred McGriff	.05
79 Tom Evans	.05
80 Scott Klingenbeck	.05
81 Chad McConnell	.05
82 Chris Eddy	.05
83 Phil Nevin	.05
84 John Kruk	.05
85 Tony Sheffield	.05
86 John Smoltz	.05
87 Trevor Humphry	.05
88 Charles Nagy	.05
89 Sean Runyan	.05
90 Mike Gulan	.05
91 Darren Daulton	.05
92 Otis Nixon	.05
93 Nomar Garciaparra	8.00
94 Larry Walker	.05
95 Hut Smith	.05
96 Rick Helling	.05
97 Roger Clemens	1.00
98 Ron Gant	.05
99 Kenny Felder	.05
100 Steve Murphy	.05
101 Mike Smith	.05
102 Terry Pendleton	.05
103 Tim Davis	.05
104 Jeff Patzke	.05
105 Craig Wilson	.05
106 Tom Glavine	.35
107 Mark Langston	.05
108 Mark Thompson	.05
109 Eric Owens RC	.05
110 Keith Johnson	.05
111 Robin Ventura	.05
112 Ed Sprague	.05
113 Jeff Schmidt RC	.05
114 Don Wengert	.05
115 Craig Biggio	.05
116 Kenny Carlyle	.05
117 Derek Jeter RC	30.00
118 Manuel Lee	.05
119 Jeff Haas	.05
120 Roger Bailey	.05
121 Sean Lowe	.05
122 Rick Aguilera	.05
123 Sandy Alomar	.05
124 Derek Wallace	.05
125 B.J. Wallace	.05
126 Greg Maddux	.85
127 Tim Moore	.05
128 Lee Smith	.05
129 Todd Steverson	.05
130 Chris Widger	.05
131 Paul Molitor	.75
132 Chris Smith	.05
133 Chris Gomez RC	.05
134 Jimmy Baron	.05
135 John Smoltz	.05
136 Pat Borders	.05
137 Donnie Leshnock	.05
138 Gus Gandarillos	.05
139 Will Clark	.05
140 Ryan Luzinski RC	.05
141 Cal Ripken, Jr.	2.50
142 B.J. Wallace	.05
143 Trey Beamon RC	.05
144 Norm Charlton	.05
145 Mike Mussina	.30
146 Billy Owens	.05
147 Ozzie Smith	.85
148 Jason Kendall RC	1.00
149 Mike Matthews RC	.05
150 David Spykstra	.05
151 Benji Grigsby	.05
152 Sean Smith	.05
153 Mark McGwire	2.00
154 David Cone	.05
155 Shon Walker RC	.05
156 Jason Giambi	.50
157 Jack McDowell	.05
158 Paxton Briley	.05
159 Edgar Martinez	.05
160 Brian Sackinsky	.05
161 Barry Bonds	2.50
162 Roberto Kelly	.05
163 Jeff Alkire	.05
164 Mike Sharperson	.05
165 Jamie Taylor	.05
166 John Saffer	.05

167 Jerry Browne	.05
168 Travis Fryman	.05
169 Brady Anderson	.05
170 Chris Roberts	.05
171 Lloyd Peever	.05
172 Francisco Cabrera	.05
173 Ramiro Martinez	.05
174 Jeff Alkire	.05
175 Ivan Rodriguez	.65
176 Kevin Brown	.05
177 Chad Roper	.05
178 Rod Henderson	.05
179 Dennis Eckersley	.65
180 Shannon Stewart RC	1.00
181 DeShawn Warren	.05
182 Lonnie Smith	.05
183 Willie Adams	.05
184 Jeff Montgomery	.05
185 Damon Hollins	.05
186 Byron Matthews	.05
187 Harold Baines	.05
188 Rick Greene	.05
189 Carlos Baerga	.05
190 Brandon Cromer	.05
191 Roberto Alomar	.20
192 Rich Ireland	.05
193 Steve Montgomery	.05
194 Brant Brown	.05
195 Ritchie Moody	.05
196 Michael Tucker	.05
197 Jason Varitek RC	6.00
198 David Manning	.05
199 Marquis Riley	.05
200 Jason Giambi	.60

Special Master Photos

Each 1993 Stadium Club Special (Jack Murphy Stadium) set included 12 Master Photos replicating cards from the set. There were nine All-Stars, two '92 rookies and a Team USA player among the Master Photos. Gold-tone prismatic foil highlights the 5" x 7" cards, decorating the large logo at top and separating the card photo from the wide white border. Backs have Stadium Club and MLB logos and copyright information printed in black. The unnumbered cards are checklisted here in alphabetical order.

	NM/M
Complete Set (12):	5.00
Common Player:	.20
(1) Sandy Alomar	.20
(2) Tom Glavine	.65
(3) Ken Griffey Jr.	2.00
(4) Tony Gwynn	1.50
(5) Chuck Knoblauch	.20
(6) Chad Mottola	.20
(7) Kirby Puckett	1.50
(8) Chris Roberts	.20
(9) Ryne Sandberg	1.50
(10) Gary Sheffield	.40
(11) Larry Walker	.20
(12) Preston Wilson	.20

Team Sets

This special edition of Stadium Club cards consists of 16

separate team sets of 30 cards each. Each blister-packed team set was priced around $6 and sold exclusively at Wal-Mart. Fronts of the UV coated cards have a player photo that is is borderless at the top, bottom and left. At right is a green stripe, at top of which is a partial baseball design and some other striping in gold-foil. Backs are basically green, with a light blue box at lower-right containing personal information and stats, along with the S.C. logo. A player photo is at upper-left, with his name superimposed on a bat. Cards are checklisted here within team set. Several of the Braves cards were authentically autographed as pack-toppers on specially marked sets.

	NM/M
Complete Set (480):	30.00
Common Player:	.10
Atlanta Braves	
Team Set:	3.00
1 Tom Glavine	.35
2 Bill Pecota	.10
3 David Justice	.10
4 Mark Lemke	.10
5 Jeff Blauser	.10
6 Ron Gant	.10
7 Greg Olson	.10
8 Francisco Cabrera	.10
9 Chipper Jones	1.00
9a Chipper Jones/Auto.	20.00
10 Steve Avery	.10
11 Kent Mercker	.10
12 John Smoltz	.35
12a John Smoltz/Auto.	6.00
13 Pete Smith	.10
14 Damon Berryhill	.10
15 Sid Bream	.10
16 Otis Nixon	.10
17 Mike Stanton	.10
18 Greg Maddux	1.00
19 Jay Howell	.10
20 Rafael Belliard	.10
21 Terry Pendleton	.10
22 Deion Sanders	.15
23 Brian Hunter	.10
24 Marvin Freeman	.10
25 Mark Wohlers	.10
26 Ryan Klesko	4.00
26a Ryan Klesko/Auto.	4.00
27a Javy Lopez/Auto.	4.00
27 Javy Lopez	.10
28 Melvin Nieves	.10
29 Tony Tarasco	.10
30 Ramon Caraballo	.10
Chicago Cubs	
Team Set:	2.50
1 Ryne Sandberg	1.50
2 Sammy Sosa	1.50
3 Greg Hibbard	.10
4 Candy Maldonado	.10
5 Willie Wilson	.10
6 Dan Plesac	.10
7 Steve Buechele	.10
8 Mark Grace	.25
9 Shawon Dunston	.10
10 Steve Lake	.10
11 Dwight Smith	.10
12 Derrick May	.10
13 Paul Assenmacher	.10
14 Mike Harkey	.10
15 Lance Dickson	.10
16 Randy Myers	.10
17 Mike Morgan	.10
18 Chuck McElroy	.10
19 Jose Guzman	.10
20 Jose Vizcaino	.10
21 Frank Castillo	.10
22 Bob Scanlon	.10
23 Rick Wilkins	.10
24 Rey Sanchez	.10
25 Phil Dauphin	.10
26 Jim Bullinger	.10
27 Jessie Hollins	.10
28 Matt Walbeck	.10
29 Fernando Ramsey	.10
30 Jose Bautista	.10
California Angels	
Team Set:	1.50
1 J.T. Snow	.25
2 Chuck Crim	.10
3 Chili Davis	.10
4 Mark Langston	.10
5 Ron Tingley	.10
6 Eduardo Perez	.10
7 Scott Sanderson	.10
8 Jorge Fabregas	.10
9 Troy Percival	.10
10 Rod Carreia	.10
11 Greg Myers	.10
12 Steve Frey	.10
13 Tim Salmon	.25
14 Scott Lewis	.10
15 Rene Gonzales	.10
16 Chuck Finley	.10
17 John Orton	.10
18 Joe Grahe	.10

19	Luis Polonia	.10
20	John Farrell	.10
21	Damion Easley	.10
22	Gene Nelson	.10
23	Chad Curtis	.10
24	Russ Springer	.10
25	De Shawn Warren	.10
26	Darryl Scott	.10
27	Gary DiSarcina	.10
28	Jerry Nielson	.10
29	Torey Lovullo	.10
30	Julio Valera	.10

Chicago White Sox
Team Set: 2.50

1	Frank Thomas	1.00
2	Bo Jackson	.25
3	Rod Bolton	.10
4	Dave Stieb	.10
5	Tim Raines	.10
6	Joey Cora	.10
7	Warren Newson	.10
8	Roberto Hernandez	.10
9	Brandon Wilson	.10
10	Wilson Alvarez	.10
11	Dan Pasqua	.10
12	Ozzie Guillen	.10
13	Robin Ventura	.25
14	Craig Grebeck	.10
15	Lance Johnson	.10
16	Carlton Fisk	.75
17	Ron Karkovice	.10
18	Jack McDowell	.10
19	Scott Radinsky	.10
20	Bobby Thigpen	.10
21	Donn Pall	.10
22	George Bell	.10
23	Alex Fernandez	.10
24	Mike Huff	.10
25	Jason Bere	.10
26	Johnny Ruffin	.10
27	Ellis Burks	.10
28	Kirk McCaskill	.10
29	Terry Leach	.10
30	Shawn Gilbert	.10

Colorado Rockies
Team Set: 1.50

1	David Nied	.10
2	Quinton McCracken	.10
3	Charlie Hayes	.10
4	Bryn Smith	.10
5	Dante Bichette	.10
6	Alex Cole	.10
7	Scott Aldred	.10
8	Roberto Mejia	.10
9	Jeff Parrett	.10
10	Joe Girardi	.10
11	Andres Galarraga	.10
12	Daryl Boston	.10
13	Jerald Clark	.10
14	Gerald Young	.10
15	Bruce Ruffin	.10
16	Rudy Seanez	.10
17	Darren Holmes	.10
18	Andy Ashby	.10
19	Chris Jones	.10
20	Mark Thompson	.10
21	Freddie Benavides	.10
22	Eric Wedge	.10
23	Vinny Castilla	.10
24	Butch Henry	.10
25	Jim Tatum	.10
26	Steve Reed	.10
27	Eric Young	.10
28	Danny Sheaffer	.10
29	Roger Bailey	.10
30	Brad Ausmus	.10

Florida Marlins
Team Set: 1.50

1	Nigel Wilson	.10
2	Bryan Harvey	.10
3	Bob McClure	.10
4	Alex Arias	.10
5	Walt Weiss	.10
6	Charlie Hough	.10
7	Scott Chiamparino	.10
8	Junior Felix	.10
9	Jack Armstrong	.10
10	Dave Magadan	.10
11	Cris Carpenter	.10
12	Benny Santiago	.10
13	Jeff Conine	.10
14	Jerry Don Gleaton	.10
15	Steve Decker	.10
16	Ryan Bowen	.10
17	Ramon Martinez	.10
18	Bret Barberie	.10
19	Monty Fariss	.10
20	Trevor Hoffman	.25
21	Scott Pose	.10
22	Mike Myers	.10
23	Geronimo Berroa	.10
24	Darrell Whitmore	.10
25	Chuck Carr	.10
26	Dave Weathers	.10
27	Matt Turner	.10
28	Jose Martinez	.10
29	Orestes Destrade	.10
30	Carl Everett	.10

Houston Astros
Team Set: 1.50

1	Doug Drabek	.10
2	Eddie Taubensee	.10
3	James Mouton	.10
4	Ken Caminiti	.10
5	Chris James	.10
6	Jeff Juden	.10
7	Eric Anthony	.10
8	Jeff Bagwell	1.00
9	Greg Swindell	.10
10	Steve Finley	.10
11	Al Osuna	.10
12	Gary Mota	.10
13	Scott Servais	.10
14	Craig Biggio	.50
15	Doug James	.10
16	Rob Mallicoat	.10
17	Darryl Kile	.10
18	Kevin Bass	.10
19	Pete Harnisch	.10
20	Andujar Cedeno	.10
21	Brian Hunter	.10
22	Brian Williams	.10
23	Chris Donnels	.10
24	Xavier Hernandez	.10
25	Todd Jones	.10
26	Luis Gonzalez	.10
27	Rick Parker	.10
28	Casey Candaele	.10
29	Tony Eusebio	.10
30	Mark Portugal	.10

Kansas City Royals
Team Set: 1.50

1	George Brett	1.00
2	Mike MacFarlane	.10
3	Tom Gordon	.15
4	Wally Joyner	.10
5	Kevin Appier	.10
6	Phil Hiatt	.10
7	Keith Miller	.10
8	Hipolito Pichardo	.10
9	Chris Gwynn	.10
10	Jose Lind	.10
11	Mark Gubicza	.10
12	Dennis Rasmussen	.10
13	Mike Magnante	.10
14	Joe Vitiello	.10
15	Kevin McReynolds	.10
16	Greg Gagne	.10
17	David Cone	.15
18	Brent Mayne	.10
19	Jeff Montgomery	.10
20	Joe Randa	.10
21	Felix Jose	.10
22	Bill Sampen	.10
23	Curt Wilkerson	.10
24	Mark Gardner	.10
25	Brian McRae	.10
26	Hubie Brooks	.10
27	Chris Eddy	.10
28	Harvey Pulliam	.10
29	Rusty Meacham	.10
30	Danny Miceli	.10

Los Angeles Dodgers
Team Set: 3.00

1	Darryl Strawberry	.10
2	Pedro Martinez	.75
3	Jody Reed	.10
4	Carlos Hernandez	.10
5	Kevin Gross	.10
6	Mike Piazza	1.50
7	Jim Gott	.10
8	Eric Karros	.10
9	Mike Sharperson	.10
10	Ramon Martinez	.10
11	Tim Wallach	.10
12	Pedro Astacio	.10
13	Lenny Harris	.10
14	Brett Butler	.10
15	Raul Mondesi	.10
16	Todd Worrell	.10
17	Jose Offerman	.10
18	Mitch Webster	.10
19	Tom Candiotti	.10
20	Eric Davis	.10
21	Michael Moore	.10
22	Billy Ashley	.10
23	Orel Hershiser	.15
24	Roger Cedeno	.10
25	Roger McDowell	.10
26	Mike James	.10
27	Steve Wilson	.10
28	Todd Hollandsworth	.10
29	Cory Snyder	.10
30	Todd Williams	.10

New York Yankees
Team Set: 2.50

1	Don Mattingly	1.25
2	Jim Abbott	.10
3	Matt Nokes	.10
4	Danny Tartabull	.10
5	Wade Boggs	1.00
6	Melido Perez	.10
7	Steve Farr	.10
8	Kevin Maas	.10
9	Randy Velarde	.10
10	Mike Humphreys	.10
11	Mike Gallego	.10
12	Mike Stanley	.10
13	Jimmy Key	.10
14	Paul O'Neill	.10
15	Spike Owen	.10
16	Pat Kelly	.10
17	Sterling Hitchcock	.10
18	Mike Witt	.10
19	Scott Kamieniecki	.10
20	John Habyan	.10
21	Bernie Williams	.20
22	Brien Taylor	.10
23	Rich Monteleone	.10
24	Mark Hutton	.10
25	Robert Eenhoorn	.10
26	Gerald Williams	.10
27	Sam Militello	.10
28	Bob Wickman	.10
29	Andy Stankiewicz	.10
30	Domingo Jean	.10

Oakland A's
Team Set: 3.00

1	Dennis Eckersley	.75
2	Lance Blankenship	.10
3	Mike Mohler	.10
4	Jerry Browne	.10
5	Kevin Seitzer	.10
6	Storm Davis	.10
7	Mark McGwire	2.00
8	Rickey Henderson	.75
9	Terry Steinbach	.10
10	Ruben Sierra	.10
11	Dave Henderson	.10
12	Bob Welch	.10
13	Rick Honeycutt	.10
14	Ron Darling	.10
15	Joe Boever	.10
16	Bobby Witt	.10
17	Izzy Molina	.10
18	Mike Bordick	.10
19	Brent Gates	.10
20	Shawn Hillegas	.10
21	Scott Hammond	.10
22	Todd Van Poppel	.10
23	Johnny Guzman	.10
24	Scott Lydy	.10
25	Scott Baker	.10
26	Todd Revenig	.10
27	Scott Brosius	.10
28	Troy Neel	.10
29	Dale Sveum	.10
30	Mike Neill	.10

Philadelphia Phillies
Team Set: 1.50

1	Darren Daulton	.10
2	Larry Anderson	.10
3	Kyle Abbott	.10
4	Chad McConnell	.10
5	Danny Jackson	.10
6	Kevin Stocker	.10
7	Jim Eisenreich	.10
8	Mickey Morandini	.10
9	Bob Ayrault	.10
10	Doug Lindsey	.10
11	Dave Hollins	.10
12	Dave West	.10
13	Wes Chamberlain	.10
14	Curt Schilling	.35
15	Len Dykstra	.10
16	Trevor Humphry	.10
17	Terry Mulholland	.10
18	Gene Schall	.10
19	Mike Lieberthal	.15
20	Ben Rivera	.10
21	Mariano Duncan	.10
22	Pete Incaviglia	.10
23	Ron Blazier	.10
24	Jeff Jackson	.10
25	Jose DeLeon	.10
26	Ron Lockett	.10
27	Tommy Greene	.10
28	Milt Thompson	.10
29	Mitch Williams	.10
30	John Kruk	.10

St. Louis Cardinals
Team Set: 1.50

1	Ozzie Smith	1.00
2	Rene Arocha	.10
3	Bernard Gilkey	.10
4	Jose Oquendo	.10
5	Mike Perez	.10
6	Tom Pagnozzi	.10
7	Rod Brewer	.10
8	Joe Magrane	.10
9	Todd Zeile	.10
10	Bob Tewksbury	.10
11	Darrel Deak	.10
12	Gregg Jefferies	.10
13	Lee Smith	.25
14	Ozzie Canseco	.10
15	Tom Urbani	.10
16	Donovan Osborne	.10
17	Ray Lankford	.10
18	Rheal Cormier	.10
19	Allen Watson	.10
20	Geronimo Pena	.10
21	Rob Murphy	.10
22	Tracy Woodson	.10
23	Basil Shabazz	.10
24	Omar Olivares	.10
25	Brian Jordan	.10
26	Les Lancaster	.10
27	Sean Lowe	.10
28	Hector Villanueva	.10
29	Brian Barber	.10
30	Aaron Holbert	.10

San Fransico Giants
Team Set: 2.50

1	Barry Bonds	2.00
2	Dave Righetti	.10
3	Matt Williams	.10
3a	Matt Williams/Auto.	10.00
4	Royce Clayton	.10
5	Salomon Torres	.10
6	Kirt Manwaring	.10
7	J.R. Phillips	.10
8	Kevin Rogers	.10
9	Will Clark	.10
10	John Burkett	.10
11	Willie McGee	.10
12	Rod Beck	.10
13	Jeff Reed	.10
14	Jeff Brantley	.10
15	Steve Hosey	.10
16	Chris Hancock	.10
17	Adell Davenport	.10
18	Mike Jackson	.10
19	Dave Martinez	.10
20	Bill Swift	.10
21	Steve Scarsone	.10
22	Trevor Wilson	.10
23	Mark Carreon	.10
24	Bud Black	.10
25	Darren Lewis	.10
26	Dan Carlson	.10
27	Craig Colbert	.10
28	Greg Brummet	.10
29	Bryan Hickerson	.10
30	Robby Thompson	.10

Seattle Mariners
Team Set: 3.00

1	Ken Griffey Jr.	1.50
2	Desi Realford	.10
3	Dave Weinhouse	.10
4	Rich Amaral	.10
5	Brian Deak	.10
6	Bret Boone	.10
7	Bill Haselman	.10
8	Dave Fleming	.10
9	Fernando Vina	.10
10	Greg Litton	.10
11	Mackey Sasser	.10
12	Lee Tinsley	.10
13	Norm Charlton	.10
14	Russ Swan	.10
15	Brian Holman	.10
16	Randy Johnson	.75
17	Erik Hanson	.10
18	Tino Martinez	.10
19	Marc Newfield	.10
20	Dave Valle	.10
21	John Cummings	.10
22	Mike Hampton	.10
23	Jay Buhner	.10
24	Edgar Martinez	.10
25	Omar Vizquel	.10
26	Pete O'Brien	.10
27	Brian Turang	.10
28	Chris Bosio	.10
29	Mike Felder	.10
30	Shawn Estes	.10

Texas Rangers
Team Set: 5.00

1	Nolan Ryan	2.50
2	Ritchie Moody	.10
3	Matt Whiteside	.10
4	David Hulse	.10
5	Roger Pavlik	.10
6	Dan Smith	.10
7	Donald Harris	.10
8	Butch Davis	.10
9	Benji Gil	.10
10	Ivan Rodriguez	.65
11	Dean Palmer	.10
12	Jeff Huson	.10
13	Rob Mauer	.10
14	Gary Redus	.10
15	Doug Dascenzo	.10
16	Charlie Liebrandt	.10
17	Tom Henke	.10
18	Manuel Lee	.10
19	Kenny Rogers	.10
20	Kevin Brown	.10
21	Juan Gonzalez	.50
22	Geno Petralli	.10
23	John Russell	.10
24	Robb Nen	.10
25	Julio Franco	.10
26	Rafael Palmeiro	.65
27	Todd Burns	.10
28	Jose Canseco	.50
29	Billy Ripken	.10
30	Dan Peltier	.10

3	Bobby Bonds	.50
4	Barry Bonds	1.00
5	Barry Bonds, Bobby Bonds	.50
6	Willie Mays	1.00
7	Barry Bonds (Business suit.)	1.00
8	Willie Mays, Bobby Bonds	1.00
9	Willie Mays	1.00
10	Barry Bonds (Tuxedo)	1.00

1994 Stadium Club Pre-Production

These sample cards introducing the 1994 Stadium Club set differ from their regular-issue counterparts only in the inclusion of a line of type vertically on the back-right, "Pre-Production Sample."

		NM/M
	Complete Set (9):	5.00
	Common Player:	.50
6	Al Martin	.50
15	Junior Ortiz	.50
36	Tim Salmon	.75
56	Jerry Spradlin	.50
122	Tom Pagnozzi	.50
123	Ron Gant	.50
125	Dennis Eckersley	1.50
135	Jose Lind	.50
238	Barry Bonds	4.00

1994 Stadium Club

cecil FIELDER

Issued in three series to a total of 720 cards, Topps' mid-price brand features a hip look and a wide range of insert specials. The regular cards feature a borderless photo with the player's name presented in a unique typewriter/label maker style at bottom. The player's last name and Topps Stadium Club logo at top are in red foil. Backs feature another player photo, some personal data and a headlined career summary. Subsets within the issue include cards annotated with Major League debut dates, 1993 awards won, home run club cards, cards featuring two or three players, and Final Tribute cards for George Brett and Nolan Ryan.

		NM/M
	Complete Set (720):	20.00
	Common Player:	.05
	1st Day:	8X
	Golden Rainbow:	2X
	Series 1, 2, 3 Pack (12):	1.00
	Series 1, 2 Wax Box (24):	15.00
1	Robin Yount	.65
2	Rick Wilkins	.05
3	Steve Scarsone	.05
4	Gary Sheffield	.40
5	George Brett	1.00
6	Al Martin	.05
7	Joe Oliver	.05
8	Stan Belinda	.05
9	Denny Hocking	.05
10	Roberto Alomar	.20
11	Luis Polonia	.05
12	Scott Hemond	.05
13	Joey Reed	.05
14	Mel Rojas	.05
15	Junior Ortiz	.05
16	Harold Baines	.05
17	Brad Pennington	.05
18	Jay Bell	.05
19	Tom Henke	.05
20	Jeff Branson	.05
21	Roberto Mejia	.05
22	Pedro Munoz	.05
23	Matt Nokes	.05
24	Jack McDowell	.05
25	Cecil Fielder	.05
26	Tony Fossas	.05
27	Jim Eisenreich	.05
28	Anthony Young	.05
29	Chuck Carr	.05
30	Jeff Treadway	.05
31	Chris Nabholz	.05
32	Tom Candiotti	.05
33	Mike Maddux	.05
34	Nolan Ryan	2.00
35	Luis Gonzalez	.05
36	Tim Salmon	.05
37	Mark Whiten	.05
38	Roger McDowell	.05
39	Royce Clayton	.05
40	Troy Neel	.05
41	Mike Harkey	.05
42	Darrin Fletcher	.05
43	Wayne Kirby	.05
44	Rich Amaral	.05
45	Robb Nen	.05
46	Tim Teufel	.05
47	Steve Cooke	.05
48	Jeff McNeely	.05
49	Jeff Montgomery	.05
50	Skeeter Barnes	.05
51	Scott Stahoviak	.05
52	Pat Kelly	.05
53	Brady Anderson	.05
54	Mariano Duncan	.05
55	Brian Bohanon	.05
56	Jerry Spradlin	.05
57	Ron Karkovice	.05
58	Jeff Gardner	.05
59	Bobby Bonilla	.05
60	Tino Martinez	.05
61	Todd Benzinger	.05
62	Steve Trachsel RC	.25
63	Brian Jordan	.05
64	Steve Bedrosian	.05
65	Brent Gates	.05
66	Shawn Green	.35
67	Sean Berry	.05
68	Joe Klink	.05
69	Fernando Valenzuela	.05
70	Andy Tomberlin	.05
71	Tony Pena	.05
72	Eric Young	.05
73	Chris Gomez	.05
74	Paul O'Neill	.05
75	Ricky Gutierrez	.05
76	Brad Holman	.05
77	Lance Painter	.05
78	Mike Butcher	.05
79	Sid Bream	.05
80	Sammy Sosa	.75
81	Felix Fermin	.05
82	Todd Hundley	.05
83	Kevin Higgins	.05
84	Todd Pratt	.05
85	Ken Griffey Jr.	1.25
86	John O'Donoghue	.05
87	Rick Renteria	.05
88	John Burkett	.05
89	Jose Vizcaino	.05
90	Kevin Seitzer	.05
91	Bobby Witt	.05
92	Chris Turner	.05
93	Omar Vizquel	.05
94	Dave Justice	.05
95	David Segui	.05
96	Dave Hollins	.05
97	Doug Strange	.05
98	Jerald Clark	.05
99	Mike Moore	.05
100	Joey Cora	.05
101	Scott Kamienicki	.05
102	Andy Benes	.05
103	Chris Bosio	.05
104	Rey Sanchez	.05
105	John Jaha	.05
106	Otis Nixon	.05
107	Rickey Henderson	.65
108	Jeff Bagwell	.65
109	Gregg Jefferies	.05
110	Topps Trios (Roberto Alomar, Paul Molitor, John Olerud)	.25
111	Topps Trios (Ron Gant, David Justice, Fred McGriff)	.05
112	Topps Trios (Juan Gonzalez, Rafael Palmeiro, Dean Palmer)	.25
113	Greg Swindell	.05
114	Bill Haselman	.05
115	Phil Plantier	.05
116	Ivan Rodriguez	.60

Ultra Pro

Special packages of plastic sheets and sleeves carrying the "Topps Stadium Club UltraPro" brand name included one of 10 special Stadium Club cards of Barry Bonds, Bobby Bonds and/or Willie Mays. Cards are typical UV coated, gold-foil quality, but because the cards were not licensed by Major League Baseball, team logos were removed from the photos.

		NM/M
	Complete Set (10):	7.00
	Common Card:	.50
1	Barry Bonds, Willie Mays, Bobby Bonds	.50
2	Willie Mays	1.00

No.	Player	Price
117	Kevin Tapani	.05
118	Mike LaValliere	.05
119	Tim Costo	.05
120	Mickey Morandini	.05
121	Brett Butler	.05
122	Tom Pagnozzi	.05
123	Ron Gant	.05
124	Damion Easley	.05
125	Dennis Eckersley	.60
126	Matt Mieske	.05
127	Cliff Floyd	.05
128	Julian Tavarez RC	.05
129	Arthur Rhodes	.05
130	Dave West	.05
131	Tim Naehring	.05
132	Freddie Benavides	.05
133	Paul Assenmacher	.05
134	David McCarty	.05
135	Jose Lind	.05
136	Reggie Sanders	.05
137	Don Slaught	.05
138	Andujar Cedeno	.05
139	Rob Deer	.05
140	Mike Piazza	1.25
141	Moises Alou	.05
142	Tom Foley	.05
143	Benny Santiago	.05
144	Sandy Alomar	.05
145	Carlos Hernandez	.05
146	Luis Alicea	.05
147	Tom Lampkin	.05
148	Ryan Klesko	.05
149	Juan Guzman	.05
150	Scott Servais	.05
151	Tony Gwynn	.75
152	Tim Wakefield	.05
153	David Nied	.05
154	Chris Haney	.05
155	Danny Bautista	.05
156	Randy Velarde	.05
157	Darrin Jackson	.05
158	J.R. Phillips RC	.05
159	Greg Gagne	.05
160	Luis Aquino	.05
161	John Vander Wal	.05
162	Randy Myers	.05
163	Ted Power	.05
164	Scott Brosius	.05
165	Len Dykstra	.05
166	Jacob Brumfield	.05
167	Bo Jackson	.10
168	Eddie Taubensee	.05
169	Carlos Baerga	.05
170	Tim Bogar	.05
171	Jose Canseco	.50
172	Greg Blosser	.05
173	Chili Davis	.05
174	Randy Knorr	.05
175	Mike Perez	.05
176	Henry Rodriguez	.05
177	Brian Turang RC	.05
178	Roger Pavlik	.05
179	Aaron Sele	.05
180	Tale of 2 Players (Fred McGriff, Gary Sheffield)	.05
181	Tale of 2 Players (J.T. Snow, Tim Salmon)	.05
182	Roberto Hernandez	.05
183	Jeff Reboulet	.05
184	John Doherty	.05
185	Danny Sheaffer	.05
186	Bip Roberts	.05
187	Denny Martinez	.05
188	Darryl Hamilton	.05
189	Eduardo Perez	.05
190	Pete Harnisch	.05
191	Rick Gossage	.05
192	Mickey Tettleton	.05
193	Lenny Webster	.05
194	Lance Johnson	.05
195	Don Mattingly	1.00
196	Gregg Olson	.05
197	Mark Gubicza	.05
198	Scott Fletcher	.05
199	Jon Shave	.05
200	Tim Mauser	.05
201	Jeromy Burnitz	.05
202	Rob Dibble	.05
203	Will Clark	.05
204	Steve Buechele	.05
205	Brian Williams	.05
206	Carlos Garcia	.05
207	Mark Clark	.05
208	Rafael Palmeiro	.60
209	Eric Davis	.05
210	Pat Meares	.05
211	Chuck Finley	.05
212	Jason Bere	.05
213	Gary DiSarcina	.05
214	Tony Fernandez	.05
215	B.J. Surhoff	.05
216	Lee Guetterman	.05
217	Tim Wallach	.05
218	Kirt Manwaring	.05
219	Albert Belle	.65
220	Dwight Gooden	.05
221	Archi Cianfrocco	.05
222	Terry Mulholland	.05
223	Hipolito Pichardo	.05
224	Kent Hrbek	.05
225	Craig Grebeck	.05
226	Todd Jones	.05
227	Mike Bordick	.05
228	John Olerud	.05
229	Jeff Blauser	.05
230	Alex Arias	.05
231	Bernard Gilkey	.05
232	Denny Neagle	.05
233	Pedro Borbon RC	.05
234	Dick Schofield	.05
235	Matias Carrillo	.05
236	Juan Bell	.05
237	Mike Hampton	.05
238	Barry Bonds	2.00
239	Cris Carpenter	.05
240	Eric Karros	.05
241	Greg McMichael	.05
242	Pat Hentgen	.05
243	Tim Pugh	.05
244	Vinny Castilla	.05
245	Charlie Hough	.05
246	Bobby Munoz	.05
247	Kevin Baez	.05
248	Todd Frohwirth	.05
249	Charlie Hayes	.05
250	Mike Macfarlane	.05
251	Danny Darwin	.05
252	Ben Rivera	.05
253	Dave Henderson	.05
254	Steve Avery	.05
255	Tim Belcher	.05
256	Dan Plesac	.05
257	Jim Thome	.60
258	Albert Belle (35+ HR Hitter)	.05
259	Barry Bonds (35+ HR Hitter)	1.00
260	Ron Gant (35+ HR Hitter)	.05
261	Juan Gonzalez (35+ HR Hitter)	.20
262	Ken Griffey Jr. (35+ HR Hitter)	.65
263	Dave Justice (35+ HR Hitter)	.05
264	Fred McGriff (35+ HR Hitter)	.05
265	Rafael Palmeiro (35+ HR Hitter)	.20
266	Mike Piazza (35+ HR Hitter)	.65
267	Frank Thomas (35+ HR Hitter)	.35
268	Matt Williams (35+ HR Hitter)	.05
269a	Checklist 1-135	.05
269b	Checklist 271-408	.05
270a	Checklist 136-270	.05
270b	Checklist 409-540	.05
271	Mike Stanley	.05
272	Tony Tarasco	.05
273	Teddy Higuera	.05
274	Ryan Thompson	.05
275	Rick Aguilera	.05
276	Ramon Martinez	.05
277	Orlando Merced	.05
278	Guillermo Velasquez	.05
279	Mark Hutton	.05
280	Larry Walker	.05
281	Kevin Gross	.05
282	Jose Offerman	.05
283	Jim Leyritz	.05
284	Jamie Moyer	.05
285	Frank Thomas	.65
286	Derek Bell	.05
287	Derrick May	.05
288	Dave Winfield	.65
289	Curt Schilling	.35
290	Carlos Quintana	.05
291	Bob Natal	.05
292	David Cone	.05
293	Al Osuna	.05
294	Bob Hamelin	.05
295	Chad Curtis	.05
296	Danny Jackson	.05
297	Bob Welch	.05
298	Felix Jose	.05
299	Jay Buhner	.05
300	Joe Carter	.05
301	Kenny Lofton	.05
302	Kirk Rueter RC	.15
303	Kim Batiste	.05
304	Mike Morgan	.05
305	Pat Borders	.05
306	Rene Arocha	.05
307	Ruben Sierra	.05
308	Steve Finley	.05
309	Travis Fryman	.05
310	Zane Smith	.05
311	Willie Wilson	.05
312	Trevor Hoffman	.05
313	Terry Pendleton	.05
314	Salomon Torres	.05
315	Robin Ventura	.05
316	Randy Tomlin	.05
317	Dave Stewart	.05
318	Mike Benjamin	.05
319	Matt Turner	.05
320	Manny Ramirez	.65
321	Kevin Young	.05
322	Ken Caminiti	.05
323	Joe Girardi	.05
324	Jeff McKnight	.05
325	Gene Harris	.05
326	Devon White	.05
327	Darryl Kile	.05
328	Craig Paquette	.05
329	Cal Eldred	.05
330	Bill Swift	.05
331	Alan Trammell	.05
332	Armando Reynoso	.05
333	Brent Mayne	.05
334	Chris Donnels	.05
335	Darryl Strawberry	.05
336	Dean Palmer	.05
337	Frank Castillo	.05
338	Jeff King	.05
339	John Franco	.05
340	Kevin Appier	.05
341	Lance Blankenship	.05
342	Mark McLemore	.05
343	Pedro Astacio	.05
344	Rich Batchelor	.05
345	Ryan Bowen	.05
346	Terry Steinbach	.05
347	Troy O'Leary	.05
348	Willie Blair	.05
349	Wade Boggs	.75
350	Tim Raines	.05
351	Scott Livingstone	.05
352	Rod Carreia	.05
353	Ray Lankford	.05
354	Pat Listach	.05
355	Milt Thompson	.05
356	Miguel Jimenez	.05
357	Marc Newfield	.05
358	Mark McGwire	1.50
359	Kirby Puckett	.75
360	Kent Mercker	.05
361	John Kruk	.05
362	Jeff Kent	.05
363	Hal Morris	.05
364	Edgar Martinez	.05
365	Dave Magadan	.05
366	Dante Bichette	.05
367	Chris Hammond	.05
368	Bret Saberhagen	.05
369	Billy Ripken	.05
370	Bill Gullickson	.05
371	Andre Dawson	.35
372	Bobby Kelly	.05
373	Cal Ripken, Jr.	2.00
374	Craig Biggio	.05
375	Dan Pasqua	.05
376	Dave Nilsson	.05
377	Duane Ward	.05
378	Greg Vaughn	.05
379	Jeff Fassero	.05
380	Jerry Dipoto	.05
381	John Patterson	.05
382	Kevin Brown	.05
383	Kevin Roberson	.05
384	Joe Orsulak	.05
385	Hilly Hathaway	.05
386	Mike Greenwell	.05
387	Orestes Destrade	.05
388	Mike Gallego	.05
389	Ozzie Guillen	.05
390	Raul Mondesi	.05
391	Scott Lydy	.05
392	Tom Urbani	.05
393	Wil Cordero	.05
394	Tony Longmire	.05
395	Todd Zeile	.05
396	Scott Cooper	.05
397	Ryne Sandberg	.75
398	Ricky Bones	.05
399	Phil Clark	.05
400	Orel Hershiser	.05
401	Mike Henneman	.05
402	Mark Lemke	.05
403	Mark Grace	.05
404	Ken Ryan	.05
405	John Smoltz	.05
406	Jeff Conine	.05
407	Greg Harris	.05
408	Doug Drabek	.05
409	Dave Fleming	.05
410	Danny Tartabull	.05
411	Chad Kreuter	.05
412	Brad Ausmus	.05
413	Ben McDonald	.05
414	Barry Larkin	.05
415	Bret Barberie	.05
416	Chuck Knoblauch	.05
417	Ozzie Smith	.75
418	Ed Sprague	.05
419	Matt Williams	.05
420	Jeremy Hernandez	.05
421	Jose Bautista	.05
422	Kevin Mitchell	.05
423	Manuel Lee	.05
424	Mike Devereaux	.05
425	Omar Olivares	.05
426	Rafael Belliard	.05
427	Richie Lewis	.05
428	Ron Darling	.05
429	Shane Mack	.05
430	Tim Hulett	.05
431	Wally Joyner	.05
432	Wes Chamberlain	.05
433	Tom Browning	.05
434	Scott Radinsky	.05
435	Rondell White	.05
436	Rod Beck	.05
437	Rheal Cormier	.05
438	Randy Johnson	.65
439	Pete Schourek	.05
440	Mo Vaughn	.05
441	Mike Timlin	.05
442	Mark Langston	.05
443	Lou Whitaker	.05
444	Kevin Stocker	.05
445	Ken Hill	.05
446	John Wetteland	.05
447	J.T. Snow	.05
448	Erik Pappas	.05
449	David Hulse	.05
450	Darren Daulton	.05
451	Chris Hoiles	.05
452	Bryan Harvey	.05
453	Darren Lewis	.05
454	Andres Galarraga	.05
455	Joe Hesketh	.05
456	Jose Valentin	.05
457*	Dan Peltier	.05
458	Joe Boever	.05
459	Kevin Rogers	.05
460	Craig Shipley	.05
461	Alvaro Espinoza	.05
462	Wilson Alvarez	.05
463	Cory Snyder	.05
464	Candy Maldonado	.05
465	Blas Minor	.05
466	Rod Bolton	.05
467	Kenny Rogers	.05
468	Greg Myers	.05
469	Jimmy Key	.05
470	Tony Castillo	.05
471	Mike Stanton	.05
472	Deion Sanders	.05
473	Tito Navarro	.05
474	Mike Gardiner	.05
475	Steve Reed	.05
476	John Roper	.05
477	Mike Trombley	.05
478	Charles Nagy	.05
479	Larry Casian	.05
480	Eric Hillman	.05
481	Bill Wertz	.05
482	Jeff Schwarz	.05
483	John Valentin	.05
484	Carl Willis	.05
485	Gary Gaetti	.05
486	Bill Pecota	.05
487	John Smiley	.05
488	Kurt Abbott RC	.25
489	Rick White RC	.05
490	Billy Brewer	.05
491	Jack Voigt	.05
492	Mike Munoz	.05
493	Lee Tinsley	.05
494	Bob Wickman	.05
495	Roger Salkeld	.05
496	Thomas Howard	.05
497	Mark Davis	.05
498	Dave Clark	.05
499	Turk Wendell	.05
500	Rafael Bournigal	.05
501	Chip Hale	.05
502	Matt Whiteside	.05
503	Brian Koelling	.05
504	Jeff Reed	.05
505	Paul Wagner	.05
506	Torey Lovullo	.05
507	Curtis Leskanic	.05
508	Derek Lilliquist	.05
509	Joe Magrane	.05
510	Mackey Sasser	.05
511	Lloyd McClendon	.05
512	Jayhawk Owens RC	.05
513	Woody Williams RC	.05
514	Gary Redus	.05
515	Tim Spehr	.05
516	Jim Abbott	.05
517	Lou Frazier	.05
518	Erik Plantenberg	.05
519	Tim Worrell	.05
520	Brian McRae	.05
521	Chan Ho Park RC	1.00
522	Mark Wohlers	.05
523	Geronimo Pena	.05
524	Andy Ashby	.05
525	Tale of 2 Players (Tim Raines, Andre Dawson)	.05
526	Tale of 2 Players (Paul Molitor, Dave Winfield)	.40
527	Joe Carter (RBI Leader)	.05
528	Frank Thomas (HR Leader)	.35
529	Ken Griffey Jr. (TB Leader)	.65
530	Dave Justice (HR Leader)	.05
531	Gregg Jefferies (AVG Leader)	.05
532	Barry Bonds (HR Leader)	1.00
533	John Kruk (Quick Start)	.05
534	Roger Clemens (Quick Start)	.50
535	Cecil Fielder (Quick Start)	.05
536	Ruben Sierra (Quick Start)	.05
537	Tony Gwynn (Quick Start)	.40
538	Tom Glavine (Quick Start)	.10
541	Ozzie Smith (Career Leader)	.40
542	Eddie Murray (Career Leader)	.30
543a	Lee Smith (Career Leader)	.05
543b	Lonnie Smith (should be #643)	.05
544	Greg Maddux	.75
545	Denis Boucher	.05
546	Mark Gardner	.05
547	Bo Jackson	.10
548	Eric Anthony	.05
549	Delino DeShields	.05
550	Turner Ward	.05
551	Scott Sanderson	.05
552	Hector Carrasco	.05
553	Tony Phillips	.05
554	Melido Perez	.05
555	Mike Felder	.05
556	Jack Morris	.05
557	Rafael Palmeiro	.60
558	Shane Reynolds	.05
559	Pete Incaviglia	.05
560	Greg Harris	.05
561	Matt Walbeck	.05
562	Todd Van Poppel	.05
563	Todd Stottlemyre	.05
564	Ricky Bones	.05
565	Mike Jackson	.05
566	Kevin McReynolds	.05
567	Melvin Nieves	.05
568	Juan Gonzalez	.35
569	Frank Viola	.05
570	Vince Coleman	.05
571	Brian Anderson RC	.25
572	Omar Vizquel	.05
573	Bernie Williams	.05
574	Tom Glavine	.35
575	Mitch Williams	.05
576	Shawon Dunston	.05
577	Mike Lansing	.05
578	Greg Pirkl	.05
579	Sid Fernandez	.05
580	Doug Jones	.05
581	Walt Weiss	.05
582	Tim Belcher	.05
583	Alex Fernandez	.05
584	Alex Cole	.05
585	Greg Cadaret	.05
586	Bob Tewksbury	.05
587	Dave Hansen	.05
588	Kurt Abbott RC	.25
589	Rick White RC	.05
590	Kevin Bass	.05
591	Geronimo Berroa	.05
592	Jaime Navarro	.05
593	Steve Farr	.05
594	Jack Armstrong	.05
595	Steve Howe	.05
596	Jose Rijo	.05
597	Otis Nixon	.05
598	Robby Thompson	.05
599	Kelly Stinnett	.05
600	Carlos Delgado	.50
601	Brian Johnson RC	.05
602	Gregg Olson	.05
603	Jim Edmonds	.05
604	Mike Blowers	.05
605	Lee Smith	.05
606	Pat Rapp	.05
607	Mike Magnante	.05
608	Karl Rhodes	.05
609	Jeff Juden	.05
610	Rusty Meacham	.05
611	Pedro Martinez	.65
612	Todd Worrell	.05
613	Stan Javier	.05
614	Mike Hampton	.05
615	Jose Guzman	.05
616	Xavier Hernandez	.05
617	David Wells	.05
618	John Habyan	.05
619	Chris Nabholz	.05
620	Bobby Jones	.05
621	Chris James	.05
622	Ellis Burks	.05
623	Erik Hanson	.05
624	Pat Meares	.05
625	Harold Reynolds	.05
626	Bob Hamelin (Rookie Rocker)	.05
627	Manny Ramirez (Rookie Rocker)	.30
628	Ryan Klesko (Rookie Rocker)	.05
629	Carlos Delgado (Rookie Rocker)	.30
630	Javier Lopez (Rookie Rocker)	.05
631	Steve Karsay (Rookie Rocket)	.05
632	Rick Helling (Rookie Rocket)	.05
633	Steve Trachsel (Rookie Rocket)	.05
634	Hector Carrasco (Rookie Rocket)	.05
635	Andy Stankiewicz	.05
636	Paul Sorrento	.05
637	Scott Erickson	.05
638	Chipper Jones	.75
639	Luis Polonia	.05
640	Howard Johnson	.05
641	John Dopson	.05
642	Jody Reed	.05
644	Mark Portugal	.05
645	Paul Molitor	.05
646	Paul Assenmacher	.05
647	Hubie Brooks	.05
648	Gary Wayne	.05
649	Sean Berry	.05
650	Roger Clemens	1.00
651	Brian Hunter	.05
652	Wally Whitehurst	.05
653	Allen Watson	.05
654	Rickey Henderson	.65
655	Sid Bream	.05
656	Dan Wilson	.05
657	Ricky Jordan	.05
658	Sterling Hitchcock	.05
659	Darrin Jackson	.05
660	Junior Felix	.05
661	Tom Brunansky	.05
662	Jose Vizcaino	.05
663	Mark Leiter	.05
664	Gil Heredia	.05
665	Fred McGriff	.05
666	Will Clark	.05
667	Al Leiter	.05
668	James Mouton	.05
669	Billy Bean	.05
670	Scott Leius	.05
671	Bret Boone	.05
672	Darren Holmes	.05
673	Dave Weathers	.05
674	Eddie Murray	.65
675	Felix Fermin	.05
676	Chris Sabo	.05
677	Billy Spiers	.05
678	Aaron Sele	.05
679	Juan Samuel	.05
680	Julio Franco	.05
681	Heathcliff Slocumb	.05
682	Denny Martinez	.05
683	Jerry Browne	.05
684	Pedro A. Martinez RC	.05
685	Rex Hudler	.05
686	Willie McGee	.05
687	Andy Van Slyke	.05
688	Pat Mahomes	.05
689	Dave Henderson	.05
690	Tony Eusebio	.05
691	Rick Sutcliffe	.05
692	Willie Banks	.05
693	Alan Mills	.05
694	Jeff Treadway	.05
695	Alex Gonzalez	.05
696	David Segui	.05
697	Rick Helling	.05
698	Bip Roberts	.05
699	Jeff Cirillo RC	.25
700	Terry Mulholland	.05
701	Marvin Freeman	.05
702	Jason Bere	.05
703	Javier Lopez	.05
704	Greg Hibbard	.05
705	Tommy Greene	.05
706	Marquis Grissom	.05
707	Brian Harper	.05
708	Steve Karsay	.05
709	Jeff Brantley	.05
710	Jeff Russell	.05
711	Bryan Hickerson	.05
712	Jim Pittsley RC	.05
713	Bobby Ayala	.05
714	John Smoltz (Fantastic Finisher)	.05
715	Jose Rijo (Fantastic Finisher)	.05
716	Greg Maddux (Fantastic Finisher)	.40
717	Matt Williams (Fantastic Finisher)	.05
718	Frank Thomas (Fantastic Finisher)	.35
719	Ryne Sandberg (Fantastic Finisher)	.40
720	Checklist	.05

Golden Rainbow

Found at the rate of one per pack, Stadium Club "Golden Rainbow" cards were issued for each of the 720 cards in the regular set. These inserts are distinguished by the use of gold prismatic foil highlights for the S.C. logo and box with the player's last name, instead of the red foil found on regular S.C. cards.

	NM/M
Complete Set (720):	60.00
Common Player:	.25
Stars:	2X

1st Day Issue

A special silver-foil embossment designating "1st Day Issue" was placed on fewer than 2,000 of each of the 720 regular cards in the '94 Stadium Club set. Inserted at the rate of one per 24 foil packs and one per 15 jumbo packs, the cards are otherwise identical to the regular TSC cards.

| Common Player: | 1.00 |
| Stars: | 8X |

Dugout Dirt

Cartoons of some of baseball's top stars are featured on the backs of this 12-card insert set. Fronts are virtually identical in format to regular S.C. cards, except the logo and box with the player's last name are in gold-foil, rather than red. Stated odds of finding a Dugout Dirt insert card were one per six packs, on average. Cards can also be found with a gold "Members Only" seal on front.

		NM/M
Complete Set (12):		5.00
Common Player:		.25
1	Mike Piazza (Catch of the Day)	1.00
2	Dave Winfield (The Road to 3,000)	.65
3	John Kruk (From Coal Mine to Gold Mine)	.25
4	Cal Ripken, Jr. (On Track)	2.00
5	Jack McDowell (Chin Music)	.25
6	Barry Bonds (The Bonds Market)	2.00
7	Ken Griffey Jr./AS (Gold Gloves)	1.00
8	Tim Salmon (The Salmon Run)	.50
9	Frank Thomas (Big Hurt)	.65
10	Jeff Kent (Super Kent)	.25
11	Randy Johnson (High Heat)	.65
12	Darren Daulton (Daulton's Gym)	.25

Finest

This insert set was included only in Series III packs of Topps Stadium Club cards, at the rate of one card per six packs, on average. Cards utilize Topps Finest technology and feature a player action photo on front, set against a red-and-gold sun-

burst background. Backs have a player portrait photo, a few stats and appropriate logos. Cards can also be found with a "Members Only" logo on front.

	NM/M
Complete Set (10):	11.00
Common Player:	.50
1	Jeff Bagwell	1.25
2	Albert Belle	.50
3	Barry Bonds	3.00
4	Juan Gonzalez	.75
5	Ken Griffey Jr.	2.00
6	Marquis Grissom	.50
7	David Justice	.50
8	Mike Piazza	2.00
9	Tim Salmon	.50
10	Frank Thomas	1.50

Finest Jumbo

Found only as a one per tub insert in special Wal-Mart repackaging of baseball packs, these 5" x 7" versions of the Series III Stadium Club inserts are identical to the smaller version. Cards utilize Topps Finest technology and feature a player action photo on front, set against a red-and-gold sunburst background. Backs have a player portrait photo, a few stats and appropriate logos.

	NM/M
Complete Set (10):	30.00
Common Player:	2.00
1	Jeff Bagwell	4.00
2	Albert Belle	2.00
3	Barry Bonds	6.50
4	Juan Gonzalez	3.00
5	Ken Griffey Jr.	5.00
6	Marquis Grissom	2.00
7	David Justice	2.00
8	Mike Piazza	5.00
9	Tim Salmon	2.00
10	Frank Thomas	4.00

Super Teams

Super Team cards were issued for each of the 28 major league teams and inserted at the rate of one per 24 regular packs and one per 15 jumbo packs. At the end of the 1995 season (the promotion was carried over when the 1994 season was ended prematurely by the players' strike), persons holding Super Team cards of the division winners, league champions and World Champions could redeem the cards for prizes. Division winning team cards could be redeemed for a set of 10 S.C. cards of that team with a special division winner embossed logo. League champion cards could be redeemed for a set of 10 Master Photos of the team with a special league logo embossed.

Persons with a Super Team card of the eventual World Series champion could trade the card in for a complete set of Stadium Club cards embossed with a World's Champion logo. Each of the Super Team cards features a small group of players on the front with the Super Team Card and S.C. logos in gold foil, and the team name in prismatic foil. Backs contain redemption rules. A version of the Super Team cards was distributed with "Members Only" sets containing such an indicia on front and team roster on back.

		NM/M
Complete Set (28):		25.00
Common Team:		.70
Expired Jan. 31, 1996.		
1	Atlanta Braves	5.00
2	Chicago Cubs	.70
3	Cincinnati Reds	1.25
4	Colorado Rockies	1.00
5	Florida Marlins	.70
6	Houston Astros	1.00
7	Los Angeles Dodgers	1.75
8	Montreal Expos	.70
9	New York Mets	.70
10	Philadelphia Phillies	.70
11	Pittsburgh Pirates	.70
12	St. Louis Cardinals	.70
13	San Diego Padres	.70
14	San Francisco Giants	1.25
15	Baltimore Orioles	1.25
16	Boston Red Sox	1.00
17	California Angels	.70
18	Chicago White Sox	1.50
19	Cleveland Indians	2.00
20	Detroit Tigers	.70
21	Kansas City Royals	1.00
22	Milwaukee Brewers	.70
23	Minnesota Twins	1.00
24	New York Yankees	1.50
25	Oakland Athletics	1.00
26	Seattle Mariners	2.00
27	Texas Rangers	1.00
28	Toronto Blue Jays	1.00

Members Only

This special gold-seal embossed version of the 1994 Topps Stadium Club set was available by a mail-in offer to club members for $230. The set includes all regular Stadium Club cards from Series I, II and III, along with the Dugout Dirt, Finest, and Super Teams insert cards. The Super Team cards, which were not eligible for the contest, have team rosters on back, rather than contest rules. All other cards are identical to the regular-issue S.C. cards except for the present of the 1/2" round gold-foil "Members Only" seal beneath or alongside of the red-foil Topps Stadium Club logo on front. There are two different checklists each numbered 269 and 270. Only 5,000 sets were produced.

	NM/M
Complete Set (770):	150.00
Common Player:	.50
Stars:	8X

Members Only Baseball

Available for purchase by Topps Stadium Club mem-

bers as a 50-card boxed set (football and basketball sets were also available), this issue features top stars, performances and career highlights from the 1993 season. Cards feature borderless action photos on front with the Topps logo and player's last name in gold-foil. Backs are horizontal and feature a black background on which the player's achievement is detailed in blue and gold. A second player photo appears on the card back. Cards #46-50 were produced in the Topps Finest-style foil-printing technology.

		NM/M
Complete Set (50):		6.00
Common Player:		.10
1	Juan Gonzalez	.25
2	Tom Henke	.10
3	John Kruk	.10
4	Paul Molitor	.50
5	Dave Justice	.10
6	Rafael Palmeiro	.45
7	John Smoltz	.10
8	Matt Williams	.10
9	John Olerud	.10
10	Mark Grace	.10
11	Joe Carter	.10
12	Wilson Alvarez	.10
13	Lenny Dykstra	.10
14	Kevin Appier	.10
15	Andres Galarraga	.10
16	Mark Langston	.10
17	Ken Griffey Jr.	.75
18	Albert Belle	.10
19	Gregg Jefferies	.10
20	Duane Ward	.10
21	Jack McDowell	.10
22	Randy Johnson	.50
23	Tom Glavine	.35
24	Barry Bonds	1.50
25	Chuck Carr	.10
26	Ron Gant	.10
27	Kenny Lofton	.10
28	Mike Piazza	.75
29	Frank Thomas	.55
30	Fred McGriff	.10
31	Bryan Harvey	.10
32	John Burkett	.10
33	Roberto Alomar	.20
34	Cecil Fielder	.10
35	Marquis Grissom	.10
36	Randy Myers	.10
37	Tony Phillips	.10
38	Rickey Henderson	.50
39	Luis Polonia	.10
40	Jose Rijo	.10
41	Jeff Montgomery	.10
42	Greg Maddux	.60
43	Tony Gwynn	.60
44	Rod Beck	.10
45	Carlos Baerga	.10
46	Wil Cordero	.10
47	Tim Salmon	.10
48	Mike Lansing	.10
49	J.T. Snow	.10
50	Jeff Conine	.10

Superstar Sampler

A small, round black-and-white "Topps Superstar Sampler" logo printed on the back is all that distinguishes these cards from regular-issue S.C. cards. This version of 45 of the top stars from the Stadium Club set was issued only in

three-card cello packs inserted into 1994 Topps retail factory sets. The packs also contained the same player's cards from the Bowman and Finest sets, similarly marked.

		NM/M
Complete Set (45):		275.00
Common Player:		2.00
4	Gary Sheffield	3.00
10	Roberto Alomar	4.00
24	Jack McDowell	2.00
25	Cecil Fielder	2.00
36	Tim Salmon	2.00
59	Bobby Bonilla	2.00
85	Ken Griffey Jr.	20.00
94	Dave Justice	2.00
108	Jeff Bagwell	12.00
109	Gregg Jefferies	2.00
127	Cliff Floyd	2.00
140	Mike Piazza	20.00
151	Tony Gwynn	12.50
165	Len Dykstra	2.00
171	Carlos Baerga	2.00
195	Jose Canseco	8.00
201	Don Mattingly	15.00
203	Will Clark	2.00
208	Rafael Palmeiro	10.00
219	Albert Belle	2.00
228	John Olerud	2.00
238	Barry Bonds	30.00
280	Larry Walker	2.00
285	Frank Thomas	12.00
300	Joe Carter	2.00
320	Manny Ramirez	12.00
359	Kirby Puckett	12.50
373	Cal Ripken Jr.	30.00
390	Raul Mondesi	2.00
397	Ryne Sandberg	12.50
403	Mark Grace	2.00
414	Barry Larkin	2.00
419	Matt Williams	2.00
438	Randy Johnson	12.00
440	Mo Vaughn	2.00
454	Darren Daulton	2.00
454	Andres Galarraga	2.00
544	Greg Maddux	12.50
568	Juan Gonzalez	6.00
574	Tom Glavine	3.00
645	Paul Molitor	2.00
650	Roger Clemens	15.00
665	Fred McGriff	2.00
687	Andy Van Slyke	2.00
706	Marquis Grissom	2.00

Team Series

Only 12 of the 28 major league teams are included in this special issue marketed in both team-set blister packs and foil packs at Wal-Mart stores around the country. Card fronts feature a player action photo bordered in the lower-right corner by a dark green mottled effect. The player's name, team and "Team Stadium Club" logo are in gold foil. Backs have a second player photo set against a background in mottled shades of green. There are a few stats and player biographical details.

		NM/M
Complete Set (360):		25.00
Common Player:		.10
Wax Box (24):		15.00
1	Barry Bonds	3.50
2	Royce Clayton	.10
3	Kirt Manwaring	.10
4	J.R. Phillips	.10
5	Robby Thompson	.10
6	Willie McGee	.10
7	Steve Hosey	.10
8	Dave Burba	.10
9	Steve Scarsone	.10
10	Salomon Torres	.10
11	Bryan Hickerson	.10
12	Mike Benjamin	.10
13	Mark Carreon	.10
14	Rich Monteleone	.10
15	Dave Martinez	.10
16	Bill Swift	.10

17	Jeff Reed	.10
18	John Patterson	.10
19	Darren Lewis	.10
20	Mark Portugal	.10
21	Trevor Wilson	.10
22	Matt Williams	.10
23	Kevin Rogers	.10
24	Luis Mercedes	.10
25	Mike Jackson	.10
26	Steve Frey	.10
27	Tony Menendez	.10
28	John Burkett	.10
29	Todd Benzinger	.10
30	Rod Beck	.10
31	Greg Maddux	1.50
32	Steve Avery	.10
33	Milt Hill	.10
34	Charlie O'Brien	.10
35	John Smoltz	.10
36	Jarvis Brown	.10
37	Dave Gallagher	.10
38	Ryan Klesko	.10
39	Kent Mercker	.10
40	Terry Pendleton	.10
41	Ron Gant	.10
42	Pedro Borbon	.10
43	Steve Bedrosian	.10
44	Ramon Caraballo	.10
45	Tyler Houston	.10
46	Mark Lemke	.10
47	Fred McGriff	.10
48	Jose Oliva	.10
49	David Justice	.10
50	Chipper Jones	1.50
51	Tony Tarasco	.10
52	Javy Lopez	.10
53	Mark Wohlers	.10
54	Deion Sanders	.10
55	Greg McMichael	.10
56	Tom Glavine	.35
57	Bill Pecota	.10
58	Mike Stanton	.10
59	Rafael Belliard	.10
60	Jeff Blauser	.10
61	Bryan Harvey	.10
62	Bret Barberie	.10
63	Rick Renteria	.10
64	Chris Hammond	.10
65	Pat Rapp	.10
66	Nigel Wilson	.10
67	Gary Sheffield	.30
68	Jerry Browne	.10
69	Charlie Hough	.10
70	Orestes Destrade	.10
71	Mario Diaz	.10
72	Ryan Bowen	.10
73	Carl Everett	.10
74	Richie Lewis	.10
75	Bob Natal	.10
76	Rich Rodriguez	.10
77	Darrell Whitmore	.10
78	Matt Turner	.10
79	Benny Santiago	.10
80	Robb Nen	.10
81	Dave Magadan	.10
82	Brian Drahman	.10
83	Mark Gardner	.10
84	Chuck Carr	.10
85	Alex Arias	.10
86	Kurt Abbott	.10
87	Joe Klink	.10
88	Jeff Mutis	.10
89	Dave Weathers	.10
90	Jeff Conine	.10
91	Andres Galarraga	.10
92	Vinny Castilla	.10
93	Roberto Mejia	.10
94	Darrell Sherman	.10
95	Mike Harkey	.10
96	Danny Sheaffer	.10
97	Pedro Castellano	.10
98	Walt Weiss	.10
99	Greg Harris	.10
100	Jayhawk Owens	.10
101	Bruce Ruffin	.10
102	Mike Munoz	.10
103	Armando Reynoso	.10
104	Eric Young	.10
105	Dante Bichette	.10
106	Marvin Freeman	.10
107	Joe Girardi	.10
108	Kent Bottenfield	.10
109	Howard Johnson	.10
110	Nelson Liriano	.10
111	David Nied	.10
112	Steve Reed	.10
113	Eric Wedge	.10
114	Charlie Hayes	.10
115	Ellis Burks	.10
116	Willie Blair	.10
117	Darren Holmes	.10
118	Curtis Leskanic	.10
119	Lance Painter	.10
120	Jim Tatum	.10
121	Frank Thomas	1.00
122	Jack McDowell	.10
123	Ron Karkovice	.10
124	Mike LaValliere	.10
125	Scott Radinsky	.10
126	Robin Ventura	.10
127	Scott Ruffcorn	.10
128	Steve Sax	.10
129	Roberto Hernandez	.10
130	Jose DeLeon	.10
131	Rod Bolton	.10
132	Wilson Alvarez	.10
133	Craig Grebeck	.10
134	Lance Johnson	.10

#	Player	Price
135	Kirk McCaskill	.10
136	Tim Raines	.10
137	Jeff Schwarz	.10
138	Warren Newson	.10
139	Norberto Martin	.10
140	Mike Huff	.10
141	Ozzie Guillen	.10
142	Alex Fernandez	.10
143	Joey Cora	.10
144	Jason Bere	.10
145	James Baldwin	.10
146	Esteban Beltre	.10
147	Julio Franco	.75
148	Matt Merullo	.10
149	Dan Pasqua	.10
150	Darrin Jackson	.10
151	Joe Carter	.10
152	Danny Cox	.10
153	Roberto Alomar	.20
154	Woody Williams	.10
155	Duane Ward	.10
156	Ed Sprague	.10
157	Domingo Martinez	.10
158	Pat Hentgen	.10
159	Shawn Green	.30
160	Dick Schofield	.10
161	Paul Molitor	1.00
162	Darnell Coles	.10
163	Willie Canate	.10
164	Domingo Cedeno	.10
165	Pat Borders	.10
166	Greg Cadaret	.10
167	Tony Castillo	.10
168	Carlos Delgado	.45
169	Scott Brow	.10
170	Juan Guzman	.10
171	Al Leiter	.10
172	John Olerud	.10
173	Todd Stottlemyre	.10
174	Devon White	.10
175	Paul Spoljaric	.10
176	Randy Knorr	.10
177	Huck Flener RC	.10
178	Rob Butler	.10
179	Dave Stewart	.10
180	Mike Timlin	.10
181	Don Mattingly	2.00
182	Mark Hutton	.10
183	Mike Gallego	.10
184	Jim Abbott	.10
185	Paul Gibson	.10
186	Scott Kamieniecki	.10
187	Sam Horn	.10
188	Melido Perez	.10
189	Randy Velarde	.10
190	Gerald Williams	.10
191	Dave Silvestri	.10
192	Jim Leyritz	.10
193	Steve Howe	.10
194	Russ Davis	.10
195	Paul Assenmacher	.10
196	Pat Kelly	.10
197	Mike Stanley	.10
198	Bernie Williams	.10
199	Paul O'Neill	.10
200	Donn Pall	.10
201	Xavier Hernandez	.10
202	James Austin	.10
203	Sterling Hitchcock	.10
204	Wade Boggs	1.50
205	Jimmy Key	.10
206	Matt Nokes	.10
207	Terry Mulholland	.10
208	Luis Polonia	.10
209	Danny Tartabull	.10
210	Bob Wickman	.10
211	Len Dykstra	.10
212	Kim Batiste	.10
213	Tony Longmire	.10
214	Bobby Munoz	.10
215	Pete Incaviglia	.10
216	Doug Jones	.10
217	Mariano Duncan	.10
218	Jeff Juden	.10
219	Milt Thompson	.10
220	Dave West	.10
221	Roger Mason	.10
222	Tommy Greene	.10
223	Larry Andersen	.10
224	Jim Eisenreich	.10
225	Dave Hollins	.10
226	John Kruk	.10
227	Todd Pratt	.10
228	Ricky Jordan	.10
229	Curt Schilling	.35
230	Mike Williams	.10
231	Heathcliff Slocumb	.10
232	Ben Rivera	.10
233	Mike Lieberthal	.10
234	Mickey Morandini	.10
235	Danny Jackson	.10
236	Kevin Foster	.10
237	Darren Daulton	.10
238	Wes Chamberlain	.10
239	Tyler Green	.10
240	Kevin Stocker	.10
241	Juan Gonzalez	.50
242	Rick Honeycutt	.10
243	Bruce Hurst	.10
244	Steve Dreyer	.10
245	Brian Bohanon	.10
246	Benji Gil	.10
247	Jon Shave	.10
248	Manuel Lee	.10
249	Donald Harris	.10
250	Jose Canseco	.50
251	David Hulse	.10
252	Kenny Rogers	.10
253	Jeff Huson	.10
254	Dan Peltier	.10
255	Mike Scioscia	.10
256	Jack Armstrong	.10
257	Rob Ducey	.10
258	Will Clark	.10
259	Cris Carpenter	.10
260	Kevin Brown	.10
261	Jeff Frye	.10
262	Jay Howell	.10
263	Roger Pavlik	.10
264	Gary Redus	.10
265	Ivan Rodriguez	.75
266	Matt Whiteside	.10
267	Doug Strange	.10
268	Billy Ripken	.10
269	Dean Palmer	.10
270	Tom Henke	.10
271	Cal Ripken Jr.	3.50
272	Mark McLemore	.10
273	Sid Fernandez	.10
274	Sherman Obando	.10
275	Paul Carey	.10
276	Mike Oquist	.10
277	Alan Mills	.10
278	Harold Baines	.10
279	Mike Mussina	.30
280	Arthur Rhodes	.10
281	Kevin McGehee	.10
282	Mark Eichhorn	.10
283	Damon Buford	.10
284	Ben McDonald	.10
285	David Segui	.10
286	Brad Pennington	.10
287	Jamie Moyer	.10
288	Chris Hoiles	.10
289	Mike Cook	.10
290	Brady Anderson	.10
291	Chris Sabo	.10
292	Jack Voigt	.10
293	Jim Poole	.10
294	Jeff Tackett	.10
295	Rafael Palmeiro	.75
296	Alex Ochoa	.10
297	John O'Donoghue	.10
298	Tim Hulett	.10
299	Mike Devereaux	.10
300	Manny Alexander	.10
301	Ozzie Smith	1.50
302	Omar Olivares	.10
303	Rheal Cormier	.10
304	Donovan Osborne	.10
305	Mark Whiten	.10
306	Todd Zeile	.10
307	Geronimo Pena	.10
308	Brian Jordan	.10
309	Luis Alicea	.10
310	Ray Lankford	.10
311	Stan Royer	.10
312	Bob Tewksbury	.10
313	Jose Oquendo	.10
314	Steve Dixon	.10
315	Rene Arocha	.10
316	Bernard Gilkey	.10
317	Gregg Jefferies	.10
318	Rob Murphy	.10
319	Tom Pagnozzi	.10
320	Mike Perez	.10
321	Tom Urbani	.10
322	Allen Watson	.10
323	Erik Pappas	.10
324	Paul Kilgus	.10
325	John Habyan	.10
326	Rod Brewer	.10
327	Rich Batchelor	.10
328	Tripp Cromer	.10
329	Gerald Perry	.10
330	Les Lancaster	.10
331	Ryne Sandberg	1.50
332	Derrick May	.10
333	Steve Buechele	.10
334	Willie Banks	.10
335	Larry Luebbers	.10
336	Tommy Shields	.10
337	Eric Yelding	.10
338	Rey Sanchez	.10
339	Mark Grace	.10
340	Jose Bautista	.10
341	Frank Castillo	.10
342	Jose Guzman	.10
343	Rafael Novoa	.10
344	Karl Rhodes	.10
345	Steve Trachsel	.10
346	Rick Wilkins	.10
347	Sammy Sosa	1.50
348	Kevin Roberson	.10
349	Mark Parent	.10
350	Randy Myers	.10
351	Glenallen Hill	.10
352	Lance Dickson	.10
353	Shawn Boskie	.10
354	Shawon Dunston	.10
355	Dan Plesac	.10
356	Jose Vizcaino	.10
357	Willie Wilson	.10
358	Turk Wendell	.10
359	Mike Morgan	.10
360	Jim Bullinger	.10

Team Series 1st Day Issue

Each of the cards in the Stadium Club Team Series can be found with a special embossed silver-foil "1st Day Issue" seal on front. Cards are otherwise identical to the regular issue.

	NM/M
Complete Set (360):	200.00
Common Player:	.50
Stars:	8X

Team Series Finest

One player from each of the 12 teams in the Stadium Club Team Series issue was printed in a chromium-metallic technology reminiscent of Topps Finest cards. These special cards are labeled "Team Stadium Club Finest." Other than the printing, the cards are in the same format as the rest of the issue.

		NM/M
Complete Set (12):		12.00
Common Player:		.50
1	Roberto Alomar	.50
2	Barry Bonds	3.00
3	Len Dykstra	.50
4	Andres Galarraga	.50
5	Juan Gonzalez	.50
6	Dave Justice	.50
7	Don Mattingly	2.00
8	Cal Ripken Jr.	3.00
9	Ryne Sandberg	1.50
10	Gary Sheffield	.65
11	Ozzie Smith	1.50
12	Frank Thomas	1.00

1995 Stadium Club

Topps' upscale brand was issued for 1995 in three series of, respectively, 270, 225 and 135 cards. Fronts have borderless color photos with a gold-foil device at bottom holding the team logo. Also in gold are the player's name at bottom and the Stadium Club logo at top. Backs have another player photo at left with a pair of computer-enhanced close-ups above it. At right are bar graphs detailing the player's '94 stats and his skills rankings. A number of specially designed subsets - "Best Seat in the House, Cover Story, MLB Debut," etc., are spread throughout the issue, which also includes a full slate of chase cards depending on the series and packaging.

	NM/M
Complete Set (630):	25.00

#	Player	Price
	Common Player:	.05
	Common First Day Production:	.50
	First Day Stars:	7X
	Series 1 or 2 Pack (14):	1.25
	Series 1 or 2 Wax Box (24):	20.00
	Series 3 Pack (13):	1.25
	Series 3 Wax Box (24):	20.00
1	Cal Ripken Jr.	2.50
2	Bo Jackson	.10
3	Bryan Harvey	.05
4	Curt Schilling	.35
5	Bruce Ruffin	.05
6	Travis Fryman	.05
7	Jim Abbott	.05
8	David McCarty	.05
9	Gary Gaetti	.05
10	Roger Clemens	1.25
11	Carlos Garcia	.05
12	Lee Smith	.05
13	Bobby Ayala	.05
14	Charles Nagy	.05
15	Lou Frazier	.05
16	Rene Arocha	.05
17	Carlos Delgado	.50
18	Steve Finley	.05
19	Ryan Klesko	.05
20	Cal Eldred	.05
21	Rey Sanchez	.05
22	Ken Hill	.05
23	Benny Santiago	.05
24	Julian Tavarez	.05
25	Jose Vizcaino	.05
26	Andy Benes	.05
27	Mariano Duncan	.05
28	Checklist A	.05
29	Shawon Dunston	.05
30	Rafael Palmeiro	.65
31	Dean Palmer	.05
32	Andres Galarraga	.05
33	Joey Cora	.05
34	Mickey Tettleton	.05
35	Barry Larkin	.05
36	Carlos Baerga	.05
37	Orel Hershiser	.05
38	Jody Reed	.05
39	Paul Molitor	.75
40	Jim Edmonds	.05
41	Bob Tewksbury	.05
42	John Patterson	.05
43	Ray McDavid	.05
44	Zane Smith	.05
45	Bret Saberhagen	.05
46	Greg Maddux	1.00
47	Frank Thomas	.75
48	Carlos Baerga	.05
49	Billy Spiers	.05
50	Stan Javier	.05
51	Rex Hudler	.05
52	Denny Hocking	.05
53	Todd Worrell	.05
54	Mark Clark	.05
55	Hipolito Pichardo	.05
56	Bob Wickman	.05
57	Raul Mondesi	.05
58	Steve Cooke	.05
59	Rod Beck	.05
60	Tim Davis	.05
61	Jeff Kent	.05
62	John Valentin	.05
63	Alex Arias	.05
64	Steve Reed	.05
65	Ozzie Smith	1.00
66	Terry Pendleton	.05
67	Kenny Rogers	.05
68	Vince Coleman	.05
69	Tom Pagnozzi	.05
70	Roberto Alomar	.20
71	Darrin Jackson	.05
72	Dennis Eckersley	.65
73	Jay Buhner	.05
74	Darren Lewis	.05
75	Dave Weathers	.05
76	Matt Walbeck	.05
77	Brad Ausmus	.05
78	Danny Bautista	.05
79	Bob Hamelin	.05
80	Steve Traschel	.05
81	Ken Ryan	.05
82	Chris Turner	.05
83	David Segui	.05
84	Ben McDonald	.05
85	Wade Boggs	1.00
86	John Vander Wal	.05
87	Sandy Alomar	.05
88	Ron Karkovice	.05
89	Doug Jones	.05
90	Gary Sheffield	.40
91	Ken Caminiti	.05
92	Chris Bosio	.05
93	Kevin Tapani	.05
94	Walt Weiss	.05
95	Erik Hanson	.05
96	Ruben Sierra	.05
97	Nomar Garciaparra	1.00
98	Terrence Long	.05
99	Jacob Shumate	.05
100	Paul Wilson	.05
101	Kevin Witt	.05
102	Paul Konerko	.15
103	Ben Grieve	.05
104	Mark Johnson RC	.05
105	Cade Gaspar RC	.05
106	Mark Farris	.05
107	Dustin Hermanson	.05
108	Scott Elarton RC	.15
109	Doug Million	.05
110	Matt Smith	.05
111	Brian Buchanan RC	.05
112	Jayson Peterson RC	.05
113	Bret Wagner	.05
114	C.J. Nitkowski	.05
115	Ramon Castro RC	.05
116	Rafael Bournigal	.05
117	Jeff Fassero	.05
118	Bobby Bonilla	.05
119	Ricky Gutierrez	.05
120	Roger Pavlik	.05
121	Mike Greenwell	.05
122	Deion Sanders	.05
123	Charlie Hayes	.05
124	Paul O'Neill	.05
125	Jay Bell	.05
126	Royce Clayton	.05
127	Willie Banks	.05
128	Mark Wohlers	.05
129	Todd Jones	.05
130	Todd Stottlemyre	.05
131	Will Clark	.05
132	Wilson Alvarez	.05
133	Chili Davis	.05
134	Dave Burba	.05
135	Chris Hoiles	.05
136	Jeff Blauser	.05
137	Jeff Reboulet	.05
138	Bret Saberhagen	.05
139	Kirk Rueter	.05
140	Dave Nilsson	.05
141	Pat Borders	.05
142	Ron Darling	.05
143	Derek Bell	.05
144	Dave Hollins	.05
145	Juan Gonzalez	.40
146	Andre Dawson	.25
147	Jim Thome	.65
148	Larry Walker	.05
149	Mike Piazza	1.50
150	Mike Perez	.05
151	Steve Avery	.05
152	Dan Wilson	.05
153	Andy Van Slyke	.05
154	Junior Felix	.05
155	Jack McDowell	.05
156	Danny Tartabull	.05
157	Willie Blair	.05
158	William Van Landingham	.05
159	Robb Nen	.05
160	Lee Tinsley	.05
161	Ismael Valdes	.05
162	Juan Guzman	.05
163	Scott Servais	.05
164	Cliff Floyd	.05
165	Allen Watson	.05
166	Eddie Taubensee	.05
167	Scott Hemond	.05
168	Jeff Tackett	.05
169	Chad Curtis	.05
170	Rico Brogna	.05
171	Luis Polonia	.05
172	Checklist B	.05
173	Lance Johnson	.05
174	Sammy Sosa	1.00
175	Mike MacFarlane	.05
176	Darryl Hamilton	.05
177	Rick Aguilera	.05
178	Dave West	.05
179	Mike Gallego	.05
180	Marc Newfield	.05
181	Steve Buechele	.05
182	David Wells	.05
183	Tom Glavine	.35
184	Joe Girardi	.05
185	Craig Biggio	.05
186	Eddie Murray	.75
187	Kevin Gross	.05
188	Sid Fernandez	.05
189	John Franco	.05
190	Bernard Gilkey	.05
191	Matt Williams	.05
192	Darrin Fletcher	.05
193	Jeff Conine	.05
194	Ed Sprague	.05
195	Eduardo Perez	.05
196	Scott Livingstone	.05
197	Ivan Rodriguez	.65
198	Orlando Merced	.05
199	Ricky Bones	.05
200	Javier Lopez	.05
201	Miguel Jimenez	.05
202	Terry McGriff	.05
203	Mike Lieberthal	.05
204	David Cone	.05
205	Todd Hundley	.05
206	Ozzie Guillen	.05
207	Alex Cole	.05
208	Tony Phillips	.05
209	Jim Eisenreich	.05
210	Greg Vaughn	.05
211	Barry Larkin	.05
212	Don Mattingly	1.00
213	Mark Grace	.05
214	Jose Canseco	.50
215	Joe Carter	.05
216	David Cone	.05
217	Sandy Alomar	.05
218	Al Martin	.05
219	Roberto Kelly	.05
220	Paul Sorrento	.05
221	Tony Fernandez	.05
222	Stan Belinda	.05
223	Mike Stanley	.05
224	Doug Drabek	.05
225	Todd Van Poppel	.05
226	Matt Mieske	.05
227	Tino Martinez	.05
228	Andy Ashby	.05
229	Midre Cummings	.05
230	Jeff Frye	.05
231	Hal Morris	.05
232	Jose Lind	.05
233	Shawn Green	.30
234	Rafael Belliard	.05
235	Randy Myers	.05
236	Frank Thomas	.45
237	Darren Daulton	.05
238	Sammy Sosa	.65
239	Cal Ripken Jr.	1.00
240	Jeff Bagwell	.40
241	Ken Griffey Jr.	1.50
242	Brett Butler	.05
243	Derrick May	.05
244	Pat Listach	.05
245	Mike Bordick	.05
246	Mark Langston	.05
247	Randy Velarde	.05
248	Julio Franco	.05
249	Chuck Knoblauch	.05
250	Bill Gullickson	.05
251	Dave Henderson	.05
252	Bret Boone	.05
253	Al Martin	.05
254	Armando Benitez	.05
255	Wil Cordero	.05
256	Al Leiter	.05
257	Luis Gonzalez	.05
258	Charlie O'Brien	.05
259	Tim Wallach	.05
260	Scott Sanders	.05
261	Tom Henke	.05
262	Otis Nixon	.05
263	Darren Daulton	.05
264	Manny Ramirez	.75
265	Bret Barberie	.05
266	Mel Rojas	.05
267	John Burkett	.05
268	Brady Anderson	.05
269	John Roper	.05
270	Shane Reynolds	.05
271	Barry Bonds	2.50
272	Alex Fernandez	.05
273	Brian McRae	.05
274	Todd Zeile	.05
275	Greg Swindell	.05
276	Johnny Ruffin	.05
277	Troy Neel	.05
278	Eric Karros	.05
279	John Hudek	.05
280	Thomas Howard	.05
281	Joe Carter	.05
282	Mike Devereaux	.05
283	Butch Henry	.05
284	Reggie Jefferson	.05
285	Mark Lemke	.05
286	Jeff Montgomery	.05
287	Ryan Thompson	.05
288	Paul Shuey	.05
289	Mark McGwire	2.00
290	Bernie Williams	.05
291	Mickey Morandini	.05
292	Scott Leius	.05
293	David Hulse	.05
294	Greg Gagne	.05
295	Moises Alou	.05
296	Geronimo Berroa	.05
297	Eddie Zambrano	.05
298	Alan Trammell	.05
299	Don Slaught	.05
300	Jose Rijo	.05
301	Joe Ausanio	.05
302	Tim Raines	.05
303	Melido Perez	.05
304	Kent Mercker	.05
305	James Mouton	.05
306	Luis Lopez	.05
307	Mike Kingery	.05
308	Willie Greene	.05
309	Cecil Fielder	.05
310	Scott Kamieniecki	.05
311	Mike Greenwell (Best Seat in the House)	.05
312	Bobby Bonilla (Best Seat in the House)	.05
313	Andres Galarraga (Best Seat in the House)	.05
314	Cal Ripken Jr. (Best Seat in the House)	1.25
315	Matt Williams (Best Seat in the House)	.05
316	Tom Pagnozzi (Best Seat in the House)	.05
317	Len Dykstra (Best Seat in the House)	.05
318	Frank Thomas (Best Seat in the House)	.40
319	Kirby Puckett (Best Seat in the House)	.50
320	Mike Piazza (Best Seat in the House)	1.00
321	Jason Jacome	.05
322	Brian Hunter	.05
323	Brent Gates	.05
324	Jim Converse	.05
325	Damion Easley	.05
326	Dante Bichette	.05
327	Kurt Abbott	.05
328	Scott Cooper	.05
329	Mike Henneman	.05
330	Orlando Miller	.05
331	John Kruk	.05
332	Jose Oliva	.05
333	Reggie Sanders	.05
334	Omar Vizquel	.05
335	Devon White	.05
336	Mike Morgan	.05

No.	Player	Price
337	J.R. Phillips	.05
338	Gary DiSarcina	.05
339	Joey Hamilton	.05
340	Randy Johnson	.75
341	Jim Leyritz	.05
342	Bobby Jones	.05
343	Jaime Navarro	.05
344	Bip Roberts	.05
345	Steve Karsay	.05
346	Kevin Stocker	.05
347	Jose Canseco	.50
348	Bill Wegman	.05
349	Rondell White	.05
350	Mo Vaughn	.05
351	Joe Orsulak	.05
352	Pat Meares	.05
353	Albie Lopez	.05
354	Edgar Martinez	.05
355	Brian Jordan	.05
356	Tommy Greene	.05
357	Chuck Carr	.05
358	Pedro Astacio	.05
359	Russ Davis	.05
360	Chris Hammond	.05
361	Gregg Jefferies	.05
362	Shane Mack	.05
363	Fred McGriff	.05
364	Pat Rapp	.05
365	Bill Swift	.05
366	Checklist	.05
367	Robin Ventura	.05
368	Bobby Witt	.05
369	Karl Rhodes	.05
370	Eddie Williams	.05
371	John Jaha	.05
372	Steve Howe	.05
373	Leo Gomez	.05
374	Hector Fajardo	.05
375	Jeff Bagwell	.75
376	Mark Acre	.05
377	Wayne Kirby	.05
378	Mark Portugal	.05
379	Jesus Tavarez	.05
380	Jim Lindeman	.05
381	Don Mattingly	1.25
382	Trevor Hoffman	.05
383	Chris Gomez	.05
384	Garret Anderson	.05
385	Bobby Munoz	.05
386	Jon Lieber	.05
387	Rick Helling	.05
388	Marvin Freeman	.05
389	Juan Castillo	.05
390	Jeff Cirillo	.05
391	Sean Berry	.05
392	Hector Carrasco	.05
393	Mark Grace	.05
394	Pat Kelly	.05
395	Tim Naehring	.05
396	Greg Pirkl	.05
397	John Smoltz	.05
398	Robby Thompson	.05
399	Rick White	.05
400	Frank Thomas	.75
401	Jeff Conine (Cover Story)	.05
402	Jose Valentin (Cover Story)	.05
403	Carlos Baerga (Cover Story)	.05
404	Rick Aguilera (Cover Story)	.05
405	Wilson Alvarez (Cover Story)	.05
406	Juan Gonzalez (Cover Story)	.20
407	Barry Larkin (Cover Story)	.05
408	Ken Hill (Cover Story)	.05
409	Chuck Carr (Cover Story)	.05
410	Tim Raines (Cover Story)	.05
411	Bryan Eversgerd	.05
412	Phil Plantier	.05
413	Josias Manzanillo	.05
414	Roberto Kelly	.05
415	Rickey Henderson	.75
416	John Smiley	.05
417	Kevin Brown	.05
418	Jimmy Key	.05
419	Wally Joyner	.05
420	Roberto Hernandez	.05
421	Felix Fermin	.05
422	Checklist	.05
423	Greg Vaughn	.05
424	Ray Lankford	.05
425	Greg Maddux	1.00
426	Mike Mussina	.30
427	Geronimo Pena	.05
428	David Nied	.05
429	Scott Erickson	.05
430	Kevin Mitchell	.05
431	Mike Lansing	.05
432	Brian Anderson	.05
433	Jeff King	.05
434	Ramon Martinez	.05
435	Kevin Seitzer	.05
436	Salomon Torres	.05
437	Brian Hunter	.05
438	Melvin Nieves	.05
439	Mike Kelly	.05
440	Marquis Grissom	.05
441	Chuck Finley	.05
442	Len Dykstra	.05
443	Ellis Burks	.05
444	Harold Baines	.05
445	Kevin Appier	.05
446	Dave Justice	.05
447	Darryl Kile	.05
448	John Olerud	.05
449	Greg McMichael	.05
450	Kirby Puckett	1.00
451	Jose Valentin	.05
452	Rick Wilkins	.05
453	Arthur Rhodes	.05
454	Pat Hentgen	.05
455	Tom Gordon	.05
456	Tom Candiotti	.05
457	Jason Bere	.05
458	Wes Chamberlain	.05
459	Greg Colbrunn	.05
460	John Doherty	.05
461	Kevin Foster	.05
462	Mark Whiten	.05
463	Terry Steinbach	.05
464	Aaron Sele	.05
465	Kirt Manwaring	.05
466	Darren Hall	.05
467	Delino DeShields	.05
468	Andujar Cedeno	.05
469	Billy Ashley	.05
470	Kenny Lofton	.05
471	Pedro Munoz	.05
472	John Wetteland	.05
473	Tim Salmon	.05
474	Denny Neagle	.05
475	Tony Gwynn	1.00
476	Vinny Castilla	.05
477	Steve Dreyer	.05
478	Jeff Shaw	.05
479	Chad Ogea	.05
480	Scott Ruffcorn	.05
481	Lou Whitaker	.05
482	J.T. Snow	.05
483	Rich Rowland	.05
484	Dennis Martinez	.05
485	Pedro Martinez	.75
486	Rusty Greer	.05
487	Dave Fleming	.05
488	John Dettmer	.05
489	Albert Belle	.05
490	Ravelo Manzanillo	.05
491	Henry Rodriguez	.05
492	Andrew Lorraine	.05
493	Dwayne Hosey	.05
494	Mike Blowers	.05
495	Turner Ward	.05
496	Fred McGriff (Extreme Corps)	.05
497	Sammy Sosa (Extreme Corps)	.50
498	Barry Larkin (Extreme Corps)	.05
499	Andres Galarraga (Extreme Corps)	.05
500	Gary Sheffield (Extreme Corps)	.15
501	Jeff Bagwell (Extreme Corps)	.40
502	Mike Piazza (Extreme Corps)	1.00
503	Moises Alou (Extreme Corps)	.05
504	Bobby Bonilla (Extreme Corps)	.05
505	Darren Daulton (Extreme Corps)	.05
506	Jeff King (Extreme Corps)	.05
507	Ray Lankford (Extreme Corps)	.05
508	Tony Gwynn (Extreme Corps)	.50
509	Barry Bonds (Extreme Corps)	1.25
510	Cal Ripken Jr. (Extreme Corps)	1.25
511	Mo Vaughn (Extreme Corps)	.05
512	Tim Salmon (Extreme Corps)	.05
513	Frank Thomas (Extreme Corps)	.45
514	Albert Belle (Extreme Corps)	.05
515	Cecil Fielder (Extreme Corps)	.05
516	Kevin Appier (Extreme Corps)	.05
517	Greg Vaughn (Extreme Corps)	.05
518	Kirby Puckett (Extreme Corps)	.50
519	Paul O'Neill (Extreme Corps)	.05
520	Ruben Sierra (Extreme Corps)	.05
521	Ken Griffey Jr. (Extreme Corps)	.75
522	Will Clark (Extreme Corps)	.05
523	Joe Carter (Extreme Corps)	.05
524	Antonio Osuna	.05
525	Glenallen Hill	.05
526	Alex Gonzalez	.05
527	Dave Stewart	.05
528	Ron Gant	.05
529	Jason Bates	.05
530	Mike Macfarlane	.05
531	Esteban Loaiza	.05
532	Joe Randa	.05
533	Dave Winfield	.75
534	Danny Darwin	.05
535	Pete Harnisch	.35
536	Joey Cora	.05
537	Jaime Navarro	.05
538	Marty Cordova	.05
539	Andujar Cedeno	.05
540	Mickey Tettleton	.05
541	Andy Van Slyke	.05
542	Carlos Perez RC	.05
543	Chipper Jones	1.00
544	Tony Fernandez	.05
545	Tom Henke	.05
546	Pat Borders	.05
547	Chad Curtis	.05
548	Ray Durham	.05
549	Joe Oliver	.05
550	Jose Mesa	.05
551	Steve Finley	.05
552	Otis Nixon	.05
553	Jacob Brumfield	.05
554	Bill Swift	.05
555	Quilvio Veras	.05
556	Hideo Nomo RC	1.50
557	Joe Vitiello	.05
558	Mike Perez	.05
559	Charlie Hayes	.05
560	Brad Radke RC	.25
561	Darren Bragg	.05
562	Orel Hershiser	.05
563	Edgardo Alfonzo	.05
564	Doug Jones	.05
565	Andy Pettitte	.25
566	Benito Santiago	.05
567	John Burkett	.05
568	Brad Clontz	.05
569	Jim Abbott	.05
570	Joe Rosselli	.05
571	Mark Grudzielanek RC	.25
572	Dustin Hermanson	.05
573	Benji Gil	.05
574	Mark Whiten	.05
575	Mike Ignasiak	.05
576	Kevin Ritz	.05
577	Paul Quantrill	.05
578	Andre Dawson	.25
579	Jerald Clark	.05
580	Frank Rodriguez	.05
581	Mark Kiefer	.05
582	Trevor Wilson	.05
583	Gary Wilson RC	.05
584	Andy Stankiewicz	.05
585	Felipe Lira	.05
586	Mike Mimbs RC	.05
587	Jon Nunnally	.05
588	Tomas Perez RC	.05
589	Checklist	.05
590	Todd Hollandsworth	.05
591	Roberto Petagine	.15
592	Mariano Rivera	.15
593	Mark McLemore	.05
594	Bobby Witt	.05
595	Jose Offerman	.05
596	Jason Christiansen	.05
597	Jeff Manto	.05
598	Jim Dougherty	.05
599	Juan Acevedo	.05
600	Troy O'Leary	.05
601	Ron Villone	.05
602	Tripp Cromer	.05
603	Steve Scarsone	.05
604	Lance Parrish	.05
605	Ozzie Timmons	.05
606	Ray Holbert	.05
607	Tony Phillips	.05
608	Phil Plantier	.05
609	Shane Andrews	.05
610	Heathcliff Slocumb	.05
611	Bobby Higginson RC	.25
612	Bob Tewksbury	.05
613	Terry Pendleton	.05
614	Scott Cooper (Trans-Action)	.05
615	John Wetteland (Trans-Action)	.05
616	Ken Hill (Trans-Action)	.05
617	Marquis Grissom (Trans-Action)	.05
618	Larry Walker (Trans-Action)	.05
619	Derek Bell (Trans-Action)	.05
620	David Cone (Trans-Action)	.05
621	Ken Caminiti (Trans-Action)	.05
622	Jack McDowell (Trans-Action)	.05
623	Vaughn Eshelman (Trans-Action)	.05
624	Brian McRae (Trans-Action)	.05
625	Gregg Jefferies (Trans-Action)	.05
626	Kevin Brown (Trans-Action)	.05
627	Lee Smith (Trans-Action)	.05
628	Tony Tarasco (Trans-Action)	.05
629	Brett Butler (Trans-Action)	.05
630	Jose Canseco (Trans-Action)	.35

1st Day Pre-Production

Stadium Club 1st Day Pre-production cards were randomly packed into one every 36 packs of Topps Series I baseball. The set of nine cards is only found in hobby packs.

		NM/M
Complete Set (9):		7.50
Common Player:		.50
29	Shawon Dunston	.50
39	Paul Molitor	1.50
79	Bob Hamelin	.50
96	Ruben Sierra	.50
131	Will Clark	.50
149	Mike Piazza	3.00
153	Andy Van Slyke	.50
166	Jeff Tackett	.50
197	Ivan Rodriguez	1.00

1st Day Issue

Series II hobby packs of Topps baseball featured a chase set of Stadium Club 1st Day Issue cards, #1-270. The FDI cards have a small gold embossed seal on front. Cards were seeded on an average of one per six packs. Ten FDI cards were also randomly inserted in each Factory set.

	NM/M
Common Player:	.50
Stars:	7X

Clear Cut

Among the most technically advanced of 1995's insert cards is the Clear Cut chase set found in Series I and II packs. Cards feature a color player action photo printed on see-through plastic. There is a rainbow-hued trapezoid behind the player with an overall background tinted in blue, green and gold. The player's name is in white in a vertical blue bar at right. Backs have a few stats and data in a blue bar vertically at left. Each of the cards can also be found in a version with the round Members Only seal embossed into the plastic at lower-left.

		NM/M
Complete Set (28):		20.00
Common Player:		.65
1	Mike Piazza	3.00
2	Ruben Sierra	.65
3	Tony Gwynn	2.50
4	Frank Thomas	2.00
5	Fred McGriff	.65
6	Rafael Palmeiro	1.50
7	Bobby Bonilla	.65
8	Chili Davis	.65
9	Hal Morris	.65
10	Jose Canseco	1.00
11	Jay Bell	.65
12	Kirby Puckett	2.50
13	Gary Sheffield	1.00
14	Bob Hamelin	.65
15	Jeff Bagwell	.65
16	Albert Belle	.65
17	Sammy Sosa	2.50
18	Ken Griffey Jr.	3.00
19	Todd Zeile	.65
20	Mo Vaughn	.65
21	Moises Alou	.65
22	Paul O'Neill	.65
23	Andres Galarraga	.65
24	Greg Vaughn	.65
25	Len Dykstra	.65
26	Joe Carter	.65
27	Barry Bonds	4.50
28	Cecil Fielder	.65

Crunch Time

Series 1 rack packs were the exclusive provenance of these cards featuring baseball's top run creators. Fronts are printed on rainbow prismatic foil. The central color action photo is repeated as an enlarged background photo, along with a team logo. At bottom in gold foil are the player name and Crunch Time logo. Backs have a positive and negative image of the same photo as background to a pie chart and stats relative to the player's runs-created stats.

		NM/M
Complete Set (20):		15.00
Common Player:		1.00
1	Jeff Bagwell	2.50
2	Kirby Puckett	3.00
3	Frank Thomas	2.50
4	Albert Belle	1.00
5	Julio Franco	1.00
6	Jose Canseco	1.50
7	Paul Molitor	2.50
8	Joe Carter	1.00
9	Ken Griffey Jr.	4.00
10	Larry Walker	1.00
11	Dante Bichette	1.00
12	Carlos Baerga	1.00
13	Fred McGriff	1.00
14	Ruben Sierra	1.00
15	Will Clark	1.00
16	Moises Alou	1.00
17	Rafael Palmeiro	2.00
18	Travis Fryman	1.00
19	Barry Bonds	5.00
20	Cal Ripken Jr.	5.00

Crystal Ball

Multi-colored swirls around a clear central circle with the player's photo, all printed on foil, are the front design for this Series 3 insert. Backs have a portrait photo in a floating crystal ball image at one side. At the other end are year-by-year minor league stats and a few words about each of the player's seasons. This insert was also produced in an edition of 4,000 bearing a gold-foil "Members Only" seal, sold in complete Stadium Club Members Only factory sets.

		NM/M
Complete Set (15):		15.00
Common Player:		.75
1	Chipper Jones	5.00
2	Dustin Hermanson	.75
3	Ray Durham	.75
4	Phil Nevin	.75
5	Billy Ashley	.75
6	Shawn Green	2.50
7	Jason Bates	.75
8	Benji Gil	.75
9	Marty Cordova	.75
10	Quilvio Veras	.75
11	Mark Grudzielanek	.75
12	Ruben Rivera	.75
13	Bill Pulsipher	.75
14	Derek Jeter	7.50
15	LaTroy Hawkins	.75

Power Zone

The performance in several parks around the league is chronicled on the back of these Series 3 inserts. Fronts are printed on foil and feature a player swinging into an exploding asteroid. His name is printed vertically down one side in prismatic glitter foil. Backs also have a portrait photo and a baseball with a weird red and green vapor trail. A special edition of 4,000 each of these inserts was included with the purchase of Stadium Club Members Only factory sets; those cards have an embossed gold-foil seal on front.

		NM/M
Complete Set (12):		9.00
Common Player:		.50
1	Jeff Bagwell	1.00
2	Albert Belle	.50
3	Barry Bonds	3.00
4	Joe Carter	.50
5	Cecil Fielder	.50
6	Andres Galarraga	.50
7	Ken Griffey Jr.	2.00
8	Paul Molitor	1.00
9	Fred McGriff	.50
10	Rafael Palmeiro	.75
11	Frank Thomas	1.00
12	Matt Williams	.50

Ring Leaders

With a background that looks like an explosion at a jewelry factory, these cards feature players who have won championship, All-Star or other award rings. Fronts are foil-printed with a player action photo on a background of flying rings and stars, and, - for some reason - an attacking eagle. Backs repeat the background motif, have a player portrait in an oval frame at top-left, photos of some of his rings and a list of rings won. Cards were random inserts in both Series 1 and 2; complete sets could also be won in Stadium Club's phone card insert contest. A version with the Members Only gold seal was also issued for each.

		NM/M
Complete Set (40):		70.00
Common Player:		.75
1	Jeff Bagwell	3.00
2	Mark McGwire	7.50
3	Ozzie Smith	4.00
4	Paul Molitor	3.00

5	Darryl Strawberry	.75
6	Eddie Murray	3.00
7	Tony Gwynn	4.00
8	Jose Canseco	2.00
9	Howard Johnson	.75
10	Andre Dawson	1.25
11	Matt Williams	.75
12	Tim Raines	.75
13	Fred McGriff	.75
14	Ken Griffey Jr.	6.00
15	Gary Sheffield	2.00
16	Dennis Eckersley	2.50
17	Kevin Mitchell	.75
18	Will Clark	.75
19	Darren Daulton	.75
20	Paul O'Neill	.75
21	Julio Franco	.75
22	Albert Belle	.75
23	Juan Gonzalez	1.50
24	Kirby Puckett	4.00
25	Joe Carter	.75
26	Frank Thomas	3.00
27	Cal Ripken Jr.	9.00
28	John Olerud	.75
29	Ruben Sierra	.75
30	Barry Bonds	9.00
31	Cecil Fielder	.75
32	Roger Clemens	5.00
33	Don Mattingly	5.00
34	Terry Pendleton	.75
35	Rickey Henderson	3.00
36	Dave Winfield	3.00
37	Edgar Martinez	.75
38	Wade Boggs	4.00
39	Willie McGee	.75
40	Andres Galarraga	.75

Ring Leaders Phone Cards

An interactive contest carrying through the "Ring Leaders" insert card set theme featured randomly inserted phone cards picturing All-Star Game players' rings. The 2-1/8" x 3/-3/8" plastic cards could be found in regular, silver and gold editions. By using the card for a long distance call, the holder could determine if it was a further winner. Regular card winners received a set of the 13 different phone cards in all three versions. Gold card winners received the genuine All-Star ring pictured on the card. Approximately 217,000 phone cards were inserted in the program; odds of finding a regular card were about one per 40 packs; silver, one per 237 packs, and, gold, one per 2,955 packs. Cards picturing the 1988 and 1989 All-Star rings were not issued. Phone cards with the number panel on back scratched off are worth 50% of values quoted.

		NM/M
Complete Set, Regular (13):		10.00
Complete Set, Silver (13):		25.00
Complete Set, Gold (13):		50.00
Common Card, Regular:		1.00
Common Card, Silver:		2.50
Common Card, Gold:		5.00
(1)	1980 All-Star Game, Los Angeles	1.00
(1s)	1980 All-Star Game, Los Angeles/Silver	2.50
(1g)	1980 All-Star Game, Los Angeles/Gold	5.00
(2)	1981 All-Star Game, Cleveland	1.00
(2s)	1981 All-Star Game, Cleveland/Silver	2.50
(2g)	1981 All-Star Game, Cleveland/Gold	5.00
(3)	1982 All-Star Game, Montreal	1.00
(3s)	1982 All-Star Game, Montreal/Silver	2.50
(3g)	1982 All-Star Game, Montreal/Gold	5.00
(4)	1983 All-Star Game, Chicago A.L.	1.00
(4s)	1983 All-Star Game, Chicago A.L./Silver	2.50
(4g)	1983 All-Star Game, Chicago A.L./Gold	5.00

(5)	1984 All-Star Game, San Francisco	1.00
(5s)	1984 All-Star Game, San Francisco/Silver	2.50
(5g)	1984 All-Star Game, San Francisco/Gold	5.00
(6)	1985 All-Star Game, Minneapolis	1.00
(6s)	1985 All-Star Game, Minneapolis/Silver	2.50
(6g)	1985 All-Star Game, Minneapolis/Gold	5.00
(7)	1986 All-Star Game, Houston	1.00
(7s)	1986 All-Star Game, Houston/Silver	2.50
(7g)	1986 All-Star Game, Houston/Gold	5.00
(8)	1987 All-Star Game, Oakland	1.00
(8s)	1987 All-Star Game, Oakland/Silver	2.50
(8g)	1987 All-Star Game, Oakland/Gold	5.00
(9)	1990 All-Star Game, Chicago N.L.	1.00
(9s)	1990 All-Star Game, Chicago N.L./Silver	2.50
(9g)	1990 All-Star Game, Chicago N.L./Gold	5.00
(10)	1991 All-Star Game, Toronto	1.00
(10s)	1991 All-Star Game, Toronto/Silver	2.50
(10g)	1991 All-Star Game, Toronto/Gold	5.00
(11)	1992 All-Star Game, San Diego	1.00
(11s)	1992 All-Star Game, San Diego/Silver	2.50
(11g)	1992 All-Star Game, San Diego/Gold	5.00
(12)	1993 All-Star Game, Baltimore	1.00
(12s)	1993 All-Star Game, Baltimore/Silver	2.50
(12g)	1993 All-Star Game, Baltimore/Gold	5.00
(13)	1994 All-Star Game, Pittsburgh	1.00
(13s)	1994 All-Star Game, Pittsburgh/Silver	2.50
(13g)	1994 All-Star Game, Pittsburgh/Gold	5.00

Super Skills

These random hobby pack inserts in both Series 1 and 2 are printed on rainbow prismatic foil which features as a background an enlarged version of the front photo. The S.C. and Super Skills logos are printed in gold foil in opposite corners, while the player's name is in blue at bottom-right. Backs repeat the enlarged background image of a close-up foreground photo, while a few words about the player's particular specialties are in white at left. Each card can also be found in a version featuring the Members Only gold-foil seal on front.

		NM/M
Complete Set (20):		30.00
Common Player:		.75
1	Roberto Alomar	1.00
2	Barry Bonds	10.00
3	Jay Buhner	.75
4	Chuck Carr	.75
5	Don Mattingly	5.00
6	Raul Mondesi	.75
7	Tim Salmon	.75
8	Deion Sanders	.75
9	Devon White	.75
10	Mark Whiten	.75
11	Ken Griffey Jr.	7.50
12	Marquis Grissom	.75
13	Paul O'Neill	.75
14	Kenny Lofton	.75
15	Larry Walker	.75
16	Scott Cooper	.75
17	Barry Larkin	.75
18	Matt Williams	.75
19	John Wetteland	.75
20	Randy Johnson	2.50

Virtual Reality

A partial parallel set found one per foil pack, two per rack pack, these cards share the

basic front and back with the corresponding card in the regular S.C. issue. On front, however, is a "Virtual Reality" seal around the team logo at bottom (gold foil in Series 1, silver-foil in Series 2). Backs differ in that instead of actual 1994 season stats, they present a bar graph of computer projected stats representing a full 162-game season instead of the strike-shortened reality. Each of these inserts can also be found in a version bearing the round gold-(Series 1) or silver-foil (Series 2) Members Only seal on the front.

		NM/M
Complete Set (270):		35.00
Common Player:		.10
1	Cal Ripken Jr.	2.50
2	Travis Fryman	.10
3	Jim Abbott	.10
4	Gary Gaetti	.10
5	Roger Clemens	1.25
6	Carlos Garcia	.10
7	Lee Smith	.10
8	Bobby Ayala	.10
9	Charles Nagy	.10
10	Rene Arocha	.10
11	Carlos Delgado	.50
12	Steve Finley	.10
13	Ryan Klesko	.10
14	Cal Eldred	.10
15	Rey Sanchez	.10
16	Ken Hill	.10
17	Jose Vizcaino	.10
18	Andy Benes	.10
19	Shawon Dunston	.10
20	Rafael Palmeiro	.65
21	Dean Palmer	.10
22	Joey Cora	.10
23	Mickey Tettleton	.10
24	Barry Larkin	.10
25	Carlos Baerga	.10
26	Orel Hershiser	.10
27	Jody Reed	.10
28	Paul Molitor	.75
29	Jim Edmonds	.10
30	Bob Tewksbury	.10
31	Ray McDavid	.10
32	Stan Javier	.10
33	Todd Worrell	.10
34	Bob Wickman	.10
35	Raul Mondesi	.10
36	Rod Beck	.10
37	Jeff Kent	.10
38	John Valentin	.10
39	Ozzie Smith	1.00
40	Terry Pendleton	.10
41	Kenny Rogers	.10
42	Vince Coleman	.10
43	Roberto Alomar	.20
44	Darrin Jackson	.10
45	Dennis Eckersley	.65
46	Jay Buhner	.10
47	Dave Weathers	.10
48	Danny Bautista	.10
49	Bob Hamelin	.10
50	Steve Trachsel	.10
51	Ben McDonald	.10
52	Wade Boggs	1.00
53	Sandy Alomar	.10
54	Ron Karkovice	.10
55	Doug Jones	.10
56	Gary Sheffield	.40
57	Ken Caminiti	.10
58	Kevin Tapani	.10
59	Ruben Sierra	.10
60	Bobby Bonilla	.10
61	Deion Sanders	.10
62	Charlie Hayes	.10
63	Paul O'Neill	.10
64	Jay Bell	.10
65	Todd Jones	.10
66	Todd Stottlemyre	.10
67	Will Clark	.10
68	Wilson Alvarez	.10
69	Chili Davis	.10
70	Chris Hoiles	.10
71	Bret Saberhagen	.10
72	Dave Nilsson	.10
73	Derek Bell	.10
74	Juan Gonzalez	.40
75	Andre Dawson	.30

76	Jim Thome	.65
77	Larry Walker	.10
78	Mike Piazza	1.50
79	Dan Wilson	.10
80	Junior Felix	.10
81	Jack McDowell	.10
82	Danny Tartabull	.10
83	William Van Landingham	.10
84	Robb Nen	.10
85	Ismael Valdes	.10
86	Juan Guzman	.10
87	Cliff Floyd	.10
88	Rico Brogna	.10
89	Luis Polonia	.10
90	Lance Johnson	.10
91	Sammy Sosa	1.00
92	Dave West	.10
93	Tom Glavine	.35
94	Joe Girardi	.10
95	Craig Biggio	.10
96	Eddie Murray	.75
97	Kevin Gross	.10
98	John Franco	.10
99	Matt Williams	.10
100	Darrin Fletcher	.10
101	Jeff Conine	.10
102	Ed Sprague	.10
103	Ivan Rodriguez	.65
104	Orlando Merced	.10
105	Ricky Bones	.10
106	David Cone	.10
107	Todd Hundley	.10
108	Alex Cole	.10
109	Tony Phillips	.10
110	Jim Eisenreich	.10
111	Paul Sorrento	.10
112	Mike Stanley	.10
113	Doug Drabek	.10
114	Matt Mieske	.10
115	Tino Martinez	.10
116	Midre Cummings	.10
117	Hal Morris	.10
118	Shawn Green	.40
119	Randy Myers	.10
120	Ken Griffey Jr.	1.50
121	Brett Butler	.10
122	Julio Franco	.10
123	Chuck Knoblauch	.10
124	Bret Boone	.10
125	Wil Cordero	.10
126	Luis Gonzalez	.10
127	Tim Wallach	.10
128	Scott Sanders	.10
129	Tom Henke	.10
130	Otis Nixon	.10
131	Darren Lewis	.10
132	Manny Ramirez	.75
133	Bret Barberie	.10
134	Brady Anderson	.10
135	Shane Reynolds	.10
136	Barry Bonds	2.50
137	Alex Fernandez	.10
138	Brian McRae	.10
139	Todd Zeile	.10
140	Greg Swindell	.10
141	Troy Neel	.10
142	Eric Karros	.10
143	John Hudek	.10
144	Joe Carter	.10
145	Mike Devereaux	.10
146	Butch Henry	.10
147	Mark Lemke	.10
148	Jeff Montgomery	.10
149	Ryan Thompson	.10
150	Bernie Williams	.10
151	Scott Leius	.10
152	Greg Gagne	.10
153	Moises Alou	.10
154	Geronimo Berroa	.10
155	Alan Trammell	.10
156	Don Slaught	.10
157	Jose Rijo	.10
158	Tim Raines	.10
159	Melido Perez	.10
160	Kent Mercker	.10
161	James Mouton	.10
162	Luis Lopez	.10
163	Mike Kingery	.10
164	Cecil Fielder	.10
165	Scott Kamieniecki	.10
166	Brent Gates	.10
167	Jason Jacome	.10
168	Dante Bichette	.10
169	Kurt Abbott	.10
170	Mike Henneman	.10
171	John Kruk	.10
172	Jose Oliva	.10
173	Reggie Sanders	.10
174	Omar Vizquel	.10
175	Devon White	.10
176	Mark McGwire	2.00
177	Gary DiSarcina	.10
178	Joey Hamilton	.10
179	Randy Johnson	.75
180	Jim Leyritz	.10
181	Bobby Jones	.10
182	Bip Roberts	.10
183	Jose Canseco	.40
184	Mo Vaughn	.10
185	Edgar Martinez	.10
186	Tommy Greene	.10
187	Chuck Carr	.10
188	Pedro Astacio	.10
189	Shane Mack	.10
190	Fred McGriff	.10
191	Pat Rapp	.10
192	Bill Swift	.10

193	Robin Ventura	.10
194	Bobby Witt	.10
195	Steve Howe	.10
196	Leo Gomez	.10
197	Hector Fajardo	.10
198	Jeff Bagwell	.75
199	Rondell White	.10
200	Don Mattingly	1.25
201	Trevor Hoffman	.10
202	Chris Gomez	.10
203	Bobby Munoz	.10
204	Marvin Freeman	.10
205	Sean Berry	.10
206	Mark Grace	.10
207	Pat Kelly	.10
208	Eddie Williams	.10
209	Frank Thomas	.75
210	Bryan Eversgerd	.10
211	Phil Plantier	.10
212	Roberto Kelly	.10
213	Rickey Henderson	.75
214	John Smiley	.10
215	Kevin Brown	.10
216	Jimmy Key	.10
217	Wally Joyner	.10
218	Roberto Hernandez	.10
219	Felix Fermin	.10
220	Greg Vaughn	.10
221	Ray Lankford	.10
222	Greg Maddux	1.00
223	Mike Mussina	.30
224	David Nied	.10
225	Scott Erickson	.10
226	Kevin Mitchell	.10
227	Brian Anderson	.10
228	Jeff King	.10
229	Ramon Martinez	.10
230	Kevin Seitzer	.10
231	Marquis Grissom	.10
232	Chuck Finley	.10
233	Len Dykstra	.10
234	Ellis Burks	.10
235	Harold Baines	.10
236	Kevin Appier	.10
237	Dave Justice	.10
238	Darryl Kile	.10
239	John Olerud	.10
240	Greg McMichael	.10
241	Kirby Puckett	1.00
242	Jose Valentin	.10
243	Rick Wilkins	.10
244	Pat Hentgen	.10
245	Tom Gordon	.10
246	Tom Candiotti	.10
247	Jason Bere	.10
248	Wes Chamberlain	.10
249	Jeff Cirillo	.10
250	Kevin Foster	.10
251	Mark Whiten	.10
252	Terry Steinbach	.10
253	Aaron Sele	.10
254	Kirt Manwaring	.10
255	Delino DeShields	.10
256	Andujar Cedeno	.10
257	Kenny Lofton	.10
258	John Wetteland	.10
259	Tim Salmon	.10
260	Denny Neagle	.10
261	Tony Gwynn	1.00
262	Lou Whitaker	.10
263	J.T. Snow	.10
264	Dennis Martinez	.10
265	Pedro Martinez	.75
266	Rusty Greer	.10
267	Dave Fleming	.10
268	John Dettmer	.10
269	Albert Belle	.10
270	Henry Rodriguez	.10

VR Extremist

A huge silver-blue metallic baseball separates the player from the background of the photo in this Series 2 insert found only in rack packs. A blue sky and clouds provides the front border. The player rises out of the clouds in a back photo in the foreground of which are some pie-in-the-sky stats. The metallic baseball is also repeated on the back, with the player's name in orange script on the sweet spot. Each card was also is-

sued in the Members Only boxed set in a version with a round silver-foil Members Only seal on front. Cards are numbered with a "VRE" prefix.

		NM/M
Complete Set (10):		25.00
Common Player:		1.50
1	Barry Bonds	7.50
2	Ken Griffey Jr.	6.00
3	Jeff Bagwell	3.50
4	Albert Belle	1.50
5	Frank Thomas	3.50
6	Tony Gwynn	4.50
7	Kenny Lofton	1.50
8	Deion Sanders	1.50
9	Ken Hill	1.50
10	Jimmy Key	1.50

Super Team Division Winners

Persons who saved 1994 Topps Stadium Club Super Team cards for the 1995 divisional winners in Major League Baseball's new playoff format were able to redeem them for a set of 10 SC cards of that team's players with a special gold-foil division series logo on front. The cards are otherwise identical to the regular-issue '95 SC versions. Included in the cellowrapped team set was a Super Team card with the gold logo on front and a white "REDEEMED" across the back.

		NM/M
Complete Set (66):		25.00
Common Player:		.15
	Atlanta Braves	
	Team Set:	7.00
1	Atlanta Braves Super Team	.30
19	Ryan Klesko	.15
128	Mark Wohlers	.15
151	Steve Avery	.15
183	Tom Glavine	.60
200	Javy Lopez	.15
393	Fred McGriff	.15
397	John Smoltz	.15
425	Greg Maddux	3.00
446	David Justice	.15
543	Chipper Jones	3.00
	Boston Red Sox	
	Team Set:	4.50
16	Boston Red Sox Super Team	.30
10	Roger Clemens	3.25
62	John Valentin	.15
121	Mike Greenwell	.15
160	Lee Tinsley	.15
347	Jose Canseco	1.25
350	Mo Vaughn	.15
395	Tim Naehring	.15
464	Aaron Sele	.15
530	Mike MacFarlane	.15
600	Troy O'Leary	.15
	Cincinnati Reds	
	Team Set:	1.50
3	Cincinnati Reds Super Team	.30
35	Barry Larkin	.15
231	Hal Morris	.15
252	Bret Boone	.15
280	Thomas Howard	.15
300	Jose Rijo	.15
333	Reggie Sanders	.15
392	Hector Carrasco	.15
416	John Smiley	.15
528	Ron Gant	.15
566	Benito Santiago	.15
	Cleveland Indians	
	Team Set:	4.50
19	Cleveland Indians Super Team	2.00
36	Carlos Baerga	.15
147	Jim Thome	1.50
186	Eddie Murray	2.00
264	Manny Ramirez	2.00
334	Omar Vizquel	.15
470	Kenny Lofton	.15

484	Dennis Martinez	.15
489	Albert Belle	.15
550	Jose Mesa	.15
562	Orel Hershiser	.15

Los Angeles Dodgers
	Team Set:	7.00
7	Los Angeles Dodgers	
	Super Team	.30
57	Raul Mondesi	.15
149	Mike Piazza	4.00
161	Ismael Valdez	.15
242	Brett Butler	.15
259	Tim Wallach	.15
278	Eric Karros	.15
434	Ramon Martinez	.15
456	Tom Candiotti	.15
467	Delino DeShields	.15
556	Hideo Nomo	1.00

Seattle Mariners
	Team Set:	6.50
26	Seattle Mariners	
	Super Team	.30
73	Jay Buhner	.15
92	Chris Bosio	.15
152	Dan Wilson	.15
227	Tino Martinez	.15
241	Ken Griffey Jr.	4.00
340	Randy Johnson	2.00
354	Edgar Martinez	.15
421	Felix Fermin	.15
494	Mike Blowers	.15
536	Joey Cora	.15

League Champion Master Photos

Persons who held onto Braves and Indians Super Team insert cards from the 1994 Stadium Club issue could redeem them following the 1995 season for special Master Photos team sets of the League Champions. Each team set included 10 player cards and a Super Team card with special gold-foil League Champion logos on the fronts. The player cards are in 5" x 7" format with the player's 1995 SC card in the center of a blue background. Backs are in black-and-white with a card number and appropriate logos and copyright. The Super Team card is 2-1/2" x 3-1/2" with a white "REDEEMED" notice overprinted on back.

		NM/M
	Complete Set (22):	15.00
	Common Player:	.35

Atlanta Braves
	Team Set:	9.00
1	Steve Avery	.40
2	Tom Glavine	.75
3	Chipper Jones	3.00
4	David Justice	.40
5	Ryan Klesko	.40
6	Javy Lopez	.40
7	Greg Maddux	3.00
8	Fred McGriff	.40
9	John Smoltz	.40
10	Mark Wohlers	.40
1	Atlanta Braves	
	Super Team	.40

Cleveland Indians
	Team Set:	7.50
11	Carlos Baerga	.40
12	Albert Belle	.40
13	Orel Hershiser	.40
14	Kenny Lofton	.40
15	Dennis Martinez	.40
16	Jose Mesa	.40
17	Eddie Murray	2.50
18	Manny Ramirez	2.50
19	Jim Thome	2.00
20	Omar Vizquel	.40
19	Cleveland Indians	
	Super Team	.40

World Series Winners

Persons who redeemed a 1994 Stadium Club Atlanta

Braves Super Team insert following the Tribe's 1995 World Series victory received a set of 1995 Stadium Club cards, each of which bears a gold-foil World's Series logo on front. The cards are otherwise identical to the regular-issue SC cards. The prize "set" contains only 585 cards, a note sent with the set explains 45 of the TSC cards - #496-523 (the Extreme Corps subset) and cards #614-630 (the Trans-Action subset) were not printed in the parallel version.

		NM/M
	Complete Set (585):	40.00
	Common Player:	.25
	Stars:	3X

Members Only

A special version of all of the regular cards from Stadium Club Series I-III, as well as many of the insert sets was offered to members of Topps' Stadium Club. Virtually identical to the regular S.C. cards, the specially boxed differs in the presence on each card front of an embossed round 1/2" gold-foil "Members Only" seal. Even the plastic Clear Cut inserts have the members' seal embossed directly into the plastic. The edition was limited to 4,000 sets.

		NM/M
	Complete Set (630):	150.00
	Common Player:	.25
	Stars:	6X
	Inserts:	50-100%

Members Only Baseball

This boxed set was sold exclusively through the newsletter for Topps Stadium Club members. Cards feature noteworthy performances and achieve-

ments of the 1994 baseball season. Borderless card fronts have a player action photo on which the background has been quartered in colors of blue, green, orange and magenta. The Members Only logo, and player name and position are presented in gold foil. Backs have another player photo at left and a description of the highlight printed in white on a blue background at right. Both front and back of each card are UV coated. The final five cards in the set are printed in Topps Finest technology and feature the company's choice of the top rookies of 1994.

		NM/M
	Complete Set (50):	9.00
	Common Player:	.20
1	Moises Alou	.20
2	Jeff Bagwell	.75
3	Albert Belle	.20
4	Andy Benes	.20
5	Dante Bichette	.20
6	Craig Biggio	.20
7	Wade Boggs	1.00
8	Barry Bonds	3.00
9	Brett Butler	.20
10	Jose Canseco	.50
11	Joe Carter	.20
12	Vince Coleman	.20
13	Jeff Conine	.20
14	Cecil Fielder	.20
15	John Franco	.20
16	Julio Franco	.20
17	Travis Fryman	.20
18	Andres Galarraga	.20
19	Ken Griffey Jr.	1.50
20	Marquis Grissom	.20
21	Tony Gwynn	1.00
22	Ken Hill	.20
23	Randy Johnson	.75
24	Lance Johnson	.20
25	Jimmy Key	.20
26	Chuck Knoblauch	.20
27	Ray Lankford	.20
28	Darren Lewis	.20
29	Kenny Lofton	.20
30	Greg Maddux	1.00
31	Fred McGriff	.20
32	Kevin Mitchell	.20
33	Paul Molitor	.75
34	Hal Morris	.20
35	Paul O'Neill	.20
36	Rafael Palmeiro	.65
37	Tony Phillips	.20
38	Mike Piazza	1.50
39	Kirby Puckett	1.00
40	Cal Ripken Jr.	3.00
41	Deion Sanders	.20
42	Lee Smith	.20
43	Frank Thomas	.75
44	Larry Walker	.20
45	Matt Williams	.20
46	Manny Ramirez	
	(Rookie Picks)	1.00
47	Joey Hamilton	
	(Rookie Picks)	.20
48	Raul Mondesi	
	(Rookie Picks)	.20
49	Bob Hamelin	
	(Rookie Picks)	.20
50	Ryan Klesko	
	(Rookie Picks)	.20

1996 Stadium Club

Consisting of 450 cards in a pair of 225-card series, Stadium Club continued Topps' 1996 tribute to Mickey Mantle with 19 Retrospective inserts. Cards feature full-bleed photos with gold-foil graphic highlights. Backs offer a TSC Skills Matrix along with another player photo, some biographical data and stats. Team TSC is the only subset with 45

cards each in Series 1 and 2. Stadium Club was issued in retail and hobby packs, with inserts found at differing ratios in each type of packaging.

		NM/M
	Complete Set (450):	25.00
	Common Player:	.05
	Series 1 or 2 Pack (10):	1.00
	Series 1 or 2 Wax Box (24):	20.00
1	Hideo Nomo	
	(Extreme Player)	.40
2	Paul Molitor	.75
3	Garret Anderson	
	(Extreme Player)	.05
4	Jose Mesa	
	(Extreme Player)	.05
5	Vinny Castilla	
	(Extreme Player)	.05
6	Mike Mussina	
	(Extreme Player)	.30
7	Ray Durham	
	(Extreme Player)	.05
8	Jack McDowell	
	(Extreme Player)	.05
9	Juan Gonzalez	
	(Extreme Player)	.40
10	Chipper Jones	
	(Extreme Player)	1.00
11	Deion Sanders	
	(Extreme Player)	.05
12	Rondell White	
	(Extreme Player)	.05
13	Tom Henke	
	(Extreme Player)	.05
14	Derek Bell	
	(Extreme Player)	.05
15	Randy Myers	
	(Extreme Player)	.05
16	Randy Johnson	
	(Extreme Player)	.75
17	Len Dykstra	
	(Extreme Player)	.05
18	Bill Pulsipher	
	(Extreme Player)	.05
19	Greg Colbrunn	
	(Extreme Player)	.05
20	David Wells	
	(Extreme Player)	.05
21	Chad Curtis	
	(Extreme Player)	.05
22	Roberto Hernandez	
	(Extreme Player)	.05
23	Kirby Puckett	
	(Extreme Player)	1.00
24	Joe Vitiello	
	(Extreme Player)	.05
25	Roger Clemens	
	(Extreme Player)	1.25
26	Al Martin	.05
27	Chad Ogea	.05
28	David Segui	.05
29	Joey Hamilton	.05
30	Dan Wilson	.05
31	Chad Fonville	
	(Extreme Player)	.05
32	Bernard Gilkey	
	(Extreme Player)	.05
33	Kevin Seitzer	
	(Extreme Player)	.05
34	Shawn Green	
	(Extreme Player)	.35
35	Rick Aguilera	
	(Extreme Player)	.05
36	Gary DiSarcina	
	(Extreme Player)	.05
37	Jaime Navarro	.05
38	Doug Jones	.05
39	Brent Gates	.05
40	Dean Palmer	
	(Extreme Player)	.05
41	Pat Rapp	.05
42	Tony Clark	.05
43	Bill Swift	.05
44	Randy Velarde	.05
45	Matt Williams	
	(Extreme Player)	.05
46	John Mabry	.05
47	Mike Fetters	.05
48	Orlando Miller	.05
49	Tom Glavine	
	(Extreme Player)	.35
50	Delino DeShields	
	(Extreme Player)	.05
51	Scott Erickson	.05
52	Andy Van Slyke	.05
53	Jim Bullinger	.05
54	Lyle Mouton	.05
55	Bret Saberhagen	.05
56	Benito Santiago	
	(Extreme Player)	.05
57	Dan Miceli	.05
58	Carl Everett	.05
59	Rod Beck	
	(Extreme Player)	.05
60	Phil Nevin	.05
61	Jason Giambi	.50
62	Paul Menhart	.05
63	Eric Karros	
	(Extreme Player)	.05
64	Allen Watson	
	(Extreme Player)	.05
65	Jeff Cirillo	.05
66	Lee Smith	
	(Extreme Player)	.05
67	Sean Berry	.05
68	Luis Sojo	.05
69	Jeff Montgomery	
	(Extreme Player)	.05
70	Todd Hundley	
	(Extreme Player)	.05
71	John Burkett	.05

72	Mark Gubicza	.05
73	Don Mattingly	
	(Extreme Player)	1.25
74	Jeff Brantley	.05
75	Matt Walbeck	.05
76	Steve Parris	.05
77	Ken Caminiti	
	(Extreme Player)	.05
78	Kirt Manwaring	.05
79	Greg Vaughn	.05
80	Pedro Martinez	
	(Extreme Player)	.75
81	Benji Gil	
	(Extreme Player)	.05
82	Heathcliff Slocumb	
	(Extreme Player)	.05
83	Joe Girardi	
	(Extreme Player)	.05
84	Sean Bergman	.05
85	Matt Karchner	.05
86	Butch Huskey	.05
87	Mike Morgan	.05
88	Todd Worrell	
	(Extreme Player)	.05
89	Mike Bordick	.05
90	Bip Roberts	
	(Extreme Player)	.05
91	Mike Hampton	.05
92	Troy O'Leary	.05
93	Wally Joyner	.05
94	Dave Stevens	.05
95	Cecil Fielder	
	(Extreme Player)	.05
96	Wade Boggs	
	(Extreme Player)	1.00
97	Hal Morris	.05
98	Mickey Tettleton	.05
99	Jeff Kent	
	(Extreme Player)	.05
100	Denny Martinez	.05
101	Luis Gonzalez	.05
102	John Jaha	.05
103	Javy Lopez	
	(Extreme Player)	.05
104	Mark McGwire	
	(Extreme Player)	2.00
105	Ken Griffey Jr.	
	(Extreme Player)	1.50
106	Darren Daulton	
	(Extreme Player)	.05
107	Bryan Rekar	.05
108	Mike Macfarlane	
	(Extreme Player)	.05
109	Gary Gaetti	
	(Extreme Player)	.05
110	Shane Reynolds	
	(Extreme Player)	.05
111	Pat Meares	.05
112	Jason Schmidt	.05
113	Otis Nixon	.05
114	John Franco	
	(Extreme Player)	.05
115	Marc Newfield	.05
116	Andy Benes	
	(Extreme Player)	.05
117	Ozzie Guillen	.05
118	Brian Jordan	.05
119	Terry Pendleton	
	(Extreme Player)	.05
120	Chuck Finley	
	(Extreme Player)	.05
121	Scott Stahoviak	.05
122	Sid Fernandez	.05
123	Derek Jeter	
	(Extreme Player)	3.00
124	John Smiley	
	(Extreme Player)	.05
125	David Bell	.05
126	Brett Butler	
	(Extreme Player)	.05
127	Doug Drabek	
	(Extreme Player)	.05
128	J.T. Snow	
	(Extreme Player)	.05
129	Joe Carter	
	(Extreme Player)	.05
130	Dennis Eckersley	
	(Extreme Player)	.65
131	Marty Cordova	
	(Extreme Player)	.05
132	Greg Maddux	
	(Extreme Player)	1.00
133	Tom Goodwin	.05
134	Andy Ashby	.05
135	Paul Sorrento	
	(Extreme Player)	.05
136	Ricky Bones	.05
137	Shawon Dunston	
	(Extreme Player)	.05
138	Moises Alou	
	(Extreme Player)	.05
139	Mickey Morandini	.05
140	Ramon Martinez	
	(Extreme Player)	.05
141	Royce Clayton	
	(Extreme Player)	.05
142	Brad Ausmus	.05
143	Kenny Rogers	
	(Extreme Player)	.05
144	Tim Naehring	
	(Extreme Player)	.05
145	Chris Gomez	
	(Extreme Player)	.05
146	Bobby Bonilla	
	(Extreme Player)	.05
147	Wilson Alvarez	.05

148	Johnny Damon	
	(Extreme Player)	.35
149	Pat Hentgen	.05
150	Andres Galarraga	
	(Extreme Player)	.05
151	David Cone	
	(Extreme Player)	.05
152	Lance Johnson	
	(Extreme Player)	.05
153	Carlos Garcia	.05
154	Doug Johns	.05
155	Midre Cummings	.05
156	Steve Sparks	.05
157	Sandy Martinez **RC**	.05
158	William	
	Van Landingham	.05
159	Dave Justice	
	(Extreme Player)	.05
160	Mark Grace	
	(Extreme Player)	.05
161	Robb Nen	
	(Extreme Player)	.05
162	Mike Greenwell	
	(Extreme Player)	.05
163	Brad Radke	.05
164	Edgardo Alfonzo	.05
165	Mark Leiter	.05
166	Walt Weiss	.05
167	Mel Rojas	
	(Extreme Player)	.05
168	Bret Boone	
	(Extreme Player)	.05
169	Ricky Bottalico	.05
170	Bobby Higginson	.05
171	Trevor Hoffman	.05
172	Jay Bell	
	(Extreme Player)	.05
173	Gabe White	.05
174	Curtis Goodwin	.05
175	Tyler Green	.05
176	Roberto Alomar	
	(Extreme Player)	.20
177	Sterling Hitchcock	.05
178	Ryan Klesko	
	(Extreme Player)	.05
179	Donne Wall **RC**	.05
180	Brian McRae	.05
181	Will Clark (Team TSC)	.05
182	Frank Thomas	
	(Team TSC)	.60
183	Jeff Bagwell	
	(Team TSC)	.60
184	Mo Vaughn (Team TSC)	.05
185	Tino Martinez	
	(Team TSC)	.05
186	Craig Biggio	
	(Team TSC)	.05
187	Chuck Knoblauch	
	(Team TSC)	.05
188	Carlos Baerga	
	(Team TSC)	.05
189	Quilvio Veras	
	(Team TSC)	.05
190	Luis Alicea (Team TSC)	.05
191	Jim Thome (Team TSC)	.40
192	Mike Blowers	
	(Team TSC)	.05
193	Robin Ventura	
	(Team TSC)	.05
194	Jeff King (Team TSC)	.05
195	Tony Phillips	
	(Team TSC)	.05
196	John Valentin	
	(Team TSC)	.05
197	Barry Larkin	
	(Team TSC)	.05
198	Cal Ripken Jr.	
	(Team TSC)	2.00
199	Omar Vizquel	
	(Team TSC)	.05
200	Kurt Abbott (Team TSC)	.05
201	Albert Belle (Team TSC)	.05
202	Barry Bonds	
	(Team TSC)	2.00
203	Ron Gant (Team TSC)	.05
204	Dante Bichette	
	(Team TSC)	.05
205	Jeff Conine (Team TSC)	.05
206	Jim Edmonds	
	(Team TSC)	.05
207	Stan Javier (Team TSC)	.05
208	Kenny Lofton	
	(Team TSC)	.05
209	Ray Lankford	
	(Team TSC)	.05
210	Bernie Williams	
	(Team TSC)	.05
211	Jay Buhner (Team TSC)	.05
212	Paul O'Neill (Team TSC)	.05
213	Tim Salmon	
	(Team TSC)	.05
214	Reggie Sanders	
	(Team TSC)	.05
215	Manny Ramirez	
	(Team TSC)	.60
216	Mike Piazza	
	(Team TSC)	1.50
217	Mike Stanley	
	(Team TSC)	.05
218	Tony Eusebio	
	(Team TSC)	.05
219	Chris Hoiles	
	(Team TSC)	.05
220	Ron Karkovice	
	(Team TSC)	.05
221	Edgar Martinez	
	(Team TSC)	.05
222	Chili Davis (Team TSC)	.05

#	Player	Price
223	Jose Canseco (Team TSC)	.35
224	Eddie Murray (Team TSC)	.60
225	Geronimo Berroa (Team TSC)	
226	Chipper Jones (Team TSC)	.75
227	Garret Anderson (Team TSC)	.05
228	Marty Cordova (Team TSC)	.05
229	Jon Nunnally (Team TSC)	.
230	Brian Hunter (Team TSC)	.05
231	Shawn Green (Team TSC)	.20
232	Ray Durham (Team TSC)	.05
233	Alex Gonzalez (Team TSC)	.05
234	Bobby Higginson (Team TSC)	.05
235	Randy Johnson (Team TSC)	.60
236	Al Leiter (Team TSC)	.05
237	Tom Glavine (Team TSC)	.10
238	Kenny Rogers (Team TSC)	.05
239	Mike Hampton (Team TSC)	.05
240	David Wells (Team TSC)	.05
241	Jim Abbott (Team TSC)	.05
242	Denny Neagle (Team TSC)	.05
243	Wilson Alvarez (Team TSC)	.05
244	John Smiley (Team TSC)	.05
245	Greg Maddux (Team TSC)	.75
246	Andy Ashby (Team TSC)	.05
247	Hideo Nomo (Team TSC)	.30
248	Pat Rapp (Team TSC)	.05
249	Tim Wakefield (Team TSC)	.05
250	John Smoltz (Team TSC)	.05
251	Joey Hamilton (Team TSC)	.05
252	Frank Castillo (Team TSC)	.05
253	Denny Martinez (Team TSC)	.05
254	Jaime Navarro (Team TSC)	.05
255	Karim Garcia (Team TSC)	.05
256	Bob Abreu (Team TSC)	.05
257	Butch Huskey (Team TSC)	.05
258	Ruben Rivera (Team TSC)	.05
259	Johnny Damon (Team TSC)	.20
260	Derek Jeter (Team TSC)	2.00
261	Dennis Eckersley (Team TSC)	.50
262	Jose Mesa (Team TSC)	.05
263	Tom Henke (Team TSC)	.05
264	Rick Aguilera (Team TSC)	.05
265	Randy Myers (Team TSC)	.05
266	John Franco (Team TSC)	.05
267	Jeff Brantley (Team TSC)	.05
268	John Wetteland (Team TSC)	.05
269	Mark Wohlers (Team TSC)	.05
270	Rod Beck (Team TSC)	.05
271	Barry Larkin	.05
272	Paul O'Neill	.05
273	Bobby Jones	.05
274	Will Clark	.05
275	Steve Avery	.05
276	Jim Edmonds	.05
277	John Olerud	.05
278	Carlos Perez	.05
279	Chris Hoiles	.05
280	Jeff Conine	.05
281	Jim Eisenreich	.05
282	Jason Jacome	.05
283	Ray Lankford	.05
284	John Wasdin	.05
285	Frank Thomas	.75
286	Jason Isringhausen	.05
287	Glenallen Hill	.05
288	Esteban Loaiza	.05
289	Bernie Williams	.05
290	Curtis Leskanic	.05
291	Scott Cooper	.05
292	Curt Schilling	.35
293	Eddie Murray	.75
294	Rick Krivda	.05
295	Domingo Cedeno	.05
296	Jeff Fassero	.05
297	Albert Belle	.05
298	Craig Biggio	.05
299	Fernando Vina	.05
300	Edgar Martinez	.05
301	Tony Gwynn	1.00
302	Felipe Lira	.05
303	Mo Vaughn	.05
304	Alex Fernandez	.05
305	Keith Lockhart	.05
306	Roger Pavlik	.05
307	Lee Tinsley	.05
308	Omar Vizquel	.05
309	Scott Servais	.05
310	Danny Tartabull	.05
311	Chili Davis	.05
312	Cal Eldred	.05
313	Roger Cedeno	.05
314	Chris Hammond	.05
315	Rusty Greer	.05
316	Brady Anderson	.05
317	Ron Villone	.05
318	Mark Carreon	.05
319	Larry Walker	.05
320	Pete Harnisch	.05
321	Robin Ventura	.05
322	Tim Belcher	.05
323	Tony Tarasco	.05
324	Juan Guzman	.05
325	Kenny Lofton	.05
326	Kevin Foster	.05
327	Wil Cordero	.05
328	Troy Percival	.05
329	Turk Wendell	.05
330	Thomas Howard	.05
331	Carlos Baerga	.05
332	B.J. Surhoff	.05
333	Jay Buhner	.05
334	Andujar Cedeno	.05
335	Jeff King	.05
336	Dante Bichette	.05
337	Alan Trammell	.05
338	Scott Leius	.05
339	Chris Snopek	.05
340	Roger Bailey	.05
341	Jacob Brumfield	.05
342	Jose Canseco	.50
343	Rafael Palmeiro	.05
344	Quilvio Veras	.05
345	Darrin Fletcher	.05
346	Carlos Delgado	.50
347	Tony Eusebio	.05
348	Ismael Valdes	.05
349	Terry Steinbach	.05
350	Orel Hershiser	.05
351	Kurt Abbott	.05
352	Jody Reed	.05
353	David Howard	.05
354	Ruben Sierra	.05
355	John Ericks	.05
356	Buck Showalter	.05
357	Jim Thome	.65
358	Geronimo Berroa	.05
359	Robby Thompson	.05
360	Jose Vizcaino	.05
361	Jeff Frye	.05
362	Kevin Appier	.05
363	Pat Kelly	.05
364	Ron Gant	.05
365	Luis Alicea	.05
366	Armando Benitez	.05
367	Rico Brogna	.05
368	Manny Ramirez	.75
369	Mike Lansing	.05
370	Sammy Sosa	1.00
371	Don Wengert	.05
372	Dave Nilsson	.05
373	Sandy Alomar	.05
374	Joey Cora	.05
375	Larry Thomas	.05
376	John Valentin	.05
377	Kevin Ritz	.05
378	Steve Finley	.05
379	Frank Rodriguez	.05
380	Ivan Rodriguez	.65
381	Alex Ochoa	.05
382	Mark Lemke	.05
383	Scott Brosius	.05
384	James Mouton	.05
385	Mark Langston	.05
386	Ed Sprague	.05
387	Joe Oliver	.05
388	Steve Ontiveros	.05
389	Rey Sanchez	.05
390	Mike Henneman	.05
391	Jose Valentin RC	.05
392	Tom Candiotti	.05
393	Damon Buford	.05
394	Erik Hanson	.05
395	Mark Smith	.05
396	Pete Schourek	.05
397	John Flaherty	.05
398	Dave Martinez	.05
399	Tommy Greene	.05
400	Gary Sheffield	.45
401	Glenn Dishman	.05
402	Barry Bonds	3.00
403	Tom Pagnozzi	.05
404	Todd Stottlemyre	.05
405	Tim Salmon	.05
406	John Hudek	.05
407	Fred McGriff	.05
408	Orlando Merced	.05
409	Brian Barber	.05
410	Ryan Thompson	.05
411	Mariano Rivera	.05
412	Eric Young	.05
413	Chris Bosio	.05
414	Chuck Knoblauch	.05
415	Jamie Moyer	.05
416	Chan Ho Park	.05
417	Mark Portugal	.05
418	Tim Raines	.05
419	Antonio Osuna	.05
420	Todd Zeile	.05
421	Steve Wojciechowski	.05
422	Marquis Grissom	.05
423	Norm Charlton	.05
424	Cal Ripken Jr.	3.00
425	Gregg Jefferies	.05
426	Mike Stanton	.05
427	Tony Fernandez	.05
428	Jose Rijo	.05
429	Jeff Bagwell	.75
430	Raul Mondesi	.05
431	Travis Fryman	.05
432	Ron Karkovice	.05
433	Alan Benes	.05
434	Tony Phillips	.05
435	Reggie Sanders	.05
436	Andy Pettitte	.25
437	Matt Lawton RC	.25
438	Jeff Blauser	.05
439	Michael Tucker	.05
440	Mark Loretta	.05
441	Charlie Hayes	.05
442	Mike Piazza	1.50
443	Shane Andrews	.05
444	Jeff Suppan	.05
445	Steve Rodriguez	.05
446	Mike Matheny	.05
447	Trenidad Hubbard	.05
448	Denny Hocking	.05
449	Mark Grudzielanek	.05
450	Joe Randa	.05

Mickey Mantle "Cereal Box" Set

This factory-set version of TSC was packaged in boxes which resembled single-serving cereal boxes. The cards are identical to the regular TSC version except for the use of silver-foil, rather than gold-foil, highlights on front.

	NM/M
Unopened Set:	30.00
Common Player:	.10

Extreme Player

A special interactive version of 179 players' cards in 1996 Stadium Club was issued as an insert set across Series 1 and 2. Specially stamped with an "Extreme Player" logo in bronze (1 per 12 packs average), silver (1:24) or gold (1:48), the cards have backs that detail a contest by which the player's on-field performance was used to rank each by position. At season's end, cards of the winning players at each position could be redeemed for special prizes. The contest cards do not have card numbers on back and are numbered here based on the regular version.

	NM/M
Complete Bronze Set (179):	40.00
Common Bronze:	.10
Silvers:	1.5X
Golds:	2.5X
1 Hideo Nomo	.50
3 Garret Anderson	.10
4 Jose Mesa	.10
5 Vinny Castilla	.10
6 Mike Mussina	.30
7 Ray Durham	.10
8 Jack McDowell	.10
9 Juan Gonzalez	.50
10 Chipper Jones	1.50
11 Deion Sanders	.10
12 Rondell White	.10
13 Tom Henke	.10
14 Derek Bell	.10
15 Randy Myers	.10
16 Randy Johnson	1.00
17 Len Dykstra	.10
18 Bill Pulsipher	.10
21 Chad Curtis	.10

#	Player	Price
22	Roberto Hernandez	.10
23	Kirby Puckett	1.50
25	Roger Clemens	1.75
31	Chad Fonville	.10
32	Bernard Gilkey	.10
34	Shawn Green	.35
35	Rick Aguilera	.10
44	Dean Palmer	.10
45	Matt Williams	.10
49	Tom Glavine	.35
50	Delino DeShields	.10
56	Benito Santiago	.10
59	Rod Beck	.10
63	Eric Karros	.10
66	Lee Smith	.10
69	Jeff Montgomery	.10
70	Todd Hundley	.10
77	Ken Caminiti	.10
80	Pedro Martinez	1.00
82	Heathcliff Slocumb	.10
83	Joe Girardi	.10
88	Todd Worrell	.10
90	Bip Roberts	.10
95	Cecil Fielder	.10
96	Wade Boggs	1.50
98	Mickey Tettleton	.10
99	Jeff Kent	.10
101	Luis Gonzalez	.10
103	Javier Lopez	.10
104	Mark McGwire	3.00
105	Ken Griffey Jr.	2.00
106	Darren Daulton	.10
108	Mike Macfarlane	.10
109	Gary Gaetti	.10
113	Shane Reynolds	.10
114	John Franco	.10
116	Andy Benes	.10
118	Brian Jordan	.10
119	Terry Pendleton	.10
120	Chuck Finley	.10
123	Derek Jeter	4.00
124	John Smiley	.10
126	Brett Butler	.10
127	Doug Drabek	.10
128	J.T. Snow	.10
129	Joe Carter	.10
130	Dennis Eckersley	.75
131	Marty Cordova	.10
132	Greg Maddux	1.50
135	Paul Sorrento	.10
137	Shawon Dunston	.10
139	Moises Alou	.10
140	Ramon Martinez	.10
142	Royce Clayton	.10
143	Kenny Rogers	.10
144	Tim Naehring	.10
145	Chris Gomez	.10
146	Bobby Bonilla	.10
148	Johnny Damon	.40
150	Andres Galarraga	.10
151	David Cone	.10
152	Lance Johnson	.10
159	Dave Justice	.10
160	Mark Grace	.10
161	Robb Nen	.10
162	Mike Greenwell	.10
167	Mel Rojas	.10
168	Bret Boone	.10
172	Jay Bell	.10
176	Roberto Alomar	.25
178	Ryan Klesko	.10
271	Barry Larkin	.10
272	Paul O'Neill	.10
274	Will Clark	.10
275	Steve Avery	.10
276	Jim Edmonds	.10
279	John Olerud	.10
280	Chris Hoiles	.10
280	Jeff Conine	.10
283	Ray Lankford	.10
285	Frank Thomas	1.00
286	Jason Isringhausen	.10
287	Glenallen Hill	.10
289	Bernie Williams	.10
290	Eddie Murray	1.00
296	Jeff Fassero	.10
297	Albert Belle	.10
298	Craig Biggio	.10
300	Edgar Martinez	.10
301	Tony Gwynn	1.50
303	Mo Vaughn	.10
304	Alex Fernandez	.10
308	Omar Vizquel	.10
310	Danny Tartabull	.10
316	Brady Anderson	.10
319	Larry Walker	.10
321	Robin Ventura	.10
325	Kenny Lofton	.10
327	Wil Cordero	.10
328	Troy Percival	.10
331	Carlos Baerga	.10
333	Jay Buhner	.10
335	Jeff King	.10
336	Dante Bichette	.10
337	Alan Trammell	.10
342	Jose Canseco	.50
343	Rafael Palmeiro	.75
344	Quilvio Veras	.10
345	Darrin Fletcher	.10
347	Tony Eusebio	.10
348	Ismael Valdes	.10
349	Terry Steinbach	.10
350	Orel Hershiser	.10
351	Kurt Abbott	.10
354	Ruben Sierra	.10
357	Jim Thome	.75
358	Geronimo Berroa	.10
359	Robby Thompson	.10
360	Jose Vizcaino	.10
362	Kevin Appier	.10
364	Ron Gant	.10
367	Rico Brogna	.10
368	Manny Ramirez	1.00
370	Sammy Sosa	1.50
373	Sandy Alomar	.10
378	Steve Finley	.10
380	Ivan Rodriguez	.75
382	Mark Lemke	.10
385	Mark Langston	.10
386	Ed Sprague	.10
388	Steve Ontiveros	.10
392	Tom Candiotti	.10
394	Erik Hanson	.10
396	Pete Schourek	.10
400	Gary Sheffield	.35
402	Barry Bonds	4.00
403	Tom Pagnozzi	.10
404	Todd Stottlemyre	.10
405	Tim Salmon	.10
407	Fred McGriff	.10
408	Orlando Merced	.10
412	Eric Young	.10
414	Chuck Knoblauch	.10
417	Mark Portugal	.10
420	Todd Zeile	.10
422	Marquis Grissom	.10
423	Norm Charlton	.10
424	Cal Ripken Jr.	4.00
425	Gregg Jefferies	.10
428	Jose Rijo	.10
429	Jeff Bagwell	1.00
430	Raul Mondesi	.10
431	Travis Fryman	.10
434	Tony Phillips	.10
435	Reggie Sanders	.10
436	Andy Pettitte	.25
438	Jeff Blauser	.10
441	Charlie Hayes	.10
442	Mike Piazza	2.00

Extreme Player - Bronze Winner

Ten-card sets of these special bronze-foil highlighted cards were the prize for those who redeemed bronze statistical winners' cards from the Stadium Club Extreme Player interactive series. Backs have statistical ratings pertinent to the game and scoring rules. Cards have an "EW" prefix to the number. The same photos and back design were used in different technologies in the bronze, silver and gold winners cards.

	NM/M
Complete Set (10):	6.00
Common Player:	.40
1 Greg Maddux	1.50
2 Mike Piazza	2.00
3 Andres Galarraga	.40
4 Chuck Knoblauch	.40
5 Ken Caminiti	.40
6 Barry Larkin	.40
7 Barry Bonds	3.00
8 Ken Griffey Jr.	2.00
9 Gary Sheffield	.75
10 Todd Worrell	.40

Extreme Player - Silver Winner

Ten-card sets of these Finest technology cards were the prize for those who redeemed statistical winners' cards from the Stadium Club Extreme Player interactive series. Backs have statistical ratings pertinent to the game and scoring rules. Cards have an "EW" prefix to the number.

	NM/M
Complete Set (10):	17.50
Common Player:	.75
1 Greg Maddux	3.00

2 Mike Piazza	4.00
3 Andres Galarraga	.75
4 Chuck Knoblauch	.75
5 Ken Caminiti	.75
6 Barry Larkin	.75
7 Barry Bonds	5.00
8 Ken Griffey Jr.	4.00
9 Gary Sheffield	1.50
10 Todd Worrell	.75

Extreme Player - Gold Winner

One of these large (2-3/4" x 3-3/4"), heavy, acrylic-coated bronze refractor cards was the prize for those who redeemed the same player's gold statistical winners' card from the Stadium Club Extreme Player interactive series. Backs have statistical ratings pertinent to the game and scoring rules. Cards have an "EW" prefix to the number. The same photos and back design were used in different technologies in the bronze, silver and gold winners cards.

	NM/M
Complete Set (10):	45.00
Common Player:	2.00
1 Greg Maddux	8.00
2 Mike Piazza	10.00
3 Andres Galarraga	2.00
4 Chuck Knoblauch	2.00
5 Ken Caminiti	2.00
6 Barry Larkin	2.00
7 Barry Bonds	15.00
8 Ken Griffey Jr.	10.00
9 Gary Sheffield	3.50
10 Todd Worrell	.75

Bash & Burn

Inserted in one per 24 retail packs and one per 48 hobby packs of Series II, Bash & Burn includes 10 players on double-fronted cards. Both sides are foil-etched with the Bash side highlighting home runs and runs batted in for 1995 and career, and the Burn side featured stolen base and runs scored leaders for 1995 and career. Cards are numbered with a "B&B" prefix.

		NM/M
Complete Set (10):		10.00
Common Player:		.75
1	Sammy Sosa	3.50
2	Barry Bonds	6.00
3	Reggie Sanders	.75
4	Craig Biggio	.75
5	Raul Mondesi	.75
6	Ron Gant	.75
7	Ray Lankford	.75
8	Glenallen Hill	.75
9	Chad Curtis	.75
10	John Valentin	.75

Mickey Mantle Retrospective

Following the success of the Mantle reprints in Topps baseball, Stadium Club produced a series of 19 Mickey Mantle Retrospective inserts; nine black-and-white cards in Series 1 and 10 color cards in Series 2. The cards chronicle Mantle's career and provide insights from baseball contemporaries. The Mantle cards are found on an average of once per 24 Series 1 packs and once per 12 Series 2 packs. Cards are numbered with an "MM" prefix.

		NM/M
Complete Set (19):		35.00
Common Series 1:		4.00
Common Series 2:		2.00
1	Mickey Mantle/1950 (minor league)	4.00
2	Mickey Mantle/1951	4.00
3	Mickey Mantle/1951	4.00
4	Mickey Mantle/1953	4.00
5	Mickey Mantle/1954 (w/ Yogi Berra)	4.00
6	Mickey Mantle/1956	4.00
7	Mickey Mantle/1957	4.00
8	Mickey Mantle/1958 (w/ Casey Stengel)	4.00
9	Mickey Mantle/1959	4.00
10	Mickey Mantle/1960 (w/ Elston Howard)	2.00
11	Mickey Mantle/1961	2.00
12	Mickey Mantle/1961 (w/ Roger Maris)	4.00
13	Mickey Mantle/1962	2.00
14	Mickey Mantle/1963	2.00
15	Mickey Mantle/1964	2.00
16	Mickey Mantle	2.00
17	Mickey Mantle/1968	2.00
18	Mickey Mantle/1969	2.00
19	Mickey Mantle (In Memoriam)	3.50

Mega Heroes

ANDRES GALARRAGA

Ten heroic players are matched with a comic book-style illustration depicting their nicknames in the Mega Heroes insert set. Printed on foilboard in a defraction tech-

nology, the cards are found, on average, once per 48 Series 1 hobby packs and twice as often in retail packs.

		NM/M
Complete Set (10):		10.00
Common Player:		1.00
1	Frank Thomas	1.50
2	Ken Griffey Jr.	3.00
3	Hideo Nomo	1.25
4	Ozzie Smith	1.75
5	Will Clark	1.00
6	Jack McDowell	1.00
7	Andres Galarraga	1.00
8	Roger Clemens	2.00
9	Deion Sanders	1.00
10	Mo Vaughn	1.00

Metalists

FRANK THOMAS

Eight players who have won two or more major awards in their careers are featured in this Series II insert. Cards are printed on foilboard and feature intricate laser-cut designs that depict the player's face. Metalist inserts are found one per 96 retail and one per 48 hobby packs, on average. Cards are numbered with an "M" prefix.

		NM/M
Complete Set (8):		12.00
Common Player:		1.00
1	Jeff Bagwell	1.25
2	Barry Bonds	3.50
3	Jose Canseco	1.00
4	Roger Clemens	2.50
5	Dennis Eckersley	1.00
6	Greg Maddux	2.00
7	Cal Ripken Jr.	3.50
8	Frank Thomas	1.25

Midsummer Matchups

These inserts salute 1995 National League and American League All-Stars on back-to-back etched-foil cards. Players are matched by position in the 10-card set. Average insertion rate is one per 48 hobby packs and one per 24 retail packs in Series 1. Cards are numbered with an "M" prefix.

		NM/M
Complete Set (10):		20.00
Common Player:		1.00
1	Hideo Nomo, Randy Johnson	2.00
2	Mike Piazza, Ivan Rodriguez	4.00
3	Fred McGriff, Frank Thomas	2.00
4	Craig Biggio, Carlos Baerga	1.00
5	Vinny Castilla, Wade Boggs	2.50
6	Barry Larkin, Cal Ripken Jr.	5.00
7	Barry Bonds, Albert Belle	5.00

8	Len Dykstra, Kenny Lofton, Tony Gwynn,	1.00
9	Kirby Puckett	3.00
10	Ron Gant, Edgar Martinez	1.00

Power Packed

JOSE CANSECO

Topps' Power Matrix technology is used to showcase 15 of the biggest, strongest players in this Series 2 insert set. Card backs feature a diagram of the player's home park with baseball graphics measuring his home runs during the 1995 season. The inserts are a one in 48 packs pick, on average, both hobby and retail. Cards are numbered with a "PP" prefix.

		NM/M
Complete Set (15):		15.00
Common Player:		1.00
1	Albert Belle	1.00
2	Mark McGwire	4.00
3	Jose Canseco	1.75
4	Mike Piazza	3.00
5	Ron Gant	1.00
6	Ken Griffey Jr.	3.00
7	Mo Vaughn	1.00
8	Cecil Fielder	1.00
9	Tim Salmon	1.00
10	Frank Thomas	2.50
11	Juan Gonzalez	1.50
12	Andres Galarraga	1.00
13	Fred McGriff	1.00
14	Jay Buhner	1.00
15	Dante Bichette	1.00

Power Streak

JIM EDMONDS

The best power hitters in baseball are featured in Power Matrix technology on these Series I inserts. Average insertion rate is one per 24 hobby and 48 retail packs. Cards are numbered with a "PS" prefix.

		NM/M
Complete Set (15):		20.00
Common Player:		1.00
1	Randy Johnson	2.00
2	Hideo Nomo	1.25
3	Albert Belle	1.00
4	Dante Bichette	1.00
5	Jay Buhner	1.00
6	Frank Thomas	2.00
7	Mark McGwire	4.00
8	Rafael Palmeiro	1.50
9	Mo Vaughn	1.00
10	Sammy Sosa	3.00
11	Larry Walker	1.00
12	Gary Gaetti	1.00
13	Tim Salmon	1.00
14	Barry Bonds	5.00
15	Jim Edmonds	1.00

Prime Cuts

The purest swings in baseball are the focus on these laser-cut, defraction-foil inserts found in Series 1 packs at an av-

erage rate of one per 36 hobby and 72 retail packs. Cards are numbered with a "PC" prefix.

		NM/M
Complete Set (8):		20.00
Common Player:		1.50
1	Albert Belle	1.50
2	Barry Bonds	6.00
3	Ken Griffey Jr.	4.00
4	Tony Gwynn	3.00
5	Edgar Martinez	1.50
6	Rafael Palmeiro	2.00
7	Mike Piazza	4.00
8	Frank Thomas	2.50

TSC Awards

TSC Awards insert cards allowed Topps' experts to honor best performances, newcomer, comeback, etc. The cards are found in Series 2 packs at an average rate of one per 24 retail and 48 hobby packs.

		NM/M
Complete Set (10):		15.00
Common Player:		.50
1	Cal Ripken Jr.	5.00
2	Albert Belle	.60
3	Tom Glavine	.50
4	Jeff Conine	.50
5	Ken Griffey Jr.	4.00
6	Hideo Nomo	1.25
7	Greg Maddux	3.00
8	Chipper Jones	3.00
9	Randy Johnson	2.00
10	Jose Mesa	.50

Members Only

DEAN PALMER

For the fourth year Topps offered a special edition of its high-end Stadium Club issue to members of its mail-order family. Each of the regular and insert cards was stamped with a gold- or silver-foil "MEMBERS ONLY" seal. The '96 edition was the scarcest ever produced, with only 750 sets offered at $200. Single "Members Only" cards paralleling the regular-issue Stadium Club cards sell for a premium while the M.O. ver-

BARRY BONDS

sions of the inserts usually sell at par or even a discount from the issued cards.

		NM/M
Complete Set (660):		150.00
Common Player:		.50
Stars:		6X
Inserts: 50-100%		

Members Only Baseball

HIDEO NOMO

This 50-card boxed set was offered to members of Topps Stadium Club at about $15 retail. The first 45 cards in the set represent Topps' choice of 1995's top players in each league. The final five cards, printed in Topps Finest technology, honor hot rookies. The basic cards feature borderless action photos on which the background has been posterized and darkened to make the color photo stand out in the foreground. A gold-foil strip at bottom has the player name and position; a "Members Only" logo is in gold foil in an upper corner. Horizontal backs once again have much of the photo background darkened with a close-up photo at right and a few sentences about the player at left. "Member's Choice" Finest rookie cards have a stylized baseball diamond in red tones as background to the action photos. Backs have a large red-shaded baseball with player write-up at bottom and - honest - a pea-green portrait photo at upper-left. Each of the Finest cards has a peel-off protective layer on front.

		NM/M
Complete Set (50):		6.00
Common Player:		.10
1	Carlos Baerga	.10
2	Derek Bell	.10
3	Albert Belle	.10
4	Dante Bichette	.10
5	Craig Biggio	.10
6	Wade Boggs	.65
7	Barry Bonds	1.50
8	Jay Buhner	.10
9	Vinny Castilla	.10
10	Jeff Conine	.10
11	Jim Edmonds	.10
12	Steve Finley	.10
13	Andres Galarraga	.10
14	Mark Grace	.10
15	Tony Gwynn	.65
16	Lance Johnson	.10
17	Randy Johnson	.50
18	Eric Karros	.10
19	Chuck Knoblauch	.10
20	Barry Larkin	.10
21	Kenny Lofton	.10
22	Greg Maddux	.65
23	Edgar Martinez	.10
24	Tino Martinez	.10
25	Mark McGwire	1.00
26	Brian McRae	.10
27	Jose Mesa	.10
28	Eddie Murray	.50
29	Mike Mussina	.30
30	Randy Myers	.10
31	Hideo Nomo	.25
32	Rafael Palmeiro	.50
33	Tony Phillips	.10
34	Mike Piazza	.75
35	Kirby Puckett	.65
36	Manny Ramirez	.50
37	Tim Salmon	.10
38	Reggie Sanders	.10
39	Sammy Sosa	.65
40	Frank Thomas	.50
41	Jim Thome	.45
42	John Valentin	.10

43	Mo Vaughn	.10
44	Quilvio Veras	.10
45	Larry Walker	.10
46	Hideo Nomo (Finest)	.50
47	Marty Cordova (Finest)	.50
48	Chipper Jones (Finest)	1.50
49	Garret Anderson (Finest)	.50
50	Andy Pettitte (Finest)	.50

1997 Stadium Club Pre-Production

These specially marked promo cards were issued in a cello wrapper.

		NM/M
Complete Set (3):		4.00
Common Player:		1.00
PP1	Chipper Jones	3.00
PP2	Kenny Lofton	1.00
PP3	Gary Sheffield	1.50

1997 Stadium Club

Stadium Club totaled 390 cards in 1997, issued in two series of 195 cards each. In Series 1 (February), cards #181-195 are a rookie subset called TSC 2000. In Series 2 (April), cards #376-390 form a subset called Stadium Slugger. Each of these subsets was short-printed and inserted about one per two packs. TSC is printed on an improved 20-point stock with Topps' Super Color process.

		NM/M
Complete Set (390):		35.00
Common Player:		.05
Series 1 or 2 Pack (9):		1.50
Series 1 or 2 Wax Box (24):		27.50
1	Chipper Jones	1.50
2	Gary Sheffield	.50
3	Kenny Lofton	.05
4	Brian Jordan	.05
5	Mark McGwire	2.50
6	Charles Nagy	.05
7	Tim Salmon	.05
8	Cal Ripken Jr.	3.00
9	Jeff Conine	.05
10	Paul Molitor	1.00
11	Mariano Rivera	.15
12	Pedro Martinez	1.00
13	Jeff Bagwell	1.00
14	Bobby Bonilla	.05
15	Barry Bonds	3.00
16	Ryan Klesko	.05
17	Barry Larkin	.05
18	Jim Thome	.65
19	Jay Buhner	.05
20	Juan Gonzalez	.50
21	Mike Mussina	.30
22	Kevin Appier	.05
23	Eric Karros	.05
24	Steve Finley	.05
25	Ed Sprague	.05
26	Bernard Gilkey	.05
27	Tony Phillips	.05
28	Henry Rodriguez	.05
29	John Smoltz	.05
30	Dante Bichette	.05
31	Mike Piazza	2.00
32	Paul O'Neill	.05
33	Billy Wagner	.05
34	Reggie Sanders	.05
35	John Jaha	.05
36	Eddie Murray	1.00
37	Eric Young	.05
38	Roberto Hernandez	.05
39	Pat Hentgen	.05
40	Sammy Sosa	1.50
41	Todd Hundley	.05
42	Mo Vaughn	.05
43	Robin Ventura	.05
44	Mark Grudzielanek	.05
45	Shane Reynolds	.05
46	Andy Pettitte	.25
47	Fred McGriff	.05
48	Rey Ordonez	.05
49	Will Clark	.05
50	Ken Griffey Jr.	2.00
51	Todd Worrell	.05
52	Rusty Greer	.05

53	Mark Grace	.05
54	Tom Glavine	.35
55	Derek Jeter	3.00
56	Rafael Palmeiro	.75
57	Bernie Williams	.05
58	Marty Cordova	.05
59	Andres Galarraga	.05
60	Ken Caminiti	.05
61	Garret Anderson	.05
62	Denny Martinez	.05
63	Mike Greenwell	.05
64	David Segui	.05
65	Julio Franco	.05
66	Rickey Henderson	1.00
67	Ozzie Guillen	.05
68	Pete Harnisch	.05
69	Chan Ho Park	.05
70	Harold Baines	.05
71	Mark Clark	.05
72	Steve Avery	.05
73	Brian Hunter	.05
74	Pedro Astacio	.05
75	Jack McDowell	.05
76	Gregg Jefferies	.05
77	Jason Kendall	.05
78	Todd Walker	.05
79	B.J. Surhoff	.05
80	Moises Alou	.05
81	Fernando Vina	.05
82	Darryl Strawberry	.05
83	Jose Rosado	.05
84	Chris Gomez	.05
85	Chili Davis	.05
86	Alan Benes	.05
87	Todd Hollandsworth	.05
88	Jose Vizcaino	.05
89	Edgardo Alfonzo	.05
90	Ruben Rivera	.05
91	Donovan Osborne	.05
92	Doug Glanville	.05
93	Gary DiSarcina	.05
94	Brooks Kieschnick	.05
95	Bobby Jones	.05
96	Raul Casanova	.05
97	Jermaine Allensworth	.05
98	Kenny Rogers	.05
99	Mark McLemore	.05
100	Jeff Fassero	.05
101	Sandy Alomar	.05
102	Chuck Finley	.05
103	Eric Owens	.05
104	Billy McMillon	.05
105	Dwight Gooden	.05
106	Sterling Hitchcock	.05
107	Doug Drabek	.05
108	Paul Wilson	.05
109	Chris Snopek	.05
110	Al Leiter	.05
111	Bob Tewksbury	.05
112	Todd Greene	.05
113	Jose Valentin	.05
114	Delino DeShields	.05
115	Mike Bordick	.05
116	Pat Meares	.05
117	Mariano Duncan	.05
118	Steve Trachsel	.05
119	Luis Castillo	.05
120	Andy Benes	.05
121	Donne Wall	.05
122	Alex Gonzalez	.05
123	Dan Wilson	.05
124	Omar Vizquel	.05
125	Devon White	.05
126	Darryl Hamilton	.05
127	Orlando Merced	.05
128	Royce Clayton	.05
129	William Van Landingham	.05
130	Terry Steinbach	.05
131	Jeff Blauser	.05
132	Jeff Cirillo	.05
133	Roger Pavlik	.05
134	Danny Tartabull	.05
135	Jeff Montgomery	.05
136	Bobby Higginson	.05
137	Mike Grace	.05
138	Kevin Elster	.05
139	Brian Giles **RC**	1.00
140	Rod Beck	.05
141	Ismael Valdes	.05
142	Scott Brosius	.05
143	Mike Fetters	.05
144	Gary Gaetti	.05
145	Mike Lansing	.05
146	Glenallen Hill	.05
147	Shawn Green	.35
148	Mel Rojas	.05
149	Joey Cora	.05
150	John Smiley	.05
151	Marvin Benard	.05
152	Curt Schilling	.35
153	Dave Nilsson	.05
154	Edgar Renteria	.05
155	Joey Hamilton	.05
156	Carlos Garcia	.05
157	Nomar Garciaparra	2.00
158	Kevin Ritz	.05
159	Keith Lockhart	.05
160	Justin Thompson	.05
161	Terry Adams	.05
162	Jamey Wright	.05
163	Otis Nixon	.05
164	Michael Tucker	.05
165	Mike Stanley	.05
166	Ben McDonald	.05
167	John Mabry	.05
168	Troy O'Leary	.05
169	Mel Nieves	.05

170	Bret Boone	.05
171	Mike Timlin	.05
172	Scott Rolen	.75
173	Reggie Jefferson	.05
174	Neifi Perez	.05
175	Brian McRae	.05
176	Tom Goodwin	.05
177	Aaron Sele	.05
178	Benny Santiago	.05
179	Frank Rodriguez	.05
180	Eric Davis	.05
181	Andruw Jones (TSC 2000)	.75
182	Todd Walker (TSC 2000)	.15
183	Wes Helms (TSC 2000)	.15
184	Nelson Figueroa **RC** (TSC 2000)	.15
185	Vladimir Guerrero (TSC 2000)	.75
186	Billy McMillon (TSC 2000)	.15
187	Todd Helton (TSC 2000)	.65
188	Nomar Garciaparra (TSC 2000)	2.00
189	Katsuhiro Maeda (TSC 2000)	.15
190	Russell Branyan (TSC 2000)	.15
191	Glendon Rusch (TSC 2000)	.15
192	Bartolo Colon (TSC 2000)	.15
193	Scott Rolen (TSC 2000)	.50
194	Angel Echevarria (TSC 2000)	.15
195	Bob Abreu (TSC 2000)	.20
196	Greg Maddux	1.50
197	Joe Carter	.05
198	Alex Ochoa	.05
199	Ellis Burks	.05
200	Ivan Rodriguez	.75
201	Marquis Grissom	.05
202	Trevor Hoffman	.05
203	Matt Williams	.05
204	Carlos Delgado	.50
205	Ramon Martinez	.05
206	Chuck Knoblauch	.05
207	Juan Guzman	.05
208	Derek Bell	.05
209	Roger Clemens	1.75
210	Vladimir Guerrero	1.00
211	Cecil Fielder	.05
212	Hideo Nomo	.50
213	Frank Thomas	1.00
214	Greg Vaughn	.05
215	Javy Lopez	.05
216	Raul Mondesi	.05
217	Wade Boggs	1.50
218	Carlos Baerga	.05
219	Tony Gwynn	1.50
220	Tino Martinez	.05
221	Vinny Castilla	.05
222	Lance Johnson	.05
223	David Justice	.05
224	Rondell White	.05
225	Dean Palmer	.05
226	Jim Edmonds	.05
227	Albert Belle	.05
228	Alex Fernandez	.05
229	Ryne Sandberg	1.50
230	Jose Mesa	.05
231	David Cone	.05
232	Troy Percival	.05
233	Edgar Martinez	.05
234	Jose Canseco	.50
235	Kevin Brown	.05
236	Ray Lankford	.05
237	Karim Garcia	.05
238	J.T. Snow	.05
239	Dennis Eckersley	.75
240	Roberto Alomar	.35
241	John Valentin	.05
242	Ron Gant	.05
243	Geronimo Berroa	.05
244	Manny Ramirez	1.00
245	Travis Fryman	.05
246	Denny Neagle	.05
247	Randy Johnson	1.00
248	Darin Erstad	.15
249	Mark Wohlers	.05
250	Ken Hill	.05
251	Larry Walker	.05
252	Craig Biggio	.05
253	Brady Anderson	.05
254	John Wetteland	.05
255	Andruw Jones	1.00
256	Turk Wendell	.05
257	Jason Isringhausen	.05
258	Jaime Navarro	.05
259	Sean Berry	.05
260	Albie Lopez	.05
261	Jay Bell	.05
262	Bobby Witt	.05
263	Tony Clark	.05
264	Tim Wakefield	.05
265	Brad Radke	.05
266	Tim Belcher	.05
267	Mark Lewis	.05
268	Roger Cedeno	.05
269	Tim Naehring	.05
270	Kevin Tapani	.05
271	Joe Randa	.05
272	Randy Myers	.05
273	Dave Burba	.05
274a	Mike Sweeney	.05

274b	Tom Pagnozzi (Should be #374.)	.05
275	Danny Graves	.05
276	Chad Mottola	.05
277	Ruben Sierra	.05
278	Norm Charlton	.05
279	Scott Servais	.05
280	Jacob Cruz	.05
281	Mike Macfarlane	.05
282	Rich Becker	.05
283	Shannon Stewart	.05
284	Gerald Williams	.05
285	Jody Reed	.05
286	Jeff D'Amico	.05
287	Walt Weiss	.05
288	Jim Leyritz	.05
289	Francisco Cordova	.05
290	F.P. Santangelo	.05
291	Scott Erickson	.05
292	Hal Morris	.05
293	Ray Durham	.05
294	Andy Ashby	.05
295	Darryl Kile	.05
296	Jose Paniagua	.05
297	Mickey Tettleton	.05
298	Joe Girardi	.05
299	Rocky Coppinger	.05
300	Bob Abreu	.05
301	John Olerud	.05
302	Paul Shuey	.05
303	Jeff Brantley	.05
304	Bob Wells	.05
305	Kevin Seitzer	.05
306	Shawon Dunston	.05
307	Jose Herrera	.05
308	Butch Huskey	.05
309	Jose Offerman	.05
310	Rick Aguilera	.05
311	Greg Gagne	.05
312	John Burkett	.05
313	Mark Thompson	.05
314	Alvaro Espinoza	.05
315	Todd Stottlemyre	.05
316	Al Martin	.05
317	James Baldwin	.05
318	Cal Eldred	.05
319	Sid Fernandez	.05
320	Mickey Morandini	.05
321	Robb Nen	.05
322	Mark Lemke	.05
323	Pete Schourek	.05
324	Marcus Jensen	.05
325	Rich Aurilia	.05
326	Jeff King	.05
327	Scott Stahoviak	.05
328	Ricky Otero	.05
329	Antonio Osuna	.05
330	Chris Hoiles	.05
331	Luis Gonzalez	.05
332	Wil Cordero	.05
333	Johnny Damon	.35
334	Mark Langston	.05
335	Orlando Miller	.05
336	Jason Giambi	.50
337	Damian Jackson	.05
338	David Wells	.05
339	Bip Roberts	.05
340	Matt Ruebel	.05
341	Tom Candiotti	.05
342	Wally Joyner	.05
343	Jimmy Key	.05
344	Tony Batista	.05
345	Paul Sorrento	.05
346	Ron Karkovice	.05
347	Wilson Alvarez	.05
348	John Flaherty	.05
349	Rey Sanchez	.05
350	John Vander Wal	.05
351a	Jermaine Dye	.05
351b	Brant Brown (Should be #361.)	.05
352	Mike Hampton	.05
353	Greg Colbrunn	.05
354	Heathcliff Slocumb	.05
355	Ricky Bottalico	.05
356	Marty Janzen	.05
357	Orel Hershiser	.05
358	Rex Hudler	.05
359	Amaury Telemaco	.05
360	Darrin Fletcher	.05
361	Not issued - see #351	
362	Russ Davis	.05
363	Allen Watson	.05
364	Mike Lieberthal	.05
365	Dave Stevens	.05
366	Jay Powell	.05
367	Tony Fossas	.05
368	Bob Wolcott	.05
369	Mark Loretta	.05
370	Shawn Estes	.05
371	Sandy Martinez	.05
372	Wendell Magee Jr.	.05
373	John Franco	.05
374	Not issued - see #274	
375	Willie Adams	.05
376	Chipper Jones (Stadium Sluggers)	2.00
377	Mo Vaughn (Stadium Sluggers)	.15
378	Frank Thomas (Stadium Sluggers)	1.50
379	Albert Belle (Stadium Sluggers)	.15
380	Andres Galarraga (Stadium Sluggers)	.15
381	Gary Sheffield (Stadium Sluggers)	.85

382	Jeff Bagwell (Stadium Sluggers)	1.50
383	Mike Piazza (Stadium Sluggers)	3.00
384	Mark McGwire (Stadium Sluggers)	3.00
385	Ken Griffey Jr. (Stadium Sluggers)	2.50
386	Barry Bonds (Stadium Sluggers)	3.50
387	Juan Gonzalez (Stadium Sluggers)	.40
388	Brady Anderson (Stadium Sluggers)	.15
389	Ken Caminiti (Stadium Sluggers)	.15
390	Jay Buhner (Stadium Sluggers)	.05

Co-Signers

Each series of Stadium Club included five different Co-Signers, with an insertion ratio of one per 168 hobby packs. These double-sided cards featured authentic autographs from each star, one per side.

		NM/M
Complete Set (10):		200.00
Common Player:		5.00
CO1	Andy Pettitte, Derek Jeter	100.00
CO2	Paul Wilson, Todd Hundley	5.00
CO3	Jermaine Dye, Mark Wohlers	6.00
CO4	Scott Rolen, Gregg Jefferies	15.00
CO5	Todd Hollandsworth, Jason Kendall	8.00
CO6	Alan Benes, Robin Ventura	8.00
CO7	Eric Karros, Raul Mondesi	15.00
CO8	Rey Ordonez, Nomar Garciaparra	45.00
CO9	Rondell White, Marty Cordova	6.00
CO10	Tony Gwynn, Karim Garcia	30.00

Firebrand Redemption

Because of production problems with its "Laser-Etched Wood" technology, Stadium Club was unable to package the Firebrand insert cards with the rest of the issue. Instead, a redemption card was substituted. The redemption card pictures the Firebrand card on its horizontal front; the back has details for exchanging the redemption card for the actual wood-printed, die-cut version. The exchange offer ended Sept. 30, 1997.

		NM/M
Complete Set (12):		15.00
Common Card:		.60
F1	Jeff Bagwell	1.25
F2	Albert Belle	.60
F3	Barry Bonds	4.00
F4	Andres Galarraga	.60
F5	Ken Griffey Jr.	2.00
F6	Brady Anderson	.60
F7	Mark McGwire	3.25
F8	Chipper Jones	2.00
F9	Frank Thomas	1.25
F10	Mike Piazza	2.50

F11	Mo Vaughn	.60
F12	Juan Gonzalez	.85

Firebrand

This 12-card insert was found only in packs sold at retail chains. Cards were inserted 1:36 packs. The hortizontal format cards are printed on thin wood stock, die-cut at top. Fronts are trimmed in gold foil. Cards are numbered with a "F" prefix.

		NM/M
Complete Set (12):		25.00
Common Player:		1.00
1	Jeff Bagwell	2.50
2	Albert Belle	1.00
3	Barry Bonds	6.50
4	Andres Galarraga	1.00
5	Ken Griffey Jr.	4.50
6	Brady Anderson	1.00
7	Mark McGwire	5.50
8	Chipper Jones	3.50
9	Frank Thomas	2.50
10	Mike Piazza	4.50
11	Mo Vaughn	1.00
12	Juan Gonzalez	1.50

Instavision

Instavision features holographic cards with exciting moments from the 1996 playoffs and World Series. Inserted one per 24 hobby packs and one per 36 retail packs, these cards are printed horizontally on plastic stock. Cards carry an "I" prefix, with the first 10 found in Series 1 and the final 12 in Series 2.

		NM/M
Complete Set (22):		10.00
Common Player:		.35
11	Eddie Murray	.75
12	Paul Molitor	.75
13	Todd Hundley	.35
14	Roger Clemens	1.50
15	Barry Bonds	3.00
16	Mark McGwire	2.00
17	Brady Anderson	.35
18	Barry Larkin	.35
19	Ken Caminiti	.35
110	Hideo Nomo	.45
111	Bernie Williams	.35
112	Juan Gonzalez	.45
113	Andy Pettitte	.45
114	Albert Belle	.35
115	John Smoltz	.35
116	Brian Jordan	.35
117	Derek Jeter	3.00
118	Ken Caminiti	.35
119	John Wetteland	.35
120	Brady Anderson	.35
121	Andruw Jones	.75
122	Jim Leyritz	.35

Millennium

Millennium was a 40-card insert that was released with 20 cards in Series I and Series II.

The set featured 40 top prospects and rookies on a silver foil, holographic front, with a Future Forecast section on the back. Cards carried an "M" prefix and were numbered consecutively M1-M40. Millennium inserts were found every 24 hobby packs and every 36 retail packs.

		NM/M
Complete Set (40):		12.50
Common Player:		.25
1	Derek Jeter	5.00
2	Mark Grudzielanek	.25
3	Jacob Cruz	.25
4	Ray Durham	.25
5	Tony Clark	.25
6	Chipper Jones	2.50
7	Luis Castillo	.25
8	Carlos Delgado	.50
9	Brant Brown	.25
10	Jason Kendall	.25
11	Alan Benes	.25
12	Rey Ordonez	.25
13	Justin Thompson	.25
14	Jermaine Allensworth	.25
15	Brian Hunter	.25
16	Marty Cordova	.25
17	Edgar Renteria	.25
18	Karim Garcia	.25
19	Todd Greene	.25
20	Paul Wilson	.25
21	Andruw Jones	1.50
22	Todd Walker	.25
23	Alex Ochoa	.25
24	Bartolo Colon	.25
25	Wendell Magee Jr.	.25
26	Jose Rosado	.25
27	Katsuhiro Maeda	.25
28	Bob Abreu	.25
29	Brooks Kieschnick	.25
30	Derrick Gibson	.25
31	Mike Sweeney	.25
32	Jeff D'Amico	.25
33	Chad Mottola	.25
34	Chris Snopek	.25
35	Jaime Bluma	.25
36	Vladimir Guerrero	1.50
37	Nomar Garciaparra	2.50
38	Scott Rolen	1.25
39	Dmitri Young	.25
40	Neifi Perez	.25

Patent Leather

Patent Leather featured 13 of the top gloves in baseball on a leather, die-cut card. The cards carry a "PL" prefix and are inerted one per 36 retail packs.

		NM/M
Complete Set (13):		25.00
Common Player:		1.00
1	Ivan Rodriguez	3.00
2	Ken Caminiti	1.00
3	Barry Bonds	6.00
4	Ken Griffey Jr.	5.00
5	Greg Maddux	4.00
6	Craig Biggio	1.00
7	Andres Galarraga	1.00
8	Kenny Lofton	1.00
9	Barry Larkin	1.00
10	Mark Grace	1.00
11	Rey Ordonez	1.00
12	Roberto Alomar	1.25
13	Derek Jeter	6.00

Pure Gold

Pure Gold featured 20 of the top players in baseball on gold, embossed foil cards. Cards carry a "PG" prefix and were inserted every 72 hobby packs and every 108 retail packs. The first 10 cards were in Series I packs, while the final 10 cards are exclusive to Series II.

		NM/M
Complete Set (20):		60.00
Common Player:		1.25
1	Brady Anderson	1.25
2	Albert Belle	1.25

3 Dante Bichette 1.25
4 Barry Bonds 12.00
5 Jay Buhner 1.25
6 Tony Gwynn 6.00
7 Chipper Jones 6.00
8 Mark McGwire 9.00
9 Gary Sheffield 2.25
10 Frank Thomas 4.50
11 Juan Gonzalez 2.50
12 Ken Caminiti 1.25
13 Kenny Lofton 1.25
14 Jeff Bagwell 4.50
15 Ken Griffey Jr. 7.50
16 Cal Ripken Jr. 12.00
17 Mo Vaughn 1.25
18 Mike Piazza 7.50
19 Derek Jeter 12.00
20 Andres Galarraga 1.25

TSC Matrix

TSC Matrix consists of 120 cards from Series I and II reprinted with Power Matrix technology. In each Series, 60 of the 190 cards were selected for inclusion in TSC Matrix and inserted every 12 hobby packs and every 18 retail packs. Each insert carries the TSC Matrix logo in a top corner of the card.

NM/M
Complete Set (120): 70.00
Common Player: .50
1 Chipper Jones 2.50
2 Gary Sheffield 1.00
3 Kenny Lofton .50
4 Brian Jordan .50
5 Mark McGwire 4.25
6 Charles Nagy .50
7 Tim Salmon .50
8 Cal Ripken Jr. 5.00
9 Jeff Conine .50
10 Paul Molitor 1.75
11 Mariano Rivera .65
12 Pedro Martinez 1.75
13 Jeff Bagwell 1.75
14 Bobby Bonilla .50
15 Barry Bonds 5.00
16 Ryan Klesko .50
17 Barry Larkin .50
18 Jim Thome 1.50
19 Jay Buhner .50
20 Juan Gonzalez 1.00
21 Mike Mussina .75
22 Kevin Appier .50
23 Eric Karros .50
24 Steve Finley .50
25 Ed Sprague .50
26 Bernard Gilkey .50
27 Tony Phillips .50
28 Henry Rodriguez .50
29 John Smoltz .50
30 Dante Bichette .50
31 Mike Piazza 3.25
32 Paul O'Neill .50
33 Billy Wagner .50
34 Reggie Sanders .50
35 John Jaha .50
36 Eddie Murray 1.75
37 Eric Young .50
38 Roberto Hernandez .50
39 Pat Hentgen .50
40 Sammy Sosa 2.50
41 Todd Hundley .50
42 Mo Vaughn .50
43 Robin Ventura .50

44 Mark Grudzielanek .50
45 Shane Reynolds .50
46 Andy Pettitte .65
47 Fred McGriff .50
48 Rey Ordonez .50
49 Will Clark .50
50 Ken Griffey Jr. 3.25
51 Todd Worrell .50
52 Rusty Greer .50
53 Mark Grace .50
54 Tom Glavine .75
55 Derek Jeter 5.00
56 Rafael Palmeiro 1.50
57 Bernie Williams .50
58 Marty Cordova .50
59 Andres Galarraga .50
60 Ken Caminiti .50
196 Greg Maddux 2.50
197 Joe Carter .50
198 Alex Ochoa .50
199 Ellis Burks .50
200 Ivan Rodriguez 1.50
201 Marquis Grissom .50
202 Trevor Hoffman .50
203 Matt Williams .50
204 Carlos Delgado 1.25
205 Ramon Martinez .50
206 Chuck Knoblauch .50
207 Juan Guzman .50
208 Dave Bell .50
209 Roger Clemens 3.00
210 Vladimir Guerrero 1.75
211 Cecil Fielder .50
212 Hideo Nomo 1.00
213 Frank Thomas 1.75
214 Greg Vaughn .50
215 Javy Lopez .50
216 Raul Mondesi .50
217 Wade Boggs 2.50
218 Carlos Baerga .50
219 Tony Gwynn 2.50
220 Tino Martinez .50
221 Vinny Castilla .50
222 Lance Johnson .50
223 David Justice .50
224 Rondell White .50
225 Dean Palmer .50
226 Jim Edmonds .50
227 Albert Belle .50
228 Alex Fernandez .50
229 Ryne Sandberg 2.50
230 Jose Mesa .50
231 David Cone .50
232 Troy Percival .50
233 Edgar Martinez .50
234 Jose Canseco 1.25
235 Kevin Brown .50
236 Ray Lankford .50
237 Karim Garcia .50
238 J.T. Snow .50
239 Dennis Eckersley 1.50
240 Roberto Alomar .75
241 John Valentin .50
242 Ron Gant .50
243 Geronimo Berroa .50
244 Manny Ramirez 1.75
245 Travis Fryman .50
246 Denny Neagle .50
247 Randy Johnson 1.75
248 Darin Erstad .65
249 Mark Wohlers .50
250 Ken Hill .50
251 Larry Walker .50
252 Craig Biggio .50
253 Brady Anderson .50
254 John Wetteland .50
255 Andruw Jones 1.75

Members Only

Production was reported at just 750 complete sets of these specially marked Stadium Club cards and inserts. Sold only as complete sets through Topps' Stadium Club program, each card differs from the regular-issue TSC version only in the presence of a subdued "MEMBERS ONLY" repeated all across the cards' backs. Star players' cards sell for a significant premium over regular-issue TSC version; inserts, depending on the scarcity of the regular version, usually sell for a significant discount in the Members Only version.

NM/M
Complete Set: 250.00
Common Player: .50
Stars: 5X
Inserts: 50-100%

Members Only Baseball

This boxed set was available only to members of Topps' Stadium Club for a price of $15, which included a year's membership in the club. Fronts feature action photos with a 2-1/2" circle behind the player, a gold-foil Members Only seal and the player's name, also in gold-foil. Backs feature another photo and a career summary on a red background which has the Members Only seal in a repeating pattern. Cards #51-55 are rookie stars and are printed in Topps Finest technologies.

NM/M
Complete Set (55): 12.00
Common Player: .10
1 Brady Anderson .10
2 Carlos Baerga .10
3 Jeff Bagwell .10
4 Albert Belle .10
5 Dante Bichette .10
6 Craig Biggio .10
7 Wade Boggs 1.00
8 Barry Bonds 2.50
9 Jay Buhner .10
10 Ellis Burks .10
11 Ken Caminiti .10
12 Jose Canseco .50
13 Joe Carter .10
14 Roger Clemens 1.25
15 Jeff Conine .10
16 Andres Galarraga .10
17 Ron Gant .10
18 Juan Gonzalez .40
19 Mark Grace .10
20 Ken Griffey Jr. 1.50
21 Tony Gwynn 1.00
22 Pat Hentgen .10
23 Todd Hollandsworth .10
24 Todd Hundley .10
25 Derek Jeter 2.50
26 Randy Johnson .75
27 Chipper Jones 1.00
28 Ryan Klesko .10
29 Chuck Knoblauch .10
30 Barry Larkin .10
31 Kenny Lofton .10
32 Greg Maddux 1.00
33 Mark McGwire 2.00
34 Paul Molitor .75
35 Raul Mondesi .10
36 Hideo Nomo .40
37 Rafael Palmeiro .65
38 Mike Piazza 1.50
39 Manny Ramirez .10
40 Cal Ripken Jr. 2.50
41 Ivan Rodriguez .65
42 Tim Salmon .10
43 Gary Sheffield .10
44 John Smoltz .10
45 Sammy Sosa 1.00
46 Frank Thomas .75
47 Jim Thome .65
48 Mo Vaughn .10
49 Bernie Williams .10
50 Matt Williams .10
51 Darin Erstad (Finest) 1.00
52 Vladimir Guerrero (Finest) 2.50
53 Andruw Jones (Finest) 2.00
54 Scott Rolen (Finest) 1.50
55 Todd Walker (Finest) 1.00

1998 Stadium Club

Stadium Club was issued in two series for 1998, with 200 odd-numbered cards in Series

1 and 200 even-numbered cards in Series 2. Retail packs contain six cards and carried an SRP of $2; hobby packs have nine cards and an SRP of $3 and HTA packs offered 15 cards at an SRP of $5. Three subsets were included: Future Stars (361-379) and Draft Picks (381-399), both being odd-numbered, and Traded (356-400) being even-numbered. Inserts in Series 1 include: First Day Issue parallels (retail), One of a Kind parallels (hobby), Printing Plates parallels (HTA), Bowman Previews, Co-Signers (hobby), In the Wings, Never Compromise, and Triumvirates (retail). Inserts in Series 2 include: First Day Issue parallels (retail), One of a Kind parallels (hobby), Printing Plates parallels (HTA), Bowman Prospect Previews, Co-Signers (hobby), Playing with Passion, Royal Court and Triumvirates (retail).

NM/M
Complete Set (400): 30.00
Common Player: .05
Hobby Pack (10): 1.50
Retail Pack (7): 1.50
Home Team Adv. Pack (16): 4.00
Hobby Box (24): 30.00
1 Chipper Jones 1.00
2 Frank Thomas .75
3 Vladimir Guerrero .75
4 Ellis Burks .05
5 John Franco .05
6 Paul Molitor .75
7 Rusty Greer .05
8 Todd Hundley .05
9 Brett Tomko .05
10 Eric Karros .05
11 Mike Cameron .05
12 Jim Edmonds .05
13 Bernie Williams .05
14 Denny Neagle .05
15 Jason Dickson .05
16 Sammy Sosa 1.00
17 Brian Jordan .05
18 Jose Vidro .05
19 Scott Spiezio .05
20 Jay Buhner .05
21 Jim Thome .65
22 Sandy Alomar .05
23 Devon White .05
24 Roberto Alomar .20
25 John Flaherty .05
26 John Wetteland .05
27 Willie Greene .05
28 Gregg Jefferies .05
29 Johnny Damon .35
30 Barry Larkin .05
31 Chuck Knoblauch .05
32 Mo Vaughn .05
33 Tony Clark .05
34 Marty Cordova .05
35 Vinny Castilla .05
36 Jeff King .05
37 Reggie Jefferson .05
38 Mariano Rivera .15
39 Jermaine Allensworth .05
40 Livan Hernandez .05
41 Heathcliff Slocumb .05
42 Jacob Cruz .05
43 Barry Bonds 2.50
44 Dave Magadan .05
45 Chan Ho Park .05
46 Jeremi Gonzalez .05
47 Jeff Cirillo .05
48 Delino DeShields .05
49 Craig Biggio .05
50 Benito Santiago .05
51 Mark Clark .05
52 Fernando Vina .05
53 F.P. Santangelo .05
54 Pep Harris RC .05
55 Edgar Renteria .05
56 Jeff Bagwell .75
57 Jimmy Key .05
58 Bartolo Colon .05
59 Curt Schilling .35

60 Steve Finley .05
61 Andy Ashby .05
62 John Burkett .05
63 Orel Hershiser .05
64 Pokey Reese .05
65 Scott Servais .05
66 Todd Jones .05
67 Javy Lopez .05
68 Robin Ventura .05
69 Miguel Tejada .15
70 Raul Casanova .05
71 Reggie Sanders .05
72 Edgardo Alfonzo .05
73 Dean Palmer .05
74 Todd Stottlemyre .05
75 David Wells .05
76 Troy Percival .05
77 Albert Belle .05
78 Pat Hentgen .05
79 Brian Hunter .05
80 Richard Hidalgo .05
81 Darren Oliver .05
82 Mark Wohlers .05
83 Cal Ripken Jr. 2.50
84 Hideo Nomo .40
85 Derrek Lee .05
86 Stan Javier .05
87 Rey Ordonez .05
88 Randy Johnson .75
89 Jeff Kent .05
90 Brian McRae .05
91 Manny Ramirez .75
92 Trevor Hoffman .05
93 Doug Glanville .05
94 Todd Walker .05
95 Andy Benes .05
96 Jason Schmidt .05
97 Mike Matheny .05
98 Tim Naehring .05
99 Jeff Blauser .05
100 Jose Rosado .05
101 Roger Clemens 1.25
102 Pedro Astacio .05
103 Mark Bellhorn .05
104 Paul O'Neill .05
105 Darin Erstad .15
106 Mike Lieberthal .05
107 Wilson Alvarez .05
108 Mike Mussina .30
109 George Williams .05
110 Cliff Floyd .05
111 Shawn Estes .05
112 Mark Grudzielanek .05
113 Tony Gwynn 1.00
114 Alan Benes .05
115 Terry Steinbach .05
116 Greg Maddux 1.00
117 Andy Pettitte .25
118 Dave Nilsson .05
119 Deivi Cruz .05
120 Carlos Delgado .50
121 Scott Hatteberg .05
122 John Olerud .05
123 Moises Alou .05
124 Garret Anderson .05
125 Royce Clayton .05
126 Dante Powell .05
127 Tom Glavine .35
128 Gary DiSarcina .05
129 Terry Adams .05
130 Raul Mondesi .05
131 Dan Wilson .05
132 Al Martin .05
133 Mickey Morandini .05
134 Rafael Palmeiro .65
135 Juan Encarnacion .05
136 Jim Pittsley .05
137 Magglio Ordonez RC 1.00
138 Will Clark .05
139 Todd Helton .65
140 Kelvim Escobar .05
141 Esteban Loaiza .05
142 John Jaha .05
143 Jeff Fassero .05
144 Harold Baines .05
145 Butch Huskey .05
146 Pat Meares .05
147 Brian Giles .05
148 Ramiro Mendoza .05
149 John Smoltz .05
150 Felix Martinez .05
151 Jose Valentin .05
152 Brad Rigby .05
153 Ed Sprague .05
154 Mike Hampton .05
155 Mike Lansing .05
156 Ray Lankford .05
157 Bobby Bonilla .05
158 Bill Mueller .05
159 Jeffrey Hammonds .05
160 Charles Nagy .05
161 Rich Loiselle .05
162 Al Leiter .05
163 Larry Walker .05
164 Chris Hoiles .05
165 Jeff Montgomery .05
166 Francisco Cordova .05
167 James Baldwin .05
168 Mark McLemore .05
169 Kevin Appier .05
170 Jamey Wright .05
171 Nomar Garciaparra 1.00
172 Matt Franco .05
173 Armando Benitez .05
174 Jeromy Burnitz .05
175 Ismael Valdes .05
176 Lance Johnson .05
177 Paul Sorrento .05

178 Rondell White .05
179 Kevin Elster .05
180 Jason Giambi .50
181 Carlos Baerga .05
182 Russ Davis .05
183 Ryan McGuire .05
184 Eric Young .05
185 Ron Gant .05
186 Manny Alexander .05
187 Scott Karl .05
188 Brady Anderson .05
189 Randall Simon .05
190 Tim Belcher .05
191 Jaret Wright .05
192 Dante Bichette .05
193 John Valentin .05
194 Darren Bragg .05
195 Mike Sweeney .05
196 Craig Counsell .05
197 Jaime Navarro .05
198 Todd Dunn .05
199 Ken Griffey Jr. 1.50
200 Juan Gonzalez .40
201 Billy Wagner .05
202 Tino Martinez .05
203 Mark McGwire 2.00
204 Jeff D'Amico .05
205 Rico Brogna .05
206 Todd Hollandsworth .05
207 Chad Curtis .05
208 Tom Goodwin .05
209 Neifi Perez .05
210 Derek Bell .05
211 Quilvio Veras .05
212 Greg Vaughn .05
213 Roberto Hernandez .05
214 Arthur Rhodes .05
215 Cal Eldred .05
216 Bill Taylor .05
217 Todd Greene .05
218 Mario Valdez .05
219 Ricky Bottalico .05
220 Frank Rodriguez .05
221 Rich Becker .05
222 Roberto Duran .05
223 Ivan Rodriguez .65
224 Mike Jackson .05
225 Deion Sanders .05
226 Tony Womack .05
227 Mark Kotsay .05
228 Steve Trachsel .05
229 Ryan Klesko .05
230 Ken Cloude .05
231 Luis Gonzalez .05
232 Gary Gaetti .05
233 Michael Tucker .05
234 Shawn Green .35
235 Ariel Prieto .05
236 Kirt Manwaring .05
237 Omar Vizquel .05
238 Matt Beech .05
239 Justin Thompson .05
240 Bret Boone .05
241 Derek Jeter 2.50
242 Ken Caminiti .05
243 Jay Bell .05
244 Kevin Tapani .05
245 Jason Kendall .05
246 Jose Guillen .05
247 Mike Bordick .05
248 Dustin Hermanson .05
249 Darrin Fletcher .05
250 Dave Hollins .05
251 Ramon Martinez .05
252 Hideki Irabu .05
253 Mark Grace .05
254 Jason Isringhausen .05
255 Jose Cruz Jr. .05
256 Brian Johnson .05
257 Brad Ausmus .05
258 Andruw Jones .75
259 Doug Jones .05
260 Jeff Shaw .05
261 Chuck Finley .05
262 Gary Sheffield .45
263 David Segui .05
264 John Smiley .05
265 Tim Salmon .05
266 J.T. Snow Jr. .05
267 Alex Fernandez .05
268 Matt Stairs .05
269 B.J. Surhoff .05
270 Keith Foulke .05
271 Edgar Martinez .05
272 Shannon Stewart .05
273 Eduardo Perez .05
274 Wally Joyner .05
275 Kevin Young .05
276 Eli Marrero .05
277 Brad Radke .05
278 Jamie Moyer .05
279 Joe Girardi .05
280 Troy O'Leary .05
281 Aaron Sele .05
282 Jose Offerman .05
283 Scott Erickson .05
284 Sean Berry .05
285 Shigetosi Hasegawa .05
286 Felix Heredia .05
287 Willie McGee .05
288 Alex Rodriguez 2.00
289 Ugueth Urbina .05
290 Jon Lieber .05
291 Fernando Tatis .05
292 Chris Stynes .05
293 Bernard Gilkey .05
294 Joey Hamilton .05
295 Matt Karchner .05

296	Paul Wilson	.05
297	Mel Nieves	.05
298	Kevin Millwood RC	.75
299	Quinton McCracken	.05
300	Jerry DiPoto	.05
301	Jermaine Dye	.05
302	Travis Lee	.05
303	Ron Coomer	.05
304	Matt Williams	.05
305	Bobby Higginson	.05
306	Jorge Fabregas	.05
307	Hal Morris	.05
308	Jay Bell	.05
309	Joe Randa	.05
310	Andy Benes	.05
311	Sterling Hitchcock	.05
312	Jeff Suppan	.05
313	Shane Reynolds	.05
314	Willie Blair	.05
315	Scott Rolen	.65
316	Wilson Alvarez	.05
317	David Justice	.05
318	Fred McGriff	.05
319	Bobby Jones	.05
320	Wade Boggs	1.00
321	Tim Wakefield	.05
322	Tony Saunders	.05
323	David Cone	.05
324	Roberto Hernandez	.05
325	Jose Canseco	.45
326	Kevin Stocker	.05
327	Gerald Williams	.05
328	Quinton McCracken	.05
329	Mark Gardner	.05
330	Ben Grieve (Prime Rookie)	.05
331	Kevin Brown	.05
332	Mike Lowell RC (Prime Rookie)	1.00
333	Jed Hansen	.05
334	Abraham Nunez (Prime Rookie)	.05
335	John Thomson	.05
336	Derrek Lee (Prime Rookie)	.05
337	Mike Piazza	1.50
338	Brad Fullmer (Prime Rookie)	.05
339	Ray Durham	.05
340	Kerry Wood (Prime Rookie)	.50
341	Kevin Polcovich RC	.05
342	Russ Johnson (Prime Rookie)	.05
343	Darryl Hamilton	.05
344	David Ortiz (Prime Rookie)	.45
345	Kevin Orie	.05
346	Sean Casey (Prime Rookie)	.25
347	Juan Guzman	.05
348	Ruben Rivera (Prime Rookie)	.05
349	Rick Aguilera	.05
350	Bobby Estalella (Prime Rookie)	.05
351	Bobby Witt	.05
352	Paul Konerko (Prime Rookie)	.25
353	Matt Morris	.05
354	Carl Pavano (Prime Rookie)	.05
355	Todd Zeile	.05
356	Kevin Brown (Transaction)	.05
357	Alex Gonzalez	.05
358	Chuck Knoblauch (Transaction)	.05
359	Joey Cora	.05
360	Mike Lansing	.05
361	Adrian Beltre (Future Stars)	.45
362	Dennis Eckersley (Transaction)	.65
363	A.J. Hinch (Future Stars)	.05
364	Kenny Lofton (Transaction)	.05
365	Alex Gonzalez (Future Stars)	.05
366	Henry Rodriguez (Transaction)	.05
367	Mike Stoner RC (Future Stars)	.05
368	Darryl Kile (Transaction)	.05
369	Carl Pavano (Future Stars)	.05
370	Walt Weiss (Transaction)	.05
371	Kris Benson (Future Stars)	.05
372	Cecil Fielder (Transaction)	.05
373	Dermal Brown (Future Stars)	.05
374	Rod Beck (Transaction)	.05
375	Eric Milton (Future Stars)	.05
376	Travis Fryman (Transaction)	.05
377	Preston Wilson (Future Stars)	.10
378	Chili Davis (Transaction)	.05
379	Travis Lee (Future Stars)	.10

380	Jim Leyritz (Transaction)	.05
381	Vernon Wells (Draft Picks)	.05
382	Joe Carter (Transaction)	.05
383	J.J. Davis (Draft Picks)	.05
384	Marquis Grissom (Transaction)	.05
385	Mike Cuddyer RC (Draft Picks)	.50
386	Rickey Henderson (Transaction)	.75
387	Chris Enochs RC (Draft Picks)	.10
388	Andres Galarraga (Transaction)	.05
389	Jason Dellaero (Draft Picks)	.05
390	Robb Nen (Transaction)	.05
391	Mark Mangum (Draft Picks)	.05
392	Jeff Blauser (Transaction)	.05
393	Adam Kennedy (Draft Picks)	.05
394	Bob Abreu (Transaction)	.05
395	Jack Cust RC (Draft Picks)	.05
396	Jose Vizcaino (Transaction)	.05
397	Jon Garland (Draft Picks)	.05
398	Pedro Martinez (Transaction)	.75
399	Aaron Akin (Draft Picks)	.05
400	Jeff Conine (Transaction)	.05

First Day Issue

	NM/M
Common Player:	2.00
Stars:	10X
Production 200 Sets	

One of a Kind

This hobby-only parallel set includes all 400 cards from Series 1 and 2 printed on a silver mirrorboard stock. Cards are sequentially numbered to 150 and inserted one per 21 Series 1 packs and one per 24 Series 2 packs.

	NM/M
Common Player:	2.00
Stars:	12X
Production 150 Sets	

Bowman Preview

This Series I insert gave collectors a sneak peak at Bowman's 50th anniversary set, with 10 top veterans displayed on the 1998 Bowman design. The cards were inserted one per 12 packs and numbered with a "BP" prefix.

		NM/M
Complete Set (10):		10.00
Common Player:		.25
Inserted 1:12		
BP1	Nomar Garciaparra	1.00
BP2	Scott Rolen	.65
BP3	Ken Griffey Jr.	1.50
BP4	Frank Thomas	.75
BP5	Larry Walker	.25
BP6	Mike Piazza	1.50
BP7	Chipper Jones	1.00
BP8	Tino Martinez	.25
BP9	Mark McGwire	2.00
BP10	Barry Bonds	2.50

Bowman Prospect Preview

Bowman Prospect Previews were inserted into Series 2 retail and hobby packs at a rate of one per 12 and HTA packs at one per four. The 10-card insert previews the upcoming 1998 Bowman set and includes top prospects that were expected to make an impact in 1998.

		NM/M
Complete Set (10):		3.00
Common Player:		.25
Inserted 1:12		
BP1	Ben Grieve	.25
BP2	Brad Fullmer	.25
BP3	Ryan Anderson	.25
BP4	Mark Kotsay	.25
BP5	Bobby Estalella	.25
BP6	Juan Encarnacion	.25
BP7	Todd Helton	2.00
BP8	Mike Lowell	.25
BP9	A.J. Hinch	.25
BP10	Richard Hidalgo	.25

Co-Signers

Co-Signers were inserted into both Series 1 and 2 hobby and HTA packs. The complete set is 36 cards, each featuring two top players along with both autographs. They were available in three levels of scarcity: Series 1 Group A 1:4,372 hobby and 1:2,623 HTA; Series 1 Group B 1:1,457 hobby and HTA 1:874; Series 1 Group C 1:121 hobby and 1:73 HTA; Series 2 Group A 1:4,702 hobby and 1:2,821 HTA; Series 2 Group B 1:1,567 hobby and 1:940 HTA, Series 2 Group C 1:1,131 hobby and 1:78 HTA. Some cards are known to bear fake autographs, despite having the Topps seal of authenticity. Those cards are believed to have been released in unsigned form in an unauthorized manner, and then signed with counterfeit signatures.

		NM/M
Common Card:		10.00
Group A 1:4,372		
Group B 1:1,457		
Group C 1:121		
CS1	Nomar Garciaparra, Scott Rolen/A	120.00
CS2	Nomar Garciaparra, Derek Jeter/B	250.00
CS3	Nomar Garciaparra, Eric Karros/C	60.00
CS4	Scott Rolen, Derek Jeter/C	100.00
CS5	Scott Rolen, Eric Karros/B	40.00
CS6	Derek Jeter, Eric Karros/A	150.00
CS7	Travis Lee, Jose Cruz Jr./B	15.00
CS8	Travis Lee, Mark Kotsay/C	10.00

CS9	Travis Lee, Paul Konerko/A	25.00
CS10	Jose Cruz Jr., Mark Kotsay/A	25.00
CS11	Jose Cruz Jr., Paul Konerko/C	12.00
CS12	Mark Kotsay, Paul Konerko/B	20.00
CS13	Tony Gwynn, Larry Walker/A	120.00
CS14	Tony Gwynn, Mark Grudzielanek/C	30.00
CS15	Tony Gwynn, Andres Galarraga/B	60.00
CS16	Larry Walker, Mark Grudzielanek/A	40.00
CS17	Larry Walker, Andres Galarraga/C	30.00
CS18	Mark Grudzielanek, Andres Galarraga/A	25.00
CS19	Sandy Alomar, Roberto Alomar/A	75.00
CS20	Sandy Alomar, Andy Pettitte/C	20.00
CS21	Sandy Alomar, Tino Martinez/B	40.00
CS22	Roberto Alomar, Andy Pettitte/B	50.00
CS23	Roberto Alomar, Tino Martinez/C	25.00
CS24	Andy Pettitte, Tino Martinez/A	75.00
CS25	Tony Clark, Todd Hundley/A	25.00
CS26	Tony Clark, Tim Salmon/B	30.00
CS27	Tony Clark, Robin Ventura/C	10.00
CS28	Todd Hundley, Tim Salmon/C	15.00
CS29	Todd Hundley, Robin Ventura/B	12.00
CS30	Tim Salmon, Robin Ventura/A	50.00
CS31	Roger Clemens, Randy Johnson/B	175.00
CS32	Roger Clemens, Jaret Wright/A	140.00
CS33	Roger Clemens, Matt Morris/C	100.00
CS34	Randy Johnson, Jaret Wright/C	50.00
CS35	Randy Johnson, Matt Morris/A	85.00
CS36	Jaret Wright, Matt Morris/B	20.00

In the Wings

In the Wings was a Series I insert found every 36 packs. It included 15 future stars on uniluster technology.

		NM/M
Complete Set (15):		6.00
Common Player:		.50
Inserted 1:36		
W1	Juan Encarnacion	.50
W2	Brad Fullmer	.50
W3	Ben Grieve	.50
W4	Todd Helton	3.00
W5	Richard Hidalgo	.50
W6	Russ Johnson	.50
W7	Paul Konerko	.75
W8	Mark Kotsay	.50
W9	Derek Lee	1.00
W10	Travis Lee	.50
W11	Eli Marrero	.50
W12	David Ortiz	.75
W13	Randall Simon	.50
W14	Shannon Stewart	.50
W15	Fernando Tatis	.50

Never Compromise

Never Compromise was a 20-card insert found in packs of Series I. Cards were inserted one per 12 packs and numbered with a "NC" prefix.

	NM/M
Complete Set (20):	10.00
Common Player:	.15
Inserted 1:12	

NC1	Cal Ripken Jr.	2.00
NC2	Ivan Rodriguez	.50
NC3	Ken Griffey Jr.	1.00
NC4	Frank Thomas	.60
NC5	Tony Gwynn	.75
NC6	Mike Piazza	1.00
NC7	Randy Johnson	.60
NC8	Greg Maddux	.75
NC9	Roger Clemens	.85
NC10	Derek Jeter	2.00
NC11	Chipper Jones	.75
NC12	Barry Bonds	2.00
NC13	Larry Walker	.15
NC14	Jeff Bagwell	.60
NC15	Barry Larkin	.15
NC16	Ken Caminiti	.15
NC17	Mark McGwire	1.50
NC18	Manny Ramirez	.60
NC19	Tim Salmon	.15
NC20	Paul Molitor	.60

Playing with Passion

This Series II insert displayed 10 players with a strong desire to win. The cards are numbered with a "P" prefix.

		NM/M
Complete Set (10):		10.00
Common Player:		.35
Inserted 1:12		
P1	Bernie Williams	.35
P2	Jim Edmonds	.35
P3	Chipper Jones	1.00
P4	Cal Ripken Jr.	3.00
P5	Craig Biggio	.35
P6	Juan Gonzalez	.45
P7	Alex Rodriguez	2.25
P8	Tino Martinez	.35
P9	Mike Piazza	1.50
P10	Ken Griffey Jr.	1.50

Printing Plates

Inserted only in Home Team Advantage boxes at a rate of approximately one per 90 packs were the actual aluminum plates used to print the fronts of the base cards. Unlike some printing plate issues, the plates were not inserted for the card backs. Each card's plate can be found in four different colors: Cyan, magenta, yellow and black. Because of their unique nature, pricing of individual player's plates cannot be provided.

	NM/M
Common Player:	25.00

Royal Court

Fifteen players were showcased on uniluster technology for this Series II insert. The set is broken up into 10 Kings (veterans) and five Princes (rookies) and inserted one per 36 packs.

		NM/M
Complete Set (15):		15.00
Common Player:		.50
Inserted 1:36		
RC1	Ken Griffey Jr.	2.00
RC2	Frank Thomas	1.25
RC3	Mike Piazza	2.00
RC4	Chipper Jones	1.50
RC5	Mark McGwire	2.50
RC6	Cal Ripken Jr.	3.00
RC7	Jeff Bagwell	1.25
RC8	Barry Bonds	3.00
RC9	Juan Gonzalez	.85
RC10	Alex Rodriguez	2.50
RC11	Travis Lee	.50
RC12	Paul Konerko	.75
RC13	Todd Helton	1.00
RC14	Ben Grieve	.50
RC15	Mark Kotsay	.50

Screen Plays Sound Chips

One of the packs in each Home Team Advantage box of TSC "Odd Series" cards contained this special "card" commemorating the home run hit by Cal Ripken, Jr. in his historic 2,131st game on Sept. 6, 1995. The item is 3-1/2" x 2-1/2" x 3/8" deep. Glued to the top is a magic motion card showing Ripken hitting the blast. When a corner of the card is squeezed, a sound chip replays the radio call of the home run by Jon Miller and President Bill Clinton. The top of the package opens to reveal a newspaper-like presentation with a picture of Ripken, details of his home run and the technology used to produce the item.

	NM/M
SC1 Cal Ripken Jr.	5.00

Triumvirate

Triumvirates were included in both series of Stadium Club and were available only in retail packs. Series 1 has 24 players, with three players from eight different teams, while Series 2 has 30 players, with three players from 10 different positions. The cards are all die-cut and fit together to form three-card panels. Three different versions of each card were available - Luminous (regular) versions were seeded one per 48 packs, Luminescent versions were seeded one per 192 packs and Illuminator versions were seeded one per 384 packs.

	NM/M
Complete Set (54):	70.00
Complete Series 1 (24):	30.00
Complete Series 2 (30):	40.00
Common Player:	.50
Luminous 1:48	
Luminescents 1:192:	1.5X
Illuminators 1:384:	2.5X

		NM/M
T1a	Chipper Jones	2.50
T1b	Andruw Jones	2.00
T1c	Kenny Lofton	.50
T2a	Derek Jeter	5.00
T2b	Bernie Williams	.50
T2c	Tino Martinez	.50
T3a	Jay Buhner	.50
T3b	Edgar Martinez	.50
T3c	Ken Griffey Jr.	3.00
T4a	Albert Belle	.50
T4b	Robin Ventura	.50
T4c	Frank Thomas	2.00
T5a	Brady Anderson	.50
T5b	Cal Ripken Jr.	5.00
T5c	Rafael Palmeiro	1.50
T6a	Mike Piazza	3.00
T6b	Raul Mondesi	.50
T6c	Eric Karros	.50
T7a	Vinny Castilla	.50
T7b	Andres Galarraga	.50
T7c	Larry Walker	.50
T8a	Jim Thome	1.50
T8b	Manny Ramirez	2.00
T8c	David Justice	.50
T9a	Mike Mussina	.75
T9b	Greg Maddux	2.50
T9c	Randy Johnson	2.00
T10a	Mike Piazza	3.00
T10b	Sandy Alomar	.50
T10c	Ivan Rodriguez	1.50
T11a	Mark McGwire	4.00
T11b	Tino Martinez	.50
T11c	Frank Thomas	2.00
T12a	Roberto Alomar	.75
T12b	Chuck Knoblauch	.50
T12c	Craig Biggio	.50
T13a	Cal Ripken Jr.	5.00
T13b	Chipper Jones	2.50
T13c	Ken Caminiti	.50
T14a	Derek Jeter	5.00
T14b	Nomar Garciaparra	2.50
T14c	Alex Rodriguez	4.00
T15a	Barry Bonds	5.00
T15b	David Justice	.50
T15c	Albert Belle	.50
T16a	Bernie Williams	.50
T16b	Ken Griffey Jr.	3.00
T16c	Ray Lankford	.50
T17a	Tim Salmon	.50
T17b	Larry Walker	.50
T17c	Tony Gwynn	2.50
T18a	Paul Molitor	2.00
T18b	Edgar Martinez	.50
T18c	Juan Gonzalez	1.00

1999 Stadium Club

Released in two series, base cards feature a full bleed design on 20-pt. stock with an embossed holographic logo. Draft Pick, Prospect and Series 2 Future Star subset cards are short-printed, seeded in every three packs. Card backs have 1998 statistics and personal information. Hobby packs consist of six cards with an S.R.P. of $2.

	NM/M
Complete Set (355):	40.00
Complete Series 1 (170):	20.00
Complete Series 2 (185):	20.00
Common Player:	.05
Common SP	
(141-160; 336-355):	.50
Inserted 1:3	
Pack (6):	1.25
Wax Box (24):	25.00

1	Alex Rodriguez	2.00
2	Chipper Jones	1.50
3	Rusty Greer	.05
4	Jim Edmonds	.05
5	Ron Gant	.05
6	Kevin Polcovich	.05
7	Darryl Strawberry	.05
8	Bill Mueller	.05
9	Vinny Castilla	.05
10	Wade Boggs	1.50
11	Jose Lima	.05
12	Darren Dreifort	.05
13	Jay Bell	.05
14	Ben Grieve	.05
15	Shawn Green	.35
16	Andres Galarraga	.05
17	Bartolo Colon	.05
18	Francisco Cordova	.05
19	Paul O'Neill	.05
20	Trevor Hoffman	.05
21	Darren Oliver	.05
22	John Franco	.05
23	Eli Marrero	.05
24	Roberto Hernandez	.05
25	Craig Biggio	.05
26	Brad Fullmer	.05
27	Scott Erickson	.05
28	Tom Gordon	.05
29	Brian Hunter	.05
30	Raul Mondesi	.05
31	Rick Reed	.05
32	Jose Canseco	.50
33	Robb Nen	.05
34	Turner Ward	.05
35	Bret Boone	.05
36	Jose Offerman	.05
37	Matt Lawton	.05
38	David Wells	.05
39	Bob Abreu	.10
40	Jeromy Burnitz	.05
41	Deivi Cruz	.05
42	Mike Cameron	.05
43	Rico Brogna	.05
44	Dmitri Young	.05
45	Chuck Knoblauch	.05
46	Johnny Damon	.35
47	Brian Meadows	.05
48	Jeremi Gonzalez	.05
49	Gary DiSarcina	.05
50	Frank Thomas	1.00
51	F.P. Santangelo	.05
52	Tom Candiotti	.05
53	Shane Reynolds	.05
54	Rod Beck	.05
55	Rey Ordonez	.05
56	Todd Helton	.75
57	Mickey Morandini	.05
58	Jorge Posada	.05
59	Mike Mussina	.30
60	Bobby Bonilla	.05
61	David Segui	.05
62	Brian McRae	.05
63	Fred McGriff	.05
64	Brett Tomko	.05
65	Derek Jeter	2.50
66	Sammy Sosa	1.50
67	Kenny Rogers	.05
68	Dave Nilsson	.05
69	Eric Young	.05
70	Mark McGwire	2.00
71	Kenny Lofton	.05
72	Tom Glavine	.35
73	Joey Hamilton	.05
74	John Valentin	.05
75	Mariano Rivera	.15
76	Ray Durham	.05
77	Tony Clark	.05
78	Livan Hernandez	.05
79	Rickey Henderson	1.00
80	Vladimir Guerrero	1.00
81	J.T. Snow Jr.	.05
82	Juan Guzman	.05
83	Darryl Hamilton	.05
84	Matt Anderson	.05
85	Travis Lee	.05
86	Joe Randa	.05
87	Dave Dellucci	.05
88	Moises Alou	.05
89	Alex Gonzalez	.05
90	Tony Womack	.05
91	Neifi Perez	.05
92	Travis Fryman	.05
93	Masato Yoshii	.05
94	Woody Williams	.05
95	Ray Lankford	.05
96	Roger Clemens	1.50
97	Dustin Hermanson	.05
98	Joe Carter	.05
99	Jason Schmidt	.05
100	Greg Maddux	1.50
101	Kevin Tapani	.05
102	Charles Johnson	.05
103	Derrek Lee	.50
104	Pete Harnisch	.05
105	Dante Bichette	.05
106	Scott Brosius	.05
107	Mike Caruso	.05
108	Eddie Taubensee	.05
109	Jeff Fassero	.05
110	Marquis Grissom	.05
111	Jose Hernandez	.05
112	Chan Ho Park	.05
113	Wally Joyner	.05
114	Bobby Estalella	.05
115	Pedro Martinez	1.00
116	Shawn Estes	.05
117	Walt Weiss	.05
118	John Mabry	.05
119	Brian Johnson	.05
120	Jim Thome	.65
121	Bill Spiers	.05
122	John Olerud	.05
123	Jeff King	.05
124	Tim Belcher	.05
125	John Wetteland	.05
126	Tony Gwynn	1.50
127	Brady Anderson	.05
128	Randy Winn	.05
129	Devon White	.05
130	Eric Karros	.05
131	Kevin Millwood	.05
132	Andy Benes	.05
133	Andy Ashby	.05
134	Ron Comer	.05
135	Juan Gonzalez	.50
136	Randy Johnson	1.00
137	Aaron Sele	.05
138	Edgardo Alfonzo	.05
139	B.J. Surhoff	.05
140	Jose Vizcaino	.05
141	Chad Moeller RC (Prospect)	.75
142	Mike Zwicka RC (Prospect)	.50
143	Angel Pena (Prospect)	.50
144	Nick Johnson RC (Prospect)	2.00
145	Giuseppe Chiaramonte RC (Prospect)	.50
146	Kit Pellow RC (Prospect)	.50
147	Clayton Andrews RC (Prospect)	.50
148	Jerry Hairston Jr. RC (Prospect)	.75
149	Jason Tyner RC (Draft Pick)	.50
150	Chip Ambres RC (Draft Pick)	.50
151	Pat Burrell RC (Draft Pick)	2.00
152	Josh McKinley RC (Draft Pick)	.75
153	Choo Freeman RC (Draft Pick)	.75
154	Rick Elder RC (Draft Pick)	.50
155	Eric Valent RC (Draft Pick)	.75
156	Jeff Winchester RC (Draft Pick)	.50
157	Mike Nannini RC (Draft Pick)	.50
158	Mamon Tucker RC (Draft Pick)	.50
159	Nate Bump RC (Draft Pick)	.50
160	Andy Brown RC (Draft Pick)	.50
161	Troy Glaus (Future Star)	1.00
162	Adrian Beltre (Future Star)	.45
163	Mitch Meluskey (Future Star)	.05
164	Alex Gonzalez (Future Star)	.05
165	George Lombard (Future Star)	.05
166	Eric Chavez (Future Star)	.25
167	Ruben Mateo (Future Star)	.05
168	Calvin Pickering (Future Star)	.05
169	Gabe Kapler (Future Star)	.05
170	Bruce Chen (Future Star)	.05
171	Darin Erstad	.15
172	Sandy Alomar	.05
173	Miguel Cairo	.05
174	Jason Kendall	.05
175	Cal Ripken Jr.	2.50
176	Darryl Kile	.05
177	David Cone	.05
178	Mike Sweeney	.05
179	Royce Clayton	.05
180	Curt Schilling	.25
181	Barry Larkin	.05
182	Eric Milton	.05
183	Ellis Burks	.05
184	A.J. Hinch	.05
185	Garret Anderson	.05
186	Sean Bergman	.05
187	Shannon Stewart	.05
188	Bernard Gilkey	.05
189	Jeff Blauser	.05
190	Andruw Jones	1.00
191	Omar Daal	.05
192	Jeff Kent	.05
193	Mark Kotsay	.05
194	Dave Burba	.05
195	Bobby Higginson	.05
196	Hideki Irabu	.05
197	Jamie Moyer	.05
198	Doug Glanville	.05
199	Quinton McCracken	.05
200	Ken Griffey Jr.	1.75
201	Mike Lieberthal	.05
202	Carl Everett	.05
203	Omar Vizquel	.05
204	Mike Lansing	.05
205	Manny Ramirez	1.00
206	Ryan Klesko	.05
207	Jeff Montgomery	.05
208	Chad Curtis	.05
209	Rick Helling	.05
210	Justin Thompson	.05
211	Tom Goodwin	.05
212	Todd Dunwoody	.05
213	Kevin Young	.05
214	Tony Saunders	.05
215	Gary Sheffield	.45
216	Jaret Wright	.05
217	Quilvio Veras	.05
218	Marty Cordova	.05
219	Tino Martinez	.05
220	Scott Rolen	.75
221	Fernando Tatis	.05
222	Damion Easley	.05
223	Aramis Ramirez	.05
224	Brad Radke	.05
225	Nomar Garciaparra	1.50
226	Magglio Ordonez	.05
227	Andy Pettitte	.20
228	David Ortiz	.45
229	Todd Jones	.05
230	Larry Walker	.05
231	Tim Wakefield	.05
232	Jose Guillen	.05
233	Gregg Olson	.05
234	Ricky Gutierrez	.05
235	Todd Walker	.05
236	Abraham Nunez	.05
237	Sean Casey	.15
238	Greg Norton	.05
239	Bret Saberhagen	.05
240	Bernie Williams	.05
241	Tim Salmon	.05
242	Jason Giambi	.50
243	Fernando Vina	.05
244	Darrin Fletcher	.05
245	Greg Vaughn	.05
246	Dennis Reyes	.05
247	Hideo Nomo	.50
248	Reggie Sanders	.05
249	Mike Hampton	.05
250	Kerry Wood	.50
251	Ismael Valdes	.05
252	Pat Hentgen	.05
253	Scott Spiezio	.05
254	Chuck Finley	.05
255	Troy Glaus	.75
256	Bobby Jones	.05
257	Wayne Gomes	.05
258	Rondell White	.05
259	Todd Zeile	.05
260	Matt Williams	.05
261	Henry Rodriguez	.05
262	Matt Stairs	.05
263	Jose Valentin	.05
264	David Justice	.05
265	Javy Lopez	.05
266	Matt Morris	.05
267	Steve Trachsel	.05
268	Edgar Martinez	.05
269	Al Martin	.05
270	Ivan Rodriguez	.75
271	Carlos Delgado	.05
272	Mark Grace	.05
273	Ugueth Urbina	.05
274	Jay Buhner	.05
275	Mike Piazza	1.75
276	Rick Aguilera	.05
277	Javier Valentin	.05
278	Brian Anderson	.05
279	Cliff Floyd	.05
280	Barry Bonds	2.50
281	Troy O'Leary	.05
282	Seth Greisinger	.05
283	Mark Grudzielanek	.05
284	Jose Cruz Jr.	.05
285	Jeff Bagwell	1.00
286	John Smoltz	.05
287	Jeff Cirillo	.05
288	Richie Sexson	.05
289	Charles Nagy	.05
290	Pedro Martinez	1.00
291	Juan Encarnacion	.05
292	Phil Nevin	.05
293	Terry Steinbach	.05
294	Miguel Tejada	.15
295	Dan Wilson	.05
296	Chris Peters	.05
297	Brian Moehler	.05
298	Jason Christiansen	.05
299	Kelly Stinnett	.05
300	Dwight Gooden	.05
301	Randy Velarde	.05
302	Kirt Manwaring	.05
303	Jeff Abbott	.05
304	Dave Hollins	.05
305	Kerry Ligtenberg	.05
306	Aaron Boone	.05
307	Carlos Hernandez	.05
308	Mike DiFelice	.05
309	Brian Meadows	.05
310	Tim Bogar	.05
311	Greg Vaughn (Transaction)	.05
312	Brant Brown (Transaction)	.05
313	Steve Finley (Transaction)	.05
314	Bret Boone (Transaction)	.05
315	Albert Belle (Transaction)	.05
316	Robin Ventura (Transaction)	.05
317	Eric Davis (Transaction)	.05
318	Todd Hundley (Transaction)	.05
319	Jose Offerman (Transaction)	.05
320	Kevin Brown (Transaction)	.05
321	Denny Neagle (Transaction)	.05
322	Brian Jordan (Transaction)	.05
323	Brian Giles (Transaction)	.05
324	Bobby Bonilla (Transaction)	.05
325	Roberto Alomar (Transaction)	.20
326	Ken Caminiti (Transaction)	.05
327	Todd Stottlemyre (Transaction)	.05
328	Randy Johnson (Transaction)	1.00
329	Luis Gonzalez (Transaction)	.05
330	Rafael Palmeiro (Transaction)	.75
331	Devon White (Transaction)	.05
332	Will Clark (Transaction)	.05
333	Dean Palmer (Transaction)	.05
334	Gregg Jefferies (Transaction)	.05
335	Mo Vaughn (Transaction)	.05
336	Brad Lidge RC (Draft Pick)	2.00
337	Chris George RC (Draft Pick)	.75
338	Austin Kearns RC (Draft Pick)	1.50
339	Matt Belisle RC (Draft Pick)	.75
340	Nate Cornejo RC (Draft Pick)	.75
341	Matt Holliday RC (Draft Pick)	4.00
342	J.M. Gold RC (Draft Pick)	.50
343	Matt Roney RC (Draft Pick)	.50
344	Seth Etherton RC (Draft Pick)	.75
345	Adam Everett RC (Draft Pick)	.75
346	Marlon Anderson (Future Star)	.50
347	Ron Belliard (Future Star)	.50
348	Fernando Seguignol (Future Star)	.50
349	Michael Barrett (Future Star)	.50
350	Dernell Stenson (Future Star)	.50
351	Ryan Anderson (Future Star)	.50
352	Ramon Hernandez (Future Star)	.50
353	Jeremy Giambi (Future Star)	.50
354	Ricky Ledee (Future Star)	.50
355	Carlos Lee (Future Star)	1.00

First Day Issue

A parallel of the 355-card set inserted exclusively in retail packs, Series I (1-170) are serially numbered to 170 at a rate of 1:75 packs. Series 2 (171-355) are serially numbered to 200 and inserted at a rate of 1:60 packs.

	NM/M
Common Player:	2.00
Stars:	8X
SP Stars:	4X

One of a Kind

This insert set parallels the 355-card base set. Cards feature a mirrorboard look and are serially numbered to 150. Inserted exclusively in hobby packs, insertion rate for Series 1 is 1:53 and Series 2 is 1:48 packs.

	NM/M
Common Player:	2.00
Stars:	8X
SP Stars:	4X

Autographs

This 10-card autographed set was issued in Series 1 and 2 with five players signing in each series. Available exclusively in retail chains, Series 1 autographs were seeded 1:1,107 packs, while series 2 were inserted in every 877 packs. Each autograph is marked with the Topps Certified Autograph Issue stamp. Card numbers have an "SCA" prefix.

		NM/M
Common Player:		10.00
Inserted 1:1,107		
1	Alex Rodriguez	75.00
2	Chipper Jones	30.00
3	Barry Bonds	150.00
4	Tino Martinez	25.00
5	Ben Grieve	10.00
6	Juan Gonzalez	15.00
7	Vladimir Guerrero	30.00
8	Albert Belle	15.00
9	Kerry Wood	25.00
10	Todd Helton	20.00

Chrome

This 40-card set was inserted in Series 1 and 2 packs, with 1-20 in first series packs and 21-40 in Series 2. Chrome appropriately utilizes chromium technology. Card numbers have an "SCC" prefix.

		NM/M
Complete Set (40):		45.00
Common Player:		.50
Inserted 1:24		
Refractors:		2X
Inserted 1:96		
1	Nomar Garciaparra	2.00
2	Kerry Wood	1.00
3	Jeff Bagwell	1.50
4	Ivan Rodriguez	1.25
5	Albert Belle	.50
6	Gary Sheffield	1.00
7	Andruw Jones	1.50
8	Kevin Brown	.50
9	David Cone	.50
10	Darin Erstad	.75
11	Manny Ramirez	1.50
12	Larry Walker	.50
13	Mike Piazza	2.50
14	Cal Ripken Jr.	4.00
15	Pedro Martinez	1.50
16	Greg Vaughn	.50
17	Barry Bonds	4.00
18	Mo Vaughn	.50
19	Bernie Williams	.50
20	Ken Griffey Jr.	2.50
21	Alex Rodriguez	3.00
22	Chipper Jones	2.00
23	Ben Grieve	.50
24	Frank Thomas	1.50
25	Derek Jeter	4.00
26	Sammy Sosa	2.00
27	Mark McGwire	3.00
28	Vladimir Guerrero	1.50
29	Greg Maddux	2.00
30	Juan Gonzalez	.75
31	Troy Glaus	1.25
32	Adrian Beltre	1.25
33	Mitch Meluskey	.50
34	Alex Gonzalez	.50
35	George Lombard	.50
36	Eric Chavez	.75
37	Ruben Mateo	.50
38	Calvin Pickering	.50
39	Gabe Kapler	.50
40	Bruce Chen	.50

Co-Signers

Co-Signers feature two autographs on each card and also for the first time includes one level of four autographs per card. Co-Signers are grouped into categories A, B, C and D. Group A Co-Signers are autographed by four players, while B-D are signed by two players. Each card features the Topps Certified Autograph Issue stamp.

		NM/M
Common Group A:		90.00
Inserted 1:18,085		
Common Group B:		20.00
Inserted 1:9043		
Common Group C:		9.00
Inserted 1:3014		
Common Group D:		6.00
Inserted 1:254		
CS1	Ben Grieve, Richie Sexson/D	15.00
CS2	Todd Helton, Troy Glaus/D	50.00
CS3	Alex Rodriguez, Scott Rolen/D	85.00
CS4	Derek Jeter, Chipper Jones/D	150.00
CS5	Cliff Floyd, Eli Marrero/D	6.00
CS6	Jay Buhner, Kevin Young/D	8.00
CS7	Ben Grieve, Troy Glaus/C	40.00
CS8	Todd Helton, Richie Sexson/C	40.00
CS9	Alex Rodriguez, Chipper Jones/C	125.00
CS10	Derek Jeter, Scott Rolen/C	125.00
CS11	Cliff Floyd, Kevin Young/C	10.00
CS12	Jay Buhner, Eli Marrero/B	10.00
CS13	Ben Grieve, Todd Helton/B	50.00
CS14	Richie Sexson, Troy Glaus/B	40.00
CS15	Alex Rodriguez, Derek Jeter/B	350.00
CS16	Chipper Jones, Scott Rolen/B	150.00
CS17	Cliff Floyd, Jay Buhner/B	15.00
CS18	Eli Marrero, Kevin Young/B	20.00
CS19	Ben Grieve, Todd Helton, Richie Sexson, Troy Glaus/A	180.00
CS20	Alex Rodriguez, Derek Jeter, Chipper Jones, Scott Rolen/A	2,500
CS21	Cliff Floyd, Jay Buhner, Eli Marrero, Kevin Young/A	100.00
CS22	Edgardo Alfonzo, Jose Guillen/D	15.00
CS23	Mike Lowell, Ricardo Rincon/D	10.00
CS24	Juan Gonzalez, Vinny Castilla/D	20.00
CS25	Moises Alou, Roger Clemens/D	60.00
CS26	Scott Spezio, Tony Womack/D	10.00
CS27	Fernando Vina, Quilvio Veras/D	10.00
CS28	Edgardo Alfonzo, Ricardo Rincon/C	10.00
CS29	Jose Guillen, Mike Lowell/C	10.00
CS30	Juan Gonzalez, Moises Alou/C	25.00
CS31	Roger Clemens, Vinny Castilla/C	85.00
CS32	Scott Spezio, Fernando Vina/C	10.00
CS33	Tony Womack, Quilvio Veras/B	20.00
CS34	Edgardo Alfonzo, Mike Lowell/B	30.00
CS35	Jose Guillen, Ricardo Rincon/B	30.00
CS36	Juan Gonzalez, Roger Clemens/B	135.00
CS37	Moises Alou, Vinny Castilla/B	30.00
CS38	Scott Spezio, Quilvio Veras/B	20.00
CS39	Tony Womack, Fernando Vina/B	20.00
CS40	Edgardo Alfonzo, Jose Guillen, Mike Lowell, Ricardo Rincon/A	90.00
CS41	Juan Gonzalez, Moises Alou, Roger Clemens, Vinny Castilla/A	900.00
CS42	Scott Spezio, Tony Womack, Fernando Vina, Quilvio Veras/A	90.00

Never Compromise

Topps selected players who bring hard work and devotion to the field every game. The first 10 cards in the set are inserted in Series 1 packs while the remaining 10 are seeded in Series 2 at a rate of 1:12 packs.

		NM/M
Complete Set (20):		10.00
Common Player:		.25
Inserted 1:12		
NC1	Mark McGwire	1.00
NC2	Sammy Sosa	.65
NC3	Ken Griffey Jr.	.75
NC4	Greg Maddux	.65
NC5	Barry Bonds	1.50
NC6	Alex Rodriguez	1.00
NC7	Darin Erstad	.35
NC8	Roger Clemens	.65
NC9	Nomar Garciaparra	1.00
NC10	Derek Jeter	1.50
NC11	Cal Ripken Jr.	1.50
NC12	Mike Piazza	.75
NC13	Greg Vaughn	.25
NC14	Andres Galarraga	.25
NC15	Vinny Castilla	.25
NC16	Jeff Bagwell	.50
NC17	Chipper Jones	.65
NC18	Eric Chavez	.35
NC19	Orlando Hernandez	.25
NC20	Troy Glaus	.40

Printing Plates

Inserted only in Home Team Advantage boxes at a rate of approximately one per 175 packs were the actual aluminum plates used to print the fronts of the base cards. Unlike some printing plate issues, the plates used for the card backs were not inserted. Each card's plate can be found in four different colors: Cyan, magenta, yellow and black. Because of their unique nature, pricing of individual player's plates cannot be provided.

	NM/M
Common Player:	25.00

Triumvirate

Three of these inserts "fuse" together to form a set of three cards, forming a Triumvirate. 48 players, 24 from each series, are available in three different technologies, Luminous, Luminescent and Illuminator.

		NM/M
Complete Set (48):		75.00
Common Player:		.50
Inserted 1:36		
Luminescents:		1.5X
Inserted 1:144		
Illuminators:		2.5X
Inserted 1:288		
T1A	Greg Vaughn	.50
T1B	Ken Caminiti	.50
T1C	Tony Gwynn	2.50
T2A	Andruw Jones	2.00
T2B	Chipper Jones	2.50
T2C	Andres Galarraga	.50
T3A	Jay Buhner	.50
T3B	Ken Griffey Jr.	3.00
T3C	Alex Rodriguez	4.00
T4A	Derek Jeter	6.00
T4B	Tino Martinez	.50
T4C	Bernie Williams	.50
T5A	Brian Jordan	.50
T5B	Ray Lankford	.50
T5C	Mark McGwire	4.00
T6A	Jeff Bagwell	2.00
T6B	Craig Biggio	.50
T6C	Randy Johnson	1.50
T7A	Nomar Garciaparra	2.50
T7B	Pedro Martinez	2.00
T7C	Mo Vaughn	.50
T8A	Mark Grace	.50
T8B	Sammy Sosa	2.50
T8C	Kerry Wood	1.00
T9A	Alex Rodriguez	4.00
T9B	Nomar Garciaparra	2.50
T9C	Derek Jeter	6.00
T10A	Todd Helton	1.50
T10B	Travis Lee	.50
T10C	Pat Burrell	1.50
T11A	Greg Maddux	2.50
T11B	Kerry Wood	1.00
T11C	Tom Glavine	.75
T12A	Chipper Jones	2.50
T12B	Vinny Castilla	.50
T12C	Scott Rolen	1.50
T13A	Juan Gonzalez	1.00
T13B	Ken Griffey Jr.	3.00
T13C	Ben Grieve	.50
T14A	Sammy Sosa	3.00
T14B	Vladimir Guerrero	2.00
T14C	Barry Bonds	6.00
T15A	Frank Thomas	2.00
T15B	Jim Thome	1.50
T15C	Tino Martinez	.50
T16A	Mark McGwire	4.00
T16B	Andres Galarraga	.50
T16C	Jeff Bagwell	2.00

Video Replay

Utilizing lenticular technology, these inserts capture highlights, such as McGwire's 70th home run, from the '98 season. By tilting the card, successive images show the selected highlight almost come to life. Video Replays are in inserted in Series 2 packs at a rate of 1:12.

		NM/M
Complete Set (5):		4.50
Common Player:		.75
Inserted 1:12		
VR1	Mark McGwire	1.50
VR2	Sammy Sosa	1.00
VR3	Ken Griffey Jr.	1.25
VR4	Kerry Wood	.75
VR5	Alex Rodriguez	1.50

Photography

The photos used on some Stadium Club Series 1 cards was available as a special issue in the format of a framed 11" x 14" color photo. The borderless action photo could be ordered from a form found in TSC packs. With a $4 shipping charge, the initial cost per picture was $23.99. The numbers here are as given on the order form.

		NM/M
Complete Set (10):		200.00
Common Player:		20.00
1	Alex Rodriguez	20.00
65	Derek Jeter	20.00
66	Sammy Sosa	20.00
135	Juan Gonzalez	20.00
NC1	Mark McGwire	20.00
NC3	Ken Griffey Jr.	20.00
SCA5	Ben Grieve	20.00
SCC1	Nomar Garciaparra	20.00
SCC2	Kerry Wood	20.00
SCC13	Mike Piazza	20.00

2000 Stadium Club

Released in one series, the base set consists of 250 cards, embossed and printed on 20-pt. stock with silver holo-foil stamping. Card backs have a small photo, with the player's vital information and 1999 season statistical breakdown. The 20-card Draft Pick subset (#231-250) are short-printed, seeded 1:5 packs.

		NM/M
Complete Set (250):		80.00
Common Player:		.15
Common SP (201-250):		2.00
Inserted 1:5		
Pack (6):		1.50
Wax Box (24):		30.00
1	Nomar Garciaparra	1.25
2	Brian Jordan	.15
3	Mark Grace	.25
4	Jeromy Burnitz	.15
5	Shane Reynolds	.15
6	Alex Gonzalez	.15
7	Jose Offerman	.15
8	Orlando Hernandez	.15
9	Mike Caruso	.15
10	Tony Clark	.15
11	Sean Casey	.25
12	Johnny Damon	.25
13	Dante Bichette	.15
14	Kevin Young	.15
15	Juan Gonzalez	.75
16	Chipper Jones	1.00
17	Quilvio Veras	.15
18	Trevor Hoffman	.15
19	Roger Cedeno	.15
20	Ellis Burks	.15
21	Richie Sexson	.15
22	Gary Sheffield	.40
23	Delino DeShields	.15
24	Wade Boggs	1.00
25	Ray Lankford	.15
26	Kevin Appier	.15
27	Roy Halladay	.15
28	Harold Baines	.15
29	Todd Zeile	.15
30	Barry Larkin	.25
31	Ron Coomer	.15
32	Jorge Posada	.15
33	Magglio Ordonez	.15
34	Brian Giles	.15
35	Jeff Kent	.15
36	Henry Rodriguez	.15
37	Fred McGriff	.15
38	Shawn Green	.50
39	Derek Bell	.15
40	Ben Grieve	.15
41	Dave Nilsson	.15
42	Mo Vaughn	.15
43	Rondell White	.15
44	Doug Glanville	.15
45	Paul O'Neill	.15
46	Carlos Lee	.15
47	Vinny Castilla	.15
48	Mike Sweeney	.15
49	Rico Brogna	.15
50	Alex Rodriguez	1.50
51	Luis Castillo	.15
52	Kevin Brown	.15
53	Jose Vidro	.15
54	John Smoltz	.15
55	Garret Anderson	.15
56	Matt Stairs	.15
57	Omar Vizquel	.15
58	Tom Goodwin	.15
59	Scott Brosius	.15
60	Robin Ventura	.15
61	B.J. Surhoff	.15
62	Andy Ashby	.15
63	Chris Widger	.15
64	Tim Hudson	.40
65	Javy Lopez	.15
66	Tim Salmon	.25
67	Warren Morris	.15
68	John Wetteland	.15
69	Gabe Kapler	.15
70	Bernie Williams	.30
71	Rickey Henderson	.75
72	Andruw Jones	.75
73	Eric Young	.15
74	Bob Abreu	.15
75	David Cone	.15
76	Rusty Greer	.15
77	Ron Belliard	.15
78	Troy Glaus	.75
79	Mike Hampton	.15
80	Miguel Tejada	.30
81	Jeff Cirillo	.15
82	Todd Hundley	.15
83	Roberto Alomar	.40
84	Charles Johnson	.15
85	Rafael Palmeiro	.65
86	Doug Mientkiewicz	.15
87	Mariano Rivera	.25
88	Neifi Perez	.15
89	Jermaine Dye	.15
90	Ivan Rodriguez	.65
91	Jay Buhner	.15
92	Pokey Reese	.15
93	John Olerud	.15
94	Brady Anderson	.15
95	Manny Ramirez	.75
96	Keith Osik	.15
97	Mickey Morandini	.15
98	Matt Williams	.15
99	Eric Karros	.15
100	Ken Griffey Jr.	1.25
101	Bret Boone	.15
102	Ryan Klesko	.15
103	Craig Biggio	.15
104	John Jaha	.15
105	Vladimir Guerrero	.75
106	Devon White	.15
107	Tony Womack	.15
108	Marvin Benard	.15
109	Kenny Lofton	.15
110	Preston Wilson	.15
111	Al Leiter	.15
112	Reggie Sanders	.15
113	Scott Williamson	.15
114	Deivi Cruz	.15
115	Carlos Beltran	.50
116	Ray Durham	.15
117	Ricky Ledee	.15
118	Torii Hunter	.15
119	John Valentin	.15
120	Scott Rolen	.65
121	Jason Kendall	.15
122	Dave Martinez	.15
123	Jim Thome	.65
124	David Bell	.15
125	Jose Canseco	.45
126	Jose Lima	.15
127	Carl Everett	.15
128	Kevin Millwood	.15
129	Bill Spiers	.15
130	Omar Daal	.15
131	Miguel Cairo	.15
132	Mark Grudzielanek	.15
133	David Justice	.15
134	Russ Ortiz	.15
135	Mike Piazza	1.25
136	Brian Meadows	.15
137	Tony Gwynn	1.00
138	Cal Ripken Jr.	2.00
139	Kris Benson	.15
140	Larry Walker	.15
141	Cristian Guzman	.15
142	Tino Martinez	.25
143	Chris Singleton	.15
144	Lee Stevens	.15
145	Rey Ordonez	.15
146	Russ Davis	.15
147	J.T. Snow Jr.	.15
148	Luis Gonzalez	.25
149	Marquis Grissom	.15
150	Greg Maddux	1.00
151	Fernando Tatis	.15
152	Jason Giambi	.50
153	Carlos Delgado	.50
154	Joe McEwing	.15
155	Raul Mondesi	.15
156	Rich Aurilia	.15
157	Alex Fernandez	.15
158	Albert Belle	.25
159	Pat Meares	.15
160	Mike Lieberthal	.15
161	Mike Cameron	.15
162	Juan Encarnacion	.15
163	Chuck Knoblauch	.15
164	Pedro Martinez	.75
165	Randy Johnson	.75
166	Shannon Stewart	.15
167	Jeff Bagwell	.75
168	Edgar Renteria	.15
169	Barry Bonds	2.00
170	Steve Finley	.15
171	Brian Hunter	.15
172	Tom Glavine	.35
173	Mark Kotsay	.15
174	Tony Fernandez	.15
175	Sammy Sosa	1.25
176	Geoff Jenkins	.15
177	Adrian Beltre	.15
178	Jay Bell	.15
179	Mike Bordick	.15
180	Ed Sprague	.15
181	Dave Roberts	.15
182	Greg Vaughn	.15
183	Brian Daubach	.15
184	Damion Easley	.15
185	Carlos Febles	.15
186	Kevin Tapani	.15
187	Frank Thomas	.75
188	Roger Clemens	1.00
189	Mike Benjamin	.15
190	Curt Schilling	.40
191	Edgardo Alfonzo	.15
192	Mike Mussina	.40
193	Todd Helton	.75
194	Todd Jones	.15
195	Dean Palmer	.15
196	John Flaherty	.15
197	Derek Jeter	2.00
198	Todd Walker	.15
199	Brad Ausmus	.15
200	Mark McGwire	1.50
201	Erubiel Durazo	2.00
202	Nick Johnson (Future Stars)	2.50
203	Ruben Mateo (Future Stars)	2.00
204	Lance Berkman (Future Stars)	2.50
205	Pat Burrell (Future Stars)	3.00
206	Pablo Ozuna (Future Stars)	2.00
207	Roosevelt Brown (Future Stars)	2.00
208	Alfonso Soriano (Future Stars)	4.00
209	A.J. Burnett (Future Stars)	2.00
210	Rafael Furcal (Future Stars)	2.00
211	Scott Morgan (Future Stars)	2.00
212	Adam Piatt (Future Stars)	2.00
213	Dee Brown (Future Stars)	2.00
214	Corey Patterson (Future Stars)	2.50
215	Mickey Lopez (Future Stars)	2.00
216	Rob Ryan (Future Stars)	2.00

#	Player	Price
217	Sean Burroughs (Future Stars)	2.00
218	Jack Cust (Future Stars)	2.00
219	John Patterson (Future Stars)	2.00
220	Kit Pellow (Future Stars)	2.00
221	Chad Hermansen (Future Stars)	2.00
222	Daryle Ward (Future Stars)	2.00
223	Jayson Werth (Future Stars)	2.00
224	Jason Standridge (Future Stars)	2.00
225	Mark Mulder (Future Stars)	2.50
226	Peter Bergeron (Future Stars)	2.00
227	Willi Mo Pena (Future Stars)	2.00
228	Aramis Ramirez (Future Stars)	2.00
229	John Sneed RC (Future Stars)	2.00
230	Wilton Veras (Future Stars)	2.00
231	Josh Hamilton (Draft Picks)	2.00
232	Eric Munson (Draft Picks)	2.00
233	Bobby Bradley RC (Draft Picks)	2.00
234	Larry Bigbie RC (Draft Picks)	2.00
235	B.J. Garbe RC (Draft Picks)	2.00
236	Brett Myers RC (Draft Picks)	6.00
237	Jason Stumm RC (Draft Picks)	2.00
238	Corey Myers RC (Draft Picks)	2.00
239	Ryan Christianson RC (Draft Picks)	2.00
240	David Walling (Draft Picks)	2.00
241	Josh Girdley (Draft Picks)	2.00
242	Omar Ortiz (Draft Picks)	2.00
243	Jason Jennings (Draft Picks)	2.00
244	Kyle Snyder RC (Draft Picks)	2.00
245	Jay Gehrke (Draft Picks)	2.00
246	Mike Paradis RC (Draft Picks)	2.00
247	Chance Caple RC (Draft Picks)	2.00
248	Ben Christiansen RC (Draft Picks)	2.00
249	Brad Baker RC (Draft Picks)	2.00
250	Rick Asadoorian RC (Draft Picks)	2.00
---	Checklist (Nomar Garciaparra)	.25

First Day Issue

Identifiable by the "First Day Issue" stamp, this retail exclusive parallel set is limited to 150 sequentially numbered sets.

Stars:	5-10X
Short-Prints:	2-3X
Production 150 Sets R	

One of a Kind

This 250-card set is a parallel to the base set, is hobby exclusive and limited to 150 serially numbered sets.

Stars:	5-10X
Short-Prints:	2-3X
Production 150 Sets H	

Bats of Brilliance

This insert set focused on 10 of baseball's top hitters.

Card fronts have a silver foil border over a black backdrop. Backs highlight the player's statistics from 1999 and his career statistics. They are numbered with a "BB" prefix and are seeded 1:12 packs. A die-cut parallel is also randomly seeded 1:60 packs.

		NM/M
Complete Set (10):		10.00
Common Player:		.50
Inserted 1:12		
1	Mark McGwire	2.50
2	Sammy Sosa	1.50
3	Jose Canseco	.50
4	Jeff Bagwell	.75
5	Ken Griffey Jr.	1.50
6	Nomar Garciaparra	1.50
7	Mike Piazza	1.50
8	Alex Rodriguez	2.50
9	Vladimir Guerrero	.75
10	Chipper Jones	1.50

Capture The Action

This 20-card set is divided into categories of Rookies, Stars, and Legends. These were seeded 1:12 packs and have the insert title, player name and logo stamped in silver foil. They are numbered with a "CA" prefix on the backs. A hobby-exclusive parallel version was also available, serially numbered to 100 and featuring a replica of the actual photo slide used to create the card.

		NM/M
Complete Set (20):		20.00
Common Player:		.50
Inserted 1:12		
Game View Stars:		3-6X
Production 100 Sets H		
1	Josh Hamilton	.50
2	Pat Burrell	.75
3	Erubiel Durazo	1.00
4	Alfonso Soriano	1.00
5	A.J. Burnett	.50
6	Alex Rodriguez	3.00
7	Sean Casey	.50
8	Derek Jeter	4.00
9	Vladimir Guerrero	1.00
10	Nomar Garciaparra	2.00
11	Mike Piazza	2.00
12	Ken Griffey Jr.	2.00
13	Sammy Sosa	2.00
14	Juan Gonzalez	1.00
15	Mark McGwire	3.00
16	Ivan Rodriguez	.75
17	Barry Bonds	4.00
18	Wade Boggs	1.50
19	Tony Gwynn	1.50
20	Cal Ripken Jr.	4.00

Co-Signers

This 15-card hobby exclusive set features two signatures on the card front, with the Topps "Certified Autograph Issue" stamp as well as the

Topps 3M sticker to ensure its authenticity. The cards are divided into three groupings with the following odds: Group A - 1:10,184; Group B - 1:5,092; and Group C - 1:508.

		NM/M
Common Card:		15.00
Group A 1:10,184		
Group B 1:5,092		
Group C 1:508		
1	Alex Rodriguez, Derek Jeter	400.00
2	Derek Jeter, Omar Vizquel	150.00
3	Alex Rodriguez, Rey Ordonez	150.00
4	Derek Jeter, Rey Ordonez	150.00
5	Omar Vizquel, Alex Rodriguez	100.00
6	Rey Ordonez, Omar Vizquel	15.00
7	Wade Boggs, Robin Ventura	30.00
8	Randy Johnson, Mike Mussina	90.00
9	Pat Burrell, Magglio Ordonez	40.00
10	Chad Hermansen, Pat Burrell	20.00
11	Magglio Ordonez, Chad Hermansen	20.00
12	Josh Hamilton, Corey Myers	20.00
13	B.J. Garbe, Josh Hamilton	20.00
14	Corey Myers, B.J. Garbe	15.00
15	Tino Martinez, Fred McGriff	60.00

Lone Star Signatures

This 16-card autographed set features the Topps "Certified Autograph Issue" stamp to verify its authenticity. The cards are divided into four groupings with the following odds: Group 1, 1:1,979 hobby; Group 2, 1:2,374 hobby; Group 3, 1:1,979; and Group 4, 1:424 hobby.

		NM/M
Common Player:		8.00
Group 1 1:1,979		
Group 2 1:2,374		
Group 3 1:1,979		
Group 4 1:424		
1	Derek Jeter	100.00
2	Alex Rodriguez	100.00
3	Wade Boggs	25.00
4	Robin Ventura	15.00
5	Randy Johnson	60.00
6	Mike Mussina	25.00
7	Tino Martinez	35.00
8	Fred McGriff	25.00
9	Omar Vizquel	15.00
10	Rey Ordonez	8.00
11	Pat Burrell	15.00
12	Chad Hermansen	8.00
13	Magglio Ordonez	10.00
14	Josh Hamilton	20.00
15	Corey Myers	8.00
16	B.J. Garbe	8.00

Onyx Extreme

This 10-card set features black styrene technology with silver foil stamping and are

seeded 1:12 packs. A die-cut parallel is also randomly inserted 1:60 hobby packs.

		NM/M
Complete Set (10):		10.00
Common Player:		.40
Inserted 1:12		
Die-Cuts:		2-3X
Inserted 1:60		
1	Ken Griffey Jr.	1.50
2	Derek Jeter	3.00
3	Vladimir Guerrero	1.00
4	Nomar Garciaparra	1.50
5	Barry Bonds	3.00
6	Alex Rodriguez	2.50
7	Sammy Sosa	1.50
8	Ivan Rodriguez	.75
9	Larry Walker	.40
10	Andruw Jones	1.50

Printing Plates

Inserted only in Home Team boxes at a rate of approximately one per 100 packs were the actual aluminum plates used to print the fronts of the base cards. Unlike some printing plate issues, the plates used for the card backs were not inserted. Each card's plate can be found in four different colors: Cyan, magenta, yellow and black. Because of their unique nature, pricing of individual player's plates cannot be provided.

	NM/M
Common Player:	60.00

Scenes

Available only in hobby and Home Team Advantage boxes, these broaden the view of the featured player and have a format sized 2 1/2" x 4 11/16". These are boxtoppers, seeded one per box.

		NM/M
Complete Set (9):		10.00
Common Player:		.50
Inserted 1:Box		
1	Mark McGwire	2.50
2	Alex Rodriguez	2.50
3	Cal Ripken Jr.	3.00
4	Sammy Sosa	3.00
5	Derek Jeter	3.00
6	Ken Griffey Jr.	2.00
7	Raul Mondesi	.50
8	Chipper Jones	1.50
9	Nomar Garciaparra	3.00

Souvenirs

These memorabilia inserts feature die-cut technology that incorporates an actual piece of a game-used uniform. Each card back contains the Topps 3M sticker to ensure its authenticity. The insert rate is 2:339 hobby packs and 2:136 HTA packs.

		NM/M
Complete Set (3):		35.00
Common Player:		8.00
Inserted 2:339		
1	Wade Boggs	20.00
2	Randy Johnson	20.00
3	Robin Ventura	8.00

3 X 3

Ten groups of three top-notch players are arranged by position on three different laser-cut technologies. The three players can be "fused" together to form one oversize card. The three versions are Luminous (1:18), Luminescent (1:72) and Illuminator (1:144).

		NM/M
Complete Set (30):		40.00
Common Player:		.75
Inserted 1:18		
Luminescent:		2X
Inserted 1:72		
Illuminator:		3-4X
Inserted 1:144		
1A	Randy Johnson	1.50
1B	Pedro Martinez	1.50
1C	Greg Maddux	2.00
2A	Mike Piazza	3.00
2B	Ivan Rodriguez	1.25
2C	Mike Lieberthal	.75
3A	Mark McGwire	4.50
3B	Jeff Bagwell	1.50
3C	Sean Casey	.75
4A	Craig Biggio	.75
4B	Roberto Alomar	1.00
4C	Jay Bell	.75
5A	Chipper Jones	2.00
5B	Matt Williams	.75
5C	Robin Ventura	.75
6A	Alex Rodriguez	4.50
6B	Derek Jeter	6.00
6C	Nomar Garciaparra	3.00
7A	Barry Bonds	6.00
7B	Luis Gonzalez	1.00
7C	Dante Bichette	1.00
8A	Ken Griffey Jr.	3.00
8B	Bernie Williams	1.50
8C	Andruw Jones	1.50
9A	Manny Ramirez	1.50
9B	Sammy Sosa	3.00
9C	Juan Gonzalez	1.50
10A	Jose Canseco	1.00
10B	Frank Thomas	1.50
10C	Rafael Palmeiro	1.50

2000 Stadium Club Chrome

The 250-card base set uses the same photography and is identical to 2000 Stadium Club besides the utilization of Chromium technology. Five-card packs had a $4 SRP.

	NM/M
Complete Set (250):	40.00
Common Player:	.15
Pack (11):	1.50
Wax Box (36):	40.00
1	Nomar Garciaparra	1.50
2	Brian Jordan	.15
3	Mark Grace	.25
4	Jeromy Burnitz	.15
5	Shane Reynolds	.15
6	Alex Gonzalez	.15
7	Jose Offerman	.15
8	Orlando Hernandez	.15
9	Mike Caruso	.15
10	Tony Clark	.15
11	Sean Casey	.25
12	Johnny Damon	.25
13	Dante Bichette	.15
14	Kevin Young	.15
15	Juan Gonzalez	.75
16	Chipper Jones	1.00
17	Quivio Veras	.15
18	Trevor Hoffman	.15
19	Roger Cedeno	.15
20	Ellis Burks	.15
21	Richie Sexson	.15
22	Gary Sheffield	.45
23	Delino DeShields	.15
24	Wade Boggs	1.00
25	Ray Lankford	.15
26	Kevin Appier	.15
27	Roy Halladay	.15
28	Harold Baines	.15
29	Todd Zeile	.15
30	Barry Larkin	.15
31	Ron Coomer	.15
32	Jorge Posada	.15
33	Magglio Ordonez	.15
34	Brian Giles	.15
35	Jeff Kent	.15
36	Henry Rodriguez	.15
37	Fred McGriff	.15
38	Shawn Green	.50
39	Derek Bell	.15
40	Ben Grieve	.15
41	Dave Nilsson	.15
42	Mo Vaughn	.15
43	Rondell White	.15
44	Doug Glanville	.15
45	Paul O'Neill	.15
46	Carlos Lee	.15
47	Vinny Castilla	.15
48	Mike Sweeney	.15
49	Rico Brogna	.15
50	Alex Rodriguez	2.50
51	Luis Castillo	.15
52	Kevin Brown	.15
53	Jose Vidro	.15
54	John Smoltz	.15
55	Garret Anderson	.15
56	Matt Stairs	.15
57	Omar Vizquel	.15
58	Tom Goodwin	.15
59	Scott Brosius	.15
60	Robin Ventura	.15
61	B.J. Surhoff	.15
62	Andy Ashby	.15
63	Chris Widger	.15
64	Tim Hudson	.40
65	Javy Lopez	.15
66	Tim Salmon	.25
67	Warren Morris	.15
68	John Wetteland	.15
69	Gabe Kapler	.15
70	Bernie Williams	.25

#	Player	Price
10	Pedro Martinez	2.00
11	Jeff Bagwell	1.50
12	Barry Bonds	6.00
13	Sammy Sosa	3.00
14	Derek Jeter	6.00
15	Mark McGwire	4.50
16	Erubiel Durazo	1.00
17	Nick Johnson	1.00
18	Pat Burrell	1.00
19	Alfonso Soriano	1.50
20	Adam Piatt	1.00

Chrome Preview

This 20-card set features Topps Chromium technology, previewing the debut of Stadium Club Chrome, a later release. The insertion odds are 1:24 packs. A Refractor parallel version is also available seeded 1:120 packs.

		NM/M
Complete Set (20):		40.00
Common Player:		1.00
Inserted 1:24		
Refractors:		2-3X
Inserted 1:120		
1	Nomar Garciaparra	3.00
2	Juan Gonzalez	2.00
3	Chipper Jones	2.00
4	Alex Rodriguez	4.50
5	Ivan Rodriguez	1.25
6	Manny Ramirez	1.50
7	Ken Griffey Jr.	3.00
8	Vladimir Guerrero	1.50
9	Mike Piazza	3.00

71	Rickey Henderson	.75
72	Andruw Jones	.75
73	Eric Young	.15
74	Bobby Abreu	.15
75	David Cone	.15
76	Rusty Greer	.15
77	Ron Belliard	.15
78	Troy Glaus	.75
79	Mike Hampton	.15
80	Miguel Tejada	.30
81	Jeff Cirillo	.15
82	Todd Hundley	.15
83	Roberto Alomar	.35
84	Charles Johnson	.15
85	Rafael Palmeiro	.65
86	Doug Mientkiewicz	.15
87	Mariano Rivera	.25
88	Neifi Perez	.15
89	Jermaine Dye	.15
90	Ivan Rodriguez	.65
91	Jay Buhner	.15
92	Pokey Reese	.15
93	John Olerud	.15
94	Brady Anderson	.15
95	Manny Ramirez	.75
96	Keith Osik	.15
97	Mickey Morandini	.15
98	Matt Williams	.15
99	Eric Karros	.15
100	Ken Griffey Jr.	1.50
101	Bret Boone	.15
102	Ryan Klesko	.15
103	Craig Biggio	.15
104	John Jaha	.15
105	Vladimir Guerrero	.75
106	Devon White	.15
107	Tony Womack	.15
108	Marvin Benard	.15
109	Kenny Lofton	.15
110	Preston Wilson	.15
111	Al Leiter	.15
112	Reggie Sanders	.15
113	Scott Williamson	.15
114	Deivi Cruz	.15
115	Carlos Beltran	.50
116	Ray Durham	.15
117	Ricky Ledee	.15
118	Torii Hunter	.15
119	John Valentin	.15
120	Scott Rolen	.65
121	Jason Kendall	.15
122	Dave Martinez	.15
123	Jim Thome	.65
124	David Bell	.15
125	Jose Canseco	.50
126	Jose Lima	.15
127	Carl Everett	.15
128	Kevin Millwood	.15
129	Bill Spiers	.15
130	Omar Daal	.15
131	Miguel Cairo	.15
132	Mark Grudzielanek	.15
133	David Justice	.15
134	Russ Ortiz	.15
135	Mike Piazza	1.50
136	Brian Meadows	.15
137	Tony Gwynn	1.00
138	Cal Ripken Jr.	3.00
139	Kris Benson	.15
140	Larry Walker	.15
141	Cristian Guzman	.15
142	Tino Martinez	.15
143	Chris Singleton	.15
144	Lee Stevens	.15
145	Rey Ordonez	.15
146	Russ Davis	.15
147	J.T. Snow Jr.	.15
148	Luis Gonzalez	.25
149	Marquis Grissom	.15
150	Greg Maddux	1.00
151	Fernando Tatis	.15
152	Jason Giambi	.50
153	Carlos Delgado	.50
154	Joe McEwing	.15
155	Raul Mondesi	.15
156	Rich Aurilia	.15
157	Alex Fernandez	.15
158	Albert Belle	.25
159	Pat Meares	.15
160	Mike Lieberthal	.15
161	Mike Cameron	.15
162	Juan Encarnacion	.15
163	Chuck Knoblauch	.15
164	Pedro Martinez	.75
165	Randy Johnson	.75
166	Shannon Stewart	.15
167	Jeff Bagwell	.75
168	Edgar Renteria	.15
169	Barry Bonds	3.00
170	Steve Finley	.15
171	Brian Hunter	.15
172	Tom Glavine	.40
173	Mark Kotsay	.15
174	Tony Fernandez	.15
175	Sammy Sosa	1.50
176	Geoff Jenkins	.15
177	Adrian Beltre	.45
178	Jay Bell	.15
179	Mike Bordick	.15
180	Ed Sprague	.15
181	Dave Roberts	.15
182	Greg Vaughn	.15
183	Brian Daubach	.15
184	Damion Easley	.15
185	Carlos Febles	.15
186	Kevin Tapani	.15
187	Frank Thomas	.75
188	Roger Clemens	1.25

189	Mike Benjamin	.15
190	Curt Schilling	.40
191	Edgardo Alfonzo	.15
192	Mike Mussina	.45
193	Todd Helton	.75
194	Todd Jones	.15
195	Dean Palmer	.15
196	John Flaherty	.15
197	Derek Jeter	3.00
198	Todd Walker	.15
199	Brad Ausmus	.15
200	Mark McGwire	2.50
201	Erubiel Durazo	.15
	(Future Stars)	
202	Nick Johnson	.15
	(Future Stars)	
203	Ruben Mateo	.15
	(Future Stars)	
204	Lance Berkman	.15
	(Future Stars)	
205	Pat Burrell	.65
	(Future Stars)	
206	Pablo Ozuna	.15
	(Future Stars)	
207	Roosevelt Brown	.15
	(Future Stars)	
208	Alfonso Soriano	1.00
	(Future Stars)	
209	A.J. Burnett	.15
	(Future Stars)	
210	Rafael Furcal	.15
	(Future Stars)	
211	Scott Morgan	.15
	(Future Stars)	
212	Adam Piatt	.15
	(Future Stars)	
213	Dee Brown	.15
	(Future Stars)	
214	Corey Patterson	.15
	(Future Stars)	
215	Mickey Lopez	.15
	(Future Stars)	
216	Rob Ryan	.15
	(Future Stars)	
217	Sean Burroughs	.15
	(Future Stars)	
218	Jack Cust	.15
	(Future Stars)	
219	John Patterson	.15
	(Future Stars)	
220	Kit Pellow	.15
	(Future Stars)	
221	Chad Hermansen	.15
	(Future Stars)	
222	Daryle Ward	.15
	(Future Stars)	
223	Jayson Werth	.15
	(Future Stars)	
224	Jason Standridge	.15
	(Future Stars)	
225	Mark Mulder	.15
	(Future Stars)	
226	Peter Bergeron	.15
	(Future Stars)	
227	Willi Mo Pena	.15
	(Future Stars)	
228	Aramis Ramirez	.15
	(Future Stars)	
229	John Sneed	.15
	(Future Stars)	
230	Wilton Veras	.15
	(Future Stars)	
231	Josh Hamilton	.15
	(Draft Picks)	
232	Eric Munson	.15
	(Draft Picks)	
233	Bobby Bradley RC	1.00
	(Draft Picks)	
234	Larry Bigbie RC	1.00
	(Draft Picks)	
235	B.J. Garbe RC	1.00
	(Draft Picks)	
236	Brett Myers RC	4.00
	(Draft Picks)	
237	Jason Stumm RC	1.00
	(Draft Picks)	
238	Corey Myers RC	1.00
	(Draft Picks)	
239	Ryan Christianson RC	1.00
	(Draft Picks)	
240	David Walling	.15
	(Draft Picks)	
241	Josh Girdley	.15
	(Draft Picks)	
242	Omar Ortiz (Draft Picks)	.15
243	Jason Jennings	.15
	(Draft Picks)	
244	Kyle Snyder	.15
	(Draft Picks)	
245	Jay Gehrke	.15
	(Draft Picks)	
246	Mike Paradis	.15
	(Draft Picks)	
247	Chance Caple RC	1.00
	(Draft Picks)	
248	Ben Christensen RC	1.00
	(Draft Picks)	
249	Brad Baker RC	1.00
	(Draft Picks)	
250	Rick Asadoorian RC	1.00
	(Draft Picks)	

Refractor

A parallel to the 250-card base set these utilize Refractor technology and have a mirror

sheen to them when held up to a light source. "Refractor" is also written under the card number on the card back. Refractors are seeded 1:12 packs.

Stars:	2-4X
Rookies:	1-2X
Inserted 1:12	

First Day Issue

A parallel to the 250-card base set. Card fronts are identical besides "First Day Issue" printed three times over the player name and Stadium Club Chrome logo. Card backs are serial numbered in an edition of 100. A Refractor First Day Issue parallel is also randomly inserted, limited to 25 serial-numbered sets.

Stars:	4-8X
Rookies:	1-3X
Production 100 Sets	
Refractor:	25-40X
Rookies:	5-10X
Production 25 Sets	

Capture The Action

This 20-card set is divided into three groups: Rookies, Stars and Legends. Card backs are numbered with a "CA" prefix. These are found 1:18 packs. A Refractor parallel version is also randomly seeded 1:90 packs and also have "Refractor" written under the card number on the back.

	NM/M
Complete Set (20):	40.00
Common Player:	1.00
Inserted 1:18	
Refractors:	2-3X
Inserted 1:90	
1 Josh Hamilton	1.00
2 Pat Burrell	1.50
3 Erubiel Durazo	1.00
4 Alfonso Soriano	1.50
5 A.J. Burnett	1.00
6 Alex Rodriguez	5.00
7 Sean Casey	1.00

8	Derek Jeter	6.00
9	Vladimir Guerrero	1.50
10	Nomar Garciaparra	3.00
11	Mike Piazza	3.00
12	Ken Griffey Jr.	3.00
13	Sammy Sosa	3.00
14	Juan Gonzalez	1.50
15	Mark McGwire	5.00
16	Ivan Rodriguez	1.50
17	Barry Bonds	6.00
18	Wade Boggs	2.00
19	Tony Gwynn	2.00
20	Cal Ripken Jr.	6.00

Clear Shots

Printed on a clear, acetate stock this 10-card insert set will depict the front of the player on the card front and the back on the card back. Card backs are numbered with a "CS" prefix. Clear Shots are inserted 1:24 packs. A die-cut Refractor parallel version is also randomly seeded 1:120 packs.

	NM/M
Complete Set (10):	10.00
Common Player:	.50
Inserted 1:24	
Refractor:	2-3X
Inserted 1:120	
1 Derek Jeter	4.00
2 Bernie Williams	.50
3 Roger Clemens	2.50
4 Chipper Jones	2.00
5 Greg Maddux	2.00
6 Andruw Jones	1.00
7 Juan Gonzalez	1.00
8 Manny Ramirez	1.00
9 Ken Griffey Jr.	3.00
10 Josh Hamilton	.50

Eyes of the Game

Printed on a clear, acetate stock this 10-card set focuses on the facial expression of the featured player. Two images are on the front with the background image a close-up shot of the player's facial expression. These were seeded 1:16. Card backs are numbered with an "EG" prefix. A Refractor parallel is randomly inserted in 1:80 packs and has "Refractor" written under the card number on the back.

	NM/M
Complete Set (10):	10.00
Common Player:	.50
Inserted 1:16	
Refractors:	2-3X
Inserted 1:80	
1 Randy Johnson	1.00
2 Mike Piazza	1.50
3 Nomar Garciaparra	1.50
4 Mark McGwire	2.50
5 Alex Rodriguez	2.50
6 Derek Jeter	3.00
7 Tony Gwynn	1.00
8 Sammy Sosa	1.50
9 Larry Walker	.50
10 Ken Griffey Jr.	1.50

True Colors

This 10-card set focuses on players Topps deemed that performed best when the game's on the line. These were inserted 1:32 and are numbered with a "TC" prefix on the card back. A Refractor parallel is randomly inserted 1:160 packs.

	NM/M
Complete Set (10):	15.00
Common Player:	1.00
Inserted 1:32	
Refractors:	2-3X
Inserted 1:160	
1 Sammy Sosa	2.00
2 Nomar Garciaparra	2.00
3 Alex Rodriguez	3.00
4 Derek Jeter	4.00
5 Mark McGwire	3.00
6 Chipper Jones	1.50
7 Mike Piazza	2.00
8 Ken Griffey Jr.	2.00
9 Manny Ramirez	1.00
10 Vladimir Guerrero	1.00

Visionaries

This 20-card set spotlights young prospects who are deemed destined for stardom. Card backs are numbered with a "V" prefix. These are found 1:18 packs. A Refractor parallel version is also seeded 1:90 packs. "Refractor" is written under the card number on the back.

	NM/M
Complete Set (20):	17.50
Common Player:	1.00
Inserted 1:18	
Refractors:	2X
Inserted 1:90	
1 Alfonso Soriano	3.00
2 Josh Hamilton	1.00
3 A.J. Burnett	1.50
4 Pat Burrell	2.50
5 Ruben Salazar	1.00
6 Aaron Rowand	1.00
7 Adam Piatt	1.00
8 Nick Johnson	1.00
9 Rafael Furcal	1.00
10 Jack Cust	1.00
11 Corey Patterson	1.00
12 Sean Burroughs	1.50
13 Pablo Ozuna	1.00
14 Dee Brown	1.00
15 John Patterson	1.00
16 Willi Mo Pena	1.00
17 Mark Mulder	1.00
18 Eric Munson	1.00
19 Alex Escobar	1.00
20 Rob Ryan	1.00

2001 Stadium Club

	NM/M
Complete Set (200):	65.00
Common Player:	.15
Common SP:	1.50
Inserted 1:6	
Pack (7):	2.00
Box (24):	35.00

1	Nomar Garciaparra	1.25
2	Chipper Jones	1.00
3	Jeff Bagwell	.75
4	Chad Kreuter	.15
5	Randy Johnson	.75
6	Mike Hampton	.15
7	Barry Larkin	.15
8	Bernie Williams	.30
9	Chris Singleton	.15
10	Larry Walker	.15
11	Brad Ausmus	.15
12	Ron Coomer	.15
13	Edgardo Alfonzo	.15
14	Delino DeShields	.15
15	Tony Gwynn	1.00
16	Andruw Jones	.75
17	Raul Mondesi	.15
18	Troy Glaus	.75
19	Ben Grieve	.15
20	Sammy Sosa	1.25
21	Fernando Vina	.15
22	Jeromy Burnitz	.15
23	Jay Bell	.15
24	Pete Harnisch	.15
25	Barry Bonds	2.00
26	Eric Karros	.15
27	Alex Gonzalez	.15
28	Mike Lieberthal	.15
29	Juan Encarnacion	.15
30	Derek Jeter	2.00
31	Bruce Aven	.15
32	Eric Milton	.15
33	Aaron Boone	.15
34	Roberto Alomar	.40
35	John Olerud	.15
36	Orlando Cabrera	.15
37	Shawn Green	.45
38	Roger Cedeno	.15
39	Garret Anderson	.15
40	Jim Thome	.65
41	Gabe Kapler	.15
42	Mo Vaughn	.15
43	Sean Casey	.25
44	Preston Wilson	.15
45	Javy Lopez	.15
46	Ryan Klesko	.15
47	Ray Durham	.15
48	Dean Palmer	.15
49	Jorge Posada	.15
50	Alex Rodriguez	1.50
51	Tom Glavine	.40
52	Ray Lankford	.15
53	Jose Canseco	.40
54	Tim Salmon	.15
55	Cal Ripken Jr.	2.00
56	Bob Abreu	.15
57	Robin Ventura	.15
58	Damion Easley	.15
59	Paul O'Neill	.15
60	Ivan Rodriguez	.65
61	Carl Everett	.15
62	Doug Glanville	.15
63	Jeff Kent	.15
64	Jay Buhner	.15
65	Cliff Floyd	.15
66	Rick Ankiel	.15
67	Mark Grace	.25
68	Brian Jordan	.15
69	Craig Biggio	.15
70	Carlos Delgado	.50
71	Brad Radke	.15
72	Greg Maddux	1.00
73	Al Leiter	.15
74	Pokey Reese	.15
75	Todd Helton	.15
76	Mariano Rivera	.25
77	Shane Spencer	.15
78	Jason Kendall	.15
79	Chuck Knoblauch	.15
80	Scott Rolen	.65
81	Jose Offerman	.15
82	J.T. Snow Jr.	.15
83	Pat Meares	.15
84	Quivio Veras	.15
85	Edgar Renteria	.15
86	Luis Matos	.15
87	Adrian Beltre	.15
88	Luis Gonzalez	.25
89	Rickey Henderson	.15
90	Brian Giles	.15
91	Carlos Febles	.15
92	Tino Martinez	.15
93	Magglio Ordonez	.15
94	Rafael Furcal	.15
95	Mike Mussina	.30
96	Gary Sheffield	.40
97	Kenny Lofton	.15
98	Fred McGriff	.15

99	Ken Caminiti	.15
100	Mark McGwire	1.50
101	Tom Goodwin	.15
102	Mark Grudzielanek	.15
103	Derek Bell	.15
104	Mike Lowell	.15
105	Jeff Cirillo	.15
106	Orlando Hernandez	.15
107	Jose Valentin	.15
108	Warren Morris	.15
109	Mike Williams	.15
110	Gregg Zaun	.15
111	Jose Vidro	.15
112	Omar Vizquel	.15
113	Vinny Castilla	.15
114	Gregg Jefferies	.15
115	Kevin Brown	.15
116	Shannon Stewart	.15
117	Marquis Grissom	.15
118	Manny Ramirez	.75
119	Albert Belle	.15
120	Bret Boone	.15
121	Johnny Damon	.25
122	Juan Gonzalez	.75
123	David Justice	.15
124	Jeffrey Hammonds	.15
125	Ken Griffey Jr.	1.25
126	Mike Sweeney	.15
127	Tony Clark	.15
128	Todd Zeile	.15
129	Mark Johnson	.15
130	Matt Williams	.15
131	Geoff Jenkins	.15
132	Jason Giambi	.50
133	Steve Finley	.15
134	Derek Lee	.15
135	Royce Clayton	.15
136	Joe Randa	.15
137	Rafael Palmeiro	.65
138	Kevin Young	.15
139	Curt Schilling	.40
140	Vladimir Guerrero	.75
141	Greg Vaughn	.15
142	Jermaine Dye	.15
143	Roger Clemens	1.00
144	Denny Hocking	.15
145	Frank Thomas	.75
146	Carlos Beltran	.50
147	Eric Young	.15
148	Pat Burrell	.50
149	Pedro Martinez	.75
150	Mike Piazza	1.25
151	Adrian Gonzalez	.50
152	Adam Johnson	.15
153	Luis Montanez **RC**	1.50
154	Mike Stodolka	.15
155	Phil Dumatrait	.15
156	Sean Burnett	.15
157	Dominic Rich **RC**	1.50
158	Adam Wainwright	.50
159	Scott Thorman	.15
160	Scott Heard	.25
161	Chad Petty **RC**	1.50
162	Matt Wheatland	2.00
163	Brad Digby	.15
164	Rocco Baldelli	1.00
165	Grady Sizemore	1.00
166	Brian Sellier **RC**	1.50
167	Rick Brosseau **RC**	1.50
168	Shawn Fagan **RC**	1.50
169	Sean Smith	1.50
170	Chris Bass **RC**	1.50
171	Corey Patterson (Future Stars)	.25
172	Sean Burroughs (Future Stars)	.25
173	Ben Petrick (Future Stars)	.15
174	Mike Glendenning (Future Stars)	.15
175	Barry Zito (Future Stars)	.50
176	Milton Bradley (Future Stars)	.15
177	Bobby Bradley (Future Stars)	.15
178	Jason Hart (Future Stars)	.15
179	Ryan Anderson (Future Stars)	.15
180	Ben Sheets (Future Stars)	.25
181	Adam Everett (Future Stars)	.15
182	Alfonso Soriano (Future Stars)	.75
183	Josh Hamilton (Future Stars)	.25
184	Eric Munson (Future Stars)	.15
185	Chin-Feng Chen (Future Stars)	.25
186	Tim Christman **RC**	1.50
187	J.R. House	.75
188	Brandon Parker **RC**	1.50
189	Sean Fesh **RC**	1.50
190	Joel Pieniero **RC**	2.00
191	Oscar Ramirez **RC**	1.50
192	Alex Santos **RC**	1.50
193	Eddy Reyes **RC**	1.50
194	Mike Jacobs **RC**	1.50
195	Erick Almonte **RC**	2.00
196	Brandon Claussen **RC**	2.00
197	Kris Keller **RC**	1.50
198	Wilson Betemit **RC**	1.50
199	Andy Phillips **RC**	1.50
200	Adam Pettyjohn **RC**	1.50
---	Derek Jeter (Checklist)	.25

Beam Team

		NM/M
Complete Set (30):		100.00
Common Player:		1.50
Production 500 Sets		
1	Sammy Sosa	6.00
2	Mark McGwire	8.00
3	Vladimir Guerrero	3.00
4	Chipper Jones	4.50
5	Manny Ramirez	3.00
6	Derek Jeter	10.00
7	Alex Rodriguez	8.00
8	Cal Ripken Jr.	10.00
9	Ken Griffey Jr.	6.00
10	Greg Maddux	4.50
11	Barry Bonds	10.00
12	Pedro Martinez	3.00
13	Nomar Garciaparra	6.00
14	Randy Johnson	3.00
15	Frank Thomas	3.00
16	Ivan Rodriguez	2.50
17	Jeff Bagwell	3.00
18	Mike Piazza	6.00
19	Todd Helton	3.00
20	Shawn Green	2.00
21	Larry Walker	1.50
22	Larry Walker	1.50
23	Tony Gwynn	4.50
24	Pat Burrell	1.50
25	Rafael Furcal	1.50
26	Corey Patterson	1.50
27	Chin-Feng Chen	1.50
28	Sean Burroughs	1.50
29	Ryan Anderson	1.50
30	Josh Hamilton	4.00

Capture The Action

		NM/M
Complete Set (15):		15.00
Common Player:		1.00
Inserted 1:8		
1	Cal Ripken Jr.	3.00
2	Alex Rodriguez	2.50
3	Mike Piazza	2.00
4	Mark McGwire	2.50
5	Greg Maddux	1.50
6	Derek Jeter	3.00
7	Chipper Jones	1.50
8	Pedro Martinez	1.00
9	Ken Griffey Jr.	2.00
10	Nomar Garciaparra	1.00
11	Randy Johnson	1.00
12	Sammy Sosa	1.50
13	Vladimir Guerrero	1.00
14	Barry Bonds	3.00
15	Ivan Rodriguez	1.00

Capture The Action Game View

		NM/M
Common Player:		10.00
Production 100 Sets		
1	Cal Ripken Jr.	30.00
2	Alex Rodriguez	25.00
3	Mike Piazza	20.00
4	Mark McGwire	25.00
5	Greg Maddux	15.00
6	Derek Jeter	30.00
7	Chipper Jones	15.00
8	Pedro Martinez	10.00
9	Ken Griffey Jr.	20.00
10	Nomar Garciaparra	20.00
11	Randy Johnson	20.00
12	Sammy Sosa	20.00
13	Vladimir Guerrero	10.00
14	Barry Bonds	30.00
15	Ivan Rodriguez	10.00

Co-Signers

		NM/M
Common Duo:		15.00
Inserted 1:1,117		
1	Nomar Garciaparra, Derek Jeter	400.00

2	Roberto Alomar, Edgardo Alfonzo	50.00
3	Rick Ankiel, Kevin Millwood	15.00
4	Chipper Jones, Troy Glaus	65.00
5	Magglio Ordonez, Bobby Abreu	20.00
6	Adam Piatt, Sean Burroughs	20.00
7	Corey Patterson, Nick Johnson	40.00
8	Adrian Gonzalez, Rocco Baldelli	40.00
9	Adam Johnson, Mike Stodolka	15.00

Diamond Pearls

		NM/M
Complete Set (20):		20.00
Common Player:		.65
Inserted 1:8		
1	Ken Griffey Jr.	2.00
2	Alex Rodriguez	2.50
3	Derek Jeter	3.00
4	Chipper Jones	1.50
5	Nomar Garciaparra	2.00
6	Vladimir Guerrero	1.00
7	Jeff Bagwell	1.00
8	Cal Ripken Jr.	3.00
9	Sammy Sosa	2.00
10	Mark McGwire	2.50
11	Frank Thomas	1.00
12	Pedro Martinez	1.00
13	Manny Ramirez	1.00
14	Randy Johnson	1.00
15	Barry Bonds	3.00
16	Ivan Rodriguez	.75
17	Greg Maddux	1.50
18	Mike Piazza	2.00
19	Todd Helton	1.00
20	Shawn Green	.65

Game-Used Cards

		NM/M
Common Player:		5.00
Inserted 1:285		
1	Chin-Feng Chen	20.00
2	Bobby Bradley	5.00
3	Tomokazu Ohka	5.00
4	Kurt Ainsworth	5.00
5	Craig Anderson	5.00
6	Josh Hamilton	10.00
7	Felipe Lopez	5.00
8	Ryan Anderson	5.00
9	Alex Escobar	5.00
10	Ben Sheets	8.00
11	Ntema Ndungidi	5.00
12	Eric Munson	5.00
13	Aaron Myette	5.00
14	Jack Cust	5.00
15	Julio Zuleta	5.00
16	Corey Patterson	10.00
17	Carlos Pena	5.00
18	Marcus Giles	5.00
19	Travis Wilson	5.00
20	Barry Zito	8.00

King of the Hill

		NM/M
Complete Set (5):		30.00
Common Player:		3.00
Inserted 1:21		
1	Pedro Martinez	10.00
2	Randy Johnson	10.00

3	Greg Maddux	15.00
4	Rick Ankiel	3.00
5	Kevin Brown	3.00

Lone Star Signatures

		NM/M
Common Player:		6.00
Inserted 1:196		
1	Nomar Garciaparra	100.00
2	Derek Jeter	120.00
3	Edgardo Alfonzo	20.00
4	Roberto Alomar	40.00
5	Magglio Ordonez	20.00
6	Bobby Abreu	40.00
7	Chipper Jones	40.00
8	Troy Glaus	30.00
9	Nick Johnson	15.00
10	Adam Piatt	8.00
11	Sean Burroughs	8.00
12	Corey Patterson	15.00
13	Rick Ankiel	6.00
14	Kevin Millwood	10.00
15	Adrian Gonzalez	15.00
16	Adam Johnson	6.00
17	Rocco Baldelli	25.00
18	Mike Stodolka	6.00

Play at the Plate

		NM/M
Common Player:		10.00
Inserted 1:8		
1	Mark McGwire	20.00
2	Sammy Sosa	15.00
3	Vladimir Guerrero	8.00
4	Ken Griffey Jr.	15.00
5	Mike Piazza	15.00
6	Chipper Jones	10.00
7	Barry Bonds	25.00
8	Alex Rodriguez	20.00
9	Jeff Bagwell	8.00
10	Nomar Garciaparra	15.00

Souvenirs

		NM/M
Common Player:		4.00
1	Scott Rolen/Bat	8.00
2	Larry Walker/Bat	5.00
3	Rafael Furcal/Bat	5.00
4	Darin Erstad/Bat	5.00
5	Mike Sweeney/Jsy	4.00
6	Matt Lawton/Jsy	4.00
7	Jose Vidro/Jsy	4.00
8	Pat Burrell/Jsy	6.00

Super Teams

These scarce exchange cards were seeded at an average rate of about one per 875 packs of TSC Hobby and Retail and one per 340 packs of Home Team Advantage. Prior to the cards' redemption deadline which expired December 1, 2001, they could be entered into drawings for various prizes including specially marked card sets, game tickets, autographs, etc.

		NM/M
Common Card:		1.00
STP1	Anaheim Angels (Troy Glaus)	2.00
STP2	Houston Astros (Jeff Bagwell)	2.00
STP3	Oakland A's (Jason Giambi)	1.25
STP4	Toronto Blue Jays (Carlos Delgado)	1.00
STP5	Atlanta Braves (Chipper Jones)	2.50
STP6	Milwaukee Brewers (Geoff Jenkins)	
STP7	St. Louis Cardinals (Mark McGwire)	4.00
STP8	Chicago Cubs (Sammy Sosa)	3.00
STP9	Tampa Bay Devil Rays (Greg Vaughn)	
STP10	Arizona Diamondbacks (Luis Gonzalez)	1.00
STP11	L.A. Dodgers (Shawn Green)	1.00
STP12	Montreal Expos (Vladimir Guerrero)	1.50
STP13	S.F. Giants (Barry Bonds)	5.00
STP14	Cleveland Indians (Roberto Alomar)	1.00
STP15	Seattle Mariners (Alex Rodriguez)	4.00
STP16	Florida Marlins (Preston Wilson)	
STP17	N.Y. Mets (Mike Piazza)	3.00
STP18	Baltimore Orioles (Mike Mussina)	1.00
STP19	S.D. Padres (Tony Gwynn)	2.00
STP20	Philadelphia Phillies (Scott Rolen)	1.25
STP21	Pittsburgh Pirates (Jason Kendall)	1.00
STP22	Texas Rangers (Ivan Rodriguez)	1.25
STP23	Boston Red Sox (Nomar Garciaparra)	3.00
STP24	Cincinnati Reds (Ken Griffey Jr.)	3.00
STP25	Colorado Rockies (Todd Helton)	1.25
STP26	K.C. Royals (Mike Sweeney)	
STP27	Detroit Tigers (Juan Gonzalez)	1.50
STP28	Minnesota Twins (Brad Radke)	1.00
STP29	Chicago White Sox (Frank Thomas)	1.50
STP30	N.Y. Yankees (Derek Jeter)	5.00

2002 Stadium Club Relic Edition

		NM/M
Complete Set (125):		
Common Player:		.15
Common SP (101-125):		5.00
Production 2,999		
Pack (6):		1.50
Box (24):		30.00
1	Pedro Martinez	.75
2	Derek Jeter	2.00
3	Chipper Jones	1.00
4	Roberto Alomar	.40
5	Albert Pujols	1.50
6	Bret Boone	.15
7	Alex Rodriguez	1.50
8	Jose Cruz	.15
9	Mike Hampton	.15
10	Vladimir Guerrero	.75
11	Jim Edmonds	.25
12	Luis Gonzalez	.25
13	Jeff Kent	.15
14	Mike Piazza	1.25
15	Ben Sheets	.15
16	Tsuyoshi Shinjo	.15
17	Pat Burrell	.40
18	Jermaine Dye	.15
19	Rafael Furcal	.15
20	Randy Johnson	.75
21	Carlos Delgado	.50
22	Roger Clemens	1.00
23	Eric Chavez	.25
24	Nomar Garciaparra	1.25
25	Ivan Rodriguez	.65
26	Juan Gonzalez	.75
27	Reggie Sanders	.15
28	Jeff Bagwell	.75
29	Kazuhiro Sasaki	.15
30	Larry Walker	.15
31	Ben Grieve	.15
32	David Justice	.15
33	David Wells	.15
34	Kevin Brown	.15
35	Miguel Tejada	.25
36	Jorge Posada	.15
37	Javy Lopez	.15
38	Cliff Floyd	.15
39	Carlos Lee	.15
40	Manny Ramirez	.75
41	Jim Thome	.65
42	Pokey Reese	.15
43	Scott Rolen	.65
44	Richie Sexson	.15
45	Dean Palmer	.15
46	Rafael Palmeiro	.65
47	Alfonso Soriano	.75
48	Craig Biggio	.15
49	Troy Glaus	.75
50	Andruw Jones	.75
51	Ichiro Suzuki	5.00
52	Kenny Lofton	.15
53	Hideo Nomo	.75
54	Magglio Ordonez	.15
55	Brad Penny	.15
56	Omar Vizquel	.15
57	Mike Sweeney	.15
58	Gary Sheffield	.25
59	Ken Griffey Jr.	1.25
60	Curt Schilling	.40
61	Bobby Higginson	.15
62	Terrence Long	.15
63	Moises Alou	.15
64	Sandy Alomar	.15
65	Cristian Guzman	.15
66	Sammy Sosa	1.25
67	Jose Vidro	.15
68	Edgar Martinez	.15
69	Jason Giambi	.50
70	Mark McGwire	1.50
71	Barry Bonds	2.00
72	Greg Vaughn	.15
73	Phil Nevin	.15
74	Jason Kendall	.15
75	Greg Maddux	1.00
76	Jeromy Burnitz	.15
77	Mike Mussina	.40
78	Johnny Damon	.25
79	Shawn Green	.40
80	Jimmy Rollins	.25
81	Edgardo Alfonzo	.15
82	Barry Larkin	.15
83	Raul Mondesi	.15
84	Preston Wilson	.15
85	Mike Lieberthal	.15
86	J.D. Drew	.40
87	Ryan Klesko	.15
88	David Segui	.15
89	Derek Bell	.15
90	Bernie Williams	.40
91	Doug Mientkiewicz	.15
92	Rich Aurilia	.15
93	Ellis Burks	.15
94	Placido Polanco	.15
95	Darin Erstad	.25
96	Brian Giles	.15
97	Geoff Jenkins	.15
98	Kerry Wood	.65
99	Mariano Rivera	.40
100	Todd Helton	.75
101	Adam Dunn	15.00
102	Grant Balfour	5.00
103	Jae Weong Seo	5.00
104	Hank Blalock	10.00
105	Chris George	5.00
106	Jack Cust	5.00
107	Juan Cruz	5.00
108	Adrian Gonzalez	5.00
109	Nick Johnson	5.00
110	Jeff Devanon **RC**	5.00
111	Juan Diaz	10.00
112	Brandon Duckworth	5.00
113	Jason Lane	5.00
114	Seung Jun Song	5.00
115	Morgan Ensberg	5.00
116	Marlyn Tisdale **RC**	5.00
117	Jason Botts **RC**	5.00
118	Henry Pichardo **RC**	5.00
119	John Rodriguez **RC**	5.00
120	Mike Peeples **RC**	5.00
121	Rob Bowen **RC**	5.00
122	Jeremy Affeldt	5.00
123	Jorge Buret **RC**	5.00
124	Manny Ravelo **RC**	10.00
125	Eudy Lajara **RC**	5.00

All-Star Relics

		NM/M
Common Player:		5.00
RA	Roberto Alomar	7.50
MA	Moises Alou	5.00
BB	Barry Bonds	40.00
BRB	Bret Boone	5.00
MC	Mike Cameron	5.00
SC	Sean Casey	7.50
CF	Cliff Floyd	5.00
BG	Brian Giles	5.00
JG	Juan Gonzalez	12.00
LG3	Luis Gonzalez	5.00
CG	Cristian Guzman	5.00
TG	Tony Gwynn	15.00
MH	Mike Hampton	5.00
TH	Todd Helton	12.00
RJ	Randy Johnson	12.00
CJ	Chipper Jones	15.00
JK	Jeff Kent	5.00
RK	Ryan Klesko	5.00
EM	Edgar Martinez	5.00

ERM	Eric Milton	5.00
JO	John Olerud	5.00
MO	Magglio Ordonez	5.00
MP	Mike Piazza	20.00
JP	Jorge Posada	5.00
AP	Albert Pujols	30.00
MR	Manny Ramirez	12.00
IR	Ivan Rodriguez	10.00
KS	Kazuhiro Sasaki	5.00
MS	Mike Sweeney	5.00
LW	Larry Walker	5.00

Chasing 500-500

NM/M
Common Player:

BB1	Barry Bonds/Dual	40.00
BB2	Barry Bonds/Jsy/600	30.00
BB3	Barry Bonds/Mult/200	75.00

Passport to the Majors

NM/M
Common Player: 5.00
Jsy 1:84
Bat 1:795

BA	Bobby Abreu/400	6.00
EA	Edgardo Alfonzo	5.00
RA	Roberto Alomar	6.00
WB	Wilson Betemit/325	4.00
BC	Bartolo Colon	5.00
RF	Rafael Furcal	5.00
AG	Andres Galarraga	5.00
JG	Juan Gonzalez	8.00
SH	Shigetoshi Hasegawa	5.00
AJ	Andruw Jones	8.00
CL	Carlos Lee	5.00
JL	Javy Lopez	5.00
PM	Pedro Martinez	10.00
RM	Raul Mondesi	5.00
MO	Magglio Ordonez	5.00
RP	Rafael Palmeiro	10.00
CP	Chan Ho Park	5.00
AP	Albert Pujols/450	40.00
MR	Manny Ramirez	10.00
IR	Ivan Rodriguez	5.00
KS	Kazuhiro Sasaki	5.00
TS	Tsuyoshi Shinjo/400	6.00
AS	Alfonso Soriano/400	10.00
MT	Miguel Tejada/375	6.00
LW	Larry Walker	5.00

Reel Time

NM/M
Complete Set (20): 25.00
Common Player: .50
Inserted 1:8

RT1	Luis Gonzalez	.50
RT2	Derek Jeter	4.00
RT3	Ken Griffey Jr.	2.50
RT4	Alex Rodriguez	3.00
RT5	Barry Bonds	4.00
RT6	Ichiro Suzuki	2.50
RT7	Carlos Delgado	1.00
RT8	Manny Ramirez	1.50
RT9	Mike Piazza	2.50
RT10	Mark McGwire	3.00
RT11	Todd Helton	1.50
RT12	Vladimir Guerrero	1.50
RT13	Jim Thome	1.50
RT14	Rich Aurilia	.50
RT15	Bret Boone	.50
RT16	Roberto Alomar	.75
RT17	Jason Giambi	1.00
RT18	Chipper Jones	2.00
RT19	Albert Pujols	3.00
RT20	Sammy Sosa	2.50

Stadium Shots

NM/M
Complete Set (10): 15.00
Common Player: 1.50
Inserted 1:12

SS1	Sammy Sosa	2.00

SS2	Manny Ramirez	1.50
SS3	Jason Giambi	1.00
SS4	Mike Piazza	2.00
SS5	Barry Bonds	4.00
SS6	Ken Griffey Jr.	2.50
SS7	Juan Gonzalez	1.50
SS8	Jeff Bagwell	1.50
SS9	Jim Thome	1.00
SS10	Mark McGwire	3.00

Stadium Slices Barrel

NM/M
Common Player: 15.00

BB	Barry Bonds	75.00
LG	Luis Gonzalez	15.00
AP	Albert Pujols	75.00
IR	Ivan Rodriguez	35.00
BW	Bernie Williams	25.00

Stadium Slices Handle

NM/M
Common Player: 15.00

BB	Barry Bonds	50.00
LG	Luis Gonzalez	15.00
AP	Albert Pujols	50.00
IR	Ivan Rodriguez	20.00
BW	Bernie Williams	15.00

Stadium Slices Trademark

NM/M
Common Player: 15.00

BB	Barry Bonds	60.00
LG	Luis Gonzalez	15.00
AP	Albert Pujols	60.00
IR	Ivan Rodriguez	20.00
BW	Bernie Williams	15.00

World Champions Relics

NM/M
Common Player: 4.00
Jersey 1:106
Bat 1:94
Pants 1:795
Spikes 1:38,400

RA	Roberto Alomar	15.00
MA	Moises Alou	8.00
DB	Don Baylor	8.00
JB	Johnny Bench	20.00
BB	Bert Blyleven	8.00
WB	Wade Boggs	15.00
BRB	Bob Boone	4.00
GB	George Brett	50.00
SB	Scot Brosius	10.00
AB	Al Bumbry	4.00
JC1	Jose Canseco	15.00
JC2	Jose Canseco	15.00
GC1	Gary Carter	15.00
GC2	Gary Carter	15.00
JC	Joe Carter	10.00
RC	Ron Cey	8.00
CC	Chris Chambliss	8.00
DC	Dave Concepcion	8.00
ED	Eric Davis	10.00
BD	Bucky Dent	8.00
GF	George Foster	8.00
PG	Phil Garner	4.00
KG1	Kirk Gibson	10.00
KG2	Kirk Gibson	10.00
TG	Tom Glavine	15.00
KG	Ken Griffey Sr.	10.00
RH	Rickey Henderson/50	80.00
GH	George Hendrick	6.00
KH	Keith Hernandez	15.00
WH	Willie Hernandez	10.00
OH	Orel Hershiser	10.00
RJ	Reggie Jackson	15.00
CWJ	Chipper Jones	15.00
DJ	David Justice	10.00
CK	Chuck Knoblauch	4.00
AL	Al Leiter	8.00
DL	Davey Lopes	8.00
JL	Javy Lopez	8.00
GL	Greg Luzinski	8.00
GM	Greg Maddux	30.00
BM	Bill Madlock	8.00
TLM	Tino Martinez	15.00
HM	Hal McRae	8.00
FM	Fred McGriff	10.00
PM	Paul Molitor	15.00
TM	Thurman Munson	50.00
EM1	Eddie Murray	15.00
EM2	Eddie Murray	15.00
JO	John Olerud	6.00
PO	Paul O'Neill	15.00
DP	Dave Parker	10.00
TP	Tony Perez	10.00
LVP	Lou Pinella	8.00
JP	Jorge Posada	10.00
KP	Kirby Puckett	20.00
WR	Willie Randolph	8.00
MJS	Mike Schmidt	50.00
MS	Mike Scoscia	10.00
OS	Ozzie Smith	30.00
JS	John Smoltz	10.00
ES	Ed Sprague	4.00
WS	Willie Stargell	15.00
AT	Alan Trammell	10.00
LW	Lou Whitaker	10.00
BW	Bernie Williams	15.00
MW	Mookie Wilson	10.00
DW	Dave Winfield	10.00
FV	Fernando Valenzuela	8.00
JV	Jose Vizcaino	4.00

2003 Stadium Club

NM/M
Complete Set (125): 30.00
Common Player: .15
Hobby Pack (6): 1.50
Hobby Box (24): 30.00

1	Rafael Furcal	.15
2	Randy Winn	.15
3	Eric Chavez	.15
4	Fernando Vina	.15
5	Pat Burrell	.25
6	Derek Jeter	2.00
7	Ivan Rodriguez	.65
8	Eric Hinske	.15
9	Roberto Alomar	.40
10	Tony Batista	.15
11	Jacque Jones	.15
12	Alfonso Soriano	.75
13	Omar Vizquel	.15
14	Paul Konerko	.25
15	Shawn Green	.45
16	Garret Anderson	.15
17	Darin Erstad	.25
18	Johnny Damon	.25
19	Juan Gonzalez	.75
20	Luis Gonzalez	.25
21	Sean Burroughs	.15
22	Mark Prior	.75
23	Javier Vazquez	.15
24	Shannon Stewart	.15
25	Jay Gibbons	.15
26	A.J. Pierzynski	.15
27	Vladimir Guerrero	.75
28	Austin Kearns	.25
29	Shea Hillenbrand	.15
30	Magglio Ordonez	.15
31	Mike Cameron	.15
32	Tim Salmon	.25
33	Brian Jordan	.15
34	Moises Alou	.15
35	Rich Aurilia	.15
36	Nick Johnson	.15
37	Junior Spivey	.15
38	Curt Schilling	.40
39	Jose Vidro	.15
40	Orlando Cabrera	.15
41	Jeff Bagwell	.75
42	Mo Vaughn	.15
43	Luis Castillo	.15
44	Vicente Padilla	.15
45	Pedro J. Martinez	.75
46	John Olerud	.15
47	Tom Glavine	.40
48	Torii Hunter	.15
49	J.D. Drew	.25
50	Alex Rodriguez	1.50
51	Randy Johnson	.75
52	Richie Sexson	.15
53	Jimmy Rollins	.15
54	Cristian Guzman	.15
55	Tim Hudson	.25
56	Mark Buehrle	.15
57	Paul LoDuca	.15
58	Aramis Ramirez	.25
59	Todd Helton	.75
60	Lance Berkman	.15
61	Josh Beckett	.25
62	Bret Boone	.15
63	Miguel Tejada	.35
64	Nomar Garciaparra	1.25
65	Albert Pujols	1.50
66	Chipper Jones	1.00
67	Scott Rolen	.65
68	Kerry Wood	.65
69	Jorge Posada	.15
70	Ichiro Suzuki	1.50
71	Jeff Kent	.15
72	David Eckstein	.15
73	Phil Nevin	.15
74	Brian Giles	.15
75	Barry Zito	.25
76	Andruw Jones	.75
77	Jim Thome	.65
78	Robert Fick	.15
79	Rafael Palmeiro	.65
80	Barry Bonds	2.00
81	Gary Sheffield	.40
82	Jim Edmonds	.25
83	Kazuhisa Ishii	.15
84	Jose Hernandez	.15
85	Jason Giambi	.40
86	Mark Mulder	.15
87	Roger Clemens	1.00
88	Troy Glaus	.75
89	Carlos Delgado	.50
90	Mike Sweeney	.15
91	Ken Griffey Jr.	1.25
92	Manny Ramirez	.75
93	Ryan Klesko	.15
94	Larry Walker	.15
95	Adam Dunn	.65
96	Raul Ibanez	.15
97	Preston Wilson	.15
98	Roy Oswalt	.15
99	Sammy Sosa	1.25
100	Mike Piazza	1.25
101	Jose Reyes	.50
102	Ed Rogers	.15
103	Hank Blalock	.75
104	Mark Teixeira	.65
105	Orlando Hudson	.15
106	Drew Henson	.25
107	Joe Mauer	.75
108	Carl Crawford	.75
109	Marlon Byrd	.15
110	Jason Stokes	.15
111	Miguel Cabrera	.50
112	Wilson Betemit	.15
113	Jerome Williams	.15
114	Walter Young	.15
115	Juan Camacho RC	.15
116	Chris Duncan RC	3.00
117	Franklin Gutierrez RC	3.00
118	Adam LaRoche	.50
119	Manuel Ramirez RC	.50
120	Il Kim RC	.50
121	Wayne Lydon RC	.50
122	Daryl Clark RC	.50
123	Sean Pierce	.50
124	Andy Marte RC	3.00
125	Matthew Peterson RC	.75

Photographer's Proof

Stars (1-100):	4-8X
Cards (101-125):	2-4X
Production 299 Sets	

Royal Gold

Stars:	1-3X
Inserted 1:1	

Beam Team

NM/M
Complete Set (20): 50.00
Common Player: 1.00
Inserted 1:12

BT1	Larry Walker	1.00

BT2	Miguel Tejada	1.50
BT3	Ichiro Suzuki	5.00
BT4	Sammy Sosa	5.00
BT5	Ivan Rodriguez	2.50
BT6	Alex Rodriguez	6.00
BT7	Mike Piazza	5.00
BT8	Jeff Kent	1.00
BT9	Chipper Jones	4.00
BT10	Derek Jeter	8.00
BT11	Todd Helton	3.00
BT12	Vladimir Guerrero	3.00
BT13	Shawn Green	1.50
BT14	Brian Giles	1.00
BT15	Jason Giambi	2.00
BT16	Nomar Garciaparra	5.00
BT17	Adam Dunn	2.00
BT18	Carlos Delgado	1.50
BT19	Barry Bonds	8.00
BT20	Lance Berkman	1.00

Born In The USA

NM/M
Common Player: 5.00
Jerseys Inserted 1:52
Bats Inserted 1:76

RA	Rich Aurilia/Jsy	5.00
JB	Jeff Bagwell/Jsy	12.00
CB	Craig Biggio/Jsy	8.00
BB	Bret Boone/Jsy	5.00
AB	A.J. Burnett/Jsy	5.00
JNB	Jeromy Burnitz/Bat	5.00
PB	Pat Burrell/Bat	10.00
SB	Sean Burroughs/Bat	6.00
EC	Eric Chavez/Jsy	6.00
TC	Tony Clark/Bat	5.00
JD	Johnny Damon/Bat	8.00
JDD	J.D. Drew/Bat	5.00
AD	Adam Dunn/Bat	12.00
JE	Jim Edmonds/Jsy	5.00
CF	Cliff Floyd/Bat	5.00
BF	Brad Fullmer/Bat	5.00
NG	Nomar Garciaparra/Bat	20.00
LG	Luis Gonzalez/Bat	6.00
MG	Mark Grace/Jsy	12.00
SG	Shawn Green/Bat	6.00
TJH	Toby Hall	5.00
JH	Josh Hamilton/Bat	8.00
TH	Todd Helton/Bat	8.00
RH	Rickey Henderson/Bat	15.00
RJ	Randy Johnson/Bat	12.00
CJ	Chipper Jones/Bat	12.00
RK	Ryan Klesko/Bat	5.00
PK	Paul Konerko/Bat	5.00
BL	Barry Larkin/Jsy	10.00
TRL	Travis Lee/Bat	5.00
TL	Terrence Long/Jsy	5.00
GM	Greg Maddux/Jsy	15.00
TM	Tino Martinez/Bat	10.00
WM	Willie Mays/Bat	40.00
EM	Eric Milton/Jsy	6.00
JO	John Olerud/Jsy	6.00
CP	Corey Patterson/Bat	8.00
MP	Mike Piazza/Jsy	15.00
AR	Alex Rodriguez/Bat	15.00
SR	Scott Rolen/Bat	15.00
RS	Richie Sexson/Bat	8.00
GS	Gary Sheffield/Bat	8.00
JS	John Smoltz/Jsy	8.00
FT	Frank Thomas/Bat	8.00
JT	Jim Thome/Bat	15.00
MV	Mo Vaughn/Bat	8.00
RV	Robin Ventura/Bat	8.00
MW	Matt Williams/Bat	8.00
PW	Preston Wilson/Bat	8.00
KW	Kerry Wood/Bat	10.00

Clubhouse Exclusive

NM/M
Jersey Inserted 1:488
Jersey & Bat 1:2,073
Jersey, Bat & Spikes 1:2,750

CE1	Albert Pujols/Jsy	15.00

CE2	Albert Pujols/Bat/Jsy	35.00
CE3	Albert Pujols/Jsy/Bat/Spike	100.00

Co-Signers

NM/M
HTA Exclusive

MI	Masanori Murakami, Kazuhisa Ishii	180.00
AM	Hank Aaron, Willie Mays	400.00

License To Drive

NM/M
Common Player: 5.00
Inserted 1:98

RA	Roberto Alomar	8.00
MA	Moises Alou	6.00
AB	Adrian Beltre	8.00
LB	Lance Berkman	6.00
EC	Eric Chavez	6.00
AD	Adam Dunn	8.00
NG	Nomar Garciaparra	15.00
JG	Juan Gonzalez	8.00
LG	Luis Gonzalez	6.00
SG	Shawn Green	8.00
TH	Todd Helton	10.00
AJ	Andruw Jones	10.00
CJ	Chipper Jones	12.00
TM	Tino Martinez	6.00
RP	Rafael Palmeiro	8.00
MP	Mike Piazza	15.00
AP	Albert Pujols	25.00
ANR	Aramis Ramirez	6.00
AR	Alex Rodriguez	20.00
IR	Ivan Rodriguez	8.00
SR	Scott Rolen	10.00
GS	Gary Sheffield	8.00
FT	Frank Thomas	10.00
LW	Larry Walker	6.00
BW	Bernie Williams	6.00

MLB Match-Ups

NM/M
Inserted 1:485

BB	Bret Boone	15.00
TH	Todd Helton	15.00
AJ	Andruw Jones	12.00
GM	Greg Maddux	30.00
AP	Albert Pujols	30.00

Stadium Shots

NM/M
Complete Set (10): 25.00
Common Player: 1.00
Inserted 1:24

SS1	Lance Berkman	1.00
SS2	Barry Bonds	6.00
SS3	Jason Giambi	2.50
SS4	Shawn Green	1.50
SS5	Vladimir Guerrero	3.00
SS6	Paul Konerko	1.00
SS7	Mike Piazza	4.50

		NM/M
SS8	Alex Rodriguez	6.00
SS9	Sammy Sosa	4.50
SS10	Jim Thome	2.00

Stadium Slices Handle

		NM/M
Common Player:		5.00
Inserted 1:237		
Trademarks:		1-1.5X
Inserted 1:415		
Barrels:		1.5-2X
Inserted 1:550		
RA	Roberto Alomar	15.00
CD	Carlos Delgado	8.00
NG	Nomar Garciaparra	20.00
TH	Todd Helton	10.00
AJ	Andruw Jones	8.00
RP	Rafael Palmeiro	10.00
MP	Mike Piazza	15.00
AP	Albert Pujols	20.00
AR	Alex Rodriguez	15.00
GS	Gary Sheffield	10.00

World Stage

		NM/M
Common Player:		5.00
Jerseys Inserted 1:118		
Bats Inserted 1:809		
AB	Adrian Beltre/Jsy	6.00
KI	Kazuhisa Ishii/Jsy	5.00
BK	Byung-Hyun Kim/Jsy	5.00
HN	Hideo Nomo/Bat	20.00
AP	Albert Pujols/Jsy	15.00
IR	Ivan Rodriguez/Jsy	8.00
KS	Kazuhiro Sasaki/Jsy	5.00
TS	Tsuyoshi Shinjo/Bat	5.00
AS	Alfonso Soriano/Bat	15.00
MT	Miguel Tejada/Jsy	8.00

1983 Star '83

Star's first baseball card issue was a 15-card tribute to Mike Schmidt, subtitled "Ten Years of Excellence." On the cards' fronts, Schmidt is shown in various posed and game-action photos, surrounded by a red border. Backs tell his story in words and numbers. The cards are the standard 2-1/2" x 3-1/2" and were sold only as complete sets through hobby dealers. Single cards are not listed because the sets are seldom broken for individual card sales.

	NM/M
Complete Set:	6.00

1984 Star '84

Star broadened the selection of its single-player collectors' issues in 1984 and adopted a new design which it used with little variation for several years. Most cards were issued in panels of three, perforated for easy separation. Each set has posed and game-action photos

surrounded by colorful borders. Team logos are in a circle at lower-left; "Star '84" is in an inset at the photo's upper-right. Backs within a set feature stats, career highlights personal information and, sometimes, puzzle pieces.

		NM/M
1-24	George Brett	7.50
1-24	Steve Carlton	6.00
1-36	Steve Garvey (7,500 sets)	3.50
1-36	Darryl Strawberry	2.00
1-24	Carl Yastrzemski (Not issued in panels.)	4.00
1-24	Carl Yastrzemski (First card autographed, edition of 500.)	20.00

1985 Star Nolan Ryan Promo

Issued to promote a set that was never issued, this promo card has on back logos and copyright information for an NBA issue.

	NM/M
Nolan Ryan	15.00

1985 Star '85

Star maintained the basic format of 1984 for its sole single-player issue of 1985. The 36-card set of Reggie Jackson has portrait and action photos surrounded by colorful borders. The logo of the A's, Orioles or Yankees appears in a circle at lower-left on front, with a "Star '85" logo at upper-right. Backs have a mix of stats, personal data and career highlights. Cards were issued in a dozen three-card panels, perforated between the cards. Production was reported as 6,000 sets, with 500 of them signed and numbered by Jackson.

	NM/M
Complete Set (36):	5.00

1986 Star Promos

Several of the 1986 Star single-player series were introduced with the issue of a promo cards, different on their backs, but otherwise similar in appearance to the regular cards.

		NM/M
Complete Set (7):		55.00
Common Player:		2.50
(1)	Rod Carew (Ad back.)	1.50
(2)	Don Mattingly (White card)(blank back.)	2.50
(3)	Don Mattingly (Yellow sticker.) (Blank back.)	3.00
(4)	Dale Murphy (Ad back.)	3.50
(5)	Jim Rice (Blank back.)	2.50
(6)	Nolan Ryan (Ad back.)	15.00
(7)	Tom Seaver (Name on back.)	2.00

1986 Star '86

The basic format of previous years' issues was retained for Star's single-player sets of 1986. Player poses and game-action photos are presented on the front, bordered in a bright color usually associated with the player's team. In standard 2-1/2" x 3-1/2" size, the cards have a circle at lower-left with the player's name - first only or first and last. At top-right, infringing on the photo is the notation, "Star '86." Backs have stats, career highlights, personal data or puzzle pieces. Most sets were issued in three-card perforated panels. Some of the player sets can also be found in a glossy edition and/or a blank-back sticker version. Single cards are seldom offered and are not listed here.

		NM/M
1-24	Wade Boggs	2.00
1-24	Wade Boggs (Glossy set.)	2.00
(1-24)	Wade Boggs (Sticker set.)	2.00
1-15	Jose Canseco (Not issued in panels.)	3.00
1-15	Jose Canseco/Auto. (Edition of 500.)	17.50
1-15	Jose Canseco (Glossy set.)	3.00
(1-15)	Jose Canseco (Sticker set.)	1.50
1-24	Rod Carew	1.50
1-15	Wally Joyner (Not issued in panels.)	1.00
1-15	Wally Joyner/Auto. (Edition of 500.)	15.00
1-15	Wally Joyner (Glossy set.)	1.50
(1-15)	Wally Joyner (Sticker set.)	2.50
1-24	Don Mattingly	5.00
1-24	Don Mattingly (Glossy set.)	7.50
(1-24)	Don Mattingly (Sticker set.)	5.00
1-24	Dale Murphy	5.00
1-20	Jim Rice (Four-card panels.)	1.00
1-20	Jim Rice/Auto. (Edition of 500.)	40.00
1-20	Jim Rice (Glossy set.)	1.50
(1-20)	Jim Rice (Sticker set.)	1.50
1-24	Nolan Ryan (4,000 sets)	9.00
1-24	Tom Seaver (8,000 sets)	3.50

1987 Star Promos

Most of Star's single-player sets issued for 1987 were preceded by the issue of blank-backed promo cards in a nearly identical format to the issued version.

		NM/M
Complete Set (6):		8.75
Common Player:		1.00
(1)	Steve Carlton	2.50
(2)	Gary Carter	2.00
(3)	Roger Clemens	4.00
(4)	Keith Hernandez	1.00
(5)	Tim Raines	1.00
(6)	Fernando Valenzuela	1.00

1987 Star '87

The single-player sets issued by Star in 1987 retain the basic format used since 1984. Standard size (2-1/2" x 3-1/2") cards were printed singly, rather than in panels, but the design remained virtually unchanged. Posed and action photos are surrounded by a colorful border which protrudes into the photo at upper-right with the logo "Star '87." At lower-left is a circle with the player's first name, or, in the case of Fernando Valenzuela, the team logo. Backs have stats, personal data or career highlights. Sets were also issued in a limited glossy version and/or as blank-back stickers. Single cards are usually not sold, so are not listed here.

		NM/M
		17.50
(1-5)	Wade Boggs, Jose Canseco (Unnumbered)	3.00
(1-5)	Wade Boggs, Jose Canseco (Glossy set.) (Unnumbered)	4.50
1-14	Steve Carlton (Glossy version only.)	3.50
1-14	Gary Carter	2.00
1-14	Gary Carter (Glossy set.)	2.25
(1-10)	Gary Carter (Sticker set.) (Different photos.)	2.50
1-12	Roger Clemens (8,500 regular sets; 500 autographed.)	
1-12	Roger Clemens (Glossy) (1,000 sets.)	2.50
(1-5)	Roger Clemens (Update) (Unnumbered)	3.00
(1-5)	Roger Clemens (Update, glossy) (Unnumbered)	4.50
1-13	Keith Hernandez (8,500 regular sets, 500 autographed.)	1.25
1-13	Keith Hernandez (Glossy; 1,000 sets.)	2.25
(1-6)	Don Mattingly (Unnumbered, five blank-back cards, one w/1986 stats.)	3.00
(1-6)	Don Mattingly (Glossy) (Unnumbered, five cards blank-back, one w/1986 stats.)	4.50
1-12	Tim Raines (8,500 regular sets; 500 autographed.)	1.00
1-12	Tim Raines (Glossy; 1,000 sets.)	1.50
1-13	Fernando Valenzuela (8,500 regular sets, 500 autographed.)	1.50
1-13	Fernando Valenzuela (Glossy; 1,000 sets.)	2.25
(1-10)	Fernando Valenzuela (Sticker set.) (Different photos.)	2.50

1988-89 Star Promos

The lengthy series of 11-card sets issued by Star in 1988-89 in the company's "new" format included one promo card for nearly every player's set. The promos are blank-backed but otherwise similar in design to the regular cards.

		NM/M
Complete Set (40):		32.50
Common Player:		.75
(1)	Alomar Brothers (Roberto Alomar)	.75
(2)	Sandy Alomar Jr. (Alomar Brothers)	.75
(3)	Sandy Alomar Jr.	.75
(4)	Wade Boggs	2.00
(5)	Jose Canseco (Blue borders.)	1.50
(6)	Jose Conseco (Canseco) (Yellow borders.)	1.50
(7)	Jose Canseco (Bay Bombers Series)	1.50
(8)	Will Clark (Purple/yellow.)	1.50
(9)	Will Clark (Clark/Mitchell set, gold borders.)	.75
(10)	Will Clark (Bay Bombers Series)	1.50
(11)	David Cone	.75
(12)	Dwight Gooden	.75
(13)	Tom Gordon	.75
(14)	Mark Grace (1,300 issued)	1.00
(15)	Mike Greenwell (Blue borders.)	.75
(16)	Mike Greenwell (Pink borders.)	.75
(17)	Ken Griffey Jr. (White-back set, blue/white borders.)	2.50
(18)	Ken Griffey Jr. (Yellow-back set, yellow borders.)	3.50
(19)	Orel Hershiser	.75
(20)	Sam Horn	.75
(21)	Bo Jackson	.75
(22)	Gregg Jefferies (Blue-border set, orange borders.)	.75
(23)	Gregg Jefferies (Orange-border set, dark blue borders, misspelled Greg.)	.75
(24)	Gregg Jefferies (Pink-border set, light blue borders, misspelled Greg.)	.75
(25)	Ricky Jordan	.75
(26)	Don Mattingly	2.00
(27)	Kevin McReynolds	.75
(28)	Kevin Mitchell (Clark/Mitchell set, gold borders.)	.75
(29)	Kevin Mitchell (Orange borders.)	.75
(30)	Matt Nokes (Yellow borders, glossy.)	.75
(31)	Kirby Puckett	1.75
(32)	Nolan Ryan	2.50
(33)	Benito Santiago	.75
(34)	Gary Sheffield	.75
(35)	Darryl Strawberry (Blue-border set, pink borders.)	.75
(36)	Darryl Strawberry (Purple-border set, orange borders.)	.75
(37)	Alan Trammell	.75
(38)	Robin Ventura	.75
(39)	Jerome Walton (Regular set, borders in two shades of blue.)	.75
(40)	Jerome Walton/Portrait (Glossy set, solid blue borders)	.75

1988-1

Late in 1988 Star introduced a new format for its single-player card sets, which it carried forward into 1989. Sets were standardized at 11 cards in the 2-1/2" x 3-1/2" format. Fronts feature posed and game-action photos that are bordered by graduating shades of a particular color, or two different colors, going from dark at top to light at bottom, or vice versa. (The first Gregg Jefferies set is an exception, having the same shade of blue on all borders.) Backs may be printed in any of a variety of colors on white, yellow, pink or green backgrounds. Stats, personal data, career highlights and team logos are found on back. Sets may carry either a 1988 or 1989 copyright date. Because the sets are seldom broken up for singles sales, individual cards are not listed here. The number of player sets for which glossy versions were issued is uncertain. Existing glossy sets should retail for 2-5X the regular version, depending on player popularity.

		NM/M
1-11	Alomar Brothers (Roberto Alomar, Sandy Alomar Jr.)	1.50
1-11	Sandy Alomar Jr.	1.50
1-11	Bay Bombers Series Jose Canseco (Solid green borders.)	3.00
1-11	Bay Bombers Series Will Clark (Solid orange borders.)	1.75
1-11	Wade Boggs (Solid red borders.)	4.00
1-11	Jose Canseco (Error set - "Conseco.")	5.00
1-11	Jose Canseco (Correct, dark green borders, white name.)	3.00
1-11	Jose Canseco (Correct, light green borders, green name.)	3.00
1-11	Will Clark	3.00
1-11	Will Clark, Kevin Mitchell	1.50
1-11	David Cone	1.50
1-11	Dwight Gooden	1.50
1-11	Tom Gordon	1.50
1-11	Mark Grace (Solid orange borders; 6,500 sets.)	1.00
1-11	Mark Grace/Auto. (500 sets)	5.00
1-11	Mike Greenwell (Purple borders.)	1.50
1-11	Mike Greenwell (Red borders.)	1.50
1-11	Ken Griffey Jr. (White backs.)	7.50
1-11	Ken Griffey Jr. (Yellow backs, different photos.)	7.50
1-11	Orel Hershiser (8,000 regular sets.)	1.50
1-11	Orel Hershiser (Glossy - 250 sets.)	2.25
1-11	Sam Horn (Solid blue borders; 4,000 sets.)	1.00
1-11	Sam Horn (Glossy - 1,000 sets.)	1.50
1-11	Bo Jackson	1.50
1-11	Gregg Jefferies (Blue borders; 8,000 sets.)	1.50
1-11	Gregg Jefferies (Orange borders.)	1.50
1-11	Gregg Jefferies (Pink borders.)	1.50
1-11	Ron Jones	1.50
1-11	Ricky Jordan (8,000 sets.)	1.00
1-11	Ricky Jordan (Glossy - 250 sets.)	2.00

Column 1 (top, torn fragments)

.../1990 ... 1.50
.../1992 ... 1.50
... green.) ... 1.50
... Jefferies/1988
(Regular blue.) ... 1.50
... ward Johnson/1990
(Regular orange.) ... 1.50
David Justice/1992
(Plastic blue/yellow.) 1.50
(20) Eric Karros/1992
(Glossy white.) 1.50
(21) Barry Larkin/1990
(Regular red.) 1.50
(22) Kevin Maas/1990
(Regular white.) 1.50
(23) Don Mattingly/1988
(Regular green.) 3.50
(24) Don Mattingly/1989
(Regular blue.) 3.50
(25) Don Mattingly/1989
(Regular gray.) 3.50
(26) Kevin Mitchell/1990
(Regular white/black.) 1.50
(27) Phil Plantier/1992
(Plastic blue/purple.) 1.50
(28) Kirby Puckett/1989
(Regular red.) 6.50
(29) Kirby Puckett/1990
(Plastic purple/blue.) 3.25
(30) Cal Ripken Jr./1992
(Regular black/
orange.) 3.50
(31) Reggie Sanders/1992
(Glossy white.) 1.50
(32) Benito Santiago/1990
(Regular purple.) 1.50
(33) Mike Scott/1989
(Regular green.) 1.50
(34) Darryl Strawberry/1991
(Regular red.) 1.50
(35g) Frank Thomas/1991
(Glossy blue/red.) 3.25
(35p) Frank Thomas/1991
(Plastic blue/red.) 3.25
(36) Frank Thomas/1992
(Plastic red/yellow.) 3.25
(37) Alan Trammell/1989
(Glossy blue.) 1.50
(38) Robin Ventura/1990
(Glossy gold.) 3.25
(39) Jerome Walton/1990
(Regular blue/red.) 1.50

1988-92 Star Ad Cards

KEVIN MAAS — NEW YORK Ad Card

These cards were distributed to give dealers and collectors basic information about Star's baseball issues. Fronts look like contemporary Star cards, but most (not all) have the notation "Ad Card" beneath the city name at lower-right. Backs have an advertising message with general information except for Horn and Jefferies, whose ads are specific to ordering those player sets. Some cards exist in both regular and glossy finish. Except for the 1992s, the Ad Cards are undated and some of the dates on this possibly incomplete checklist are only best estimates. The unnumbered cards are checklisted here alphabetically.

	NM/M
Complete Set (45):	70.00
Common Player:	1.50

(1) Sandy Alomar Jr./1989 (Regular gray.) 1.50
(1g) Sandy Alomar Jr./1989 (Glossy gray.) 1.50
(2) Steve Avery/1992 (Plastic red/blue.) 1.50
(3) Jeff Bagwell/1992 (Plastic orange/green.) 1.50
(4) Wade Boggs/1989 (Regular pink.) 3.25
(5) Bobby Bonilla/1991 (Regular purple.) 1.50
(5g) Bobby Bonilla/1991 (Glossy purple.) 1.50
(6) Will Clark/1988 (Regular green.) 1.50
(6g) Will Clark/1988 (Glossy green.) 1.50
(7) Roger Clemens/1988 (Regular) 2.50
(8) Eric Davis/1989 (Glossy red.) 1.50
(9) Ken Griffey Jr./1989 (Regular purple.) 3.50
(10) Ken Griffey Jr./1990 (Regular green.) 2.50
(10g) Ken Griffey Jr./1990 (Glossy green.) 3.50
(11) Rickey Henderson/1991 (Regular green/yellow.) 1.50
(11g) Rickey Henderson/1991 (Glossy green/yellow.) 1.50
(12) Keith Hernandez/1989 (Regular orange.) 1.50
(13) Orel Hershiser/1989 (Regular purple.) 1.50
(14) Sam Horn/1988 (Regular purple.) 1.50

1988-89 Star Gold Edition

KIRBY PUCKETT — GOLD EDITION

This 180-card set was released from late 1988 into 1989 (though all cards bear 1988 copyright date) in a format matching the regular-issue player sets of the 1988-89 issue. Eighteen single-player sets of 10 cards each are included. The high quality photographs on front feature a special gold embossing. The cards devoted to each player are noted by number in the corresponding listings. Single cards are not checklisted because the issue is usually sold only as complete single-player sets. Fifteen hundred of each set were produced, plus 300 black-bordered, blank-back "promo" cards of each player.

	NM/M
Complete Set (180):	22.50
Common Player Set (10):	1.00
Complete Promo Set:	32.50
Common Promo Card:	1.50

1-10 Gregg Jefferies 1.00
Gregg Jefferies/PC 1.50
11-20 Sam Horn 1.00
Sam Horn/PC 1.50
21-30 Don Mattingly 6.00
Don Mattingly/PC 7.50

ABBREVIATIONS
PC - Promo Card

31-40 Matt Nokes 1.00
Matt Nokes/PC 1.50
41-50 Darryl Strawberry 1.00
Darryl Strawberry/PC 1.50
51-60 Will Clark 2.00
Will Clark/PC 3.00
61-70 Wade Boggs 3.00
Wade Boggs/PC 3.00
71-80 Mark Grace 1.50
Mark Grace/PC 2.00
81-90 Bo Jackson 1.50
Bo Jackson/PC 1.50
91-100 Jose Canseco 3.00
Jose Canseco/PC 3.00
101-110 Eric Davis 1.50
Eric Davis/PC 1.50
110-119 Orel Hershiser (#120 misnumbered #110) 1.00
Orel Hershiser/PC 1.50
121-130 Mike Greenwell 1.00
Mike Greenwell/PC 1.50
131-140 Dave Winfield 2.00
Dave Winfield/PC 3.00
141-150 Alan Trammell 1.00
Alan Trammell/PC 1.50
151-160 Roger Clemens 4.00
Roger Clemens/PC 3.50
161-170 Kirby Puckett 3.50
Kirby Puckett/PC 3.50
171-180 Kevin Seitzer 1.00
Kevin Seitzer/PC 1.50

1988-89 Star Nova Edition

JOSE CANSECO — Major League Stats

With production limited to just 500 sets and 40 promo cards of each player, these are the most limited of the regular Star issues of 1989. Cards follow the format of the regular-issue Star single-player sets of the 1988-89 issue. Each of the 9-card player sets is listed here in alphabetical order. Single cards are not listed because complete player sets are seldom broken for individual card sales. The Nova promo cards have blue borders at the top and red at bottom. Cards #109-117 were not issued. Ryne Sandberg cards #154-161 have his name misspelled Sanberg on front and back.

	NM/M
Complete Set (153):	85.00
Common Player Set (9):	3.00
Complete Promo Card Set (17):	225.00
Common Promo Card:	7.50

1-9 Mike Greenwell 3.00
Mike Greenwell/PC 7.50
10-18 Darryl Strawberry 3.00
Darryl Strawberry/PC 7.50
19-27 Don Mattingly 11.00
Don Mattingly/PC 30.00
28-36 Eric Davis 3.00
Eric Davis/PC 7.50
37-45 Jose Canseco 7.50
Jose Canseco/PC 22.50
46-54 Sandy Alomar Jr. 3.00
Sandy Alomar Jr./PC 7.50
55-63 Kirby Puckett 9.00
Kirby Puckett/PC 25.00
64-72 Orel Hershiser 3.00
Orel Hershiser/PC 7.50
73-81 Wade Boggs 3.00
Wade Boggs/PC 17.50
82-90 Rickey Henderson 5.00
Rickey Henderson/PC 9.00
91-99 Will Clark 3.50
Will Clark/PC 15.00
100-108 Bo Jackson 3.50
Bo Jackson/PC 12.50
118-126 Ken Griffey Jr. 15.00
Ken Griffey Jr./PC 30.00
127-135 Mike Schmidt 11.00
Mike Schmidt/PC 30.00

136-144 Gary Sheffield 3.50
Gary Sheffield/PC 9.00
145-153 Cal Ripken Jr. 12.50
Cal Ripken Jr./PC 35.00
154-162 Ryne Sandberg 7.50
Ryne Sandberg/PC 20.00

1988 Star Platinum Edition

DWIGHT GOODEN — PLATINUM — The Future

Twelve single-player sets make up the 1988 Star Platinum series. Ten cards were devoted to each player. While the cards were sold as individual player sets, they were numbered continuously. Fronts feature photos with various colorful borders (by player), highlighted in silver foil. No single card prices are quoted because the cards are usually sold only as complete player sets. One thousand sets of each player were issued, along with 200 gold-bordered promo cards per player.

	NM/M
Complete Set (120):	27.50
Common Player Set (10):	1.50
Complete Promo Set (12):	32.50
Common Promo Player:	2.00

1-10 Don Mattingly 6.00
Don Mattingly/PC 10.00
11-20 Dwight Gooden 1.50
Dwight Gooden/PC 2.00
21-30 Roger Clemens 3.50
Roger Clemens/PC 3.50
31-40 Mike Schmidt 3.50
Mike Schmidt/PC 4.00
41-50 Wade Boggs 2.50
Wade Boggs/PC 3.00
51-60 Mark McGwire 6.00
Mark McGwire/PC 5.00
61-70 Andre Dawson 1.50
Andre Dawson/PC 2.50
71-80 Jose Canseco 2.50
Jose Canseco/PC 4.00
81-90 Eric Davis 1.50
Eric Davis/PC 2.00
91-100 George Brett 3.50
George Brett/Throwing/PC 4.00
101-110 Darryl Strawberry 1.50
Darryl Strawberry/PC (Blue uniform.) 2.00
111-120 Dale Murphy 1.50
Dale Murphy/PC 2.00

1988-89 Star Platinum

GEORGE BRETT — PLATINUM — 1980 MVP

Fourteen of baseball's top players are featured in 10-card single-player sets within this issue. Cards #21-30 were devoted to Gregg Jefferies, but a contract dispute prevented their release. While sold as single-player sets, the cards are numbered contiguously. Card numbers are provided for each player in the checklist below. Single cards are not checklisted be-

cause the issue is generally sold only as complete player sets. A thousand sets of each player were produced, along with 200 promo cards of each player. The cards follow the format of the regular-issue Star 1988-89 player sets.

	NM/M
Complete Set (140):	17.50
Common Player Set (10):	1.00
Complete Promo Set (14):	22.50
Common Promo Card:	1.50

1-10 Jose Canseco 2.00
Jose Canseco/PC 2.00
11-20 Mike Greenwell 1.50
Mike Greenwell/PC 1.50
31-40 Wade Boggs 2.50
Wade Boggs/PC 3.00
41-50 Don Mattingly 3.25
Don Mattingly/PC 3.75
51-60 Kirby Puckett 2.50
Kirby Puckett/PC 3.00
61-70 Dwight Gooden 1.00
Dwight Gooden/PC 1.50
71-80 Alan Trammell 1.00
Alan Trammell/PC 1.50
81-90 Darryl Strawberry 1.50
Darryl Strawberry/PC (White uniform.) 1.50
91-100 Orel Hershiser 1.00
Orel Hershiser/PC 1.50
101-110 Will Clark 1.50
Will Clark/PC 2.50
111-120 Roger Clemens 2.00
Roger Clemens/PC 3.50
121-130 Eric Davis 1.00
Eric Davis/PC 1.50
131-140 George Brett 3.00
George Brett/Batting/PC 3.50
141-150 Frank Viola 1.00
Frank Viola/PC 1.50

1988-89 Star Silver Edition

RICKY JORDAN — SILVER SERIES — Career Stats

This 90-card issue features 10 single-player sets. Only 2,000 serial numbered sets were printed (plus 400 "promo" cards of each player, featuring black borders fading to white at the middle). Single-card values are not quoted because the player sets are seldom broken for individual card sales. Cards follow the format of the regular-issue 1988-89 Star player sets.

	NM/M
Complete Set (90):	35.00
Common Player Set:	1.50
Complete Promo Card Set (10):	37.50
Common Promo Card:	3.00

1-9 Ken Griffey Jr. 17.50
Ken Griffey Jr./PC 9.00
10-18 Wade Boggs 5.00
Wade Boggs/PC 6.00
19-27 Ricky Jordan 1.50
Ricky Jordan/PC 3.00
28-36 Mike Greenwell 1.50
Mike Greenwell/PC 3.00
37-45 Sandy Alomar Jr. 1.50
Sandy Alomar Jr./PC 3.00
46-54 Mike Schmidt 6.00
Mike Schmidt/PC 7.50
55-63 Gary Sheffield 2.25
Gary Sheffield/PC 3.00
64-72 Will Clark 2.25
Will Clark/PC 3.50
73-81 Ron Jones 1.50
Ron Jones/PC 3.00
82-90 Kirby Puckett 6.00
Kirby Puckett/PC 6.00

1988 Star '88 Promos

Most of the Star '88 single- and dual-player card sets also had a promo card issued; blank-

backed but otherwise nearly identical to the regular cards.

	NM/M
Complete Set (23):	35.00
Common Player:	1.00

(1) George Bell 1.00
(2) Wade Boggs 2.00
(3) Wade Boggs, Tony Gwynn 1.50
(4) Gary Carter 1.50
(5) Will Clark 1.50
(6) Roger Clemens, Dwight Gooden 1.50
(7) Eric Davis 1.00
(8) Andre Dawson 1.50
(9) Dwight Gooden 1.00
(10) Tony Gwynn 2.00
(11) Bo Jackson 1.50
(12) Don Mattingly 3.00
(13) Don Mattingly, Mike Schmidt 1.75
(14) Mark McGwire (Yellow-border set, green-border promo.) 4.00
(15) Mark McGwire (Aqua-border set, yellow-border promo.) 2.50
(16) Mark McGwire (Green-border set, white-border promo.) 4.00
(17) Eddie Murray 2.00
(18) Cal Ripken Jr. 3.50
(19) Mike Schmidt 2.50
(20) Mike Scott 1.00
(21) Kevin Seitzer 1.00
(22) Cory Snyder 1.00
(23) Dave Winfield 2.50

1988 Star '88

ANDRE DAWSON — THE HAWK

For the fifth straight year Star utilized the same basic format for its single-player card sets of 1988. Fronts have player posed and game-action photos surrounded by a brightly colored border. Pushing into the top-right of the photo is a "Star '88" logo. A circle at the lower-left contains the player name or logo. Backs have stats, personal data, career highlights or a checklist. Single cards are not listed because sets are seldom broken. Many player sets were also issued in a more limited glossy edition, and some sets were produced with the first card authentically autographed.

	NM/M
1-11 George Bell (7,500 sets)	1.50
(1-10) George Bell (Sticker set.)	2.00
1-11 Wade Boggs (10,000 sets)	2.50
1-11 Wade Boggs (#1 autographed.)	25.00
1-11 Wade Boggs (Glossy - 1,000 sets.)	4.00
1-11 Wade Boggs, Tony Gwynn	2.50
1-11 Gary Carter (6,000 sets)	2.00
1-11 Gary Carter (Glossy - 1,000 sets.)	3.00
1-11 Will Clark (7,500 sets)	1.75
1-11 Will Clark (#1 autographed)	15.00
1-11 Roger Clemens, Dwight Gooden	2.00
1-12 Eric Davis	1.50
1-11 Eric Davis (Glossy - 1,000 sets.)	1.50
1-11 Eric Davis, Mark McGwire	2.25
1-11 Andre Dawson (4,500 sets)	1.50
1-11 Andre Dawson (Glossy - 1,000 sets.)	2.50
1-11 Andre Dawson/Auto. (500 sets)	12.50
1-12 Dwight Gooden (5,600 sets)	1.50

1-12	Dwight Gooden (Glossy - 1,000 sets.)	2.25
1-12	Dwight Gooden/Auto. (400 sets)	10.00
1-11	Tony Gwynn (5,000 sets)	2.50
1-11	Tony Gwynn (Glossy - 1,000 sets.)	4.50
1-11	Tony Gwynn/Auto. (500 sets)	15.00
1-16	Bo Jackson (Set includes four blank-back cards as Auburn football player; 6,000 sets.)	3.00
1-16	Bo Jackson (Glossy - 1,000 sets.)	4.50
1-11	Don Mattingly (Card #3 exists with fielding or batting pose, 10,000 sets.)	6.00
1-11	Don Mattingly (Glossy - 1,000 sets.)	7.00
1-11	Don Mattingly, Mike Schmidt (2,000 sets)	4.00
1-11	Don Mattingly, Mike Schmidt (Glossy - 1,000 sets.)	4.50
1-12	Mark McGwire (Yellow borders; 12,000 sets.)	3.50
1-12	Mark McGwire (Yellow borders; glossy - 1,000 sets.)	4.50
1-12	Mark McGwire/Auto. (Yellow borders; 500 sets)	50.00
1-11	Mark McGwire (Aqua borders.)	7.50
1-11	Mark McGwire (Green borders; 6,000 sets.)	3.50
1-11	Mark McGwire (Green borders; glossy - 1,000 sets.)	5.00
1-12	Eddie Murray (Glossy version only.)	2.00
1-12	Cal Ripken Jr.	6.00
1-12	Mike Schmidt (Glossy version only.)	4.00
1-11	Mike Scott	1.50
1-11	Kevin Seitzer (6,000 sets)	1.50
1-11	Kevin Seitzer (Glossy - 1,000 sets.)	2.25
1-11	Cory Snyder (8,500 sets)	1.50
1-11	Cory Snyder (Glossy - 1,000 sets.)	2.25
1-11	Cory Snyder/Auto. (500 sets)	5.00
(1-8)	Cory Snyder (Sticker set; 4,000 sets.)	2.00
1-12	Dave Winfield (5,000 sets)	2.00
1-12	Dave Winfield (Glossy - 1,000 sets.)	3.00
1-12	Dave Winfield/Auto. (500 sets)	16.00
(1-10)	Dave Winfield (Sticker set; 3,000.)	2.00

1989-90 Star Rookies

Two-card "sets" of each of 12 promising players were produced in an edition of 10,000 each as an exclusive for a New York comic book dealer. Cards have player photos on front with a few stats on back. Cards #1-12 have borders of red and gold and backs printed in red and tan. The 1990 cards, #13-24, are bordered in purple and yellow with backs printed in purple on yellow. All cards have 1989 copyright dates. Unlike most other contemporary Star sets, no glossy or promo cards were made.

		NM/M
	Complete Set (24):	2.50
	Common Player:	.15
1	Eric Anthony	.15
2	Eric Anthony	.15

3	Mark Lewis	.15
4	Mark Lewis	.15
5	Pete Rose, Jr.	.25
6	Pete Rose, Jr.	.25
7	Robin Ventura	.40
8	Robin Ventura	.40
9	Beau Allred	.15
10	Beau Allred	.15
11	Pat Combs	.15
12	Pat Combs	.15
13	Deion Sanders	.25
14	Deion Sanders	.25
15	Bob Hamelin	.15
16	Bob Hamelin	.15
17	Andy Benes	.20
18	Andy Benes	.20
19	Bam Bam Muelens	.15
20	Bam Bam Muelens	.15
21	Trey McCoy	.15
22	Trey McCoy	.15
23	Sandy Alomar Jr.	.25
24	Sandy Alomar Jr.	.25

1990-91 Star Promos

Most of the 1990-91 series of Star player sets feature a promo card in the same format. They are blank-backed and have the word "Promo" on front beneath the city name. Regular and glossy promos exist for most cards.

		NM/M
	Complete Set (44):	75.00
	Common Player:	1.50
(1)	Jim Abbott	1.50
(2)	Andy Benes	1.50
(3)	Barry Bonds (Correct)	6.00
(4)	Bobby Bonds (Photo actually Barry.)	6.00
(5)	Bobby Bonilla	1.50
(6)	Jose Canseco (Blue borders, from purple set.)	1.50
(7)	Jose Canseco (Orange borders, from yellow set.)	1.50
(8)	Jose Canseco (Green borders, from yellow set.)	1.50
(9)	Will Clark (Black borders.)	1.50
(10)	Will Clark (Purple)	1.50
(11)	Will Clark (Orange, from Clark/Grace set.)	1.50
(12)	Mark Davis	1.50
(13)	Cecil Fielder (Purple, from blue set.)	1.50
(14)	Cecil Fielder (Yellow glossy, from blue set.)	12.50
(15)	Ken Griffey Jr. (Purple, from blue set.)	2.25
(16)	Ken Griffey Jr. (Blue on yellow, from blue set.)	1.50
(17)	Ken Griffey Jr. (Red, batting with "S" on helmet, from yellow set.)	1.50
(18)	Ken Griffey Jr. (Red, no "S" on helmet, from aqua Jr./Sr. set.)	2.25
(19)	Ken Griffey Jr. (Red on yellow, from red Jr./Sr. set.)	2.25
(20)	Ken Griffey Sr. (Blue, from aqua set.)	1.50
(21)	Ken Griffey Sr. (Yellow, from red set.)	1.50
(22)	Rickey Henderson (Blue, 1990)	1.50
(23)	Rickey Henderson/Running (Green, 1990)	1.50
(24)	Rickey Henderson/Btg (Green, 1991)	1.50
(25)	Bo Jackson/Running	1.50
(26)	Bo Jackson/Portrait	1.50
(27)	Bo Jackson (Diamond Terror, yellow)	1.50
(28)	David Justice	1.50
(29)	Barry Larkin	1.50
(30)	Kevin Maas	1.50
(31)	Ben McDonald	1.50
(32)	Kevin Mitchell	1.50
(33)	Gregg Olson	1.50
(34)	Cal Ripken Jr.	3.00
(35)	Nolan Ryan (Blue, from Rangers set.)	4.00
(36)	Nolan Ryan (Yellow, from all-team set.)	3.00
(37)	Bret Saberhagen	1.50
(38)	Ryne Sandberg	1.50
(39)	Darryl Strawberry	1.50
(40)	Frank Thomas	1.50
(41)	Jerome Walton	1.50
(42)	Matt Williams	1.50
(43)	Robin Yount (Brown on yellow, from Mitchell/Yount set.)	1.50
(44)	Robin Yount (Blue on yellow.)	1.50

1990-91 Star

Issued as single-player sets over the two-year span these sets maintain a design continuity despite the fact some have a 1990 copyright line on back and some have a 1991 date. Fronts of all cards have posed and game-action photos which are bordered in a single bright color, by player. That border color is darkest at top and bottom and fades to white at the center. Backs are printed in one of several colors on white cardboard and feature personal data, stats, career highlights, checklists and team logos. Single cards are not listed because sets are seldom broken for individual card sales. Glossy versions are known for most, but not all, player sets.

		NM/M
1-11	Jim Abbott	1.50
1-11	Andy Benes	1.50
1-11	Barry Bonds (Error, cards #2-11 say "Bobby Bonds.")	9.00
1-11	Barry Bonds (Corrected)	9.00
1-11	Bobby Bonila	1.50
1-11	Jose Canseco (Purple borders.)	1.50
1-11	Jose Canseco (Yellow borders.)	1.50
1-11	Will Clark	1.50
1-11	Will Clark, Mark Grace	1.50
1-11	Cecil Fielder (Blue borders.)	1.50
1-11	Cecil Fielder (Orange borders.)	1.50
1-11	Ken Griffey Jr. (Blue borders.)	3.00
1-11	Ken Griffey Jr. (Yellow borders.)	2.00
1-11	Ken Griffey Jr., Ken Griffey Sr. (Aqua borders.)	2.00
1-11	Ken Griffey Jr., Ken Griffey Sr. (Red borders.)	2.00
1-11	Rickey Henderson/ 1990	4.00
1-11	Rickey Henderson (Glossy - 250 sets.)	4.50
1-11	Rickey Henderson/ 1991	4.00
1-11	Bo Jackson	1.50
1-11	Bo Jackson, Barry Larkin (Diamond Terror)	1.50
1	Howard Johnson (Autographed card numbered to 400.)	
1-11	Dave Justice	1.50
1-11	Dave Justice, Kevin Maas	1.50
1-11	Barry Larkin	1.50
1-11	Kevin Maas	1.50
1-11	Ben McDonald	1.50
1-11	Kevin Mitchell, Robin Yount	1.50
1-11	Cal Ripken Jr.	6.00
1-11	Nolan Ryan (Card #1 pitching, all Rangers photos.)	2.50

1-11	Nolan Ryan (Card #1 portrait, all four teams.)	2.50
1-11	Bret Saberhagen, Mark Davis	1.50
1-11	Ryne Sandberg	2.00
1-11	Ryne Sandberg (Glossy)	10.00
1-11	Darryl Strawberry	1.50
1-11	Frank Thomas	1.50
1-11	Jerome Walton, Gregg Olson	1.50
1-11	Matt Williams	1.50
1-11	Robin Yount	1.50

1990-93 Star "Career Stats"

These unnumbered cards are not part of any Star sets. They share a common design of two-color graduated borders on front, with color photos both front and back. The words "Career Stats" are prominently displayed on both front and back. Some players were sold in both autographed and unautographed versions, while some are known only in one version or the other.

		NM/M
	Complete Set (26):	65.00
	Common Player:	1.50
(1)	Ken Griffey Jr./1990	3.50
(2)	Barry Bonds/1991	4.00
(2a)	Barry Bonds/1991 (autographed)	15.00
(3)	Bobby Bonilla/1991	1.50
(4)	Scott Erickson/1991	1.50
(4a)	Scott Erickson/1991/ Auto.	3.00
(5)	Chuck Knoblauch/ 1991	1.50
(5a)	Chuck Knoblauch/1991/ Auto.	3.00
(6)	Frank Thomas/1991	3.00
(6a)	Frank Thomas/1991/ Auto.	10.00
(6g)	Frank Thomas/ 1991/Glossy	3.00
(7)	Matt Williams/1991	1.50
(7a)	Matt Williams/1991/ Auto.	3.00
(8)	Jeff Bagwell/1992	2.00
(9a)	Pat Kelly/1992/Auto.	3.00
(10a)	Mark Lewis/1992/ Auto.	3.00
(11a)	John Olerud/1992/ Auto.	3.00
(12)	Jim Abbott/1993	1.50
(12a)	Jim Abbott/1993/ Auto.	3.00
(13)	Bret Barberie/1993	1.50
(13a)	Bret Barberie/1993/ Auto.	3.00
(14)	Andy Benes/1993	1.50
(14a)	Andy Benes/1993/ Auto.	3.00
(15)	Rickey Henderson/ 1993	2.00
(16a)	Eric Karros/1993/Auto.	3.00
(17)	Ryan Klesko/1993	1.50
(18)	Kevin Mass/1993 (Maas)	1.50
(19)	Dean Palmer/1993	1.50

1990-91 Star Gold Edition

Only 1,500 of each 9-card, single-player set was produced in Star's 1990-91 Gold Edition. Single cards are not listed or priced because the issue is almost exclusively traded in complete player sets. Cards were numbered contiguously as noted in the alphabetical checklist presented here. Suggested retail price at issue was $15-20

per set. An edition of 300 gray-bordered promo cards was issued for each player.

		NM/M
	Complete Set (180):	40.00
	Common Player:	1.50
	Complete Promo Set (20):	50.00
	Common Promo Card:	2.00
(1)	Wade Boggs (#136-144)	2.25
(1)	Wade Boggs/PC	4.00
(2)	Bobby Bonilla (#145-153)	1.50
(2)	Bobby Bonilla/PC	2.00
(3)	Jose Canseco (#19-27)	2.25
(3)	Jose Canseco/PC	3.00
(4)	Will Clark (#64-72)	2.25
(4)	Will Clark/PC	3.00
(5)	Dwight Gooden (#109-117)	1.50
(5)	Dwight Gooden/PC	2.00
(6)	Mark Grace (#154-162)	1.50
(6)	Mark Grace/PC	2.00
(7)	Ken Griffey Jr. (#10-18)	7.50
(7)	Ken Griffey Jr./PC	10.00
(8)	Rickey Henderson (#82-90)	3.00
(8)	Rickey Henderson/PC	4.00
(9)	Bo Jackson (#1-9)	1.50
(9)	Bo Jackson/PC	2.00
(10)	Howard Johnson (#163-171)	1.50
(10)	Howard Johnson/PC	2.00
(11)	David Justice (#118-126)	1.50
(11)	David Justice/PC	2.00
(12)	Barry Larkin (#91-99)	1.50
(12)	Barry Larkin/PC	2.00
(13)	Kevin Maas (#127-135)	1.50
(13)	Kevin Maas/PC	2.00
(14)	Don Mattingly (#100-108)	4.50
(14)	Don Mattingly/PC	4.50
(15)	Kirby Puckett (#55-63)	4.00
(15)	Kirby Puckett/PC	6.00
(16)	Tim Raines (#37-45)	1.50
(16)	Tim Raines/PC	2.00
(17)	Cal Ripken Jr. (#73-81)	7.50
(17)	Cal Ripken Jr./PC	10.00
(18)	Ryne Sandberg (#46-54)	3.00
(18)	Ryne Sandberg/PC	4.00
(19)	Darryl Strawberry (#172-180)	1.50
(19)	Darryl Strawberry/PC	2.00
(20)	Robin Yount (#28-36)	1.50
(20)	Robin Yount/PC	2.00

1990-91 Star Nova Edition

With just 500 of each nine-card single-player set produced, the Nova Edition was Star's top of the line in 1990. Player sets are listed alphabetically. Single cards are not listed because sets are seldom broken. Each set is also represented by an issue of 100 promo cards, featuring black borders at top and yellow at bottom.

		NM/M
	Complete Set (180):	50.00
	Common Player Set:	2.25
	Complete Promo Set (20):	65.00
	Common Promo Card:	3.00
(1)	Wade Boggs (#28-36)	5.00
(1)	Wade Boggs/PC	6.00
(2)	Jose Canseco (#55-63)	3.75
(2)	Jose Canseco/PC	5.00
(3)	Joe Carter (#118-126)	2.25
(3)	Joe Carter/PC	3.00
(4)	Will Clark (#46-54)	2.25
(4)	Will Clark/PC	4.00
(5)	Roger Clemens (#109-117)	6.50

(5)	Roger Clemens	
(6)	Glenn Davis	
	(#127-135)	
(6)	Glenn Davis	
(7)	Len Dykstra	
	(#163-171)	
(7)	Len Dykstra/PC	
(8)	Cecil Fielder	
	(#154-162)	
(8)	Cecil Fielder/PC	
(9)	Ken Griffey Jr.	
	(#172-180)	
(9)	Ken Griffey Jr./PC	
(10)	Rickey Henderson	
	(#73-81)	
(10)	Rickey Henderson/PC	
(11)	Bo Jackson (#64-72)	2.
(11)	Bo Jackson/PC	3.
(12)	Howard Johnson (#37-45)	2.25
(12)	Howard Johnson/PC	3.00
(13)	Barry Larkin (#100-108)	2.25
(13)	Barry Larkin/PC	3.00
(14)	Don Mattingly (#1-9)	6.50
(14)	Don Mattingly/PC	9.00
(15)	Kevin Mitchell (#145-153)	2.25
(15)	Kevin Mitchell/PC	3.00
(16)	Nolan Ryan (#19-27)	7.50
(16)	Nolan Ryan/PC	10.00
(17)	Ryne Sandberg (#136-144)	5.00
(17)	Ryne Sandberg/PC	6.00
(18)	Dave Stewart (#91-99)	2.25
(18)	Dave Stewart/PC	3.00
(19)	Darryl Strawberry (#82-90)	2.25
(19)	Darryl Strawberry/PC	3.00
(20)	Robin Yount (#10-18)	2.25
(20)	Robin Yount/PC	3.00

1990-91 Star Platinum Edition

The stars in Star's Platinum Edition were featured in nine-card sets with production of 1,000 each (plus 200 black-bordered promo cards of each player). Suggested retail price at the time of issue was about $20. The player sets are checklisted here in alphabetical order. Single cards are not listed because the sets are almost never broken up. Cards are numbered contiguously as noted in the alphabetical checklisted.

		NM/M
	Complete Set (180):	40.00
	Common Player Set:	1.50
	Complete Promo Set (21):	50.00
	Common Promo Card:	2.00
(1)	Jim Abbott (#19-27)	1.50
(1)	Jim Abbott/PC	2.00
(2)	Wade Boggs (#145-153)	3.00
(2)	Wade Boggs/PC	4.00
(3)	Jose Canseco (#91-99)	3.50
(3)	Jose Canseco/PC	4.00
(4)	Will Clark (#1-9)	2.50
(4)	Will Clark/PC	4.00
(5)	Roger Clemens (#46-54)	3.50
(5)	Roger Clemens/PC	7.50
(6)	Eric Davis (#55-63)	1.50
(6)	Eric Davis/PC	2.00
(7)	Dwight Gooden (#82-90)	1.50
(7)	Dwight Gooden/PC	2.00
(8)	Mark Grace (#172-180)	
(8)	(#172 says "Silver Series")	2.25
(8)	Mark Grace/PC	3.00
(9)	Mike Greenwell (#64-72)	1.50
(9)	Mike Greenwell/PC	2.00
(10)	Ken Griffey Jr. (#100-108)	7.00
(10)	Ken Griffey Jr./PC	8.00
(11)	Tony Gwynn (#28-36)	4.50
(11)	Tony Gwynn/PC	6.00

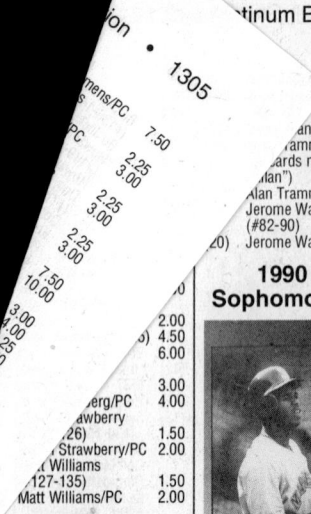

Platinum Edition

ld/PC	1.00	
ens/PC		.75
	7.50	
antiago/PC	1.00	
rammell (#46-54)	2.25	
	3.00	
ards misspelled	3.00	
lan")		.75
Alan Trammell/PC	1.00	
Jerome Walton	2.25	
(#82-90)	3.00	
20) Jerome Walton/PC	1.00	
	2.25	
	3.00	
	7.50	
	10.00	
	2.00	
	4.50	
	6.00	
	3.00	
erg/PC	4.00	
rawberry		
Strawberry/PC	2.00	
t Williams		
127-135)	1.50	
Matt Williams/PC	2.00	

1990-91 Star Silver Edition

Many of 1990's biggest stars are represented in nine-card single-player sets within Star Co.'s Silver Edition. Production of each silver-foil trimmed set was limited to 2,000. Because single cards are seldom offered, only complete player sets are priced. Cards are numbered contiguously as noted in the alphabetical checklist presented here. Retail price at issue was $10-15. Each player is also represented by an issue of 400 black-bordered promo cards.

		NM/M
Complete Set (180):		17.50
Common Player Set:		.75
Complete Promo Set:		22.50
Common Promo Card:		1.00
(1)	Jim Abbott (#1-9)	.75
(1)	Jim Abbott/PC	1.00
(2)	Sandy Alomar Jr. (#55-63)	.75
(2)	Sandy Alomar Jr./PC	1.00
(3)	Andy Benes (#19-27)	.75
(3)	Andy Benes/PC	1.00
(4)	Barry Bonds (#172-180)	3.00
(4)	Barry Bonds/PC	4.00
(5)	Bobby Bonilla (#154-162)	.75
(5)	Bobby Bonilla/PC	1.00
(6)	Jose Canseco (#127-135)	1.25
(6)	Jose Canseco/PC	1.50
(7)	Will Clark (#73-81)	1.25
(7)	Will Clark/PC	1.50
(8)	Delino DeShields (#145-153)	.75
(8)	Delino DeShields/PC	1.00
(9)	Tom Gordon (#37-45)	.75
(9)	Tom Gordon/PC	1.00
(10)	Mark Grace (#10-18)	1.25
(10)	Mark Grace/PC	1.50
(11)	Ken Griffey Jr. (#91-99)	3.50
(11)	Ken Griffey Jr./PC	5.00
(12)	Mike Harkey (#163-171)	1.00
(12)	Mike Harkey/PC	1.00
(13)	Wally Joyner (#28-36)	.75
(13)	Wally Joyner/PC	1.00
(14)	David Justice (#118-126)	.75
(14)	David Justice/PC	1.00
(15)	Kevin Maas (#109-117)	.75
(15)	Kevin Maas/PC	1.00
(16)	Don Mattingly (#136-144)	2.50
(16)	Don Mattingly/PC	3.00
(17)	Ben McDonald (#100-108)	.75

1990 Star Sophomore Stars

This special six-card set was distributed only at the 1990 Arlington 11th National Sports Collectors Convention. The set came polybagged with a DC comic book in exchange for a $2 donation to the Arthritis Foundation. The 2-1/2" x 3-1/2" cards feature a border that changes from dark blue at the top to red at the bottom. Backs are printed in blue-on-white and include team and MLB logos along with major and minor league career stats. Production was reported as 10,000 sets.

		NM/M
Complete Set (6):		4.50
Common Player:		.15
1	Ken Griffey Jr./ Batting Cage	2.00
2	Ken Griffey Jr./Sitting	2.00
3	Gary Sheffield/Portrait	.30
4	Gary Sheffield/Btg	.30
5	Jerome Walton/Portrait	.15
6	Jerome Walton/Btg	.15

1991 Star

A common design is again shared by the single-player card sets released by Star for 1991. Cards feature posed and action photos on front with borders that graduate from one color at top to another at bottom (yellow to blue; green to gray, etc.). The player name is at left beneath the photo, his city at right and the card name beneath that. Backs are printed in one of several colors on white stock and feature personal data, stats, career highlights, checklist or team logo. Each set was also produced in a high-gloss version, which carries a 4-5X premium today. Single cards are not listed here because player sets are seldom broken for individual card sales. All promo cards except Clemens have a solid-color border.

	NM/M
Complete Set (88):	10.00
Common Player Set:	1.25

Complete Promo Set (6):		11.00
Common Promo Card:		1.50
(1)	Roger Clemens	1.50
	Roger Clemens/PC	2.50
1-11	Rickey Henderson	1.50
1-11	Bo Jackson	1.25
	Bo Jackson/PC	1.50
1-11	Pat Kelly (Glossy version only.)	1.25
	Pat Kelly/PC	1.50
1-11	Cal Ripken Jr.	2.50
	Cal Ripken Jr./PC	3.25
1-11	Nolan Ryan	2.00
	Nolan Ryan/PC	3.25
1-11	Darryl Strawberry	1.25
1-11	Frank Thomas (Glossy version only.)	2.50
	Frank Thomas/PC	3.00

All-Stars

This Star issue is comprised of 500 sets and 100 promo cards of each player. (Except Jackson who has 200.) The checklist is arranged alphabetically.

		NM/M
Complete Set (135):		80.00
Common Player Set:		3.75
Complete Promo Set (15):		110.00
Common Promo Card:		5.00
(1)	Wade Boggs (#109-117)	7.50
(1)	Wade Boggs/PC	10.00
(2)	Jose Canseco (#37-45)	7.50
(2)	Jose Canseco/PC	10.00
(3)	Roger Clemens (#64-72)	7.50
(3)	Roger Clemens/PC	10.00
(4)	Lenny Dykstra (#91-99)	3.75
(4)	Lenny Dykstra/PC	5.00
(5)	Cecil Fielder (#118-126)	3.75
(5)	Cecil Fielder/PC	5.00
(6)	Dwight Gooden (#82-90)	3.75
(6)	Dwight Gooden/PC	5.00
(7)	Ken Griffey Jr. (#1-9)	10.00
(7)	Ken Griffey Jr./PC	15.00
(8)	Rickey Henderson (#19-27)	7.50
(8)	Rickey Henderson/PC	10.00
(9)	Bo Jackson (#46-54)	3.75
(9)	Bo Jackson/PC	5.00
(10)	Don Mattingly (#73-81)	9.00
(10)	Don Mattingly/PC	12.00
(11)	Kirby Puckett (#100-108)	7.50
(11)	Kirby Puckett/PC	12.00
(12)	Cal Ripken Jr. (#55-63)	9.00
(12p)	Cal Ripken Jr. (#55-63) (Plastic test issue.)	12.00
(12)	Cal Ripken Jr./PC	12.00
(12p)	Cal Ripken Jr./ Plastic/PC	16.00
(13)	Nolan Ryan (#10-18)	9.00
(13)	Nolan Ryan/PC	12.00
(14)	Ryne Sandberg (#28-36)	7.50
(14)	Ryne Sandberg/PC	10.00

Diamond Series

Production of these nine-card, single-player sets was limited to 2,000 of each (plus 400 promo cards each), with a suggested retail price at issue of $25. Players in the edition are listed here in alphabetical order. Cards are numbered contiguously throughout the issue, as noted in the alpha-order listings here. Single cards are not priced because the sets are seldom broken up.

	NM/M
Complete Set (126):	22.50
Common Player Set:	1.00
Complete Promo Set:	27.50

Common Promo Card:		1.50
(1)	Barry Bonds (#10-18)	5.00
(1)	Barry Bonds/PC	5.00
(2)	Bobby Bonilla (#46-54)	1.00
(2)	Bobby Bonilla/PC	1.50
(3)	Jose Canseco (#37-45)	2.00
(3)	Jose Canseco/PC	2.50
(4)	Roger Clemens (#64-72)	2.50
(4)	Roger Clemens/PC	2.50
(5)	Cecil Fielder (#118-126)	1.00
(5)	Cecil Fielder/PC	1.50
(6)	Ken Griffey Jr. (#55-63)	3.50
(6)	Ken Griffey Jr./PC	5.00
(7)	Tony Gwynn (#100-108)	1.75
(7)	Tony Gwynn/PC	2.00
(8)	Bo Jackson (#1-9)	1.00
(8)	Bo Jackson/PC	1.50
(9)	Don Mattingly (#19-27)	5.00
(9)	Don Mattingly/PC	6.00
(10)	Kirby Puckett (#82-90)	2.50
(10)	Kirby Puckett/PC	5.00
(11)	Cal Ripken Jr. (#28-36)	7.50
(11)	Cal Ripken Jr./PC	3.50
(12)	Nolan Ryan (#109-117)	6.00
(12)	Nolan Ryan/PC	7.50
(13)	Darryl Strawberry (#73-81)	1.00
(13)	Darryl Strawberry/PC	1.50
(14)	Frank Thomas (#91-99)	2.25
(14)	Frank Thomas/PC	3.00

Gold Edition

Only 1,500 of each nine-card, single-player set was produced - along with 300 promo cards of each player - in Star's 1991 Gold Edition. Cards are numbered contiguously throughout the issue, as noted in the alphabetical checklist shown here. Single cards are not listed or priced because the issue is almost exclusively traded in complete-player sets.

		NM/M
Complete Set (144):		40.00
Common Player Set:		2.00
Complete Promo Set (16):		40.00
Common Promo Card:		2.00
(1)	Albert Belle (#118-126)	2.00
(1)	Albert Belle/PC	2.00
(2)	Barry Bonds (#73-81)	7.00
(2)	Barry Bonds/PC	7.00
(3)	Bobby Bonilla (#127-135)	2.00
(3)	Bobby Bonilla/PC	2.00
(4)	Jose Canseco (#55-63)	3.00
(4)	Jose Canseco/PC	3.00
(5)	Will Clark (#28-36)	2.00
(5)	Will Clark/PC	2.00
(6)	Roger Clemens (#64-72)	6.00
(6)	Roger Clemens/PC	6.00
(7)	Ken Griffey Jr. (#19-27)	5.00
(7)	Ken Griffey Jr./PC	5.00
(8)	Bo Jackson (#37-45)	2.00
(8)	Bo Jackson/PC	2.00
(9)	David Justice (#82-90)	2.00
(9)	David Justice/PC	2.00
(10)	Don Mattingly (#91-99)	6.00
(10)	Don Mattingly/PC	6.00
(11)	Fred McGriff (#136-144)	2.00
(11)	Fred McGriff/PC	2.00
(12)	Kirby Puckett (#1-9)	4.50
(12)	Kirby Puckett/PC	4.50
(13)	Nolan Ryan (#109-117)	6.00
(13)	Nolan Ryan/PC	6.00
(14)	Ryne Sandberg (#10-18)	4.00
(14)	Ryne Sandberg/PC	4.00
(15)	Darryl Strawberry (#46-54)	2.00
(15)	Darryl Strawberry/PC	2.00
(16)	Frank Thomas (#100-108)	3.00
(16)	Frank Thomas/PC	3.00

Home Run Series

With a suggested retail price at issue of $25 or so, and an edition limit of 1,500 each of the single-player, nine-card sets (plus 300 promo cards of each player), these are among the scarcer of the 1991 Star issues. Numbers on individual

BALTIMORE · Honors & Awards - 2 · CAL RIPKEN, Jr.

player cards run contiguously throughout the issue and are noted in the alphabetical checklist. Because sets are seldom available as singles, individual cards are not listed here.

		NM/M
Complete Set (126):		65.00
Common Player Set:		3.75
Complete Promo Set (14):		85.00
Common Promo Card:		5.00
(1)	Wade Boggs (#91-99)	5.50
(1)	Wade Boggs/PC	7.50
(2)	Barry Bonds (#64-72)	9.00
(2)	Barry Bonds/PC	12.00
(3)	Bobby Bonilla (#10-18)	3.75
(3)	Bobby Bonilla/PC	5.00
(4)	Jose Canseco (#1-9)	5.50
(4)	Jose Canseco/PC	7.50
(5)	Dwight Gooden (#73-81)	3.75
(5)	Dwight Gooden/PC	5.00
(6)	Ken Griffey Jr. (#37-45)	5.00
(6)	Ken Griffey Jr./PC	7.50
(7)	Rickey Henderson (#19-27)	6.00
(7)	Rickey Henderson/PC	8.00
(8)	Bo Jackson (#82-90)	3.00
(8)	Bo Jackson/PC	4.50
(9)	Don Mattingly (#46-54)	9.00
(9)	Don Mattingly/PC	10.00
(10)	Cal Ripken Jr. (#109-117)	9.00
(10)	Cal Ripken Jr./PC	12.00
(11)	Nolan Ryan (#55-63)	9.00
(11)	Nolan Ryan/PC	12.00
(12)	Ryne Sandberg (#100-108)	7.50
(12)	Ryne Sandberg/PC	7.50
(13)	Darryl Strawberry (#28-36)	3.75
(13)	Darryl Strawberry/PC	5.00
(14)	Frank Thomas (#118-126)	7.50
(14)	Frank Thomas/PC	10.00

Millennium Edition

DON MATTINGLY · NEW YORK · Minor League Stats

As the name suggests, production of each of these nine-card, single-player sets was pegged at 1,000 (plus 200 promo cards of each player). Suggested retail price at issue was about $30. Cards are numbered contiguously throughout the issue, as noted in the alphabetical checklist (part of each Ripken and Gooden set are misnumbered). Individual cards are not listed or priced because the sets are almost never broken down for singles sales.

		NM/M
Complete Set (126):		50.00
Common Player Set:		1.50
Complete Promo Set (14):		50.00
Common Promo Card:		1.50
(1)	Wade Boggs (#55-63)	7.50
(1)	Wade Boggs/PC	7.50
(2)	Will Clark (#46-54)	3.00

(2)	Will Clark/PC	3.00
(3)	Cecil Fielder (#109-117)	1.50
(3)	Cecil Fielder/PC	1.50
(4)	Dwight Gooden (#10-14, 78-81)	1.50
(4)	Dwight Gooden/PC	1.50
(5)	Ken Griffey Jr. (#91-99)	6.00
(5)	Ken Griffey Jr./PC	6.00
(6)	Howard Johnson (#64-72)	1.50
(6)	Howard Johnson/PC	1.50
(7)	Dave Justice (#100-108)	1.50
(7)	David Justice/PC	1.50
(8)	Kevin Maas (#82-90)	1.50
(8)	Kevin Maas/PC	1.50
(9)	Don Mattingly (#37-45)	7.50
(9)	Don Mattingly/PC	7.50
(10)	Kirby Puckett (#19-27)	7.50
(10)	Kirby Puckett/PC	7.50
(11)	Cal Ripken Jr. (#15-18, 73-77)	7.50
(11)	Cal Ripken Jr./PC	7.50
(12)	Ryne Sandberg (#28-36)	6.00
(12)	Ryne Sandberg/PC	6.00
(13)	Frank Thomas (#118-126)	6.00
(13)	Frank Thomas/PC	6.00
(14)	Robin Yount (#1-9)	3.00
(14)	Robin Yount/PC	3.00

Nova Edition

Rickey Henderson · OAKLAND · Minor League Stats

Production of these nine-card, single-player sets was limited to 500 of each (plus 100 promo cards of each player). Sets are checklisted here in alphabetical order. Individual cards are numbered contiguously throughout the issue, as noted. Single cards are not priced because sets are seldom broken up for sale of individual cards.

		NM/M
Complete Set (144):		60.00
Common Player Set:		2.50
Complete Promo Set (16):		60.00
Common Promo Card:		2.50
(1)	Wade Boggs (#82-90)	6.00
(1)	Wade Boggs/PC	6.00
(2)	Jose Canseco (#55-63)	5.00
(2)	Jose Canseco/PC	5.00
(3)	Vince Coleman (#127-135)	2.50
(3)	Vince Coleman/PC	2.50
(4)	Cecil Fielder (#136-144)	2.50
(4)	Cecil Fielder/PC	2.50
(5)	Dwight Gooden (#10-18)	2.50
(5)	Dwight Gooden/PC	2.50
(6)	Ken Griffey Jr. (#91-99)	7.50
(6)	Ken Griffey Jr./PC	7.50
(7)	Tony Gwynn (#100-108)	5.00
(7)	Tony Gwynn/PC	5.00
(8)	Rickey Henderson (#1-9)	5.00
(8)	Rickey Henderson/PC	5.00
(9)	Bo Jackson (#28-36)	2.50
(9)	Bo Jackson/PC	2.50
(10)	Howard Johnson (#118-126)	2.50
(10)	Howard Johnson/PC	2.50
(11)	Don Mattingly (#64-72)	7.50
(11)	Don Mattingly/PC	7.50
(12)	Kirby Puckett (#109-117)	5.00
(12)	Kirby Puckett/PC	5.00
(13)	Cal Ripken Jr. (#46-54)	9.00

ABBREVIATIONS

PC - Promo Card

(13)	Cal Ripken Jr./PC	9.00
(14)	Nolan Ryan (#19-27)	10.00
(14)	Nolan Ryan/PC	10.00
(15)	Ryne Sandberg (#73-81)	6.00
(15)	Ryne Sandberg/PC	6.00
(16)	Darryl Strawberry (#37-45)	2.50
(16)	Darryl Strawberry/PC	2.50

Platinum Edition

These nine-card, single-player sets were produced in an edition of 1,000 each (plus 200 promo cards per player). Sets are checklisted here alphabetically, with individual card numbers shown for each player. Single cards are not listed because the sets are seldom offered as singles.

		NM/M
	Complete Set (108):	45.00
	Common Player Set:	2.00
	Complete Promo Set (14):	60.00
	Common Promo Card:	2.50
(1)	Wade Boggs (#109-117)	5.00
(1)	Wade Boggs/PC	5.00
(2)	Barry Bonds (#28-36)	5.00
(2)	Barry Bonds/PC	7.50
(3)	Bobby Bonilla (#73-81)	2.00
(3)	Bobby Bonilla/PC	2.50
(4)	Jose Canseco (#19-27)	5.00
(4)	Jose Canseco/PC	6.00
(5)	Will Clark (#118-126)	3.75
(5)	Will Clark/PC	5.00
(6)	Roger Clemens (#10-18)	5.00
(6)	Roger Clemens/PC	8.00
(7)	Mark Grace (#1-9)	2.00
(7)	Mark Grace/PC	2.50
(8)	Ken Griffey Jr. (#55-63)	3.75
(8)	Ken Griffey Jr./PC	6.00
(9)	Rickey Henderson (#46-54)	3.75
(9)	Rickey Henderson/PC	5.00
(10)	Kevin Maas (#37-45)	2.00
(10)	Kevin Maas/PC	2.50
(11)	Don Mattingly (#82-90)	6.00
(11)	Don Mattingly/PC	6.50
(12)	Cal Ripken Jr. (#91-99)	7.50
(12)	Cal Ripken Jr./PC	7.50
(13)	Nolan Ryan (#64-72)	7.50
(13)	Nolan Ryan/PC	10.00
(14)	Frank Thomas (#100-108)	3.75
(14)	Frank Thomas/PC	5.00

Cal Ripken Promo Set

This unusual Star set has five solid orange-bordered cards of Ripken. Unlike the other Star promo cards, which are blank-backed, the backs of these glossy-finish cards says "1 of 1,000 Promo Sets," and include stats and other information.

		NM/M
1-5	Cal Ripken Jr.	10.00

Rookie Guild Prototypes

Labeled as "Prototype" cards, these unnumbered blank-back cards can be found in a confusing variety of regular, glossy and plastic finish for the six players in the Rookie Guild set. Only those cards confirmed to exist are listed here.

	NM/M
Complete Set, Regular (3):	4.00

MARK LEWIS — CLEVELAND — Prototype

	Complete Set, Glossy (3):	6.00
	Complete Set, Plastic (4):	8.00
(1g)	Jeff Bagwell/Glossy	2.00
(1p)	Jeff Bagwell/Plastic	2.50
(2)	Albert Belle	1.50
(3g)	Juan Gonzalez/Glossy	2.00
(3p)	Juan Gonzalez/Plastic	2.50
(4a)	Chris Knoblauch (Chuck)	2.50
(4bp)	Chuck Knoblauch/ Plastic	2.00
(5)	Mark Lewis	1.00
(6g)	Frank Thomas/Glossy	3.75
(6p)	Frank Thomas/Plastic	4.50

Rookie Guild Promos

A confusing variety of regular, glossy and plastic finish promo cards were issued in different combinations for the six players in Star's 1991 Rookie Guild issue. The blank-back, unnumbered cards are checklisted here in alphabetical order. Only those cards confirmed to have been issued are listed.

		NM/M
	Complete Set, Regular (3):	4.00
	Complete Set, Glossy (6):	12.50
	Complete Set, Plastic (4):	9.00
(1g)	Jeff Bagwell/Glossy	2.25
(1p)	Jeff Bagwell/Plastic	2.50
(2)	Albert Belle	1.50
(2g)	Albert Belle/Glossy	3.00
(3g)	Juan Gonzalez/Glossy	2.25
(3p)	Juan Gonzalez/Plastic	2.50
(4a)	Chris Knoblauch (Chuck)	1.75
(4ag)	Chris Knoblauch/Glossy (Chuck)	3.25
(4bp)	Chuck Knoblauch/ Plastic	2.00
(5)	Mark Lewis	.70
(5g)	Mark Lewis/Glossy	1.50
(6g)	Frank Thomas/Glossy	2.50
(6p)	Frank Thomas/Plastic	3.25

Rookie Guild

ALBERT BELLE — CLEVELAND — Career Info - 1

Late in the 1991 baseball season, Star introduced yet another series of single-player card sets. The emphasis was on young stars in 11-card sets. Most player sets were produced in some combination of regular and glossy finish, or glossy and plastic finish. Each player was also represented with some combination of 1,000 each promotional (border other than white) and prototype cards and 50 glossy and/or plastic promo cards. Single cards are not listed because sets are seldom broken for individual card sales.

	NM/M
Common Player Set, Regular: 1.00
Common Player Set, Glossy: 1.50
Common Player Set, Plastic: 2.00
(1) Albert Belle (#1-11) 1.00

(1g)	Albert Belle/Glossy	3.00
(2a)	Chris Knoblauch (Chuck)	3.00
(2ag)	Chris Knoblauch/Glossy (Chuck)	4.50
(2bg)	Chuck Knoblauch (#12-22) (Glossy only.)	1.50
(3g)	Mark Lewis (#23-33)	1.00
(3g)	Mark Lewis/Glossy	3.00
(4g)	Frank Thomas/Glossy (#33-44)	1.75
(4p)	Frank Thomas/Plastic	5.00
(5g)	Juan Gonzalez/Glossy (#45-55)	1.50
(5p)	Juan Gonzalez/Plastic	4.00
(6g)	Jeff Bagwell/Glossy (#56-66)	1.50
(6p)	Jeff Bagwell/Plastic	4.00

Silver Edition

SILVER — VINCE COLEMAN — NEW YORK — Career Highlights

Two thousand of each nine-card player set was produced in Star's silver-enhanced set, along with 400 promo cards of each player. Players are listed here in alphabetical order. Individual cards are not listed because the sets are seldom offered as singles.

		NM/M
	Complete Set (126):	35.00
	Common Player Set:	1.50
	Complete Promo Set (15):	45.00
	Common Promo Card:	2.00
(1)	Wade Boggs (#10-18)	4.00
(1)	Wade Boggs/PC	4.00
(2)	Bobby Bonilla (#37-45)	1.50
(2)	Bobby Bonilla/PC	2.00
(3)	Jose Canseco (#109-117)	3.00
(3)	Jose Canseco/PC	4.00
(4)	Vince Coleman (#1-9)	1.50
(4)	Vince Coleman/PC	2.00
(5)	Dwight Gooden (#73-81)	1.50
(5)	Dwight Gooden/PC	2.00
(6)	Ken Griffey Jr. (#91-99)	6.00
(6)	Ken Griffey Jr./PC	4.00
(7)	Tony Gwynn (#46-54)	4.00
(7)	Tony Gwynn/PC	5.00
(8)	Rickey Henderson (#82-90)	3.00
(8)	Rickey Henderson/PC	4.00
(9)	Bo Jackson (#100-108)	1.50
(9)	Bo Jackson/PC	2.00
(10)	Kevin Maas (#28-36)	1.50
(10)	Kevin Maas/PC	2.00
(11)	Don Mattingly (#19-27)	4.50
(11)	Don Mattingly/PC	6.00
(12)	Nolan Ryan (#55-63)	6.00
(12)	Nolan Ryan/PC	8.00
(13)	Ryne Sandberg (#64-72)	4.00
(13)	Ryne Sandberg/PC	5.00
(14)	Frank Thomas (#118-126)	3.75
(14)	Frank Thomas/PC	5.00
(15)	Albert Belle (Promo card only, produced in error.)	3.00

Stellar Edition

The same players who appear in other Star sets for 1991 are repackaged into this edition of 500 sets of each player. One hundred promo cards of each player were also issued.

		NM/M
	Complete Set (126):	50.00
	Common Player Set:	2.00
	Complete Promo Set (14):	65.00
	Common Promo Card:	2.50
(1)	Bobby Bonilla (#55-63)	2.00
(1)	Bobby Bonilla/PC	2.50
(2)	Will Clark (#37-45)	5.00
(2)	Will Clark/PC	5.00

---

(3)	Roger Clemens (#10-18)	6.50
(3)	Roger Clemens/PC	8.00
(4)	Vince Coleman (#73-81)	2.00
(4)	Vince Coleman/PC	2.50
(5)	Ken Griffey Jr. (#1-9)	7.50
(5)	Ken Griffey Jr./PC	10.00
(6)	Tony Gwynn (#46-54)	5.00
(6)	Tony Gwynn/PC	6.50
(7)	Rickey Henderson (#118-126)	5.00
(7)	Rickey Henderson/PC	6.50
(8)	Howard Johnson (#100-108)	2.00
(8)	Rickey Henderson/PC	2.50
(9)	Don Mattingly (#109-117)	6.00
(9)	Don Mattingly/PC	6.00
(10)	Kirby Puckett (#64-72)	6.00
(10)	Kirby Puckett/PC	6.00
(11)	Cal Ripken Jr. (#82-90)	7.50
(11)	Cal Ripken Jr./PC	8.00
(12)	Nolan Ryan (#19-27)	7.50
(12)	Nolan Ryan/PC	8.00
(13)	Ryne Sandberg (#91-99)	6.00
(13)	Ryne Sandberg/PC	6.50
(14)	Robin Yount (#28-36)	4.50
(14)	Robin Yount/PC	5.00

The Future

the FUTURE — PAT KELLY — NEW YORK — Checklist

A few players who had not yet been included among the flood of 1991 Star issues joined the others in this post-season issue. Production was put at 1,000 nine-card sets per player, plus 200 promo cards of each. Players are listed here in alphabetical order. Individual cards are not listed because the sets are usually never sold as singles.

		NM/M
	Complete Set (90):	15.00
	Common Player Set:	1.50
	Complete Promo Set (10):	20.00
	Common Promo Card:	2.00
(1)	Jeff Bagwell (#28-36)	3.00
(1)	Jeff Bagwell/PC	4.00
(2)	Albert Belle (#55-63)	2.00
(2)	Albert Belle/PC	2.75
(3)	Scott Erickson (#82-90)	1.50
(3)	Scott Erickson/PC	2.00
(4)	Juan Gonzalez (#1-9)	2.25
(4)	Juan Gonzalez/PC	3.50
(5)	Pat Kelly (#10-18)	1.50
(5)	Pat Kelly/PC	2.00
(6)	Mark Lewis (#73-81)	1.50
(6)	Mark Lewis/PC	2.00
(7)	Ramon Martinez (#46-54)	1.50
(7)	Ramon Martinez/PC	2.00
(8)	Brian McRae (#64-72)	1.50
(8)	Brian McRae/PC	2.00
(9)	Frank Thomas (#37-45)	3.50
(9)	Frank Thomas/PC	5.00
(10)	Mo Vaughn (#19-27)	1.50
(10)	Mo Vaughn/PC	2.00

'92

STAR '92 — TODD VAN POPPEL — OAKLAND — A's

Though labeled "Star '92" on front, these single-player 11-card sets were produced in 1991. Fronts feature borders which fade from one color at top to gray at the bottom. The photos at center are a mix of poses and game-action shots. Backs have a small color portrait photo - the same on all cards within a set - at upper-left. Stats, personal data, highlights, checklists and team logos are printed in color on yellow cardboard. The cards carry a 1991 copyright line at bottom center. Each set can be found in a glossy version, which carries a premium of 2X.

		NM/M
	Complete Set (22):	5.00
	Common Player Set:	2.50
	Complete Promo Set (2):	4.00
	Common Promo Card:	2.00
1-11	Scott Erickson	1.50
	Scott Erickson/PC	2.00
1-11	Todd Van Poppel	1.50
	Todd Van Poppel/PC	2.00

1992 Star '92

STAR '92 — DAVE JUSTICE — ATLANTA — Career Stats

Utilizing a design introduced the previous year, the Star '92 single-player card sets produced in 1992 are printed on cardboard laminated with thin high-gloss plastic surfaces front and back. Each player's cards are bordered with a single bright color at top which fades to gray at bottom. Photos are a mix of poses and game-action shots. Backs have a yellow background with a small color portrait (the same throughout the player's set) at upper-left. Stats, personal data, career highlights, checklist or team logo are printed in colored ink. The cards carry a 1992 copyright date and each set has a large capital letter in the lower-right corner. It is not known whether sets were issued for the letters missing in the checklist below, though prototype cards are known for some. Production was reported as 4,000 of each player set and 800 of each promo and prototype card. Only confirmed cards are listed. Single cards are not listed because sets are seldom broken for individual card sales.

		NM/M
	Common Player Set:	1.00
	Common Promo Card:	1.75
	Common Prototype Card:	1.75
A1-11	Jeff Bagwell	2.00
	Jeff Bagwell/PC	3.00
	Jeff Bagwell (Prototype)	3.00
B1-11	Albert Belle	1.50
	Albert Belle/PC	2.00
C1-11	Ron Gant	1.00
	Ron Gant/PC	1.75
	Ron Gant (Prototype)	1.75
D1-11	Bo Jackson	1.00
	Bo Jackson/PC	1.75
	Bo Jackson (Prototype)	1.75
E1-11	Dave Justice	1.00
	David Justice/PC	1.75
	David Justice (Prototype)	1.75
F1-11	Chuck Knoblauch	1.00
	Chuck Knoblauch/PC	1.75
	Chuck Knoblauch (Prototype)	1.75
G1-11	Kirby Puckett	2.50

	Kirby Puckett	
	Kirby Puckett (Prototype)	
H1-11	Ryne Sandberg	
	Ryne Sandberg/PC	
	Ryne Sandberg (Prototype)	
I1-11	Steve Avery	
	Steve Avery/PC	
	Steve Avery (Prototype)	
J1-11	Phil Plantier	
	Phil Plantier/PC	
	Phil Plantier (Prototype)	
K	Wade Boggs (Prototype)	
M1-11	Will Clark	
	Will Clark/PC	
N1-11	Ken Griffey Jr.	5.
	Ken Griffey Jr./PC	6.
	Ken Griffey Jr. (Prototype)	6.25
O	Cal Ripken Jr. (Prototype)	3.75
P	Nolan Ryan (Prototype, regular finish.)	4.50
	Nolan Ryan (Plastic prototype.)	6.00
R	Frank Thomas (Prototype)	4.50
S	Bobby Bonilla (Prototype)	1.75
T	Kevin Mitchell (Prototype)	1.75
U1-11	Danny Tartabull (Prototype)	1.00
	Danny Tartabull/PC	1.75
V1-11	Dean Palmer	1.00
	Dean Palmer/PC	1.75
	Dean Palmer (Prototype)	1.75

Gold Edition

GOLD '92 by STAR — DON MATTINGLY — NEW YORK — Yankee Captain

The 12 players in Star's 1992 Gold Edition are represented in an issue of 750 sets each, plus 150 promo cards. The checklist is arranged alphabetically. Single cards are not listed because sets are not often broken up for individual card sales.

		NM/M
	Complete Set (108):	55.00
	Common Player Set:	3.00
	Complete Promo Set (12):	75.00
	Common Promo Card:	5.00
(1)	Steve Avery (#91-99)	3.00
(1)	Steve Avery/PC	5.00
(2)	Jose Canseco (#19-27)	6.00
(2)	Jose Canseco/PC	8.00
(3)	Will Clark (#28-36)	5.00
(3)	Will Clark/PC	8.00
(4)	Ken Griffey Jr. (#82-90)	9.00
(4)	Ken Griffey Jr./PC	9.00
(5)	Bo Jackson (#46-54)	3.00
(5)	Bo Jackson/PC	4.00
(6)	David Justice (#10-18)	3.50
(6)	David Justice/PC	5.00
(7)	Don Mattingly (#1-9)	7.50
(7)	Don Mattingly/PC	10.00
(8)	Cal Ripken Jr. (#64-72)	9.00
(8)	Cal Ripken Jr./PC	12.00
(9)	Nolan Ryan (#37-45)	9.00
(9)	Nolan Ryan/PC	12.00
(10)	Ryne Sandberg (#55-63)	6.00
(10)	Ryne Sandberg/PC	8.00
(11)	Darryl Strawberry (#100-108)	3.50
(11)	Darryl Strawberry/PC	5.00
(12)	Frank Thomas (#73-81)	7.50
(12)	Frank Thomas/PC	10.00

Millenium Edition

Star's Millenium Edition for 1992 included an issue of 750 sets and 150 promo cards for each of 12 players, listed alphabetically in the checklist here. Single cards are not list-

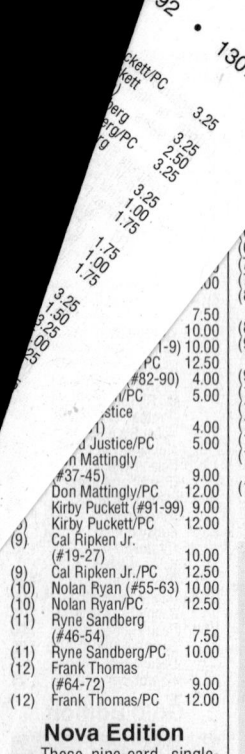

(partially obscured price list, top-left)

```
...ckett/PC            5.00
...kett                6.50
.../PC                 3.25
...(#100-108)          5.00
...PC                  4.00
...lemens
...99                  5.00
  Roger Clemens/PC     6.50
  Ken Griffey Jr.
   (#37-45)            7.50
  Ken Griffey Jr./PC  10.00
  Bo Jackson (28-36)   2.50
  Bo Jackson/PC        3.00
  David Justice (#10-18) 2.50
  David Justice/PC     3.00
  Don Mattingly
   (#64-72)            7.50
  Don Mattingly/PC    10.00
  Cal Ripken Jr.
   (#46-54)            7.50
  Cal Ripken Jr./PC   10.00
  Nolan Ryan (#82-90)  7.50
  Nolan Ryan/PC       10.00
  Ryne Sandberg (#1-9) 5.00
  Ryne Sandberg/PC     6.50
  Frank Thomas
   (#19-27)            6.00
  Frank Thomas/PC      8.00
```

```
   (1-9)              10.00
   ... /PC            12.50
   ...(#82-90)         4.00
   ... /PC
                       4.00
   ...Justice/PC       5.00
   Don Mattingly
    (#37-45)           9.00
   Don Mattingly/PC    9.00
   Kirby Puckett (#91-99) 9.00
   Kirby Puckett/PC   12.00
   Cal Ripken Jr.
    (#19-27)          10.00
   Cal Ripken Jr./PC  12.50
   Nolan Ryan (#55-63) 10.00
   Nolan Ryan/PC      12.50
   Ryne Sandberg
    (#46-54)           7.50
   Ryne Sandberg/PC   10.00
   Frank Thomas
    (#64-72)           9.00
   Frank Thomas/PC    12.00
```

Nova Edition

These nine-card, single-player sets were limited to an edition of 500 for each player, plus 100 promo cards. Numbering errors occurred on the Avery and Strawberry cards. The former were supposed to be numbered 10-18; the latter 64-72.

		NM/M
Complete Set (108):		75.00
Common Player Set:		4.50
Complete Promo Set:		100.00
Common Promo Card:		6.00
(1)	Nolan Ryan (#1-9)	6.00
(1)	Nolan Ryan/PC	15.00
(2)	Steve Avery (#10-14, 69-72)	4.50
(2)	Steve Avery/PC	6.00
(3)	Frank Thomas (#19-27)	9.00
(3)	Frank Thomas/PC	12.00
(4)	Don Mattingly (#28-36)	12.50
(4)	Don Mattingly/PC	15.00
(5)	Ken Griffey Jr. (#37-45)	12.50
(5)	Ken Griffey Jr./PC	15.00
(6)	David Justice (#46-54)	4.50
(6)	David Justice/PC	6.00
(7)	Ryne Sandberg (#55-63)	9.00
(7)	Ryne Sandberg/PC	12.00
(8)	Darryl Strawberry (#64-68, 15-18)	4.50
(8)	Darryl Strawberry/PC	6.00
(9)	Cal Ripken Jr. (#73-81)	12.50
(9)	Cal Ripken Jr./PC	15.00
(10)	Bo Jackson (#82-90)	4.50
(10)	Bo Jackson/PC	6.00
(11)	Jose Canseco (#91-99)	7.50
(11)	Jose Canseco/PC	10.00
(12)	Roger Clemens (#100-108)	9.00
(12)	Roger Clemens/PC	12.00

Platinum Edition

A dozen established stars are featured in the '92 Star Platinum issue, each in nine-card sets, contiguously numbered. One thousand sets of each player were issued, along with 200 promo cards. The cards are listed here in alphabetical order. Single cards are not listed because the player sets are not often broken up for individual sales.

		NM/M
Complete Set (108):		50.00
Common Player Set:		2.50
Complete Promo Set (12):		65.00
Common Promo Card:		3.00
(1)	Jeff Bagwell (#55-63)	5.00
(1)	Jeff Bagwell/PC	6.00

(3)	Will Clark/PC	4.00
(4)	Ken Griffey Jr. (#28-36)	6.00
(4)	Ken Griffey Jr./PC	8.00
(5)	Bo Jackson (#37-45)	3.00
(5)	Bo Jackson/PC	4.00
(6)	David Justice (#19-27)	3.00
(7)	David Justice/PC	4.00
(7)	Don Mattingly (#100-108)	6.00
(7)	Don Mattingly/PC	8.00
(8)	Cal Ripken Jr. (#82-90)	6.00
(8)	Cal Ripken Jr./PC	8.00
(9)	Nolan Ryan (#73-81)	6.00
(9)	Nolan Ryan/PC	8.00
(10)	Ryne Sandberg (#10-18)	6.00
(10)	Ryne Sandberg/PC	7.50
(11)	Darryl Strawberry (#91-99)	3.00
(11)	Darryl Strawberry/PC	4.00
(12)	Frank Thomas (#55-63)	5.00
(12)	Frank Thomas/PC	8.00

Rookie Guild

ROOKIE GUILD '92
LOS ANGELES — ERIC KARROS
Ad Card

Each of the four players in the '92 Rookie Guild issue is represented by an 11-card set, a promo card and a gold preview card. The first 10 cards in each player's set have blue borders, while the last card has white borders. Cards are seldom available as singles since the sets are rarely broken up.

		NM/M
Complete Set (44):		6.00
Complete Promo Set:		8.00
Complete Preview Set:		12.00
1-11	Reggie Sanders	1.50
	Reggie Sanders/PC	2.00
	Reggie Sanders (Gold preview.)	3.00
12-22	Phil Plantier	1.50
	Phil Plantier/PC	2.00
	Phil Plantier (Gold preview.)	3.00
23-33	Dean Palmer	1.50
	Dean Palmer/PC	2.00
	Dean Palmer (Gold preview.)	3.00
34-44	Eric Karros	1.50
	Eric Karros/PC	2.00
	Eric Karros (Gold preview.)	3.00
	Eric Karros (Ad card.)	3.00

Silver Edition

Nearly the same line-up as found in other special edition Star nine-card player sets is found in the silver version. Announced production was 1,000 sets of each player along with 200 promo cards. The cards are listed here in alphabetical order. Single cards are not listed because the player sets are not often broken up for individual sales.

ABBREVIATIONS

PC - Promo Card

Stellar Edition

Among the scarcer of Star's 1992 single-player, nine-card sets, the Stellar Edition was produced in an issue of 500 sets and 100 promo cards of each player, contiguously numbered. The cards are listed here in alphabetical order. Single cards are not listed because the player sets are not often broken up for individual sales.

		NM/M
Complete Set (108):		65.00
Common Player Set:		4.50
Complete Promo Set (12):		90.00
Common Promo Card:		6.00
(1)	Jeff Bagwell (#19-27)	6.00
(1)	Jeff Bagwell/PC	10.00
(2)	Jose Canseco (#100-108)	7.50
(2)	Jose Canseco/PC	7.50
(3)	Will Clark (#37-45)	6.00
(3)	Will Clark/PC	6.00
(4)	Roger Clemens (#10-18)	7.50
(4)	Roger Clemens/PC	10.00
(5)	Ken Griffey Jr. (#55-63)	7.50
(5)	Ken Griffey Jr./PC	12.00
(6)	Bo Jackson (#73-81)	4.50
(6)	Bo Jackson/PC	6.00
(7)	David Justice (#64-72)	4.50
(7)	David Justice/PC	6.00
(8)	Don Mattingly (#91-99)	9.00
(8)	Don Mattingly/PC	12.00
(9)	Cal Ripken Jr. (#46-54)	9.00
(9)	Cal Ripken Jr./PC	12.00
(10)	Nolan Ryan (#82-90)	9.00
(10)	Nolan Ryan/PC	12.00
(11)	Ryne Sandberg (#46-54)	7.50
(11)	Ryne Sandberg/PC	10.00
(12)	Frank Thomas (#1-9)	7.50
(12)	Frank Thomas/PC	10.00

The Kid

This five-card set was reportedly produced in an edition of 1,000 as a value-added with Star's porcelain statue of Ken Griffey, Jr. One card set was given with the purchase of five statues at $125 each. No promo cards or glossy version were issued.

		NM/M
Complete Set (5):		50.00
1-5	Ken Griffey Jr.	10.00

1993 Star '93 Andy Benes

STAR '93 — ANDY BENES

It is unknown whether the usual 11-card set was produced for this continuation of the Star single-player series, or whether this represents a promotional card. In format similar to the Star '92 issues, the card has a red top border which morphs to yellow at bottom. Back repeats a detail of the front photo and has career stats printed in red on a yellow background. There is a 1993 copyright date, but no card number. The card does not have the high-gloss plastic coating found on the earlier series.

	NM/M
Andy Benes	2.00
Andy Benes/ Auto. w/COA	3.00

1995 Star Cal Ripken, Jr.

Cal, Ripken, Jr. — They Pinch hit for Cal

A major design fault apparently prevented this issue from being widely circulated. Each of the 80 cards in the boxed set has an extraneous comma between "Cal" and "Ripken." That fatal flaw aside, the set does a creditable job of detailing Ripken's major league career through his record 2, 131st consecutive game in 1995. Glossy card fronts have color photos at center with orange and brown graphic highlights. Each card has him identified as "Cal, Ripken, Jr." at bottom, below which there is a card title. Backs have a baseball at center with career highlights, stats, personal information or trivia. The name error is repeated in orange script at bottom. The set was fully licensed by Ripken and Major League Baseball.

	NM/M
Complete Boxed Set (80):	10.00
Common Card:	.25

1989 Starline Prototypes

MARK GRACE

Prior to its first major baseball card issue, Starline produced six variations of a prototype issue. The seven-card sets feature game-action photos on the front, surrounded by colorful borders and with a combination of up to three logos in the bottom border. Cards were produced with just the Starline logo, with the Starline and Coca-Cola logos and with the card company and soft drink logos in con-junction with those of McDonald's, 7-11, Burger King or Dominos pizza. Backs repeat the logos at bottom, along with that of Major League Baseball. At top is a color player photo, along with biographical data, complete major and minor league stats and career highlights. The unnumbered cards are checklisted here alphabetically.

		NM/M
Complete Set (7):		45.00
Common Player:		6.00
(1)	Eric Davis	6.00
(2)	Mark Grace	6.00
(3)	Tony Gwynn	10.00
(4)	Gregg Jefferies	6.00
(5)	Don Mattingly	12.00
(6)	Mark McGwire	13.50
(7)	Darryl Strawberry	6.00

1990 Starline

MARK GRACE

Five-card cello packs of this Coca-Cola sponsored issue were given away with the purchase of dinner and a soft drink at Long John Silver fish restaurants. Cards feature game-action photos on front, bordered in team colors. Backs repeat the team-color scheme and feature a portrait photo along with major league stats and career highlights. Most of the players had two or more cards in the 40-card issue. A header card in each pack offered a 2' x 3' poster of one of 18 players in set for $3.99.

		NM/M
Complete Set (40):		3.00
Common Player:		.10
1	Don Mattingly	.40
2	Mark Grace	.10
3	Eric Davis	.10
4	Tony Gwynn	.30
5	Bobby Bonilla	.10
6	Wade Boggs	.30
7	Frank Viola	.10
8	Ruben Sierra	.10
9	Mark McGwire	.50
10	Alan Trammell	.10
11	Mark McGwire	.50
12	Gregg Jefferies	.10
13	Nolan Ryan	.60
14	John Smoltz	.10
15	Glenn Davis	.10
16	Mark Grace	.10
17	Wade Boggs	.30
18	Frank Viola	.10
19	Bret Saberhagen	.10
20	Chris Sabo	.10
21	Darryl Strawberry	.10
22	Wade Boggs	.30
23	Tim Raines	.10
24	Alan Trammell	.10
25	Chris Sabo	.10
26	Nolan Ryan	.60
27	Mark McGwire	.50
28	Don Mattingly	.40
29	Tony Gwynn	.30
30	Glenn Davis	.10
31	Bobby Bonilla	.10
32	Gregg Jefferies	.10
33	Ruben Sierra	.10
34	John Smoltz	.10
35	Don Mattingly	.40
36	Bret Saberhagen	.10
37	Darryl Strawberry	.10
38	Eric Davis	.10
39	Tim Raines	.10
40	Mark Grace	.10
---	Header Card/ Poster Offer	.05

1990 Starline Americana

Several baseball players were among the subjects fea-

Americana — Babe Ruth

tured in a set of "Americana" quiz cards. The 2-1/2" x 3-1/2" cards are printed in full-color front and back. Backs repeat the front photo in miniature and provide "Historical Highlights" along with a trivia question and the answer to the question on another card.

		NM/M
237	Jackie Robinson	2.00
245	Babe Ruth	2.00

1991 Starline Prototypes

GEORGE BELL

These sample cards were produced for submission to baseball licensing authorities for approval, and to prospective sponsors. Only 60 of each card were reported produced. Card fronts have color action photos and a team logo set against a black background. The player's name appears in white and red at top and along the side. Backs have a smaller player photo at upper-right. All of the prototypes have back stats and biography of Nolan Ryan, with a gray diagonal "PROTOTYPE" across them. The Starline, MLB and Player Association logo appear across the bottom.

		NM/M
Complete Set (5):		50.00
Common Player:		10.00
(1)	George Bell	10.00
(2)	Bobby Bonilla	10.00
(3)	Roger Clemens	20.00
(4)	Tim Raines	10.00
(5)	Darryl Strawberry	10.00

1983 Starliner Stickers

This unauthorized collector's issue is based on 16 of the cards issued by Dexter Press in 1967 as Coca-Cola premiums. In July 1983, a Midwestern card dealer produced these stickers by reprinting the 5-1/2" x 7" Dexter Press cards in 2-7/16" x 3-1/4" format and eliminating the white border. The stickers can be found with either white ("Mactac Starliner") or tan ("Tuchdown Splitless") paper on back. By the early 1990s, the story of the true origins of these stickers had been largely forgotten within the hobby and some dealers were charging between $10-50 apiece for them. The unnumbered stickers are checklisted here in alphabetical order. Production of the white-back stickers was reported at 2,000 sets, with Mantle and Rose double printed.

		NM/M
Complete Set (16):		40.00
Common Player:		1.00
(1)	Hank Aaron	7.50
(2)	Ernie Banks	1.50
(3)	Roberto Clemente	10.00
(4)	Rocky Colavito	1.00
(5)	Al Kaline	1.50
(6)	Harmon Killebrew	1.00
(7)	Mickey Mantle/DP	20.00
(8)	Willie Mays	7.50
(9)	Willie McCovey	1.00
(10)	Joe Morgan	1.00
(11)	Jim Palmer	1.00
(12)	Brooks Robinson	1.00
(13)	Frank Robinson	1.00
(14)	Pete Rose/DP	7.50
(15)	Willie Stargell	1.00
(16)	Carl Yastrzemski	1.50

1988 Starting Lineup Talking Baseball

Measuring 2-5/8" x 3", these cards were part of the Starting Lineup Talking Baseball game produced by Kenner Parker Toys Inc. The electronic game, with a computer memory and keyboard to respond to a particular baseball game situation, retailed for more than $100. However, several hobby dealers sold the cards separately from the game. The set includes seven instruction cards that do not picture players.

		NM/M
Complete Set (42):		25.00
Common Player:		.25
11a	Terry Kennedy	1.25
11b	Gary Carter	1.25
12a	Carlton Fisk	1.25
12b	Steve Sax	.25
13a	Eddie Murray	1.25
13b	Jack Clark	.25
14a	Don Mattingly	2.50
14b	Keith Hernandez	.25
15a	Willie Randolph	.25
15b	Buddy Bell	.25
16a	Cal Ripken	4.00
16b	Ryne Sandberg	2.00
17a	Lou Whitaker	.25
17b	Ozzie Smith	2.00
18a	Wade Boggs	2.00
18b	Dale Murphy	.75
19a	George Brett	2.50
19b	Mike Schmidt	2.50
20a	Alan Trammell	.25
20b	Eric Davis	.25
21a	Kirby Puckett	2.00
21b	Tony Gwynn	2.00
22a	George Bell	.25
22b	Darryl Strawberry	.25
23a	Rickey Henderson	1.25
23b	Tim Raines	.25
24a	Dave Winfield	1.25
24b	Andre Dawson	.75

ABBREVIATIONS
DP - Double Print

25a	Jack Morris	.25
25b	Mike Scott	.25
26a	Robin Yount	1.25
26b	Jody Davis	.25
27a	Roger Clemens	2.50
27b	Todd Worrell	.25
28a	Bret Saberhagen	.25
28b	Fernando Valenzuela	.25
29a	Dave Righetti	.25
29b	Dwight Gooden	.25
30a	Dan Quisenberry	.25
30b	Nolan Ryan	4.00
---	American League checklist	.25
---	National League checklist	.25

Team Sets

Similar in format to the cards issued with the Parker Brothers game, these accessory cards could be purchased in groups of three team sets. The team-set cards share the format (2-5/8" x 3") and design of the boxed-set cards, but differ in that the player portraits are presented as colored drawings rather than photos. Because the issue was licensed only by the players' union, and not MLB, the caps have no team logos. Backs are in black-and-white. Each team set has 20 player cards (the Indians have only 19) plus a batting order/checklist card. Several players appear in more than one set as a result of trades. The cards are checklisted here alphabetically within team.

		NM/M
Complete Set (545):		60.00
Common Player:		.10

Atlanta Braves
Team Set: 4.00
(1)	Jim Acker	.10
(2)	Paul Assenmacher	.10
(3)	Jeff Blauser	.10
(4)	Jeff Dedmon	.10
(5)	Ron Gant	.10
(6)	Tom Glavine	.75
(7)	Ken Griffey	.10
(8)	Albert Hall	.10
(9)	Glenn Hubbard	.10
(10)	Dion James	.10
(11)	Rick Mahler	.10
(12)	Dale Murphy	1.00
(13)	Ken Oberkfell	.10
(14)	Gerald Perry	.10
(15)	Gary Roenicke	.10
(16)	Paul Runge	.10
(17)	Ted Simmons	.10
(18)	Pete Smith	.10
(19)	Andres Thomas	.10
(20)	Ozzie Virgil	.10
(21)	Batting order/checklist	.05

Baltimore Orioles
Team Set: 12.00
(1)	Eric Bell	.10
(2)	Mike Boddicker	.10
(3)	Jim Dwyer	.10
(4)	Ken Gerhart	.10
(5)	Rene Gonzalez	.10
(6)	Terry Kennedy	.10
(7)	Ray Knight	.10
(8)	Lee Lacy	.10
(9)	Fred Lynn	.10
(10)	Eddie Murray	3.00
(11)	Tom Niedenfuer	.10
(12)	Billy Ripken (Ripken)	.10
(13)	Cal Ripken Jr.	7.50
(14)	Dave Schmidt	.10
(15)	Larry Sheets	.10
(16)	Pete Stanicek	.10
(17)	Mark Thurmond	.10
(18)	Ron Washington	.10
(19)	Mark Williamson	.10
(20)	Mike Young	.10
(21)	Batting order/checklist	.05

Boston Red Sox
Team Set: 7.50
(1)	Marty Barrett	.10
(2)	Todd Benzinger	.10
(3)	Wade Boggs	4.00
(4)	Dennis Boyd	.10
(5)	Ellis Burks	.10
(6)	Roger Clemens	4.50
(7)	Dwight Evans	.10
(8)	Wes Gardner	.10
(9)	Rich Gedman	.10
(10)	Mike Greenwell	.10
(11)	Sam Horn	.10
(12)	Bruce Hurst	.10
(13)	John Marzano	.10
(14)	Spike Owen	.10
(15)	Jody Reed	.10
(16)	Jim Rice	.35
(17)	Ed Romero	.10
(18)	Kevin Romine	.10
(19)	Lee Smith	.10
(20)	Bob Stanley	.10
(21)	Batting order/checklist	.05

California Angels
Team Set: 2.25
(1)	Tony Armas	.10
(2)	Bob Boone	.10
(3)	Bill Buckner	.10
(4)	DeWayne Buice	.10
(5)	Brian Downing	.10
(6)	Chuck Finley	.10
(7)	Willie Fraser	.10
(8)	George Hendrick	.10
(9)	Jack Howell	.10
(10)	Ruppert Jones	.10
(11)	Wally Joyner	.10
(12)	Kirk McCaskill	.10
(13)	Mark McLemore	.10
(14)	Darrell Miller	.10
(15)	Greg Minton	.10
(16)	Gary Pettis	.10
(17)	Johnny Ray	.10
(18)	Dick Schofield	.10
(19)	Devon White	.10
(20)	Mike Witt	.10
(21)	Batting order/checklist	.05

Chicago Cubs
Team Set: 6.00
(1)	Jody Davis	.10
(2)	Andre Dawson	.35
(3)	Bob Dernier	.10
(4)	Frank DiPino	.10
(5)	Shawon Dunston	.10
(6)	Leon Durham	.10
(7)	Dave Martinez	.10
(8)	Keith Moreland	.10
(9)	Jamie Moyer	.10
(10)	Jerry Mumphrey	.10
(11)	Paul Noce	.10
(12)	Rafael Palmeiro	2.50
(13)	Luis Quinones	.10
(14)	Ryne Sandberg	4.00
(15)	Scott Sanderson	.10
(16)	Calvin Schiraldi	.10
(17)	Lee Smith	.10
(18)	Jim Sundberg	.10
(19)	Rick Sutcliffe	.10
(20)	Manny Trillo	.10
(21)	Batting order/checklist	.05

Chicago White Sox
Team Set: 4.00
(1)	Harold Baines	.10
(2)	Floyd Bannister	.10
(3)	Daryl Boston	.10
(4)	Ivan Calderon	.10
(5)	Jose DeLeon	.10
(6)	Rich Dotson	.10
(7)	Carlton Fisk	3.00
(8)	Ozzie Guillen	.10
(9)	Jerry Hairston Sr.	.10
(10)	Donnie Hill	.10
(11)	Dave LaPoint	.10
(12)	Steve Lyons	.10
(13)	Fred Manrique	.10
(14)	Dan Pasqua	.10
(15)	Gary Redus	.10
(16)	Mark Salas	.10
(17)	Ray Searage	.10
(18)	Bobby Thigpen	.10
(19)	Greg Walker	.10
(20)	Ken Williams	.10
(21)	Batting order/checklist	.05

Cincinnati Reds
Team Set: 2.25
(1)	Buddy Bell	.10
(2)	Tom Browning	.10
(3)	Dave Collins	.10
(4)	Dave Concepcion	.10
(5)	Kal Daniels	.10
(6)	Eric Davis	.10
(7)	Bo Diaz	.10
(8)	Nick Esasky	.10
(9)	John Franco	.10
(10)	Terry Francona	.10
(11)	Tracy Jones	.10
(12)	Barry Larkin	.10
(13)	Rob Murphy	.10
(14)	Paul O'Neill	.10
(15)	Dave Parker	.10
(16)	Ted Power	.10
(17)	Dennis Rasmussen	.10
(18)	Kurt Stillwell	.10
(19)	Jeff Treadway	.10
(20)	Frank Williams	.10
(21)	Batting order/checklist	.05

Cleveland Indians
Team Set: 2.25
(1)	Andy Allanson	.10
(2)	Scott Bailes	.10
(3)	Chris Bando	.10
(4)	Jay Bell	.10
(5)	Brett Butler	.10
(6)	Tom Candiotti	.10
(7)	Joe Carter	.10
(8)	Carmen Castillo	.10
(9)	Dave Clark	.10
(10)	John Farrell	.10
(11)	Julio Franco	.10
(12)	Mel Hall	.10
(13)	Tom Hinzo	.10
(14)	Brook Jacoby	.10
(15)	Doug Jones	.10
(16)	Junior Noboa	.10
(17)	Ken Schrom	.10
(18)	Cory Snyder	.10
(19)	Pat Tabler	.10
(20)	Batting order/checklist	.05

Detroit Tigers
Team Set: 2.25
(1)	Doyle Alexander	.10
(2)	Dave Bergman	.10
(3)	Tom Brookens	.10
(4)	Darrell Evans	.10
(5)	Kirk Gibson	.10
(6)	Mike Heath	.10
(7)	Mike Henneman	.10
(8)	Willie Hernandez	.10
(9)	Larry Herndon	.10
(10)	Eric King	.10
(11)	Ray Knight	.10
(12)	Chet Lemon	.10
(13)	Bill Madlock	.10
(14)	Jack Morris	.10
(15)	Jim Morrison	.10
(16)	Matt Nokes	.10
(17)	Pat Sheridan	.10
(18)	Frank Tanana	.10
(19)	Alan Trammell	.10
(20)	Lou Whitaker	.10
(21)	Batting order/checklist	.05

Houston Astros
Team Set: 6.00
(1)	Juan Agosto	.10
(2)	Larry Andersen	.10
(3)	Alan Ashby	.10
(4)	Kevin Bass	.10
(5)	Ken Caminiti	.10
(6)	Jose Cruz	.10
(7)	Danny Darwin	.10
(8)	Glenn Davis	.10
(9)	Bill Doran	.10
(10)	Billy Hatcher	.10
(11)	Jim Pankovitz	.10
(12)	Terry Puhl	.10
(13)	Rafael Ramirez	.10
(14)	Craig Reynolds	.10
(15)	Nolan Ryan	7.50
(16)	Mike Scott	.10
(17)	Dave Smith	.10
(18)	Marc Sullivan	.10
(19)	Dennis Walling	.10
(20)	Eric Young	.10
(21)	Batting order/checklist	.05

Kansas City Royals
Team Set: 6.00
(1)	Steve Balboni	.10
(2)	George Brett	4.50
(3)	Jim Eisenreich	.10
(4)	Gene Garber	.10
(5)	Jerry Don Gleaton	.10
(6)	Mark Gubicza	.10
(7)	Bo Jackson	.50
(8)	Charlie Leibrandt	.10
(9)	Mike Macfarlane	.10
(10)	Larry Owen	.10
(11)	Bill Pecota	.10
(12)	Jamie Quirk	.10
(13)	Dan Quisenberry	.10
(14)	Bret Saberhagen	.10
(15)	Kevin Seitzer	.10
(16)	Kurt Stillwell	.10
(17)	Danny Tartabull	.10
(18)	Gary Thurman	.10
(19)	Frank White	.10
(20)	Willie Wilson	.10
(21)	Batting order/checklist	.05

Los Angeles Dodgers
Team Set: 2.50
(1)	Dave Anderson	.10
(2)	Mike Davis	.10
(3)	Mariano Duncan	.10
(4)	Kirk Gibson	.10
(5)	Alfredo Griffin	.10
(6)	Pedro Guerrero	.10
(7)	Mickey Hatcher	.10
(8)	Orel Hershiser	.10
(9)	Glenn Hoffman	.10
(10)	Brian Holton	.10
(11)	Mike Marshall	.10
(12)	Jesse Orosco	.10
(13)	Alejandro Pena	.10
(14)	Steve Sax	.10
(15)	Mike Scioscia	.10
(16)	John Shelby	.10
(17)	Franklin Stubbs	.10
(18)	Don Sutton	2.00
(19)	Alex Trevino	.10
(20)	Fernando Valenzuela	.10
(21)	Batting order/checklist	.05

Milwaukee Brewers
Team Set: 6.00
(1)	Chris Bosio	.10
(2)	Glenn Braggs	.10
(3)	Greg Brock	.10
(4)	Juan Castillo	.10
(5)	Chuck Crim	.10
(6)	Rob Deer	.10
(7)	Mike Felder	.10
(8)	Jim Gantner	.10
(9)	Teddy Higuera	.10
(10)	Steve Kiefer	.10
(11)	Paul Molitor	3.00
(12)	Juan Nieves	.10
(13)	Dan Plesac	.10
(14)	Ernie Riles	.10
(15)	Billy Jo Robidoux	.10
(16)	Bill Schroeder	.10
(17)	B.J. Surhoff	.10
(18)	Dale Sveum	.10
(19)	Bill Wegman	.10
(20)	Robin Yount	3.00
(21)	Batting order/checklist	.05

Minnesota Twins
Team Set: 6.00
(1)	Don Baylor	.10
(2)	Juan Berenguer	.10
(3)	Bert Blyleven	.10
(4)	Tom Brunansky	.10
(5)	Randy Bush	.10
(6)	Mark Davidson	.10
(7)	Gary Gaetti	.10
(8)	Greg Gagne	.10
(9)	Dan Gladden	.10
(10)	Kent Hrbek	.10
(11)	Gene Larkin	.10
(12)	Tim Laudner	.10
(13)	Steve Lombardozzi	.10
(14)	Al Newman	.10
(15)	Kirby Puckett	4.00
(16)	Jeff Reardon	.10
(17)	Dan Schatzeder	.10
(18)	Roy Smalley	.10
(19)	Les Straker	.10
(20)	Frank Viola	.10
(21)	Batting order/checklist	.05

Montreal Expos
Team Set: 9.00
(1)	Hubie Brooks	.10
(2)	Tim Burke	.10
(3)	Casey Candaele	.10
(4)	Mike Fitzgerald	.10
(5)	Tom Foley	.10
(6)	Andres Galarraga	.10
(7)	Neal Heaton	.10
(8)	Randy Johnson	7.50
(9)	Vance Law	.10
(10)	Bob McClure	.10
(11)	Andy McGaffigan	.10
(12)	Dennis Powell	.10
(13)	Tim Raines	.10
(14)	Jeff Reed	.10
(15)	Luis Rivera	.10
(16)	Bryn Smith	.10
(17)	Tim Wallach	.10
(18)	Mitch Webster	.10
(19)	Herm Winningham	.10
(20)	Floyd Youmans	.10
(21)	Batting order/checklist	.05

New York Mets Team Issue: 4.00
(1)	Bill Almon	.10
(2)	Wally Backman	.10
(3)	Gary Carter	3.00
(4)	David Cone	.10
(5)	Ron Darling	.10
(6)	Lenny Dykstra	.10
(7)	Sid Fernandez	.10
(8)	Dwight Gooden	.10
(9)	Keith Hernandez	.10
(10)	Howard Johnson	.10
(11)	Barry Lyons	.10
(12)	Dave Magadan	.10
(13)	Lee Mazzilli	.10
(14)	Roger McDowell	.10
(15)	Kevin McReynolds	.10
(16)	Jesse Orosco	.10
(17)	Rafael Santana	.10
(18)	Darryl Strawberry	.10
(19)	Tim Teufel	.10
(20)	Mookie Wilson	.10
(21)	Batting order/checklist	.05

New York Yankees
Team Set: 9.00
(1)	Rick Cerone	.10
(2)	Jack Clark	.10
(3)	Pat Clements	.10
(4)	Mike Easler	.10
(5)	Ron Guidry	.10
(6)	Rickey Henderson	3.00
(7)	Tommy John	.10
(8)	Don Mattingly	4.50
(9)	Bobby Meacham	.10
(10)	Mike Pagliarulo	.10
(11)	Willie Randolph	.10
(12)	Rick Rhoden	.10
(13)	Dave Righetti	.10
(14)	Jerry Royster	.10
(15)	Don Slaught	.10
(16)	Tim Stoddard	.10
(17)	Wayne Tolleson	.10
(18)	Gary Ward	.10
(19)	Claudell Washington	.10
(20)	Dave Winfield	3.00
(21)	Batting order/checklist	.05

Oakland A's
Team Set: 15.00
(1)	Tony Bernazard	.10
(2)	Jose Canseco	1.50
(3)	Mike Davis	.10
(4)	Dennis Eckersley	2.00
(5)	Mike Gallego	.10
(6)	Alfredo Griffin	.10
(7)	Rickey Henderson	3.00
(8)	Reggie Jackson	4.50
(9)	Carney Lansford	.10
(10)	Mark McGwire	6.00
(11)	Gene Nelson	.10
(12)	Steve Ontiveros	.10
(13)	Dave Parker	.10
(14)	Tony Phillips	.10
(15)	Luis Polonia	.10
(16)	Terry Steinbach	.10
(17)	Dave Stewart	.10
(18)	Mickey Tettleton	.10
(19)	Bob Welch	.10
(20)	Curt Young	.10
(21)	Batting order/checklist	.05

Philadelphia Phillies
Team Set: 5.00
(1)	Luis Aguayo	.10
(2)	Steve Bedrosian	.10
(3)	Phil Bradley	.10
(4)	Jeff Calhoun	.10
(5)	Don Carman	.10
(6)	Darren Daulton	.10
(7)	Bob Dernier	.10
(8)	Greg Gross	.10
(9)	Von Hayes	.10
(10)	Chris James	.10
(11)	Steve Jeltz	.10
(12)	Lance Parrish	.10
(13)	Shane Rawley	.10
(14)	Bruce Ruffin	.10
(15)	Juan Samuel	.10
(16)	Mike Schmidt	4.50
(17)	Rick Schu	.10
(18)	Kent Tekulve	.10
(19)	Milt Thompson	.10
(20)	Glenn Wilson	.10
(21)	Batting order/checklist	.05

Pittsburgh Pirates
Team Set: 9.00
(1)	Rafael Belliard	.10
(2)	Barry Bonds	7.50
(3)	Bobby Bonilla	.10
(4)	Sid Bream	.10
(5)	John Cangelosi	.10
(6)	Darnell Coles	.10
(7)	Mike Diaz	.10
(8)	Doug Drabek	.10
(9)	Mike Dunne	.10
(10)	Felix Fermin	.10
(11)	Brian Fisher	.10
(12)	Jim Gott	.10
(13)	Mike LaValliere	.10
(14)	Jose Lind	.10
(15)	Junior Ortiz	.10
(16)	Al Pedrique	.10
(17)	R.J. Reynolds	.10
(18)	Jeff Robinson	.10
(19)	John Smiley	.10
(20)	Andy Van Slyke	.10
(21)	Batting order/checklist	.05

San Diego Padres
Team Set: 5.00
(1)	Shawn Abner	.10
(2)	Roberto Alomar	.25
(3)	Bobby Brown	.10
(4)	Joey Cora	.10
(5)	Mark Davis	.10
(6)	Tim Flannery	.10
(7)	Goose Gossage	.10
(8)	Mark Grant	.10
(9)	Tony Gwynn	4.00
(10)	Stan Jefferson	.10
(11)	John Kruk	.10
(12)	Shane Mack	.10
(13)	Carmelo Martinez	.10
(14)	Lance McCullers	.10
(15)	Randy Ready	.10
(16)	Benito Santiago	.10
(17)	Eric Show	.10
(18)	Garry Templeton	.10
(19)	Ed Whitson	.10
(20)	Marvell Wynne	.10
(21)	Batting order/checklist	.05

San Francisco Giants
Team Set: 2.50
(1)	Mike Aldrete	.10
(2)	Bob Brenly	.10
(3)	Brett Butler	.10
(4)	Will Clark	.10
(5)	Chili Davis	.10
(6)	Dave Dravecky	.10
(7)	Scott Garrelts	.10
(8)	Atlee Hammaker	.10
(9)	Craig Lefferts	.10
(10)	Jeffrey Leonard	.10
(11)	Candy Maldonado	.10
(12)	Bob Melvin	.10
(13)	Kevin Mitchell	.10
(14)	Rick Reuschel	.10
(15)	Don Robinson	.10
(16)	Chris Speier	.10
(17)	Chris Spielman	.10
(18)	Robby Thompson	.10
(19)	Jose Uribe	.10
(20)	Matt Williams	.10
(21)	Batting order/checklist	.05

Seattle Mariners
Team Set: 2.25
(1)	Phil Bradley	.10
(2)	Scott Bradley	.10
(3)	Mickey Brantley	.10
(4)	Mike Campbell	.10
(5)	Henry Cotto	.10
(6)	Alvin Davis	.10
(7)	Mike Kingery	.10
(8)	Mark Langston	.10
(9)	Mike Moore	.10
(10)	John Moses	.10
(11)	Donell Nixon	.10
(12)	Ed Nunez	.10
(13)	Ken Phelps	.10
(14)	Jim Presley	.10
(15)	Rey Quinones	.10
(16)	Jerry Reed	.10
(17)	Harold Reynolds	.10
(18)	Dave Valle	.10
(19)	Bill Wilkinson	.10

(20) Glenn Wilson .10
(21) Batting order/checklist .05
St. Louis Cardinals
Team Set: 4.50
(1) Greg Booker .10
(2) Jack Clark .10
(3) Vince Coleman .10
(4) Danny Cox .10
(5) Ken Dayley .10
(6) Curt Ford .10
(7) Tom Herr .10
(8) Bob Horner .10
(9) Ricky Horton .10
(10) Lance Johnson .10
(11) Steve Lake .10
(12) Jim Lindeman .10
(13) Greg Mathews .10
(14) Willie McGee .10
(15) Jose Oquendo .10
(16) Tony Pena .10
(17) Terry Pendleton .10
(18) Ozzie Smith 4.00
(19) John Tudor .10
(20) Todd Worrell .10
(21) Batting order/checklist .05
Texas Rangers
Team Set: 2.25
(1) Jerry Browne .10
(2) Bob Brower .10
(3) Steve Buechele .10
(4) Scott Fletcher .10
(5) Juan Guzman .10
(6) Charlie Hough .10
(7) Pete Incaviglia .10
(8) Oddibe McDowell .10
(9) Dale Mohorcic .10
(10) Pete O'Brien .10
(11) Tom O'Malley .10
(12) Larry Parrish .10
(13) Geno Petralli .10
(14) Jeff Russell .10
(15) Ruben Sierra .10
(16) Don Slaught .10
(17) Mike Stanley .10
(18) Curt Wilkerson .10
(19) Mitch Williams .10
(20) Bobby Witt .10
(21) Batting order/checklist .05
Toronto Blue Jays
Team Set: 2.25
(1) Jesse Barfield .10
(2) George Bell .10
(3) Juan Beniquez .10
(4) Jim Clancy .10
(5) Mark Eichhorn .10
(6) Tony Fernandez .10
(7) Cecil Fielder .10
(8) Tom Henke .10
(9) Garth Iorg .10
(10) Jimmy Key .10
(11) Rick Leach .10
(12) Manny Lee .10
(13) Nelson Liriano .10
(14) Fred McGriff .10
(15) Lloyd Moseby .10
(16) Rance Mulliniks .10
(17) Jeff Musselman .10
(18) Dave Steib .10
(19) Willie Upshaw .10
(20) Ernie Whitt .10
(21) Batting order/checklist .05

1995 Stouffer's Legends of Baseball

To promote its French bread frozen pizza, this Nestle's subsidiary issued a series of five three-dimensional cards featuring current and future Hall of Famers. The 2-1/2" x 3-1/2" cards have a die-cut action photo on front connected to a tab at the card top. When the tab is pulled, the player figure stands up. The back of the card has another player photo and a few career highlights. Because the promotion was licensed only by individuals, and not Major League Baseball, uniform and cap logos have been airbrushed off the photos.

NM/M
Complete Set (6): 4.00
Common Player: 1.00
1 Yogi Berra 2.00
1a Yogi Berra/Auto. 20.00
2 Gary Carter 1.50
3 Don Drysdale 2.00
4 Bob Feller 2.00
5 Willie Stargell 2.00

1983 Stuart Expos

This set of Montreal Expos players and coaches was issued by a Montreal area baking company for inclusion in packages of snack cakes. The 30 cards feature full-color player photos, with the player name, number and team logo also on the card fronts. The backs list brief player biographies in both English and French. Twenty-five players are pictured on the 2-1/2" x 3-1/2" cards.

NM/M
Complete Set (30): 10.00
Common Player: .25
1 Bill Virdon .25
2 Woodie Fryman .25
3 Vern Rapp .25
4 Andre Dawson 2.00
5 Jeff Reardon .35
6 Al Oliver .50
7 Doug Flynn .25
8 Gary Carter 5.00
9 Tim Raines 1.00
10 Steve Rogers .25
11 Billy DeMars .25
12 Tim Wallach .25
13 Galen Cisco .25
14 Terry Francona .25
15 Bill Gullickson .25
16 Ray Burris .25
17 Scott Sanderson .25
18 Warren Cromartie .25
19 Jerry White .25
20 Bobby Ramos .25
21 Jim Wolhford .25
22 Dan Schatzeder .25
23 Charlie Lea .25
24 Bryan Little .25
25 Mel Wright .25
26 Tim Blackwell .25
27 Chris Speier .25
28 Randy Lerch .25
29 Bryn Smith .25
30 Brad Mills .25

1984 Stuart Expos

For the second year in a row, Stuart Cakes issued a full-color card set of the Montreal Expos. The 2-1/2"x3-1/2" cards again list the player name and number along with the team and company logos on the card fronts. The backs are bilingual with biographical information in both English and French. The 40-card set was issued in two series. Card numbers 21-40, issued late in the summer, are more difficult to find than the first 20 cards. The 40 cards include players, the manager, coaches and team mascot.

NM/M
Complete Set (40): 15.00
Common Player (1-20): .25
Common Player (21-40): .35
Album: 6.00
1 Youppi!/Mascot .25
2 Bill Virdon .25
3 Billy DeMars .25
4 Galen Cisco .25
5 Russ Nixon .25
6 Felipe Alou .75
7 Dan Schatzeder .25
8 Charlie Lea .25
9 Bobby Ramos .25
10 Bob James .25
11 Andre Dawson 2.00
12 Gary Lucas .25
13 Jeff Reardon .35
14 Tim Wallach .35
15 Gary Carter 5.00
16 Bill Gullickson .25
17 Pete Rose 6.00
18 Terry Francona .25
19 Steve Rogers .25
20 Tim Raines 1.00
21 Bryn Smith .25
22 Greg Harris .35
23 David Palmer .35
24 Jim Wohlford .35
25 Miguel Dilone .35
26 Mike Stenhouse .35
27 Chris Speier .35
28 Derrel Thomas .35
29 Doug Flynn .35
30 Bryan Little .35
31 Argenis Salazar .35
32 Mike Fuentes .35
33 Joe Kerrigan .35
34 Andy McGaffigan .35
35 Fred Breining .35
36 Expos 1983 All-Stars (Gary Carter, Andre Dawson, Tim Raines, Steve Rogers) .75
37 Co-Players Of The Year (Andre Dawson, Tim Raines) .75
38 Expos' Coaching Staff (Felipe Alou, Galen Cisco, Billy DeMars, Joe Kerrigan, Russ Nixon, Bill Virdon) .35
39 Team Photo .50
40 Checklist .10

1987 Stuart

Twenty-eight four-part folding panels make up the 1987 Stuart Super Stars set, which was issued only in Canada. Three player cards and a sweepstakes entry form card comprise each panel. All 26 major league teams are included with the Montreal Expos and Toronto Blue Jays being represented twice. The cards, which are full color and measure 2-1/2" x 3-1/2", are written in both English and French. The card backs contain the player's previous year's statistics. All team insignias have been airbrushed away.

NM/M
Complete Panel Set (28): 15.00
Complete Singles Set (84): 10.00
Common Panel: .35
Common Single Player: .05
Panel (New York Mets) .60
1a Gary Carter .50
1b Keith Hernandez .10
1c Darryl Strawberry .05
Panel (Atlanta Braves) .60
2a Bruce Benedict .05
2b Ken Griffey .05
2c Dale Murphy .25
Panel (Chicago Cubs) .50
3a Jody Davis .05
3b Andre Dawson .35
3c Leon Durham .05
Panel (Cincinnati Reds)
4a Buddy Bell .05
4b Eric Davis .05
4c Dave Parker .05
Panel (Houston Astros) 1.75
5a Glenn Davis .05
5b Nolan Ryan .75
5c Mike Scott .05
Panel (Los Angeles Dodgers) .35
6a Pedro Guerrero .05
6b Mike Marshall .05
6c Fernando Valenzuela .05
Panel (Montreal Expos) 1.00
7a Tim Raines .25
7b Tim Wallach .10
7c Mitch Webster .10
Panel (Montreal Expos) .75
8a Hubie Brooks .10
8b Bryn Smith .10
8c Floyd Youmans .10
Panel (Philadelphia Phillies) 1.25
9a Shane Rawley .05
9b Juan Samuel .05
9c Mike Schmidt .60
Panel (Pittsburgh Pirates) .35
10a Jim Morrison .05
10b Johnny Ray .05
10c R.J. Reynolds .05
Panel (St. Louis Cardinals) 1.00
11a Jack Clark .05
11b Vince Coleman .05
11c Ozzie Smith .50
Panel (San Diego Padres) 1.00
12a Steve Garvey .15
12b Tony Gwynn .50
12c John Kruk .05
Panel (San Francisco Giants) .35
13a Chili Davis .05
13b Jeffrey Leonard .05
13c Robbie Thompson .05
Panel (Baltimore Orioles) 2.50
14a Fred Lynn .05
14b Eddie Murray .50
14c Cal Ripken, Jr. 1.00
Panel (Boston Red Sox) 1.75
15a Don Baylor .05
15b Wade Boggs .50
15c Roger Clemens .60
Panel (California Angels) .40
16a Doug DeCinces .05
16b Wally Joyner .05
16c Mike Witt .05
Panel (Chicago White Sox) .70
17a Harold Baines .05
17b Carlton Fisk .50
17c Ozzie Guillen .05
Panel (Cleveland Indians) .35
18a Joe Carter .50
18b Julio Franco .05
18c Pat Tabler .05
Panel (Detroit Tigers) .35
19a Kirk Gibson .05
19b Jack Morris .05
19c Alan Trammell .05
Panel (Kansas City Royals) 1.25
20a George Brett .50
20b Bret Saberhagen .05
20c Willie Wilson .05
Panel (Milwaukee Brewers) 1.50
21a Cecil Cooper .05
21b Paul Molitor .40
21c Robin Yount .40
Panel (Minnesota Twins) .70
22a Tom Brunansky .05
22b Kent Hrbek .05
22c Kirby Puckett .50
Panel (New York Yankees) 2.50
23a Rickey Henderson .40
23b Don Mattingly .60
23c Dave Winfield .40
Panel (Oakland A's) 1.00
24a Jose Canseco .35
24b Alfredo Griffin .05
24c Carney Lansford .05
Panel (Seattle Mariners) .35
25a Phil Bradley .05
25b Alvin Davis .05
25c Mark Langston .05
Panel (Texas Rangers) .35
26a Pete Incaviglia .05
26b Pete O'Brien .05
26c Larry Parrish .05
Panel (Toronto Blue Jays) .75
27a Jesse Barfield .10
27b George Bell .10
27c Tony Fernandez .10
Panel (Toronto Blue Jays) .75
28a Lloyd Moseby .10
28b Dave Steib .10
28c Ernie Whitt .10

1991 Studio Preview

Each 1991 Donruss set packaged for the retail trade included a pack of four cards previewing the debut Studio set. The cards are in the same format as the regular set, 2-1/2" x 3-1/2" with evocative black-and-white photos bordered in maroon on front, and a biographical write-up on the back.

NM/M
Complete Set (18): 5.00

Common Player: .50
1 Juan Bell .50
2 Roger Clemens 3.00
3 Dave Parker .50
4 Tim Raines .50
5 Kevin Seitzer .50
6 Teddy Higuera .50
7 Bernie Williams .50
8 Harold Baines .50
9 Gary Pettis .50
10 Dave Justice .50
11 Eric Davis .50
12 Andujar Cedeno .50
13 Tom Foley .50
14 Dwight Gooden .50
15 Doug Drabek .50
16 Steve Decker .50
17 Joe Torre .75
18 Header Card .10

1991 Studio

Donruss introduced this 264-card set in 1991. The cards feature maroon borders surrounding black and white posed player photos. The card backs are printed in black and white and feature personal data, career highlights, hobbies and interests and the player's hero. The cards were released in foil packs only and feature a special Rod Carew puzzle.

NM/M
Complete Set (264): 7.50
Common Player: .05
Foil Pack (10): .75
Foil Box (48): 12.50
1 Glenn Davis .05
2 Dwight Evans .05
3 Leo Gomez .05
4 Chris Hoiles .05
5 Sam Horn .05
6 Ben McDonald .05
7 Randy Milligan .05
8 Gregg Olson .05
9 Cal Ripken, Jr. 1.00
10 David Segui .05
11 Wade Boggs .40
12 Ellis Burks .05
13 Jack Clark .05
14 Roger Clemens .45
15 Mike Greenwell .05
16 Tim Naehring .05
17 Tony Pena .05
18 Phil Plantier RC .05
19 Jeff Reardon .05
20 Mo Vaughn .05
21 Jimmy Reese .05
22 Jim Abbott .05
23 Bert Blyleven .05
24 Chuck Finley .05
25 Gary Gaetti .05
26 Wally Joyner .05
27 Mark Langston .05
28 Kirk McCaskill .05
29 Lance Parrish .05
30 Dave Winfield .30
31 Alex Fernandez .05
32 Carlton Fisk .30
33 Scott Fletcher .05
34 Greg Hibbard .05
35 Charlie Hough .05
36 Jack McDowell .05
37 Tim Raines .05
38 Sammy Sosa .40
39 Bobby Thigpen .05
40 Frank Thomas .30
41 Sandy Alomar .05
42 John Farrell .05
43 Glenallen Hill .05
44 Brook Jacoby .05
45 Chris James .05
46 Doug Jones .05
47 Eric King .05
48 Mark Lewis .05
49 Greg Swindell .05
50 Mark Whiten .05
51 Milt Cuyler .05
52 Rob Deer .05
53 Cecil Fielder .05
54 Travis Fryman .05
55 Bill Gullickson .05
56 Lloyd Moseby .05
57 Frank Tanana .05
58 Mickey Tettleton .05
59 Alan Trammell .05
60 Lou Whitaker .05
61 Mike Boddicker .05
62 George Brett .45
63 Jeff Conine .05
64 Warren Cromartie .05
65 Storm Davis .05
66 Kirk Gibson .05
67 Mark Gubicza .05
68 Brian McRae RC .05
69 Bret Saberhagen .05
70 Kurt Stillwell .05
71 Tim McIntosh .05
72 Candy Maldonado .05
73 Paul Molitor .30
74 Willie Randolph .05
75 Ron Robinson .05
76 Gary Sheffield .20
77 Franklin Stubbs .05
78 B.J. Surhoff .05
79 Greg Vaughn .05
80 Robin Yount .30
81 Rick Aguilera .05
82 Steve Bedrosian .05
83 Scott Erickson .05
84 Greg Gagne .05
85 Dan Gladden .05
86 Brian Harper .05
87 Kent Hrbek .05
88 Shane Mack .05
89 Jack Morris .05
90 Kirby Puckett .40
91 Jesse Barfield .05
92 Steve Farr .05
93 Steve Howe .05
94 Roberto Kelly .05
95 Tim Leary .05
96 Kevin Maas .05
97 Don Mattingly .45
98 Hensley Meulens .05
99 Scott Sanderson .05
100 Steve Sax .05
101 Jose Canseco .20
102 Dennis Eckersley .05
103 Dave Henderson .05
104 Rickey Henderson .30
105 Rick Honeycutt .05
106 Mark McGwire .75
107 Dave Stewart .05
108 Eric Show .05
109 Todd Van Poppel RC .05
110 Bob Welch .05
111 Alvin Davis .05
112 Ken Griffey Jr. .50
113 Ken Griffey Sr. .05
114 Erik Hanson .05
115 Brian Holman .05
116 Randy Johnson .30
117 Edgar Martinez .05
118 Tino Martinez .05
119 Harold Reynolds .05
120 David Valle .05
121 Kevin Belcher .05
122 Scott Chiamparino .05
123 Julio Franco .05
124 Juan Gonzalez .20
125 Rich Gossage .05
126 Jeff Kunkel .05
127 Rafael Palmeiro .05
128 Nolan Ryan 1.00
129 Ruben Sierra .05
130 Bobby Witt .05
131 Roberto Alomar .10
132 Tom Candiotti .05
133 Joe Carter .05
134 Ken Dayley .05
135 Kelly Gruber .05
136 John Olerud .05
137 Dave Steib .05
138 Turner Ward .05
139 Devon White .05
140 Mookie Wilson .05
141 Steve Avery .05
142 Sid Bream .05
143 Nick Esasky .05
144 Ron Gant .05
145 Tom Glavine .05
146 Dave Justice .20
147 Kelly Mann .05
148 Terry Pendleton .05
149 John Smoltz .05
150 Jeff Treadway .05
151 George Bell .05
152 Shawn Boskie .05
153 Andre Dawson .20
154 Lance Dickson .05
155 Shawon Dunston .05

156	Joe Girardi	.05
157	Mark Grace	.05
158	Ryne Sandberg	.40
159	Gary Scott	.05
160	Dave Smith	.05
161	Tom Browning	.05
162	Eric Davis	.05
163	Rob Dibble	.05
164	Mariano Duncan	.05
165	Chris Hammond	.05
166	Billy Hatcher	.05
167	Barry Larkin	.05
168	Hal Morris	.05
169	Paul O'Neill	.05
170	Chris Sabo	.05
171	Eric Anthony	.05
172	Jeff Bagwell RC	1.50
173	Craig Biggio	.05
174	Ken Caminitti	.05
175	Jim Deshaies	.05
176	Steve Finley	.05
177	Pete Harnisch	.05
178	Darryl Kile	.05
179	Curt Schilling	.20
180	Mike Scott	.05
181	Brett Butler	.05
182	Gary Carter	.30
183	Orel Hershiser	.05
184	Ramon Martinez	.05
185	Eddie Murray	.30
186	Jose Offerman	.05
187	Bob Ojeda	.05
188	Juan Samuel	.05
189	Mike Scioscia	.05
190	Darryl Strawberry	.05
191	Moises Alou	.05
192	Brian Barnes	.05
193	Oil Can Boyd	.05
194	Ivan Calderon	.05
195	Delino DeShields	.05
196	Mike Fitzgerald	.05
197	Andres Galarraga	.05
198	Marquis Grissom	.05
199	Bill Sampen	.05
200	Tim Wallach	.05
201	Daryl Boston	.05
202	Vince Coleman	.05
203	John Franco	.05
204	Dwight Gooden	.05
205	Tom Herr	.05
206	Gregg Jefferies	.05
207	Howard Johnson	.05
208	Dave Magadan	.05
209	Kevin McReynolds	.05
210	Frank Viola	.05
211	Wes Chamberlain	.05
212	Darren Daulton	.05
213	Len Dykstra	.05
214	Charlie Hayes	.05
215	Ricky Jordan	.05
216	Steve Lake	.05
217	Roger McDowell	.05
218	Mickey Morandini	.05
219	Terry Mulholland	.05
220	Dale Murphy	.15
221	Jay Bell	.05
222	Barry Bonds	1.00
223	Bobby Bonilla	.05
224	Doug Drabek	.05
225	Bill Landrum	.05
226	Mike LaValliere	.05
227	Jose Lind	.05
228	Don Slaught	.05
229	John Smiley	.05
230	Andy Van Slyke	.05
231	Bernard Gilkey	.05
232	Pedro Guerrero	.05
233	Rex Hudler	.05
234	Ray Lankford	.05
235	Joe Magrane	.05
236	Jose Oquendo	.05
237	Lee Smith	.05
238	Ozzie Smith	.40
239	Milt Thompson	.05
240	Todd Zeile	.05
241	Larry Andersen	.05
242	Andy Benes	.05
243	Paul Faries	.05
244	Tony Fernandez	.05
245	Tony Gwynn	.40
246	Atlee Hammaker	.05
247	Fred McGriff	.05
248	Bip Roberts	.05
249	Benito Santiago	.05
250	Ed Whitson	.05
251	Dave Anderson	.05
252	Mike Benjamin	.05
253	John Burkett	.05
254	Will Clark	.05
255	Scott Garrelts	.05
256	Willie McGee	.05
257	Kevin Mitchell	.05
258	Dave Righetti	.05
259	Matt Williams	.05
260	Black & Decker (Bud Black, Steve Decker)	.10
261	Checklist	.03
262	Checklist	.03
263	Checklist	.03
---	Header Card	.03

1992 Studio Preview

To introduce its 1992 Studio brand, Leaf produced 22 preview cards in format virtually

CAL RIPKEN, JR. PREVIEW — Baltimore Orioles

identical to the issued versions of the same cards. The only differences are the appearance of the word "PREVIEW" in the lower-right corner of the card front, in place of the player's position, and the number "X of 22 / Preview Card" on the back where regular cards have the card number in the upper-right corner. The cards were distributed on a very limited basis to members of the Donruss dealers' network.

		NM/M
Complete Set (22):		75.00
Common Player:		1.50
1	Ruben Sierra	1.50
2	Kirby Puckett	6.00
3	Ryne Sandberg	6.00
4	John Kruk	1.50
5	Cal Ripken, Jr.	12.00
6	Robin Yount	4.50
7	Dwight Gooden	1.50
8	David Justice	1.50
9	Don Mattingly	7.50
10	Wally Joyner	1.50
11	Will Clark	1.50
12	Rob Dibble	1.50
13	Roberto Alomar	2.50
14	Wade Boggs	6.00
15	Barry Bonds	12.00
16	Jeff Bagwell	4.50
17	Mark McGwire	9.00
18	Frank Thomas	6.00
19	Brett Butler	1.50
20	Ozzie Smith	6.00
21	Jim Abbott	1.50
22	Tony Gwynn	6.00

1992 Studio

PETE HARNISCH RHP — Houston Astros

Donruss introduced the Studio line in 1991 and released another 264-card set entitled Leaf Studio for 1992. The cards feature a color player closeup with a large, rough-textured black-and-white photo of the player in the background. Tan borders surround the photos. The cards were only released in foil packs. Special Heritage insert cards featuring top players in vintage uniforms could be found in foil and jumbo packs.

		NM/M
Complete Set (264):		8.00
Common Player:		.05
Pack (10):		.65
Wax Box (48):		15.00
1	Steve Avery	.05
2	Sid Bream	.05
3	Ron Gant	.05
4	Tom Glavine	.25
5	Dave Justice	.05
6	Mark Lemke	.05
7	Greg Olson	.05
8	Terry Pendleton	.05
9	Deion Sanders	.25
10	John Smoltz	.05
11	Doug Dascenzo	.05
12	Andre Dawson	.25
13	Joe Girardi	.05
14	Mark Grace	.05
15	Greg Maddux	.50
16	Chuck McElroy	.05
17	Mike Morgan	.05
18	Ryne Sandberg	.50
19	Gary Scott	.05
20	Sammy Sosa	.50
21	Norm Charlton	.05
22	Rob Dibble	.05
23	Barry Larkin	.05
24	Hal Morris	.05
25	Paul O'Neill	.05
26	Jose Rijo	.05
27	Bip Roberts	.05
28	Chris Sabo	.05
29	Reggie Sanders	.05
30	Greg Swindell	.05
31	Jeff Bagwell	.45
32	Craig Biggio	.05
33	Ken Caminiti	.05
34	Andujar Cedeno	.05
35	Steve Finley	.05
36	Pete Harnisch	.05
37	Butch Henry	.05
38	Doug Jones	.05
39	Darryl Kile	.05
40	Eddie Taubensee	.05
41	Brett Butler	.05
42	Tom Candiotti	.05
43	Eric Davis	.05
44	Orel Hershiser	.05
45	Eric Karros	.05
46	Ramon Martinez	.05
47	Jose Offerman	.05
48	Mike Scioscia	.05
49	Mike Sharperson	.05
50	Darryl Strawberry	.05
51	Bret Barbarie	.05
52	Ivan Calderon	.05
53	Gary Carter	.45
54	Delino DeShields	.05
55	Marquis Grissom	.05
56	Ken Hill	.05
57	Dennis Martinez	.05
58	Spike Owen	.05
59	Larry Walker	.05
60	Tim Wallach	.05
61	Bobby Bonilla	.05
62	Tim Burke	.05
63	Vince Coleman	.05
64	John Franco	.05
65	Dwight Gooden	.05
66	Todd Hundley	.05
67	Howard Johnson	.05
68	Eddie Murray	.45
69	Bret Saberhagen	.05
70	Anthony Young	.05
71	Kim Batiste	.05
72	Wes Chamberlain	.05
73	Darren Daulton	.05
74	Mariano Duncan	.05
75	Len Dykstra	.05
76	John Kruk	.05
77	Mickey Morandini	.05
78	Terry Mulholland	.05
79	Dale Murphy	.20
80	Mitch Williams	.05
81	Jay Bell	.05
82	Barry Bonds	1.00
83	Steve Buechele	.05
84	Doug Drabek	.05
85	Mike LaValliere	.05
86	Jose Lind	.05
87	Denny Neagle	.05
88	Randy Tomlin	.05
89	Andy Van Slyke	.05
90	Gary Varsho	.05
91	Pedro Guerrero	.05
92	Rex Hudler	.05
93	Brian Jordan	.05
94	Felix Jose	.05
95	Donovan Osborne	.05
96	Tom Pagnozzi	.05
97	Lee Smith	.05
98	Ozzie Smith	.50
99	Todd Worrell	.05
100	Todd Zeile	.05
101	Andy Benes	.05
102	Jerald Clark	.05
103	Tony Fernandez	.05
104	Tony Gwynn	.50
105	Greg Harris	.05
106	Fred McGriff	.05
107	Benito Santiago	.05
108	Gary Sheffield	.30
109	Kurt Stillwell	.05
110	Tim Teufel	.05
111	Kevin Bass	.05
112	Jeff Brantley	.05
113	John Burkett	.05
114	Will Clark	.05
115	Royce Clayton	.05
116	Mike Jackson	.05
117	Darren Lewis	.05
118	Bill Swift	.05
119	Robby Thompson	.05
120	Matt Williams	.05
121	Brady Anderson	.05
122	Glenn Davis	.05
123	Mike Devereaux	.05
124	Chris Hoiles	.05
125	Sam Horn	.05
126	Ben McDonald	.05
127	Mike Mussina	.25
128	Gregg Olson	.05
129	Cal Ripken, Jr.	1.00
130	Rick Sutcliffe	.05
131	Wade Boggs	.50
132	Roger Clemens	.60
133	Greg Harris	.05
134	Tim Naehring	.05
135	Tony Pena	.05
136	Phil Plantier	.05
137	Jeff Reardon	.05
138	Jody Reed	.05
139	Mo Vaughn	.05
140	Frank Viola	.05
141	Jim Abbott	.05
142	Hubie Brooks	.05
143	Chad Curtis RC	.05
144	Gary DiSarcina	.05
145	Chuck Finley	.05
146	Bryan Harvey	.05
147	Von Hayes	.05
148	Mark Langston	.05
149	Lance Parrish	.05
150	Lee Stevens	.05
151	George Bell	.05
152	Alex Fernandez	.05
153	Greg Hibbard	.05
154	Lance Johnson	.05
155	Kirk McCaskill	.05
156	Tim Raines	.05
157	Steve Sax	.05
158	Bobby Thigpen	.05
159	Frank Thomas	.45
160	Robin Ventura	.05
161	Sandy Alomar, Jr.	.05
162	Jack Armstrong	.05
163	Carlos Baerga	.05
164	Albert Belle	.05
165	Alex Cole	.05
166	Glenallen Hill	.05
167	Mark Lewis	.05
168	Kenny Lofton	.05
169	Paul Sorrento	.05
170	Mark Whiten	.05
171	Milt Cuyler (Color photo is Lou Whitaker.)	.05
172	Rob Deer	.05
173	Cecil Fielder	.05
174	Travis Fryman	.05
175	Mike Henneman	.05
176	Tony Phillips	.05
177	Frank Tanana	.05
178	Mickey Tettleton	.05
179	Alan Trammell	.05
180	Lou Whitaker	.05
181	George Brett	.60
182	Tom Gordon	.05
183	Mark Gubicza	.05
184	Gregg Jefferies	.05
185	Wally Joyner	.05
186	Brent Mayne	.05
187	Brian McRae	.05
188	Kevin McReynolds	.05
189	Keith Miller	.05
190	Jeff Montgomery	.05
191	Dante Bichette	.05
192	Ricky Bones	.05
193	Scott Fletcher	.05
194	Paul Molitor	.45
195	Jaime Navarro	.05
196	Franklin Stubbs	.05
197	B.J. Surhoff	.05
198	Greg Vaughn	.05
199	Bill Wegman	.05
200	Robin Yount	.45
201	Rick Aguilera	.05
202	Scott Erickson	.05
203	Greg Gagne	.05
204	Brian Harper	.05
205	Kent Hrbek	.05
206	Scott Leius	.05
207	Shane Mack	.05
208	Pat Mahomes	.05
209	Kirby Puckett	.50
210	John Smiley	.05
211	Mike Gallego	.05
212	Charlie Hayes	.05
213	Pat Kelly	.05
214	Roberto Kelly	.05
215	Kevin Maas	.05
216	Don Mattingly	.60
217	Matt Nokes	.05
218	Melido Perez	.05
219	Scott Sanderson	.05
220	Danny Tartabull	.05
221	Harold Baines	.05
222	Jose Canseco	.30
223	Dennis Eckersley	.35
224	Dave Henderson	.05
225	Carney Lansford	.05
226	Mark McGwire	.75
227	Mike Moore	.05
228	Randy Ready	.05
229	Terry Steinbach	.05
230	Dave Stewart	.05
231	Jay Buhner	.05
232	Ken Griffey Jr.	.65
233	Erik Hanson	.05
234	Randy Johnson	.45
235	Edgar Martinez	.05
236	Tino Martinez	.05
237	Kevin Mitchell	.05
238	Pete O'Brien	.05
239	Harold Reynolds	.05
240	David Valle	.05
241	Julio Franco	.05
242	Juan Gonzalez	.25
243	Jose Guzman	.05
244	Rafael Palmeiro	.35
245	Dean Palmer	.05
246	Ivan Rodriguez	.35
247	Jeff Russell	.05
248	Nolan Ryan	1.00
249	Ruben Sierra	.05
250	Dickie Thon	.05
251	Roberto Alomar	.20
252	Derek Bell	.05
253	Pat Borders	.05
254	Joe Carter	.05
255	Kelly Gruber	.05
256	Juan Guzman	.05
257	Jack Morris	.05
258	John Olerud	.05
259	Devon White	.05
260	Dave Winfield	.45
261	Checklist	.05
262	Checklist	.05
263	Checklist	.05
264	History card	.05

Heritage

HERITAGE SERIES — RYNE SANDBERG

Superstars of 1992 were photographed in vintage-style uniforms in this 14-card insert set found in packages of Studio's 1992 issue. Cards #1-8 could be found in standard foil packs while #9-14 were inserted in Studio jumbos. Cards featured a sepia-tone photo bordered in turquoise and highlighted with copper foil. Cards carry a "BC" prefix to the card number on back.

		NM/M
Complete Set (14):		6.00
Common Player:		.50
1	Ryne Sandberg	1.00
2	Carlton Fisk	.75
3	Wade Boggs	1.00
4	Jose Canseco	.65
5	Don Mattingly	1.25
6	Darryl Strawberry	.50
7	Cal Ripken, Jr.	1.50
8	Will Clark	.50
9	Andre Dawson	.50
10	Andy Van Slyke	.50
11	Paul Molitor	.75
12	Jeff Bagwell	.75
13	Darren Daulton	.50
14	Kirby Puckett	1.00

1993 Studio Promos

Though unmarked as such, a pair of promo cards was produced in advance of '93 Studio. At first glance the cards appear identical to the same players' issued versions, but there are noticeable cropping differences. On the back of the Thomas card, the promo has a smaller projection of his face, with much more of his hair showing at top and the last line of type about even with the bottom of his nose. The issued card shows almost no hair at top and has the last line even with his top lip. The Sandberg cropping difference appears on front. On the promo his right ear is well clear of the left border; on the issued version his ear touches the border.

		NM/M
Complete Set (2):		6.00
Common Player:		2.00
139	Frank Thomas	2.00
176	Ryne Sandberg	5.00

1993 Studio

This 220-card set features full-bleed photos. The player's portrait appears against one of several backgrounds featuring his team's uniform. His signature and the Studio logo are

printed in gold foil. Backs have an extreme closeup partial portrait of the player and insights into his personality.

		NM/M
Complete Set (220):		15.00
Common Player:		.05
Pack (12):		.75
Wax Box (36):		12.50
1	Dennis Eckersley	.35
2	Chad Curtis	.05
3	Eric Anthony	.05
4	Roberto Alomar	.20
5	Steve Avery	.05
6	Cal Eldred	.05
7	Bernard Gilkey	.05
8	Steve Buechele	.05
9	Brett Butler	.05
10	Terry Mulholland	.05
11	Moises Alou	.05
12	Barry Bonds	1.00
13	Sandy Alomar Jr.	.05
14	Chris Bosio	.05
15	Scott Sanderson	.05
16	Bobby Bonilla	.05
17	Brady Anderson	.05
18	Derek Bell	.05
19	Wes Chamberlain	.05
20	Jay Bell	.05
21	Kevin Brown	.05
22	Roger Clemens	.60
23	Roberto Kelly	.05
24	Dante Bichette	.05
25	George Brett	.60
26	Rob Deer	.05
27	Brian Harper	.05
28	George Bell	.05
29	Jim Abbott	.05
30	Dave Henderson	.05
31	Wade Boggs	.50
32	Chili Davis	.05
33	Ellis Burks	.05
34	Jeff Bagwell	.40
35	Kent Hrbek	.05
36	Pat Borders	.05
37	Cecil Fielder	.05
38	Sid Bream	.05
39	Greg Gagne	.05
40	Darryl Hamilton	.05
41	Jerald Clark	.05
42	Mark Grace	.05
43	Barry Larkin	.05
44	John Burkett	.05
45	Scott Cooper	.05
46	Mike Lansing RC	.25
47	Jose Canseco	.30
48	Will Clark	.05
49	Carlos Garcia	.05
50	Carlos Baerga	.05
51	Darren Daulton	.05
52	Jay Buhner	.05
53	Andy Benes	.05
54	Jeff Conine	.05
55	Mike Devereaux	.05
56	Vince Coleman	.05
57	Terry Steinbach	.05
58	J.T. Snow RC	.40
59	Greg Swindell	.05
60	Devon White	.05
61	John Smoltz	.05
62	Todd Zeile	.05
63	Rick Wilkins	.05
64	Tim Wallach	.05
65	John Wetteland	.05
66	Matt Williams	.05
67	Paul Sorrento	.05
68	David Valle	.05
69	Walt Weiss	.05
70	John Franco	.05
71	Nolan Ryan	1.00
72	Frank Viola	.05
73	Chris Sabo	.05
74	David Nied	.05
75	Kevin McReynolds	.05
76	Lou Whitaker	.05
77	Dave Winfield	.40
78	Robin Ventura	.05
79	Spike Owen	.05
80	Cal Ripken, Jr.	1.00
81	Dan Walter	.05
82	Mitch Williams	.05
83	Tim Wakefield	.05
84	Rickey Henderson	.40
85	Gary DiSarcina	.05
86	Craig Biggio	.05
87	Joe Carter	.05

#	Player	NM/M
88	Ron Gant	.05
89	John Jaha	.05
90	Gregg Jefferies	.05
91	Jose Guzman	.05
92	Eric Karros	.05
93	Wil Cordero	.05
94	Royce Clayton	.05
95	Albert Belle	.05
96	Ken Griffey Jr.	.65
97	Orestes Destrade	.15
98	Tony Fernandez	.05
99	Leo Gomez	.05
100	Tony Gwynn	.50
101	Len Dykstra	.05
102	Jeff King	.05
103	Julio Franco	.05
104	Andre Dawson	.25
105	Randy Milligan	.05
106	Alex Cole	.05
107	Phil Hiatt	.05
108	Travis Fryman	.05
109	Chuck Knoblauch	.05
110	Bo Jackson	.10
111	Pat Kelly	.05
112	Bret Saberhagen	.05
113	Ruben Sierra	.05
114	Tim Salmon	.05
115	Doug Jones	.05
116	Ed Sprague	.05
117	Terry Pendleton	.05
118	Robin Yount	.40
119	Mark Whiten	.05
120	Checklist	.05
121	Sammy Sosa	.50
122	Darryl Strawberry	.05
123	Larry Walker	.05
124	Robby Thompson	.05
125	Carlos Martinez	.05
126	Edgar Martinez	.05
127	Benito Santiago	.05
128	Howard Johnson	.05
129	Harold Reynolds	.05
130	Craig Shipley	.05
131	Curt Schilling	.30
132	Andy Van Slyke	.05
133	Ivan Rodriguez	.35
134	Mo Vaughn	.05
135	Bip Roberts	.05
136	Charlie Hayes	.05
137	Brian McRae	.05
138	Mickey Tettleton	.05
139	Frank Thomas	.40
140	Paul O'Neill	.05
141	Mark McGwire	.75
142	Damion Easley	.05
143	Ken Caminiti	.05
144	Juan Guzman	.05
145	Tom Glavine	.25
146	Pat Listach	.05
147	Lee Smith	.05
148	Derrick May	.05
149	Ramon Martinez	.05
150	Delino DeShields	.05
151	Kirt Manwaring	.05
152	Reggie Jefferson	.05
153	Randy Johnson	.40
154	Dave Magadan	.05
155	Dwight Gooden	.05
156	Chris Hoiles	.05
157	Fred McGriff	.05
158	Dave Hollins	.05
159	Al Martin	.05
160	Juan Gonzalez	.20
161	Mike Greenwell	.05
162	Kevin Mitchell	.05
163	Andres Galarraga	.05
164	Wally Joyner	.05
165	Kirk Gibson	.05
166	Pedro Munoz	.05
167	Ozzie Guillen	.05
168	Jimmy Key	.05
169	Kevin Seitzer	.05
170	Luis Polonia	.05
171	Luis Gonzalez	.05
172	Paul Molitor	.40
173	Dave Justice	.05
174	B.J. Surhoff	.05
175	Ray Lankford	.05
176	Ryne Sandberg	.50
177	Jody Reed	.05
178	Marquis Grissom	.05
179	Willie McGee	.05
180	Kenny Lofton	.05
181	Junior Felix	.05
182	Jose Offerman	.05
183	John Kruk	.05
184	Orlando Merced	.05
185	Rafael Palmeiro	.35
186	Billy Hatcher	.05
187	Joe Oliver	.05
188	Joe Girardi	.05
189	Jose Lind	.05
190	Harold Baines	.05
191	Mike Pagliarulo	.05
192	Lance Johnson	.05
193	Don Mattingly	.60
194	Doug Drabek	.05
195	John Olerud	.05
196	Greg Maddux	.50
197	Greg Vaughn	.05
198	Tom Pagnozzi	.05
199	Willie Wilson	.05
200	Jack McDowell	.05
201	Mike Piazza	.65
202	Mike Mussina	.30
203	Charles Nagy	.05
204	Tino Martinez	.05
205	Charlie Hough	.05
206	Todd Hundley	.05
207	Gary Sheffield	.30
208	Mickey Morandini	.05
209	Don Slaught	.05
210	Dean Palmer	.05
211	Jose Rijo	.05
212	Vinny Castilla	.05
213	Tony Phillips	.05
214	Kirby Puckett	.50
215	Tim Raines	.05
216	Otis Nixon	.05
217	Ozzie Smith	.50
218	Jose Vizcaino	.05
220	Checklist	.05

Heritage

All types of 1993 Leaf Studio packs were candidates for having one of 12 Heritage cards inserted in them. The fronts feature the player posing in an old-time uniform, framed in turquoise with copper highlights. The backs have a mug shot surrounded by an ornate frame and describe the uniform on the front. Team trivia is also included.

		NM/M
Complete Set (12):		12.00
Common Player:		.50
1	George Brett	2.00
2	Juan Gonzalez	.75
3	Roger Clemens	2.00
4	Mark McGwire	4.00
5	Mark Grace	.50
6	Ozzie Smith	1.50
7	Barry Larkin	.50
8	Frank Thomas	1.00
9	Carlos Baerga	.50
10	Eric Karros	.50
11	J.T. Snow	.50
12	John Kruk	.50

Silhouettes

These insert cards were randomly included in jumbo packs only. The card fronts feature a ghosted image of the player against an action silhouette on a gray background. The player's name is in bronze foil at bottom. Backs have a player action photo and description of career highlights.

		NM/M
Complete Set (10):		7.00
Common Player:		.15
1	Frank Thomas	.65
2	Barry Bonds	3.00
3	Jeff Bagwell	.65
4	Juan Gonzalez	.40
5	Travis Fryman	.15
6	J.T. Snow	.15
7	John Kruk	.15
8	Jeff Blauser	.15
9	Mike Piazza	2.00
10	Nolan Ryan	3.00

Superstars on Canvas

Ten players are featured on these insert cards, which were available in hobby and

retail packs. The cards show player portraits which mix photography and artwork.

		NM/M
Complete Set (10):		8.00
Common Player:		.25
1	Ken Griffey Jr.	1.50
2	Jose Canseco	.60
3	Mark McGwire	2.00
4	Mike Mussina	.50
5	Joe Carter	.25
6	Frank Thomas	1.00
7	Darren Daulton	.25
8	Mark Grace	.25
9	Andres Galarraga	.25
10	Barry Bonds	2.50

Frank Thomas

FRANK THOMAS

This five-card set is devoted to Frank Thomas. Cards were randomly included in all types of 1993 Leaf Studio packs. Topics covered on the cards include Thomas' childhood, his baseball memories, his family, his performance and being a role model.

		NM/M
Complete Set (5):		5.00
Common Card:		1.00
1	Childhood	1.00
2	Baseball Memories	1.00
3	Importance of Family	1.00
4	Performance	1.00
5	On Being a Role Model	1.00

1994 Studio Samples

To introduce its "locker-room look" issue for 1994, Leaf's Studio brand produced this three-star sample set and distributed it to its hobby dealer network. The cards are basically the same as the regular-issue cards of those players except for the addition of a "Promotional Sample" over-printed diagonally on front and back. The "Up Close" biographies on the cards' backs are different between the promos and the regular cards and there is a slight difference in front photo cropping on the Gonzalez card.

		NM/M
Complete Set (3):		6.00
83	Barry Bonds	3.00
154	Juan Gonzalez	1.00
209	Frank Thomas	2.00

1994 Studio

Studio baseball from Donruss returned in mid-August, 1994, with a three-time MVP spokesman, several jazzy and short-printed inserts subsets and a reduced overall production figure that represents a sharp drop from 1993. Barry Bonds is the MVP whose mug adorns Studio counter boxes and advertisements. According to Donruss officials, production was limited to 8,000 cases of 20 boxes each, which represents a 35 percent decrease from 1993 and works out to about 315,000 of each card. Only 2,000 cases were earmarked for retail distribution and no jumbo packs were produced. Studio 1994 features 220 cards issued in one series, once again with close-up personal portraits of the top stars in the game. Each card is foil-stamped with a borderless design and UV coating front and back. The front of the card features the player in the foreground with his locker in the background. As in the previous three Studio offerings, the backs of the cards contain personal information about the players.

#	Player	NM/M
Complete Set (220):		7.50
Common Player:		.05
Pack (12):		.45
Wax Box (36):		10.00
1	Dennis Eckersley	.45
2	Brent Gates	.05
3	Rickey Henderson	.55
4	Mark McGwire	1.00
5	Troy Neel	.05
6	Ruben Sierra	.05
7	Terry Steinbach	.05
8	Chad Curtis	.05
9	Chili Davis	.05
10	Gary DiSarcina	.05
11	Damion Easley	.05
12	Bo Jackson	.10
13	Mark Langston	.05
14	Eduardo Perez	.05
15	Tim Salmon	.05
16	Jeff Bagwell	.55
17	Craig Biggio	.05
18	Ken Caminiti	.05
19	Andujar Cedeno	.05
20	Doug Drabek	.05
21	Steve Finley	.05
22	Luis Gonzalez	.05
23	Darryl Kile	.05
24	Roberto Alomar	.20
25	Pat Borders	.05
26	Joe Carter	.05
27	Carlos Delgado	.40
28	Pat Hentgen	.05
29	Paul Molitor	.55
30	John Olerud	.05
31	Ed Sprague	.05
32	Devon White	.05
33	Steve Avery	.05
34	Tom Glavine	.25
35	David Justice	.05
36	Roberto Kelly	.05
37	Ryan Klesko	.05
38	Javier Lopez	.05
39	Greg Maddux	.60
40	Fred McGriff	.05
41	Terry Pendleton	.05
42	Ricky Bones	.05
43	Darryl Hamilton	.05
44	Brian Harper	.05
45	John Jaha	.05
46	Dave Nilsson	.05
47	Kevin Seitzer	.05
48	Greg Vaughn	.05
49	Turner Ward	.05
50	Bernard Gilkey	.05
51	Gregg Jefferies	.05
52	Ray Lankford	.05
53	Tom Pagnozzi	.05
54	Ozzie Smith	.60
55	Bob Tewksbury	.05
56	Mark Whiten	.05
57	Todd Zeile	.05
58	Steve Buechele	.05
59	Shawon Dunston	.05
60	Mark Grace	.05
61	Derrick May	.05
62	Tuffy Rhodes	.05
63	Ryne Sandberg	.60
64	Sammy Sosa	.60
65	Rick Wilkins	.05
66	Brett Butler	.05
67	Delino DeShields	.05
68	Orel Hershiser	.05
69	Eric Karros	.05
70	Raul Mondesi	.05
71	Jose Offerman	.05
72	Mike Piazza	.75
73	Tim Wallach	.05
74	Moises Alou	.05
75	Sean Berry	.05
76	Wil Cordero	.05
77	Cliff Floyd	.05
78	Marquis Grissom	.05
79	Ken Hill	.05
80	Larry Walker	.05
81	John Wetteland	.05
82	Rod Beck	.05
83	Barry Bonds	1.50
84	Royce Clayton	.05
85	Darren Lewis	.05
86	Willie McGee	.05
87	Bill Swift	.05
88	Robby Thompson	.05
89	Matt Williams	.05
90	Sandy Alomar Jr.	.05
91	Carlos Baerga	.05
92	Albert Belle	.05
93	Kenny Lofton	.05
94	Eddie Murray	.55
95	Manny Ramirez	.55
96	Paul Sorrento	.05
97	Jim Thome	.45
98	Rich Amaral	.05
99	Eric Anthony	.05
100	Jay Buhner	.05
101	Ken Griffey Jr.	.75
102	Randy Johnson	.55
103	Edgar Martinez	.05
104	Tino Martinez	.05
105	Kurt Abbott RC	.05
106	Bret Barberie	.05
107	Chuck Carr	.05
108	Jeff Conine	.05
109	Chris Hammond	.05
110	Bryan Harvey	.05
111	Benito Santiago	.05
112	Gary Sheffield	.30
113	Bobby Bonilla	.05
114	Dwight Gooden	.05
115	Todd Hundley	.05
116	Bobby Jones	.05
117	Jeff Kent	.05
118	Kevin McReynolds	.05
119	Bret Saberhagen	.05
120	Ryan Thompson	.05
121	Harold Baines	.05
122	Mike Devereaux	.05
123	Jeffrey Hammonds	.05
124	Ben McDonald	.05
125	Mike Mussina	.45
126	Rafael Palmeiro	.45
127	Cal Ripken, Jr.	1.50
128	Lee Smith	.05
129	Brad Ausmus	.05
130	Derek Bell	.05
131	Andy Benes	.05
132	Tony Gwynn	.60
133	Trevor Hoffman	.05
134	Scott Livingstone	.05
135	Phil Plantier	.05
136	Darren Daulton	.05
137	Mariano Duncan	.05
138	Len Dykstra	.05
139	Dave Hollins	.05
140	Pete Incaviglia	.05
141	Danny Jackson	.05
142	John Kruk	.05
143	Kevin Stocker	.05
144	Jay Bell	.05
145	Carlos Garcia	.05
146	Jeff King	.05
147	Al Martin	.05
148	Orlando Merced	.05
149	Don Slaught	.05
150	Andy Van Slyke	.05
151	Kevin Brown	.05
152	Jose Canseco	.40
153	Will Clark	.05
154	Juan Gonzalez	.30
155	David Hulse	.05
156	Dean Palmer	.05
157	Ivan Rodriguez	.45
158	Kenny Rogers	.05
159	Roger Clemens	.65
160	Scott Cooper	.05
161	Andre Dawson	.25
162	Mike Greenwell	.05
163	Otis Nixon	.05
164	Aaron Sele	.05
165	John Valentin	.05
166	Mo Vaughn	.05
167	Bret Boone	.05
168	Barry Larkin	.05
169	Kevin Mitchell	.05
170	Hal Morris	.05
171	Jose Rijo	.05
172	Deion Sanders	.05
173	Reggie Sanders	.05
174	John Smiley	.05
175	Dante Bichette	.05
176	Ellis Burks	.05
177	Andres Galarraga	.05
178	Joe Girardi	.05
179	Charlie Hayes	.05
180	Roberto Mejia	.05
181	Walt Weiss	.05
182	David Cone	.05
183	Gary Gaetti	.05
184	Greg Gagne	.05
185	Felix Jose	.05
186	Wally Joyner	.05
187	Mike Macfarlane	.05
188	Brian McRae	.05
189	Eric Davis	.05
190	Cecil Fielder	.05
191	Travis Fryman	.05
192	Tony Phillips	.05
193	Mickey Tettleton	.05
194	Alan Trammell	.05
195	Lou Whitaker	.05
196	Kent Hrbek	.05
197	Chuck Knoblauch	.05
198	Shane Mack	.05
199	Pat Meares	.05
200	Kirby Puckett	.60
201	Matt Walbeck	.05
202	Dave Winfield	.55
203	Wilson Alvarez	.05
204	Alex Fernandez	.05
205	Julio Franco	.05
206	Ozzie Guillen	.05
207	Jack McDowell	.05
208	Tim Raines	.05
209	Frank Thomas	.55
210	Robin Ventura	.05
211	Jim Abbott	.05
212	Wade Boggs	.60
213	Pat Kelly	.05
214	Jimmy Key	.05
215	Don Mattingly	.65
216	Paul O'Neill	.05
217	Mike Stanley	.05
218	Danny Tartabull	.05
219	Checklist	.05
220	Checklist	.05

Editor's Choice

Printed in similitude to a strip of color slide film, each of the cards in this insert set feature a complete player photo at center, with partial "frames" at top and bottom. Printed on acetate, the back of the card shows a reversed image of the front. Stated odds of finding an Editor's Choice insert card are about one per box of 36 packs.

		NM/M
Complete Set (8):		12.00
Common Player:		.50
1	Barry Bonds	3.00
2	Frank Thomas	1.50
3	Ken Griffey Jr.	2.50
4	Andres Galarraga	.50
5	Juan Gonzalez	.75
6	Tim Salmon	.50
7	Paul O'Neill	.50
8	Mike Piazza	2.50

Heritage

Besides picturing today's players in vintage uniforms, the 1994 Studio Heritage inserts have the player portraits set against sepia-toned photos of

old ballparks. Fronts are enhanced by copper-foil logos and by a round device at upper-left containing the player's name, team and year represented. Backs have a second color player photo and a short write-up about the team represented. Unlike the other cards in the set, the Heritage cards are printed on a porous cardboard stock to enhance the image of antiquity. Stated odds of finding a Heritage Collection insert card are one in nine packs.

	NM/M
Complete Set (8):	9.00
Common Player:	.50
1 Barry Bonds	4.00
2 Frank Thomas	1.50
3 Joe Carter	.50
4 Don Mattingly	3.00
5 Ryne Sandberg	2.00
6 Javier Lopez	.50
7 Gregg Jefferies	.50
8 Mike Mussina	.65

Silver Stars

Each of the 10 players in this insert set was produced in an edition of 10,000 cards. Printed on acetate, fronts feature action photos set against a clear plastic background with a silver-foil seal at bottom. Within the player silhouette on back, a second photo is printed. The back also features a black-and-white version of the seal, including the card's unique serial number. Stated odds of picking a Silver Series Star are one per 60 packs, on average.

	NM/M
Complete Set (10):	35.00
Common Player:	1.50
1 Tony Gwynn	3.50
2 Barry Bonds	7.50
3 Frank Thomas	2.50
4 Ken Griffey Jr.	4.50
5 Joe Carter	1.50
6 Mike Piazza	4.50
7 Cal Ripken, Jr.	7.50
8 Greg Maddux	3.50
9 Juan Gonzalez	2.00
10 Don Mattingly	4.00

Gold Stars

The scarcest of the 1994 Studio chase cards, only 5,000 cards of each of the 10 players were produced. Printed on acetate, fronts feature an action photo set against a clear plastic background. At bottom is a large gold-foil seal. Backs have another player photo, within the silhouette

of the front photo, and a black-and-white version of the seal, including the card's unique serial number. According to the series wrapper, odds of finding a Gold Series Star card are one in 120 packs.

	NM/M
Complete Set (10):	80.00
Common Player:	4.50
1 Tony Gwynn	9.00
2 Barry Bonds	16.00
3 Frank Thomas	7.50
4 Ken Griffey Jr.	12.50
5 Joe Carter	4.50
6 Mike Piazza	12.50
7 Cal Ripken, Jr.	16.00
8 Greg Maddux	9.00
9 Juan Gonzalez	5.00
10 Don Mattingly	10.00

1995 Studio

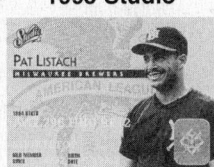

Known since its inception as a brand name for its innovative design, Studio did not disappoint in 1995, unveiling a baseball card with a credit card look. In horizontal format the cards feature embossed stats and data on front, plus a team logo hologram. Backs have a color player photo, facsimile autograph and simulated magnetic data strip to carry through the credit card impression.

	NM/M
Complete Set (200):	25.00
Common Player:	.05
Pack (5):	1.00
Wax Box (36):	20.00
1 Frank Thomas	.75
2 Jeff Bagwell	.75
3 Don Mattingly	1.25
4 Mike Piazza	1.50
5 Ken Griffey Jr.	1.50
6 Greg Maddux	1.00
7 Barry Bonds	2.50
8 Cal Ripken Jr.	2.50
9 Jose Canseco	.40
10 Paul Molitor	.75
11 Kenny Lofton	.05
12 Will Clark	.05
13 Tim Salmon	.05
14 Joe Carter	.05
15 Albert Belle	.05
16 Roger Clemens	1.25
17 Roberto Alomar	.30
18 Alex Rodriguez	2.00
19 Raul Mondesi	.05
20 Deion Sanders	.05
21 Juan Gonzalez	.40
22 Kirby Puckett	1.00
23 Fred McGriff	.05
24 Matt Williams	.05
25 Tony Gwynn	1.00
26 Cliff Floyd	.05
27 Travis Fryman	.05
28 Shawn Green	.30
29 Mike Mussina	.35
30 Bob Hamelin	.05
31 Dave Justice	.05
32 Manny Ramirez	.75
33 David Cone	.05
34 Marquis Grissom	.05
35 Moises Alou	.05
36 Carlos Baerga	.05
37 Barry Larkin	.05
38 Robin Ventura	.05
39 Mo Vaughn	.05
40 Jeffrey Hammonds	.05
41 Ozzie Smith	1.00
42 Andres Galarraga	.05

43 Carlos Delgado	.50
44 Lenny Dykstra	.05
45 Cecil Fielder	.05
46 Wade Boggs	1.00
47 Gregg Jefferies	.05
48 Randy Johnson	.75
49 Rafael Palmeiro	.05
50 Craig Biggio	.05
51 Steve Avery	.05
52 Ricky Bottalico	.05
53 Chris Gomez	.05
54 Carlos Garcia	.05
55 Brian Anderson	.05
56 Wilson Alvarez	.05
57 Roberto Kelly	.05
58 Larry Walker	.05
59 Dean Palmer	.05
60 Rick Aguilera	.05
61 Javy Lopez	.05
62 Shawon Dunston	.05
63 William	.05
Van Landingham	
64 Jeff Kent	.05
65 David McCarty	.05
66 Armando Benitez	.05
67 Brett Butler	.05
68 Bernard Gilkey	.05
69 Joey Hamilton	.05
70 Chad Curtis	.05
71 Dante Bichette	.05
72 Chuck Carr	.05
73 Pedro Martinez	.75
74 Ramon Martinez	.05
75 Rondell White	.05
76 Alex Fernandez	.05
77 Dennis Martinez	.05
78 Sammy Sosa	1.00
79 Bernie Williams	.05
80 Lou Whitaker	.05
81 Kurt Abbott	.05
82 Tino Martinez	.05
83 Willie Greene	.05
84 Garret Anderson	.05
85 Jose Rijo	.05
86 Jeff Montgomery	.05
87 Mark Langston	.05
88 Reggie Sanders	.05
89 Rusty Greer	.05
90 Delino DeShields	.05
91 Jason Bere	.05
92 Lee Smith	.05
93 Devon White	.05
94 John Wetteland	.05
95 Luis Gonzalez	.05
96 Greg Vaughn	.05
97 Lance Johnson	.05
98 Alan Trammell	.05
99 Bret Saberhagen	.05
100 Jack McDowell	.05
101 Trevor Hoffman	.05
102 Dave Nilsson	.05
103 Bryan Harvey	.05
104 Chuck Knoblauch	.05
105 Bobby Bonilla	.05
106 Hal Morris	.05
107 Mark Whiten	.05
108 Phil Plantier	.05
109 Ryan Klesko	.05
110 Greg Gagne	.05
111 Ruben Sierra	.05
112 J.R. Phillips	.05
113 Terry Steinbach	.05
114 Jay Buhner	.05
115 Ken Caminiti	.05
116 Gary DiSarcina	.05
117 Ivan Rodriguez	.65
118 Bip Roberts	.05
119 Jay Bell	.05
120 Ken Hill	.05
121 Mike Greenwell	.05
122 Rick Wilkins	.05
123 Rickey Henderson	.75
124 Dave Hollins	.05
125 Terry Pendleton	.05
126 Rich Becker	.05
127 Billy Ashley	.05
128 Derek Bell	.05
129 Dennis Eckersley	.65
130 Andujar Cedeno	.05
131 John Jaha	.05
132 Chuck Finley	.05
133 Steve Finley	.05
134 Danny Tartabull	.05
135 Jeff Conine	.05
136 Jon Lieber	.05
137 Jim Abbott	.05
138 Steve Traschel	.05
139 Bret Boone	.05
140 Charles Johnson	.05
141 Mark McGwire	2.00
142 Eddie Murray	.75
143 Doug Drabek	.05
144 Steve Cooke	.05
145 Kevin Seitzer	.05
146 Rod Beck	.05
147 Eric Karros	.05
148 Tim Raines	.05
149 Joe Girardi	.05
150 Aaron Sele	.05
151 Robby Thompson	.05
152 Chan Ho Park	.05
153 Ellis Burks	.05
154 Brian McRae	.05
155 Jimmy Key	.05
156 Rico Brogna	.05
157 Ozzie Guillen	.05
158 Chili Davis	.05
159 Darren Daulton	.05

160 Chipper Jones	1.00
161 Walt Weiss	.05
162 Paul O'Neill	.05
163 Al Martin	.05
164 John Valentin	.05
165 Tim Wallach	.05
166 Scott Erickson	.05
167 Ryan Thompson	.05
168 Todd Zeile	.05
169 Scott Cooper	.05
170 Matt Mieske	.05
171 Allen Watson	.05
172 Brian Hunter	.05
173 Kevin Stocker	.05
174 Cal Eldred	.05
175 Tony Phillips	.05
176 Ben McDonald	.05
177 Mark Grace	.05
178 Midre Cummings	.05
179 Orlando Merced	.05
180 Jeff King	.05
181 Gary Sheffield	.40
182 Tom Glavine	.35
183 Edgar Martinez	.05
184 Terry Karsay	.05
185 Pat Listach	.05
186 Wil Cordero	.05
187 Brady Anderson	.05
188 Bobby Jones	.05
189 Andy Benes	.05
190 Ray Lankford	.05
191 John Doherty	.05
192 Wally Joyner	.05
193 Jim Thome	.65
194 Royce Clayton	.05
195 John Olerud	.05
196 Steve Buechele	.05
197 Harold Baines	.05
198 Geronimo Berroa	.05
199 Checklist	.05
200 Checklist	.05

Gold

The chase cards in 1995 Studio are plastic versions of some of the regular cards. The round-cornered plastic format of the inserts gives them an even greater similitude to credit cards. The first 50 numbers in the regular set are reproduced in a parallel Studio Gold plastic version, found one per pack, except for those packs which have a platinum card.

	NM/M
Complete Set (50):	25.00
Common Player:	.15
1 Frank Thomas	1.00
2 Jeff Bagwell	1.00
3 Don Mattingly	1.75
4 Mike Piazza	2.00
5 Ken Griffey Jr.	2.00
6 Greg Maddux	1.50
7 Barry Bonds	3.00
8 Cal Ripken Jr.	3.00
9 Jose Canseco	.50
10 Paul Molitor	1.00
11 Kenny Lofton	.15
12 Will Clark	.15
13 Tim Salmon	.15
14 Joe Carter	.15
15 Albert Belle	.15
16 Roger Clemens	1.75
17 Roberto Alomar	.35
18 Alex Rodriguez	2.50
19 Raul Mondesi	.15
20 Deion Sanders	.15
21 Juan Gonzalez	.50
22 Kirby Puckett	1.50
23 Fred McGriff	.15
24 Matt Williams	.15
25 Tony Gwynn	1.50
26 Cliff Floyd	.15
27 Travis Fryman	.15
28 Shawn Green	.40
29 Mike Mussina	.35
30 Bob Hamelin	.15
31 Dave Justice	.15
32 Manny Ramirez	1.00
33 David Cone	.15
34 Marquis Grissom	.15
35 Moises Alou	.15
36 Carlos Baerga	.15
37 Barry Larkin	.15
38 Robin Ventura	.15
39 Mo Vaughn	.15
40 Jeffrey Hammonds	.15
41 Ozzie Smith	1.50
42 Andres Galarraga	.15
43 Carlos Delgado	.50
44 Lenny Dykstra	.15
45 Cecil Fielder	.15
46 Wade Boggs	1.50

47 Gregg Jefferies	.15
48 Randy Johnson	1.00
49 Rafael Palmeiro	.75
50 Craig Biggio	.15

Platinum

Found at the rate of one per 10 packs, Studio Platinum cards are silver-toned plastic versions of the first 25 cards from the regular set.

	NM/M
Complete Set (25):	25.00
Common Player:	.50
1 Frank Thomas	2.00
2 Jeff Bagwell	2.00
3 Don Mattingly	3.25
4 Mike Piazza	3.50
5 Ken Griffey Jr.	3.50
6 Greg Maddux	3.00
7 Barry Bonds	5.00
8 Cal Ripken Jr.	5.00
9 Jose Canseco	1.00
10 Paul Molitor	2.00
11 Kenny Lofton	.50
12 Will Clark	.50
13 Tim Salmon	.50
14 Joe Carter	.50
15 Albert Belle	.50
16 Roger Clemens	3.25
17 Roberto Alomar	.75
18 Alex Rodriguez	4.00
19 Raul Mondesi	.50
20 Deion Sanders	.50
21 Juan Gonzalez	1.00
22 Kirby Puckett	3.00
23 Fred McGriff	.50
24 Matt Williams	.50
25 Tony Gwynn	3.00

1996 Studio

The 1996 Studio set is the first Donruss product to be released under the Pinnacle Brands flagship. The 150-card set has three parallel sets - Bronze Press Proofs (2,000 sets), Silver Press Proofs (found only in magazine packs, 100 sets), and Gold Press Proofs (500 sets). Three insert sets were also made - Hit Parade, Masterstrokes and Stained Glass Stars.

	NM/M
Complete Set (150):	9.00
Common Player:	.05
Bronze Press Proofs:	3X
Gold Press Proofs:	7X
Silver Press Proofs:	25X
Pack (7):	1.25
Wax Box (24):	20.00
1 Cal Ripken Jr.	1.50
2 Alex Gonzalez	.05
3 Roger Cedeno	.05
4 Todd Hollandsworth	.05
5 Gregg Jefferies	.05
6 Ryne Sandberg	.65
7 Eric Karros	.05
8 Jeff Conine	.05
9 Rafael Palmeiro	.45
10 Bip Roberts	.05
11 Roger Clemens	.70
12 Tom Glavine	.30
13 Jason Giambi	.40
14 Rey Ordonez	.25
15 Chan Ho Park	.15
16 Vinny Castilla	.05
17 Butch Huskey	.05
18 Greg Maddux	.65
19 Bernard Gilkey	.05
20 Marquis Grissom	.05
21 Chuck Knoblauch	.05

22 Ozzie Smith	.65
23 Garret Anderson	.05
24 J.T. Snow	.05
25 John Valentin	.05
26 Barry Larkin	.05
27 Bobby Bonilla	.05
28 Todd Zeile	.05
29 Roberto Alomar	.20
30 Ramon Martinez	.05
31 Jeff King	.05
32 Dennis Eckersley	.45
33 Derek Jeter	1.50
34 Edgar Martinez	.05
35 Geronimo Berroa	.05
36 Hal Morris	.05
37 Troy Percival	.05
38 Jason Isringhausen	.05
39 Greg Vaughn	.05
40 Robin Ventura	.05
41 Craig Biggio	.05
42 Will Clark	.05
43 Sammy Sosa	.65
44 Bernie Williams	.05
45 Kenny Lofton	.05
46 Wade Boggs	.65
47 Javy Lopez	.05
48 Reggie Sanders	.05
49 Jeff Bagwell	.55
50 Fred McGriff	.05
51 Charles Johnson	.05
52 Darren Daulton	.05
53 Jose Canseco	.40
54 Cecil Fielder	.05
55 Hideo Nomo	.30
56 Tim Salmon	.05
57 Carlos Delgado	.40
58 David Cone	.05
59 Tim Raines	.05
60 Lyle Mouton	.05
61 Wally Joyner	.05
62 Bret Boone	.05
63 Raul Mondesi	.05
64 Gary Sheffield	.05
65 Alex Rodriguez	1.00
66 Russ Davis	.05
67 Checklist	.05
68 Marty Cordova	.05
69 Ruben Sierra	.05
70 Jose Mesa	.05
71 Matt Williams	.05
72 Chipper Jones	.65
73 Randy Johnson	.55
74 Kirby Puckett	.65
75 Jim Edmonds	.05
76 Barry Bonds	1.50
77 David Segui	.05
78 Larry Walker	.05
79 Jason Kendall	.05
80 Mike Piazza	.75
81 Brian Hunter	.05
82 Julio Franco	.05
83 Jay Bell	.05
84 Kevin Seitzer	.05
85 John Smoltz	.05
86 Joe Carter	.05
87 Ray Durham	.05
88 Carlos Baerga	.05
89 Ron Gant	.05
90 Orlando Merced	.05
91 Lee Smith	.05
92 Pedro Martinez	.55
93 Frank Thomas	.55
94 Al Martin	.05
95 Chad Curtis	.05
96 Eddie Murray	.55
97 Rusty Greer	.05
98 Jay Buhner	.05
99 Rico Brogna	.05
100 Todd Hundley	.05
101 Moises Alou	.05
102 Chili Davis	.05
103 Ismael Valdes	.05
104 Mo Vaughn	.55
105 Juan Gonzalez	.30
106 Mark Grudzielanek	.05
107 Derek Bell	.05
108 Shawn Green	.30
109 David Justice	.05
110 Paul O'Neill	.05
111 Kevin Appier	.05
112 Ray Lankford	.05
113 Travis Fryman	.05
114 Manny Ramirez	.55
115 Brooks Kieschnick	.05
116 Ken Griffey Jr.	.75
117 Jeffrey Hammonds	.05
118 Mark McGwire	1.00
119 Denny Neagle	.05
120 Quivilo Veras	.05
121 Alan Benes	.05
122 Rondell White	.05
123 Osvaldo Fernandez RC	.20
124 Andres Galarraga	.05
125 Johnny Damon	.35
126 Lenny Dykstra	.05
127 Jason Schmidt	.05
128 Mike Mussina	.30
129 Ken Caminiti	.05
130 Michael Tucker	.05
131 LaTroy Hawkins	.05
132 Checklist	.05
133 Delino DeShields	.05
134 Dave Nilsson	.05
135 Jack McDowell	.05
136 Joey Hamilton	.05
137 Dante Bichette	.05
138 Paul Molitor	.55
139 Ivan Rodriguez	.45

140	Mark Grace	.05
141	Paul Wilson	.05
142	Orel Hershiser	.05
143	Albert Belle	.05
144	Tino Martinez	.05
145	Tony Gwynn	.65
146	George Arias	.05
147	Brian Jordan	.05
148	Brian McRae	.05
149	Rickey Henderson	.55
150	Ryan Klesko	.05

Press Proofs

The basic 150-card 1996 Studio set was also produced in three parallel press proof versions. Each is basically identical to the regular-issue cards except for appropriately colored foil highlights on front and a notation of edition size in the circle around the portrait photo on back. Bronze press proofs were issued in an edition of 2,000 each and were inserted at an average rate of one per six packs. Gold press proofs were an edition of 500 with an average insertion rate of one per 24 packs. The silver press proofs were inserted only into magazine packs and limited to just 100 cards of each.

	NM/M
Common Player, Bronze:	.50
Bronze Stars:	3X
Common Player, Gold:	1.00
Gold Stars:	7X
Common Player, Silver:	4.00
Silver Stars:	25X

Hit Parade

These die-cut inserts resemble an album with half of the record pulled out of the sleeve. Hit Parade cards, which feature top long ball hitters, were seeded one per every 36 packs. The cards were individually numbered up to 7,500. Each card can also be found in a sample version which has a "XXXX/5000" serial number on back.

		NM/M
		10.00
Complete Set (10):		10.00
Common Player:		.75
1	Tony Gwynn	1.50
2	Ken Griffey Jr.	2.00
3	Frank Thomas	1.00
4	Jeff Bagwell	1.00
5	Kirby Puckett	1.50
6	Mike Piazza	2.00
7	Barry Bonds	2.50
8	Albert Belle	.75
9	Tim Salmon	.75
10	Mo Vaughn	.75

Masterstrokes

Only 5,000 each of these 1996 Studio insert cards were made. The cards simulate oil painting detail on an embossed canvas-feel front. Backs are glossy and individually serial numbered. They are found on average of once per 70 packs. Sample versions of each card

---

tion shot, along with a short career summary. The "pack" for '97 Studio is something totally new to the hobby. An 8-1/2" x 12" cardboard envelope, complete with a zip strip opener in the style of an express-mail envelope, contains a cello pack of five standard-size cards plus either an 8" x 10" Studio Portrait card or an 8" x 10" version of the Master Strokes insert. Suggested retail price at issue was $2.49 per pack. Regular-size Master Strokes cards are one of several insert series which includes silver and gold press proofs and die-cut plastic Hard Hats.

	NM/M
Complete Set (165):	17.50
Common Player:	.05
Silver Press Proofs:	4X
Gold Press Proofs:	8X
Pack (5):	3.00
Wax Box (18):	40.00

1	Frank Thomas	.65
2	Gary Sheffield	.45
3	Jason Isringhausen	.05
4	Ron Gant	.05
5	Andy Pettitte	.25
6	Todd Hollandsworth	.05
7	Troy Percival	.05
8	Mark McGwire	1.50
9	Barry Larkin	.05
10	Ken Caminiti	.05
11	Paul Molitor	.65
12	Travis Fryman	.05
13	Kevin Brown	.05
14	Robin Ventura	.05
15	Andres Galarraga	.05
16	Ken Griffey Jr.	1.00
17	Roger Clemens	.85
18	Alan Benes	.05
19	David Justice	.05
20	Damon Buford	.05
21	Mike Piazza	1.00
22	Ray Durham	.05
23	Billy Wagner	.05
24	Dean Palmer	.05
25	David Cone	.05
26	Ruben Sierra	.05
27	Henry Rodriguez	.05
28	Ray Lankford	.05
29	Jamey Wright	.05
30	Brady Anderson	.05
31	Tino Martinez	.05
32	Manny Ramirez	.65
33	Jeff Conine	.05
34	Dante Bichette	.05
35	Jose Canseco	.50
36	Mo Vaughn	.05
37	Sammy Sosa	.75
38	Mark Grudzielanek	.05
39	Mike Mussina	.35
40	Bill Pulsipher	.05
41	Ryne Sandberg	.75
42	Rickey Henderson	.65
43	Alex Rodriguez	1.50
44	Eddie Murray	.65
45	Ernie Young	.05
46	Joey Hamilton	.05
47	Wade Boggs	.75
48	Rusty Greer	.05
49	Carlos Delgado	.50
50	Ellis Burks	.05
51	Cal Ripken Jr.	2.00
52	Alex Fernandez	.05
53	Wally Joyner	.05
54	James Baldwin	.05
55	Juan Gonzalez	.35
56	John Smoltz	.05
57	Omar Vizquel	.05
58	Shane Reynolds	.05
59	Barry Bonds	2.00
60	Jason Kendall	.05
61	Marty Cordova	.05
62	Charles Johnson	.05
63	John Jaha	.05
64	Chan Ho Park	.05
65	Jermaine Allensworth	.05
66	Mark Grace	.05
67	Tim Salmon	.05
68	Edgar Martinez	.05
69	Marquis Grissom	.05
70	Craig Biggio	.05
71	Bobby Higginson	.05
72	Kevin Seitzer	.05
73	Hideo Nomo	.35
74	Dennis Eckersley	.60
75	Bobby Bonilla	.05
76	Dwight Gooden	.05
77	Jeff Cirillo	.05
78	Brian McRae	.05
79	Chipper Jones	.75
80	Jeff Fassero	.05
81	Fred McGriff	.05
82	Garret Anderson	.05
83	Eric Karros	.05
84	Derek Bell	.05
85	Kenny Lofton	.05
86	John Mabry	.05
87	Pat Hentgen	.05
88	Greg Maddux	.75
89	Jason Giambi	.45

---

overprinted as such on the back and numbered "PROMO/5000" were also issued.

		NM/M
Complete Set (8):		30.00
Common Player:		4.00
Samples: 75%		
1	Tony Gwynn	6.00
2	Mike Piazza	8.00
3	Jeff Bagwell	4.00
4	Manny Ramirez	4.00
5	Cal Ripken Jr.	12.00
6	Frank Thomas	4.00
7	Ken Griffey Jr.	8.00
8	Greg Maddux	6.00

Stained Glass Stars

Twelve superstars are featured on these clear, die-cut plastic cards which resemble stained glass windows. These 1996 Studio inserts were seeded one per every 30 packs.

		NM/M
Complete Set (12):		24.00
Common Player:		1.00
1	Cal Ripken Jr.	5.00
2	Ken Griffey Jr.	3.50
3	Frank Thomas	2.00
4	Greg Maddux	2.50
5	Chipper Jones	2.50
6	Mike Piazza	3.50
7	Albert Belle	1.00
8	Jeff Bagwell	2.00
9	Hideo Nomo	1.00
10	Barry Bonds	5.00
11	Manny Ramirez	1.00
12	Kenny Lofton	1.00

1997 Studio

Innovations in both product and packaging marked the seventh annual issue of Donruss' Studio brand. As in the past, the 165 cards in the base set rely on high-quality front photos to bring out the players' personalities. For '97, the photos are set against a background of variously shaded gray horizontal stripes. Backs have a second player photo, often an ac-

---

90	Al Martin	.05
91	Derek Jeter	2.00
92	Rey Ordonez	.05
93	Will Clark	.05
94	Kevin Appier	.05
95	Roberto Alomar	.30
96	Joe Carter	.05
97	Bernie Williams	.05
98	Albert Belle	.05
99	Greg Vaughn	.05
100	Tony Clark	.05
101	Matt Williams	.05
102	Jeff Bagwell	.65
103	Reggie Sanders	.05
104	Mariano Rivera	.15
105	Larry Walker	.05
106	Shawn Green	.30
107	Alex Ochoa	.05
108	Ivan Rodriguez	.60
109	Eric Young	.05
110	Javier Lopez	.05
111	Brian Hunter	.05
112	Raul Mondesi	.05
113	Randy Johnson	.65
114	Tony Phillips	.05
115	Carlos Garcia	.05
116	Moises Alou	.05
117	Paul O'Neill	.05
118	Jim Thome	.60
119	Jermaine Dye	.05
120	Wilson Alvarez	.05
121	Rondell White	.05
122	Michael Tucker	.05
123	Mike Lansing	.05
124	Tony Gwynn	.75
125	Ryan Klesko	.05
126	Jim Edmonds	.05
127	Chuck Knoblauch	.05
128	Rafael Palmeiro	.60
129	Jay Buhner	.05
130	Tom Glavine	.35
131	Julio Franco	.05
132	Cecil Fielder	.05
133	Paul Wilson	.05
134	Deion Sanders	.05
135	Alex Gonzalez	.05
136	Charles Nagy	.05
137	Andy Ashby	.05
138	Edgar Renteria	.05
139	Pedro Martinez	.65
140	Brian Jordan	.05
141	Todd Hundley	.05
142	Marc Newfield	.05
143	Darryl Strawberry	.05
144	Dan Wilson	.05
145	Brian Giles **RC**	.50
146	Bartolo Colon	.05
147	Shannon Stewart	.05
148	Scott Spiezio	.05
149	Andruw Jones	.65
150	Karim Garcia	.05
151	Vladimir Guerrero	.65
152	George Arias	.05
153	Brooks Kieschnick	.05
154	Todd Walker	.05
155	Scott Rolen	.60
156	Todd Greene	.05
157	Dmitri Young	.05
158	Ruben Rivera	.05
159	Trey Beamon	.05
160	Nomar Garciaparra	.75
161	Bob Abreu	.05
162	Darin Erstad	.15
163	Ken Griffey Jr. (checklist)	.50
164	Frank Thomas (Checklist)	.35
165	Alex Rodriguez (Checklist)	.75

Press Proofs

Each of the 165 cards in the base set of '97 Studio was also produced in a pair of Press Proof versions as random pack inserts. Fronts of the Press Proofs have either silver or gold holographic foil replacing the silver foil graphics found on regular cards, as well as foil strips down each side. Backs are identical to the regular issue. The silver Press Proofs were is-

---

sued in an edition of 1,500 of each player; the golds are limited to 500 of each.

	NM/M
Common Player, Silver:	.50
Silver Stars:	4X
Common Player, Gold:	1.00
Gold Stars:	8X

Hard Hats

Die-cut plastic is used to represent a player's batting helmet in this set of '97 Studio inserts. A player action photo appears in the foreground with his name and other graphic elements in silver foil. Backs feature a small portrait photo, short career summary and a serial number from within the edition of 5,000 of each card.

		NM/M
Complete Set (24):		50.00
Common Player:		1.50
1	Ivan Rodriguez	3.00
2	Albert Belle	1.50
3	Ken Griffey Jr.	6.00
4	Chuck Knoblauch	1.50
5	Frank Thomas	4.00
6	Cal Ripken Jr.	8.00
7	Todd Walker	1.50
8	Alex Rodriguez	7.00
9	Jim Thome	3.00
10	Mike Piazza	6.00
11	Barry Larkin	1.50
12	Chipper Jones	5.00
13	Derek Jeter	8.00
14	Jermaine Dye	1.50
15	Jason Giambi	2.00
16	Tim Salmon	1.50
17	Brady Anderson	1.50
18	Rondell White	1.50
19	Bernie Williams	1.50
20	Juan Gonzalez	2.00
21	Karim Garcia	1.50
22	Scott Rolen	3.00
23	Darin Erstad	2.00
24	Brian Jordan	1.50

Master Strokes

The look and feel of a painting on canvas is the effect presented by '97 Studio's Master Strokes inserts. Card fronts feature unique player action art and are highlighted by gold-foil graphics. Each card has a facsimile autograph on front. UV-coated backs are team-color coordinated and have a few sentences about the player. Gold-foil serial numbering identifies the card from an edition of 2,000 of each player.

		NM/M
Complete Set (24):		120.00
Common Player:		2.00
1	Derek Jeter	12.00
2	Jeff Bagwell	4.50
3	Ken Griffey Jr.	8.00
4	Barry Bonds	12.00
5	Frank Thomas	4.50
6	Andy Pettitte	2.25
7	Mo Vaughn	2.00
8	Alex Rodriguez	10.00
9	Andruw Jones	4.50
10	Kenny Lofton	2.00
11	Cal Ripken Jr.	12.00
12	Greg Maddux	6.00
13	Manny Ramirez	4.50

14	Mike Piazza	8.00
14p	Mike Piazza (Promo)	3.50
15	Vladimir Guerrero	4.50
16	Albert Belle	2.00
17	Chipper Jones	6.00
18	Hideo Nomo	2.50
19	Sammy Sosa	6.00
20	Tony Gwynn	6.00
21	Gary Sheffield	2.50
22	Mark McGwire	10.00
23	Juan Gonzalez	2.50
24	Paul Molitor	4.50

Master Strokes 8x10

The look and feel of a painting on canvas is the effect presented by the 8" x 10" version of '97 Studio's Master Strokes inserts. Card fronts feature unique player action art and are highlighted by gold-foil graphics. Each card has a facsimile autograph on front. UV-coated backs are team-color coordinated and have a few sentences about the player. Gold-foil serial numbering identifies the card from an edition of 5,000 of each player — making the super-size version more than twice as common as the 2-1/2" x 3-1/2" version.

		NM/M
Complete Set (24):		45.00
Common Player:		.75
1	Derek Jeter	5.00
2	Jeff Bagwell	2.00
3	Ken Griffey Jr.	3.00
4	Barry Bonds	5.00
5	Frank Thomas	2.00
6	Andy Pettitte	1.00
7	Mo Vaughn	.75
8	Alex Rodriguez	4.00
9	Andruw Jones	2.00
10	Kenny Lofton	.75
11	Cal Ripken Jr.	5.00
12	Greg Maddux	2.50
13	Manny Ramirez	2.50
14	Mike Piazza	3.00
15	Vladimir Guerrero	2.00
16	Albert Belle	.75
17	Chipper Jones	2.50
18	Hideo Nomo	1.50
19	Sammy Sosa	2.50
20	Tony Gwynn	2.50
21	Gary Sheffield	1.50
22	Mark McGwire	4.00
23	Juan Gonzalez	1.50
24	Paul Molitor	2.00

Portraits

Perhaps the most innovative feature of '97 Studio is the 8" x 10" Portrait cards which come one per pack (except when a pack contains a Master Strokes 8x10). Virtually identical to the player's regular-size Studio card, the jumbo version has the word "PORTRAIT" in black beneath the team name on front. Backs have different card numbers than the same player's card in the regular set. The Portrait cards are produced with a special UV coating on front to facilitate autographing. Pre-autographed cards of three youngsters in the series were included as random pack inserts.

		NM/M
Complete Set (24):		10.00
Common Player:		.25
1	Ken Griffey Jr.	1.00
1s	Frank Thomas/OPS	.75
2	Frank Thomas	.65
3	Alex Rodriguez	1.50
4	Andruw Jones	.65
5	Cal Ripken Jr.	2.00
6	Greg Maddux	.75
7	Mike Piazza	1.00
8	Chipper Jones	.75
9	Albert Belle	.25
10	Derek Jeter	2.00
11	Juan Gonzalez	.45
12	Todd Walker	.25
12a	Todd Walker (Autographed edition of 1,250.)	10.00
13	Mark McGwire	1.50
14	Barry Bonds	2.00
15	Jeff Bagwell	.65
16	Manny Ramirez	.65
17	Kenny Lofton	.25
18	Mo Vaughn	.25
19	Hideo Nomo	.45
20	Tony Gwynn	.75
21	Vladimir Guerrero	.65
21a	Vladimir Guerrero (Autographed edition of 500.)	30.00
22	Gary Sheffield	.45
23	Ryne Sandberg	.75
24	Scott Rolen	.50
24a	Scott Rolen (Autographed edition of 1,000.)	12.00

Portrait Collection

In a departure from traditional sportscard marketing, the 1997 Studio program offered a pair of specially framed editions directly to consumers. The offer was made in a color brochure found in about half the packs advertising the "Portrait Collection." The offer includes one standard-size card and an 8" x 10" Portrait or Master card similar to those in the regular issue. These cards differ from the regular issue in that they are trimmed in platinum holographic foil, individually handnumbered and signed by the photographer. The cards were sold framed with a metal plaque, also numbered, attesting to the limited-edition status. The framed Studio Portrait piece was produced in an edition of 500 of each player; the Master Strokes piece was limited to 100 for each player on the checklist. The former was issued at $159; the latter at $299.

		NM/M
Complete Set, Studio Portrait (24):		2,850
Complete Set, Master Strokes (24):		5,250
Common Plaque, Studio Portrait:		125.00
Common Plaque, Master Strokes:		225.00
P1	Ken Griffey Jr.	125.00
P2	Frank Thomas	125.00
P3	Alex Rodriguez	125.00
P4	Andruw Jones	125.00
P5	Cal Ripken Jr.	125.00
P6	Greg Maddux	125.00
P7	Mike Piazza	125.00
P8	Chipper Jones	125.00
P9	Albert Belle	125.00
P10	Derek Jeter	125.00
P11	Juan Gonzalez	125.00
P12	Todd Walker	125.00
P13	Mark McGwire	125.00
P14	Barry Bonds	125.00
P15	Jeff Bagwell	125.00
P16	Manny	125.00
P17	Kenny Lofton	125.00
P18	Mo Vaughn	125.00
P19	Hideo Nomo	125.00
P20	Tony Gwynn	125.00
P21	Vladimir Guerrero	125.00
P22	Gary Sheffield	125.00
P23	Ryne Sandberg	125.00

ABBREVIATIONS

OPS - Overprinted "Promotional Sample"

P24	Scott Rolen	125.00
M1	Derek Jeter	225.00
M2	Jeff Bagwell	225.00
M3	Ken Griffey Jr.	225.00
M4	Barry Bonds	225.00
M5	Frank Thomas	225.00
M6	Andy Pettitte	225.00
M7	Mo Vaughn	225.00
M8	Alex Rodriguez	225.00
M9	Andruw Jones	225.00
M10	Kenny Lofton	225.00
M11	Cal Ripken Jr.	225.00
M12	Greg Maddux	225.00
M13	Manny Ramirez	225.00
M14	Mike Piazza	225.00
M15	Vladimir Guerrero	225.00
M16	Albert Belle	225.00
M17	Chipper Jones	225.00
M18	Hideo Nomo	225.00
M19	Sammy Sosa	225.00
M20	Tony Gwynn	225.00
M21	Gary Sheffield	225.00
M22	Mark McGwire	225.00
M23	Juan Gonzalez	225.00
M24	Paul Molitor	225.00

1998 Studio

The Donruss Studio base set consists of 220 regular-sized cards and 36 8-x-10 portraits. The base cards feature a posed photo with an action shot in the background, surrounded by a white border. Silver Studio Proofs (numbered to 1,000) and Gold Studio Proofs (300) parallel the regular-size base set. Inserts included Freeze Frame, Hit Parade and Masterstrokes.

		NM/M
Complete Set (220):		25.00
Common Player:		.05
Silver Proofs:		3X
Gold Proofs:		6X
Pack (7 Cards+8x10):		2.00
Wax Box (18):		20.00
1	Tony Clark	.05
2	Jose Cruz Jr.	.05
3	Ivan Rodriguez	.65
4	Mo Vaughn	.05
5	Kenny Lofton	.05
6	Will Clark	.05
7	Barry Larkin	.05
8	Jay Bell	.05
9	Kevin Young	.05
10	Francisco Cordova	.05
11	Justin Thompson	.05
12	Paul Molitor	.75
13	Jeff Bagwell	.05
14	Jose Canseco	.45
15	Scott Rolen	.65
16	Wilton Guerrero	.05
17	Shannon Stewart	.05
18	Hideki Irabu	.05
19	Michael Tucker	.05
20	Joe Carter	.05
21	Gabe Alvarez	.05
22	Ricky Ledee	.05
23	Karim Garcia	.05
24	Eli Marrero	.05
25	Scott Elarton	.05
26	Mario Valdez	.05
27	Ben Grieve	.05
28	Paul Konerko	.15
29	Esteban Yan RC	.05
30	Esteban Loaiza	.05
31	Delino DeShields	.05
32	Bernie Williams	.05
33	Joe Randa	.05
34	Randy Johnson	.75
35	Brett Tomko	.05
36	Todd Erdos RC	.05
37	Bobby Higginson	.05
38	Jason Kendall	.05
39	Ray Lankford	.05
40	Mark Grace	.05
41	Andy Pettitte	.25
42	Alex Rodriguez	2.00
43	Hideo Nomo	.45
44	Sammy Sosa	1.00
45	J.T. Snow	.05
46	Jason Varitek	.05
47	Vinny Castilla	.05
48	Neifi Perez	.05

49	Todd Walker	.05
50	Mike Cameron	.05
51	Jeffrey Hammonds	.05
52	Deivi Cruz	.05
53	Brian Hunter	.05
54	Al Martin	.05
55	Ron Coomer	.05
56	Chan Ho Park	.05
57	Pedro Martinez	.75
58	Darin Erstad	.15
59	Albert Belle	.05
60	Nomar Garciaparra	1.00
61	Tony Gwynn	1.00
62	Mike Piazza	1.50
63	Todd Helin	.65
64	David Ortiz	.45
65	Todd Dunwoody	.05
66	Orlando Cabrera	.05
67	Ken Cloude	.05
68	Andy Benes	.05
69	Mariano Rivera	.15
70	Cecil Fielder	.05
71	Brian Jordan	.05
72	Darryl Kile	.05
73	Reggie Jefferson	.05
74	Shawn Estes	.05
75	Bobby Bonilla	.05
76	Denny Neagle	.05
77	Robin Ventura	.05
78	Omar Vizquel	.05
79	Craig Biggio	.05
80	Moises Alou	.05
81	Garret Anderson	.05
82	Eric Karros	.05
83	Dante Bichette	.05
84	Charles Johnson	.05
85	Rusty Greer	.05
86	Travis Fryman	.05
87	Fernando Tatis	.05
88	Wilson Alvarez	.05
89	Carl Pavano	.05
90	Brian Rose	.05
91	Geoff Jenkins	.05
92	Magglio Ordonez RC	1.50
93	David Segui	.05
94	David Cone	.05
95	John Smoltz	.05
96	Jim Thome	.65
97	Gary Sheffield	.45
98	Barry Bonds	2.50
99	Andres Galarraga	.05
100	Brad Fullmer	.05
101	Bobby Estalella	.05
102	Enrique Wilson	.05
103	Frank Catalanotto RC	.25
104	Mike Lowell RC	1.00
105	Kevin Orie	.05
106	Matt Morris	.05
107	Pokey Reese	.05
108	Shawn Green	.35
109	Tony Womack	.05
110	Ken Caminiti	.20
111	Roberto Alomar	.20
112	Ken Griffey Jr.	1.50
113	Cal Ripken Jr.	2.50
114	Lou Collier	.05
115	Larry Walker	.05
116	Fred McGriff	.05
117	Jim Edmonds	.05
118	Edgar Martinez	.05
119	Matt Williams	.05
120	Ismael Valdes	.05
121	Bartolo Colon	.05
122	Jeff Cirillo	.05
123	Steve Woodard RC	.25
124	Kevin Millwood RC	1.00
125	Derrick Gibson	.05
126	Jacob Cruz	.05
127	Russell Branyan	.05
128	Sean Casey	.15
129	Derrek Lee	.50
130	Paul O'Neill	.05
131	Brad Radke	.05
132	Kevin Appier	.05
133	John Olerud	.05
134	Alan Benes	.05
135	Todd Greene	.05
136	Carlos Mendoza RC	.05
137	Wade Boggs	1.00
138	Jose Guillen	.05
139	Tino Martinez	.05
140	Aaron Boone	.05
141	Abraham Nunez	.05
142	Preston Wilson	.05
143	Randall Simon	.05
144	Dennis Reyes	.05
145	Mark Kotsay	.05
146	Richard Hidalgo	.05
147	Travis Lee	.05
148	Hanley Frias RC	.05
149	Ruben Rivera	.05
150	Rafael Medina	.05
151	Dave Nilsson	.05
152	Curt Schilling	.35
153	Brady Anderson	.05
154	Carlos Delgado	.50
155	Jason Giambi	.45
156	Pat Hentgen	.05
157	Tom Glavine	.35
158	Ryan Klesko	.05
159	Chipper Jones	1.00
160	Juan Gonzalez	.45
161	Mark McGwire	2.00
162	Vladimir Guerrero	.75
163	Derek Jeter	2.50
164	Manny Ramirez	.75
165	Mike Mussina	.30
166	Rafael Palmeiro	.65

167	Henry Rodriguez	.05
168	Jeff Suppan	.05
169	Eric Milton	.05
170	Scott Spiezio	.05
171	Wilson Delgado	.05
172	Bubba Trammell	.05
173	Ellis Burks	.05
174	Jason Dickson	.05
175	Butch Huskey	.05
176	Edgardo Alfonzo	.05
177	Eric Young	.05
178	Marquis Grissom	.05
179	Lance Johnson	.05
180	Kevin Brown	.05
181	Sandy Alomar Jr.	.05
182	Todd Hundley	.05
183	Rondell White	.05
184	Javier Lopez	.05
185	Damian Jackson	.05
186	Raul Mondesi	.05
187	Rickey Henderson	.75
188	David Justice	.05
189	Jay Buhner	.05
190	Jaret Wright	.05
191	Miguel Tejada	.25
192	Ron Wright	.05
193	Livan Hernandez	.05
194	A.J. Hinch	.05
195	Richie Sexson	.05
196	Bob Abreu	.05
197	Luis Castillo	.05
198	Michael Coleman	.05
199	Greg Maddux	1.00
200	Frank Thomas	.75
201	Andruw Jones	.75
202	Roger Clemens	1.25
203	Tim Salmon	.05
204	Chuck Knoblauch	.05
205	Wes Helms	.05
206	Juan Encarnacion	.05
207	Russ Davis	.05
208	John Valentin	.05
209	Tony Saunders	.05
210	Mike Sweeney	.05
211	Steve Finley	.05
212	David Dellucci RC	.25
213	Edgar Renteria	.05
214	Jeremi Gonzalez	.05
215	Checklist (Jeff Bagwell)	.40
216	Checklist (Mike Piazza)	1.00
217	Checklist (Greg Maddux)	.50
218	Checklist (Cal Ripken Jr.)	1.25
219	Checklist (Frank Thomas)	.45
220	Checklist (Ken Griffey Jr.)	.75

Silver Proofs

This parallel set includes all 220 cards in Studio baseball. Cards are identified by a silver holographic strip around the borders. Silver versions are limited to 1,000 sets.

	NM/M
Common Player:	1.00
Silver Stars:	3X

Gold Proofs

Gold proofs is a parallel of the 220-card base set. Card fronts feature gold holo-foil

---

highlights. Backs are sequentially numbered to 300 each.

	NM/M
Common Player:	3.00
Stars:	6X

Autographs

Three top rookies signed a number of 8x10s for this product. Cards have a Donruss "Authentic Signature" stamp on front.

		NM/M
1	Travis Lee/500	20.00
2	Todd Helton/1000	20.00
3	Ben Grieve/1000	10.00

Freeze Frame

Freeze Frame is a 30-card insert sequentially numbered to 5,000. The cards are designed to look like a piece of film with a color action photo. The first 500 of each card are die-cut.

		NM/M
Complete Set (30):		75.00
Common Player:		1.25
Production 4,500 Sets		
Die-Cuts:		1.5X
Production 500 Sets		
1	Ken Griffey Jr.	5.00
2	Derek Jeter	7.50
3	Ben Grieve	1.25
4	Cal Ripken Jr.	7.50
5	Alex Rodriguez	6.00
6	Greg Maddux	4.00
7	David Justice	1.25
8	Mike Piazza	5.00
9	Chipper Jones	4.00
10	Randy Johnson	3.00
11	Jeff Bagwell	3.00
12	Nomar Garciaparra	3.00
13	Andruw Jones	3.00
14	Frank Thomas	3.00
15	Scott Rolen	2.50
16	Barry Bonds	7.50
17	Kenny Lofton	1.25
18	Ivan Rodriguez	2.50
19	Chuck Knoblauch	1.25
20	Jose Cruz Jr.	1.25
21	Bernie Williams	1.25
22	Tony Gwynn	4.00
23	Juan Gonzalez	2.00
24	Gary Sheffield	2.25
25	Roger Clemens	4.50
26	Travis Lee	1.25
27	Brad Fullmer	1.25
28	Tim Salmon	1.25
29	Raul Mondesi	1.25
30	Roberto Alomar	1.25

Hit Parade

These 20 cards are printed on micro-etched foil board. This set honors baseball's top hitters and is sequentially numbered to 5,000.

		NM/M
Complete Set (20):		30.00
Common Player:		1.00
Production 5,000 Sets		

1	Tony Gwynn	2.50
2	Larry Walker	1.00
3	Mike Piazza	3.00
4	Frank Thomas	2.00
5	Manny Ramirez	1.00
6	Ken Griffey Jr.	3.00
7	Todd Helton	1.50
8	Vladimir Guerrero	2.00
9	Albert Belle	1.00
10	Jeff Bagwell	2.00
11	Juan Gonzalez	1.25
12	Jim Thome	1.50
13	Scott Rolen	1.50
14	Tino Martinez	1.00
15	Mark McGwire	4.00
16	Barry Bonds	5.00
17	Tony Clark	1.00
18	Mo Vaughn	1.00
19	Darin Erstad	1.25
20	Paul Konerko	1.25

Masterstrokes

Printed on a canvas-like material, these 20 cards are numbered to 1,000.

		NM/M
Complete Set (20):		95.00
Common Player:		2.00
Production 1,000 Sets		
Samples:		3X
1	Travis Lee	2.00
2	Kenny Lofton	2.00
3	Mo Vaughn	2.00
4	Ivan Rodriguez	3.50
5	Roger Clemens	6.50
6	Mark McGwire	10.00
7	Hideo Nomo	2.50
8	Andruw Jones	4.50
9	Nomar Garciaparra	6.00
10	Juan Gonzalez	2.50
11	Jeff Bagwell	4.50
12	Derek Jeter	12.50
13	Tony Gwynn	6.00
14	Chipper Jones	6.00
15	Mike Piazza	7.50
16	Greg Maddux	6.00
17	Alex Rodriguez	10.00
18	Cal Ripken Jr.	12.50
19	Frank Thomas	4.50
20	Ken Griffey Jr.	7.50

Sony MLB 99

Twenty Sony MLB '99 sweepstakes cards were inserted one per two Studio packs. The fronts feature a color action shot and the backs have sweepstakes rules and a MLB '99 tip.

		NM/M
Complete Set (20):		8.00
Common Player:		.15
1	Cal Ripken Jr.	1.50
2	Nomar Garciaparra	.75
3	Barry Bonds	1.50
4	Mike Mussina	.35
5	Pedro Martinez	.60
6	Derek Jeter	1.50
7	Andruw Jones	.60
8	Kenny Lofton	.15
9	Gary Sheffield	.45
10	Raul Mondesi	.15
11	Jeff Bagwell	.60
12	Tim Salmon	.15

13 Tom Glavine .35
14 Ben Grieve .15
15 Matt Williams .15
16 Juan Gonzalez .35
17 Mark McGwire 1.00
18 Bernie Williams .15
19 Andres Galarraga .15
20 Jose Cruz Jr. .15

8x10 Portraits Samples

Sample versions of the 8x10 cards which would be found in '98 Studio packs were also issued. They are identical in format to the issued cards, with UV coating and silver-foil graphics on fronts. Backs have a large black "SAMPLE" overprinted diagonally.

NM/M
001 Travis Lee 2.00
002 Todd Helton 3.00

8x10 Portraits

One Studio 8-x-10 was included in each pack. The cards were blown-up versions of the regular-size base cards, which were inserted seven per pack. The large portraits are paralleled in the Gold Proofs set, which adds gold holo-foil to the cards. Gold Proofs are numbered to 300.

NM/M
Complete Set (36): 65.00
Common Player: .50
Inserted 1:1
1 Travis Lee .50
2 Todd Helton 1.50
3 Ben Grieve .50
4 Paul Konerko .65
5 Jeff Bagwell 2.00
6 Derek Jeter 7.00
7 Ivan Rodriguez 1.50
8 Cal Ripken Jr. 7.00
9 Mike Piazza 4.00
10 Chipper Jones 3.00
11 Frank Thomas 2.00
12 Tony Gwynn 3.00
13 Nomar Garciaparra 3.00
14 Juan Gonzalez 1.00
15 Greg Maddux 3.00
16 Hideo Nomo 1.00
17 Scott Rolen 1.50
18 Barry Bonds 7.00
19 Ken Griffey Jr. 4.00
20 Alex Rodriguez 5.00
21 Roger Clemens 3.50
22 Mark McGwire 5.00
23 Jose Cruz Jr. .50
24 Andruw Jones 2.00
25 Tino Martinez .50
26 Mo Vaughn .50
27 Vladimir Guerrero 2.00
28 Tony Clark .50
29 Andy Pettitte .65
30 Jaret Wright .50
31 Paul Molitor 2.00
32 Darin Erstad .65
33 Larry Walker .50
34 Chuck Knoblauch .50
35 Barry Larkin .50
36 Kenny Lofton .50

8x10 Portraits Gold Proofs

This parallel of the 8x10 base set adds gold holo-foil treatments to the 36 cards, which are sequentially numbered to 300 and randomly inserted in packs.

NM/M
Common Player: 5.00
Stars: 6X

1995 Summit Samples

Nine-card cello packs of Summit cards, including "Big Bang" inserts, were released to dealers to debut the new Score brand. Cards are specially marked as promotional samples.

NM/M
Complete Set (9): 5.00
Common Player: .50
10 Barry Larkin .50
11 Albert Belle .50
79 Cal Ripken Jr. 3.00
80 David Cone .50
125 Alex Gonzalez (Rookie) .50
130 Charles Johnson (Rookie) .50
BB12 Jose Canseco (Big Bang) 1.00
BB17 Fred McGriff (Big Bang) .50
--- Information card .05

1995 Summit

A late-season release, Summit introduced the Score label to a premium brand card. Printed on extra heavy cardboard stock and UV coated on both sides the veteran player cards (#1-111) feature horizontal or vertical action photos with the player's name and team logo printed in gold-foil on front. Backs have a player portrait photo along with his 1994 stats in monthly charted form. The rookie cards subset (#112-173) have a large black "ROOKIE" on top-front while the back has a short career summary instead of stats. Other subsets include "BAT SPEED" (#174-188), honoring top hitters, and "SPECIAL DELIVERY" (#189-193), featuring top pitchers. Each are designated on front with spe-

cial gold-foil logos. Seven checklists close out the regular 200-card set. The Summit issued featured a four-tiered chase card program, including a parallel "Nth Degree" set. Summit was a hobby-only issue sold in 7-card foil packs.

NM/M
Complete Set (200): 10.00
Common Player: .05
Pack (7): 1.00
Wax Box (24): 12.50
1 Ken Griffey Jr. 1.00
2 Alex Fernandez .05
3 Fred McGriff .05
4 Ben McDonald .05
5 Rafael Palmeiro .60
6 Tony Gwynn .75
7 Jim Thome .60
8 Ken Hill .05
9 Barry Bonds 2.00
10 Barry Larkin .05
11 Albert Belle .05
12 Billy Ashley .05
13 Matt Williams .05
14 Andy Benes .05
15 Midre Cummings .05
16 J.R. Phillips .05
17 Edgar Martinez .05
18 Manny Ramirez .65
19 Jose Canseco .40
20 Chili Davis .05
21 Don Mattingly .85
22 Bernie Williams .05
23 Tom Glavine .35
24 Robin Ventura .05
25 Jeff Conine .05
26 Mark Grace .05
27 Mark McGwire 1.50
28 Carlos Delgado .45
29 Greg Colbrunn .05
30 Greg Maddux .75
31 Craig Biggio .05
32 Kirby Puckett .75
33 Derek Bell .05
34 Lenny Dykstra .05
35 Tim Salmon .05
36 Deion Sanders .05
37 Moises Alou .05
38 Ray Lankford .05
39 Willie Greene .05
40 Ozzie Smith .75
41 Roger Clemens .85
42 Andres Galarraga .05
43 Gary Sheffield .35
44 Sammy Sosa .75
45 Larry Walker .05
46 Kevin Appier .05
47 Raul Mondesi .05
48 Kenny Lofton .05
49 Darryl Hamilton .05
50 Roberto Alomar .20
51 Hal Morris .05
52 Cliff Floyd .05
53 Brent Gates .05
54 Rickey Henderson .65
55 John Olerud .05
56 Gregg Jefferies .05
57 Cecil Fielder .05
58 Paul Molitor .65
59 Bret Boone .05
60 Greg Vaughn .05
61 Wally Joyner .05
62 Jeffrey Hammonds .05
63 James Mouton .05
64 Omar Vizquel .05
65 Wade Boggs .75
66 Terry Steinbach .05
67 Wil Cordero .05
68 Joey Hamilton .05
69 Rico Brogna .05
70 Darren Daulton .05
71 Chuck Knoblauch .05
72 Bob Hamelin .05
73 Carl Everett .05
74 Joe Carter .05
75 Dave Winfield .65
76 Bobby Bonilla .05
77 Paul O'Neill .05
78 Javier Lopez .05
79 Cal Ripken Jr. 2.00
80 David Cone .05
81 Bernard Gilkey .05
82 Ivan Rodriguez .60
83 Dean Palmer .05
84 Jason Bere .05
85 Will Clark .05
86 Scott Cooper .05
87 Royce Clayton .05
88 Mike Piazza 1.00
89 Ryan Klesko .05
90 Juan Gonzalez .35
91 Travis Fryman .05
92 Frank Thomas .65
93 Eduardo Perez .05
94 Mo Vaughn .05
95 Jay Bell .05
96 Jeff Bagwell .65
97 Randy Johnson .65
98 Jimmy Key .05
99 Dennis Eckersley .60
100 Carlos Baerga .05
101 Eddie Murray .65
102 Mike Mussina .30
103 Brian Anderson .05

104 Jeff Cirillo .05
105 Dante Bichette .05
106 Bret Saberhagen .05
107 Jeff Kent .05
108 Ruben Sierra .05
109 Kirk Gibson .05
110 Reggie Sanders .05
111 Dave Justice .05
112 Benji Gil .05
113 Vaughn Eshelman .05
114 Carlos Perez RC .05
115 Chipper Jones .75
116 Shane Andrews .05
117 Orlando Miller .05
118 Scott Ruffcorn .05
119 Jose Oliva .05
120 Joe Vitiello .05
121 Jon Nunnally .05
122 Garret Anderson .05
123 Curtis Goodwin .05
124 Mark Grudzielanek RC .25
125 Alex Gonzalez .05
126 David Bell .05
127 Dustin Hermanson .05
128 Dave Nilsson .05
129 Wilson Heredia .05
130 Charles Johnson .05
131 Frank Rodriguez .05
132 Alex Ochoa .05
133 Alex Rodriguez 1.50
134 Bobby Higginson RC .25
135 Edgardo Alfonzo .05
136 Armando Benitez .05
137 Rich Aude .05
138 Tim Naehring .05
139 Joe Randa .05
140 Quilvio Veras .05
141 Hideo Nomo RC 1.00
142 Ray Holbert .05
143 Michael Tucker .05
144 Chad Mottola .05
145 John Valentin .05
146 James Baldwin .05
147 Esteban Loaiza .05
148 Marty Cordova .05
149 Juan Acevedo RC .05
150 Tim Unroe RC .05
151 Brad Clontz .05
152 Steve Rodriguez .05
153 Rudy Pemberton .05
154 Ozzie Timmons .05
155 Ricky Otero .05
156 Allen Battle .05
157 Joe Roselli .05
158 Roberto Petagine .05
159 Todd Hollandsworth .05
160 Shannon Penn .05
161 Antonio Osuna .05
162 Russ Davis .05
163 Jason Giambi .40
164 Terry Bradshaw .05
165 Ray Durham .05
166 Todd Steverson .05
167 Tim Belk .05
168 Andy Pettitte .25
169 Roger Cedeno .05
170 Jose Parra .05
171 Scott Sullivan .05
172 LaTroy Hawkins .05
173 Jeff McCurry .05
174 Ken Griffey Jr. (Bat Speed) .50
175 Frank Thomas (Bat Speed) .30
176 Cal Ripken Jr. (Bat Speed) 1.00
177 Jeff Bagwell (Bat Speed) .30
178 Mike Piazza (Bat Speed) .50
179 Barry Bonds (Bat Speed) 1.00
180 Matt Williams (Bat Speed) .05
181 Don Mattingly (Bat Speed) .45
182 Will Clark (Bat Speed) .05
183 Tony Gwynn (Bat Speed) .40
184 Kirby Puckett (Bat Speed) .40
185 Jose Canseco (Bat Speed) .25
186 Paul Molitor (Bat Speed) .30
187 Albert Belle (Bat Speed) .05
188 Joe Carter (Bat Speed) .05
189 Greg Maddux (Special Delivery) .40
190 Roger Clemens (Special Delivery) .45
191 David Cone (Special Delivery) .05
192 Mike Mussina (Special Delivery) .15
193 Randy Johnson (Special Delivery) .30
194 Checklist (Frank Thomas) .30
195 Checklist (Ken Griffey Jr.) .50
196 Checklist (Cal Ripken Jr.) .75
197 Checklist (Jeff Bagwell) .30
198 Checklist (Mike Piazza) .50
199 Checklist (Barry Bonds) .75
200 Checklist (Mo Vaughn, Matt Williams) .05

Big Bang

The game's top sluggers are featured in this insert set. The front is printed on prismatic metallic foil, a process which Score calls "Spectroetch," with large and small action photos. Backs are conventionally printed and have a large photo with a career highlight printed beneath. The toughest of the Summit chase cards, these are found on the average of once every two boxes (72 packs). Cards are numbered with a "BB" prefix.

NM/M
Complete Set (20): 45.00
Common Player: 1.00
1 Ken Griffey Jr. 6.00
2 Frank Thomas 3.25
3 Cal Ripken Jr. 8.00
4 Jeff Bagwell 3.25
5 Mike Piazza 6.00
6 Barry Bonds 8.00
7 Matt Williams 1.00
8 Don Mattingly 4.50
9 Will Clark 1.00
10 Tony Gwynn 4.00
11 Kirby Puckett 4.00
12 Jose Canseco 2.00
13 Paul Molitor 3.25
14 Albert Belle 1.00
15 Joe Carter 1.00
16 Rafael Palmeiro 3.00
17 Fred McGriff 1.00
18 Dave Justice 1.00
19 Tim Salmon 1.00
20 Mo Vaughn 1.00

New Age

Printed on metallic foil in a horizontal format, the New Age inserts were seeded at a rate of about one per 18 packs. Red and silver colors predominate on front, while the backs are printed in standard technology and feature a second photo and career summary.

NM/M
Complete Set (15): 10.00
Common Player: .25
1 Cliff Floyd .25
2 Manny Ramirez 2.00
3 Raul Mondesi .25
4 Alex Rodriguez 5.00
5 Billy Ashley .25
6 Alex Gonzalez .25
7 Michael Tucker .25
8 Charles Johnson .25
9 Carlos Delgado 1.00
10 Benji Gil .25
11 Chipper Jones 3.00
12 Todd Hollandsworth .25
13 Frank Rodriguez .25
14 Shawn Green .60
15 Ray Durham .25

Nth Degree

A prismatic foil background differentiates the Nth Degree parallel inserts from the Summit base cards. Nth Degree inserts are found on a 1:4 pack ratio.

NM/M
Complete Set (200): 50.00
Common Player: .25
Stars: 2X

21 Club

Metallic foil printing on front and back distinguishes this set of chase cards. A large red-foil "21 / CLUB" logo on each side identifies the theme of this set as players who professed to be that age during the 1955 baseball season. The players are pictured in action pose on front and a portrait on back. On average the 21 Club cards are seeded one per box (36 packs). Cards are numbered with a "TC" prefix.

NM/M
Complete Set (9): 4.00
Common Player: .50
1 Bob Abreu .65
2 Pokey Reese .50
3 Edgardo Alfonzo .50
4 Jim Pittsley .50
5 Ruben Rivera .50
6 Chan Ho Park .50
7 Julian Tavarez .50
8 Ismael Valdes .50
9 Dmitri Young .50

1996 Summit

Pinnacle's 1996 Summit baseball has 200 cards, including 35 rookies, four checklists and 10 Deja Vu subset cards. Each card is also reprinted in three parallel versions - Above and Beyond (one per seven packs), Artist's Proofs (one in 36) and a retail-only silver foil-bordered version. Above and Beyond cards use an all-prismatic foil design; Artist's Proof cards have holographic foil stamping. Five insert sets were produced: Big Bang; Mirage (a parallel set to Big Bang); Hitters, Inc.; Ballparks; and Positions (found one per every 50 magazine packs).

NM/M
Complete Set (200): 10.00
Common Player: .05
Pack (7): 1.25
Wax Box (18): 15.00
1 Mike Piazza 1.25
2 Matt Williams .05
3 Tino Martinez .05
4 Reggie Sanders .05
5 Ray Durham .05
6 Brad Radke .05

7 Jeff Bagwell .65
8 Ron Gant .05
9 Lance Johnson .05
10 Kevin Seitzer .05
11 Dante Bichette .05
12 Ivan Rodriguez .60
13 Jim Abbott .05
14 Greg Colbrunn .05
15 Rondell White .40
16 Shawn Green .40
17 Gregg Jefferies .05
18 Omar Vizquel .05
19 Cal Ripken Jr. 2.00
20 Mark McGwire 1.50
21 Wally Joyner .05
22 Chili Davis .05
23 Jose Canseco .40
24 Royce Clayton .05
25 Jay Bell .05
26 Travis Fryman .05
27 Jeff King .05
28 Todd Hundley .05
29 Joe Vitiello .05
30 Russ Davis .05
31 Mo Vaughn .05
32 Raul Mondesi .05
33 Ray Lankford .05
34 Mike Stanley .05
35 B.J. Surhoff .05
36 Greg Vaughn .05
37 Todd Stottlemyre .05
38 Carlos Delgado .50
39 Kenny Lofton .05
40 Hideo Nomo .35
41 Sterling Hitchcock .05
42 Pete Schourek .05
43 Edgardo Alfonzo .05
44 Ken Hill .05
45 Ken Caminiti .05
46 Bobby Higginson .05
47 Michael Tucker .05
48 David Cone .05
49 Cecil Fielder .05
50 Brian Hunter .05
51 Charles Johnson .05
52 Bobby Bonilla .05
53 Eddie Murray .65
54 Kenny Rogers .05
55 Jim Edmonds .05
56 Trevor Hoffman .05
57 Kevin Mitchell .05
58 Ruben Sierra .05
59 Benji Gil .05
60 Juan Gonzalez .35
61 Larry Walker .05
62 Jack McDowell .05
63 Shawon Dunston .05
64 Andy Benes .05
65 Jay Buhner .05
66 Rickey Henderson .65
67 Alex Gonzalez .05
68 Mike Kelly .05
69 Fred McGriff .05
70 Ryne Sandberg .75
71 Ernie Young .05
72 Kevin Appier .05
73 Moises Alou .05
74 John Jaha .05
75 J.T. Snow .05
76 Jim Thome .60
77 Kirby Puckett .75
78 Hal Morris .05
79 Robin Ventura .05
80 Ben McDonald .05
81 Tim Salmon .05
82 Albert Belle .05
83 Marquis Grissom .05
84 Alex Rodriguez 1.50
85 Manny Ramirez .65
86 Ken Griffey Jr. 1.25
87 Sammy Sosa .75
88 Frank Thomas .65
89 Lee Smith .05
90 Marty Cordova .05
91 Greg Maddux .75
92 Lenny Dykstra .05
93 Butch Huskey .05
94 Garret Anderson .05
95 Mike Bordick .05
96 Dave Justice .05
97 Chad Curtis .05
98 Carlos Baerga .05
99 Jason Isringhausen .05
100 Gary Sheffield .35
101 Roger Clemens 1.00
102 Ozzie Smith .75
103 Ramon Martinez .05
104 Paul O'Neill .05
105 Will Clark .05
106 Tom Glavine .35
107 Barry Bonds 2.00
108 Barry Larkin .05
109 Derek Bell .05
110 Randy Johnson .65
111 Jeff Conine .05
112 John Mabry .05
113 Julian Tavarez .05
114 Gary DiSarcina .05
115 Andres Galarraga .05
116 Marc Newfield .05
117 Frank Rodriguez .05
118 Brady Anderson .05
119 Mike Mussina .30
120 Orlando Merced .05
121 Melvin Nieves .05
122 Brian Jordan .05
123 Rafael Palmeiro .60
124 Johnny Damon .35

125 Wil Cordero .05
126 Chipper Jones .75
127 Eric Karros .05
128 Darren Daulton .05
129 Vinny Castilla .05
130 Joe Carter .05
131 Bernie Williams .05
132 Bernard Gilkey .05
133 Bret Boone .05
134 Tony Gwynn .75
135 Dave Nilsson .05
136 Ryan Klesko .05
137 Paul Molitor .65
138 John Olerud .05
139 Craig Biggio .05
140 John Valentin .05
141 Chuck Knoblauch .05
142 Edgar Martinez .05
143 Rico Brogna .05
144 Dean Palmer .05
145 Mark Grace .05
146 Roberto Alomar .20
147 Alex Fernandez .05
148 Andre Dawson .25
149 Wade Boggs .75
150 Mark Lewis .05
151 Gary Gaetti .05
152 Paul Wilson, Roger Clemens .45
153 Rey Ordonez, Ozzie Smith (Deja Vu) .35
154 Derek Jeter, Cal Ripken Jr. (Deja Vu) 1.00
155 Alan Benes, Andy Benes (Deja Vu) .05
156 Jason Kendall, Mike Piazza (Deja Vu) .75
157 Ryan Klesko, Frank Thomas (Deja Vu) .30
158 Johnny Damon, Ken Griffey Jr. (Deja Vu) .65
159 Karim Garcia, Sammy Sosa (Deja Vu) .40
160 Raul Mondesi, Tim Salmon (Deja Vu) .05
161 Chipper Jones, Matt Williams (Deja Vu) .40
162 Rey Ordonez .05
163 Bob Wolcott .05
164 Brooks Kieschnick .05
165 Steve Gibralter .05
166 Bob Abreu .05
167 Gregg Zaun .05
168 Tavo Alvarez .05
169 Sal Fasano .05
170 George Arias .05
171 Derek Jeter .05
172 Livan Hernandez RC .25
173 Alan Benes .05
174 George Williams .05
175 John Wasdin .05
176 Chan Ho Park .05
177 Paul Wilson .05
178 Jeff Suppan .05
179 Quinton McCracken .05
180 Wilton Guerrero RC .05
181 Eric Owens .05
182 Felipe Crespo .05
183 LaTroy Hawkins .05
184 Jason Schmidt .05
185 Terrell Wade .05
186 Mike Grace RC .05
187 Chris Snopek .05
188 Jason Kendall .05
189 Todd Hollandsworth .05
190 Jim Pittsley .05
191 Jermaine Dye .05
192 Mike Busby RC .05
193 Richard Hidalgo .05
194 Tyler Houston .05
195 Jimmy Haynes .05
196 Karim Garcia .05
197 Ken Griffey Jr. (Checklist) .50
198 Frank Thomas (Checklist) .30
199 Greg Maddux (Checklist) .40
200 Cal Ripken Jr. (Checklist) 1.00

Artist's Proof

Holographic-foil highlights and an "ARTIST'S PROOF" notation on the front photo distinguish the cards in this parallel edition. The AP cards are found once per 36 packs.

	NM/M
Complete Set (200):	100.00
Common Player:	1.00
Stars:	8X

Foil

This parallel issue was an exclusive in Summit seven-card magazine retail packaging. The black borders of the regular Summit versions have been replaced on these cards by silver foil.

	NM/M
Complete Set (200):	30.00
Common Player:	.25
Stars:	3X

Above & Beyond

These 200 insert cards parallel Pinnacle's 1996 Summit set, using all-prismatic foil for each card. The cards were seeded one per every four packs.

	NM/M
Complete Set (200):	50.00
Common Player:	.25
Stars:	3X

Ballparks

These 18 cards feature images of players superimposed over their respective teams' ballparks. The cards were seeded one per every 18 packs of 1996 Pinnacle Summit baseball and are serially within an edition of 8,000 each.

	NM/M
Complete Set (18):	45.00
Common Player:	1.00
1 Cal Ripken Jr.	7.50
2 Albert Belle	1.00
3 Dante Bichette	1.00
4 Mo Vaughn	1.00
5 Ken Griffey Jr.	6.00
6 Derek Jeter	7.50
7 Juan Gonzalez	1.50
8 Greg Maddux	4.00
9 Frank Thomas	3.00
10 Ryne Sandberg	4.00
11 Mike Piazza	6.00
12 Johnny Damon	1.50
13 Barry Bonds	7.50
14 Jeff Bagwell	3.00
15 Paul Wilson	1.00
16 Tim Salmon	1.00
17 Kirby Puckett	4.00
18 Tony Gwynn	4.00

Big Bang

Sixteen of the biggest hitters are featured on these 1996 Pinnacle Summit insert cards. The cards, seeded one per every 72 packs, use Spectroetched backgrounds with foil highlights.

	NM/M
Complete Set (16):	60.00
Common Player:	1.50
1 Frank Thomas	4.00
2 Ken Griffey Jr.	7.50
3 Albert Belle	1.50
4 Mo Vaughn	1.50
5 Barry Bonds	12.00
6 Cal Ripken Jr.	12.00
7 Jeff Bagwell	4.00
8 Mike Piazza	7.50
9 Ryan Klesko	1.50
10 Manny Ramirez	4.00
11 Tim Salmon	1.50
12 Dante Bichette	1.50
13 Sammy Sosa	6.00
14 Raul Mondesi	1.50
15 Chipper Jones	6.00
16 Garret Anderson	1.50

Big Bang Mirage

These 16 cards form a parallel version to Summit's Big Bang inserts. The cards use an innovative technology that creates a floating background behind the player's image. By holding the card in direct sunlight or under an incandescent bulb, a collector can see three dimensions and a floating baseball that seems to levitate in the background. Mirage cards are serially numbered in an edition of 600 each.

	NM/M
Complete Set (16):	115.00
Common Player:	3.50
1 Frank Thomas	10.00
2 Ken Griffey Jr.	15.00
3 Albert Belle	3.50
4 Mo Vaughn	3.50
5 Barry Bonds	20.00
6 Cal Ripken Jr.	20.00
7 Jeff Bagwell	10.00
8 Mike Piazza	15.00
9 Ryan Klesko	3.50
10 Manny Ramirez	10.00
11 Tim Salmon	3.50
12 Dante Bichette	3.50
13 Sammy Sosa	12.50
14 Raul Mondesi	3.50
15 Chipper Jones	12.50
16 Garret Anderson	3.50

ABBREVIATIONS

OPS - Overprinted "Promotional Sample"

Hitters, Inc.

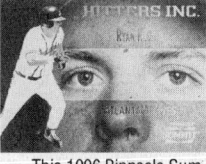

This 1996 Pinnacle Summit set honors 16 top hitters. The cards, seeded one per 36 packs, put an embossed highlight on an enlarged photo of the player's eyes. Backs are serially numbered within an edition of 4,000 each.

	NM/M
Complete Set (16):	40.00
Common Player:	1.25
1 Tony Gwynn	4.00
2 Mo Vaughn	1.25
3 Tim Salmon	1.25
4 Ken Griffey Jr.	5.00
5 Sammy Sosa	4.00
6 Frank Thomas	3.00
7 Wade Boggs	4.00
8 Albert Belle	1.25
9 Cal Ripken Jr.	8.00
10 Manny Ramirez	3.00
11 Ryan Klesko	1.25
11p Ryan Klesko/OPS	1.25
12 Dante Bichette	1.25
13 Mike Piazza	5.00
14 Chipper Jones	4.00
15 Ryne Sandberg	4.00
16 Matt Williams	1.25

Positions

This insert issue features top players at each position. It is an exclusive magazine pack find, seeded about one per 50 packs. Fronts have action photos of three top players at the position on a baseball infield background at top. Close-ups of those players appear at bottom, separated by a gold-foil strip. Backs have narrow action photos of each player, a few stats and a serial number from within an edition of 1,500 each.

	NM/M
Complete Set (9):	100.00
Common Card:	6.00
1 Jeff Bagwell, Mo Vaughn, Frank Thomas/ First Base	10.00
2 Roberto Alomar, Craig Biggio, Chuck Knoblauch/ Second Base	6.00
3 Matt Williams, Jim Thome, Chipper Jones/ Third Base	12.50
4 Barry Larkin, Cal Ripken Jr., Alex Rodriguez/ Short Stop	20.00
5 Mike Piazza, Ivan Rodriguez, Charles Johnson/ Catcher	15.00
6 Hideo Nomo, Greg Maddux, Randy Johnson/ Pitcher	12.50
7 Barry Bonds, Albert Belle, Ryan Klesko/ Left Field	20.00
8 Johnny Damon, Jim Edmonds, Ken Griffey Jr./ Center Field	15.00
9 Manny Ramirez, Gary Sheffield, Sammy Sosa/ Right Field	12.50

1987 Sun Foods Milwaukee Brewers

Though they are nowhere identified on the cards, Sun Foods was the sponsor of this team set, issuing four cards per week. Measuring 6" x 9", the cards were licensed only by the Players' Association and so do not feature team uniform logos. Bare-headed players are photographed against a blue background with a black facsimile autograph at bottom. An MLBPA logo appears in the upper-left. Backs are blank. The unnumbered cards are checklisted here in alphabetical order.

	NM/M
Complete Set (16):	15.00
Common Player:	.50
(1) Glenn Braggs	.50
(2) Greg Brock	.50
(3) Mark Clear	.50
(4) Cecil Cooper	.50
(5) Rob Deer	.50
(6) Jim Gantner	.50
(7) Ted Higuera	.50
(8) Paul Molitor	5.00
(9) Juan Nieves	.50
(10) Dan Plesac	.50
(11) Billy Jo Robidoux	.50
(12) Bill Schroeder	.50
(13) B.J. Surhoff	.50
(14) Dale Sveum	.50
(15) Bill Wegman	.50
(16) Robin Yount	5.00

2001 Sunoco Dream Team

Twenty-four former stars are depicted two per card on this "Dream Team" set. Horizontal format cards have action photos (or in the case of two cards, Jim Trusilo artwork) with a city name at top and player names at left and right. A gold-foil Sunoco Dream Team logo is at lower-right. Backs have career stats and highlights, a card title, Sunoco, Coca-Cola and MLB Players Alumni logos. Cards were available in three-card packs for 49 cents with a gasoline or Coke purchase.

	NM/M
Complete Set (12):	5.00
Common Card:	.50
1 Game Seven Slams (Bill Mazeroski, Willie Stargell)	1.00
2 Philly Phenoms (Mike Schmidt, Steve Carlton)	1.50
3 Red Hot Heroes (Tony Perez, Joe Morgan)	1.00
4 Bronx Legends (Yogi Berra, Don Mattingly)	1.50
5 Outstanding O's (Jim Palmer, Frank Robinson)	1.00
6 Dynamic Duo (Carlton Fisk, Luis Tiant)	1.00

7	Beantown Beginnings (Fred Lynn, Jim Rice)	1.00
8	Tiger Tough (Sparky Anderson, Al Kaline)	1.00
9	Whiz Kids Robin Roberts, Richie Ashburn (Artwork)	1.00
10	Amazin' Championships (Tug McGraw, Gary Carter)	1.00
11	Top of the Tribe Lou Boudreau, Bob Feller (Artwork)	1.00
12	In Tribute (Roger Maris, Catfish Hunter)	1.50

1994 SuperSlam

An innovative issued felled by the 1994 baseball strike, SuperSlams are a 5-1/2" x 7-1/2" tent-fold display card. Front and back have a gridded silver metallic background. At center on front is a 3-3/4" x 5-1/4" color photo on which is superimposed a 3-D action pose of the player. Backs have extensive "This is my life" biographical information about the player. The cards are skip-numbered. Promo cards of Jack McDowell were issued with either silver or gold background. Cards were sold for $7.95 apiece with reported production between 2,000 and 50,000, depending on player.

		NM/M
Complete Set (18):		60.00
Common Player:		2.50
3	Greg Maddux	5.00
4	Fred McGriff	2.50
5	Moises Alou	2.50
19	Roberto Alomar	3.00
27	Cal Ripken Jr.	8.00
28	Roger Clemens	5.50
40	Mike Piazza	6.00
42	Barry Bonds	8.00
47	Tony Gwynn	5.00
53	Rickey Henderson	4.00
58	Tim Salmon	2.50
60	Ken Griffey Jr.	6.00
65	Juan Gonzalez	3.00
67	Jeff Bagwell	4.00
83	Albert Belle	2.50
84	Kenny Lofton	2.50
90	Kirby Puckett	5.00
95	Frank Thomas	5.00
P1	Jack McDowell/Gold	2.50
P2	Jack McDowell/Silver	2.50

1982 Superstar

AL KALINE

A second series of Superstar collector cards was produced in 1982. Similar in format to the 1980 issue, they also feature black-and-white photos. Surrounding graphics on the second series are in red, white and blue. Backs are numbered from 45-90 in continuation of

the first series and contain career narratives. Many players are again featured on multiple cards, and the second series contains sports stars other than baseball players. Issue price was again $3.50.

		NM/M
Complete Set (45):		10.00
Common Player:		.40
46	Duke Snider	.40
47	Al Kaline	.40
48	Stan Musial	.60
49	Frank Robinson	.40
50	Jim Brown	.40
51	Bobby Orr	.60
52	Roger Staubach	.40
53	Honus Wagner	.40
54	Willie Mays	.80
55	Roy Campanella	.40
56	Mickey Mantle	2.50
57	Hank Aaron	.80
58	Ernie Banks	.60
59	Babe Ruth, Lou Gehrig	1.50
60	Ted Williams	.80
61	Babe Ruth	1.50
62	Lou Gehrig	.80
63	Sandy Koufax	.80
64	Fran Tarkenton	.40
65	Gordie Howe	.60
66	Roberto Clemente	1.25
67	Ty Cobb	.40
68	Lou Brock	.40
69	Joe Namath	.60
70	O.J. Simpson	.60
71	Whitey Ford	.40
72	Jackie Robinson	.80
73	Bill Russell	.60
74	Johnny Unitas	.40
75	Bobby Hull	.60
76	Bob Cousy	.60
77	Walter Johnson	.40
78	Satchel Paige	.50
79	Joe DiMaggio	1.25
80	Yogi Berra	.40
81	Jerry West	.60
82	Rod Gilbert	.60
83	Sadaharu Oh	.40
84	Wilt Chamberlain	.60
85	Frank Gifford	.40
86	Casey Stengel	.40
87	Eddie Mathews	.40
88	Hank Aaron, Sandy Koufax	.80
89	Ted Williams, Mickey Mantle	1.25
90	Casey Stengel, Mickey Mantle	1.50

1987 Super Stars Discs

Produced by Mike Schecter Associates, the Super Stars disc set was released as part of a promotion for various brands of iced tea mixes in many parts of the country. Among the brands participating in the promotion were Acme, Alpha Beta, Bustelo, Key, King Kullen, Lady Lee, Our Own, and Weis. The discs were issued in three-part folding panels with each disc measuring 2-1/2" in diameter. Fronts feature a full-color photo inside a bright yellow border. Two player discs were included in each panel along with a coupon disc offering either an uncut press sheet of the set or a facsimile autographed ball. Because the series was licensed only by the players' union, and not MLB, cap logos were removed.

		NM/M
Complete Panel Set (10):		7.50
Complete Singles Set (20):		4.50
Common Panel:		.25
Common Single Player:		.10
	Panel (1)	1.00
1	Darryl Strawberry	.10
2	Roger Clemens	.50
	Panel (2)	.25
3	Ron Darling	.10
4	Keith Hernandez	.10
	Panel (3)	1.00
5	Tony Pena	.10
6	Don Mattingly	.50
	Panel (4)	.75
7	Eric Davis	.10
8	Gary Carter	.25
	Panel (5)	.75
9	Dave Winfield	.25
10	Wally Joyner	.10
	Panel (6)	1.00
11	Mike Schmidt	.50
12	Robby Thompson	.10
	Panel (7)	2.00
13	Wade Boggs	.35
14	Cal Ripken Jr.	.75
	Panel (8)	1.00
15	Dale Murphy	.25
16	Tony Gwynn	.35
	Panel (9)	1.00
17	Jose Canseco	.80
18	Rickey Henderson	.25
	Panel (10)	.25
19	Lance Parrish	.10
20	Leo Righetti	.10

1988 Super Stars Discs

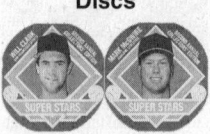

The "Second Annual Collector's Edition" of Super Stars discs is similar to the 1987 issue. A set of 20 discs (2-1/2" diameter) featuring full-color player photos was inserted in specially marked cannisters of iced tea and fruit drinks. Each triple-fold insert consists of two player discs and one redemption card. Player discs are bright blue, yellow, red and green with a diamond design framing the player portrait. The player name appears upper left, the set logo appears upper right. Personalized disc series were issued for Tetley, Weis, Key Food and A&P supermarkets (untitled series were also sold at Lucky, Skaggs, Alpha Beta, Acme King Kullen, Laneco and Krasdale stores). The series name (i.e. Weis Winners) is printed below the player photo. Backs are in red with a few personal data and stats. Because the discs are licensed only through the players' union, cap logos have been airbrushed off the photos.

		NM/M
Complete Panel Set (10):		7.50
Complete Singles Set (20):		4.50
Common Panel:		.25
Common Single Player:		.10
	Panel (1)	2.00
1	Wade Boggs	.50
9	Roger Clemens	.60
	Panel (2)	1.25
3	Don Mattingly	.60
13	Dave Magadan	.10
	Panel (3)	1.50
4	Mark McGwire	.65
10	Will Clark	.10
	Panel (4)	.25
5	Matt Nokes	.10
11	Vince Coleman	.10
	Panel (5)	.10
8	Kevin Seitzer	.10
2	Ellis Burks	.10
	Panel (6)	1.25
12	Eric Davis	.10
1	Kirby Puckett	.50
	Panel (7)	.25
15	Benito Santiago	.10
20	Fernando Valenzuela	.10
	Panel (8)	1.50
16	Mike Schmidt	.60
14	Dale Murphy	.25
	Panel (9)	.25
17	Darryl Strawberry	.10
10	Dwight Gooden	.10
	Panel (10)	.25
8	Steve Bedrosian	.10
7	Billy Ripken	.10

1989 Super Stars Discs

SUPER STARS
MARK McGWIRE
OAKLAND ATHLETICS

The third annual series of Super Stars perforated disc folders again offered two play-

ers and an offer for a a facsimile autographed baseball or an uncut sheet of discs. The 2-3/4" diameter discs have a yellow border with a red star at center. A player portrait photo is in the star. Backs are printed in black and have a few previous season stats and biographical bits. As in previous years, the discs were produced by Michael Schechter Associates, which does business only with the players' union, precluding the use of MLB logos on the player photos.

		NM/M
Complete Panel Set (10):		9.00
Complete Singles Set (20):		5.00
Common Panel:		.25
Common Player:		.10
	Panel (1)	1.25
1	Don Mattingly	.50
2	David Cone	.25
	Panel (2)	2.00
3	Mark McGwire	.65
4	Will Clark	.25
	Panel (3)	.25
5	Darryl Strawberry	.10
6	Dwight Gooden	.10
	Panel (4)	2.00
7	Wade Boggs	.45
8	Roger Clemens	.50
	Panel (5)	.25
9	Benito Santiago	.10
10	Orel Hershiser	.10
	Panel (6)	1.25
11	Eric Davis	.10
12	Kirby Puckett	.45
	Panel (7)	1.25
13	Dave Winfield	.40
14	Andre Dawson	.10
	Panel (8)	2.00
15	Steve Bedrosian	.10
16	Cal Ripken Jr.	.75
	Panel (9)	1.00
17	Andy Van Slyke	.10
18	Jose Canseco	.35
	Panel (10)	.75
19	Jose Oquendo	.10
20	Dale Murphy	.25

1990 Super Stars Discs

SUPER STARS
BO JACKSON
KANSAS CITY ROYALS

In its fourth annual edition the Super Stars discs continued the three-piece perforated folder format. Each panel consists of two player discs and a disc offering a 1990-1991 calendar at the center of an uncut sheet of the discs. Discs have a red border with a player portrait photo in the center of a tombstone-shaped yellow frame. A few 1989 stats and biographical notes are printed in black on the back. Because the discs are licensed only by the players' union, and not Major League Baseball, the player photos have had team logos excised.

		NM/M
Complete Panel Set (10):		9.00
Complete Set, Singles (20):		4.50
Common Panel:		.25
Common Player:		.10
	Panel (1)	.50
1	Will Clark	.10
2	Howard Johnson	.10
	Panel (2)	1.00
3	Chris Sabo	.10
4	Jose Canseco	.40
	Panel (3)	.50
5	Bo Jackson	.15
6	Kevin Mitchell	.10
	Panel (4)	.50
7	Wade Boggs	.50
8	Ken Griffey Jr.	.65
	Panel (5)	.25
9	George Bell	.10
10	Dwight Gooden	.10
	Panel (6)	1.00
11	Bobby Bonilla	.10
12	Ryne Sandberg	.50
	Panel (7)	2.00
13	Kirby Puckett	.50
14	Don Mattingly	.60
	Panel (8)	1.50
15	Mark McGwire	.75
16	Frank Viola	.10
	Panel (9)	.25
17	Bret Saberhagen	.10
18	Mike Greenwell	.10
	Panel (10)	2.00
19	Steve Sax	.10
20	Nolan Ryan	1.00

1989 Swell Baseball Greats

TED WILLIAMS
OUTFIELD
HALL OF FAME
SWELL

Collectors Marketing Corp. handled the distribution of Philadelphia Gum Company's debut "old-timers" set. Most cards featured color photos, though some of the older players were represented in sepia shots. Red-and-white backs featured career stats, a baseball biography and a few vital statistics.

		NM/M
Complete Set (135):		12.00
Common Player:		.15
Wax Pack (10):		.65
Wax Box (36):		15.00
1	Babe Ruth	3.50
2	Ty Cobb	1.50
3	Walter Johnson	.75
4	Honus Wagner	.75
5	Cy Young	.75
6	Joe Adcock	.15
7	Jim Bunning	.15
8	Orlando Cepeda	.15
9	Harvey Kuenn	.15
10	Catfish Hunter	.15
11	Johnny VanderMeer	.15
12	Tony Oliva	.15
13	Harvey Haddix (Reversed negative.)	.15
14	Dick McAuliffe	.15
15	Lefty Grove	.15
16	Bo Belinski	.15
17	Claude Osteen	.15
18	Doc Medich	.15
19	Del Ennis	.15
20	Rogers Hornsby	.40
21	Bob Buhl	.15
22	Phil Niekro	.15
23	Don Zimmer	.15
24	Greg Luzinski	.15
25	Lou Gehrig	2.50
26	Ken Singleton	.15
27	Bob Allison	.15
28	Ed Kranepool	.15
29	Manny Sanguillen	.15
30	Luke Appling	.15
31	Ralph Terry	.15
32	Smoky Burgess	.15
33	Gil Hodges	.40
34	Harry Walker	.15
35	Edd Roush	.15
36	Ron Santo	.15
37	Jim Perry	.15
38	Jose Morales	.15
39	Stan Bahnsen	.15
40	Al Kaline	.40
41	Mel Harder	.15
42	Ralph Houk	.15
43	Jack Billingham	.15
44	Carl Erskine	.15
45	Hoyt Wilhelm	.15
46	Dick Radatz	.15
47	Roy Sievers	.15
48	Jim Lonborg	.15
49	Bobby Richardson	.25
50	Whitey Ford	.40
51	Roy Face	.15
52	Tom Tresh	.15
53	Joe Nuxhall	.15
54	Mickey Vernon	.15
55	Johnny Mize	.15
56	Scott McGregor	.15
57	Billy Pierce	.15
58	Dave Giusti	.15
59	Minnie Minoso	.15
60	Early Wynn	.15
61	Jose Cardenal	.15
62	Sam Jethroe	.15
63	Sal Bando	.15
64	Elrod Hendricks	.15
65	Enos Slaughter	.15
66	Jim Bouton	.15
67	Bill Mazeroski	.25
68	Tony Kubek	.25
69	Joe Black	.15
70	Harmon Killebrew	.40
71	Sam McDowell	.15
72	Bucky Dent	.15
73	Virgil Trucks	.15
74	Andy Pafko	.15
75	Bob Feller	.40
76	Tito Francona	.15
77	Al Dark	.15
78	Larry Dierker	.15
79	Nellie Briles	.15
80	Lou Boudreau	.15
81	Wally Moon	.15
82	Hank Bauer	.15
83	Jim Piersall	.15
84	Jim Grant	.15
85	Richie Ashburn	.15
86	Bob Friend	.15
87	Ken Keltner	.15
88	Jim Kaat	.15
89	Dean Chance	.15
90	Al Lopez	.15
91	Dick Groat	.15
92	Johnny Blanchard	.15
93	Chuck Hinton	.15
94	Clete Boyer	.15
95	Steve Carlton	.40
96	Tug McGraw	.15
97	Mickey Lolich	.15
98	Earl Weaver	.15
99	Sal Maglie	.15
100	Ted Williams	2.25
101	Allie Reynolds (Photo actually Marius Russo.)	.15
102	Gene Woodling (Photo actually Irv Noren.)	.15
103	Moe Drabowsky	.15
104	Mickey Stanley	.15
105	Jim Palmer	.15
106	Bill Freehan	.15
107	Bob Robertson	.15
108	Walt Dropo	.15
109	Jerry Koosman	.15
110	Bobby Doerr	.15
111	Phil Rizzuto	.40
112	Don Kessinger	.15
113	Milt Pappas	.15
114	Herb Score	.15
115	Larry Doby	.15
116	Glenn Beckert	.15
117	Andre Thornton	.15
118	Gary Matthews	.15
119	Bill Virdon	.15
120	Billy Williams	.15
121	Johnny Sain	.15
122	Don Newcombe	.15
123	Rico Petrocelli	.15
124	Dick Bosman	.15
125	Roberto Clemente	3.00
126	Rocky Colavito	.15
127	Wilbur Wood	.15
128	Duke Sims	.15
129	Ken Holtzman	.15
130	Casey Stengel	.15
131	Bobby Shantz	.15
132	Del Crandall	.15
133	Bobby Thomson	.15
134	Brooks Robinson	.40
135	Checklist	.15

1990 Swell Baseball Greats

BASEBALL GREATS
BILL ROBINSON
OUTFIELD/1ST BASE
SWELL

In its second year of "old-timers" set production, Swell moved its "Baseball Greats" banner to the card front, above a color player photo. Where color photos were unavailable, sepia pictures were used. Backs were virtually identical to the previous year, with a line of lifetime stats, a career highlights write-up and a few bits of personal data. Also nearly identical is player selection within the 135-card set.

	NM/M
Complete Set (135):	12.00

Common Player: .15
Wax Pack (10): .75
Wax Box (36): 12.50

1 Tom Seaver .50
2 Hank Aaron 2.50
3 Mickey Cochrane .15
4 Rod Carew .15
5 Carl Yastrzemski .40
6 Dizzy Dean .50
7 Sal Bando .15
8 Whitey Ford .40
9 Bill White .15
10 Babe Ruth 3.50
11 Robin Roberts .15
12 Warren Spahn .15
13 Billy Williams .15
14 Joe Garagiola .40
15 Ty Cobb 1.50
16 Boog Powell .15
17 Tom Tresh .15
18 Luke Appling .15
19 Tommie Agee .15
20 Roberto Clemente 3.00
21 Bobby Thomson .15
22 Charlie Keller .15
23 George Bamberger .15
24 Eddie Lopat .15
25 Lou Gehrig 2.50
26 Manny Mota .15
27 Steve Stone .15
28 Orlando Cepeda .15
29 Al Bumbry .15
30 Grover Alexander .15
31 Lou Boudreau .15
32 Herb Score .15
33 Harry Walker .15
34 Deron Johnson .15
35 Edd Roush .15
36 Carl Erskine .15
37 Ken Forsch .15
38 Sal Maglie .15
39 Al Rosen .15
40 Casey Stengel .15
41 Cesar Cedeno .15
42 Roy White .15
43 Larry Doby .15
44 Rod Kanehl .15
45 Tris Speaker .40
46 Ralph Garr .15
47 Andre Thornton .15
48 Frankie Crosetti .15
49 Dick Groat .15
50 Honus Wagner .75
51 Rogers Hornsby .40
52 Ken Brett .15
53 Lenny Randle .15
54 Enos Slaughter .15
55 Mel Ott .15
56 Rico Petrocelli .15
57 Walt Dropo .15
58 Bob Grich .15
59 Billy Herman .15
60 Bob Feller .40
61 Davey Johnson .15
62 Don Drysdale .15
63 Larry Sorensen .15
64 Ron Santo .15
65 Eddie Mathews .15
66 Gaylord Perry .15
67 Lee May .15
68 Johnnie LeMaster .15
69 Don Kessinger .15
70 Lefty Grove .15
71 Lou Brock .15
72 Don Cardwell .15
73 Harvey Haddix .15
74 Frank Torre .15
75 Walter Johnson .75
76 Don Newcombe .15
77 Marv Throneberry .15
78 Jim Northrup .15
79 Fritz Peterson .15
80 Ralph Kiner .15
81 Mickey Lolich .15
82 Donn Clendenon .15
83 Pete Vuckovich .15
84 Lefty Gomez .15
85 Monte Irvin .15
86 Rick Ferrell .15
87 Tommy Hutton .15
88 Julio Cruz .15
89 Vida Blue .15
90 Johnny Mize .15
91 Rusty Staub .15
92 Jimmy Piersall .15
93 Bill Mazeroski .15
94 Lee Lacy .15
95 Ernie Banks .40
96 Bobby Doerr .15
97 George Foster .15
98 Eric Soderholm .15
99 Johnny VanderMeer .15
100 Cy Young .75
101 Jimmie Foxx .40
102 Clete Boyer .15
103 Steve Garvey .15
104 Johnny Podres .15
105 Yogi Berra .40
106 Bill Monbouquette .15
107 Milt Pappas .15
108 Dave LaRoche .15
109 Elliott Maddox .15
110 Steve Carlton .15
111 Bud Harrelson .15
112 Mark Littell .15
113 Frank J. Thomas .15
114 Bill Robinson .15
115 Satchel Paige .75
116 John Denny .15
117 Clyde King .15
118 Billy Sample .15
119 Rocky Colavito .15
120 Bob Gibson .15
121 Bert Campaneris .15
122 Mark Fidrych .15
123 Ed Charles .15
124 Jim Lonborg .15
125 Ted Williams 2.50
126 Manny Sanguillen .15
127 Matt Keough .15
128 Vern Ruhle .15
129 Bob Skinner .15
130 Joe Torre .15
131 Ralph Houk .15
132 Gil Hodges .40
133 Ralph Branca .15
134 Christy Mathewson .75
135 Checklist .15

1991 Swell Baseball Greats

The last of three "old-timers" sets issued by Philadelphia Gum Co., this 150-card set was marketed by Impel. Cards are 2-1/2" x 3-1/2" and feature red and yellow borders around color player photos. In the case of some older players, sepia-toned photos are used instead of color. Backs are printed in red and black and include career stats and a few vital statistics.

NM/M
Complete Set (150): 17.50
Common Player: .15
Wax Pack (10): .75
Wax Box (36): 15.00

1 Tommie Agee .15
2 Matty Alou .15
3 Luke Appling .15
4 Richie Ashburn .15
5 Ernie Banks .40
6 Don Baylor .15
7 Buddy Bell .15
8 Yogi Berra .40
9 Joe Black .15
10 Vida Blue .15
11 Bobby Bonds .15
12 Lou Boudreau .15
13 Lou Brock .15
14 Ralph Branca .15
15 Bobby Brown .15
16 Lou Burdette .15
17 Steve Carlton .25
18 Rico Carty .15
19 Jerry Coleman .15
20 Frankie Crosetti .15
21 Julio Cruz .15
22 Alvin Dark .15
23 Doug DeCinces .15
24 Larry Doby .15
25 Bobby Doerr .15
26 Don Drysdale .15
27 Carl Erskine .15
28 Elroy Face .15
29 Rick Ferrell .15
30 Rollie Fingers .15
31 Joe Garagiola .40
32 Steve Garvey .15
33 Bob Gibson .15
34 Mudcat Grant .15
35 Dick Groat .15
36 Jerry Grote .15
37 Toby Harrah .15
38 Bud Harrelson .15
39 Billy Herman .15
40 Ken Holtzman .15
41 Willie Horton .15
42 Ralph Houk .15
43 Al Hrabosky .15
44 Monte Irvin .15
45 Fergie Jenkins .15
46 Davey Johnson .15
47 George Kell .15
48 Charlie Keller .15
49 Harmon Killebrew .25
50 Ralph Kiner .15
51 Clyde King .15
52 Dave Kingman .15
53 Al Kaline .40
54 Clem Labine .15
55 Vern Law .15
56 Mickey Lolich .15
57 Jim Lonborg .15
58 Eddie Lopat .15
59 Sal Maglie .15
60 Bill Mazeroski .25
61 Johnny VanderMeer .15
62 Johnny Mize .15
63 Manny Mota .15
64 Wally Moon .15
65 Rick Monday .15
66 Tom Tresh .15
67 Graig Nettles .15
68 Don Newcombe .15
69 Milt Pappas .15
70 Gaylord Perry .15
71 Rico Petrocelli .15
72 Jimmy Piersall .15
73 Johnny Podres .15
74 Boog Powell .15
75 Bobby Richardson .25
76 Vern Ruhle .15
77 Robin Roberts .15
78 Al Rosen .15
79 Billy Sample .15
80 Manny Sanguillen .15
81 Ron Santo .15
82 Herb Score .15
83 Bobby Shantz .15
84 Enos Slaughter .15
85 Eric Soderholm .15
86 Warren Spahn .15
87 Rusty Staub .15
88 Bobby Thomson .15
89 Marv Throneberry .15
90 Luis Tiant .15
91 Frank Torre .15
92 Joe Torre .25
93 Bill Virdon .15
94 Harry Walker .15
95 Earl Weaver .15
96 Bill White .15
97 Roy White .15
98 Billy Williams .15
99 Dick Williams .15
100 Ted Williams 2.50
101 Gene Woodling .15
102 Hank Aaron 2.50
103 Rod Carew .15
104 Cesar Cedeno .15
105 Orlando Cepeda .15
106 Willie Mays 2.50
107 Tom Seaver .40
108 Carl Yastrzemski .40
109 Clete Boyer .15
110 Bert Campaneris .15
111 Walt Dropo .15
112 George Foster .15
113 Phil Garner .15
114 Harvey Kuenn .15
115 Don Kessinger .15
116 Rocky Colavito .15
117 Bobby Murcer .15
118 Mel Parnell .15
119 Ken Reitz .15
120 Earl Wilson .15
121 Wilbur Wood .15
122 Ed Yost .15
123 Jim Bouton .15
124 Babe Ruth 3.50
125 Lou Gehrig 2.50
126 Honus Wagner .75
127 Ty Cobb 1.50
128 Grover C. Alexander .15
129 Lefty Gomez .15
130 Walter Johnson .75
131 Gil Hodges .40
132 Roberto Clemente 3.00
133 Satchel Paige .75
134 Edd Roush .15
135 Cy Young .75
136 Casey Stengel .15
137 Rogers Hornsby .40
138 Dizzy Dean .50
139 Lefty Grove .15
140 Tris Speaker .40
141 Christy Mathewson .75
142 Mickey Cochrane .40
143 Jimmie Foxx .40
144 Mel Ott .15
145 Bob Feller .25
146 Brooks Robinson .40
147 Eddie Mathews .15
148 Pie Traynor .15
149 Thurman Munson .25
150 Checklist .15

2003 Sycuan Casino-Resort Tony Gwynn

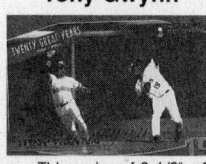

This series of 3-1/2" x 5" cards commemorating the career of Padres icon Tony Gwynn was issued on a one-per-month basis between April-September by a San Diego area tribal entertainment complex. Cards are UV coated and feature silver-foil highlights on front. Posed or action photos are framed in dark green. Backs have a ghosted photo of the player, a few sentences about him and logos of the team and casino.

NM/M
Complete Set (6): 50.00
Common Card: 10.00

1 Tony Gwynn (Twenty Great Years) 10.00
2 Tony Gwynn (Eight Batting Titles) 10.00
3 Tony Gwynn (Five Gold Gloves) 10.00
4 Tony Gwynn (3,000th Hit) 10.00
5 Tony Gwynn (Hitting Machine) 10.00
6 Tony Gwynn (Last At Bat.) 10.00

T

1988 T & M Sports Umpires

The first umpires to be featured on baseball cards since the 1955 Bowman set are the arbiters included in this boxed set issued T & M and licensed by the umps' union. Cards have posed photos framed in red (American League) green (National League) with a black border on front. The correct league logo is in a lower corner. The umpire's uniform number and name are in white at bottom. The back has a blue background with personal data, career summary, service record and card number, along with licensor logos.

NM/M
Complete Set (64): 5.00
Common Card: .15

1 Doug Harvey .15
2 Lee Weyer .15
3 Billy Williams .15
4 John Kibler .15
5 Bob Engel .15
6 Harry Wendelstedt .15
7 Larry Barnett .15
8 Don Denkinger .15
9 Dave Phillips .15
10 Larry McCoy .15
11 Bruce Froemming .15
12 John McSherry .15
13 Jim Evans .15
14 Frank Pulli .15
15 Joe Brinkman .15
16 Terry Tata .15
17 Paul Runge .15
18 Dutch Rennert .15
19 Nick Bremigan .15
20 Jim McKean .15
21 Terry Cooney .15
22 Rich Garcia .15
23 Dale Ford .15
24 Al Clark .15
25 Greg Koso .15
26 Jim Quick .15
27 Ed Montague .15
28 Jerry Crawford .15
29 Steve Palermo .15
30 Durwood Merrill .15
31 Ken Kaiser .15
32 Vic Voltaggio .15
33 Mike Reilly .15
34 Eric Gregg .15
35 Ted Hendry .15
36 Joe West .15
37 Dave Pallone .15
38 Fred Brocklander .15
39 John Shulock .15
40 Derryl Cousins .15
41 Charlie Williams .15
42 Rocky Roe .15
43 Randy Marsh .15
44 Bob Davidson .15
45 Drew Coble .15
46 Tim McClelland .15
47 Dan Morrison .15
48 Rick Reed .15
49 Steve Rippley .15
50 John Hirschbeck .15
51 Mark Johnson .15
52 Gerry Davis .15
53 Dana DeMuth .15
54 Larry Young .15
55 Tim Welke .15
56 Greg Bonin .15
57 Tom Hallion .15
58 Dale Scott .15
59 Tim Tschida .15
60 Dick Stello .15
61 1987 All-Star Game (Derryl Cousins, Bob Davidson, Don Denkinger, Dick Stello, Vic Voltaggio, Joe West) .15
62 1987 World Series (Ken Kaiser, Greg Kosc, John McSherry, Dave Phillips, Terry Tata, Lee Weyer) .15
63 Jocko Conlan .30
64 Checklist .15

1989 T & M Sports Senior League

The 120-card 1989-90 T&M Sports Senior League set features a full-color photo of the player on the front on a borderless card. A red stripe separates the photo from the black bottom with the player's name, team logo and position. The cards are printed on heavy, white cardboard stock and sold as a boxed set. The backs have a red border across the top and bio and career notes, along with a summary of the player's career. Included in the set are eight static-cling puzzle pieces which, when put together, show a drawing of a prominent player from each team.

NM/M
Complete Set (120): 4.00
Common Player: .05

1 Curt Flood (Commissioner) .10
2 Willie Aikens .05
3 Gary Allenson .05
4 Stan Bahnsen .05
5 Alan Bannister .05
6 Juan Beniquez .05
7 Jim Bibby .05
8 Paul Blair .05
9 Vida Blue .10
10 Bobby Bonds .10
11 Pedro Borbon .05
12 Clete Boyer .05
13 Gates Brown .05
14 Al Bumbry .05
15 Sal Butera .05
16 Bert Campaneris .10
17 Bill Campbell .05
18 Bernie Carbo .05
19 Dave Cash .05
20 Cesar Cedeno .05
21 Gene Clines .05
22 Dave Collins .05
23 Cecil Cooper .05
24 Doug Corbett .05
25 Al Cowens .05
26 Jose Cruz .05
27 Mike Cuellar .05
28 Pat Dobson .05
29 Dick Drago .05
30 Dan Driessen .05
31 Jamie Easterly .05
32 Juan Eichelberger .05
33 Dock Ellis .05
34 Ed Figueroa .05
35 Rollie Fingers .50
36 George Foster .15
37 Oscar Gamble .05
38 Wayne Garland .05
39 Wayne Garrett .05
40 Ross Grimsley .05
41 Jerry Grote .05
42 Johnny Grubb .05
43 Mario Guerrero .05
44 Toby Harrah .05
45 Steve Henderson .05
46 George Hendrick .05
47 Butch Hobson .05
48 Roy Howell .05
49 Al Hrabosky .05
50 Clint Hurdle .05
51 Garth Iorg .05
52 Tim Ireland .05
53 Grant Jackson .05
54 Ron Jackson .05
55 Ferguson Jenkins .50
56 Odell Jones .05
57 Mike Kekich .05
58 Steve Kemp .05
59 Dave Kingman .10
60 Bruce Kison .05
61 Lee Lacy .05
62 Rafael Landestoy .05
63 Ken Landreaux .05
64 Tito Landrum .05
65 Dave LaRoche .05
66 Bill Lee .05
67 Ron LeFlore .05
68 Dennis Leonard .05
69 Bill Madlock .10
70 Mickey Mahler .05
71 Rick Manning .05
72 Tippy Martinez .05
73 Jon Matlack .05
74 Bake McBride .05
75 Steve McCarty .05
76 Hal McRae .10
77 Dan Meyer .05
78 Felix Millan .05
79 Paul Mirabella .05
80 Omar Moreno .05
81 Jim Morrison .05
82 Graig Nettles .05
83 Al Oliver .10
84 Amos Otis .05
85 Tom Paciorek .05
86 Lowell Plamer .05
87 Pat Putnam .05
88 Lenny Randle .05
89 Ken Reitz .05
90 Gene Richards .05
91 Mickey Rivers .05
92 Leon Roberts .05
93 Joe Sambito .05
94 Rodney Scott .05
95 Bob Shirley .05
96 Jim Slaton .05
97 Elias Sosa .05
98 Fred Stanley .05
99 Bill Stein .05
100 Rennie Stennett .05
101 Sammy Stewart .05
102 Tim Stoddard .05
103 Champ Summers .05
104 Derrell Thomas .05
105 Luis Tiant .10
106 Bobby Tolan .05
107 Bill Travers .05
108 Tom Underwood .05
109 Rick Waits .05
110 Ron Washington .05
111 U.L. Washington .05
112 Earl Weaver .25
113 Jerry White .05
114 Milt Wilcox .05
115 Dick Williams .05
116 Walt Williams .05
117 Rick Wise .05
118 Favorite Suns (Luis Tiant, Cesar Cedeno) .05
119 Home Run Legends (George Foster, Bobby Bonds) .05
120 Sunshine Skippers (Earl Weaver, Dick Williams) .25

1989 T & M Sports Umpires

A second edition of umpires' cards from T & M was also sold as a boxed set. Fronts of the 2-1/2" x 3-1/2" cards have color photos which are borderless at top and sides. At bottom is a strip with the ump's name and uniform number at right and league logo at left. Backs have personal data and a career summary, along with logos of MLB and the Umpires' Association.

LARRY McCOY 10

		NM/M
Complete Set (63):		7.50
Common Card:		.15
1	Doug Harvey	.25
2	John Kibler	.15
3	Bob Engel	.15
4	Harry Wendelstedt	.15
5	Larry Barnett	.15
6	Don Denkinger	.15
7	Dave Phillips	.15
8	Larry McCoy	.15
9	Bruce Froemming	.15
10	John McSherry	.20
11	Jim Evans	.15
12	Frank Pulli	.15
13	Joe Brinkman	.15
14	Terry Tata	.15
15	Nick Bremigan	.15
16	Jim McKean	.15
17	Paul Runge	.15
18	Dutch Rennert	.15
19	Terry Cooney	.15
20	Rich Garcia	.15
21	Dale Ford	.15
22	Al Clark	.15
23	Greg Kosc	.15
24	Jim Quick	.15
25	Ed Montague	.15
26	Jerry Crawford	.15
27	Steve Palermo	.35
28	Durwood Merrill	.15
29	Ken Kaiser	.20
30	Vic Voltaggio	.15
31	Mike Reilly	.15
32	Eric Gregg	.25
33	Ted Hendry	.15
34	Joe West	.15
35	Dave Pallone	.25
36	Fred Brocklander	.15
37	John Shulock	.15
38	Derryl Cousins	.15
39	Charlie Williams	.15
40	Rocky Roe	.15
41	Randy Marsh	.15
42	Bob Davidson	.15
43	Drew Coble	.15
44	Tim McClelland	.15
45	Dan Morrison	.15
46	Rick Reed	.15
47	Steve Rippley	.15
48	John Hirschbeck	.15
49	Mark Johnson	.15
50	Gerry Davis	.15
51	Dana DeMuth	.15
52	Larry Young	.15
53	Tim Welke	.15
54	Greg Bonin	.15
55	Tom Hallion	.15
56	Dale Scott	.15
57	Tim Tschida	.15
58	Gary Darling	.15
59	Mark Hirschbeck	.15
60	All-Star Crew	.15
61	World Series Crew	.15
62	Lee Weyer	.15
63	Tom Connolly, Bill Klem	.25

1990 T & M Sports Umpires

DUTCH RENNERT 16

Puzzle piece inserts and a send-away premium card offer are featured in the 1990 umpires set. Card fronts have action photos of the arbiters with league insignia in a home plate-shaped frame in a lower corner. Above the photo, the umpire's name and uniform number are printed in a banner. Backs have biographical data, a baseball rules trivia question and the logos of MLB and the Major League Umpires Association. Card #71, Hall of Fame umpire Al Barlick, was only available by sending in the four puzzle pieces overprinted with the National League logo.

		NM/M
Complete Set		
(70, no Barlick):		6.00
Common Card:		.10
1	Doug Harvey	.10
2	John Kibler	.10
3	Bob Engel	.10
4	Harry Wendelstedt	.10
5	Larry Barnett	.10
6	Don Denkinger	.10
7	Dave Phillips	.10
8	Larry McCoy	.10
9	Bruce Froemming	.10
10	John McSherry	.10
11	Jim Evans	.10
12	Frank Pulli	.10
13	Joe Brinkman	.10
14	Terry Tata	.10
15	Jim McKean	.10
16	Dutch Rennert	.10
17	Paul Runge	.10
18	Terry Cooney	.10
19	Rich Garcia	.10
20	Dale Ford	.10
21	Al Clark	.10
22	Greg Kosc	.10
23	Jim Quick	.10
24	Eddie Montague	.10
25	Jerry Crawford	.10
26	Steve Palermo	.10
27	Durwood Merrill	.10
28	Ken Kaiser	.10
29	Vic Voltaggio	.10
30	Mike Reilly	.10
31	Eric Gregg	.10
32	Ted Hendry	.10
33	Joe West	.10
34	Fred Brocklander	.10
35	John Shulock	.10
36	Derryl Cousins	.10
37	Charlie Williams	.10
38	Rocky Roe	.10
39	Randy Marsh	.10
40	Bob Davidson	.10
41	Drew Coble	.10
42	Tim McClelland	.10
43	Dan Morrison	.10
44	Rick Reed	.10
45	Steve Rippley	.10
46	John Hirschbeck	.10
47	Mark Johnson	.10
48	Gerry Davis	.10
49	Dana DeMuth	.10
50	Larry Young	.10
51	Tim Welke	.10
52	Greg Bonin	.10
53	Tom Hallion	.10
54	Dale Scott	.10
55	Tim Tschida	.10
56	Gary Darling	.10
57	Mark Hirschbeck	.10
58	Jerry Layne	.10
59	Jim Joyce	.10
60	Bill Hohn	.10
61	All-Star Game	.10
62	World Series	.10
63	Nick Bremigan	.10
64	The Runges (Ed Runge, Paul Runge)	.10
65	A. Bartlett Giamatti	.10
66	Puzzle Piece #1	.10
66a	Puzzle Piece #1 (w/N.L. logo on back)	.10
67	Puzzle Piece #2	.10
67a	Puzzle Piece #3 (N.L. Logo)	.10
68	Puzzle Piece #3	.10
68a	Puzzle Piece #3 (N.L. Logo)	.10
69	Puzzle Piece #4	.10
69a	Puzzle piece #4 (N.L. Logo)	.10
70	Checklist	.05
71	Al Barlick	4.00

1990 Target Dodgers

Virtually every player who appeared in the uniform of the Brooklyn or Los Angeles Dodgers between 1890-1990 was included in this 1,100-card issue. Quality of the photo varies wildly from sharp to barely identifiable. Cards measure 2-1/16" x 3" and are perforated on two, three or four sides, depending where they were positioned on the 15-card perforated sheets in

CASEY STENGEL – MGR

TARGET

which the cards were distributed at various Dodgers home games. Player photos are in dark blue and white, bordered in speckled blue. Name and position appear in black in a light blue banner at top. At lower-left is the Dodgers 100th anniversary logo, with the Target stores logo at lower-right. On back the player's name and position reappear at top, with the logos below and the card number in a banner at bottom. Cards were numbered roughly alphabetically, though many are out of order. Some cards have duplicated numbers and there were some numbers skipped in the issue. All back printing is in blue on white. Career major league stats and the years in which the player was with the Dodgers are also noted on back. According to figures released by the team, production was to be about 50,000 sets.

		NM/M
Complete Set (1,103):		150.00
Common Player:		.25
1	Bert Abbey	.25
2	Cal Abrams	.50
3	Hank Aguirre	.25
4	Eddie Ainsmith	.25
5	Ed Albosta	.25
6	Luis Alcaraz	.25
7	Doyle Alexander	.25
8	Dick Allen	2.50
9	Frank Allen	.25
10	Johnny Allen	.25
11	Mel Almada	1.25
12	Walter Alston	1.25
13	Ed Amelung	.25
14	Sandy Amoros	1.25
15	Dave Anderson	.25
16	Ferrell Anderson	.25
17	John Anderson	.25
18	Stan Andrews	.25
19	Bill Antonello	.25
20	Jimmy Archer	.25
21	Bob Aspromonte	.25
22	Rick Auerbach	.25
23	Charlie Babb	.25
24	Johnny Babich	.25
25	Bob Bailey	.25
26	Bob Bailor	.25
27	Dusty Baker	1.25
28	Tom Baker	.25
29	Dave Bancroft	.75
30	Dan Bankhead	.25
31	Jack Banta	.25
32	Jim Barbieri	.25
33	Red Barkley	.25
34	Jesse Barnes	.25
35	Rex Barney	.75
36	Billy Barnie	.25
37	Bob Barrett	.25
38	Jim Baxes	.25
39	Billy Bean	.25
40	Boom Boom Beck	.25
41	Joe Beckwith	.25
42	Hank Behrman	.25
43	Mark Belanger	.25
44	Wayne Belardi	.25
45	Tim Belcher	.25
46	George Bell	.25
47	Ray Benge	.25
48	Moe Berg	4.00
49	Bill Bergen	.25
50	Ray Berres	.25
51	Don Bessent	.25
52	Steve Bilko	.25
53	Jack Billingham	.25
54	Babe Birrer	.25
55	Del Bissonette	.25
56	Joe Black	1.25
57	Lu Blue	.25
58	George Boehler	.25
59	Sammy Bohne	1.50
60	John Boiling	.25
61	Ike Boone	.25
62	Frenchy Bordagaray	.25
63	Ken Boyer	1.25
64	Buzz Boyle	.25
65	Mark Bradley	.25
66	Bobby Bragan	.25
67	Ralph Branca	1.25
68	Ed Brandt	.25
69	Sid Bream	.25
70	Marv Breeding	.25
71	Tom Brennan	.25
72	William Brennan	.25
73	Rube Bressler	.25
74	Ken Brett	.25
75	Jim Brewer	.25
76	Tony Brewer	.25
77	Rocky Bridges	.25
78	Greg Brock	.25
79	Dan Brouthers	.25
80	Eddie Brown	.25
81	Elmer Brown	.25
82	Lindsay Brown	.25
83	Lloyd Brown	.25
84	Mace Brown	.25
85	Tommy Brown	.25
86	Pete Browning	.25
87	Ralph Bryant	.25
88	Jim Bucher	.25
89	Bill Buckner	1.25
90	Jim Bunning	1.25
91	Jack Burdock	.25
92	Glenn Burke	.25
93	Buster Burrell	.25
94	Larry Burright	.25
95	Doc Bushong	.25
96	Max Butcher	.25
97	Johnny Butler	.25
98	Enos Cabell	.25
99	Leon Cadore	.25
100	Bruce Caldwell	.25
101	Dick Calmus	.25
102	Dolf Camilli	.25
103	Doug Camilli	.25
104	Roy Campanella	9.00
105	Al Campanis	.25
106	Jim Campanis	.25
107A	Leo Callahan	.25
107B	Gilly Campbell	.25
108	Jimmy Canavan	.25
109	Chris Cannizzaro	.25
110	Guy Cantrell	.25
111	Ben Cantwell	.25
112	Andy Carey	.25
113	Max Carey	.25
114	Tex Carleton	.25
115	Ownie Carroll	.25
116	Bob Caruthers	.25
117	Doc Casey	.25
118	Hugh Casey	.25
119	Bobby Castillo	.25
120	Cesar Cedeno	.25
121	Ron Cey	1.25
122	Ed Chandler	.25
123	Ben Chapman	.25
124	Larry Cheney	.25
125	Bob Chipman	.25
126	Chuck Churn	.25
127	Gino Cimoli	.25
128	Moose Clabaugh	.25
129	Bud Clancy	.25
130	Bob Clark	.25
131	Watty Clark	.25
132	Alta Cohen	.25
133	Rocky Colavito	5.00
134	Jackie Collum	.25
135	Chuck Connors	5.00
136	Jack Coombs	.25
137	Johnny Cooney	.25
138	Tommy Corcoran	.25
139	Pop Corkhill	.25
140	John Corriden	.25
141	Pete Coscarart	.25
142	Wes Covington	.25
143	Billy Cox	1.25
144	Roger Craig	.75
145	Cannonball Crane	.25
146	Willie Crawford	.25
147	Tim Crews	.25
148	John Cronin	.25
149	Lave Cross	.25
150	Bill Crouch	.25
151	Don Crow	.25
152	Henry Cruz	.25
153	Tony Cuccinello	.25
154	Roy Cullenbine	.25
155	George Culver	.25
156	Nick Cullop	.25
157	George Cutshaw	.25
158	Kiki Cuyler	.25
159	Bill Dahlen	.25
160	Babe Dahlgren	.25
161	Jack Dalton	.25
162	Tom Daly	.25
163	Cliff Dapper	.25
164	Bob Darnell	.25
165	Bobby Darwin	.25
166	Jake Daubert	.25
167	Vic Davalillo	.25
168	Curt Davis	.25
169	Mike Davis	.25
170	Ron Davis	.25
171	Tommy Davis	1.25
172	Willie Davis	1.25
173	Pea Ridge Day	.25
174	Tommy Dean	.25
175	Hank DeBerry	.25
176	Art Decatur	.25
177	Raoul Dedeaux	.25
178	Ivan DeJesus	.25
179	Don Demeter	.25
180	Gene DeMontreville	.25
181	Rick Dempsey	.25
182	Eddie Dent	.25
183	Mike Devereaux	.25
184	Carlos Diaz	.25
185	Dick Dietz	.25
186	Pop Dillon	.25
187	Bill Doak	.25
188	John Dobbs	.25
189	George Dockins	.25
190	Cozy Dolan	.25
191	Patsy Donovan	.25
192	Wild Bill Donovan	.25
193	Mickey Doolan	.25
194	Jack Doscher	.25
195	Phil Douglas	.25
196	Snooks Dowd	.25
197	Al Downing	.25
198	Red Downs	.25
199	Jack Doyle	.25
200	Solly Drake	.25
201	Tom Drake	.25
202	Chuck Dressen	.75
203	Don Drysdale	5.00
204	Clise Dudley	.25
205	Mariano Duncan	.25
206	Jack Dunn	.25
207	Bull Durham	.25
208	Leo Durocher	1.25
209	Billy Earle	.25
210	George Earnshaw	.25
211	Ox Eckhardt	.25
212	Bruce Edwards	.25
213	Hank Edwards	.25
214	Dick W. Egan	.25
215	Harry Eisenstat	.25
216	Kid Elberfeld	.25
217	Jumbo Elliot	.25
218	Don Elston	.25
219	Gil English	.25
220	Johnny Enzmann	.25
221	Al Epperly	.25
222	Carl Erskine	1.25
223	Tex Erwin	.25
224	Cecil Espy	.25
225	Chuck Essegian	.25
226	Dude Esterbrook	.25
227	Red Evans	.25
228	Bunny Fabrique	.25
229	Jim Fairey	.25
230	Ron Fairly	1.25
231	George Fallon	.25
232	Turk Farrell	.25
233	Duke Farrel	.25
234	Jim Faulkner	.25
235	Alex Ferguson	.25
236	Joe Ferguson	.25
237	Chico Fernandez	.25
238	Sid Fernandez	.25
239	Al Ferrara	.25
240	Wes Ferrell	.25
241	Lou Fette	.25
242	Chick Fewster	.25
243	Jack Fimple	.25
244	Neal "Mickey" Finn	.25
245	Bob Fisher	.25
246	Freddie Fitzsimmons	.25
247	Tim Flood	.25
248	Jake Flowers	.25
249	Hod Ford	.25
250	Terry Forster	.75
251	Alan Foster	.25
252	Jack Fournier	.25
253	Dave Foutz	.25
254	Art Fowler	.25
255	Fred Frankhouse	.25
256	Herman Franks	.25
257	Johnny Frederick	.25
258	Larry French	.25
259	Lonny Frey	.25
260	Pepe Frias	.25
261	Charlie Fuchs	.25
262	Carl Furillo	4.00
263	Len Gabrielson	.25
264	Augie Galan	.25
265	Joe Gallagher	.25
266	Phil Gallivan	.25
267	Balvino Galvez	.25
268	Mike Garman	.25
269	Phil Garner	.25
270	Steve Garvey	2.50
271	Ned Garvin	.25
272	Hank Gastright	.25
273	Sid Gautreaux	.25
274	Jim Gentile	.25
275	Greek George	.25
276	Ben Geraghty	.25
277	Gus Getz	.25
278	Bob Giallombardo	.25
279	Kirk Gibson	1.25
280	Charlie Gilbert	.25
281	Jim Gilliam	1.25
282	Al Gionfriddo	.50
283	Tony Giuliani	.25
284	Al Glossop	.25
285	John Gochnaur	.25
286	Jim Golden	.25
287	Dave Goltz	.25
288	Jose Gonzalez	.25
289	Johnny Gooch	.25
290	Ed Goodson	.25
291	Bill Grabarkewitz	.25
292	Jack Graham	.25
293	Mudcat Grant	.25
294	Dick Gray	.25
295	Kent Greenfield	.25
296	Hal Gregg	.25
297	Alfredo Griffin	.25
298	Mike Griffin	.25
299	Derrell Griffith	.25
300	Tommy Griffith	.25
301	Burleigh Grimes	.25
302	Lee Grissom	.25
303	Jerry Grote	.25
304	Pedro Guerrero	.75
305	Brad Gulden	.25
306	Ad Gumbert	.25
307	Chris Gwynn	.25
308	Bert Haas	.25
309	John Hale	.25
310	Tom Haller	.25
311	Bill Hallman	.25
312	Jeff Hamilton	.25
313	Luke Hamlin	.25
314	Ned Hanlon	.25
315	Gerald Hannahs	.25
316	Charlie Hargreaves	.25
317	Tim Harkness	.25
318	Harry Harper	.25
319	Joe Harris	.25
320	Lenny Harris	.25
321	Bill F. Hart	.25
322	Buddy Hassett	.25
323	Mickey Hatcher	.25
324	Joe Hatten	.25
325	Phil Haugstad	.25
326	Brad Havens	.25
327	Ray Hayworth	.25
328	Ed Head	.25
329	Danny Heep	.25
330	Fred Heimach	.25
331	Harvey Hendrick	.25
332	Weldon Henley	.25
333	Butch Henline	.25
334	Dutch Henry	.25
335	Roy Henshaw	.25
336	Babe Herman	.75
337	Billy Herman	.75
338	Gene Hermanski	.25
339	Enzo Hernandez	.25
340	Art Herring	.25
341	Orel Hershiser	1.25
342	Dave J. Hickman	.25
343	Jim Hickman	.25
344	Kirby Higbe	.25
345	Andy High	.25
346	George Hildebrand	.25
347	Hunkey Hines	.25
348	Don Hoak	.75
349	Oris Hockett	.25
350	Gil Hodges	5.00
351	Glenn Hoffman	.25
352	Al Hollingsworth	.25
353	Tommy Holmes	.25
354	Brian Holton	.25
355	Rick Honeycutt	.25
356	Burt Hooton	.25
357	Gail Hopkins	.25
358	Johnny Hopp	.25
359	Charlie Hough	.75
360	Frank Howard	1.25
361	Steve Howe	.75
362	Dixie Howell	.25
363	Harry Howell	.25
364	Jay Howell	.25
365	Ken Howell	.25
366	Waite Hoyt	.25
367	Johnny Hudson	.25
368	Jim J. Hughes	.25
369	Jim R. Hughes	.25
370	Mickey Hughes	.25
371	John Hummel	.25
372	Ron Hunt	.25
373	Willard Hunter	.25
374	Ira Hutchinson	.25
375	Tom Hutton	.25
376	Charlie Irwin	.25
377	Fred Jacklitsch	.25
378	Randy Jackson	.25
379	Merwin Jacobson	.25
380	Cleo James	.25
381	Hal Janvrin	.25
382	Roy Jarvis	.25
383	George Jeffcoat	.25
384	Jack Jenkins	.25
385	Hughie Jennings	.25
386	Tommy John	1.25
387	Lou Johnson	.25
388	Fred Ivy Johnston	.25
389	Jimmy Johnston	.25
390	Jay Johnstone	.75
391	Fielder Jones	.25
392	Oscar Jones	.25
393	Tim Jordan	.25
394	Spider Jorgensen	.25
395	Von Joshua	.25
396	Bill Joyce	.25
397	Joe Judge	.25
398	Alex Kampouris	.25
399	Willie Keeler	.25
400	Mike Kekich	.25
401	John Kelleher	.25
402	Frank Kellert	.25
403	Joe Kelley	.25
404	George Kelly	.25
405	Bob Kennedy	.25
406	Brickyard Kennedy	.25
407	John Kennedy	.25
408	Newt Kimball	.25
409	Clyde King	.25
410	Enos Kirkpatrick	.25
411	Franky Kitson	.25
412	Johnny Klippstein	.25
413	Elmer Klumpp	.25
414	Len Koenecke	.25

No.	Player	Price
416	Ed Konetchy	.25
417	Andy Kosco	.25
418	Sandy Koufax	15.00
419	Ernie Koy	.25
420	Charlie Kress	.25
421	Bill Krueger	.25
422	Ernie Krueger	.25
423	Clem Labine	.75
424	Candy LaChance	.25
425	Lee Lacy	.25
426	Lerrin LaGrow	.25
427	Bill Lamar	.25
428	Wayne LaMaster	.25
429	Ray Lamb	.25
430	Rafael Landestoy	.25
431	Ken Landreaux	.25
432	Tito Landrum	.25
433	Norm Larker	.75
434	Lyn Lary	.25
435	Tom Lasorda	1.25
436	Cookie Lavagetto	.25
437	Rudy Law	.25
438	Tony Lazzeri	.25
439	Tim Leary	.25
440	Bob Lee	.25
441	Hall Lee	.25
442	Leron Lee	.25
443	Jim Lefebvre	.25
444	Ken Lehman	.25
445	Don LeJohn	.25
446	Steve Lembo	.25
447	Ed Lennox	.25
448	Dutch Leonard	.25
449	Jeffery Leonard	.25
450	Sam Leslie	.25
451	Dennis Lewallyn	.25
452	Bob Lillis	.25
453	Jim Lindsey	.25
454	Fred Lindstrom	.25
455	Billy Loes	.50
456	Bob Logan	.25
457	Bill Lohrman	.25
459	Vic Lombardi	.25
460	Davey Lopes	.75
461	Al Lopez	.25
462	Ray Lucas	.25
464	Harry Lumley	.25
465	Don Lund	.25
466	Dolf Luque	.25
467	Jim Lyttle	.25
468	Max Macon	.25
469	Bill Madlock	.75
470	Lee Magee	.25
471	Sal Maglie	.75
472	George Magoon	.25
473	Duster Mails	.25
474	Candy Maldonado	.25
475	Tony Malinosky	.25
476	Lew Malone	.25
477	Al Mamaux	.25
478	Gus Mancuso	.25
479	Charlie Manuel	.25
480	Heinie Manush	.25
481	Rabbit Maranville	.25
482	Juan Marichal	2.50
483	Rube Marquard	.25
484	Bill Marriott	.25
485	Buck Marrow	.25
486	Mike A. Marshall	.75
487	Mike G. Marshall	.75
488	Morrie Martin	.25
489	Ramon Martinez	1.25
490	Teddy Martinez	.25
491	Earl Mattingly	.25
492	Len Matuszek	.25
493	Gene Mauch	.25
494	Al Maul	.25
495	Carmen Mauro	.25
496	Alvin McBean	.25
497	Bill McCarren	.25
498	Jack McCarthy	.25
499	Tommy McCarthy	.25
500	Lew McCarty	.25
501	Mike J. McCormick	.25
502	Judge McCreedie	.25
503	Tom McCreery	.25
504	Danny McDevitt	.25
505	Chappie McFarland	.25
506	Joe McGinnity	.25
507	Bob McGraw	.25
508	Deacon McGuire	.25
509	Bill McGunnigle	.25
510	Harry McIntyre	.25
511	Cal McLish	.25
512	Ken McMullen	.25
513	Dough McWeeny	.25
514	Joe Medwick	.25
515	Rube Melton	.25
516	Fred Merkle	.25
517	Orlando Mercado	.25
518	Andy Messersmith	.25
519	Irish Meusel	.25
520	Benny Meyer	.25
521	Russ Meyer	.25
522	Chief Meyers	.25
523	Gene Michael	.25
524	Pete Mikkelsen	.25
525	Eddie Miksis	.25
526	Johnny Miljus	.25
527	Bob Miller	.25
528	Larry Miller	.25
529	Otto Miller	.25
530	Ralph Miller	.25
531	Walt Miller	.25
532	Wally Millies	.25
533	Bob Milliken	.25
534	Buster Mills	.25
535	Paul Minner	.25
536	Bobby Mitchell	.25
537	Clarence Mitchell	.25
538	Dale Mitchell	.25
539	Fred Mitchell	.25
540	Johnny Mitchell	.25
541	Joe Moeller	.25
542	Rick Monday	.75
543	Wally Moon	.75
544	Cy Moore	.25
545	Dee Moore	.25
546	Eddie Moore	.25
547	Gene Moore	.25
548	Randy Moore	.25
549	Ray Moore	.25
550	Jose Morales	.25
551	Bobby Morgan	.25
552	Eddie Morgan	.25
553	Mike Morgan	.25
554	Johnny Morrison	.25
555	Walt Moryn	.25
556	Ray Moss	.25
557	Manny Mota	.75
558	Joe Mulvey	.25
559	Van Lingle Mungo	.25
560	Les Munns	.25
561	Mike Munoz	.25
562	Simmy Murch	.25
563	Eddie Murray	4.00
564	Hy Myers	.25
565	Sam Nahem	.25
566	Earl Naylor	.25
567	Charlie Neal	.75
568	Ron Negray	.25
569	Bernie Neis	.25
570	Rocky Nelson	.25
571	Dick Nen	.25
572	Don Newcombe	2.50
573	Bobo Newsom	.25
574	Doc Newton	.25
575	Tom Niedenfuer	.25
576	Otho Nitcholas	.25
577	Al Nixon	.25
578	Jerry Nops	.25
579	Irv Noren	.25
580	Fred Norman	.25
581	Bill North	.25
582	Johnny Oates	.25
583	Bob O'Brien	.25
584	John O'Brien	.25
585	Lefty O'Doul	.25
586	Joe Oeschger	.25
587	Al Oliver	.75
588	Nate Oliver	.25
589	Luis Olmo	.25
590	Ivy Olson	.25
591	Mickey O'Neil	.25
592	Joe Orengo	.25
593	Jesse Orosco	.25
594	Frank O'Rourke	.25
595	Jorge Orta	.25
596	Phil Ortega	.25
597	Claude Osteen	.25
598	Fritz Ostermueller	.25
599	Mickey Owen	.25
600	Tom Paciorek	.25
601	Don Padgett	.25
602	Andy Pafko	.75
603	Erv Palica	.25
604	Ed Palmquist	.25
605	Wes Parker	.25
606	Jay Partridge	.25
607	Camilo Pascual	.25
608	Kevin Pasley	.25
609	Dave Patterson	.25
610	Harley Payne	.25
611	Johnny Peacock	.25
612	Hal Peck	.25
613	Stu Pederson	.25
614	Alejandro Pena	.25
615	Jose Pena	.25
616	Jack Perconte	.25
617	Charlie Perkins	.25
618	Ron Perranoski	.50
619	Jim Peterson	.25
620	Jesse Petty	.25
621	Jeff Pfeffer	.25
622	Babe Phelps	.25
623	Val Picinich	.25
624	Joe Pignatano	.25
625	George Pinckney	.25
626	Ed Pipgras	.25
627	Bud Podbielan	.25
628	Johnny Podres	.75
629	Boots Poffenberger	.25
630	Nick Polly	.25
631	Paul Popovich	.25
632	Bill Posedel	.25
633	Boog Powell	.50
634	Dennis Powell	.25
635	Paul Ray Powell	.25
636	Ted Power	.25
637	Tot Pressnell	.25
638	John Purdin	.25
639	Jack Quinn	.25
640	Marv Rackley	.25
641	Jack Radtke	.25
642	Pat Ragan	.25
643	Ed Rakow	.25
644	Bob Ramazzotti	.25
645	Willie Ramsdell	.25
646	Mike James Ramsey	.25
647	Mike Jeffery Ramsey	.25
648	Willie Randolph	.25
649	Doug Rau	.25
650	Lance Rautzhan	.25
651	Howie Reed	.25
652	Pee Wee Reese	9.00
653	Phil Regan	.25
654	Bill Reidy	.25
655	Bobby Reis	.25
656	Pete Reiser	.75
657	Rip Repulski	.25
658	Ed Reulbach	.25
659	Jerry Reuss	.50
660	R.J. Reynolds	.25
661	Billy Rhiel	.25
662	Rick Rhoden	.25
663	Paul Richards	.25
664	Danny Richardson	.25
665	Pete Richert	.25
666	Harry Riconda	.25
667	Joe Riggert	.25
668	Lew Riggs	.25
669	Jimmy Ripple	.25
670	Lou Ritter	.25
671	German Rivera	.25
672	Johnny Rizzo	.25
673	Jim Roberts	.25
674	Earl Robinson	.25
675	Frank Robinson	5.00
676	Jackie Robinson	15.00
677a	Wilbert Robinson	.25
677b	Sergio Robles	.25
678	Rich Rodas	.25
679	Ellie Rodriguez	.25
680	Preacher Roe	.75
681	Ed Roebuck	.25
682	Ron Roenicke	.25
683	Oscar Roettger	.25
684	Lee Rogers	.25
685	Packy Rogers	.25
686	Stan Rojek	.25
687	Vicente Romo	.25
688	Johnny Roseboro	.75
689	Goody Rosen	.25
690	Don Ross	.25
691	Ken Rowe	.25
692	Schoolboy Rowe	.25
693	Luther Roy	.25
694	Jerry Royster	.50
695	Nap Rucker	.25
696	Dutch Ruether	.25
697	Bill Russell	.75
698	Jim Russell	.25
699	John Russell	.25
700	Johnny Rutherford	.25
701	John Ryan	.25
702	Rosy Ryan	.25
703	Mike Sandlock	.25
704	Ted Savage	.25
705	Dave Sax	.25
706	Steve Sax	.75
707	Bill Sayles	.25
708	Bill Schardt	.25
709	Johnny Schmitz	.25
710	Dick Schofield	.25
711	Howie Schultz	.25
712	Ferdie Schupp	.25
713	Mike Scioscia	.75
714	Dick Scott	.25
715	Tom Seats	.25
716	Jimmy Sebring	.25
717	Larry See	.25
718	Dave Sells	.25
719	Greg Shanahan	.25
720	Mike Sharperson	.25
721	Joe Shaute	.25
722	Merv Shea	.25
723	Jimmy Sheckard	.25
724	Jack Sheehan	.25
725	John Shelby	.25
726	Vince Sherlock	.25
727	Larry Sherry	.25
728	Norm Sherry	.75
729	Bill Shindle	.25
730	Craig Shipley	.25
731	Bart Shirley	.25
732	Steve Shirley	.25
733	Burt Shotton	.25
734	George Shuba	.50
735	Dick Siebert	.25
736	Joe Simpson	.25
737	Duke Sims	.25
738	Bill Singer	.25
739	Fred Sington	.25
740	Ted Sizemore	.25
741	Frank Skaff	.25
742	Bill Skowron	1.25
743	Gordon Slade	.25
744	Dwain Lefty Sloat	.25
745	Charley Smith	.25
746	Dick Smith	.25
747	George Smith	.25
748	Germany Smith	.25
749	Jack Smith	.25
750	Reggie Smith	.75
751	Sherry Smith	.25
752	Harry Smythe	.25
753	Duke Snider	9.00
754	Eddie Solomon	.25
755	Elias Sosa	.25
756	Daryl Spencer	.25
757	Roy Spencer	.25
758	Karl Spooner	.50
759	Eddie Stack	.25
760	Tuck Stainback	.25
761	George Stallings	.25
762	Jerry Standaert	.25
763	Don Stanhouse	.25
764	Eddie Stanky	.25
765	Dolly Stark	.25
766	Jigger Statz	.25
767	Casey Stengel	1.25
768	Jerry Stephenson	.25
769	Ed Stevens	.25
770	Dave Stewart	.75
771	Stuffy Stewart	.25
772	Bob Stinson	.25
773	Milt Stock	.25
774	Harry Stovey	.25
775	Mike Strahler	.25
776	Sammy Strang	.25
777	Elmer Stricklett	.25
778	Joe Stripp	.25
779	Dick Stuart	.50
780	Franklin Stubbs	.25
781	Bill Sudakis	.25
782	Clyde Sukeforth	.25
783	Billy Sullivan	.25
784	Tom Sunkel	.25
785	Rick Sutcliffe	.25
786	Don Sutton	4.00
787	Bill Swift	.25
788	Vito Tamulis	.25
789	Danny Taylor	.25
790	Harry Taylor	.25
791	Zack Taylor	.25
792	Chuck Templeton	.25
793	Wayne Terwilliger	.25
794	Derrel Thomas	.25
795	Fay Thomas	.25
796	Gary Thomasson	.25
797	Don Thompson	.25
798	Fresco Thompson	.25
799	Tim Thompson	.25
800	Hank Thormahlen	.25
801	Sloppy Thurston	.25
802	Cotton Tierney	.25
803	Al Todd	.25
804	Bert Tooley	.25
805	Jeff Torborg	.25
806	Dick Tracewski	.25
807	Nick Tremark	.25
808	Alex Trevino	.25
809	Tommy Tucker	.25
810	John Tudor	.25
811	Mike Vail	.25
812	Rene Valdes (Valdez)	.25
813	Bobby Valentine	.25
814	Fernando Valenzuela	.25
815	Elmer Valo	.25
816	Dazzy Vance	.75
817	Sandy Vance	.25
818	Chris Van Cuyk	.25
819	Ed VandeBerg	.25
820	Arky Vaughan	.25
821	Zoilo Versalles	.25
822	Joe Vosmik	.25
823	Ben Wade	.25
824	Dixie Walker	.25
825	Rube Walker	.50
826	Stan Wall	.25
827	Lee Walls	.25
828	Danny Walton	.25
829	Lloyd Waner	.25
830	Paul Waner	.25
831	Chuck Ward	.25
832	John Monte Ward	.25
833	Preston Ward	.25
834	Jack Warner	.25
835	Tommy Warren	.25
836	Carl Warwick	.25
837	Jimmy Wasdell	.25
838	Ron Washington	.25
839	George Watkins	.25
840	Hank Webb	.25
841	Les Webber	.25
842	Gary Weiss	.25
843	Bob Welch	.75
844	Brad Wellman	.25
845	John Werhas	.25
846	Max West	.25
847	Gus Weyhing	.25
848	Mack Wheat	.25
849	Zack Wheat	.25
850	Ed Wheeler	.25
851	Larry White	.25
852	Myron White	.25
853	Terry Whitfield	.25
854	Dick Whitman	.25
855	Possum Whitted	.25
856	Kemp Wicker	.25
857	Hoyt Wilhelm	.75
858	Kaiser Wilhelm	.25
859	Nick Willhite	.25
860	Dick Williams	.75
861	Reggie Williams	.25
862	Stan Williams	.25
863	Woody Williams	.25
864	Maury Wills	.75
865	Hack Wilson	.75
866	Robert Wilson	.25
867	Gordon Windhorn	.25
868	Jim Winford	.25
869	Lave Winham	.25
870	Tom Winsett	.25
871	Hank Winston	.25
872	Whitey Witt	.25
873	Pete Wojey	.25
874	Tracy Woodson	.25
875	Clarence Wright	.25
876	Glenn Wright	.25
877	Ricky Wright	.25
878	Whit Wyatt	.25
879	Jimmy Wynn	.25
880	Joe Yeager	.25
881	Steve Yeager	.25
882	Matt Young	.25
883	Tom Zachary	.25
884	Pat Zachry	.25
885	Geoff Zahn	.25
886	Don Zimmer	.25
887	Morrie Aderholt	.25
888	Raleigh Aitchison	.25
889	Whitey Alperman	.25
890	Whitey Alperman	.25
891	Orlando Alvarez	.25
892	Pat Ankeman	.25
893	Ed Appleton	.25
894	Doug Baird	.25
895	Lady Baldwin	.25
896	Win Ballou	.25
897	Bob Barr	.25
898	Boyd Bartley	.25
899	Eddie Basinski	.25
900	Erve Beck	.25
901	Ralph Birkofer	.25
903	Joe Bradshaw	.25
904	Bruce Brubaker	.25
905	Oyster Burns	.25
906	John Butler	.25
908	Kid Carsey	.25
909	Pete Cassidy	.25
910	Tom Catterson	.25
911	Glenn Chapman	.25
912	Paul Chervinko	.25
913	George Cisar	.25
914	Wally Clement	.25
915	Bill Collins	.25
916	Chuck Corgan	.25
917	Dick Cox	.25
918	George Crable	.25
919	Sam Crane	.25
920	Cliff Curtis	.25
921	Fats Dantonio	.25
922	Con Daily	.25
923	Jud Daley	.25
924	Jake Daniel	.25
925	Kal Daniels	.25
926	Dan Daub	.25
927	Lindsay Deal	.25
928	Artie Dede	.25
929	Pat Deisel	.25
930	Bert Delmas	.25
931	Rube Dessau	.25
932	Leo Dickerman	.25
933	John Douglas	.25
934	Red Downey	.25
935	Carl Doyle	.25
936	John Duffie	.25
937	Dick Durning	.25
938	Red Durrett	.25
939	Mal Eason	.25
940	Charlie Ebbetts	.75
941	Rube Ehardt	.25
942	Rowdy Elliot	.25
943	Bones Ely	.25
944	Woody English	.25
945	Roy Evans	.25
946	Gus Felix	.25
947	Bill Fischer	.25
948	Jeff Fischer	.25
949	Chauncey Fisher	.25
950	Tom Fitzsimmons	.25
951	Darrin Fletcher	.25
952	Wes Flowers	.25
953	Howard Freigau	.25
954	Nig Fuller	.25
955	John Gaddy	.25
956	Welcome Gaston	.25
957	Frank Gatins	.25
958	Pete Gilbert	.25
959	Wally Wilbert	.25
960	Carden Gillenwater	.25
961	Roy Gleason	.25
962	Harvey Green	.25
963	Nelson Greene	.25
964	John Grim	.25
965	Dan Griner	.25
967	Bill Hall	.25
968	Johnny Hall	.25
970	Pat Hanifin	.25
971	Bill Harris	.25
972	Bill W. Hart	.25
973	Chris Hartje	.25
974	Mike Hartley	.25
975	Gil Hatfield	.25
976	Chris Haughey	.25
977	Hugh Hearne	.25
978	Mike Hechinger	.25
979	Jake Hehl	.25
980	Bob Higgins	.25
981	Still Bill Hill	.25
982	Shawn Hillegas	.25
983	Wally Hood	.25
984	Lefty Hopper	.25
985	Ricky Horton	.25
986	Ed Householder	.25
987	Bill Hubbell	.25
988	Al Humphrey	.25
989	Bernie Hungling	.25
990	George Hunter	.25
991	Pat Hurley	.25
992	Joe Hutcheson	.25
993	Roy Hutson	.25
994	Bert Inks	.25
995	Dutch Jordan	.25
997	Frank Kane	.25
998	Chet Kehn	.25
999	Maury Kent	.25
1000	Tom Kinslow	.25
1001	Fred Kipp	.25
1002	Joe Klugman	.25
1003	Elmer Knetzer	.25
1004	Barney Koch	.25
1005	Jim Korwan	.25
1006	Joe Koukalik	.25
1007	Lou Koupal	.25
1008	Joe Kustus	.25
1009	Frank Lamanske	.25
1010	Tacks Latimer	.25
1011	Bill Leard	.25
1012	Phil Lewis	.25
1013	Mickey Livingston	.25
1014	Dick Loftus	.25
1015	Charlie Loudenslager	.25
1016	Tom Lovett	.25
1017	Charlie Malay	.25
1018	Mal Mallett	.25
1019	Ralph Mauriello	.25
1020	Bill McCabe	.25
1021	Gene McCann	.25
1022	Mike McCormick	.25
1023	Terry McDermott	.25
1024	John McDougal	.25
1025	Pryor McElveen	.25
1026	Dan McGann	.25
1027	Pat McGlothin	.25
1028	Doc McJames	.25
1029	Kit McKenna	.25
1030	Sadie McMahon	.25
1032	Tommy McMillan	.25
1033	Glenn Mickens	.25
1034	Don Miles	.25
1035	Hack Miller	.25
1036	John Miller	.25
1037	Lemmie Miller	.25
1038	George Mohart	.25
1039	Gary Moore	.25
1040	Herbie Moran	.25
1041	Earl Mossor	.25
1042	Glen Moulder	.25
1043	Billy Mullen	.25
1044	Hub Northen	.25
1045	Curly Onis	.25
1046	Tiny Osbourne	.25
1047	Jim Pastorius	.25
1048	Art Parks	.25
1049	Chink Outen	.25
1050	Jimmy Pattison	.25
1051	Norman Pitt	.25
1052	Doc Reisling	.25
1053	Gilberto Reyes	.25
1055	Lou Rochelli	.25
1057	Max Rosenfeld	.25
1058	Andy Rush	.25
1059	Jack Ryan	.25
1060	Jack Savage	.25
1062	Ray Schmandt	.25
1063	Henry Schmidt	.25
1064	Charlie Schmutz	.25
1065	Joe Schultz	.25
1066	Ray Searage	.25
1067	Elmer Sexauer	.25
1068	George Sharrott	.25
1069	Tommy Sheehan	.25
1071	George Shoch	.25
1072	Broadway Aleck Smith	.25
1073	Hap Smith	.25
1074	Red Smith	.25
1075	Tony Smith	.25
1076	Gene Snyder	.25
1077	Denny Sothern	.25
1078	Bill Steele	.25
1080	Farmer Steelman	.25
1081	Dutch Stryker	.25
1082	Tommy Tatum	.25
1084	Adonis Terry	.25
1085	Ray Thomas	.25
1086	George Treadway	.25
1087	Overton Tremper	.25
1088	Ty Tyson	.25
1089	Rube Vickers	.25
1090	Jose Vizcaino	.25
1091	Bull Wagner	.25
1092	Butts Wagner	.25
1093	Rube Ward	.25
1094	John Wetteland	.25
1095	Eddie Wilson	.25
1096	Tex Wilson	.25
1097	Zeke Wrigley	.25
1099	Rube Yarrison	.25
1100	Earl Yingling	.25
1101	Chink Zachary	.25
1102	Lefty Davis	.25
1103	Bob Hall	.25
1104	Darby O'Brien	.25
1105	Larry LeJeune	.25

1989 Taystee Kansas City Royals

PAT TABLER
KANSAS CITY ROYALS

The 1989 Royals are featured on this set of discs distributed by a K.C. area bakery. The 2-3/4" discs have color player photos at center. The team logo has been airbrushed off the caps because the issue was licensed only by the players, and not by Major League Baseball. In the white border is the issuer's logo in red at top, player identification at bottom in a yellow banner and "AL STARS" in blue stars at each side. Backs are printed in blue with player data, 1988 stats and copyright information.

		NM/M
Complete Set (12):		9.00
Common Player:		.50
1	George Brett	4.00
2	Kevin Seitzer	.50
3	Pat Tabler	.50
4	Danny Tartabull	.50
5	Willie Wilson	.75
6	Bo Jackson	1.00
7	Frank White	.50
8	Kurt Stillwell	.50
9	Mark Gubicza	.50
10	Charlie Leibrandt	.50
11	Bret Saberhagen	.75
12	Steve Farr	.50

1981 TCMA The 1960's, Series 2

A second series of cards depicting major and minor league players of the 1960s was produced by TCMA in 1981. The cards continued in the same 2-1/2" x 3-1/2" format as the earlier series. Fronts are unadorned color photos, backs have player identification, data and career summary printed in green on white. The numbering of the cards continues at #294, where the first series concluded, but only about one-third the quantity was produced of this series, compared with the first series.

		NM/M
Complete Set (189):		75.00
Common Player:		.50
294	Fritzie Brickell	.50
295	Craig Anderson	.50
296	Cliff Cook	.50
297	Pumpsie Green	.50
298	Choo Choo Coleman	.50
299	Don Buford	.50
300	Sparky Anderson	1.00
301	John Anderson	.50
302	Ted Beard	.50
303	Mickey Mantle, Roger Maris	15.00
304	Gene Freese	.50
305	Don Wilkinson	.50
306	Walter Alston	1.00
307	George Bamberger	.50
308	Nelson Briles	.50
309	Dave Baldwin	.50
310	Bob Bailey	.50
311	Paul Blair	.50
312	Ken Boswell	.50
313	Sam Bowens	.50
314	Ray Barker	.50
315	Tommie Agee, Gil Hodges	
316	Elmer Valo	.50
317	Ken Walters	.50
318	Joel Horlen	.50
320	Charlie Maxwell	.50
321	Joe Foy	.50
322	Tommie Agee, Cleon Jones, Ron Swoboda	.50
323	Paul Foytack	.50
324	Ron Fairly	.50
325	Wilbur Wood	.50
327	Felix Mantilla	.50
328a	Ed Bouchee	.50
328b	Don Wilson	.50
329	Sandy Valdespino	.50
330	Al Ferrera	.50
331	Jose Tartabull	.50
332*	Dick Kenworthy	.50
333	Don Pavletich	.50
334	Jim Fairey	.50
335	Rico Petrocelli	.50
336	Gary Roggenburk	.50

337	Rick Reichardt	.50
338	Ken McMullen	.50
339	Dooley Womack	.50
340	Joe Moock	.50
341	Lou Brock	1.00
342	Hector Torres	.50
343	Ted Savage	.50
344	Hobie Landrith	.50
345	Ed Lopat	.50
346	Mel Nelson	.50
347	Mickey Lolich	.50
348	Al Lopez	1.00
349	Frederico Olivo	.50
350	Bob Moose	.50
351	Bill McCool	.50
352	Ernie Bowman	.50
353	Tom McCraw	.50
354	Sam Mele	.50
355	Len Boehmer	.50
356	Hank Aaron	9.00
357	Ron Hunt	.50
358	Luis Aparicio	1.00
359	Gene Mauch	.50
360	Barry Moore	.50
361	John Buzhardt	.50
362	Spring Training (St. Louis Cardinals)	.50
363	Duke Snider	3.00
364	Billy Martin	1.00
365	Wes Parker	.50
366	Dick Stuart	.50
367	Glenn Beckert	.50
368	Ollie Brown	.50
369	Stan Bahnsen	.50
370	Lee Bales	.50
371	Johnny Keane	.50
372	Wally Moon	.50
373	Larry Miller	.50
374	Fred Newman	.50
375	John Orsino	.50
376	Joe Pactwa	.50
377	John O'Donoghue	.50
378	Jim Ollom	.50
379	Ray Oyler	.50
380	Ron Nischwitz	.50
381	Ron Paul	.50
382	Yogi Berra, John Blanchard, Roger Maris	2.00
383	Jim McKnight	.50
384	Gene Michael	.50
385	Dave May	.50
386	Tim McCarver	1.00
387	Larry Mason	.50
388	Don Hoak	.50
389	Nate Oliver	.50
390	Phil Ortega	.50
391	Billy Madden	.50
392	John Miller	.50
393	Danny Murtaugh	.50
394	Nelson Mathews	.50
395	Red Schoendienst	1.00
396	Roger Nelson	.50
397	Tom Matchick	.50
398	Dennis Musgraves	.50
399	Tommy Harper	.50
400	Fracis Peters	.50
401	Tony Pierce	.50
402	Billy Williams	1.00
403	Dave Boswell	.50
404	Ray Washburn	.50
405	Al Worthington	.50
406	Jesus Alou	.50
407	Yogi Berra, Gil Hodges, Joe Pignatano, Eddie Yost	1.00
408	Wally Bunker	.50
409	Jim Brenneman	.50
410	Bobby Bragan	.50
411	Cal McLish	.50
412	Curt Blefary	.50
413	Jim Bethke	.50
414	Infield 1964 (St. Louis Cardinals)	
415	Richie Allen	1.00
416	Larry Brown	.50
417	Mike Andrews	.50
418	Don Mossi	.50
419	J.C. Martin	.50
420	Dick Rusteck	.50
421	Elly Rodriguez	.50
422	Casey Stengel	1.00
423	Gil Hodges, Ed Vargo	.50
424	Johnny Briggs	.50
425	Bud Harrelson, Al Weis	.50
426	Doc Edwards	.50
427	Joe Hague	.50
428	Lee Elia	.50
429	Billy Moran	.50
431	Pete Mikkelsen	.50
432a	Al Moran (Should be #430.)	.50
432b	Aurelio Monteagudo	.50
433	Ken MacKenzie	.50
434	Dick Egan	.50
435	Al McBean	.50
436	Mike Ferraro	.50
437	Gary Wagner	.50
438	Jerry Grote, J.C. Martin	.50
439	Ted Kluszewski	1.00
440	Jerry Johnson	.50
441	Ross Moschitto	.50
442	Zoilo Versalles	.50
443	Dennis Ribant	.50
444	Ted Williams	9.00
445	Steve Whitaker	.50
446	Frank Bertaina	.50
447	Bo Belinsky	.50

448	Joe Moeller	.50
449	Don Shaw, Ron Taylor	.50
450	Al Downing, Whitey Ford, Fritz Peterson, Mel Stottlemyre	1.00
451	Jack Tracy	.50
452	Tony Curry	.50
453	Roy White	.50
454	Jim Bunning	1.00
455	Ralph Houk	.50
456	Bobby Shantz	.50
457	Bill Rigney	.50
458	Roger Repoz	.50
459	Robin Roberts, Bob Turley	1.00
460	Gordon Richardson	.50
461	Dick Tracewski	.50
462	Thad Tillotson	.50
463	Larry Osborne	.50
464	Larry Burright	.50
465	Alan Foster	.50
466	Ron Taylor	.50
467	Fred Talbot	.50
468	Bob Miller	.50
469	Frank Tepedino	.50
470	Danny Frisella	.50
471	Cecil Perkins	.50
472	Danny Napoleon	.50
473	John Upham	.50
474	Yogi Berra, Elston Howard, Mickey Mantle, Roger Maris, Bill Skowron	6.00
475	Al Weis	.50
476	Rich Beck	.50
477	Clete Boyer, Tony Kubek, Joe Pepitone, Bobby Richardson	3.00
478	Jack Fisher	.50
479	Archie Moore	.50
480	Roger Craig	.50
481	Frank Crosetti, Mike Hegan, Ralph Houk, Wally Moses	.50
482	Roger Craig, Gil Hodges, Clem Labine, Cookie Lavagetto	.50

1959 Chicago White Sox

JIM McANANY OF.

The A.L. Champion Chicago White Sox are featured in this collectors' issue. The 2-1/2" x 3-1/2" cards have black-and-white player photos with dark blue borders. Backs are in black-and-white with a few bits of player data, career information, 1959 and lifetime stats, along with a TCMA copyright line.

		NM/M
Complete Set (45):		45.00
Common Player:		1.00
1	Earl Torgeson	1.00
2	Nellie Fox	5.00
3	Luis Aparicio	5.00
4	Bubba Phillips	1.00
5	Jim McAnany	1.00
6	Jim Landis	1.00
7	Al Smith	1.00
8	Sherman Lollar	1.00
9	Billy Goodman	1.00
10	Jim Rivera	1.00
11	Sammy Esposito	1.00
12	Norm Cash	2.50
13	Johnny Romano	1.00
14	Johnny Callison	1.00
15	Harry Simpson	1.00
16	Ted Kluszewski	4.00
17	Del Ennis	1.00
18	Earl Battey	1.00
19	Larry Doby	4.00
20	Ron Jackson	1.00
21	Ray Boone	1.00
22	Lou Skizas	1.00
23	Joe Hicks	1.00
24	Don Mueller	1.00
25	J.C. Martin	1.00
26	Cam Carreon	1.00
27	Early Wynn	3.00
28	Bob Shaw	1.00
29	Billy Pierce	1.50
30	Turk Lown	1.00

31	Dick Donovan	1.00
32	Gerry Staley	1.00
33	Barry Latman	1.00
34	Ray Moore	1.00
35	Rudy Arias	1.00
36	Joe Stanka	1.00
37	Ken McBride	1.00
38	Don Rudolph	1.00
39	Claude Raymond	1.00
40	Gary Peters	1.00
41	Al Lopez	1.50
42	Don Gutteridge	1.00
43	Ray Berres	1.00
44	Tony Cuccinello	1.00
45	John Cooney	1.00

1962 San Francisco Giants

CAP PETERSON IN

The National League Champions for 1962 are featured in this collector's edition card set. The 2-1/2" x 3-1/2" cards have orange borders on front, around black-and-white player photos. Backs are in black-and-white with personal data, career information and 1982 stats.

		NM/M
Complete Set (35):		45.00
Common Player:		1.00
1	Alvin Dark	1.00
2	Whitey Lockman	1.00
3	Larry Jansen	1.00
4	Wes Westrum	1.00
5	Ed Bailey	1.00
6	Tom Haller	1.00
7	Harvey Kuenn	1.00
8	Willie Mays	15.00
9	Felipe Alou	1.50
10	Orlando Cepeda	4.00
11	Chuck Hiller	1.00
12	Jose Pagan	1.00
13	Jim Davenport	1.00
14	Willie McCovey	4.00
15	Matty Alou	1.00
16	Manny Mota	1.50
17	Ernie Bowman	1.00
18	Carl Boles	1.00
19	John Orsino	1.00
20	Joe Pignatano	1.00
21	Gaylord Perry	2.50
22	Jim Duffalo	1.00
23	Dick LeMay	1.00
24	Bob Garibaldi	1.00
25	Bobby Bolin	1.00
26	Don Larsen	1.25
27	Mike McCormick	1.00
28	Stu Miller	1.00
29	Jack Sanford	1.00
30	Billy O'Dell	1.00
31	Juan Marichal	2.50
32	Billy Pierce	1.00
33	Dick Phillips	1.00
34	Cap Peterson	1.00
35	Bob Nieman	1.00

1982 TCMA Baseball's Greatest Hitters

HITTERS — JOE DiMAGGIO

Baseball's hit kings of the past are featured in this collectors set. Fronts of the 2-1/2" x 3-1/2" cards have a color or

black-and-white photo surrounded by a colored frame. Backs are in black-and-white with a career summary, lifetime stats and Major League Baseball licensee logo.

		NM/M
Complete Set (45):		8.00
Common Player:		.25
1	Ted Williams	1.00
2	Stan Musial	1.00
3	Joe DiMaggio	2.00
4	Roberto Clemente	2.00
5	Jackie Robinson	1.00
6	Willie Mays	1.00
7	Lou Brock	.25
8	Al Kaline	.25
9	Richie Ashburn	.25
10	Tony Oliva	.25
11	Harvey Kuenn	.25
12	Mickey Vernon	.25
13	Tommy Davis	.25
14	Ty Cobb	.75
15	Rogers Hornsby	.25
16	Joe Jackson	2.00
17	Willie Keeler	.25
18	Tris Speaker	.25
19	Babe Ruth	2.50
20	Harry Heilmann	.25
21	Bill Terry	.25
22	George Sisler	.25
23	Lou Gehrig	1.00
24	Nap Lajoie	.25
25	Riggs Stephenson	.25
26	Al Simmons	.25
27	Cap Anson	.25
28	Paul Waner	.25
29	Eddie Collins	.25
30	Heinie Manush	.25
31	Honus Wagner	.50
32	Earle Combs	.25
33	Sam Rice	.25
34	Charlie Gehringer	.25
35	Chick Hafey	.25
36	Zack Wheat	.25
37	Frank Frisch	.25
38	Bill Dickey	.25
39	Ernie Lombardi	.25
40	Joe Cronin	.25
41	Lefty O'Doul	.25
42	Luke Appling	.25
43	Ferris Fain	.25
44	Arky Vaughan	.25
45	Joe Medwick	.25

Baseball's Greatest Pitchers

PITCHERS — DON DRYSDALE

The best pitchers who were no longer active are featured in this collectors issue. Color or black-and-white photos are presented at center of the 2-1/2" x 3-1/2" cards, with a colored frame surrounding the title, name and position. Backs are printed in dark blue and have a career summary and lifetime stats.

		NM/M
Complete Set (45):		6.00
Common Player:		.25
1	Bob Feller	.35
2	Bob Lemon	.25
3	Whitey Ford	.75
4	Joe Page	.25
5	Wilbur Wood	.25
6	Robin Roberts	.25
7	Warren Spahn	.25
8	Sandy Koufax	3.00
9	Juan Marichal	.25
10	Don Newcombe	.25
11	Hoyt Wilhelm	.25
12	Roy Face	.25
13	Allie Reynolds	.25
14	Don Drysdale	.25
15	Bob Gibson	.25
16	Cy Young	.25
17	Walter Johnson	.25
18	Grover Alexander	.25
19	Jack Chesbro	.25
20	Lefty Gomez	.25
21	Wes Ferrell	.25
22	Hal Newhouser	.25
23	Early Wynn	.25

24	Denny McLain	.25
25	Catfish Hunter	.25
26	Jim Lonborg	.25
27	Frank Lary	.25
28	Red Ruffing	.25
29	Lefty Grove	.25
30	Herb Pennock	.25
31	Satchel Paige	1.50
32	Iron Man McGinnity	.25
33	Christy Mathewson	.50
34	Mordecai Brown	.25
35	Eppa Rixey	.25
36	Dizzy Dean	.40
37	Carl Hubbell	.25
38	Dazzy Vance	.25
39	Jim Bunning	.25
40	Smokey Joe Wood	.25
41	Freddie Fitzsimmons	.25
42	Rube Waddell	.25
43	Addie Joss	.25
44	Burleigh Grimes	.25
45	Chief Bender	.25

Baseball's Greatest Sluggers

SLUGGERS — BABE RUTH

The heaviest hitters in baseball history are featured in this collectors issue. The 2-1/2" x 3-1/2" cards have color or black-and-white photos on front framed in red or green and bordered in white. Backs have a few personal data, career stats and career summary along with a logo indicating licensing by Major League Baseball, all in black-and-white, or blue-and-white. Cards can be found printed on either white or gray cardboard.

		NM/M
Complete Set (45):		8.00
Common Player:		.25
1	Harmon Killebrew	.25
2	Roger Maris	.50
3	Mickey Mantle	3.00
4	Hank Aaron	1.50
5	Ralph Kiner	.25
6	Willie McCovey	.25
7	Eddie Mathews	.25
8	Ernie Banks	.25
9	Duke Snider	.50
10	Frank Howard	.25
11	Ted Kluszewski	.25
12	Frank Robinson	.25
13	Billy Williams	.25
14	Gil Hodges	.50
15	Yogi Berra	.25
16	Richie Allen	.25
17	Joe Adcock	.25
18	Babe Ruth	2.50
19	Lou Gehrig	2.00
20	Jimmie Foxx	.25
21	Rogers Hornsby	.25
22	Ted Williams	1.50
23	Hack Wilson	.25
24	Al Simmons	.25
25	John Mize	.25
26	Chuck Klein	.25
27	Hank Greenberg	.25
28	Babe Herman	.25
29	Norm Cash	.25
30	Rudy York	.25
31	Gavvy Cravath	.25
32	Mel Ott	.25
33	Orlando Cepeda	.25
34	Dolf Camilli	.25
35	Frank Baker	.25
36	Larry Doby	.25
37	Jim Gentile	.25
38	Harry Davis	.25
39	Rocco Colavito	.25
40	Cy Williams	.25
41	Roy Sievers	.25
42	Boog Powell	.25
43	Willie Mays	1.50
44	Joe DiMaggio	2.00
45	Earl Averill	.25

Great Players of the 1950's & 60's: Series 1

These large-format (3-3/4" x 5-3/4") cards have white-bordered color poses on front, with no extraneous graphics. Backs have a black-and-white head shot of the player with lifetime stats, career highlights and personal data in a red border.

		NM/M
Complete Set (20):		15.00
Common Player:		.60
1	Roberto Clemente	3.00
2	Sandy Koufax	2.50
3	Phil Rizzuto	1.00
4	Bob Feller	.60
5	Duke Snider	1.00
6	Hank Aaron	2.50
7	Eddie Mathews	.60
8	Roy Campanella	1.50
9	Willie Mays	2.50
10	Robin Roberts	.60
11	Nelson Fox	.60
12	Early Wynn	.60
13	Ted Williams	2.50
14	Warren Spahn	.60
15	Jackie Robinson	2.00
16	Joe DiMaggio	2.50
17	Frank Robinson	.60
18	Yogi Berra	1.25
19	Mickey Mantle	3.50
20	Stan Musial	2.00

"1952" Bowman

A find of player paintings evidently intended for use in Bowman's 1952 baseball card set allowed TCMA to produce this collectors' issue of 15 Bowman "high numbers that never were." The 2-1/8" x 3-1/8" cards approximate the size of the originals. Fronts have only the color picture with a white border around; the facsimile signatures found on original 1952 Bowmans are not present. Backs are printed in red and black and have layout and style similar to the 1952 cards, along with a 1982 TCMA copyright. The issue was numbered consecutively from #253, beginning where the original issue ended.

		NM/M
Complete Set (15):		12.00
Common Player:		1.00
253	Bob Kennedy	1.00
254	Barney McCosky	1.00
255	Chris Van Cuyk	1.00
256	Morrie Martin	1.00
257	Jim Wilson	1.00
258	Bob Thorpe	1.00
259	Bill Henry	1.00
260	Bob Addis	1.00
261	Terry Moore	1.00
262	Joe Dobson	1.00
263	Jack Merson	1.00
264	Virgil Trucks	1.00
265	Johnny Hopp	1.00
266	Cookie Lavagetto	1.00
267	George Shuba	1.00

1983 TCMA All-Time Athletics

ALL-TIME ATHLETICS
Mule Haas OF

This was one of several early 1980s collectors issues from TCMA depicting an All-Time team. The 2-1/2" x 3-1/2" cards have black-and-white photos on front with red graphics. Backs are printed in blue and offer personal data, a career summary and lifetime stats.

		NM/M
Complete Set (12):		12.00
Common Player:		.75
1	Jimmie Foxx	1.50
2	Eddie Collins	1.25
3	Frank Baker	1.25
4	Jack Barry	.75
5	Al Simmons	1.25
6	Mule Haas	.75
7	Bing Miller	.75
8	Mickey Cochrane	1.25
9	Chief Bender	1.25
10	Lefty Grove	1.25
11	John Wyatt	.75
12	Connie Mack	1.25

All-Time Cardinals

ALL-TIME CARDINALS
Jim Bottomley 1B

A picked team of Cardinal greats through the 1970s is featured on this collectors' issue. The 2-1/2" x 3-1/2" cards have black-and-white photos on front, with the set title printed in red in the white bottom border. Backs have player data and a career summary printed in purple on gray or blue on white.

		NM/M
Complete Set (12):		18.00
Common Player:		1.00
1	Jim Bottomley	1.00
2	Rogers Hornsby	1.25
3	Ken Boyer	1.50
4	Marty Marion	1.00
5	Ducky Medwick	1.00
6	Chick Hafey	1.00
7	Stan Musial	6.00
8	Tim McCarver	1.25
9	Robert "Bob" Gibson	1.50
10	Harry Brecheen	1.00
11	Alpha Brazle	1.00
12	Red Schoendienst	1.25

All-Time Pirates

This was one of several early 1980s collectors' issues from TCMA depicting an All-Time team. The 2-1/2" x 3-1/2" cards have black-and-white photos on front with blue graphics. Backs are printed in blue and offer personal data, a career summary and lifetime stats.

		NM/M
Complete Set (12):		12.00
Common Player:		1.00
1	Willie Stargell	2.00
2	Bill Mazeroski	1.50

DEACON PHILLIPPE P

3	Pie Traynor	1.00
4	Honus Wagner	2.00
5	Roberto Clemente	6.00
6	Lloyd Waner, Paul Waner	1.50
7	Ralph Kiner	1.00
8	Manny Sanguillen	1.00
9	Deacon Phillippe	1.00
10	Bob Veale	1.00
11	Elroy Face	1.00
12	Danny Murtaugh	1.00

Play Ball Postcards

These 5-1/2" x 3-1/2" postcards have vintage photos in sepia with white borders and player identification on front. The postcard-style backs have a write-up about the team represented.

		NM/M
Complete Set (18):		25.00
Common Card:		2.00
1	1949 Indians (Lou Boudreau, Joe Gordon)	2.00
2	1948 Red Sox (Murrell Jones, Bobby Doerr, Junior Stephens, Johnny Pesky)	2.00
3	1948 Red Sox (Sam Mele, Ted Williams, Stan Spence, Dom DiMaggio)	4.00
4	1948 Yankees (Joe DiMaggio, Johnny Lindell, Charlie Keller, Tommy Henrich)	5.00
5	Pittsburgh 1947 (Happy Chandler, Hank Greenberg)	2.00
6	1948 Phillies (Eddie Miller, Emil Verban)	2.00
7	1948 Cardinals (Howie Pollett, Red Munger, Murry Dickson, Harry Brecheen, Ken Burkhart)	2.00
8	1948 Braves (Warren Spahn, Johnny Sain)	2.50
9	1948 Braves (Alvin Dark, Eddie Stanky)	2.00
10	1948 Braves (Bob Elliott, Tommy Holmes)	2.00
11	1941 Yankees Team Photo	3.00
12	1943 Yankees Team Photo	3.00
13	1947 Yankees Team Photo	3.00
14	1948 Spring Training (Yankees) (Eddie Lopat, Spec Shea, Vic Raschi, Red Embree, Bill Bevens)	3.00
15	1948 A's (Lou Brissie, Connie Mack)	2.00
16	1948 Tigers (Ted Gray, Hal Newhouser, Virgil Trucks,	

	Art Houtteman, Fred Hutchinson, Dizzy Trout)	2.00
17	Yankees (Phil Rizzuto, Joe Gordon)	3.00
18	1944 Browns (Ellis Clary, Floyd Baker, Vern Stephens, Mark Christman, Don Gutteridge, George McQuinn)	2.00

50 Years of Yankees All-Stars

Yankees' players who participated in the first 50 years of All-Star Games (1933-1983) are featured in this collectors' issue. The 2-3/4" x 3-1/2" cards feature on front the art of Robert Stephen Simon.

		NM/M
Complete Set (50):		12.50
Common Player:		.40
1	Checklist (Mickey Mantle)	1.25
2	Luis Arroyo	.40
3	Hank Bauer	.40
4	Yogi Berra	.75
5	Tommy Byrne	.40
6	Spud Chandler	.40
7	Ben Chapman	.40
8	Jim Coates	.40
9	Bill Dickey	.50
10	Joe DiMaggio	3.00
11	Al Downing	.40
12	Ryne Duren	.40
13	Whitey Ford	.75
14	Whitey Ford	.75
15	Lou Gehrig	3.00
16	Lefty Gomez	.40
17	Bob Grim	.40
18	Tommy Henrich	.40
19	Elston Howard	.40
20	Catfish Hunter	.40
21	Billy Johnson	.40
22	Charlie Keller	.40
23	Johnny Kucks	.40
24	Ed Lopat	.40
25	Sparky Lyle	.40
26	Mickey Mantle	4.00
27	Roger Maris	.75
28	Billy Martin	.50
29	Johnny Mize	.50
30	Bobby Murcer	.40
31	Irv Noren	.40
32	Joe Pepitone	.40
33	Fritz Peterson	.40
34	Vic Raschi	.40
35	Allie Reynolds	.40
36	Bobby Richardson	.40
37	Phil Rizzuto	.75
38	Marius Russo	.40
39	Babe Ruth	3.50
40	Johnny Sain	.40
41	George Selkirk	.40
42	Bobby Shantz	.40
43	Spec Shea	.40
44	Moose Skowron	.40
45	Casey Stengel	.60
46	Mel Stottlemyre	.40
47	Ralph Terry	.40
48	Tom Tresh	.40
49	Bob Turley	.40
50	Roy White	.40

1936-1939 Yankee Dynasty

Many of the players who participated in one or more of the Yankees' four consecutive World Champion seasons in the late 1930s are included in this collectors' edition. Cards are 2-3/4" x 4" and feature black-and-white photos on front. In the white borders at top and bottom, the set name and player identification are printed in blue. Backs have stats for each season and are printed in black-and-white on a brown background. This set

is a virtual reprint of the set made in 1974, with two player cards added. The unnumbered cards are checklisted here alphabetically.

		NM/M
Complete Set (56):		45.00
Common Player:		1.00
(1)	"Poison Ivy" Andrews	1.00
(2)	Joe Beggs	1.00
(3)	Marv Breuer	1.00
(4)	Johnny Broaca	1.00
(5)	"Jumbo" Brown	1.00
(6)	"Spud" Chandler	1.00
(7)	Ben Chapman	1.00
(8)	Earle Combs	1.00
(9)	Frankie Crosetti	1.00
(10)	"Babe" Dahlgren	1.00
(11)	Bill Dickey	1.50
(12)	Joe DiMaggio	8.00
(13)	Atley Donald	1.00
(14)	Wes Ferrell	1.00
(15)	Artie Fletcher	1.00
(16)	Joe Gallagher	1.00
(17)	Lou Gehrig	8.00
(18)	Joe Glenn	1.00
(19)	"Lefty" Gomez	1.00
(20)	Joe Gordon	1.00
(21)	"Bump" Hadley	1.00
(22)	Don Heffner	1.00
(23)	Tommy Henrich	1.00
(24)	Oral Hildebrand	1.00
(25)	Myril Hoag	1.00
(26)	Roy Johnson	1.00
(27)	Arndt Jorgens	1.00
(28)	Charlie Keller	1.00
(29)	Ted Kleinhans	1.00
(30)	Billy Knickerbocker	1.00
(31)	Tony Lazzeri	1.00
(32)	Frank Makosky	1.00
(33)	"Pat" Malone	1.00
(34)	Johnny Murphy	1.00
(35)	"Monty" Pearson	1.00
(36)	"Jake" Powell	1.00
(37)	"Red" Rolfe	1.00
(38)	"Buddy" Rosar	1.00
(39)	"Red" Ruffing	1.00
(40)	Marius Russo	1.00
(41)	"Jack" Saltzgaver	1.00
(42)	Paul Schreiber	1.00
(43)	Johnny Schulte	1.00
(44)	Bob Seeds	1.00
(45)	"Twinkletoes" Selkirk	1.00
(46)	Lee Stine	1.00
(47)	Steve Sundra	1.00
(48)	"Sandy" Vance	1.00
(49)	Dixie Walker	1.00
(50)	Kemp Wicker	1.00
(51)	Joe McCarthy, Jacob Ruppert	1.00
(52)	Joe DiMaggio, Frank Crosetti, Tony Lazzeri, Bill Dickey, Lou Gehrig, Jake Powell, George Selkirk	3.00
(53)	Lou Gehrig, Joe DiMaggio	5.00
(54)	Gehrig Hits Another	5.00
(55)	Red Rolfe, Tony Lazzeri, Lou Gehrig, Frank Crosetti	3.00
(56)	World Champions - 1936	3.00

1942-46 St. Louis Cardinals

This set is a virtual re-issue of the 1975 set, except for some minor changes in player selection, the use of a slightly smaller (2-1/2" x 3-1/2) format, gray cardboard backs instead of white and which include biographical information as well as stats and the appearance on a black line around the black-and-white player photos. Highlight printing on front is again in red. This version of the set includes card numbers.

		NM/M
Complete Set (68):		24.00
Common Player:		.25
1	Jimmy Brown	.25
2	Jeff Cross	.25
3	Lou Klein	.25
4	Danny Litwhiler	.25
5	Sam Narron	.25
6	Estel Crabtree	.25
7	Buzzy Wares	.25
8	Ken O'Dea	.25
9	Buddy Blattner	.25
10	Erv Dusak	.25
11	Ray Sanders	.25
12	Harry Walker	.25
13	Coaker Triplett	.25
14	Stan Musial	4.00
15	Walker Cooper	.25
16	Whitey Kurowski	.25
17	Enos Slaughter	1.50
18	Terry Moore	.35
19	Johnny Hopp	.25

20	Creepy Crespi	.25
21	Marty Marion	.50
22	Debs Garms	.25
23	Frank Demaree	.25
24	George Fallon	.25
25	Buster Adams	.25
26	Emil Verban	.25
27	Augie Bergamo	.50
28	Pepper Martin	.50
29	Mike Gonzalez	.50
30	Leo Durocher	
	Eddie Dyer	.50
31	Red Schoendienst	1.50
32	Del Rice	.25
33	Joe Garagiola	2.00
34	Dick Sisler	.25
35	Clyde Kluttz	.25
36	Bill Endicott	.25
37	Nippy Jones	.25
38	Walt Sessi	.25
39	Del Wilber	.25
40	Mort Cooper	.25
41	John Beazley	.25
42	Howie Krist	.25
43	Max Lanier	.25
44	Harry Grumbert (Gumbert)	
45	Howie Pollet	.25
46	Ernie White	.25
47	Murray Dickson (Murry)	.25
48	Lon Warneke	.25
49	Bill Lohrman	.25
50	Clyde Shoun	.25
51	Red Munger	.25
52	Harry Brecheen	.25
53	Al Brazle	.25
54	Bud Byerly	.25
55	Ted Wilks	.25
56	Fred Schmidt	.25
57	Al Jurisich	.25
58	Red Barrett	.25
59	Ken Burkhart	.25
60	Blix Donnelly	.25
61	Johnny Grodzicki	.25
62	Billy Southworth	.25
63	Eddie Dyer	.25
64	Red Ruffing, Johnny Beazley	.25
65	Stan Musial, Billy Southworth, Johnny Hopp	1.00
66	Sportsman's Park (5' x 3-1/2')	2.00
67	1942 St. Louis Cardinals (5" x 3-1/2')	2.00
68	Stan Musial, Billy Southworth, Ray Sanders	1.00

1942 Play Ball

Between 1983-85, TCMA produced eight sets of collectors' cards resurrecting the Play Ball brand name which had been active in the field from 1939-41. The TCMA sets attempt to replicate the style and substance of the earlier Play Ball cards as if the company had continued production through World War II and the end of the 1940s. The "1942" set features sepia-toned photos on front, with black graphics. Backs are printed on gray stock in blue ink. Size approximates the original Play Balls at 2-1/2" x 3-1/4".

		NM/M
Complete Set (45):		30.00
Common Player:		1.50
1	Joe Gordon	1.50
2	Joe DiMaggio	6.50
3	Bill Dickey	2.00
4	Joe McCarthy	1.50
5	Tex Hughson	1.50
6	Ted Williams	5.00
7	Walt Judnich	1.50
8	Vern Stephens	1.50
9	Denny Galehouse	1.50
10	Lou Boudreau	1.50
11	Ken Keltner	1.50
12	Jim Bagby	1.50
13	Rudy York	1.50
14	Barney McCosky	1.50
15	Schoolboy Rowe	1.50
16	Luke Appling	1.50
17	Taft Wright	1.50
18	Ted Lyons	1.50
19	Mickey Vernon	1.50
20	George Case	1.50
21	Bobo Newsom	1.50
22	Bob Johnson	1.50
23	Buddy Blair	1.50
24	Pete Suder	1.50
25	Terry Moore	1.50
26	Stan Musial	5.00
27	Marty Marion	1.50
28	Pee Wee Reese	3.50
29	Arky Vaughan	1.50
30	Larry French	1.50
31	Johnny Mize	2.00
32	Mel Ott	2.00
33	Willard Marshall	1.50

34	Carl Hubbell	2.00
35	Frank McCormick	1.50
36	Linus Frey	1.50
37	Bob Elliott	1.50
38	Vince DiMaggio	1.50
39	Al Lopez	1.50
40	Stan Hack	1.50
41	Lou Novikoff	1.50
42	Casey Stengel	2.00
43	Tommy Holmes	1.50
44	Ron Northey	1.50
45	Rube Melton	1.50

1943 Play Ball

JOE MEDWICK

Between 1983-85, TCMA produced eight sets of collectors' cards resurrecting the Play Ball brand name which had been active in the field from 1939-41. The TCMA sets attempt to replicate the style and substance of the earlier Play Ball cards as if the company had continued production through World War II and the end of the 1940s. The "1943" set features sepia-toned photos on front, with black graphics. Backs are printed on gray stock in purple ink. Size approximates the original Play Balls at 2-1/2" x 3-1/4".

		NM/M
Complete Set (45):		25.00
Common Player:		1.50
1	Spud Chandler	1.50
2	Frank Crosetti	1.50
3	Johnny Lindell	1.50
4	Emil "Dutch" Leonard	1.50
5	Stan Spence	1.50
6	Ray Mack	1.50
7	Hank Edwards	1.50
8	Al Smith	1.50
9	Mike Tresh	1.50
10	Don Kolloway	1.50
11	Orval Grove	1.50
12	Doc Cramer	1.50
13	Pinky Higgins	1.50
14	Dick Wakefield	1.50
15	Harland Clift (Harland)	1.50
16	Chet Laabs	1.50
17	George McQuinn	1.50
18	Tony Lupien	1.50
19	Oscar Judd	1.50
20	Roy Partee	1.50
21	Lum Harris	1.50
22	Roger Wolf	1.50
23	Dick Siebert	1.50
24	Walker Cooper	1.50
25	Mort Cooper	1.50
26	Whitey Kurowski	1.50
27	Eddie Miller	1.50
28	Elmer Riddle	1.50
29	Bucky Walters	1.50
30	Whitlow Wyatt	1.50
31	Dolf Camilli	1.50
32	Elbie Fletcher	1.50
33	Frank Gustine	1.50
34	Rip Sewell	1.50
35	Phil Cavarretta	1.50
36	Bill "Swish" Nicholson	1.50
37	Peanuts Lowrey	1.50
38	Phil Masi	1.50
39	Al Javery	1.50
40	Jim Tobin	1.50
41	Glen Stewart	1.50
42	Mickey Livingston	1.50
43	Ace Adams	1.50
44	Joe Medwick	2.50
45	Sid Gordon	1.50

1944 Play Ball

Between 1983-85, TCMA produced eight sets of collectors' cards resurrecting the Play Ball brand name which had been active in the field from 1939-41. The TCMA sets attempt to replicate the style and substance of the earlier Play Ball cards as if the company had continued production through World War II and the end of the 1940s. The

BOB CHIPMAN

"1944" set features black-and-white photos on front, with blue graphics. Backs are printed on gray stock in black ink. Size approximates the original Play Balls at 2-1/2" x 3-1/4".

		NM/M
Complete Set (45):		25.00
Common Player:		1.50
1	Don Gutteridge	1.50
2	Mark Christman	1.50
3	Mike Kreevich	1.50
4	Jimmy Outlaw	1.50
5	Paul Richards	1.50
6	Hal Newhouser	2.50
7	Bud Metheny	1.50
8	Mike Garbark	1.50
9	Hersh Martin	1.50
10	Bob Johnson	1.50
11	Mike Ryba	1.50
12	Oris Hockett	1.50
13	Ed Kleiman	1.50
14	Ford Garrison	1.50
15	Irv Hall	1.50
16	Ed Busch	1.50
17	Ralph Hogdin	1.50
18	Thurman Tucker	1.50
19	Bill Dietrich	1.50
20	Rick Ferrell	2.00
21	John Sullivan	1.50
22	Mickey Haefner	1.50
23	Ray Sanders	1.50
24	Johnny Hopp	1.50
25	Ted Wilks	1.50
26	John Barrett	1.50
27	Jim Russell	1.50
28	Nick Strincevich	1.50
29	Eric Tipton	1.50
30	Jim Konstanty	1.50
31	Gee Walker	1.50
32	Dom Dellessandro	1.50
33	Bob Chipman	1.50
34	Hank Wyse	1.50
35	Phil Weintraub	1.50
36	George Hausmann	1.50
37	Bill Voiselle	1.50
38	Whitey Wietelmann	1.50
39	Clyde Kluttz	1.50
40	Connie Ryan	1.50
41	Eddie Stanky	1.50
42	Augie Galan	1.50
43	Mickey Owen	1.50
44	Charlie Schanz	1.50
45	Bob Finley	1.50

1945 Play Ball

JOHNNY DICKSHOT

Between 1983-85, TCMA produced eight sets of collectors' cards resurrecting the Play Ball brand name which had been active in the field from 1939-41. The TCMA sets attempt to replicate the style and substance of the earlier Play Ball cards as if the company had continued production through World War II and the end of the 1940s. The "1945" set features black-and-white photos on front, with blue graphics. Backs are printed on gray stock in black ink. Size approximates the original Play Balls at 2-1/2" x 3-1/4".

	NM/M
Complete Set (45):	25.00
Common Player:	1.50

1	Eddie Mayo	1.50
2	Dizzy Trout	1.50
3	Roy Cullenbine	1.50
4	Joe Kuhel	1.50
5	George Binks	1.50
6	Roger Wolff	1.50
7	Gene Moore	1.50
8	Frank Mancuso	1.50
9	Bob Muncrief	1.50
10	Tuck Stainback	1.50
11	Bill Bevens	1.50
12	Snuffy Stirnweiss	1.50
13	Don Ross	1.50
14	Felix Mackiewicz	1.50
15	Jeff Heath	1.50
16	John Dickshot	1.50
17	Ed Lopat	2.00
18	Skeeter Newsom (Newsome)	1.50
19	Eddie Lake	1.50
20	John Lazor	1.50
21	Hal Peck	1.50
22	Al Brancato	1.50
23	Paul Derringer	1.50
24	Stan Hack	1.50
25	Len Merullo	1.50
26	Emil Verban	1.50
27	Ken O'Dea	1.50
28	Red Barrett	1.50
29	Eddie Basinski	1.50
30	Dixie Walker	1.50
31	Goody Rosen	1.50
32	Preacher Roe	1.50
33	Pete Coscarat	1.50
34	Frankie Frisch	2.50
35	Napoleon Reyes	1.50
36	Dan Gardella	1.50
37	Buddy Kerr	1.50
38	Dick Culler	1.50
39	Tommy Holmes	1.50
40	Al Libke	1.50
41	Howie Fox	1.50
42	Johnny Riddle	1.50
43	Andy Seminick	1.50
44	Andy Karl	1.50
45	Rene Monteguedo	1.50

1984 TCMA American League All-Stars

LOU BOUDREAU

The American League "players who compiled the greatest All-Star Game Records" are included in this collectors' edition - one at each position. In standard 2-1/2" x 3-1/2" size, the cards have black-and-white photos with blue frames. Backs have career All-Star Game stats and a copyright line. The unnumbered cards are listed here in alphabetical order.

		NM/M
Complete Set (9):		6.00
Common Player:		.25
(1)	Lou Boudreau	.25
(2)	Rocky Colavito	.50
(3)	Bill Dickey	.50
(4)	Nellie Fox	.50
(5)	Jimmie Foxx	.50
(6)	Mel Harder	.25
(7)	Al Kaline	1.00
(8)	Brooks Robinson	1.00
(9)	Ted Williams	2.50

Roberto Clemente

This one-card set was produced in the same format as the four-card 1984 Hall of Fame Induction set and was probably printed on the same sheet in the same quantity (fewer than 500). Front has a black-and-white photo, back has lifetime stats.

	NM/M
Roberto Clemente	7.50

Great Players of the 1950's & 60's: Series 2

AL KALINE

These large-format (3-3/4" x 5-3/4") cards have color photos bordered in white with a green stripe at bottom bearing the player (or team) name. Backs have a black-and-white head shot of the player, his identification, personal data, career stats and a short biography, all framed in blue with decorative top corners.

		NM/M
Complete Set (33):		75.00
Common Player:		2.00
1	Brooks Robinson	6.00
2	Al Kaline	6.00
3	Tony Oliva	2.00
4	Frank Howard	2.00
5	Richie Ashburn	6.00
6	Harmon Killebrew	6.00
7	George Kell	6.00
8	Larry Doby	6.00
9	Ernie Banks	7.50
10	Maury Wills	4.00
11	Roger Maris	10.00
12	Al Rosen	2.00
13	Willie McCovey	6.00
14	Luis Aparicio	6.00
15	Ron Santo	4.00
16	Harvey Kuenn	2.00
17	Lou Brock	6.00
18	1960 Pittsburgh Pirates (Murtaugh on back)	7.50
19	1966 N.Y. Yankees (Westrum on back)	7.50
20	1950 Philadelphia Phillies (Sawyer on back)	6.00
21	1955 Brooklyn Dodgers (Alston on back)	7.50
22	1957 Milwaukee Braves (Haney on back)	7.50
23	Bob Gibson	6.00
24	Don Drysdale	6.00
25	Whitey Ford	6.00
26	Mickey Mantle, Roger Maris, Mrs. Babe Ruth	7.50
27	Harmon Killebrew, Willie Mays, Mickey Mantle	10.00
28	Willie Mays, Don Drysdale	7.50
29	1961 Yankees, Manager and Coaches	7.50
30	1964 Mets, Manager and Coaches	6.00
31	Ken Boyer, Stan Musial, Red Schoendienst	3.50
32	1952 Giants Pitching Staff	2.00
33	Vada Pinson	2.00

Hall of Fame Induction

While the production of Induction cards in the larger format continued for several years, TCMA's issue of standard 2-1/2" x 3-1/2" format cards was exclusive to 1984. The black-and-white cards have lifetime stats on back. It is reported that fewer than 500 sets were made.

		NM/M
Complete Set (4):		20.00
Common Player:		4.00
(1)	Luis Aparicio	6.00
(2)	Don Drysdale	8.00
(3)	Rick Ferrell	4.00
(4)	Harmon Killebrew	8.00

Hall of Fame Induction 8x10s

For four years TCMA produced 8" x 10" cards for the cur-

rent inductees to the Baseball Hall of Fame. There are no TCMA markings on the cards, which were distributed by Baseball Nostalgia of Cooperstown, N.Y. The cards are blank-backed and unnumbered. They were printed in black-and-white in 1984, 1986-1987; the 1985 cards are blue-and-white. Only 500 of each card were issued.

		NM/M
Complete Set (18):		250.00
Common Player:		15.00
(1)	Luis Aparicio	15.00
(2)	Don Drysdale	15.00
(3)	Rick Ferrell	15.00
(4)	Harmon Killebrew	15.00
(5)	Pee Wee Reese	20.00
(6)	Composite (Luis Aparicio, Don Drysdale, Rick Ferrell, Harmon Killebrew, Pee Wee Reese)	20.00
(7)	Lou Brock	15.00
(8)	Enos Slaughter	15.00
(9)	Hoyt Wilhelm	15.00
(10)	Composite (Lou Brock, Enos Slaughter, Arky Vaughn (Vaughan), Hoyt Wilhelm)	20.00
(11)	Bobby Doerr	15.00
(12)	Willie McCovey	15.00
(13)	Composite (Bobby Doerr, Ernie Lombardi, Willie McCovey)	20.00
(14)	50th Anniversary Composite (Ty Cobb, Walter Johnson, Christy Mathewson, Babe Ruth, Honus Wagner (Edition of 300.)	75.00
(15)	Ray Dandridge	15.00
(16)	Jim "Catfish" Hunter	15.00
(17)	Billy Williams	15.00
(18)	Composite (Ray Dandridge, Jim "Catfish" Hunter, Billy Williams)	15.00

National League All-Stars

DICK GROAT

The National League "players who compiled the greatest All-Star Game Records" are included in this collectors' edition - one at each position. In standard 2-1/2" x 3-1/2" size, the cards have black-and-white photos with red frames. Backs have career All-Star Game stats and a copyright line. The unnumbered cards are listed here in alphabetical order.

		NM/M
Complete Set (9):		6.00
Common Player:		.25
(1)	Ernie Banks	1.00
(2)	Ken Boyer	.25
(3)	Roberto Clemente	2.50
(4)	Dick Groat	.25
(5)	Billy Herman	.25
(6)	Ernie Lombardi	.25
(7)	Juan Marichal	.25
(8)	Willie Mays	2.00
(9)	Stan Musial	1.00

Bruce Stark Postcards

Color artwork by Bruce Stark is featured on these 3-3/4" x 5-3/4" postcards.

		NM/M
Complete Set (5):		9.00
Common Player:		1.25
BS1	Joe DiMaggio	4.50
BS2	Ted Williams	3.00
BS3	Ted Kluzewski (Kluszewski)	1.75

JOE DI MAGGIO

BS4	Mickey Vernon	1.25
BS5	Stan Musial	2.50

1946 Play Ball

HANK GREENBERG

Between 1983-85, TCMA produced eight sets of collectors' cards resurrecting the Play Ball brand name which had been active in the field from 1939-41. The TCMA sets attempt to replicate the style and substance of the earlier Play Ball cards as if the company had continued production through World War II and the end of the 1940s. The "1946" set features black-and-white photos on front, with green graphics. Backs are printed on white stock in black ink. Size approximates the originals at 2-1/2" x 3-1/4".

		NM/M
Complete Set (45):		20.00
Common Player:		1.00
1	Dom DiMaggio	1.25
2	Boo Ferriss	1.00
3	Johnny Pesky	1.00
4	Hank Greenberg	2.00
5	George Kell	1.00
6	Virgil Trucks	1.00
7	Phil Rizzuto	1.75
8	Charlie Keller	1.25
9	Tommy Henrich	1.25
10	Cecil Travis	1.00
11	Al Evans	1.00
12	Buddy Lewis	1.00
13	Edgar Smith	1.00
14	Dario Lodigiani	1.00
15	Earl Caldwell	1.00
16	Jim Hegan	1.00
17	Bob Feller	1.75
18	John Berardino	1.25
19	Jack Kramer	1.00
20	John Lucadello	1.00
21	Hank Majeski	1.00
22	Elmer Valo	1.00
23	Buddy Rosar	1.00
24	Red Schoendienst	1.25
25	Dick Sisler	1.00
26	John Beazley	1.00
27	Vic Lombardi	1.00
28	Dick Whitman	1.00
29	Carl Furillo	1.75
30	Bill Jurges	1.00
31	Marv Rickert	1.00
32	Clyde McCullough	1.00
33	Johnny Hopp	1.00
34	Mort Cooper	1.00
35	Johnny Sain	1.25
36	Del Ennis	1.00
37	Roy Hughes	1.00
38	Bert Haas	1.00
39	Grady Hatton	1.00
40	Ed Bahr	1.00
41	Billy Cox	1.00
42	Lee Handley	1.00
43	Bill Rigney	1.00
44	Babe Young	1.00
45	Buddy Blattner	1.00

1985 TCMA Cy Young Award Winners

This polybagged set of 2-1/2" x 3-1/2" cards is formatted

on two perforated strips. Fronts have color photos with orange borders while backs detail the player's CY season(s). The header card presents the history of the award. The unnumbered cards are listed here alphabetically.

		NM/M
Complete Set (10):		6.00
Common Player:		.25
(1)	Don Drysdale	.75
(2)	Whitey Ford	1.50
(3)	Bob Gibson	.50
(4)	Catfish Hunter	.40
(5)	Sandy Koufax	4.00
(6)	Vern Law	.25
(7)	Sparky Lyle	.25
(8)	Denny McLain	.35
(9)	Jim Palmer	.50
(10a)	Warren Spahn (Boston Braves)	.50
(10b)	Warren Spahn (Milwaukee Braves)	.50

Home Run Champs

This polybagged set of 2-1/2" x 3-1/2" cards is formatted on two perforated strips. Fronts have color photos with reddish-brown borders while backs detail the player's slugging prowess. The header cards presents the history of the award. The unnumbered cards are listed here alphabetically.

		NM/M
Complete Set (10):		6.00
Common Player:		.30
(1)	Hank Aaron	1.50
(2)	Orlando Cepeda	.60
(3)	Joe DiMaggio	2.00
(4)	Larry Doby	.60
(5)	Ralph Kiner	.60
(6)	Eddie Mathews	.60
(7)	Willie McCovey	.60
(8)	Al Rosen	.30
(9)	Duke Snider	.60
(10)	Ted Williams	1.50

Most Valuable Players - A.L.

This polybagged set of 2-1/2" x 3-1/2" cards is formatted on two perforated strips. Fronts have color photos with green borders while backs detail the player's MVP season(s). The header card presents the history of the award. The unnumbered cards are listed here alphabetically.

		NM/M
Complete Set (10):		9.00
Common Player:		.40
(1)	Richie Allen	.40
(2)	Yogi Berra	.75
(3)	Elston Howard	.40
(4)	Jackie Jensen	.40
(5)	Harmon Killebrew	.75
(6)	Mickey Mantle	4.00
(7)	Roger Maris	1.50
(8)	Boog Powell	.40
(9)	Brooks Robinson	.75
(10)	Carl Yastrzemski	1.25

Most Valuable Players - N.L.

This polybagged set of 2-1/2" x 3-1/2" cards is formatted on two perforated strips. Fronts have color photos with blue borders while backs detail the player's MVP season(s). The header card presents the history of the award. The unnumbered cards are listed here alphabetically.

		NM/M
Complete Set (10):		9.00
Common Player:		.40
(1)	Ernie Banks	1.00
(2)	Johnny Bench	1.00
(3)	Roy Campanella	.90
(4)	Roberto Clemente	3.00
(5)	Dick Groat	.40
(6)	Willie Mays	2.50
(7)	Stan Musial	1.50
(8)	Frank Robinson	1.00
(9)	Willie Stargell	.75
(10)	Maury Wills	.40

N.Y. Mets Postcards

A certain sameness of poses, generally belt-to-cap, marks

the cards in this color player postcard issue produced by TCMA for team issue. The 3-1/2" x 5-1/2" cards have borderless color photos with a glossy finish and no extraneous graphics. Backs have a large, light blue team logo at left, with player ID at top and a line of 1984 stats at bottom. A TCMA copyright line is vertically at center. The postcard indicia at right includes a card number at the bottom of the stamp box; the number is preceded by an "NYM85-" prefix.

		NM/M
Complete Set (40):		12.50
Common Player:		.50
1	Davey Johnson	.75
2	Vern Hoscheit	.50
3	Bill Robinson	.50
4	Mel Stottlemyre	.75
5	Bobby Valentine	.50
6	Bruce Berenyi	.50
7	Jeff Bettendorf	.50
8	Ron Darling	.50
9	Sid Fernandez	.50
10	Brent Gaff	.50
11	Wes Gardner	.50
12	Dwight Gooden	1.50
13	Tom Gorman	.50
14	Ed Lynch	.50
15	Jesse Orosco	.50
16	Calvin Schiraldi	.50
17	Doug Sisk	.50
18	Gary Carter	2.00
19	John Gibbons	.50
20	Ronn Reynolds	.50
21	Wally Backman	.50
22	Kelvin Chapman	.50
23	Ron Gardenhire	.50
24	Keith Hernandez	1.00
25	Howard Johnson	.75
26	Ray Knight	.75
27	Kevin Mitchell	.75
28	Terry Blocker	.50
29	Rafael Santana	.50
30	Billy Beane	.50
31	John Christensen	.50
32	Len Dykstra	1.00
33	George Foster	1.00
34	Danny Heep	.50
35	Darryl Strawberry	1.00
36	Mookie Wilson	.75
37	Jeff Bittiger	.50
38	Clint Hurdle	.50
39	Laschelle Tarver	.50
40	Roger McDowell	.50

N.Y. Yankees Postcards

In 1985-86, TCMA produced color player postcard sets for the two New York teams. The 1985 Yankees set is 3-1/2" x 5-1/2" with borderless color poses on front. Backs have a light blue Yan-

kees logo at left. Player identification and data is at top-left with 1984 stats at bottom. A TCMA copyright lines is vertically at center. Cards are numbered in the stamp box NYY85-1 through NYY85-40.

		NM/M
Complete Set (40):		12.50
Common Player:		.50
1	Yogi Berra	1.75
2	Mark Connor	.50
3	Stump Merrill	.50
4	Gene Michael	.50
5	Lou Piniella	.75
6	Jeff Torborg	.50
7	Mike Armstrong	.50
8	Rich Bordi	.50
9	Clay Christensen	.50
10	Joe Cowley	.50
11	Jim Deshaies	.50
12	Ron Guidry	.75
13	John Montefusco	.50
14	Dale Murray	.50
15	Phil Niekro	1.00
16	Alfonso Pulido	.50
17	Dennis Rasmussen	.50
18	Dave Righetti	.50
19	Bob Shirley	.50
20	Ed Whitson	.50
21	Scott Bradley	.50
22	Ron Hassey	.50
23	Butch Wynegar	.50
24	Dale Berra	.50
25	Billy Sample	.50
26	Rex Hudler	.50
27	Don Mattingly	3.00
28	Bobby Meacham	.50
29	Mike Pagliarulo	.50
30	Willie Randolph	.75
31	Andre Robertson	.50
32	Henry Cotto	.50
33	Don Baylor	.75
34	Ken Griffey	.50
35	Rickey Henderson	2.00
36	Vic Mata	.50
37	Omar Moreno	.50
38	Dan Pasqua	.50
39	Dave Winfield	2.00
40	Brian Fisher	.50

Photo Classics Postcards

Teammate pairings and other groupings are featured in this collector's issue set of black-and-white postcards. In 3-1/2" x 5-1/2" format, the postcard-style backs identify the players on front.

		NM/M
Complete Set (40):		45.00
Common Card:		1.00
1	Warren Spahn, Johnny Sain	1.50
2	Jackie Robinson	3.00
3	President Eisenhower w/ Yankees	1.50
4	Babe Ruth	4.00
5	Joe McCarthy, Lou Gehrig, Joe DiMaggio	2.00
6	Bob Feller	1.50
7	Johnny Lindell, Johnny Murphy	1.00
8	Babe Ruth, Claire Ruth	1.50
9	Babe Ruth, Joe Cook	1.50
10	Bobo Newsom	1.00
11	Johnny Antonelli, Robin Roberts	1.00
12	Joe Adcock, Eddie Mathews	1.50
13	Al Lopez, Mike Garcia, Bob Lemon, Early Wynn	2.00
14	Gil McDougald, Roy Campanella	1.50
15	Ralph Branca, Bobby Thomson	2.00
16	Lou Gehrig	2.50
17	Johnny Mize, Bill Rigney, Mel Ott	1.50

18	Spider Jorgensen, Pee Wee Reese, Eddie Stanky, Jackie Robinson	2.00
19	Tommy Holmes, Earl Torgeson, Jeff Heath, Connie Ryan, Billy Southworth	1.50
20	Ted Williams, Bobby Doerr, Dom DiMaggio, Vern Stephens	1.50
21	Chuck Schilling, Carl Yastrzemski	1.50
22	Roger Maris, Mickey Mantle	3.00
23	Rogers Hornsby, Gil McDougald	1.00
24	Jim Gentile, Gus Triandos	1.00
25	Bobby Avila, Willie Mays	1.50
26	Joe Garagiola, Ralph Kiner	1.00
27	Jim Gentile, Willie Mays	1.50
28	Red Schoendienst, Marty Marion	1.00
29	Charlie Keller	1.00
30	House of David Team	1.00
31	Harvey Kuenn, Al Kaline	1.50
32	Hank Sauer	1.00
33	Enos Slaughter	1.00
34	Stan Musial	2.00
35	Willie Mays	2.00
36	William Bendix, Babe Ruth	1.50
37	Whitey Lockman, Davey Williams, Hank Thompson, Alvin Dark, Don Mueller, Willie Mays, Monte Irvin, Wes Westrum	1.00
38	Pete Runnels, Vic Wertz	1.00
39	Stan Musial	2.00
40	Dom DiMaggio	1.00

Rookies of the Year

This polybagged set of 2-1/2" x 3-1/2" cards is formatted on two perforated strips. Fronts have color photos while backs detail the player's ROY season. The header card presents the history of the award. The unnumbered cards are listed here alphabetically.

		NM/M
Complete Set (10):		6.00
Common Player:		.25
(1)	Tommy Agee	.25
(2)	Luis Aparicio	.50
(3)	Frank Howard	.25
(4)	Harvey Kuenn	.25
(5)	Thurman Munson	3.00
(6)	Don Newcombe	.25
(7)	Tony Oliva	.25
(8)	Jackie Robinson	3.00
(9)	Herb Score	.25
(10)	Billy Williams	.50

1947 Play Ball

Between 1983-85, TCMA produced eight sets of collectors' cards resurrecting the Play Ball brand name which had

been active in the field from 1939-41. The TCMA sets attempt to replicate the style and substance of the earlier Play Ball cards as if the company had continued production through World War II and the end of the 1940s. The "1947" set features black-and-white photos on front, with green graphics. Backs are printed on white stock in black ink. Size approximates the originals at 2-1/2" x 3-1/4".

		NM/M
Complete Set (45):		30.00
Common Player:		1.00
1	Hal Wagner	1.00
2	Jake Jones	1.00
3	Bobby Doerr	1.00
4	Fred Hutchinson	1.00
5	Bob Swift	1.00
6	Pat Mullin	1.00
7	Joe Page	1.00
8	Allie Reynolds	1.00
9	Billy Johnson	1.00
10	Early Wynn	1.00
11	Eddie Yost	1.00
12	Floyd Baker	1.00
13	Dave Philley	1.00
14	George Dickey	1.00
15	Dale Mitchell	1.00
16	Bob Lemon	1.00
17	Jerry Witte	1.00
18	Paul Lehner	1.00
19	Sam Zoldak	1.00
20	Sam Chapman	1.00
21	Eddie Joost	1.00
22	Ferris Fain	1.00
23	Erv Dusak	1.00
24	Joe Garagiola	1.00
25	Vernal "Nippy" Jones	1.00
26	Bobby Bragan	1.00
27	Jackie Robinson	6.00
28	Spider Jorgensen	1.00
29	Bob Scheffing	1.00
30	Johnny Schmitz	1.00
31	Doyle Lade	1.00
32	Earl Torgeson	1.00
33	Warren Spahn	1.00
34	Walt Lanfranconi	1.00
35	Johnny Wyrostek	1.00
36	Oscar Judd	1.00
37	Ewell Blackwell	1.00
38	Ed Lukon	1.00
39	Benny Zientara	1.00
40	Gene Woodling	1.00
41	Ernie Bonham	1.00
42	Hank Greenberg	3.00
43	Bobby Thomson	1.00
44	Jack "Lucky" Lohrke	1.00
45	Dave Koslo	1.00

1948 Play Ball

Between 1983-85, TCMA produced eight sets of collectors' cards resurrecting the Play Ball brand name which had been active in the field from 1939-41. The TCMA sets attempt to replicate the style and substance of the earlier Play Ball cards as if the company had continued production through World War II and the end of the 1940s. The "1948" set features black-and-white photos on front, with red graphics. Backs are printed on white stock in black ink. Size approximates the originals at 2-1/2" x 3-1/4".

		NM/M
Complete Set (45):		50.00
Common Player:		1.00
1	Murry Dickson	1.00
2	Enos Slaughter	1.50
3	Don Lang	1.00
4	Joe Hatten	1.00
5	Gil Hodges	2.00
6	Gene Hermanski	1.00
7	Eddie Waitkus	1.00
8	Jess Dobernic	1.00
9	Andy Pafko	1.00
10	Vern Bickford	1.00

11	Mike McCormick	1.00
12	Harry Walker	1.00
13	Putsy Caballero	1.00
14	Hubert "Dutch" Leonard	1.00
15	Frankie Baumholtz	1.00
16	Ted Kluszewski	1.50
17	Virgil Stallcup	1.00
18	Bob Chesnes	1.00
19	Ted Beard	1.00
20	Wes Westrum	1.00
21	Clint Hartung	1.00
22	Whitey Lockman	1.00
23	Billy Goodman	1.00
24	Jack Kramer	1.00
25	Mel Parnell	1.00
26	George Vico	1.00
27	Walter "Hoot" Evers	1.00
28	Vic Wertz	1.00
29	Yogi Berra	2.00
30	Joe DiMaggio	8.00
31	Tommy Byrne	1.00
32	Al Kozar	1.00
33	Jake Early	1.00
34	Gil Coan	1.00
35	Pat Seerey	1.00
36	Ralph Hodgin	1.00
37	Allie Clark	1.00
38	Gene Bearden	1.00
39	Steve Gromek	1.00
40	Al Zarilla	1.00
41	Fred Sanford	1.00
42	Les Moss	1.00
43	Don White	1.00
44	Carl Scheib	1.00
45	Lou Brissie	1.00

1949 Play Ball

Between 1983-85, TCMA produced eight sets of collectors' cards resurrecting the Play Ball brand name which had been active in the field from 1939-41. The TCMA sets attempt to replicate the style and substance of the earlier Play Ball cards as if the company had continued production through World War II and the end of the 1940s. The "1949" set features black-and-white photos on front, with red graphics. Backs are printed on white stock in black ink. Size approximates the originals at 2-1/2" x 3-1/4".

		NM/M
Complete Set (45):		40.00
Common Player:		1.00
1	Al Brazle	1.00
2	Harry Brecheen	1.00
3	Howie Pollett	1.00
4	Cal Abrams	1.00
5	Ralph Branca	1.00
6	Duke Snider	2.50
7	Charlie Grimm	1.00
8	Clarence Maddern	1.00
9	Hal Jeffcoat	1.00
10	Johnny Antonelli	1.00
11	Alvin Dark	1.00
12	Nelson Potter	1.00
13	Granny Hamner	1.00
14	Willie Jones	1.00
15	Robin Roberts	1.50
16	Lloyd Merriman	1.00
17	Bobby Adams	1.00
18	Herman Wehmeier	1.00
19	Ralph Kiner	1.00
20	Dino Restelli	1.00
21	Larry Jansen	1.00
22	Sheldon Jones	1.00
23	Red Webb	1.00
24	Vern Stephens	1.00
25	Tex Hughson	1.00
26	Ellis Kinder	1.00
27	Neil Berry	1.00
28	Johnny Groth	1.00
29	Art Houtteman	1.00
30	Hank Bauer	1.00
31	Vic Raschi	1.00
32	Bobby Brown	1.00
33	Joe Haynes	1.00
34	Eddie Robinson	1.00
35	Sam Dente	1.00
36	Herb Adams	1.00
37	Don Wheeler	1.00
38	Randy Gumpert	1.00

39	Ray Boone	1.00
40	Larry Doby	1.50
41	Jack Graham	1.00
42	Bob Dillinger	1.00
43	Dick Kokos	1.00
44	Wally Moses	1.00
45	Mike Guerra	1.00

1986 TCMA All Time Teams

Similar to TCMA sets of 1980-83, these sets feature 11 all-time great players and a manager from each team. In standard 2-1/2" x 3-1/2" format, most of the cards utilize black-and-white player photos, though some more recent stars are pictured in color. Several decorative borders, varying by team, surround the front photos. On most team sets there is an "All Time" designation at top, with the player name and (usually) position at bottom. Backs are fairly uniform, printed in blue, and offering a few biographical details and career highlights. Besides hobby sales, these old-timers' sets were also sold in several major retails chains, originally priced at about $4.

All Time Angels

		NM/M
Complete Set (12):		4.50
Common Player:		.50
1-ANG	Rod Carew	2.00
2-ANG	Sandy Alomar	.50
3-ANG	Jim Fregosi	.50
4-ANG	Dave Chalk	.50
5-ANG	Leon Wagner	.50
6-ANG	Albie Pearson	.50
7-ANG	Rick Reichardt	.50
8-ANG	Bob Rodgers	.50
9-ANG	Dean Chance	.50
10-ANG	Clyde Wright	.50
11-ANG	Bob Lee	.50
12-ANG	Bill Rigney	.50

All Time Astros

		NM/M
Complete Set (12):		6.00
Common Player:		.50
1-AST	Bob Watson	.50
2-AST	Joe Morgan	1.75
3-AST	Roger Metzger	.50
4-AST	Doug Rader	.50
5-AST	Jimmy Wynn	.70
6-AST	Cesar Cedeno	.70
7-AST	Rusty Staub	.70
8-AST	Johnny Edwards	.50
9-AST	J.R. Richard	.80
10-AST	Dave Roberts	.50
11-AST	Fred Gladding	.50
12-AST	Bill Virdon	.50

All Time Blue Jays

		NM/M
Complete Set (12):		5.00
Common Player:		.50
1-BLU	John Mayberry	.50
2-BLU	Bob Bailor	.50
3-BLU	Luis Gomez	.50
4-BLU	Roy Howell	.50
5-BLU	Otto Velez	.50
6-BLU	Rick Bosetti	.50
7-BLU	Al Woods	.50
8-BLU	Rick Cerone	.50
9-BLU	Dave Lemanczyk	.50
10-BLU	Tom Underwood	.50
11-BLU	Joey McLaughlin	.50
12-BLU	Bobby Cox	.75

All Time Boston/ Milwaukee Braves

DEL CRANDALL C

		NM/M
Complete Set (12):		7.50
Common Player:		.50
1B	Joe Adcock	.70

All Time Brewers

HARVEY KUENN M

		NM/M
Complete Set (12):		6.00
Common Player:		.50
1-BRE	George Scott	.75
2-BRE	Pedro Garcia	.50
3-BRE	Tim Johnson	.50
4-BRE	Don Money	.50
5-BRE	Sixto Lezcano	.50
6-BRE	John Briggs	.50
7-BRE	Dave May	.50
8-BRE	Darrell Porter	.50
9-BRE	Jim Colborn	.50
10-BRE	Mike Caldwell	.50
11-BRE	Rollie Fingers	1.50
12-BRE	Harvey Kuenn	.50

All Time Expos

JIM FANNING M

		NM/M
Complete Set (12):		5.00
Common Player:		.50
1-EXP	Ron Fairly	.50
2-EXP	Dave Cash	.50
3-EXP	Tim Foley	.50
4-EXP	Bob Bailey	.50
5-EXP	Ken Singleton	.75
6-EXP	Ellis Valentine	.50
7-EXP	Rusty Staub	.75
8-EXP	John Bateman	.50
9-EXP	Steve Rogers	.50
10-EXP	Woodie Fryman	.50
11-EXP	Mike Marshall	.50
12-EXP	Jim Fanning	.50

All Time Indians

JOE JACKSON OF

		NM/M
Complete Set (12):		7.00
Common Player:		.50
1-IND	Hal Trosky	.50
2-IND	Nap Lajoie	.50
3-IND	Lou Boudreau	.50
4-IND	Al Rosen	.50
5-IND	Joe Jackson	6.00
6-IND	Tris Speaker	.75
7-IND	Larry Doby	1.00
8-IND	Jim Hegan	.50

2B	Felix Millan	.50
3B	Rabbit Maranville	.50
4B	Eddie Mathews	2.00
5B	Hank Aaron	6.00
6B	Wally Berger	.50
7B	Tommy Holmes	.50
8B	Del Crandall	.50
9B	Warren Spahn	2.00
10B	Charles "Kid" Nichols	.50
11B	Cecil Upshaw	.50
12B	Fred Haney	.50

All Time Mariners

		NM/M
Complete Set (12):		5.00
Common Player:		.50
1-MAR	Pat Putnam	.50
2-MAR	Larry Milbourne	.50
3-MAR	Todd Cruz	.50
4-MAR	Bill Stein	.50
5-MAR	Leon Roberts	.50
6-MAR	Leroy Stanton	.50
7-MAR	Dan Meyer	.50
8-MAR	Bob Stinson	.50
9-MAR	Glenn Abbott	.50
10-MAR	John Montague	.50
11-MAR	Bryan Clark	.50
12-MAR	Rene Lachemann	.50

All Time Mets

		NM/M
Complete Set (12):		7.50
Common Player:		.50
1M	Ed Kranepool	.50
2M	Ron Hunt	.50
3M	Bud Harrelson	.75
4M	Wayne Garrett	.50
5M	Cleon Jones	.75
6M	Tommie Agee	.75
7M	Rusty Staub	1.00
8M	Jerry Grote	.50
9M	Gary Gentry	.50
10M	Jerry Koosman	.75
11M	Tug McGraw	.75
12M	Gil Hodges	2.00

All Time Oakland A's

JIM "CATFISH" HUNTER P

		NM/M
Complete Set (12):		7.00
Common Player:		.50
1-ATH	Gene Tenace	.50
2-ATH	Dick Green	.50
3-ATH	Bert Campaneris	.75
4-ATH	Sal Bando	.50
5-ATH	Joe Rudi	.75
6-ATH	Rick Monday	.50
7-ATH	Bill North	.50
8-ATH	Dave Duncan	.50
9-ATH	Jim "Catfish" Hunter	1.50
10-ATH	Ken Holtzman	.50
11-ATH	Rollie Fingers	1.50
12-ATH	Alvin Dark	.50

All Time Orioles

FRANK ROBINSON OF

		NM/M
Complete Set (12):		14.00
Common Player:		.50
1BA	Hoyt Wilhelm	.50
2BA	Hank Bauer	.50
3BA	Jim Palmer	2.00
4BA	Dave McNally	.50
5BA	Paul Blair	.50
6BA	Gus Triandos	.50
7BA	Frank Robinson	3.00
8BA	Ken Singleton	.50
9BA	Luis Aparicio	2.50
10BA	Brooks Robinson	4.00
11BA	John "Boog" Powell	1.00
12BA	Dave Johnson	.50

9-IND	Cy Young	1.00
10-IND	Sam McDowell	.60
11-IND	Ray Narleski	.50
12-IND	Al Lopez	.50

All Time Padres

		NM/M
Complete Set (12):		6.00
Common Player:		.50
1-PAD	Nate Colbert	.50
2-PAD	Tito Fuentes	.50
3-PAD	Enzo Hernandez	.50
4-PAD	Dave Roberts	.50
5-PAD	Gene Richards	.50
6-PAD	Ollie Brown	.50
7-PAD	Clarence Gaston	.50
8-PAD	Fred Kendall	.50
9-PAD	Gaylord Perry	1.50
10-PAD	Randy Jones	.50
11-PAD	Rollie Fingers	1.50
12-PAD	Preston Gomez	.50

All Time Phillies

RICHIE ALLEN 3B

		NM/M
Complete Set (12):		7.00
Common Player:		.35
1PP	Chuck Klein	.50
2PP	Richie Ashburn	3.00
3PP	Del Ennis	.35
4PP	Spud Davis	.35
5PP	Grover Alexander	.50
6PP	Chris Short	.35
7PP	Jim Konstanty	.35
8PP	Danny Ozark	.35
9PP	Larry Bowa	.50
10PP	Richie Allen	1.00
11PP	Don Hurst	.35
12PP	Tony Taylor	.35

All Time Pirates

		NM/M
Complete Set (12):		14.00
Common Player:		.50
1-PIR	Willie Stargell	2.50
2-PIR	Bill Mazeroski	2.50
3-PIR	Honus Wagner	2.50
4-PIR	Pie Traynor	.50
5-PIR	Ralph Kiner	.75
6-PIR	Paul Waner	.50
7-PIR	Roberto Clemente	5.00
8-PIR	Manny Sanguillen	.50
9-PIR	Vic Willis	.50
10-PIR	Wilbur Cooper	.50
11-PIR	Roy Face	.50
12-PIR	Danny Murtaugh	.50

Time Rangers

		NM/M
Complete Set (12):		6.00
Common Player:		.50
1-RAN	Gaylord Perry	2.00
2-RAN	Jon Matlack	.50
3-RAN	Jim Kern	.50
4-RAN	Billy Hunter	.50
5-RAN	Mike Hargrove	.75
6-RAN	Bump Wills	.50
7-RAN	Toby Harrah	.75
8-RAN	Lenny Randle	.50
9-RAN	Al Oliver	.75
10-RAN	Mickey Rivers	.50
11-RAN	Jeff Burroughs	.50
12-RAN	Dick Billings	.50

All Time Reds

		NM/M
Complete Set (12):		9.00
Common Player:		.50
1CR	Clay Carroll	.50
2CR	Bill McKechnie	.50
3CR	Paul Derringer	.50
4CR	Eppa Rixey	.50
5CR	Frank Robinson	2.50
6CR	Vada Pinson	1.00
7CR	Leo Cardenas	.50
8CR	Heinie Groh	.50
9CR	Ted Kluszewski	2.00
10CR	Joe Morgan	1.50
11CR	Edd Roush	.50
12CR	Johnny Bench	3.00

All Time Red Sox

		NM/M
Complete Set (12):		10.00
Common Player:		.50
1BRS	Sammy White	.50
2BRS	Lefty Grove	.50
3BRS	Cy Young	1.00
4BRS	Jimmie Foxx	1.00
5BRS	Bobby Doerr	.50

ALL TIME RED SOX

JIMMIE FOXX 1B

6BRS	Joe Cronin	.50
7BRS	Frank Malzone	.50
8BRS	Ted Williams	6.00
9BRS	Carl Yastrzemski	4.00
10BRS	Tris Speaker	1.00
11BRS	Dick Radatz	.50
12BRS	Dick Williams	.50

All Time Royals

		NM/M
Complete Set (12):		5.00
Common Player:		.50
1-ROY	John Mayberry	.50
2-ROY	Cookie Rojas	.50
3-ROY	Fred Patek	.50
4-ROY	Paul Schall	.50
5-ROY	Lou Piniella	1.00
6-ROY	Amos Otis	.50
7-ROY	Tom Poquette	.50
8-ROY	Ed Kirkpatrick	.50
9-ROY	Steve Busby	.50
10-ROY	Paul Splittorff	.50
11-ROY	Mark Littell	.50
12-ROY	Jim Frey	.50

All Time Twins

		NM/M
Complete Set (12):		9.00
Common Player:		.50
1-TWI	Harmon Killebrew	2.50
2-TWI	Rod Carew	4.00
3-TWI	Zoilo Versalles	.50
4-TWI	Cesar Tovar	.50
5-TWI	Bob Allison	.50
6-TWI	Larry Hisle	.50
7-TWI	Tony Oliva	.50
8-TWI	Earl Battey	.50
9-TWI	Jim Perry	.50
10-TWI	Jim Kaat	.75
11-TWI	Allan Worthington	.50
12-TWI	Sam Mele	.50

N.Y. Mets Postcards

For a second, and final, year TCMA produced a set of color player postcards for the Mets. The 3-1/2" x 5-1/2" cards have borderless player poses on their glossy fronts; there are no other graphic elements. Backs have a large, light blue team 25th anniversary logo at left, with player ID above and a line of 1985 stats below. There is a TCMA copyright line vertically at center. Among the postcard indicia at right, a card number prefixed with "NYM86-" appears within the stamp box. Cards were sold only as complete sets, for $7.95.

		NM/M
Complete Set (40):		7.50
Common Player:		.50
1	Rick Aguilera	.50
2	Bruce Berenyi	.50
3	Ron Darling	.50
4	Sid Fernandez	.50
5	Dwight Gooden	.75
6	Tom Gorman	.50
7	Ed Lynch	.50

8	Roger McDowell	.50
9	Randy Myers	.60
10	Bob Ojeda	.50
11	Jesse Orosco	.50
12	Doug Sisk	.50
13	Gary Carter	2.00
14	John Gibbons	.50
15	Barry Lyons	.50
16	Wally Backman	.50
17	Ron Gardenhire	.50
18	Keith Hernandez	.75
19	Howard Johnson	.75
20	Ray Knight	.50
21	Kevin Mitchell	.50
22	Rafael Santana	.50
23	Tim Teufel	.50
24	Lenny Dykstra	.75
25	George Foster	.75
26	Danny Heep	.50
27	Mel Stottlemyre	.50
28	Darryl Strawberry	.75
29	Mookie Wilson	.75
30	Randy Nieman	.50
32	Ed Hearn	.50
33	Stan Jefferson	.50
34	Bill Robinson	.50
35	Shawn Abner	.50
36	Terry Blocker	.50
37	Davey Johnson	.50
38	Bud Harrelson	.50
39	Vern Hoscheit	.50
40	Greg Pavlick	.50
43	Tim Corcoran	.50

N.Y. Yankees Postcards

For a second consecutive year, TCMA produced a set of color player postcards for team issue. Similar in format to the 1985 cards, the 1986 version is in 3-1/2" x 5-1/2" format. Fronts have borderless color poses with no other graphics and a high-gloss finish. Backs have a Yankee logo in light blue at left and (usually) a line of 1985 stats at lower-left. Player ID is at upper left. A TCMA copyright line is vertically at center. Among the postcard indicia at right is a card number within the stamp box; cards are skip-numbered with an "NYY86-" prefix; there are two #18. The cards were sold only as complete sets, for $7.95.

		NM/M
Complete Set (40):		9.00
Common Player:		.50
1	Tommy John	1.00
2	Brad Arnsburg (Arnsberg)	.50
3	Al Holland (Al)	.50
4	Mike Armstrong	.50
5	Marty Bystrom	.50
6	Doug Drabek	.50
7	Brian Fisher	.50
8	Stump Merrill	.50
9	Ron Guidry	.75
10	Joe Niekro	.50
11	Dennis Rasmussen	.50
12	Dave Righetti	.50
13	Rod Scurry	.50
14	Bob Shirley	.50
15	Bob Tewksbury	.50
16	Ed Whitson	.50
18a	Britt Burns	.50
18b	Gene Michael	.50
19	Butch Wynegar	.50
20	Ron Hassey	.50
21	Dale Berra	.50
22	Jeff Torborg	.50
23	Mike Fischlin	.50
24	Don Mattingly	3.00
25	Bobby Meacham	.50
26	Mike Pagliarulo	.50
27	Willie Randolph	.50
28	Andre Robertson	.50
29	Roy White	.75
31	Henry Cotto	.50

32	Ken Griffey	.50
33	Rickey Henderson	2.00
34	Vic Mata	.50
35	Dan Pasqua	.50
36	Dave Winfield	2.00
37	Gary Roenicke	.50
38	Lou Piniella	.75
39	Joe Altobelli	.50
40	Sammy Ellis	.50
45	Mike Easler	.50

Premium Autographs

This three-card set was made available with the purchase of other items from TCMA. The 2-1/2" x 3-1/2" cards have a glossy front finish and each card is personally autographed by the player depicted. Backs have a message about card collecting from the player and 1985 stats, along with TCMA advertising.

		NM/M
Complete Set (3):		175.00
Common Player:		45.00
(1)	Gary Carter	60.00
(2)	Tony Gwynn	90.00
(3)	Bret Saberhagen	30.00

Simon's Super Stars

The paintings of sports artist Robert Stephen Simon are reproduced in an unusually sized (2-13/16" x 3-1/2") card issue marketed to collectors. Fronts have color pictures with no extraneous graphics, bordered in white. Backs, printed in blue and white, have biographical and career information.

		NM/M
Complete Set (50):		35.00
Common Player:		.50
1	Carl Erskine	.50
2	Babe Ruth, Henry Aaron	1.50
3	Ted Williams	1.50
4	Mickey Mantle	2.00
5	Gil Hodges	.75
6	Roberto Clemente	1.50
7	Mickey Mantle	2.00
8	Walter Johnson	.50
9	N.Y. Yankees stars	1.50
10	Carl Yastrzemski, Ted Williams	1.50
11	Mickey Mantle	2.00
12	Harmon Killebrew	.50
13	Warren Spahn	.50
14	Ralph Kiner, Babe Ruth	1.00
15	Bob Gibson	.50
16	Pee Wee Reese	.50
17	Billy Martin	.50
18	Joe DiMaggio, Mickey Mantle	2.00
19	Phil Rizzuto	.50
20	Sandy Koufax	1.00
21	Jackie Robinson	1.00
22	Don Drysdale	.50
23	Mickey Mantle	2.00
24	Mickey Mantle	2.00
25	Joe DiMaggio	1.50
26	Robin Roberts	.50
27	Lou Brock	.50
28	Lou Gehrig	1.50
29	Willie Mays	1.00
30	Brooks Robinson	.50
31	Thurman Munson	.50
32	Roger Maris	1.00
33	Jim Palmer	.50
34	Stan Musial	.75
35	Roy Campanella	.50
36	Joe Pepitone	.50
37	Ebbets Field	.50
38	Honus Wagner	.50
39	Yogi Berra	.50
40	Eddie Mathews	.50
41	Carl Yastrzemski	.50
42	Babe Ruth	1.50
43	Babe Ruth	1.50
44	Pete Reiser	.50
45	Don Larsen	.50
46	Ernie Banks	.50
47	Casey Stengel	.50
48	Jackie Robinson	1.00
49	Duke Snider	.50
50	Checklist (Duke Snider)	.50

1987 TCMA All Time N.Y. Yankees

Mickey Mantle

Essentially a reprint of its 1980 team set, this TCMA collectors issue can be distinguished by the presence on back of a Major League Baseball logo. The earlier set has a TCMA date line on back. Fronts of the 2-1/2" x 3-1/2" cards have black-and-white player photos with an ornate blue frame and white border. Backs are in black-and-white and include the All Time team roster.

		NM/M
Complete Set (12):		33.00
Common Player:		.35
1	Lou Gehrig	7.00
2	Tony Lazzeri	.50
3	Red Rolfe	.40
4	Phil Rizzuto	1.25
5	Babe Ruth	7.50
6	Mickey Mantle	9.00
7	Joe DiMaggio	7.00
8	Bill Dickey	.70
9	Red Ruffing	.40
10	Whitey Ford	1.25
11	Johnny Murphy	.40
12	Casey Stengel	.60

Baseball's Greatest Teams

'69 Mets — TUG McGRAW P

Ten of the greatest lineups in baseball history are featured in this collectors' series. Each of the nine-card team sets features a different front design while backs share a common format offering player biographical details. The earlier teams picture players in black-and-white photos, while the later sets have color photos. Original issue price was about $1 per set, retail.

		NM/M
Complete Set (90):		70.00
Common Team Set (9):		4.50
Common Player:		.25
1907 Chicago Cubs		
Team Set:		4.50
1	Harry Steinfeldt	.25
2	Three-Finger Brown	.75
3	Ed Reulbach	.25
4	Johnny Kling	.25
5	Orvie Overall	.25
6	Joe Tinker	.75
7	Wildfire Schulte	.25
8	Frank Chance	.75
9	Johnny Evers	.75
1927 N.Y. Yankees		
Team Set:		20.00
1	Miller Huggins	.25
2	Herb Pennock	.25
3	Tony Lazzeri	.25
4	Waite Hoyt	.25
5	Wilcy Moore	.25
6	Earle Combs	.25
7	Bob Meusel	.25
8	Lou Gehrig	6.00
9	Babe Ruth	9.00
1934 St. Louis Cardinals		
Team Set:		4.50
1	Dizzy Dean	1.50
2	Daffy Dean	.60
3	Pepper Martin	.50
4	Rip Collins	.25
5	Frank Frisch	.50
6	Leo Durocher	.50
7	Ducky Medwick	.50
8	Tex Carleton	.25
9	Spud Davis	.25
1946 Boston Red Sox		
Team Set:		7.50
1	Joe Cronin	.50
2	Rudy York	.25
3	Bobby Doerr	.25
4	Johnny Pesky	.25
5	Dom DiMaggio	.60
6	Ted Williams	4.50
7	Boo Ferriss	.25
8	Tex Hughson	.25
9	Mickey Harris	.25
1950 Philadelphia Phillies		
Team Set:		4.50
1	Eddie Sawyer	.25
2	Curt Simmons	.25
3	Jim Konstanty	.50
4	Eddie Waitkus	.25
5	Granny Hamner	.25
6	Del Ennis	.25
7	Richie Ashburn	.60
8	Dick Sisler	.25
9	Robin Roberts	.60
1955 Brooklyn Dodgers		
Team Set:		7.50
1	Duke Snider, Walt Alston	.75
2	Roy Campanella	1.50
3	Jackie Robinson	3.00
4	Carl Furillo	.60
5	Gil Hodges	.75
6	Pee Wee Reese, Jim Gilliam	.75
7	Don Newcombe	.60
8	Ed Roebuck, Clem Labine	.50
9	Carl Erskine	.50
1957 Milwaukee Braves		
Team Set:		7.50
1	Hank Aaron	4.50
2	Eddie Mathews	.60
3	Bob Hazle	.25
4	Johnny Logan	.25
5	Red Schoendienst	.25
6	Wes Covington	.25
7	Lew Burdette	.35
8	Warren Spahn	.60
9	Bob Buhl	.25
1960 Pittsburgh Pirates		
Team Set:		7.50
1	Dick Stuart	.25
2	Bill Mazeroski	.75
3	Dick Groat	.25
4	Roberto Clemente	6.00
5	Bob Skinner	.25
6	Smoky Burgess	.35
7	Roy Face	.25
8	Bob Friend	.25
9	Vernon Law	.35
1961 N.Y. Yankees		
Team Set:		20.00
1	Bill Skowron	.50
2	Mickey Mantle	10.00
3	Bobby Richardson	.50
4	Tony Kubek	.50
5	Elston Howard	.50
6	Yogi Berra	2.25
7	Whitey Ford	2.25
8	Roger Maris	4.50
9	Ralph Houk	.25
1969 N.Y. Mets		
Team Set:		4.50
1	Ed Kranepool	.35
2	Bud Harrelson	.35
3	Cleon Jones, Tommie Agee, Ron Swoboda	.25
4	Jerry Koosman	.25
5	Gary Gentry	.25
6	Tug McGraw	.35
7	Ron Taylor	.25
8	Jerry Grote	.25
9	Ken Boswell	.25

1996 Team Metal Ken Griffey Jr.

CUI, the parent firm of the company that produces Metallic Images sports and non-sports cards, created this set of metal cards for sale in large retail chains. The four cards come packaged in a lithographed steel box about the size and shape of a Band-aid tin. The 2-5/8" x 3-9/16" cards have a blue and teal background with a color game-action photo at center. Backs have rolled metal edges with a photo at left. A few sentences about the player are printed at right. Logos and copyright data are at bottom. Issue price of the four-card set was just under $10.

		NM/M
Complete Set (4):		7.50
Common Card:		2.00
1	Ken Griffey Jr. (Home run trot.)	2.00
2	Ken Griffey Jr./Sliding	2.00
3	Ken Griffey Jr. (Batting follow-through.)	2.00
4	Ken Griffey Jr. (Batting follow-through.)	2.00

1996 Team Metal Cal Ripken, Jr.

CUI, the parent firm of the company that produces Metallic Impressions sports and non-sports cards, created this set of metal cards for sale in large retail chains. The four cards come packaged in a lithographed steel box about the size and shape of a Band-aid tin. The 2-5/8" x 3-9/16" cards have a green and orange background with a color game-action photo at center. Backs have rolled metal edges with a photo at left. A few sentences about the player are printed at right. Logos and copyright data are at bottom. Issue price of the four-card set was just under $10.

		NM/M
Complete Set (4):		7.50
Common Card:		2.00
1	Cal Ripken Jr./Btg (Black jersey.)	2.00
2	Cal Ripken Jr./Btg (Follow-through.)	2.00
3	Cal Ripken Jr./Fielding	2.00
4	Cal Ripken Jr./Btg (White jersey.)	2.00

1996 Team Out! Game

This baseball card game is sold as a boxed set containing 37 of the 91 different player cards, plus an assortment of 23 of the 10 cartoon "action" cards used to play the game. Cards are 2-1/4" x 3-1/2" with rounded corners and glossy surfaces. Backs have a close-up photo of a baseball with product and censor logos and copyright information. Fronts of the player photo cards are bordered in black; the cartoon action cards have red or blue borders. The unnumbered cards are checklisted here in alphabetical order.

		NM/M
Complete Set (101):		40.00
Common Player:		.25
(1)	Roberto Alomar	.35
(2)	Brady Anderson	.25
(3)	Kevin Appier	.25
(4)	Carlos Baerga	.25
(5)	Jeff Bagwell	1.50
(6)	Albert Belle	.25
(7)	Dante Bichette	.25
(8)	Craig Biggio	.25
(9)	Wade Boggs	2.00
(10)	Barry Bonds	3.00
(11)	Kevin Brown	.25
(12)	Jay Buhner	.25
(13)	Ellis Burks	.25
(14)	Ken Caminiti	.25
(15)	Joe Carter	.25
(16)	Vinny Castilla	.25
(17)	Jeff Cirillo	.25
(18)	Will Clark	.25
(19)	Jeff Conine	.25
(20)	Joey Cora	.25
(21)	Marty Cordova	.25
(22)	Eric Davis	.25
(23)	Ray Durham	.25
(24)	Jim Edmonds	.25
(25)	Cecil Fielder	.25
(26)	Travis Fryman	.25
(27)	Jason Giambi	.60
(28)	Bernard Gilkey	.25
(29)	Tom Glavine	.45
(30)	Juan Gonzalez	.75
(31)	Mark Grace	.25
(32)	Ken Griffey Jr.	2.25
(33)	Marquis Grissom	.25
(34)	Mark Grudzielanek	.25
(35)	Ozzie Guillen	.25
(36)	Tony Gwynn	2.00
(37)	Bobby Higginson	.25
(38)	Todd Hundley	.25
(39)	Derek Jeter	3.00
(40)	Lance Johnson	.25
(41)	Randy Johnson	1.50
(42)	Chipper Jones	2.00
(43)	Brian Jordan	.25
(44)	Wally Joyner	.25
(45)	Jason Kendall	.25
(46)	Chuck Knoblauch	.25
(47)	Ray Lankford	.25
(48)	Mike Lansing	.25
(49)	Barry Larkin	.25
(50)	Kenny Lofton	.25
(51)	Javier Lopez	.25
(52)	Mike MacFarlane	.25
(53)	Greg Maddux	2.00
(54)	Al Martin	.25
(55)	Brian McRae	.25
(56)	Mark McGwire	2.50
(57)	Raul Mondesi	.25
(58)	Denny Neagle	.25
(59)	Hideo Nomo	.25
(60)	John Olerud	.25
(61)	Rey Ordonez	.25
(62)	Troy Percival	.25
(63)	Mike Piazza	2.25
(64)	Andy Pettitte	.35
(65)	Manny Ramirez	1.50
(66)	Cal Ripken Jr.	3.00
(67)	Alex Rodriguez	2.50
(68)	Ivan Rodriguez	1.00
(69)	Ryne Sandberg	2.00
(70)	Tim Salmon	.25
(71)	Benito Santiago	.25
(72)	Kevin Seitzer	.25
(73)	Scott Servais	.25
(74)	Gary Sheffield	.60
(75)	Ozzie Smith	2.00
(76)	John Smoltz	.25
(77)	Sammy Sosa	2.00
(78)	Mike Stanley	.25
(79)	Terry Steinbach	.25
(80)	Frank Thomas	1.50
(81)	Steve Trachsel	.25
(82)	Jose Valentin	.25
(83)	Mo Vaughn	.25
(84)	Jose Vizcaino	.25
(85)	Robin Ventura	.25
(86)	Larry Walker	.25
(87)	Walt Weiss	.25
(88)	Bernie Williams	.25
(89)	Matt Williams	.25
(90)	Eric Young	.25
(91)	Todd Zeile	.25
(92)	Double Play/Roberto Alomar (Cartoon)	.25
(93)	Free Agent Acquisition/ Barry Bonds (Cartoon)	1.50
(94)	No Trade - Infield/ Mark McGwire, Ozzie Smith, Mo Vaughn (Cartoon)	.75
(95)	No Trade - Outfield/ Albert Belle, Raul Mondesi (Cartoon)	.25
(96)	Out!/Mike Piazza, Matt Williams (Cartoon)	.75
(97)	Pitcher Bombed (Cartoon)	.25
(98)	Pitcher Stays/ Greg Maddux (Cartoon)	1.00
(99)	Safe!/Frank Thomas (Cartoon)	.75
(100)	Trade - Infield/Cal Ripken Jr., Alex Rodriguez (Cartoon)	.75
(101)	Trade - Outfield/ Ken Griffey Jr., Sammy Sosa (Cartoon)	.65

1988 Tetley Tea Discs

The Tetley iced tea discs are virtually identical in format to the 1988 Baseball Super Stars discs, but are labeled "FIRST ANNUAL COLLECTORS' EDITION," rather than Second and appear to have slight differences in the player pairs which make up each folder. Values for these can be extrapolated by combining the values of individual discs shown under the 1988 Baseball Super Stars listing.

1989 Tetley Tea Discs

The Tetley iced tea discs are virtually identical in format to the 1989 Baseball Super Stars discs, but are labeled "SECOND ANNUAL COLLECTORS' EDITION." The tri-fold panels were distributed in canisters of iced tea mix in the East.

1990 Tetley Tea Discs

The Tetley iced tea discs are virtually identical in format to the 1990 Baseball Super Stars discs, but are labeled "THIRD ANNUAL COLLECTORS' EDITION." The tri-fold panels were distributed in canisters of iced tea mix in the East.

1986 Texas Gold Ice Cream Reds

(14) PETE ROSE MANAGER

One of the last regional baseball card sets produced during the 1986 season was a 28-card team set sponsored by a Cincinnati-area ice cream company and given to fans attending the September 19 game. Photos on the 2-1/2" x 3-1/2" cards are game-action shots, and include three different cards of playing manager Pete Rose. The set is also notable for the inclusion of first cards of some of the Reds' young prospects.

	NM/M
Complete Set (28):	16.00
Common Player:	.50
6 Bo Diaz	.50
9 Max Venable	.50
11 Kurt Stillwell	.50
12 Nick Esasky	.50
13 Dave Concepcion	.75
14a Pete Rose (Commemorative)	4.00
14b Pete Rose/Infield	6.00
14c Pete Rose/Manager	4.00
16 Ron Oester	.50
20 Eddie Milner	.50
22 Sal Butera	.50
24 Tony Perez	1.50
25 Buddy Bell	.75
28 Kal Daniels	.50
29 Tracy Jones	.50
31 John Franco	.50
32 Tom Browning	.50
33 Ron Robinson	.50
34 Bill Gullickson	.50
36 Mario Soto	.50
39 Dave Parker	.75
40 John Denny	.50
44 Eric Davis	1.00
45 Chris Welsh	.50
48 Ted Power	.50
49 Joe Price	.50
--- Reds coaches (Scott Breeden, Billy Demars, Tommy Helms, Bruce Kimm, Jim Lett, George Scherger)	
--- Logo/Coupon card	.20

1987 Texas Rangers Fire Safety

Co-sponsored by the team, U.S. and Texas Forest Services, the set was given out to fans at special promotions at Arlington Stadium. Cards measure 4-1/4" x 6" and feature color action photos. Backs contain brief player personal information along with a Smokey the Bear wildfire prevention message. Cards of Mike Mason and Tom Paciorek were withdrawn from the sets given out by the Rangers and are quite scarce.

	NM/M
Complete Set (32):	45.00
Common Player:	.30
1 Charlie Hough	.30
2 Greg Harris	.30
3 Jose Guzman	.30
4 Mike Mason	20.00
5 Dale Mohorcic	.30
6 Bobby Witt	.30
7 Mitch Williams	.30
8 Geno Petralli	.30
9 Don Slaught	.30
10 Darrell Porter	.30
11 Steve Beuchele	.30
12 Pete O'Brien	.30
13 Scott Fletcher	.30
14 Tom Paciorek	20.00
15 Pete Incaviglia	.30
16 Oddibe McDowell	.30
17 Ruben Sierra	.30

18 Larry Parrish	.30
19 Bobby Valentine	.30
20 Tom House	.30
21 Tom Robson	.30
22 Edwin Correa	.30
23 Mike Stanley	.30
24 Joe Ferguson	.30
25 Art Howe	.30
26 Bob Brower	.30
27 Mike Loynd	.30
28 Curtis Wilkerson	.30
29 Tim Foli	.30
30 Dave Oliver	.30
31 Jerry Browne	.30
32 Jeff Russell	.30

1988 Texas Rangers Fire Safety

This oversized (3-1/2" x 5") set was distributed to Rangers' fans at Smokey Bear Game Day on August 7. Fronts feature full-color action photos framed in an oval blue and red border on a white background. A nameplate above the photo identifies the player and a "Wildfire Prevention" logo is printed beneath the photo. Rangers (left) and Smokey (right) logos fill the upper corners of the card face. The card backs are black-and-white and include player info, U.S. and Texas Forest Service logos, and fire prevention tips.

	NM/M
Complete Set (21):	5.00
Common Player:	.30
1 Tom O'Malley	.30
2 Pete O'Brien	.30
3 Geno Petralli	.30
4 Pete Incaviglia	.30
5 Oddibe McDowell	.30
6 Dale Mohorcic	.30
7 Bobby Witt	.30
8 Bobby Valentine	.30
9 Ruben Sierra	.30
10 Scott Fletcher	.30
11 Mike Stanley	.30
12 Steve Buechele	.30
13 Charlie Hough	.30
14 Larry Parrish	.30
15 Jerry Browne	.30
16 Bob Brower	.30
17 Jeff Russell	.30
18 Edwin Correa	.30
19 Mitch Williams	.30
20 Jose Guzman	.30
21 Curtis Wilkerson	.30

1989 Texas Rangers Fire Safety

Given away at a Rangers home game in 1989, this large-format (4-1/4" x 6") set features player portrait photos within an oval frame on a white border. The team logo is at upper-left; Smokey the Bear at upper-right. Backs have minimal biographical data and stats and a cartoon

fire prevention tip. The unnumbered cards are checklisted here alphabetically.

	NM/M
Complete Set (34):	20.00
Common Player:	.25
(1) Darrel Akerfelds	.25
(2) Brad Arnsberg	.25
(3) Buddy Bell	.25
(4) Kevin Brown	.25
(5) Steve Buechele	.25
(6) Dick Egan	.25
(7) Cecil Espy	.25
(8) Scott Fletcher	.25
(9) Julio Franco	.25
(10) Cecilio Guante	.25
(11) Jose Guzman	.25
(12) Drew Hall	.25
(13) Toby Harrah	.25
(14) Charlie Hough	.25
(15) Tom House	.25
(16) Pete Incaviglia	.25
(17) Chad Kreuter	.25
(18) Jeff Kunkel	.25
(19) Rick Leach	.25
(20) Davey Lopes	.25
(21) Craig McMurtry	.25
(22) Jamie Moyer	.25
(23) Dave Oliver	.25
(24) Rafael Palmeiro	2.00
(25) Geno Petralli	.25
(26) Tom Robson	.25
(27) Kenny Rogers	.25
(28) Jeff Russell	.25
(29) Nolan Ryan	15.00
(30) Ruben Sierra	.25
(31) Mike Stanley	.25
(32) Jim Sundberg	.25
(33) Bobby Valentine	.25
(34) Bobby Witt	.25

1990 Texas Rangers Fire Safety

This stadium giveaway set is identical in design to the 1989 issue, but at 3-1/2" x 5", is slightly smaller. Backs have a cartoon fire safety tip and a bit of player personal data.

	NM/M
Complete Set (24):	30.00
Common Player:	.50
(1) Harold Baines	.50
(2) Brian Bohannon	.50
(3) Thad Bosley	.50
(4) Kevin Brown	.75
(5) Jack Daugherty	.50
(6) Cecil Espy	.50
(7) Julio Franco	.75
(8) Jeff Huson	.50
(9) Pete Incaviglia	.50
(10) Mike Jeffcoat	.50
(11) Chad Kreuter	.50
(12) Jeff Kunkel	.50
(13) Gary Mielke	.50
(14) Jamie Moyer	.50
(15) Rafael Palmeiro	3.00
(16) Gary Pettis	.50
(17) Kenny Rogers	.50
(18) Jeff Russell	.50
(19) John Russell	.50
(20) Nolan Ryan	25.00
(21) Ruben Sierra	.50
(22) Bobby Valentine	.50
(23) Bobby Witt	.50
(24) Arlington Stadium	1.00

1983 Thorn Apple Valley Cubs

This set of 27 cards was issued in conjuction with a "Baseball Card Day" promotion at Wrigley Field in 1983. Thorn Apple Valley was the meat company which produced the hot dogs sold at the ballpark. The cards feature borderless color photos with the player's name, uniform number (also the card's number in the checklist) and an abbreviation for their po-

#33 JOE CARTER OF

sition. Card backs feature annual statistics. Of the 27 cards, which measure 2-1/4" x 3-1/2", 25 feature players, one is a team card, and one features the manager and coaches.

	NM/M
Complete Set (27):	25.00
Common Player:	.50
1 Larry Bowa	.50
6 Keith Moreland	.50
7 Jody Davis	.50
10 Leon Durham	.50
11 Ron Cey	.50
16 Steve Lake	.50
20 Thad Bosley	.50
21 Jay Johnstone	.50
22 Bill Buckner	1.00
23 Ryne Sandberg	15.00
24 Jerry Morales	.50
25 Gary Woods	.50
27 Mel Hall	.50
29 Tom Veryzer	.50
30 Chuck Rainey	.50
31 Fergie Jenkins	4.00
32 Craig Lefferts	.50
33 Joe Carter	2.00
34 Steve Trout	.50
36 Mike Proly	.50
39 Bill Campbell	.50
41 Warren Brusstar	.50
44 Dick Ruthven	.50
46 Lee Smith	1.50
48 Dickie Noles	.50
--- Coaching Staff (Ruben Amaro, Billy Connors, Duffy Dyer, Lee Elia, Fred Koenig, John Vukovich)	.50
--- Team Photo	.50

1994 Tombstone Pizza

Score produced a special 30-card set which could be obtained by eating a lot of frozen pizzas (one card per pizza) or by sending in a dollar and five proofs of purchase. Titled "'94 Tombstone Super-Pro Series," the cards are black-bordered and UV coated on front and back. Because the set is licensed only by the players' union and not by Major League Baseball, the uniform logos on the front action photos and back portraits have been airbrushed away. Cards feature the Tombstone logo on both front and back. Backs have recent and career stats, a facsimile autograph and a card number.

	NM/M
Complete Set (30):	4.00
Common Player:	.25
1 Frank Thomas	.50
2 David Cone	.25
3 Bob Hamelin	.25
4 Jeff Bagwell	.50
5 Greg Maddux	.65
6 Raul Mondesi	.25
7 Chili Davis	.25
8 Cecil Fielder	.25
9 Ken Griffey Jr.	.75
10 Jimmy Key	.25
11 Kenny Lofton	.25
12 Paul Molitor	.50
13 Kirby Puckett	.65
14 Cal Ripken Jr.	1.50
15 Ivan Rodriguez	.40
16 Kevin Seitzer	.25
17 Ruben Sierra	.25
18 Mo Vaughn	.25
19 Moises Alou	.25
20 Barry Bonds	1.50
21 Jeff Conine	.25
22 Lenny Dykstra	.25
23 Andres Galarraga	.25
24 Tony Gwynn	.65
25 Barry Larkin	.25
26 Fred McGriff	.25
27 Orlando Merced	.25
28 Bret Saberhagen	.25
29 Ozzie Smith	.65
30 Sammy Sosa	.25

1981 Topps

This is another 726-card set of 2-1/2" x 3-1/2" cards from Topps. The cards have the usual color photo with all cards from the same team sharing the same color borders. Player names appear

4 Bobby Bonilla	.25
5 Andres Galarraga	.25
6 Mark Grace	.25
7 Marquis Grissom	.25
8 Tony Gwynn	.65
9 Bryan Harvey	.25
10 Gregg Jefferies	.25
11 David Justice	.25
12 John Kruk	.25
13 Barry Larkin	.25
14 Greg Maddux	.65
15 Mike Piazza	.75
16 Jim Abbott	.25
17 Albert Belle	.25
18 Cecil Fielder	.25
19 Juan Gonzalez	.35
20 Mike Greenwell	.25
21 Ken Griffey Jr.	.75
22 Jack McDowell	.25
23 Jeff Montgomery	.25
24 John Olerud	.25
25 Kirby Puckett	.65
26 Cal Ripken, Jr.	1.50
27 Tim Salmon	.50
28 Ruben Sierra	.25
29 Frank Thomas	.50
30 Robin Yount	.50

1995 Tombstone Pizza

Tombstone's second annual baseball card issue was available either singly in frozen pizza packages, or as a 30-card boxed set via a mail-in offer. Cards feature action player photos on front and portrait photos on back; both have had uniform logos airbrushed for lack of a MLB license. There is a graduated red to black border on each side. On front at lower-right are the player and team name and the Tombstone logo. Backs have biographical data, recent stats and career highlights. At bottom is a card number and the players' association logo.

under the photo with team and position on a baseball cap at lower-left. The Topps logo returned in a small baseball in the lower-right. Card backs include the usual stats along with a headline and a cartoon if there was room. Specialty cards include previous season record-breakers, highlights of the playoffs and World Series, along with the final appearance of team cards. Eleven cards on each of the six press sheets were double-printed.

	NM/M
Complete Set (726):	45.00
Common Player:	.10
Wax Pack (15):	3.00
Wax Box (36):	85.00
Cello Pack (28):	3.00
Cello Box (24):	75.00
Rack Pack (48):	6.00
Rack Box (24):	120.00
Vending Box (500):	40.00
1 Batting Leaders (George Brett, Bill Buckner)	.75
2 Home Run Leaders (Reggie Jackson, Ben Oglivie, Mike Schmidt)	.75
3 RBI Leaders (Cecil Cooper, Mike Schmidt)	.25
4 Stolen Base Leaders (Rickey Henderson, Ron LeFlore)	.50
5 Victory Leaders (Steve Carlton, Steve Stone)	.15
6 Strikeout Leaders (Len Barker, Steve Carlton)	.15
7 ERA Leaders (Rudy May, Don Sutton)	
8 Leading Firemen (Rollie Fingers, Tom Hume, Dan Quisenberry)	.10
9 Pete LaCock/DP	.10
10 Mike Flanagan	.10
11 Jim Wohlford/DP	.10
12 Mark Clear	.10
13 Joe Charboneau RC	.50
14 John Tudor RC	.20
15 Larry Parrish	.10
16 Ron Davis	.10
17 Cliff Johnson	.10
18 Glenn Adams	.10
19 Jim Clancy	.10
20 Jeff Burroughs	.10
21 Ron Oester	.10
22 Danny Darwin	.10
23 Alex Trevino	.10
24 Don Stanhouse	.10
25 Sixto Lezcano	.10
26 U.L. Washington	.10
27 Champ Summers/DP	.10
28 Enrique Romo	.10
29 Gene Tenace	.10
30 Jack Clark	.10
31 Checklist 1-121/DP	.10
32 Ken Oberkfell	.10
33 Rick Honeycutt	.10
34 Aurelio Rodriguez	.10
35 Mitchell Page	.10
36 Ed Farmer	.10
37 Gary Roenicke	.10
38 Win Remmerswaal	.10
39 Tom Veryzer	.10
40 Tug McGraw	.10
41 Rangers Future Stars (Bob Babcock, John Butcher, Jerry Don Gleaton)	.10
42 Jerry White/DP	.10
43 Jose Morales	.10
44 Larry McWilliams	.10
45 Enos Cabell	.10

ABBREVIATIONS
DP - Double Print

#	Card	Price
46	Rick Bosetti	.10
47	Ken Brett	.10
48	Dave Skaggs	.10
49	Bob Shirley	.10
50	Dave Lopes	.10
51	Bill Robinson/DP	.10
52	Hector Cruz	.10
53	Kevin Saucier	.10
54	Ivan DeJesus	.10
55	Mike Norris	.10
56	Buck Martinez	.10
57	Dave Roberts	.10
58	Joel Youngblood	.10
59	Dan Petry	.10
60	Willie Randolph	.10
61	Butch Wynegar	.10
62	Joe Pettini	.10
63	Steve Renko/DP	.10
64	Brian Asselstine	.10
65	Scott McGregor	.10
66	Royals Future Stars (Manny Castillo, Tim Ireland, Mike Jones)	.10
67	Ken Kravec	.10
68	Matt Alexander/DP	.10
69	Ed Halicki	.10
70	Al Oliver/DP	.10
71	Hal Dues	.10
72	Barry Evans/DP	.10
73	Doug Bair	.10
74	Mike Hargrove	.10
75	Reggie Smith	.10
76	Mario Mendoza	.10
77	Mike Barlow	.10
78	Steve Dillard	.10
79	Bruce Robbins	.10
80	Rusty Staub	.15
81	Dave Stapleton	.10
82	Astros Future Stars (Danny Heep, Alan Knicely, Bobby Sprowl/DP)	.10
83	Mike Proly	.10
84	Johnnie LeMaster	.10
85	Mike Caldwell	.10
86	Wayne Gross	.10
87	Rick Camp	.10
88	Joe Lefebvre	.10
89	Darrell Jackson	.10
90	Bake McBride	.10
91	Tim Stoddard/DP	.10
92	Mike Easler	.10
93	Ed Glynn/DP	.10
94	Harry Spilman/DP	.10
95	Jim Sundberg	.10
96	A's Future Stars (Dave Beard, Ernie Camacho RC, Pat Dempsey)	.10
97	Chris Speier	.10
98	Clint Hurdle	.10
99	Eric Wilkins	.10
100	Rod Carew	2.00
101	Benny Ayala	.10
102	Dave Tobik	.10
103	Jerry Martin	.10
104	Terry Forster	.10
105	Jose Cruz	.10
106	Don Money	.10
107	Rich Wortham	.10
108	Bruce Benedict	.10
109	Mike Scott	.10
110	Carl Yastrzemski	2.00
111	Greg Minton	.10
112	White Sox Future Stars (Rusty Kuntz, Fran Mullins, Leo Sutherland)	.10
113	Mike Phillips	.10
114	Tom Underwood	.10
115	Roy Smalley	.10
116	Joe Simpson	.10
117	Pete Falcone	.10
118	Kurt Bevacqua	.10
119	Tippy Martinez	.10
120	Larry Bowa	.10
121	Larry Harlow	.10
122	John Denny	.10
123	Al Cowens	.10
124	Jerry Garvin	.10
125	Andre Dawson	1.50
126	Charlie Leibrandt RC	.40
127	Rudy Law	.10
128	Gary Allenson/DP	.10
129	Art Howe	.10
130	Larry Gura	.10
131	Keith Moreland RC	.20
132	Tommy Boggs	.10
133	Jeff Cox	.10
134	Steve Mura	.10
135	Gorman Thomas	.10
136	Doug Capilla	.10
137	Hosken Powell	.10
138	Rich Dotson/DP RC	.20
139	Oscar Gamble	.10
140	Bob Forsch	.10
141	Miguel Dilone	.10
142	Jackson Todd	.10
143	Dan Meyer	.10
144	Allen Ripley	.10
145	Mickey Rivers	.10
146	Bobby Castillo	.10
147	Dale Berra	.10
148	Randy Niemann	.10
149	Joe Nolan	.10
150	Mark Fidrych	.15
151	Claudell Washington/DP	.10
152	John Urrea	.10
153	Tom Poquette	.10
154	Rick Langford	.10
155	Chris Chambliss	.10
156	Bob McClure	.10
157	Jim Wathan	.10
158	Fergie Jenkins	1.00
159	Brian Doyle	.10
160	Garry Maddox	.10
161	Dan Graham	.10
162	Doug Corbett	.10
163	Billy Almon	.10
164	Lamarr Hoyt (LaMarr) RC	.15
165	Tony Scott	.10
166	Floyd Bannister	.10
167	Terry Whitfield	.10
168	Don Robinson/DP	.10
169	John Mayberry	.10
170	Ross Grimsley	.10
171	Gene Richards	.10
172	Gary Woods	.10
173	Bump Wills	.10
174	Doug Rau	.10
175	Dave Collins	.10
176	Mike Krukow	.10
177	Rick Peters	.10
178	Jim Essian/DP	.10
179	Rudy May	.10
180	Pete Rose	5.00
181	Elias Sosa	.10
182	Bob Grich	.10
183	Dick Davis/DP	.10
184	Jim Dwyer	.10
185	Dennis Leonard	.10
186	Wayne Nordhagen	.10
187	Mike Parrott	.10
188	Doug DeCinces	.10
189	Craig Swan	.10
190	Cesar Cedeno	.10
191	Rick Sutcliffe	.10
192	Braves Future Stars (Terry Harper RC, Ed Miller, Rafael Ramirez RC)	.10
193	Pete Vuckovich	.10
194	Rod Scurry RC	.10
195	Rich Murray	.10
196	Duffy Dyer	.10
197	Jim Kern	.10
198	Jerry Dybzinski	.10
199	Chuck Rainey	.10
200	George Foster	.10
201	Johnny Bench (Record Breaker)	.45
202	Steve Carlton (Record Breaker)	.25
203	Bill Gullickson (Record Breaker)	.10
204	Ron LeFlore, Rodney Scott (Record Breaker)	.10
205	Pete Rose (Record Breaker)	1.50
206	Mike Schmidt (Record Breaker)	1.00
207	Ozzie Smith (Record Breaker)	1.00
208	Willie Wilson (Record Breaker)	.10
209	Dickie Thon/DP	.10
210	Jim Palmer	1.50
211	Derrel Thomas	.10
212	Steve Nicosia	.10
213	Al Holland RC	.10
214	Angels Future Stars (Ralph Botting, Jim Dorsey, John Harris)	.10
215	Larry Hisle	.10
216	John Henry Johnson	.10
217	Rich Hebner	.10
218	Paul Splittorff	.10
219	Ken Landreaux	.10
220	Tom Seaver	2.00
221	Bob Davis	.10
222	Jorge Orta	.10
223	Roy Lee Jackson	.10
224	Pat Zachry	.10
225	Ruppert Jones	.10
226	Manny Sanguillen/DP	.10
227	Fred Martinez	.10
228	Tom Paciorek	.10
229	Rollie Fingers	1.00
230	George Hendrick	.10
231	Joe Beckwith	.10
232	Mickey Klutts	.10
233	Skip Lockwood	.10
234	Lou Whitaker	.10
235	Scott Sanderson	.10
236	Mike Ivie	.10
237	Charlie Moore	.10
238	Willie Hernandez	.10
239	Rick Miller/DP	.10
240	Nolan Ryan	5.00
241	Checklist 122-242/DP	.10
242	Chet Lemon	.10
243	Sal Butera	.10
244	Cardinals Future Stars (Tito Landrum RC, Al Olmsted, Andy Rincon)	.10
245	Ed Figueroa	.10
246	Ed Ott/DP	.10
247	Glenn Hubbard/DP	.10
248	Joey McLaughlin	.10
249	Larry Cox	.10
250	Ron Guidry	.15
251	Tom Brookens	.10
252	Victor Cruz	.10
253	Dave Bergman	.10
254	Ozzie Smith	3.00
255	Mark Littell	.10
256	Bombo Rivera	.10
257	Rennie Stennett	.10
258	Joe Price RC	.10
259	Mets Future Stars (Juan Berenguer, Hubie Brooks RC, Mookie Wilson RC)	.75
260	Ron Cey	.10
261	Rickey Henderson	4.50
262	Sammy Stewart	.10
263	Brian Downing	.10
264	Jim Norris	.10
265	John Candelaria	.10
266	Tom Herr	.10
267	Stan Bahnsen	.10
268	Jerry Royster	.10
269	Ken Forsch	.10
270	Greg Luzinski	.10
271	Bill Castro	.10
272	Bruce Kimm	.10
273	Stan Papi	.10
274	Craig Chamberlain	.10
275	Dwight Evans	.10
276	Dan Spillner	.10
277	Alfredo Griffin	.10
278	Rick Sofield	.10
279	Bob Knepper	.10
280	Ken Griffey	.10
281	Fred Stanley	.10
282	Mariners Future Stars (Rick Anderson, Greg Biercevicz, Rodney Craig)	.10
283	Billy Sample	.10
284	Brian Kingman	.10
285	Jerry Turner	.10
286	Dave Frost	.10
287	Lenn Sakata	.10
288	Bob Clark	.10
289	Mickey Hatcher	.10
290	Bob Boone/DP	.10
291	Aurelio Lopez	.10
292	Mike Squires	.10
293	Charlie Lea RC	.15
294	Mike Tyson/DP	.10
295	Hal McRae	.10
296	Bill Nahorodny/DP	.10
297	Bob Bailor	.10
298	Buddy Solomon	.10
299	Elliott Maddox	.10
300	Paul Molitor	2.00
301	Matt Keough	.10
302	Dodgers Future Stars (Jack Perconte RC, Mike Scioscia RC, Fernando Valenzuela RC)	2.00
303	Johnny Oates	.10
304	John Castino	.10
305	Ken Clay	.10
306	Juan Beniquez/DP	.10
307	Gene Garber	.10
308	Rick Manning	.10
309	Luis Salazar RC	.10
310	Vida Blue/DP	.10
311	Freddie Patek	.10
312	Rick Rhoden	.10
313	Luis Pujols	.10
314	Rich Dauer	.10
315	Kirk Gibson RC	3.00
316	Craig Minetto	.10
317	Lonnie Smith	.10
318	Steve Yeager	.10
319	Rowland Office	.10
320	Tom Burgmeier	.10
321	Leon Durham RC	.15
322	Neil Allen	.10
323	Jim Morrison/DP	.10
324	Mike Willis	.10
325	Ray Knight	.10
326	Biff Pocoroba	.10
327	Moose Haas	.10
328	Twins Future Stars (Dave Engle RC, Greg Johnston, Gary Ward)	.15
329	Joaquin Andujar	.10
330	Frank White	.10
331	Dennis Lamp	.10
332	Lee Lacy/DP	.10
333	Sid Monge	.10
334	Dane Iorg	.10
335	Rick Cerone	.10
336	Eddie Whitson	.10
337	Lynn Jones	.10
338	Checklist 243-363	.10
339	John Ellis	.10
340	Bruce Kison	.10
341	Dwayne Murphy	.10
342	Eric Rasmussen/DP	.10
343	Frank Taveras	.10
344	Byron McLaughlin	.10
345	Warren Cromartie	.10
346	Larry Christenson/DP	.10
347	Harold Baines RC	4.00
348	Bob Sykes	.10
349	Glenn Hoffman	.10
350	J.R. Richard	.10
351	Otto Velez	.10
352	Dick Tidrow/DP	.10
353	Terry Kennedy	.10
354	Mario Soto	.10
355	Bob Horner	.10
356	Padres Future Stars (George Stablein, Craig Stimac, Tom Tellmann)	.10
357	Jim Slaton	.10
358	Mark Wagner	.10
359	Tom Hausman	.10
360	Willie Wilson	.10
361	Joe Strain	.10
362	Bo Diaz	.10
363	Geoff Zahn	.10
364	Mike Davis RC	.10
365	Graig Nettles/DP	.15
366	Mike Ramsey	.10
367	Denny Martinez	.10
368	Leon Roberts	.10
369	Frank Tanana	.10
370	Dave Winfield	2.00
371	Charlie Hough	.10
372	Jay Johnstone	.10
373	Pat Underwood	.10
374	Tom Hutton	.10
375	Dave Concepcion	.10
376	Ron Reed	.10
377	Jerry Morales	.10
378	Dave Rader	.10
379	Lary Sorensen	.10
380	Willie Stargell	2.00
381	Cubs Future Stars (Carlos Lezcano, Steve Macko, Randy Martz)	.10
382	Paul Mirabella RC	.10
383	Eric Soderholm/DP	.10
384	Mike Sadek	.10
385	Joe Sambito	.10
386	Dave Edwards	.10
387	Phil Niekro	1.00
388	Andre Thornton	.10
389	Marty Pattin	.10
390	Cesar Geronimo	.10
391	Dave Lemanczyk/DP	.10
392	Lance Parrish	.10
393	Broderick Perkins	.10
394	Woodie Fryman	.10
395	Scot Thompson	.10
396	Bill Campbell	.10
397	Julio Cruz	.10
398	Ross Baumgarten	.10
399	Orioles Future Stars (Mike Boddicker RC, Mark Corey, Floyd Rayford RC)	.20
400	Reggie Jackson	3.00
401	A.L. Championships (Royals Sweep Yankees)	.50
402	N.L. Championships (Phillies Squeak Past Astros)	.25
403	World Series (Phillies Beat Royals In 6)	.25
404	World Series Summary (Phillies Win First World Series)	.25
405	Nino Espinosa	.10
406	Dickie Noles	.10
407	Ernie Whitt	.10
408	Fernando Arroyo	.10
409	Larry Herndon	.10
410	Bert Campaneris	.10
411	Terry Puhl	.10
412	Britt Burns RC	.10
413	Tony Bernazard	.10
414	John Pacella/DP	.10
415	Ben Oglivie	.10
416	Gary Alexander	.10
417	Dan Schatzeder	.10
418	Bobby Brown	.10
419	Tom Hume	.10
420	Keith Hernandez	.10
421	Bob Stanley	.10
422	Dan Ford	.10
423	Shane Rawley	.10
424	Yankees Future Stars (Tim Lollar, Bruce Robinson, Dennis Werth)	.10
425	Al Bumbry	.10
426	Warren Brusstar	.10
427	John D'Acquisto	.10
428	John Stearns	.10
429	Mick Kelleher	.10
430	Jim Bibby	.10
431	Dave Roberts	.10
432	Len Barker	.10
433	Rance Mulliniks	.10
434	Roger Erickson	.10
435	Jim Spencer	.10
436	Gary Lucas	.10
437	Mike Heath/DP	.10
438	John Montefusco	.10
439	Denny Walling	.10
440	Jerry Reuss	.10
441	Ken Reitz	.10
442	Ron Pruitt	.10
443	Jim Beattie/DP	.10
444	Garth Iorg	.10
445	Ellis Valentine	.10
446	Checklist 364-484	.10
447	Junior Kennedy/DP	.10
448	Tim Corcoran	.10
449	Paul Mitchell	.10
450	Dave Kingman/DP	.10
451	Indians Future Stars (Chris Bando, Tom Brennan, Sandy Wihtol)	.10
452	Renie Martin	.10
453	Rob Wilfong/DP	.10
454	Andy Hassler	.10
455	Rick Burleson	.10
456	Jeff Reardon RC	1.50
457	Mike Lum	.10
458	Randy Jones	.10
459	Greg Gross	.10
460	Rich Gossage	.10
461	Dave McKay	.10
462	Jack Brohamer	.10
463	Milt May	.10
464	Adrian Devine	.10
465	Bill Russell	.10
466	Bob Molinaro	.10
467	Dave Stieb	.10
468	Johnny Wockenfuss	.10
469	Jeff Leonard	.10
470	Manny Trillo	.10
471	Mike Vail	.10
472	Dyar Miller/DP	.10
473	Jose Cardenal	.10
474	Mike LaCoss	.10
475	Buddy Bell	.10
476	Jerry Koosman	.10
477	Luis Gomez	.10
478	Juan Eichelberger	.10
479	Expos Future Stars (Bobby Pate RC, Tim Raines RC, Roberto Ramos RC)	3.00
480	Carlton Fisk	2.00
481	Bob Lacey/DP	.10
482	Jim Gantner	.10
483	Mike Griffin	.10
484	Max Venable/DP	.10
485	Garry Templeton	.10
486	Marc Hill	.10
487	Dewey Robinson	.10
488	Damaso Garcia RC	.10
489	John Littlefield (Photo actually Mark Riggins)	.10
490	Eddie Murray	2.00
491	Gordy Pladson	.10
492	Barry Foote	.10
493	Dan Quisenberry	.10
494	Bob Walk RC	.20
495	Dusty Baker	.15
496	Paul Dade	.10
497	Fred Norman	.10
498	Pat Putnam	.10
499	Frank Pastore	.10
500	Jim Rice	.25
501	Tim Foli/DP	.10
502	Giants Future Stars (Chris Bourjos, Al Hargesheimer, Mike Rowland)	.10
503	Steve McCatty	.10
504	Dale Murphy	.75
505	Jason Thompson	.10
506	Phil Huffman	.10
507	Jamie Quirk	.10
508	Rob Dressler	.10
509	Pete Mackanin	.10
510	Lee Mazzilli	.10
511	Wayne Garland	.10
512	Gary Thomasson	.10
513	Frank LaCorte	.10
514	George Riley	.10
515	Robin Yount	2.00
516	Doug Bird	.10
517	Richie Zisk	.10
518	Grant Jackson	.10
519	John Tamargo/DP	.10
520	Steve Stone	.10
521	Sam Mejias	.10
522	Mike Colbern	.10
523	John Fulgham	.10
524	Willie Aikens	.10
525	Mike Torrez	.10
526	Phillies Future Stars (Marty Bystrom, Jay Loviglio, Jim Wright)	.10
527	Danny Goodwin	.10
528	Gary Matthews	.10
529	Dave LaRoche	.10
530	Steve Garvey	.75
531	John Curtis	.10
532	Bill Stein	.10
533	Jesus Figueroa	.10
534	Dave Smith RC	.10
535	Omar Moreno	.10
536	Bob Owchinko/DP	.10
537	Ron Hodges	.10
538	Tom Griffin	.10
539	Rodney Scott	.10
540	Mike Schmidt/DP	3.00
541	Steve Swisher	.10
542	Larry Bradford/DP	.10
543	Terry Crowley	.10
544	Rich Gale	.10
545	Johnny Grubb	.10
546	Paul Moskau	.10
547	Mario Guerrero	.10
548	Dave Goltz	.10
549	Jerry Remy	.10
550	Tommy John	.20
551	Pirates Future Stars (Vance Law RC, Tony Pena RC, Pascual Perez RC)	.75
552	Steve Trout	.10
553	Tim Blackwell	.10
554	Bert Blyleven	.10
555	Cecil Cooper	.10
556	Jerry Mumphrey	.10
557	Chris Knapp	.10
558	Barry Bonnell	.10
559	Willie Montanez	.10
560	Joe Morgan	2.00
561	Dennis Littlejohn	.10
562	Checklist 485-605	.10
563	Jim Kaat	.15
564	Ron Hassey/DP	.10
565	Burt Hooton	.10
566	Del Unser	.10
567	Mark Bomback	.10
568	Dave Revering	.10
569	Al Williams/DP	.10
570	Ken Singleton	.10
571	Todd Cruz	.10
572	Jack Morris	.10
573	Phil Garner	.10
574	Bill Caudill	.10
575	Tony Perez	1.00
576	Reggie Cleveland	.10
577	Blue Jays Future Stars (Luis Leal, Brian Milner, Ken Schrom)	.10
578	Bill Gullickson RC	.20
579	Tim Flannery	.10
580	Don Baylor	.15
581	Roy Howell	.10
582	Gaylord Perry	1.00
583	Larry Milbourne	.10
584	Randy Lerch	.10
585	Amos Otis	.10
586	Silvio Martinez	.10
587	Jeff Newman	.10
588	Gary Lavelle	.10
589	Lamar Johnson	.10
590	Bruce Sutter	1.00
591	John Lowenstein	.10
592	Steve Comer	.10
593	Steve Kemp	.10
594	Preston Hanna/DP	.10
595	Butch Hobson	.10
596	Jerry Augustine	.10
597	Rafael Landestoy	.10
598	George Vukovich/DP	.10
599	Dennis Kinney	.10
600	Johnny Bench	2.00
601	Don Aase	.10
602	Bobby Murcer	.10
603	John Verhoeven	.10
604	Rob Picciolo	.10
605	Don Sutton	1.00
606	Reds Future Stars (Bruce Berenyi, Geoff Combe, Paul Householder/DP)	.10
607	Dave Palmer	.10
608	Greg Pryor	.10
609	Lynn McGlothen	.10
610	Darrell Porter	.10
611	Rick Matula (DP)	.10
612	Duane Kuiper	.10
613	Jim Anderson	.10
614	Dave Rozema	.10
615	Rick Dempsey	.10
616	Rick Wise	.10
617	Craig Reynolds	.10
618	John Milner	.10
619	Steve Henderson	.10
620	Dennis Eckersley	1.00
621	Tom Donohue	.10
622	Randy Moffitt	.10
623	Sal Bando	.10
624	Bob Welch	.10
625	Bill Buckner	.10
626	Tigers Future Stars (Dave Steffen, Jerry Ujdur, Roger Weaver)	.10
627	Luis Tiant	.10
628	Vic Correll	.10
629	Tony Armas	.10
630	Steve Carlton	2.00
631	Ron Jackson	.10
632	Alan Bannister	.10
633	Bill Lee	.10
634	Doug Flynn	.10
635	Bobby Bonds	.10
636	Al Hrabosky	.10
637	Jerry Narron	.10
638	Checklist 606	.10
639	Carney Lansford	.10
640	Dave Parker	.10
641	Mark Belanger	.10
642	Vern Ruhle	.10
643	Lloyd Moseby RC	.20
644	Ramon Aviles/DP	.10
645	Rick Reuschel	.10
646	Marvis Foley	.10
647	Dick Drago	.10
648	Darrell Evans	.10
649	Manny Sarmiento	.10
650	Bucky Dent	.10
651	Pedro Guerrero	.10
652	John Montague	.10
653	Bill Fahey	.10
654	Ray Burris	.10
655	Dan Driessen	.10
656	Jon Matlack	.10
657	Mike Cubbage/DP	.10
658	Milt Wilcox	.10
659	Brewers Future Stars (John Flinn, Ed Romero, Ned Yost)	.10
660	Gary Carter	2.00
661	Orioles Team (Earl Weaver)	.25
662	Red Sox Team (Ralph Houk)	.20

663	Angels Team (Jim Fregosi)	.10
664	White Sox Team (Tony LaRussa)	.25
665	Indians Team (Dave Garcia)	.10
666	Tigers Team (Sparky Anderson)	.25
667	Royals Team (Jim Frey)	.10
668	Brewers Team (Bob Rodgers)	.10
669	Twins Team (John Goryl)	.10
670	Yankees Team (Gene Michael)	.15
671	A's Team (Billy Martin)	.25
672	Mariners Team (Maury Wills)	.20
673	Rangers Team (Don Zimmer)	.20
674	Blue Jays Team (Bobby Mattick)	.10
675	Braves Team (Bobby Cox)	.25
676	Cubs Team (Joe Amalfitano)	.10
677	Reds Team (John McNamara)	.10
678	Astros Team (Bill Virdon)	.10
679	Dodgers Team (Tom Lasorda)	.25
680	Expos Team (Dick Williams)	.20
681	Mets Team (Joe Torre)	.25
682	Phillies Team (Dallas Green)	.15
683	Pirates Team (Chuck Tanner)	.10
684	Cardinals Team (Whitey Herzog)	.15
685	Padres Team (Frank Howard)	.20
686	Giants Team (Dave Bristol)	.10
687	Jeff Jones	.10
688	Kiko Garcia	.10
689	Red Sox Future Stars (Bruce Hurst RC, Keith MacWhorter, Reid Nichols RC)	.30
690	Bob Watson	.10
691	Dick Ruthven	.10
692	Lenny Randle	.10
693	Steve Howe RC	.20
694	Bud Harrelson/DP	.10
695	Kent Tekulve	.10
696	Alan Ashby	.10
697	Rick Waits	.10
698	Mike Jorgensen	.10
699	Glenn Abbott	.10
700	George Brett	3.50
701	Joe Rudi	.10
702	George Medich	.10
703	Alvis Woods	.10
704	Bill Travers/DP	.10
705	Ted Simmons	.10
706	Dave Ford	.10
707	Dave Cash	.10
708	Doyle Alexander	.10
709	Alan Trammell/DP	.10
710	Ron LeFlore/DP	.10
711	Joe Ferguson	.10
712	Bill Bonham	.10
713	Bill North	.10
714	Pete Redfern	.10
715	Bill Madlock	.10
716	Glenn Borgmann	.10
717	Jim Barr/DP	.10
718	Larry Biittner	.10
719	Sparky Lyle	.10
720	Fred Lynn	.10
721	Toby Harrah	.10
722	Joe Niekro	.10
723	Bruce Bochte	.10
724	Lou Piniella	.15
725	Steve Rogers	.10
726	Rick Monday	.10

Traded

The 132 cards in this extension set are numbered from 727 to 858, technically making them a high-numbered series of the regular Topps set. The set was not packaged in gum packs, but rather sold in a specially designed red box through baseball card dealers only. The set features not only mid-season trades, but also single-player rookie cards of some of the hottest prospects. The cards measure 2-1/2" x 3-1/2".

		NM/M
Complete Set (132):		15.00
Common Player:		.10
727	Danny Ainge RC	2.00
728	Doyle Alexander	.10
729	Gary Alexander	.10
730	Billy Almon	.10
731	Joaquin Andujar	.10
732	Bob Bailor	.10
733	Juan Beniquez	.10
734	Dave Bergman	.10
735	Tony Bernazard	.10
736	Larry Biittner	.10
737	Doug Bird	.10
738	Bert Blyleven	.25
739	Mark Bomback	.10
740	Bobby Bonds	.15
741	Rick Bosetti	.10
742	Hubie Brooks	.15
743	Rick Burleson	.10
744	Ray Burris	.10
745	Jeff Burroughs	.10
746	Enos Cabell	.10
747	Ken Clay	.10
748	Mark Clear	.10
749	Larry Cox	.10
750	Hector Cruz	.10
751	Victor Cruz	.10
752	Mike Cubbage	.10
753	Dick Davis	.10
754	Brian Doyle	.10
755	Dick Drago	.10
756	Leon Durham	.10
757	Jim Dwyer	.10
758	Dave Edwards	.10
759	Jim Essian	.10
760	Bill Fahey	.10
761	Rollie Fingers	1.00
762	Carlton Fisk	2.00
763	Barry Foote	.10
764	Ken Forsch	.10
765	Kiko Garcia	.10
766	Cesar Geronimo	.10
767	Gary Gray	.10
768	Mickey Hatcher	.10
769	Steve Henderson	.10
770	Marc Hill	.10
771	Butch Hobson	.10
772	Rick Honeycutt	.10
773	Roy Howell	.10
774	Mike Ivie	.10
775	Roy Lee Jackson	.10
776	Cliff Johnson	.10
777	Randy Jones	.10
778	Ruppert Jones	.10
779	Mick Kelleher	.10
780	Terry Kennedy	.10
781	Dave Kingman	.10
782	Bob Knepper	.10
783	Ken Kravec	.10
784	Bob Lacey	.10
785	Dennis Lamp	.10
786	Rafael Landestoy	.10
787	Ken Landreaux	.10
788	Carney Lansford	.10
789	Dave LaRoche	.10
790	Joe Lefebvre	.10
791	Ron LeFlore	.10
792	Randy Lerch	.10
793	Sixto Lezcano	.10
794	John Littlefield	.10
795	Mike Lum	.10
796	Greg Luzinski	.10
797	Fred Lynn	.10
798	Jerry Martin	.10
799	Buck Martinez	.10
800	Gary Matthews	.10
801	Mario Mendoza	.10
802	Larry Milbourne	.10
803	Rick Miller	.10
804	John Montefusco	.10
805	Jerry Morales	.10
806	Jose Morales	.10
807	Joe Morgan	2.00
808	Jerry Mumphrey	.10
809	Gene Nelson RC	.10
810	Ed Ott	.10
811	Bob Owchinko	.10
812	Gaylord Perry	1.00
813	Mike Phillips	.10
814	Darrell Porter	.10
815	Mike Proly	.10
816	Tim Raines	3.00
817	Lenny Randle	.10
818	Doug Rau	.10
819	Jeff Reardon	.10
820	Ken Reitz	.10
821	Steve Renko	.10
822	Rick Reuschel	.10
823	Dave Revering	.10
824	Dave Roberts	.10
825	Leon Roberts	.10
826	Joe Rudi	.10
827	Kevin Saucier	.10
828	Tony Scott	.10
829	Bob Shirley	.10
830	Ted Simmons	.10
831	Lary Sorensen	.10
832	Jim Spencer	.10
833	Harry Spilman	.10
834	Fred Stanley	.10
835	Rusty Staub	.25
836	Bill Stein	.10
837	Joe Strain	.10
838	Bruce Sutter	1.00
839	Don Sutton	1.00
840	Steve Swisher	.10
841	Frank Tanana	.10
842	Gene Tenace	.10
843	Jason Thompson	.10
844	Dickie Thon	.10
845	Bill Travers	.10
846	Tom Underwood	.10
847	John Urrea	.10
848	Mike Vail	.10
849	Ellis Valentine	.10
850	Fernando Valenzuela	2.00
851	Pete Vuckovich	.10
852	Mark Wagner	.10
853	Bob Walk	.10
854	Claudell Washington	.10
855	Dave Winfield	4.00
856	Geoff Zahn	.10
857	Richie Zisk	.10
858	Checklist 727-858	.05

Team Card Sheet

Via a special mail-in offer, uncut sheets of team cards from the 1981 Topps issue were made available to collectors.

	NM/M
Team card sheet	20.00

Giant Photo Cards

Once again testing the popularity of large-format cards, Topps issued 4-7/8" x 6-7/8" cards in two different sets. The team-set cards feature a large color photo, facsimile autograph and white border on the front. Backs have the player's name, team, position and a checklist at the bottom. The 102 cards were sold in limited areas corresponding to the teams' geographic home. Cards were sold in one-card wax packs with 36 packs per box. Boxes contained either the cards of a single team, or of two teams from the same city or state. It was also possible to order the whole set by mail. Ten teams are involved in the issue, with the number of players from each team ranging from 6 to 12.

		NM/M
Complete Set (102):		25.00
Common Player:		.25
Angels-Dodgers Wax Box:		6.00
Astros-Rangers Wax Box:		7.50
Cubs-White Sox Wax Box:		6.00
Mets-Yankees Wax Box:		9.00
Phillies Wax Box:		9.00
Reds Wax Box:		7.50
Red Sox Wax Box:		7.50
(1)	Tom Burgmeier	.25
(2)	Dennis Eckersley	1.00
(3)	Dwight Evans	.35
(4)	Carlton Fisk	1.00
(5)	Glenn Hoffman	.25
(6)	Carney Lansford	.25
(7)	Tony Perez	1.00
(8)	Jim Rice	.75
(9)	Bob Stanley	.25
(10)	Dave Stapleton	.25
(11)	Frank Tanana	.25
(12)	Carl Yastrzemski	1.50
(1)	Don Baylor	.35
(2)	Rick Burleson	.25
(3)	Rod Carew	1.00
(4)	Bobby Grich	.35
(5)	Butch Hobson	.25
(6)	Fred Lynn	.35
(1)	Tim Blackwell	.25
(2)	Bill Buckner	.35
(3)	Ivan DeJesus	.25
(4)	Leon Durham	.25
(5)	Dave Kingman	.40
(6)	Mike Krukow	.25
(7)	Ken Reitz	.25
(8)	Rick Reuschel	.25
(9)	Mike Tyson	.25
(1)	Britt Burns	.25
(2)	Rich Dotson	.25
(3)	Ed Farmer	.25
(4)	Lamar Johnson	.25
(5)	Ron LeFlore	.25
(6)	Chet Lemon	.25
(7)	Bob Molinaro	.25
(8)	Jim Morrison	.25
(9)	Wayne Nordhagen	.25
(1)	Johnny Bench	1.00
(2)	Dave Collins	.25
(3)	Dave Concepcion	.25
(4)	Dan Driessen	.25
(5)	George Foster	.35
(6)	Ken Griffey	.35
(7)	Tom Hume	.25
(8)	Ray Knight	.25
(9)	Joe Nolan	.25
(10)	Ron Oester	.25
(11)	Tom Seaver	1.00
(12)	Mario Soto	.25
(2)	Cesar Cedeno	.25
(3)	Jose Cruz	.25
(4)	Art Howe	.25
(5)	Terry Puhl	.25
(6)	Nolan Ryan	3.00
(7)	Don Sutton	1.00
(1)	Dusty Baker	.35
(2)	Ron Cey	.25
(3)	Steve Garvey	.75
(4)	Burt Hooton	.25
(5)	Steve Howe	.25
(6)	Davey Lopes	.25
(7)	Rick Monday	.25
(8)	Jerry Reuss	.25
(9)	Bill Russell	.25
(10)	Reggie Smith	.25
(11)	Bob Welch	.25
(12)	Steve Yeager	.25
(2)	Neil Allen	.25
(3)	Doug Flynn	.25
(4)	Lee Mazzilli	.25
(5)	Rusty Staub	.40
(6)	Alex Taveras	.25
(7)	Alex Trevino	.25
(1)	Rick Cerone	.25
(2)	Bucky Dent	.35
(3)	Rich Gossage	.50
(4)	Ron Guidry	.35
(5)	Reggie Jackson	1.50
(6)	Tommy John	.35
(7)	Ruppert Jones	.25
(8)	Rudy May	.25
(9)	Graig Nettles	.25
(10)	Willie Randolph	.25
(11)	Bob Watson	.25
(12)	Dave Winfield	1.00
(1)	Bob Boone	.35
(2)	Larry Bowa	.25
(3)	Steve Carlton	1.00
(4)	Greg Luzinski	.25
(5)	Garry Maddox	.25
(6)	Bake McBride	.25
(7)	Tug McGraw	.25
(8)	Pete Rose	3.00
(9)	Dick Ruthven	.25
(10)	Mike Schmidt	2.00
(11)	Manny Trillo	.25
(12)	Del Unser	.25
(1)	Buddy Bell	.25
(2)	Jon Matlack	.25
(3)	Al Oliver	.35
(4)	Mickey Rivers	.25
(5)	Jim Sundberg	.25
(6)	Bump Wills	.25

National 5x7 Photos

This set is the other half of Topps' efforts with large cards in 1981. Measuring 4-7/8" x 6-7/8", the National photo issue was limited to 15 cards. They were sold in areas not covered by the team-set issues. The set includes 10 cards which carry the same photos found in the team sets, but with no checklist on the backs. Five cards are unique to the National set: Brett, Cooper, Palmer, Parker and Simmons.

		NM/M
Complete Set (15):		4.00
Common Player:		.15
(1)	Buddy Bell	.15
(2)	Johnny Bench	.50
(3)	George Brett	.75
(4)	Rod Carew	.50
(5)	Cecil Cooper	.15
(6)	Steve Garvey	.35
(7)	Rich Gossage	.15
(8)	Reggie Jackson	.60
(9)	Jim Palmer	.50
(10)	Dave Parker	.15
(11)	Jim Rice	.30
(12)	Pete Rose	1.00
(13)	Mike Schmidt	.75
(14)	Tom Seaver	.50
(15)	Ted Simmons	.15

Mets Magic Memories

Celebrating 20 years of N.Y. Mets baseball, the team issued a set of "Magic Memories" cards. Topps produced 20,000 each of the 6-7/8" x 4-7/8" cards. The cards were individually cello wrapped. Cards #1-2 were distributed at the team's August 27 game; cards #3-4 at the September 22 contest. The first card is a sepia team photo of the 1962 Mets. Card #2-3 are color team photos from 1969 and 1973. The team photo cards have player stats on back. The fourth card depicts four of the Mets managers on front, with biographies on back.

		NM/M
Complete Set (4):		24.00
Common Player:		6.00
1	1962 Mets team photo	6.00
2	1969 Mets team photo	6.00
3	1973 Mets team photo	6.00
4	New York Mets managers (Casey Stengel, Gil Hodges, Yogi Berra, Joe Torre)	12.00

Scratchoffs

Sold as a separate issue with bubble gum, this 108-card set was issued in three-card panels that measure 3-1/4" x 5-1/4". Each individual card measures 1-13/16" x 3-1/4" and contains a small player photo alongside a series of black dots designed to be scratched off as part of a baseball game. Cards of National League players have a green background, while American League players have a red background. While there are 108 different players in the set, there are 144 possible panel combinations. An intact panel of three cards is valued approximately 20-25 percent more the sum of the individual cards.

		NM/M
Complete Set (108):		10.00
Common Player:		.15
Wax Pack:		.75
Wax Box (36):		15.00
1	George Brett	1.00
2	Cecil Cooper	.15
3	Reggie Jackson	.50
4	Al Oliver	.15
5	Fred Lynn	.15
6	Tony Armas	.15
7	Ben Oglivie	.15
8	Tony Perez	.25
9	Eddie Murray	.25
10	Robin Yount	.25
11	Steve Kemp	.15
12	Joe Charboneau	.15
13	Jim Rice	.20
14	Lance Parrish	.25
15	John Mayberry	.15
16	Richie Zisk	.15
17	Ken Singleton	.15
18	Rod Carew	.25
19	Rick Manning	.15
20	Willie Wilson	.15
21	Buddy Bell	.15
22	Dave Revering	.15
23	Tom Paciorek	.15
24	Champ Summers	.15
25	Carney Lansford	.15
26	Lamar Johnson	.15
27	Willie Aikens	.15
28	Rick Cerone	.15
29	Al Bumbry	.15
30	Bruce Bochte	.15
31	Mickey Rivers	.15
32	Mike Hargrove	.15
33	John Castino	.15
34	Chet Lemon	.15
35	Paul Molitor	.15
36	Willie Randolph	.15
37	Rick Burleson	.15
38	Alan Trammell	.15
39	Rickey Henderson	.25
40	Dan Meyer	.15
41	Ken Landreaux	.15
42	Damaso Garcia	.15
43	Roy Smalley	.15
44	Otto Velez	.15
45	Sixto Lezcano	.15
46	Toby Harrah	.15
47	Frank White	.15
48	Dave Stapleton	.15
49	Steve Stone	.15
50	Jim Palmer	.25
51	Larry Gura	.15
52	Tommy John	.15
53	Mike Norris	.15
54	Ed Farmer	.15
55	Bill Buckner	.15
56	Steve Garvey	.20
57	Reggie Smith	.15
58	Bake McBride	.15
59	Dave Parker	.15
60	Mike Schmidt	1.00
61	Bob Horner	.15
62	Pete Rose	2.00
63	Ted Simmons	.15
64	Johnny Bench	.25
65	George Foster	.15
66	Gary Carter	.25
67	Keith Hernandez	.25
68	Ozzie Smith	.35
69	Dave Kingman	.15
70	Jack Clark	.15
71	Dusty Baker	.15
72	Dale Murphy	.20
73	Ron Cey	.15
74	Greg Luzinski	.15
75	Lee Mazzilli	.15
76	Gary Matthews	.15
77	Cesar Cedeno	.15
78	Warren Cromartie	.15
79	Steve Henderson	.15
80	Ellis Valentine	.15
81	Mike Easler	.15
82	Garry Templeton	.15
83	Jose Cruz	.15
84	Dave Collins	.15
85	George Hendrick	.15
86	Gene Richards	.15
87	Terry Whitfield	.15
88	Terry Puhl	.15
89	Larry Parrish	.15
90	Andre Dawson	.20
91	Ken Griffey	.15
92	Dave Lopes	.15
93	Doug Flynn	.15
94	Ivan DeJesus	.15
95	Dave Concepcion	.15
96	John Stearns	.15
97	Jerry Mumphrey	.15
98	Jerry Martin	.15
99	Art Howe	.15
100	Omar Moreno	.15
101	Ken Reitz	.15
102	Phil Garner	.15
103	Jerry Reuss	.15
104	Steve Carlton	.25
105	Jim Bibby	.15
106	Steve Rogers	.15
107	Tom Seaver	.25
108	Vida Blue	.15

Stickers

The 262 stickers in this full-color set measure 1-15/16" x 2-9/16" and are numbered on both the front and back. They were produced for Topps by the Panini Co. of Italy. The set includes a series of "All-Star" stickers printed on silver or gold "foil." An album to house the stickers was also available.

	NM/M
Complete Set (262):	9.00
Common Player:	.05
Sticker Album:	2.00
Wax Pack (5):	.40
Wax Box (100):	15.00

1	Steve Stone	.05
2	Tommy John, Mike Norris	.05
3	Rudy May	.05
4	Mike Norris	.05
5	Len Barker	.05
6	Mike Norris	.05
7	Dan Quisenberry	.05
8	Rich Gossage	.05
9	George Brett	.30
10	Cecil Cooper	.05
11	Reggie Jackson, Ben Oglivie	.05
12	Gorman Thomas	.05
13	Cecil Cooper	.05
14	George Brett, Ben Oglivie	.05
15	Rickey Henderson	.25
16	Willie Wilson	.05
17	Bill Buckner	.05
18	Keith Hernandez	.05
19	Mike Schmidt	.30
20	Bob Horner	.05
21	Mike Schmidt	.30
22	George Hendrick	.05
23	Ron LeFlore	.05
24	Omar Moreno	.05
25	Steve Carlton	.20
26	Joe Niekro	.05
27	Don Sutton	.20
28	Steve Carlton	.20
29	Steve Carlton	.20
30	Nolan Ryan	.50
31	Rollie Fingers, Tom Hume	.05
32	Bruce Sutter	.20
33	Ken Singleton	.05
34	Eddie Murray	.25
35	Al Bumbry	.05
36	Rich Dauer	.05
37	Scott McGregor	.05
38	Rick Dempsey	.05
39	Jim Palmer	.25
40	Steve Stone	.05
41	Jim Rice	.15
42	Fred Lynn	.05
43	Carney Lansford	.05
44	Tony Perez	.25
45	Carl Yastrzemski	.25
46	Carlton Fisk	.25
47	Dave Stapleton	.05
48	Dennis Eckersley	.20
49	Rod Carew	.25
50	Brian Downing	.05
51	Don Baylor	.05
52	Rick Burleson	.05
53	Bobby Grich	.05
54	Butch Hobson	.05
55	Andy Hassler	.05
56	Frank Tanana	.05
57	Chet Lemon	.05
58	Lamar Johnson	.05
59	Wayne Nordhagen	.05
60	Jim Morrison	.05
61	Bob Molinaro	.05
62	Rich Dotson	.05
63	Britt Burns	.05
64	Ed Farmer	.05
65	Toby Harrah	.05
66	Joe Charboneau	.25
67	Miguel Dilone	.05
68	Mike Hargrove	.05
69	Rick Manning	.05
70	Andre Thornton	.05
71	Ron Hassey	.05
72	Len Barker	.05
73	Lance Parrish	.05
74	Steve Kemp	.05
75	Alan Trammell	.05

76	Champ Summers	.05
77	Rick Peters	.05
78	Kirk Gibson	.05
79	Johnny Wockenfuss	.05
80	Jack Morris	.05
81	Willie Wilson	.05
82	George Brett	.30
83	Frank White	.05
84	Willie Aikens	.05
85	Clint Hurdle	.05
86	Hal McRae	.05
87	Dennis Leonard	.05
88	Larry Gura	.05
89	American League Pennant Winner (Kansas City Royals Team)	.05
90	American League Pennant Winner (Kansas City Royals Team)	.05
91	Paul Molitor	.25
92	Ben Oglivie	.05
93	Cecil Cooper	.05
94	Ted Simmons	.05
95	Robin Yount	.25
96	Gorman Thomas	.05
97	Mike Caldwell	.05
98	Moose Haas	.05
99	John Castino	.05
100	Roy Smalley	.05
101	Ken Landreaux	.05
102	Butch Wynegar	.05
103	Ron Jackson	.05
104	Jerry Koosman	.05
105	Roger Erickson	.05
106	Doug Corbett	.05
107	Reggie Jackson	.30
108	Willie Randolph	.05
109	Rick Cerone	.05
110	Bucky Dent	.05
111	Dave Winfield	.25
112	Ron Guidry	.10
113	Rich Gossage	.05
114	Tommy John	.10
115	Rickey Henderson	.25
116	Tony Armas	.05
117	Dave Revering	.05
118	Wayne Gross	.05
119	Dwayne Murphy	.05
120	Jeff Newman	.05
121	Rick Langford	.05
122	Mike Norris	.05
123	Bruce Bochte	.05
124	Tom Paciorek	.05
125	Dan Meyer	.05
126	Julio Cruz	.05
127	Richie Zisk	.05
128	Floyd Bannister	.05
129	Shane Rawley	.05
130	Buddy Bell	.05
131	Al Oliver	.05
132	Mickey Rivers	.05
133	Jim Sundberg	.05
134	Bump Wills	.05
135	Jon Matlack	.05
136	Danny Darwin	.05
137	Damaso Garcia	.05
138	Otto Velez	.05
139	John Mayberry	.05
140	Alfredo Griffin	.05
141	Alvis Woods	.05
142	Dave Stieb	.05
143	Jim Clancy	.05
144	Gary Matthews	.05
145	Bob Horner	.05
146	Dale Murphy	.25
147	Chris Chambliss	.05
148	Phil Niekro	.20
149	Glenn Hubbard	.05
150	Rick Camp	.05
151	Dave Kingman	.05
152	Bill Caudill	.05
153	Bill Buckner	.05
154	Barry Foote	.05
155	Mike Tyson	.05
156	Ivan DeJesus	.05
157	Rick Reuschel	.05
158	Ken Reitz	.05
159	George Foster	.05
160	Johnny Bench	.25
161	Dave Concepcion	.05
162	Dave Collins	.05
163	Ken Griffey	.05
164	Dan Driessen	.05
165	Tom Seaver	.25
166	Tom Hume	.05
167	Cesar Cedeno	.05
168	Rafael Landestoy	.05
169	Jose Cruz	.05
170	Art Howe	.05
171	Terry Puhl	.05
172	Joe Sambito	.05
173	Nolan Ryan	.50
174	Joe Niekro	.05
175	Dave Lopes	.05
176	Steve Garvey	.15
177	Ron Cey	.05
178	Reggie Smith	.05
179	Bill Russell	.05
180	Burt Hooton	.05
181	Jerry Reuss	.05
182	Dusty Baker	.05
183	Larry Parrish	.05
184	Gary Carter	.25
185	Rodney Scott	.05
186	Ellis Valentine	.05
187	Andre Dawson	.20
188	Warren Cromartie	.05
189	Chris Speier	.05

190	Steve Rogers	.05
191	Lee Mazzilli	.05
192	Doug Flynn	.05
193	Steve Henderson	.05
194	John Stearns	.05
195	Joel Youngblood	.05
196	Frank Taveras	.05
197	Pat Zachry	.05
198	Neil Allen	.05
199	Mike Schmidt	.30
200	Pete Rose	.50
201	Larry Bowa	.05
202	Bake McBride	.05
203	Bob Boone	.05
204	Garry Maddox	.05
205	Tug McGraw	.05
206	Steve Carlton	.20
207	National League Pennant Winner (Philadelphia Phillies Team)	.05
208	National League Pennant Winner (Philadelphia Phillies Team)	.05
209	Phil Garner	.05
210	Dave Parker	.05
211	Omar Moreno	.05
212	Mike Easler	.05
213	Bill Madlock	.05
214	Ed Ott	.05
215	Willie Stargell	.25
216	Jim Bibby	.05
217	Garry Templeton	.05
218	Sixto Lezcano	.05
219	Keith Hernandez	.05
220	George Hendrick	.05
221	Bruce Sutter	.20
222	Ken Oberkfell	.05
223	Tony Scott	.05
224	Darrell Porter	.05
225	Gene Richards	.05
226	Broderick Perkins	.05
227	Jerry Mumphrey	.05
228	Luis Salazar	.05
229	Jerry Turner	.05
230	Ozzie Smith	.30
231	John Curtis	.05
232	Rick Wise	.05
233	Terry Whitfield	.05
234	Jack Clark	.05
235	Darrell Evans	.05
236	Larry Herndon	.05
237	Milt May	.05
238	Greg Minton	.05
239	Vida Blue	.05
240	Eddie Whitson	.05
241	Cecil Cooper	.05
242	Willie Randolph	.05
243	George Brett	.30
244	Robin Yount	.25
245	Reggie Jackson	.30
246	Al Oliver	.05
247	Willie Wilson	.05
248	Rick Cerone	.05
249	Steve Stone	.05
250	Tommy John	.05
251	Rich Gossage	.05
252	Steve Garvey	.15
253	Phil Garner	.05
254	Mike Schmidt	.30
255	Garry Templeton	.05
256	George Hendrick	.05
257	Dave Parker	.05
258	Cesar Cedeno	.05
259	Gary Carter	.25
260	Jim Bibby	.05
261	Steve Carlton	.20
262	Tug McGraw	.05

Thirst Break Comics

These 2-1/2" x 1-5/8" wax paper comics were the wrapper for Thirst Break Gum, a Topps test issue distributed to parts of Ohio and Pennsylvania. Each orange foil pack contained five comics (labeled as "Sport Facts") which were folded and wrapped around five soft gum pieces. A total of 56 different comics were produced, 20 of which were baseball players. The great majority of comics found today are slightly wrinkled and stained by the gum, but are usually considered to be in Near Mint condition.

	NM/M
Complete (Baseball) Set (20):	1.00
Common Player:	1.00
Wax Pack (5):	4.00
Wax Box (48):	110.00

1	Shortest Game	.50
2	Lefty Gomez	1.00

3	Bob Gibson	1.00
4	Hoyt Wilhelm	1.00
5	Babe Ruth	5.00
6	Toby Harrah	1.00
7	Carl Hubbell	1.00
8	Harvey Haddix	1.00
9	Steve Carlton	1.50
10	Nolan Ryan, Tom Seaver, Steve Carlton	3.50
11	Lou Brock	1.00
12	Mickey Mantle	6.00
13	Tom Seaver	2.50
14	Don Drysdale	1.00
15	Billy Williams	1.00
20	Christy Mathewson	1.00
21	Hank Aaron	4.00
22	Ron Blomberg	1.00
23	Joe Nuxhall	1.00
24	Reggie Jackson	3.00

1982 Topps

At 792 cards, this was the largest issue produced up to that time, eliminating the need for double-printed cards. The 2-1/2" x 3-1/2" cards feature a front color photo with a pair of stripes down the left side. Under the player's photo are found his name, team and position. A facsimile autograph runs across the front of the picture. Specialty cards include great performances of the previous season, All-Stars, statistical leaders and "In Action" cards (indicated by "IA" in listings below). Managers and hitting/pitching leaders have cards, while rookies are shown as "Future Stars" on group cards.

	NM/M
Unopened Fact. Set (792):	180.00
Complete Set (792):	70.00
Common Player:	.10
Wax Pack (15):	5.00
Wax Box (36):	140.00
Cello Pack (28):	6.00
Cello Box (24):	130.00
Rack Pack (51):	8.00
Rack Box (24):	210.00
Vending Box (500):	60.00

1	Steve Carlton (1981 Highlight)	.25
2	Ron Davis (1981 Highlight)	.10
3	Tim Raines (1981 Highlight)	.10
4	Pete Rose (1981 Highlight)	.75
5	Nolan Ryan (1981 Highlight)	3.00
6	Fernando Valenzuela (1981 Highlight)	.10
7	Scott Sanderson	.10
8	Rich Dauer	.10
9	Ron Guidry	.15
10	Ron Guidry/IA	.10
11	Gary Alexander	.10
12	Moose Haas	.10
13	Lamar Johnson	.10
14	Steve Howe	.10
15	Ellis Valentine	.10
16	Steve Comer	.10
17	Darrell Evans	.10
18	Fernando Arroyo	.10
19	Ernie Whitt	.10
20	Garry Maddox	.10
21	Orioles Future Stars (Bob Bonner RC, Cal Ripken, Jr. RC, Jeff Schneider RC)	50.00
22	Jim Beattie	.10
23	Willie Hernandez	.10
24	Dave Frost	.10
25	Jerry Remy	.10
26	Jorge Orta	.10
27	Tom Herr	.10
28	John Urrea	.10
29	Dwayne Murphy	.10
30	Tom Seaver	1.50
31	Tom Seaver/IA	1.00
32	Gene Garber	.10

33	Jerry Morales	.10
34	Joe Sambito	.10
35	Willie Aikens	.10
36	Rangers Batting/Pitching Leaders (George Medich, Al Oliver)	.10
37	Dan Graham	.10
38	Charlie Lea	.10
39	Lou Whitaker	.10
40	Dave Parker	.10
41	Dave Parker/IA	.10
42	Rick Sofield	.10
43	Mike Cubbage	.10
44	Britt Burns	.10
45	Rick Cerone	.10
46	Jerry Augustine	.10
47	Jeff Leonard	.10
48	Bobby Castillo	.10
49	Alvis Woods	.10
50	Buddy Bell	.10
51	Chicago Cubs Future Stars (Jay Howell RC, Carlos Lezcano RC, Ty Waller RC)	.40
52	Larry Andersen	.10
53	Greg Gross	.10
54	Ron Hassey	.10
55	Rick Burleson	.10
56	Mark Littell	.10
57	Craig Reynolds	.10
58	John D'Acquisto	.10
59	Rich Gedman RC	.10
60	Tony Armas	.10
61	Tommy Boggs	.10
62	Mike Tyson	.10
63	Mario Soto	.10
64	Lynn Jones	.10
65	Terry Kennedy	.10
66	Astros Batting/Pitching Leaders (Art Howe, Nolan Ryan)	.75
67	Rich Gale	.10
68	Roy Howell	.10
69	Al Williams	.10
70	Tim Raines	.50
71	Roy Lee Jackson	.10
72	Rick Auerbach	.10
73	Buddy Solomon	.10
74	Bob Clark	.10
75	Tommy John	.20
76	Greg Pryor	.10
77	Miguel Dilone	.10
78	George Medich	.10
79	Bob Bailor	.10
80	Jim Palmer	1.00
81	Jim Palmer/IA	.30
82	Bob Welch	.10
83	Yankees Future Stars (Steve Balboni RC, Andy McGaffigan RC, Andre Robertson RC)	.15
84	Rennie Stennett	.10
85	Lynn McGlothen	.10
86	Dane Iorg	.10
87	Matt Keough	.10
88	Biff Pocoroba	.10
89	Steve Henderson	.10
90	Nolan Ryan	4.00
91	Carney Lansford	.10
92	Brad Havens	.10
93	Larry Hisle	.10
94	Andy Hassler	.10
95	Ozzie Smith	2.00
96	Royals Batting/Pitching Leaders (George Brett, Larry Gura)	.35
97	Paul Moskau	.10
98	Terry Bulling	.10
99	Barry Bonnell	.10
100	Mike Schmidt	3.00
101	Mike Schmidt/IA	1.50
102	Dan Briggs	.10
103	Bob Lacey	.10
104	Rance Mulliniks	.10
105	Kirk Gibson	.10
106	Enrique Romo	.10
107	Wayne Krenchicki	.10
108	Bob Sykes	.10
109	Dave Revering	.10
110	Carlton Fisk	1.50
111	Carlton Fisk/IA	.65
112	Billy Sample	.10
113	Steve McCatty	.10
114	Ken Landreaux	.10
115	Gaylord Perry	1.00
116	Jim Wohlford	.10
117	Rawly Eastwick	.10
118	Expos Future Stars (Terry Francona RC, Brad Mills RC, Bryn Smith RC)	.20
119	Joe Pittman	.10
120	Gary Lucas	.10
121	Ed Lynch	.10
122	Jamie Easterly	.10
123	Danny Goodwin	.10
124	Reid Nichols	.10
125	Danny Ainge	1.00
126	Braves Batting/Pitching Leaders (Rick Mahler, Claudell Washington)	.10
127	Lonnie Smith	.10
128	Frank Pastore	.10
129	Checklist 1-132	.10
130	Julio Cruz	.10
131	Stan Bahnsen	.10
132	Lee May	.10
133	Pat Underwood	.10

134	Dan Ford	.10
135	Andy Rincon	.10
136	Lenn Sakata	.10
137	George Cappuzzello	.10
138	Tony Pena	.10
139	Jeff Jones	.10
140	Ron LeFlore	.10
141	Indians Future Stars (Chris Bando, Tom Brennan, Von Hayes RC)	.20
142	Dave LaRoche	.10
143	Mookie Wilson	.10
144	Fred Breining	.10
145	Bob Horner	.10
146	Mike Griffin	.10
147	Denny Walling	.10
148	Mickey Klutts	.10
149	Pat Putnam	.10
150	Ted Simmons	.10
151	Dave Edwards	.10
152	Ramon Aviles	.10
153	Roger Erickson	.10
154	Dennis Werth	.10
155	Otto Velez	.10
156	A's Batting/Pitching Leaders (Rickey Henderson, Steve McCatty)	.10
157	Steve Crawford	.10
158	Brian Downing	.10
159	Larry Biittner	.10
160	Luis Tiant	.10
161	Batting Leaders (Carney Lansford, Bill Madlock)	.10
162	Home Run Leaders (Tony Armas, Dwight Evans, Bobby Grich, Eddie Murray, Mike Schmidt)	.25
163	RBI Leaders (Eddie Murray, Mike Schmidt)	.40
164	Stolen Base Leaders (Rickey Henderson, Tim Raines)	.35
165	Victory Leaders (Denny Martinez, Steve McCatty, Jack Morris, Tom Seaver, Pete Vuckovich)	.10
166	Strikeout Leaders (Len Barker, Fernando Valenzuela)	.10
167	ERA Leaders (Steve McCatty, Nolan Ryan)	1.50
168	Leading Relievers (Rollie Fingers, Bruce Sutter)	.15
169	Charlie Leibrandt	.10
170	Jim Bibby	.10
171	Giants Future Stars (Bob Brenly RC, Chili Davis RC, Bob Tufts RC)	2.00
172	Bill Gullickson	.10
173	Jamie Quirk	.10
174	Dave Ford	.10
175	Jerry Mumphrey	.10
176	Dewey Robinson	.10
177	John Ellis	.10
178	Dyar Miller	.10
179	Steve Garvey	.75
180	Steve Garvey/IA	.30
181	Silvio Martinez	.10
182	Larry Herndon	.10
183	Mike Proly	.10
184	Mick Kelleher	.10
185	Phil Niekro	1.00
186	Cardinals Batting/Pitching Leaders (Bob Forsch, Keith Hernandez)	.10
187	Jeff Newman	.10
188	Randy Martz	.10
189	Glenn Hoffman	.10
190	J.R. Richard	.05
191	Tim Wallach RC	2.00
192	Broderick Perkins	.10
193	Darrell Jackson	.10
194	Mike Vail	.10
195	Paul Molitor	1.50
196	Willie Upshaw	.10
197	Shane Rawley	.10
198	Chris Speier	.10
199	Don Aase	.10
200	George Brett	3.00
201	George Brett/IA	2.00
202	Rick Manning	.10
203	Blue Jays Future Stars (Jesse Barfield RC, Brian Milner, Boomer Wells)	.50
204	Gary Roenicke	.10
205	Neil Allen	.10
206	Tony Bernazard	.10
207	Rod Scurry	.10
208	Bobby Murcer	.10
209	Gary Lavelle	.10
210	Keith Hernandez	.10
211	Dan Petry	.10
212	Mario Mendoza	.10
213	Dave Stewart RC	4.00
214	Brian Asselstine	.10
215	Mike Krukow	.10
216	White Sox Batting/Pitching Leaders (Dennis Lamp, Chet Lemon)	.10
217	Bo McLaughlin	.10

No.	Name	Price
218	Dave Roberts	.10
219	John Curtis	.10
220	Manny Trillo	.10
221	Jim Slaton	.10
222	Butch Wynegar	.10
223	Lloyd Moseby	.10
224	Bruce Bochte	.10
225	Mike Torrez	.10
226	Checklist 133-264	.10
227	Ray Burris	.10
228	Sam Mejias	.10
229	Geoff Zahn	.10
230	Willie Wilson	.10
231	Phillies Future Stars (Mark Davis RC, Bob Dernier RC, Ozzie Virgil RC)	.20
232	Terry Crowley	.10
233	Duane Kuiper	.10
234	Ron Hodges	.10
235	Mike Easler	.10
236	John Martin	.10
237	Rusty Kuntz	.10
238	Kevin Saucier	.10
239	Jon Matlack	.10
240	Bucky Dent	.10
241	Bucky Dent/IA	.10
242	Milt May	.10
243	Bob Owchinko	.10
244	Rufino Linares	.10
245	Ken Reitz	.10
246	Mets Batting/Pitching Leaders (Hubie Brooks, Mike Scott)	.10
247	Pedro Guerrero	.10
248	Frank LaCorte	.10
249	Tim Flannery	.10
250	Tug McGraw	.10
251	Fred Lynn	.10
252	Fred Lynn/IA	.10
253	Chuck Baker	.10
254	George Bell RC	1.00
255	Tony Perez	1.00
256	Tony Perez/IA	.10
257	Larry Harlow	.10
258	Bo Diaz	.10
259	Rodney Scott	.10
260	Bruce Sutter	1.00
261	Tigers Future Stars (Howard Bailey, Marty Castillo, Dave Rucker)	.10
262	Doug Bair	.10
263	Victor Cruz	.10
264	Dan Quisenberry	.10
265	Al Bumbry	.10
266	Rick Leach	.10
267	Kurt Bevacqua	.10
268	Rickey Keeton	.10
269	Jim Essian	.10
270	Rusty Staub	.15
271	Larry Bradford	.10
272	Bump Wills	.10
273	Doug Bird	.10
274	Bob Ojeda RC	.50
275	Bob Watson	.10
276	Angels Batting/Pitching Leaders (Rod Carew, Ken Forsch)	.25
277	Terry Puhl	.10
278	John Littlefield	.10
279	Bill Russell	.10
280	Ben Oglivie	.10
281	John Verhoeven	.10
282	Ken Macha	.10
283	Brian Allard	.10
284	Bob Grich	.10
285	Sparky Lyle	.10
286	Bill Fahey	.10
287	Alan Bannister	.10
288	Garry Templeton	.10
289	Bob Stanley	.10
290	Ken Singleton	.10
291	Pirates Future Stars (Vance Law, Bob Long, Johnny Ray RC)	.15
292	Dave Palmer	.10
293	Rob Picciolo	.10
294	Mike LaCoss	.10
295	Jason Thompson	.10
296	Bob Walk	.10
297	Clint Hurdle	.10
298	Danny Darwin	.10
299	Steve Trout	.10
300	Reggie Jackson	2.00
301	Reggie Jackson/IA	1.50
302	Doug Flynn	.10
303	Bill Caudill	.10
304	Johnnie LeMaster	.10
305	Don Sutton	1.00
306	Don Sutton/IA	.20
307	Randy Bass	.10
308	Charlie Moore	.10
309	Pete Redfern	.10
310	Mike Hargrove	.10
311	Dodgers Batting/Pitching Leaders (Dusty Baker, Burt Hooton)	.10
312	Lenny Randle	.10
313	John Harris	.10
314	Buck Martinez	.10
315	Burt Hooton	.10
316	Steve Braun	.10
317	Dick Ruthven	.10
318	Mike Heath	.10
319	Dave Rozema	.10
320	Chris Chambliss	.10
321	Chris Chambliss/IA	.10
322	Garry Hancock	.10
323	Bill Lee	.10
324	Steve Dillard	.10
325	Jose Cruz	.10
326	Pete Falcone	.10
327	Joe Nolan	.10
328	Ed Farmer	.10
329	U.L. Washington	.10
330	Rick Wise	.10
331	Benny Ayala	.10
332	Don Robinson	.10
333	Brewers Future Stars (Frank DiPino RC, Marshall Edwards, Chuck Porter)	.10
334	Aurelio Rodriguez	.10
335	Jim Sundberg	.10
336	Mariners Batting/Pitching Leaders (Glenn Abbott, Tom Paciorek)	.10
337	Pete Rose/AS	1.50
338	Dave Lopes/AS	.10
339	Mike Schmidt/AS	1.00
340	Dave Concepcion/AS	.10
341	Andre Dawson/AS	.25
342a	George Foster/AS (no autograph)	2.00
342b	George Foster/AS (autograph on front)	.10
343	Dave Parker/AS	.10
344	Gary Carter/AS	.60
345	Fernando Valenzuela/AS	.10
346	Tom Seaver/AS	.75
347	Bruce Sutter/AS	.50
348	Derrel Thomas	.10
349	George Frazier	.10
350	Thad Bosley	.10
351	Reds Future Stars (Scott Brown, Geoff Combe, Paul Householder)	.10
352	Dick Davis	.10
353	Jack O'Connor	.10
354	Roberto Ramos	.10
355	Dwight Evans	.10
356	Denny Lewallyn	.10
357	Butch Hobson	.10
358	Mike Parrott	.10
359	Jim Dwyer	.10
360	Len Barker	.10
361	Rafael Landestoy	.10
362	Jim Wright	.10
363	Bob Molinaro	.10
364	Doyle Alexander	.10
365	Bill Madlock	.10
366	Padres Batting/Pitching Leaders (Juan Eichelberger, Luis Salazar)	.10
367	Jim Kaat	.10
368	Alex Trevino	.10
369	Champ Summers	.10
370	Mike Norris	.10
371	Jerry Don Gleaton	.10
372	Luis Gomez	.10
373	Gene Nelson RC	.10
374	Tim Blackwell	.10
375	Dusty Baker	.15
376	Chris Welsh	.10
377	Kiko Garcia	.10
378	Mike Caldwell	.10
379	Rob Wilfong	.10
380	Dave Stieb	.10
381	Red Sox Future Stars (Bruce Hurst, Dave Schmidt, Julio Valdez)	.25
382	Joe Simpson	.10
383a	Pascual Perez (No position on front)	20.00
383b	Pascual Perez ("Pitcher" on front)	.10
384	Keith Moreland	.10
385	Ken Forsch	.10
386	Jerry White	.10
387	Tom Veryzer	.10
388	Joe Rudi	.10
389	George Vukovich	.10
390	Eddie Murray	1.50
391	Dave Tobik	.10
392	Rick Bosetti	.10
393	Al Hrabosky	.10
394	Checklist 265-396	.10
395	Omar Moreno	.10
396	Twins Batting/Pitching Leaders (Fernando Arroyo, John Castino)	.10
397	Ken Brett	.10
398	Mike Squires	.10
399	Pat Zachry	.10
400	Johnny Bench	1.50
401	Johnny Bench/IA	.45
402	Bill Stein	.10
403	Jim Tracy	.10
404	Dickie Thon	.10
405	Rick Reuschel	.10
406	Al Holland	.10
407	Danny Boone	.10
408	Ed Romero	.10
409	Don Cooper	.10
410	Ron Cey	.10
411	Ron Cey/IA	.10
412	Luis Leal	.10
413	Dan Meyer	.10
414	Elias Sosa	.10
415	Don Baylor	.15
416	Marty Bystrom	.10
417	Pat Kelly	.10
418	Rangers Future Stars (John Butcher, Bobby Johnson, Dave Schmidt RC)	.10
419	Steve Stone	.10
420	George Hendrick	.10
421	Mark Clear	.10
422	Cliff Johnson	.10
423	Stan Papi	.10
424	Bruce Benedict	.10
425	John Candelaria	.10
426	Orioles Batting/Pitching Leaders (Eddie Murray, Sammy Stewart)	.25
427	Ron Oester	.10
428	Lamarr Hoyt (LaMarr)	.10
429	John Wathan	.10
430	Vida Blue	.10
431	Vida Blue/IA	.10
432	Mike Scott	.10
433	Alan Ashby	.10
434	Joe Lefebvre	.10
435	Robin Yount	1.50
436	Joe Strain	.10
437	Juan Berenguer	.10
438	Pete Mackanin	.10
439	Dave Righetti RC	.75
440	Jeff Burroughs	.10
441	Astros Future Stars (Danny Heep, Billy Smith, Bobby Sprowl)	.10
442	Bruce Kison	.10
443	Mark Wagner	.10
444	Terry Forster	.10
445	Larry Parrish	.10
446	Wayne Garland	.10
447	Darrell Porter	.10
448	Darrell Porter/IA	.10
449	Luis Aguayo RC	.10
450	Jack Morris	.10
451	Ed Miller	.10
452	Lee Smith RC	4.00
453	Art Howe	.10
454	Rick Langford	.10
455	Tom Burgmeier	.10
456	Cubs Batting & Pitching Ldrs. (Bill Buckner, Randy Martz)	.10
457	Tim Stoddard	.10
458	Willie Montanez	.10
459	Bruce Berenyi	.10
460	Jack Clark	.10
461	Rich Dotson	.10
462	Dave Chalk	.10
463	Jim Kern	.10
464	Juan Bonilla	.10
465	Lee Mazzilli	.10
466	Randy Lerch	.10
467	Mickey Hatcher	.10
468	Floyd Bannister	.10
469	Ed Ott	.10
470	John Mayberry	.10
471	Royals Future Stars (Atlee Hammaker RC, Mike Jones, Darryl Motley)	.15
472	Oscar Gamble	.10
473	Mike Stanton	.10
474	Ken Oberkfell	.10
475	Alan Trammell	.10
476	Brian Kingman	.10
477	Steve Yeager	.10
478	Ray Searage	.10
479	Rowland Office	.10
480	Steve Carlton	1.50
481	Steve Carlton/IA	.40
482	Glenn Hubbard	.10
483	Gary Woods	.10
484	Ivan DeJesus	.10
485	Kent Tekulve	.10
486	Yankees Batting & Pitching Ldrs. (Tommy John, Jerry Mumphrey)	.10
487	Bob McClure	.10
488	Ron Jackson	.10
489	Rick Dempsey	.10
490	Dennis Eckersley	1.00
491	Checklist 397-528	.10
492	Joe Price	.10
493	Chet Lemon	.10
494	Hubie Brooks	.10
495	Dennis Leonard	.10
496	Johnny Grubb	.10
497	Jim Anderson	.10
498	Dave Bergman	.10
499	Paul Mirabella	.10
500	Rod Carew	1.50
501	Rod Carew/IA	.40
502	Braves Future Stars (Steve Bedrosian RC, Brett Butler RC, Larry Owen)	2.00
503	Julio Gonzalez	.10
504	Rick Peters	.10
505	Graig Nettles	.10
506	Graig Nettles/IA	.10
507	Terry Harper	.10
508	Jody Davis RC	.15
509	Harry Spilman	.10
510	Fernando Valenzuela	.10
511	Ruppert Jones	.10
512	Jerry Dybzinski	.10
513	Rick Rhoden	.10
514	Joe Ferguson	.10
515	Larry Bowa	.10
516	Larry Bowa/IA	.10
517	Mark Brouhard	.10
518	Garth Iorg	.10
519	Glenn Adams	.10
520	Mike Flanagan	.10
521	Billy Almon	.10
522	Chuck Rainey	.10
523	Gary Gray	.10
524	Tom Hausman	.10
525	Ray Knight	.10
526	Expos Batting & Pitching Ldrs. (Warren Cromartie, Bill Gullickson)	.10
527	John Henry Johnson	.10
528	Matt Alexander	.10
529	Allen Ripley	.10
530	Dickie Noles	.10
531	A's Future Stars (Rich Bordi, Mark Budaska, Kelvin Moore)	.10
532	Toby Harrah	.10
533	Joaquin Andujar	.10
534	Dave McKay	.10
535	Lance Parrish	.10
536	Rafael Ramirez	.10
537	Doug Capilla	.10
538	Lou Piniella	.10
539	Vern Ruhle	.10
540	Andre Dawson	.75
541	Barry Evans	.10
542	Ned Yost	.10
543	Bill Robinson	.10
544	Larry Christenson	.10
545	Reggie Smith	.10
546	Reggie Smith/IA	.10
547	Rod Carew/AS	.25
548	Willie Randolph/AS	.10
549	George Brett/AS	1.50
550	Bucky Dent/AS	.10
551	Reggie Jackson/AS	.75
552	Ken Singleton/AS	.10
553	Dave Winfield/AS	.60
554	Carlton Fisk/AS	.25
555	Scott McGregor/AS	.10
556	Jack Morris/AS	.10
557	Rich Gossage/AS	.10
558	John Tudor	.10
559	Indians Batting & Pitching Ldrs. (Bert Blyleven, Mike Hargrove)	.10
560	Doug Corbett	.10
561	Cardinals Future Stars (Glenn Brummer, Luis DeLeon, Gene Roof)	.10
562	Mike O'Berry	.10
563	Ross Baumgarten	.10
564	Doug DeCinces	.10
565	Jackson Todd	.10
566	Mike Jorgensen	.10
567	Bob Babcock	.10
568	Joe Pettini	.10
569	Willie Randolph	.10
570	Willie Randolph/IA	.10
571	Glenn Abbott	.10
572	Juan Beniquez	.10
573	Rick Waits	.10
574	Mike Ramsey	.10
575	Al Cowens	.10
576	Giants Batting & Pitching Ldrs. (Vida Blue, Milt May)	.10
577	Rick Monday	.10
578	Shooty Babitt	.10
579	Rick Mahler RC	.10
580	Bobby Bonds	.10
581	Ron Reed	.10
582	Luis Pujols	.10
583	Tippy Martinez	.10
584	Hosken Powell	.10
585	Rollie Fingers	1.00
586	Rollie Fingers/IA	.15
587	Tim Lollar	.10
588	Dale Berra	.10
589	Dave Stapleton	.10
590	Al Oliver	.10
591	Al Oliver/IA	.10
592	Craig Swan	.10
593	Billy Smith	.10
594	Renie Martin	.10
595	Dave Collins	.10
596	Damaso Garcia	.10
597	Wayne Nordhagen	.10
598	Bob Galasso	.10
599	White Sox Future Stars (Jay Loviglio, Reggie Patterson, Leo Sutherland)	.10
600	Dave Winfield	1.50
601	Sid Monge	.10
602	Freddie Patek	.10
603	Rich Hebner	.10
604	Orlando Sanchez	.10
605	Steve Rogers	.10
606	Blue Jays Batting & Pitching Ldrs. (John Mayberry, Dave Stieb)	.10
607	Leon Durham	.10
608	Jerry Royster	.10
609	Rick Sutcliffe	.10
610	Rickey Henderson	1.50
611	Joe Niekro	.10
612	Gary Ward	.10
613	Jim Gantner	.10
614	Juan Eichelberger	.10
615	Bob Boone	.10
616	Bob Boone/IA	.10
617	Scott McGregor	.10
618	Tim Foli	.10
619	Bill Campbell	.10
620	Ken Griffey	.10
621	Ken Griffey/IA	.10
622	Dennis Lamp	.10
623	Mets Future Stars (Ron Gardenhire, Terry Leach RC, Tim Leary RC)	.20
624	Fergie Jenkins	1.00
625	Hal McRae	.10
626	Randy Jones	.10
627	Enos Cabell	.10
628	Bill Travers	.10
629	Johnny Wockenfuss	.10
630	Joe Charboneau	.10
631	Gene Tenace	.10
632	Bryan Clark	.10
633	Mitchell Page	.10
634	Checklist 529-660	.10
635	Ron Davis	.10
636	Phillies Batting & Pitching Ldrs. (Steve Carlton, Pete Rose)	.50
637	Rick Camp	.10
638	John Milner	.10
639	Ken Kravec	.10
640	Cesar Cedeno	.10
641	Steve Mura	.10
642	Mike Scioscia	.10
643	Pete Vuckovich	.10
644	John Castino	.10
645	Frank White	.10
646	Frank White/IA	.10
647	Warren Brusstar	.10
648	Jose Morales	.10
649	Ken Clay	.10
650	Carl Yastrzemski	1.50
651	Carl Yastrzemski/IA	.65
652	Steve Nicosia	.10
653	Angels Future Stars (Tom Brunansky RC, Luis Sanchez RC, Daryl Sconiers RC)	.40
654	Jim Morrison	.10
655	Joel Youngblood	.10
656	Eddie Whitson	.10
657	Tom Poquette	.10
658	Tito Landrum	.10
659	Fred Martinez	.10
660	Dave Concepcion	.10
661	Dave Concepcion/IA	.10
662	Luis Salazar	.10
663	Hector Cruz	.10
664	Dan Spillner	.10
665	Jim Clancy	.10
666	Tigers Batting & Pitching Ldrs. (Steve Kemp, Dan Petry)	.10
667	Jeff Reardon	.15
668	Dale Murphy	.75
669	Larry Milbourne	.10
670	Steve Kemp	.10
671	Mike Davis	.10
672	Bob Knepper	.10
673	Keith Drumright	.10
674	Dave Goltz	.10
675	Cecil Cooper	.10
676	Sal Butera	.10
677	Alfredo Griffin	.10
678	Tom Paciorek	.10
679	Sammy Stewart	.10
680	Gary Matthews	.10
681	Dodgers Future Stars (Mike Marshall RC, Ron Roenicke RC, Steve Sax RC)	.75
682	Jesse Jefferson	.10
683	Phil Garner	.10
684	Harold Baines	.05
685	Bert Blyleven	.10
686	Gary Allenson	.10
687	Greg Minton	.10
688	Leon Roberts	.10
689	Lary Sorensen	.10
690	Dave Kingman	.10
691	Dan Schatzeder	.10
692	Wayne Gross	.10
693	Cesar Geronimo	.10
694	Dave Wehrmeister	.10
695	Warren Cromartie	.10
696	Pirates Batting & Pitching Ldrs. (Bill Madlock, Buddy Solomon)	.10
697	John Montefusco	.10
698	Tony Scott	.10
699	Dick Tidrow	.10
700	George Foster	.10
701	George Foster/IA	.10
702	Steve Renko	.10
703	Brewers Batting & Pitching Ldrs. (Cecil Cooper, Pete Vuckovich)	.10
704	Mickey Rivers	.10
705	Mickey Rivers/IA	.10
706	Barry Foote	.10
707	Mark Bomback	.10
708	Gene Richards	.10
709	Don Money	.10
710	Jerry Reuss	.10
711	Mariners Future Stars (Dave Edler RC, Dave Henderson RC, Reggie Walton RC)	.25
712	Denny Martinez	.10
713	Del Unser	.10
714	Jerry Koosman	.10
715	Willie Stargell	1.50
716	Willie Stargell/IA	.30
717	Rick Miller	.10
718	Charlie Hough	.10
719	Jerry Narron	.10
720	Greg Luzinski	.10
721	Greg Luzinski/IA	.10
722	Jerry Martin	.10
723	Junior Kennedy	.10
724	Dave Rosello	.10
725	Amos Otis	.10
726	Amos Otis/IA	.10
727	Sixto Lezcano	.10
728	Aurelio Lopez	.10
729	Jim Spencer	.10
730	Gary Carter	1.50
731	Padres Future Stars (Mike Armstrong, Doug Gwosdz, Fred Kuhaulua)	.10
732	Mike Lum	.10
733	Larry McWilliams	.10
734	Mike Ivie	.10
735	Rudy May	.10
736	Jerry Turner	.10
737	Reggie Cleveland	.10
738	Dave Engle	.10
739	Joey McLaughlin	.10
740	Dave Lopes	.10
741	Dave Lopes/IA	.10
742	Dick Drago	.10
743	John Stearns	.10
744	Mike Witt RC	.25
745	Bake McBride	.10
746	Andre Thornton	.10
747	John Lowenstein	.10
748	Marc Hill	.10
749	Bob Shirley	.10
750	Jim Rice	.20
751	Rick Honeycutt	.10
752	Lee Lacy	.10
753	Tom Brookens	.10
754	Joe Morgan	1.50
755	Joe Morgan/IA	.25
756	Reds Batting & Pitching Ldrs. (Ken Griffey, Tom Seaver)	.25
757	Tom Underwood	.10
758	Claudell Washington	.10
759	Paul Splittorff	.10
760	Bill Buckner	.10
761	Dave Smith	.10
762	Mike Phillips	.10
763	Tom Hume	.10
764	Steve Swisher	.10
765	Gorman Thomas	.10
766	Twins Future Stars (Lenny Faedo RC, Kent Hrbek RC, Tim Laudner RC)	2.00
767	Roy Smalley	.10
768	Jerry Garvin	.10
769	Richie Zisk	.10
770	Rich Gossage	.10
771	Rich Gossage/IA	.10
772	Bert Campaneris	.10
773	John Denny	.10
774	Jay Johnstone	.10
775	Bob Forsch	.10
776	Mark Belanger	.10
777	Tom Griffin	.10
778	Kevin Hickey	.10
779	Grant Jackson	.10
780	Pete Rose	3.50
781	Pete Rose/IA	2.00
782	Frank Taveras	.10
783	Greg Harris RC	.10
784	Milt Wilcox	.10
785	Dan Driessen	.10
786	Red Sox Batting & Pitching Ldrs. (Carney Lansford, Mike Torrez)	.10
787	Fred Stanley	.10
788	Woodie Fryman	.10
789	Checklist 661-792	.10
790	Larry Gura	.10
791	Bobby Brown	.10
792	Frank Tanana	.10

"Blackless"

PHILLIES PETE ROSE

ABBREVIATIONS

AS - All-Star
IA - In Action

Whether through faulty pre-production work or the simple fact that the black ink may have run dry during printing, exactly half of the 1982 Topps cards can be found in a "blackless" version. All cards on the set's A, B and C press sheets can be found blackless. On regular player's cards the lack of black printing is most obvious in the absence of the facsimile autograph on front. The thin black pinstripe around the player photo is also missing on those cards. On cards in which the position was supposed to be printed in black, it will be missing on these variations. All-Star cards affected by this error will be missing the player's name. It is estimated fewer than 100 of each "blackless" card were released. Originally cards from the A and B sheets were found in metro New York, while the C cards turned up most often in the Midwest. Cards from the C sheet are much scarcer than those from the A and B sheets, although limited collector demand for full sets has kept prices in relative parity.

#	Player	NM/M
	Complete Set (396):	5,500.
	Common Player:	12.50
8	Rich Dauer	12.50
9	Ron Guidry	20.00
10	Ron Guidry/IA	12.50
11	Gary Alexander	12.50
12	Moose Haas	12.50
13	Lamar Johnson	12.50
14	Steve Howe	12.50
17	Darrell Evans	12.50
18	Fernando Arroyo	12.50
20	Garry Maddox	12.50
24	Dave Frost	12.50
26	Jorge Orta	12.50
28	John Urrea	12.50
31	Tom Seaver/IA	22.50
35	Willie Aikens	12.50
37	Dan Graham	12.50
38	Charlie Lea	12.50
39	Lou Whitaker	12.50
40	Dave Parker	12.50
42	Rick Sofield	12.50
48	Bobby Castillo	12.50
49	Alvis Woods	12.50
50	Buddy Bell	12.50
52	Larry Andersen	12.50
54	Ron Hassey	12.50
55	Rick Burleson	12.50
60	Tony Armas	12.50
64	Lynn Jones	12.50
65	Terry Kennedy	12.50
67	Rich Gale	12.50
68	Roy Howell	12.50
70	Tim Raines	12.50
71	Roy Lee Jackson	12.50
72	Rick Auerbach	12.50
73	Buddy Solomon	12.50
74	Bob Clark	12.50
77	Miguel Dilone	12.50
78	George Medich	12.50
80	Jim Palmer	40.00
81	Jim Palmer/IA	15.00
84	Rennie Stennett	12.50
87	Matt Keough	12.50
88	Biff Pocoroba	12.50
89	Steve Henderson	12.50
90	Nolan Ryan	425.00
91	Carney Lansford	12.50
92	Brad Havens	12.50
94	Andy Hassler	12.50
95	Ozzie Smith	60.00
98	Terry Bulling	12.50
99	Barry Bonnell	12.50
100	Mike Schmidt	185.00
101	Mike Schmidt/IA	130.00
105	Kirk Gibson	12.50
107	Wayne Krenchicki	12.50
109	Dave Revering	12.50
110	Carlton Fisk	45.00
112	Billy Sample	12.50
113	Steve McCatty	12.50
114	Ken Landreaux	12.50
115	Gaylord Perry	35.00
116	Jim Wohlford	12.50
117	Rawly Eastwick	12.50
118	Joe Pittman	12.50
120	Gary Lucas	12.50
122	Jamie Easterley	12.50
123	Danny Goodwin	12.50
123	Danny Ainge	22.50
127	Lonnie Smith	12.50
128	Frank Pastore	12.50
130	Julio Cruz	12.50
131	Stan Bahnsen	12.50
134	Lee May	12.50
134	Dan Ford	12.50
135	Andy Rincon	12.50

#	Player	NM/M
136	Lenn Sakata	12.50
137	George Cappuzzello	12.50
138	Tony Pena	12.50
140	Ron LeFlore	12.50
143	Mookie Wilson	12.50
147	Denny Walling	12.50
155	Ted Simmons	12.50
155	Otto Velez	12.50
157	Steve Crawford	12.50
158	Brian Downing	12.50
159	Larry Biittner	12.50
160	Luis Tiant	12.50
170	Jim Bibby	12.50
172	Bill Gullickson	12.50
173	Jamie Quirk	12.50
174	Dave Ford	12.50
175	Jerry Mumphrey	12.50
177	John Ellis	12.50
178	Dyar Miller	12.50
179	Steve Garvey	30.00
181	Silvio Martinez	12.50
183	Mike Proly	12.50
185	Phil Niekro	35.00
189	Glenn Hoffman	12.50
190	J.R. Richard	12.50
192	Broderick Perkins	12.50
198	Chris Speier	12.50
200	George Brett	150.00
201	George Brett/IA	55.00
204	Gary Roenicke	12.50
209	Gary Lavelle	12.50
210	Keith Hernandez	12.50
211	Dan Petry	12.50
212	Mario Mendoza	12.50
215	Mike Krukow	12.50
220	Manny Trillo	12.50
221	Jim Slaton	12.50
222	Butch Wynegar	12.50
223	Lloyd Moseby	12.50
224	Bruce Bochte	12.50
225	Mike Torrez	12.50
228	Sam Mejias	12.50
230	Willie Wilson	12.50
232	Terry Crowley	12.50
233	Duane Kuiper	12.50
234	Ron Hodges	12.50
235	Mike Easler	12.50
237	Rusty Kuntz	12.50
238	Kevin Saucier	12.50
239	Jon Matlack	12.50
240	Bucky Dent	12.50
241	Bucky Dent/IA	12.50
245	Ken Reitz	12.50
247	Pedro Guerrero	12.50
251	Fred Lynn	12.50
255	Tony Perez	35.00
256	Tony Perez/IA	12.50
257	Larry Harlow	12.50
258	Bo Diaz	12.50
259	Rodney Scott	12.50
260	Bruce Sutter	35.00
262	Doug Bair	12.50
264	Dan Quisenberry	12.50
265	Al Bumbry	12.50
267	Kurt Bevacqua	12.50
270	Rusty Staub	15.00
272	Bump Wills	12.50
275	Bob Watson	12.50
278	John Littlefield	12.50
280	Ben Oglivie	12.50
281	John Verhoeven	12.50
283	Brian Allard	12.50
285	Sparky Lyle	12.50
287	Alan Bannister	12.50
288	Garry Templeton	12.50
289	Bob Stanley	12.50
290	Ken Singleton	12.50
297	Clint Hurdle	12.50
299	Steve Trout	12.50
300	Reggie Jackson	65.00
302	Doug Flynn	12.50
305	Don Sutton	30.00
307	Randy Bass	12.50
308	Charlie Moore	12.50
310	Mike Hargrove	12.50
312	Lenny Randle	12.50
313	John Harris	12.50
315	Burt Hooton	12.50
317	Dick Ruthven	12.50
321	Bill Lee	12.50
324	Steve Dillard	12.50
328	Jose Cruz	12.50
328	Ed Farmer	12.50
329	U.L. Washington	12.50
330	Rick Wise	12.50
332	Don Robinson	12.50
334	Aurelio Rodriguez	12.50
335	Jim Sundberg	12.50
339	Mike Schmidt/AS	130.00
340	Dave Concepcion/AS	12.50
341	Andre Dawson/AS	15.00
342	George Foster/AS	12.50
343	Dave Parker/AS	12.50
344	Gary Carter/AS	15.00
345	Fernando Valenzuela/AS	12.50
349	George Frazier	12.50
352	Dick Davis	12.50
354	Roberto Ramos	12.50

ABBREVIATIONS

AS - All-Star
IA - In Action

#	Player	NM/M
355	Dwight Evans	12.50
357	Butch Hobson	12.50
359	Jim Dwyer	12.50
360	Len Barker	12.50
363	Bob Molinaro	12.50
365	Bill Madlock	12.50
370	Mike Norris	12.50
380	Dave Stieb	12.50
382	Joe Simpson	12.50
385	Ken Forsch	12.50
387	Tom Veryzer	12.50
388	Joe Rudi	12.50
390	Eddie Murray	45.00
397	Ken Brett	12.50
398	Mike Squires	12.50
399	Pat Zachry	12.50
405	Johnny Bench	50.00
406	Al Holland	12.50
408	Don Cooper	12.50
412	Luis Leal	12.50
413	Dan Meyer	12.50
415	Don Baylor	12.50
417	Pat Kelly	12.50
419	Steve Stone	12.50
420	George Hendrick	12.50
421	Mark Clear	12.50
422	Cliff Johnson	12.50
423	Stan Papi	12.50
424	Bruce Benedict	12.50
425	John Candelaria	12.50
426	Vida Blue	12.50
440	Jeff Burroughs	12.50
442	Bruce Kison	12.50
443	Mark Wagner	12.50
446	Larry Parrish	12.50
446	Wayne Garland	12.50
448	Darrell Porter/IA	12.50
450	Jack Morris	12.50
451	Ed Miller	12.50
459	Bruce Berenyi	12.50
460	Jack Clark	12.50
461	Rich Dotson	12.50
462	Dave Chalk	12.50
463	Jim Kern	12.50
465	Juan Bonilla	12.50
465	Lee Mazzilli	12.50
467	Mickey Hatcher	12.50
468	Floyd Bannister	12.50
472	Oscar Gamble	12.50
475	Alan Trammell	12.50
476	Brian Kingman	12.50
477	Steve Yeager	12.50
480	Steve Carlton	35.00
481	Steve Carlton/IA	15.00
484	Ivan DeJesus	12.50
490	Dennis Eckersley	35.00
492	Joe Price	12.50
493	Chet Lemon	12.50
495	Dennis Leonard	12.50
496	Johnny Grubb	12.50
498	Dave Bergman	12.50
499	Paul Mirabella	12.50
500	Rod Carew	45.00
501	Rod Carew/IA	15.00
503	Julio Gonzalez	12.50
507	Terry Harper	12.50
511	Fernando Valenzuela	17.50
511	Ruppert Jones	12.50
512	Jerry Dybzinski	12.50
515	Larry Bowa	12.50
518	Garth Iorg	12.50
520	Glenn Adams	12.50
520	Mike Flanagan	12.50
521	Bill Almon	12.50
523	Gary Gray	12.50
528	Tom Hausman	12.50
532	Toby Harrah	12.50
534	Dave McKay	12.50
539	Rafael Ramirez	12.50
540	Andre Dawson	30.00
541	Barry Evans	12.50
542	Ned Yost	12.50
545	Bill Robinson	12.50
547	Rod Carew/AS	25.00
548	Willie Randolph/AS	12.50
549	George Brett/AS	150.00
550	Bucky Dent/AS	15.00
552	Reggie Jackson/AS	30.00
552	Ken Singleton/AS	12.50
553	Dave Winfield/AS	25.00
554	Carlton Fisk/AS	25.00
555	Scott McGregor/AS	12.50
557	Jack Morris/AS	12.50
557	Rich Gossage/AS	12.50
560	Doug Corbett	12.50
563	Ross Baumgarten	12.50
565	Doug DeCinces	12.50
565	Jackson Todd	12.50
567	Bob Babcock	12.50
569	Joe Pettini	12.50
569	Willie Randolph	12.50
573	Rick Waits	12.50
574	Mike Ramsey	12.50
579	Al Cowens	12.50
579	Rick Mahler	12.50
580	Bobby Bonds	12.50
581	Ron Reed	12.50
582	Luis Pujols	12.50
588	Rollie Fingers	35.00
590	Dale Berra	12.50
594	Al Oliver	12.50
594	Renie Martin	12.50
600	Dave Winfield	50.00
601	Sid Monge	12.50
602	Freddie Patek	12.50
605	Richie Hebner	12.50
608	Jerry Royster	12.50

#	Player	NM/M
610	Rickey Henderson	150.00
611	Joe Niekro	12.50
612	Gary Ward	12.50
613	Jim Gantner	12.50
615	Bob Boone	12.50
616	Bob Boone/IA	12.50
622	Dennis Lamp	12.50
624	Fergie Jenkins	35.00
625	Hal McRae	12.50
626	Randy Jones	12.50
627	Enos Cabell	12.50
629	Johnny Wockenfuss	12.50
630	Joe Charboneau	25.00
632	Bryan Clark	12.50
635	Ron Davis	12.50
637	Rick Camp	12.50
640	Cesar Cedeno	12.50
645	Frank White	12.50
646	Frank White/IA	12.50
648	Jose Morales	12.50
649	Ken Clay	12.50
654	Jim Morrison	12.50
655	Joel Youngblood	12.50
656	Eddie Whitson	12.50
661	Dave Concepcion/IA	12.50
663	Hector Cruz	12.50
664	Dan Spillner	12.50
665	Jim Clancy	12.50
668	Dale Murphy	35.00
669	Larry Milbourne	12.50
670	Steve Kemp	12.50
672	Bob Knepper	12.50
675	Cecil Cooper	12.50
677	Alfredo Griffin	12.50
678	Tom Paciorek	12.50
684	Harold Baines	12.50
685	Bert Blyleven	12.50
686	Gary Allenson	12.50
690	Dave Kingman	12.50
691	Dan Schatzeder	12.50
694	Dave Wehrmeister	12.50
695	Warren Cromartie	12.50
700	George Foster	12.50
702	Steve Renko	12.50
704	Mickey Rivers	12.50
705	Mickey Rivers/IA	12.50
706	Barry Foote	12.50
707	Mark Bomback	12.50
708	Gene Richards	12.50
710	Jerry Reuss	12.50
713	Del Unser	12.50
715	Willie Stargell	45.00
716	Willie Stargell/IA	15.00
718	Charlie Hough	12.50
720	Greg Luzinski	12.50
721	Greg Luzinski/IA	12.50
722	Jerry Martin	12.50
724	Dave Rosello	12.50
725	Amos Otis	12.50
730	Gary Carter	45.00
735	Rudy May	12.50
737	Reggie Cleveland	12.50
738	Dave Engle	12.50
739	Joey McLaughlin	12.50
740	Dave Lopes	12.50
741	Dave Lopes/IA	12.50
742	Dick Drago	12.50
743	John Stearns	12.50
745	Bake McBride	12.50
747	John Lowenstein	12.50
748	Marc Hill	12.50
751	Rick Honeycutt	12.50
753	Tom Brookens	12.50
754	Joe Morgan	45.00
757	Tom Underwood	12.50
760	Bill Buckner	12.50
761	Dave Smith	12.50
764	Steve Swisher	12.50
765	Gorman Thomas	12.50
767	Roy Smalley	12.50
768	Jerry Garvin	12.50
769	Richie Zisk	12.50
771	Rich Gossage/IA	12.50
775	Bob Forsch	12.50
776	Mark Belanger	12.50
777	Tom Griffin	12.50
778	Kevin Hickey	12.50
780	Pete Rose	225.00
781	Pete Rose/IA	100.00
782	Frank Taveras	12.50
784	Milt Wilcox	12.50
788	Woodie Fryman	12.50
790	Larry Gura	12.50
792	Frank Tanana	12.50

Traded

Topps released its second straight 132-card Traded set in September of 1982. Again, the 2-1/2" x 3-1/2" cards feature not only players who had been traded during the season, but also promising rookies who were given their first individual cards. The cards follow the basic design of the regular issues, but have their backs printed in red rather than the regular-issue green. As in 1981, the cards were not available in normal retail outlets and could only be purchased through regular baseball card dealers. Unlike the previous year, the cards are numbered 1-132 with the letter "T" following the number.

#	Player	NM/M
	Complete Set (132):	175.00
	Common Player:	.10
1T	Doyle Alexander	.10
2T	Jesse Barfield	.10
3T	Ross Baumgarten	.10
4T	Steve Bedrosian	.10
5T	Mark Belanger	.10
6T	Kurt Bevacqua	.10
7T	Tim Blackwell	.10
8T	Vida Blue	.10
9T	Bob Boone	.30
10T	Larry Bowa	.10
11T	Dan Briggs	.10
12T	Bobby Brown	.10
13T	Tom Brunansky	.10
14T	Jeff Burroughs	.10
15T	Enos Cabell	.10
16T	Bill Campbell	.10
17T	Bobby Castillo	.10
18T	Bill Caudill	.10
19T	Cesar Cedeno	.10
20T	Dave Collins	.10
21T	Doug Corbett	.10
22T	Al Cowens	.10
23T	Chili Davis	.50
24T	Dick Davis	.10
25T	Ron Davis	.10
26T	Doug DeCinces	.10
27T	Ivan DeJesus	.10
28T	Bob Dernier	.10
29T	Bo Diaz	.10
30T	Roger Erickson	.10
31T	Jim Essian	.10
32T	Ed Farmer	.10
33T	Doug Flynn	.10
34T	Tim Foli	.10
35T	Dan Ford	.10
36T	George Foster	.10
37T	Dave Frost	.10
38T	Rich Gale	.10
39T	Ron Gardenhire	.10
40T	Ken Griffey	.10
41T	Greg Harris	.10
42T	Von Hayes	.10
43T	Larry Herndon	.10
44T	Kent Hrbek	2.00
45T	Mike Ivie	.10
46T	Grant Jackson	.10
47T	Reggie Jackson	5.00
48T	Ron Jackson	.10
49T	Fergie Jenkins	2.00
50T	Lamar Johnson	.10
51T	Randy Johnson	.10
52T	Jay Johnstone	.10
53T	Mick Kelleher	.10
54T	Steve Kemp	.10
55T	Junior Kennedy	.10
56T	Jim Kern	.10
57T	Ray Knight	.10
58T	Wayne Krenchicki	.10
59T	Mike Krukow	.10
60T	Duane Kuiper	.10
61T	Mike LaCoss	.10
62T	Chet Lemon	.10
63T	Sixto Lezcano	.10
64T	Dave Lopes	.10
65T	Jerry Martin	.10
66T	Renie Martin	.10
67T	John Mayberry	.10
68T	Lee Mazzilli	.10
69T	Bake McBride	.10
70T	Dan Meyer	.10
71T	Larry Milbourne	.10
72T	Eddie Milner RC	.10
73T	Sid Monge	.10
74T	John Montefusco	.10
75T	Jose Morales	.10
76T	Keith Moreland	.10
77T	Jim Morrison	.10
78T	Rance Mulliniks	.10
79T	Steve Mura	.10
80T	Gene Nelson	.10
81T	Joe Nolan	.10
82T	Dickie Noles	.10
83T	Al Oliver	.10
84T	Jorge Orta	.10
85T	Tom Paciorek	.10
86T	Larry Parrish	.10
87T	Jack Perconte	.10
88T	Gaylord Perry	2.00
89T	Rob Picciolo	.10
90T	Joe Pittman	.10
91T	Hosken Powell	.10
92T	Mike Proly	.10
93T	Greg Pryor	.10
94T	Charlie Puleo RC	.10
95T	Shane Rawley	.10
96T	Johnny Ray	.10
97T	Dave Revering	.10
98T	Cal Ripken, Jr.	140.00
99T	Allen Ripley	.10
100T	Bill Robinson	.10
101T	Aurelio Rodriguez	.10
102T	Joe Rudi	.10
103T	Steve Sax	.50
104T	Dan Schatzeder	.10
105T	Bob Shirley	.10
106T	Eric Show RC	.10
107T	Roy Smalley	.10
108T	Lonnie Smith	.10
109T	Ozzie Smith	20.00
110T	Reggie Smith	.10
111T	Lary Sorensen	.10
112T	Elias Sosa	.10
113T	Mike Stanton	.10
114T	Steve Stroughter	.10
115T	Champ Summers	.10
116T	Rick Sutcliffe	.10
117T	Frank Tanana	.10
118T	Frank Taveras	.10
119T	Garry Templeton	.10
120T	Alex Trevino	.10
121T	Jerry Turner	.10
122T	Ed Vande Berg RC	.10
123T	Tom Veryzer	.10
124T	Ron Washington	.10
125T	Bob Watson	.10
126T	Dennis Werth	.10
127T	Eddie Whitson	.10
128T	Rob Wilfong	.10
129T	Bump Wills	.10
130T	Gary Woods	.10
131T	Butch Wynegar	.10
132T	Checklist 1-132	.10

Team Leaders Sheet

Available via a special mail-in offer, this 10-1/2" x 23" uncut sheet contained the 26 team batting and pitching leaders cards plus a card offering Topps collectors boxes. The team leader cards are identical to those issued in packs.

	NM/M
Team Leaders sheet	10.00

Insert Stickers

85
WILLIE STARGELL
1st Base
ALBUMS COMING SOON! SAVE THIS STICKER ... and place it in your new 1982 Topps Baseball Sticker Album. Albums and ALL stickers are sold where Topps Baseball cards are available.
IT'S Topps FOR SPORTS
© 1982 TOPPS CHEWING GUM, INC.

This 48-player set is actually an abbreviated version of the regular 1982 Topps sticker set with different backs. Used to promote the 1982 sticker set, Topps inserted these stickers in its baseball card wax packs. They are identical to the regular 1982 stickers, except for the backs, which advertise that the Topps sticker album will be "Coming Soon." The 48 stickers retain the same names used in the regular sticker set, resulting in the smaller set being skip-numbered.

#	Player	NM/M
	Complete Set (48):	3.00
	Common Player:	.05
17	Chris Chambliss	.05
21	Bruce Benedict	.05
25	Leon Durham	.05
29	Bill Buckner	.05
33	Dave Collins	.05

37 Dave Concepcion .05
41 Nolan Ryan 1.00
45 Bob Knepper .05
49 Ken Landreaux .05
53 Burt Hooton .05
57 Andre Dawson .15
61 Gary Carter .25
65 Joel Youngblood .05
69 Ellis Valentine .05
73 Garry Maddox .05
77 Bob Boone .50
81 Omar Moreno .05
85 Willie Stargell .25
89 Ken Oberkfell .05
93 Darrell Porter .05
97 Juan Eichelberger .05
101 Luis Salazar .05
105 Enos Cabell .05
109 Larry Herndon .05
143 Scott McGregor .05
148 Mike Flanagan .05
151 Mike Torrez .05
156 Carney Lansford .05
161 Fred Lynn .05
166 Rich Dotson .05
171 Tony Bernazard .05
176 Bo Diaz .05
181 Alan Trammell .05
186 Milt Wilcox .05
191 Dennis Leonard .05
196 Willie Aikens .05
201 Ted Simmons .05
206 Hosken Powell .05
211 Roger Erickson .05
215 Graig Nettles .05
216 Reggie Jackson .45
221 Rickey Henderson .25
226 Cliff Johnson .05
231 Jeff Burroughs .05
236 Tom Paciorek .05
241 Pat Putnam .05
246 Lloyd Moseby .05
251 Barry Bonnell .05

Stickers

The 1982 Topps sticker set is complete at 260 stickers and includes another series of "foil" All-Stars. The stickers measure 1-15/16" x 2-9/16" and feature full-color photos surrounded by a red border for American League players or a blue border for National League players. They are numbered on both the front and back and were designed to be mounted in a special album.

NM/M
Complete Set (260): 7.50
Common Player: .05
Sticker Album: 2.00
Wax Pack (5): .25
Wax Box (100): 15.00
1 Bill Madlock .05
2 Carney Lansford .05
3 Mike Schmidt .30
4 Tony Armas, Dwight Evans, Bobby Grich, Eddie Murray .05
5 Mike Schmidt .30
6 Eddie Murray .25
7 Tim Raines .05
8 Rickey Henderson .25
9 Tom Seaver .25
10 Denny Martinez, Steve McCatty, Jack Morris, Pete Vuckovich .05
11 Fernando Valenzuela .05
12 Len Barker .05
13 Nolan Ryan .50
14 Steve McCatty .05
15 Bruce Sutter .20
16 Rollie Fingers .20
17 Chris Chambliss .05
18 Bob Horner .05
19 Dale Murphy .15
20 Phil Niekro .20
21 Bruce Benedict .05
22 Claudell Washington .05
23 Glenn Hubbard .05
24 Rick Camp .05
25 Leon Durham .05
26 Ken Reitz .05

27 Dick Tidrow .05
28 Tim Blackwell .05
29 Bill Buckner .05
30 Steve Henderson .05
31 Mike Krukow .05
32 Ivan DeJesus .05
33 Dave Collins .05
34 Ron Oester .05
35 Johnny Bench .25
36 Tom Seaver .25
37 Dave Concepcion .05
38 Ken Griffey .05
39 Ray Knight .05
40 George Foster .05
41 Nolan Ryan .50
42 Terry Puhl .05
43 Art Howe .05
44 Jose Cruz .05
45 Bob Knepper .05
46 Craig Reynolds .05
47 Cesar Cedeno .05
48 Alan Ashby .05
49 Ken Landreaux .05
50 Fernando Valenzuela .05
51 Ron Cey .05
52 Dusty Baker .05
53 Burt Hooton .05
54 Steve Garvey .15
55 Pedro Guerrero .05
56 Jerry Reuss .05
57 Andre Dawson .20
58 Chris Speier .05
59 Steve Rogers .05
60 Warren Cromartie .05
61 Gary Carter .25
62 Tim Raines .05
63 Scott Sanderson .05
64 Larry Parrish .05
65 Joel Youngblood .05
66 Neil Allen .05
67 Lee Mazzilli .05
68 Hubie Brooks .05
69 Ellis Valentine .05
70 Doug Flynn .05
71 Pat Zachry .05
72 Dave Kingman .05
73 Garry Maddox .05
74 Mike Schmidt .30
75 Steve Carlton .25
76 Manny Trillo .05
77 Bob Boone .05
78 Pete Rose .40
79 Gary Matthews .05
80 Larry Bowa .05
81 Omar Moreno .05
82 Rick Rhoden .05
83 Bill Madlock .05
84 Mike Easler .05
85 Willie Stargell .25
86 Jim Bibby .05
87 Dave Parker .05
88 Tim Foli .05
89 Ken Oberkfell .05
90 Bob Forsch .05
91 George Hendrick .05
92 Keith Hernandez .05
93 Darrell Porter .05
94 Bruce Sutter .20
95 Sixto Lezcano .05
96 Garry Templeton .05
97 Juan Eichelberger .05
98 Broderick Perkins .05
99 Ruppert Jones .05
100 Terry Kennedy .05
101 Luis Salazar .05
102 Gary Lucas .05
103 Gene Richards .05
104 Ozzie Smith .30
105 Enos Cabell .05
106 Jack Clark .05
107 Greg Minton .05
108 Johnnie LeMaster .05
109 Larry Herndon .05
110 Milt May .05
111 Vida Blue .05
112 Darrell Evans .05
113 Len Barker .05
114 Julio Cruz .05
115 Billy Martin .05
116 Tim Raines .05
117 Pete Rose .40
118 Bill Stein .05
119 Fernando Valenzuela .05
120 Carl Yastrzemski .25
121 Pete Rose .40
122 Manny Trillo .05
123 Mike Schmidt .30
124 Dave Concepcion .05
125 Andre Dawson .20
126 George Foster .05
127 Dave Parker .05
128 Gary Carter .25
129 Steve Carlton .25
130 Bruce Sutter .05
131 Rod Carew .25
132 Jerry Remy .05
133 George Brett .30
134 Rick Burleson .05
135 Dwight Evans .05
136 Ken Singleton .05
137 Dave Winfield .25
138 Carlton Fisk .25
139 Jack Morris .05
140 Rich Gossage .05
141 Al Bumbry .05
142 Doug DeCinces .05
143 Scott McGregor .05
144 Ken Singleton .05

145 Eddie Murray .25
146 Jim Palmer .20
147 Rich Dauer .05
148 Mike Flanagan .05
149 Jerry Remy .05
150 Jim Rice .15
151 Mike Torrez .05
152 Tony Perez .25
153 Dwight Evans .05
154 Mark Clear .05
155 Carl Yastrzemski .25
156 Carney Lansford .05
157 Rick Burleson .05
158 Don Baylor .10
159 Ken Forsch .05
160 Rod Carew .25
161 Fred Lynn .05
162 Bob Grich .05
163 Dan Ford .05
164 Butch Hobson .05
165 Greg Luzinski .05
166 Rich Dotson .05
167 Billy Almon .05
168 Chet Lemon .05
169 Steve Trout .05
170 Carlton Fisk .25
171 Tony Bernazard .05
172 Ron LeFlore .05
173 Bert Blyleven .05
174 Andre Thornton .05
175 Jorge Orta .05
176 Bo Diaz .05
177 Toby Harrah .05
178 Len Barker .05
179 Rick Manning .05
180 Mike Hargrove .05
181 Alan Trammell .05
182 Al Cowens .05
183 Jack Morris .05
184 Kirk Gibson .05
185 Steve Kemp .05
186 Milt Wilcox .05
187 Lou Whitaker .05
188 Lance Parrish .05
189 Willie Wilson .05
190 George Brett .30
191 Dennis Leonard .05
192 John Wathan .05
193 Frank White .05
194 Amos Otis .05
195 Larry Gura .05
196 Willie Aikens .05
197 Ben Oglivie .05
198 Rollie Fingers .20
199 Cecil Cooper .05
200 Paul Molitor .20
201 Ted Simmons .05
202 Pete Vuckovich .05
203 Robin Yount .25
204 Gorman Thomas .05
205 Rob Wilfong .05
206 Hosken Powell .05
207 Roy Smalley .05
208 Butch Wynegar .05
209 John Castino .05
210 Doug Corbett .05
211 Roger Erickson .05
212 Mickey Hatcher .05
213 Dave Winfield .25
214 Tommy John .10
215 Graig Nettles .05
216 Reggie Jackson .25
217 Rich Gossage .05
218 Rick Cerone .05
219 Willie Randolph .05
220 Jerry Mumphrey .05
221 Rickey Henderson .25
222 Mike Norris .05
223 Jim Spencer .05
224 Tony Armas .05
225 Matt Keough .05
226 Cliff Johnson .05
227 Dwayne Murphy .05
228 Steve McCatty .05
229 Richie Zisk .05
230 Lenny Randle .05
231 Jeff Burroughs .05
232 Bruce Bochte .05
233 Gary Gray .05
234 Floyd Bannister .05
235 Julio Cruz .05
236 Tom Paciorek .05
237 Danny Darwin .05
238 Buddy Bell .05
239 Al Oliver .05
240 Jim Sundberg .05
241 Pat Putnam .05
242 Steve Comer .05
243 Mickey Rivers .05
244 Bump Wills .05
245 Damaso Garcia .05
246 Lloyd Moseby .05
247 Ernie Whitt .05
248 John Mayberry .05
249 Otto Velez .05
250 Dave Stieb .05
251 Barry Bonnell .05
252 Alfredo Griffin .05
253 1981 N.L. Championship (Gary Carter) .10
254 1981 A.L. Championship (Mike Heath, Larry Milbourne) .05
255 1981 World Champions (Los Angeles Dodgers Team) .05

256 1981 World Champions (Los Angeles Dodgers Team) .05
257 1981 World Series - Game 3 (Fernando Valenzuela) .05
258 1981 World Series - Game 4 (Steve Garvey) .10
259 1981 World Series - Game 5 (Jerry Reuss, Steve Yeager) .05
260 1981 World Series - Game 6 (Pedro Guerrero) .05

1983 Topps

The 1983 Topps set totals 792 cards. Missing among the regular 2-1/2" x 3-1/2" cards are some form of future stars cards, as Topps was saving them for the now-established late season "Traded" set. The 1983 cards carry a large color photo as well as a smaller color photo on the front, quite similar in design to the 1963 set. Team colors frame the card, which, at the bottom, have the player's name, position and team. At the upper right-hand corner is a Topps Logo. The backs are horizontal and include statistics, personal information and 1982 highlights. Specialty cards include record-breaking performances, league leaders, All-Stars, numbered checklists "Team Leaders" and "Super Veteran" cards which are horizontal with a current and first-season picture of the honored player.

NM/M
Complete Set (792): 60.00
Common Player: .05
Wax Pack (15): 3.00
Wax Box (36): 110.00
Crimp-End Test Pack (15): 4.00
Crimp-End Test Box (36): 110.00
Cello Pack (28): 5.00
Cello Box (24): 125.00
Rack Pack (51): 7.50
Rack Box (24): 175.00
Vending Box (500): 65.00
1 Tony Armas (Record Breaker) .05
2 Rickey Henderson (Record Breaker) .75
3 Greg Minton (Record Breaker) .05
4 Lance Parrish (Record Breaker) .05
5 Manny Trillo (Record Breaker) .05
6 John Wathan (Record Breaker) .05
7 Gene Richards .05
8 Steve Balboni .05
9 Joey McLaughlin .05
10 Gorman Thomas .05
11 Billy Gardner .05
12 Paul Mirabella .05
13 Larry Herndon .05
14 Frank LaCorte .05
15 Ron Cey .05
16 George Vukovich .05
17 Kent Tekulve .05
18 Kent Tekulve (Super Veteran) .05
19 Oscar Gamble .05
20 Carlton Fisk 2.00
21 Orioles Batting & Pitching Ldrs. (Eddie Murray, Jim Palmer, ...)
22 Randy Martz .05
23 Mike Heath .05
24 Steve Mura .05
25 Hal McRae .05
26 Jerry Royster .05
27 Doug Corbett .05
28 Bruce Bochte .05

29 Randy Jones .05
30 Jim Rice .15
31 Bill Gullickson .05
32 Dave Bergman .05
33 Jack O'Connor .05
34 Paul Householder .05
35 Rollie Fingers .75
36 Rollie Fingers (Super Veteran) .15
37 Darrell Johnson .05
38 Tim Flannery .05
39 Terry Puhl .05
40 Fernando Valenzuela .05
41 Jerry Turner .05
42 Dale Murray .05
43 Bob Dernier .05
44 Don Robinson .05
45 John Mayberry .05
46 Richard Dotson .05
47 Dave McKay .05
48 Lary Sorensen .05
49 Willie McGee RC 1.50
50 Bob Horner .05
51 Cubs Batting & Pitching Ldrs. (Leon Durham, Fergie Jenkins, ...) .05
52 Onix Concepcion RC .05
53 Mike Witt .05
54 Jim Maler .05
55 Mookie Wilson .05
56 Chuck Rainey .05
57 Tim Blackwell .05
58 Al Holland .05
59 Benny Ayala .05
60 Johnny Bench 2.00
61 Johnny Bench (Super Veteran) .75
62 Bob McClure .05
63 Rick Monday .05
64 Bill Stein .05
65 Jack Morris .05
66 Bob Lillis .05
67 Sal Butera .05
68 Eric Show RC .05
69 Lee Lacy .05
70 Steve Carlton 2.00
71 Steve Carlton (Super Veteran) .30
72 Tom Paciorek .05
73 Allen Ripley .05
74 Julio Gonzalez .05
75 Amos Otis .05
76 Rick Mahler .05
77 Hosken Powell .05
78 Bill Caudill .05
79 Mick Kelleher .05
80 George Foster .05
81 Yankees Batting & Pitching Ldrs. (Jerry Mumphrey, Dave Righetti) .05
82 Bruce Hurst .05
83 Ryne Sandberg RC 15.00
84 Milt May .05
85 Ken Singleton .05
86 Tom Hume .05
87 Joe Rudi .05
88 Jim Gantner .05
89 Leon Roberts .05
90 Jerry Reuss .05
91 Larry Milbourne .05
92 Mike LaCoss .05
93 John Castino .05
94 Dave Edwards .05
95 Alan Trammell .05
96 Dick Howser .05
97 Ross Baumgarten .05
98 Vance Law .05
99 Dickie Noles .05
100 Pete Rose 4.00
101 Pete Rose (Super Veteran) 2.00
102 Dave Beard .05
103 Darrell Porter .05
104 Bob Walk .05
105 Don Baylor .15
106 Gene Nelson .05
107 Mike Jorgensen .05
108 Glenn Hoffman .05
109 Luis Leal .05
110 Ken Griffey .05
111 Expos Batting & Pitching Ldrs. (Al Oliver, Steve Rogers) .05
112 Bob Shirley .05
113 Ron Roenicke .05
114 Jim Slaton .05
115 Chili Davis .05
116 Dave Schmidt .05
117 Alan Knicely .05
118 Chris Welsh .05
119 Tom Brookens .05
120 Len Barker .05
121 Mickey Hatcher .05
122 Jimmy Smith .05
123 George Frazier .05
124 Marc Hill .05
125 Leon Durham .05
126 Joe Torre .25
127 Preston Hanna .05
128 Mike Ramsey .05
129 Checklist 1-132 .05
130 Dave Stieb .05
131 Ed Ott .05
132 Todd Cruz .05
133 Jim Barr .05
134 Hubie Brooks .05
135 Dwight Evans .05
136 Willie Aikens .05

137 Woodie Fryman .05
138 Rick Dempsey .05
139 Bruce Berenyi .05
140 Willie Randolph .05
141 Indians Batting & Pitching Ldrs. (Toby Harrah, Rick Sutcliffe) .05
142 Mike Caldwell .05
143 Joe Pettini .05
144 Mark Wagner .05
145 Don Sutton .75
146 Don Sutton (Super Veteran) .20
147 Rick Leach .05
148 Dave Roberts .05
149 Johnny Ray .05
150 Bruce Sutter .75
151 Bruce Sutter (Super Veteran) .50
152 Jay Johnstone .05
153 Jerry Koosman .05
154 Johnnie LeMaster .05
155 Dan Quisenberry .05
156 Billy Martin .15
157 Steve Bedrosian .05
158 Rob Wilfong .05
159 Mike Stanton .05
160 Dave Kingman .05
161 Dave Kingman (Super Veteran) .05
162 Mark Clear .05
163 Cal Ripken, Jr. 6.00
164 Dave Palmer .05
165 Dan Driessen .05
166 John Pacella .05
167 Mark Brouhard .05
168 Juan Eichelberger .05
169 Doug Flynn .05
170 Steve Howe .05
171 Giants Batting & Pitching Ldrs. (Bill Laskey, Joe Morgan) .05
172 Vern Ruhle .05
173 Jim Morrison .05
174 Jerry Ujdur .05
175 Bo Diaz .05
176 Dave Righetti .05
177 Harold Baines .05
178 Luis Tiant .05
179 Luis Tiant (Super Veteran) .05
180 Rickey Henderson 2.00
181 Terry Felton .05
182 Mike Fischlin .05
183 Ed Vande Berg RC .05
184 Bob Clark .05
185 Tim Lollar .05
186 Whitey Herzog .05
187 Terry Leach .05
188 Rick Miller .05
189 Dan Schatzeder .05
190 Cecil Cooper .05
191 Joe Price .05
192 Floyd Rayford .05
193 Harry Spilman .05
194 Cesar Geronimo .05
195 Bob Stoddard .05
196 Bill Fahey .05
197 Jim Eisenreich RC .50
198 Kiko Garcia .05
199 Marty Bystrom .05
200 Rod Carew 2.00
201 Rod Carew (Super Veteran) .35
202 Blue Jays Batting & Pitching Ldrs. (Damaso Garcia, Dave Stieb) .05
203 Mike Morgan .05
204 Junior Kennedy .05
205 Dave Parker .05
206 Ken Oberkfell .05
207 Rick Camp .05
208 Dan Meyer .05
209 Mike Moore RC .15
210 Jack Clark .05
211 John Denny .05
212 John Stearns .05
213 Tom Burgmeier .05
214 Jerry White .05
215 Mario Soto .05
216 Tony LaRussa .05
217 Tim Stoddard .05
218 Roy Howell .05
219 Mike Armstrong .05
220 Dusty Baker .05
221 Joe Niekro .05
222 Damaso Garcia .05
223 John Montefusco .05
224 Mickey Rivers .05
225 Enos Cabell .05
226 Enrique Romo .05
227 Chris Bando .05
228 Joaquin Andujar .05
229 Phillies Batting/Pitching Leaders (Steve Carlton, Bo Diaz) .15
230 Fergie Jenkins .75
231 Fergie Jenkins (Super Veteran) .20
232 Tom Brunansky .05
233 Wayne Gross .05
234 Larry Andersen .05
235 Claudell Washington .05
236 Steve Renko .05
237 Dan Norman .05
238 Bud Black RC .25
239 Dave Stapleton .05

No.	Player	Price
240	Rich Gossage	.05
241	Rich Gossage (Super Veteran)	.05
242	Joe Nolan	.05
243	Duane Walker	.05
244	Dwight Bernard	.05
245	Steve Sax	.05
246	George Bamberger	.05
247	Dave Smith	.05
248	Bake McBride	.05
249	Checklist 133-264	.05
250	Bill Buckner	.05
251	Alan Wiggins RC	.05
252	Luis Aguayo	.05
253	Larry McWilliams	.05
254	Rick Cerone	.05
255	Gene Garber	.05
256	Gene Garber (Super Veteran)	.05
257	Jesse Barfield	.05
258	Manny Castillo	.05
259	Jeff Jones	.05
260	Steve Kemp	.05
261	Tigers Batting & Pitching Ldrs. (Larry Herndon, Dan Petry)	.05
262	Ron Jackson	.05
263	Renie Martin	.05
264	Jamie Quirk	.05
265	Joel Youngblood	.05
266	Paul Boris	.05
267	Terry Francona	.05
268	Storm Davis RC	.05
269	Ron Oester	.05
270	Dennis Eckersley	.75
271	Ed Romero	.05
272	Frank Tanana	.05
273	Mark Belanger	.05
274	Terry Kennedy	.05
275	Ray Knight	.05
276	Gene Mauch	.05
277	Rance Mulliniks	.05
278	Kevin Hickey	.05
279	Greg Gross	.05
280	Bert Blyleven	.05
281	Andre Robertson	.05
282	Reggie Smith	.05
283	Reggie Smith (Super Veteran)	.05
284	Jeff Lahti	.05
285	Lance Parrish	.05
286	Rick Langford	.05
287	Bobby Brown	.05
288	Joe Cowley RC	.05
289	Jerry Dybzinski	.05
290	Jeff Reardon	.05
291	Pirates Batting & Pitching Ldrs. (John Candelaria, Bill Madlock)	.05
292	Craig Swan	.05
293	Glenn Gulliver	.05
294	Dave Engle	.05
295	Jerry Remy	.05
296	Greg Harris	.05
297	Ned Yost	.05
298	Floyd Chiffer	.05
299	George Wright	.05
300	Mike Schmidt	3.00
301	Mike Schmidt (Super Veteran)	1.50
302	Ernie Whitt	.05
303	Miguel Dilone	.05
304	Dave Rucker	.05
305	Larry Bowa	.05
306	Tom Lasorda	.25
307	Lou Piniella	.05
308	Jesus Vega	.05
309	Jeff Leonard	.05
310	Greg Luzinski	.05
311	Glenn Brummer	.05
312	Brian Kingman	.05
313	Gary Gray	.05
314	Ken Dayley RC	.05
315	Rick Burleson	.05
316	Paul Splittorff	.05
317	Gary Rajsich	.05
318	John Tudor	.05
319	Lenn Sakata	.05
320	Steve Rogers	.05
321	Brewers Batting & Pitching Ldrs. (Pete Vuckovich, Robin Yount)	.10
322	Dave Van Gorder	.05
323	Luis DeLeon	.05
324	Mike Marshall	.05
325	Von Hayes	.05
326	Garth Iorg	.05
327	Bobby Castillo	.05
328	Craig Reynolds	.05
329	Randy Niemann	.05
330	Buddy Bell	.05
331	Mike Krukow	.05
332	Glenn Wilson RC	.05
333	Dave LaRoche	.05
334	Dave LaRoche (Super Veteran)	.05
335	Steve Henderson	.05
336	Rene Lachemann	.05
337	Tito Landrum	.05
338	Bob Owchinko	.05
339	Terry Harper	.05
340	Larry Gura	.05
341	Doug DeCinces	.05
342	Atlee Hammaker	.05
343	Bob Bailor	.05
344	Roger LaFrancois	.05
345	Jim Clancy	.05
346	Joe Pittman	.05
347	Sammy Stewart	.05
348	Alan Bannister	.05
349	Checklist 265-396	.05
350	Robin Yount	2.00
351	Reds Batting & Pitching Ldrs. (Cesar Cedeno, Mario Soto)	.05
352	Mike Scioscia	.05
353	Steve Comer	.05
354	Randy S. Johnson	.05
355	Jim Bibby	.05
356	Gary Woods	.05
357	Len Matuszek RC	.05
358	Jerry Garvin	.05
359	Dave Collins	.05
360	Nolan Ryan	5.00
361	Nolan Ryan (Super Veteran)	4.00
362	Bill Almon	.05
363	John Stuper RC	.05
364	Brett Butler	.05
365	Dave Lopes	.05
366	Dick Williams	.05
367	Bud Anderson	.05
368	Richie Zisk	.05
369	Jesse Orosco	.05
370	Gary Carter	2.00
371	Mike Richardt	.05
372	Terry Crowley	.05
373	Kevin Saucier	.05
374	Wayne Krenchicki	.05
375	Pete Vuckovich	.05
376	Ken Landreaux	.05
377	Lee May	.05
378	Lee May (Super Veteran)	.05
379	Guy Sularz	.05
380	Ron Davis	.05
381	Red Sox Batting & Pitching Ldrs. (Jim Rice, Bob Stanley)	.05
382	Bob Knepper	.05
383	Ozzie Virgil	.05
384	Dave Dravecky RC	.50
385	Mike Easler	.05
386	Rod Carew/AS	.35
387	Bob Grich/AS	.05
388	George Brett/AS	1.50
389	Robin Yount/AS	.60
390	Reggie Jackson/AS	1.00
391	Rickey Henderson/AS	.50
392	Fred Lynn/AS	.05
393	Carlton Fisk/AS	.35
394	Pete Vuckovich/AS	.05
395	Larry Gura/AS	.05
396	Dan Quisenberry/AS	.05
397	Pete Rose/AS	2.00
398	Manny Trillo/AS	.05
399	Mike Schmidt/AS	1.50
400	Dave Concepcion/AS	.05
401	Dale Murphy/AS	.20
402	Andre Dawson/AS	.35
403	Tim Raines/AS	.05
404	Gary Carter/AS	.35
405	Steve Rogers/AS	.30
406	Steve Carlton/AS	.30
407	Bruce Sutter/AS	.25
408	Rudy May	.05
409	Marvis Foley	.05
410	Phil Niekro	.75
411	Phil Niekro (Super Veteran)	.25
412	Rangers Batting & Pitching Ldrs. (Buddy Bell, Charlie Hough)	.05
413	Matt Keough	.05
414	Julio Cruz	.05
415	Bob Forsch	.05
416	Joe Ferguson	.05
417	Tom Hausman	.05
418	Greg Pryor	.05
419	Steve Crawford	.05
420	Al Oliver	.05
421	Al Oliver (Super Veteran)	.05
422	George Cappuzzello	.05
423	Tom Lawless RC	.05
424	Jerry Augustine	.05
425	Pedro Guerrero	.25
426	Earl Weaver	.25
427	Roy Lee Jackson	.05
428	Champ Summers	.05
429	Eddie Whitson	.05
430	Kirk Gibson	.05
431	Gary Gaetti RC	.75
432	Porfirio Altamirano	.05
433	Dale Berra	.05
434	Dennis Lamp	.05
435	Tony Armas	.05
436	Bill Campbell	.05
437	Rick Sweet	.05
438	Dave LaPoint RC	.05
439	Rafael Ramirez	.05
440	Ron Guidry	.05
441	Astros Batting & Pitching Ldrs. (Ray Knight, Joe Niekro)	.05
442	Brian Downing	.05
443	Don Hood	.05
444	Wally Backman RC	.05
445	Mike Flanagan	.05
446	Reid Nichols	.05
447	Bryn Smith	.05
448	Darrell Evans	.05
449	Eddie Milner RC	.05
450	Ted Simmons	.05
451	Ted Simmons (Super Veteran)	.05
452	Lloyd Moseby	.05
453	Lamar Johnson	.05
454	Bob Welch	.05
455	Sixto Lezcano	.05
456	Lee Elia	.05
457	Milt Wilcox	.05
458	Ron Washington	.05
459	Ed Farmer	.05
460	Roy Smalley	.05
461	Steve Trout	.05
462	Steve Nicosia	.05
463	Gaylord Perry	.75
464	Gaylord Perry (Super Veteran)	.20
465	Lonnie Smith	.05
466	Tom Underwood	.05
467	Rufino Linares	.05
468	Dave Goltz	.05
469	Ron Gardenhire	.05
470	Greg Minton	.05
471	Royals Batting & Pitching Ldrs. (Vida Blue, Willie Wilson)	.05
472	Gary Allenson	.05
473	John Lowenstein	.05
474	Ray Burris	.05
475	Cesar Cedeno	.05
476	Rob Picciolo	.05
477	Tom Niedenfuer RC	.05
478	Phil Garner	.05
479	Charlie Hough	.05
480	Toby Harrah	.05
481	Scot Thompson	.05
482	Tony Gwynn RC	25.00
483	Lynn Jones	.05
484	Dick Ruthven	.05
485	Omar Moreno	.05
486	Clyde King	.05
487	Jerry Hairston Sr.	.05
488	Alfredo Griffin	.05
489	Tom Herr	.05
490	Jim Palmer	1.50
491	Jim Palmer (Super Veteran)	.20
492	Paul Serna	.05
493	Steve McCatty	.05
494	Bob Brenly	.05
495	Warren Cromartie	.05
496	Tom Veryzer	.05
497	Rick Sutcliffe	.05
498	Wade Boggs RC	15.00
499	Jeff Little	.05
500	Reggie Jackson	2.00
501	Reggie Jackson (Super Veteran)	.75
502	Braves Batting & Pitching Ldrs. (Dale Murphy, Phil Niekro)	.20
503	Moose Haas	.05
504	Don Werner	.05
505	Garry Templeton	.05
506	Jim Gott RC	.25
507	Tony Scott	.05
508	Tom Filer	.05
509	Lou Whitaker	.05
510	Tug McGraw	.05
511	Tug McGraw (Super Veteran)	.05
512	Doyle Alexander	.05
513	Fred Stanley	.05
514	Rudy Law	.05
515	Gene Tenace	.05
516	Bill Virdon	.05
517	Gary Ward	.05
518	Bill Laskey	.05
519	Terry Bulling	.05
520	Fred Lynn	.05
521	Bruce Benedict	.05
522	Pat Zachry	.05
523	Carney Lansford	.05
524	Tom Brennan	.05
525	Frank White	.05
526	Checklist 397-528	.05
527	Larry Biittner	.05
528	Jamie Easterly	.05
529	Tim Laudner	.05
530	Eddie Murray	2.00
531	Athletics Batting & Pitching Ldrs. (Rickey Henderson, Rick Langford)	.15
532	Dave Stewart	.05
533	Luis Salazar	.05
534	John Butcher	.05
535	Manny Trillo	.05
536	Johnny Wockenfuss	.05
537	Rod Scurry	.05
538	Danny Heep	.05
539	Roger Erickson	.05
540	Ozzie Smith	2.00
541	Britt Burns	.05
542	Jody Davis	.05
543	Alan Fowlkes	.05
544	Larry Whisenton	.05
545	Floyd Bannister	.05
546	Dave Garcia	.05
547	Geoff Zahn	.05
548	Brian Giles	.05
549	Charlie Puleo RC	.05
550	Carl Yastrzemski	2.00
551	Carl Yastrzemski (Super Veteran)	.50
552	Tim Wallach	.05
553	Denny Martinez	.05
554	Mike Vail	.05
555	Steve Yeager	.05
556	Willie Upshaw	.05
557	Rick Honeycutt	.05
558	Dickie Thon	.05
559	Pete Redfern	.05
560	Ron LeFlore	.05
561	Cardinals Batting & Pitching Ldrs. (Joaquin Andujar, Lonnie Smith)	.05
562	Dave Rozema	.05
563	Juan Bonilla	.05
564	Sid Monge	.05
565	Bucky Dent	.05
566	Manny Sarmiento	.05
567	Joe Simpson	.05
568	Willie Hernandez	.05
569	Jack Perconte	.05
570	Vida Blue	.05
571	Mickey Klutts	.05
572	Bob Watson	.05
573	Andy Hassler	.05
574	Glenn Adams	.05
575	Neil Allen	.05
576	Frank Robinson	.25
577	Luis Aponte	.05
578	David Green	.05
579	Rich Dauer	.05
580	Tom Seaver	2.00
581	Tom Seaver (Super Veteran)	.50
582	Marshall Edwards	.05
583	Terry Forster	.05
584	Dave Hostetler	.05
585	Jose Cruz	.05
586	Frank Viola RC	1.50
587	Ivan DeJesus	.05
588	Pat Underwood	.05
589	Alvis Woods	.05
590	Tony Pena	.05
591	White Sox Batting & Pitching Ldrs. (LaMarr Hoyt, Greg Luzinski)	.05
592	Shane Rawley	.05
593	Broderick Perkins	.05
594	Eric Rasmussen	.05
595	Tim Raines	.05
596	Randy S. Johnson	.05
597	Mike Proly	.05
598	Dwayne Murphy	.05
599	Don Aase	.05
600	George Brett	3.00
601	Ed Lynch	.05
602	Rich Gedman	.05
603	Joe Morgan	2.00
604	Joe Morgan (Super Veteran)	.35
605	Gary Roenicke	.05
606	Bobby Cox	.05
607	Charlie Leibrandt	.05
608	Don Money	.05
609	Danny Darwin	.05
610	Steve Garvey	.50
611	Bert Roberge	.05
612	Steve Swisher	.05
613	Mike Ivie	.05
614	Ed Glynn	.05
615	Garry Maddox	.05
616	Bill Nahorodny	.05
617	Butch Wynegar	.05
618	LaMarr Hoyt	.05
619	Keith Moreland	.05
620	Mike Norris	.05
621	Mets Batting & Pitching Ldrs. (Craig Swan, Mookie Wilson)	.05
622	Dave Edler	.05
623	Luis Sanchez	.05
624	Glenn Hubbard	.05
625	Ken Forsch	.05
626	Jerry Martin	.05
627	Doug Bair	.05
628	Julio Valdez	.05
629	Charlie Lea	.05
630	Paul Molitor	2.00
631	Tippy Martinez	.05
632	Alex Trevino	.05
633	Vicente Romo	.05
634	Max Venable	.05
635	Graig Nettles	.05
636	Graig Nettles (Super Veteran)	.05
637	Pat Corrales	.05
638	Dan Petry	.05
639	Art Howe	.05
640	Andre Thornton	.05
641	Billy Sample	.05
642	Checklist 529-660	.05
643	Bump Wills	.05
644	Joe Lefebvre	.05
645	Bill Madlock	.05
646	Jim Essian	.05
647	Bobby Mitchell	.05
648	Jeff Burroughs	.05
649	Tommy Boggs	.05
650	George Hendrick	.05
651	Angels Batting & Pitching Ldrs. (Rod Carew, Mike Witt)	.05
652	Butch Hobson	.05
653	Ellis Valentine	.05
654	Bob Ojeda	.05
655	Al Bumbry	.05
656	Dave Frost	.05
657	Mike Gates	.05
658	Frank Pastore	.05
659	Charlie Moore	.05
660	Mike Hargrove	.05
661	Bill Russell	.05
662	Joe Sambito	.05
663	Tom O'Malley	.05
664	Bob Molinaro	.05
665	Jim Sundberg	.05
666	Sparky Anderson	.25
667	Dick Davis	.05
668	Larry Christenson	.05
669	Mike Squires	.05
670	Jerry Mumphrey	.05
671	Lenny Faedo	.05
672	Jim Kaat	.10
673	Jim Kaat (Super Veteran)	.05
674	Kurt Bevacqua	.05
675	Jim Beattie	.05
676	Biff Pocoroba	.05
677	Dave Revering	.05
678	Juan Beniquez	.05
679	Mike Scott	.05
680	Andre Dawson	.60
681	Dodgers Batting & Pitching Ldrs. (Pedro Guerrero, Fernando Valenzuela)	.05
682	Bob Stanley	.05
683	Dan Ford	.05
684	Rafael Landestoy	.05
685	Lee Mazzilli	.05
686	Randy Lerch	.05
687	U.L. Washington	.05
688	Jim Wohlford	.05
689	Ron Hassey	.05
690	Kent Hrbek	.05
691	Dave Tobik	.05
692	Denny Walling	.05
693	Sparky Lyle	.05
694	Sparky Lyle (Super Veteran)	.05
695	Ruppert Jones	.05
696	Chuck Tanner	.05
697	Barry Foote	.05
698	Tony Bernazard	.05
699	Lee Smith	.05
700	Keith Hernandez	.05
701	Batting Leaders (Al Oliver, Willie Wilson)	.05
702	Home Run Leaders (Reggie Jackson, Dave Kingman, Gorman Thomas)	.15
703	Runs Batted In Leaders (Hal McRae, Dale Murphy, Al Oliver)	.05
704	Stolen Base Leaders (Rickey Henderson, Tim Raines)	.10
705	Victory Leaders (Steve Carlton, LaMarr Hoyt)	.05
706	Strikeout Leaders (Floyd Bannister, Steve Carlton)	.05
707	Earned Run Average Leaders (Steve Rogers, Rick Sutcliffe)	.05
708	Leading Firemen (Dan Quisenberry, Bruce Sutter)	.10
709	Jimmy Sexton	.05
710	Willie Wilson	.05
711	Mariners Batting & Pitching Ldrs. (Jim Beattie, Bruce Bochte)	.05
712	Bruce Kison	.05
713	Ron Hodges	.05
714	Wayne Nordhagen	.05
715	Tony Perez	1.50
716	Tony Perez (Super Veteran)	.05
717	Scott Sanderson	.05
718	Jim Dwyer	.05
719	Rich Gale	.05
720	Dave Concepcion	.05
721	John Martin	.05
722	Jorge Orta	.05
723	Randy Moffitt	.05
724	Johnny Grubb	.05
725	Dan Spillner	.05
726	Harvey Kuenn	.05
727	Chet Lemon	.05
728	Ron Reed	.05
729	Jerry Morales	.05
730	Jason Thompson	.05
731	Al Williams	.05
732	Dave Henderson	.05
733	Buck Martinez	.05
734	Steve Braun	.05
735	Tommy John	.20
736	Tommy John (Super Veteran)	.05
737	Mitchell Page	.05
738	Tim Foli	.05
739	Rick Ownbey	.05
740	Rusty Staub	.05
741	Rusty Staub (Super Veteran)	.05
742	Padres Batting & Pitching Ldrs. (Terry Kennedy, Tim Lollar)	.05
743	Mike Torrez	.05
744	Brad Mills	.05
745	Scott McGregor	.05
746	John Wathan	.05
747	Fred Breining	.05
748	Derrel Thomas	.05
749	Jon Matlack	.05
750	Ben Oglivie	.05
751	Brad Havens	.05
752	Luis Pujols	.05
753	Elias Sosa	.05
754	Bill Robinson	.05
755	John Candelaria	.05
756	Russ Nixon	.05
757	Rick Manning	.05
758	Aurelio Rodriguez	.05
759	Doug Bird	.05
760	Dale Murphy	.60
761	Gary Lucas	.05
762	Cliff Johnson	.05
763	Al Cowens	.05
764	Pete Falcone	.05
765	Bob Boone	.05
766	Barry Bonnell	.05
767	Duane Kuiper	.05
768	Chris Speier	.05
769	Checklist 661-792	.05
770	Dave Winfield	2.00
771	Twins Batting & Pitching Ldrs. (Bobby Castillo, Kent Hrbek)	.05
772	Jim Kern	.05
773	Larry Hisle	.05
774	Alan Ashby	.05
775	Burt Hooton	.05
776	Larry Parrish	.05
777	John Curtis	.05
778	Rich Hebner	.05
779	Rick Waits	.05
780	Gary Matthews	.05
781	Rick Rhoden	.05
782	Bobby Murcer	.05
783	Bobby Murcer (Super Veteran)	.05
784	Jeff Newman	.05
785	Dennis Leonard	.05
786	Ralph Houk	.05
787	Dick Tidrow	.05
788	Dane Iorg	.05
789	Bryan Clark	.05
790	Bob Grich	.05
791	Gary Lavelle	.05
792	Chris Chambliss	.05

Traded

These 2-1/2" x 3-1/2" cards mark a continuation of the traded set introduced in 1981. The 132 cards retain the basic design of the year's regular issue, with their numbering being 1-132 with the "T" suffix. Cards in the set include traded players, new managers and promising rookies. Sold only through dealers, the set was in heavy demand as it contained the first cards of Darryl Strawberry, Ron Kittle, Julio Franco, and Mel Hall. While some of those cards were very hot in 1983, it seems likely that some of the rookies may not live up to their initial promise.

	NM/M
Complete Set (132):	20.00
Common Player:	.05
1T Neil Allen	.05
2T Bill Almon	.05
3T Joe Altobelli	.05
4T Tony Armas	.05
5T Doug Bair	.05
6T Steve Baker	.05
7T Floyd Bannister	.05
8T Don Baylor	.25
9T Tony Bernazard	.05
10T Larry Biittner	.05
11T Dann Bilardello	.05
12T Doug Bird	.05
13T Steve Boros	.05
14T Greg Brock RC	.05
15T Mike Brown	.05
16T Tom Burgmeier	.05
17T Randy Bush RC	.05
18T Bert Campaneris	.05
19T Ron Cey	.05
20T Chris Codiroli RC	.05
21T Dave Collins	.05
22T Terry Crowley	.05
23T Julio Cruz	.05
24T Mike Davis	.05
25T Frank DiPino	.05
26T Bill Doran RC	.05
27T Jerry Dybzinski	.05
28T Jamie Easterly	.05
29T Juan Eichelberger	.05
30T Jim Essian	.05

31T	Pete Falcone	.05
32T	Mike Ferraro	.05
33T	Terry Forster	.05
34T	Julio Franco RC	3.00
35T	Rich Gale	.05
36T	Kiko Garcia	.05
37T	Steve Garvey	1.00
38T	Johnny Grubb	.05
39T	Mel Hall RC	.05
40T	Von Hayes	.05
41T	Danny Heep	.05
42T	Steve Henderson	.05
43T	Keith Hernandez	.15
44T	Leo Hernandez	.05
45T	Willie Hernandez	.05
46T	Al Holland	.05
47T	Frank Howard	.05
48T	Bobby Johnson	.05
49T	Cliff Johnson	.05
50T	Odell Jones	.05
51T	Mike Jorgensen	.05
52T	Bob Kearney	.05
53T	Steve Kemp	.05
54T	Matt Keough	.05
55T	Ron Kittle RC	.05
56T	Mickey Klutts	.05
57T	Alan Knicely	.05
58T	Mike Krukow	.05
59T	Rafael Landestoy	.05
60T	Carney Lansford	.05
61T	Joe Lefebvre	.05
62T	Bryan Little	.05
63T	Aurelio Lopez	.05
64T	Mike Madden	.05
65T	Rick Manning	.05
66T	Billy Martin	.25
67T	Lee Mazzilli	.05
68T	Andy McGaffigan	.05
69T	Craig McMurtry RC	.05
70T	John McNamara	.05
71T	Orlando Mercado	.05
72T	Larry Milbourne	.05
73T	Randy Moffitt	.05
74T	Sid Monge	.05
75T	Jose Morales	.05
76T	Omar Moreno	.05
77T	Joe Morgan	4.00
78T	Mike Morgan	.05
79T	Dale Murray	.05
80T	Jeff Newman	.05
81T	Pete O'Brien RC	.05
82T	Jorge Orta	.05
83T	Alejandro Pena RC	.05
84T	Pascual Perez	.05
85T	Tony Perez	1.00
86T	Broderick Perkins	.05
87T	Tony Phillips RC	.15
88T	Charlie Puleo	.05
89T	Pat Putnam	.05
90T	Jamie Quirk	.05
91T	Doug Rader	.05
92T	Chuck Rainey	.05
93T	Bobby Ramos	.05
94T	Gary Redus	.05
95T	Steve Renko	.05
96T	Leon Roberts	.05
97T	Aurelio Rodriguez	.05
98T	Dick Ruthven	.05
99T	Daryl Sconiers	.05
100T	Mike Scott	.05
101T	Tom Seaver	6.00
102T	John Shelby RC	.05
103T	Bob Shirley	.05
104T	Joe Simpson	.05
105T	Doug Sisk RC	.05
106T	Mike Smithson RC	.05
107T	Elias Sosa	.05
108T	Darryl Strawberry RC	10.00
109T	Tom Tellmann	.05
110T	Gene Tenace	.05
111T	Gorman Thomas	.05
112T	Dick Tidrow	.05
113T	Dave Tobik	.05
114T	Wayne Tolleson RC	.05
115T	Mike Torrez	.05
116T	Manny Trillo	.05
117T	Steve Trout	.05
118T	Lee Tunnell RC	.05
119T	Mike Vail	.05
120T	Ellis Valentine	.05
121T	Tom Veryzer	.05
122T	George Vukovich	.05
123T	Rick Waits	.05
124T	Greg Walker RC	.05
125T	Chris Welsh	.05
126T	Len Whitehouse	.05
127T	Eddie Whitson	.05
128T	Jim Wohlford	.05
129T	Matt Young RC	.05
130T	Joel Youngblood	.05
131T	Pat Zachry	.05
132T	Checklist 1-132	.05

Traded Steve Carlton Bronze

The first in a series of 1/4-size metal replicas of Topps star cards was issued to dealers who purchased cases of 1983 Topps Traded sets. Each detail of the 1983 Steve Carlton card is reproduced on the 1-1/4" x 1-3/4" bronze metal mini-card, right down to the stats.

NM/M
70 Steve Carlton 6.00

1982 League Leaders Sheet

The leaders in various major statistical categories in 1982 are featured on this 7-1/2" x 10-1/2" blank-back sheet. Most of the cards on the sheet are identical to the players' regular 1983 Topps cards except for a white strip at upper-left identifying their statistical accomplishment. Reggie Jackson and Gorman Thomas who shared the A.L. home run record for 1982 share a card on this sheet. Available via a mail-in offer, huge quantities of these sheets are readily available.

NM/M
Uncut Sheet:
Willie Wilson, Reggie Jackson, Gorman Thomas, Al Oliver, LaMarr Hoyt, Steve Carlton, Dan Quisenberry, Dave Kingman, Bruce Sutter 1.00

All-Star Glossy Set of 40

This set was a "consolation prize" in a scratch-off contest in regular packs of 1983 cards. The 2-1/2" x 3-1/2" cards have a large color photo surrounded by a yellow frame on the front. In very small type on a white border is printed the player's name. Backs carry the player's name, team, position and the card number along with a Topps identification. A major feature is that the surface of the front is glossy, which most collectors find very attractive. With many top stars, the set is a popular one, but the price has not moved too far above the issue price.

		NM/M
Complete Set (40):		3.00
Common Player:		.05
1	Carl Yastrzemski	.25
2	Mookie Wilson	.05
3	Andre Thornton	.05
4	Keith Hernandez	.05
5	Robin Yount	.25
6	Terry Kennedy	.05
7	Dave Winfield	.25
8	Mike Schmidt	.50
9	Buddy Bell	.05
10	Fernando Valenzuela	.05
11	Rich Gossage	.05
12	Bob Horner	.05
13	Toby Harrah	.05
14	Pete Rose	.75
15	Cecil Cooper	.05
16	Dale Murphy	.15
17	Carlton Fisk	.25
18	Ray Knight	.05
19	Jim Palmer	.25
20	Gary Carter	.25
21	Richard Zisk	.05
22	Dusty Baker	.05
23	Willie Wilson	.05
24	Bill Buckner	.05
25	Dave Stieb	.05
26	Bill Madlock	.05
27	Lance Parrish	.05
28	Nolan Ryan	1.00
29	Rod Carew	.25
30	Al Oliver	.05
31	George Brett	.50
32	Jack Clark	.05
33	Rickey Henderson	.25
34	Dave Concepcion	.05
35	Kent Hrbek	.25
36	Steve Carlton	.25
37	Eddie Murray	.25
38	Ruppert Jones	.05
39	Reggie Jackson	.30
40	Bruce Sutter	.20

Foldouts

Another Topps test issue, these 3-1/2" x 5-5/16" cards were printed in booklets like souvenir postcards. Each of the booklets have a theme of currently playing statistical leaders in a specific category such as home runs. The cards feature a color player photo on each side. A black strip at the bottom gives the player's name, position and team along with statistics in the particular category. A facsimile autograph crosses the photograph. Booklets carry nine cards, with eight having players on both sides and one doubling as the back cover, for a total of 17 cards per booklet. There are 85 cards in the set, although some players appear in more than one category. Naturally, most of the players pictured are stars. Even so, the set is a problem as it seems to be most valuable when complete and unseparated, so the cards are difficult to display.

	NM/M
Complete Set (5):	9.00
Common Folder:	3.00
1 Pitching Leaders (Vida Blue, Bert Blyleven, Steve Carlton, Fergie Jenkins, Tommy John, Jim Kaat, Jerry Koosman, Joe Niekro, Phil Niekro, Jim Palmer, Gaylord Perry, Jerry Reuss, Nolan Ryan, Tom Seaver, Paul Splittorff, Don Sutton, Mike Torrez)	6.00
2 Home Run Leaders (Johnny Bench, Ron Cey, Darrell Evans, George Foster, Reggie Jackson, Dave Kingman, Greg Luzinski, John Mayberry, Rick Monday, Joe Morgan, Bobby Murcer, Graig Nettles, Tony Perez, Jim Rice, Mike Schmidt, Rusty Staub, Carl Yastrzemski)	4.50
3 Batting Leaders (George Brett, Rod Carew, Cecil Cooper, Steve Garvey, Ken Griffey, Pedro Guerrero, Keith Hernandez, Dane Iorg, Fred Lynn, Bill Madlock, Bake McBride, Al Oliver, Dave Parker, Jim Rice, Pete Rose, Lonnie Smith, Willie Wilson)	4.50
4 Relief Aces (Tom Burgmeier, Bill Campbell, Ed Farmer, Rollie Fingers, Terry Forster, Gene Garber, Rich Gossage, Jim Kern, Gary Lavelle, Tug McGraw, Greg Minton, Randy Moffitt, Dan Quisenberry, Ron Reed, Elias Sosa, Bruce Sutter, Kent Tekulve)	3.00
5 Stolen Base Leaders (Don Baylor, Larry Bowa, Al Bumbry, Rod Carew, Cesar Cedeno, Dave Concepcion, Jose Cruz, Julio Cruz, Rickey Henderson, Ron LeFlore, Davey Lopes, Garry Maddox, Omar Moreno, Joe Morgan, Amos Otis, Mickey Rivers, Willie Wilson)	3.00

Stickers

Topps increased the number of stickers in its set to 330 in 1983, but retained the same 1-15/16" x 2-9/16" size. The stickers are again numbered on both the front and back. Similar in style to previous sticker issues, the set includes 28 "foil" stickers, and various special stickers highlighting the 1982 season, playoffs and World Series. An album was also available.

		NM/M
Complete Set (330):		15.00
Common Player:		.05
Sticker Album:		2.00
Wax Pack (5):		.25
Wax Box (100):		16.00
1	Hank Aaron	1.00
2	Babe Ruth	2.00
3	Willie Mays	1.00
4	Frank Robinson	.15
5	Reggie Jackson	.50
6	Carl Yastrzemski	.25
7	Johnny Bench	.25
8	Tony Perez	.25
9	Lee May	.05
10	Mike Schmidt	.50
11	Dave Kingman	.05
12	Reggie Smith	.05
13	Graig Nettles	.05
14	Rusty Staub	.05
15	Willie Wilson	.05
16	LaMarr Hoyt	.05
17	Reggie Jackson, Gorman Thomas	.10
18	Floyd Bannister	.05
19	Hal McRae	.05
20	Rick Sutcliffe	.05
21	Rickey Henderson	.25
22	Dan Quisenberry	.05
23	Jim Palmer	.25
24	John Lowenstein	.05
25	Mike Flanagan	.05
26	Cal Ripken, Jr.	1.00
27	Rich Dauer	.05
28	Ken Singleton	.05
29	Eddie Murray	.25
30	Rick Dempsey	.05
31	Carl Yastrzemski	.05
32	Carney Lansford	.05
33	Jerry Remy	.05
34	Dennis Eckersley	.20
35	Dave Stapleton	.05
36	Mark Clear	.05
37	Jim Rice	.15
38	Dwight Evans	.05
39	Rod Carew	.25
40	Don Baylor	.10
41	Reggie Jackson	.50
42	Geoff Zahn	.05
43	Bobby Grich	.05
44	Fred Lynn	.05
45	Bob Boone	.05
46	Doug DeCinces	.05
47	Tom Paciorek	.05
48	Britt Burns	.05
49	Tony Bernazard	.05
50	Steve Kemp	.05
51	Greg Luzinski	.05
52	Harold Baines	.05
53	LaMarr Hoyt	.05
54	Carlton Fisk	.25
55	Andre Thornton	.05
56	Mike Hargrove	.05
57	Len Barker	.05
58	Toby Harrah	.05
59	Dan Spillner	.05
60	Rick Manning	.05
61	Rick Sutcliffe	.05
62	Ron Hassey	.05
63	Lance Parrish	.05
64	John Wockenfuss	.05
65	Lou Whitaker	.05
66	Alan Trammell	.05
67	Kirk Gibson	.05
68	Larry Herndon	.05
69	Jack Morris	.05
70	Dan Petry	.05
71	Frank White	.05
72	Amos Otis	.05
73	Willie Wilson	.05
74	Dan Quisenberry	.05
75	Hal McRae	.05
76	George Brett	.60
77	Larry Gura	.05
78	John Wathan	.05
79	Rollie Fingers	.20
80	Cecil Cooper	.05
81	Robin Yount	.25
82	Ben Oglivie	.05
83	Paul Molitor	.25
84	Gorman Thomas	.05
85	Ted Simmons	.05
86	Pete Vuckovich	.05
87	Gary Gaetti	.05
88	Kent Hrbek	.05
89	John Castino	.05
90	Tom Brunansky	.05
91	Bobby Mitchell	.05
92	Gary Ward	.05
93	Tim Laudner	.05
94	Ron Davis	.05
95	Willie Randolph	.05
96	Roy Smalley	.05
97	Jerry Mumphrey	.05
98	Ken Griffey	.05
99	Dave Winfield	.25
100	Rich Gossage	.05
101	Butch Wynegar	.05
102	Ron Guidry	.05
103	Rickey Henderson	.25
104	Mike Heath	.05
105	Dave Lopes	.05
106	Rick Langford	.05
107	Dwayne Murphy	.05
108	Tony Armas	.05
109	Matt Keough	.05
110	Dan Meyer	.05
111	Bruce Bochte	.05
112	Julio Cruz	.05
113	Floyd Bannister	.05
114	Gaylord Perry	.20
115	Al Cowens	.05
116	Richie Zisk	.05
117	Jim Essian	.05
118	Bill Caudill	.05
119	Buddy Bell	.05
120	Larry Parrish	.05
121	Danny Darwin	.05
122	Bucky Dent	.05
123	Johnny Grubb	.05
124	George Wright	.05
125	Charlie Hough	.05
126	Jim Sundberg	.05
127	Dave Stieb	.05
128	Willie Upshaw	.05
129	Alfredo Griffin	.05
130	Lloyd Moseby	.05
131	Ernie Whitt	.05
132	Jim Clancy	.05
133	Barry Bonnell	.05
134	Damaso Garcia	.05
135	Jim Kaat	.05
136	Jim Kaat	.05
137	Greg Minton	.05
138	Greg Minton	.05
139	Paul Molitor	.20
140	Paul Molitor	.20
141	Manny Trillo	.05
142	Manny Trillo	.05
143	Joel Youngblood	.05
144	Joel Youngblood	.05
145	Robin Yount	.20
146	Robin Yount	.20
147	Willie McGee	.05
148	Darrell Porter	.05
149	Darrell Porter	.05
150	Robin Yount	.20
151	Bruce Benedict	.05
152	Bruce Benedict	.05
153	George Hendrick	.05
154	Bruce Benedict	.05
155	Doug DeCinces	.05
156	Paul Molitor	.05
157	Charlie Moore	.05
158	Fred Lynn	.05
159	Rickey Henderson	.25
160	Dale Murphy	.15
161	Willie Wilson	.05
162	Jack Clark	.05
163	Reggie Jackson	.50
164	Andre Dawson	.15
165	Dan Quisenberry	.05
166	Bruce Sutter	.20
167	Robin Yount	.25
168	Ozzie Smith	.25
169	Frank White	.05
170	Phil Garner	.05
171	Doug DeCinces	.05
172	Mike Schmidt	.50
173	Cecil Cooper	.05
174	Al Oliver	.05
175	Jim Palmer	.25
176	Steve Carlton	.25
177	Carlton Fisk	.25
178	Gary Carter	.25
179	Joaquin Andujar	.05
180	Ozzie Smith	.25
181	Cecil Cooper	.05
182	Darrell Porter	.05
183	Darrell Porter	.05
184	Mike Caldwell	.05
185	Mike Caldwell	.05
186	Ozzie Smith	.25
187	Bruce Sutter	.20
188	Keith Hernandez	.05
189	Dane Iorg	.05
190	Dane Iorg	.05
191	Tony Armas	.05
192	Tony Armas	.05
193	Lance Parrish	.05
194	Lance Parrish	.05
195	John Wathan	.05
196	John Wathan	.05
197	Rickey Henderson	.20
198	Rickey Henderson	.20
199	Rickey Henderson	.20
200	Rickey Henderson	.20
201	Rickey Henderson	.20
202	Rickey Henderson	.20
203	Steve Carlton	.20
204	Steve Carlton	.20
205	Al Oliver	.05
206	Dale Murphy, Al Oliver	.05
207	Dave Kingman	.05
208	Steve Rogers	.05
209	Bruce Sutter	.20
210	Tim Raines	.05
211	Dale Murphy	.15
212	Chris Chambliss	.05
213	Gene Garber	.05
214	Bob Horner	.05
215	Glenn Hubbard	.05
216	Claudell Washington	.05
217	Bruce Benedict	.05
218	Phil Niekro	.20
219	Leon Durham	.05
220	Jay Johnstone	.05
221	Larry Bowa	.05
222	Keith Moreland	.05
223	Bill Buckner	.05
224	Fergie Jenkins	.20
225	Dick Tidrow	.05
226	Jody Davis	.05
227	Dave Concepcion	.05
228	Dan Driessen	.05
229	Johnny Bench	.25
230	Ron Oester	.05
231	Cesar Cedeno	.05
232	Alex Trevino	.05
233	Tom Seaver	.25
234	Mario Soto	.05
235	Nolan Ryan	1.00
236	Art Howe	.05
237	Phil Garner	.05
238	Ray Knight	.05
239	Terry Puhl	.05
240	Joe Niekro	.05
241	Alan Ashby	.05
242	Jose Cruz	.05
243	Steve Garvey	.15
244	Ron Cey	.05
245	Dusty Baker	.05
246	Ken Landreaux	.05
247	Jerry Reuss	.05
248	Pedro Guerrero	.05
249	Bill Russell	.05
250	Fernando Valenzuela	.05
251	Al Oliver	.05
252	Andre Dawson	.15
253	Tim Raines	.05
254	Jeff Reardon	.05
255	Gary Carter	.25
256	Steve Rogers	.05
257	Tim Wallach	.05
258	Chris Speier	.05

259	Dave Kingman	.05
260	Bob Bailor	.05
261	Hubie Brooks	.05
262	Craig Swan	.05
263	George Foster	.05
264	John Stearns	.05
265	Neil Allen	.05
266	Mookie Wilson	.05
267	Steve Carlton	.20
268	Manny Trillo	.05
269	Gary Matthews	.05
270	Mike Schmidt	.50
271	Ivan DeJesus	.05
272	Pete Rose	.75
273	Bo Diaz	.05
274	Sid Monge	.05
275	Bill Madlock	.05
276	Jason Thompson	.05
277	Don Robinson	.05
278	Omar Moreno	.05
279	Dale Berra	.05
280	Dave Parker	.05
281	Tony Pena	.05
282	John Candelaria	.05
283	Lonnie Smith	.05
284	Bruce Sutter	.20
285	George Hendrick	.05
286	Tom Herr	.05
287	Ken Oberkfell	.05
288	Ozzie Smith	.25
289	Bob Forsch	.05
290	Keith Hernandez	.05
291	Garry Templeton	.05
292	Broderick Perkins	.05
293	Terry Kennedy	.05
294	Gene Richards	.05
295	Ruppert Jones	.05
296	Tim Lollar	.05
297	John Montefusco	.05
298	Sixto Lezcano	.05
299	Greg Minton	.05
300	Jack Clark	.05
301	Milt May	.05
302	Reggie Smith	.05
303	Joe Morgan	.25
304	John LeMaster	.05
305	Darrell Evans	.05
306	Al Holland	.05
307	Jesse Barfield	.05
308	Wade Boggs	.60
309	Tom Brunansky	.05
310	Storm Davis	.05
311	Von Hayes	.05
312	Dave Hostetler	.05
313	Kent Hrbek	.05
314	Tim Laudner	.05
315	Cal Ripken, Jr.	1.00
316	Andre Robertson	.05
317	Ed Vande Berg	.05
318	Glenn Wilson	.05
319	Chili Davis	.05
320	Bob Dernier	.05
321	Terry Francona	.05
322	Brian Giles	.05
323	David Green	.05
324	Atlee Hammaker	.05
325	Bill Laskey	.05
326	Willie McGee	.05
327	Johnny Ray	.05
328	Ryne Sandberg	.75
329	Steve Sax	.05
330	Eric Show	.05

Stickers Boxes

RICKEY HENDERSON

These eight cards were printed on the back panels of 1983 Topps sticker boxes, one card per box. The blank-backed cards measure the standard 2-1/2" x 3-1/2" and feature a full-color photo with the player's name at the top. The rest of the back panel advertises the sticker album, while the front of the box has an action photo of Reggie Jackson. The boxes are numbered on the front. Prices in the checklist that follows are for complete boxes.

		NM/M
Complete Set (8):		6.50
Common Player:		.75
1	Fernando Valenzuela	.75

2	Gary Carter	1.00
3	Mike Schmidt	1.50
4	Reggie Jackson	1.25
5	Jim Palmer	.75
6	Rollie Fingers	.75
7	Pete Rose	2.00
8	Rickey Henderson	1.00

1952 Reprint Set

The first of several reprint/retro sets in different sports issued by Topps, the 402-card reprinting of its classic 1952 baseball card set was controversial at the time of issue, but has since gained hobby acceptance and market value. To avoid possible confusion of the reprints for originals, the reprints were done in the now-standard 2-1/2" x 3-1/2" format instead of the original 2-5/8" x 3-3/4". Backs, printed in red, carry a line "Topps 1952 Reprint Series" at bottom, though there is no indication of the year of reprinting. Fronts have a semi-gloss finish, which also differs from the originals. Because of inability to come to terms with five of the players from the original 1952 Topps set, they were not included in the reprint series. Those cards which weren't issued are: #20 Billy Loes, #22 Dom DiMaggio, #159 Saul Rogovin, #196 Solly Hemus, and #289 Tommy Holmes. The '52 reprints were available only as a complete boxed set with a retail price of about $40 at issue.

		NM/M
Complete Sealed Boxed Set:		175.00
Complete Set (402):		150.00
Common Player:		.25
Minor Stars:		.35
Typical Hall of Famers:		2.00
Superstar Hall of Famers:		8.00
311	Mickey Mantle	30.00
407	Eddie Mathews (Sample card.)	8.00

1984 Topps

WILLIE McGEE OF

Another 792-card regular set from Topps. For the second straight year, the 2-1/2" x 3-1/2" cards featured a color action photo on the front along with a small portrait photo in the lower-left. The team name runs in big letters down the left side, while the player's name and position appear under the action photo. Backs have a team logo in the upper-right, along with statistics, personal information and a few highlights, all in a hard-to-read red and purple coloring. Specialty cards include past season highlights, team leaders, statistical leaders, All-Stars, active career leaders and numbered checklists. Again, promising rookies were saved for the traded set. The six 132-card uncut sheets which comprise the set were made available to collectors at about $30 for the set.

		NM/M
Complete Set (792):		40.00
Common Player:		.05
Wax Pack (15):		2.00
Wax Box (36):		50.00
Cello Pack (28):		2.50
Cello Box (24):		50.00
Rack Pack (54+1):		3.50
Rack Box (24):		60.00
Vending Box (500):		20.00
1	Steve Carlton (1983 Highlight)	.25
2	Rickey Henderson (1983 Highlight)	.25
3	Dan Quisenberry (1983 Highlight)	.05
4	Steve Carlton, Gaylord Perry, Nolan Ryan (1983 Highlight)	.50
5	Bob Forsch, Dave Righetti, Mike Warren (1983 Highlight)	.05
6	Johnny Bench, Gaylord Perry, Carl Yastrzemski (1983 Highlight)	.25
7	Gary Lucas	.05
8	Don Mattingly RC	15.00
9	Jim Gott	.05
10	Robin Yount	1.00
11	Twins Batting & Pitching Leaders (Kent Hrbek, Ken Schrom)	.05
12	Billy Sample	.05
13	Scott Holman	.05
14	Tom Brookens	.05
15	Burt Hooton	.05
16	Omar Moreno	.05
17	John Denny	.05
18	Dale Berra	.05
19	Ray Fontenot RC	.05
20	Greg Luzinski	.05
21	Joe Altobelli	.05
22	Bryan Clark	.05
23	Keith Moreland	.05
24	John Martin	.05
25	Glenn Hubbard	.05
26	Bud Black	.05
27	Daryl Sconiers	.05
28	Frank Viola	.05
29	Danny Heep	.05
30	Wade Boggs	3.00
31	Andy McGaffigan	.05
32	Bobby Ramos	.05
33	Tom Burgmeier	.05
34	Eddie Milner	.05
35	Don Sutton	.65
36	Denny Walling	.05
37	Rangers Batting & Pitching Leaders (Buddy Bell, Rick Honeycutt)	.05
38	Luis DeLeon	.05
39	Garth Iorg	.05
40	Dusty Baker	.05
41	Tony Bernazard	.05
42	Johnny Grubb	.05
43	Ron Reed	.05
44	Jim Morrison	.05
45	Jerry Mumphrey	.05
46	Ray Smith	.05
47	Rudy Law	.05
48	Julio Franco	.05
49	John Stuper	.05
50	Chris Chambliss	.05
51	Jim Frey	.05
52	Paul Splittorff	.05
53	Juan Beniquez	.05
54	Jesse Orosco	.05
55	Dave Concepcion	.05
56	Gary Allenson	.05
57	Dan Schatzeder	.05
58	Max Venable	.05
59	Sammy Stewart	.05
60	Paul Molitor	1.00
61	Chris Codiroli RC	.05
62	Dave Hostetler	.05
63	Ed Vande Berg	.05
64	Mike Scioscia	.05
65	Kirk Gibson	.05
66	Astros Batting & Pitching Leaders (Jose Cruz, Nolan Ryan)	.25
67	Gary Ward	.05
68	Luis Salazar	.05
69	Rod Scurry	.05
70	Gary Matthews	.05
71	Leo Hernandez	.05
72	Mike Squires	.05
73	Jody Davis	.05
74	Jerry Martin	.05
75	Bob Forsch	.05
76	Alfredo Griffin	.05
77	Brett Butler	.05
78	Mike Torrez	.05
79	Rob Wilfong	.05
80	Steve Rogers	.05
81	Billy Martin	.15
82	Doug Bird	.05
83	Richie Zisk	.05
84	Lenny Faedo	.05
85	Atlee Hammaker	.05
86	John Shelby RC	.05
87	Frank Pastore	.05
88	Rob Picciolo	.05
89	Mike Smithson RC	.05
90	Pedro Guerrero	.05
91	Dan Spillner	.05
92	Lloyd Moseby	.05
93	Bob Knepper	.05
94	Mario Ramirez	.05
95	Aurelio Lopez	.05
96	Royals Batting & Pitching Leaders (Larry Gura, Hal McRae)	.05
97	LaMarr Hoyt	.05
98	Steve Nicosia	.05
99	Craig Lefferts RC	.25
100	Reggie Jackson	1.50
101	Porfirio Altamirano	.05
102	Ken Oberkfell	.05
103	Dwayne Murphy	.05
104	Ken Dayley	.05
105	Tony Armas	.05
106	Tim Stoddard	.05
107	Ned Yost	.05
108	Randy Moffitt	.05
109	Brad Wellman	.05
110	Ron Guidry	.05
111	Bill Virdon	.05
112	Tom Niedenfuer	.05
113	Kelly Paris	.05
114	Checklist 1-132	.25
115	Andre Thornton	.05
116	George Bjorkman	.05
117	Tom Veryzer	.05
118	Charlie Hough	.05
119	Johnny Wockenfuss	.05
120	Keith Hernandez	.05
121	Pat Sheridan RC	.05
122	Cecilio Guante RC	.05
123	Butch Wynegar	.05
124	Damaso Garcia	.05
125	Britt Burns	.05
126	Braves Batting & Pitching Leaders (Craig McMurtry, Dale Murphy)	.05
127	Mike Madden	.05
128	Rick Manning	.05
129	Bill Laskey	.05
130	Ozzie Smith	2.00
131	Batting Leaders (Wade Boggs, Bill Madlock)	.25
132	Home Run Leaders (Jim Rice, Mike Schmidt)	.25
133	RBI Leaders (Cecil Cooper, Dale Murphy, Jim Rice)	.10
134	Stolen Base Leaders (Rickey Henderson, Tim Raines)	.25
135	Victory Leaders (John Denny, LaMarr Hoyt)	.05
136	Strikeout Leaders (Steve Carlton, Jack Morris)	.05
137	Earned Run Average Leaders (Atlee Hammaker, Rick Honeycutt)	.05
138	Leading Firemen (Al Holland, Dan Quisenberry)	.05
139	Bert Campaneris	.05
140	Storm Davis	.05
141	Pat Corrales	.05
142	Rich Gale	.05
143	Jose Morales	.05
144	Brian Harper RC	.20
145	Gary Lavelle	.05
146	Ed Romero	.05
147	Dan Petry	.05
148	Joe Lefebvre	.05
149	Jon Matlack	.05
150	Dale Murphy	.50
151	Steve Trout	.05
152	Glenn Brummer	.05
153	Dick Tidrow	.05
154	Dave Henderson	.05
155	Frank White	.05
156	Athletics Batting & Pitching Leaders (Tim Conroy, Rickey Henderson)	.15
157	Gary Gaetti	.05
158	John Curtis	.05
159	Darryl Cias	.05
160	Mario Soto	.05
161	Junior Ortiz RC	.05
162	Bob Ojeda	.05
163	Lorenzo Gray	.05
164	Scott Sanderson	.05
165	Ken Singleton	.05
166	Jamie Nelson	.05
167	Marshall Edwards	.05
168	Juan Bonilla	.05
169	Larry Parrish	.05
170	Jerry Reuss	.05
171	Frank Robinson	.25
172	Frank DiPino	.05
173	Marvell Wynne RC	.05
174	Juan Berenguer	.05
175	Graig Nettles	.05
176	Lee Smith	.05
177	Jerry Hairston Sr.	.05
178	Bill Krueger	.05
179	Buck Martinez	.05
180	Manny Trillo	.05
181	Roy Thomas	.05
182	Darryl Strawberry	.25
183	Al Williams	.05
184	Mike O'Berry	.05
185	Sixto Lezcano	.05
186	Cardinals Batting & Pitching Leaders (Lonnie Smith, John Stuper)	.05
187	Luis Aponte	.05
188	Bryan Little	.05
189	Tim Conroy RC	.05
190	Ben Oglivie	.05
191	Mike Boddicker	.05
192	Nick Esasky RC	.05
193	Darrell Brown	.05
194	Domingo Ramos	.05
195	Jack Morris	.05
196	Don Slaught RC	.05
197	Garry Hancock	.05
198	Bill Doran	.05
199	Willie Hernandez	.05
200	Andre Dawson	.60
201	Bruce Kison	.05
202	Bobby Cox	.05
203	Matt Keough	.05
204	Bobby Meacham RC	.05
205	Greg Minton	.05
206	Andy Van Slyke RC	.75
207	Donnie Moore	.05
208	Jose Oquendo RC	.05
209	Manny Sarmiento	.05
210	Joe Morgan	1.00
211	Rick Sweet	.05
212	Broderick Perkins	.05
213	Bruce Hurst	.05
214	Paul Householder	.05
215	Tippy Martinez	.05
216	White Sox Batting & Pitching Leaders (Richard Dotson, Carlton Fisk)	.05
217	Alan Ashby	.05
218	Rick Waits	.05
219	Joe Simpson	.05
220	Fernando Valenzuela	.05
221	Cliff Johnson	.05
222	Rick Honeycutt	.05
223	Wayne Krenchicki	.05
224	Sid Monge	.05
225	Lee Mazzilli	.05
226	Juan Eichelberger	.05
227	Steve Braun	.05
228	John Rabb	.05
229	Paul Owens	.05
230	Rickey Henderson	1.00
231	Gary Woods	.05
232	Tim Wallach	.05
233	Checklist 133-264	.05
234	Rafael Ramirez	.05
235	Matt Young RC	.05
236	Ellis Valentine	.05
237	John Castino	.05
238	Reid Nichols	.05
239	Jay Howell	.05
240	Eddie Murray	1.00
241	Billy Almon	.05
242	Alex Trevino	.05
243	Pete Ladd	.05
244	Candy Maldonado RC	.05
245	Rick Sutcliffe	.05
246	Mets Batting & Pitching Leaders (Tom Seaver, Mookie Wilson)	.25
247	Onix Concepcion	.05
248	Bill Dawley RC	.05
249	Jay Johnstone	.05
250	Bill Madlock	.05
251	Tony Gwynn	4.00
252	Larry Christenson	.05
253	Jim Wohlford	.05
254	Shane Rawley	.05
255	Bruce Benedict	.05
256	Dave Geisel	.05
257	Julio Cruz	.05
258	Luis Sanchez	.05
259	Sparky Anderson	.15
260	Scott McGregor	.05
261	Bobby Brown	.05
262	Tom Candiotti RC	.25
263	Jack Fimple	.05
264	Doug Frobel	.05
265	Donnie Hill RC	.05
266	Steve Lubratich	.05
267	Carmelo Martinez RC	.05
268	Jack O'Connor	.05
269	Aurelio Rodriguez	.05
270	Jeff Russell RC	.05
271	Moose Haas	.05
272	Rick Dempsey	.05
273	Charlie Puleo	.05
274	Rick Monday	.05
275	Len Matuszek	.05
276	Angels Batting & Pitching Leaders (Rod Carew, Geoff Zahn)	.10
277	Eddie Whitson	.05
278	Jorge Bell	.05
279	Ivan DeJesus	.05
280	Floyd Bannister	.05
281	Larry Milbourne	.05
282	Jim Barr	.05
283	Larry Biittner	.05
284	Howard Bailey	.05
285	Darrell Porter	.05
286	Lary Sorensen	.05
287	Warren Cromartie	.05
288	Jim Beattie	.05
289	Randy S. Johnson	.05
290	Dave Dravecky	.05
291	Chuck Tanner	.05
292	Tony Scott	.05
293	Ed Lynch	.05
294	U.L. Washington	.05
295	Mike Flanagan	.05
296	Jeff Newman	.05
297	Bruce Berenyi	.05
298	Jim Gantner	.05
299	John Butcher	.05
300	Pete Rose	5.00
301	Frank LaCorte	.05
302	Barry Bonnell	.05
303	Marty Castillo	.05
304	Warren Brusstar	.05
305	Roy Smalley	.05
306	Dodgers Batting & Pitching Leaders (Pedro Guerrero, Bob Welch)	.05
307	Bobby Mitchell	.05
308	Ron Hassey	.05
309	Tony Phillips	.05
310	Willie McGee	.05
311	Jerry Koosman	.05
312	Jorge Orta	.05
313	Mike Jorgensen	.05
314	Orlando Mercado	.05
315	Bob Grich	.05
316	Mark Bradley	.05
317	Greg Pryor	.05
318	Bill Gullickson	.05
319	Al Bumbry	.05
320	Bob Stanley	.05
321	Harvey Kuenn	.05
322	Ken Schrom	.05
323	Alan Knicely	.05
324	Alejandro Pena RC	.05
325	Darrell Evans	.05
326	Bob Kearney	.05
327	Ruppert Jones	.05
328	Vern Ruhle	.05
329	Pat Tabler RC	.05
330	John Candelaria	.05
331	Bucky Dent	.05
332	Kevin Gross RC	.05
333	Larry Herndon	.05
334	Chuck Rainey	.05
335	Don Baylor	.15
336	Mariners Batting & Pitching Leaders (Pat Putnam, Matt Young)	.05
337	Kevin Hagen	.05
338	Mike Warren	.05
339	Roy Lee Jackson	.05
340	Hal McRae	.05
341	Dave Tobik	.05
342	Tim Foli	.05
343	Mark Davis	.05
344	Rick Miller	.05
345	Kent Hrbek	.05
346	Kurt Bevacqua	.05
347	Allan Ramirez	.05
348	Toby Harrah	.05
349	Bob L. Gibson	.05
350	George Foster	.05
351	Russ Nixon	.05
352	Dave Stewart	.05
353	Jim Anderson	.05
354	Jeff Burroughs	.05
355	Jason Thompson	.05
356	Glenn Abbott	.05
357	Ron Cey	.05
358	Bob Dernier	.05
359	Jim Acker RC	.05
360	Willie Randolph	.05
361	Dave Smith	.05
362	David Green	.05
363	Tim Laudner	.05
364	Scott Fletcher RC	.05
365	Steve Bedrosian	.05
366	Padres Batting & Pitching Leaders (Dave Dravecky, Terry Kennedy)	.05
367	Jamie Easterly	.05
368	Hubie Brooks	.05
369	Steve McCatty	.05
370	Tim Raines	.05
371	Dave Gumpert	.05
372	Gary Roenicke	.05
373	Bill Scherrer	.05
374	Don Money	.05
375	Dennis Leonard	.05
376	Dave Anderson RC	.05
377	Danny Darwin	.05
378	Bob Brenly	.05
379	Checklist 265-396	.05
380	Steve Garvey	.45
381	Ralph Houk	.05
382	Chris Nyman	.05
383	Terry Puhl	.05
384	Lee Tunnell RC	.05
385	Tony Perez	1.00
386	George Hendrick/AS	.05
387	Johnny Ray/AS	.05
388	Mike Schmidt/AS	.75
389	Ozzie Smith/AS	.50
390	Tim Raines/AS	.05
391	Dale Murphy/AS	.20
392	Andre Dawson/AS	.25
393	Gary Carter/AS	.30

394	Steve Rogers/AS	.05
395	Steve Carlton/AS	.25
396	Jesse Orosco/AS	.05
397	Eddie Murray/AS	.40
398	Lou Whitaker/AS	.05
399	George Brett/AS	.75
400	Cal Ripken, Jr./AS	4.00
401	Jim Rice/AS	.05
402	Dave Winfield/AS	.30
403	Lloyd Moseby/AS	.05
404	Ted Simmons/AS	.05
405	LaMarr Hoyt/AS	.05
406	Ron Guidry/AS	.05
407	Dan Quisenberry/AS	.05
408	Lou Piniella	.05
409	Juan Agosto RC	.05
410	Claudell Washington	.05
411	Houston Jimenez	.05
412	Doug Rader	.05
413	Spike Owen RC	.05
414	Mitchell Page	.05
415	Tommy John	.15
416	Dane Iorg	.05
417	Mike Armstrong	.05
418	Ron Hodges	.05
419	John Henry Johnson	.05
420	Cecil Cooper	.05
421	Charlie Lea	.05
422	Jose Cruz	.05
423	Mike Morgan	.05
424	Dann Bilardello	.05
425	Steve Howe	.05
426	Orioles Batting & Pitching Leaders (Mike Boddicker, Cal Ripken, Jr.)	.50
427	Rick Leach	.05
428	Fred Breining	.05
429	Randy Bush RC	.05
430	Rusty Staub	.05
431	Chris Bando	.05
432	Charlie Hudson RC	.05
433	Rich Hebner	.05
434	Harold Baines	.05
435	Neil Allen	.05
436	Rick Peters	.05
437	Mike Proly	.05
438	Biff Pocoroba	.05
439	Bob Stoddard	.05
440	Steve Kemp	.05
441	Bob Lillis	.05
442	Byron McLaughlin	.05
443	Benny Ayala	.05
444	Steve Renko	.05
445	Jerry Remy	.05
446	Luis Pujols	.05
447	Tom Brunansky	.05
448	Ben Hayes	.05
449	Joe Pettini	.05
450	Gary Carter	1.00
451	Bob Jones	.05
452	Chuck Porter	.05
453	Willie Upshaw	.05
454	Joe Beckwith	.05
455	Terry Kennedy	.05
456	Cubs Batting & Pitching Leaders (Fergie Jenkins, Keith Moreland)	.05
457	Dave Rozema	.05
458	Kiko Garcia	.05
459	Kevin Hickey	.05
460	Dave Winfield	1.00
461	Jim Maler	.05
462	Lee Lacy	.05
463	Dave Engle	.05
464	Jeff Jones	.05
465	Mookie Wilson	.05
466	Gene Garber	.05
467	Mike Ramsey	.05
468	Geoff Zahn	.05
469	Tom O'Malley	.05
470	Nolan Ryan	6.00
471	Dick Howser	.05
472	Mike Brown	.05
473	Jim Dwyer	.05
474	Greg Bargar	.05
475	Gary Redus RC	.05
476	Tom Tellmann	.05
477	Rafael Landestoy	.05
478	Alan Bannister	.05
479	Frank Tanana	.05
480	Ron Kittle RC	.05
481	Mark Thurmond RC	.05
482	Enos Cabell	.05
483	Fergie Jenkins	.65
484	Ozzie Virgil	.05
485	Rick Rhoden	.05
486	Yankees Batting & Pitching Leaders (Don Baylor, Ron Guidry)	.05
487	Ricky Adams	.05
488	Jesse Barfield	.05
489	Dave Von Ohlen	.05
490	Cal Ripken, Jr.	6.00
491	Bobby Castillo	.05
492	Tucker Ashford	.05
493	Mike Norris	.05
494	Chili Davis	.05
495	Rollie Fingers	.65
496	Terry Francona	.05
497	Bud Anderson	.05
498	Rich Gedman	.05
499	Mike Witt	.05
500	George Brett	2.00
501	Steve Henderson	.05
502	Joe Torre	.05
503	Elias Sosa	.05
504	Mickey Rivers	.05
505	Pete Vuckovich	.05

506	Ernie Whitt	.05
507	Mike LaCoss	.05
508	Mel Hall	.05
509	Brad Havens	.05
510	Alan Trammell	.05
511	Marty Bystrom	.05
512	Oscar Gamble	.05
513	Dave Beard	.05
514	Floyd Rayford	.05
515	Gorman Thomas	.05
516	Expos Batting & Pitching Leaders (Charlie Lea, Al Oliver)	.05
517	John Moses	.05
518	Greg Walker RC	.05
519	Ron Davis	.05
520	Bob Boone	.05
521	Pete Falcone	.05
522	Dave Bergman	.05
523	Glenn Wilson	.05
524	Carlos Diaz	.05
525	Willie Wilson	.05
526	Ron Oester	.05
527	Checklist 397-528	.05
528	Mark Brouhard	.05
529	Keith Atherton RC	.05
530	Dan Ford	.05
531	Steve Boros	.05
532	Eric Show	.05
533	Ken Landreaux	.05
534	Pete O'Brien	.05
535	Bo Diaz	.05
536	Doug Bair	.05
537	Johnny Ray	.05
538	Kevin Bass	.05
539	George Frazier	.05
540	George Hendrick	.05
541	Dennis Lamp	.05
542	Duane Kuiper	.05
543	Craig McMurtry RC	.05
544	Cesar Geronimo	.05
545	Bill Buckner	.05
546	Indians Batting & Pitching Leaders (Mike Hargrove, Lary Sorensen)	.05
547	Mike Moore	.05
548	Ron Jackson	.05
549	Walt Terrell RC	.05
550	Jim Rice	.15
551	Scott Ullger	.05
552	Ray Burris	.05
553	Joe Nolan	.05
554	Ted Power RC	.05
555	Greg Brock	.05
556	Joey McLaughlin	.05
557	Wayne Tolleson	.05
558	Mike Davis	.05
559	Mike Scott	.05
560	Carlton Fisk	1.00
561	Whitey Herzog	.05
562	Manny Castillo	.05
563	Glenn Wilson	.05
564	Al Holland	.05
565	Leon Durham	.05
566	Jim Bibby	.05
567	Mike Heath	.05
568	Pete Filson	.05
569	Bake McBride	.05
570	Dan Quisenberry	.05
571	Bruce Bochy	.05
572	Jerry Royster	.05
573	Dave Kingman	.05
574	Brian Downing	.05
575	Jim Clancy	.05
576	Giants Batting & Pitching Leaders (Atlee Hammaker, Jeff Leonard)	.05
577	Mark Clear	.05
578	Lenn Sakata	.05
579	Bob James	.05
580	Lonnie Smith	.05
581	Jose DeLeon RC	.05
582	Bob McClure	.05
583	Derrel Thomas	.05
584	Dave Schmidt	.05
585	Dan Driessen	.05
586	Joe Niekro	.05
587	Von Hayes	.05
588	Milt Wilcox	.05
589	Mike Easler	.05
590	Dave Stieb	.05
591	Tony LaRussa	.05
592	Andre Robertson	.05
593	Jeff Lahti	.05
594	Gene Richards	.05
595	Jeff Reardon	.05
596	Ryne Sandberg	3.00
597	Rick Camp	.05
598	Rusty Kuntz	.05
599	Doug Sisk RC	.05
600	Rod Carew	1.00
601	John Tudor	.05
602	John Wathan	.05
603	Renie Martin	.05
604	John Lowenstein	.05
605	Mike Caldwell	.05
606	Blue Jays Batting & Pitching Leaders (Lloyd Moseby, Dave Stieb)	.05
607	Tom Hume	.05
608	Bobby Johnson	.05
609	Dan Meyer	.05
610	Steve Sax	.05
611	Chet Lemon	.05
612	Harry Spilman	.05
613	Greg Gross	.05
614	Len Barker	.05

615	Garry Templeton	.05
616	Don Robinson	.05
617	Rick Cerone	.05
618	Dickie Noles	.05
619	Jerry Dybzinski	.05
620	Al Oliver	.05
621	Frank Howard	.05
622	Al Cowens	.05
623	Ron Washington	.05
624	Terry Harper	.05
625	Larry Gura	.05
626	Bob Clark	.05
627	Dave LaPoint	.05
628	Ed Jurak	.05
629	Rick Langford	.05
630	Ted Simmons	.05
631	Denny Martinez	.05
632	Tom Foley	.05
633	Mike Krukow	.05
634	Mike Marshall	.05
635	Dave Righetti	.05
636	Pat Putnam	.05
637	Phillies Batting & Pitching Leaders (John Denny, Gary Matthews)	.05
638	George Vukovich	.05
639	Rick Lysander	.05
640	Lance Parrish	.05
641	Mike Richardt	.05
642	Tom Underwood	.05
643	Mike Brown	.05
644	Tim Lollar	.05
645	Tony Pena	.05
646	Checklist 529-660	.05
647	Ron Roenicke	.05
648	Len Whitehouse	.05
649	Tom Herr	.05
650	Phil Niekro	.65
651	John McNamara	.05
652	Rudy May	.05
653	Dave Stapleton	.05
654	Bob Bailor	.05
655	Amos Otis	.05
656	Bryn Smith	.05
657	Thad Bosley	.05
658	Jerry Augustine	.05
659	Duane Walker	.05
660	Ray Knight	.05
661	Steve Yeager	.05
662	Tom Brennan	.05
663	Johnnie LeMaster	.05
664	Dave Stegman	.05
665	Buddy Bell	.05
666	Tigers Batting & Pitching Leaders (Jack Morris, Lou Whitaker)	.05
667	Vance Law	.05
668	Larry McWilliams	.05
669	Dave Lopes	.05
670	Rich Gossage	.05
671	Jamie Quirk	.05
672	Ricky Nelson	.05
673	Mike Walters	.05
674	Tim Flannery	.05
675	Pascual Perez	.05
676	Brian Giles	.05
677	Doyle Alexander	.05
678	Chris Speier	.05
679	Art Howe	.05
680	Fred Lynn	.05
681	Tom Lasorda	.15
682	Dan Morogiello	.05
683	Marty Barrett RC	.05
684	Bob Shirley	.05
685	Willie Aikens	.05
686	Joe Price	.05
687	Roy Howell	.05
688	George Wright	.05
689	Mike Fischlin	.05
690	Jack Clark	.05
691	Steve Lake RC	.05
692	Dickie Thon	.05
693	Alan Wiggins	.05
694	Mike Stanton	.05
695	Lou Whitaker	.05
696	Pirates Batting & Pitching Leaders (Bill Madlock, Rick Rhoden)	.05
697	Dale Murray	.05
698	Marc Hill	.05
699	Dave Rucker	.05
700	Mike Schmidt	2.00
701	NL Active Career Batting Leaders (Bill Madlock, Dave Parker, Pete Rose)	.25
702	NL Active Career Hit Leaders (Tony Perez, Pete Rose, Rusty Staub)	.25
703	NL Active Career Home Run Leaders (Dave Kingman, Tony Perez, Mike Schmidt)	.15
704	NL Active Career RBI Leaders (Al Oliver, Tony Perez, Rusty Staub)	.05
705	NL Active Career Stolen Bases Leaders (Larry Bowa, Cesar Cedeno, Joe Morgan)	.05
706	NL Active Career Victory Leaders (Steve Carlton, Fergie Jenkins, Tom Seaver)	.05

707	NL Active Career Strikeout Leaders (Steve Carlton, Nolan Ryan, Tom Seaver)	.35
708	NL Active Career ERA Leaders (Steve Carlton, Steve Rogers, Tom Seaver)	.05
709	NL Active Career Save Leaders (Gene Garber, Tug McGraw, Bruce Sutter)	.10
710	AL Active Career Batting Leaders (George Brett, Rod Carew, Cecil Cooper)	.25
711	AL Active Career Hit Leaders (Bert Campaneris, Rod Carew, Reggie Jackson)	.15
712	AL Active Career Home Run Leaders (Reggie Jackson, Greg Luzinski, Graig Nettles)	.15
713	AL Active Career RBI Leaders (Reggie Jackson, Graig Nettles, Ted Simmons)	.15
714	AL Active Career Stolen Bases Leaders (Bert Campaneris, Dave Lopes, Omar Moreno)	.05
715	AL Active Career Victory Leaders (Tommy John, Jim Palmer, Don Sutton)	.05
716	AL Active Strikeout Leaders (Bert Blyleven, Jerry Koosman, Don Sutton)	.05
717	AL Active Career ERA Leaders (Rollie Fingers, Ron Guidry, Jim Palmer)	.05
718	AL Active Career Save Leaders (Rollie Fingers, Rich Gossage, Dan Quisenberry)	.05
719	Andy Hassler	.05
720	Dwight Evans	.05
721	Del Crandall	.05
722	Bob Welch	.05
723	Rich Dauer	.05
724	Eric Rasmussen	.05
725	Cesar Cedeno	.05
726	Brewers Batting & Pitching Leaders (Moose Haas, Ted Simmons)	.05
727	Joel Youngblood	.05
728	Tug McGraw	.05
729	Gene Tenace	.05
730	Bruce Sutter	.75
731	Lynn Jones	.05
732	Terry Crowley	.05
733	Dave Collins	.05
734	Odell Jones	.05
735	Rick Burleson	.05
736	Dick Ruthven	.05
737	Jim Essian	.05
738	Bill Schroeder RC	.05
739	Bob Watson	.05
740	Tom Seaver	1.00
741	Wayne Gross	.05
742	Dick Williams	.05
743	Don Hood	.05
744	Jamie Allen	.05
745	Dennis Eckersley	.65
746	Mickey Hatcher	.05
747	Pat Zachry	.05
748	Jeff Leonard	.05
749	Doug Flynn	.05
750a	Jim Palmer	1.00
750b	Jim Palmer (Missing 1980-82 losses on back.)	3.00
750c	Jim Palmer (Missing 1979-83 losses on back.)	4.00
751	Charlie Moore	.05
752	Phil Garner	.05
753	Doug Gwosdz	.05
754	Kent Tekulve	.05
755	Garry Maddox	.05
756	Reds Batting & Pitching Leaders (Ron Oester, Mario Soto)	.05
757	Larry Bowa	.05
758	Bill Stein	.05
759	Richard Dotson	.05
760	Bob Horner	.05
761	John Montefusco	.05
762	Rance Mulliniks	.05
763	Craig Swan	.05
764	Mike Hargrove	.05
765	Ken Forsch	.05
766	Mike Vail	.05
767	Carney Lansford	.05
768	Champ Summers	.05
769	Bill Caudill	.05
770	Ken Griffey	.05
771	Billy Gardner	.05
772	Jim Slaton	.05
773	Todd Cruz	.05
774	Tom Gorman	.05
775	Dave Parker	.05
776	Craig Reynolds	.05
777	Tom Paciorek	.05
778	Andy Hawkins RC	.05
779	Jim Sundberg	.05

780	Steve Carlton	1.00
781	Checklist 661-792	.05
782	Steve Balboni	.05
783	Luis Leal	.05
784	Leon Roberts	.05
785	Joaquin Andujar	.05
786	Red Sox Batting & Pitching Leaders (Wade Boggs, Bob Ojeda)	.25
787	Bill Campbell	.05
788	Milt May	.05
789	Bert Blyleven	.05
790	Doug DeCinces	.05
791	Terry Forster	.05
792	Bill Russell	.05

Tiffany

In 1984 Topps introduced a specially boxed, limited edition version of its baseball card set. Sold only through hobby dealers, the cards differed from regular-issue 1984 Topps cards in their use of white cardboard stock and the application of a high-gloss finish to the front of the card. Production was limited to a reported 10,000 sets. The nickname "Tiffany" was coined by collectors to identify the glossy collectors edition.

	NM/M
Unopened Set (792):	175.00
Complete Set (792):	95.00
Common Player:	.15
Stars:	6X
8 Don Mattingly	80.00

Traded

The popular Topps Traded set returned for its fourth year in 1984 with another 132-card set. The 2-1/2" x 3-1/2" cards have an identical design to the regular Topps cards except that the back cardboard is white and card numbers carry a "T" suffix. As before, the set was sold only through hobby dealers. Also as before, players who changed teams, new managers and promising rookies are included in the set. A glossy-finish "Tiffany" version of the set was also issued.

		NM/M
Complete Set (132):		17.50
Common Player:		.05
1T	Willie Aikens	.05
2T	Luis Aponte	.05
3T	Mike Armstrong	.05
4T	Bob Bailor	.05
5T	Dusty Baker	.15
6T	Steve Balboni	.05
7T	Alan Bannister	.05
8T	Dave Beard	.05
9T	Joe Beckwith	.05
10T	Bruce Berenyi	.05
11T	Dave Bergman	.05
12T	Tony Bernazard	.05
13T	Yogi Berra	.25
14T	Barry Bonnell	.05
15T	Phil Bradley RC	.05
16T	Fred Breining	.05
17T	Bill Buckner	.05
18T	Ray Burris	.05
19T	John Butcher	.05
20T	Brett Butler	.05
21T	Enos Cabell	.05
22T	Bill Campbell	.05
23T	Bill Caudill	.05
24T	Bob Clark	.05
25T	Bryan Clark	.05
26T	Jaime Cocanower	.05
27T	Ron Darling RC	.50
28T	Alvin Davis RC	.05
29T	Ken Dayley	.05
30T	Jeff Dedmon RC	.05
31T	Bob Dernier	.05
32T	Carlos Diaz	.05
33T	Mike Easler	.05
34T	Dennis Eckersley	1.50
35T	Jim Essian	.05
36T	Darrell Evans	.05
37T	Mike Fitzgerald RC	.05
38T	Tim Foli	.05
39T	George Frazier	.05
40T	Rich Gale	.05
41T	Barbaro Garbey	.05
42T	Dwight Gooden RC	3.00
43T	Rich Gossage	.05
44T	Wayne Gross	.05
45T	Mark Gubicza RC	.25
46T	Jackie Gutierrez	.05
47T	Mel Hall	.05
48T	Toby Harrah	.05
49T	Ron Hassey	.05
50T	Rich Hebner	.05
51T	Willie Hernandez	.05
52T	Ricky Horton RC	.05
53T	Art Howe	.05
54T	Dane Iorg	.05
55T	Brook Jacoby RC	.05
56T	Mike Jeffcoat RC	.05
57T	Dave Johnson	.05
58T	Lynn Jones	.05
59T	Ruppert Jones	.05
60T	Mike Jorgensen	.05
61T	Bob Kearney	.05
62T	Jimmy Key RC	.50
63T	Dave Kingman	.05
64T	Jerry Koosman	.05
65T	Wayne Krenchicki	.05
66T	Rusty Kuntz	.05
67T	Rene Lachemann	.05
68T	Frank LaCorte	.05
69T	Dennis Lamp	.05
70T	Mark Langston RC	.50
71T	Rick Leach	.05
72T	Craig Lefferts	.05
73T	Gary Lucas	.05
74T	Jerry Martin	.05
75T	Carmelo Martinez	.05
76T	Mike Mason RC	.05
77T	Gary Matthews	.05
78T	Andy McGaffigan	.05
79T	Larry Milbourne	.05
80T	Sid Monge	.05
81T	Jackie Moore	.05
82T	Joe Morgan	2.00
83T	Graig Nettles	.05
84T	Phil Niekro	1.00
85T	Ken Oberkfell	.05
86T	Mike O'Berry	.05
87T	Al Oliver	.05
88T	Jorge Orta	.05
89T	Amos Otis	.05
90T	Dave Parker	.05
91T	Tony Perez	1.00
92T	Gerald Perry RC	.05
93T	Gary Pettis RC	.05
94T	Rob Picciolo	.05
95T	Vern Rapp	.05
96T	Floyd Rayford	.05
97T	Randy Ready RC	.05
98T	Ron Reed	.05
99T	Gene Richards	.05
100T	Jose Rijo RC	.25
101T	Jeff Robinson RC	.05
102T	Ron Romanick RC	.05
103T	Pete Rose	7.50
104T	Bret Saberhagen RC	3.00
105T	Juan Samuel RC	.05
106T	Scott Sanderson	.05
107T	Dick Schofield RC	.05
108T	Tom Seaver	3.00
109T	Jim Slaton	.05
110T	Mike Smithson	.05
111T	Lary Sorensen	.05
112T	Tim Stoddard	.05
113T	Champ Summers	.05
114T	Jim Sundberg	.05
115T	Rick Sutcliffe	.05
116T	Craig Swan	.05
117T	Tim Teufel RC	.05
118T	Derrel Thomas	.05
119T	Gorman Thomas	.05
120T	Alex Trevino	.05
121T	Manny Trillo	.05
122T	John Tudor	.05
123T	Tom Underwood	.05
124T	Mike Vail	.05
125T	Tom Waddell	.05
126T	Gary Ward	.05
127T	Curt Wilkerson	.05
128T	Frank Williams RC	.05
129T	Glenn Wilson	.05
130T	Johnny Wockenfuss	.05
131T	Ned Yost	.05
132T	Checklist 1-132	.05

Traded Tiffany

Following up on its inaugural Tiffany collectors' edition, Topps produced a special glossy version of its Traded set for 1984, as well. Cards in this special boxed set differ from regular Traded cards only in the use of white cardboard stock with a high-gloss finish coat on front.

	NM/M
Complete Set (132):	35.00
Common Player:	.25
Stars:	2X

Traded Darryl Strawberry Bronze

This 1/4-size metal replica of Strawberry's first-ever Topps card was issued to dealers who purchased cases of 1984 Topps Traded sets. Each detail of the 1983 Topps Traded Strawberry card is reproduced on the 1-1/4" x 1-3/4" bronze metal mini-card, right down to the stats.

	NM/M
108T Darryl Strawberry	3.00

Proofs

Though still small in terms of actual numbers, the quantity of 1984 Topps proofs from the "A" sheet which have made their way into the hobby is relatively large. More precisely, 66 cards (half a production press sheet) are frequently seen in proof version. Like other true proofs, they are blank-backed but these have a very discernible difference from the issued 1984 Topps cards. On the proofs, the portrait photo at lower-left is completely within the black frame of the box. On issued cards, the cap extends above the box border. On the proofs, portrait photos of Steve Carlton and Gary Matthews are found on each other's cards and Manny Trillo is pictured in an Indians uniform, rather than the Expos livery on which he appears in the regularly issued version. Single proofs in the market have been cut from half-sheets.

		NM/M
Uncut Sheet (66):		650.00
Complete Set, Singles (66):		800.00
Common Player:		10.00
(1)	Buddy Bell	10.00
(2)	Wade Boggs	50.00
(3)	Bob Boone	12.50
(4)	Greg Brock	10.00
(5)	Hubie Brooks	10.00
(6)	Steve Carlton (Inset photo Gary Matthews.)	150.00
(7)	Gary Carter	20.00
(8)	Cecil Cooper	10.00
(9)	Andre Dawson	20.00
(10)	Storm Davis	10.00
(11)	Doug DeCinces	10.00
(12)	Ivan DeJesus	10.00
(13)	Rick Dempsey	10.00
(14)	Dwight Evans	10.00
(15)	Rollie Fingers	20.00
(16)	Carlton Fisk	50.00
(17)	Ken Forsch	10.00
(18)	George Foster	10.00
(19)	Julio Franco	10.00
(20)	Jim Gantner	10.00
(21)	Damaso Garcia	10.00
(22)	Ken Griffey	12.50
(23)	Alfredo Griffin	10.00
(24)	Bill Gullickson	10.00
(25)	Moose Haas	10.00
(26)	Rickey Henderson	50.00
(27)	Kent Hrbek	12.50
(28)	Reggie Jackson	50.00
(29)	Roy Lee Jackson	10.00
(30)	Cliff Johnson	10.00
(31)	Ron Kittle	10.00
(32)	Charlie Lea	10.00
(33)	Luis Leal	10.00
(34)	Bill Madlock	10.00
(35)	Buck Martinez	10.00
(36)	Gary Matthews (Inset photo is Steve Carlton.)	75.00
(37)	Willie McGee	12.50
(38)	Greg Minton	10.00
(39)	Paul Molitor	30.00
(40)	Joe Morgan	30.00
(41)	Lloyd Moseby	10.00
(42)	Rance Mulliniks	10.00
(43)	Graig Nettles	10.00
(44)	Al Oliver	15.00
(45)	Lou Piniella	15.00
(46)	Bobby Ramos	10.00
(47)	Johnny Ray	10.00
(48)	Jeff Reardon	10.00
(49)	Jim Rice	20.00
(50)	Andre Robertson	10.00
(51)	Nolan Ryan	300.00
(52)	Scott Sanderson	10.00
(53)	Steve Sax	10.00
(54)	Dan Schatzeder	10.00
(55)	Tom Seaver	60.00
(56)	Lee Smith	15.00
(57)	Don Sutton	20.00
(58)	Jason Thompson	10.00
(59)	Alan Trammell	15.00
(60)	Manny Trillo (Indians)	100.00
(61)	Willie Upshaw	10.00
(62)	Fernando Valenzuela	15.00
(63)	Tim Wallach	10.00
(64)	Ernie Whitt	10.00
(65)	Glenn Wilson	10.00
(66)	Robin Yount	30.00

All-Star Glossy Set of 22

These 2-1/2" x 3-1/2" cards were a result of the success of Topps' efforts the previous year with glossy cards on a mail-in basis. The set is divided evenly between the two leagues. Each All-Star Game starter for both leagues, the managers and the honorary team captains have an All-Star Glossy card. Cards feature a large color photo on the front with an All-Star banner across the top and the league emblem in the lower-left. Player identification appears below the photo. Backs have a name, team, position and card number along with the phrase "1983 All-Star Game Commemorative Set." The '84 Glossy All-Stars were distributed one card per rack pack.

		NM/M
Complete Set (22):		4.00
Common Player:		.10
1	Harvey Kuenn	.10
2	Rod Carew	.50
3	Manny Trillo	.10
4	George Brett	1.00
5	Robin Yount	.50
6	Jim Rice	.25
7	Fred Lynn	.10
8	Dave Winfield	.50
9	Ted Simmons	.10
10	Dave Stieb	.10
11	Carl Yastrzemski	.50
12	Whitey Herzog	.10
13	Al Oliver	.10
14	Steve Sax	.10
15	Mike Schmidt	1.00
16	Ozzie Smith	.50
17	Tim Raines	.10
18	Andre Dawson	.25
19	Dale Murphy	.50
20	Gary Carter	.50
21	Mario Soto	.10
22	Johnny Bench	.50

All-Star Glossy Set of 40

For the second straight year in 1984, Topps produced a 40-card All-Star "Collector's Edition" set as a "consolation prize" for its sweepstakes game. By collecting game cards and sending them in with a bit of cash, the collector could receive one of eight different five-card series.

As the previous year, the 2-1/2" x 3-1/2" cards feature a nearly full-frame color photo on its glossy finish front. Backs are printed in red and blue.

		NM/M
Complete Set (40):		6.00
Common Player:		.10
1	Pete Rose	1.00
2	Lance Parrish	.10
3	Steve Rogers	.10
4	Eddie Murray	.40
5	Johnny Ray	.10
6	Rickey Henderson	.40
7	Atlee Hammaker	.10
8	Wade Boggs	.50
9	Gary Carter	.40
10	Jack Morris	.10
11	Darrell Evans	.10
12	George Brett	1.00
13	Bob Horner	.10
14	Ron Guidry	.10
15	Nolan Ryan	1.50
16	Dave Winfield	.40
17	Ozzie Smith	.50
18	Ted Simmons	.10
19	Bill Madlock	.10
20	Tony Armas	.10
21	Al Oliver	.10
22	Jim Rice	.25
23	George Hendrick	.10
24	Dave Stieb	.10
25	Pedro Guerrero	.10
26	Rod Carew	.40
27	Steve Carlton	.40
28	Dave Righetti	.10
29	Darryl Strawberry	.10
30	Lou Whitaker	.10
31	Dale Murphy	.25
32	LaMarr Hoyt	.10
33	Jesse Orosco	.10
34	Cecil Cooper	.10
35	Andre Dawson	.25
36	Robin Yount	.40
37	Tim Raines	.10
38	Dan Quisenberry	.10
39	Mike Schmidt	1.00
40	Carlton Fisk	.40

Cereal Series

The Topps-produced 1984 Cereal Series set is identical to the Ralston Purina set from the same year in nearly all aspects. On the card fronts the words "Ralston Purina Company" were replaced by "Cereal Series" and Topps logos were substituted for Ralston checkerboard logos. The set is comprised of 33 cards, each measuring 2-1/2" x 3-1/2." The cards were inserted in unmarked boxes of Chex brand cereals.

		NM/M
Complete Set (33):		4.00
Common Player:		.05
1	Eddie Murray	.25
2	Ozzie Smith	.30
3	Ted Simmons	.05
4	Pete Rose	.75
5	Greg Luzinski	.05
6	Andre Dawson	.15
7	Dave Winfield	.25

8	Tom Seaver	.25
9	Jim Rice	.15
10	Fernando Valenzuela	.05
11	Wade Boggs	.30
12	Dale Murphy	.15
13	George Brett	.50
14	Nolan Ryan	1.00
15	Rickey Henderson	.25
16	Steve Carlton	.25
17	Rod Carew	.25
18	Steve Garvey	.15
19	Reggie Jackson	.35
20	Dave Concepcion	.05
21	Robin Yount	.25
22	Mike Schmidt	.50
23	Jim Palmer	.25
24	Bruce Sutter	.05
25	Dan Quisenberry	.05
26	Bill Madlock	.05
27	Cecil Cooper	.05
28	Gary Carter	.25
29	Fred Lynn	.05
30	Pedro Guerrero	.05
31	Ron Guidry	.05
32	Keith Hernandez	.05
33	Carlton Fisk	.25

"Darryl Palmer"

For use as a prop in the 1985 movie "The Slugger's Wife," Topps produced this 1984-style card of actor Michael O'Keefe as Darryl Palmer. (O'Keefe is better remembered as caddy Danny Noonan in "Caddyshack.") Front and back are in the '84T format, complete with personal data, stats and Topps copyrights.

		NM/M
801	Darryl Palmer	15.00

Gallery of Immortals

The Gallery of Immortals bronze and silver replicas were the first metal miniature set from Topps and the start of an annual tradition (in 1985, the name was changed to Gallery of Champions). Each mini is an exact one-quarter scale replica of the featured player's 1984 Topps baseball card, both front and back, in minute detail. The three-dimensional metal cards were packaged in a velvet-lined case that bears the title of the set in gold-embossed letters. A certificate of authenticity is included with each set. A Tom Seaver pewter metal mini-card was given as a premium to dealers who purchsed sets. Issue price was about $100 for the cased bronze set, $500 for the silver edition of 1,000.

		NM/M
Complete Bronze Set (12):		40.00
Complete Silver Set (12):		190.00
(1b)	George Brett/Bronze	12.50
(1s)	George Brett/Silver	45.00
(2b)	Rod Carew/Bronze	6.00
(2s)	Rod Carew/Silver	15.00
(3b)	Steve Carlton/Bronze	6.00
(3s)	Steve Carlton/Silver	15.00
(4b)	Rollie Fingers/Bronze	4.00
(4s)	Rollie Fingers/Silver	12.50
(5b)	Steve Garvey/Bronze	4.00
(5s)	Steve Garvey/Silver	12.50
(6b)	Reggie Jackson/Bronze	7.50
(6s)	Reggie Jackson/Silver	17.50
(7b)	Joe Morgan/Bronze	5.00
(7s)	Joe Morgan/Silver	5.00
(8b)	Jim Palmer/Bronze	5.00
(8s)	Jim Palmer/Silver	12.50
(9b)	Pete Rose/Bronze	20.00
(9s)	Pete Rose/Silver	50.00
(10b)	Nolan Ryan/Bronze	25.00
(10s)	Nolan Ryan/Silver	60.00
(11b)	Mike Schmidt/Bronze	12.50
(11s)	Mike Schmidt/Silver	45.00
(12b)	Tom Seaver/Bronze	12.50
(12s)	Tom Seaver/Silver	15.00
(12p)	Tom Seaver/Pewter	15.00

Topps "Pewter" Gallery Ingots

All of the Topps Gallery of Immortals (1984) and Gallery of Champions (1985-1989) miniature ingots have been counterfeited in a pewter or pot metal alloy designed to look like the genuine silver pieces. The fakes are cast, rather than die-struck, have a porous surface upon magnification and sometimes the casting seam is visible despite the filing done to remove it. These are often sold on eBay as "pewter." Topps did did make one genuine pewter piece each year 1984-1991, as an ordering incentive; they are listed within each year's Gallery checklist.

Rub Downs

This set consists of 32 "Rub Down" sheets featuring 112 different players. Each sheet measures 2-3/8" x 3-15/16" and includes small, color baseball player figures along with bats, balls and gloves. The pictures can be transferred to another surface by rubbing the paper backing. The sheets, which were sold as a separate issue, are somewhat reminiscent of earlier tattoo sets issued by Topps. The sheets are not numbered.

	NM/M
Complete Set (32):	7.50
Common Sheet:	.50
Pack (2):	.50
Box (36):	9.00

(1)	Steve Bedrosian, Bruce Benedict, Tony Armas, Harold Baines, Lonnie Smith	.50
(2)	Chris Chambliss, Bob Horner, Don Baylor, George Hendrick, Ron Kittle, Johnnie LeMaster	.50
(3)	Glenn Hubbard, Rafael Ramirez, Buddy Bell, Ray Knight, Lloyd Moseby	.50
(4)	Craig McMurtry, Bruce Benedict, Atlee Hammaker, Frank White	.50
(5)	Wade Boggs, Rick Dempsey, Keith Hernandez	.75
(6)	George Brett, Andre Dawson, Paul Molitor, Alan Wiggins	1.00
(7)	Tom Brunansky, Pedro Guerrero, Darryl Strawberry	.50
(8)	Bill Buckner, Rich Gossage, Dave Stieb, Rick Sutcliffe	.50
(9)	Rod Carew, Carlton Fisk, Johnny Ray, Matt Young	.60
(10)	Steve Carlton, Bob Horner, Dan Quisenberry	.60
(11)	Gary Carter, Phil Garner, Ron Guidry	.60
(12)	Ron Cey, Steve Kemp, Greg Luzinski, Kent Tekulve	.50
(13)	Chris Chambliss, Dwight Evans, Julio Franco	.50
(14)	Jack Clark, Damaso Garcia, Hal McRae, Lance Parrish	.50
(15)	Dave Concepcion, Cecil Cooper, Fred Lynn, Jesse Orosco	.50
(16)	Jose Cruz, Gary Matthews, Jack Morris, Jim Rice	.50
(17)	Ron Davis, Kent Hrbek, Tom Seaver	.60
(18)	John Denny, Carney Lansford, Mario Soto, Lou Whitaker	.50
(19)	Leon Durham, Dave Lopes, Steve Sax	.50
(20)	George Foster, Gary Gaetti, Bobby Grich, Gary Redus	.50
(21)	Steve Garvey, Bill Russell, Jerry Remy, George Wright	.50
(22)	Moose Haas, Bruce Sutter, Dickie Thon, Andre Thornton	.50
(23)	Toby Harrah, Pat Putnam, Tim Raines, Mike Schmidt	1.00
(24)	Rickey Henderson, Dave Righetti, Pete Rose	1.00
(25)	Steve Henderson, Bill Madlock, Alan Trammell	.50
(26)	LaMarr Hoyt, Larry Parrish, Nolan Ryan	1.50
(27)	Reggie Jackson, Eric Show, Jason Thompson	.60
(28)	Tommy John, Terry Kennedy, Eddie Murray, Ozzie Smith	.60
(29)	Jeff Leonard, Dale Murphy, Ken Singleton, Dave Winfield	.60
(30)	Craig McMurtry, Cal Ripken, Steve Rogers, Willie Upshaw	1.50
(31)	Ben Oglivie, Jim Palmer, Darrell Porter	.50
(32)	Tony Pena, Fernando Valenzuela, Robin Yount	.60

Stickers

The largest sticker set issued by Topps, the 1984 set consists of 386 stickers, each measuring 1-15/16" x 2-9/16". The full color photos have stars in each of the corners and are numbered on both the front and the back. The back includes information about the sticker album and a promotion to order stickers through the mail. The back of the album is a tribute to Carl Yastrzemski, including a large photo and re-productions of his 1960-1983 cards in miniature.

	NM/M
Complete Set (386):	12.00
Common Player:	.05
Sticker Album:	3.00
Box (35):	6.00

#	Player	Price
1	Steve Carlton	.25
2	Steve Carlton	.25
3	Rickey Henderson	.25
4	Rickey Henderson	.25
5	Fred Lynn	.05
6	Fred Lynn	.05
7	Greg Luzinski	.05
8	Greg Luzinski	.05
9	Dan Quisenberry	.05
10	Dan Quisenberry	.05
11	1983 Championship (LaMarr Hoyt)	.05
12	1983 Championship (Mike Flanagan)	.05
13	1983 Championship (Mike Boddicker)	.05
14	1983 Championship (Tito Landrum)	.05
15	1983 Championship (Steve Carlton)	.10
16	1983 Championship (Fernando Valenzuela)	.05
17	1983 Championship (Charlie Hudson)	.05
18	1983 Championship (Gary Matthews)	.05
19	1983 World Series (John Denny)	.05
20	1983 World Series (John Lowenstein)	.05
21	1983 World Series (Jim Palmer)	.10
22	1983 World Series (Benny Ayala)	.05
23	1983 World Series (Rick Dempsey)	.05
24	1983 World Series (Cal Ripken)	.50
25	1983 World Series (Sammy Stewart)	.05
26	1983 World Series (Eddie Murray)	.10
27	Dale Murphy	.15
28	Chris Chambliss	.05
29	Glenn Hubbard	.05
30	Bob Horner	.05
31	Phil Niekro	.20
32	Claudell Washington	.05
33	Rafael Ramirez	.05
34	Bruce Benedict	.05
35	Gene Garber	.05
36	Pascual Perez	.05
37	Jerry Royster	.05
38	Steve Bedrosian	.05
39	Keith Moreland	.05
40	Leon Durham	.05
41	Ron Cey	.05
42	Bill Buckner	.05
43	Jody Davis	.05
44	Lee Smith	.05
45	Ryne Sandberg	.30
46	Larry Bowa	.05
47	Chuck Rainey	.05
48	Fergie Jenkins	.20
49	Dick Ruthven	.05
50	Jay Johnstone	.05
51	Mario Soto	.05
52	Gary Redus	.05
53	Ron Oester	.05
54	Cesar Cedeno	.05
55	Dan Driessen	.05
56	Dave Concepcion	.05
57	Dann Bilardello	.05
58	Joe Price	.05
59	Tom Hume	.05
60	Eddie Milner	.05
61	Paul Householder	.05
62	Bill Scherrer	.05
63	Phil Garner	.05
64	Dickie Thon	.05
65	Jose Cruz	.05
66	Nolan Ryan	.60
67	Terry Puhl	.05
68	Ray Knight	.05
69	Joe Niekro	.05
70	Jerry Mumphrey	.05
71	Bill Dawley	.05
72	Alan Ashby	.05
73	Denny Walling	.05
74	Frank DiPino	.05
75	Pedro Guerrero	.05
76	Ken Landreaux	.05
77	Bill Russell	.05
78	Steve Sax	.05
79	Fernando Valenzuela	.05
80	Dusty Baker	.05
81	Jerry Reuss	.05
82	Alejandro Pena	.05
83	Rick Monday	.05
84	Rick Honeycutt	.05
85	Mike Marshall	.05
86	Steve Yeager	.05
87	Al Oliver	.05
88	Steve Rogers	.05
89	Jeff Reardon	.05
90	Gary Carter	.25
91	Tim Raines	.05
92	Andre Dawson	.15
93	Manny Trillo	.05
94	Tim Wallach	.05
95	Chris Speier	.05
96	Bill Gullickson	.05
97	Doug Flynn	.05
98	Charlie Lea	.05
99	Bill Madlock	.05
100	Wade Boggs	.25
101	Mike Schmidt	.40
102a	Jim Rice	.15
102b	Reggie Jackson	.25
103	Hubie Brooks	.05
104	Jesse Orosco	.05
105	George Foster	.05
106	Tom Seaver	.25
107	Keith Hernandez	.05
108	Mookie Wilson	.05
109	Bob Bailor	.05
110	Walt Terrell	.05
111	Brian Giles	.05
112	Jose Oquendo	.05
113	Mike Torrez	.05
114	Junior Ortiz	.05
115	Pete Rose	.50
116	Joe Morgan	.25
117	Mike Schmidt	.40
118	Gary Matthews	.05
119	Steve Carlton	.25
120	Bo Diaz	.05
121	Ivan DeJesus	.05
122	John Denny	.05
123	Garry Maddox	.05
124	Von Hayes	.05
125	Al Holland	.05
126	Tony Perez	.25
127	John Candelaria	.05
128	Jason Thompson	.05
129	Tony Pena	.05
130	Dave Parker	.05
131	Bill Madlock	.05
132	Kent Tekulve	.05
133	Larry McWilliams	.05
134	Johnny Ray	.05
135	Marvell Wynne	.05
136	Dale Berra	.05
137	Mike Easler	.05
138	Lee Lacy	.05
139	George Hendrick	.05
140	Lonnie Smith	.05
141	Willie McGee	.05
142	Tom Herr	.05
143	Darrell Porter	.05
144	Ozzie Smith	.40
145	Bruce Sutter	.20
146	Dave LaPoint	.05
147	Neil Allen	.05
148	Ken Oberkfell	.05
149	David Green	.05
150	Andy Van Slyke	.05
151	Garry Templeton	.05
152	Juan Bonilla	.05
153	Alan Wiggins	.05
154	Terry Kennedy	.05
155	Dave Dravecky	.05
156	Steve Garvey	.10
157	Bobby Brown	.05
158	Ruppert Jones	.05
159	Luis Salazar	.05
160	Tony Gwynn	.40
161	Gary Lucas	.05
162	Eric Show	.05
163	Darrell Evans	.05
164	Gary Lavelle	.05
165	Atlee Hammaker	.05
166	Jeff Leonard	.05
167	Jack Clark	.05
168	Johnny LeMaster	.05
169	Duane Kuiper	.05
170	Tom O'Malley	.05
171	Chili Davis	.05
172	Bill Laskey	.05
173	Joel Youngblood	.05
174	Bob Brenly	.05
175	Atlee Hammaker	.05
176	Rick Honeycutt	.05
177	John Denny	.05
178	LaMarr Hoyt	.05
179	Tim Raines	.05
180	Dale Murphy	.15
181	Andre Dawson	.15
182	Steve Rogers	.05
183	Gary Carter	.25
184	Steve Carlton	.25
185	George Hendrick	.05
186	Johnny Ray	.05
187	Ozzie Smith	.40
188	Mike Schmidt	.40
189	Jim Rice	.15
190	Dave Winfield	.25
191	Lloyd Moseby	.05
192	LaMarr Hoyt	.05
193	Ted Simmons	.05
194	Ron Guidry	.05
195	Eddie Murray	.25
196	Lou Whitaker	.05
197	Cal Ripken, Jr.	.60
198	George Brett	.40
199	Dale Murphy	.15
200a	Cecil Cooper	.05
200b	Jim Rice	.15
201	Tim Raines	.05
202	Rickey Henderson	.25
203	Eddie Murray	.25
204	Cal Ripken	.60
205	Gary Roenicke	.05
206	Ken Singleton	.05
207	Scott McGregor	.05
208	Tippy Martinez	.05
209	John Lowenstein	.05
210	Mike Flanagan	.05
211	Jim Palmer	.20
212	Dan Ford	.05
213	Rick Dempsey	.05
214	Rich Dauer	.05
215	Jerry Remy	.05
216	Wade Boggs	.25
217	Jim Rice	.15
218	Tony Armas	.05
219	Dwight Evans	.05
220	Bob Stanley	.05
221	Dave Stapleton	.05
222	Rich Gedman	.05
223	Glenn Hoffman	.05
224	Dennis Eckersley	.20
225	John Tudor	.05
226	Bruce Hurst	.05
227	Rod Carew	.25
228	Bobby Grich	.05
229	Doug DeCinces	.05
230	Fred Lynn	.05
231	Reggie Jackson	.25
232	Tommy John	.05
233	Luis Sanchez	.05
234	Bob Boone	.05
235	Bruce Kison	.05
236	Brian Downing	.05
237	Ken Forsch	.05
238	Rick Burleson	.05
239	Dennis Lamp	.05
240	LaMarr Hoyt	.05
241	Richard Dotson	.05
242	Harold Baines	.05
243	Carlton Fisk	.25
244	Greg Luzinski	.05
245	Rudy Law	.05
246	Tom Paciorek	.05
247	Floyd Bannister	.05
248	Julio Cruz	.05
249	Vance Law	.05
250	Scott Fletcher	.05
251	Toby Harrah	.05
252	Pat Tabler	.05
253	Gorman Thomas	.05
254	Rick Sutcliffe	.05
255	Andre Thornton	.05
256	Bake McBride	.05
257	Alan Bannister	.05
258	Jamie Easterly	.05
259	Lary Sorenson	.05
260	Mike Hargrove	.05
261	Bert Blyleven	.05
262	Ron Hassey	.05
263	Jack Morris	.05
264	Larry Herndon	.05
265	Lance Parrish	.05
266	Alan Trammell	.05
267	Lou Whitaker	.05
268	Aurelio Lopez	.05
269	Dan Petry	.05
270	Glenn Wilson	.05
271	Chet Lemon	.05
272	Kirk Gibson	.05
273	Enos Cabell	.05
274	Johnny Wockenfuss	.05
275	George Brett	.40
276	Willie Aikens	.05
277	Frank White	.05
278	Hal McRae	.05
279	Dan Quisenberry	.05
280	Willie Wilson	.05
281	Paul Splitorff	.05
282	U.L. Washington	.05
283	Bud Black	.05
284	John Wathan	.05
285	Larry Gura	.05
286	Pat Sheridan	.05
287a	Rusty Staub	.05
287b	Dave Righetti	.05
288a	Bob Forsch	.05
288b	Mike Warren	.05
289	Al Holland	.05
290	Dan Quisenberry	.05
291	Cecil Cooper	.05
292	Moose Haas	.05
293	Paul Molitor	.25
294	Paul Molitor	.25
295	Robin Yount	.05
296	Ben Oglivie	.05
297	Tom Tellmann	.05
298	Jim Gantner	.05
299	Rick Manning	.05
300	Don Sutton	.20
301	Charlie Moore	.05
302	Jim Slaton	.05
303	Gary Ward	.05
304	Tom Brunansky	.05
305	Kent Hrbek	.05
306	Gary Gaetti	.05
307	John Castino	.05
308	Ken Schrom	.05
309	Ron Davis	.05
310	Lenny Faedo	.05
311	Darrell Brown	.05
312	Frank Viola	.05
313	Dave Engle	.05
314	Randy Bush	.05
315	Dave Righetti	.05
316	Rich Gossage	.05
317	Ken Griffey	.05
318	Ron Guidry	.05
319	Dave Winfield	.25
320	Don Baylor	.10
321	Butch Wynegar	.05
322	Omar Moreno	.05
323	Andre Robertson	.05
324	Willie Randolph	.05
325	Don Mattingly	.60
326	Graig Nettles	.05
327	Rickey Henderson	.25
328	Carney Lansford	.05
329	Jeff Burroughs	.05
330	Chris Codiroli	.05
331	Dave Lopes	.05
332	Dwayne Murphy	.05
333	Wayne Gross	.05
334	Bill Almon	.05
335	Tom Underwood	.05
336	Dave Beard	.05
337	Mike Heath	.05
338	Mike Davis	.05
339	Pat Putnam	.05
340	Tony Bernazard	.05
341	Steve Henderson	.05
342	Richie Zisk	.05
343	Dave Henderson	.05
344	Al Cowens	.05
345	Bill Caudill	.05
346	Jim Beattie	.05
347	Ricky Nelson	.05
348	Roy Thomas	.05
349	Spike Owen	.05
350	Jamie Allen	.05
351	Buddy Bell	.05
352	Billy Sample	.05
353	George Wright	.05
354	Larry Parrish	.05
355	Jim Sundberg	.05
356	Charlie Hough	.05
357	Pete O'Brien	.05
358	Wayne Tolleson	.05
359	Danny Darwin	.05
360	Dave Stewart	.05
361	Mickey Rivers	.05
362	Bucky Dent	.05
363	Willie Upshaw	.05
364	Damaso Garcia	.05
365	Lloyd Moseby	.05
366	Cliff Johnson	.05
367	Jim Clancy	.05
368	Dave Stieb	.05
369	Alfredo Griffin	.05
370	Barry Bonnell	.05
371	Luis Leal	.05
372	Jesse Barfield	.05
373	Ernie Whitt	.05
374	Rance Mulliniks	.05
375	Mike Boddicker	.05
376	Greg Brock	.05
377	Bill Doran	.05
378	Nick Esasky	.05
379	Julio Franco	.05
380	Mel Hall	.05
381	Bob Kearney	.05
382	Ron Kittle	.05
383	Carmelo Martinez	.05
384	Craig McMurtry	.05
385	Darryl Strawberry	.05
386	Matt Young	.05

Stickers Boxes

For the second straight year, Topps printed baseball cards on the back of its sticker boxes. The 1984 set, titled "The Super Bats" features 24 hitting leaders. The cards are blank-backed and measure 2-1/2" x 3-1/2". Two cards were printed on each of 12 different boxes. The player's name appears inside a bat above his photo. Prices listed are for complete boxes.

		NM/M
Complete Set (12):		8.50
Common Player:		.75
1	Al Oliver, Lou Whitaker	.75
2	Ken Oberkfell, Ted Simmons	.75
3	Hal McRae, Alan Wiggins	.75
4	Lloyd Moseby, Tim Raines	.75
5	Lonnie Smith, Willie Wilson	.75
6	Keith Hernandez, Robin Yount	1.00
7	Wade Boggs, Johnny Ray	1.00
8	Willie McGee, Ken Singleton	.75
9	Ray Knight, Alan Trammell	.75

		NM/M
11	Rod Carew, George Hendrick	1.00
12	Bill Madlock, Eddie Murray	1.00
13	Jose Cruz, Cal Ripken, Jr.	3.00

Super

A new generation in Topps' experiments to market large-format cards, these 4-7/8" x 6-7/8" cards were sold in single-card plastic-wrap packs with a complete set being 30 cards. Other than their size and the change in card number on the back, there is nothing to distinguish the Supers from the regular 1984 Topps cards of the same players. One plus is that the players are all big name stars, and are likely to remain in demand.

	NM/M
Complete Set (30):	10.00
Common Player:	.25
Wax Pack (1):	.50
Wax Box (36):	9.00
1	Cal Ripken, Jr.	3.00
2	Dale Murphy	.40
3	LaMarr Hoyt	.25
4	John Denny	.25
5	Jim Rice	.40
6	Mike Schmidt	1.00
7	Wade Boggs	.60
8	Bill Madlock	.25
9	Dan Quisenberry	.25
10	Al Holland	.25
11	Ron Kittle	.25
12	Darryl Strawberry	.35
13	George Brett	1.00
14	Bill Buckner	.25
15	Carlton Fisk	.50
16	Steve Carlton	.50
17	Ron Guidry	.25
18	Gary Carter	.50
19	Rickey Henderson	.50
20	Andre Dawson	.40
21	Reggie Jackson	.75
22	Steve Garvey	.30
23	Fred Lynn	.25
24	Pedro Guerrero	.25
25	Eddie Murray	.50
26	Keith Hernandez	.25
27	Dave Winfield	.50
28	Nolan Ryan	3.00
29	Robin Yount	.50
30	Fernando Valenzuela	.25

the 1984 U.S. Olympic Baseball Team members and a set featuring #1 draft choices since the inception of the baseball draft in 1965. Large numbers of uncut sheets were made available within the hobby, originally selling around $60 for a set of six.

	NM/M
Unopened Fact. Set (792):	140.00
Complete Set (792):	70.00
Common Player:	.05
Wax Pack (15):	4.50
Wax Box (36):	150.00
Cello Pack (28):	6.50
Cello Box (24):	150.00
Rack Pack (51+1):	9.00
Rack Box (24):	180.00
Vending Box (500):	60.00

1	Carlton Fisk (Record Breaker)	.25
2	Steve Garvey (Record Breaker)	.05
3	Dwight Gooden (Record Breaker)	.05
4	Cliff Johnson (Record Breaker)	.05
5	Joe Morgan (Record Breaker)	.10
6	Pete Rose (Record Breaker)	.50
7	Nolan Ryan (Record Breaker)	1.50
8	Juan Samuel RC (Record Breaker)	.05
9	Bruce Sutter (Record Breaker)	.10
10	Don Sutton (Record Breaker)	.05
11	Ralph Houk	.05
12	Dave Lopes	.05
13	Tim Lollar	.05
14	Chris Bando	.05
15	Jerry Koosman	.05
16	Bobby Meacham	.05
17	Mike Scott	.05
18	Mickey Hatcher	.05
19	George Frazier	.05
20	Chet Lemon	.05
21	Lee Tunnell	.05
22	Duane Kuiper	.05
23	Bret Saberhagen	.05
24	Jesse Barfield	.05
25	Steve Bedrosian	.05
26	Roy Smalley	.05
27	Bruce Berenyi	.05
28	Dann Bilardello	.05
29	Odell Jones	.05
30	Cal Ripken, Jr.	4.00
31	Terry Whitfield	.05
32	Chuck Porter	.05
33	Tito Landrum	.05
34	Ed Nunez RC	.05
35	Graig Nettles	.05
36	Fred Breining	.05
37	Reid Nichols	.05
38	Jackie Moore	.05
39	Johnny Wockenfuss	.05
40	Phil Niekro	.60
41	Mike Fischlin	.05
42	Luis Sanchez	.05
43	Andre David	.05
44	Dickie Thon	.05
45	Greg Minton	.05
46	Gary Woods	.05
47	Dave Rozema	.05
48	Tony Fernandez RC	.05
49	Butch Davis	.05
50	John Candelaria	.05
51	Bob Watson	.05
52	Jerry Dybzinski	.05
53	Tom Gorman	.05
54	Cesar Cedeno	.05
55	Frank Tanana	.05
56	Jim Dwyer	.05
57	Pat Zachry	.05
58	Orlando Mercado	.05
59	Rick Waits	.05
60	George Hendrick	.05
61	Curt Kaufman	.05
62	Mike Ramsey	.05
63	Steve McCatty	.05
64	Mark Bailey RC	.05
65	Bill Buckner	.05
66	Dick Williams	.05
67	Rafael Santana RC	.05
68	Von Hayes	.05
69	Jim Winn RC	.05
70	Don Baylor	.10
71	Tim Laudner	.05
72	Rick Sutcliffe	.05
73	Rusty Kuntz	.05
74	Mike Krukow	.05
75	Willie Upshaw	.05
76	Alan Bannister	.05
77	Joe Beckwith	.05
78	Scott Fletcher	.05
79	Rick Mahler	.05
80	Keith Hernandez	.05
81	Lenn Sakata	.05
82	Joe Price	.05
83	Charlie Moore	.05
84	Spike Owen	.05
85	Mike Marshall	.05
86	Don Aase	.05
87	David Green	.05
88	Bryn Smith	.05
89	Jackie Gutierrez	.05
90	Rich Gossage	.05
91	Jeff Burroughs	.05
92	Paul Owens	.05
93	Don Schulze RC	.05
94	Toby Harrah	.05
95	Jose Cruz	.05
96	Johnny Ray	.05
97	Pete Filson	.05
98	Steve Lake	.05
99	Milt Wilcox	.05
100	George Brett	2.00
101	Jim Acker	.05
102	Tommy Dunbar	.05
103	Randy Lerch	.05
104	Mike Fitzgerald	.05
105	Ron Kittle	.05
106	Pascual Perez	.05
107	Tom Foley	.05
108	Darnell Coles RC	.05
109	Gary Roenicke	.05
110	Alejandro Pena	.05
111	Doug DeCinces	.05
112	Tom Tellmann	.05
113	Tom Herr	.05
114	Bob James	.05
115	Rickey Henderson	.75
116	Dennis Boyd RC	.05
117	Greg Gross	.05
118	Eric Show	.05
119	Pat Corrales	.05
120	Steve Kemp	.05
121	Checklist 1-132	.05
122	Tom Brunansky	.05
123	Dave Smith	.05
124	Rich Hebner	.05
125	Kent Tekulve	.05
126	Ruppert Jones	.05
127	Mark Gubicza	.05
128	Ernie Whitt	.05
129	Gene Garber	.05
130	Al Oliver	.05
131	Father - Son (Buddy Bell, Gus Bell)	.05
132	Father - Son (Dale Berra, Yogi Berra)	.10
133	Father - Son (Bob Boone, Ray Boone)	.05
134	Father - Son (Terry Francona, Tito Francona)	.05
135	Father - Son (Bob Kennedy, Terry Kennedy)	.05
136	Father - Son (Bill Kunkel, Jeff Kunkel RC)	.05
137	Father - Son (Vance Law, Vern Law)	.05
138	Father - Son (Dick Schofield, Dick Schofield, Jr.)	.05
139	Father - Son (Bob Skinner, Joel Skinner)	.05
140	Father - Son (Roy Smalley, Jr., Roy Smalley III)	.05
141	Father - Son (Dave Stenhouse, Mike Stenhouse)	.05
142	Father - Son (Dizzy Trout, Steve Trout)	.05
143	Father - Son (Ozzie Virgil, Ozzie Virgil)	.05
144	Ron Gardenhire	.05
145	Alvin Davis	.05
146	Gary Redus	.05
147	Bill Swaggerty	.05
148	Steve Yeager	.05
149	Dickie Noles	.05
150	Jim Rice	.15
151	Moose Haas	.05
152	Steve Braun	.05
153	Frank LaCorte	.05
154	Argenis Salazar RC	.05
155	Yogi Berra	.10
156	Craig Reynolds	.05
157	Tug McGraw	.05
158	Pat Tabler	.05
159	Carlos Diaz	.05
160	Lance Parrish	.05
161	Ken Schrom	.05
162	Benny Distefano RC	.05
163	Dennis Eckersley	.60
164	Jorge Orta	.05
165	Dusty Baker	.05
166	Keith Atherton	.05
167	Rufino Linares	.05
168	Garth Iorg	.05
169	Dan Spillner	.05
170	George Foster	.05
171	Bill Stein	.05
172	Jack Perconte	.05
173	Mike Young RC	.05
174	Rick Honeycutt	.05
175	Dave Parker	.05
176	Bill Schroeder	.05
177	Dave Von Ohlen	.05
178	Miguel Dilone	.05
179	Tommy John	.10
180	Dave Winfield	.75
181	Roger Clemens	30.00
182	Tim Flannery	.05
183	Larry McWilliams	.05
184	Carmen Castillo RC	.05
185	Al Holland	.05
186	Bob Lillis	.05
187	Mike Walters	.05
188	Greg Pryor	.05
189	Warren Brusstar	.05
190	Rusty Staub	.05
191	Steve Nicosia	.05
192	Howard Johnson	.05
193	Jimmy Key	.05
194	Dave Stegman	.05
195	Glenn Hubbard	.05
196	Pete O'Brien	.05
197	Mike Warren	.05
198	Eddie Milner	.05
199	Denny Martinez	.05
200	Reggie Jackson	1.50
201	Burt Hooton	.05
202	Gorman Thomas	.05
203	Bob McClure	.05
204	Art Howe	.05
205	Steve Rogers	.05
206	Phil Garner	.05
207	Mark Clear	.05
208	Champ Summers	.05
209	Bill Campbell	.05
210	Gary Matthews	.05
211	Clay Christiansen	.05
212	George Vukovich	.05
213	Billy Gardner	.05
214	John Tudor	.05
215	Bob Brenly	.05
216	Jerry Don Gleaton	.05
217	Leon Roberts	.05
218	Doyle Alexander	.05
219	Gerald Perry	.05
220	Fred Lynn	.05
221	Ron Reed	.05
222	Hubie Brooks	.05
223	Tom Hume	.05
224	Al Cowens	.05
225	Mike Boddicker	.05
226	Juan Beniquez	.05
227	Danny Darwin	.05
228	Dion James RC	.05
229	Dave LaPoint	.05
230	Gary Carter	.75
231	Dwayne Murphy	.05
232	Dave Beard	.05
233	Ed Jurak	.05
234	Jerry Narron	.05
235	Garry Maddox	.05
236	Mark Thurmond	.05
237	Julio Franco	.05
238	Jose Rijo	.05
239	Tim Teufel	.05
240	Dave Stieb	.05
241	Jim Frey	.05
242	Greg Harris	.05
243	Barbaro Garbey	.05
244	Mike Jones	.05
245	Chili Davis	.05
246	Mike Norris	.05
247	Wayne Tolleson	.05
248	Terry Forster	.05
249	Harold Baines	.05
250	Jesse Orosco	.05
251	Brad Gulden	.05
252	Dan Ford	.05
253	Sid Bream RC	.10
254	Pete Vuckovich	.05
255	Lonnie Smith	.05
256	Mike Stanton	.05
257	Brian Little (Bryan)	.05
258	Mike Brown	.05
259	Gary Allenson	.05
260	Dave Righetti	.05
261	Checklist 133-264	.05
262	Greg Booker RC	.05
263	Mel Hall	.05
264	Joe Sambito	.05
265	Juan Samuel RC	.05
266	Frank Viola	.05
267	Henry Cotto RC	.05
268	Chuck Tanner	.05
269	Doug Baker RC	.05
270	Dan Quisenberry	.05
271	Tim Foli (#1 Draft Pick)	.05
272	Jeff Burroughs (#1 Draft Pick)	.05
273	Bill Almon (#1 Draft Pick)	.05
274	Floyd Bannister (#1 Draft Pick)	.05
275	Harold Baines (#1 Draft Pick)	.10
276	Bob Horner (#1 Draft Pick)	.10
277	Al Chambers (#1 Draft Pick)	.05
278	Darryl Strawberry (#1 Draft Pick)	.30
279	Mike Moore RC (#1 Draft Pick)	.05
280	Shawon Dunston RC (#1 Draft Pick)	.40
281	Tim Belcher RC (#1 Draft Pick)	.30
282	Shawn Abner RC (#1 Draft Pick)	.05
283	Fran Mullins	.05
284	Marty Bystrom	.05
285	Dan Driessen	.05
286	Rudy Law	.05
287	Walt Terrell	.05
288	Jeff Kunkel RC	.05
289	Tom Underwood	.05
290	Cecil Cooper	.05
291	Bob Welch	.10
292	Brad Komminsk RC	.05
293	Curt Young RC	.05
294	Tom Nieto RC	.05
295	Joe Niekro	.05
296	Ricky Nelson	.05
297	Gary Lucas	.05
298	Marty Barrett	.05
299	Andy Hawkins	.05
300	Rod Carew	.75
301	John Montefusco	.05
302	Tim Corcoran	.05
303	Mike Jeffcoat RC	.05
304	Gary Gaetti	.05
305	Dale Berra	.05
306	Rick Reuschel	.05
307	Sparky Anderson	.10
308	John Wathan	.05
309	Mike Witt	.05
310	Manny Trillo	.05
311	Jim Gott	.05
312	Marc Hill	.05
313	Dave Schmidt	.05
314	Ron Oester	.05
315	Doug Sisk	.05
316	John Lowenstein	.05
317	Jack Lazorko RC	.05
318	Ted Simmons	.05
319	Jeff Jones	.05
320	Dale Murphy	.35
321	Ricky Horton RC	.05
322	Dave Stapleton	.05
323	Andy McGaffigan	.05
324	Bruce Bochy	.05
325	John Denny	.05
326	Kevin Bass	.05
327	Brook Jacoby	.05
328	Bob Shirley	.05
329	Ron Washington	.05
330	Leon Durham	.05
331	Bill Laskey	.05
332	Brian Harper	.05
333	Willie Hernandez	.05
334	Dick Howser	.05
335	Bruce Benedict	.05
336	Rance Mulliniks	.05
337	Billy Sample	.05
338	Britt Burns	.05
339	Danny Heep	.05
340	Robin Yount	.75
341	Floyd Rayford	.05
342	Ted Power	.05
343	Bill Russell	.05
344	Dave Henderson	.05
345	Charlie Lea	.05
346	Terry Pendleton RC	.75
347	Rick Langford	.05
348	Bob Boone	.05
349	Domingo Ramos	.05
350	Wade Boggs	1.00
351	Juan Agosto	.05
352	Joe Morgan	.75
353	Julio Solano	.05
354	Andre Robertson	.05
355	Bert Blyleven	.05
356	Dave Meier	.05
357	Rich Bordi	.05
358	Tony Pena	.05
359	Pat Sheridan	.05
360	Steve Carlton	.75
361	Alfredo Griffin	.05
362	Craig McMurtry	.05
363	Ron Hodges	.05
364	Richard Dotson	.05
365	Danny Ozark	.05
366	Todd Cruz	.05
367	Keefe Cato	.05
368	Dave Bergman	.05
369	R.J. Reynolds RC	.05
370	Bruce Sutter	.65
371	Mickey Rivers	.05
372	Roy Howell	.05
373	Mike Moore	.05
374	Brian Downing	.05
375	Jeff Reardon	.05
376	Jeff Newman	.05
377	Checklist 265-396	.05
378	Alan Wiggins	.05
379	Charles Hudson	.05
380	Ken Griffey	.05
381	Roy Smith	.05
382	Denny Walling	.05
383	Rick Lysander	.05
384	Jody Davis	.05
385	Jose DeLeon	.05
386	Dan Gladden RC	.30
387	Buddy Biancalana RC	.05
388	Bert Roberge	.05
389	Rod Dedeaux (Team USA)	.05
390	Sid Akins RC (Team USA)	.05
391	Flavio Alfaro (Team USA)	.05
392	Don August RC (Team USA)	.05
393	Scott Bankhead RC (Team USA)	.10
394	Bob Caffrey RC (Team USA)	.05
395	Mike Dunne RC (Team USA)	.05
396	Gary Green RC (Team USA)	.05
397	John Hoover RC (Team USA)	.05
398	Shane Mack RC (Team USA)	.10
399	John Marzano RC (Team USA)	.05
400	Oddibe McDowell RC (Team USA)	.05
401	Mark McGwire RC (Team USA)	20.00
402	Pat Pacillo RC (Team USA)	.30
403	Cory Snyder RC (Team USA)	.30
404	Billy Swift RC (Team USA)	.40
405	Tom Veryzer	.05
406	Len Whitehouse	.05
407	Bobby Ramos	.05
408	Sid Monge	.05
409	Brad Wellman	.05
410	Bob Horner	.05
411	Bobby Cox	.05
412	Bud Black	.05
413	Vance Law	.05
414	Gary Ward	.05
415	Ron Darling	.05
416	Wayne Gross	.05
417	John Franco RC	.45
418	Ken Landreaux	.05
419	Mike Caldwell	.05
420	Andre Dawson	.50
421	Dave Rucker	.05
422	Carney Lansford	.05
423	Barry Bonnell	.05
424	Al Nipper RC	.05
425	Mike Hargrove	.05
426	Verne Ruhle	.05
427	Mario Ramirez	.05
428	Larry Andersen	.05
429	Rick Cerone	.05
430	Ron Davis	.05
431	U.L. Washington	.05
432	Thad Bosley	.05
433	Jim Morrison	.05
434	Gene Richards	.05
435	Dan Petry	.05
436	Willie Aikens	.05
437	Al Jones	.05
438	Joe Torre	.10
439	Junior Ortiz	.05
440	Fernando Valenzuela	.05
441	Duane Walker	.05
442	Ken Forsch	.05
443	George Wright	.05
444	Tony Phillips	.05
445	Tippy Martinez	.05
446	Jim Sundberg	.05
447	Jeff Lahti	.05
448	Derrel Thomas	.05
449	Phil Bradley RC	.10
450	Steve Garvey	.25
451	Bruce Hurst	.05
452	John Castino	.05
453	Tom Waddell	.05
454	Glenn Wilson	.05
455	Bob Knepper	.05
456	Tim Foli	.05
457	Cecilio Guante	.05
458	Randy S. Johnson	.05
459	Charlie Leibrandt	.05
460	Ryne Sandberg	1.00
461	Marty Castillo	.05
462	Gary Lavelle	.05
463	Dave Collins	.05
464	Mike Mason RC	.05
465	Bob Grich	.05
466	Tony LaRussa	.10
467	Ed Lynch	.05
468	Wayne Krenchicki	.05
469	Sammy Stewart	.05
470	Steve Sax	.05
471	Pete Ladd	.05
472	Jim Essian	.05
473	Tim Wallach	.05
474	Kurt Kepshire	.05
475	Andre Thornton	.05
476	Jeff Stone RC	.05
477	Bob Ojeda	.05
478	Kurt Bevacqua	.05
479	Mike Madden	.05
480	Lou Whitaker	.05
481	Dale Murray	.05
482	Harry Spilman	.05
483	Mike Smithson	.05
484	Larry Bowa	.05
485	Matt Young	.05
486	Steve Balboni	.05
487	Frank Williams RC	.05
488	Joel Skinner	.05
489	Bryan Clark	.05
490	Jason Thompson	.05
491	Rick Camp	.05
492	Dave Johnson	.05
493	Orel Hershiser RC	1.50
494	Rich Dauer	.05
495	Mario Soto	.05
496	Donnie Scott	.05
497	Gary Pettis	.05
498	Ed Romero	.05
499	Danny Cox RC	.05
500	Mike Schmidt	2.00
501	Dan Schatzeder	.05
502	Rick Miller	.05
503	Tim Conroy	.05
504	Jerry Willard	.05
505	Jim Beattie	.05
506	Franklin Stubbs RC	.05
507	Ray Fontenot	.05
508	John Shelby	.05
509	Milt May	.05
510	Kent Hrbek	.05
511	Lee Smith	.05
512	Tom Brookens	.05
513	Lynn Jones	.05
514	Jeff Cornell	.05
515	Dave Concepcion	.05
516	Roy Lee Jackson	.05
517	Jerry Martin	.05
518	Chris Chambliss	.05
519	Doug Rader	.05
520	LaMarr Hoyt	.05
521	Rick Dempsey	.05
522	Paul Molitor	.75
523	Candy Maldonado	.05
524	Rob Wilfong	.05
525	Darrell Porter	.05
526	Dave Palmer	.05
527	Checklist 397-528	.05
528	Bill Krueger	.05
529	Rich Gedman	.05
530	Dave Dravecky	.05
531	Joe Lefebvre	.05
532	Frank DiPino	.05
533	Tony Bernazard	.05
534	Brian Dayett RC	.05
535	Pat Putnam	.05
536	Kirby Puckett	7.50
537	Don Robinson	.05
538	Keith Moreland	.05
539	Aurelio Lopez	.05
540	Claudell Washington	.05
541	Mark Davis	.05
542	Don Slaught	.05
543	Mike Squires	.05
544	Bruce Kison	.05
545	Lloyd Moseby	.05
546	Brent Gaff	.05
547	Pete Rose	1.50
548	Larry Parrish	.05
549	Mike Scioscia	.05
550	Scott McGregor	.05
551	Andy Van Slyke	.05
552	Chris Codiroli	.05
553	Bob Clark	.05
554	Doug Flynn	.05
555	Bob Stanley	.05
556	Sixto Lezcano	.05
557	Len Barker	.05
558	Carmelo Martinez	.05
559	Jay Howell	.05
560	Bill Madlock	.05
561	Darryl Motley	.05
562	Houston Jimenez	.05
563	Dick Ruthven	.05
564	Alan Ashby	.05
565	Kirk Gibson	.05
566	Ed Vande Berg	.05
567	Joel Youngblood	.05
568	Cliff Johnson	.05
569	Ken Oberkfell	.05
570	Darryl Strawberry	.10
571	Charlie Hough	.05
572	Tom Paciorek	.05
573	Jay Tibbs RC	.05
574	Joe Altobelli	.05
575	Pedro Guerrero	.05
576	Jaime Cocanower	.05
577	Chris Speier	.05
578	Terry Francona	.05
579	Ron Romanick RC	.05
580	Dwight Evans	.05
581	Mark Wagner	.05
582	Ken Phelps RC	.05
583	Bobby Brown	.05
584	Kevin Gross	.05
585	Butch Wynegar	.05
586	Bill Scherrer	.05
587	Doug Frobel	.05
588	Bobby Castillo	.05
589	Bob Dernier	.05
590	Ray Knight	.05
591	Larry Herndon	.05
592	Jeff Robinson RC	.05
593	Rick Leach	.05
594	Curt Wilkerson RC	.05
595	Larry Gura	.05
596	Jerry Hairston Sr.	.05
597	Brad Lesley	.05
598	Jose Oquendo	.05
599	Storm Davis	.05
600	Pete Rose	3.00
601	Tom Lasorda	.10
602	Jeff Dedmon RC	.05
603	Rick Manning	.05
604	Daryl Sconiers	.05
605	Ozzie Smith	1.00
606	Rich Gale	.05
607	Bill Almon	.05
608	Craig Lefferts	.05
609	Broderick Perkins	.05
610	Jack Morris	.05
611	Ozzie Virgil	.05
612	Mike Armstrong	.05
613	Terry Puhl	.05
614	Al Williams	.05
615	Marvell Wynne	.05
616	Scott Sanderson	.05
617	Willie Wilson	.05
618	Pete Falcone	.05
619	Jeff Leonard	.05
620	Dwight Gooden	.50
621	Marvis Foley	.05
622	Luis Leal	.05
623	Greg Walker	.05
624	Benny Ayala	.05
625	Mark Langston	.05
626	German Rivera	.05
627	Eric Davis RC	.45
628	Rene Lachemann	.05
629	Dick Schofield	.05
630	Tim Raines	.05

631	Bob Forsch	.05
632	Bruce Bochte	.05
633	Glenn Hoffman	.05
634	Bill Dawley	.05
635	Terry Kennedy	.05
636	Shane Rawley	.05
637	Brett Butler	.05
638	Mike Pagliarulo RC	.10
639	Ed Hodge	.05
640	Steve Henderson	.05
641	Rod Scurry	.05
642	Dave Owen	.05
643	Johnny Grubb	.05
644	Mark Huismann RC	.05
645	Damaso Garcia	.05
646	Scot Thompson	.05
647	Rafael Ramirez	.05
648	Bob Jones	.05
649	Sid Fernandez RC	.05
650	Greg Luzinski	.05
651	Jeff Russell	.05
652	Joe Nolan	.05
653	Mark Brouhard	.05
654	Dave Anderson	.05
655	Joaquin Andujar	.05
656	Chuck Cottier	.05
657	Jim Slaton	.05
658	Mike Stenhouse	.05
659	Checklist 529-660	.05
660	Tony Gwynn	1.00
661	Steve Crawford	.05
662	Mike Heath	.05
663	Luis Aguayo	.05
664	Steve Farr RC	.05
665	Don Mattingly	2.00
666	Mike LaCoss	.05
667	Dave Engle	.05
668	Steve Trout	.05
669	Lee Lacy	.05
670	Tom Seaver	.75
671	Dane Iorg	.05
672	Juan Berenguer	.05
673	Buck Martinez	.05
674	Atlee Hammaker	.05
675	Tony Perez	.75
676	Albert Hall RC	.05
677	Wally Backman	.05
678	Joey McLaughlin	.05
679	Bob Kearney	.05
680	Jerry Reuss	.05
681	Ben Oglivie	.05
682	Doug Corbett	.05
683	Whitey Herzog	.05
684	Bill Doran	.05
685	Bill Caudill	.05
686	Mike Easler	.05
687	Bill Gullickson	.05
688	Len Matuszek	.05
689	Luis DeLeon	.05
690	Alan Trammell	.05
691	Dennis Rasmussen RC	.05
692	Randy Bush	.05
693	Tim Stoddard	.05
694	Joe Carter	.05
695	Rick Rhoden	.05
696	John Rabb	.05
697	Onix Concepcion	.05
698	Jorge Bell	.05
699	Donnie Moore	.05
700	Eddie Murray	.75
701	Eddie Murray/AS	.40
702	Damaso Garcia/AS	.05
703	George Brett/AS	.50
704	Cal Ripken, Jr./AS	1.50
705	Dave Winfield/AS	.40
706	Rickey Henderson/AS	.35
707	Tony Armas/AS	.05
708	Lance Parrish/AS	.05
709	Mike Boddicker/AS	.05
710	Frank Viola/AS	.05
711	Dan Quisenberry/AS	.05
712	Keith Hernandez/AS	.05
713	Ryne Sandberg/AS	.40
714	Mike Schmidt/AS	.75
715	Ozzie Smith/AS	.50
716	Dale Murphy/AS	.15
717	Tony Gwynn/AS	.75
718	Jeff Leonard/AS	.05
719	Gary Carter/AS	.35
720	Rick Sutcliffe/AS	.05
721	Bob Knepper/AS	.05
722	Bruce Sutter/AS	.30
723	Dave Stewart	.05
724	Oscar Gamble	.05
725	Floyd Bannister	.05
726	Al Bumbry	.05
727	Frank Pastore	.05
728	Bob Bailor	.05
729	Don Sutton	.60
730	Dave Kingman	.05
731	Neil Allen	.05
732	John McNamara	.05
733	Tony Scott	.05
734	John Henry Johnson	.05
735	Garry Templeton	.05
736	Jerry Mumphrey	.05
737	Bo Diaz	.05
738	Omar Moreno	.05
739	Ernie Camacho	.05
740	Jack Clark	.05
741	John Butcher	.05
742	Ron Hassey	.05
743	Frank White	.05
744	Doug Bair	.05
745	Buddy Bell	.05
746	Jim Clancy	.05
747	Alex Trevino	.05
748	Lee Mazzilli	.05

749	Julio Cruz	.05
750	Rollie Fingers	.60
751	Kelvin Chapman	.05
752	Bob Owchinko	.05
753	Greg Brock	.05
754	Larry Milbourne	.05
755	Ken Singleton	.05
756	Rob Picciolo	.05
757	Willie McGee	.05
758	Ray Burris	.05
759	Jim Fanning	.05
760	Nolan Ryan	4.00
761	Jerry Remy	.05
762	Eddie Whitson	.05
763	Kiko Garcia	.05
764	Jamie Easterly	.05
765	Willie Randolph	.05
766	Paul Mirabella	.05
767	Darrell Brown	.05
768	Ron Cey	.05
769	Joe Cowley	.05
770	Carlton Fisk	.75
771	Geoff Zahn	.05
772	Johnnie LeMaster	.05
773	Hal McRae	.05
774	Dennis Lamp	.05
775	Mookie Wilson	.05
776	Jerry Royster	.05
777	Ned Yost	.05
778	Mike Davis	.05
779	Nick Esasky	.05
780	Mike Flanagan	.05
781	Jim Gantner	.05
782	Tom Niedenfuer	.05
783	Mike Jorgensen	.05
784	Checklist 661-792	.05
785	Tony Armas	.05
786	Enos Cabell	.05
787	Jim Wohlford	.05
788	Steve Comer	.05
789	Luis Salazar	.05
790	Ron Guidry	.10
791	Ivan DeJesus	.05
792	Darrell Evans	.05

Tiffany

In its second year of producing a high-gloss collectors' edition of its regular baseball card set, Topps cut production to a reported 5,000 sets. Other than the use of white cardboard stock and the glossy front coating, the cards in this specially boxed set are identical to regular 1985 Topps cards.

	NM/M
Complete Unopened Set (792):	500.00
Complete Set, Opened (792):	325.00
Common Player:	.25
Stars:	4X
181 Roger Clemens	100.00
401 Mark McGwire	90.00

Traded

Topps continued the annual Traded set tradition with another 132-card set. The 2-1/2" x 3-1/2" cards follow the pattern of being virtually identical in design to the regular cards of that year. Sold only through hobby dealers, the set features traded veterans and promising rookies. A glossy-finish "Tiffany" edition of the set was also issued. Cards are numbered with a "T" suffix.

	NM/M
Complete Set (132):	10.00
Common Player:	.05
Wax Test Pack (8):	10.00
Wax Test Wax Box (36):	150.00
1 Don Aase	.05
2 Bill Almon	.05
3 Benny Ayala	.05
4 Dusty Baker	.25
5 George Bamberger	.05
6 Dale Berra	.05
7 Rich Bordi	.05

8	Daryl Boston RC	.05
9	Hubie Brooks	.05
10	Chris Brown RC	.05
11	Tom Browning RC	.05
12	Al Bumbry	.05
13	Ray Burris	.05
14	Jeff Burroughs	.05
15	Bill Campbell	.05
16	Don Carman RC	.05
17	Gary Carter	1.50
18	Bobby Castillo	.05
19	Bill Caudill	.05
20	Rick Cerone	.05
21	Bryan Clark	.05
22	Jack Clark	.05
23	Pat Clements RC	.05
24	Vince Coleman RC	.50
25	Dave Collins	.05
26	Danny Darwin	.05
27	Jim Davenport	.05
28	Jerry Davis	.05
29	Brian Dayett	.05
30	Ivan DeJesus	.05
31	Ken Dixon	.05
32	Mariano Duncan RC	.05
33	John Felske	.05
34	Mike Fitzgerald	.05
35	Ray Fontenot	.05
36	Greg Gagne RC	.05
37	Oscar Gamble	.05
38	Scott Garrelts RC	.05
39	Bob L. Gibson	.05
40	Jim Gott	.05
41	David Green	.05
42	Alfredo Griffin	.05
43	Ozzie Guillen RC	3.00
44	Eddie Haas	.05
45	Terry Harper	.05
46	Toby Harrah	.05
47	Greg Harris	.05
48	Ron Hassey	.05
49	Rickey Henderson	2.50
50	Steve Henderson	.05
51	George Hendrick	.05
52	Joe Hesketh RC	.05
53	Teddy Higuera RC	.05
54	Donnie Hill	.05
55	Al Holland	.05
56	Burt Hooton	.05
57	Jay Howell	.05
58	Ken Howell RC	.05
59	LaMarr Hoyt	.05
60	Tim Hulett RC	.05
61	Bob James	.05
62	Steve Jeltz RC	.05
63	Cliff Johnson	.05
64	Howard Johnson	.05
65	Ruppert Jones	.05
66	Steve Kemp	.05
67	Bruce Kison	.05
68	Alan Knicely	.05
69	Mike LaCoss	.05
70	Lee Lacy	.05
71	Dave LaPoint	.05
72	Gary Lavelle	.05
73	Vance Law	.05
74	Johnnie LeMaster	.05
75	Sixto Lezcano	.05
76	Tim Lollar	.05
77	Fred Lynn	.05
78	Billy Martin	.25
79	Ron Mathis	.05
80	Len Matuszek	.05
81	Gene Mauch	.05
82	Oddibe McDowell	.05
83	Roger McDowell RC	.05
84	John McNamara	.05
85	Donnie Moore	.05
86	Gene Nelson	.05
87	Steve Nicosia	.05
88	Al Oliver	.05
89	Joe Orsulak RC	.05
90	Rob Picciolo	.05
91	Chris Pittaro	.05
92	Jim Presley RC	.05
93	Rick Reuschel	.05
94	Bert Roberge	.05
95	Bob Rodgers	.05
96	Jerry Royster	.05
97	Dave Rozema	.05
98	Dave Rucker	.05
99	Vern Ruhle	.05
100	Paul Runge RC	.05
101	Mark Salas RC	.05
102	Luis Salazar	.05
103	Joe Sambito	.05
104	Rick Schu RC	.05
105	Donnie Scott	.05
106	Larry Sheets RC	.05
107	Don Slaught	.05
108	Roy Smalley	.05
109	Lonnie Smith	.05
110	Nate Snell	.05
111	Chris Speier	.05
112	Mike Stenhouse	.05
113	Tim Stoddard	.05
114	Jim Sundberg	.05
115	Bruce Sutter	1.00
116	Don Sutton	.50
117	Kent Tekulve	.05
118	Tom Tellmann	.05
119	Walt Terrell	.05
120	Mickey Tettleton RC	1.00
121	Derrel Thomas	.05
122	Rich Thompson	.05
123	Alex Trevino	.05
124	John Tudor	.05
125	Jose Uribe RC	.05

126	Bobby Valentine	.05
127	Dave Von Ohlen	.05
128	U.L. Washington	.05
129	Earl Weaver	.05
130	Eddie Whitson	.05
131	Herm Winningham RC	.05
132	Checklist 1-132	.05

Traded Tiffany

This specially boxed collectors version of the Topps Traded sets features cards that differ only in the use of a high-gloss finish coat on the fronts.

	NM/M
Complete Set (132):	35.00
Common Player:	.25
Stars:	4X

Traded Pete Rose Bronze

This 1/4-size metal replica was issued to dealers who purchased cases of 1985 Topps Traded sets. Each detail of the 1985 Topps Pete Rose card is reproduced on the 1-3/4" x 1-3/4" bronze metal mini-card, right down to the stats.

	NM/M
600 Pete Rose	10.00

All-Star Glossy Set of 22

This was the second straight year for this set of 22 cards featuring the starting players, honorary captains and managers in the All-Star Game. The set is virtually identical to that of the previous year in design with a color photo, All-Star banner, league emblem, and player ID on the front. Fronts have a high-gloss finish. The cards were available as inserts in Topps rack packs.

	NM/M
Complete Set (22):	5.00
Common Player:	.10
1 Paul Owens	.10
2 Steve Garvey	.30
3 Ryne Sandberg	.50
4 Mike Schmidt	1.00
5 Ozzie Smith	.50
6 Tony Gwynn	.50
7 Dale Murphy	.30
8 Darryl Strawberry	.40
9 Gary Carter	.40
10 Charlie Lea	.10
11 Willie McCovey	.30
12 Joe Altobelli	.10
13 Rod Carew	.40
14 Lou Whitaker	.10
15 George Brett	1.00
16 Cal Ripken, Jr.	1.50
17 Dave Winfield	.40
18 Chet Lemon	.10
19 Reggie Jackson	.50
20 Lance Parrish	.10

21	Dave Stieb	.10
22	Hank Greenberg	.25

All-Star Glossy Set of 40

Similar to previous years' glossy sets, the 1985 All-Star "Collector's Edition" set of 40 could be obtained through the mail in eight five-card subsets. To obtain the 2-1/2" x 3-1/2" cards, collectors had to accumulate sweepstakes insert cards from Topps packs, and pay 75¢ postage and handling. Under the circumstances, the complete set of 40 cards was not inexpensive.

	NM/M
Complete Set (40):	8.00
Common Player:	.10
1 Dale Murphy	.30
2 Jesse Orosco	.10
3 Bob Brenly	.10
4 Mike Boddicker	.10
5 Dave Kingman	.10
6 Jim Rice	.20
7 Frank Viola	.10
8 Alvin Davis	.10
9 Rick Sutcliffe	.10
10 Pete Rose	2.00
11 Leon Durham	.10
12 Joaquin Andujar	.10
13 Keith Hernandez	.10
14 Dave Winfield	.40
15 Reggie Jackson	.50
16 Alan Trammell	.10
17 Bert Blyleven	.10
18 Tony Armas	.10
19 Rich Gossage	.10
20 Jose Cruz	.10
21 Ryne Sandberg	.50
22 Bruce Sutter	.30
23 Mike Schmidt	1.00
24 Cal Ripken, Jr.	3.00
25 Dan Petry	.10
26 Jack Morris	.10
27 Don Mattingly	1.00
28 Eddie Murray	.40
29 Tony Gwynn	.50
30 Charlie Lea	.10
31 Juan Samuel	.10
32 Phil Niekro	.30
33 Alejandro Pena	.10
34 Harold Baines	.10
35 Dan Quisenberry	.10
36 Gary Carter	.40
37 Mario Soto	.10
38 Dwight Gooden	.40
39 Tom Brunansky	.10
40 Dave Stieb	.10

All-Time Record Holders

ALL-TIME RECORD HOLDER
STEVE CARLTON
Philadelphia Phillies

Gallery of Champions

This second annual metallic miniatures issue honors 12 award winners from the previous season (MVP, Cy Young, Rookie of Year, Fireman, etc.).

YANKEES
1B
DON MATTINGLY

Each mini is an exact reproduction at one-quarter scale of the player's 1985 Topps card, both front and back. The sets (editions of 1,000) were issued in a specially-designed velvet-like case. A Dwight Gooden pewter replica was given as a premium to dealers who bought the sets.

	NM/M
Complete Bronze Set (12):	60.00
Complete Silver Set (12):	280.00
(1b) Tony Armas/Bronze	3.00
(1s) Tony Armas/Silver	10.00
(2b) Alvin Davis/Bronze	3.00
(2s) Alvin Davis/Silver	10.00
(3b) Dwight Gooden/Bronze	5.00
(3s) Dwight Gooden/Silver	15.00
(3p) Dwight Gooden/Pewter	6.00
(4b) Tony Gwynn/Bronze	15.00
(4s) Tony Gwynn/Silver	50.00
(5b) Willie Hernandez/Bronze	3.00
(5s) Willie Hernandez/Silver	10.00
(6b) Don Mattingly/Bronze	30.00
(6s) Don Mattingly/Silver	75.00
(7b) Dale Murphy/Bronze	30.00
(7s) Dale Murphy/Silver	45.00
(8b) Dan Quisenberry/Bronze	3.00
(8s) Dan Quisenberry/Silver	10.00
(9b) Ryne Sandberg/Bronze	15.00
(9s) Ryne Sandberg/Silver	50.00
(10b) Mike Schmidt/Silver	25.00
(10s) Mike Schmidt/Silver	60.00
(11b) Rick Sutcliffe/Bronze	3.00
(11s) Rick Sutcliffe/Silver	10.00
(12b) Bruce Sutter/Bronze	6.00
(12s) Bruce Sutter/Silver	20.00

Minis

CARDINALS
1B
ANDY VAN SLYKE

Never released for public sale, quantities of these enigmatic cards nevertheless reached the hobby market. Smaller than the standard 2-1/2" x 3-1/2" Topps cards, the "mini" version measures 2-3/8" x 3-9/32", 10 percent smaller than regular cards. Printed in Canada, the minis use a whiter cardboard stock than the regular '85 Topps, making the color printing more vibrant. The minis were the result of a test of new printing equipment by O-Pee-Chee, Topps' Canadian licensee. Only 132 of the 792 cards in the '85 Topps set are found in mini version. Only about 100 of each mini card are known, including about 15 percent blank-backs.

	NM/M
Complete Set (132):	1,500

Common Player: 5.00
Blank-backs: 50%

#	Player	Price
12	Dave Lopes	5.00
15	Jerry Koosman	5.00
17	Mike Scott	5.00
25	Steve Bedrosian	5.00
44	Dickie Thon	5.00
65	Bill Buckner	5.00
68	Von Hayes	5.00
72	Rick Sutcliffe	5.00
75	Willie Upshaw	5.00
82	Joe Price	5.00
88	Bryn Smith	5.00
91	Jeff Burroughs	5.00
95	Jose Cruz	5.00
96	Johnny Ray	5.00
109	Gary Roenicke	5.00
113	Tom Herr	5.00
114	Bob James	5.00
117	Greg Gross	5.00
120	Steve Kemp	5.00
121	Checklist 1-132	3.00
128	Ernie Whitt	5.00
148	Steve Yeager	5.00
150	Jim Rice	15.00
151	Moose Haas	5.00
154	Argenis Salazar	5.00
156	Craig Reynolds	5.00
160	Lance Parrish	5.00
170	Dusty Baker	5.00
170	George Foster	5.00
178	Miguel Dilone	5.00
185	Al Holland	5.00
190	Rusty Staub	5.00
198	Eddie Milner	5.00
201	Burt Hooton	5.00
205	Steve Rogers	5.00
209	Bill Campbell	5.00
210	Gary Matthews	5.00
218	Doyle Alexander	5.00
222	Hubie Brooks	5.00
223	Tom Hume	5.00
225	Mike Boddicker	5.00
229	Dave LaPoint	5.00
230	Gary Carter	45.00
235	Garry Maddox	5.00
236	Mark Thurmond	5.00
237	Julio Franco	5.00
239	Tim Teufel	5.00
248	Terry Forster	5.00
250	Jesse Orosco	5.00
251	Brad Gulden	5.00
255	Lonnie Smith	5.00
261	Checklist 133-264	3.00
263	Mel Hall	5.00
266	Frank Viola	5.00
287	Walt Terrell	5.00
306	Rick Reuschel	5.00
310	Manny Trillo	5.00
313	Dave Schmidt	5.00
325	John Denny	5.00
330	Leon Durham	5.00
333	Willie Hernandez	5.00
340	Robin Yount	45.00
343	Bill Russell	5.00
345	Charlie Lea	5.00
352	Joe Morgan	45.00
355	Bert Blyleven	5.00
358	Tony Pena	5.00
360	Steve Carlton	45.00
362	Craig McMurtry	5.00
375	Jeff Reardon	5.00
379	Charles Hudson	5.00
415	Ron Darling	5.00
445	Tippy Martinez	5.00
446	Jim Sundberg	5.00
450	Steve Garvey	7.50
452	John Castino	5.00
464	Mike Mason	5.00
470	Steve Sax	5.00
485	Matt Young	5.00
487	Frank Williams	5.00
489	Bryan Clark	5.00
491	Rick Camp	5.00
495	Mario Soto	5.00
500	Mike Schmidt	250.00
501	Dan Schatzeder	5.00
504	Jerry Willard	5.00
511	Lee Smith	5.00
515	Dave Concepcion	5.00
520	LaMarr Hoyt	5.00
526	Dave Palmer	5.00
530	Dave Dravecky	5.00
538	Keith Moreland	5.00
545	Lloyd Moseby	5.00
551	Andy Van Slyke	5.00
554	Doug Flynn	5.00
556	Sixto Lezcano	5.00
563	Bill Madlock	5.00
563	Dick Ruthven	5.00
566	Ed Vande Berg	5.00
568	Cliff Johnson	5.00
569	Ken Oberkfell	5.00
575	Pedro Guerrero	5.00
580	Dwight Evans	5.00
592	Bob Dernier	5.00
592	Jeff Robinson	5.00
603	Rick Manning	5.00
608	Craig Lefferts	5.00
610	Jack Morris	5.00
613	Terry Puhl	5.00
615	Marvell Wynne	5.00
619	Jeff Leonard	5.00
625	Mark Langston	5.00
630	Tim Raines	5.00
634	Bill Dawley	5.00
670	Tom Seaver	45.00
673	Buck Martinez	5.00
674	Atlee Hammaker	5.00
685	Bill Caudill	5.00
700	Eddie Murray	45.00
725	Floyd Bannister	5.00
729	Don Sutton	10.00
731	Neil Allen	5.00
736	Jerry Mumphrey	5.00
748	Lee Mazzilli	5.00
753	Greg Brock	5.00
755	Ken Singleton	5.00
757	Willie McGee	5.00
760	Nolan Ryan	650.00
762	Eddie Whitson	5.00
775	Mookie Wilson	5.00
780	Mike Flanagan	5.00
782	Tom Niedenfuer	5.00

Rub Downs

Similar in size and design to the Rub Downs of the previous year, the 1985 set again consisted of 32 unnumbered sheets featuring 112 different players. The set was sold by Topps as a separate issue.

		NM/M
Complete Set (32):		5.00
Common Sheet:		.25
Pack (2):		.50
Wax Box (36):		7.50

(1) Tony Armas, Harold Baines, Lonnie Smith .25
(2) Don Baylor, George Hendrick, Ron Kittle .25
(3) Buddy Bell, Tony Gwynn, Lloyd Moseby .75
(4) Bruce Benedict, Atlee Hammaker, Frank White .25
(5) Mike Boddicker, Rod Carew, Carlton Fisk, Johnny Ray .60
(6) Wade Boggs, Rick Dempsey, Keith Hernandez .60
(7) George Brett, Andre Dawson, Paul Molitor, Alan Wiggins 1.00
(8) Tom Brunansky, Pedro Guerrero, Darryl Strawberry .25
(9) Bill Buckner, Tim Raines, Ryne Sandberg, Mike Schmidt 1.00
(10) Steve Carlton, Bob Horner, Dan Quisenberry .60
(11) Gary Carter, Phil Garner, Ron Guidry .60
(12) Jack Clark, Damaso Garcia, Hal McRae, Lance Parrish .25
(13) Dave Concepcion, Cecil Cooper, Fred Lynn, Jesse Orosco .25
(14) Jose Cruz, Jack Morris, Jim Rice, Rick Sutcliffe .25
(15) Alvin Davis, Steve Kemp, Greg Luzinski, Kent Tekulve .25
(16) Ron Davis, Kent Hrbek, Juan Samuel .25
(17) John Denny, Carney Lansford, Mario Soto, Lou Whitaker .25
(18) Leon Durham, Willie Hernandez, Steve Sax .25
(19) Dwight Evans, Julio Franco, Dwight Gooden .25
(20) George Foster, Gary Gaetti, Bobby Grich, Gary Redus .25
(21) Steve Garvey, Jerry Remy, Bill Russell, George Wright .25
(22) Kirk Gibson, Rich Gossage, Don Mattingly, Dave Stieb 1.00
(23) Moose Haas, Bruce Sutter, Dickie Thon, Andre Thornton .25
(24) Rickey Henderson, Dave Righetti, Pete Rose 1.50
(25) Steve Henderson, Bill Madlock, Alan Trammell .25
(26) LaMarr Hoyt, Larry Parrish, Nolan Ryan 2.00
(27) Reggie Jackson, Eric Show, Jason Thompson .75
(28) Terry Kennedy, Eddie Murray, Tom Seaver, Ozzie Smith .75
(29) Mark Langston, Ben Oglivie, Darrell Porter .25
(30) Jeff Leonard, Gary Matthews, Dale Murphy, Dave Winfield .60
(31) Craig McMurtry, Cal Ripken, Jr., Steve Rogers, Willie Upshaw 2.00
(32) Tony Pena, Fernando Valenzuela, Robin Yount .60

Stickers

Topps went to a larger size for its stickers in 1985. Produced by Panini, each of the 376 stickers measures 2-1/8" x 3" and is numbered on both the front and the back. The backs contain either an offer to obtain an autographed team ball or a poster. An album was also available.

		NM/M
Complete Set (376):		12.50
Common Player:		.05
Sticker Album:		2.00
Pack (5):		.25
Box (100):		15.00

#	Player	Price
1	Steve Garvey	.15
2	Steve Garvey	.15
3	Dwight Gooden	.05
4	Dwight Gooden	.05
5	Joe Morgan	.30
6	Joe Morgan	.30
7	Don Sutton	.30
8	Don Sutton	.30
9	1984 A.L. Championships (Jack Morris)	.05
10	1984 A.L. Championships (Milt Wilcox)	.05
11	1984 A.L. Championships (Kirk Gibson)	.05
12	1984 N.L. Championships (Gary Matthews)	.05
13	1984 N.L. Championships (Steve Garvey)	.05
14	1984 N.L. Championships (Steve Garvey)	.05
15	1984 World Series (Jack Morris)	.05
16	1984 World Series (Kurt Bevacqua)	.05
17	1984 World Series (Milt Wilcox)	.05
18	1984 World Series (Alan Trammell)	.05
19	1984 World Series (Kirk Gibson)	.05
20	1984 World Series (Alan Trammell)	.05
21	1984 World Series (Chet Lemon)	.05
22	Dale Murphy	.25
23	Steve Bedrosian	.05
24	Bob Horner	.05
25	Claudell Washington	.05
26	Rick Mahler	.05
27	Rafael Ramirez	.05
28	Craig McMurtry	.05
29	Chris Chambliss	.05
30	Alex Trevino	.05
31	Bruce Benedict	.05
32	Ken Oberkfell	.05
33	Glenn Hubbard	.05
34	Ryne Sandberg	.40
35	Rick Sutcliffe	.05
36	Leon Durham	.05
37	Jody Davis	.05
38	Bob Dernier	.05
39	Keith Moreland	.05
40	Scott Sanderson	.05
41	Lee Smith	.05
42	Ron Cey	.05
43	Steve Trout	.05
44	Gary Matthews	.05
45	Larry Bowa	.05
46	Mario Soto	.05
47	Dave Parker	.05
48	Dave Concepcion	.05
49	Gary Redus	.05
50	Ted Power	.05
51	Nick Esasky	.05
52	Duane Walker	.05
53	Eddie Milner	.05
54	Ron Oester	.05
55	Cesar Cedeno	.05
56	Joe Price	.05
57	Pete Rose	.65
58	Nolan Ryan	.75
59	Jose Cruz	.05
60	Jerry Mumphrey	.05
61	Enos Cabell	.05
62	Bob Knepper	.05
63	Dickie Thon	.05
64	Phil Garner	.05
65	Craig Reynolds	.05
66	Frank DiPino	.05
67	Terry Puhl	.05
68	Bill Doran	.05
69	Joe Niekro	.05
70	Pedro Guerrero	.05
71	Fernando Valenzuela	.05
72	Mike Marshall	.05
73	Alejandro Pena	.05
74	Orel Hershiser	.10
75	Ken Landreaux	.05
76	Bill Russell	.05
77	Steve Sax	.05
78	Rick Honeycutt	.05
79	Mike Scioscia	.05
80	Tom Niedenfuer	.05
81	Candy Maldonado	.05
82	Tim Raines	.05
83	Gary Carter	.30
84	Charlie Lea	.05
85	Jeff Reardon	.05
86	Andre Dawson	.15
87	Tim Wallach	.05
88	Terry Francona	.05
89	Steve Rogers	.05
90	Bryn Smith	.05
91	Bill Gullickson	.05
92	Dan Driessen	.05
93	Doug Flynn	.05
94	Mike Schmidt	.50
95	Tony Armas	.05
96	Dale Murphy	.15
97	Rick Sutcliffe	.05
98	Keith Hernandez	.05
99	George Foster	.05
100	Darryl Strawberry	.05
101	Jesse Orosco	.05
102	Mookie Wilson	.05
103	Doug Sisk	.05
104	Hubie Brooks	.05
105	Ron Darling	.05
106	Wally Backman	.05
107	Dwight Gooden	.05
108	Mike Fitzgerald	.05
109	Walt Terrell	.05
110	Ozzie Virgil	.05
111	Mike Schmidt	.50
112	Steve Carlton	.30
113	Al Holland	.05
114	Juan Samuel	.05
115	Von Hayes	.05
116	Jeff Stone	.05
117	Jerry Koosman	.05
118	Al Oliver	.05
119	John Denny	.05
120	Charles Hudson	.05
121	Garry Maddox	.05
122	Bill Madlock	.05
123	John Candelaria	.05
124	Tony Pena	.05
125	Jason Thompson	.05
126	Lee Lacy	.05
127	Rick Rhoden	.05
128	Doug Frobel	.05
129	Kent Tekulve	.05
130	Johnny Ray	.05
131	Marvell Wynne	.05
132	Larry McWilliams	.05
133	Dale Berra	.05
134	George Hendrick	.05
135	Bruce Sutter	.20
136	Joaquin Andujar	.05
137	Ozzie Smith	.50
138	Andy Van Slyke	.05
139	Lonnie Smith	.05
140	Darrell Porter	.05
141	Willie McGee	.05
142	Tom Herr	.05
143	Dave LaPoint	.05
144	Neil Allen	.05
145	David Green	.05
146	Tony Gwynn	.50
147	Rich Gossage	.05
148	Terry Kennedy	.05
149	Steve Garvey	.15
150	Alan Wiggins	.05
151	Garry Templeton	.05
152	Ed Whitson	.05
153	Tim Lollar	.05
154	Dave Dravecky	.05
155	Graig Nettles	.05
156	Eric Show	.05
157	Carmelo Martinez	.05
158	Bob Brenly	.05
159	Gary Lavelle	.05
160	Jack Clark	.05
161	Jeff Leonard	.05
162	Chili Davis	.05
163	Mike Krukow	.05
164	Johnnie LeMaster	.05
165	Atlee Hammaker	.05
166	Dan Gladden	.05
167	Greg Minton	.05
168	Joel Youngblood	.05
169	Frank Williams	.05
170	Tony Gwynn	.50
171	Don Mattingly	.60
172	Bruce Sutter	.05
173	Dan Quisenberry	.05
174	Tony Gwynn	.50
175	Ryne Sandberg	.40
176	Steve Garvey	.15
177	Dale Murphy	.15
178	Mike Schmidt	.50
179	Darryl Strawberry	.05
180	Gary Carter	.30
181	Ozzie Smith	.50
182	Charlie Lea	.05
183	Lou Whitaker	.05
184	Rod Carew	.30
185	Cal Ripken, Jr.	.75
186	Dave Winfield	.40
187	Reggie Jackson	.40
188	George Brett	.50
189	Lance Parrish	.05
190	Chet Lemon	.05
191	Dave Stieb	.05
192	Gary Carter	.30
193	Mike Schmidt	.50
194	Tony Armas	.05
195	Mike Witt	.05
196	Eddie Murray	.25
197	Cal Ripken, Jr.	.75
198	Scott McGregor	.05
199	Rick Dempsey	.05
200	Tippy Martinez	.05
201	Ken Singleton	.05
202	Mike Boddicker	.05
203	Rich Dauer	.05
204	John Shelby	.05
205	Al Bumbry	.05
206	John Lowenstein	.05
207	Mike Flanagan	.05
208	Jim Rice	.10
209	Tony Armas	.05
210	Wade Boggs	.40
211	Bruce Hurst	.05
212	Dwight Evans	.05
213	Mike Easler	.05
214	Bill Buckner	.05
215	Bob Stanley	.05
216	Jackie Gutierrez	.05
217	Rich Gedman	.05
218	Jerry Remy	.05
219	Marty Barrett	.05
220	Reggie Jackson	.40
221	Geoff Zahn	.05
222	Doug DeCinces	.05
223	Rod Carew	.30
224	Brian Downing	.05
225	Fred Lynn	.05
226	Gary Pettis	.05
227	Mike Witt	.05
228	Bob Boone	.05
229	Tommy John	.05
230	Bobby Grich	.05
231	Ron Romanick	.05
232	Ron Kittle	.05
233	Richard Dotson	.05
234	Harold Baines	.05
235	Tom Seaver	.40
236	Greg Walker	.05
237	Roy Smalley	.05
238	Greg Luzinski	.05
239	Julio Cruz	.05
240	Scott Fletcher	.05
241	Rudy Law	.05
242	Vance Law	.05
243	Carlton Fisk	.30
244	Andre Thornton	.05
245	Julio Franco	.05
246	Brett Butler	.05
247	Bert Blyleven	.05
248	Mike Hargrove	.05
249	George Vukovich	.05
250	Pat Tabler	.05
251	Brook Jacoby	.05
252	Tony Bernazard	.05
253	Ernie Camacho	.05
254	Mel Hall	.05
255	Carmen Castillo	.05
256	Jack Morris	.05
257	Willie Hernandez	.05
258	Alan Trammell	.05
259	Lance Parrish	.05
260	Chet Lemon	.05
261	Lou Whitaker	.05
262	Howard Johnson	.05
263	Barbaro Garbey	.05
264	Dan Petry	.05
265	Aurelio Lopez	.05
266	Larry Herndon	.05
267	Kirk Gibson	.05
268	George Brett	.50
269	Dan Quisenberry	.05
270	Hal McRae	.05
271	Steve Balboni	.05
272	Pat Sheridan	.05
273	Jorge Orta	.05
274	Frank White	.05
275	Bud Black	.05
276	Darryl Motley	.05
277	Willie Wilson	.05
278	Larry Gura	.05
279	Don Slaught	.05
280	Dwight Gooden	.05
281	Mark Langston	.05
282	Tim Raines	.05
283	Rickey Henderson	.30
284	Robin Yount	.30
285	Rollie Fingers	.30
286	Jim Sundberg	.05
287	Cecil Cooper	.05
288	Jaime Cocanower	.05
289	Mike Caldwell	.05
290	Don Sutton	.30
291	Rick Manning	.05
292	Ben Oglivie	.05
293	Moose Haas	.05
294	Ted Simmons	.05
295	Jim Gantner	.05
296	Kent Hrbek	.05
297	Ron Davis	.05
298	Dave Engle	.05
299	Tom Brunansky	.05
300	Frank Viola	.05
301	Mike Smithson	.05
302	Gary Gaetti	.05
303	Tim Teufel	.05
304	Mickey Hatcher	.05
305	John Butcher	.05
306	Darrell Brown	.05
307	Kirby Puckett	.50
308	Dave Winfield	.40
309	Phil Niekro	.30
310	Don Mattingly	.60
311	Don Baylor	.05
312	Willie Randolph	.05
313	Ron Guidry	.05
314	Dave Righetti	.05
315	Bobby Meacham	.05
316	Butch Wynegar	.05
317	Mike Pagliarulo	.05
318	Joe Cowley	.05
319	John Montefusco	.05
320	Dave Kingman	.05
321	Rickey Henderson	.30
322	Bill Caudill	.05
323	Dwayne Murphy	.05
324	Steve McCatty	.05
325	Joe Morgan	.30
326	Mike Heath	.05
327	Chris Codiroli	.05
328	Ray Burris	.05
329	Tony Phillips	.05
330	Carney Lansford	.05
331	Bruce Bochte	.05
332	Alvin Davis	.05
333	Al Cowens	.05
334	Jim Beattie	.05
335	Bob Kearney	.05
336	Ed Vande Berg	.05
337	Mark Langston	.05
338	Dave Henderson	.05
339	Spike Owen	.05
340	Matt Young	.05
341	Jack Perconte	.05
342	Barry Bonnell	.05
343	Mike Stanton	.05
344	Pete O'Brien	.05
345	Charlie Hough	.05
346	Larry Parrish	.05
347	Buddy Bell	.05
348	Frank Tanana	.05
349	Curt Wilkerson	.05
350	Jeff Kunkel	.05
351	Billy Sample	.05
352	Danny Darwin	.05
353	Gary Ward	.05
354	Mike Mason	.05
355	Mickey Rivers	.05
356	Dave Stieb	.05
357	Damaso Garcia	.05
358	Willie Upshaw	.05
359	Lloyd Moseby	.05
360	George Bell	.05
361	Luis Leal	.05
362	Jesse Barfield	.05
363	Dave Collins	.05
364	Roy Lee Jackson	.05
365	Doyle Alexander	.05
366	Alfredo Griffin	.05
367	Cliff Johnson	.05
368	Alvin Davis	.05
369	Juan Samuel	.05
370	Brook Jacoby	.05
371	Dwight Gooden	.05
	Mark Langston	.05
372	Mike Fitzgerald	.05
373	Jackie Gutierrez	.05
374	Dan Gladden	.05
375	Carmelo Martinez	.05
376	Kirby Puckett	.50

Super

Still trying to sell collectors on the idea of jumbo-sized cards, Topps returned for a second year with its 4-7/8" x 6-7/8" "Super" set. In fact, the set size was doubled from the previous year, to 60 cards. The Supers are identical to the regular-issue 1985 cards of the same players, only the card numbers on back were changed. The cards were sold three per pack for 50 cents.

		NM/M
	Complete Set (60):	12.00
	Common Player:	.25
	Wax Pack (1):	.25
	Wax Box (24):	6.00
1	Ryne Sandberg	1.00
2	Willie Hernandez	.25
3	Rick Sutcliffe	.25
4	Don Mattingly	1.50
5	Tony Gwynn	1.00
6	Alvin Davis	.25
7	Dwight Gooden	.50
8	Dan Quisenberry	.25
9	Bruce Sutter	.65
10	Tony Armas	.25
11	Dale Murphy	.50
12	Mike Schmidt	1.50
13	Gary Carter	.75
14	Rickey Henderson	.75
15	Tim Raines	.25
16	Mike Boddicker	.25
17	Alejandro Pena	.25
18	Eddie Murray	.75
19	Gary Matthews	.25
20	Mark Langston	.25
21	Mario Soto	.25
22	Dave Stieb	.25
23	Nolan Ryan	3.00
24	Steve Carlton	.75
25	Alan Trammell	.25
26	Steve Garvey	.40
27	Kirk Gibson	.25
28	Juan Samuel	.25
29	Reggie Jackson	1.00
30	Darryl Strawberry	.25
31	Tom Seaver	.75
32	Pete Rose	2.00
33	Dwight Evans	.25
34	Jose Cruz	.25
35	Bert Blyleven	.25
36	Keith Hernandez	.25
37	Robin Yount	.75
38	Joaquin Andujar	.25
39	Lloyd Moseby	.25
40	Chili Davis	.25
41	Kent Hrbek	.25
42	Dave Parker	.25
43	Jack Morris	.25
44	Pedro Guerrero	.25
45	Mike Witt	.25
46	George Brett	1.50
47	Ozzie Smith	1.00
48	Cal Ripken, Jr.	3.00
49	Rich Gossage	.25
50	Jim Rice	.35
51	Harold Baines	.25
52	Fernando Valenzuela	.25
53	Buddy Bell	.25
54	Jesse Orosco	.25
55	Lance Parrish	.25
56	Jason Thompson	.25
57	Tom Brunansky	.25
58	Dave Righetti	.25
59	Dave Kingman	.25
60	Dave Winfield	.75

3-D

These 4-1/4" x 6" cards were something new. Printed on plastic, rather than paper, the player picture on the card is actually raised above the surface much like might be found on a relief map; a true 3-D baseball card. The plastic cards include the player's name, a Topps logo and card number across the top, and a team logo on the side. The backs are blank but have two peel-off adhesive strips so that the card may be attached to a flat surface. There are 30 cards in the set, mostly stars. Cards were sold one per pack for 50 cents.

		NM/M
	Complete Set (30)	12.00
	Common Player:	.25
	Wax Pack (1):	.50
	Wax Box (24):	12.50
1	Mike Schmidt	2.00
2	Eddie Murray	.75
3	Dale Murphy	.50
4	George Brett	2.00
5	Pete Rose	2.50
6	Jim Rice	.35
7	Ryne Sandberg	1.50
8	Don Mattingly	2.00
9	Darryl Strawberry	.25
10	Rickey Henderson	.75
11	Keith Hernandez	.25
12	Dave Kingman	.25
13	Tony Gwynn	1.50
14	Reggie Jackson	1.50
15	Gary Carter	.75
16	Cal Ripken, Jr.	3.00
17	Tim Raines	.25
18	Dave Winfield	.75
19	Dwight Gooden	.35
20	Dave Stieb	.25
21	Fernando Valenzuela	.25
22	Mark Langston	.25
23	Bruce Sutter	.65
24	Dan Quisenberry	.25
25	Steve Carlton	.75
26	Mike Boddicker	.25
27	Goose Gossage	.25
28	Jack Morris	.25
29	Rick Sutcliffe	.25
30	Tom Seaver	.75

1986 Topps

The 1986 Topps set consists of 792 cards. Fronts of the 2-1/2" x 3-1/2" cards feature color photos with the Topps logo in the upper right-hand corner while the player's position is in the lower left-hand corner. Above the picture is the team name, while below it is the player's name. The borders are a departure from previous practice, as the top 7/8" is black, while the remainder is white. Once again, a 5,000-set glossy-finish "Tiffany" edition was produced.

		NM/M
	Unopened Fact. Set, Retail (792):	65.00
	Unopened Fact. Set, Hobby (792):	30.00
	Complete Set (792):	25.00
	Common Player:	.05
	Wax Pack (15):	.75
	Wax Box (36):	20.00
	Cello Pack (28):	1.00
	Cello Box (20):	20.00
	Rack Pack (51):	1.25
	Rack Box (24):	25.00
	Vending Box (500):	10.00
1	Pete Rose	1.50
2	Pete Rose (Special 1963-66)	.50
3	Pete Rose (Special 1967-70)	.50
4	Pete Rose (Special 1971-74)	.50
5	Pete Rose (Special 1975-78)	.50
6	Pete Rose (Special 1972-82)	.50
7	Pete Rose (Special 1983-85)	.50
8	Dwayne Murphy	.05
9	Roy Smith	.05
10	Tony Gwynn	.75
11	Bob Ojeda	.05
12	Jose Uribe RC	.05
13	Bob Kearney	.05
14	Julio Cruz	.05
15	Eddie Whitson	.05
16	Rick Schu RC	.05
17	Mike Stenhouse	.05
18	Brent Gaff	.05
19	Rich Hebner	.05
20	Lou Whitaker	.05
21	George Bamberger	.05
22	Duane Walker	.05
23	Manny Lee RC	.05
24	Len Barker	.05
25	Willie Wilson	.05
26	Frank DiPino	.05
27	Ray Knight	.05
28	Eric Davis	.05
29	Tony Phillips	.05
30	Eddie Murray	.50
31	Jamie Easterly	.05
32	Steve Yeager	.05
33	Jeff Lahti	.05
34	Ken Phelps RC	.05
35	Jeff Reardon	.25
36	Tigers Leaders (Lance Parrish)	.05
37	Mark Thurmond	.05
38	Glenn Hoffman	.05
39	Dave Rucker	.05
40	Ken Griffey	.05
41	Brad Wellman	.05
42	Geoff Zahn	.05
43	Dave Engle	.05
44	Lance McCullers RC	.05
45	Damaso Garcia	.05
46	Billy Hatcher RC	.05
47	Juan Berenguer	.05
48	Bill Almon	.05
49	Rick Manning	.05
50	Dan Quisenberry	.05
51	Chris Welsh	.05
52	Len Dykstra RC	.50
53	John Franco	.05
54	Fred Lynn	.05
55	Tom Niedenfuer	.05
56	Bill Doran	.05
57a	Bobby Wine	.05
57b	Bobby Wine (Supposed to be #51.)	.05
58	Bill Krueger	.05
59	Andre Thornton	.05
60	Dwight Evans	.05
61	Karl Best	.05
62	Bob Boone	.05
63	Ron Roenicke	.05
64	Floyd Bannister	.05
65	Dan Driessen	.05
66	Cardinals Leaders (Bob Forsch)	.05
67	Carmelo Martinez	.05
68	Ed Lynch	.05
69	Luis Aguayo	.05
70	Dave Winfield	.50
71	Ken Schrom	.05
72	Shawon Dunston	.05
73	Randy O'Neal RC	.05
74	Rance Mulliniks	.05
75	Jose DeLeon	.05
76	Dion James	.05
77	Charlie Leibrandt	.05
78	Bruce Benedict	.05
79	Dave Schmidt	.05
80	Darryl Strawberry	.05
81	Gene Mauch	.05
82	Tippy Martinez	.05
83	Phil Garner	.05
84	Curt Young	.05
85	Tony Perez	.40
86	Tom Waddell	.05
87	Candy Maldonado	.05
88	Tom Nieto	.05
89	Randy St. Claire RC	.05
90	Garry Templeton	.05
91	Steve Crawford	.05
92	Al Cowens	.05
93	Scot Thompson	.05
94	Rich Bordi	.05
95	Ozzie Virgil	.05
96	Blue Jay Leaders (Jim Clancy)	.05
97	Gary Gaetti	.05
98	Dick Ruthven	.05
99	Buddy Biancalana	.05
100	Nolan Ryan	2.00
101	Dave Bergman	.05
102	Joe Orsulak RC	.15
103	Luis Salazar	.05
104	Sid Fernandez	.05
105	Gary Ward	.05
106	Ray Burris	.05
107	Rafael Ramirez	.05
108	Ted Power	.05
109	Len Matuszek	.05
110	Scott McGregor	.05
111	Roger Craig	.05
112	Bill Campbell	.05
113	U.L. Washington	.05
114	Mike Brown	.05
115	Jay Howell	.05
116	Brook Jacoby	.05
117	Bruce Kison	.05
118	Jerry Royster	.05
119	Barry Bonnell	.05
120	Steve Carlton	.50
121	Nelson Simmons	.05
122	Pete Filson	.05
123	Greg Walker	.05
124	Luis Sanchez	.05
125	Dave Lopes	.05
126	Mets Leaders (Mookie Wilson)	.05
127	Jack Howell RC	.05
128	John Wathan	.05
129	Jeff Dedmon RC	.05
130	Alan Trammell	.05
131	Checklist 1-132	.05
132	Razor Shines	.05
133	Andy McGaffigan	.05
134	Carney Lansford	.05
135	Joe Niekro	.05
136	Mike Hargrove	.05
137	Charlie Moore	.05
138	Mark Davis	.05
139	Daryl Boston	.05
140	John Candelaria	.05
141a	Chuck Cottier	.05
141b	Bob Rodgers (Supposed to be #171.)	.05
142	Bob Jones	.05
143	Dave Van Gorder	.05
144	Doug Sisk	.05
145	Pedro Guerrero	.05
146	Jack Perconte	.05
147	Larry Sheets	.05
148	Mike Heath	.05
149	Brett Butler	.05
150	Joaquin Andujar	.05
151	Dave Stapleton	.05
152	Mike Morgan	.05
153	Ricky Adams	.05
154	Bert Roberge	.05
155	Bob Grich	.05
156	White Sox Leaders (Richard Dotson)	.05
157	Ron Hassey	.05
158	Derrel Thomas	.05
159	Orel Hershiser	.05
160	Chet Lemon	.05
161	Lee Tunnell	.05
162	Greg Gagne	.05
163	Pete Ladd	.05
164	Steve Balboni	.05
165	Mike Davis	.05
166	Dickie Thon	.05
167	Zane Smith RC	.05
168	Jeff Burroughs	.05
169	George Wright	.05
170	Gary Carter	.50
171	Jerry Reed	.05
172	Wayne Gross	.05
173	Brian Snyder	.05
174	Steve Sax	.05
175	Jay Tibbs	.05
176	Joel Youngblood	.05
177	Ivan DeJesus	.05
178	Stu Cliburn RC	.05
180	Don Mattingly	1.00
181	Al Nipper	.05
182	Bobby Brown	.05
183	Larry Andersen	.05
184	Tim Laudner	.05
185	Rollie Fingers	.40
186	Astros Leaders (Jose Cruz)	.05
187	Scott Fletcher	.05
188	Bob Dernier	.05
189	Mike Mason	.05
190	George Hendrick	.05
191	Wally Backman	.05
192	Milt Wilcox	.05
193	Daryl Sconiers	.05
194	Craig McMurtry	.05
195	Dave Concepcion	.05
196	Doyle Alexander	.05
197	Enos Cabell	.05
198	Ken Dixon	.05
199	Dick Howser	.05
200	Mike Schmidt	1.00
201	Vince Coleman	.08
202	Dwight Gooden (Record Breaker)	.05
203	Keith Hernandez (Record Breaker)	.05
204	Phil Niekro (Record Breaker)	.05
205	Tony Perez (Record Breaker)	.05
206	Pete Rose (Record Breaker)	.25
207	Fernando Valenzuela (Record Breaker)	.05
208	Ramon Romero	.05
209	Randy Ready	.05
210	Calvin Schiraldi RC	.05
211	Ed Wojna	.05
212	Chris Speier	.05
213	Bob Shirley	.05
214	Randy Bush	.05
215	Frank White	.05
216	A's Leaders (Dwayne Murphy)	.05
217	Bill Scherrer	.05
218	Randy Hunt	.05
219	Dennis Lamp	.05
220	Bob Horner	.05
221	Dave Henderson	.05
222	Craig Gerber	.05
223	Atlee Hammaker	.05
224	Cesar Cedeno	.05
225	Ron Darling	.05
226	Lee Lacy	.05
227	Al Jones	.05
228	Tom Lawless	.05
229	Bill Gullickson	.05
230	Terry Kennedy	.05
231	Jim Frey	.05
232	Rick Rhoden	.05
233	Steve Lyons RC	.05
234	Doug Corbett	.05
235	Butch Wynegar	.05
236	Frank Eufemia	.05
237	Ted Simmons	.05
238	Larry Parrish	.05
239	Joel Skinner	.05
240	Tommy John	.10
241	Tony Fernandez	.05
242	Rich Thompson	.05
243	Johnny Grubb	.05
244	Craig Lefferts	.05
245	Jim Sundberg	.05
246	Phillies Leaders (Steve Carlton)	.10
247	Terry Harper	.05
248	Spike Owen	.05
249	Rob Deer RC	.05
250	Dwight Gooden	.05
251	Rich Dauer	.05
252	Bobby Castillo	.05
253	Dann Bilardello	.05
254	Ozzie Guillen RC	.30
255	Tony Armas	.05
256	Kurt Kepshire	.05
257	Doug DeCinces	.05
258	Tim Burke RC	.05
259	Dan Pasqua RC	.05
260	Tony Pena	.05
261	Bobby Valentine	.05
262	Mario Ramirez	.05
263	Checklist 133-264	.05
264	Darren Daulton	.05
265	Ron Davis	.05
266	Keith Moreland	.05
267	Paul Molitor	.50
268	Mike Scott	.05
269	Dane Iorg	.05
270	Jack Morris	.05
271	Dave Collins	.05
272	Tim Tolman	.05
273	Jerry Willard	.05
274	Ron Gardenhire	.05
275	Charlie Hough	.05
276	Yankees Leaders (Willie Randolph)	.05
277	Jaime Cocanower	.05
278	Sixto Lezcano	.05
279	Al Pardo	.05
280	Tim Raines	.05
281	Steve Mura	.05
282	Jerry Mumphrey	.05
283	Mike Fischlin	.05
284	Brian Dayett	.05
285	Buddy Bell	.05
286	Luis DeLeon	.05
287	John Christensen RC	.05
288	Don Aase	.05
289	Johnnie LeMaster	.05
290	Carlton Fisk	.50
291	Tom Lasorda	.10
292	Chuck Porter	.05
293	Chris Chambliss	.05
294	Danny Cox	.05
295	Kirk Gibson	.05
296	Geno Petralli RC	.05
297	Tim Lollar	.05
298	Craig Reynolds	.05
299	Bryn Smith	.05
300	George Brett	1.00
301	Dennis Rasmussen	.05
302	Greg Gross	.05
303	Curt Wardle	.05
304	Mike Gallego RC	.10
305	Phil Bradley	.05
306	Padres Leaders (Terry Kennedy)	.05
307	Dave Sax	.05
308	Ray Fontenot	.05
309	John Shelby	.05
310	Greg Minton	.05
311	Dick Schofield	.05
312	Tom Filer	.05
313	Joe DeSa	.05
314	Frank Pastore	.05
315	Mookie Wilson	.05
316	Sammy Khalifa	.05
317	Ed Romero	.05
318	Terry Whitfield	.05
319	Rick Camp	.05
320	Jim Rice	.15
321	Earl Weaver	.10
322	Bob Forsch	.05
323	Jerry Davis	.05
324	Dan Schatzeder	.05
325	Juan Beniquez	.05
326	Kent Tekulve	.05
327	Mike Pagliarulo	.05
328	Pete O'Brien	.05
329	Kirby Puckett	.75
330	Rick Sutcliffe	.05
331	Alan Ashby	.05
332	Darryl Motley	.05
333	Tom Henke RC	.05
334	Ken Oberkfell	.05
335	Don Sutton	.40
336	Indians Leaders (Andre Thornton)	.05
337	Darnell Coles	.05
338	Jorge Bell	.05
339	Bruce Berenyi	.05
340	Cal Ripken, Jr.	2.00
341	Frank Williams	.05
342	Gary Redus	.05
343	Carlos Diaz	.05
344	Jim Wohlford	.05
345	Donnie Moore	.05
346	Bryan Little	.05
347	Teddy Higuera RC	.10
348	Cliff Johnson	.05
349	Mark Clear	.05
350	Jack Clark	.05
351	Chuck Tanner	.05
352	Harry Spilman	.05
353	Keith Atherton	.05
354	Tony Bernazard	.05
355	Lee Smith	.05
356	Mickey Hatcher	.05
357	Ed Vande Berg	.05
358	Rick Dempsey	.05
359	Mike LaCoss	.05
360	Lloyd Moseby	.05
361	Shane Rawley	.05
362	Tom Paciorek	.05
363	Terry Forster	.05
364	Reid Nichols	.05
365	Mike Flanagan	.05
366	Reds Leaders (Dave Concepcion)	.05
367	Aurelio Lopez	.05
368	Greg Brock	.05
369	Al Holland	.05
370	Vince Coleman	.35
371	Bill Stein	.05
372	Ben Oglivie	.05
373	Urbano Lugo RC	.05
374	Terry Francona	.05
375	Rich Gedman	.05
376	Bill Dawley	.05
377	Joe Carter	.05
378	Bruce Bochte	.05
379	Bobby Meacham	.05
380	LaMarr Hoyt	.05
381	Ray Miller	.05
382	Ivan Calderon RC	.05
383	Chris Brown RC	.05
384	Steve Trout	.05
385	Cecil Cooper	.05
386	Cecil Fielder RC	.75
387	Steve Kemp	.05
388	Dickie Noles	.05
389	Glenn Davis RC	.05
390	Tom Seaver	.60
391	Julio Franco	.05
392	John Russell RC	.05
393	Chris Pittaro	.05
394	Checklist 265-396	.05
395	Scott Garrelts	.05
396	Red Sox Leaders (Dwight Evans)	.05
397	Steve Buechele RC	.10
398	Earnie Riles RC	.05
399	Bill Swift	.05
400	Rod Carew	.50
401	Fernando Valenzuela (Turn Back the Clock)	.05
402	Tom Seaver (Turn Back the Clock)	.25
403	Willie Mays (Turn Back the Clock)	.35
404	Frank Robinson (Turn Back the Clock)	.10
405	Roger Maris (Turn Back the Clock)	.30
406	Scott Sanderson	.05
407	Sal Butera	.05
408	Dave Von Ohlen	.05
409	Paul Runge RC	.05
410	Dave Kingman	.05
411	Sparky Anderson	.10
412	Jim Clancy	.05
413	Tim Flannery	.05
414	Tom Gorman	.05
415	Hal McRae	.05
416	Denny Martinez	.05
417	R.J. Reynolds	.05
418	Alan Knicely	.05
419	Frank Wills	.05
420	Von Hayes	.05
421	Dave Palmer	.05
422	Mike Jorgensen	.05
423	Dan Spillner	.05
424	Rick Miller	.05
425	Larry McWilliams	.05
426	Brewers Leaders (Charlie Moore)	.05
427	Joe Cowley	.05
428	Max Venable	.05
429	Greg Booker	.05
430	Kent Hrbek	.05
431	George Frazier	.05
432	Mark Bailey	.05
433	Chris Codiroli	.05
434	Curt Wilkerson	.05
435	Bill Caudill	.05
436	Doug Flynn	.05
437	Rick Mahler	.05
438	Clint Hurdle	.05
439	Rick Honeycutt	.05
440	Alvin Davis	.05
441	Whitey Herzog	.05
442	Ron Robinson RC	.05
443	Bill Buckner	.05
444	Alex Trevino	.05
445	Bert Blyleven	.05
446	Lenn Sakata	.05
447	Jerry Don Gleaton	.05

#	Player	Price
448	Herm Winningham RC	.05
449	Rod Scurry	.05
450	Graig Nettles	.05
451	Mark Brown	.05
452	Bob Clark	.05
453	Steve Jeltz	.05
454	Burt Hooton	.05
455	Willie Randolph	.05
456	Braves Leaders (Dale Murphy)	.10
457	Mickey Tettleton	.05
458	Kevin Bass	.05
459	Luis Leal	.05
460	Leon Durham	.05
461	Walt Terrell	.05
462	Domingo Ramos	.05
463	Jim Gott	.05
464	Ruppert Jones	.05
465	Jesse Orosco	.05
466	Tom Foley	.05
467	Bob James	.05
468	Mike Scioscia	.05
469	Storm Davis	.05
470	Bill Madlock	.05
471	Bobby Cox	.05
472	Joe Hesketh	.05
473	Mark Brouhard	.05
474	John Tudor	.05
475	Juan Samuel	.05
476	Ron Mathis	.05
477	Mike Easler	.05
478	Andy Hawkins	.05
479	Bob Melvin RC	.05
480	Oddibe McDowell RC	.05
481	Scott Bradley RC	.05
482	Rick Lysander	.05
483	George Vukovich	.05
484	Donnie Hill	.05
485	Gary Matthews	.05
486	Angels Leaders (Bob Grich)	.05
487	Bret Saberhagen	.05
488	Lou Thornton	.05
489	Jim Winn	.05
490	Jeff Leonard	.05
491	Pascual Perez	.05
492	Kelvin Chapman	.05
493	Gene Nelson	.05
494	Gary Roenicke	.05
495	Mark Langston	.05
496	Jay Johnstone	.05
497	John Stuper	.05
498	Tito Landrum	.05
499	Bob L. Gibson	.05
500	Rickey Henderson	.50
501	Dave Johnson	.05
502	Glen Cook	.05
503	Mike Fitzgerald	.05
504	Denny Walling	.05
505	Jerry Koosman	.05
506	Bill Russell	.05
507	Steve Ontiveros RC	.05
508	Alan Wiggins	.05
509	Ernie Camacho	.05
510	Wade Boggs	.75
511	Ed Nunez	.05
512	Thad Bosley	.05
513	Ron Washington	.05
514	Mike Jones	.05
515	Darrell Evans	.05
516	Giants Leaders (Greg Minton)	.05
517	Milt Thompson RC	.05
518	Buck Martinez	.05
519	Danny Darwin	.05
520	Keith Hernandez	.05
521	Nate Snell	.05
522	Bob Bailor	.05
523	Joe Price	.05
524	Darrell Miller RC	.05
525	Marvell Wynne	.05
526	Charlie Lea	.05
527	Checklist 397-528	.05
528	Terry Pendleton	.05
529	Marc Sullivan	.05
530	Rich Gossage	.05
531	Tony LaRussa	.05
532	Don Carman RC	.05
533	Billy Sample	.05
534	Jeff Calhoun	.05
535	Toby Harrah	.05
536	Jose Rijo	.05
537	Mark Salas	.05
538	Dennis Eckersley	.40
539	Glenn Hubbard	.05
540	Dan Petry	.05
541	Jorge Orta	.05
542	Don Schulze	.05
543	Jerry Narron	.05
544	Eddie Milner	.05
545	Jimmy Key	.05
546	Mariners Leaders (Dave Henderson)	.05
547	Roger McDowell	.05
548	Mike Young	.05
549	Bob Welch	.05
550	Tom Herr	.05
551	Dave LaPoint	.05
552	Marc Hill	.05
553	Jim Morrison	.05
554	Paul Householder	.05
555	Hubie Brooks	.05
556	John Denny	.05
557	Gerald Perry	.05
558	Tim Stoddard	.05
559	Tommy Dunbar	.05
560	Dave Righetti	.05
561	Bob Lillis	.05
562	Joe Beckwith	.05
563	Alejandro Sanchez	.05
564	Warren Brusstar	.05
565	Tom Brunansky	.05
566	Alfredo Griffin	.05
567	Jeff Barkley	.05
568	Donnie Scott	.05
569	Jim Acker	.05
570	Rusty Staub	.10
571	Mike Jeffcoat	.05
572	Paul Zuvella	.05
573	Tom Hume	.05
574	Ron Kittle	.05
575	Mike Boddicker	.05
576	Expos Leaders (Andre Dawson)	.05
577	Jerry Reuss	.05
578	Lee Mazzilli	.05
579	Jim Slaton	.05
580	Willie McGee	.05
581	Bruce Hurst	.05
582	Jim Gantner	.05
583	Al Bumbry	.05
584	Brian Fisher RC	.05
585	Garry Maddox	.05
586	Greg Harris	.05
587	Rafael Santana	.05
588	Steve Lake	.05
589	Sid Bream	.05
590	Bob Knepper	.05
591	Jackie Moore	.05
592	Frank Tanana	.05
593	Jesse Barfield	.05
594	Chris Bando	.05
595	Dave Parker	.05
596	Onix Concepcion	.05
597	Sammy Stewart	.05
598	Jim Presley	.05
599	Rick Aguilera RC	.25
600	Dale Murphy	.25
601	Gary Lucas	.05
602	Mariano Duncan	.05
603	Bill Laskey	.05
604	Gary Pettis	.05
605	Dennis Boyd	.05
606	Royals Leaders (Hal McRae)	.05
607	Ken Dayley	.05
608	Bruce Bochy	.05
609	Barbaro Garbey	.05
610	Ron Guidry	.05
611	Gary Woods	.05
612	Richard Dotson	.05
613	Roy Smalley	.05
614	Rick Waits	.05
615	Johnny Ray	.05
616	Glenn Brummer	.05
617	Lonnie Smith	.05
618	Jim Pankovits	.05
619	Danny Heep	.05
620	Bruce Sutter	.40
621	John Felske	.05
622	Gary Lavelle	.05
623	Floyd Rayford	.05
624	Steve McCatty	.05
625	Bob Brenly	.05
626	Roy Thomas	.05
627	Ron Oester	.05
628	Kirk McCaskill RC	.15
629	Mitch Webster RC	.05
630	Fernando Valenzuela	.05
631	Steve Braun	.05
632	Dave Von Ohlen	.05
633	Jackie Gutierrez	.05
634	Roy Lee Jackson	.05
635	Jason Thompson	.05
636	Cubs Leaders (Lee Smith)	.05
637	Rudy Law	.05
638	John Butcher	.05
639	Bo Diaz	.05
640	Jose Cruz	.05
641	Wayne Tolleson	.05
642	Ray Searage	.05
643	Tom Brookens	.05
644	Mark Gubicza	.05
645	Dusty Baker	.05
646	Mike Moore	.05
647	Mel Hall	.05
648	Steve Bedrosian	.05
649	Ronn Reynolds	.05
650	Dave Stieb	.05
651	Billy Martin	.10
652	Tom Browning	.05
653	Jim Dwyer	.05
654	Ken Howell	.05
655	Manny Trillo	.05
656	Brian Harper	.05
657	Juan Agosto	.05
658	Rob Wilfong	.05
659	Checklist 529-660	.05
660	Steve Garvey	.20
661	Roger Clemens	3.00
661	Roger Clemens (Blue streak upper-right.)	7.50
662	Bill Schroeder	.05
663	Neil Allen	.05
664	Tim Corcoran	.05
665	Alejandro Pena	.05
666	Rangers Leaders (Charlie Hough)	.05
667	Tim Teufel	.05
668	Cecilio Guante	.05
669	Ron Cey	.05
670	Willie Hernandez	.05
671	Lynn Jones	.05
672	Rob Picciolo	.05
673	Ernie Whitt	.05
674	Pat Tabler	.05
675	Claudell Washington	.05
676	Matt Young	.05
677	Nick Esasky	.05
678	Dan Gladden	.05
679	Britt Burns	.05
680	George Foster	.05
681	Dick Williams	.05
682	Andy Van Slyke	.05
683	Bob McClure	.05
684	Tim Wallach	.05
685	Jeff Stone	.05
686	Mike Trujillo	.05
687	Larry Herndon	.05
688	Dave Stewart	.05
689	Ryne Sandberg	.75
690	Mike Madden	.05
691	Dale Berra	.05
692	Tom Tellmann	.05
693	Garth Iorg	.05
694	Mike Smithson	.05
695	Dodgers Leaders (Bill Russell)	.05
696	Bud Black	.05
697	Brad Komminsk	.05
698	Pat Corrales	.05
699	Reggie Jackson	.75
700	Keith Hernandez/AS	.05
701	Tom Herr/AS	.05
702	Tim Wallach/AS	.05
703	Ozzie Smith/AS	.35
704	Dale Murphy/AS	.10
705	Pedro Guerrero/AS	.05
706	Willie McGee/AS	.05
707	Gary Carter/AS	.25
708	Dwight Gooden/AS	.05
709	John Tudor/AS	.05
710	Jeff Reardon/AS	.05
711	Don Mattingly/AS	.50
712	Damaso Garcia/AS	.05
713	George Brett/AS	.45
714	Cal Ripken, Jr./AS	1.00
715	Rickey Henderson/AS	.25
716	Dave Winfield/AS	.25
717	George Bell/AS	.05
718	Carlton Fisk/AS	.20
719	Bret Saberhagen/AS	.05
720	Ron Guidry/AS	.05
721	Dan Quisenberry/AS	.05
722	Marty Bystrom	.05
723	Tim Hulett	.05
724	Mario Soto	.05
725	Orioles Leaders (Rick Dempsey)	.05
726	David Green	.05
727	Mike Marshall	.05
728	Jim Beattie	.05
729	Ozzie Smith	.75
730	Don Robinson	.05
731	Floyd Youmans RC	.05
732	Ron Romanick	.05
733	Marty Barrett	.05
734	Dave Dravecky	.05
735	Glenn Wilson	.05
736	Pete Vuckovich	.05
737	Andre Robertson	.05
738	Dave Rozema	.05
739	Lance Parrish	.05
740	Steve Bedrosian	.05
741	Pete Rose	1.00
742	Frank Viola	.05
743	Pat Sheridan	.05
744	Lary Sorensen	.05
745	Willie Upshaw	.05
746	Denny Gonzalez	.05
747	Rick Cerone	.05
748	Steve Henderson	.05
749	Ed Jurak	.05
750	Gorman Thomas	.05
751	Howard Johnson	.05
752	Mike Krukow	.05
753	Dan Ford	.05
754	Pat Clements RC	.05
755	Harold Baines	.05
756	Pirates Leaders (Rick Rhoden)	.05
757	Darrell Porter	.05
758	Dave Anderson	.05
759	Moose Haas	.05
760	Andre Dawson	.30
761	Don Slaught	.05
762	Eric Show	.05
763	Terry Puhl	.05
764	Kevin Gross	.05
765	Don Baylor	.05
766	Rick Langford	.05
767	Jody Davis	.05
768	Vern Ruhle	.05
769	Harold Reynolds RC	.25
770	Vida Blue	.05
771	John McNamara	.05
772	Brian Downing	.05
773	Greg Pryor	.05
774	Terry Leach	.05
775	Al Oliver	.05
776	Gene Garber	.05
777	Wayne Krenchicki	.05
778	Jerry Hairston Sr.	.05
779	Rick Reuschel	.05
780	Robin Yount	.50
781	Joe Nolan	.05
782	Ken Landreaux	.05
783	Ricky Horton	.05
784	Alan Bannister	.05
785	Bob Stanley	.05
786	Twins Leaders (Mickey Hatcher)	.05
787	Vance Law	.05
788	Marty Castillo	.05
789	Kurt Bevacqua	.05
790	Phil Niekro	.40
791	Checklist 661-792	.05
792	Charles Hudson	.05

Tiffany

A total of only 5,000 of these specially boxed collectors' edition sets were reported produced. Sold only through hobby dealers' the cards differ from the regular-issue 1986 Topps cards only in the use of white cardboard stock and the application of a high-gloss finish on the cards' fronts.

	NM/M
Unopened Set (792):	100.00
Complete Set (792):	45.00
Common Player:	.25

Traded

JOSE CANSECO

This 132-card set of 2-1/2" x 3-1/2" cards was, at issue, one of the most popular sets of recent times. As always, the set features traded veterans, and a better than usual crop of rookies. As in the previous two years, a glossy-finish "Tiffany" edition of 5,000 Traded sets was produced.

	NM/M
Unopened Set (132):	30.00
Complete Set (132):	25.00
Common Player:	.05

#	Player	Price
1T	Andy Allanson RC	.05
2T	Neil Allen	.05
3T	Joaquin Andujar	.05
4T	Paul Assenmacher RC	.05
5T	Scott Bailes RC	.05
6T	Don Baylor	.15
7T	Steve Bedrosian	.05
8T	Juan Beniquez	.05
9T	Juan Berenguer	.05
10T	Mike Bielecki RC	.05
11T	Barry Bonds RC	20.00
12T	Bobby Bonilla RC	.50
13T	Juan Bonilla	.05
14T	Rich Bordi	.05
15T	Steve Boros	.05
16T	Rick Burleson	.05
17T	Bill Campbell	.05
18T	Tom Candiotti	.05
19T	John Cangelosi RC	.05
20T	Jose Canseco RC	4.00
21T	Carmen Castillo	.05
22T	Rick Cerone	.05
23T	John Cerutti RC	.05
24T	Will Clark RC	1.50
25T	Mark Clear	.05
26T	Darnell Coles	.05
27T	Dave Collins	.05
28T	Tim Conroy	.05
29T	Joe Cowley	.05
30T	Joel Davis RC	.05
31T	Rob Deer	.05
32T	John Denny	.05
33T	Mike Easler	.05
34T	Mark Eichhorn RC	.05
35T	Steve Farr	.05
36T	Scott Fletcher	.05
37T	Terry Forster	.05
38T	Terry Francona	.05
39T	Jim Fregosi	.05
40T	Andres Galarraga RC	.35
41T	Ken Griffey	.05
42T	Bill Gullickson	.05
43T	Jose Guzman RC	.05
44T	Moose Haas	.05
45T	Billy Hatcher	.05
46T	Mike Heath	.05
47T	Tom Hume	.05
48T	Pete Incaviglia RC	.20
49T	Dane Iorg	.05
50T	Bo Jackson RC	1.50
51T	Wally Joyner RC	.40
52T	Charlie Kerfeld RC	.05
53T	Eric King RC	.05
54T	Bob Kipper RC	.05
55T	Wayne Krenchicki	.05
56T	John Kruk RC	.35
57T	Mike LaCoss	.05
58T	Pete Ladd	.05
59T	Mike Laga	.05
60T	Hal Lanier	.05
61T	Dave LaPoint	.05
62T	Rudy Law	.05
63T	Rick Leach	.05
64T	Tim Leary	.05
65T	Dennis Leonard	.05
66T	Jim Leyland	.05
67T	Steve Lyons	.05
68T	Mickey Mahler	.05
69T	Candy Maldonado	.05
70T	Roger Mason RC	.05
71T	Bob McClure	.05
72T	Andy McGaffigan	.05
73T	Gene Michael	.05
74T	Kevin Mitchell RC	.25
75T	Omar Moreno	.05
76T	Jerry Mumphrey	.05
77T	Phil Niekro	.25
78T	Randy Niemann	.05
79T	Juan Nieves RC	.05
80T	Otis Nixon RC	.05
81T	Bob Ojeda	.05
82T	Jose Oquendo	.05
83T	Tom Paciorek	.05
84T	Dave Palmer	.05
85T	Frank Pastore	.05
86T	Lou Piniella	.05
87T	Dan Plesac RC	.05
88T	Darrell Porter	.05
89T	Rey Quinones RC	.05
90T	Gary Redus	.05
91T	Bip Roberts	.05
92T	Billy Jo Robidoux RC	.05
93T	Jeff Robinson	.05
94T	Gary Roenicke	.05
95T	Ed Romero	.05
96T	Argenis Salazar	.05
97T	Joe Sambito	.05
98T	Billy Sample	.05
99T	Dave Schmidt	.05
100T	Ken Schrom	.05
101T	Tom Seaver	.50
102T	Ted Simmons	.05
103T	Sammy Stewart	.05
104T	Kurt Stillwell RC	.05
105T	Franklin Stubbs	.05
106T	Dale Sveum RC	.05
107T	Chuck Tanner	.05
108T	Danny Tartabull RC	.05
109T	Tim Teufel	.05
110T	Bob Tewksbury RC	.05
111T	Andres Thomas RC	.05
112T	Milt Thompson	.05
113T	Robby Thompson RC	.05
114T	Jay Tibbs	.05
115T	Wayne Tolleson	.05
116T	Alex Trevino	.05
117T	Manny Trillo	.05
118T	Ed Vande Berg	.05
119T	Ozzie Virgil	.05
120T	Bob Walk	.05
121T	Gene Walter RC	.05
122T	Claudell Washington	.05
123T	Bill Wegman RC	.05
124T	Dick Williams	.05
125T	Mitch Williams RC	.05
126T	Bobby Witt RC	.05
127T	Todd Worrell RC	.05
128T	George Wright	.05
129T	Ricky Wright	.05
130T	Steve Yeager	.05
131T	Paul Zuvella	.05
132T	Checklist	.05

Traded Tiffany

This collectors' edition differs from the regular 1986 Topps Traded set only in the use of a high-gloss front finish. The set was sold only through hobby channels in a specially design box.

	NM/M
Unopened Set (132):	700.00
Complete Set (132):	450.00
Common Player:	.25
11T	Barry Bonds	325.00

Traded Mickey Mantle Bronze

This 1/4-size metal replica of Mantle's first-ever Topps card was issued to dealers who purchased cases of 1986 Topps Traded sets. Each detail of the 1952 Topps Mantle card is reproduced on the 1-1/4" x 1-3/4" bronze metal mini-card, right down to the stats.

		NM/M
311	Mickey Mantle	9.00

Box Panels

Following the lead of Donruss, which introduced the concept in 1985, Topps produced special cards on the bottom panels of wax boxes. Individual cards measure 2-1/2" x 3-1/2", the same as regular cards. Design of the cards is virtually identical with regular '86 Topps, though the top border is in red, rather than black. The cards are lettered "A" through "P," rather than numbered on the back.

		NM/M
Complete Panel Set:		7.00
Complete Singles Set:		6.00
Common Panel:		1.00
Common Single Player:		.10
Panel		2.00
A	Jorge Bell	.10
B	Wade Boggs	.75
C	George Brett	1.00
D	Vince Coleman	.25
Panel		1.00
E	Carlton Fisk	.50
F	Dwight Gooden	.10
G	Pedro Guerrero	.10
H	Ron Guidry	.10
Panel		2.00
I	Reggie Jackson	.75
J	Don Mattingly	1.00
K	Oddibe McDowell	.10
L	Willie McGee	.10
Panel		2.50
M	Dale Murphy	.35
N	Pete Rose	1.50
O	Bret Saberhagen	.10
P	Fernando Valenzuela	.10

All-Star Glossy Set of 22

As in previous years, Topps continued to make the popular glossy-surfaced cards as an insert in rack packs. The All-Star Glossy set of 2-1/2" x 3-1/2" cards shows little design change from previous years. Cards feature a front color photo and All-Star banner at the top. The bottom has the player's name and position. The set includes the All-Star starting teams as well as the managers and honorary captains.

	NM/M
Complete Set (22):	2.50

	Common Player:	.05
1	Sparky Anderson	.05
2	Eddie Murray	.35
3	Lou Whitaker	.05
4	George Brett	.50
5	Cal Ripken, Jr.	.65
6	Jim Rice	.25
7	Rickey Henderson	.35
8	Dave Winfield	.35
9	Carlton Fisk	.25
10	Jack Morris	.05
11	A.L. All-Star Team	.05
12	Dick Williams	.05
13	Steve Garvey	.15
14	Tom Herr	.05
15	Graig Nettles	.05
16	Ozzie Smith	.45
17	Tony Gwynn	.45
18	Dale Murphy	.25
19	Darryl Strawberry	.05
20	Terry Kennedy	.05
21	LaMarr Hoyt	.05
22	N.L. All-Star Team	.05

All-Star Glossy Set of 60

The Topps All-Star & Hot Prospects glossy set of 60 cards represents an expansion of a good idea. The 2-1/2" x 3-1/2" cards had a good following when they were limited to stars, but Topps realized that the addition of top young players would spice up the set even further, so in 1986 it was expanded from 40 to 60 cards. The cards themselves are basically all color glossy pictures with the player's name in very small print in the lower left-hand corner. To obtain the set, it was necessary to send $1 plus six special offer cards from wax packs to Topps for each series. At 60 cards, that meant the process had to be repeated six times as there were 10 cards in each series, making the set quite expensive from the outset.

		NM/M
	Complete Set (60):	8.00
	Common Player:	.10
1	Oddibe McDowell	.10
2	Reggie Jackson	.50
3	Fernando Valenzuela	.10
4	Jack Clark	.10
5	Rickey Henderson	.40
6	Steve Balboni	.10
7	Keith Hernandez	.10
8	Lance Parrish	.10
9	Willie McGee	.10
10	Chris Brown	.10
11	Darryl Strawberry	.10
12	Ron Guidry	.10
13	Dave Parker	.10
14	Cal Ripken	1.00
15	Tim Raines	.10
16	Rod Carew	.40
17	Mike Schmidt	.75
18	George Brett	.75
19	Joe Hesketh	.10
20	Dan Pasqua	.10
21	Vince Coleman	.10
22	Tom Seaver	.40
23	Gary Carter	.40
24	Orel Hershiser	.10
25	Pedro Guerrero	.10
26	Wade Boggs	.50
27	Bret Saberhagen	.10
28	Carlton Fisk	.40
29	Kirk Gibson	.10
30	Brian Fisher	.10
31	Don Mattingly	.75
32	Tom Herr	.10
33	Eddie Murray	.40
34	Ryne Sandberg	.30
35	Dan Quisenberry	.10
36	Jim Rice	.30
37	Dale Murphy	.30
38	Steve Garvey	.25

39	Roger McDowell	.10
40	Earnie Riles	.10
41	Dwight Gooden	.10
42	Dave Winfield	.40
43	Dave Stieb	.10
44	Bob Horner	.10
45	Nolan Ryan	1.00
46	Ozzie Smith	.50
47	Jorge Bell	.10
48	Gorman Thomas	.10
49	Tom Browning	.10
50	Larry Sheets	.10
51	Pete Rose	.90
52	Brett Butler	.10
53	John Tudor	.10
54	Phil Bradley	.10
55	Jeff Reardon	.10
56	Rich Gossage	.10
57	Tony Gwynn	.50
58	Ozzie Guillen	.10
59	Glenn Davis	.10
60	Darrell Evans	.10

Gallery of Champions

For the third consecutive year Topps issued 12 metal "mini cards," adding an aluminum version to the bronze and silver. The metal replicas were minted 1/4-size (approximately 1-1/4" x 1-3/4") of the regular cards. The bronze and silver sets were issued in leather-like velvet-lined display cases, the aluminum in individual poly packs. A pewter Don Mattingly was issued as a premium to those ordering the sets.

		NM/M
	Complete Aluminum Set:	15.00
	Complete Bronze Set:	50.00
	Complete Silver Set:	200.00
(1a)	Wade Boggs/Aluminum	2.00
(1b)	Wade Boggs/Bronze	15.00
(1s)	Wade Boggs/Silver	35.00
(2a)	Vince Coleman/Aluminum	1.50
(2b)	Vince Coleman/Bronze	4.00
(2s)	Vince Coleman/Silver	12.00
(3a)	Darrell Evans/Aluminum	1.00
(3b)	Darrell Evans/Bronze	4.00
(3s)	Darrell Evans/Silver	12.00
(4a)	Dwight Gooden/Aluminum	1.00
(4b)	Dwight Gooden/Bronze	4.00
(4s)	Dwight Gooden/Silver	12.00
(5a)	Ozzie Guillen/Aluminum	1.00
(5b)	Ozzie Guillen/Bronze	4.00
(5s)	Ozzie Guillen/Silver	12.00
(6a)	Don Mattingly/Aluminum	4.00
(6b)	Don Mattingly/Bronze	20.00
(6s)	Don Mattingly/Silver	75.00
(6p)	Don Mattingly/Pewter	45.00
(7a)	Willie McGee/Aluminum	1.00
(7b)	Willie McGee/Bronze	4.00
(7s)	Willie McGee/Silver	12.00
(8a)	Dale Murphy/Aluminum	1.50
(8b)	Dale Murphy/Bronze	7.50
(8s)	Dale Murphy/Silver	30.00
(9a)	Dan Quisenberry/Aluminum	1.00
(9b)	Dan Quisenberry/Bronze	4.00
(9s)	Dan Quisenberry/Silver	12.00
(10a)	Jeff Reardon/Aluminum	1.00
(10b)	Jeff Reardon/Bronze	4.00
(10s)	Jeff Reardon/Silver	12.00
(11a)	Pete Rose/Aluminum	5.00
(11b)	Pete Rose/Bronze	25.00
(11s)	Pete Rose/Silver	90.00
(12a)	Bret Saberhagen/Aluminum	1.00
(12b)	Bret Saberhagen/Bronze	4.00
(12s)	Bret Saberhagen/Silver	12.00

Mini League Leaders

MIKE SCHMIDT

Topps had long experimented with bigger cards, but in 1986, they also decided to try smaller ones. These 2-1/8" x 2-15/16" cards feature top players in a number of categories. Sold in plastic packs as a regular Topps issue, the 66-card set is attractive as well as innovative. The cards feature color photos and a minimum of added information on the fronts where only the player's name and Topps logo appear. Backs limited information as well, but do feature enough to justify the player's inclusion in a set of league leaders.

		NM/M
	Complete Set (66):	5.00
	Common Player:	.05
	Wax Pack (6):	.50
	Wax Box (36):	10.00
	Vend Box (500):	15.00
1	Eddie Murray	.35
2	Cal Ripken, Jr.	1.00
3	Wade Boggs	.45
4	Dennis Boyd	.05
5	Dwight Evans	.05
6	Bruce Hurst	.05
7	Gary Pettis	.05
8	Harold Baines	.05
9	Floyd Bannister	.05
10	Britt Burns	.05
11	Carlton Fisk	.35
12	Brett Butler	.05
13	Darrell Evans	.05
14	Jack Morris	.05
15	Lance Parrish	.05
16	Walt Terrell	.05
17	Steve Balboni	.05
18	George Brett	.75
19	Charlie Leibrandt	.05
20	Bret Saberhagen	.05
21	Lonnie Smith	.05
22	Willie Wilson	.05
23	Bert Blyleven	.05
24	Mike Smithson	.05
25	Frank Viola	.05
26	Ron Guidry	.05
27	Rickey Henderson	.35
28	Don Mattingly	.75
29	Dave Winfield	.35
30	Mike Moore	.05
31	Gorman Thomas	.05
32	Toby Harrah	.05
33	Charlie Hough	.05
34	Doyle Alexander	.05
35	Jimmy Key	.05
36	Dave Stieb	.05
37	Dale Murphy	.20
38	Keith Moreland	.05
39	Ryne Sandberg	.45
40	Tom Browning	.05
41	Dave Parker	.05
42	Mario Soto	.05
43	Nolan Ryan	1.00
44	Pedro Guerrero	.05
45	Orel Hershiser	.05
46	Mike Scioscia	.05
47	Fernando Valenzuela	.05
48	Bob Welch	.05
49	Tim Raines	.05
50	Gary Carter	.35
51	Sid Fernandez	.05
52	Dwight Gooden	.05
53	Keith Hernandez	.05
54	Juan Samuel	.05
55	Mike Schmidt	.75
56	Glenn Wilson	.05
57	Rick Reuschel	.05
58	Joaquin Andujar	.05
59	Jack Clark	.05
60	Vince Coleman	.05
61	Danny Cox	.05
62	Tom Herr	.05

Stickers

The 1986 Topps stickers are 2-1/8" x 3". The 200-piece set features 316 different subjects, with some stickers including two or three players. Numbers run only to 315, however. The set includes some specialty stickers such as League Championships and World Series themes. Stickers are numbered both front and back and included a chance to win a trip to spring training as well as an offer to buy a complete 1986 Topps regular set. An album for the stickers was available in stores. It features Pete Rose in action on the front cover and reproductions of his Topps cards on back.

		NM/M
	Complete Set (315):	6.00
	Common Player:	.05
	Sticker Album:	1.50
	Wax Pack (5):	.30
	Wax Box (100):	11.00
1	Pete Rose	.60
2	Pete Rose	.60
3	George Brett	.50
4	Rod Carew	.40
5	Vince Coleman	.05
6	Dwight Gooden	.05
7	Phil Niekro	.20
8	Tony Perez	.30
9	Nolan Ryan	.75
10	Tom Seaver	.40
11	N.L. Championship Series (Ozzie Smith)	.10
12	N.L. Championship Series (Bill Madlock)	.05
13	N.L. Championship Series (Cardinals Celebrate)	.05
14	A.L. Championship Series (Al Oliver)	.05
15	A.L. Championship Series (Jim Sundberg)	.05
16	A.L. Championship Series (George Brett)	.10
17	World Series (Bret Saberhagen)	.05
18	World Series (Dane Iorg)	.05
19	World Series (Tito Landrum)	.05
20	World Series (John Tudor)	.05
21	World Series (Buddy Biancalana)	.05
22	World Series (Darryl Motley, Darrell Porter)	.05
23	World Series (George Brett, Frank White)	.05
24	Nolan Ryan	.75
25	Bill Doran	.05
26	Jose Cruz	.05
27	Mike Scott	.05
28	Kevin Bass	.05
29	Glenn Davis	.05
30	Mark Bailey	.05
31	Dave Smith	.05
32	Phil Garner	.05
33	Dickie Thon	.05
34	Bob Horner	.05
35	Dale Murphy	.25
36	Glenn Hubbard	.05
37	Bruce Sutter	.20
38	Ken Oberkfell	.05
39	Claudell Washington	.05
40	Steve Bedrosian	.05
41	Terry Harper	.05
42	Rafael Ramirez	.05
43	Rick Mahler	.05
44	Joaquin Andujar	.05
45	Willie McGee	.05
46	Ozzie Smith	.50
47	Vince Coleman	.05
48	Danny Cox	.05
49	Tom Herr	.05
50	Jack Clark	.05
51	Andy Van Slyke	.05
52	John Tudor	.05
53	Terry Pendleton	.05
54	Keith Moreland	.05
55	Ryne Sandberg	.40
56	Lee Smith	.05
57	Steve Trout	.05
58	Jody Davis	.05
59	Gary Matthews	.05
60	Leon Durham	.05
61	Rick Sutcliffe	.05
62	Dennis Eckersley	.30
63	Bob Dernier	.05
64	Fernando Valenzuela	.05
65	Pedro Guerrero	.05
66	Jerry Reuss	.05
67	Greg Brock	.05
68	Mike Scioscia	.05
69	Ken Howell	.05
70	Bill Madlock	.05
71	Mike Marshall	.05
72	Steve Sax	.05
73	Orel Hershiser	.05
74	Andre Dawson	.25
75	Tim Raines	.05
76	Jeff Reardon	.05
77	Hubie Brooks	.05
78	Bill Gullickson	.05
79	Bryn Smith	.05
80	Terry Francona	.05
81	Vance Law	.05
82	Tim Wallach	.05
83	Herm Winningham	.05
84	Jeff Leonard	.05
85	Chris Brown	.05
86	Scott Garrelts	.05
87	Jose Uribe	.05
88	Manny Trillo	.05
89	Dan Driessen	.05
90	Dan Gladden	.05
91	Mark Davis	.05
92	Bob Brenly	.05
93	Mike Krukow	.05
94	Dwight Gooden	.05
95	Darryl Strawberry	.05
96	Gary Carter	.40
97	Wally Backman	.05
98	Ron Darling	.05
99	Keith Hernandez	.05
100	George Foster	.05
101	Howard Johnson	.05
102	Rafael Santana	.05
103	Roger McDowell	.05
104	Steve Garvey	.15
105	Tony Gwynn	.50
106	Graig Nettles	.05
107	Rich Gossage	.05
108	Andy Hawkins	.05
109	Carmelo Martinez	.05
110	Garry Templeton	.05
111	Terry Kennedy	.05
112	Tim Flannery	.05
113	LaMarr Hoyt	.05
114	Mike Schmidt	.50
115	Ozzie Virgil	.05
116	Steve Carlton	.40
117	Garry Maddox	.05
118	Glenn Wilson	.05
119	Kevin Gross	.05
120	Von Hayes	.05
121	Juan Samuel	.05
122	Rick Schu	.05
123	Shane Rawley	.05
124	Johnny Ray	.05
125	Tony Pena	.05
126	Rick Reuschel	.05
127	Sammy Khalifa	.05
128	Marvell Wynne	.05
129	Jason Thompson	.05
130	Rick Rhoden	.05
131	Bill Almon	.05
132	Joe Orsulak	.05
133	Jim Morrison	.05
134	Pete Rose	.60
135	Dave Parker	.05
136	Mario Soto	.05
137	Dave Concepcion	.05
138	Ron Oester	.05
139	Buddy Bell	.05
140	Ted Power	.05
141	Tom Browning	.05
142	John Franco	.05
143	Tony Perez	.30
144	Willie McGee	.05
145	Dale Murphy	.50
146	Tony Gwynn	.50
147	Tom Herr	.05
148	Steve Garvey	.15
149	Dale Murphy	.25
150	Darryl Strawberry	.05
151	Graig Nettles	.05
152	Terry Kennedy	.05
153	Ozzie Smith	.50
154	LaMarr Hoyt	.05
155	Rickey Henderson	.40
156	Lou Whitaker	.05
157	George Brett	.50
158	Eddie Murray	.40
159	Cal Ripken, Jr.	.75
160	Dave Winfield	.40
161	Jim Rice	.15
162	Carlton Fisk	.40
163	Jack Morris	.05
164	Wade Boggs	.40
165	Darrell Evans	.05
166	Mike Davis	.05
167	Dave Kingman	.05
168	Alfredo Griffin	.05
169	Carney Lansford	.05
170	Bruce Bochte	.05
171	Dwayne Murphy	.05
172	Dave Collins	.05
173	Chris Codiroli	.05
174	Mike Heath	.05
175	Jay Howell	.05
176	Rod Carew	.40
177	Reggie Jackson	.50
178	Doug DeCinces	.05
179	Bob Boone	.05
180	Ron Romanick	.05
181	Bob Grich	.05
182	Donnie Moore	.05
183	Brian Downing	.05
184	Ruppert Jones	.05
185	Juan Beniquez	.05
186	Dave Stieb	.05
187	Jorge Bell	.05
188	Willie Upshaw	.05
189	Tom Henke	.05
190	Damaso Garcia	.05
191	Jimmy Key	.05
192	Jesse Barfield	.05
193	Dennis Lamp	.05
194	Tony Fernandez	.05
195	Lloyd Moseby	.05
196	Cecil Cooper	.05
197	Robin Yount	.40
198	Rollie Fingers	.20
199	Ted Simmons	.05
200	Ben Oglivie	.05
201	Moose Haas	.05
202	Jim Gantner	.05
203	Paul Molitor	.40
204	Charlie Moore	.05
205	Danny Darwin	.05
206	Brett Butler	.05
207	Brook Jacoby	.05
208	Andre Thornton	.05
209	Tom Waddell	.05
210	Tony Bernazard	.05
211	Julio Franco	.05
212	Pat Tabler	.05
213	Joe Carter	.05
214	George Vukovich	.05
215	Rich Thompson	.05
216	Gorman Thomas	.05
217	Phil Bradley	.05
218	Alvin Davis	.05
219	Jim Presley	.05
220	Matt Young	.05
221	Mike Moore	.05
222	Dave Henderson	.05
223	Ed Nunez	.05
224	Spike Owen	.05
225	Mark Langston	.05
226	Cal Ripken, Jr.	.75
227	Eddie Murray	.40
228	Fred Lynn	.05
229	Lee Lacy	.05
230	Scott McGregor	.05
231	Storm Davis	.05
232	Rick Dempsey	.05
233	Mike Boddicker	.05
234	Mike Young	.05
235	Sammy Stewart	.05
236	Pete O'Brien	.05
237	Oddibe McDowell	.05
238	Toby Harrah	.05
239	Gary Ward	.05
240	Larry Parrish	.05
241	Charlie Hough	.05
242	Burt Hooton	.05
243	Don Slaught	.05
244	Curt Wilkerson	.05
245	Greg Harris	.05
246	Jim Rice	.15
247	Wade Boggs	.40
248	Rich Gedman	.05
249	Dennis Boyd	.05
250	Marty Barrett	.05
251	Dwight Evans	.05
252	Bill Buckner	.05
253	Bob Stanley	.05
254	Tony Armas	.05
255	Mike Easler	.05
256	George Brett	.50
257	Dan Quisenberry	.05
258	Willie Wilson	.05
259	Jim Sundberg	.05
260	Bret Saberhagen	.05
261	Bud Black	.05
262	Charlie Leibrandt	.05
263	Frank White	.05
264	Lonnie Smith	.05
265	Steve Balboni	.05
266	Kirk Gibson	.05
267	Alan Trammell	.05
268	Jack Morris	.05
269	Darrell Evans	.05
270	Dan Petry	.05
271	Larry Herndon	.05
272	Lou Whitaker	.05
273	Lance Parrish	.05
274	Chet Lemon	.05
275	Willie Hernandez	.05
276	Tom Brunansky	.05
277	Kent Hrbek	.05
278	Mark Salas	.05
279	Bert Blyleven	.05
280	Tim Teufel	.05
281	Ron Davis	.05
282	Mike Smithson	.05
283	Gary Gaetti	.05
284	Frank Viola	.05
285	Kirby Puckett	.50
286	Carlton Fisk	.40
287	Tom Seaver	.40
288	Harold Baines	.05
289	Ron Kittle	.05
290	Bob James	.05
291	Rudy Law	.05
292	Britt Burns	.05
293	Greg Walker	.05
294	Ozzie Guillen	.05

295	Tim Hulett	.05
296	Don Mattingly	.50
297	Rickey Henderson	.40
298	Dave Winfield	.40
299	Butch Wynegar	.05
300	Don Baylor	.05
301	Eddie Whitson	.05
302	Ron Guidry	.05
303	Dave Righetti	.05
304	Bobby Meacham	.05
305	Willie Randolph	.05
306	Vince Coleman	.05
307	Oddibe McDowell	.05
308	Larry Sheets	.05
309	Ozzie Guillen	.05
310	Earnie Riles	.05
311	Chris Brown	.05
312	Brian Fisher, Roger McDowell	.05
313	Tom Browning	.05
314	Glenn Davis	.05
315	Mark Salas	.05

Super Sample

EDDIE MURRAY

To preview its oversize Super set for 1986, Topps issued a sample card of Eddie Murray. Front of the 4-7/8" x 6-7/8" card is the same as the issued version. On back, however, is this message: "topps / SPECIAL / COLLECTOR / SAMPLE / ACTUAL PRODUCT TO HAVE / STATISTICS PRINTED ON / WHITE-BOARD CARD BACK."

	NM/M
Eddie Murray	6.00

Super

REGGIE JACKSON

A third year of oversize (4-7/8" x 6-7/8") versions of Topps' regular issue cards saw the set once again hit the 60-card mark. Besides being four times the size of a normal card, the Supers differ only in the number on the back of the card.

		NM/M
Complete Set (60):		9.00
Common Player:		.25
1	Don Mattingly	1.00
2	Willie McGee	.25
3	Bret Saberhagen	.25
4	Dwight Gooden	.25
5	Dan Quisenberry	.25
6	Jeff Reardon	.25
7	Ozzie Guillen	.25
8	Vince Coleman	.25
9	Harold Baines	.25
10	Jorge Bell	.25
11	Bert Blyleven	.25
12	Wade Boggs	.60
13	Phil Bradley	.25
14	George Brett	1.00
15	Hubie Brooks	.25
16	Tom Browning	.25
17	Bill Buckner	.25
18	Brett Butler	.25
19	Gary Carter	.45
20	Cecil Cooper	.25
21	Darrell Evans	.25
22	Dwight Evans	.25
23	Carlton Fisk	.45

24	Steve Garvey	.35
25	Kirk Gibson	.25
26	Rich Gossage	.25
27	Pedro Guerrero	.25
28	Ron Guidry	.25
29	Tony Gwynn	.60
30	Rickey Henderson	.45
31	Keith Hernandez	.25
32	Tom Herr	.25
33	Orel Hershiser	.25
34	Jay Howell	.25
35	Reggie Jackson	.75
36	Bob James	.25
37	Charlie Leibrandt	.25
38	Jack Morris	.25
39	Dale Murphy	.35
40	Eddie Murray	.45
41	Dave Parker	.25
42	Tim Raines	.25
43	Jim Rice	.35
44	Dave Righetti	.25
45	Cal Ripken, Jr.	2.00
46	Pete Rose	1.50
47	Nolan Ryan	2.00
48	Ryne Sandberg	.60
49	Mike Schmidt	1.00
50	Tom Seaver	.45
51	Bryn Smith	.25
52	Lee Smith	.25
53	Ozzie Smith	.60
54	Dave Stieb	.25
55	Darryl Strawberry	.25
56	Gorman Thomas	.25
57	John Tudor	.25
58	Fernando Valenzuela	.25
59	Willie Wilson	.25
60	Dave Winfield	.45

Super Star

FRED LYNN

Tattoos

Topps returned to tattoos in 1986, marketing a set of 24 different tattoo sheets. Each sheet of tattoos measures 3-7/16" x 14" and includes both player and smaller action tattoos. As the action tattoos were uniform and not of any particular player, they add little value to the sheet. The

player tattoos measure 1-1/2" x 2-1/2". With 24 sheets, eight players per sheet, there are 192 players represented in the set. The sheets are numbered.

	NM/M
Complete Set (24):	9.00
Common Sheet:	.40
Pack (1):	.60
Wax Box (36):	13.50

1	Julio Franco, Rich Gossage, Keith Hernandez, Charlie Leibrandt, Jack Perconte, Lee Smith, Dickie Thon, Dave Winfield	.60
2	Jesse Barfield, Shawon Dunston, Dennis Eckersley, Brian Fisher, Moose Haas, Mike Moore, Dale Murphy, Bret Saberhagen	.50
3	George Bell, Bob Brenly, Steve Carlton, Jose DeLeon, Bob Horner, Bob James, Dan Quisenberry, Andre Thornton	.60
4	Mike Davis, Leon Durham, Darrell Evans, Glenn Hubbard, Johnny Ray, Cal Ripken, Ted Simmons	1.50
5	John Candelaria, Rick Dempsey, Steve Garvey, Ozzie Guillen, Gary Matthews, Jesse Orosco, Tony Pena	.45
6	Bruce Bochte, George Brett, Cecil Cooper, Sammy Khalifa, Ron Kittle, Scott McGregor, Pete Rose, Mookie Wilson	1.25
7	John Franco, Carney Lansford, Don Mattingly, Graig Nettles, Rick Reuschel, Mike Schmidt, Larry Sheets, Don Sutton	1.50
8	Cecilio Guante, Willie Hernandez, Mike Krukow, Fred Lynn, Phil Niekro, Ed Nunez, Ryne Sandberg, Pat Tabler	.75
9	Brett Butler, Chris Codiroli, Jim Gantner, Charlie Hough, Dave Parker, Rick Rhoden, Glenn Wilson, Robin Yount	.50
10	Tom Browning, Ron Darling, Von Hayes, Chet Lemon, Tom Seaver, Mike Smithson, Bruce Sutter, Alan Trammell	.60
11	Tony Armas, Jose Cruz, Jay Howell, Rick Mahler, Jack Morris, Rafael Ramirez, Dave Righetti, Mike Young	.40
12	Alvin Davis, Doug DeCinces, Andy Hawkins, Dennis Lamp, Keith Moreland, Jim Presley, Mario Soto, John Tudor	.40
13	Hubie Brooks, Jody Davis, Dwight Evans, Ron Hassey, Charles Hudson, Kirby Puckett, Jose Uribe	1.00
14	Tony Bernazard, Phil Bradley, Bill Buckner, Brian Downing, Dan Driessen, Ron Guidry, LaMarr Hoyt, Garry Maddox	.40
15	Buddy Bell, Joe Carter, Tony Fernandez, Tito Landrum, Jeff Leonard, Hal McRae, Willie Randolph, Juan Samuel	.40
16	Dennis Boyd, Vince Coleman, Scott Garrelts, Alfredo Griffin, Donnie Moore, Tony Perez, Ozzie Smith, Frank White	1.00
17	Rich Gedman, Kent Hrbek, Reggie Jackson, Mike Marshall, Terry Pendleton, Tim Raines, Mark Salas, Claudell Washington	1.00

18	Chris Brown, Tom Brunansky, Glenn Davis, Ron Davis, Burt Hooton, Darryl Strawberry, Frank Viola, Tim Wallach	.40
19	Jack Clark, Bill Doran, Toby Harrah, Bill Madlock, Pete O'Brien, Larry Parrish, Mike Scioscia, Garry Templeton	.40
20	Gary Carter, Andre Dawson, Dwight Gooden, Orel Hershiser, Oddibe McDowell, Roger McDowell, Dwayne Murphy, Jim Rice	.40
21	Steve Balboni, Mike Easler, Charlie Lea, Lloyd Moseby, Steve Sax, Rick Sutcliffe, Gary Ward, Willie Wilson	.40
22	Wade Boggs, Dave Concepcion, Kirk Gibson, Tom Herr, Lance Parrish, Jeff Reardon, Bryn Smith, Gorman Thomas	.75
23	Carlton Fisk, Bob Grich, Pedro Guerrero, Willie McGee, Paul Molitor, Mike Scott, Dave Stieb, Lou Whitaker	.60
24	Bert Blyleven, Damaso Garcia, Phil Garner, Tony Gwynn, Rickey Henderson, Ben Oglivie, Nolan Ryan, Fernando Valenzuela	1.50

3-D

DON MATTINGLY

This set is a second effort in the production of over-size (4-1/2" x 6") plastic cards on which the player figure is embossed. Cards were sold one per pack for 50¢. The 30 players in the set are among the game's top stars. The embossed color photo is bordered at bottom by a strip of contrasting color on which the player name appears. At the top, a row of white baseballs each contain a letter of the team nickname. Backs have no printing, and contain two self-adhesive strips with which the cards can be attached to a hard surface.

	NM/M
Complete Set (30):	9.00
Common Player:	.25
Wax Pack (1):	1.00
Wax Box (24):	15.00

1	Bert Blyleven	.25
2	Gary Carter	.60
3	Wade Boggs	.75
4	Dwight Gooden	.25
5	George Brett	1.50
6	Rich Gossage	.25
7	Darrell Evans	.25
8	Pedro Guerrero	.25
9	Ron Guidry	.25
10	Keith Hernandez	.25
11	Rickey Henderson	.60
12	Orel Hershiser	.25
13	Reggie Jackson	1.00
14	Willie McGee	.25
15	Don Mattingly	1.50
16	Dale Murphy	.45
17	Jack Morris	.25
18	Dave Parker	.25
19	Eddie Murray	.60
20	Jeff Reardon	.25
21	Dan Quisenberry	.25
22	Pete Rose	2.00
23	Jim Rice	.45
24	Mike Schmidt	1.50
25	Bret Saberhagen	.25
26	Darryl Strawberry	.25
27	Dave Stieb	.25
28	John Tudor	.25

29	Dave Winfield	.60
30	Fernando Valenzuela	.25

1987 Topps

MARIANO DUNCAN

The design of Topps' set of 792 2-1/2" x 3-1/2" cards is closely akin to the 1962 set in that the player photo is set against a woodgrain border. Instead of a rolling corner, as in 1962, the player photos in '87 feature a couple of clipped corners at top left and bottom right, where the team logo and player name appear. The player's position is not given on the front of the card. For the first time in several years, the trophy which designates members of Topps All-Star Rookie Team returned to the card design. As in the previous three years, Topps issued a glossy-finish "Tiffany" edition of their 792-card set. However, it was speculated that as many as 30,000 sets were produced as opposed to the 5,000 sets printed in 1985 and 1986.

	NM/M
Unopened Factory Set, Retail (792):	30.00
Unopened Factory Set, Hobby (792):	25.00
Complete Set (792):	20.00
Uncut Sheet Set (6):	45.00
Common Player:	.05
Wax Pack (15):	.75
Wax Box (36):	20.00
Cello Pack (31):	1.00
Cello Box (24):	20.00
Rack Pack (49):	1.50
Rack Box (24):	25.00
Vending Box (500):	12.00

1	Roger Clemens (Record Breaker)	.45
2	Jim Deshaies (Record Breaker)	.05
3	Dwight Evans (Record Breaker)	.05
4	Dave Lopes (Record Breaker)	.05
5	Dave Righetti (Record Breaker)	.05
6	Ruben Sierra (Record Breaker)	.05
7	Todd Worrell (Record Breaker)	.05
8	Terry Pendleton	.05
9	Jay Tibbs	.05
10	Cecil Cooper	.05
11	Indians Leaders (Jack Aker, Chris Bando, Phil Niekro)	.05
12	Jeff Sellers **RC**	.05
13	Nick Esasky	.05
14	Dave Stewart	.05
15	Claudell Washington	.05
16	Pat Clements	.05
17	Pete O'Brien	.05
18	Dick Howser	.05
19	Matt Young	.05
20	Gary Carter	.40
21	Mark Davis	.05
22	Doug DeCinces	.05
23	Lee Smith	.05
24	Tony Walker	.05
25	Bert Blyleven	.05
26	Greg Brock	.05
27	Joe Cowley	.05
28	Rick Dempsey	.05
29	Jimmy Key	.05
30	Tim Raines	.05
31	Braves Leaders (Glenn Hubbard, Rafael Ramirez)	.05
32	Tim Leary	.05
33	Andy Van Slyke	.05
34	Jose Rijo	.05
35	Sid Bream	.05
36	Eric King **RC**	.05
37	Marvell Wynne	.05
38	Dennis Leonard	.05
39	Marty Barrett	.05

40	Dave Righetti	.05
41	Bo Diaz	.05
42	Gary Redus	.05
43	Gene Michael	.05
44	Greg Harris	.05
45	Jim Presley	.05
46	Danny Gladden	.05
47	Dennis Powell	.05
48	Wally Backman	.05
49	Terry Harper	.05
50	Dave Smith	.05
51	Mel Hall	.05
52	Keith Atherton	.05
53	Ruppert Jones	.05
54	Bill Dawley	.05
55	Tim Wallach	.05
56	Brewers Leaders (Jamie Cocanower, Paul Molitor, Charlie Moore, Herm Starrette)	.10
57	Scott Nielsen **RC**	.05
58	Thad Bosley	.05
59	Ken Dayley	.05
60	Tony Pena	.05
61	Bobby Thigpen **RC**	.05
62	Bobby Meacham	.05
63	Fred Toliver **RC**	.05
64	Harry Spilman	.05
65	Tom Browning	.05
66	Marc Sullivan	.05
67	Bill Swift	.05
68	Tony LaRussa	.05
69	Lonnie Smith	.05
70	Charlie Hough	.05
71	Mike Aldrete **RC**	.05
72	Walt Terrell	.05
73	Dave Anderson	.05
74	Dan Pasqua	.05
75	Ron Darling	.05
76	Rafael Ramirez	.05
77	Bryan Oelkers	.05
78	Tom Foley	.05
79	Juan Nieves	.05
80	Wally Joyner **RC**	.35
81	Padres Leaders (Andy Hawkins, Terry Kennedy)	.05
82	Rob Murphy **RC**	.05
83	Mike Davis	.05
84	Steve Lake	.05
85	Kevin Bass	.05
86	Nate Snell	.05
87	Mark Salas	.05
88	Ed Wojna	.05
89	Ozzie Guillen	.05
90	Dave Stieb	.05
91	Harold Reynolds	.05
92a	Urbano Lugo (No trademark on front.)	.10
92b	Urbano Lugo (Trademark on front.)	.05
93	Jim Leyland	.05
94	Calvin Schiraldi	.05
95	Oddibe McDowell	.05
96	Frank Williams	.05
97	Glenn Wilson	.05
98	Bill Scherrer	.05
99	Darryl Motley	.05
100	Steve Garvey	.15
101	Carl Willis **RC**	.05
102	Paul Zuvella	.05
103	Rick Aguilera	.05
104	Billy Sample	.05
105	Floyd Youmans	.05
106	Blue Jays Leaders (George Bell, Willie Upshaw)	.05
107	John Butcher	.05
108	Jim Gantner (Photo reversed.)	.05
109	R.J. Reynolds	.05
110	John Tudor	.05
111	Alfredo Griffin	.05
112	Alan Ashby	.05
113	Neil Allen	.05
114	Billy Beane	.05
115	Donnie Moore	.05
116	Mike Stanley **RC**	.05
117	Jim Beattie	.05
118	Bobby Valentine	.05
119	Ron Robinson	.05
120	Eddie Murray	.40
121	Kevin Romine **RC**	.05
122	Jim Clancy	.05
123	John Kruk	.05
124	Ray Fontenot	.05
125	Bob Brenly	.05
126	Mike Loynd **RC**	.05
127	Vance Law	.05
128	Checklist 1-132	.05
129	Rick Cerone	.05
130	Dwight Gooden	.05
131	Pirates Leaders (Sid Bream, Tony Pena)	.05
132	Paul Assenmacher **RC**	.05
133	Jose Oquendo	.05
134	Rich Yett **RC**	.05
135	Mike Easler	.05
136	Ron Romanick	.05
137	Jerry Willard	.05
138	Roy Lee Jackson	.05
139	Devon White **RC**	.40
140	Bret Saberhagen	.05
141	Herm Winningham	.05
142	Rick Sutcliffe	.05
143	Steve Boros	.05
144	Mike Scioscia	.05

No.	Player	Price
145	Charlie Kerfeld	.05
146	Tracy Jones RC	.05
147	Randy Niemann	.05
148	Dave Collins	.05
149	Ray Searage	.05
150	Wade Boggs	.45
151	Mike LaCoss	.05
152	Toby Harrah	.05
153	Duane Ward RC	.05
154	Tom O'Malley	.05
155	Eddie Whitson	.05
156	Mariners Leaders (Bob Kearney, Phil Regan, Matt Young)	.05
157	Danny Darwin	.05
158	Tim Teufel	.05
159	Ed Olwine	.05
160	Julio Franco	.05
161	Steve Ontiveros	.05
162	Mike LaValliere RC	.10
163	Kevin Gross	.05
164	Sammy Khalifa	.05
165	Jeff Reardon	.05
166	Bob Boone	.05
167	Jim Deshaies RC	.10
168	Lou Piniella	.05
169	Ron Washington	.05
170	Bo Jackson (Future Stars)	.35
171	Chuck Cary RC	.05
172	Ron Oester	.05
173	Alex Trevino	.05
174	Henry Cotto	.05
175	Bob Stanley	.05
176	Steve Buechele	.05
177	Keith Moreland	.05
178	Cecil Fielder	.05
179	Bill Wegman	.05
180	Chris Brown	.05
181	Cardinals Leaders (Mike LaValliere, Ozzie Smith, Ray Soff)	.10
182	Lee Lacy	.05
183	Andy Hawkins	.05
184	Bobby Bonilla	.05
185	Roger McDowell	.05
186	Bruce Benedict	.05
187	Mark Huismann	.05
188	Tony Phillips	.05
189	Joe Hesketh	.05
190	Jim Sundberg	.05
191	Charles Hudson	.05
192	Cory Snyder RC	.05
193	Roger Craig	.05
194	Kirk McCaskill	.05
195	Mike Pagliarulo	.05
196	Randy O'Neal	.05
197	Mark Bailey	.05
198	Lee Mazzilli	.05
199	Mariano Duncan	.05
200	Pete Rose	.75
201	John Cangelosi RC	.05
202	Ricky Wright	.05
203	Mike Kingery RC	.05
204	Sammy Stewart	.05
205	Graig Nettles	.05
206	Twins Leaders (Tim Laudner, Frank Viola)	.05
207	George Frazier	.05
208	John Shelby	.05
209	Rick Schu	.05
210	Lloyd Moseby	.05
211	John Morris RC	.05
212	Mike Fitzgerald	.05
213	Randy Myers RC	.20
214	Omar Moreno	.05
215	Mark Langston	.05
216	B.J. Surhoff RC (Future Stars)	.20
217	Chris Codiroli	.05
218	Sparky Anderson	.10
219	Cecilio Guante	.05
220	Joe Carter	.05
221	Vern Ruhle	.05
222	Denny Walling	.05
223	Charlie Leibrandt	.05
224	Wayne Tolleson	.05
225	Mike Smithson	.05
226	Max Venable	.05
227	Jamie Moyer RC	.05
228	Curt Wilkerson	.05
229	Mike Birkbeck RC	.05
230	Don Baylor	.05
231	Giants Leaders (Bob Brenly, Mike Krukow)	.05
232	Reggie Williams RC	.05
233	Russ Morman RC	.05
234	Pat Sheridan	.05
235	Alvin Davis	.05
236	Tommy John	.10
237	Jim Morrison	.05
238	Bill Krueger	.05
239	Juan Espino	.05
240	Steve Balboni	.05
241	Danny Heep	.05
242	Rick Mahler	.05
243	Whitey Herzog	.05
244	Dickie Noles	.05
245	Willie Upshaw	.05
246	Jim Dwyer	.05
247	Jeff Reed RC	.05
248	Gene Walter	.05
249	Jim Pankovits	.05
250	Teddy Higuera	.05
251	Rob Wilfong	.05
252	Denny Martinez	.05
253	Eddie Milner	.05
254	Bob Tewksbury RC	.20
255	Juan Samuel	.05
256	Royals Leaders (George Brett, Frank White)	.15
257	Bob Forsch	.05
258	Steve Yeager	.05
259	Mike Greenwell RC	.25
260	Vida Blue	.05
261	Ruben Sierra	.05
262	Jim Winn	.05
263	Stan Javier RC	.05
264	Checklist 133-264	.05
265	Darrell Evans	.05
266	Jeff Hamilton RC	.05
267	Howard Johnson	.05
268	Pat Corrales	.05
269	Cliff Speck	.05
270	Jody Davis	.05
271	Mike Brown	.05
272	Andres Galarraga	.05
273	Gene Nelson	.05
274	Jeff Hearron RC	.05
275	LaMarr Hoyt	.05
276	Jackie Gutierrez	.05
277	Juan Agosto	.05
278	Gary Pettis	.05
279	Dan Plesac RC	.05
280	Jeffrey Leonard	.05
281	Reds Leaders (Bo Diaz, Bill Gullickson, Pete Rose)	.10
282	Jeff Calhoun	.05
283	Doug Drabek RC	.25
284	John Moses	.05
285	Dennis Boyd	.05
286	Mike Woodard RC	.05
287	Dave Von Ohlen	.05
288	Tito Landrum	.05
289	Bob Kipper	.05
290	Leon Durham	.05
291	Mitch Williams	.05
292	Franklin Stubbs	.05
293	Bob Rodgers	.05
294	Steve Jeltz	.05
295	Len Dykstra	.05
296	Andres Thomas RC	.05
297	Don Schulze	.05
298	Larry Herndon	.05
299	Joel Davis	.05
300	Reggie Jackson	.50
301	Luis Aquino RC	.05
302	Bill Schroeder	.05
303	Juan Berenguer	.05
304	Phil Garner	.05
305	John Franco	.05
306	Red Sox Leaders (Rich Gedman, John McNamara, Tom Seaver)	.10
307	Lee Guetterman RC	.05
308	Don Slaught	.05
309	Mike Young	.05
310	Frank Viola	.05
311	Rickey Henderson (Turn Back the Clock)	.10
312	Reggie Jackson (Turn Back the Clock)	.10
313	Roberto Clemente (Turn Back the Clock)	.50
314	Carl Yastrzemski (Turn Back the Clock)	.10
315	Maury Wills (Turn Back the Clock)	.05
316	Brian Fisher	.05
317	Clint Hurdle	.05
318	Jim Fregosi	.05
319	Greg Swindell RC	.10
320	Barry Bonds	8.00
321	Mike Laga	.05
322	Chris Bando	.05
323	Al Newman RC	.05
324	Dave Palmer	.05
325	Garry Templeton	.05
326	Mark Gubicza	.05
327	Dale Sveum RC	.05
328	Bob Welch	.05
329	Ron Roenicke	.05
330	Mike Scott	.05
331	Mets Leaders (Gary Carter, Keith Hernandez, Dave Johnson, Darryl Strawberry)	.10
332	Joe Price	.05
333	Ken Phelps	.05
334	Ed Correa RC	.05
335	Candy Maldonado	.05
336	Allan Anderson RC	.05
337	Darrell Miller	.05
338	Tim Conroy	.05
339	Donnie Hill	.05
340	Roger Clemens	.65
341	Mike Brown	.05
342	Bob James	.05
343	Hal Lanier	.05
344a	Joe Niekro (Copyright outside yellow on back.)	.05
344b	Joe Niekro (Copyright inside yellow on back.)	.05
645	Andre Dawson	.25
346	Shawon Dunston	.05
347	Mickey Brantley RC	.05
348	Carmelo Martinez	.05
349	Storm Davis	.05
350	Keith Hernandez	.05
351	Gene Garber	.05
352	Mike Felder RC	.05
353	Ernie Camacho	.05
354	Jamie Quirk	.05
355	Don Carman	.05
356	White Sox Leaders (Ed Brinkman, Julio Cruz)	.05
357	Steve Fireovid RC	.05
358	Sal Butera	.05
359	Doug Corbett	.05
360	Pedro Guerrero	.05
361	Mark Thurmond	.05
362	Luis Quinones RC	.05
363	Jose Guzman	.05
364	Randy Bush	.05
365	Rick Rhoden	.05
366	Mark McGwire	3.00
367	Jeff Lahti	.05
368	John McNamara	.05
369	Brian Dayett	.05
370	Fred Lynn	.05
371	Mark Eichhorn RC	.05
372	Jerry Mumphrey	.05
373	Jeff Dedmon	.05
374	Glenn Hoffman	.05
375	Ron Guidry	.10
376	Scott Bradley	.05
377	John Henry Johnson	.05
378	Rafael Santana	.05
379	John Russell	.05
380	Rich Gossage	.05
381	Expos Leaders (Mike Fitzgerald, Bob Rodgers)	.05
382	Rudy Law	.05
383	Ron Davis	.05
384	Johnny Grubb	.05
385	Orel Hershiser	.05
386	Dickie Thon	.05
387	T.R. Bryden RC	.05
388	Geno Petralli	.05
389	Jeff Robinson	.05
390	Gary Matthews	.05
391	Jay Howell	.05
392	Checklist 265-396	.05
393	Pete Rose	.60
394	Mike Bielecki	.05
395	Damaso Garcia	.05
396	Tim Lollar	.05
397	Greg Walker	.05
398	Brad Havens	.05
399	Curt Ford	.05
400	George Brett	.50
401	Billy Jo Robidoux	.05
402	Mike Trujillo	.05
403	Jerry Royster	.05
404	Doug Sisk	.05
405	Brook Jacoby	.05
406	Yankees Leaders (Rickey Henderson, Don Mattingly)	.25
407	Jim Acker	.05
408	John Mizerock	.05
409	Milt Thompson	.05
410	Fernando Valenzuela	.05
411	Darnell Coles	.05
412	Eric Davis	.05
413	Moose Haas	.05
414	Joe Orsulak	.05
415	Bobby Witt RC	.05
416	Tom Nieto	.05
417	Pat Perry RC	.05
418	Dick Williams	.05
419	Mark Portugal RC	.10
420	Will Clark	.40
421	Jose DeLeon	.05
422	Jack Howell	.05
423	Jaime Cocanower	.05
424	Chris Speier	.05
425	Tom Seaver	.40
426	Floyd Rayford	.05
427	Ed Nunez	.05
428	Bruce Bochy	.05
429	Tim Pyznarski RC (Future Stars)	.05
430	Mike Schmidt	.50
431	Dodgers Leaders (Tom Niedenfuer, Ron Perranoski, Alex Trevino)	.05
432	Jim Slaton	.05
433	Ed Hearn RC	.05
434	Mike Fischlin	.05
435	Bruce Sutter	.35
436	Andy Allanson RC	.05
437	Ted Power	.05
438	Kelly Downs RC	.05
439	Karl Best	.05
440	Willie McGee	.05
441	Dave Leiper RC	.05
442	Mitch Webster	.05
443	John Felske	.05
444	Jeff Russell	.05
445	Dave Lopes	.05
446	Chuck Finley RC	.25
447	Bill Almon	.05
448	Chris Bosio RC	.10
449	Pat Dodson RC (Future Stars)	.05
450	Kirby Puckett	.45
451	Joe Sambito	.05
452	Dave Henderson	.05
453	Scott Terry RC	.05
454	Luis Salazar	.05
455	Mike Boddicker	.05
456	A's Leaders (Carney Lansford, Tony LaRussa, Mickey Tettleton, Dave Von Ohlen)	.05
457	Len Matuszek	.05
458	Kelly Gruber RC	.05
459	Dennis Eckersley	.35
460	Darryl Strawberry	.05
461	Craig McMurtry	.05
462	Scott Fletcher	.05
463	Tom Candiotti	.05
464	Butch Wynegar	.05
465	Todd Worrell	.05
466	Kal Daniels RC	.05
467	Randy St. Claire	.05
468	George Bamberger	.05
469	Mike Diaz RC	.05
470	Dave Dravecky	.05
471	Ronn Reynolds	.05
472	Bill Doran	.05
473	Steve Farr	.05
474	Jerry Narron	.05
475	Scott Garrelts	.05
476	Danny Tartabull	.05
477	Ken Howell	.05
478	Tim Laudner	.05
479	Bob Sebra RC	.05
480	Jim Rice	.15
481	Phillies Leaders (Von Hayes, Juan Samuel, Glenn Wilson)	.05
482	Daryl Boston	.05
483	Dwight Lowry	.05
484	Jim Traber RC	.05
485	Tony Fernandez	.05
486	Otis Nixon	.05
487	Dave Gumpert	.05
488	Ray Knight	.05
489	Bill Gullickson	.05
490	Dale Murphy	.20
491	Ron Karkovice RC	.05
492	Mike Heath	.05
493	Tom Lasorda	.10
494	Barry Jones RC	.05
495	Gorman Thomas	.05
496	Bruce Bochte	.05
497	Dale Mohorcic RC	.05
498	Bob Kearney	.05
499	Bruce Ruffin RC	.05
500	Don Mattingly	.65
501	Craig Lefferts	.05
502	Dick Schofield	.05
503	Larry Andersen	.05
504	Mickey Hatcher	.05
505	Bryn Smith	.05
506	Orioles Leaders (Rich Bordi, Rick Dempsey, Earl Weaver)	.05
507	Dave Stapleton	.05
508	Scott Bankhead RC	.05
509	Enos Cabell	.05
510	Tom Henke	.05
511	Steve Lyons	.05
512	Dave Magadan RC (Future Stars)	.20
513	Carmen Castillo	.05
514	Orlando Mercado	.05
515	Willie Hernandez	.05
516	Ted Simmons	.05
517	Mario Soto	.05
518	Gene Mauch	.05
519	Curt Young	.05
520	Jack Clark	.05
521	Rick Reuschel	.05
522	Checklist 397-528	.05
523	Earnie Riles	.05
524	Bob Shirley	.05
525	Phil Bradley	.05
526	Roger Mason	.05
527	Jim Wohlford	.05
528	Ken Dixon	.05
529	Alvaro Espinoza RC	.05
530	Tony Gwynn	.45
531	Astros Leaders (Yogi Berra, Hal Lanier, Denis Menke, Gene Tenace)	.05
532	Jeff Stone	.05
533	Argenis Salazar	.05
534	Scott Sanderson	.05
535	Tony Armas	.05
536	Terry Mulholland RC	.15
537	Rance Mulliniks	.05
538	Tom Niedenfuer	.05
539	Reid Nichols	.05
540	Terry Kennedy	.05
541	Rafael Belliard RC	.05
542	Ricky Horton	.05
543	Dave Johnson	.05
544	Zane Smith	.05
545	Buddy Bell	.05
546	Mike Morgan	.05
547	Rob Deer	.05
548	Bill Mooneyham RC	.05
549	Bob Melvin	.05
550	Pete Incaviglia	.05
551	Frank Wills	.05
552	Larry Sheets	.05
553	Mike Maddux RC	.05
554	Buddy Biancalana	.05
555	Dennis Rasmussen	.05
556	Angels Leaders (Bob Boone, Marcel Lachemann, Mike Witt)	.05
557	John Cerutti RC	.05
558	Greg Gagne	.05
559	Lance McCullers	.05
560	Glenn Davis	.05
561	Rey Quinones RC	.05
562	Bryan Clutterbuck RC	.05
563	John Stefero	.05
564	Larry McWilliams	.05
565	Dusty Baker	.05
566	Tim Hulett	.05
567	Greg Mathews RC	.05
568	Earl Weaver	.10
569	Wade Rowdon RC	.05
570	Sid Fernandez	.05
571	Ozzie Virgil	.05
572	Pete Ladd	.05
573	Hal McRae	.05
574	Manny Lee	.05
575	Pat Tabler	.05
576	Frank Pastore	.05
577	Dann Bilardello	.05
578	Billy Hatcher	.05
579	Rick Burleson	.05
580	Mike Krukow	.05
581	Cubs Leaders (Ron Cey, Steve Trout)	.05
582	Bruce Berenyi	.05
583	Junior Ortiz	.05
584	Ron Kittle	.05
585	Scott Bailes RC	.05
586	Ben Oglivie	.05
587	Eric Plunk RC	.05
588	Wallace Johnson	.05
589	Steve Crawford	.05
590	Vince Coleman	.05
591	Spike Owen	.05
592	Chris Welsh	.05
593	Chuck Tanner	.05
594	Rick Anderson	.05
595	Keith Hernandez/AS	.05
596	Steve Sax/AS	.05
597	Mike Schmidt/AS	.35
598	Ozzie Smith/AS	.30
599	Tony Gwynn/AS	.30
600	Dave Parker/AS	.05
601	Darryl Strawberry/AS	.05
602	Gary Carter/AS	.25
603a	(No trademark on front)	.25
603b	Dwight Gooden/AS (Trademark on front)	.05
604	Fernando Valenzuela/AS	.05
605	Todd Worrell/AS	.05
606a	Don Mattingly/AS (No trademark on front)	.75
606b	Don Mattingly/AS (Trademark on front)	.35
607	Tony Bernazard/AS	.05
608	Wade Boggs/AS	.30
609	Cal Ripken, Jr./AS	.45
610	Jim Rice/AS	.05
611	Kirby Puckett/AS	.30
612	George Bell/AS	.05
613	Lance Parrish/AS	.05
614	Roger Clemens/AS	.35
615	Teddy Higuera/AS	.05
616	Dave Righetti/AS	.05
617	Al Nipper	.05
618	Tom Kelly	.05
619	Jerry Reed	.05
620	Jose Canseco	.60
621	Danny Cox	.05
622	Glenn Braggs RC	.05
623	Kurt Stillwell RC	.05
624	Tim Burke	.05
625	Mookie Wilson	.05
626	Joel Skinner	.05
627	Ken Oberkfell	.05
628	Bob Walk	.05
629	Larry Parrish	.05
630	John Candelaria	.05
631	Tigers Leaders (Sparky Anderson, Mike Heath, Willie Hernandez)	.05
632	Rob Woodward RC	.05
633	Jose Uribe	.05
634	Rafael Palmeiro RC	2.00
635	Ken Schrom	.05
636	Darren Daulton	.05
637	Bip Roberts RC	.10
638	Rich Bordi	.05
639	Gerald Perry	.05
640	Mark Clear	.05
641	Domingo Ramos	.05
642	Al Pulido	.05
643	Ron Shepherd	.05
644	John Denny	.05
645	Dwight Evans	.05
646	Mike Mason	.05
647	Tom Lawless	.05
648	Barry Larkin RC	.60
649	Mickey Tettleton	.05
650	Hubie Brooks	.05
651	Benny Distefano	.05
652	Terry Forster	.05
653	Kevin Mitchell	.05
654	Checklist 529-660	.05
655	Jesse Barfield	.05
656	Rangers Leaders (Bobby Valentine, Rickey Wright)	.05
657	Tom Waddell	.05
658	Robby Thompson RC	.05
659	Aurelio Lopez	.05
660	Bob Horner	.05
661	Lou Whitaker	.05
662	Frank DiPino	.05
663	Cliff Johnson	.05
664	Mike Marshall	.05
665	Rod Scurry	.05
666	Von Hayes	.05
667	Ron Hassey	.05
668	Juan Bonilla	.05
669	Bud Black	.05
670	Jose Cruz	.05
671a	Ray Soff (No "D*" before copyright line.)	.20
671b	Ray Soff ("D*" before copyright line.)	.05
672	Chili Davis	.05
673	Don Sutton	.35
674	Bill Campbell	.05
675	Ed Romero	.05
676	Charlie Moore	.05
677	Bob Grich	.05
678	Carney Lansford	.05
679	Kent Hrbek	.05
680	Ryne Sandberg	.45
681	George Bell	.05
682	Jerry Reuss	.05
683	Gary Roenicke	.05
684	Kent Tekulve	.05
685	Jerry Hairston Sr.	.05
686	Doyle Alexander	.05
687	Alan Trammell	.05
688	Juan Beniquez	.05
689	Darrell Porter	.05
690	Dane Iorg	.05
691	Dave Parker	.05
692	Frank White	.05
693	Terry Puhl	.05
694	Phil Niekro	.05
695	Chico Walker	.05
696	Gary Lucas	.05
697	Ed Lynch	.05
698	Ernie Whitt	.05
699	Ken Landreaux	.05
700	Dave Bergman	.05
701	Willie Randolph	.05
702	Greg Gross	.05
703	Dave Schmidt	.05
704	Jesse Orosco	.05
705	Bruce Hurst	.05
706	Rick Manning	.05
707	Bob McClure	.05
708	Scott McGregor	.05
709	Dave Kingman	.05
710	Gary Gaetti	.05
711	Ken Griffey	.05
712	Don Robinson	.05
713	Tom Brookens	.05
714	Dan Quisenberry	.05
715	Bob Dernier	.05
716	Rick Leach	.05
717	Ed Vande Berg	.05
718	Steve Carlton	.40
719	Tom Hume	.05
720	Richard Dotson	.05
721	Tom Herr	.05
722	Bob Knepper	.05
723	Brett Butler	.05
724	Greg Minton	.05
725	George Hendrick	.05
726	Frank Tanana	.05
727	Mike Moore	.05
728	Tippy Martinez	.05
729	Tom Paciorek	.05
730	Eric Show	.05
731	Dave Concepcion	.05
732	Manny Trillo	.05
733	Bill Caudill	.05
734	Bill Madlock	.05
735	Rickey Henderson	.40
736	Steve Bedrosian	.05
737	Floyd Bannister	.05
738	Jorge Orta	.05
739	Chet Lemon	.05
740	Rich Gedman	.05
741	Paul Molitor	.40
742	Andy McGaffigan	.05
743	Dwayne Murphy	.05
744	Roy Smalley	.05
745	Glenn Hubbard	.05
746	Bob Ojeda	.05
747	Johnny Ray	.05
748	Mike Flanagan	.05
749	Ozzie Smith	.45
750	Steve Trout	.05
751	Garth Iorg	.05
752	Dan Petry	.05
753	Rick Honeycutt	.05
754	Dave LaPoint	.05
755	Luis Aguayo	.05
756	Carlton Fisk	.05
757	Nolan Ryan	.75
758	Tony Bernazard	.05
759	Joel Youngblood	.05
760	Mike Witt	.05
761	Greg Pryor	.05
762	Gary Ward	.05
763	Tim Flannery	.05
764	Bill Buckner	.05
765	Kirk Gibson	.05
766	Don Aase	.05
767	Ron Cey	.05
768	Dennis Lamp	.05
769	Steve Sax	.05
770	Dave Winfield	.40
771	Shane Rawley	.05
772	Harold Baines	.05
773	Robin Yount	.40
774	Wayne Krenchicki	.05
775	Joaquin Andujar	.05
776	Tom Brunansky	.05
777	Chris Chambliss	.05
778	Jack Morris	.05
779	Craig Reynolds	.05
780	Andre Thornton	.05

#	Player	Price
781	Atlee Hammaker	.05
782	Brian Downing	.05
783	Willie Wilson	.05
784	Cal Ripken, Jr.	.75
785	Terry Francona	.05
786	Jimy Williams	.05
787	Alejandro Pena	.05
788	Tim Stoddard	.05
789	Dan Schatzeder	.05
790	Julio Cruz	.05
791	Lance Parrish	.05
792	Checklist 661-792	.05

Tiffany

Produced in much greater quantity (reportedly 30,000 sets) than the previous years' sets, this specially boxed collectors' edition differs from the regular 1987 Topps cards only in its use of white cardboard stock and a high-gloss finish on the cards' fronts.

	NM/M
Unopened Set (792):	90.00
Complete Set (792):	50.00
Common Player:	.15
320 Barry Bonds	35.00

Traded

KEVIN McREYNOLDS

The Topps Traded set consists of 132 cards as did all Traded sets issued by Topps since 1981. Cards measure the standard 2-1/2" x 3-1/2" and are identical in design to the regular edition set. The purpose of the set is to update player trades and feature rookies not included in the regular issue. As they had done the previous three years, Topps produced a glossy-coated "Tiffany" edition of the Traded set. Cards are numbered with a "T" suffix.

		NM/M
Complete Set (132):		4.00
Common Player:		.05
1	Bill Almon	.05
2	Scott Bankhead	.05
3	Eric Bell RC	.05
4	Juan Beniquez	.05
5	Juan Berenguer	.05
6	Greg Booker	.05
7	Thad Bosley	.05
8	Larry Bowa	.05
9	Greg Brock	.05
10	Bob Brower RC	.05
11	Jerry Browne RC	.05
12	Ralph Bryant RC	.05
13	DeWayne Buice RC	.05
14	Ellis Burks RC	.50
15	Ivan Calderon	.05
16	Jeff Calhoun	.05
17	Casey Candaele RC	.05
18	John Cangelosi	.05
19	Steve Carlton	.25
20	Juan Castillo RC	.05
21	Rick Cerone	.05
22	Ron Cey	.05
23	John·Christensen	.05
24	Dave Cone RC	.15
25	Chuck Crim RC	.05
26	Storm Davis	.05
27	Andre Dawson	.25
28	Rick Dempsey	.05
29	Doug Drabek	.05
30	Mike Dunne	.05
31	Dennis Eckersley	.25
32	Lee Elia	.05
33	Brian Fisher	.05
34	Terry Francona	.05
35	Willie Fraser RC	.05
36	Billy Gardner	.05
37	Ken Gerhart RC	.05
38	Danny Gladden	.05
39	Jim Gott	.05
40	Cecilio Guante	.05
41	Albert Hall	.05
42	Terry Harper	.05
43	Mickey Hatcher	.05
44	Brad Havens	.05

#	Player	Price
45	Neal Heaton	.05
46	Mike Henneman RC	.20
47	Donnie Hill	.05
48	Guy Hoffman	.05
49	Brian Holton RC	.05
50	Charles Hudson	.05
51	Danny Jackson RC	.05
52	Reggie Jackson	.40
53	Chris James RC	.05
54	Dion James	.05
55	Stan Jefferson RC	.05
56	Joe Johnson RC	.05
57	Terry Kennedy	.05
58	Mike Kingery	.05
59	Ray Knight	.05
60	Gene Larkin RC	.05
61	Mike LaValliere	.05
62	Jack Lazorko	.05
63	Terry Leach	.05
64	Tim Leary	.05
65	Jim Lindeman RC	.05
66	Steve Lombardozzi RC	.05
67	Bill Long RC	.05
68	Barry Lyons RC	.05
69	Shane Mack RC	.05
70	Greg Maddux RC	3.00
71	Bill Madlock	.05
72	Joe Magrane RC	.05
73	Dave Martinez RC	.05
74	Fred McGriff RC	.25
75	Mark McLemore RC	.05
76	Kevin McReynolds RC	.05
77	Dave Meads RC	.05
78	Eddie Milner	.05
79	Greg Minton	.05
80	John Mitchell RC	.05
81	Kevin Mitchell	.05
82	Charlie Moore	.05
83	Jeff Musselman RC	.05
84	Gene Nelson	.05
85	Graig Nettles	.05
86	Al Newman	.05
87	Reid Nichols	.05
88	Tom Niedenfuer	.05
89	Joe Niekro	.05
90	Tom Nieto	.05
91	Matt Nokes RC	.10
92	Dickie Noles	.05
93	Pat Pacillo	.05
94	Lance Parrish	.05
95	Tony Pena	.05
96	Luis Polonia RC	.05
97	Randy Ready	.05
98	Jeff Reardon	.05
99	Gary Redus	.05
100	Jeff Reed	.05
101	Rick Rhoden	.05
102	Cal Ripken, Sr.	.05
103	Wally Ritchie RC	.05
104	Jeff Robinson RC	.05
105	Gary Roenicke	.05
106	Jerry Royster	.05
107	Mark Salas	.05
108	Luis Salazar	.05
109	Benny Santiago RC	.15
110	Dave Schmidt	.05
111	Kevin Seitzer RC	.05
112	John Shelby	.05
113	Steve Shields RC	.05
114	John Smiley RC	.20
115	Chris Speier	.05
116	Mike Stanley RC	.05
117	Terry Steinbach RC	.15
118	Les Straker RC	.05
119	Jim Sundberg	.05
120	Danny Tartabull	.05
121	Tom Trebelhorn RC	.05
122	Dave Valle RC	.05
123	Ed Vande Berg	.05
124	Andy Van Slyke	.05
125	Gary Ward	.05
126	Alan Wiggins	.05
127	Bill Wilkinson RC	.05
128	Frank Williams	.05
129	Matt Williams RC	.75
130	Jim Winn	.05
131	Matt Young	.05
132	Checklist 1T-132T	.05

Traded Tiffany

The cards in this specially boxed limited edition version of the Traded set differ from the regular-issue cards only in the application of a high-gloss finish to the cards' fronts. Production was reported as 30,000 sets.

	NM/M
Complete Set (132):	30.00
Common Player:	.15

Traded Willie Mays Bronze

This 1/4-size metal replica was issued to dealers who purchased cases of 1987 Topps Traded sets. Each detail of the 1953 Topps Mays card is reproduced on the 1-1/4" x 1-3/4" bronze metal mini-card, right down to the stats.

WILLIE MAYS
Outfield · New York Giants

		NM/M
244	Willie Mays	10.00

Box Panels

Offering baseball cards on retail boxes for a second straight year, Topps reduced the size of the cards to 2-1/8" x 3". Four different wax pack boxes are available, each featuring two cards that were placed on the sides of the boxes. The card fronts are identical in design to the regular issue cards. The backs are printed in blue and yellow and carry a commentary imitating a newspaper format. The cards are numbered A through H.

		NM/M
Complete Singles Set (8):		2.00
Complete Panel Set (4):		2.50
Common Panel:		.50
Common Single Player:		.15
Panel		.50
A	Don Baylor	.15
B	Steve Carlton	.30
Panel		.50
C	Ron Cey	.15
D	Cecil Cooper	.15
Panel		.75
E	Rickey Henderson	.40
F	Jim Rice	.20
Panel		.75
G	Don Sutton	.25
H	Dave Winfield	.40

All-Star Glossy Set of 22

ROGER CLEMENS

For the fourth consecutive year, Topps produced an All-Star Game commemorative set of 22 cards. The glossy cards, 2-1/2" x 3-1/2", were included in rack packs. Using the same basic design as in previous efforts with a few minor changes, the 1987 edition features American and National League logos on the card fronts. Cards #1-12 feature representatives from the American League, while #13-22 are National Leaguers.

		NM/M
Complete Set (22):		2.50
Common Player:		.05
1	Whitey Herzog	.05
2	Keith Hernandez	.05
3	Ryne Sandberg	.35

#	Player	Price
4	Mike Schmidt	.50
5	Ozzie Smith	.35
6	Tony Gwynn	.35
7	Dale Murphy	.20
8	Darryl Strawberry	.05
9	Gary Carter	.30
10	Dwight Gooden	.05
11	Fernando Valenzuela	.05
12	Dick Howser	.05
13	Wally Joyner	.05
14	Lou Whitaker	.05
15	Wade Boggs	.35
16	Cal Ripken, Jr.	.60
17	Dave Winfield	.30
18	Rickey Henderson	.30
19	Kirby Puckett	.35
20	Lance Parrish	.05
21	Roger Clemens	.40
22	Teddy Higuera	.05

All-Star Glossy Set of 60

Using the same design as the previous year, the 1987 Topps All-Star glossy set includes 48 All-Star performers plus 12 potential superstars branded as "Hot Prospects." The card fronts are uncluttered, save the player's name found in very small print at the bottom. The set was available via a mail-in offer. Six subsets make up the 60-card set, with each subset being available for $1.00 plus six special offer cards that were found in wax packs.

		NM/M
Complete Set (60):		15.00
Common Player:		.10
1	Don Mattingly	.75
2	Tony Gwynn	.50
3	Gary Gaetti	.10
4	Glenn Davis	.10
5	Roger Clemens	.65
6	Dale Murphy	.25
7	Lou Whitaker	.10
8	Roger McDowell	.10
9	Cory Snyder	.10
10	Todd Worrell	.10
11	Gary Carter	.40
12	Eddie Murray	.40
13	Bob Knepper	.10
14	Harold Baines	.10
15	Jeff Reardon	.10
16	Joe Carter	.10
17	Dave Parker	.10
18	Wade Boggs	.50
19	Danny Tartabull	.10
20	Jim Deshaies	.10
21	Rickey Henderson	.40
22	Rob Deer	.10
23	Ozzie Smith	.50
24	Dave Righetti	.10
25	Kent Hrbek	.10
26	Keith Hernandez	.10
27	Don Baylor	.10
28	Mike Schmidt	.85
29	Pete Incaviglia	.10
30	Barry Bonds	9.00
31	George Brett	.85
32	Darryl Strawberry	.10
33	Mike Witt	.10
34	Kevin Bass	.10
35	Jesse Barfield	.10
36	Bob Ojeda	.10
37	Cal Ripken, Jr.	2.00
38	Vince Coleman	.10
39	Wally Joyner	.10
40	Robby Thompson	.10
41	Pete Rose	1.00
42	Jim Rice	.25
43	Tony Bernazard	.10
44	Eric Davis	.10
45	George Bell	.10
46	Hubie Brooks	.10
47	Jack Morris	.10
48	Tim Raines	.10
49	Mark Eichhorn	.10
50	Kevin Mitchell	.10
51	Dwight Gooden	.10
52	Doug DeCinces	.10
53	Fernando Valenzuela	.10
54	Reggie Jackson	.50
55	Johnny Ray	.10
56	Mike Pagliarulo	.10
57	Kirby Puckett	.50
58	Lance Parrish	.10
59	Jose Canseco	.50
60	Greg Mathews	.10

Baseball Highlights

The "Baseball Highlights" boxed set of 33 cards was prepared by Topps for distribution at stores in the Woolworth's chain, although the retailer's name does not appear on the cards. Each card measures 2-1/2" x 3-1/2" in size and features a memorable baseball event that occurred during the 1986 season. The glossy set sold for $1.99.

Coins

For the first time since 1971, Topps issued a set of baseball "coins." Similar in design to the 1964 edition, the metal discs measure 1-1/2" in diameter. The aluminum coins were sold on a limited basis in retail outlets. Three coins and three sticks of gum were found in a pack. The coin fronts feature a full-color photo along with the player's name, team and position in a white band at the bottom. Gold-colored rims are found for American League players; National League players have silver-colored rims. Backs are silvered and carry the coin number, player's name and personal and statistical information.

		NM/M
Complete Set (48):		7.50
Common Player:		.10
Wax Pack (3):		1.00
Wax Box (24):		15.00
1	Harold Baines	.10
2	Jesse Barfield	.10
3	George Bell	.10
4	Wade Boggs	.45
5	George Brett	1.00
6	Jose Canseco	.25
7	Joe Carter	.10
8	Roger Clemens	.60
9	Alvin Davis	.10
10	Rob Deer	.10
11	Kirk Gibson	.10
12	Rickey Henderson	.35
13	Kent Hrbek	.10
14	Pete Incaviglia	.10
15	Reggie Jackson	.60
16	Wally Joyner	.10
17	Don Mattingly	.75
18	Jack Morris	.10
19	Eddie Murray	.35
20	Kirby Puckett	.40
21	Jim Rice	.25
22	Dave Righetti	.10
23	Cal Ripken, Jr.	1.50
24	Cory Snyder	.10
25	Danny Tartabull	.10
26	Dave Winfield	.35
27	Hubie Brooks	.10

#	Player	Price
28	Gary Carter	.35
29	Vince Coleman	.10
30	Eric Davis	.10
31	Glenn Davis	.10
32	Steve Garvey	.15
33	Dwight Gooden	.10
34	Tony Gwynn	.45
35	Von Hayes	.10
36	Keith Hernandez	.10
37	Dale Murphy	.20
38	Dave Parker	.10
39	Tony Pena	.10
40	Nolan Ryan	1.50
41	Ryne Sandberg	.45
42	Steve Sax	.10
43	Mike Schmidt	1.00
44	Mike Scott	.10
45	Ozzie Smith	.45
46	Darryl Strawberry	.10
47	Fernando Valenzuela	.10
48	Todd Worrell	.10

Gallery of Champions

ROGER CLEMENS

Designed as a tribute to 1986's winners of baseball's most prestigious awards, the Gallery of Champions are metal "cards" that are one-quarter size replicas of the regular issue Topps cards. The bronze and silver sets were issued in leather-like velvet-lined display cases; the aluminum sets came cello-wrapped. Hobby dealers who purchased one bronze set or a 16-set case of aluminum "cards" received one free Jose Canseco pewter metal mini-card. The purchase of a silver set included five Canseco pewters.

	NM/M
Complete Aluminum Set (12):	17.50
Complete Bronze Set (12):	75.00
Complete Silver Set (12):	250.00
(1a) Jesse Barfield/ Aluminum	2.00
(1b) Jesse Barfield/Bronze	6.00
(1s) Jesse Barfield/Silver	15.00
(2a) Wade Boggs/ Aluminum	4.50
(2b) Wade Boggs/Bronze	15.00
(2s) Wade Boggs/Silver	30.00
(3a) Jose Canseco/ Aluminum	3.50
(3b) Jose Canseco/Bronze	10.00
(3s) Jose Canseco/Silver	25.00
(3p) Jose Canseco/Pewter	12.50
(4a) Joe Carter/Aluminum	2.00
(4b) Joe Carter/Bronze	6.00
(4s) Joe Carter/Silver	15.00
(5a) Roger Clemens/ Aluminum	5.00
(5b) Roger Clemens/ Bronze	16.00
(5s) Roger Clemens/Silver	40.00
(6a) Tony Gwynn/ Aluminum	4.50
(6b) Tony Gwynn/Bronze	15.00
(6s) Tony Gwynn/Silver	30.00
(7a) Don Mattingly/ Aluminum	5.00
(7b) Don Mattingly/Bronze	17.50
(7s) Don Mattingly/Silver	45.00
(8a) Tim Raines/Aluminum	2.00
(8b) Tim Raines/Bronze	6.00
(8s) Tim Raines/Silver	15.00
(9a) Dave Righetti/ Aluminum	2.00
(9b) Dave Righetti/Bronze	6.00
(9s) Dave Righetti/Silver	15.00
(10a) Mike Schmidt/ Aluminum	6.00
(10b) Mike Schmidt/Bronze	20.00
(10s) Mike Schmidt/Silver	50.00
(11a) Mike Scott/Aluminum	2.00
(11b) Mike Scott/Bronze	6.00
(11s) Mike Scott/Silver	15.00
(12a) Todd Worrell/ Aluminum	2.00
(12b) Todd Worrell/Bronze	6.00
(12s) Todd Worrell/Silver	15.00

Glossy Rookies

The 1987 Topps Glossy Rookies set of 22 cards was introduced with Topps' new 100-card "Jumbo Packs." Intended for sale in supermarkets, the jumbo packs contained one glossy card. Measuring the standard 2-1/2" x 3-1/2" size, the special insert cards feature the top rookies from the previous season.

		NM/M
Complete Set (22):		3.00
Common Player:		.05
1	Andy Allanson	.05
2	John Cangelosi	.05
3	Jose Canseco	1.00
4	Will Clark	.25
5	Mark Eichhorn	.05
6	Pete Incaviglia	.05
7	Wally Joyner	.05
8	Eric King	.05
9	Dave Magadan	.05
10	John Morris	.05
11	Juan Nieves	.05
12	Rafael Palmeiro	2.50
13	Billy Jo Robidoux	.05
14	Bruce Ruffin	.05
15	Ruben Sierra	.05
16	Cory Snyder	.05
17	Kurt Stillwell	.05
18	Dale Sveum	.05
19	Danny Tartabull	.05
20	Andres Thomas	.05
21	Robby Thompson	.05
22	Todd Worrell	.05

Bobby Grich Night Sheet

In conjunction with a Bobby Grich Night sponsored by the California Angels on May 1, 1987, Sheraton Hotels of Los Angeles and radio station KLAC issued this sheet bearing reproductions of each of Grich's regular issue Topps cards from 1971-1987. The sheet measures 10" x 17-1/2", while the perforated cards, if removed from the sheet, measure the standard 2-1/2" x 3-1/2".

		NM/M
Complete Sheet:		10.00
Common Card:		.75
1971	Bob Grich #193	1.50
1972	Bob Grich #338	.75
1973	Bob Grich #418	.75
1974	Bob Grich #109	.75
1975	Bob Grich #225	.75
1976	Bob Grich #335	.75
1977	Bob Grich #521	.75
1978	Bob Grich #18	.75
1979	Bob Grich #477	.75
1980	Bob Grich #621	.75
1981	Bob Grich #182	.75
1982	Bob Grich #284	.75
1983	Bob Grich #790	.75
1984	Bob Grich #315	.75
1985	Bob Grich #465	.75
1986	Bob Grich #155	.75
1987	Bob Grich #677	.75

Mini League Leaders

Returning for 1987, the Topps "Major League Leaders" set was increased in size from 66 to 76 cards. The 2-1/8" x 3" cards feature woodgrain borders that encompass a white-bordered color photo. Backs are printed in yellow, orange and brown and list the player's official ranking based on his 1986 American or National League statistics. The players

DENNIS RASMUSSEN

featured are those who finished the top five in their leagues' various batting and pitching categories. The cards were sold in plastic-wrapped packs, seven cards plus a game card per pack.

		NM/M
Complete Set (77):		4.00
Common Player:		.05
Wax Pack (7):		.50
Wax Box (36):		10.00
1	Bob Horner	.05
2	Dale Murphy	.15
3	Lee Smith	.05
4	Eric Davis	.05
5	John Franco	.05
6	Dave Parker	.05
7	Kevin Bass	.05
8	Glenn Davis	.05
9	Bill Doran	.05
10	Bob Knepper	.05
11	Mike Scott	.05
12	Dave Smith	.05
13	Mariano Duncan	.05
14	Orel Hershiser	.05
15	Steve Sax	.05
16	Fernando Valenzuela	.05
17	Tim Raines	.05
18	Jeff Reardon	.05
19	Floyd Youmans	.05
20	Gary Carter	.25
21	Ron Darling	.05
22	Sid Fernandez	.05
23	Dwight Gooden	.05
24	Keith Hernandez	.05
25	Bob Ojeda	.05
26	Darryl Strawberry	.05
27	Steve Bedrosian	.05
28	Von Hayes	.05
29	Juan Samuel	.05
30	Mike Schmidt	.75
31	Rick Rhoden	.05
32	Vince Coleman	.05
33	Danny Cox	.05
34	Todd Worrell	.05
35	Tony Gwynn	.35
36	Mike Krukow	.05
37	Candy Maldonado	.05
38	Don Aase	.05
39	Eddie Murray	.25
40	Cal Ripken, Jr.	1.00
41	Wade Boggs	.40
42	Roger Clemens	.40
43	Bruce Hurst	.05
44	Jim Rice	.15
45	Wally Joyner	.05
46	Donnie Moore	.05
47	Gary Pettis	.05
48	Mike Witt	.05
49	John Cangelosi	.05
50	Tom Candiotti	.05
51	Joe Carter	.05
52	Pat Tabler	.05
53	Kirk Gibson	.05
54	Willie Hernandez	.05
55	Jack Morris	.05
56	Alan Trammell	.05
57	George Brett	.75
58	Willie Wilson	.05
59	Rob Deer	.05
60	Teddy Higuera	.05
61	Bert Blyleven	.05
62	Gary Gaetti	.05
63	Kirby Puckett	.35
64	Rickey Henderson	.05
65	Don Mattingly	.50
66	Dennis Rasmussen	.05
67	Dave Righetti	.05
68	Jose Canseco	.20
69	Dave Kingman	.05
70	Phil Bradley	.05
71	Mark Langston	.05
72	Pete O'Brien	.05
73	Jesse Barfield	.05
74	George Bell	.05
75	Tony Fernandez	.05
76	Tom Henke	.05
77	Checklist	

Stickers - Hardback Test

In addition to its regular issue of Panini-produced paper-backed stickers, Topps in 1987

produced a very limited version of the same issue with a hard cardboard back. The Topps hard-back version is virtually identical to the more common Panini version except for the copyright line printed on back. Production of the hard-back version was reported to be 1/10 of 1 percent of the Panini version.

		NM/M
Complete Set (313):		75.00
Common Player:		.50
Wax Pack (5):		1.00
Wax Box (48):		25.00

Stickers - Panini

For the seventh consecutive year, Topps issued stickers produced by Panini in Italy for use in a special album or yearbook. The 2-1/8" x 3" stickers offer a full-color front with a peel-off paper back. Fronts feature either one full-size player picture or two half-size individual stickers. The yearbook contains 36 glossy, magazine-style pages, all printed in full color. Mike Schmidt, 1986 N.L. MVP, is featured on the covers. The yearbook sold in retail outlets for \$.35, while stickers were sold five in a pack for \$.25. The number in parentheses in this checklist is the sticker number the player shares the sticker with. Besides the common soft-back sticker made for Topps by Panini, there was a test issue of hard-back stickercards.

		NM/M
Complete Set (313):		15.00
Common Player:		.05
Sticker Album:		1.50
Wax Pack (5):		.25
Wax Box (100):		15.00
1	1986 Highlights	
	Jim Deshaies/172	.05
2	1986 Highlights	
	Roger Clemens/175	.25
3	1986 Highlights	
	Roger Clemens/176	.25
4	1986 Highlights	
	Dwight Evans/177	.05
5	1986 Highlights	
	Dwight Gooden/178	.05
6	1986 Highlights	
	Dwight Gooden/180	.05
7	1986 Highlights	
	Dave Lopes/181	.05
8	1986 Highlights	
	Dave Righetti/182	.05
9	1986 Highlights	
	Dave Righetti/183)	.05
10	1986 Highlights	
	Ruben Sierra/185	.05
11	1986 Highlights	
	Todd Worrell/186	.05
12	1986 Highlights	
	Todd Worrell/187	.05
13	N.L. Championship Series	
	(Lenny Dykstra)	.05
14	N.L. Championship Series	
	(Gary Carter)	.15
15	N.L. Championship Series	
	(Mike Scott)	.05
16	A.L. Championship Series	
	(Gary Pettis)	.05
17	A.L. Championship Series	
	(Jim Rice)	.05
18	A.L. Championship Series	
	(Bruce Hurst)	.05
19	1986 World Series	
	(Bruce Hurst)	.05
20	1986 World Series	
	(Wade Boggs)	.15
21	1986 World Series	
	(Lenny Dykstra)	.05
22	1986 World Series	
	(Gary Carter)	.15
23	1986 World Series	
	(Dave Henderson)	.05
24	1986 World Series	
	(Howard Johnson)	.05
25	1986 World Series	
	(Mets Celebrate)	.05
26	Glenn Davis	.05
27	Nolan Ryan/188	.60
28	Charlie Kerfeld/189	.05
29	Jose Cruz/190	.05
30	Phil Garner/191	.05
31	Bill Doran/192	.05
32	Bob Knepper/195	.05
33	Denny Walling/196	.05
34	Kevin Bass/197	.05
35	Mike Scott	.05
36	Dale Murphy	.20
37	Paul Assenmacher/198	.05
38	Ken Oberkfell/200	.05
39	Andres Thomas/201	.05
40	Gene Garber/202	.05
41	Bob Horner	.05
42	Rafael Ramirez/203	.05
43	Rick Mahler/204	.05
44	Omar Moreno/205	.05
45	Dave Palmer/206	.05
46	Ozzie Smith	.35
47	Bob Forsch/207	.05
48	Willie McGee/209	.05
49	Tom Herr/210	.05
50	Vince Coleman/211	.05
51	Andy Van Slyke/212	.05
52	Jack Clark/215	.05
53	John Tudor/216	.05
54	Terry Pendleton/217	.05
55	Todd Worrell	.05
56	Lee Smith	.05
57	Leon Durham/218	.05
58	Jerry Mumphrey/219	.05
59	Shawon Dunston/220	.05
60	Scott Sanderson/221	.05
61	Ryne Sandberg	.35
62	Gary Matthews/222	.05
63	Dennis Eckersley/225	.25
64	Jody Davis/226	.05
65	Keith Moreland/227	.05
66	Mike Marshall/228	.05
67	Bill Madlock/229	.05
68	Greg Brock/230	.05
69	Pedro Guerrero/231	.05
70	Steve Sax	.05
71	Rick Honeycutt/232	.05
72	Franklin Stubbs/235	.05
73	Mike Scioscia/236	.05
74	Mariano Duncan/237	.05
75	Fernando Valenzuela	.05
76	Hubie Brooks	.05
77	Andre Dawson/238	.20
78	Tim Burke/240	.05
79	Floyd Youmans/241	.05
80	Tim Wallach/242	.05
81	Jeff Reardon/243	.05
82	Mitch Webster/244	.05
83	Bryn Smith/245	.05
84	Andres Galarraga/246	.05
85	Tim Raines	.05
86	Chris Brown	.05
87	Bob Brenly/247	.05
88	Will Clark/249	.10
89	Scott Garrelts/250	.05
90	Jeffrey Leonard/251	.05
91	Robby Thompson/252	.05
92	Mike Krukow/255	.05
93	Danny Gladden/256	.05
94	Candy Maldonado/257	.05
95	Chili Davis	.05
96	Dwight Gooden	.25
97	Sid Fernandez/258	.05
98	Len Dykstra/259	.05
99	Bob Ojeda/260	.05
100	Wally Backman/261	.05
101	Gary Carter	.30
102	Keith Hernandez/262	.05
103	Darryl Strawberry/265	.05
104	Roger McDowell/266	.05
105	Ron Darling/267	.05
106	Tony Gwynn	.35
107	Dave Dravecky/268	.05
108	Terry Kennedy/269	.05
109	Rich Gossage/270	.05
110	Garry Templeton/271	.05
111	Lance McCullers/272	.05
112	Eric Show/275	.05
113	John Kruk/276	.05
114	Tim Flannery/277	.05
115	Steve Garvey	.15
116	Mike Schmidt	.45
117	Glenn Wilson/278	.05
118	Kent Tekulve/280	.05
119	Gary Redus/281	.05
120	Shane Rawley/282	.05
121	Von Hayes	.05
122	Don Carman/283	.05
123	Bruce Ruffin/285	.05
124	Steve Bedrosian/286	.05
125	Juan Samuel/287	.05
126	Sid Bream/288	.05
127	Cecilio Guante/289	.05
128	Rick Reuschel/290	.05
129	Tony Pena/291	.05
130	Rick Rhoden	.05
131	Barry Bonds/292	5.00
132	Joe Orsulak/295	.05
133	Jim Morrison/296	.05
134	R.J. Reynolds/297	.05
135	Johnny Ray	.05
136	Eric Davis	.05
137	Tom Browning/298	.05
138	John Franco/300	.05
139	Pete Rose/301	.35
140	Bill Gullickson/302	.05
141	Ron Oester/303	.05
142	Bo Diaz/304	.05
143	Buddy Bell/305	.05
144	Eddie Milner/306	.05
145	Dave Parker	.05
146	Kirby Puckett	.35
147	Rickey Henderson	.30
148	Wade Boggs	.35
149	Lance Parrish	.05
150	Wally Joyner	.05
151	Cal Ripken, Jr.	.75
152	Dave Winfield	.30
153	Lou Whitaker	.05
154	Roger Clemens	.40
155	Tony Gwynn	.35
156	Ryne Sandberg	.35
157	Keith Hernandez	.05
158	Gary Carter	.30
159	Darryl Strawberry	.05
160	Mike Schmidt	.45
161	Dale Murphy	.15
162	Ozzie Smith	.35
163	Dwight Gooden	.05
164	Jose Canseco	.25
165	Curt Young/307	.05
166	Alfredo Griffin/308	.05
167	Dave Stewart/309	.05
168	Mike Davis/310	.05
169	Bruce Bochte/311	.05
170	Dwayne Murphy/312	.05
171	Carney Lansford/313	.05
172	Joaquin Andujar/1	.05
173	Dave Kingman	.05
174	Wally Joyner	.05
175	Gary Pettis/2	.05
176	Dick Schofield/3	.05
177	Donnie Moore/4	.05
178	Brian Downing/5	.05
179	Mike Witt	.05
180	Bob Boone/6	.05
181	Kirk McCaskill/7	.05
182	Doug DeCinces/8	.05
183	Don Sutton/9	.25
184	Jessie Barfield	.05
185	Tom Henke/10	.05
186	Willie Upshaw/11	.05
187	Mark Eichhorn/12	.05
188	Damaso Garcia/27	.05
189	Jim Clancy/28	.05
190	Lloyd Moseby/29	.05
191	Tony Fernandez/30	.05
192	Jimmy Key/31	.05
193	George Bell	.05
194	Rob Deer	.05
195	Mark Clear/32	.05
196	Robin Yount/33	.20
197	Jim Gantner/34	.05
198	Cecil Cooper/37	.05
199	Teddy Higuera	.05
200	Paul Molitor/38	.25
201	Dan Plesac/39	.05
202	Billy Jo Robidoux/40	.05
203	Earnie Riles/42	.05
204	Ken Schrom/43	.05
205	Pat Tabler/44	.05
206	Mel Hall/45	.05
207	Tony Bernazard/47	.05
208	Joe Carter	.05
209	Ernie Camacho/48	.05
210	Julio Franco/47	.05
211	Tom Candiotti/50	.05
212	Brook Jacoby/51	.05
213	Cory Snyder	.05
214	Jim Presley	.05
215	Mike Moore/52	.05
216	Harold Reynolds/53	.05
217	Scott Bradley/54	.05
218	Matt Young/57	.05
219	Mark Langston/58	.05
220	Alvin Davis/59	.05
221	Phil Bradley/60	.05
222	Ken Phelps/62	.05
223	Danny Tartabull	.05
224	Eddie Murray	.30
225	Rick Dempsey/63	.05
226	Mike Boddicker/65	.05
227	Don Aase/66	.05
228	Larry Sheets/67	.05
229	Larry Sheets/67	.05
230	Storm Davis/68	.05
231	Lee Lacy/69	.05
232	Jim Traber/71	.05
233	Cal Ripken, Jr.	.75
234	Larry Parrish	.05
235	Gary Ward/72	.05
236	Pete Incaviglia/73	.05
237	Scott Fletcher/74	.05
238	Greg Harris/77	.05
239	Pete O'Brien	.05
240	Charlie Hough/78	.05
241	Don Slaught/79	.05
242	Steve Buechele/80	.05
243	Oddibe McDowell/81	.05
244	Roger Clemens/82	.30
245	Bob Stanley/83	.05
246	Tom Seaver/84	.20
247	Rich Gedman/87	.05
248	Jim Rice	.15
249	Dennis Boyd/88	.05
250	Bill Buckner/89	.05
251	Dwight Evans/90	.05
252	Don Baylor/91	.05
253	Wade Boggs	.35
254	George Brett	.45
255	Steve Farr/92	.05
256	Jim Sundberg/93	.05
257	Dan Quisenberry/94	.05
258	Charlie Leibrandt/97	.05
259	Argenis Salazar/98	.05
260	Frank White/99	.05
261	Willie Wilson/100	.05
262	Lonnie Smith/102	.05
263	Steve Balboni	.05
264	Darrell Evans	.05
265	Johnny Grubb/103	.05
266	Jack Morris/104	.05
267	Lou Whitaker/105	.05
268	Chet Lemon/107	.05
269	Lance Parrish/108	.05
270	Alan Trammell/109	.05
271	Darnell Coles/110	.05
272	Willie Hernandez/111	.05
273	Kirk Gibson	.05
274	Kirby Puckett	.35
275	Mike Smithson/112	.05
276	Mickey Hatcher/113	.05
277	Frank Viola/114	.05
278	Bert Blyleven/117	.05
279	Gary Gaetti	.05
280	Tom Brunansky/118	.05
281	Kent Hrbek/119	.05
282	Roy Smalley/120	.05
283	Greg Gagne/122	.05
284	Harold Baines	.05
285	Ron Hassey/123	.05
286	Floyd Bannister/124	.05
287	Ozzie Guillen/125	.05
288	Carlton Fisk/126	.25
289	Tim Hulett/127	.05
290	Joe Cowley/128	.05
291	Greg Walker/129	.05
292	Neil Allen/131	.05
293	John Cangelosi	.05
294	Don Mattingly	.45
295	Mike Easler/132	.05
296	Rickey Henderson/133	.20
297	Dan Pasqua/134	.05
298	Dave Winfield/137	.20
299	Dave Righetti	.05
300	Mike Pagliarulo/138	.05
301	Ron Guidry/139	.05
302	Willie Randolph/140	.05
303	Dennis Rasmussen/141	.05
304	Jose Canseco/142	.20
305	Andres Thomas/143	.05
306	Danny Tartabull/144	.05
307	Robby Thompson/165	.05
308	Pete Incaviglia,	
	Cory Snyder/166	.05
309	Dale Sveum/167	.05
310	Todd Worrell/168	.05
311	Andy Allanson/169	.05
312	Bruce Ruffin/170	.05
313	Wally Joyner/171	.05

1988 Topps

The 1988 Topps set features a clean, attractive design of a player photo surrounded by a thin colored frame which is encompassed by a white border. The player's name appears in the lower-right corner in a diagonal colored strip. The team nickname is in large letters at the top of the card. Backs feature black print on orange and gray stock and include the usual player personal and career statistics. Many of the cards contain a new feature titled "This Way To The Clubhouse," which explains how the player joined his current team. The 792-card set includes a number of special subsets including "Future Stars," "Turn Back The Clock," All-Star teams, All-Star rookie selections, and Record Breakers.

NM/M

Unopened Factory Set, Retail (792):	17.50
Unopened Factory Set, Hobby (792):	16.00
Complete Set (792):	12.50
Common Player:	.05
Wax Pack (15):	.40
Wax Box (36):	15.00
Cello Pack (28):	.70
Cello Box (24):	13.50
Rack Pack (43):	.75
Rack Box (24):	15.00
Vending Box (500):	7.50

1	Vince Coleman (Record Breakers)	.05
2	Don Mattingly (Record Breakers)	.25
3a	Mark McGwire (Record Breakers, white triangle by left foot)	1.00
3b	Mark McGwire (Record Breakers, no white triangle)	.40
4a	Eddie Murray (Record Breakers, no mention of record on front)	.25
4b	Eddie Murray (Record Breakers, record in box on front)	.20
5	Joe Niekro, Phil Niekro (Record Breakers)	.05
6	Nolan Ryan (Record Breakers)	.40
7	Benito Santiago (Record Breakers)	.05
8	Kevin Elster RC (Future Stars)	.05
9	Andy Hawkins	.05
10	Ryne Sandberg	.50
11	Mike Young	.05
12	Bill Schroeder	.05
13	Andres Thomas	.05
14	Sparky Anderson	.10
15	Chili Davis	.05
16	Kirk McCaskill	.05
17	Ron Oester	.05
18a	Al Leiter RC (Actually Steve George. Future Stars, no "NY" on shirt, photo.)	.40
18b	Al Leiter RC (Photo. Future Stars, "NY" on shirt, correct.)	.20
19	Mark Davidson RC	.05
20	Kevin Gross	.05
21	Red Sox Leaders (Wade Boggs, Spike Owen)	.10
22	Greg Swindell	.05
23	Ken Landreaux	.05
24	Jim Deshaies	.05
25	Andres Galarraga	.05
26	Mitch Williams	.05
27	R.J. Reynolds	.05
28	Jose Nunez RC	.05
29	Argenis Salazar	.05
30	Sid Fernandez	.05
31	Bruce Bochy	.05
32	Mike Morgan	.05
33	Rob Deer	.05
34	Ricky Horton	.05
35	Harold Baines	.05
36	Jamie Moyer	.05
37	Ed Romero	.05
38	Jeff Calhoun	.05
39	Gerald Perry	.05
40	Orel Hershiser	.05
41	Bob Melvin	.05
42	Bill Landrum RC	.05
43	Dick Schofield	.05
44	Lou Piniella	.05
45	Kent Hrbek	.05
46	Darnell Coles	.05
47	Joaquin Andujar	.05
48	Alan Ashby	.05
49	Dave Clark RC	.05
50	Hubie Brooks	.05
51	Orioles Leaders (Eddie Murray, Cal Ripken, Jr.)	.25
52	Don Robinson	.05
53	Curt Wilkerson	.05
54	Jim Clancy	.05
55	Phil Bradley	.05
56	Ed Hearn	.05
57	Tim Crews RC	.05
58	Dave Magadan	.05
59	Danny Cox	.05
60	Rickey Henderson	.40
61	Mark Knudson RC	.05
62	Jeff Hamilton	.05
63	Jimmy Jones RC	.05
64	Ken Caminiti RC	.25
65	Leon Durham	.05
66	Shane Rawley	.05
67	Ken Oberkfell	.05

68	Dave Dravecky	.05
69	Mike Hart RC	.05
70	Roger Clemens	.60
71	Gary Pettis	.05
72	Dennis Eckersley	.30
73	Randy Bush	.05
74	Tom Lasorda	.05
75	Joe Carter	.25
76	Denny Martinez	.05
77	Tom O'Malley	.05
78	Dan Petry	.05
79	Ernie Whitt	.05
80	Mark Langston	.05
81	Reds Leaders (John Franco, Ron Robinson)	.05
82	Darrel Akerfelds RC	.05
83	Jose Oquendo	.05
84	Cecilio Guante	.05
85	Howard Johnson	.05
86	Ron Karkovice	.05
87	Mike Mason	.05
88	Earnie Riles	.05
89	Gary Thurman RC	.05
90	Dale Murphy	.20
91	Joey Cora RC	.10
92	Len Matuszek	.05
93	Bob Sebra	.05
94	Chuck Jackson RC	.05
95	Lance Parrish	.05
96	Todd Benzinger RC	.05
97	Scott Garrelts	.05
98	Rene Gonzales RC	.05
99	Chuck Finley	.05
100	Jack Clark	.05
101	Allan Anderson	.05
102	Barry Larkin	.05
103	Curt Young	.05
104	Dick Williams	.05
105	Jesse Orosco	.05
106	Jim Walewander RC	.05
107	Scott Bailes	.05
108	Steve Lyons	.05
109	Joel Skinner	.05
110	Teddy Higuera	.05
111	Expos Leaders (Hubie Brooks, Vance Law)	.05
112	Les Lancaster RC	.05
113	Kelly Gruber	.05
114	Jeff Russell	.05
115	Johnny Ray	.05
116	Jerry Don Gleaton	.05
117	James Steels RC	.05
118	Bob Welch	.05
119	Robbie Wine RC	.05
120	Kirby Puckett	.50
121	Checklist 1-132	.05
122	Tony Bernazard	.05
123	Tom Candiotti	.05
124	Ray Knight	.05
125	Bruce Hurst	.05
126	Steve Jeltz	.05
127	Jim Gott	.05
128	Johnny Grubb	.05
129	Greg Minton	.05
130	Buddy Bell	.05
131	Don Schulze	.05
132	Donnie Hill	.05
133	Greg Mathews	.05
134	Chuck Tanner	.05
135	Dennis Rasmussen	.05
136	Brian Dayett	.05
137	Chris Bosio	.05
138	Mitch Webster	.05
139	Jerry Browne	.05
140	Jesse Barfield	.05
141	Royals Leaders (George Brett, Bret Saberhagen)	.20
142	Andy Van Slyke	.05
143	Mickey Tettleton	.05
144	Don Gordon RC	.05
145	Bill Madlock	.05
146	Donell Nixon RC	.05
147	Bill Buckner	.05
148	Carmelo Martinez	.05
149	Ken Howell	.05
150	Eric Davis	.05
151	Bob Knepper	.05
152	Jody Reed RC	.10
153	John Habyan	.05
154	Jeff Stone	.05
155	Bruce Sutter	.30
156	Gary Matthews	.05
157	Atlee Hammaker	.05
158	Tim Hulett	.05
159	Brad Arnsberg RC	.05
160	Willie McGee	.05
161	Bryn Smith	.05
162	Mark McLemore	.05
163	Dale Mohorcic	.05
164	Dave Johnson	.05
165	Robin Yount	.40
166	Rick Rodriguez RC	.05
167	Rance Mulliniks	.05
168	Barry Jones	.05
169	Ross Jones RC	.05
170	Rich Gossage	.05
171	Cubs Leaders (Shawon Dunston, Manny Trillo)	.05
172	Lloyd McClendon RC	.05
173	Eric Plunk	.05
174	Phil Garner	.05
175	Kevin Bass	.05
176	Jeff Reed	.05
177	Frank Tanana	.05

178	Dwayne Henry RC	.05
179	Charlie Puleo	.05
180	Terry Kennedy	.05
181	Dave Cone	.05
182	Ken Phelps	.05
183	Tom Lawless	.05
184	Ivan Calderon	.05
185	Rick Rhoden	.05
186	Rafael Palmeiro	.35
187	Steve Kiefer RC	.05
188	John Russell	.05
189	Wes Gardner RC	.05
190	Candy Maldonado	.05
191	John Cerutti	.05
192	Devon White	.05
193	Brian Fisher	.05
194	Tom Kelly	.05
195	Dan Quisenberry	.05
196	Dave Engle	.05
197	Lance McCullers	.05
198	Franklin Stubbs	.05
199	Dave Meads RC	.05
200	Wade Boggs	.50
201	Rangers Leaders (Steve Buechele, Pete Incaviglia, Pete O'Brien, Bobby Valentine)	.05
202	Glenn Hoffman	.05
203	Fred Toliver	.05
204	Paul O'Neill RC	.05
205	Nelson Liriano RC	.05
206	Domingo Ramos	.05
207	John Mitchell RC	.05
208	Steve Lake	.05
209	Richard Dotson	.05
210	Willie Randolph	.05
211	Frank DiPino	.05
212	Greg Brock	.05
213	Albert Hall	.05
214	Dave Schmidt	.05
215	Von Hayes	.05
216	Jerry Reuss	.05
217	Harry Spilman	.05
218	Dan Schatzeder	.05
219	Mike Stanley	.05
220	Tom Henke	.05
221	Rafael Belliard	.05
222	Steve Farr	.05
223	Stan Jefferson	.05
224	Tom Trebelhorn	.05
225	Mike Scioscia	.05
226	Dave Lopes	.05
227	Ed Correa	.05
228	Wallace Johnson	.05
229	Jeff Musselman	.05
230	Pat Tabler	.05
231	Pirates Leaders (Barry Bonds, Bobby Bonilla)	.50
232	Bob James	.05
233	Rafael Santana	.05
234	Ken Dayley	.05
235	Gary Ward	.05
236	Ted Power	.05
237	Mike Heath	.05
238	Luis Polonia RC	.10
239	Roy Smalley	.05
240	Lee Smith	.05
241	Damaso Garcia	.05
242	Tom Niedenfuer	.05
243	Mark Ryal RC	.05
244	Jeff Robinson	.05
245	Rich Gedman	.05
246	Mike Campbell RC (Future Stars)	.05
247	Thad Bosley	.05
248	Storm Davis	.05
249	Mike Marshall	.05
250	Nolan Ryan	.75
251	Tom Foley	.05
252	Bob Brower	.05
253	Checklist 133-264	.05
254	Lee Elia	.05
255	Mookie Wilson	.05
256	Ken Schrom	.05
257	Jerry Royster	.05
258	Ed Nunez	.05
259	Ron Kittle	.05
260	Vince Coleman	.05
261	Giants Leaders (Will Clark, Candy Maldonado, Kevin Mitchell, Robby Thompson, Jose Uribe)	.05
262	Drew Hall RC	.05
263	Glenn Braggs	.05
264	Les Straker RC	.05
265	Bo Diaz	.05
266	Paul Assenmacher	.05
267	Billy Bean RC	.05
268	Bruce Ruffin	.05
269	Ellis Burks	.05
270	Mike Witt	.05
271	Ken Gerhart	.05
272	Steve Ontiveros	.05
273	Garth Iorg	.05
274	Junior Ortiz	.05
275	Kevin Seitzer	.05
276	Luis Salazar	.05
277	Alejandro Pena	.05
278	Jose Cruz	.05
279	Randy St. Claire	.05
280	Pete Incaviglia	.05
281	Jerry Hairston Sr.	.05
282	Pat Perry	.05
283	Phil Lombardi RC	.05
284	Larry Bowa	.05

285	Jim Presley	.05
286	Chuck Crim RC	.05
287	Manny Trillo	.05
288	Pat Pacillo RC	.05
289	Dave Bergman	.05
290	Tony Fernandez	.05
291	Astros Leaders (Kevin Bass, Billy Hatcher)	.05
292	Carney Lansford	.05
293	Doug Jones RC	.05
294	Al Pedrique RC	.05
295	Bert Blyleven	.05
296	Floyd Rayford	.05
297	Zane Smith	.05
298	Milt Thompson	.05
299	Steve Crawford	.05
300	Don Mattingly	.60
301	Bud Black	.05
302	Jose Uribe	.05
303	Eric Show	.05
304	George Hendrick	.05
305	Steve Sax	.05
306	Billy Hatcher	.05
307	Mike Trujillo	.05
308	Lee Mazzilli	.05
309	Bill Long RC	.05
310	Tom Herr	.05
311	Scott Sanderson	.05
312	Joey Meyer RC (Future Stars)	.05
313	Bob McClure	.05
314	Jimy Williams	.05
315	Dave Parker	.05
316	Jose Rijo	.05
317	Tom Nieto	.05
318	Mel Hall	.05
319	Mike Loynd	.05
320	Alan Trammell	.05
321	White Sox Leaders (Harold Baines, Carlton Fisk)	.05
322	Vicente Palacios RC	.05
323	Rick Leach	.05
324	Danny Jackson	.05
325	Glenn Hubbard	.05
326	Al Nipper	.05
327	Larry Sheets	.05
328	Greg Cadaret RC	.05
329	Chris Speier	.05
330	Eddie Whitson	.05
331	Brian Downing	.05
332	Jerry Reed	.05
333	Wally Backman	.05
334	Dave LaPoint	.05
335	Claudell Washington	.05
336	Ed Lynch	.05
337	Jim Gantner	.05
338	Brian Holton	.05
339	Kurt Stillwell	.05
340	Jack Morris	.05
341	Carmen Castillo	.05
342	Larry Andersen	.05
343	Greg Gagne	.05
344	Tony LaRussa	.05
345	Scott Fletcher	.05
346	Vance Law	.05
347	Joe Johnson	.05
348	Jim Eisenreich	.05
349	Bob Walk	.05
350	Will Clark	.05
351	Cardinals Leaders (Tony Pena, Red Schoendienst)	.05
352	Billy Ripken RC	.05
353	Ed Olwine	.05
354	Marc Sullivan	.05
355	Roger McDowell	.05
356	Luis Aguayo	.05
357	Floyd Bannister	.05
358	Rey Quinones	.05
359	Tim Stoddard	.05
360	Tony Gwynn	.50
361	Greg Maddux	.50
362	Juan Castillo	.05
363	Willie Fraser	.05
364	Nick Esasky	.05
365	Floyd Youmans	.05
366	Chet Lemon	.05
367	Tim Leary	.05
368	Gerald Young RC	.05
369	Greg Harris	.05
370	Jose Canseco	.25
371	Joe Hesketh	.05
372	Matt Williams	.05
373	Checklist 265-396	.05
374	Doc Edwards	.05
375	Tom Brunansky	.05
376	Bill Wilkinson RC	.05
377	Sam Horn RC	.05
378	Todd Frohwirth RC	.05
379	Rafael Ramirez	.05
380	Joe Magrane RC	.05
381	Angels Leaders (Jack Howell, Wally Joyner)	.05
382	Keith Miller RC	.05
383	Eric Bell	.05
384	Neil Allen	.05
385	Carlton Fisk	.40
386	Don Mattingly/AS	.30
387	Willie Randolph/AS	.05
388	Wade Boggs/AS	.20
389	Alan Trammell/AS	.05
390	George Bell/AS	.05
391	Kirby Puckett/AS	.25
392	Dave Winfield/AS	.20
393	Matt Nokes/AS	.05

394	Roger Clemens/AS	.35
395	Jimmy Key/AS	.05
396	Tom Henke/AS	.05
397	Jack Clark/AS	.05
398	Juan Samuel/AS	.05
399	Tim Wallach/AS	.05
400	Ozzie Smith/AS	.25
401	Andre Dawson/AS	.15
402	Tony Gwynn/AS	.25
403	Tim Raines/AS	.05
404	Benny Santiago/AS	.05
405	Dwight Gooden/AS	.05
406	Shane Rawley/AS	.05
407	Steve Bedrosian/AS	.05
408	Dion James	.05
409	Joel McKeon RC	.05
410	Tony Pena	.05
411	Wayne Tolleson	.05
412	Randy Myers	.05
413	John Christensen	.05
414	John McNamara	.05
415	Don Carman	.05
416	Keith Moreland	.05
417	Mark Ciardi RC	.05
418	Joel Youngblood	.05
419	Scott McGregor	.05
420	Wally Joyner	.05
421	Ed Vande Berg	.05
422	Dave Concepcion	.05
423	John Smiley	.05
424	Dwayne Murphy	.05
425	Jeff Reardon	.05
426	Randy Ready	.05
427	Paul Kilgus RC	.05
428	John Shelby	.05
429	Tigers Leaders (Kirk Gibson, Alan Trammell)	.05
430	Glenn Davis	.05
431	Casey Candaele	.05
432	Mike Moore	.05
433	Bill Pecota RC	.05
434	Rick Aguilera	.05
435	Mike Pagliarulo	.05
436	Mike Bielecki	.05
437	Fred Manrique RC	.05
438	Rob Ducey RC	.05
439	Dave Martinez	.05
440	Steve Bedrosian	.05
441	Rick Manning	.05
442	Tom Bolton RC	.05
443	Ken Griffey	.05
444	Cal Ripken, Sr.	.05
445	Mike Krukow	.05
446	Doug DeCinces	.05
447	Jeff Montgomery RC	.20
448	Mike Davis	.05
449	Jeff Robinson RC	.05
450	Barry Bonds	.75
451	Keith Atherton	.05
452	Willie Wilson	.05
453	Dennis Powell	.05
454	Marvell Wynne	.05
455	Shawn Hillegas RC	.05
456	Dave Anderson	.05
457	Terry Leach	.05
458	Ron Hassey	.05
459	Yankees Leaders (Willie Randolph, Dave Winfield)	.05
460	Ozzie Smith	.50
461	Danny Darwin	.05
462	Don Slaught	.05
463	Fred McGriff	.05
464	Jay Tibbs	.05
465	Paul Molitor	.40
466	Jerry Mumphrey	.05
467	Don Aase	.05
468	Darren Daulton	.05
469	Jeff Dedmon	.05
470	Dwight Evans	.05
471	Donnie Moore	.05
472	Robby Thompson	.05
473	Joe Niekro	.05
474	Tom Brookens	.05
475	Pete Rose	.65
476	Dave Stewart	.05
477	Jamie Quirk	.05
478	Sid Bream	.05
479	Brett Butler	.05
480	Dwight Gooden	.05
481	Mariano Duncan	.05
482	Mark Davis	.05
483	Rod Booker RC	.05
484	Pat Clements	.05
485	Harold Reynolds	.05
486	Pat Keedy RC	.05
487	Jim Pankovits	.05
488	Andy McGaffigan	.05
489	Dodgers Leaders (Pedro Guerrero, Fernando Valenzuela)	.05
490	Larry Parrish	.05
491	B.J. Surhoff	.05
492	Doyle Alexander	.05
493	Mike Greenwell	.05
494	Wally Ritchie RC	.05
495	Eddie Murray	.40
496	Guy Hoffman	.05
497	Kevin Mitchell	.05
498	Bob Boone	.05
499	Eric King	.05
500	Andre Dawson	.25
501	Tim Birtsas RC	.05
502	Danny Gladden	.05
503	Junior Noboa RC	.05
504	Bob Rodgers	.05
505	Willie Upshaw	.05

506	John Cangelosi	.05
507	Mark Gubicza	.05
508	Tim Teufel	.05
509	Bill Dawley	.05
510	Dave Winfield	.40
511	Joel Davis	.05
512	Alex Trevino	.05
513	Tim Flannery	.05
514	Pat Sheridan	.05
515	Juan Nieves	.05
516	Jim Sundberg	.05
517	Ron Robinson	.05
518	Greg Gross	.05
519	Mariners Leaders (Phil Bradley, Harold Reynolds)	.05
520	Dave Smith	.05
521	Jim Dwyer	.05
522	Bob Patterson RC	.05
523	Gary Roenicke	.05
524	Gary Lucas	.05
525	Marty Barrett	.05
526	Juan Berenguer	.05
527	Steve Henderson	.05
528a	Checklist 397-528 (#455 is Steve Carlton)	.05
528b	Checklist 397-528 (#455 is Shawn Hillegas)	
529	Tim Burke	.05
530	Gary Carter	.40
531	Rich Yett	.05
532	Mike Kingery	.05
533	John Farrell RC	.05
534	John Wathan	.05
535	Ron Guidry	.05
536	John Morris	.05
537	Steve Buechele	.05
538	Bill Wegman	.05
539	Mike LaValliere	.05
540	Bret Saberhagen	.05
541	Juan Beniquez	.05
542	Paul Noce RC	.05
543	Kent Tekulve	.05
544	Jim Traber	.05
545	Don Baylor	.05
546	John Candelaria	.05
547	Felix Fermin RC	.05
548	Shane Mack	.05
549	Braves Leaders (Ken Griffey, Dion James, Dale Murphy, Gerald Perry)	.05
550	Pedro Guerrero	.05
551	Terry Steinbach	.05
552	Mark Thurmond	.05
553	Tracy Jones	.05
554	Mike Smithson	.05
555	Brook Jacoby	.05
556	Stan Clarke RC	.05
557	Craig Reynolds	.05
558	Bob Ojeda	.05
559	Ken Williams RC	.05
560	Tim Wallach	.05
561	Rick Cerone	.05
562	Jim Lindeman	.05
563	Jose Guzman	.05
564	Frank Lucchesi	.05
565	Lloyd Moseby	.05
566	Charlie O'Brien RC	.05
567	Mike Diaz	.05
568	Chris Brown	.05
569	Charlie Leibrandt	.05
570	Jeffrey Leonard	.05
571	Mark Williamson RC	.05
572	Chris James	.05
573	Bob Stanley	.05
574	Graig Nettles	.05
575	Don Sutton	.30
576	Tommy Hinzo RC	.05
577	Tom Browning	.05
578	Gary Gaetti	.05
579	Mets Leaders (Gary Carter, Kevin McReynolds)	.05
580	Mark McGwire	.65
581	Tito Landrum	.05
582	Mike Henneman	.05
583	Dave Valle RC	.05
584	Steve Trout	.05
585	Ozzie Guillen	.05
586	Bob Forsch	.05
587	Terry Puhl	.05
588	Jeff Parrett RC	.05
589	Geno Petralli	.05
590	George Bell	.05
591	Doug Drabek	.05
592	Dale Sveum	.05
593	Bob Tewksbury	.05
594	Bobby Valentine	.05
595	Frank White	.05
596	John Kruk	.05
597	Gene Garber	.05
598	Lee Lacy	.05
599	Calvin Schiraldi	.05
600	Mike Schmidt	.60
601	Jack Lazorko	.05
602	Mike Aldrete	.05
603	Rob Murphy	.05
604	Chris Bando	.05
605	Kirk Gibson	.05
606	Moose Haas	.05
607	Mickey Hatcher	.05
608	Charlie Kerfeld	.05
609	Twins Leaders (Gary Gaetti, Kent Hrbek)	.05
610	Keith Hernandez	.05
611	Tommy John	.05
612	Curt Ford	.05
613	Bobby Thigpen	.05

614 Herm Winningham .05
615 Jody Davis .05
616 Jay Aldrich RC .05
617 Oddibe McDowell .05
618 Cecil Fielder .05
619 Mike Dunne RC .05
620 Cory Snyder .05
621 Gene Nelson .05
622 Kal Daniels .05
623 Mike Flanagan .05
624 Jim Leyland .05
625 Frank Viola .05
626 Glenn Wilson .05
627 Joe Boever RC .05
628 Dave Henderson .05
629 Kelly Downs .05
630 Darrell Evans .05
631 Jack Howell .05
632 Steve Shields RC .05
633 Barry Lyons RC .05
634 Jose DeLeon .05
635 Terry Pendleton .05
636 Charles Hudson .05
637 Jay Bell RC .25
638 Steve Balboni .05
639 Brewers Leaders (Glenn Braggs, Tony Muser) .05
640 Garry Templeton .05
641 Rick Honeycutt .05
642 Bob Dernier .05
643 Rocky Childress RC .05
644 Terry McGriff RC .05
645 Matt Nokes .05
646 Checklist 529-660 .05
647 Pascual Perez .05
648 Al Newman .05
649 DeWayne Buice RC .05
650 Cal Ripken, Jr. .75
651 Mike Jackson RC .05
652 Bruce Benedict .05
653 Jeff Sellers .05
654 Roger Craig .05
655 Len Dykstra .05
656 Lee Guetterman .05
657 Gary Redus .05
658 Tim Conroy .05
659 Bobby Meacham .05
660 Rick Reuschel .05
661 Nolan Ryan (Turn Back the Clock) .35
662 Jim Rice (Turn Back the Clock) .05
663 Ron Blomberg (Turn Back the Clock) .05
664 Bob Gibson (Turn Back the Clock) .10
665 Stan Musial (Turn Back the Clock) .20
666 Mario Soto .05
667 Luis Quinones .05
668 Walt Terrell .05
669 Phillies Leaders (Lance Parrish, Mike Ryan) .05
670 Dan Plesac .05
671 Tim Laudner .05
672 John Davis RC .05
673 Tony Phillips .05
674 Mike Fitzgerald .05
675 Jim Rice .20
676 Ken Dixon .05
677 Eddie Milner .05
678 Jim Acker .05
679 Darrell Miller .05
680 Charlie Hough .05
681 Bobby Bonilla .05
682 Jimmy Key .05
683 Julio Franco .05
684 Hal Lanier .05
685 Ron Darling .05
686 Terry Francona .05
687 Mickey Brantley .05
688 Jim Winn .05
689 Tom Pagnozzi RC .05
690 Jay Howell .05
691 Dan Pasqua .05
692 Mike Birkbeck .05
693 Benny Santiago .05
694 Eric Nolte RC .05
695 Shawon Dunston .05
696 Duane Ward .05
697 Steve Lombardozzi .05
698 Brad Havens .05
699 Padres Leaders (Tony Gwynn, Benny Santiago) .15
700 George Brett .60
701 Sammy Stewart .05
702 Mike Gallego .05
703 Bob Brenly .05
704 Dennis Boyd .05
705 Juan Samuel .05
706 Rick Mahler .05
707 Fred Lynn .05
708 Gus Polidor RC .05
709 George Frazier .05
710 Darryl Strawberry .05
711 Bill Gullickson .05
712 John Moses .05
713 Willie Hernandez .05
714 Jim Fregosi .05
715 Todd Worrell .05
716 Lenn Sakata .05
717 Jay Baller RC .05
718 Mike Felder .05
719 Denny Walling .05
720 Tim Raines .05

721 Pete O'Brien .05
722 Manny Lee .05
723 Bob Kipper .05
724 Danny Tartabull .05
725 Mike Boddicker .05
726 Alfredo Griffin .05
727 Greg Booker .05
728 Andy Allanson .05
729 Blue Jays Leaders (George Bell, Fred McGriff) .05
730 John Franco .05
731 Rick Schu .05
732 Dave Palmer .05
733 Spike Owen .05
734 Craig Lefferts .05
735 Kevin McReynolds .05
736 Matt Young .05
737 Butch Wynegar .05
738 Scott Bankhead .05
739 Daryl Boston .05
740 Rick Sutcliffe .05
741 Mike Easler .05
742 Mark Clear .05
743 Larry Herndon .05
744 Whitey Herzog .05
745 Bill Doran .05
746 Gene Larkin RC .05
747 Bobby Witt .05
748 Reid Nichols .05
749 Mark Eichhorn .05
750 Bo Jackson .10
751 Jim Morrison .05
752 Mark Grant .05
753 Danny Heep .05
754 Mike LaCoss .05
755 Ozzie Virgil .05
756 Mike Maddux .05
757 John Marzano RC .05
758 Eddie Williams RC .05
759 A's Leaders (Jose Canseco, Mark McGwire) .35
760 Mike Scott .05
761 Tony Armas .05
762 Scott Bradley .05
763 Doug Sisk .05
764 Greg Walker .05
765 Neal Heaton .05
766 Henry Cotto .05
767 Jose Lind RC (Future Stars) .10
768 Dickie Noles .05
769 Cecil Cooper .05
770 Lou Whitaker .05
771 Ruben Sierra .05
772 Sal Butera .05
773 Frank Williams .05
774 Gene Mauch .05
775 Dave Stieb .05
776 Checklist 661-792 .05
777 Lonnie Smith .05
778a Keith Comstock RC (White team letters.) .40
778b Keith Comstock RC (Blue team letters, white name.) .10
778c Keith Comstock RC (Blue team letters, yellow name.) 2.00
779 Tom Glavine RC .75
780 Fernando Valenzuela .05
781 Keith Hughes RC .05
782 Jeff Ballard RC .05
783 Ron Roenicke .05
784 Joe Sambito .05
785 Alvin Davis .05
786 Joe Price .05
787 Bill Almon .05
788 Ray Searage .05
789 Indians Leaders (Joe Carter, Cory Snyder) .05
790 Dave Righetti .05
791 Ted Simmons .05
792 John Tudor .05

Tiffany

Sharing a checklist with the regular issue 1988 Topps baseball set, this specially boxed, limited-edition (25,000 sets) features cards printed on white cardboard stock with high-gloss front finish. Topps offered the sets directly to the public in ads in USA Today and Sporing News at a price of $99.

NM/M
Complete Set (792): 40.00
Common Player: .15

Traded

In addition to new players and traded veterans, 21 members of the U.S.A. Olympic Baseball team are showcased in this 132-card set, numbered 1T-132T. The 2-1/2" x 3-1/2" cards follow the same design as the basic Topps issue - white borders, large full-color photos, team name (or U.S.A.) in large bold letters at the top of the card face, player name on a diagonal stripe across the lower-right corner. Topps had issued its traded series each year since 1981 in boxed complete sets available only through hobby dealers.

NM/M
Complete Set (132): 5.00
Common Player: .05
1 Jim Abbott RC (USA) .25
2 Juan Agosto .05
3 Luis Alicea RC .05
4 Roberto Alomar RC 1.50
5 Brady Anderson RC .25
6 Jack Armstrong .05
7 Don August .05
8 Floyd Bannister .05
9 Bret Barberie (USA) .05
10 Jose Bautista RC .05
11 Don Baylor .05
12 Tim Belcher .05
13 Buddy Bell .05
14 Andy Benes RC (USA) .25
15 Damon Berryhill .05
16 Bud Black .05
17 Pat Borders .05
18 Phil Bradley .05
19 Jeff Branson RC (USA) .05
20 Tom Brunansky .05
21 Jay Buhner RC .75
22 Brett Butler .05
23 Jim Campanis RC (USA) .05
24 Sil Campusano RC .05
25 John Candelaria .05
26 Jose Cecena RC .05
27 Rick Cerone .05
28 Jack Clark .05
29 Kevin Coffman RC .05
30 Pat Combs (USA) .05
31 Henry Cotto .05
32 Chili Davis .05
33 Mike Davis .05
34 Jose DeLeon .05
35 Richard Dotson .05
36 Cecil Espy .05
37 Tom Filer .05
38 Mike Fiore RC (USA) .05
39 Ron Gant RC .25
40 Kirk Gibson .05
41 Rich Gossage .05
42 Mark Grace RC 1.00
43 Alfredo Griffin .05
44 Ty Griffin RC (USA) .05
45 Bryan Harvey .05
46 Ron Hassey .05
47 Ray Hayward RC .05
48 Dave Henderson .05
49 Tom Herr .05
50 Bob Horner .05
51 Ricky Horton .05
52 Jay Howell .05
53 Glenn Hubbard .05
54 Jeff Innis RC .05
55 Danny Jackson .05
56 Darrin Jackson .05
57 Roberto Kelly .05
58 Ron Kittle .05
59 Ray Knight .05
60 Vance Law .05
61 Jeffrey Leonard .05
62 Mike Macfarlane RC .05
63 Scotti Madison RC .05
64 Kirt Manwaring RC .05
65 Mark Marquess RC (USA) .05
66 Tino Martinez RC (USA) .75
67 Billy Masse RC (USA) .05
68 Jack McDowell RC .25
69 Jack McKeon .05
70 Larry McWilliams .05
71 Mickey Morandini (USA) .05
72 Keith Moreland .05
73 Mike Morgan .05
74 Charles Nagy (USA) .10
75 Al Nipper .05
76 Russ Nixon .05
77 Jesse Orosco .05
78 Joe Orsulak .05
79 Dave Palmer .05
80 Mark Parent RC .05
81 Dave Parker .05
82 Dan Pasqua .05
83 Melido Perez .05
84 Steve Peters RC .05
85 Dan Petry .05
86 Gary Pettis .05
87 Jeff Pico RC .05
88 Jim Poole (USA) .05
89 Ted Power .05
90 Rafael Ramirez .05
91 Dennis Rasmussen .05
92 Jose Rijo .05
93 Earnie Riles .05
94 Luis Rivera RC .05
95 Doug Robbins RC (USA) .05
96 Frank Robinson .15
97 Cookie Rojas .05
98 Chris Sabo RC .10
99 Mark Salas .05
100 Luis Salazar .05
101 Rafael Santana .05
102 Nelson Santovenia RC .05
103 Mackey Sasser RC .05
104 Calvin Schiraldi .05
105 Mike Schooler RC .05
106 Scott Servais RC (USA) .05
107 Dave Silvestri (USA) .05
108 Don Slaught .05
109 Joe Slusarski RC (USA) .05
110 Lee Smith .05
111 Pete Smith RC .05
112 Jim Snyder .05
113 Ed Sprague RC (USA) .05
114 Pete Stanicek RC .05
115 Kurt Stillwell .05
116 Todd Stottlemyre .05
117 Bill Swift .05
118 Pat Tabler .05
119 Scott Terry RC .05
120 Mickey Tettleton .05
121 Dickie Thon .05
122 Jeff Treadway .05
123 Willie Upshaw .05
124 Robin Ventura RC .05
125 Ron Washington .05
126 Walt Weiss RC .05
127 Bob Welch .05
128 David Wells RC .05
129 Glenn Wilson .05
130 Ted Wood RC (USA) .05
131 Don Zimmer .05
132 Checklist 1T-132T .05

Traded Tiffany

The high-gloss front surface is all that distinguishes this limited-edition, hobby-only collectors version from the regular Topps Traded boxed set.

NM/M
Complete Set (132): 25.00
Common Player: .15

Traded Duke Snider Bronze

This 1/4-size metal replica was issued to dealers who purchased cases of 1988 Topps Traded sets. Each detail of the 1955 Topps Snider card is reproduced on the 1-3/4" x 1-1/4" bronze metal mini-card, right down to the stats.

NM/M
210 Duke Snider 7.50

Box Panels

After a one-year hiatus during which they appeared on the sides of Topps wax pack display boxes, Topps retail box cards returned to box bottoms in 1988. The series includes 16 standard-size baseball cards, four cards per each of four different display boxes. Card fronts follow the same design as the 1988 Topps basic issue; full-color player photos, framed in yellow, surrounded by a white border; diagonal player name lower-right; team name in large letters at the top. Card backs are "numbered" A through P and are printed in black and orange.

NM/M
Complete Panel Set (4): 3.00
Complete Singles Set (16): 3.00
Common Panel: .50
Common Single Player: .10
A Don Baylor .10
B Steve Bedrosian .10
C Juan Beniquez .10
D. Bob Boone .10
Panel .75
E Darrell Evans .10
F Tony Gwynn .50
G John Kruk .10
H Marvell Wynne .10
Panel .60
I Joe Carter .10
J Eric Davis .10
K Howard Johnson .10
L Darryl Strawberry .10
Panel 2.00
M Rickey Henderson .40
N Nolan Ryan 1.00
O Mike Schmidt .75
P Kent Tekulve .10

All-Star Glossy Set of 22

The fifth edition of Topps' special All-Star inserts was included in the company's 1988 rack packs. The 1987 American and National League All-Star lineup, plus honorary captains Jim Hunter and Billy Williams, are featured on the 2-1/2" x 3-1/2" cards. The glossy full-color fronts contain player photos centered between a red and yellow "1987 All-Star" logo at top and the player name (also red and yellow) which is printed in the bottom margin. A league logo is in the lower-left corner. Card backs are printed in red and blue on a white background, with the title and All-Star logo emblem printed above the player name and card number.

NM/M
Complete Set (22): 3.00
Common Player: .05
1 John McNamara .05
2 Don Mattingly .75
3 Willie Randolph .05
4 Wade Boggs .65
5 Cal Ripken, Jr. 1.00
6 George Bell .05
7 Rickey Henderson .50
8 Dave Winfield .50
9 Terry Kennedy .05
10 Bret Saberhagen .05
11 Catfish Hunter .05
12 Davey Johnson .05
13 Jack Clark .05
14 Ryne Sandberg .65
15 Mike Schmidt .75
16 Ozzie Smith .65
17 Eric Davis .05
18 Andre Dawson .20
19 Darryl Strawberry .05
20 Gary Carter .50
21 Mike Scott .05
22 Billy Williams .05

All-Star Glossy Set of 60

This collectors' set includes 60 full-color glossy cards featuring All-Stars and Prospects in six separate 10-card sets. Card fronts have a white border and a thin red line framing the player photo, with the player's name in the lower-left corner. Backs, in red and blue, include basic player identification along with the set logo and card number. Sets were marketed via a special offer printed on a card packaged in all Topps wax packs. For six special offer cards and $1.25, collectors received one of the six 10-card sets; 18 special offer cards and $7.50 earned the entire 60-card collection.

NM/M
Complete Set (60): 4.00
Common Player: .10
1 Andre Dawson .20
2 Jesse Barfield .10
3 Mike Schmidt .75
4 Ruben Sierra .10
5 Mike Scott .10
6 Cal Ripken, Jr. 1.00
7 Gary Carter .50
8 Kent Hrbek .10
9 Kevin Seitzer .10
10 Mike Henneman .10
11 Don Mattingly .65
12 Tim Raines .10
13 Roger Clemens .65
14 Ryne Sandberg .60
15 Tony Fernandez .10
16 Eric Davis .10
17 Jack Morris .10
18 Tim Wallach .10
19 Mike Dunne .10
20 Mike Greenwell .10
21 Dwight Evans .10
22 Darryl Strawberry .10
23 Cory Snyder .10
24 Pedro Guerrero .10
25 Rickey Henderson .50
26 Dale Murphy .20
27 Kirby Puckett .60
28 Steve Bedrosian .10
29 Devon White .10
30 Benny Santiago .10
31 George Bell .10
32 Keith Hernandez .10
33 Dave Stewart .10
34 Dave Parker .10
35 Tom Henke .10
36 Willie McGee .10
37 Alan Trammell .10
38 Tony Gwynn .60
39 Mark McGwire .85
40 Joe Magrane .10
41 Jack Clark .10
42 Willie Randolph .10
43 Juan Samuel .10
44 Joe Carter .10
45 Shane Rawley .10
46 Dave Winfield .50
47 Ozzie Smith .60
48 Wally Joyner .10
49 B.J. Surhoff .10
50 Ellis Burks .10
51 Wade Boggs .60
52 Howard Johnson .10
53 George Brett .75
54 Dwight Gooden .10
55 Jose Canseco .35
56 Lee Smith .10
57 Paul Molitor .50
58 Andres Galarraga .10
59 Matt Nokes .10
60 Casey Candaele .10

American Baseball

This set, ostensibly issued for sale in the United Kingdom, was also made available for distribution by U.S. hobby dealers.

DWIGHT EVANS OF/1B — BOSTON RED SOX

Cards were packaged in checklist-backed boxes with an American flag on the top flap. The 2-1/4" x 3" cards feature full-color photos printed on white stock. The team name, printed in team colors, intersects the red frame at the top of the card. A yellow name banner appears below the photo. Backs have blue borders and cartoon-style horizontal layouts which include a team logo, stats, caricature of the player and a one-line caption. Below the cartoon, a short "Talkin' Baseball" paragraph provides elementary information, designed to acquaint soccer-playing European collectors with baseball rules and terminology. Uncut sheets of all 88 cards are not uncommon.

	NM/M
Complete Set (88):	6.00
Common Player:	.05
Uncut Sheet:	12.00
Wax Box (48):	7.50

No.	Player	Price
1	Harold Baines	.05
2	Steve Bedrosian	.05
3	George Bell	.05
4	Wade Boggs	.60
5	Barry Bonds	1.00
6	Bob Boone	.05
7	George Brett	.75
8	Hubie Brooks	.05
9	Ivan Calderon	.05
10	Jose Canseco	.35
11	Gary Carter	.50
12	Joe Carter	.05
13	Jack Clark	.05
14	Will Clark	.05
15	Roger Clemens	.75
16	Vince Coleman	.05
17	Alvin Davis	.05
18	Eric Davis	.05
19	Glenn Davis	.05
20	Andre Dawson	.20
21	Mike Dunne	.05
22	Dwight Evans	.05
23	Tony Fernandez	.05
24	John Franco	.05
25	Gary Gaetti	.05
26	Kirk Gibson	.05
27	Dwight Gooden	.05
28	Pedro Guerrero	.05
29	Tony Gwynn	.60
30	Billy Hatcher	.05
31	Rickey Henderson	.50
32	Tom Henke	.05
33	Keith Hernandez	.05
34	Orel Hershiser	.05
35	Teddy Higuera	.05
36	Charlie Hough	.05
37	Kent Hrbek	.05
38	Brook Jacoby	.05
39	Dion James	.05
40	Wally Joyner	.05
41	John Kruk	.05
42	Mark Langston	.05
43	Jeffrey Leonard	.05
44	Candy Maldonaldo	.05
45	Don Mattingly	.75
46	Willie McGee	.05
47	Mark McGwire	.85
48	Kevin Mitchell	.05
49	Paul Molitor	.50
50	Jack Morris	.05
51	Lloyd Moseby	.05
52	Dale Murphy	.20
53	Eddie Murray	.50
54	Matt Nokes	.05
55	Dave Parker	.05
56	Larry Parrish	.05
57	Kirby Puckett	.60
58	Tim Raines	.05
59	Willie Randolph	.05
60	Harold Reynolds	.05
61	Cal Ripken, Jr.	1.00
62	Nolan Ryan	1.00
63	Bret Saberhagen	.05
64	Juan Samuel	.05
65	Ryne Sandberg	.60
66	Benny Santiago	.05
67	Mike Schmidt	.75
68	Mike Scott	.05
69	Kevin Seitzer	.05
70	Larry Sheets	.05
71	Ruben Sierra	.05
72	Ozzie Smith	.60
73	Zane Smith	.05
74	Cory Snyder	.05
75	Dave Stewart	.05
76	Darryl Strawberry	.05
77	Rick Sutcliffe	.05
78	Danny Tartabull	.05
79	Alan Trammell	.05
80	Fernando Valenzuela	.05
81	Andy Van Slyke	.05
82	Frank Viola	.05
83	Greg Walker	.05
84	Tim Wallach	.05
85	Dave Winfield	.50
86	Mike Witt	.05
87	Robin Yount	.50
88	Checklist	.05

American Baseball Tiffany

This glossy "Tiffany" edition of the Topps American Baseball set is a complete parallel of the regular-issue.

	NM/M
Complete Set (88):	15.00
Common Player:	.40

Big Baseball

ALAN TRAMMELL

Topps Big Baseball cards (2-5/8" x 3-3/4") were issued in three series, 88 cards per series (a total set of 264 cards) sold in seven-card packs. The glossy cards are similar in format, both front and back, to the 1956 Topps set. Each card features a portrait and a game-action photo on the front, framed by a wide white border. A white outline highlights the portrait. The player's name appears at bottom on a splash of color that fades from yellow to orange to red to pink. On the card back, the player's name is printed in large red letters across the top, followed by his team name and position printed in a red rectangle beside a Topps baseball logo bearing the card number. A triple cartoon strip, in full-color, illustrates career highlights, performance, personal background, etc. A red, white and blue statistics box (pitching, batting, fielding) is printed across the bottom.

	NM/M
Complete Set (264):	9.00
Common Player:	.05
Wax Pack (7):	.50
Wax Box, Series 1-3 (36):	9.00

No.	Player	Price
1	Paul Molitor	.45
2	Milt Thompson	.05
3	Billy Hatcher	.05
4	Mike Witt	.05
5	Vince Coleman	.05
6	Dwight Evans	.05
7	Tim Wallach	.05
8	Alan Trammell	.05
9	Will Clark	.05
10	Jeff Reardon	.05
11	Dwight Gooden	.05
12	Benny Santiago	.05
13	Jose Canseco	.35
14	Dale Murphy	.20
15	George Bell	.05
16	Ryne Sandberg	.60
17	Brook Jacoby	.05
18	Fernando Valenzuela	.05
19	Scott Fletcher	.05
20	Eric Davis	.05
21	Willie Wilson	.05
22	B.J. Surhoff	.05
23	Steve Bedrosian	.05
24	Dave Winfield	.45
25	Bobby Bonilla	.05
26	Larry Sheets	.05
27	Ozzie Guillen	.05
28	Checklist 1-88	.05
29	Nolan Ryan	1.50
30	Bob Boone	.05
31	Tom Herr	.05
32	Wade Boggs	.60
33	Neal Heaton	.05
34	Doyle Alexander	.05
35	Candy Maldonado	.05
36	Kirby Puckett	.60
37	Gary Carter	.45
38	Lance McCullers	.05
39a	Terry Steinbach (Black Topps logo on front.)	.10
39b	Terry Steinbach (White Topps logo on front.)	.10
40	Gerald Perry	.05
41	Tom Henke	.05
42	Leon Durham	.05
43	Cory Snyder	.05
44	Dale Sveum	.05
45	Lance Parrish	.05
46	Steve Sax	.05
47	Charlie Hough	.05
48	Kal Daniels	.05
49	Bo Jackson	.10
50	Ron Guidry	.05
51	Bill Doran	.05
52	Wally Joyner	.05
53	Terry Pendleton	.05
54	Marty Barrett	.05
55	Andres Galarraga	.05
56	Larry Herndon	.05
57	Kevin Mitchell	.05
58	Greg Gagne	.05
59	Keith Hernandez	.05
60	John Kruk	.05
61	Mike LaValliere	.05
62	Cal Ripken, Jr.	1.50
63	Ivan Calderon	.05
64	Alvin Davis	.05
65	Luis Polonia	.05
66	Robin Yount	.45
67	Juan Samuel	.05
68	Andres Thomas	.05
69	Jeff Musselman	.05
70	Jerry Mumphrey	.05
71	Joe Carter	.05
72	Mike Scioscia	.05
73	Pete Incaviglia	.05
74	Barry Larkin	.05
75	Frank White	.05
76	Willie Randolph	.05
77	Kevin Bass	.05
78	Brian Downing	.05
79	Willie McGee	.05
80	Ellis Burks	.05
81	Hubie Brooks	.05
82	Darrell Evans	.05
83	Robby Thompson	.05
84	Kent Hrbek	.05
85	Ron Darling	.05
86	Stan Jefferson	.05
87	Teddy Higuera	.05
88	Mike Schmidt	.75
89	Barry Bonds	1.50
90	Jim Presley	.05
91	Orel Hershiser	.05
92	Jesse Barfield	.05
93	Tom Candiotti	.05
94	Bret Saberhagen	.05
95	Jose Uribe	.05
96	Tom Browning	.05
97	Johnny Ray	.05
98	Mike Morgan	.05
99	Jim Sundberg	.05
100	Roger McDowell	.05
101	Randy Ready	.05
102	Mike Gallego	.05
103	Steve Buechele	.05
104	Greg Walker	.05
105	Jose Lind	.05
106	Steve Trout	.05
107	Rick Rhoden	.05
108	Jim Pankovits	.05
109	Ken Griffey	.05
110	Danny Cox	.05
111	Franklin Stubbs	.05
112	Lloyd Moseby	.05
113	Mel Hall	.05
114	Kevin Seitzer	.05
115	Tim Raines	.05
116	Juan Castillo	.05
117	Roger Clemens	.75
118	Mike Aldrete	.05
119	Mario Soto	.05
120	Jack Howell	.05
121	Rick Schu	.05
122	Jeff Robinson	.05
123	Doug Drabek	.05
124	Henry Cotto	.05
125	Checklist 89-176	.05
126	Gary Gaetti	.05
127	Rick Sutcliffe	.05
128	Howard Johnson	.05
129	Chris Brown	.05
130	Dave Henderson	.05
131	Curt Wilkerson	.05
132	Mike Marshall	.05
133	Kelly Gruber	.05
134	Julio Franco	.05
135	Kurt Stillwell	.05
136	Donnie Hill	.05
137	Mike Pagliarulo	.05
138	Von Hayes	.05
139	Mike Scott	.05
140	Bob Kipper	.05
141	Harold Reynolds	.05
142	Bob Brenly	.05
143	Dave Concepcion	.05
144	Devon White	.05
145	Devon White	.05
146	Jeff Stone	.05
147	Chet Lemon	.05
148	Ozzie Virgil	.05
149	Todd Worrell	.05
150	Mitch Webster	.05
151	Rob Deer	.05
152	Rich Gedman	.05
153	Andre Dawson	.20
154	Mike Davis	.05
155	Nelson Liriano	.05
156	Greg Swindell	.05
157	George Brett	.75
158	Kevin McReynolds	.05
159	Brian Fisher	.05
160	Mike Kingery	.05
161	Tony Gwynn	.60
162	Don Baylor	.05
163	Jerry Browne	.05
164	Dan Pasqua	.05
165	Rickey Henderson	.45
166	Brett Butler	.05
167	Nick Esasky	.05
168	Kirk McCaskill	.05
169	Fred Lynn	.05
170	Jack Morris	.05
171	Pedro Guerrero	.05
172	Dave Stieb	.05
173	Pat Tabler	.05
174	Floyd Bannister	.05
175	Rafael Belliard	.05
176	Mark Langston	.05
177	Greg Mathews	.05
178	Claudell Washington	.05
179	Mark McGwire	1.00
180	Bert Blyleven	.05
181	Jim Rice	.15
182	Mookie Wilson	.05
183	Willie Fraser	.05
184	Andy Van Slyke	.05
185	Matt Nokes	.05
186	Eddie Whitson	.05
187	Tony Fernandez	.05
188	Rick Reuschel	.05
189	Ken Phelps	.05
190	Juan Nieves	.05
191	Kirk Gibson	.05
192	Glenn Davis	.05
193	Zane Smith	.05
194	Jose DeLeon	.05
195	Gary Ward	.05
196	Pascual Perez	.05
197	Carlton Fisk	.45
198	Oddibe McDowell	.05
199	Mark Gubicza	.05
200	Glenn Hubbard	.05
201	Frank Viola	.05
202	Jody Reed	.05
203	Len Dykstra	.05
204	Dick Schofield	.05
205	Sid Bream	.05
206	Guillermo Hernandez	.05
207	Keith Moreland	.05
208	Mark Eichhorn	.05
209	Rene Gonzales	.05
210	Dave Valle	.05
211	Tom Brunansky	.05
212	Charles Hudson	.05
213	John Farrell	.05
214	Jeff Treadway	.05
215	Eddie Murray	.45
216	Checklist 177-264	.05
217	Greg Brock	.05
218	John Shelby	.05
219	Craig Reynolds	.05
220	Dion James	.05
221	Carney Lansford	.05
222	Juan Berenguer	.05
223	Luis Rivera	.05
224	Harold Baines	.05
225	Shawon Dunston	.05
226	Luis Aguayo	.05
227	Pete O'Brien	.05
228	Ozzie Smith	.60
229	Don Mattingly	.75
230	Danny Tartabull	.05
231	Andy Allanson	.05
232	John Franco	.05
233	Mike Greenwell	.05
234	Bob Ojeda	.05
235	Chili Davis	.05
236	Mike Dunne	.05
237	Jim Morrison	.05
238	Carmelo Martinez	.05
239	Ernie Whitt	.05
240	Scott Garrelts	.05
241	Mike Moore	.05
242	Dave Parker	.05
243	Tim Laudner	.05
244	Bill Wegman	.05
245	Bob Horner	.05
246	Rafael Santana	.05
247	Alfredo Griffin	.05
248	Mark Bailey	.05
249	Ron Gant	.05
250	Bryn Smith	.05
251	Lance Johnson	.05
252	Sam Horn	.05
253	Darryl Strawberry	.05
254	Chuck Finley	.05
255	Darnell Coles	.05
256	Mike Henneman	.05
257	Andy Hawkins	.05
258	Jim Clancy	.05
259	Atlee Hammaker	.05
260	Glenn Wilson	.05
261	Larry McWilliams	.05
262	Jack Clark	.05
263	Walt Weiss	.05
264	Gene Larkin	.05

Cloth Experimental

PIRATES — FutureStars

This is a true experimental issue from Topps: Baseball cards printed on heavy textured paper, much like high-quality paper towels. The cloth cards are the standard 2-1/2" x 3-1/2" in size and feature the fronts as used on Topps' regular '88 baseball card issue. Overprinted across the fronts of some cards are parts of the legend, "SAMPLE ONLY NOT FOR SALE." Backs are blank, and unlike earlier Topps cloth issues, are not gummed for use as stickers. The checklist is presented here in alphabetical order.

No.	Player	Price
	Complete Set (121):	600.00
	Uncut Sheet (121):	500.00
	Common Player:	8.00
(1)	A's Team Leaders (Jose Canseco, Mark McGwire)	30.00
(2)	Rick Aguilera	8.00
(3)	Andy Allanson	8.00
(4)	Tony Armas	8.00
(5)	Keith Atherton	8.00
(6)	Steve Balboni	8.00
(7)	Billy Bean	8.00
(8)	Steve Bedrosian/AS	8.00
(9)	George Bell/AS	8.00
(10)	Bruce Benedict	8.00
(11)	Dave Bergman	8.00
(12)	Mike Bielecki	8.00
(13)	Tim Birtsas	8.00
(14)	Bruce Bochy	8.00
(15)	Wade Boggs/AS	40.00
(16)	Rod Booker	8.00
(17)	Dennis Boyd	8.00
(18)	Braves Leaders (Ken Griffey, Dion James, Dale Murphy, Gerald Perry)	15.00
(19)	Tom Browning	8.00
(20)	Carmen Castillo	8.00
(21)	Rick Cerone	8.00
(22)	Jack Clark/AS	8.00
(23)	Mark Clear	8.00
(24)	Roger Clemens/AS	75.00
(25)	Pat Clements	8.00
(26)	Keith Comstock	8.00
(27)	Cecil Cooper	8.00
(28)	Joey Cora	8.00
(29)	Ed Correa	8.00
(30)	Mark Davidson	8.00
(31)	Mark Davis	8.00
(32)	Jeff Dedmon	8.00
(33)	Jim Dwyer	8.00
(34)	Doc Edwards	8.00
(35)	John Farrell	8.00
(36)	Mike Felder	8.00
(37)	Curt Ford	8.00
(38)	Bob Forsch	8.00
(39)	Damaso Garcia	8.00
(40)	Tom Glavine	45.00
(41)	Mark Grant	8.00
(42)	Tony Gwynn/AS	40.00
(43)	Drew Hall	8.00
(44)	Jeff Hamilton	8.00
(45)	Mike Hart	8.00
(46)	Andy Hawkins	8.00
(47)	Ed Hearn	8.00
(48)	Tom Henke/AS	8.00
(49)	Whitey Herzog	8.00
(50)	Shawn Hillegas	8.00
(51)	Charles Hudson	8.00
(52)	Dave Johnson	8.00
(53)	Ron Karkovice	8.00
(54)	Pat Keedy	8.00
(55)	Jimmy Key/AS	8.00
(56)	Mark Kiefer	8.00
(57)	Bob Kipper	8.00
(58)	Les Lancaster	8.00
(59)	Ken Landreaux	8.00
(60)	Craig Lefferts	8.00
(61)	Jim Leyland	8.00
(62)	Jose Lind	8.00
(63)	Gary Lucas	8.00
(64)	Frank Lucchesi	8.00
(65)	Barry Lyons	8.00
(66)	John Marzano	8.00
(67)	Greg Mathews	8.00
(68)	Don Mattingly/AS	75.00
(69)	Len Matuszek	8.00
(70)	Kirk McCaskill	8.00
(71)	Terry McGriff	8.00
(72)	Joey Meyer	8.00
(73)	John Mitchell	8.00
(74)	Jeff Montgomery	8.00
(75)	John Morris	8.00
(76)	John Moses	8.00
(77)	Tom Nieto	8.00
(78)	Matt Nokes/AS	8.00
(79)	Charlie O'Brien	8.00
(80)	Ed Olwine	8.00
(81)	Paul O'Neill	8.00
(82)	Steve Ontiveros	8.00
(83)	Pat Pacillo	8.00
(84)	Tom Pagnozzi	8.00
(85)	Jim Pankovitz	8.00
(86)	Bill Pecota	8.00
(87)	Geno Petralli	8.00
(88)	Eric Plunk	8.00
(89)	Gus Polidor	8.00
(90)	Dennis Powell	8.00
(91)	Terry Puhl	8.00
(92)	Charlie Puleo	8.00
(93)	Shane Rawley/AS	8.00
(94)	Rick Rodriguez	8.00
(95)	Ron Roenicke	8.00
(96)	Pete Rose	200.00
(97)	Lenn Sakata	8.00
(98)	Joe Sambito	8.00
(99)	Juan Samuel/AS	8.00
(100)	Rafael Santana	8.00
(101)	Dan Schatzeder	8.00
(102)	Pat Sheridan	8.00
(103)	Steve Shields	8.00
(104)	Ted Simmons	8.00
(105)	Doug Sisk	8.00
(106)	Joel Skinner	8.00
(107)	Ozzie Smith/AS	40.00
(108)	Chris Speier	8.00
(109)	Jim Sundberg	8.00
(110)	Don Sutton	15.00
(111)	Chuck Tanner	8.00
(112)	Mickey Tettleton	8.00
(113)	Tim Teufel	8.00
(114)	Gary Thurman	8.00
(115)	Alex Trevino	8.00
(116)	Mike Trujillo	8.00
(117)	Twins Leaders (Gary Gaetti, Kent Hrbek)	20.00
(118)	Tim Wallach/AS	8.00
(119)	Frank Williams	8.00
(120)	Dave Winfield/AS	25.00
(121)	Butch Wynegar	8.00

Coins

CAL RIPKEN — SHORTSTOP • ORIOLES

This edition of 60 lightweight metal coins is similar in design to Topps' 1964 set. The 1988 coins are 1-1/2" in diameter and feature full-color player portraits under crimped edges in silver, gold and pink. Curved under the photo is a red and white player name banner pinned by two gold stars. Coin backs list the coin number, player name, personal information and career summary in black letters on a silver background.

No.	Player	Price
	Factory Boxed Set (60):	20.00
	Complete Set (60):	10.00
	Common Player:	.15
	Wax Pack (3):	.45
	Wax Box (36):	10.00
1	George Bell	.15
2	Roger Clemens	1.00
3	Mark McGwire	1.25
4	Wade Boggs	.75
5	Harold Baines	.15
6	Ivan Calderon	.15
7	Jose Canseco	.45
8	Joe Carter	.15
9	Jack Clark	.15
10	Alvin Davis	.15
11	Dwight Evans	.15
12	Tony Fernandez	.15
13	Gary Gaetti	.15
14	Mike Greenwell	.15
15	Charlie Hough	.15
16	Wally Joyner	.15
17	Jimmy Key	.15
18	Mark Langston	.15
19	Don Mattingly	1.00
20	Paul Molitor	.60
21	Jack Morris	.15

22	Eddie Murray	.60
23	Kirby Puckett	.75
24	Cal Ripken, Jr.	1.50
25	Bret Saberhagen	.15
26	Ruben Sierra	.15
27	Cory Snyder	.15
28	Terry Steinbach	.15
29	Danny Tartabull	.15
30	Alan Trammell	.15
31	Devon White	.15
32	Robin Yount	.60
33	Andre Dawson	.30
34	Steve Bedrosian	.15
35	Benny Santiago	.15
36	Tony Gwynn	.75
37	Bobby Bonilla	.15
38	Will Clark	.15
39	Eric Davis	.15
40	Mike Dunne	.15
41	John Franco	.15
42	Dwight Gooden	.15
43	Pedro Guerrero	.15
44	Dion James	.15
45	John Kruk	.15
46	Jeffrey Leonard	.15
47	Carmelo Martinez	.15
48	Dale Murphy	.30
49	Tim Raines	.15
50	Nolan Ryan	1.50
51	Juan Samuel	.15
52	Ryne Sandberg	.75
53	Mike Schmidt	1.00
54	Mike Scott	.15
55	Ozzie Smith	.75
56	Darryl Strawberry	.15
57	Rick Sutcliffe	.15
58	Fernando Valenzuela	.15
59	Tim Wallach	.15
60	Todd Worrell	.15

Gallery of Champions

These metal replicas are exact reproductions at one-quarter scale of Topps 1988 cards, both front and back. The set includes 12 three-dimensional raised metal cards packaged in a velvet-lined case that bears the title of the set in gold embossed letters. A deluxe limited edition of the set (1,000) was produced in in sterling silver and an economy version in aluminum. A Mark McGwire pewter replica was given as a premium to dealers ordering the aluminum, bronze and silver sets. The special pewter card is distinguished from the regular issue by a diagonal name banner in the lower-right corner; regular replicas have a rectangular name banner parallel to the lower edge of the card.

		NM/M
Complete Aluminum Set (12):		10.00
Complete Bronze Set (12):		60.00
Complete Silver Set (12):		140.00
(1a)	Steve Bedrosian/Aluminum	.50
(1b)	Steve Bedrosian/Bronze	1.50
(1s)	Steve Bedrosian/Silver	6.00
(2a)	George Bell/Aluminum	.50
(2b)	George Bell/Bronze	1.50
(2s)	George Bell/Silver	6.00
(3a)	Wade Boggs/Aluminum	1.50
(3b)	Wade Boggs/Bronze	6.00
(3s)	Wade Boggs/Silver	20.00
(4a)	Jack Clark/Aluminum	.50
(4b)	Jack Clark/Bronze	1.50
(4s)	Jack Clark/Silver	6.00
(5a)	Roger Clemens/Aluminum	2.00
(5b)	Roger Clemens/Bronze	10.00
(5s)	Roger Clemens/Silver	25.00
(6a)	Andre Dawson/Aluminum	1.00
(6b)	Andre Dawson/Bronze	2.50
(6s)	Andre Dawson/Silver	9.00
(7a)	Tony Gwynn/Aluminum	1.50
(7b)	Tony Gwynn/Bronze	6.00
(7s)	Tony Gwynn/Silver	20.00
(8a)	Mark Langston/Aluminum	.50
(8b)	Mark Langston/Bronze	1.50
(8s)	Mark Langston/Silver	6.00
(9a)	Mark McGwire/Aluminum	2.50
(9b)	Mark McGwire/Bronze	12.50
(9s)	Mark McGwire/Silver	25.00
(9p)	Mark McGwire/Pewter	13.50
(10a)	Dave Righetti/Aluminum	.50
(10b)	Dave Righetti/Bronze	1.50
(10s)	Dave Righetti/Silver	6.00
(11a)	Nolan Ryan/Aluminum	3.00
(11b)	Nolan Ryan/Bronze	15.00
(11s)	Nolan Ryan/Silver	30.00
(12a)	Benny Santiago/Aluminum	.50
(12b)	Benny Santiago/Bronze	1.50
(12s)	Benny Santiago/Silver	6.00

Glossy Rookies

The Topps 1988 Rookies special insert cards follow the same basic design as the All-Star inserts. The set consists of 22 standard-size cards found one per pack in 100-card jumbo cellos. Large, glossy color player photos are printed on a white background below a red, yellow and blue "1987 Rookies" banner. A red and yellow player name appears beneath the photo. Red, white and blue card backs bear the title of the special insert set, the Rookies logo emblem, player name and card number.

		NM/M
Complete Set (22):		3.00
Common Player:		.05
1	Billy Ripken	.05
2	Ellis Burks	.05
3	Mike Greenwell	.05
4	DeWayne Buice	.05
5	Devon White	.05
6	Fred Manrique	.05
7	Mike Henneman	.05
8	Matt Nokes	.05
9	Kevin Seitzer	.05
10	B.J. Surhoff	.05
11	Casey Candaele	.05
12	Randy Myers	.05
13	Mark McGwire	2.50
14	Luis Polonia	.05
15	Terry Steinbach	.05
16	Mike Dunne	.05
17	Al Pedreque	.05
18	Benny Santiago	.05
19	Kelly Downs	.05
20	Joe Magrane	.05
21	Jerry Browne	.05
22	Jeff Musselman	.05

Mini League Leaders

The third consecutive issue of Topps mini-cards (2-1/8" x 3") includes 77 cards spotlighting the top five ranked pitchers and batters. This set is unique in that it was the first time Topps included full-color player photos on both the front and back. Glossy action shots on the card fronts fade into a white border with a Topps logo in an upper corner. The player's name is printed in bold black letters beneath the photo. Horizontal re-

WADE BOGGS

verses feature circular player photos on a blue and white background with the card number, player name, personal information, 1987 ranking and lifetime/1987 stats printed in red, black and yellow lettering.

		NM/M
Complete Set (77):		3.00
Common Player:		.05
Wax Pack (7):		.30
Wax Box (36):		6.00
1	Wade Boggs	.60
2	Roger Clemens	.65
3	Dwight Evans	.05
4	DeWayne Buice	.05
5	Brian Downing	.05
6	Wally Joyner	.05
7	Ivan Calderon	.05
8	Carlton Fisk	.50
9	Gary Redus	.05
10	Darrell Evans	.05
11	Jack Morris	.05
12	Alan Trammell	.05
13	Lou Whitaker	.05
14	Bret Saberhagen	.05
15	Kevin Seitzer	.05
16	Danny Tartabull	.05
17	Willie Wilson	.05
18	Teddy Higuera	.05
19	Paul Molitor	.50
20	Dan Plesac	.05
21	Robin Yount	.50
22	Kent Hrbek	.05
23	Kirby Puckett	.60
24	Jeff Reardon	.05
25	Frank Viola	.05
26	Rickey Henderson	.50
27	Don Mattingly	.65
28	Willie Randolph	.05
29	Dave Righetti	.05
30	Jose Canseco	.35
31	Mark McGwire	.75
32	Dave Stewart	.05
33	Phil Bradley	.05
34	Mark Langston	.05
35	Harold Reynolds	.05
36	Charlie Hough	.05
37	George Bell	.05
38	Tom Henke	.05
39	Jimmy Key	.05
40	Dion James	.05
41	Dale Murphy	.20
42	Zane Smith	.05
43	Andre Dawson	.20
44	Lee Smith	.05
45	Rick Sutcliffe	.05
46	Eric Davis	.05
47	John Franco	.05
48	Dave Parker	.05
49	Billy Hatcher	.05
50	Nolan Ryan	1.00
51	Mike Scott	.05
52	Pedro Guerrero	.05
53	Orel Hershiser	.05
54	Fernando Valenzuela	.05
55	Bob Welch	.05
56	Andres Galarraga	.05
57	Tim Raines	.05
58	Tim Wallach	.05
59	Len Dykstra	.05
60	Dwight Gooden	.05
61	Howard Johnson	.05
62	Roger McDowell	.05
63	Darryl Strawberry	.05
64	Steve Bedrosian	.05
65	Shane Rawley	.05
66	Juan Samuel	.05
67	Mike Schmidt	.65
68	Mike Dunne	.05
69	Jack Clark	.05
70	Vince Coleman	.05
71	Willie McGee	.05
72	Ozzie Smith	.50
73	Todd Worrell	.05
74	Tony Gwynn	.60
75	John Kruk	.05
76	Rick Rueschel	.05
77	Checklist	

Stickercards

Actually a part of the 1988 Topps Stickers issue, this set consists of 67 cards. The cards

SUPER STAR

TONY GWYNN

are the backs of the peel-off stickers and measure 2-1/8" x 3". To determine total value, combine the prices of the stickers (found in the 1988 Topps Stickers checklist) on the stickercard front with the value assigned to the stickercard in the following checklist.

		NM/M
Complete Set (67):		3.00
Common Player:		.05
1	Jack Clark	.05
2	Andres Galarraga	.05
3	Keith Hernandez	.05
4	Tom Herr	.05
5	Juan Samuel	.05
6	Ryne Sandberg	.50
7	Terry Pendleton	.05
8	Mike Schmidt	.60
9	Tim Wallach	.05
10	Hubie Brooks	.05
11	Shawon Dunston	.05
12	Ozzie Smith	.50
13	Andre Dawson	.20
14	Eric Davis	.05
15	Pedro Guerrero	.05
16	Tony Gwynn	.50
17	Jeffrey Leonard	.05
18	Dale Murphy	.20
19	Dave Parker	.05
20	Tim Raines	.05
21	Darryl Strawberry	.05
22	Gary Carter	.40
23	Jody Davis	.05
24	Ozzie Virgil	.05
25	Dwight Gooden	.05
26	Mike Scott	.05
27	Rick Sutcliffe	.05
28	Sid Fernandez	.05
29	Neal Heaton	.05
30	Fernando Valenzuela	.05
31	Steve Bedrosian	.05
32	John Franco	.05
33	Lee Smith	.05
34	Wally Joyner	.05
35	Don Mattingly	.65
36	Mark McGwire	.65
37	Willie Randolph	.05
38	Lou Whitaker	.05
39	Frank White	.05
40	Wade Boggs	.50
41	George Brett	.60
42	Paul Molitor	.40
43	Tony Fernandez	.05
44	Cal Ripken, Jr.	.75
45	Alan Trammell	.05
46	Jesse Barfield	.05
47	George Bell	.05
48	Jose Canseco	.35
49	Joe Carter	.05
50	Dwight Evans	.05
51	Rickey Henderson	.40
52	Kirby Puckett	.50
53	Cory Snyder	.05
54	Dave Winfield	.40
55	Terry Kennedy	.05
56	Matt Nokes	.05
57	B.J. Surhoff	.05
58	Roger Clemens	.60
59	Jack Morris	.05
60	Bret Saberhagen	.05
61	Ron Guidry	.05
62	Bruce Hurst	.05
63	Mark Langston	.05
64	Tom Henke	.05
65	Dan Plesac	.05
66	Dave Righetti	.05
67	Checklist	

Stickers

This set of 313 stickers (on 198 cards) offers an addition for 1988 - 66 different players are pictured on the backs of the sticker cards. The stickers come in two sizes (2-1/8" x 3" or 1-1/2" x 2-1/8"). Larger stickers fill an entire card, smaller ones are attached in pairs. A 36-page sticker yearbook with Mark McGwire on the cover has a designated space inside for each sticker,

with one page per team and special pages of 1987 Highlights, World Series, All-Stars and future Stars. No printing appears on the full-color action shot stickers except for a small black number in the lower left corner. Stickers were sold in packs of five (with gum) for 25 cents per pack. Unlike the 1987 Topps Stickers set, different pairings can be found, rather than the same two players/numbers always sharing the same sticker. To determine total value, combine the value of the stickercard (found in the 1988 Topps Stickercard checklist) with the values assigned the stickers in the following checklist.

		NM/M
Complete Set (313):		10.00
Common Player:		.05
Sticker Album:		1.50
Wax Pack (5):		.25
Wax Box (48):		7.00
1-263	1987 Highlights (Mark McGwire, Willie Wilson)	.25
2-304	1987 Highlights (Benny Santiago, Al Pedreque (Future Star))	.05
3-187	1987 Highlights (Don Mattingly, Ernie Whitt)	.20
4-223	1987 Highlights (Vince Coleman, Gary Matthews)	.05
5-272	1987 Highlights (Bob Boone, Jim Morrison)	.05
6-278	1987 Highlights (Steve Bedrosian, Tim Laudner)	.05
7-276	1987 Highlights (Nolan Ryan, Bert Blyleven)	.30
8-306	1987 Highlights (Darrell Evans, Kevin Seitzer (Future Star))	.05
9-255	1987 Highlights (Mike Schmidt, Frank White)	.15
10-256	1987 Highlights (Don Baylor, Dan Quisenberry)	.05
11-145	1987 Highlights (Eddie Murray, Dennis Rasmussen)	.10
12-237	1987 Highlights (Juan Beniquez, Oddibe McDowell)	.05
13	1987 Championship Series (John Tudor)	.05
14	1987 Championship Series (Jeff Reardon)	.05
15	1987 Championship Series (Tom Brunansky)	.05
16	1987 Championship Series (Jeffrey Leonard)	.05
17	1987 Championship Series (Gary Gaetti)	.05
18	1987 Championship Series (Cardinals Celebrate)	.05
19	1987 World Series (Danny Gladden)	.05
20	1987 World Series (Bert Blyleven)	.05
21	1987 World Series (John Tudor)	.05
22	1987 World Series (Tom Lawless)	.05
23	1987 World Series (Curt Ford)	.05
24	1987 World Series (Kent Hrbek)	.05
25	1987 World Series (Frank Viola)	.05

26-216	Dave Smith, Edwin Nunez	.05
27-240	Jim Deshaies, Pete O'Brien	.05
28-171	Billy Hatcher, Mike Davis	.05
29-196	Kevin Bass, Teddy Higuera	.05
30	Mike Scott	.05
31-224	Danny Walling, Eric Bell	.05
32-185	Alan Ashby, Willie Upshaw	.05
33-292	Ken Caminiti, Greg Walker	.05
34-245	Bill Doran, Dwight Evans	.05
35	Glenn Davis	.05
36	Ozzie Virgil	.05
37-260	Ken Oberkfell, Charlie Leibrandt	.05
38-183	Ken Griffey, Devon White	.05
39-287	Albert Hall, Ken Williams	.05
40-310	Zane Smith, Ellis Burks (Future Star)	.05
41-207	Andres Thomas, Julio Franco	.05
42-178	Dion James, Gary Pettis	.05
43-249	Jim Acker, Mike Greenwell	.05
44-226	Tom Glavine, Dave Schmidt	.20
45	Dale Murphy	.20
46	Jack Clark	.05
47-269	Vince Coleman, Matt Nokes	.05
48-221	Ricky Horton, Harold Reynolds	.05
49-303	Terry Pendleton, Gary Ward	.05
50-271	Tom Herr, Eric King	.05
51-265	Joe Magrane, Darrell Evans	.05
52-211	Tony Pena, Brook Jacoby	.05
53-298	Ozzie Smith, Rick Rhoden	.40
54-169	Todd Worrell, Alfredo Griffin	.05
55	Willie McGee	.05
56	Andre Dawson	.25
57-225	Ryne Sandberg, Terry Kennedy	.35
58-291	Keith Moreland, Richard Dotson	.05
59-198	Greg Maddux, Rob Deer	.40
60-290	Jody Davis, Carlton Fisk	.25
61	Rick Sutcliffe	.05
62-295	Jamie Moyer, Mike Pagliarulo	.05
63-172	Leon Durham, Luis Polonia	.05
64-313	Lee Smith, Devon White (Future Star)	.05
65-250	Shawon Dunston, Ellis Burks	.05
66-257	Franklin Stubbs, Danny Tartabull	.05
67-235	Mike Scioscia, Steve Buechele	.05
68-177	Orel Hershiser, Dick Schofield	.05
69-289	Mike Marshall, Bob James	.05
70	Fernando Valenzuela	.05
71-281	Mickey Hatcher, Danny Gladden	.05
72-166	Matt Young, Jay Howell	.05
73-236	Bob Welch, Charlie Hough	.05
74-170	Steve Sax, Dennis Eckersley	.25
75	Pedro Guerrero	.05
76	Tim Raines	.05
77-252	Casey Candaele, Rich Gedman	.05
78-248	Mike Fitzgerald, Marty Barrett	.05
79-301	Andres Galarraga, Claudell Washington	.05
80-212	Neal Heaton, Brett Butler	.05
81-296	Hubie Brooks, Ron Guidry	.05
82-258	Floyd Youmans, Bo Jackson	.10
83-201	Herm Winningham, Robin Yount	.25
84-307	Denny Martinez, Mike Dunne (Future Star)	.05
85	Tim Wallach	.05
86	Jeffrey Leonard	.05
87-251	Will Clark, Roger Clemens	.45
88-288	Kevin Mitchell, Jim Winn	.05
89-267	Mike Aldrete, Kirk Gibson	.05
90-191	Scott Garrelts, Dave Steib	.05

91-231 Jose Uribe, Mike Boddicker .05
92-246 Bob Brenly, Sam Horn .05
93-189 Robby Thompson, Lloyd Moseby .05
94-217 Don Robinson, Jim Presley .05
95 Candy Maldonado .05
96 Darryl Strawberry .05
97-192 Keith Hernandez, Jesse Barfield .05
98-220 Ron Darling, Dave Valle .05
99-218 Howard Johnson, Phil Bradley .05
100-190 Roger McDowell, Jimmy Key .05
101 Dwight Gooden .05
102-165 Kevin McReynolds, Tony Phillips .05
103-275 Sid Fernandez, Tom Brunansky .05
104-241 Dave Magadan, Scott Fletcher .05
105-167 Gary Carter, Carney Lansford .25
106-302 Carmelo Martinez, Dave Winfield .05
107-205 Eddie Whitson, Mel Hall .05
108-180 Tim Flannery, DeWayne Buice .05
109-266 Stan Jefferson, Bill Madlock .05
110 John Kruk .05
111-168 Chris Brown, Dave Stewart .05
112-215 Benny Santiago, Rey Quinones .05
113-270 Garry Templeton, Lou Whitaker .05
114-186 Lance McCullers, Tom Henke .05
115 Tony Gwynn .50
116 Steve Bedrosian .05
117-247 Von Hayes, Jim Rice .10
118-279 Kevin Gross, Gene Larkin .05
119-238 Bruce Ruffin, Mike Stanley .05
120-184 Juan Samuel, Jim Clancy .05
121-182 Shane Rawley, Bob Boone .05
122-222 Chris James, Scott Bradley .05
123-199 Lance Parrish, Dale Sveum .05
124-181 Glenn Wilson, Brian Downing .05
125 Mike Schmidt .60
126 Andy Van Slyke .05
127-297 Jose Lind, Rickey Henderson .05
128-176 Al Pedrique, Greg Minton .05
129-277 Bobby Bonilla, Gary Gaetti .05
130-175 Sid Bream, Jack Howell .05
131-230 Mike LaValliere, Larry Sheets .05
132-197 Mike Dunne, Glenn Braggs .05
133-232 Jeff Robinson, Tom Niedenfuer .05
134-195 Doug Drabek, Jim Gantner .05
135 Barry Bonds .75
136 Dave Parker .05
137-208 Nick Esasky, Cory Snyder .05
138-280 Buddy Bell, Jeff Reardon .05
139-239 Kal Daniels, Pete Incaviglia .05
140-285 Barry Larkin, Ivan Calderon .05
141 Eric Davis .05
142-227 John Franco, Billy Ripken .05
143-229 Bo Diaz, Ray Knight .05
144-261 Ron Oester, Kevin Seitzer .05
146 Eric Davis/AS .05
147 Ryne Sandberg/AS .15
148 Andre Dawson/AS .15
149 Mike Schmidt/AS .40
150 Jack Clark/AS .05
151 Darryl Strawberry/AS .05
152 Gary Carter/AS .35
153 Ozzie Smith/AS .35
154 Mike Scott/AS .35
155 Rickey Henderson/AS .35
156 Don Mattingly/AS .40
157 Wade Boggs/AS .30
158 George Bell/AS .05
159 Dave Winfield/AS .35
160 Cal Ripken, Jr./AS .50

161 Terry Kennedy/AS .05
162 Willie Randolph/AS .05
163 Bret Saberhagen/AS .05
164 Mark McGwire .65
173 Jose Canseco .35
174 Mike Witt .05
179 Wally Joyner .05
188 George Bell .05
193 Tony Fernandez .05
194 Paul Molitor .40
200-308 Bill Wegman, Jeff Musselman (Future Star) .05
202-309 B.J. Surhoff, Mark McGwire (Future Star) .50
203 Dan Plesac .05
204 Pat Tabler .05
206-305 Scott Bailes, Casey Candaele (Future Star) .05
209-312 Chris Bando, Mike Greenwell (Future Star) .05
210-311 Greg Swindell, Matt Nokes (Future Star) .05
213 Joe Carter .05
214 Mark Langston .05
219 Alvin Davis .05
228 Cal Ripken, Jr. .75
233 Eddie Murray .40
234 Ruben Sierra .50
242-300 Dale Mohorcic, Dave Righetti .05
243 Larry Parrish .05
244 Wade Boggs .40
253 Bruce Hurst .05
254 Bret Saberhagen .05
259 George Brett .50
262-282 Mark Gubicza, Frank Viola .05
264-286 Frank Tanana, Donnie Hill .05
268 Jack Morris .05
273 Alan Trammell .05
274 Kent Hrbek .05
283 Kirby Puckett .50
284 Ozzie Guillen .05
293 Harold Baines .05
294 Willie Randolph .05
299 Don Mattingly .50

Campbell's Richie Ashburn Tribute Sheet

Longtime Phillies star, Hall of Famer and broadcaster Richie Ashburn was honored for his 40 years in baseball by the issue of a commemorative card set in the form of a 10" x 14" poster given away as a stadium promotion. A 5" x 7" card picturing the 61-year old Ashburn was at center, with his complete major league stats on back. Surrounding the center card and separated by perforations are reproductions of 12 of Ashburn's baseball cards. The cards are reduced to about 75 percent of actual size and shown on an American flag background. The back of each card is also reproduced, with a cartoon figure of the Campbell's Kid baseball player included on front and back.

NM/M
Complete Set (Sheet): 25.00
Complete Set, Singles (13): 20.00
Common Card:
1952 Bowman 2.00
1952 Topps 2.00
1954 Topps 2.00
1956 Topps 2.00
1957 Topps 2.00
1958 Topps 2.00
1959 Topps 2.00
1959 Topps (N.L. Hitting Kings) 2.00
1960 Topps 2.00
1961 Topps 2.00

1962 Topps 2.00
1963 Topps 2.00
Richie Ashburn (1988 Portrait) 2.00

Sports Shots Portfolios

One hundred and thirty of the biggest names from Topps' 1988 baseball card set were reproduced in the form of 9-1/2" x 11-3/4" cardboard folders. The folders reproduce both front and back of the '88 Topps cards and open to offer two pockets for storage. Various manufacturer and licensor logos are the only printing inside. The folders carried a suggested retail price of $1 apiece and were distributed in either team packs or all-star assortments of 50 pieces each. By 1992, the folders were being wholesaled within the hobby at less than 30 cents apiece.

NM/M
Complete Set (130): 60.00
Common Player: .50
10 Ryne Sandberg 2.50
15 Chili Davis .50
25 Andres Galarraga .50
35 Harold Baines .50
39 Gerald Perry .50
40 Orel Hershiser .50
45 Kent Hrbek .50
50 Hubie Brooks .50
55 Phil Bradley .50
60 Rickey Henderson 2.00
70 Roger Clemens 3.00
75 Joe Carter .50
80 Mark Langston .50
90 Dale Murphy 1.00
95 Lance Parrish .50
100 Jack Clark .50
102 Barry Larkin .50
110 Teddy Higuera .50
118 Bob Welch .50
120 Kirby Puckett 2.50
130 Buddy Bell .50
138 Mitch Webster .50
140 Jesse Barfield .50
142 Andy Van Slyke .50
150 Eric Davis .50
165 Robin Yount 2.00
170 Goose Gossage .50
180 Terry Kennedy .50
184 Ivan Calderon .50
192 Devon White .50
193 Brian Fisher .50
195 Dan Quisenberry .50
197 Lance McCullers .50
200 Wade Boggs 2.50
210 Willie Randolph .50
215 Von Hayes .50
230 Pat Tabler .50
238 Luis Polonia .50
240 Lee Smith .50
250 Nolan Ryan 4.00
260 Vince Coleman .50
265 Bo Diaz .50
270 Mike Witt .50
280 Pete Incaviglia .50
285 Jim Presley .50
297 Zane Smith .50
300 Don Mattingly 3.00
305 Steve Sax .50
306 Billy Hatcher .50
320 Alan Trammell .50
327 Larry Sheets .50
331 Brian Downing .50
340 Jack Morris .50
343 Greg Gagne .50
350 Will Clark .50
360 Tony Gwynn 2.50
370 Jose Canseco 1.00
385 Carlton Fisk .50
408 Dion James .50
410 Tony Pena .50
420 Wally Joyner .50
424 Dwayne Murphy .50
430 Glenn Davis .50
440 Steve Bedrosian .50
450 Barry Bonds 4.00

452 Willie Wilson .50
460 Ozzie Smith 2.50
465 Paul Molitor 2.00
470 Dwight Evans .50
476 Dave Stewart .50
479 Brett Butler .50
480 Dwight Gooden .50
485 Harold Reynolds .50
490 Larry Parrish .50
491 B.J. Surhoff .50
495 Eddie Murray 2.00
497 Kevin Mitchell .50
500 Andre Dawson 1.00
510 Dave Winfield .50
525 Marty Barrett .50
530 Gary Carter 2.00
540 Bret Saberhagen .50
550 Pedro Guerrero .50
555 Brook Jacoby .50
560 Tim Wallach .50
565 Lloyd Moseby .50
570 Jeffrey Leonard .50
578 Gary Gaetti .50
580 Mark McGwire 3.50
590 George Bell .50
596 John Kruk .50
600 Mike Schmidt 3.00
605 Kirk Gibson .50
610 Keith Hernandez .50
613 Bobby Thigpen .50
615 Jody Davis .50
619 Mike Dunne .50
620 Cory Snyder .50
625 Frank Viola .50
645 Matt Nokes .50
649 De Wayne Buice .50
650 Cal Ripken Jr. 4.00
660 Rick Reuschel .50
670 Dan Plesac .50
675 Jim Rice 1.00
680 Charlie Hough .50
681 Bobby Bonilla .50
682 Jimmy Key .50
685 Ron Darling .50
693 Benito Santiago .50
705 George Brett 3.00
710 Juan Samuel .50
715 Darryl Strawberry .50
720 Todd Worrell .50
721 Tim Raines .50
721 Pete O'Brien .50
725 Mike Boddicker .50
730 John Franco .50
740 Rick Sutcliffe .50
745 Bill Doran .50
750 Bo Jackson 1.00
755 Ozzie Virgil .50
760 Mike Scott .50
764 Greg Walker .50
770 Lou Whitaker .50
771 Ruben Sierra .50
775 Dave Steib .50
780 Fernando Valenzuela .50
785 Alvin Davis .50
790 Dave Righetti .50

1989 Topps

Ten top young players from the June 1988 draft are featured on "#1 Draft Pick" cards in this full-color basic set of 792 standard-size baseball cards. An additional five cards salute 1989 Future Stars, 22 cards highlight All-Stars, seven contain Record Breakers, five are designated Turn Back The Clock, and six contain checklists. This set features the familiar white borders, but upper-left and lower-right photo corners have been rounded off. A curved name banner in bright red or blue is beneath the team name in large script in the lower-right corner. The card backs are printed in black on a red background and include personal information and complete minor and major league stats. Another new addition in this set is the special Monthly Scoreboard chart that lists monthly stats (April through September) in two of several categories (hits, run, home runs, stolen bases, RBIs, wins, strikeouts, games or saves).

NM/M
Unopened Factory Set, Retail (792): 25.00
Unopened Factory Set, Hobby (792): 25.00
Complete Set (792): 15.00
Common Player: .05
Wax Pack (15): .75
Wax Box (36): 12.00
Cello Pack (29): 1.00
Cello Box (24): 18.00
Rack Pack (43): .75
Rack Box (24): 15.00
Vending Box (500): 6.00
1 George Bell (Record Breaker) .05
2 Wade Boggs (Record Breaker) .25
3 Gary Carter (Record Breaker) .20
4 Andre Dawson (Record Breaker) .10
5 Orel Hershiser (Record Breaker) .05
6 Doug Jones (Record Breaker) .05
7 Kevin McReynolds (Record Breaker) .05
8 Dave Eiland RC .05
9 Tim Teufel .05
10 Andre Dawson .25
11 Bruce Sutter .35
12 Dale Sveum .05
13 Doug Sisk .05
14 Tom Kelly .05
15 Robby Thompson .05
16 Ron Robinson .05
17 Brian Downing .05
18 Rick Rhoden .05
19 Greg Gagne .05
20 Steve Bedrosian .05
21 White Sox Leaders (Greg Walker) .05
22 Tim Crews .05
23 Mike Fitzgerald .05
24 Larry Andersen .05
25 Frank White .05
26 Dale Mohorcic .05
27 Orestes Destrade RC .05
28 Mike Moore .05
29 Kelly Gruber .05
30 Dwight Gooden .05
31 Terry Francona .05
32 Dennis Rasmussen .05
33 B.J. Surhoff .05
34 Ken Williams .05
35 John Tudor .05
36 Mitch Webster .05
37 Bob Stanley .05
38 Paul Runge .05
39 Mike Maddux .05
40 Steve Sax .05
41 Terry Mulholland .05
42 Jim Eppard RC .05
43 Guillermo Hernandez .05
44 Jim Snyder .05
45 Kal Daniels .05
46 Mark Portugal .05
47 Carney Lansford .05
48 Tim Burke .05
49 Craig Biggio .05
50 George Bell .05
51 Angels Leaders (Mark McLemore) .05
52 Bob Brenly .05
53 Ruben Sierra .05
54 Steve Trout .05
55 Julio Franco .05
56 Pat Tabler .05
57 Alejandro Pena .05
58 Lee Mazzilli .05
59 Mark Davis .05
60 Tom Brunansky .05
61 Neil Allen .05
62 Alfredo Griffin .05
63 Mark Clear .05
64 Alex Trevino .05
65 Rick Reuschel .05
66 Manny Trillo .05
67 Dave Palmer .05
68 Darrell Miller .05
69 Jeff Ballard .05
70 Mark McGwire .65
71 Mike Boddicker .05
72 John Moses .05
73 Pascual Perez .05
74 Nick Leyva .05
75 Tom Henke .05
76 Terry Blocker RC .05
77 Doyle Alexander .05
78 Jim Sundberg .05
79 Scott Bankhead .05
80 Cory Snyder .05
81 Expos Leaders (Tim Raines) .05
82 Dave Leiper .05
83 Jeff Blauser RC .05
84 Bill Bene RC (#1 Draft Pick) .05
85 Kevin McReynolds .05
86 Al Nipper .05

87 Larry Owen .05
88 Darryl Hamilton RC .05
89 Dave LaPoint .05
90 Vince Coleman .05
91 Floyd Youmans .05
92 Jeff Kunkel .05
93 Ken Howell .05
94 Chris Speier .05
95 Gerald Young .05
96 Rick Cerone .05
97 Greg Mathews .05
98 Larry Sheets .05
99 Sherman Corbett RC .05
100 Mike Schmidt .50
101 Les Straker .05
102 Mike Gallego .05
103 Tim Birtsas .05
104 Dallas Green .05
105 Ron Darling .05
106 Willie Upshaw .05
107 Jose DeLeon .05
108 Fred Manrique .05
109 Hipolito Pena RC .05
110 Paul Molitor .40
111 Reds Leaders (Eric Davis) .05
112 Jim Presley .05
113 Lloyd Moseby .05
114 Bob Kipper .05
115 Jody Davis .05
116 Jeff Montgomery .05
117 Dave Anderson .05
118 Checklist 1-132 .05
119 Terry Puhl .05
120 Frank Viola .05
121 Garry Templeton .05
122 Lance Johnson RC .05
123 Spike Owen .05
124 Jim Traber .05
125 Mike Krukow .05
126 Sid Bream .05
127 Walt Terrell .05
128 Milt Thompson .05
129 Terry Clark RC .05
130 Gerald Perry .05
131 Dave Otto RC .05
132 Curt Ford .05
133 Bill Long .05
134 Don Zimmer .05
135 Jose Rijo .05
136 Joey Meyer .05
137 Geno Petralli .05
138 Wallace Johnson .05
139 Mike Flanagan .05
140 Shawon Dunston .05
141 Indians Leaders (Brook Jacoby) .05
142 Mike Diaz .05
143 Mike Campbell .05
144 Jay Bell .05
145 Dave Stewart .05
146 Gary Pettis .05
147 DeWayne Buice .05
148 Bill Pecota .05
149 Doug Dascenzo RC .05
150 Fernando Valenzuela .05
151 Terry McGriff .05
152 Mark Thurmond .05
153 Jim Pankovits .05
154 Don Carman .05
155 Marty Barrett .05
156 Dave Gallagher RC .05
157 Tom Glavine .25
158 Mike Aldrete .05
159 Pat Clements .05
160 Jeffrey Leonard .05
161 Gregg Olson RC (#1 Draft Pick) .05
162 John Davis .05
163 Bob Forsch .05
164 Hal Lanier .05
165 Mike Dunne .05
166 Doug Jennings RC .05
167 Steve Searcy RC (Future Star) .05
168 Willie Wilson .05
169 Mike Jackson .05
170 Tony Fernandez .05
171 Braves Leaders (Andres Thomas) .05
172 Frank Williams .05
173 Mel Hall .05
174 Todd Burns RC .05
175 John Shelby .05
176 Jeff Parrett .05
177 Monty Fariss RC (#1 Draft Pick) .05
178 Mark Grant .05
179 Ozzie Virgil .05
180 Mike Scott .05
181 Craig Worthington RC .05
182 Bob McClure .05
183 Oddibe McDowell .05
184 John Costello RC .05
185 Claudell Washington .05
186 Pat Perry .05
187 Darren Daulton .05
188 Dennis Lamp .05
189 Kevin Mitchell .05
190 Mike Witt .05
191 Sil Campusano RC .05
192 Paul Mirabella .05
193 Sparky Anderson .10
194 Greg Harris RC .05
195 Ozzie Guillen .05
196 Denny Walling .05
197 Neal Heaton .05
198 Danny Heep .05

No.	Player	Price
199	Mike Schooler RC	.05
200	George Brett	.50
201	Blue Jays Leaders (Kelly Gruber)	.05
202	Brad Moore RC	.05
203	Rob Ducey	.05
204	Brad Havens •	.05
205	Dwight Evans	.05
206	Roberto Alomar	.35
207	Terry Leach	.05
208	Tom Pagnozzi	.05
209	Jeff Bittiger RC	.05
210	Dale Murphy	.15
211	Mike Pagliarulo	.05
212	Scott Sanderson	.05
213	Rene Gonzales	.05
214	Charlie O'Brien	.05
215	Kevin Gross	.05
216	Jack Howell	.05
217	Joe Price	.05
218	Mike LaValliere	.05
219	Jim Clancy	.05
220	Gary Gaetti	.05
221	Cecil Espy	.05
222	Mark Lewis RC (#1 Draft Pick)	.05
223	Jay Buhner	.05
224	Tony LaRussa	.05
225	Ramon Martinez RC	.25
226	Bill Doran	.05
227	John Farrell	.05
228	Nelson Santovenia RC	.05
229	Jimmy Key	.05
230	Ozzie Smith	.45
231	Padres Leaders (Roberto Alomar)	.05
232	Ricky Horton	.05
233	Gregg Jefferies (Future Star)	.20
234	Tom Browning	.05
235	John Kruk	.05
236	Charles Hudson	.05
237	Glenn Hubbard	.05
238	Eric King	.05
239	Tim Laudner	.05
240	Greg Maddux	.45
241	Brett Butler	.05
242	Ed Vande Berg	.05
243	Bob Boone	.05
244	Jim Acker	.05
245	Jim Rice	.15
246	Rey Quinones	.05
247	Shawn Hillegas	.05
248	Tony Phillips	.05
249	Tim Leary	.05
250	Cal Ripken, Jr.	.75
251	John Dopson RC	.05
252	Billy Hatcher	.05
253	Jose Alvarez RC	.05
254	Tom LaSorda	.05
255	Ron Guidry	.10
256	Benny Santiago	.05
257	Rick Aguilera	.05
258	Checklist 133-264	.05
259	Larry McWilliams	.05
260	Dave Winfield	.40
261	Cardinals Leaders (Tom Brunansky)	.05
262	Jeff Pico RC	.05
263	Mike Felder	.05
264	Rob Dibble RC	.10
265	Kent Hrbek	.05
266	Luis Aquino	.05
267	Jeff Robinson	.05
268	Keith Miller	.05
269	Tom Bolton	.05
270	Wally Joyner	.05
271	Jay Tibbs	.05
272	Ron Hassey	.05
273	Jose Lind	.05
274	Mark Eichhorn	.05
275	Danny Tartabull	.05
276	Paul Kilgus	.05
277	Mike Davis	.05
278	Andy McGaffigan	.05
279	Scott Bradley	.05
280	Bob Knepper	.05
281	Gary Redus	.05
282	Cris Carpenter RC	.05
283	Andy Allanson	.05
284	Jim Leyland	.05
285	John Candelaria	.05
286	Darrin Jackson	.05
287	Juan Nieves	.05
288	Pat Sheridan	.05
289	Ernie Whitt	.05
290	John Franco	.05
291	Mets Leaders (Darryl Strawberry)	.05
292	Jim Corsi RC	.05
293	Glenn Wilson	.05
294	Juan Berenguer	.05
295	Scott Fletcher	.05
296	Ron Gant	.05
297	Oswald Peraza RC	.05
298	Chris James	.05
299	Steve Ellsworth RC	.05
300	Darryl Strawberry	.05
301	Charlie Leibrandt	.05
302	Gary Ward	.05
303	Felix Fermin	.05
304	Joel Youngblood	.05
305	Dave Smith	.05
306	Tracy Woodson RC	.05
307	Lance McCullers	.05
308	Ron Karkovice	.05
309	Mario Diaz RC	.05
310	Rafael Palmeiro	.35
311	Chris Bosio	.05
312	Tom Lawless	.05
313	Denny Martinez	.05
314	Bobby Valentine	.05
315	Greg Swindell	.05
316	Walt Weiss	.05
317	Jack Armstrong RC	.05
318	Gene Larkin	.05
319	Greg Booker	.05
320	Lou Whitaker	.05
321	Red Sox Leaders (Jody Reed)	.05
322	John Smiley	.05
323	Gary Thurman	.05
324	Bob Milacki RC	.05
325	Jesse Barfield	.05
326	Dennis Boyd	.05
327	Mark Lemke RC	.05
328	Rick Honeycutt	.05
329	Bob Melvin	.05
330	Eric Davis	.05
331	Curt Wilkerson	.05
332	Tony Armas	.05
333	Bob Ojeda	.05
334	Steve Lyons	.05
335	Dave Righetti	.05
336	Steve Balboni	.05
337	Calvin Schiraldi	.05
338	Jim Adduci RC	.05
339	Scott Bailes	.05
340	Kirk Gibson	.05
341	Jim Deshaies	.05
342	Tom Brookens	.05
343	Gary Sheffield RC (Future Star)	1.50
344	Tom Trebelhorn	.05
345	Charlie Hough	.05
346	Rex Hudler RC	.05
347	John Cerutti	.05
348	Ed Hearn	.05
349	Ron Jones RC	.05
350	Andy Van Slyke	.05
351	Giants Leaders (Bob Melvin)	.05
352	Rick Schu	.05
353	Marvell Wynne	.05
354	Larry Parrish	.05
355	Mark Langston	.05
356	Kevin Elster	.05
357	Jerry Reuss	.05
358	Ricky Jordan RC	.05
359	Tommy John	.10
360	Ryne Sandberg	.45
361	Kelly Downs	.05
362	Jack Lazorko	.05
363	Rich Yett	.05
364	Rob Deer	.05
365	Mike Henneman	.05
366	Herm Winningham	.05
367	Johnny Paredes RC	.05
368	Brian Holton	.05
369	Ken Caminiti	.05
370	Dennis Eckersley	.35
371	Manny Lee	.05
372	Craig Lefferts	.05
373	Tracy Jones	.05
374	John Wathan	.05
375	Terry Pendleton	.05
376	Steve Lombardozzi	.05
377	Mike Smithson	.05
378	Checklist 265-396	.05
379	Tim Flannery	.05
380	Rickey Henderson	.40
381	Orioles Leaders (Larry Sheets)	.05
382	John Smoltz	.50
383	Howard Johnson	.05
384	Mark Salas	.05
385	Von Hayes	.05
386	Andres Galarraga/AS	.05
387	Ryne Sandberg/AS	.20
388	Bobby Bonilla/AS	.05
389	Ozzie Smith/AS	.25
390	Darryl Strawberry/AS	.05
391	Andre Dawson/AS	.05
392	Andy Van Slyke/AS	.05
393	Gary Carter/AS	.05
394	Orel Hershiser/AS	.05
395	Danny Jackson/AS	.05
396	Kirk Gibson/AS	.05
397	Don Mattingly/AS	.30
398	Julio Franco/AS	.05
399	Wade Boggs/AS	.05
400	Alan Trammell/AS	.05
401	Jose Canseco/AS	.15
402	Mike Greenwell/AS	.05
403	Kirby Puckett/AS	.25
404	Bob Boone/AS	.05
405	Roger Clemens/AS	.30
406	Frank Viola/AS	.05
407	Dave Winfield/AS	.20
408	Greg Walker	.05
409	Ken Dayley	.05
410	Jack Clark	.05
411	Mitch Williams	.05
412	Barry Lyons	.05
413	Mike Kingery	.05
414	Jim Fregosi	.05
415	Rich Gossage	.05
416	Fred Lynn	.05
417	Mike LaCoss	.05
418	Bob Dernier	.05
419	Tom Filer	.05
420	Joe Carter	.05
421	Kirk McCaskill	.05
422	Bo Diaz	.05
423	Brian Fisher	.05
424	Luis Polonia	.05
425	Jay Howell	.05
426	Danny Gladden	.05
427	Eric Show	.05
428	Craig Reynolds	.05
429	Twins Leaders (Greg Gagne)	.05
430	Mark Gubicza	.05
431	Luis Rivera	.05
432	Chad Kreuter RC	.10
433	Albert Hall	.05
434	Ken Patterson RC	.05
435	Len Dykstra	.05
436	Bobby Meacham	.05
437	Andy Benes (#1 Draft Pick)	.05
438	Greg Gross	.05
439	Frank DiPino	.05
440	Bobby Bonilla	.05
441	Jerry Reed	.05
442	Jose Oquendo	.05
443	Rod Nichols RC	.05
444	Moose Stubing	.05
445	Matt Nokes	.05
446	Rob Murphy	.05
447	Donell Nixon	.05
448	Eric Plunk	.05
449	Carmelo Martinez	.05
450	Roger Clemens	.50
451	Mark Davidson	.05
452	Israel Sanchez RC	.05
453	Tom Prince RC	.05
454	Paul Assenmacher	.05
455	Johnny Ray	.05
456	Tim Belcher	.05
457	Mackey Sasser	.05
458	Donn Pall RC	.05
459	Mariners Leaders (Dave Valle)	.05
460	Dave Stieb	.05
461	Buddy Bell	.05
462	Jose Guzman	.05
463	Steve Lake	.05
464	Bryn Smith	.05
465	Mark Grace	.05
466	Chuck Crim	.05
467	Jim Walewander	.05
468	Henry Cotto	.05
469	Jose Bautista RC	.05
470	Lance Parrish	.05
471	Steve Curry RC	.05
472	Brian Harper	.05
473	Don Robinson	.05
474	Bob Rodgers	.05
475	Dave Parker	.05
476	Jon Perlman RC	.05
477	Dick Schofield	.05
478	Doug Drabek	.05
479	Mike Macfarlane	.05
480	Keith Hernandez	.05
481	Chris Brown	.05
482	Steve Peters RC	.05
483	Mickey Hatcher	.05
484	Steve Shields	.05
485	Hubie Brooks	.05
486	Jack McDowell	.05
487	Scott Lusader RC	.05
488	Kevin Coffman	.05
489	Phillies Leaders (Mike Schmidt)	.15
490	Chris Sabo	.05
491	Mike Birkbeck	.05
492	Alan Ashby	.05
493	Todd Benzinger	.05
494	Shane Rawley	.05
495	Candy Maldonado	.05
496	Dwayne Henry	.05
497	Pete Stanicek	.05
498	Dave Valle	.05
499	Don Heinkel RC	.05
500	Jose Canseco	.35
501	Vance Law	.05
502	Duane Ward	.05
503	Al Newman	.05
504	Bob Walk	.05
505	Pete Rose	.65
506	Kirt Manwaring	.05
507	Steve Farr	.05
508	Wally Backman	.05
509	Bud Black	.05
510	Bob Horner	.05
511	Richard Dotson	.05
512	Donnie Hill	.05
513	Jesse Orosco	.05
514	Chet Lemon	.05
515	Barry Larkin	.05
516	Eddie Whitson	.05
517	Greg Brock	.05
518	Bruce Ruffin	.05
519	Yankees Leaders (Willie Randolph)	.05
520	Rick Sutcliffe	.05
521	Mickey Tettleton	.05
522	Randy Kramer RC	.05
523	Andres Thomas	.05
524	Checklist 397-528	.05
525	Chili Davis	.05
526	Wes Gardner	.05
527	Dave Henderson	.05
528	Luis Medina RC	.05
529	Tom Foley	.05
530	Nolan Ryan	.75
531	Dave Hengel RC	.05
532	Jerry Browne	.05
533	Andy Hawkins	.05
534	Doc Edwards	.05
535	Todd Worrell	.05
536	Joel Skinner	.05
537	Pete Smith	.05
538	Juan Castillo	.05
539	Barry Jones	.05
540	Bo Jackson	.10
541	Cecil Fielder	.05
542	Todd Frohwirth	.05
543	Damon Berryhill	.05
544	Jeff Sellers	.05
545	Mookie Wilson	.05
546	Mark Williamson	.05
547	Mark McLemore	.05
548	Bobby Witt	.05
549	Cubs Leaders (Jamie Moyer)	.05
550	Orel Hershiser	.05
551	Randy Ready	.05
552	Greg Cadaret	.05
553	Luis Salazar	.05
554	Nick Esasky	.05
555	Bert Blyleven	.05
556	Bruce Fields RC	.05
557	Keith Miller RC	.05
558	Dan Pasqua	.05
559	Juan Agosto	.05
560	Tim Raines	.05
561	Luis Aguayo	.05
562	Danny Cox	.05
563	Bill Schroeder	.05
564	Russ Nixon	.05
565	Jeff Russell	.05
566	Al Pedrique	.05
567	David Wells	.05
568	Mickey Brantley	.05
569	German Jimenez RC	.05
570	Tony Gwynn	.45
571	Billy Ripken	.05
572	Atlee Hammaker	.05
573	Jim Abbott (#1 Draft Pick)	.10
574	Dave Clark	.05
575	Juan Samuel	.05
576	Greg Minton	.05
577	Randy Bush	.05
578	John Morris	.05
579	Astros Leaders (Glenn Davis)	.05
580	Harold Reynolds	.05
581	Gene Nelson	.05
582	Mike Marshall	.05
583	Paul Gibson RC	.05
584	Randy Velarde RC	.05
585	Harold Baines	.05
586	Joe Boever	.05
587	Mike Stanley	.05
588	Luis Alicea RC	.05
589	Dave Meads	.05
590	Andres Galarraga	.05
591	Jeff Musselman	.05
592	John Cangelosi	.05
593	Drew Hall	.05
594	Jimy Williams	.05
595	Teddy Higuera	.05
596	Kurt Stillwell	.05
597	Terry Taylor RC	.05
598	Ken Gerhart	.05
599	Tom Candiotti	.05
600	Wade Boggs	.45
601	Dave Dravecky	.05
602	Devon White	.05
603	Frank Tanana	.05
604	Paul O'Neill	.05
605a	Bob Welch (Missing Complete Major League Pitching Record line.)	3.00
605b	Bob Welch (Contains Complete Major League Pitching Record line.)	.05
606	Rick Dempsey	.05
607	Willie Ansley RC (#1 Draft Pick)	.05
608	Phil Bradley	.05
609	Tigers Leaders (Frank Tanana)	.05
610	Randy Myers	.05
611	Don Slaught	.05
612	Dan Quisenberry	.05
613	Gary Varsho RC	.05
614	Joe Hesketh	.05
615	Robin Yount	.40
616	Steve Rosenberg RC	.05
617	Mark Parent RC	.05
618	Rance Mulliniks	.05
619	Checklist 529-660	.05
620	Barry Bonds	.75
621	Rick Mahler	.05
622	Stan Javier	.05
623	Fred Toliver	.05
624	Jack McKeon	.05
625	Eddie Murray	.40
626	Jeff Reed	.05
627	Greg Harris	.05
628	Matt Williams	.05
629	Pete O'Brien	.05
630	Mike Greenwell	.05
631	Dave Bergman	.05
632	Bryan Harvey RC	.10
633	Daryl Boston	.05
634	Marvin Freeman RC	.05
635	Willie Randolph	.05
636	Bill Wilkinson	.05
637	Carmen Castillo	.05
638	Floyd Bannister	.05
639	Athletics Leaders (Walt Weiss)	.05
640	Willie McGee	.05
641	Curt Young	.05
642	Argenis Salazar	.05
643	Louie Meadows RC	.05
644	Lloyd McClendon	.05
645	Jack Morris	.05
646	Kevin Bass	.05
647	Randy Johnson RC	3.00
648	Sandy Alomar RC (Future Star)	.25
649	Stewart Cliburn	.05
650	Kirby Puckett	.45
651	Tom Niedenfuer	.05
652	Rich Gedman	.05
653	Tommy Barrett RC	.05
654	Whitey Herzog	.05
655	Dave Magadan	.05
656	Ivan Calderon	.05
657	Joe Magrane	.05
658	R.J. Reynolds	.05
659	Al Leiter	.05
660	Will Clark	.05
661	Dwight Gooden (Turn Back the Clock)	.05
662	Lou Brock (Turn Back the Clock)	.05
663	Hank Aaron (Turn Back the Clock)	.15
664	Gil Hodges (Turn Back the Clock)	.05
665a	Tony Oliva (No copyright line.)	12.50
665b	Tony Oliva (With copyright line.)	.05
666	Randy St. Claire	.05
667	Dwayne Murphy	.05
668	Mike Bielecki	.05
669	Dodgers Leaders (Orel Hershiser)	.05
670	Kevin Seitzer	.05
671	Jim Gantner	.05
672	Allan Anderson	.05
673	Don Baylor	.05
674	Otis Nixon	.05
675	Bruce Hurst	.05
676	Ernie Riles	.05
677	Dave Schmidt	.05
678	Dion James	.05
679	Willie Fraser	.05
680	Gary Carter	.40
681	Jeff Robinson	.05
682	Rick Leach	.05
683	Jose Cecena RC	.05
684	Dave Johnson	.05
685	Jeff Treadway	.05
686	Scott Terry	.05
687	Alvin Davis	.05
688	Zane Smith	.05
689a	Stan Jefferson (Pink triangle at bottom-left photo.)	.05
689b	Stan Jefferson (Pink/purple triangle.)	.05
689c	Stan Jefferson (Purple triangle.)	.05
690	Doug Jones	.05
691	Roberto Kelly	.05
692	Steve Ontiveros	.05
693	Pat Borders RC	.05
694	Les Lancaster	.05
695	Carlton Fisk	.40
696	Don August	.05
697	Franklin Stubbs	.05
698	Keith Atherton	.05
699	Pirates Leaders (Al Pedrique)	.05
700	Don Mattingly	.50
701	Storm Davis	.05
702	Jamie Quirk	.05
703	Scott Garrelts	.05
704	Carlos Quintana RC	.05
705	Terry Kennedy	.05
706	Pete Incaviglia	.05
707	Steve Jeltz	.05
708	Chuck Finley	.05
709	Tom Herr	.05
710	Dave Cone	.05
711	Candy Sierra RC	.05
712	Bill Swift	.05
713	Ty Griffin RC (#1 Draft Pick)	.05
714	Joe M. Morgan	.05
715	Tony Pena	.05
716	Wayne Tolleson	.05
717	Jamie Moyer	.05
718	Glenn Braggs	.05
719	Danny Darwin	.05
720	Tim Wallach	.05
721	Ron Tingley RC	.05
722	Todd Stottlemyre	.05
723	Rafael Belliard	.05
724	Jerry Don Gleaton	.05
725	Terry Steinbach	.05
726	Dickie Thon	.05
727	Joe Orsulak	.05
728	Charlie Puleo	.05
729	Rangers Leaders (Steve Buechele)	.05
730	Danny Jackson	.05
731	Mike Young	.05
732	Steve Buechele	.05
733	Randy Bockus RC	.05
734	Jody Reed	.05
735	Roger McDowell	.05
736	Jeff Hamilton	.05
737	Norm Charlton RC	.05
738	Darnell Coles	.05
739	Brook Jacoby	.05
740	Dan Plesac	.05
741	Ken Phelps	.05
742	Mike Harkey RC (Future Star)	.05
743	Mike Heath	.05
744	Roger Craig	.05
745	Fred McGriff	.05
746	German Gonzalez RC	.05
747	Wil Tejada RC	.05
748	Jimmy Jones	.05
749	Rafael Ramirez	.05
750	Bret Saberhagen	.05
751	Ken Oberkfell	.05
752	Jim Gott	.05
753	Jose Uribe	.05
754	Bob Brower	.05
755	Mike Scioscia	.05
756	Scott Medvin RC	.05
757	Brady Anderson	.05
758	Gene Walter	.05
759	Brewers Leaders (Rob Deer)	.05
760	Lee Smith	.05
761	Dante Bichette RC	.25
762	Bobby Thigpen	.05
763	Dave Martinez	.05
764	Robin Ventura (#1 Draft Pick)	.25
765	Glenn Davis	.05
766	Cecilio Guante	.05
767	Mike Capel RC	.05
768	Bill Wegman	.05
769	Junior Ortiz	.05
770	Alan Trammell	.05
771	Ron Kittle	.05
772	Ron Oester	.05
773	Keith Moreland	.05
774	Frank Robinson	.15
775	Jeff Reardon	.05
776	Nelson Liriano	.05
777	Ted Power	.05
778	Bruce Benedict	.05
779	Craig McMurtry	.05
780	Pedro Guerrero	.05
781	Greg Briley RC	.05
782	Checklist 661-792	.05
783	Trevor Wilson RC	.05
784	Steve Avery RC (#1 Draft Pick)	.15
785	Ellis Burks	.05
786	Melido Perez	.05
787	Dave West RC	.05
788	Mike Morgan	.05
789	Royals Leaders (Bo Jackson)	.05
790	Sid Fernandez	.05
791	Jim Lindeman	.05
792	Rafael Santana	.05

Tiffany

This special hobby-only edition shares the checklist with the regular 1989 Topps set. Cards are identical except for the use of white cardboard stock and the high-gloss front coating. Production has been reported as 25,000 sets.

NM/M

Unopened Set (792):	75.00
Complete Set (792):	40.00
Common Player:	.10

Traded

For the ninth straight year, Topps issued its annual 132-card "Traded" set at the end of the 1989 baseball season. The set, which was packaged in a special box and sold by hobby dealers, includes traded players and rookies who were not in the regular 1989 Topps set.

NM/M

Unopened Set, Retail (132):	12.50
Unopened Set, Hobby (132):	10.00
Complete Set (132):	7.50
Common Player:	.05

No.	Player	Price
1T	Don Aase	.05
2T	Jim Abbott	.05
3T	Kent Anderson RC	.05
4T	Keith Atherton	.05
5T	Wally Backman	.05
6T	Steve Balboni	.05
7T	Jesse Barfield	.05
8T	Steve Bedrosian	.05
9T	Todd Benzinger	.05
10T	Geronimo Berroa	.05

11T	Bert Blyleven	.05
12T	Bob Boone	.05
13T	Phil Bradley	.05
14T	Jeff Brantley RC	.05
15T	Kevin Brown RC	.05
16T	Jerry Browne	.05
17T	Chuck Cary	.05
18T	Carmen Castillo	.05
19T	Jim Clancy	.05
20T	Jack Clark	.05
21T	Bryan Clutterbuck	.05
22T	Jody Davis	.05
23T	Mike Devereaux	.05
24T	Frank DiPino	.05
25T	Benny Distefano	.05
26T	John Dopson	.05
27T	Len Dykstra	.05
28T	Jim Eisenreich	.05
29T	Nick Esasky	.05
30T	Alvaro Espinoza	.05
31T	Darrell Evans	.05
32T	Junior Felix	.05
33T	Felix Fermin	.05
34T	Julio Franco	.05
35T	Terry Francona	.05
36T	Cito Gaston	.05
37T	Bob Geren RC (Photo actually Mike Fennell.)	.05
38T	Tom Gordon RC	.10
39T	Tommy Gregg RC	.05
40T	Ken Griffey	.05
41T	Ken Griffey Jr. RC	6.00
42T	Kevin Gross	.05
43T	Lee Guetterman	.05
44T	Mel Hall	.05
45T	Erik Hanson RC	.05
46T	Gene Harris RC	.05
47T	Andy Hawkins	.05
48T	Rickey Henderson	.40
49T	Tom Herr	.05
50T	Ken Hill RC	.05
51T	Brian Holman RC	.05
52T	Brian Holton	.05
53T	Art Howe	.05
54T	Ken Howell	.05
55T	Bruce Hurst	.05
56T	Chris James	.05
57T	Randy Johnson	1.50
58T	Jimmy Jones	.05
59T	Terry Kennedy	.05
60T	Paul Kilgus	.05
61T	Eric King	.05
62T	Ron Kittle	.05
63T	John Kruk	.05
64T	Randy Kutcher RC	.05
65T	Steve Lake	.05
66T	Mark Langston	.05
67T	Dave LaPoint	.05
68T	Rick Leach	.05
69T	Terry Leach	.05
70T	Jim Levebvre	.05
71T	Al Leiter	.05
72T	Jeffrey Leonard	.05
73T	Derek Lilliquist RC	.05
74T	Rick Mahler	.05
75T	Tom McCarthy RC	.05
76T	Lloyd McClendon	.05
77T	Lance McCullers	.05
78T	Oddibe McDowell	.05
79T	Roger McDowell	.05
80T	Larry McWilliams	.05
81T	Randy Milligan	.05
82T	Mike Moore	.05
83T	Keith Moreland	.05
84T	Mike Morgan	.05
85T	Jamie Moyer	.05
86T	Rob Murphy	.05
87T	Eddie Murray	.40
88T	Pete O'Brien	.05
89T	Gregg Olson	.05
90T	Steve Ontiveros	.05
91T	Jesse Orosco	.05
92T	Spike Owen	.05
93T	Rafael Palmeiro	.35
94T	Clay Parker RC	.05
95T	Jeff Parrett	.05
96T	Lance Parrish	.05
97T	Dennis Powell	.05
98T	Rey Quinones	.05
99T	Doug Rader	.05
100T	Willie Randolph	.05
101T	Shane Rawley	.05
102T	Randy Ready	.05
103T	Bip Roberts	.05
104T	Kenny Rogers RC	.10
105T	Ed Romero	.05
106T	Nolan Ryan	1.00
107T	Luis Salazar	.05
108T	Juan Samuel	.05
109T	Alex Sanchez RC	.05
110T	Deion Sanders	.50
111T	Steve Sax	.05
112T	Rick Schu	.05
113T	Dwight Smith RC	.05
114T	Lonnie Smith	.05
115T	Billy Spiers RC	.05
116T	Kent Tekulve	.05
117T	Walt Terrell	.05
118T	Milt Thompson	.05
119T	Dickie Thon	.05
120T	Jeff Torborg	.05
121T	Jeff Treadway	.05
122T	Omar Vizquel RC	.50
123T	Jerome Walton RC	.05
124T	Gary Ward	.05
125T	Claudell Washington	.05
126T	Curt Wilkerson	.05
127T	Eddie Williams	.05
128T	Frank Williams	.05
129T	Ken Williams	.05
130T	Mitch Williams	.05
131T	Steve Wilson RC	.05
---	Topps Magazine subscription offer card	.05

Traded Tiffany

The Topps Traded set was issued in a specially boxed, hobby-only edition. Cards are identical to the regular-issue Topps Traded cards except for the application of a high-gloss to the fronts. Production has been reported as 15,000 sets.

NM/M
Unopened Set (132):	85.00
Complete Set (132):	50.00
Common Player:	.10

Traded Jackie Robinson Bronze

This 1/4-size metal replica of Robinson's first-ever Topps card was issued to dealers who purchased cases of 1989 Topps Traded sets. Each detail of the 1952 Topps Robinson card is reproduced on the 1-1/4" x 1-3/4" bronze metal mini-card, right down to the stats.

NM/M
312	Jackie Robinson	10.00

Box Panels

Continuing its practice of printing baseball cards on the bottom panels of its wax pack boxes, Topps in 1989 issued a special 16-card set, printing four cards on each of four different box-bottom panels. The cards are identical in design to the regular 1989 Topps cards. They are designated by letter (from A through P) rather than by number.

NM/M
Complete Panel Set (4):		7.50
Complete Singles Set: (16):		7.50
Common Panel:		1.50
Common Single Player:		.10
PANEL		1.50
A	George Bell	.10
B	Bill Buckner	.10
C	Darrell Evans	.10
D	Goose Gossage	.10
PANEL		1.50
E	Greg Gross	.10
F	Rickey Henderson	.60
G	Keith Hernandez	.10
H	Tommy Lasorda	.10
PANEL		7.50
I	Jim Rice	.20
J	Cal Ripken Jr.	2.00
K	Nolan Ryan	2.00
L	Mike Schmidt	.75
PANEL		2.00
M	Bruce Sutter	.30
N	Don Sutton	.30
O	Kent Tekulve	.10
P	Dave Winfield	.60

All-Star Glossy Set of 22

The glossy All-Stars were included in the Topps 1989 rack packs. Format was very similar to the sets produced since 1984. Besides the starting lineups of the 1988 All-Star Game, the set included the managers and honorary team captains, Bobby Doerr and Willie Stargell.

NM/M
Complete Set (22):		3.00
Common Player:		.05
1	Tom Kelly	.05
2	Mark McGwire	.75
3	Paul Molitor	.40
4	Wade Boggs	.50
5	Cal Ripken, Jr.	1.00
6	Jose Canseco	.30
7	Rickey Henderson	.40
8	Dave Winfield	.40
9	Terry Steinbach	.05
10	Frank Viola	.05
11	Bobby Doerr	.05
12	Whitey Herzog	.05
13	Will Clark	.50
14	Ryne Sandberg	.50
15	Bobby Bonilla	.05
16	Ozzie Smith	.50
17	Vince Coleman	.05
18	Andre Dawson	.25
19	Darryl Strawberry	.40
20	Gary Carter	.40
21	Dwight Gooden	.05
22	Willie Stargell	.10

All-Star Glossy Set of 60

For the seventh straight year Topps issued this "sendaway" glossy set. Divided into six 10-card sets, it was available only by sending in special offer cards from wax packs. The 2-1/2" x 3-1/2" cards feature full-color photos bordered in white with a thin yellow frame. The player's name appears in small print in the lower-right corner. Red-and-blue-printed flip sides provide basic information. Any of the six 10-card sets were available for $1.25 and six special offer cards. The set was also made available in its complete 60-card set form for $7.50 and 18 special offer cards.

NM/M
Complete Set (60):		6.00
Common Player:		.05
1	Kirby Puckett	.60
2	Eric Davis	.05
3	Joe Carter	.05
4	Andy Van Slyke	.05
5	Wade Boggs	.60
6	Dave Cone	.05
7	Kent Hrbek	.05
8	Darryl Strawberry	.05
9	Jay Buhner	.05
10	Ron Gant	.05
11	Will Clark	.05
12	Jose Canseco	.35
13	Juan Samuel	.05
14	George Brett	.75
15	Benny Santiago	.05
16	Dennis Eckersley	.40
17	Gary Carter	.50
18	Frank Viola	.05
19	Roberto Alomar	.15
20	Paul Gibson	.05
21	Dave Winfield	.50
22	Howard Johnson	.05
23	Roger Clemens	.65
24	Bobby Bonilla	.05
25	Alan Trammell	.05
26	Kevin McReynolds	.05
27	George Bell	.05
28	Bruce Hurst	.05
29	Mark Grace	.05
30	Tim Belcher	.05
31	Mike Greenwell	.05
32	Glenn Davis	.05
33	Gary Gaetti	.05
34	Ryne Sandberg	.60
35	Rickey Henderson	.50
36	Dwight Evans	.05
37	Doc Gooden	.05
38	Robin Yount	.50
39	Damon Berryhill	.05
40	Chris Sabo	.05
41	Mark McGwire	1.00
42	Ozzie Smith	.60
43	Paul Molitor	.50
44	Andres Galarraga	.05
45	Dave Stewart	.05
46	Tom Browning	.05
47	Cal Ripken, Jr.	1.50
48	Orel Hershiser	.05
49	Dave Gallagher	.05
50	Walt Weiss	.05
51	Don Mattingly	.65
52	Tony Fernandez	.05
53	Tim Raines	.05
54	Jeff Reardon	.05
55	Kirk Gibson	.05
56	Jack Clark	.05
57	Danny Jackson	.05
58	Tony Gwynn	.60
59	Cecil Espy	.05
60	Jody Reed	.05

American Baseball

For the second consecutive year Topps released an 88-card set of baseball cards available in both the United States and the United Kingdom. The mini-sized cards (2-1/4" x 3") are printed on white stock with a low-gloss finish. The game-action color player photo is outlined in red, white and blue and framed in white. Backs are horizontal and include a characterization cartoon along with biographical information and statistics. The cards were sold in packs of five with a stick of bubble gum for 12 pence.

NM/M
Complete Set (88):		6.00
Common Player:		.05
Wax Pack (5):		.50
Wax Box (48):		8.00
1	Brady Anderson	.05
2	Harold Baines	.05
3	George Bell	.05
4	Wade Boggs	.60
5	Barry Bonds	1.50
6	Bobby Bonilla	.05
7	George Brett	.75
8	Hubie Brooks	.05
9	Tom Brunansky	.05
10	Jay Buhner	.05
11	Brett Butler	.05
12	Jose Canseco	.30
13	Joe Carter	.05
14	Jack Clark	.05
15	Will Clark	.05
16	Roger Clemens	.65
17	Dave Cone	.05
18	Alvin Davis	.05
19	Eric Davis	.05
20	Glenn Davis	.05
21	Andre Dawson	.25
22	Bill Doran	.05
23	Dennis Eckersley	.35
24	Dwight Evans	.05
25	Tony Fernandez	.05
26	Carlton Fisk	.45
27	John Franco	.05
28	Andres Galarraga	.05
29	Ron Gant	.05
30	Kirk Gibson	.05
31	Dwight Gooden	.05
32	Mike Greenwell	.05
33	Mark Gubicza	.05
34	Pedro Gurrero	.05
35	Ozzie Guillen	.05
36	Tony Gwynn	.60
37	Rickey Henderson	.45
38	Orel Hershiser	.05
39	Teddy Higuera	.05
40	Charlie Hough	.05
41	Kent Hrbek	.05
42	Bruce Hurst	.05
43	Bo Jackson	.10
44	Gregg Jefferies	.05
45	Ricky Jordan	.05
46	Wally Joyner	.05
47	Mark Langston	.05
48	Mike Marshall	.05
49	Don Mattingly	.75
50	Fred McGriff	.05
51	Mark McGwire	1.00
52	Kevin McReynolds	.05
53	Paul Molitor	.45
54	Jack Morris	.05
55	Dale Murphy	.20
56	Eddie Murray	.45
57	Pete O'Brien	.05
58	Rafael Palmeiro	.35
59	Gerald Perry	.05
60	Kirby Puckett	.60
61	Tim Raines	.05
62	Johnny Ray	.05
63	Rick Reuschel	.05
64	Cal Ripken	1.50
65	Chris Sabo	.05
66	Juan Samuel	.05
67	Ryne Sandberg	.60
68	Benny Santiago	.05
69	Steve Sax	.05
70	Mike Schmidt	.75
71	Ruben Sierra	.05
72	Ozzie Smith	.60
73	Cory Snyder	.05
74	Dave Stewart	.05
75	Darryl Strawberry	.05
76	Greg Swindell	.05
77	Alan Trammell	.05
78	Fernando Valenzuela	.05
79	Andy Van Slyke	.05
80	Frank Viola	.05
81	Claudell Washington	.05
82	Walt Weiss	.05
83	Lou Whitaker	.05
84	Dave Winfield	.45
85	Mike Witt	.05
86	Gerald Young	.05
87	Robin Yount	.45
88	Checklist	.05

Batting Leaders

The active career batting leaders are showcased in this 22-card set. The 2-1/2" x 3-1/2" cards are printed on super glossy stock with full-color photos and bright red borders. A "Top Active Career Batting Leaders" cup is displayed in the lower corner. The player's name appears above the photo. This set is specially numbered in accordance to career batting average. Wade Boggs is featured on card #1 as the top active career batting leader. The flip sides present batting statistics. One batting leader card was included in each K-Mart blister pack, which also includes 100 cards from the 1989 regular Topps set.

NM/M
Complete Set (22):		90.00
Common Player:		1.50
1	Wade Boggs	12.00
2	Tony Gwynn	12.00
3	Don Mattingly	16.00
4	Kirby Puckett	12.00
5	George Brett	16.00
6	Pedro Guerrero	1.50
7	Tim Raines	1.50
8	Keith Hernandez	1.50
9	Jim Rice	3.00
10	Paul Molitor	8.00
11	Eddie Murray	8.00
12	Willie McGee	1.50
13	Dave Parker	1.50
14	Julio Franco	1.50
15	Rickey Henderson	8.00
16	Kent Hrbek	1.50
17	Willie Wilson	1.50
18	Johnny Ray	1.50
19	Pat Tabler	1.50
20	Carney Lansford	1.50
21	Robin Yount	8.00
22	Alan Trammell	1.50

Big Baseball

Known by collectors as Topps "Big Baseball," the cards in this 330-card set measure 2-5/8" x 3-3/4" and are patterned after the 1956 Topps cards. The glossy card fronts are horizontally-designed and include two photos of each player, a portrait alongside an action photo. The backs include 1988 and career stats, but are dominated by a color cartoon featuring the player. Members of the 1988 Team U.S.A. Olympic baseball team are included in the set, which was issued in three series of 110 cards each.

NM/M
Complete Set (330):		9.00
Common Player:		.05
Wax Pack:		.40
Wax Box (36):		7.50
1	Orel Hershiser	.05
2	Harold Reynolds	.05
3	Jody Davis	.05
4	Greg Walker	.05
5	Barry Bonds	1.00
6	Bret Saberhagen	.05
7	Johnny Ray	.05
8	Mike Fiore	.05
9	Juan Castillo	.05
10	Todd Burns	.05
11	Carmelo Martinez	.05
12	Geno Petralli	.05
13	Mel Hall	.05
14	Tom Browning	.05
15	Fred McGriff	.05
16	Kevin Elster	.05
17	Tim Leary	.05
18	Jim Rice	.20
19	Bret Barberie	.05
20	Jay Buhner	.05
21	Atlee Hammaker	.05
22	Lou Whitaker	.05
23	Paul Runge	.05
24	Carlton Fisk	.40
25	Jose Lind	.05
26	Mark Gubicza	.05
27	Billy Ripken	.05
28	Mike Pagliarulo	.05
29	Jim Deshaies	.05
30	Mark McLemore	.05
31	Scott Terry	.05
32	Franklin Stubbs	.05
33	Don August	.05
34	Mark McGwire	.75
35	Eric Show	.05
36	Cecil Espy	.05
37	Ron Tingley	.05
38	Mickey Brantley	.05
39	Paul O'Neill	.05
40	Ed Sprague	.05
41	Len Dykstra	.05
42	Roger Clemens	.60
43	Ron Gant	.05
44	Dan Pasqua	.05
45	Jeff Robinson	.05
46	George Brett	.65
47	Bryn Smith	.05
48	Mike Marshall	.05
49	Doug Robbins	.05

#	Player	Price		#	Player	Price		#	Player	Price
50	Don Mattingly	.65		169	Dennis Lamp	.05		287	Randy Johnson	.50
51	Mike Scott	.05		170	Ty Griffin	.05		288	Julio Franco	.05
52	Steve Jeltz	.05		171	Ron Hassey	.05		289	Ivan Calderon	.05
53	Dick Schofield	.05		172	Dale Murphy	.15		290	Rich Yett	.05
54	Tom Brunansky	.05		173	Andres Galarraga	.05		291	Scott Servais	.05
55	Gary Sheffield	.45		174	Tim Flannery	.05		292	Bill Pecota	.05
56	Dave Valle	.05		175	Cory Snyder	.05		293	Ken Phelps	.05
57	Carney Lansford	.05		176	Checklist	.05		294	Chili Davis	.05
58	Tony Gwynn	.50		177	Tommy Barrett	.05		295	Manny Trillo	.05
59	Checklist	.05		178	Dan Petry	.05		296	Mike Boddicker	.05
60	Damon Berryhill	.05		179	Billy Masse	.05		297	Geronimo Berroa	.05
61	Jack Morris	.05		180	Terry Kennedy	.05		298	Todd Stottlemyre	.05
62	Brett Butler	.05		181	Joe Orsulak	.05		299	Kirk Gibson	.05
63	Mickey Hatcher	.05		182	Doyle Alexander	.05		300	Wally Backman	.05
64	Bruce Sutter	.35		183	Willie McGee	.05		301	Hubie Brooks	.05
65	Robin Ventura	.05		184	Jim Gantner	.05		302	Von Hayes	.05
66	Junior Ortiz	.05		185	Keith Hernandez	.05		303	Matt Nokes	.05
67	Pat Tabler	.05		186	Greg Gagne	.05		304	Dwight Gooden	.05
68	Greg Swindell	.05		187	Kevin Bass	.05		305	Walt Weiss	.05
69	Jeff Branson	.05		188	Mark Eichhorn	.05		306	Mike LaValliere	.05
70	Manny Lee	.05		189	Mark Grace	.15		307	Cris Carpenter	.05
71	Dave Magadan	.05		190	Jose Canseco	.35		308	Ted Wood	.05
72	Rich Gedman	.05		191	Bobby Witt	.05		309	Jeff Russell	.05
73	Tim Raines	.05		192	Rafael Santana	.05		310	Dave Gallagher	.05
74	Mike Maddux	.05		193	Dwight Evans	.05		311	Andy Allanson	.05
75	Jim Presley	.05		194	Greg Booker	.05		312	Craig Reynolds	.05
76	Chuck Finley	.05		195	Brook Jacoby	.05		313	Kevin Seitzer	.05
77	Jose Oquendo	.05		196	Rafael Belliard	.05		314	Dave Winfield	.40
78	Rob Deer	.05		197	Candy Maldonado	.05		315	Andy McGaffigan	.05
79	Jay Howell	.05		198	Mickey Tettleton	.05		316	Nick Esasky	.05
80	Terry Steinbach	.05		199	Barry Larkin	.05		317	Jeff Blauser	.05
81	Eddie Whitson	.05		200	Frank White	.05		318	George Bell	.05
82	Ruben Sierra	.05		201	Wally Joyner	.05		319	Eddie Murray	.40
83	Bruce Benedict	.05		202	Chet Lemon	.05		320	Mark Davidson	.05
84	Fred Manrique	.05		203	Joe Magrane	.05		321	Juan Samuel	.05
85	John Smiley	.05		204	Glenn Braggs	.05		322	Jim Abbott	.05
86	Mike Macfarlane	.05		205	Scott Fletcher	.05		323	Kal Daniels	.05
87	Rene Gonzales	.05		206	Gary Ward	.05		324	Mike Brumley	.05
88	Charles Hudson	.05		207	Nelson Liriano	.05		325	Gary Carter	.40
89	Les Straker	.05		208	Howard Johnson	.05		326	Dave Henderson	.05
90	Carmen Castillo	.05		209	Kent Hrbek	.05		327	Checklist	.05
91	Tracy Woodson	.05		210	Ken Caminiti	.05		328	Garry Templeton	.05
92	Tino Martinez	.15		211	Mike Greenwell	.05		329	Pat Perry	.05
93	Herm Winningham	.05		212	Ryne Sandberg	.50		330	Paul Molitor	.40
94	Herm Winningham	.05		213	Joe Slusarski	.05				
95	Kelly Gruber	.05		214	Donnell Nixon	.05				
96	Terry Leach	.05		215	Tim Wallach	.05				
97	Jody Reed	.05		216	John Kruk	.05				
98	Nelson Santovenia	.05		217	Charles Nagy	.05				
99	Tony Armas	.05		218	Alvin Davis	.05				
100	Greg Brock	.05		219	Oswald Peraza	.05				
101	Dave Stewart	.05		220	Mike Schmidt	.65				
102	Roberto Alomar	.20		221	Spike Owen	.05				
103	Jim Sundberg	.05		222	Mike Smithson	.05				
104	Albert Hall	.05		223	Dion James	.05				
105	Steve Lyons	.05		224	Ernie Whitt	.05				
106	Sid Bream	.05		225	Mike Davis	.05				
107	Danny Tartabull	.05		226	Gene Larkin	.05				
108	Rick Dempsey	.05		227	Pat Combs	.05				
109	Rich Renteria	.05		228	Jack Howell	.05				
110	Ozzie Smith	.50		229	Ron Oester	.05				
111	Steve Sax	.05		230	Paul Gibson	.05				
112	Kelly Downs	.05		231	Mookie Wilson	.05				
113	Larry Sheets	.05		232	Glenn Hubbard	.05				
114	Andy Benes	.05		233	Shawon Dunston	.05				
115	Pete O'Brien	.05		234	Otis Nixon	.05				
116	Kevin McReynolds	.05		235	Melido Perez	.05				
117	Juan Berenguer	.05		236	Jerry Browne	.05				
118	Billy Hatcher	.05		237	Rick Rhoden	.05				
119	Rick Cerone	.05		238	Bo Jackson	.10				
120	Andre Dawson	.15		239	Randy Velarde	.05				
121	Storm Davis	.05		240	Jack Clark	.05				
122	Devon White	.05		241	Wade Boggs	.50				
123	Alan Trammell	.05		242	Lonnie Smith	.05				
124	Vince Coleman	.05		243	Mike Flanagan	.05				
125	Al Leiter	.05		244	Willie Randolph	.05				
126	Dale Sveum	.05		245	Oddibe McDowell	.05				
127	Pete Incaviglia	.05		246	Ricky Jordan	.05				
128	Dave Stieb	.05		247	Greg Briley	.05				
129	Kevin Mitchell	.05		248	Rex Hudler	.05				
130	Dave Schmidt	.05		249	Robin Yount	.40				
131	Gary Redus	.05		250	Lance Parrish	.05				
132	Ron Robinson	.05		251	Chris Sabo	.05				
133	Darnell Coles	.05		252	Mike Henneman	.05				
134	Benny Santiago	.05		253	Gregg Jefferies	.05				
135	John Farrell	.05		254	Curt Young	.05				
136	Willie Wilson	.05		255	Andy Van Slyke	.05				
137	Steve Bedrosian	.05		256	Rod Booker	.05				
138	Don Slaught	.05		257	Rafael Palmeiro	.35				
139	Darryl Strawberry	.05		258	Jose Uribe	.05				
140	Frank Viola	.05		259	Ellis Burks	.05				
141	Dave Silvestri	.05		260	John Smoltz	.05				
142	Carlos Quintana	.05		261	Tom Foley	.05				
143	Vance Law	.05		262	Lloyd Moseby	.05				
144	Dave Parker	.05		263	Jim Poole	.05				
145	Tim Belcher	.05		264	Gary Gaetti	.05				
146	Will Clark	.05		265	Bob Dernier	.05				
147	Mark Williamson	.05		266	Harold Baines	.05				
148	Ozzie Guillen	.05		267	Tom Candiotti	.05				
149	Kirk McCaskill	.05		268	Rafael Ramirez	.05				
150	Pat Sheridan	.05		269	Bob Boone	.05				
151	Terry Pendleton	.05		270	Buddy Bell	.05				
152	Roberto Kelly	.05		271	Rickey Henderson	.40				
153	Joey Meyer	.05		272	Willie Fraser	.05				
154	Mark Grant	.05		273	Eric Davis	.05				
155	Joe Carter	.05		274	Jeff Robinson	.05				
156	Steve Buechele	.05		275	Damaso Garcia	.05				
157	Tony Fernandez	.05		276	Sid Fernandez	.05				
158	Jeff Reed	.05		277	Stan Javier	.05				
159	Bobby Bonilla	.05		278	Marty Barrett	.05				
160	Henry Cotto	.05		279	Gerald Perry	.05				
161	Kurt Stillwell	.05		280	Rob Ducey	.05				
162	Mickey Morandini	.05		281	Mike Scioscia	.05				
163	Robby Thompson	.05		282	Randy Bush	.05				
164	Rick Schu	.05		283	Tom Herr	.05				
165	Stan Jefferson	.05		284	Glenn Wilson	.05				
166	Ron Darling	.05		285	Pedro Guerrero	.05				
167	Kirby Puckett	.50		286	Cal Ripken, Jr.	1.00				
168	Bill Doran	.05								

#	Player	Price
34	George Brett	.75
35	Jay Buhner	.10
36	Joe Carter	.10
37	Roger Clemens	.60
38	Alvin Davis	.10
39	Tony Fernandez	.10
40	Carlton Fisk	.40
41	Mike Greenwell	.10
42	Kent Hrbek	.10
43	Don Mattingly	.75
44	Fred McGriff	.10
45	Mark McGwire	1.00
46	Paul Molitor	.40
47	Rafael Palmeiro	.35
48	Kirby Puckett	.50
49	Johnny Ray	.10
50	Cal Ripken, Jr.	1.50
51	Ruben Sierra	.10
52	Pete Stanicek	.10
53	Dave Stewart	.10
54	Greg Swindell	.10
55	Danny Tartabull	.10
56	Alan Trammell	.10
57	Lou Whitaker	.10
58	Dave Winfield	.40
59	Mike Witt	.10
60	Robin Yount	.40

Double Headers All-Stars

This scarce test issue was produced in two versions, an All-Stars set and a set of exclusively Mets and Yankees players. The "cards" are two-sided miniature (1-5/8" x 2-1/4") reproductions of the player's 1989 Topps card and his Topps rookie card, encased in a clear plastic stand.

	NM/M
Complete Set (24):	9.00
Common Player:	.50
Wax Pack (1):	.50
Wax Box (24):	9.00
(1) Alan Ashby	.50
(2) Wade Boggs	1.00
(3) Bobby Bonilla	.50
(4) Jose Canseco	.65
(5) Will Clark	.50
(6) Roger Clemens	1.25
(7) Andre Dawson	.60
(8) Dennis Eckersley	.65
(9) Carlton Fisk	.75
(10) John Franco	.50
(11) Julio Franco	.50
(12) Kirk Gibson	.50
(13) Mike Greenwell	.50
(14) Orel Hershiser	.50
(15) Danny Jackson	.50
(16) Don Mattingly	1.25
(17) Mark McGwire	2.00
(18) Kirby Puckett	1.00
(19) Ryne Sandberg	1.00
(20) Ozzie Smith	1.00
(21) Darryl Strawberry	.50
(22) Alan Trammell	.50
(23) Andy Van Slyke	.50
(24) Frank Viola	.50

Double Headers Mets/Yankees Proofs

In advance of its special Mets/Yankees Double Headers novelty issue, Topps prepared a series of proof versions featuring four players from each of the New York teams. Like the later issues, these Double Headers feature miniature versions of the players' Topps rookie cards in a small plastic stand-up frame. However, the proof versions have the rookie cards back-to-back with the players' 1988 Topps cards, rather than 1989 as on the regularly issued pieces. Two different types of wrappers are found for the proofs, an opaque paper enve-

Coins

RUBEN SIERRA RANGERS

Similar in format to previous Topps coins, this 60-piece set features 1-1/2" diameter coins with rolled colored edges. A shooting star device printed over the player photo gives his name, team and position. Backs have a few biographical details and a summary of the player's previous season performance printed in black on silver. The coins were sold three per pack, with each pack including an offer card for an album to house the pieces.

	NM/M
Factory Boxed Set (60):	15.00
Complete Set (60):	7.50
Common Player:	.10
Wax Pack (3):	.50
Wax Box (36):	8.00
1 Kirk Gibson	.10
2 Orel Herhiser	.10
3 Chris Sabo	.10
4 Tony Gwynn	.50
5 Brett Butler	.10
6 Bobby Bonilla	.10
7 Jack Clark	.10
8 Will Clark	.10
9 Eric Davis	.10
10 Glenn Davis	.15
11 Andre Dawson	.15
12 John Franco	.10
13 Andres Galarraga	.10
14 Dwight Gooden	.10
15 Mark Grace	.10
16 Pedro Guerrero	.10
17 Ricky Jordan	.10
18 Mike Marshall	.10
19 Dale Murphy	.15
20 Eddie Murray	.10
21 Gerald Perry	.10
22 Tim Raines	.10
23 Juan Samuel	.10
24 Benito Santiago	.10
25 Ozzie Smith	.50
26 Darryl Strawberry	.10
27 Andy Van Slyke	.10
28 Gerald Young	.10
29 Jose Canseco	.35
30 Frank Viola	.10
31 Walt Weiss	.10
32 Wade Boggs	.50
33 Harold Baines	.10

lope picturing Gary Carter's piece and a cellophane wrapper with the proof issue's checklist.

	NM/M
Complete Set (8):	425.00
Common Player:	50.00
(1) Gary Carter	125.00
(2) Ron Darling	50.00
(3) Dwight Gooden	50.00
(4) Darryl Strawberry	50.00
(1) Rickey Henderson	125.00
(2) Don Mattingly	200.00
(3) Dave Righetti	50.00
(4) Dave Winfield	125.00

Double Headers Mets/Yankees

This was a regionally issued test for the concept of two "mini" baseball cards of a player encapsulated in clear plastic. Only New York players are represented in the set. Each double header plastic frame holds miniature (1-5/8" x 2-1/4") versions of the player's 1989 Topps card, and his first Topps card, printed on thin paper. The Double Headers of players who also appeared in the All-Star issue are indistinguishable in this version. The stand-ups were sold in boxes of 24 paper-wrapped pieces. It is reported that each box contains a full set. The unnumbered pieces are checklisted here in alphabetical order by team.

	NM/M
Complete Set (24):	150.00
Common Player:	10.00
New York Mets Team Set:	85.00
(1) Gary Carter	25.00
(2) David Cone	10.00
(3) Ron Darling	10.00
(4) Len Dykstra	10.00
(5) Doc Gooden	10.00
(6) Keith Hernandez	10.00
(7) Gregg Jefferies	10.00
(8) Howard Johnson	10.00
(9) Kevin McReynolds	10.00
(10) Randy Myers	10.00
(11) Darryl Strawberry	.50
(12) Tim Teufel	10.00
(13) Mookie Wilson	10.00
New York Yankees Team Set:	65.00
(14) Richard Dotson	10.00
(15) Rickey Henderson	25.00
(16) Don Mattingly	3.00
(17) Mike Pagliarulo	10.00
(18) Ken Phelps	10.00
(19) Rick Rhoden	10.00
(20) Dave Righetti	10.00
(21) Rafael Santana	10.00
(22) Steve Sax	10.00
(23) Claudell Washington	10.00
(24) Dave Winfield	25.00

Gallery of Champions

Dodgers KIRK GIBSON

Topps continued its issue of 1/4-size metallic ingot reproductions of current-year base-

ball cards with aluminum, bronze and sterling silver sets in 1989. Again the players represented major award winners from the previous season. The metal mini-cards were sold only as complete sets. Dealers who ordered bronze and silver sets could receive as a bonus a pewter version of the Jose Canseco ingot.

	NM/M
Complete Aluminum Set (12):	12.50
Complete Bronze Set (12):	50.00
Complete Silver Set (12):	120.00
(1a) Wade Boggs/ Aluminum	3.50
(1b) Wade Boggs/Bronze	5.00
(1s) Wade Boggs/Silver	25.00
(2a) Jose Canseco/ Aluminum	2.00
(2b) Jose Canseco/Bronze	5.00
(2s) Jose Canseco/Silver	15.00
(2p) Jose Canseco/Pewter	7.50
(3a) Will Clark/Aluminum	1.00
(3b) Will Clark/Bronze	3.50
(3s) Will Clark/Silver	7.50
(4a) Dennis Eckersley/ Aluminum	1.50
(4b) Dennis Eckersley/ Bronze	5.00
(4s) Dennis Eckersley/ Silver	10.00
(5a) John Franco/ Aluminum	1.00
(5b) John Franco/Bronze	3.50
(5s) John Franco/Silver	7.50
(6a) Kirk Gibson/Aluminum	1.00
(6b) Kirk Gibson/Bronze	3.50
(6s) Kirk Gibson/Silver	7.50
(7a) Tony Gwynn/ Aluminum	3.50
(7b) Tony Gwynn/Bronze	10.00
(7s) Tony Gwynn/Silver	25.00
(8a) Orel Hershiser/ Aluminum	1.00
(8b) Orel Hershiser/Bronze	3.50
(8s) Orel Hershiser/Silver	7.50
(9a) Chris Sabo/Aluminum	1.00
(9b) Chris Sabo/Bronze	3.50
(9s) Chris Sabo/Silver	7.50
(10a) Darryl Strawberry/ Aluminum	1.00
(10b) Darryl Strawberry/ Bronze	3.50
(10s) Darryl Strawberry/ Silver	7.50
(11a) Frank Viola/Aluminum	1.00
(11b) Frank Viola/Bronze	3.50
(11s) Frank Viola/Silver	7.50
(12a) Walt Weiss/Aluminum	1.00
(12b) Walt Weiss/Bronze	3.50
(12s) Walt Weiss/Silver	7.50

Glossy Rookies Set of 22

1988 ROOKIES DAVID WELLS

Bearing the same design and style of the past two years, Topps featured the top first-year players from the 1988 season in this glossy set. The full-color player photo appears beneath the "1988 Rookies" banner. The player's name is displayed beneath the photo. The flip side features the "1988 Rookies Commemorative Set" logo followed by the player ID and card number. Glossy rookies were found only in 100-card jumbo cello packs.

	NM/M
Complete Set (22):	5.00
Common Player:	.15
1 Roberto Alomar	.50
2 Brady Anderson	.15
3 Tim Belcher	.15
4 Damon Berryhill	.15
5 Jay Buhner	.25
6 Kevin Elster	.15

		NM/M
7	Cecil Espy	.15
8	Dave Gallagher	.15
9	Ron Gant	.25
10	Paul Gibson	.15
11	Mark Grace	.50
12	Darrin Jackson	.15
13	Gregg Jefferies	.25
14	Ricky Jordan	.15
15	Al Leiter	.15
16	Melido Perez	.15
17	Chris Sabo	.15
18	Nelson Santovenia	.15
19	Mackey Sasser	.15
20	Gary Sheffield	2.00
21	Walt Weiss	.15
22	David Wells	.15

Heads Up! Test Issue

Much rarer than the 1990 issue, this 24-card test set debuted the bizarre "shrunken head" format of a die-cut player's head and cap printed on heavy cardboard, approximately 4-1/2" x 6-1/2" in size and sold one per pack. Backs feature both a small plastic suction cup and an adhesive strip for hanging the card. The player's name and team are printed in black on the back. Except for the copyright date on back, the cards of players from the 1989 test set which were repeated in the 1990 regular issue are virtually identical and often sell for much less than those players who were unique to the 1989 set.

		NM/M
Complete Set (24):		600.00
Common Player:		12.00
1	Tony Gwynn	65.00
2	Will Clark	17.50
3	Dwight Gooden	12.00
4	Ricky Jordan	12.00
5	Ken Griffey Jr.	150.00
6	Darryl Strawberry	17.50
7	Frank Viola	17.50
8	Bo Jackson	15.00
9	Ryne Sandberg	65.00
10	Gregg Jefferies	17.50
11	Wade Boggs	65.00
12	Ellis Burks	17.50
13	Gary Sheffield	25.00
14	Mark McGwire	150.00
15	Mark Grace	17.50
16	Jim Abbott	12.00
17	Ozzie Smith	65.00
18	Jose Canseco	25.00
19	Don Mattingly	75.00
20	Kirby Puckett	65.00
21	Eric Davis	17.50
22	Mike Greenwell	17.50
23	Dale Murphy	30.00
24	Mike Schmidt	125.00

Mini League Leaders

This 77-card set features baseball's statistical leaders from the 1988 season. It is referred to as a "mini" set because

of the cards' small (2-1/8" x 3") size. The glossy cards feature action photos that have a soft focus on all edges. The player's team and name appear along the bottom of the card. The back features a head- shot of the player along with his 1988 season ranking and stats.

		NM/M
Complete Set (77):		3.00
Common Player:		.05
Wax Pack (7):		.25
Wax Box (36):		6.00
1	Dale Murphy	.20
2	Gerald Perry	.05
3	Andre Dawson	.25
4	Greg Maddux	.65
5	Rafael Palmeiro	.45
6	Tom Browning	.05
7	Kal Daniels	.05
8	Eric Davis	.05
9	John Franco	.05
10	Danny Jackson	.05
11	Barry Larkin	.05
12	Jose Rijo	.05
13	Chris Sabo	.05
14	Nolan Ryan	1.00
15	Mike Scott	.05
16	Gerald Young	.05
17	Kirk Gibson	.05
18	Orel Hershiser	.05
19	Steve Sax	.05
20	John Tudor	.05
21	Hubie Brooks	.05
22	Andres Galarraga	.05
23	Otis Nixon	.05
24	Dave Cone	.05
25	Sid Fernandez	.05
26	Dwight Gooden	.05
27	Kevin McReynolds	.05
28	Darryl Strawberry	.05
29	Juan Samuel	.05
30	Bobby Bonilla	.05
31	Sid Bream	.05
32	Jim Gott	.05
33	Andy Van Slyke	.05
34	Vince Coleman	.05
35	Jose DeLeon	.05
36	Joe Magrane	.05
37	Ozzie Smith	.65
38	Todd Worrell	.05
39	Tony Gwynn	.65
40	Brett Butler	.05
41	Will Clark	.05
42	Rick Reuschel	.05
43	Checklist	.05
44	Eddie Murray	.50
45	Wade Boggs	.65
46	Roger Clemens	.70
47	Dwight Evans	.05
48	Mike Greenwell	.05
49	Bruce Hurst	.05
50	Johnny Ray	.05
51	Doug Jones	.05
52	Greg Swindell	.05
53	Gary Pettis	.05
54	George Brett	.70
55	Mark Gubicza	.05
56	Willie Wilson	.05
57	Teddy Higuera	.05
58	Paul Molitor	.50
59	Robin Yount	.50
60	Allan Anderson	.05
61	Gary Gaetti	.05
62	Kirby Puckett	.65
63	Jeff Reardon	.05
64	Frank Viola	.05
65	Jack Clark	.05
66	Rickey Henderson	.50
67	Dave Winfield	.50
68	Jose Canseco	.35
69	Dennis Eckersley	.45
70	Mark McGwire	.75
71	Dave Stewart	.05
72	Alvin Davis	.05
73	Mark Langston	.05
74	Harold Reynolds	.05
75	George Bell	.05
76	Tony Fernandez	.05
77	Fred McGriff	.05

Stickercards

Once again in 1989 Topps used a stickercard as cardboard backing for its paper sticker issue. Measuring 2-1/8" x 3", the cards are found with either one or two player stickers on back. The stickercards have a player photo on a background of graduated color. Minimal stats and biographic data are presented at the bottom. Values shown are for complete stickercard/sticker(s), without regard to which stickers are on back.

		NM/M
Complete Set (66):		5.00
Common Player:		.05
Wax Pack (5):		.25
Wax Box (48):		6.00
1	George Brett	.65
2	Don Mattingly	.65
3	Mark McGwire	.75
4	Julio Franco	.05
5	Harold Reynolds	.05
6	Lou Whitaker	.05
7	Wade Boggs	.50
8	Gary Gaetti	.05
9	Paul Molitor	.45
10	Tony Fernandez	.05
11	Cal Ripken Jr.	1.00
12	Alan Trammell	.05
13	Jose Canseco	.30
14	Joe Carter	.05
15	Dwight Evans	.05
16	Mike Greenwell	.05
17	Dave Henderson	.05
18	Rickey Henderson	.45
19	Kirby Puckett	.50
20	Dave Winfield	.45
21	Robin Yount	.45
22	Bob Boone	.05
23	Carlton Fisk	.45
24	Geno Petralli	.05
25	Roger Clemens	.65
26	Mark Gubicza	.05
27	Dave Stewart	.05
28	Teddy Higuera	.05
29	Bruce Hurst	.05
30	Frank Viola	.05
31	Dennis Eckersley	.40
32	Doug Jones	.05
33	Jeff Reardon	.05
34	Will Clark	.05
35	Glenn Davis	.05
36	Andres Galarraga	.05
37	Juan Samuel	.05
38	Ryne Sandberg	.50
39	Steve Sax	.05
40	Bobby Bonilla	.05
41	Howard Johnson	.05
42	Vance Law	.05
43	Shawon Dunston	.05
44	Barry Larkin	.05
45	Ozzie Smith	.50
46	Barry Bonds	1.00
47	Eric Davis	.05
48	Andre Dawson	.25
49	Kirk Gibson	.05
50	Tony Gwynn	.50
51	Kevin McReynolds	.05
52	Rafael Palmeiro	.40
53	Darryl Strawberry	.05
54	Andy Van Slyke	.05
55	Gary Carter	.45
56	Mike LaValliere	.05
57	Benito Santiago	.05
58	David Cone	.05
59	Dwight Gooden	.05
60	Orel Hershiser	.05
61	Tom Browning	.05
62	Danny Jackson	.05
63	Bob Knepper	.05
64	Mark Davis	.05
65	John Franco	.05
66	Randy Myers	.05

Stickers

Topps' 1989 stickers were produced in two formats. Some measure 2-1/8" x 3" while there are 128 pairs of half-size (1-1/2" x 2-1/8") stickers. All stickers are attached to Super Star stickercards from which they can be peeled and affixed in a special Yearbook which was sold separately for 50 cents. Stickers have large center photos with white borders. Above and below are zipping fastball graphics trailing

graduated color bars (blues for N.L., reds for A.L.) A tiny black sticker number is in the lower-right corner. There is no player name on the stickers; the albums have a box under each space with player data. The half-size stickers are printed in pairs and are checklisted in that fashion. Values given are for complete sticker(s)/stickercard combinations, but without regard for which stickercard is on back.

		NM/M
Complete Set (326):		11.00
Common Player/Pair:		.05
Album:		2.00
1-230	George Bell, Jeff Ballard	.05
2-272	Gary Carter, Steve Farr	.25
3-324	Doug Jones, Mark Grace	.05
4-320	John Franco, Cecil Espy	.05
5-322	Andre Dawson, Ron Gant	.15
6-326	Pat Tabler, Walt Weiss	.05
7-317	Tom Browning, Tim Belcher	.05
8-239	Jeff Reardon, Larry Sheets	.05
9-325	Wade Boggs, Chris Sabo	.30
10-319	Kevin McReynolds, Jay Buhner	.05
11-323	Jose Canseco, Paul Gibson	.30
12-318	Orel Hershiser, Damon Berryhill	.05
13-231	Dave Smith, Mickey Tettleton	.05
14-302	Kevin Bass, Jack McDowell	.05
15-232	Mike Scott, Pete Stanicek	.05
16-256	Bill Doran, Jim Rice	.10
17-207	Rafael Ramirez, Andy Allanson	.05
18-181	Buddy Bell, Jack Howell	.05
19-214	Billy Hatcher, John Farrell	.05
20-275	Nolan Ryan, Frank Tanana	.50
21	Glenn Davis	.05
22	Bob Knepper	.05
23-211	Gerald Young, Tom Candiotti	.05
24-208	Dion James, Julio Franco	.05
25-243	Bruce Sutter, Jeff Russell	.20
26-310	Andres Thomas, Tommy John	.05
27-200	Zane Smith, B.J. Surhoff	.05
28-198	Ozzie Virgil, Teddy Higuera	.05
29-269	Rick Mahler, Floyd Bannister	.05
30-219	Albert Hall, Mickey Brantley	.05
31-203	Pete Smith, Jim Gantner	.05
32	Dale Murphy	.20
33	Gerald Perry	.05
34-177	Ron Gant, Chili Davis	.05
35-244	Bob Horner, Mike Stanley	.05
36-313	Willie McGee, Rafael Santana	.05
37-288	Luis Alicea, Greg Gagne	.05
38-279	Tony Pena, Gary Pettis	.05
39-184	Todd Worrell, Kirk McCaskill	.05
40-228	Pedro Guerrero, Bill Swift	.05
41-174	Tom Brunansky, Dick Schofield	.05
42-262	Terry Pendleton, Frank White	.05
43	Vince Coleman	.05
44	Ozzie Smith	.60
45-240	Jose Oquendo, Cecil Espy	.05
46-191	Vance Law, Pat Borders	.05
47-258	Rafael Palmeiro, Bob Stanley	.25
48-213	Greg Maddux, Greg Swindell	.30
49-229	Shawon Dunston, Jose Bautista	.05
50-210	Mark Grace, Cory Snyder	.05
51-187	Damon Berryhill, Kelly Gruber	.05
52-192	Rick Sutcliffe, Rance Mulliniks	.05

		NM/M
53-291	Jamie Moyer, Juan Berenguer	.05
54	Andre Dawson	.25
55	Ryne Sandberg	.60
56-284	Calvin Schiraldi, Jeff Reardon	.05
57-308	Steve Sax, Jack Clark	.05
58-263	Mike Scioscia, Bret Saberhagen	.05
59-298	Alfredo Griffin, Steve Lyons	.05
60-202	Fernando Valenzuela, Rob Deer	.05
61-286	Jay Howell, Dan Gladden	.05
62-305	Tim Leary, Bobby Thigpen	.05
63-212	John Shelby, Brook Jacoby	.05
64-306	John Tudor, John Candelaria	.05
65	Orel Hershiser	.05
66	Kirk Gibson	.05
67-223	Mike Marshall, Jim Presley	.05
68-206	Luis Rivera, Dale Sveum	.05
69-311	Tim Burke, Mike Pagliarulo	.05
70-253	Tim Wallach, Rich Gedman	.05
71-265	Pascual Perez, Bo Jackson	.05
72-185	Hubie Brooks, Fred McGriff	.05
73-250	Jeff Parrett, Steve Buechele	.05
74-316	Dennis Martinez, Rich Dotson	.05
75-285	Andy McGaffigan, Bert Blyleven	.05
76	Andres Galarraga	.05
77	Rock Raines	.05
78-287	Nelson Santovenia, Kent Hrbek	.05
79-261	Rick Reuschel, Mike Boddicker	.05
80-276	Mike Aldrete, Luis Salazar	.05
81-247	Kelly Downs, Mitch Williams	.05
82-283	Jose Uribe, Chet Lemon	.05
83-190	Mike Krukow, Mike Flanagan	.05
84-179	Kevin Mitchell, Devon White	.05
85-195	Brett Butler, Tom Henke	.05
86-252	Don Robinson, Dwight Evans	.05
87	Robby Thompson	.05
88	Will Clark	.05
89-188	Candy Maldonado, Lloyd Moseby	.05
90-180	Len Dykstra, Bryan Harvey	.05
91-234	Howard Johnson, Rene Gonzalez	.05
92-266	Roger McDowell, Kurt Stillwell	.05
93-222	Keith Hernandez, Steve Balboni	.05
94-178	Gary Carter, Brian Downing	.05
95-277	Kevin McReynolds, Jack Morris	.05
96-307	David Cone, Dave Righetti	.05
97-175	Randy Myers, Bob Boone	.05
98	Darryl Strawberry	.05
99	Doc Gooden	.05
100-257	Ron Darling, Marty Barrett	.05
101-201	Benny Santiago, Greg Brock	.05
102-273	John Kruk, Mike Henneman	.05
103-242	Chris Brown, Ruben Sierra	.05
104-255	Roberto Alomar, Mike Greenwell	.10
105-290	Keith Moreland, Tim Laudner	.05
106-217	Randy Ready, Scott Bailes	.05
107-267	Marvell Wynne, Danny Tartabull	.05
108-176	Lance McCullers, Mike Witt	.05
109	Tony Gwynn	.60
110	Mark Davis	.05
111-236	Andy Hawkins, Tom Niedenfuer	.05
112-233	Steve Bedrosian, Jim Traber	.05
113-196	Phil Bradley, Glenn Braggs	.05
114-189	Steve Jeltz, Tony Fernandez	.05
115-209	Von Hayes, Bud Black	.05
116-245	Kevin Gross, Charlie Hough	.05
117-218	Juan Samuel, Henry Cotto	.05

		NM/M
118-274	Shane Rawley, Doyle Alexander	.05
119-186	Chris James, Jimmy Key	.05
120	Mike Schmidt	.65
121	Don Carman	.05
122-280	Bruce Ruffin, Matt Nokes	.05
123-246	Bob Walk, Scott Fletcher	.05
124-278	John Smiley, Tom Brookens	.05
125-301	Sid Bream, Dan Pasqua	.05
126-251	Jose Lind, Lee Smith	.05
127-309	Barry Bonds, Willie Randolph	.40
128-294	Mike LaValliere, Gene Larkin	.05
129-225	Jeff D. Robinson, Scott Bradley	.05
130-295	Mike Dunne, Dave Gallagher	.05
131	Bobby Bonilla	.05
132	Andy Van Slyke	.05
133-241	Rafael Belliard, Jose Guzman	.05
134-197	Nick Esasky, Dan Plesac	.05
135-300	Bo Diaz, Fred Manrique	.05
136-221	John Franco, Mark Langston	.05
137-312	Barry Larkin, Rickey Henderson	.25
138-173	Eric Davis, Ron Hassey	.05
139-299	Jeff Treadway, Carlton Fisk	.05
140-254	Jose Rijo, Ellis Burks	.05
141-220	Tom Browning, Mike Moore	.05
142	Chris Sabo	.05
143	Danny Jackson	.05
144-199	Kal Daniels, Jeffrey Leonard	.05
145	Rickey Henderson/AS	.50
146	Paul Molitor/AS	.25
147	Wade Boggs/AS	.35
148	Jose Canseco/AS	.20
149	Dave Winfield/AS	.30
150	Cal Ripken Jr./AS	.50
151	Mark McGwire/AS	.40
152	Terry Steinbach/AS	.05
153	Frank Viola/AS	.05
154	Vince Coleman/AS	.05
155	Ryne Sandberg/AS	.35
156	Andre Dawson/AS	.15
157	Darryl Strawberry/AS	.05
158	Bobby Bonilla/AS	.05
159	Will Clark/AS	.05
160	Gary Carter/AS	.05
161	Ozzie Smith/AS	.35
162	Doc Gooden/AS	.05
163-268	Dave Stewart, Willie Wilson	.05
164-297	Dave Henderson, Ivan Calderon	.05
165-321	Terry Steinbach, Dave Gallagher	.05
166-264	Bob Welch, Kevin Seitzer	.05
167-224	Dennis Eckersley, Rey Quinones	.30
168-235	Walt Weiss, Terry Kennedy	.05
169-296	Dave Parker, Melido Perez	.05
170-289	Carney Lansford, Gary Gaetti	.05
171	Jose Canseco	.35
172	Mark McGwire	.75
182	Johnny Ray	.05
193	George Bell	.05
194	Dave Steib	.05
204	Paul Molitor	.50
205	Robin Yount	.50
215	Doug Jones	.05
216	Joe Carter	.05
226	Harold Reynolds	.05
227	Alvin Davis	.05
237	Cal Ripken Jr.	1.00
238	Eddie Murray	.50
248	Pete O'Brien	.05
249	Pete Incaviglia	.05
259	Roger Clemens	.65
260	Wade Boggs	.60
270	George Brett	.65
271	Mark Gubicza	.05
281	Alan Trammell	.05
282	Lou Whitaker	.05
292	Frank Viola	.05
293	Kirby Puckett	.60
303	Ozzie Guillen	.05
304	Harold Baines	.05
314	Don Mattingly	.65
315	Dave Winfield	.50

LJN Baseball Talk

Another generation of "talking baseball cards" was produced by Topps and the LJN Toy Co. in 1989. After purchasing a hand-held player, collectors could buy sets of four

"Baseball Talk Collection" cards for about $4. The 3-1/4" x 5-1/4" cards have a plastic sheet laminated on their backs containing information about the player which could be heard by inserting the card into the player. Fronts of the cards of players active in 1989 reproduce their 1989 Topps cards. The cards of earlier stars reproduce various older Topps cards of those players. Narrators on the cards were Don Drysdale, Joe Torre and Mel Allen.

		NM/M
	Complete Set (164):	125.00
	Common Player:	1.00
	Record Player:	30.00
1	1975 World Series Game 6	1.00
2	1986 World Series Game 6	1.00
3	1986 ALCS Game 6	1.00
4	1956 World Series Game 5	1.00
5	1986 NLCS Game 6	1.00
6	1969 World Series Game 5	1.00
7	1984 World Series Game 5	1.00
8	1988 World Series Game 1	1.00
9	Reggie Jackson	4.00
10	Brooks Robinson	1.50
11	Billy Williams	1.50
12	Bobby Thomson	1.00
13	Harmon Killebrew	1.50
14	Johnny Bench	2.00
15	Tom Seaver	2.00
16	Willie Stargell	1.50
17	Ernie Banks	4.00
18	Gaylord Perry	1.50
19	Bill Mazeroski	1.50
20	Babe Ruth	7.50
21	Lou Gehrig	6.00
22	Ty Cobb	5.00
23	Bob Gibson	1.50
24	Al Kaline	1.50
25	Rod Carew	1.50
26	Lou Brock	1.50
27	Stan Musial	4.00
28	Joe Morgan	1.50
29	Willie McCovey	1.50
30	Duke Snider	4.00
31	Whitey Ford	4.00
32	Eddie Mathews	1.50
33	Carl Yastrzemski	2.00
34	Pete Rose	7.50
35	Hank Aaron/1976	6.00
36	Ralph Kiner	1.50
37	Steve Carlton	1.50
38	Roberto Clemente	7.50
39	Don Drysdale	1.50
40	Robin Roberts	1.50
41	Hank Aaron/1954	6.00
42	Dave Winfield	2.00
43	Alan Trammell	1.00
44	Darryl Strawberry	1.00
45	Ozzie Smith	3.00
46	Kirby Puckett	3.00
47	Will Clark	1.00
48	Keith Hernandez	1.00
49	Wally Joyner	1.00
50	Mike Scott	1.00
51	Eric Davis	1.00
52	George Brett	4.00
53	George Bell	1.00
54	Tommy Lasorda	1.00
55	Rickey Henderson	2.00
56	Robin Yount	3.00
57	Wade Boggs	3.00
58	Roger Clemens	4.00
59	Vince Coleman	1.00
60	Jose Canseco	1.50
61	Fernando Valenzuela	1.00
62	Tony Gwynn	3.00
63	Dwight Gooden	1.00
64	Mark McGwire	6.00
65	Jack Clark	1.00
66	Dale Murphy	1.25
67	Kirk Gibson	1.00
68	Jack Morris	1.00
69	Ryne Sandberg	3.00
70	Nolan Ryan	9.00
71	John Tudor	1.00
72	Mike Schmidt	4.00
73	Dave Righetti	1.00
74	Pedro Guerrero	1.00
75	Rick Sutcliffe	1.00
76	Gary Carter	2.00
77	Cal Ripken Jr.	9.00
78	Andre Dawson	1.25
79	Andy Van Slyke	1.00
80	Tim Raines	1.00
81	Frank Viola	1.00
82	Don Mattingly	4.00
83	Rick Reuschel	1.00
84	Willie McGee	1.00
85	Mark Langston	1.00
86	Ron Darling	1.00
87	Gregg Jefferies	1.00
88	Harold Baines	1.00
89	Eddie Murray	2.00
90	Barry Larkin	1.00
91	Gary Gaetti	1.00
92	Bret Saberhagen	1.00
93	Roger McDowell	1.00
94	Joe Magrane	1.00
95	Juan Samuel	1.00
96	Bert Blyleven	1.00
97	Kal Daniels	1.00
98	Kevin Bass	1.00
99	Glenn Davis	1.00
100	Steve Sax	1.00
101	Rich Gossage	1.00
102	Roger Craig	1.00
103	Carney Lansford	1.00
104	Joe Carter	1.00
105	Bruce Sutter	2.00
106	Barry Bonds	9.00
107	Danny Jackson	1.00
108	Mike Flanagan	1.00
109	Dwight Evans	1.00
110	Ron Guidry	1.00
111	Bruce Hurst	1.00
112	Jim Rice	1.25
113	Oddibe McDowell	1.00
114	Bobby Bonilla	1.00
115	Bob Welch	1.00
116	Dave Parker	1.00
117	Tim Wallach	1.00
118	Tom Henke	1.00
119	Mike Greenwell	1.00
120	Kevin Seitzer	1.00
121	Randy Myers	1.00
122	Andres Galarraga	1.00
123	Orel Hershiser	1.00
124	Cory Snyder	1.00
125	Mike Witt	1.00
126	Mike LaValliere	1.00
127	Pete Incaviglia	1.00
128	Dennis Eckersley	2.00
129	Jimmy Key	1.00
130	John Franco	1.00
131	Dan Plesac	1.00
132	Tony LaRussa	1.00
133	Hubie Brooks	1.00
134	Chili Davis	1.00
135	Bob Boone	1.00
136	Jeff Reardon	1.00
137	Candy Maldonado	1.00
138	Mike Marshall	1.00
139	Tommy John	1.00
140	Chris Sabo	1.00
141	Alvin Davis	1.00
142	Frank White	1.00
143	Harold Reynolds	1.00
144	Lee Smith	1.00
145	John Kruk	1.00
146	Tony Fernandez	1.00
147	Steve Bedrosian	1.00
148	Benito Santiago	1.00
149	Ozzie Guillen	1.00
150	Gerald Perry	1.00
151	Carlton Fisk	2.00
152	Tom Brunansky	1.00
153	Paul Molitor	2.00
154	Todd Worrell	1.00
155	Brett Butler	1.00
156	Sparky Anderson	1.00
157	Kent Hrbek	1.00
158	Frank Tanana	1.00
159	Kevin Mitchell	1.00
160	Charlie Hough	1.00
161	Doug Jones	1.00
162	Lou Whitaker	1.00
163	Fred Lynn	1.00
---	Checklist	.50

Sport Shots Portfolios

In its second year, the number of baseball card folders produced by Shaeffer Eaton reproducing current Topps baseball cards was drastically reduced, from 130 to 39. The format remains the same, a 9-1/2" x 11-3/4" cardboard two-pocket folder. The 1989 portfolios are considerably scarcer than the 1988s.

	NM/M
Complete Set (39):	40.00
Common Player:	1.00

1989 Topps (Sport Shots)

No.	Player	Price
10	Andre Dawson	1.25
30	Doc Gooden	1.00
70	Mark McGwire	4.00
85	Kevin McReynolds	1.00
110	Paul Molitor	1.50
120	Frank Viola	1.00
145	Dave Stewart	1.00
180	Mike Scott	1.00
200	George Brett	2.50
205	Dwight Evans	1.00
230	Ozzie Smith	2.00
233	Gregg Jefferies	1.00
260	Dave Winfield	1.50
300	Darryl Strawberry	1.00
330	Eric Davis	1.00
335	Dave Righetti	1.00
340	Kirk Gibson	1.00
370	Dennis Eckersley	1.25
380	Rickey Henderson	1.50
425	Jay Howell	1.00
450	Roger Clemens	2.50
480	Keith Hernandez	1.00
500	Jose Canseco	1.25
527	Dave Henderson	1.00
550	Orel Hershiser	1.00
570	Tony Gwynn	2.00
582	Mike A. Marshall	1.00
590	Andres Galarraga	1.00
600	Wade Boggs	2.00
630	Mike Greenwell	1.00
650	Kirby Puckett	2.00
660	Will Clark	1.00
700	Don Mattingly	2.50
710	David Cone	1.00
725	Terry Steinbach	1.00
730	Danny Jackson	1.00
755	Mike Scioscia	1.00
770	Alan Trammell	1.00
785	Ellis Burks	1.00

1990 Topps

JOEY BELLE

The 1990 Topps set again included 792 cards, and sported a newly-designed front that featured six different color schemes. The set led off with a special four-card salute to Nolan Ryan, and sported other specials including All-Stars, Number 1 Draft Picks, Record Breakers, managers, rookies, and "Turn Back the Clock" cards. The set also includes a special card commemorating A. Bartlett Giamatti, the late baseball commissioner. Backs are printed in black on a chartreuse background. The set features 725 different individual player cards, the most ever, including 138 players' first appearance in a regular Topps set.

	NM/M
Unopened Factory Set, Retail (792):	25.00
Unopened Factory Set, Hobby (792):	20.00
Complete Set (792):	15.00
Common Player:	.05
Wax Pack (16):	.60
Wax Box (36):	12.00
Cello Pack (31):	1.00
Cello Box (24):	15.00
Rack Box (45):	1.00
Rack Box (24):	16.00
Vending Box (500):	7.50

No.	Player	Price
1	Nolan Ryan	.75
2	Nolan Ryan/Mets	.35
3	Nolan Ryan/Angels	.25
4	Nolan Ryan/Astros	.25
5	Nolan Ryan/Rangers	.25
6	Vince Coleman (Record Breaker)	.05
7	Rickey Henderson (Record Breaker)	.20
8	Cal Ripken, Jr. (Record Breaker)	.40
9	Eric Plunk	.05
10	Barry Larkin	.05
11	Paul Gibson	.05
12	Joe Girardi RC	.05
13	Mark Williamson	.05
14	Mike Fetters RC	.05
15	Teddy Higuera	.05
16	Kent Anderson RC	.05
17	Kelly Downs	.05
18	Carlos Quintana	.05
19	Al Newman	.05
20	Mark Gubicza	.05
21	Jeff Torborg	.05
22	Bruce Ruffin	.05
23	Randy Velarde	.05
24	Joe Hesketh	.05
25	Willie Randolph	.05
26	Don Slaught	.05
27	Rick Leach	.05
28	Duane Ward	.05
29	John Cangelosi	.05
30	David Cone	.05
31	Henry Cotto	.05
32	John Farrell	.05
33	Greg Walker	.05
34	Tony Fossas RC	.05
35	Benito Santiago	.05
36	John Costello	.05
37	Domingo Ramos	.05
38	Wes Gardner	.05
39	Curt Ford	.05
40	Jay Howell	.05
41	Matt Williams	.05
42	Jeff Robinson	.05
43	Dante Bichette	.05
44	Roger Salkeld RC (#1 Draft Pick)	.10
45	Dave Parker	.05
46	Rob Dibble	.05
47	Brian Harper	.05
48	Zane Smith	.05
49	Tom Lawless	.05
50	Glenn Davis	.05
51	Doug Rader	.05
52	Jack Daugherty RC	.05
53	Mike LaCoss	.05
54	Joel Skinner	.05
55	Darrell Evans	.05
56	Franklin Stubbs	.05
57	Greg Vaughn	.05
58	Keith Miller	.05
59	Ted Power	.05
60	George Brett	.50
61	Deion Sanders	.05
62	Ramon Martinez	.05
63	Mike Pagliarulo	.05
64	Danny Darwin	.05
65	Devon White	.05
66	Greg Litton RC	.05
67	Scott Sanderson	.05
68	Dave Henderson	.05
69	Todd Frohwirth	.05
70	Mike Greenwell	.05
71	Allan Anderson	.05
72	Jeff Huson RC	.05
73	Bob Milacki	.05
74	Jeff Jackson RC (#1 Draft Pick)	.05
75	Doug Jones	.05
76	Dave Valle	.05
77	Dave Bergman	.05
78	Mike Flanagan	.05
79	Ron Kittle	.05
80	Jeff Russell	.05
81	Bob Rodgers	.05
82	Scott Terry	.05
83	Hensley Meulens	.05
84	Ray Searage	.05
85	Juan Samuel	.05
86	Paul Kilgus	.05
87	Rick Luecken RC	.05
88	Glenn Braggs	.05
89	Clint Zavaras RC	.05
90	Jack Clark	.05
91	Steve Frey RC	.05
92	Mike Stanley	.05
93	Shawn Hillegas	.05
94	Herm Winningham	.05
95	Todd Worrell	.05
96	Jody Reed	.05
97	Curt Schilling	.25
98	Jose Gonzalez RC	.05
99	Rich Monteleone RC	.05
100	Will Clark	.25
101	Shane Rawley	.05
102	Stan Javier	.05
103	Marvin Freeman	.05
104	Bob Knepper	.05
105	Randy Myers	.05
106	Charlie O'Brien	.05
107	Fred Lynn	.05
108	Rod Nichols	.05
109	Roberto Kelly	.05
110	Tommy Helms	.05
111	Ed Whited	.05
112	Glenn Wilson	.05
113	Manny Lee	.05
114	Mike Bielecki	.05
115	Tony Pena	.05
116	Floyd Bannister	.05
117	Mike Sharperson RC	.05
118	Erik Hanson	.05
119	Billy Hatcher	.05
120	John Franco	.05
121	Robin Ventura	.05
122	Shawn Abner	.05
123	Rich Gedman	.05
124	Dave Dravecky	.05
125	Kent Hrbek	.05
126	Randy Kramer	.05
127	Mike Devereaux	.05
128	Checklist 1-132	.05
129	Ron Jones	.05
130	Bert Blyleven	.05
131	Matt Nokes	.05
132	Lance Blankenship RC	.05
133	Ricky Horton	.05
134	Earl Cunningham RC (#1 Draft Pick)	.05
135	Dave Magadan	.05
136	Kevin Brown	.05
137	Marty Pevey RC	.05
138	Al Leiter	.05
139	Greg Brock	.05
140	Andre Dawson	.25
141	John Hart	.05
142	Jeff Wetherby RC	.05
143	Rafael Belliard	.05
144	Bud Black	.05
145	Terry Steinbach	.05
146	Rob Richie RC	.05
147	Chuck Finley	.05
148	Edgar Martinez RC	.05
149	Steve Farr	.05
150	Kirk Gibson	.05
151	Rick Mahler	.05
152	Lonnie Smith	.05
153	Randy Milligan	.05
154	Mike Maddux	.05
155	Ellis Burks	.05
156	Ken Patterson	.05
157	Craig Biggio	.05
158	Craig Lefferts	.05
159	Mike Felder	.05
160	Dave Righetti	.05
161	Harold Reynolds	.05
162	Todd Zeile RC	.20
163	Phil Bradley	.05
164	Jeff Juden RC (#1 Draft Pick)	.05
165	Walt Weiss	.05
166	Bobby Witt	.05
167	Kevin Appier RC	.05
168	Jose Lind	.05
169	Richard Dotson	.05
170	George Bell	.05
171	Russ Nixon	.05
172	Tom Lampkin RC	.05
173	Tim Belcher	.05
174	Jeff Kunkel	.05
175	Mike Moore	.05
176	Luis Quinones	.05
177	Mike Henneman	.05
178	Chris James	.05
179	Brian Holton	.05
180	Rock Raines	.05
181	Juan Agosto	.05
182	Mookie Wilson	.05
183	Steve Lake	.05
184	Danny Cox	.05
185	Ruben Sierra	.05
186	Dave LaPoint	.05
187	Rick Wrona RC	.05
188	Mike Smithson	.05
189	Dick Schofield	.05
190	Rick Reuschel	.05
191	Pat Borders	.05
192	Don August	.05
193	Andy Benes	.05
194	Glenallen Hill RC	.05
195	Tim Burke	.05
196	Gerald Young	.05
197	Doug Drabek	.05
198	Mike Marshall	.05
199	Sergio Valdez RC	.05
200	Don Mattingly	.50
201	Cito Gaston	.05
202	Mike Macfarlane	.05
203	Mike Roesler RC	.05
204	Bob Dernier	.05
205	Mark Davis	.05
206	Nick Esasky	.05
207	Bob Ojeda	.05
208	Brook Jacoby	.05
209	Greg Mathews	.05
210	Ryne Sandberg	.45
211	John Cerutti	.05
212	Joe Orsulak	.05
213	Scott Bankhead	.05
214	Terry Francona	.05
215	Kirk McCaskill	.05
216	Ricky Jordan	.05
217	Don Robinson	.05
218	Wally Backman	.05
219	Donn Pall	.05
220	Barry Bonds	.75
221	Gary Mielke RC	.05
222	Kurt Stillwell	.05
223	Tommy Gregg	.05
224	Delino DeShields RC	.15
225	Jim Deshaies	.05
226	Mickey Hatcher	.05
227	Kevin Tapani RC	.15
228	Dave Martinez	.05
229	David Wells	.05
230	Keith Hernandez	.05
231	Jack McKeon	.05
232	Darnell Coles	.05
233	Ken Hill RC	.05
234	Mariano Duncan	.05
235	Jeff Reardon	.05
236	Hal Morris RC	.05
237	Kevin Ritz RC	.05
238	Felix Jose RC	.05
239	Eric Show	.05
240	Mark Grace	.05
241	Mike Krukow	.05
242	Fred Manrique	.05
243	Barry Jones	.05
244	Bill Schroeder	.05
245	Roger Clemens	.50
246	Jim Eisenreich	.05
247	Jerry Reed	.05
248	Dave Anderson	.05
249	Mike Smith RC	.05
250	Jose Canseco	.25
251	Jeff Blauser	.05
252	Otis Nixon	.05
253	Mark Portugal	.05
254	Francisco Cabrera	.05
255	Bobby Thigpen	.05
256	Marvell Wynne	.05
257	Jose DeLeon	.05
258	Barry Lyons	.05
259	Lance McCullers	.05
260	Eric Davis	.05
261	Whitey Herzog	.05
262	Checklist 133-264	.05
263	Mel Stottlemyre, Jr. RC	.10
264	Bryan Clutterbuck	.05
265	Pete O'Brien	.05
266	German Gonzalez	.05
267	Mark Davidson	.05
268	Rob Murphy	.05
269	Dickie Thon	.05
270	Dave Stewart	.05
271	Chet Lemon	.05
272	Bryan Harvey	.05
273	Bobby Bonilla	.05
274	Goose Gozzo RC	.05
275	Mickey Tettleton	.05
276	Gary Thurman	.05
277	Lenny Harris RC	.05
278	Pascual Perez	.05
279	Steve Buechele	.05
280	Lou Whitaker	.05
281	Kevin Bass	.05
282	Derek Lilliquist	.05
283	Albert Belle	.15
284	Mark Gardner RC	.05
285	Willie McGee	.05
286	Lee Guetterman	.05
287	Vance Law	.05
288	Greg Briley	.05
289	Norm Charlton	.05
290	Robin Yount	.35
291	Dave Johnson	.05
292	Jim Gott	.05
293	Mike Gallego	.05
294	Craig McMurtry	.05
295	Fred McGriff	.05
296	Jeff Ballard	.05
297	Tom Herr	.05
298	Danny Gladden	.05
299	Adam Peterson RC	.05
300	Bo Jackson	.10
301	Don Aase	.05
302	Marcus Lawton RC	.05
303	Rick Cerone	.05
304	Marty Clary RC	.05
305	Eddie Murray	.35
306	Tom Niedenfuer	.05
307	Bip Roberts	.05
308	Jose Guzman	.05
309	Eric Yelding RC	.05
310	Steve Bedrosian	.05
311	Dwight Smith	.05
312	Dan Quisenberry	.05
313	Gus Polidor	.05
314	Donald Harris RC (#1 Draft Pick)	.05
315	Bruce Hurst	.05
316	Carney Lansford	.05
317	Mark Guthrie RC	.05
318	Wallace Johnson	.05
319	Dion James	.05
320	Dave Steib	.05
321	Joe M. Morgan	.05
322	Junior Ortiz	.05
323	Willie Wilson	.05
324	Pete Harnisch	.05
325	Robby Thompson	.05
326	Tom McCarthy RC	.05
327	Ken Williams	.05
328	Curt Young	.05
329	Oddibe McDowell	.05
330	Ron Darling	.05
331	Juan Gonzalez RC	1.50
332	Paul O'Neill	.05
333	Bill Wegman	.05
334	Johnny Ray	.05
335	Andy Hawkins	.05
336	Ken Griffey Jr.	.75
337	Lloyd McClendon	.05
338	Dennis Lamp	.05
339	Dave Clark	.05
340	Fernando Valenzuela	.05
341	Tom Foley	.05
342	Alex Trevino	.05
343	Frank Tanana	.05
344	George Canale RC	.05
345	Harold Baines	.05
346	Jim Presley	.05
347	Junior Felix RC	.05
348	Gary Wayne RC	.05
349	Steve Finley RC	.15
350	Bret Saberhagen	.05
351	Roger Craig	.05
352	Bryn Smith	.05
353	Sandy Alomar	.05
354	Stan Belinda RC	.05
355	Marty Barrett	.05
356	Randy Ready	.05
357	Dave West	.05
358	Andres Thomas	.05
359	Jimmy Jones	.05
360	Paul Molitor	.35
361	Randy McCament RC	.05
362	Damon Berryhill	.05
363	Dan Petry	.05

#	Player	Price
364	Rolando Roomes RC	.05
365	Ozzie Guillen	.05
366	Mike Heath	.05
367	Mike Morgan	.05
368	Bill Doran	.05
369	Todd Burns	.05
370	Tim Wallach	.05
371	Jimmy Key	.05
372	Terry Kennedy	.05
373	Alvin Davis	.05
374	Steve Cummings RC	.05
375	Dwight Evans	.05
376	Checklist 265-396	.05
377	Mickey Weston RC	.05
378	Luis Salazar	.05
379	Steve Rosenberg	.05
380	Dave Winfield	.35
381	Frank Robinson	.10
382	Jeff Musselman	.05
383	John Morris	.05
384	Pat Combs RC	.05
385	Fred McGriff/AS	.05
386	Julio Franco/AS	.05
387	Wade Boggs/AS	.20
388	Cal Ripken, Jr./AS	.40
389	Robin Yount/AS	.20
390	Ruben Sierra/AS	.20
391	Kirby Puckett/AS	.25
392	Carlton Fisk/AS	.20
393	Bret Saberhagen/AS	.05
394	Jeff Ballard/AS	.05
395	Jeff Russell/AS	.05
396	A. Bartlett Giamatti	.20
397	Will Clark/AS	.20
398	Ryne Sandberg/AS	.20
399	Howard Johnson/AS	.05
400	Ozzie Smith/AS	.20
401	Kevin Mitchell/AS	.05
402	Eric Davis/AS	.05
403	Tony Gwynn/AS	.25
404	Craig Biggio/AS	.05
405	Mike Scott/AS	.05
406	Joe Magrane/AS	.05
407	Mark Davis/AS	.05
408	Trevor Wilson	.05
409	Tom Brunansky	.05
410	Joe Boever	.05
411	Ken Phelps	.05
412	Jamie Moyer	.05
413	Brian DuBois RC	.05
414a	Frank Thomas No Name (No name on front.)	450.00
414b	Frank Thomas RC (Name on front.)	2.00
415	Shawon Dunston	.05
416	Dave Johnson RC	.05
417	Jim Gantner	.05
418	Tom Browning	.05
419	Beau Allred RC	.05
420	Carlton Fisk	.35
421	Greg Minton	.05
422	Pat Sheridan	.05
423	Fred Toliver	.05
424	Jerry Reuss	.05
425	Bill Landrum	.05
426	Jeff Hamilton	.05
427	Carmem Castillo	.05
428	Steve Davis RC	.05
429	Tom Kelly	.05
430	Pete Incaviglia	.05
431	Randy Johnson	.35
432	Damaso Garcia	.05
433	Steve Olin RC	.05
434	Mark Carreon RC	.05
435	Kevin Seitzer	.05
436	Mel Hall	.05
437	Les Lancaster	.05
438	Greg Myers RC	.05
439	Jeff Parrett	.05
440	Alan Trammell	.05
441	Bob Kipper	.05
442	Jerry Browne	.05
443	Cris Carpenter	.05
444	Kyle Abbott RC (FDP)	.10
445	Danny Jackson	.05
446	Dan Pasqua	.05
447	Atlee Hammaker	.05
448	Greg Gagne	.05
449	Dennis Rasmussen	.05
450	Rickey Henderson	.35
451	Mark Lemke	.05
452	Luis de los Santos RC	.05
453	Jody Davis	.05
454a	Jeff King RC (No white on back.)	100.00
454b	Jeff King (Correct use of white.)	.05
455	Jeffrey Leonard	.05
456	Chris Gwynn RC	.05
457	Gregg Jefferies	.05
458	Bob McClure	.05
459	Jim Lefebvre	.05
460	Mike Scott	.05
461	Carlos Martinez RC	.05
462	Denny Walling	.05
463	Drew Hall	.05
464	Jerome Walton RC	.05
465	Kevin Gross	.05
466	Rance Mulliniks	.05
467	Juan Nieves	.05

ABBREVIATIONS

AS - All-Star

#	Player	Price
468	Billy Ripken	.05
469	John Kruk	.05
470	Frank Viola	.05
471	Mike Brumley	.05
472	Jose Uribe	.05
473	Joe Price	.05
474	Rich Thompson	.05
475	Bob Welch	.05
476	Brad Komminsk	.05
477	Willie Fraser	.05
478	Mike LaValliere	.05
479	Frank White	.05
480	Sid Fernandez	.05
481	Garry Templeton	.05
482	Steve Carter RC	.05
483	Alejandro Pena	.05
484	Mike Fitzgerald	.05
485	John Candelaria	.05
486	Jeff Treadway	.05
487	Steve Searcy	.05
488	Ken Oberkfell	.05
489	Nick Leyva	.05
490	Dan Plesac	.05
491	Dave Cochrane RC	.05
492	Ron Oester	.05
493	Jason Grimsley RC	.05
494	Terry Puhl	.05
495	Lee Smith	.05
496	Cecil Espy	.05
497	Dave Schmidt	.05
498	Rick Schu	.05
499	Bill Long	.05
500	Kevin Mitchell	.05
501	Matt Young	.05
502	Mitch Webster	.05
503	Randy St. Claire	.05
504	Tom O'Malley	.05
505	Kelly Gruber	.05
506	Tom Glavine	.25
507	Gary Redus	.05
508	Terry Leach	.05
509	Tom Pagnozzi	.05
510	Dwight Gooden	.05
511	Clay Parker	.05
512	Gary Pettis	.05
513	Mark Eichhorn	.05
514	Andy Allanson	.05
515	Len Dykstra	.05
516	Tim Leary	.05
517	Roberto Alomar	.15
518	Bill Krueger	.05
519	Bucky Dent	.05
520	Mitch Williams	.05
521	Craig Worthington	.05
522	Mike Dunne	.05
523	Jay Bell	.05
524	Daryl Boston	.05
525	Wally Joyner	.05
526	Checklist 397-528	.05
527	Ron Hassey	.05
528	Kevin Wickander RC	.05
529	Greg Harris	.05
530	Mark Langston	.05
531	Ken Caminiti	.05
532	Cecilio Guante	.05
533	Tim Jones RC	.05
534	Louie Meadows	.05
535	John Smoltz	.05
536	Bob Geren RC	.05
537	Mark Grant	.05
538	Billy Spiers RC	.05
539	Neal Heaton	.05
540	Danny Tartabull	.05
541	Pat Perry	.05
542	Darren Daulton	.05
543	Nelson Liriano	.05
544	Dennis Boyd	.05
545	Kevin McReynolds	.05
546	Kevin Hickey	.05
547	Jack Howell	.05
548	Pat Clements	.05
549	Don Zimmer	.05
550	Julio Franco	.05
551	Tim Crews	.05
552	Mike Smith RC	.05
553	Scott Scudder RC	.05
554	Jay Buhner	.05
555	Jack Morris	.05
556	Gene Larkin	.05
557	Jeff Innis RC	.05
558	Rafael Ramirez	.05
559	Andy McGaffigan	.05
560	Steve Sax	.05
561	Ken Dayley	.05
562	Chad Kreuter	.05
563	Alex Sanchez	.05
564	Tyler Houston RC (#1 Draft Pick)	.10
565	Scott Fletcher	.05
566	Mark Knudson	.05
567	Ron Gant	.05
568	John Smiley	.05
569	Ivan Calderon	.05
570	Cal Ripken, Jr.	.75
571	Brett Butler	.05
572	Greg Harris	.05
573	Danny Heep	.05
574	Bill Swift	.05
575	Lance Parrish	.05
576	Mike Dyer RC	.05
577	Charlie Hayes RC	.05
578	Joe Magrane	.05
579	Art Howe	.05
580	Joe Carter	.05
581	Ken Griffey	.05
582	Rick Honeycutt	.05
583	Bruce Benedict	.05
584	Phil Stephenson RC	.05

#	Player	Price
585	Kal Daniels	.05
586	Ed Nunez	.05
587	Lance Johnson	.05
588	Rick Rhoden	.05
589	Mike Aldrete	.05
590	Ozzie Smith	.45
591	Todd Stottlemyre	.05
592	R.J. Reynolds	.05
593	Scott Bradley	.05
594	Luis Sojo RC	.05
595	Greg Swindell	.05
596	Jose DeJesus RC	.05
597	Chris Bosio	.05
598	Brady Anderson	.05
599	Frank Williams	.05
600	Darryl Strawberry	.05
601	Luis Rivera	.05
602	Scott Garrelts	.05
603	Tony Armas	.05
604	Ron Robinson	.05
605	Mike Scioscia	.05
606	Storm Davis	.05
607	Steve Jeltz	.05
608	Eric Anthony RC	.10
609	Sparky Anderson	.10
610	Pedro Guerrero	.05
611	Walt Terrell	.05
612	Dave Gallagher	.05
613	Jeff Pico	.05
614	Nelson Santovenia	.05
615	Rob Deer	.05
616	Brian Holman	.05
617	Geronimo Berroa	.05
618	Eddie Whitson	.05
619	Rob Ducey	.05
620	Tony Castillo RC	.05
621	Melido Perez	.05
622	Sid Bream	.05
623	Jim Corsi	.05
624	Darrin Jackson	.05
625	Roger McDowell	.05
626	Bob Melvin	.05
627	Jose Rijo	.05
628	Candy Maldonado	.05
629	Eric Hetzel RC	.05
630	Gary Gaetti	.05
631	John Wetteland RC	.15
632	Scott Lusader	.05
633	Dennis Cook RC	.05
634	Luis Polonia	.05
635	Brian Downing	.05
636	Jesse Orosco	.05
637	Craig Reynolds	.05
638	Jeff Montgomery	.05
639	Tony LaRussa	.05
640	Rick Sutcliffe	.05
641	Doug Strange RC	.05
642	Jack Armstrong	.05
643	Alfredo Griffin	.05
644	Paul Assenmacher	.05
645	Jose Oquendo	.05
646	Checklist 529-660	.05
647	Rex Hudler	.05
648	Jim Clancy	.05
649	Dan Murphy RC	.05
650	Mike Witt	.05
651	Rafael Santana	.05
652	Mike Boddicker	.05
653	John Moses	.05
654	Paul Coleman RC (#1 Draft Pick)	.05
655	Gregg Olson	.05
656	Mackey Sasser	.05
657	Terry Mulholland	.05
658	Donell Nixon	.05
659	Greg Cadaret	.05
660	Vince Coleman	.05
661	Dick Howser (Turn Back the Clock)	.05
662	Mike Schmidt (Turn Back the Clock)	.10
663	Fred Lynn (Turn Back the Clock)	.05
664	Johnny Bench (Turn Back the Clock)	.05
665	Sandy Koufax (Turn Back the Clock)	.15
666	Brian Fisher	.05
667	Curt Wilkerson	.05
668	Joe Oliver RC	.05
669	Tom Lasorda	.05
670	Dennis Eckersley	.30
671	Bob Boone	.05
672	Roy Smith	.05
673	Joey Meyer	.05
674	Spike Owen	.05
675	Jim Abbott	.05
676	Randy Kutcher RC	.05
677	Jay Tibbs	.05
678	Kirt Manwaring	.05
679	Gary Ward	.05
680	Howard Johnson	.05
681	Mike Schooler	.05
682	Dann Bilardello	.05
683	Kenny Rogers	.05
684	Julio Machado RC	.05
685	Tony Fernandez	.05
686	Carmelo Martinez	.05
687	Tim Birtsas	.05
688	Milt Thompson	.05
689	Rich Yett	.05
690	Mark McGwire	.65
691	Chuck Cary	.05
692	Sammy Sosa RC	4.00
693	Calvin Schiraldi	.05
694	Mike Stanton RC	.05
695	Tom Henke	.05
696	B.J. Surhoff	.05

#	Player	Price
697	Mike Davis	.05
698	Omar Vizquel	.05
699	Jim Leyland	.05
700	Kirby Puckett	.45
701	Bernie Williams RC	1.00
702	Tony Phillips	.05
703	Jeff Brantley	.05
704	Chip Hale RC	.05
705	Claudell Washington	.05
706	Geno Petralli	.05
707	Luis Aquino	.05
708	Larry Sheets	.05
709	Juan Berneguer	.05
710	Von Hayes	.05
711	Rick Aguilera	.05
712	Todd Benzinger	.05
713	Tim Drummond RC	.05
714	Marquis Grissom RC	.25
715	Greg Maddux	.45
716	Steve Balboni	.05
717	Ron Kakovice	.05
718	Gary Sheffield	.30
719	Wally Whitehurst RC	.05
720	Andres Galarraga	.05
721	Lee Mazzilli	.05
722	Felix Fermin	.05
723	Jeff Robinson	.05
724	Juan Bell RC	.05
725	Terry Pendleton	.05
726	Gene Nelson	.05
727	Pat Tabler	.05
728	Jim Acker	.05
729	Bobby Valentine	.05
730	Tony Gwynn	.45
731	Don Carman	.05
732	Ernie Riles	.05
733	John Dopson	.05
734	Kevin Elster	.05
735	Charlie Hough	.05
736	Rick Dempsey	.05
737	Chris Sabo	.05
738	Gene Harris RC	.05
739	Dale Sveum	.05
740	Jesse Barfield	.05
741	Steve Wilson	.05
742	Ernie Whitt	.05
743	Tom Candiotti	.05
744	Kelly Mann RC	.05
745	Hubie Brooks	.05
746	Dave Smith	.05
747	Randy Bush	.05
748	Doyle Alexander	.05
749	Mark Parent	.05
750	Dale Murphy	.15
751	Steve Lyons	.05
752	Tom Gordon	.05
753	Chris Speier	.05
754	Bob Walk	.05
755	Rafael Palmeiro	.30
756	Ken Howell	.05
757	Larry Walker RC	.75
758	Mark Thurmond	.05
759	Tom Trebelhorn	.05
760	Wade Boggs	.45
761	Mike Jackson	.05
762	Doug Dascenzo	.05
763	Denny Martinez	.05
764	Tim Teufel	.05
765	Chili Davis	.05
766	Brian Meyer RC	.05
767	Tracy Jones	.05
768	Chuck Crim	.05
769	Greg Hibbard RC	.05
770	Cory Snyder	.05
771	Pete Smith	.05
772	Jeff Reed	.05
773	Dave Leiper	.05
774	Ben McDonald RC	.20
775	Andy Van Slyke	.05
776	Charlie Leibrandt	.05
777	Tim Laudner	.05
778	Mike Jeffcoat	.05
779	Lloyd Moseby	.05
780	Orel Hershiser	.05
781	Mario Diaz	.05
782	Jose Alvarez	.05
783	Checklist 661-792	.05
784	Scott Bailes	.05
785	Jim Rice	.15
786	Eric King	.05
787	Rene Gonzales	.05
788	Frank DiPino	.05
789	John Wathan	.05
790	Gary Carter	.35
791	Alvaro Espinoza	.05
792	Gerald Perry	.05

Tiffany

This specially boxed version of Topps' 1990 baseball card set was sold through hobby channels only. The checklist is identical to the regular-issue Topps set and the cards are nearly so. The Tiffany version features white cardboard stock and a high-gloss finish on the fronts.

	NM/M
Unopened Set (792):	115.00
Complete Set (792):	90.00
Common Player:	.10

Traded

For the first time, Topps "Traded" series cards were

made available nationwide in retail wax packs. The 132-card set was also sold in complete boxed form as it has been in recent years. The wax pack traded cards feature gray backs, while the boxed set cards feature white backs. Each of the gray-back wax-pack cards can be found with copyright lines preceded by one or two asterisks. The cards are numbered 1T-132T and showcase rookies, players who changed teams and new managers.

	NM/M
Complete Set, Retail (132):	6.00
Complete Set, Hobby (132):	4.00
Common Player:	.05
Wax Pack (7):	.05
Wax Box (36):	9.00

#	Player	Price
1	Darrel Akerfelds	.05
2	Sandy Alomar, Jr.	.05
3	Brad Arnsberg	.05
4	Steve Avery	.05
5	Wally Backman	.05
6	Carlos Baerga RC	.10
7	Kevin Bass	.05
8	Willie Blair RC	.05
9	Mike Blowers RC	.05
10	Shawn Boskie RC	.05
11	Daryl Boston	.05
12	Dennis Boyd	.05
13	Glenn Braggs	.05
14	Hubie Brooks	.05
15	Tom Brunansky	.05
16	John Burkett RC	.05
17	Casey Candaele	.05
18	John Candelaria	.05
19	Gary Carter	.75
20	Joe Carter	.05
21	Rick Cerone	.05
22	Scott Coolbaugh RC	.05
23	Bobby Cox	.05
24	Mark Davis	.05
25	Storm Davis	.05
26	Edgar Diaz RC	.05
27	Wayne Edwards RC	.05
28	Mark Eichhorn	.05
29	Scott Erickson RC	.05
30	Nick Esasky	.05
31	Cecil Fielder	.05
32	John Franco	.05
33	Travis Fryman RC	.25
34	Bill Gullickson	.05
35	Darryl Hamilton	.05
36	Mike Harkey	.05
37	Bud Harrelson	.05
38	Billy Hatcher	.05
39	Keith Hernandez	.05
40	Joe Hesketh	.05
41	Dave Hollins RC	.05
42	Sam Horn	.05
43	Steve Howard RC	.05
44	Todd Hundley RC	.15
45	Jeff Huson	.05
46	Chris James	.05
47	Stan Javier	.05
48	Dave Justice RC	.75
49	Jeff Kaiser RC	.05
50	Dana Kiecker RC	.05
51	Joe Klink RC	.05
52	Brent Knackert RC	.05
53	Brad Komminsk	.05
54	Mark Langston	.05
55	Tim Layana RC	.05
56	Rick Leach	.05
57	Terry Leach	.05
58	Tim Leary	.05
59	Craig Lefferts	.05
60	Charlie Leibrandt	.05
61	Jim Leyritz RC	.05
62	Fred Lynn	.05
63	Kevin Maas RC	.05
64	Shane Mack	.05
65	Candy Maldonado	.05
66	Fred Manrique	.05
67	Mike Marshall	.05
68	Carmelo Martinez	.05
69	John Marzano	.05
70	Ben McDonald	.05
71	Jack McDowell	.05
72	John McNamara	.05
73	Orlando Mercado	.05
74	Stump Merrill	.05

#	Player	Price
75	Alan Mills	.05
76	Hal Morris	.05
77	Lloyd Moseby	.05
78	Randy Myers	.05
79	Tim Naehring RC	.05
80	Junior Noboa	.05
81	Matt Nokes	.05
82	Pete O'Brien	.05
83	John Olerud RC	.75
84	Greg Olson RC	.05
85	Junior Ortiz	.05
86	Dave Parker	.05
87	Rick Parker RC	.05
88	Bob Patterson	.05
89	Alejandro Pena	.05
90	Tony Pena	.05
91	Pascual Perez	.05
92	Gerald Perry	.05
93	Dan Perry	.05
94	Gary Pettis	.05
95	Tony Phillips	.05
96	Lou Pinella	.05
97	Luis Polonia	.05
98	Jim Presley	.05
99	Scott Radinsky RC	.05
100	Willie Randolph	.05
101	Jeff Reardon	.05
102	Greg Riddoch	.05
103	Jeff Robinson	.05
104	Ron Robinson	.05
105	Kevin Romine	.05
106	Scott Ruskin RC	.05
107	John Russell	.05
108	Bill Sampen RC	.05
109	Juan Samuel	.05
110	Scott Sanderson	.05
111	Jack Savage RC	.05
112	Dave Schmidt	.05
113	Red Schoendienst	.10
114	Terry Shumpert RC	.05
115	Matt Sinatro	.05
116	Don Slaught	.05
117	Bryn Smith	.05
118	Lee Smith	.05
119	Paul Sorrento RC	.05
120	Franklin Stubbs	.05
121	Russ Swan RC	.05
122	Bob Tewksbury	.05
123	Wayne Tolleson	.05
124	John Tudor	.05
125	Randy Veres RC	.05
126	Hector Villanueva RC	.05
127	Mitch Webster	.05
128	Ernie Whitt	.05
129	Frank Wills	.05
130	Dave Winfield	.75
131	Matt Young	.05
132	Checklist	.05

Traded Tiffany

Identical to the regular Topps Traded issue except for the glossy front surface, this special hobby-only boxed set shares the same checklist.

	NM/M
Complete Set (132):	25.00
Common Player:	.15

Traded Hank Aaron Bronze

This 1/4-size metal replica of Aaron's first-ever Topps card was issued to dealers who purchased cases of 1990 Topps Traded sets. Each detail of the 1954 Aaron card is reproduced on the 1-1/4" x 1-3/4" bronze metal mini-card, right down to the stats.

	NM/M
128	Hank Aaron	15.00

Box Panels

This special 16-card set features four cards on four different box-bottom panels. The cards are identical in design to the regular 1990 Topps cards. The cards are designated by letter.

		NM/M
Complete Panel Set (4):		7.00
Complete Singles Set (16):		6.00
Common Panel:		1.00
Common Player:		.10
Panel		2.00
A	Wade Boggs	.60
B	George Brett	.75
C	Andre Dawson	.15
D	Darrell Evans	.10
Panel		1.00
E	Dwight Gooden	.10
F	Rickey Henderson	.45
G	Tom Lasorda	.10
H	Fred Lynn	.10
Panel		1.50
I	Mark McGwire	1.00
J	Dave Parker	.10
K	Jeff Reardon	.10
L	Rick Reuschel	.10
Panel		4.00
M	Jim Rice	.20
N	Cal Ripken, Jr.	1.50
O	Nolan Ryan	1.50
P	Ryne Sandberg	.60

All-Star Glossy Set of 22

One glossy All-Star card was included in each 1990 Topps rack pack. The cards measure 2-1/2" x 3-1/2" and feature a similar style to past glossy All-Star cards. Special cards of All-Star team captains Carl Yastrzemski and Don Drysdale are included in the set.

		NM/M
Complete Set (22):		4.00
Common Player:		.05
1	Tom Lasorda	.05
2	Will Clark	.05
3	Ryne Sandberg	.50
4	Howard Johnson	.05
5	Ozzie Smith	.40
6	Kevin Mitchell	.05
7	Eric Davis	.05
8	Tony Gwynn	.50
9	Benny Santiago	.05
10	Rick Rueschel	.05
11	Don Drysdale	.10
12	Tony LaRussa	.05
13	Mark McGwire	.75
14	Julio Franco	.05
15	Wade Boggs	.50
16	Cal Ripken, Jr.	1.00
17	Bo Jackson	.10
18	Kirby Puckett	.50
19	Ruben Sierra	.05
20	Terry Steinbach	.05
21	Dave Stewart	.05
22	Carl Yastrzemski	.10

All-Star Glossy Set of 60

Sharp color photographs and a clutter-free design are features of the cards in this 60-card send away set. Topps initiated the redemption series in 1983. Six special offer cards, included in Topps baseball wax packs, were necessary to obtain each of the six 10-card sets in the series.

		NM/M
Complete Set (60):		9.00
Common Player:		.10
1	Ryne Sandberg	.75
2	Nolan Ryan	2.00
3	Glenn Davis	.10
4	Dave Stewart	.10
5	Barry Larkin	.10
6	Carney Lansford	.10
7	Darryl Strawberry	.10
8	Steve Sax	.10
9	Carlos Martinez	.10
10	Gary Sheffield	.50
11	Don Mattingly	1.00
12	Mark Grace	.10
13	Bret Saberhagen	.10
14	Mike Scott	.10
15	Robin Yount	.60
16	Ozzie Smith	.75
17	Jeff Ballard	.10
18	Rick Reuschel	.10
19	Greg Briley	.10
20	Ken Griffey Jr.	1.25
21	Kevin Mitchell	.10
22	Wade Boggs	.75
23	Dwight Gooden	.10
24	George Bell	.10
25	Eric Davis	.10
26	Ruben Sierra	.10
27	Roberto Alomar	.20
28	Gary Gaetti	.10
29	Gregg Olson	.10
30	Tom Gordon	.10
31	Jose Canseco	.45
32	Pedro Guerrero	.10
33	Joe Carter	.10
34	Mike Scioscia	.10
35	Julio Franco	.10
36	Joe Magrane	.10
37	Rickey Henderson	.60
38	Tim Raines	.10
39	Jerome Walton	.10
40	Bob Geren	.10
41	Andre Dawson	.10
42	Mark McGwire	1.50
43	Howard Johnson	.10
44	Bo Jackson	.20
45	Shawon Dunston	.10
46	Carlton Fisk	.60
47	Mitch Williams	.10
48	Kirby Puckett	.75
49	Craig Worthington	.10
50	Jim Abbott	.75
51	Cal Ripken, Jr.	2.00
52	Will Clark	.75
53	Dennis Eckersley	.55
54	Craig Biggio	.10
55	Fred McGriff	.75
56	Tony Gwynn	.75
57	Mickey Tettleton	.10
58	Mark Davis	.10
59	Omar Vizquel	.10
60	Gregg Jefferies	.10

Glossy Rookies

While the size of the annual glossy rookies set increased to 33 cards from previous years' issues of 22, the format remained identical in 1990. Above the player photo is a colored banner with "1989 Rookies." The player's name appears in red in a yellow bar beneath the photo. Backs are printed in red and blue and contain a shield design with the notation, "1989 Rookies Commemorative Set." The player's name, position and team are listed below, along with a card number. Cards are numbered alphabetically in the set. The glossy rookies were found one per pack in jumbo (100-card) cello packs.

		NM/M
Complete Set (33):		6.00
Common Player:		.10
1	Jim Abbott	.50
2	Joey Belle	.50
3	Andy Benes	.10
4	Greg Briley	.10
5	Kevin Brown	.10
6	Mark Carreon	.10
7	Mike Devereaux	.10
8	Junior Felix	.10
9	Bob Geren	.10
10	Tom Gordon	.10
11	Ken Griffey Jr.	5.00
12	Pete Harnisch	.10
13	Greg W. Harris	.10
14	Greg Hibbard	.10
15	Ken Hill	.10
16	Gregg Jefferies	.10
17	Jeff King	.10
18	Derek Lilliquist	.10
19	Carlos Martinez	.10
20	Ramon Martinez	.10
21	Bob Milacki	.10
22	Gregg Olson	.10
23	Donn Pall	.10
24	Kenny Rogers	.10
25	Gary Sheffield	1.50
26	Dwight Smith	.10
27	Billy Spiers	.10
28	Omar Vizquel	.10
29	Jerome Walton	.10
30	Dave West	.10
31	John Wetteland	.10
32	Steve Wilson	.10
33	Craig Worthington	.10

Glossy Rookies Foil-Test Cards

To test the use of metallic-foil highlights which it would debut on its 1991 Stadium Club and Desert Shield cards, Topps made a test run using as base cards the 33-piece "1989 Rookies Commemorative Set." The test consists of a 2-1/4" x 1/4" metallic strip with a "topps" logotype punched out of the center. Cards can be found with the strip in many different locations horizontally on the cards' fronts, and in many colors including silver, gold, red, green, blue and purple. Color of foil does not affect values, though a complete set in matching color might command a premium.

		NM/M
Complete Set (33):		40.00
Common Player:		1.00
1	Jim Abbott	1.00
2	Joey Belle	2.00
3	Andy Benes	1.00
4	Greg Briley	1.00
5	Kevin Brown	1.00
6	Mark Carreon	1.00
7	Mike Devereaux	1.00
8	Junior Felix	1.00
9	Bob Geren	1.00
10	Tom Gordon	1.00
11	Ken Griffey Jr.	20.00
12	Pete Harnisch	1.00
13	Greg W. Harris	1.00
14	Greg Hibbard	1.00
15	Ken Hill	1.00
16	Gregg Jefferies	1.00
17	Jeff King	1.00
18	Derek Lilliquist	1.00
19	Carlos Martinez	1.00
20	Ramon Martinez	1.00
21	Bob Milacki	1.00
22	Gregg Olson	1.00
23	Donn Pall	1.00
24	Kenny Rogers	1.00
25	Gary Sheffield	5.00
26	Dwight Smith	1.00
27	Billy Spiers	1.00
28	Omar Vizquel	1.00
29	Jerome Walton	1.00
30	Dave West	1.00
31	John Wetteland	1.00
32	Steve Wilson	1.00
33	Craig Worthington	1.00

Award Winners Commemorative Sheet

Six of 1989's top award winners are pictured in the style of 1990 Topps baseball cards on this sheet issued with blister packed sets of Topps baseball stickers. The cards are blank-backed and use photos which are different from those found on the same players' regular 1990 cards. Each player's award is noted in the panel beneath his name. The sheet measures 8-3/4" x 8-1/8" with individual cards measuring the standard 2-1/2" x 3-1/2".

		NM/M
Complete Set, Sheet:		3.00
Complete Set, Singles (6):		2.00
Common Player:		.10
(1)	Mark Davis (N.L. Cy Young)	.10
(2)	Kevin Mitchell (N.L. MVP)	.10
(3)	Gregg Olson (A.L. R.O.Y.)	.10
(4)	Bret Saberhagen (A.L. Cy Young)	.10
(5)	Jerome Walton (N.L. R.O.Y.)	.10
(6)	Robin Yount (A.L. MVP)	1.50

Batting Leaders

Once again produced as an exclusive insert in jumbo blister packs for K-Mart stores, the 1990 career batting leaders cards are similar in concept and design to the previous year's issue; in fact, some of the same player photos were used. The 22 cards in the set are arranged roughly in order of the players' standings in lifetime batting average. Cards fronts are bordered in bright green; backs are printed in red, white and dark green.

		NM/M
Complete Set (22):		110.00
Common Player:		1.50
1	Wade Boggs	12.50
2	Tony Gwynn	15.00
3	Kirby Puckett	15.00
4	Don Mattingly	20.00
5	George Brett	20.00
6	Pedro Guerrero	1.50
7	Tim Raines	1.50
8	Paul Molitor	12.50
9	Jim Rice	3.00
10	Keith Hernandez	1.50
11	Julio Franco	1.50
12	Carney Lansford	1.50
13	Dave Parker	1.50
14	Willie McGee	1.50
15	Robin Yount	12.50
16	Tony Fernandez	1.50
17	Eddie Murray	12.50
18	Johnny Ray	1.50
19	Lonnie Smith	1.50
20	Phil Bradley	1.50
21	Rickey Henderson	12.50
22	Kent Hrbek	1.50

Big Baseball

For the third consecutive year, Topps issued a 330-card set of oversized cards (2-5/8" x 3-3/4") in three 110-card series. The cards are reminiscent of Topps cards from the mid-1950s, featuring players in portrait and action shots. As in previous years, the cards are printed on white front stock with a glossy front finish. Backs include 1989 and career hitting, fielding and pitching stats and a player cartoon. Series 3 cards (#221-330) are believed to have been somewhat scarcer than the first two series.

		NM/M
Complete Set (330):		15.00
Common Player:		.05
Wax Pack (8):		.50
Wax Box, Series 1-2 (36):		7.50
Wax Box, Series 3 (36):		20.00
1	Dwight Evans	.05
2	Kirby Puckett	.60
3	Kevin Gross	.05
4	Ron Hassey	.05
5	Lloyd McClendon	.05
6	Bo Jackson	.10
7	Lonnie Smith	.05
8	Alvaro Espinoza	.05
9	Roberto Alomar	.15
10	Glenn Braggs	.05
11	David Cone	.05
12	Claudell Washington	.05
13	Pedro Guerrero	.05
14	Todd Benzinger	.05
15	Jeff Russell	.05
16	Terry Kennedy	.05
17	Kelly Gruber	.05
18	Alfredo Griffin	.05
19	Mark Grace	.05
20	Dave Winfield	.50
21	Bret Saberhagen	.05
22	Roger Clemens	.65
23	Bob Walk	.05
24	Dave Magadan	.05
25	Spike Owen	.05
26	Jody Davis	.05
27	Kent Merek	.05
28	Mark McGwire	1.00
29	Eddie Murray	.50
30	Paul O'Neill	.05
31	Jose DeLeon	.05
32	Steve Lyons	.05
33	Dan Plesac	.05
34	Jack Howell	.05
35	Greg Briley	.05
36	Andy Hawkins	.05
37	Cecil Espy	.05
38	Rick Sutcliffe	.05
39	Jack Clark	.05
40	Dale Murphy	.15
41	Mike Henneman	.05
42	Rick Honeycutt	.05
43	Willie Randolph	.05
44	Marty Barrett	.05
45	Willie Wilson	.05
46	Wallace Johnson	.05
47	Greg Brock	.05
48	Tom Browning	.05
49	Gerald Young	.05
50	Dennis Eckersley	.40
51	Scott Garrelts	.05
52	Gary Redus	.05
53	Al Newman	.05
54	Darryl Boston	.05
55	Ron Oester	.05
56	Danny Tartabull	.05
57	Gregg Jefferies	.05
58	Tom Foley	.05
59	Robin Yount	.50
60	Pat Borders	.05
61	Mike Greenwell	.05
62	Shawon Dunston	.05
63	Steve Buechele	.05
64	Dave Stewart	.05
65	Jose Oquendo	.05
66	Ron Gant	.05
67	Mike Scioscia	.05
68	Randy Velarde	.05
69	Charlie Hayes	.05
70	Tim Wallach	.05
71	Eric Show	.05
72	Eric Davis	.05
73	Mike Gallego	.05
74	Rob Deer	.05
75	Ryne Sandberg	.60
76	Kevin Seitzer	.05
77	Wade Boggs	.60
78	Greg Gagne	.05
79	John Smiley	.05
80	Ivan Calderon	.05
81	Pete Incaviglia	.05
82	Orel Hershiser	.05
83	Carney Lansford	.05
84	Mike Fitzgerald	.05
85	Don Mattingly	.65
86	Chet Lemon	.05
87	Rolando Roomes	.05
88	Bill Spiers	.05
89	Pat Tabler	.05
90	Danny Heep	.05
91	Andre Dawson	.25
92	Randy Bush	.05
93	Tony Gwynn	.60
94	Tom Brunansky	.05
95	Johnny Ray	.05
96	Matt Williams	.05
97	Barry Lyons	.05
98	Jeff Hamilton	.05
99	Tom Glavine	.20
100	Ken Griffey Sr.	.05
101	Tom Henke	.05
102	Dave Righetti	.05
103	Paul Molitor	.50
104	Mike LaValliere	.05
105	Frank White	.05
106	Bob Welch	.05
107	Ellis Burks	.05
108	Andres Galarraga	.05
109	Mitch Williams	.05
110	Checklist	.05
111	Craig Biggio	.05
112	Dave Steib	.05
113	Ron Darling	.05
114	Bert Blyleven	.05
115	Dickie Thon	.05
116	Carlos Martinez	.05
117	Jeff King	.05
118	Terry Steinbach	.05
119	Frank Tanana	.05
120	Mark Lemke	.05
121	Chris Sabo	.05
122	Glenn Davis	.05
123	Mel Hall	.05
124	Jim Gantner	.05
125	Benito Santiago	.05
126	Milt Thompson	.05
127	Rafael Palmeiro	.40
128	Barry Bonds	1.50
129	Mike Bielecki	.05
130	Lou Whitaker	.05
131	Bob Ojeda	.05
132	Dion James	.05
133	Denny Martinez	.05
134	Fred McGriff	.05
135	Terry Pendleton	.05
136	Pat Combs	.05
137	Kevin Mitchell	.05
138	Marquis Grissom	.05
139	Chris Bosio	.05
140	Omar Vizquel	.05
141	Steve Sax	.05
142	Nelson Liriano	.05
143	Kevin Elster	.05
144	Dan Pasqua	.05
145	Dave Smith	.05
146	Craig Worthington	.05
147	Dan Gladden	.05
148	Oddibe McDowell	.05
149	Bip Roberts	.05
150	Randy Ready	.05
151	Dwight Smith	.05
152	Ed Whitson	.05
153	George Bell	.05
154	Tim Raines	.05
155	Sid Fernandez	.05
156	Henry Cotto	.05
157	Harold Baines	.05
158	Willie McGee	.05
159	Bill Doran	.05
160	Steve Balboni	.05
161	Pete Smith	.05
162	Frank Viola	.05
163	Gary Sheffield	.35
164	Bill Landrum	.05
165	Tony Fernandez	.05
166	Mike Heath	.05
167	Jody Reed	.05
168	Wally Joyner	.05
169	Robby Thompson	.05
170	Ken Caminiti	.05
171	Nolan Ryan	1.50
172	Ricky Jordan	.05
173	Lance Blankenship	.05
174	Dwight Gooden	.05
175	Ruben Sierra	.05
176	Carlton Fisk	.50
177	Garry Templeton	.05
178	Mike Devereaux	.05

179	Mookie Wilson	.05
180	Jeff Blauser	.05
181	Scott Bradley	.05
182	Luis Salazar	.05
183	Rafael Ramirez	.05
184	Vince Coleman	.05
185	Doug Drabek	.05
186	Darryl Strawberry	.05
187	Tim Burke	.05
188	Jesse Barfield	.05
189	Barry Larkin	.05
190	Alan Trammell	.05
191	Steve Lake	.05
192	Derek Lilliquist	.05
193	Don Robinson	.05
194	Kevin McReynolds	.05
195	Melido Perez	.05
196	Jose Lind	.05
197	Eric Anthony	.05
198	B.J. Surhoff	.05
199	John Olerud	.05
200	Mike Moore	.05
201	Mark Gubicza	.05
202	Phil Bradley	.05
203	Ozzie Smith	.60
204	Greg Maddux	.60
205	Julio Franco	.05
206	Tom Herr	.05
207	Scott Fletcher	.05
208	Bobby Bonilla	.05
209	Bob Geren	.05
210	Junior Felix	.05
211	Dick Schofield	.05
212	Jim Deshaies	.05
213	Jose Uribe	.05
214	John Kruk	.05
215	Ozzie Guillen	.05
216	Howard Johnson	.05
217	Andy Van Slyke	.05
218	Tim Laudner	.05
219	Manny Lee	.05
220	Checklist	.05
221	Cory Snyder	.05
222	Billy Hatcher	.05
223	Bud Black	.05
224	Will Clark	.05
225	Kevin Tapani	.05
226	Mike Pagliarulo	.05
227	Dave Parker	.05
228	Ben McDonald	.05
229	Carlos Baerga	.05
230	Roger McDowell	.05
231	Delino DeShields	.05
232	Mark Langston	.05
233	Wally Backman	.05
234	Jim Eisenreich	.05
235	Mike Schooler	.05
236	Kevin Bass	.05
237	John Farrell	.05
238	Kal Daniels	.05
239	Tony Phillips	.05
240	Todd Stottlemyre	.05
241	Greg Olson	.05
242	Charlie Hough	.05
243	Mariano Duncan	.05
244	Billy Ripken	.05
245	Joe Carter	.05
246	Tim Belcher	.05
247	Roberto Kelly	.05
248	Candy Maldonado	.05
249	Mike Scott	.05
250	Ken Griffey Jr.	.75
251	Nick Esasky	.05
252	Tom Gordon	.05
253	John Tudor	.05
254	Gary Gaetti	.05
255	Neal Heaton	.05
256	Jerry Browne	.05
257	Jose Rijo	.05
258	Mike Boddicker	.05
259	Brett Butler	.05
260	Andy Benes	.05
261	Kevin Brown	.05
262	Hubie Brooks	.05
263	Randy Milligan	.05
264	John Franco	.05
265	Sandy Alomar	.05
266	Dave Valle	.05
267	Jerome Walton	.05
268	Bob Boone	.05
269	Ken Howell	.05
270	Jose Canseco	.30
271	Joe Magrane	.05
272	Brian DuBois	.05
273	Carlos Quintana	.05
274	Lance Johnson	.05
275	Steve Bedrosian	.05
276	Brook Jacoby	.05
277	Fred Lynn	.05
278	Jeff Ballard	.05
279	Otis Nixon	.05
280	Chili Davis	.05
281	Joe Oliver	.05
282	Brian Holman	.05
283	Juan Samuel	.05
284	Rick Aguilera	.05
285	Jeff Reardon	.05
286	Sammy Sosa	3.00
287	Carmelo Martinez	.05
288	Greg Swindell	.05
289	Erik Hanson	.05
290	Tony Pena	.05
291	Pascual Perez	.05
292	Rickey Henderson	.50
293	Kurt Stillwell	.05
294	Todd Zeile	.05
295	Bobby Thigpen	.05
296	Larry Walker	.05

297	Rob Murphy	.05
298	Mitch Webster	.05
299	Devon White	.05
300	Len Dykstra	.05
301	Keith Hernandez	.05
302	Gene Larkin	.05
303	Jeffrey Leonard	.05
304	Jim Presley	.05
305	Lloyd Moseby	.05
306	John Smoltz	.05
307	Sam Horn	.05
308	Greg Litton	.05
309	Dave Henderson	.05
310	Mark McLemore	.05
311	Gary Pettis	.05
312	Mark Davis	.05
313	Cecil Fielder	.05
314	Jack Armstrong	.05
315	Alvin Davis	.05
316	Doug Jones	.05
317	Eric Yelding	.05
318	Joe Orsulak	.05
319	Chuck Finley	.05
320	Glenn Wilson	.05
321	Harold Reynolds	.05
322	Teddy Higuera	.05
323	Lance Parrish	.05
324	Bruce Hurst	.05
325	Dave West	.05
326	Kirk Gibson	.05
327	Cal Ripken, Jr.	1.50
328	Rick Reuschel	.05
329	Jim Abbott	.05
330	Checklist	.05

George Bush

GEORGE BUSH

As a favor to President George Bush, Topps produced a special run of 100 cards in its 1990 design featuring a photo of the president in his Yale University baseball uniform. At least a few of the cards reportedly were inadvertently included in regular Topps packages and made their way into the hobby.

	NM/M
USA1 George Bush (7/05 auction)	2,000

Coins

Sixty top stars and promising rookies are featured in this fourth annual coin set. Fronts of the 1-1/2" diameter coins feature a portrait photo with a symbolic infield. Player name and team appear below. Most coins feature natural aluminum coloring on the rolled edges and on the back. Special coins of major award winners have different colors in the background and edges. Backs feature a coin number, minimal biographical data and a previous season career summary. Coins were sold three per pack which included an offer card for a coin holder and Topps magazine subscription offer.

	NM/M
Factory Set (60):	15.00
Complete Set (60):	7.50
Common Player:	.15
Wax Pack (3):	.75

Wax Box (36):		9.00
1	Robin Yount	.50
2	Bret Saberhagen	.15
3	Gregg Olson	.15
4	Kirby Puckett	.65
5	George Bell	.15
6	Wade Boggs	.65
7	Jerry Browne	.15
8	Ellis Burks	.15
9	Ivan Calderon	.15
10	Tom Candiotti	.15
11	Alvin Davis	.15
12	Chili Davis	.15
13	Chuck Finley	.15
14	Gary Gaetti	.15
15	Tom Gordon	.15
16	Ken Griffey Jr.	.75
17	Rickey Henderson	.50
18	Kent Hrbek	.15
19	Bo Jackson	.20
20	Carlos Martinez	.15
21	Don Mattingly	.75
22	Fred McGriff	.15
23	Paul Molitor	.15
24	Cal Ripken, Jr.	1.00
25	Nolan Ryan	1.00
26	Steve Sax	.15
27	Gary Sheffield	.30
28	Ruben Sierra	.15
29	Dave Stewart	.15
30	Mickey Tettleton	.15
31	Alan Trammell	.15
32	Lou Whitaker	.15
33	Kevin Mitchell	.15
34	Mark Davis	.15
35	Jerome Walton	.15
36	Tony Gwynn	.65
37	Roberto Alomar	.25
38	Tim Belcher	.15
39	Craig Biggio	.15
40	Barry Bonds	1.00
41	Bobby Bonilla	.15
42	Joe Carter	.15
43	Will Clark	.15
44	Eric Davis	.15
45	Glenn Davis	.15
46	Sid Fernandez	.15
47	Pedro Guerrero	.15
48	Von Hayes	.15
49	Tom Herr	.15
50	Howard Johnson	.15
51	Barry Larkin	.15
52	Joe Magrane	.15
53	Dale Murphy	.25
54	Tim Raines	.15
55	Willie Randolph	.15
56	Ryne Sandberg	.65
57	Dwight Smith	.15
58	Lonnie Smith	.15
59	Robby Thompson	.15
60	Tim Wallach	.15

Double Headers

WHITE SOX

CARLTON FISK

For a second (and final) year, Topps produced an issue of mini cards encased in plastic stands and marketed as Double Headers. Each piece features a 1-5/8" x 2-1/4" reproduction of the player's Topps rookie card, backed by a reproduction of his card from the regular 1990 Topps set. The size of the DH set was increased from 24 in 1989 to 72 for 1990. The novelties were sold for 50 cents apiece. The unnumbered cards are checklisted here alphabetically.

	NM/M
Complete Set (72):	25.00
Common Player:	.25
Wax Pack (1):	.50
Wax Box (36):	15.00
(1) Jim Abbott	.25
(2) Jeff Ballard	.25
(3) George Bell	.25
(4) Wade Boggs	1.00
(5) Barry Bonds	2.50
(6) Bobby Bonilla	.25
(7) Ellis Burks	.25
(8) Jose Canseco	.50
(9) Joe Carter	.25
(10) Will Clark	.25
(11) Roger Clemens	1.25
(12) Vince Coleman	.25

(13)	Alvin Davis	.25
(14)	Eric Davis	.25
(15)	Glenn Davis	.25
(16)	Mark Davis	.25
(17)	Andre Dawson	.40
(18)	Shawon Dunston	.25
(19)	Dennis Eckersley	.60
(20)	Sid Fernandez	.25
(21)	Tony Fernandez	.25
(22)	Chuck Finley	.25
(23)	Carlton Fisk	.75
(24)	Julio Franco	.25
(25)	Gary Gaetti	.25
(26)	Dwight Gooden	.25
(27)	Mark Grace	.25
(28)	Mike Greenwell	.25
(29)	Ken Griffey Jr.	1.50
(30)	Pedro Guerrero	.25
(31)	Tony Gwynn	1.00
(32)	Von Hayes	.25
(33)	Rickey Henderson	.75
(34)	Orel Hershiser	.25
(35)	Bo Jackson	.25
(36)	Gregg Jefferies	.25
(37)	Howard Johnson	.25
(38)	Ricky Jordan	.25
(39)	Carney Lansford	.25
(40)	Barry Larkin	.25
(41)	Greg Maddux	1.00
(42)	Joe Magrane	.25
(43)	Don Mattingly	1.25
(44)	Fred McGriff	.25
(45)	Mark McGwire	2.00
(46)	Kevin McReynolds	.25
(47)	Kevin Mitchell	.25
(48)	Gregg Olson	.25
(49)	Kirby Puckett	1.00
(50)	Tim Raines	.25
(51)	Harold Reynolds	.25
(52)	Cal Ripken, Jr.	2.50
(53)	Nolan Ryan	2.50
(54)	Bret Saberhagen	.25
(55)	Ryne Sandberg	1.00
(56)	Benito Santiago	.25
(57)	Steve Sax	.25
(58)	Mike Scioscia	.25
(59)	Mike Scott	.25
(60)	Ruben Sierra	.25
(61)	Lonnie Smith	.25
(62)	Ozzie Smith	1.00
(63)	Dave Stewart	.25
(64)	Darryl Strawberry	.25
(65)	Greg Swindell	.25
(66)	Alan Trammell	.25
(67)	Frank Viola	.25
(68)	Tim Wallach	.25
(69)	Jerome Walton	.25
(70)	Lou Whitaker	.25
(71)	Mitch Williams	.25
(72)	Robin Yount	.75

Experimental Mylar Stickers

PADRES

JOE CARTER

Testing the concept of refractive printing, with stars in the background of these stickers, Topps produced a trial run of Mylar stickers using fronts from its 1990 Traded card set. Fronts of the 2-1/2" x 3-1/2" stickers are printed on metallic foil. Backs are blank.

	NM/M
Complete Set (6):	400.00
Common Player:	60.00
(1) Joe Carter	60.00
(2) Shane Mack	60.00
(3) Alan Mills	60.00
(4) Alejandro Pena	60.00
(5) Gerald Perry	60.00
(6) Dave Winfield	175.00

Gallery of Champions

The 1990 Topps 1/4-size metal baseball mini-cards were issued only as complete sets in a special display case. As with earlier editions, the 1-1/4" x 1-3/4" ingots do a creditable job of reproducing the players' 1990 Topps cards, right down to the tiny stats on the back. Players in

BLUE JAYS

FRED McGRIFF

the set represent the winners of major awards and statistical leaders from the previous season. A pewter Nolan Ryan 1/4-size card was issued as a sales incentive for dealers purchasing the Gallery of Champions sets.

	NM/M
Complete Aluminum Set (12):	15.00
Complete Bronze Set (12):	50.00
Complete Silver Set (12):	100.00
(1a) Mark Davis/Aluminum	1.00
(1b) Mark Davis/Bronze	2.50
(1s) Mark Davis/Silver	5.00
(2a) Jose DeLeon/ Aluminum	1.00
(2b) Jose DeLeon/Bronze	2.50
(2s) Jose DeLeon/Silver	5.00
(3a) Tony Gwynn/ Aluminum	3.00
(3b) Tony Gwynn/Bronze	7.50
(3s) Tony Gwynn/Silver	20.00
(4a) Fred McGriff/ Aluminum	1.00
(4b) Fred McGriff/Bronze	2.50
(4s) Fred McGriff/Silver	5.00
(5a) Kevin Mitchell/ Aluminum	1.00
(5b) Kevin Mitchell/Bronze	2.50
(5s) Kevin Mitchell/Silver	5.00
(6a) Gregg Olson/ Aluminum	1.00
(6b) Gregg Olson/Bronze	2.50
(6s) Gregg Olson/Silver	5.00
(7a) Kirby Puckett/ Aluminum	3.00
(7b) Kirby Puckett/Bronze	7.50
(7s) Kirby Puckett/Silver	20.00
(8a) Jeff Russell/Aluminum	1.00
(8b) Jeff Russell/Bronze	2.50
(8s) Jeff Russell/Silver	5.00
(9a) Nolan Ryan/ Aluminum	10.00
(9b) Nolan Ryan/Bronze	20.00
(9s) Nolan Ryan/Silver	40.00
(9p) Nolan Ryan/Pewter	35.00
(10a) Bret Saberhagen/ Aluminum	1.00
(10b) Bret Saberhagen/ Bronze	2.50
(10s) Bret Saberhagen/Silver	5.00
(11a) Jerome Walton/ Aluminum	1.00
(11b) Jerome Walton/Bronze	2.50
(11s) Jerome Walton/Silver	5.00
(12a) Robin Yount/ Aluminum	2.00
(12b) Robin Yount/Bronze	5.00
(12s) Robin Yount/Silver	15.00

Golden Spikes Award

Chicago

AUGUST 2, 1990

ALEX FERNANDEZ

This one-card "set" was given out at the United States Baseball Federation awards luncheon in New York City on November 14, 1990, honoring Alex Fernandez as the outstanding amateur baseball player of the year and winner of the Golden Spikes Award. The rough borders found on

many of these cards indicates they were cut from the press sheet by hand. Production was reported as 600 cards.

	NM/M
Alex Fernandez	85.00

Heads Up!

Following up a much rarer test issue of the previous year, the Heads Up! Baseball Stars of 1990 was a 24-piece set which received much wider distribution, but proved unpopular with collectors. On heavy cardboard, die-cut to approximately 5" x 6", these novelties featured only a head-and-cap photo of the player. Backs have the player's name and team, along with an adhesive strip and plastic suction cup which could be used to "hang" the player.

	NM/M
Complete Set (24):	10.00
Common Player:	.50
Wax Pack (1):	.75
Wax Box (24):	10.00
1 Tony Gwynn	2.00
2 Will Clark	.50
3 Dwight Gooden	.50
4 Dennis Eckersley	1.25
5 Ken Griffey Jr.	3.00
6 Craig Biggio	.50
7 Bret Saberhagen	.50
8 Bo Jackson	.75
9 Ryne Sandberg	2.00
10 Gregg Olson	.50
11 John Franco	.50
12 Rafael Palmeiro	1.25
13 Gary Sheffield	1.00
14 Mark McGwire	4.00
15 Kevin Mitchell	.50
16 Jim Abbott	.50
17 Harold Reynolds	.50
18 Jose Canseco	1.00
19 Don Mattingly	2.50
20 Kirby Puckett	2.00
21 Tom Gordon	.50
22 Craig Worthington	.50
23 Dwight Smith	.50
24 Jerome Walton	.50

Magazine

ROYCE

GIANTS

Beginning with its debut issue dated Winter, 1990, Topps Magazine included sportscards in each quarterly issue. Generally printed on perforated panels which could be easily separated from the magazine and the other cards, six to eight cards were included in most issues. Most of the cards were original designs, but some depicted then-current players on Topps designs from previous years. For the duration of their issue, the cards were numbered consecutively with a "TM" prefix.

	NM/M
Complete Set (112):	50.00

Common Player: .25
1 Dave Staton .25
2 Dan Peltier .25
3 Ken Griffey Jr. 2.00
4 Ruben Sierra .25
5 Bret Saberhagen .25
6 Jerome Walton .25
7 Kevin Mitchell .25
8 Mike Scott .25
9 Bo Jackson .30
10 Nolan Ryan 3.00
11 Will Clark .25
12 Robin Yount .75
13 Joe Morgan .75
14 Jim Palmer .75
15 Ben McDonald .25
16 John Olerud .25
17 Don Mattingly 1.50
18 Eric Davis, Barry Larkin, Chris Sabo .25
19 Jim Abbott .25
20 Sandy Alomar Jr. .25
21 Jose Canseco .50
22 Delino DeShields .25
23 Wade Boggs 1.00
24 Kirby Puckett 1.00
25 Ryne Sandberg 1.00
26 Roger Clemens 1.25
27 Ken Griffey Jr.,
   Ken Griffey Sr. 1.00
28 Cecil Fielder .25
29 Steve Avery .25
30 Rickey Henderson .75
31 Kevin Maas .25
32 Len Dykstra .25
33 Darryl Strawberry .25
34 Mark McGwire 2.25
35 Matt Williams .25
36 David Justice .25
37 Cincinnati Reds .25
38 Todd Van Poppel .25
39 Jose Offerman .25
40 Alex Fernandez .25
41 Carlton Fisk .75
42 Barry Bonds 3.00
43 Bobby Bonilla .25
44 Bob Welch .25
45 Mo Vaughn .25
46 Tino Martinez .25
47 D.J. Dozier .25
48 Frank Thomas .75
49 Cal Ripken Jr.
   ('75 Topps style) 3.00
50 Dave Winfield
   ('75 Topps style) .75
51 Dwight Gooden
   ('75 Topps style) .25
52 Bo Jackson
   ('75 Topps style) .30
53 Kirk Dressendorfer .25
54 Gary Scott .25
55 Steve Decker .25
56 Ray Lankford .25
57 Ozzie Smith
   ('86 Topps style) 1.00
58 Joe Carter
   ('86 Topps style) .25
59 Dave Henderson
   ('86 Topps style) .25
60 Tony Gwynn
   ('86 Topps style) 1.00
61 Jeff Bagwell .75
62 Scott Erickson .25
63 Pat Kelly .25
64 Orlando Merced .40
65 Andre Dawson .25
66 Reggie Sanders .25
67 Phil Plantier .25
68 Paul Molitor .75
69 Terry Pendleton .25
70 Julio Franco .25
71 Lee Smith .25
72 '91 Minnesota Twins .25
73 Royce Clayton .25
74 Tom Glavine .45
75 Roger Salkeld .25
76 Robin Ventura .25
77 John Goodman
   (As Babe Ruth.) .25
78 Jack Morris .25
79 Brien Taylor .25
80 Howard Johnson .25
81 Barry Larkin .25
82 Deion Sanders .30
83 Mike Mussina .60
84 Juan Gonzalez .50
85 Roberto Alomar .50
86 Fred McGriff .25
87 Doug Drabek .25
88 George Brett 1.25
89 Otis Nixon .25
90 Brady Anderson .25
91 Gary Sheffield .50
92 Dave Fleming .25
93 Jeff Reardon .25
94 Mark McGwire 2.25
95 Larry Walker .25
96 John Kruk .25
97 Carlos Baerga .25
98 Pat Listach .25
99 '92 Toronto Blue Jays .25
100 Eric Karros .25
101 Bret Boone .25
102 Al Martin .25
103 Wil Cordero .25
104 Tim Salmon .25
105 Danny Tartabull .25
106 J.T. Snow .25

107 Mike Piazza 1.50
108 Frank Viola .25
109 Nolan Ryan/Mets 2.25
110 Nolan Ryan/Angels 2.25
111 Nolan Ryan/Astros 2.25
112 Nolan Ryan/Rangers 2.25

Mini League Leaders

The last in a five-year string of mini cards, the 1990 league leaders' set offers players who were in the top five in major batting and pitching stats during the 1989 season. Fronts of the 2-1/8" x 3" cards mimic the regular Topps' design for 1990; featuring an action photo with multi-colored borders. Backs offer a round player portrait photo and information about the statistical achievement, all printed in full color. Cards are numbered alphabetically within teams. The 1990 minis are considerably scarcer than the previous years' offerings.

NM/M
Complete Set (88): 5.00
Common Player: .05
1 Jeff Ballard .05
2 Phil Bradley .05
3 Wade Boggs .65
4 Roger Clemens .75
5 Nick Esasky .05
6 Jody Reed .05
7 Bert Blyleven .05
8 Chuck Finley .05
9 Kirk McCaskill .05
10 Devon White .05
11 Ivan Calderon .05
12 Bobby Thigpen .05
13 Joe Carter .05
14 Gary Pettis .05
15 Tom Gordon .05
16 Bo Jackson .10
17 Bret Saberhagen .05
18 Kevin Seitzer .05
19 Chris Bosio .05
20 Paul Molitor .50
21 Dan Plesac .05
22 Robin Yount .50
23 Kirby Puckett .65
24 Don Mattingly .75
25 Steve Sax .05
26 Storm Davis .05
27 Dennis Eckersley .40
28 Rickey Henderson .50
29 Carney Lansford .05
30 Mark McGwire 1.00
31 Mike Moore .05
32 Dave Stewart .05
33 Alvin Davis .05
34 Harold Reynolds .05
35 Mike Schooler .05
36 Cecil Espy .05
37 Julio Franco .05
38 Jeff Russell .05
39 Nolan Ryan 1.50
40 Ruben Sierra .05
41 George Bell .05
42 Tony Fernandez .05
43 Fred McGriff .05
44 Dave Steib .05
45 Checklist .05
46 Lonnie Smith .05
47 John Smoltz .05
48 Mike Bielecki .05
49 Mark Grace .05
50 Greg Maddux .65
51 Ryne Sandberg .65
52 Mitch Williams .05
53 Eric Davis .05
54 John Franco .05
55 Glenn Davis .05
56 Mike Scott .05
57 Tim Belcher .05
58 Orel Hershiser .05
59 Jay Howell .05
60 Eddie Murray .50
61 Tim Burke .05
62 Mark Langston .05
63 Tim Raines .05

64 Tim Wallach .05
65 David Cone .05
66 Sid Fernandez .05
67 Howard Johnson .05
68 Juan Samuel .05
69 Von Hayes .05
70 Barry Bonds 1.50
71 Bobby Bonilla .05
72 Andy Van Slyke .05
73 Vince Coleman .05
74 Jose DeLeon .05
75 Pedro Guerrero .05
76 Joe Magrane .05
77 Roberto Alomar .20
78 Jack Clark .05
79 Mark Davis .05
80 Tony Gwynn .65
81 Bruce Hurst .05
82 Eddie Whitson .05
83 Brett Butler .05
84 Will Clark .05
85 Scott Garrelts .05
86 Kevin Mitchell .05
87 Rick Reuschel .05
88 Robby Thompson .05

Nolan Ryan Bronze

This full-size bronze reproduction of Ryan's 1990 Topps card was given to dealers who made early orders for Topps' 1991 "Tiffany" sets. A 2,500 piece limit was announced.

NM/M
Nolan Ryan 50.00

Senior League

Topps was among several companies to produce a Senior League set in 1990. The set includes 132 cards and was sold as a boxed set. The card fronts have the Senior Baseball and Topps logo on top and the player's name and team logo on the bottom, with a woodgrain-like border surrounding the front photo. The backs of the card include traditional biographical information, plus career major league statistics, career ML bests and stats from any Senior League experience.

NM/M
Complete Set (132): 5.00
Common Player: .05
1 George Foster .15
2 Dwight Lowry .05
3 Bob Jones .05
4 Clete Boyer .05
5 Rafael Landestoy .05
6 Bob Shirley .05
7 Ivan Murrell .05
8 Jerry White .05
9 Steve Henderson .05
10 Marty Castillo .05
11 Bruce Kison .05
12 George Hendrick .05
13 Bernie Carbo .05
14 Jerry Martin .05
15 Al Hrabosky .05
16 Luis Gomez .05
17 Dick Drago .05
18 Bobby Ramos .05
19 Joe Pittman .05
20 Ike Blessitt .05
21 Bill Travers .05
22 Dick Williams .05
23 Randy Lerch .05
24 Tom Spencer .05
25 Graig Nettles .05
26 Jim Gideon .05
27 Al Bumbry .05
28 Tom Murphy .05
29 Rodney Scott .05
30 Alan Bannister .05
31 John D'Acquisto .05
32 Bert Campaneris .05
33 Bill Lee .05
34 Jerry Grote .05

35 Ken Reitz .05
36 Al Oliver .15
37 Tim Stoddard .05
38 Lenny Randle .05
39 Rick Manning .05
40 Bobby Bonds .15
41 Rick Wise .05
42 Sal Butera .05
43 Ed Figueroa .05
44 Ron Washington .05
45 Elias Sosa .05
46 Dan Driessen .05
47 Wayne Nordhagen .05
48 Vida Blue .15
49 Butch Hobson .05
50 Randy Bass .05
51 Paul Mirabella .05
52 Steve Kemp .05
53 Kim Allen .05
54 Stan Cliburn .05
55 Derrel Thomas .05
56 Pete Falcone .05
57 Willie Aikens .05
58 Toby Harrah .05
59 Bob Tolan .05
60 Rick Waits .05
61 Jim Morrison .05
62 Stan Bahnsen .05
63 Gene Richards .05
64 Dave Cash .05
65 Rollie Fingers .50
66 Butch Benton .05
67 Tim Ireland .05
68 Rick Lysander .05
69 Cesar Cedeno .05
70 Jim Willoughby .05
71 Bill Madlock .15
72 Lee Lacy .05
73 Milt Wilcox .05
74 Ron Pruitt .05
75 Wayne Krenchicki .05
76 Earl Weaver .25
77 Pedro Borbon .05
78 Jose Cruz .15
79 Steve Ontiveros .05
80 Mike Easler .05
81 Amos Otis .05
82 Mickey Mahler .05
83 Orlando Gonzalez .05
84 Doug Simunic .05
85 Felix Millan .05
86 Garth Iorg .05
87 Pete Broberg .05
88 Roy Howell .05
89 Dave LaRoche .05
90 Jerry Manuel .05
91 Tony Scott .05
92 Larvell Blanks .05
93 Joaquin Andujar .05
94 Tito Landrum .05
95 Joe Sambito .05
96 Pat Dobson .05
97 Dan Meyer .05
98 Clint Hurdle .05
99 Pete LaCock .05
100 Bob Galasso .05
101 Dave Kingman .15
102 Jon Matlack .05
103 Larry Harlow .05
104 Rick Peterson .05
105 Joe Hicks .05
106 Bill Campbell .05
107 Tom Paciorek .05
108 Ray Burris .05
109 Ken Landreaux .05
110 Steve McCatty .05
111 Ron LeFlore .05
112 Joe Decker .05
113 Leon Roberts .05
114 Doug Corbett .05
115 Mickey Rivers .05
116 Dock Ellis .05
117 Ron Jackson .05
118 Bob Molinaro .05
119 Fergie Jenkins .50
120 U.L. Washington .05
121 Roy Thomas .05
122 Hal McRae .15
123 Juan Eichelberger .05
124 Gary Rajsich .05
125 Dennis Leonard .05
126 Walt Williams .05
127 Rennie Stennett .05
128 Jim Bibby .05
129 Dyar Miller .05
130 Luis Pujols .05
131 Juan Beniquez .05
132 Checklist .05

Stickercards

Providing a cardboard backing for its annual series of player stickers, the stickercards are a collectible in themselves. Each 2-1/8" x 3" card is backed by one or two player stickers which could be removed and placed into a special album. The card portion features a player photo set against a solid-color background. A few vitae plus 1989 and career stats are presented in a graduated-color box toward the bottom. The stickercards are sequenced by position within league.

KEN GRIFFEY, JR. • OF
SUPER STAR

NM/M
Complete Set (67): 5.00
Common Player: .05
Wax Pack (5): .25
Wax Box (48): 10.00
1 Will Clark .05
2 Glenn Davis .05
3 Pedro Guerrero .05
4 Roberto Alomar .15
5 Gregg Jefferies .05
6 Ryne Sandberg .60
7 Bobby Bonila .05
8 Howard Johnson .05
9 Tim Wallach .05
10 Shawon Dunston .05
11 Barry Larkin .05
12 Ozzie Smith .60
13 Eric Davis .05
14 Andre Dawson .25
15 Tony Gwynn .60
16 Von Hayes .05
17 Kevin Mitchell .05
18 Rock Raines .05
19 Lonnie Smith .05
20 Darryl Strawberry .05
21 Jerome Walton .05
22 Craig Biggio .05
23 Benito Santiago .05
24 Mike Scioscia .05
25 Doc Gooden .05
26 Rick Reuschel .05
27 Mike Scott .05
28 Sid Fernandez .05
29 Mark Langston .05
30 Joe Magrane .05
31 Mark Davis .05
32 Jay Howell .05
33 Mitch Williams .05
34 Don Mattingly .65
35 Fred McGriff .05
36 Mark McGwire .85
37 Julio Franco .05
38 Steve Sax .05
39 Lou Whitaker .05
40 Wade Boggs .60
41 Gary Gaetti .05
42 Carney Lansford .05
43 Tony Fernandez .05
44 Cal Ripken Jr. 1.00
45 Alan Trammell .05
46 George Bell .05
47 Jose Canseco .35
48 Joe Carter .05
49 Ken Griffey Jr. .75
50 Rickey Henderson .45
51 Bo Jackson .10
52 Kirby Puckett .60
53 Ruben Sierra .05
54 Robin Yount .45
55 Carlton Fisk .45
56 Terry Steinbach .05
57 Mickey Tettleton .05
58 Nolan Ryan 1.00
59 Bret Saberhagen .05
60 Dave Stewart .05
61 Jeff Ballard .05
62 Chuck Finley .05
63 Greg Swindell .05
64 Dennis Eckersley .40
65 Gregg Olson .05
66 Jeff Russell .05
67 Checklist .05

OPC Stickers

Topps' 1990 stickers were produced in two formats. Some measure 2-1/8" x 3" while there are many pairs of half-size (1-1/2" x 2-1/8") stickers. All stickers are attached to Super Star stickercards from which they can be peeled and affixed in a special yearbook. Stickers have large center photos with a shadowbox effect in the borders, (blues for N.L., reds for A.L.). A tiny black sticker number is in the lower-right corner. There is no player name on the stickers; the albums have a box under each space with player data. The half-size stickers are printed in pairs and are checklisted in that fashion. Values given are for complete sticker(s)/stickercard combinations, but without regard for which stickercard is on back. The checklist and values for the O-Pee-Chee version of this set are identical to those for the Topps brand. Packs of five stickers sold for a quarter; the album with Don Mattingly on the cover retailed for 50 cents. Numbers in parentheses in this checklist indicate with which other sticker the named sticker is paired in the smaller format.

NM/M
Complete Set (328): 7.50
Common Sticker: .05
Album: 2.00
1 Rick Cerone/HL/321 .05
2 Kevin Elster/HL/322 .05
3 Nolan Ryan/HL/323 .45
4 Vince Coleman/HL/319 .05
5 Cal Ripken Jr./HL/240 .45
6 Jeff Reardon/HL/328 .05
7 Rickey Henderson/
   HL/320 .15
8 Wade Boggs/HL/324 .30
9 Barry Bonds/HL/325 .45
10 Gregg Olson/HL/236 .05
11 Tony Fernandez/HL/327 .05
12 Ryne Sandberg/HL/326 .30
13 Glenn Davis .05
14 Danny Darwin/316 .05
15 Bill Doran/298 .05
16 Dave Smith/225 .05
17 Kevin Bass/278 .05
18 Rafael Ramirez/177 .05
19 Mike Scott .05
20 Ken Caminiti/235 .05
21 Jim Deshaies/272 .05
22 Gerald Young/314 .05
23 Craig Biggio/186 .05
24 Lonnie Smith .05
25 Dale Murphy/210 .10
26 Tom Glavine .15
27 Gerald Perry/313 .05
28 Jeff Blauser/269 .05
29 Jeff Treadway/252 .05
30 John Smoltz/299 .05
31 Darrell Evans/295 .05
32 Oddibe McDowell/265 .05
33 Andres Thomas/304 .05
34 Joe Boever/191 .05
35 Pedro Guerrero .05
36 Ken Dayley/226 .05
37 Milt Thompson/188 .05
38 Jose DeLeon/180 .05
39 Vince Coleman/293 .05
40 Terry Pendleton/225 .05
41 Joe Magrane .05
42 Ozzie Smith/179 .30
43 Todd Worrell/195 .05
44 Jose Oquendo/238 .05
45 Tom Brunansky/287 .05
46 Ryne Sandberg .05
47 Andre Dawson/268 .15
48 Mitch Williams .05
49 Damon Berryhill/204 .05
50 Jerome Walton/274 .05
51 Greg Maddux/315 .30
52 Dwight Smith/248 .05
53 Shawon Dunston/194 .05
54 Mike Bielecki/239 .05
55 Rick Sutcliffe/305 .05
56 Mark Grace/228 .05
57 Eddie Murray .40
58 Alfredo Griffin/197 .05
59 Fernando Valenzuela/
   277 .05
60 Kirk Gibson/201 .05
61 Ramon Martinez/190 .05
62 Mike Marshall/309 .05
63 Orel Hershiser .05
64 Mike Scioscia/271 .05
65 Jay Howell/279 .05
66 Willie Randolph/283 .05
67 Jeff Hamilton/280 .05
68 Denny Martinez .05
69 Tim Raines/184 .05

No.	Player	Price
70	Mark Langston	.05
71	Dave Martinez/301	.05
72	Tim Burke/258	.05
73	Spike Owen/232	.05
74	Tim Wallach/254	.05
75	Andres Galarraga/208	.05
76	Kevin Gross/234	.05
77	Hubie Brooks/263	.05
78	Bryn Smith/207	.05
79	Kevin Mitchell	.05
80	Craig Lefferts/256	.05
81	Ernest Riles/247	.05
82	Scott Garrelts/185	.05
83	Robby Thompson/251	.05
84	Don Robinson/282	.05
85	Will Clark	.05
86	Steve Bedrosian/183	.05
87	Brett Butler/284	.05
88	Matt Williams/227	.05
89	Rick Reuschel/291	.05
90	Howard Johnson	.05
91	Darryl Strawberry/246	.05
92	Sid Fernandez	.05
93	David Cone/189	.05
94	Kevin McReynolds/311	.05
95	Frank Viola/229	.05
96	Dwight Gooden/206	.05
97	Kevin Elster/267	.05
98	Ron Darling/289	.05
99	Dave Magadan/257	.05
100	Randy Myers/192	.05
101	Tony Gwynn	.60
102	Mark Davis/312	.05
103	Bip Roberts/212	.05
104	Jack Clark/205	.05
105	Chris James/211	.05
106	Mike Pagliarulo/199	.05
107	Ed Whitson	.05
108	Bruce Hurst/245	.05
109	Roberto Alomar/202	.15
110	Benito Santiago/224	.05
111	Eric Show/307	.05
112	Ricky Jordan	.05
113	Steve Jeltz/203	.05
114	Von Hayes	.05
115	Dickie Thon/182	.05
116	Ken Howell/213	.05
117	John Kruk/306	.05
118	Lenny Dykstra/302	.05
119	Jeff Parrett/300	.05
120	Randy Ready/230	.05
121	Roger McDowell/262	.05
122	Tom Herr/250	.05
123	Barry Bonds	.90
124	Andy Van Slyke/219	.05
125	Bob Walk/216	.05
126	R.J. Reynolds/243	.05
127	Gary Redus/249	.05
128	Bill Landrum/276	.05
129	Bobby Bonilla	.05
130	Doug Drabek/218	.05
131	Jose Lind/221	.05
132	John Smiley/241	.05
133	Mike LaValliere/214	.05
134	Eric Davis	.05
135	Tom Browning/270	.05
136	Barry Larkin	.05
137	Jose Rijo/318	.05
138	Todd Benzinger/292	.05
139	Rick Mahler/217	.05
140	Chris Sabo/196	.05
141	Paul O'Neill/175	.05
142	Danny Jackson/273	.05
143	Rolando Roomes/261	.05
144	John Franco/233	.05
145	Ozzie Smith/AS	.30
146	Tony Gwynn/AS	.30
147	Will Clark/AS	.35
148	Kevin Mitchell/AS	.05
149	Eric Davis/AS	.05
150	Howard Johnson/AS	.05
151	Pedro Guerrero/AS	.05
152	Ryne Sandberg/AS	.35
153	Benito Santiago/AS	.05
154	Rick Reuschel/AS	.05
155	Bo Jackson/AS	.05
156	Wade Boggs/AS	.35
157	Kirby Puckett/AS	.30
158	Harold Baines/AS	.05
159	Julio Franco/AS	.05
160	Cal Ripken Jr./AS	.45
161	Ruben Sierra(AS)	.05
162	Mark McGwire/AS	.40
163	Terry Steinbach/AS	.05
164	Dave Stewart/AS	.05
165	Bert Blyleven	.05
166	Wally Joyner/285	.05
167	Kirk McCaskill/290	.05
168	Devon White/223	.05
169	Brian Downing/294	.05
170	Lance Parrish/296	.05
171	Chuck Finley	.05
172	Jim Abbott/317	.05
173	Chili Davis/181	.05
174	Johnny Ray/260	.05
175	Bryan Harvey/141	.05
176	Mark McGwire	.75
177	Jose Canseco/18	.15
178	Mike Moore	.05
179	Dave Parker/42	.05
180	Bob Welch/38	.05
181	Rickey Henderson/173	.05
182	Dennis Eckersley/115	.20
183	Carney Lansford/86	.05
184	Dave Henderson/69	.05
185	Dave Stewart/82	.05
186	Terry Steinbach/23	.05
187	Fred McGriff	.05

No.	Player	Price
188	Junior Felix/37	.05
189	Ernie Whitt/93	.05
190	Dave Smith/61	.65
191	Jimmy Key/34	.05
192	George Bell/100	.05
193	Kelly Gruber	.05
194	Tony Fernandez/53	.05
195	John Cerutti/43	.05
196	Tom Henke/140	.05
197	Nelson Liriano/58	.05
198	Robin Yount	.40
199	Paul Molitor/106	.05
200	Dan Plesac	.05
201	Teddy Higuera/60	.05
202	Gary Sheffield/109	.15
203	B.J. Surhoff/113	.05
204	Rob Deer/49	.05
205	Chris Bosio/104	.05
206	Glenn Braggs/96	.05
207	Jim Gantner/78	.05
208	Greg Brock/75	.05
209	Joe Carter	.05
210	Jerry Browne/25	.05
211	Cory Snyder/105	.05
212	Joey Belle/103	.10
213	Bud Black/116	.05
214	Greg Swindell/133	.05
215	Doug Jones	.05
216	Tom Candiotti/125	.05
217	John Farrell/139	.05
218	Pete O'Brien/130	.05
219	Brook Jacoby/124	.05
220	Alvin Davis	.05
221	Harold Reynolds/131	.05
222	Scott Bankhead	.05
223	Jeffrey Leonard/168	.05
224	Jim Presley/110	.05
225	Ken Griffey Jr./40	.40
226	Greg Briley/36	.05
227	Darnell Coles/88	.05
228	Mike Schooler/56	.05
229	Scott Bradley/95	.05
230	Randy Johnson/120	.25
231	Cal Ripken Jr.	.90
232	Jeff Ballard/73	.05
233	Randy Milligan/144	.05
234	Joe Orsulak/76	.05
235	Billy Ripken/20	.05
236	Mark Williamson/10	.05
237	Mickey Tettleton	.05
238	Gregg Olson/44	.05
239	Craig Worthington/54	.05
240	Bob Milacki/5	.05
241	Phil Bradley/132	.05
242	Nolan Ryan	.90
243	Julio Franco/126	.05
244	Ruben Sierra	.05
245	Harold Baines/128	.05
246	Jeff Kunkel/91	.05
247	Pete Incaviglia/81	.05
248	Kevin Brown/7	.05
249	Cecil Espy/127	.05
250	Rafael Palmeiro/122	.20
251	Steve Buechele/83	.05
252	Jeff Russell/29	.05
253	Wade Boggs	.60
254	Mike Greenwell/74	.05
255	Roger Clemens/16	.35
256	Marty Barrett/80	.05
257	Dwight Evans/99	.05
258	Mike Boddicker/72	.05
259	Ellis Burks	.05
260	John Dopson/174	.05
261	Rob Murphy/143	.05
262	Lee Smith/121	.05
263	Nick Esasky/77	.05
264	Bo Jackson	.10
265	George Brett/32	.35
266	Bret Saberhagen	.05
267	Kevin Seitzer/97	.05
268	Tom Gordon/47	.05
269	Kurt Stillwell/28	.05
270	Steve Farr/135	.05
271	Jim Eisenreich/64	.05
272	Mark Gubicza/21	.05
273	Jeff Montgomery/142	.05
274	Danny Tartabull/50	.05
275	Lou Whitaker	.05
276	Jack Morris/128	.05
277	Frank Tanana/59	.05
278	Chet Lemon/17	.05
279	Fred Lynn/65	.05
280	Mike Heath/67	.05
281	Alan Trammell	.05
282	Mike Henneman/84	.05
283	Gary Pettis/56	.05
284	Jeff Robinson/87	.05
285	Dave Bergman/166	.05
286	Kirby Puckett	.60
287	Kent Hrbek/45	.05
288	Gary Gaetti	.05
289	Jeff Reardon/98	.05
290	Brian Harper/167	.05
291	Gene Larkin/89	.05
292	Dan Gladden/138	.05
293	Al Newman/39	.05
294	Randy Bush/169	.05
295	Greg Gagne/31	.05
296	Allan Anderson/170	.05
297	Bobby Thigpen	.05
298	Ozzie Guillen/15	.05
299	Ivan Calderon/30	.05
300	Carlos Martinez/119	.05
301	Steve Lyons/71	.05
302	Ron Kittle/118	.05
303	Carlton Fisk	.40
304	Melido Perez/33	.05
305	Dave Gallagher/55	.05

No.	Player	Price
306	Dan Pasqua/117	.05
307	Scott Fletcher/111	.05
308	Don Mattingly	.65
309	Dave Righetti/62	.05
310	Steve Sax	.05
311	Alvaro Espinoza/94	.05
312	Roberto Kelly/102	.05
313	Mel Hall/27	.05
314	Jesse Barfield/22	.05
315	Chuck Cary/51	.05
316	Bob Geren/14	.05
317	Andy Hawkins/172	.05
318	Don Slaught/137	.05
319	Jim Abbott/4 (Future Star)	.05
320	Greg Briley/7 (Future Star)	.05
321	Bob Geren/1 (Future Star)	.05
322	Tom Gordon/2 (Future Star)	.05
323	Ken Griffey Jr./3 (Future Star)	.30
324	Gregg Jefferies/8 (Future Star)	.10
325	Carlos Martinez/9 (Future Star)	.05
326	Gary Sheffield/12 (Future Star)	.15
327	Jerome Walton/11 (Future Star)	.05
328	Craig Worthington/6 (Future Star)	.05

TV All-Stars

MARK McGWIRE

This 66-card boxed set was sold only through a television offer in limited markets. Consequently, production numbers are relatively low and single cards are seldom offered in the hobby market. Most of the game's top stars are included in the issue. Fronts feature a high-gloss surface. On the red-bordered backs there are several lines of biographical data plus each player's "Career Bests" in various statistical categories, set against a pastel background shield. Issue price was $22.90.

		NM/M
	Complete Set (66):	45.00
	Common Player:	.25
1	Mark McGwire	6.50
2	Julio Franco	.25
3	Ozzie Guillen	.25
4	Carney Lansford	.25
5	Bo Jackson	.75
6	Kirby Puckett	.25
7	Ruben Sierra	.25
8	Carlton Fisk	3.00
9	Nolan Ryan	9.00
10	Rickey Henderson	3.00
11	Jose Canseco	1.50
12	Mark Davis	.25
13	Dennis Eckersley	2.25
14	Chuck Finley	.25
15	Bret Saberhagen	.25
16	Dave Stewart	.25
17	Don Mattingly	5.00
18	Steve Sax	.25
19	Cal Ripken, Jr.	9.00
20	Wade Boggs	3.50
21	George Bell	.25
22	Mike Greenwell	.25
23	Robin Yount	3.00
24	Mickey Tettleton	.25
25	Roger Clemens	5.00
26	Fred McGriff	.25
27	Jeff Ballard	.25
28	Dwight Evans	.25
29	Paul Molitor	3.00
30	Gregg Olson	.25
31	Dan Plesac	.25
32	Greg Swindell	.25
33	Cito Gaston	.25
	Tony LaRussa	.25
34	Will Clark	.25
35	Roberto Alomar	.25
36	Barry Larkin	.25
37	Ken Caminiti	.25
38	Eric Davis	.25
39	Tony Gwynn	3.50
40	Kevin Mitchell	.25
41	Craig Biggio	.25
42	Mike Scott	.25
43	Joe Carter	.25
44	Jack Clark	.25
45	Glenn Davis	.25
46	Orel Hershiser	.25
47	Jay Howell	.25
48	Bruce Hurst	.25
49	Dave Smith	.25
50	Pedro Guerrero	.25
51	Ryne Sandberg	3.50
52	Ozzie Smith	3.50
53	Howard Johnson	.25
54	Von Hayes	.25
55	Tim Raines	.25
56	Darryl Strawberry	.25
57	Mike LaValliere	.25
58	Dwight Gooden	.25
59	Bobby Bonilla	.25
60	Tim Burke	.25
61	Sid Fernandez	.25
62	Andres Galarraga	.25
63	Mark Grace	.25
64	Joe Magrane	.25
65	Mitch Williams	.25
66	Roger Craig, Don Zimmer	.25

TV Cardinals Team Set

RAY LANKFORD

Available only as a boxed set via a limited television offer, this team set includes cards of all players on the opening day roster plus the manager, selected coaches and many of the organization's top prospects. In many cases this is the first card of a player in major league uniform, and in some cases represents the only card which will ever be issued of the player as a major leaguer. Cards feature a high-gloss front surface. Backs have a red border and feature a "ghost image" of the photo on the front as a background to the statistical and biographical data. Because of the relatively limited production and the fact it was sold as a boxed set only, single cards are seldom available.

		NM/M
	Complete Set (66):	20.00
	Common Player:	.25
1	Whitey Herzog	.25
2	Steve Braun	.25
3	Rich Hacker	.25
4	Dave Ricketts	.25
5	Jim Riggleman	.25
6	Mike Roarke	.25
7	Cris Carpenter	.25
8	John Costello	.25
9	Danny Cox	.25
10	Ken Dayley	.25
11	Jose DeLeon	.25
12	Frank DiPino	.25
13	Ken Hill	.25
14	Howard Hilton	.25
15	Ricky Horton	.25
16	Joe Magrane	.25
17	Greg Mathews	.25
18	Bryn Smith	.25
19	Scott Terry	.25
20	Bob Tewksbury	.25
21	John Tudor	.25
22	Todd Worrell	.25
23	Tom Pagnozzi	.25
24	Todd Zeile	.50
25	Pedro Guerrero	.25
26	Tim Jones	.25
27	Jose Oquendo	.25
28	Terry Pendleton	.25
29	Ozzie Smith	15.00
30	Denny Walling	.25
31	Tom Brunansky	.25
32	Vince Coleman	.50
33	Dave Collins	.25
34	Willie McGee	.50
35	John Morris	.25
36	Milt Thompson	.25
37	Gibson Alba	.25
38	Scott Arnold	.25
39	Rod Brewer	.25
40	Greg Carmona	.25
41	Mark Clark	.25
42	Stan Clarke	.25
43	Paul Coleman	.25
44	Todd Crosby	.25
45	Brad DuVall	.25
46	John Ericks	.25
47	Bien Figueroa	.25
48	Terry Francona	.25
49	Ed Fulton	.25
50	Bernard Gilkey	1.00
51	Ernie Camacho	.25
52	Mike Hinkle	.25
53	Ray Lankford	1.00
54	Julian Martinez	.25
55	Jesus Mendez	.25
56	Mike Milchin	.25
57	Mauricio Nunez	.25
58	Omar Olivares	.25
59	Geronimo Pena	.25
60	Mike Perez	.25
61	Gaylen Pitts	.25
62	Mark Riggins	.25
63	Tim Sherrill	.25
64	Roy Silver	.25
65	Ray Stephens	.25
66	Craig Wilson	.25

TV Cubs Team Set

GREG MADDUX

Sold only in boxed set form via a limited television offer, this 66-card issue includes all players on the team's 1990 opening day roster as well as the manager, selected coaches and some of the organization's top minor league prospects. For the latter group, this sets offers the first - and in many cases the only - card of the player in a major league uniform. The cards have a high-gloss front surface. Card backs feature a "ghost image" of the color photo used on the front as a background to the stats and biographical information. A red border completes the back design. Because the set was sold only in boxed form, and production was relatively low, single cards are seldom seen in the market.

		NM/M
	Complete Set (66):	45.00
	Common Player:	.35
1	Don Zimmer	.35
2	Joe Altobelli	.35
3	Chuck Cottier	.35
4	Jose Martinez	.35
5	Dick Pole	.35
6	Phil Roof	.35
7	Paul Assenmacher	.35
8	Mike Bielecki	.35
9	Mike Harkey	.35
10	Joe Kraemer	.35
11	Les Lancaster	.35
12	Greg Maddux	20.00
13	Jose Nunez	.35
14	Jeff Pico	.35
15	Rick Sutcliffe	.75
16	Dean Wilkins	.35
17	Mitch Williams	.35
18	Steve Wilson	.35
19	Damon Berryhill	.35
20	Joe Girardi	.35
21	Rick Wrona	.35
22	Shawon Dunston	.50
23	Mark Grace	5.00
24	Domingo Ramos	.35
25	Luis Salazar	.35
26	Ryne Sandberg	20.00
27	Greg Smith	.35
28	Curtis Wilkerson	.35
29	Dave Clark	.35
30	Doug Dascenzo	.35
31	Andre Dawson	7.50
32	Lloyd McClendon	.35
33	Dwight Smith	.35
34	Jerome Walton	.35
35	Marvell Wynne	.35
36	Alex Arias	.35
37	Bob Bafia	.35
38	Brad Bierley	.35
39	Shawn Boskie	.35
40	Danny Clay	.35
41	Rusty Crockett	.35
42	Earl Cunningham	.35
43	Len Damian	.35
44	Darrin Duffy	.35
45	Ty Griffin	.35
46	Brian Guinn	.35
47	Phil Hannon	.35
48	Phil Harrison	.35
49	Jeff Hearron	.35
50	Greg Kallevig	.35
51	Cedric Landrum	.35
52	Bill Long	.35
53	Derrick May	.35
54	Ray Mullino	.35
55	Erik Pappas	.35
56	Steve Parker	.35
57	Dave Pavlas	.35
58	Laddie Renfroe	.35
59	Jeff Small	.35
60	Doug Strange	.35
61	Gary Varsho	.35
62	Hector Villanueva	.35
63	Rick Wilkins	.35
64	Dana Williams	.35
65	Bill Wrona	.35
66	Fernando Zarranz	.35

TV Mets Team Set

CRAIG SHIPLEY

This late-season issue, sold only as a boxed set via a television offer in limited areas, features all of the players on the 1990 opening day roster, plus the manager, selected coaches and many of the organization's top minor league prospects. For many of the prospects, this is the first, if not the only, card on which they appear in major league uniform. A highlight of the back design is a "ghost image" full-color reproduction of the front photo, used as a background to the statistical and biographical information. A red border dominates the remainder of the back design. Because it was sold only as a boxed set, and production was relatively limited, single cards are seldom available.

		NM/M
	Complete Set (66):	10.00
	Common Player:	.35
1	Dave Johnson	.35
2	Mike Cubbage	.35
3	Doc Edwards	.35
4	Bud Harrelson	.35
5	Greg Pavlick	.35
6	Mel Stottlemyre, Sr.	.35
7	Blaine Beatty	.35
8	David Cone	1.00
9	Ron Darling	.35
10	Sid Fernandez	.50
11	John Franco	.50
12	Dwight Gooden	.50
13	Jeff Innis	.35
14	Julio Machado	.35
15	Jeff Musselman	.35
16	Bob Ojeda	.35
17	Alejandro Pena	.35
18	Frank Viola	.50
19	Wally Whitehurst	.35
20	Barry Lyons	.35
21	Orlando Mercado	.35
22	Mackey Sasser	.35
23	Kevin Elster	.35
24	Gregg Jefferies	.50
25	Howard Johnson	.50
26	Dave Magadan	.35
27	Mike Marshall	.35
28	Tom O'Malley	.35
29	Tim Teufel	.35
30	Mark Carreon	.35

#	Player	
31	Kevin McReynolds	.35
32	Keith Miller	.35
33	Darryl Strawberry	.50
34	Lou Thornton	.35
35	Shawn Barton	.35
36	Tim Bogar	.35
37	Terry Bross	.35
38	Kevin Brown	.35
39	Mike DeButch	.35
40	Alex Diaz	.35
41	Chris Donnels	.35
42	Jeff Gardner	.35
43	Denny Gonzalez	.35
44	Kenny Graves	.35
45	Manny Hernandez	.35
46	Keith Hughes	.35
47	Todd Hundley	.50
48	Chris Jelic	.35
49	Dave Liddell	.35
50	Terry McDaniel	.35
51	Cesar Mejia	.35
52	Scott Nielsen	.35
53	Dale Plummer	.35
54	Darren Reed	.35
55	Gil Roca	.35
56	Jaime Roseboro	.35
57	Roger Samuels	.35
58	Zoilo Sanchez	.35
59	Pete Schourek	.35
60	Craig Shipley	.35
61	Ray Soff	.35
62	Steve Swisher	.35
63	Kelvin Torve	.35
64	Dave Trautwein	.35
65	Julio Valera	.35
66	Alan Zinter	.35

TV Red Sox Team Set

This 66-card set was available only via a television offer in certain limited areas. Production was relatively low and single cards are hard to find. Player selection includes all those on the team's opening day roster in 1990, plus the manager, selected coaches and the team's top minor league prospects. In many cases this represents the first, or even the only, appearance of these prospects on major league baseball cards. Fronts have a high-gloss surface. On back, bordered in red, feature a "ghost image" reproduction of the front photo as a background to the statistics and biographical data.

		NM/M
Complete Set (66):		40.00
Common Player:		.35
1	Joe Morgan	.35
2	Dick Berardino	.35
3	Al Bumbry	.35
4	Bill Fischer	.35
5	Richie Hebner	.35
6	Rac Slider	.35
7	Mike Boddicker	.35
8	Roger Clemens	25.00
9	John Dopson	.35
10	Wes Gardner	.35
11	Greg Harris	.35
12	Dana Kiecker	.35
13	Dennis Lamp	.35
14	Rob Murphy	.35
15	Jeff Reardon	.35
16	Mike Rochford	.35
17	Lee Smith	.50
18	Rich Gedman	.35
19	John Marzano	.35
20	Tony Pena	.35
21	Marty Barrett	.35
22	Wade Boggs	15.00
23	Bill Buckner	.50
24	Danny Heep	.35
25	Jody Reed	.35
26	Luis Rivera	.35
27	Billy Jo Robidoux	.35
28	Ellis Burks	.35
29	Dwight Evans	.35
30	Mike Greenwell	.35
31	Randy Kutcher	.35

#	Player	
32	Carlos Quintana	.35
33	Kevin Romine	.35
34	Ed Nottle	.35
35	Mark Meleski	.35
36	Steve Bast	.35
37	Greg Blosser	.35
38	Tom Bolton	.35
39	Scott Cooper	.35
40	Zach Crouch	.35
41	Steve Curry	.35
42	Mike Dalton	.35
43	John Flaherty	.35
44	Angel Gonzalez	.35
45	Eric Hetzel	.35
46	Daryl Irvine	.35
47	Joe Johnson	.35
48	Rick Lancellotti	.35
49	John Leister	.35
50	Derek Livernois	.35
51	Josias Manzanillo	.35
52	Kevin Morton	.35
53	Julius McDougal	.35
54	Tim Naehring	.35
55	Jim Pankovits	.35
56	Mickey Pina	.35
57	Phil Plantier	.35
58	Jerry Reed	.35
59	Larry Shikles	.35
60	Tito Stewart	.35
61	Jeff Stone	.35
62	John Trautwein	.35
63	Gary Tremblay	.35
64	Mo Vaughn	2.50
65	Scott Wade	.35
66	Eric Wedge	.35

TV Yankees Team Set

DON MATTINGLY

The first - and in many cases the only - baseball card appearance of top minor league prospects occurs in this special 66-card boxed set which was sold only via a special television offer in limited markets. The set also includes all players on the team's opening day roster, plus the manager and selected coaches. Card fronts have a high-gloss surface. On back, framed by a red border, the design features a "ghost image" of the color front photo, used as a background to the statistical and biographical information. Because the cards were sold only as a complete set, single cards are seldom available.

		NM/M
Complete Set (66):		60.00
Common Player:		.35
1	Bucky Dent	.35
2	Mark Connor	.35
3	Billy Connors	.35
4	Mike Ferraro	.35
5	Joe Sparks	.35
6	Champ Summers	.35
7	Greg Cadaret	.35
8	Chuck Cary	.35
9	Lee Guetterman	.35
10	Andy Hawkins	.35
11	Dave LaPoint	.35
12	Tim Leary	.35
13	Lance McCullers	.35
14	Alan Mills	.35
15	Clay Parker	.35
16	Pascual Perez	.35
17	Eric Plunk	.35
18	Dave Righetti	.35
19	Jeff Robinson	.35
20	Rick Cerone	.35
21	Bob Geren	.35
22	Steve Balboni	.35
23	Mike Blowers	.35
24	Alvaro Espinoza	.35
25	Don Mattingly	40.00
26	Steve Sax	.35
27	Wayne Tolleson	.35
28	Randy Velarde	.35
29	Jesse Barfield	.35
30	Mel Hall	.35
31	Roberto Kelly	.35
32	Luis Polonia	.35

#	Player	
33	Deion Sanders	1.00
34	Dave Winfield	15.00
35	Steve Adkins	.35
36	Oscar Azocar	.35
37	Bob Brower	.35
38	Britt Burns	.35
39	Bob Davidson	.35
40	Brian Dorsett	.35
41	Dave Eiland	.35
42	John Fishel	.35
43	Andy Fox	.35
44	John Habyan	.35
45	Cullen Hartzog	.35
46	Sterling Hitchcock	.35
47	Brian Johnson	.35
48	Jimmy Jones	.35
49	Scott Kamieniecki	.35
50	Mark Leiter	.35
51	Jim Leyritz	.35
52	Jason Maas	.35
53	Kevin Maas	.35
54	Hensley Meulens	.35
55	Kevin Mmahat	.35
56	Rich Monteleone	.35
57	Vince Phillips	.35
58	Carlos Rodriguez	.35
59	Dave Sax	.35
60	Willie Smith	.35
61	Van Snider	.35
62	Andy Stankiewicz	.35
63	Wade Taylor	.35
64	Ricky Torres	.35
65	Jim Walewander	.35
66	Bernie Williams	4.00

1989 Major League Debut

SEPTEMBER 1, 1989 MAJOR LEAGUE DEBUT — MIKE BLOWERS

This 150-card set chronicles the debut date of all 1989 Major League rookies. Two checklist cards are also included in this boxed set, listing the players in order of debut date, though the cards are numbered alphabetically. The card fronts resemble the 1990 Topps cards in style. A debut banner appears in an upper corner. The flip sides are horizontal and are printed in black on yellow stock, providing an overview of the player's first game. The set is packaged in a special collectors box and was only available through hobby dealers.

		NM/M
Complete Set (150):		9.00
Common Player:		.05
1	Jim Abbott	.05
2	Beau Allred	.05
3	Wilson Alvarez	.05
4	Kent Anderson	.05
5	Eric Anthony	.05
6	Kevin Appier	.05
7	Larry Arndt	.05
8	John Barfield	.05
9	Billy Bates	.05
10	Kevin Batiste	.05
11	Blaine Beatty	.05
12	Stan Belinda	.05
13	Juan Bell	.05
14	Joey Belle	.25
15	Andy Benes	.05
16	Mike Benjamin	.05
17	Geronimo Berroa	.05
18	Mike Blowers	.05
19	Brian Brady	.05
20	Francisco Cabrera	.05
21	George Canale	.05
22	Jose Cano	.05
23	Steve Carter	.05
24	Pat Combs	.05
25	Scott Coolbaugh	.05
26	Steve Cummings	.05
27	Pete Dalena	.05
28	Jeff Datz	.05
29	Bobby Davidson	.05
30	Drew Denson	.05
31	Gary DiSarcina	.05
32	Brian DuBois	.05
33	Mike Dyer	.05
34	Wayne Edwards	.05
35	Junior Felix	.05

#	Player	
36	Mike Fetters	.05
37	Steve Finley	.05
38	Darren Fletcher	.05
39	LaVel Freeman	.05
40	Steve Frey	.05
41	Mark Gardner	.05
42	Joe Girardi	.05
43	Juan Gonzalez	.50
44	Goose Gozzo	.05
45	Tommy Greene	.05
46	Ken Griffey Jr.	3.00
47	Jason Grimsley	.05
48	Marquis Grissom	.05
49	Mark Guthrie	.05
50	Chip Hale	.05
51	John Hardy	.05
52	Gene Harris	.05
53	Mike Hartley	.05
54	Scott Hemond	.05
55	Xavier Hernandez	.05
56	Eric Hetzel	.05
57	Greg Hibbard	.05
58	Mark Higgins	.05
59	Glenallen Hill	.05
60	Chris Hoiles	.05
61	Shawn Holman	.05
62	Dann Howitt	.05
63	Mike Huff	.05
64	Terry Jorgenson	.05
65	Dave Justice	.25
66	Jeff King	.05
67	Matt Kinzer	.05
68	Joe Kraemer	.05
69	Marcus Lawton	.05
70	Derek Lilliquist	.05
71	Scott Little	.05
72	Greg Litton	.05
73	Rick Lueken	.05
74	Julio Machado	.05
75	Tom Magrann	.05
76	Kelly Mann	.05
77	Randy McCament	.05
78	Ben McDonald	.05
79	Chuck McElroy	.05
80	Jeff McKnight	.05
81	Kent Mercker	.05
82	Matt Merullo	.05
83	Hensley Meulens	.05
84	Kevin Mmahat	.05
85	Mike Munoz	.05
86	Dan Murphy	.05
87	Jaime Navarro	.05
88	Randy Nosek	.05
89	John Olerud	.15
90	Steve Olin	.05
91	Joe Oliver	.05
92	Francisco Oliveras	.05
93	Greg Olson	.05
94	John Orton	.05
95	Dean Palmer	.05
96	Ramon Pena	.05
97	Jeff Peterek	.05
98	Marty Pevey	.05
99	Rusty Richards	.05
100	Jeff Richardson	.05
101	Rob Richie	.05
102	Kevin Ritz	.05
103	Rosario Rodriguez	.05
104	Mike Roesler	.05
105	Kenny Rogers	.05
106	Bobby Rose	.05
107	Alex Sanchez	.05
108	Deion Sanders	.25
109	Jeff Schaefer	.05
110	Jeff Schulz	.05
111	Mike Schwabe	.05
112	Dick Scott	.05
113	Scott Scudder	.05
114	Rudy Seanez	.05
115	Joe Skalski	.05
116	Dwight Smith	.05
117	Greg Smith	.05
118	Mike Smith	.05
119	Paul Sorrento	.05
120	Sammy Sosa	3.00
121	Billy Spiers	.05
122	Mike Stanton	.05
123	Phil Stephenson	.05
124	Doug Strange	.05
125	Russ Swan	.05
126	Kevin Tapani	.05
127	Stu Tate	.05
128	Greg Vaughn	.05
129	Robin Ventura	.15
130	Randy Veres	.05
131	Jose Vizcaino	.05
132	Omar Vizquel	.05
133	Larry Walker	.25
134	Jerome Walton	.05
135	Gary Wayne	.05
136	Lenny Webster	.05
137	Mickey Weston	.05
138	Jeff Wetherby	.05
139	John Wetteland	.05
140	Ed Whited	.05
141	Wally Whitehurst	.05
142	Kevin Wickander	.05
143	Dean Wilkins	.05
144	Dana Williams	.05
145	Paul Wilmet	.05
146	Craig Wilson	.05
147	Matt Winters	.05
148	Eric Yelding	.05
149	Clint Zavaras	.05
150	Todd Zeile	.05
----	Checklist (1 of 2)	.05
----	Checklist (2 of 2)	.05

1991 Topps Pre-Production Sample Sheet

To preview its 40th anniversary set, Topps distributed this 7-1/2" x 10-1/2" uncut sheet. Fronts are identical to the issued versions of each player's card while backs are printed in blue with a large anniversary logo, the player's name, a copyright line and "1991 PRE-PRODUCTION / SAMPLE."

		NM/M
Uncut Sheet:		15.00
Complete Set (9):		15.00
Common Player:		1.00
(1)	Wade Boggs	3.00
(2)	Jose Canseco	2.00
(3)	Roger Clemens	6.00
(4)	Rickey Henderson	2.50
(5)	Bo Jackson	1.50
(6)	Kirt Manwaring	1.00
(7)	Willie Randolph	1.00
(8)	Benny Santiago	1.00
(9)	Walt Weiss	1.00

1991 Topps

Topps celebrated its 40th anniversary in 1991 with the biggest promotional campaign in baseball card history. More than 300,000 vintage Topps cards (or certificates redeemable for valuable older cards) produced from 1952 to 1990 were randomly inserted in packs. Also a grand prize winner received a complete set from each year, and others received a single set from 1952-1990. The 1991 Topps card fronts feature the "Topps 40 Years of Baseball" logo in the upper-left corner. Colored borders frame the player photos. All players of the same team have cards with the same frame/border colors. Both action and posed shots appear in full-color on the card fronts. The flip sides are printed horizontally and feature complete statistics. Record Breakers and other special cards were once again included in the set. The cards measure 2-1/2" x 3-1/2". Many cards can be found with variations in the sheet-letter (A-F) designations in the copyright line on back.

	NM/M
Unopened Factory Set, Retail (792):	30.00
Unopened Factory Set, Hobby (792):	25.00
Complete Set (792):	20.00
Common Player:	.05

Wax Pack (15):		.50
Wax Box (36):		12.50
Cello Pack (34):		1.00
Cello Box (24):		15.00
Rack Pack (45):		1.00
Rack Box (24):		15.00
Vending Box (500):		7.50
1	Nolan Ryan	.75
2	George Brett (Record Breaker)	.25
3	Carlton Fisk (Record Breaker)	.20
4	Kevin Maas (Record Breaker)	.05
5	Cal Ripken, Jr. (Record Breaker)	.40
6	Nolan Ryan (Record Breaker)	.40
7	Ryne Sandberg (Record Breaker)	.30
8	Bobby Thigpen (Record Breaker)	.05
9	Darrin Fletcher RC	.05
10	Gregg Olson	.05
11	Roberto Kelly	.05
12	Paul Assenmacher	.05
13	Mariano Duncan	.05
14	Dennis Lamp	.05
15	Von Hayes	.05
16	Mike Heath	.05
17	Jeff Brantley	.05
18	Nelson Liriano	.05
19	Jeff Robinson	.05
20	Pedro Guerrero	.05
21	Joe M. Morgan	.05
22	Storm Davis	.05
23	Jim Gantner	.05
24	Dave Martinez	.05
25	Tim Belcher	.05
26	Luis Sojo	.05
27	Bobby Witt	.05
28	Alvaro Espinoza	.05
29	Bob Walk	.05
30	Gregg Jefferies	.05
31	Colby Ward RC	.05
32	Mike Simms RC	.05
33	Barry Jones	.05
34	Atlee Hammaker	.05
35	Greg Maddux	.50
36	Donnie Hill	.05
37	Tom Bolton	.05
38	Scott Bradley	.05
39	Jim Neidlinger RC	.05
40	Kevin Mitchell	.05
41	Ken Dayley	.05
42a	Chris Hoiles RC (White inner photo frame.)	.20
42b	Chris Hoiles RC (Gray inner photo frame.)	.10
43	Roger McDowell	.05
44	Mike Felder	.05
45	Chris Sabo	.05
46	Tim Drummond	.05
47	Brook Jacoby	.05
48	Dennis Boyd	.05
49a	Pat Borders (40 stolen bases in Kinston 1986)	.20
49b	Pat Borders (0 stolen bases in Kinston 1986)	.10
50	Bob Welch	.05
51	Art Howe	.05
52	Francisco Oliveras RC	.05
53	Mike Sharperson	.05
54	Gary Mielke	.05
55	Jeffrey Leonard	.05
56	Jeff Parrett	.05
57	Jack Howell	.05
58	Mel Stottlemyre	.05
59	Eric Yelding	.05
60	Frank Viola	.05
61	Stan Javier	.05
62	Lee Guetterman	.05
63	Milt Thompson	.05
64	Tom Herr	.05
65	Bruce Hurst	.05
66	Terry Kennedy	.05
67	Rick Honeycutt	.05
68	Gary Sheffield	.25
69	Steve Wilson	.05
70	Ellis Burks	.05
71	Jim Acker	.05
72	Junior Ortiz	.05
73	Craig Worthington	.05
74	Shane Andrews RC (#1 Draft Pick)	.10
75	Jack Morris	.05
76	Jerry Browne	.05
77	Drew Hall	.05
78	Geno Petralli	.05
79	Frank Thomas	.35
80a	Fernando Valenzuela (No diamond after 104 ER in 1990.)	.05
80b	Fernando Valenzuela (Diamond after 104 ER in 1990.)	.05
81	Cito Gaston	.05
82	Tom Glavine	.20
83	Daryl Boston	.05
84	Bob McClure	.05
85	Jesse Barfield	.05
86	Les Lancaster	.05
87	Tracy Jones	.05
88	Bob Tewksbury	.05
89	Darren Daulton	.05
90	Danny Tartabull	.05
91	Greg Colbrunn RC (Future Star)	.05

No.	Player	Price
92	Danny Jackson	.05
93	Ivan Calderon	.05
94	John Dopson	.05
95	Paul Molitor	.35
96	Trevor Wilson	.05
97a	Brady Anderson (3H, 2RBI in Sept. scoreboard)	.25
97b	Brady Anderson (14H, 3 RBI in Sept. scoreboard)	.05
98	Sergio Valdez	.05
99	Chris Gwynn	.05
100a	Don Mattingly (10 hits 1990)	.50
100b	Don Mattingly (101 hits in 1990)	.50
101	Rob Ducey	.05
102	Gene Larkin	.05
103	Tim Costo RC (#1 Draft Pick)	.05
104	Don Robinson	.05
105	Kevin McReynolds	.05
106	Ed Nunez	.05
107	Luis Polonia	.05
108	Matt Young	.05
109	Greg Riddoch	.05
110	Tom Henke	.05
111	Andres Thomas	.05
112	Frank DiPino	.05
113	Carl Everett RC (#1 Draft Pick)	.50
114	Lance Dickson RC (Future Star)	.05
115	Hubie Brooks	.05
116	Mark Davis	.05
117	Dion James	.05
118	Tom Edens RC	.05
119	Carl Nichols RC	.05
120	Joe Carter	.05
121	Eric King	.05
122	Paul O'Neill	.05
123	Greg Harris	.05
124	Randy Bush	.05
125	Steve Bedrosian	.05
126	Bernard Gilkey RC	.10
127	Joe Price	.05
128	Travis Fryman	.05
129	Mark Eichhorn	.05
130	Ozzie Smith	.50
131a	Checklist 1 (Phil Bradley #727)	.05
131b	Checklist 1 (Phil Bradley #717)	.05
132	Jamie Quirk	.05
133	Greg Briley	.05
134	Kevin Elster	.05
135	Jerome Walton	.05
136	Dave Schmidt	.05
137	Randy Ready	.05
138	Jamie Moyer	.05
139	Jeff Treadway	.05
140	Fred McGriff	.05
141	Nick Leyva	.05
142	Curtis Wilkerson	.05
143	John Smiley	.05
144	Dave Henderson	.05
145	Lou Whitaker	.05
146	Dan Plesac	.05
147	Carlos Baerga	.05
148	Rey Palacios	.05
149	Al Osuna RC	.05
150	Cal Ripken, Jr.	.75
151	Tom Browning	.05
152	Mickey Hatcher	.05
153	Bryan Harvey	.05
154	Jay Buhner	.05
155a	Dwight Evans (Diamond after 162 G 1982.)	.10
155b	Dwight Evans (No diamond after 162 G 1982.)	.05
156	Carlos Martinez	.05
157	John Smoltz	.05
158	Jose Uribe	.05
159	Joe Boever	.05
160	Vince Coleman	.05
161	Tim Leary	.05
162	Ozzie Canseco RC	.10
163	Dave Johnson	.05
164	Edgar Diaz	.05
165	Sandy Alomar	.05
166	Harold Baines	.05
167a	Randy Tomlin RC ("Harriburg" 1989-90.)	.10
167b	Randy Tomlin RC ("Harrisburg" 1989-90.)	.05
168	John Olerud	.05
169	Luis Aquino	.05
170	Carlton Fisk	.35
171	Tony LaRussa	.05
172	Pete Incaviglia	.05
173	Jason Grimsley	.05
174	Ken Caminiti	.05
175	Jack Armstrong	.05
176	John Orton	.05
177	Reggie Harris RC	.05
178	Dave Valle	.05
179	Pete Harnisch	.05
180	Tony Gwynn	.50
181	Duane Ward	.05
182	Junior Noboa	.05
183	Clay Parker	.05
184	Gary Green	.05
185	Joe Magrane	.05
186	Rod Booker	.05
187	Greg Cadaret	.05
188	Damon Berryhill	.05
189	Daryl Irvine RC	.05
190	Matt Williams	.05
191	Willie Blair RC	.05
192	Rob Deer	.05
193	Felix Fermin	.05
194	Xavier Hernandez RC	.05
195	Wally Joyner	.05
196	Jim Vatcher RC	.05
197	Chris Nabholz RC	.05
198	R.J. Reynolds	.05
199	Mike Hartley RC	.05
200	Darryl Strawberry	.05
201	Tom Kelly	.05
202	Jim Leyritz RC	.20
203	Gene Harris	.05
204	Herm Winningham	.05
205	Mike Perez RC	.05
206	Carlos Quintana	.05
207	Gary Wayne	.05
208	Willie Wilson	.05
209	Ken Howell	.05
210	Lance Parrish	.05
211	Brian Barnes RC (Future Star)	.05
212	Steve Finley	.05
213	Frank Wills	.05
214	Joe Girardi	.05
215	Dave Smith	.05
216	Greg Gagne	.05
217	Chris Bosio	.05
218	Rick Parker RC	.05
219	Jack McDowell	.05
220	Tim Wallach	.05
221	Don Slaught	.05
222	Brian McRae RC	.10
223	Allan Anderson	.05
224	Juan Gonzalez	.20
225	Randy Johnson	.35
226	Alfredo Griffin	.05
227	Steve Avery	.05
228	Rex Hudler	.05
229	Rance Mulliniks	.05
230	Sid Fernandez	.05
231	Doug Rader	.05
232	Jose DeJesus	.05
233	Al Leiter	.05
234	Scott Erickson RC	.10
235	Dave Parker	.05
236a	Frank Tanana (No diamond after 269 SO 1975.)	.10
236b	Frank Tanana (Diamond after 269 SO 1975.)	.05
237	Rick Cerone	.05
238	Mike Dunne	.05
239	Darren Lewis RC	.05
240	Mike Scott	.05
241	Dave Clark	.05
242	Mike LaCoss	.05
243	Lance Johnson	.05
244	Mike Jeffcoat	.05
245	Kal Daniels	.05
246	Kevin Wickander	.05
247	Jody Reed	.05
248	Tom Gordon	.05
249	Bob Melvin	.05
250	Dennis Eckersley	.30
251	Mark Lemke	.05
252	Mel Rojas RC	.05
253	Garry Templeton	.05
254	Shawn Boskie RC	.05
255	Brian Downing	.05
256	Greg Hibbard	.05
257	Tom O'Malley	.05
258	Chris Hammond RC	.05
259	Hensley Meulens	.05
260	Harold Reynolds	.05
261	Bud Harrelson	.05
262	Tim Jones	.05
263	Checklist 2	.05
264	Dave Hollins RC	.05
265	Mark Gubicza	.05
266	Carmen Castillo	.05
267	Mark Knudson	.05
268	Tom Brookens	.05
269	Joe Hesketh	.05
270a	Mark McGwire (1987 SLG .618)	.75
270b	Mark McGwire (1987 SLG 618)	.75
271	Omar Olivares RC	.05
272	Jeff King	.05
273	Johnny Ray	.05
274	Ken Williams	.05
275	Alan Trammell	.05
276	Bill Swift	.05
277	Scott Coolbaugh	.05
278	Alex Fernandez RC (#1 Draft Pick)	.10
279a	Jose Gonzalez (Photo of Billy Bean, left-handed batter.)	.75
279b	Jose Gonzalez (Correct photo, right-handed batter.)	.05
280	Bret Saberhagen	.05
281	Larry Sheets	.05
282	Don Carman	.05
283	Marquis Grissom	.05
284	Bill Spiers	.05
285	Jim Abbott	.05
286	Ken Oberkfell	.05
287	Mark Grant	.05
288	Derrick May RC	.05
289	Tim Birtsas	.05
290	Steve Sax	.05
291	John Wathan	.05
292	Bud Black	.05
293	Jay Bell	.05
294	Mike Moore	.05
295	Rafael Palmeiro	.30
296	Mark Williamson	.05
297	Manny Lee	.05
298	Omar Vizquel	.05
299	Scott Radinsky RC	.05
300	Kirby Puckett	.50
301	Steve Farr	.05
302	Tim Teufel	.05
303	Mike Boddicker	.05
304	Kevin Reimer RC	.05
305	Mike Scioscia	.05
306a	Lonnie Smith (136 G 1990)	.10
306b	Lonnie Smith (135 G 1990)	.05
307	Andy Benes	.05
308	Tom Pagnozzi	.05
309	Norm Charlton	.05
310	Gary Carter	.35
311	Jeff Pico	.05
312	Charlie Hayes	.05
313	Ron Robinson	.05
314	Gary Pettis	.05
315	Roberto Alomar	.15
316	Gene Nelson	.05
317	Mike Fitzgerald	.05
318	Rick Aguilera	.05
319	Jeff McKnight RC	.05
320	Tony Fernandez	.05
321	Bob Rodgers	.05
322	Terry Shumpert RC	.05
323	Cory Snyder	.05
324a	Ron Kittle ("6 Home Runs" in career summary)	.10
324b	Ron Kittle ("7 Home Runs" in career summary)	.05
325	Brett Butler	.05
326	Ken Patterson	.05
327	Ron Hassey	.05
328	Walt Terrell	.05
329	Dave Justice	.05
330	Dwight Gooden	.05
331	Eric Anthony	.05
332	Kenny Rogers	.05
333	Chipper Jones RC (#1 Draft Pick)	2.00
334	Todd Benzinger	.05
335	Mitch Williams	.05
336	Matt Nokes	.05
337a	Keith Comstock (Mariners logo.)	.05
337b	Keith Comstock (Cubs logo.)	1.50
338	Luis Rivera	.05
339	Larry Walker	.05
340	Ramon Martinez	.05
341	John Moses	.05
342	Mickey Morandini RC	.10
343	Jose Oquendo	.05
344	Jeff Russell	.05
345	Len Dykstra	.05
346	Jesse Orosco	.05
347	Greg Vaughn	.05
348	Todd Stottlemyre	.05
349	Dave Gallagher	.05
350	Glenn Davis	.05
351	Joe Torre	.05
352	Frank White	.05
353	Tony Castillo	.05
354	Sid Bream	.05
355	Chili Davis	.05
356	Mike Marshall	.05
357	Jack Savage	.05
358	Mark Parent	.05
359	Chuck Cary	.05
360	Tim Raines	.05
361	Scott Garrelts	.05
362	Hector Villanueva RC	.05
363	Rick Mahler	.05
364	Dan Pasqua	.05
365	Mike Schooler	.05
366a	Checklist 3 (Carl Nichols #19.)	.05
366b	Checklist 3 (Carl Nichols #119.)	.05
367	Dave Walsh RC	.05
368	Felix Jose	.05
369	Steve Searcy	.05
370	Kelly Gruber	.05
371	Jeff Montgomery	.05
372	Spike Owen	.05
373	Darrin Jackson	.05
374	Larry Casian RC	.05
375	Tony Pena	.05
376	Mike Harkey	.05
377	Rene Gonzales	.05
378a	Wilson Alvarez RC (No 1989 Port Charlotte stats.)	.50
378b	Wilson Alvarez RC (1989 Port Charlotte stats)	.20
379	Randy Velarde	.05
380	Willie McGee	.05
381	Jim Leyland	.05
382	Mackey Sasser	.05
383	Pete Smith	.05
384	Gerald Perry	.05
385	Mickey Tettleton	.05
386	Cecil Fielder	.05
387	Julio Franco/AS	.05
388	Kelly Gruber/AS	.05
389	Alan Trammell/AS	.05
390	Jose Canseco/AS	.15
391	Rickey Henderson/AS	.20
392	Ken Griffey Jr./AS	.35
393	Carlton Fisk/AS	.20
394	Bob Welch/AS	.05
395	Chuck Finley/AS	.05
396	Bobby Thigpen/AS	.05
397	Eddie Murray/AS	.20
398	Ryne Sandberg/AS	.30
399	Matt Williams/AS	.05
400	Barry Larkin/AS	.05
401	Barry Bonds/AS	.40
402	Darryl Strawberry/AS	.05
403	Bobby Bonilla/AS	.05
404	Mike Scoscia/AS	.05
405	Doug Drabek/AS	.05
406	Frank Viola/AS	.05
407	John Franco/AS	.05
408	Ernie Riles	.05
409	Mike Stanley	.05
410	Dave Righetti	.05
411	Lance Blankenship	.05
412	Dave Bergman	.05
413	Terry Mulholland	.05
414	Sammy Sosa	.60
415	Rick Sutcliffe	.05
416	Randy Milligan	.05
417	Bill Krueger	.05
418	Nick Esasky	.05
419	Jeff Reed	.05
420	Bobby Thigpen	.05
421	Alex Cole RC	.05
422	Rick Rueschel	.05
423	Rafael Ramirez	.05
424	Calvin Schiraldi	.05
425	Andy Van Slyke	.05
426	Joe Grahe RC	.05
427	Rick Dempsey	.05
428	John Barfield RC	.05
429	Stump Merrill	.05
430	Gary Gaetti	.05
431	Paul Gibson	.05
432	Delino DeShields	.05
433	Pat Tabler	.05
434	Julio Machado RC	.05
435	Kevin Maas	.05
436	Scott Bankhead	.05
437	Doug Dascenzo	.05
438	Vicente Palacios	.05
439	Dickie Thon	.05
440	George Bell	.05
441	Zane Smith	.05
442	Charlie O'Brien	.05
443	Jeff Innis	.05
444	Glenn Braggs	.05
445	Greg Swindell	.05
446	Craig Grebeck RC	.05
447	John Burkett	.05
448	Craig Lefferts	.05
449	Juan Berenguer	.05
450	Wade Boggs	.50
451	Neal Heaton	.05
452	Bill Schroeder	.05
453	Lenny Harris	.05
454a	Kevin Appier (No 1990 Omaha stats.)	.15
454b	Kevin Appier (1990 Omaha stats)	.05
455	Walt Weiss	.05
456	Charlie Leibrandt	.05
457	Todd Hundley	.05
458	Brian Holman	.05
459	Tom Trebelhorn	.05
460	Dave Steib	.05
461a	Robin Ventura (Gray inner photo frame at left.)	.15
461b	Robin Ventura (Red inner photo frame at left.)	.05
462	Steve Frey	.05
463	Dwight Smith	.05
464	Steve Buechele	.05
465	Ken Griffey	.05
466	Charles Nagy RC	.05
467	Dennis Cook	.05
468	Tim Hulett	.05
469	Chet Lemon	.05
470	Howard Johnson	.05
471	Mike Lieberthal RC (#1 Draft Pick)	.50
472	Kirt Manwaring	.05
473	Curt Young	.05
474	Phil Plantier RC	.10
475	Teddy Higuera	.05
476	Glenn Wilson	.05
477	Mike Fetters	.05
478	Kurt Stillwell	.05
479	Bob Patterson	.05
480	Dave Magadan	.05
481	Eddie Whitson	.05
482	Tino Martinez	.05
483	Mike Aldrete	.05
484	Dave LaPoint	.05
485	Terry Pendleton	.05
486	Tommy Greene RC	.05
487	Rafael Belliard	.05
488	Jeff Manto RC	.05
489	Bobby Valentine	.05
490	Kirk Gibson	.05
491	Kurt Miller RC (#1 Draft Pick)	.05
492	Ernie Whitt	.05
493	Jose Rijo	.05
494	Chris James	.05
495	Charlie Hough	.05
496	Marty Barrett	.05
497	Ben McDonald	.05
498	Mark Salas	.05
499	Melido Perez	.05
500	Will Clark	.05
501	Mike Bielecki	.05
502	Carney Lansford	.05
503	Roy Smith	.05
504	Julio Valera RC	.05
505	Chuck Finley	.05
506	Darnell Coles	.05
507	Steve Jeltz	.05
508	Mike York RC	.05
509	Glenallen Hill	.05
510	John Franco	.05
511	Steve Balboni	.05
512	Jose Mesa RC	.05
513	Jerald Clark	.05
514	Mike Stanton	.05
515	Alvin Davis	.05
516	Karl Rhodes RC	.05
517	Joe Oliver	.05
518	Cris Carpenter	.05
519	Sparky Anderson	.10
520	Mark Grace	.05
521	Joe Orsulak	.05
522	Stan Belinda	.05
523	Rodney McCray RC	.05
524	Darrel Akerfelds	.05
525	Willie Randolph	.05
526a	Moises Alou (37 R 1990 Pirates)	.20
526b	Moises Alou (0 R 1990 Pirates)	.15
527a	Checklist 4 (Kevin McReynolds #719)	.05
527b	Checklist 4 (Kevin McReynolds #105)	.05
528	Denny Martinez	.05
529	Mark Newfield RC (#1 Draft Pick)	.05
530	Roger Clemens	.60
531	Dave Rhode RC	.05
532	Kirk McCaskill	.05
533	Oddibe McDowell	.05
534	Mike Jackson	.05
535	Ruben Sierra	.05
536	Mike Witt	.05
537	Jose Lind	.05
538	Bip Roberts	.05
539	Scott Terry	.05
540	George Brett	.60
541	Domingo Ramos	.05
542	Rob Murphy	.05
543	Junior Felix	.05
544	Alejandro Pena	.05
545	Dale Murphy	.15
546	Jeff Ballard	.05
547	Mike Pagliarulo	.05
548	Jaime Navarro	.05
549	John McNamara	.05
550	Eric Davis	.05
551	Bob Kipper	.05
552	Jeff Hamilton	.05
553	Joe Klink RC	.05
554	Brian Harper	.05
555	Turner Ward RC	.05
556	Gary Ward	.05
557	Wally Whitehurst	.05
558	Otis Nixon	.05
559	Adam Peterson	.05
560	Greg Smith RC	.05
561	Tim McIntosh RC (Future Star)	.05
562	Jeff Kunkel	.05
563	Brent Knackert RC	.05
564	Dante Bichette	.05
565	Craig Biggio	.05
566	Craig Wilson RC	.05
567	Dwayne Henry	.05
568	Ron Karkovice	.05
569	Curt Schilling	.05
570	Barry Bonds	.75
571	Pat Combs	.05
572	Dave Anderson	.05
573	Rich Rodriguez RC	.05
574	John Marzano	.05
575	Robin Yount	.35
576	Jeff Kaiser	.05
577	Bill Doran	.05
578	Dave West	.05
579	Roger Craig	.05
580	Dave Stewart	.05
581	Luis Quinones	.05
582	Marty Clary	.05
583	Tony Phillips	.05
584	Kevin Brown	.05
585	Pete O'Brien	.05
586	Fred Lynn	.05
587	Jose Offerman RC (Future Star)	.05
588a	Mark Whiten RC (Hand inside left border.)	.15
588b	Mark Whiten RC (Hand over left border.)	.20
589	Scott Ruskin RC	.05
590	Eddie Murray	.35
591	Ken Hill	.05
592	B.J. Surhoff	.05
593a	Mike Walker RC (No 1990 Canton-Akron stats.)	.15
593b	Mike Walker RC (1990 Canton-Akron stats)	.05
594	Rich Garces RC (Future Star)	.05
595	Bill Landrum	.05
596	Ronnie Walden RC (#1 Draft Pick)	.05
597	Jerry Don Gleaton	.05
598	Sam Horn	.05
599a	Greg Myers (No 1990 Syracuse stats.)	.10
599b	Greg Myers (1990 Syracuse stats)	.05
600	Bo Jackson	.10
601	Bob Ojeda	.05
602	Casey Candaele	.05
603a	Wes Chamberlain RC (Photo of Louie Meadows, no bat.)	.75
603b	Wes Chamberlain RC (Correct photo, holding bat.)	.05
604	Billy Hatcher	.05
605	Jeff Reardon	.05
606	Jim Gott	.05
607	Edgar Martinez	.05
608	Todd Burns	.05
609	Jeff Torborg	.05
610	Andres Galarraga	.05
611	Dave Eiland	.05
612	Steve Lyons	.05
613	Eric Show	.05
614	Luis Salazar	.05
615	Bert Blyleven	.05
616	Todd Zeile	.05
617	Bill Wegman	.05
618	Sil Campusano	.05
619	David Wells	.05
620	Ozzie Guillen	.05
621	Ted Power	.05
622	Jack Daugherty	.05
623	Jeff Blauser	.05
624	Tom Candiotti	.05
625	Terry Steinbach	.05
626	Gerald Young	.05
627	Tim Layana RC	.05
628	Greg Litton	.05
629	Wes Gardner	.05
630	Dave Winfield	.35
631	Mike Morgan	.05
632	Lloyd Moseby	.05
633	Kevin Tapani	.05
634	Henry Cotto	.05
635	Andy Hawkins	.05
636	Geronimo Pena RC	.05
637	Bruce Ruffin	.05
638	Mike Macfarlane	.05
639	Frank Robinson	.05
640	Andre Dawson	.20
641	Mike Henneman	.05
642	Hal Morris	.05
643	Jim Presley	.05
644	Chuck Crim	.05
645	Juan Samuel	.05
646	Andujar Cedeno RC	.05
647	Mark Portugal	.05
648	Lee Stevens RC	.05
649	Bill Sampen RC	.05
650	Jack Clark	.05
651	Alan Mills RC	.05
652	Kevin Romine	.05
653	Anthony Telford RC	.05
654	Paul Sorrento RC	.05
655	Erik Hanson	.05
656a	Checklist 5 (Vincente Palacios #348.)	.05
656b	Checklist 5 (Palacios #433.)	.05
656c	Checklist 5 (Palacios #438.)	.05
657	Mike Kingery	.05
658	Scott Aldred RC	.05
659	Oscar Azocar RC	.05
660	Lee Smith	.05
661	Steve Lake	.05
662	Rob Dibble	.05
663	Greg Brock	.05
664	John Farrell	.05
665	Mike LaValliere	.05
666	Danny Darwin	.05
667	Kent Anderson	.05
668	Bill Long	.05
669	Lou Pinella	.05
670	Rickey Henderson	.35
671	Andy McGaffigan	.05
672	Shane Mack	.05
673	Greg Olson RC	.05
674a	Kevin Gross (No diamond after 89 BB 1988.)	.10
674b	Kevin Gross (Diamond after 89 BB 1988.)	.05
675	Tom Brunansky	.05
676	Scott Chiamparino RC	.05
677	Billy Ripken	.05
678	Mark Davidson	.05
679	Bill Bathe RC	.05
680	David Cone	.05
681	Jeff Schaefer RC	.05
682	Ray Lankford RC	.15
683	Derek Lilliquist	.05
684	Milt Cuyler RC	.05
685	Doug Drabek	.05
686	Mike Gallego	.05
687a	John Cerutti (4.46 ERA 1990)	.05
687b	John Cerutti (4.76 ERA 1990)	.05
688	Rosario Rodriguez RC	.05
689	John Kruk	.05
690	Orel Hershiser	.05
691	Mike Blowers	.05
692a	Efrain Valdez RC (No text below stats.)	.15
692b	Efrain Valdez RC (Two lines of text below stats.)	.05
693	Francisco Cabrera	.05
694	Randy Veres	.05
695	Kevin Seitzer	.05
696	Steve Olin	.05
697	Shawn Abner	.05
698	Mark Guthrie	.05
699	Jim Lefebvre	.05
700	Jose Canseco	.25
701	Pascual Perez	.05

702	Tim Naehring **RC**	.05
703	Juan Agosto	.05
704	Devon White	.05
705	Robby Thompson	.05
706a	Brad Arnsberg (68.2 IP Rangers 1990)	.05
706b	Brad Arnsberg (62.2 IP Rangers 1990)	.05
707	Jim Eisenreich	.05
708	John Mitchell **RC**	.05
709	Matt Sinatro	.05
710	Kent Hrbek	.05
711	Jose DeLeon	.05
712	Ricky Jordan	.05
713	Scott Scudder	.05
714	Marvell Wynne	.05
715	Tim Burke	.05
716	Bob Geren	.05
717	Phil Bradley	.05
718	Steve Crawford	.05
719	Keith Miller	.05
720	Cecil Fielder	.05
721	Mark Lee **RC**	.05
722	Wally Backman	.05
723	Candy Maldonado	.05
724	David Segui **RC**	.10
725	Ron Gant	.05
726	Phil Stephenson	.05
727	Mookie Wilson	.05
728	Scott Sanderson	.05
729	Don Zimmer	.05
730	Barry Larkin	.05
731	Jeff Gray **RC**	.05
732	Franklin Stubbs	.05
733	Kelly Downs	.05
734	John Russell	.05
735	Ron Darling	.05
736	Dick Schofield	.05
737	Tim Crews	.05
738	Mel Hall	.05
739	Russ Swan **RC**	.05
740	Ryne Sandberg	.50
741	Jimmy Key	.05
742	Tommy Gregg	.05
743	Bryn Smith	.05
744	Nelson Santovenia	.05
745	Doug Jones	.05
746	John Shelby	.05
747	Tony Fossas	.05
748	Al Newman	.05
749	Greg Harris	.05
750	Bobby Bonilla	.05
751	Wayne Edwards **RC**	.05
752	Kevin Bass	.05
753	Paul Marak **RC**	.05
754	Bill Pecota	.05
755	Mark Langston	.05
756	Jeff Huson	.05
757	Mark Gardner	.05
758	Mike Devereaux	.05
759	Bobby Cox	.05
760	Benny Santiago	.05
761	Larry Andersen	.05
762	Mitch Webster	.05
763	Dana Kiecker **RC**	.05
764	Mark Carreon	.05
765	Shawon Dunston	.05
766	Jeff Robinson	.05
767	Dan Wilson **RC** (#1 Draft Pick)	.10
768	Donn Pall	.05
769	Tim Sherrill **RC**	.05
770	Jay Howell	.05
771	Gary Redus	.05
772	Kent Mercker **RC**	.05
773	Tom Foley	.05
774	Dennis Rasmussen	.05
775	Julio Franco	.05
776	Brent Mayne **RC**	.05
777	John Candelaria	.05
778	Danny Gladden	.05
779	Carmelo Martinez	.05
780a	Randy Myers (Career losses 15.)	.10
780b	Randy Myers (Career losses 19.)	.05
781	Darryl Hamilton	.05
782	Jim Deshaies	.05
783	Joel Skinner	.05
784	Willie Fraser	.05
785	Scott Fletcher	.05
786	Eric Plunk	.05
787	Checklist 6	.05
788	Bob Milacki	.05
789	Tom Lasorda	.05
790	Ken Griffey Jr.	.60
791	Mike Benjamin **RC**	.05
792	Mike Greenwell	.05

Tiffany

Topps ended its annual run of special collectors' edition boxed sets in 1991, producing the glossy sets inconsiderably more limited quantity than in previous years. Cards are identical to the regular 1991 Topps set except for the use of white cardboard stock and a high-gloss front finish.

	NM/M
Unopened Set (792):	135.00
Complete Set (792):	85.00
Common Player:	.10

Desert Shield

As a special treat for U.S. armed services personnel serving in the Persian Gulf prior to and during the war with Iraq, Topps produced a special edition featuring a gold-foil overprint honoring the military effort. Enough cards were produced to equal approximately 6,800 sets. While some cards actually reached the troops in the Middle East, many were shortstopped by military supply personnel stateside and sold into the hobby. Many of the cards sent to Saudi Arabia never returned to the U.S., however, making the supply of available cards somewhat scarce. The checklist cards in the set were not overprinted. At least two types of counterfeit overprint have been seen on genuine Topps cards in an attempt to cash in on the scarcity of these war "veterans."

	NM/M
Complete Set (792):	1,200
Common Player:	1.00
Wax Pack:	60.00

Traded

"Team USA" players are featured in the 1991 Topps Traded set. The cards feature the same style as the regular 1991 issue, including the 40th anniversary logo. The set includes 132 cards and showcases rookies and traded players along with "Team USA." The cards are numbered with a "T" designation in alphabetical order. Wax-pack versions have a gray cardboard stock (unlike the box-set's white stock). Each of the wax-pack cards can be found with one or two asterisks preceding the copyright line on back.

		NM/M
Unopened Retail or Hobby Set (132):		12.00
Complete Set (132):		10.00
Common Player:		.05
Wax Pack (7):		.65
Wax Box (36):		15.00
1	Juan Agosto	.05
2	Roberto Alomar	.15
3	Wally Backman	.05
4	Jeff Bagwell **RC**	3.00
5	Skeeter Barnes **RC**	.05
6	Steve Bedrosian	.05
7	Derek Bell **RC**	.05
8	George Bell	.05
9	Rafael Belliard	.05
10	Dante Bichette	.05
11	Bud Black	.05
12	Mike Boddicker	.05
13	Sid Bream	.05
14	Hubie Brooks	.05
15	Brett Butler	.05
16	Ivan Calderon	.05
17	John Candelaria	.05
18	Tom Candiotti	.05
19	Gary Carter	.50
20	Joe Carter	.05
21	Rick Cerone	.05
22	Jack Clark	.05
23	Vince Coleman	.05
24	Scott Coolbaugh	.05
25	Danny Cox	.05
26	Danny Darwin	.05
27	Chili Davis	.05
28	Glenn Davis	.05
29	Steve Decker **RC**	.05
30	Rob Deer	.05
31	Rich DeLucia **RC**	.05
32	John Dettmer **RC** (USA)	.05
33	Brian Downing	.05
34	Darren Dreifort **RC** (USA)	.25
35	Kirk Dressendorfer **RC**	.05
36	Jim Essian	.05
37	Dwight Evans	.05
38	Steve Farr	.05
39	Jeff Fassero **RC**	.05
40	Junior Felix	.05
41	Tony Fernandez	.05
42	Steve Finley	.05
43	Jim Fregosi	.05
44	Gary Gaetti	.05
45	Jason Giambi **RC** (USA)	4.00
46	Kirk Gibson	.05
47	Leo Gomez **RC**	.05
48	Luis Gonzalez **RC**	1.00
49	Jeff Granger **RC** (USA)	.10
50	Todd Greene **RC** (USA)	.05
51	Jeffrey Hammonds **RC** (USA)	.15
52	Mike Hargrove	.05
53	Pete Harnisch	.05
54	Rick Helling **RC** (USA)	.10
55	Glenallen Hill	.05
56	Charlie Hough	.05
57	Pete Incaviglia	.05
58	Bo Jackson	.10
59	Danny Jackson	.05
60	Reggie Jefferson **RC**	.05
61	Charles Johnson **RC** (USA)	.15
62	Jeff Johnson **RC**	.05
63	Todd Johnson **RC**	.05
64	Barry Jones	.05
65	Chris Jones	.05
66	Scott Kamienecki	.05
67	Pat Kelly **RC**	.05
68	Darryl Kile **RC**	.05
69	Chuck Knoblauch **RC**	.05
70	Bill Krueger	.05
71	Scott Leius **RC**	.05
72	Donnie Leshnock **RC** (USA)	.05
73	Mark Lewis	.05
74	Candy Maldonado	.05
75	Jason McDonald **RC** (USA)	.05
76	Willie McGee	.05
77	Fred McGriff	.05
78	Billy McMillon **RC** (USA)	.05
79	Hal McRae	.05
80	Dan Melendez **RC** (USA)	.05
81	Orlando Merced **RC**	.05
82	Jack Morris	.05
83	Phil Nevin **RC** (USA)	.50
84	Otis Nixon	.05
85	Johnny Oates	.05
86	Bob Ojeda	.05
87	Mike Pagliarulo	.05
88	Dean Palmer **RC**	.05
89	Dave Parker	.05
90	Terry Pendleton	.05
91	Tony Phillips **RC** (USA)	.10
92	Doug Piatt **RC**	.05
93	Ron Polk (U.S.A.)	.05
94	Tim Raines	.05
95	Willie Randolph	.05
96	Dave Righetti	.05
97	Ernie Riles	.05
98	Chris Roberts **RC** (USA)	.05
99	Jeff Robinson/Angels	.05
100	Jeff Robinson/Orioles	.05
101	Ivan Rodriguez **RC**	3.00
102	Steve Rodriguez **RC** (USA)	.05
103	Tom Runnells	.05
104	Scott Sanderson	.05
105	Bob Scanlan **RC**	.05
106	Pete Schourek **RC**	.05
107	Gary Scott **RC**	.05
108	Paul Shuey **RC** (USA)	.10
109	Doug Simons **RC**	.05
110	Dave Smith	.05
111	Cory Snyder	.05
112	Luis Sojo	.05
113	Kennie Steenstra **RC** (USA)	.05
114	Darryl Strawberry	.05
115	Franklin Stubbs	.05
116	Todd Taylor **RC** (USA)	.05
117	Wade Taylor **RC**	.05
118	Garry Templeton	.05
119	Mickey Tettleton	.05
120	Tim Teufel	.05
121	Mike Timlin	.05
122	David Tuttle **RC** (USA)	.05
123	Mo Vaughn **RC**	.25
124	Jeff Ware **RC** (USA)	.05
125	Devon White	.05
126	Mark Whiten	.05
127	Mitch Williams	.05
128	Craig Wilson **RC** (USA)	.05
129	Willie Wilson	.05
130	Chris Wimmer **RC** (USA)	.05
131	Ivan Zweig **RC** (USA)	.05
132	Checklist	.05

Traded Tiffany

The final year of production for Topps "Tiffany" parallel boxed sets saw production levels slashed for the 132-card Traded version. Value of the sets has risen dramatically with the hobby's perception of the set's scarcity and the development of key rookies such as Bagwell, Giambi and I-Rod. Like the regular Traded set, cards are numbered in alphabetical order with a "T" suffix.

	NM/M
Unopened Set (132):	165.00
Complete Set (132):	90.00
Common Player:	.25
Stars and Rookies:	4X

Traded Brooks Robinson Bronze

This 1/4-size metal replica of Robinson's first-ever Topps card was issued to dealers who purchased cases of 1991 Topps Traded sets. Each detail of the 1957 Robinson card is reproduced on the 1-1/4" x 1-3/4" bronze metal mini-card, right down to the stats.

		NM/M
328	Brooks Robinson	15.00

Box Panel Cards

Styled like the standard 1991 Topps cards, this 16-card set honors milestones of the featured players. The cards were found on the bottom of wax pack boxes. The cards are designated in alphabetical order by (A-P) and are not numbered.

		NM/M
Complete Set (16):		6.00
Common Player:		.15
A	Bert Blyleven	.15
B	George Brett	1.25
C	Brett Butler	.15
D	Andre Dawson	.50
E	Dwight Evans	.15
F	Carlton Fisk	.75
G	Alfredo Griffin	.15
H	Rickey Henderson	.75
I	Willie McGee	.15
J	Dale Murphy	.50
K	Eddie Murray	.75
L	Dave Parker	.15
M	Jeff Reardon	.15
N	Nolan Ryan	2.25
O	Juan Samuel	.15
P	Robin Yount	.75

All-Star Glossy Set of 22

Continuing the same basic format used since 1984, these glossy-front rack-pack inserts honor the players, manager and honorary captains of the previous year's All-Star Game. Fronts have a league logo in the lower-left corner, a 1990 All-Star banner above the photo and a Topps 40th anniversary logo superimposed over the photo. Backs have a shield and star design and the legend "1990 All-Star Commemorative Set" above the player's name, position and card number. Backs are printed in red and blue.

		NM/M
Complete Set (22):		3.00
Common Player:		.05
1	Tony LaRussa	.05
2	Mark McGwire	.85
3	Steve Sax	.05
4	Wade Boggs	.50
5	Cal Ripken, Jr.	1.00
6	Rickey Henderson	.40
7	Ken Griffey Jr.	.75
8	Jose Canseco	.30
9	Sandy Alomar, Jr.	.05
10	Bob Welch	.05
11	Al Lopez	.05
12	Roger Craig	.05
13	Will Clark	.50
14	Ryne Sandberg	.50
15	Chris Sabo	.05
16	Ozzie Smith	.50
17	Kevin Mitchell	.05
18	Len Dykstra	.05
19	Andre Dawson	.15
20	Mike Scoscia	.05
21	Jack Armstrong	.05
22	Juan Marichal	.05

Glossy Rookies

Similar in format to previous years' glossy rookies sets, this 33-card issue was available one per pack in 100-card jumbo cello packs. Card fronts have a colored "1990 Rookies" banner above the player photo, with the player's name in red in a yellow bar beneath. The Topps 40th anniversary logo appears in one of the upper corners of the photo. Backs are printed in red and blue and feature a "1990 Rook-

ies Commemorative Set" shield logo. The player's name, position, team and card number are printed beneath. Cards are numbered alphabetically.

		NM/M
Complete Set (33):		2.00
Common Player:		.10
1	Sandy Alomar, Jr.	.10
2	Kevin Appier	.10
3	Steve Avery	.10
4	Carlos Baerga	.10
5	John Burkett	.10
6	Alex Cole	.10
7	Pat Combs	.10
8	Delino DeShields	.10
9	Travis Fryman	.10
10	Marquis Grissom	.10
11	Mike Harkey	.10
12	Glenallen Hill	.10
13	Jeff Huson	.10
14	Felix Jose	.10
15	Dave Justice	.25
16	Jim Leyritz	.10
17	Kevin Maas	.10
18	Ben McDonald	.10
19	Kent Mercker	.10
20	Hal Morris	.10
21	Chris Nabholz	.10
22	Tim Naehring	.10
23	Jose Offerman	.10
24	John Olerud	.25
25	Scott Radinsky	.10
26	Scott Ruskin	.10
27	Kevin Tapani	.10
28	Frank Thomas	1.50
29	Randy Tomlin	.10
30	Greg Vaughn	.10
31	Robin Ventura	.25
32	Larry Walker	.10
33	Todd Zeile	.10

East Coast National Reprints

Produced in Topps' 40th anniversary year, this four-card set was issued at the 1991 East Coast National card show, the first card show in which Topps had ever participated. A total of 40,000 sets were reportedly issued in the now-standard 2-1/2" x 3-1/2" format. Fronts reproduce first Topps cards of four baseball greats while backs, printed in blue, carry a reprint notice, ad for the card show and Topps copyright.

		NM/M
Complete Set (4):		7.50
Common Card:		1.50
(1)	Mickey Mantle/1952	5.00
(2)	Hank Aaron/1954	3.00
(3)	Frank Robinson/1957	1.50
(4)	Stan Musial/1958	1.50

Gallery of Champions

Topps final issue of metallic mini-cards continued the theme of honoring the previous year's winners of major awards. The 1/4-size (1-1/4" x 1-3/4") ingots were issued in complete boxed sets of aluminum, bronze and silver in special display cases. To promote quantity sales, Topps offered a special pewter version of the Rickey Henderson ingot.

		NM/M
Complete Aluminum Set (12):		22.50
Complete Bronze Set (12):		45.00
Complete Silver Set (12):		180.00
(1a)	Sandy Alomar Jr./ Aluminum	1.00
(1b)	Sandy Alomar Jr./ Bronze	2.50

(1s)	Sandy Alomar Jr./ Silver	6.00
(2a)	Barry Bonds/ Aluminum	10.00
(2b)	Barry Bonds/Bronze	15.00
(2s)	Barry Bonds/Silver	65.00
(3a)	George Brett/ Aluminum	7.50
(3b)	George Brett/Bronze	10.00
(3s)	George Brett/Silver	50.00
(4a)	Doug Drabek/ Aluminum	1.00
(4b)	Doug Drabek/Bronze	2.50
(4s)	Doug Drabek/Silver	6.00
(5a)	Cecil Fielder/ Aluminum	1.00
(5b)	Cecil Fielder/Bronze	2.50
(5s)	Cecil Fielder/Silver	6.00
(6a)	John Franco/ Aluminum	1.00
(6b)	John Franco/Bronze	2.50
(6s)	John Franco/Silver	6.00
(7a)	Rickey Henderson/ Aluminum	3.00
(7b)	Rickey Henderson/ Bronze	6.00
(7s)	Rickey Henderson/ Silver	35.00
(7p)	Rickey Henderson/ Pewter	15.00
(8a)	Dave Justice/ Aluminum	1.25
(8b)	Dave Justice/Bronze	3.00
(8s)	Dave Justice/Silver	9.00
(9a)	Willie McGee/ Aluminum	1.00
(9b)	Willie McGee/Bronze	2.50
(9s)	Willie McGee/Silver	6.00
(10a)	Ryne Sandberg/ Aluminum	6.00
(10b)	Ryne Sandberg/ Bronze	7.50
(10s)	Ryne Sandberg/Silver	40.00
(11a)	Bobby Thigpen/ Aluminum	1.00
(11b)	Bobby Thigpen/Bronze	2.50
(11s)	Bobby Thigpen/Silver	6.00
(12a)	Bob Welch/Aluminum	1.00
(12b)	Bob Welch/Bronze	2.50
(12s)	Bob Welch/Silver	6.00

Golden Spikes Award

Each year the United States Baseball Federation honors the outstanding amateur player with the Golden Spikes Award. This card was handed out at the Nov. 20, 1991 awards banquet honoring Arizona State star Mike Kelly. Production was reported as 600 cards.

	NM/M
Mike Kelly	85.00

Joe Garagiola

Virtually identical to the personal business card which Topps produced for long-time NBC announcer and former major leaguer Joe Garagiola in 1976, this 1991 version makes mention of the Today Show on

both front and back. The front is in the format of a 1973 Topps card and has a color portrait. The back resembles the 1976 Topps card, is in black-and-white and provides contact information.

		NM/M
1	Joe Garagiola	8.00

Micro

	NM/M
Complete Set (792):	9.00
Common Player:	.05
Stars/Rookies:	1-1.5X

Babe Ruth

This 11-card set by Topps was released in honor of the NBC movie about Babe Ruth. The cards were released on a limited basis. The card fronts feature full-color photos from the movie, while the flip sides are printed horizontally and describe the front photo. The cards are numbered on the back.

		NM/M
Complete Set (11):		12.50
Common Player:		1.00
1	Sunday Oct. 6, NBC	1.00
2	Stephen Lang as Babe Ruth	1.00
3	Bruce Weitz as Miller Huggins	1.00
4	Lisa Zane as Claire Ruth	1.00
5	Donald Moffat as Jacob Ruppert	1.00
6	Neil McDonough as Lou Gehrig	1.00
7	Pete Rose as Ty Cobb	5.00
8	Baseball Consultant (Rod Carew)	2.50
9	Miller Huggins, Babe Ruth	1.00
10	Ruth In Action	1.00
11	Babe Calls His Shot	1.00

Superstar Stand-Ups

Another of Topps' efforts over the years to market candy containers with a baseball player theme, the 1991 Superstar Stand-Ups were a test issue. Sold in a color-printed paper envelope, Stand-Ups are a hard plastic container filled with candy tablets. In bright see-through colors, the containers measure 2-1/16" x 2-9/16" and are vaguely shaped like a head and shoulders. A paper label attached to the front of the plastic has a player portrait with his team in a banner above and his name in a strip at bottom. Backs

have a baseball design on the label with the Topps 40th anniversary logo at top. The player's name, team and position are in color bars at the bottom, with the item number at left. At center are the player's height, weight, birth date, batting and throwing preference and the year and number of his Topps rookie card. Clear (non-colored) plastic containers are also known for each player, though their relative scarcity to the colored pieces is currently undetermined.

	NM/M
Complete Set (36):	45.00
Common Player:	1.00
Wax Pack (1):	1.50
Wax Box (36):	30.00
1	Jim Abbott	1.00
2	Sandy Alomar	1.00
3	Wade Boggs	2.50
4	Barry Bonds	5.00
5	Bobby Bonilla	1.00
6	George Brett	3.00
7	Jose Canseco	1.50
8	Will Clark	1.00
9	Roger Clemens	3.00
10	Eric Davis	1.00
11	Andre Dawson	1.50
12	Len Dykstra	1.00
13	Cecil Fielder	1.00
14	Carlton Fisk	2.00
15	Dwight Gooden	1.00
16	Mark Grace	1.00
17	Ken Griffey Jr.	3.50
18	Tony Gwynn	2.50
19	Rickey Henderson	2.00
20	Bo Jackson	1.50
21	Dave Justice	1.00
22	Kevin Maas	1.00
23	Ramon Martinez	1.00
24	Don Mattingly	3.00
25	Ben McDonald	1.00
26	Mark McGwire	4.00
27	Kevin Mitchell	1.00
28	Cal Ripken, Jr.	5.00
29	Nolan Ryan	5.00
30	Ryne Sandberg	2.50
31	Ozzie Smith	2.50
32	Dave Stewart	1.00
33	Darryl Strawberry	1.00
34	Frank Viola	1.00
35	Matt Williams	1.00
36	Robin Yount	2.00

"1953" Topps Archives Promos

This nine-card set was issued to promote Topps' 1953 Archives set. Besides seven of the cards being reprinted from the '53 set, the promo set included two of the "new" 1953-style cards which were included in the Archives issue - cards of Hank Aaron and Eleanor Engle, the first woman to sign a minor league contract in modern times. Card fronts are identical to the issued Archives cards, while the backs are white with red Archives logo and "Pre-production Sample" notation.

	NM/M
Complete Set (9):	75.00
Common Player:	7.50
(1)	Hank Aaron	12.00
(2)	Roy Campanella	7.50
(3)	Eleanor Engle	7.50
(4)	Bob Feller	7.50
(5)	Whitey Ford	7.50
(6)	Mickey Mantle	20.00
(7)	Willie Mays	12.00
(8)	Jackie Robinson	10.00
(9)	Satchell Paige	10.00

"1953" Topps Archives

Billed as "The Ultimate 1953 Set," this issue reproduced 273 of the original 274-card 1953 Topps set. (Card #174, Billy Loes, was not reproduced due to lack of permission from the former Dodgers pitcher, though cards with #174 are known with a Loes back and another player on the front.) The Archives issue downsized the cards from their original 2-5/8" x 3-3/4" size to the now-standard 2-1/2" x 3-1/2" format. More than 50 cards of players who were not included in the 1953 Topps set were created as part of the Archives issue. Because Topps chose to use black-and-white photos and colorized backgrounds for most of the "extended" cards, rather than paintings as on the originals, collector interest in the Archives issue was diminished. Only 18,000 cases were reportedly produced.

	NM/M
Complete Set (337):	45.00
Common Player:	.10
Wax Pack (12):	1.50
Wax Box (36):	35.00
1	Jackie Robinson	7.50
2	Luke Easter	.10
3	George Crowe	.10
4	Ben Wade	.10
5	Joe Dobson	.10
6	Sam Jones	.10
7	Bob Borkowski	.10
8	Clem Koshorek	.10
9	Joe Collins	.10
10	Smoky Burgess	.10
11	Sal Yvars	.10
12	Howie Judson	.10
13	Conrado Marrero	.10
14	Clem Labine	.10
15	Bobo Newsom	.10
16	Peanuts Lowrey	.10
17	Billy Hitchcock	.10
18	Ted Lepcio	.10
19	Mel Parnell	.10
20	Hank Thompson	.10
21	Billy Johnson	.10
22	Howie Fox	.10
23	Toby Atwell	.10
24	Ferris Fain	.10
25	Ray Boone	.10
26	Dale Mitchell	.10
27	Roy Campanella	1.50
28	Eddie Pellagrini	.10
29	Hal Jeffcoat	.10
30	Willard Nixon	.10
31	Ewell Blackwell	.10
32	Clyde Vollmer	.10
33	Bob Kennedy	.10
34	George Shuba	.10
35	Irv Noren	.10
36	Johnny Groth	.10
37	Eddie Mathews	1.00
38	Jim Hearn	.10
39	Eddie Miksis	.10
40	John Lipon	.10
41	Enos Slaughter	.50
42	Gus Zernial	.10
43	Gil McDougald	.30
44	Ellis Kinder	.10
45	Grady Hatton	.10
46	Johnny Klippstein	.10
47	Bubba Church	.10
48	Bob Del Greco	.10
49	Faye Throneberry	.10
50	Chuck Dressen	.10
51	Frank Campos	.10
52	Ted Gray	.10
53	Sherman Lollar	.10
54	Bob Feller	1.00
55	Maurice McDermott	.10
56	Gerald Staley	.10
57	Carl Scheib	.10
58	George Metkovich	.10
59	Karl Drews	.10
60	Cloyd Boyer	.10
61	Early Wynn	.50
62	Monte Irvin	.50
63	Gus Niarhos	.10
64	Dave Philley	.10
65	Earl Harrist	.10
66	Orestes Minoso	.25
67	Roy Sievers	.10
68	Del Rice	.10
69	Dick Brodowski	.10
70	Ed Yuhas	.10
71	Tony Bartirome	.10
72	Fred Hutchinson	.10
73	Eddie Robinson	.10
74	Joe Rossi	.10
75	Mike Garcia	.10
76	Pee Wee Reese	1.00
77	John Mize	.75
78	Al Schoendienst	.50
79	Johnny Wyrostek	.10
80	Jim Hegan	.10
81	Joe Black	.10
82	Mickey Mantle	12.50
83	Howie Pollet	.10
84	Bob Hooper	.10
85	Bobby Morgan	.10
86	Billy Martin	.35
87	Ed Lopat	.20
88	Willie Jones	.10
89	Chuck Stobbs	.10
90	Hank Edwards	.10
91	Ebba St. Claire	.10
92	Paul Minner	.10
93	Hal Rice	.10
94	William Kennedy	.10
95	Willard Marshall	.10
96	Virgil Trucks	.10
97	Don Kolloway	.10
98	Cal Abrams	.10
99	Dave Madison	.10
100	Bill Miller	.10
101	Ted Wilks	.10
102	Connie Ryan	.10
103	Joe Astroth	.10
104	Yogi Berra	1.50
105	Joe Nuxhall	.10
106	John Antonelli	.10
107	Danny O'Connell	.10
108	Bob Porterfield	.10
109	Alvin Dark	.10
110	Herman Wehmeier	.10
111	Hank Sauer	.10
112	Ned Garver	.10
113	Jerry Priddy	.10
114	Phil Rizzuto	1.00
115	George Spencer	.10
116	Frank Smith	.10
117	Sid Gordon	.10
118	Gus Bell	.10
119	John Sain	.25
120	Davey Williams	.10
121	Walt Dropo	.10
122	Elmer Valo	.10
123	Tommy Byrne	.10
124	Sibby Sisti	.10
125	Dick Williams	.20
126	Bill Connelly	.10
127	Clint Courtney	.10
128	Wilmer Mizell	.10
129	Keith Thomas	.10
130	Turk Lown	.10
131	Harry Byrd	.10
132	Tom Morgan	.10
133	Gil Coan	.10
134	Rube Walker	.10
135	Al Rosen	.25
136	Ken Heintzelman	.10
137	John Rutherford	.10
138	George Kell	.50
139	Sammy White	.10
140	Tommy Glaviano	.10
141	Allie Reynolds	.10
142	Vic Wertz	.10
143	Billy Pierce	.20
144	Bob Schultz	.10
145	Harry Dorish	.10
146	Granville Hamner	.10
147	Warren Spahn	1.00
148	Mickey Grasso	.10
149	Dom DiMaggio	.25
150	Harry Simpson	.10
151	Hoyt Wilhelm	.50
152	Bob Adams	.10
153	Andy Seminick	.10
154	Dick Groat	.20
155	Dutch Leonard	.10
156	Jim Rivera	.10
157	Bob Addis	.10
158	John Logan	.10
159	Wayne Terwilliger	.10
160	Bob Young	.10
161	Vern Bickford	.10
162	Ted Kluszewski	.35
163	Fred Hatfield	.10
164	Frank Shea	.10
165	Billy Hoeft	.10
166	Bill Hunter	.10
167	Art Schult	.10
168	Willard Schmidt	.10
169	Dizzy Trout	.10
170	Bill Werle	.10
171	Bill Glynn	.10
172	Rip Repulski	.10
173	Preston Ward	.10
175	Ron Kline	.10
176	Don Hoak	.10
177	Jim Dyck	.10
178	Jim Waugh	.10
179	Gene Hermanski	.10
180	Virgil Stallcup	.10
181	Al Zarilla	.10
182	Bob Hofman	.10
183	Stu Miller	.10
184	Hal Brown	.10
185	Jim Pendleton	.10
186	Charlie Bishop	.10
187	Jim Fridley	.10
188	Andy Carey	.10
189	Ray Jablonski	.10
190	Dixie Walker	.10
191	Ralph Kiner	.50
192	Wally Westlake	.10
193	Mike Clark	.10
194	Eddie Kazak	.10
195	Ed McGhee	.10
196	Bob Keegan	.10
197	Del Crandall	.10
198	Forrest Main	.10
199	Marion Fricano	.10
200	Gordon Goldsberry	.10
201	Paul La Palme	.10
202	Carl Sawatski	.10
203	Cliff Fannin	.10
204	Dick Bokelmann	.10
205	Vern Benson	.10
206	Ed Bailey	.10
207	Whitey Ford	1.00
208	Jim Wilson	.10
209	Jim Greengrass	.10
210	Bob Cerv	.10
211	J.W. Porter	.10
212	Jack Dittmer	.10
213	Ray Scarborough	.10
214	Bill Bruton	.10
215	Gene Conley	.10
216	Jim Hughes	.10
217	Murray Wall	.10
218	Les Fusselman	.10
219	Pete Runnels	.10
220	Satchell Paige	4.00
221	Bob Milliken	.10
222	Vic Janowicz	.10
223	John O'Brien	.10
224	Lou Sleater	.10
225	Bobby Shantz	.20
226	Ed Erautt	.10
227	Morris Martin	.10
228	Hal Newhouser	.10
229	Rocky Krshnich	.10
230	Johnny Lindell	.10
231	Solly Hemus	.10
232	Dick Kokos	.10
233	Al Aber	.10
234	Ray Murray	.10
235	John Hetki	.10
236	Harry Perkowski	.10
237	Clarence Podbielan	.10
238	Cal Hogue	.10
239	Jim Delsing	.10
240	Freddie Marsh	.10
241	Al Sima	.10
242	Charlie Silvera	.10
243	Carlos Bernier	.10
244	Willie Mays	7.50
245	Bill Norman	.10
246	Roy Face	.10
247	Mike Sandlock	.10
248	Gene Stephens	.10
249	Ed O'Brien	.10
250	Bob Wilson	.10
251	Sid Hudson	.10
252	Henry Foiles	.10
254	Preacher Roe	.10
255	Dixie Howell	.10
256	Les Peden	.10
257	Bob Boyd	.10
258	Jim Gilliam	.35
259	Roy McMillan	.10
260	Sam Calderone	.10
262	Bob Oldis	.10
263	John Podres	.35
264	Gene Woodling	.35
265	Jackie Jensen	.35
266	Bob Cain	.10
269	Duane Pillette	.10
270	Vern Stephens	.10
272	Bill Antonello	.10
273	Harvey Haddix	.10
274	John Riddle	.10
276	Ken Raffensberger	.10
277	Don Lund	.10
278	Willie Miranda	.10
279	Joe Coleman	.10
280	Milt Bolling	.10
281	Jimmie Dykes	.10
282	Ralph Houk	.35
283	Frank Thomas	.10
284	Bob Lemon	.50
285	Joe Adcock	.10
286	Jimmy Piersall	.10
287	Mickey Vernon	.10
288	Robin Roberts	.50
289	Rogers Hornsby	.50
290	Hank Bauer	.10
291	Hoot Evers	.10
292	Whitey Lockman	.10
293	Ralph Branca	.25
294	Wally Post	.10
295	Phil Cavarretta	.10
296	Gil Hodges	.35
297	Roy Smalley	.10
298	Bob Friend	.10
299	Dusty Rhodes	.25
300	Eddie Stanky	.10
301	Harvey Kuenn	.25

302	Marty Marion	.10
303	Sal Maglie	.10
304	Lou Boudreau	.50
305	Carl Furillo	.35
306	Bobo Holloman	.10
307	Steve O'Neill	.10
308	Carl Erskine	.25
309	Leo Durocher	.25
310	Lew Burdette	.10
311	Richie Ashburn	.50
312	Hoyt Wilhelm	.50
313	Bucky Harris	.50
314	Joe Garagiola	.50
315	Johnny Pesky	.10
316	Fred Haney	.10
317	Hank Aaron	7.50
318	Curt Simmons	.10
319	Ted Williams	7.50
320	Don Newcombe	.35
321	Charlie Grimm	.10
322	Paul Richards	.10
323	Wes Westrum	.10
324	Vern Law	.10
325	Casey Stengel	1.00
326	Hall of Fame Inductees (Dizzy Dean, Al Simmons)	1.00
327	Duke Snider	1.00
328	Bill Rigney	.10
329	Al Lopez	.50
330	Bobby Thomson	.35
331	Nellie Fox	.50
332	Eleanor Engle	.10
333	Larry Doby	.50
334	Billy Goodman	.10
335	Checklist 1-140	.10
336	Checklist 141-280	.10
337	Checklist 281-337	.10

1990 Major League Debut

This 171-card set features the players who made their Major League debut in 1990. The cards are styled like the 1991 Topps cards and are numbered in alphabetical order. The card backs are printed horizontally and feature information about the player's debut and statistics. The issue was sold only as a boxed set through hobby channels.

		NM/M
Complete Set (171):		5.00
Common Player:		.05
1	Paul Abbott	.05
2	Steve Adkins	.05
3	Scott Aldred	.05
4	Gerald Alexander	.05
5	Moises Alou	.25
6	Steve Avery	.05
7	Oscar Azocar	.05
8	Carlos Baerga	.05
9	Kevin Baez	.05
10	Jeff Baldwin	.05
11	Brian Barnes	.05
12	Kevin Bearse	.05
13	Kevin Belcher	.05
14	Mike Bell	.05
15	Sean Berry	.05
16	Joe Bitker	.05
17	Willie Blair	.05
18	Brian Bohanon	.05
19	Mike Bordick	.05
20	Shawn Boskie	.05
21	Rod Brewer	.05
22	Kevin Brown	.10
23	Dave Burba	.05
24	Jim Campbell	.05
25	Ozzie Canseco	.05
26	Chuck Carr	.05
27	Larry Casian	.05
28	Andujar Cedeno	.05
29	Wes Chamberlain	.05
30	Scott Chiamparino	.05
31	Steve Chitren	.05
32	Pete Coachman	.05
33	Alex Cole	.05
34	Jeff Conine	.10
35	Scott Cooper	.05
36	Milt Cuyler	.05
37	Steve Decker	.05
38	Rich DeLucia	.05
39	Delino DeShields	.05
40	Mark Dewey	.05
41	Carlos Diaz	.05
42	Lance Dickson	.05
43	Narciso Elvira	.05
44	Luis Encarnacion	.05
45	Scott Erickson	.05
46	Paul Faries	.05
47	Howard Farmer	.05
48	Alex Fernandez	.05
49	Travis Fryman	.50
50	Rich Garces	.05
51	Carlos Garcia	.05
52	Mike Gardiner	.05
53	Bernard Gilkey	.05
54	Tom Gilles	.05
55	Jerry Goff	.05
56	Leo Gomez	.05
57	Luis Gonzalez	.75
58	Joe Grahe	.05
59	Craig Grebeck	.05
60	Kip Gross	.05
61	Eric Gunderson	.05
62	Chris Hammond	.05
63	Dave Hansen	.05
64	Reggie Harris	.05
65	Bill Haselman	.05
66	Randy Hennis	.05
67	Carlos Hernandez	.05
68	Howard Hilton	.05
69	Dave Hollins	.05
70	Darren Holmes	.05
71	John Hoover	.05
72	Steve Howard	.05
73	Thomas Howard	.05
74	Todd Hundley	.05
75	Daryl Irvine	.05
76	Chris Jelic	.05
77	Dana Kiecker	.05
78	Brent Knackert	.05
79	Jimmy Kremers	.05
80	Jerry Kutzler	.05
81	Ray Lankford	.05
82	Tim Layana	.05
83	Terry Lee	.05
84	Mark Leiter	.05
85	Scott Leius	.05
86	Mark Leonard	.05
87	Darren Lewis	.05
88	Scott Lewis	.05
89	Jim Leyritz	.05
90	Dave Liddell	.05
91	Luis Lopez	.05
92	Kevin Maas	.05
93	Bob MacDonald	.05
94	Carlos Maldonado	.05
95	Chuck Malone	.05
96	Ramon Manon	.05
97	Jeff Manto	.05
98	Paul Marak	.05
99	Tino Martinez	.25
100	Derrick May	.05
101	Brent Mayne	.05
102	Paul McClellan	.05
103	Rodney McCray	.05
104	Tim McIntosh	.05
105	Brian McRae	.05
106	Jose Melendez	.05
107	Orlando Merced	.05
108	Alan Mills	.05
109	Gino Minutelli	.05
110	Mickey Morandini	.05
111	Pedro Munoz	.05
112	Chris Nabholz	.05
113	Tim Naehring	.05
114	Charles Nagy	.05
115	Jim Neidlinger	.05
116	Rafael Novoa	.05
117	Jose Offerman	.05
118	Omar Olivares	.05
119	Javier Ortiz	.05
120	Al Osuna	.05
121	Rick Parker	.05
122	Dave Pavlas	.05
123	Geronimo Pena	.05
124	Mike Perez	.05
125	Phil Plantier	.05
126	Jim Poole	.05
127	Tom Quinlan	.05
128	Scott Radinsky	.05
129	Darren Reed	.05
130	Karl Rhodes	.05
131	Jeff Richardson	.05
132	Rich Rodriguez	.05
133	Dave Rohde	.05
134	Mel Rojas	.05
135	Vic Rosario	.05
136	Rich Rowland	.05
137	Scott Ruskin	.05
138	Bill Sampen	.05
139	Andres Santana	.05
140	David Segui	.05
141	Jeff Shaw	.05
142	Tim Sherrill	.05
143	Terry Shumpert	.05
144	Mike Simms	.05
145	Daryl Smith	.05
146	Luis Sojo	.05
147	Steve Springer	.05
148	Ray Stephens	.05
149	Lee Stevens	.05
150	Mel Stottlemyre, Jr.	.05
151	Glenn Sutko	.05
152	Anthony Telford	.05
153	Frank Thomas	3.00
154	Randy Tomlin	.05
155	Brian Traxler	.05
156	Efrain Valdez	.05
157	Rafael Valdez	.05
158	Julio Valera	.05
159	Jim Vatcher	.05
160	Hector Villanueva	.05
161	Hector Wagner	.05
162	Dave Walsh	.05
163	Steve Wapnick	.05
164	Colby Ward	.05
165	Turner Ward	.05
166	Terry Wells	.05
167	Mark Whiten	.05
168	Mike York	.05
169	Cliff Young	.05
170	Checklist	.05
171	Checklist	.05

1992 Topps Pre-Production

To preview its 1992 card set for dealers, Topps distributed a nine-card sheet in the basic format of its 1992 issue. The 8" x 10" sheets are often found cut into standard 2-1/2" x 3-1/2" singles. Card numbers on the backs of these promo cards do not correspond to the same cards in the regular set, and the stats for 1991 are not included. The preview cards have an orange oval on back, with the words, "1992 Pre-Production Sample."

		NM/M
Uncut Sheet:		6.00
Complete Set (9):		6.00
Common Player:		1.00
3	Shawon Dunston	1.00
16	Mike Heath	1.00
18	Todd Frowirth	1.00
20	Bip Roberts	1.00
131	Rob Dibble	1.00
174	Otis Nixon	1.00
273	Dennis Martinez	1.00
325	Brett Butler	1.00
798	Tom Lasorda	1.00

1992 Topps

This 792-card set features white stock much like the 1991 issue. The card fronts feature full-color action and posed photos with a gray inner frame and the player name and position at bottom. Backs feature biographical information, statistics and stadium photos on player cards where space is available. All-Star cards and #1 Draft Pick cards are once again included. Topps brought back four-player rookie cards in 1992. Nine Top Prospect cards of this nature can be found within the set. "Match the Stats" game cards were inserted into packs of 1992 Topps cards. Special bonus cards were given away to winners of this insert game. This was the first Topps regular-issue baseball card set since 1951 which was sold without bubblegum.

		NM/M
Unopened Fact. Set (802):		30.00
Complete Set (792):		20.00
Common Player:		.05
Golds:		4X
Wax Pack (14):		.50
Wax Box (36):		12.50
Cello Pack (34):		1.00
Cello Box (24):		16.00
Vending Box (500):		6.00
1	Nolan Ryan	.75
2	Rickey Henderson (Record Breaker)	.20
3	Jeff Reardon (Record Breaker)	.05
4	Nolan Ryan (Record Breaker)	.40
5	Dave Winfield (Record Breaker)	.20
6	Brien Taylor RC (Draft Pick)	.05
7	Jim Olander RC	.05
8	Bryan Hickerson RC	.05
9	John Farrell (Draft Pick)	.05
10	Wade Boggs	.45
11	Jack McDowell	.05
12	Luis Gonzalez	.05
13	Mike Scioscia	.05
14	Wes Chamberlain	.05
15	Denny Martinez	.05
16	Jeff Montgomery	.05
17	Randy Milligan	.05
18	Greg Cadaret	.05
19	Jamie Quirk	.05
20	Bip Roberts	.05
21	Buck Rodgers	.05
22	Bill Wegman	.05
23	Chuck Knoblauch	.05
24	Randy Myers	.05
25	Ron Gant	.05
26	Mike Bielecki	.05
27	Juan Gonzalez	.20
28	Mike Schooler	.05
29	Mickey Tettleton	.05
30	John Kruk	.05
31	Bryn Smith	.05
32	Chris Nabholz	.05
33	Carlos Baerga	.05
34	Jeff Juden	.05
35	Dave Righetti	.05
36	Scott Ruffcorn RC (Draft Pick)	.05
37	Luis Polonia	.05
38	Tom Candiotti	.05
39	Greg Olson	.05
40	Cal Ripken, Jr.	.75
41	Craig Lefferts	.05
42	Mike Macfarlane	.05
43	Jose Lind	.05
44	Rick Aguilera	.05
45	Gary Carter	.35
46	Steve Farr	.05
47	Rex Hudler	.05
48	Scott Scudder	.05
49	Damon Berryhill	.05
50	Ken Griffey Jr.	.55
51	Tom Runnells	.05
52	Juan Bell	.05
53	Tommy Gregg	.05
54	David Wells	.05
55	Rafael Palmeiro	.30
56	Charlie O'Brien	.05
57	Donn Pall	.05
58	Top Prospects-Catchers (Brad Ausmus RC, Jim Campanis RC, Dave Nilsson RC, Doug Robbins RC)	.15
59	Mo Vaughn	.05
60	Tony Fernandez	.05
61	Paul O'Neill	.05
62	Gene Nelson	.05
63	Randy Ready	.05
64	Bob Kipper	.05
65	Willie McGee	.05
66	Scott Stahoviak RC (Draft Pick)	.05
67	Luis Salazar	.05
68	Marvin Freeman	.05
69	Kenny Lofton	.05
70	Gary Gaetti	.05
71	Erik Hanson	.05
72	Eddie Zosky RC	.05
73	Brian Barnes	.05
74	Scott Leius	.05
75	Bret Saberhagen	.05
76	Mike Gallego	.05
77	Jack Armstrong	.05
78	Ivan Rodriguez	.35
79	Jesse Orosco	.05
80	Dave Justice	.05
81	Ced Landrum RC	.05
82	Doug Simons RC	.05
83	Tommy Greene	.05
84	Leo Gomez	.05
85	Jose DeLeon	.05
86	Steve Finley	.05
87	Bob MacDonald RC	.05
88	Darrin Jackson	.05
89	Neal Heaton	.05
90	Robin Yount	.35
91	Jeff Reed	.05
92	Lenny Harris	.05
93	Reggie Jefferson	.05
94	Sammy Sosa	.45
95	Scott Bailes	.05
96	Tom McKinnon RC (Draft Pick)	.05
97	Luis Rivera	.05
98	Mike Harkey	.05
99	Jeff Treadway	.05
100	Jose Canseco	.25
101	Omar Vizquel	.05
102	Scott Kamieniecki RC	.05
103	Ricky Jordan	.05
104	Jeff Ballard	.05
105	Felix Jose	.05
106	Mike Boddicker	.05
107	Dan Pasqua	.05
108	Mike Timlin RC	.10
109	Roger Craig	.05
110	Ryne Sandberg	.45
111	Mark Carreon	.05
112	Oscar Azocar	.05
113	Mike Greenwell	.05
114	Mark Portugal	.05
115	Terry Pendleton	.05
116	Willie Randolph	.05
117	Scott Terry	.05
118	Chili Davis	.05
119	Mark Gardner	.05
120	Alan Trammell	.05
121	Derek Bell	.05
122	Gary Varsho	.05
123	Bob Ojeda	.05
124	Shawn Livsey RC (Draft Pick)	.05
125	Chris Hoiles	.05
126	Top Prospects-1st Baseman (Rico Brogna, John Jaha, Ryan Klesko, Dave Staton)	.05
127	Carlos Quintana	.05
128	Kurt Stillwell	.05
129	Melido Perez	.05
130	Alvin Davis	.05
131	Checklist 1	.05
132	Eric Show	.05
133	Rance Mulliniks	.05
134	Darryl Kile	.05
135	Von Hayes	.05
136	Bill Doran	.05
137	Jeff Robinson	.05
138	Monty Fariss	.05
139	Jeff Innis	.05
140	Mark Grace	.05
141	Jim Leyland	.05
142	Todd Van Poppel	.05
143	Paul Gibson	.05
144	Bill Swift	.05
145	Danny Tartabull	.05
146	Al Newman	.05
147	Cris Carpenter	.05
148	Anthony Young RC	.05
149	Brian Bohanon RC	.05
150	Roger Clemens	.50
151	Jeff Hamilton	.05
152	Charlie Leibrandt	.05
153	Ron Karkovice	.05
154	Hensley Meulens	.05
155	Scott Bankhead	.05
156	Manny Ramirez RC (Draft Pick)	3.00
157	Keith Miller	.05
158	Todd Frowirth	.05
159	Darrin Fletcher	.05
160	Bobby Bonilla	.05
161	Casey Candaele	.05
162	Paul Faries RC	.05
163	Dana Kiecker	.05
164	Shane Mack	.05
165	Mark Langston	.05
166	Geronimo Pena	.05
167	Andy Allanson	.05
168	Dwight Smith	.05
169	Chuck Crim	.05
170	Alex Cole	.05
171	Bill Plummer	.05
172	Juan Berenguer	.05
173	Brian Downing	.05
174	Steve Frey	.05
175	Orel Hershiser	.05
176	Ramon Garcia RC	.05
177	Danny Gladden	.05
178	Jim Acker	.05
179	Top Prospects-2nd Baseman (Cesar Bernhardt RC, Bobby DeJardin RC, Armando Moreno RC, Andy Stankiewicz RC)	.05
180	Kevin Mitchell	.05
181	Hector Villanueva	.05
182	Jeff Reardon	.05
183	Brent Mayne	.05
184	Jimmy Jones	.05
185	Benny Santiago	.05
186	Cliff Floyd RC (Draft Pick)	.50
187	Ernie Riles	.05
188	Jose Guzman	.05
189	Junior Felix	.05
190	Glenn Davis	.05
191	Charlie Hough	.05
192	Dave Fleming RC	.05
193	Omar Oliveras RC	.05
194	Eric Karros	.05
195	David Cone	.05
196	Frank Castillo RC	.05
197	Glenn Braggs	.05
198	Scott Aldred	.05
199	Jeff Blauser	.05
200	Len Dykstra	.05
201	Buck Showalter	.05
202	Rick Honeycutt	.05
203	Greg Myers	.05
204	Trevor Wilson	.05
205	Jay Howell	.05
206	Luis Sojo	.05
207	Jack Clark	.05
208	Julio Machado	.05
209	Lloyd McClendon	.05
210	Ozzie Guillen	.05
211	Jeremy Hernandez RC	.05
212	Randy Velarde	.05
213	Les Lancaster	.05
214	Andy Mota	.05
215	Rich Gossage	.05
216	Brent Gates RC (Draft Pick)	.05
217	Brian Harper	.05
218	Mike Flanagan	.05
219	Jerry Browne	.05
220	Jose Rijo	.05
221	Skeeter Barnes	.05
222	Jaime Navarro	.05
223	Mel Hall	.05
224	Brett Barberie RC	.05
225	Roberto Alomar	.15
226	Pete Smith	.05
227	Daryl Boston	.05
228	Eddie Whitson	.05
229	Shawn Boskie	.05
230	Dick Schofield	.05
231	Brian Drahman RC	.05
232	John Smiley	.05
233	Mitch Webster	.05
234	Terry Steinbach	.05
235	Jack Morris	.05
236	Bill Pecota	.05
237	Jose Hernandez RC	.05
238	Greg Litton	.05
239	Brian Holman	.05
240	Andres Galarraga	.05
241	Gerald Young	.05
242	Mike Mussina	.30
243	Alvaro Espinoza	.05
244	Darren Daulton	.05
245	John Smoltz	.05
246	Jason Pruitt RC (Draft Pick)	.05
247	Chuck Finley	.05
248	Jim Gantner	.05
249	Tony Fossas	.05
250	Ken Griffey	.05
251	Kevin Elster	.05
252	Dennis Rasmussen	.05
253	Terry Kennedy	.05
254	Ryan Bowen RC	.05
255	Robin Ventura	.05
256	Mike Aldrete	.05
257	Jeff Russell	.05
258	Jim Lindeman	.05
259	Ron Darling	.05
260	Devon White	.05
261	Tom Lasorda	.05
262	Terry Lee RC	.05
263	Bob Patterson	.05
264	Checklist 2	.05
265	Teddy Higuera	.05
266	Roberto Kelly	.05
267	Steve Bedrosian	.05
268	Brady Anderson	.05
269	Ruben Amaro RC	.05
270	Tony Gwynn	.45
271	Tracy Jones	.05
272	Jerry Don Gleaton	.05
273	Craig Grebeck	.05
274	Bob Scanlan RC	.05
275	Todd Zeile	.05
276	Shawn Green RC (Draft Pick)	1.50
277	Scott Chiamparino	.05
278	Darryl Hamilton	.05
279	Jim Clancy	.05
280	Carlos Martinez	.05
281	Kevin Appier	.05
282	John Wehner RC	.05
283	Reggie Sanders	.05
284	Gene Larkin	.05
285	Bob Welch	.05
286	Gilberto Reyes	.05
287	Pete Schourek	.05
288	Andujar Cedeno	.05
289	Mike Morgan	.05
290	Bo Jackson	.10
291	Phil Garner	.05
292	Ray Lankford	.05
293	Mike Henneman	.05
294	Dave Valle	.05
295	Alonzo Powell RC	.05
296	Tom Brunansky	.05
297	Kevin Brown	.05
298	Kelly Gruber	.05
299	Charles Nagy	.05
300	Don Mattingly	.50
301	Kirk McCaskill	.05
302	Joey Cora	.05
303	Dan Plesac	.05
304	Joe Oliver	.05
305	Tom Glavine	.25
306	Al Shirley RC (Draft Pick)	.05
307	Bruce Ruffin	.05
308	Craig Shipley RC	.05
309	Dave Martinez	.05
310	Jose Mesa	.05
311	Henry Cotto	.05

No.	Player	Price
312	Mike LaValliere	.05
313	Kevin Tapani	.05
314	Jeff Huson	.05
315	Juan Samuel	.05
316	Curt Schilling	.25
317	Mike Bordick RC	.05
318	Steve Howe	.05
319	Tony Phillips	.05
320	George Bell	.05
321	Lou Pinella	.05
322	Tim Burke	.05
323	Milt Thompson	.05
324	Danny Darwin	.05
325	Joe Orsulak	.05
326	Eric King	.05
327	Jay Buhner	.05
328	Joel Johnston RC	.05
329	Franklin Stubbs	.05
330	Will Clark	.05
331	Steve Lake	.05
332	Chris Jones RC	.05
333	Pat Tabler	.05
334	Kevin Gross	.05
335	Dave Henderson	.05
336	Greg Anthony RC (Draft Pick)	.05
337	Alejandro Pena	.05
338	Shawn Abner	.05
339	Tom Browning	.05
340	Otis Nixon	.05
341	Bob Geren	.05
342	Tim Spehr RC	.05
343	Jon Vander Wal RC	.20
344	Jack Daugherty	.05
345	Zane Smith	.05
346	Rheal Cormier RC	.05
347	Kent Hrbek	.05
348	Rick Wilkins RC	.10
349	Steve Lyons	.05
350	Gregg Olson	.05
351	Greg Riddoch	.05
352	Ed Nunez	.05
353	Braulio Castillo RC	.05
354	Dave Bergman	.05
355	Warren Newson RC	.05
356	Luis Quinones	.05
357	Mike Witt	.05
358	Ted Wood RC	.05
359	Mike Moore	.05
360	Lance Parrish	.05
361	Barry Jones	.05
362	Javier Ortiz RC	.05
363	John Candelaria	.05
364	Glenallen Hill	.05
365	Duane Ward	.05
366	Checklist 3	.05
367	Rafael Belliard	.05
368	Bill Krueger	.05
369	Steve Whitaker RC (Draft Pick)	.05
370	Shawon Dunston	.05
371	Dante Bichette	.05
372	Kip Gross RC	.05
373	Don Robinson	.05
374	Bernie Williams	.05
375	Bert Blyleven	.05
376	Chris Donnels RC	.05
377	Bob Zupcic RC	.05
378	Joel Skinner	.05
379	Steve Chitren	.05
380	Barry Bonds	.75
381	Sparky Anderson	.10
382	Sid Fernandez	.05
383	Dave Hollins	.05
384	Mark Lee	.05
385	Tim Wallach	.05
386	Will Clark/AS	.05
387	Ryne Sandberg/AS	.20
388	Howard Johnson/AS	.05
389	Barry Larkin/AS	.05
390	Barry Bonds/AS	.40
391	Ron Gant/AS	.05
392	Bobby Bonilla/AS	.05
393	Craig Biggio/AS	.05
394	Denny Martinez/AS	.05
395	Tom Glavine/AS	.05
396	Lee Smith/AS	.05
397	Cecil Fielder/AS	.05
398	Julio Franco/AS	.05
399	Wade Boggs/AS	.20
400	Cal Ripken, Jr./AS	.05
401	Jose Canseco/AS	.15
402	Joe Carter/AS	.05
403	Ruben Sierra/AS	.05
404	Matt Nokes/AS	.05
405	Roger Clemens/AS	.25
406	Jim Abbott/AS	.05
407	Bryan Harvey/AS	.05
408	Bob Milacki	.05
409	Geno Petralli	.05
410	Dave Stewart	.05
411	Mike Jackson	.05
412	Luis Aquino	.05
413	Tim Teufel	.05
414	Jeff Ware (Draft Pick)	.05
415	Jim Deshaies	.05
416	Ellis Burks	.05
417	Allan Anderson	.05
418	Alfredo Griffin	.05
419	Wally Whitehurst	.05
420	Sandy Alomar	.05
421	Juan Agosto	.05
422	Sam Horn	.05
423	Jeff Fassero RC	.05
424	Paul McClellan RC	.05
425	Cecil Fielder	.05
426	Tim Raines	.05
427	Eddie Taubensee RC	.05
428	Dennis Boyd	.05
429	Tony LaRussa	.05
430	Steve Sax	.05
431	Tom Gordon	.05
432	Billy Hatcher	.05
433	Cal Eldred	.05
434	Wally Backman	.05
435	Mark Eichhorn	.05
436	Mookie Wilson	.05
437	Scott Servais RC	.10
438	Mike Maddux	.05
439	Chico Walker RC	.05
440	Doug Drabek	.05
441	Rob Deer	.05
442	Dave West	.05
443	Spike Owen	.05
444	Tyrone Hill RC (Draft Pick)	.05
445	Matt Williams	.05
446	Mark Lewis	.05
447	David Segui	.05
448	Tom Pagnozzi	.05
449	Jeff Johnson RC	.05
450	Mark McGwire	.65
451	Tom Henke	.05
452	Wilson Alvarez	.05
453	Gary Redus	.05
454	Darren Holmes	.05
455	Pete O'Brien	.05
456	Pat Combs	.05
457	Hubie Brooks	.05
458	Frank Tanana	.05
459	Tom Kelly	.05
460	Andre Dawson	.25
461	Doug Jones	.05
462	Rich Rodriguez	.05
463	Mike Simms RC	.05
464	Mike Jeffcoat	.05
465	Barry Larkin	.05
466	Stan Belinda	.05
467	Lonnie Smith	.05
468	Greg Harris	.05
469	Jim Eisenreich	.05
470	Pedro Guerrero	.05
471	Jose DeJesus	.05
472	Rich Rowland RC	.05
473	Top Prospects-3rd Baseman (Frank Bolick RC, Craig Paquette RC, Tom Redington RC, Paul Russo RC)	.05
474	Mike Rossiter RC (Draft Pick)	.05
475	Robby Thompson	.05
476	Randy Bush	.05
477	Greg Hibbard	.05
478	Dale Sveum	.05
479	Chito Martinez RC	.05
480	Scott Sanderson	.05
481	Tino Martinez	.05
482	Jimmy Key	.05
483	Terry Shumpert	.05
484	Mike Hartley	.05
485	Chris Sabo	.05
486	Bob Walk	.05
487	John Cerutti	.05
488	Scott Cooper RC	.05
489	Bobby Cox	.05
490	Julio Franco	.05
491	Jeff Brantley	.05
492	Mike Devereaux	.05
493	Jose Offerman	.05
494	Gary Thurman	.05
495	Carney Lansford	.05
496	Joe Grahe	.05
497	Andy Ashby RC	.10
498	Gerald Perry	.05
499	Dave Otto	.05
500	Vince Coleman	.05
501	Rob Mallicoat RC	.05
502	Greg Briley	.05
503	Pascual Perez	.05
504	Aaron Sele RC (Draft Pick)	.25
505	Bobby Thigpen	.05
506	Todd Benzinger	.05
507	Candy Maldonado	.05
508	Bill Gullickson	.05
509	Doug Dascenzo	.05
510	Frank Viola	.05
511	Kenny Rogers	.05
512	Mike Heath	.05
513	Kevin Bass	.05
514	Kim Batiste RC	.05
515	Delino DeShields	.05
516	Ed Sprague RC	.05
517	Jim Gott	.05
518	Jose Melendez RC	.05
519	Hal McRae	.05
520	Jeff Bagwell	.35
521	Joe Hesketh	.05
522	Milt Cuyler	.05
523	Shawn Hillegas	.05
524	Don Slaught	.05
525	Randy Johnson	.35
526	Doug Piatt RC	.05
527	Checklist 4	.05
528	Steve Foster RC	.05
529	Joe Girardi	.05
530	Jim Abbott	.05
531	Larry Walker	.05
532	Mike Huff	.05
533	Mackey Sasser	.05
534	Benji Gil RC (Draft Pick)	.05
535	Dave Stieb	.05
536	Willie Wilson	.05
537	Mark Leiter RC	.05
538	Jose Uribe	.05
539	Thomas Howard	.05
540	Ben McDonald	.05
541	Jose Tolentino RC	.05
542	Keith Mitchell RC	.05
543	Jerome Walton	.05
544	Cliff Brantley RC	.05
545	Andy Van Slyke	.05
546	Paul Sorrento	.05
547	Herm Winningham	.05
548	Mark Guthrie	.05
549	Joe Torre	.05
550	Darryl Strawberry	.05
551	Top Prospects-Shortstops (Manny Alexander, Alex Arias, Wil Cordero, Chipper Jones)	.25
552	Dave Gallagher	.05
553	Edgar Martinez	.05
554	Donald Harris	.05
555	Frank Thomas	.35
556	Storm Davis	.05
557	Dickie Thon	.05
558	Scott Garrelts	.05
559	Steve Olin	.05
560	Rickey Henderson	.35
561	Jose Vizcaino	.05
562	Wade Taylor RC	.05
563	Pat Borders	.05
564	Jimmy Gonzalez RC (Draft Pick)	.05
565	Lee Smith	.05
566	Bill Sampen	.05
567	Dean Palmer	.05
568	Bryan Harvey	.05
569	Tony Pena	.05
570	Lou Whitaker	.05
571	Randy Tomlin	.05
572	Greg Vaughn	.05
573	Kelly Downs	.05
574	Steve Avery	.05
575	Kirby Puckett	.45
576	Heathcliff Slocumb RC	.05
577	Kevin Seitzer	.05
578	Lee Guetterman	.05
579	Johnny Oates	.05
580	Greg Maddux	.45
581	Stan Javier	.05
582	Vicente Palacios	.05
583	Mel Rojas	.05
584	Wayne Rosenthal RC	.05
585	Lenny Webster RC	.05
586	Rod Nichols	.05
587	Mickey Morandini	.05
588	Russ Swan	.05
589	Mariano Duncan	.05
590	Howard Johnson	.05
591	Top Prospects-Outfielders (Jacob Brumfield RC, Jeromy Burnitz RC, Alan Cockrell RC, D.J. Dozier RC)	.25
592	Denny Neagle RC	.05
593	Steve Decker	.05
594	Brian Barber RC (Draft Pick)	.05
595	Bruce Hurst	.05
596	Kent Mercker	.05
597	Mike Magnante RC	.05
598	Jody Reed	.05
599	Steve Searcy	.05
600	Paul Molitor	.35
601	Dave Smith	.05
602	Mike Fetters	.05
603	Luis Mercedes RC	.05
604	Chris Gwynn	.05
605	Scott Erickson	.05
606	Brook Jacoby	.05
607	Todd Stottlemyre	.05
608	Scott Bradley	.05
609	Mike Hargrove	.05
610	Eric Davis	.05
611	Brian Hunter RC	.05
612	Pat Kelly	.05
613	Pedro Munoz RC	.05
614	Al Osuna	.05
615	Matt Merullo	.05
616	Larry Andersen	.05
617	Junior Ortiz	.05
618	Top Prospects-Outfielders (Cesar Hernandez RC, Steve Hosey RC, Dan Peltier RC, Jeff McNeely RC)	.10
619	Danny Jackson	.05
620	George Brett	.50
621	Dan Gakeler RC	.05
622	Steve Buechele	.05
623	Bob Tewksbury	.05
624	Shawn Estes RC (Draft Pick)	.25
625	Kevin McReynolds	.05
626	Chris Haney RC	.05
627	Mike Sharperson	.05
628	Mark Williamson	.05
629	Wally Joyner	.05
630	Carlton Fisk	.35
631	Armando Reynoso RC	.05
632	Felix Fermin	.05
633	Mitch Williams	.05
634	Manuel Lee	.05
635	Harold Baines	.05
636	Greg Harris	.05
637	Orlando Merced	.05
638	Chris Bosio	.05
639	Wayne Housie RC	.05
640	Xavier Hernandez	.05
641	David Howard RC	.05
642	Tim Crews	.05
643	Rick Cerone	.05
644	Terry Leach	.05
645	Deion Sanders	.10
646	Craig Wilson	.05
647	Marquis Grissom	.05
648	Scott Fletcher	.05
649	Norm Charlton	.05
650	Jesse Barfield	.05
651	Joe Slusarski RC	.05
652	Bobby Rose	.05
653	Dennis Lamp	.05
654	Allen Watson RC (Draft Pick)	.05
655	Brett Butler	.05
656	Top Prospects-Outfielders (Rudy Pemberton RC, Henry Rodriguez RC, Lee Tinsley RC, Gerald Williams RC)	.10
657	Dave Johnson	.05
658	Checklist 5	.05
659	Brian McRae	.05
660	Fred McGriff	.05
661	Bill Landrum	.05
662	Juan Guzman	.05
663	Greg Gagne	.05
664	Ken Hill	.05
665	Dave Haas RC	.05
666	Tom Foley	.05
667	Roberto Hernandez RC	.10
668	Dwayne Henry	.05
669	Jim Fregosi	.05
670	Harold Reynolds	.05
671	Mark Whiten	.05
672	Eric Plunk	.05
673	Todd Hundley	.05
674	Mo Sanford RC	.05
675	Bobby Witt	.05
676	Top Prospects-Pitchers (Pat Mahomes RC, Sam Militello RC, Roger Salkeld, Turk Wendell RC)	.15
677	John Marzano	.05
678	Joe Klink	.05
679	Pete Incaviglia	.05
680	Dale Murphy	.15
681	Rene Gonzales	.05
682	Andy Benes	.05
683	Jim Poole RC	.05
684	Trever Miller RC (Draft Pick)	.10
685	Scott Livingstone RC	.05
686	Rich DeLucia	.05
687	Harvey Pulliam RC	.05
688	Tim Belcher	.05
689	Mark Lemke	.05
690	John Franco	.05
691	Walt Weiss	.05
692	Scott Ruskin	.05
693	Jeff King	.05
694	Mike Gardiner RC	.05
695	Gary Sheffield	.30
696	Joe Boever	.05
697	Mike Felder	.05
698	John Habyan	.05
699	Cito Gaston	.05
700	Ruben Sierra	.05
701	Scott Radinsky	.05
702	Lee Stevens	.05
703	Mark Wohlers RC	.05
704	Curt Young	.05
705	Dwight Evans	.05
706	Rob Murphy	.05
707	Gregg Jefferies	.05
708	Tom Bolton	.05
709	Chris James	.05
710	Kevin Maas	.05
711	Ricky Bones RC	.05
712	Curt Wilkerson	.05
713	Roger McDowell	.05
714	Calvin Reese RC (Draft Pick)	.10
715	Craig Biggio	.05
716	Kirk Dressendorfer RC	.05
717	Ken Dayley	.05
718	B.J. Surhoff	.05
719	Terry Mulholland	.05
720	Kirk Gibson	.05
721	Mike Pagliarulo	.05
722	Walt Terrell	.05
723	Jose Oquendo	.05
724	Kevin Morton RC	.05
725	Dwight Gooden	.05
726	Kirt Manwaring	.05
727	Chuck McElroy	.05
728	Dave Burba RC	.05
729	Art Howe	.05
730	Ramon Martinez	.05
731	Donnie Hill	.05
732	Nelson Santovenia	.05
733	Bob Melvin	.05
734	Scott Hatteberg RC (Draft Pick)	.10
735	Greg Swindell	.05
736	Lance Johnson	.05
737	Kevin Reimer	.05
738	Dennis Eckersley	.35
739	Rob Ducey	.05
740	Ken Caminiti	.05
741	Mark Gubicza	.05
742	Billy Spiers	.05
743	Darren Lewis	.05
744	Chris Hammond	.05
745	Dave Magadan	.05
746	Bernard Gilkey	.05
747	Willie Banks RC	.05
748	Matt Nokes	.05
749	Jerald Clark	.05
750	Travis Fryman	.05
751	Steve Wilson	.05
752	Billy Ripken	.05
753	Paul Assenmacher	.05
754	Charlie Hayes	.05
755	Alex Fernandez	.05
756	Gary Pettis	.05
757	Rob Dibble	.05
758	Tim Naehring	.05
759	Jeff Torborg	.05
760	Ozzie Smith	.45
761	Mike Fitzgerald	.05
762	John Burkett	.05
763	Kyle Abbott	.05
764	Tyler Green RC (Draft Pick)	.05
765	Pete Harnisch	.05
766	Mark Davis	.05
767	Kal Daniels	.05
768	Jim Thome	.35
769	Jack Howell	.05
770	Sid Bream	.05
771	Arthur Rhodes RC	.10
772	Garry Templeton	.05
773	Hal Morris	.05
774	Bud Black	.05
775	Ivan Calderon	.05
776	Doug Henry RC	.05
777	John Olerud	.05
778	Tim Leary	.05
779	Jay Bell	.05
780	Eddie Murray	.35
781	Paul Abbott RC	.05
782	Phil Plantier	.05
783	Joe Magrane	.05
784	Ken Patterson	.05
785	Albert Belle	.05
786	Royce Clayton	.05
787	Checklist 6	.05
788	Mike Stanton	.05
789	Bobby Valentine	.05
790	Joe Carter	.05
791	Danny Cox	.05
792	Dave Winfield	.35

cards were random inserts in all forms of packs. Additionally, factory sets of Gold cards were sold which included an autographed card of Yankees #1 draft pick Brien Taylor, and which had the checklist cards replaced with player cards. Several errors connected with the gold name/team strips are noted; no corrected versions were issued.

	NM/M
Unopened Fact. Set (793):	75.00
Complete Set (792):	35.00
Common Player:	.20
86 Steve Finley (Incorrect name, Mark Davidson, on gold strip)	.20
131 Terry Mathews	.20
264 Rod Beck	1.00
288 Andujar Cedeno (Incorrect team, Yankees, listed on gold strip)	.60
366 Tony Perezchica	.20
465 Barry Larkin (Incorrect team, Astros, listed on gold strip)	2.50
527 Terry McDaniel	.20
532 Mike Huff (Incorrect team, Red Sox, listed on gold strip)	.20
658 John Ramos	.20
787 Brian Williams	.20
793 Brien Taylor (Autographed edition of 12,000; factory sets only.)	7.50

Gold Promo Sheet

Similar in form and function to the nine-card promo sheet issued for the regular 1992 Topps set, this 8" x 11" sheet previewed the Topps Gold cards for dealers. Fronts are identical to the regular-issue '92 Topps cards. Backs differ in that actual 1991 stats are not printed, and there is a diamond over the stat box which reads, "1992 Pre-Production Sample." Card numbers on the gold preview cards correspond to the regular Topps cards. Single cards in the standard 2-1/2" x 3-1/2" size are frequently offered cut from these sheets.

	NM/M
Complete Set (Sheet):	8.00
Complete Set (9):	8.00
Common Player:	1.00
1 Nolan Ryan	4.00
15 Dennis Martinez	1.00
20 Bip Roberts	1.00
40 Cal Ripken, Jr.	4.00
261 Tom Lasorda	1.00
370 Shawon Dunston	1.00
512 Mike Heath	1.00
655 Brett Butler	1.00
757 Rob Dibble	1.00

Gold Winners

A second gold-foil enhanced parallel version of the regular 1992 Topps issue was the Gold Winner cards awarded as prizes in a scratch-off contest found in each pack. Winner cards are identical to the Topps Gold cards except for the addition of a gold-foil "Winner" and star added above the team name. Due to a flaw in the design of the scratch-off game cards, it was easy to win every time and the Winner cards had to be produced in quantities far greater than originally planned, making them rather common. Six checklist cards from the regular issue were replaced with player cards in the Winners edition. Cards were sent to winners in 10-card cello packs.

	NM/M
Complete Set (792):	30.00
Common Player:	.10
Cello Pack (10):	.75
131 Terry Mathews	.15
264 Rod Beck	.25
366 Tony Perezchica	.15
465a Barry Larkin (Team name incorrect, Astros.)	2.00
465b Barry Larkin (Team name correct, Reds.)	.75

Gold

Topps Gold cards share a checklist and format with the regular-issue 1992 Topps baseball issue except the color bars with the player's name and team printed beneath the photo have been replaced with gold foil. On back the light blue Topps logo printed beneath the stats has been replaced with a gold "ToppsGold" logo. Topps Gold

527 Terry McDaniel .15
658 John Ramos .15
787 Brian Williams .15

Traded

Members of the United States baseball team are featured in this 132-card boxed set released by Topps. The cards are styled after the regular 1992 Topps cards and are numbered alphabetically. Several United States baseball players featured in this set were also featured in the 1991 Topps Traded set.

	NM/M
Complete Set (132):	50.00
Common Player:	.05
Golds:	2-4X

1 Willie Adams RC (USA) .05
2 Jeff Alkire (USA) .05
3 Felipe Alou .05
4 Moises Alou .10
5 Ruben Amaro RC .05
6 Jack Armstrong .05
7 Scott Bankhead .05
8 Tim Belcher .05
9 George Bell .05
10 Freddie Benavides RC .05
11 Todd Benzinger .05
12 Joe Boever .05
13 Ricky Bones .05
14 Bobby Bonilla .05
15 Hubie Brooks .05
16 Jerry Browne .05
17 Jim Bullinger .05
18 Dave Burba .05
19 Kevin Campbell RC .05
20 Tom Candiotti .05
21 Mark Carreon .05
22 Gary Carter .75
23 Archi Cianfrocco .05
24 Phil Clark .05
25 Chad Curtis RC .50
26 Eric Davis .05
27 Tim Davis (USA) .05
28 Gary DiSarcina .05
29 Darren Dreifort (USA) .05
30 Mariano Duncan .05
31 Mike Fitzgerald .05
32 John Flaherty RC .05
33 Darrin Fletcher .05
34 Scott Fletcher .05
35 Ron Fraser (USA) .05
36 Andres Galarraga .05
37 Dave Gallagher .05
38 Mike Gallego .05
39 Nomar Garciaparra RC (USA) 30.00
40 Jason Giambi (USA) 1.00
41 Danny Gladden .05
42 Rene Gonzales .05
43 Jeff Granger (USA) .05
44 Rick Greene (USA) .05
45 Jeffrey Hammonds (USA) .05
46 Charlie Hayes .05
47 Von Hayes .05
48 Rick Helling (USA) .05
49 Butch Henry RC .05
50 Carlos Hernandez RC .05
51 Ken Hill .05
52 Butch Hobson .05
53 Vince Horsman RC .05
54 Pete Incaviglia .05
55 Gregg Jefferies .05
56 Charles Johnson (USA) .05
57 Doug Jones .05
58 Brian Jordan RC 2.00
59 Wally Joyner .05
60 Daron Kirkreit RC (USA) .20
61 Bill Krueger .05
62 Gene Lamont .05
63 Jim Lefebvre .05
64 Danny Leon RC .05
65 Pat Listach .05
66 Kenny Lofton .05
67 Dave Martinez .05
68 Derrick May .05
69 Kirk McCaskill .05
70 Chad McConnell RC (USA) .05
71 Kevin McReynolds .05
72 Rusty Meacham RC .05

73 Keith Miller .05
74 Kevin Mitchell .05
75 Jason Moler RC (USA) .05
76 Mike Morgan .05
77 Jack Morris .05
78 Calvin Murray RC (USA) .05
79 Eddie Murray .75
80 Randy Myers .05
81 Denny Neagle RC .05
82 Phil Nevin (USA) .10
83 Dave Nilsson .05
84 Junior Ortiz .05
85 Donovan Osborne .05
86 Bill Pecota .05
87 Melido Perez .05
88 Mike Perez RC .05
89 Hipolito Pena RC .05
90 Willie Randolph .05
91 Darren Reed RC .05
92 Bip Roberts .05
93 Chris Roberts (USA) .05
94 Steve Rodriguez (USA) .05
95 Bruce Ruffin .05
96 Scott Ruskin .05
97 Bret Saberhagen .05
98 Rey Sanchez RC .05
99 Steve Sax .05
100 Curt Schilling .25
101 Dick Schofield .05
102 Gary Scott .05
103 Kevin Seitzer .05
104 Frank Seminara RC .05
105 Gary Sheffield .35
106 John Smiley .05
107 Cory Snyder .05
108 Paul Sorrento .05
109 Sammy Sosa 1.50
110 Matt Stairs RC .25
111 Andy Stankiewicz .05
112 Kurt Stillwell .05
113 Rick Sutcliffe .05
114 Bill Swift .05
115 Jeff Tackett RC .05
116 Danny Tartabull .05
117 Eddie Taubensee RC .05
118 Dickie Thon .05
119 Michael Tucker RC (USA) .25
120 Scooter Tucker RC .05
121 Marc Valdes RC (USA) .05
122 Julio Valera RC .05
123 Jason Varitek RC (USA) 15.00
124 Ron Villone RC (USA) .05
125 Frank Viola .05
126 B.J. Wallace RC (USA) .05
127 Dan Walters RC .05
128 Craig Wilson (USA) .05
129 Chris Wimmer (USA) .05
130 Dave Winfield .05
131 Herm Winningham .05
132 Checklist .05

Traded Gold

A reported 6,000 sets of 1992 Topps Traded were produced in a gold edition, with gold-foil strips on front bearing the player and team names. The cards are in all other respects identical to the regular boxed Traded issue.

	NM/M
Complete Unopened Set (132):	75.00
Complete Set (132):	65.00
Common Player:	.25
Stars/Rookies:	4X

Golden Spikes Award

At a Nov. 17, 1992 awards ceremony, Phil Nevin was presented with the U.S. Baseball Federation's Golden Spikes Award, emblematic of his selection as the outstanding amateur player in the nation. Topps created and handed out at the affair a reported 600 of these cards.

Phil Nevin 45.00

Kids

In a market which had increasingly become the province of adult collectors, Topps in 1992 offered an issue unashamedly aimed at the youngster. Called "Topps Kids," the 132-card set features bright colors, garish graphics and the game's top stars. Sold at 35 cents per pack (with bubble gum), the issue was even priced for the young collector. Unfortunately, the concept was a flop and was not repeated in subsequent years. Card fronts feature player photos, sometimes only the player's head on a cartoon body, against a background of wild designs or cartoon ballpark action. Player names at bottom were rendered in superhero comic-book style. Backs feature a few 1991 and career stats, and/or a cartoon or two about the player or baseball trivia.

	NM/M
Complete Set (132):	7.50
Common Player:	.05
Wax Pack (7):	.40
Wax Box (36):	6.00

1 Ryne Sandberg .45
2 Andre Dawson .25
3 George Bell .05
4 Mark Grace .05
5 Shawon Dunston .05
6 Tim Wallach .05
7 Ivan Calderon .05
8 Marquis Grissom .05
9 Delino DeShields .05
10 Denny Martinez .05
11 Dwight Gooden .05
12 Howard Johnson .05
13 John Franco .05
14 Gregg Jefferies .05
15 Kevin McReynolds .05
16 David Cone .05
17 Len Dykstra .05
18 John Kruk .05
19 Von Hayes .05
20 Mitch Williams .05
21 Barry Bonds .75
22 Bobby Bonilla .05
23 Andy Van Slyke .05
24 Doug Drabek .05
25 Ozzie Smith .45
26 Pedro Guerrero .05
27 Todd Zeile .05
28 Lee Smith .05
29 Felix Jose .05
30 Jose DeLeon .05
31 David Justice .05
32 Ron Gant .05
33 Terry Pendleton .05
34 Tom Glavine .25
35 Otis Nixon .05
36 Steve Avery .05
37 Barry Larkin .05
38 Eric Davis .05

39 Chris Sabo .05
40 Rob Dibble .05
41 Paul O'Neill .05
42 Jose Rijo .05
43 Craig Biggio .05
44 Jeff Bagwell .05
45 Ken Caminiti .05
46 Steve Finley .05
47 Darryl Strawberry .05
48 Ramon Martinez .05
49 Brett Butler .05
50 Eddie Murray .35
51 Kal Daniels .05
52 Orel Hershiser .05
53 Tony Gwynn .45
54 Benny Santiago .05
55 Fred McGriff .05
56 Bip Roberts .05
57 Tony Fernandez .05
58 Will Clark .05
59 Kevin Mitchell .05
60 Matt Williams .05
61 Willie McGee .05
62 Dave Righetti .05
63 Cal Ripken, Jr. .75
64 Ben McDonald .05
65 Glenn Davis .05
66 Gregg Olson .05
67 Roger Clemens .50
68 Wade Boggs .45
69 Mike Greenwell .05
70 Ellis Burks .05
71 Sandy Alomar .05
72 Greg Swindell .05
73 Albert Belle .05
74 Mark Whiten .05
75 Alan Trammell .05
76 Cecil Fielder .05
77 Lou Whitaker .05
78 Travis Fryman .05
79 Tony Phillips .05
80 Robin Yount .35
81 Paul Molitor .05
82 B.J. Surhoff .05
83 Greg Vaughn .05
84 Don Mattingly .50
85 Steve Sax .05
86 Kevin Maas .05
87 Mel Hall .05
88 Roberto Kelly .05
89 Joe Carter .05
90 Roberto Alomar .15
91 Dave Stieb .05
92 Kelly Gruber .05
93 Tom Henke .05
94 Chuck Finley .05
95 Wally Joyner .05
96 Dave Winfield .35
97 Jim Abbott .05
98 Mark Langston .05
99 Frank Thomas .35
100 Ozzie Guillen .05
101 Bobby Thigpen .05
102 Robin Ventura .05
103 Bo Jackson .10
104 Tim Raines .05
105 George Brett .50
106 Danny Tartabull .05
107 Bret Saberhagen .05
108 Brian McRae .05
109 Kirby Puckett .45
110 Scott Erickson .05
111 Kent Hrbek .05
112 Chuck Knoblauch .05
113 Chili Davis .05
114 Rick Aguilera .05
115 Jose Canseco .25
116 Dave Henderson .05
117 Dave Stewart .05
118 Rickey Henderson .35
119 Dennis Eckersley .30
120 Harold Baines .05
121 Mark McGwire .60
122 Ken Griffey Jr. .60
123 Harold Reynolds .05
124 Erik Hanson .05
125 Edgar Martinez .05
126 Randy Johnson .35
127 Nolan Ryan .75
128 Ruben Sierra .05
129 Julio Franco .05
130 Rafael Palmeiro .30
131 Juan Gonzalez .20
132 Checklist .05

Micro

Topps returned for a second year with a micro parallel of its regular-issue baseball set, in a format about 40 percent the size of the standard cards. Sold only in complete-set form, the 1" x 1-3/8" cards also included a dozen gold-enhanced star cards. Stars and rookies among the micros are valued at a percentage of the corresponding regular card.

	NM/M
Complete Set (804):	9.00
Common Player:	.05
Stars/Rookies:	50-100%

1 Nolan Ryan (Record Breaker) 2.00
2 Rickey Henderson (Record Breaker) .65
10 Wade Boggs .75
50 Ken Griffey Jr. 1.00
100 Jose Canseco .60
270 Tony Gwynn .75
300 Don Mattingly .90
380 Barry Bonds 2.00
397 Cecil Fielder/AS .50
403 Ruben Sierra/AS .50
460 Andre Dawson .55
725 Dwight Gooden .50

Triple Header Photo Balls

Picture a slightly oversize ping pong ball painted like a baseball with the heads and facsimile autographs of three different players on it and you've got the idea behind the Triple Headers test issue. Very limited in distribution, the team balls were sold in a small box with a package of candy.

	NM/M
Complete Set (26):	100.00
Common Ball:	3.50

(1) California Angels (Chuck Finley, Dave Winfield, Wally Joyner) 4.00
(2) Houston Astros (Jeff Bagwell, Craig Biggio, Ken Caminiti) 4.50
(3) Oakland Athletics (Dave Henderson, Jose Canseco, Rickey Henderson) 4.50
(4) Toronto Blue Jays (Roberto Alomar, Kelly Gruber, Joe Carter) 4.00
(5) Atlanta Braves (Ron Gant, Tom Glavine, Dave Justice) 4.00
(6) Milwaukee Brewers (Greg Vaughn, Paul Molitor, Robin Yount) 4.50
(7) St. Louis Cardinals (Todd Zeile, Pedro Guerrero, Ozzie Smith) 4.50
(8) Chicago Cubs (Ryne Sandberg, George Bell, Mark Grace) 4.50
(9) Los Angeles Dodgers (Ramon Martinez, Eddie Murray, Darryl Strawberry) 4.50
(10) Montreal Expos (Delino DeShields, Dennis Martinez, Ivan Calderon) 3.50
(11) San Francisco Giants (Will Clark, Kevin Mitchell, Matt Williams) 3.50
(12) Cleveland Indians (Sandy Alomar Jr., Alex Cole, Mark Lewis) 3.50
(13) Seattle Mariners (Ken Griffey Jr., Harold Reynolds, Ken Griffey Sr.) 10.00
(14) New York Mets (Vince Coleman, Dwight Gooden, Howard Johnson) 3.50
(15) Baltimore Orioles (Ben McDonald, Cal Ripken Jr., Gregg Olson) 12.50
(16) San Diego Padres (Benito Santiago, Fred McGriff, Tony Gwynn) 5.00
(17) Philadelphia Phillies (Len Dykstra, John Kruk, Dale Murphy) 3.50
(18) Pittsburgh Pirates (Andy Van Slyke, Barry Bonds, Bobby Bonilla) 12.50
(19) Cincinnati Reds (Chris Sabo, Eric Davis, Barry Larkin) 3.50
(20) Boston Red Sox (Wade Boggs, Mike Greenwell, Roger Clemens) 6.00
(21) Kansas City Royals (George Brett, Danny Tartabull, Bret Saberhagen) 6.00
(22) Texas Rangers (Julio Franco, Nolan Ryan, Juan Gonzalez) 12.50
(23) Minnesota Twins (Scott Erickson, Kirby Puckett, Kent Hrbek) 3.50
(24) Detroit Tigers (Cecil Fielder, Tony Phillips, Alan Trammell) 3.50
(25) Chicago White Sox (Carlton Fisk, Robin Ventura, Frank Thomas) 5.00
(26) New York Yankees (Don Mattingly, Steve Sax, Willie Randolph) 6.00

1991 Major League Debut

This 194-card set highlights the debut date of 1991 Major League rookies. Two checklist cards are also included in this boxed set. The card fronts resemble the 1992 Topps cards. A debut banner appears in the lower-right corner of the card front. The set is packaged in an attractive collector box and the cards are numbered alphabetically. This set was available only through hobby dealers.

	NM/M
Complete Set (194):	12.50
Common Player:	.05

1 Kyle Abbott .05
2 Dana Allison .05
3 Rich Amaral .05
4 Ruben Amaro .05
5 Andy Ashby .05
6 Jim Austin .05
7 Jeff Bagwell 4.00
8 Jeff Banister .05
9 Willie Banks .05
10 Bret Barberie .05
11 Kim Batiste .05
12 Chris Beasley .05
13 Rod Beck .05
14 Derek Bell .05
15 Esteban Beltre .05
16 Freddie Benavides .05
17 Rickey Bones .05
18 Denis Boucher .05
19 Ryan Bowen .05
20 Cliff Brantley .05
21 John Briscoe .05
22 Scott Brosius .05
23 Terry Bross .05
24 Jarvis Brown .05
25 Scott Bullett .05
26 Kevin Campbell .05
27 Amalio Carreno .05
28 Matias Carrillo .05
29 Jeff Carter .05
30 Vinny Castilla .05
31 Braulio Castillo .05
32 Frank Castillo .05

No.	Player	Price
33	Darrin Chapin	.05
34	Mike Christopher	.05
35	Mark Clark	.05
36	Royce Clayton	.05
37	Stu Cole	.05
38	Gary Cooper	.05
39	Archie Corbin	.05
40	Rheal Cormier	.05
41	Chris Cron	.05
42	Mike Dalton	.05
43	Mark Davis	.05
44	Francisco de la Rosa	.05
45	Chris Donnels	.05
46	Brian Drahman	.05
47	Tom Drees	.05
48	Kirk Dressendorfer	.05
49	Bruce Egloff	.05
50	Cal Eldred	.05
51	Jose Escobar	.05
52	Tony Eusebio	.05
53	Hector Fajardo	.05
54	Monty Farriss	.05
55	Jeff Fassero	.05
56	Dave Fleming	.05
57	Kevin Flora	.05
58	Steve Foster	.05
59	Dan Gakeler	.05
60	Ramon Garcia	.05
61	Chris Gardner	.05
62	Jeff Gardner	.05
63	Chris George	.05
64	Ray Giannelli	.05
65	Tom Goodwin	.05
66	Mark Grater	.05
67	Johnny Guzman	.05
68	Juan Guzman	.05
69	Dave Haas	.05
70	Chris Haney	.05
71	Shawn Hare	.05
72	Donald Harris	.05
73	Doug Henry	.05
74	Pat Hentgen	.05
75	Gil Heredia	.05
76	Jeremy Hernandez	.05
77	Jose Hernandez	.05
78	Roberto Hernandez	.05
79	Bryan Hickerson	.05
80	Milt Hill	.05
81	Vince Horsman	.05
82	Wayne Housie	.05
83	Chris Howard	.05
84	David Howard	.05
85	Mike Humphreys	.05
86	Brian Hunter	.05
87	Jim Hunter	.05
88	Mike Ignasiak	.05
89	Reggie Jefferson	.05
90	Jeff Johnson	.05
91	Joel Johnson	.05
92	Calvin Jones	.05
93	Chris Jones	.05
94	Stacy Jones	.05
95	Jeff Juden	.05
96	Scott Kamieniecki	.05
97	Eric Karros	.05
98	Pat Kelly	.05
99	John Kiely	.05
100	Darryl Kile	.05
101	Wayne Kirby	.05
102	Garland Kiser	.05
103	Chuck Knoblauch	.05
104	Randy Knorr	.05
105	Tom Kramer	.05
106	Ced Landrum	.05
107	Patrick Lennon	.05
108	Jim Lewis	.05
109	Mark Lewis	.05
110	Doug Lindsey	.05
111	Scott Livingstone	.05
112	Kenny Lofton	.10
113	Ever Magallanes	.05
114	Mike Magnante	.05
115	Barry Manuel	.05
116	Josias Manzanillo	.05
117	Chito Martinez	.05
118	Terry Mathews	.05
119	Rob Mauer	.05
120	Tim Mauser	.05
121	Terry McDaniel	.05
122	Rusty Meacham	.05
123	Luis Mercedes	.05
124	Paul Miller	.05
125	Keith Mitchell	.05
126	Bobby Moore	.05
127	Kevin Morton	.05
128	Andy Mota	.05
129	Jose Mota	.05
130	Mike Mussina	2.00
131	Jeff Mutis	.05
132	Denny Neagle	.05
133	Warren Newson	.05
134	Jim Olander	.05
135	Erik Pappas	.05
136	Jorge Pedre	.05
137	Yorkis Perez	.05
138	Mark Petkovsek	.05
139	Doug Piatt	.05
140	Jeff Plympton	.05
141	Harvey Pulliam	.05
142	John Ramos	.05
143	Mike Remlinger	.05
144	Laddie Renfroe	.05
145	Armando Reynoso	.05
146	Arthur Rhodes	.05
147	Pat Rice	.05
148	Nikco Riesgo	.05
149	Carlos Rodriguez	.05
150	Ivan Rodriguez	3.00
151	Wayne Rosenthal	.05
152	Rico Rossy	.05
153	Stan Royer	.05
154	Rey Sanchez	.05
155	Reggie Sanders	.05
156	Mo Sanford	.05
157	Bob Scanlan	.05
158	Pete Schourek	.05
159	Gary Scott	.05
160	Tim Scott	.05
161	Tony Scruggs	.05
162	Scott Servais	.05
163	Doug Simons	.05
164	Heathcliff Slocumb	.05
165	Joe Slusarski	.05
166	Tim Spehr	.05
167	Ed Sprague	.05
168	Jeff Tackett	.05
169	Eddie Taubensee	.05
170	Wade Taylor	.05
171	Jim Thome	2.50
172	Mike Timlin	.05
173	Jose Tolentino	.05
174	John Vander Wal	.05
175	Todd Van Poppel	.05
176	Mo Vaughn	.50
177	Dave Wainhouse	.05
178	Don Wakamatsu	.05
179	Bruce Walton	.05
180	Kevin Ward	.05
181	Dave Weathers	.05
182	Eric Wedge	.05
183	John Wehner	.05
184	Rick Wilkins	.05
185	Bernie Williams	.50
186	Brian Williams	.05
187	Ron Witmeyer	.05
188	Mark Wohlers	.05
189	Ted Wood	.05
190	Anthony Young	.05
191	Eddie Zosky	.05
192	Bob Zupcic	.05
193	Checklist	.05
194	Checklist	.05

1993 Topps Pre-Production

Specially marked 1992 Topps factory sets included this nine-card preview of the coming year's issue. The preview cards are identical to the regular-issue versions except the backs have a gray oval over the stats box with the notation, "1993 Pre-Production Sample."

		NM/M
Complete Set (9):		7.50
Common Player:		.35
1	Robin Yount	.75
2	Barry Bonds	3.00
11	Eric Karros	.50
32	Don Mattingly	1.00
100	Mark McGwire	2.00
150	Frank Thomas	.75
179	Ken Griffey Jr.	1.50
230	Carlton Fisk	.75
250	Chuck Knoblauch	.50

1993 Topps Pre-Production Sheet

Originally produced as an 8" x 11" nine-card sheet, these pre-production sample cards are rarely found as singles. Cards are in the same basic format as the regular-issue 1993 Topps cards. Backs differ in that all cards are numbered "000" with all zeroes for 1992 stats and bogus career highlights. A large gray circle over the stats box reads "1993 Pre-Production Sample For General Look Only."

		NM/M
Uncut Sheet:		6.00
Complete Set (9):		6.00
Common Player:		.50
(1)	Roberto Alomar	.60
(2)	Bobby Bonilla	.60
(3)	Gary Carter	1.00
(4)	Andre Dawson	.75
(5)	Dave Fleming	.50
(6)	Ken Griffey Jr.	3.00
(7)	Pete Incaviglia	.50
(8)	Spike Owen	.50
(9)	Larry Walker	.50

1993 Topps

Topps issued in a two-series format in 1993. Series I includes cards #1-396; Series II comprises #397-825. The card fronts feature full-color photos enclosed by a white border. The player's name and team appear at the bottom. The backs feature an additional player photo and biographical information at the top. The bottom box includes statistics and player information. The cards are numbered in red in a yellow flag on the back. The factory set includes the regular 825 cards plus 10 gold parallels, three Black Gold inserts and nine 1994 preview cards.

	NM/M
Unopened Fact. Set (847):	40.00
Complete Set (825):	30.00
Common Player:	.05
Golds:	3X
Series 1 Wax Pack (15):	1.00
Series 1 Wax Box (36):	25.00
Series 2 Wax Pack (15):	.75
Series 2 Wax Box (36):	15.00
Series 1 Jumbo Pack (41):	2.00
Series 1 Jumbo Box (24):	30.00
Series 2 Jumbo Pack (41):	1.50
Series 2 Jumbo Box (24):	20.00

No.	Player	Price
1	Robin Yount	.50
2	Barry Bonds	1.00
3	Ryne Sandberg	.60
4	Roger Clemens	.65
5	Tony Gwynn	.60
6	Jeff Tackett RC	.05
7	Pete Incaviglia	.05
8	Mark Wohlers	.05
9	Kent Hrbek	.05
10	Will Clark	.05
11	Eric Karros	.05
12	Lee Smith	.05
13	Esteban Beltre	.05
14	Greg Briley	.05
15	Marquis Grissom	.05
16	Dan Plesac	.05
17	Dave Hollins	.05
18	Terry Steinbach	.05
19	Ed Nunez	.05
20	Tim Salmon	.05
21	Luis Salazar	.05
22	Jim Eisenreich	.05
23	Todd Stottlemyre	.05
24	Tim Naehring	.05
25	John Franco	.05
26	Skeeter Barnes	.05
27	Carlos Garcia RC	.05
28	Joe Orsulak	.05
29	Dwayne Henry	.05
30	Fred McGriff	.05
31	Derek Lilliquist	.05
32	Don Mattingly	.65
33	B.J. Wallace (1992 Draft Pick)	.05
34	Juan Gonzalez	.25
35	John Smoltz	.05
36	Scott Servais	.05
37	Lenny Webster	.05
38	Chris James	.05
39	Roger McDowell	.05
40	Ozzie Smith	.60
41	Alex Fernandez	.05
42	Spike Owen	.05
43	Ruben Amaro	.05
44	Kevin Seitzer	.05
45	Dave Fleming	.05
46	Eric Fox RC	.05
47	Bob Scanlan	.05
48	Bert Blyleven	.05
49	Brian McRae	.05
50	Roberto Alomar	.20
51	Mo Vaughn	.05
52	Bobby Bonilla	.05
53	Frank Tanana	.05
54	Mike LaValliere	.05
55	Mark McLemore	.05
56	Chad Mottola RC (1992 Draft Pick)	.10
57	Norm Charlton	.05
58	Jose Melendez	.05
59	Carlos Martinez	.05
60	Roberto Kelly	.05
61	Gene Larkin	.05
62	Rafael Belliard	.05
63	Al Osuna	.05
64	Scott Chiamparino	.05
65	Brett Butler	.05
66	John Burkett	.05
67	Felix Jose	.05
68	Omar Vizquel	.05
69	John Vander Wal	.05
70	Roberto Hernandez	.05
71	Ricky Bones	.05
72	Jeff Grotewold RC	.05
73	Mike Moore	.05
74	Steve Buechele	.05
75	Juan Guzman	.05
76	Kevin Appier	.05
77	Junior Felix	.05
78	Greg Harris	.05
79	Dick Schofield	.05
80	Cecil Fielder	.05
81	Lloyd McClendon	.05
82	David Segui	.05
83	Reggie Sanders	.05
84	Kurt Stillwell	.05
85	Sandy Alomar	.05
86	John Habyan	.05
87	Kevin Reimer	.05
88	Mike Stanton	.05
89	Eric Anthony	.05
90	Scott Erickson	.05
91	Craig Colbert	.05
92	Tom Pagnozzi	.05
93	Pedro Astacio RC	.10
94	Lance Johnson	.05
95	Larry Walker	.05
96	Russ Swan	.05
97	Scott Fletcher	.05
98	Derek Jeter RC (1992 Draft Pick)	10.00
99	Mike Williams RC	.05
100	Mark McGwire	.85
101	Jim Bullinger RC	.05
102	Brian Hunter	.05
103	Jody Reed	.05
104	Mike Butcher RC	.05
105	Gregg Jefferies	.05
106	Howard Johnson	.05
107	John Kiely	.05
108	Jose Lind	.05
109	Sam Horn	.05
110	Barry Larkin	.05
111	Bruce Hurst	.05
112	Brian Barnes	.05
113	Thomas Howard	.05
114	Mel Hall	.05
115	Robby Thompson	.05
116	Mark Lemke	.05
117	Eddie Taubensee	.05
118	David Hulse	.05
119	Pedro Munoz	.05
120	Ramon Martinez	.05
121	Todd Worrell	.05
122	Joey Cora	.05
123	Moises Alou	.05
124	Franklin Stubbs	.05
125	Pete O'Brien	.05
126	Bob Ayrault RC	.05
127	Carney Lansford	.05
128	Kal Daniels	.05
129	Joe Grahe	.05
130	Jeff Montgomery	.05
131	Dave Winfield	.50
132	Preston Wilson RC (1992 Draft Pick)	.75
133	Steve Wilson	.05
134	Lee Guetterman	.05
135	Mickey Tettleton	.05
136	Jeff King	.05
137	Alan Mills	.05
138	Joe Oliver	.05
139	Gary Gaetti	.05
140	Gary Sheffield	.30
141	Dennis Cook	.05
142	Charlie Hayes	.05
143	Jeff Huson	.05
144	Kent Mercker	.05
145	Eric Young RC	.10
146	Scott Leius	.05
147	Bryan Hickerson	.05
148	Steve Finley	.05
149	Rheal Cormier	.05
150	Frank Thomas	.50
151	Archi Cianfrocco RC	.05
152	Rich DeLucia	.05
153	Greg Vaughn	.05
154	Wes Chamberlain	.05
155	Dennis Eckersley	.40
156	Sammy Sosa	.60
157	Gary DiSarcina	.05
158	Kevin Koslofski RC	.05
159	Doug Linton RC	.05
160	Lou Whitaker	.05
161	Chad McDonnell (1992 Draft Pick)	.05
162	Joe Hesketh	.05
163	Tim Wakefield RC	.10
164	Leo Gomez	.05
165	Jose Rijo	.05
166	Tim Scott RC	.05
167	Steve Olin	.05
168	Kevin Maas	.05
169	Kenny Rogers	.05
170	Dave Justice	.05
171	Doug Jones	.05
172	Jeff Reboulet RC	.05
173	Andres Galarraga	.05
174	Randy Velarde	.05
175	Kirk McCaskill	.05
176	Darren Lewis	.05
177	Lenny Harris	.05
178	Jeff Fassero	.05
179	Ken Griffey Jr.	.75
180	Darren Daulton	.05
181	John Jaha	.05
182	Ron Darling	.05
183	Greg Maddux	.05
184	Damion Easley RC	.10
185	Jack Morris	.05
186	Mike Magnante	.05
187	John Dopson	.05
188	Sid Fernandez	.05
189	Tony Phillips	.05
190	Doug Drabek	.05
191	Sean Lowe RC (1992 Draft Pick)	.05
192	Bob Milacki	.05
193	Steve Foster RC	.05
194	Jerald Clark	.05
195	Pete Harnisch	.05
196	Pat Kelly	.05
197	Jeff Frye	.05
198	Alejandro Pena	.05
199	Junior Ortiz	.05
200	Kirby Puckett	.60
201	Jose Uribe	.05
202	Mike Scioscia	.05
203	Bernard Gilkey	.05
204	Dan Pasqua	.05
205	Gary Carter	.50
206	Henry Cotto	.05
207	Paul Molitor	.50
208	Mike Hartley	.05
209	Jeff Parrett	.05
210	Mark Langston	.05
211	Doug Dascenzo	.05
212	Rick Reed	.05
213	Candy Maldonado	.05
214	Danny Darwin	.05
215	Pat Howell RC	.05
216	Mark Leiter	.05
217	Kevin Mitchell	.05
218	Ben McDonald	.05
219	Bip Roberts	.05
220	Benny Santiago	.05
221	Carlos Baerga	.05
222	Bernie Williams	.05
223	Roger Pavlik RC	.05
224	Sid Bream	.05
225	Matt Williams	.05
226	Willie Banks	.05
227	Jeff Bagwell	.50
228	Tom Goodwin	.05
229	Mike Perez	.05
230	Carlton Fisk	.50
231	John Wetteland	.05
232	Tino Martinez	.05
233	Rick Greene RC (1992 Draft Pick)	.05
234	Tim McIntosh	.05
235	Mitch Williams	.05
236	Kevin Campbell RC	.05
237	Jose Vizcaino	.05
238	Chris Donnels	.05
239	Mike Boddicker	.05
240	John Olerud	.05
241	Mike Gardiner	.05
242	Charlie O'Brien	.05
243	Rob Deer	.05
244	Denny Neagle	.05
245	Chris Sabo	.05
246	Gregg Olson	.05
247	Frank Seminara	.05
248	Scott Scudder	.05
249	Tim Burke	.05
250	Chuck Knoblauch	.05
251	Mike Bielecki	.05
252	Xavier Hernandez	.05
253	Jose Guzman	.05
254	Cory Snyder	.05
255	Orel Hershiser	.05
256	Wil Cordero	.05
257	Luis Alicea	.05
258	Mike Schooler	.05
259	Craig Grebeck	.05
260	Duane Ward	.05
261	Bill Wegman	.05
262	Mickey Morandini	.05
263	Vince Horsman RC	.05
264	Paul Sorrento	.05
265	Andre Dawson	.25
266	Rene Gonzales	.05
267	Keith Miller	.05
268	Derek Bell	.05
269	Todd Steverson RC (1992 Draft Pick)	.05
270	Frank Viola	.05
271	Wally Whitehurst	.05
272	Kurt Knudsen RC	.05
273	Dan Walters RC	.05
274	Rick Sutcliffe	.05
275	Andy Van Slyke	.05
276	Paul O'Neill	.05
277	Mark Whiten	.05
278	Chris Nabholz	.05
279	Todd Burns	.05
280	Tom Glavine	.25
281	Butch Henry RC	.05
282	Shane Mack	.05
283	Mike Jackson	.05
284	Henry Rodriguez	.05
285	Bob Tewksbury	.05
286	Ron Karkovice	.05
287	Mike Gallego	.05
288	Dave Cochrane	.05
289	Jesse Orosco	.05
290	Dave Stewart	.05
291	Tommy Greene	.05
292	Rey Sanchez	.05
293	Rob Ducey	.05
294	Brent Mayne	.05
295	Dave Stieb	.05
296	Luis Rivera	.05
297	Jeff Innis	.05
298	Scott Livingstone	.05
299	Bob Patterson	.05
300	Cal Ripken, Jr.	1.00
301	Cesar Hernandez	.05
302	Randy Myers	.05
303	Brook Jacoby	.05
304	Melido Perez	.05
305	Rafael Palmeiro	.40
306	Damon Berryhill	.05
307	Dan Serafini RC (1992 Draft Pick)	.05
308	Darryl Kile	.05
309	J.T. Bruett RC	.05
310	Dave Righetti	.05
311	Jay Howell	.05
312	Geronimo Pena	.05
313	Greg Hibbard	.05
314	Mark Gardner	.05
315	Edgar Martinez	.05
316	Dave Nilsson	.05
317	Kyle Abbott	.05
318	Willie Wilson	.05
319	Paul Assenmacher	.05
320	Tim Fortugno RC	.05
321	Rusty Meacham	.05
322	Pat Borders	.05
323	Mike Greenwell	.05
324	Willie Randolph	.05
325	Bill Gullickson	.05
326	Gary Varsho	.05
327	Tim Hulett	.05
328	Scott Ruskin	.05
329	Mike Maddux	.05
330	Danny Tartabull	.05
331	Kenny Lofton	.05
332	Geno Petralli	.05
333	Otis Nixon	.05
334	Jason Kendall RC (1992 Draft Pick)	.50
335	Mark Portugal	.05
336	Mike Pagliarulo	.05
337	Kirt Manwaring	.05
338	Bob Ojeda	.05
339	Mark Clark RC	.05
340	John Kruk	.05
341	Mel Rojas	.05
342	Erik Hanson	.05
343	Doug Henry	.05
344	Jack McDowell	.05
345	Harold Baines	.05
346	Chuck McElroy	.05
347	Luis Sojo	.05
348	Andy Stankiewicz	.05
349	Hipolito Pichardo RC	.05
350	Joe Carter	.05
351	Ellis Burks	.05
352	Pete Schourek	.05
353	Buddy Groom RC	.05
354	Jay Bell	.05
355	Brady Anderson	.05
356	Freddie Benavides	.05
357	Phil Stephenson	.05
358	Kevin Wickander	.05
359	Mike Stanley	.05
360	Ivan Rodriguez	.40
361	Scott Bankhead	.05
362	Luis Gonzalez	.05
363	John Smiley	.05
364	Trevor Wilson	.05
365	Tom Candiotti	.05
366	Craig Wilson	.05
367	Steve Sax	.05
368	Delino DeShields	.05
369	Jaime Navarro	.05
370	Dave Valle	.05
371	Mariano Duncan	.05
372	Rod Nichols	.05
373	Mike Morgan	.05
374	Julio Valera	.05
375	Wally Joyner	.05
376	Tom Henke	.05
377	Herm Winningham	.05
378	Orlando Merced	.05

379 Mike Munoz .05
380 Todd Hundley .05
381 Mike Flanagan .05
382 Tim Belcher .05
383 Jerry Browne .05
384 Mike Benjamin .05
385 Jim Leyritz .05
386 Ray Lankford .05
387 Devon White .05
388 Jeremy Hernandez .05
389 Brian Harper .05
390 Wade Boggs .60
391 Derrick May .05
392 Travis Fryman .05
393 Ron Gant .05
394 Checklist 1-132 .05
395 Checklist 133-264 .05
396 Checklist 265-396 .05
397 George Brett .65
398 Bobby Witt .05
399 Daryl Boston .05
400 Bo Jackson .10
401 Fred McGriff, Frank Thomas/AS .20
402 Ryne Sandberg, Carlos Baerga/AS .30
403 Gary Sheffield, Edgar Martinez/AS .05
404 Barry Larkin, Travis Fryman/AS .05
405 Andy Van Slyke, Ken Griffey Jr./AS .40
406 Larry Walker, Kirby Puckett/AS .20
407 Barry Bonds, Joe Carter/AS .50
408 Darren Daulton, Brian Harper/AS .05
409 Greg Maddux, Roger Clemens/AS .25
410 Tom Glavine, Dave Fleming/AS .05
411 Lee Smith, Dennis Eckersley/AS .15
412 Jamie McAndrew .05
413 Pete Smith .05
414 Juan Guerrero .05
415 Todd Frohwirth .05
416 Randy Tomlin .05
417 B.J. Surhoff .05
418 Jim Gott .05
419 Mark Thompson (1992 Draft Pick) .05
420 Kevin Tapani .05
421 Curt Schilling .25
422 J.T. Snow RC .40
423 Top Prospects 1B (Ryan Klesko, Ivan Cruz, Bubba Smith, Larry Sutton) .05
424 John Valentin .05
425 Joe Girardi .05
426 Nigel Wilson RC .05
427 Bob MacDonald .05
428 Todd Zeile .05
429 Milt Cuyler .05
430 Eddie Murray .50
431 Rich Amaral .05
432 Pete Young .05
433 Rockies Future Stars (Roger Bailey, Tom Schmidt) .05
434 Jack Armstrong .05
435 Willie McGee .05
436 Greg Harris .05
437 Chris Hammond .05
438 Ritchie Moody RC (1992 Draft Pick) .05
439 Bryan Harvey .05
440 Ruben Sierra .05
441 Marlins Future Stars (Don Lemon, Todd Pridy) .05
442 Kevin McReynolds .05
443 Terry Leach .05
444 David Nied .05
445 Dale Murphy .15
446 Luis Mercedes .05
447 Keith Shepherd RC .05
448 Ken Caminiti .05
449 James Austin .05
450 Darryl Strawberry .05
451 Top Prospects 2B (Ramon Caraballo, Jon Shave, Brent Gates, Quinton McCracken RC) .10
452 Bob Wickman .05
453 Victor Cole .05
454 John Johnstone RC .05
455 Chili Davis .05
456 Scott Taylor .05
457 Tracy Woodson .05
458 David Wells .05
459 Derek Wallace RC (1992 Draft Pick) .05
460 Randy Johnson .50
461 Steve Reed RC .05
462 Felix Fermin .05
463 Scott Aldred .05
464 Greg Colbrunn .05
465 Tony Fernandez .05
466 Mike Felder .05
467 Lee Stevens .05
468 Matt Whiteside .05
469 Dave Hansen .05
470 Rob Dibble .05
471 Dave Gallagher .05
472 Chris Gwynn .05

473 Dave Henderson .05
474 Ozzie Guillen .05
475 Jeff Reardon .05
476 Rockies Future Stars (Mark Voisard, Will Scalzitti) .05
477 Jimmy Jones .05
478 Greg Cadaret .05
479 Todd Pratt .05
480 Pat Listach .05
481 Ryan Luzinski RC (1992 Draft Pick) .05
482 Darren Reed .05
483 Brian Griffiths RC (1992 Draft Pick) .05
484 John Wehner .05
485 Glenn Davis .05
486 Eric Wedge RC .05
487 Jesse Hollins .05
488 Manuel Lee .05
489 Scott Fredrickson RC .05
490 Omar Olivares .05
491 Shawn Hare .05
492 Tom Lampkin .05
493 Jeff Nelson .05
494 Top Prospects 3B (Kevin Young, Adell Davenport, Eduardo Perez, Lou Lucca) .05
495 Ken Hill .05
496 Reggie Jefferson .05
497 Marlins Future Stars (Matt Petersen, Willie Brown) .05
498 Bud Black .05
499 Chuck Crim .05
500 Jose Canseco .30
501 Major League Managers (Johnny Oates, Bobby Cox) .05
502 Major League Managers (Butch Hobson, Jim Lefebvre) .05
503 Major League Managers (Buck Rodgers, Tony Perez) .05
504 Major League Managers (Gene Lamont, Don Baylor) .05
505 Major League Managers (Mike Hargrove, Rene Lachemann) .05
506 Major League Managers (Sparky Anderson, Art Howe) .10
507 Major League Managers (Hal McRae, Tommy Lasorda) .05
508 Major League Manager (Phil Garner, Felipe Alou) .05
509 Major League Managers (Tom Kelly, Jeff Torborg) .05
510 Major League Managers (Buck Showalter, Jim Fregosi) .05
511 Major League Managers (Tony LaRussa, Jim Leyland) .10
512 Major League Managers (Lou Piniella, Joe Torre) .10
513 Major League Managers (Toby Harrah, Jim Riggleman) .05
514 Major League Managers (Cito Gaston, Dusty Baker) .05
515 Greg Swindell .05
516 Alex Arias .05
517 Bill Pecota .05
518 Benji Grigsby RC (1992 Draft Pick) .05
519 David Howard .05
520 Charlie Hough .05
521 Kevin Flora .05
522 Shane Reynolds .05
523 Doug Bochtler RC .05
524 Chris Hoiles .05
525 Scott Sanderson .05
526 Mike Sharperson .05
527 Mike Fetters .05
528 Paul Quantrill .05
529 Top Propsects SS (Dave Silvestri, Chipper Jones, Benji Gil, Jeff Patzke) .25
530 Sterling Hitchcock .05
531 Joe Millette .05
532 Tom Brunansky .05
533 Frank Castillo .05
534 Randy Knorr .05
535 Jose Oquendo .05
536 Dave Haas .05
537 Rockies Future Stars (Jason Hutchins, Ryan Turner) .05
538 Jimmy Baron (1992 Draft Pick) .05
539 Kerry Woodson .05
540 Ivan Calderon .05
541 Denis Boucher .05
542 Royce Clayton .05
543 Reggie Williams .05
544 Steve Decker .05
545 Dean Palmer .05
546 Hal Morris .05
547 Ryan Thompson RC .05

548 Lance Blankenship .05
549 Hensley Meulens .05
550 Scott Radinsky .05
551 Eric Young RC .10
552 Jeff Blauser .05
553 Andujar Cedeno .05
554 Arthur Rhodes .05
555 Terry Mulholland .05
556 Darryl Hamilton .05
557 Pedro Martinez .50
558 Marlins Future Stars (Ryan Whitman, Mark Skeels) .05
559 Jamie Arnold RC (1992 Draft Pick) .05
560 Zane Smith .05
561 Matt Nokes .05
562 Bob Zupcic .05
563 Shawn Boskie .05
564 Mike Timlin .05
565 Jerald Clark .05
566 Rod Brewer .05
567 Mark Carreon .05
568 Andy Benes .05
569 Shawn Barton .05
570 Tim Wallach .05
571 Dave Mlicki .05
572 Trevor Hoffman .05
573 John Patterson .05
574 DeShawn Warren (1992 Draft Pick) .05
575 Monty Fariss .05
576 Top Prospects OF (Darrell Sherman, Damon Buford, Cliff Floyd, Michael Moore) .05
577 Tim Costo .05
578 Dave Magadan .05
579 Rockies Future Stars (Neil Garret, Jason Bates) .05
580 Walt Weiss .05
581 Chris Haney .05
582 Shawn Abner .05
583 Marvin Freeman .05
584 Casey Candaele .05
585 Ricky Jordan .05
586 Jeff Tabaka .05
587 Manny Alexander .05
588 Mike Trombley .05
589 Carlos Hernandez .05
590 Cal Eldred .05
591 Alex Cole .05
592 Phil Plantier .05
593 Brett Merriman .05
594 Jerry Nielsen .05
595 Shawon Dunston .05
596 Jimmy Key .05
597 Gerald Perry .05
598 Rico Brogna .05
599 Marlins Future Stars (Clemente Nunez, Dan Robinson) .05
600 Bret Saberhagen .05
601 Craig Shipley .05
602 Henry Mercedes .05
603 Jim Thome .40
604 Rod Beck .05
605 Chuck Finley .05
606 J. Owens .05
607 Dan Smith .05
608 Bill Doran .05
609 Lance Parrish .05
610 Denny Martinez .05
611 Tom Gordon .05
612 Byron Mathews (1992 Draft Pick) .05
613 Joel Adamson .05
614 Brian Williams .05
615 Steve Avery .05
616 Top Prospects OF (Matt Mieske, Tracy Sanders, Midre Cummings, Ryan Freeburg) .05
617 Craig Lefferts .05
618 Tony Pena .05
619 Billy Spiers .05
620 Todd Benzinger .05
621 Rockies Future Stars (Mike Kotarski, Greg Boyd) .05
622 Ben Rivera .05
623 Al Martin RC .05
624 Sam Militello .05
625 Rick Aguilera .05
626 Danny Gladden .05
627 Andres Berumen .05
628 Kelly Gruber .05
629 Cris Carpenter .05
630 Mark Grace .05
631 Jeff Brantley .05
632 Chris Widger (1992 Draft Pick) .05
633 Russian Angels (Rodolf Razjigaev, Evgenyi Puchkov, Ilya Bogatyrev) .10
634 Mo Sanford .05
635 Albert Belle .05
636 Tim Teufel .05
637 Greg Myers .05
638 Brian Bohanon .05
639 Mike Bordick .05
640 Dwight Gooden .05
641 Marlins Future Stars (Pat Leahy, Gavin Baugh) .05

642 Milt Hill .05
643 Luis Aquino .05
644 Dante Bichette .05
645 Bobby Thigpen .05
646 Rich Scheid .05
647 Brian Sackinsky (1992 Draft Pick) .05
648 Ryan Hawblitzel .05
649 Tom Marsh .05
650 Terry Pendleton .05
651 Rafael Bournigal RC .05
652 Dave West .05
653 Steve Hosey .05
654 Gerald Williams .05
655 Scott Cooper .05
656 Gary Scott .05
657 Mike Harkey .05
658 Top Prospects OF (Jeromy Burnitz, Melvin Nieves, Rich Becker, Shon Walker) .05
659 Ed Sprague .05
660 Alan Trammell .05
661 Rockies Future Stars (Garvin Alston, Mike Case) .05
662 Donovan Osborne .05
663 Jeff Gardner .05
664 Calvin Jones .05
665 Darrin Fletcher .05
666 Glenallen Hill .05
667 Jim Rosenbohm (1992 Draft Pick) .05
668 Scott Lewis .05
669 Kip Yaughn .05
670 Julio Franco .05
671 Dave Martinez .05
672 Kevin Bass .05
673 Todd Van Poppel .05
674 Mark Gubicza .05
675 Tim Raines .05
676 Rudy Seanez .05
677 Charlie Leibrandt .05
678 Randy Milligan .05
679 Kim Batiste .05
680 Craig Biggio .05
681 Darren Holmes .05
682 John Candelaria .05
683 Marlins Future Stars (Jerry Stafford, Eddie Christian) .05
684 Pat Mahomes .05
685 Bob Walk .05
686 Russ Springer .05
687 Tony Sheffield (1992 Draft Picks) .05
688 Dwight Smith .05
689 Eddie Zosky .05
690 Bien Figueroa .05
691 Jim Tatum .05
692 Chad Kreuter .05
693 Rich Rodriguez .05
694 Shane Turner .05
695 Kent Bottenfield .05
696 Jose Mesa .05
697 Darrell Whitmore RC .05
698 Ted Wood .05
699 Chad Curtis .05
700 Nolan Ryan 1.00
701 Top Prospects C (Mike Piazza, Carlos Delgado, Brook Fordyce, Donnie Leshnock) .85
702 Tim Pugh RC .05
703 Jeff Kent .05
704 Rockies Future Stars (Jon Goodrich, Danny Figueroa) .05
705 Bob Welch .05
706 Sherard Clinkscales (1992 Draft Pick) .05
707 Donn Pall .05
708 Greg Olson .05
709 Jeff Juden .05
710 Mike Mussina .30
711 Scott Chiamparino .05
712 Stan Javier .05
713 John Doherty .05
714 Kevin Gross .05
715 Greg Gagne .05
716 Steve Cooke .05
717 Steve Farr .05
718 Jay Buhner .05
719 Butch Henry .05
720 David Cone .05
721 Rick Wilkins .05
722 Chuck Carr .05
723 Kenny Felder RC (1992 Draft Pick) .05
724 Guillermo Velasquez .05
725 Billy Hatcher .05
726 Marlins Future Stars (Mike Veneziale, Ken Kendrena) .05
727 Jonathan Hurst .05
728 Steve Frey .05
729 Mark Leonard .05
730 Charles Nagy .05
731 Donald Harris .05
732 Travis Buckley .05
733 Tom Browning .05
734 Anthony Young .05
735 Steve Shifflett .05
736 Jeff Russell .05
737 Wilson Alvarez .05
738 Lance Painter .05

739 Dave Weathers .05
740 Len Dykstra .05
741 Mike Devereaux .05
742 Top Prospects/SP (Rene Arocha, Alan Embree, Tim Crabtree RC, Brien Taylor) .05
743 Dave Landaker (1992 Draft Pick) .05
744 Chris George .05
745 Eric Davis .05
746 Rockies Future Stars (Mark Strittmatter RC, LaMarr Rogers) .05
747 Carl Willis .05
748 Stan Belinda .05
749 Scott Kamieniecki .05
750 Rickey Henderson .50
751 Eric Hillman .05
752 Pat Hentgen .05
753 Jim Corsi .05
754 Brian Jordan .05
755 Bill Swift .05
756 Mike Henneman .05
757 Harold Reynolds .05
758 Sean Berry .05
759 Charlie Hayes .05
760 Luis Polonia .05
761 Darrin Jackson .05
762 Mark Lewis .05
763 Rob Maurer .05
764 Willie Greene .05
765 Vince Coleman .05
766 Todd Revenig .05
767 Rich Ireland (1992 Draft Pick) .05
768 Mike MacFarlane .05
769 Francisco Cabrera .05
770 Robin Ventura .05
771 Kevin Ritz .05
772 Chito Martinez .05
773 Cliff Brantley .05
774 Curtis Leskanic .05
775 Chris Bosio .05
776 Jose Offerman .05
777 Mark Guthrie .05
778 Don Slaught .05
779 Rich Monteleone .05
780 Jim Abbott .05
781 Jack Clark .05
782 Marlins Future Stars (Rafael Mendoza, Dan Roman) .05
783 Heathcliff Slocumb .05
784 Jeff Branson .05
785 Kevin Brown .05
786 Top Prospects RP (Mike Christopher, Ken Ryan, Aaron Taylor, Gus Gandarillas) .05
787 Mike Matthews (1992 Draft Pick) .05
788 Mackey Sasser .05
789 Jeff Conine .05
790 George Bell .05
791 Pat Rapp .05
792 Joe Boever .05
793 Jim Poole .05
794 Andy Ashby .05
795 Deion Sanders .10
796 Scott Brosius .05
797 Brad Pennington (Coming Attraction) .05
798 Greg Blosser (Coming Attraction) .05
799 Jim Edmonds RC (Coming Attraction) 1.00
800 Shawn Jeter (Coming Attraction) .05
801 Jesse Levis (Coming Attraction) .05
802 Phil Clark (Coming Attraction) .05
803 Ed Pierce (Coming Attraction) .05
804 Jose Valentin RC (Coming Attraction) .05
805 Terry Jorgensen (Coming Attraction) .05
806 Mark Hutton (Coming Attraction) .05
807 Troy Neel (Coming Attraction) .05
808 Bret Boone (Coming Attraction) .05
809 Chris Colon (Coming Attraction) .05
810 Domingo Martinez RC (Coming Attraction) .05
811 Javier Lopez (Coming Attraction) .05
812 Matt Walbeck (Coming Attraction) .05
813 Dan Wilson (Coming Attraction) .05
814 Scooter Tucker (Coming Attraction) .05
815 Billy Ashley RC (Coming Attraction) .05
816 Tim Laker RC (Coming Attraction) .05
817 Bobby Jones (Coming Attraction) .05
818 Brad Brink (Coming Attraction) .05
819 William Pennyfeather (Coming Attraction) .05

820 Stan Royer (Coming Attraction) .05
821 Doug Brocail (Coming Attraction) .05
822 Kevin Rogers (Coming Attraction) .05
823 Checklist 397-528 .05
824 Checklist 541-691 .05
825 Checklist 692-825 .05

Gold

Expanding on the concept begun in 1992, Topps issued a "gold" version of each of its regular 1993 cards as a package insert. One Gold card was found in each wax pack; three per rack-pack and five per jumbo cello pack. Ten Gold cards were included in each factory set. Identical in format to the regular-issue 1993 Topps cards, the Gold version replaces the black or white Topps logo on front with a "ToppsGold" logo in gold-foil. The color bars and angled strips beneath the player photo which carry the player and team ID on regular cards are replaced with a gold-foil version on the insert cards. Backs are identical to the regular cards. The six checklist cards in the regular issue were replaced in the Gold version with cards of players who do not appear in the 1993 Topps set.

	NM/M
Complete Set (825):	40.00
Common Player:	.15
394 Bernardo Brito	.25
395 Jim McNamara	.25
396 Rich Sauveur	.25
823 Keith Brown	.25
824 Russ McGinnis	.25
825 Mike Walker	.25

Black Gold

Randomly inserted in regular 1993 Topps packs, as well as 10 per factory set, Black Gold cards are found in both single-player versions and "Winner" cards. The single-player cards feature an action photo set against a black background and highlighted at top and bottom with gold foil. Backs have another player photo at left, again on a black background. A career summary is printed in a blue box at right. A "Topps Black Gold" logo appears at top-left, and the player's name is printed in gold foil in an art deco device at top-right. The Winner cards picture tiny versions of the Black Gold player cards for which they could be redeemed by mail.

Some, perhaps all, of the mail-in cards can also be found on which the miniature card pictures on front do not correspond to the players named on back. In addition, with each mail-in redemption set, a non-redeemable version of the Winner card was also sent.

	NM/M
Complete Set (44):	7.50
Common Player:	.10
Winner A (1-11):	1.00
Winner B (12-22):	1.00
Winner C (23-33):	1.00
Winner D (34-44):	1.00
Winner AB (1-22):	3.00
Winner CD (23-44):	3.00
Winner ABCD (1-44):	5.00
1 Barry Bonds	1.50
2 Will Clark	.10
3 Darren Daulton	.10
4 Andre Dawson	.25
5 Delino DeShields	.10
6 Tom Glavine	.20
7 Marquis Grissom	.10
8 Tony Gwynn	.75
9 Eric Karros	.10
10 Ray Lankford	.10
11 Barry Larkin	.10
12 Greg Maddux	.75
13 Fred McGriff	.10
14 Joe Oliver	.10
15 Terry Pendleton	.10
16 Bip Roberts	.10
17 Ryne Sandberg	.75
18 Gary Sheffield	.40
19 Lee Smith	.10
20 Ozzie Smith	.75
21 Andy Van Slyke	.10
22 Larry Walker	.10
23 Roberto Alomar	.20
24 Brady Anderson	.10
25 Carlos Baerga	.10
26 Joe Carter	.10
27 Roger Clemens	.85
28 Mike Devereaux	.10
29 Dennis Eckersley	.60
30 Cecil Fielder	.10
31 Travis Fryman	.10
32 Juan Gonzalez	.35
33 Ken Griffey Jr.	1.00
34 Brian Harper	.10
35 Pat Listach	.10
36 Kenny Lofton	.10
37 Edgar Martinez	.10
38 Jack McDowell	.10
39 Mark McGwire	1.00
40 Kirby Puckett	.75
41 Mickey Tettleton	.10
42 Frank Thomas	.65
43 Robin Ventura	.10
44 Dave Winfield	.65

Colorado Rockies Inaugural Year

To mark the team's inaugural year in the Major Leagues, Topps produced a special run of 10,000 of its 1993 factory sets in which each card was embossed with a special gold seal incorporating the Rockies logo. Sets sold for $100 at the team's normal souvenir outlets. The factory sets were sealed with a sticker featuring the inaugural year logo.

	NM/M
Complete Set (825):	80.00
Common Player:	.50

Florida Marlins Inaugural Year

To commemorate the team's inaugural year in the Major Leagues, Topps produced a special edition of 6,000 of its 1993 factory sets in which every card was embossed with a special gold seal incorporating the Marlins logo. The sets were sold for $100 at the team's normal souvenir outlets. Factory sets are sealed with a sticker incorporating the inaugural year logo.

	NM/M
Complete Set (825):	100.00
Common Player:	.50

Traded

The 1993 Topps Traded baseball set features many players in their new uniforms as a result of trades, free agent signings and rookie call-ups. The set also features 35 expansion players from the Colorado Rockies and Florida Marlins, as well as 22 Team USA members exclusive to Topps. The 132-card set is packed in a color deluxe printed box.

	NM/M
Complete Set (132):	20.00
Common Player:	.05
1 Barry Bonds	2.00
2 Rich Renteria	.05
3 Aaron Sele	.05
4 Carlton Loewer RC (USA)	.10
5 Erik Pappas	.05
6 Greg McMichael RC	.05
7 Freddie Benavides	.05
8 Kirk Gibson	.05
9 Tony Fernandez	.05
10 Jay Gainer RC (USA)	.05
11 Orestes Destrade	.05
12 A.J. Hinch RC (USA)	.40
13 Bobby Munoz	.05
14 Tom Henke	.05
15 Rob Butler	.05
16 Gary Wayne	.05
17 David McCarty	.05
18 Walt Weiss	.05
19 Todd Helton RC (USA)	15.00
20 Mark Whiten	.05
21 Ricky Gutierrez	.05
22 Dustin Hermanson RC (USA)	.40
23 Sherman Obando RC	.05
24 Mike Piazza	2.00
25 Jeff Russell	.05
26 Jason Bere	.05
27 Jack Voight RC	.05
28 Chris Bosio	.05
29 Phil Hiatt	.05
30 Matt Beaumont RC (USA)	.05
31 Andres Galarraga	.05
32 Greg Swindell	.05
33 Vinny Castilla	.05
34 Pat Clougherty RC (USA)	.05
35 Greg Briley	.05
36 Dallas Green	.05
37 Davey Johnson	.05
38 Tyler Green	.05
39 Craig Paquette	.05
40 Danny Sheaffer	.05

41 Terry Harvey	.05
42 Phil Plantier	.05
43 Doug Saunders RC	.05
44 Benny Santiago	.05
45 Dante Powell RC (USA)	.10
46 Jeff Parrett	.05
47 Wade Boggs	.85
48 Paul Molitor	.75
49 Turk Wendell	.05
50 David Wells	.05
51 Gary Sheffield	.35
52 Kevin Young	.05
53 Nelson Liriano	.05
54 Greg Maddux	.85
55 Derek Bell	.05
56 Matt Turner RC	.05
57 Charlie Nelson RC (USA)	.05
58 Mike Hampton	.05
59 Troy O'Leary RC	.10
60 Benji Gil	.05
61 Mitch Lyden RC	.05
62 J.T. Snow	.05
63 Damon Buford	.05
64 Gene Harris	.05
65 Randy Myers	.05
66 Felix Jose	.05
67 Todd Dunn RC (USA)	.05
68 Jimmy Key	.05
69 Pedro Castellano	.05
70 Mark Merila RC (USA)	.05
71 Rich Rodriguez	.05
72 Matt Mieske	.05
73 Pete Incaviglia	.05
74 Carl Everett	.05
75 Jim Abbott	.05
76 Luis Aquino	.05
77 Rene Arocha RC	.05
78 Jon Shave RC	.05
79 Todd Walker RC (USA)	1.00
80 Jack Armstrong	.05
81 Jeff Richardson	.05
82 Blas Minor	.05
83 Dave Winfield	.75
84 Paul O'Neill	.05
85 Steve Reich RC (USA)	.10
86 Chris Hammond	.05
87 Hilly Hathaway RC	.05
88 Fred McGriff	.05
89 Dave Telgheder RC	.05
90 Richie Lewis RC	.05
91 Brent Gates	.05
92 Andre Dawson	.15
93 Andy Barkett RC (USA)	.05
94 Doug Drabek	.05
95 Joe Klink	.05
96 Willie Blair	.05
97 Danny Graves RC (USA)	.05
98 Pat Meares	.05
99 Mike Lansing	.05
100 Marcos Armas RC	.05
101 Darren Grass RC (USA)	.05
102 Chris Jones	.05
103 Ken Ryan RC	.05
104 Ellis Burks	.05
105 Bobby Kelly	.05
106 Dave Magadan	.05
107 Paul Wilson RC (USA)	.25
108 Rob Natal	.05
109 Paul Wagner	.05
110 Jeromy Burnitz	.05
111 Monty Fariss	.05
112 Kevin Mitchell	.05
113 Scott Pose RC	.05
114 Dave Stewart	.05
115 Russ Johnson RC (USA)	.10
116 Armando Reynoso	.05
117 Geronimo Berroa	.05
118 Woody Williams RC	.15
119 Tim Bogar RC	.05
120 Bob Scafa RC (USA)	.05
121 Henry Cotto	.05
122 Gregg Jefferies	.05
123 Norm Charlton	.05
124 Bret Wagner RC (USA)	.05
125 David Cone	.05
126 Daryl Boston	.05
127 Tim Wallach	.05
128 Mike Martin RC (USA)	.05
129 John Cummings RC	.05
130 Ryan Bowen	.05
131 John Powell RC (USA)	.05
132 Checklist	.05

Full Shot Super

Just as rivals Upper Deck and Donruss did, Topps issued a set of 21 oversized cards (3-1/2" x 5") that was available in retail outlets in packages that contained one of the large cards and two packs of regular issue Topps cards from the same year. The Topps Full Shot cards feature many of the top players in the game, and unlike the Upper Deck oversized cards, the Topps cards were not enlarged versions of existing cards but rather photos and a design that appeared only in this format.

	NM/M
Complete Set (21):	65.00
Common Player:	2.00
1 Frank Thomas	4.00
2 Ken Griffey Jr.	6.50
3 Barry Bonds	9.00
4 Juan Gonzalez	2.50
5 Roberto Alomar	2.50
6 Mike Piazza	6.50
7 Tony Gwynn	4.50
8 Jeff Bagwell	3.50
9 Tim Salmon	2.00
10 John Olerud	2.00
11 Cal Ripken, Jr.	9.00
12 David McCarty	2.00
13 Darren Daulton	2.00
14 Carlos Baerga	2.00
15 Roger Clemens	5.00
16 John Kruk	2.00
17 Barry Larkin	2.00
18 Gary Sheffield	2.50
19 Tom Glavine	2.50
20 Andres Galarraga	2.00
21 Fred McGriff	2.00

Golden Spikes Award

Darren Dreifort was the 1993 recipient of the U.S. Baseball Federation's Golden Spikes Award, emblematic of his selection as the outstanding amateur player in the nation. Topps created and handed out at the awards ceremony this special card.

	NM/M
Darren Dreifort	125.00

Magazine Jumbo Rookies

The final four issues of Topps' Magazine in 1993 substituted a 5-1/2" x 8" enlargement of a player's Topps rookie card in place of four of the standard-size inserts found previously. The jumbo rookie cards are identical, front and back, to the original rookie cards but carry a reprint notice on front. In an attempt to increase sales to subscribers and at the newsstands, the stars pictured autographed 100 of their cards to be randomly bound into the magazine and given away in prize drawings.

	NM/M
Complete Set (4):	7.50
Common Player:	1.00
(1) Dennis Eckersley (1976 Topps)	1.00
(2) Dave Winfield (1974 Topps)	1.00
(3) George Brett (1975 Topps)	2.00
(4) Jerry Koosman, Nolan Ryan (1968 Topps)	4.00

Micro

Topps returned for a final year with a micro parallel of its regular-issue baseball set, in a format about 40% the size of the standard cards. Sold only in complete-set form, the 1" x 1-3/8" cards also included a dozen prismatic-foil bordered star cards. Stars and rookies among the micros are valued at a percentage of the corresponding regular card.

	NM/M
Complete Set (837):	11.00
Common Player:	.05
Stars/Rookies:	1-1.5X
1 Robin Yount	.75
20 Tim Salmon	.50
32 Don Mattingly	1.25
50 Roberto Alomar	.60
150 Frank Thomas	.75
155 Dennis Eckersley	.65
179 Ken Griffey Jr.	1.50
200 Kirby Puckett	1.00
397 George Brett	1.25
426 Nigel Wilson	.50
444 David Nied	.50
700 Nolan Ryan	2.00

1994 Topps Preview

Two different versions of this nine-card set exist. A cello-wrapped version, designated (a) in the checklist, was given away to dealers and the hobby press. A second version, designated (b), was included in 1993 Topps factory sets. It is currently unknown which version, if either, will become more valuable due to demand and perceived scarcity. Both versions are similar to the regular-issue '94 Topps cards, except for the sample notation on back.

	NM/M
Complete Set (a)(9):	10.00
Complete Set (b)(9):	10.00

Common Player (a):	.30
Common Player (b):	.30
2a Barry Bonds (Vertical format.)	4.00
2b Barry Bonds (Horizontal)	4.00
6a Jeff Tackett (Full bat label visible.)	.30
6b Jeff Tackett (Partial bat label.)	.30
34a Juan Gonzalez (Green triangle behind "Juan.")	.75
34b Juan Gonzalez (Brown triangle.)	.75
225a Matt Williams (Green triangle behind "Matt.")	.30
225b Matt Williams (Blue triangle.)	.30
294a Carlos Quintana (Team/position yellow.)	.30
294b Carlos Quintana (Team/position black.)	.30
331a Ken Lofton (Team/position white.)	.30
331b Ken Lofton (Team/position black.)	.30
390a Wade Boggs (Team/position yellow.)	2.00
390b Wade Boggs (Team/position black.)	2.00
397a George Brett (Vertical format.)	3.00
397b George Brett (Horizontal)	3.00
700a Nolan Ryan (Vertical format.)	4.00
700b Nolan Ryan (Horizontal)	4.00

1994 Topps

Once again released in two 396-card series, Topps' basic issue for 1994 offers a standard mix of regular player cards, Future Stars, multi-player rookie cards and double-header All-Star cards. On most cards the player photo on front is framed in a home-plate shaped design. The player's name appears in script beneath the photo and a team color-coded strip at bottom carries the team name and position designation. On back is a player photo, a red box at top with biographical details and a marbled panel which carries the stats and a career highlight. Cards are UV coated on each side. Inserts include a gold-foil enhanced parallel card in every pack, plus random Black Gold cards. Factory hobby sets include the 792 base cards plus 10 gold parallels, three Black Gold inserts and three Finest pre-production cards. Factory retails sets have the 792 base cards, 10 Gold, three Black Gold, 10 1995 Topps pre-production cards and three Superstar Sampler cards.

	NM/M
Unopened Retail Set (818):	60.00
Unopened Hobby Set (808):	50.00
Complete Set (792):	35.00
Common Player:	.05
Golds:	2X
Series 1 or 2 Pack (12):	.50
Series 1 or 2 Wax Box (36):	15.00
1 Mike Piazza (All-Star Rookie)	.85
2 Bernie Williams	.05
3 Kevin Rogers	.05
4 Paul Leyton (Future Star)	.05
5 Ozzie Guillen	.05
6 Derrick May	.05
7 Jose Mesa	.05
8 Todd Hundley	.05
9 Chris Haney	.05
10 John Olerud	.05
11 Andujar Cedeno	.05

No.	Player	Price
12	John Smiley	.05
13	Phil Plantier	.05
14	Willie Banks	.05
15	Jay Bell	.05
16	Doug Henry	.05
17	Lance Blankenship	.05
18	Greg Harris	.05
19	Scott Livingstone	.05
20	Bryan Harvey	.05
21	Wil Cordero (All-Star Rookie)	.05
22	Roger Pavlik	.05
23	Mark Lemke	.05
24	Jeff Nelson	.05
25	Todd Zeile	.05
26	Billy Hatcher	.05
27	Joe Magrane	.05
28	Tony Longmire (Future Star)	.05
29	Omar Daal	.05
30	Kirt Manwaring	.05
31	Melido Perez	.05
32	Tim Hulett	.05
33	Jeff Schwarz	.05
34	Nolan Ryan	1.00
35	Jose Guzman	.05
36	Felix Fermin	.05
37	Jeff Innis	.05
38	Brent Mayne	.05
39	Huck Flener RC	.05
40	Jeff Bagwell	.50
41	Kevin Wickander	.05
42	Ricky Gutierrez	.05
43	Pat Mahomes	.05
44	Jeff King	.05
45	Cal Eldred	.05
46	Craig Paquette	.05
47	Richie Lewis	.05
48	Tony Phillips	.05
49	Armando Reynoso	.05
50	Moises Alou	.05
51	Manuel Lee	.05
52	Otis Nixon	.05
53	Billy Ashley (Future Star)	.05
54	Mark Whiten	.05
55	Jeff Russell	.05
56	Chad Curtis	.05
57	Kevin Stocker	.05
58	Mike Jackson	.05
59	Matt Nokes	.05
60	Chris Bosio	.05
61	Damon Buford	.05
62	Tim Belcher	.05
63	Glenallen Hill	.05
64	Bill Wertz	.05
65	Eddie Murray	.50
66	Tom Gordon	.05
67	Alex Gonzalez (Future Star)	.05
68	Eddie Taubensee	.05
69	Jacob Brumfield	.05
70	Andy Benes	.05
71	Rich Becker (Future Star)	.05
72	Steve Cooke (All-Star Rookie)	.05
73	Billy Spiers	.05
74	Scott Brosius	.05
75	Alan Trammell	.05
76	Luis Aquino	.05
77	Jerald Clark	.05
78	Mel Rojas	.05
79	OF Prospects (Billy Masse, Stanton Cameron, Tim Clark, Craig McClure)	.05
80	Jose Canseco	.30
81	Greg McMichael (All-Star Rookie)	.05
82	Brian Turang	.05
83	Tom Urban	.05
84	Garret Anderson (Future Star)	.05
85	Tony Pena	.05
86	Ricky Jordan	.05
87	Jim Gott	.05
88	Pat Kelly	.05
89	Bud Black	.05
90	Robin Ventura	.05
91	Rick Sutcliffe	.05
92	Jose Bautista	.05
93	Bob Ojeda	.05
94	Phil Hiatt	.05
95	Tim Pugh	.05
96	Randy Knorr	.05
97	Todd Jones (Future Star)	.05
98	Ryan Thompson	.05
99	Tim Mauser	.05
100	Kirby Puckett	.60
101	Mark Dewey	.05
102	B.J. Surhoff	.05
103	Sterling Hitchcock	.05
104	Alex Arias	.05
105	David Wells	.05
106	Daryl Boston	.05
107	Mike Stanton	.05
108	Gary Redus	.05
109a	Delino DeShields (Red "Expos, 2B.")	2.00
109b	Delino DeShields (Yellow "Expos, 2B.")	.05
110	Lee Smith	.05
111	Greg Litton	.05
112	Frank Rodriguez (Future Star)	.05
113	Russ Springer	.05
114	Mitch Williams	.05
115	Eric Karros	.05
116	Jeff Brantley	.05
117	Jack Voight	.05
118	Jason Bere	.05
119	Kevin Roberson	.05
120	Jimmy Key	.05
121	Reggie Jefferson	.05
122	Jeromy Burnitz	.05
123	Billy Brewer (Future Star)	.05
124	Willie Canate	.05
125	Greg Swindell	.05
126	Hal Morris	.05
127	Brad Ausmus	.05
128	George Tsamis	.05
129	Denny Neagle	.05
130	Pat Listach	.05
131	Steve Karsay	.05
132	Bret Barberie	.05
133	Mark Leiter	.05
134	Greg Colbrunn	.05
135	David Nied	.05
136	Dean Palmer	.05
137	Steve Avery	.05
138	Bill Haselman	.05
139	Tripp Cromer (Future Star)	.05
140	Frank Viola	.05
141	Rene Gonzales	.05
142	Curt Schilling	.25
143	Tim Wallach	.05
144	Bobby Munoz	.05
145	Brady Anderson	.05
146	Rod Beck	.05
147	Mike LaValliere	.05
148	Greg Hibbard	.05
149	Kenny Lofton	.05
150	Dwight Gooden	.05
151	Greg Gagne	.05
152	Ray McDavid (Future Star)	.05
153	Chris Donnels	.05
154	Dan Wilson	.05
155	Todd Stottlemyre	.05
156	David McCarty	.05
157	Paul Wagner	.05
158	SS Prospects (Orlando Miller, Brandon Wilson, Derek Jeter, Mike Neal)	1.00
159	Mike Fetters	.05
160	Scott Lydy	.05
161	Darrell Whitmore	.05
162	Bob MacDonald	.05
163	Vinny Castilla	.05
164	Denis Boucher	.05
165	Ivan Rodriguez	.40
166	Ron Gant	.05
167	Tim Davis	.05
168	Steve Dixon	.05
169	Scott Fletcher	.05
170	Terry Mulholland	.05
171	Greg Myers	.05
172	Brett Butler	.05
173	Bob Wickman	.05
174	Dave Martinez	.05
175	Fernando Valenzuela	.05
176	Craig Grebeck	.05
177	Shawn Boskie	.05
178	Albie Lopez	.05
179	Butch Huskey (Future Star)	.05
180	George Brett	.65
181	Juan Guzman	.05
182	Eric Anthony	.05
183	Bob Dibble	.05
184	Craig Shipley	.05
185	Kevin Tapani	.05
186	Marcus Moore	.05
187	Graeme Lloyd	.05
188	Mike Bordick	.05
189	Chris Hammond	.05
190	Cecil Fielder	.05
191	Curtis Leskanic	.05
192	Lou Frazier	.05
193	Steve Dreyer	.05
194	Javier Lopez (Future Star)	.05
195	Edgar Martinez	.05
196	Allen Watson	.05
197	John Flaherty	.05
198	Kurt Stillwell	.05
199	Danny Jackson	.05
200	Cal Ripken, Jr.	1.00
201	Mike Bell (Draft Pick)	.05
202	Alan Benes RC (Draft Pick)	.10
203	Matt Farner (Draft Pick)	.05
204	Jeff Granger RC (Draft Pick)	.05
205	Brooks Kieschnick RC (Draft Pick)	.05
206	Jeremy Lee (Draft Pick)	.05
207	Charles Peterson RC (Draft Pick)	.05
208	Andy Rice (Draft Pick)	.05
209	Billy Wagner RC (Draft Pick)	.25
210	Kelly Wunsch (Draft Pick)	.05
211	Tom Candiotti	.05
212	Domingo Jean (Draft Pick)	.05
213	John Burkett	.05
214	George Bell	.05
215	Dan Plesac	.05
216	Manny Ramirez (Future Star)	.60
217	Mike Maddux	.05
218	Kevin McReynolds	.05
219	Pat Borders	.05
220	Doug Drabek	.05
221	Larry Luebbers	.05
222	Trevor Hoffman	.05
223	Pat Meares	.05
224	Danny Miceli (Future Star)	.05
225	Greg Vaughn	.05
226	Scott Hemond	.05
227	Pat Rapp	.05
228	Kirk Gibson	.05
229	Lance Painter	.05
230	Larry Walker	.05
231	Benji Gil (Future Star)	.05
232	Mark Wohlers	.05
233	Rich Amaral	.05
234	Erik Pappas	.05
235	Scott Cooper	.05
236	Mike Butcher	.05
237	OF Prospects (Curtis Pride RC, Shawn Green, Mark Sweeney, Eddie Davis)	.35
238	Kim Batiste	.05
239	Paul Assenmacher	.05
240	Will Clark	.05
241	Jose Offerman	.05
242	Todd Frohwirth	.05
243	Tim Raines	.05
244	Rick Wilkins	.05
245	Bret Saberhagen	.05
246	Thomas Howard	.05
247	Stan Belinda	.05
248	Rickey Henderson	.50
249	Brian Williams	.05
250	Barry Larkin	.05
251	Jose Valentin (Future Star)	.05
252	Lenny Webster	.05
253	Blas Minor	.05
254	Tim Teufel	.05
255	Bobby Witt	.05
256	Walt Weiss	.05
257	Chad Kreuter	.05
258	Roberto Mejia	.05
259	Cliff Floyd (Future Star)	.05
260	Julio Franco	.05
261	Rafael Belliard	.05
262	Marc Newfield	.05
263	Gerald Perry	.05
264	Ken Ryan	.05
265	Chili Davis	.05
266	Dave West	.05
267	Royce Clayton	.05
268	Pedro Martinez	.50
269	Mark Hutton	.05
270	Frank Thomas	.50
271	Brad Pennington	.05
272	Mike Harkey	.05
273	Sandy Alomar	.05
274	Dave Gallagher	.05
275	Wally Joyner	.05
276	Ricky Trlicek	.05
277	Al Osuna	.05
278	Calvin Reese (Future Star)	.05
279	Kevin Higgins	.05
280	Rick Aguilera	.05
281	Orlando Merced	.05
282	Mike Mohler	.05
283	John Jaha	.05
284	Robb Nen	.05
285	Travis Fryman	.05
286	Mark Thompson (Future Star)	.05
287	Mike Lansing (All-Star Rookie)	.05
288	Craig Lefferts	.05
289	Damon Berryhill	.05
290	Randy Johnson	.50
291	Jeff Reed	.05
292	Danny Darwin	.05
293	J.T. Snow (All-Star Rookie)	.05
294	Tyler Green	.05
295	Chris Hoiles	.05
296	Roger McDowell	.05
297	Spike Owen	.05
298	Salomon Torres (Future Star)	.05
299	Wilson Alvarez	.05
300	Ryne Sandberg	.60
301	Derek Lilliquist	.05
302	Howard Johnson	.05
303	Greg Cadaret	.05
304	Pat Hentgen	.05
305	Craig Biggio	.05
306	Scott Service	.05
307	Melvin Nieves	.05
308	Mike Trombley	.05
309	Carlos Garcia (All-Star Rookie)	.05
310	Robin Yount	.50
311	Marcos Armas	.05
312	Rich Rodriguez	.05
313	Justin Thompson (Future Star)	.05
314	Danny Sheaffer	.05
315	Ken Hill	.05
316	P Prospects (Chad Ogea RC, Duff Brumley RC, Terrell Wade RC, Chris Michalak RC)	.10
317	Cris Carpenter	.05
318	Jeff Blauser	.05
319	Ted Power	.05
320	Ozzie Smith	.60
321	John Dopson	.05
322	Chris Turner	.05
323	Pete Incaviglia	.05
324	Alan Mills	.05
325	Jody Reed	.05
326	Rich Monteleone	.05
327	Mark Carreon	.05
328	Donn Pall	.05
329	Matt Walbeck (Future Star)	.05
330	Charles Nagy	.05
331	Jeff McKnight	.05
332	Jose Lind	.05
333	Mike Timlin	.05
334	Doug Jones	.05
335	Kevin Mitchell	.05
336	Luis Lopez	.05
337	Shane Mack	.05
338	Randy Tomlin	.05
339	Matt Mieske	.05
340	Mark McGwire	.85
341	Nigel Wilson (Future Star)	.05
342	Danny Gladden	.05
343	Mo Sanford	.05
344	Sean Berry	.05
345	Kevin Brown	.05
346	Greg Olson	.05
347	Dave Magadan	.05
348	Rene Arocha	.05
349	Carlos Quintana	.05
350	Jim Abbott	.05
351	Gary DiSarcina	.05
352	Ben Rivera	.05
353	Carlos Hernandez	.05
354	Darren Lewis	.05
355	Harold Reynolds	.05
356	Scott Ruffcorn (Future Star)	.05
357	Mark Gubicza	.05
358	Paul Sorrento	.05
359	Anthony Young	.05
360	Mark Grace	.05
361	Rob Butler	.05
362	Kevin Bass	.05
363	Eric Helfand (Future Star)	.05
364	Derek Bell	.05
365	Scott Erickson	.05
366	Al Martin	.05
367	Ricky Bones	.05
368	Jeff Branson	.05
369	3B Prospects (Luis Ortiz, David Bell, Jason Giambi, George Arias RC)	.30
370a	Benny Santiago	.05
370b	Mark McLemore (Originally checklisted as #379.)	.05
371	John Doherty	.05
372	Joe Girardi	.05
373	Tim Scott	.05
374	Marvin Freeman	.05
375	Deion Sanders	.10
376	Roger Salkeld	.05
377	Bernard Gilkey	.05
378	Tony Fossas	.05
380	Darren Daulton	.05
381	Chuck Finley	.05
382	Mitch Webster	.05
383	Gerald Williams	.05
384	Frank Thomas, Fred McGriff/AS	.30
385	Roberto Alomar, Robby Thompson/AS	.05
386	Wade Boggs, Matt Williams/AS	.35
387	Cal Ripken, Jr., Jeff Blauser/AS	.50
388	Ken Griffey Jr., Len Dykstra/AS	.40
389	Juan Gonzalez, Dave Justice/AS	.10
390	Albert Belle, Barry Bonds/AS	.45
391	Mike Stanley, Mike Piazza/AS	.45
392	Jack McDowell, Greg Maddux/AS	.35
393	Jimmy Key, Tom Glavine/AS	.05
394	Jeff Montgomery, Randy Myers/AS	.05
395	Checklist 1	.05
396	Checklist 2	.05
397	Tim Salmon (All-Star Rookie)	.10
398	Todd Benzinger	.05
399	Frank Castillo	.05
400	Ken Griffey Jr.	.75
401	John Kruk	.05
402	Dave Telgheder	.05
403	Gary Gaetti	.05
404	Jim Edmonds	.05
405	Don Slaught	.05
406	Jose Oquendo	.05
407	Bruce Ruffin	.05
408	Phil Clark	.05
409	Joe Klink	.05
410	Lou Whitaker	.05
411	Kevin Seitzer	.05
412	Darrin Fletcher	.05
413	Kenny Rogers	.05
414	Bill Pecota	.05
415	Dave Fleming	.05
416	Luis Alicea	.05
417	Paul Quantrill	.05
418	Damion Easley	.05
419	Wes Chamberlain	.05
420	Harold Baines	.05
421	Scott Radinsky	.05
422	Rey Sanchez	.05
423	Junior Ortiz	.05
424	Jeff Kent	.05
425	Brian McRae	.05
426	Ed Sprague	.05
427	Tom Edens	.05
428	Willie Greene	.05
429	Bryan Hickerson	.05
430	Dave Winfield	.50
431	Pedro Astacio	.05
432	Mike Gallego	.05
433	Dave Burba	.05
434	Bob Walk	.05
435	Darryl Hamilton	.05
436	Vince Horsman	.05
437	Bob Natal	.05
438	Mike Henneman	.05
439	Willie Blair	.05
440	Denny Martinez	.05
441	Dan Peltier	.05
442	Tony Tarasco	.05
443	John Cummings	.05
444	Geronimo Pena	.05
445	Aaron Sele	.05
446	Stan Javier	.05
447	Mike Williams	.05
448	1B Prospects (Greg Pirkl, Roberto Petagine, D.J. Boston, Shawn Wooten)	.05
449	Jim Poole	.05
450	Carlos Baerga	.05
451	Bob Scanlan	.05
452	Lance Johnson	.05
453	Eric Hillman	.05
454	Keith Miller	.05
455	Dave Stewart	.05
456	Pete Harnisch	.05
457	Roberto Kelly	.05
458	Tim Worrell	.05
459	Pedro Munoz	.05
460	Orel Hershiser	.05
461	Randy Velarde	.05
462	Trevor Wilson	.05
463	Jerry Goff	.05
464	Bill Wegman	.05
465	Dennis Eckersley	.40
466	Jeff Conine (All-Star Rookie)	.05
467	Joe Boever	.05
468	Dante Bichette	.05
469	Jeff Shaw	.05
470	Rafael Palmeiro	.40
471	Phil Leftwich RC	.05
472	Jay Buhner	.05
473	Bob Tewksbury	.05
474	Tim Naehring	.05
475	Tom Glavine	.25
476	Dave Hollins	.05
477	Arthur Rhodes	.05
478	Joey Cora	.05
479	Mike Morgan	.05
480	Albert Belle	.05
481	John Franco	.05
482	Hipolito Pichardo	.05
483	Duane Ward	.05
484	Luis Gonzalez	.05
485	Joe Oliver	.05
486	Wally Whitehurst	.05
487	Mike Benjamin	.05
488	Eric Davis	.05
489	Scott Kamieniecki	.05
490	Kent Hrbek	.05
491	John Hope RC	.05
492	Jesse Orosco	.05
493	Troy Neel	.05
494	Ryan Bowen	.05
495	Mickey Tettleton	.05
496	Chris Jones	.05
497	John Wetteland	.05
498	David Hulse	.05
499	Greg Maddux	.60
500	Bo Jackson	.10
501	Donovan Osborne	.05
502	Mike Greenwell	.05
503	Steve Frey	.05
504	Jim Eisenreich	.05
505	Robby Thompson	.05
506	Leo Gomez	.05
507	Dave Staton	.05
508	Wayne Kirby (All-Star Rookie)	.05
509	Tim Bogar	.05
510	David Cone	.05
511	Devon White	.05
512	Xavier Hernandez	.05
513	Tim Costo	.05
514	Gene Harris	.05
515	Jack McDowell	.05
516	Kevin Gross	.05
517	Scott Leius	.05
518	Lloyd McClendon	.05
519	Alex Diaz RC	.05
520	Wade Boggs	.60
521	Bob Welch	.05
522	Henry Cotto	.05
523	Mike Moore	.05
524	Tim Laker	.05
525	Andres Galarraga	.05
526	Jamie Moyer	.05
527	2B Prospects (Norberto Martin, Ruben Santana, Jason Hardtke, Chris Sexton)	.05
528	Sid Bream	.05
529	Erik Hanson	.05
530	Ray Lankford	.05
531	Rob Deer	.05
532	Rod Correia	.05
533	Roger Mason	.05
534	Mike Devereaux	.05
535	Jeff Montgomery	.05
536	Dwight Smith	.05
537	Jeremy Hernandez	.05
538	Ellis Burks	.05
539	Bobby Jones	.05
540	Paul Molitor	.50
541	Jeff Juden	.05
542	Chris Sabo	.05
543	Larry Casian	.05
544	Jeff Gardner	.05
545	Ramon Martinez	.05
546	Paul O'Neill	.05
547	Steve Hosey	.05
548	Dave Nilsson	.05
549	Ron Darling	.05
550	Matt Williams	.05
551	Jack Armstrong	.05
552	Bill Krueger	.05
553	Freddie Benavides	.05
554	Jeff Fassero	.05
555	Chuck Knoblauch	.05
556	Guillermo Velasquez	.05
557	Joel Johnston	.05
558	Tom Lampkin	.05
559	Todd Van Poppel	.05
560	Gary Sheffield	.30
561	Skeeter Barnes	.05
562	Darren Holmes	.05
563	John Vander Wal	.05
564	Mike Ignasiak	.05
565	Fred McGriff	.05
566	Luis Polonia	.05
567	Mike Perez	.05
568	John Valentin	.05
569	Mike Felder	.05
570	Tommy Greene	.05
571	David Segui	.05
572	Roberto Hernandez	.05
573	Steve Wilson	.05
574	Willie McGee	.05
575	Randy Myers	.05
576	Darrin Jackson	.05
577	Eric Plunk	.05
578	Mike MacFarlane	.05
579	Doug Brocail	.05
580	Steve Finley	.05
581	John Roper	.05
582	Danny Cox	.05
583	Chip Hale	.05
584	Scott Bullett	.05
585	Kevin Reimer	.05
586	Brent Gates	.05
587	Matt Turner	.05
588	Rich Rowland	.05
589	Kent Bottenfield	.05
590	Marquis Grissom	.05
591	Doug Strange	.05
592	Jay Howell	.05
593	Omar Vizquel	.05
594	Rheal Cormier	.05
595	Andre Dawson	.25
596	Hilly Hathaway	.05
597	Todd Pratt	.05
598	Mike Mussina	.30
599	Alex Fernandez	.05
600	Don Mattingly	.65
601	Frank Thomas (Measures of Greatness)	.25
602	Ryne Sandberg (Measures of Greatness)	.30
603	Wade Boggs (Measures of Greatness)	.30
604	Cal Ripken, Jr. (Measures of Greatness)	.50
605	Barry Bonds (Measures of Greatness)	.50
606	Ken Griffey Jr. (Measures of Greatness)	.40
607	Kirby Puckett (Measures of Greatness)	.35
608	Darren Daulton (Measures of Greatness)	.05
609	Paul Molitor (Measures of Greatness)	.25
610	Terry Steinbach	.05
611	Todd Worrell	.05
612	Jim Thome	.40
613	Chuck McElroy	.05
614	John Habyan	.05
615	Sid Fernandez	.05
616	OF Prospects (Eddie Zambrano, Glenn Murray, Chad Mottola, Jermaine Allensworth RC)	.05
617	Steve Bedrosian	.05
618	Rob Ducey	.05
619	Tom Browning	.05
620	Tony Gwynn	.60
621	Carl Willis	.05
622	Kevin Young	.05
623	Rafael Novoa	.05

624	Jerry Browne	.05
625	Charlie Hough	.05
626	Chris Gomez	.05
627	Steve Reed	.05
628	Kirk Rueter	.05
629	Matt Whiteside	.05
630	Dave Justice	.05
631	Brad Holman	.05
632	Brian Jordan	.05
633	Scott Bankhead	.05
634	Torey Lovullo	.05
635	Len Dykstra	.05
636	Ben McDonald	.05
637	Steve Howe	.05
638	Jose Vizcaino	.05
639	Bill Swift	.05
640	Darryl Strawberry	.05
641	Steve Farr	.05
642	Tom Kramer	.05
643	Joe Orsulak	.05
644	Tom Henke	.05
645	Joe Carter	.05
646	Ken Caminiti	.05
647	Reggie Sanders	.05
648	Andy Ashby	.05
649	Derek Parks	.05
650	Andy Van Slyke	.05
651	Juan Bell	.05
652	Roger Smithberg	.05
653	Chuck Carr	.05
654	Bill Gullickson	.05
655	Charlie Hayes	.05
656	Chris Nabholz	.05
657	Karl Rhodes	.05
658	Pete Smith	.05
659	Bret Boone	.05
660	Gregg Jefferies	.05
661	Bob Zupcic	.05
662	Steve Sax	.05
663	Mariano Duncan	.05
664	Jeff Tackett	.05
665	Mark Langston	.05
666	Steve Buechele	.05
667	Candy Maldonado	.05
668	Woody Williams	.05
669	Tim Wakefield	.05
670	Danny Tartabull	.05
671	Charlie O'Brien	.05
672	Felix Jose	.05
673	Bobby Ayala	.05
674	Scott Servais	.05
675	Roberto Alomar	.15
676	Pedro Martinez	.05
677	Eddie Guardado	.05
678	Mark Lewis	.05
679	Jaime Navarro	.05
680	Ruben Sierra	.05
681	Rick Renteria	.05
682	Storm Davis	.05
683	Cory Snyder	.05
684	Ron Karkovice	.05
685	Juan Gonzalez	.25
686	C Prospects (Chris Howard, Carlos Delgado, Jason Kendall, Paul Bako)	.40
687	John Smoltz	.05
688	Brian Dorsett	.05
689	Omar Olivares	.05
690	Mo Vaughn	.05
691	Joe Grahe	.05
692	Mickey Morandini	.05
693	Tino Martinez	.05
694	Brian Barnes	.05
695	Mike Stanley	.05
696	Mark Clark	.05
697	Dave Hansen	.05
698	Willie Wilson	.05
699	Pete Schourek	.05
700	Barry Bonds	1.00
701	Kevin Appier	.05
702	Tony Fernandez	.05
703	Darryl Kile	.05
704	Archi Cianfrocco	.05
705	Jose Rijo	.05
706	Brian Harper	.05
707	Zane Smith	.05
708	Dave Henderson	.05
709	Angel Miranda	.05
710	Orestes Destrade	.05
711	Greg Gohr	.05
712	Eric Young	.05
713	P Prospects (Todd Williams, Ron Watson, Kirk Bullinger, Mike Welch)	.05
714	Tim Spehr	.05
715	Hank Aaron (20th Anniversary #715)	.50
716	Nate Minchey	.05
717	Mike Blowers	.05
718	Kent Mercker	.05
719	Tom Pagnozzi	.05
720	Roger Clemens	.65
721	Eduardo Perez	.05
722	Milt Thompson	.05
723	Gregg Olson	.05
724	Kirk McCaskill	.05
725	Sammy Sosa	.60
726	Alvaro Espinoza	.05
727	Henry Rodriguez	.05
728	Jim Leyritz	.05
729	Steve Scarsone	.05
730	Bobby Bonilla	.05
731	Chris Gwynn	.05
732	Al Leiter	.05
733	Bip Roberts	.05

734	Mark Portugal	.05
735	Terry Pendleton	.05
736	Dave Valle	.05
737	Paul Kilgus	.05
738	Greg Harris	.05
739	Jon Ratliff RC (Draft Pick)	.05
740	Kirk Presley RC (Draft Pick)	.05
741	Josue Estrada RC (Draft Pick)	.05
742	Wayne Gomes RC (Draft Pick)	.10
743	Pat Watkins RC (Draft Pick)	.05
744	Jamey Wright RC (Draft Pick)	.05
745	Jay Powell RC (Draft Pick)	.05
746	Ryan McGuire RC (Draft Pick)	.05
747	Marc Barcelo RC (Draft Pick)	.05
748	Sloan Smith RC (Draft Pick)	.05
749	John Wasdin RC (Draft Pick)	.05
750	Marc Valdes (Draft Pick)	.05
751	Dan Ehler RC (Draft Pick)	.05
752	Andre King RC (Draft Pick)	.05
753	Greg Keagle RC (Draft Pick)	.05
754	Jason Myers RC (Draft Pick)	.05
755	Dax Winslett RC (Draft Pick)	.05
756	Casey Whitten RC (Draft Pick)	.05
757	Tony Fuduric RC (Draft Pick)	.05
758	Greg Norton RC (Draft Pick)	.05
759	Jeff D'Amico RC (Draft Pick)	.05
760	Ryan Hancock RC (Draft Pick)	.05
761	David Cooper RC (Draft Pick)	.05
762	Kevin Orie RC (Draft Pick)	.05
763	John O'Donoghue, Mike Oquist (Coming Attractions)	.05
764	Cory Bailey, Scott Hatteberg (Coming Attractions)	.05
765	Mark Holzemer, Paul Swingle (Coming Attractions)	.05
766	James Baldwin, Rod Bolton (Coming Attractions)	.05
767	Jerry DiPoto RC, Julian Tavarez RC (Coming Attractions)	.10
768	Danny Bautista, Sean Bergman (Coming Attractions)	.05
769	Bob Hamelin, Joe Vitiello (Coming Attractions)	.05
770	Mark Kiefer, Troy O'Leary (Coming Attractions)	.05
771	Denny Hocking, Oscar Munoz (Coming Attractions)	.05
772	Russ Davis, Brien Taylor (Coming Attractions)	.05
773	Kurt Abbott, Miguel Jimenez (Coming Attractions)	.05
774	Kevin King, Eric Plantenberg (Coming Attractions)	.05
775	Jon Shave, Desi Wilson (Coming Attractions)	.05
776	Domingo Cedeno, Paul Spoljaric (Coming Attractions)	.05
777	Chipper Jones, Ryan Klesko (Coming Attractions)	.60
778	Steve Trachsel, Turk Wendell (Coming Attractions)	.05
779	Johnny Ruffin, Jerry Spradlin (Coming Attractions)	.05
780	Jason Bates, John Burke (Coming Attractions)	.05
781	Carl Everett, Dave Weathers (Coming Attractions)	.05
782	Gary Mota, James Mouton (Coming Attractions)	.05
783	Raul Mondesi, Ben Van Ryn (Coming Attractions)	.05
784	Gabe White, Rondell White (Coming Attractions)	.05
785	Brook Fordyce, Bill Pulsipher (Coming Attractions)	.05
786	Kevin Foster, Gene Schall (Coming Attractions)	.05

787	Rich Aude, Midre Cummings (Coming Attractions)	.05
788	Brian Barber, Richard Batchelor (Coming Attractions)	.05
789	Brian Johnson RC, Scott Sanders (Coming Attractions)	.05
790	Rikkert Faneyte, J.R. Phillips (Coming Attractions)	.05
791	Checklist 3	.05
792	Checklist 4	.05

Gold

This premium parallel set was issued as inserts in virtually all forms of Topps packaging. Identical in all other ways to the regular Topps cards, the Gold version replaces the white or black Topps logo on front with a gold-foil "Topps Gold" logo, and prints either the player name or card title in gold foil. The four checklist cards from the regular issue are replaced with cards of players not found in the regular Topps set.

	NM/M
Complete Set (792):	50.00
Common Player:	.15

Black Gold

Black Gold inserts returned for 1994 randomly included in all types of Topps packaging. Single cards, as well as cards redeemable by mail for 11, 22 or 44 Black Gold cards, were produced. The basic single-player card features an action photo, the background of which has been almost completely blacked out. At top is the team name in black letters against a gold prismatic foil background. The player name at bottom is in the same gold foil. On back, bordered in white, is a background which fades from black at top to gray at the bottom and is gridded with white lines. At left is another player action photo. The Topps Black Gold logo and player name appear in gold foil; the latter printed on a simulated wooden board "hanging" from the top of the card. A second hanging plank has player stats and rankings from the 1993 season. The multi-card redemption cards come in two versions. The type found in packs has all 11, 22 or 44 of the cards pictured on front in miniature and redemption details printed on back. A second ver-

sion, returned with the single cards won, has on back a checklist and non-redemption notice. Stated odds of winning Black Gold cards were one in 72 packs for single cards; one in 180 packs for 11-card winners and one in 720 packs (one per foil-pack case) for a 22-card winner.

	NM/M
Complete Set (44):	10.00
Complete Series 1 (22):	6.00
Complete Series 2 (22):	4.00
Common Player:	.10
1	Roberto Alomar	.20
2	Carlos Baerga	.10
3	Albert Belle	.10
4	Joe Carter	.10
5	Cecil Fielder	.10
6	Travis Fryman	.10
7	Juan Gonzalez	.25
8	Ken Griffey Jr.	.75
9	Chris Hoiles	.10
10	Randy Johnson	.45
11	Kenny Lofton	.10
12	Jack McDowell	.10
13	Paul Molitor	.45
14	Jeff Montgomery	.10
15	John Olerud	.10
16	Rafael Palmeiro	.45
17	Kirby Puckett	.60
18	Cal Ripken, Jr.	1.50
19	Tim Salmon	.10
20	Mike Stanley	.10
21	Frank Thomas	.50
22	Robin Ventura	.10
23	Jeff Bagwell	.45
24	Jay Bell	.10
25	Craig Biggio	.10
26	Jeff Blauser	.10
27	Barry Bonds	1.50
28	Darren Daulton	.10
29	Len Dykstra	.10
30	Andres Galarraga	.10
31	Ron Gant	.10
32	Tom Glavine	.10
33	Mark Grace	.10
34	Marquis Grissom	.10
35	Gregg Jefferies	.10
36	Dave Justice	.10
37	John Kruk	.10
38	Greg Maddux	.60
39	Fred McGriff	.10
40	Randy Myers	.10
41	Mike Piazza	1.00
42	Sammy Sosa	.60
43	Robby Thompson	.10
44	Matt Williams	.10
---	Winner A	.50
---	Winner B	.50
---	Winner C	.50
---	Winner D	.50
---	Winner A/B	.60
---	Winner C/D	.60
---	Winner A/B/C/D	.75

Traded

Topps Traded features top prospects and rookies as well as traded veterans. Also included in the boxed set is an eight-card Topps Finest subset of six MVPs and two Rookie of the Year cards. Regular cards have the same design as the previously released '94 Topps set. "Anatomy of a Trade" is a two-card subset that includes Roberto Kelly/Deion Sanders and Pedro Martinez/Delino DeShields on a split, puzzle-like front. There is also a Prospect card, showcasing a top prospect from AAA, AA and A, as well as a top-rated draft pick. In addition, there are 12 Draft Pick cards included in the Traded set. Finally, two cards pay tribute to Ryne Sandberg, one in a Phillies uniform, one with the Cubs.

	NM/M
Complete Set (140):	30.00

	Common Player:	.05
1	Paul Wilson (Draft Pick)	.05
2	Bill Taylor	.05
3	Dan Wilson	.05
4	Mark Smith	.05
5	Toby Borland	.05
6	Dave Clark	.05
7	Denny Martinez	.05
8	Dave Gallagher	.05
9	Josias Manzanillo	.05
10	Brian Anderson	.05
11	Damon Berryhill	.05
12	Alex Cole	.05
13	Jacob Shumate (Draft Pick)	.05
14	Oddibe McDowell	.05
15	Willie Banks	.05
16	Jerry Browne	.05
17	Donnie Elliott	.05
18	Ellis Burks	.05
19	Chuck McElroy	.05
20	Luis Polonia	.05
21	Brian Harper	.05
22	Mark Portugal	.05
23	Dave Henderson	.05
24	Mark Acre	.05
25	Julio Franco	.05
26	Darren Hall	.05
27	Eric Anthony	.05
28	Sid Fernandez	.05
29	Rusty Greer RC	.25
30	Riccardo Ingram	.05
31	Gabe White	.05
32	Tim Belcher	.05
33	Terrence Long RC (Draft Pick)	1.00
34	Mark Dalesandro RC	.05
35	Mike Kelly	.05
36	Jack Morris	.05
37	Jeff Brantley	.05
38	Larry Barnes RC (Draft Pick)	.05
39	Brian Hunter	.05
40	Otis Nixon	.05
41	Bret Wagner (Draft Pick)	.05
42	Anatomy of a Trade (Pedro Martinez/Delino DeShields)	.25
43	Heathcliff Slocumb	.05
44	Ben Grieve (Draft Pick)	.35
45	John Hudek	.05
46	Shawon Dunston	.05
47	Greg Colbrunn	.05
48	Joey Hamilton	.05
49	Marvin Freeman	.05
50	Terry Mulholland	.05
51	Keith Mitchell	.05
52	Dwight Smith	.05
53	Shawn Boskie	.05
54	Kevin Witt (Draft Pick)	.05
55	Ron Gant	.05
56	1994 Prospects (Trenidad Hubbard, Jason Schmidt RC, Larry Sutton, Stephen Larkin)	10.00
57	Jody Reed	.05
58	Rick Helling	.05
59	John Powell (Draft Pick)	.05
60	Eddie Murray	.60
61	Joe Hall	.05
62	Jorge Fabregas	.05
63	Mike Mordecai	.05
64	Ed Vosberg	.05
65	Rickey Henderson	.60
66	Tim Grieve (Draft Pick)	.05
67	Jon Lieber	.05
68	Chris Howard	.05
69	Matt Walbeck	.05
70	Chan Ho Park	.15
71	Bryan Eversgerd	.05
72	John Dettmer	.05
73	Erik Hanson	.05
74	Mike Thurman (Draft Pick)	.05
75	Bobby Ayala	.05
76	Rafael Palmeiro	.50
77	Bret Boone	.05
78	Paul Shuey (Future Star)	.05
79	Kevin Foster	.05
80	Dave Magadan	.05
81	Bip Roberts	.05
82	Howard Johnson	.05
83	Xavier Hernandez	.05
84	Ross Powell	.05
85	Doug Million RC (Draft Pick)	.05
86	Geronimo Berroa	.05
87	Mark Farris RC (Draft Pick)	.05
88	Butch Henry	.05
89	Junior Felix	.05
90	Bo Jackson	.10
91	Hector Carrasco	.05
92	Charlie O'Brien	.05
93	Omar Vizquel	.05
94	David Segui	.05
95	Dustin Hermanson (Draft Pick)	.05
96	Gar Finnvold	.05
97	Dave Stevens	.05
98	Corey Pointer (Draft Pick)	.05

99	Felix Fermin	.05
100	Lee Smith	.05
101	Reid Ryan (Draft Pick)	.15
102	Bobby Munoz	.05
103	Anatomy of a Trade (Deion Sanders, Roberto Kelly)	.05
104	Turner Ward	.05
105	William Van Landingham	.05
106	Vince Coleman	.05
107	Stan Javier	.05
108	Darrin Jackson	.05
109	C.J. Nitkowski (Draft Pick)	.05
110	Anthony Young	.05
111	Kurt Miller	.05
112	Paul Konerko RC (Draft Pick)	15.00
113	Walt Weiss	.05
114	Daryl Boston	.05
115	Will Clark	.05
116	Matt Smith RC (Draft Pick)	.05
117	Mark Leiter	.05
118	Gregg Olson	.05
119	Tony Pena	.05
120	Jose Vizcaino	.05
121	Rick White	.05
122	Rich Rowland	.05
123	Jeff Reboulet	.05
124	Greg Hibbard	.05
125	Chris Sabo	.05
126	Doug Jones	.05
127	Tony Fernandez	.05
128	Carlos Reyes	.05
129	Kevin Brown (Draft Pick)	.05
130	Commemorative (Ryne Sandberg)	1.00
131	Commemorative (Ryne Sandberg)	1.00
132	Checklist 1-132	.05

Traded Finest Inserts

Eight Finest cards were included in the 1994 Topps Traded set. Cards picture the player on a blue and gold background. Either Rookie of the Year or MVP is printed across the bottom opposite the player's name, indicating the player's candidacy for such an award in 1994. Backs offer a portrait photo, stats through the All-Star break and comments on the player's season to that point.

	NM/M
Complete Set (8):	6.00
Common Player:	.25
1	Greg Maddux	1.50
2	Mike Piazza	2.00
3	Matt Williams	.25
4	Raul Mondesi	.25
5	Ken Griffey Jr.	2.00
6	Kenny Lofton	.25
7	Frank Thomas	1.25
8	Manny Ramirez	1.00

Bilingual

Produced in a limited edition said to be 5,000 sets, this

issue is a close parallel to the regular 1994 Topps baseball card issue. Each card is virtually identical to the regular Topps card except that backs are printed in English and Spanish. The set was test marketed in areas with a high percentage of Hispanic population and was also sold through Topps' Stadium Club. The bilingual edition was sold only in factory set form. A special feature of the set was the inclusion of 10 "Topps Leyendas/Legends" cards of former Latin stars.

		NM/M
Factory Set (792+10):		225.00
Common Player:		.50
1	Felipe Alou	3.00
2	Ruben Amaro	1.00
3	Luis Aparicio	7.50
4	Rod Carew	7.50
5	Chico Carrasquel	1.50
6	Orlando Cepeda	7.50
7	Juan Marichal	7.50
8	Minnie Minoso	6.00
9	Cookie Rojas	1.00
10	Luis Tiant	2.00

"1954" Archives

Marketed as "The Ultimate 1954 Series," the Archives set was a virtual reproduction of the popular 1954 Topps issue. Of the 250 cards in the original set, 248 were included in the Archives release. Ted Williams, who was on cards #1 and 250 in the '54 set, was contractually prohibited by Upper Deck from appearing in the Archives issue. Eight "1954 Prospect" cards featuring future Hall of Famers and star players were appended to the reproduction cards to create a 256-card Archives issue. Cards were sold in 12-card packs, with one Gold card in each pack. There were 1,954 personally autographed cards of Henry Aaron inserted at random, along with cards that could be redeemed for genuine 1954 Topps cards and complete sets of Gold Archives cards. The Archives cards were produced in the now-standard 2-1/2" x 3-1/2" size, instead of the original 1954 dimensions of 2-5/8" x 3-3/4". That format allowed the Archives cards to have a white border at top which the originals lack. While the card backs identify the Archives issue, they do not specify a 1994 production date anywhere.

		NM/M
Complete Set (256):		90.00
Common Player:		.25
Wax Pack (12):		4.00
Wax Box (24):		65.00
2	Gus Zernial	.25
3	Monte Irvin	.75
4	Hank Sauer	.25
5	Ed Lopat	.40
6	Pete Runnels	.25
7	Ted Kluszewski	.60
8	Bobby Young	.25
9	Harvey Haddix	.25
10	Jackie Robinson	4.50
11	Paul Smith	.25
12	Del Crandall	.25
13	Billy Martin	.75
14	Preacher Roe	.40
15	Al Rosen	.25
16	Vic Janowicz	.25

17	Phil Rizzuto	1.00
18	Walt Dropo	.25
19	Johnny Lipon	.25
20	Warren Spahn	.75
21	Bobby Shantz	.25
22	Jim Greengrass	.25
23	Luke Easter	.25
24	Granny Hamner	.25
25	Harvey Kuenn	.25
26	Ray Jablonski	.25
27	Ferris Fain	.25
28	Paul Minner	.25
29	Jim Hegan	.25
30	Eddie Mathews	.75
31	Johnny Klippstein	.25
32	Duke Snider	1.50
33	Johnny Schmitz	.25
34	Jim Rivera	.25
35	Junior Gilliam	.40
36	Hoyt Wilhelm	.75
37	Whitey Ford	1.25
38	Eddie Stanky	.25
39	Sherman Lollar	.25
40	Mel Parnell	.25
41	Willie Jones	.25
42	Don Mueller	.25
43	Dick Groat	.25
44	Ned Garver	.25
45	Richie Ashburn	.75
46	Ken Raffensberger	.25
47	Ellis Kinder	.25
48	Billy Hunter	.25
49	Ray Murray	.25
50	Yogi Berra	1.50
51	Johnny Lindell	.25
52	Vic Power	.25
53	Jack Dittmer	.25
54	Vern Stephens	.25
55	Phil Cavarretta	.25
56	Willie Miranda	.40
57	Luis Aloma	.25
58	Bob Wilson	.25
59	Gene Conley	.25
60	Frank Baumholtz	.25
61	Bob Cain	.25
62	Eddie Robinson	.40
63	Johnny Pesky	.25
64	Hank Thompson	.25
65	Bob Swift	.25
66	Ted Lepcio	.25
67	Jim Willis	.25
68	Sam Calderone	.25
69	Bud Podbielan	.25
70	Larry Doby	.75
71	Frank Smith	.25
72	Preston Ward	.25
73	Wayne Terwilliger	.25
74	Bill Taylor	.25
75	Fred Haney	.25
76	Bob Scheffing	.25
77	Ray Boone	.25
78	Ted Kazanski	.25
79	Andy Pafko	.25
80	Jackie Jensen	.40
81	Dave Hoskins	.25
82	Milt Bolling	.25
83	Joe Collins	.40
84	Dick Cole	.25
85	Bob Turley	.75
86	Billy Herman	.40
87	Roy Face	.25
88	Matt Batts	.25
89	Howie Pollet	.25
90	Willie Mays	4.50
91	Bob Oldis	.25
92	Wally Westlake	.25
93	Sid Hudson	.25
94	Ernie Banks	4.50
95	Hal Rice	.25
96	Charlie Silvera	.40
97	Jerry Lane	.25
98	Joe Black	.25
99	Bob Hofman	.25
100	Bob Keegan	.25
101	Gene Woodling	.25
102	Gil Hodges	1.25
103	Jim Lemon	.25
104	Mike Sandlock	.25
105	Andy Carey	.25
106	Dick Kokos	.25
107	Duane Pillette	.25
108	Thornton Kipper	.25
109	Bill Bruton	.25
110	Harry Dorish	.25
111	Jim Delsing	.25
112	Bill Renna	.25
113	Bob Boyd	.25
114	Dean Stone	.25
115	"Rip" Repulski	.25
116	Steve Bilko	.25
117	Solly Hemus	.25
118	Carl Scheib	.25
119	Johnny Antonelli	.25
120	Roy McMillan	.25
121	Clem Labine	.40
122	Johnny Logan	.25
123	Bobby Adams	.25
124	Marion Fricano	.25
125	Harry Perkowski	.25
126	Ben Wade	.25
127	Steve O'Neill	.25
128	Hank Aaron	7.50
129	Forrest Jacobs	.25
130	Hank Bauer	.75
131	Reno Bertoia	.25
132	Tom Lasorda	3.00
133	Del Baker	.25
134	Cal Hogue	.25

135	Joe Presko	.25
136	Connie Ryan	.25
137	Wally Moon	.25
138	Bob Borkowski	.25
139	Ed & Johnny O'Brien	.60
140	Tom Wright	.25
141	Joe Jay	.25
142	Tom Poholsky	.25
143	Rollie Hemsley	.25
144	Bill Werle	.25
145	Elmer Valo	.25
146	Don Johnson	.25
147	John Riddle	.25
148	Bob Trice	.25
149	Jim Robertson	.25
150	Dick Kryhoski	.25
151	Alex Grammas	.25
152	Mike Blyzka	.25
153	Rube Walker	.25
154	Mike Fornieles	.25
155	Bob Kennedy	.25
156	Joe Coleman	.25
157	Don Lenhardt	.25
158	Peanuts Lowrey	.25
159	Dave Philley	.25
160	Red Kress	.25
161	John Hetki	.25
162	Herman Wehmeier	.25
163	Frank House	.25
164	Stu Miller	.25
165	Jim Pendleton	.25
166	Johnny Podres	.40
167	Don Lund	.25
168	Morrie Martin	.25
169	Jim Hughes	.25
170	Dusty Rhodes	.25
171	Leo Kiely	.25
172	Hal Brown	.25
173	Jack Harshman	.25
174	Tom Qualters	.25
175	Frank Leja	.40
176	Bob Keely	.25
177	Bob Milliken	.25
178	Bill Glynn	.25
179	Gair Allie	.25
180	Wes Westrum	.25
181	Mel Roach	.25
182	Chuck Harmon	.25
183	Earle Combs	.25
184	Ed Bailey	.25
185	Chuck Stobbs	.25
186	Karl Olson	.25
187	Heinie Manush	.25
188	Dave Jolly	.25
189	Bob Ross	.25
190	Ray Herbert	.25
191	Dick Schofield	.25
192	Cot Deal	.25
193	Johnny Hopp	.25
194	Bill Sarni	.25
195	Bill Consolo	.25
196	Stan Jok	.25
197	Schoolboy Rowe	.25
198	Carl Sawatski	.25
199	Rocky Nelson	.25
200	Larry Jansen	.25
201	Al Kaline	4.50
202	Bob Purkey	.25
203	Harry Brecheen	.25
204	Angel Scull	.25
205	Johnny Sain	.40
206	Ray Crone	.25
207	Tom Oliver	.25
208	Grady Hatton	.25
209	Charlie Thompson	.25
210	Bob Buhl	.40
211	Don Hoak	.25
212	Mickey Micelotta	.25
213	John Fitzpatrick	.25
214	Arnold Portocarrero	.25
215	Ed McGhee	.25
216	Al Sima	.25
217	Paul Schreiber	.25
218	Fred Marsh	.25
219	Charlie Kress	.25
220	Ruben Gomez	.25
221	Dick Brodowski	.25
222	Bill Wilson	.25
223	Joe Haynes	.25
224	Dick Weik	.25
225	Don Liddle	.25
226	Jehosie Heard	.25
227	Buster Mills	.25
228	Gene Hermanski	.25
229	Bob Talbot	.25
230	Bob Kuzava	.40
231	Roy Smalley	.25
232	Lou Limmer	.25
233	Augie Galan	.25
234	Jerry Lynch	.25
235	Vern Law	.25
236	Paul Penson	.25
237	Mike Ryba	.25
238	Al Aber	.25
239	Bill Skowron	.75
240	Sam Mele	.25
241	Bob Miller	.25
242	Curt Roberts	.25
243	Ray Blades	.25
244	Leroy Wheat	.25
245	Roy Sievers	.25
246	Howie Fox	.25
247	Eddie Mayo	.25
248	Al Smith	.25
249	Wilmer Mizell	.25
251	Roberto Clemente	7.50
252	Bob Grim	.40
253	Elston Howard	.75

254	Harmon Killebrew	1.25
255	Camilo Pascual	.25
256	Herb Score	.25
257	Bill Virdon	.25
258	Don Zimmer	.50

"1954" Archives Gold

Issued as a premium insert at the rate of one per foil pack, gold versions of each of the cards in the 1954 Archives set differ from the regular cards only in that the team logo at top and player facsimile autograph on bottom are printed in gold foil. Redemption cards for complete Archives gold sets were also randomly inserted into Archives packs.

		NM/M
Complete Set (256):		150.00
Common Player:		.45
128	Hank Aaron/Auto.	125.00

1995 Topps Pre-production

The "Baker's Dozen" version of Topps' 1994 factory baseball card set includes a 10-card pre-production sample of the company's 1995 issue. The sample features nine regular-issue cards and one of them in its Spectralite foil-printed version, as used on the Cyberstats insert cards. Cards are virtually identical to the regular '95 Topps except the backs have a "PP" prefix to the card number and "PRE-PRODUCTION SAMPLE" instead of 1994 season stats.

		NM/M
Complete Set (9):		6.00
Complete Set, Cyberstats (9):		20.00
1	Larry Walker	.50
1	Larry Walker (Spectralite)	1.50
2	Mike Piazza	2.50
2	Mike Piazza (Spectralite)	7.50
3	Greg Vaughn	.50
3	Greg Vaughn (Spectralite)	1.50
4	Sandy Alomar Jr.	.50
4	Sandy Alomar Jr. (Spectralite)	1.50
5	Travis Fryman	.50
5	Travis Fryman (Spectralite)	1.50
6	Ken Griffey Jr.	2.50
6	Ken Griffey Jr. (Spectralite)	7.50
7	Mike Devereaux	.25
7	Mike Devereaux (Spectralite)	1.50
8	Roberto Hernandez	.25
8	Roberto Hernandez (Spectralite)	1.50
9	Alex Fernandez	.25

9	Alex Fernandez (Spectralite)	1.50

1995 Topps

Topps 1995 baseball arrived offering Cyberstats, which projected full-season statistics for the strike shortened year, as well as League Leaders and Stadium Club First Day Issue pre-production inserts. Series 1 comprises 396 cards, including subsets of Draft Picks, Star Tracks, a Babe Ruth commemorative card and the Topps All-Stars, featuring two players per card at each position. Regular cards have a ragged white border around the player photo, with his name in gold foil under the picture. Series 2 concluded the Cyberstats inserts and added 264 cards to the regular set. Subsets in Series 2 include a continuation of the Draft Picks as well as two-player On Deck cards and four-player Prospects cards, arranged by position. Besides the 660 base cards, hobby-version factory sets include 10 Stadium Club 1st Day previews and seven Cyberstat Season in Review cards. Two versions of the retail factory sets were made. One has 660 regular cards, 20 Cyberstats parallels and four League Leader inserts. The other has the base set of 660 plus 10 Opening Day cards and seven Cyberstat Season in Review.

		NM/M
Unopened Hobby Set (677):		100.00
Unopened Retail Set (684):		75.00
Unopened Retail Set (677):		85.00
Complete Set (660):		45.00
Common Player:		.05
Series 1 or 2 Pack (15):		1.25
Series 1 or 2 Wax Box (36):		25.00
1	Frank Thomas	.75
2	Mickey Morandini	.05
3a	Babe Ruth (100th Birthday, no gold "Topps" logo)	2.00
3b	Babe Ruth (100th Birthday, gold "Topps" logo)	2.00
4	Scott Cooper	.05
5	David Cone	.05
6	Jacob Shumate (Draft Pick)	.05
7	Trevor Hoffman	.05
8	Shane Mack	.05
9	Delino DeShields	.05
10	Matt Williams	.05
11	Sammy Sosa	1.00
12	Gary DiSarcina	.05
13	Kenny Rogers	.05
14	Jose Vizcaino	.05
15	Lou Whitaker	.05
16	Ron Darling	.05
17	Dave Nilsson	.05
18	Chris Hammond	.05
19	Sid Bream	.05
20	Denny Martinez	.05
21	Orlando Merced	.05
22	John Wetteland	.05
23	Mike Devereaux	.05
24	Rene Arocha	.05
25	Jay Buhner	.05
26	Darren Holmes	.05
27	Hal Morris	.05
28	Brian Buchanan RC (Draft Pick)	.10
29	Keith Miller	.05
30	Paul Molitor	.75
31	Dave West	.05
32	Tony Tarasco	.05
33	Scott Sanders	.05
34	Eddie Zambrano	.05
35	Ricky Bones	.05
36	John Valentin	.05

37	Kevin Tapani	.05
38	Tim Wallach	.05
39	Darren Lewis	.05
40	Travis Fryman	.05
41	Mark Leiter	.05
42	Jose Bautista	.05
43	Pete Smith	.05
44	Bret Barberie	.05
45	Dennis Eckersley	.65
46	Ken Hill	.05
47	Chad Ogea (Star Track)	.05
48	Pete Harnisch	.05
49	James Baldwin (Future Star)	.05
50	Mike Mussina	.45
51	Al Martin	.05
52	Mark Thompson (Star Track)	.05
53	Matt Smith (Draft Pick)	.05
54	Joey Hamilton (All-Star Rookie)	.05
55	Edgar Martinez	.05
56	John Smiley	.05
57	Rey Sanchez	.05
58	Mike Timlin	.05
59	Ricky Bottalico (Star Track)	.05
60	Jim Abbott	.05
61	Mike Kelly	.05
62	Brian Jordan	.05
63	Ken Ryan	.05
64	Matt Mieske	.05
65	Rick Aguilera	.05
66	Ismael Valdes	.05
67	Royce Clayton	.05
68	Junior Felix	.05
69	Harold Reynolds	.05
70	Juan Gonzalez	.35
71	Kelly Stinnett	.05
72	Carlos Reyes	.05
73	Dave Weathers	.05
74	Mel Rojas	.05
75	Doug Drabek	.05
76	Charles Nagy	.05
77	Tim Raines	.05
78	Midre Cummings	.05
79	1B Prospects (Gene Schall, Scott Talanoa RC, Harold Williams RC, Ray Brown RC)	.05
80	Rafael Palmeiro	.65
81	Charlie Hayes	.05
82	Ray Lankford	.05
83	Tim Davis	.05
84	C.J. Nitkowski RC (Draft Pick)	.05
85	Andy Ashby	.05
86	Gerald Williams	.05
87	Terry Shumpert	.05
88	Heathcliff Slocumb	.05
89	Domingo Cedeno	.05
90	Mark Grace	.05
91	Brad Woodall RC (Star Track)	.10
92	Gar Finnvold	.05
93	Jaime Navarro	.05
94	Carlos Hernandez	.05
95	Mark Langston	.05
96	Chuck Carr	.05
97	Mike Gardiner	.05
98	David McCarty	.05
99	Cris Carpenter	.05
100	Barry Bonds	2.00
101	David Segui	.05
102	Scott Brosius	.05
103	Mariano Duncan	.05
104	Kenny Lofton	.05
105	Ken Caminiti	.05
106	Darrin Jackson	.05
107	Jim Poole	.05
108	Wil Cordero	.05
109	Danny Miceli	.05
110	Walt Weiss	.05
111	Tom Pagnozzi	.05
112	Terrence Long (Draft Pick)	.05
113	Bret Boone	.05
114	Daryl Boston	.05
115	Wally Joyner	.05
116	Rob Butler	.05
117	Rafael Belliard	.05
118	Luis Lopez	.05
119	Tony Fossas	.05
120	Len Dykstra	.05
121	Mike Morgan	.05
122	Denny Hocking	.05
123	Kevin Gross	.05
124	Todd Benzinger	.05
125	John Doherty	.05
126	Eduardo Perez	.05
127	Dan Smith	.05
128	Joe Orsulak	.05
129	Brent Gates	.05
130	Jeff Conine	.05
131	Doug Henry	.05
132	Paul Sorrento	.05
133	Mike Hampton	.05
134	Tim Spehr	.05
135	Julio Franco	.05
136	Mike Dyer	.05
137	Chris Sabo	.05
138	Rheal Cormier	.05
139	Paul Konerko (Draft Pick)	.25
140	Dante Bichette	.05
141	Chuck McElroy	.05
142	Mike Stanley	.05

143 Bob Hamelin
(All-Star Rookie) .05
144 Tommy Greene .05
145 John Smoltz .05
146 Ed Sprague .05
147 Ray McDavid
(Star Track) .05
148 Otis Nixon .05
149 Turk Wendell .05
150 Chris James .05
151 Derek Parks .05
152 Jose Offerman .05
153 Tony Clark (Future Star) .05
154 Chad Curtis .05
155 Mark Portugal .05
156 Bill Pulsipher
(Future Star) .05
157 Troy Neel .05
158 Dave Winfield .75
159 Bill Wegman .05
160 Benny Santiago .05
161 Jose Mesa .05
162 Luis Gonzalez .05
163 Alex Fernandez .05
164 Freddie Benavides .05
165 Ben McDonald .05
166 Blas Minor .05
167 Bret Wagner
(Draft Pick) .05
168 Mac Suzuki
(Future Star) .05
169 Roberto Mejia .05
170 Wade Boggs 1.00
171 Calvin Reese
(Future Star) .05
172 Hipolito Pichardo .05
173 Kim Batiste .05
174 Darren Hall .05
175 Tom Glavine .25
176 Phil Plantier .05
177 Chris Howard .05
178 Karl Rhodes .05
179 LaTroy Hawkins
(Future Star) .05
180 Raul Mondesi
(All-Star Rookie) .05
181 Jeff Reed .05
182 Milt Cuyler .05
183 Jim Edmonds .05
184 Hector Fajardo .05
185 Jeff Kent .05
186 Wilson Alvarez .05
187 Geronimo Berroa .05
188 Billy Spiers .05
189 Derek Lilliquist .05
190 Craig Biggio .05
191 Roberto Hernandez .05
192 Bob Natal .05
193 Bobby Ayala .05
194 Travis Miller RC
(Draft Pick) .10
195 Bob Tewksbury .05
196 Rondell White .05
197 Steve Cooke .05
198 Jeff Branson .25
199 Derek Jeter
(Future Star) 2.00
200 Tim Salmon .05
201 Steve Frey .05
202 Kent Mercker .05
203 Randy Johnson .75
204 Todd Worrell .05
205 Mo Vaughn .05
206 Howard Johnson .05
207 John Wasdin
(Future Star) .05
208 Eddie Williams .05
209 Tim Belcher .05
210 Jeff Montgomery .05
211 Kirt Manwaring .05
212 Ben Grieve (Draft Pick) .05
213 Pat Hentgen .05
214 Shawon Dunston .05
215 Mike Greenwell .05
216 Alex Diaz .05
217 Pat Mahomes .05
218 Dave Hanson .05
219 Kevin Rogers .05
220 Cecil Fielder .05
221 Andrew Lorraine
(Star Track) .05
222 Jack Armstrong .05
223 Todd Hundley .05
224 Mark Acre .05
225 Darrell Whitmore .05
226 Randy Milligan .05
227 Wayne Kirby .05
228 Darryl Kile .05
229 Bob Zupcic .05
230 Jay Bell .05
231 Dustin Hermanson
(Draft Pick) .05
232 Harold Baines .05
233 Alan Benes
(Future Star) .05
234 Felix Fermin .05
235 Ellis Burks .05
236 Jeff Brantley .05
237 OF Prospects
(Brian Hunter,
Jose Malave, Shane Pullen,
Karim Garcia RC) .40
238 Matt Nokes .05
239 Ben Rivera .05
240 Joe Carter .05
241 Jeff Granger
(Star Track) .05
242 Terry Pendleton .05

243 Melvin Nieves .05
244 Frank Rodriguez
(Future Star) .05
245 Darryl Hamilton .05
246 Brooks Kieschnick
(Future Star) .05
247 Todd Hollandsworth
(Future Star) .05
248 Joe Rosselli
(Future Star) .05
249 Bill Gullickson .05
250 Chuck Knoblauch .05
251 Kurt Miller (Star Track) .05
252 Bobby Jones .05
253 Lance Blankenship .05
254 Matt Whiteside .05
255 Darrin Fletcher .05
256 Eric Plunk .05
257 Shane Reynolds .05
258 Norberto Martin .05
259 Mike Thurman
(Draft Pick) .05
260 Andy Van Slyke .05
261 Dwight Smith .05
262 Allen Watson .05
263 Dan Wilson .05
264 Brent Mayne .05
265 Bip Roberts .05
266 Sterling Hitchcock .05
267 Alex Gonzalez
(Star Track) .05
268 Greg Harris .05
269 Ricky Jordan .05
270 Johnny Ruffin .05
271 Mike Stanton .05
272 Rich Rowland .05
273 Steve Trachsel .05
274 Pedro Munoz .05
275 Ramon Martinez .05
276 Dave Henderson .05
277 Chris Gomez
(All-Star Rookie) .05
278 Joe Grahe .05
279 Rusty Greer .05
280 John Franco .05
281 Mike Bordick .05
282 Jeff D'Amico
(Future Star) .05
283 Dave Magadan .05
284 Tony Pena .05
285 Greg Swindell .05
286 Doug Million
(Draft Pick) .05
287 Gabe White (Star Track) .05
288 Trey Beamon
(Future Star) .05
289 Arthur Rhodes .05
290 Juan Guzman .05
291 Jose Oquendo .05
292 Willie Blair .05
293 Eddie Taubensee .05
294 Steve Howe .05
295 Greg Maddux 1.00
296 Mike MacFarlane .05
297 Curt Schilling .25
298 Phil Clark .05
299 Woody Williams .05
300 Jose Canseco .40
301 Aaron Sele .05
302 Carl Willis .05
303 Steve Buechele .05
304 Dave Burba .05
305 Orel Hershiser .05
306 Damion Easley .05
307 Mike Henneman .05
308 Josias Manzanillo .05
309 Kevin Seitzer .05
310 Ruben Sierra .05
311 Bryan Harvey .05
312 Jim Thome .45
313 Ramon Castro RC
(Draft Pick) .05
314 Lance Johnson .05
315 Marquis Grissom .05
316 SP Prospects
(Terrell Wade,
Juan Acevedo,
Matt Arrandale,
Eddie Priest RC) .05
317 Paul Wagner .05
318 Jamie Moyer .05
319 Todd Zeile .05
320 Chris Bosio .05
321 Steve Reed .05
322 Erik Hanson .05
323 Luis Polonia .05
324 Ryan Klesko .05
325 Kevin Appier .05
326 Jim Eisenreich .05
327 Randy Knorr .05
328 Craig Shipley .05
329 Tim Naehring .05
330 Randy Myers .05
331 Alex Cole .05
332 Jim Gott .05
333 Mike Jackson .05
334 John Flaherty .05
335 Chili Davis .05
336 Benji Gil (Star Track) .05
337a Jason Jacome
(No Diamond Vision
logo on back photo.) .25
337b Jason Jacome
(Diamond Vision logo
on back photo.) .05
338 Stan Javier .05
339 Mike Fetters .05
340 Rick Renteria .05

341 Kevin Witt (Draft Pick) .05
342 Scott Servais .05
343 Craig Grebeck .05
344 Kirk Rueter .05
345 Don Slaught .05
346 Armando Benitez RC
(Star Track) .15
347 Ozzie Smith 1.00
348 Mike Blowers .05
349 Armando Reynoso .05
350 Barry Larkin .05
351 Mike Williams .05
352 Scott Kamieniecki .05
353 Gary Gaetti .05
354 Todd Stottlemyre .05
355 Fred McGriff .05
356 Tim Mauser .05
357 Chris Gwynn .05
358 Frank Castillo .05
359 Jeff Reboulet .05
360 Roger Clemens 1.00
361 Mark Carreon .05
362 Chad Kreuter .05
363 Mark Farris (Draft Pick) .05
364 Bob Welch .05
365 Dean Palmer .05
366 Jeromy Burnitz .05
367 B.J. Surhoff .05
368 Mike Butcher .05
369 RP Prospects (Brad Clontz,
Steve Phoenix,
Scott Gentile,
Bucky Buckles) .05
370 Eddie Murray .75
371 Orlando Miller
(Star Track) .05
372 Ron Karkovice .05
373 Richie Lewis .05
374 Lenny Webster .05
375 Jeff Tackett .05
376 Tom Urbani .05
377 Tino Martinez .05
378 Mark Dewey .05
379 Charlie O'Brien .05
380 Terry Mulholland .05
381 Thomas Howard .05
382 Chris Haney .05
383 Billy Hatcher .05
384 Jeff Bagwell,
Frank Thomas/AS .45
385 Bret Boone,
Carlos Baerga/AS .05
386 Matt Williams,
Wade Boggs/AS .30
387 Wil Cordero,
Cal Ripken Jr./AS 1.00
388 Barry Bonds,
Ken Griffey Jr./AS 1.00
389 Tony Gwynn,
Albert Belle/AS .50
390 Dante Bichette,
Kirby Puckett/AS .50
391 Mike Piazza,
Mike Stanley/AS .75
392 Greg Maddux,
David Cone/AS .50
393 Danny Jackson,
Jimmy Key/AS .05
394 John Franco,
Lee Smith/AS .05
395 Checklist 1-198 .05
396 Checklist 199-396 .05
397 Ken Griffey Jr. 1.25
398 Rick Heiserman RC
(Draft Pick) .05
399 Don Mattingly 1.00
400 Henry Rodriguez .05
401 Lenny Harris .05
402 Ryan Thompson .05
403 Darren Oliver .05
404 Omar Vizquel .05
405 Jeff Bagwell .75
406 Doug Webb RC
(Draft Pick) .05
407 Todd Van Poppel .05
408 Leo Gomez .05
409 Mark Whiten .05
410 Pedro Martinez .05
411 Reggie Sanders .05
412 Kevin Foster .05
413 Danny Tartabull .05
414 Jeff Blauser .05
415 Mike Magnante .05
416 Tom Candiotti .05
417 Rod Beck .05
418 Jody Reed .05
419 Vince Coleman .05
420 Danny Jackson .05
421 Ryan Nye RC
(Draft Pick) .05
422 Larry Walker .05
423 Russ Johnson
(Draft Pick) .05
424 Pat Borders .05
425 Lee Smith .05
426 Paul O'Neill .05
427 Devon White .05
428 Jim Bullinger .05
429 SP Prospects
(Greg Hansell,
Brian Sackinsky,
Carey Paige,
Rob Welch) .05
430 Steve Avery .05
431 Tony Gwynn 1.00
432 Pat Meares .05
433 Bill Swift .05
434 David Wells .05

435 John Briscoe .05
436 Roger Pavlik .05
437 Jayson Peterson RC
(Draft Pick) .05
438 Roberto Alomar .15
439 Billy Brewer .05
440 Gary Sheffield .40
441 Lou Frazier .05
442 Terry Steinbach .05
443 Jay Payton RC
(Draft Pick) .25
444 Jason Bere .05
445 Denny Neagle .05
446 Andres Galarraga .05
447 Hector Carrasco .05
448 Bill Risley .05
449 Andy Benes .05
450 Jim Leyritz .05
451 Jose Oliva .05
452 Greg Vaughn .05
453 Rich Monteleone .05
454 Tony Eusebio .05
455 Chuck Finley .05
456 Kevin Brown .05
457 Joe Boever .05
458 Bobby Munoz .05
459 Bret Saberhagen .05
460 Kurt Abbott .05
461 Bobby Witt .05
462 Cliff Floyd .05
463 Mark Clark .05
464 Andujar Cedeno .05
465 Marvin Freeman .05
466 Mike Piazza 1.25
467 Willie Greene .05
468 Pat Kelly .05
469 Carlos Delgado .40
470 Willie Banks .05
471 Matt Walbeck .05
472 Mark McGwire 1.50
473 McKay Christensen
(Draft Pick) .05
474 Alan Trammell .05
475 Tom Gordon .05
476 Greg Colbrunn .05
477 Darren Daulton .05
478 Albie Lopez .05
479 Robin Ventura .05
480 C Prospects
(Eddie Perez RC,
Jason Kendall,
Einar Diaz RC,
Bret Hemphill) .20
481 Bryan Eversgerd .05
482 Dave Fleming .05
483 Scott Livingstone .05
484 Pete Schourek .05
485 Bernie Williams .05
486 Mark Lemke .05
487 Eric Karros .05
488 Scott Ruffcorn .05
489 Billy Ashley .05
490 Rico Brogna .05
491 John Burkett .05
492 Cade Gaspar RC
(Draft Pick) .05
493 Jorge Fabregas .05
494 Greg Gagne .05
495 Doug Jones .05
496 Troy O'Leary .05
497 Pat Rapp .05
498 Butch Henry .05
499 John Olerud .05
500 John Hudek .05
501 Jeff King .05
502 Bobby Bonilla .05
503 Albert Belle .05
504 Rick Wilkins .05
505 John Jaha .05
506 Nigel Wilson .05
507 Sid Fernandez .05
508 Deion Sanders .05
509 Gil Heredia .05
510 Scott Elarton RC
(Draft Pick) .10
511 Melido Perez .05
512 Greg McMichael .05
513 Rusty Meacham .05
514 Shawn Green .35
515 Carlos Garcia .05
516 Dave Stevens .05
517 Eric Young .05
518 Omar Daal .05
519 Kirk Gibson .05
520 Spike Owen .05
521 Jacob Cruz RC
(Draft Pick) .05
522 Sandy Alomar .05
523 Steve Bedrosian .05
524 Ricky Gutierrez .05
525 Dave Veres .05
526 Gregg Jefferies .05
527 Jose Valentin .05
528 Robb Nen .05
529 Jose Rijo .05
530 Sean Berry .05
531 Mike Gallego .05
532 Roberto Kelly .05
533 Kevin Stocker .05
534 Kirby Puckett 1.00
535 Chipper Jones 1.00
536 Russ Davis .05
537 Jon Lieber .05
538 Trey Moore RC
(Draft Pick) .05
539 Joe Girardi .05

540 2B Prospects
(Quilvio Veras,
Arquimedez Pozo,
Miguel Cairo,
Jason Camilli) .05
541 Tony Phillips .05
542 Brian Anderson .05
543 Ivan Rodriguez .65
544 Jeff Cirillo .05
545 Joey Cora .05
546 Chris Hoiles .05
547 Bernard Gilkey .05
548 Mike Lansing .05
549 Jimmy Key .05
550 Mark Wohlers .05
551 Chris Clemons
(Draft Pick) .05
552 Vinny Castilla .05
553 Mark Guthrie .05
554 Mike Lieberthal .05
555 Tommy Davis RC
(Draft Pick) .05
556 Robby Thompson .05
557 Danny Bautista .05
558 Will Clark .05
559 Rickey Henderson .75
560 Todd Jones .05
561 Jack McDowell .05
562 Carlos Rodriguez .05
563 Mark Eichhorn .05
564 Jeff Nelson .05
565 Eric Anthony .05
566 Randy Velarde .05
567 Javy Lopez .05
568 Kevin Mitchell .05
569 Steve Karsay .05
570 Brian Meadows RC
(Draft Pick) .10
571 SS Prospects
(Rey Ordonez RC,
Mike Metcalfe, Ray Holbert,
Kevin Orie) .40
572 John Kruk .05
573 Scott Leius .05
574 John Patterson .05
575 Kevin Brown .05
576 Mike Moore .05
577 Manny Ramirez .75
578 Jose Lind .05
579 Derrick May .05
580 Cal Eldred .05
581 3B Prospects (David Bell,
Joel Chelmis, Lino Diaz,
Aaron Boone RC) .15
582 J.T. Snow .05
583 Luis Sojo .05
584 Moises Alou .05
585 Dave Clark .05
586 Dave Hollins .05
587 Nomar Garciaparra
(Draft Pick) 2.00
588 Cal Ripken Jr. 2.00
589 Pedro Astacio .05
590 J.R. Phillips .05
591 Jeff Frye .05
592 Bo Jackson .10
593 Steve Ontiveros .05
594 David Nied .05
595 Brad Ausmus .05
596 Carlos Baerga .05
597 James Mouton .05
598 Ozzie Guillen .05
599 OF Prospects
(Ozzie Timmons,
Curtis Goodwin,
Johnny Damon,
Jeff Abbott RC) .25
600 Yorkis Perez .05
601 Rich Rodriguez .05
602 Mark McLemore .05
603 Jeff Fassero .05
604 John Roper .05
605 Mark Johnson RC
(Draft Pick) .10
606 Wes Chamberlain .05
607 Felix Jose .05
608 Tony Longmire .05
609 Duane Ward .05
610 Brett Butler .05
611 William
Van Landingham .05
612 Mickey Tettleton .05
613 Brady Anderson .05
614 Reggie Jefferson .05
615 Mike Kingery .05
616 Derek Bell .05
617 Scott Erickson .05
618 Bob Wickman .05
619 Phil Leftwich .05
620 Dave Justice .05
621 Paul Wilson (Draft Pick) .05
622 Pedro Martinez .75
623 Terry Mathews .05
624 Brian McRae .05
625 Bruce Ruffin .05
626 Steve Finley .05
627 Ron Gant .05
628 Rafael Bournigal .05
629 Darryl Strawberry .05
630 Luis Alicea .05
631 Mark Smith,
Scott Klingenbeck
(On Deck) .05
632 Cory Bailey,
Scott Hatteberg
(On Deck) .05
633 Todd Greene, Troy Percival
(On Deck) .05

634 Rod Bolton, Olmedo Saenz
(On Deck) .05
635 Herb Perry, Steve Kline
(On Deck) .05
636 Sean Bergman,
Shannon Penn
(On Deck) .05
637 Joe Vitiello, Joe Randa
(On Deck) .05
638 Jose Mercedes,
Duane Singleton
(On Deck) .05
639 Marty Cordova,
Marc Barcelo (On Deck) .10
640 Ruben Rivera, Andy Pettitte
(On Deck) .10
641 Willie Adams, Scott Spiezio
(On Deck) .05
642 Eddie Diaz, Desi Relaford
(On Deck) .05
643 Jon Shave, Terrell Lowery
(On Deck) .05
644 Paul Spoljaric,
Angel Martinez
(On Deck) .05
645 Damon Hollins,
Tony Graffanino
(On Deck) .05
646 Darron Cox, Doug Glanville
(On Deck) .05
647 Tim Belk, Pat Watkins
(On Deck) .05
648 Rod Pedraza,
Phil Schneider
(On Deck) .05
649 Marc Valdes,
Vic Darensbourg
(On Deck) .05
650 Rick Huisman,
Roberto Petagine
(On Deck) .05
651 Ron Coomer,
Roger Cedeno
(On Deck) .05
652 Carlos Perez RC,
Shane Andrews
(On Deck) .10
653 Jason Isringhausen,
Chris Roberts
(On Deck) .05
654 Kevin Jordan,
Wayne Gomes
(On Deck) .05
655 Esteban Loaiza,
Steve Pegues (On Deck) .05
656 John Frascatore,
Terry Bradshaw
(On Deck) .05
657 Bryce Florie,
Andres Berumen
(On Deck) .05
658 Keith Williams,
Dan Carlson (On Deck) .05
659 Checklist .05
660 Checklist .05

Cyberstats

Inserted into all types of Topps packaging at the rate of about one per 15 cards, this special series attempted to "complete" the statistics from the strike-shortened 1994 baseball season for nearly 400 players. Topps used computer modeling to predict how each player would have ended the season. Fronts of the cards are the same as found in the regular Topps set, except they have been printed on metallic foil. Backs have a black background.

	NM/M
Complete Set (396):	25.00
Common Player:	.10
1 Frank Thomas	.75
2 Mickey Morandini	.10
3 Todd Worrell	.10
4 David Cone	.10
5 Trevor Hoffman	.10
6 Shane Mack	.10
7 Delino DeShields	.10
8 Matt Williams	.10
9 Sammy Sosa	1.00

#	Player	
10	Gary DiSarcina	.10
11	Kenny Rogers	.10
12	Jose Vizcaino	.10
13	Lou Whitaker	.10
14	Ron Darling	.10
15	Dave Nilsson	.10
16	Dennis Martinez	.10
17	Orlando Merced	.10
18	John Wetteland	.10
19	Mike Devereaux	.10
20	Rene Arocha	.10
21	Jay Buhner	.10
22	Hal Morris	.10
23	Paul Molitor	.75
24	Dave West	.10
25	Scott Sanders	.10
26	Eddie Zambrano	.10
27	Ricky Bones	.10
28	John Valentin	.10
29	Kevin Tapani	.10
30	Tim Wallach	.10
31	Darren Lewis	.10
32	Travis Fryman	.10
33	Bret Barberie	.10
34	Dennis Eckersley	.65
35	Ken Hill	.10
36	Pete Harnisch	.10
37	Mike Mussina	.50
38	Dave Winfield	.75
39	Joey Hamilton	.10
40	Edgar Martinez	.10
41	John Smiley	.10
42	Jim Abbott	.10
43	Mike Kelly	.10
44	Brian Jordan	.10
45	Ken Ryan	.10
46	Matt Mieske	.10
47	Rick Aguilera	.10
48	Ismael Valdes	.10
49	Royce Clayton	.10
50	Juan Gonzalez	.35
51	Mel Rojas	.10
52	Doug Drabek	.10
53	Charles Nagy	.10
54	Tim Raines	.10
55	Midre Cummings	.10
56	Rafael Palmeiro	.65
57	Charlie Hayes	.10
58	Ray Lankford	.10
59	Tim Davis	.10
60	Andy Ashby	.10
61	Mark Grace	.10
62	Mark Langston	.10
63	Chuck Carr	.10
64	Barry Bonds	2.00
65	David Segui	.10
66	Mariano Duncan	.10
67	Kenny Lofton	.10
68	Ken Caminiti	.10
69	Darrin Jackson	.10
70	Wil Cordero	.10
71	Walt Weiss	.10
72	Tom Pagnozzi	.10
73	Bret Boone	.10
74	Wally Joyner	.10
75	Luis Lopez	.10
76	Len Dykstra	.10
77	Pedro Munoz	.10
78	Kevin Gross	.10
79	Eduardo Perez	.10
80	Brent Gates	.10
81	Jeff Conine	.10
82	Paul Sorrento	.10
83	Julio Franco	.10
84	Chris Sabo	.10
85	Dante Bichette	.10
86	Mike Stanley	.10
87	Bob Hamelin	.10
88	Tommy Greene	.10
89	Jeff Brantley	.10
90	Ed Sprague	.10
91	Otis Nixon	.10
92	Chad Curtis	.10
93	Chuck McElroy	.10
94	Troy Neel	.10
95	Benito Santiago	.10
96	Jose Mesa	.10
97	Luis Gonzalez	.10
98	Alex Fernandez	.10
99	Ben McDonald	.10
100	Wade Boggs	1.00
101	Tom Glavine	.35
102	Phil Plantier	.10
103	Raul Mondesi	.10
104	Jim Edmonds	.10
105	Jeff Kent	.10
106	Wilson Alvarez	.10
107	Geronimo Berroa	.10
108	Craig Biggio	.10
109	Roberto Hernandez	.10
110	Bobby Ayala	.10
111	Bob Tewksbury	.10
112	Rondell White	.10
113	Steve Cooke	.10
114	Tim Salmon	.10
115	Kent Mercker	.10
116	Randy Johnson	.75
117	Mo Vaughn	.10
118	Eddie Williams	.10
119	Jeff Montgomery	.10
120	Kirt Manwaring	.10
121	Pat Hentgen	.10
122	Shawon Dunston	.10
123	Tim Belcher	.10
124	Cecil Fielder	.10
125	Todd Hundley	.10
126	Mark Acre	.10
127	Darrell Whitmore	.10
128	Darryl Kile	.10
129	Jay Bell	.10
130	Harold Baines	.10
131	Felix Fermin	.10
132	Ellis Burks	.10
133	Joe Carter	.10
134	Terry Pendleton	.10
135	Junior Felix	.10
136	Bill Gullickson	.10
137	Melvin Nieves	.10
138	Chuck Knoblauch	.10
139	Bobby Jones	.10
140	Darrin Fletcher	.10
141	Andy Van Slyke	.10
142	Allen Watson	.10
143	Dan Wilson	.10
144	Bip Roberts	.10
145	Sterling Hitchcock	.10
146	Johnny Ruffin	.10
147	Steve Trachsel	.10
148	Ramon Martinez	.10
149	Dave Henderson	.10
150	Chris Gomez	.10
151	Rusty Greer	.10
152	John Franco	.10
153	Mike Bordick	.10
154	Dave Magadan	.10
155	Greg Swindell	.10
156	Arthur Rhodes	.10
157	Juan Guzman	.10
158	Greg Maddux	1.00
159	Mike Macfarlane	.10
160	Curt Schilling	.35
161	Jose Canseco	.40
162	Aaron Sele	.10
163	Steve Buechele	.10
164	Orel Hershiser	.10
165	Mike Henneman	.10
166	Kevin Seitzer	.10
167	Ruben Sierra	.10
168	Alex Cole	.10
169	Jim Thome	.65
170	Lance Johnson	.10
171	Marquis Grissom	.10
172	Jamie Moyer	.10
173	Todd Zeile	.10
174	Chris Bosio	.10
175	Steve Howe	.10
176	Luis Polonia	.10
177	Ryan Klesko	.10
178	Kevin Appier	.10
179	Tim Naehring	.10
180	Randy Myers	.10
181	Mike Jackson	.10
182	Chili Davis	.10
183	Jason Jacome	.10
184	Stan Javier	.10
185	Scott Servais	.10
186	Kirk Rueter	.10
187	Don Slaught	.10
188	Ozzie Smith	1.00
189	Barry Larkin	.10
190	Gary Gaetti	.10
191	Fred McGriff	.10
192	Roger Clemens	1.00
193	Dean Palmer	.10
194	Jeromy Burnitz	.10
195	Scott Kamieniecki	.10
196	Eddie Murray	.75
197	Ron Karkovice	.10
198	Tino Martinez	.10
199	Ken Griffey Jr.	1.25
200	Don Mattingly	1.00
201	Henry Rodriguez	.10
202	Lenny Harris	.10
203	Ryan Thompson	.10
204	Darren Oliver	.10
205	Omar Vizquel	.10
206	Jeff Bagwell	.75
207	Todd Van Poppel	.10
208	Leo Gomez	.10
209	Mark Whiten	.10
210	Pedro Martinez	.10
211	Reggie Sanders	.10
212	Kevin Foster	.10
213	Danny Tartabull	.10
214	Jeff Blauser	.10
215	Mike Magnante	.10
216	Tom Candiotti	.10
217	Rod Beck	.10
218	Jody Reed	.10
219	Vince Coleman	.10
220	Danny Jackson	.10
221	Larry Walker	.10
222	Pat Borders	.10
223	Lee Smith	.10
224	Paul O'Neill	.10
225	Devon White	.10
226	Jim Bullinger	.10
227	Steve Avery	.10
228	Tony Gwynn	1.00
229	Pat Meares	.10
230	Bill Swift	.10
231	David Wells	.10
232	John Briscoe	.10
233	Roger Pavlik	.10
234	Roberto Alomar	.30
235	Billy Brewer	.10
236	Gary Sheffield	.40
237	Lou Frazier	.10
238	Terry Steinbach	.10
239	Omar Daal	.10
240	Jason Bere	.10
241	Denny Neagle	.10
242	Danny Bautista	.10
243	Hector Carrasco	.10
244	Bill Risley	.10
245	Andy Benes	.10
246	Jim Leyritz	.10
247	Jose Oliva	.10
248	Greg Vaughn	.10
249	Rich Monteleone	.10
250	Tony Eusebio	.10
251	Chuck Finley	.10
252	Joe Boever	.10
253	Bobby Munoz	.10
254	Bret Saberhagen	.10
255	Kurt Abbott	.10
256	Bobby Witt	.10
257	Cliff Floyd	.10
258	Mark Clark	.10
259	Andujar Cedeno	.10
260	Marvin Freeman	.10
261	Mike Piazza	1.25
262	Pat Kelly	.10
263	Carlos Delgado	.45
264	Willie Banks	.10
265	Matt Walbeck	.10
266	Mark McGwire	1.50
267	Alan Trammell	.10
268	Tom Gordon	.10
269	Greg Colbrunn	.10
270	Darren Daulton	.10
271	Albie Lopez	.10
272	Robin Ventura	.10
273	Bryan Eversgerd	.10
274	Dave Fleming	.10
275	Scott Livingstone	.10
276	Pete Schourek	.10
277	Bernie Williams	.10
278	Mark Lemke	.10
279	Eric Karros	.10
280	Billy Ashley	.10
281	Rico Brogna	.10
282	John Burkett	.10
283	Jorge Fabregas	.10
284	Greg Gagne	.10
285	Doug Jones	.10
286	Troy O'Leary	.10
287	Pat Rapp	.10
288	Butch Henry	.10
289	John Olerud	.10
290	John Hudek	.10
291	Jeff King	.10
292	Bobby Bonilla	.10
293	Albert Belle	.10
294	Rick Wilkins	.10
295	John Jaha	.10
296	Sid Fernandez	.10
297	Deion Sanders	.10
298	Gil Heredia	.10
299	Melido Perez	.10
300	Greg McMichael	.10
301	Rusty Meacham	.10
302	Shawn Green	.35
303	Carlos Garcia	.10
304	Dave Stevens	.10
305	Eric Young	.10
306	Kirk Gibson	.10
307	Spike Owen	.10
308	Sandy Alomar	.10
309	Ricky Gutierrez	.10
310	Dave Veres	.10
311	Gregg Jefferies	.10
312	Jose Valentin	.10
313	Robb Nen	.10
314	Jose Rijo	.10
315	Sean Berry	.10
316	Mike Gallego	.10
317	Roberto Kelly	.10
318	Kevin Stocker	.10
319	Kirby Puckett	1.00
320	Jon Lieber	.10
321	Joe Girardi	.10
322	Tony Phillips	.10
323	Brian Anderson	.10
324	Ivan Rodriguez	.65
325	Jeff Cirillo	.10
326	Joey Cora	.10
327	Chris Hoiles	.10
328	Bernard Gilkey	.10
329	Mike Lansing	.10
330	Jimmy Key	.10
331	Vinny Castilla	.10
332	Mark Guthrie	.10
333	Mike Lieberthal	.10
334	Will Clark	.10
335	Rickey Henderson	.75
336	Todd Jones	.10
337	Jack McDowell	.10
338	Carlos Rodriguez	.10
339	Mark Eichhorn	.10
340	Jeff Nelson	.10
341	Eric Anthony	.10
342	Randy Velarde	.10
343	Javier Lopez	.10
344	Kevin Mitchell	.10
345	Steve Bedrosian	.10
346	John Kruk	.10
347	Scott Leius	.10
348	John Patterson	.10
349	Kevin Brown	.10
350	Mike Moore	.10
351	Manny Ramirez	.75
352	Jose Lind	.10
353	Derrick May	.10
354	Cal Eldred	.10
355	J.T. Snow	.10
356	Luis Sojo	.10
357	Moises Alou	.10
358	Dave Clark	.10
359	Dave Hollins	.10
360	Cal Ripken Jr.	2.00
361	Pedro Astacio	.10
362	Tony Longmire	.10
363	Jeff Frye	.10
364	Bo Jackson	.20
365	Steve Ontiveros	.10
366	David Nied	.10
367	Brad Ausmus	.10
368	Carlos Baerga	.10
369	James Mouton	.10
370	Ozzie Guillen	.10
371	Yorkis Perez	.10
372	Rich Rodriguez	.10
373	Mark McLemore	.10
374	Jeff Fassero	.10
375	John Roper	.10
376	Wes Chamberlain	.10
377	Felix Jose	.10
378	Brett Butler	.10
379	William Van Landingham	.10
380	Mickey Tettleton	.10
381	Brady Anderson	.10
382	Reggie Jefferson	.10
383	Mike Kingery	.10
384	Derek Bell	.10
385	Scott Erickson	.10
386	Bob Wickman	.10
387	Phil Leftwich	.10
388	Dave Justice	.10
389	Pedro Martinez	.75
390	Terry Mathews	.10
391	Brian McRae	.10
392	Bruce Ruffin	.10
393	Steve Finley	.10
394	Rafael Bournigal	.10
395	Darryl Strawberry	.10
396	Luis Alicea	.10

Cyberstat Season in Review

This special edition of Cyberstat cards was available only in Topps factory sets. Carrying forward the idea of computerized projections to complete the strike-shortened 1994 season, the Season in Review cards speculate on career milestones and the playoffs that never happened. The Season in Review cards have player action photos printed on a foil background resembling the U.S. flag. Names are in gold foil. Backs have a black background and a recap of the computer simulation.

		NM/M
Complete Set (7):		10.00
Common Player:		1.00
1	Barry Bonds (61 Home Runs)	6.00
2	Jose Canseco (AL One-Game Playoff)	2.00
3	Juan Gonzalez (AL Divisional Playoffs)	1.50
4	Fred McGriff (NL Divisional Playoffs)	1.00
5	Carlos Baerga (ALCS MVP)	1.00
6	Ryan Klesko (NLCS MVP)	1.00
7	Kenny Lofton (World Series MVP)	1.00

League Leaders

League Leaders is a 50-card insert set found in one of every six retail packs only of both Series I and II. The set includes the top five players in each league across 10 statistical categories. Cards featured the statistical category running up the right side, with the player's name across the bottom. Photo backgrounds have been darkened and posterized to make the player action stand out. Backs have the player's stat rankings within his division and league, and a bar graph at bottom gives his performance in that statistical category for the previous five seasons.

		NM/M
Complete Set (50):		20.00
Common Player:		.15
1	Albert Belle	.15
2	Kevin Mitchell	.15
3	Wade Boggs	1.50
4	Tony Gwynn	1.50
5	Moises Alou	.15
6	Andres Galarraga	.15
7	Matt Williams	.15
8	Barry Bonds	4.00
9	Frank Thomas	.75
10	Jose Canseco	.50
11	Jeff Bagwell	.75
12	Kirby Puckett	1.50
13	Julio Franco	.15
14	Albert Belle	.15
15	Fred McGriff	.15
16	Kenny Lofton	.15
17	Otis Nixon	.15
18	Brady Anderson	.15
19	Deion Sanders	.15
20	Chuck Carr	.15
21	Pat Hentgen	.15
22	Andy Benes	.15
23	Roger Clemens	1.75
24	Greg Maddux	1.50
25	Pedro Martinez	.75
26	Paul O'Neill	.15
27	Jeff Bagwell	.75
28	Frank Thomas	.75
29	Hal Morris	.15
30	Kenny Lofton	.15
31	Ken Griffey Jr.	2.00
32	Jeff Bagwell	.75
33	Albert Belle	.15
34	Fred McGriff	.15
35	Cecil Fielder	.15
36	Matt Williams	.15
37	Joe Carter	.15
38	Dante Bichette	.15
39	Frank Thomas	.75
40	Mike Piazza	2.00
41	Craig Biggio	.15
42	Vince Coleman	.15
43	Marquis Grissom	.15
44	Chuck Knoblauch	.15
45	Darren Lewis	.15
46	Randy Johnson	.75
47	Jose Rijo	.15
48	Chuck Finley	.15
49	Bret Saberhagen	.15
50	Kevin Appier	.15

Total Bases Finest

Printed in Topps Finest technology, including a peel-off plastic protector coating on the front, these cards honor the 1994 statistical leaders in total bases. The cards have a silver waffle-texture background on front as a background to the color action photo. At bottom is a team logo and team-color bar with the player's name. Backs feature a portrait photo and the player's total base stats. These inserts are found in Series II Topps packs at an average rate of one per 36 packs (one box).

	NM/M
Complete Set (15):	12.00
Common Player:	.50
1 Jeff Bagwell	1.25
2 Albert Belle	.50
3 Ken Griffey Jr.	2.00
4 Frank Thomas	1.25
5 Matt Williams	.50
6 Dante Bichette	.50
7 Barry Bonds	2.50
8 Moises Alou	.50
9 Andres Galarraga	.50
10 Kenny Lofton	.50
11 Rafael Palmeiro	1.00
12 Tony Gwynn	1.50
13 Kirby Puckett	1.50
14 Jose Canseco	.75
15 Jeff Conine	.50

1995 Topps Traded and Rookies

Traded players, free agents signed by new teams and all the up-and-coming rookies are the meat of the 1995 Topps Traded and Rookies set, sold for the first time exclusively in foil-pack form. Maintaining the same format used in Series 1 and 2 Topps, the updates also reused the Future Star, Draft Pick and Star Track subsets, along with four-player Prospects cards. New subsets included Rookie of the Year Candidates, All-Stars, On Deck and "At the Break," 10 cards chronicling star players' performances through the first half of the 1995 season. A double-thick, foil-printed version of the "At the Break" cards called "Power Boosters" were the only inserts in the Traded/Rookies set.

		NM/M
Complete Set (165):		30.00
Common Player:		.05
Pack (11):		2.50
Wax Box (36):		60.00
1	Frank Thomas (At the Break)	.50
2	Ken Griffey Jr. (At the Break)	.65
3	Barry Bonds (At the Break)	1.00
4	Albert Belle (At The Break)	.05
5	Cal Ripken Jr. (At The Break)	1.00
6	Mike Piazza (At the Break)	.75
7	Tony Gwynn (At the Break)	.60
8	Jeff Bagwell (At the Break)	.45
9	Mo Vaughn (At The Break)	.05
10	Matt Williams (At the Break)	.05
11	Ray Durham	.05
12	Juan LeBron (Photo Carlos Beltran.) RC (Draft Pick)	5.00
13	Shawn Green (Rookie of the Year Candidate)	.50
14	Kevin Gross	.05
15	Jon Nunnally	.05
16	Brian Maxcy RC	.05
17	Mark Kiefer	.05
18	Carlos Beltran RC (Draft Pick)(Photo actually Juan Beltran.)	20.00
19	Mike Mimbs RC	.05
20	Larry Walker	.05
21	Chad Curtis	.05
22	Jeff Barry	.05
23	Joe Oliver	.05
24	Tomas Perez RC	.05
25	Michael Barrett RC (Draft Pick)	1.50
26	Brian McRae	.05
27	Derek Bell	.05

28	Ray Durham (Rookie of the Year Candidate)	.05
29	Todd Williams	.05
30	Ryan Jaroncyk **RC** (Draft Pick)	.05
31	Todd Steverson	.05
32	Mike Devereaux	.05
33	Rheal Cormier	.05
34	Benny Santiago	.05
35	Bobby Higginson **RC**	.50
36	Jack McDowell	.05
37	Mike Macfarlane	.05
38	Tony McKnight **RC** (Draft Pick)	.05
39	Brian Hunter (Rookie of the Year Candidate)	.05
40	Hideo Nomo **RC** (Star Track)	2.00
41	Brett Butler	.05
42	Donovan Osborne	.05
43	Scott Karl	.05
44	Tony Phillips	.05
45	Marty Cordova (Rookie of the Year Candidate)	.20
46	Dave Mlicki	.05
47	Bronson Arroyo **RC** (Draft Pick)	4.00
48	John Burkett	.05
49	J.D. Smart **RC** (Draft Pick)	.05
50	Mickey Tettleton	.05
51	Todd Stottlemyre	.05
52	Mike Perez	.05
53	Terry Mulholland	.05
54	Edgardo Alfonzo	.05
55	Zane Smith	.05
56	Jacob Brumfield	.05
57	Andujar Cedeno	.05
58	Jose Parra	.05
59	Manny Alexander	.05
60	Tony Tarasco	.05
61	Orel Hershiser	.05
62	Tim Scott	.05
63	Felix Rodriguez **RC**	.05
64	Ken Hill	.05
65	Marquis Grissom	.05
66	Lee Smith	.05
67	Jason Bates (Rookie of the Year Candidate)	.05
68	Felipe Lira	.05
69	Alex Hernandez **RC** (Draft Pick)	.10
70	Tony Fernandez	.05
71	Scott Radinsky	.05
72	Jose Canseco	.50
73	Mark Grudzielanek **RC**	.50
74	Ben Davis **RC** (Draft Pick)	.25
75	Jim Abbott	.05
76	Roger Bailey	.05
77	Gregg Jefferies	.05
78	Erik Hanson	.05
79	Brad Radke **RC**	1.50
80	Jaime Navarro	.05
81	John Wetteland	.05
82	Chad Fonville **RC**	.10
83	John Mabry	.05
84	Glenallen Hill	.05
85	Ken Caminiti	.05
86	Tom Goodwin	.05
87	Darren Bragg	.05
88	1995 Prospects/Pitchers (Pat Ahearne **RC**, Gary Rath **RC**, Larry Wimberly **RC**, Robbie Bell **RC**)	.10
89	Jeff Russell	.05
90	Dave Gallagher	.05
91	Steve Finley	.05
92	Vaughn Eshelman	.05
93	Kevin Jarvis	.05
94	Mark Gubicza	.05
95	Tim Wakefield	.05
96	Bob Tewksbury	.05
97	Sid Roberson **RC**	.05
98	Tom Henke	.05
99	Michael Tucker (Future Star)	.05
100	Jason Bates	.05
101	Otis Nixon	.05
102	Mark Whiten	.05
103	Dilson Torres	.05
104	Melvin Bunch **RC**	.05
105	Terry Pendleton	.05
106	Corey Jenkins **RC** (Draft Pick)	.05
107	On Deck (Glenn Dishman **RC**, Rob Grable **RC**)	.05
108	Reggie Taylor **RC** (Draft Pick)	.05
109	Curtis Goodwin (Rookie of the Year Candidate)	.05
110	David Cone	.05
111	Antonio Osuna	.05
112	Paul Shuey	.05
113	Doug Jones	.05
114	Mark McLemore	.05
115	Kevin Ritz	.05
116	John Kruk	.05
117	Trevor Wilson	.05
118	Jerald Clark	.05
119	Julian Tavarez	.05
120	Tim Pugh	.05
121	Todd Zeile	.05

122	1995 Prospects/Fielders (Mark Sweeney **RC**, George Arias, Richie Sexson **RC**, Brian Schneider **RC**)	4.00
123	Bobby Witt	.05
124	Hideo Nomo (Rookie of the Year Candidate)	1.00
125	Joey Cora	.05
126	Jim Scharrer **RC** (Draft Pick)	.05
127	Paul Quantrill	.05
128	Chipper Jones (Rookie of the Year Candidate)	.75
129	Kenny James **RC** (Draft Pick)	.05
130	On Deck (Lyle Mouton, Mariano Rivera)	.15
131	Tyler Green (Rookie of the Year Candidate)	.05
132	Brad Clontz	.05
133	Jon Nunnally (Rookie of the Year Candidate)	.05
134	Dave Magadan	.05
135	Al Leiter	.05
136	Bret Barberie	.05
137	Bill Swift	.05
138	Scott Cooper	.05
139	Roberto Kelly	.05
140	Charlie Hayes	.05
141	Pete Harnisch	.05
142	Rich Amaral	.05
143	Rudy Seanez	.05
144	Pat Listach	.05
145	Quilvio Veras (Rookie of the Year Candidate)	.05
146	Jose Olmeda **RC** (Draft Pick)	.05
147	Roberto Petagine	.05
148	Kevin Brown	.05
149	Phil Plantier	.05
150	Carlos Perez **RC** (Rookie of the Year Candidate)	.05
151	Pat Borders	.05
152	Tyler Green	.05
153	Stan Belinda	.05
154	Dave Stewart	.05
155	Andre Dawson	.25
156	Frank Thomas, Fred McGriff/AS	.30
157	Carlos Baerga, Craig Biggio/AS	.05
158	Wade Boggs, Matt Williams/AS	.35
159	Cal Ripken Jr., Ozzie Smith/AS	.75
160	Ken Griffey Jr., Tony Gwynn/AS	.40
161	Albert Belle, Barry Bonds/AS	.75
162	Kirby Puckett, Len Dykstra/AS	.35
163	Ivan Rodriguez, Mike Piazza/AS	.40
164	Randy Johnson, Hideo Nomo/AS	.25
165	Checklist	.05

Power Boosters

Virtually identical to the first 10 cards of the 1995 Topps Traded and Rookies issue, the "At the Break" subset is the only insert found in Traded packs. Cards are printed on double-thick cardboard stock on metallized foil. The chase cards are found at an average rate of one per 36 packs.

		NM/M
Complete Set (10):		20.00
Common Player:		.75
1	Frank Thomas	1.50
2	Ken Griffey Jr.	3.00
3	Barry Bonds	5.00
4	Albert Belle	.75
5	Cal Ripken Jr.	5.00
6	Mike Piazza	3.00
7	Tony Gwynn	2.50

Abbreviations

AS - All-Star

8	Jeff Bagwell	1.50
9	Mo Vaughn	.75
10	Matt Williams	.75

Opening Day

This 10-card set featuring top performers on the belated opening day of the 1995 season was available exclusively in retail factory sets. Card fronts feature color action photos printed on textured foil in a U.S. flag-like design. A large colorful Opening Day logo appears in an upper corner while the player's key stats from that game appear in a foil box at lower-right. Backs have a portrait photo along with complete details and a stats line of the opening day performance.

		NM/M
Complete Set (10):		7.50
Common Player:		.75
1	Kevin Appier	.75
2	Dante Bichette	.75
3	Ken Griffey Jr.	3.50
4	Todd Hundley	.75
5	John Jaha	.75
6	Fred McGriff	.75
7	Raul Mondesi	.75
8	Manny Ramirez	2.50
9	Danny Tartabull	.75
10	Devon White	.75

Archives Brooklyn Dodgers

In a departure from its program of complete set reissues, Topps' Archives baseball series for 1995 was a tribute to the 40th anniversary of the Brooklyn Dodgers' 1955 World Series victory over the archrival Yankees. Besides reprinting all of the Dodgers' cards from the 1952-56 Topps sets and the 1955 Bowman issue, the Archives release included some 30 "cards that never were," done in the styles of the 1952-55 Topps issues. Those cards are designated with an "N" suffix in parentheses. The old larger format of the vintage cards has been reduced to the standard 2-1/2 x 3-1/2" format for the Archives versions. Cards are UV coated on each side. Each card carries its original or an "extended" card number in the normal location, plus a tiny Archives series card number at the bottom in the fine print. The numbers on cards #97-109 do not coincide with those listed on the checklist card. The only chase cards in the issue were autographed versions of Sandy Koufax's 1956

Archives card. Cards #111-165 are short-printed in relation to cards #1-110.

		NM/M
Complete Set (165):		75.00
Common Player:		.10
Wax Pack (10):		5.00
Wax Box (24):		110.00
1	Andy Pafko/52T	.25
2	Wayne Terwilliger/52T	.10
3	Billy Loes/52T	.25
4	Gil Hodges/52T	.50
5	Duke Snider/52T	.75
6	Jim Russell/52T	.10
7	Chris Van Cuyk/52T	.10
8	Preacher Roe/52T	.10
9	Johnny Schmitz/52T	.10
10	Bud Podbielan/52T	.10
11	Phil Haugstad/52T	.10
12	Clyde King/52T	.10
13	Billy Cox/52T	.10
14	Rocky Bridges/52T	.10
15	Carl Erskine/52T	.10
16	Erv Palica/52T	.10
17	Ralph Branca/52T	.10
18	Jackie Robinson/52T	2.00
19	Roy Campanella/52T	.75
20	Rube Walker/52T	.10
21	Johnny Rutherford/52T	.10
22	Joe Black/52T	.25
23	George Shuba/52T	.10
24	Pee Wee Reese/52T	.75
25	Clem Labine/52T	.10
26	Bobby Morgan/52T	.10
27	Cookie Lavagetto/52T	.10
28	Chuck Dressen/52T	.10
29	Ben Wade/52T	.10
30	Rocky Nelson/52T	.10
31	Billy Herman/52T	.10
32	Jake Pitler/52T	.10
33	Dick Williams/52T	.10
34	Cal Abrams/52N	.25
35	Carl Furillo/52N	.25
36	Don Newcombe/52N	.25
37	Jackie Robinson/53T	2.00
38	Ben Wade/53T	.10
39	Clem Labine/53T	.10
40	Roy Campanella/53T	.75
41	George Shuba/53T	.10
42	Chuck Dressen/53T	.10
43	Pee Wee Reese/53T	.75
44	Joe Black/53T	.25
45	Bobby Morgan/53T	.10
46	Dick Williams/53T	.10
47	Rube Walker/53T	.10
48	Johnny Rutherford/53T	.10
49	Billy Loes/53T	.15
50	Don Hoak/53T	.10
51	Jim Hughes/53T	.10
52	Bob Milliken/53T	.10
53	Preacher Roe/53T	.10
54	Dixie Howell/53T	.10
55	Junior Gilliam/53T	.25
56	Johnny Podres/53T	.25
57	Bill Antonello/53T	.10
58	Ralph Branca/53T	.10
59	Gil Hodges/53N	.60
60	Carl Furillo/53N	.45
61	Carl Erskine/53N	.25
62	Don Newcombe/53N	.35
63	Duke Snider/53N	.75
64	Billy Cox/53N	.25
65	Russ Meyer/53N	.25
66	Jackie Robinson/54T	2.00
67	Preacher Roe/54T	.25
68	Duke Snider/54T	.75
69	Junior Gilliam/54T	.25
70	Billy Herman/54T	.10
71	Joe Black/54T	.15
72	Gil Hodges/54T	.50
73	Clem Labine/54T	.10
74	Ben Wade/54T	.10
75	Tommy Lasorda/54T	1.00
76	Rube Walker/54T	.10
77	Johnny Podres/54T	.10
78	Jim Hughes/54T	.10
79	Bob Milliken/54T	.10
80	Charlie Thompson/54T	.10
81	Don Hoak/54T	.10
82	Roberto Clemente/54N	1.00
83	Don Zimmer/54N	.25
84	Roy Campanella/54N	.50
85	Billy Cox/54N	.45
86	Carl Erskine/54N	.45
87	Carl Furillo/54N	.45
88	Don Newcombe/54N	.45
89	Pee Wee Reese/54N	1.00
90	George Shuba/54N	.10
91	Junior Gilliam/55T	.10
92	Billy Herman/55T	.10
93	Johnny Podres/55T	.10
94	Don Hoak/55T	.10
95	Jackie Robinson/55T	2.00
96	Jim Hughes/55T	.10
97	Bob Borkowski/55N	.10
98	Sandy Amoros/55T	.10
99	Karl Spooner/55T	.10
100	Don Zimmer/55T	.10
101	Rube Walker/55T	.10
102	Bob Milliken/55T	.10
103	Sandy Koufax/55T	2.00
104	Joe Black/55T	.20
105	Clem Labine/55T	.10
106	Gil Hodges/55T	.50
107	Ed Roebuck/55T	.10
108	Bert Hamric/55T	.10

109	Duke Snider/55T	.75
110	Walter Alston/55N	.25
111	Roger Craig/55N	.75
112	Don Drysdale/55N	3.00
113	Dixie Howell/55N	.50
114	Frank Kellert/55N	.50
115	Tommy Lasorda/55N	2.50
116	Chuck Templeton/55N	.50
117	World Series Game 3, Dodgers Stay Alive (Jackie Robinson/55N)	1.00
118	World Series Game 4, Series Knotted (Gil Hodges/55N)	1.00
119	World Series Game 5, Dodgers Lead (Duke Snider/55N)	1.00
120	World Series Game 7, Dodgers Reign (Johnny Podres/55N)	1.00
121	Don Hoak/55B	.35
122	Roy Campanella/55B	2.00
123	Pee Wee Reese/55B	2.00
124	Bob Darnell/55B	.50
125	Don Zimmer/55B	.50
126	George Shuba/55B	.50
127	Johnny Podres/55B	.50
128	Junior Gilliam/55B	.65
129	Don Newcombe/55B	.65
130	Jim Hughes/55B	.50
131	Gil Hodges/55B	2.00
132	Carl Furillo/55B	1.00
133	Carl Erskine/55B	.50
134	Erv Palica/55B	.50
135	Russ Meyer/55B	.50
136	Billy Loes/55B	.50
137	Walt Moryn/55B	.50
138	Chico Fernandez/55B	.50
139	Charley Neal/55B	.50
140	Ken Lehman/55B	.50
141	Walter Alston/56T	1.00
142	Jackie Robinson/56T	6.00
143	Sandy Amoros/56T	.50
144	Ed Roebuck/56T	.50
145	Roger Craig/56T	.50
146	Sandy Koufax/56T	5.00
146a	Sandy Koufax/56T, autographed	650.00
147	Karl Spooner/56T	.50
148	Don Zimmer/56T	.50
149	Roy Campanella/56T	3.00
150	Gil Hodges/56T	2.50
151	Duke Snider/56T	4.50
152	Team photo/56T	5.00
153	Johnny Podres/56T	.50
154	Don Bessent/56T	.50
155	Carl Furillo/56T	.75
156	Randy Jackson/56T	.50
157	Carl Erskine/56T	.50
158	Don Newcombe/56T	.65
159	Pee Wee Reese/56T	2.50
160	Billy Loes/56T	.50
161	Junior Gilliam/56T	.65
162	Clem Labine/56T	.50
163	Charley Neal/56T	.50
164	Rube Walker/56T	.50
165	Checklist	.05

1995 Topps DIII

Describing its cards as featuring "infinite depth perspectives" with game-action photos, Topps entered the 3-D card market with its Dimension III product. Utilizing "super thick laminated construction" to provide the illusion of depth, the cards feature borderless action photos on front. Backs are conventionally printed with a color portrait photo and several sets of stats that go beyond the usual to the provide a more in-depth look at the player's performance.

		NM/M
Complete Set (59):		10.00
Common Player:		.15
Retail Pack (3):		.50
Retail Wax Box (24):		9.00
Hobby Pack (5):		.65
Hobby Wax Box (24):		12.50
1	Dave Justice	.25
2	Cal Ripken Jr.	2.50
3	Ruben Sierra	.15

4	Roberto Alomar	.25
5	Dennis Martinez	.15
6	Todd Zeile	.15
7	Albert Belle	.15
8	Chuck Knoblauch	.15
9	Roger Clemens	1.25
10	Cal Eldred	.15
11	Dennis Eckersley	.75
12	Andy Benes	.15
13	Moises Alou	.15
14	Andres Galarraga	.15
15	Jim Thome	.65
16	Tim Salmon	.15
17	Carlos Garcia	.15
18	Scott Leius	.15
19	Jeff Montgomery	.15
20	Brian Anderson	.15
21	Will Clark	.15
22	Bobby Bonilla	.15
23	Mike Stanley	.15
24	Barry Bonds	2.50
25	Jeff Conine	.15
26	Paul O'Neill	.15
27	Mike Piazza	1.50
28	Tom Glavine	.35
29	Jim Edmonds	.15
30	Lou Whitaker	.15
31	Jeff Frye	.15
32	Ivan Rodriguez	.75
33	Bret Boone	.15
34	Mike Greenwell	.15
35	Mark Grace	.15
36	Darren Lewis	.15
37	Don Mattingly	1.25
38	Jose Rijo	.15
39	Robin Ventura	.15
40	Bob Hamelin	.15
41	Tim Wallach	.15
42	Tony Gwynn	1.00
43	Ken Griffey Jr.	1.50
44	Doug Drabek	.15
45	Rafael Palmeiro	.75
46	Dean Palmer	.15
47	Bip Roberts	.15
48	Barry Larkin	.15
49	Dave Nilsson	.15
50	Wil Cordero	.15
51	Travis Fryman	.15
52	Chuck Carr	.15
53	Rey Sanchez	.15
54	Walt Weiss	.15
55	Joe Carter	.15
56	Len Dykstra	.15
57	Orlando Merced	.15
58	Ozzie Smith	1.00
59	Chris Gomez	.15

Zone

A barrage of baseballs in the background, behind a player action photo, are featured on the front of this DIII chase set. Backs have a blazing baseball across the top and a description and stats of the pictured player's hot streaks of the previous season -- those times when athletes are said to be "in the zone." The inserts are found on average of one per six packs.

		NM/M
Complete Set (6):		4.00
Common Player:		.50
1	Frank Thomas	1.00
2	Kirby Puckett	1.50
3	Jeff Bagwell	1.00
4	Fred McGriff	.50
5	Raul Mondesi	.50
6	Kenny Lofton	.50

1995 Topps Embossed

Taking the embossed sportscard idea which Action Packed developed years earlier to a new level, Topps Embossed baseball features the tactile image on both sides of the card. Fronts have a lightly textured border while the central player photo is deeply embossed. The player name is embossed in gold-foil letters at bottom. Backs have another embossed player photo and various levels of embossing around the borders and boxes which contain stats and trivia.

	NM/M
Complete Set (140):	7.50
Common Player:	.10
Embossed Golds:	2X
Wax Pack (6+1):	1.50
Wax Box (24):	22.50

1	Kenny Lofton	.10
2	Gary Sheffield	.35
3	Hal Morris	.10
4	Cliff Floyd	.10
5	Pat Hentgen	.10
6	Tony Gwynn	.75
7	Jose Valentin	.10
8	Jason Bere	.10
9	Jeff Kent	.10
10	John Valentin	.10
11	Brian Anderson	.10
12	Deion Sanders	.10
13	Ryan Thompson	.10
14	Ruben Sierra	.10
15	Jay Bell	.10
16	Chuck Carr	.10
17	Brent Gates	.10
18	Bret Boone	.10
19	Paul Molitor	.60
20	Chili Davis	.10
21	Ryan Klesko	.10
22	Will Clark	.10
23	Greg Vaughn	.10
24	Moises Alou	.10
25	Ray Lankford	.10
26	Jose Rijo	.10
27	Bobby Jones	.10
28	Rick Wilkins	.10
29	Cal Eldred	.10
30	Juan Gonzalez	.30
31	Royce Clayton	.10
32	Bryan Harvey	.10
33	Dave Nilsson	.10
34	Chris Hoiles	.10
35	David Nied	.10
36	Javy Lopez	.10
37	Tim Wallach	.10
38	Bobby Bonilla	.10
39	Danny Tartabull	.10
40	Andy Benes	.10
41	Dean Palmer	.10
42	Chris Gomez	.10
43	Kevin Appier	.10
44	Brady Anderson	.10
45	Alex Fernandez	.10
46	Roberto Kelly	.10
47	Dave Hollins	.10
48	Chuck Finley	.10
49	Wade Boggs	.75
50	Travis Fryman	.10
51	Ken Griffey Jr.	1.00
52	John Olerud	.10
53	Delino DeShields	.10
54	Ivan Rodriguez	.50
55	Tommy Greene	.10
56	Tom Pagnozzi	.10
57	Bip Roberts	.10
58	Luis Gonzalez	.10
59	Rey Sanchez	.10
60	Ken Ryan	.10
61	Darren Daulton	.10
62	Rick Aguilera	.10
63	Wally Joyner	.10
64	Mike Greenwell	.10
65	Jay Buhner	.10
66	Craig Biggio	.10
67	Charles Nagy	.10
68	Devon White	.10
69	Randy Johnson	.60
70	Shawon Dunston	.10
71	Kirby Puckett	.75
72	Paul O'Neill	.10
73	Tino Martinez	.10
74	Carlos Garcia	.10
75	Ozzie Smith	.75
76	Cecil Fielder	.10
77	Mike Stanley	.10
78	Lance Johnson	.10
79	Tony Phillips	.10
80	Bobby Munoz	.10
81	Kevin Tapani	.10
82	William	
	Van Landingham	.10
83	Dante Bichette	.10

84	Tom Candiotti	.10
85	Wil Cordero	.10
86	Jeff Conine	.10
87	Joey Hamilton	.10
88	Mark Whiten	.10
89	Jeff Montgomery	.10
90	Andres Galarraga	.10
91	Roberto Alomar	.20
92	Orlando Merced	.10
93	Mike Mussina	.35
94	Pedro Martinez	.60
95	Carlos Baerga	.10
96	Steve Trachsel	.10
97	Lou Whitaker	.10
98	David Cone	.10
99	Chuck Knoblauch	.10
100	Frank Thomas	.60
101	Dave Justice	.10
102	Raul Mondesi	.10
103	Rickey Henderson	.60
104	Doug Drabek	.10
105	Sandy Alomar	.10
106	Roger Clemens	.85
107	Mark McGwire	1.20
108	Tim Salmon	.10
109	Greg Maddux	.75
110	Mike Piazza	1.00
111	Tom Glavine	.30
112	Walt Weiss	.10
113	Cal Ripken Jr.	1.50
114	Eddie Murray	.60
115	Don Mattingly	.85
116	Ozzie Guillen	.10
117	Bob Hamelin	.10
118	Jeff Bagwell	.60
119	Eric Karros	.10
120	Barry Bonds	1.50
121	Mickey Tettleton	.10
122	Mark Langston	.10
123	Robin Ventura	.10
124	Bret Saberhagen	.10
125	Albert Belle	.10
126	Rafael Palmeiro	.50
127	Fred McGriff	.10
128	Jimmy Key	.10
129	Barry Larkin	.10
130	Tim Raines	.10
131	Len Dykstra	.10
132	Todd Zeile	.10
133	Joe Carter	.10
134	Matt Williams	.10
135	Terry Steinbach	.10
136	Manny Ramirez	.60
137	John Wetteland	.10
138	Rod Beck	.10
139	Mo Vaughn	.10
140	Darren Lewis	.10

Golden Idols

The only insert in the Topps Embossed baseball set was a parallel set of the 140 cards rendered in gold tones on front and inserted at the rate of one per pack. Backs are identical to the regular version.

	NM/M
Complete Set (140):	25.00
Common Player:	.25

Legends of the '60s

Twelve of the true superstars of the 1960s are featured on one of their best Topps card designs in this collection of 6-

oz. bronze metal cards. In 2-1/2" x 3-1/2" size, the ingots' fronts reproduce one of the player's 1960s Topps cards. Backs have been modified to present entire career stats. The set was sold in a mail-order subscription plan and included a custom wood box to house the collection.

		NM/M
Complete Set (12):		100.00
Common Player:		7.50
(1)	Hank Aaron/1965	10.00
(2)	Roberto Clemente/	
	1965	10.00
(3)	Don Drysdale/1964	7.50
(4)	Bob Gibson/1965	7.50
(5)	Harmon Killebrew/	
	1968	7.50
(6)	Juan Marichal/1966	7.50
(7)	Willie Mays/1964	10.00
(8)	Willie McCovey/1961	7.50
(9)	Brooks Robinson/	
	1969	7.50
(10)	Frank Robinson/1962	7.50
(11)	Billy Williams/1967	7.50
(12)	Carl Yastrzemski/1966	7.50

Own the Game Instant Winner

Randomly packaged at a rate between 1:60 and 1:120, depending on type of packaging, Instant Winner cards were available in 1995 Topps baseball. The grand prize was a $40,000 "Baseball Passport" good for games, flights, hotels, etc., for 60 days during the 1996 season. Other prizes included personalized Topps baseball cards picturing the winner and Topps Spectra Light cards in team sets, league sets or a complete set. Prize cards had to be redeemed by Jan. 31, 1996.

Ted Williams Tunnel Opening Commemorative

This card was produced as the header for a 13-card set distributed at a luncheon in conjunction with Dec. 15, 1995 opening day ceremonies for the Ted Williams Tunnel, connecting South Boston with the city's airport, running beneath Boston Harbor. Just 3,000 sets were reported produced. This card is in the style of Topps' regular 1996 baseball card set and features gold-foil highlights on front. A career summary is on back. The card was later offered free with a $75 purchase from Topps Sta-

dium Club. (See also 1995 Choice Marketing Ted Williams Tunnel Opening Day Set.)

		NM/M
9	Ted Williams	35.00

"1952" Gold Mickey Mantle

This down-sized (2-1/2" x 3-1/2") version of Topps' first Mickey Mantle card was produced with embossed 22K gold-foil design on front and back and individually serial numbered within an edition of 50,000.

		NM/M
311	Mickey Mantle	10.00

1996 Topps Pre-Production

This set of promo cards was reportedly included in some 1995 Topps factory Hobby sets as an unadvertised insert. Cards are in the format of the forthcoming 1996 issue but do not have 1995 stats or career updates, and are numbered with a "PP" prefix.

		NM/M
Complete Set (9):		25.00
Common Player:		2.00
PP1	Cal Ripken Jr.	10.00
PP2	Thomas Howard	2.00
PP3	Rafael Bournigal	2.00
PP4	Ron Gant	2.00
PP5	Chipper Jones	7.50
PP6	Frank Thomas	6.00
PP7	Barry Bonds	10.00
PP8	Fred McGriff	2.00
PP9	Hideo Nomo	6.00

1996 Topps

At 440 cards, the basic Topps set for 1996 was the smallest regular-issue from the company since it adopted the 2-1/2" x 3-1/2" format in 1957. Honoring the late Mickey Mantle on card No. 7, Topps announced

it would hereafter retire that card number. Subsets in the 220-card Series 1 are Star Power, Commemoratives, Draft Picks, Tribute, AAA Stars and Future Stars. Series 2 subsets repeat Star Power and Draft Picks and add Prospects, Now Appearing and Rookie All-Stars. Three different factory sets were available with each including the 440-card base set and various inserts. The "Cereal Box" set, so named because of the resemblance of its four component boxes to single-serving cereal boxes, has four of the Mantle inserts. The Retail and Hobby sets each include seven randomly packed chase cards, a plastic-cased #7 Mantle card labeled "Last Day Production" and a Mantle Foundation card. In addition the Retail version has one of the 19 Mantle reprints.

	NM/M
Unopened Hobby Set (449):	40.00
Unopened Retail Set (450):	40.00
Unopened Cereal Box Set	
(444):	35.00
Complete Set (440):	25.00
Common Player:	.05
Wax Pack (12):	1.50
Wax Box (36):	35.00
Cello Pack (17):	2.50
Cello Box (24):	40.00
Vending Box (500):	12.50

1	Tony Gwynn	
	(Star Power)	.50
2	Mike Piazza	
	(Star Power)	.75
3	Greg Maddux	
	(Star Power)	.50
4	Jeff Bagwell	
	(Star Power)	.40
5	Larry Walker	
	(Star Power)	.05
6	Barry Larkin	
	(Star Power)	.05
7	Mickey Mantle	
	(Commemorative)	4.00
8	Tom Glavine	
	(Star Power)	.05
9	Craig Biggio	
	(Star Power)	.05
10	Barry Bonds	
	(Star Power)	1.00
11	Heathcliff Slocumb	
	(Star Power)	.05
12	Matt Williams	
	(Star Power)	.05
13	Todd Helton	
	(Draft Pick)	.75
14	Mark Redman	
	(Draft Pick)	.05
15	Michael Barrett	
	(Draft Pick)	.05
16	Ben Davis (Draft Pick)	.05
17	Juan LeBron	
	(Draft Pick)	.05
18	Tony McKnight	
	(Draft Pick)	.05
19	Ryan Jaroncyk	
	(Draft Pick)	.05
20	Corey Jenkins	
	(Draft Pick)	.05
21	Jim Scharrer	
	(Draft Pick)	.05
22	Mark Bellhorn RC	
	(Draft Pick)	.10
23	Jarrod Washburn RC	
	(Draft Pick)	.50
24	Geoff Jenkins RC	
	(Draft Pick)	1.00
25	Sean Casey RC	
	(Draft Pick)	3.00
26	Brett Tomko RC	
	(Draft Pick)	.10
27	Tony Fernandez	.05
28	Rich Becker	.05
29	Andujar Cedeno	.05
30	Paul Molitor	.75
31	Brent Gates	.05
32	Glenallen Hill	.05
33	Mike MacFarlane	.05
34	Manny Alexander	.05
35	Todd Zeile	.05
36	Joe Girardi	.05
37	Tony Tarasco	.05
38	Tim Belcher	.05
39	Tom Goodwin	.05
40	Orel Hershiser	.05
41	Tripp Cromer	.05
42	Sean Bergman	.05
43	Troy Percival	.05
44	Kevin Stocker	.05
45	Albert Belle	.05
46	Tony Eusebio	.05
47	Sid Roberson	.05
48	Todd Hollandsworth	.05
49	Mark Wohlers	.05
50	Kirby Puckett	1.00
51	Darren Holmes	.05

52	Ron Karkovice	.05
53	Al Martin	.05
54	Pat Rapp	.05
55	Mark Grace	.05
56	Greg Gagne	.05
57	Stan Javier	.05
58	Scott Sanders	.05
59	J.T. Snow	.05
60	David Justice	.05
61	Royce Clayton	.05
62	Kevin Foster	.05
63	Tim Naehring	.05
64	Orlando Miller	.05
65	Mike Mussina	.35
66	Jim Eisenreich	.05
67	Felix Fermin	.05
68	Bernie Williams	.05
69	Robb Nen	.05
70	Ron Gant	.05
71	Felipe Lira	.05
72	Jacob Brumfield	.05
73	John Mabry	.05
74	Mark Carreon	.05
75	Carlos Baerga	.05
76	Doug Dougherty	.05
77	Ryan Thompson	.05
78	Scott Leius	.05
79	Roger Pavlik	.05
80	Gary Sheffield	.45
81	Julian Tavarez	.05
82	Andy Ashby	.05
83	Mark Lemke	.05
84	Omar Vizquel	.05
85	Darren Daulton	.05
86	Mike Lansing	.05
87	Rusty Greer	.05
88	Dave Stevens	.05
89	Jose Offerman	.05
90	Tom Henke	.05
91	Troy O'Leary	.05
92	Michael Tucker	.05
93	Marvin Freeman	.05
94	Alex Diaz	.05
95	John Wetteland	.05
96	Cal Ripken Jr.	
	(Tribute Card)	1.00
97	Mike Mimbs	.05
98	Bobby Higginson	.05
99	Edgardo Alfonzo	.05
100	Frank Thomas	.75
101	Steve Gibralter, Bob Abreu	
	(AAA Stars)	.05
102	Brian Givens, T.J. Mathews	
	(AAA Stars)	.05
103	Chris Pritchett,	
	Trenidad Hubbard	
	(AAA Stars)	.05
104	Eric Owens, Butch Huskey	
	(AAA Stars)	.05
105	Doug Drabek	.05
106	Tomas Perez	.05
107	Mark Leiter	.05
108	Joe Oliver	.05
109	Tony Castillo	.05
110	Checklist	.05
111	Kevin Seitzer	.05
112	Pete Schourek	.05
113	Sean Berry	.05
114	Todd Stottlemyre	.05
115	Joe Carter	.05
116	Jeff King	.05
117	Dan Wilson	.05
118	Kurt Abbott	.05
119	Lyle Mouton	.05
120	Jose Rijo	.05
121	Curtis Goodwin	.05
122	Jose Valentin RC	.05
123	Ellis Burks	.05
124	David Cone	.05
125	Eddie Murray	.75
126	Brian Jordan	.05
127	Darrin Fletcher	.05
128	Curt Schilling	.25
129	Ozzie Guillen	.05
130	Kenny Rogers	.05
131	Tom Pagnozzi	.05
132	Garret Anderson	.05
133	Bobby Jones	.05
134	Chris Gomez	.05
135	Mike Stanley	.05
136	Hideo Nomo	.35
137	Jon Nunnally	.05
138	Tim Wakefield	.05
139	Steve Finley	.05
140	Ivan Rodriguez	.65
141	Quilvio Veras	.05
142	Mike Fetters	.05
143	Mike Greenwell	.05
144	Bill Pulsipher	.05
145	Mark McGwire	1.50
146	Frank Castillo	.05
147	Greg Vaughn	.05
148	Pat Hentgen	.05
149	Walt Weiss	.05
150	Randy Johnson	.75
151	David Segui	.05
152	Benji Gil	.05
153	Tom Candiotti	.05
154	Geronimo Berroa	.05
155	John Franco	.05
156	Jay Bell	.05
157	Mark Gubicza	.05
158	Hal Morris	.05
159	Wilson Alvarez	.05
160	Derek Bell	.05
161	Ricky Bottalico	.05
162	Bret Boone	.05
163	Brad Radke	.05

164	John Valentin	.05
165	Steve Avery	.05
166	Mark McLemore	.05
167	Danny Jackson	.05
168	Tino Martinez	.05
169	Shane Reynolds	.05
170	Terry Pendleton	.05
171	Jim Edmonds	.05
172	Esteban Loaiza	.05
173	Ray Durham	.05
174	Carlos Perez	.05
175	Raul Mondesi	.05
176	Steve Ontiveros	.05
177	Chipper Jones	1.00
178	Otis Nixon	.05
179	John Burkett	.05
180	Gregg Jefferies	.05
181	Denny Martinez	.05
182	Ken Caminiti	.05
183	Doug Jones	.05
184	Brian McRae	.05
185	Don Mattingly	1.00
186	Mel Rojas	.05
187	Marty Cordova	.05
188	Vinny Castilla	.05
189	John Smoltz	.05
190	Travis Fryman	.05
191	Chris Hoiles	.05
192	Chuck Finley	.05
193	Ryan Klesko	.05
194	Alex Fernandez	.05
195	Dante Bichette	.05
196	Eric Karros	.05
197	Roger Clemens	1.00
198	Randy Myers	.05
199	Tony Phillips	.05
200	Cal Ripken Jr.	2.00
201	Rod Beck	.05
202	Chad Curtis	.05
203	Jack McDowell	.05
204	Gary Gaetti	.05
205	Ken Griffey Jr.	1.25
206	Ramon Martinez	.05
207	Jeff Kent	.05
208	Brad Ausmus	.05
209	Devon White	.05
210	Jason Giambi (Future Star)	.45
211	Nomar Garciaparra (Future Star)	1.00
212	Billy Wagner (Future Star)	.05
213	Todd Greene (Future Star)	.05
214	Paul Wilson (Future Star)	.05
215	Johnny Damon (Future Star)	.25
216	Alan Benes (Future Star)	.05
217	Karim Garcia (Future Star)	.10
218	Dustin Hermanson (Future Star)	.05
219	Derek Jeter (Future Star)	2.00
220	Checklist	.05
221	Kirby Puckett (Star Power)	.50
222	Cal Ripken Jr. (Star Power)	1.00
223	Albert Belle (Star Power)	.05
224	Randy Johnson (Star Power)	.40
225	Wade Boggs (Star Power)	.50
226	Carlos Baerga (Star Power)	.05
227	Ivan Rodriguez (Star Power)	.30
228	Mike Mussina (Star Power)	.25
229	Frank Thomas (Star Power)	.40
230	Ken Griffey Jr. (Star Power)	.75
231	Jose Mesa (Star Power)	.05
232	Matt Morris RC (Draft Pick)	1.00
233	Craig Wilson RC (Draft Pick)	.50
234	Alvie Shepherd RC (Draft Pick)	.05
235	Randy Winn RC (Draft Pick)	.05
236	David Yocum RC (Draft Pick)	.05
237	Jason Brester RC (Draft Pick)	.05
238	Shane Monahan RC (Draft Pick)	.05
239	Brian McNichol RC (Draft Pick)	.05
240	Reggie Taylor (Draft Pick)	.05
241	Garrett Long (Draft Pick)	.05
242	Jonathan Johnson RC (Draft Pick)	.05
243	Jeff Liefer RC (Draft Pick)	.05
244	Brian Powell RC (Draft Pick)	.05
245	Brian Buchanan (Draft Pick)	.05
246	Mike Piazza	1.25
247	Edgar Martinez	.05

248	Chuck Knoblauch	.05
249	Andres Galarraga	.05
250	Tony Gwynn	1.00
251	Lee Smith	.05
252	Sammy Sosa	1.00
253	Jim Thome	.45
254	Frank Rodriguez	.05
255	Charlie Hayes	.05
256	Bernard Gilkey	.05
257	John Smiley	.05
258	Brady Anderson	.05
259	Rico Brogna	.05
260	Kirt Manwaring	.05
261	Len Dykstra	.05
262	Tom Glavine	.25
263	Vince Coleman	.05
264	John Olerud	.05
265	Orlando Merced	.05
266	Kent Mercker	.05
267	Terry Steinbach	.05
268	Brian Hunter	.05
269	Jeff Fassero	.05
270	Jay Buhner	.05
271	Jeff Brantley	.05
272	Tim Raines	.05
273	Jimmy Key	.05
274	Mo Vaughn	.05
275	Andre Dawson	.25
276	Jose Mesa	.05
277	Brett Butler	.05
278	Luis Gonzalez	.05
279	Steve Sparks	.05
280	Chili Davis	.05
281	Carl Everett	.05
282	Jeff Cirillo	.05
283	Thomas Howard	.05
284	Paul O'Neill	.05
285	Pat Meares	.05
286	Mickey Tettleton	.05
287	Rey Sanchez	.05
288	Bip Roberts	.05
289	Roberto Alomar	.15
290	Ruben Sierra	.05
291	John Flaherty	.05
292	Bret Saberhagen	.05
293	Barry Larkin	.05
294	Sandy Alomar	.05
295	Ed Sprague	.05
296	Gary DiSarcina	.05
297	Marquis Grissom	.05
298	John Frascatore	.05
299	Will Clark	.05
300	Barry Bonds	2.00
301	Ozzie Smith	1.00
302	Dave Nilsson	.05
303	Pedro Martinez	.75
304	Joey Cora	.05
305	Rick Aguilera	.05
306	Craig Biggio	.05
307	Jose Vizcaino	.05
308	Jeff Montgomery	.05
309	Moises Alou	.05
310	Robin Ventura	.05
311	David Wells	.05
312	Delino DeShields	.05
313	Trevor Hoffman	.05
314	Andy Benes	.05
315	Deion Sanders	.05
316	Jim Bullinger	.05
317	John Jaha	.05
318	Greg Maddux	1.00
319	Tim Salmon	.05
320	Ben McDonald	.05
321	Sandy Martinez RC	.05
322	Dan Miceli	.05
323	Wade Boggs	1.00
324	Ismael Valdes	.05
325	Juan Gonzalez	.35
326	Charles Nagy	.05
327	Ray Lankford	.05
328	Mark Portugal	.05
329	Bobby Bonilla	.05
330	Reggie Sanders	.05
331	Jamie Brewington	.05
332	Aaron Sele	.05
333	Pete Harnisch	.05
334	Cliff Floyd	.05
335	Cal Eldred	.05
336	Jason Bates	.05
337	Tony Clark (Now Appearing)	.05
338	Jose Herrera (Now Appearing)	.05
339	Alex Ochoa (Now Appearing)	.05
340	Mark Loretta (Now Appearing)	.05
341	Donne Wall RC (Now Appearing)	.05
342	Jason Kendall (Now Appearing)	.05
343	Shannon Stewart (Now Appearing)	.05
344	Brooks Kieschnick (Now Appearing)	.05
345	Chris Snopek (Now Appearing)	.05
346	Ruben Rivera (Now Appearing)	.05
347	Jeff Suppan (Now Appearing)	.05
348	Phil Nevin (Now Appearing)	.05
349	John Wasdin (Now Appearing)	.05
350	Jay Payton (Now Appearing)	.05

351	Tim Crabtree (Now Appearing)	.05
352	Rick Krivda (Now Appearing)	.05
353	Bob Wolcott (Now Appearing)	.05
354	Jimmy Haynes (Now Appearing)	.05
355	Herb Perry (Now Appearing)	.05
356	Ryne Sandberg	1.00
357	Harold Baines	.05
358	Chad Ogea	.05
359	Lee Tinsley	.05
360	Matt Williams	.05
361	Randy Velarde	.05
362	Jose Canseco	.40
363	Larry Walker	.05
364	Kevin Appier	.05
365	Darryl Hamilton	.05
366	Jose Lima	.05
367	Javy Lopez	.05
368	Dennis Eckersley	.65
369	Jason Isringhausen	.05
370	*Mickey Morandini	.05
371	Scott Cooper	.05
372	Jim Abbott	.05
373	Paul Sorrento	.05
374	Chris Hammond	.05
375	Lance Johnson	.05
376	Kevin Brown	.05
377	Luis Alicea	.05
378	Andy Pettitte	.25
379	Dean Palmer	.05
380	Jeff Bagwell	.75
381	Jaime Navarro	.05
382	Rondell White	.05
383	Erik Hanson	.05
384	Pedro Munoz	.05
385	Heathcliff Slocumb	.05
386	Wally Joyner	.05
387	Bob Tewksbury	.05
388	David Bell	.05
389	Fred McGriff	.05
390	Mike Henneman	.05
391	Robby Thompson	.05
392	Norm Charlton	.05
393	Cecil Fielder	.05
394	Benito Santiago	.05
395	Rafael Palmeiro	.65
396	Ricky Bones	.05
397	Rickey Henderson	.75
398	C.J. Nitkowski	.05
399	Shawon Dunston	.05
400	Manny Ramirez	.75
401	Bill Swift	.05
402	Chad Fonville	.05
403	Joey Hamilton	.05
404	Alex Gonzalez	.05
405	Roberto Hernandez	.05
406	Jeff Blauser	.05
407	LaTroy Hawkins	.05
408	Greg Colbrunn	.05
409	Todd Hundley	.05
410	Glenn Dishman	.05
411	Joe Vitiello	.05
412	Todd Worrell	.05
413	Wil Cordero	.05
414	Ken Hill	.05
415	Carlos Garcia	.05
416	Bryan Rekar	.05
417	Shawn Green (Topps Rookie All-Star)	.40
418	Tyler Green	.05
419	Mike Blowers	.05
420	Kenny Lofton	.05
421	Denny Neagle	.05
422	Jeff Conine	.05
423	Mark Langston	.05
424	Steve Cox, Jesse Ibarra RC, Derrek Lee, Ron Wright RC (Prospects)	.10
425	Jim Bonnici RC, Billy Owens, Richie Sexson, Daryle Ward RC (Prospects)	.10
426	Kevin Jordan, Bobby Morris RC, Desi Relaford, Adam Riggs RC (Prospects)	.10
427	Tim Harkrider, Rey Ordonez, Neifi Perez, Enrique Wilson (Prospects)	.05
428	Bartolo Colon, Doug Million, Rafael Orellano, Ray Ricken RC (Prospects)	.05
429	Jeff D'Amico, Marty Janzen RC, Gary Rath, Clint Sodowsky (Prospects)	.05
430	Matt Drews, Rich Hunter RC, Matt Ruebel RC, Bret Wagner (Prospects)	.05
431	Jaime Bluma, Dave Coggin RC, Steve Montgomery, Brandon Reed (Prospects)	.05

432	Mike Figga, Raul Ibanez RC, Paul Konerko, Julio Mosquera (Prospects)	.25
433	Brian Barber, Marc Kroon, Marc Valdes, Don Wengert (Prospects)	.05
434	George Arias, Chris Haas RC, Scott Rolen, Scott Spiezio (Prospects)	.50
435	Brian Banks RC, Vladimir Guerrero, Andruw Jones, Billy McMillon (Prospects)	.50
436	Roger Cedeno, Derrick Gibson, Ben Grieve, Shane Spencer RC (Prospects)	.50
437	Anton French, Demond Smith, Darond Stovall RC, Keith Williams (Prospects)	.10
438	Michael Coleman RC, Jacob Cruz, Richard Hidalgo, Charles Peterson (Prospects)	.10
439	Trey Beamon, Yamil Benitez, Jermaine Dye, Angel Echevarria (Prospects)	.05
440	Checklist	.05

Confrontations

Head-to-head stats among baseball's top pitchers and hitters are featured in this insert set. The cards were seeded one per pack in the special 50-cent packs sold exclusively at Wal-Mart during the T206 Honus Wagner card giveaway promotion. Fronts have player action poses against a granite background and are highlighted in gold foil. Backs have a portrait photo and stats.

		NM/M
Complete Set (15):		3.50
Common Player:		.06
1	Ken Griffey Jr.	.65
2	Cal Ripken Jr.	1.00
3	Edgar Martinez	.05
4	Kirby Puckett	.45
5	Frank Thomas	.35
6	Barry Bonds	1.00
7	Reggie Sanders	.05
8	Andres Galarraga	.05
9	Tony Gwynn	.45
10	Mike Piazza	.65
11	Randy Johnson	.35
12	Mike Mussina	.25
13	Roger Clemens	.50
14	Tom Glavine	.25
15	Greg Maddux	.45

Mickey Mantle Commemorative Last Day

To mark the last day on which Topps would produce a #7 baseball card, the Mantle card from its 1996 set was issued in this sealed plastic case with a gold-foil logo on back.

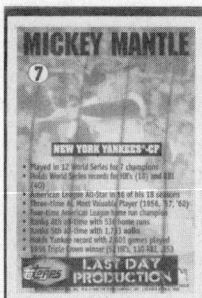

		NM/M
7	Mickey Mantle	5.00

Mickey Mantle Reprints

One of Mickey Mantle's regular-issue Bowman or Topps cards from each year 1951-1969 was reproduced in 2-1/2" x 3-1/2" format as a Series 1 insert. Each card carries a gold-foil commemorative seal in one corner of the front. The reprints are found one per six retail packs and, in hobby, once per nine packs. The 1965-69 reprints were somewhat short-printed (four 1965-69 cards for each 1951-1964) and are 20 percent scarcer.

		NM/M
Complete Set (19):		80.00
Common Mantle:		5.00
Common SP Mantle (15-19):		8.00
1	1951 Bowman #253	15.00
2	1952 Topps #311	15.00
3	1953 Topps #82	5.00
4	1954 Bowman #65	5.00
5	1955 Bowman #202	5.00
6	1956 Topps #135	5.00
7	1957 Topps #95	5.00
8	1958 Topps #150	5.00
9	1959 Topps #10	5.00
10	1960 Topps #350	5.00
11	1961 Topps #300	5.00
12	1962 Topps #200	5.00
13	1963 Topps #200	5.00
14	1964 Topps #50	5.00
15	1965 Topps #350	8.00
16	1966 Topps #50	8.00
17	1967 Topps #150	8.00
18	1968 Topps #280	8.00
19	1969 Topps #500	8.00

Mickey Mantle Finest Reprints

Nineteen of Mickey Mantle's regular-issue Bowman and Topps cards from 1951-1969 were printed in Finest technology for this Series 2 insert set. Each card's chrome front is protected with a peel-off plastic layer. Average insertion rate for the Mantle Finest reprints is one per 18 packs. The 1965-69 reprints were printed in a ratio of four for every five 1951-64 reprints, making them 20 percent scarcer. Unmarked Refractor versions of each card were inserted at an average rate of 1:144 packs.

		NM/M
Complete Set (19):		90.00
Common Card (1-14):		6.00
Common Shortprint (15-19):		8.00
Refractors:		3X
Inserted 1:144		
1	1951 Bowman #253	15.00
2	1952 Topps #311	15.00
3	1953 Topps #82	6.00
4	1954 Bowman #65	6.00
5	1955 Bowman #202	6.00
6	1956 Topps #135	6.00
7	1957 Topps #95	6.00
8	1958 Topps #150	6.00
9	1959 Topps #10	6.00
10	1960 Topps #350	6.00
11	1961 Topps #300	6.00
12	1962 Topps #200	6.00
13	1963 Topps #200	6.00
14	1964 Topps #50	6.00
15	1965 Topps #350	8.00
16	1966 Topps #50	8.00
17	1967 Topps #150	8.00
18	1968 Topps #280	8.00
19	1969 Topps #500	8.00

Mickey Mantle Case Inserts

Inserted one per case of Series 2 Topps, these special versions of the 19 Mickey Mantle reprint cards come sealed in a soft plastic holder. The plastic sleeve has a gold-foil stamp at bottom-back which reads "FACTORY TOPPS SEAL 1996." Like the other Mantle reprints, the 1965-69 cards are somewhat scarcer due to short-printing.

		NM/M
Complete Set (19):		375.00
Common Mantle:		20.00
Common SP Mantle (15-19):		30.00
1	1951 Bowman #253	60.00
2	1952 Topps #311	60.00
3	1953 Topps #82	30.00
4	1954 Bowman #65	20.00
5	1955 Bowman #202	20.00
6	1956 Topps #135	20.00
7	1957 Topps #95	20.00
8	1958 Topps #150	20.00
9	1959 Topps #10	20.00
10	1960 Topps #350	20.00
11	1961 Topps #300	20.00
12	1962 Topps #200	20.00
13	1963 Topps #200	20.00
14	1964 Topps #50	20.00
15	1965 Topps #350	30.00
16	1966 Topps #50	30.00
17	1967 Topps #150	30.00
18	1968 Topps #280	30.00
19	1969 Topps #500	30.00

Mickey Mantle Redemption

Each of the 19 Mantle reprint cards, minus the commemorative gold-foil stamp on front, was also issued in a sweepstakes insert. Seeded one per 108 packs, these cards could be sent in for a chance to win the authentic Mantle card pictured on front. Between one and 10 genuine Mantles were awarded for each of the 19 years. Cards entered in the sweepstakes were not returned when the contest ended Oct. 15, 1996. The sweepstakes cards are a Series 2 exclusive insert.

		NM/M
Complete Set (19):		200.00
Common Mantle:		10.00
Inserted 1:108 Series 2 Retail		
1	1951 Bowman #253	35.00
2	1952 Topps #311	35.00
3	1953 Topps #82	15.00
4	1954 Bowman #65	10.00
5	1955 Bowman #202	10.00
6	1956 Topps #135	10.00
7	1957 Topps #95	10.00
8	1958 Topps #150	10.00
9	1959 Topps #10	10.00
10	1960 Topps #350	10.00
11	1961 Topps #300	10.00
12	1962 Topps #200	10.00
13	1963 Topps #200	10.00
14	1964 Topps #50	10.00
15	1965 Topps #350	10.00
16	1966 Topps #50	10.00
17	1967 Topps #150	10.00
18	1968 Topps #280	10.00
19	1969 Topps #500	10.00

Mickey Mantle Commemorative Card Sheet

In conjunction with its program of reprinting most of the Mick's Topps and Bowman cards of the 1950s-1960s, Topps created this limited edition (numbered to 10,000) framed sheet depicting 20 cards surrounding an enlarged portrait from his famed 1952 Topps card. The sheet is embossed with a gold-foil #7 seal and was sold with a certificate of authenticity from Topps' president. The framed sheet measures about 19-1/2" x 25".

	NM/M
Framed Sheet:	80.00

Mickey Mantle Foundation

This black-and-white card was an insert exclusive to specially marked 1996 Topps factory sets. In standard 2-1/2" x 3-1/2" format, the card offers on its back information about the foundation and its work in health care and organ donation causes.

	NM/M
Mickey Mantle	4.00

Masters of the Game

Appearing at a one per 18 pack rate, these inserts are exclusive to Series 1 hobby packs.

		NM/M
Complete Set (20):		20.00
Common Player:		.35
1	Dennis Eckersley	.75
2	Denny Martinez	.35
3	Eddie Murray	1.00
4	Paul Molitor	1.00
5	Ozzie Smith	1.50
6	Rickey Henderson	1.00
7	Tim Raines	.35
8	Lee Smith	.35
9	Cal Ripken Jr.	4.00
10	Chili Davis	.35
11	Wade Boggs	1.50
12	Tony Gwynn	1.50
13	Don Mattingly	2.00
14	Bret Saberhagen	.35
15	Kirby Puckett	1.50
16	Joe Carter	.35
17	Roger Clemens	2.00
18	Barry Bonds	4.00
19	Greg Maddux	1.50
20	Frank Thomas	1.00

Mystery Finest

Each Mystery Finest insert has an opaque black film over the card front, concealing the identity of the player until removed. The inserts are seeded at the rate of one per 36 packs.

		NM/M
Complete Set (21)		25.00
Common Player:		.50
Refractors:		1.5X
M1	Hideo Nomo	1.00
M2	Greg Maddux	2.00
M3	Randy Johnson	1.50
M4	Chipper Jones	2.00
M5	Marty Cordova	.50
M6	Garret Anderson	.50
M7	Cal Ripken Jr.	4.00
M8	Kirby Puckett	2.00
M9	Tony Gwynn	2.00
M10	Manny Ramirez	1.50
M11	Jim Edmonds	.50
M12	Mike Piazza	2.50
M13	Barry Bonds	4.00
M14	Raul Mondesi	.50
M15	Sammy Sosa	2.00
M16	Ken Griffey Jr.	2.50
M17	Albert Belle	.50
M18	Dante Bichette	.50
M19	Mo Vaughn	.50
M20	Jeff Bagwell	1.50
M21	Frank Thomas	1.50

5-Star Mystery Finest

The 5-Star Mystery Finest inserts have an opaque black film over the card front, like the regular Mystery Finest, but has the words "5-Star" in large letters across the background. They are inserted at the average rate of one per 36 packs.

		NM/M
Complete Set (5):		12.50
Common Player:		2.00
Refractors:		2X
M22	Hideo Nomo	2.00
M23	Cal Ripken Jr.	5.00
M24	Mike Piazza	3.00
M25	Ken Griffey Jr.	3.00
M26	Frank Thomas	2.50

Power Boosters

This insert set is printed in Topps' "Power Matrix" technology, replacing two regular cards when found on the average of once per 36 packs. The Power Boosters reproduce the Star Power and Draft Picks subsets on a double-thick card.

		NM/M
Complete Set (26):		30.00
Common Player:		1.00
1	Tony Gwynn (Star Power)	2.00
2	Mike Piazza (Star Power)	3.00
3	Greg Maddux (Star Power)	2.00
4	Jeff Bagwell (Star Power)	1.50
5	Larry Walker (Star Power)	1.00
6	Barry Larkin (Star Power)	1.00
7	Tom Glavine (Star Power)	1.25
9	Craig Biggio (Star Power)	1.00
10	Barry Bonds (Star Power)	4.00
11	Heathcliff Slocumb (Star Power)	1.00
12	Matt Williams (Star Power)	1.00
13	Todd Helton (Draft Pick)	4.00
14	Mark Redman (Draft Pick)	1.00
15	Michael Barrett (Draft Pick)	1.00
16	Ben Davis (Draft Pick)	1.00
17	Juan LeBron (Draft Pick)	1.00
18	Tony McKnight (Draft Pick)	1.00
19	Ryan Jaroncyk (Draft Pick)	1.00
20	Corey Jenkins (Draft Pick)	1.00
21	Jim Scharrer (Draft Pick)	1.00
22	Mark Bellhorn (Draft Pick)	1.00
23	Jarrod Washburn (Draft Pick)	1.00
24	Geoff Jenkins (Draft Pick)	1.00
25	Sean Casey (Draft Pick)	2.00
26	Brett Tomko (Draft Pick)	1.00

Profiles-AL

Ten cards from this insert issue can be found in each of Topps Series 1 and 2. Analyzing an up-and-coming star, the cards are found every 12th pack, on average.

		NM/M
Complete Set (20):		8.00
Common Player:		.25
1	Roberto Alomar	.30
2	Carlos Baerga	.25
3	Albert Belle	.25
4	Cecil Fielder	.25
5	Ken Griffey Jr.	1.00
6	Randy Johnson	.60
7	Paul O'Neill	.25
8	Cal Ripken Jr.	1.50
9	Frank Thomas	.60
10	Mo Vaughn	.25
11	Jay Buhner	.25
12	Marty Cordova	.25
13	Jim Edmonds	.25
14	Juan Gonzalez	.35
15	Kenny Lofton	.25
16	Edgar Martinez	.25
17	Don Mattingly	.25
18	Mark McGwire	1.25
19	Rafael Palmeiro	.50
20	Tim Salmon	.25

Profiles-NL

Projected future stars of the National League are featured in this insert set. Ten players each are found in Series 1 and 2 packs at the rate of one per 12, on average.

		NM/M
Complete Set (20):		7.00
Common Player:		.25
1	Jeff Bagwell	.60
2	Derek Bell	.25
3	Barry Bonds	1.50
4	Greg Maddux	.75
5	Fred McGriff	.25
6	Raul Mondesi	.25
7	Mike Piazza	1.00
8	Reggie Sanders	.25
9	Sammy Sosa	.75
10	Larry Walker	.25
11	Dante Bichette	.25
12	Andres Galarraga	.25
13	Ron Gant	.25
14	Tom Glavine	.35
15	Chipper Jones	.75
16	David Justice	.25
17	Barry Larkin	.25
18	Hideo Nomo	.40
19	Gary Sheffield	.40
20	Matt Williams	.25

Road Warriors

These inserts feature top hitters and were only found in Series 2 packs sold at Wal-Mart stores. Cards have an RW prefix to their number. Fronts have action photos and gold foil highlights. Backs feature a portrait photo and hitting stats from the player's favorite out-of-town ballparks.

		NM/M
Complete Set (20):		9.00
Common Player:		.25
1	Derek Bell	.25
2	Albert Belle	.25
3	Craig Biggio	.25
4	Barry Bonds	2.50
5	Jay Buhner	.25
6	Jim Edmonds	.25
7	Gary Gaetti	.25
8	Ron Gant	.25
9	Edgar Martinez	.25
10	Tino Martinez	.25
11	Mark McGwire	1.50
12	Mike Piazza	1.25
13	Manny Ramirez	1.00
14	Tim Salmon	.25
15	Reggie Sanders	.25
16	Frank Thomas	1.00
17	John Valentin	.25
18	Mo Vaughn	.25
19	Robin Ventura	.25
20	Matt Williams	.25

Wrecking Crew

Printed on foilboard stock, cards of 15 players known for their hitting prowess are featured in this insert set. Found only in Series 2 hobby packs, the inserts are a one per 72 packs find, on average. Cards are numbered with a "WC" prefix.

		NM/M
Complete Set (15):		20.00
Common Player:		.50
1	Jeff Bagwell	1.50
2	Albert Belle	.50
3	Barry Bonds	5.00
4	Jose Canseco	.75
5	Joe Carter	.50
6	Cecil Fielder	.50
7	Ron Gant	.50
8	Juan Gonzalez	.75
9	Ken Griffey Jr.	3.00
10	Fred McGriff	.50
11	Mark McGwire	4.00
12	Mike Piazza	3.00
13	Frank Thomas	1.50
14	Mo Vaughn	.50
15	Matt Williams	.50

Team Topps

Some of baseball's most popular players and their teammates are featured on specially marked cards sold in blister packed team sets along with a jumbo "Big Topps" version of the team superstar's card. The team sets were a Wal-Mart exclusive, selling for around $5. Most of the Team Topps cards are identical to the regular-issue versions except for the addition of a gold-foil Team Topps logo on the card front. Several cards in this team set issue have had their regular and Star Power backs transposed.

		NM/M
Complete Set (84):		25.00
Common Player:		.10
Orioles Team Set (19):		8.00
Cal Ripken, Jr. Big Topps:		4.00
34	Manny Alexander	.10
65	Mike Mussina (Star Power front, regular back.)	.50
96	Cal Ripken Jr. (2,131)	1.25
121	Curtis Goodwin	.10
183	Doug Jones	.10
191	Chris Hoiles	.10
200	Cal Ripken Jr.	2.50
222	Cal Ripken Jr. (Star Power)	1.25
228	Mike Mussina (Regular-card front, Star Power back.)	.50
234	Alvie Shepherd (Draft Pick)	.10
258	Brady Anderson	.10
320	Ben McDonald	.10
329	Bobby Bonilla	.10
	Rick Krivda (Now Appearing)	.10
354	Jimmy Haynes (Now Appearing)	.10
357	Harold Baines	.10
376	Kevin Brown	.10
395	Rafael Palmeiro	.65
Cubs Team Set (16):		5.00
Ryne Sandberg Big Topps:		3.00
35	Todd Zeile	.10
55	Mark Grace	.10
62	Kevin Foster	.10
146	Frank Castillo	.10
184	Brian McRae	.10
198	Randy Myers	.10
239	Brian McNichol (Draft Pick)	.10
252	Sammy Sosa	1.00
278	Luis Gonzalez	.10
287	Rey Sanchez	.10
316	Jim Bullinger	.10
344	Brooks Kieshnick (Now Appearing)	.10
356	Ryne Sandberg	1.00
381	Jaime Navarro	.10
399	Shawon Dunston	.10
White Sox Team Set (15):		5.00
Frank Thomas Big Topps:		2.50
52	Ron Karkovice	.10
100	Frank Thomas	.75
119	Lyle Mouton	.10
	Ozzie Guillen	.10
159	Wilson Alvarez	.10
173	Ray Durham (All-Star Rookie)	.10
194	Alex Fernandez	.10
	Frank Thomas (Star Power)	.40
243	Jeff Liefer (Draft Pick)	.10
272	Tim Raines	.10
310	Robin Ventura	.10
345	Chris Snopek (Now Appearing)	.10
375	Lance Johnson	.10
405	Roberto Hernandez	.10
Yankees Team Set (19):		8.00
Derek Jeter Big Topps:		4.00
7	Mickey Mantle	3.00
27	Tony Fernandez	.10
68	Bernie Williams	.10
95	John Wetteland	.10
124	David Cone	.10
135	Mike Stanley	.10
185	Don Mattingly	1.25
203	Jack McDowell	.10
219	Derek Jeter (Future Star)	2.50
225	Wade Boggs (Star Power)	.50
245	Brian Buchanan (Draft Pick)	.10
273	Jimmy Key	.10
284	Paul O'Neill	.10
290	Ruben Sierra	.10
323	Wade Boggs	1.00
346	Ruben Rivera (Now Appearing)	.10
361	Randy Velarde	.10
378	Andy Pettitte	.35
Rangers Team Set (15):		5.00
Juan Gonzalez Big Topps:		2.00
79	Roger Pavlik	.10
87	Rusty Greer	.10
130	Kenny Rogers	.10
140	Ivan Rodriguez	.65
152	Benji Gil	.10
166	Mark McLemore	.10
178	Otis Nixon	.10
227	Ivan Rodriguez (Star Power)	.35
242	Jonathan Johnson (Draft Pick)	.10
286	Mickey Tettleton	.10
299	Will Clark	.10
325	Juan Gonzalez	.35
387	Bob Tewksbury	.10
379	Dean Palmer	.10

American League Champion Cleveland Indians

Sold in a blister pack at Wal-Mart stores, this team set features specially overprinted versions of the Indians' regular' per-size "Big Topps" card of Albert Belle. Each card carries a color logo recognizing the Tribe's A.L. Championship season of 1995. Sets sold for around $5.

JIM THOME

MIKE PIAZZA

	NM/M
Complete Set (21):	4.00
Common Player:	.10
Albert Belle Big Topps:	2.00
25 Sean Casey	1.50
40 Orel Hershiser	.10
45 Albert Belle	.10
75 Carlos Baerga	.10
81 Julian Tavarez	.10
84 Omar Vizquel	.10
125 Eddie Murray	.75
181 Denny Martinez	.10
223 Albert Belle (Star Power)	.10
226 Carlos Baerga (Star Power)	.10
231 Jose Mesa (Star Power)	.10
253 Jim Thome	.65
276 Jose Mesa	.10
294 Sandy Alomar	.10
326 Charles Nagy	.10
355 Herb Perry	.10
358 Chad Ogea	.10
373 Paul Sorrento	.10
400 Manny Ramirez	.75
414 Ken Hill	.10
420 Kenny Lofton	.10

A.L. West Champion Seattle Mariners

JOEY CORA

These specially marked versions of Topps' regular '96 cards were sold for around $5 in a blister pack with a Ken Griffey, Jr. "Big Topps" card. The team sets were a Wal-Mart exclusive. Each of the Mariners' cards is overprinted with a color A.L. West Champions logo. Cards are otherwise identical to the regular set.

	NM/M
Complete Set (18):	3.50
Common Player:	.10
Ken Griffey, Jr. Big Topps:	3.50
38 Tim Belcher	.10
67 Felix Fermin	.10
94 Alex Diaz	.10
117 Dan Wilson	.10
150 Randy Johnson	.75
168 Tino Martinez	.10
205 Ken Griffey Jr.	1.50
224 Randy Johnson (Star Power)	.40
230 Ken Griffey Jr. (Star Power)	.75
238 Shane Monahan (Draft Pick)	.10
247 Edgar Martinez	.10
263 Vince Coleman	.10
270 Jay Buhner	.10
304 Joey Cora	.10
314 Andy Benes	.10
353 Bob Wolcott (Now Appearing)	.10
392 Norm Charlton	.10
419 Mike Blowers	.10

Dodger Stadium 35th Anniversary L.A. Dodgers

Celebrating 35 seasons of play in Chavez Ravine, this team

318 Greg Maddux	1.00
367 Javy Lopez	.10
389 Fred McGriff	.10
406 Jeff Blauser	.10

Big Topps

BIG TOPPS

KEN GRIFFEY JR.

These double-size (3-1/2" x 5") cards are found exclusively in team-set blister packs prepared by Treat Entertainments for sale at Wal-Mart stores. Suggested retail price was just under $5. The Big Topps cards feature the fronts of the players' regular 1996 Topps card set against a marbled green background. Backs are in black-and-white with copyright data and licensors' logos. The unnumbered cards are checklisted here alphabetically.

	NM/M
Complete Set (9):	20.00
Common Player:	2.00
(1) Albert Belle	2.00
(2) Juan Gonzalez	2.00
(3) Ken Griffey Jr.	3.50
(4) Derek Jeter	4.00
(5) Greg Maddux	3.00
(6) Hideo Nomo	2.00
(7) Cal Ripken Jr.	4.00
(8) Ryne Sandberg	3.00
(9) Frank Thomas	2.50

1996 Topps Chrome Promo Sheet

This promotional sheet was issued to promote the first annual issue of Topps Chrome baseball cards. The 8" x 5" sheet reproduces three of the card fronts from the forthcoming set in Topps' "Brilliant Chromium" technology. Back of the sheet is conventionally printed and advertises the set and its chase cards.

	NM/M
Sheet:	5.00

1996 Topps Chrome

JAY BUHNER

In conjunction with baseball's postseason, Topps introduced the premiere edition of Chrome Baseball. The set has 165 of the elite players from 1996 Topps Series 1 and 2. Card #7 is a Mickey Mantle tribute card. There are two insert

sets: Masters of the Game and Wrecking Crew, and scarcer Refractor versions, for each.

	NM/M
Complete Set (165):	40.00
Common Player:	.10
Refractors:	3X
Pack (4):	2.00
Wax Box (24):	30.00
1 Tony Gwynn (Star Power)	1.00
2 Mike Piazza (Star Power)	1.25
3 Greg Maddux (Star Power)	1.00
4 Jeff Bagwell (Star Power)	.75
5 Larry Walker (Star Power)	.10
6 Barry Larkin (Star Power)	.10
7 Mickey Mantle (Commemorative)	9.00
8 Tom Glavine (Star Power)	.10
9 Craig Biggio (Star Power)	.10
10 Barry Bonds (Star Power)	2.00
11 Heathcliff Slocumb (Star Power)	.10
12 Matt Williams (Star Power)	.10
13 Todd Helton (Draft Pick)	2.00
14 Paul Molitor	1.50
15 Glenallen Hill	.10
16 Troy Percival	.10
17 Albert Belle	.10
18 Mark Wohlers	.10
19 Kirby Puckett	2.00
20 Mark Grace	.10
21 J.T. Snow	.10
22 David Justice	.10
23 Mike Mussina	.75
24 Bernie Williams	.10
25 Ron Gant	.10
26 Carlos Baerga	.10
27 Gary Sheffield	.65
28 Cal Ripken Jr. (Tribute Card)	2.00
29 Frank Thomas	1.50
30 Kevin Seitzer	.10
31 Joe Carter	.10
32 Jeff King	.10
33 David Cone	.10
34 Eddie Murray	1.50
35 Brian Jordan	.10
36 Garret Anderson	.10
37 Hideo Nomo	.75
38 Steve Finley	.10
39 Ivan Rodriguez	1.25
40 Quilvio Veras	.10
41 Mark McGwire	3.00
42 Greg Vaughn	.10
43 Randy Johnson	1.50
44 David Segui	.10
45 Derek Bell	.10
46 John Valentin	.10
47 Steve Avery	.10
48 Tino Martinez	.10
49 Shane Reynolds	.10
50 Jim Edmonds	.10
51 Raul Mondesi	.10
52 Chipper Jones	2.00
53 Gregg Jefferies	.10
54 Ken Caminiti	.10
55 Brian McRae	.10
56 Don Mattingly	2.25
57 Marty Cordova	.10
58 Vinny Castilla	.10
59 John Smoltz	.10
60 Travis Fryman	.10
61 Ryan Klesko	.10
62 Alex Fernandez	.10
63 Dante Bichette	.10
64 Eric Karros	.10
65 Roger Clemens	2.25
66 Randy Myers	.10
67 Cal Ripken Jr.	4.00
68 Rod Beck	.10
69 Jack McDowell	.10
70 Ken Griffey Jr.	2.50
71 Ramon Martinez	.10
72 Jason Giambi (Future Star)	.75
73 Nomar Garciaparra (Future Star)	2.00
74 Billy Wagner (Future Star)	.10
75 Todd Greene (Future Star)	.10
76 Paul Wilson (Future Star)	.10
77 Johnny Damon (Future Star)	.35
78 Alan Benes (Future Star)	.10
79 Karim Garcia (Future Star)	.25
80 Derek Jeter (Future Star)	4.00
81 Kirby Puckett (Star Power)	1.00
82 Cal Ripken Jr. (Star Power)	2.00

83 Albert Belle (Star Power)	.10
84 Randy Johnson (Star Power)	.40
85 Wade Boggs (Star Power)	1.00
86 Carlos Baerga (Star Power)	.10
87 Ivan Rodriguez (Star Power)	.35
88 Mike Mussina (Star Power)	.30
89 Frank Thomas (Star Power)	.75
90 Ken Griffey Jr. (Star Power)	1.25
91 Jose Mesa (Star Power)	.10
92 Matt Morris RC (Draft Pick)	1.00
93 Mike Piazza	2.50
94 Edgar Martinez	.10
95 Chuck Knoblauch	.10
96 Andres Galarraga	.10
97 Tony Gwynn	2.00
98 Lee Smith	.10
99 Sammy Sosa	2.00
100 Jim Thome	1.25
101 Bernard Gilkey	.10
102 Brady Anderson	.10
103 Rico Brogna	.10
104 Lenny Dykstra	.10
105 Tom Glavine	.35
106 John Olerud	.10
107 Terry Steinbach	.10
108 Brian Hunter	.10
109 Jay Buhner	.10
110 Mo Vaughn	.10
111 Jose Mesa	.10
112 Brett Butler	.10
113 Chili Davis	.10
114 Paul O'Neill	.10
115 Roberto Alomar	.35
116 Barry Larkin	.10
117 Marquis Grissom	.10
118 Will Clark	.10
119 Barry Bonds	4.00
120 Ozzie Smith	2.00
121 Pedro Martinez	1.50
122 Craig Biggio	.10
123 Moises Alou	.10
124 Robin Ventura	.10
125 Greg Maddux	2.00
126 Tim Salmon	.10
127 Wade Boggs	2.00
128 Ismael Valdes	.10
129 Juan Gonzalez	.75
130 Ray Lankford	.10
131 Bobby Bonilla	.10
132 Reggie Sanders	.10
133 Alex Ochoa (Now Appearing)	.10
134 Mark Loretta (Now Appearing)	.10
135 Jason Kendall (Now Appearing)	.10
136 Brooks Kieschnick (Now Appearing)	.10
137 Chris Snopek (Now Appearing)	.10
138 Ruben Rivera (Now Appearing)	.10
139 Jeff Suppan (Now Appearing)	.10
140 John Wasdin (Now Appearing)	.10
141 Jay Payton (Now Appearing)	.10
142 Rick Krivda (Now Appearing)	.10
143 Jimmy Haynes (Now Appearing)	.10
144 Ryne Sandberg	2.00
145 Matt Williams	.10
146 Jose Canseco	.65
147 Larry Walker	.10
148 Kevin Appier	.10
149 Javy Lopez	.10
150 Dennis Eckersley	1.25
151 Jason Isringhausen	.10
152 Dean Palmer	.10
153 Jeff Bagwell	1.50
154 Rondell White	.10
155 Wally Joyner	.10
156 Fred McGriff	.10
157 Cecil Fielder	.10
158 Rafael Palmeiro	1.25
159 Rickey Henderson	1.50
160 Shawon Dunston	.10
161 Manny Ramirez	1.50
162 Alex Gonzalez	.10
163 Shawn Green	.45
164 Kenny Lofton	.10
165 Jeff Conine	.10

Masters of the Game

These 1996 Topps Chrome inserts were seeded one per every 12 packs. Each of the cards is also reprinted in a Refractor version; these cards are seeded one per every 36 packs.

	NM/M
Complete Set (20):	35.00

MASTER OF THE GAME

ROGER CLEMENS

	NM/M
Common Player:	1.00
Refractors:	1.5X
1 Dennis Eckersley	2.00
2 Denny Martinez	1.00
3 Eddie Murray	2.50
4 Paul Molitor	2.50
5 Ozzie Smith	3.50
6 Rickey Henderson	2.50
7 Tim Raines	1.00
8 Lee Smith	1.00
9 Cal Ripken Jr.	6.00
10 Chili Davis	1.00
11 Wade Boggs	3.50
12 Tony Gwynn	3.50
13 Don Mattingly	4.00
14 Bret Saberhagen	1.00
15 Kirby Puckett	3.50
16 Joe Carter	1.00
17 Roger Clemens	4.00
18 Barry Bonds	6.00
19 Greg Maddux	3.50
20 Frank Thomas	2.50

Wrecking Crew

WRECKING CREW

BARRY BONDS

Wrecking Crew insert cards were inserted one per every 24 packs of 1996 Topps Chrome Baseball. Refractor versions were also made for these cards; they are seeded one per every 72 packs. Cards are numbered with a "WC" prefix.

	NM/M
Complete Set (15):	25.00
Common Player:	1.00
Refractors:	1.5X
1 Jeff Bagwell	2.50
2 Albert Belle	1.00
3 Barry Bonds	5.00
4 Jose Canseco	1.50
5 Joe Carter	1.00
6 Cecil Fielder	1.00
7 Ron Gant	1.00
8 Juan Gonzalez	1.25
9 Ken Griffey Jr.	3.50
10 Fred McGriff	1.00
11 Mark McGwire	4.00
12 Mike Piazza	4.00
13 Frank Thomas	2.50
14 Mo Vaughn	1.00
15 Matt Williams	1.00

1996 Topps Gallery

MARQUIS GRISSOM

This 180-card set is printed on 24-point stock utilizing metallic inks and a high-definition printing process. Then a high-gloss film is applied to each card, followed by foil stamping. The regular set is broken down into five subsets - The Classics, The Modernists, The Futurists, The Masters and New Editions.

set of specially marked cards was issued in a blister pack with a jumbo Hideo Nomo "Big Topps" card. Selling for about $5, the team set was a Wal-Mart exclusive. Otherwise identical to the regular '96 Topps cards, these are overprinted with a colorful 35 Seasons logo. The backs of the two Mike Piazza cards in the set were switched. His regular card has the Star Power back (#2) while his Star Power card (#246) has the regular-issue back.

	NM/M
Complete Set (16):	5.00
Common Player:	.10
Hideo Nomo Big Topps:	2.00
2 Mike Piazza (Star Power back.)	2.50
48 Todd Hollandsworth	.10
89 Jose Offerman	.10
136 Hideo Nomo (All-Star Rookie)	1.00
153 Tom Candiotti	.10
175 Raul Mondesi	.10
196 Eric Karros	.10
206 Ramon Martinez	.10
217 Karim Garcia (Future Star)	.25
236 David Yocum (Draft Pick)	.10
246 Mike Piazza (Star Power front.)	2.50
277 Brett Butler	.10
312 Delino DeShields	.10
324 Ismael Valdes	.10
402 Chad Fonville	.10
412 Todd Worrell	.10

World Champions Atlanta Braves

CHIPPER JONES

These specially marked versions of Topps regular 1996 cards feature a color World Champions logo overprinted on the front of each card. They were sold as a team set along with a 3-1/2" x 5" "Big Topps" card at Wal-Mart stores for around $5.

	NM/M
Complete Set (17):	4.00
Common Player:	.10
Greg Maddux Big Topps:	3.00
3 Greg Maddux (Star Power)	.50
8 Tom Glavine (Star Power)	.15
12 Jim Scharrer (Draft Pick)	.10
49 Mark Wohlers	.10
60 David Justice	.10
83 Mark Lemke	.10
165 Steve Avery	.10
177 Chipper Jones (All-Star Rookie)	2.00
189 John Smoltz	.10
193 Ryan Klesko	.10
262 Tom Glavine	.30
266 Kent Mercker	.10
297 Marquis Grissom	.10

Each theme has a different design. Gallery also has four insert sets. Player's Private Issue cards are a parallel set to the main issue; these cards are seeded one per every 12 packs. The backs are sequentially numbered from 0-999, with the first 100 cards sent to the players; the rest are inserted into packs. The backs are UV coated on the photo only, to allow for autographing. The other insert sets are Expressionists, Photo Gallery and a Mickey Mantle Masterpiece card.

	NM/M
Complete Set (180):	20.00
Common Player:	.10
Private Issue:	8X
Pack (8):	1.50
Wax Box (24):	27.50
1 Tom Glavine	.35
2 Carlos Baerga	.10
3 Dante Bichette	.10
4 Mark Langston	.10
5 Ray Lankford	.10
6 Moises Alou	.10
7 Marquis Grissom	.10
8 Ramon Martinez	.10
8p Ramon Martinez (Unmarked promo, "Pitcher" spelled out under photo on back.)	2.50
9 Steve Finley	.10
10 Todd Hundley	.10
11 Brady Anderson	.10
12 John Valentin	.10
13 Heathcliff Slocumb	.10
14 Ruben Sierra	.10
15 Jeff Conine	.10
16 Jay Buhner	.10
16p Jay Buhner (Unmarked promo; height, weight and "Bats" on same line.)	2.50
17 Sammy Sosa	1.00
18 Doug Drabek	.10
19 Jose Mesa	.10
20 Jeff King	.10
21 Mickey Tettleton	.10
22 Jeff Montgomery	.10
23 Alex Fernandez	.10
24 Greg Vaughn	.10
25 Chuck Finley	.10
26 Terry Steinbach	.10
27 Rod Beck	.10
28 Jack McDowell	.10
29 Mark Wohlers	.10
30 Lenny Dykstra	.10
31 Bernie Williams	.10
32 Travis Fryman	.10
33 Jose Canseco	.45
34 Ken Caminiti	.10
35 Devon White	.10
36 Bobby Bonilla	.10
37 Paul Sorrento	.10
38 Ryne Sandberg	1.00
39 Derek Bell	.10
40 Bobby Jones	.10
41 J.T. Snow	.10
42 Denny Neagle	.10
43 Tim Wakefield	.10
44 Andres Galarraga	.10
45 David Segui	.10
46 Lee Smith	.10
47 Mel Rojas	.10
48 John Franco	.10
49 Pete Schourek	.10
50 John Wetteland	.10
51 Paul Molitor	.75
52 Ivan Rodriguez	.65
53 Chris Hoiles	.10
54 Mike Greenwell	.10
55 Orel Hershiser	.10
56 Brian McRae	.10
57 Geronimo Berroa	.10
58 Craig Biggio	.10
59 David Justice	.10
59p David Justice (Unmarked promo; height,weight and "Bats" on same line.)	2.50
60 Lance Johnson	.10
61 Andy Ashby	.10
62 Randy Myers	.10
63 Gregg Jefferies	.10
64 Kevin Appier	.10
65 Rick Aguilera	.10
66 Shane Reynolds	.10
67 John Smoltz	.10
68 Ron Gant	.10
69 Eric Karros	.10
70 Jim Thome	.65
71 Terry Pendleton	.10
72 Kenny Rogers	.10
73 Robin Ventura	.10
74 Dave Nilsson	.10
75 Brian Jordan	.10
76 Glenallen Hill	.10
77 Greg Colbrunn	.10
78 Roberto Alomar	.25
79 Rickey Henderson	.75
80 Carlos Garcia	.10
81 Dean Palmer	.10
82 Mike Stanley	.10

83 Hal Morris	.10
84 Wade Boggs	1.00
85 Chad Curtis	.10
86 Roberto Hernandez	.10
87 John Olerud	.10
88 Frank Castillo	.10
89 Rafael Palmeiro	.65
90 Trevor Hoffman	.10
91 Marty Cordova	.10
92 Hideo Nomo	.35
93 Johnny Damon	.30
94 Bill Pulsipher	.10
95 Garret Anderson	.10
96 Ray Durham	.10
97 Ricky Bottalico	.10
98 Carlos Perez	.10
99 Troy Percival	.10
100 Chipper Jones	1.00
101 Esteban Loaiza	.10
102 John Mabry	.10
103 Jon Nunnally	.10
104 Andy Pettitte	.35
105 Lyle Mouton	.10
106 Jason Isringhausen	.10
107 Brian Hunter	.10
108 Quilvio Veras	.10
109 Jim Edmonds	.10
110 Ryan Klesko	.10
111 Pedro Martinez	.75
112 Joey Hamilton	.10
113 Vinny Castilla	.10
114 Alex Gonzalez	.10
115 Raul Mondesi	.10
116 Rondell White	.10
117 Dan Miceli	.10
118 Tom Goodwin	.10
119 Bret Boone	.10
120 Shawn Green	.35
121 Jeff Cirillo	.10
122 Rico Brogna	.10
123 Chris Gomez	.10
124 Ismael Valdes	.10
125 Javy Lopez	.10
126 Manny Ramirez	.75
127 Paul Wilson	.10
128 Billy Wagner	.10
129 Eric Owens	.10
130 Todd Greene	.10
131 Karim Garcia	.10
132 Jimmy Haynes	.10
133 Michael Tucker	.10
134 John Wasdin	.10
135 Brooks Kieschnick	.10
136 Alex Ochoa	.10
137 Ariel Prieto	.10
138 Tony Clark	.10
139 Mark Loretta	.10
140 Rey Ordonez	.10
141 Chris Snopek	.10
142 Roger Cedeno	.10
143 Derek Jeter	2.00
144 Jeff Suppan	.10
145 Greg Maddux	1.00
146 Ken Griffey Jr.	1.25
147 Tony Gwynn	1.00
148 Darren Daulton	.10
149 Will Clark	.10
150 Mo Vaughn	.10
151 Reggie Sanders	.10
152 Kirby Puckett	1.00
153 Paul O'Neill	.10
154 Tim Salmon	.10
155 Mark McGwire	1.50
156 Barry Bonds	2.00
157 Albert Belle	.10
158 Edgar Martinez	.10
159 Mike Mussina	.35
160 Cecil Fielder	.10
161 Kenny Lofton	.10
162 Randy Johnson	.75
163 Juan Gonzalez	.35
164 Jeff Bagwell	.75
165 Joe Carter	.10
166 Mike Piazza	1.25
167 Eddie Murray	.10
168 Cal Ripken Jr.	2.00
169 Barry Larkin	.10
170 Chuck Knoblauch	.10
171 Chili Davis	.10
172 Fred McGriff	.10
173 Matt Williams	.10
174 Roger Clemens	1.00
175 Frank Thomas	.75
176 Dennis Eckersley	.10
177 Gary Sheffield	.40
178 David Cone	.10
179 Larry Walker	.10
180 Mark Grace	.10

Players Private Issue

The first 999 examples of each of the base cards in the Gallery issue are designated on the front with a gold-foil stamp as "Players Private Issue." The first 100 of those cards were given to the depicted player, the others are randomly packed. Besides the logo on front, the PPI cards are identified on back with an individual serial number.

	NM/M
Complete Set (180):	200.00
Common Player:	1.00
Stars:	8X

Gallery Expressionists

These 1996 Topps Gallery inserts feature 20 team leaders printed on triple foil-stamped and texture-embossed cards. Cards are seeded one per every 24 packs.

	NM/M
Complete Set (20):	20.00
Common Player:	.35
1 Mike Piazza	3.00
2 J.T. Snow	.35
3 Ken Griffey Jr.	3.00
4 Kirby Puckett	2.00
5 Carlos Baerga	.35
6 Chipper Jones	2.00
7 Hideo Nomo	.75
8 Mark McGwire	4.00
9 Gary Sheffield	.75
10 Randy Johnson	1.25
11 Ray Lankford	.35
12 Sammy Sosa	2.00
13 Denny Martinez	.35
14 Jose Canseco	.75
15 Tony Gwynn	2.00
16 Edgar Martinez	.35
17 Reggie Sanders	.35
18 Andres Galarraga	.35
19 Albert Belle	.35
20 Barry Larkin	.35

Masterpiece

Topps continues its tribute to Mickey Mantle with this 1996 Topps Gallery insert card. The card, seeded one per every 48 packs, has three photos of Mantle on the front, with his comprehensive career statistics on the back.

	NM/M
MP1 Mickey Mantle	6.00

Photo Gallery

Photo Gallery is a collection of 15 cards featuring photography of baseball's biggest stars and greatest moments from the last season. The text on the card includes details of the card's front and back photos. The cards are seeded one per every 30 packs. Cards are numbered with a "PG" prefix.

	NM/M
Complete Set (180):	200.00
Common Player:	1.00
Stars:	8X

	NM/M
Complete Set (15):	20.00
Common Player:	.75
1 Eddie Murray	2.00
2 Randy Johnson	2.00
3 Cal Ripken Jr.	5.00
4 Bret Boone	.75
5 Frank Thomas	2.00
6 Jeff Conine	.75
7 Johnny Damon	.85
8 Roger Clemens	3.00
9 Albert Belle	.75
10 Ken Griffey Jr.	4.00
11 Kirby Puckett	2.50
12 David Justice	.75
13 Bobby Bonilla	.75
14 Larry Walker, Andres Galarraga, Vinny Castilla, Dante Bichette	1.00
15 Mark Wohlers, Javier Lopez	.75

Derek Jeter Panel

The method of issue for this triple-size (about 7-1/2" x 3-1/2") panel is uncertain. It has been reported that the piece was inserted into some 1995 Topps Hobby factory sets as an unadvertised bonus. The front has an action sequence showing the Yankees shortstop turning a double play. On back is personal data, minor and major league stats, a repeat of the center photo and a few sentences about the budding superstar.

	NM/M
Derek Jeter	7.50

Landmark Medallions

Milestones of the 1995 season are recalled in this set of limited edition (2,000) medallions. Each of the 2-1/2" x 3-1/2" pieces features a Topps Finest technology card bonded to a 1/8" thick, 4-oz. burnished bronze ingot, then clear-coated. Backs have career stats and a description of the milestone minted into the bronze. The issue was sold only as complete sets through Topps Stadium Club; issue price was $100.

	NM/M
Complete Set (4):	75.00
Common Player:	10.00
1 Greg Maddux (4th straight Cy Young)	20.00

2 Albert Belle (First 50 HR/50 2B season.)	10.00
3 Cal Ripken, Jr. (2,131 consecutive games)	35.00
4 Eddie Murray (3,000 hits)	15.00

1996 Topps Laser

Topps' 1996 Laser Baseball was the first set to use laser-cut technology on every card, creating surgically-precise latticework across the entire card. Every card in the 128-card regular issue set features one of four designs laser-cut into 20-point stock. One card from each of the four different designs is found in each four-card pack. Three different laser-cut insert sets were also produced: Bright Spots, Power Cuts and Stadium Stars. Cards 1-8 from each insert set were in Series 1 packs; cards 9-16 were seeded in Series 2 packs. A slightly oversize (1-5/8" x 3-5/8") checklist card in each pack helped protect the delicate die-cut details from damage.

	NM/M
Complete Set (128):	27.50
Common Player:	.10
Series 1 or 2 Pack (4):	1.50
Series 1 or 2 Wax Box (24):	22.50
1 Moises Alou	.10
2 Derek Bell	.10
3 Joe Carter	.10
4 Jeff Conine	.10
5 Darren Daulton	.10
6 Jim Edmonds	.10
7 Ron Gant	.10
8 Juan Gonzalez	.50
9 Brian Jordan	.10
10 Ryan Klesko	.10
11 Paul Molitor	1.00
12 Tony Phillips	.10
13 Manny Ramirez	1.00
14 Sammy Sosa	1.50
15 Devon White	.10
16 Bernie Williams	.10
17 Garret Anderson	.10
18 Jay Bell	.10
19 Craig Biggio	.10
20 Bobby Bonilla	.10
21 Ken Caminiti	.10
22 Shawon Dunston	.10
23 Mark Grace	.10
23p Mark Grace (Unmarked promo, plain, rather than brushed, gold foil.)	2.00
24 Gregg Jefferies	.10
25 Jeff King	.10
26 Javy Lopez	.10
27 Edgar Martinez	.10
28 Dean Palmer	.10
29 J.T. Snow	.10
30 Mike Stanley	.10
30p Mike Stanley (Unmarked promo; plain, rather than brushed, gold foil.)	1.00
31 Terry Steinbach	.10
32 Robin Ventura	.10
33 Roberto Alomar	.20
34 Jeff Bagwell	.75
35 Dante Bichette	.10
36 Wade Boggs	1.50
37 Barry Bonds	3.00
38 Jose Canseco	.50
39 Vinny Castilla	.10
40 Will Clark	.10
41 Marty Cordova	.10
42 Ken Griffey Jr.	2.00
43 Tony Gwynn	1.50
44 Rickey Henderson	1.00
45 Chipper Jones	1.50
46 Mark McGwire	2.50
47 Brian McRae	.10
48 Ryne Sandberg	1.50
49 Andy Ashby	.10
50 Alan Benes	.10
51 Andy Benes	.10

52 Roger Clemens	1.75
53 Doug Drabek	.10
54 Dennis Eckersley	.75
55 Tom Glavine	.35
56 Randy Johnson	1.00
57 Mark Langston	.10
58 Denny Martinez	.10
59 Jack McDowell	.10
60 Hideo Nomo	.50
61 Shane Reynolds	.10
62 John Smoltz	.10
63 Paul Wilson	.10
64 Mark Wohlers	.10
65 Shawn Green	.35
66 Marquis Grissom	.10
67 Dave Hollins	.10
68 Todd Hundley	.10
69 David Justice	.10
70 Eric Karros	.10
71 Ray Lankford	.10
72 Fred McGriff	.10
73 Hal Morris	.10
74 Eddie Murray	1.00
75 Paul O'Neill	.10
76 Rey Ordonez	.10
77 Reggie Sanders	.10
78 Gary Sheffield	.45
79 Jim Thome	.75
80 Rondell White	.10
81 Travis Fryman	.10
82 Derek Jeter	3.00
83 Chuck Knoblauch	.10
84 Barry Larkin	.10
85 Tino Martinez	.10
86 Raul Mondesi	.10
87 John Olerud	.10
88 Rafael Palmeiro	.75
89 Mike Piazza	2.00
90 Cal Ripken Jr.	3.00
91 Ivan Rodriguez	.75
92 Frank Thomas	1.00
93 John Valentin	.10
94 Mo Vaughn	.10
95 Quilvio Veras	.10
96 Matt Williams	.10
97 Brady Anderson	.10
98 Carlos Baerga	.10
99 Albert Belle	.10
100 Jay Buhner	.10
101 Johnny Damon	.35
102 Chili Davis	.10
103 Ray Durham	.10
104 Lenny Dykstra	.10
105 Cecil Fielder	.10
106 Andres Galarraga	.10
107 Brian Hunter	.10
108 Kenny Lofton	.10
109 Kirby Puckett	1.50
110 Tim Salmon	.10
111 Greg Vaughn	.10
112 Larry Walker	.10
113 Rick Aguilera	.10
114 Kevin Appier	.10
115 Kevin Brown	.10
116 David Cone	.10
117 Alex Fernandez	.10
118 Chuck Finley	.10
119 Joey Hamilton	.10
120 Jason Isringhausen	.10
121 Greg Maddux	1.50
122 Pedro Martinez	1.00
123 Jose Mesa	.10
124 Jeff Montgomery	.10
125 Mike Mussina	.50
126 Randy Myers	.10
127 Kenny Rogers	.10
128 Ismael Valdes	.10
Series 1 checklist	.10
Series 2 Checklist	.05

Bright Spots

Top young stars are featured on these insert cards, which use etched silver and gold diffraction foil. The cards are seeded one per 20 packs. Numbers 1-8 are in Series 1 packs; cards 9-16 are in Series 2 packs.

	NM/M
Complete Set (16):	17.50
Common Player:	.50
1 Brian Hunter	.50
2 Derek Jeter	4.50
3 Jason Kendall	.50
4 Brooks Kieschnick	.50
5 Rey Ordonez	.50

6	Jason Schmidt	.50
7	Chris Snopek	.50
8	Bob Wolcott	.50
9	Alan Benes	.50
10	Marty Cordova	.50
11	Jimmy Haynes	.50
12	Todd Hollandsworth	.50
13	Derek Jeter	4.50
14	Chipper Jones	3.00
15	Hideo Nomo	1.00
16	Paul Wilson	.50

Power Cuts

This insert set spotlights 16 of the game's top power hitters on etched foil and gold diffraction foil cards. These cards were seeded one per 40 packs; numbers 1-8 were in Series 1 packs; cards 9-16 were in Series 2 packs.

		NM/M
Complete Set (16):		20.00
Common Player:		.75
1	Albert Belle	.75
2	Jay Buhner	.75
3	Fred McGriff	.75
4	Mike Piazza	3.00
5	Tim Salmon	.75
6	Frank Thomas	2.00
7	Mo Vaughn	.75
8	Matt Williams	.75
9	Jeff Bagwell	2.00
10	Barry Bonds	5.00
11	Jose Canseco	1.00
12	Cecil Fielder	.75
13	Juan Gonzalez	1.00
14	Ken Griffey Jr.	3.00
15	Sammy Sosa	2.50
16	Larry Walker	.75

Stadium Stars

These 1996 Topps Laser cards are the most difficult to find; they are seeded one per every 60 packs. The 16 cards feature a laser-sculpted cover that folds back to reveal striated silver and gold etched diffraction foil on each card front. Cards 1-8 were in Series I packs; numbers 9-16 were Series II inserts.

		NM/M
Complete Set (16):		45.00
Common Player:		1.50
1	Carlos Baerga	1.50
2	Barry Bonds	10.00
3	Andres Galarraga	1.50
4	Ken Griffey Jr.	7.50
5	Barry Larkin	1.50
6	Raul Mondesi	1.50
7	Kirby Puckett	5.00
8	Cal Ripken Jr.	10.00
9	Will Clark	1.50
10	Roger Clemens	6.00
11	Tony Gwynn	5.00
12	Randy Johnson	4.00
13	Kenny Lofton	1.50
14	Edgar Martinez	1.50
15	Ryne Sandberg	5.00
16	Frank Thomas	4.00

League Leaders Finest Bronze

Specially designed Topps Finest cards are bedded to a slab of bronze and clear-coated in this set honoring major award winners from the 1995 season. A "League Leaders" logo at top has the player's award inscribed. Backs of the 2-3/4" x 3-3/4" ingots are silk-screened with season and career stats. The issue was sold only in complete sets (2,000 limit) through Topps Stadium Club for $80.

		NM/M
Complete Set (6):		75.00
Common Player:		10.00
(1)	Mo Vaughn (A.L. MVP)	10.00
(2)	Barry Larkin (N.L. MVP)	10.00
(3)	Randy Johnson (A.L. CY)	15.00
(4)	Greg Maddux (N.L. CY)	30.00
(5)	Marty Cordova (A.L. ROY)	10.00
(6)	Hideo Nomo (N.L. ROY)	15.00

Legends of the '50s

A dozen of the greatest players of the 1950s ever to grace a Topps card are featured in this set of bronze replicas. Each player's card is reproduced in a 4-oz. bronze version in 2-1/2" x 3-1/2" format. The card fronts are faithfully reproduced on each ingot, while the backs have been modified to present the player's lifetime stats. The ingots were sold through Topps' Stadium Club for about $45 apiece through a monthly subscription plan. The complete set was housed in a special wooden display case. The ingots are checklisted here alphabetically, with the year of Topps card reproduced noted parenthetically.

		NM/M
Complete Set (12):		275.00
Common Player:		20.00
(1)	Ernie Banks/1954	20.00
(2)	Yogi Berra/1952	20.00
(3)	Roy Campanella/1952	20.00
(4)	Whitey Ford/1953	20.00
(5)	Mickey Mantle/1952	35.00
(6)	Eddie Mathews/1952	25.00
(7)	Willie Mays/1953	25.00
(8)	Stan Musial/1959	20.00
(9)	Jackie Robinson/1952	20.00
(10)	Duke Snider/1955	20.00
(11)	Warren Spahn/1952	20.00
(12)	Ted Williams/1954, #250	30.00

"1952" Gold Willie Mays

This reproduction of Topps' 1952 card #261 is embossed and covered in 22 karat gold foil. Each full-size replica card is serially numbered within an edition of 50,000.

		NM/M
261	Willie Mays	12.00

"1954" Ted Williams Gold

This reproduction of Topps' 1954 card #1, Ted Williams, is embossed and covered in 22 karat gold foil. Each full-size replica card is serially numbered within an edition of 50,000.

		NM/M
1	Ted Williams	12.00

"1959" Stan Musial Gold

Topps' first regular-issue card of Stan Musial was reproduced in a full-size (2-1/2" x 3-1/2") 22-karat gold foil edition sold through Topps' Stadium Club. Each of the gold replicas bears a unique serial number. Issue price of the card was about $30.

		NM/M
150	Stan Musial	10.00

1997 Topps

Topps' 1997 set includes the first-ever player cards of the expansion Diamondbacks and Devil Rays; 16 Mickey Mantle reprints; a special Jackie Robinson tribute card; 27 Willie Mays Topps and Bowman reprints; randomly-inserted Willie Mays autographed reprint cards; and Inter-League Finest and Finest Refractors cards. The base set has 275 cards in Series 1 and 220 cards in Series 2. Each card front has a glossy coating on the photo and a spot matte finish on the border, with gold-foil graphics. Card backs have informative text, complete player stats and biographies, and a second photo. Mantle reprints, seeded one per 12 packs, feature the 16 remaining Mantle cards which were not reprinted in 1996, stamped with a gold foil logo, and numbered from #21 to #36. Willie Mays has 27 of his cards reprinted and seeded one per eight packs. Each card also has a gold foil stamp. As a special hobby-exclusive bonus, 1,000 Mays reprints were autographed and randomly inserted in packs. Five other insert sets were made: All-Stars, Inter-League Finest and Inter-League Finest Refractors, Sweet Strokes and Hobby Masters. Two factory sets, comprising the 495 base cards and either seven or eight random inserts were produced and currently enjoy a significant premium over hand-collated sets.

		NM/M
Unopened Fact. Set (504):		110.00
Unopened Fact. Set (503):		145.00
Complete Set (495):		65.00
Common Player:		.05
Ser. 1 or 2 Pack (11):		1.00
Ser. 1 or 2 Wax Box (36):		20.00
Ser. 1 or 2 Vending Box (500):		12.00
1	Barry Bonds	2.00
2	Tom Pagnozzi	.05
3	Terrell Wade	.05
4	Jose Valentin	.05
5	Mark Clark	.05
6	Brady Anderson	.05
7	Wade Boggs	1.00
8	Scott Stahoviak	.05
9	Andres Galarraga	.05
10	Steve Avery	.05
11	Joey Hamilton	.05
12	Rusty Greer	.05
13	Derek Jeter	2.00
14	Ricky Bottalico	.05
15	Andy Ashby	.05
16	Paul Shuey	.05
17	F.P. Santangelo	.05
18	Royce Clayton	.05
19	Mike Mohler	.05
20	Mike Piazza	1.50
21	Jaime Navarro	.05
22	Billy Wagner	.05
23	Mike Timlin	.05
24	Garret Anderson	.05
25	Ben McDonald	.05
26	Mel Rojas	.05
27	John Burkett	.05
28	Jeff King	.05
29	Reggie Jefferson	.05
30	Kevin Appier	.05
31	Felipe Lira	.05
32	Kevin Tapani	.05
33	Mark Portugal	.05
34	Carlos Garcia	.05
35	Joey Cora	.05
36	David Segui	.05
37	Mark Grace	.05
38	Erik Hanson	.05
39	Jeff D'Amico	.05
40	Jay Buhner	.05
41	B.J. Surhoff	.05
42	Jackie Robinson	1.50
43	Roger Pavlik	.05
44	Hal Morris	.05
45	Mariano Duncan	.05
46	Harold Baines	.05
47	Jorge Fabregas	.05
48	Jose Herrera	.05
49	Jeff Cirillo	.05
50	Tom Glavine	.25
51	Pedro Astacio	.05
52	Mark Gardner	.05
53	Arthur Rhodes	.05
54	Troy O'Leary	.05
55	Bip Roberts	.05
56	Mike Lieberthal	.05
57	Shane Andrews	.05
58	Scott Karl	.05
59	Gary DiSarcina	.05
60	Andy Pettitte	.25
61a	Kevin Elster (Should be #84.)	.05
61b	Mike Fetters	.05
62	Mark McGwire	1.75
63	Dan Wilson	.05
64	Mickey Morandini	.05
65	Chuck Knoblauch	.05
66	Tim Wakefield	.05
67	Raul Mondesi	.05
68	Todd Jones	.05
69	Albert Belle	.05
70	Trevor Hoffman	.05
71	Eric Young	.05
72	Robert Perez	.05
73	Butch Huskey	.05
74	Brian McRae	.05
75	Jim Edmonds	.05
76	Mike Henneman	.05
77	Frank Rodriguez	.05
78	Danny Tartabull	.05
79	Robby Nen	.05
80	Reggie Sanders	.05
81	Ron Karkovice	.05
82	Benny Santiago	.05
83	Mike Lansing	.05
84	Craig Biggio	.05
85	Mike Bordick	.05
86	Ray Lankford	.05
87	Charles Nagy	.05
88	Paul Wilson	.05
89	John Wetteland	.05
90	Tom Candiotti	.05
91	Carlos Delgado	.45
92	Derek Bell	.05
93	Mark Lemke	.05
94	Edgar Martinez	.05
95	Rickey Henderson	.75
96	Greg Myers	.05
97	Jim Leyritz	.05
98	Mark Johnson	.05
99	Dwight Gooden (Season Highlights)	.05
100	Al Leiter (Season Highlights)	.15
101	John Mabry (ends "... Mabry") (Season Highlights) (Last line on back.)	.05
102a	John Mabry (Season Highlights) (Last line on back ends "...walked.")	.05
102b	John Mabry (Season Highlights) (Last line on back ends "...walked.")	.05
103	Alex Ochoa (Season Highlights)	.05
104	Mike Piazza (Season Highlights)	.75
105	Jim Thome	.65
106	Ricky Otero	.05
107	Jamey Wright	.05
108	Frank Thomas	.75
109	Jody Reed	.05
110	Orel Hershiser	.05
111	Terry Steinbach	.05
112	Mark Loretta	.05
113	Turk Wendell	.05
114	Marvin Benard	.05
115	Kevin Brown	.05
116	Robert Person	.05
117	Joey Hamilton	.05
118	Francisco Cordova	.05
119	John Smiley	.05
120	Travis Fryman	.05
121	Jimmy Key	.05
122	Tom Goodwin	.05
123	Mike Greenwell	.05
124	Juan Gonzalez	.35
125	Pete Harnisch	.05
126	Roger Cedeno	.05
127	Ron Gant	.05
128	Mark Langston	.05
129	Tim Crabtree	.05
130	Greg Maddux	1.00
131	William Van Landingham	.05
132	Wally Joyner	.05
133	Randy Myers	.05
134	John Valentin	.05
135	Bret Boone	.05
136	Bruce Ruffin	.05
137	Chris Snopek	.05
138	Paul Molitor	.75
139	Mark McLemore	.05
140	Rafael Palmeiro	.65
141	Herb Perry	.05
142	Luis Gonzalez	.05
143	Doug Drabek	.05
144	Ken Ryan	.05
145	Todd Hundley	.05
146	Ellis Burks	.05
147	Ozzie Guillen	.05
148	Rich Becker	.05
149	Sterling Hitchcock	.05
150	Bernie Williams	.05
151	Mike Stanley	.05
152	Roberto Alomar	.25
153	Jose Mesa	.05
154	Steve Trachsel	.05
155	Alex Gonzalez	.05
156	Troy Percival	.05
157	John Smoltz	.05
158	Pedro Martinez	.75
159	Jeff Conine	.05
160	Bernard Gilkey	.05
161	Jim Eisenreich	.05
162	Mickey Tettleton	.05
163	Justin Thompson	.05
164	Jose Offerman	.05
165	Tony Phillips	.05
166	Ismael Valdes	.05
167	Ryne Sandberg	1.00
168	Matt Mieske	.05
169	Geronimo Berroa	.05
170	Otis Nixon	.05
171	John Mabry	.05
172	Shawon Dunston	.05
173	Omar Vizquel	.05
174	Chris Holles	.05
175	Doc Gooden	.05
176	Wilson Alvarez	.05
177	Todd Hollandsworth	.05
178	Roger Salkeld	.05
179	Rey Sanchez	.05
180	Rey Ordonez	.05
181	Denny Martinez	.05
182	Ramon Martinez	.05
183	Dave Nilsson	.05
184	Marquis Grissom	.05
185	Randy Velarde	.05
186	Ron Coomer	.05
187	Tino Martinez	.05
188	Jeff Brantley	.05
189	Steve Finley	.05
190	Andy Benes	.05
191	Terry Adams	.05
192	Mike Blowers	.05
193	Russ Davis	.05
194	Darryl Hamilton	.05
195	Jason Kendall	.05
196	Johnny Damon	.25
197	Dave Martinez	.05
198	Mike Macfarlane	.05
199	Norm Charlton	.05
200	Doug Million, Damian Moss, Bobby Rodgers (Prospect)	.05
201	Geoff Jenkins, Raul Ibanez, Mike Cameron (Prospect)	.05
202	Sean Casey, Jim Bonnici, Dmitri Young (Prospect)	.15
203	Jed Hansen, Homer Bush, Felipe Crespo (Prospect)	.05
204	Kevin Orie, Gabe Alvarez, Aaron Boone (Prospect)	.05
205	Ben Davis, Kevin Brown, Bobby Estalella (Prospect)	.05
206	Billy McMillon, Bubba Trammell RC, Dante Powell (Prospect)	.25
207	Jarrod Washburn, Marc Wilkins RC, Glendon Rusch (Prospect)	.05
208	Brian Hunter	.05
209	Jason Giambi	.45
210	Henry Rodriguez	.05
211	Edgar Renteria	.05
212	Edgardo Alfonzo	.05
213	Fernando Vina	.05
214	Shawn Green	.40
215	Ray Durham	.05
216	Joe Randa	.05
217	Armando Reynoso	.05
218	Eric Davis	.05
219	Bob Tewksbury	.05
220	Jacob Cruz	.05
221	Glenallen Hill	.05
222	Gary Gaetti	.05
223	Donne Wall	.05
224	Brad Clontz	.05
225	Marty Janzen	.05
226	Todd Worrell	.05
227	John Franco	.05
228	David Wells	.05
229	Gregg Jefferies	.05
230	Tim Naehring	.05
231	Thomas Howard	.05
232	Roberto Hernandez	.05
233	Kevin Ritz	.05
234	Julian Tavarez	.05
235	Ken Hill	.05
236	Greg Gagne	.05
237	Bobby Chouinard	.05
238	Joe Carter	.05
239	Jermaine Dye	.05
240	Antonio Osuna	.05
241	Julio Franco	.05
242	Mike Grace	.05
243	Aaron Sele	.05
244	David Justice	.05
245	Sandy Alomar	.05
246	Jose Canseco	.45
247	Paul O'Neill	.05
248	Sean Berry	.05
249	Nick Bierbrodt RC, Kevin Sweeney RC (Diamond Backs)	.05
250	Larry Rodriguez RC, Vladimir Nunez RC (Diamond Backs)	.10
251	Ron Hartman, David Hayman (Diamond Backs)	.05
252	Alex Sanchez, Matt Quatraro (Devil Rays)	.05
253	Ronni Seberino, Pablo Ortega RC (Devil Rays)	.05
254	Rex Hudler	.05
255	Orlando Miller	.05
256	Mariano Rivera	.10
257	Brad Radke	.05
258	Bobby Higginson	.05
259	Jay Bell	.05
260	Mark Grudzielanek	.05
261	Lance Johnson	.05
262	Ken Caminiti	.05
263	J.T. Snow	.05
264	Gary Sheffield	.45
265	Darrin Fletcher	.05
266	Eric Owens	.05
267	Luis Castillo	.05
268	Scott Rolen	.65
269	Todd Noel RC, John Oliver (Draft Pick)	.05
270	Robert Stratton RC, Corey Lee RC (Draft Pick)	.05
271	Gil Meche RC, Matt Halloran RC (Draft Pick)	.50
272	Eric Milton RC, Dermal Brown (Draft Pick)	.25
273	Josh Garrett RC, Chris Reitsma RC (Draft Pick)	.10
274	A.J. Zapp RC, Jason Marquis RC (Draft Pick)	.50
275	Checklist	.05
276a	Checklist	.05
276b	Chipper Jones (Should be #277.)	1.00
278	Orlando Merced	.05
279	Ariel Prieto	.05
280	Al Leiter	.05
281	Pat Meares	.05
282	Darryl Strawberry	.05
283	Jamie Moyer	.05
284	Scott Servais	.05
285	Delino DeShields	.05
286	Danny Graves	.05
287	Gerald Williams	.05
288	Todd Greene	.05
289	Rico Brogna	.05
290	Derrick Gibson	.05
291	Joe Girardi	.05
292	Darren Lewis	.05
293	Nomar Garciaparra	1.00
294	Greg Colbrunn	.05
295	Jeff Bagwell	.75
296	Brent Gates	.05
297	Jose Vizcaino	.05
298	Alex Ochoa	.05
299	Sid Fernandez	.05
300	Ken Griffey Jr.	1.50
301	Chris Gomez	.05
302	Wendell Magee	.05
303	Darren Oliver	.05
304	Mel Nieves	.05
305	Sammy Sosa	1.00
306	George Arias	.05
307	Jack McDowell	.05
308	Stan Javier	.05
309	Kimera Bartee	.05
310	James Baldwin	.05
311	Rocky Coppinger	.05
312	Keith Lockhart	.05
313	C.J. Nitkowski	.05
314	Allen Watson	.05
315	Darryl Kile	.05
316	Amaury Telemaco	.05
317	Jason Isringhausen	.05
318	Manny Ramirez	.75
319	Terry Pendleton	.05
320	Tim Salmon	.05
321	Eric Karros	.05
322	Mark Whiten	.05

323	Rick Krivda	.05
324	Brett Butler	.05
325	Randy Johnson	.75
326	Eddie Taubensee	.05
327	Mark Leiter	.05
328	Kevin Gross	.05
329	Ernie Young	.05
330	Pat Hentgen	.05
331	Rondell White	.05
332	Bobby Witt	.05
333	Eddie Murray	.75
334	Tim Raines	.05
335	Jeff Fassero	.05
336	Chuck Finley	.05
337	Willie Adams	.05
338	Chan Ho Park	.05
339	Jay Powell	.05
340	Ivan Rodriguez	.65
341	Jermaine Allensworth	.05
342	Jay Payton	.05
343	T.J. Mathews	.05
344	Tony Batista	.05
345	Ed Sprague	.05
346	Jeff Kent	.05
347	Scott Erickson	.05
348	Jeff Suppan	.05
349	Pete Schourek	.05
350	Kenny Lofton	.05
351	Alan Benes	.05
352	Fred McGriff	.05
353	Charlie O'Brien	.05
354	Darren Bragg	.05
355	Alex Fernandez	.05
356	Al Martin	.05
357	Bob Wells	.05
358	Chad Mottola	.05
359	Devon White	.05
360	David Cone	.05
361	Bobby Jones	.05
362	Scott Sanders	.05
363	Karim Garcia	.15
364	Kirt Manwaring	.05
365	Chili Davis	.05
366	Mike Hampton	.05
367	Chad Ogea	.05
368	Curt Schilling	.25
369	Phil Nevin	.05
370	Roger Clemens	1.25
371	Willie Greene	.05
372	Kenny Rogers	.05
373	Jose Rijo	.05
374	Bobby Bonilla	.05
375	Mike Mussina	.35
376	Curtis Pride	.05
377	Todd Walker	.05
378	Jason Bere	.05
379	Heathcliff Slocumb	.05
380	Dante Bichette	.05
381	Carlos Baerga	.05
382	Livan Hernandez	.05
383	Jason Schmidt	.05
384	Kevin Stocker	.05
385	Matt Williams	.05
386	Bartolo Colon	.05
387	Will Clark	.05
388	Dennis Eckersley	.65
389	Brooks Kieschnick	.05
390	Ryan Klesko	.05
391	Mark Carreon	.05
392	Tim Worrell	.05
393	Dean Palmer	.05
394	Wil Cordero	.05
395	Javy Lopez	.05
396	Rich Aurilia	.05
397	Greg Vaughn	.05
398	Vinny Castilla	.05
399	Jeff Montgomery	.05
400	Cal Ripken Jr.	2.00
401	Walt Weiss	.05
402	Brad Ausmus	.05
403	Ruben Rivera	.05
404	Mark Wohlers	.05
405	Rick Aguilera	.05
406	Tony Clark	.05
407	Lyle Mouton	.05
408	Bill Pulsipher	.05
409	Jose Rosado	.05
410	Tony Gwynn	1.00
411	Cecil Fielder	.05
412	John Flaherty	.05
413	Lenny Dykstra	.05
414	Ugueth Urbina	.05
415	Brian Jordan	.05
416	Bob Abreu	.05
417	Craig Paquette	.05
418	Sandy Martinez	.05
419	Jeff Blauser	.05
420	Barry Larkin	.05
421	Kevin Seitzer	.05
422	Tim Belcher	.05
423	Paul Sorrento	.05
424	Cal Eldred	.05
425	Robin Ventura	.05
426	John Olerud	.05
427	Bob Wolcott	.05
428	Matt Lawton	.05
429	Rod Beck	.05
430	Shane Reynolds	.05
431	Mike James	.05
432	Steve Wojciechowski	.05
433	Vladimir Guerrero	.75
434	Dustin Hermanson	.05
435	Marty Cordova	.05
436	Marc Newfield	.05
437	Todd Stottlemyre	.05
438	Jeffrey Hammonds	.05
439	Dave Stevens	.05
440	Hideo Nomo	.35

441	Mark Thompson	.05
442	Mark Lewis	.05
443	Quinton McCracken	.05
444	Cliff Floyd	.05
445	Denny Neagle	.05
446	John Jaha	.05
447	Mike Sweeney	.05
448	John Wasdin	.05
449	Chad Curtis	.05
450	Mo Vaughn	.05
451	Donovan Osborne	.05
452	Ruben Sierra	.05
453	Michael Tucker	.05
454	Kurt Abbott	.05
455	Andruw Jones	.75
456	Shannon Stewart	.05
457	Scott Brosius	.05
458	Juan Guzman	.05
459	Ron Villone	.05
460	Moises Alou	.05
461	Larry Walker	.05
462	Eddie Murray (Season Highlights)	.40
463	Paul Molitor (Season Highlights)	.40
464	Hideo Nomo (Season Highlights)	.20
465	Barry Bonds (Season Highlights)	1.00
466	Todd Hundley (Season Highlights)	.05
467	Rheal Cormier	.05
468	Jason Conti RC	.05
469	Rod Barajas RC	.05
470	Jared Sandberg, Cedric Bowers RC	.05
471	Paul Wilders, Chie Gunner RC	.05
472	Mike Decelle, Marcus McCain RC	.05
473	Todd Zeile	.05
474	Neifi Perez	.05
475	Jeromy Burnitz	.05
476	Trey Beamon	.05
477	John Patterson, Braden Looper RC (Draft Picks)	.15
478	Danny Peoples RC, Jake Westbrook RC (Draft Picks)	.25
479	Eric Chavez RC, Adam Eaton (Draft Picks)	.75
480	Joe Lawrence RC, Pete Tucci (Draft Picks)	.05
481	Kris Benson, Billy Koch RC (Draft Picks)	.25
482	John Nicholson, Andy Prater (Draft Picks)	.05
483	Mark Kotsay RC, Mark Johnson (Draft Picks)	.25
484	Armando Benitez	.05
485	Mike Matheny	.05
486	Jeff Reed	.05
487	Mark Bellhorn, Russ Johnson, Enrique Wilson (Prospects)	.05
488	Ben Grieve, Richard Hidalgo, Scott Morgan RC (Prospects)	.05
489	Paul Konerko, Derek Lee, Ron Wright (Prospects)	.50
490	Wes Helms, Bill Mueller RC, Brad Seitzer (Prospects)	.50
491	Jeff Abbott, Shane Monahan, Edgard Velazquez (Prospects)	.05
492	Jimmy Anderson RC, Ron Blazier, Gerald Witasick Jr. (Prospects)	.05
493	Darin Blood, Heath Murray, Carl Pavano (Prospects)	.05
494	Mark Redman, Mike Villano RC, Nelson Figueroa (Prospects)	.05
495	Checklist	.05
496	Checklist	.05

All-Stars

Ivan Rodriguez

Topps' 1997 All-Stars insert cards, printed on a dazzling rainbow foilboard, feature the top players from each position. There are 22 cards, 11 from each league, which showcase the top three players from each position as voted by Topps' sports department. On the front of each card is a photo of a "first team" all-star player; the back has a different photo of that player, who appears alongside the "second team" and "third team" selections. These cards are seeded one per every 18 1997 Topps Series I packs. Cards are numbered with an "AS" prefix.

		NM/M
Complete Set (22):		12.00
Common Player:		.25
1	Ivan Rodriguez	.75
2	Todd Hundley	.25
3	Frank Thomas	1.00
4	Andres Galarraga	.25
5	Chuck Knoblauch	.25
6	Eric Young	.25
7	Jim Thome	.25
8	Chipper Jones	1.50
9	Cal Ripken Jr.	3.00
10	Barry Larkin	.25
11	Albert Belle	.25
12	Barry Bonds	3.00
13	Ken Griffey Jr.	2.00
14	Ellis Burks	.25
15	Juan Gonzalez	.60
16	Gary Sheffield	.50
17	Andy Pettitte	.35
18	Tom Glavine	.35
19	Pat Hentgen	.25
20	John Smoltz	.25
21	Roberto Hernandez	.25
22	Mark Wohlers	.25

Awesome Impact

This flashy insert exclusive to Series 2 retail packaging features young players who have quickly made their mark in the big leagues. Fronts have player action photos against a background of silver primatic geometric shapes. Backs are horizontal with a player portrait photo, recent stats and a few words about the player's current and projected impact. Stated odds of finding this insert are one per 18 packs. Cards are numbered with an "AI" prefix.

		NM/M
Complete Set (20):		20.00
Common Player:		.40
1	Jaime Bluma	.40
2	Tony Clark	.40
3	Jermaine Dye	.40
4	Nomar Garciaparra	4.50
5	Vladimir Guerrero	3.00
6	Todd Hollandsworth	.40
7	Derek Jeter	6.00
8	Andruw Jones	3.00
9	Chipper Jones	4.50
10	Jason Kendall	.40
11	Brooks Kieschnick	.40
12	Alex Ochoa	.40
13	Rey Ordonez	.40
14	Neifi Perez	.40
15	Edgar Renteria	.40
16	Mariano Rivera	.40
17	Ruben Rivera	.40
18	Scott Rolen	2.25
19	Billy Wagner	.40
20	Todd Walker	.40

Inter-League Match Ups

The double-sided Inter-League Finest and Inter-League Finest Refractors (seeded one in

36 and one in 216 Topps Series 1 packs respectively) feature top individual matchups from inter-league rivalries. One player from each major league team is represented, for a total of 28 players on 14 different cards. Each card is covered with a Finest clear protector. Cards are numbered with an "ILM" prefix.

		NM/M
Complete Set (14):		16.00
Common Card:		.50
Refractors:		1.5X
1	Mark McGwire, Barry Bonds	3.00
2	Tim Salmon, Mike Piazza	2.00
3	Ken Griffey Jr., Dante Bichette	2.00
4	Juan Gonzalez, Tony Gwynn	1.50
5	Frank Thomas, Sammy Sosa	1.50
6	Albert Belle, Barry Larkin	.50
7	Johnny Damon, Brian Jordan	.75
8	Paul Molitor, Jeff King	1.00
9	John Jaha, Jeff Bagwell	1.00
10	Bernie Williams, Todd Hundley	.50
11	Joe Carter, Henry Rodriguez	.50
12	Cal Ripken Jr., Gregg Jefferies	3.00
13	Mo Vaughn, Chipper Jones	1.50
14	Travis Fryman, Gary Sheffield	.75

Derek Jeter Autograph

An authentically autographed card honoring Derek Jeter as Rookie of the Year was a random insert found on average of one per 576 packs of Topps Series 2.

	NM/M
Derek Jeter	130.00

Hobby Masters

These 20 cards lead the way as dealers' top selections. The cards, printed on 28-point diffraction foilboard, replace two regular cards in every 36th pack of 1997 Topps Series 1 product. Cards are numbered with a "HM" prefix.

		NM/M
Complete Set (20):		30.00
Common Player:		.75
1	Ken Griffey Jr.	3.00
2	Cal Ripken Jr.	4.50
3	Greg Maddux	2.25
4	Albert Belle	.75
5	Tony Gwynn	2.25
6	Jeff Bagwell	1.50
7	Randy Johnson	1.50
8	Raul Mondesi	.75
9	Juan Gonzalez	1.00
10	Kenny Lofton	.75
11	Frank Thomas	1.50
12	Mike Piazza	3.00
13	Chipper Jones	2.25
14	Brady Anderson	.75
15	Ken Caminiti	.75
16	Barry Bonds	4.50
17	Mo Vaughn	.75
18	Derek Jeter	4.50
19	Sammy Sosa	2.25
20	Andres Galarraga	.75

Mickey Mantle Reprints

All 16 remaining Mickey Mantle cards that were not re-printed in 1996 Topps Baseball are found in this insert, seeded every 12 packs of Series I Topps. The set starts off with No. 21 and runs through No. 36 since the '96 reprints were numbered 1-20.

		NM/M
Complete Set (16):		60.00
Common Card:		3.00
Inserted 1:12 Series 1		
21	1953 Bowman #44	5.00
22	1953 Bowman #59	5.00
23	1957 Topps #407	5.00
24	1958 Topps #418	5.00
25	1958 Topps #487	5.00
26	1959 Topps #461	5.00
27	1959 Topps #564	5.00
28	1960 Topps #160	5.00
29	1960 Topps #563	5.00
30	1961 Topps #406	5.00
31	1961 Topps #475	5.00
32	1961 Topps #578	5.00
33	1962 Topps #18	5.00
34	1962 Topps #318	5.00
35	1962 Topps #471	5.00
36	1964 Topps #331	5.00

Mickey Mantle Finest

The Mickey Mantle reprint inserts found in Series 1 were re-issued in Series 2 in Finest technology, found on average

of every 24 packs. Refractor versions of each Finest reprint were inserted at a 1:216 rate.

		NM/M
Complete Set (16):		70.00
Common Card:		5.00
Inserted 1:24 Series 2		
Refractor:		4X
Inserted 1:216		
21	1953 Bowman #44	5.00
22	1953 Bowman #59	7.50
23	1957 Topps #407	5.00
24	1958 Topps #418	5.00
25	1958 Topps #487	5.00
26	1959 Topps #461	5.00
27	1959 Topps #564	5.00
28	1960 Topps #160	5.00
29	1960 Topps #563	5.00
30	1961 Topps #406	5.00
31	1961 Topps #475	5.00
32	1961 Topps #578	5.00
33	1962 Topps #18	5.00
34	1962 Topps #318	5.00
35	1962 Topps #471	5.00
36	1964 Topps #331	5.00

Mickey Mantle Case Inserts

Inserted one per case of Series 1 Topps, these reprints of 16 Mickey Mantle special cards of the 1950s-1960s come sealed in a soft plastic holder. The plastic sleeve has a gold-foil stamp at bottom-back which reads "FACTORY TOPPS SEAL 1997."

		NM/M
Complete Set (16):		160.00
Common Card:		12.50
21	1953 Bowman #44	12.50
22	1953 Bowman #59	18.00
23	1957 Topps #407	12.50
24	1958 Topps #418	12.50
25	1958 Topps #487	12.50
26	1959 Topps #461	12.50
27	1959 Topps #564	12.50
28	1960 Topps #160	12.50
29	1960 Topps #563	12.50
30	1961 Topps #406	12.50
31	1961 Topps #475	12.50
32	1961 Topps #578	12.50
33	1962 Topps #18	12.50
34	1962 Topps #318	12.50
35	1962 Topps #471	12.50
36	1964 Topps #331	12.50

Willie Mays Reprints

Willie Mays

There are 27 different Willie Mays cards reprinted in Series 1 and seeded every eight packs. The inserts form a collection of Topps and Bowman cards from throughout Mays' career and each is highlighted by a special commemorative gold foil stamp. Many of the Mays reprints can also be found in an

autographed edition, bearing a special "Certified Autograph Issue" gold-foil logo.

		NM/M
Complete Set (27):		50.00
Common Card:		3.00
Autographed Card:		120.00
1	1951 Bowman #305	6.00
2	1952 Topps #261	4.00
3	1953 Topps #244	3.00
4	1954 Bowman #89	3.00
5	1954 Topps #90	3.00
6	1955 Bowman #184	3.00
7	1955 Topps #194	3.00
8	1956 Topps #130	3.00
9	1957 Topps #10	3.00
10	1958 Topps #5	3.00
11	1959 Topps #50	3.00
12	1960 Topps #200	3.00
13	1960 Topps #564	3.00
14	1961 Topps #150	3.00
15	1961 Topps #579	3.00
16	1962 Topps #300	3.00
17	1963 Topps #300	3.00
18	1964 Topps #150	3.00
19	1965 Topps #250	3.00
20	1966 Topps #1	3.00
21	1967 Topps #200	3.00
22	1968 Topps #50	3.00
23	1969 Topps #190	3.00
24	1970 Topps #600	3.00
25	1971 Topps #600	3.00
26	1972 Topps #49	3.00
27	1973 Topps #305	3.00

Willie Mays Reprint Autographs

According to Topps, only 19 of the 27 different Willie Mays cards reprinted in Series 1 exist in authentically autographed form, bearing a special "Certified Autograph Issue" gold-foil logo.

		NM/M
Common Card:		120.00
1	1951 Bowman #305	150.00
2	1952 Topps #261	120.00
3	1953 Topps #244	120.00
6	1955 Bowman #184	120.00
7	1955 Topps #194	120.00
9	1957 Topps #10	120.00
10	1958 Topps #5	120.00
12	1960 Topps #200	120.00
13	1960 Topps #564	120.00
14	1961 Topps #150	120.00
15	1961 Topps #579	120.00
17	1963 Topps #300	120.00
18	1964 Topps #150	120.00
19	1965 Topps #250	120.00
20	1966 Topps #1	120.00
23	1969 Topps #190	120.00
24	1970 Topps #600	120.00
26	1972 Topps #49	120.00
27	1973 Topps #305	120.00

Willie Mays Finest

Series 2 offered collectors a chance to find Finest technology versions of each of the 27 commemorative reprint Topps and Bowman cards from throughout Mays' career. The Finest reprints are found one in every 30 packs, on average, with Refractor versions seeded 1:180.

		NM/M
Complete Set (27):		60.00
Common Card:		3.00
Refractor:		3X
Inserted 1:180		
1	1951 Bowman #305	6.00
2	1952 Topps #261	4.00
3	1953 Topps #244	3.00
4	1954 Bowman #89	3.00
5	1954 Topps #90	3.00
6	1955 Bowman #184	3.00
7	1955 Topps #194	3.00
8	1956 Topps #130	3.00

9	1957 Topps #10	3.00
10	1958 Topps #5	3.00
11	1959 Topps #50	3.00
12	1960 Topps #200	3.00
13	1960 Topps #564	3.00
14	1961 Topps #150	3.00
15	1961 Topps #579	3.00
16	1962 Topps #300	3.00
17	1963 Topps #300	3.00
18	1964 Topps #150	3.00
19	1965 Topps #250	3.00
20	1966 Topps #1	3.00
21	1967 Topps #200	3.00
22	1968 Topps #50	3.00
23	1969 Topps #190	3.00
24	1970 Topps #600	3.00
25	1971 Topps #600	3.00
26	1972 Topps #49	3.00
27	1973 Topps #305	3.00

Willie Mays Commemorative Super

This oversize (4-1/4" x 5-3/4") version of card #2 (1952 Topps) in the Willie Mays Commemorative Reprint series was available exclusively in a special retail packaging of 10 1997 Topps Series 1 foil packs. Like the regular-size reprints, it has a gold-foil commemorative stamp on front.

		NM/M
2	Willie Mays (1952 Topps)	5.00

Season's Best

Season's Best features 25 players on prismatic illusion foilboard, and can be found every six packs. The set has the top five players from five statistical categories: home runs, RBIs, batting average, steals, and wins. Season's Best were found in packs of Topps Series II, and later reprinted on chromium stock as part of Topps Chrome.

		NM/M
Complete Set (25):		12.00
Common Player:		.25
1	Tony Gwynn	1.50
2	Frank Thomas	1.25
3	Ellis Burks	.25
4	Paul Molitor	1.25
5	Chuck Knoblauch	.25
6	Mark McGwire	3.00
7	Brady Anderson	.25
8	Ken Griffey Jr.	2.00
9	Albert Belle	.25
10	Andres Galarraga	.25
11	Andres Galarraga	.25
12	Albert Belle	.25
13	Juan Gonzalez	.75
14	Mo Vaughn	.25
15	Rafael Palmeiro	1.00
16	John Smoltz	.25
17	Andy Pettitte	.50
18	Pat Hentgen	.25
19	Mike Mussina	.50

(Column 3 top)

20	Andy Benes	.25
21	Kenny Lofton	.25
22	Tom Goodwin	.25
23	Otis Nixon	.25
24	Eric Young	.25
25	Lance Johnson	.25

Series 2 Supers

At 3-3/4" x 5-1/4", these premium cards are nearly identical to the regular-issue versions except for size. Also, whereas the regular cards have a front format which combines a high-gloss central area with a matte finish near the borders, the supers have just one finish on the front which is a semi-gloss. The supers also have different card numbers on back. One of the supers was included in each boxed lot of 15 Series II foil packs sold at large retail outlets with a price tag of about $15.

		NM/M
Complete Set (3):		10.00
1	Chipper Jones	3.00
2	Ken Griffey Jr.	4.00
3	Cal Ripken Jr.	5.00

Sweet Strokes

These retail-exclusive Sweet Strokes insert cards consist of 15 Power Matrix foil cards of the top hitters in the game. These players have the swings to produce game winning-hits. The cards were seeded one per every 12 1997 Topps Series I retail packs. Cards are numbered with a "SS" prefix.

		NM/M
Complete Set (15):		15.00
Common Player:		.35
1	Roberto Alomar	.50
2	Jeff Bagwell	1.25
3	Albert Belle	.35
4	Barry Bonds	3.00
5	Mark Grace	.35
6	Ken Griffey Jr.	2.00
7	Tony Gwynn	1.50
8	Chipper Jones	1.50
9	Edgar Martinez	.35
10	Mark McGwire	2.50
11	Rafael Palmeiro	1.00
12	Mike Piazza	2.00
13	Gary Sheffield	.75
14	Frank Thomas	1.25
15	Mo Vaughn	.35

Team Timber

Team Timber was a 16-card insert that was exclusive to retail packs and inserted one per 36. The set displays the game's top sluggers on laminated litho wood cards. Cards are numbered with a "TT" prefix.

		NM/M
Complete Set (16):		24.00
Common Player:		.50
1	Ken Griffey Jr.	3.00
2	Ken Caminiti	.50
3	Bernie Williams	.50
4	Jeff Bagwell	1.50
5	Frank Thomas	1.50
6	Andres Galarraga	.50

(Column 4 top — Team Timber image)

7	Barry Bonds	5.00
8	Rafael Palmeiro	1.25
9	Brady Anderson	.50
10	Juan Gonzalez	.75
11	Mo Vaughn	.50
12	Mark McGwire	4.00
13	Gary Sheffield	.90
14	Albert Belle	.50
15	Chipper Jones	2.50
16	Mike Piazza	3.00

1997 Topps Chrome

Chrome Baseball reprinted the top 165 cards from Topps Series I and II baseball on a chromium, metallized stock. Chrome sold in four-card packs and included three insert sets: Diamond Duos, which was created exclusively for this product, Season's Best and Topps All-Stars, which were both reprinted from Topps products. Refractor versions of each card were found every 12 packs.

		NM/M
Complete Set (165):		35.00
Common Player:		.10
Refractors:		2X
Pack (4):		1.50
Wax Box (24):		25.00
1	Barry Bonds	3.00
2	Jose Valentin	.10
3	Brady Anderson	.10
4	Wade Boggs	1.50
5	Andres Galarraga	.10
6	Rusty Greer	.10
7	Derek Jeter	3.00
8	Ricky Bottalico	.10
9	Mike Piazza	2.00
10	Garret Anderson	.10
11	Jeff King	.10
12	Kevin Appier	.10
13	Mark Grace	.10
14	Jeff D'Amico	.10
15	Jay Buhner	.10
16	Hal Morris	.10
17	Harold Baines	.10
18	Jeff Cirillo	.10
19	Tom Glavine	.35
20	Andy Pettitte	.35
21	Mark McGwire	2.50
22	Chuck Knoblauch	.10
23	Raul Mondesi	.10
24	Albert Belle	.10
25	Trevor Hoffman	.10
26	Eric Young	.10
27	Brian McRae	.10
28	Jim Edmonds	.10
29	Robb Nen	.10
30	Reggie Sanders	.10
31	Mike Lansing	.10
32	Craig Biggio	.10
33	Ray Lankford	.10
34	Charles Nagy	.10
35	Paul Wilson	.10
36	John Wetteland	.10
37	Derek Bell	.10
38	Edgar Martinez	.10
39	Rickey Henderson	1.00
40	Jim Thome	.75
41	Frank Thomas	1.00
42	Jackie Robinson (Tribute)	2.00
43	Terry Steinbach	.10

44	Kevin Brown	.10
45	Joey Hamilton	.10
46	Travis Fryman	.10
47	Juan Gonzalez	.50
48	Ron Gant	.10
49	Greg Maddux	1.50
50	Wally Joyner	.10
51	John Valentin	.10
42	Bret Boone	.10
53	Paul Molitor	1.00
54	Rafael Palmeiro	.75
55	Todd Hundley	.10
56	Ellis Burks	.10
57	Bernie Williams	.10
58	Roberto Alomar	.25
59	Jose Mesa	.10
60	Troy Percival	.10
61	John Smoltz	.10
62	Jeff Conine	.10
63	Bernard Gilkey	.10
64	Mickey Tettleton	.10
65	Justin Thompson	.10
66	Tony Phillips	.10
67	Ryne Sandberg	1.50
68	Geronimo Berroa	.10
69	Todd Hollandsworth	.10
70	Rey Ordonez	.10
71	Marquis Grissom	.10
72	Tino Martinez	.10
73	Steve Finley	.10
74	Andy Benes	.10
75	Jason Kendall	.10
76	Johnny Damon	.35
77	Jason Giambi	.50
78	Henry Rodriguez	.10
79	Edgar Renteria	.10
80	Ray Durham	.10
81	Gregg Jefferies	.10
82	Roberto Hernandez	.10
83	Joe Carter	.10
84	Jermaine Dye	.10
85	Julio Franco	.10
86	David Justice	.10
87	Jose Canseco	.50
88	Paul O'Neill	.10
89	Mariano Rivera	.15
90	Bobby Higginson	.10
91	Mark Grudzielanek	.10
92	Lance Johnson	.10
93	Ken Caminiti	.10
94	Gary Sheffield	.50
95	Luis Castillo	.10
96	Scott Rolen	.75
97	Chipper Jones	1.50
98	Darryl Strawberry	.10
99	Nomar Garciaparra	1.50
100	Jeff Bagwell	1.00
101	Ken Griffey Jr.	2.00
102	Sammy Sosa	1.50
103	Jack McDowell	.10
104	James Baldwin	.10
105	Rocky Coppinger	.10
106	Manny Ramirez	1.00
107	Tim Salmon	.10
108	Eric Karros	.10
109	Brett Butler	.10
110	Randy Johnson	1.00
111	Pat Hentgen	.10
112	Rondell White	.10
113	Eddie Murray	1.00
114	Ivan Rodriguez	.75
115	Jermaine Allensworth	.10
116	Ed Sprague	.10
117	Kenny Lofton	.10
118	Alan Benes	.10
119	Fred McGriff	.10
120	Alex Fernandez	.10
121	Al Martin	.10
122	Devon White	.10
123	David Cone	.10
124	Karim Garcia	.25
125	Chili Davis	.10
126	Roger Clemens	1.75
127	Bobby Bonilla	.10
128	Mike Mussina	.50
129	Todd Walker	.10
130	Dante Bichette	.10
131	Carlos Baerga	.10
132	Matt Williams	.10
133	Will Clark	.10
134	Dennis Eckersley	.75
135	Ryan Klesko	.10
136	Dean Palmer	.10
137	Javy Lopez	.10
138	Greg Vaughn	.10
139	Vinny Castilla	.10
140	Cal Ripken Jr.	3.00
141	Ruben Rivera	.10
142	Mark Wohlers	.10
143	Tony Clark	.10
144	Jose Rosado	.10
145	Tony Gwynn	1.50
146	Cecil Fielder	.10
147	Brian Jordan	.10
148	Bob Abreu	.10
149	Barry Larkin	.10
150	Robin Ventura	.10
151	John Olerud	.10
152	Rod Beck	.10
153	Vladimir Guerrero	1.00
154	Marty Cordova	.10
155	Todd Stottlemyre	.10
156	Hideo Nomo	.50
157	Denny Neagle	.10
158	John Jaha	.10
159	Mo Vaughn	.10
160	Andruw Jones	1.00
161	Moises Alou	.10

162	Larry Walker	.10
163	Eddie Murray (Season Highlights)	.75
164	Paul Molitor (Season Highlights)	.75
165	Checklist	.10

Chrome All-Stars

Topps Chrome All-Stars display the same 22 cards found in Topps Series I, however these are reprinted on a Chrome stock. Regular versions are seeded every 24 packs, while Refractor versions arrive every 72 packs. Cards are numbered with an "AS" prefix.

		NM/M
Complete Set (22):		25.00
Common Player:		.75
Refractors:		1.5X
1	Ivan Rodriguez	1.50
2	Todd Hundley	.75
3	Frank Thomas	2.00
4	Andres Galarraga	.75
5	Chuck Knoblauch	.75
6	Eric Young	.75
7	Jim Thome	1.50
8	Chipper Jones	3.00
9	Cal Ripken Jr.	6.00
10	Barry Larkin	.75
11	Albert Belle	.75
12	Barry Bonds	6.00
13	Ken Griffey Jr.	4.00
14	Ellis Burks	.75
15	Juan Gonzalez	1.00
16	Gary Sheffield	1.25
17	Andy Pettitte	1.00
18	Tom Glavine	1.00
19	Pat Hentgen	.75
20	John Smoltz	.75
21	Roberto Hernandez	.75
22	Mark Wohlers	.75

Diamond Duos

Diamond Duos is the only one of the three insert sets in Chrome Baseball that was developed exclusively for this product. The set has 10 cards featuring two superstar teammates on double-sided chromium cards. Diamond Duos are found every 36 packs, while Refractor versions are found every 108 packs. Cards are numbered with a "DD" prefix.

		NM/M
Complete Set (10):		17.50
Common Player:		.50
Refractors:		1.5X
1	Chipper Jones, Andruw Jones	2.00
2	Derek Jeter, Bernie Williams	4.00
3	Ken Griffey Jr., Jay Buhner	2.50
4	Kenny Lofton, Manny Ramirez	1.50
5	Jeff Bagwell, Craig Biggio	1.50
6	Juan Gonzalez, Ivan Rodriguez	1.25

7	Cal Ripken Jr., Brady Anderson	4.00
8	Mike Piazza, Hideo Nomo	2.50
9	Andres Galarraga, Dante Bichette	.50
10	Frank Thomas, Albert Belle	1.50

Season's Best

Season's Best includes the 25 players found in Topps Series II, but in a chromium version. The top five players from five statistical categories, including Leading Looters, Bleacher Reachers and Kings of Swing. Regular versions are seeded every 18 packs, with Refractors every 54 packs.

		NM/M
Complete Set (25):		17.50
Common Player:		.50
Refractors:		1.5X
1	Tony Gwynn	2.00
2	Frank Thomas	1.50
3	Ellis Burks	.50
4	Paul Molitor	1.50
5	Chuck Knoblauch	.50
6	Mark McGwire	4.00
7	Brady Anderson	.50
8	Ken Griffey Jr.	3.00
9	Albert Belle	.50
10	Andres Galarraga	.50
11	Andres Galarraga	.50
12	Albert Belle	.50
13	Juan Gonzalez	.75
14	Mo Vaughn	.50
15	Rafael Palmeiro	1.25
16	John Smoltz	.50
17	Andy Pettitte	.75
18	Pat Hentgen	.50
19	Mike Mussina	.75
20	Andy Benes	.50
21	Kenny Lofton	.50
22	Tom Goodwin	.50
23	Otis Nixon	.50
24	Eric Young	.50
25	Lance Johnson	.50

Jumbos

These large-format (3-3/4" x 5-1/4") Topps Chrome cards were produced for sale in special retail packaging offering one jumbo card and five packs of Topps Chrome for about $15. The jumbos are identical in design to the regular-issue Chrome cards of the same players. Because they were offered in a windowed retail package, it was easy for collectors to pick the card they wanted.

		NM/M
Complete Set (6):		10.00
Common Player:		.75
9	Mike Piazza	2.00
94	Gary Sheffield	.75
97	Chipper Jones	1.50
101	Ken Griffey Jr.	2.00
102	Sammy Sosa	1.50
140	Cal Ripken Jr.	3.00

1997 Topps Gallery Pre-Production

In its second year Topps Gallery was produced in a greatly improved combination of card stock, graphic highlights and inserts. To reintroduce the hobby to the issue, Topps distributed these promotional samples to dealers and the press. Except for the "PP" prefix

to the card number on front, the samples are virtually identical to the issued versions.

		NM/M
Complete Set (4):		25.00
Common Player:		3.00
1	Andruw Jones	5.00
2	Derek Jeter	9.00
3	Mike Piazza	10.00
4	Craig Biggio	3.00

1997 Topps Gallery

The second year of Gallery features 180 cards printed on extra-thick 24-point stock. Card fronts feature a player photo surrounded by an embossed foil "frame" to give each card the look of a piece of artwork. Backs contain career stats and biographical information on each player. Inserts include Peter Max Serigraphs, Signature Series Serigraphs, Player's Private Issue (parallel set), Photo Gallery and Gallery of Heroes. Cards were sold exclusively in hobby shops in eight-card packs for $4 each.

		NM/M
Complete Set (180):		20.00
Common Player:		.10
Pack (8):		1.50
Wax Box (24):		25.00
1	Paul Molitor	.75
2	Devon White	.10
3	Andres Galarraga	.10
4	Cal Ripken Jr.	3.00
5	Tony Gwynn	1.50
6	Mike Stanley	.10
7	Orel Hershiser	.10
8	Jose Canseco	.25
9	Chili Davis	.10
10	Harold Baines	.10
11	Rickey Henderson	.75
12	Darryl Strawberry	.10
13	Todd Worrell	.10
14	Cecil Fielder	.10
15	Gary Gaetti	.10
16	Bobby Bonilla	.10
17	Will Clark	.25
18	Kevin Brown	.10
19	Tom Glavine	.35
20	Wade Boggs	1.50
21	Edgar Martinez	.10
22	Lance Johnson	.10
23	Gregg Jefferies	.10
24	Bip Roberts	.10
25	Tony Phillips	.10
26	Greg Maddux	1.50
27	Mickey Tettleton	.10
28	Terry Steinbach	.10
29	Ryne Sandberg	1.50
30	Wally Joyner	.10
31	Joe Carter	.10
32	Ellis Burks	.10
33	Fred McGriff	.10
34	Barry Larkin	.10
35	John Franco	.10
36	Rafael Palmeiro	.65
37	Mark McGwire	2.50
38	Ken Caminiti	.10
39	David Cone	.10
40	Julio Franco	.10
41	Roger Clemens	1.75
42	Barry Bonds	3.00
43	Dennis Eckersley	.65
44	Eddie Murray	.75
45	Paul O'Neill	.10
46	Craig Biggio	.50
47	Roberto Alomar	.20
48	Mark Grace	.50
49	Matt Williams	.10
50	Jay Buhner	.10
51	John Smoltz	.10
52	Randy Johnson	.75
53	Ramon Martinez	.10
54	Curt Schilling	.35
55	Gary Sheffield	.50
56	Jack McDowell	.10
57	Brady Anderson	.10
58	Dante Bichette	.10
59	Ron Gant	.10

60	Alex Fernandez	.10
61	Moises Alou	.10
62	Travis Fryman	.10
63	Dean Palmer	.10
64	Todd Hundley	.10
65	Jeff Brantley	.10
66	Bernard Gilkey	.10
67	Geronimo Berroa	.10
68	John Wetteland	.10
69	Robin Ventura	.10
70	Ray Lankford	.10
71	Kevin Appier	.10
72	Juan Gonzalez	.40
73	Jeff King	.10
74	Greg Vaughn	.10
75	Steve Finley	.10
76	Brian McRae	.10
77	Paul Sorrento	.10
78	Ken Griffey Jr.	2.00
79	Omar Vizquel	.10
80	Jose Mesa	.10
81	Albert Belle	.10
82	Glenallen Hill	.10
83	Sammy Sosa	1.50
84	Andy Benes	.10
85	David Justice	.10
86	Marquis Grissom	.10
87	John Olerud	.10
88	Tino Martinez	.10
89	Frank Thomas	.75
90	Raul Mondesi	.10
91	Steve Trachsel	.10
92	Jim Edmonds	.10
93	Rusty Greer	.10
94	Joey Hamilton	.10
95	Ismael Valdes	.10
96	Dave Nilsson	.10
97	John Jaha	.10
98	Alex Gonzalez	.10
99	Javy Lopez	.10
100	Ryan Klesko	.10
101	Tim Salmon	.10
102	Bernie Williams	.10
103	Roberto Hernandez	.10
104	Chuck Knoblauch	.10
105	Mike Lansing	.10
106	Vinny Castilla	.10
107	Reggie Sanders	.10
108	Mo Vaughn	.10
109	Rondell White	.10
110	Ivan Rodriguez	.65
111	Mike Mussina	.40
112	Carlos Baerga	.10
113	Jeff Conine	.10
114	Jim Thome	.65
115	Manny Ramirez	.75
116	Kenny Lofton	.10
117	Wilson Alvarez	.10
118	Eric Karros	.10
119	Robb Nen	.10
120	Mark Wohlers	.10
121	Ed Sprague	.10
122	Pat Hentgen	.10
123	Juan Guzman	.10
124	Derek Bell	.10
125	Jeff Bagwell	.75
126	Eric Young	.10
127	John Valentin	.10
128	Al Martin (Photo actually Javy Lopez.)	.10
129	Trevor Hoffman	.10
130	Henry Rodriguez	.10
131	Pedro Martinez	.75
132	Mike Piazza	2.00
133	Brian Jordan	.10
134	Jose Valentin	.10
135	Jeff Cirillo	.10
136	Chipper Jones	1.50
137	Ricky Bottalico	.10
138	Hideo Nomo	.40
139	Troy Percival	.10
140	Rey Ordonez	.10
141	Edgar Renteria	.10
142	Luis Castillo	.10
143	Vladimir Guerrero	.75
144	Jeff D'Amico	.10
145	Andruw Jones	.75
146	Darin Erstad	.25
147	Bob Abreu	.10
148	Carlos Delgado	.45
149	Jamey Wright	.10
150	Nomar Garciaparra	1.50
151	Jason Kendall	.10
152	Jermaine Allensworth	.10
153	Scott Rolen	.65
154	Rocky Coppinger	.10
155	Paul Wilson	.10
156	Garret Anderson	.10
157	Mariano Rivera	.15
158	Ruben Rivera	.10
159	Andy Pettitte	.35
160	Derek Jeter	3.00
161	Neifi Perez	.10
162	Ray Durham	.10
163	James Baldwin	.10
164	Marty Cordova	.10
165	Tony Clark	.10
166	Michael Tucker	.10
167	Mike Sweeney	.10
168	Johnny Damon	.25
169	Jermaine Dye	.10
170	Alex Ochoa	.10
171	Jason Isringhausen	.10
172	Mark Grudzielanek	.10
173	Jose Rosado	.10
174	Todd Hollandsworth	.10
175	Alan Benes	.10

176	Jason Giambi	.45
177	Billy Wagner	.10
178	Justin Thompson	.10
179	Todd Walker	.10

Players Private Issue

A parallel version of the Gallery issue called Players Private Issue was produced as a 1:12 pack insert. The PPI cards differ from the regular version in the use of a "PPI-" prefix to the card number on front and the application of a small silver PPI seal in a lower corner. On back, the line "One of 250 Issued" has been added.

		NM/M
Common Player:		1.00
Stars:		5X

Of Heroes

This 10-card die-cut insert features a design resembling stained glass. Cards were inserted 1:36 packs. Cards are numbered with a "GH" prefix.

		NM/M
Complete Set (10):		30.00
Common Player:		1.50
1	Derek Jeter	6.00
2	Chipper Jones	6.00
3	Frank Thomas	2.50
4	Ken Griffey Jr.	4.00
5	Cal Ripken Jr.	6.00
6	Mark McGwire	5.00
7	Mike Piazza	4.00
8	Jeff Bagwell	2.50
9	Tony Gwynn	3.00
10	Mo Vaughn	1.50

Peter Max

Noted artist Peter Max has painted renditions of 10 superstar players and offered his commentary about those players on the backs. Cards were inserted 1:24 packs. In addition, Max-autographed

cards signed and numbered from an edition of 40 are inserted 1:1,200 packs.

		NM/M
Complete Set (10):		60.00
Common Player:		2.00
Peter Max Autographed:		100.00
1	Derek Jeter	9.00
2	Albert Belle	3.00
3	Ken Caminiti	3.00
4	Chipper Jones	6.00
5	Ken Griffey Jr.	7.50
6	Frank Thomas	5.00
7	Cal Ripken Jr.	10.00
8	Mark McGwire	9.00
9	Barry Bonds	10.00
10	Mike Piazza	7.50

Photo Gallery

This 21-card set features full-bleed, high-gloss action photos of some of the game's top stars. Cards were inserted 1:24 packs. They are numbered with a "PG" prefix.

		NM/M
Complete Set (16):		15.00
Common Player:		.50
1	World Series	.50
2	Paul Molitor	1.00
3	Eddie Murray	1.00
4	Ken Griffey Jr.	2.50
5	Chipper Jones	1.50
6	Derek Jeter	3.50
7	Frank Thomas	1.00
8	Mark McGwire	3.00
9	Kenny Lofton	.50
10	Gary Sheffield	.65
11	Mike Piazza	2.50
12	Vinny Castilla	.50
13	Andres Galarraga	.50
14	Andy Pettitte	.50
15	Robin Ventura	.50
16	Barry Larkin	.50

Screenplays

Twenty of the game's top stars were featured in this multi-part collectible. The packaging is a 5-1/8" diameter lithographed steel can. The can was shrink-wrapped at the factory with a round checklist disc covering the color player photo on top of the can. The top has a woodgrain border around the photo and a gold facsimile autograph. The back of the topper disc has a career summary of the player. Inside the tin is a 2-1/2" x 3-1/2" plastic motion card with several seconds of game action shown as the angle of view changes. The card is covered by a peel-off protective layer on front and back. Foam pieces in the package allow both the can and card to be displayed upright. Issue price was about $10 per can. The unnumbered cans are checklisted here alphabetically. Values shown are for can/card combinations.

		NM/M
Complete Set (20):		25.00
Common Player:		1.00
Pack (1):		2.50
Wax Box (21):		30.00
(1)	Jeff Bagwell	2.00
(2)	Albert Belle	1.00
(3)	Barry Bonds	5.00
(4)	Andres Galarraga	1.00
(5)	Nomar Garciaparra	2.50
(6)	Juan Gonzalez	1.25

(7)	Ken Griffey Jr.	3.00
(8)	Tony Gwynn	2.50
(9)	Derek Jeter	5.00
(10)	Randy Johnson	2.00
(11)	Andruw Jones	2.00
(12)	Chipper Jones	2.50
(13)	Kenny Lofton	1.00
(14)	Mark McGwire	4.00
(15)	Paul Molitor	2.00
(16)	Hideo Nomo	1.25
(17)	Cal Ripken Jr.	5.00
(18)	Sammy Sosa	2.50
(19)	Frank Thomas	2.00
(20)	Jim Thome	1.50

Screenplays Inserts

		NM/M
Complete Set (6):		35.00
Common Player:		2.00
1	Larry Walker	2.00
2	Cal Ripken Jr	12.50
3	Chipper Jones	6.00
4	Frank Thomas	5.00
5	Mike Piazza	7.50
6	Ken Griffey Jr.	7.50

1997 Topps Stars Promos

These promo cards introduced Topps' new line of premium cards. They are in the same basic format as the regular issue, but are marked "PRE-PRODUCTION / SAMPLE" in the stats box on back.

		NM/M
Complete Set (3):		5.00
Common Player:		1.00
PP1	Larry Walker	1.00
PP2	Roger Clemens	3.00
PP3	Frank Thomas	2.00

1997 Topps Stars

The premiere version of this product was sold only to hobby shops that were members of the Topps Home Team Advantage program. Each of the 125 regular cards in the set is printed on 20-point stock. Card fronts feature spot UV coating with a textured star pattern running down one side of the card. Inserts include the parallel Always Mint set, as well as '97 All-Stars, Future All-Stars, All-Star memories, and Autographed Rookie Reprints. Cards were sold in seven-card packs for $3 each.

		NM/M
Complete Set (125):		30.00
Common Player:		.10
Always Mint Stars, RC's:		8X
Pack (7):		3.00
Wax Box (24):		65.00
1	Larry Walker	.10
2	Tino Martinez	.10
3	Cal Ripken Jr.	3.00
4	Ken Griffey Jr.	2.00
5	Chipper Jones	1.50

6	David Justice	.10
7	Mike Piazza	2.00
8	Jeff Bagwell	1.00
9	Ron Gant	.10
10	Sammy Sosa	2.00
11	Tony Gwynn	1.50
12	Carlos Baerga	.10
13	Frank Thomas	1.00
14	Moises Alou	.10
15	Barry Larkin	.10
16	Ivan Rodriguez	.75
17	Greg Maddux	1.50
18	Jim Edmonds	.10
19	Jose Canseco	.50
20	Rafael Palmeiro	.75
21	Paul Molitor	1.00
22	Kevin Appier	.10
23	Raul Mondesi	.10
24	Lance Johnson	.10
25	Edgar Martinez	.10
26	Andres Galarraga	.10
27	Mo Vaughn	.10
28	Ken Caminiti	.10
29	Cecil Fielder	.10
30	Harold Baines	.10
31	Roberto Alomar	.25
32	Shawn Estes	.10
33	Tom Glavine	.35
34	Dennis Eckersley	.10
35	Manny Ramirez	1.00
36	John Olerud	.10
37	Juan Gonzalez	.50
38	Chuck Knoblauch	.10
39	Albert Belle	.10
40	Vinny Castilla	.10
41	John Smoltz	.10
42	Barry Bonds	3.00
43	Randy Johnson	.10
44	Brady Anderson	.10
45	Jeff Blauser	.10
46	Craig Biggio	.10
47	Jeff Conine	.10
48	Marquis Grissom	.10
49	Mark Grace	.10
50	Roger Clemens	1.75
51	Mark McGwire	2.50
52	Fred McGriff	.10
53	Gary Sheffield	.50
54	Bobby Jones	.10
55	Eric Young	.10
56	Robin Ventura	.10
57	Wade Boggs	1.50
58	Joe Carter	.10
59	Ryne Sandberg	1.50
60	Matt Williams	.10
61	Todd Hundley	.10
62	Dante Bichette	.10
63	Chili Davis	.10
64	Kenny Lofton	.10
65	Jay Buhner	.10
66	Will Clark	.10
67	Travis Fryman	.10
68	Pat Hentgen	.10
69	Ellis Burks	.10
70	Mike Mussina	.40
71	Hideo Nomo	.50
72	Sandy Alomar	.10
73	Bobby Bonilla	.10
74	Rickey Henderson	1.00
75	David Cone	.10
76	Terry Steinbach	.10
77	Pedro Martinez	1.00
78	Jim Thome	.75
79	Rod Beck	.10
80	Randy Myers	.10
81	Charles Nagy	.10
82	Mark Wohlers	.10
83	Paul O'Neill	.10
84	Curt Schilling	.35
85	Joey Cora	.10
86	John Franco	.10
87	Kevin Brown	.10
88	Benito Santiago	.10
89	Ray Lankford	.10
90	Bernie Williams	.10
91	Jason Dickson	.10
92	Jeff Cirillo	.10
93	Nomar Garciaparra	2.00
94	Mariano Rivera	.15
95	Javy Lopez	.10
96	Tony Womack RC	.25
97	Jose Rosado	.10
98	Denny Neagle	.10
99	Darryl Kile	.10
100	Justin Thompson	.10
101	Juan Encarnacion	.10
102	Brad Fullmer	.10
103	Kris Benson RC	.75
104	Todd Helton	1.00
105	Paul Konerko	.10
106	Travis Lee RC	1.00
107	Todd Greene	.10
108	Mark Kotsay RC	.50
109	Carl Pavano	.10
110	Kerry Wood RC	4.00
111	Jason Romano RC	.10
112	Geoff Goetz RC	.10
113	Scott Hodges RC	.10
114	Aaron Akin RC	.10
115	Vernon Wells RC	6.00
116	Chris Stowe RC	.10
117	Brett Caradonna RC	.10
118	Adam Kennedy RC	1.00
119	Jayson Werth RC	.10
120	Glenn Davis RC	.10
121	Troy Cameron RC	.10
122	J.J. Davis RC	.10
123	Jason Dellaero RC	.10

Always Mint

This set parallels the regular Topps Stars issue and was inserted at the announced rate of one card per 12 packs. Identical in design to the regular version, the Always Mint cards have metallic foil background on the player portion of the front photos. Backs of the Always Mint parallels have a shiny metallic silver background.

		NM/M
Complete Set (125):		250.00
Common Player:		.50
Stars/Rookies:		8X

All-Star Memories

This 10-card insert features stars who have had memorable performances in previous All-Star Games. Cards feature a laser-cut cascade of stars on a foilboard stock. Backs have another photo and a description of the All-Star memory. The cards were inserted 1:24 packs. Cards are numbered with an "ASM" prefix.

		NM/M
Complete Set (10):		20.00
Common Player:		1.00
1	Cal Ripken Jr.	6.00
2	Jeff Conine	1.00
3	Mike Piazza	4.00
4	Randy Johnson	2.00
5	Ken Griffey Jr.	4.00
6	Fred McGriff	1.00
7	Moises Alou	1.00
8	Hideo Nomo	1.25
9	Larry Walker	1.00
10	Sandy Alomar	1.00

Future All-Stars

This 15-card set showcases the top candidates to make their All-Star Game debut in 1998. Cards feature a prismatic rainbow foil back-

---

ground and were inserted 1:12 packs. Cards are numbered with a "FAS" prefix.

		NM/M
Complete Set (15):		17.50
Common Player:		.75
1	Derek Jeter	4.00
2	Andruw Jones	2.50
3	Vladimir Guerrero	3.00
4	Scott Rolen	2.50
5	Jose Guillen	.75
6	Jose Cruz, Jr.	.75
7	Darin Erstad	2.50
8	Tony Clark	.75
9	Scott Spiezio	.75
10	Kevin Orie	.75
11	Calvin Reese	.75
12	Billy Wagner	.75
13	Matt Morris	.75
14	Jeremi Gonzalez	.75
15	Hideki Irabu	.75

Rookie Reprints

Fifteen Topps rookie cards of Hall of Famers were reprinted as a one-per-six-packs insert. Regardless of original size, all reprints are 2-1/2" x 3-1/2" with a reprint notice on back.

		NM/M
Complete Set (15):		25.00
Common Player:		2.00
(1)	Luis Aparicio	2.00
(2)	Richie Ashburn	2.00
(3)	Jim Bunning	2.00
(4)	Bob Feller	2.00
(5)	Rollie Fingers	2.00
(6)	Monte Irvin	2.00
(7)	Al Kaline	3.00
(8)	Ralph Kiner	2.00
(9)	Eddie Mathews	3.00
(10)	Hal Newhouser	2.00
(11)	Gaylord Perry	2.00
(12)	Robin Roberts	2.00
(13)	Brooks Robinson	3.00
(14)	Enos Slaughter	2.00
(15)	Earl Weaver	2.00

Autographed Rookie Reprints

Fourteen different Hall of Famers autographed reprinted versions of their Topps rookie cards as a one-per-30-pack insert. Each card features a special certified stamp. Richie Ashburn was to have been card #2, but he died before he could autograph them.

		NM/M
Common Player:		15.00
(1)	Luis Aparicio	20.00
(3)	Jim Bunning	30.00
(4)	Bob Feller	35.00
(5)	Rollie Fingers	15.00
(6)	Monte Irvin	15.00
(7)	Al Kaline	30.00
(8)	Ralph Kiner	25.00
(9)	Eddie Mathews	75.00
(10)	Hal Newhouser	40.00
(11)	Gaylord Perry	15.00
(12)	Robin Roberts	30.00

---

(13)	Brooks Robinson	40.00
(14)	Enos Slaughter	30.00
(15)	Earl Weaver	20.00

1997 All-Stars

This 20-card insert honors, participants of the 1997 All-Star Game in Cleveland. Cards were inserted 1:24 packs. Fronts are printed on prismatic foil with hundreds of stars in the background. On back is another player photo and his All-Star Game 1997 and career stats. Cards are numbered with an "AS" prefix.

		NM/M
Complete Set (20):		60.00
Common Player:		1.50
1	Greg Maddux	6.00
2	Randy Johnson	4.50
3	Tino Martinez	1.50
4	Jeff Bagwell	4.50
5	Ivan Rodriguez	3.50
6	Mike Piazza	7.50
7	Cal Ripken Jr.	12.00
8	Ken Caminiti	1.50
9	Tony Gwynn	6.00
10	Edgar Martinez	1.50
11	Craig Biggio	1.50
12	Roberto Alomar	2.00
13	Larry Walker	1.50
14	Brady Anderson	1.50
15	Barry Bonds	12.00
16	Ken Griffey Jr.	7.50
17	Ray Lankford	1.50
18	Paul O'Neill	1.50
19	Jeff Blauser	1.50
20	Sandy Alomar	1.50

Dodger Rookie of the Year Collection

Available only through Topps Stadium Club and at Dodger Stadium, this set of special cards honors the five consecutive (1992-96) N.L. Rookies of the Year - all L.A. Dodgers - as well as the first-ever Rookie of the Year, Jackie Robinson. The cards feature reproductions of the players' rookie cards printed on front in metallic foil and with an N.L. Rookie of the Year logo and year banner. Backs are virtually identical to the regular-issue cards, but include a reprint line in the fine print. Raul Mondesi's card is a different version of the '94 Topps Coming Attractions subset card which he shared with Ben Van Ryn. Production was reported at 4,000 sets.

		NM/M
Complete Set (6):		35.00
Common Player:		3.00
1	Jackie Robinson	
	(1952 Topps)	20.00

---

(13)	Brooks Robinson	40.00
(14)	Enos Slaughter	30.00
(15)	Earl Weaver	20.00

2	Mike Piazza	
	(1992 Bowman)	10.00
3	Eric Karros	
	(1993 Topps)	3.00
4	Raul Mondesi	
	(1994 Topps)	3.00
5	Hideo Nomo	
	(1995 Topps Traded)	7.50
6	Todd Hollandsworth	
	(1996 Topps)	3.00

"Pro Shooters" Photo Marbles

This limited distribution test issue was another attempt to market baseball player photos with baseball player photos. The hard plastic 1" diameter marbles have a black composite band around the circumference. On one side is a player portrait, on the other is a team logo at center with the player name in a strip below and a number "... of 60" in a strip above. The Topps name does not appear. They were sold two per pack.

		NM/M
Complete Set (60):		1,000
Common Player:		10.00
1	Roberto Alomar	15.00
2	Brady Anderson	10.00
3	Carlos Baerga	10.00
4	Jeff Bagwell	30.00
5	Albert Belle	10.00
6	Dante Bichette	10.00
7	Craig Biggio	10.00
8	Wade Boggs	40.00
9	Barry Bonds	60.00
10	Jay Buhner	10.00
11	Ken Caminiti	10.00
12	Jose Canseco	15.00
13	Roger Clemens	42.50
14	David Cone	10.00
15	Cecil Fielder	10.00
16	Travis Fryman	10.00
17	Andres Galarraga	10.00
18	Ron Gant	10.00
19	Bernard Gilkey	10.00
20	Tom Glavine	12.50
21	Juan Gonzalez	15.00
22	Mark Grace	10.00
23	Ken Griffey Jr.	45.00
24	Tony Gwynn	40.00
25	Todd Hundley	10.00
26	John Jaha	10.00
27	Derek Jeter	60.00
28	Lance Johnson	10.00
29	Randy Johnson	30.00
30	Andruw Jones	30.00
31	Chipper Jones	40.00
32	Brian Jordan	10.00
33	Jason Kendall	10.00
34	Chuck Knoblauch	10.00
35	Ray Lankford	10.00
36	Barry Larkin	10.00
37	Kenny Lofton	10.00
38	Greg Maddux	40.00
39	Edgar Martinez	10.00
40	Fred McGriff	10.00
41	Mark McGwire	50.00
42	Paul Molitor	30.00
43	Raul Mondesi	10.00
44	Eddie Murray	30.00
45	Mike Mussina	15.00
46	Hideo Nomo	15.00
47	Rafael Palmeiro	25.00
48	Andy Pettitte	15.00
49	Mike Piazza	45.00
50	Cal Ripken Jr.	60.00
51	Ivan Rodriguez	25.00
52	Tim Salmon	10.00
53	Ryne Sandberg	40.00
54	Gary Sheffield	15.00
55	John Smoltz	10.00
56	Sammy Sosa	40.00
57	Frank Thomas	30.00
58	Mo Vaughn	10.00
59	Bernie Williams	10.00
60	Matt Williams	10.00
1 of 2	Checklist card 1-30	30.00
2 of 2	Checklist card 31-60	30.00

22k Gold

These 22-karat gold-foil cards were created for direct sale by Topps. They reproduce, front and back, Griffey's and

---

Ripken's regular-issue 1997 Topps cards, and feature a 1997-style card of Irabu, who did not appear on a regular Topps card that year. The 2-1/2" x 3-1/2" cards are individually serial numbered and were sold in a protective display holder. Initially priced at $30 apiece, they were discounted in a later offer to $19.95.

		NM/M
Complete Set (3):		60.00
Common Player:		20.00
300	Ken Griffey Jr.	15.00
400	Cal Ripken Jr.	20.00
----	Hideki Irabu	15.00

1998 Topps Pre-Production

To give potential customers a feel for its 1998 baseball cards, Topps issued this series of pre-production samples. Cards are identical in format to the issued versions except they are numbered with a "PP" prefix and the 1997 stats line reads "PRE-PRODUCTIONSAMPLE."

		NM/M
Complete Set (6):		4.00
Common Player:		.25
PP1	Carlos Baerga	.25
PP2	Jeff Bagwell	.75
PP3	Marquis Grissom	.25
PP4	Derek Jeter	1.50
PP5	Randy Johnson	.75
PP6	Mike Piazza	1.00

1998 Topps

Topps issued two series in 1998, a total of 503 base cards; 282 in Series 1 and 221 in Series 2. Cards feature a gold border instead of the traditional white of past years. The product features Roberto Clemente inserts and a tribute card No. 21 in the base set. Series 1 subsets Series Highlights, Expansion Team Prospects, Interleague Highlights, Season Highlights, Prospects and Draft Picks. Subsets in Series II included: Expansion Teams, InterLeague Preview, Season Highlights, Prospects and Draft Picks. Every card in the set is paralleled in a Minted in Cooperstown insert that was stamped on-site at the Baseball Hall of Fame in Cooperstown. Inserts in Series 1 include: Roberto Clemente Reprints, Clemente Finest, Clemente Tribute, Memorabilia Madness, Etch a Sketch, Mystery Finest, Flashback and Baby Boomers. Inserts in Series 2 included: Clemente Reprints, Clemente Finest, 1998 Rookie Class, Mystery Finest, Milestones, Focal Points, and Clout 9. A factory set includes the 503 base cards, eight randomly selected inserts and one Clemente card sealed in a gold-foil stamped soft plastic case.

		NM/M
Unopened Fact. Set (511):		85.00
Complete Set (503):		40.00
Common Player:		.05
Minted:		6X
Inserted 1:8		
Series 1 or 2 Pack (11):		1.00
Series 1 or 2 Wax Box (36):		25.00

1	Tony Gwynn	1.00
2	Larry Walker	.05
3	Billy Wagner	.05
4	Denny Neagle	.05
5	Vladimir Guerrero	.75
6	Kevin Brown	.05
8	Mariano Rivera	.10
9	Tony Clark	.05
10	Deion Sanders	.05
11	Francisco Cordova	.05
12	Matt Williams	.05
13	Carlos Baerga	.05
14	Mo Vaughn	.05
15	Bobby Witt	.05
16	Matt Stairs	.05
17	Chan Ho Park	.05
18	Mike Bordick	.05
19	Michael Tucker	.05
20	Frank Thomas	.75
21	Roberto Clemente	1.50
22	Dmitri Young	.05
23	Steve Trachsel	.05
24	Jeff Kent	.05
25	Scott Rolen	.50
26	John Thomson	.05
27	Joe Vitiello	.05
28	Eddie Guardado	.05
29	Charlie Hayes	.05
30	Juan Gonzalez	.40
31	Garret Anderson	.05
32	John Jaha	.05
33	Omar Vizquel	.05
34	Brian Hunter	.05
35	Jeff Bagwell	.75
36	Mark Lemke	.05
37	Doug Glanville	.05
38	Dan Wilson	.05
39	Steve Cooke	.05
40	Chili Davis	.05
41	Mike Cameron	.05
42	F.P. Santangelo	.05
43	Brad Ausmus	.05
44	Gary DiSarcina	.05
45	Pat Hentgen	.05
46	Wilton Guerrero	.05
47	Devon White	.05
48	Danny Patterson	.05
49	Pat Meares	.05
50	Rafael Palmeiro	.65
51	Mark Gardner	.05
52	Jeff Blauser	.05
53	Dave Hollins	.05
54	Carlos Garcia	.05
55	Ben McDonald	.05
56	John Mabry	.05
57	Trevor Hoffman	.05
58	Tony Fernandez	.05
59	Rich Loiselle	.05
60	Mark Leiter	.05
61	Pat Kelly	.05
62	John Flaherty	.05
63	Roger Bailey	.05
64	Tom Gordon	.05
65	Ryan Klesko	.05
66	Darryl Hamilton	.05
67	Jim Eisenreich	.05
68	Butch Huskey	.05
69	Mark Grudzielanek	.05
70	Marquis Grissom	.05
71	Mark McLemore	.05
72	Gary Gaetti	.05
73	Greg Gagne	.05
74	Lyle Mouton	.05
75	Jim Edmonds	.05
76	Shawn Green	.25
77	Greg Vaughn	.05
78	Terry Adams	.05
79	Kevin Polcovich RC	.05
80	Troy O'Leary	.05
81	Jeff Shaw	.05
82	Rich Becker	.05
83	David Wells	.05
84	Steve Karsay	.05
85	Charles Nagy	.05
86	B.J. Surhoff	.05
87	Jamey Wright	.05
88	James Baldwin	.05
89	Edgardo Alfonzo	.05
90	Jay Buhner	.05
91	Brady Anderson	.05
92	Scott Servais	.05
93	Edgar Renteria	.05
94	Mike Lieberthal	.05
95	Rick Aguilera	.05
96	Walt Weiss	.05
97	Deivi Cruz	.05
98	Kurt Abbott	.05
99	Henry Rodriguez	.05

100	Mike Piazza	1.25
101	Bill Taylor	.05
102	Todd Zeile	.05
103	Rey Ordonez	.05
104	Willie Greene	.05
105	Tony Womack	.05
106	Mike Sweeney	.05
107	Jeffrey Hammonds	.05
108	Kevin Orie	.05
109	Alex Gonzalez	.05
110	Jose Canseco	.50
111	Paul Sorrento	.05
112	Joey Hamilton	.05
113	Brad Radke	.05
114	Steve Avery	.05
115	Esteban Loaiza	.05
116	Stan Javier	.05
117	Chris Gomez	.05
118	Royce Clayton	.05
119	Orlando Merced	.05
120	Kevin Appier	.05
121	Mel Nieves	.05
122	Joe Girardi	.05
123	Rico Brogna	.05
124	Kent Mercker	.05
125	Manny Ramirez	.75
126	Jeromy Burnitz	.05
127	Kevin Foster	.05
128	Matt Morris	.05
129	Jason Dickson	.05
130	Tom Glavine	.25
131	Wally Joyner	.05
132	Rick Reed	.05
133	Todd Jones	.05
134	Dave Martinez	.05
135	Sandy Alomar	.05
136	Mike Lansing	.05
137	Sean Berry	.05
138	Doug Jones	.05
139	Todd Stottlemyre	.05
140	Jay Bell	.05
141	Jaime Navarro	.05
142	Chris Hoiles	.05
143	Joey Cora	.05
144	Scott Spiezio	.05
145	Joe Carter	.05
146	Jose Guillen	.05
147	Damion Easley	.05
148	Lee Stevens	.05
149	Alex Fernandez	.05
150	Randy Johnson	.75
151	J.T. Snow	.05
152	Chuck Finley	.05
153	Bernard Gilkey	.05
154	David Segui	.05
155	Dante Bichette	.05
156	Kevin Stocker	.05
157	Carl Everett	.05
158	Jose Valentin	.05
159	Pokey Reese	.05
160	Derek Jeter	2.00
161	Roger Pavlik	.05
162	Mark Wohlers	.05
163	Ricky Bottalico	.05
164	Ozzie Guillen	.05
165	Mike Mussina	.50
166	Gary Sheffield	.50
167	Hideo Nomo	.40
168	Mark Grace	.05
169	Aaron Sele	.05
170	Darryl Kile	.05
171	Shawn Estes	.05
172	Vinny Castilla	.05
173	Ron Coomer	.05
174	Jose Rosado	.05
175	Kenny Lofton	.05
176	Jason Giambi	.50
177	Hal Morris	.05
178	Darren Bragg	.05
179	Orel Hershiser	.05
180	Ray Lankford	.05
181	Hideki Irabu	.05
182	Kevin Young	.05
183	Javy Lopez	.05
184	Jeff Montgomery	.05
185	Mike Holtz	.05
186	George Williams	.05
187	Cal Eldred	.05
188	Tom Candiotti	.05
189	Glenallen Hill	.05
190	Brian Giles	.05
191	Dave Mlicki	.05
192	Garrett Stephenson	.05
193	Jeff Frye	.05
194	Joe Oliver	.05
195	Bob Hamelin	.05
196	Luis Sojo	.05
197	LaTroy Hawkins	.05
198	Kevin Elster	.05
199	Jeff Reed	.05
200	Dennis Eckersley	.65
201	Bill Mueller	.05
202	Russ Davis	.05
203	Armando Benitez	.05
204	Quilvio Veras	.05
205	Tim Naehring	.05
206	Quinton McCracken	.05
207	Raul Casanova	.05
208	Matt Lawton	.05
209	Luis Alicea	.05
210	Luis Gonzalez	.05
211	Allen Watson	.05
212	Gerald Williams	.05
213	David Bell	.05
214	Todd Hollandsworth	.05
215	Wade Boggs	1.00
216	Jose Mesa	.05
217	Jamie Moyer	.05

218	Darren Daulton	.05
219	Mickey Morandini	.05
220	Rusty Greer	.05
221	Jim Bullinger	.05
222	Jose Offerman	.05
223	Matt Karchner	.05
224	Woody Williams	.05
225	Mark Loretta	.05
226	Mike Hampton	.05
227	Willie Adams	.05
228	Scott Hatteberg	.05
229	Rich Amaral	.05
230	Terry Steinbach	.05
231	Glendon Rusch	.05
232	Bret Boone	.05
233	Robert Person	.05
234	Jose Hernandez	.05
235	Doug Drabek	.05
236	Jason McDonald	.05
237	Chris Widger	.05
238	Tom Martin RC	.05
239	Dave Burba	.05
240	Pete Rose II	.05
241	Bobby Ayala	.05
242	Tim Wakefield	.05
243	Dennis Springer	.05
244	Tim Belcher	.05
245	Jon Garland, Geoff Goetz (Draft Pick)	.05
246	Glenn Davis, Lance Berkman (Draft Pick)	.10
247	Vernon Wells, Aaron Akin (Draft Pick)	.10
248	Adam Kennedy, Jason Romano (Draft Pick)	.10
249	Jason Dellaero, Troy Cameron (Draft Pick)	.05
250	Alex Sanchez, Jared Sandberg RC (Expansion Team Prospects)	.10
251	Pablo Ortega, Jim Manias (Expansion Team Prospects)	.05
252	Jason Conti, Mike Stoner RC (Expansion Team Prospects)	.10
253	John Patterson, Larry Rodriguez (Expansion Team Prospects)	.05
254	Adrian Beltre, Ryan Minor RC, Aaron Boone (Prospect)	.15
255	Ben Grieve, Brian Buchanan, Dermal Brown (Prospect)	.05
256	Carl Pavano, Kerry Wood, Gil Meche (Prospect)	.15
257	David Ortiz, Daryle Ward, Richie Sexson (Prospect)	.50
258	Randy Winn, Juan Encarnacion, Andrew Vessel (Prospect)	.05
259	Kris Benson, Travis Smith, Courtney Duncan (Prospect)	.05
260	Chad Hermansen, Brent Butler, Warren Morris RC (Prospect)	.05
261	Ben Davis, Elieser Marrero, Ramon Hernandez (Prospect)	.05
262	Eric Chavez, Russell Branyan, Russ Johnson (Prospect)	.20
263	Todd Dunwoody, John Barnes, Ryan Jackson RC (Prospect)	.10
264	Matt Clement, Roy Halladay, Brian Fuentes RC (Prospect)	.05
265	Randy Johnson (Season Highlight)	.15
266	Kevin Brown (Season Highlight)	.05
267	Ricardo Rincon, Francisco Cordova (Season Highlight)	.05
268	Nomar Garciaparra (Season Highlight)	.50
269	Tino Martinez (Season Highlight)	.05
270	Chuck Knoblauch (Interleague)	.05
271	Pedro Martinez (Interleague)	.40
272	Denny Neagle (Interleague)	.05
273	Juan Gonzalez (Interleague)	.20
274	Andres Galarraga (Interleague)	.05
275	Checklist	.05
276	Checklist	.05
277	Moises Alou (World Series)	.05

278	Sandy Alomar (World Series)	.05
279	Gary Sheffield (World Series)	.05
280	Matt Williams (World Series)	.05
281	Livan Hernandez (World Series)	.05
282	Chad Ogea (World Series)	.05
283	Marlins Win (World Series)	.05
284	Tino Martinez	.05
285	Roberto Alomar	.20
286	Jeff King	.05
287	Brian Jordan	.05
288	Darin Erstad	.15
289	Ken Caminiti	.05
290	Jim Thome	.60
291	Paul Molitor	.75
292	Ivan Rodriguez	.65
293	Bernie Williams	.05
294	Todd Hundley	.05
295	Andres Galarraga	.05
296	Greg Maddux	1.00
297	Edgar Martinez	.05
298	Ron Gant	.05
299	Derek Bell	.05
300	Roger Clemens	1.00
301	Rondell White	.05
302	Barry Larkin	.05
303	Robin Ventura	.05
304	Jason Kendall	.05
305	Chipper Jones	1.00
306	John Franco	.05
307	Sammy Sosa	1.00
308	Troy Percival	.05
309	Chuck Knoblauch	.05
310	Ellis Burks	.05
311	Al Martin	.05
312	Tim Salmon	.05
313	Moises Alou	.05
314	Lance Johnson	.05
315	Justin Thompson	.05
316	Will Clark	.05
317	Barry Bonds	2.00
318	Craig Biggio	.05
319	John Smoltz	.05
320	Cal Ripken Jr.	2.00
321	Ken Griffey Jr.	1.25
322	Paul O'Neill	.05
323	Todd Helton	.65
324	John Olerud	.05
325	Mark McGwire	1.50
326	Jose Cruz Jr.	.05
327	Jeff Cirillo	.05
328	Dean Palmer	.05
329	John Wetteland	.05
330	Steve Finley	.05
331	Albert Belle	.05
332	Curt Schilling	.25
333	Raul Mondesi	.05
334	Andruw Jones	.75
335	Nomar Garciaparra	1.00
336	David Justice	.05
337	Andy Pettitte	.25
338	Pedro Martinez	.75
339	Travis Miller	.05
340	Chris Stynes	.05
341	Gregg Jefferies	.05
342	Jeff Fassero	.05
343	Craig Counsell	.05
344	Wilson Alvarez	.05
345	Bip Roberts	.05
346	Kelvim Escobar	.05
347	Mark Bellhorn	.05
348	Cory Lidle RC	.05
349	Fred McGriff	.05
350	Chuck Carr	.05
351	Bob Abreu	.05
352	Juan Guzman	.05
353	Fernando Vina	.05
354	Andy Benes	.05
355	Dave Nilsson	.05
356	Bobby Bonilla	.05
357	Ismael Valdes	.05
358	Carlos Perez	.05
359	Kirk Rueter	.05
360	Bartolo Colon	.05
361	Mel Rojas	.05
362	Johnny Damon	.25
363	Geronimo Berroa	.05
364	Reggie Sanders	.05
365	Jermaine Allensworth	.05
366	Orlando Cabrera	.05
367	Jorge Fabregas	.05
368	Scott Stahoviak	.05
369	Ken Cloude	.05
370	Donovan Osborne	.05
371	Roger Cedeno	.05
372	Neifi Perez	.05
373	Chris Holt	.05
374	Cecil Fielder	.05
375	Marty Cordova	.05
376	Tom Goodwin	.05
377	Jeff Suppan	.05
378	Jeff Brantley	.05
379	Mark Langston	.05
380	Shane Reynolds	.05
381	Mike Fetters	.05
382	Todd Greene	.05
383	Ray Durham	.05
384	Carlos Delgado	.30
385	Jeff D'Amico	.05
386	Brian McRae	.05
387	Alan Benes	.05
388	Heathcliff Slocumb	.05
389	Eric Young	.05

390	Travis Fryman	.05
391	David Cone	.05
392	Otis Nixon	.05
393	Jeremi Gonzalez	.05
394	Jeff Juden	.05
395	Jose Vizcaino	.05
396	Ugueth Urbina	.05
397	Ramon Martinez	.05
398	Robb Nen	.05
399	Harold Baines	.05
400	Delino DeShields	.05
401	John Burkett	.05
402	Sterling Hitchcock	.05
403	Mark Clark	.05
404	Terrell Wade	.05
405	Scott Brosius	.05
406	Chad Curtis	.05
407	Brian Johnson	.05
408	Roberto Kelly	.05
409	Dave Dellucci RC	.15
410	Michael Tucker	.05
411	Mark Kotsay	.05
412	Mark Lewis	.05
413	Ryan McGuire	.05
414	Shawon Dunston	.05
415	Brad Rigby	.05
416	Scott Erickson	.05
417	Bobby Jones	.05
418	Darren Oliver	.05
419	John Smiley	.05
420	T.J. Mathews	.05
421	Dustin Hermanson	.05
422	Mike Timlin	.05
423	Willie Blair	.05
424	Manny Alexander	.05
425	Bob Tewksbury	.05
426	Pete Schourek	.05
427	Reggie Jefferson	.05
428	Ed Sprague	.05
429	Jeff Conine	.05
430	Roberto Hernandez	.05
431	Tom Pagnozzi	.05
432	Jaret Wright	.05
433	Livan Hernandez	.05
434	Andy Ashby	.05
435	Todd Dunn	.05
436	Bobby Higginson	.05
437	Rod Beck	.05
438	Jim Leyritz	.05
439	Matt Williams	.05
440	Brett Tomko	.05
441	Joe Randa	.05
442	Chris Carpenter	.05
443	Dennis Reyes	.05
444	Al Leiter	.05
445	Jason Schmidt	.05
446	Ken Hill	.05
447	Shannon Stewart	.05
448	Enrique Wilson	.05
449	Fernando Tatis	.05
450	Jimmy Key	.05
451	Darrin Fletcher	.05
452	John Valentin	.05
453	Kevin Tapani	.05
454	Eric Karros	.05
455	Jay Bell	.05
456	Walt Weiss	.05
457	Devon White	.05
458	Carl Pavano	.05
459	Mike Lansing	.05
460	John Flaherty	.05
461	Richard Hidalgo	.05
462	Quinton McCracken	.05
463	Karim Garcia	.15
464	Miguel Cairo	.05
465	Edwin Diaz	.05
466	Bobby Smith	.05
467	Yamil Benitez	.05
468	Rich Butler RC	.05
469	Ben Ford RC	.05
470	Bubba Trammell	.05
471	Brent Brede	.05
472	Brooks Kieschnick	.05
473	Carlos Castillo	.05
474	Brad Radke (Season Highlight)	.05
475	Roger Clemens (Season Highlight)	.50
476	Curt Schilling (Season Highlight)	.05
477	John Olerud (Season Highlight)	.05
478	Mark McGwire (Season Highlight)	.75
479	Mike Piazza, Ken Griffey Jr. (Interleague)	.75
480	Jeff Bagwell, Frank Thomas (Interleague)	.50
481	Chipper Jones, Nomar Garciaparra (Interleague)	.65
482	Larry Walker, Juan Gonzalez (Interleague)	.30
483	Gary Sheffield, Tino Martinez (Interleague)	.05
484	Derrick Gibson, Michael Coleman, Norm Hutchins (Prospect)	.05
485	Braden Looper, Cliff Politte, Brian Rose (Prospect)	.05
486	Eric Milton, Jason Marquis, Corey Lee (Prospect)	.05
487	A.J. Hinch, Mark Osborne, Robert Fick RC (Prospect)	.10

488	Aramis Ramirez, Alex Gonzalez, Sean Casey (Prospect)	.15
489	Donnie Bridges RC, Tim Drew RC (Draft Pick)	.10
490	Ntema Ndungidi RC, Darnell McDonald RC (Draft Pick)	.10
491	Ryan Anderson RC, Mark Mangum (Draft Pick)	.25
492	J.J. Davis, Troy Glaus RC (Draft Pick)	2.00
493	Jayson Werth, Dan Reichert RC (Draft Pick)	.10
494	John Curtice RC, Mike Cuddyer RC (Draft Pick)	.25
495	Jack Cust RC, Jason Standridge RC (Draft Pick)	.15
496	Brian Anderson (Expansion Team Prospect)	.05
497	Tony Saunders (Expansion Team Prospect)	.05
498	Vladimir Nunez, Jhensy Sandoval RC (Expansion Team Prospect)	.10
499	Brad Penny, Nick Bierbrodt (Expansion Team Prospect)	.05
500	Dustin Carr RC, Luis Cruz RC (Expansion Team Prospect)	.05
501	Marcus McCain RC, Cedrick Bowers RC (Expansion Team Prospect)	.05
502	Checklist	.05
503	Checklist	.05
504	Alex Rodriguez	1.50

Minted in Cooperstown

As part of an effort to promote interest in the various major sports' halls of fame, Topps produced this parallel version of its Series 1 baseball set. A special embossing machine was set up at the National Baseball Hall of Fame in Cooperstown to apply a bronze-foil "MINTED IN COOPERSTOWN" logo to cards. Twenty-card sheets of the logoed cards were sold on the premises and single cards were inserted into foil packs.

	NM/M
Common Card:	.50
Stars/Rookies:	6X

Arizona Diamondbacks Inaugural Season

To mark the team's inaugural year in the Major Leagues, Topps produced a special run of 5,000 factory sets in which each card was embossed with a special gold seal incorporating the D-Backs logo. Sets were sold only at the team's normal souvenir outlets.

	NM/M
Complete Set (503):	80.00

Common Player: .50
Stars/Rookies: 6X

Tampa Bay Devil Rays Inaugural Season

To mark the team's inaugural year in the Major Leagues, Topps produced a special run of 5,000 factory sets in which each card was embossed with a special gold seal incorporating the D-Rays logo. Sets were sold only at the team's normal souvenir outlets.

	NM/M
Complete Set (503):	100.00
Common Player:	.50
Stars/Rookies:	6X

Baby Boomers

This 15-card retail exclusive insert was seeded one per 36 packs of Series 1. It featured some of the top young players in the game and was numbered with a "BB" prefix.

		NM/M
Complete Set (15):		15.00
Common Player:		.75
Inserted 1:36 retail		
1	Derek Jeter	6.00
2	Scott Rolen	1.00
3	Nomar Garciaparra	3.50
4	Jose Cruz Jr.	.75
5	Darin Erstad	.85
6	Todd Helton	1.50
7	Tony Clark	.75
8	Jose Guillen	.75
9	Andruw Jones	1.00
10	Vladimir Guerrero	1.50
11	Mark Kotsay	.75
12	Todd Greene	.75
13	Andy Pettitte	.85
14	Justin Thompson	.75
15	Alan Benes	.75

Roberto Clemente Reprints

Nineteen different Topps Clemente cards were reprinted with a gold foil stamp and in-

cluded 1998 Topps. Odd numbers were included in Series I, while even numbers were inserted into Series II, both at a rate of one per 18 packs. The insert was created to honor the memory of the 25th anniversary of Clemente's death.

		NM/M
Complete Set (19):		50.00
Common Card:		2.50
Inserted 1:18		
1	1955	4.00
2	1956	2.50
3	1957	2.50
4	1958	2.50
5	1959	2.50
6	1960	2.50
7	1961	2.50
8	1962	2.50
9	1963	2.50
10	1964	2.50
11	1965	2.50
12	1966	2.50
13	1967	2.50
14	1968	2.50
15	1969	2.50
16	1970	2.50
17	1971	2.50
18	1972	2.50
19	1973	2.50

Roberto Clemente Finest

Clemente Finest inserts were included in both Series I and II at a rate of one per 72 packs. There were a total of 19 different, with odd numbers in Series I and even numbers in Series II. The insert helped honor the memory of the 25th anniversary of his death.

		NM/M
Complete Set (19):		60.00
Common Card:		3.50
Inserted 1:72		
Refractors:		2X
Inserted 1:288		
1	1955	6.00
2	1956	3.50
3	1957	3.50
4	1958	3.50
5	1959	3.50
6	1960	3.50
7	1961	3.50
8	1962	3.50
9	1963	3.50
10	1964	3.50
11	1965	3.50
12	1966	3.50
13	1967	3.50
14	1968	3.50
15	1969	3.50
16	1970	3.50
17	1971	3.50
18	1972	3.50
19	1973	3.50

Roberto Clemente "Tin" Reprints

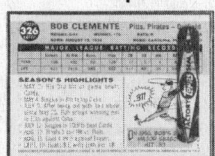

Each of the 19 basic Clemente reprint cards can also be found in a factory-sealed, gold-foil stamped soft plastic case. These were inserted in special retail-only tin boxes and one per factory set of 1998 Topps.

	NM/M
Complete Set (19):	60.00

Roberto Clemente Commemorative Tins

This series of commemorative tin card "packs" reproduces in an enlarged (about 3" x 4-5/8" x 3/4") format the front and back of four of Roberto Clemente's Topps cards. Each tin, originally retailing for about $5, contains a plastic-sealed Clemente reprint card.

	NM/M
Complete Set (4):	10.00
Roberto Clemente/ 1955	3.50
Roberto Clemente/ 1956	2.50
Roberto Clemente/ 1965	2.50
Roberto Clemente/ 1971	2.50

Roberto Clemente Tribute

Five Clemente Tribute cards were produced for Series I and inserted in one per 12 packs. The set features some classic photos of Clemente and honor his memory in the 25th anniversary of his death. Clemente Tribute cards are numbered with a "RC" prefix.

		NM/M
Complete Set (5):		3.00
Common Clemente:		.75
Inserted 1:12		
1-5	Roberto Clemente	.75

Clout 9

Clout 9 captured nine players known for their statistical supremacy. Cards were numbered with a "C" prefix and inserted one per 72 packs of Series 2.

		NM/M
Complete Set (9):		17.50
Common Player:		1.00
Inserted 1:72		
1	Edgar Martinez	1.00
2	Mike Piazza	5.00
3	Frank Thomas	2.00
4	Craig Biggio	1.00
5	Vinny Castilla	1.00
6	Jeff Blauser	1.00

		NM/M
Common Card:		4.00
1	1955	8.00
2	1956	4.00
3	1957	4.00
4	1958	4.00
5	1959	4.00
6	1960	4.00
7	1961	4.00
8	1962	4.00
9	1963	4.00
10	1964	4.00
11	1965	4.00
12	1966	4.00
13	1967	4.00
14	1968	4.00
15	1969	4.00
16	1970	4.00
17	1971	4.00
18	1972	4.00
19	1973	4.00
7	Barry Bonds	7.50
8	Ken Griffey Jr.	5.00
9	Larry Walker	1.00

Etch-A-Sketch

Etch-a-Sketch featured nine different players depicted by nationally acclaimed artist George Vlosich III. Known as "The Etch-a-Sketch Kid," Vlosich created each one of these Series I inserts, which were inserted at a rate of one per 36 packs. Cards are numbered with an "ES" prefix.

		NM/M
Complete Set (9):		20.00
Common Player:		1.00
Inserted 1:36		
1	Juan Gonzalez	.85
2	Nomar Garciaparra	2.50
3	Jose Cruz Jr.	.75
4	Cal Ripken Jr.	5.00
5	Ken Griffey Jr.	3.50
6	Ivan Rodriguez	1.00
7	Larry Walker	.75
8	Barry Bonds	5.00
9	Roger Clemens	3.00
10	Frank Thomas	1.50
11	Chuck Knoblauch	.75
12	Mike Piazza	3.50
13	Greg Maddux	2.50
14	Vladimir Guerrero	1.50
15	Andruw Jones	1.50

Hallbound

Hall Bound features players who were considered locks to be inducted into the Hall of Fame when their career was over. This insert was exclusive to Series 1 hobby packs and seeded one per 36. Cards are numbered with a "HB" prefix.

		NM/M
Complete Set (15):		45.00
Common Player:		1.50
1	Paul Molitor	2.50
2	Tony Gwynn	3.50
3	Wade Boggs	3.50
4	Roger Clemens	4.00
5	Dennis Eckersley	2.00
6	Cal Ripken Jr.	7.50
7	Greg Maddux	3.50
8	Rickey Henderson	2.50
9	Ken Griffey Jr.	5.00
10	Frank Thomas	2.50
11	Mark McGwire	6.00
12	Barry Bonds	7.50
13	Mike Piazza	5.00
14	Juan Gonzalez	1.50
15	Randy Johnson	2.50

Inter-League Mystery Finest

Five of the 1997 season's most intriguing inter-league matchups are showcased with four cards each in Inter-League Mystery Finest. Regular versions of this Series 1 insert are seeded one per 36 packs, while Refractor versions are seeded one per 144 packs. Cards are numbered with an "ILM" prefix.

		NM/M
Complete Set (20):		35.00
Common Player:		.75
Inserted 1:36		
Refractors:		1.5X
Inserted 1:144		
1	Chipper Jones	3.00
2	Cal Ripken Jr.	6.50
3	Greg Maddux	3.00
4	Rafael Palmeiro	1.50
5	Todd Hundley	.75
6	Derek Jeter	6.50
7	John Olerud	.75
8	Tino Martinez	.75
9	Larry Walker	.75
10	Ken Griffey Jr.	4.00
11	Andres Galarraga	.75
12	Randy Johnson	2.00
13	Mike Piazza	4.00
14	Jim Edmonds	.75
15	Eric Karros	.75
16	Tim Salmon	.75
17	Sammy Sosa	3.00
18	Frank Thomas	2.00
19	Mark Grace	.75
20	Albert Belle	.75

Milestones

Milestones features 10 records that could be broken during the 1998 season and the players who have the best shot at breaking them. This retail exclusive insert is seeded one per 36 packs and is numbered with a "MS" prefix.

		NM/M
Complete Set (10):		17.50
Common Player:		.75
MS1	Barry Bonds	5.00
MS2	Roger Clemens	2.50
MS3	Dennis Eckersley	1.00
MS4	Juan Gonzalez	.75
MS5	Ken Griffey Jr.	3.00
MS6	Tony Gwynn	2.00
MS7	Greg Maddux	2.00
MS8	Mark McGwire	4.00
MS9	Cal Ripken Jr.	5.00
MS10	Frank Thomas	1.25

Mystery Finest

This 20-card insert set features top players on bordered and borderless designs, with Refractor versions of each. Exclusive to Series 2 packs, bordered cards are seeded 1:36 packs, borderless are seeded 1:72 packs, bordered Refractors are 1:108 and borderless Refractors are seeded 1:288 packs. Mystery Finest inserts are numbered with a "M" prefix.

	NM/M
Complete Set (20):	25.00
Common Player:	.50
Inserted 1:36	
Borderless 1:72:	1.5X
Bordered Refractors 1:108:	1.5X

Flashback

This double-sided insert offers "then and now" photos of 10 top major leaguers. One side pictures the player circa 1998, while the other side shows him at the beginning of his major league career. Flashback inserts were seeded one per 72 packs and numbered with a "FB" prefix.

		NM/M
Complete Set (10):		22.50
Common Player:		1.00
Inserted 1:72		
1	Barry Bonds	7.50
2	Ken Griffey Jr.	5.00
3	Paul Molitor	2.00
4	Randy Johnson	2.00
5	Cal Ripken Jr.	7.50
6	Tony Gwynn	3.00
7	Kenny Lofton	1.00
8	Gary Sheffield	1.50
9	Deion Sanders	1.00
10	Brady Anderson	1.00

Focal Point

This hobby exclusive insert focuses on the skills that have made the players great. Focal Point inserts were avail-

able in Series 2 packs, seeded one per 36, and are numbered with a "FP" prefix.

	NM/M
Complete Set (15):	25.00
Common Player:	.75
Inserted 1:36	

Borderless Refractors 1:288: 2X

#	Player	Price
1	Nomar Garciaparra	1.50
2	Chipper Jones	1.50
3	Scott Rolen	.75
4	Albert Belle	.50
5	Mo Vaughn	.50
6	Jose Cruz Jr.	.50
7	Mark McGwire	3.00
8	Derek Jeter	3.50
9	Tony Gwynn	1.50
10	Frank Thomas	1.00
11	Tino Martinez	.50
12	Greg Maddux	1.50
13	Juan Gonzalez	.75
14	Larry Walker	.50
15	Mike Piazza	2.50
16	Cal Ripken Jr.	3.50
17	Jeff Bagwell	1.00
18	Andruw Jones	1.00
19	Barry Bonds	3.50
20	Ken Griffey Jr.	2.50

Rookie Class

Rookie Class features 10 young stars from 1998 and was exclusive to Series II packs. The cards were inserted one per 12 packs and numbered with a "R" prefix.

		NM/M
Complete Set (10):		4.00
Common Player:		.25
Inserted 1:12		
1	Travis Lee	.50
2	Richard Hidalgo	.25
3	Todd Helton	2.00
4	Paul Konerko	.75
5	Mark Kotsay	.25
6	Derrek Lee	1.50
7	Eli Marrero	.25
8	Fernando Tatis	.25
9	Juan Encarnacion	.25
10	Ben Grieve	.25

1998 Topps Chrome

All 502 1998 Topps cards were reprinted in chromium versions for Topps Chrome. Chrome was released in two series; Series 1 containing 282 cards and Series 2 including 220 cards. Four-card packs had a suggested retail price of $3. Card fronts include a Topps Chrome logo. The issue offers a sampling of the inserts from Topps, along with Refractor versions of every card and insert. Series 1 inserts included: Flashbacks, Baby Boomers and Hallbound. Series 2 inserts included: Milestones, '98 Rookie Class and Clout 9.

		NM/M
Complete Set (502):		100.00
Common Player:		.10
Refractors:		5X
Inserted 1:12		
Foil Pack (4):		1.50
Foil Box (24):		25.00
1	Tony Gwynn	2.00
2	Larry Walker	.10
3	Billy Wagner	.10
4	Denny Neagle	.10
5	Vladimir Guerrero	1.50
6	Kevin Brown	.10
7	Mariano Rivera	.10
8	Tony Clark	.10
9	Deion Sanders	.10
10	Francisco Cordova	.10
11	Matt Williams	.10
12	Carlos Baerga	.10
13	Mo Vaughn	.10
14	Bobby Witt	.10
15	Matt Stairs	.10
16	Chan Ho Park	.10
17	Mike Bordick	.10
18	Michael Tucker	.10
19	Frank Thomas	1.50
20	Roberto Clemente (Tribute)	2.50
21	Dmitri Young	.10
22	Steve Trachsel	.10
23	Jeff Kent	.10
24	Scott Rolen	.75
25	John Thomson	.10
26	Joe Vitiello	.10
27	Eddie Guardado	.10
28	Charlie Hayes	.10
29	Juan Gonzalez	.75
30	Garret Anderson	.10
31	John Jaha	.10
32	Omar Vizquel	.10
33	Brian Hunter	.10
34	Jeff Bagwell	1.50
35	Mark Lemke	.10
36	Doug Glanville	.10
37	Dan Wilson	.10
38	Steve Cooke	.10
39	Chili Davis	.10
40	Mike Cameron	.10
41	F.P. Santangelo	.10
42	Brad Ausmus	.10
43	Gary DiSarcina	.10
44	Pat Hentgen	.10
45	Wilton Guerrero	.10
46	Devon White	.10
47	Danny Patterson	.10
48	Pat Meares	.10
49	Rafael Palmeiro	1.00
50	Mark Gardner	.10
51	Jeff Blauser	.10
52	Dave Hollins	.10
53	Carlos Garcia	.10
54	Ben McDonald	.10
55	John Mabry	.10
56	Trevor Hoffman	.10
57	Tony Fernandez	.10
58	Rich Loiselle	.10
59	Mark Leiter	.10
60	Pat Kelly	.10
61	John Flaherty	.10
62	Roger Bailey	.10
63	Tom Gordon	.10
64	Ryan Klesko	.10
65	Darryl Hamilton	.10
66	Jim Eisenreich	.10
67	Butch Huskey	.10
68	Mark Grudzielanek	.10
69	Marquis Grissom	.10
70	Mark McLemore	.10
71	Gary Gaetti	.10
72	Greg Gagne	.10
73	Lyle Mouton	.10
74	Jim Edmonds	.10
75	Shawn Green	.35
76	Terry Vaughn	.10
77	Terry Adams	.10
78	Kevin Polcovich RC	.10
79	Troy O'Leary	.10
80	Jeff Shaw	.10
81	Rich Becker	.10
82	David Wells	.10
83	Steve Karsay	.10
84	Charles Nagy	.10
85	B.J. Surhoff	.10
86	Jamey Wright	.10
87	James Baldwin	.10
88	Edgardo Alfonzo	.10
89	Jay Buhner	.10
90	Brady Anderson	.10
91	Scott Servais	.10
92	Edgar Renteria	.10
93	Mike Lieberthal	.10
94	Rick Aguilera	.10
95	Walt Weiss	.10
96	Deivi Cruz	.10
97	Kurt Abbott	.10
98	Henry Rodriguez	.10
99	Mike Piazza	2.25
100	Bill Taylor	.10
101	Todd Zeile	.10
102	Rey Ordonez	.10
103	Willie Greene	.10
104	Tony Womack	.10
105	Mike Sweeney	.10
106	Jeffrey Hammonds	.10
107	Kevin Orie	.10
108	Alex Gonzalez	.10
109	Jose Canseco	.60
110	Paul Sorrento	.10
111	Joey Hamilton	.10
112	Brad Radke	.10
113	Steve Avery	.10
114	Esteban Loaiza	.10
115	Stan Javier	.10
116	Chris Gomez	.10
117	Royce Clayton	.10
118	Orlando Merced	.10
119	Kevin Appier	.10
120	Kevin Appier	.10
121	Mel Nieves	.10
122	Joe Girardi	.10
123	Rico Brogna	.10
124	Kent Mercker	.10
125	Manny Ramirez	1.50
126	Jeromy Burnitz	.10
127	Kevin Foster	.10
128	Matt Morris	.10
129	Jason Dickson	.10
130	Tom Glavine	.35
131	Wally Joyner	.10
132	Rick Reed	.10
133	Todd Jones	.10
134	Dave Martinez	.10
135	Sandy Alomar	.10
136	Mike Lansing	.10
137	Sean Berry	.10
138	Doug Jones	.10
139	Todd Stottlemyre	.10
140	Jay Bell	.10
141	Jaime Navarro	.10
142	Chris Hoiles	.10
143	Joey Cora	.10
144	Scott Spiezio	.10
145	Joe Carter	.10
146	Jose Guillen	.10
147	Damion Easley	.10
148	Lee Stevens	.10
149	Alex Fernandez	.10
150	Randy Johnson	1.50
151	J.T. Snow	.10
152	Chuck Finley	.10
153	Bernard Gilkey	.10
154	David Segui	.10
155	Dante Bichette	.10
156	Kevin Stocker	.10
157	Carl Everett	.10
158	Jose Valentin	.10
159	Pokey Reese	.10
160	Derek Jeter	3.00
161	Roger Pavlik	.10
162	Mark Wohlers	.10
163	Ricky Bottalico	.10
164	Ozzie Guillen	.10
165	Mike Mussina	.60
166	Gary Sheffield	.50
167	Hideo Nomo	.75
168	Mark Grace	.10
169	Aaron Sele	.10
170	Darryl Kile	.10
171	Shawn Estes	.10
172	Vinny Castilla	.10
173	Ron Coomer	.10
174	Jose Rosado	.10
175	Kenny Lofton	.10
176	Jason Giambi	.65
177	Hal Morris	.10
178	Darren Bragg	.10
179	Orel Hershiser	.10
180	Ray Lankford	.10
181	Hideki Irabu	.10
182	Kevin Young	.10
183	Javy Lopez	.10
184	Jeff Montgomery	.10
185	Mike Holtz	.10
186	George Williams	.10
187	Cal Eldred	.10
188	Tom Candiotti	.10
189	Glenallen Hill	.10
190	Brian Giles	.10
191	Dave Mlicki	.10
192	Garrett Stephenson	.10
193	Jeff Frye	.10
194	Joe Oliver	.10
195	Bob Hamelin	.10
196	Luis Sojo	.10
197	LaTroy Hawkins	.10
198	Kevin Elster	.10
199	Jeff Reed	.10
200	Dennis Eckersley	1.00
201	Bill Mueller	.10
202	Russ Davis	.10
203	Armando Benitez	.10
204	Quilvio Veras	.10
205	Tim Naehring	.10
206	Quinton McCracken	.10
207	Raul Casanova	.10
208	Matt Lawton	.10
209	Luis Alicea	.10
210	Luis Gonzalez	.10
211	Allen Watson	.10
212	Gerald Williams	.10
213	David Bell	.10
214	Todd Hollandsworth	.10
215	Wade Boggs	2.00
216	Jose Mesa	.10
217	Jamie Moyer	.10
218	Darren Daulton	.10
219	Mickey Morandini	.10
220	Rusty Greer	.10
221	Jim Bullinger	.10
222	Jose Offerman	.10
223	Matt Karchner	.10
224	Woody Williams	.10
225	Mark Loretta	.10
226	Mike Hampton	.10
227	Willie Adams	.10
228	Scott Hatteberg	.10
229	Rich Amaral	.10
230	Terry Steinbach	.10
231	Glendon Rusch	.10
232	Bret Boone	.10
233	Robert Person	.10
234	Jose Hernandez	.10
235	Doug Drabek	.10
236	Jason McDonald	.10
237	Chris Widger	.10
238	Tom Martin RC	.10
239	Dave Burba	.10
240	Pete Rose	.10
241	Bobby Ayala	.10
242	Tim Wakefield	.10
243	Dennis Springer	.10
244	Tim Belcher	.10
245	Jon Garland, Geoff Goetz (Draft Pick)	.25
246	Glenn Davis, Lance Berkman (Draft Pick)	.25
247	Vernon Wells, Aaron Akin (Draft Pick)	.15
248	Adam Kennedy, Jason Romano (Draft Pick)	.10
249	Jason Dellaero, Troy Cameron (Draft Pick)	.10
250	Alex Sanchez, Jared Sandberg RC (Expansion)	.25
251	Pablo Ortega, James Manias RC (Expansion)	.10
252	Jason Conti, Mike Stoner RC (Expansion)	.10
253	John Patterson, Larry Rodriguez (Expansion)	.10
254	Adrian Beltre, Ryan Minor RC, Aaron Boone (Prospect)	.25
255	Ben Grieve, Brian Buchanan, Dermal Brown (Prospect)	.10
256	Carl Pavano, Kerry Wood, Gil Meche (Prospect)	.75
257	David Ortiz, Daryle Ward, Richie Sexson (Prospect)	.65
258	Randy Winn, Juan Encarnacion, Andrew Vessel (Prospect)	.10
259	Kris Benson, Travis Smith, Courtney Duncan (Prospect)	.15
260	Chad Hermansen, Brent Butler, Warren Morris RC (Prospect)	.15
261	Ben Davis, Elieser Marrero, Ramon Hernandez (Prospect)	.10
262	Eric Chavez, Russell Branyan, Russ Johnson (Prospect)	.25
263	Todd Dunwoody, John Barnes, Ryan Jackson RC (Prospect)	.10
264	Matt Clement, Roy Halladay, Brian Fuentes (Prospect)	.20
265	Randy Johnson (Season Highlight)	.50
266	Kevin Brown (Season Highlight)	.10
267	Francisco Cordova, Ricardo Rincon (Season Highlight)	.10
268	Nomar Garciaparra (Season Highlight)	.75
269	Tino Martinez (Season Highlight)	.10
270	Chuck Knoblauch (Inter-League)	.10
271	Pedro Martinez (Inter-League)	.40
272	Denny Neagle (Inter-League)	.10
273	Juan Gonzalez (Inter-League)	.20
274	Andres Galarraga (Inter-League)	.10
275	Checklist	.10
276	Checklist	.10
277	Moises Alou (World Series)	.10
278	Sandy Alomar (World Series)	.10
279	Gary Sheffield (World Series)	.10
280	Matt Williams (World Series)	.10
281	Livan Hernandez (World Series)	.10
282	Chad Ogea (World Series)	.10
283	Marlins Win (World Series)	.10
284	Tino Martinez	.10
285	Roberto Alomar	.35
286	Jeff King	.10
287	Brian Jordan	.10
288	Darin Erstad	.30
289	Ken Caminiti	.10
290	Jim Thome	.90
291	Paul Molitor	1.50
292	Ivan Rodriguez	1.00
293	Bernie Williams	.10
294	Todd Hundley	.10
295	Andres Galarraga	.10
296	Greg Maddux	2.00
297	Edgar Martinez	.10
298	Ron Gant	.10
299	Derek Bell	.10
300	Roger Clemens	2.00
301	Rondell White	.10
302	Barry Larkin	.10
303	Robin Ventura	.10
304	Jason Kendall	.10
305	Chipper Jones	2.00
306	John Franco	.10
307	Sammy Sosa	2.00
308	Troy Percival	.10
309	Chuck Knoblauch	.10
310	Ellis Burks	.10
311	Al Martin	.10
312	Tim Salmon	.10
313	Moises Alou	.10
314	Lance Johnson	.10
315	Justin Thompson	.10
316	Will Clark	.10
317	Barry Bonds	3.00
318	Craig Biggio	.10
319	John Smoltz	.10
320	Cal Ripken Jr.	3.00
321	Ken Griffey Jr.	2.25
322	Paul O'Neill	.10
323	Todd Helton	1.50
324	John Olerud	.10
325	Mark McGwire	2.50
326	Jose Cruz Jr.	.10
327	Jeff Cirillo	.10
328	Dean Palmer	.10
329	John Wetteland	.10
330	Steve Finley	.10
331	Albert Belle	.10
332	Curt Schilling	.35
333	Raul Mondesi	.10
334	Andruw Jones	1.50
335	Nomar Garciaparra	2.00
336	David Justice	.10
337	Andy Pettitte	.30
338	Pedro Martinez	1.50
339	Travis Miller	.10
340	Chris Stynes	.10
341	Gregg Jefferies	.10
342	Jeff Fassero	.10
343	Craig Counsell	.10
344	Wilson Alvarez	.10
345	Bip Roberts	.10
346	Kelvim Escobar	.10
347	Mark Bellhorn	.10
348	Cory Lidle	.10
349	Fred McGriff	.10
350	Chuck Carr	.10
351	Bob Abreu	.10
352	Juan Guzman	.10
353	Fernando Vina	.10
354	Andy Benes	.10
355	Dave Nilsson	.10
356	Bobby Bonilla	.10
357	Ismael Valdes	.10
358	Carlos Perez	.10
359	Kirk Rueter	.10
360	Bartolo Colon	.10
361	Mel Rojas	.10
362	Johnny Damon	.35
363	Geronimo Berroa	.10
364	Reggie Sanders	.10
365	Jermaine Allensworth	.10
366	Orlando Cabrera	.10
367	Jorge Fabregas	.10
368	Scott Stahoviak	.10
369	Ken Cloude	.10
370	Donovan Osborne	.10
371	Roger Cedeno	.10
372	Neifi Perez	.10
373	Chris Holt	.10
374	Cecil Fielder	.10
375	Marty Cordova	.10
376	Tom Goodwin	.10
377	Jeff Suppan	.10
378	Jeff Brantley	.10
379	Mark Langston	.10
380	Shane Reynolds	.10
381	Mike Fetters	.10
382	Todd Greene	.10
383	Ray Durham	.10
384	Carlos Delgado	.35
385	Jeff D'Amico	.10
386	Brian McRae	.10
387	Alan Benes	.10
388	Heathcliff Slocumb	.10
389	Eric Young	.10
390	Travis Fryman	.10
391	David Cone	.10
392	Otis Nixon	.10
393	Jeremi Gonzalez	.10
394	Jeff Juden	.10
395	Jose Vizcaino	.10
396	Ugueth Urbina	.10
397	Ramon Martinez	.10
398	Robb Nen	.10
399	Harold Baines	.10
400	Delino DeShields	.10
401	John Burkett	.10
402	Sterling Hitchcock	.10
403	Mark Clark	.10
404	Terrell Wade	.10
405	Scott Brosius	.10
406	Chad Curtis	.10
407	Brian Johnson	.10
408	Roberto Kelly	.10
409	Dave Dellucci RC	.25
410	Michael Tucker	.10
411	Mark Kotsay	.10
412	Mark Lewis	.10
413	Ryan McGuire	.10
414	Shawon Dunston	.10
415	Brad Rigby	.10
416	Scott Erickson	.10
417	Bobby Jones	.10
418	Darren Oliver	.10
419	John Smiley	.10
420	T.J. Mathews	.10
421	Dustin Hermanson	.10
422	Mike Timlin	.10
423	Willie Blair	.10
424	Manny Alexander	.10
425	Bob Tewksbury	.10
426	Pete Schourek	.10
427	Reggie Jefferson	.10
428	Ed Sprague	.10
429	Jeff Conine	.10
430	Roberto Hernandez	.10
431	Tom Pagnozzi	.10
432	Jaret Wright	.10
433	Livan Hernandez	.10
434	Andy Ashby	.10
435	Todd Dunn	.10
436	Bobby Higginson	.10
437	Rod Beck	.10
438	Jim Leyritz	.10
439	Matt Williams	.10
440	Brett Tomko	.10
441	Joe Randa	.10
442	Chris Carpenter	.10
443	Dennis Reyes	.10
444	Al Leiter	.10
445	Jason Schmidt	.10
446	Ken Hill	.10
447	Shannon Stewart	.10
448	Enrique Wilson	.10
449	Fernando Tatis	.10
450	Jimmy Key	.10
451	Darrin Fletcher	.10
452	John Valentin	.10
453	Kevin Tapani	.10
454	Eric Karros	.10
455	Jay Bell	.10
456	Walt Weiss	.10
457	Devon White	.10
458	Carl Pavano	.10
459	Mike Lansing	.10
460	John Flaherty	.10
461	Richard Hidalgo	.10
462	Quinton McCracken	.10
463	Karim Garcia	.20
464	Miguel Cairo	.10
465	Edwin Diaz	.10
466	Bobby Smith	.10
467	Yamil Benitez	.10
468	Rich Butler RC	.10
469	Ben Ford RC	.10
470	Bubba Trammell	.10
471	Brent Brede	.10
472	Brooks Kieschnick	.10
473	Carlos Castillo	.10
474	Brad Radke (Season Highlight)	.10
475	Roger Clemens (Season Highlight)	1.00
476	Curt Schilling (Season Highlight)	.15
477	John Olerud (Season Highlight)	.10
478	Mark McGwire (Season Highlight)	1.25
479	Mike Piazza, Ken Griffey Jr. (Interleague)	1.25
480	Jeff Bagwell, Frank Thomas (Interleague)	1.00
481	Chipper Jones, Nomar Garciaparra (Interleague)	1.00
482	Larry Walker, Juan Gonzalez (Interleague)	.20
483	Gary Sheffield, Tino Martinez (Interleague)	.10
484	Derrick Gibson, Michael Coleman, Norm Hutchins (Prospect)	.10
485	Braden Looper, Cliff Politte, Brian Rose (Prospect)	.15
486	Eric Milton, Jason Marquis, Corey Lee (Prospect)	.25
487	A.J. Hinch, Mark Osborne, Robert Fick RC (Prospect)	.25
488	Aramis Ramirez, Alex Gonzalez, Sean Casey (Prospect)	.25
489	Donnie Bridges RC, Tim Drew RC (Draft Pick)	.20
490	Ntema Ndungidi RC, Darnell McDonald RC (Draft Pick)	.50
491	Ryan Anderson RC, Mark Mangum (Draft Pick)	.50
492	J.J. Davis, Troy Glaus RC (Draft Pick)	3.00
493	Jayson Werth, Dan Reichert (Draft Pick)	.10
494	John Curtice RC, Mike Cuddyer RC (Draft Pick)	.50
495	Jack Cust RC, Jason Standridge (Draft Pick)	.50

496 Brian Anderson (Expansion Team Prospect) .10
497 Tony Saunders (Expansion Team Prospect) .10
498 Vladimir Nunez, Jhensy Sandoval **RC** (Expansion Team Prospect) .10
499 Brad Penny, Nick Bierbrodt (Expansion Team Prospect) .10
500 Dustin Carr **RC**, Luis Cruz **RC** (Expansion Team Prospect) .10
501 Marcus McCain **RC**, Cedrick Bowers **RC** (Expansion Team Prospect) .10
502 Checklist .10
503 Checklist .10
504 Alex Rodriguez 2.50

Refractors

Each card in the regular Topps Series 1 and Series 2 Chrome issue could also be found in a refractor version seeded approximately one per 12 packs. Refractor versions are so designated above the card number on back.

	NM/M
Common Player:	.50
Stars/Rookies:	5X

Baby Boomers

This 15-card insert featured players with less than three years of experience. Cards were inserted one per 24 packs, with Refractor versions found every 72 packs of Series I. Cards were numbered with a "BB" prefix.

	NM/M
Complete Set (15):	16.00
Common Player:	.75
Inserted 1:24	
Refractors:	1.5X
Inserted 1:72	
1 Derek Jeter	6.00
2 Scott Rolen	.90
3 Nomar Garciaparra	3.50
4 Jose Cruz Jr.	.75
5 Darin Erstad	.90
6 Todd Helton	1.50
7 Tony Clark	.75
8 Jose Guillen	.75
9 Andruw Jones	1.50
10 Vladimir Guerrero	1.50
11 Mark Kotsay	.75
12 Todd Greene	.75
13 Andy Pettitte	.90
14 Justin Thompson	.75
15 Alan Benes	.75

Clout 9

This nine-card insert included players for their statistical supremacy. Clout 9 cards were found in Series II packs at a rate of one per 24 packs, with Refractor versions every 72 packs. Cards are numbered with a "C" prefix.

	NM/M
Complete Set (9):	15.00
Common Player:	.75
Inserted 1:24	
Refractors:	1.5X
Inserted 1:72	
1 Edgar Martinez	.75
2 Mike Piazza	3.50
3 Frank Thomas	1.50
4 Craig Biggio	.75
5 Vinny Castilla	.75
6 Jeff Blauser	.75
7 Barry Bonds	6.00
8 Ken Griffey Jr.	3.50
9 Larry Walker	.75

Flashback

This 10-card double-sided insert features top players as they looked in 1998 on one side, and how they looked when they first appeared in the majors on the other side. Flashback inserts were seeded one per 24 packs of Series I, with Refractors every 72 packs. This insert was numbered with a "FB" prefix.

	NM/M
Complete Set (10):	16.00
Common Player:	.75
Inserted 1:24	
Refractors:	1.5X
Inserted 1:72	
1 Barry Bonds	6.00
2 Ken Griffey Jr.	3.50
3 Paul Molitor	1.50
4 Randy Johnson	1.50
5 Cal Ripken Jr.	6.00
6 Tony Gwynn	2.50
7 Kenny Lofton	.75
8 Gary Sheffield	.85
9 Deion Sanders	.75
10 Brady Anderson	.75

Hallbound

Hallbound highlighted 15 players destined for the Hall of Fame on die-cut cards. Inserted at a rate of one per 24 packs of Series I, with Refractors every 72 packs, these were numbered with a "HB" prefix.

	NM/M
Complete Set (15):	35.00
Common Player:	1.50
Inserted 1:24	
Refractors:	1.5X
Inserted 1:72	
1 Paul Molitor	2.00
2 Tony Gwynn	2.50
3 Wade Boggs	2.50
4 Roger Clemens	3.00
5 Dennis Eckersley	1.50
6 Cal Ripken Jr.	6.00
7 Greg Maddux	2.50
8 Rickey Henderson	2.00
9 Ken Griffey Jr.	3.50
10 Frank Thomas	2.00
11 Mark McGwire	4.50
12 Barry Bonds	6.00
13 Mike Piazza	3.50
14 Juan Gonzalez	1.50
15 Randy Johnson	2.00

Milestones

Ten superstars who were within reach of major records for the 1998 season are featured in Milestones. This Series II insert was seeded one per 24 packs, with Refractor versions seeded one per 72 packs. Milestones were numbered with a "MS" prefix.

	NM/M
Complete Set (10):	25.00
Common Player:	1.00
Inserted 1:24	
Refractors:	1.5X
Inserted 1:72	
1 Barry Bonds	6.00
2 Roger Clemens	3.00
3 Dennis Eckersley	1.00
4 Juan Gonzalez	1.00
5 Ken Griffey Jr.	3.50
6 Tony Gwynn	2.50
7 Greg Maddux	2.50
8 Mark McGwire	4.50
9 Cal Ripken Jr.	6.00
10 Frank Thomas	1.50

Rookie Class

This insert featured 10 players with less than one year of major league experience. Inserted in Series II packs at a rate of one per 12 packs, with Refractors every 24 packs, '98 Rookie Class inserts were numbered with a "R" prefix.

	NM/M
Complete Set (10):	10.00
Common Player:	.75
Inserted 1:12	
Refractors:	1.5X
Inserted 1:24	
1 Travis Lee	1.00
2 Richard Hidalgo	.75
3 Todd Helton	4.50
4 Paul Konerko	1.50
5 Mark Kotsay	.75
6 Derrek Lee	3.00
7 Eli Marrero	.75
8 Fernando Tatis	.75
9 Juan Encarnacion	.75
10 Ben Grieve	.75

Super Chrome

This 36-card oversized set featured some of the top players from Chrome on 4-1/8" x 5-3/4" cards. The product sold in three-card packs and featured the same photography as Topps and Topps Chrome before it, but added a Super Chrome logo. Refractor versions of each card were also available, inserted one per 12 packs.

	NM/M
Complete Set (36):	20.00
Common Player:	.25
Refractors:	1.5X
Inserted 1:12	
Pack (3):	2.50
Wax Box (12):	25.00
1 Tony Gwynn	1.00
2 Larry Walker	.25
3 Vladimir Guerrero	.25
4 Mo Vaughn	.25
5 Frank Thomas	.75
6 Barry Larkin	.25
7 Scott Rolen	.25
8 Juan Gonzalez	.75
9 Jeff Bagwell	.75
10 Ryan Klesko	.25
11 Mike Piazza	1.50
12 Randy Johnson	.75
13 Derek Jeter	3.00
14 Gary Sheffield	.50
15 Hideo Nomo	.50
16 Tino Martinez	.25
17 Ivan Rodriguez	.65
18 Bernie Williams	.25
19 Greg Maddux	1.00
20 Roger Clemens	1.25
21 Roberto Clemente	2.00
22 Chipper Jones	1.00
23 Sammy Sosa	1.00
24 Tony Clark	.25
25 Barry Bonds	3.00
26 Craig Biggio	.25
27 Cal Ripken Jr.	3.00
28 Ken Griffey Jr.	1.50
29 Todd Helton	.65
30 Mark McGwire	3.00
31 Jose Cruz	.25
32 Albert Belle	.25
33 Andruw Jones	.75
34 Nomar Garciaparra	1.00
35 Andy Pettitte	.45
36 Alex Rodriguez	2.00

1998 Topps Gallery Pre-Production Samples

To introduce its premium Gallery line for 1998, Topps issued this set of pre-production samples showcasing several of the different technologies to be found in the issue. The samples are virtually identical to the issued versions except for the use of a "PP" prefix to the card number.

	NM/M
Complete Set (5):	7.50
Common Player:	1.50
PP1 Andruw Jones (Portraits)	1.50
PP2 Juan Gonzalez (Permanent Collection)	1.00
PP3 Barry Bonds (Expressionists)	3.00
PP4 Derek Jeter (Exhibitions)	3.00
PP5 Nomar Garciaparra (Impressions)	2.00

1998 Topps Gallery

Gallery returned in 1998 with a 150-card set broken up into five different subsets - Exhibitions, Impressions, Expressionists, Portraits and Permanent Collection. The set was paralleled twice - first in a Player's Private Issue set and, second in Gallery Proofs. Gallery cards were made to look like works of art instead of simply a photo of the player on cardboard, and were sold in six-card packs. Inserts in this single-series product include: Photo Gallery, Gallery of Heroes and Awards Gallery.

	NM/M
Complete Set (150):	15.00
Common Player:	.10
Pack (6):	1.50
Wax Box (24):	25.00
1 Andruw Jones	1.00
2 Fred McGriff	.10
3 Wade Boggs	1.50
4 Pedro Martinez	1.00
5 Matt Williams	.10
6 Wilson Alvarez	.10
7 Henry Rodriguez	.10
8 Jay Bell	.10
9 Marquis Grissom	.10
10 Darryl Kile	.10
11 Chuck Knoblauch	.10
12 Kenny Lofton	.10
13 Quinton McCracken	.10
14 Andres Galarraga	.10
15 Brian Jordan	.10
16 Mike Lansing	.10
17 Travis Fryman	.10
18 Tony Saunders	.10
19 Moises Alou	.10
20 Travis Lee	.10
21 Garret Anderson	.10
22 Ken Caminiti	.10
23 Pedro Astacio	.10
24 Ellis Burks	.10
25 Albert Belle	.10
26 Alan Benes	.10
27 Jay Buhner	.10
28 Derek Bell	.10
29 Jeromy Burnitz	.10
30 Kevin Appier	.10
31 Jeff Cirillo	.10
32 Bernard Gilkey	.10
33 David Cone	.10
34 Jason Dickson	.10
35 Jose Cruz Jr.	.10
36 Marty Cordova	.10
37 Ray Durham	.10
38 Jaret Wright	.10
39 Billy Wagner	.10
40 Roger Clemens	1.75
41 Juan Gonzalez	.50
42 Jeremi Gonzalez	.10
43 Mark Grudzielanek	.10
44 Tom Glavine	.35
45 Barry Larkin	.10
46 Lance Johnson	.10
47 Bobby Higginson	.10
48 Mike Mussina	.50
49 Al Martin	.10
50 Mark McGwire	2.50
51 Todd Hundley	.10
52 Ray Lankford	.10
53 Jason Kendall	.10
54 Javy Lopez	.10
55 Ben Grieve	.10
56 Randy Johnson	1.00
57 Jeff King	.10
58 Mark Grace	.10
59 Rusty Greer	.10
60 Greg Maddux	1.50
61 Jeff Kent	.10
62 Rey Ordonez	.10
63 Hideo Nomo	.50
64 Charles Nagy	.10
65 Rondell White	.10
66 Todd Helton	.75
67 Jim Thome	.75
68 Denny Neagle	.10
69 Ivan Rodriguez	.75
70 Vladimir Guerrero	1.00
71 Jorge Posada	.10
72 J.T. Snow Jr.	.10
73 Reggie Sanders	.10
74 Scott Rolen	.75
75 Robin Ventura	.10
76 Mariano Rivera	.15
77 Cal Ripken Jr.	3.00
78 Justin Thompson	.10
79 Mike Piazza	2.00
80 Kevin Brown	.10
81 Sandy Alomar	.10
82 Craig Biggio	.10
83 Vinny Castilla	.10
84 Eric Young	.10
85 Bernie Williams	.10
86 Brady Anderson	.10
87 Bobby Bonilla	.10
88 Tony Clark	.10
89 Dan Wilson	.10
90 John Wetteland	.10
91 Barry Bonds	3.00
92 Chan Ho Park	.10
93 Carlos Delgado	.35
94 David Justice	.10
95 Chipper Jones	1.50
96 Shawn Estes	.10
97 Jason Giambi	.60
98 Ron Gant	.10
99 John Olerud	.10
100 Frank Thomas	1.00
101 Jose Guillen	.10
102 Brad Radke	.10
103 Troy Percival	.10
104 John Smoltz	.10
105 Edgardo Alfonzo	.10
106 Dante Bichette	.10
107 Larry Walker	.10
108 John Valentin	.10
109 Roberto Alomar	.30
110 Mike Cameron	.10
111 Eric Davis	.10
112 Johnny Damon	.35
113 Darin Erstad	.30
114 Omar Vizquel	.10
115 Derek Jeter	3.00
116 Tony Womack	.10
117 Edgar Renteria	.10
118 Raul Mondesi	.10
119 Tony Gwynn	1.50
120 Ken Griffey Jr.	2.00
121 Jim Edmonds	.10
122 Brian Hunter	.10
123 Neifi Perez	.10
124 Dean Palmer	.10
125 Alex Rodriguez	2.50
126 Tim Salmon	.10
127 Curt Schilling	.35
128 Kevin Orie	.10
129 Andy Pettitte	.30
130 Gary Sheffield	.50
131 Jose Rosado	.10
132 Manny Ramirez	1.00
133 Rafael Palmeiro	.75
134 Sammy Sosa	1.50
135 Jeff Bagwell	1.00
136 Delino DeShields	.10
137 Ryan Klesko	.10
138 Mo Vaughn	.10
139 Steve Finley	.10
140 Nomar Garciaparra	1.50
141 Paul Molitor	1.00
142 Pat Hentgen	.10
143 Eric Karros	.10
144 Bobby Jones	.10
145 Tino Martinez	.10
146 Matt Morris	.10
147 Livan Hernandez	.10
148 Edgar Martinez	.10
149 Paul O'Neill	.10
150 Checklist	.10

Player's Private Issue

Player's Private Issue inserts parallel the 150-card base set with a distinct design and embossing. The average insertion rate is one per 12 packs.

	NM/M
Common Player:	1.00
Stars/Rookies:	4X
Production 250 Sets	

Player's Private Issue Auction Cards

These special auction points cards were seeded one per pack of Gallery. Fronts are identical to the much scarcer PPI cards. Backs, however, differ greatly. Where regular PPI cards have a player photo, serial number, etc., these auction points cards have details of the procedure by which points could be accumulated and used to bid for original photos and printing plates. The redemption period ended Oct. 16, 1998.

	NM/M
Complete Set (150):	60.00
Common Player:	.25
Stars/Rookies:	1.5X

Gallery Proofs

This hobby-only parallel set included all 150 cards in the base set. Gallery Proofs were sequentially numbered to 125 sets.

	NM/M
Common Player:	1.50
Stars/Rookies:	4X
Production 125 Sets	

Awards Gallery

Awards Gallery featured 10 players who earned the highest honors in the game on a horizontal design. Fronts featured a shot of the player and the award he won on silver foilboard. These were inserted every 24 packs and numbered with an "AG" prefix.

		NM/M
Complete Set (10):		18.00
Common Player:		1.00
Inserted 1:24		
1	Ken Griffey Jr.	4.00
2	Larry Walker	1.00
3	Roger Clemens	2.50
4	Pedro Martinez	1.50
5	Nomar Garciaparra	2.00
6	Scott Rolen	1.00
7	Frank Thomas	1.50
8	Tony Gwynn	2.00
9	Mark McGwire	5.00
10	Livan Hernandez	1.00

Heroes

Gallery of Heroes is a 15-card insert printed on colored, die-cut plastic that resembles a stained glass window. Cards were inserted one per 24 packs and numbered with a "GH" prefix. More is less in the case in the jumbo (3-1/4" x 4-1/2") version of the cards which were inserted one per hobby box. Cards are numbered with a "GH" prefix.

		NM/M
Complete Set (15):		80.00
Common Player:		1.25
Inserted 1:24		
Jumbo Version (1:24): 75%		
1	Ken Griffey Jr.	8.00
2	Derek Jeter	15.00
3	Barry Bonds	15.00
4	Alex Rodriguez	12.00
5	Frank Thomas	4.00
6	Nomar Garciaparra	12.00
7	Mark McGwire	12.00
8	Mike Piazza	8.00
9	Cal Ripken Jr.	15.00
10	Jose Cruz Jr.	1.25
11	Jeff Bagwell	4.00
12	Chipper Jones	6.00
13	Juan Gonzalez	2.00
14	Hideo Nomo	2.00
15	Greg Maddux	6.00

Photo Gallery

This 10-card insert captured unique shots of players on a silver foilboard design. Photo Gallery inserts were seeded one per 24 packs and numbered with a "PG" prefix.

	NM/M
Complete Set (10):	25.00
Common Player:	1.00

Inserted 1:24

1	Alex Rodriguez	3.00
2	Frank Thomas	2.00
3	Derek Jeter	4.00
4	Cal Ripken Jr.	4.00
5	Ken Griffey Jr.	2.50
6	Mike Piazza	2.50
7	Nomar Garciaparra	2.25
8	Tim Salmon	1.00
9	Jeff Bagwell	2.00
10	Barry Bonds	4.00

Printing Plates

The aluminum press plates used to print the Gallery cards were issued as random pack inserts. Each card's front and back can be found in four different color variations. Because of the unique nature of each plate, assignment of catalog values is not feasible.

	NM/M
Common Player, Front:	50.00
Common Player, Back:	35.00

Gold Label Class 1 (Fielding, Follow-Thru)

Topps debuted its Gold Label brand with 100 cards printed on 30-point "spectral-reflective stock" with gold foil stamping and two shots of the player on each card front. Cards arrived in Gold Label, Black Label and Red Label versions, each with varying levels of scarcity. The rarity of the cards was determined by the photo and foil stamping on the cards. In the foreground of each card front, the photograph is the same, but in the background one of three shots is featured. Class 1, fielding, are considered base cards; Class 2: running (inserted 1:4 packs) and Class 3, hitting (inserted 1:8 packs) are seeded levels. For pitching the levels are: Class 1, set position (base); Class 2, throwing (inserted 1:4 packs) and Class 3, follow-through (inserted 1:8 packs). Black Label cards are scarcer, while Red Label cards are scarcer yet. In addition, 1 of 1 cards exist for each Class and version. Class 1 cards have matte gold-foil graphic highlights on front. Black Label Class 1 cards were inserted one per eight packs. Red Label Class 1 cards are a 1:99 insert and are serially numbered to 100.

	NM/M
Complete Set (100):	12.00

Gold Label Common Player:		.10
Black Label Common Player:		.35
Black Label Stars/RC's:		4X
Red Label Common Player:		1.50
Red Label Stars/RC's:		12X
Pack (5):		2.00
Wax Box (24):		50.00
1	Kevin Brown	.10
2	Greg Maddux	1.25
3	Albert Belle	.10
4	Andres Galarraga	.10
5	Craig Biggio	.10
6	Matt Williams	.10
7	Derek Jeter	3.00
8	Randy Johnson	1.00
9	Jay Bell	.10
10	Jim Thome	.75
11	Roberto Alomar	.30
12	Tom Glavine	.35
13	Reggie Sanders	.10
14	Tony Gwynn	1.25
15	Mark McGwire	2.00
16	Jeromy Burnitz	.10
17	Andruw Jones	1.00
18	Jay Buhner	.10
19	Robin Ventura	.10
20	Jeff Bagwell	1.00
21	Roger Clemens	1.25
22	Masato Yoshii RC	.25
23	Travis Fryman	.10
24	Rafael Palmeiro	.75
25	Alex Rodriguez	2.00
26	Sandy Alomar	.10
27	Chipper Jones	1.25
28	Rusty Greer	.10
29	Cal Ripken Jr.	3.00
30	Tony Clark	.10
31	Derek Bell	.10
32	Fred McGriff	.10
33	Paul O'Neill	.10
34	Moises Alou	.10
35	Henry Rodriguez	.10
36	Steve Finley	.10
37	Marquis Grissom	.10
38	Jason Giambi	.60
39	Javy Lopez	.10
40	Damion Easley	.10
41	Mariano Rivera	.15
42	Mo Vaughn	.40
43	Mike Mussina	.40
44	Jason Kendall	.10
45	Pedro Martinez	1.00
46	Frank Thomas	1.00
47	Jim Edmonds	.10
48	Hideki Irabu	.10
49	Eric Karros	.10
50	Juan Gonzalez	.50
51	Ellis Burks	.10
52	Dean Palmer	.10
53	Scott Rolen	.60
54	Raul Mondesi	.10
55	Quinton McCracken	.10
56	John Olerud	.10
57	Ken Caminiti	.10
58	Brian Jordan	.10
59	Wade Boggs	1.25
60	Mike Piazza	1.50
61	Darin Erstad	.10
62	Curt Schilling	.35
63	David Justice	.10
64	Kenny Lofton	.10
65	Barry Bonds	3.00
66	Ray Lankford	.10
67	Brian Hunter	.10
68	Chuck Knoblauch	.10
69	Vinny Castilla	.10
70	Vladimir Guerrero	1.00
71	Tim Salmon	.10
72	Larry Walker	.10
73	Paul Molitor	1.00
74	Barry Larkin	.10
75	Edgar Martinez	.10
76	Bernie Williams	.10
77	Dante Bichette	.10
78	Nomar Garciaparra	1.25
79	Ben Grieve	.10
80	Ivan Rodriguez	.10
81	Todd Helton	.75
82	Ryan Klesko	.10
83	Sammy Sosa	1.25
84	Travis Lee	.10
85	Jose Cruz	.10
86	Mark Kotsay	.10
87	Richard Hidalgo	.10
88	Rondell White	.10
89	Greg Vaughn	.10
90	Gary Sheffield	.50
91	Paul Konerko	.25
92	Mark Grace	.10
93	Kevin Millwood RC	1.00
94	Manny Ramirez	1.00
95	Tino Martinez	.10
96	Brad Fullmer	.10
97	Todd Walker	.10
98	Carlos Delgado	.45
99	Kerry Wood	.60
100	Ken Griffey Jr.	1.50

Gold Label Class 2 (Running, Set Position)

Class 2 Gold Label and parallels feature background photos on front of position players running and pitchers in the set position. Class 2 cards have sparkling silver-foil graphic highlights on front and were inserted one per two packs. Black Label Class 2 cards were inserted one per 16 packs. Red Label Class 2 cards are a 1:198 insert and are serially numbered to 50.

	NM/M
Complete Set (100):	50.00
Gold Label Common Player:	.35
Gold Label Stars/RC's:	2X
Black Label Common Player:	1.00
Black Label Stars/RC's:	4X
Red Label Common Player:	4.00
Red Label Stars/RC's:	25X

Gold Label Class 3 (Hitting, Throwing)

Class 3 Gold Label and parallels feature background photos on front of position players hitting and pitchers throwing. Class 3 cards have sparkling gold-foil graphic highlights on front and were inserted one per four packs. Black Label Class 3 cards were inserted one per 32 packs. Red Label Class 3 cards are a 1:396 insert and are serially numbered to 25.

	NM/M
Complete Set (100):	120.00
Common Player:	.75
Gold Label Stars/RC's:	2.5X
Black Label Common Player:	2.00
Black Label Stars/RC's	6X
Red Label Common Player:	6.00
Red Label Stars/RC's:	35X

Gold Label 1 of 1

Each of the Classes and color versions of Topps Gold Label cards was paralleled in a 1 of 1 insert which was to be found on average of one per 1,085 packs. Each player, thus, can be found on nine different 1 of 1 cards in the issue.

Gold Label Home Run Race

Home Run Race of '98 was a four-card insert set. Each of the current players' cards features a background photo of Roger Maris, while the fourth card features two shots of Maris. Gold, Black and Red Label versions are identified by the different foil-stamp logos. Gold cards were inserted 1:12 packs, Black Label cards were inserted 1:48 packs and Red Label cards were sequentially numbered to 61 and inserted 1:4,055 packs. The Home Run Race inserts are exclusive to Topps Home Team Advantage boxes.

		NM/M
Complete Set (4):		7.50
Common Player:		2.00
Black Label:		2X
Red Label:		4X
HR1	Roger Maris	3.00
HR2	Mark McGwire	3.00
HR3	Ken Griffey Jr.	2.50
HR4	Sammy Sosa	2.00

Opening Day

Topps Opening Day was a retail exclusive product comprising 165 cards, with 110 from Series 1 and 55 from Series 2. The cards from Series 2 were available in this product prior to the regular-issue cards being released. Opening Day cards feature a silver border vs. the gold border in the regular set, and include a silver-foil Opening Day stamp.

	NM/M
Complete Set (165):	10.00
Common Player:	.05
Wax Pack (7):	.65
Wax Box (22):	10.00

1	Tony Gwynn	.65
2	Larry Walker	.05
3	Billy Wagner	.05
4	Denny Neagle	.05
5	Vladimir Guerrero	.50
6	Kevin Brown	.05
7	Mariano Rivera	.15
8	Tony Clark	.05
9	Deion Sanders	.05
10	Matt Williams	.05
11	Carlos Baerga	.05
12	Mo Vaughn	.25
13	Chan Ho Park	.05
14	Frank Thomas	.50
15	John Jaha	.05
16	Steve Trachsel	.05
17	Jeff Kent	.05
18	Scott Rolen	.40
19	Juan Gonzalez	.25
20	Garret Anderson	.05
21	Roberto Clemente	1.00
22	Omar Vizquel	.05
23	Brian Hunter	.05
24	Jeff Bagwell	.50
25	Chili Davis	.05
26	Mike Cameron	.05
27	Pat Hentgen	.05
28	Wilton Guerrero	.05
29	Devon White	.05
30	Rafael Palmeiro	.40
31	Jeff Blauser	.05
32	Dave Hollins	.05
33	Trevor Hoffman	.05
34	Ryan Klesko	.05
35	Butch Huskey	.05
36	Mark Grudzielanek	.05
37	Marquis Grissom	.05
38	Jim Edmonds	.05
39	Greg Vaughn	.05
40	David Wells	.05
41	Charles Nagy	.05
42	B.J. Surhoff	.05
43	Edgardo Alfonzo	.05
44	Jay Buhner	.05
45	Brady Anderson	.05
46	Edgar Renteria	.05
47	Rick Aguilera	.05
48	Henry Rodriguez	.05
49	Mike Piazza	.75
50	Todd Zeile	.05
51	Rey Ordonez	.05
52	Tony Womack	.05
53	Mike Sweeney	.05
54	Jeffrey Hammonds	.05
55	Kevin Orie	.05
56	Alex Gonzalez	.05
57	Jose Canseco	.35
58	Joey Hamilton	.05
59	Brad Radke	.05
60	Kevin Appier	.05
61	Manny Ramirez	.50
62	Jeromy Burnitz	.05
63	Matt Morris	.05
64	Jason Dickson	.05
65	Tom Glavine	.25
66	Wally Joyner	.05
67	Todd Jones	.05
68	Sandy Alomar	.05
69	Mike Lansing	.05
70	Todd Stottlemyre	.05
71	Jay Bell	.05
72	Joey Cora	.05
73	Scott Spiezio	.05
74	Joe Carter	.05
75	Jose Guillen	.05
76	Damion Easley	.05
77	Alex Fernandez	.05
78	Randy Johnson	.50
79	J.T. Snow	.05
80	Bernard Gilkey	.05
81	David Segui	.05
82	Dante Bichette	.05
83	Derek Jeter	1.50
84	Mark Wohlers	.05
85	Ricky Bottalico	.05
86	Mike Mussina	.35
87	Gary Sheffield	.35
88	Hideo Nomo	.25
89	Mark Grace	.05
90	Darryl Kile	.05
91	Shawn Estes	.05
92	Vinny Castilla	.05
93	Jose Rosado	.05
94	Kenny Lofton	.05
95	Jason Giambi	.35
96	Ray Lankford	.05
97	Hideki Irabu	.05
98	Javy Lopez	.05
99	Jeff Montgomery	.05
100	Dennis Eckersley	.40
101	Armando Benitez	.05
102	Tim Naehring	.05
103	Luis Gonzalez	.05
104	Todd Hollandsworth	.05
105	Wade Boggs	.65
106	Mickey Morandini	.05
107	Rusty Greer	.05
108	Terry Steinbach	.05
109	Pete Rose II	.05
110	Checklist	.05
111	Tino Martinez	.05
112	Roberto Alomar	.20
113	Jeff King	.05
114	Brian Jordan	.05
115	Darin Erstad	.25
116	Ken Caminiti	.05
117	Jim Thome	.60
118	Paul Molitor	.50
119	Ivan Rodriguez	.40
120	Bernie Williams	.05
121	Todd Hundley	.05
122	Andres Galarraga	.05
123	Greg Maddux	.65
124	Edgar Martinez	.05
125	Ron Gant	.05
126	Derek Bell	.05
127	Roger Clemens	.70
128	Rondell White	.05
129	Barry Larkin	.05
130	Robin Ventura	.05
131	Jason Kendall	.05
132	Chipper Jones	.65
133	John Franco	.05
134	Sammy Sosa	.65
135	Chuck Knoblauch	.05
136	Ellis Burks	.05
137	Al Martin	.05
138	Tim Salmon	.05
139	Moises Alou	.05
140	Lance Johnson	.05

141	Justin Thompson	.05
142	Will Clark	.05
143	Barry Bonds	1.50
144	Craig Biggio	.05
145	John Smoltz	.05
146	Cal Ripken Jr.	1.50
147	Ken Griffey Jr.	.75
148	Paul O'Neill	.05
149	Todd Helton	.40
150	John Olerud	.05
151	Mark McGwire	1.00
152	Jose Cruz Jr.	.05
153	Jeff Cirillo	.05
154	Dean Palmer	.05
155	John Wetteland	.05
156	Eric Karros	.05
157	Steve Finley	.05
158	Albert Belle	.05
159	Curt Schilling	.25
160	Raul Mondesi	.05
161	Andruw Jones	.50
162	Nomar Garciaparra	.65
163	David Justice	.05
164	Andy Pettitte	.20
165	Pedro Martinez	.05

SportzCubz Prototypes

This rare "Product Prototype" (says so right on the back) was designed to allow collectors to get creative in making 3-D structures featuring their favorite ballplayers. About 3" square, the plastic pieces have slots and tabs which would allow them to be connected in a variety of ways. Fronts have action photos on a large team logo. Backs have a portrait photo, personal data, recent stats, a career highlight or two and essential licensing data. The product was never rolled out for public consumption and it is unknown to what extent the prototypes were produced or have found their way into collectors' hands. Therefore, no pricing is provided.

Complete Set (25)

1998 Topps Stars Pre-Production

These promotional cards introduced the new Stars brand from Topps to dealers and the hobby press. The cards are virtually identical to the regularly-issued version except for the numbering on back, which has a "PP" prefix and serial numbers "000/000."

		NM/M
Complete Set (6):		5.00
Common Player:		.50
PP1	Mike Piazza	3.00
PP2	Darin Erstad	.60
PP3	Vinny Castilla	.50
PP4	Craig Biggio	.50
PP5	Ivan Rodriguez	.50
PP6	Pedro Martinez	1.00

1998 Topps Stars

Topps Stars adopted an all-sequential numbering format in 1998 with a 150-card set. Every card was available in a bronze (numbered to 9,799), red (9,799), silver (4,399), gold (2,299) and gold rainbow format (99) with different color foil to distinguish the groups. Players were each judged in five categories: arm strength, hit for average, power, defense and speed. Inserts in the product include: Galaxy, Luminaries, Supernovas, Rookie Reprints and Rookie Reprint Autographs. All regular-issue cards and inserts were individually numbered except the Rookie Reprints.

		NM/M
Complete Set, Red or Bronze (150):		24.00
Common Player, Red or Bronze:		.10
Production 9,799 sets each.		
Pack (6):		1.25
Wax Box (24):		25.00
1	Greg Maddux	1.50
2	Darryl Kile	.10
3	Rod Beck	.10
4	Ellis Burks	.10
5	Gary Sheffield	.40
6	David Ortiz	.10
7	Marquis Grissom	.10
8	Tony Womack	.10
9	Mike Mussina	.60
10	Bernie Williams	.10
11	Andy Benes	.10
12	Rusty Greer	.10
13	Carlos Delgado	.35
14	Jim Edmonds	.10
15	Raul Mondesi	.10
16	Andres Galarraga	.10
17	Wade Boggs	1.50
18	Paul O'Neill	.10
19	Edgar Renteria	.10
20	Tony Clark	.10
21	Vladimir Guerrero	1.00
22	Moises Alou	.10
23	Bernard Gilkey	.10
24	Lance Johnson	.10
25	Ben Grieve	.10
26	Sandy Alomar	.10
27	Ray Durham	.10
28	Shawn Estes	.10
29	David Segui	.10
30	Javy Lopez	.10
31	Steve Finley	.10
32	Rey Ordonez	.10
33	Derek Jeter	3.00
34	Henry Rodriguez	.10
35	Mo Vaughn	.10
36	Richard Hidalgo	.10
37	Omar Vizquel	.10
38	Johnny Damon	.35
39	Brian Hunter	.10
40	Matt Williams	.10
41	Chuck Finley	.10
42	Jeromy Burnitz	.10
43	Livan Hernandez	.10
44	Delino DeShields	.10
45	Charles Nagy	.10
46	Scott Rolen	.75
47	Neifi Perez	.10
48	John Wetteland	.10
49	Eric Milton	.10
50	Mike Piazza	2.00
51	Cal Ripken Jr.	3.00
52	Mariano Rivera	.25
53	Butch Huskey	.10
54	Quinton McCracken	.10
55	Jose Cruz Jr.	.10
56	Brian Jordan	.10
57	Hideo Nomo	.50
58	Masato Yoshii	.10
59	Cliff Floyd	.10
60	Jose Guillen	.10
61	Jeff Shaw	.10
62	Edgar Martinez	.10
63	Rondell White	.10
64	Hal Morris	.10
65	Barry Larkin	.10
66	Eric Young	.10
67	Ray Lankford	.10
68	Derek Bell	.10
69	Charles Johnson	.10
70	Robin Ventura	.10
71	Chuck Knoblauch	.10
72	Kevin Brown	.10
73	Jose Valentin	.10
74	Jay Buhner	.10
75	Tony Gwynn	1.50
76	Andy Pettitte	.30
77	Edgardo Alfonzo	.10
78	Kerry Wood	.40
79	Darin Erstad	.30
80	Paul Konerko	.15
81	Jason Kendall	.10
82	Tino Martinez	.10
83	Brad Radke	.10
84	Jeff King	.10
85	Travis Lee	.10
86	Jeff Kent	.10
87	Trevor Hoffman	.10

88	David Cone	.10
89	Jose Canseco	.40
90	Juan Gonzalez	.50
91	Todd Hundley	.10
92	John Valentin	.10
93	Sammy Sosa	1.50
94	Jason Giambi	.40
95	Chipper Jones	1.50
96	Jeff Blauser	.10
97	Brad Fullmer	.10
98	Derek Lee	.60
99	Denny Neagle	.10
100	Ken Griffey Jr.	2.00
101	David Justice	.10
102	Tim Salmon	.10
103	J.T. Snow	.10
104	Fred McGriff	.10
105	Brady Anderson	.10
106	Larry Walker	.10
107	Jeff Cirillo	.10
108	Andruw Jones	1.00
109	Manny Ramirez	1.00
110	Justin Thompson	.10
111	Vinny Castilla	.10
112	Chan Ho Park	.10
113	Mark Grudzielanek	.10
114	Mark Grace	.10
115	Ken Caminiti	.10
116	Ryan Klesko	.10
117	Rafael Palmeiro	.75
118	Pat Hentgen	.10
119	Eric Karros	.10
120	Randy Johnson	1.00
121	Roberto Alomar	.25
122	John Olerud	.10
123	Paul Molitor	1.00
124	Dean Palmer	.10
125	Nomar Garciaparra	1.50
126	Curt Schilling	.30
127	Jay Bell	.10
128	Craig Biggio	.10
129	Marty Cordova	.10
130	Ivan Rodriguez	.75
131	Todd Helton	.75
132	Jim Thome	.65
133	Albert Belle	.10
134	Mike Lansing	.10
135	Mark McGwire	2.50
136	Roger Clemens	1.75
137	Tom Glavine	.30
138	Ron Gant	.10
139	Alex Rodriguez	2.50
140	Jeff Bagwell	1.00
141	John Smoltz	.10
142	Kenny Lofton	.10
143	Dante Bichette	.10
144	Pedro Martinez	1.00
145	Barry Bonds	3.00
146	Travis Fryman	.10
147	Bobby Jones	.10
148	Bobby Higginson	.10
149	Reggie Sanders	.10
150	Frank Thomas	1.00
	Checklist	.05

Silver

	NM/M
Common Silver:	.50
Silver Stars:	1.5X
Production 4,399 Sets	

Gold

	NM/M
Common Gold:	1.00
Gold Stars:	2X
Production 2,299 Sets	

Gold Rainbow

Each card in Topps Stars was available in a Gold Rainbow version. This was the most limited of the five parallels and was numbered to 99. Cards featured gold prismatic foil on the front and were seeded every 46 packs.

	NM/M
Common Gold Rainbow:	4.00
Gold Rainbow Stars:	8X
Production 99 Sets	

Galaxy

Galaxy featured 10 players who possess all five skills featured in Topps Stars Baseball. Four versions were available and sequentially numbered, including: Bronze (numbered to 100, inserted 1:682 packs), Silver (numbered to 75, inserted 1:910), Gold (numbered to 50, inserted 1:1,364) and Gold Rainbow (numbered to 5, inserted 1:13,643).

		NM/M
Complete Set (10):		150.00
Common Player:		7.50
Production 100 Sets		
Silvers:		1.5X
Production 75 Sets		
Golds:		2X
Production 50 Sets		
Gold Rainbows:		
Values Undetermined		
Production 5-Sets		
G1	Barry Bonds	40.00
G2	Jeff Bagwell	15.00
G3	Nomar Garciaparra	20.00
G4	Chipper Jones	20.00
G5	Ken Griffey Jr.	25.00
G6	Sammy Sosa	20.00
G7	Larry Walker	7.50
G8	Alex Rodriguez	35.00
G9	Craig Biggio	7.50
G10	Raul Mondesi	7.50

Luminaries

Luminaries feature three top players in each "tool" group. The 15-card insert has four parallel sequentially numbered versions inserted as follows: bronze (numbered to 100, inserted 1:455), silver (numbered to 75, inserted 1:606), gold (numbered to 50, inserted 1:910) and gold rainbow (numbered to 5, inserted 1:9,095).

	NM/M
Complete Set (15):	140.00
Common Player:	4.00
Production 100 Sets	
Silver (75 Sets):	1.5X
Gold (50 Sets):	1.5X
Gold Rainbow (5 Sets):	
Values Undetermined	

L1	Ken Griffey Jr.	15.00
L2	Mark McGwire	20.00
L3	Juan Gonzalez	5.00
L4	Tony Gwynn	12.50
L5	Frank Thomas	15.00
L6	Mike Piazza	15.00
L7	Chuck Knoblauch	4.00
L8	Kenny Lofton	4.00
L9	Barry Bonds	25.00
L10	Matt Williams	4.00
L11	Raul Mondesi	4.00
L12	Ivan Rodriguez	7.50
L13	Alex Rodriguez	20.00
L14	Nomar Garciaparra	12.50
L15	Ken Caminiti	4.00

Supernovas

Supernovas was a 10-card insert in Topps Stars and included rookies and prospects who either have all five tools focused on in the product, or excel dramatically in one of the five. Four sequentially numbered levels were available, with insert rates as follows: bronze (numbered to 100, inserted 1:682), silver (numbered to 75, inserted 1:910), gold (numbered to 50, inserted 1:1,364) and gold rainbow (numbered to 5, inserted 1:13,643).

		NM/M
Complete Set (10):		35.00
Common Player:		2.00
Production 100 Sets		
Silver:		1.5X
Production 75 Sets		
Gold:		1.5X
Production 50 Sets		
Gold Rainbow:		
Values Undetermined		
Production 5 Sets		
S1	Ben Grieve	2.00
S2	Travis Lee	4.00
S3	Todd Helton	10.00
S4	Adrian Beltre	2.50
S5	Derrek Lee	6.00
S6	David Ortiz	6.00
S7	Brad Fullmer	2.00
S8	Mark Kotsay	2.00
S9	Paul Konerko	2.50
S10	Kerry Wood	6.00

Rookie Reprints

Topps reprinted the rookie cards of five Hall of Famers in Rookie Reprints. The cards are inserted one per 24 packs and have UV coating.

		NM/M
Complete Set (5):		7.00
Common Player:		1.50
1968	Johnny Bench	1.50
1953	Whitey Ford	1.50
1965	Joe Morgan	1.50
1973	Mike Schmidt	2.50
1960	Carl Yastrzemski	2.00

Rookie Reprints Autographs

Autographed versions of all five Rookie Reprint inserts were available and seeded one per 273 packs. Each card arrive with a Topps "Certified Autograph Issue" stamp to ensure its authenticity.

	NM/M
Complete Set (5):	175.00

Common Player:		25.00
1968	Johnny Bench	75.00
1953	Whitey Ford	50.00
1965	Joe Morgan	25.00
1973	Mike Schmidt	90.00
1960	Carl Yastrzemski	90.00

Stars 'N Steel

Stars 'N Steel was a 44-card set printed on four-colored textured film laminate bonded to a sheet of 25-gauge metal. Regular cards featured a silver colored border while gold versions were also available and seeded one per 12 packs. Stars 'N Steel was available only to Home Team Advantage members and was packaged in three-card packs that arrived in a sturdy, tri-fold stand-up display unit. A second parallel version was also available featuring gold holographic technology and was seeded one per 40 packs.

		NM/M
Complete Set (44):		40.00
Common Player:		.25
Golds:		2X
Holographics:		7X
Pack (3):		3.50
Wax Box (12):		30.00
1	Roberto Alomar	.50
2	Jeff Bagwell	1.25
3	Albert Belle	.25
4	Dante Bichette	.25
5	Barry Bonds	4.00
6	Jay Buhner	.25
7	Ken Caminiti	.25
8	Vinny Castilla	.25
9	Roger Clemens	2.25
10	Jose Cruz Jr.	.25
11	Andres Galarraga	.25
12	Nomar Garciaparra	2.00
13	Juan Gonzalez	.65
14	Mark Grace	.25
15	Ken Griffey Jr.	2.50
16	Tony Gwynn	2.00
17	Todd Hundley	.25
18	Derek Jeter	4.00
19	Randy Johnson	1.25
20	Andruw Jones	1.25
21	Chipper Jones	2.00
22	David Justice	.25
23	Ray Lankford	.25
24	Barry Larkin	.25
25	Kenny Lofton	.25
26	Greg Maddux	2.00
27	Edgar Martinez	.25
28	Tino Martinez	.25
29	Mark McGwire	3.00
30	Paul Molitor	1.25
31	Rafael Palmeiro	1.00
32	Mike Piazza	2.50
33	Manny Ramirez	1.25
34	Cal Ripken Jr.	4.00
35	Ivan Rodriguez	1.00
36	Scott Rolen	.75
37	Tim Salmon	.25
38	Gary Sheffield	.50
39	Sammy Sosa	2.00
40	Frank Thomas	1.25
41	Jim Thome	1.00
42	Mo Vaughn	.25
43	Larry Walker	.25
44	Bernie Williams	.25

1998 Topps TEK Pre-Production

Each of three players' Tek cards can also be found in two versions marked diagonally across the card number on back "Pre-production." The gold-foil version is much scarcer than the silver.

	NM/M
Complete Set, Silver (3):	10.00
Complete Set, Gold (3):	45.00
23 Mark McGwire/Silver	6.00

23	Mark McGwire/Gold	30.00
45	Roger Clemens/Silver	5.00
45	Roger Clemens/Gold	20.00
?	Raul Mondesi/Silver	.50
?	Raul Mondesi/Gold	2.50

1998 Topps TEK

A myriad of collecting methods was created with this innovative product which features 90 different players each printed on an acetate stock with 90 different background patterns. A parallel series utilizing Diffraction technology was inserted at the rate of one per six packs. Each of the 8,100 different cards was created in the same quantity, so there is no differentiation in value among patterns.

		NM/M
Complete Set (90):		75.00
Common Player:		.25
Pack (4):		4.00
Wax Box (20):		80.00
1	Ben Grieve	.25
2	Kerry Wood	1.50
3	Barry Bonds	8.00
4	John Olerud	.25
5	Ivan Rodriguez	2.00
6	Frank Thomas	2.50
7	Bernie Williams	.25
8	Dante Bichette	.25
9	Alex Rodriguez	6.00
10	Tom Glavine	.50
11	Eric Karros	.25
12	Craig Biggio	.25
13	Mark McGwire	6.00
14	Derek Jeter	8.00
15	Nomar Garciaparra	4.00
16	Brady Anderson	.25
17	Vladimir Guerrero	2.50
18	David Justice	.25
19	Chipper Jones	4.00
20	Jim Edmonds	.25
21	Roger Clemens	4.50
22	Mark Kotsay	.25
23	Tony Gwynn	4.00
24	Todd Walker	.25
25	Tino Martinez	.25
26	Andruw Jones	2.50
27	Sandy Alomar	.25
28	Sammy Sosa	4.00
29	Gary Sheffield	1.50
30	Ken Griffey Jr.	5.00
31	Aramis Ramirez	.25
32	Curt Schilling	.50
33	Robin Ventura	.25
34	Larry Walker	.25
35	Darin Erstad	1.25
36	Todd Dunwoody	.25
37	Paul O'Neill	.25
38	Vinny Castilla	.25
39	Randy Johnson	2.50
40	Rafael Palmeiro	2.00
41	Pedro Martinez	2.50
42	Derek Bell	.25
43	Carlos Delgado	.50
44	Matt Williams	.25
45	Kenny Lofton	.25
46	Edgar Renteria	.25
47	Albert Belle	.25
48	Jeromy Burnitz	.25
49	Adrian Beltre	.40

50	Greg Maddux	4.00
51	Cal Ripken Jr.	8.00
52	Jason Kendall	.25
53	Ellis Burks	.25
54	Paul Molitor	2.50
55	Moises Alou	.25
56	Raul Mondesi	.25
57	Barry Larkin	.25
58	Tony Clark	.25
59	Travis Lee	.25
60	Juan Gonzalez	1.25
61	Troy Glaus RC	3.00
62	Jose Cruz Jr.	.25
63	Paul Konerko	.40
64	Edgar Martinez	.25
65	Javy Lopez	.25
66	Manny Ramirez	2.50
67	Roberto Alomar	.75
68	Ken Caminiti	.25
69	Todd Helton	1.50
70	Chuck Knoblauch	.25
71	Kevin Brown	.25
72	Tim Salmon	.25
73	Orlando Hernandez RC	1.00
74	Jeff Bagwell	2.50
75	Brian Jordan	.25
76	Derek Lee	1.50
77	Brad Fullmer	.25
78	Mark Grace	.25
79	Jeff King	.25
80	Mike Mussina	1.50
81	Jay Buhner	.25
82	Quinton McCracken	.25
83	A.J. Hinch	.25
84	Richard Hidalgo	.25
85	Andres Galarraga	.25
86	Mike Piazza	5.00
87	Mo Vaughn	.25
88	Scott Rolen	1.50
89	Jim Thome	2.00
90	Ray Lankford	.25

Diffraction

Not only can each of the 90 cards in Topps TEK be found in 90 different background patterns, but each can be found in a parallel edition printed with diffraction foil. The parallels are inserted on an average of one per six packs. Like the regular issue TEKs, all patterns were produced equally and there is no value differentiation among them.

		NM/M
Complete Set (90):		400.00
Common Player:		4.00
Stars/RC's:		4X

1999 Topps Pre-Production

To give potential customers a feel for its 1999 baseball cards, Topps issued this series of pre-production samples. Cards are identical in format to the issued versions except they are numbered with a "PP" prefix and the 1998 stats line reads "PRE-PRODUCTION SAMPLE."

		NM/M
Complete Set (6):		7.00
Common Player:		.50
PP1	Roger Clemens	2.00
PP2	Sammy Sosa	2.00
PP3	Derek Jeter	2.50
PP4	Walt Weiss	.50
PP5	Darin Erstad	.75
PP6	Jason Kendall	.50

1999 Topps

Released in two series, the 462-card set includes two home run record subsets, featuring McGwire and Sosa. McGwire's subset card #220 has 70 different versions, commemorating each of his home runs, including where it was hit, the pitcher, date and estimated distance. Sosa's subset card #461 has 66 different versions. Other subsets include World Series Highlights, Prospects, Draft Picks and Season Highlights. Each pack contains 11 cards with an SRP of $1.29. MVPs are the only parallel. They feature a special Topps MVP logo; 100 cards of each player exist. If the player on the card was named a weekly Topps MVP, collectors won a special set of redemption cards.

		NM/M
Unop. Hobby Set (462):		40.00
Unop. Retail Set (463):		50.00
Complete Set (462):		35.00
Common Player:		.05
MVP Stars/Rookies:		20X
Ser. 1 or 2 Hobby Pack (11):		1.25
Ser. 1 or 2 Hobby Box (36):		40.00
Ser. 1 or 2 Retail Pack (8):		1.00
Ser. 1 or 2 Retail Box (22):		20.00
Ser. 1 or 2 Jumbo Pack (40):		3.50
Ser. 1 or 2 Jumbo Box (12):		30.00
1	Roger Clemens	1.00
2	Andres Galarraga	.05
3	Scott Brosius	.05
4	John Flaherty	.05
5	Jim Leyritz	.05
6	Ray Durham	.05
7	Joe Vizcaino	.05
8	Will Clark	.05
9	David Wells	.05
10	Jose Guillen	.05
11	Scott Hatteberg	.05
12	Edgardo Alfonzo	.05
13	Mike Bordick	.05
14	Manny Ramirez	.75
15	Greg Maddux	1.00
16	David Segui	.05
17	Darryl Strawberry	.05
18	Brad Radke	.05
19	Kerry Wood	.40
20	Matt Anderson	.05
21	Derek Lee	.60
22	Mickey Morandini	.05
23	Paul Konerko	.15
24	Travis Lee	.15
25	Ken Hill	.05
26	Kenny Rogers	.05
27	Paul Sorrento	.05
28	Quilvio Veras	.05
29	Todd Walker	.05
30	Ryan Jackson	.05
31	John Olerud	.05
32	Doug Glanville	.05
33	Nolan Ryan	2.00
34	Ray Lankford	.05
35	Mark Loretta	.05
36	Jason Dickson	.05
37	Sean Bergman	.05
38	Quinton McCracken	.05
39	Bartolo Colon	.05
40	Brady Anderson	.05
41	Chris Stynes	.05
42	Jorge Posada	.05
43	Justin Thompson	.05
44	Johnny Damon	.30
45	Armando Benitez	.05
46	Brant Brown	.05
47	Charlie Hayes	.05
48	Darren Dreifort	.05
49	Juan Gonzalez	.40

51	Chuck Knoblauch	.05
52	Todd Helton	.05
	(Rookie All-Star)	.75
53	Rick Reed	.05
54	Chris Gomez	.05
55	Gary Sheffield	.45
56	Rod Beck	.05
57	Rey Sanchez	.05
58	Garret Anderson	.05
59	Jimmy Haynes	.05
60	Steve Woodard	.05
61	Rondell White	.05
62	Vladimir Guerrero	.75
63	Eric Karros	.05
64	Russ Davis	.05
65	Mo Vaughn	.05
66	Sammy Sosa	1.00
67	Troy Percival	.05
68	Kenny Lofton	.05
69	Bill Taylor	.05
70	Mark McGwire	1.50
71	Roger Cedeno	.05
72	Javy Lopez	.05
73	Damion Easley	.05
74	Andy Pettitte	.05
75	Tony Gwynn	1.00
76	Ricardo Rincon	.05
77	F.P. Santangelo	.05
78	Jay Bell	.05
79	Scott Servais	.05
80	Jose Canseco	.40
81	Roberto Hernandez	.05
82	Todd Dunwoody	.05
83	John Wetteland	.05
84	Mike Caruso		
	(Rookie All-Star)	.05
85	Derek Jeter	2.00
86	Aaron Sele	.05
87	Jose Lima	.05
88	Ryan Christenson	.05
89	Jeff Cirillo	.05
90	Jose Hernandez	.05
91	Mark Kotsay		
	(Rookie All-Star)	.05
92	Darren Bragg	.05
93	Albert Belle	.05
94	Matt Lawton	.05
95	Pedro Martinez	.75
96	Greg Vaughn	.05
97	Neifi Perez	.05
98	Gerald Williams	.05
99	Derek Bell	.05
100	Ken Griffey Jr.	1.25
101	David Cone	.05
102	Brian Johnson	.05
103	Dean Palmer	.05
104	Javier Valentin	.05
105	Trevor Hoffman	.05
106	Butch Huskey	.05
107	Dave Martinez	.05
108	Billy Wagner	.05
109	Shawn Green	.30
110	Ben Grieve		
	(Rookie All-Star)	.05
111	Tom Goodwin	.05
112	Jaret Wright	.05
113	Aramis Ramirez	.05
114	Dmitri Young	.05
115	Hideki Irabu	.05
116	Roberto Kelly	.05
117	Jeff Fassero	.05
118	Mark Clark	.05
119	Jason McDonald	.05
120	Matt Williams	.05
121	Dave Burba	.05
122	Bret Saberhagen	.05
123	Deivi Cruz	.05
124	Chad Curtis	.05
125	Scott Rolen	.65
126	Lee Stevens	.05
127	J.T. Snow Jr.	.05
128	Rusty Greer	.05
129	Brian Meadows	.05
130	Jim Edmonds	.05
131	Ron Gant	.05
132	A.J. Hinch		
	(Rookie All-Star)	.10
133	Shannon Stewart	.05
134	Brad Fullmer	.05
135	Cal Eldred	.05
136	Matt Walbeck	.05
137	Carl Everett	.05
138	Walt Weiss	.05
139	Fred McGriff	.05
140	Darin Erstad	.25
141	Dave Nilsson	.05
142	Eric Young	.05
143	Dan Wilson	.05
144	Jeff Reed	.05
145	Brett Tomko	.05
146	Terry Steinbach	.05
147	Seth Greisinger	.05
148	Pat Meares	.05
149	Livan Hernandez	.05
150	Jeff Bagwell	.75
151	Bob Wickman	.05
152	Omar Vizquel	.05
153	Eric Davis	.05
154	Larry Sutton	.05
155	Magglio Ordonez		
	(Rookie All-Star)	.40
156	Eric Milton	.05
157	Darren Lewis	.05
158	Rick Aguilera	.05
159	Mike Lieberthal	.05
160	Robb Nen	.05
161	Brian Giles	.05
162	Jeff Brantley	.05

163	Gary DiSarcina	.05
164	John Valentin	.05
165	David Dellucci	.05
166	Chan Ho Park	.05
167	Masato Yoshii	.05
168	Jason Schmidt	.05
169	LaTroy Hawkins	.05
170	Bret Boone	.05
171	Jerry DiPoto	.05
172	Mariano Rivera	.10
173	Mike Cameron	.05
174	Scott Erickson	.05
175	Charles Johnson	.05
176	Bobby Jones	.05
177	Francisco Cordova	.05
178	Todd Jones	.05
179	Jeff Montgomery	.05
180	Mike Mussina	.40
181	Bob Abreu	.05
182	Ismael Valdes	.05
183	Andy Fox	.05
184	Woody Williams	.05
185	Denny Neagle	.05
186	Jose Valentin	.05
187	Darrin Fletcher	.05
188	Gabe Alvarez	.05
189	Eddie Taubensee	.05
190	Edgar Martinez	.05
191	Jason Kendall	.05
192	Darryl Kile	.05
193	Jeff King	.05
194	Rey Ordonez	.05
195	Andruw Jones	.75
196	Tony Fernandez	.05
197	Jamey Wright	.05
198	B.J. Surhoff	.05
199	Vinny Castilla	.05
200	David Wells	.05
201	Mark McGwire (Season Highlight)	.75
202	Sammy Sosa (Season Highlight)	.50
203	Roger Clemens (Season Highlight)	.50
204	Kerry Wood (Season Highlight)	.15
205	Lance Berkman, Mike Frank, Gabe Kapler (Prospects)	.15
206	Alex Escobar RC, Ricky Ledee, Mike Stoner (Prospects)	.25
207	Peter Bergeron RC, Jeremy Giambi, George Lombard (Prospects)	.30
208	Michael Barrett, Ben Davis, Robert Fick (Prospects)	.05
209	Pat Cline, Ramon Hernandez, Jayson Werth (Prospects)	.05
210	Bruce Chen, Chris Enochs, Ryan Anderson (Prospects)	.05
211	Mike Lincoln, Octavio Dotel, Brad Penny (Prospects)	.05
212	Chuck Abbott, Brent Butler, Danny Klassen (Prospects)	.05
213	Chris Jones, Jeff Urban RC (Draft Pick)	.05
214	Arturo McDowell RC, Tony Torcato RC (Draft Pick)	.25
215	Josh McKinley RC, Jason Tyner RC (Draft Pick)	.25
216	Matt Burch RC, Seth Etherton RC (Draft Pick)	.05
217	Mamon Tucker RC, Rick Elder RC (Draft Pick)	.10
218	J.M. Gold RC, Ryan Mills RC (Draft Pick)	.10
219	Adam Brown RC, Choo Freeman RC (Draft Pick)	.25
220	Home Run Record #1 (M. McGwire)	20.00
220	HR Record #1 -60 (M. McGwire)	6.00
220	HR Record #1-62 (M. McGwire)	10.00
220	HR Record #63-69 (M. McGwire)	15.00
220	HR Record #70 (Mark McGwire)	40.00
221	Larry Walker (League Leader)	.05
222	Bernie Williams (League Leader)	.05
223	Mark McGwire (League Leader)	.75
224	Ken Griffey Jr. (League Leader)	.65
225	Sammy Sosa (League Leader)	.50
226	Juan Gonzalez (League Leader)	.20
227	Dante Bichette (League Leader)	.05
228	Alex Rodriguez (League Leader)	.75

229	Sammy Sosa (League Leader)	.50
230	Derek Jeter (League Leader)	1.00
231	Greg Maddux (League Leader)	.50
232	Roger Clemens (League Leader)	.50
233	Ricky Ledee (World Series)	.05
234	Chuck Knoblauch (World Series)	.05
235	Bernie Williams (World Series)	.05
236	Tino Martinez (World Series)	.05
237	Orlando Hernandez (World Series)	.05
238	Scott Brosius (World Series)	.05
239	Andy Pettitte (World Series)	.05
240	Mariano Rivera (World Series)	.05
241	Checklist	.05
242	Checklist	.05
243	Tom Glavine	.25
244	Andy Benes	.05
245	Sandy Alomar	.05
246	Wilton Guerrero	.05
247	Alex Gonzalez	.05
248	Roberto Alomar	.30
249	Ruben Rivera	.05
250	Eric Chavez	.15
251	Ellis Burks	.05
252	Richie Sexson	.05
253	Steve Finley	.05
254	Dwight Gooden	.05
255	Dustin Hermanson	.05
256	Kirk Rueter	.05
257	Steve Trachsel	.05
258	Gregg Jefferies	.05
259	Matt Stairs	.05
260	Shane Reynolds	.05
261	Gregg Olson	.05
262	Kevin Tapani	.05
263	Matt Morris	.05
264	Carl Pavano	.05
265	Nomar Garciaparra	1.00
266	Kevin Young	.05
267	Rick Helling	.05
268	Mark Leiter	.05
269	Brian McRae	.05
270	Cal Ripken Jr.	2.00
271	Jeff Abbott	.05
272	Tony Batista	.05
273	Bill Simas	.05
274	Brian Hunter	.05
275	John Franco	.05
276	Devon White	.05
277	Rickey Henderson	.75
278	Chuck Finley	.05
279	Mike Blowers	.05
280	Mark Grace	.05
281	Randy Winn	.05
282	Bobby Bonilla	.05
283	David Justice	.05
284	Shane Monahan	.05
285	Kevin Brown	.05
286	Todd Zeile	.05
287	Al Martin	.05
288	Troy O'Leary	.05
289	Darryl Hamilton	.05
290	Tino Martinez	.05
291	David Ortiz	.45
292	Tony Clark	.05
293	Ryan Minor	.05
294	Reggie Sanders	.05
295	Wally Joyner	.05
296	Cliff Floyd	.05
297	Shawn Estes	.05
298	Pat Hentgen	.05
299	Scott Elarton	.05
300	Alex Rodriguez	1.50
301	Ozzie Guillen	.05
302	Manny Martinez	.05
303	Ryan McGuire	.05
304	Brad Ausmus	.05
305	Alex Gonzalez	.05
306	Brian Jordan	.05
307	John Jaha	.05
308	Mark Grudzielanek	.05
309	Juan Guzman	.05
310	Tony Womack	.05
311	Dennis Reyes	.05
312	Marty Cordova	.05
313	Ramiro Mendoza	.05
314	Robin Ventura	.05
315	Rafael Palmeiro	.60
316	Ramon Martinez	.05
317	John Mabry	.05
318	Dave Hollins	.05
319	Tom Candiotti	.05
320	Al Leiter	.05
321	Rico Brogna	.05
322	Jimmy Key	.05
323	Bernard Gilkey	.05
324	Jason Giambi	.45
325	Craig Biggio	.05
326	Troy Glaus	.65
327	Delino DeShields	.05
328	Fernando Vina	.05
329	John Smoltz	.05
330	Jeff Kent	.05
331	Roy Halladay	.05
332	Andy Ashby	.05
333	Tim Wakefield	.05
334	Tim Belcher	.05

Common Player: .50

335 Bernie Williams .05
336 Desi Relaford .05
337 John Burkett .05
338 Mike Hampton .05
339 Royce Clayton .05
340 Mike Piazza 1.25
341 Jeremi Gonzalez .05
342 Mike Lansing .05
343 Jamie Moyer .05
344 Ron Coomer .05
345 Barry Larkin .05
346 Fernando Tatis .05
347 Chili Davis .05
348 Bobby Higginson .05
349 Hal Morris .05
350 Larry Walker .05
351 Carlos Guillen .05
352 Miguel Tejada .05
353 Travis Fryman .05
354 Jarrod Washburn .05
355 Chipper Jones 1.00
356 Todd Stottlemyre .05
357 Henry Rodriguez .05
358 Eli Marrero .05
359 Alan Benes .05
360 Tim Salmon .05
361 Luis Gonzalez .05
362 Scott Spiezio .05
363 Chris Carpenter .05
364 Bobby Howry .05
365 Raul Mondesi .05
366 Ugueth Urbina .05
367 Tom Evans .05
368 Kerry Ligtenberg RC .15
369 Adrian Beltre .15
370 Ryan Klesko .05
371 Wilson Alvarez .05
372 John Thomson .05
373 Tony Saunders .05
374 Mike Stanley .05
375 Ken Caminiti .05
376 Jay Buhner .05
377 Bill Mueller .05
378 Jeff Blauser .05
379 Edgar Renteria .05
380 Jim Thome .60
381 Joey Hamilton .05
382 Calvin Pickering .05
383 Marquis Grissom .05
384 Omar Daal .05
385 Curt Schilling .25
386 Jose Cruz Jr. .05
387 Chris Widger .05
388 Pete Harnisch .05
389 Charles Nagy .05
390 Tom Gordon .05
391 Bobby Smith .05
392 Derrick Gibson .05
393 Jeff Conine .05
394 Carlos Perez .05
395 Barry Bonds 2.00
396 Mark McLemore .05
397 Juan Encarnacion .05
398 Wade Boggs 1.00
399 Ivan Rodriguez .65
400 Moises Alou .05
401 Jeromy Burnitz .05
402 Sean Casey .10
403 Jose Offerman .05
404 Joe Fontenot .05
405 Kevin Millwood .05
406 Lance Johnson .05
407 Richard Hidalgo .05
408 Mike Jackson .05
409 Brian Anderson .05
410 Jeff Shaw .05
411 Preston Wilson .05
412 Todd Hundley .05
413 Jim Parque .05
414 Justin Baughman .05
415 Dante Bichette .05
416 Paul O'Neill .05
417 Miguel Cairo .05
418 Randy Johnson .75
419 Jesus Sanchez .05
420 Carlos Delgado .30
421 Ricky Ledee .05
422 Orlando Hernandez .05
423 Frank Thomas .75
424 Pokey Reese .05
425 Carlos Lee, Mike Lowell, Kit Pellow RC (Prospect) .25
426 Michael Cuddyer, Mark DeRosa, Jerry Hairston Jr. (Prospect) .05
427 Marlon Anderson, Ron Belliard, Orlando Cabrera (Prospect) .10
428 Micah Bowie RC, Phil Norton RC, Randy Wolf (Prospect) .10
429 Jack Cressend, Jason Rakers, John Rocker (Prospect) .10
430 Ruben Mateo, Scott Morgan, Mike Zywica RC (Prospect) .10
431 Jason LaRue, Matt LeCroy RC, Mitch Meluskey (Prospect) .10

432 Gabe Kapler, Armando Rios, Fernando Seguignol (Prospect) .05
433 Adam Kennedy, Mickey Lopez RC, Jackie Rexrode (Prospect) .10
434 Jose Fernandez RC, Jeff Liefer, Chris Truby (Prospect) .10
435 Corey Koskie, Doug Mientkiewicz, Damon Minor (Prospect) .10
436 Roosevelt Brown RC, Dernell Stenson, Vernon Wells (Prospect) .10
437 A.J. Burnett RC, John Nicholson, Billy Koch (Prospect) .25
438 Matt Belisle RC, Matt Roney RC (Draft Pick) .10
439 Austin Kearns RC, Chris George RC (Draft Pick) 2.50
440 Nate Bump RC, Nate Cornejo RC (Draft Pick) .40
441 Brad Lidge RC, Mike Nannini RC (Draft Pick) .25
442 Matt Holiday RC, Jeff Winchester RC (Draft Pick) .25
443 Adam Everett RC, Chip Ambres RC (Draft Pick) .25
444 Pat Burrell RC, Eric Valent RC (Draft Pick) 1.50
445 Roger Clemens (Strikeout Kings) .50
446 Kerry Wood (Strikeout Kings) .15
447 Curt Schilling (Strikeout Kings) .05
448 Randy Johnson (Strikeout Kings) .40
449 Pedro Martinez (Strikeout Kings) .40
450 Jeff Bagwell, Andres Galarraga, Mark McGwire (All-Topps) .50
451 John Olerud, Jim Thome, Tino Martinez (All-Topps) .30
452 Alex Rodriguez, Nomar Garciaparra, Derek Jeter (All-Topps) .60
453 Vinny Castilla, Chipper Jones, Scott Rolen (All-Topps) .40
454 Sammy Sosa, Ken Griffey Jr., Juan Gonzalez (All-Topps) .50
455 Barry Bonds, Manny Ramirez, Larry Walker (All-Topps) .60
456 Frank Thomas, Tim Salmon, David Justice (All-Topps) .30
457 Travis Lee, Todd Helton, Ben Grieve (All-Topps) .30
458 Vladimir Guerrero, Greg Vaughn, Bernie Williams (All-Topps) .25
459 Mike Piazza, Ivan Rodriguez, Jason Kendall (All-Topps) .50
460 Roger Clemens, Kerry Wood, Greg Maddux (All-Topps) .45
461 Home Run Parade #1 (Sammy Sosa) 10.00
461 HR Parade #2-60 (Sammy Sosa) 4.00
461 HR Parade #61-62 (Sammy Sosa) 10.00
461 HR Parade #63-65 (Sammy Sosa) 6.00
461 HR Parade #66 (Sammy Sosa) 20.00
462 Checklist .05
463 Checklist .05

MVP Promotion

Each of the 198 regular-issue players' cards in Series 1 and cards #243-444 in Series 2 were issued in a parallel version of 100 each for use in an MVP of the Week sweepstakes. Overprinted with a large gold-foil seal on front, the MVP cards have contest rules on back. The MVP cards were inserted at ratios of between 1:142 (HTA) and 1:515

(Hobby) packs. Cards of players who won MVP of the Week during the 1999 season could be redeemed for a special set of MVP cards prior to the Dec. 31, 1999 deadline. Winning players' cards are checklisted here according to their regular-issue card number. Because they were not returned when redeemed, they are in shorter supply than non-winning cards, though market value is not significantly affected.

	NM/M
Common Player:	3.00
Stars/Rookies:	20X

MVP Redemption

Person redeeming winning MVP contest cards prior to Dec. 31, 1999, received this set of 25 cards corresponding to the weekly winners. Cards have an MVP prefix.

		NM/M
Complete Set (25):		30.00
Common Player:		.50
1	Raul Mondesi	.50
2	Tim Salmon	.50
3	Fernando Tatis	.50
4	Larry Walker	.50
5	Fred McGriff	.50
6	Nomar Garciaparra	3.00
7	Rafael Palmeiro	1.50
8	Randy Johnson	2.00
9	Mike Lieberthal	.50
10	B.J. Surhoff	.50
11	Todd Helton	2.00
12	Tino Martinez	.50
13	Scott Rolen	1.50
14	Mike Piazza	4.00
15	David Cone	.50
16	Tony Clark	.50
17	Roberto Alomar	.60
18	Miguel Tejada	.75
19	Alex Rodriguez	5.00
20	J.T. Snow	.50
21	Ray Lankford	.50
22	Mo Vaughn	.50
23	Paul O'Neill	.50
24	Chipper Jones	3.00
25	Mark McGwire	5.00

All-Matrix

This 30-card set features holo-foil card fronts and features the top stars in the game. Each card is numbered with an "AM" prefix on card backs and are seeded 1:18 packs.

		NM/M
Complete Set (30):		45.00
Common Player:		.75
Inserted 1:18		
AM1	Mark McGwire	6.00
AM2	Sammy Sosa	3.50
AM3	Ken Griffey Jr.	4.50
AM4	Greg Vaughn	.75
AM5	Albert Belle	.75
AM6	Vinny Castilla	.75
AM7	Jose Canseco	1.25
AM8	Juan Gonzalez	1.25
AM9	Manny Ramirez	2.50
AM10	Andres Galarraga	.75
AM11	Rafael Palmeiro	2.00
AM12	Alex Rodriguez	6.00
AM13	Mo Vaughn	.75
AM14	Eric Chavez	1.25
AM15	Gabe Kapler	.75
AM16	Calvin Pickering	.75
AM17	Ruben Mateo	.75
AM18	Roy Halladay	1.25
AM19	Jeremy Giambi	.75
AM20	Alex Gonzalez	.75
AM21	Ron Belliard	.75
AM22	Marlon Anderson	.75
AM23	Carlos Lee	.75
AM24	Kerry Wood	1.25
AM25	Roger Clemens	3.50
AM26	Curt Schilling	1.25
AM27	Kevin Brown	.75
AM28	Randy Johnson	2.50
AM29	Pedro Martinez	2.50
AM30	Orlando Hernandez	.75

All-Topps Mystery Finest

This 33-card set features a black opaque covering that collectors peel off to reveal the player. Each card is numbered with an "M" prefix and inserted 1:36 packs. A parallel Refractor version is also randomly seeded and inserted 1:144 packs.

		NM/M
Complete Set (33):		100.00
Common Player:		1.00
Inserted 1:36		
Refractors:		1.5X
Inserted 1:144		
M1	Jeff Bagwell	4.25
M2	Andres Galarraga	1.00
M3	Mark McGwire	9.00
M4	John Olerud	1.00
M5	Jim Thome	2.50
M6	Tino Martinez	1.00
M7	Alex Rodriguez	9.00
M8	Nomar Garciaparra	4.00
M9	Derek Jeter	12.50
M10	Vinny Castilla	1.00
M11	Chipper Jones	5.00
M12	Scott Rolen	3.00
M13	Sammy Sosa	5.00
M14	Ken Griffey Jr.	7.50
M15	Juan Gonzalez	2.00
M16	Barry Bonds	12.50
M17	Manny Ramirez	4.50
M18	Larry Walker	1.00
M19	Frank Thomas	4.50
M20	Tim Salmon	1.00
M21	David Justice	1.00
M22	Travis Lee	1.50
M23	Todd Helton	4.50
M24	Ben Grieve	1.00
M25	Vladimir Guerrero	4.50
M26	Greg Vaughn	1.00
M27	Bernie Williams	1.00
M28	Mike Piazza	7.50
M29	Ivan Rodriguez	3.50
M30	Jason Kendall	1.00
M31	Roger Clemens	6.00
M32	Kerry Wood	2.00
M33	Greg Maddux	5.00

Autographs

Autographs were inserted exclusively in hobby packs in both Topps series 1 and 2. Each series had eight cards with each one carrying the Topps Certified Autograph Issue stamp. Series 1 Autographs were seeded 1:532 packs while Series 2 were found 1:501 packs.

		NM/M
Common Player:		8.00
Series 1 Inserted 1:532 H		
Series 2 Inserted 1:501 H		
A1	Roger Clemens	100.00
A2	Chipper Jones	40.00
A3	Scott Rolen	25.00

A4	Alex Rodriguez	100.00
A5	Andres Galarraga	8.00
A6	Rondell White	8.00
A7	Ben Grieve	8.00
A8	Troy Glaus	20.00
A9	Moises Alou	15.00
A10	Barry Bonds	180.00
A11	Vladimir Guerrero	35.00
A12	Andruw Jones	20.00
A13	Darin Erstad	12.00
A14	Shawn Green	16.00
A15	Eric Chavez	20.00
A16	Pat Burrell	25.00

Hall of Fame

Found exclusively in hobby packs, Hall of Fame Collection is a 10-card set featured on cards that silhouette their images against their respective Hall of Fame plaques. These were seeded 1:12 packs.

		NM/M
Complete Set (10):		8.00
Common Player:		.50
Inserted 1:12 H		
HOF1	Mike Schmidt	1.50
HOF2	Brooks Robinson	.75
HOF3	Stan Musial	1.50
HOF4	Willie McCovey	.50
HOF5	Eddie Mathews	.75
HOF6	Reggie Jackson	1.50
HOF7	Ernie Banks	1.00
HOF8	Whitey Ford	.75
HOF9	Bob Feller	.50
HOF10	Yogi Berra	1.00

Lords of the Diamond

Inserted in every 18 packs this 15-card set features the top players in the game including Barry Bonds and Ken Griffey Jr. Card fronts include a holographic look with die-cutting across the top of the card on a silver background.

		NM/M
Complete Set (15):		13.00
Common Player:		.25
Inserted 1:18		
LD1	Ken Griffey Jr.	1.25
LD2	Chipper Jones	1.00
LD3	Sammy Sosa	1.00
LD4	Frank Thomas	.75
LD5	Mark McGwire	1.50
LD6	Jeff Bagwell	.75
LD7	Alex Rodriguez	1.50
LD8	Juan Gonzalez	.40
LD9	Barry Bonds	2.00
LD10	Nomar Garciaparra	1.00
LD11	Darin Erstad	.35
LD12	Tony Gwynn	1.00
LD13	Andres Galarraga	.25
LD14	Mike Piazza	1.25
LD15	Greg Maddux	1.00

New Breed

The next generation of stars are featured in this 15-card set that showcases the young talent on a silver foil card. These are seeded 1:18 packs.

		NM/M
Complete Set (15):		9.00
Common Player:		.25
Inserted 1:18		
NB1	Darin Erstad	.50
NB2	Brad Fullmer	.25
NB3	Kerry Wood	.50
NB4	Nomar Garciaparra	1.50
NB5	Travis Lee	.35
NB6	Scott Rolen	.75
NB7	Todd Helton	.75
NB8	Vladimir Guerrero	1.00
NB9	Derek Jeter	3.00
NB10	Alex Rodriguez	2.00
NB11	Ben Grieve	.25
NB12	Andruw Jones	1.00
NB13	Paul Konerko	.40
NB14	Aramis Ramirez	.25
NB15	Adrian Beltre	.35

Picture Perfect

This 10-card set features a full bleed photo of baseball's biggest stars, including Derek Jeter and Ken Griffey Jr. These are found one per eight packs.

		NM/M
Complete Set (10):		5.00
Common Player:		.25
Inserted 1:8		
P1	Ken Griffey Jr.	.75
P2	Kerry Wood	.30
P3	Pedro Martinez	.45
P4	Mark McGwire	.90
P5	Greg Maddux	.60
P6	Sammy Sosa	.60
P7	Greg Vaughn	.25
P8	Juan Gonzalez	.30
P9	Jeff Bagwell	.25
P10	Derek Jeter	1.50

Power Brokers

This 20-card set features baseball's biggest superstars including McGwire, Sosa and Chipper Jones. The cards are die-cut at the top and printed on Finest technology. Power Brokers are inserted in every 36 packs. A Refractor parallel version also exists, which are seeded 1:144 packs.

POWER BROKERS

Andres Galarraga

		NM/M
Complete Set (20):		20.00
Common Player:		.25
Inserted 1:36		
Refractors:		1.5X
Inserted 1:144		
PB1	Mark McGwire	3.00
PB2	Andres Galarraga	.25
PB3	Ken Griffey Jr.	2.00
PB4	Sammy Sosa	1.50
PB5	Juan Gonzalez	.50
PB6	Alex Rodriguez	3.00
PB7	Frank Thomas	1.00
PB8	Jeff Bagwell	1.00
PB9	Vinny Castilla	.25
PB10	Mike Piazza	2.00
PB11	Greg Vaughn	.25
PB12	Barry Bonds	4.00
PB13	Mo Vaughn	.25
PB14	Jim Thome	.65
PB15	Larry Walker	.25
PB16	Chipper Jones	1.50
PB17	Nomar Garciaparra	1.50
PB18	Manny Ramirez	1.00
PB19	Roger Clemens	1.75
PB20	Kerry Wood	.65

Record Numbers

RECORD NUMBERS
KEN GRIFFEY JR.

This 10-card set highlights achievements from the game's current stars, including Nomar Garciaparra's 30 game hitting streak, the longest by a rookie in major league history. These inserts are randomly seeded 1:8 packs, each card is numbered on the back with a "RN" prefix.

		NM/M
Complete Set (10):		7.50
Common Player:		.35
Inserted 1:8		
RN1	Mark McGwire	1.50
RN2	Mike Piazza	1.00
RN3	Curt Schilling	.35
RN4	Ken Griffey Jr.	1.00
RN5	Sammy Sosa	.65
RN6	Nomar Garciaparra	.65
RN7	Kerry Wood	.40
RN8	Roger Clemens	.75
RN9	Cal Ripken Jr.	2.00
RN10	Mark McGwire	1.50

Record Numbers Gold

This is a parallel of the Record Numbers insert set, each card features the appropriate sequential numbering based on the featured players' highlighted record. Each card is numbered with a "RN" prefix on the back.

		NM/M
Complete Set (10):		500.00
Common Player:		5.00
RN1	Mark McGwire/70	125.00
RN2	Mike Piazza/362	25.00
RN3	Curt Schilling/319	15.00
RN4	Ken Griffey Jr./350	20.00
RN5	Sammy Sosa/20	125.00

RN6	Nomar Garciaparra/30	75.00
RN7	Kerry Wood/20	40.00
RN8	Roger Clemens/20	125.00
RN9	Cal Ripken Jr./2,632	12.50
RN10	Mark McGwire/162	60.00

Nolan Ryan Reprints

ANGELS
NOLAN RYAN

Topps reprinted all 27 of Nolan Ryan's basic Topps cards, with 14 odd numbers appearing in Series 1 and the remaining 13 even cards inserted into Series 2 packs. Each card is stamped with a gold Topps commemorative stamp on the front for identification. Reprints were seeded in every 18 packs. Ryan also autographed a number of the reprints for both series. Series 1 Ryan autographs are seeded 1:4,260, with Series 2 autographs found 1:5,007 packs. Ryan autographs were inserted exclusively in hobby packs.

		NM/M
Complete Set (27):		40.00
Common Ryan:		3.00
Inserted 1:18		
Nolan Ryan Autograph:		150.00
1	Nolan Ryan/1968	7.50
2	Nolan Ryan/1969	4.50
3	Nolan Ryan/1970	3.00
4	Nolan Ryan/1971	3.00
5	Nolan Ryan/1972	3.00
6	Nolan Ryan/1973	3.00
7	Nolan Ryan/1974	3.00
8	Nolan Ryan/1975	3.00
9	Nolan Ryan/1976	3.00
10	Nolan Ryan/1977	3.00
11	Nolan Ryan/1978	3.00
12	Nolan Ryan/1979	3.00
13	Nolan Ryan/1980	3.00
14	Nolan Ryan/1981	3.00
15	Nolan Ryan/1982	3.00
16	Nolan Ryan/1983	3.00
17	Nolan Ryan/1984	3.00
18	Nolan Ryan/1985	3.00
19	Nolan Ryan/1986	3.00
20	Nolan Ryan/1987	3.00
21	Nolan Ryan/1988	3.00
22	Nolan Ryan/1989	3.00
23	Nolan Ryan/1990	3.00
24	Nolan Ryan/1991	3.00
25	Nolan Ryan/1992	3.00
26	Nolan Ryan/1993	3.00
27	Nolan Ryan/1994	3.00

Nolan Ryan Reprint Autographs

NOLAN RYAN
ANGELS

Topps reprinted all 27 of Nolan Ryan's basic Topps cards, with 14 odd numbers appearing in Series 1 and the remaining 13 even cards inserted into Series 2 packs. Each card is stamped with a gold Topps commemorative stamp on the

front for identification. Ryan-autographed reprints, found exclusively in hobby packs, are seeded 1:4,260 in Series 1, with Series 2 autographs found 1:5,007 packs.

		NM/M
Common Card:		150.00
1	Nolan Ryan/1968	200.00
2	Nolan Ryan/1969	150.00
3	Nolan Ryan/1970	150.00
4	Nolan Ryan/1971	150.00
5	Nolan Ryan/1972	150.00
6	Nolan Ryan/1973	150.00
7	Nolan Ryan/1974	150.00
8	Nolan Ryan/1975	150.00
9	Nolan Ryan/1976	150.00
10	Nolan Ryan/1977	150.00
11	Nolan Ryan/1978	150.00
12	Nolan Ryan/1979	150.00
13	Nolan Ryan/1980	150.00
14	Nolan Ryan/1981	150.00
15	Nolan Ryan/1982	150.00
16	Nolan Ryan/1983	150.00
17	Nolan Ryan/1984	150.00
18	Nolan Ryan/1985	150.00
19	Nolan Ryan/1986	150.00
20	Nolan Ryan/1987	150.00
21	Nolan Ryan/1988	150.00
22	Nolan Ryan/1989	150.00
23	Nolan Ryan/1990	150.00
24	Nolan Ryan/1991	150.00
25	Nolan Ryan/1992	150.00
26	Nolan Ryan/1993	150.00
27	Nolan Ryan/1994	150.00

Nolan Ryan Finest Reprints

CALIFORNIA   PITCHER

NOLAN RYAN   ANGELS

This 27-card set reprinted all 27 of Ryan's basic Topps cards. Odd numbers were distributed in Series 1 packs, with even numbers distributed in Series 2 packs. These are seeded 1:72 packs in both series 1 and 2 packs. A Refractor parallel version is inserted 1:288 packs.

		NM/M
Complete Set (27):		125.00
Common Card:		5.00
Inserted 1:72		
Refractors:		2X
Inserted 1:288		
1	1968	12.50
2	1969	7.50
3	1970	5.00
4	1971	5.00
5	1972	5.00
6	1973	5.00
7	1974	5.00
8	1975	5.00
9	1976	5.00
10	1977	5.00
11	1978	5.00
12	1979	5.00
13	1980	5.00
14	1981	5.00
15	1982	5.00
16	1983	5.00
17	1984	5.00
18	1985	5.00
19	1986	5.00
20	1987	5.00
21	1988	5.00
22	1989	5.00
23	1990	5.00
24	1991	5.00
25	1992	5.00
26	1992	5.00
27	1992	5.00

1999 Topps Traded and Rookies

Identical in design to the base 1999 Topps cards the 121-card set includes players involved in pre and mid-season transactions as well as top prospects and 1999 Draft Picks. Released in a boxed set, each set

Topps

ADAM DUNN

also includes one autographed card from the 75 rookie/draft pick cards in the set.

		NM/M
Unopened Set (122):		30.00
Complete Set, No Autograph (121):		10.00
Common Player:		.10
1	Seth Etherton	.10
2	Mark Harriger RC	.10
3	Matt Wise RC	.25
4	Carlos Hernandez RC	.15
5	Julio Lugo RC	.25
6	Mike Nannini	.10
7	Justin Bowles RC	.10
8	Mark Mulder RC	1.00
9	Roberto Vaz RC	.10
10	Felipe Lopez RC	.50
11	Matt Belisle	.10
12	Micah Bowie	.10
13	Ruben Quevedo RC	.10
14	Jose Garcia RC	.10
15	David Kelton RC	.25
16	Phillip Norton	.10
17	Corey Patterson RC	1.00
18	Ron Walker RC	.10
19	Paul Hoover RC	.10
20	Ryan Rupe RC	.15
21	J.D. Closser RC	.10
22	Rob Ryan RC	.10
23	Steve Colyer RC	.10
24	Bubba Crosby RC	.50
25	Luke Prokopec RC	.10
26	Matt Blank RC	.10
27	Josh McKinley	.10
28	Nate Bump	.10
29	Giuseppe Chiaramonte RC	.10
30	Arturo McDowell	.10
31	Tony Torcato	.10
32	Dave Roberts	.10
33	C.C. Sabathia RC	.75
34	Sean Spencer RC	.10
35	Chip Ambres	.10
36	A.J. Burnett	.15
37	Mo Bruce RC	.10
38	Jason Tyner	.10
39	Mamon Tucker	.10
40	Sean Burroughs RC	1.00
41	Kevin Eberwein RC	.10
42	Junior Herndon RC	.10
43	Bryan Wolff RC	.10
44	Pat Burrell	.50
45	Eric Valent	.10
46	Carlos Pena RC	.50
47	Mike Zywica	.10
48	Adam Everett	.10
49	Juan Pena RC	.50
50	Adam Dunn RC	3.00
51	Austin Kearns	.75
52	Jacobo Sequea RC	.10
53	Choo Freeman	.10
54	Jeff Winchester	.10
55	Matt Burch	.10
56	Chris George	.10
57	Scott Mullen RC	.10
58	Kit Pellow	.10
59	Mark Quinn RC	.15
60	Nate Cornejo	.10
61	Ryan Mills RC	.25
62	Kevin Beirne RC	.10
63	Kip Wells RC	.50
64	Juan Rivera RC	.25
65	Alfonso Soriano RC	4.00
66	Josh Hamilton RC	4.00
67	Josh Girdley RC	.10
68	Kyle Snyder RC	.15
69	Mike Paradis RC	.10
70	Jason Jennings RC	.25
71	David Walling RC	.10
72	Omar Ortiz RC	.10
73	Jay Gehrke RC	.10
74	Casey Burns RC	.10
75	Carl Crawford RC	2.00
76	Reggie Sanders	.10
77	Will Clark	.10
78	David Wells	.10
79	Paul Konerko	.20
80	Armando Benitez	.10
81	Brant Brown	.10
82	Mo Vaughn	.10
83	Jose Canseco	.30
84	Albert Belle	.10
85	Dean Palmer	.10
86	Greg Vaughn	.10
87	Mark Clark	.10
88	Pat Meares	.10
89	Eric Davis	.10
90	Brian Giles	.10
91	Jeff Brantley	.10
92	Bret Boone	.10
93	Ron Gant	.10
94	Mike Cameron	.10
95	Charles Johnson	.10
96	Denny Neagle	.10
97	Brian Hunter	.10
98	Jose Hernandez	.10
99	Rick Aguilera	.10
100	Tony Batista	.10
101	Roger Cedeno	.10
102	Creighton Gubanich	.10
103	Tim Belcher	.10
104	Bruce Aven	.10
105	Brian Daubach RC	.30
106	Ed Sprague	.10
107	Michael Tucker	.10
108	Homer Bush	.10
109	Armando Reynoso	.10
110	Brook Fordyce	.10
111	Matt Mantei	.10
112	Jose Guillen	.10
113	Kenny Rogers	.10
114	Livan Hernandez	.10
115	Butch Huskey	.10
116	David Segui	.10
117	Darryl Hamilton	.10
118	Jim Leyritz	.10
119	Randy Velarde	.10
120	Bill Taylor	.10
121	Kevin Appier	.10

Autographs

Cincinnati Reds

These autographs have identical photos and design from the Traded and Rookies set. Seeded one per boxed set, each card has a "Topps Certified Autograph Issue" stamp ensuring its authenticity. Cards of the first 75 rookies/draft picks included in the 121-card boxed set can be found in this autographed version.

		NM/M
Common Player:		3.00
Inserted 1:Set		
1	Seth Etherton	3.00
2	Mark Harriger	3.00
3	Matt Wise	5.00
4	Carlos Hernandez	5.00
5	Julio Lugo	15.00
6	Mike Nannini	3.00
7	Justin Bowles	3.00
8	Mark Mulder	50.00
9	Roberto Vaz	3.00
10	Felipe Lopez	40.00
11	Matt Belisle	3.00
12	Micah Bowie	3.00
13	Ruben Quevedo	5.00
14	Jose Garcia	3.00
15	David Kelton	10.00
16	Phillip Norton	5.00
17	Corey Patterson	25.00
18	Ron Walker	3.00
19	Paul Hoover	3.00
20	Ryan Rupe	8.00
21	J.D. Closser	4.00
22	Rob Ryan	3.00
23	Steve Colyer	5.00
24	Bubba Crosby	15.00
25	Luke Prokopec	3.00
26	Matt Blank	3.00
27	Josh McKinley	5.00
28	Nate Bump	3.00
29	Giuseppe Chiaramonte	3.00
30	Arturo McDowell	3.00
31	Tony Torcato	5.00
32	Dave Roberts	10.00
33	C.C. Sabathia	30.00
34	Sean Spencer	3.00
35	Chip Ambres	3.00
36	A.J. Burnett	25.00
37	Mo Bruce	3.00
38	Jason Tyner	3.00
39	Mamon Tucker	3.00
40	Sean Burroughs	10.00
41	Kevin Eberwein	3.00
42	Junior Herndon	3.00
43	Bryan Wolff	3.00
44	Pat Burrell	50.00
45	Eric Valent	8.00
46	Carlos Pena	10.00
47	Mike Zywica	3.00
48	Adam Everett	15.00
49	Juan Pena	5.00
50	Adam Dunn	100.00
51	Austin Kearns	30.00
52	Jacobo Sequea	3.00
53	Choo Freeman	8.00
54	Jeff Winchester	3.00
55	Matt Burch	3.00
56	Chris George	4.00
57	Scott Mullen	3.00
58	Kit Pellow	3.00
59	Mark Quinn	3.00
60	Nate Cornejo	8.00
61	Ryan Mills	3.00
62	Kevin Beirne	4.00
63	Kip Wells	8.00
64	Juan Rivera	10.00
65	Alfonso Soriano	240.00
66	Josh Hamilton	150.00
67	Josh Girdley	3.00
68	Kyle Snyder	5.00
69	Mike Paradis	3.00
70	Jason Jennings	10.00
71	David Walling	3.00
72	Omar Ortiz	3.00
73	Jay Gehrke	5.00
74	Casey Burns	3.00
75	Carl Crawford	90.00

Supers

These oversize (3-1/2" x 5") versions of Topps cards were issued one per box in hobby and Home Team Advantage boxes. Eight cards were issued in each of Series 1 and 2. Other than their size and the card numbers on back, the supers are identical to the regular versions.

		NM/M
Complete Set (16):		17.50
Common Player:		.50
1	Roger Clemens	1.25
2	Greg Maddux	1.25
3	Kerry Wood	.75
4	Juan Gonzalez	.75
5	Sammy Sosa	1.25
6	Mark McGwire	2.50
7	Ken Griffey Jr.	2.00
8	Ben Grieve	.50
1	Nomar Garciaparra	1.25
2	Cal Ripken Jr.	3.00
3	Alex Rodriguez	2.00
4	Mike Piazza	1.50
5	Larry Walker	.50
6	Chipper Jones	1.25
7	Barry Bonds	3.00
8	Frank Thomas	1.00

Action Flats

"Dynamic action poses... painstakingly capturing one of their signature plays" are featured in this issue of plastic player figures. The figures are about 3" tall by 2-1/2" wide and stand on a plastic base. In the manner of early 20th Century tin soldiers, there is little depth to the figures. Each handpainted figure is sold in a plastic-windowed box which includes a special foil-stamped version of the player's 1999 Topps card inside. Each figure was also produced in a short-printed "away" jersey version, with 10 of the players seeded at the rate of one per 12 figures, Sosa at a 1:24 rate and McGwire at a 1:36 rate. Suggested retail price at issue was $2.99. Values shown are for unopened packages.

	NM/M
Complete Set, "Home" (12):	6.00
Complete Set, "Away" (12):	12.00
Common Player, "Home":	.50
Common Player, "Away":	.75

#	Player	Price
1	Chipper Jones	.50
2	Greg Maddux	.50
3	Mark McGwire	1.00
4	Sammy Sosa	.50
5	Kerry Wood	.50
6	Barry Bonds	1.50
7	Alex Rodriguez	1.00
8	Ken Griffey Jr.	.75
9	Cal Ripken Jr.	1.50
10	Juan Gonzalez	.50
11	Nomar Garciaparra	.50
12	Derek Jeter	1.50
1	Chipper Jones	.75
2	Greg Maddux	.75
3	Mark McGwire	1.50
4	Sammy Sosa	.75
5	Kerry Wood	.75
6	Barry Bonds	2.00
7	Alex Rodriguez	1.50
8	Ken Griffey Jr.	1.00
9	Cal Ripken Jr.	2.00
10	Juan Gonzalez	.75
11	Nomar Garciaparra	.75
12	Derek Jeter	2.00

1999 Topps Chrome

The 462-card base set is a chromium parallel version of Topps baseball. Included are the Mark McGwire #220 and Sammy Sosa #461 home run subset cards, which commemorate each of their home runs. Each pack contains four cards with a S.R.P. of $3.00 per pack.

		NM/M
Complete Set (461):		75.00
Common Player:		.15
Refractors:		4X
Inserted 1:12		
Ser. 1 or 2 Pack (4):		1.50
Ser. 1 or 2 Box (24):		30.00

#	Player	Price
1	Roger Clemens	1.75
2	Andres Galarraga	.15
3	Scott Brosius	.15
4	John Flaherty	.15
5	Jim Leyritz	.15
6	Ray Durham	.15
7	Joe Vizcaino	.15
8	Will Clark	.15
9	David Wells	.15
10	Jose Guillen	.15
11	Scott Hatteberg	.15
12	Edgardo Alfonzo	.15
13	Mike Bordick	.15
14	Manny Ramirez	1.00
15	Greg Maddux	1.50
16	David Segui	.15
17	Darryl Strawberry	.15
18	Brad Radke	.15
19	Kerry Wood	.40
20	Matt Anderson	.15
21	Derek Lee	.60
22	Mickey Morandini	.15
23	Paul Konerko	.30
24	Travis Lee	.15
25	Ken Hill	.15
26	Kenny Rogers	.15
27	Paul Sorrento	.15
28	Quilvio Veras	.15
29	Todd Walker	.15
30	Ryan Jackson	.15
31	John Olerud	.15
32	Doug Glanville	.15
33	Nolan Ryan	3.00
34	Ray Lankford	.15
35	Mark Loretta	.15
36	Jason Dickson	.15
37	Sean Bergman	.15
38	Quinton McCracken	.15
39	Bartolo Colon	.15
40	Brady Anderson	.15
41	Chris Stynes	.15
42	Jorge Posada	.15
43	Justin Thompson	.15
44	Johnny Damon	.40
45	Armando Benitez	.15
46	Brant Brown	.15
47	Charlie Hayes	.15
48	Darren Dreifort	.15
49	Juan Gonzalez	.50
50	Chuck Knoblauch	.15
51	Todd Helton (Rookie All-Star)	1.00
52	Rick Reed	.15
53	Chris Gomez	.15
55	Gary Sheffield	.50
56	Rod Beck	.15
57	Rey Sanchez	.15
58	Garret Anderson	.15
59	Jimmy Haynes	.15
60	Steve Woodard	.15
61	Rondell White	.15
62	Vladimir Guerrero	1.00
63	Eric Karros	.15
64	Russ Davis	.15
65	Mo Vaughn	.15
66	Sammy Sosa	1.50
67	Troy Percival	.15
68	Kenny Lofton	.15
69	Bill Taylor	.15
70	Mark McGwire	2.50
71	Roger Cedeno	.15
72	Javy Lopez	.15
73	Damion Easley	.15
74	Andy Pettitte	.35
75	Tony Gwynn	1.50
76	Ricardo Rincon	.15
77	F.P. Santangelo	.15
78	Jay Bell	.15
79	Scott Servais	.15
80	Jose Canseco	.50
81	Roberto Hernandez	.15
82	Todd Dunwoody	.15
83	John Wetteland	.15
84	Mike Caruso (Rookie All-Star)	.15
85	Derek Jeter	3.00
86	Aaron Sele	.15
87	Jose Lima	.15
88	Ryan Christenson	.15
89	Jeff Cirillo	.15
90	Jose Hernandez	.15
91	Mark Kotsay (Rookie All-Star)	.15
92	Darren Bragg	.15
93	Albert Belle	.15
94	Matt Lawton	.15
95	Pedro Martinez	1.00
96	Greg Vaughn	.15
97	Neifi Perez	.15
98	Gerald Williams	.15
99	Derek Bell	.15
100	Ken Griffey Jr.	2.00
101	David Cone	.15
102	Brian Johnson	.15
103	Dean Palmer	.15
104	Javier Valentin	.15
105	Trevor Hoffman	.15
106	Butch Huskey	.15
107	Dave Martinez	.15
108	Billy Wagner	.15
109	Shawn Green	.35
110	Ben Grieve (Rookie All-Star)	.15
111	Tom Goodwin	.15
112	Jaret Wright	.15
113	Aramis Ramirez	.15
114	Dmitri Young	.15
115	Hideki Irabu	.15
116	Roberto Kelly	.15
117	Jeff Fassero	.15
118	Mark Clark	.15
119	Jason McDonald	.15
120	Matt Williams	.15
121	Dave Burba	.15
122	Jeff Saberhagen	.15
123	Deivi Cruz	.15
124	Chad Curtis	.15
125	Scott Rolen	.75
126	Lee Stevens	.15
127	J.T. Snow Jr.	.15
128	Rusty Greer	.15
129	Brian Meadows	.15
130	Jim Edmonds	.15
131	Ron Gant	.15
132	A.J. Hinch (Rookie All-Star)	.15
133	Shannon Stewart	.15
134	Brad Fullmer	.15
135	Cal Eldred	.15
136	Matt Walbeck	.15
137	Carl Everett	.15
138	Walt Weiss	.15
139	Fred McGriff	.15
140	Darin Erstad	.40
141	Dave Nilsson	.15
142	Eric Young	.15
143	Dan Wilson	.15
144	Jeff Reed	.15
145	Brett Tomko	.15
146	Terry Steinbach	.15
147	Seth Greisinger	.15
148	Pat Meares	.15
149	Livan Hernandez	.15
150	Jeff Bagwell	1.00
151	Bob Wickman	.15
152	Omar Vizquel	.15
153	Eric Davis	.15
154	Larry Sutton	.15
155	Magglio Ordonez (Rookie All-Star)	.45
156	Eric Milton	.15
157	Darren Lewis	.15
158	Rick Aguilera	.15
159	Mike Lieberthal	.15
160	Robb Nen	.15
161	Brian Giles	.15
162	Jeff Brantley	.15
163	Gary DiSarcina	.15
164	John Valentin	.15
165	David Dellucci	.15
166	Chan Ho Park	.15
167	Masato Yoshii	.15
168	Jason Schmidt	.15
169	LaTroy Hawkins	.15
170	Bret Boone	.15
171	Jerry DiPoto	.15
172	Mariano Rivera	.25
173	Mike Cameron	.15
174	Scott Erickson	.15
175	Charles Johnson	.15
176	Bobby Jones	.15
177	Francisco Cordova	.15
178	Todd Jones	.15
179	Jeff Montgomery	.15
180	Mike Mussina	.50
181	Bob Abreu	.15
182	Ismael Valdes	.15
183	Andy Fox	.15
184	Woody Williams	.15
185	Denny Neagle	.15
186	Jose Valentin	.15
187	Darrin Fletcher	.15
188	Gabe Alvarez	.15
189	Eddie Taubensee	.15
190	Edgar Martinez	.15
191	Jason Kendall	.15
192	Darryl Kile	.15
193	Jeff King	.15
194	Rey Ordonez	.15
195	Andruw Jones	1.00
196	Tony Fernandez	.15
197	Jamey Wright	.15
198	B.J. Surhoff	.15
199	Vinny Castilla	.15
200	David Wells (Season Highlight)	.15
201	Mark McGwire (Season Highlight)	1.25
202	Sammy Sosa (Season Highlight)	.75
203	Roger Clemens (Season Highlight)	.85
204	Kerry Wood (Season Highlight)	.20
205	Lance Berkman, Mike Frank, Gabe Kapler (Prospects)	.15
206	Alex Escobar RC, Ricky Ledee, Mike Stoner (Prospects)	.50
207	Peter Bergeron RC, Jeremy Johnson, George Lombard (Prospects)	.15
208	Michael Barrett, Ben Davis, Robert Fick (Prospects)	.15
209	Pat Cline, Ramon Hernandez, Jayson Werth (Prospects)	.20
210	Bruce Chen, Chris Enochs, Ryan Anderson (Prospects)	.15
211	Mike Lincoln, Octavio Dotel, Brad Penny (Prospects)	.15
212	Chuck Abbott, Brent Butler, Danny Klassen (Prospects)	.15
213	Chris Jones, Jeff Urban RC (Draft Pick)	.25
214	Arturo McDowell RC, Tony Torcato RC (Draft Pick)	.25
215	Josh McKinley RC, Jason Tyner RC (Draft Pick)	.30
216	Matt Burch RC, Seth Etherton RC (Draft Pick)	.20
217	Mamon Tucker RC, Rick Elder RC (Draft Pick)	.20
218	J.M. Gold RC, Ryan Mills RC (Draft Pick)	.15
219	Adam Brown RC, Choo Freeman RC (Draft Pick)	.20
220	Mark McGwire HR #1 (Record Breaker)	15.00
220	Mark McGwire HR #2-60	10.00
220	McGwire HR #61-62	15.00
220	McGwire HR #63-69	12.50
220	McGwire HR #70	40.00
221	Larry Walker (League Leader)	.15
222	Bernie Williams (League Leader)	.15
223	Mark McGwire (League Leader)	1.25
224	Ken Griffey Jr. (League Leader)	1.00
225	Sammy Sosa (League Leader)	.75
226	Juan Gonzalez (League Leader)	.35
227	Dante Bichette (League Leader)	.15
228	Alex Rodriguez (League Leader)	1.25
229	Sammy Sosa (League Leader)	.75
230	Derek Jeter (League Leader)	1.50
231	Greg Maddux (League Leader)	.75
232	Roger Clemens (League Leader)	.75
233	Ricky Ledee (World Series)	.15
234	Chuck Knoblauch (World Series)	.15
235	Bernie Williams (World Series)	.15
236	Tino Martinez (World Series)	.15
237	Orlando Hernandez (World Series)	.15
238	Scott Brosius (World Series)	.15
239	Andy Pettitte (World Series)	.15
240	Mariano Rivera (World Series)	.15
241	Checklist	.15
242	Checklist	.15
243	Tom Glavine	.35
244	Andy Benes	.15
245	Sandy Alomar	.15
246	Wilton Guerrero	.15
247	Alex Gonzalez	.15
248	Roberto Alomar	.30
249	Ruben Rivera	.15
250	Eric Chavez	.15
251	Ellis Burks	.15
252	Richie Sexson	.15
253	Steve Finley	.15
254	Dwight Gooden	.15
255	Dustin Hermanson	.15
256	Kirk Rueter	.15
257	Steve Trachsel	.15
258	Gregg Jefferies	.15
259	Matt Stairs	.15
260	Shane Reynolds	.15
261	Gregg Olson	.15
262	Kevin Tapani	.15
263	Matt Morris	.15
264	Carl Pavano	.15
265	Nomar Garciaparra	1.50
266	Kevin Young	.15
267	Rick Helling	.15
268	Matt Franco	.15
269	Brian McRae	.15
270	Cal Ripken Jr.	3.00
271	Jeff Abbott	.15
272	Tony Batista	.15
273	Bill Simas	.15
274	Brian Hunter	.15
275	John Franco	.15
276	Devon White	.15
277	Rickey Henderson	1.00
278	Chuck Finley	.15
279	Mike Blowers	.15
280	Mark Grace	.15
281	Randy Winn	.15
282	Bobby Bonilla	.15
283	David Justice	.15
284	Shane Monahan	.15
285	Kevin Brown	.15
286	Todd Zeile	.15
287	Al Martin	.15
288	Troy O'Leary	.15
289	Darryl Hamilton	.15
290	Tino Martinez	.50
291	David Ortiz	.50
292	Tony Clark	.15
293	Ryan Minor	.15
294	Reggie Sanders	.15
295	Wally Joyner	.15
296	Cliff Floyd	.15
297	Shawn Estes	.15
298	Pat Hentgen	.15
299	Scott Elarton	.15
300	Alex Rodriguez	2.50
301	Ozzie Guillen	.15
302	Hideo Martinez	.15
303	Ryan McGuire	.15
304	Brad Ausmus	.15
305	Alex Gonzalez	.15
306	Brian Jordan	.15
307	John Jaha	.15
308	Mark Grudzielanek	.15
309	Juan Guzman	.15
310	Tony Womack	.15
311	Dennis Reyes	.15
312	Marty Cordova	.15
313	Ramiro Mendoza	.15
314	Robin Ventura	.15
315	Rafael Palmeiro	.65
316	Ramon Martinez	.15
317	Pedro Astacio	.15
318	Dave Hollins	.15
319	Tom Candiotti	.15
320	Al Leiter	.15
321	Rico Brogna	.15
322	Reggie Jefferson	.15
323	Bernard Gilkey	.15
324	Jason Giambi	.40
325	Craig Biggio	.15
326	Troy Glaus	.75
327	Delino DeShields	.15
328	Fernando Vina	.15
329	John Smoltz	.15
330	Jeff Kent	.15
331	Roy Halladay	.15
332	Andy Ashby	.15
333	Tim Wakefield	.15
334	Roger Clemens	1.75
335	Bernie Williams	.15
336	Desi Relaford	.15
337	John Burkett	.15
338	Mike Hampton	.15
339	Royce Clayton	.15
340	Mike Piazza	2.00
341	Jeremi Gonzalez	.15
342	Mike Lansing	.15
343	Jamie Moyer	.15
344	Ron Coomer	.15
345	Barry Larkin	.15
346	Fernando Tatis	.15
347	Chili Davis	.15
348	Bobby Higginson	.15
349	Hal Morris	.15
350	Larry Walker	.15
351	Carlos Guillen	.15
352	Miguel Tejada	.30
353	Travis Fryman	.15
354	Jarrod Washburn	.15
355	Chipper Jones	1.50
356	Todd Stottlemyre	.15
357	Henry Rodriguez	.15
358	Eli Marrero	.15
359	Alan Benes	.15
360	Tim Salmon	.15
361	Luis Gonzalez	.15
362	Scott Spiezio	.15
363	Chris Carpenter	.15
364	Bobby Howry	.15
365	Raul Mondesi	.15
366	Ugueth Urbina	.15
367	Tom Evans	.15
368	Kerry Ligtenberg RC	.40
369	Adrian Beltre	.35
370	Ryan Klesko	.15
371	Wilson Alvarez	.15
372	John Thomson	.15
373	Tony Saunders	.15
374	Mike Stanley	.15
375	Ken Caminiti	.15
376	Jay Buhner	.15
377	Bill Mueller	.15
378	Jeff Blauser	.15
379	Edgar Renteria	.15
380	Jim Thome	.60
381	Joey Hamilton	.15
382	Calvin Pickering	.15
383	Marquis Grissom	.15
384	Omar Daal	.15
385	Curt Schilling	.35
386	Jose Cruz Jr.	.15
387	Chris Widger	.15
388	Pete Harnisch	.15
389	Charles Nagy	.15
390	Tom Gordon	.15
391	Bobby Smith	.15
392	Derrick Gibson	.15
393	Jeff Conine	.15
394	Carlos Perez	.15
395	Barry Bonds	3.00
396	Mark McLemore	.15
397	Juan Encarnacion	.15
398	Wade Boggs	1.50
399	Ivan Rodriguez	.75
400	Moises Alou	.15
401	Jeromy Burnitz	.15
402	Sean Casey	.25
403	Jose Offerman	.15
404	Joe Fontenot	.15
405	Kevin Millwood	.15
406	Lance Johnson	.15
407	Richard Hidalgo	.15
408	Mike Jackson	.15
409	Brian Anderson	.15
410	Jeff Shaw	.15
411	Preston Wilson	.15
412	Todd Hundley	.15
413	Jim Parque	.15
414	Justin Baughman	.15
415	Dante Bichette	.15
416	Paul O'Neill	.15
417	Miguel Cairo	.15
418	Randy Johnson	1.00
419	Jesus Sanchez	.15
420	Carlos Delgado	.35
421	Ricky Ledee	.15
422	Orlando Hernandez	.15
423	Frank Thomas	1.00
424	Pokey Reese	.15
425	Carlos Lee, Mike Lowell, Kit Pellow RC (Prospect)	.30
426	Michael Cuddyer, Mark DeRosa, Jerry Hairston Jr. RC (Prospect)	.60
427	Marlon Anderson, Ron Belliard, Orlando Cabrera (Prospect)	.45
428	Micah Bowie RC, Phil Norton RC, Randy Wolf (Prospect)	.35
429	Jack Cressend, Jason Rakers, John Rocker (Prospect)	.25
430	Ruben Mateo, Scott Morgan, Mike Zywica RC (Prospect)	.25
431	Jason LaRue, Matt LeCroy RC, Mitch Meluskey RC (Prospect)	.25
432	Gabe Kapler, Armando Rios RC, Fernando Seguignol (Prospect)	.25
433	Adam Kennedy, Mickey Lopez RC, Jackie Rexrode (Prospect)	.25
434	Jose Fernandez RC, Jeff Liefer, Chris Truby (Prospect)	.25
435	Corey Koskie, Doug Mientkiewicz RC, Damon Minor (Prospect)	.60
436	Roosevelt Brown RC, Dernell Stenson, Vernon Wells (Prospect)	.25
437	A.J. Burnett RC, John Nicholson, Billy Koch (Prospect)	.75
438	Matt Belisle RC, Matt Roney RC (Draft Pick)	.30
439	Austin Kearns RC, Chris George RC (Draft Pick)	3.00
440	Nate Bump RC, Nate Cornejo RC (Draft Pick)	.40
441	Brad Lidge RC, Mike Nannini RC (Draft Pick)	.60
442	Matt Holliday RC, Jeff Winchester RC (Draft Pick)	5.00
443	Adam Everett RC, Chip Ambres RC (Draft Pick)	.30
444	Pat Burrell RC, Eric Valent RC (Draft Pick)	3.00
445	Roger Clemens (Strikeout Kings)	.85
446	Kerry Wood (Strikeout Kings)	.20
447	Curt Schilling (Strikeout Kings)	.15
448	Randy Johnson (Strikeout Kings)	.50
449	Pedro Martinez (Strikeout Kings)	.50
450	Jeff Bagwell, Andres Galarraga, Mark McGwire (All-Tops)	1.25
451	John Olerud, Jim Thome, Tino Martinez (All-Tops)	.40
452	Alex Rodriguez, Nomar Garciaparra, Derek Jeter (All-Tops)	1.50
453	Vinny Castilla, Chipper Jones, Scott Rolen (All-Tops)	.75
454	Sammy Sosa, Ken Griffey Jr., Juan Gonzalez (All-Tops)	1.00
455	Barry Bonds, Manny Ramirez, Larry Walker (All-Tops)	1.50
456	Frank Thomas, Tim Salmon, David Justice (All-Tops)	.60
457	Travis Lee, Todd Helton, Ben Grieve (All-Tops)	.50
458	Vladimir Guerrero, Greg Vaughn, Bernie Williams (All-Tops)	.50
459	Mike Piazza, Ivan Rodriguez, Jason Kendall (All-Tops)	1.00
460	Roger Clemens, Kerry Wood, Greg Maddux (All-Tops)	1.00
461	Sammy Sosa #1 (Home Run Parade)	10.00
461	Sammy Sosa HR #2-60	6.00
461	S. Sosa HR #61-62	10.00
461	S. Sosa HR #63-65	7.50
461	S. Sosa HR #66	20.00
---	Checklist 1-100	.15
---	Checklist - inserts	.15

All-Etch

Inserted in Series 2 packs, All-Etch has three different styles of inserts. '99 Rookie Rush features rookies who have the best shot of winning '99

Rookie of the Year. Club 40 features 13 players who hit 40 homers or more in 1998, and Club K features seven pitchers known for their strikeout abilities. Each is inserted 1:6 packs, while Refractor versions are seeded 1:24 packs.

		NM/M
Complete Set (30):		15.00
Common Player:		.35
Inserted 1:6		
Refractors:		1.5X
Inserted 1:24		
1	Mark McGwire	3.00
2	Sammy Sosa	1.50
3	Ken Griffey Jr.	2.00
4	Greg Vaughn	.25
5	Albert Belle	.25
6	Vinny Castilla	.25
7	Jose Canseco	.50
8	Juan Gonzalez	.50
9	Manny Ramirez	1.00
10	Andres Galarraga	.25
11	Rafael Palmeiro	.75
12	Alex Rodriguez	3.00
13	Mo Vaughn	.25
14	Eric Chavez	.40
15	Gabe Kapler	.25
16	Calvin Pickering	.25
17	Ruben Mateo	.25
18	Roy Halladay	.40
19	Jeremy Giambi	.25
20	Alex Gonzalez	.25
21	Ron Belliard	.25
22	Marlon Anderson	.25
23	Carlos Lee	.25
24	Kerry Wood	.50
25	Roger Clemens	1.50
26	Curt Schilling	.50
27	Kevin Brown	.25
28	Randy Johnson	1.00
29	Pedro Martinez	1.00
30	Orlando Hernandez	.25

Early Road to the Hall

This insert set spotlights players with less than 10 years in the Majors but who are gunning towards their respective spots in Cooperstown. The cards feature chromium technology, with an insert rate of 1:12 packs. A Refractor parallel edition, numbered to 100 each, was a 1:944 hobby-only insert.

		NM/M
Complete Set (10):		12.00
Common Player:		.50
Inserted 1:12		
Refractors (#'d to 100):		6X
ER1	Nomar Garciaparra	4.00
ER2	Derek Jeter	3.00
ER3	Alex Rodriguez	2.50
ER4	Juan Gonzalez	.50
ER5	Ken Griffey Jr.	2.00
ER6	Chipper Jones	1.50
ER7	Vladimir Guerrero	1.00
ER8	Jeff Bagwell	1.00
ER9	Ivan Rodriguez	.75
ER10	Frank Thomas	1.00

Fortune 15

Fortune 15 showcases the baseball's best players and hot rookies. They are inserted in Series 2 packs at a rate of 1:12. A Refractor version also exists found exclusively in hobby packs at a rate of 1:627 packs. Refractors are sequentially numbered to 100.

		NM/M
Complete Set (15):		17.50
Common Player:		.50
Inserted 1:12		
Refractors (#'d to 100):		4X
1	Alex Rodriguez	2.25
2	Nomar Garciaparra	1.25

3	Derek Jeter	3.00
4	Troy Glaus	.75
5	Ken Griffey Jr.	1.50
6	Vladimir Guerrero	1.00
7	Kerry Wood	.65
8	Eric Chavez	.65
9	Greg Maddux	1.25
10	Mike Piazza	1.50
11	Sammy Sosa	1.25
12	Mark McGwire	2.25
13	Ben Grieve	.50
14	Chipper Jones	1.25
15	Manny Ramirez	1.00

Home Run Heroes

These cards were part of an unannounced multi-manufacturer (Fleer, Upper Deck, Topps, Pacific) insert program exclusive to Wal-Mart. Each company produced cards of Mark McGwire and Sammy Sosa, along with two other premier sluggers. Each company's cards share a "Power Elite" logo at top and "Home Run Heroes" logo vertically at right.

		NM/M
Complete Set (4):		5.00
Common Player:		1.00
9	Mark McGwire	2.00
10	Sammy Sosa	1.50
11	Alex Rodriguez	2.00
12	Vladimir Guerrero	1.00

Lords of the Diamond

Parallel to the Topps version, this insert set features die-cutting across the card top and is seeded 1:8 in Series 1 packs. Refractor versions can be found 1:24 packs.

		NM/M
Complete Set (15):		20.00
Common Player:		.40
Inserted 1:8		
Refractors:		2X
Inserted 1:24		
LD1	Ken Griffey Jr.	2.00
LD2	Chipper Jones	1.50
LD3	Sammy Sosa	1.50
LD4	Frank Thomas	1.25

LD5	Mark McGwire	2.50
LD6	Jeff Bagwell	1.25
LD7	Alex Rodriguez	2.25
LD8	Juan Gonzalez	.65
LD9	Barry Bonds	3.00
LD10	Nomar Garciaparra	1.50
LD11	Darin Erstad	.50
LD12	Tony Gwynn	1.50
LD13	Andres Galarraga	.40
LD14	Mike Piazza	1.50
LD15	Greg Maddux	1.50

New Breed

A parallel version utilizing chromium technology, this insert set features the top young stars in the game and is seeded 1:24 packs. A Refractor version also exists, found 1:72 packs.

		NM/M
Complete Set (15):		30.00
Common Player:		.50
Inserted 1:24		
Refractors:		1.5X
Inserted 1:72		
NB1	Darin Erstad	.75
NB2	Brad Fullmer	.50
NB3	Kerry Wood	.75
NB4	Nomar Garciaparra	5.00
NB5	Travis Lee	.65
NB6	Scott Rolen	2.00
NB7	Todd Helton	3.00
NB8	Vladimir Guerrero	7.50
NB9	Derek Jeter	7.50
NB10	Alex Rodriguez	6.00
NB11	Ben Grieve	.50
NB12	Andruw Jones	3.00
NB13	Paul Konerko	.75
NB14	Aramis Ramirez	.75
NB15	Adrian Beltre	.75

Record Numbers

This insert set salutes nine record-setters who have earned a mark of distinction, including Cal Ripken Jr. for his record setting consecutive game streak. Inserted randomly in Series 2 packs at a rate of 1:36 packs. Refractor parallel versions are seeded 1:144 packs.

		NM/M
Complete Set (10):		20.00
Common Player:		.50
Inserted 1:36		
Refractors:		1.5X
Inserted 1:144		
1	Mark McGwire	3.00
2	Craig Biggio	.50
3	Barry Bonds	4.00
4	Ken Griffey Jr.	2.50
5	Sammy Sosa	2.00
6	Alex Rodriguez	3.00
7	Kerry Wood	1.00
8	Roger Clemens	2.00
9	Cal Ripken Jr.	4.00
10	Mark McGwire	3.00

Traded and Rookies

Actually issued in 2000, this parallel of the Topps Traded set utilizing Chromium

technology was issued only in complete set form.

		NM/M
Complete Set (121):		60.00
Common Player:		.15
1	Seth Etherton	.15
2	Mark Harriger RC	.25
3	Matt Wise RC	.25
4	Carlos Hernandez RC	.50
5	Julio Lugo RC	1.50
6	Mike Nannini	.15
7	Justin Bowles RC	.25
8	Mark Mulder RC	5.00
9	Roberto Vaz RC	.15
10	Felipe Lopez RC	3.00
11	Matt Belisle	.15
12	Micah Bowie	.15
13	Ruben Quevedo RC	.25
14	Jose Garcia RC	.15
15	David Kelton RC	1.00
16	Phillip Norton	.15
17	Corey Patterson RC	2.50
18	Ron Walker RC	.15
19	Paul Hoover RC	.15
20	Ryan Rupe RC	.25
21	J.D. Closser RC	.15
22	Rob Ryan RC	.15
23	Steve Colyer RC	.15
24	Bubba Crosby RC	1.00
25	Luke Prokopec RC	.15
26	Matt Blank RC	.15
27	Josh McKinley	.15
28	Nate Bump	.15
29	Giuseppe Chiaramonte RC	.15
30	Arturo McDowell	.15
31	Tony Torcato	.15
32	Dave Roberts	.15
33	C.C. Sabathia RC	3.00
34	Sean Spencer RC	.15
35	Chip Ambres	.15
36	A.J. Burnett	.50
37	Mo Bruce RC	.15
38	Jason Tyner	.15
39	Mamon Tucker	.15
40	Sean Burroughs RC	.75
41	Kevin Eberwein RC	.15
42	Junior Herndon RC	.25
43	Bryan Wolff RC	.15
44	Pat Burrell	1.00
45	Eric Valent	.15
46	Carlos Pena RC	1.00
47	Mike Zywica	.15
48	Adam Everett	.15
49	Juan Pena RC	.75
50	Adam Dunn RC	10.00
51	Austin Kearns	2.00
52	Jacobo Sequea RC	.15
53	Choo Freeman	.50
54	Jeff Winchester	.15
55	Matt Burch	.15
56	Chris George	.25
57	Scott Mullen RC	.15
58	Kit Pellow	.15
59	Mark Quinn RC	.75
60	Nate Cornejo	.15
61	Ryan Mills RC	.15
62	Kevin Beirne RC	.15
63	Kip Wells RC	.75
64	Juan Rivera RC	.50
65	Alfonso Soriano RC	10.00
66	Josh Hamilton RC	12.00
67	Josh Girdley RC	.15
68	Kyle Snyder RC	.25
69	Mike Paradis RC	.25
70	Jason Jennings RC	.25
71	David Walling RC	.25
72	Omar Ortiz RC	.15
73	Jay Gehrke RC	.15
74	Casey Burns RC	.15
75	Carl Crawford RC	8.00
76	Reggie Sanders	.15
77	Will Clark	.15
78	David Wells	.15
79	Paul Konerko	.30
80	Armando Benitez	.15
81	Brant Brown	.15
82	Mo Vaughn	.15
83	Jose Canseco	.75
84	Albert Belle	.25
85	Dean Palmer	.15
86	Greg Vaughn	.15
87	Mark Clark	.15
88	Pat Meares	.15
89	Eric Davis	.15
90	Brian Giles	.15
91	Jeff Brantley	.15
92	Bret Boone	.15
93	Ron Gant	.15
94	Mike Cameron	.15
95	Charles Johnson	.15
96	Denny Neagle	.15
97	Brian Hunter	.15
98	Jose Hernandez	.15
99	Rick Aguilera	.15
100	Tony Batista	.15
101	Roger Cedeno	.15
102	Creighton Gubanich	.15
103	Tim Belcher	.15
104	Bruce Aven	.15
105	Brian Daubach RC	.75
106	Ed Sprague	.15
107	Michael Tucker	.15
108	Homer Bush	.15
109	Armando Reynoso	.15
110	Brook Fordyce	.15
111	Matt Mantei	.15
112	Jose Guillen	.15
113	Kenny Rogers	.15
114	Livan Hernandez	.15
115	Butch Huskey	.15
116	David Segui	.15
117	Darryl Hamilton	.15
118	Jim Leyritz	.15
119	Randy Velarde	.15
120	Bill Taylor	.15
121	Kevin Appier	.15

Super Chrome

Using identical photos from Topps Chrome Baseball, Topps supersized 36 players to 4-1/8" x 5-3/4" card size. The cards are done on standard chromium technology. Each pack contains three oversized cards and sells for S.R.P. of $4.99. There also is a Refractor parallel set, which are seeded 1:12 packs.

		NM/M
Complete Set (36):		45.00
Common Player:		.50
Refractors:		2X
Inserted 1:12		
Pack (3):		4.50
Wax Box (12):		48.00
1	Roger Clemens	2.25
2	Andres Galarraga	.50
3	Manny Ramirez	1.50
4	Greg Maddux	2.00
5	Kerry Wood	.75
6	Travis Lee	.75
7	Nolan Ryan	4.50
8	Juan Gonzalez	.75
9	Vladimir Guerrero	1.50
10	Sammy Sosa	2.00
11	Mark McGwire	3.00
12	Javy Lopez	.50
13	Tony Gwynn	2.00
14	Derek Jeter	4.50
15	Albert Belle	.50
16	Pedro Martinez	1.50
17	Greg Vaughn	.50
18	Ken Griffey Jr.	2.50
19	Ben Grieve	.50
20	Vinny Castilla	.50
21	Moises Alou	.50
22	Barry Bonds	4.50
23	Nomar Garciaparra	2.00
24	Chipper Jones	2.00
25	Mike Piazza	2.50
26	Alex Rodriguez	3.00
27	Ivan Rodriguez	1.25
28	Frank Thomas	1.50
29	Larry Walker	.50
30	Troy Glaus	1.00
31	David Wells (Season Highlight)	.50
32	Roger Clemens (Season Highlight)	1.00
33	Kerry Wood (Season Highlight)	.50
34	Mark McGwire (Home Run Record)	3.00
35	Sammy Sosa (Home Run Parade)	2.00
36	World Series	.50

1999 Topps Gallery Pre-Production

Topps debuted its 1999 Gallery set with this trio of sample cards. Format is virtually identical to issued cards except for the use of a "PP" prefix to the card numbers on back.

		NM/M
Complete Set (3):		5.00
Common Player:		2.00
PP1	Scott Rolen	2.00
PP2	Andres Galarraga (Masters)	2.00
PP3	Brad Fullmer (Artisans)	2.00

1999 Topps Gallery

This 150-card base set features a white textured border surrounding the player image with the player's name, team name and Topps Gallery logo stamped in gold foil. The first 100 cards in the set portray veteran players while the final 50 cards are short-printed in three subsets: Masters, Artisans and Apprentices. Card backs have a monthly batting or pitching record from the '98 season, a player photo and vital information.

		NM/M
Complete Set (150):		60.00
Common Player (1-100):		.10
Common Player (101-150):		.25
Player's Private Issue:		5X
PPI SP's:		3X
Production 250 Sets		
Pack (6):		3.00
Wax Box (24):		45.00
1	Mark McGwire	1.50
2	Jim Thome	.35
3	Bernie Williams	.10
4	Larry Walker	.10
5	Juan Gonzalez	.30
6	Ken Griffey Jr.	1.00
7	Raul Mondesi	.10
8	Sammy Sosa	.75
9	Greg Maddux	.75
10	Jeff Bagwell	.60
11	Vladimir Guerrero	.60
12	Scott Rolen	.50
13	Nomar Garciaparra	.75
14	Mike Piazza	1.00
15	Travis Lee	.15
16	Carlos Delgado	.35
17	Darin Erstad	.25
18	David Justice	.10
19	Cal Ripken Jr.	2.00
20	Derek Jeter	2.00
21	Tony Clark	.10
22	Barry Larkin	.10
23	Greg Vaughn	.10
24	Jeff Kent	.10
25	Wade Boggs	.75
26	Andres Galarraga	.10
27	Ken Caminiti	.10
28	Jason Kendall	.10
29	Todd Helton	.60
30	Chuck Knoblauch	.10

31	Roger Clemens	.85
32	Jeromy Burnitz	.10
33	Javy Lopez	.10
34	Roberto Alomar	.25
35	Eric Karros	.10
36	Ben Grieve	.10
37	Eric Davis	.10
38	Rondell White	.10
39	Dmitri Young	.10
40	Ivan Rodriguez	.50
41	Paul O'Neill	.10
42	Jeff Cirillo	.10
43	Kerry Wood	.30
44	Albert Belle	.10
45	Frank Thomas	.60
46	Manny Ramirez	.60
47	Tom Glavine	.25
48	Mo Vaughn	.10
49	Jose Cruz Jr.	.10
50	Sandy Alomar	.10
51	Edgar Martinez	.10
52	John Olerud	.10
53	Todd Walker	.10
54	Tim Salmon	.10
55	Derek Bell	.10
56	Matt Williams	.10
57	Alex Rodriguez	1.50
58	Rusty Greer	.10
59	Vinny Castilla	.10
60	Jason Giambi	.30
61	Mark Grace	.10
62	Jose Canseco	.40
63	Gary Sheffield	.40
64	Brad Fullmer	.10
65	Trevor Hoffman	.10
66	Mark Kotsay	.10
67	Mike Mussina	.25
68	Johnny Damon	.30
69	Tino Martinez	.25
70	Curt Schilling	.25
71	Jay Buhner	.10
72	Kenny Lofton	.10
73	Randy Johnson	.60
74	Kevin Brown	.10
75	Brian Jordan	.10
76	Craig Biggio	.25
77	Barry Bonds	2.00
78	Tony Gwynn	.75
79	Jim Edmonds	.10
80	Shawn Green	.35
81	Todd Hundley	.10
82	Cliff Floyd	.10
83	Jose Guillen	.10
84	Dante Bichette	.10
85	Moises Alou	.10
86	Chipper Jones	.75
87	Ray Lankford	.10
88	Fred McGriff	.10
89	Rod Beck	.10
90	Dean Palmer	.10
91	Pedro Martinez	.60
92	Andruw Jones	.60
93	Robin Ventura	.10
94	Ugueth Urbina	.10
95	Orlando Hernandez	.10
96	Sean Casey	.15
97	Denny Neagle	.10
98	Troy Glaus	.60
99	John Smoltz	.10
100	Al Leiter	.10
101	Ken Griffey Jr.	1.50
102	Frank Thomas	.75
103	Mark McGwire	2.00
104	Sammy Sosa	1.00
105	Chipper Jones	1.00
106	Alex Rodriguez	2.00
107	Nomar Garciaparra	1.00
108	Juan Gonzalez	.40
109	Derek Jeter	3.00
110	Mike Piazza	1.50
111	Barry Bonds	3.00
112	Tony Gwynn	1.00
113	Cal Ripken Jr.	3.00
114	Greg Maddux	1.00
115	Roger Clemens	1.25
116	Brad Fullmer	.25
117	Kerry Wood	.50
118	Ben Grieve	.25
119	Todd Helton	.65
120	Kevin Millwood	.25
121	Sean Casey	.35
122	Vladimir Guerrero	.75
123	Travis Lee	.25
124	Troy Glaus	.65
125	Bartolo Colon	.25
126	Andruw Jones	.75
127	Scott Rolen	.60
128	Alfonso Soriano **RC**	4.00
129	Nick Johnson **RC**	1.00
130	Matt Belisle **RC**	.25
131	Jorge Toca **RC**	.25
132	Masao Kida **RC**	.25
133	Carlos Pena **RC**	1.00
134	Adrian Beltre	.40
135	Eric Chavez	.40
136	Carlos Beltran	.65
137	Alex Gonzalez	.25
138	Ryan Anderson	.25
139	Ruben Mateo	.25
140	Bruce Chen	.25
141	Pat Burrell **RC**	3.00
142	Michael Barrett	.25
143	Carlos Lee	.25
144	Mark Mulder **RC**	1.00
145	Choo Freeman **RC**	.50
146	Gabe Kapler	.25
147	Juan Encarnacion	.25
148	Jeremy Giambi	.25

149	Jason Tyner **RC**	.35
150	George Lombard	.25
		.10
	Checklist folder 1	
	(1:3 packs)	.10
	Checklist folder 2 (1:3)	.10
	Checklist folder 3 (1:3)	.10
	Checklist folder 4 (1:12)	.25
	Checklist folder 5	
	(1:240)	1.50
	Checklist folder 6	
	(1:640)	3.00

Player's Private Issue

This parallel to the 150 regular cards in 1999 Gallery is limited to 250 serially numbered cards of each. Stated odds of insertion were one per 17 packs.

	NM/M
Common Player:	1.00
Stars:	5X
SP's:	3X
Production 250 Sets	

Autograph Cards

Three of baseball's top young third basemen are featured in this autographed set. The insertion odds are 1:209.

	NM/M
Common Player:	10.00
Inserted 1:209	
GA1 Troy Glaus	15.00
GA2 Adrian Beltre	10.00
GA3 Eric Chavez	10.00

Awards Gallery

This 10-card set features players who have earned the highest honors in baseball. Each insert commemorates the player's award by stamping his achievement on the bottom of the card front. Card fronts have silver borders surrounding the player's image. These are seeded 1:12 and card numbers have a "AG" prefix.

	NM/M
Complete Set (10):	12.50

Common Player:		.50
Inserted 1:12		
AG1	Kerry Wood	.75
AG2	Ben Grieve	.50
AG3	Roger Clemens	2.50
AG4	Tom Glavine	.75
AG5	Juan Gonzalez	.75
AG6	Sammy Sosa	3.00
AG7	Ken Griffey Jr.	3.00
AG8	Mark McGwire	4.00
AG9	Bernie Williams	.50
AG10	Larry Walker	.50

Exhibitions

This 20-card set is done on textured 24-point stock and features baseball's top stars. Exhibitions are seeded 1:48 packs.

		NM/M
Complete Set (20):		75.00
Common Player:		2.00
Inserted 1:48		
E1	Sammy Sosa	4.50
E2	Mark McGwire	7.50
E3	Greg Maddux	4.50
E4	Roger Clemens	5.00
E5	Ben Grieve	2.00
E6	Kerry Wood	2.25
E7	Ken Griffey Jr.	6.00
E8	Tony Gwynn	4.50
E9	Cal Ripken Jr.	10.00
E10	Frank Thomas	4.00
E11	Jeff Bagwell	4.00
E12	Derek Jeter	10.00
E13	Alex Rodriguez	7.50
E14	Nomar Garciaparra	4.50
E15	Manny Ramirez	4.00
E16	Vladimir Guerrero	4.00
E17	Darin Erstad	2.25
E18	Scott Rolen	3.00
E19	Mike Piazza	6.00
E20	Andres Galarraga	2.00

Gallery of Heroes

This 10-card set is done on card stock that simulates medieval stained glass. Gallery of Heroes are found 1:24 packs.

		NM/M
Complete Set (10):		30.00
Common Player:		.75
Inserted 1:24		
GH1	Mark McGwire	6.00
GH2	Sammy Sosa	3.50
GH3	Ken Griffey Jr.	4.50
GH4	Mike Piazza	4.50
GH5	Derek Jeter	7.50
GH6	Nomar Garciaparra	4.50
GH7	Kerry Wood	1.50
GH8	Ben Grieve	.75
GH9	Chipper Jones	3.50
GH10	Alex Rodriguez	6.00

Heritage

Nineteen contemporary legends and Hall-of-Famer Hank Aaron are artistically depicted using the 1953 Topps design as a template. For a chance to bid on the original art used in the development of this insert set, collectors were

able to enter the Topps Gallery Auction. Collectors could accumulate auction points found in Topps Gallery packs. Heritages are seeded 1:12 packs. A parallel called Heritage Proofs are also randomly inserted in 1:48 packs and have a chrome styrene finish.

		NM/M
Complete Set (20):		100.00
Common Player:		2.50
Inserted 1:12		
Heritage Proofs:		1.5X
Inserted 1:48		
TH1	Hank Aaron	10.00
TH2	Ben Grieve	2.50
TH3	Nomar Garciaparra	7.50
TH4	Roger Clemens	8.50
TH5	Travis Lee	2.50
TH6	Tony Gwynn	7.50
TH7	Alex Rodriguez	12.50
TH8	Ken Griffey Jr.	10.00
TH9	Derek Jeter	15.00
TH10	Sammy Sosa	7.50
TH11	Scott Rolen	2.50
TH12	Chipper Jones	7.50
TH13	Cal Ripken Jr.	15.00
TH14	Kerry Wood	3.00
TH15	Barry Bonds	15.00
TH16	Juan Gonzalez	3.00
TH17	Mike Piazza	10.00
TH18	Greg Maddux	7.50
TH19	Frank Thomas	6.00
TH20	Mark McGwire	12.50

Heritage Proofs

Heritage Proofs are a parallel to the 1953-style inserts. Printed on chrome styrene, the proofs have a silver metallic background on front and the notation on bottom-back, "1953 TOPPS HERITAGE PROOF." The proof versions are found on average of one per 48 packs.

		NM/M
Complete Set (20):		175.00
TH1	Hank Aaron	15.00
TH2	Ben Grieve	3.00
TH3	Nomar Garciaparra	10.00
TH4	Roger Clemens	11.50
TH5	Travis Lee	3.00
TH6	Tony Gwynn	10.00
TH7	Alex Rodriguez	15.00
TH8	Ken Griffey Jr.	12.50
TH9	Derek Jeter	20.00
TH10	Sammy Sosa	12.50
TH11	Scott Rolen	5.00
TH12	Chipper Jones	10.00
TH13	Cal Ripken Jr.	20.00
TH14	Kerry Wood	4.00
TH15	Barry Bonds	20.00
TH16	Juan Gonzalez	5.00
TH17	Mike Piazza	12.50
TH18	Greg Maddux	10.00
TH19	Frank Thomas	7.50
TH20	Mark McGwire	15.00

Heritage Lithographs

Eight of the paintings used to create the Heritage in-

serts for 1999 Topps Gallery were reproduced as enlarged limited-edition offset lithographs. The paintings of Bill Purdom and James Fiorentino were reproduced in an 18" x 25" serially-numbered, artist-signed edition of 600 pieces each. The lithos were offered through Bill Goff Inc / Good Sports at $60 each unframed.

		NM/M
Complete Set (8):		480.00
Single Player:		60.00
(1)	Roger Clemens	60.00
(2)	Nomar Garciaparra	60.00
(3)	Ken Griffey Jr.	60.00
(4)	Derek Jeter	60.00
(5)	Mark McGwire	60.00
(6)	Mike Piazza	60.00
(7)	Cal Ripken Jr.	60.00
(8)	Sammy Sosa	60.00

Heritage Super Promos

Actually issued as a Topps handout at the 2000 National Sports Collectors Convention Corporate Block Party, this set depicts eight of the 1953 Topps-style cards which had been created for the Gallery Heritage insert series in 1999. The super-size (3-3/4" x 5-1/8") promos are printed on thin, glossy stock. Fronts have card-style artwork by Bill Goff or Bill Purdom. Backs are in black-and-white with player information and advertising by the artists, along with MLB and MLBPA licensor logos. The unnumbered cards are checklisted here alphabetically.

		NM/M
Complete Set (8):		40.00
Common Player:		4.00
(1)	Roger Clemens	4.50
(2)	Nomar Garciaparra	4.00
(3)	Ken Griffey Jr.	5.00
(4)	Derek Jeter	7.50
(5)	Mark McGwire	6.00
(6)	Mike Piazza	5.00
(7)	Cal Ripken Jr.	7.50
(8)	Sammy Sosa	4.00

Press Plates

The aluminum press plates used to print the Gallery cards were inserted at a rate of one per 985 packs. Each card's front and back can be found in four different color variations. Because of the unique nature of each plate, assignment of catalog values is not feasible.

	NM/M
Common Player:	25.00

Gold Label Pre-Production

This trio of pre-production samples previews Topps' 1999 version of its high-end Gold Label brand. Cards are nearly identical in format to the issued version except for the "PP" prefix to card numbers on back.

		NM/M
Complete Set (3):		3.00
Common Player:		1.00
PP1	Tom Glavine	1.00
PP2	Tino Martinez	1.00
PP3	Jim Thome	2.00

Gold Label Class 1

This set consists of 100 cards on 35-point spectral-reflective rainbow stock with gold foil stamping. All cards are available in three versions each with the same foreground photo, but with different background photos that vary by category: Class 1 (fielding), Class 2 (running, 1:2), Class 3 (hitting, 1:4), In addition each variation has a different version of the player's team logo in the background. Variations for pitchers are Class 1, set position; Class 2, wind-up, and Class 3, throwing. Black Label parallels were inserted at the rate of between 1:8 and 1:12, depending on packaging. Red Label parallels, serially numbered to 100 each were inserted at rates from 1:118 to 1:148. A One to One parallel version also exists and is limited to one numbered card for each variation and color (Gold, Black and Red), for a total of 900 cards inserted about one per 1,500 packs.

		NM/M
Complete Set (100):		30.00
Common Gold Label:		.10
Common Black Label:		.50
Black Label Stars:		3X
Common Red Label:		2.00
Red Label Stars:		12X
Pack (5):		3.00
Wax Box (24):		50.00
1	Mike Piazza	2.00
2	Andres Galarraga	.10
3	Mark Grace	.10
4	Tony Clark	.10
5	Jim Thome	.10
6	Tony Gwynn	1.50
7	Kelly Dransfeldt **RC**	.15
8	Eric Chavez	.25
9	Brian Jordan	.10
10	Todd Hundley	.10
11	Rondell White	.10
12	Dmitri Young	.10

13	Jeff Kent	.10
14	Derek Bell	.10
15	Todd Helton	.75
16	Chipper Jones	1.50
17	Albert Belle	.10
18	Barry Larkin	.10
19	Dante Bichette	.10
20	Gary Sheffield	.50
21	Cliff Floyd	.10
22	Derek Jeter	3.00
23	Jason Giambi	.50
24	Ray Lankford	.10
25	Alex Rodriguez	2.50
26	Ruben Mateo	.10
27	Wade Boggs	1.50
28	Carlos Delgado	.45
29	Tim Salmon	.10
30	Alfonso Soriano RC	5.00
31	Javy Lopez	.10
32	Jason Kendall	.10
33	Nick Johnson RC	1.00
34	A.J. Burnett RC	1.00
35	Troy Glaus	.75
36	Pat Burrell RC	3.00
37	Jeff Cirillo	.10
38	David Justice	.10
39	Ivan Rodriguez	.75
40	Bernie Williams	.10
41	Jay Buhner	.10
42	Mo Vaughn	.10
43	Randy Johnson	1.00
44	Pedro Martinez	1.00
45	Larry Walker	.10
46	Todd Walker	.10
47	Roberto Alomar	.25
48	Kevin Brown	.10
49	Mike Mussina	.40
50	Tom Glavine	.25
51	Curt Schilling	.25
52	Ken Caminiti	.10
53	Brad Fullmer	.10
54	Bobby Seay RC	.10
55	Orlando Hernandez	.10
56	Sean Casey	.10
57	Al Leiter	.10
58	Sandy Alomar	.10
59	Mark Kotsay	.10
60	Matt Williams	.10
61	Raul Mondesi	.10
62	Joe Crede RC	5.00
63	Jim Edmonds	.10
64	Jose Cruz Jr.	.10
65	Juan Gonzalez	.50
66	Sammy Sosa	1.50
67	Cal Ripken Jr.	3.00
68	Vinny Castilla	.10
69	Craig Biggio	.10
70	Mark McGwire	2.50
71	Greg Vaughn	.10
72	Greg Maddux	1.50
73	Paul O'Neill	.10
74	Scott Rolen	.65
75	Ben Grieve	.10
76	Vladimir Guerrero	1.00
77	John Olerud	.10
78	Eric Karros	.10
79	Jeromy Burnitz	.10
80	Jeff Bagwell	1.00
81	Kenny Lofton	.10
82	Manny Ramirez	1.00
83	Andruw Jones	1.00
84	Travis Lee	.15
85	Darin Erstad	.25
86	Nomar Garciaparra	1.50
87	Frank Thomas	1.00
88	Moises Alou	.10
89	Tino Martinez	.10
90	Carlos Pena RC	1.00
91	Shawn Green	.40
92	Rusty Greer	.10
93	Matt Belisle RC	.25
94	Adrian Beltre	.25
95	Roger Clemens	1.75
96	John Smoltz	.10
97	Mark Mulder RC	1.00
98	Kerry Wood	.50
99	Barry Bonds	3.00
100	Ken Griffey Jr.	2.00
	Checklist folder	.05

Gold Label Class 2

Background photos for Class 2 Gold Label and color parallels show position players running and pitchers in their windup. Class 2 Gold Label cards are inserted at the rate of one in two Home Team Advantage packs, and one in four retail packs. Black Label versions are inserted 1:16 HTA and 1:24 R. Red Labels, numbered to 50 each, are found in HTA at a 1:237 rate, and in retail at 1:296.

	NM/M
Complete Set (100):	75.00
Common Gold Label:	.25
Gold Label Stars:	1.5X
Common Black Label:	2.00
Black Label Stars:	4X
Common Red Label:	6.00
Red Label Stars:	15X

Gold Label Class 3

Background photos for Class 3 Gold Label and color parallels show position players hitting and pitchers pitching. Class 3 Gold Label cards are inserted at the rate of one in four Home Team Advantage packs, and one in eight retail packs. Black Label versions are inserted 1:32 HTA and 1:48 R. Red Labels, numbered to 25 each, are found in HTA at a 1:473 rate, and in retail at 1:591.

	NM/M
Complete Set (100):	125.00
Common Gold Label:	.50
Gold Label Stars:	2
Common Black Label:	3.00
Black Label Stars:	6X
Common Red Label:	12.00
Red Label Stars:	35X

Gold Label One to One

Depending on type of packaging, these rare parallels are found at the rate of only one per approximately 1,200-1,600 packs. Each of the three Classes in Gold, Red and Black versions can be found as a One to One insert, for a total of nine "unique" cards for each player in the base set and three in the Race to Aaron insert series. Backs of the One to One cards are printed in silver foil with a "1/1" foil serial number.

	NM/M
Common Player, Base Set:	50.00
Common Player, Race to Aaron:	150.00

Gold Label Race to Aaron

This 10-card set features the best current players who are chasing Hank Aaron's career home run and career RBI records. Each player is pictured in the foreground with Aaron silhouetted in the background on the card front. These are seeded 1:12 packs. Two parallel versions also exist: Black and Red. Blacks have black foil stamping and are seeded 1:48 packs. Reds have red foil stamping and are limited to 44 sequentially numbered sets.

		NM/M
Complete Set (10):		20.00
Common Player:		1.00
Blacks:		2X
Reds:		12X
1	Mark McGwire	4.50
2	Ken Griffey Jr.	3.00
3	Alex Rodriguez	4.50
4	Vladimir Guerrero	1.50
5	Albert Belle	1.00
6	Nomar Garciaparra	2.50
7	Ken Griffey Jr.	3.00
8	Alex Rodriguez	4.50
9	Juan Gonzalez	1.00
10	Barry Bonds	7.50

Gold Label Name Mismatches

Because of faulty alignment when the gold-foil logo and player name were applied to card fronts, some Gold Label cards are found with the wrong name on front. Because each of these error cards is rare or possibly unique, and the demand is dependent on the combination of photo and name, it is not possible to assign values.

Opening Day

This retail exclusive product is comprised of 165 cards. Base cards have a silver bor-

der, and the Opening Day logo stamped with silver foil. Packs are pre-priced at $.99, each pack has seven cards. Hank Aaron autographs are randomly seeded and are stamped with the Topps "Certified Autograph Issue" stamp. The insertion rate for the autograph is 1:29,642 packs.

		NM/M
Complete Set (165):		20.00
Common Player:		.10
Hank Aaron Autograph:		150.00
Pack (7):		1.50
Wax Box (24):		20.00
1	Hank Aaron	3.00
2a	Roger Clemens	1.25
2b	Andres Galarraga (should be #3)	.10
4	Scott Brosius	.10
5	Ray Durham	.10
6	Will Clark	.10
7	David Wells	.10
8	Jose Guillen	.10
9	Edgardo Alfonzo	.10
10	Manny Ramirez	.75
11	Greg Maddux	1.00
12	David Segui	.10
13	Darryl Strawberry	.10
14	Brad Radke	.10
15	Kerry Wood	.35
16	Paul Konerko	.30
17	Travis Lee	.10
18	Kenny Rogers	.10
19	Todd Walker	.10
20	John Olerud	.10
21	Nolan Ryan	2.00
22	Ray Lankford	.10
23	Bartolo Colon	.10
24	Brady Anderson	.10
25	Jorge Posada	.10
26	Justin Thompson	.10
27	Juan Gonzalez	.40
28	Chuck Knoblauch	.10
29	Todd Helton	.65
30	Gary Sheffield	.40
31	Rod Beck	.10
32	Garret Anderson	.10
33	Rondell White	.10
34	Vladimir Guerrero	.75
35	Eric Karros	.10
36	Mo Vaughn	.10
37	Sammy Sosa	1.00
38	Kenny Lofton	.10
39	Mark McGwire	2.00
40	Javy Lopez	.10
41	Damion Easley	.10
42	Andy Pettitte	.30
43	Tony Gwynn	1.00
44	Jay Bell	.10
45	Jose Canseco	.45
46	John Wetteland	.10
47	Mike Caruso	.10
48	Derek Jeter	3.00
49	Aaron Sele	.10
50	Jeff Cirillo	.10
51	Mark Kotsay	.10
52	Albert Belle	.10
53	Matt Lawton	.10
54	Pedro Martinez	.75
55	Greg Vaughn	.10
56	Neifi Perez	.10
57	Derek Bell	.10
58	Ken Griffey Jr.	1.50
59	David Cone	.10
60	Dean Palmer	.10
61	Trevor Hoffman	.10
62	Billy Wagner	.10
63	Shawn Green	.25
64	Ben Grieve	.10
65	Tom Goodwin	.10
66	Jaret Wright	.10
67	Dmitri Young	.10
68	Hideki Irabu	.10
69	Jeff Fassero	.10
70	Matt Williams	.10
71	Bret Saberhagen	.10
72	Chad Curtis	.10
73	Scott Rolen	.60
74	J.T. Snow Jr.	.10
75	Rusty Greer	.10
76	Jim Edmonds	.10
77	Ron Gant	.10
78	A.J. Hinch	.10
79	Shannon Stewart	.10
80	Brad Fullmer	.10
81	Walt Weiss	.10
82	Fred McGriff	.10
83	Darin Erstad	.25
84	Eric Young	.10
85	Livan Hernandez	.10
86	Jeff Bagwell	.75
87	Omar Vizquel	.10
88	Eric Davis	.10
89	Magglio Ordonez	.25
90	John Valentin	.10
91	Dave Dellucci	.10
92	Chan Ho Park	.10
93	Masato Yoshii	.10
94	Bret Boone	.10
95	Mariano Rivera	.20
96	Bobby Jones	.10
97	Francisco Cordova	.10
98	Mike Mussina	.40
99	Denny Neagle	.10
100	Edgar Martinez	.10
101	Jason Kendall	.10
102	Jeff King	.10
103	Rey Ordonez	.10
104	Andruw Jones	.75
105	Vinny Castilla	.10
106	Troy Glaus	.65
107	Tom Glavine	.40
108	Moises Alou	.10
109	Carlos Delgado	.40
110	Raul Mondesi	.10
111	Shane Reynolds	.10
112	Jason Giambi	.60
113	Jose Cruz Jr.	.10
114	Craig Biggio	.10
115	Tim Salmon	.10
116	Chipper Jones	1.00
117	Andy Benes	.10
118	John Smoltz	.10
119	Jeromy Burnitz	.10
120	Randy Johnson	.75
121	Mark Grace	.25
122	Henry Rodriguez	.10
123	Ryan Klesko	.10
124	Kevin Millwood	.10
125	Sean Casey	.20
126	Brian Jordan	.10
127	Kevin Brown	.10
128	Orlando Hernandez	.10
129	Barry Bonds	3.00
130	David Justice	.10
131	Carlos Perez	.10
132	Andy Ashby	.10
133	Paul O'Neill	.10
134	Curt Schilling	.40
135	Alex Rodriguez	2.00
136	Cliff Floyd	.10
137	Rafael Palmeiro	.60
138	Nomar Garciaparra	1.00
139	Mike Piazza	1.50
140	Roberto Alomar	.30
141	Todd Hundley	.10
142	Jeff Kent	.10
143	Barry Larkin	.10
144	Cal Ripken Jr.	3.00
145	Jay Buhner	.10
146	Kevin Young	.10
147	Ivan Rodriguez	.65
148	Al Leiter	.10
149	Sandy Alomar	.10
150	Bernie Williams	.10
151	Ellis Burks	.10
152	Wally Joyner	.10
153	Bobby Higginson	.10
154	Tony Clark	.10
155	Larry Walker	.10
156	Frank Thomas	.75
157	Tino Martinez	.10
158	Jim Thome	.60
159	Dante Bichette	.10
160	David Wells (Season Highlights)	.10
161	Roger Clemens (Season Highlights)	.50
162	Kerry Wood (Season Highlights)	.15
163	Mark McGwire (HR Record #70)	4.00
164	Sammy Sosa (HR Record #66)	1.50
165	Checklist	.10

1999 Topps Stars Pre-Production

Five-card cello packs of pre-production samples were distributed to introduce Topps' new concept for its Stars brand. The samples follow the format of the issued versions except for the use of a "PP" prefix to the card number on back.

		NM/M
Complete Set (5):		5.00
Common Player:		.75
PP1	Paul O'Neill (Base card.)	.75
PP2	Vinny Castilla (One-star.)	.75
PP3	Darin Erstad (Two-star.)	1.00
PP4	Kerry Wood (Three-star.)	1.50
PP5	Chipper Jones (Four-star.)	3.00

1999 Topps Stars

Topps Stars consists of 180 cards on 20-point stock with foil stamping and metallic inks. The set is comprised of 150 base cards and 30 subset cards: Luminaries and Supernovas. Packs contain six cards; three base cards, two One-Star cards and one Two-Star card on the average.

		NM/M
Complete Set (180):		20.00
Common Player:		.05
Pack (6):		1.50
Wax Box (24):		25.00
1	Ken Griffey Jr.	.75
2	Chipper Jones	.50
3	Mike Piazza	.75
4	Nomar Garciaparra	.50
5	Derek Jeter	1.50
6	Frank Thomas	.40
7	Ben Grieve	.05
8	Mark McGwire	1.00
9	Sammy Sosa	.50
10	Alex Rodriguez	1.00
11	Troy Glaus	.35
12	Eric Chavez	.25
13	Kerry Wood	.30
14	Barry Bonds	1.50
15	Vladimir Guerrero	.40
16	Albert Belle	.05
17	Juan Gonzalez	.20
18	Roger Clemens	.60
19	Ruben Mateo	.05
20	Cal Ripken Jr.	1.50
21	Darin Erstad	.25
22	Jeff Bagwell	.40
23	Roy Halladay	.10
24	Todd Helton	.35
25	Michael Barrett	.05
26	Manny Ramirez	.40
27	Fernando Seguignol	.05
28	Pat Burrell RC	2.00
29	Andruw Jones	.40
30	Randy Johnson	.40
31	Jose Canseco	.30
32	Brad Fullmer	.05
33	Alex Escobar RC	.10
34	Alfonso Soriano RC	3.00
35	Larry Walker	.05
36	Matt Clement	.05
37	Mo Vaughn	.05
38	Bruce Chen	.05
39	Travis Lee	.20
40	Adrian Beltre	.10
41	Alex Gonzalez	.05
42	Jason Tyner RC	.10
43	George Lombard	.05
44	Scott Rolen	.25
45	Mark Mulder RC	.50
46	Gabe Kapler	.05
47	Choo Freeman RC	.10
48	Tony Gwynn	.50
49	A.J. Burnett RC	.25
50	Matt Belisle RC	.10
51	Greg Maddux	.50
52	John Smoltz	.05
53	Mark Grace	.05
54	Wade Boggs	.50
55	Bernie Williams	.05
56	Pedro Martinez	.40
57	Barry Larkin	.05
58	Orlando Hernandez	.05
59	Jason Kendall	.05
60	Mark Kotsay	.05
61	Jim Thome	.35
62	Gary Sheffield	.30
63	Preston Wilson	.05
64	Rafael Palmeiro	.35
65	David Wells	.05
66	Shawn Green	.30
67	Tom Glavine	.05
68	Jeromy Burnitz	.05
69	Kevin Brown	.05
70	Rondell White	.05
71	Roberto Alomar	.25
72	Cliff Floyd	.05
73	Craig Biggio	.05
74	Greg Vaughn	.05
75	Ivan Rodriguez	.35
76	Vinny Castilla	.05
77	Todd Walker	.05
78	Paul Konerko	.15
79	Andy Brown RC	.05

No.	Player	Price
80	Todd Hundley	.05
81	Dmitri Young	.05
82	Tony Clark	.05
83	Nick Johnson RC	.50
84	Mike Caruso	.05
85	David Ortiz	.35
86	Matt Williams	.05
87	Raul Mondesi	.05
88	Kenny Lofton	.05
89	Miguel Tejada	.10
90	Dante Bichette	.05
91	Jorge Posada	.05
92	Carlos Beltran	.05
93	Carlos Delgado	.30
94	Javy Lopez	.05
95	Aramis Ramirez	.05
96	Neifi Perez	.05
97	Marlon Anderson	.05
98	David Cone	.05
99	Moises Alou	.05
100	John Olerud	.05
101	Tim Salmon	.05
102	Jason Giambi	.30
103	Sandy Alomar	.05
104	Curt Schilling	.25
105	Andres Galarraga	.05
106	Rusty Greer	.05
107	Bobby Seay RC	.05
108	Eric Young	.05
109	Brian Jordan	.05
110	Eric Davis	.05
111	Will Clark	.05
112	Andy Ashby	.05
113	Edgardo Alfonzo	.05
114	Paul O'Neill	.05
115	Denny Neagle	.05
116	Eric Karros	.05
117	Ken Caminiti	.05
118	Garret Anderson	.05
119	Todd Stottlemyre	.05
120	David Justice	.05
121	Francisco Cordova	.05
122	Robin Ventura	.05
123	Mike Mussina	.25
124	Hideki Irabu	.05
125	Justin Thompson	.05
126	Mariano Rivera	.15
127	Delino DeShields	.05
128	Steve Finley	.05
129	Jose Cruz Jr.	.05
130	Ray Lankford	.05
131	Jim Edmonds	.05
132	Charles Johnson	.05
133	Al Leiter	.05
134	Jose Offerman	.05
135	Eric Milton	.05
136	Dean Palmer	.05
137	Johnny Damon	.25
138	Andy Pettitte	.05
139	Ray Durham	.05
140	Ugueth Urbina	.05
141	Marquis Grissom	.05
142	Ryan Klesko	.05
143	Brady Anderson	.05
144	Bobby Higginson	.05
145	Chuck Knoblauch	.05
146	Rickey Henderson	.40
147	Kevin Millwood	.05
148	Fred McGriff	.05
149	Damion Easley	.05
150	Tino Martinez	.05
151	Greg Maddux (Luminaries)	.30
152	Scott Rolen (Luminaries)	.20
153	Pat Burrell (Luminaries)	.75
154	Roger Clemens (Luminaries)	.35
155	Albert Belle (Luminaries)	.05
156	Troy Glaus (Luminaries)	.25
157	Cal Ripken Jr. (Luminaries)	.75
158	Alfonso Soriano (Luminaries)	.75
159	Manny Ramirez (Luminaries)	.25
160	Eric Chavez (Luminaries)	.10
161	Kerry Wood (Luminaries)	.20
162	Tony Gwynn (Luminaries)	.30
163	Barry Bonds (Luminaries)	.75
164	Ruben Mateo (Luminaries)	.05
165	Todd Helton (Luminaries)	.20
166	Darin Erstad (Luminaries)	.05
167	Jeff Bagwell (Luminaries)	.25
168	Juan Gonzalez (Luminaries)	.15
169	Mo Vaughn (Luminaries)	.05
170	Vladimir Guerrero (Luminaries)	.25
171	Nomar Garciaparra (Supernovas)	.35
172	Derek Jeter (Supernovas)	.75
173	Alex Rodriguez (Supernovas)	.50
174	Ben Grieve (Supernovas)	.05
175	Mike Piazza (Supernovas)	.40
176	Chipper Jones (Supernovas)	.35
177	Frank Thomas (Supernovas)	.25
178	Ken Griffey Jr. (Supernovas)	.40
179	Sammy Sosa (Supernovas)	.35
180	Mark McGwire (Supernovas)	.50
	Checklist 1 (1-45)	.05
	Checklist 2 (46-136)	.05
	Checklist 3 (137-150, inserts)	.05

Foil

MIGUEL TEJADA

Metallic foil in the background and a serial number on back from within a specific edition identifies this parallel. Stated odds of insertion were one in 15 packs for parallels of the 180 base cards, numbered to 299 each. One-Star foil parallels are numbered to 249 and inserted 1:33. The Two-Star Foils are numbered to 199 each and found on average of one per 82 packs. With insertion odds of 1:410, the Three-Star Foil parallels are numbered within an edition of 99. At the top of the scarcity scale, the Foil Four-Star parallels are sequentially numbered to 49 and are a one per 650-pack find.

	NM/M
Complete Base Set (180):	90.00
Common Foil Player:	.15
Foil Stars:	3X

One-Star

ALEX RODRIGUEZ

One-Star inserts include card numbers 1-100 from the base set and have silver foil stamping with one star on the bottom left portion of the card front. These are seeded two per pack. A foil One-Star parallel also is randomly seeded and sequentially numbered to 249 sets. These are a 1:33 pack insert.

	NM/M
Complete Set (100):	25.00
Common Player:	.10
Foils (249 Each):	2X
1 Ken Griffey Jr.	1.25
2 Chipper Jones	1.00
3 Mike Piazza	1.25
4 Nomar Garciaparra	1.00
5 Derek Jeter	2.00
6 Frank Thomas	.75
7 Ben Grieve	.10
8 Mark McGwire	1.50
9 Sammy Sosa	1.00
10 Alex Rodriguez	1.50
11 Troy Glaus	.65
12 Eric Chavez	.25

No.	Player	Price
13	Kerry Wood	.35
14	Barry Bonds	2.00
15	Vladimir Guerrero	.75
16	Albert Belle	.10
17	Juan Gonzalez	.40
18	Roger Clemens	1.00
19	Ruben Mateo	.10
20	Cal Ripken Jr.	2.00
21	Darin Erstad	.30
22	Jeff Bagwell	.75
23	Roy Halladay	.20
24	Todd Helton	.65
25	Michael Barrett	.10
26	Manny Ramirez	.75
27	Fernando Seguignol	.10
28	Pat Burrell	1.00
29	Andruw Jones	.75
30	Randy Johnson	.75
31	Jose Canseco	.40
32	Brad Fullmer	.10
33	Alex Escobar	.10
34	Alfonso Soriano	1.00
35	Larry Walker	.10
36	Matt Clement	.25
37	Mo Vaughn	.10
38	Bruce Chen	.10
39	Travis Lee	.15
40	Adrian Beltre	.20
41	Alex Gonzalez	.10
42	Jason Tyner	.10
43	George Lombard	.10
44	Scott Rolen	.50
45	Mark Mulder	.50
46	Gabe Kapler	.10
47	Choo Freeman	.10
48	Tony Gwynn	1.00
49	A.J. Burnett	.15
50	Matt Belisle	.10
51	Greg Maddux	1.00
52	John Smoltz	.10
53	Mark Grace	.10
54	Wade Boggs	1.00
55	Bernie Williams	.10
56	Pedro Martinez	.75
57	Barry Larkin	.10
58	Orlando Hernandez	.10
59	Jason Kendall	.10
60	Mark Kotsay	.10
61	Jim Thome	.45
62	Gary Sheffield	.40
63	Preston Wilson	.10
64	Rafael Palmeiro	.60
65	David Wells	.10
66	Shawn Green	.30
67	Tom Glavine	.30
68	Jeromy Burnitz	.10
69	Kevin Brown	.10
70	Rondell White	.10
71	Roberto Alomar	.25
72	Cliff Floyd	.10
73	Craig Biggio	.10
74	Greg Vaughn	.10
75	Ivan Rodriguez	.60
76	Vinny Castilla	.10
77	Todd Walker	.10
78	Paul Konerko	.20
79	Andy Brown	.10
80	Todd Hundley	.10
81	Dmitri Young	.10
82	Tony Clark	.10
83	Nick Johnson	.50
84	Mike Caruso	.10
85	David Ortiz	.40
86	Matt Williams	.10
87	Raul Mondesi	.10
88	Kenny Lofton	.10
89	Miguel Tejada	.20
90	Dante Bichette	.10
91	Jorge Posada	.10
92	Carlos Beltran	.20
93	Carlos Delgado	.25
94	Javy Lopez	.10
95	Aramis Ramirez	.10
96	Neifi Perez	.10
97	Marlon Anderson	.10
98	David Cone	.10
99	Moises Alou	.10
100	John Olerud	.10

Two-Star

Two-Stars are inserted one per pack and feature light gold metallic inks and foil stamping. Two-Stars include card numbers 1-50 from the base set. A Two-Star parallel is also randomly seeded and limited to 199 sequentially numbered sets.

	NM/M
Complete Set (50):	50.00
Common Player:	.25
Foils:	3X
1 Ken Griffey Jr.	2.00
2 Chipper Jones	1.50
3 Mike Piazza	2.00
4 Nomar Garciaparra	1.50
5 Derek Jeter	3.00
6 Frank Thomas	1.00
7 Ben Grieve	.25
8 Mark McGwire	2.50
9 Sammy Sosa	1.50
10 Alex Rodriguez	2.50
11 Troy Glaus	.75
12 Eric Chavez	.30
13 Kerry Wood	.40
14 Barry Bonds	3.00
15 Vladimir Guerrero	1.00
16 Albert Belle	.25
17 Juan Gonzalez	.50
18 Roger Clemens	1.75
19 Ruben Mateo	.25
20 Cal Ripken Jr.	3.00
21 Darin Erstad	.75
22 Jeff Bagwell	1.00
23 Roy Halladay	.40
24 Todd Helton	.75
25 Michael Barrett	.25
26 Manny Ramirez	1.00
27 Fernando Seguignol	.25
28 Pat Burrell	1.50
29 Andruw Jones	1.00
30 Randy Johnson	1.00
31 Jose Canseco	.50
32 Brad Fullmer	.25
33 Alex Escobar	.25
34 Alfonso Soriano	1.50
35 Larry Walker	.25
36 Matt Clement	.30
37 Mo Vaughn	.25
38 Bruce Chen	.25
39 Travis Lee	.30
40 Adrian Beltre	.30
41 Alex Gonzalez	.25
42 Jason Tyner	.25
43 George Lombard	.25
44 Scott Rolen	.65
45 Mark Mulder	.45
46 Gabe Kapler	.25
47 Choo Freeman	.25
48 Tony Gwynn	1.50
49 A.J. Burnett	.30
50 Matt Belisle	.25

Three-Star

Three-Star inserts are a partial parallel from the base set including cards 1-20. Inserted 1:5 packs, these cards feature refractive silver foil stamping along with gold metallic inks. A Three-Star parallel also is randomly inserted featuring gold stamping and limited to 99 serial numbered sets, inserted one per 410 packs.

	NM/M
Complete Set (20):	30.00
Common Player:	.50
Foils:	4X
1 Ken Griffey Jr.	2.50
2 Chipper Jones	2.00
3 Mike Piazza	2.50
4 Nomar Garciaparra	2.00
5 Derek Jeter	4.00
6 Frank Thomas	1.50
7 Ben Grieve	.50
8 Mark McGwire	3.00
9 Sammy Sosa	2.00
10 Alex Rodriguez	3.00
11 Troy Glaus	1.25
12 Eric Chavez	.60
13 Kerry Wood	.75
14 Barry Bonds	4.00
15 Vladimir Guerrero	1.50
16 Albert Belle	.50
17 Juan Gonzalez	.75
18 Roger Clemens	2.25
19 Ruben Mateo	.50
20 Cal Ripken Jr.	4.00

Four-Star

Four-Star inserts include cards numbered 1-10 from the base set and are seeded 1:10 packs. The cards feature dark metallic inks and refractive foil stamping on front. A Four-Star parallel is also randomly seeded and has gold metallic inks. Sequentially numbered to 49, it is inserted at the rate of one per 650 packs.

	NM/M
Complete Set (10):	30.00
Common Player:	1.00
Foils:	2X
1 Ken Griffey Jr.	4.00
2 Chipper Jones	3.00
3 Mike Piazza	4.00
4 Nomar Garciaparra	3.00
5 Derek Jeter	6.00
6 Frank Thomas	2.50
7 Ben Grieve	1.00
8 Mark McGwire	5.00
9 Sammy Sosa	3.00
10 Alex Rodriguez	5.00

Bright Futures

This 10-card set features top prospects with a brilliant future ahead of them. Each card features foil stamping and is sequentially numbered to 1,999. Cards have a "BF" prefix to the number. A metallized foil parallel version is also randomly seeded (1:2,702) and limited to 30 numbered sets.

	NM/M
Complete Set (10):	20.00
Common Player:	1.50
Production 1,999 Sets	
Foil (30 Each):	8X
1 Troy Glaus	3.00
2 Eric Chavez	2.00
3 Adrian Beltre	2.00
4 Michael Barrett	1.50
5 Fernando Seguignol	1.50
6 Alex Gonzalez	1.50
7 Matt Clement	1.50
8 Pat Burrell	6.00
9 Ruben Mateo	1.50
10 Alfonso Soriano	6.00

Galaxy

This 10-card set highlights the top players in baseball with foil stamping and limited to 1,999 numbered sets, inserted at the rate of one per 41 packs. Each card is numbered on the back with a "G" prefix. A Galaxy foil parallel version is also randomly seeded (1:2,702) and sequentially numbered to 30 sets.

	NM/M
Complete Set (10):	25.00
Common Player:	1.00
Production 1,999 Sets	
Foil (30 Each):	8X
1 Mark McGwire	5.00
2 Roger Clemens	3.00
3 Nomar Garciaparra	4.00
4 Alex Rodriguez	5.00
5 Kerry Wood	1.50
6 Ben Grieve	1.00
7 Derek Jeter	6.00
8 Vladimir Guerrero	2.50
9 Ken Griffey Jr.	4.00
10 Sammy Sosa	3.00

Rookie Reprints

bob gibson

ST. LOUIS CARDINALS
PITCHER

Topps reprinted five Hall of Famers' rookie cards. The rookie reprints are inserted 1:65 packs and limited to 2,500 numbered sets.

	NM/M
Complete Set (5):	10.00
Common Player:	2.00
Production 2,500 Sets	
1 Frank Robinson	2.00
2 Ernie Banks	3.00
3 Yogi Berra	3.00
4 Bob Gibson	2.00
5 Tom Seaver	3.00

Rookie Reprints Autographs

METS 1967 ROOKIE STARS
BILL DENEHY • P   TOM SEAVER • P

These foil stamped inserts feature the "Topps Certified Autograph Issue" stamp and are inserted 1:406 packs. The Ernie Banks autograph is inserted 1:812 packs.

	NM/M
Complete Set (5):	150.00
Common Player:	20.00
Inserted 1:406	
Banks Inserted 1:812	
1 Frank Robinson	25.00
2 Ernie Banks	70.00
3 Yogi Berra	35.00
4 Bob Gibson	20.00
5 Tom Seaver	65.00

'N Steel

IVAN RODRIGUEZ

Using Serilusion technology, each borderless card features a four-colored textured film laminate bonded to a sheet of strong 25-gauge metal. Each pack contains three cards, packaged in a stand-up tri-fold display unit, at an S.R.P. of $9.99. There are two parallels to the 44-card set, Gold and Domed Holographics. Golds are seeded 1:12 packs, Holographics are found every 24 packs.

1999 Topps Stars

		NM/M
Complete Set (44):		65.00
Common Player:		.50
Gold:		4X
Inserted 1:12		
Holographic Dome:		6X
Inserted 1:24		
Pack (3):		4.00
Wax Box (12):		40.00
1	Kerry Wood	1.00
2	Ben Grieve	.50
3	Chipper Jones	3.00
4	Alex Rodriguez	5.00
5	Mo Vaughn	.50
6	Bernie Williams	.50
7	Juan Gonzalez	1.00
8	Vinny Castilla	.50
9	Tony Gwynn	3.00
10	Manny Ramirez	2.00
11	Raul Mondesi	.50
12	Roger Clemens	3.50
13	Darin Erstad	.75
14	Barry Bonds	6.00
15	Cal Ripken Jr.	6.00
16	Barry Larkin	.50
17	Scott Rolen	1.00
18	Albert Belle	.50
19	Craig Biggio	.50
20	Tony Clark	.50
21	Mark McGwire	5.00
22	Andres Galarraga	.50
23	Kenny Lofton	.50
24	Pedro Martinez	.50
25	Paul O'Neill	.50
26	Ken Griffey Jr.	4.00
27	Travis Lee	75.00
28	Tim Salmon	.50
29	Frank Thomas	2.00
30	Larry Walker	.50
31	Moises Alou	.50
32	Vladimir Guerrero	2.00
33	Ivan Rodriguez	1.50
34	Derek Jeter	6.00
35	Greg Vaughn	.50
36	Gary Sheffield	1.00
37	Carlos Delgado	1.00
38	Greg Maddux	3.00
39	Sammy Sosa	3.00
40	Mike Piazza	4.00
41	Nomar Garciaparra	3.00
42	Dante Bichette	.50
43	Jeff Bagwell	2.00
44	Jim Thome	1.50

'N Steel Gold Domed Holographics

This parallel edition was inserted at a rate of one per box. Cards are basically the same as the regular-issue, except for the use of holographic foil highlights on front and the presence of a thick plastic dome which covers the front.

	NM/M
Complete Set (44):	600.00
Common Player:	6.00
Stars:	8X

1999 Topps TEK Pre-Production

The second edition of Topps TEK was introduced with this trio of star cards. The preview cards are virtually identical in format to the issued version, except for the use of "PP" prefixes to card numbers on back.

		NM/M
Complete Set (3):		5.00
Common Player:		1.00
PP1A	Derek Jeter	4.00
PP2A	Moises Alou	1.00
PP3A	Tony Clark	1.00

1999 Topps TEK

Topps TEK baseball contains 45 players, with all cards printed on a transparent, 27-point stock. Each player is featured in two different versions (A & B), which are noted on the card back. The versions are differentiated by type of player uniform (home is version A and away uniforms are version B). Each version also has 30 different baseball focused background patterns; as a result every player in the 45-card set has 60 total cards. There is also a Gold parallel set that has a gold design and all versions are paralleled. Each gold card is numbered to 10, with an insertion rate of 1:15 packs.

		NM/M
Complete Set (45):		30.00
Common Player:		.25
Common Gold		
(10 Each Variation):		2.00
Gold Stars:		10X
Pack (4):		3.00
Wax Box (20):		45.00
1	Ben Grieve	.25
2	Andres Galarraga	.25
3	Travis Lee	.35
4	Larry Walker	.50
5	Ken Griffey Jr.	2.50
6	Sammy Sosa	2.00
7	Mark McGwire	3.00
8	Roberto Alomar	.40
9	Wade Boggs	2.00
10	Troy Glaus	.75
11	Craig Biggio	.25
12	Kerry Wood	.50
13	Vladimir Guerrero	1.00
14	Albert Belle	.25
15	Mike Piazza	2.50
16	Chipper Jones	2.00
17	Randy Johnson	1.00
18	Adrian Beltre	.45
19	Barry Bonds	4.00
20	Jim Thome	.65
21	Greg Vaughn	.25
22	Scott Rolen	.75
23	Ivan Rodriguez	.75
24	Derek Jeter	4.00
25	Cal Ripken Jr.	4.00
26	Mark Grace	.25
27	Bernie Williams	.75
28	Darin Erstad	.75
29	Eric Chavez	.35
30	Tom Glavine	.50
31	Jeff Bagwell	1.00
32	Manny Ramirez	1.00
33	Tino Martinez	.75
34	Todd Helton	.75
35	Jason Kendall	.25
36	Pat Burrell RC	2.50
37	Tony Gwynn	2.00
38	Nomar Garciaparra	2.00
39	Frank Thomas	1.00
40	Orlando Hernandez	1.00
41	Juan Gonzalez	.50
42	Alex Rodriguez	3.00
43	Greg Maddux	2.00
44	Mo Vaughn	.50
45	Roger Clemens	2.25
	Version A checklist folder (orange)	.05
	Version B checklist folder (green)	.05

Gold

Each of the two player versions on each of the 30 background patterns was paralleled in a gold insert version. Cards share the same front and back designs and photos but feature gold graphics. Each card is serially numbered to an edition of just 10. Insertion rate is one per 15 packs.

	NM/M
Common Gold:	2.00
Gold Stars:	10X

Fantastek Phenoms

This 10-card set highlights top young prospects on a transparent plastic stock with silver and blue highlighting. These are inserted 1:18 packs.

		NM/M
Complete Set (10):		15.00
Common Player:		.75
Inserted 1:18		
F1	Eric Chavez	1.50
F2	Troy Glaus	4.00
F3	Pat Burrell	4.00
F4	Alex Gonzalez	.75
F5	Carlos Lee	1.00
F6	Ruben Mateo	.75
F7	Carlos Beltran	2.00
F8	Adrian Beltre	1.50
F9	Bruce Chen	.75
F10	Ryan Anderson	.75

Teknicians

This 10-card set focuses on baseball's top stars on a clear, plastic stock utilizing metallic blue, silver and red inks. These are inserted 1:18 packs.

		NM/M
Complete Set (10):		24.00
Common Player:		1.00
Inserted 1:18		
T1	Ken Griffey Jr.	3.00
T2	Mark McGwire	4.00
T3	Kerry Wood	1.00
T4	Ben Grieve	1.00
T5	Sammy Sosa	2.50
T6	Derek Jeter	6.00
T7	Alex Rodriguez	4.00
T8	Roger Clemens	2.50
T9	Nomar Garciaparra	2.50
T10	Vladimir Guerrero	1.50

2000 Topps Pre-Production

Though carrying a "PP" prefix as previous years' pre-production samples, this three-card issue was not distributed until July-August at the National and SportsFest conventions. The three-card cello packs contain cards which differ from the regular issued versions only in their numbers and the fact that they have white borders, rather than the pewter borders found on regular-issue cards.

		NM/M
Complete Set (3):		5.00
Common Player:		2.00
PP1	Brady Anderson	2.00
PP2	Jason Kendall	2.00
PP3	Ryan Klesko	2.00

2000 Topps

Released in two series the card fronts have a silver border with the Topps logo, player name and position stamped with gold foil. Card backs have complete year-by-year statistics along with a small photo in the upper right portion and the player's vital information. Subsets within the first series 239-card set include Draft Picks, Prospects, Magic Moments, Season Highlights and 20th Century's Best. The Topps MVP promotion is a parallel of 200 of the base cards, excluding subsets, with a special Topps MVP logo. 100 cards of each player was produced and if the featured player is named MVP for a week, collectors win a prize.

		NM/M
Complete Set (478):		50.00
Complete Series I Set (239):		25.00
Complete Series II Set (239):		25.00
Common Player:		.10
MVP Stars:		20-40X
Yng Stars & RC's:		10-20X
Production 100 Sets		
5 Versions for 236-240, 475-479		
Pack (11):		1.00
Wax Box (36):		30.00
1	Mark McGwire	1.00
2	Tony Gwynn	.75
3	Wade Boggs	.75
4	Cal Ripken Jr.	1.50
5	Matt Williams	.10
6	Jay Buhner	.10
7	Jeff Conine	.10
8	Todd Greene	.10
9	Mike Lieberthal	.10
10	Steve Avery	.10
11	Bret Saberhagen	.10
12	Maggio Ordonez	.20
13	Brad Radke	.10
14	Derek Jeter	1.50
15	Javy Lopez	.10
16	Russ David	.10
17	Russ David	.10
18	Armando Benitez	.10
19	B.J. Surhoff	.10
20	Darryl Kile	.10
21	Mark Lewis	.10
22	Mike Williams	.10
23	Mark McLemore	.10
24	Sterling Hitchcock	.10
25	Darin Erstad	.20
26	Ricky Gutierrez	.10
27	John Jaha	.10
28	Homer Bush	.10
29	Darrin Fletcher	.10
30	Mark Grace	.10
31	Fred McGriff	.10
32	Omar Daal	.10
33	Eric Karros	.10
34	Orlando Cabrera	.15
35	J.T. Snow Jr.	.10
36	Luis Castillo	.10
37	Rey Ordonez	.10
38	Bob Abreu	.20
39	Warren Morris	.10
40	Juan Gonzalez	.20
41	Mike Lansing	.10
42	Chili Davis	.10
43	Dean Palmer	.10
44	Hank Aaron	1.00
45	Jeff Bagwell	.60
46	Jose Valentin	.10
47	Shannon Stewart	.10
48	Kent Bottenfield	.10
49	Jeff Shaw	.10
50	Sammy Sosa	.75
51	Randy Johnson	.60
52	Benny Agbayani	.10
53	Dante Bichette	.10
54	Pete Harnisch	.10
55	Frank Thomas	.60
56	Jorge Posada	.10
57	Todd Walker	.10
58	Juan Encarnacion	.15
59	Mike Sweeney	.10
60	Pedro Martinez	.60
61	Lee Stevens	.10
62	Brian Giles	.10
63	Chad Ogea	.10
64	Ivan Rodriguez	.50
65	Roger Cedeno	.10
66	David Justice	.10
67	Steve Trachsel	.10
68	Eli Marrero	.10
69	Dave Nilsson	.10
70	Ken Caminiti	.10
71	Tim Raines	.10
72	Brian Jordan	.10
73	Jeff Blauser	.10
74	Bernard Gilkey	.10
75	John Flaherty	.10
76	Brent Mayne	.10
77	Jose Vidro	.10
78	Jeff Fassero	.10
79	Bruce Aven	.10
80	John Olerud	.10
81	Pokey Reese	.10
82	Woody Williams	.10
83	Ed Sprague	.10
84	Joe Girardi	.10
85	Barry Larkin	.10
86	Mike Caruso	.10
87	Bobby Higginson	.10
88	Roberto Kelly	.10
89	Edgar Martinez	.10
90	Mark Kotsay	.10
91	Paul Sorrento	.10
92	Eric Young	.10
93	Carlos Delgado	.10
94	Troy Glaus	.50
95	Ben Grieve	.10
96	Jose Lima	.10
97	Garret Anderson	.10
98	Luis Gonzalez	.10
99	Carl Pavano	.10
100	Alex Rodriguez	1.25
101	Preston Wilson	.10
102	Ron Gant	.10
103	Harold Baines	.10
104	Rickey Henderson	.60
105	Gary Sheffield	.40
106	Mickey Morandini	.10
107	Jim Edmonds	.10
108	Kris Benson	.10
109	Adrian Beltre	.20
110	Alex Fernandez	.10
111	Dan Wilson	.10
112	Mark Clark	.10
113	Greg Vaughn	.10
114	Neifi Perez	.10
115	Paul O'Neill	.10
116	Jermaine Dye	.10
117	Todd Jones	.10
118	Terry Steinbach	.10
119	Greg Norton	.10
120	Curt Schilling	.25
121	Todd Zeile	.10
122	Edgardo Alfonzo	.10
123	Ryan McGuire	.10
124	Stan Javier	.10
125	John Smoltz	.10
126	Bob Wickman	.10
127	Richard Hidalgo	.10
128	Chuck Finley	.10
129	Billy Wagner	.10
130	Todd Hundley	.10
131	Dwight Gooden	.10
132	Russ Ortiz	.10
133	Mike Lowell	.10
134	Reggie Sanders	.10
135	John Valentin	.10
136	Brad Ausmus	.10
137	Chad Kreuter	.10
138	David Cone	.10
139	Brook Fordyce	.10
140	Roberto Alomar	.25
141	Charles Nagy	.10
142	Brian Hunter	.10
143	Mike Mussina	.30
144	Robin Ventura	.10
145	Kevin Brown	.10
146	Pat Hentgen	.10
147	Ryan Klesko	.10
148	Derek Bell	.10
149	Andy Sheets	.10
150	Larry Walker	.10
151	Scott Williamson	.10
152	Jose Offerman	.10
153	Doug Mientkiewicz	.10
154	John Snyder RC	.10
155	Sandy Alomar	.10
156	Joe Nathan	.10
157	Lance Johnson	.10
158	Odalis Perez	.10
159	Hideo Nomo	.25
160	Steve Finley	.10
161	Dave Martinez	.10
162	Matt Walbeck	.10
163	Bill Spiers	.10
164	Fernando Tatis	.10
165	Kenny Lofton	.10
166	Paul Byrd	.10
167	Aaron Sele	.10
168	Eddie Taubensee	.10
169	Reggie Jefferson	.10
170	Roger Clemens	.85
171	Francisco Cordova	.10
172	Mike Bordick	.10
173	Wally Joyner	.10
174	Marvin Benard	.10
175	Jason Kendall	.10
176	Mike Stanley	.10
177	Chad Allen	.10
178	Carlos Beltran	.25
179	Deivi Cruz	.10
180	Chipper Jones	.75
181	Vladimir Guerrero	.60
182	Dave Burba	.10
183	Tom Goodwin	.10
184	Brian Daubach	.10
185	Jay Bell	.10
186	Roy Halladay	.25
187	Miguel Tejada	.10
188	Armando Rios	.10
189	Fernando Vina	.10
190	Eric Davis	.10
191	Henry Rodriguez	.10
192	Joe McEwing	.10
193	Jeff Kent	.10
194	Mike Jackson	.10
195	Mike Morgan	.10
196	Jeff Montgomery	.10
197	Jeff Zimmerman	.10
198	Tony Fernandez	.10
199	Jason Giambi	.40
200	Jose Canseco	.40
201	Alex Gonzalez	.10
202	Jack Cust, Mike Colangelo, Dee Brown	.10
203	Felipe Lopez, Alfonso Soriano, Pablo Ozuna	.75
204	Erubiel Durazo, Pat Burrell, Nick Johnson	.25
205	John Sneed RC, Kip Wells, Matt Blank	
206	Josh Kalinowski RC, Michael Tejera RC, Chris Mears	.10
207	Roosevelt Brown, Corey Patterson, Lance Berkman	.25
208	Kit Pellow, Kevin Barker, Russ Branyan	.10
209	B.J. Garbe RC, Larry Bigbie RC	1.00
210	Eric Munson, Bobby Bradley RC	.25
211	Josh Girdley, Kyle Snyder	.10
212	Chance Caple RC, Jason Jennings	.25
213	Ryan Christiansen RC, Brett Myers RC	1.50
214	Jason Stumm RC, Rob Purvis RC	
215	David Walling, Mike Paradis	
216	Omar Ortiz, Jay Gehrke	.10
217	David Cone (Season Highlights)	
218	Jose Jimenez (Season Highlights)	
219	Chris Singleton (Season Highlights)	
220	Fernando Tatis (Season Highlights)	
221	Todd Helton (Season Highlights)	.20
222	Kevin Millwood (Post-Season Highlights)	.15
223	Todd Pratt (Post-Season Highlights)	
224	Orlando Hernandez (Post-Season Highlights)	.25
225	(Post-Season Highlights)	
226	(Post-Season Highlights)	
227	Bernie Williams (Post-Season Highlights)	.25
228	Mariano Rivera (Post-Season Highlights)	.20
229	Tony Gwynn (20th Century's Best)	.50
230	Wade Boggs (20th Century's Best)	.25
231	Tim Raines (20th Century's Best)	.10

232	Mark McGwire (20th Century's Best)	2.00
233	Rickey Henderson (20th Century's Best)	.25
234	Rickey Henderson (20th Century's Best)	.25
235	Roger Clemens (20th Century's Best)	1.50
236	Mark McGwire (Magic Moments)	2.00
237	Hank Aaron (Magic Moments)	2.00
238	Cal Ripken Jr. (Magic Moments)	3.00
239	Wade Boggs (Magic Moments)	.75
240	Tony Gwynn (Magic Moments)	1.00
	Series 1 checklist (1-201)	.05
	Series 1 checklist (202-240, inserts)	.05
241	Tom Glavine	.25
242	David Wells	.10
243	Kevin Appier	.10
244	Troy Percival	.10
245	Ray Lankford	.10
246	Marquis Grissom	.10
247	Randy Winn	.10
248	Miguel Batista	.10
249	Darren Dreifort	.10
250	Barry Bonds	1.50
251	Harold Baines	.10
252	Cliff Floyd	.10
253	Freddy Garcia	.10
254	Kenny Rogers	.10
255	Ben Davis	.10
256	Charles Johnson	.10
257	John Burkett	.10
258	Desi Relaford	.10
259	Al Martin	.10
260	Andy Pettitte	.20
261	Carlos Lee	.10
262	Matt Lawton	.10
263	Andy Fox	.10
264	Chan Ho Park	.10
265	Billy Koch	.10
266	Dave Roberts	.10
267	Carl Everett	.10
268	Orel Hershiser	.10
269	Trot Nixon	.10
270	Rusty Greer	.10
271	Will Clark	.10
272	Quilvio Veras	.10
273	Rico Brogna	.10
274	Devon White	.10
275	Tim Hudson	.25
276	Mike Hampton	.10
277	Miguel Cairo	.10
278	Darren Oliver	.10
279	Jeff Cirillo	.10
280	Al Leiter	.10
281	Brant Brown	.10
282	Carlos Febles	.10
283	Pedro Astacio	.10
284	Juan Guzman	.10
285	Orlando Hernandez	.20
286	Paul Konerko	.15
287	Tony Clark	.10
288	Aaron Boone	.10
289	Ismael Valdes	.10
290	Moises Alou	.10
291	Kevin Tapani	.10
292	John Franco	.10
293	Todd Zeile	.10
294	Jason Schmidt	.15
295	Johnny Damon	.25
296	Scott Brosius	.10
297	Travis Fryman	.10
298	Jose Vizcaino	.10
299	Eric Chavez	.20
300	Mike Piazza	1.00
301	Matt Clement	.10
302	Cristian Guzman	.10
303	Darryl Strawberry	.10
304	Jeff Abbott	.10
305	Brett Tomko	.10
306	Mike Lansing	.10
307	Eric Owens	.10
308	Livan Hernandez	.10
309	Rondell White	.10
310	Todd Stottlemyre	.10
311	Chris Carpenter	.10
312	Ken Hill	.10
313	Mark Loretta	.10
314	John Rocker	.10
315	Richie Sexson	.25
316	Ruben Mateo	.10
317	Joe Randa	.10
318	Mike Sirotka	.10
319	Jose Rosado	.10
320	Matt Mantei	.10
321	Kevin Millwood	.10
322	Gary DiSarcina	.10
323	Dustin Hermanson	.10
324	Mike Stanton	.10
325	Kirk Rueter	.10
326	Damian Miller	.10
327	Doug Glanville	.10
328	Scott Rolen	.50
329	Ray Durham	.10
330	Butch Huskey	.10
331	Mariano Rivera	.20
332	Darren Lewis	.10
333	Ramiro Mendoza	.10
334	Mark Grudzielanek	.10
335	Mike Cameron	.10
336	Kelvim Escobar	.10

337	Bret Boone	.10
338	Mo Vaughn	.10
339	Craig Biggio	.10
340	Michael Barrett	.10
341	Marlon Anderson	.10
342	Bobby Jones	.10
343	John Halama	.10
344	Todd Ritchie	.10
345	Chuck Knoblauch	.10
346	Rick Reed	.10
347	Kelly Stinnett	.10
348	Tim Salmon	.10
349	A.J. Hinch	.10
350	Jose Cruz Jr.	.10
351	Roberto Hernandez	.10
352	Edgar Renteria	.10
353	Jose Hernandez	.10
354	Brad Fullmer	.10
355	Trevor Hoffman	.10
356	Troy O'Leary	.10
357	Justin Thompson	.10
358	Kevin Young	.10
359	Hideki Irabu	.10
360	Jim Thome	.50
361	Todd Dunwoody	.10
362	Octavio Dotel	.10
363	Omar Vizquel	.10
364	Raul Mondesi	.10
365	Shane Reynolds	.10
366	Bartolo Colon	.10
367	Chris Widger	.10
368	Gabe Kapler	.10
369	Bill Simas	.10
370	Tino Martinez	.10
371	John Thomson	.10
372	Delino DeShields	.10
373	Carlos Perez	.10
374	Eddie Perez	.10
375	Jeromy Burnitz	.10
376	Jimmy Haynes	.10
377	Travis Lee	.10
378	Darryl Hamilton	.10
379	Jamie Moyer	.10
380	Alex Gonzalez	.10
381	John Wetteland	.10
382	Vinny Castilla	.10
383	Jeff Suppan	.10
384	Chad Curtis	.10
385	Robb Nen	.10
386	Wilson Alvarez	.10
387	Andres Galarraga	.10
388	Mike Remlinger	.10
389	Geoff Jenkins	.10
390	Matt Stairs	.10
391	Bill Mueller	.10
392	Mike Lowell	.10
393	Andy Ashby	.10
394	Ruben Rivera	.10
395	Todd Helton	.50
396	Bernie Williams	.10
397	Royce Clayton	.10
398	Manny Ramirez	.60
399	Kerry Wood	.25
400	Ken Griffey Jr.	.75
401	Enrique Wilson	.10
402	Joey Hamilton	.10
403	Shawn Estes	.10
404	Ugueth Urbina	.10
405	Albert Belle	.10
406	Rick Helling	.10
407	Steve Parris	.10
408	Eric Milton	.10
409	Dave Mlicki	.10
410	Shawn Green	.25
411	Jaret Wright	.10
412	Tony Womack	.10
413	Vernon Wells	.15
414	Ron Belliard	.10
415	Ellis Burks	.10
416	Scott Erickson	.10
417	Rafael Palmeiro	.35
418	Damion Easley	.10
419	Jamey Wright	.10
420	Corey Koskie	.10
421	Bobby Howry	.10
422	Ricky Ledee	.10
423	Dmitri Young	.10
424	Sidney Ponson	.10
425	Greg Maddux	.75
426	Jose Guillen	.10
427	Jon Lieber	.10
428	Andy Benes	.10
429	Randy Velarde	.10
430	Sean Casey	.20
431	Torii Hunter	.20
432	Ryan Rupe	.10
433	David Segui	.10
434	Rich Aurilia	.10
435	Nomar Garciaparra	.75
436	Denny Neagle	.10
437	Ron Coomer	.10
438	Chris Singleton	.10
439	Tony Batista	.10
440	Andruw Jones	.60
441	Adam Piatt, Aubrey Huff, Sean Burroughs (Prospects)	.20
442	Rafael Furcal, Jason Dallero, Travis Dawkins (Prospects)	.20
443	Wilton Veras, Joe Crede, Mike Lamb **RC** (Prospects)	.10
444	Julio Zuleta **RC**, Dernell Stenson, Jorge Toca (Prospects)	.20

445	Tim Raines Jr., Gary Mathews Jr., Garry Maddox Jr. **RC** (Prospects)	.20
446	Matt Riley, Mark Mulder, C.C. Sabathia (Prospects)	.10
447	Scott Downs **RC**, Chris George, Matt Belisle (Prospects)	.10
448	Doug Mirabelli, Ben Petrick, Jayson Werth (Prospects)	.10
449	Josh Hamilton, Corey Myers **RC** (Draft Picks)	.25
450	Ben Christensen **RC**, Brett Myers (Draft Picks)	.20
451	Barry Zito **RC**, Ben Sheets **RC** (Draft Picks)	2.00
452	Ty Howington **RC**, Kurt Ainsworth **RC** (Draft Picks)	.25
453	Rick Asadoorian **RC**, Vince Faison **RC** (Draft Picks)	.10
454	Keith Reed **RC**, Jeff Heaverlo **RC** (Draft Picks)	.25
455	Mike MacDougal **RC**, Jay Gehrke (Draft Picks)	.25
456	Mark McGwire (Season Highlights)	.75
457	Cal Ripken Jr. (Season Highlights)	1.00
458	Wade Boggs (Season Highlights)	.25
459	Tony Gwynn (Season Highlights)	.50
460	Jesse Orosco (Season Highlights)	.10
461	Nomar Garciaparra, Larry Walker (League Leaders)	.50
462	Mark McGwire, Ken Griffey Jr. (League Leaders)	.50
463	Mark McGwire, Manny Ramirez (League Leaders)	.50
464	Randy Johnson, Pedro Martinez (League Leaders)	.25
465	Randy Johnson, Pedro Martinez (League Leaders)	.25
466	Luis Gonzalez, Derek Jeter (League Leaders)	.50
467	Manny Ramirez, Larry Walker (League Leaders)	.25
468	Tony Gwynn (20th Century's Best)	.75
469	Mark McGwire (20th Century's Best)	2.00
470	Frank Thomas (20th Century's Best)	.50
471	Harold Baines (20th Century's Best)	.10
472	Roger Clemens (20th Century's Best)	.75
473	John Franco (20th Century's Best)	.10
474	John Franco (20th Century's Best)	.10
475	Ken Griffey Jr. (Magic Moments)	1.50
476	Barry Bonds (Magic Moments)	2.00
477	Sammy Sosa (Magic Moments)	1.25
478	Derek Jeter (Magic Moments)	2.50
479	Alex Rodriguez (Magic Moments)	2.00

Hank Aaron Reprints

This 23-card set reprints all of Aaron's 23-regular issued Topps cards and are seeded 1:18 packs.

	NM/M
Complete Set (23):	60.00

Hank Aaron Chrome Reprints

This 23-card set reprints Aaron's regular issued Topps cards utilizing Chromium technology. Each card has a commemorative logo and are seeded 1:72 packs. A Refractor parallel version is also randomly inserted 1:288 packs and have Refractor printed underneath the number on the card back.

		NM/M
Complete Set (23):		90.00
Common Aaron:		5.00
Inserted 1:72		
Refractors:		3X
Inserted 1:288		
1	Hank Aaron/1954	10.00
2	Hank Aaron/1955	5.00
3	Hank Aaron/1956	5.00
4	Hank Aaron/1957	5.00
5	Hank Aaron/1958	5.00
6	Hank Aaron/1959	5.00
7	Hank Aaron/1960	5.00
8	Hank Aaron/1961	5.00
9	Hank Aaron/1962	5.00
10	Hank Aaron/1963	5.00
11	Hank Aaron/1964	5.00
12	Hank Aaron/1965	5.00
13	Hank Aaron/1966	5.00
14	Hank Aaron/1967	5.00
15	Hank Aaron/1968	5.00
16	Hank Aaron/1969	5.00
17	Hank Aaron/1970	5.00
18	Hank Aaron/1971	5.00
19	Hank Aaron/1972	5.00
20	Hank Aaron/1973	5.00
21	Hank Aaron/1974	5.00
22	Hank Aaron/1975	5.00
23	Hank Aaron/1976	5.00

All-Star Rookie Team

Common Aaron:		3.00
Inserted 1:18		
Autographed:		300.00
"Limited Edition" 4,000 Sets:		1X
1	Hank Aaron/1954	8.00
2	Hank Aaron/1955	3.00
3	Hank Aaron/1956	3.00
4	Hank Aaron/1957	3.00
5	Hank Aaron/1958	3.00
6	Hank Aaron/1959	3.00
7	Hank Aaron/1960	3.00
8	Hank Aaron/1961	3.00
9	Hank Aaron/1962	3.00
10	Hank Aaron/1963	3.00
11	Hank Aaron/1964	3.00
12	Hank Aaron/1965	3.00
13	Hank Aaron/1966	3.00
14	Hank Aaron/1967	3.00
15	Hank Aaron/1968	3.00
16	Hank Aaron/1969	3.00
17	Hank Aaron/1970	3.00
18	Hank Aaron/1971	3.00
19	Hank Aaron/1972	3.00
20	Hank Aaron/1973	3.00
21	Hank Aaron/1974	3.00
22	Hank Aaron/1975	3.00
23	Hank Aaron/1976	3.00

All-Topps Team

This insert set spotlights 10 National League (Series 1) and 10 A.L. (Series 2) players who are deemed the best at their respective position. On front, a Hall of Fame style plaque design features gold-foil highlights. Backs offer stat comparisons to contemporary players and Hall of Fame greats at their position. These were seeded 1:12 packs. Cards are numbered with an "AT" prefix.

		NM/M
Complete Set (20):		15.00
Common Player:		.25
Inserted 1:12		
"Limited Edition" 4,000 Sets:		1X
1	Greg Maddux	1.50
2	Mike Piazza	1.50
3	Mark McGwire	2.50
4	Craig Biggio	.40
5	Chipper Jones	1.50
6	Barry Larkin	.40
7	Barry Bonds	2.50
8	Andruw Jones	.75
9	Sammy Sosa	1.50
10	Larry Walker	.40
11	Pedro Martinez	1.00
12	Ivan Rodriguez	.50
13	Rafael Palmeiro	.50
14	Roberto Alomar	.50
15	Cal Ripken Jr.	3.00
16	Derek Jeter	3.00
17	Albert Belle	.25
18	Ken Griffey Jr.	1.50
19	Manny Ramirez	.75
20	Jose Canseco	.50

Autographs

Inserted exclusively in Series 1 and 2 hobby packs, each card features the "Topps Certified Autograph Issue" stamp and is autographed on the card front.

		NM/M
Common Player:		8.00
Group A 1:7,589		
Group B 1:4,553		
Group C 1:518		
Group D 1:911		
Group E 1:1,138		
1	Alex Rodriguez/A	100.00
2	Tony Gwynn/A	50.00
3	Vinny Castilla/B	15.00
4	Sean Casey/B	15.00

Common Aaron:		.25
Inserted 1:36		
"Limited Edition" 4,000 Sets:		1X
1	Mark McGwire	3.00
2	Chuck Knoblauch	.25
3	Chipper Jones	2.00
4	Cal Ripken Jr.	4.00
5	Manny Ramirez	1.00
6	Jose Canseco	.75
7	Ken Griffey Jr.	2.00
8	Mike Piazza	2.00
9	Dwight Gooden	.25
10	Billy Wagner	.25

5	Shawn Green/C	25.00
6	Rey Ordonez/C	8.00
7	Matt Lawton/C	15.00
8	Tony Womack/C	8.00
9	Gabe Kapler/D	10.00
10	Pat Burrell/D	20.00
11	Preston Wilson/D	15.00
12	Troy Glaus/D	30.00
13	Carlos Beltran/D	40.00
14	Josh Girdley/E	8.00
15	B.J. Garbe/E	8.00
16	Derek Jeter (A)	125.00
17	Cal Ripken Jr./A	150.00
18	Ivan Rodriguez/B	40.00
19	Rafael Palmeiro/B	40.00
20	Vladimir Guerrero/E	45.00
21	Raul Mondesi/C	15.00
22	Scott Rolen/C	40.00
23	Billy Wagner/C	8.00
24	Fernando Tatis/C	8.00
25	Ruben Mateo/D	8.00
26	Carlos Febles/D	8.00
27	Mike Sweeney/E	10.00
28	Alex Gonzalez/D	10.00
29	Miguel Tejada/D	40.00
30	Josh Hamilton/E	30.00

Century Best

		NM/M
Common Player:		2.00
Ser. 1 1:869 H		
Ser. 2 1:362		
CB1	Tony Gwynn/339	8.00
CB2	Wade Boggs/4	4.00
CB3	Lance Johnson/117	2.00
CB4	Mark McGwire/522	20.00
CB5	Rickey Henderson/ 1,334	4.00
CB6	Rickey Henderson/ 2,103	4.00
CB7	Roger Clemens/247	12.00
CB8	Tony Gwynn/3,067	6.00
CB9	Mark McGwire/587	20.00
CB10	Frank Thomas/440	6.00
CB11	Harold Baines/1,583	2.00
CB12	Roger Clemens/3,316	8.00
CB13	John Franco/264	2.00
CB14	John Franco/416	2.00

Combos

		NM/M
Complete Set (10):		15.00
Common Card:		1.00
Inserted 1:18		
"Limited Edition" 4,000 Sets:		1X
1	Roberto Alomar, Manny Ramirez, Kenny Lofton, Jim Thome	1.00
2	Tom Glavine, Greg Maddux, John Smoltz	1.50
3	Derek Jeter, Bernie Williams, Tino Martinez	3.00
4	Ivan Rodriguez, Mike Piazza	1.50
5	Nomar Garciaparra, Alex Rodriguez, Derek Jeter	3.00
6	Sammy Sosa, Mark McGwire	3.00
7	Pedro Martinez, Randy Johnson	1.00
8	Barry Bonds, Ken Griffey Jr.	2.50

9	Chipper Jones, Ivan Rodriguez	1.50
10	Cal Ripken Jr., Tony Gwynn, Wade Boggs	3.00

Hands of Gold

This seven-card insert set highlights players who have won at least five gold gloves. Each card is foil stamped and die-cut and is seeded 1:18 packs.

		NM/M
Complete Set (7):		5.00
Common Player:		.25
Inserted 1:18		
"Limited Edition" 4,000 Sets:		1X
1	Barry Bonds	2.50
2	Ivan Rodriguez	.75
3	Ken Griffey Jr.	1.50
4	Roberto Alomar	.75
5	Tony Gwynn	1.00
6	Omar Vizquel	.25
7	Greg Maddux	1.50

Mark McGwire 1985 Rookie Reprint

This insert pays tribute to baseball's reigning single season home run record holder by reprinting his '85 Topps Rookie card. Card fronts have a commemorative gold stamp and is seeded 1:36 packs.

		NM/M
Complete Set (1):		6.00
	Mark McGwire	6.00

Own the Game

		NM/M
Complete Set (30):		15.00
Common Player:		.15
Inserted 1:12		
"Limited Edition" 4,000 Sets:		1X
1	Derek Jeter	2.00
2	B.J. Surhoff	.15
3	Luis Gonzalez	.25
4	Manny Ramirez	.50
5	Rafael Palmeiro	.40
6	Mark McGwire	1.50

7	Mark McGwire	1.50
8	Sammy Sosa	1.00
9	Ken Griffey Jr.	1.00
10	Larry Walker	.25
11	Nomar Garciaparra	1.50
12	Derek Jeter	2.00
13	Larry Walker	.25
14	Mark McGwire	1.50
15	Manny Ramirez	.50
16	Pedro Martinez	.75
17	Randy Johnson	.75
18	Kevin Millwood	.25
19	Pedro Martinez	.75
20	Randy Johnson	.75
21	Kevin Brown	.25
22	Chipper Jones	1.00
23	Ivan Rodriguez	.50
24	Mariano Rivera	.25
25	Scott Williamson	.15
26	Carlos Beltran	.25
27	Randy Johnson	.75
28	Pedro Martinez	.75
29	Sammy Sosa	1.00
30	Manny Ramirez	.50

Perennial All-Stars

This 10-card set highlights 10 superstars who have consistently achieved All-Star recognition. Card fronts feature a silver holographic foil throughout, while card backs have the featured player's career All-Star statistics. These were seeded 1:18 packs. Cards are numbered with a "PA" prefix.

		NM/M
Complete Set (10):		10.00
Common Player:		.50
Inserted 1:18		
"Limited Edition" 4,000 Sets:		1X
1	Ken Griffey Jr.	1.00
2	Derek Jeter	2.00
3	Sammy Sosa	1.00
4	Cal Ripken Jr.	2.00
5	Mike Piazza	1.00
6	Nomar Garciaparra	1.50
7	Jeff Bagwell	.50
8	Barry Bonds	1.50
9	Alex Rodriguez	1.50
10	Mark McGwire	1.50

Power Players

This 20-card set highlights the top power hitters in the game and are printed on a holographic silver foil front. They are numbered with a "P" prefix and are seeded 1:8 packs.

		NM/M
Complete Set (20):		10.00
Common Player:		.25
Inserted 1:8		
"Limited Edition" 4,000 Sets:		1X
1	Juan Gonzalez	.50
2	Ken Griffey Jr.	1.00
3	Mark McGwire	1.50
4	Nomar Garciaparra	1.50
5	Barry Bonds	1.50
6	Mo Vaughn	.25
7	Larry Walker	.25
8	Alex Rodriguez	1.50
9	Jose Canseco	.25

10	Jeff Bagwell	.50
11	Manny Ramirez	.50
12	Albert Belle	.25
13	Frank Thomas	.50
14	Mike Piazza	1.00
15	Chipper Jones	1.00
16	Sammy Sosa	1.00
17	Vladimir Guerrero	.50
18	Scott Rolen	.50
19	Raul Mondesi	.25
20	Derek Jeter	2.00

Stadium Relics

Inserted exclusively in Home-Team Advantage packs, this five-card set features historical baseball stadiums and the autograph of the players who made them sacred. Besides the player autograph, the cards also have a piece of base from the featured stadium embedded into each card. These were seeded 1:165 HTA packs and are numbered with a "SR" prefix.

		NM/M
Common Player:		40.00
Inserted 1:165 HTA		
1	Don Mattingly	150.00
2	Carl Yastrzemski	100.00
3	Ernie Banks	75.00
4	Johnny Bench	75.00
5	Willie Mays	150.00
6	Mike Schmidt	100.00
7	Lou Brock	50.00
8	Al Kaline	75.00
9	Paul Molitor	60.00
10	Eddie Matthews	75.00

Supers

Each box of Topps foil packs includes one upwrapped box-topper card in an oversize (3-1/2" x 5") format. Except for its size, the super version differs from the same players' issued cards only in the numbering on back which designates each card "x of 8."

		NM/M
Complete Set (16):		35.00
Common Player:		1.00
Inserted 1:Box		
1	Mark McGwire	5.00
2	Hank Aaron	5.00
3	Derek Jeter	3.00
4	Sammy Sosa	3.00
5	Alex Rodriguez	3.00
6	Chipper Jones	4.00
7	Cal Ripken Jr.	3.00
1	Pedro Martinez	2.00
2	Orlando Hernandez	1.00
3	Mike Piazza	3.00
4	Manny Ramirez	1.50
5	Ken Griffey Jr.	4.00
6	Rafael Palmeiro	1.00
7	Greg Maddux	2.50
8	Nomar Garciaparra	3.00

21st Century Topps

Printed on a silver holographic foil front, this 10-card set highlights young players who are poised to thrive into the next millenium. These are seeded 1:18 packs are numbered on the card backs with a "C" prefix.

		NM/M
Complete Set (10):		5.00
Common Player:		.25
"Limited Edition" 4,000 Sets:		1X
1	Ben Grieve	.25
2	Alex Gonzalez	.25
3	Derek Jeter	2.00
4	Sean Casey	.25
5	Nomar Garciaparra	1.50
6	Alex Rodriguez	1.50
7	Scott Rolen	.50
8	Andruw Jones	.50
9	Vladimir Guerrero	.50
10	Todd Helton	.50

2000 Topps Traded and Rookies

		NM/M
Complete Set (135):		25.00
Common Player:		.10
Unopened Set (136):		50.00
1	Mike MacDougal RC	.20
2	Andy Tracy RC	.20
3	Brandon Phillips RC	.50
4	Brandon Inge RC	.75
5	Robbie Morrison RC	.25
6	Josh Pressley RC	.20
7	Todd Moser RC	.25
8	Rob Purvis RC	.25
9	Chance Caple RC	.25
10	Ben Sheets	.75
11	Russ Jacobson RC	.10
12	Brian Cole RC	.10
13	Brad Baker RC	.25
14	Alex Cintron RC	.40
15	Lyle Overbay RC	1.00
16	Mike Edwards RC	.20
17	Sean McGowan RC	.25
18	Jose Molina RC	.25
19	Marcos Castillo RC	.20
20	Josue Espada RC	.20
21	Alex Gordon RC	.10
22	Rob Pugmire RC	.10
23	Jason Stumm RC	.25
24	Ty Howington RC	.40
25	Brett Myers RC	.50
26	Maicer Izturis RC	.10
27	John McDonald RC	.10
28	Wilfredo Rodriguez RC	.25
29	Carlos Zambrano RC	3.00
30	Alejandro Diaz RC	.20
31	Geraldo Guzman RC	.20
32	J.R. House RC	.50
33	Elvin Nina RC	.20
34	Juan Pierre RC	.50
35	Ben Johnson RC	.50
36	Jeff Bailey RC	.20
37	Miguel Olivo RC	.10
38	Francisco Rodriguez RC	2.00
39	Tony Pena Jr. RC	1.00
40	Miguel Cabrera RC	15.00
41	Asdrubal Oropeza RC	.10
42	Junior Zamora RC	.10
43	Jovanny Cedeno RC	.25
44	John Sneed RC	.10
45	Josh Kalinowski RC	.10
46	Mike Young RC	3.00
47	Rico Washington RC	.10
48	Chad Durbin RC	.40
49	Junior Brignac RC	.40
50	Carlos Hernandez RC	.40
51	Cesar Izturis RC	.50
52	Oscar Salazar RC	.25
53	Pat Strange RC	.25
54	Rick Asadoorian	.15

55	Keith Reed RC	.25
56	Leo Estrella RC	.10
57	Wascar Serrano RC	.10
58	Richard Gomez RC	.25
59	Ramon Santiago RC	.25
60	Jovanny Sosa RC	.25
61	Aaron Rowand RC	.50
62	Junior Guerrero RC	.25
63	Luis Terrero RC	.25
64	Brian Sanches RC	.10
65	Scott Sobkowiak RC	.10
66	Gary Majewski RC	.10
67	Barry Zito RC	.75
68	Ryan Christianson RC	.40
69	Cristian Guerrero RC	.40
70	Tomas de la Rosa RC	.10
71	Andrew Beinbrink RC	.25
72	Ryan Knox RC	.10
73	Alex Graman RC	.25
74	Juan Guzman RC	.10
75	Ruben Salazar RC	.40
76	Luis Matos RC	.40
77	Tony Mota RC	.10
78	Doug Davis RC	.50
79	Ben Christensen RC	.25
80	Mike Lamb RC	.10
81	Adrian Gonzalez RC (Draft Picks)	1.50
82	Mike Stodolka RC (Draft Picks)	.25
83	Adam Johnson RC (Draft Picks)	.25
84	Matt Wheatland RC (Draft Picks)	.25
85	Corey Smith RC (Draft Picks)	.50
86	Rocco Baldelli RC (Draft Picks)	1.50
87	Keith Bucktrot RC (Draft Picks)	.25
88	Adam Wainwright RC (Draft Picks)	1.50
89	Scott Thorman RC (Draft Picks)	1.50
90	Tripper Johnson RC (Draft Picks)	.50
91	Jim Edmonds	.25
92	Masato Yoshii	.10
93	Adam Kennedy	.10
94	Darryl Kile	.10
95	Mark McLemore	.10
96	Ricky Gutierrez	.10
97	Juan Gonzalez	.40
98	Melvin Mora	.10
99	Dante Bichette	.10
100	Lee Stevens	.10
101	Roger Cedeno	.10
102	John Olerud	.25
103	Eric Young	.10
104	Mickey Morandini	.10
105	Travis Lee	.10
106	Greg Vaughn	.10
107	Todd Zeile	.10
108	Chuck Finley	.10
109	Ismael Valdes	.10
110	Ron Henika	.10
111	Pat Hentgen	.10
112	Ryan Klesko	.10
113	Derek Bell	.10
114	Hideo Nomo	.40
115	Aaron Sele	.10
116	Fernando Vina	.10
117	Wally Joyner	.10
118	Brian Hunter	.10
119	Joe Girardi	.10
120	Omar Daal	.10
121	Brook Fordyce	.10
122	Jose Valentin	.10
123	Curt Schilling	.40
124	B.J. Surhoff	.10
125	Henry Rodriguez	.10
126	Mike Bordick	.10
127	David Justice	.25
128	Charles Johnson	.10
129	Will Clark	.25
130	Dwight Gooden	.10
131	David Segui	.10
132	Denny Neagle	.10
133	Andy Ashby	.10
134	Bruce Chen	.10
135	Jason Bere	.10

Autographs

		NM/M
Common Player:		4.00
Inserted 1:set		
1	Mike MacDougal	8.00

2	Andy Tracy	4.00
3	Brandon Phillips	20.00
4	Brandon Inge	30.00
5	Robbie Morrison	4.00
6	Josh Pressley	4.00
7	Todd Moser	4.00
8	Rob Purvis	4.00
9	Chance Caple	4.00
10	Ben Sheets	40.00
11	Russ Jacobson	4.00
12	Brian Cole	4.00
13	Brad Baker	4.00
14	Alex Cintron	10.00
15	Lyle Overbay	30.00
16	Mike Edwards	4.00
17	Sean McGowan	4.00
18	Jose Molina	4.00
19	Marcos Castillo	4.00
20	Alex Gordon	4.00
21	Rob Pugmire	4.00
22	Jason Stumm	4.00
23	Ty Howington	4.00
24	Brett Myers	25.00
25	Maicer Izturis	8.00
26	John McDonald	4.00
27	Wilfredo Rodriguez	4.00
28	Carlos Zambrano	125.00
29	Alejandro Diaz	4.00
30	Geraldo Guzman	4.00
31	J.R. House	8.00
32	Elvin Nina	4.00
33	Juan Pierre	25.00
34	Ben Johnson	12.00
35	Jeff Bailey	4.00
36	Miguel Olivo	10.00
37	Francisco Rodriguez	50.00
38	Tony Pena Jr.	4.00
39	Miguel Cabrera	600.00
40	Asdrubal Oropeza	4.00
41	Junior Zamora	4.00
42	Jovanny Cedeno	4.00
43	John Sneed	4.00
44	Josh Kalinowski	8.00
45	Mike Young	100.00
46	Rico Washington	4.00
47	Chad Durbin	4.00
48	Junior Brignac	4.00
49	Carlos Hernandez	8.00
50	Cesar Izturis	15.00
51	Oscar Salazar	4.00
52	Pat Strange	4.00
53	Rick Asadoorian	4.00
54	Keith Reed	4.00
55	Leo Estrella	4.00
56	Wascar Serrano	4.00
57	Richard Gomez	4.00
58	Ramon Santiago	4.00
59	Jovanny Sosa	4.00
60	Aaron Rowand	35.00
61	Junior Guerrero	4.00
62	Luis Terrero	10.00
63	Brian Sanches	4.00
64	Scott Sobkowiak	4.00
65	Gary Majewski	8.00
66	Barry Zito	40.00
67	Ryan Christianson	8.00
68	Cristian Guerrero	8.00
69	Tomas de la Rosa	4.00
70	Andrew Beinbrink	4.00
71	Ryan Knox	4.00
72	Alex Graman	4.00
73	Juan Guzman	4.00
74	Ruben Salazar	4.00
75	Luis Matos	10.00
76	Tony Mota	4.00
77	Doug Davis	15.00
78	Ben Christensen	4.00
79	Mike Lamb	10.00

2000 Topps Opening Day

Essentially identical in design to 2000 Topps regular cards, Opening Day has a silver border with "2000 Opening Day" stamped in silver foil on the card front. The checklist is made up of cards from Series 1 and 2 from Topps base set with identical photos. The rookie reprint card of Hank Aaron was intended to carry card #110, but it does not appear, only the original '54 Topps card #128.

		NM/M
	Complete Set (165):	30.00
	Common Player:	.15
	Pack (8):	1.00
	Wax Box (36):	25.00
1	Mark McGwire	2.00
2	Tony Gwynn	1.00
3	Wade Boggs	.40
4	Cal Ripken Jr.	2.50
5	Matt Williams	.20
6	Jay Buhner	.15
7	Mike Lieberthal	.15
8	Magglio Ordonez	.25
9	Derek Jeter	2.00
10	Javy Lopez	.25
11	Armando Benitez	.15
12	Darin Erstad	.25
13	Mark Grace	.25
14	Eric Karros	.15
15	J.T. Snow Jr.	.15
16	Luis Castillo	.15
17	Rey Ordonez	.15
18	Bob Abreu	.25
19	Warren Morris	.15
20	Juan Gonzalez	.75
21	Dean Palmer	.15
22	Hank Aaron	2.00
23	Jeff Bagwell	.75
24	Sammy Sosa	1.50
25	Randy Johnson	.75
26	Dante Bichette	.25
27	Frank Thomas	.75
28	Pedro Martinez	.75
29	Brian Giles	.15
30	Ivan Rodriguez	.50
31	Roger Cedeno	.15
32	David Justice	.25
33	Ken Caminiti	.15
34	Brian Jordan	.15
35	John Olerud	.25
36	Pokey Reese	.15
37	Barry Larkin	.25
38	Edgar Martinez	.25
39	Carlos Delgado	.50
40	Troy Glaus	.40
41	Ben Grieve	.15
42	Jose Lima	.15
43	Luis Gonzalez	.15
44	Alex Rodriguez	2.00
45	Preston Wilson	.20
46	Rickey Henderson	.40
47	Gary Sheffield	.25
48	Jim Edmonds	.25
49	Greg Vaughn	.15
50	Neifi Perez	.15
51	Paul O'Neill	.25
52	Jermaine Dye	.15
53	Curt Schilling	.25
54	Edgardo Alfonzo	.25
55	John Smoltz	.20
56	Chuck Finley	.15
57	Billy Wagner	.15
58	David Cone	.25
59	Roberto Alomar	.50
60	Charles Nagy	.15
61	Mike Mussina	.50
62	Robin Ventura	.15
63	Kevin Brown	.15
64	Pat Hentgen	.15
65	Ryan Klesko	.15
66	Derek Bell	.15
67	Larry Walker	.25
68	Scott Williamson	.15
69	Jose Offerman	.15
70	Doug Mientkiewicz	.15
71	John Snyder	.15
72	Sandy Alomar	.15
73	Joe Nathan	.15
74	Steve Finley	.15
75	Dave Martinez	.15
76	Fernando Tatis	.15
77	Kenny Lofton	.20
78	Paul Byrd	.15
79	Aaron Sele	.15
80	Roger Clemens	1.50
81	Francisco Cordova	.15
82	Wally Joyner	.15
83	Jason Kendall	.25
84	Carlos Beltran	.15
85	Chipper Jones	1.50
86	Vladimir Guerrero	.75
87	Tom Goodwin	.15
88	Brian Daubach	.15
89	Jay Bell	.15
90	Roy Halladay	.15
91	Miguel Tejada	.40
92	Eric Davis	.15
93	Henry Rodriguez	.15
94	Joe McEwing	.15
95	Jeff Kent	.15
96	Jeff Zimmerman	.15
97	Tony Fernandez	.15
98	Jason Giambi	.75
99	Jose Canseco	.40
100	Alex Gonzalez	.15
101	Erubiel Durazo, Pat Burrell, Nick Johnson (Prospects)	.40
102	Corey Patterson, Roosevelt Brown, Lance Berkman (Prospects)	.25

103	Eric Munson, Bobby Bradley RC (Draft Picks)	.25
104	Josh Hamilton, Corey Myers RC (Draft Picks)	.25
105	Mark McGwire (Magic Moments)	2.00
106	Hank Aaron (Magic Moments)	2.00
107	Cal Ripken Jr. (Magic Moments)	2.50
108	Wade Boggs (Magic Moments)	.40
109	Tony Gwynn (Magic Moments)	1.00
(110)	Hank Aaron (Rookie Reprint)	2.00
111	Tom Glavine	.40
112	Mo Vaughn	.20
113	Tino Martinez	.25
114	Craig Biggio	.25
115	Tim Hudson	.25
116	John Wetteland	.15
117	Ellis Burks	.15
118	David Wells	.15
119	Rico Brogna	.15
120	Greg Maddux	1.50
121	Jeromy Burnitz	.15
122	Raul Mondesi	.25
123	Rondell White	.25
124	Barry Bonds	2.00
125	Orlando Hernandez	.25
126	Bartolo Colon	.15
127	Tim Salmon	.25
128	Kevin Young	.15
129	Troy O'Leary	.15
130	Jim Thome	.50
131	Ray Durham	.15
132	Tony Clark	.15
133	Mariano Rivera	.25
134	Omar Vizquel	.15
135	Ken Griffey Jr.	1.50
136	Shawn Green	.40
137	Cliff Floyd	.15
138	Al Leiter	.15
139	Mike Hampton	.15
140	Mike Piazza	1.50
141	Andy Pettitte	.25
142	Albert Belle	.20
143	Scott Rolen	.75
144	Rusty Greer	.15
145	Kevin Millwood	.25
146	Ivan Rodriguez	.75
147	Nomar Garciaparra	1.50
148	Denny Neagle	.15
149	Manny Ramirez	.75
150	Vinny Castilla	.15
151	Andruw Jones	.50
152	Johnny Damon	.25
153	Eric Milton	.15
154	Todd Helton	.50
155	Rafael Palmeiro	.25
156	Damion Easley	.15
157	Carlos Febles	.15
158	Paul Konerko	.25
159	Bernie Williams	.50
160	Ken Griffey Jr. (Magic Moments)	1.50
161	Barry Bonds (Magic Moments)	2.00
162	Sammy Sosa (Magic Moments)	2.00
163	Derek Jeter (Magic Moments)	2.00
164	Alex Rodriguez (Magic Moments)	2.00
165	Checklist (Magic Moments)	.15

Autographs

EDGARDO ALFONZO

		NM/M
	Common Player:	25.00
1	Edgardo Alfonzo	25.00
2	Wade Boggs	60.00
3	Robin Ventura	25.00
4	Josh Hamilton	25.00
5	Vernon Wells	30.00

2000 Topps Chrome

The base set consists of 478 cards utilizing Topps Chromium technology and features the same photos and basic design as the 2000 Topps base set. Subsets include Prospects,

JOSE CANSECO

Draft Picks, 20th Century's Best, Magic Moments and Post Season Highlights. A parallel Refractor version is also available 1:12 packs.

		NM/M
	Complete Set (478)	100.00
	Complete Series I Set (239):	50.00
	Complete Series II Set (239):	50.00
	Common Player:	.25
	Pack (4):	1.50
	Wax Box (24):	30.00
1	Mark McGwire	3.00
2	Tony Gwynn	1.50
3	Wade Boggs	.75
4	Cal Ripken Jr.	4.00
5	Matt Williams	.40
6	Jay Buhner	.40
7	Jeff Conine	.25
8	Todd Greene	.25
9	Mike Lieberthal	.25
10	Steve Avery	.25
11	Bret Saberhagen	.25
12	Magglio Ordonez	.50
13	Brad Radke	.25
14	Derek Jeter	4.00
15	Javy Lopez	.50
16	Russ David	.25
17	Armando Benitez	.25
18	B.J. Surhoff	.25
19	Darryl Kile	.25
20	Mark Lewis	.25
21	Mike Williams	.25
22	Mark McLemore	.25
23	Sterling Hitchcock	.25
24	Darin Erstad	.50
25	Ricky Gutierrez	.25
26	John Jaha	.25
27	Homer Bush	.25
28	Darrin Fletcher	.25
29	Mark Grace	.75
30	Fred McGriff	.50
31	Omar Daal	.25
32	Eric Karros	.40
33	Orlando Cabrera	.40
34	J.T. Snow Jr.	.25
35	Luis Castillo	.25
36	Rey Ordonez	.25
37	Bob Abreu	.40
38	Warren Morris	.25
39	Juan Gonzalez	1.00
40	Mike Lansing	.25
41	Chili Davis	.25
42	Dean Palmer	.25
43	Hank Aaron	3.00
44	Jeff Bagwell	1.00
45	Jose Valentin	.25
46	Shannon Stewart	.25
47	Kent Bottenfield	.25
48	Jeff Shaw	.25
49	Sammy Sosa	2.00
50	Randy Johnson	1.50
51	Benny Agbayani	.25
52	Dante Bichette	.25
53	Pete Harnisch	.25
54	Frank Thomas	1.00
55	Jorge Posada	.75
56	Todd Walker	.25
57	Juan Encarnacion	.40
58	Mike Sweeney	.25
59	Pedro Martinez	1.50
60	Lee Stevens	.25
61	Brian Giles	.50
62	Chad Ogea	.25
63	Ivan Rodriguez	1.00
64	Roger Cedeno	.25
65	David Justice	.50
66	Steve Trachsel	.25
67	Eli Marrero	.25
68	Dave Nilsson	.25
69	Ken Caminiti	.25
70	Tim Raines	.25
71	Brian Jordan	.25
72	Jeff Blauser	.25
73	Bernard Gilkey	.25
74	John Flaherty	.25
75	Brent Mayne	.25
76	Jose Vidro	.25
77	Jeff Fassero	.25
78	Bruce Aven	.25
79	John Olerud	.50
80	Juan Guzman	.25
81	Woody Williams	.25
82	Ed Sprague	.25
83	Joe Girardi	.25

85	Barry Larkin	.50
86	Mike Caruso	.25
87	Bobby Higginson	.25
88	Roberto Kelly	.25
89	Edgar Martinez	.40
90	Mark Kotsay	.25
91	Paul Sorrento	.25
92	Eric Young	.25
93	Carlos Delgado	1.00
94	Troy Glaus	1.00
95	Ben Grieve	.25
96	Jose Lima	.25
97	Garret Anderson	.50
98	Luis Gonzalez	.50
99	Carl Pavano	.25
100	Alex Rodriguez	3.00
101	Preston Wilson	.40
102	Ron Gant	.40
103	Harold Baines	.25
104	Rickey Henderson	.50
105	Gary Sheffield	.75
106	Mickey Morandini	.25
107	Jim Edmonds	.50
108	Kris Benson	.25
109	Adrian Beltre	.25
110	Alex Fernandez	.25
111	Dan Wilson	.25
112	Mark Clark	.25
113	Greg Vaughn	.25
114	Neifi Perez	.25
115	Paul O'Neill	.50
116	Jermaine Dye	.25
117	Todd Jones	.25
118	Terry Steinbach	.25
119	Greg Norton	.25
120	Curt Schilling	.75
121	Todd Zeile	.25
122	Edgardo Alfonzo	.25
123	Ryan McGuire	.25
124	Stan Javier	.25
125	John Smoltz	.40
126	Bob Wickman	.25
127	Richard Hidalgo	.25
128	Chuck Finley	.25
129	Billy Wagner	.25
130	Todd Hundley	.25
131	Dwight Gooden	.40
132	Russ Ortiz	.25
133	Mike Lowell	.25
134	Reggie Sanders	.25
135	John Valentin	.25
136	Brad Ausmus	.25
137	Chad Kreuter	.25
138	David Cone	.40
139	Brook Fordyce	.25
140	Roberto Alomar	.75
141	Charles Nagy	.25
142	Brian Hunter	.25
143	Mike Mussina	.75
144	Robin Ventura	.40
145	Kevin Brown	.40
146	Pat Hentgen	.25
147	Ryan Klesko	.40
148	Derek Bell	.25
149	Andy Sheets	.25
150	Larry Walker	.50
151	Scott Williamson	.25
152	Jose Offerman	.25
153	Doug Mientkiewicz	.25
154	John Snyder RC	.40
155	Sandy Alomar	.25
156	Joe Nathan	.25
157	Lance Johnson	.25
158	Odalis Perez	.25
159	Hideo Nomo	.75
160	Steve Finley	.25
161	Dave Martinez	.25
162	Matt Walbeck	.25
163	Bill Spiers	.25
164	Fernando Tatis	.25
165	Kenny Lofton	.40
166	Paul Byrd	.25
167	Aaron Sele	.25
168	Eddie Taubensee	.25
169	Reggie Jefferson	.25
170	Roger Clemens	2.50
171	Francisco Cordova	.25
172	Mike Bordick	.25
173	Wally Joyner	.25
174	Marvin Benard	.25
175	Jason Kendall	.40
176	Mike Stanley	.25
177	Chad Allen	.25
178	Carlos Beltran	.50
179	Deivi Cruz	.25
180	Chipper Jones	2.00
181	Vladimir Guerrero	1.50
182	Dave Burba	.25
183	Tom Goodwin	.25
184	Brian Daubach	.25
185	Jay Bell	.25
186	Roy Halladay	.25
187	Miguel Tejada	.50
188	Armando Rios	.25
189	Fernando Vina	.25
190	Eric Davis	.40
191	Henry Rodriguez	.25
192	Joe McEwing	.25
193	Jeff Kent	.50
194	Mike Jackson	.25
195	Mike Morgan	.25
196	Jeff Montgomery	.25
197	Jeff Zimmerman	.25
198	Tony Fernandez	.25
199	Jason Giambi	1.00
200	Jose Canseco	.75
201	Alex Gonzalez	.25

202	Jack Cust, Mike Colangelo	.25
	Dee Brown	.50
203	Felipe Lopez, Alfonso Soriano, Pablo Ozuna	3.00
204	Erubiel Durazo, Pat Burrell, Nick Johnson	.75
205	John Sneed RC, Kip Wells, Matt Blank	.50
206	Josh Kalinowski RC, Michael Tejera RC, Chris Mears	.50
207	Roosevelt Brown, Corey Patterson, Lance Berkman	.40
208	Kit Pellow, Kevin Barker, Russ Branyan	.40
209	B.J. Garbe RC, Larry Bigbie RC	3.00
210	Eric Munson, Bobby Bradley RC	.75
211	Josh Girdley, Kyle Snyder	.50
212	Chance Caple RC, Jason Jennings	.50
213	Ryan Christiansen RC, Brett Myers RC	6.00
214	Jason Stumm RC, Rob Purvis RC	.75
215	David Walling, Mike Paradis	.40
216	Omar Ortiz, Jay Gehrke	.40
217	David Cone (Season Highlights)	.40
218	Jose Jimenez (Season Highlights)	.25
219	Chris Singleton (Season Highlights)	.25
220	Fernando Tatis (Season Highlights)	.25
221	Todd Helton (Season Highlights)	1.00
222	Kevin Millwood (Post-Season Highlights)	.50
223	Todd Pratt (Post-Season Highlights)	.25
224	Orlando Hernandez (Post-Season Highlights)	.25
225	Post-Season Highlights	.25
226	Post-Season Highlights	.25
227	Bernie Williams (Post-Season Highlights)	.75
228	Mariano Rivera (Post-Season Highlights)	.50
229	Tony Gwynn (20th Century's Best)	1.50
230	Wade Boggs (20th Century's Best)	.50
231	Tim Raines (20th Century's Best)	.25
232	Mark McGwire (20th Century's Best)	3.00
233	Rickey Henderson (20th Century's Best)	.75
234	Rickey Henderson (20th Century's Best)	.75
235	Roger Clemens (20th Century's Best)	2.00
236	Mark McGwire (Magic Moments)	5.00
237	Hank Aaron (Magic Moments)	5.00
238	Cal Ripken Jr. (Magic Moments)	6.00
239	Wade Boggs (Magic Moments)	1.00
240	Tony Gwynn (Magic Moments)	3.00
	Series 1 checklist (1-201)	.05
	Series 1 checklist (202-240, inserts)	.05
241	Tom Glavine	.50
242	David Wells	.25
243	Kevin Appier	.25
244	Troy Percival	.25
245	Ray Lankford	.25
246	Marquis Grissom	.25
247	Randy Winn	.25
248	Miguel Batista	.25
249	Darren Dreifort	.25
250	Barry Bonds	3.00
251	Harold Baines	.25
252	Cliff Floyd	.25
253	Freddy Garcia	.40
254	Kenny Rogers	.25
255	Ben Davis	.25
256	Charles Johnson	.25
257	John Burkett	.25
258	Desi Relaford	.25
259	Al Martin	.25
260	Andy Pettitte	.50
261	Carlos Lee	.25
262	Matt Lawton	.25
263	Andy Fox	.25
264	Chan Ho Park	.25
265	Billy Koch	.25
266	Dave Roberts	.25
267	Carl Everett	.25
268	Orel Hershiser	.25
269	Trot Nixon	.25
270	Rusty Greer	.25
271	Will Clark	.75
272	Quivilo Veras	.25
273	Rico Brogna	.25
274	Devon White	.25
275	Tim Hudson	.50
276	Mike Hampton	.25

277	Miguel Cairo	.25
278	Darren Oliver	.25
279	Jeff Cirillo	.25
280	Al Leiter	.25
281	Brant Brown	.25
282	Carlos Febles	.25
283	Pedro Astacio	.25
284	Juan Guzman	.25
285	Orlando Hernandez	.25
286	Paul Konerko	.25
287	Tony Clark	.25
288	Aaron Boone	.50
289	Ismael Valdes	.50
290	Moises Alou	.50
291	Kevin Tapani	.25
292	John Franco	.25
293	Todd Zeile	.25
294	Jason Schmidt	.25
295	Johnny Damon	.40
296	Scott Brosius	.25
297	Travis Fryman	.40
298	Jose Vizcaino	.25
299	Eric Chavez	.50
300	Mike Piazza	2.00
301	Matt Clement	.25
302	Cristian Guzman	.25
303	Darryl Strawberry	.40
304	Jeff Abbott	.25
305	Brett Tomko	.25
306	Mike Lansing	.25
307	Eric Owens	.25
308	Livan Hernandez	.25
309	Rondell White	.40
310	Todd Stottlemyre	.25
311	Chris Carpenter	.25
312	Ken Hill	.25
313	Mark Loretta	.25
314	John Rocker	.25
315	Richie Sexson	.75
316	Ruben Mateo	.25
317	Ramon Martinez	.25
318	Mike Sirotka	.25
319	Jose Rosado	.25
320	Matt Mantei	.25
321	Kevin Millwood	.50
322	Gary DiSarcina	.25
323	Dustin Hermanson	.25
324	Mike Stanton	.25
325	Kirk Rueter	.25
326	Damian Miller	.25
327	Doug Glanville	.25
328	Scott Rolen	1.00
329	Ray Durham	.25
330	Butch Huskey	.25
331	Mariano Rivera	.50
332	Darren Lewis	.25
333	Ramiro Mendoza	.25
334	Mark Grudzielanek	.25
335	Mike Cameron	.25
336	Kelvim Escobar	.25
337	Bret Boone	.40
338	Mo Vaughn	.40
339	Craig Biggio	.40
340	Michael Barrett	.25
341	Marlon Anderson	.25
342	Bobby Jones	.25
343	John Halama	.25
344	Todd Ritchie	.25
345	Chuck Knoblauch	.25
346	Rick Reed	.25
347	Kelly Stinnett	.25
348	Tim Salmon	.50
349	A.J. Hinch	.25
350	Jose Cruz Jr.	.25
351	Roberto Hernandez	.25
352	Edgar Renteria	.25
353	Jose Hernandez	.25
354	Brad Fullmer	.25
355	Trevor Hoffman	.25
356	Troy O'Leary	.25
357	Justin Thompson	.25
358	Kevin Young	.25
359	Hideki Irabu	.25
360	Jim Thome	1.00
361	Todd Dunwoody	.25
362	Octavio Dotel	.25
363	Omar Vizquel	.40
364	Raul Mondesi	.40
365	Shane Reynolds	.25
366	Bartolo Colon	.25
367	Chris Widger	.25
368	Gabe Kapler	.25
369	Bill Simas	.25
370	Tino Martinez	.50
371	John Thomson	.25
372	Delino DeShields	.25
373	Carlos Perez	.25
374	Eddie Perez	.25
375	Jeromy Burnitz	.25
376	Jimmy Haynes	.25
377	Travis Lee	.25
378	Darryl Hamilton	.25
379	Jamie Moyer	.25
380	Alex Gonzalez	.25
381	John Wetteland	.25
382	Vinny Castilla	.40
383	Jeff Suppan	.25
384	Chad Curtis	.25
385	Robb Nen	.25
386	Wilson Alvarez	.25
387	Andres Galarraga	.50
388	Mike Remlinger	.25
389	Geoff Jenkins	.40
390	Matt Stairs	.25
391	Bill Mueller	.25
392	Mike Lowell	.25
393	Andy Ashby	.25
394	Ruben Rivera	.25

395	Todd Helton	1.00
396	Bernie Williams	.75
397	Royce Clayton	.25
398	Manny Ramirez	1.00
399	Kerry Wood	.75
400	Ken Griffey Jr.	2.00
401	Enrique Wilson	.25
402	Joey Hamilton	.25
403	Shawn Estes	.25
404	Ugueth Urbina	.25
405	Albert Belle	.30
406	Rick Helling	.25
407	Steve Parris	.25
408	Eric Milton	.25
409	Dave Mlicki	.25
410	Shawn Green	.50
411	Jaret Wright	.25
412	Tony Womack	.25
413	Vernon Wells	.50
414	Ron Belliard	.25
415	Ellis Burks	.25
416	Scott Erickson	.25
417	Rafael Palmeiro	.75
418	Damion Easley	.25
419	Jamey Wright	.25
420	Corey Koskie	.25
421	Bobby Howry	.25
422	Ricky Ledee	.25
423	Dmitri Young	.25
424	Sidney Ponson	.25
425	Greg Maddux	2.00
426	Jose Guillen	.25
427	Jon Lieber	.25
428	Andy Benes	.25
429	Randy Velarde	.25
430	Sean Casey	.40
431	Torii Hunter	.25
432	Ryan Rupe	.25
433	David Segui	.25
434	Rich Aurilia	.25
435	Nomar Garciaparra	3.00
436	Denny Neagle	.25
437	Ron Coomer	.25
438	Chris Singleton	.25
439	Tony Batista	.25
440	Andruw Jones	1.00
441	Adam Piatt, Aubrey Huff, Sean Burroughs (Prospects)	.50
442	Rafael Furcal, Jason Dallero, Travis Dawkins (Prospects)	.50
443	Wilton Veras, Joe Crede, Mike Lamb RC (Prospects)	.25
444	Julio Zuleta RC, Dernell Stenson, Jorge Toca (Prospects)	.25
445	Tim Raines Jr., Gary Mathews Jr., Garry Maddox Jr. RC (Prospects)	.50
446	Matt Riley, Mark Mulder, C.C. Sabathia (Prospects)	.25
447	Scott Downs RC, Chris George, Matt Belisle (Prospects)	.50
448	Doug Mirabelli, Ben Petrick, Jayson Werth (Prospects)	.25
449	Josh Hamilton, Corey Myers RC (Draft Picks)	.50
450	Ben Christensen RC, Brett Myers (Draft Picks)	.50
451	Barry Zito RC, Ben Sheets RC (Draft Picks)	10.00
452	Ty Howington RC, Kurt Ainsworth RC (Draft Picks)	2.00
453	Rick Asadoorian RC, Vince Faison RC (Draft Picks)	.50
454	Keith Reed RC, Jeff Heaverlo RC (Draft Picks)	.50
455	Mike MacDougal RC, Jay Gehrke (Draft Picks)	1.50
456	Mark McGwire (Season Highlights)	3.00
457	Cal Ripken Jr. (Season Highlights)	4.00
458	Wade Boggs (Season Highlights)	.75
459	Tony Gwynn (Season Highlights)	1.50
460	Jesse Orosco (Season Highlights)	.25
461	Nomar Garciaparra, Larry Walker (League Leaders)	1.50
462	Mark McGwire, Ken Griffey Jr. (League Leaders)	1.50
463	Mark McGwire, Manny Ramirez (League Leaders)	1.50
464	Randy Johnson, Pedro Martinez (League Leaders)	1.00
465	Randy Johnson, Pedro Martinez (League Leaders)	
466	Luis Gonzalez, Derek Jeter (League Leaders)	2.00
467	Manny Ramirez, Larry Walker (League Leaders)	.75
468	Tony Gwynn (20th Century's Best)	1.50
469	Mark McGwire (20th Century's Best)	3.00
470	Frank Thomas (20th Century's Best)	.75
471	Harold Baines (20th Century's Best)	.25
472	Roger Clemens (20th Century's Best)	1.50
473	John Franco (20th Century's Best)	.25
474	John Franco (20th Century's Best)	.25
475	Ken Griffey Jr. (Magic Moments)	3.00
476	Barry Bonds (Magic Moments)	5.00
477	Sammy Sosa (Magic Moments)	4.00
478	Derek Jeter (Magic Moments)	6.00
479	Alex Rodriguez (Magic Moments)	5.00

Refractors

A parallel to the base set, Refractors have a reflective sheen to them when held up to light. They are seeded 1:12 packs and have "Refractor" written underneath the card number on the back.

Stars: 3-5X
Young Stars/RC's: 1-2X
Inserted 1:12

All-Star Rookie Team

This 10-card set highlights players who lived up to the high expectations placed on them during their rookie season. These are seeded 1:16 packs and are numbered with an "RT" prefix on the card back. A Refractor parallel is also randomly inserted, seeded 1:80 packs. "Refractor" is printed under the card number on the back.

		NM/M
Complete Set (10):		10.00
Common Player:		.50
Inserted 1:16		
Refractors:		2-3X
Inserted 1:80		
1	Mark McGwire	3.00
2	Chuck Knoblauch	.50
3	Chipper Jones	2.00
4	Cal Ripken Jr.	4.00
5	Manny Ramirez	1.00
6	Jose Canseco	.75
7	Ken Griffey Jr.	2.00
8	Mike Piazza	2.00
9	Dwight Gooden	.50
10	Billy Wagner	.50

All-Topps Team

These feature top National League players and picks a top player for each position. They have a brown border utilizing Topps Chromium technology. Card backs have a small photo along with statistical comparisons made to current and former greats for their respective position. Backs are numbered with an "AT" prefix and are seeded 1:32 packs. A Refractor parallel is inserted 1:160 packs.

		NM/M
Complete Set (20):		40.00
Complete Series I Set (10):		20.00
Complete Series II Set (10):		20.00
Common Player:		.50
Inserted 1:32		
Refractors:		2-3X
Inserted 1:160		
1	Greg Maddux	3.00
2	Mike Piazza	3.00
3	Mark McGwire	5.00
4	Craig Biggio	1.00
5	Chipper Jones	3.00
6	Barry Larkin	1.00
7	Barry Bonds	5.00
8	Andruw Jones	1.50
9	Sammy Sosa	3.00
10	Larry Walker	1.00
11	Pedro Martinez	2.00
12	Ivan Rodriguez	1.00
13	Rafael Palmeiro	1.00
14	Roberto Alomar	1.00
15	Cal Ripken Jr.	6.00
16	Derek Jeter	6.00
17	Albert Belle	.50
18	Ken Griffey Jr.	3.00
19	Manny Ramirez	1.50
20	Jose Canseco	1.00

Allegiance

Allegiance features 20 stars who have spent their entire career with one team. They are seeded 1:16 and are numbered with a "TA" prefix. There is also a hobby-exclusive Refractor parallel version, sequentially numbered to 100 and inserted 1:424 packs.

		NM/M
Complete Set (20):		30.00
Common Player:		.75
Inserted 1:16		
Refractors:		5X
Inserted 1:424		
1	Derek Jeter	6.00
2	Ivan Rodriguez	1.00
3	Alex Rodriguez	5.00
4	Cal Ripken Jr.	6.00
5	Mark Grace	1.00
6	Tony Gwynn	2.00
7	Juan Gonzalez	1.50
8	Frank Thomas	1.50
9	Manny Ramirez	1.50
10	Barry Larkin	.75
11	Bernie Williams	1.50
12	Raul Mondesi	.75
13	Vladimir Guerrero	1.50
14	Craig Biggio	.75
15	Nomar Garciaparra	4.00
16	Andruw Jones	1.50
17	Jim Thome	1.50
18	Scott Rolen	1.50
19	Chipper Jones	3.00
20	Ken Griffey Jr.	3.00

Combos

Ten player combinations linked by a common element are featured in this set. Combos are found 1:16 packs and are numbered with a "TC" prefix on the card back. A Refractor parallel is randomly seeded 1:80 packs and have "Refractor" printed under the card number on the back.

		NM/M
Complete Set (10):		20.00
Common Player:		1.00
Inserted 1:16		
Refractors:		2-3X
Inserted 1:80		
1	Roberto Alomar, Manny Ramirez, Kenny Lofton, Jim Thome	1.00
2	Tom Glavine, Greg Maddux, John Smoltz	2.00
3	Derek Jeter, Bernie Williams, Tino Martinez	4.00
4	Ivan Rodriguez, Mike Piazza	2.00
5	Nomar Garciaparra, Alex Rodriguez, Derek Jeter	4.00
6	Sammy Sosa, Mark McGwire	4.00
7	Pedro Martinez, Randy Johnson	1.50
8	Barry Bonds, Ken Griffey Jr.	3.00
9	Chipper Jones, Ivan Rodriguez	2.00
10	Cal Ripken Jr., Tony Gwynn, Wade Boggs	4.00

Kings

This 10-card set spotlights hitters who have averaged 30 or more homeruns per season for their career. Kings are seeded 1:32 packs and are numbered with an "CK" prefix on the card back. A Refractor parallel is also randomly inserted and are serially numbered to the featured player's career homerun total.

		NM/M
Complete Set (10):		25.00
Common Player:		1.50
Inserted 1:32		
1	Mark McGwire	5.00
2	Sammy Sosa	3.00
3	Ken Griffey Jr.	3.00
4	Mike Piazza	3.00
5	Alex Rodriguez	5.00
6	Manny Ramirez	1.50
7	Barry Bonds	6.00
8	Nomar Garciaparra	4.00
9	Chipper Jones	3.00
10	Vladimir Guerrero	1.50

Mark McGwire 1985 Rookie Reprint

This insert is a chromium reprinted version of McGwire's 1985 Topps rookie card. Each card features a commemorative gold-foil stamp. The insertion rate is 1:32 packs. A hobby-exclusive Refractor version is also inserted, limited to 70 sequentially numbered sets and seeded 1:12,116 packs.

	NM/M
Complete Set (1):	5.00
Inserted 1:32	
Refractor:	50.00
Production 70 cards	
Mark McGwire	5.00

Millennium Stars

This 10-card set features stars who had less than three years major league experience in 2000. Millennium Stars are seeded 1:32 packs and are numbered with an "NMS" prefix. A Refractor parallel is randomly inserted in 1:160 packs and has "Refractor" printed under the card number on the back.

		NM/M
Complete Set (10):		10.00
Common Player:		.50
Inserted 1:32		
Refractors:		2-3X
Inserted 1:160		
1	Nomar Garciaparra	4.00
2	Vladimir Guerrero	1.50
3	Sean Casey	.75
4	Richie Sexson	1.00
5	Todd Helton	1.50
6	Carlos Beltran	.75
7	Kevin Millwood	.75
8	Ruben Mateo	.50
9	Pat Burrell	1.00
10	Alfonso Soriano	2.00

Own the Game

This 30-card set spotlights statistical stars and 1999 Major League Baseball award winners. These were seeded 1:11 packs and are numbered with an "OTG" prefix on the card back. A Refractor parallel is randomly inserted 1:55 packs and has "Refractor" written under the card number on the back.

		NM/M
Complete Set (30):		30.00
Common Player:		.25
Inserted 1:12		
Refractors:		2-3X
Inserted 1:55		
1	Derek Jeter	4.00
2	B.J. Surhoff	.25
3	Luis Gonzalez	.50
4	Manny Ramirez	1.00
5	Rafael Palmeiro	1.00
6	Mark McGwire	3.00
7	Mark McGwire	3.00
8	Sammy Sosa	2.00
9	Ken Griffey Jr.	2.00
10	Larry Walker	.50
11	Nomar Garciaparra	3.00
12	Derek Jeter	4.00
13	Larry Walker	.50
14	Mark McGwire	3.00
15	Manny Ramirez	1.00
16	Pedro Martinez	1.50
17	Randy Johnson	1.50
18	Kevin Millwood	.50
19	Pedro Martinez	1.50
20	Randy Johnson	1.50
21	Kevin Brown	.50
22	Chipper Jones	2.00
23	Ivan Rodriguez	1.00
24	Mariano Rivera	.50
25	Scott Williamson	.25
26	Carlos Beltran	.50
27	Randy Johnson	1.50
28	Pedro Martinez	1.50
29	Sammy Sosa	2.00
30	Manny Ramirez	1.00

Power Players

Twenty of the leading power hitters are featured on a colorful design. They are seeded 1:8 packs and are numbered with a "P" prefix. A Refractor parallel is also randomly seeded 1:40 packs.

		NM/M
Complete Set (20):		25.00
Common Player:		.25
Inserted 1:8		
Refractors:		2-3X
Inserted 1:40		
1	Juan Gonzalez	1.00
2	Ken Griffey Jr.	2.00
3	Mark McGwire	3.00
4	Nomar Garciaparra	3.00
5	Barry Bonds	3.00
6	Mo Vaughn	.40
7	Larry Walker	.50
8	Alex Rodriguez	3.00
9	Jose Canseco	.75
10	Jeff Bagwell	1.00
11	Manny Ramirez	1.00
12	Albert Belle	.25
13	Frank Thomas	1.00
14	Mike Piazza	2.00
15	Chipper Jones	2.00
16	Sammy Sosa	2.00
17	Vladimir Guerrero	1.00
18	Scott Rolen	1.00
19	Raul Mondesi	.40
20	Derek Jeter	4.00

21st Century Topps

This 10-card set focuses on the top young stars in baseball heading into the next century. These were seeded 1:16

packs and are numbered with a "C" prefix on the card back. A Refractor parallel version is also seeded 1:80 packs.

	NM/M
Complete Set (10):	10.00
Common Player:	.25
Inserted 1:16	
Refractors:	2-3X
Inserted 1:80	
1 Ben Grieve	.25
2 Alex Gonzalez	.25
3 Derek Jeter	4.00
4 Sean Casey	.50
5 Nomar Garciaparra	3.00
6 Alex Rodriguez	3.00
7 Scott Rolen	1.00
8 Andruw Jones	1.00
9 Vladimir Guerrero	1.00
10 Todd Helton	1.00

Traded and Rookies

	NM/M
Complete Set (135):	60.00
Common Player:	.25
1 Mike MacDougal RC	1.00
2 Andy Tracy RC	.50
3 Brandon Phillips RC	1.50
4 Brandon Inge RC	1.50
5 Robbie Morrison RC	.50
6 Josh Pressley RC	.50
7 Todd Moser RC	.50
8 Rob Purvis RC	.50
9 Chance Caple RC	.50
10 Ben Sheets	2.00
11 Russ Jacobson RC	.50
12 Brian Cole RC	.50
13 Brad Baker RC	.50
14 Alex Cintron RC	.25
15 Lyle Overbay RC	2.00
16 Mike Edwards RC	.50
17 Sean McGowan RC	.50
18 Jose Molina RC	.50
19 Marcos Castillo RC	.50
20 Josue Espada RC	.50
21 Alex Gordon RC	.50
22 Rob Pugmire RC	.50
23 Jason Stumm RC	.50
24 Ty Howington RC	1.00
25 Brett Myers	1.00
26 Maicer Izturis RC	.50
27 John McDonald RC	.50
28 Wilfredo Rodriguez RC	.50
29 Carlos Zambrano RC	6.00
30 Alejandro Diaz RC	.50
31 Geraldo Guzman RC	.50
32 J.R. House RC	.75
33 Elvin Nina RC	.50
34 Juan Pierre RC	2.00
35 Ben Johnson RC	1.00
36 Jeff Bailey RC	.50
37 Miguel Olivo RC	.50
38 Francisco Rodriguez RC	4.00
39 Tony Pena Jr. RC	.50
40 Miguel Cabrera RC	50.00
41 Asdrubal Oropeza RC	.50
42 Junior Zamora RC	.50
43 Jovanny Cedeno RC	.50
44 John Sneed RC	.50
45 Josh Kalinowski RC	.50
46 Mike Young RC	8.00
47 Rico Washington RC	.50
48 Chad Durbin RC	.50
49 Junior Brignac RC	.50
50 Carlos Hernandez RC	.50
51 Cesar Izturis RC	1.00
52 Oscar Salazar RC	.50
53 Pat Strange RC	.50
54 Rick Asadoorian RC	.50
55 Keith Reed RC	.50
56 Leo Estrella RC	.50
57 Wascar Serrano RC	.50
58 Richard Gomez RC	.50
59 Ramon Santiago RC	.50
60 Jovanny Sosa RC	.50
61 Aaron Rowand RC	3.00
62 Junior Guerrero RC	.50
63 Luis Terrero RC	.75
64 Brian Sanches RC	.50
65 Scott Sobkowiak RC	.50
66 Gary Majewski RC	.50
67 Barry Zito	2.00
68 Ryan Christianson RC	.50
69 Cristian Guerrero RC	.50
70 Tomas de la Rosa RC	.50

71 Andrew Beinbrink RC	.50
72 Ryan Knox RC	.50
73 Alex Graman RC	.50
74 Juan Guzman RC	.50
75 Ruben Salazar RC	.50
76 Luis Matos RC	.75
77 Tony Mota RC	.50
78 Doug Davis RC	.75
79 Ben Christensen RC	.50
80 Mike Lamb	.50
81 Adrian Gonzalez RC (Draft Picks)	5.00
82 Mike Stodolka RC (Draft Picks)	.50
83 Adam Johnson RC (Draft Picks)	.50
84 Matt Wheatland RC (Draft Picks)	.50
85 Corey Smith RC (Draft Picks)	.75
86 Rocco Baldelli RC (Draft Picks)	4.00
87 Keith Bucktrot RC (Draft Picks)	.50
88 Adam Wainwright RC (Draft Picks)	5.00
89 Scott Thorman RC (Draft Picks)	2.00
90 Tripper Johnson RC (Draft Picks)	.75
91 Jim Edmonds	.50
92 Masato Yoshii	.25
93 Adam Kennedy	.25
94 Darryl Kile	.25
95 Mark McLemore	.25
96 Ricky Gutierrez	.25
97 Juan Gonzalez	.50
98 Melvin Mora	.25
99 Dante Bichette	.25
100 Lee Stevens	.25
101 Roger Cedeno	.25
102 John Olerud	.40
103 Eric Young	.25
104 Mickey Morandini	.25
105 Travis Lee	.25
106 Greg Vaughn	.25
107 Todd Zeile	.25
108 Chuck Finley	.25
109 Ismael Valdes	.25
110 Ron Henika	.25
111 Pat Hentgen	.25
112 Ryan Klesko	.40
113 Derek Bell	.25
114 Hideo Nomo	1.00
115 Aaron Sele	.25
116 Fernando Vina	.25
117 Wally Joyner	.25
118 Brian Hunter	.25
119 Joe Girardi	.25
120 Omar Daal	.25
121 Brook Fordyce	.25
122 Jose Valentin	.25
123 Curt Schilling	.75
124 B.J. Surhoff	.25
125 Henry Rodriguez	.25
126 Mike Bordick	.25
127 David Justice	.50
128 Charles Johnson	.25
129 Will Clark	.75
130 Dwight Gooden	.25
131 David Segui	.25
132 Denny Neagle	.25
133 Andy Ashby	.25
134 Bruce Chen	.25
135 Jason Bere	.25

FanFest Honus Wagner T206 Reprint

WAGNER, PITTSBURG

In conjunction with the forthcoming sale of the finest-known T206 Honus Wagner card in July, 2000, Topps produced this reprint as a promotional device for the seller (Robert Edwards Auction) and principal venue (eBay). The card was distributed at the All-Star FanFest in Atlanta. Front of the 1-1/2" x 2-5/8" card re-

produces the 1909 Wagner card. The black-and-white back details the history of the card and makes note of the upcoming sale.

	NM/M
Honus Wagner	5.00

2000 Topps Gallery

The base set consists of 150 cards. Cards 101-150 are broken down into two subsets Masters of the Game (20 cards) and Students of the Game (30 cards). The subset cards are found one per pack. Card fronts have a tan textured border around the player photo with the player name, team and Gallery logo stamped in gold foil. Card backs have a small photo, brief career note and the featured player's '99 statistics. Gallery was a hobby exclusive product. Five-card packs carried a $3 SRP.

	NM/M
Complete Set (150):	40.00
Common Player:	.15
Common (101-150):	.50
Inserted 1:1	
Pack (6):	2.00
Wax Box (24):	40.00
1 Nomar Garciaparra	1.50
2 Kevin Millwood	.25
3 Jay Bell	.15
4 Rusty Greer	.15
5 Bernie Williams	.50
6 Barry Larkin	.25
7 Carlos Beltran	.25
8 Damion Easley	.15
9 Magglio Ordonez	.25
10 Matt Williams	.20
11 Shannon Stewart	.15
12 Ray Lankford	.15
13 Vinny Castilla	.20
14 Miguel Tejada	.25
15 Craig Biggio	.25
16 Chipper Jones	1.00
17 Albert Belle	.20
18 Doug Glanville	.15
19 Brian Giles	.25
20 Shawn Green	.25
21 J.T. Snow Jr.	.15
22 Luis Gonzalez	.25
23 Carlos Delgado	.50
24 J.D. Drew	.25
25 Ivan Rodriguez	.50
26 Tino Martinez	.25
27 Erubiel Durazo	.20
28 Scott Rolen	.50
29 Gary Sheffield	.40
30 Manny Ramirez	.50
31 Luis Castillo	.15
32 Fernando Tatis	.15
33 Darin Erstad	.25
34 Tim Hudson	.25
35 Sammy Sosa	1.00
36 Jason Kendall	.25
37 Todd Walker	.15
38 Orlando Hernandez	.25
39 Pokey Reese	.15
40 Mike Piazza	1.00
41 B.J. Surhoff	.15
42 Tony Gwynn	.75
43 Kevin Brown	.25
44 Preston Wilson	.25
45 Kenny Lofton	.25
46 Rondell White	.20
47 Frank Thomas	.50
48 Neifi Perez	.15
49 Edgardo Alfonzo	.25
50 Ken Griffey Jr.	1.00
51 Barry Bonds	1.50
52 Brian Jordan	.15
53 Raul Mondesi	.25
54 Troy Glaus	.50
55 Curt Schilling	.40
56 Mike Mussina	.50
57 Brian Daubach	.15
58 Roger Clemens	1.00
59 Carlos Febles	.15

60 Todd Helton	.50
61 Mark Grace	.40
62 Randy Johnson	.75
63 Jeff Bagwell	.50
64 Tom Glavine	.25
65 Adrian Beltre	.20
66 Rafael Palmeiro	.50
67 Paul O'Neill	.25
68 Robin Ventura	.25
69 Ray Durham	.15
70 Mark McGwire	1.50
71 Greg Vaughn	.15
72 Javy Lopez	.25
73 Jeromy Burnitz	.15
74 Mike Lieberthal	.15
75 Cal Ripken Jr.	2.00
76 Juan Gonzalez	.50
77 Sean Casey	.25
78 Jermaine Dye	.15
79 John Olerud	.25
80 Jose Canseco	.40
81 Eric Karros	.20
82 Roberto Alomar	.40
83 Ben Grieve	.15
84 Greg Maddux	1.00
85 Pedro Martinez	.75
86 Tony Clark	.15
87 Richie Sexson	.25
88 Cliff Floyd	.15
89 Eric Chavez	.25
90 Andruw Jones	.50
91 Vladimir Guerrero	.50
92 Alex Gonzalez	.15
93 Jim Thome	.50
94 Bob Abreu	.25
95 Derek Jeter	2.00
96 Larry Walker	.25
97 John Smoltz	.25
98 Mo Vaughn	.20
99 Jason Giambi	.50
100 Alex Rodriguez	1.50
101 Mark McGwire (Masters of the Game)	2.50
102 Sammy Sosa (Masters of the Game)	1.50
103 Alex Rodriguez (Masters of the Game)	2.50
104 Derek Jeter (Masters of the Game)	3.00
105 Greg Maddux (Masters of the Game)	1.50
106 Jeff Bagwell (Masters of the Game)	.75
107 Nomar Garciaparra (Masters of the Game)	2.00
108 Mike Piazza (Masters of the Game)	1.50
109 Pedro Martinez (Masters of the Game)	1.00
110 Chipper Jones (Masters of the Game)	1.50
111 Randy Johnson (Masters of the Game)	1.00
112 Barry Bonds (Masters of the Game)	2.50
113 Ken Griffey Jr. (Masters of the Game)	1.50
114 Manny Ramirez (Masters of the Game)	.75
115 Ivan Rodriguez (Masters of the Game)	.75
116 Juan Gonzalez (Masters of the Game)	.75
117 Vladimir Guerrero (Masters of the Game)	.75
118 Tony Gwynn (Masters of the Game)	1.00
119 Larry Walker (Masters of the Game)	.50
120 Cal Ripken Jr. (Masters of the Game)	3.00
121 Josh Hamilton (Students of the Game)	.50
122 Corey Patterson (Students of the Game)	.50
123 Pat Burrell (Students of the Game)	.50
124 Nick Johnson (Students of the Game)	.50
125 Adam Piatt (Students of the Game)	.50
126 Rick Ankiel (Students of the Game)	.50
127 A.J. Burnett (Students of the Game)	.50
128 Ben Petrick (Students of the Game)	.50
129 Rafael Furcal (Students of the Game)	.75
130 Alfonso Soriano (Students of the Game)	2.00
131 Dee Brown (Students of the Game)	.50
132 Ruben Mateo (Students of the Game)	.50
133 Pablo Ozuna (Students of the Game)	.50
134 Sean Burroughs (Students of the Game)	.75
135 Mark Mulder (Students of the Game)	.75
136 Jason Jennings (Students of the Game)	.50
137 Eric Munson (Students of the Game)	.50
138 Vernon Wells (Students of the Game)	.50

139 Brett Myers RC (Students of the Game)	3.00
140 Ben Christensen RC (Students of the Game)	.50
141 Bobby Bradley RC (Students of the Game)	.50
142 Ruben Salazar RC (Students of the Game)	.50
143 Ryan Christianson RC (Students of the Game)	.50
144 Corey Myers RC (Students of the Game)	.50
145 Aaron Rowand RC (Students of the Game)	1.00
146 Julio Zuleta RC (Students of the Game)	.50
147 Kurt Ainsworth RC (Students of the Game)	1.00
148 Scott Downs RC (Students of the Game)	.50
149 Larry Bigbie RC (Students of the Game)	1.50
150 Chance Caple RC (Students of the Game)	.50

Players Private Issue

A parallel to the 150-card base set, Players Private Issue differ from the base cards with silver foil stamping on the card front and "Players Private Issue" stamped in silver foil across the card bottom. Card backs are serial numbered in an edition of 250 sets.

Stars (1-100):	4-8X
SPs (101-150):	2-4X
Production 250 Sets	

Autographs

This five-card set features top prospects. Each card is stamped with the Topps Certified Autograph Issue logo and the Topps Authentication sticker. Autographs are seeded 1:153 packs.

	NM/M
Common Player:	5.00
Inserted 1:153	
RA Rick Ankiel	5.00
RM Ruben Mateo	5.00
CP Corey Patterson	20.00
BP Ben Petrick	5.00
VW Vernon Wells	15.00

Gallery Exhibits

This 30-card set traces the history of art from medieval to contemporary. Card fronts have gold foil stamping and the card backs are numbered with a "GE" prefix and are found 1:18 packs.

	NM/M
Complete Set (30):	50.00
Common Player:	.50
Inserted 1:18	

1 Mark McGwire	5.00
2 Jeff Bagwell	1.50
3 Mike Piazza	3.00
4 Alex Rodriguez	4.00
5 Nomar Garciaparra	4.00
6 Ivan Rodriguez	1.50
7 Chipper Jones	3.00
8 Cal Ripken Jr.	6.00
9 Tony Gwynn	2.00
10 Jose Canseco	1.00
11 Albert Belle	.50
12 Greg Maddux	3.00
13 Barry Bonds	5.00
14 Ken Griffey Jr.	3.00
15 Juan Gonzalez	1.50
16 Rickey Henderson	1.00
17 Craig Biggio	.75
18 Vladimir Guerrero	1.50
19 Rey Ordonez	.50
20 Roberto Alomar	1.00
21 Derek Jeter	6.00
22 Manny Ramirez	1.50
23 Shawn Green	1.00
24 Sammy Sosa	3.00
25 Larry Walker	1.00
26 Pedro Martinez	2.00
27 Randy Johnson	2.00
28 Pat Burrell	1.00
29 Josh Hamilton	1.00
30 Corey Patterson	1.00

Heroes

This 10-card set is printed on an acetate stock that simulates stained glass. Gallery of Heroes are found on the average of 1:24 packs and are numbered with a "GH" prefix on the card back.

	NM/M
Complete Set (10):	20.00
Common Player:	1.00
Inserted 1:24	
1 Alex Rodriguez	3.00
2 Chipper Jones	2.00
3 Pedro Martinez	1.50
4 Sammy Sosa	2.00
5 Mark McGwire	3.00
6 Nomar Garciaparra	3.00
7 Vladimir Guerrero	1.00
8 Ken Griffey Jr.	2.00
9 Mike Piazza	2.00
10 Derek Jeter	4.00

Press Plates

The aluminum press plates used to print the Gallery cards were inserted at a rate of one per 1,200 packs. Each card's front and back can be found in four different color variations. Because of the unique nature of each plate, assignment of catalog values in not feasible.

	NM/M
Common Player:	50.00

Proof Positive

This 10-card set features both positive and negative photography. Done on a horizontal format the inserts pair a current star with a top prospect at the same position. Printed on a clear polycarbonate stock they were inserted 1:48 packs and are numbered with a "P" prefix.

		NM/M
Complete Set (10):		40.00
Common Player:		3.00
Inserted 1:48		
1	Ken Griffey Jr., Ruben Mateo	4.00
2	Derek Jeter, Alfonso Soriano	6.00
3	Mark McGwire, Pat Burrell	6.00
4	Pedro Martinez, A.J. Burnett	3.00
5	Alex Rodriguez, Rafael Furcal	6.00
6	Sammy Sosa, Corey Patterson	4.00
7	Randy Johnson, Rick Ankiel	3.00
8	Chipper Jones, Adam Piatt	4.00
9	Nomar Garciaparra, Pablo Ozuna	6.00
10	Mike Piazza, Eric Munson	4.00

Topps Heritage

Twenty current players are artistically depicted using the 1954 Topps card design as a template. They are seeded 1:12 packs and are numbered on the card back with a "TGH" prefix. As an added bonus the original artwork used in the development of the set is available through the Topps Gallery Auction. Auction points cards are found in every pack of Gallery.

		NM/M
Complete Set (20):		100.00
Common Player:		2.00
Inserted 1:12		
Proofs:		1-2X
Inserted 1:27		
1	Mark McGwire	12.00
2	Sammy Sosa	8.00
3	Greg Maddux	8.00
4	Mike Piazza	8.00
5	Ivan Rodriguez	4.00
6	Manny Ramirez	4.00
7	Jeff Bagwell	4.00
8	Sean Casey	2.00
9	Orlando Hernandez	4.00
10	Randy Johnson	5.00
11	Pedro Martinez	5.00
12	Vladimir Guerrero	4.00
13	Shawn Green	2.50
14	Ken Griffey Jr.	8.00
15	Alex Rodriguez	12.00
16	Nomar Garciaparra	10.00
17	Derek Jeter	15.00
18	Tony Gwynn	5.00
19	Chipper Jones	8.00
20	Cal Ripken Jr.	15.00

Lithos

Eight cards from the Topps Gallery set were issued in the form of limited edition lithographs by Bill Goff Inc. Measuring 18" x 25", the lithographs were each produced in an edition of 600, with 60 artist's proofs. Issue price on the lithos was $80 for single-player pieces and $100 for the multi-player prints.

		NM/M
Complete Set (8):		675.00
Common Player:		80.00
(1)	Shawn Green (1954 Topps Style)	80.00
(2)	Ken Griffey Jr. (1954 Topps Style)	80.00
(3)	Chipper Jones (1954 Topps Style)	80.00
(4)	Pedro Martinez (1954 Topps Style)	80.00
(5)	Alex Rodriguez (1954 Topps Style)	80.00
(6)	Ivan Rodriguez (1954 Topps Style)	80.00
(7)	Three of a Kind (Nomar Garciaparra, Alex Rodriguez, Derek Jeter)	100.00
(8)	Torre's Terrors (Paul O'Neill, Derek Jeter, Bernie Williams, Tino Martinez)	100.00

2000 Topps Gold Label Pre-Production

A Derek Jeter card in each of the three classes of Gold Label was produced as a promo and distributed in three-card cello packs.

		NM/M
Complete Set (3):		7.50
Common Card:		3.00
PP1	Derek Jeter/Btg	3.00
PP2	Derek Jeter/Fielding	3.00
PP3	Derek Jeter/Running	3.00

2000 Topps Gold Label Class 1

Each base card in the 100-card set has three different classes, each noted on the card back below the featured player's team logo. Each base card is also printed on 35-point rainbow styrene stock with gold foil stamping. Besides the notation on the card back, Class 1's can also be identified by the action in the background photo. Hitters are hitting and pitchers are at the start of their wind-up. A Gold die-cut parallel is also randomly numbered to 100.

	NM/M
Complete Set (100):	25.00
Common Player:	.25
Gold Parallel:	4-8X
Production 100 Sets	
Pack (3):	2.00
Wax Box (24):	30.00
1 Sammy Sosa	1.50
2 Greg Maddux	1.50
3 Dee Brown	.25
4 Rondell White	.40
5 Fernando Tatis	.25
6 Troy Glaus	.75
7 Nick Johnson	.40
8 Albert Belle	.30
9 Scott Rolen	.75
10 Rafael Palmeiro	.50
11 Tony Gwynn	1.00
12 Kevin Brown	.40
13 Roberto Alomar	.50
14 John Olerud	.40
15 Rick Ankiel	.25
16 Chipper Jones	1.50
17 Craig Biggio	.40
18 Mark Mulder	.40
19 Carlos Delgado	.75
20 Alex Gonzalez	.25
21 Gabe Kapler	.25
22 Derek Jeter	3.00
23 Carlos Beltran	.40
24 Todd Helton	.75
25 Mark McGwire	2.50
26 Ben Grieve	.25
27 Rafael Furcal	.25
28 Vernon Wells	.40
29 Greg Vaughn	.25
30 Vladimir Guerrero	.75
31 Mike Piazza	1.50
32 Roger Clemens	2.00
33 Barry Larkin	.40
34 Pedro Martinez	1.00
35 Matt Williams	.30
36 Mo Vaughn	.30
37 Tim Hudson	.40
38 Andruw Jones	.75
39 Vinny Castilla	.25
40 Frank Thomas	1.50
41 Pokey Reese	.25
42 Corey Patterson	.40
43 Jeromy Burnitz	.25
44 Preston Wilson	.40
45 Juan Gonzalez	.75
46 Brian Giles	.40
47 Todd Walker	.25
48 Magglio Ordonez	.40
49 Alfonso Soriano	1.00
50 Ken Griffey Jr.	1.50
51 Michael Barrett	.25
52 Shawn Green	.50
53 Erubiel Durazo	.40
54 Adam Piatt	.25
55 Pat Burrell	.50
56 Mike Mussina	.50
57 Bernie Williams	.75
58 Sean Casey	.40
59 Randy Johnson	1.00
60 Jeff Bagwell	.75
61 Eric Chavez	.50
62 Josh Hamilton	.50
63 A.J. Burnett	.25
64 Jim Thome	.75
65 Raul Mondesi	.40
66 Jason Kendall	.40
67 Mike Lieberthal	.25
68 Robin Ventura	.40
69 Ivan Rodriguez	.50
70 Larry Walker	.40
71 Eric Munson	.25
72 Brian Jordan	.25
73 Edgardo Alfonzo	.25
74 Curt Schilling	.50
75 Nomar Garciaparra	2.00
76 Mark Grace	.50
77 Shannon Stewart	.25
78 J.D. Drew	.40
79 Jack Cust	.25
80 Cal Ripken Jr.	3.00
81 Bob Abreu	.40
82 Ruben Mateo	.25
83 Orlando Hernandez	.25
84 Kris Benson	.25
85 Barry Bonds	2.50
86 Manny Ramirez	.75
87 Jose Canseco	.50
88 Sean Burroughs	.50
89 Kevin Millwood	.40
90 Alex Rodriguez	2.50
91 Brett Myers RC	3.00
92 Rick Asadoorian RC	.40
93 Ben Christensen RC	.40
94 Bobby Bradley RC	.50
95 Corey Myers RC	.50
96 Brad Baisley RC	.50
97 Aaron McNeal RC	.50
98 Aaron Rowand RC	.75
99 Scott Downs RC	.40
100 Michael Tejera RC	.40

Class 2

Each base card in the 100-card set has three different classes, each noted on the card back below the featured player's team logo. Each base card is also printed on 35-point rainbow styrene stock with gold foil stamping. Besides the notation on the card back, Class 2's can also be identified by the action in the background photo. Hitters are fielding and pitchers are in a throwing motion. A Gold

die-cut parallel is also randomly seeded and are serially numbered to 100.

Same prices as Class 1.
| Gold Parallel: | 4-8X |

Class 3

Each base card in the 100-card set has three different classes, each noted on the card back below the featured player's team logo. Each base card is also printed on 35-point rainbow styrene stock with gold foil stamping. Besides the notation on the card back, Class 3's can also be identified by the action in the background photo. Hitters are running and pitchers are in their follow through. A Gold die-cut parallel is also randomly seeded and are serially numbered to 100.

Same prices as Class 1.
| Gold Parallel: | 4-8X |
| Production 100 Sets | |

Bullion

This 10-card set features three teammates superimposed over their team logo on a gold holo-foiled front with gold foil stamping. They are seeded 1:53 packs and are numbered on the card back with a "B" prefix.

		NM/M
Complete Set (10):		125.00
Common Player:		4.00
Inserted 1:53		
1	Jim Thome, Manny Ramirez, Roberto Alomar	6.00
2	Derek Jeter, Orlando Hernandez, Bernie Williams	15.00
3	Chipper Jones, Andruw Jones, Greg Maddux	12.00
4	Alex Rodriguez, Jay Buhner, John Olerud	20.00
5	Nomar Garciaparra, Pedro Martinez, Brian Daubach	15.00
6	Mark McGwire, J.D. Drew, Rick Ankiel	20.00
7	Sammy Sosa, Mark Grace, Kerry Wood	15.00
8	Ken Griffey Jr., Sean Casey, Barry Larkin	20.00
9	Mike Piazza, Edgardo Alfonzo, Robin Ventura	15.00
10	Randy Johnson, Matt Williams, Erubiel Durazo	6.00

End of the Rainbow

This 15-card set highlights some of baseball's top prospects on a silver holo foiled card front with gold foil stamping. Card backs are numbered with an "ER" prefix and are seeded 1:11 packs.

		NM/M
Complete Set (15):		8.00
Common Player:		.50
Inserted 1:11		
1	Pat Burrell	1.50
2	Corey Patterson	1.00
3	Josh Hamilton	1.00
4	Eric Munson	.50
5	Sean Burroughs	.75
6	Jack Cust	.50
7	Rafael Furcal	.75
8	Ruben Salazar	.50
9	Brett Myers	1.00
10	Wes Anderson	.50
11	Nick Johnson	1.00
12	Scott Downs	.50
13	Choo Freeman	.50
14	Brad Baisley	.50
15	A.J. Burnett	.75

Prospector's Dream

These inserts feature 10 players whose success was projected early in their careers. Card fronts feature gold holo foil with the player name, Gold Label logo and insert name stamped in gold foil. Card backs are numbered with an "PD" prefix. They are inserted 1:26 packs.

		NM/M
Complete Set (10):		15.00
Common Player:		.50
Inserted 1:26		
1	Mark McGwire	3.00
2	Alex Rodriguez	3.00
3	Nomar Garciaparra	3.00
4	Pat Burrell	.75
5	Todd Helton	1.00
6	Derek Jeter	4.00
7	Adam Piatt	.50
8	Chipper Jones	2.00
9	Shawn Green	.75
10	Josh Hamilton	1.00

The Treasury

This 25-card set spotlights 15 veterans and 10 prospects on a silver holo foiled front with gold foil stamping. They have an insertion ratio of 1:21 packs and are numbered on the card back with a "T" prefix.

		NM/M
Complete Set (25):		40.00
Common Player:		.50
Inserted 1:21		
1	Ken Griffey Jr.	3.00
2	Derek Jeter	6.00
3	Chipper Jones	3.00
4	Manny Ramirez	1.50
5	Nomar Garciaparra	4.00
6	Sammy Sosa	3.00
7	Cal Ripken Jr.	6.00
8	Alex Rodriguez	5.00
9	Mike Piazza	3.00
10	Pedro Martinez	2.00
11	Vladimir Guerrero	1.50
12	Jeff Bagwell	1.50
13	Shawn Green	1.00
14	Greg Maddux	3.00
15	Mark McGwire	5.00
16	Josh Hamilton	1.00
17	Corey Patterson	1.00
18	Dee Brown	.50
19	Rafael Furcal	.75
20	Pat Burrell	1.00
21	Alfonso Soriano	3.00
22	Adam Piatt	.50
23	A.J. Burnett	.75
24	Mark Mulder	.75
25	Ruben Mateo	.50

Name Mismatches

Because of faulty alignment when the gold-foil logo and player name were applied to card fronts, some Gold Label cards are found with the wrong name on front. Because each of these error cards is rare or possibly unique, and the demand is dependent on the combination of photo and name, it is not possible to assign values.

2000 Topps HD

This super-premium product consists of 100 regular base cards comprised of 88 veterans and 12 rookies. The base cards feature hyper-color technology and printed on a very thick 50-pt. card stock. Card backs have a small photo, career highlight and complete year-by-year statistics. A Platinum parallel to the base set is also randomly seeded and are sequentially numbered to 99 sets.

	NM/M
Complete Set (100):	30.00
Common Player:	.25

Platinums:	4-8X
Production 99 Sets	
Pack (4):	1.50
Wax Box (20):	30.00
1 Derek Jeter	3.00
2 Andruw Jones	.75
3 Ben Grieve	.25
4 Carlos Beltran	.40
5 Randy Johnson	1.00
6 Javy Lopez	.40
7 Gary Sheffield	.50
8 John Olerud	.25
9 Vinny Castilla	.25
10 Barry Larkin	.40
11 Tony Clark	.25
12 Roberto Alomar	.50
13 Brian Jordan	.25
14 Wade Boggs	.50
15 Carlos Febles	.25
16 Alfonso Soriano	1.50
17 A.J. Burnett	.25
18 Matt Williams	.25
19 Alex Gonzalez	.25
20 Larry Walker	.40
21 Jeff Bagwell	.75
22 Al Leiter	.25
23 Ken Griffey Jr.	1.50
24 Ruben Mateo	.25
25 Mark Grace	.40
26 Carlos Delgado	.75
27 Vladimir Guerrero	.75
28 Kenny Lofton	.40
29 Rusty Greer	.25
30 Pedro Martinez	1.00
31 Todd Helton	.75
32 Ray Lankford	.25
33 Jose Canseco	.50
34 Raul Mondesi	.40
35 Mo Vaughn	.40
36 Eric Chavez	.40
37 Manny Ramirez	.75
38 Jason Kendall	.40
39 Mike Mussina	.50
40 Dante Bichette	.25
41 Troy Glaus	.75
42 Rickey Henderson	.50
43 Pablo Ozuna	.25
44 Michael Barrett	.25
45 Tony Gwynn	1.00
46 John Smoltz	.40
47 Rafael Palmeiro	.50
48 Curt Schilling	.50
49 Todd Walker	.25
50 Greg Vaughn	.25
51 Orlando Hernandez	.25
52 Jim Thome	.75
53 Pat Burrell	.50
54 Tim Salmon	.40
55 Tom Glavine	.40
56 Travis Lee	.25
57 Gabe Kapler	.25
58 Greg Maddux	1.50
59 Scott Rolen	.75
60 Cal Ripken Jr.	3.00
61 Preston Wilson	.40
62 Ivan Rodriguez	.50
63 Johnny Damon	.40
64 Bernie Williams	.50
65 Barry Bonds	2.50
66 Sammy Sosa	1.50
67 Robin Ventura	.40
68 Tony Fernandez	.25
69 Jay Bell	.25
70 Mark McGwire	2.50
71 Jeromy Burnitz	.25
72 Chipper Jones	1.50
73 Josh Hamilton	.25
74 Darin Erstad	.40
75 Alex Rodriguez	2.50
76 Sean Casey	.40
77 Tino Martinez	.40
78 Juan Gonzalez	.75
79 Cliff Floyd	.25
80 Craig Biggio	.40
81 Shawn Green	.50
82 Adrian Beltre	.25
83 Mike Piazza	1.50
84 Nomar Garciaparra	2.00
85 Kevin Brown	.40
86 Roger Clemens	2.00
87 Frank Thomas	.75
88 Albert Belle	.25
89 Erubiel Durazo	.25
90 David Walling	.50
91 John Sneed RC	.50
92 Larry Bigbie RC	1.50
93 B.J. Garbe RC	.75
94 Bobby Bradley RC	.75
95 Ryan Christianson RC	.50
96 Jay Gerhke RC	.50
97 Jason Stumm RC	.50
98 Brett Myers RC	4.00
99 Chance Caple RC	.50
100 Corey Myers RC	.75

Autographs

This two-card set features Cal Ripken Jr. and Derek Jeter. Card fronts include the Topps "Certified Autograph Issue" logo stamp as well as the Topps 3M authentication sticker to verify its authenticity. The insert rate for Jeter is 1:859 and Ripken Jr. 1:4,386.

NM/M
Jeter 1:859
Ripken 1:4,386

1 Derek Jeter	150.00
2 Cal Ripken Jr.	250.00

Ballpark Figures

This 10-card set features a baseball field designed die-cut. These are seeded 1:11 packs and are numbered with a "BF" prefix on the card back.

		NM/M
Complete Set (10):		15.00
Common Player:		.50
Inserted 1:11		
1	Mark McGwire	3.00
2	Ken Griffey Jr.	2.00
3	Nomar Garciaparra	3.00
4	Derek Jeter	4.00
5	Sammy Sosa	2.00
6	Mike Piazza	2.00
7	Juan Gonzalez	1.00
8	Larry Walker	.75
9	Ben Grieve	.50
10	Barry Bonds	3.00

Clearly Refined

This 10-card set focuses on baseball's top young stars heading into the 2000 season. They are printed on high definition card stock and are seeded 1:20 packs. These are numbered with a "CR" prefix on the card back.

		NM/M
Complete Set (10):		8.00
Common Player:		.50
Inserted 1:20		
1	Alfonso Soriano	3.00
2	Ruben Mateo	.50
3	Josh Hamilton	.75
4	Chad Hermansen	.50
5	Ryan Anderson	.50
6	Nick Johnson	1.00
7	Octavio Dotel	.50
8	Peter Bergeron	.50
9	Adam Piatt	.50
10	Pat Burrell	2.00

Image

This 10-card insert set highlights those batters with the best eyes at the plate. These were seeded 1:44 packs and are numbered with a "HD" prefix on the card back.

		NM/M
Complete Set (10):		30.00
Common Player:		1.00
Inserted 1:44		
1	Sammy Sosa	3.00
2	Mark McGwire	5.00
3	Derek Jeter	6.00
4	Albert Belle	1.00
5	Vladimir Guerrero	1.50
6	Ken Griffey Jr.	3.00
7	Mike Piazza	3.00
8	Alex Rodriguez	5.00
9	Barry Bonds	5.00
10	Nomar Garciaparra	4.00

HD On The Cutting Edge

This 10-card insert set is die-cut down the right hand side of the card highlighting the five-tool stars top five baseball attributes. These are inserted 1:22 packs and are numbered with a "CE" prefix on the card back.

		NM/M
Complete Set (10):		15.00
Common Player:		.50
Inserted 1:22		
1	Andruw Jones	1.00
2	Nomar Garciaparra	3.00
3	Barry Bonds	3.00
4	Larry Walker	.50
5	Vladimir Guerrero	1.00
6	Jeff Bagwell	1.00
7	Derek Jeter	4.00
8	Sammy Sosa	2.00
9	Alex Rodriguez	3.00
10	Ken Griffey Jr.	2.00

Opening Day 2K

As part of a multi-manufacturer promotion, Topps issued eight cards of an "Opening Day 2K" set. Packages containing some of the 32 cards in the issue were distributed by MLB teams early in the season. The cards were also available exclusively as inserts in Topps Opening Day packs sold at KMart stores early in the season. The Topps OD2K cards have goldfoil graphic highlights on front. Backs have portrait photos, stats and are numbered with an "OD" prefix.

		NM/M
Complete Set (8):		6.00
Common Player:		.50
1	Mark McGwire	2.00
2	Barry Bonds	.75
3	Ivan Rodriguez	.75
4	Sean Casey	.65
5	Derek Jeter	1.00
6	Vladimir Guerrero	1.00
7	Preston Wilson	.65
8	Ben Grieve	.20

2000 Topps Stars

The base set consists of 200 cards, including a 50-card Spotlights subset (151-200). Card fronts have a shadow image of the featured player in the background of the player photo. The Topps Stars logo, player name, team logo and position are stamped in silver foil.

	NM/M
Complete Set (200):	35.00
Common Player:	.10
Pack (6):	2.00
Box (24):	40.00
1 Vladimir Guerrero	.75
2 Eric Karros	.10
3 Omar Vizquel	.20
4 Ken Griffey Jr.	1.50
5 Preston Wilson	.20
6 Albert Belle	.20
7 Ryan Klesko	.10
8 Bob Abreu	.10
9 Warren Morris	.10
10 Rafael Palmeiro	.40
11 Nomar Garciaparra	2.00
12 Dante Bichette	.10
13 Jeff Cirillo	.10
14 Carlos Beltran	.10
15 Tony Clark	.10
16 Ray Durham	.10
17 Mark McGwire	2.00
18 Jim Thome	.50
19 Todd Walker	.10
20 Richie Sexson	.40
21 Adrian Beltre	.10
22 Jay Bell	.10
23 Craig Biggio	.25
24 Ben Grieve	.15
25 Greg Maddux	1.50
26 Fernando Tatis	.10
27 Jeromy Burnitz	.10
28 Vinny Castilla	.10
29 Mark Grace	.25
30 Derek Jeter	2.00
31 Larry Walker	.25
32 Ivan Rodriguez	.50
33 Curt Schilling	.40
34 Mike Lamb RC	.25
35 Kevin Brown	.20
36 Andruw Jones	.40
37 Chris Mears RC	.10
38 Bartolo Colon	.10
39 Edgardo Alfonzo	.15
40 Brady Anderson	.20
41 Andres Galarraga	.25
42 Scott Rolen	.50
43 Manny Ramirez	.75
44 Carlos Delgado	.50
45 David Cone	.10
46 Carl Everett	.10
47 Chipper Jones	1.50
48 Barry Bonds	2.00
49 Dean Palmer	.10
50 Frank Thomas	.75
51 Paul O'Neill	.25
52 Mo Vaughn	.20
53 Todd Helton	.50
54 Jason Giambi	1.00
55 Brian Jordan	.10
56 Luis Gonzalez	.20
57 Alex Rodriguez	2.00
58 J.D. Drew	.10
59 Javy Lopez	.20
60 Tony Gwynn	1.00
61 Jason Kendall	.10
62 Pedro Martinez	.75
63 Matt Williams	.20
64 Gary Sheffield	.25
65 Roberto Alomar	.40
66 Lyle Overbay RC	1.00
67 Jeff Bagwell	.75
68 Tim Hudson	.40
69 Sammy Sosa	1.50
70 Keith Reed RC	.10
71 Robin Ventura	.20
72 Cal Ripken Jr.	2.50
73 Alex Gonzalez	.10
74 Aaron McNeal RC	.10
75 Mike Lieberthal	.10
76 Brian Giles	.25
77 Kevin Millwood	.20
78 Troy O'Leary	.10
79 Raul Mondesi	.20
80 John Olerud	.20
81 David Justice	.25
82 Erubiel Durazo	.10
83 Shawn Green	.40
84 Tino Martinez	.20
85 Greg Vaughn	.15
86 Tom Glavine	.25
87 Jose Canseco	.40
88 Kenny Lofton	.25
89 Brian Daubach	.10
90 Mike Piazza	1.50
91 Randy Johnson	.75
92 Pokey Reese	.10
93 Troy Glaus	.50
94 Kerry Wood	.25
95 Sean Casey	.20
96 Magglio Ordonez	.40
97 Bernie Williams	.50
98 Juan Gonzalez	.75
99 Barry Larkin	.25
100 Orlando Hernandez	.20
101 Roger Clemens	1.50
102 Bob Gibson (Retired Stars)	.40
103 Gary Carter (Retired Stars)	.10
104 Willie Stargell (Retired Stars)	.10
105 Joe Morgan (Retired Stars)	.40
106 Brooks Robinson (Retired Stars)	.50
107 Ozzie Smith (Retired Stars)	.50
108 Carl Yastrzemski (Retired Stars)	.25
109 Al Kaline (Retired Stars)	.40
110 Frank Robinson (Retired Stars)	.40
111 Lance Berkman (Shining Prospects)	.10
112 Adam Piatt (Shining Prospects)	.20
113 Vernon Wells (Shining Prospects)	.25
114 Rafael Furcal (Shining Prospects)	.25
115 Rick Ankiel (Shining Prospects)	.25
116 Corey Patterson (Shining Prospects)	.40
117 Josh Hamilton (Shining Prospects)	.25
118 Jack Cust (Shining Prospects)	.20
119 Josh Girdley (Shining Prospects)	.10
120 Pablo Ozuna (Shining Prospects)	.10
121 Sean Burroughs (Shining Prospects)	.25
122 Pat Burrell (Shining Prospects)	.25
123 Chad Hermansen (Shining Prospects)	.10
124 Ruben Mateo (Shining Prospects)	.10
125 Ben Petrick (Shining Prospects)	.10
126 Dee Brown (Shining Prospects)	.10
127 Eric Munson (Shining Prospects)	.10
128 Ruben Salazar (Shining Prospects)	.10
129 Kip Wells (Shining Prospects)	.10
130 Alfonso Soriano (Shining Prospects)	1.00
131 Mark Mulder (Shining Prospects)	.25
132 Roosevelt Brown (Shining Prospects)	.10
133 Nick Johnson (Shining Prospects)	.40
134 Kyle Snyder (Shining Prospects)	.10
135 David Walling (Shining Prospects)	.10
136 Geraldo Guzman RC	.25
137 John Sneed RC	.25
138 Ben Christensen RC	.40
139 Corey Myers RC	.25
140 Jose Ortiz RC	3.00
141 Ryan Christianson RC	.25
142 Brett Myers RC	3.00
143 Bobby Bradley RC	.25
144 Rick Asadoorian RC	.25
145 Julio Zuleta RC	.40
146 Ty Howington RC	1.00
147 Josh Kalinowski RC	.40
148 B.J. Garbe RC	.25
149 Scott Downs RC	.40
150 Dan Wright RC	.25
151 Jeff Bagwell (Veterans)	.40
152 Vladimir Guerrero (Veterans)	.50
153 Mike Piazza (Veterans)	1.00
154 Juan Gonzalez (Veterans)	.40
155 Ivan Rodriguez (Veterans)	.40
156 Manny Ramirez (Veterans)	.40
157 Sammy Sosa (Veterans)	1.00
158 Chipper Jones (Veterans)	.75
159 Shawn Green (Veterans)	.20
160 Ken Griffey Jr. (Veterans)	.75
161 Cal Ripken Jr. (Veterans)	1.25
162 Nomar Garciaparra (Veterans)	1.00
163 Derek Jeter (Veterans)	1.00
164 Barry Bonds (Veterans)	1.00
165 Greg Maddux (Veterans)	.75
166 Mark McGwire (Veterans)	1.00
167 Roberto Alomar (Veterans)	.25
168 Alex Rodriguez (Veterans)	1.25
169 Randy Johnson (Veterans)	.40
170 Tony Gwynn (Veterans)	.50
171 Pedro Martinez (Veterans)	.40
172 Bob Gibson (Retired Stars)	.25
173 Gary Carter (Retired Stars)	.10
174 Willie Stargell (Retired Stars)	.25
175 Joe Morgan (Retired Stars)	.25
176 Brooks Robinson (Retired Stars)	.40
177 Ozzie Smith (Retired Stars)	.50
178 Carl Yastrzemski (Retired Stars)	.20
179 Al Kaline (Retired Stars)	.25
180 Frank Robinson (Retired Stars)	.40
181 Adam Piatt (Prospects)	.20
182 Alfonso Soriano (Prospects)	.75
183 Corey Patterson (Prospects)	.25
184 Vernon Wells (Prospects)	.40
185 Pat Burrell (Prospects)	.20
186 Mark Mulder (Prospects)	.10
187 Eric Munson (Prospects)	.10
188 Rafael Furcal (Prospects)	.15
189 Rick Ankiel (Prospects)	.20
190 Ruben Mateo (Prospects)	.10
191 Sean Burroughs (Prospects)	.20
192 Josh Hamilton (Prospects)	.40
193 Brett Myers	1.00
194 Ben Christensen	.20
195 Ty Howington	.25
196 Rick Asadoorian	.20
197 Josh Kalinowski	.20
198 Corey Myers	.25
199 Ryan Christianson	.25
200 John Sneed	.25

Blue

A parallel to the 200-card base set the player shadow has blue tint and the Topps Stars logo, player name, team logo and position are stamped in blue foil. Cards 1-150 are serially numbered on the card back to 299 and cards 151-200 are serially numbered to 99.

Stars (1-150):	3-5X
Production 299 Sets	
Stars (151-180):	4-8X
Rookies (181-200):	2-4X
Production 99 Sets	

All-Star Authority

This 14-card set features a gold and silver holo foiled front with gold etching. Card backs are numbered with an "AS" prefix. They are found on the the average of 1:13 packs.

		NM/M
Complete Set (14):		25.00
Common Player:		1.00
Inserted 1:13		
1	Mark McGwire	3.00
2	Sammy Sosa	2.00
3	Ken Griffey Jr.	2.00
4	Cal Ripken Jr.	4.00
5	Tony Gwynn	1.50
6	Barry Bonds	4.00
7	Mike Piazza	2.00
8	Pedro Martinez	1.50
9	Chipper Jones	2.00
10	Manny Ramirez	1.00
11	Alex Rodriguez	3.00
12	Derek Jeter	4.00
13	Nomar Garciaparra	3.00
14	Roberto Alomar	1.00

Autographs

A combination of retired and current players make up this 13-card set. The set is broken down into two levels: A and B. Level A autographs are seeded 1:382 packs and Level B autographs are found 1:1,636 packs. Each card features the Topps "Certified Autograph Issue" stamp and the Topps "Genuine Issue" sticker on the card back. Card backs are numbered with the featured player's initials.

		NM/M
Common Player:		10.00
Group A 1:382		
Group B 1:1,636		
RA	Rick Ankiel/A	10.00
GC	Gary Carter/B	60.00
RF	Rafael Furcal/A	15.00
BG	Bob Gibson/A	25.00
DJ	Derek Jeter/A	90.00
AK	Al Kaline/B	50.00
KM	Kevin Millwood/A	15.00
JM	Joe Morgan/B	40.00
BR	Brooks Robinson/B	40.00
FR	Frank Robinson/B	20.00
OS	Ozzie Smith/B	35.00
WS	Willie Stargell/B	50.00
CY	Carl Yastrzemski/B	65.00

Game Gear Bats

A piece of the featured player's game-used bat is embedded into the card front and are seeded 1:175 packs.

		NM/M
Common Player:		10.00
Group A 1:2,289		
Group B 1:1,153		
Group C 1:409		
1	Rafael Furcal/C	10.00
2	Sean Burroughs/B	10.00
3	Corey Patterson/B	10.00
4	Chipper Jones/B	40.00
5	Vernon Wells/C	15.00
6	Alfonso Soriano/B	25.00
7	Eric Munson/C	10.00
8	Ben Petrick/A	10.00
9	Dee Brown/A	10.00
10	Lance Berkman/C	15.00

Game Gear Jersey

A piece of the featured player's game-used jersey is

---

embedded into the card front and are seeded 1:382 packs.

		NM/M
Common Player:		10.00
Inserted 1:382		
1	Kevin Millwood	10.00
2	Brad Penny	10.00
3	J.D. Drew	15.00

Progression

Each of the nine cards features three players on a horizontal format, progressing from past, present and future stars at each of the nine positions. They were seeded 1:13 packs and are numbered on the back with an "P" prefix.

		NM/M
Complete Set (9):		15.00
Common Player:		1.00
Inserted 1:13		
1	Bob Gibson, Pedro Martinez, Rick Ankiel	1.50
2	Gary Carter, Mike Piazza, Ben Petrick	2.00
3	Willie Stargell, Mark McGwire, Pat Burrell	3.00
4	Joe Morgan, Roberto Alomar, Ruben Salazar	1.00
5	Brooks Robinson, Chipper Jones, Sean Burroughs	2.00
6	Ozzie Smith, Derek Jeter, Rafael Furcal	3.00
7	Carl Yastrzemski, Barry Bonds, Josh Hamilton	4.00
8	Al Kaline, Ken Griffey Jr., Ruben Mateo	2.00
9	Frank Robinson, Manny Ramirez, Corey Patterson	1.50

Walk of Fame

This 15-card set spotlights the top stars on a silver and gold holo foiled card front. Card backs feature comparative commentary with the all-time best at their respective positions and are numbered with an "WF" prefix. They are seeded 1:8 packs.

		NM/M
Complete Set (15):		15.00
Common Player:		.75
Inserted 1:8		
1	Cal Ripken Jr.	3.00
2	Ken Griffey Jr.	1.50
3	Mark McGwire	2.00
4	Sammy Sosa	1.50
5	Alex Rodriguez	2.00
6	Derek Jeter	2.50
7	Nomar Garciaparra	2.00
8	Chipper Jones	1.50
9	Manny Ramirez	1.00
10	Mike Piazza	1.50

11	Vladimir Guerrero	1.00
12	Barry Bonds	3.00
13	Tony Gwynn	1.00
14	Roberto Alomar	.75
15	Pedro Martinez	1.00

2000 Topps Subway Series Parade Promos

During the October 30 World Series victory parade in New York, Topps randomly distributed a pair of special cards promoting its forthcoming Subway Series boxed set. Besides regular versions of each card, a foil version was also produced in a hand-numbered edition of 1,000 each, with 500 given to Topps employees. Cards have group photos of the team's celebrating on front, with the title in a black band on top, along with a team logo and the subway station number. Backs are in blue and orange on white and have a team logo printed beneath a short post-season summary. At bottom are ads for Topps' Subway Series commemorative set and information on a sweepstakes for 2001 Yankees or Mets tickets.

	NM/M
N.L. Champs	3.00
N.L. Champs (Foil)	6.00
Yankees Win Subway Series	5.00
Yankees Win Subway Series (Foil)	10.00

2000 Topps Subway Series Parade Promos - Mets Win

To cover themselves in the event the Mets had won the 2000 Subway Series against the Yankees, Topps printed up a "Mets Win" card for distribution as a promo for its Subway Series set. When the Yankees won, the Mets Win card was not released. Early in 2002, a quantity (50) of these cards surfaced, reportedly having been given to a Topps employee in 2000. The Mets Win cards are nearly identical to the issued Yankees version, with an on-field celebration group hug on front and information about the Series on back, along with information about the Subway Series card set and other Topps products.

	NM/M
Mets Win Subway Series	90.00

2000 Topps Subway Series

	NM/M
Complete Fact. Set (101):	70.00
Complete Set (100):	20.00
Common Player:	.20
1	Mike Piazza	3.00
2	Jay Payton	.20
3	Edgardo Alfonzo	.40
4	Todd Pratt	.20
5	Todd Zeile	.20
6	Mike Bordick	.20
7	Robin Ventura	.40

Rick Reed — P — 2000 New York City Subway Series

8	Benny Agbayani	.20
9	Timo Perez	.50
10	Kurt Abbott	.20
11	Matt Franco	.20
12	Bubba Trammell	.20
13	Darryl Hamilton	.20
14	Lenny Harris	.20
15	Joe McEwing	.20
16	Mike Hampton	.40
17	Al Leiter	.40
18	Rick Reed	.20
19	Bobby Jones	.20
20	Glendon Rusch	.20
21	Armando Benitez	.20
22	John Franco	.20
23	Rick White	.20
24	Dennis Cook	.20
25	Turk Wendell	.20
26	Bobby Valentine	.20
27	Derek Jeter	4.00
28	Chuck Knoblauch	.40
29	Tino Martinez	.30
30	Jorge Posada	.40
31	Luis Sojo	.20
32	Scott Brosius	.20
33	Chris Turner	.20
34	Bernie Williams	.75
35	David Justice	.75
36	Paul O'Neill	.40
37	Glenallen Hill	.20
38	Jose Vizcaino	.20
39	Luis Polonia	.20
40	Clay Bellinger	.20
41	Orlando Hernandez	.40
42	Roger Clemens	1.50
43	Andy Pettitte	.50
44	Denny Neagle	.20
45	Dwight Gooden	.30
46	David Cone	.20
47	Mariano Rivera	.50
48	Jeff Nelson	.20
49	Mike Stanton	.20
50	Jason Grimsley	.20
51	Jose Canseco	.75
52	Joe Torre	.50
53	Edgardo Alfonzo	.40
54	Darryl Hamilton	.20
55	John Franco	.20
56	Benny Agbayani	.20
57	Bobby Jones	.20
58	New York Mets	.20
59	Bobby Valentine	.20
60	Mike Piazza	3.00
61	Armando Benitez	.20
62	Mike Piazza	3.00
63	Mike Piazza	3.00
64	Todd Zeile	.20
65	Timo Perez	.50
66	Timo Perez	.50
67	Mike Hampton	.40
68	Andy Pettitte	.50
69	Tino Martinez	.30
70	Joe Torre	.50
71	New York Yankees	.40
72	Orlando Hernandez	.40
73	Bernie Williams	.75
74	Andy Pettitte	.50
75	Mariano Rivera	.50
76	New York Yankees	.40
77	Roger Clemens	1.50
78	Derek Jeter	4.00
79	David Justice	.75
80	Mariano Rivera	.50
81	Tino Martinez	.30
82	New York Yankees	.40
83	Jorge Posada	.40
84	Chuck Knoblauch	.40
85	Jose Vizcaino	.20
86	Roger Clemens	1.50
87	Mike Piazza	3.00
88	Clay Bellinger	.20
89	Robin Ventura	.40
90	Benny Agbayani	.20
91	Orlando Hernandez	.40
92	Derek Jeter	4.00
93	Mike Piazza	3.00
94	Mariano Rivera	.50
95	Derek Jeter	3.00
96	Luis Sojo	.20
97	New York Yankees	.40
98	Mike Hampton	.40
99	David Justice	.75
100	Derek Jeter	4.00

Fan Fare

	NM/M
Common Player:	25.00

Mike Piazza — Catcher

	Inserted 1:Set	
1	Timo Perez	35.00
2	Edgardo Alfonzo	40.00
3	Mike Piazza	120.00
4	Robin Ventura	35.00
5	Todd Zeile	25.00
6	Benny Agbayani	25.00
7	Jay Payton	25.00
8	Mike Bordick	25.00
9	Matt Franco	25.00
10	Mike Hampton	40.00
11	Al Leiter	40.00
12	Rick Reed	25.00
13	Bobby Jones	25.00
14	Glendon Rusch	25.00
15	Darryl Hamilton	25.00
16	Turk Wendell	25.00
17	John Franco	25.00
18	Armando Benitez	25.00
19	Chuck Knoblauch	35.00
20	Derek Jeter	200.00
21	David Justice	40.00
22	Bernie Williams	50.00
23	Jorge Posada	40.00
24	Paul O'Neill	50.00
25	Tino Martinez	35.00
26	Luis Sojo	25.00
27	Scott Brosius	25.00
28	Jose Canseco	50.00
29	Orlando Hernandez	35.00
30	Roger Clemens	100.00
31	Andy Pettitte	40.00
32	Denny Neagle	25.00
33	David Cone	25.00
34	Jeff Nelson	25.00
35	Mike Stanton	25.00
36	Mariano Rivera	60.00

2000 Topps TEK

Mike Piazza

Forty-five players make up this set including 5 rookies (41-45). Each card is printed on a transparent, polycarbonate stock with patterns 1-15 featuring silver foil metalization. All 45 players are featured on 20 different player focused background patterns. Card backs have two numbers, the first is the player's card number within the set and the second is the pattern number. Patterns 16-20 have color variations and have an insertion rate of 1:10 packs. Each pack contains 4 TEK cards with an SRP of $5.

		NM/M
Complete Set (45):		25.00
Common Player:		.40
Common Rookie (41-45):		.75
2,000 serial numbered rookies		
Pack (4):		2.00
Box (20):		30.00
1	Mike Piazza	1.50
2	Chipper Jones	1.50
3	Juan Gonzalez	.75
4	Ivan Rodriguez	.50
5	Cal Ripken Jr.	3.00
6	A.J. Burnett	.40
7	Jim Thome	.75
8	Mo Vaughn	.40
9	Andruw Jones	.75
10	Mark McGwire	2.00
11	Jose Canseco	.50
12	Shawn Green	.50
13	Barry Bonds	3.00
14	Bernie Williams	.50
15	Manny Ramirez	.75
16	Greg Maddux	1.50
17	Carlos Beltran	.40
18	Pedro Martinez	1.00
19	Jeff Bagwell	.75

20	Sammy Sosa	2.00
21	J.D. Drew	.40
22	Randy Johnson	1.00
23	Larry Walker	.40
24	Frank Thomas	.75
25	Orlando Hernandez	.40
26	Scott Rolen	.75
27	Tony Gwynn	1.00
28	Rick Ankiel	.40
29	Roberto Alomar	.75
30	Ken Griffey Jr.	1.50
31	Vladimir Guerrero	1.00
32	Derek Jeter	3.00
33	Nomar Garciaparra	2.00
34	Alex Rodriguez	2.50
35	Sean Casey	.40
36	Adam Piatt (Prospects)	.40
37	Corey Patterson (Prospects)	.40
38	Josh Hamilton (Prospects)	.40
39	Pat Burrell (Prospects)	.50
40	Eric Munson (Prospects)	.40
41	Ruben Salazar RC (Rookies)	.75
42	John Sneed RC (Rookies)	.75
43	Josh Girdley RC (Rookies)	.75
44	Brett Myers RC (Rookies)	4.00
45	Rick Asadoorian RC (Rookies)	.75

Color

Ruben Salazar

Color variations make up patterns 16-20 of the base set and instead of metallic silver foil they have a different color background. They are seeded on the average of 1:10 packs.

Patterns 16-20:		1-2X
Inserted 1:10		

Gold

Alex Rodriguez

This parallel to the base set has a rounded top corner and rounded bottom corner with a gold background. Each pattern is serially numbered on the card back in an edition of 10 sets.

Stars:	8-15X
Rookies:	4-8X
Production 10 Sets	

ArchiTEKs

Printed on a clear, polycarbonate card stock the TEK logo, and player name are stamped in gold foil. Card backs are numbered with an "A" prefix. They are found on the average of 1:5 packs.

		NM/M
Complete Set (18):		20.00
Common Player:		.50
Inserted 1:5		
1	Nomar Garciaparra	2.00
2	Derek Jeter	3.00
3	Chipper Jones	1.50
4	Vladimir Guerrero	1.00

ArchiTEKs

5	Mark McGwire	2.50
6	Ken Griffey Jr.	1.50
7	Mike Piazza	1.50
8	Jeff Bagwell	1.00
9	Larry Walker	.50
10	Manny Ramirez	1.00
11	Alex Rodriguez	2.00
12	Sammy Sosa	2.00
13	Shawn Green	.50
14	Juan Gonzalez	.75
15	Barry Bonds	3.00
16	Pedro Martinez	1.00
17	Cal Ripken Jr.	3.00
18	Ivan Rodriguez	.75

DramaTEK Performers

Printed on a clear, polycarbonate stock, the insert name and TEK logo are stamped in blue foil. Card backs are numbered with a "DP" prefix and are seeded 1:10 packs.

		NM/M
Complete Set (9):		15.00
Common Player:		1.00
Inserted 1:10		
1	Mark McGwire	3.00
2	Sammy Sosa	2.50
3	Ken Griffey Jr.	2.00
4	Nomar Garciaparra	3.00
5	Chipper Jones	2.00
6	Mike Piazza	2.00
7	Alex Rodriguez	3.00
8	Derek Jeter	3.00
9	Vladimir Guerrero	1.50

TEKtonics

This nine-card set features baseball's top hitters on a die-cut design on a clear, polycarbonate stock. Card backs are numbered with a "TT" prefix and are inserted 1:30 packs.

		NM/M
Complete Set (9):		35.00
Common Player:		4.00
Inserted 1:30		
1	Derek Jeter	6.00
2	Mark McGwire	6.00
3	Ken Griffey Jr.	4.00
4	Mike Piazza	4.00
5	Alex Rodriguez	6.00
6	Chipper Jones	4.00
7	Nomar Garciaparra	6.00
8	Sammy Sosa	5.00
9	Cal Ripken Jr.	8.00

2001 Topps Promo Cards

Since a 50th anniversary only comes around once, Topps made a big deal in promoting its 2001 baseball card issue with an oversize promo pack. Each gold-foil finfold pack contains eight 9" x 12-1/2" glossy promo cards. Fronts reproduce various cards from the base set, subsets and inserts while backs provide further photos and details.

		NM/M
Complete Set (8):		25.00
Common Player:		3.00
(1)	Hank Aaron (1954 Topps)	7.50
(2)	Johnny Bench (Golden Anniversary Great)	4.00
(3)	Mark McGwire (Base card.)	5.00
(4)	Nolan Ryan (King of Kings)	15.00
(5)	Mike Schmidt (Golden Greats)	4.00
(6)	Bob Gibson, Pedro Martinez (Topps Combos)	3.00
(7)	Checklist	.50
(8)	Header	.50

2001 Topps

		NM/M
Complete Set (790):		70.00
Complete Ser. 1 Set (405):		30.00
Complete Ser. 2 Set (385):		40.00
Common Player:		.10
Complete Factory Set, Blue (795):		75.00
Complete Factory Set, Gold (795):		75.00
Ser. 1 Pack (10):		1.50
Ser. 1 Box (36):		45.00
Ser. 2 Pack (10):		1.50
Ser. 2 Box (36):		45.00
1	Cal Ripken Jr.	1.50
2	Chipper Jones	1.00
3	Roger Cedeno	.10
4	Garret Anderson	.10
5	Robin Ventura	.20
6	Daryle Ward	.10
7	Not Issued	.10
8	Ron Gant	.20
9	Phil Nevin	.10
10	Jermaine Dye	.10
11	Chris Singleton	.10
12	Mike Stanton	.10
13	Brian Hunter	.10
14	Mike Redmond	.10
15	Jim Thome	.25
16	Brian Jordan	.10
17	Joe Girardi	.10
18	Steve Woodard	.10
19	Dustin Hermanson	.10
20	Shawn Green	.30
21	Todd Stottlemyre	.10
22	Dan Wilson	.10
23	Todd Pratt	.10
24	Derek Lowe	.10
25	Juan Gonzalez	.40
26	Clay Bellinger	.10
27	Jeff Fassero	.10
28	Pat Meares	.10
29	Eddie Taubensee	.10
30	Paul O'Neill	.25
31	Jeffrey Hammonds	.10
32	Pokey Reese	.10
33	Mike Mussina	.30
34	Rico Brogna	.10
35	Jay Buhner	.10
36	Steve Cox	.10
37	Quilvio Veras	.10
38	Marquis Grissom	.10
39	Shigetoshi Hasegawa	.10
40	Shane Reynolds	.10
41	Adam Piatt	.10
42	Luis Polonia	.10
43	Brook Fordyce	.10
44	Preston Wilson	.10
45	Ellis Burks	.10
46	Armando Rios	.10
47	Chuck Finley	.10
48	Dan Plesac	.10
49	Shannon Stewart	.10
50	Mark McGwire	1.00
51	Mark Loretta	.10
52	Gerald Williams	.10
53	Eric Young	.10
54	Peter Bergeron	.10
55	Dave Hansen	.10
56	Arthur Rhodes	.10
57	Bobby Jones	.10
58	Matt Clement	.10
59	Mike Benjamin	.10
60	Pedro Martinez	.50
61	Jose Canseco	.40
62	Matt Anderson	.10
63	Torii Hunter	.10
64	Carlos Lee	.10
65	David Cone	.10
66	Ray Sanchez	.10
67	Eric Chavez	.20
68	Rick Helling	.10
69	Manny Alexander	.10
70	John Franco	.10
71	Mike Bordick	.10
72	Andres Galarraga	.25
73	Jose Cruz Jr.	.10
74	Mike Matheny	.10
75	Randy Johnson	.50
76	Richie Sexson	.10
77	Vladimir Nunez	.10
78	Harold Baines	.10
79	Aaron Boone	.10
80	Darin Erstad	.40
81	Alex Gonzalez	.10
82	Gil Heredia	.10
83	Shane Andrews	.10
84	Todd Hundley	.10
85	Bill Mueller	.10
86	Mark McLemore	.10
87	Scott Spiezio	.10
88	Kevin McGlinchy	.10
89	Bubba Trammell	.10
90	Manny Ramirez	.50
91	Mike Lamb	.10
92	Scott Karl	.10
93	Brian Buchanan	.10
94	Chris Turner	.10
95	Mike Sweeney	.10
96	John Wetteland	.10
97	Rob Bell	.10
98	Pat Rapp	.10
99	John Burkett	.10
100	Derek Jeter	1.50
101	J.D. Drew	.25
102	Jose Offerman	.10
103	Rick Reed	.10
104	Will Clark	.30
105	Rickey Henderson	.25
106	Dave Berg	.10
107	Kirk Rueter	.10
108	Lee Stevens	.10
109	Jay Bell	.10
110	Fred McGriff	.20
111	Julio Zuleta	.10
112	Brian Anderson	.10
113	Orlando Cabrera	.10
114	Alex Fernandez	.10
115	Derek Bell	.10
116	Eric Owens	.10
117	Brian Bohannon	.10
118	Dennys Reyes	.10
119	Mike Stanley	.10
120	Jorge Posada	.20
121	Rich Becker	.10
122	Paul Konerko	.10
123	Mike Remlinger	.10
124	Travis Lee	.10
125	Ken Caminiti	.10
126	Kevin Barker	.10
127	Paul Quantrill	.10
128	Ozzie Guillen	.10
129	Kevin Tapani	.10
130	Mark Johnson	.10
131	Randy Wolf	.10
132	Michael Tucker	.10
133	Darren Lewis	.10
134	Joe Randa	.10
135	Jeff Cirillo	.10
136	David Ortiz	.10
137	Herb Perry	.10
138	Jeff Nelson	.10
139	Chris Stynes	.10
140	Johnny Damon	.10
141	Desi Relaford	.10
142	Jason Schmidt	.10
143	Charles Johnson	.10
144	Pat Burrell	.40
145	Gary Sheffield	.25
146	Tom Glavine	.25
147	Jason Isringhausen	.10
148	Chris Carpenter	.10
149	Jeff Suppan	.10
150	Ivan Rodriguez	.50
151	Luis Sojo	.10
152	Ron Villone	.10
153	Mike Sirotka	.10
154	Chuck Knoblauch	.20
155	Jason Kendall	.10
156	Dennis Cook	.10
157	Bobby Estalella	.10
158	Jose Guillen	.10
159	Thomas Howard	.10
160	Carlos Delgado	.50
161	Benji Gil	.10
162	Tim Bogar	.10
163	Kevin Elster	.10
164	Scott Downs	.10
165	Andy Benes	.10
166	Adrian Beltre	.10
167	David Bell	.10
168	Turk Wendell	.10
169	Pete Harnisch	.10
170	Roger Clemens	.75
171	Scott Williamson	.10
172	Kevin Jordan	.10
173	Brad Penny	.10
174	John Flaherty	.10
175	Troy Glaus	.50
176	Kevin Appier	.10
177	Walt Weiss	.10
178	Tyler Houston	.10
179	Michael Barrett	.10
180	Mike Hampton	.10
181	Francisco Cordova	.10
182	Mike Jackson	.10
183	David Segui	.10
184	Carlos Febles	.10
185	Roy Halladay	.10
186	Seth Etherton	.10
187	Charlie Hayes	.10
188	Fernando Tatis	.10
189	Steve Trachsel	.10
190	Livan Hernandez	.10
191	Joe Oliver	.10
192	Stan Javier	.10
193	B.J. Surhoff	.10
194	Rob Ducey	.10
195	Barry Larkin	.25
196	Danny Patterson	.10
197	Bobby Howry	.10
198	Dmitri Young	.10
199	Brian Hunter	.10
200	Alex Rodriguez	1.00
201	Hideo Nomo	.25
202	Luis Alicea	.10
203	Warren Morris	.10
204	Antonio Alfonseca	.10
205	Edgardo Alfonzo	.20
206	Mark Grudzielanek	.10
207	Fernando Vina	.10
208	Willie Greene	.10
209	Homer Bush	.10
210	Jason Giambi	.30
211	Mike Morgan	.10
212	Steve Karsay	.10
213	Matt Lawton	.10
214	Wendell Magee Jr.	.10
215	Rusty Greer	.10
216	Keith Lockhart	.10
217	Billy Koch	.10
218	Todd Hollandsworth	.10
219	Raul Ibanez	.10
220	Tony Gwynn	.75
221	Carl Everett	.20
222	Hector Carrasco	.10
223	Jose Valentin	.10
224	Deivi Cruz	.10
225	Bret Boone	.10
226	Kurt Abbott	.10
227	Melvin Mora	.10
228	Danny Graves	.10
229	Jose Jimenez	.10
230	James Baldwin	.10
231	C.J. Nitkowski	.10
232	Jeff Zimmerman	.10
233	Mike Lowell	.10
234	Hideki Irabu	.10
235	Greg Vaughn	.20
236	Omar Daal	.10
237	Darren Dreifort	.10
238	Gil Meche	.10
239	Damian Jackson	.10
240	Frank Thomas	.75
241	Travis Miller	.10
242	Jeff Frye	.10
243	Dave Magadan	.10
244	Luis Castillo	.10
245	Bartolo Colon	.10
246	Steve Kline	.10
247	Shawon Dunston	.10
248	Rick Aguilera	.10
249	Omar Olivares	.10
250	Craig Biggio	.20
251	Scott Schoeneweis	.10
252	Dave Veres	.10
253	Ramon Martinez	.10
254	Jose Vidro	.10
255	Todd Helton	.50
256	Greg Norton	.10
257	Jacque Jones	.10
258	Jason Grimsley	.10
259	Dan Reichert	.10
260	Robb Nen	.10
261	Mark Clark	.10
262	Scott Hatteberg	.10
263	Doug Brocail	.10
264	Mark Johnson	.10
265	Eric Davis	.20
266	Terry Shumpert	.10
267	Kevin Millar	.10
268	Ismael Valdes	.10
269	Richard Hidalgo	.20
270	Randy Velarde	.10
271	Bengie Molina	.10
272	Tony Womack	.10
273	Enrique Wilson	.10
274	Jeff Brantley	.10
275	Rick Ankiel	.25
276	Terry Mulholland	.10
277	Ron Belliard	.10
278	Terrence Long	.10
279	Alberto Castillo	.10
280	Royce Clayton	.10
281	Joe McEwing	.10
282	Jason McDonald	.10
283	Ricky Bottalico	.10
284	Keith Foulke	.10
285	Brad Radke	.10
286	Gabe Kapler	.10
287	Pedro Astacio	.10
288	Armando Reynoso	.10
289	Darryl Kile	.10
290	Reggie Sanders	.10
291	Esteban Yan	.10
292	Joe Nathan	.10
293	Jay Payton	.10
294	Francisco Cordero	.10
295	Gregg Jefferies	.10
296	LaTroy Hawkins	.10
297	Jeff Tam	.10
298	Jacob Cruz	.10
299	Chris Holt	.10
300	Vladimir Guerrero	.75
301	Marvin Benard	.10
302	Matt Franco	.10
303	Mike Williams	.10
304	Sean Bergman	.10
305	Juan Encarnacion	.10
306	Russ Davis	.10
307	Hanley Frias	.10
308	Ramon Hernandez	.10
309	Matt Walbeck	.10
310	Bill Spiers	.10
311	Bob Wickman	.10
312	Sandy Alomar	.10
313	Eddie Guardado	.10
314	Shane Halter	.10
315	Geoff Jenkins	.20
316	Gerald Witasick	.10
317	Damian Miller	.10
318	Darrin Fletcher	.10
319	Rafael Furcal	.25
320	Mark Grace	.25
321	Mark Mulder	.10
322	Joe Torre (Managers)	.10
323	Bobby Cox (Managers)	.10
324	Mike Scioscia (Managers)	.10
325	Mike Hargrove (Managers)	.10
326	Jimy Williams (Managers)	.10
327	Jerry Manuel (Managers)	.10
328	Buck Showalter (Managers)	.10
329	Charlie Manuel (Managers)	.10
330	Don Baylor (Managers)	.10
331	Phil Garner (Managers)	.10
332	Jack McKeon (Managers)	.10
333	Tony Muser (Managers)	.10
334	Buddy Bell (Managers)	.10
335	Tom Kelly (Managers)	.10
336	John Boles (Managers)	.10
337	Art Howe (Managers)	.10
338	Larry Dierker (Managers)	.10
339	Lou Pinella (Managers)	.10
340	Davey Johnson (Managers)	.10
341	Larry Rothschild (Managers)	.10
342	Davey Lopes (Managers)	.10
343	Johnny Oates (Managers)	.10
344	Felipe Alou (Managers)	.10
345	Jim Fregosi (Managers)	.10
346	Bobby Valentine (Managers)	.10
347	Terry Francona (Managers)	.10
348	Gene Lamont (Managers)	.10
349	Tony LaRussa (Managers)	.10
350	Bruce Bochy (Managers)	.10
351	Dusty Baker (Managers)	.10
352	Adrian Gonzalez, Adam Johnson (Draft Picks)	.75
353	Matt Wheatland, Brian Digby (Draft Picks)	.40
354	Tripper Johnson, Scott Thorman (Draft Picks)	.40
355	Phil Dumatrait, Adam Wainwright (Draft Picks)	.50
356	Scott Heard, David Parrish RC (Draft Picks)	.40
357	Rocco Baldelli, Mark Folsom RC (Draft Picks)	.40
358	Dominic Rich RC, Aaron Herr (Draft Picks)	.40
359	Mike Stodolka, Sean Burnett (Draft Picks)	.25
360	Derek Thompson, Corey Smith (Draft Picks)	.40
361	Danny Borrell RC, Jason Bourgeois RC (Draft Picks)	.40
362	Chin-Feng Chen, Corey Patterson, Josh Hamilton (Prospects)	.25
363	Ryan Anderson, Barry Zito, C.C. Sabathia (Prospects)	.50
364	Scott Sobkowiak, David Walling, Ben Sheets (Prospects)	.50
365	Ty Howington, Josh Kalinowski, Josh Girdley (Prospects)	.10
366	Hee Seop Choi RC, Aaron McNeal, Jason Hart (Prospects)	1.00
367	Bobby Bradley, Kurt Ainsworth, Chin-Hui Tsao (Prospects)	.40
368	Mike Glendenning, Kenny Kelly, Juan Silvestri RC (Prospects)	.25
369	J.R. House, Ramon Castro, Ben Davis (Prospects)	.25
370	Chance Caple, Rafael Soriano RC, Pasqual Coco (Prospects)	.50
371	Travis Hafner RC, Eric Munson, Bucky Jacobsen (Prospects)	1.50
372	Jason Conti, Chris Wakeland, Brian Cole (Prospects)	.20
373	Scott Seabol, Aubrey Huff, Joe Crede (Prospects)	.40
374	Adam Everett, Jose Ortiz, Keith Ginter (Prospects)	.25
375	Carlos Hernandez, Geraldo Guzman, Adam Eaton (Prospects)	.25
376	Bobby Kielty, Milton Bradley, Juan Rivera (Prospects)	.25
377	Mark McGwire (Golden Moments)	.75
378	Don Larsen (Golden Moments)	.20
379	Bobby Thomson (Golden Moments)	.10
380	Bill Mazeroski (Golden Moments)	.20
381	Reggie Jackson (Golden Moments)	.40
382	Kirk Gibson (Golden Moments)	.10
383	Roger Maris (Golden Moments)	.40
384	Cal Ripken Jr. (Golden Moments)	.75
385	Hank Aaron (Golden Moments)	.75
386	Joe Carter (Golden Moments)	.10
387	Cal Ripken Jr. (Season Highlights)	.75
388	Randy Johnson (Season Highlights)	.30
389	Ken Griffey Jr. (Season Highlights)	.50
390	Troy Glaus (Season Highlights)	.30
391	Kazuhiro Sasaki (Season Highlights)	.40
392	Sammy Sosa, Troy Glaus (League Leaders)	.50
393	Todd Helton, Edgar Martinez (League Leaders)	.25
394	Nomar Garciaparra, Todd Helton (League Leaders)	.50
395	Barry Bonds, Jason Giambi (League Leaders)	.40
396	Todd Helton, Manny Ramirez (League Leaders)	.25
397	Todd Helton, Darin Erstad (League Leaders)	.25

398	Kevin Brown, Pedro Martinez (League Leaders)	.25
399	Randy Johnson, Pedro Martinez (League Leaders)	.25
400	Will Clark (Playoff Highlights)	.20
401	NY Mets Divisional Highlight	.10
402	NY Yankees Divisional Highlight	.10
403	Seattle Mariners Divisional Highlight	.10
404	Mike Hampton (Playoff Highlights)	.10
405	NY Yankees ALCS Highlight	.75
406	World Series Highlight	1.00
407	Jeff Bagwell	.50
408	Brant Brown	.10
409	Brad Fullmer	.10
410	Dean Palmer	.10
411	Gregg Zaun	.10
412	Jose Vizcaino	.10
413	Jeff Abbott	.10
414	Travis Fryman	.15
415	Mike Cameron	.10
416	Matt Mantei	.10
417	Alan Benes	.10
418	Mickey Morandini	.10
419	Troy Percival	.10
420	Eddie Perez	.10
421	Vernon Wells	.10
422	Ricky Gutierrez	.10
423	Carlos Hernandez	.10
424	Chan Ho Park	.15
425	Armando Benitez	.10
426	Sidney Ponson	.10
427	Adrian Brown	.10
428	Ruben Mateo	.20
429	Alex Ochoa	.10
430	Jose Rosado	.10
431	Masato Yoshii	.10
432	Corey Koskie	.10
433	Andy Pettitte	.20
434	Brian Daubach	.10
435	Sterling Hitchcock	.10
436	Timo Perez	.10
437	Shawn Estes	.10
438	Tony Armas Jr.	.10
439	Danny Bautista	.10
440	Randy Winn	.10
441	Wilson Alvarez	.10
442	Rondell White	.15
443	Jeromy Burnitz	.10
444	Kelvim Escobar	.10
445	Paul Bako	.10
446	Javier Vazquez	.10
447	Eric Gagne	.10
448	Kenny Lofton	.20
449	Mark Kotsay	.10
450	Jamie Moyer	.10
451	Delino DeShields	.10
452	Rey Ordonez	.10
453	Russ Ortiz	.10
454	Dave Burba	.10
455	Eric Karros	.15
456	Felix Martinez	.10
457	Tony Batista	.10
458	Bobby Higginson	.10
459	Jeff D'Amico	.10
460	Shane Spencer	.10
461	Brent Mayne	.10
462	Glendon Rusch	.10
463	Chris Gomez	.10
464	Jeff Shaw	.10
465	Damon Buford	.10
466	Mike DiFelice	.10
467	Jimmy Haynes	.10
468	Billy Wagner	.10
469	A.J. Hinch	.10
470	Gary DiSarcina	.10
471	Tom Lampkin	.10
472	Adam Eaton	.10
473	Brian Giles	.15
474	John Thomson	.10
475	Cal Eldred	.10
476	Ramiro Mendoza	.10
477	Scott Sullivan	.10
478	Scott Rolen	.25
479	Todd Ritchie	.10
480	Pablo Ozuna	.10
481	Carl Pavano	.10
482	Matt Morris	.10
483	Matt Stairs	.10
484	Tim Belcher	.10
485	Lance Berkman	.15
486	Brian Meadows	.10
487	Bobby Abreu	.15
488	John Vander Wal	.10
489	Donnie Sadler	.10
490	Damion Easley	.10
491	David Justice	.25
492	Ray Durham	.10
493	Todd Zeile	.10
494	Desi Relaford	.10
495	Cliff Floyd	.10
496	Scott Downs	.10
497	Barry Bonds	1.00
498	Jeff D'Amico	.10
499	Octavio Dotel	.10
500	Kent Mercker	.10
501	Craig Grebeck	.10
502	Roberto Hernandez	.10
503	Matt Williams	.15
504	Bruce Aven	.10
505	Brett Tomko	.10
506	Kris Benson	.10
507	Neifi Perez	.10
508	Alfonso Soriano	.50
509	Keith Osik	.10
510	Matt Franco	.10
511	Steve Finley	.10
512	Olmedo Saenz	.10
513	Esteban Loaiza	.10
514	Adam Kennedy	.10
515	Scott Elarton	.10
516	Moises Alou	.15
517	Bryan Rekar	.10
518	Darryl Hamilton	.10
519	Osvaldo Fernandez	.10
520	Kip Wells	.10
521	Bernie Williams	.40
522	Mike Darr	.10
523	Marlon Anderson	.10
524	Derrek Lee	.10
525	Ugueth Urbina	.10
526	Vinny Castilla	.10
527	David Wells	.10
528	Jason Marquis	.10
529	Orlando Palmeiro	.10
530	Carlos Perez	.10
531	J.T. Snow Jr.	.10
532	Al Leiter	.15
533	Jimmy Anderson	.10
534	Brett Laxton	.10
535	Butch Huskey	.10
536	Orlando Hernandez	.20
537	Magglio Ordonez	.15
538	Willie Blair	.10
539	Kevin Sefcik	.10
540	Chad Curtis	.10
541	John Halama	.10
542	Andy Fox	.10
543	Juan Guzman	.10
544	Frank Menechino	.10
545	Raul Mondesi	.15
546	Tim Salmon	.15
547	Ryan Rupe	.10
548	Jeff Reed	.10
549	Mike Mordecai	.10
550	Jeff Kent	.15
551	Wiki Gonzalez	.10
552	Kenny Rogers	.10
553	Kevin Young	.10
554	Brian Johnson	.10
555	Tom Goodwin	.10
556	Tony Clark	.10
557	Mac Suzuki	.10
558	Brian Moehler	.10
559	Jim Parque	.10
560	Mariano Rivera	.20
561	Trot Nixon	.10
562	Mike Mussina	.30
563	Nelson Figueroa	.10
564	Alex Gonzalez	.10
565	Benny Agbayani	.10
566	Ed Sprague	.10
567	Scott Erickson	.10
568	Abraham Nunez	.10
569	Jerry DiPoto	.10
570	Sean Casey	.10
571	Wilton Veras	.10
572	Joe Mays	.10
573	Bill Simas	.10
574	Doug Glanville	.10
575	Scott Sauerbeck	.10
576	Ben Davis	.10
577	Jesus Sanchez	.10
578	Ricardo Rincon	.10
579	John Olerud	.15
580	Curt Schilling	.10
581	Alex Cora	.10
582	Pat Hentgen	.10
583	Javy Lopez	.15
584	Ben Grieve	.10
585	Frank Castillo	.10
586	Kevin Stocker	.10
587	Mark Sweeney	.10
588	Ray Lankford	.10
589	Turner Ward	.10
590	Felipe Crespo	.10
591	Omar Vizquel	.10
592	Mike Lieberthal	.10
593	Ken Griffey Jr.	1.00
594	Troy O'Leary	.10
595	Dave Mlicki (Front photo actually Brian Moehler.)	.10
596	Manny Ramirez	.50
597	Mike Lansing	.10
598	Rich Aurilia	.10
599	Russ Branyan	.10
600	Russ Johnson	.10
601	Gregg Colbrunn	.10
602	Andruw Jones	.40
603	Henry Blanco	.10
604	Jarrod Washburn	.10
605	Tony Eusebio	.10
606	Aaron Sele	.10
607	Charles Nagy	.10
608	Ryan Klesko	.10
609	Dante Bichette	.10
610	Bill Haselman	.10
611	Jerry Spradlin	.10
612	Alex Rodriguez	1.00
613	Jose Silva	.10
614	Darren Oliver	.10
615	Pat Mahomes	.10
616	Roberto Alomar	.40
617	Edgar Renteria	.10
618	Jon Lieber	.10
619	John Rocker	.10
620	Miguel Tejada	.15
621	Mo Vaughn	.10
622	Jose Lima	.10
623	Kerry Wood	.15
624	Mike Timlin	.10
625	Wil Cordero	.10
626	Albert Belle	.15
627	Bobby Jones	.10
628	Doug Mirabelli	.10
629	Jason Tyner	.10
630	Andy Ashby	.10
631	Jose Hernandez	.10
632	Devon White	.10
633	Ruben Rivera	.10
634	Steve Parris	.10
635	David McCarty	.10
636	Jose Canseco	.25
637	Todd Walker	.10
638	Stan Spencer	.10
639	Wayne Gomes	.10
640	Freddy Garcia	.10
641	Jeremy Giambi	.10
642	Luis Lopez	.10
643	John Smoltz	.10
644	Kelly Stinnett	.10
645	Kevin Brown	.10
646	Wilton Guerrero	.10
647	Al Martin	.10
648	Woody Williams	.10
649	Brian Rose	.10
650	Rafael Palmeiro	.30
651	Pete Schourek	.10
652	Kevin Jarvis	.10
653	Mark Redman	.10
654	Ricky Ledee	.10
655	Larry Walker	.20
656	Paul Byrd	.10
657	Jason Bere	.10
658	Rick White	.10
659	Calvin Murray	.10
660	Greg Maddux	1.00
661	Ron Gant	.10
662	Eli Marrero	.10
663	Graeme Lloyd	.10
664	Trevor Hoffman	.10
665	Nomar Garciaparra	1.00
666	Glenallen Hill	.10
667	Matt LeCroy	.10
668	Justin Thompson	.10
669	Brady Anderson	.10
670	Miguel Batista	.10
671	Erubiel Durazo	.10
672	Kevin Millwood	.10
673	Mitch Meluskey	.10
674	Luis Gonzalez	.15
675	Edgar Martinez	.10
676	Robert Person	.10
677	Benito Santiago	.10
678	Todd Jones	.10
679	Tino Martinez	.15
680	Carlos Beltran	.10
681	Gabe White	.10
682	Bret Saberhagen	.10
683	Jeff Conine	.10
684	Jaret Wright	.10
685	Bernard Gilkey	.10
686	Garrett Stephenson	.10
687	Jamey Wright	.10
688	Sammy Sosa	1.00
689	John Jaha	.10
690	Ramon Martinez	.10
691	Robert Fick	.10
692	Eric Milton	.10
693	Denny Neagle	.10
694	Ron Coomer	.10
695	John Valentin	.10
696	Placido Polanco	.10
697	Tim Hudson	.15
698	Marty Cordova	.10
699	Chad Kreuter	.10
700	Frank Catalanotto	.10
701	Tim Wakefield	.15
702	Jim Edmonds	.15
703	Michael Tucker	.10
704	Cristian Guzman	.10
705	Joey Hamilton	.10
706	Mike Piazza	1.00
707	Dave Martinez	.10
708	Mike Hampton	.15
709	Bobby Bonilla	.10
710	Juan Pierre	.10
711	John Parrish	.10
712	Kory DeHaan	.10
713	Brian Tollberg	.10
714	Chris Truby	.10
715	Emil Brown	.10
716	Ryan Dempster	.10
717	Rich Garces	.10
718	Mike Myers	.10
719	Luis Ordaz	.10
720	Kazuhiro Sasaki	.10
721	Mark Quinn	.10
722	Ramon Ortiz	.10
723	Kerry Ligtenberg	.10
724	Rolando Arrojo	.10
725	Tsuyoshi Shinjo RC	1.00
726	Ichiro Suzuki RC	15.00
727	Roy Oswalt, Pat Strange, Jon Rauch (Prospects)	.25
728	Phil Wilson RC, Jake Peavy RC, Darwin Cubillan RC (Prospects)	.75
729	Steve Smyth RC, Mike Bynum, Nathan Haynes (Prospects)	.40
730	Michael Cuddyer, Joe Lawrence, Choo Freeman (Prospects)	.10
731	Carlos Pena, Larry Barnes, Dewayne Wise (Prospects)	.10
732	Gookie Dawkins, Erick Almonte RC, Felipe Lopez (Prospects)	.40
733	Alex Escobar, Eric Valent, Brad Wilkerson (Prospects)	.10
734	Toby Hall, Rod Barajas, Jeff Goldbach RC (Prospects)	.10
735	Jason Romano, Marcus Giles, Pablo Ozuna (Prospects)	.10
736	Dee Brown, Jack Cust, Vernon Wells (Prospects)	.10
737	David Espinosa, Luis Montanez RC (Draft Picks)	.40
738	John Lackey, Justin Wayne RC (Draft Picks)	.50
739	Josh Axelson RC, Carmen Cali RC (Draft Picks)	.50
740	Shaun Boyd RC, Chris Morris RC (Draft Picks)	.50
741	Tommy Arko RC, Dan Moylan RC (Draft Picks)	.50
742	Luis Cotto RC, Luis Escobar (Draft Picks)	.40
743	Brandon Mims RC, Blake Williams RC (Draft Picks)	.40
744	Chris Russ RC, Bryan Edwards (Draft Picks)	.10
745	Joe Torres, Ben Diggins (Draft Picks)	.10
746	Mark Dalesandro, Edwin Encarnacion RC (Draft Picks)	.50
747	Brian Bass RC, Odannis Ayala RC (Draft Picks)	.10
748	Jason Kaanoi RC, Michael Mathews RC (Draft Picks)	.10
749	Stuart McFarland RC, Adam Sterrett RC (Draft Picks)	.40
750	David Krynzel, Grady Sizemore (Draft Picks)	.10
751	Keith Bucktrot, Dane Sardinha (Draft Picks)	.10
752	Anaheim Angels	.10
753	Arizona Diamondbacks	.10
754	Atlanta Braves	.10
755	Baltimore Orioles	.10
756	Boston Red Sox	.10
757	Chicago Cubs	.10
758	Chicago White Sox	.10
759	Cincinnati Reds	.10
760	Cleveland Indians	.10
761	Colorado Rockies	.10
762	Detroit Tigers	.10
763	Florida Marlins	.10
764	Houston Astros	.10
765	Kansas City Royals	.10
766	Los Angeles Dodgers	.10
767	Milwaukee Brewers	.10
768	Minnesota Twins	.10
769	Montreal Expos	.10
770	New York Mets	.10
771	New York Yankees	.75
772	Oakland Athletics	.10
773	Philadelphia Phillies	.10
774	Pittsburgh Pirates	.10
775	San Diego Padres	.10
776	San Francisco Giants	.10
777	Seattle Mariners	.10
778	St. Louis Cardinals	.10
779	Tampa Bay Devil Rays	.10
780	Texas Rangers	.10
781	Toronto Blue Jays	.10
782	Bucky Dent (Golden Moments)	.10
783	Jackie Robinson (Golden Moments)	1.00
784	Roberto Clemente (Golden Moments)	1.00
785	Nolan Ryan (Golden Moments)	1.50
786	Kerry Wood (Golden Moments)	.10
787	Rickey Henderson (Golden Moments)	.10
788	Lou Brock (Golden Moments)	.25
789	David Wells (Golden Moments)	.10
790	Andruw Jones (Golden Moments)	.25
791	Carlton Fisk (Golden Moments)	.10

Prospects and RC's: 3-6X
Inserted 1:17

Home Team Advantage

Cards which bear a bright, embossed gold-foil "Topps Home Team Advantage" seal in a lower corner originated in the Topps factory set. Individual cards may command a small premium from single-player specialist collectors.

Common Player:
Star: +25%

A Look Ahead

NM/M

Complete Set (10): 15.00
Common Player: .50
Inserted 1:25

1	Vladimir Guerrero	1.50
2	Derek Jeter	4.00
3	Todd Helton	1.00
4	Alex Rodriguez	3.00
5	Ken Griffey Jr.	2.00
6	Nomar Garciaparra	3.00
7	Chipper Jones	2.00
8	Ivan Rodriguez	1.00
9	Pedro Martinez	2.00
10	Rick Ankiel	.50

A Tradition Continued

NM/M

Complete Set (30): 50.00
Common Player: .50
Inserted 1:17

Gold

Stars: 8-15X

1	Chipper Jones	3.00
2	Cal Ripken Jr.	6.00
3	Mike Piazza	3.00
4	Ken Griffey Jr.	3.00
5	Randy Johnson	1.50
6	Derek Jeter	5.00
7	Scott Rolen	1.50
8	Nomar Garciaparra	4.00
9	Roberto Alomar	1.00
10	Greg Maddux	3.00
11	Ivan Rodriguez	1.50
12	Jeff Bagwell	1.50
13	Ivan Rodriguez	1.50
14	Pedro Martinez	2.00
15	Sammy Sosa	4.00
16	Jim Edmonds	1.00
17	Mo Vaughn	.50
18	Barry Bonds	5.00
19	Larry Walker	.75
20	Mark McGwire	4.00
21	Vladimir Guerrero	2.00
22	Andruw Jones	1.50
23	Todd Helton	1.50
24	Kevin Brown	.75
25	Tony Gwynn	2.00
26	Manny Ramirez	1.50
27	Roger Clemens	4.00
28	Frank Thomas	1.50
29	Shawn Green	.75
30	Jim Thome	1.50

Autographs

Rafael Furcal
GOLDEN ANNIVERSARY STAR

NM/M

Common Player:
Group A 1:22,866
Group B 1:3,054
Group C 1:1,431
Group D 1:18,339
Group E 1:13,737
Group F 1:11,015
Group G 1:625

HA	Hank Aaron	250.00
DA	Dick Allen	25.00
RA	Rick Ankiel	10.00
RB	Rocco Baldelli	30.00
EB	Ernie Banks	100.00
YB	Yogi Berra	80.00
LB	Lou Brock	50.00
PB	Pat Burrell	15.00
RC	Rod Carew	50.00
MC	Mike Cuellar	15.00
WF	Whitey Ford	40.00
RF	Rafael Furcal	25.00
BG	Bob Gibson	40.00
AG	Adrian Gonzalez	15.00
SH	Scott Heard	15.00
WH	Willie Hernandez	10.00
AJ	Adam Johnson	10.00
CJ	Chipper Jones	80.00
SK	Sandy Koufax	500.00
ML	Mike Lamb	15.00
VL	Vernon Law	15.00
JM	Jason Marquis	10.00
WM	Willie Mays	250.00
MO	Magglio Ordonez	20.00
AP	Andy Pafko	30.00
BR	Brooks Robinson	80.00
JR	Joe Rudi	15.00
MS	Mike Schmidt	100.00
MS	Mike Stodolka	15.00
RS	Ron Swoboda	30.00
GT	Garry Templeton	30.00
JV	Jose Vidro	20.00
MW	Matt Wheatland	20.00
TZ	Todd Zeile	20.00

Autographs Series 2

Justin Wayne
GOLDEN ANNIVERSARY PROSPECT

		NM/M
Common Player:		10.00
DA	Denny Abreu	10.00
TA	Tony Alvarez	10.00
RB	Rocco Baldelli	30.00
GB	George Bell	10.00
JB	Johnny Bench	60.00
BB	Barry Bonds	180.00
MB	Milton Bradley	15.00
GHB	George Brett	175.00
MAB	Mike Bynum	10.00
EB	Eric Byrnes	10.00
JC	Jorge Cantu	10.00
CC	Chris Clapinski	10.00
WD	Willie Davis	40.00
JDD	J.D. Drew	30.00
TDLR	Tomas de la Rosa	10.00
CD	Chad Durbin	10.00
CE	Carl Erskine	25.00
BE	Brian Esposito	15.00
WF	Whitey Ford	40.00
EF	Eddy Furniss	10.00
BG	Bob Gibson	40.00
MG	Mike Glendenning	15.00
AG	Adrian Gonzalez	20.00
NG	Nick Green	10.00
KG	Kevin Gregg	10.00
DG	Dick Groat	25.00
GG	Geraldo Guzman	10.00
YH	Yamid Haad	10.00
TH	Todd Helton	40.00
AH	Aaron Herr	15.00
KH	Ken Holtzman	20.00
RJ	Reggie Jackson	100.00
NJ	Neil Jenkins	15.00
AJ	Adam Johnson	10.00
TJ	Tripper Johnson	15.00
BK	Bobby Kielty	10.00
JL	John Lackey	10.00
ML	Matt Lawton	15.00
CL	Colby Lewis	10.00
MFL	Mike Lockwood	10.00
GM	Gary Matthews	20.00
LM	Luis Montanez	15.00
EM	Eric Munson	15.00
SM	Stan Musial	150.00
BO	Ben Oglivie	15.00
AO	Augie Ojeda	10.00
ER	Erasmo Ramirez	15.00
CR	Chris Richard	10.00
JR	Juan Rincon	10.00
LR	Luis Rivas	20.00
SR	Scott Rolen	35.00
NR	Nolan Ryan	200.00
JS	Juan Salas	10.00
TS	Tom Seaver	150.00
CS	Carlos Silva	10.00
GS	Grady Sizemore	125.00
CCS	Corey Smith	10.00
MS	Mike Stodolka	15.00
MS	Mike Sweeney	15.00
KT	Kent Tekulve	20.00
DT	Derek Thompson	10.00
ST	Scott Thorman	10.00
BT	Brian Tollberg	15.00
JW	Justin Wayne	20.00
MW	Michael Wenner	15.00
MJW	Matt Wheatland	15.00
WW	Wilbur Wood	20.00
CY	Carl Yastrzemski	75.00

Base Hit

		NM/M
Complete Set (28):		450.00
Common Player:		25.00
BH1	Mike Scioscia	35.00
BH2	Larry Dierker	25.00
BH3	Art Howe	25.00
BH4	Jim Fregosi	25.00
BH5	Bobby Cox	35.00
BH6	Davey Lopes	25.00
BH7	Tony LaRussa	30.00
BH8	Don Baylor	35.00
BH9	Larry Rothschild	30.00
BH10	Buck Showalter	30.00
BH11	Davey Johnson	30.00
BH12	Felipe Alou	30.00
BH13	Charlie Manuel	25.00
BH14	Lou Piniella	30.00
BH15	John Boles	25.00
BH16	Bobby Valentine	30.00
BH17	Mike Hargrove	25.00
BH18	Bruce Bochy	25.00
BH19	Terry Francona	25.00
BH20	Gene Lamont	25.00
BH21	Johnny Oates	25.00
BH22	Jimy Williams	25.00
BH23	Jack McKeon	25.00
BH24	Buddy Bell	25.00
BH25	Tony Muser	25.00
BH26	Phil Garner	25.00
BH27	Tom Kelly	25.00
BH28	Jerry Manuel	25.00

Before There Was Topps

Lou Gehrig

		NM/M
Complete Set (10):		20.00
Common Player:		1.50
Inserted 1:25		
BT1	Lou Gehrig	4.00
BT2	Babe Ruth	5.00
BT3	Cy Young	2.00
BT4	Walter Johnson	2.00
BT5	Ty Cobb	4.00
BT6	Tris Speaker	1.50
BT7	Honus Wagner	2.00
BT8	Christy Mathewson	1.50
BT9	Grover Alexander	1.50
BT0	Joe DiMaggio	4.00

Combos

		NM/M
Complete Set (20):		25.00
Common Player:		1.50
Inserted 1:12		
1	Yogi Berra, Whitey Ford, Reggie Jackson, Don Mattingly, Derek Jeter	3.00
2	Brooks Robinson, Cal Ripken Jr.	3.00
3	Barry Bonds, Willie Mays	3.00
4	Bob Gibson, Pedro Martinez	1.50
5	Ivan Rodriguez, Johnny Bench	2.00
6	Ernie Banks, Alex Rodriguez	2.50
7	Joe Morgan, Ken Griffey Jr., Barry Larkin, Johnny Bench	2.50
8	Vladimir Guerrero, Roberto Clemente	2.50
9	Ted Williams, Carl Yastrzemski, Nomar Garciaparra	3.00
10	Joe Torre, Casey Stengel	1.50
11	Kevin Brown, Sandy Koufax, Don Drysdale	3.00
12	Mark McGwire, Sammy Sosa, Roger Maris, Babe Ruth	3.00
13	Ted Williams, Carl Yastrzemski, Nomar Garciaparra	3.00
14	Greg Maddux, Roger Clemens, Cy Young	2.00
15	Tony Gwynn, Ted Williams	3.00
16	Cal Ripken Jr., Lou Gehrig	4.00
17	Sandy Koufax, Randy Johnson, Warren Spahn, Steve Carlton	3.00
18	Mike Piazza, Josh Gibson	2.00
19	Barry Bonds, Willie Mays	3.00
20	Jackie Robinson, Larry Doby	2.50

Future Archives Gold Bordered Reprints

		NM/M
Complete Set (20):		60.00
Common Player:		2.00
Inserted five per factory set.		
1	Barry Bonds/1987	6.00
2	Chipper Jones/1991	8.00
3	Cal Ripken Jr./1982	12.00
4	Shawn Green/1992	4.00
5	Frank Thomas/1990	5.00
6	Derek Jeter/1993	9.00
7	Geoff Jenkins/1996	2.00
8	Jim Edmonds/1993	2.00
9	Bernie Williams/1990	2.00
10	Sammy Sosa/1990	6.00
11	Rickey Henderson/1980	2.00
12	Tony Gwynn/1983	6.00
13	Randy Johnson/1989	3.00
14	Juan Gonzalez/1990	3.00
15	Gary Sheffield/1989	3.00
16	Manny Ramirez/1992	3.00
17	Pokey Reese/1992	2.00
18	Preston Wilson/1993	2.00
19	Jay Payton/1995	2.00
20	Rafael Palmeiro/1987	3.00

Golden Anniversary

		NM/M
Complete Set (50):		60.00
Common Player:		.50
Inserted 1:10		
1	Hank Aaron	3.00
2	Ernie Banks	1.50
3	Mike Schmidt	3.00
4	Willie Mays	4.00
5	Johnny Bench	1.50
6	Tom Seaver	1.00
7	Frank Robinson	1.00
8	Sandy Koufax	3.00
9	Bob Gibson	1.00
10	Ted Williams	4.00
11	Cal Ripken Jr.	5.00
12	Tony Gwynn	1.50
13	Mark McGwire	3.00
14	Ken Griffey Jr.	2.00
15	Greg Maddux	2.00
16	Roger Clemens	3.00
17	Barry Bonds	4.00
18	Rickey Henderson	.75
19	Mike Piazza	2.00
20	Jose Canseco	1.00
21	Derek Jeter	4.00
22	Nomar Garciaparra	3.00
23	Alex Rodriguez	3.00
24	Sammy Sosa	2.50
25	Ivan Rodriguez	1.00
26	Vladimir Guerrero	1.50
27	Chipper Jones	2.00
28	Jeff Bagwell	1.00
29	Pedro Martinez	1.50
30	Randy Johnson	1.50
31	Pat Burrell	1.00
32	Josh Hamilton	.50
33	Nick Johnson	.50
34	Corey Patterson	.50
35	Eric Munson	.50
36	Sean Burroughs	.50
37	Alfonso Soriano	1.50
38	Chin-Feng Chen	.50
39	Barry Zito	.75
40	Adrian Gonzalez	.50
41	Mark McGwire	3.00
42	Nomar Garciaparra	3.00
43	Todd Helton	1.00
44	Matt Williams	.50
45	Troy Glaus	.75
46	Geoff Jenkins	.50
47	Frank Thomas	1.00
48	Mo Vaughn	.50
49	Barry Larkin	.75
50	J.D. Drew	.50

Hit Parade

Reggie Jackson

		NM/M
Complete Set (6):		25.00
Common Player:		25.00
1:2,600 Retail		
HP1	Reggie Jackson	40.00
HP2	Dave Winfield	25.00
HP3	Eddie Murray	25.00
HP4	Rickey Henderson	25.00
HP5	Robin Yount	25.00
HP6	Carl Yastrzemski	65.00

King of Kings

		NM/M
Common Card:		25.00
Inserted 1:2,056		
1	Hank Aaron	50.00
2	Nolan Ryan	50.00
3	Rickey Henderson	30.00
4	Mark McGwire	100.00
5	Bob Gibson	25.00
6	Nolan Ryan	50.00

King of Kings Golden Edition

		NM/M
Production 50 cards		
KKGE	Hank Aaron, Nolan Ryan, Rickey Henderson	250.00
KKLE2	Mark McGwire, Bob Gibson, Nolan Ryan	300.00

Noteworthy

bob gibson

		NM/M
Complete Set (50):		40.00

Originals

Roberto Clemente

		NM/M
Common Player:		10.00
Series 1 1:1,172		
Series 2 1:1,023		
1	Roberto Clemente/1955	80.00
2	Carl Yastrzemski/1960	30.00
3	Mike Schmidt/1974	30.00
4	Wade Boggs/1983	15.00
5	Chipper Jones/1991	15.00
6	Willie Mays	40.00
7	Lou Brock	15.00
8	Dave Parker	10.00
9	Barry Bonds	40.00
10	Alex Rodriguez	25.00

The Shot Heard Round The World Autograph

		NM/M
B. Thomson/R. Branca		
	Ralph Branca, Bobby Thomson	40.00

Through the Years

		NM/M
Complete Set (50):		100.00
Common Player:		1.50
Inserted 1:8		
1	Yogi Berra	2.00
2	Roy Campanella	2.00
3	Willie Mays	5.00
4	Andy Pafko	1.50
5	Jackie Robinson	4.00
6	Stan Musial	4.00
7	Duke Snider	2.00
8	Warren Spahn	2.50
9	Ted Williams	6.00

Common Player:		.50
Inserted 1:8		
TN1	Mark McGwire	2.00
TN2	Derek Jeter	2.50
TN3	Sammy Sosa	2.00
TN4	Todd Helton	1.00
TN5	Alex Rodriguez	2.00
TN6	Chipper Jones	1.50
TN7	Barry Bonds	2.00
TN8	Ken Griffey Jr.	1.50
TN9	Nomar Garciaparra	2.00
TN10	Frank Thomas	1.00
TN11	Randy Johnson	1.00
TN12	Cal Ripken Jr.	3.00
TN13	Mike Piazza	1.50
TN14	Ivan Rodriguez	1.00
TN15	Jeff Bagwell	1.00
TN16	Vladimir Guerrero	1.00
TN17	Greg Maddux	1.50
TN18	Tony Gwynn	1.00
TN19	Larry Walker	.50
TN20	Juan Gonzalez	.75
TN21	Scott Rolen	1.00
TN22	Jason Giambi	1.00
TN23	Jeff Kent	.50
TN24	Pat Burrell	.75
TN25	Pedro Martinez	1.00
TN26	Willie Mays	2.00
TN27	Whitey Ford	.75
TN28	Jackie Robinson	2.00
TN29	Ted Williams	2.50
TN30	Babe Ruth	3.00
TN31	Warren Spahn	1.00
TN32	Nolan Ryan	3.00
TN33	Yogi Berra	1.00
TN34	Mike Schmidt	2.00
TN35	Steve Carlton	.75
TN36	Brooks Robinson	1.00
TN37	Bob Gibson	1.00
TN38	Reggie Jackson	1.00
TN39	Johnny Bench	1.50
TN40	Ernie Banks	1.00
TN41	Eddie Mathews	.50
TN42	Don Mattingly	2.00
TN43	Duke Snider	.75
TN44	Hank Aaron	2.00
TN45	Roberto Clemente	2.00
TN46	Harmon Killebrew	1.00
TN47	Frank Robinson	1.00
TN48	Stan Musial	2.00
TN49	Lou Brock	.50
TN50	Joe Morgan	.50

Don Mattingly OF-1B

10	Eddie Matthews	2.00
11	Willie McCovey	1.50
12	Frank Robinson	2.00
13	Ernie Banks	3.00
14	Hank Aaron	5.00
15	Sandy Koufax	4.00
16	Bob Gibson	2.00
17	Harmon Killebrew	2.00
18	Whitey Ford	2.00
19	Roberto Clemente	5.00
20	Juan Marichal	1.50
21	Johnny Bench	3.00
22	Willie Stargell	1.50
23	Joe Morgan	1.50
24	Carl Yastrzemski	2.00
25	Reggie Jackson	2.00
26	Tom Seaver	1.50
27	Steve Carlton	1.50
28	Jim Palmer	1.50
29	Rod Carew	1.50
30	George Brett	5.00
31	Roger Clemens	5.00
32	Don Mattingly	5.00
33	Ryne Sandberg	3.00
34	Mike Schmidt	4.00
35	Cal Ripken Jr.	6.00
36	Tony Gwynn	2.00
37	Ozzie Smith	3.00
38	Wade Boggs	1.50
39	Nolan Ryan	6.00
40	Robin Yount	2.00
41	Mark McGwire	5.00
42	Ken Griffey Jr.	4.00
43	Sammy Sosa	4.00
44	Alex Rodriguez	4.00
45	Barry Bonds	6.00
46	Mike Piazza	3.00
47	Chipper Jones	3.00
48	Greg Maddux	3.00
49	Nomar Garciaparra	4.00
50	Derek Jeter	5.00

Two of a Kind

		NM/M
Inserted 1:30,167		
TK	Bo Jackson, Deion Sanders	75.00

What Could've Been

		NM/M
Complete Set (10):		15.00
Common Player:		1.00
Inserted 1:25		
WCB1	Josh Gibson	3.00
WCB2	Leroy "Satchel" Paige	3.00
WCB3	Walter "Buck" Leonard	2.00
WCB4	James "Cool Papa" Bell	2.00
WCB5	Andrew "Rube" Foster	2.00
WCB6	Martin Dihigo	1.50
WCB7	William "Judy" Johnson	1.50
WCB8	Mule Suttles	1.00
WCB9	Ray Dandridge	1.00
WCB10	John Henry "Pop" Lloyd	2.00

2001 Topps Opening Day

Cal Ripken

		NM/M
Complete Set (165):		35.00

Common Player: .15
Pack (7): 1.00
Box (24): 20.00
1 Cal Ripken Jr. 2.50
2 Chipper Jones 1.50
3 Garret Anderson .40
4 Robin Ventura .20
5 Jermaine Dye .15
6 Jim Thome .75
7 Brian Jordan .15
8 Shawn Green .40
9 Juan Gonzalez .75
10 Paul O'Neill .25
11 Pokey Reese .15
12 Mike Mussina .40
13 Jay Buhner .15
14 Shane Reynolds .15
15 Adam Piatt .15
16 Preston Wilson .15
17 Ellis Burks .15
18 Chuck Finley .15
19 Shannon Stewart .15
20 Mark McGwire 2.00
21 Mark Loretta .15
22 Bobby Jones .15
23 Matt Clement .15
24 Pedro J. Martinez 1.00
25 Carlos Lee .15
26 John Franco .15
27 Andres Galarraga .25
28 Jose Cruz Jr. .15
29 Randy Johnson .75
30 Richie Sexson .40
31 Darin Erstad .30
32 Manny Ramirez .75
33 Mike Sweeney .15
34 John Wetteland .15
35 Derek Jeter 2.50
36 J.D. Drew .15
37 Rick Reed .15
38 Jay Bell .15
39 Fred McGriff .25
40 Orlando Cabrera .15
41 Eric Owens .15
42 Jorge Posada .40
43 Jeff Cirillo .15
44 Johnny Damon .25
45 Charles Johnson .15
46 Pat Burrell .40
47 Gary Sheffield .40
48 Tom Glavine .30
49 Ivan Rodriguez .75
50 Chuck Knoblauch .15
51 Jason Kendall .15
52 Carlos Delgado .60
53 Roger Clemens 1.50
54 Brad Penny .15
55 Troy Glaus .75
56 Mike Hampton .15
57 Carlos Febles .15
58 Seth Etherton .15
59 Fernando Tatis .15
60 Livan Hernandez .15
61 Barry Larkin .30
62 Alex Rodriguez 2.00
63 Warren Morris .15
64 Antonio Alfonseca .15
65 Edgardo Alfonzo .15
66 Fernando Vina .15
67 Jason Giambi .75
68 Matt Lawton .15
69 Rusty Greer .15
70 Tony Gwynn 1.00
71 Carl Everett .15
72 Bret Boone .25
73 James Baldwin .15
74 Greg Vaughn .15
75 Darren Dreifort .15
76 Frank Thomas 1.00
77 Luis Castillo .15
78 Bartolo Colon .25
79 Craig Biggio .25
80 Jose Vidro .15
81 Todd Helton .75
82 Jacque Jones .15
83 Robb Nen .15
84 Richard Hidalgo .15
85 Tony Womack .15
86 Rick Ankiel .15
87 Terrence Long .15
88 Brad Radke .15
89 Gabe Kapler .15
90 Pedro Astacio .15
91 Darryl Kile .15
92 Jay Payton .15
93 Vladimir Guerrero 1.00
94 Juan Encarnacion .15
95 Ramon Hernandez .15
96 Sandy Alomar .15
97 Geoff Jenkins .25
98 Rafael Furcal .25
99 Mark Grace .25
100 Mark Mulder .25
101 Jim Edmonds .25
102 Tim Salmon .25
103 Jeff Bagwell .75
104 Jose Canseco .40
105 Ben Grieve .15
106 Ryan Klesko .25
107 Javy Lopez .25
108 Greg Maddux 1.50
109 Andruw Jones .50
110 Jeromy Burnitz .15
111 Ray Lankford .15
112 Sammy Sosa 1.50
113 Raul Mondesi .25
114 Mike Piazza 1.50
115 Todd Zeile .15

116 Eric Karros .15
117 Barry Bonds 2.50
118 J.T. Snow .15
119 Jeff Kent .15
120 David Justice .25
121 Matt Williams .25
122 Brian Giles .25
123 Edgar Martinez .15
124 Ken Griffey Jr. 1.50
125 Al Leiter .25
126 Kevin Brown .25
127 John Olerud .25
128 Roberto Alomar .50
129 Rafael Palmeiro .40
130 Steve Finley .15
131 Tim Hudson .40
132 Scott Rolen .75
133 Nomar Garciaparra 1.50
134 Mo Vaughn .15
135 Larry Walker .30
136 Albert Belle .15
137 Ray Durham .15
138 Andy Pettitte .40
139 Mariano Rivera .25
140 Bernie Williams .50
141 David Wells .15
142 Magglio Ordonez .40
143 Kevin Millwood .15
144 Cliff Floyd .15
145 Rich Aurilia .15
146 Eric Chavez .15
147 Scott Elarton .15
148 Tony Armas Jr. .15
149 Mark Redman .15
150 Javier Vazquez .15
151 Adrian Gonzalez, Adam Johnson .50
152 Mike Stodolka, Sean Burnett .15
153 David Walling, Ben Sheets .50
154 Chin-Feng Chen, Corey Patterson, Josh Hamilton .25
155 Mark McGwire (Golden Moments) 1.00
156 Bobby Thomson (Golden Moments) .15
157 Bill Mazeroski (Golden Moments) .15
158 Cal Ripken Jr. (Golden Moments) 1.00
159 Hank Aaron (Golden Moments) 1.00
160 Bucky Dent (Golden Moments) .15
161 Jackie Robinson (Golden Moments) 1.00
162 Roberto Clemente (Golden Moments) 1.00
163 Nolan Ryan (Golden Moments) 1.00
164 Kerry Wood (Golden Moments) .25
165 Checklist .15

Autographs
NM/M
Common Autograph: 20.00
TH Todd Helton 40.00
CJ Chipper Jones 100.00
MO Magglio Ordonez 25.00
CP Corey Patterson 20.00

Team Logo Stickers
NM/M
Complete Set (30): 6.00
Sticker: .25
Each team represented.

2001 Topps American Pie

NM/M
Complete Set (150): 30.00
Common Player: .20
Pack (5): 3.00
Box (24): 60.00
1 Al Kaline .40
2 Al Oliver .20
3 Andre Dawson .20
4 Bert Blyleven .20
5 Bill Buckner .20
6 Bill Mazeroski .20
7 Bob Gibson .50

8 Bill Freeman .20
9 Bobby Grich .20
10 Bobby Murcer .20
11 Bobby Richardson .20
12 Boog Powell .20
13 Brooks Robinson .20
14 Carl Yastrzemski .75
15 Carlton Fisk .40
16 Clete Boyer .20
17 Curt Flood .20
18 Dale Murphy .30
19 Tony Conigliaro .20
20 Dave Parker .20
21 Dave Winfield .50
22 Dick Allen .20
23 Dick Groat .20
24 Don Drysdale .50
25 Don Sutton .20
26 Dwight Evans .20
27 Eddie Mathews .75
28 Elston Howard .20
29 Frank Howard .20
30 Frank Robinson .50
31 Fred Lynn .20
32 Gary Carter .20
33 Gaylord Perry .20
34 Norm Cash .20
35 George Brett 1.50
36 George Foster .20
37 Goose Gossage .20
38 Graig Nettles .20
39 Greg Luzinski .20
40 Harmon Killebrew .75
41 Jack Clark .20
42 Jack Morris .20
43 Jim Wynn .20
44 Jim Kaat .20
45 Jim Palmer .20
46 Joe Pepitone .20
47 Joe Rudi .20
48 Johnny Bench 1.00
49 Juan Marichal .40
50 Keith Hernandez .20
51 Bucky Dent .20
52 Lou Brock .40
53 Ron Cey .20
54 Luis Aparicio .20
55 Luis Tiant .20
56 Mark Fidrych .20
57 Maury Wills .20
58 Mickey Lolich .20
59 Mickey Rivers .20
60 Mike Schmidt 1.00
61 Moose Skowron .20
62 Nolan Ryan 3.00
63 Orlando Cepeda .20
64 Ozzie Smith .75
65 Phil Niekro .20
66 Reggie Jackson .75
67 Reggie Smith .20
68 Rico Carty .20
69 Roberto Clemente 2.00
70 Robin Yount .75
71 Roger Maris 1.50
72 Rollie Fingers .20
73 Ron Guidry .20
74 Ron Santo .20
75 Ron Swoboda .20
76 Sal Bando .20
77 Sam McDowell .20
78 Steve Carlton .40
79 Thurman Munson 1.00
80 Tim McCarver .20
81 Tom Seaver .75
82 Mike Cuellar .20
83 Tony Kubek .20
84 Tommy John .20
85 Tony Perez .20
86 Tug McGraw .20
87 Vida Blue .20
88 Warren Spahn .75
89 Whitey Ford .50
90 Willie Mays 2.00
91 Willie McCovey .50
92 Willie Stargell .50
93 Yogi Berra 1.00
94 Stan Musial 1.00
95 Jim Piersall .20
96 Duke Snider .50
97 Bruce Sutter .30
98 Dave Concepcion .20
99 Darrell Evans .20
100 Dennis Eckersley .40
101 Hoyt Wilhelm .20
102 Minnie Minoso .20
103 Don Newcombe .20
104 Richie Ashburn .20
105 Alan Trammell .20
106 Jim "Catfish" Hunter .20
107 Lou Whitaker .20
108 Johnny Podres .20
109 Denny Martinez .20
110 Willie Horton .20
111 Dean Chance .20
112 Fergie Jenkins .20
113 Cecil Cooper .20
114 Rick Reuschel .20
115 Space Race (Events) .20
116 Man On The Moon (Events) .50
117 Woodstock (Events) .50
118 Peace Movement/Flower Power (Events) .20
119 N.Y. Worlds Fair (Events) .20
120 Vietnam War (Events) .20
121 Vietnam Cease Fire (Events) .20

123 Kennedy Elected President (Events) .50
124 Kennedy Assassination (Events) .20
125 Malcom X (Events) .20
126 Nixon Elected President (Events) .20
127 Watergate (Events) .20
128 Nixon Resigns (Events) .20
129 Cuban Missile Crisis (Events) .20
130 Astrodome (Events) .20
131 Secretariat (Events) .20
132 Lyndon Johnson Signs Civil Rights Bill (Events) .20
133 Atomic Bomb Test Ban Treaty (Events) .20
134 Bi Centennial (Events) .20
135 String Bikini (Events) .20
136 Birth Control Pill (Events) .20
137 Studio 54 (Events) .20
138 Motown (Events) .20
139 Microsoft Started (Events) .20
140 Internet Developed (Events) .20
141 John F. Kennedy (Personalities) 1.50
142 Marilyn Monroe (Personalities) 1.50
143 Elvis Presley (Personalities) 1.50
144 Jimi Hendrix (Personalities) 1.00
145 Arthur Ashe (Personalities) .20
146 Richard Nixon (Personalities) .20
147 James Dean (Personalities) 1.00
148 Janis Joplin (Personalities) .50
149 Frank Sinatra (Personalities) 1.00
150 Malcom X (Personalities) .50

Autoproofs Baseball Legends
No pricing due to scarcity.
Production 25 Sets

Decade Leaders

NM/M
Complete Set (10): 15.00
Common Player: 1.00
Inserted 1:12
DL1 Willie Stargell 1.50
DL2 Harmon Killebrew 1.50
DL3 Johnny Bench 2.00
DL4 Hank Aaron 3.00
DL5 Rod Carew 1.50
DL6 Roberto Clemente 3.00
DL7 Nolan Ryan 4.00
DL8 Bob Gibson 1.50
DL9 Jim Palmer 1.00
DL10 Juan Marichal 1.00

Entertainment Stars
NM/M
Production 500 Sets
1 Lou Ferrigno (Incredible Hulk) 50.00
2 Adam West (Batman) 60.00
3 Danny Bonaduce (Partridge Family) 30.00

Legends Autographs
NM/M
Common Player: 10.00
Inserted 1:211
TT1R Willie Mays 100.00
TT14R Johnny Bench 60.00
TT48R Bobby Richardson 20.00
TT8R Carl Yastrzemski 50.00
TT13R Warren Spahn 25.00
TT15R Reggie Jackson 50.00
TT18R Bob Gibson 20.00
TT25R Luis Tiant 10.00
TT29R Moose Skowron 10.00
TT31R Clete Boyer 10.00

TT33R Vida Blue 15.00
TT35R Joe Pepitone 10.00
TT37R Tug McGraw 15.00
TT47R Frank Howard 10.00
TT49R Tony Kubek 40.00
TT50R Mickey Lolich 10.00

Profiles In Courage

TOM SEAVER

NM/M
Complete Set (20): 25.00
Common Player: 1.00
Inserted 1:8
PIC1 Roger Maris 2.00
PIC2 Lou Brock 1.00
PIC3 Brooks Robinson 1.50
PIC4 Carl Yastrzemski 1.50
PIC5 Mike Schmidt 2.50
PIC6 Hank Aaron 3.00
PIC7 Tom Seaver 1.50
PIC8 Willie Mays 3.00
PIC9 Graig Nettles 1.00
PIC10 Frank Robinson 1.50
PIC11 Rollie Fingers 1.00
PIC12 Tony Perez 1.00
PIC13 George Brett 3.00
PIC14 Robin Yount 1.50
PIC15 Nolan Ryan 4.00
PIC16 Warren Spahn 1.50
PIC17 Johnny Bench 2.00
PIC18 Vida Blue 1.00
PIC19 Roberto Clemente 3.00
PIC20 Thurman Munson 2.00

Rookie Reprint Relics

ROBIN YOUNT

NM/M
Common Player: 10.00
Inserted 1:116
JB Johnny Bench 20.00
GB George Brett 40.00
SC Steve Carlton 15.00
GC Gary Carter 10.00
AD Andre Dawson 10.00
DE Dennis Eckersley 10.00
MF Mark Fidrych 10.00
BG Bobby Grich 10.00
RJ Reggie Jackson 15.00
JK Jim Kaat 10.00
TMC Tim McCarver 10.00
TM Thurman Munson 35.00
BM Bobby Murcer 10.00
AO Al Oliver 10.00
BP Boog Powell 10.00
OS Ozzie Smith 10.00
DS Don Sutton 10.00
DW Dave Winfield 10.00
RY Robin Yount 20.00

Timeless Classics Relics

NM/M
Common Player: 8.00
Inserted 1:80
Sam McDowell 8.00
Frank Howard 8.00
Dick Groat 8.00
Roger Maris 50.00
Orlando Cepeda 8.00
Willie Mays 40.00
Carl Yastrzemski 30.00
Roberto Clemente 60.00
Harmon Killebrew 20.00
Brooks Robinson 20.00
Tony Conigliaro 15.00
Frank Robinson 15.00
Hank Aaron 40.00
Willie McCovey 15.00
Rico Carty 8.00
Johnny Bench 20.00
Willie Stargell 15.00
Steve Carlton 15.00
Norm Cash 8.00
Reggie Jackson 15.00
Mike Schmidt 30.00
Mickey Rivers 8.00
Tom Seaver 20.00
George Brett 40.00
George Foster 8.00
Graig Nettles 8.00
Nolan Ryan 40.00
Dave Parker 10.00
Dick Allen 8.00
Fred Lynn 8.00
Keith Hernandez 8.00
Dave Winfield 15.00

Woodstock Relics
NM/M
Common Player: 8.00
Inserted 1:138
GB George Brett 40.00
BB Bill Buckner 8.00
OC Orlando Cepeda 10.00
DE Dwight Evans 8.00
CF Carlton Fisk 15.00
BF Bill Freehan 8.00
DG Dick Groat 8.00
RJ Reggie Jackson 15.00
TK Ted Kluszewski 8.00
FL Fred Lynn 8.00
WM Willie Mays 45.00
SM Stan Musial 40.00
TP Tony Perez 8.00
JP Jimmy Piersall 8.00
BR Brooks Robinson 15.00
FR Frank Robinson 15.00
JR Joe Rudi 8.00
DS Duke Snider 15.00
WS Willie Stargell 15.00
MW Maury Wills 8.00
DW Dave Winfield 15.00
WS Woodstock 15.00
JW Jim Wynn 8.00
CY Carl Yastrzemski 30.00
RY Robin Yount 20.00

2001 Topps Archives

ROGER MARIS

NM/M
Common Player: 10.00
Complete Set (450): 150.00
Complete Series 1 (225): 75.00
Complete Series 2 (225): 75.00
Common Player: .40
Pack (8): 4.50
Box (20): 80.00
1 Johnny Antonelli .40
2 Yogi Berra 2.50
3 Dom DiMaggio .40
4 Carl Erskine .40
5 Joe Garagiola .50
6 Monte Irvin .40
7 Vernon Law .40
8 Eddie Mathews 2.00

#	Player	Price
9	Willie Mays	5.00
10	Gil McDougald	.40
11	Andy Pafko	.40
12	Phil Rizzuto	.75
13	Preacher Roe	.40
14	Hank Sauer	.50
15	Bobby Shantz	.40
16	Enos Slaughter	.50
17	Warren Spahn	2.00
18	Mickey Vernon	.40
19	Early Wynn	.40
20	Whitey Ford	1.00
21	Johnny Podres	.40
22	Ernie Banks	2.00
23	Moose Skowron	.40
24	Harmon Killebrew	2.00
25	Ted Williams	6.00
26	Jimmy Piersall	.40
27	Frank Thomas	.40
28	Bill Mazeroski	.50
29	Bobby Richardson	.40
30	Frank Robinson	1.50
31	Stan Musial	3.00
32	Johnny Callison	.40
33	Bob Gibson	2.00
34	Frank Howard	.50
35	Willie McCovey	.40
36	Carl Yastrzemski	2.00
37	Jim Maloney	.40
38	Ron Santo	.40
39	Lou Brock	.75
40	Tim McCarver	.50
41	Joe Pepitone	.40
42	Boog Powell	.50
43	Bill Freehan	.40
44	Dick Allen	.40
45	Willie Horton	.40
46	Mickey Lolich	.40
47	Wilbur Wood	.40
48	Bert Campaneris	.40
49	Rod Carew	1.50
50	Tug McGraw	.40
51	Tony Perez	.75
52	Luis Tiant	.40
53	Bobby Murcer	.40
54	Don Sutton	.75
55	Ken Holtzman	.40
56	Reggie Smith	.40
57	Hal McRae	.40
58	Roy White	.40
59	Reggie Jackson	3.00
60	Graig Nettles	.40
61	Joe Rudi	.40
62	Vida Blue	.50
63	Darrell Evans	.40
64	David Concepcion	.40
65	Bobby Grich	.40
66	Greg Luzinski	.40
67	Cecil Cooper	.40
68	George Hendrick	.40
69	Dwight Evans	.40
70	Gary Matthews	.40
71	Mike Schmidt	3.00
72	Dave Parker	.40
73	Dave Winfield	1.00
74	Gary Carter	.40
75	Dennis Eckersley	.75
76	Kent Tekulve	.40
77	Andre Dawson	.75
78	Denny Martinez	.40
79	Bruce Sutter	.75
80	Jack Morris	.40
81	Ozzie Smith	1.50
82	Lee Smith	.40
83	Don Mattingly	4.00
84	Joe Carter	.40
85	Kirby Puckett	3.00
86	Joe Adcock	.40
87	Gus Bell	.40
88	Roy Campanella	2.00
89	Jackie Jensen	.40
90	Johnny Mize	.75
91	Allie Reynolds	.40
92	Al Rosen	.40
93	Hal Newhouser	.40
94	Harvey Kuenn	.40
95	Nellie Fox	.75
96	Elston Howard	.40
97	Sal Maglie	.40
98	Roger Maris	3.00
99	Norm Cash	.40
100	Thurman Munson	2.50
101	Roy Campanella	1.50
102	Joe Garagiola	.75
103	Dom DiMaggio	.40
104	Johnny Mize	.50
105	Allie Reynolds	.40
106	Preacher Roe	.40
107	Hal Newhouser	.40
108	Monte Irvin	.40
109	Carl Erskine	.40
110	Enos Slaughter	.40
111	Gil McDougald	.40
112	Andy Pafko	.40
113	Sal Maglie	.40
114	Johnny Antonelli	.40
115	Phil Rizzuto	.50
116	Yogi Berra	1.50
117	Early Wynn	.40
118	Mickey Vernon	.40
119	Gus Bell	.40
120	Ted Williams	4.00
121	Frank Thomas	.40
122	Bobby Richardson	.40
123	Whitey Ford	1.00
124	Vernon Law	.40
125	Jimmy Piersall	.40
126	Moose Skowron	.40
127	Joe Adcock	.40
128	Johnny Podres	.40
129	Ernie Banks	1.50
130	Jim Maloney	.40
131	Johnny Callison	.40
132	Eddie Mathews	1.50
133	Joe Pepitone	.40
134	Warren Spahn	1.50
135	Bill Mazeroski	.40
136	Norm Cash	.40
137	Bob Gibson	1.00
138	Harmon Killebrew	1.50
139	Frank Robinson	1.00
140	Ron Santo	.40
141	Hank Sauer	.40
142	Bobby Shantz	.40
143	Nellie Fox	.50
144	Elston Howard	.40
145	Jackie Jensen	.40
146	Al Rosen	.40
147	Dick Allen	.40
148	Bill Freehan	.40
149	Boog Powell	.40
150	Lou Brock	.75
151	Rod Carew	.75
152	Wilbur Wood	.40
153	Thurman Munson	1.50
154	Ken Holtzman	.40
155	Willie Horton	.40
156	Mickey Lolich	.40
157	Tim McCarver	.40
158	Willie McCovey	.40
159	Roy White	.40
160	Bobby Murcer	.40
161	Joe Rudi	.40
162	Reggie Smith	.40
163	Luis Tiant	.40
164	Bert Campaneris	.40
165	Frank Howard	.40
166	Harvey Kuenn	.50
167	Greg Luzinski	.40
168	Tug McGraw	.40
169	Willie Mays	3.00
170	Roger Maris	2.00
171	Vida Blue	.40
172	Bobby Grich	.40
173	Reggie Jackson	2.00
174	Hal McRae	.40
175	Carl Yastrzemski	1.00
176	David Concepcion	.40
177	Cecil Cooper	.40
178	George Hendrick	.40
179	Gary Matthews	.40
180	Stan Musial	3.00
181	Graig Nettles	.40
182	Don Sutton	.50
183	Kent Tekulve	.40
184	Bruce Sutter	.75
185	Darrell Evans	.40
186	Mike Schmidt	2.00
187	Dave Parker	.40
188	Dwight Evans	.40
189	Gary Carter	.40
190	Jack Morris	.40
191	Tony Perez	.50
192	Dave Winfield	.75
193	Andre Dawson	.50
194	Lee Smith	.40
195	Ozzie Smith	1.00
196	Denny Martinez	.40
197	Don Mattingly	2.50
198	Joe Carter	.40
199	Dennis Eckersley	.75
200	Kirby Puckett	2.00
201	Walter Alston	.40
202	Casey Stengel	.75
203	Sparky Anderson	.40
204	Tommy Lasorda	.75
205	Whitey Herzog	.40
206	Harmon Killebrew, Frank Howard, Reggie Jackson (League Leader)	.40
207	Hank Aaron, Early Wynn, Ron Santo, Willie McCovey (League Leader)	2.50
208	Frank Robinson, Harmon Killebrew, Boog Powell (League Leader)	1.50
209	Tony Oliva, Frank Robinson, Frank Howard (League Leader)	.75
210	Hank Aaron, Willie McCovey, Willie Mays, Orlando Cepeda (League Leader)	2.50
211	Hank Aaron, Frank Robinson, Willie Mays, Ernie Banks (League Leaders)	2.50
212	Carl Yastrzemski, Harmon Killebrew, Frank Howard (League Leaders)	1.50
213	Ernie Banks/HL	1.50
214	Hank Aaron/HL	2.50
215	Willie Mays/HL	2.50
216	Al Kaline/HL	.75
217	Stan Musial/HL	2.00
218	Duke Snider/HL	.75
219	Frank Robinson, Hank Bauer, Frank Robinson/HL	.50
220	Willie Mays, Stan Musial/HL	1.50
221	Whitey Ford (World Series Highlight)	.75
222	Jerry Koosman (World Series Highlight)	.40
223	Bob Gibson (World Series Highlight)	.75
224	Gil Hodges (World Series Highlight)	.40
225	Reggie Jackson (World Series Highlight)	1.50
226	Hank Bauer	.40
227	Ralph Branca	.40
228	Joe Garagiola	.75
229	Bob Feller	2.00
230	Dick Groat	.40
231	George Kell	.40
232	Bob Boone	.40
233	Minnie Minoso	.40
234	Billy Pierce	.40
235	Robin Roberts	.50
236	Johnny Sain	.40
237	Red Schoendienst	.40
238	Curt Simmons	.40
239	Duke Snider	2.00
240	Bobby Thomson	.40
241	Hoyt Wilhelm	.40
242	Elroy Face	.40
243	Ralph Kiner	.75
244	Hank Aaron	4.00
245	Al Kaline	2.00
246	Don Larsen	1.50
247	Tug McGraw	.40
248	Don Newcombe	.75
249	Herb Score	.40
250	Clete Boyer	.40
251	Lindy McDaniel	.40
252	Brooks Robinson	2.50
253	Orlando Cepeda	.60
254	Larry Bowa	.40
255	Mike Cuellar	.40
256	Jim Perry	.40
257	Dave Parker	.40
258	Maury Wills	.40
259	Willie Davis	.40
260	Juan Marichal	.60
261	Jim Bouton	.40
262	Dean Chance	.40
263	Sam McDowell	.40
264	Whitey Ford	3.00
265	Bob Uecker	2.00
266	Willie Stargell	2.00
267	Rico Carty	.40
268	Tommy John	.40
269	Phil Niekro	.60
270	Paul Blair	.40
271	Steve Carlton	3.00
272	Jim Lonborg	.40
273	Tony Perez	.60
274	Ron Swoboda	.40
275	Fergie Jenkins	.75
276	Jim Palmer	1.50
277	Sal Bando	.40
278	Tom Seaver	4.00
279	Johnny Bench	4.00
280	Nolan Ryan	6.00
281	Rollie Fingers	.50
282	Sparky Lyle	.40
283	Al Oliver	.40
284	Bob Watson	.40
285	Bill Buckner	.40
286	Bert Blyleven	.40
287	George Foster	.40
288	Al Hrabosky	.40
289	Cecil Cooper	.40
290	Carlton Fisk	1.00
291	Mickey Rivers	.40
292	Goose Gossage	.40
293	Bucky Dent	.40
294	Bucky Dent	.40
295	Frank Tanana	.40
296	George Brett	4.00
297	Keith Hernandez	.40
298	Fred Lynn	.40
299	Robin Yount	3.00
300	Ron Guidry	.40
301	Jack Clark	.40
302	Mark Fidrych	.40
303	Dale Murphy	1.50
304	Willie Hernandez	.40
305	Lou Whitaker	.40
306	Kirk Gibson	.75
307	Wade Boggs	3.00
308	Ryne Sandberg	4.00
309	Orel Hershiser	.40
310	Jimmy Key	.40
311	Richie Ashburn	.40
312	Smoky Burgess	.40
313	Gil Hodges	1.50
314	Ted Kluszewski	.40
315	Pee Wee Reese	1.00
316	Jackie Robinson	4.00
317	Harvey Haddix	.40
318	Satchel Paige	3.00
319	Roberto Clemente	5.00
320	Carl Furillo	.40
321	Don Drysdale	2.00
322	Curt Flood	.40
323	Bob Allison	.40
324	Tony Conigliaro	.40
325	Dan Quisenberry	.40
326	Ralph Branca	.40
327	Bob Feller	1.00
328	Satchel Paige	3.00
329	George Kell	.40
330	Pee Wee Reese	1.00
331	Bobby Thomson	.40
332	Carl Furillo	.40
333	Hank Bauer	.40
334	Herb Score	.40
335	Richie Ashburn	.40
336	Billy Pierce	.40
337	Duke Snider	2.00
338	Harvey Haddix	.40
339	Robin Roberts	.40
340	Dick Groat	.40
341	Curt Simmons	.40
342	Bob Uecker	1.00
343	Smoky Burgess	.40
344	Jim Bouton	.40
345	Elroy Face	.40
346	Don Drysdale	1.00
347	Bob Allison	.40
348	Clete Boyer	.40
349	Dean Chance	.40
350	Tony Conigliaro	.40
351	Curt Flood	.40
352	Hoyt Wilhelm	.40
353	Ron Swoboda	.40
354	Roberto Clemente	3.00
355	Tug McGraw	.40
356	Orlando Cepeda	.40
357	Joe Garagiola	.40
358	Juan Marichal	.50
359	Sam McDowell	.40
360	Johnny Sain	.40
361	Ted Kluszewski	.40
362	Al Kaline	2.00
363	Lindy McDaniel	.40
364	Don Newcombe	.40
365	Jim Perry	.40
366	Hank Aaron	4.00
367	Don Larsen	1.00
368	Mike Cuellar	.40
369	Willie Davis	.40
370	Ralph Kiner	.40
371	Minnie Minoso	.40
372	Larry Bowa	.40
373	Brooks Robinson	1.00
374	Bob Boone	.40
375	Jim Lonborg	.40
376	Paul Blair	.40
377	Rico Carty	.40
378	Sal Bando	.40
379	Mark Fidrych	.40
380	Al Hrabosky	.40
381	Willie Stargell	1.00
382	Johnny Bench	2.50
383	Dave Parker	.40
384	Sparky Lyle	.40
385	Fergie Jenkins	.50
386	Jim Palmer	1.00
387	Whitey Ford	2.00
388	Tony Perez	.40
389	Mickey Rivers	.40
390	Bob Watson	.40
391	Rollie Fingers	.40
392	George Foster	.40
393	Al Oliver	.40
394	Tom Seaver	3.00
395	Maury Wills	.40
396	Steve Carlton	1.00
397	Cecil Cooper	.40
398	Bill Buckner	.40
399	Phil Niekro	.40
400	Ron Guidry	.40
401	Willie Hernandez	.40
402	Willie Hernandez	.40
403	Tommy John	.40
404	Gil Hodges	.40
405	Bucky Dent	.40
406	Keith Hernandez	.40
407	Dan Quisenberry	.40
408	Fred Lynn	.40
409	Rick Reuschel	.40
410	Jackie Robinson	3.00
411	Goose Gossage	.40
412	Bert Blyleven	.40
413	Jack Clark	.40
414	Carlton Fisk	.50
415	Dale Murphy	.75
416	Frank Tanana	.40
417	George Brett	3.00
418	Robin Yount	2.50
419	Kirk Gibson	.50
420	Lou Whitaker	.40
421	Ryne Sandberg	2.50
422	Jimmy Key	.40
423	Nolan Ryan	5.00
424	Wade Boggs	.75
425	Orel Hershiser	.40
426	Billy Martin (Managers)	.40
427	Ralph Houk (Managers)	.40
428	Chuck Tanner (Managers)	.40
429	Earl Weaver (Managers)	.40
430	Leo Durocher (Managers)	.40
431	Tony Conigliaro, Norm Cash, Willie Horton (League Leaders)	.40
432	Ernie Banks, Hank Aaron, Eddie Mathews, Clete Boyer (League Leaders)	1.50
433	Norm Cash, Frank Howard, Al Kaline, Jimmy Piersall (League Leaders)	.40
434	Goose Gossage, Rollie Fingers (League Leaders)	.40
435	Nolan Ryan, Tom Seaver	.40
436	Reggie Jackson, Willie Stargell (League Leaders)	.75
437	Johnny Bench, Dick Allen (League Leaders)	.75
438	Roger Maris (Decade Highlights)	3.00
439	Carl Yastrzemski (Decade Highlights)	2.00
440	Nolan Ryan (Decade Highlights)	4.00
441	Cincinnati Reds (Decade Highlights)	.75
442	Tony Perez (Decade Highlights)	.40
443	Steve Carlton (Decade Highlights)	.75
444	Wade Boggs (Decade Highlights)	.75
445	Andre Dawson (Decade Highlights)	.75
446	Whitey Ford (World Series Highlights)	1.50
447	Hank Aaron (World Series Highlights)	4.00
448	Bob Gibson (World Series Highlights)	4.00
449	Roberto Clemente (World Series Highlights)	4.00
450	Orioles/Jackie Robinson (World Series Highlights)	1.50

Autographs

DON MATTINGLY OF-1B

NM/M

Common Player: 10.00
Inserted 1:Box

#	Player	Price
TAA1	Johnny Antonelli	15.00
TAA2	Hank Bauer	20.00
TAA3	Yogi Berra/50	350.00
TAA4	Ralph Branca	20.00
TAA5	Dom DiMaggio	50.00
TAA6	Joe Garagiola	40.00
TAA7	Carl Erskine	25.00
TAA8	Bob Feller	25.00
TAA10	Dick Groat	50.00
TAA11	Monte Irvin	25.00
TAA12	George Kell	20.00
TAA13	Vernon Law	15.00
TAA14	Bob Boone	10.00
TAA16	Willie Mays/50	500.00
TAA17	Gil McDougald	20.00
TAA18	Minnie Minoso	30.00
TAA19	Andy Pafko	30.00
TAA20	Billy Pierce	10.00
TAA21	Phil Rizzuto/200	100.00
TAA22	Robin Roberts	20.00
TAA23	Preacher Roe	20.00
TAA24	Johnny Sain	20.00
TAA25	Hank Sauer	20.00
TAA26	Red Schoendienst	25.00
TAA27	Bobby Shantz	10.00
TAA28	Curt Simmons	10.00
TAA29	Enos Slaughter	30.00
TAA30	Duke Snider	80.00
TAA31	Warren Spahn	120.00
TAA32	Bobby Thomson	20.00
TAA33	Mickey Vernon	15.00
TAA34	Hoyt Wilhelm	30.00
TAA35	Jim Wynn	10.00
TAA36	Elroy Face	10.00
TAA37	Gaylord Perry	35.00
TAA38	Ralph Kiner	50.00
TAA39	Johnny Podres	10.00
TAA40	Hank Aaron/50	400.00
TAA41	Ernie Banks/50	450.00
TAA42	Al Kaline	150.00
TAA43	Moose Skowron	15.00
TAA44	Don Larsen	140.00
TAA45	Harmon Killebrew	140.00
TAA46	Tug McGraw	30.00
TAA47	Don Newcombe	20.00
TAA48	Jimmy Piersall	15.00
TAA49	Herb Score	15.00
TAA50	Frank Thomas	10.00
TAA51	Clete Boyer	15.00
TAA52	Bill Mazeroski	60.00
TAA53	Lindy McDaniel	10.00
TAA54	Bobby Richardson	15.00
TAA55	Brooks Robinson/SP	200.00
TAA56	Frank Robinson	80.00
TAA57	Orlando Cepeda	40.00
TAA58	Stan Musial/50	300.00
TAA59	Larry Bowa	25.00
TAA60	Johnny Callison	15.00
TAA61	Mike Cuellar	15.00
TAA62	Bob Gibson/SP/50	180.00
TAA63	Jim Perry	10.00
TAA64	Frank Howard	15.00
TAA65	David Palmer	15.00
TAA67	Willie McCovey	80.00
TAA68	Maury Wills	15.00
TAA69	Carl Yastrzemski	200.00
TAA70	Willie Davis	10.00
TAA71	Jim Maloney	10.00
TAA73	Ron Santo	30.00
TAA74	Jim Bouton	25.00
TAA75	Lou Brock/50	180.00
TAA76	Dean Chance	10.00
TAA77	Tim McCarver/200	50.00
TAA78	Sam McDowell	15.00
TAA79	Joe Pepitone	10.00
TAA80	Whitey Ford	120.00
TAA81	Boog Powell	10.00
TAA83	Bill Freehan	15.00
TAA85	Dick Allen	30.00
TAA86	Rico Carty	10.00
TAA87	Willie Horton	10.00
TAA88	Tommy John	15.00
TAA89	Mickey Lolich	10.00
TAA90	Phil Niekro	30.00
TAA91	Wilbur Wood	10.00
TAA92	Paul Blair	10.00
TAA93	Bert Campaneris	10.00
TAA94	Steve Carlton	100.00
TAA96	Jim Lonborg	10.00
TAA97	Luis Aparicio	40.00
TAA98	Tony Perez	40.00
TAA99	Joe Morgan/200	90.00
TAA100	Ron Swoboda	25.00
TAA101	Luis Tiant	15.00
TAA102	Fergie Jenkins	15.00
TAA103	Bobby Murcer	30.00
TAA104	Jim Palmer	75.00
TAA106	Sal Bando	10.00
TAA107	Ken Holtzman	10.00
TAA108	Tom Seaver/50	200.00
TAA110	Johnny Bench	225.00
TAA111	Hal McRae	10.00
TAA112	Nolan Ryan	400.00
TAA113	Roy White	10.00
TAA114	Rollie Fingers	25.00
TAA115	Reggie Jackson/50	200.00
TAA116	Sparky Lyle	15.00
TAA117	Graig Nettles	10.00
TAA118	Al Oliver	10.00
TAA119	Joe Rudi	15.00
TAA120	Bob Watson	10.00
TAA121	Vida Blue	10.00
TAA122	Bill Buckner	10.00
TAA123	Darrell Evans	10.00
TAA124	Bert Blyleven	25.00
TAA125	David Concepcion	15.00
TAA126	George Foster	10.00
TAA127	Bobby Grich	10.00
TAA128	Al Hrabosky	10.00
TAA129	Greg Luzinski	20.00
TAA130	Cecil Cooper	10.00
TAA131	Ron Cey	10.00
TAA132	Carlton Fisk	90.00
TAA133	George Hendrick	10.00
TAA134	Mickey Rivers	10.00
TAA135	Dwight Evans	20.00
TAA136	Goose Gossage	20.00
TAA137	Gary Matthews	10.00
TAA138	Rick Reuschel	10.00
TAA139	Mike Schmidt	300.00
TAA140	Bucky Dent	25.00
TAA141	Jim Kaat	25.00
TAA142	Frank Tanana	10.00
TAA143	Dave Winfield/200	90.00
TAA144	George Brett	300.00
TAA145	Gary Carter/200	30.00
TAA146	Keith Hernandez	25.00
TAA147	Fred Lynn	25.00
TAA148	Robin Yount/SP/200	150.00
TAA149	Dennis Eckersley/SP/200	80.00
TAA150	Ron Guidry	30.00
TAA151	Kent Tekulve	15.00
TAA152	Jack Clark	10.00
TAA153	Andre Dawson/SP/200	60.00
TAA154	Mark Fidrych	20.00
TAA155	Denny Martinez/SP/200	40.00
TAA156	Dale Murphy	50.00
TAA157	Bruce Sutter	35.00
TAA158	Willie Hernandez	35.00
TAA160	Lou Whitaker	15.00
TAA162	Kirk Gibson	30.00
TAA163	Lee Smith	15.00
TAA164	Wade Boggs	80.00
TAA165	Ryne Sandberg/SP/200	160.00
TAA166	Don Mattingly	125.00
TAA167	Joe Carter/SP/200	40.00
TAA168	Orel Hershiser	40.00
TAA169	Kirby Puckett	150.00
TAA170	Jimmy Key	10.00

Baseball Bucks

NM/M

Valid to 3/02 for Topps merchandise:

		NM/M
TB1	Willie Mays ($1/15,000)	2.00
TB2	Roberto Clemente ($5/1,000)	4.00
TB3	Jackie Robinson ($10/500)	10.00

Game-Used Bat

		NM/M
	Common Player:	15.00
1	Johnny Bench	30.00
2	George Brett	50.00
3	Fred Lynn	15.00
4	Reggie Jackson	25.00
5	Mike Schmidt	50.00
6	Willie Stargell	20.00

Game-Used Bat Autograph

		NM/M
	Common Player:	120.00
	Production 25 Sets	
1	Johnny Bench	150.00
2	George Brett	200.00
3	Fred Lynn	75.00

Topps Final Autoproof

	NM/M
Common Player:	30.00
Carlton Fisk	60.00
Wade Boggs	40.00
Willie Mays	120.00
Willie McCovey	30.00
Jim Palmer	30.00
Robin Roberts	30.00
Duke Snider	40.00
Warren Spahn	40.00
Hoyt Wilhelm	30.00
Carl Yastrzemski	80.00

Reserve

		NM/M
	Complete Set (100):	90.00
	Common Player:	.75
	Hobby Pack (5):	10.00
	Hobby Box (10 + Auto. Ball):	150.00
1	Joe Adcock	.75
2	Brooks Robinson	3.00
3	Luis Aparicio	.75
4	Richie Ashburn	.75
5	Hank Bauer	.75
6	Johnny Bench	4.00
7	Wade Boggs	2.00
8	Moose Skowron	.75
9	George Brett	5.00
10	Lou Brock	2.00
11	Roy Campanella	4.00
12	Willie Hernandez	.75
13	Steve Carlton	2.00
14	Gary Carter	.75
15	Hoyt Wilhelm	.75
16	Orlando Cepeda	.75
17	Roberto Clemente	8.00
18	Dale Murphy	1.50
19	Dave Concepcion	.75
20	Dom DiMaggio	.75
21	Larry Doby	.75
22	Don Drysdale	4.00
23	Dennis Eckersley	.75
24	Bob Feller	2.00
25	Rollie Fingers	.75
26	Carlton Fisk	2.00
27	Nellie Fox	1.50
28	Mickey Rivers	.75
29	Tommy John	.75
30	Johnny Sain	.75
31	Keith Hernandez	.75
32	Gil Hodges	.75
33	Elston Howard	3.00
34	Frank Howard	.75
35	Bob Gibson	5.00
36	Fergie Jenkins	.75
37	Jackie Jensen	.75
38	Al Kaline	3.00
39	Harmon Killebrew	5.00
40	Ralph Kiner	.75
41	Dick Groat	.75
42	Don Larsen	.75
43	Ralph Branca	.75
44	Mickey Lolich	.75
45	Juan Marichal	3.00
46	Roger Maris	6.00
47	Bobby Thomson	.75
48	Eddie Mathews	4.00
49	Don Mattingly	8.00
50	Willie McCovey	2.00
51	Gil McDougald	.75
52	Tug McGraw	.75
53	Billy Pierce	.75
54	Minnie Minoso	.75
55	Johnny Mize	2.00
56	Elroy Face	.75
57	Joe Morgan	1.50
58	Thurman Munson	5.00
59	Stan Musial	5.00
60	Phil Niekro	.75
61	Paul Blair	.75
62	Andy Pafko	.75
63	Satchel Paige	5.00
64	Tony Perez	.75
65	Sal Bando	.75
66	Jimmy Piersall	.75
67	Kirby Puckett	5.00
68	Phil Rizzuto	3.00
69	Robin Roberts	.75
70	Jackie Robinson	8.00
71	Ryne Sandberg	3.00
72	Mike Schmidt	4.00
73	Red Schoendienst	.75
74	Herb Score	.75
75	Enos Slaughter	.75
76	Ozzie Smith	3.00
77	Warren Spahn	2.00
78	Don Sutton	.75
79	Luis Tiant	.75
80	Ted Kluszewski	.75
81	Whitey Ford	3.00
82	Maury Wills	.75
83	Dave Winfield	2.00
84	Early Wynn	.75
85	Carl Yastrzemski	3.00
86	Robin Yount	4.00
87	Bob Allison	.75
88	Clete Boyer	.75
89	Reggie Jackson	3.00
90	Yogi Berra	5.00
91	Willie Mays	8.00
92	Jim Palmer	.75
93	Pee Wee Reese	2.00
94	Frank Robinson	2.00
95	Boog Powell	.75
96	Willie Stargell	2.00
97	Nolan Ryan	10.00
98	Tom Seaver	4.00
99	Duke Snider	3.00
100	Bill Mazeroski	.75

Reserve Autographs

	NM/M
Common Autograph:	10.00
Inserted 1:10	
1 Willie Mays	160.00
2 Whitey Ford	60.00
3 Nolan Ryan	175.00
4 Carl Yastrzemski	90.00
5 Frank Robinson	40.00
6 Tom Seaver	80.00
7 Warren Spahn	75.00
8 Johnny Bench	100.00
9 Reggie Jackson	80.00
10 Bob Gibson	40.00
11 Bob Feller	20.00
12 Gil McDougald	15.00
13 Luis Tiant	10.00
14 Minnie Minoso	10.00
15 Herb Score	10.00
16 Moose Skowron	15.00
17 Maury Wills	10.00
18 Clete Boyer	15.00
19 Don Larsen	20.00
23 Tug McGraw	20.00
25 Robin Roberts	20.00
26 Frank Howard	10.00
27 Mickey Lolich	10.00
31 Tommy John	10.00
32 Dick Groat	15.00
33 Elroy Face	10.00
34 Paul Blair	10.00

Reserve Autographed Baseball

	NM/M
Common Autograph:	15.00
Inserted 1:Box	
1 Johnny Bench/100	80.00
2 Paul Blair/1,000	15.00
3 Clete Boyer/1,000	15.00
4 Ralph Branca/400	25.00
5 Elroy Face/1,000	15.00
6 Bob Feller/1,000	25.00
7 Whitey Ford/1,000	60.00
8 Bob Gibson/1,000	30.00
9 Dick Groat/1,000	15.00
10 Frank Howard/1,000	15.00
11 Reggie Jackson/100	75.00
12 Don Larsen/1,000	30.00
13 Mickey Lolich/500	15.00
14 Willie Mays/100	150.00
15 Gil McDougald/500	20.00
16 Tug McGraw/1,000	15.00
17 Minnie Minoso/1,000	15.00
18 Andy Pafko/500	25.00
19 Joe Pepitone/1,000	15.00
20 Robin Roberts/1,000	25.00
21 Frank Robinson/100	50.00
22 Nolan Ryan/100	150.00
23 Herb Score/500	20.00
24 Tom Seaver/100	80.00
25 Moose Skowron/1,000	15.00
26 Warren Spahn/100	50.00
27 Bobby Thomson/400	20.00
28 Luis Tiant/500	20.00
29 Carl Yastrzemski/100	100.00
30 Maury Wills/1,000	20.00

Reserve Bat Relics

	NM/M
Common Player:	8.00
Overall Relic Odds 1:10	
21 Al Kaline	20.00
22 Carl Yastrzemski	25.00
23 Carlton Fisk	15.00
24 Dale Murphy	15.00
25 Dave Winfield	10.00
26 Dick Groat	8.00
27 Dom DiMaggio	15.00
28 Don Mattingly	40.00
29 Gary Carter	8.00
30 George Kell	15.00
31 Harmon Killebrew	20.00
32 Jackie Jensen	15.00
33 Jackie Robinson	75.00
34 Jimmy Piersall	8.00
35 Joe Adcock	8.00
36 Joe Carter	8.00
37 Johnny Mize	10.00
38 Kirk Gibson	8.00
39 Mickey Vernon	8.00
40 Mike Schmidt	40.00
41 Ryne Sandberg	40.00
42 Ozzie Smith	20.00
43 Ted Kluszewski	10.00
44 Wade Boggs	15.00
45 Willie Mays	60.00
46 Duke Snider	15.00
47 Harvey Kuenn	8.00
48 Robin Yount	20.00
49 Red Schoendienst	8.00
50 Elston Howard	10.00
51 Bob Allison	8.00

Reserve Jersey Relics

	NM/M
Common Player:	8.00
Overall Relic Odds 1:10	
1 Brooks Robinson	15.00
2 Tony Conigliaro	15.00
3 Frank Howard	8.00
4 Don Sutton	10.00
5 Ferguson Jenkins	8.00
6 Frank Robinson	15.00
7 Don Mattingly	40.00
8 Willie Stargell	15.00
9 Moose Skowron	15.00
10 Fred Lynn	8.00
11 George Brett	40.00
12 Nolan Ryan	50.00
13 Orlando Cepeda	10.00
14 Reggie Jackson	15.00
15 Steve Carlton	15.00
16 Tom Seaver	20.00
17 Thurman Munson	25.00
18 Yogi Berra	20.00
19 Willie McCovey	10.00
20 Robin Yount	20.00

Chicago Cubs Reprints

This series of reprints of popular Cubs players' cards was part of Topps' 50th Anniversary celebration in 2001. Each card was printed in a serially-numbered edition of 30,000 and given to fans at special promotional dates. About 200 of each player's card were autographed and randomly distributed.

	NM/M
Complete Set (10):	75.00
Common Player:	5.00
1952 Andy Pafko	7.50
1952 Andy Pafko/Auto.	25.00
1958 Ernie Banks	20.00
1958 Ernie Banks/Auto.	75.00
1961 Ron Santo	7.50
1961 Ron Santo/Auto.	45.00
1971 Fergie Jenkins	7.50
1971 Fergie Jenkins/Auto.	45.00
1972 Billy Williams	7.50
1972 Billy Williams/Auto.	45.00
1979 Bruce Sutter	7.50
1979 Bruce Sutter/Auto.	45.00
1984 Ryne Sandberg	20.00
1984 Ryne Sandberg/Auto.	75.00
1985 Rick Sutcliffe	5.00
1985 Rick Sutcliffe/Auto.	25.00
1988 Andre Dawson	6.00
1988 Andre Dawson/Auto.	45.00
1998 Sammy Sosa	20.00
1998 Sammy Sosa/Auto.	75.00

2001 Topps Chrome

		NM/M
	Complete Set (660):	225.00
	Complete Series 1 (330):	100.00
	Complete Series 2 (330):	125.00
	Common Player:	.25
	Series 1 Pack (4):	2.50
	Series 1 Box (24):	45.00
	Series 2 Pack (4):	7.00
	Series 2 Box (24):	140.00
1	Cal Ripken Jr.	3.00
2	Chipper Jones	1.00
3	Roger Cedeno	.25
4	Garret Anderson	.50
5	Robin Ventura	.40
6	Daryle Ward	.25
7	Phil Nevin	.25
8	Jermaine Dye	.25
9	Chris Singleton	.25
10	Mike Redmond	.25
11	Jim Thome	1.00
12	Brian Jordan	.25
13	Dustin Hermanson	.25
14	Shawn Green	.50
15	Todd Stottlemyre	.25
16	Dan Wilson	.25
17	Derek Lowe	.25
18	Juan Gonzalez	.75
19	Pat Meares	.25
20	Paul O'Neill	.50
21	Jeffrey Hammonds	.25
22	Pokey Reese	.25
23	Mike Mussina	.75
24	Rico Brogna	.25
25	Jay Buhner	.25
26	Steve Cox	.25
27	Quilvio Veras	.25
28	Marquis Grissom	.25
29	Shigetoshi Hasegawa	.25
30	Shane Reynolds	.25
31	Adam Piatt	.25
32	Preston Wilson	.25
33	Ellis Burks	.25
34	Armando Rios	.25
35	Chuck Finley	.25
36	Shannon Stewart	.25
37	Mark McGwire	2.50
38	Gerald Williams	.25
39	Eric Young	.25
40	Peter Bergeron	.25
41	Arthur Rhodes	.25
42	Bobby Jones	.25
43	Matt Clement	.25
44	Pedro Martinez	1.00
45	Jose Canseco	.75
46	Matt Anderson	.25
47	Torii Hunter	.25
48	Carlos Lee	.50
49	Eric Chavez	.50
50	Rick Helling	.25
51	John Franco	.25
52	Mike Bordick	.25
53	Andres Galarraga	.40
54	Jose Cruz Jr.	.25
55	Mike Matheny	.25
56	Randy Johnson	1.00
57	Richie Sexson	.75
58	Vladimir Nunez	.25
59	Aaron Boone	.25
60	Darin Erstad	.50
61	Alex Gonzalez	.25
62	Gil Heredia	.25
63	Shane Andrews	.25
64	Todd Hundley	.25
65	Bill Mueller	.25
66	Mark McLemore	.25
67	Scott Spiezio	.25
68	Kevin McGlinchy	.25
69	Manny Ramirez	1.00
70	Mike Lamb	.25
71	Brian Buchanan	.25
72	Mike Sweeney	.25
73	John Wetteland	.25
74	Rob Bell	.25
75	John Burkett	.25
76	Derek Jeter	3.00
77	J.D. Drew	.50
78	Jose Offerman	.25
79	Rick Reed	.25
80	Will Clark	.25
81	Rickey Henderson	.75
82	Kirk Rueter	.25
83	Lee Stevens	.25
85	Jay Bell	.25
86	Fred McGriff	.50
87	Julio Zuleta	.25
88	Brian Anderson	.25
89	Orlando Cabrera	.25
90	Alex Fernandez	.25
91	Derek Bell	.25
92	Eric Owens	.25
93	Dennys Reyes	.25
94	Mike Stanley	.25
95	Jorge Posada	.75
96	Paul Konerko	.50
97	Mike Remlinger	.25
98	Travis Lee	.25
99	Ken Caminiti	.25
100	Kevin Barker	.25
101	Ozzie Guillen	.25
102	Randy Wolf	.25
103	Michael Tucker	.25
104	Darren Lewis	.25
105	Joe Randa	.25
106	Jeff Cirillo	.25
107	David Ortiz	1.00
108	Herb Perry	.25
109	Jeff Nelson	.25
110	Chris Stynes	.25
111	Johnny Damon	1.00
112	Jason Schmidt	.50
113	Charles Johnson	.25
114	Pat Burrell	.50
115	Gary Sheffield	.75
116	Tom Glavine	.50
117	Jason Isringhausen	.25
118	Chris Carpenter	.25
119	Jeff Suppan	.25
120	Ivan Rodriguez	1.00
121	Luis Sojo	.25
122	Ron Villone	.25
123	Mike Sirotka	.25
124	Chuck Knoblauch	.25
125	Jason Kendall	.25
126	Bobby Estalella	.25
127	Jose Guillen	.25
128	Carlos Delgado	1.00
129	Benji Gil	.25
130	Einar Diaz	.25
131	Andy Benes	.25
132	Adrian Beltre	.50
133	Roger Clemens	3.00
134	Scott Williamson	.25
135	Brad Penny	.25
136	Troy Glaus	.50
137	Kevin Appier	.25
138	Walt Weiss	.25
139	Michael Barrett	.25
140	Mike Hampton	.25
141	Francisco Cordova	.25
142	David Segui	.25
143	Carlos Febles	.25
144	Roy Halladay	.50
145	Seth Etherton	.25
146	Fernando Tatis	.25
147	Livan Hernandez	.25
148	B.J. Surhoff	.25
149	Barry Larkin	.50
150	Bobby Howry	.25
151	Dmitri Young	.25
152	Brian Hunter	.25
153	Alex Rodriguez	3.00
154	Hideo Nomo	.75
155	Warren Morris	.25
156	Antonio Alfonseca	.25
157	Edgardo Alfonzo	.25
158	Mark Grudzielanek	.25
159	Fernando Vina	.25
160	Homer Bush	.25
161	Jason Giambi	1.00
162	Steve Karsay	.25
163	Matt Lawton	.25
164	Rusty Greer	.25
165	Billy Koch	.25
166	Todd Hollandsworth	.25
167	Raul Ibanez	.25
168	Tony Gwynn	1.00
169	Carl Everett	.25
170	Hector Carrasco	.25
171	Jose Valentin	.25
172	Deivi Cruz	.25
173	Bret Boone	.25
174	Melvin Mora	.25
175	Danny Graves	.25
176	Jose Jimenez	.25
177	James Baldwin	.25
178	C.J. Nitkowski	.25
179	Jeff Zimmerman	.25
180	Mike Lowell	.25
181	Hideki Irabu	.25
182	Greg Vaughn	.25
183	Omar Daal	.25
184	Darren Dreifort	.25
185	Gil Meche	.25
186	Damian Jackson	.25
187	Frank Thomas	1.00
188	Luis Castillo	.25
189	Bartolo Colon	.50
190	Craig Biggio	.50
191	Scott Schoeneweis	.25
192	Dave Veres	.25
193	Ramon Martinez	.25
194	Jose Vidro	.25
195	Todd Helton	.75
196	Greg Norton	.25
197	Jacque Jones	.25
198	Jason Grimsley	.25
199	Dan Reichert	.25
200	Robb Nen	.25
201	Scott Hatteberg	.25
202	Terry Shumpert	.25

203 Kevin Millar .25
204 Ismael Valdes .25
205 Richard Hidalgo .25
206 Randy Velarde .25
207 Bengie Molina .25
208 Tony Womack .25
209 Enrique Wilson .25
210 Jeff Brantley .25
211 Rick Ankiel .25
212 Terry Mulholland .25
213 Ron Belliard .25
214 Terrence Long .25
215 Alberto Castillo .25
216 Royce Clayton .25
217 Joe McEwing .25
218 Jason McDonald .25
219 Ricky Bottalico .25
220 Keith Foulke .25
221 Brad Radke .25
222 Gabe Kapler .25
223 Pedro Astacio .25
224 Armando Reynoso .25
225 Darryl Kile .25
226 Reggie Sanders .25
227 Esteban Yan .25
228 Joe Nathan .25
229 Jay Payton .25
230 Francisco Cordero .25
231 Gregg Jefferies .25
232 LaTroy Hawkins .25
233 Jacob Cruz .25
234 Chris Holt .25
235 Vladimir Guerrero 1.00
236 Marvin Benard .25
237 Alex Ramirez .25
238 Mike Williams .25
239 Sean Bergman .25
240 Juan Encarnacion .25
241 Russ Davis .25
242 Ramon Hernandez .25
243 Sandy Alomar .25
244 Eddie Guardado .25
245 Shane Halter .25
246 Geoff Jenkins .50
247 Brian Meadows .25
248 Damian Miller .25
249 Darrin Fletcher .25
250 Rafael Furcal .50
251 Mark Grace .75
252 Mark Mulder .50
253 Joe Torre (Managers) .75
254 Bobby Cox (Managers) .25
255 Mike Scioscia (Managers) .25
256 Mike Hargrove (Managers) .25
257 Jimy Williams (Managers) .25
258 Jerry Manuel (Managers) .25
259 Charlie Manuel (Managers) .25
260 Don Baylor (Managers) .25
261 Phil Garner (Managers) .25
262 Tony Muser (Managers) .25
263 Buddy Bell (Managers) .25
264 Tom Kelly (Managers) .25
265 John Boles (Managers) .25
266 Art Howe (Managers) .25
267 Larry Dierker (Managers) .25
268 Lou Piniella (Managers) .25
269 Larry Rothschild (Managers) .25
270 Davey Lopes (Managers) .25
271 Johnny Oates (Managers) .25
272 Felipe Alou (Managers) .25
273 Bobby Valentine (Managers) .25
274 Tony LaRussa (Managers) .25
275 Bruce Bochy (Managers) .25
276 Dusty Baker (Managers) .25
277 Adrian Gonzalez, Adam Johnson (Draft Picks and Prospects) 1.00
278 Matt Wheatland, Brian Digby (Draft Picks and Prospects) .50
279 Tripper Johnson, Scott Thorman (Draft Picks and Prospects) 1.00
280 Phil Dumatrait, Adam Wainwright (Draft Picks and Prospects) 1.00
281 Scott Heard, David Parrish RC (Draft Picks and Prospects) .75
282 Rocco Baldelli, Mark Folsom RC (Draft Picks and Prospects) 1.00
283 Dominic Rich RC, Aaron Herr (Draft Picks and Prospects) .75
284 Mike Stodolka, Sean Burnett (Draft Picks and Prospects) .75
285 Derek Thompson, Corey Smith (Draft Picks and Prospects) .75
286 Danny Borrell RC, Jason Bourgeois RC (Draft Picks and Prospects) .75

287 Chin-Feng Chen, Corey Patterson, Josh Hamilton (Draft Picks and Prospects) .75
288 Ryan Anderson, Barry Zito, C.C. Sabathia (Draft Picks and Prospects) .75
289 Scott Sobkowiak, David Walling, Ben Sheets (Draft Picks and Prospects) .75
290 Ty Howington, Josh Kalinowski, Josh Girdley (Draft Picks and Prospects) .50
291 Hee Seop Choi RC, Aaron McNeal, Jason Hart (Draft Picks and Prospects) 1.00
292 Bobby Bradley, Kurt Ainsworth, Chin-Hui Tsao (Draft Picks and Prospects) .75
293 Mike Glendenning, Kenny Kelly, Juan Silvestri (Draft Picks and Prospects) .50
294 J.R. House, Ramon Castro, Ben Davis (Draft Picks and Prospects) .50
295 Chance Caple, Rafael Soriano RC, Pascual Coco (Draft Picks and Prospects) 1.00
296 Travis Hafner RC, Eric Munson, Bucky Jacobsen (Draft Picks and Prospects) 6.00
297 Jason Conti, Chris Wakeland, Brian Cole (Draft Picks and Prospects) .75
298 Scott Seabol, Aubrey Huff, Joe Crede (Draft Picks and Prospects) .50
299 Adam Everett, Jose Ortiz, Keith Ginter (Draft Picks and Prospects) .50
300 Carlos Hernandez, Geraldo Guzman, Adam Eaton (Draft Picks and Prospects) .75
301 Bobby Kielty, Milton Bradley, Juan Rivera (Draft Picks and Prospects) .50
302 Mark McGwire (Golden Moments) 2.00
303 Don Larsen (Golden Moments) .75
304 Bobby Thomson (Golden Moments) .25
305 Bill Mazeroski (Golden Moments) .25
306 Reggie Jackson (Golden Moments) 1.00
307 Kirk Gibson (Golden Moments) .25
308 Roger Maris (Golden Moments) 1.50
309 Cal Ripken Jr. (Golden Moments) 3.00
310 Hank Aaron (Golden Moments) 3.00
311 Joe Carter (Golden Moments) .25
312 Cal Ripken Jr. (Season Highlights) 3.00
313 Randy Johnson (Season Highlights) 1.00
314 Ken Griffey Jr. (Season Highlights) 2.00
315 Troy Glaus (Season Highlights) .75
316 Kazuhiro Sasaki (Season Highlights) .25
317 Sammy Sosa, Troy Glaus (League Leaders) 1.00
318 Todd Helton, Edgar Martinez (League Leaders) .50
319 Todd Helton, Nomar Garciaparra (League Leaders) 1.00
320 Barry Bonds, Jason Giambi (League Leaders) 1.50
321 Todd Helton, Manny Ramirez (League Leaders) .50
322 Todd Helton, Darin Erstad (League Leaders) .50
323 Kevin Brown, Pedro Martinez (League Leaders) .75
324 Randy Johnson, Pedro Martinez (League Leaders) .75
325 Will Clark (Post Season Highlights) .40
326 New York Mets (Post Season Highlights) .25
327 New York Yankees (Post Season Highlights) 1.00
328 Seattle Mariners (Post Season Highlights) .25
329 Mike Hampton (Post Season Highlights) .25

330 New York Yankees (Post Season Highlights) 1.00
331 World Series (Post Season Highlights) 1.50
332 Jeff Bagwell 1.00
333 Andy Pettitte .75
334 Tony Armas Jr. .25
335 Jeromy Burnitz .25
336 Javier Vazquez .25
337 Eric Karros .25
338 Brian Giles .50
339 Scott Rolen 1.00
340 David Justice .50
341 Ray Durham .25
342 Todd Zeile .25
343 Cliff Floyd .25
344 Barry Bonds 3.00
345 Matt Williams .25
346 Steve Finley .25
347 Scott Elarton .25
348 Bernie Williams .75
349 David Wells .25
350 J.T. Snow .25
351 Al Leiter .40
352 Magglio Ordonez .50
353 Raul Mondesi .25
354 Tim Salmon .50
355 Jeff Kent .40
356 Mariano Rivera .50
357 John Olerud .50
358 Javy Lopez .25
359 Ben Grieve .25
360 Ray Lankford .25
361 Ken Griffey Jr. 2.00
362 Rich Aurilia .25
363 Andruw Jones 1.00
364 Ryan Klesko .50
365 Roberto Alomar .50
366 Miguel Tejada .50
367 Mo Vaughn .25
368 Albert Belle .25
369 Jose Canseco .75
370 Kevin Brown .25
371 Rafael Palmeiro .75
372 Mark Redman .25
373 Larry Walker .50
374 Greg Maddux 2.00
375 Nomar Garciaparra 1.00
376 Kevin Millwood .50
377 Edgar Martinez .50
378 Sammy Sosa 1.50
379 Tim Hudson .50
380 Jim Edmonds .50
381 Mike Piazza 1.50
382 Brant Brown .25
383 Brad Fullmer .25
384 Alex Benes .25
385 Mickey Morandini .25
386 Troy Percival .25
387 Eddie Perez .25
388 Vernon Wells .50
389 Ricky Gutierrez .25
390 Rondell White .25
391 Kevin Escobar .25
392 Tony Batista .25
393 Jimmy Haynes .25
394 Billy Wagner .50
395 A.J. Hinch .25
396 Matt Morris .25
397 Lance Berkman .75
398 Jeff D'Amico .25
399 Octavio Dotel .25
400 Olmedo Saenz .25
401 Esteban Loaiza .25
402 Adam Kennedy .25
403 Moises Alou .25
404 Orlando Palmeiro .25
405 Kevin Young .25
406 Tom Goodwin .25
407 Mac Suzuki .25
408 Pat Hentgen .25
409 Kevin Stocker .25
410 Mark Sweeney .25
411 Tony Eusebio .25
412 Edgar Renteria .25
413 John Rocker .25
414 Jose Lima .25
415 Kerry Wood .50
416 Mike Timlin .25
417 Jose Hernandez .25
418 Jeremy Giambi .25
419 Luis Lopez .25
420 Mitch Meluskey .25
421 Garrett Stephenson .25
422 Jamey Wright .25
423 John Jaha .25
424 Placido Polanco .25
425 Marty Cordova .25
426 Joey Hamilton .25
427 Travis Fryman .25
428 Mike Cameron .25
429 Matt Mantei .25
430 Chan Ho Park .25
431 Shawn Estes .25
432 Danny Bautista .25
433 Wilson Alvarez .25
434 Kenny Lofton .40
435 Russ Ortiz .25
436 Dave Burba .25
437 Felix Martinez .25
438 Jeff Shaw .25
439 Mike Difelice .25
440 Roberto Hernandez .25
441 Bryan Rekar .25
442 Ugueth Urbina .25
443 Vinny Castilla .25
444 Carlos Perez .25
445 Juan Guzman .25

446 Ryan Rupe .25
447 Mike Mordecai .25
448 Ricardo Rincon .25
449 Curt Schilling 1.00
450 Alex Cora .25
451 Turner Ward .25
452 Omar Vizquel .40
453 Russ Branyan .25
454 Russ Johnson .25
455 Gregg Colbrunn .25
456 Charles Nagy .25
457 Wil Cordero .25
458 Jason Tyner .25
459 Devon White .25
460 Kelly Stinnett .25
461 Wilton Guerrero .25
462 Jason Bere .25
463 Calvin Murray .25
464 Miguel Batista .25
465 Erubiel Durazo .25
466 Luis Gonzalez .50
467 Jaret Wright .25
468 Chad Kreuter .25
469 Armando Benitez .25
470 Sidney Ponson .25
471 Adrian Brown .25
472 Sterling Hitchcock .25
473 Timoniel Perez .25
474 Jamie Moyer .25
475 Delino DeShields .25
476 Glendon Rusch .25
477 Chris Gomez .25
478 Adam Eaton .25
479 Pablo Ozuna .25
480 Bob Abreu .50
481 Kris Benson .25
482 Keith Osik .25
483 Darryl Hamilton .25
484 Marlon Anderson .25
485 Jimmy Anderson .25
486 John Halama .25
487 Nelson Figueroa .25
488 Alex Gonzalez .25
489 Benny Agbayani .25
490 Ed Sprague .25
491 Scott Erickson .25
492 Doug Glanville .25
493 Jesus Sanchez .25
494 Mike Lieberthal .25
495 Aaron Sele .25
496 Pat Mahomes .25
497 Ruben Rivera .25
498 Wayne Gomes .25
499 Freddy Garcia .25
500 Al Martin .25
501 Woody Williams .25
502 Paul Byrd .25
503 Rick White .25
504 Trevor Hoffman .25
505 Brady Anderson .25
506 Robert Person .25
507 Jeff Conine .25
508 Chris Truby .25
509 Emil Brown .25
510 Ryan Dempster .25
511 Ruben Mateo .25
512 Alex Ochoa .25
513 Jose Rosado .25
514 Masato Yoshii .25
515 Brian Daubach .25
516 Jeff D'Amico .25
517 Brent Mayne .25
518 John Thomson .25
519 Todd Ritchie .25
520 John Vander Wal .25
521 Neifi Perez .25
522 Chad Curtis .25
523 Kenny Rogers .25
524 Trot Nixon .25
525 Sean Casey .25
526 Wilton Veras .25
527 Troy O'Leary .25
528 Dante Bichette .25
529 Jose Silva .25
530 Darren Oliver .25
531 Steve Parris .25
532 David McCarty .25
533 Todd Walker .25
534 Brian Rose .25
535 Pete Schourek .25
536 Ricky Ledee .25
537 Justin Thompson .25
538 Benito Santiago .25
539 Carlos Beltran .40
540 Gabe White .25
541 Bret Saberhagen .25
542 Ramon Martinez .25
543 John Valentin .25
544 Frank Catalanotto .25
545 Tim Wakefield .25
546 Michael Tucker .25
547 Juan Pierre .25
548 Rich Garces .25
549 Luis Ordaz .25
550 Jerry Spradlin .25
551 Corey Koskie .25
552 Cal Eldred .25
553 Alfonso Soriano 1.00
554 Kip Wells .25
555 Orlando Hernandez .40
556 Bill Simas .25
557 Jim Parque .25
558 Joe Mays .25
559 Tim Belcher .25
560 Shane Spencer .25
561 Glenallen Hill .25
562 Matt LeCroy .25
563 Tino Martinez .25

564 Eric Milton .25
565 Ron Coomer .25
566 Cristian Guzman .25
567 Kazuhiro Sasaki .25
568 Mark Quinn .25
569 Eric Gagne .25
570 Kerry Ligtenberg .25
571 Rolando Arrojo .25
572 Jon Lieber .25
573 Jose Vizcaino .25
574 Jeff Abbott .25
575 Carlos Hernandez .25
576 Scott Sullivan .25
577 Matt Stairs .25
578 Tom Lampkin .25
579 Donnie Sadler .25
580 Desi Relaford .25
581 Scott Downs .25
582 Mike Mussina .75
583 Ramon Ortiz .25
584 Mike Myers .25
585 Frank Castillo .25
586 Manny Ramirez 1.00
587 Alex Rodriguez 3.00
588 Andy Ashby .25
589 Felipe Crespo .25
590 Bobby Bonilla .25
591 Denny Neagle .25
592 Dave Martinez .25
593 Mike Hampton .25
594 Gary DiSarcina .25
595 Tsuyoshi Shinjo RC .75
596 Albert Pujols RC 80.00
597 Roy Oswalt, Pat Strange, Jon Rauch (Prospects) .75
598 Phil Wilson RC, Jake Peavy RC, Darwin Cubillan RC (Prospects) 10.00
599 Nathan Haynes, Steve Smyth RC, Mike Bynum (Prospects) .75
600 Joe Lawrence, Choo Freeman, Michael Cuddyer (Prospects) .50
601 Larry Barnes, Dewayne Wise, Carlos Pena (Prospects) .25
602 Felipe Lopez, Gookie Dawkins, Erick Almonte RC (Prospects) 1.00
603 Brad Wilkerson, Alex Escobar, Eric Valent (Prospects) .25
604 Jeff Goldbach RC, Toby Hall, Rod Barajas (Prospects) .25
605 Marcus Giles, Pablo Ozuna, Jason Romano (Prospects) .25
606 Vernon Wells, Jack Cust, Dee Brown (Prospects) .25
607 Luis Montanez RC, David Espinosa (Draft Picks) 1.00
608 John Lackey, Justin Wayne RC (Draft Picks) 1.00
609 Josh Axelson RC, Carmen Cali RC (Draft Picks) 1.00
610 Shaun Boyd RC, Chris Morris RC (Draft Picks) .25
611 Dan Moylan RC, Tommy Arko RC (Draft Picks) 1.00
612 Luis Cotto RC, Luis Escobar (Draft Picks) 1.00
613 Blake Williams RC, Brandon Mims RC (Draft Picks) 1.00
614 Chris Russ RC, Bryan Edwards (Draft Picks) 1.00
615 Joe Torres, Ben Diggins (Draft Picks) .25
616 Mike Dalesandro, Edwin Encarnacion RC (Draft Picks) 5.00
617 Brian Bass RC, Odannis Ayala RC (Draft Picks) 1.00
618 Jason Kaanoi RC, Michael Mathews RC (Draft Picks) .50
619 Stuart McFarland RC, Adam Sterrett RC (Draft Picks) 1.00
620 David Krynzel, Grady Sizemore (Draft Picks) 1.00
621 Keith Bucktrot, Dane Sardinha (Draft Picks) .25
622 Anaheim Angels .25
623 Arizona Diamondbacks .25
624 Atlanta Braves .25
625 Baltimore Orioles .25
626 Boston Red Sox .25
627 Chicago Cubs .25
628 Chicago White Sox .25
629 Cincinnati Reds .25

630 Cleveland Indians .25
631 Colorado Rockies .25
632 Detroit Tigers .25
633 Florida Marlins .25
634 Houston Astros .25
635 Kansas City Royals .25
636 Los Angeles Dodgers .25
637 Milwaukee Brewers .25
638 Minnesota Twins .25
639 Montreal Expos .25
640 New York Mets .25
641 New York Yankees 1.50
642 Oakland Athletics .25
643 Philadelphia Phillies .25
644 Pittsburgh Pirates .25
645 San Diego Padres .25
646 San Francisco Giants .25
647 Seattle Mariners .25
648 St. Louis Cardinals .25
649 Tampa Bay Devil Rays .25
650 Texas Rangers .25
651 Toronto Blue Jays .25
652 Bucky Dent (Golden Moments) .25
653 Jackie Robinson (Golden Moments) 1.50
654 Roberto Clemente (Golden Moments) 1.50
655 Nolan Ryan (Golden Moments) 2.50
656 Kerry Wood (Golden Moments) .50
657 Rickey Henderson (Golden Moments) .50
658 Lou Brock (Golden Moments) .25
659 David Wells (Golden Moments) .25
660 Andruw Jones (Golden Moments) .75
661 Carlton Fisk (Golden Moments) .25

Retrofractors

Stars: 3-5X
Inserted 1:12

Before There Was Topps

Joe DiMaggio

	NM/M
Complete Set (10):	40.00
Common Player:	3.00
Inserted 1:20	
Refractors:	2-4X
Inserted 1:200	
BT1 Lou Gehrig	8.00
BT2 Babe Ruth	10.00
BT3 Cy Young	5.00
BT4 Walter Johnson	3.00
BT5 Ty Cobb	8.00
BT6 Rogers Hornsby	3.00
BT7 Honus Wagner	4.00
BT8 Christy Mathewson	3.00
BT9 Grover Alexander	3.00
BT10 Joe DiMaggio	8.00

Combos

MOUND MARKSMEN BOB GIBSON PEDRO MARTINEZ

	NM/M
Complete Set (20):	80.00
Common Card:	2.00
Inserted 1:12	
Refractors:	2-4X
Inserted 1:120	
1 Derek Jeter, Yogi Berra, Whitey Ford, Don Mattingly, Reggie Jackson	6.00

2	Chipper Jones, Mike Schmidt	6.00
3	Brooks Robinson, Cal Ripken Jr.	8.00
4	Bob Gibson, Pedro Martinez	3.00
5	Ivan Rodriguez, Johnny Bench	4.00
6	Ernie Banks, Alex Rodriguez	6.00
7	Joe Morgan, Ken Griffey Jr., Barry Larkin	5.00
8	Vladimir Guerrero, Roberto Clemente	6.00
9	Ken Griffey Jr., Hank Aaron	6.00
10	Casey Stengel, Joe Torre	2.00
TC11	Kevin Brown, Sandy Koufax, Don Drysdale	5.00
TC12	Mark McGwire, Sammy Sosa, Roger Marris, Babe Ruth	8.00
TC13	Ted Williams, Carl Yastrzelmski, Nomar Garciaparra	8.00
TC14	Greg Maddux, Roger Clemens, Cy Young	5.00
TC15	Tony Gwynn, Ted Williams	6.00
TC16	Cal Ripken Jr., Lou Gehrig	10.00
TC17	Sandy Koufax, Randy Johnson, Warren Spahn, Steve Carlton	4.00
TC18	Mike Piazza, Josh Gibson	5.00
TC19	Barry Bonds, Willie Mays	8.00
TC20	Jackie Robinson, Larry Doby	5.00

Golden Anniversary

NM/M
Complete Set (50): 120.00
Common Player: 1.00
Inserted 1:10
Refractors: 2-4X
Inserted 1:100

1	Hank Aaron	6.00
2	Ernie Banks	3.00
3	Mike Schmidt	5.00
4	Willie Mays	6.00
5	Johnny Bench	4.00
6	Tom Seaver	3.00
7	Frank Robinson	2.00
8	Sandy Koufax	3.00
9	Bob Gibson	3.00
10	Ted Williams	8.00
11	Cal Ripken Jr.	8.00
12	Tony Gwynn	3.00
13	Mark McGwire	6.00
14	Ken Griffey Jr.	4.00
15	Greg Maddux	6.00
16	Roger Clemens	6.00
17	Barry Bonds	8.00
18	Rickey Henderson	1.50
19	Mike Piazza	4.00
20	Jose Canseco	2.00
21	Derek Jeter	6.00
22	Nomar Garciaparra	5.00
23	Alex Rodriguez	5.00
24	Sammy Sosa	5.00
25	Ivan Rodriguez	2.00
26	Vladimir Guerrero	3.00
27	Chipper Jones	4.00
28	Jeff Bagwell	2.00
29	Pedro Martinez	3.00
30	Randy Johnson	3.00
31	Pat Burrell	1.50
32	Josh Hamilton	1.00
33	Ryan Anderson	1.00
34	Corey Patterson	1.50
35	Eric Munson	1.00
36	Sean Burroughs	1.00
37	C.C. Sabathia	1.00
38	Chin-Feng Chen	1.00
39	Barry Zito	1.50
40	Adrian Gonzalez	1.00
41	Mark McGwire	6.00
42	Nomar Garciaparra	5.00
43	Todd Helton	2.00
44	Matt Williams	1.00
45	Troy Glaus	1.50
46	Geoff Jenkins	1.00
47	Frank Thomas	2.00
48	Mo Vaughn	1.00
49	Barry Larkin	1.50
50	J.D. Drew	1.00

King of Kings

NM/M
Common Player: 40.00
Inserted 1:5,175 H
Inserted 1:5,209 R

KKR1	Hank Aaron	80.00
KKR2	Nolan Ryan	120.00
KKR3	Rickey Henderson	40.00
KKR5	Bob Gibson	40.00
KKR6	Nolan Ryan	120.00

King of Kings Golden Edition

Inserted 1:59,220 H

Past To Present

NM/M
Complete Set (10): 20.00
Common Player: 1.50
Inserted 1:18
Refractors: 1.5-3X
Inserted 1:180

1	Phil Rizzuto, Derek Jeter	6.00
2	Warren Spahn, Greg Maddux	4.00
3	Yogi Berra, Jorge Posada	3.00
4	Willie Mays, Barry Bonds	6.00
5	Red Schoendienst, Fernando Vina	1.50
6	Duke Snider, Shawn Green	2.00
7	Bob Feller, Bartolo Colon	1.50
8	Johnny Mize, Tino Martinez	1.50
9	Larry Doby, Manny Ramirez	2.00
10	Eddie Mathews, Chipper Jones	3.00

Through The Years

NM/M
Complete Set (50): 200.00
Common Player: 2.00
Inserted 1:10
Refractors: 2-4X
Inserted 1:100

1	Yogi Berra	4.00
2	Roy Campanella	4.00
3	Willie Mays	8.00
4	Andy Pafko	2.00
5	Jackie Robinson	8.00
6	Stan Musial	5.00
7	Duke Snider	4.00
8	Warren Spahn	4.00
9	Ted Williams	10.00
10	Eddie Matthews	4.00
11	Willie McCovey	2.00
12	Frank Robinson	4.00
13	Ernie Banks	5.00
14	Hank Aaron	8.00
15	Sandy Koufax	6.00
16	Bob Gibson	4.00
17	Harmon Killebrew	3.00
18	Whitey Ford	3.00
19	Roberto Clemente	8.00
20	Juan Marichal	2.00
21	Johnny Bench	5.00
22	Willie Stargell	3.00
23	Joe Morgan	2.00
24	Carl Yastrzemski	5.00
25	Reggie Jackson	4.00
26	Tom Seaver	4.00
27	Steve Carlton	3.00
28	Jim Palmer	2.00
29	Rod Carew	3.00
30	George Brett	8.00
31	Roger Clemens	8.00
32	Don Mattingly	5.00
33	Ryne Sandberg	6.00
34	Mike Schmidt	8.00
35	Cal Ripken Jr.	10.00
36	Tony Gwynn	4.00
37	Ozzie Smith	5.00
38	Wade Boggs	3.00
39	Nolan Ryan	10.00
40	Robin Yount	4.00
41	Mark McGwire	8.00
42	Ken Griffey Jr.	5.00
43	Sammy Sosa	6.00
44	Alex Rodriguez	6.00
45	Barry Bonds	8.00
46	Mike Piazza	5.00
47	Chipper Jones	5.00
48	Greg Maddux	5.00
49	Nomar Garciaparra	5.00
50	Derek Jeter	8.00

Topps Originals

NM/M
Common Player: 15.00
Inserted 1:1,783 H
Inserted 1:1,788 R
Refractors 10 sets produced

1	Roberto Clemente	180.00
2	Carl Yastrzemski	60.00
3	Mike Schmidt	75.00
4	Wade Boggs	20.00
5	Chipper Jones	40.00
6	Lou Brock	20.00
7	Dave Parker	15.00
8	Barry Bonds	80.00
10	Alex Rodriguez	50.00

What Could've Been

NM/M
Complete Set (10): 25.00
Common Player: 2.00
Inserted 1:30
Refractors: 2-4X
Inserted 1:300

WCB1	Josh Gibson	6.00
WCB2	Satchel Paige	6.00
WCB3	Buck Leonard	3.00
WCB4	James "Cool Pap Bell	4.00
WCB5	Andrew "Rube" Foster	3.00
WCB6	Martin Dihigo	2.00
WCB7	William "Judy" Johnson	3.00
WCB8	Mule Suttles	2.00
WCB9	Ray Dandridge	2.00
WCB10	John Henry Lloyd	2.00

2001 Topps Traded & Rookies

NM/M
Complete Topps Set (265): 140.00
Common Player: .10
Chrome Cards: 2-3X
Pack (8 + 2 Chrome): 8.00
Box (24): 175.00

T1	Sandy Alomar Jr.	.10
T2	Kevin Appier	.10
T3	Brad Ausmus	.10
T4	Derek Bell	.10
T5	Bret Boone	.20
T6	Rico Brogna	.10
T7	Ellis Burks	.10
T8	Ken Caminiti	.10
T9	Roger Cedeno	.10
T10	Royce Clayton	.10
T11	Enrique Wilson	.10
T12	Rheal Cormier	.10
T13	Eric Davis	.10
T14	Shawon Duston	.10
T15	Andres Galarraga	.20
T16	Tom Gordon	.10
T17	Mark Grace	.50
T18	Jeffrey Hammonds	.10
T19	Dustin Hermanson	.10
T20	Quinton McCracken	.10
T21	Todd Hundley	.10
T22	Charles Johnson	.10
T23	Marquis Grissom	.10
T24	Jose Mesa	.10
T25	Terry Mulholland	.10
T26	John Rocker	.10
T27	Jeff Frye	.10
T28	Reggie Sanders	.10
T29	David Segui	.10
T30	Shawn Sirotka	.10
T31	Fernando Tatis	.10
T32	Steve Trachsel	.10
T33	Ismael Valdes	.10
T34	Randy Velarde	.10
T35	Brian Boehringer	.10
T36	Mike Bordick	.10
T37	Ken Bottenfield	.10
T38	Pat Rapp	.10
T39	Jeff Nelson	.10
T40	Ricky Bottalico	.10
T41	Deion Sanders	.20
T42	Hideo Nomo	.50
T43	Bill Mueller	.10
T44	Roberto Kelly	.10
T45	Chris Holt	.10
T46	Mike Jackson	.10
T47	Devon White	.10
T48	Gerald Williams	.10
T49	Eddie Taubensee	.10
T50	Brian Hunter	.10
T51	Nelson Cruz	.10
T52	Jeff Fassero	.10
T53	Bubba Trammell	.10
T54	Bo Porter	.10
T55	Greg Norton	.10
T56	Benito Santiago	.10
T57	Ruben Rivera	.10
T58	Dee Brown	.10
T59	Jose Canseco	.50
T60	Chris Michalak	.10
T61	Tim Worrell	.10
T62	Matt Clement	.10
T63	Bill Pulsipher	.10
T64	Troy Brohawn	.10
T65	Mark Kotsay	.10
T66	Jose Lima	.10
T67	Shea Hillenbrand	.10
T68	Ted Lilly	.10
T69	Jermaine Dye	.10
T70	Jerry Hairston Jr.	.10
T71	John Mabry	.10
T72	Kurt Abbott	.10
T73	Eric Owens	.10
T74	Jeff Brantley	.10
T75	Vinny Castilla	.10
T76	Ron Villone	.10
T77	Ricky Henderson	.40
T78	Jason Grimsley	.10
T79	Christian Parker RC	.10
T80	Donnie Wall	.10
T81	Alex Arias	.10
T82	Willis Roberts	.10
T83	Ryan Minor	.10
T84	Jason LaRue	.10
T85	Ruben Sierra	.10
T86	Johnny Damon	.75
T87	Juan Gonzalez	.40
T88	Mac Suzuki	.10
T89	Tony Batista	.10
T90	Jay Witasick	.10
T91	Brent Abernathy	.10
T92	Paul LoDuca	.10
T93	Wes Helms	.10
T94	Milton Bradley	.10
T95	Matt LeCroy	.10
T96	A.J. Hinch	.10
T97	Bud Smith RC	.10
T98	Adam Dunn	.50
T99	Albert Pujols, Ichiro Suzuki	15.00
T100	Carlton Fisk	.25
T101	Tim Raines	.25
T102	Juan Marichal	.25
T103	Dave Winfield	.50
T104	Reggie Jackson	1.00
T105	Cal Ripken Jr.	3.00
T106	Ozzie Smith	1.00
T107	Tom Seaver	1.00
T108	Lou Piniella	.25
T109	Dwight Gooden	.25
T110	Bret Saberhagen	.25
T111	Gary Carter	.25
T112	Jack Clark	.25
T113	Rickey Henderson	.75
T114	Barry Bonds	3.00
T115	Bobby Bonilla	.25
T116	Jose Canseco	.75
T117	Will Clark	.25
T118	Andres Galarraga	.25
T119	Bo Jackson	.75
T120	Wally Joyner	.25
T121	Ellis Burks	.25
T122	David Cone	.25
T123	Greg Maddux	1.00
T124	Willie Randolph	.25
T125	Dennis Eckersley	.25
T126	Matt Williams	.40
T127	Joe Morgan	.50
T128	Fred McGriff	.40
T129	Roberto Alomar	.25
T130	Lee Smith	.25
T131	David Wells	.25
T132	Ken Griffey Jr.	2.00
T133	Deion Sanders	.50
T134	Nolan Ryan	2.00
T135	David Justice	.25
T136	Joe Carter	.25
T137	Jack Morris	.25
T138	Mike Piazza	1.50
T139	Barry Bonds	2.00
T140	Terrence Long	.10
T141	Ben Grieve	.10
T142	Richie Sexson	.25
T143	Sean Burroughs	.10
T144	Alfonso Soriano	.50
T145	Bob Boone	.10
T146	Larry Bowa	.10
T147	Bob Brenly	.10
T148	Buck Martinez	.10
T149	Lloyd McClendon	.10
T150	Jim Tracy	.10
T151	Jared Abruzzo RC	.50
T152	Kurt Ainsworth	.10
T153	Willie Bloomquist	.10
T154	Ben Broussard	.10
T155	Bobby Bradley	.10
T156	Mike Bynum	.10
T157	Ken Harvey	.10
T158	Ryan Christianson	.10
T159	Ryan Kohlmeier	.10
T160	Joe Crede	.50
T161	Jack Cust	.10
T162	Ben Diggins	.10
T163	Phil Dumatrait	.10
T164	Alex Escobar	.10
T165	Miguel Olivo	.10
T166	Chris George	.10
T167	Marcus Giles	.10
T168	Keith Ginter	.10
T169	Josh Girdley	.10
T170	Tony Alvarez	.10
T171	Scott Seabol	.10
T172	Josh Hamilton	.10
T173	Jason Hart	.10
T174	Israel Alcantara	.10
T175	Jake Peavy	2.50
T176	Stubby Clapp RC	.10
T177	D'Angelo Jimenez	.10
T178	Nick Johnson	.10
T179	Ben Johnson	.10
T180	Larry Bigbie	.10
T181	Allen Levrault	.10
T182	Felipe Lopez	.10
T183	Sean Burnett	.10
T184	Nick Neugebauer	.10
T185	Austin Kearns	.25
T186	Corey Patterson	.25
T187	Carlos Pena	.10
T188	Ricardo Rodriguez RC	.50
T189	Juan Rivera	.10
T190	Grant Roberts	.10
T191	Adam Pettyjohn RC	.25
T192	Jared Sandberg	.10
T193	Xavier Nady	.25
T194	Dane Sardinha	.10
T195	Shawn Sonnier	.10
T196	Rafael Soriano	.25
T197	Brian Specht RC	.10
T198	Aaron Myette	.10
T199	Juan Uribe RC	.40
T200	Jayson Werth	.10
T201	Brad Wilkerson	.10
T202	Horacio Estrada	.10
T203	Joel Pineiro	.10
T204	Matt LeCroy	.10
T205	Michael Coleman	.10
T206	Ben Sheets	.40
T207	Eric Byrnes	.10
T208	Sean Burroughs	.10
T209	Ken Harvey	.10
T210	Travis Hafner	2.50
T211	Erick Almonte	.10
T212	Jason Belcher RC	.50
T213	Wilson Betemit RC	.75
T214	Hank Blalock RC	2.00
T215	Danny Borrell	.10
T216	John Buck RC	.50
T217	Freddie Bynum RC	.50
T218	Noel Devarez RC	.10
T219	Juan Diaz RC	.25
T220	Felix Diaz RC	.25
T221	Josh Fogg RC	.50
T222	Matt Ford RC	.25
T223	Scott Heard	.10
T224	Ben Hendrickson RC	.25
T225	Cody Ross RC	.25
T226	Adrian Hernandez RC	.40
T227	Alfredo Amezaga RC	.25
T228	Bob Keppel RC	.25
T229	Ryan Madson RC	.50
T230	Octavio Martinez RC	.25
T231	Hee Seop Choi	.40
T232	Thomas Mitchell	.10
T233	Luis Montanez	.10
T234	Andy Morales RC	.40
T235	Justin Morneau RC	5.00
T236	Greg "Toe" Nash RC	.25
T237	Valentino Pasucci RC	.25
T238	Roy Smith RC	.25
T239	Antonio Perez RC	.40
T240	Chad Petty RC	.50
T241	Steve Smyth	.10
T242	Jose Reyes RC	20.00
T243	Eric Reynolds RC	.40
T244	Dominic Rich	.10
T245	Jason Richardson RC	.25
T246	Ed Rogers RC	.25
T247	Albert Pujols RC	50.00
T248	Esix Snead RC	.25
T249	Luis Torres RC	.25
T250	Matt White RC	.40
T251	Blake Williams	.10
T252	Chris Russ	.10
T253	Joe Kennedy RC	.25
T254	Jeff Randazzo RC	.25
T255	Beau Hale RC	.25
256	Brad Hennessey RC	.25
257	Jake Gautreau RC	.25
258	Jeff Mathis RC	.75
259	Aaron Heilman RC	.50
260	Bronson Sardinha RC	.50
261	Irvin Guzman RC	4.00
262	Gabe Gross RC	.50
263	J.D. Martin RC	.40
264	Chris Smith RC	.40
265	Kenny Baugh RC	.40

Autographs

NM/M
Common Autograph: 15.00

JD	Johnny Damon	30.00
MM	Mike Mussina	25.00

Legends Autographs

NM/M
Common Player: 15.00

TT51	Ralph Branca	15.00
TTF47	Frank Howard	25.00
TTF50	Mickey Lolich	15.00
TT37	Tug McGraw	15.00
TT48F	Bobby Richardson	20.00
TT36F	Enos Slaughter	25.00
TT13	Warren Spahn	40.00
TT43	Bobby Thomson	20.00

Relics

NM/M
Common Player: 4.00
Inserted 1:29

SA	Sandy Alomar Jr.	4.00
DB	Derek Jeter	4.00
BB	Bobby Bonilla	4.00
BB	Bret Boone	4.00
RB	Rico Brogna	4.00
KC	Ken Caminiti	4.00
JC	Jose Canseco	8.00
ROC	Roger Cedeno	4.00
RSC	Royce Clayton	4.00
JD	Johnny Damon	10.00
ED	Eric Davis	4.00
JD	Jermaine Dye	4.00
AG	Andres Galarraga	4.00
RG	Ron Gant	4.00
JG	Juan Gonzalez	6.00
MG	Mark Grace	8.00
MG	Marquis Grissom	4.00
JH	Jeffrey Hammonds	4.00
MH	Mike Hampton	4.00
DH	Dustin Hermanson	4.00
TH	Todd Hundley	4.00
CJ	Charles Johnson	4.00
FM	Fred McGriff	5.00
BM	Bill Mueller	4.00
DN	Denny Neagle	4.00
HR	Hideo Nomo	25.00
NP	Neifi Perez	4.00
TR	Tim Raines	4.00
RS	Ruben Sierra	4.00
MS	Matt Stairs	4.00
KS	Kelly Stinnett	4.00
FT	Fernando Tatis	4.00
DW	David Wells	4.00
GW	Gerald Williams	4.00
EW	Enrique Wilson	4.00

Dual-Traded Relics

NM/M
Common Player: 4.00

DB	Derek Bell	4.00
MG	Mark Grace	10.00
BG	Ben Grieve	4.00
DH	Dustin Hermanson	4.00
MR	Manny Ramirez	15.00

Farewell Dual Relic

NM/M
Inserted 1:4,693

RG	Cal Ripken, Tony Gwynn	80.00

Hall of Fame Relics

NM/M
Complete Set (1):

PW	Kirby Puckett, Dave Winfield	40.00

Rookie Relics

		NM/M
Common Player:		4.00
Inserted 1:91		
AP	Albert Pujols	150.00
TS	Tsuyoshi Shinjo	4.00
AB	Angel Berroa	6.00
BO	Bill Ortega	4.00
HC	Humberto Cota	4.00
JL	Jason Lane	4.00
JS	Jamal Strong	4.00
JV	Jose Valverde	4.00
JY	Jason Young	4.00
NC	Nate Cornejo	4.00
NN	Nick Neugebauer	4.00
PF	Pedro Feliz	4.00
RS	Richard Stahl	4.00
SB	Sean Burroughs	4.00
SS	Jae Weong Seo	6.00
WB	Wilson Betemit	8.00
WR	Wilken Ruan	4.00

Who Would Have Thought

		NM/M
Complete Set (20):		15.00
Common Player:		.75
Inserted 1:8		
WWH1	Nolan Ryan	3.00
WWH2	Ozzie Smith	1.50
WWH3	Tom Seaver	1.50
WWH4	Steve Carlton	.75
WWH5	Reggie Jackson	1.50
WWH6	Frank Robinson	1.00
WWH7	Keith Hernandez	.75
WWH8	Andre Dawson	.75
WWH9	Lou Brock	.75
WWH10	Dennis Eckersley	.75
WWH11	Dave Winfield	1.00
WWH12	Rod Carew	1.00
WWH13	Willie Randolph	.75
WWH14	Doc Gooden	.75
WWH15	Carlton Fisk	1.00
WWH16	Dale Murphy	.75
WWH17	Paul Molitor	1.00
WWH18	Gary Carter	.75
WWH19	Wade Boggs	1.00
WWH20	Willie Mays	3.00

eTopps

Operating along the lines of a stock exchange, with collectors able to buy and sell the cards without ever taking physical possession, eTopps was launched in October and had about 10 "Initial Player Offerings" (new cards) issued per week to a total of 75. Issue price and quantity available were announced at the time of release. If a card was not sold out during its five-day order period, the unsold cards were destroyed. Fronts have portrait and action photos, player identification and an eTopps logo, printed on refractive metallic foil. Backs, labeled, "Inaugural Edition," have a portrait photo, personal data and stats, along with 2000 highlights and a projection for the 2001 season. A circular holographic seal at top-right has a serial number. Each card is issued in a thick plastic holder that is sealed with an eTopps holographic sticker. Cards are skip-numbered between 1-150, as it was originally intended that 150 cards would be issued the first year. Shown in parentheses for each player are the initial offering price and the quantity reported issued by Topps. Values shown are for cards in a virtual portfolio, rather than

"in hand." Taking physical possession of a card from an eTopps portfolio requires payment of a delivery fee of $7.

		NM/M
Complete Set (75):		1,350
Common Player:		1.50
1	Nomar Garciaparra ($9.50 / 1,315)	10.00
2	Chipper Jones ($9.50 / 674)	90.00
3	Jeff Bagwell ($9.50 / 485)	35.00
4	Randy Johnson ($6.50 / 1,499)	20.00
7	Adam Dunn ($6.50 / 4,197)	5.00
8	J.D. Drew ($6.50 / 767)	10.00
9	Larry Walker ($6.50 / 420)	25.00
10	Edgardo Alfonzo ($6.50 / 338)	65.00
11	Lance Berkman ($6.50 / 595)	35.00
12	Tony Gwynn ($6.50 / 828)	30.00
13	Andruw Jones ($6.50 / 908)	22.50
15	Troy Glaus ($6.50 / 862)	10.00
17	Sammy Sosa ($9.50 / 2,487)	5.00
21	Darin Erstad ($3.50 / 664)	10.00
22	Barry Bonds ($9.50 / 1,567)	95.00
27	Derek Jeter ($9.50 / 1,041)	50.00
29	Curt Schilling ($6.50 / 2,125)	5.00
30	Roberto Alomar ($6.50 / 448)	20.00
31	Luis Gonzalez ($6.50 / 1,104)	3.00
32	Jimmy Rollins ($3.50 / 1,307)	5.00
34	Joe Crede ($3.50 / 1,050)	10.00
39	Sean Casey ($6.50 / 537)	30.00
46	Alex Rodriguez ($9.50 / 2,212)	35.00
47	Tom Glavine ($6.50 / 437)	35.00
	Jose Ortiz ($3.50 / 738)	5.00
51	Cal Ripken Jr. ($9.50 / 2,201)	30.00
52	Bobby Abreu ($3.50 / 677)	27.50
55	Alex Escobar ($3.50 / 931)	4.00
56	Ivan Rodriguez ($6.50 / 698)	15.00
59	Jeff Kent ($6.50 / 452)	20.00
62	Rick Ankiel ($6.50 / 752)	6.00
65	Craig Biggio ($6.50 / 410)	40.00
66	Carlos Delgado ($6.50 / 398)	40.00
68	Greg Maddux ($6.50 / 1,031)	15.00
69	Kerry Wood ($3.50 / 1,056)	9.00
71	Todd Helton ($6.50 / 978)	20.00
72	Mariano Rivera ($6.50 / 824)	20.00
73	Jason Kendall ($3.50 / 672)	10.00
75	Scott Rolen ($6.50 / 498)	40.00
76	Kazuhiro Sasaki ($6.50 / 5,000)	2.00
77	Roy Oswalt ($6.50 / 915)	20.00
78	C.C. Sabathia ($6.50 / 1,974)	3.00
83	Brian Giles ($6.50 / 400)	25.00
87	Rafael Furcal ($3.50 / 646)	9.00
88	Mike Mussina ($6.50 / 793)	12.50
89	Gary Sheffield ($6.50 / 359)	50.00
92	Mark McGwire ($9.50 / 2,908)	10.00
94	Tsuyoshi Shinjo ($3.50 / 3,000)	1.50
99	Jose Vidro ($3.50 / 443)	25.00
100	Ichiro Suzuki ($6.50 / 10,000)	12.50
105	Manny Ramirez ($6.50 / 1,074)	15.00
109	Juan Gonzalez ($6.50 / 558)	9.00
112	Ken Griffey Jr. ($9.50 / 2,398)	12.00
114	Tim Hudson ($6.50 / 663)	17.50
115	Nick Johnson ($6.50 / 1,217)	5.00
118	Jason Giambi ($9.50 / 897)	10.00
122	Rafael Palmeiro ($6.50 / 464)	20.00
124	Vladimir Guerrero ($6.50 / 854)	30.00
125	Vernon Wells ($6.50 / 349)	80.00
127	Roger Clemens ($9.50 / 1,462)	30.00
128	Frank Thomas ($6.50 / 834)	15.00
129	Carlos Beltran ($3.50 / 489)	50.00
130	Pat Burrell ($3.50 / 1,253)	15.00
131	Pedro Martinez ($9.50 / 1,038)	15.00
132	Mike Piazza ($9.50 / 1,379)	10.00
135	Luis Montanez ($3.50 / 5,000)	1.50
140	Sean Burroughs ($3.50 / 5,000)	1.50
141	Barry Zito ($6.50 / 843)	22.50
142	Bobby Bradley ($3.50 / 5,000)	1.50
143	Albert Pujols ($6.50 / 1,699)	45.00
143a	Albert Pujols (32 autographed pieces sold by Topps 6/05 for $199 each)	1,500
144	Ben Sheets ($3.50 / 1,713)	5.00
145	Alfonso Soriano ($6.50 / 1,699)	15.00
146	Josh Hamilton ($3.50 / 5,000)	1.50
147	Eric Munson ($3.50 / 5,000)	1.50
150	Mark Mulder ($3.50 / 4,335)	2.00

2001 Topps Fusion

		NM/M
Complete Set (250):		150.00
Common Player:		.25
Pack (5):		2.50
Box (24):		50.00
1	Albert Belle	.25
2	Albert Belle	.25
3	Albert Belle	.25
4	Nick Bierbrodt	.25
5	Alex Rodriguez	2.50
6	Alex Rodriguez	2.50
7	Alex Rodriguez	2.50
8	Alex Rodriguez	2.50
9	Eric Munson	.25
10	Barry Bonds	3.00
11	Andruw Jones	.75
12	Antonio Alfonseca	.25
13	Andres Galarraga	.40
14	Joe Crede	.25
15	Barry Larkin	.40
16	Barry Bonds	3.00
17	Barry Bonds	3.00
18	Andruw Jones	.75
19	C.C. Sabathia	.25
20	Bobby Higginson	.25
21	Barry Larkin	.40
22	Ben Grieve	.25
23	Barry Bonds	3.00
24	Corey Patterson	.25
25	Carlos Delgado	.75
26	Bernie Williams	.50
27	Brian Giles	.40
28	Barry Larkin	.40
29	Gookie Dawkins	.25
30	Chipper Jones	1.50
31	Brian Giles	.40
32	Carlos Delgado	.75
33	Ben Grieve	.25
34	Geoff Goetz	.25
35	Cristian Guzman	.25
36	Cal Ripken Jr.	3.00
37	Chipper Jones	1.50
38	Bernie Williams	.50
39	Pablo Ozuna	.25
40	Dante Bichette	.25
41	Carlos Delgado	.75
42	Craig Biggio	.25
43	Cal Ripken Jr.	3.00
44	Tim Redding	.25
45	Darin Erstad	.50
46	Chipper Jones	1.50
47	Darin Erstad	.50
48	Carlos Delgado	.75
49	Josh Hamilton	.25
50	Derek Jeter	3.00
51	Darin Erstad	.50
52	Dean Palmer	.25
53	Chipper Jones	1.50
54	Chin-Feng Chen	.25
55	Edgar Martinez	.25
56	Derek Jeter	3.00
57	Derek Jeter	3.00
58	Craig Biggio	.25
59	Keith Ginter	.25
60	Edgardo Alfonzo	.25
61	Edgar Martinez	.25
62	Edgardo Alfonzo	.25
63	David Justice	.50
64	Roy Oswalt	.25
65	Eric Karros	.25
66	Edgardo Alfonzo	.25
67	Frank Thomas	1.00
68	Dean Palmer	.25
69	Alfonso Soriano	1.00
70	Fernando Vina	.25
71	Frank Thomas	1.00
72	Garret Anderson	.40
73	Derek Jeter	.25
74	Bobby Bradley	.25
75	Frank Thomas	1.00
76	Gary Sheffield	.50
77	Geoff Jenkins	.25
78	Edgar Martinez	.25
79	Nick Johnson	.25
80	Fred McGriff	.40
81	Geoff Jenkins	.25
82	Greg Maddux	1.50
83	Edgardo Alfonzo	.25
84	Hee Seop Choi RC	2.00
85	Garret Anderson	.50
86	Greg Maddux	1.50
87	Ivan Rodriguez	.75
88	Eric Karros	.25
89	Scott Seabol	.25
90	Ivan Rodriguez	.75
91	Ivan Rodriguez	.75
92	J.D. Drew	.25
93	Frank Thomas	1.00
94	Ryan Anderson	.25
95	Jason Giambi	.75
96	Jason Giambi	.75
97	Jason Kendall	.25
98	Gary Sheffield	.50
99	Milton Bradley	.25
100	Jason Kendall	.25
101	Jason Kendall	.25
102	Jeff Bagwell	.75
103	Greg Maddux	1.50
104	Sean Burroughs	.25
105	Jay Bell	.25
106	Jeff Bagwell	.75
107	Jeffrey Hammonds	.25
108	Ivan Rodriguez	.75
109	Ben Petrick	.25
110	Jeff Bagwell	.75
111	Jeff Cirillo	.25
112	Jermaine Dye	.25
113	J.T. Snow Jr.	.25
114	Ben Davis	.25
115	Jeff Cirillo	.25
116	Jeff Kent	.25
117	Jeromy Burnitz	.25
118	Jay Bell	.25
119	Jason Hart	.25
120	Jeff Kent	.25
121	Jermaine Dye	.25
122	John Olerud	.25
123	Jeff Bagwell	.75
124	Jeff Segar RC	.25
125	Jeromy Burnitz	.25
126	Jeromy Burnitz	.25
127	Johnny Damon	.25
128	Jim Edmonds	.40
129	Tim Christman RC	.25
130	Jim Thome	.75
131	Jim Edmonds	.40
132	Jorge Posada	.75
133	Jim Thome	.75
134	Danny Borrell RC	.50
135	Johnny Damon	.25
136	Jim Thome	.75
137	Jose Vidro	.25
138	Ken Griffey Jr.	1.50
139	Sean Burnett	.25
140	Larry Walker	.40
141	Jose Vidro	.25
142	Ken Griffey Jr.	1.50
143	Larry Walker	.40
144	Robert Keppell RC	1.00
145	Luis Castillo	.25
146	Ken Griffey Jr.	1.50
147	Kevin Brown	.40
148	Manny Ramirez	.75
149	David Parrish RC	.25
150	Manny Ramirez	.75
151	Kevin Brown	.40
152	Luis Castillo	.25
153	Mark Grace	.50
154	Mike Jacobs RC	.50
155	Mark Grace	.50
156	Larry Walker	.40
157	Magglio Ordonez	.50
158	Mark McGwire	2.00
159	Adam Johnson	.25
160	Mark McGwire	2.00
161	Magglio Ordonez	.50
162	Mark McGwire	2.00
163	Matt Williams	.40
164	Oscar Ramirez RC	.50
165	Mike Piazza	1.50
166	Manny Ramirez	.75
167	Mike Piazza	1.50
168	Mike Mussina	.50
169	Odannis Ayala RC	.25
170	Mike Sweeney	.25
171	Mark McGwire	2.00
172	Nomar Garciaparra	2.50
173	Mike Piazza	1.50
174	J.R. House	.25
175	Neifi Perez	.25
176	Mike Piazza	1.50
177	Pedro Martinez	1.00
178	Mo Vaughn	.25
179	Shawn Fagan RC	.50
180	Nomar Garciaparra	2.50
181	Mo Vaughn	.25
182	Rafael Palmeiro	.50
183	Nomar Garciaparra	2.50
184	Chris Bass RC	.75
185	Raul Mondesi	.25
186	Nomar Garciaparra	2.50
187	Randy Johnson	1.00
188	Omar Vizquel	.25
189	Erick Almonte RC	1.00
190	Ray Durham	.25
191	Pedro Martinez	1.00
192	Robb Nen	.25
193	Pedro Martinez	1.00
194	Luis Montanez RC	.25
195	Ray Lankford	.25
196	Rafael Palmeiro	.50
197	Roberto Alomar	.75
198	Rafael Palmeiro	.50
199	Chad Petty RC	.25
200	Richard Hidalgo	.25
201	Randy Johnson	1.00
202	Robin Ventura	.25
203	Randy Johnson	1.00
204	Derek Thompson	.25
205	Sammy Sosa	2.00
206	Roberto Alomar	.75
207	Sammy Sosa	2.00
208	Raul Mondesi	.25
209	Scott Heard	.25
210	Scott Rolen	.75
211	Sammy Sosa	2.00
212	Scott Rolen	.75
213	Roberto Alomar	.75
214	Dominic Rich RC	.50
215	Sean Casey	.25
216	Scott Rolen	.75
217	Sean Casey	.25
218	Robin Ventura	.25
219	William Smith RC	.50
220	Tim Salmon	.40
221	Sean Casey	.25
222	Shannon Stewart	.25
223	Sammy Sosa	2.00
224	Joel Pieniero RC	.50
225	Tino Martinez	.25
226	Shawn Green	.40
227	Shawn Green	.40
228	Scott Rolen	.50
229	Greg Morrison RC	.50
230	Tony Gwynn	1.00
231	Todd Helton	.75
232	Steve Finley	.25
233	Scott Williamson	.25
234	Talmadge Nunnari	.25
235	Tony Womack	.25
236	Tony Batista	.25
237	Tim Salmon	.40
238	Shawn Green	.40
239	Carlos Villalobos RC	.25
240	Troy Glaus	.50
241	Troy Glaus	.50
242	Todd Helton	.75
243	Tim Salmon	.40
244	Marco Scutaro RC	.50
245	Troy O'Leary	.25
246	Vladimir Guerrero	1.00
247	Vladimir Guerrero	1.00
248	Vladimir Guerrero	1.00
249	Horacio Estrada	.25
250	Vladimir Guerrero	1.00

Autographs

		NM/M
Common Player:		5.00
Inserted 1:23		
1	Rafael Furcal	10.00
2	Mike Lamb	5.00
3	Jason Marquis	5.00
4	Milton Bradley	5.00
5	Barry Zito	20.00
6	Derek Lee	20.00
7	Corey Patterson	10.00
8	Josh Hamilton	30.00
9	Sean Burroughs	8.00
10	Jason Hart	5.00
11	Luis Montanez	5.00
12	Robert Keppell	5.00
13	Blake Williams	10.00
14	Phil Wilson	5.00
15	Jake Peavy	40.00
16	Alex Rodriguez	70.00
17	Ivan Rodriguez	20.00
18	Don Larsen	20.00
19	Todd Helton	20.00
20	Carlos Delgado	15.00
21	Geoff Jenkins	10.00
22	Willie Stargell	30.00
23	Frank Robinson	30.00
24	Warren Spahn	40.00
25	Harmon Killebrew	30.00
26	Chipper Jones	30.00
27	Chipper Jones	30.00
28	Chipper Jones	30.00
29	Chipper Jones	30.00
30	Chipper Jones	30.00
31	Rocco Baldelli	25.00
32	Keith Ginter	5.00
33	J.R. House	8.00
34	Alex Cabrera	5.00
35	Tony Alvarez	5.00
36	Pablo Ozuna	5.00
37	Juan Salas	5.00

Feature

		NM/M
Common Player:		4.00
Inserted 1:51		
1	Ivan Rodriguez	8.00
2	Rickey Henderson	15.00
3	John Smoltz	5.00
4	Tom Glavine	8.00
5	Willie Stargell	8.00
6	Frank Thomas	8.00
7	Carlos Delgado	8.00
8	Todd Helton	8.00
9	Adrian Gonzalez	5.00
10	Pat Burrell	8.00
11	Jose Vidro	4.00
12	Roberto Alomar	8.00
13	Chipper Jones	10.00
14	Robin Ventura	5.00
15	J.D. Drew	5.00
16	Matt Lawton	4.00
17	Josh Hamilton	8.00
18	Chin-Feng Chen	25.00
19	Rafael Furcal	8.00
20	Miguel Tejada	8.00
21	Josh Beckett	8.00
22	Ryan Anderson	4.00

Double Feature

		NM/M
Common Duo:		10.00
1	Ivan Rodriguez, Rickey Henderson	40.00
2	John Smoltz, Tom Glavine	15.00
3	Willie Stargell, Frank Thomas	20.00
4	Carlos Delgado, Todd Helton	15.00
5	Adrian Gonzalez, Pat Burrell	15.00
6	Jose Vidro, Roberto Alomar	15.00
7	Chipper Jones, Robin Ventura	20.00
8	J.D. Drew, Matt Lawton	10.00
9	Josh Hamilton, Chin-Feng Chen	25.00
10	Rafael Furcal, Miguel Tejada	15.00
11	Josh Beckett, Ryan Anderson	15.00

2001 Topps Gallery

		NM/M
Complete Set (152):		120.00
Common Player:		.15
Common Rookie:		1.50
Inserted 1:3.5		
Common Prospect:		.50

ICHIRO SUZUKI
Seattle Mariners

Inserted 1:2.5
Common Retired: 1.00
Inserted 1:5
Pack (6): 5.00
Box (24): 100.00
Set price includes one Suzuki rookie.

1	Darin Erstad	.40
2	Chipper Jones	1.50
3	Nomar Garciaparra	2.50
4	Fernando Vina	.15
5	Bartolo Colon	.25
6	Bobby Higginson	.15
7	Antonio Alfonseca	.15
8	Mike Sweeney	.15
9	Kevin Brown	.25
10	Jose Vidro	.15
11	Derek Jeter	3.00
12	Jason Giambi	.75
13	Pat Burrell	.50
14	Jeff Kent	.25
15	Alex Rodriguez	2.50
16	Rafael Palmeiro	.50
17	Garret Anderson	.40
18	Brad Fullmer	.15
19	Doug Glanville	.15
20	Mark Quinn	.15
21	Mo Vaughn	.25
22	Andruw Jones	.75
23	Pedro Martinez	1.00
24	Ken Griffey Jr.	1.50
25	Roberto Alomar	.75
26	Dean Palmer	.15
27	Jeff Bagwell	.75
28	Jermaine Dye	.15
29	Chan Ho Park	.15
30	Vladimir Guerrero	1.00
31	Bernie Williams	.15
32	Ben Grieve	.15
33	Jason Kendall	.15
34	Barry Bonds	3.00
35	Jim Edmonds	.40
36	Ivan Rodriguez	.75
37	Javy Lopez	.25
38	J.T. Snow	.15
39	Erubiel Durazo	.15
40	Terrence Long	.15
41	Tim Salmon	.25
42	Greg Maddux	1.50
43	Sammy Sosa	2.00
44	Sean Casey	.25
45	Jeff Cirillo	.15
46	Juan Gonzalez	.75
47	Richard Hidalgo	.25
48	Shawn Green	.25
49	Jeromy Burnitz	.15
50	Willie Mays	15.00
51	David Justice	.25
52	Tim Hudson	.40
53	Brian Giles	.15
54	Robb Nen	.15
55	Fernando Tatis	.15
56	Tony Batista	.15
57	Pokey Reese	.15
58	Ray Durham	.15
59	Greg Vaughn	.15
60	Kazuhiro Sasaki	.15
61	Troy Glaus	.50
62	Rafael Furcal	.40
63	Magglio Ordonez	.40
64	Jim Thome	.75
65	Todd Helton	.75
66	Preston Wilson	.15
67	Moises Alou	.25
68	Gary Sheffield	.40
69	Geoff Jenkins	.25
70	Mike Piazza	1.50
71	Jorge Posada	.50
72	Bobby Abreu	.25
73	Phil Nevin	.15
74	John Olerud	.25
75	Mark McGwire	2.00
76	Jose Cruz Jr.	.15
77	David Segui	.15
78	Neifi Perez	.15
79	Omar Vizquel	.25
80	Rick Ankiel	.15
81	Randy Johnson	1.00
82	Albert Belle	.15
83	Frank Thomas	.75
84	Manny Ramirez	.75
85	Larry Walker	.15
86	Luis Castillo	.15
87	Johnny Damon	.25
88	Adrian Beltre	.25
89	Cristian Guzman	.15
90	Jay Payton	.15
91	Miguel Tejada	.40
92	Scott Rolen	.75

93	Ryan Klesko	.40
94	Edgar Martinez	.25
95	Fred McGriff	.25
96	Carlos Delgado	.75
97	Barry Zito	.50
98	Mike Lieberthal	.15
99	Trevor Hoffman	.15
100	Gabe Kapler	.15
101	Edgardo Alfonzo	.25
102	Corey Patterson	.50
103	Alfonso Soriano	1.00
104	Keith Ginter	.50
105	Keith Reed	.50
106	Nick Johnson	.50
107	Carlos Pena	.50
108	Vernon Wells	.50
109	Roy Oswalt	.75
110	Alex Escobar	.50
111	Adam Everett	.50
112	Jimmy Rollins	.50
113	Marcus Giles	.50
114	Jack Cust	.50
115	Chin-Feng Chen	1.00
116	Pablo Ozuna	.50
117	Ben Sheets	.50
118	Adrian Gonzalez	.50
119	Ben Davis	.50
120	Eric Valent	.50
121	Scott Heard	.50
122	David Parrish RC	1.50
123	Sean Burnett	.50
124	Derek Thompson	.50
125	Tim Christman RC	1.50
126	Mike Jacobs RC	1.50
127	Luis Montanez RC	1.50
128	Chris Bass RC	1.50
129	William Smith RC	1.50
130	Justin Wayne RC	2.00
131	Shawn Fagan RC	1.50
132	Chad Petty RC	1.50
133	J.R. House	.50
134	Joel Pineiro	.50
135	Albert Pujols RC	75.00
136	Carmen Cali RC	1.50
137	Steve Smyth RC	1.50
138	John Lackey	.50
139	Bob Keppel RC	1.50
140	Dominic Rich RC	1.50
141	Josh Hamilton	.50
142	Nolan Ryan	5.00
143	Tom Seaver	1.50
144	Reggie Jackson	1.50
145	Johnny Bench	1.50
146	Warren Spahn	1.50
147	Brooks Robinson	1.50
148	Carl Yastrzemski	1.00
149	Al Kaline	1.00
150	Bob Feller	1.00
151a	Ichiro Suzuki/ English RC	25.00
151b	Ichiro Suzuki/ Japanese RC	25.00

Autographs

		NM/M
Common Autograph:		15.00
Inserted 1:232		
GA-RA	Rick Ankiel	15.00
GA-BB	Barry Bonds	150.00
GA-PB	Pat Burrell	20.00
GA-AG	Adrian Gonzalez	15.00
GA-AR	Alex Rodriguez	100.00
GA-IR	Ivan Rodriguez	50.00

Baseball Bucks

		NM/M
1:102 insert; used in Gallery Auction:		
$5	Johnny Bench	1.50

Heritage

		NM/M
Complete Set (10):		30.00
Common Player:		2.00
Inserted 1:12		
GH1	Todd Helton	3.00
GH2	Greg Maddux	4.00

DEREK JETER
YANKEES
SHORTSTOP

GH3	Pedro Martinez	3.00
GH4	Orlando Cepeda	2.00
GH5	Willie McCovey	2.00
GH6	Ken Griffey Jr.	4.00
GH7	Alex Rodriguez	6.00
GH8	Derek Jeter	8.00
GH9	Mark McGwire	6.00
GH10	Vladimir Guerrero	3.00

Heritage Relic

GREG MADDUX
PITCHER

		NM/M
Common Player:		10.00
Inserted 1:133		
	Orlando Cepeda	10.00
	Greg Maddux	25.00
	Pedro Martinez	20.00
	Willie McCovey	10.00

Heritage Autographed Relic

	NM/M
Production 25 Sets	
Orlando Cepeda	75.00
Willie McCovey	100.00

Star Gallery

		NM/M
Complete Set (10):		15.00
Common Player:		1.00
Inserted 1:8		
SG1	Vladimir Guerrero	1.00
SG2	Alex Rodriguez	2.50
SG3	Derek Jeter	3.00
SG4	Nomar Garciaparra	2.50
SG5	Ken Griffey Jr.	1.50
SG6	Mark McGwire	2.00
SG7	Chipper Jones	1.50
SG8	Sammy Sosa	2.00
SG9	Barry Bonds	3.00
SG10	Mike Piazza	1.50

Originals Relics

	NM/M
Common Player:	8.00
Inserted 1:133	

GR-RA	Roberto Alomar	10.00
GR-JD	Jermaine Dye	8.00
GR-DE	Darin Erstad	8.00
GR-JG	Jason Giambi	10.00
GR-AG	Adrian Gonzalez	8.00
GR-SG	Shawn Green	10.00
GR-AJ	Andruw Jones	10.00
GR-JK	Jason Kendall	8.00
GR-JFK	Jeff Kent	8.00
GR-RP	Rafael Palmeiro	10.00
GR-PR	Pokey Reese	8.00
GR-SS	Sammy Sosa	20.00
GR-RV	Robin Ventura	8.00
GR-BW	Bernie Williams	10.00
GR-PW	Preston Wilson	8.00

Press Plates

The aluminum press plates used to print the Gallery cards were inserted at a rate of one per 1,200 packs. Each card's front and back can be found in four different color variations. Because of the unique nature of each plate, assignment of catalog values in not feasible.

| | NM/M |
| Common Player: | 50.00 |

Team Topps Legends Autographs

	NM/M
Common Autograph:	10.00
Inserted 1:286	
TT23R	Gil McDougald	10.00
TT27F	Andy Pafko	20.00
TT10R	Frank Robinson	20.00
TT28F	Herb Score	10.00
TT25R	Luis Tiant	10.00

2001 Topps Gold Label

	NM/M
Complete Set (115):	80.00
Common Player:	.25
Common Rookie:	4.00
Production 999	
Golds:	2-3X
Production 999	
Gold Rookies:	2-3X
Production 99	
Pack (5):	3.00

Box (24):		50.00
1	Adrian Beltre	.40
2	Danny Borrell RC	4.00
3	Albert Belle	.25
4	Alex Cabrera	.25
5	Alex Rodriguez	2.50
6	Andruw Jones	.75
7	Antonio Alfonseca	.25
8	Barry Bonds	3.00
9	Barry Larkin	.50
10	Ben Grieve	.25
11	Ben Molina	.25
12	Bernie Williams	.50
13	Bobby Abreu	.40
14	Bobby Higginson	.25
15	Brad Fullmer	.25
16	Brian Giles	.40
17	Cal Ripken Jr.	3.00
18	Carlos Delgado	.75
19	Chad Petty RC	4.00
20	Charles Johnson	.25
21	Chipper Jones	1.50
22	Cristian Guzman	.25
23	Darin Erstad	.40
24	David Justice	.40
25	David Segui	.25
26	Derek Jeter	2.50
27	Edgar Martinez	.40
28	Edgardo Alfonzo	.25
29	Fernando Tatis	.25
30	Eric Karros	.25
31	Eric Munson	.25
32	Eric Young	.25
33	Frank Thomas	.75
34	Fernando Vina	.25
35	Garret Anderson	.50
36	Gary Sheffield	.50
37	Geoff Jenkins	.40
38	Greg Maddux	1.50
39	Ivan Rodriguez	.75
40	J.D. Drew	.40
41	J.R. House	.25
42	J.T. Snow Jr.	.25
43	Jason Giambi	.75
44	Jason Kendall	.40
45	Jay Payton	.25
46	Jeff Bagwell	.75
47	Jeff Cirillo	.25
48	Jeff Kent	.40
49	Chan Ho Park	.25
50	Jermaine Dye	.25
51	Jeromy Burnitz	.25
52	Jim Edmonds	.50
53	Jim Thome	.75
54	John Olerud	.25
55	Johnny Damon	.40
56	Jorge Posada	.50
57	Jose Cruz Jr.	.25
58	Jose Vidro	.25
59	Josh Hamilton	.25
60	Juan Gonzalez	.75
61	Steve Smyth RC	4.00
62	Justin Wayne RC	8.00
63	Kazuhiro Sasaki	.25
64	Ken Griffey Jr.	1.50
65	Kevin Brown	.40
66	Kevin Young	.25
67	Larry Walker	.40
68	Luis Castillo	.25
69	Steve Finley	.25
70	Magglio Ordonez	.50
71	Manny Ramirez	.75
72	Mark McGwire	2.50
73	Mark Quinn	.25
74	Miguel Tejada	.50
75	Mike Piazza	1.50
76	Mike Sweeney	.25
77	Mo Vaughn	.40
78	Moises Alou	.25
79	Nomar Garciaparra	2.00
80	Pat Burrell	.50
81	Paul Konerko	.25
82	Pedro Martinez	1.00
83	Phil Nevin	.25
84	Preston Wilson	.25
85	Rafael Furcal	.50
86	Todd Zeile	.25
87	Randy Johnson	1.00
88	Travis Lee	.25
89	Carl Everett	.25
90	Quilvio Veras	.25
91	Rick Ankiel	.25
92	Rick Brosseau RC	4.00
93	Robert Keppell RC	4.00
94	Roberto Alomar	.50
95	Ryan Klesko	.40
96	Sammy Sosa	2.00
97	Scott Heard	.25
98	Scott Rolen	.75
99	Sean Casey	.50
100	Shawn Green	.40
101	Terrence Long	.25
102	Tim Salmon	.40
103	Todd Helton	.75
104	Tom Glavine	.50
105	Tony Batista	.25
106	Travis Baptist RC	4.00
107	Troy Glaus	.50
108	Victor Hall RC	4.00
109	Vladimir Guerrero	1.00
110	Tim Hudson	.50
111	Brian Roberts RC	2.00
112	Virgil Chevalier RC	4.00
113	Fernando Rodney RC	4.00
114	Paul Phillips RC	4.00
115	Cesar Bolivar RC	4.00

Class 2

Stars:	1-2X
Inserted 1:4	
Rookies:	1-1.5X
Production 699	
Golds:	2-3X
Production 699	
Gold Rookies:	2-3X
Production 69	

Class 3

Stars:	2-3X
Inserted 1:12	
Rookies:	1-2X
Production 299	
Golds:	3-5X
Production 299	
Gold Rookies:	2-4X
Production 29	

Masterpiece

A 1-of-1 "masterpiece" card was created for each card in each of the three Classes of Topps Gold Label. Because of scarcity and widely varying demand, catalog values cannot be given.

| | NM/M |
| Common Player: | 50.00 |

Gold Fixtures

GOLD FIXTURES

	NM/M
Complete Set (10):	150.00
Common Player:	8.00

Inserted 1:374
1	Alex Rodriguez	20.00
2	Mark McGwire	20.00
3	Derek Jeter	25.00
4	Nomar Garciaparra	20.00
5	Chipper Jones	15.00
6	Sammy Sosa	20.00
7	Ken Griffey Jr.	15.00
8	Carlos Delgado	8.00
9	Frank Thomas	10.00
10	Barry Bonds	25.00

MLB Awards Ceremony

		NM/M
	Common Player:	4.00
	Inserted 1:24	
SA	Sandy Alomar/Bat	4.00
JB	Jeff Bagwell/Bat	8.00
AB	Albert Belle/Bat	4.00
CB	Carlos Beltran/Bat	4.00
DB	Dante Bichette	4.00
BB	Barry Bonds/Jsy	25.00
BB	Barry Bonds/Bat	25.00
SB	Scott Brosius/Bat	4.00
JC	Jose Canseco/Bat	6.00
JC	Jose Canseco/Bat	6.00
WC	Will Clark/Jsy	6.00
RC	Roger Clemens/Jsy	20.00
MC	Marty Cordova/Bat	4.00
RF	Rafael Furcal/Bat	4.00
AG	Andres Galarraga/Bat	4.00
NG	Nomar Garciaparra/Jsy	20.00
NG	Nomar Garciaparra/Bat	20.00
JG	Jason Giambi/Bat	8.00
TG	Troy Glaus/Bat	8.00
TG	Tom Glavine/Jsy	6.00
JG	Juan Gonzalez/Bat	8.00
JG	Juan Gonzalez/Bat	8.00
DG	Dwight Gooden/Jsy	4.00
BG	Ben Grieve/Jsy	4.00
KG	Ken Griffey Jr./Jsy	15.00
KG	Ken Griffey Jr./Bat	15.00
TG	Tony Gwynn/Bat	10.00
TH	Todd Helton/Bat	8.00
RH	Rickey Henderson/Jsy	15.00
TH	Todd Hollandsworth/Bat	4.00
DJ	Derek Jeter/Bat	25.00
RJ	Randy Johnson/Jsy	10.00
CJ	Chipper Jones/Jsy	10.00
DJ	David Justice/Jsy	5.00
JK	Jeff Kent/Bat	4.00
CK	Chuck Knoblauch/Bat	4.00
BL	Barry Larkin/Bat	8.00
GM	Greg Maddux/Jsy	15.00
EM	Edgar Martinez/Bat	6.00
PM	Pedro Martinez/Jsy	10.00
FM	Fred McGriff/Bat	5.00
MM	Mark McGwire/Jsy	60.00
MM	Mark McGwire/Jsy	60.00
RM	Raul Mondesi/Bat	4.00
HN	Hideo Nomo/Jsy	25.00
JO	John Olerud/Bat	4.00
PO	Paul O'Neill/Bat	5.00
MP	Mike Piazza/Bat	12.00
CR	Cal Ripken Jr./Jsy	35.00
AR	Alex Rodriguez/Bat	15.00
IR	Ivan Rodriguez/Jsy	8.00
SR	Scott Rolen/Jsy	8.00
TS	Tim Salmon/Jsy	4.00
KS	Kazuhiro Sasaki/Jsy	5.00
GS	Gary Sheffield/Jsy	6.00
JS	John Smoltz/Jsy	4.00
SS	Sammy Sosa/Jsy/Bat	15.00
SS	Sammy Sosa/Jsy	15.00
DS	Darryl Strawberry/Jsy	4.00
DS	Darryl Strawberry/Bat	4.00
FT	Frank Thomas/Bat	8.00
FT	Frank Thomas/Jsy	8.00
MV	Mo Vaughn/Bat	4.00
MV	Mo Vaughn/Bat	4.00
LW	Larry Walker/Bat	4.00
LW	Larry Walker/Bat	5.00
JW	John Wetteland/Bat	4.00
BW	Bernie Williams/Bat	8.00
MW	Matt Williams/Bat	5.00

2001 Topps HD

		NM/M
	Complete Set (120):	50.00
	Common Player:	.25
	Common (101-120):	1.00
	Inserted 1:6	
	Pack (4):	2.50
	Box (20):	40.00
1	Derek Jeter	3.00
2	Magglio Ordonez	.50
3	Eric Munson	.25
4	Jermaine Dye	.25
5	Larry Walker	.40
6	Pokey Reese	.25
7	Pedro Martinez	1.00
8	Rafael Palmeiro	.75
9	Jason Kendall	.40
10	Mike Lieberthal	.25
11	Ryan Klesko	.40
12	Cal Ripken Jr.	3.00
13	Mike Piazza	1.50
14	Adam Sterrett RC	.75
15	John Olerud	.40
16	Manny Ramirez	.75
17	Chad Petty RC	.75
18	Vladimir Guerrero	1.00
19	Kevin Brown	.40
20	Luis Cotto RC	.50
21	Josh Hamilton	.25
22	Mark Grace	.40
23	Mark McGwire	2.50
24	Jeromy Burnitz	.25
25	Andruw Jones	.75
26	Raul Mondesi	.40
27	Stuart McFarland RC	.50
28	Craig Biggio	.40
29	Troy Glaus	.50
30	Carlos Delgado	.75
31	Rafael Furcal	.40
32	J.D. Drew	.25
33	Corey Patterson	.40
34	Gary Sheffield	.40
35	Jeff Kent	.40
36	Alex Rodriguez	2.50
37	Edgardo Alfonzo	.25
38	Jeff Segar RC	.25
39	Bobby Abreu	.40
40	Brian Giles	.40
41	Jason Smith RC	.40
42	Mo Vaughn	.25
43	Pat Burrell	.40
44	Barry Larkin	.50
45	Carlos Beltran	.50
46	Eric Mosley RC	.50
47	Alfonso Soriano	1.00
48	Tim Salmon	.40
49	Jason Giambi	.75
50	Greg Maddux	1.50
51	Randy Johnson	1.00
52	Jose Vidro	.25
53	Edgar Martinez	.40
54	Albert Belle	.25
55	Ivan Rodriguez	.50
56	Sean Casey	.25
57	Jorge Posada	.25
58	Preston Wilson	.25
59	Paul Konerko	.25
60	Todd Helton	.75
61	Dominic Rich RC	.50
62	Tony Gwynn	1.00
63	Bernie Williams	.75
64	Anthony Brewer RC	.50
65	Shawn Green	.50
66	Jeff Bagwell	.50
67	Jose Cruz Jr.	.25
68	Darin Erstad	.40
69	Jim Edmonds	.50
70	Frank Thomas	.75
71	Ryan Anderson	.75
72	Scott Rolen	.75
73	Jeff Cirillo	.25
74	Chris Bass RC	.50
75	William Smith RC	.50
76	Trot Nixon	.25
77	Bobby Bradley	.25
78	Odannis Ayala RC	.50
79	Jim Thome	.75
80	Sammy Sosa	2.00
81	Geoff Jenkins	.40
82	Ben Grieve	.40
83	Andres Galarraga	.40
84	Rick Ankiel	.25
85	Barry Bonds	3.00
86	Alex Gonzalez	.25
87	Sean Burroughs	.40
88	Nomar Garciaparra	2.00
89	Ken Griffey Jr.	1.50
90	Tim Hudson	.50
91	Chipper Jones	1.50
92	Matt Williams	.40
93	Roberto Alomar	.75
94	Adrian Gonzalez	.50
95	Juan Gonzalez	.75
96	Brian Bass RC	.50
97	Rick Brosseau RC	.50
98	Mariano Rivera	.40
99	James Baldwin	.25
100	Dean Palmer	.25
101	Pedro Martinez	2.00
102	Randy Johnson	2.00
103	Greg Maddux	3.00
104	Sammy Sosa	4.00
105	Mark McGwire	5.00
106	Ivan Rodriguez	1.50
107	Mike Piazza	3.00
108	Chipper Jones	3.00
109	Vladimir Guerrero	2.00
110	Alex Rodriguez	5.00
111	Ken Griffey Jr.	3.00
112	Cal Ripken Jr.	6.00
113	Derek Jeter	6.00
114	Barry Bonds	6.00
115	Nomar Garciaparra	4.00
116	Jeff Bagwell	1.50
117	Todd Helton	1.50
118	Darin Erstad	1.00
119	Shawn Green	1.00
120	Roberto Alomar	1.00

Platinum
Stars (1-100): 4-8X
Stars (101-120): 2-4X
Production 199 Sets

Autographed Cards

		NM/M
	Common Player:	10.00
	Inserted 1:431	
1	Todd Helton	25.00
2	Rick Ankiel	10.00
3	Mark Quinn	10.00
4	Adrian Gonzalez	10.00

Game Defined

		NM/M
	Complete Set (10):	25.00
	Common Player:	1.50
	Inserted 1:24	
	Platinum	1.5-2X
	Inserted 1:72	
1	Ken Griffey Jr.	3.00
2	Derek Jeter	5.00
3	Sammy Sosa	3.00
4	Mark McGwire	4.00
5	Todd Helton	1.50
6	Mike Piazza	3.00
7	Chipper Jones	2.50
8	Vladimir Guerrero	1.50
9	Alex Rodriguez	4.00
10	Nomar Garciaparra	3.00

Game-Worn Jersey

		NM/M
	Common Card:	5.00
	Inserted 1:108	
	Cards 5-8 are redemptions.	
1	Grant Roberts	5.00
2	Vernon Wells	10.00
3	Travis Dawkins	5.00
4	Ramon Ortiz	5.00
5	Steve Finley	5.00
6	Ramon Hernandez	5.00
7	Jay Payton	8.00
8	Jeromy Burnitz	5.00

Images of Excellence

		NM/M
	Complete Set (10):	15.00
	Common Player:	1.00
	Inserted 1:8	
	Platinum	1.5-2X
	Inserted 1:24	
1	Willie Mays	2.50
2	Reggie Jackson	1.00

3	Ernie Banks	1.50
4	Hank Aaron	2.50
5	Ted Williams	2.50
6	Mike Schmidt	2.00
7	Tom Seaver	1.00
8	Johnny Bench	1.50
9	George Brett	2.50
10	Nolan Ryan	3.00

20-20

		NM/M
	Complete Set (10):	15.00
	Common Player:	.50
	Inserted 1:12	
	Platinum	1.5-2X
	Inserted 1:36	
1	Barry Bonds	4.00
2	Chipper Jones	2.00
3	Ken Griffey Jr.	2.00
4	Alex Rodriguez	3.00
5	Ivan Rodriguez	1.00
6	Sammy Sosa	2.50
7	Roberto Alomar	.75
8	Larry Walker	.50
9	Shawn Green	.75
10	Jeff Bagwell	1.00

2001 Topps Heritage Pre-Production

To introduce its retro-look 2001 Heritage baseball set, Topps issued a cello-packaged, three-card promo set. The cards are in the same format as the regular-issue Heritage series, except that all the stats on back are zeroes and the cards are numbered with a "PP" prefix.

		NM/M
	Complete Set (3):	6.00
	Common Player:	2.00
PP1	Kevin Brown	2.00
PP2	Andres Galarraga	2.00
PP3	Roger Clemens	4.00

2001 Topps Heritage

		NM/M
	Complete Set (407):	300.00
	Complete Master Set (487):	375.00
	Common Player:	.50
	Common SP (311-407):	2.50
	Inserted 1:2	
	Pack (8):	13.00
	Box (24):	275.00
1	Kris Benson	.50
2	Brian Jordan	.50
3	Fernando Vina	.50
4	Mike Sweeney	.50
5	Rafael Palmeiro	2.00
6	Paul O'Neill	1.00
7	Todd Helton	2.50
8	Ramiro Mendoza	.50
9	Kevin Millwood	1.00
10	Chuck Knoblauch	.75
11	Derek Jeter	10.00
12	Alex Rodriguez	8.00
13	Geoff Jenkins	.75
14	David Justice	1.00
15	David Cone	1.00
16	Andres Galarraga	1.00
17	Garret Anderson	.50
18	Roger Cedeno	.50
19	Randy Velarde	.50
20	Carlos Delgado	2.00
21	Quilvio Veras	.50
22	Jose Vidro	.50
23	Corey Patterson	.75
24	Jorge Posada	1.00
25	Eddie Perez	.50
26	Jack Cust	.50
27	Sean Burroughs	.75
28	Randy Wolf	.50
29	Mike Lamb	.50
30	Rafael Furcal	.50
31	Barry Bonds	8.00
32	Tim Hudson	.75
33	Tom Glavine	1.50
34	Javy Lopez	.75
35	Aubrey Huff	.50
36	Wally Joyner	.50
37	Magglio Ordonez	1.00
38	Matt Lawton	.50
39	Mariano Rivera	1.00
40	Andy Ashby	.50
41	Mark Buehrle	3.00
42	Esteban Loaiza	.50
43	Mark Redman	.50
44	Mark Quinn	.50
45	Tino Martinez	.50
46	Joe Mays	.50
47	Walt Weiss	.50
48	Roger Clemens	6.00
49	Greg Maddux	5.00
50	Richard Hidalgo	.50
51	Orlando Hernandez	.75
52	Chipper Jones	.50
53	Ben Grieve	.50
54	Jimmy Haynes	.50
55	Ken Caminiti	.50
56	Tim Salmon	.50
57	Andy Pettitte	1.00
58	Darin Erstad	1.00
59	Marquis Grissom	.50
60	Raul Mondesi	.75
61	Bengie Molina	.50
62	Miguel Tejada	1.00
63	Jose Cruz Jr.	.50
64	Billy Koch	.50
65	Troy Glaus	2.00
66	Cliff Floyd	.50
67	Tony Batista	.50
68	Jeff Bagwell	2.50
69	Billy Wagner	.50
70	Eric Chavez	.75
71	Troy Percival	.50
72	Andruw Jones	2.50
73	Shane Reynolds	.50
74	Barry Zito	2.50
75	Roy Halladay	1.00
76	David Wells	.50
77	Jason Giambi	1.50
78	Scott Elarton	.50
79	Moises Alou	.75
80	Adam Piatt	.50
81	Wilton Veras	.50
82	Darryl Kile	.50
83	Johnny Damon	.50
84	Tony Armas Jr.	.50
85	Ellis Burks	.50
86	Jamey Wright	.50
87	Jose Vizcaino	.50
88	Bartolo Colon	.50
89	Carmen Cali RC	.50
90	Kevin Brown	.75
91	Josh Hamilton	.50
92	Jay Buhner	.50
93	Scott Pratt RC	.50
94	Alex Cora	.50
95	Luis Montanez RC	1.00
96	Dmitri Young	.50
97	J.T. Snow Jr.	.50
98	Damion Easley	.50
99	Greg Norton	.50
100	Matt Wheatland	.50
101	Chin-Feng Chen	.50
102	Tony Womack	.50
103	Adam Kennedy	.50

104	J.D. Drew	.50
105	Carlos Febles	.50
106	Jim Thome	1.00
107	Danny Graves	.50
108	Dave Mlicki	.50
109	Ron Coomer	.50
110	James Baldwin	.50
111	Shaun Boyd RC	.75
112	Brian Bohannon	.50
113	Jacque Jones	.50
114	Alfonso Soriano	1.50
115	Tony Clark	.50
116	Terrence Long	.50
117	Todd Hundley	.50
118	Kazuhiro Sasaki	.50
119	Brian Sellier RC	.50
120	John Olerud	.75
121	Javier Vazquez	.50
122	Sean Burnett	.50
123	Matt LeCroy	.50
124	Erubiel Durazo	.50
125	Juan Encarnacion	.50
126	Pablo Ozuna	.50
127	Russ Ortiz	.50
128	David Segui	.50
129	Mark McGwire	3.00
130	Mark Grace	1.00
131	Fred McGriff	.75
132	Carl Pavano	.50
133	Derek Thompson	.50
134	Shawn Green	.75
135	B.J. Surhoff	.50
136	Michael Tucker	.50
137	Jason Isringhausen	.50
138	Eric Milton	.50
139	Mike Stodolka	.50
140	Milton Bradley	.50
141	Curt Schilling	.75
142	Sandy Alomar	.50
143	Brent Mayne	.50
144	Todd Jones	.50
145	Charles Johnson	.50
146	Dean Palmer	.50
147	Masato Yoshii	.50
148	Edgar Renteria	.50
149	Joe Randa	.50
150	Adam Johnson	.50
151	Greg Vaughn	.50
152	Adrian Beltre	.75
153	Glenallen Hill	.50
154	David Parrish RC	.75
155	Neifi Perez	.50
156	Pete Harnisch	.50
157	Paul Konerko	.50
158	Dennys Reyes	.50
159	Jose Lima	.50
160	Eddie Taubensee	.50
161	Miguel Cairo	.50
162	Jeff Kent	.75
163	Dustin Hermanson	.50
164	Alex Gonzalez	.50
165	Hideo Nomo	.75
166	Sammy Sosa	2.00
167	C.J. Nitkowski	.50
168	Cal Eldred	.50
169	Jeff Abbott	.50
170	Jim Edmonds	.75
171	Mark Mulder	.75
172	Dominic Rich RC	.50
173	Ray Lankford	.50
174	Danny Borrell RC	.75
175	Rick Aguilera	.50
176	Shannon Stewart	.50
177	Steve Finley	.50
178	Jim Parque	.50
179	Kevin Appier	.50
180	Adrian Gonzalez	.75
181	Tom Goodwin	.50
182	Kevin Tapani	.50
183	Fernando Tatis	.50
184	Mark Grudzielanek	.50
185	Ryan Anderson	.50
186	Jeffrey Hammonds	.50
187	Corey Koskie	.50
188	Brad Fullmer	.50
189	Rey Sanchez	.50
190	Michael Barrett	.50
191	Rickey Henderson	1.00
192	Jermaine Dye	.50
193	Scott Brosius	.50
194	Matt Anderson	.50
195	Brian Buchanan	.50
196	Derrek Lee	.50
197	Larry Walker	.75
198	David Krynzel	.50
199	Vinny Castilla	.50
200	Ken Griffey Jr.	2.00
201	Matt Stairs	.50
202	Ty Howington	.50
203	Andy Benes	.50
204	Luis Gonzalez	.75
205	Brian Moehler	.50
206	Harold Baines	.50
207	Pedro Astacio	.50
208	Cristian Guzman	.50
209	Kip Wells	.50
210	Frank Thomas	1.00
211	Jose Rosado	.50
212	Vernon Wells	.50
213	Bobby Higginson	.50
214	Juan Gonzalez	.50
215	Omar Vizquel	.75
216	Bernie Williams	1.00
217	Aaron Sele	.50
218	Shawn Estes	.50
219	Roberto Alomar	1.00
220	Rick Ankiel	.50
221	Josh Kalinowski	.50

222	David Bell	.50
223	Keith Foulke	.50
224	Craig Biggio	.75
225	Shawn Fagan RC	.50
226	Scott Williamson	.50
227	Ron Belliard	.50
228	Chris Singleton	.50
229	Alex Serrano	.50
230	Deivi Cruz	.50
231	Eric Munson	.50
232	Luis Castillo	.50
233	Edgar Martinez	.75
234	Jeff Shaw	.50
235	Jeromy Burnitz	.50
236	Richie Sexson	.75
237	Will Clark	1.00
238	Ron Villone	.50
239	Kerry Wood	1.00
240	Rich Aurilia	.50
241	Mo Vaughn	.50
242	Travis Fryman	.75
243	Manny Ramirez	1.00
244	Chris Stynes	.50
245	Ray Durham	.50
246	Juan Uribe RC	.50
247	Juan Guzman	.50
248	Lee Stevens	.50
249	Devon White	.50
250	Kyle Lohse RC	1.50
251	Bryan Wolff	.50
252	Rick Brousseau RC	.50
253	Eric Young	.50
254	Freddy Garcia	.50
255	Jay Bell	.50
256	Steve Cox	.50
257	Torii Hunter	.75
258	Jose Canseco	.75
259	Brad Ausmus	.50
260	Jeff Cirillo	.50
261	Brad Penny	.50
262	Antonio Alfonseca	.50
263	Russ Branyan	.50
264	Scott Heard	.50
265	John Lackey	.50
266	Justin Wayne RC	1.00
267	Brad Radke	.50
268	Todd Stottlemyre	.50
269	Mark Loretta	.50
270	Matt Williams	.50
271	Kenny Lofton	.50
272	Jeff D'Amico	.50
273	Jamie Moyer	.50
274	Darren Dreifort	.50
275	Denny Neagle	.50
276	Orlando Cabrera	.50
277	Chuck Finley	.50
278	Miguel Batista	.50
279	Carlos Beltran	.50
280	Eric Karros	.50
281	Mark Kotsay	.50
282	Ryan Dempster	.50
283	Barry Larkin	.75
284	Jeff Suppan	.50
285	Gary Sheffield	.75
286	Jose Valentin	.50
287	Robb Nen	.50
288	Chan Ho Park	.50
289	John Halama	.50
290	Steve Smyth RC	.50
291	Gerald Williams	.50
292	Preston Wilson	.50
293	Victor Hall RC	.75
294	Ben Sheets	.50
295	Eric Davis	.50
296	Kirk Rueter	.50
297	Chad Petty RC	.75
298	Kevin Millar	.50
299	Marvin Benard	.50
300	Vladimir Guerrero	1.00
301	Livan Hernandez	.50
302	Travis Baptist RC	.75
303	Bill Mueller	.50
304	Mike Cameron	.50
305	Randy Johnson	1.50
306	Alan Mahaffey RC	.50
307	Timo Perez (No facsimile autograph.)	.50
308	Pokey Reese	.50
309	Ryan Rupe	.50
310	Carlos Lee	.50
311	Doug Glanville	2.50
312	Jay Payton	2.50
313	Troy O'Leary	2.50
314	Francisco Cordero	2.50
315	Rusty Greer	2.50
316	Cal Ripken Jr.	25.00
317	Ricky Ledee	2.50
318	Brian Daubach	2.50
319	Robin Ventura	3.00
320	Todd Zeile	3.00
321	Francisco Cordova	2.50
322	Henry Rodriguez	2.50
323	Pat Meares	2.50
324	Glendon Rusch	2.50
325	Keith Osik	2.50
326	Robert Keppell RC	4.00
327	Bobby Jones	2.50
328	Alex Ramirez	2.50
329	Robert Person	2.50
330	Ruben Mateo	2.50
331	Rob Bell	2.50
332	Carl Everett	2.50
333	Jason Schmidt	3.00
334	Scott Rolen	5.00
335	Jimmy Anderson	2.50
336	Bret Boone	3.00
337	Delino DeShields	2.50
338	Trevor Hoffman	2.50

339	Bob Abreu	3.00
340	Mike Williams	2.50
341	Mike Hampton	3.00
342	John Wetteland	2.50
343	Scott Erickson	2.50
344	Enrique Wilson	2.50
345	Tim Wakefield	2.50
346	Mike Lowell	2.50
347	Todd Pratt	2.50
348	Brook Fordyce	2.50
349	Benny Agbayani	2.50
350	Gabe Kapler	3.00
351	Sean Casey	3.00
352	Darren Oliver	2.50
353	Todd Ritchie	2.50
354	Kenny Rogers	2.50
355	Jason Kendall	3.00
356	John Vander Wal	2.50
357	Ramon Martinez	2.50
358	Edgardo Alfonzo	2.50
359	Phil Nevin	2.50
360	Albert Belle	2.50
361	Ruben Rivera	2.50
362	Pedro Martinez	10.00
363	Derek Lowe	2.50
364	Pat Burrell	5.00
365	Mike Mussina	5.00
366	Brady Anderson	2.50
367	Darren Lewis	2.50
368	Sidney Ponson	2.50
369	Adam Eaton	2.50
370	Eric Owens	2.50
371	Aaron Boone	2.50
372	Matt Clement	2.50
373	Derek Bell	2.50
374	Trot Nixon	2.50
375	Travis Lee	2.50
376	Mike Benjamin	2.50
377	Jeff Zimmerman	2.50
378	Mike Lieberthal	2.50
379	Rick Reed	2.50
380	Nomar Garciaparra	15.00
381	Omar Daal	2.50
382	Ryan Klesko	3.00
383	Rey Ordonez	2.50
384	Kevin Young	2.50
385	Rick Helling	2.50
386	Brian Giles	4.00
387	Tony Gwynn	8.00
388	Ed Sprague	2.50
389	J.R. House	2.50
390	Scott Hatteberg	2.50
391	John Valentin	2.50
392	Melvin Mora	2.50
393	Royce Clayton	2.50
394	Jeff Fassero	2.50
395	Manny Alexander	2.50
396	John Franco	2.50
397	Luis Alicea	2.50
398	Ivan Rodriguez	5.00
399	Kevin Jordan	2.50
400	Jose Offerman	2.50
401	Jeff Conine	2.50
402	Seth Etherton	2.50
403	Mike Bordick	2.50
404	Al Leiter	3.00
405	Mike Piazza	10.00
406	Armando Benitez	2.50
407	Warren Morris	2.50

Chrome

DAVID WELLS

		NM/M
Common Player:		3.00
1	Cal Ripken Jr.	40.00
2	Jim Thome	10.00
3	Derek Jeter	40.00
4	Andres Galarraga	4.00
5	Carlos Delgado	8.00
6	Roberto Alomar	8.00
7	Tom Glavine	5.00
8	Gary Sheffield	5.00
9	Mo Vaughn	3.00
10	Preston Wilson	3.00
11	Mike Mussina	8.00
12	Greg Maddux	30.00
13	Ivan Rodriguez	10.00
14	Al Leiter	3.00
15	Seth Etherton	3.00
16	Edgardo Alfonzo	3.00
17	Richie Sexson	3.00
18	Andruw Jones	10.00
19	Bartolo Colon	3.00
20	Darin Erstad	5.00
21	Kevin Brown	4.00
22	Mike Sweeney	3.00
23	Mike Piazza	30.00
24	Rafael Palmeiro	10.00
25	Terrence Long	3.00
26	Kazuhiro Sasaki	3.00
27	John Olerud	5.00
28	Mark McGwire	30.00
29	Fred McGriff	5.00
30	Todd Helton	10.00
31	Curt Schilling	5.00
32	Alex Rodriguez	30.00
33	Jeff Kent	4.00
34	Pat Burrell	8.00
35	Jim Edmonds	6.00
36	Mark Mulder	3.00
37	Troy Glaus	8.00
38	Jay Payton	3.00
39	Jermaine Dye	3.00
40	Larry Walker	5.00
41	Ken Griffey Jr.	30.00
42	Jeff Bagwell	10.00
43	Rick Ankiel	3.00
44	Mark Redman	3.00
45	Edgar Martinez	3.00
46	Mike Hampton	4.00
47	Manny Ramirez	10.00
48	Ray Durham	3.00
49	Rafael Furcal	3.00
50	Sean Casey	4.00
51	Jose Canseco	3.00
52	Barry Bonds	40.00
53	Tim Hudson	5.00
54	Barry Zito	10.00
55	Chuck Finley	3.00
56	Magglio Ordonez	4.00
57	David Wells	3.00
58	Jason Giambi	8.00
59	Tony Gwynn	15.00
60	Vladimir Guerrero	15.00
61	Randy Johnson	15.00
62	Bernie Williams	8.00
63	Craig Biggio	5.00
64	Jason Kendall	3.00
65	Pedro Martinez	15.00
66	Mark Quinn	3.00
67	Frank Thomas	15.00
68	Nomar Garciaparra	30.00
69	Brian Giles	5.00
70	Shawn Green	5.00
71	Roger Clemens	25.00
72	Sammy Sosa	30.00
73	Juan Gonzalez	10.00
74	Orlando Hernandez	4.00
75	Chipper Jones	20.00
76	Josh Hamilton	3.00
77	Adam Johnson	3.00
78	Shaun Boyd	3.00
79	Alfonso Soriano	15.00
80	Derek Thompson	3.00
81	Adrian Gonzalez	3.00
82	Ryan Anderson	3.00
83	Corey Patterson	5.00
84	J.R. House	3.00
85	Sean Burroughs	3.00
86	Scott Heard	3.00
87	John Lackey	3.00
88	Ben Sheets	4.00
89	Wilson Betemit	3.00
90	Robert Keppell	3.00
91	Luis Montanez	3.00
92	Sean Burnett	3.00
93	Justin Wayne	5.00
94	Eric Munson	3.00
95	Steve Smyth	3.00
96	Rick Brousseau	3.00
97	Carmen Cali	3.00
98	Brian Sellier	3.00
99	David Parrish	3.00
100	Danny Borrell	3.00
101	Chad Petty	3.00
102	Dominic Rich	3.00
103	Shawn Fagan	3.00
104	Alex Serrano	3.00
105	Juan Uribe	3.00
106	Travis Baptist	3.00
107	Alan Mahaffey	3.00
108	Kyle Lohse	4.00
109	Victor Hall	3.00
110	Scott Pratt	3.00

Classic Renditions

Nomar Garciaparra
Boston Red Sox®

		NM/M
Complete Set (10):		15.00
Common Player:		1.00
Inserted 1:5		
1	Mark McGwire	2.50
2	Nomar Garciaparra	2.00
3	Barry Bonds	3.00
4	Sammy Sosa	2.00
5	Chipper Jones	1.50
6	Pat Burrell	1.00
7	Frank Thomas	1.00
8	Manny Ramirez	1.00
9	Derek Jeter	3.00
10	Ken Griffey Jr.	2.00

Classic Renditions Autographs

Classic Renditions

Chipper Jones • Atlanta Braves

		NM/M
Production 25 Sets		
BB	Barry Bonds	650.00
CJ	Chipper Jones	350.00
NG	Nomar Garciaparra	450.00

Clubhouse Collection Autographs

		NM/M
Common Player:		
MM	Minnie Monoso/25	120.00
RS	Red Schoendienst/25	150.00

Clubhouse Collection Game-Used

CLUBHOUSE COLLECTION

3B

CHIPPER JONES

		NM/M
Common Player:		25.00
MM	Minnie Monoso	25.00
RS	Red Schoendienst	30.00
DS	Duke Snider	40.00
EM	Eddie Mathews	40.00
CJ	Chipper Jones	40.00
RA	Richie Ashburn	30.00
FT	Frank Thomas	40.00
FV	Fernando Vina	25.00
SG	Shawn Green	30.00
WM	Willie Mays	150.00
BB	Barry Bonds	80.00
SR	Scott Rolen	40.00

Clubhouse Collection Dual Game-used

		NM/M
Common Card:		75.00
Production 52 Sets		
MMFT	Minnie Monoso, Frank Thomas	100.00
RSFV	Red Schoendienst, Fernando Vina	75.00
DSSG	Duke Snider, Shawn Green	150.00
RAPB	Richie Ashburn, Scott Rolen	100.00
EMCJ	Eddie Mathews, Chipper Jones	125.00
WMBB	Willie Mays, Barry Bonds	250.00

Grandstand Glory

GRANDSTAND GLORY

Jackie Robinson • 2B
EBBETTS FIELD • BROOKLYN DODGERS

		NM/M
Common Player:		20.00
Inserted 1:211		
PR	Phil Rizzuto	30.00
YB	Yogi Berra	30.00
RA	Richie Ashburn	20.00
RR	Robin Roberts	20.00
WM	Willie Mays	60.00
NF	Nellie Fox	20.00
JR	Jackie Robinson	50.00

New Age Performers

new age performers ★ ★ ★

Derek Jeter
NEW YORK YANKEES

		NM/M
Complete Set (15):		20.00
Common Player:		1.00
Inserted 1:8		
1	Mike Piazza	1.50
2	Sammy Sosa	2.00
3	Alex Rodriguez	2.50
4	Barry Bonds	3.00
5	Ken Griffey Jr.	1.50
6	Chipper Jones	1.50
7	Randy Johnson	1.00
8	Derek Jeter	3.00
9	Nomar Garciaparra	2.00
10	Mark McGwire	2.50
11	Jeff Bagwell	1.00
12	Pedro Martinez	1.00
13	Todd Helton	1.00
14	Vladimir Guerrero	1.00
15	Greg Maddux	2.00

Real One Autographs

GIANTS

		NM/M
Common Player:		30.00
Current MLB Players		
200 Blue-inked produced		
52 Red-inked produced		
Prices listed for Blue sigs.		
RH	Richard Hidalgo	30.00
TL	Terrence Long	30.00
CD	Carlos Delgado	60.00
CJ	Chipper Jones	150.00
TG	Tom Glavine	100.00
GJ	Geoff Jenkins	40.00
JM	Joe Mays	30.00
FV	Fernando Vina	30.00
CP	Corey Patterson	40.00
JV	Jose Vidro	30.00
BB	Barry Bonds	275.00
AR	Alex Rodriguez	200.00
AH	Aubrey Huff	40.00
SPB	Sean Burroughs	30.00
RW	Randy Wolf	30.00
KB	Kris Benson	30.00
ML	Mike Lamb	30.00
TH	Todd Helton	80.00
MQ	Mark Quinn	30.00
MS	Mike Sweeney	30.00
ML	Matt Lawton	35.00
MO	Magglio Ordonez	40.00
MB	Mark Buehrle	50.00
MR	Mark Redman	30.00
CF	Cliff Floyd	30.00
NG	Nomar Garciaparra	150.00
1952 MLB Players		
MV	Mickey Vernon	40.00
HB	Hank Bauer	80.00
DD	Dom DiMaggio	100.00
LD	Larry Doby	90.00
JG	Joe Garagiola	75.00
DG	Dick Groat	60.00
MI	Monte Irvin	75.00
VL	Vernon Law	50.00
EM	Eddie Matthews	200.00
WM	Willie Mays	200.00
GM	Gil McDougald	60.00
MM	Minnie Monoso	80.00
AP	Andy Pafko	75.00
PFR	Phil Rizzuto	120.00
PR	Preacher Roe	100.00
JS	Johnny Sain	60.00
HS	Hank Sauer	60.00
RS	Red Schoendienst	75.00
BS	Bobby Shantz	40.00
CS	Curt Simmons	40.00
ES	Enos Slaughter	100.00
DS	Duke Snider	180.00
WS	Warren Spahn	120.00
BT	Bobby Thomson	85.00
HW	Hoyt Wilhelm	90.00
RR	Robin Roberts	80.00

Then and Now

Then and Now

SHORTSTOP

Pee Wee Reese
Brooklyn Dodgers®

Nomar Garciaparra
Boston Red Sox™

		NM/M
Complete Set (10):		15.00
Common Player:		1.50
Inserted 1:8		
1	Yogi Berra, Mike Piazza	1.50
2	Duke Snider, Sammy Sosa	2.00
3	Willie Mays, Ken Griffey Jr.	2.00
4	Phil Rizzuto, Derek Jeter	3.00
5	Pee Wee Reese, Nomar Garciaparra	2.00
6	Jackie Robinson, Alex Rodriguez	2.50
7	Johnny Mize, Mark McGwire	2.50
8	Bob Feller, Pedro Martinez	1.50
9	Robin Roberts, Greg Maddux	2.00
10	Warren Spahn, Randy Johnson	1.50

Time Capsule

TED WILLIAMS

		NM/M
Common Player:		20.00
Inserted 1:369		
WM	Willie Mays	75.00
TW	Ted Williams	85.00
DN	Don Newcombe	20.00
WF	Whitey Ford	30.00
WMTW	Ted Williams, Willie Mays/52	200.00

2001 Topps Reserve

		NM/M
Complete Set (151):		
Common Player:		.40
Common SP (101-150):		4.00
Production 1,500		
Sealed Hobby Box (10):		150.00
1	Darin Erstad	.50
2	Moises Alou	.40
3	Tony Batista	.40
4	Andruw Jones	.75
5	Edgar Renteria	.40
6	Eric Young	.40
7	Steve Finley	.40
8	Adrian Beltre	.40
9	Vladimir Guerrero	.40

JASON GIAMBI

10	Barry Bonds	3.00
11	Juan Gonzalez	.75
12	Jay Buhner	.40
13	Luis Castillo	.40
14	Cal Ripken Jr.	3.00
15	Bob Abreu	.40
16	Ivan Rodriguez	.75
17	Nomar Garciaparra	2.00
18	Todd Helton	.75
19	Bobby Higginson	.40
20	Jorge Posada	.50
21	Tim Salmon	.50
22	Jason Giambi	.75
23	Jose Cruz Jr.	.40
24	Chipper Jones	1.50
25	Jim Edmonds	.50
26	Gerald Williams	.40
27	Randy Johnson	1.00
28	Gary Sheffield	.50
29	Jeff Kent	.40
30	Jim Thome	.75
31	John Olerud	.50
32	Cliff Floyd	.40
33	Mike Lowell	.40
34	Phil Nevin	.40
35	Scott Rolen	.75
36	Alex Rodriguez	2.50
37	Ken Griffey Jr.	2.00
38	Neifi Perez	.40
39	Christian Guzman	.40
40	Mariano Rivera	.40
41	Troy Glaus	.75
42	Johnny Damon	.40
43	Rafael Furcal	.40
44	Jeromy Burnitz	.40
45	Mark McGwire	2.00
46	Fred McGriff	.40
47	Matt Williams	.40
48	Kevin Brown	.40
49	J.T. Snow	.40
50	Kenny Lofton	.40
51	Al Martin	.40
52	Antonio Alfonseca	.40
53	Edgardo Alfonzo	.40
54	Ryan Klesko	.40
55	Pat Burrell	.50
56	Rafael Palmeiro	.75
57	Sean Casey	.40
58	Jeff Cirillo	.40
59	Ray Durham	.40
60	Derek Jeter	3.00
61	Jeff Bagwell	.75
62	Carlos Delgado	.75
63	Tom Glavine	.50
64	Richie Sexson	.50
65	J.D. Drew	.40
66	Ben Grieve	.40
67	Mark Grace	.50
68	Shawn Green	.40
69	Robb Nen	.40
70	Omar Vizquel	.40
71	Edgar Martinez	.40
72	Preston Wilson	.40
73	Mike Piazza	1.50
74	Tony Gwynn	1.00
75	Jason Kendall	.40
76	Manny Ramirez	.75
77	Pokey Reese	.40
78	Mike Sweeney	.40
79	Magglio Ordonez	.50
80	Bernie Williams	.75
81	Richard Hidalgo	.40
82	Brad Fullmer	.40
83	Greg Maddux	2.00
84	Geoff Jenkins	.40
85	Sammy Sosa	2.00
86	Luis Gonzalez	.50
87	Eric Karros	.40
88	Jose Vidro	.40
89	Rich Aurilia	.40
90	Roberto Alomar	.75
91	Mike Cameron	.40
92	Mike Mussina	.60
93	Albert Belle	.40
94	Mike Lieberthal	.40
95	Brian Giles	.40
96	Pedro Martinez	1.00
97	Barry Larkin	.50
98	Jermaine Dye	.40
99	Frank Thomas	.75
100	David Justice	.50
101	Gary Johnson RC	4.00
102	Matt Ford RC	4.00
103	Albert Pujols RC	140.00
104	Brad Cresse RC	4.00
105	Valentino Pascucci RC	4.00
106	Bob Keppel RC	4.00
107	Luis Torres RC	4.00

108	Tony Blanco RC	6.00
109	Ronnie Corona RC	4.00
110	Phil Wilson RC	4.00
111	John Buck RC	4.00
112	Jim Journell RC	4.00
113	Victor Hall RC	4.00
114	Jeff Andra RC	4.00
115	Greg Nash RC	4.00
116	Travis Hafner RC	25.00
117	Casey Fossum RC	4.00
118	Miguel Olivo RC	4.00
119	Elpidio Guzman RC	4.00
120	Jason Belcher RC	4.00
121	Esix Snead RC	4.00
122	Joe Thurston RC	4.00
123	Rafael Soriano RC	6.00
124	Ed Rogers RC	4.00
125	Omar Beltre RC	4.00
126	Brett Gray RC	4.00
127	Deivi Mendez RC	4.00
128	Freddie Bynum RC	4.00
129	David Krynzel RC	4.00
130	Blake Williams RC	4.00
131	Reggie Abercrombie RC	8.00
132	Miguel Villio RC	4.00
133	Ryan Madson RC	10.00
134	Matt Thompson RC	4.00
135	Mark Burnett RC	4.00
136	Andy Beal RC	4.00
137	Ryan Ludwick RC	6.00
138	Roberto Miniel RC	4.00
139	Steve Smyth RC	4.00
140	Ben Washburn RC	4.00
141	Marvin Seale RC	4.00
142	Reggie Griggs RC	4.00
143	Seung Song RC	4.00
144	Chad Petty RC	4.00
145	Noel Devarez RC	4.00
146	Matt Butler RC	4.00
147	Brett Evert RC	4.00
148	Cesar Izturis RC	4.00
149	Troy Farnsworth RC	4.00
150	Brian Schmitt RC	4.00
151	Ichiro Suzuki RC	50.00

Game-Used Bat

NM/M
Common Player: 4.00
Inserted 1:Box

JB	Jeff Bagwell	8.00
BB	Barry Bonds	25.00
CD	Carlos Delgado	6.00
JE	Jim Edmonds	6.00
DE	Darin Erstad	4.00
RF	Rafael Furcal	4.00
NG	Nomar Garciaparra	20.00
VG	Vladimir Guerrero	10.00
TG	Tony Gwynn	10.00
CJ	Chipper Jones	15.00
MP	Mike Piazza	15.00
AR	Alex Rodriguez	15.00
IR	Ivan Rodriguez	8.00
BW	Bernie Williams	8.00

Game-Worn Uniform

NM/M
Common Player: 4.00
Inserted 1:Box

RA	Roberto Alomar	8.00
BB	Barry Bonds	25.00
CD	Carlos Delgado	8.00
JE	Jim Edmonds	6.00
NG	Nomar Garciaparra	15.00
JG	Juan Gonzalez	8.00
SG	Shawn Green	5.00
VG	Vladimir Guerrero	8.00
TG	Tony Gwynn	10.00
TH	Todd Helton	8.00
RJ	Randy Johnson	8.00
CJ	Chipper Jones	10.00
DJ	David Justice	4.00
GM	Greg Maddux	15.00
PM	Pedro Martinez	8.00
RP	Rafael Palmeiro	8.00
AR	Alex Rodriguez	15.00
IR	Ivan Rodriguez	8.00
SR	Scott Rolen	8.00
FT	Frank Thomas	8.00

Rookie Autographed Baseballs

NM/M
Common Player: 10.00
Inserted 1:Box w/holder.

Reggie Abercrombie	10.00
Jeff Andra	10.00
Andy Beal	10.00
Jason Belcher	10.00
Omar Beltre	10.00
Tony Blanco	15.00
John Buck	15.00
Mark Burnett	10.00
Freddie Bynum	10.00
Ronnie Corona	10.00
Noel Devarez	10.00
Matt Ford	10.00
Casey Fossum	15.00
Brett Gray	10.00
Reggie Griggs	10.00
Elpidio Guzman	10.00
Travis Hafner	60.00
Victor Hall	10.00
Gary Johnson	10.00
Jim Journell	10.00
Bob Keppel	15.00
David Krynzel	15.00
Ryan Ludwick	15.00
Ryan Madson	15.00
Deivi Mendez	10.00
Roberto Miniel	10.00
Greg Nash	10.00
Chad Petty	10.00
Albert Pujols	400.00
Ed Rogers	10.00
Marvin Seale	10.00
Steve Smyth	10.00
Esix Snead	10.00
Seung Song	10.00
Rafael Soriano	15.00
Matt Thompson	10.00
Joe Thurston	10.00
Luis Torres	10.00
Miguel Villio	10.00
Ben Washburn	10.00

Rookie Graded Autograph

NM/M
Common Rookie: 10.00
Inserted 1:Box
Prices for PSA 8
PSA 9's: 1.5X

Reggie Abercrombie	10.00
Jeff Andra	10.00
Andy Beal	10.00
Jason Belcher	10.00
Omar Beltre	10.00
Tony Blanco	10.00
John Buck	10.00
Mark Burnett	10.00
Freddie Bynum	10.00
Ronnie Corona	10.00
Noel Devarez	10.00
Matt Ford	10.00
Casey Fossum	15.00
Brett Gray	10.00
Reggie Griggs	10.00
Elpidio Guzman	10.00
Travis Hafner	65.00
Victor Hall	10.00
Gary Johnson	10.00
Jim Journell	10.00
David Krynzel	10.00
Ryan Ludwick	20.00
Ryan Madson	10.00

ALBERT PUJOLS

2001 Topps Stars

Deivi Mendez		10.00
Roberto Miniel		10.00
Greg Nash		10.00
Miguel Olivo		10.00
Valentino Pascucci		10.00
Chad Petty		10.00
Albert Pujols		375.00
Ed Rogers		10.00
Marvin Seale		10.00
Steve Smyth		10.00
Esix Snead		10.00
Seung Song		10.00
Rafael Soriano		15.00
Matt Thompson		10.00
Joe Thurston		15.00
Luis Torres		10.00
Miguel Villio		10.00
Ben Washburn		10.00
Blake Williams		10.00
Phil Wilson		10.00

NM/M
Complete Set (200): 90.00
Common Player: .15
Pack (6): 5.00
Box (24): 100.00

1	Darin Erstad	.25
2	Luis Gonzalez	.25
3	Rafael Furcal	.25
4	Dante Bichette	.25
5	Sammy Sosa	1.25
6	Ken Griffey Jr.	1.00
7	Jim Thome	.50
8	Bobby Higginson	.15
9	Cliff Floyd	.25
10	Lance Berkman	.25
11	Eric Karros	.25
12	Jeromy Burnitz	.15
13	Jose Vidro	.15
14	Benny Agbayani	.15
15	Jorge Posada	.40
16	Ramon Hernandez	.15
17	Jason Kendall	.25
18	Jeff Kent	.25
19	John Olerud	.25
20	Al Martin	.15
21	Gerald Williams	.15
22	Gabe Kapler	.15
23	Carlos Delgado	.50
24	Mariano Rivera	.25
25	Javy Lopez	.25
26	Paul Konerko	.15
27	Daryle Ward	.15
28	Mike Lieberthal	.15
29	Tom Goodwin	.15
30	Garret Anderson	.40
31	Steve Finley	.15
32	Brian Jordan	.15
33	Nomar Garciaparra	1.50
34	Ray Durham	.15
35	Sean Casey	.25
36	Kenny Lofton	.25
37	Dean Palmer	.15
38	Jeff Bagwell	.50
39	Mike Sweeney	.25
40	Adrian Beltre	.25
41	Richie Sexson	.25
42	Vladimir Guerrero	.75
43	Derek Jeter	2.00
44	Miguel Tejada	.25
45	Doug Glanville	.15
46	Brian Giles	.25
47	Marvin Benard	.15
48	Edgar Martinez	.25
49	Edgar Renteria	.15
50	Fred McGriff	.25
51	Ivan Rodriguez	.50
52	Brad Fullmer	.15
53	Antonio Alfonseca	.15
54	Tom Glavine	.40
55	Warren Morris	.15
56	Johnny Damon	.25
57	Dmitri Young	.15
58	Mo Vaughn	.15
59	Randy Johnson	.75
60	Greg Maddux	1.00
61	Carl Everett	.15
62	Magglio Ordonez	.25
63	Pokey Reese	.15
64	Todd Helton	.50
65	Preston Wilson	.15
66	Richard Hidalgo	.15
67	Jermaine Dye	.25
68	Gary Sheffield	.40
69	Geoff Jenkins	.25
70	Edgardo Alfonzo	.15

71	Paul O'Neill	.25
72	Terrence Long	.15
73	Bob Abreu	.25
74	Kevin Young	.15
75	J.T. Snow	.15
76	Alex Rodriguez	1.50
77	Jim Edmonds	.25
78	Mark McGwire	1.50
79	Tony Batista	.15
80	Darrin Fletcher	.15
81	Robb Nen	.15
82	Jose Offerman	.15
83	Travis Fryman	.25
84	Joe Randa	.15
85	Omar Vizquel	.25
86	Tim Salmon	.25
87	Andruw Jones	.50
88	Albert Belle	.25
89	Manny Ramirez	.50
90	Frank Thomas	.50
91	Barry Larkin	.25
92	Neifi Perez	.15
93	Luis Castillo	.25
94	Moises Alou	.25
95	Mark Quinn	.15
96	Kevin Brown	.25
97	Cristian Guzman	.15
98	Mike Piazza	1.00
99	Bernie Williams	.40
100	Jason Giambi	.50
101	Scott Rolen	.75
102	Phil Nevin	.15
103	Rich Aurilia	.15
104	Mike Cameron	.15
105	Fernando Vina	.15
106	Greg Vaughn	.15
107	Jose Cruz	.15
108	Raul Mondesi	.15
109	Ben Molina	.15
110	Pedro Martinez	.75
111	Todd Hollandsworth	.15
112	Jacque Jones	.15
113	Rickey Henderson	.25
114	Troy Glaus	.25
115	Chipper Jones	1.00
116	Delino DeShields	.15
117	Eric Young	.15
118	Jose Valentin	.15
119	Roberto Alomar	.40
120	Jeff Cirillo	.15
121	Mike Lowell	.15
122	Julio Lugo	.15
123	Shawn Green	.15
124	Marquis Grissom	.15
125	Matt Lawton	.15
126	Jay Payton	.15
127	David Justice	.25
128	Eric Chavez	.15
129	Pat Burrell	.50
130	Ryan Klesko	.15
131	Barry Bonds	2.00
132	Jay Bulner	.15
133	J.D. Drew	.25
134	Rafael Palmeiro	.50
135	Shannon Stewart	.15
136	Juan Gonzalez	.50
137	Tony Womack	.15
138	Carlos Lee	.15
139	Derrek Lee	.15
140	Ben Grieve	.15
141	Ron Belliard	.15
142	Stan Musial	1.50
143	Ernie Banks	1.00
144	Jim Palmer	.50
145	Tony Perez	.25
146	Duke Snider	.50
147	Rod Carew	.40
148	Warren Spahn	.75
149	Yogi Berra	.75
150	Juan Marichal	.15
151	Eric Munson	.15
152	Carlos Pena	.15
153	Joe Crede	.15
154	Ryan Anderson	.15
155	Milton Bradley	.15
156	Sean Burroughs	.15
157	Corey Patterson	.25
158	C.C. Sabathia	.15
159	Ben Petrick	.15
160	Aubrey Huff	.15
161	Gookie Dawkins	.15
162	Ben Sheets	.25
163	Pablo Ozuna	.15
164	Eric Valent	.15
165	Rod Barajas	.15
166	Chin-Feng Chen	.40
167	Josh Hamilton	.15
168	Keith Ginter	.15
169	Vernon Wells	.15
170	Dernell Stenson	.15
171	Alfonso Soriano	.75
172	Jason Marquis	.15
173	Nick Johnson	.15
174	Adam Everett	.15
175	Jimmy Rollins	.25
176	Ben Diggins	.15
177	John Lackey	.15
178	Scott Heard	.15
179	Brian Hitchcox RC	.50
180	Odannis Ayala RC	.50
181	Scott Pratt RC	.50
182	Greg Runser RC	.50
183	Chris Russ RC	.50
184	Derek Thompson RC	.50
185	Jason Jones RC	.50
186	Dominic Rich RC	.50
187	Chad Petty RC	.50
188	Steve Smyth RC	.50

189	Bryan Hebson RC	.50
190	Danny Borrell RC	.50
191	Bob Keppel RC	.50
192	Justin Wayne RC	1.00
193	Reggie Abercrombie RC	1.00
194	Travis Baptist RC	.50
195	Shawn Fagan RC	.50
196	Jose Reyes RC	25.00
197	Chris Bass RC	.50
198	Albert Pujols RC	75.00
199	Luis Cotto RC	.50
200	Jake Peavy RC	4.00

Elimination

Stars: 5-10X
Production 100 Sets
Redemp. deadline 10/19/01.

Gold

BERNIE WILLIAMS

Stars: 2-5X
Production 499 Sets

Onyx

Stars: 6-12X
Rookies: 4-6X
Production 99 Sets

Autographs

ERIC MUNSON

NM/M
Common Player: 15.00
Inserted 1:353

EB	Ernie Banks	50.00
YB	Yogi Berra	40.00
RC	Rod Carew	30.00
CD	Carlos Delgado	15.00
TH	Todd Helton	30.00
JM	Juan Marichal	30.00
EM	Eric Munson	10.00
SM	Stan Musial	80.00
JP	Jim Palmer	25.00
TP	Tony Perez	25.00
IR	Ivan Rodriguez	30.00
DS	Duke Snider	35.00
WS	Warren Spahn	40.00

Game Gear Bats

GAME GEAR

ERIC MUNSON

NM/M
Common Player: 5.00
Inserted 1:187

AB	Adrian Beltre	5.00
LB	Lance Berkman	6.00
SB	Sean Burroughs	5.00
MC	Michael Cuddyer	5.00
BD	Ben Davis	5.00
JDD	J.D. Drew	5.00
ED	Erubiel Durazo	5.00
JE	Juan Encarnacion	5.00
RF	Rafael Furcal	8.00
AK	Adam Kennedy	5.00
GL	George Lombard	5.00
TL	Terrence Long	5.00
FL	Felipe Lopez	5.00
GM	Gary Mathews	5.00
CP	Corey Patterson	8.00
NP	Neifi Perez	5.00

AP	Adam Piatt	5.00
SR	Scott Rolen	15.00
FS	Fernando Seguignol	5.00
RS	Richie Sexson	10.00

Game Gear Bats Autographs

Inserted 1:12,240
No pricing due to scarcity.

Game Gear Jerseys

NM/M

Common Player: 4.00
Inserted 1:61

EA	Edgardo Alfonzo	4.00
RA	Roberto Alomar	8.00
BB	Barry Bonds	25.00
LC	Luis Castillo	4.00
TG	Tony Gwynn	10.00
TH	Todd Helton	8.00
AJ	Andruw Jones	8.00
CJ	Chipper Jones	10.00
EM	Edgar Martinez	8.00
MO	Magglio Ordonez	5.00
MP	Mike Piazza	15.00
SS	Sammy Sosa	25.00
SHS	Shannon Stewart	4.00
FT	Frank Thomas	8.00
JV	Jose Vidro	4.00

Game Gear Jerseys Autographs

Inserted 1:19,288
No pricing due to scarcity.

Progression

NM/M

Complete Set (9): 10.00
Common Player: 1.00
Inserted 1:8

P1	Ernie Banks, Alex Rodriguez, Felipe Lopez	3.00
P2	Yogi Berra, Ivan Rodriguez, Ramon Hernandez	2.00
P3	Tony Perez, Carlos Delgado, Eric Munson	1.00
P4	Rod Carew, Roberto Alomar, Jose Ortiz	1.00
P5	Stan Musial, Darin Erstad, Alex Escobar	2.00
P6	Jim Palmer, Kevin Brown, Kurt Ainsworth	1.00
P7	Duke Snider, Jim Edmonds, Vernon Wells	1.00
P8	Warren Spahn, Randy Johnson, Ryan Anderson	1.50
P9	Juan Marichal, Bartolo Colon, Bobby Bradley	1.00

Players Choice Award Nominees

NM/M

Complete Set (10): 15.00
Common Player: 1.50
Inserted 1:12

1	Barry Bonds, Carlos Delgado, Todd Helton	4.00
2	Gary Sheffield, Eric Davis, Turk Wendell	1.50
3	Alex Rodriguez, Carlos Delgado, Frank Thomas	3.00
4	David Wells, Pedro Martinez, Andy Pettitte	2.00
5	Mark Quinn, Terrence Long, Kazuhiro Sasaki	1.50
6	Jay Buhner, Frank Thomas, Bobby Higginson	1.50
7	Barry Bonds, Todd Helton, Jeff Kent	4.00
8	Tom Glavine, Randy Johnson, Greg Maddux	2.50
9	Rick Ankiel, Rafael Furcal, Jay Payton	1.50
10	Moises Alou, Andres Galarraga, Jeff D'Amico	1.50

Player Choice Awards Relics

NM/M

Common Player: 10.00
Inserted 1:1,530

1	Carlos Delgado	15.00
2	Eric Davis	10.00
3	Carlos Delgado	15.00
4	Pedro Martinez	25.00
5	Terrence Long	10.00
6	Frank Thomas	20.00
7	Todd Helton	15.00
8	Randy Johnson	25.00
9	Rafael Furcal	15.00
10	Andres Galarraga	10.00

2001 Topps Tribute

NM/M

Complete Set (90): 300.00
Common Player: 2.00
Pack (3): 75.00
Box (6): 425.00

1	Pee Wee Reese	2.00
2	Babe Ruth	15.00
3	Ralph Kiner	2.00
4	Brooks Robinson	5.00
5	Don Sutton	2.00
6	Carl Yastrzemski	8.00
7	Roger Maris	10.00
8	Andre Dawson	2.00
9	Luis Aparicio	2.00
10	Wade Boggs	4.00
11	Johnny Bench	8.00
12	Ernie Banks	6.00
13	Thurman Munson	5.00
14	Harmon Killebrew	5.00
15	Ted Kluszewski	2.00
16	Bob Feller	3.00
17	Mike Schmidt	10.00
18	Warren Spahn	4.00
19	Jim Palmer	3.00
20	Don Mattingly	12.00
21	Willie Mays	10.00
22	Gil Hodges	2.00
23	Juan Marichal	2.00
24	Robin Yount	6.00
25	Nolan Ryan	12.00
26	Dave Winfield	3.00
27	Hank Greenberg	2.00
28	Honus Wagner	8.00
29	Nolan Ryan	12.00
30	Phil Niekro	2.00
31	Robin Roberts	2.00
32	Casey Stengel	3.00
33	Willie McCovey	2.00
34	Roy Campanella	4.00
35	Rollie Fingers	2.00
36	Tom Seaver	5.00
37	Jackie Robinson	10.00
38	Hank Aaron	10.00
39	Bob Gibson	4.00
40	Carlton Fisk	4.00
41	Hank Aaron	10.00
42	George Brett	10.00
43	Orlando Cepeda	2.00
44	Red Schoendienst	2.00
45	Don Drysdale	4.00
46	Mel Ott	2.00
47	Casey Stengel	3.00
48	Al Kaline	4.00
49	Reggie Jackson	5.00
50	Tony Perez	2.00
51	Ozzie Smith	6.00
52	Billy Martin	4.00
53	Bill Dickey	2.00
54	Catfish Hunter	2.00
55	Duke Snider	4.00
56	Dale Murphy	2.00
57	Bobby Doerr	2.00
58	Earl Averill	2.00
59	Carlton Fisk	4.00
60	Tom Lasorda	2.00
61	Lou Gehrig	12.00
62	Enos Slaughter	2.00
63	Jim Bunning	2.00
64	Rollie Fingers	2.00
65	Frank Robinson	4.00
66	Earl Weaver	2.00
67	Eddie Mathews	5.00
68	Kirby Puckett	5.00
69	Phil Rizzuto	4.00
70	Lou Brock	4.00
71	Walt Alston	2.00
72	Bill Pierce	2.00
73	Joe Morgan	2.00
74	Roberto Clemente	12.00
75	Whitey Ford	4.00
76	Richie Ashburn	2.00
77	Elston Howard	2.00
78	Gary Carter	2.00
79	Carl Hubbell	2.00
80	Yogi Berra	6.00
81	Ken Boyer	2.00
82	Nolan Ryan	12.00
83	Bill Mazeroski	2.00
84	Dizzy Dean	4.00
85	Nellie Fox	2.00
86	Stan Musial	10.00
87	Steve Carlton	4.00
88	Willie Stargell	4.00
89	Hal Newhouser	2.00
90	Frank Robinson	4.00

Franchise Figures

NM/M

Inserted 1:34

AL	Walt Alston, Tommy Lasorda	50.00
AFF	Luis Aparicio, Nellie Fox, Carlton Fisk	125.00
BPKR	Johnny Bench, Tony Perez, Ted Kluszewski, Frank Robinson, Joe Morgan	150.00
CD	Gary Carter, Andre Dawson	40.00
HDB	Bill Dickey, Elston Howard, Yogi Berra	150.00
FY	Carlton Fisk, Carl Yastrzemski	150.00
HSS	Gil Hodges, Casey Stengel, Tom Seaver	150.00
JM	Reggie Jackson, Billy Martin	125.00
KG	Al Kaline, Hank Greenberg	150.00
MMC	Willie Mays, Willie McCovey, Orlando Cepeda	200.00
MCS	Bill Mazeroski, Roberto Clemente, Willie Stargell	185.00
MM	Thurman Munson, Don Mattingly	200.00
MMA	Dale Murphy, Ed Mathews, Hank Aaron	185.00
PK	Kirby Puckett, Harmon Killebrew	100.00
RSC	Pee Wee Reese, Duke Snider, Roy Campanella	160.00
RR	Brooks Robinson, Frank Robinson	75.00
RG	Babe Ruth, Lou Gehrig	500.00
SAC	Mike Schmidt, Richie Ashburn, Steve Carlton	125.00
SBSM	Ozzie Smith, Lou Brock, Red Schoendienst, Stan Musial	125.00

Game-Used Bat Relics

NM/M

Common Player: 20.00
Inserted 1:2

HA	Hank Aaron	50.00
LA	Luis Aparicio	20.00
RA	Richie Ashburn	25.00
KB	Ken Boyer	20.00
GB	George Brett	40.00
LB	Lou Brock	20.00
RC	Roy Campanella	30.00
RCL	Roberto Clemente	80.00
CF	Carlton Fisk	25.00
LG	Lou Gehrig	160.00
HG	Hank Greenberg	50.00
GH	Gil Hodges	25.00
RJ	Reggie Jackson	30.00
AK	Al Kaline	30.00
HK	Harmon Killebrew	30.00
RM	Roger Maris	50.00
BM	Billy Martin	20.00
DM	Don Mattingly	50.00
WM	Willie McCovey	25.00
TM	Thurman Munson	35.00
PWR	Pee Wee Reese	20.00
BRO	Brooks Robinson	30.00
FRR	Frank Robinson	30.00
BR	Babe Ruth	200.00
OS	Ozzie Smith	35.00
CS	Casey Stengel	20.00
HW	Honus Wagner	200.00
CY	Carl Yastrzemski	40.00

Game-Worn Patch And Number Relics

NM/M

Common Player: 60.00
Inserted 1:61

WA	Walt Alston	60.00
JB	Johnny Bench	180.00
YB	Yogi Berra	150.00
WB	Wade Boggs	80.00
LB	Lou Brock	60.00
BD	Bill Dickey	150.00
BDO	Bobby Doerr	100.00
HK	Harmon Killebrew	250.00
TL	Tom Lasorda	80.00
JM	Juan Marichal	75.00
EM	Eddie Mathews	150.00
KB	Kirby Puckett	250.00
NR	Nolan Ryan	300.00
MS	Mike Schmidt	250.00
RS	Red Schoendienst	80.00
DW	Dave Winfield	80.00
CY	Carl Yastrzemski	100.00
RY	Robin Yount	100.00

Retired Game-Worn Relics

NM/M

Common Player: 20.00
Inserted 1:2

WA	Walt Alston	20.00
EB	Ernie Banks	30.00
EBA	Ernie Banks	30.00
JB	Johnny Bench	30.00
YB	Yogi Berra	30.00
WB	Wade Boggs	20.00
GB	George Brett	50.00
LB	Lou Brock	25.00
SC	Steve Carlton	25.00
DD	Dizzy Dean	40.00
BD	Bill Dickey	40.00
BDO	Bobby Doerr	25.00
NF	Nellie Fox	30.00
HK	Harmon Killebrew	30.00
TL	Tom Lasorda	20.00
JMG	Juan Marichal	30.00
EM	Eddie Mathews	40.00
DM	Don Mattingly	50.00
WMF	Willie Mays	75.00
WMW	Willie Mays	75.00
SM	Stan Musial	75.00
JP	Jim Palmer	20.00
KP	Kirby Puckett	30.00
FR	Frank Robinson	25.00
NRA	Nolan Ryan	80.00
NRH	Nolan Ryan	80.00
NRR	Nolan Ryan	80.00
MSB	Mike Schmidt	50.00
MSW	Mike Schmidt	50.00
RS	Red Schoendienst	20.00
WST	Willie Stargell	20.00
CS	Casey Stengel	20.00
DW	Dave Winfield	20.00
CY	Carl Yastrzemski/White	40.00
CYA	Carl Yastrzemski/Gray	40.00
RY	Robin Yount	30.00

Frank Robinson Dual Relic

NM/M

Inserted 1:860

FR-RO	Frank Robinson	90.00

Nolan Ryan Tri-Relic

NM/M

Randomly inserted.

NR	Nolan Ryan	475.00

Casey Stengel Dual Relic

NM/M

Inserted 1:860

CS	Casey Stengel	100.00

Vintage Buy-Back Cards

No pricing due to scarcity.

Post Collector's Series

Baseball cards returned to boxes of Post cereals in 2001 with a special edition of Topps cards. The baseball cards were issued two per cello pack along with an introductory "pass" to the cereal company's web site for kids. The top card in each pack was visible through a win-

FIRST BASE
MARK McGWIRE

dow cut in the specially marked cereal boxes. The 2-1/2" x 3-1/2" cards have game-action photos which are borderless at the top and sides. At bottom are color strips with the player's position and name. A team logo in the lower-left corner of the photo and the Topps 50th anniversary logo is at upper-left. Backs have a portrait photo, facsimile autograph, biographical data, recent stats and various league, and sponsor logos.

NM/M

Complete Set (18): 10.00
Common Player: .25

1	Alex Rodriguez	1.50
2	Barry Bonds	2.00
3	Bernie Williams	.35
4	Frank Thomas	.75
5	Greg Maddux	1.50
6	Mark McGwire	1.50
7	Manny Ramirez	.75
8	Orlando Hernandez	.25
9	Pedro Martinez	.25
10	Gary Sheffield	.45
11	Jermaine Dye	.25
12	Mike Piazza	1.50
13	Barry Larkin	.25
14	Brad Radke	.25
15	Ivan Rodriguez	.60
16	Moises Alou	.25
17	Tony Gwynn	1.00
18	Todd Helton	.75

500 Home Run Club

WILLIE McCOVEY
INDUCTED IN 1986
521 CAREER HOME RUNS

Baseball cards returned to boxes of Post cereals in 2001 with a special edition of Topps cards. The baseball cards were issued two per cello pack. The top card in each pack was visible through a window cut in the specially marked cereal boxes. The 2-1/2" x 3-1/2" cards have player photos in a white diamond on a wood-look background. Player name is in a red strip below. At center-left is a Hall of Fame logo, with a 500 Home Run Club logo opposite. The Topps 50th anniversary logo is at upper-left. Backs have complete major league stats, biographical data and various league and sponsor logos.

NM/M

Complete Set (8): 7.50
Common Player: 1.00

1	Babe Ruth	2.00
2	Ernie Banks	1.50
3	Jimmie Foxx	1.00
4	Willie McCovey	1.00
5	Frank Robinson	1.00
6	Harmon Killebrew	1.00
7	Mike Schmidt	1.50
8	Reggie Jackson	1.50

2002 Topps Promos

Topps previewed the format of its 2002 base set with a three-card promo issue.

	NM/M
Complete Set (3):	6.00
Common Player:	2.00
P1 Sammy Sosa	3.00
P2 Jason Giambi	2.00
P3 Curt Schilling	2.00

2002 Topps

	NM/M
Complete Set (718):	70.00
Complete Factory Set (723):	80.00
Complete Series 1 (365):	35.00
Complete Series 2 (354):	35.00
Common Player:	.10
Pack (10):	1.50
Box (36):	40.00

1	Pedro Martinez	.50
2	Mike Stanton	.10
3	Brad Penny	.10
4	Mike Matheny	.10
5	Johnny Damon	.20
6	Bret Boone	.20
7	Not Issued (Retired)	
8	Chris Truby	.10
9	B.J. Surhoff	.10
10	Mike Hampton	.10
11	Juan Pierre	.10
12	Mark Buehrle	.10
13	Bob Abreu	.20
14	David Cone	.10
15	Aaron Sele	.10
16	Fernando Tatis	.10
17	Bobby Jones	.10
18	Rick Helling	.10
19	Dmitri Young	.10
20	Mike Mussina	.40
21	Mike Sweeney	.10
22	Cristian Guzman	.10
23	Ryan Kohlmeier	.10
24	Adam Kennedy	.10
25	Larry Walker	.25
26	Eric Davis	.10
27	Jason Tyner	.10
28	Eric Young	.10
29	Jason Marquis	.10
30	Luis Gonzalez	.20
31	Kevin Tapani	.10
32	Orlando Cabrera	.10
33	Marty Cordova	.10
34	Brad Ausmus	.10
35	Livan Hernandez	.10
36	Alex Gonzalez	.10
37	Edgar Renteria	.20
38	Bengie Molina	.10
39	Frank Menechino	.10
40	Rafael Palmeiro	.40
41	Brad Fullmer	.10
42	Julio Zuleta	.10
43	Darren Dreifort	.10
44	Trot Nixon	.10
45	Trevor Hoffman	.10
46	Vladimir Nunez	.10
47	Mark Kotsay	.10
48	Kenny Rogers	.10
49	Ben Petrick	.10
50	Jeff Bagwell	.40
51	Juan Encarnacion	.10
52	Ramiro Mendoza	.10
53	Brian Meadows	.10
54	Chad Curtis	.10
55	Aramis Ramirez	.25
56	Mark McLemore	.10
57	Dante Bichette	.10
58	Scott Schoeneweis	.10
59	Jose Cruz Jr.	.10
60	Roger Clemens	1.00
61	Jose Guillen	.10
62	Darren Oliver	.10
63	Chris Reitsma	.10
64	Jeff Abbott	.10
65	Robin Ventura	.10
66	Denny Neagle	.10
67	Al Martin	.10
68	Benito Santiago	.10
69	Roy Oswalt	.20
70	Juan Gonzalez	.40
71	Garret Anderson	.25
72	Bobby Bonilla	.10
73	Danny Bautista	.10
74	J.T. Snow Jr.	.10
75	Derek Jeter	1.50
76	John Olerud	.20
77	Kevin Appier	.10
78	Phil Nevin	.20
79	Sean Casey	.20
80	Troy Glaus	.40
81	Joe Randa	.10
82	Jose Valentin	.10
83	Ricky Bottalico	.10
84	Todd Zeile	.10
85	Barry Larkin	.25
86	Bob Wickman	.10
87	Jeff Shaw	.10
88	Greg Vaughn	.10
89	Fernando Vina	.10
90	Mark Mulder	.25
91	Paul Bako	.10
92	Aaron Boone	.10
93	Esteban Loaiza	.10
94	Richie Sexson	.40
95	Alfonso Soriano	.50
96	Tony Womack	.10
97	Paul Shuey	.10
98	Melvin Mora	.10
99	Tony Gwynn	.50
100	Vladimir Guerrero	.50
101	Keith Osik	.10
102	Randy Velarde	.10
103	Scott Williamson	.10
104	Daryle Ward	.10
105	Doug Mientkiewicz	.10
106	Stan Javier	.10
107	Russ Ortiz	.10
108	Wade Miller	.10
109	Luke Prokopec	.10
110	Andruw Jones	.40
111	Ron Coomer	.10
112	Dan Wilson	.10
113	Luis Castillo	.10
114	Derek Bell	.10
115	Gary Sheffield	.20
116	Ruben Rivera	.10
117	Paul O'Neill	.10
118	Craig Paquette	.10
119	Chris Michalak	.10
120	Brad Radke	.10
121	Jorge Fabregas	.10
122	Randy Winn	.10
123	Tom Goodwin	.10
124	Jaret Wright	.10
125	Manny Ramirez	.40
126	Al Leiter	.20
127	Ben Davis	.10
128	Frank Catalanotto	.10
129	Jose Cabrera	.10
130	Magglio Ordonez	.20
131	Jose Macias	.10
132	Ted Lilly	.10
133	Chris Holt	.10
134	Eric Milton	.10
135	Shannon Stewart	.10
136	Omar Olivares	.10
137	David Segui	.10
138	Jeff Nelson	.10
139	Matt Williams	.25
140	Ellis Burks	.10
141	Jason Bere	.10
142	Jimmy Haynes	.10
143	Ramon Hernandez	.10
144	Craig Counsell (Front photo actually Greg Colbrunn.)	.10
145	John Smoltz	.25
146	Homer Bush	.10
147	Quilvio Veras	.10
148	Esteban Yan	.10
149	Ramon Ortiz	.10
150	Carlos Delgado	.30
151	Lee Stevens	.10
152	Wil Cordero	.10
153	Mike Bordick	.10
154	John Flaherty	.10
155	Omar Daal	.10
156	Todd Ritchie	.10
157	Carl Everett	.10
158	Scott Sullivan	.10
159	Deivi Cruz	.10
160a	Albert Pujols (Back photo is Placido Polanco.) (In cap.)	1.00
160b	Albert Pujols (Back photo corrected.)(No cap.)	10.00
161	Royce Clayton	.10
162	Jeff Suppan	.10
163	C.C. Sabathia	.10
164	Jimmy Rollins	.25
165	Rickey Henderson	.25
166	Rey Ordonez	.10
167	Shawn Estes	.10
168	Reggie Sanders	.10
169	Jon Lieber	.10
170	Armando Benitez	.10
171	Mike Remlinger	.10
172	Billy Wagner	.10
173	Troy Percival	.10
174	Devon White	.10
175	Ivan Rodriguez	.40
176	Dustin Hermanson	.10
177	Brian Anderson	.10
178	Graeme Lloyd	.10
179	Russ Branyan	.10
180	Bobby Higginson	.10
181	Alex Gonzalez	.10
182	John Franco	.10
183	Sidney Ponson	.10
184	Jose Mesa	.10
185	Todd Hollandsworth	.10
186	Kevin Young	.10
187	Tim Wakefield	.10
188	Craig Biggio	.20
189	Jason Isringhausen	.10
190	Mark Quinn	.10
191	Glendon Rusch	.10
192	Damian Miller	.10
193	Sandy Alomar	.10
194	Scott Brosius	.10
195	Dave Martinez	.10
196	Danny Graves	.10
197	Shea Hillenbrand	.10
198	Jimmy Anderson	.10
199	Travis Lee	.10
200	Randy Johnson	.50
201	Carlos Beltran	.25
202	Jerry Hairston Jr.	.10
203	Jesus Sanchez	.10
204	Eddie Taubensee	.10
205	David Wells	.10
206	Russ Davis	.10
207	Michael Barrett	.10
208	Marquis Grissom	.10
209	Byung-Hyun Kim	.10
210	Hideo Nomo	.25
211	Ryan Rupe	.10
212	Ricky Gutierrez	.10
213	Darryl Kile	.10
214	Rico Brogna	.10
215	Terrence Long	.10
216	Mike Jackson	.10
217	Jamey Wright	.10
218	Adrian Beltre	.20
219	Benny Agbayani	.10
220	Chuck Knoblauch	.10
221	Randy Wolf	.10
222	Andy Ashby	.10
223	Corey Koskie	.10
224	Roger Cedeno	.10
225	Ichiro Suzuki	1.00
226	Keith Foulke	.10
227	Ryan Minor	.10
228	Shawon Dunston	.10
229	Alex Cora	.10
230	Jeromy Burnitz	.10
231	Mark Grace	.25
232	Aubrey Huff	.10
233	Jeffrey Hammonds	.10
234	Olmedo Saenz	.10
235	Brian Jordan	.10
236	Jeremy Giambi	.10
237	Joe Girardi	.10
238	Eric Gagne	.25
239	Masato Yoshii	.10
240	Greg Maddux	.75
241	Bryan Rekar	.10
242	Ray Durham	.10
243	Torii Hunter	.20
244	Derrek Lee	.20
245	Jim Edmonds	.25
246	Einar Diaz	.10
247	Brian Bohanon	.10
248	Ron Belliard	.10
249	Mike Lowell	.20
250	Sammy Sosa	1.00
251	Richard Hidalgo	.10
252	Bartolo Colon	.10
253	Jorge Posada	.25
254	LaTroy Hawkins	.10
255	Paul LoDuca	.10
256	Carlos Febles	.10
257	Nelson Cruz	.10
258	Edgardo Alfonzo	.10
259	Joey Hamilton	.10
260	Cliff Floyd	.10
261	Wes Helms	.10
262	Jay Bell	.10
263	Mike Cameron	.10
264	Paul Konerko	.10
265	Jeff Kent	.20
266	Robert Fick	.10
267	Allen Levrault	.10
268	Placido Polanco	.10
269	Marlon Anderson	.10
270	Mariano Rivera	.20
271	Chan Ho Park	.10
272	Jose Vizcaino	.10
273	Jeff D'Amico	.10
274	Mark Gardner	.10
275	Travis Fryman	.10
276	Darren Lewis	.10
277	Jerry Manuel	.10
278	Bruce Bochy	.10
279	Bob Brenly	.10
280	Don Baylor	.10
281	Davey Lopes	.10
282	Jerry Narron	.10
283	Tony Muser	.10
284	Hal McRae	.10
285	Bobby Cox	.10
286	Larry Dierker	.10
287	Phil Garner	.10
288	Jimy Williams	.10
289	Bobby Valentine	.10
290	Dusty Baker	.10
291	Lloyd McLendon	.10
292	Mike Scioscia	.10
293	Buck Martinez	.10
294	Larry Bowa	.10
295	Tony LaRussa	.10
296	Jeff Torborg	.10
297	Tom Kelly	.10
298	Mike Hargrove	.10
299	Art Howe	.10
300	Lou Pinella	.10
301	Charlie Manuel	.10
302	Buddy Bell	.10
303	Tony Perez	.10
304	Bob Boone	.10
305	Joe Torre	.25
306	Jim Tracy	.10
307	Jason Lane	.10
308	Chris George	.10
309	Hank Blalock	.25
310	Joe Borchard	.10
311	Marlon Byrd	.10
312	Raymond Cabrera **RC**	.25
313	Freddy Sanchez **RC**	.40
314	Scott Wiggins **RC**	.40
315	Jason Maule **RC**	.30
316	Dionys Cesar **RC**	.40
317	Boof Bonser	.10
318	Juan Tolentino **RC**	.40
319	Earl Snyder **RC**	.25
320	Travis Wade **RC**	.25
321	Napoleon Calzado **RC**	.40
322	Eric Glaser **RC**	.40
323	Craig Kuzmic **RC**	.40
324	Nic Jackson **RC**	.50
325	Mike Rivera	.10
326	Jason Bay **RC**	1.00
327	Chris Smith	.10
328	Jake Gautreau	.10
329	Gabe Gross	.10
330	Kenny Baugh	.10
331	J.D. Martin	.10
332	Barry Bonds	1.00
333	Rickey Henderson	.25
334	Bud Smith	.10
335	Rickey Henderson	.25
336	Barry Bonds	1.00
337	Ichiro Suzuki, Jason Giambi, Roberto Alomar	.50
338	Alex Rodriguez, Ichiro Suzuki, Bret Boone	.50
339	Alex Rodriguez, Jim Thome, Rafael Palmeiro	.40
340	Bret Boone, Juan Gonzalez, Alex Rodriguez	.40
341	Freddy Garcia, Mike Mussina, Joe Mays	.15
342	Hideo Nomo, Mike Mussina, Roger Clemens	.40
343	Larry Walker, Todd Helton, Moises Alou	.25
344	Sammy Sosa, Todd Helton, Barry Bonds	.40
345	Barry Bonds, Sammy Sosa, Luis Gonzalez	.40
346	Sammy Sosa, Todd Helton, Luis Gonzalez	.40
347	Curt Schilling, Randy Johnson, John Burkett	.20
348	Randy Johnson, Curt Schilling, Chan Ho Park	.20
349	Seattle Mariners	.25
350	Oakland A's	.10
351	New York Yankees	.50
352	Cleveland Indians	.10
353	Arizona Diamondbacks	.10
354	Atlanta Braves	.10
355	St. Louis Cardinals	.10
356	Houston Astros	.10
357	D'backs vs. Rockies	.10
358	Mets vs. Pirates	.10
359	Braves vs. Phillies	.10
360	D'backs vs. Phillies	.10
361	Yankees vs. White Sox	.10
362	Cubs vs. Reds	.10
363	Angels vs. Mariners	.10
364	Astros vs. Giants	.10
365	Barry Bonds Race to 70 #1	10.00
365	Barry Bonds HR #2-69	8.00
365	Barry Bonds HR #70	15.00
365	Barry Bonds HR #71	10.00
365	Barry Bonds HR #72	10.00
365	Barry Bonds HR #73	50.00
366	Pat Meares	.10
367	Mike Lieberthal	.10
368	Scott Erickson	.10
369	Ron Gant	.10
370	Moises Alou	.25
371	Chad Kreuter	.10
372	Willis Roberts	.10
373	Toby Hall	.10
374	Miguel Batista	.10
375	John Burkett	.10
376	Cory Lidle	.10
377	Nick Neugebauer	.10
378	Jay Payton	.10
379	Steve Karsay	.10
380	Eric Chavez	.20
381	Kelly Stinnett	.10
382	Jarrod Washburn	.10
383	C.J. Nitkowski	.10
384	Jeff Conine	.10
385	Fred McGriff	.25
386	Marvin Benard	.10
387	Dave Burba	.10
388	Dennis Cook	.10
389	Rick Reed	.10
390	Tom Glavine	.25
391	Rondell White	.15
392	Matt Morris	.20
393	Pat Rapp	.10
394	Robert Person	.10
395	Omar Vizquel	.15
396	Jeff Cirillo	.10
397	Dave Mlicki	.10
398	Jose Ortiz	.10
399	Ryan Dempster	.10
400	Curt Schilling	.25
401	Peter Bergeron	.10
402	Kyle Lohse	.10
403	Craig Wilson	.10
404	David Justice	.20
405	Darin Erstad	.20
406	Jose Mercedes	.10
407	Carl Pavano	.10
408	Albie Lopez	.10
409	Alex Ochoa	.10
410	Chipper Jones	.50
411	Tyler Houston	.10
412	Dean Palmer	.10
413	Damian Jackson	.10
414	Josh Towers	.10
415	Rafael Furcal	.20
416	Ken Caminiti	.10
417	Herb Perry	.10
418	Mike Sirotka	.10
419	Mark Wohlers	.10
420	Nomar Garciaparra	1.00
421	Felipe Lopez	.10
422	Joe McEwing	.10
423	Jacque Jones	.10
424	Julio Franco	.10
425	Frank Thomas	.40
426	So Taguchi **RC**	.50
427	Kazuhisa Ishii **RC**	1.00
428	D'Angelo Jimenez	.10
429	Chris Stynes	.10
430	Kerry Wood	.50
431	Chris Singleton	.10
432	Erubiel Durazo	.10
433	Matt Lawton	.10
434	Bill Mueller	.10
435	Jose Canseco	.25
436	Ben Grieve	.10
437	Terry Mulholland	.10
438	David Bell	.10
439	A.J. Pierzynski	.10
440	Adam Dunn	.40
441	Jon Garland	.10
442	Jeff Fassero	.10
443	Julio Lugo	.10
444	Carlos Guillen	.10
445	Orlando Hernandez	.20
446	Mark Loretta	.10
447	Scott Spiezio	.10
448	Kevin Millwood	.10
449	Jamie Moyer	.10
450	Todd Helton	.40
451	Todd Walker	.10
452	Jose Lima	.10
453	Brook Fordyce	.10
454	Aaron Rowand	.10
455	Barry Zito	.20
456	Eric Owens	.10
457	Charles Nagy	.10
458	Raul Ibanez	.10
459	Joe Mays	.10
460	Jim Thome	.50
461	Adam Eaton	.10
462	Felix Martinez	.10
463	Vernon Wells	.20
464	Donnie Sadler	.10
465	Tony Clark	.10
466	Jose Hernandez	.10
467	Ramon Martinez	.10
468	Rusty Greer	.10
469	Rod Barajas	.10
470	Lance Berkman	.25
471	Brady Anderson	.10
472	Pedro Astacio	.10
473	Shane Halter	.10
474	Bret Prinz	.10
475	Edgar Martinez	.20
476	Steve Trachsel	.10
477	Gary Matthews Jr.	.10
478	Ismael Valdes	.10
479	Juan Uribe	.10
480	Shawn Green	.20
481	Kirk Rueter	.10
482	Damion Easley	.10
483	Chris Carpenter	.10
484	Kris Benson	.10
485	Antonio Alfonseca	.10
486	Kyle Farnsworth	.10
487	Brandon Lyon	.10
488	Hideki Irabu	.10
489	David Ortiz	.25
490	Mike Piazza	1.00
491	Derek Lowe	.10
492	Chris Gomez	.10
493	Mark Johnson	.10
494	John Rocker	.10
495	Eric Karros	.10
496	Bill Haselman	.10
497	Dave Veres	.10
498	Gil Heredia	.10
499	Tomokazu Ohka	.10
500	Barry Bonds	1.50
501	David Dellucci	.10
502	Ed Sprague	.10
503	Tom Gordon	.10
504	Javier Vazquez	.10
505	Ben Sheets	.25
506	Wilton Guerrero	.10
507	John Halama	.10
508	Mark Redman	.10
509	Jack Wilson	.10
510	Bernie Williams	.40
511	Miguel Cairo	.10
512	Denny Hocking	.10
513	Tony Batista	.10
514	Mark Grudzielanek	.10
515	Jose Vidro	.10
516	Sterling Hitchcock	.10
517	Billy Koch	.10
518	Matt Clement	.10
519	Bruce Chen	.10
520	Roberto Alomar	.40
521	Orlando Palmeiro	.10
522	Steve Finley	.10
523	Danny Patterson	.10
524	Terry Adams	.10
525	Tino Martinez	.10
526	Tony Armas Jr.	.10
527	Geoff Jenkins	.20
528	Chris Michalak	.10
529	Corey Patterson	.20
530	Brian Giles	.10
531	Jose Jimenez	.10
532	Joe Kennedy	.10
533	Armando Rios	.10
534	Osvaldo Fernandez	.10
535	Ruben Sierra	.10
536	Octavio Dotel	.10
537	Luis Sojo	.10
538	Brent Butler	.10
539	Pablo Ozuna	.10
540	Freddy Garcia	.10
541	Chad Durbin	.10
542	Orlando Merced	.10
543	Michael Tucker	.10
544	Roberto Hernandez	.10
545	Pat Burrell	.25
546	A.J. Burnett	.10
547	Bubba Trammell	.10
548	Scott Elarton	.10
549	Mike Darr	.10
550	Ken Griffey Jr.	1.00
551	Ugueth Urbina	.10
552	Todd Jones	.10
553	Delino DeShields	.10
554	Adam Piatt	.10
555	Jason Kendall	.10
556	Hector Ortiz	.10
557	Turk Wendell	.10
558	Rob Bell	.10
559	Sun-Woo Kim	.10
560	Raul Mondesi	.10
561	Brent Abernathy	.10
562	Seth Etherton	.10
563	Shawn Wooten	.10
564	Jay Buhner	.10
565	Andres Galarraga	.10
566	Shane Reynolds	.10
567	Rod Beck	.10
568	Dee Brown	.10
569	Pedro Feliz	.10
570	Ryan Klesko	.10
571	John Vander Wal	.10
572	Nick Bierbrodt	.10
573	Joe Nathan	.10
574	James Baldwin	.10
575	J.D. Drew	.20
576	Greg Colbrunn	.10
577	Doug Glanville	.10
578	Rey Sanchez	.10
579	Todd Van Poppel	.10
580	Rich Aurilia	.10
581	Chuck Finley	.10
582	Abraham Nunez	.10
583	Kenny Lofton	.20
584	Brian Daubach	.10
585	Miguel Tejada	.25
586	Nate Cornejo	.10
587	Kazuhiro Sasaki	.10
588	Chris Richard	.10
589	Armando Reynoso	.10
590	Tim Hudson	.20
591	Neifi Perez	.10
592	Steve Cox	.10
593	Henry Blanco	.10
594	Ricky Ledee	.10
595	Tim Salmon	.20
596	Luis Rivas	.10
597	Jeff Zimmerman	.10
598	Matt Stairs	.10
599	Preston Wilson	.10
600	Mark McGwire	1.50
601	Timo Perez	.10
602	Matt Anderson	.10
603	Todd Hundley	.10
604	Rick Ankiel	.10
605	Tsuyoshi Shinjo	.10
606	Woody Williams	.10
607	Jason LaRue	.10
608	Carlos Lee	.10
609	Russ Johnson	.10
610	Scott Rolen	.50
611	Brent Mayne	.10
612	Darrin Fletcher	.10
613	Ray Lankford	.10
614	Troy O'Leary	.10
615	Javier Lopez	.20

616 Randy Velarde .10
617 Vinny Castilla .10
618 Milton Bradley .10
619 Ruben Mateo .10
620 Jason Giambi .40
621 Andy Benes .10
622 Tony Eusebio .10
623 Andy Pettitte .20
624 Jose Offerman .10
625 Mo Vaughn .20
626 Steve Sparks .10
627 Mike Matthews .10
628 Robb Nen .10
629 Kip Wells .10
630 Kevin Brown .20
631 Arthur Rhodes .10
632 Gabe Kapler .10
633 Jermaine Dye .10
634 Josh Beckett .25
635 Pokey Reese .10
636 Benji Gil .10
637 Marcus Giles .10
638 Julian Tavarez .10
639 Jason Schmidt .25
640 Alex Rodriguez 1.25
641 Anaheim Angels .10
642 Arizona Diamondbacks .10
643 Atlanta Braves .10
644 Baltimore Orioles .10
645 Boston Red Sox .10
646 Chicago Cubs .10
647 Chicago White Sox .10
648 Cincinnati Reds .10
649 Cleveland Indians .10
650 Colorado Rockies .10
651 Detroit Tigers .10
652 Florida Marlins .10
653 Houston Astros .10
654 Kansas City Royals .10
655 Los Angeles Dodgers .10
656 Milwaukee Brewers .10
657 Minnesota Twins .10
658 Montreal Expos .10
659 New York Mets .10
660 New York Yankees .10
661 Oakland Athletics .10
662 Philadelphia Phillies .10
663 Pittsburgh Pirates .10
664 San Diego Padres .10
665 San Francisco Giants .10
666 Seattle Mariners .10
667 St. Louis Cardinals .10
668 Tampa Bay Devil Rays .10
669 Texas Rangers .10
670 Toronto Blue Jays .10
671 Juan Cruz .25
672 Kevin Cash RC .50
673 Jimmy Gobble RC .75
674 Mike Hill RC .40
675 Taylor Buchholz RC .10
676 Bill Hall .10
677 Brett Roneberg RC .40
678 Royce Huffman RC .40
679 Chris Tritle RC .40
680 Nate Espy RC .40
681 Nick Alvarez RC .50
682 Jason Botts RC .40
683 Ryan Gripp RC .40
684 Dan Phillips RC .50
685 Pablo Arias RC .50
686 John Rodriguez RC .40
687 Rich Harden RC 3.00
688 Neal Frendling RC .50
689 Rich Thompson RC .40
690 Greg Montalbano RC .40
691 Leonard Dinardo RC .40
692 Ryan Raburn RC .40
693 Josh Barfield 1.00
694 David Bacani RC .40
695 Dan Johnson RC .50
696 Mike Mussina (Gold Glove Award Winners) .25
697 Ivan Rodriguez (Gold Glove Award Winners) .25
698 Doug Mientkiewicz (Gold Glove Award Winners) .10
699 Roberto Alomar (Gold Glove Award Winners) .25
700 Eric Chavez (Gold Glove Award Winners) .15
701 Omar Vizquel (Gold Glove Award Winners) .10
702 Mike Cameron (Gold Glove Award Winners) .10
703 Torii Hunter (Gold Glove Award Winners) .10
704 Ichiro Suzuki (Gold Glove Award Winners) .50
705 Greg Maddux (Gold Glove Award Winners) .50
706 Brad Ausmus (Gold Glove Award Winners) .10
707 Todd Helton (Gold Glove Award Winners) .25
708 Fernando Vina (Gold Glove Award Winners) .10
709 Scott Rolen (Gold Glove Award Winners) .40
710 Orlando Cabrera (Gold Glove Award Winners) .10
711 Andruw Jones (Gold Glove Award Winners) .15
712 Jim Edmonds (Gold Glove Award Winners) .10
713 Larry Walker (Gold Glove Award Winners) .15
714 Roger Clemens (Cy Young Award Winners) .50
715 Randy Johnson (Cy Young Award Winners) .25
716 Ichiro Suzuki (MVP Award Winners) .50
717 Barry Bonds (MVP Award Winners) .75
718 Ichiro Suzuki (ROY Award Winners) .50
719 Albert Pujols (ROY Award Winners) .50

Gold

Complete Set (659) 700.00
Stars: 5-10X
Production 2,002 Sets

Limited

NM/M
Complete Set (790): 165.00
Includes all 73 B. Bonds #365 HR cards.

Aces

NM/M
Common Player: 10.00
Inserted 1:1,180
MH Mike Hampton 10.00
RJ Randy Johnson 20.00
GM Greg Maddux 30.00
PM Pedro Martinez 20.00
MM Mark Mulder 10.00

All-World Team

NM/M
Complete Set (25): 25.00
Common Player: .50
Inserted 1:12
AW-1 Ichiro Suzuki 3.00
AW-2 Barry Bonds 4.00
AW-3 Pedro Martinez 1.50
AW-4 Juan Gonzalez 1.00
AW-5 Larry Walker .50
AW-6 Sammy Sosa 3.00
AW-7 Mariano Rivera .75
AW-8 Vladimir Guerrero 1.50
AW-9 Alex Rodriguez 3.00
AW-10 Albert Pujols 3.00
AW-11 Luis Gonzalez .50
AW-12 Ken Griffey Jr. 2.50
AW-13 Kazuhiro Sasaki .50
AW-14 Bob Abreu .50
AW-15 Todd Helton 1.00
AW-16 Nomar Garciaparra 2.50
AW-17 Miguel Tejada .75
AW-18 Roger Clemens 3.00
AW-19 Mike Piazza 2.50
AW-20 Carlos Delgado 1.00
AW-21 Derek Jeter 4.00
AW-22 Hideo Nomo .75
AW-23 Randy Johnson 1.50
AW-24 Ivan Rodriguez 1.00
AW-25 Chan Ho Park .50

Autographs

NM/M
Common Player: 10.00
TA1 Carlos Delgado 40.00
TA2 Ivan Rodriguez 50.00
TA3 Miguel Tejada 30.00
TA4 Geoff Jenkins 10.00
TA5 Johnny Damon 40.00
TA6 Tim Hudson 25.00
TA7 Terrence Long 10.00
TA8 Gabe Kapler 10.00
TA9 Magglio Ordonez 20.00
TA10 Barry Bonds 180.00
TA11 Pat Burrell 20.00
TA12 Mike Mussina 40.00
TA13 Eric Valent 5.00
TA14 Xavier Nady 8.00
TA15 Cristian Guerrero 5.00
TA16 Ben Sheets 15.00
TA17 Corey Patterson 15.00
TA18 Carlos Pena 5.00
TA19 Alex Rodriguez 80.00
Series 2
TA-AB Adrian Beltre 25.00
TA-JD Jermaine Dye 15.00
TA-AE Alex Escobar 8.00
TA-CF Cliff Floyd 15.00
TA-RF Rafael Furcal 20.00
TA-BG Brian Giles 20.00
TA-KG Keith Ginter 8.00
TA-TG Troy Glaus 40.00
TA-BGR Ben Grieve 20.00
TA-CG Cristian Guzman 15.00
TA-JH Josh Hamilton 25.00
TA-NJ Nick Johnson 15.00
TA-RK Ryan Klesko 20.00
TA-JO Jose Ortiz 10.00
TA-RO Roy Oswalt 15.00
TA-RP Rafael Palmeiro 50.00
TA-AR Alex Rodriguez 80.00
TA-JR Jimmy Rollins 25.00
TA-RS Richie Sexson 25.00
TA-MS Mike Sweeney 20.00
TA-JW Justin Wayne 10.00
TA-BW Brad Wilkerson 10.00

Battery Mates Relic

NM/M
Inserted 1:4,401
ML Greg Maddux, Javy Lopez 30.00
LP Al Leiter, Mike Piazza 30.00

Coaches Collection Relics

NM/M
Common Card 8.00
Inserted 1:236 Retail
AH Art Howe 8.00
AT Alan Trammell 15.00
BB Bruce Bochy 8.00
BM Buck Martinez 8.00
BV Bobby Valentine 15.00
BW Billy Williams 15.00
BBE Buddy Bell 15.00
BBR Bob Brenly 15.00
DB Dusty Baker 20.00
DL Davey Lopes 15.00
DBA Don Baylor 15.00
EH Elrod Hendricks 8.00
EM Eddie Murray 40.00
FW Frank White 15.00
HM Hal McRae 8.00
JT Joe Torre 10.00
KG Ken Griffey Sr. 8.00
LB Larry Bowa 15.00
LP Lance Parrish 15.00
MH Mike Hargrove 10.00
MS Mike Scioscia 10.00
MW Mookie Wilson 10.00
PG Phil Garner 10.00
PM Paul Molitor 40.00
TP Tony Perez 10.00
WR Willie Randolph 15.00

Draft Picks

NM/M
Complete Set (10): 40.00
1-5 in Green Factory Sets
6-10 in Holiday Factory Sets
1 Scott Moore 6.00
2 Val Majewski 6.00
3 Brian Slocum 4.00
4 Chris Gruler 6.00
5 Mark Schramek 6.00
6 Joe Saunders 4.00
7 Jeff Francis 8.00
8 Royce Ring 6.00
9 Greg Miller 8.00
10 Brandon Weeden 4.00

Dueces Are Wild

NM/M
Common Card: 15.00
Inserted 1:1,962
JG Randy Johnson, Luis Gonzalez 30.00
BK Barry Bonds, Jeff Kent 40.00
TA Jim Thome, Roberto Alomar 30.00
WH Larry Walker, Todd Helton 25.00
BG Bret Boone, Freddy Garcia 15.00

East Meets West

NM/M
Complete Set (8): 6.00
Common Player: 1.00
Inserted 1:24
EW-HN Hideo Nomo, Masanori Murakami 2.00
EW-HI Hideki Irabu, Masanori Murakami 1.00
EW-SH Shigetoshi Hasegawa, Masanori Murakami 1.00
EW-MY Masato Yoshii, Masanori Murakami 1.00
EW-TS Tsuyoshi Shinjo, Masanori Murakami 1.00
EW-KS Kazuhiro Sasaki, Masanori Murakami 1.00
EW-MS Mac Suzuki, Masanori Murakami 1.00
EW-TO Tomo Ohka, Masanori Murakami 1.00

East Meets West Relics

NM/M
Common Player: 15.00
Inserted 1:3,419
HN Hideo Nomo 40.00
KS Kazuhiro Sasaki 15.00
TS Tsuyoshi Shinjo 15.00

Ebbets Field Seat Relics

NM/M
Inserted 1:9,116
JB Joe Black 100.00
RC Roy Campanella 250.00
BC Billy Cox 100.00
CF Carl Furillo 100.00
GH Gil Hodges 250.00
AP Andy Pafko 100.00
PWR Pee Wee Reese 250.00
JR Jackie Robinson 250.00
DS Duke Snider 200.00

Dual Ebbets/Yankee Seat Relic

NM/M
Complete Set (1):

Dual Ebbets/Yankee Autographed Seat Relic

NM/M
Complete Set (1):

Ebbets Field/Yankee Stadium Seat Dual Relic

NM/M
Complete Set (1):

Hall of Fame Vintage BuyBacks AutoProofs

NM/M
Common Autograph: 15.00
BR16 Brooks Robinson
EW10 Earl Weaver 87/100 15.00
FJ33 Fergie Jenkins 84/100 15.00
GP26 Gaylord Perry 82/100 15.00
GP29 Gaylord Perry 83/100 15.00
GP30 Gaylord Perry 83 SV/200 15.00
OC1 Orlando Cepeda 82 KM/200 15.00
RF15 Rollie Fingers 81/300 15.00
RF16 Rollie Fingers 81 LL/100 15.00
RF18 Rollie Fingers 82/200 15.00
RF19 Rollie Fingers 82 IA/200 15.00
RF21 Rollie Fingers 82 KM/300 15.00
RF22 Rollie Fingers 83/200 15.00
RF24 Rollie Fingers 84/200 15.00
RF27 Rollie Fingers 85/300 15.00
RF28 Rollie Fingers 86/100 15.00
SC5 Steve Carlton 84 LL/100 25.00
SC6 Steve Carlton 85/200 25.00
SC8 Steve Carlton 87/200 25.00

Heart of the Order Relic

NM/M
Inserted 1:4,247
KBA Jeff Kent, Barry Bonds, Rich Aurilia 75.00
TGA Jim Thome, Juan Gonzalez, Roberto Alomar 50.00
ARB Bob Abreu, Scott Rolen, Pat Burrell 50.00
OWM Paul O'Neill, Bernie Williams, Tino Martinez 50.00

Hit and Run Relic

NM/M
Inserted 1:4,241
JD Johnny Damon 10.00
DE Darin Erstad 10.00
RF Rafael Furcal 10.00

Hobby Masters

NM/M
Complete Set (20): 40.00
Common Player: 1.00
Inserted 1:25
1 Mark McGwire 5.00
2 Derek Jeter 5.00
3 Chipper Jones 2.00
4 Roger Clemens 4.00
5 Vladimir Guerrero 2.00
6 Ichiro Suzuki 3.00
7 Todd Helton 1.50
8 Alex Rodriguez 4.00
9 Albert Pujols 4.00
10 Sammy Sosa 3.00
11 Ken Griffey Jr. 3.00
12 Randy Johnson 2.00
13 Nomar Garciaparra 3.00
14 Ivan Rodriguez 1.50
15 Manny Ramirez 1.50
16 Barry Bonds 5.00
17 Mike Piazza 3.00
18 Pedro Martinez 1.50
19 Jeff Bagwell 1.50
20 Luis Gonzalez 1.00

Jack of All Trades

NM/M
Inserted 1:1,350
RO Roberto Alomar/Bat 20.00
BB Barry Bonds/Jsy 35.00
AJ Andruw Jones/Jsy 10.00
IR Ivan Rodriguez/Jsy 15.00
BW Bernie Williams/Jsy 15.00

Kings of the Clubhouse

NM/M
Common Player: 10.00
Inserted 1:1,449 Ser. 2
TG Tom Glavine/Jsy 15.00
TH Todd Helton/Jsy 15.00
RJ Randy Johnson/Jsy 20.00
EM Edgar Martinez/Jsy 10.00
PO Paul O'Neill/Bat 20.00

Like Father Like Son Relic

NM/M
Common Duo:
Inserted 1:1,304 Retail
AL Roberto Alomar, Sandy Alomar, Sandy Alomar Jr. 40.00
BE Dale Berra, Yogi Berra 50.00
BON Bobby Bonds, Barry Bonds 80.00
BOO Bob Boone, Bret Boone, Aaron Boone 40.00
CR Jose Cruz, Jose Cruz Jr. 40.00

Own The Game

NM/M
Complete Set (30): 25.00
Common Player: .50
Inserted 1:12
OG1 Moises Alou .75
OG2 Roberto Alomar .75
OG3 Luis Gonzalez .50
OG4 Bret Boone .75
OG5 Barry Bonds 4.00
OG6 Jim Thome 1.50
OG7 Jimmy Rollins .75
OG8 Cristian Guzman .50
OG9 Lance Berkman .75
OG10 Mike Sweeney .50
OG11 Rich Aurilia .50
OG12 Ichiro Suzuki 2.50
OG13 Luis Gonzalez .50
OG14 Ichiro Suzuki 2.50
OG15 Jimmy Rollins .75
OG16 Roger Cedeno .50
OG17 Barry Bonds 4.00
OG18 Jim Thome 1.50
OG19 Curt Schilling 1.00
OG20 Roger Clemens 3.00
OG21 Curt Schilling 1.00
OG22 Brad Radke .50
OG23 Greg Maddux 2.00
OG24 Mark Mulder .75
OG25 Jeff Shaw .50
OG26 Mariano Rivera .75
OG27 Randy Johnson 1.50
OG28 Pedro Martinez 1.50
OG29 John Burkett .50
OG30 Tim Hudson .75

Prime Cuts Pine Tar Series

NM/M
Common Player: 15.00
Inserted 1:4,420
BB Barry Bonds 60.00
LG Luis Gonzalez 20.00
TG Tony Gwynn 40.00
TH Todd Helton 25.00
AP Albert Pujols 40.00
Series 2
Inserted 1:1,043
Trademark Series: 1.5-2X
Inserted 1:2,087 Ser. 2
Prime Cuts Barrel: 2-4X
Inserted 1:7,824 Ser. 2
WB Wilson Betemit 15.00
SB Sean Burroughs 15.00
JC Joe Crede 20.00
AD Adam Dunn 30.00
AE Alex Escobar 15.00
MG Marcus Giles 15.00
AG Alexis Gomez 15.00
TH Toby Hall 15.00
JH Josh Hamilton 15.00
NJ Nick Johnson 15.00
XN Xavier Nady 15.00
CP Corey Patterson 20.00
CPE Carlos Pena 15.00
AR Aaron Rowand 25.00
RS Ruben Salazar 15.00

Prime Cuts Autograph Series

No Pricing

Prime Cuts Pine Tar Series

NM/M
Common Player: 15.00
Inserted 1:4,420
BB Barry Bonds 60.00
LG Luis Gonzalez 20.00
TG Tony Gwynn 40.00
TH Todd Helton 25.00
AP Albert Pujols 40.00
Series 2
Inserted 1:1,043
Trademark Series: 1.5-2X
Inserted 1:2,087 Ser. 2
Prime Cuts Barrel: 2-4X
Inserted 1:7,824 Ser. 2
WB Wilson Betemit 15.00
SB Sean Burroughs 15.00
JC Joe Crede 20.00
AD Adam Dunn 30.00
AE Alex Escobar 15.00
MG Marcus Giles 15.00
AG Alexis Gomez 15.00
TH Toby Hall 15.00
JH Josh Hamilton 15.00
NJ Nick Johnson 15.00
XN Xavier Nady 15.00
CP Corey Patterson 20.00
CPE Carlos Pena 15.00
AR Aaron Rowand 25.00
RS Ruben Salazar 15.00

Ring Masters

NM/M
Complete Set (10): 15.00
Common Player: .50
Inserted 1:25
1 Derek Jeter 4.00
2 Mark McGwire 4.00
3 Mariano Rivera 1.00
4 Gary Sheffield .75
5 Al Leiter .50
6 Chipper Jones 1.50
7 Roger Clemens 3.00
8 Greg Maddux 2.00
9 Roberto Alomar 1.00
10 Paul O'Neill .50

Team Topps Legends Autographs

NM/M
Common Player: 25.00
TT6R Whitey Ford 60.00
TT8R Bob Gibson 40.00
TT47R Frank Howard 25.00
TT46F Robin Roberts 25.00
TT13F Warren Spahn 40.00
Series 2

Three of a Kind

NM/M
Common Card:
Inserted 1:2,039
SPA Tsuyoshi Shinjo, Mike Piazza, Edgardo Alfonzo 50.00
LOC Carlos Lee, Magglio Ordonez, Jose Canseco 50.00
FBJ Rafael Furcal, Wilson Betemit, Andruw Jones 40.00
PSW Jorge Posada, Alfonso Soriano, Bernie Williams 50.00
BDB A.J. Burnett, Ryan Dempster, Josh Beckett 40.00

Trademark Series

NM/M
Common Player:

Turn Two Relic

NM/M
Inserted 1:4,401
TW Alan Trammell, Lou Whitaker 40.00
VA Omar Vizquel, Roberto Alomar 40.00

Yankee Stadium Seat Relics

NM/M
Inserted 1:579

HB	Hank Bauer	100.00
YB	Yogi Berra	250.00
JC	Joe Collins	100.00
BM	Billy Martin	250.00
GM	Gil McDougald	100.00
JM	Johnny Mize	100.00
AR	Allie Reynolds	100.00
PR	Phil Rizzuto	250.00
GW	Gene Woodling	100.00

2 Bagger Relic
NM/M
Inserted 1:3,733

TG	Tony Gwynn	30.00
TH	Todd Helton	20.00
SR	Scott Rolen	20.00

1952 Player Autographs
NM/M
Inserted 1:7,524

HBA	Hank Bauer	75.00
YBA	Yogi Berra	100.00
PRA	Preacher Roe	70.00

1952 Reprint Autographs
NM/M
Common Autograph: 25.00
Inserted 1:10,268

JBA	Joe Black	90.00
CEA	Carl Erskine	50.00
GMA	Gil McDougal	40.00
APA	Andy Pafko	60.00
PRA	Phil Rizzuto	80.00
DSA	Duke Snider	100.00

1952 World Series Highlights

NM/M
Complete Set (7): 10.00
Common Player: 2.00
Inserted 1:25

52WS-1	Dodgers' Game 1 Starting Line Up	3.00
52WS-2	Dodgers Celebrate Game 3 Win!	2.00
52WS-3	Carl Erskine Wins Game 5	2.00

Series 2

52WS-2	Game 2	2.00
52WS-4	Game 4	2.00
52WS-6	Game 6	2.00
52WS-7	Game 7	2.00

1952 World Series Tribute

NM/M
Complete Set (19): 50.00
Common Player: 3.00
Inserted 1:25

1	Roy Campanella	4.00
2	Duke Snider	4.00
3	Carl Erskine	3.00
4	Andy Pafko	3.00
5	Johnny Mize	3.00
6	Billy Martin	4.00
7	Phil Rizzuto	4.00
8	Gil McDougal	3.00
9	Allie Reynolds	4.00
10	Jackie Robinson	4.00

Series 2

11	Preacher Roe	3.00
12	Gil Hodges	3.00
13	Billy Cox	3.00
14	Yogi Berra	4.00
15	Gene Woodling	3.00
16	Jerry Sain	3.00
17	Ralph Houk	3.00
18	Joe Collins	3.00
19	Hank Bauer	3.00

American Pie American Sluggers

NM/M
Complete Set (25): 25.00
Common Player: .50
Inserted 1:1
Each card issued in blue, gold, silver and red; no value differential.

AD	Andre Dawson	.50
AK	Al Kaline	1.00
BR	Brooks Robinson	1.00
CC	Cecil Cooper	.50
CF	Carlton Fisk	1.00
CY	Carl Yastrzemski	2.00
DS	Duke Snider	1.00
DW	Dave Winfield	1.00
EM	Eddie Mathews	1.00
FH	Frank Howard	.50
FL	Fred Lynn	.50
FR	Frank Robinson	1.00
GB	George Brett	3.00
GF	George Foster	.50
HK	Harmon Killebrew	1.00
JC	Jack Clark	.50
JCC	Joe Carter	.50
KG	Kirk Gibson	.50
MI	Monte Irvin	.50
MS	Mike Schmidt	3.00
RC	Rod Carew	1.00
RJ	Reggie Jackson	2.50
RS	Ryne Sandberg	2.00
TK	Ted Kluszewski	1.00
WM	Willie Mays	4.00

American Pie Spirit of America

NM/M
Complete Set (150): 30.00
Common Player: .25
Pack (7): 5.00
Box (24): 100.00

1	Warren Spahn	.75
2	Reggie Jackson	.75
3	Bill Mazeroski	.25
4	Carl Yastrzemski	.75
5	Whitey Ford	.75
6	Ralph Houk	.25
7	Rod Carew	.50
8	Kirk Gibson	.25
9	Bobby Thomson	.25
10	Don Newcombe	.25
11	Gaylord Perry	.25
12	Bruce Sutter	.40
13	Bob Gibson	.50
14	Brooks Robinson	1.00
15	Steve Carlton	.50
16	Robin Yount	1.00
17	Ernie Banks	.75
18	Lou Brock	.75
19	Al Kaline	.75
20	Carlton Fisk	.75
21	Frank Robinson	.75
22	Bobby Bonds	.25
23	Andre Dawson	.25
24	Rich "Goose" Gossage	.25
25	Fred Lynn	.25
26	Keith Hernandez	.25
27	Rollie Fingers	.25
28	Juan Marichal	.25
29	Maury Wills	.25
30	Dave Winfield	.50
31	Frank Howard	.25
32	Tony Gwynn	1.00
33	Jim Palmer	.50
34	Mike Schmidt	1.50
35	Bo Jackson	.75
36	Ferguson Jenkins	.25
37	Bobby Richardson	.25
38	Harmon Killebrew	.75
39	Monte Irvin	.25
40	Jim Abbott	.50
41	Wade Boggs	.75
42	Jackie Robinson	2.00
43	Ralph Branca	.25
44	Minnie Minoso	.25
45	Tug McGraw	.25
46	Willie Mays	2.00
47	Nolan Ryan	3.00
48	Duke Snider	1.00
49	Tom Seaver	1.00
50	Casey Stengel	.50
51	D-Day	.75
52	Gulf War	.25
53	Vietnam War	.25
54	Korean War	.25
55	Secret Service	.25
56	Crayons	.25
57	Hoover Dam	.25
58	Penicillin	.25
59	Polio Vaccine	.25
60	Empire State Building	.25
61	Television	.25
62	Free Speech	.25
63	Voyager Mission	.25
64	Space Shuttle	.25
65	Ellis Island	.25
66	Statue of Liberty	.25
67	Battle of the Bulge	.25
68	Battle of Midway	.25
69	Iwo Jima	.25
70	Panama Canal	.25
71	Spirit of St. Louis/Lindbergh	.25
72	Civil Rights/We Shall Overcome	.25
73	Space Race	.25
74	Alaska Pipeline	.25
75	Teddy Bear	.25
76	Sea Biscuit	.25
77	Bazooka Joe	.25
78	Mt. Rushmore	.25
79	Yellowstone Park	.25
80	Niagara Falls	.25
81	Grand Canyon	.25
82	Hoola Hoop	.25
83	George Patton	.50
84	Audie Murphy	.25
85	Amelia Earhart	.25
86	Glen Miller	.25
87	Rick Monday	.25
88	Buzz Aldrin	.25
89	Rosa Parks	.25
90	Edward R. Murrow	.25
91	Susan B. Anthony	.25
92	Bobby Kennedy	.25
93	Gloria Steinem	.25
94	Hank Greenberg	.75
95	Jimmy Doolittle	.25
96	Thurgood Marshall	.25
97	Ernest Hemingway	.75
98	Henry Ford	.25
99	Wright Brothers	.25
100	Thomas Edison	.25
101	Albert Einstein	.75
102	Will Rogers	.25
103	George Gershwin	.25
104	Irving Berlin	.25
105	Frank Lloyd Wright	.25
106	Howard Hughes	.25
107	George M. Cohan	.25
108	Jack Kerouac	.25
109	Harry Houdini	.25
110	Helen Keller	.25
111	John McCain	.25
112	Andrew Carnegie	.25
113	Sandra Day O'Connor	.25
114	Brooklyn Bridge	.25
115	Douglas MacArthur	.25
116	Elvis Presley	1.00
117	George Burns	.25
118	Judy Garland	.50
119	Buddy Holly	.25
120	Don McLean	.25
121	Marilyn Monroe	1.00
122	Humphrey Bogart	.50
123	Gary Cooper	.25
124	The Andrews Sisters	.25
125	Jim Thorpe	1.00
126	Joe Louis	.75
127	Jesse Owens	.50
128	Kate Smith	.25
129	W.C. Fields	.25
130	Bette Davis	.25
131	Jayne Mansfield	.25
132	Teddy Roosevelt	.25
133	Franklin D. Roosevelt	.75
134	Harry Truman	.25
135	Dwight Eisenhower	.50
136	George H.W. Bush	.50
137	George W. Bush	.50
138	John F. Kennedy	1.00
139	Lyndon B. Johnson	.25
140	William Taft	.25
141	Horace Harding	.25
142	Woodrow Wilson	.25
143	Richard Nixon	.25
144	Bill Clinton	.25
145	Jimmy Carter	.25
146	Herbert Hoover	.25
147	Gerald Ford	.25
148	Ronald Reagan	.25
149	Calvin Coolidge	.25
150	William McKinley	.25

American Pie Through the Years Relics

NM/M
Common Player: 8.00
Inserted 1:11

JA	Jim Abbott	15.00
DA	Dick Allen	8.00
JB	Johnny Bench	20.00
WB	Wade Boggs	10.00
BB	Bill Buckner	8.00
JC	Jack Clark	8.00
AD	Andre Dawson	10.00
KT	Jim Kaat	10.00
EM	Eddie Mathews	15.00
DM	Don Mattingly	40.00
WM	Willie Mays	15.00
MM	Minnie Minoso	15.00
RM	Rick Monday	10.00
JM	Joe Morgan	10.00
TM	Thurman Munson	30.00
AL	Al Oliver	8.00
DP	Dave Parker	10.00
GP	Gaylord Perry	15.00
FR	Frank Robinson	15.00
JR	Joe Rudi	10.00
NR	Nolan Ryan	40.00
TS	Tom Seaver	20.00
WS	Willie Stargell	15.00
DS	Darryl Strawberry	15.00
DW	Dave Winfield	12.00
CY	Carl Yastrzemski	20.00

2002 Topps Archives

NM/M
Complete Set (200): 70.00
Common Player: .40
Pack (8): 3.00
Box (20): 50.00

1	Willie Mays	3.00
2	Dale Murphy	.40
3	Dave Winfield	.75
4	Roger Maris	2.00
5	Ron Cey	.40
6	Lee Smith	.40
7	Len Dykstra	.40
8	Ray Fosse	.40
9	Warren Spahn	1.00
10	Herb Score	.40
11	Jim Wynn	.40
12	Sam McDowell	.40
13	Fred Lynn	.40
14	Yogi Berra	1.50
15	Ron Santo	.40
16	Alvin Dark	.40
17	Bill Buckner	.40
18	Rollie Fingers	.60
19	Tony Gwynn	1.50
20	Red Schoendienst	.40
21	Gaylord Perry	.40
22	Jose Cruz	.40
23	Dennis Martinez	.40
24	Dave McNally	.40
25	Norm Cash	.40
26	Ted Kluszewski	.40
27	Rick Reuschel	.40
28	Bruce Sutter	.75
29	Don Larsen	.40
30	Claudell Washington	.40
31	Luis Aparicio	.40
32	Clete Boyer	.40
33	Rich "Goose" Gossage	.40
34	Ray Knight	.40
35	Roy Campanella	1.50
36	Tug McGraw	.40
37	Bob Lemon	.40
38	Willie Stargell	1.00
39	Roberto Clemente	3.00
40	Jim Fregosi	.40
41	Reggie Smith	.40
42	Dave Parker	.40
43	Darrell Evans	.40
44	Ryne Sandberg	2.00
45	Manny Mota	.40
46	Dennis Eckersley	.60
47	Nellie Fox	.40
48	Gil Hodges	.40
49	Reggie Jackson	1.50
50	Bobby Shantz	.40
51	Cecil Cooper	.40
52	Jim Kaat	.40
53	George Hendrick	.40
54	Johnny Podres	.40
55	Bob Gibson	1.00
56	Vern Law	.40
57	Joe Adcock	.40
58	Jack Clark	.40
59	Bill Mazeroski	.40
60	Carl Yastrzemski	1.50
61	Bobby Murcer	.40
62	Davey Johnson	.40
63	Jim Palmer	.75
64	Roy Face	.40
65	Dean Chance	.40
66	Bill "Moose" Skowron	.40
67	Dwight Evans	.40
68	Kirk Gibson	.40
69	Sal Bando	.40
70	Mike Schmidt	2.00
71	Bo Jackson	.40
72	Chris Chambliss	.40
73	Fergie Jenkins	.40
74	Brooks Robinson	1.50
75	Bobby Richardson	.40
76	Duke Snider	1.50
77	Allie Reynolds	.40
78	Harmon Killebrew	1.50
79	Steve Carlton	1.00
80	Bert Blyleven	.40
81	Phil Niekro	.40
82	Lew Burdette	.40
83	Hoyt Wilhelm	.40
84	Curt Flood	.40
85	Guillermo Hernandez	.40
86	Robin Yount	1.50
87	Robin Roberts	.40
88	Whitey Ford	1.00
89	Tony Oliva	.75
90	Don Newcombe	.40
91	Al Oliver	.40
92	Mike Cuellar	.40
93	Mike Scott	.40
94	Dick Allen	.40
95	Jimmy Piersall	.40
96	Bill Freehan	.40
97	Willie Horton	.40
98	Bob Friend	.40
99	Ken Holtzman	.40
100	Rico Carty	.40
101	Gil McDougald	.40
102	Lee May	.40
103	Joe Pepitone	.40
104	Gene Tenace	.40
105	Gary Carter	.40
106	Tim McCarver	.40
107	Ernie Banks	1.50
108	George Foster	.40
109	Lou Brock	1.00
110	Dick Groat	.40
111	Graig Nettles	.40
112	Boog Powell	.40
113	Joe Carter	.40
114	Juan Marichal	.75
115	Larry Doby	.40
116	Fernando Valenzuela	.40
117	Luis Tiant	.40
118	Early Wynn	.40
119	Bill Madlock	.40
120	Eddie Mathews	1.50
121	George Brett	3.00
122	Al Kaline	1.50
123	Frank Howard	.40
124	Mickey Lolich	.40
125	Kirby Puckett	3.00
126	Bob Cerv	.40
127	Will Clark	1.00
128	Vida Blue	.40
129	Kevin Mitchell	.40
130	Bucky Dent	.40
131	Tom Seaver	2.00
132	Jerry Koosman	.40
133	Orlando Cepeda	.40
134	Nolan Ryan	4.00
135	Tony Kubek	.40
136	Don Drysdale	1.00
137	Paul Blair	.40
138	Elston Howard	.40
139	Joe Rudi	.40
140	Tommie Agee	.40
141	Richie Ashburn	.40
142	Jim Bunning	.40
143	Hank Sauer	.40
144	Greg Luzinski	.40
145	Ron Guidry	.40
146	Rod Carew	1.00
147	Andre Dawson	.40
148	Keith Hernandez	.40
149	Carlton Fisk	1.00
150	Cleon Jones	.40
151	Don Mattingly	3.00
152	Vada Pinson	.40
153	Ozzie Smith	1.50
154	Dave Concepcion	.40
155	Al Rosen	.40
156	Tommy John	.40
157	Bob Ojeda	.40
158	Frank Robinson	1.50
159	Darryl Strawberry	.40
160	Bobby Bonds	.40
161	Bert Campaneris	.40
162	Jim "Catfish" Hunter	.40
163	Bud Harrelson	.40
164	Dwight Gooden	.40
165	Wade Boggs	1.00
166	Joe Morgan	1.00
167	Ron Swoboda	.40
168	Hank Aaron	4.00
169	Steve Garvey	.40
170	Mickey Rivers	.40
171	Johnny Bench	3.00
172	Ralph Terry	.40
173	Billy Pierce	.40
174	Thurman Munson	2.50
175	Don Sutton	.40
176	Sparky Anderson	.40
177	Gil Hodges	.40
178	Davey Johnson	.40
179	Frank Robinson	1.50
180	Red Schoendienst	.40
181	Roger Maris	2.00
182	Willie Mays	.40
183	Luis Aparicio	.40
184	Nellie Fox	.40
185	Ernie Banks	1.50
186	Orlando Cepeda	.75
187	Whitey Ford	1.00
188	Bob Gibson	1.00
189	Bill Mazeroski	.40
190	Hank Aaron	3.00
191	League Leaders (Elston Howard, Harmon Killebrew, Carl Yastrzemski)	.75
192	League Leaders (Orlando Cepeda, Jackie Robinson, Willie Mays)	2.00
193	League Leaders (Hank Aaron, Roberto Clemente, Dick Allen)	2.00
194	League Leaders (Tom Seaver, Phil Niekro, Fergie Jenkins, Juan Marichal)	1.00
195	League Leaders (Jim Palmer, Jim Hunter, Dennis Eckersley)	.65
196	Hank Aaron	3.00
197	Brooks Robinson	1.50
198	Tom Seaver	1.50
199	Jim Palmer	.75
200	Lou Brock	1.00

Autographs
NM/M
Common Autograph: 10.00
Inserted 1:22

HA	Hank Aaron	250.00
DA	Dick Allen	25.00
SB	Sal Bando	20.00
EB	Ernie Banks	125.00
BB	Bobby Bonds	25.00
GB	George Brett	250.00
JBU	Jim Bunning	40.00
LB	Lew Burdette	20.00
BC	Bert Campaneris	10.00
GC	Gary Carter	50.00
RCE	Ron Cey	15.00
CC	Chris Chambliss	15.00
JCR	Jose Cruz	15.00
AD	Alvin Dark	25.00
BD	Bucky Dent	20.00
LD	Len Dykstra	20.00
DEV	Darrell Evans	15.00
GF	George Foster	15.00
JF	Jim Fregosi	10.00
SG	Steve Garvey	15.00
DG	Dwight Gooden	25.00
DGR	Dick Groat	15.00
BH	Bud Harrelson	15.00
WH	Willie Hernandez	10.00
KH	Keith Hernandez	15.00
BJ	Bo Jackson	80.00
FJ	Fergie Jenkins	20.00
TJ	Tommy John	15.00
JK	Jim Kaat	20.00
AK	Al Kaline	125.00
HK	Harmon Killebrew	110.00
JKO	Jerry Koosman	65.00
GL	Greg Luzinski	20.00
FL	Fred Lynn	20.00
DM	Dave McNally	20.00
KM	Kevin Mitchell	20.00
DN	Don Newcombe	15.00
TO	Tony Oliva	30.00
JP	Jim Palmer	50.00
DP	Dave Parker	20.00
GP	Gaylord Perry	20.00
BP	Billy Pierce	10.00

JPI	Jimmy Piersall	15.00
JPO	Johnny Podres	15.00
BPO	Boog Powell	25.00
KP	Kirby Puckett	150.00
MR	Mickey Rivers	10.00
BRO	Brooks Robinson	80.00
JR	Joe Rudi	15.00
RS	Ron Santo	30.00
MS	Mike Schmidt	150.00
LS	Lee Smith	20.00
RSM	Reggie Smith	15.00
BS	Bruce Sutter	35.00
RT	Ralph Terry	25.00
HW	Hoyt Wilhelm	15.00
DW	Dave Winfield	85.00
RY	Robin Yount	100.00

AutoProofs
NM/M

Quantity produced listed

1	Gary Carter/80	40.00
2	Jose Cruz/95	25.00
4	Bo Jackson/300	50.00
5	Kevin Mitchell/65	25.00
6	Kirby Puckett/65	75.00
7	Mike Schmidt/147	90.00
8	Ozzie Smith/105	75.00
9	Darryl Strawberry/181	40.00
11	Robin Yount/39	100.00

Game-Used Bat
NM/M

Common Player:
Group A 1:106
Group B 1:282

JB	Johnny Bench	20.00
GB	George Brett	40.00
GC	Gary Carter	10.00
JC	Joe Carter	10.00
NC	Norm Cash	10.00
AD	Andre Dawson	8.00
DE	Dwight Evans	8.00
BF	Bill Freehan	8.00
WH	Willie Horton	8.00
RJ	Reggie Jackson	15.00
DM	Don Mattingly	50.00
RM	Roger Maris	50.00
JM	Joe Morgan	10.00
DP	Dave Parker	10.00
BR	Brooks Robinson	20.00
RS	Ron Santo	20.00
WS	Willie Stargell	15.00
CY	Carl Yastrzemski	40.00
RY	Robin Yount	20.00

Game-Worn Uniform

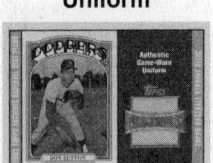

NM/M

Common Player: 8.00
Inserted 1:28

SA	Sparky Anderson	10.00
WB	Wade Boggs	15.00
BB	Bobby Bonds	8.00
GB	George Brett	30.00
OC	Orlando Cepeda	14.00
WC	Will Clark	20.00
DC	Dave Concepcion	8.00
DE	Dennis Eckersley	10.00
SG	Steve Garvey	10.00
FL	Fred Lynn	8.00
DM	Dale Murphy	20.00
PN	Phil Niekro	10.00
GP	Gaylord Perry	10.00
KP	Kirby Puckett	20.00
FR	Frank Robinson	15.00
NR	Nolan Ryan	40.00
RS	Ryne Sandberg	30.00
OS	Ozzie Smith	20.00
DS	Don Sutton	10.00
DW	Dave Winfield	10.00

Stadium Seat
NM/M

Common Player: 8.00

RA	Richie Ashburn	15.00
SA	Sparky Anderson	10.00
EB	Ernie Banks	25.00
YB	Yogi Berra	20.00
JB	Jim Bunning	15.00
RC	Rod Carew	20.00
JC	Joe Carter	10.00
NF	Nellie Fox	15.00
RG	Ron Guidry	10.00
TK	Ted Kluszewski	15.00
BL	Bob Lemon	10.00
ML	Mickey Lolich	10.00
EM	Eddie Mathews	20.00
SM	Sam McDowell	8.00
JP	Jim Palmer	10.00
DP	Dave Parker	10.00
HS	Herb Score	8.00
DS	Duke Snider	20.00
WS	Warren Spahn	15.00

Reserve

HANK Aaron MILWAUKEE BRAVES OUTFIELD

NM/M

Complete Set (100): 100.00
Common Player: .75
Box (10 Packs + Auto. Baseball): 125.00

1	Lee Smith	.75
2	Gaylord Perry	.75
3	Al Oliver	.75
4	Rich "Goose" Gossage	.75
5	Bill Madlock	.75
6	Rod Carew	1.50
7	Fred Lynn	.75
8	Frank Robinson	2.00
9	Al Kaline	2.50
10	Len Dykstra	.75
11	Carlton Fisk	1.50
12	Nellie Fox	1.00
13	Reggie Jackson	3.00
14	Bob Gibson	2.00
15	Bill Buckner	.75
16	Harmon Killebrew	2.00
17	Gary Carter	1.50
18	Dave Winfield	1.50
19	Ozzie Smith	2.50
20	Dwight Evans	.75
21	Dave Concepcion	.75
22	Joe Morgan	1.00
23	Clete Boyer	.75
24	Will Clark	1.50
25	Lee May	.75
26	Kevin Mitchell	.75
27	Roger Maris	3.00
28	Mickey Lolich	.75
29	Luis Aparicio	.75
30	George Foster	.75
31	Don Mattingly	6.00
32	Fernando Valenzuela	.75
33	Bobby Bonds	.75
34	Jim Palmer	1.50
35	Dennis Eckersley	1.00
36	Kirby Puckett	3.00
37	Jose Cruz	.75
38	Richie Ashburn	.75
39	Whitey Ford	2.00
40	Robin Roberts	.75
41	Don Newcombe	.75
42	Roy Campanella	2.50
43	Dennis Martinez	.75
44	Larry Doby	1.00
45	Steve Garvey	.75
46	Thurman Munson	3.00
47	Dale Murphy	1.50
48	Bill "Moose" Skowron	.75
49	Tom Seaver	3.00
50	Orlando Cepeda	.75
51	Graig Nettles	.75
52	Willie Stargell	1.50
53	Yogi Berra	2.50
54	Steve Carlton	1.50
55	Don Sutton	.75
56	Brooks Robinson	1.50
57	Vida Blue	.75
58	Rollie Fingers	1.00
59	Jim Bunning	.75
60	Nolan Ryan	8.00
61	Hank Aaron	6.00
62	Fergie Jenkins	.75
63	Andre Dawson	1.00
64	Ernie Banks	2.50
65	Early Wynn	.75
66	Duke Snider	1.50
67	Red Schoendienst	.75
68	Don Drysdale	1.00
69	Jim "Catfish" Hunter	1.00
70	George Brett	6.00
71	Elston Howard	1.00
72	Wade Boggs	1.50
73	Keith Hernandez	.75
74	Billy Pierce	.75
75	Ted Kluszewski	.75
76	Carl Yastrzemski	4.00
77	Bert Blyleven	.75
78	Tony Oliva	.75
79	Joe Carter	.75
80	Johnny Bench	3.00
81	Tony Gwynn	3.00
82	Mike Schmidt	4.00
83	Phil Niekro	.75
84	Juan Marichal	.75
85	Eddie Mathews	2.50
86	Boog Powell	.75
87	Dwight Gooden	.75
88	Darryl Strawberry	.75
89	Roberto Clemente	6.00
90	Ryne Sandberg	5.00
91	Jack Clark	.75
92	Willie Mays	6.00
93	Ron Guidry	.75
94	Kirk Gibson	.75
95	Lou Brock	1.00
96	Robin Yount	2.50
97	Bill Mazeroski	.75
98	Dave Parker	.75
99	Hoyt Wilhelm	.75
100	Warren Spahn	1.50

Reserve Autographed Baseballs

NM/M

Common Auto. Ball: 15.00
Inserted 1:Box

Luis Aparicio/1,600	25.00
Ernie Banks/50	75.00
Yogi Berra/100	85.00
Lou Brock/400	40.00
Jim Bunning/500	35.00
Gary Carter/500	40.00
Rich Gossage/500	20.00
Fergie Jenkins/1,000	20.00
Al Kaline/250	75.00
Harmon Killebrew/250	60.00
Joe Morgan/250	40.00
Graig Nettles/1,600	15.00
Jim Palmer/400	25.00
Gaylord Perry/500	15.00
Brooks Robinson/500	40.00
Mike Schmidt/250	125.00
Duke Snider/100	65.00
Dave Winfield/1650	30.00
Robin Yount/250	90.00

Reserve Best Years Autographs

GAYLORD PERRY S.F. GIANTS

NM/M

Common Autograph: 12.00
Inserted 1:15 Hobby

LA	Luis Aparicio	15.00
EB	Ernie Banks	70.00
YB	Yogi Berra	60.00
LB	Lou Brock	25.00
GC	Gary Carter	20.00
FJ	Fergie Jenkins	12.00
AK	Al Kaline	40.00
HK	Harmon Killebrew	40.00
WM	Willie Mays	120.00
JM	Joe Morgan	25.00
GN	Graig Nettles	12.00
GP	Gaylord Perry	15.00
BR	Brooks Robinson	25.00
MS	Mike Schmidt	60.00
LS	Lee Smith	12.00
DS	Duke Snider	60.00
RY	Robin Yount	80.00

Reserve Best Years Game-Used Bat

NM/M

Common Player: 10.00
Inserted 1:22

HAB	Hank Aaron	40.00
GBB	George Brett	25.00
OC	Orlando Cepeda	10.00
CF	Carlton Fisk	10.00
RM	Roger Maris	70.00
EMB	Eddie Mathews	20.00
DMB	Don Mattingly	30.00
TM	Thurman Munson	30.00
DW	Dave Winfield	10.00
CYB	Carl Yastrzemski	25.00

Reserve Best Years Game-Worn Uniform

NM/M

Common Player: 10.00
Inserted 1:7 Hobby

EB	Ernie Banks	25.00
JBU	Johnny Bench	15.00
WBJ	Wade Boggs	10.00
GCJ	Gary Carter	12.00
WC	Will Clark	15.00
NF	Nellie Fox	15.00
TG	Tony Gwynn	15.00
JM	Juan Marichal	12.00
WM	Willie Mays	35.00
KPJ	Kirby Puckett	15.00
BR	Brooks Robinson	12.00
NR	Nolan Ryan	30.00
RSJ	Red Schoendienst	10.00
WS	Willie Stargell	15.00
RYU	Robin Yount	12.00

Reserve Team Topps Legends Autographs

GAYLORD PERRY S.F. GIANTS

NM/M

Common Player:

Rich "Goose" Gossage	10.00
Graig Nettles	10.00
Jim Palmer	15.00
Gaylord Perry	15.00

2002 Topps Chrome

TODD HELTON

NM/M

Complete Set (685): 200.00
Common Player: .25
Pack (4): 2.00
Box (24): 40.00

1	Pedro Martinez	1.25
2	Mike Stanton	.25
3	Brad Penny	.25
4	Mike Matheny	.25
5	Johnny Damon	.40
6	Bret Boone	.40
7	Retired # not issued	
8	Chris Truby	.25
9	B.J. Surhoff	.25
10	Mike Hampton	.40
11	Juan Pierre	.25
12	Mark Buehrle	.25
13	Bob Abreu	.50
14	David Cone	.25
15	Aaron Sele	.25
16	Fernando Tatis	.25
17	Bobby Jones	.25
18	Rick Helling	.25
19	Dmitri Young	.25
20	Mike Mussina	1.00
21	Mike Sweeney	.25
22	Cristian Guzman	.25
23	Ryan Kohlmeier	.25
24	Adam Kennedy	.25
25	Larry Walker	.50
26	Eric Davis	.40
27	Jason Tyner	.25
28	Eric Young	.25
29	Jason Marquis	.25
30	Luis Gonzalez	.50
31	Kevin Tapani	.25
32	Orlando Cabrera	.25
33	Marty Cordova	.25
34	Brad Ausmus	.25
35	Livan Hernandez	.25
36	Alex Gonzalez	.25
37	Edgar Renteria	.50
38	Bengie Molina	.25
39	Frank Menechino	.25
40	Rafael Palmeiro	1.00
41	Brad Fullmer	.25
42	Julio Zuleta	.25
43	Darren Dreifort	.25
44	Trot Nixon	.50
45	Trevor Hoffman	.25
46	Vladimir Nunez	.25
47	Mark Kotsay	.25
48	Kenny Rogers	.25
49	Ben Petrick	.25
50	Jeff Bagwell	1.00
51	Juan Encarnacion	.25
52	Ramiro Mendoza	.25
53	Brian Meadows	.25
54	Chad Curtis	.25
55	Aramis Ramirez	.50
56	Mark McLemore	.25
57	Dante Bichette	.25
58	Scott Schoeneweis	.25
59	Jose Cruz	.25
60	Roger Clemens	3.00
61	Jose Guillen	.25
62	Darren Oliver	.25
63	Chris Reitsma	.25
64	Jeff Abbott	.25
65	Robin Ventura	.25
66	Denny Neagle	.25
67	Al Martin	.25
68	Benito Santiago	.25
69	Roy Oswalt	.50
70	Juan Gonzalez	1.00
71	Garret Anderson	.75
72	Bobby Bonilla	.25
73	Danny Bautista	.25
74	J.T. Snow	.25
75	Derek Jeter	4.00
76	John Olerud	.50
77	Kevin Appier	.25
78	Phil Nevin	.25
79	Sean Casey	.50
80	Troy Glaus	.75
81	Joe Randa	.25
82	Jose Valentin	.25
83	Ricky Bottalico	.25
84	Todd Zeile	.25
85	Barry Larkin	.75
86	Bob Wickman	.25
87	Jeff Shaw	.25
88	Greg Vaughn	.25
89	Fernando Vina	.25
90	Mark Mulder	.50
91	Paul Bako	.25
92	Aaron Boone	.25
93	Esteban Loaiza	.25
94	Richie Sexson	.75
95	Alfonso Soriano	.25
96	Tony Womack	.25
97	Paul Shuey	.25
98	Melvin Mora	.25
99	Tony Gwynn	1.50
100	Vladimir Guerrero	1.50
101	Keith Osik	.25
102	Randy Velarde	.25
103	Scott Williamson	.25
104	Daryle Ward	.25
105	Doug Mientkiewicz	.25
106	Stan Javier	.25
107	Russ Ortiz	.25
108	Wade Miller	.25
109	Luke Prokopec	.25
110	Andruw Jones	1.00
111	Ron Coomer	.25
112	Dan Wilson	.25
113	Luis Castillo	.25
114	Derek Bell	.25
115	Gary Sheffield	.75
116	Ruben Rivera	.25
117	Paul O'Neill	.50
118	Craig Paquette	.25
119	Kelvim Escobar	.25
120	Brad Radke	.25
121	Jorge Fabregas	.25
122	Randy Winn	.25
123	Tom Goodwin	.25
124	Jaret Wright	.25
125	Bonds-Race to 73	40.00
126	Al Leiter	.50
127	Ben Davis	.25
128	Frank Catalanotto	.25
129	Jose Cabrera	.25
130	Magglio Ordonez	.50
131	Jose Macias	.25
132	Ted Lilly	.25
133	Chris Holt	.25
134	Eric Milton	.25
135	Shannon Stewart	.25
136	Omar Olivares	.25
137	David Segui	.25
138	Jeff Nelson	.25
139	Matt Williams	.25
140	Ellis Burks	.25
141	Jason Bere	.25
142	Jimmy Haynes	.25
143	Ramon Hernandez	.25
144	Craig Counsell	.25
145	John Smoltz	.50
146	Homer Bush	.25
147	Quilvio Veras	.25
148	Esteban Yan	.25
149	Ramon Ortiz	.25
150	Carlos Delgado	.75
151	Lee Stevens	.25
152	Wil Cordero	.25
153	Mike Bordick	.25
154	John Flaherty	.25
155	Omar Daal	.25
156	Todd Ritchie	.25
157	Carl Everett	.25
158	Scott Sullivan	.25
159	Deivi Cruz	.25
160	Albert Pujols	3.00
161	Royce Clayton	.25
162	Jeff Suppan	.25
163	C.C. Sabathia	.25
164	Jimmy Rollins	.50
165	Rickey Henderson	.50
166	Rey Ordonez	.25
167	Shawn Estes	.25
168	Reggie Sanders	.25
169	Jon Lieber	.25
170	Armando Benitez	.25
171	Mike Remlinger	.25
172	Billy Wagner	.25
173	Troy Percival	.25
174	Devon White	.25
175	Ivan Rodriguez	1.00
176	Dustin Hermanson	.25
177	Brian Anderson	.25
178	Graeme Lloyd	.25
179	Russell Branyan	.25
180	Bobby Higginson	.25
181	Alex Gonzalez	.25
182	John Franco	.25
183	Sidney Ponson	.25
184	Jose Mesa	.25
185	Todd Hollandsworth	.25
186	Kevin Young	.25
187	Tim Wakefield	.25
188	Craig Biggio	.50
189	Jason Isringhausen	.25
190	Mark Quinn	.25
191	Glendon Rusch	.25
192	Damian Miller	.25
193	Sandy Alomar	.25
194	Scott Brosius	.25
195	Dave Martinez	.25
196	Danny Graves	.25
197	Shea Hillenbrand	.25
198	Jimmy Anderson	.25
199	Travis Lee	.25
200	Randy Johnson	1.50
201	Carlos Beltran	.50
202	Jerry Hairston Jr.	.25
203	Jesus Sanchez	.25
204	Eddie Taubensee	.25
205	David Wells	.25
206	Russ Davis	.25
207	Michael Barrett	.25
208	Marquis Grissom	.25
209	Byung-Hyun Kim	.25
210	Hideo Nomo	.75
211	Ryan Rupe	.25
212	Ricky Gutierrez	.25
213	Darryl Kile	.25
214	Rico Brogna	.25
215	Terrence Long	.25
216	Mike Jackson	.25
217	Jamey Wright	.25
218	Adrian Beltre	.50
219	Benny Agbayani	.25
220	Chuck Knoblauch	.25
221	Randy Wolf	.25
222	Andy Ashby	.25
223	Corey Koskie	.25
224	Roger Cedeno	.25
225	Ichiro Suzuki	3.00
226	Keith Foulke	.25
227	Ryan Minor	.25
228	Shawon Dunston	.25
229	Alex Cora	.25
230	Jeromy Burnitz	.25
231	Mark Grace	.75
232	Aubrey Huff	.25
233	Jeffrey Hammonds	.25
234	Olmedo Saenz	.25
235	Brian Jordan	.25
236	Jeremy Giambi	.25
237	Joe Girardi	.25
238	Eric Gagne	.50
239	Masato Yoshii	.25
240	Greg Maddux	2.00
241	Bryan Rekar	.25
242	Ray Durham	.25
243	Torii Hunter	.25
244	Derrek Lee	.50
245	Jim Edmonds	.75
246	Einar Diaz	.25
247	Brian Bohanon	.25
248	Ron Belliard	.25
249	Mike Lowell	.50
250	Sammy Sosa	2.50

#	Player	Price
251	Richard Hidalgo	.40
252	Bartolo Colon	.25
253	Jorge Posada	.50
254	LaTroy Hawkins	.25
255	Paul LoDuca	.25
256	Carlos Febles	.25
257	Nelson Cruz	.25
258	Edgardo Alfonzo	.25
259	Joey Hamilton	.25
260	Cliff Floyd	.25
261	Wes Helms	.25
262	Jay Bell	.25
263	Mike Cameron	.25
264	Paul Konerko	.25
265	Jeff Kent	.50
266	Robert Fick	.25
267	Allen Levrault	.25
268	Placido Polanco	.25
269	Marlon Anderson	.25
270	Mariano Rivera	.50
271	Chan Ho Park	.25
272	Jose Vizcaino	.25
273	Jeff D'Amico	.25
274	Mark Gardner	.25
275	Travis Fryman	.25
276	Darren Lewis	.25
277	Bruce Bochy	.25
278	Jerry Manuel	.25
279	Bob Brenly	.25
280	Don Baylor	.25
281	Davey Lopes	.25
282	Jerry Narron	.25
283	Tony Muser	.25
284	Hal McRae	.25
285	Bobby Cox	.25
286	Larry Dierker	.25
287	Phil Garner	.25
288	Jimy Williams	.25
289	Bobby Valentine	.25
290	Dusty Baker	.25
291	Lloyd McLendon	.25
292	Mike Scioscia	.25
293	Buck Martinez	.25
294	Larry Bowa	.25
295	Tony LaRussa	.25
296	Jeff Torborg	.25
297	Tom Kelly	.25
298	Mike Hargrove	.25
299	Art Howe	.25
300	Lou Piniella	.25
301	Charlie Manuel	.25
302	Buddy Bell	.25
303	Tony Perez	.25
304	Bob Boone	.25
305	Joe Torre	.25
306	Jim Tracy	.25
307	Jason Lane	1.00
308	Chris George	.25
309	Hank Blalock	2.00
310	Joe Borchard	.25
311	Marlon Byrd	.50
312	Raymond Cabrera RC	1.00
313	Freddy Sanchez RC	4.00
314	Scott Wiggins RC	1.00
315	Jason Maule RC	1.00
316	Dionys Cesar RC	1.50
317	Boof Bonser	.25
318	Juan Tolentino RC	1.50
319	Earl Snyder RC	1.50
320	Travis Wade RC	1.50
321	Napoleon Calzado RC	1.50
322	Eric Glaser RC	1.50
323	Craig Kuzmic RC	1.50
324	Nic Jackson RC	1.50
325	Mike Rivera	.25
326	Jason Bay RC	8.00
327	Chris Smith	.25
328	Jake Gautreau	.25
329	Gabe Gross	.25
330	Kenny Baugh	.25
331	J.D. Martin	.25
366	Pat Meares	.25
367	Mike Lieberthal	.25
368	Scott Erickson	.25
369	Ron Gant	.25
370	Moises Alou	.50
371	Chad Kreuter	.25
372	Willis Roberts	.25
373	Toby Hall	.25
374	Miguel Batista	.25
375	John Burkett	.25
376	Cory Lidle	.25
377	Nick Neugebauer	.25
378	Jay Payton	.25
379	Steve Karsay	.25
380	Eric Chavez	.50
381	Kelly Stinnett	.25
382	Jarrod Washburn	.25
383	C.J. Nitkowski	.25
384	Jeff Conine	.25
385	Fred McGriff	.50
386	Marvin Benard	.25
387	Dave Burba	.25
388	Dennis Cook	.25
389	Rick Reed	.25
390	Tom Glavine	.75
391	Rondell White	.25
392	Matt Morris	.50
393	Pat Rapp	.25
394	Robert Person	.25
395	Omar Vizquel	.40
396	Jeff Cirillo	.25
397	Dave Mlicki	.25
398	Jose Ortiz	.25
399	Ryan Dempster	.25
400	Curt Schilling	.75
401	Peter Bergeron	.25
402	Kyle Lohse	.25
403	Craig Wilson	.25
404	David Justice	.75
405	Darin Erstad	.50

#	Player	Price
406	Jose Mercedes	.25
407	Carl Pavano	.25
408	Albie Lopez	.25
409	Alex Ochoa	.25
410	Chipper Jones	1.50
411	Tyler Houston	.25
412	Dean Palmer	.25
413	Damian Jackson	.25
414	Josh Towers	.25
415	Rafael Furcal	.50
416	Mike Morgan	.25
417	Herb Perry	.25
418	Mike Sirotka	.25
419	Mark Wohlers	.25
420	Nomar Garciaparra	2.50
421	Felipe Lopez	.25
422	Joe McEwing	.25
423	Jacque Jones	.25
424	Julio Franco	.25
425	Frank Thomas	1.00
426	Kent Bottenfield	.25
427	Mac Suzuki	.25
428	D'Angelo Jimenez	.25
429	Chris Stynes	.25
430	Kerry Wood	1.50
431	Chris Singleton	.25
432	Erubiel Durazo	.25
433	Matt Lawton	.25
434	Bill Mueller	.25
435	Jose Canseco	.50
436	Ben Grieve	.25
437	Terry Mulholland	.25
438	David Bell	.25
439	A.J. Pierzynski	.25
440	Adam Dunn	1.00
441	Jon Garland	.25
442	Jeff Fassero	.25
443	Julio Lugo	.25
444	Carlos Guillen	.25
445	Orlando Hernandez	.25
446	Mark Loretta	.25
447	Scott Spiezio	.25
448	Kevin Millwood	.50
449	Jamie Moyer	.25
450	Todd Helton	1.00
451	Todd Walker	.25
452	Jose Lima	.25
453	Brook Fordyce	.25
454	Aaron Rowand	.25
455	Barry Zito	.50
456	Eric Owens	.25
457	Charles Nagy	.25
458	Raul Ibanez	.25
459	Joe Mays	.25
460	Jim Thome	1.50
461	Adam Eaton	.25
462	Felix Martinez	.25
463	Vernon Wells	.25
464	Donnie Sadler	.25
465	Tony Clark	.25
466	Jose Hernandez	.25
467	Ramon Martinez	.25
468	Rusty Greer	.25
469	Rod Barajas	.25
470	Lance Berkman	.75
471	Brady Anderson	.25
472	Pedro Astacio	.25
473	Shane Halter	.25
474	Bret Prinz	.25
475	Edgar Martinez	.50
476	Steve Trachsel	.25
477	Gary Matthews Jr.	.25
478	Ismael Valdes	.25
479	Juan Uribe	.25
480	Shawn Green	.75
481	Kirk Rueter	.25
482	Damion Easley	.25
483	Chris Carpenter	.25
484	Kris Benson	.25
485	Antonio Alfonseca	.25
486	Kyle Farnsworth	.25
487	Brandon Lyon	.25
488	Hideki Irabu	.25
489	David Ortiz	.50
490	Mike Piazza	2.50
491	Derek Lowe	.25
492	Chris Gomez	.25
493	Mark Johnson	.25
494	John Rocker	.25
495	Eric Karros	.25
496	Bill Haselman	.25
497	Dave Veres	.25
498	Gil Heredia	.25
499	Tomokazu Ohka	.25
500	Barry Bonds	4.00
501	David Dellucci	.25
502	Ed Sprague	.25
503	Tom Gordon	.25
504	Javier Vazquez	.25
505	Ben Sheets	.75
506	Wilton Guerrero	.25
507	John Halama	.25
508	Mark Redman	.25
509	Jack Wilson	.25
510	Bernie Williams	.75
511	Miguel Cairo	.25
512	Denny Hocking	.25
513	Tony Batista	.25
514	Mark Grudzielanek	.25
515	Jose Vidro	.25
516	Sterling Hitchcock	.25
517	Billy Koch	.25
518	Matt Clement	.25
519	Bruce Chen	.25
520	Roberto Alomar	1.00
521	Orlando Palmeiro	.25
522	Steve Finley	.25
523	Danny Patterson	.25
524	Terry Adams	.25
525	Tino Martinez	.25
526	Tony Armas Jr.	.25

#	Player	Price
527	Geoff Jenkins	.50
528	Chris Michalak	.25
529	Corey Patterson	.25
530	Brian Giles	.50
531	Jose Jimenez	.25
532	Joe Kennedy	.25
533	Armando Rios	.25
534	Osvaldo Fernandez	.25
535	Ruben Sierra	.25
536	Octavio Dotel	.25
537	Luis Sojo	.25
538	Brent Butler	.25
539	Pablo Ozuna	.25
540	Freddy Garcia	.25
541	Chad Durbin	.25
542	Orlando Merced	.25
543	Michael Tucker	.25
544	Roberto Hernandez	.25
545	Pat Burrell	.50
546	A.J. Burnett	.25
547	Bubba Trammell	.25
548	Scott Elarton	.25
549	Mike Darr	.25
550	Ken Griffey Jr.	2.00
551	Ugueth Urbina	.25
552	Todd Jones	.25
553	Delino DeShields	.25
554	Adam Piatt	.25
555	Jason Kendall	.25
556	Hector Ortiz	.25
557	Turk Wendell	.25
558	Rob Bell	.25
559	Sun-Woo Kim	.25
560	Raul Mondesi	.50
561	Brent Abernathy	.25
562	Seth Etherton	.25
563	Shawn Wooten	.25
564	Jay Buhner	.50
565	Andres Galarraga	.50
566	Shane Reynolds	.25
567	Rod Beck	.25
568	Dee Brown	.25
569	Pedro Feliz	.25
570	Ryan Klesko	.25
571	John Vander Wal	.25
572	Nick Bierbrodt	.25
573	Joe Nathan	.25
574	James Baldwin	.25
575	J.D. Drew	.75
576	Greg Colbrunn	.25
577	Doug Glanville	.25
578	Rey Sanchez	.25
579	Todd Van Poppel	.25
580	Rich Aurilia	.25
581	Chuck Finley	.25
582	Abraham Nunez	.25
583	Kenny Lofton	.50
584	Brian Daubach	.25
585	Miguel Tejada	.75
586	Nate Cornejo	.25
587	Kazuhiro Sasaki	.50
588	Chris Richard	.25
589	Armando Reynoso	.25
590	Tim Hudson	.75
591	Neifi Perez	.25
592	Steve Cox	.25
593	Henry Blanco	.25
594	Ricky Ledee	.25
595	Tim Salmon	.50
596	Luis Rivas	.25
597	Jeff Zimmerman	.25
598	Matt Stairs	.25
599	Preston Wilson	.25
600	Mark McGwire	4.00
601	Timo Perez	.25
602	Matt Anderson	.25
603	Todd Hundley	.25
604	Rick Ankiel	.25
605	Tsuyoshi Shinjo	.25
606	Woody Williams	.25
607	Jason LaRue	.25
608	Carlos Lee	.25
609	Russ Johnson	.25
610	Scott Rolen	1.50
611	Brent Mayne	.25
612	Darrin Fletcher	.25
613	Ray Lankford	.25
614	Troy O'Leary	.25
615	Javier Lopez	.50
616	Randy Velarde	.25
617	Vinny Castilla	.25
618	Milton Bradley	.25
619	Ruben Mateo	.25
620	Jason Giambi	1.00
621	Andy Benes	.25
622	Joe Mauer RC	12.00
623	Andy Pettitte	.75
624	Jose Offerman	.25
625	Mo Vaughn	.50
626	Steve Sparks	.25
627	Mike Matthews	.25
628	Robb Nen	.25
629	Kip Wells	.25
630	Kevin Brown	.50
631	Arthur Rhodes	.25
632	Gabe Kapler	.25
633	Jermaine Dye	.25
634	Josh Beckett	.75
635	Pokey Reese	.25
636	Benji Gil	.25
637	Marcus Giles	.25
638	Julian Tavarez	.25
639	Jason Schmidt	.50
640	Alex Rodriguez	3.00
641	Anaheim Angels	.25
642	Arizona Diamondbacks	.25
643	Atlanta Braves	.25
644	Baltimore Orioles	.25
645	Boston Red Sox	.25
646	Chicago Cubs	.25
647	Chicago White Sox	.25

#	Player	Price
648	Cincinnati Reds	.25
649	Cleveland Indians	.25
650	Colorado Rockies	.25
651	Detroit Tigers	.25
652	Florida Marlins	.25
653	Houston Astros	.25
654	Kansas City Royals	.25
655	Los Angeles Dodgers	.25
656	Milwaukee Brewers	.25
657	Minnesota Twins	.25
658	Montreal Expos	.25
659	New York Mets	.25
660	New York Yankees	1.00
661	Oakland Athletics	.25
662	Philadelphia Phillies	.25
663	Pittsburgh Pirates	.25
664	San Diego Padres	.25
665	San Francisco Giants	.25
666	Seattle Mariners	.25
667	St. Louis Cardinals	.25
668	Tampa Bay Devil Rays	.25
669	Texas Rangers	.25
670	Toronto Blue Jays	.25
671	Juan Cruz	.25
672	Kevin Cash RC	1.00
673	Jimmy Gobble RC	3.00
674	Mike Hill RC	.75
675	Taylor Buchholz RC	.75
676	Bill Hall	.75
677	Brett Roneberg RC	.75
678	Royce Huffman RC	.75
679	Chris Tritle RC	1.00
680	Nate Espy RC	.50
681	Nick Alvarez RC	1.00
682	Jason Botts RC	1.50
683	Ryan Gripp RC	.75
684	Dan Phillips RC	.50
685	Pablo Arias RC	.75
686	John Rodriguez RC	.75
687	Rich Harden RC	10.00
688	Neal Frendling RC	1.00
689	Rich Thompson RC	.50
690	Greg Montalbano RC	1.00
691	Leonard Dinardo RC	.75
692	Ryan Raburn RC	.75
693	Josh Barfield RC	5.00
694	David Bacani RC	.75
695	Dan Johnson RC	2.00
696	Mike Mussina	.50
697	Ivan Rodriguez	.75
698	Doug Mientkiewicz	.25
699	Roberto Alomar	.50
700	Eric Chavez	.25
701	Omar Vizquel	.25
702	Mike Cameron	.25
703	Torii Hunter	.25
704	Ichiro Suzuki	1.50
705	Greg Maddux	1.00
706	Brad Ausmus	.25
707	Todd Helton	.75
708	Fernando Vina	.25
709	Scott Rolen	.75
710	Orlando Cabrera	.25
711	Andruw Jones	.50
712	Jim Edmonds	.25
713	Larry Walker	.25
714	Roger Clemens	1.50
715	Randy Johnson	.75
716	Ichiro Suzuki	1.50
717	Barry Bonds	2.00
718	Ichiro Suzuki	1.50
719	Albert Pujols	1.50

Black Refractor

CHRIS HOLT

Stars:	5-10X
Production 50 Sets	

Gold Refractor

RANDY JOHNSON

Stars:	2-4X
Inserted 1:4	

Aces

		NM/M
	Common Player:	10.00
KB	Kevin Brown	10.00
TH	Tim Hudson	10.00
AL	Al Leiter	10.00
CS	Curt Schilling	15.00
BZ	Barry Zito	10.00

Batterymates

		NM/M
Inserted 1:349		
GL	Tom Glavine, Javy Lopez	20.00
HP	Mike Hampton, Ben Petrick	10.00

Deuces Are Wild

		NM/M
Common Card:		
Inserted 1:428		
CA	Andruw Jones, Chipper Jones	40.00
BT	Bernie Williams, Tino Martinez	25.00
RC	Ryan Dempster, Cliff Floyd	10.00

Jack of All Trades

		NM/M
	Common Player:	10.00
CJ	Chipper Jones	20.00
MO	Magglio Ordonez	10.00
AR	Alex Rodriguez	25.00

Kings of the Clubhouse

		NM/M
	Common Player:	15.00
JB	Jeff Bagwell	15.00
TG	Tony Gwynn	20.00
AR	Alex Rodriguez	25.00

Like Father, Like Son Relics

		NM/M
Inserted 1:790		
WI	Preston Wilson, Mookie Wilson	10.00

Three of a Kind

		NM/M
Common Card		
AIR	Alex Rodriguez, Ivan Rodriguez, Rafael Palmeiro	50.00
BEJ	Bret Boone, Edgar Martinez, John Olerud	25.00
JCL	Jeff Bagwell, Craig Biggio, Lance Berkman	40.00

Top Of The Order

		NM/M
	Common Player:	8.00
Inserted 1:106		
BA	Benny Agbayani/Jsy	8.00
PB	Peter Bergeron/Jsy	8.00
CB	Craig Biggio/Jsy	15.00
JD	Johnny Damon/Bat	10.00
RF	Rafael Furcal/Bat	10.00
RH	Rickey Henderson/Bat	20.00
JK	Jason Kendall/Bat	10.00
CK	Chuck Knoblauch/Bat	8.00
PL	Paul LoDuca/Bat	8.00
KL	Kenny Lofton/Jsy	10.00
JP	Juan Pierre/Bat	10.00
SS	Shannon Stewart/Jsy	10.00

1952 Player Reprints

PREACHER ROE

		NM/M
Complete Set (19):		50.00
Common Card:		3.00
Inserted 1:8		
Refractors:		2X
Inserted 1:24		
52R-1	Roy Campanella	4.00
52R-2	Duke Snider	4.00
52R-3	Carl Erskine	3.00
52R-4	Andy Pafko	3.00
52R-5	Johnny Mize	3.00
52R-6	Billy Martin	4.00
52R-7	Phil Rizzuto	4.00
52R-8	Gil McDougald	3.00
52R-9	Allie Reynolds	3.00
52R-10	Jackie Robinson	5.00
52R-11	Preacher Roe	3.00
52R-12	Gil Hodges	3.00
52R-13	Billy Cox	3.00
52R-14	Yogi Berra	4.00
52R-15	Gene Woodling	3.00
52R-16	Johnny Sain	3.00
52R-17	Ralph Houk	3.00
52R-18	Joe Collins	3.00
52R-19	Hank Bauer	3.00

2002 Topps eTopps

ERIC HINSKE
eTopps
TORONTO BLUE JAYS

Topps continued its on-line card program with a second annual eTopps edition in 2002. Initial Player Offerings were again made for only one week with allocations having to be made for some cards in high demand. After the IPO, cards could be bought and sold within portfolios, or physically delivered (for a fee) for more traditional venues. The 2-1/2" x 3-1/2" cards are printed on metallic foil with vertical portrait and action photos on front. Horizontal backs have another portrait photo, a 2001 recap and 2002 "prospectus," and a few biographical bits and stats. The listings here include the initial offering price and the number of cards sold during the open ordering period. Values shown are for cards in a virtual portfolio, rather than "in hand." Taking physical possession of a card from an eTopps portfolio costs about $7.

		NM/M
Complete Set (107):		185.00
Common Player:		1.50
1	Ichiro Suzuki ($9.50 / 9,477)	2.00
2	Jason Giambi ($9.50 / 5,142)	1.50
3	Roberto Alomar ($6.50 / 2,711)	1.50
4	Bret Boone ($4 / 2,000)	6.00
5	Frank Catalanotto ($6.50 / 2,000)	6.00
6	Alex Rodriguez ($9.50 / 6,393)	3.00
7	Jim Thome ($6.50 / 2,927)	2.00
8	Toby Hall ($6.50 / 2,000)	1.50
9	Troy Glaus ($6.50 / 4,323)	1.50
10	Derek Jeter ($9.50 / 8,000)	4.00
11	Alfonso Soriano ($6.50 / 5,000)	1.50
12	Eric Chavez ($6.50 / 4,334)	1.50
13	Preston Wilson ($4 / 2,000)	1.50
14	Bernie Williams ($6.50 / 4,436)	1.50
15	Larry Walker ($6.50 / 2,546)	1.50
16	Todd Helton ($9.50 / 3,430)	1.50
17	Moises Alou ($6.50 / 2,856)	1.50
18	Lance Berkman ($6.50 / 5,000)	1.50
19	Chipper Jones ($6.50 / 4,734)	1.50
20	Andruw Jones ($6.50 / 4,849)	1.50
21	Barry Bonds ($9.50 / 6,658)	7.50

#	Player	Value
22	Sammy Sosa ($9.50 / 8,000)	1.50
23	Luis Gonzalez ($6.50 / 2,671)	1.50
24	Shawn Green ($6.50 / 4,438)	1.50
25	Jeff Bagwell ($9.50 / 3,359)	1.50
26	Albert Pujols ($6.50 / 5,531)	4.00
27	Rafael Palmeiro ($6.50 / 2,700)	1.50
28	Jimmy Rollins ($4 / 5,000)	1.50
29	Vladimir Guerrero ($6.50 / 6,000)	1.50
30	Jeff Kent ($6.50 / 3,000)	1.50
31	Ken Griffey Jr. ($9.50 / 4,569)	2.00
32	Magglio Ordonez ($6.50 / 4,000)	1.50
33	Mike Piazza ($9.50 / 4,202)	1.50
34	Pedro Martinez ($9.50 / 6,000)	1.50
35	Mark Mulder ($6.50 / 4,000)	1.50
36	Roger Clemens ($9.50 / 4,567)	2.50
37	Freddy Garcia ($6.50 / 4,986)	1.50
38	Tim Hudson ($6.50 / 2,000)	1.50
39	Mike Mussina ($6.50 / 3,708)	1.50
40	Joe Mays ($4 / 3,000)	1.50
41	Barry Zito ($6.50 / 3,590)	1.50
42	Jermaine Dye ($6.50 / 2,693)	1.50
43	Mariano Rivera ($6.50 / 3,709)	1.50
44	Randy Johnson ($9.50 / 6,211)	1.50
45	Curt Schilling ($6.50 / 5,190)	1.50
46	Greg Maddux ($9.50 / 4,008)	1.50
47	Javier Vazquez ($6.50 / 3,000)	1.50
48	Kerry Wood ($6.50 / 3,346)	1.50
49	Wilson Betemit ($6.50 / 2,377)	1.50
50	Adam Dunn ($6.50 / 6,000)	1.50
51	Josh Beckett ($6.50 / 5,000)	2.00
52	Paul LoDuca ($4 / 3,998)	1.50
53	Ben Sheets ($4 / 3,842)	1.50
54	Eric Valent ($4 / 5,000)	1.50
55	Brian Giles ($6.50 / 2,000)	1.50
56	Mo Vaughn ($6.50 / 2,772)	1.50
57	C.C. Sabathia ($6.50 / 2,525)	1.50
58	Nick Johnson ($6.50 / 5,000)	1.50
59	Miguel Tejada ($6.50 / 4,000)	1.50
60	Carlos Delgado ($6.50 / 3,604)	1.50
61	Tsuyoshi Shinjo ($4 / 3,000)	1.50
62	Juan Gonzalez ($6.50 / 2,361)	1.50
63	Mike Sweeney ($6.50 / 3,175)	1.50
64	Ivan Rodriguez ($9.50 / 3,000)	1.50
65	Bud Smith ($4.00 / 3,000)	2.00
66	Brandon Duckworth ($6.50 / 2,000)	4.00
67	Xavier Nady ($4 / 4,000)	1.50
68	D'Angelo Jimenez ($4 / 1,725)	1.50
69	Roy Oswalt ($6.50 / 3,523)	1.50
70	J.D. Drew ($9.50 / 3,195)	1.50
71	Cliff Floyd ($6.50 / 3,575)	1.50
72	Kevin Brown ($6.50 / 3,000)	1.50
73	Gary Sheffield ($6.50 / 2,593)	2.00
74	Aramis Ramirez ($6.50 / 3,000)	1.50
75	Nomar Garciaparra ($9.50 / 5,090)	1.50
76	Phil Nevin ($6.50 / 2,348)	1.50
77	Juan Cruz ($4 / 4,000)	1.50
78	Hideo Nomo ($6.50 / 2,857)	1.50
79	Chris George ($4 / 3,000)	1.50
80	Matt Morris ($4 / 3,000)	1.50
81	Corey Patterson ($6.50 / 4,000)	1.50
82	Joel Pineiro ($6.50 / 4,776)	1.50
83	Mark Buehrle ($4 / 3,000)	4.00
84	Shannon Stewart ($4 / 1,992)	1.50
85	Kazuhiro Sasaki ($6.50 / 4,000)	1.50
86	Carlos Pena ($4 / 4,000)	1.50
87	Brad Penny ($6.50 / 3,000)	1.50
88	Rich Aurilia ($6.50 / 2,795)	2.00
89	Wade Miller ($4 / 4,000)	1.50
90	Tim Raines Jr. ($4 / 5,000)	1.50
91	Kazuhisa Ishii ($6.50 / 6,000)	1.50
92	Hank Blalock ($6.50 / 5,000)	3.00
93	So Taguchi ($4 / 5,000)	1.50
94	Mark Prior ($9.50 / 5,000)	9.00
95	Rickey Henderson ($9.50 / 4,013)	3.50
96	Austin Kearns ($6.50 / 6,000)	1.50
97	Tom Glavine ($9.50 / 3,000)	1.50
98	Manny Ramirez ($6.50 / 4,905)	1.50
99	Shea Hillenbrand ($6.50 / 4,000)	1.50
100	Junior Spivey ($6.50 / 5,000)	1.50
101	Derek Lowe ($6.50 / 4,911)	1.50
102	Torii Hunter ($6.50 / 4,000)	1.50
103	Juan Rivera ($6.50 / 4,000)	1.50
104	Eric Hinske ($6.50 / 5,000)	1.50
105	Bobby Hill ($6.50 / 3,000)	1.50
106	Rafael Soriano ($6.50 / 4,000)	1.50
107	Jim Edmonds ($6.50 / 3,851)	2.00

Classics

Topps expanded its eTopps line-up in 2002 with the issue of 20 cards of former greats. Like regular eTopps cards, they could only be ordered during a one-week Initial Player Offering period. Cards were issued in a quantity of 4,000 each at $12.50. Fronts have a color or colorized action photo, backs have a picture of one of that player's Topps cards, along with career notes, stats, etc. Values shown are latest auction prices realized on the date cited and represent cards in a virtual portfolio rather than "in hand". The cost to physically move a card from an eTopps portfolio into one's possession is about $7.

		NM/M
Complete Set (20):		90.00
Common Player:		3.50
1	Babe Ruth	15.00
2	Tom Seaver	3.50
3	Honus Wagner	4.00
4	Warren Spahn	3.50
5	Frank Robinson	3.50
6	Whitey Ford	3.50
7	Bob Gibson	3.50
8	Reggie Jackson	5.00
9	Joe Morgan	3.50
10	Harmon Killebrew	3.50
11	Eddie Mathews	3.50
12	Willie Mays	9.00
12a	Willie Mays (2004 autographed edition of 100)	135.00

#	Player	Value
13	Brooks Robinson	3.50
14	Ty Cobb	5.00
15	Carl Yastrzemski	4.00
16	Jackie Robinson	7.00
17	Mike Schmidt	4.50
18	Nolan Ryan	9.00
19	Duke Snider	3.50
20	Stan Musial	4.50

Events

Special events during the 2002 season were commemorated by Topps with the issue of special eTopps cards. Like the regular-issue eTopps, the cards were only available directly from Topps on-line. Five thousand of each card were issued with an initial order price of $8 each. Only the baseball related Events cards are listed here. Values shown are for cards in a virtual portfolio. Taking physical possession of a card from an eTopps portfolio costs about $7 apiece.

			NM/M
1	Mike Cameron/5,000 (Four HR)		1.00
2	Shawn Green/5,000 (Four HR, 19 TB)		1.00
4	Oakland A's/5,000 (20 Straight Wins)		1.00
5	Greg Maddux/3,851 (15+ Wins, 15 Years)		1.50

2002 Topps Gallery

		NM/M
Complete Set (200):		60.00
Common Player:		.25
Common (151-200):		.75
Inserted 1:1		
Pack (6):		1.50
Box (24):		30.00
1	Jason Giambi	.50
2	Mark Grace	.40
3	Bret Boone	.40
4	Antonio Alfonseca	.25
5	Kevin Brown	.40
6	Cristian Guzman	.25
7	Magglio Ordonez	.40
8	Luis Gonzalez	.40
9	Jorge Posada	.40
10	Roberto Alomar	.50
11	Mike Sweeney	.25
12	Jeff Kent	.40
13	Matt Morris	.40
14	Alfonso Soriano	.75
15	Adam Dunn	.50
16	Neifi Perez	.25
17	Todd Walker	.25
18	J.D. Drew	.40
19	Eric Chavez	.40
20	Alex Rodriguez	1.50
21	Ray Lankford	.25
22	Roger Cedeno	.25
23	Chipper Jones	.75
24	Jose Canseco	.50
25	Mike Piazza	1.50
26	Freddy Garcia	.25
27	Todd Helton	.50
28	Tino Martinez	.40
29	Kazuhiro Sasaki	.25

#	Player	Value
30	Curt Schilling	.50
31	Mark Buehrle	.25
32	John Olerud	.40
33	Brad Radke	.25
34	Steve Sparks	.25
35	Jason Tyner	.25
36	Jeff Shaw	.25
37	Mariano Rivera	.40
38	Russ Ortiz	.25
39	Richard Hidalgo	.25
40	Barry Bonds	2.00
41	John Burkett	.25
42	Tim Hudson	.25
43	Mike Hampton	.25
44	Orlando Cabrera	.25
45	Barry Zito	.40
46	C.C. Sabathia	.25
47	Chan Ho Park	.25
48	Tom Glavine	.50
49	Aramis Ramirez	.25
50	Lance Berkman	.40
51	Al Leiter	.25
52	Phil Nevin	.25
53	Javier Vazquez	.25
54	Troy Glaus	.25
55	Tsuyoshi Shinjo	.25
56	Albert Pujols	.40
57	John Smoltz	.40
58	Derek Jeter	2.00
59	Robb Nen	.25
60	Jason Kendall	.25
61	Eric Gagne	.25
62	Vladimir Guerrero	.75
63	Corey Patterson	.40
64	Rickey Henderson	.50
65	Jack Wilson	.25
66	Jason LaRue	.25
67	Sammy Sosa	1.50
68	Ken Griffey Jr.	1.00
69	Randy Johnson	.75
70	Nomar Garciaparra	.75
71	Ivan Rodriguez	.50
72	J.T. Snow	.25
73	Darryl Kile	.25
74	Andruw Jones	.50
75	Brian Giles	.40
76	Pedro Martinez	.75
77	Jeff Bagwell	.50
78	Rafael Palmeiro	.50
79	Ryan Dempster	.25
80	Jeff Cirillo	.25
81	Geoff Jenkins	.40
82	Brandon Duckworth	.25
83	Roger Clemens	1.50
84	Fred McGriff	.50
85	Hideo Nomo	.50
86	Larry Walker	.50
87	Sean Casey	.40
88	Trevor Hoffman	.25
89	Robert Fick	.25
90	Armando Benitez	.25
91	Jeromy Burnitz	.25
92	Bernie Williams	.50
93	Carlos Delgado	.25
94	Troy Percival	.25
95	Nate Cornejo	.25
96	Derrek Lee	.40
97	Jose Ortiz	.25
98	Brian Jordan	.25
99	Jose Cruz	.25
100	Ichiro Suzuki	1.50
101	Jose Mesa	.25
102	Tim Salmon	.40
103	Bud Smith	.25
104	Paul LoDuca	.25
105	Juan Pierre	.25
106	Ben Grieve	.25
107	Russell Branyan	.25
108	Bobby Abreu	.40
109	Moises Alou	.25
110	Richie Sexson	.50
111	Jerry Hairston Jr.	.25
112	Marlon Anderson	.25
113	Juan Gonzalez	.50
114	Craig Biggio	.50
115	Carlos Beltran	.50
116	Eric Milton	.25
117	Cliff Floyd	.25
118	Rich Aurilia	.25
119	Adrian Beltre	.25
120	Jason Bere	.25
121	Darin Erstad	.40
122	Ben Sheets	.40
123	Johnny Damon	.40
124	Jimmy Rollins	.25
125	Shawn Green	.40
126	Greg Maddux	1.00
127	Mark Mulder	.40
128	Bartolo Colon	.25
129	Shannon Stewart	.25
130	Ramon Ortiz	.25
131	Kerry Wood	.75
132	Ryan Klesko	.25
133	Preston Wilson	.25
134	Roy Oswalt	.40
135	Rafael Furcal	.25
136	Eric Karros	.25
137	Nick Neugebauer	.25
138	Doug Mientkiewicz	.25
139	Paul Konerko	.40
140	Bobby Higginson	.25
141	Garret Anderson	.40
142	Wes Helms	.25
143	Brent Abernathy	.25
144	Scott Rolen	.75
145	Dmitri Young	.25
146	Jim Thome	.75
147	Raul Mondesi	.25
148	Pat Burrell	.40
149	Gary Sheffield	.40
150	Miguel Tejada	.40
151	Brandon Inge	.75
152	Carlos Pena	.75
153	Jason Lane	.75
154	Nathan Haynes	.75
155	Hank Blalock	1.50
156	Juan Cruz	.75
157	Morgan Ensberg	.75
158	Sean Burroughs	.75
159	Ed Rogers	.75
160	Nick Johnson	.75
161	Orlando Hudson	.75
162	Anastacio Martinez RC	.75
163	Jeremy Affeldt	.75
164	Brandon Claussen	.75
165	Deivis Santos	.75
166	Mike Rivera	.75
167	Carlos Silva	.75
168	Valentino Pascucci	.75
169	Xavier Nady	.75
170	David Espinosa	.75
171	Dan Phillips RC	.75
172	Tony Fontana RC	.75
173	Juan Silvestre	.75
174	Henry Pichardo RC	.75
175	Pablo Arias RC	.75
176	Brett Roneberg RC	.75
177	Chad Qualls RC	.75
178	Greg Sain RC	.75
179	Rene Reyes RC	.75
180	So Taguchi RC	2.00
181	Dan Johnson RC	2.50
182	Justin Backsmeyer RC	.75
183	Juan Gonzalez	.75
184	Jason Ellison RC	.75
185	Kazuhisa Ishii RC	3.00
186	Joe Mauer RC	8.00
187	James Shanks RC	.75
188	Kevin Cash RC	.75
189	J.J. Trujillo RC	.75
190	Jorge Padilla RC	1.00
191	Nolan Ryan	4.00
192	George Brett	3.00
193	Ryne Sandberg	2.00
194	Robin Yount	1.50
195	Tom Seaver	1.00
196	Mike Schmidt	2.00
197	Frank Robinson	1.00
198	Harmon Killebrew	1.00
199	Kirby Puckett	2.00
200	Don Mattingly	4.00

Autographs

		NM/M
Common Player:		8.00
Inserted 1:192		
LB	Lance Berkman	30.00
BBO	Bret Boone	20.00
JD	J.D. Drew	25.00
LG	Luis Gonzalez	20.00
SG	Shawn Green	25.00
JL	Jason Lane	8.00
MO	Magglio Ordonez	20.00
JP	Jorge Posada	40.00
JS	Juan Silvestre	8.00

Baseball Bucks

		NM/M
Used for gallery original art auctions:		
$5	Nolan Ryan	2.50

Originals Relics

		NM/M
Common Player:		8.00
Inserted 1:169		
BBO	Bret Boone	8.00
JC	Jose Canseco	10.00
CD	Carlos Delgado	8.00
JG	Juan Gonzalez	10.00
LG	Luis Gonzalez	8.00
TG	Tony Gwynn	15.00
TH	Todd Helton	12.00
AJ	Andruw Jones	8.00
CJ	Chipper Jones	10.00
TM	Tino Martinez	10.00
MP	Mike Piazza	20.00
AP	Albert Pujols	35.00
AR	Alex Rodriguez	15.00
AS	Alfonso Soriano	10.00
BW	Bernie Williams	10.00

Heritage

		NM/M
Complete Set (25):		100.00

Common Player:		2.00
Inserted 1:12		
GH-RA	Roberto Alomar	4.00
GH-BBO	Bret Boone	2.00
GH-RC	Roger Clemens	8.00
GH-JG	Jason Giambi	3.00
GH-LG	Luis Gonzalez	3.00
GH-SG	Shawn Green	3.00
GH-KG	Ken Griffey Jr.	6.00
GH-TG	Tony Gwynn	4.00
GH-RJ	Reggie Jackson	4.00
GH-CJ	Chipper Jones	4.00
GH-AK	Al Kaline	4.00
GH-GM	Greg Maddux	5.00
GH-PM	Pedro Martinez	5.00
GH-MM	Mark McGwire	10.00
GH-SM	Stan Musial	4.00
GH-MP	Mike Piazza	6.00
GH-BR	Brooks Robinson	5.00
GH-AR	Alex Rodriguez	8.00
GH-NR	Nolan Ryan	10.00
GH-MS	Mike Schmidt	4.00
GH-TS	Tom Seaver	4.00
GH-TSH	Tsuyoshi Shinjo	4.00
GH-SS	Sammy Sosa	8.00
GH-CY	Carl Yastrzemski	5.00
GH-RY	Robin Yount	5.00

Heritage Autographs

		NM/M
Inserted 1:240		
BBO	Bret Boone	20.00
LG	Luis Gonzalez	25.00
SG	Shawn Green	25.00

Heritage Relics

		NM/M
Common Player:		8.00
Inserted 1:85		
BBO	Bret Boone	8.00
LG	Luis Gonzalez	8.00
TG	Tony Gwynn	15.00
CJ	Chipper Jones	10.00
GM	Greg Maddux	15.00
PM	Pedro Martinez	15.00
MP	Mike Piazza	15.00
AR	Alex Rodriguez	15.00
TS	Tsuyoshi Shinjo	8.00

Press Plates

The aluminum press plates used to print the Gallery cards were inserted at a rate of one per 1,200 packs. Each card's front and back can be found in four different color variations. Because of the unique nature of each plate, assignment of catalog values in not feasible.

		NM/M
Common Player:		50.00

Team Topps Legends Autographs

		NM/M
Inserted 1:1,019		
	Luis Aparicio	15.00
	Jim Bunning	20.00
	Fergie Jenkins	15.00
	Carl Yastrzemski	65.00

2002 Topps Gold Label

		NM/M
Complete Set (200):		60.00
Common Player:		.25
Pack (4):		3.00
Box (18):		40.00
1	Alex Rodriguez	1.50
2	Derek Jeter	2.00
3	Luis Gonzalez	.40
4	Troy Glaus	.40
5	Albert Pujols	1.50
6	Lance Berkman	.40
7	J.D. Drew	.75
8	Chipper Jones	.75
9	Miguel Tejada	.75
10	Randy Johnson	.75
11	Mike Cameron	.25
12	Brian Giles	.25
13	Roger Cedeno	.25
14	Kerry Wood	.75
15	Ken Griffey Jr.	1.00
16	Carlos Lee	.50
17	Todd Helton	.50
18	Gary Sheffield	.40
19	Richie Sexson	.40
20	Vladimir Guerrero	.75
21	Bobby Higginson	.25
22	Roger Clemens	1.50
23	Barry Zito	.40
24	Juan Pierre	.25
25	Pedro Martinez	.75
26	Sean Casey	.25
27	David Segui	.25
28	Jose Garcia	.25
29	Curt Schilling	.50
30	Bernie Williams	.40
31	Ben Grieve	.25
32	Hideo Nomo	.40
33	Aramis Ramirez	.25
34	Cristian Guzman	.25
35	Rich Aurilia	.25
36	Greg Maddux	1.00
37	Eric Chavez	.40
38	Shawn Green	.40
39	Luis Rivas	.25
40	Magglio Ordonez	.40
41	Jose Vidro	.25
42	Mariano Rivera	.40
43	Chris Tritle RC	.50
44	C.C. Sabathia	.25
45	Larry Walker	.40
46	Raul Mondesi	.25
47	Kevin Brown	.25
48	Jeff Bagwell	.50
49	Earl Snyder RC	.50
50	Jason Giambi	.50
51	Ichiro Suzuki	1.50
52	Andruw Jones	.50
53	Ivan Rodriguez	.50
54	Jim Edmonds	.40
55	Preston Wilson	.25
56	Greg Vaughn	.25
57	Jon Lieber	.25
58	Justin Sherrod RC	.50
59	Marcus Giles	.25
60	Roberto Alomar	.40
61	Pat Burrell	.50
62	Doug Mientkiewicz	.25
63	Mark Mulder	.40
64	Mike Hampton	.25
65	Adam Dunn	.50
66	Moises Alou	.25
67	Jose Cruz Jr.	.25
68	Derek Bell	.25
69	Sammy Sosa	1.50
70	Joe Mays	.25
71	Phil Nevin	.25
72	Edgardo Alfonzo	.25
73	Barry Bonds	2.00
74	Edgar Martinez	.40
75	Juan Encarnacion	.25
76	Jason Tyner	.25
77	Edgar Renteria	.40
78	Bret Boone	.40
79	Scott Rolen	.50
80	Nomar Garciaparra	1.50
81	Frank Thomas	.50
82	Roy Oswalt	.40
83	Tsuyoshi Shinjo	.25
84	Ben Sheets	.40
85	Hank Blalock	.50
86	Carlos Delgado	.50
87	Tim Hudson	.40
88	Alfonso Soriano	.75
89	Michael Hill RC	.50
90	Jim Thome	.75
91	Craig Biggio	.40
92	Ryan Klesko	.25
93	Geoff Jenkins	.40
94	Matt Morris	.40
95	Jorge Posada	.40
96	Cliff Floyd	.40
97	Jimmy Rollins	.40
98	Mike Sweeney	.25
99	Frank Catalanotto	.25
100	Mike Piazza	1.25
101	Mark Quinn	.25
102	Torii Hunter	.40
103	Lee Stevens	.25
104	Byung-Hyug Kim	.25
105	Freddy Sanchez RC	.50
106	David Cone	.25
107	Jerry Hairston Jr.	.25
108	Kyle Farnsworth	.25
109	Rafael Furcal	.25
110	Bartolo Colon	.25
111	Juan Rivera	.25
112	Kevin Young	.25
113	Chris Narveson RC	1.00
114	Richard Hidalgo	.25
115	Andy Pettitte	.40
116	Darin Erstad	.40
117	Corey Koskie	.25
118	Rickey Henderson	.50
119	Derrek Lee	.40
120	Sean Burroughs	.25
121	Paul Konerko	.25
122	Ross Peeples RC	.50
123	Terrence Long	.25
124	John Smoltz	.40
125	Brandon Duckworth	.25
126	Luis Maza	.25
127	Morgan Ensberg	.25
128	Eric Valent	.25
129	Shannon Stewart	.25
130	D'Angelo Jimenez	.25
131	Jeff Cirillo	.25
132	Jack Cust	.25
133	Dmitri Young	.25
134	Darryl Kile	.25
135	Reggie Sanders	.25
136	Marlon Byrd	.25
137	Napoleon Calzado RC	.50
138	Javy Lopez	.25
139	Orlando Cabrera	.25
140	Mike Mussina	.40
141	Josh Beckett	.40
142	Kazuhiro Sasaki	.25
143	Jermaine Dye	.25
144	Carlos Beltran	.40
145	Trevor Hoffman	.25
146	Kazuhisa Ishii RC	2.00
147	Alex Gonzalez	.25
148	Marty Cordova	.25
149	Kevin Deaton RC	.50
150	Toby Hall	.25
151	Rafael Palmeiro	.50
152	John Olerud	.40
153	David Eckstein	.25
154	Doug Glanville	.25
155	Johnny Damon	.40
156	Javier Vazquez	.25
157	Jason Bay RC	2.00
158	Robb Nen	.25
159	Rafael Soriano	.25
160	Placido Polanco	.25
161	Garret Anderson	.40
162	Aaron Boone	.25
163	Mike Lieberthal	.25
164	Joe Mauer RC	10.00
165	Matt Lawton	.25
166	Juan Tolentino RC	.50
167	Alex Gonzalez	.25
168	Steve Finley	.25
169	Troy Percival	.25
170	Bud Smith	.25
171	Freddie Garcia	.25
172	Ray Lankford	.25
173	Tim Redding	.25
174	Ryan Dempster	.25
175	Travis Lee	.25
176	Jeff Kent	.40
177	Ramon Hernandez	.25
178	Carl Everett	.25
179	Tom Glavine	.40
180	Juan Gonzalez	.50
181	Nick Johnson	.25
182	Mike Lowell	.40
183	Al Leiter	.25
184	Jason Maule RC	.50
185	Wilson Betemit	.25
186	Tino Martinez	.40
187	Jason Standridge	.25
188	Mike Peeples RC	.50
189	Jason Kendall	.25
190	Fred McGriff	.50
191	John Rodriguez RC	.50
192	Brett Roneberg RC	.50
193	Marlyn Tisdale RC	.50
194	J.T. Snow	.25
195	Craig Kuzmic RC	.75
196	Cory Lidle	.25
197	Alex Cintron	.25
198	Fernando Vina	.25
199	Austin Kearns	.50
200	Paul LoDuca	.25

Class One Gold

Stars: 2-4X
Production 500 Sets

Class Two Platinum

Stars: 4-8X
Production 250 Sets

Class Three Titanium

Stars: 6-10X
Production 100 Sets

Platinum Memorabilia

Platinum: .75-1.5X
Titanium Memorabilia: 1-2X

All-Star MVP Winners

		NM/M
Common Player:		8.00
RA	Roberto Alomar	10.00
SA	Sandy Alomar	8.00
BLB	Bobby Bonds	8.00
DC	Dave Concepcion	8.00
SG2	Steve Garvey	10.00
KG	Ken Griffey Sr.	8.00
BM1	Bill Madlock	8.00
FM	Fred McGriff	10.00
DP3	Dave Parker	8.00
TP	Tony Perez	10.00
MP	Mike Piazza	15.00
KP2	Kirby Puckett	15.00
TR	Tim Raines	8.00

Batting Average

		NM/M
Common Player:		8.00
WB	Wade Boggs	15.00
BB	Bill Buckner	8.00
RC2	Rod Carew	15.00
RAC	Rico Carty	8.00
NC	Norm Cash	15.00
TG1	Tony Gwynn	15.00
TG2	Tony Gwynn	15.00
BM2	Bill Madlock	8.00
DP4	Dave Parker	8.00
KP3	Kirby Puckett	15.00
LW	Larry Walker	8.00
CY2	Carl Yastrzemski	30.00

Cy Young Winners

		NM/M
Common Player:		8.00
RWC	Roger Clemens	15.00
DE	Dennis Eckersley	8.00
RJ	Randy Johnson	12.00
BS	Bret Saberhagen	8.00
JS	John Smoltz	8.00

Home Run Champions

		NM/M
Common Player:		8.00
BB2	Barry Bonds	20.00
GF	George Foster	8.00
TK2	Ted Kluszewski	15.00
KM2	Kevin Mitchell	8.00
DM2	Dale Murphy	40.00
AR	Alex Rodriguez	15.00
DS1	Darryl Strawberry	10.00

League Championship MVP Winners

		NM/M
Common Player:		8.00
GB2	George Brett	40.00
WC	Will Clark	15.00
CC	Craig Counsell	8.00
RH	Rickey Henderson	15.00
JL	Javier Lopez	8.00
AEP	Andy Pettitte	12.00
KP1	Kirby Puckett	15.00
FW	Frank White	8.00
BFW	Bernie Williams	10.00

MLB Moments in Time

		NM/M
Common Player:		8.00
BLB	Barry Bonds	20.00
BB1	Bret Boone	8.00
BB2	Bret Boone	8.00
CD	Carlos Delgado	8.00
TG	Tony Gwynn	15.00
TH	Toby Hall	8.00
CL	Carlos Lee	8.00
JL	Javy Lopez	8.00
MO	Magglio Ordonez	10.00
RP1	Rafael Palmeiro	10.00
RP2	Rafael Palmeiro	10.00
AR	Alex Rodriguez	15.00

MVP Winners

		NM/M
Common Player:		8.00
EB	Ernie Banks	20.00
DB	Don Baylor	8.00
YB	Yogi Berra	15.00
BB1	Barry Bonds	20.00
GB1	George Brett	40.00
SG1	Steve Garvey	8.00
KHG	Kirk Gibson	8.00
KH	Keith Hernandez	10.00
RJ1	Reggie Jackson	15.00
DM	Don Mattingly	40.00
KM1	Kevin Mitchell	8.00
JM	Joe Morgan	8.00
DM1	Dale Murphy	40.00
DP1	Dave Parker	8.00
BR	Brooks Robinson	15.00
FR	Frank Robinson	12.00
RS	Ryne Sandberg	40.00
HS	Hank Sauer	8.00
WS	Willie Stargell	15.00
JT	Joe Torre	10.00
MW	Maury Wills	8.00
CY1	Carl Yastrzemski	30.00
RY	Robin Yount	20.00

RBI Leaders

		NM/M
Common Player:		8.00
BRB	Bret Boone	8.00
BRB2	Bret Boone	8.00
GC	Gary Carter	8.00
GL	Greg Luzinski	8.00
EM1	Eddie Murray	12.00
AO	Al Oliver	8.00
DP2	Dave Parker	8.00
DW	Dave Winfield	12.00

Rookie of the Year Winners

		NM/M
Common Player:		8.00
DA	Dick Allen	15.00
AB	Al Bumbry	8.00
RC1	Rod Carew	15.00
CF	Carlton Fisk	15.00
MH	Mike Hargrove	8.00
DJ	Dave Justice	10.00
EM2	Eddie Murray	12.00
LP	Lou Piniella	8.00
AP	Albert Pujols	20.00
DS2	Darryl Strawberry	15.00
FV	Fernando Valenzuela	8.00
BW	Billy Williams	8.00

World Series MVP Winners

		NM/M
Common Player:		8.00
JB	Johnny Bench	15.00
RCC	Ron Cey	8.00
RJ2	Reggie Jackson	15.00
PM	Paul Molitor	15.00
MR	Mariano Rivera	10.00

2002 Topps Heritage

		NM/M
Complete Set (440):		325.00
Common Player:		.25
Common (364-446):		3.00
Inserted 1:2		
Pack (8):		4.00
Box (24):		90.00
1	Ichiro Suzuki/SP	10.00
2	Darin Erstad	.50
3	Rod Beck	.25
4	Doug Mientkiewicz	.25
5	Mike Sweeney	.25
6	Roger Clemens	2.50
7	Jason Tyner	.25
8	Alex Gonzalez	.25
9	Eric Young	.25
10	Randy Johnson	1.50
11	Randy Johnson/SP	6.00
12	Aaron Sele	.25
13	Tony Clark	.25
14	C.C. Sabathia	.25
15	Melvin Mora	.25
16	Tim Hudson	.50
17	Ben Petrick	.25
18	Tom Glavine	.75
19	Jason Lane	.25
20	Larry Walker	.50
21	Mark Mulder	.50
22	Steve Finley	.25
23	Bengie Molina	.25
24	Rob Bell	.25
25	Nathan Haynes	.25
26	Rafael Furcal	.50
27	Rafael Furcal/SP	3.00
28	Mike Mussina	1.00
29	Paul LoDuca	.25
30	Torii Hunter	.50
31	Carlos Lee	.25
32	Jimmy Rollins	.50
33	Arthur Rhodes	.25
34	Ivan Rodriguez	1.00
35	Wes Helms	.25
36	Cliff Floyd	.25
37	Julian Tavarez	.25
38	Mark McGwire	4.00
39	Chipper Jones/SP	6.00
40	Denny Neagle	.25
41	Odalis Perez	.25
42	Antonio Alfonseca	.25
43	Edgar Renteria	.50
44	Troy Glaus	.75
45	Scott Brosius	.25
46	Abraham Nunez	.25
47	Jamey Wright	.25
48	Bobby Bonilla	.25
49	Ismael Valdes	.25
50	Chris Reitsma	.25
51	Kevin Brown	.50
52	Ben Grieve	.25
53	Alex Rodriguez/SP	10.00
54	Charles Nagy	.25
55	Reggie Sanders	.25
56	Nelson Figueroa	.25
57	Felipe Lopez	.25
58	Bill Ortega	.25
59	Mac Suzuki	.25
60	Johnny Estrada	.25
61	Bob Wickman	.25
62	Doug Glanville	.25
63	Jeff Cirillo	.50
63	Jeff Cirillo/SP	3.00
64	Corey Patterson	.50
65	Aaron Myette	.25
66	Magglio Ordonez	.50
67	Ellis Burks	.25
68	Miguel Tejada	.50
69	John Olerud	.50
69	John Olerud/SP	4.00
70	Greg Vaughn	.25
71	Andy Pettitte	.75
72	Mike Matheny	.25
73	Brandon Duckworth	.25
74	Scott Schoeneweis	.25
75	Mike Lowell	.50
76	Einar Diaz	.25
77	Tino Martinez	.50
78	Matt Williams	.50
79	Jason Young RC	1.00
80	Nate Cornejo	.25
81	Andres Galarraga	.40
82	Bernie Williams/SP	6.00
83	Ryan Klesko	.25
84	Dan Wilson	.25
85	Henry Pichardo RC	.50
86	Ray Durham	.25
87	Omar Daal	.25
88	Derrek Lee	.25
89	Al Leiter	.50
90	Darrin Fletcher	.25
91	Josh Beckett	.75
92	Johnny Damon	.25
92	Johnny Damon/SP	5.00
93	Abraham Nunez	.25
94	Ricky Ledee	.25
95	Richie Sexson	.75
96	Adam Kennedy	.25
97	Raul Mondesi	.25
98	John Burkett	.25
99	Ben Sheets	.50
99	Ben Sheets/SP	4.00
100	Preston Wilson	.25
100	Preston Wilson/SP	3.00
101	Boof Bonser	.25
102	Shigetoshi Hasegawa	.25
103	Carlos Febles	.25
104	Jorge Posada/SP	5.00
105	Michael Tucker	.25
106	Roberto Hernandez	.25
107	John Rodriguez RC	.75
108	Danny Graves	.25
109	Rich Aurilia	.25
110	Jon Lieber	.25
111	Tim Hummel RC	.50
112	J.T. Snow	.25
113	Kris Benson	.25
114	Derek Jeter	4.00
115	John Franco	.25
116	Matt Stairs	.25
117	Ben Davis	.25
118	Darryl Kile	.25
119	Mike Peeples RC	.50
120	Kevin Tapani	.25
121	Armando Benitez	.25
122	Damian Miller	.25
123	Jose Jimenez	.25
124	Pedro Astacio	.25
125	Marlyn Tisdale RC	.50
126	Deivi Cruz	.25
127	Paul O'Neill	.75
128	Jermaine Dye	.25
129	Marcus Giles	.25
130	Mark Loretta	.25
131	Garret Anderson	.25
132	Todd Ritchie	.25
133	Joe Crede	.25
134	Kevin Millwood	.50
135	Shane Reynolds	.25
136	Mark Grace	.75
137	Shannon Stewart	.25
138	Nick Neugebauer	.25
139	Nic Jackson RC	.75
140	Robb Nen	.25
141	Dmitri Young	.25
142	Kevin Appier	.25
143	Jack Cust	.25
144	Andres Torres	.25
145	Frank Thomas	1.00
146	Jason Kendall	.25
147	Greg Maddux	2.00
148	David Justice	.50
149	Hideo Nomo	.75
150	Bret Boone	.50
151	Wade Miller	.25
152	Jeff Kent	.50
153	Scott Williamson	.25
154	Julio Lugo	.25
155	Bobby Higginson	.25
156	Geoff Jenkins	.25
157	Darren Dreifort	.25
158	Freddy Sanchez RC	.75
159	Bud Smith	.25
160	Phil Nevin	.25
161	Cesar Izturis	.25
162	Sean Casey	.50
163	Jose Ortiz	.25
164	Brent Abernathy	.25
165	Kevin Young	.25
166	Daryle Ward	.25
167	Trevor Hoffman	.25
168	Rondell White	.25
169	Kip Wells	.25
170	John Vander Wal	.25
171	Jose Lima	.25
172	Wilton Guerrero	.25
173	Aaron Dean	.25
174	Rick Helling	.25
175	Juan Pierre	.25
176	Jay Bell	.25
177	Craig House	.25
178	David Bell	.25
179	Pat Burrell	.25
180	Eric Gagne	.75
181	Adam Pettyjohn	.25
182	Ugueth Urbina	.25
183	Peter Bergeron	.25
184	Adrian Gonzalez	.25
184	Adrian Gonzalez/SP	4.00
185	Damion Easley	.25
186	Gookie Dawkins	.25
187	Matt Lawton	.25
188	Frank Catalanotto	.25
189	David Wells	.25
190	Roger Cedeno	.25
191	Brian Giles	.50
192	Julio Zuleta	.25

#	Player	Price
193	Timo Perez	.25
194	Billy Wagner	.25
195	Craig Counsell	.25
196	Bart Miadich	.25
197	Gary Sheffield	.75
198	Richard Hidalgo	.50
199	Juan Uribe	.25
200	Curt Schilling	1.00
201	Javy Lopez	.50
202	Jimmy Haynes	.25
203	Jim Edmonds	.75
204	Pokey Reese	.25
204	Pokey Reese/SP	3.00
205	Matt Clement	.25
206	Dean Palmer	.25
207	Nick Johnson	.25
208	Nate Espy RC	.75
209	Pedro Feliz	.25
210	Aaron Rowand	.25
211	Masato Yoshii	.25
212	Jose Cruz	.25
213	Paul Byrd	.25
214	Mark Phillips RC	1.00
215	Benny Agbayani	.25
216	Frank Menechino	.25
217	John Flaherty	.25
218	Brian Boehringer	.25
219	Todd Hollandsworth	.25
220	Sammy Sosa/SP	8.00
221	Steve Sparks	.25
222	Homer Bush	.25
223	Mike Hampton	.50
224	Bobby Abreu	.50
225	Barry Larkin	.75
226	Ryan Rupe	.25
227	Bubba Trammell	.25
228	Todd Zeile	.25
229	Jeff Shaw	.25
230	Alex Ochoa	.25
231	Orlando Cabrera	.25
232	Jeremy Giambi	.25
233	Tomo Ohka	.25
234	Luis Castillo	.25
235	Chris Holt	.25
236	Shawn Green	.50
237	Sidney Ponson	.25
238	Lee Stevens	.25
239	Hank Blalock	.50
240	Randy Winn	.25
241	Pedro Martinez	1.50
242	Vinny Castilla	.25
243	Steve Karsay	.25
244	Barry Bonds/SP	15.00
245	Jason Bere	.25
246	Scott Rolen	1.50
246	Scott Rolen/SP	6.00
247	Ryan Kohlmeier	.25
248	Kerry Wood	1.50
249	Aramis Ramirez	.50
250	Lance Berkman	.75
251	Omar Vizquel	.50
252	Juan Encarnacion	.25
254	David Segui	.25
255	Brian Anderson	.25
256	Jay Payton	.25
257	Mark Grudzielanek	.25
258	Jimmy Anderson	.25
259	Eric Valent	.25
260	Chad Durbin	.25
261	Alex Gonzalez	.25
262	Scott Dunn	.25
263	Scott Elarton	.25
264	Tom Gordon	.25
265	Moises Alou	.50
266	Mark Buehrle	.25
269	Jerry Hairston Jr.	.25
270	Luke Prokopec	.25
272	Graeme Lloyd	.25
273	Bret Prinz	.25
274	Chris Carpenter	.25
276	Ryan Minor	.25
277	Jeff D'Amico	.25
278	Raul Ibanez	.25
279	Joe Mays	.25
280	Livan Hernandez	.25
281	Robin Ventura	.40
282	Gabe Kapler	.40
283	Tony Batista	.25
284	Ramon Hernandez	.25
285	Craig Paquette	.25
286	Mark Kotsay	.25
287	Mike Lieberthal	.25
288	Joe Borchard	.25
289	Cristian Guzman	.25
290	Craig Biggio	.50
291	Joaquin Benoit	.25
292	Ken Caminiti	.25
293	Sean Burroughs	.25
294	Eric Karros	.50
295	Eric Chavez	.50
296	LaTroy Hawkins	.25
297	Alfonso Soriano	1.00
298	John Smoltz	.50
299	Adam Dunn	1.00
300	Ryan Dempster	.25
301	Travis Hafner	.50
302	Russell Branyan	.25
303	Dustin Hermanson	.25
304	Jim Thome	1.50
305	Carlos Beltran	.75
306	Jason Botts RC	.25
307	David Cone	.25
308	Ivanon Coffie	.25
309	Brian Jordan	.25
310	Todd Walker	.25
311	Jeromy Burnitz	.25
312	Tony Armas	.25
313	Jeff Conine	.25
314	Jeff Conine	.25
315	Todd Jones	.25
316	Roy Oswalt	.50
317	Aubrey Huff	.25
318	Josh Fogg	.25
319	Jose Vidro	.25
320	Jace Brewer	.25
321	Mike Redmond	.25
322	Noochie Varner RC	1.00
323	Russ Ortiz	.25
324	Edgardo Alfonzo	.25
325	Ruben Sierra	.25
326	Calvin Murray	.25
327	Marlon Anderson	.25
328	Albie Lopez	.25
329	Chris Gomez	.25
330	Fernando Tatis	.25
331	Stubby Clapp	.25
332	Rickey Henderson	.75
333	Brad Radke	.25
334	Brent Mayne	.25
335	Cory Lidle	.25
336	Edgar Martinez	.50
337	Aaron Boone	.25
338	Jay Witasick	.25
339	Benito Santiago	.25
340	Jose Mercedes	.25
341	Fernando Vina	.25
342	A.J. Pierzynski	.25
343	Jeff Bagwell	1.00
344	Brian Bohanon	.25
345	Adrian Beltre	.50
346	Troy Percival	.25
347	Napoleon Calzado RC	.75
348	Ruben Rivera	.25
349	Rafael Soriano	.25
350	Damian Jackson	.25
351	Joe Randa	.25
352	Chan Ho Park	.25
353	Dante Bichette	.25
354	Bartolo Colon	.25
355	Jason Bay RC	5.00
356	Shea Hillenbrand	.25
357	Matt Morris	.50
358	Brad Penny	.25
359	Mark Quinn	.25
360	Marquis Grissom	.25
361	Henry Blanco	.25
362	Billy Koch	.25
363	Mike Cameron	.25
364	Albert Pujols	10.00
365	Paul Konerko	.50
366	Eric Milton	.25
367	Nick Bierbrodt	.25
368	Rafael Palmeiro	5.00
369	Jorge Padilla RC	4.00
370	Jason Giambi	4.00
371	Mike Piazza	10.00
372	Alex Cora	3.00
373	Todd Helton	6.00
374	Juan Gonzalez	6.00
375	Mariano Rivera	4.00
376	Jason LaRue	3.00
377	Tony Gwynn	6.00
378	Wilson Betemit	3.00
379	J.J. Trujillo RC	3.00
380	Brad Ausmus	3.00
381	Chris George	3.00
382	Jose Canseco	5.00
383	Ramon Ortiz	3.00
384	John Rocker	3.00
385	Rey Ordonez	3.00
386	Ken Griffey Jr.	10.00
387	Juan Pena	3.00
388	Michael Barrett	3.00
389	J.D. Drew	4.00
390	Corey Koskie	3.00
391	Vernon Wells	3.00
392	Juan Tolentino RC	3.00
393	Luis Gonzalez	3.00
394	Terrance Long	3.00
395	Travis Lee	3.00
396	Earl Snyder RC	3.00
397	Nomar Garciaparra	10.00
398	Jason Schmidt	4.00
399	David Espinosa	3.00
400	Steve Green	3.00
401	Jack Wilson	3.00
402	Chris Tritle RC	3.00
403	Angel Berroa	3.00
404	Josh Towers	3.00
405	Andruw Jones	4.00
406	Brent Butler	3.00
407	Craig Kuzmic RC	3.00
408	Derek Bell	3.00
409	Eric Glaser RC	3.00
410	Joel Pineiro	3.00
411	Alexis Gomez	3.00
412	Mike Rivera	3.00
413	Shawn Estes	3.00
414	Milton Bradley	3.00
415	Carl Everett	3.00
416	Kazuhiro Sasaki	3.00
417	Tony Fontana RC	3.00
418	Josh Pearce	3.00
419	Gary Matthews Jr.	3.00
420	Raymond Cabrera RC	3.00
421	Joe Kennedy	3.00
422	Jason Maule RC	3.00
423	Casey Fossum	3.00
424	Christian Parker	3.00
425	Laynce Nix RC	5.00
426	Byung-Hyun Kim	3.00
427	Freddy Garcia	3.00
428	Herbert Perry	3.00
429	Jason Marquis	3.00
430	Sandy Alomar Jr.	3.00
431	Roberto Alomar	5.00
432	Tsuyoshi Shinjo	3.00
433	Tim Wakefield	3.00
434	Robert Fick	3.00
435	Vladimir Guerrero	6.00
436	Jose Mesa	3.00
437	Scott Spiezio	3.00
438	Jose Hernandez	3.00
439	Jose Acevedo	3.00
440	Brian West RC	3.00
441	Barry Zito	4.00
442	Luis Maza	3.00
443	Marlon Byrd	4.00
444	A.J. Burnett	3.00
445	Dee Brown	3.00
446	Carlos Delgado	5.00

Chrome

Stars (1-100): 6-10X
RC's: 3-6X
Production 553 Sets

Classic Renditions

	NM/M
Complete Set (10):	10.00
Common Player:	.50

Inserted 1:12

CR-1	Kerry Wood	2.00
CR-2	Brian Giles	1.00
CR-3	Roger Cedeno	.50
CR-4	Jason Giambi	1.50
CR-5	Albert Pujols	4.00
CR-6	Mark Buehrle	.50
CR-7	Cristian Guzman	.50
CR-8	Jimmy Rollins	.50
CR-9	Jim Thome	2.00
CR-10	Shawn Green	1.00

Classic Renditions Autographs

Production 25 Sets

Clubhouse Collection

	NM/M
Common Player:	15.00

Jersey 1:332
Bat 1:498

RA	Rich Aurilia/Bat	15.00
YB	Yogi Berra/Jsy	40.00
BB	Barry Bonds/Bat	60.00
AD	Alvin Dark/Bat	25.00
NG	Nomar Garciaparra/Bat	50.00
GK	George Kell/Jsy	25.00
GM	Greg Maddux/Jsy	30.00
EM	Eddie Mathews/Jsy	35.00
WM	Willie Mays/Bat	75.00
CP	Corey Patterson/bat	20.00
JP	Jorge Posada/Bat	25.00
HS	Hank Sauer/Bat	20.00

Clubhouse Collection Autograph Relics

No Pricing
Production 25 Sets

Clubhouse Collection Dual Relics

	NM/M

Production 53 Sets

SM	Eddie Mathews, Greg Maddux	150.00
BP	Yogi Berra, Jorge Posada	125.00
SP	Hank Sauer, Corey Patterson	75.00
KR	George Kell, Nomar Garciaparra	100.00
DA	Alvin Dark, Rich Aurilia	100.00
MB	Willie Mays, Barry Bonds	200.00

Grandstand Glory Stadium Seat

	NM/M
Common Player:	10.00

Inserted 1:133

| RC | Roy Campanella | 25.00 |
| BF | Bob Feller | 20.00 |

New Age Performers

	NM/M
Complete Set (15):	30.00
Common Player:	1.00

Inserted 1:15

NA-1	Luis Gonzalez	1.00
NA-2	Mark McGwire	5.00
NA-3	Barry Bonds	5.00
NA-4	Ken Griffey Jr.	3.00
NA-5	Ichiro Suzuki	3.00
NA-6	Sammy Sosa	3.00
NA-7	Andruw Jones	1.00
NA-8	Derek Jeter	5.00
NA-9	Todd Helton	1.50
NA-10	Alex Rodriguez	4.00
NA-11	Jason Giambi	1.50
NA-12	Bret Boone	1.00
NA-13	Roberto Alomar	1.00
NA-14	Albert Pujols	4.00
NA-15	Vladimir Guerrero	1.50

Real One Autographs

	NM/M
Common Autograph:	20.00

Inserted 1:180
Red Ink: .75-1.5X
Production 53

YB	Yogi Berra	100.00
JB	Joe Black	50.00
RB	Ray Boone	60.00
AC	Andy Carey	40.00
RCL	Roger Clemens	125.00
AD	Alvin Dark	60.00
DD	Dom DiMaggio	80.00
JE	Jim Edmonds	50.00
RF	Roy Face	60.00
BF	Bob Feller	60.00
WF	Whitey Ford	80.00
CG	Brian Giles	25.00
CG	Cristian Guzman	20.00
MI	Monte Irvin	60.00
GK	George Kell	60.00
WM	Willie Mays	200.00
GM	Gil McDougald	75.00
OM	Orestes Minoso	60.00
JP	John Podres	60.00
PR	Phil Rizzuto	80.00
ARO	Alex Rodriguez	140.00
PRO	Preacher Roe	60.00
AR	Al Rosen	75.00
ASC	Al Schoendienst	50.00
BS	Bobby Shantz	50.00
ES	Enos Slaughter	80.00
WS	Warren Spahn	100.00
HW	Hoyt Wilhelm	60.00
WF	Whitey Ford	20.00
TK	Ted Kluszewski	20.00
BM	Billy Martin	25.00
HN	Hal Newhouser	15.00
SP	Satchel Paige	40.00
BP	Billy Pierce	15.00
HS	Hank Sauer	10.00
BS	Bobby Shantz	15.00
WS	Warren Spahn	20.00
EW	Early Wynn	15.00

Real One Autographs Red Ink

Red Ink: .75-1.5X
Production 53 Sets

Team Topps Legends Autographs

	NM/M

Inserted 1:613

Vida Blue	20.00
Frank Howard	30.00
Mickey Lolich	25.00
Frank Robinson	40.00
Bobby Thomson	30.00

Then and Now

	NM/M
Complete Set (10):	15.00
Common Player:	1.00

Inserted 1:15

TN-1	Ed Mathews, Barry Bonds	4.00
TN-2	Al Rosen, Alex Rodriguez	4.00
TN-3	Carl Furillo, Larry Walker	1.00
TN-4	Mickey Vernon, Ichiro Suzuki	3.00
TN-5	Roy Campanella, Sammy Sosa	3.00
TN-6	Al Rosen, Bret Boone	1.00
TN-7	Warren Spahn, Randy Johnson	2.00
TN-8	Ed Lopat, Freddy Garcia	1.00
TN-9	Robin Roberts, Randy Johnson	2.00
TN-10	Billy Pierce, Hideo Nomo	1.50

2002 Topps Opening Day

	NM/M
Complete Set (165):	40.00
Common Player:	.10
Pack (7):	1.00
Box (36):	30.00

#	Player	Price
1	Roy Oswalt	.25
2	Derek Jeter	2.00
3	Dmitri Young	.10
4	Ramon Hernandez	.10
5	Albert Pujols	1.50
6	Sean Casey	.25
7	Joe Randa	.10
8	Craig Counsell	.10
9	John Olerud	.25
10	Troy Glaus	.40
11	Adam Kennedy	.10
12	Carlos Delgado	.40
13	Bobby Abreu	.10
14	J.T. Snow Jr.	.10
15	Ivan Rodriguez	.50
16	Mike Lowell	.10
17	Juan Pierre	.10
18	Magglio Ordonez	.30
19	Greg Maddux	1.00
20	Jorge Posada	.25
21	Johnny Damon	.25
22	Mike Hampton	.10
23	Paul LoDuca	.10
24	Terrence Long	.10
25	Jeff Bagwell	.50
26	Shannon Stewart	.10
27	Brad Radke	.10
28	Brian Jordan	.10
29	Lee Stevens	.10
30	Cliff Floyd	.10
31	Roger Clemens	1.00
32	Mike Matheny	.10
33	Alfonso Soriano	.50
34	Randy Johnson	.75
35	Mike Sweeney	.10
36	Jose Cruz Jr.	.20
37	Fernando Tatis	.10
38	Eric Young	.10
39	Ruben Rivera	.10
40	Mike Mussina	.50
41	Alex Gonzalez	.10
42	Edgardo Alfonzo	.10
43	Torii Hunter	.25
44	Richie Sexson	.25
45	Bret Boone	.25
46	John Smoltz	.10
47	Bengie Molina	.10
48	Trot Nixon	.10
49	Mike Cameron	.10
50	Mariano Rivera	.20
51	Ichiro Suzuki	1.50
52	Cristian Guzman	.10
53	Andruw Jones	.40
54	Jerry Hairston Jr.	.10
55	Brad Fullmer	.10
56	Luis Gonzalez	.25
57	Placido Polanco	.10
58	Jason Tyner	.10
59	Dan Wilson	.10
60	Jim Edmonds	.25
61	Larry Walker	.25
62	Edgar Renteria	.10
63	Orlando Cabrera	.10
64	Sammy Sosa	1.50
65	Derrek Lee	.20
66	C.C. Sabathia	.20
67	Aaron Boone	.10
68	Royce Clayton	.10
69	Darryl Kile	.10
70	Vladimir Guerrero	.75
71	Bud Smith	.10
72	Adrian Beltre	.25
73	Barry Bonds	15.00
74	Ben Petrick	.10
75	Derek Bell	.10
76	Jeff Kent	.20
77	Ricky Gutierrez	.10
78	Rafael Palmeiro	.50
79	Doug Mientkiewicz	.10
80	Fernando Vina	.10
81	Mark Mulder	.25
82	Carlos Beltran	.25
83	Juan Encarnacion	.10
84	Jimmy Rollins	.25
85	Pedro J. Martinez	.50
86	Aramis Ramirez	.10
87	Reggie Sanders	.10
88	Gary Sheffield	.25
89	Bartolo Colon	.10
90	Jose Macias	.10
91	Bobby Higginson	.10
92	Craig Biggio	.20
93	Al Leiter	.20
94	Juan Gonzalez	.50
95	Jose Valentin	.10
96	Jon Lieber	.10
97	Alex Gonzalez	.10
98	Jose Mesa	.10
99	Sandy Alomar	.10
100	Barry Bonds	2.00
101	Todd Walker	.10
102	Kevin Young	.10
103	Ken Griffey Jr.	1.00
104	Mark McGwire	2.00
105	Jason Giambi	.50
106	Todd Helton	.50
107	Mike Piazza	1.00
108	Nomar Garciaparra	1.50
109	Bernie Williams	.40
110	Shawn Wooten	.10
111	Eric Chavez	.20
112	Curt Schilling	.25
113	Roberto Alomar	.50
114	Chipper Jones	.75
115	Edgar Martinez	.25
116	Shawn Green	.25
117	Ben Grieve	.10
118	Jermaine Dye	.10
119	Steve Finley	.10
120	Adam Dunn	.25
121	Preston Wilson	.10
122	Lance Berkman	.25
123	Ben Sheets	.10
124	Ryan Klesko	.20
125	Brian Giles	.20
126	Marcus Giles	.10
127	Craig Wilson	.10
128	Miguel Tejada	.25
129	Andres Galarraga	.20
130	Alex Rodriguez	1.50
131	David Justice	.20
132	Barry Zito	.25
133	Scott Rolen	.75
134	Brent Abernathy	.10
135	Raul Mondesi	.20
136	Josh Towers	.10
137	Rafael Furcal	.25
138	Gabe Kapler	.10
139	Fred McGriff	.25
140	Jeff Conine	.10
141	Mike Lieberthal	.10
142	Frank Thomas	.75
143	Jason Kendall	.10
144	Toby Hall	.10
145	Pat Burrell	.30
146	J.D. Drew	.25
147	Javier Lopez	.10
148	Carlos Lee	.20
149	Doug Glanville	.10
150	Ruben Sierra	.10
151	Julio Franco	.10
152	Tim Hudson	.25
153	Rich Aurilia	.10
154	Geoff Jenkins	.10
155	Tsuyoshi Shinjo	.20
156	Moises Alou	.20
157	Jim Thome	.75
158	Steve Cox	.10
159	Kevin Brown	.25

#	Player	Price
160	Barry Bonds	.50
161	Rickey Henderson	.20
162	Bud Smith	.10
163	Rickey Henderson	.20
164	Barry Bonds	.50
165	Checklist	.10

Autographs

		NM/M
	Common Auto.:	10.00
GJ	Geoff Jenkins	15.00
NJ	Nick Johnson	10.00
BS	Ben Sheets	25.00

2002 Topps Pristine

SAMMY SOSA CHICAGO CUBS

		NM/M
Complete Set (210):		
Common Player:		.75
Common Uncommon RC:		3.00
Production 1,999		
Common Rare RC:		5.00
Production 799		
Pack (8):		30.00
Box (5):		125.00
1	Alex Rodriguez	5.00
2	Carlos Delgado	1.50
3	Jimmy Rollins	.75
4	Jason Kendall	.75
5	John Olerud	1.00
6	Albert Pujols	5.00
7	Curt Schilling	2.00
8	Gary Sheffield	1.00
9	Johnny Damon	1.00
10	Ichiro Suzuki	4.00
11	Pat Burrell	1.00
12	Garret Anderson	1.00
13	Andruw Jones	1.50
14	Kerry Wood	2.00
15	Kenny Lofton	1.00
16	Adam Dunn	1.50
17	Juan Pierre	.75
18	Josh Beckett	1.00
19	Roy Oswalt	1.00
20	Derek Jeter	6.00
21	Jose Vidro	.75
22	Richie Sexson	1.50
23	Mike Sweeney	.75
24	Jeff Kent	1.00
25	Jason Giambi	1.50
26	Bret Boone	1.00
27	J.D. Drew	1.00
28	Shannon Stewart	.75
29	Miguel Tejada	1.00
30	Barry Bonds	6.00
31	Randy Johnson	2.00
32	Pedro J. Martinez	2.00
33	Magglio Ordonez	1.00
34	Todd Helton	1.50
35	Craig Biggio	1.00
36	Shawn Green	1.00
37	Vladimir Guerrero	2.00
38	Mo Vaughn	1.00
39	Alfonso Soriano	2.00
40	Barry Zito	1.00
41	Aramis Ramirez	1.00
42	Ryan Klesko	1.00
43	Ruben Sierra	.75
44	Tino Martinez	.75
45	Toby Hall	.75
46	Ivan Rodriguez	1.50
47	Raul Mondesi	.75
48	Carlos Pena	.75
49	Darin Erstad	1.00
50	Sammy Sosa	4.00
51	Bartolo Colon	1.00
52	Robert Fick	.75
53	Cliff Floyd	.75
54	Brian Jordan	.75
55	Torii Hunter	1.00
56	Roberto Alomar	1.00
57	Roger Clemens	4.00
58	Mark Mulder	1.00
59	Brian Giles	1.00
60	Mike Piazza	4.00
61	Rich Aurilia	.75
62	Freddy Garcia	.75
63	Jim Edmonds	1.50
64	Eric Hinske	.75
65	Jeremy Giambi	.75
66	Javier Vazquez	.75
67	Cristian Guzman	.75
68	Paul LoDuca	.75
69	Bobby Abreu	1.00
70	Nomar Garciaparra	4.00
71	Troy Glaus	1.00
72	Chipper Jones	2.00
73	Scott Rolen	2.00
74	Lance Berkman	1.00
75	C.C. Sabathia	.75
76	Bernie Williams	1.00
77	Rafael Palmeiro	1.50
78	Phil Nevin	.75
79	Kazuhiro Sasaki	.75
80	Eric Chavez	1.00
81	Jorge Posada	1.00
82	Edgardo Alfonzo	.75
83	Geoff Jenkins	.75
84	Preston Wilson	.75
85	Jim Thome	2.00
86	Frank Thomas	1.50
87	Jeff Bagwell	1.50
88	Greg Maddux	3.00
89	Mark Prior	3.00
90	Larry Walker	1.00
91	Luis Gonzalez	1.00
92	Tim Hudson	1.00
93	Tsuyoshi Shinjo	.75
94	Juan Gonzalez	1.50
95	Shea Hillenbrand	.75
96	Paul Konerko	.75
97	Tom Glavine	1.50
98	Marty Cordova	1.00
99	Moises Alou	1.00
100	Ken Griffey Jr.	4.00
101	Hank Blalock	1.50
102	Matt Morris	1.00
103	Robb Nen	.75
104	Mike Cameron	.75
105	Mark Buehrle	.75
106	Sean Burroughs	.75
107	Orlando Cabrera	.75
108	Jeromy Burnitz	.75
109	Juan Uribe	.75
110	Eric Milton	.75
111	Carlos Lee	.75
112	Jose Mesa	.75
113	Morgan Ensberg	.75
114	Mike Rivera	.75
115	Juan Cruz	.75
116	Mike Lieberthal	.75
117	Armando Benitez	.75
118	Vinny Castilla	.75
119	Russ Ortiz	.75
120	Mike Lowell	1.00
121	Corey Patterson	1.00
122	Mike Mussina	1.50
123	Rafael Furcal	.75
124	Mark Grace	1.50
125	Ben Sheets	1.00
126	John Smoltz	1.00
127	Fred McGriff	1.00
128	Nick Johnson	.75
129	J.T. Snow	.75
130	Jeff Cirillo	.75
131	Trevor Hoffman	.75
132	Kevin Brown	1.00
133	Mariano Rivera	1.50
134	Marlon Anderson	.75
135	Al Leiter	.75
136	Doug Mientkiewicz	.75
137	Eric Karros	.75
138	Bobby Higginson	.75
139	Sean Casey	1.00
140	Troy Percival	.75
141	Willie Mays	5.00
142	Carl Yastrzemski	3.00
143	Stan Musial	4.00
144	Harmon Killebrew	3.00
145	Mike Schmidt	5.00
146	Duke Snider	2.00
147	Brooks Robinson	3.00
148	Frank Robinson	2.00
149	Nolan Ryan	8.00
150	Reggie Jackson	3.00
151	Joe Mauer/C RC	20.00
152	Joe Mauer/U RC	25.00
153	Joe Mauer/R RC	35.00
154	Colt Griffin/C	3.00
155	Colt Griffin/U	5.00
156	Colt Griffin/U	8.00
157	Jason Simontacchi/C RC	2.00
158	Jason Simontacchi/U RC	3.00
159	Jason Simontacchi/R RC	5.00
160	Casey Kotchman/C	5.00
161	Casey Kotchman/U	8.00
162	Casey Kotchman/R	15.00
163	Greg Sain/C RC	1.50
164	Greg Sain/U RC	3.00
165	Greg Sain/R RC	5.00
166	David Wright/C	40.00
167	David Wright/U	50.00
168	David Wright/R	60.00
169	Scott Hairston/C	4.00
170	Scott Hairston/U	6.00
171	Scott Hairston/R	8.00
172	Rolando Viera/C RC	1.50
173	Rolando Viera/U RC	3.00
174	Rolando Viera/R RC	5.00
175	Tyrell Godwin/C	1.50
176	Tyrell Godwin/U	3.00
177	Tyrell Godwin/R	5.00
178	Jesus Cota/C RC	1.50
179	Jesus Cota/U RC	3.00
180	Jesus Cota/R RC	5.00
181	Dan Johnson/C RC	5.00
182	Dan Johnson/U RC	10.00
183	Dan Johnson/R RC	15.00
184	Mario Ramos/C	1.50
185	Mario Ramos/U	3.00
186	Mario Ramos/R	5.00
187	Jason Dubois/C RC	4.00
188	Jason Dubois/U RC	6.00
189	Jason Dubois/R RC	10.00
190	Jonny Gomes/C RC	8.00
191	Jonny Gomes/U RC	15.00
192	Jonny Gomes/R RC	20.00
193	Chris Snelling/C RC	2.00
194	Chris Snelling/U RC	4.00
195	Chris Snelling/R RC	6.00
196	Hansel Izquierdo/C RC	2.00
197	Hansel Izquierdo/U RC	4.00
198	Hansel Izquierdo/R RC	6.00
199	So Taguchi/C RC	3.00
200	So Taguchi/U RC	4.00
201	So Taguchi/R RC	6.00
202	Kazuhisa Ishii/C RC	3.00
203	Kazuhisa Ishii/U RC	5.00
204	Kazuhisa Ishii/R RC	8.00
205	Jorge Padilla/C RC	1.50
206	Jorge Padilla/U RC	3.00
207	Jorge Padilla/R RC	5.00
208	Earl Snyder/C RC	2.00
209	Earl Snyder/U RC	4.00
210	Earl Snyder/R RC	6.00

Refractors

JAVIER VAZQUEZ MONTREAL EXPOS

Stars (1-150):	2-4X
Production 149	
Common Rookies:	.75-1.5X
Production 1,999	
Uncommon Rookies:	1-2X
Production 799	
Rare Rookies:	2-3X
Production 149	
Gold Refractors (1-150):	3-5X
Gold Common RC's:	4-8X
Gold Uncommon RC's:	2-4X
Gold Rare RC's:	1-2X
Production 70 Sets	

All Refractors are Uncirculated

Fall Memories

FALL MEMORIES — LUIS GONZALEZ, ARIZONA DIAMONDBACKS

		NM/M
Common Player:		5.00
Varying quantities produced		
JB	Johnny Bench	15.00
BB	Barry Bonds	30.00
GB	George Brett	25.00
TG	Tom Glavine	5.00
LG	Luis Gonzalez	5.00
MG	Mark Grace	12.00
SG	Shawn Green	6.00
TH	Todd Helton	8.00
RJ	Reggie Jackson	15.00
AJ	Andruw Jones	8.00
CP	Chipper Jones	10.00
TM	Tino Martinez	8.00
WM	Willie Mays	40.00
EM	Eddie Murray	15.00
JP	Jorge Posada	8.00
KP	Kirby Puckett	15.00
CS	Curt Schilling	8.00
GS	Gary Sheffield	5.00
AS	Alfonso Soriano	10.00
BW	Bernie Williams	8.00

In The Gap

IN THE GAP — BERNIE WILLIAMS

		NM/M
Common Player:		5.00
Varying quantities produced		
RA	Roberto Alomar	10.00
LB	Lance Berkman	8.00
WBE	Wilson Betemit	5.00
WB	Wade Boggs	8.00
BBO	Barry Bonds	25.00
BB	Bret Boone	6.00
EC	Eric Chavez	8.00
CD	Carlos Delgado	6.00
AD	Adam Dunn	10.00
JE	Jim Edmonds	8.00
DE	Darin Erstad	5.00
NG	Nomar Garciaparra	15.00
TG	Tony Gwynn	15.00
TH	Todd Helton	8.00
RH	Rickey Henderson	10.00
AJ	Andruw Jones	8.00
JK	Jeff Kent	8.00
RK	Ryan Klesko	8.00
PL	Paul LoDuca	10.00
RP	Rafael Palmeiro	10.00
MP	Mike Piazza	15.00
AP	Albert Pujols	15.00
ARA	Aramis Ramirez	8.00
AR	Alex Rodriguez	15.00
IR	Ivan Rodriguez	8.00
TS	Tsuyoshi Shinjo	8.00
AS	Alfonso Soriano	10.00
LW	Larry Walker	8.00
BW	Bernie Williams	15.00
PW	Preston Wilson	5.00

Patches

No Pricing
Production 25 Sets

Personal Endorsements

		NM/M
Common Autograph:		8.00
Inserted 1:Box		
RA	Roberto Alomar	30.00
KB	Kenny Baugh	8.00
LB	Lance Berkman	30.00
BB	Barry Bonds	180.00
DB	Dewon Brazelton	15.00
JD	Johnny Damon	30.00
GF	Gavin Floyd	25.00
CG	Cristian Guzman	10.00
IG	Irvin Guzman	10.00
OH	Orlando Hudson	10.00
KI	Kazuhisa Ishii	30.00
CK	Casey Kotchman	20.00
JL	Jason Lane	8.00
CW	Corwin Malone	8.00
NN	Nick Neugebauer	8.00
AP	Albert Pujols	125.00
JR	Jimmy Rollins	20.00
BS	Ben Sheets	20.00
JS	Juan Silvestre	8.00
ST	So Taguchi	15.00
MT	Marcus Thames	8.00

Popular Demand

POPULAR DEMAND — jeff bagwell

		NM/M
Common Player:		5.00
Varying quantities produced		
RA	Roberto Alomar	10.00
JB	Jeff Bagwell	10.00
WB	Wade Boggs	8.00
BBO	Barry Bonds	25.00
BB	Bret Boone	5.00
CD	Carlos Delgado	5.00
AD	Adam Dunn	8.00
NG	Nomar Garciaparra	15.00
SG	Shawn Green	5.00
TG	Tony Gwynn	12.00
TH	Todd Helton	5.00
CJ	Chipper Jones	12.00
DM	Don Mattingly	35.00
MP	Mike Piazza	15.00
AP	Albert Pujols	20.00
AR	Alex Rodriguez	15.00
IR	Ivan Rodriguez	8.00
CS	Curt Schilling	5.00
FT	Frank Thomas	10.00
LW	Larry Walker	5.00

Portions

PRINCIPAL PORTIONS — BRET BOONE, SECOND BASE, SEATTLE MARINERS

		NM/M
Common Player:		5.00
Varying quantities produced		
RA	Roberto Alomar	10.00
JB	Jeff Bagwell	10.00
LB	Lance Berkman	10.00
CB	Craig Biggio	8.00
BBO	Barry Bonds	20.00
BB	Bret Boone	5.00
CD	Carlos Delgado	5.00
RD	Ryan Dempster	5.00
AD	Adam Dunn	8.00
CF	Cliff Floyd	5.00
RF	Rafael Furcal	5.00
NG	Nomar Garciaparra	15.00
CG	Cristian Guzman	5.00
TH	Todd Helton	8.00
NJ	Nick Johnson	5.00
LD	Paul LoDuca	5.00
GM	Greg Maddux	10.00
EM	Edgar Martinez	5.00
MM	Mike Mussina	10.00
MO	Magglio Ordonez	5.00
RP	Rafael Palmeiro	8.00
MP	Mike Piazza	15.00
JP	Jorge Posada	8.00
AP	Albert Pujols	15.00
AR	Alex Rodriguez	15.00
IR	Ivan Rodriguez	8.00
NR	Nolan Ryan	30.00
KS	Kazuhiro Sasaki	5.00

2002 Topps Reserve

KEARNS — REDS

		NM/M
Complete Set (150):		120.00
Common Player:		.25
Common (136-150):		4.00
Production 999		
Silver parallel (1-135):		4-8X
Silver (136-150):		.75-1.5X
Production 150		
Box:10 Packs & 1 Auto.		
Helmet:		100.00
1	Alex Rodriguez	2.50
2	Tsuyoshi Shinjo	.25
3	Craig Biggio	.40
4	Troy Glaus	.50
5	Mike Rivera	.25
6	Curt Schilling	.50
7	Garret Anderson	.50
8	Ben Sheets	.50
9	Todd Helton	.75
10	Paul Konerko	.50
11	Sammy Sosa	2.00
12	Bud Smith	.25
13	Jeff Bagwell	.75
14	Albert Pujols	2.00
15	Jose Vidro	.50
16	Carlos Delgado	.50
17	Torii Hunter	.50
18	Jerry Hairston Jr.	.25
19	Troy Percival	.25
20	Vladimir Guerrero	1.00
21	Geoff Jenkins	.40
22	Carlos Pena	.25
23	Juan Gonzalez	.75
24	Raul Mondesi	.25
25	Jimmy Rollins	.40
26	Mariano Rivera	.50
27	Jorge Posada	.50
28	Magglio Ordonez	.50
29	Roberto Alomar	.50
30	Randy Johnson	1.00
31	Xavier Nady	.25
32	Terrence Long	.25
33	Chipper Jones	1.00
34	Rich Aurilia	.25
35	Aramis Ramirez	.25
36	Jim Thome	1.00
37	Bret Boone	.50
38	Angel Berroa	.25
39	Jeff Conine	.25
40	Cliff Floyd	.25
41	Pedro J. Martinez	1.00
42	J.D. Drew	.50
43	Kazuhiro Sasaki	.25
44	Jon Rauch	.25
45	Orlando Hudson	.25
46	Scott Rolen	1.00
47	Rafael Furcal	.25
48	Brad Penny	.25
49	Miguel Tejada	.50
50	Orlando Cabrera	.25
51	Bobby Abreu	.50
52	Darin Erstad	.25
53	Edgar Martinez	.40
54	Ben Grieve	.25
55	Shawn Green	.50
56	Ivan Rodriguez	.75
57	Josh Beckett	.25
58	Ray Durham	.25
59	Jason Hart	.25
60	Nathan Haynes	.25
61	Jason Giambi	.75
62	Eric Chavez	.50
63	Matt Morris	.40
64	Lance Berkman	.50
65	Jeff Kent	.40
66	Andruw Jones	.50
67	Brian Giles	.50
68	Morgan Ensberg	.25
69	Pat Burrell	.50
70	Ken Griffey Jr.	2.00
71	Carlos Beltran	.50
72	Ichiro Suzuki	2.00
73	Larry Walker	.50
74	J.J. Putz RC	.50
75	Mike Piazza	2.00
76	Rafael Palmeiro	.75
77	Mark Prior	2.00
78	Toby Hall	.25
79	Pokey Reese	.25
80	Mike Mussina	.50
81	Omar Vizquel	.25
82	Shannon Stewart	.25
83	Jeromy Burnitz	.25
84	Bernie Williams	.50
85	C.C. Sabathia	.25
86	Mike Hampton	.25
87	Kevin Brown	.50
88	Juan Cruz	.25
89	Jeff Weaver	.25
90	Jason Lane	.25
91	Adam Dunn	.75
92	Jose Cruz Jr.	.25
93	Marlon Anderson	.25
94	Jeff Cirillo	.25
95	Mark Buehrle	.25
96	Austin Kearns	.50
97	Tim Hudson	.50
98	Brian Jordan	.25
99	Phil Nevin	.25
100	Barry Bonds	3.00
101	Derek Jeter	3.00
102	Javier Vazquez	.25
103	Jason Kendall	.40
104	Jim Edmonds	.50
105	Kenny Kelly	.25
106	Juan Pena	.25
107	Mark Grace	.50
108	Roger Clemens	2.00
109	Barry Zito	.50
110	Greg Vaughn	.25
111	Greg Maddux	1.50
112	Richie Sexson	.50
113	Jermaine Dye	.25
114	Kerry Wood	1.00
115	Matt Lawton	.25
116	Sean Casey	.25
117	Gary Sheffield	.50
118	Preston Wilson	.25
119	Cristian Guzman	.25
120	Mike Sweeney	.25
121	Neifi Perez	.25
122	Paul LoDuca	.50
123	Luis Gonzalez	.50
124	Ryan Klesko	.25
125	Alfonso Soriano	1.00
126	Bobby Higginson	.25
127	Juan Pierre	.25
128	Moises Alou	.50
129	Roy Oswalt	.50
130	Nomar Garciaparra	2.00
131	Fred McGriff	.40
132	Edgardo Alfonzo	.25
133	Johnny Damon	.40
134	Dewon Brazelton	.25
135	Mark Mulder	.50
136	So Taguchi RC	.50
137	Mario Ramos	4.00
138	Dan Johnson RC	15.00
139	Hansel Izquierdo RC	8.00
140	Kazuhisa Ishii RC	10.00
141	Jon Switzer	
142	Chris Tritle RC	6.00
143	Chris Snelling RC	8.00
144	Chone Figgins RC	8.00
145	Dan Phillips RC	4.00
146	John Rodriguez RC	4.00
147	Colt Griffin	8.00
148	Jonny Gomes RC	15.00
149	Josh Barfield	10.00
150	Joe Mauer RC	30.00

Silver

Stars (1-135):	4-8X
SP's (136-150):	.75-1.5X

Autographed Mini-Helmets

		NM/M
Common Helmet:		20.00
1:Box		
Gold Ink Autographs:		No Pricing
Production 25		
	Roberto Alomar	45.00
	Moises Alou	25.00
	Lance Berkman	35.00

Bret Boone	25.00
Eric Chavez	30.00
Adam Dunn	40.00
Cliff Floyd	20.00
Troy Glaus	40.00
Luis Gonzalez	30.00
Todd Helton	50.00
Magglio Ordonez	25.00
Rafael Palmeiro	40.00
Albert Pujols	100.00
Alex Rodriguez	100.00
Scott Rolen	35.00
Jimmy Rollins	50.00
Alfonso Soriano	30.00
Barry Zito	30.00

Game-Used Baseball

NM/M
Inserted 1:1,761

I	Ichiro Suzuki	65.00

Game-Used Bat

NM/M
Common Player: 5.00
Inserted 1:12

RA	Roberto Alomar	10.00
JB	Jeff Bagwell	10.00
BB	Barry Bonds	20.00
CD	Carlos Delgado	8.00
JG	Juan Gonzalez	8.00
LG	Luis Gonzalez	5.00
TG	Tony Gwynn	12.00
RH	Rickey Henderson	10.00
CJ	Chipper Jones	10.00
AJ	Andruw Jones	8.00
TM	Tino Martinez	8.00
RP	Rafael Palmeiro	8.00
MB	Mike Piazza	15.00
AP	Albert Pujols	15.00
AR	Alex Rodriguez	12.00
IR	Ivan Rodriguez	8.00
TS	Tsuyoshi Shinjo	5.00
AS	Alfonso Soriano	8.00
FT	Frank Thomas	8.00
BW	Bernie Williams	8.00

Game-Worn Patch

No Pricing
Production 25 Sets

Game-Worn Uniform

NM/M
Common Player: 5.00
Inserted 1:5

BB	Barry Bonds	20.00
BBO	Bret Boone	5.00
DE	Darin Erstad	5.00
NG	Nomar Garciaparra	15.00
LG	Luis Gonzalez	5.00
TG	Tony Gwynn	10.00
TH	Todd Helton	8.00
RJ	Randy Johnson	8.00
AJ	Andruw Jones	6.00
CJ	Chipper Jones	10.00
GM	Greg Maddux	12.00
PM	Pedro Martinez	10.00
MM	Mark Mulder	5.00
MO	Magglio Ordonez	8.00
RP	Rafael Palmeiro	8.00
MP	Mike Piazza	12.00
AP	Albert Pujols	15.00
AR	Alex Rodriguez	12.00
IR	Ivan Rodriguez	8.00
SR	Scott Rolen	10.00
KS	Kazuhiro Sasaki	8.00
CS	Curt Schilling	8.00
FT	Frank Thomas	8.00
KW	Kerry Wood	10.00

2002 Topps Super Teams

NM/M
Complete Set: 40.00
Common Player: .25
Pack (7): 3.50
Box (20): 60.00

1	Leo Durocher	.25
2	Whitey Lockman	.25
3	Alvin Dark	.25
4	Monte Irvin	.50
5	Willie Mays	2.50
6	Wes Westrum	.25
7	Johnny Antonelli	.25
8	Sal Maglie	.25
9	Dusty Rhodes	.25
10	Davey Williams	.25
11	Hoyt Wilhelm	.25
12	Don Mueller	.25
13	Dusty Rhodes	.25
14	Willie Mays, Monte Irvin, Dusty Rhodes	.75
15	Walt Alston	.25
16	Gil Hodges	.75
17	Jim Gilliam	.25
18	Pee Wee Reese	.50
19	Jackie Robinson	2.00
20	Duke Snider	1.00
21	Carl Furillo	.25
22	Roy Campanella	1.00
23	Don Newcombe	.25
24	Don Hoak	.25
25	Johnny Podres	.25
26	Clem Labine	.25
27	Johnny Podres	.25
28	Pee Wee Reese, Jackie Robinson, Duke Snider	1.00
29	Fred Haney	.25
30	Joe Adcock	.25
31	Frank Torre	.25
32	Red Schoendienst	.25
33	Johnny Logan	.25
34	Eddie Mathews	1.00
35	Hank Aaron	3.00
36	Andy Pafko	.25
37	Wes Covington	.25
38	Lew Burdette	.25
39	Warren Spahn	1.00
40	Del Crandall	.25
41	Lew Burdette	.25
42	Warren Spahn, Eddie Mathews, Hank Aaron	1.50
43	Danny Murtaugh	.25
44	Dick Stuart	.25
45	Bill Mazeroski	.25
46	Dick Groat	.25
47	Don Hoak	.25
48	Gino Cimoli	.25
49	Bill Virdon	.25
50	Roberto Clemente	2.50
51	Smoky Burgess	.25
52	Bob Friend	.25
53	Vernon Law	.25
54	Roy Face	.25
55	Bill Mazeroski	.25
56	Roberto Clemente,	
57	Bill Mazeroski, Dick Groat	1.00
58	Ralph Houk	.25
59	Bill "Moose" Skowron	.50
60	Bobby Richardson	.25
61	Tony Kubek	.25
62	Clete Boyer	.25
63	Yogi Berra	1.50
64	Bob Cerv	.25
65	Roger Maris	1.50
66	Elston Howard	.25
67	Whitey Ford	1.00
68	Ralph Terry	.25
69	Johnny Blanchard	.25
70	Whitey Ford	1.00
71	Yogi Berra, Roger Maris, Elston Howard, Bill "Moose" Skowron	1.00
72	Red Schoendienst	.25
73	Orlando Cepeda	.40
74	Julian Javier	.25
75	Dal Maxvill	.25
76	Mike Shannon	.25
77	Lou Brock	.75
78	Roger Maris	1.50
79	Curt Flood	.25
80	Tim McCarver	.25
81	Steve Carlton	.75
82	Bob Gibson	1.00
83	Nelson Briles	.25
84	Bobby Tolan	.25
85	Bob Gibson	1.00
86	Bob Gibson, Steve Carlton, Orlando Cepeda	.50
87	Lou Brock	.50
88	Gil Hodges	.25
89	Ed Kranepool	.25
90	Buddy Harrelson	.25
91	Wayne Garrett	.25
92	Tommie Agee	.25
93	Ron Swoboda	.25
94	Al Weis	.25
95	Jerry Grote	.25
96	Tom Seaver	1.00
97	Jerry Koosman	.25
98	Tug McGraw	.25
99	Nolan Ryan	3.00
100	Donn Clendenon	.25
101	Tom Seaver, Jerry Koosman, Tug McGraw, Nolan Ryan	1.00
102	Earl Weaver	.25
103	Boog Powell	.25
104	Davey Johnson	.25
105	Mark Belanger	.25
106	Brooks Robinson	1.00
107	Don Buford	.25
108	Paul Blair	.25
109	Frank Robinson	1.00
110	Dick Hall	.25
111	Jim Palmer	.75
112	Mike Cuellar	.25
113	Dave McNally	.25
114	Andy Etchebarren	.25
115	Brooks Robinson	1.00
116	Dick Hall, Jim Palmer, Mike Cuellar, Dave McNally	.40
117	Alvin Dark	.25
118	Gene Tenace	.25
119	Dick Green	.25
120	Bert Campaneris	.25
121	Sal Bando	.25
122	Reggie Jackson	1.00
123	Joe Rudi	.25
124	Claudell Washington	.25
125	Ray Fosse	.25
126	Vida Blue	.40
127	Rollie Fingers	.25
128	Jim "Catfish" Hunter	.50
129	Ken Holtzman	.25
130	Rollie Fingers	.25
131	Jim "Catfish" Hunter, Sal Bando, Reggie Jackson, Rollie Fingers	.50
132	Davey Johnson	.25
133	Keith Hernandez	.25
134	Wally Backman	.25
135	Rafael Santana	.25
136	Ray Knight	.25
137	Len Dykstra	.25
138	Darryl Strawberry	.25
139	Kevin Mitchell	.25
140	Dwight Gooden	.25
141	Bob Ojeda	.25
142	Sid Fernandez	.25
143	Ron Darling	.25
144	Gary Carter	.25
145	Ray Knight	.25
146	Darryl Strawberry, Dwight Gooden, Keith Hernandez	.25

Retrofractor

Cards (1-146): 2-4X
#'d to year team won World Series

Autographs

NM/M
Common Autograph: 10.00
Inserted 1:19

YB	Yogi Berra	60.00
VB	Vida Blue	15.00
CB	Clete Boyer	15.00
SC	Steve Carlton	25.00
MI	Monte Irvin	15.00
RJ	Reggie Jackson	50.00
TK	Tony Kubek	30.00
TM	Tug McGraw	15.00
AP	Andy Pafko	20.00
JP	Jim Palmer	25.00
JPO	Johnny Podres	15.00
BR	Bobby Richardson	15.00
BRO	Brooks Robinson	30.00
NR	Nolan Ryan	150.00
TS	Tom Seaver	40.00
MS	Bill "Moose" Skowron	20.00
WS	Warren Spahn	40.00
HW	Hoyt Wilhelm	15.00

A View To a Thrill Seat Relics

NM/M
Common Player: 10.00
Inserted 1:30

HA	Hank Aaron	20.00
YB	Yogi Berra	15.00
LB	Lew Burdette	10.00
RC	Roberto Clemente	50.00
WF	Whitey Ford	15.00
BG	Bob Gibson	15.00
RMB	Roger Maris/ Cardinals	20.00
RMY	Roger Maris/Yanks	40.00
EM	Eddie Mathews	15.00
WM	Willie Mays	30.00
BM	Bill Mazeroski	10.00
JP	Jim Palmer	10.00
BP	Boog Powell	10.00
BR	Brooks Robinson	15.00
FR	Frank Robinson	15.00
RS	Red Schoendienst	15.00
DS	Duke Snider	15.00
WS	Warren Spahn	15.00

A View To A Thrill Autograph Relics

NM/M
Produced listed

WFA	Whitey Ford/61	100.00
BGA	Bob Gibson/67	60.00
WMA	Willie Mays/54	150.00
DSA	Duke Snider/55	80.00
WSA	Warren Spahn/57	60.00

Classic Combos

NM/M
Common Card: 40.00
Inserted 1:865

AJ	Tommie Agee, Cleon Jones	40.00
JR	Reggie Jackson, Joe Rudi	40.00
RR	Brooks Robinson, Frank Robinson	50.00
SK	Tom Seaver, Jerry Koosman	50.00
SRBK	"Moose" Skowron, Bobby Richardson, Clete Boyer, Tony Kubek	80.00

Relics

NM/M
Common Player: 10.00

TA	Tommie Agee/Bat	20.00
SBB	Sal Bando/Bat	10.00
SBJ	Sal Bando/Jsy	10.00
MB	Mark Belanger/Bat	10.00
PB	Paul Blair/Bat	10.00
CB	Clete Boyer/Bat	10.00
LB	Lew Burdette/Jsy	15.00
SB	Smoky Burgess/Bat	10.00
BC	Bert Campaneris/Jsy	15.00
GC	Gary Carter/Jkt	20.00
GCB	Gary Carter/Jsy	15.00
GCJ	Gary Carter/Jsy	15.00
OC	Orlando Cepeda/Bat	15.00
BCE	Bob Cerv/Bat	10.00
GCI	Gino Cimoli/Bat	10.00
DC	Del Crandel/Bat	10.00
MC	Mike Cuellar/Jsy	10.00
RD	Ron Darling/Jsy	10.00
LD	Len Dykstra/Bat	15.00
RF	Ray Fosse/Bat	10.00
BF	Bob Friend/Jsy	10.00
WG	Wayne Garrett/Bat	10.00
DG	Dwight Gooden/Jsy	15.00
DH	Don Hoak/Bat	10.00
RH	Ralph Houk/Jsy	10.00
RJ	Reggie Jackson/Bat	35.00
DJ	Davey Johnson/Bat	10.00
CJ	Cleon Jones/Bat	20.00
RK	Ray Knight/Bat	10.00
JK	Jerry Koosman/Jsy	10.00
EK	Ed Kranepool/Jsy	15.00
TK	Tony Kubek/Bat	25.00
TM	Tug McGraw/Jsy	15.00
DM	Dave McNally/Jsy	10.00
KM	Kevin Mitchell/Bat	10.00
AP	Andy Pafko/Bat	10.00
BR	Bobby Richardson/ Bat	25.00
BRO	Brooks Robinson/ Bat	25.00
FR	Frank Robinson/Bat	20.00
JR	Joe Rudi/Bat	10.00
NR	Nolan Ryan/Bat	75.00
RS	Red Schoendienst/ Bat	10.00
TS	Tom Seaver/bat	20.00
MS	"Moose" Skowron/ Bat	20.00
DS	Darryl Strawberry/ Bat	20.00
CW	Claudell Washington/ Bat	10.00

Super Teammates

NM/M
Complete Set (5): 10.00
Common Card: 2.00
Inserted 1:10

ST-BG	Lou Brock, Bob Gibson	2.00
ST-FB	Whitey Ford, Yogi Berra	4.00
ST-MI	Willie Mays, Monte Irvin	4.00

ST-RR	Brooks Robinson, Frank Robinson	3.00
ST-SRBK	Bill "Moose" Skowron, Bobby Richardson, Clete Boyer, Tony Kubek	2.00

Super Teammates Autographs

NM/M
Production 50 Sets

BGA	Lou Brock, Bob Gibson	100.00
FBA	Whitey Ford, Yogi Berra	150.00
MIA	Willie Mays, Monte Irvin	180.00
RRA	Brooks Robinson, Frank Robinson	100.00
SRBKA	Bill "Moose" Skowron, Bobby Richardson, Clete Boyer, Tony Kubek	200.00

2002 Topps Ten

NM/M
Complete Set (200): 40.00
Common Player: .15
Pack (7): 2.00
Box (24): 40.00

1	Ichiro Suzuki	1.00
2	Rich Aurilia	.15
3	Bret Boone	.15
4	Juan Pierre	.15
5	Shannon Stewart	.15
6	Alex Rodriguez	1.00
7	Luis Gonzalez	.25
8	Todd Helton	.25
9	Garret Anderson	.25
10	Albert Pujols	1.00
11	Lance Berkman	.25
12	Todd Helton	.50
13	Jeff Kent	.15
14	Bob Abreu	.25
15	Jason Giambi	.40
16	Albert Pujols	1.00
17	Mike Sweeney	.15
18	Vladimir Guerrero	.50
19	Cliff Floyd	.15
20	Shannon Stewart	.15
21	Cristian Guzman	.15
22	Roberto Alomar	.25
23	Carlos Beltran	.25
24	Jimmy Rollins	.25
25	Roger Cedeno	.15
26	Juan Pierre	.15
27	Juan Uribe	.15
28	Luis Castillo	.15
29	Ray Durham	.15
30	Mark McLemore	.15
31	Barry Bonds	1.50
32	Sammy Sosa	1.00
33	Luis Gonzalez	.25
34	Alex Rodriguez	1.00
35	Shawn Green	.25
36	Todd Helton	.50
37	Jim Thome	.50
38	Rafael Palmeiro	.40
39	Richie Sexson	.25
40	Phil Nevin	.15
41	Troy Glaus	.40
42	Sammy Sosa	1.00
43	Todd Helton	.50
44	Luis Gonzalez	.25
45	Bret Boone	.25
46	Juan Gonzalez	.40
47	Barry Bonds	1.50
48	Alex Rodriguez	1.00
49	Jeff Bagwell	.50
50	Albert Pujols	1.00
51	Phil Nevin	.15
52	Ichiro Suzuki	1.00
53	Larry Walker	.25
54	Jason Giambi	.40
55	Roberto Alomar	.25
56	Todd Helton	.50
57	Moises Alou	.25
58	Lance Berkman	.25
59	Bret Boone	.25
60	Frank Catalanotto	.15
61	Chipper Jones	.25
62	Barry Bonds	1.50
63	Sammy Sosa	1.00
64	Luis Gonzalez	.25
65	Todd Helton	.50
66	Larry Walker	.25
67	Jason Giambi	.40
68	Jim Thome	.25
69	Alex Rodriguez	1.00
70	Lance Berkman	.25
71	Albert Pujols	1.00
72	Ichiro Suzuki	1.00
73	Roger Cedeno	.15
74	Juan Pierre	.15
75	Jimmy Rollins	.15
76	Alfonso Soriano	.50
77	Mark McLemore	.15
78	Chuck Knoblauch	.15
79	Vladimir Guerrero	.50
80	Bob Abreu	.25
81	Mike Cameron	.15
82	Sammy Sosa	1.00
83	Alex Rodriguez	1.00
84	Todd Helton	.50
85	Barry Bonds	1.50
86	Luis Gonzalez	.25
87	Ichiro Suzuki	1.00
88	Jeff Bagwell	.50
89	Cliff Floyd	.15
90	Shawn Green	.15
91	Craig Biggio	.15
92	Juan Pierre	.15
93	Fernando Vina	.15
94	Paul LoDuca	.15
95	Mark Grace	.15
96	Eric Young	.15
97	Placido Polanco	.15
98	Jason Kendall	.15
99	Ichiro Suzuki	1.00
100	Orlando Cabrera	.15
101	Rey Sanchez	.15
102	Ichiro Suzuki	1.00
103	Edgar Martinez	.25
104	Bret Boone	.25
105	Barry Bonds	1.50
106	Ivan Rodriguez	1.00
107	Mike Piazza	1.00
108	Sammy Sosa	1.00
109	John Olerud	.25
110	Roberto Alomar	.40
111	Roberto Alomar	.25
112	Mark McGwire	1.50
113	Barry Larkin	.25
114	Ken Griffey Jr.	1.00
115	Rickey Henderson	.25
116	Barry Bonds	1.50
117	Ivan Rodriguez	.40
118	Mike Piazza	.25
119	Roger Clemens	1.00
120	Randy Johnson	1.00
121	Albert Pujols	1.00
122	Ichiro Suzuki	1.00
123	Roy Oswalt	.25
124	C.C. Sabathia	.15
125	Jimmy Rollins	.25
126	Alfonso Soriano	.50
127	David Eckstein	.25
128	Adam Dunn	.50
129	Bud Smith	.15
130	Tsuyoshi Shinjo	.15
131	Matt Morris	.15
132	Curt Schilling	.25
133	Randy Johnson	.50
134	Mark Mulder	.25
135	Roger Clemens	1.00
136	Jon Lieber	.15
137	Jamie Moyer	.15
138	Freddy Garcia	.15
139	Tim Hudson	.15
140	C.C. Sabathia	.15
141	Randy Johnson	.25
142	Curt Schilling	.25
143	John Burkett	.15
144	Freddy Garcia	.15
145	Greg Maddux	.75
146	Darryl Kile	.25
147	Mike Mussina	.40
148	Joe Mays	.15
149	Matt Morris	.25
150	Russ Ortiz	.15
151	Randy Johnson	.50
152	Curt Schilling	.25
153	Hideo Nomo	.25
154	Chan Ho Park	.25
155	Kerry Wood	.50
156	Mike Mussina	.40
157	Roger Clemens	1.00
158	Javier Vazquez	.15
159	Barry Zito	.25
160	Bartolo Colon	.15
161	Mariano Rivera	.25
162	Robb Nen	.15
163	Kazuhiro Sasaki	.15
164	Armando Benitez	.15

165	Trevor Hoffman	.15
166	Jeff Shaw	.15
167	Keith Foulke	.15
168	Jose Mesa	.15
169	Troy Percival	.15
170	Billy Wagner	.15
171	Pat Burrell	.25
172	Raul Mondesi	.15
173	Gary Sheffield	.25
174	Carlos Beltran	.25
175	Vladimir Guerrero	.50
176	Torii Hunter	.25
177	Jeromy Burnitz	.15
178	Tim Salmon	.15
179	Jim Edmonds	.25
180	Tsuyoshi Shinjo	.15
181	Greg Maddux	.75
182	Roberto Alomar	.40
183	Ken Griffey Jr.	1.00
184	Ivan Rodriguez	.40
185	Omar Vizquel	.15
186	Barry Bonds	1.50
187	Devon White	.15
188	J.T. Snow	.15
189	Larry Walker	.25
190	Robin Ventura	.15
191	Mark Phillips **RC**	3.00
192	Clint Nageotte **RC**	2.00
193	Mauricio Lara **RC**	.75
194	Nic Jackson **RC**	.75
195	Chris Tritle **RC**	.75
196	Ryan Gripp **RC**	.75
197	Greg Montalbano **RC**	.75
198	Noochie Varner **RC**	.75
199	Nick Alvarez **RC**	.75
200	Craig Kuzmic **RC**	.75

Die-Cut

Stars (1-200): 2-4X
Inserted 1:4

Autographs

NM/M
Common Autograph: 10.00
Inserted 1:67

BB	Barry Bonds	180.00
BBO	Bret Boone	20.00
RCL	Roger Clemens	100.00
JE	Jim Edmonds	25.00
CF	Cliff Floyd	10.00
LG	Luis Gonzalez	15.00
CG	Cristian Guzman	10.00
RO	Roy Oswalt	15.00
JR	Jimmy Rollins	15.00
BZ	Barry Zito	20.00

Relics

NM/M
Common Player: 8.00
Bat Relic 1:27
Jersey Relic 1:26

BA	Bob Abreu/Bat	12.00
RA	Roberto Alomar/Bat	15.00
MA	Moises Alou/Bat	8.00
GA	Garret Anderson/Bat	10.00
JBA	Jeff Bagwell/Jsy	15.00
CB	Carlos Beltran/Bat	10.00
AB	Armando Benitez/Jsy	8.00
LB	Lance Berkman/Bat	10.00
CBI	Craig Biggio/Jsy	15.00
BB	Barry Bonds/Jsy	25.00
BBO	Bret Boone/Bat	8.00
JBU	John Burkett/Jsy	8.00
JB	Jeromy Burnitz/Jsy	8.00
MC	Mike Cameron/Bat	10.00
LC	Luis Castillo/Bat	8.00
RC	Roger Cedeno/Bat	8.00
BC	Bartolo Colon/Bat	8.00
RD	Ray Durham/Bat	8.00
JE	Jim Edmonds/Bat	15.00
CF	Cliff Floyd/Jsy	8.00
FG	Freddy Garcia/Jsy	8.00
JGO	Juan Gonzalez/Bat	8.00
LG	Luis Gonzalez/Bat	8.00
MG	Mark Grace/Bat	'20.00
SG	Shawn Green/Bat	8.00
CG	Cristian Guzman/Bat	8.00
TH	Todd Helton/Bat	15.00
THO	Trevor Hoffman/Jsy	8.00
THU	Torii Hunter/Bat	-15.00
RJ	Randy Johnson/Jsy	20.00
CJ	Chipper Jones/Bat	20.00
JK	Jason Kendall/Jsy	10.00
JKE	Jeff Kent/Jsy	10.00
CK	Chuck Knoblauch/Jsy	8.00
PL	Paul LoDuca/Bat	10.00
GM	Greg Maddux/Jsy	25.00
EM	Edgar Martinez/Jsy	10.00
MM	Mark McLemore/Bat	8.00
PM	Raul Mondesi/Bat	8.00
PN	Phil Nevin/Bat	8.00
JO	John Olerud/Jsy	8.00
RP	Rafael Palmeiro/Jsy	12.00
CP	Chan Ho Park/Jsy	8.00
MP	Mike Piazza/Jsy	20.00
JP	Juan Pierre/Jsy	10.00
PP	Placido Polanco/Bat	10.00
AP	Albert Pujols/Bat	25.00
AR	Alex Rodriguez/Jsy	15.00
TS	Tim Salmon/Bat	10.00
CS	Curt Schilling/Jsy	15.00
RS	Richie Sexson/Bat	10.00
GS	Gary Sheffield/Jsy	10.00
TSH	Tsuyoshi Shinjo/Bat	10.00
JS	J.T. Snow/Bat	8.00
AS	Alfonso Soriano/Bat	15.00
SS	Shannon Stewart/Bat	8.00
MS	Mike Sweeney/Bat	15.00
JT	Jim Thome/Bat	20.00
RV	Robin Ventura/Bat	8.00
FV	Fernando Vina/Bat	10.00
OV	Omar Vizquel/Bat	10.00
BW	Billy Wagner/Jsy	10.00
LW	Larry Walker/Bat	10.00
DW	Devon White/Bat	8.00
BZ	Barry Zito/Jsy	10.00

Team Topps Legends Autographs

NM/M
Common Player:
Carl Yastrzemski 65.00

2002 Topps Total Pre-Production

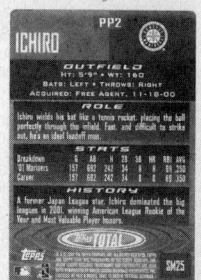

NM/M
Complete Set (3): 6.00
Common Player: 2.00

PP1	Barry Bonds	2.00
PP2	Ichiro	2.00
PP3	Hank Blalock	2.00

2002 Topps Total

NM/M
Complete Set (990): 125.00
Common Player: .10
Pack (10): 1.00
Box (36): 30.00

1	Joe Mauer **RC**	5.00
2	Derek Jeter	2.00
3	Shawn Green	.25
4	Vladimir Guerrero	.50
5	Mike Piazza	1.50
6	Brandon Duckworth	.10
7	Aramis Ramirez	.10
8	Josh Barfield	1.00
9	Troy Glaus	.40
10	Sammy Sosa	1.00
11	Rod Barajas	.10
12	Tsuyoshi Shinjo	.25
13	Larry Bigbie	.10
14	Tino Martinez	.10
15	Craig Biggio	.25
16	Anastacio Martinez **RC**	.40
17	John McDonald	.10
18	Kyle Kane **RC**	.30
19	Aubrey Huff	.10
20	Juan Cruz	.10
21	Doug Creek	.10
22	Luther Hackman	.10
23	Rafael Furcal	.10
24	Andres Torres	.10
25	Jason Giambi	.50
26	Jose Paniagua	.10
27	Jose Offerman	.10
28	Alex Arias	.10
29	J.M. Gold	.10
30	Jeff Bagwell	.50
31	Brent Cookson **RC**	.20
32	Kelly Wunsch	.10
33	Larry Walker	.25
34	Luis Gonzalez	.25
35	John Franco	.10
36	Roy Oswalt	.25
37	Tom Glavine	.25
38	C.C. Sabathia	.25
39	Jay Gibbons	.10
40	Wilson Betemit	.10
41	Tony Armas	.10
42	Mo Vaughn	.10
43	Gerard Oakes **RC**	.40
44	Dmitri Young	.10
45	Tim Salmon	.10
46	Barry Zito	.10
47	Adrian Gonzalez	.10
48	Joe Davenport	.10
49	Adrian Hernandez	.10
50	Randy Johnson	.50
51	Benito Baez	.10
52	Adam Pettyjohn	.10
53	Alex Escobar	.10
54	Stevenson Agosto **RC**	.25
55	Omar Daal	.10
56	Mike Buddie	.10
57	Dave Williams	.10
58	Marquis Grissom	.10
59	Pat Burrell	.25
60	Mark Prior	2.00
61	Mike Bynum	.10
62	Mike Hill **RC**	.25
63	Brandon Backe **RC**	.25
64	Dan Wilson	.10
65	Nick Johnson	.10
66	Jason Grimsley	.10
67	Russ Johnson	.10
68	Todd Walker	.10
69	Kyle Farnsworth	.10
70	Ben Broussard	.10
71	Garrett Guzman **RC**	.50
72	Terry Mulholland	.10
73	Tyler Houston	.10
74	Jace Brewer	.10
75	Chris Baker **RC**	.25
76	Frank Catalanotto	.10
77	Mike Redmond	.10
78	Matt Wise	.10
79	Fernando Vina	.10
80	Kevin Brown	.10
81	Grant Balfour	.10
82	Clint Nageotte **RC**	.75
83	Jeff Tam	.10
84	Steve Trachsel	.10
85	Tomokazu Ohka	.10
86	Keith McDonald	.10
87	Jose Ortiz	.10
88	Rusty Greer	.10
89	Jeff Suppan	.10
90	Moises Alou	.10
91	Juan Encarnacion	.10
92	Tyler Yates **RC**	.40
93	Scott Strickland	.10
94	Brent Butler	.10
95	Jon Rauch	.10
96	Brian Mallette **RC**	.25
97	Joe Randa	.10
98	Cesar Crespo	.10
99	Felix Rodriguez	.10
100	Chipper Jones	.75
101	Victor Martinez	.10
102	Danny Graves	.10
103	Brandon Berger **RC**	.10
104	Carlos Garcia	.10
105	Alfonso Soriano	.75
106	Allan Simpson **RC**	.10
107	Brad Thomas	.10
108	Devon White	.10
109	Scott Chiasson	.10
110	Cliff Floyd	.10
111	Scott Williamson	.10
112	Julio Zuleta	.10
113	Terry Adams	.10
114	Zach Day	.10
115	Ben Grieve	.10
116	Mark Ellis	.10
117	Bobby Jenks **RC**	.75
118	LaTroy Hawkins	.10
119	Tim Raines Jr.	.10
120	Juan Uribe	.10
121	Bob Scanlan	.10
122	Brad Nelson **RC**	1.50
123	Adam Johnson	.10
124	Raul Casanova	.10
125	Jeff D'Amico	.10
126	Aaron Cook **RC**	.50
127	Alan Benes	.10
128	Mark Little	.10
129	Randy Wolf	.10
130	Phil Nevin	.10
131	Guillermo Mota	.10
132	Nick Neugebauer	.10
133	Pedro Borbon	.10
134	Doug Mientkiewicz	.10
135	Edgardo Alfonzo	.10
136	Dustan Mohr	.10
137	Dan Reichert	.10
138	Dewon Brazelton	.10
139	Orlando Cabrera	.10
140	Todd Hollandsworth	.10
141	Darren Dreifort	.10
142	Jose Valentin	.10
143	Josh Kalinowski	.10
144	Randy Keisler	.10
145	Bret Boone	.10
146	Roosevelt Brown	.10
147	Brent Abernathy	.10
148	Jorge Julio	.10
149	Alex Gonzalez	.10
150	Juan Pierre	.10
151	Roger Cedeno	.10
152	Javier Vazquez	.10
153	Armando Benitez	.10
154	Dave Burba	.10
155	Brad Penny	.10
156	Ryan Jensen	.10
157	Jeromy Burnitz	.10
158	Matt Childers **RC**	.40
159	Wilmy Caceres	.10
160	Roger Clemens	.10
161	Michael Tejera	.10
162	Jason Christiansen	.10
163	Pokey Reese	.10
164	Ivanon Coffie	.10
165	Joaquin Benoit	.10
166	Mike Matheny	.10
167	Eric Cammack	.10
168	Alex Graman	.10
169	Brook Fordyce	.10
170	Mike Lieberthal	.10
171	Giovanni Carrara	.10
172	Antonio Perez	.10
173	Fernando Tatis	.10
174	Jason Bay **RC**	2.00
175	Jason Botts **RC**	.50
176	Danys Baez	.10
177	Shea Hillenbrand	.10
178	Jack Cust	.10
179	Clay Bellinger	.10
180	Roberto Alomar	.10
181	Graeme Lloyd	.10
182	Clint Weibl **RC**	.10
183	Royce Clayton	.10
184	Ben Davis	.10
185	Brian Adams	.25
186	Jack Wilson	.10
187	David Coggin	.10
188	Derrick Turnbow	.10
189	Vladimir Nunez	.10
190	Mariano Rivera	.10
191	Wilson Guzman	.10
192	Michael Barrett	.10
193	Corey Patterson	.10
194	Luis Sojo	.10
195	Scott Elarton	.10
196	Charles Thomas	.25
197	Ricky Bottalico	.10
198	Wilfredo Rodriguez	.10
199	Ricardo Rincon	.10
200	John Smoltz	.10
201	Travis Miller	.10
202	Ben Weber	.10
203	T.J. Tucker	.10
204	Terry Shumpert	.10
205	Bernie Williams	.10
206	Russ Ortiz	.10
207	Nate Rolison	.10
208	Jose Cruz Jr.	.10
209	Bill Ortega	.10
210	Carl Everett	.10
211	Luis Lopez	.10
212	Brian Wolfe **RC**	.25
213	Doug Davis	.10
214	Troy Mattes	.10
215	Al Leiter	.10
216	Joe Mays	.10
217	Bobby Smith	.10
218	J.J. Trujillo **RC**	.25
219	Hideo Nomo	.20
220	Jimmy Rollins	.25
221	Bobby Seay	.10
222	Mike Thurman	.10
223	Bartolo Colon	.10
224	Jesus Sanchez	.10
225	Ray Durham	.10
226	Juan Diaz	.10
227	Lee Stevens	.10
228	Ben Howard **RC**	.75
229	James Moulton	.10
230	Paul Quantrill	.10
231	Randy Knorr	.10
232	Abraham Nunez	.10
233	Mike Fetters	.10
234	Mario Encarnacion	.10
235	Jeremy Fikac	.10
236	Travis Lee	.10
237	Bob File	.10
238	Pete Harnisch	.10
239	Randy Galvez **RC**	.25
240	Geoff Goetz	.10
241	Gary Glover	.10
242	Troy Percival	.10
243	Lenny Dinardo **RC**	.40
244	Jonny Gomes **RC**	2.00
245	Jesus Medrano **RC**	.25
246	Rey Ordonez	.10
247	Juan Gonzalez	.50
248	Jose Guillen	.10
249	Franklin German **RC**	.25
250	Mike Mussina	.40
251	Ugueth Urbina	.10
252	Melvin Mora	.10
253	Gerald Williams	.10
254	Jared Sandberg	.10
255	Darrin Fletcher	.10
256	A.J. Pierzynski	.10
257	Lenny Harris	.10
258	Blaine Neal	.10
259	Denny Neagle	.10
260	Jason Hart	.10
261	Henry Mateo	.10
262	Rheal Cormier	.10
263	Luis Terrero	.10
264	Shigetoshi Hasegawa	.10
265	Bill Haselman	.10
266	Scott Hatteberg	.10
267	Adam Hyzdu	.10
268	Mike Williams	.10
269	Marlon Anderson	.10
270	Bruce Chen	.10
271	Eli Marrero	.10
272	Jimmy Haynes	.10
273	Bronson Arroyo	.10
274	Kevin Jordan	.10
275	Rick Helling	.10
276	Mark Loretta	.10
277	Dustin Hermanson	.10
278	Pablo Ozuna	.10
279	Syketo Anderson **RC**	.25
280	Jermaine Dye	.10
281	Will Smith	.10
282	Brian Daubach	.10
283	Eric Hinske	.10
284	Joe Jiannetti **RC**	.40
285	Chan Ho Park	.10
286	Curtis Legendre **RC**	.25
287	Jeff Reboulet	.10
288	Scott Rolen	.50
289	Chris Richard	.10
290	Eric Chavez	.25
291	Scot Shields	.10
292	Donnie Sadler	.10
293	Dave Veres	.10
294	Craig Counsell	.10
295	Armando Reynoso	.10
296	Kyle Lohse	.10
297	Arthur Rhodes	.10
298	Sidney Ponson	.10
299	Trevor Hoffman	.10
300	Kerry Wood	.25
301	Danny Bautista	.10
302	Scott Sauerbeck	.10
303	Johnny Estrada	.10
304	Mike Timlin	.10
305	Orlando Hernandez	.10
306	Tony Clark	.10
307	Tomas Perez	.10
308	Marcus Giles	.10
309	Mike Bordick	.10
310	Jorge Posada	.25
311	Jason Conti	.10
312	Kevin Millar	.10
313	Paul Shuey	.10
314	Jake Mauer **RC**	.75
315	Luke Hudson	.10
316	Angel Berroa	.10
317	Fred Bastardo **RC**	.25
318	Shawn Estes	.10
319	Andy Ashby	.10
320	Ryan Klesko	.10
321	Kevin Appier	.10
322	Juan Pena	.10
323	Alex Herrera	.10
324	Robb Nen	.10
325	Orlando Hudson	.10
326	Lyle Overbay	.10
327	Ben Sheets	.25
328	Mike DiFelice	.10
329	Pablo Arias **RC**	.25
330	Mike Sweeney	.10
331	Rick Ankiel	.10
332	Tomas De La Rosa	.10
333	Kazuhisa Ishii **RC**	1.00
334	Jose Reyes	.10
335	Jeremy Giambi	.10
336	Jose Mesa	.10
337	Ralph Roberts **RC**	.25
338	Jose Nunez	.10
339	Curt Schilling	.40
340	Sean Casey	.10
341	Bob Wells	.10
342	Carlos Beltran	.10
343	Alexis Gomez	.10
344	Brandon Claussen	.25
345	Buddy Groom	.10
346	Mark Phillips **RC**	.50
347	Francisco Cordova	.10
348	Joe Oliver	.10
349	Danny Patterson	.10
350	Joel Pineiro	.10
351	J.R. House	.10
352	Benny Agbayani	.10
353	Jose Vidro	.10
354	Reed Johnson **RC**	.10
355	Mike Lowell	.10
356	Scott Schoeneweis	.10
357	Brian Jordan	.10
358	Steve Finley	.10
359	Randy Choate	.10
360	Jose Lima	.10
361	Miguel Olivo	.10
362	Kenny Rogers	.10
363	David Justice	.20
364	Brandon Knight	.10
365	Joe Kennedy	.10
366	Eric Valent	.10
367	Nelson Cruz	.10
368	Brian Giles	.25
369	Charles Gibson Jr.	.10
370	Juan Pena	.10
371	Mark Redman	.10
372	Billy Koch	.10
373	Ted Lilly	.10
374	Craig Paquette	.10
375	Kevin Jarvis	.10
376	Scott Erickson	.10
377	Josh Paul	.10
378	Darwin Cubillan	.10
379	Nelson Figueroa	.10
380	Darin Erstad	.20
381	Jeremy Hill **RC**	.25
382	Elvin Nina	.10
383	David Wells	.25
384	Jay Caliguiri **RC**	.10
385	Freddy Garcia	.10
386	Damian Miller	.10
387	Bobby Higginson	.10
388	Alejandro Giron **RC**	.25
389	Ivan Rodriguez	.40
390	Ed Rogers	.10
391	Andy Benes	.10
392	Matt Blank	.10
393	Ryan Vogelsong	.10
394	Kelly Ramos **RC**	.25
395	Eric Karros	.10
396	Bobby Jones	.10
397	Omar Vizquel	.25
398	Matt Perisho	.10
399	Delino DeShields	.10
400	Carlos Hernandez	.10
401	Derrek Lee	.10
402	Kirk Rueter	.10
403	David Wright	30.00
404	Paul LoDuca	.10
405	Brian Schneider	.10
406	Milton Bradley	.10
407	Daryle Ward	.10
408	Cody Ransom	.10
409	Fernando Rodney	.10
410	John Suomi **RC**	.20
411	Joe Girardi	.10
412	Demetrius Heath **RC**	.25
413	John Foster **RC**	.25
414	Doug Glanville	.10
415	Ryan Kohlmeier	.10
416	Mike Matthews	.10
417	Craig Wilson	.10
418	Jay Witasick	.10
419	Jay Payton	.10
420	Andruw Jones	.40
421	Benji Gil	.10
422	Jeff Liefer	.10
423	Kevin Young	.10
424	Richie Sexson	.25
425	Cory Lidle	.10
426	Shane Halter	.10
427	Jesse Foppert	.40
428	Jose Molina	.10
429	Nick Alvarez **RC**	.40
430	Brian L. Hunter	.10
431	Clifford Bartosh **RC**	.25
432	Junior Spivey	.10
433	Eric Good **RC**	.25
434	Chin-Feng Chen	.10
435	T.J. Mathews	.10
436	Rich Rodriguez	.10
437	Bobby Abreu	.20
438	Joe McEwing	.10
439	Michael Tucker	.10
440	Preston Wilson	.10
441	Mike MacDougal	.10
442	Shannon Stewart	.10
443	Bob Howry	.10
444	Mike Benjamin	.10
445	Erik Hiljus	.10
446	Ryan Gripp **RC**	.25
447	Jose Vizcaino	.10
448	Shawn Wooten	.10
449	Steve Kent **RC**	.25
450	Ramiro Mendoza	.10
451	Jake Westbrook	.10
452	Joe Lawrence	.10
453	Jae Weong Seo	.10
454	Ryan Fry **RC**	.20
455	Darren Lewis	.10
456	Brad Wilkerson	.10
457	Gustavo Chacin **RC**	.25
458	Adrian Brown	.10
459	Mike Cameron	.10
460	Bud Smith	.10
461	Derrick Lewis	.10
462	Derek Lowe	.10
463	Matt Williams	.10
464	Jason Jennings	.10
465	Albie Lopez	.10
466	Felipe Lopez	.10
467	Luke Allen	.10
468	Brian Anderson	.10
469	Matt Riley	.10
470	Ryan Dempster	.10
471	Matt Ginter	.10
472	David Ortiz	.10
473	Cole Barthel	.10
474	Damian Jackson	.10
475	Andy Van Hekken	.10
476	Doug Brocail	.10
477	Denny Hocking	.10
478	Sean Douglass	.10
479	Eric Owens	.10
480	Ryan Ludwick	.10
481	Todd Pratt	.10
482	Aaron Sele	.10
483	Edgar Renteria	.10
484	Raymond Cabrera **RC**	.25
485	Brandon Lyon	.10
486	Chase Utley	.10
487	Robert Fick	.10
488	Wilfredo Cordero	.10
489	Octavio Dotel	.10
490	Paul Abbott	.10
491	Jason Kendall	.10
492	Jarrod Washburn	.10
493	Dane Sardinha	.10
494	Jung Bong	.10
495	J.D. Drew	.10
496	Jason Schmidt	.10
497	Mike Magnante	.10
498	Jorge Padilla **RC**	.50
499	Eric Gagne	.10
500	Todd Helton	.50
501	Jeff Weaver	.10
502	Alex Sanchez	.10
503	Ken Griffey Jr.	.10
504	Abraham Nunez	.10

#	Player	Price
505	Reggie Sanders	.10
506	Casey Kotchman	2.00
507	Jim Mann	.10
508	Matt LeCroy	.10
509	Frank Castillo	.10
510	Geoff Jenkins	.10
511	Jayson Durocher RC	.20
512	Ellis Burks	.10
513	Aaron Fultz	.10
514	Hiram Bocachica	.10
515	Nate Espy	.10
516	Placido Polanco	.10
517	Kerry Ligtenberg	.10
518	Doug Nickle	.10
519	Ramon Ortiz	.10
520	Greg Swindell	.10
521	J.J. Davis	.10
522	Sandy Alomar	.10
523	Chris Carpenter	.10
524	Vance Wilson	.10
525	Nomar Garciaparra	1.00
526	Jim Mecir	.10
527	Taylor Buchholz RC	.25
528	Brent Mayne	.10
529	John Rodriguez RC	.25
530	David Segui	.10
531	Nate Cornejo	.10
532	Gil Heredia	.10
533	Esteban Loaiza	.10
534	Pat Mahomes	.10
535	Matt Morris	.10
536	Todd Stottlemyre	.10
537	Brian Lesher	.10
538	Arturo McDowell	.10
539	Felix Diaz	.10
540	Mark Mulder	.10
541	Kevin Frederick RC	.25
542	Andy Fox	.10
543	Dionys Cesar RC	.10
544	Justin Miller	.10
545	Keith Osik	.10
546	Shane Reynolds	.10
547	Mike Myers	.10
548	Raul Chavez RC	.25
549	Joe Nathan	.10
550	Ryan Anderson	.10
551	Jason Marquis	.10
552	Marty Cordova	.10
553	Kevin Tapani	.10
554	Jimmy Anderson	.10
555	Pedro Martinez	.50
556	Rocky Biddle	.10
557	Alex Ochoa	.10
558	D'Angelo Jimenez	.10
559	Wilkin Ruan	.10
560	Terrence Long	.10
561	Mark Lukasiewicz	.10
562	Jose Santiago	.10
563	Brad Fullmer	.10
564	Corky Miller	.10
565	Matt White	.10
566	Mark Grace	.30
567	Raul Ibanez	.10
568	Josh Towers	.10
569	Juan Gonzalez	.40
570	Brian Buchanan	.10
571	Ken Harvey	.10
572	Jeffrey Hammonds	.10
573	Wade Miller	.10
574	Elpidio Guzman	.10
575	Kevin Olsen	.10
576	Austin Kearns	.40
577	Tim Kalita RC	.40
578	David Dellucci	.10
579	Alex Gonzalez	.10
580	Joe Orloski RC	.20
581	Gary Matthews Jr.	.10
582	Ryan Mills	.10
583	Erick Almonte	.10
584	Jeremy Affeldt	.10
585	Chris Tritle RC	1.00
586	Michael Cuddyer	.10
587	Kris Foster	.10
588	Russell Branyan	.10
589	Darren Oliver	.10
590	Freddie Money RC	.25
591	Carlos Lee	.10
592	Tim Wakefield	.10
593	Bubba Trammell	.10
594	John Koronka RC	3.00
595	Geoff Blum	.10
596	Darryl Kile	.10
597	Neifi Perez	.10
598	Torii Hunter	.10
599	Luis Castillo	.10
600	Mark Buehrle	.10
601	Jeff Zimmerman	.10
602	Mike DeJean	.10
603	Julio Lugo	.10
604	Chad Hermansen	.10
605	Keith Foulke	.10
606	Lance Davis	.10
607	Jeff Austin RC	.25
608	Brandon Inge	.10
609	Orlando Merced	.10
610	Johnny Damon	.10
611	Doug Henry	.10
612	Adam Kennedy	.10
613	Wiki Gonzalez	.10
614	Brian West RC	.25
615	Andy Pettitte	.25
616	Chone Figgins RC	.25
617	Matt Lawton	.10
618	Paul Rigdon	.10
619	Keith Lockhart	.10
620	Tim Redding	.10
621	John Parrish	.10
622	Chad Hutchinson	.10
623	Todd Greene	.10
624	David Eckstein	.10
625	Greg Montalbano RC	1.00
626	Joe Beimel	.10
627	Adrian Beltre	.20
628	Charles Nagy	.10
629	Cristian Guzman	.10
630	Toby Hall	.10
631	Jose Hernandez	.10
632	Jose Macias	.10
633	Jaret Wright	.10
634	Steve Parris	.10
635	Gene Kingsdale	.10
636	Tim Worrell	.10
637	Billy Martin	.10
638	Jovanny Cedeno	.10
639	Curt Leskanic	.10
640	Tim Hudson	.20
641	Juan Castro	.10
642	Rafael Soriano	.10
643	Juan Rincon	.10
644	Mark DeRosa	.10
645	Carlos Pena	.10
646	Robin Ventura	.20
647	Odalis Perez	.10
648	Damion Easley	.10
649	Benito Santiago	.10
650	Alex Rodriguez	1.50
651	Aaron Rowand	.10
652	Alex Cora	.10
653	Bobby Kielty	.10
654	Jose Rodriguez	.10
655	Herbert Perry	.10
656	Jeff Urban	.10
657	Paul Bako	.10
658	Shane Spencer	.10
659	Pat Hentgen	.10
660	Jeff Kent	.20
661	Mark McLemore	.10
662	Chuck Knoblauch	.10
663	Blake Stein	.10
664	Brett Roneberg RC	.25
665	Josh Phelps	.10
666	Byung-Hyun Kim	.10
667	Dave Martinez	.10
668	Mike Maroth	.10
669	Shawn Chacon	.10
670	Billy Wagner	.10
671	Luis Alicea	.10
672	Sterling Hitchcock	.10
673	Adam Piatt	.10
674	Ryan Franklin	.10
675	Luke Prokopec	.10
676	Alfredo Amezega	.10
677	Gookie Dawkins	.10
678	Eric Byrnes	.10
679	Barry Larkin	.25
680	Albert Pujols	1.00
681	Edwards Guzman	.10
682	Jason Bere	.10
683	Adam Everett	.10
684	Greg Colbrunn	.10
685	Brandon Puffer RC	.40
686	Mark Kotsay	.10
687	Willie Bloomquist	.10
688	Hank Blalock	.25
689	Travis Hafner	.10
690	Lance Berkman	.40
691	Joe Crede	.10
692	Chuck Finley	.10
693	John Grabow	.10
694	Randy Winn	.10
695	Mike James	.10
696	Kris Benson	.10
697	Bret Prinz	.10
698	Jeff Williams	.10
699	Eric Munson	.10
700	Mike Hampton	.10
701	Ramon E. Martinez	.10
702	Hansel Izquierdo RC	.25
703	Nathan Haynes	.10
704	Eddie Taubensee	.10
705	Esteban German	.10
706	Ross Gload	.10
707	Matthew Merricks RC	.10
708	Chris Piersoll RC	.25
709	Seth Greisinger	.10
710	Ichiro Suzuki	1.00
711	Cesar Izturis	.10
712	Brad Cresse	.10
713	Carl Pavano	.10
714	Steve Sparks	.10
715	Dennis Tankersley	.10
716	Kelvim Escobar	.10
717	Jason LaRue	.10
718	Corey Koskie	.10
719	Vinny Castilla	.10
720	Tim Drew	.10
721	Chin-Hui Tsao	.10
722	Paul Byrd	.10
723	Alex Cintron	.10
724	Orlando Palmeiro	.10
725	Ramon Hernandez	.10
726	Mark Johnson	.10
727	B.J. Ryan	.10
728	Wendell Magee	.10
729	Michael Coleman	.10
730	Mario Ramos	.50
731	Mike Stanton	.10
732	Dee Brown	.10
733	Brad Ausmus	.10
734	Napoleon Calzado RC	.25
735	Woody Williams	.10
736	Paxton Crawford	.10
737	Jason Karnuth	.10
738	Michael Restovich	.10
739	Ramon Castro	.10
740	Magglio Ordonez	.25
741	Tom Gordon	.10
742	Mark Grudzielanek	.10
743	Jamie Moyer	.10
744	Marlyn Tisdale RC	.20
745	Steve Kline	.10
746	Adam Eaton	.10
747	Eric Glaser RC	.25
748	Sean DePaula	.10
749	Greg Norton	.10
750	Steve Reed	.10
751	Ricardo Aramboles	.10
752	Matt Mantei	.10
753	Gene Stechschulte	.10
754	Chuck McElroy	.10
755	Barry Bonds	1.50
756	Matt Anderson	.10
757	Yorvit Torrealba	.10
758	Jason Standridge	.10
759	Desi Relaford	.10
760	Jolbert Cabrera	.10
761	Chris George	.10
762	Erubiel Durazo	.10
763	Paul Konerko	.25
764	Tike Redman	.10
765	Chad Ricketts RC	.20
766	Roberto Hernandez	.10
767	Mark Lewis	.10
768	Livan Hernandez	.10
769	Carlos Brackley RC	.25
770	Kazuhiro Sasaki	.10
771	Bill Hall	.10
772	Nelson Castro RC	.25
773	Eric Milton	.10
774	Tom Davey	.10
775	Todd Ritchie	.10
776	Seth Etherton	.10
777	Chris Singleton	.10
778	Robert Averette RC	.20
779	Robert Person	.10
780	Fred McGriff	.25
781	Richard Hidalgo	.10
782	Kris Wilson	.10
783	John Rocker	.10
784	Justin Kaye	.10
785	Glendon Rusch	.10
786	Greg Vaughn	.10
787	Mike Lamb	.10
788	Greg Myers	.10
789	Nate Field RC	.25
790	Jim Edmonds	.25
791	Olmedo Saenz	.10
792	Jason Johnson	.10
793	Mike Lincoln	.10
794	Todd Coffey	.10
795	Jesus Sanchez	.10
796	Aaron Myette	.10
797	Tony Womack	.10
798	Chad Kreuter	.10
799	Brady Clark	.10
800	Adam Dunn	.50
801	Jacque Jones	.10
802	Kevin Millwood	.10
803	Mike Rivera	.10
804	Jim Thome	.40
805	Jeff Conine	.10
806	Elmer Dessens	.10
807	Randy Velarde	.10
808	Carlos Delgado	.30
809	Steve Karsay	.10
810	Casey Fossum	.10
811	J.C. Romero	.10
812	Chris Truby	.10
813	Tony Graffanino	.10
814	Wascar Serrano	.10
815	Delvin James	.10
816	Pedro Feliz	.10
817	Damian Rolls	.10
818	Scott Linebrink	.10
819	Rafael Palmeiro	.40
820	Javy Lopez	.10
821	Larry Barnes	.10
822	Brian Lawrence	.10
823	Scotty Layfield RC	.25
824	Jeff Cirillo	.10
825	Willis Roberts	.10
826	Rich Harden RC	4.00
827	Chris Snelling RC	1.00
828	Gary Sheffield	.25
829	Jeff Heaverlo	.10
830	Matt Clement	.10
831	Rich Garces	.10
832	Rondell White	.10
833	Henry Pichardo RC	.25
834	Aaron Boone	.10
835	Ruben Sierra	.10
836	Deivis Santos	.10
837	Tony Batista	.10
838	Rob Bell	.10
839	Frank Thomas	.50
840	Jose Silva	.10
841	Dan Johnson RC	.50
842	Steve Cox	.10
843	Jose Acevedo	.10
844	Jay Bell	.10
845	Mike Sirotka	.10
846	Garret Anderson	.10
847	James Shanks RC	.25
848	Trot Nixon	.10
849	Keith Ginter	.10
850	Tim Spooneybarger	.10
851	Matt Stairs	.10
852	Chris Stynes	.10
853	Marvin Bernard	.10
854	Raul Mondesi	.20
855	Jeremy Owens	.10
856	Jon Garland	.10
857	Mitch Meluskey	.10
858	Chad Durbin	.10
859	John Burkett	.10
860	Jon Switzer	.10
861	Peter Bergeron	.10
862	Jesus Colome	.10
863	Todd Hundley	.10
864	Ben Petrick	.10
865	So Taguchi RC	.75
866	Ryan Drese	.10
867	Mike Trombley	.10
868	Rick Reed	.10
869	Mark Teixeira	.20
870	Corey Thurman RC	.10
871	Brian Roberts	.10
872	Mike Timlin	.10
873	Chris Reitsma	.10
874	Jeff Fassero	.10
875	Carlos Valderrama	.10
876	John Lackey	.10
877	Travis Fryman	.10
878	Ismael Valdes	.10
879	Rick White	.10
880	Edgar Martinez	.10
881	Dean Palmer	.10
882	Matt Allegra RC	.20
883	Greg Sain RC	.25
884	Carlos Silva	.10
885	Jose Valverde RC	.25
886	Dernell Stenson	.10
887	Todd Van Poppel	.10
888	Wes Anderson	.10
889	Bill Mueller	.10
890	Morgan Ensberg	.10
891	Marcus Thames	.10
892	Adam Walker RC	.10
893	John Halama	.10
894	Frank Menechino	.10
895	Greg Maddux	1.00
896	Gary Bennett	.10
897	Mauricio Lara RC	.25
898	Mike Young	.10
899	Travis Phelps	.10
900	Rich Aurilia	.10
901	Henry Blanco	.10
902	Carlos Febles	.10
903	Scott MacRae	.10
904	Lou Merloni	.10
905	Dicky Gonzalez	.10
906	Jeff DaVanon	.10
907	A.J. Burnett	.10
908	Einar Diaz	.10
909	Julio Franco	.10
910	John Olerud	.25
911	Mark Hamilton RC	.10
912	David Riske	.10
913	Jason Tyner	.10
914	Britt Reames	.10
915	Vernon Wells	.10
916	Eddie Perez	.10
917	Edwin Almonte RC	.25
918	Enrique Wilson	.10
919	Chris Gomez	.10
920	Jayson Werth	.10
921	Jeff Nelson	.10
922	Freddy Sanchez RC	.75
923	John Vander Wal	.10
924	Chad Qualls RC	.25
925	Gabe White	.10
926	Chad Harville	.10
927	Ricky Gutierrez	.10
928	Carlos Guillen	.10
929	B.J. Surhoff	.10
930	Chris Woodard	.10
931	Ricardo Rodriguez	.10
932	Jimmy Gobble RC	1.00
933	Jon Lieber	.10
934	Craig Kuzmic RC	.25
935	Eric Young	.10
936	Gregg Zaun	.10
937	Miguel Batista	.10
938	Danny Wright	.10
939	Todd Zeile	.10
940	Chad Zerbe	.10
941	Jason Young RC	.50
942	Ronnie Belliard	.10
943	John Ennis RC	.10
944	John Flaherty	.10
945	Jerry Hairston Jr.	.10
946	Al Levine	.10
947	Antonio Alfonseca	.10
948	Brian Moehler	.10
949	Calvin Murray	.10
950	Nick Bierbrodt	.10
951	Sun-Woo Kim	.10
952	Noochie Varner RC	.50
953	Luis Rivas	.10
954	Donnie Bridges	.10
955	Ramon Vazquez	.10
956	Luis Garcia	.10
957	Mark Quinn	.10
958	Armando Rios	.10
959	Chad Fox	.10
960	Hee Seop Choi	.10
961	Turk Wendell	.10
962	Adam Roller RC	.20
963	Grant Roberts	.10
964	Ben Molina	.10
965	Juan Rivera	.10
966	Matt Kinney	.10
967	Rod Beck	.10
968	Xavier Nady	.10
969	Masato Yoshii	.10
970	Miguel Tejada	.25
971	Danny Kolb	.10
972	Mike Remlinger	.10
973	Ray Lankford	.10
974	Ryan Minor	.10
975	J.T. Snow	.10
976	Brad Radke	.10
977	Jason Lane	.10
978	Jamey Wright	.10
979	Tom Goodwin	.10
980	Erik Bedard	.10
981	Gabe Kapler	.10
982	Brian Reith	.10
983	Nic Jackson RC	.50
984	Kurt Ainsworth	.10
985	Jason Isringhausen	.10
986	Willie Harris	.10
987	David Cone	.10
988	Bob Wickman	.10
989	Wes Helms	.10
990	Josh Beckett	.25

Award Winners

JORGE POSADA

	NM/M
Complete Set (30):	25.00
Common Player:	.75
Inserted 1:6	
AW1 Ichiro Suzuki	2.00
AW2 Albert Pujols	2.00
AW3 Barry Bonds	3.00
AW4 Ichiro Suzuki	2.00
AW5 Randy Johnson	1.00
AW6 Roger Clemens	2.00
AW7 Jason Giambi	.75
AW8 Bret Boone	.50
AW9 Troy Glaus	.75
AW10 Alex Rodriguez	2.50
AW11 Juan Gonzalez	.75
AW12 Ichiro Suzuki	.75
AW13 Jorge Posada	.75
AW14 Edgar Martinez	.75
AW15 Todd Helton	.75
AW16 Jeff Kent	.50
AW17 Albert Pujols	2.00
AW18 Rich Aurilia	.50
AW19 Barry Bonds	3.00
AW20 Luis Gonzalez	.50
AW21 Sammy Sosa	2.00
AW22 Mike Piazza	2.00
AW23 Mike Hampton	.50
AW24 Ruben Sierra	.50
AW25 Matt Morris	.50
AW26 Curt Schilling	.75
AW27 Alex Rodriguez	2.50
AW28 Barry Bonds	3.00
AW29 Jim Thome	1.00
AW30 Barry Bonds	3.00

Total Production

MAGGLIO ORDONEZ

	NM/M
Complete Set (10):	15.00
Common Player:	.75
Inserted 1:12	
TP1 Alex Rodriguez	3.00
TP2 Barry Bonds	3.00
TP3 Ichiro Suzuki	2.00
TP4 Edgar Martinez	.75
TP5 Jason Giambi	1.00
TP6 Todd Helton	1.00
TP7 Nomar Garciaparra	2.50
TP8 Vladimir Guerrero	2.00
TP9 Sammy Sosa	2.00
TP10 Chipper Jones	2.00

Total Topps

	NM/M
Complete Set (50):	35.00
Common Player:	.50
Inserted 1:3	
TT1 Roberto Alomar	.75
TT2 Moises Alou	.50
TT3 Jeff Bagwell	1.00
TT4 Lance Berkman	.75
TT5 Barry Bonds	2.00
TT6 Bret Boone	.50
TT7 Kevin Brown	.50
TT8 Eric Chavez	.50
TT9 Roger Clemens	1.50
TT10 Carlos Delgado	.50
TT11 Cliff Floyd	.50
TT12 Nomar Garciaparra	2.50
TT13 Jason Giambi	1.00
TT14 Brian Giles	.75
TT15 Troy Glaus	.75
TT16 Tom Glavine	.50
TT17 Luis Gonzalez	.50
TT18 Juan Gonzalez	.75
TT19 Shawn Green	.50
TT20 Ken Griffey Jr.	2.50
TT21 Vladimir Guerrero	1.00
TT22 Jorge Posada	.50
TT23 Todd Helton	.75
TT24 Tim Hudson	.50
TT25 Derek Jeter	4.00
TT26 Randy Johnson	1.00
TT27 Andruw Jones	.75
TT28 Chipper Jones	2.00
TT29 Jeff Kent	.50
TT30 Greg Maddux	2.00
TT31 Edgar Martinez	.50
TT32 Pedro Martinez	1.00
TT33 Magglio Ordonez	.50
TT34 Rafael Palmeiro	.50
TT35 Mike Piazza	3.00
TT36 Albert Pujols	2.00
TT37 Aramis Ramirez	.50
TT38 Manny Ramirez	.50
TT39 Alex Rodriguez	3.00
TT40 Ivan Rodriguez	.75
TT41 Curt Schilling	.75
TT42 Gary Sheffield	.50
TT43 Sammy Sosa	2.00
TT44 Ichiro Suzuki	4.00
TT45 Miguel Tejada	.50
TT46 Frank Thomas	1.00
TT47 Jim Thome	.75
TT48 Larry Walker	.50
TT49 Bernie Williams	.50
TT50 Kerry Wood	.50

2002 Topps Traded & Rookies

SHAWN RIGGANS

	NM/M
Complete Set (275):	125.00
Common Player:	.15
Common SP (1-110):	.50
Chrome Cards:	2-4X
2:Pack	
Pack (10):	3.00
Box (24):	60.00
T1 Jeff Weaver	.50
T2 Jay Powell	.50
T3 Alex Gonzalez	.50
T4 Jason Isringhausen	.50
T5 Darren Oliver	.50
T6 Hector Ortiz	.50
T7 Chuck Knoblauch	.50
T8 Brian L. Hunter	.50
T9 Dustan Mohr	.50
T10 Eric Hinske	.50
T11 Roger Cedeno	.50
T12 Eddie Perez	.50
T13 Jeromy Burnitz	.50
T14 Bartolo Colon	.50
T15 Rick Helling	.50
T16 Dan Plesac	.50
T17 Scott Strickland	.50
T18 Antonio Alfonseca	.50
T19 Ricky Gutierrez	.50
T20 John Valentin	.50
T21 Raul Mondesi	.50
T22 Ben Davis	.50
T23 Nelson Figueroa	.50
T24 Earl Snyder	.50
T25 Robin Ventura	.50
T26 Jimmy Haynes	.50
T27 Kenny Kelly	.50
T28 Morgan Ensberg	.50
T29 Reggie Sanders	.50
T30 Shigetoshi Hasegawa	.50
T31 Allen Levrault	.50
T32 Russell Branyan	.50
T33 Jose Guillen	.50
T34 Jose Paniagua	.50
T35 Kent Mercker	.50
T36 Jesse Orosco	.50
T37 Gregg Zaun	.50
T38 Reggie Taylor	.50
T39 Andres Galarraga	.50
T40 Chris Truby	.50

T41	Bruce Chen		.50
T42	Darren Lewis		.50
T43	Ryan Kohlmeier		.50
T44	John McDonald		.50
T45	Omar Daal		.50
T46	Matt Clement		.50
T47	Glendon Rusch		.50
T48	Chan Ho Park		.50
T49	Benny Agbayani		.50
T50	Juan Gonzalez		1.50
T51	Carlos Baerga		.50
T52	Tim Raines		.50
T53	Kevin Appier		.50
T54	Marty Cordoua		.50
T55	Jeff D'Amico		.50
T56	Dmitri Young		.50
T57	Roosevelt Brown		.50
T58	Dustin Hermanson		.50
T59	Jose Rijo		.50
T60	Todd Ritchie		.50
T61	Lee Stevens		.50
T62	Shane Heams		.50
T63	Eric Young		.50
T64	Chuck Finley		.50
T65	Dicky Gonzalez		.50
T66	Jose Macias		.50
T67	Gabe Kapler		.50
T68	Sandy Alomar Jr.		.50
T69	Henry Blanco		.50
T70	Julian Tavarez		.50
T71	Paul Bako		.50
T72	Dave Burba		.50
T73	Brian Jordan		.50
T74	Rickey Henderson		1.00
T75	Kevin Mench		.50
T76	Hideo Nomo		1.00
T77	Mark Sweeney		.50
T78	Brad Fullmer		.50
T79	Carl Everett		.50
T80	David Wells		.50
T81	Aaron Sele		.50
T82	Todd Hollandsworth		.50
T83	Vicente Padilla		.50
T84	Chris Latham		.50
T85	Corky Miller		.50
T86	Josh Fogg		.50
T87	Calvin Murray		.50
T88	Craig Paquette		.50
T89	Jay Payton		.50
T90	Carlos Pena		.50
T91	Juan Encarnacion		.50
T92	Rey Sanchez		.50
T93	Ryan Dempster		.50
T94	Mario Encarnacion		.50
T95	Jorge Julio		.50
T96	John Mabry		.50
T97	Todd Zeile		.50
T98	Johnny Damon		.50
T99	Deivi Cruz		.50
T100	Gary Sheffield		1.00
T101	Ted Lilly		.50
T102	Todd Van Poppel		.50
T103	Shawn Estes		.50
T104	Cesar Izturis		.50
T105	Ron Coomer		.50
T106	Grady Little		.50
T107	Jimy Williams		.50
T108	Tony Pena		.50
T109	Frank Robinson		.50
T110	Ron Gardenhire		.50
T111	Dennis Tankersley		.15
T112	Alejandro Cadena	RC	.25
T113	Justin Reid	RC	.25
T114	Nate Field	RC	.25
T115	Rene Reyes	RC	.25
T116	Nelson Castro	RC	.15
T117	Miguel Olivo		.15
T118	David Espinosa		.15
T119	Chris Bootcheck	RC	.40
T120	Rob Henkel	RC	.25
T121	Steve Bechler	RC	.25
T122	Mark Outlaw	RC	.25
T123	Henry Pichardo	RC	.25
T124	Michael Floyd	RC	.25
T125	Richard Lane	RC	.25
T126	Peter Zamora	RC	.25
T127	Javier Colina		.15
T128	Greg Sain	RC	.25
T129	Ronnie Merrill	RC	.25
T130	Gavin Floyd		1.50
T131	Josh Bonifay	RC	.25
T132	Tommy Marx	RC	.25
T133	Gary Cates Jr.	RC	.25
T134	Neal Cotts		.25
T135	Angel Berroa		.25
T136	Elio Serrano	RC	.25
T137	J.J. Putz	RC	.25
T138	Ruben Gotay	RC	.25
T139	Eddie Rogers	RC	.25
T140	Wily Mo Pena		.25
T141	Tyler Yates	RC	.25
T142	Colin Young	RC	.25
T143	Chance Caple		.15
T144	Ben Howard	RC	.25
T145	Ryan Bukvich	RC	.25
T146	Clifford Bartosh	RC	.25
T147	Brandon Claussen		.25
T148	Cristian Guerrero		.15
T149	Derrick Lewis		.15
T150	Eric Miller	RC	.25
T151	Justin Huber	RC	.75
T152	Adrian Gonzalez		.15
T153	Brian West	RC	.25
T154	Chris Baker	RC	.25
T155	Drew Henson		.75
T156	Scott Hairston		.75
T157	Jason Simontacchi	RC	.75
T158	Jason Arnold		.40
T159	Brandon Phillips		.15
T160	Adam Roller	RC	.25
T161	Scotty Layfield	RC	.25
T162	Freddie Money	RC	.25
T163	Noochie Varner	RC	.50
T164	Terrance Hill	RC	.25
T165	Jeremy Hill	RC	.25
T166	Carlos Cabrera	RC	.25
T167	Jose Morban	RC	.25
T168	Kevin Frederick	RC	.25
T169	Mark Teixeira		.40
T170	Brian Rogers		.15
T171	Anastacio Martinez	RC	.25
T172	Bobby Jenks	RC	.75
T173	David Gil	RC	.25
T174	Andres Torres		.15
T175	James Barrett	RC	.25
T176	Jimmy Journell		.15
T177	Brett Kay	RC	.25
T178	Jason Young	RC	.25
T179	Mark Hamilton	RC	.25
T180	Jose Bautista	RC	.50
T181	Blake McGinley	RC	.25
T182	Ryan Mottl	RC	.25
T183	Jeff Austin	RC	.25
T184	Xavier Nady		.15
T185	Kyle Kane	RC	.15
T186	Travis Foley		.15
T187	Nathan Kaup	RC	.25
T188	Eric Cyr	RC	.25
T189	Josh Cisneros	RC	.25
T190	Brad Nelson	RC	.75
T191	Clint Weibl	RC	.25
T192	Ron Calloway	RC	.25
T193	Jung Bong		.15
T194	Rolando Viera	RC	.25
T195	Jason Bulger	RC	.25
T196	Chone Figgins	RC	.75
T197	Jimmy Alvarez	RC	.25
T198	Joel Crump	RC	.25
T199	Ryan Doumit	RC	1.50
T200	Demetrius Heath	RC	.25
T201	John Ennis	RC	.25
T202	Doug Sessions	RC	.25
T203	Clinton Hosford	RC	.25
T204	Chris Narveson	RC	.25
T205	Ross Peeples	RC	.25
T206	Alexander Requena	RC	.25
T207	Matt Erickson	RC	.25
T208	Brian Forystek	RC	.25
T209	Dewon Brazelton		.15
T210	Nathan Haynes		.15
T211	Jack Cust		.15
T212	Jesse Foppert		.75
T213	Jesus Cota	RC	.25
T214	Juan Gonzalez		.15
T215	Tim Kalita	RC	.25
T216	Manny Delcarmen	RC	2.00
T217	Jim Kavourias		.15
T218	C.J. Wilson	RC	.25
T219	Edwin Yan	RC	.25
T220	Andy Van Hekken		.25
T221	Michael Cuddyer		.15
T222	Jeff Verplancke	RC	.25
T223	Mike Wilson	RC	.25
T224	Corwin Malone		.15
T225	Chris Snelling	RC	.50
T226	Joe Rogers	RC	.25
T227	Jason Bay		.50
T228	Ezequiel Astacio	RC	.25
T229	Joey Hammond	RC	.25
T230	Chris Duffy	RC	.25
T231	Mark Prior		1.00
T232	Hansel Izquierdo	RC	.25
T233	Franklyn German	RC	.25
T234	Alexis Gomez		.15
T235	Jorge Padilla	RC	.25
T236	Ryan Snare	RC	.25
T237	Deivis Santos		.15
T238	Taggert Bozied	RC	1.00
T239	Mike Peeples	RC	.25
T240	Ronald Acuna	RC	.25
T241	Koyie Hill		.15
T242	Garrett Guzman	RC	.25
T243	Ryan Church	RC	1.00
T244	Tony Fontana	RC	.25
T245	Keto Anderson	RC	.25
T246	Brad Bouras	RC	.25
T247	Jason Dubois	RC	1.00
T248	Angel Guzman	RC	2.00
T249	Joel Hanrahan	RC	.50
T250	Joe Jiannetti	RC	.25
T251	Sean Pierce	RC	.25
T252	Jake Mauer	RC	.25
T253	Marshall McDougall	RC	.50
T254	Edwin Almonte	RC	.25
T255	Shawn Riggans	RC	.25
T256	Steven Shell		.15
T257	Kevin Hooper	RC	.40
T258	Michael Frick	RC	.25
T259	Travis Chapman	RC	.40
T260	Tim Hummel	RC	.25
T261	Adam Morrissey	RC	.25
T262	Dontrelle Willis	RC	5.00
T263	Justin Sherrod	RC	.25
T264	Gerald Smiley	RC	.25
T265	Tony Miller	RC	.25
T266	Nolan Ryan		1.50
T267	Reggie Jackson		.50
T268	Steve Garvey		.15
T269	Wade Boggs		.25
T270	Sammy Sosa		1.00
T271	Curt Schilling		.25
T272	Mark Grace		.25
T273	Jason Giambi		.50
T274	Ken Griffey Jr.		.75
T275	Roberto Alomar		.40

Gold

Gold Stars:	2-4X
Production 2,002 Sets	
Chrome Refractors:	3-5X
Inserted 1:12	

Farewell Relics

NM/M

Randomly inserted.

JC	Jose Canseco	10.00

Hall of Fame Relics

NM/M

Randomly inserted.

HOF-OS	Ozzie Smith	25.00

Signature Moves Autographs

NM/M

Common Autograph: 8.00
Inserted 1:91

RA	Roberto Alomar	30.00
MA	Moises Alou	15.00
TBL	Tony Blanco	8.00
BB	Boof Bonser	8.00
AC	Antoine Cameron	10.00
BC	Brandon Claussen	15.00
MC	Matt Cooper	8.00
JD	Johnny Damon	30.00
JDA	Jeff DaVanon	8.00
VD	Victor Diaz	12.00
RH	Ryan Hannaman	8.00
KI	Kazuhisa Ishii	40.00
FJ	Forrest Johnson	8.00
TL	Todd Linden	15.00
CM	Corwin Malone	8.00
JM	Jake Mauer	8.00
AM	Andy Morales	8.00
RM	Ramon Moreta	8.00
JMO	Justin Morneau	30.00
JP	Juan Pena	8.00
JS	Juan Silvestre	8.00
CS	Chris Smith	8.00
DT	Dennis Tankersley	8.00
MT	Marcus Thames	8.00
CU	Chase Utley	70.00
JW	Justin Wayne	8.00

Team Topps Legends Autographs

NM/M

Common Autograph: 10.00
Inserted 1:1,097

	Johnny Bench	40.00
	Vida Blue	10.00
	Clete Boyer	12.00
	Whitey Ford	30.00
	Bob Gibson	25.00
	Joe Pepitone	10.00
	Bobby Richardson	10.00
	Bill "Moose" Skowron	10.00
	Enos Slaughter	18.00
	Carl Yastrzemski	60.00

Tools of the Trade Relics

NM/M

Common Player: 5.00
Bat Relics 1:34
Jersey Relics 1:426

RAB	Roberto Alomar/Bat	8.00
MA	Moises Alou/Bat	8.00
DB	David Bell/Bat	5.00
JBU	Jeromy Burnitz/Bat	5.00
JC	Jose Canseco/Bat	10.00
VC	Vinny Castilla/Bat	5.00
JCI	Jeff Cirillo/Bat	5.00
TC	Tony Clark/Bat	5.00
JDB	Johnny Damon/Bat	6.00
CE	Carl Everett/Bat	5.00
BF	Brad Fullmer/Bat	5.00
AG	Andres Galarraga/Bat	5.00
JG	Juan Gonzalez/Jsy	8.00
RHB	Rickey Henderson/Bat	10.00
BJ	Brian Jordan/Bat	5.00
DJ	David Justice/Bat	5.00
CK	Chuck Knoblauch/Bat	5.00
MLB	Matt Lawton/Bat	5.00
KL	Kenny Lofton/Bat	5.00
TM	Tino Martinez/Bat	6.00
CP	Carlos Pena/Bat	6.00
JP	Josh Phelps/Jsy	6.00
TR	Tim Raines/Bat	5.00
RS	Reggie Sanders/Bat	5.00
GS	Gary Sheffield/Bat	5.00
TS	Tsuyoshi Shinjo/Bat	5.00
RSI	Ruben Sierra/Bat	5.00
MT	Michael Tucker/Bat	5.00
MV	Mo Vaughn/Jsy	6.00
MVB	Mo Vaughn/Bat	6.00
RV	Robin Ventura/Bat	6.00
RW	Rondell White/Bat	5.00
EY	Eric Young/Bat	5.00

Topps of the Trade Dual Relics

NM/M

Common Card: 8.00
Inserted 1:539

MA	Moises Alou	10.00
HN	Hideo Nomo	35.00
CP	Chan Ho Park	8.00

2002 Topps Tribute

NM/M

Complete Set (90):	120.00
Common Player:	1.50
Pack (5):	35.00
Box (6):	150.00

1	Hank Aaron	6.00
2	Rogers Hornsby	2.50
3	Bobby Thomson	1.50
4	Eddie Collins	1.50
5	Joe Carter	1.50
6	Jim Palmer	1.50
7	Willie Mays	6.00
8	Willie Stargell	2.50
9	Vida Blue	1.50
10	Whitey Ford	3.00
11	Bob Gibson	3.00
12	Nellie Fox	2.00
13	Napoleon Lajoie	2.00
14	Frankie Frisch	1.50
15	Nolan Ryan	10.00
16	Brooks Robinson	2.50
17	Kirby Puckett	1.50
18	Fergie Jenkins	1.50
19	Edd Roush	1.50
20	Honus Wagner	6.00
21	Richie Ashburn	1.50
22	Bob Feller	1.50
23	Joe Morgan	1.50
24	Orlando Cepeda	1.50
25	Steve Garvey	1.50
26	Hank Greenberg	1.50
27	Stan Musial	5.00
28	Sam Crawford	1.50
29	Jim Rice	1.50
30	Hack Wilson	2.50
31	Lou Brock	1.50
32	Mickey Vernon	1.50
33	Chuck Klein	1.50
34	Joe Jackson	6.00
35	Duke Snider	3.00
36	Ryne Sandberg	1.50
37	Johnny Bench	5.00
38	Sam Rice	1.50
39	Lou Gehrig	8.00
40	Robin Yount	3.00
41	Don Sutton	1.50
42	Jim Bottomley	1.50
43	Billy Herman	1.50
44	Zach Wheat	1.50
45	Juan Marichal	1.50
46	Bert Blyleven	1.50
47	Jackie Robinson	6.00
48	Gil Hodges	1.50
49	Mike Schmidt	6.00
50	Dale Murphy	1.50
51	Phil Rizzuto	1.50
52	Ty Cobb	6.00
53	Andre Dawson	1.50
54	Fred Lindstrom	1.50
55	Roy Campanella	3.00
56	Don Larsen	2.00
57	Harry Heilmann	1.50
58	Jim "Catfish" Hunter	1.50
59	Frank Robinson	2.00
60	Bill Mazeroski	1.50
61	Roger Maris	2.50
62	Dave Winfield	2.50
63	Warren Spahn	2.50
64	Babe Ruth	10.00
65	Ernie Banks	4.00
66	Wade Boggs	2.00
67	Carl Yastrzemski	3.00
68	Ron Santo	1.50
69	Dennis Martinez	1.50
70	Yogi Berra	4.00
71	Paul Waner	1.50
72	George Brett	6.00
73	Eddie Mathews	1.50
74	Bill Dickey	1.50
75	Carlton Fisk	2.00
76	Thurman Munson	4.00
77	Reggie Jackson	4.00
78	Phil Niekro	1.50
79	Luis Aparicio	1.50
80	Steve Carlton	1.50
81	Tris Speaker	1.50
82	Johnny Mize	1.50
83	Tom Seaver	4.00
84	Heinie Manush	1.50
85	Tommy John	1.50
86	Joe Cronin	1.50
87	Don Mattingly	8.00
88	Kirk Gibson	1.50
89	Bo Jackson	3.00
90	Mel Ott	1.50

First Impressions

NM/M

Cards #'d 51-86:	3-5X
Cards #'d 26-50:	4-8X

#'d to last two digits of RK year

Lasting Impressions

Cards #'d 51-96:	3-5X
Cards #'d 26-50:	4-8X

#'d to last two digits of final season
Production under 25 not priced.

Marks of Excellence

NM/M

Inserted 1:61

LB	Lou Brock	50.00
SC	Steve Carlton	50.00
DL	Don Larsen	50.00
SM	Stan Musial	100.00
MS	Mike Schmidt	85.00
WS	Warren Spahn	65.00

Marks of Excellence Relics

NM/M

Inserted 1:61

FJ	Fergie Jenkins	40.00
DM	Don Mattingly	120.00
JP	Jim Palmer	40.00
BR	Brooks Robinson	75.00
DS	Duke Snider	60.00
RY	Robin Yount	70.00

Matching Marks Dual

NM/M

Common Card: 10.00
Inserted 1:11

SBA	Ron Santo, Ernie Banks	25.00
YK	Carl Yastrzemski, Chuck Klein	65.00
WY	Dave Winfield, Carl Yastrzemski	25.00
WYO	Dave Winfield, Robin Yount	20.00
SM	Duke Snider, Willie Mays	85.00
RJ	Frank Robinson, Reggie Jackson	50.00
BMA	George Brett, Don Mattingly	90.00
GH	Steve Garvey, Gil Hodges	20.00
AR	Hank Aaron, Babe Ruth	300.00
GA	Hank Greenberg, Richie Ashburn	80.00
PJ	Jim Palmer, Tommy John	20.00
NS	Phil Niekro, Tom Seaver	15.00
SR	Willie Stargell, Jim Rice	15.00
BF	Johnny Bench, Carlton Fisk	50.00
RS	Nolan Ryan, Tom Seaver	125.00
JS	Fergie Jenkins, Tom Seaver	35.00
YP	Robin Yount, Kirby Puckett	60.00
SB	Tris Speaker, George Brett	100.00
BM	Vida Blue, Dennis Martinez	10.00
BB	Wade Boggs, George Brett	40.00
MA	Willie Mays, Hank Aaron	200.00
BS	Bert Blyleven, Don Sutton	15.00

Memorable Materials

NM/M

Common Player:	10.00
Season parallel:	1.5-3X

#'d to last two digits yr event occurred Jsy Number para.#'d

40-75:	1.5-3X

Under 40 not priced.
Numbered to jersey #.

HA	Hank Aaron	40.00
GB	George Brett	35.00
RC	Roy Campanella	30.00
JC	Joe Carter	10.00
CF	Carlton Fisk	20.00
KG	Kirk Gibson	15.00
BJ	Bo Jackson	15.00
RJ	Reggie Jackson	20.00
CK	Chuck Klein	25.00
RM	Roger Maris	75.00
DM	Don Mattingly	40.00
BM	Bill Mazeroski	15.00
JM	Joe Morgan	15.00
TM	Thurman Munson	50.00
KP	Kirby Puckett	30.00
PR	Phil Rizzuto	25.00
JR	Jackie Robinson	50.00
NR	Nolan Ryan	50.00
BT	Bobby Thomson	15.00
HW	Hack Wilson	40.00
CY	Carl Yastrzemski	30.00

Milestone Materials

NM/M

Common Player:	10.00
Inserted 1:4	
Season parallel #'d 51-95:	1.5-3X

#'d to last two digits milestone season
Jersey Number par.#'d

51-95:	1.5-3X

Numbered to Jersey Number.
Under 50 not priced yet.

LA	Luis Aparicio	15.00
EB	Ernie Banks	30.00
JB	Johnny Bench	20.00
YB	Yogi Berra	25.00
WB	Wade Boggs	15.00
JBO	Jim Bottomley	20.00
OC	Orlando Cepeda	15.00
TC	Ty Cobb	150.00
EC	Eddie Collins	15.00
SC	Sam Crawford	25.00
JC	Joe Cronin	20.00
AD	Andre Dawson	15.00
BD	Bill Dickey	15.00
BF	Bob Feller	15.00
WF	Whitey Ford	25.00

NF	Nellie Fox	30.00
FF	Frankie Frisch	25.00
LG	Lou Gehrig	150.00
BG	Bob Gibson	15.00
HH	Harry Heilmann	20.00
BH	Billy Herman	10.00
RH	Rogers Hornsby	50.00
CH	Jim "Catfish" Hunter	12.00
RJ	Reggie Jackson	20.00
NL	Napoleon Lajoie	60.00
FL	Fred Lindstrom	15.00
HM	Heinie Manush	20.00
JMA	Juan Marichal	15.00
EM	Eddie Mathews	20.00
WH	Willie Mays	45.00
JM	Johnny Mize	15.00
DM	Dale Murphy	20.00
MO	Mel Ott	40.00
JP	Jim Palmer	15.00
SR	Sam Rice	20.00
BRO	Brooks Robinson	20.00
FR	Frank Robinson	20.00
ER	Edd Roush	25.00
BR	Babe Ruth	160.00
NR	Nolan Ryan	50.00
RS	Ryne Sandberg	30.00
TS	Tom Seaver	15.00
DS	Duke Snider	20.00
TSP	Tris Speaker	65.00
WS	Willie Stargell	15.00
MV	Mickey Vernon	15.00
HW	Honus Wagner	140.00
PW	Paul Waner	30.00
ZW	Zach Wheat	40.00
RY	Robin Yount	25.00

Pasttime Patches

NM/M
Inserted 1:92

JB	Johnny Bench	125.00
WB	Wade Boggs	90.00
GB	George Brett	200.00
BD	Bill Dickey	100.00
EM	Eddie Mathews	125.00
DM	Don Mattingly	160.00
JP	Jim Palmer	75.00
KP	Kirby Puckett	125.00
NRA	Nolan Ryan	200.00
NRR	Nolan Ryan	200.00
DW	Dave Winfield	100.00
CY	Carl Yastrzemski	180.00
RY	Robin Yount	100.00

Signature Cuts

NM/M
Reported production 2 each.
Inserted 1:9936

SC-TC	Ty Cobb (4/04 auction)	4,725

"The Catch" Dual

NM/M
Inserted 1:1,023

MW	Willie Mays, Vic Wertz	250.00
MW	Willie Mays, Vic Wertz/54	300.00

2002 Topps206

NM/M
Complete Set (456): 150.00
Common Player: .20
Common (141-155, 271-285): 1.00
Inserted 1:2
Series I Pack (8): 6.00
Series I Box (20): 100.00
Series II Pack (8): 4.00
Series II Box (20): 60.00
Series III Pack (8): 6.00
Series III Box (20): 100.00

1	Vladimir Guerrero	.75
2	Sammy Sosa	1.50
3	Garret Anderson	.40
4	Rafael Palmeiro	.50
5	Juan Gonzalez	.50
6	John Smoltz	.40
7	Mark Mulder	.40
8	Jon Lieber	.20
9	Greg Maddux	1.00
10	Moises Alou	.40
11	Joe Randa	.20
12	Bobby Abreu	.40
13	Ryan Kohlmeier	.20
14	Kerry Wood	.75
15	Craig Biggio	.40
16	Curt Schilling	.50
17	Brian Jordan	.20
18	Edgardo Alfonzo	.20
19	Darren Dreifort	.20
20	Todd Helton	.50
21	Ramon Ortiz	.20
22	Ichiro Suzuki	1.50
23	Jimmy Rollins	.50
24	Darin Erstad	.40
25	Shawn Green	.40
26	Tino Martinez	.30
27	Bret Boone	.40
28	Alfonso Soriano	.75
29	Chan Ho Park	.40
30	Roger Clemens	1.50
31	Cliff Floyd	.20
32	Johnny Damon	.40
33	Frank Thomas	.75
34	Barry Bonds	2.00
35	Luis Gonzalez	.40
36	Carlos Lee	.20
37	Roberto Alomar	.50
38	Carlos Delgado	.20
39	Nomar Garciaparra	1.50
40	Jason Kendall	.40
41	Scott Rolen	.75
42	Tom Glavine	.40
43	Ryan Klesko	.40
44	Brian Giles	.40
45	Bud Smith	.20
46	Charles Nagy	.20
47	Tony Gwynn	.75
48	C.C. Sabathia	.40
49	Manny Ramirez	.75
50	Jerry Hairston Jr.	.20
51	Jeromy Burnitz	.20
52	David Justice	.40
53	Bartolo Colon	.20
54	Andres Galarraga	.30
55	Jeff Weaver	.20
56	Terrance Long	.20
57	Tsuyoshi Shinjo	.40
58	Barry Zito	.20
59	Mariano Rivera	.40
60	John Olerud	.20
61	Randy Johnson	.75
62	Kenny Lofton	.40
63	Jermaine Dye	.20
64	Troy Glaus	.40
65	Larry Walker	.40
66	Hideo Nomo	.40
67	Mike Mussina	.40
68	Paul LoDuca	.20
69	Magglio Ordonez	.40
70	Paul O'Neill	.40
71	Sean Casey	.20
72	Lance Berkman	.40
73	Adam Dunn	.50
74	Aramis Ramirez	.20
75	Rafael Furcal	.40
76	Gary Sheffield	.40
77	Todd Hollandsworth	.20
78	Chipper Jones	.75
79	Bernie Williams	.40
80	Richard Hidalgo	.25
81	Eric Chavez	.40
82	Mike Piazza	1.50
83	J.D. Drew	.40
84	Ken Griffey Jr.	1.00
85	Joe Kennedy	.20
86	Joel Pineiro	.20
87	Josh Towers	.20
88	Andruw Jones	.50
89	Carlos Beltran	.40
90	Mike Cameron	.20
91	Albert Pujols	1.50
92	Alex Rodriguez	1.50
93	Omar Vizquel	.30
94	Juan Encarnacion	.20
95	Jeff Bagwell	.50
96	Jose Canseco	.40
97	Ben Sheets	.40
98	Mark Grace	.40
99	Mike Sweeney	.20
100	Mark McGwire	2.00
101	Ivan Rodriguez	.75
102	Rich Aurilia	.20
103	Cristian Guzman	.20
104	Roy Oswalt	.40
105	Tim Hudson	.40
106	Brent Abernathy	.20
107	Mike Hampton	.40
108	Miguel Tejada	.40
109	Bobby Higginson	.20
110	Edgar Martinez	.40
111	Jorge Posada	.40
112	Jason Giambi	.50
113	Pedro Astacio	.20
114	Kazuhisa Sasaki	.20
115	Preston Wilson	.20
116	Jason Bere	.20
117	Mark Quinn	.20
118	Pokey Reese	.20
119	Derek Jeter	2.00
120	Shannon Stewart	.20
121	Jeff Kent	.40
122	Jeremy Giambi	.20
123	Pat Burrell	.40
124	Jim Edmonds	.40
125	Mark Buehrle	.20
126	Kevin Brown	.40
127	Raul Mondesi	.20
128	Pedro Martinez	.75
129	Jim Thome	.75
130	Russ Ortiz	.20
131	Brandon Duckworth	.20
132	Ryan Jamison RC	.50
133	Brandon Inge	.20
134	Felipe Lopez	.20
135	Jason Lane	.20
136	Forrest Johnson RC	.50
137	Greg Nash	.20
138	Covelli Crisp	.20
139	Nick Neugebauer	.20
140	Dustan Mohr	.20
141	Freddy Sanchez RC	1.00
142	Justin Backsmeyer RC	1.00
143	Jorge Julio	1.00
144	Ryan Mottl RC	1.00
145	Chris Tritle RC	1.00
146	Noochie Varner RC	1.00
147	Brian Rogers	1.00
148	Michael Hill RC	1.00
149	Luis Pineda	1.00
150	Rich Thompson RC	1.00
151	Bill Hall	1.00
152	Jose Dominguez RC	1.50
153	Justin Woodrow RC	1.00
154	Nic Jackson RC	1.00
155	Laynce Nix RC	4.00
156	Hank Aaron	3.00
157	Ernie Banks	1.50
158	Johnny Bench	1.50
159	George Brett	4.00
160	Carlton Fisk	.50
161	Bob Gibson	.75
162	Reggie Jackson	1.00
163	Don Mattingly	4.00
164	Kirby Puckett	1.50
165	Frank Robinson	1.00
166	Nolan Ryan	5.00
167	Tom Seaver	1.00
168	Mike Schmidt	1.50
169	Dave Winfield	.50
170	Carl Yastrzemski	1.00
171	Frank Chance	.75
172	Ty Cobb	3.00
173	Sam Crawford	.75
174	Johnny Evers	.75
175	John McGraw	1.00
176	Eddie Plank	.50
177	Tris Speaker	1.00
178	Joe Tinker	.50
179	Honus Wagner	5.00
180	Cy Young	2.50
181	Javier Vazquez	.20
182	Mark Mulder	.40
183	Roger Clemens	1.50
184	Kazuhisa Ishii RC	1.50
185	Roberto Alomar	.50
186	Lance Berkman	.40
187	Adam Dunn	.50
188	Aramis Ramirez	.40
189	Chuck Knoblauch	.20
190	Nomar Garciaparra	1.50
191	Brad Penny	.20
192	Gary Sheffield	.40
193	Alfonso Soriano	.75
194	Andruw Jones	.50
195	Randy Johnson	.75
196	Corey Patterson	.40
197	Milton Bradley	.20
198	Johnny Damon	.40
199	Paul LoDuca	.20
200	Albert Pujols	1.50
201	Scott Rolen	.75
202	J.D. Drew	.40
203	Vladimir Guerrero	.75
204	Jason Giambi	.40
205	Moises Alou	.40
206	Magglio Ordonez	.40
207	Carlos Febles	.20
208	So Taguchi RC	.50
209	Rafael Palmeiro	.50
210	David Wells	.20
211	Orlando Cabrera	.20
212	Sammy Sosa	1.50
213	Armando Benitez	.20
214	Wes Helms	.20
215	Mariano Rivera	.40
216	Jimmy Rollins	.40
217	Matt Lawton	.20
218	Shawn Green	.40
219	Bernie Williams	.50
220	Bret Boone	.40
221	Alex Rodriguez	2.00
222	Roger Cedeno	.20
223	Marty Cordova	.20
224	Fred McGriff	.40
225	Chipper Jones	.75
226	Kerry Wood	.75
227	Larry Walker	.40
228	Robin Ventura	.40
229	Robert Fick	.20
230	Tino Martinez	.40
231	Ben Petrick	.20
232	Neifi Perez	.20
233	Pedro Martinez	.75
234	Brian Jordan	.20
235	Freddy Garcia	.20
236	Derek Jeter	2.00
237	Ben Grieve	.20
238	Barry Bonds	2.00
239	Luis Gonzalez	.40
240	Shane Halter	.20
241	Brian Giles	.40
242	Bud Smith	.20
243	Richie Sexson	.40
244	Barry Zito	.20
245	Eric Milton	.20
246	Ivan Rodriguez	.50
247	Toby Hall	.20
248	Mike Piazza	1.50
249	Ruben Sierra	.20
250	Tsuyoshi Shinjo	.20
251	Jermaine Dye	.20
252	Roy Oswalt	.40
253	Todd Helton	.50
254	Adrian Beltre	.40
255	Doug Mientkiewicz	.20
256	Ichiro Suzuki	1.50
257	C.C. Sabathia	.20
258	Paul Konerko	.20
259	Ken Griffey Jr.	1.00
260	Jeromy Burnitz	.20
261	Hank Blalock	.50
262	Mark Prior	1.50
263	Josh Beckett	.50
264	Carlos Pena	.20
265	Sean Burroughs	.20
266	Austin Kearns	.40
267	Chin-Hui Tsao	.20
268	Dewon Brazelton	.20
269	J.D. Martin	.20
270	Marlon Byrd	.20
271	Joe Mauer RC	8.00
272	Jason Botts RC	1.00
273	Mauricio Lara RC	1.00
274	Jonny Gomes RC	3.00
275	Gavin Floyd	1.50
276	Alexander Requena RC	1.00
277	Jimmy Gobble RC	1.00
278	Chris Duffy RC	1.00
279	Colt Griffin	1.00
280	Ryan Church RC	1.50
281	Beltran Perez	1.00
282	Clint Nageotte RC	1.50
283	Justin Schuda RC	1.00
284	Scott Hairston	1.50
285	Mario Ramos	1.00
286	Tom Seaver	2.00
287	Hank Aaron	3.00
288	Mike Schmidt	3.00
289	Robin Yount	1.50
290	Joe Morgan	1.00
291	Frank Robinson	1.00
292	Reggie Jackson	2.00
293	Nolan Ryan	4.00
294	Dave Winfield	1.00
295	Willie Mays	3.00
296	Brooks Robinson	1.50
297	Mark McGwire	3.00
298	Honus Wagner	3.00
299	Sherry Magee	1.00
300	Frank Chance	1.00
301	Larry Doyle	1.00
302	John McGraw	2.00
303	Jimmy Collins	1.00
304	Buck Herzog	1.00
305	Sam Crawford	1.00
306	Cy Young	2.50
307	Honus Wagner	3.00
308	Alex Rodriguez	2.00
308	Alex Rodriguez/SP Blue Jsy	4.00
309	Vernon Wells	.20
310	Barry Bonds	2.00
310	Barry Bonds/SP Cream Jsy	6.00
311	Vicente Padilla	.20
312	Alfonso Soriano	.75
312	A.Soriano/SP No wristband	1.50
313	Mike Piazza	1.50
314	Jacque Jones	.20
315	Shawn Green/SP	1.50
316	Paul Byrd	.20
317	Lance Berkman	.40
318	Larry Walker	.40
319	Ken Griffey Jr./SP	3.00
320	Shea Hillenbrand	.20
321	Jay Gibbons	.20
322	Andruw Jones	.50
323	Luis Gonzalez/SP	1.50
324	Garret Anderson	.40
325	Roy Halladay	.40
326	Randy Winn	.20
327	Matt Morris	.40
328	Robb Nen	.20
329	Trevor Hoffman	.20
330	Kip Wells	.20
331	Orlando Hernandez	.30
332	Rey Ordonez	.20
333	Torii Hunter	.40
334	Geoff Jenkins	.40
335	Eric Karros	.20
336	Mike Lowell	.40
337	Nick Johnson	.20
338	Randall Simon	.20
339	Ellis Burks	.20
340	Sammy Sosa	1.50
340	Sammy Sosa/SP Blue Jsy	4.00
341	Pedro J. Martinez	.75
342	Junior Spivey	.20
343	Vinny Castilla	.20
344	Randy Johnson/SP	2.00
345	Chipper Jones/SP	1.50
346	Orlando Hudson	.20
347	Albert Pujols/SP	5.00
348	Rondell White	.20
349	Vladimir Guerrero	.75
350	Mark Prior	1.00
350	Mark Prior/SP Red background	3.00
351	Eric Gagne	.50
352	Todd Zeile	.20
353	Manny Ramirez/SP	2.00
354	Kevin Millwood	.40
355	Troy Percival	.20
356	Jason Giambi	.50
356	Jason Giambi/SP White Jsy	1.50
357	Bartolo Colon	.20
358	Jeremy Giambi	.20
359	Jose Cruz Jr.	.20
360	Ichiro Suzuki	1.50
360	Ichiro/SP Blue warm-up	3.00
361	Eddie Guardado	.20
362	Ivan Rodriguez	.50
363	Carl Crawford	.20
364	Jason Simontacchi RC	.20
365	Kenny Lofton	.40
366	Raul Mondesi	.20
367	A.J. Pierzynski	.20
368	Ugueth Urbina	.20
369	Rodrigo Lopez	.20
370	Nomar Garciaparra	1.50
370	N. Garciaparra/SP 1 Bat	3.00
371	Craig Counsell	.20
372	Barry Larkin	.40
373	Carlos Pena	.20
374	Luis Castillo	.20
375	Raul Ibanez	.20
376	Kazuhisa Ishii/SP	1.50
377	Derek Lowe	.20
378	Curt Schilling	.50
379	Jim Thome	.75
380	Derek Jeter	2.00
380	D. Jeter/SP Blue background	5.00
381	Pat Burrell	.50
382	Jamie Moyer	.20
383	Eric Hinske	.20
384	Scott Rolen	.75
385	Miguel Tejada/SP	1.50
386	Andy Pettitte	.40
387	Mike Lieberthal	.20
388	Al Leiter	.20
389	Todd Helton/SP	2.00
390	Adam Dunn	.50
390	Adam Dunn/SP with bat	1.00
391	Cliff Floyd	.20
392	Tim Salmon	.40
393	Joe Torre	.20
394	Bobby Cox	.20
395	Tony LaRussa	.20
396	Art Howe	.20
397	Bob Brenly	.20
398	Ron Gardenhire	.20
399	Mike Cuddyer	.20
400	Joe Mauer	2.50
401	Mark Teixeira	.50
402	Hee Seop Choi	.20
403	Angel Berroa	.20
404	Jesse Foppert	.50
405	Bobby Crosby	.50
406	Jose Reyes	.50
407	Casey Kotchman	1.00
408	Aaron Heilman	.20
409	Adrian Gonzalez	.20
410	Delwyn Young RC	.75
411	Brett Myers	.20
412	Justin Huber RC	1.00
413	Drew Henson	.20
414	Taggert Bozied RC	.50
415	Dontrelle Willis RC	6.00
416	Rocco Baldelli	.50
417	Jason Stokes RC	2.50
418	Brandon Phillips	.20
419	Jake Blalock/SP RC	2.00
420	Micah Schilling/SP RC	1.00
421	Denard Span/SP RC	1.00
422	James Loney/SP RC	4.00
423	Wes Bankston/SP RC	1.50
424	Jeremy Hermida/ SP RC	6.00
425	Curtis Granderson/ SP RC	1.00
426	Jason Pridie/SP RC	1.00
427	Larry Broadway/ SP RC	1.00
428	Khalil Greene/SP RC	5.00
429	Joey Votto/SP RC	2.50
430	B.J. Upton/SP RC	8.00
431	Sergio Santos/SP RC	2.00
432	Brian Dopirak/SP RC	2.00
433	Ozzie Smith/SP	2.00
434	Wade Boggs/SP	1.00
435	Yogi Berra/SP	3.00
436	Al Kaline/SP	2.00
437	Robin Roberts/SP	1.00
438	Roberto Clemente/SP	8.00
439	Gary Carter/SP	1.00
440	Fergie Jenkins/SP	1.00
441	Orlando Cepeda/SP	1.00
442	Rod Carew/SP	1.50
443	Harmon Killebrew/SP	2.50
444	Duke Snider/SP	1.00
445	Stan Musial/SP	5.00
446	Hank Greenberg/SP	1.00
447	Lou Brock/SP	1.00
448	Jim Palmer	.50
449	John McGraw	.75
450	Mordecai Brown	.50
451	Christy Mathewson	1.00
452	Sam Crawford	.50
453	Bill O'Hara	.50
454	Joe Tinker	.50
455	Napoleon Lajoie	.75
456	Honus Wagner	3.00

T206 Mini Parallel

MONDESI, TORONTO

Polar Bear:	2-3X
Tolstoi Black:	2-5X
Average 4:Box	
Tolstoi Red:	4-8X
Average 2:Box	
Cycle:	6-12X
Average 1:Box	
Series 2	
Polar Bear:	2-3X
Piedmont Black:	3-5X
Piedmond Red:	4-8X
Carolina Brights:	6-12X
Series 3	
Polar Bear:	2-3X
Sweet Caporal Red:	3-5X
Sweet Caporal Blue or Black:	4-6X
Uzit:	6-12X
Bazooka Backs:	No Pricing
Production 30	
Drum Backs:	No Pricing
Production 20	
Lenox variations:	No Pricing
Production 10	
American Beauty variation:	No Pricing
Production 5	

Autographs

NM/M
Common Player: 8.00
Inserted 1:41

BB	Barry Bonds	200.00
RC	Roger Clemens	150.00
JE	Jim Edmonds	30.00
BG	Brian Giles	15.00
CG	Cristian Guzman	15.00
BI	Brandon Inge	10.00
RJ	Ryan Jamison	8.00
FJ	Forrest Johnson	8.00
JJ	Jorge Julio	10.00
FL	Felipe Lopez	15.00
GN	Greg Nash	8.00
MO	Magglio Ordonez	20.00
AR	Alex Rodriguez	100.00
JR	Jimmy Rollins	20.00
BZ	Barry Zito	20.00

Autographs Series 2

NM/M
Common Player: 8.00
Inserted 1:55

MA	Moises Alou	30.00
LB	Lance Berkman	35.00
HB	Hank Blalock	30.00
DB	Dewon Brazelton	8.00
MB	Marlon Byrd	10.00
EC	Eric Chavez	30.00

ABBREVIATIONS

SP - Short Print

JD	Johnny Damon	25.00
GF	Gavin Floyd	20.00
LG	Luis Gonzalez	20.00
KI	Kazuhisa Ishii	40.00
JDM	J.D. Martin	8.00
JM	Joe Mauer	100.00
MP	Mark Prior	40.00
AP	Albert Pujols	140.00
SR	Scott Rolen	40.00
RS	Richie Sexson	15.00
BS	Ben Sheets	20.00
BSM	Bud Smith	10.00
ST	So Taguchi	25.00
CT	Chris Tritle	10.00

Autographs Series 3

NM/M

	Common Autograph:	8.00
MB	Milton Bradley	10.00
JC	Jose Cruz Jr.	15.00
DE	David Eckstein	8.00
DH	Drew Henson	15.00
ML	Mike Lamb	8.00
MT	Marcus Thames	8.00
JV	Jose Vidro	10.00

Relics

NM/M

	Common Player:	5.00
	Overall Relics 1:11	
RA	Roberto Alomar/Jsy	10.00
JB	Jeff Bagwell/Jsy	10.00
CB	Craig Biggio/Jsy	8.00
BB	Barry Bonds/Jsy	25.00
BBO	Bret Boone/Jsy	8.00
MC	Mike Cameron/Jsy	5.00
JC	Jose Canseco/Bat	10.00
CD	Carlos Delgado/Jsy	8.00
JED	Jim Edmonds/Jsy	10.00
CF	Cliff Floyd/Jsy	5.00
JGI	Jason Giambi/Jsy	8.00
JG	Jeremy Giambi/Jsy	5.00
TG	Tom Glavine/Jsy	8.00
SG	Shawn Green/Jsy	8.00
TGW	Tony Gwynn/Jsy	15.00
TH	Todd Helton/Jsy	10.00
RJ	Randy Johnson/Jsy	15.00
AJ	Andruw Jones/Jsy	8.00
CJ	Chipper Jones/Jsy	10.00
CL	Carlos Lee/Jsy	5.00
KL	Kenny Lofton/Jsy	5.00
GM	Greg Maddux/Jsy	15.00
EM	Edgar Martinez/Jsy	10.00
TM	Tino Martinez/Jsy	5.00
JO	John Olerud/Jsy	5.00
PO	Paul O'Neill/Jsy	5.00
MO	Magglio Ordonez/Jsy	6.00
CP	Chan Ho Park/Bat	5.00
MP	Mike Piazza/Jsy	15.00
AP	Albert Pujols/Bat	25.00
IR	Ivan Rodriguez/Jsy	8.00
AS	Alfonso Soriano/Bat	10.00
SS	Shannon Stewart/Bat	8.00
FT	Frank Thomas/Jsy	15.00
JT	Jim Thome/Jsy	20.00
LW	Larry Walker/Jsy	5.00
JW	Jeff Weaver/Jsy	5.00
BW	Bernie Williams/Jsy	8.00
BZ	Barry Zito/Jsy	8.00

Relics Series 2

NM/M

	Common Player:	5.00
	Jerseys 1:18	
	Bats 1:40	
RA	Roberto Alomar/Jsy	10.00
JB	Jeff Bagwell/Jsy	8.00
BB	Barry Bonds/Jsy	20.00
BBO	Bret Boone/Jsy	6.00
KB	Kevin Brown/Jsy	6.00
AB	A.J. Burnett/Jsy	5.00
SB	Sean Burroughs/Bat	5.00
EC	Eric Chavez/Bat	8.00
TC	Ty Cobb/Bat	400.00
JC	Jimmy Collins/Bat	45.00
SCR	Sam Crawford/Bat	50.00
JD	Jimmy Damon/Bat	12.00
RD	Ryan Dempster/Jsy	5.00
BD	Brandon Duckworth/Jsy	5.00
AD	Adam Dunn/Bat	10.00
DE	Darin Erstad/Jsy	5.00
JEV	Johnny Evers/Bat	50.00
CF	Cliff Floyd/Jsy	5.00
TGL	Tom Glavine/Jsy	8.00

JG	Juan Gonzalez/Bat	10.00
MG	Mark Grace/Bat	10.00
SG	Shawn Green/Jsy	6.00
CG	Cristian Guzman/Jsy	5.00
TG	Tony Gwynn/Jsy	15.00
TH	Toby Hall/Jsy	5.00
JH	Josh Hamilton/Bat	10.00
THE	Todd Helton/Bat	15.00
RH	Rickey Henderson/Bat	15.00
BH	Buck Herzog/Bat	30.00
JJ	Jason Jennings/Jsy	5.00
RJ	Randy Johnson/Jsy	15.00
AJ	Andruw Jones/Jsy	8.00
CJO	Chipper Jones/Jsy	10.00
JK	Jeff Kent/Jsy	5.00
BL	Barry Larkin/Jsy	8.00
TL	Travis Lee/Bat	5.00
GM	Greg Maddux/Bat	12.00
EM	Edgar Martinez/Jsy	10.00
TM	Tino Martinez/Bat	10.00
JM	Joe Mays/Jsy	5.00
JMC	John McGraw/Bat	60.00
FM	Fred McGriff/Bat	8.00
JO	John Olerud/Jsy	5.00
RP	Rafael Palmeiro/Jsy	8.00
BP	Brad Penny/Jsy	5.00
MP	Mike Piazza/Jsy	15.00
AP	Albert Pujols/Jsy	15.00
ARA	Aramis Ramirez/Bat	10.00
AR	Alex Rodriguez/Bat	20.00
IR	Ivan Rodriguez/Jsy	8.00
CS	Curt Schilling/Bat	15.00
GS	Gary Sheffield/Bat	8.00
TS	Tsuyoshi Shinjo/Bat	5.00
AS	Alfonso Soriano/Bat	10.00
MT	Miguel Tejada/Bat	8.00
FT	Frank Thomas/Jsy	8.00
JTH	Jim Thome/Bat	15.00
JT	Joe Tinker/Bat	40.00
MV	Mo Vaughn/Bat	8.00
RV	Robin Ventura/Bat	5.00
HWA	Honus Wagner/Bat	400.00
LW	Larry Walker/Jsy	5.00
BW	Bernie Williams/Jsy	5.00
MW	Matt Williams/Jsy	5.00
PW	Preston Wilson/Jsy	5.00

Relics Series 3

NM/M

	Common Player:	5.00
RA	Roberto Alomar/Bat	8.00
JB	Jeff Bagwell/Bat	5.00
WB	Wilson Betemit/Bat	5.00
PB	Pat Burrell/Bat	10.00
EC	Eric Chavez/Jsy	8.00
AD	Adam Dunn/Bat	10.00
JE	Jim Edmonds/Jsy	8.00
NG	Nomar Garciaparra/Bat	20.00
LG	Luis Gonzalez/Jsy	5.00
TG	Tony Gwynn/Jsy	10.00
TH	Todd Helton/Jsy	8.00
RH	Rickey Henderson/Bat	15.00
NJ	Nick Johnson/Bat	5.00
RJ	Randy Johnson/Jsy	10.00
AJ	Andruw Jones/Bat	8.00
CJ	Chipper Jones/Jsy	8.00
PM	Pedro Martinez/Jsy	12.00
DM	Doug Mientkiewicz/Jsy	6.00
RP	Rafael Palmeiro/Bat	8.00
CP	Corey Patterson/Bat	6.00
MP	Mike Piazza/Jsy	15.00
AP	Albert Pujols/Bat	20.00
AR	Alex Rodriguez/Bat	15.00
IR	Ivan Rodriguez/Bat	8.00
SR	Scott Rolen/Bat	10.00
CS	Curt Schilling/Bat	8.00
GS	Gary Sheffield/Bat	8.00
TS	Tsuyoshi Shinjo/Bat	5.00
AS	Alfonso Soriano/Bat	10.00
MTE	Miguel Tejada/Bat	8.00
FT	Frank Thomas/Bat	8.00
JT	Jim Thome/Jsy	10.00
MV	Mo Vaughn/Jsy	5.00
BW	Bernie Williams/Jsy	8.00
BZ	Barry Zito/Jsy	6.00

Reprint Relics

NM/M

	Common Player:	75.00
SC	Sam Crawford	90.00
JE	Johnny Evers	90.00
JM	John McGraw	75.00
TS	Tris Speaker	140.00
HW	Honus Wagner	400.00

Team Topps Legends Autographs

NM/M

Inserted 1:7,093

	Nolan Ryan	400.00

Team Topps Legends Autographs Series 2

NM/M

Inserted 1:260

	Ralph Branca	25.00
	Andy Pafko	20.00

	Joe Pepitone	10.00
	Tom Seaver	60.00
	Warren Spahn	25.00
	Luis Tiant	10.00

Team 206

NM/M

	Complete Set (20):	10.00
	Common Player:	.25
	Inserted 1:Pack	
1	Barry Bonds	2.00
2	Ivan Rodriguez	.50
3	Luis Gonzalez	.25
4	Jason Giambi	.50
5	Pedro Martinez	.75
6	Larry Walker	.25
7	Bobby Abreu	.40
8	Derek Jeter	2.00
9	Bret Boone	.40
10	Mike Piazza	1.00
11	Alex Rodriguez	1.50
12	Roger Clemens	1.50
13	Albert Pujols	1.50
14	Randy Johnson	.75
15	Sammy Sosa	1.50
16	Cristian Guzman	.25
17	Shawn Green	.40
18	Curt Schilling	.50
19	Ichiro Suzuki	1.00
20	Chipper Jones	.75

Team 206 Series 2

RODRIGUEZ, TEXAS

NM/M

	Complete Set (25):	10.00
	Common Player:	.25
	Inserted 1:1	
1	Alex Rodriguez	1.50
2	Sammy Sosa	1.50
3	Jason Giambi	.50
4	Nomar Garciaparra	1.25
5	Ichiro Suzuki	.75
6	Chipper Jones	.75
7	Derek Jeter	2.00
8	Barry Bonds	2.00
9	Mike Piazza	1.50
10	Randy Johnson	.75
11	Shawn Green	.25
12	Todd Helton	.50
13	Luis Gonzalez	.25
14	Albert Pujols	.75
15	Curt Schilling	.50
16	Scott Rolen	.75
17	Ivan Rodriguez	.50
18	Roberto Alomar	.50
19	Cristian Guzman	.25
20	Bret Boone	.25
21	Barry Zito	.25
22	Larry Walker	.25
23	Eric Chavez	.25
24	Roger Clemens	1.50
25	Pedro Martinez	.75

Team 206 Series 3

N.Y.

MATHEWSON, N.Y. NAT'L

NM/M

	Complete Set (30):	10.00
	Common Player:	.25
	Inserted 1:1	
1	Ichiro Suzuki	1.00
2	Kazuhisa Ishii	.25
3	Alex Rodriguez	1.50
4	Mark Prior	1.00
5	Derek Jeter	2.00
6	Sammy Sosa	1.00
7	Nomar Garciaparra	1.25
8	Mike Piazza	1.00
9	Jason Giambi	.50
10	Vladimir Guerrero	.75
11	Curt Schilling	.50
12	Jim Thome	.75
13	Adam Dunn	.50
14	Albert Pujols	1.50
15	Pat Burrell	.50
16	Chipper Jones	.75
17	Randy Johnson	.50
18	Todd Helton	.50
19	Luis Gonzalez	.25
20	Alfonso Soriano	.75
21	Shawn Green	.40
22	Pedro J. Martinez	.75
23	Lance Berkman	.40
24	Ivan Rodriguez	.50
25	Larry Walker	.25
26	Andruw Jones	.40
27	Ken Griffey Jr.	1.00
28	Eric Hinske	.25
29	Mike Sweeney	.25
30	Miguel Tejada	.50

1982 California Angels Reprints

DON BAYLOR DH-OUTFIELD ANGELS

Commemorating the 20th anniversary of the A.L. West Championship Angels, Fox Sport Net issued this reprint set of the team's stars. Fronts are identical to the originals. Backs also closely reproduce the 1982 versions, but have a shaded box at the right end with a card number and updated copyright information. Fifteen thousand sets, cello-wrapped with a sponsor's header card, were given to fans attending an Anaheim game.

NM/M

	Complete Set (10):	10.00
	Common Player:	.50
1	Don Baylor	1.00
2	Rod Carew	2.00
3	Doug DeCinces	.50
4	Brian Downing	.50
5	Reggie Jackson	5.00
6	Fred Lynn	.75
7	Geoff Zahn	.50
8	Bob Boone	1.00
9	Bob Grich	.75
--	Header Card	.05

Chicago Cubs Reprints

DON CARDWELL Chicago Cubs

For a second year the Cubs contracted with Topps to provide a series of reprint cards for use as give-aways at special games throughout the season. Each reprint features a Wrigley Field logo on front and is sequentially numbered to 20,000 in a strip of gold foil on back. Each card was distributed in a cello wrapper with the date of the promotion and names of the sponsor(s).

NM/M

	Complete Set (11):	35.00
	Common Player:	2.50
1954	Ernie Banks	12.50
1961	Don Cardwell	2.50
1961	Billy Williams	5.00
1962	Ken Hubbs	3.50
1969	Ken Holtzman	2.50
1972	Milt Pappas	2.50
1979	Dave Kingman	3.00
1980	Bill Buckner	3.00
1984	Lee Smith	4.00
1998	Kerry Wood	3.00
2002	Sammy Sosa	3.00

Milwaukee Brewers Reprints

MICHAEL PAUL MOLITOR Brewers

Topps cards of former Brewers favorites were reprinted and distributed one per month at selected home games. The cards are nearly identical to the originals except for a sponsor's (St. Michael Hospital) logo on front and a reprint notice on back.

NM/M

	Complete Set (6):	25.00
	Common Player:	4.00
(1)	Don Money/1978	4.00
(2)	Cecil Cooper/1979	4.00
(3)	Ben Oglivie/1980	4.00
(4)	Gorman Thomas/1981	4.00
(5)	Robin Yount/1982	7.50
(6)	Paul Molitor/1992	7.50

Post Collector's Series

FRANK THOMAS First Base

For a second consecutive year in 2002, Post cereals packaged a special edition of Topps cards. The baseball cards were issued two per cello pack. The 2-1/2" x 3-1/2" cards have game-action photos with the background printed in a matte finish. The player portion of the photo and the surrounding team-color coded graphics at the sides and bottom have spot gloss. At bottom-right are the player's position and name. A team logo in the lower-left corner and the Topps logo is at upper-left. Backs have a portrait photo, biographical data, 2001 monthly stats and various league and sponsor logos. An album to house the collection was available by mail for $8.95 and two proofs of purchase.

NM/M

	Complete Set (30):	10.00
	Common Player:	.25
	Album:	9.00
1	Alex Rodriguez	1.50
2	Pedro Martinez	.50
3	Bernie Williams	.35
4	Mike Piazza	1.00
5	Jim Edmonds	.25
6	Rich Aurilia	.25
7	Sammy Sosa	1.25
8	Sean Casey	.25
9	Ichiro	2.00
10	Jason Giambi	.40
11	Todd Helton	.40
12	Chipper Jones	1.00
13	Frank Thomas	.65
14	Scott Rolen	.35
15	Carlos Delgado	.35
16	Jeff Bagwell	.65
17	Jim Thome	.25
18	Shawn Green	.35
19	Luis Gonzales	.50
20	Vladimir Guerrero	.65
21	Troy Glaus	.50
22	Ryan Klesko	.25
23	Jeromy Burnitz	.25
24	Bobby Higginson	.25
25	Jason Kendall	.25
26	Cliff Floyd	.25
27	Greg Vaughn	.25
28	Brad Radke	.25
29	Mike Sweeney	.25
30	Jeff Conine	.25

2003 Topps

	Complete Set (720):	70.00
	Sealed Factory Set (725):	70.00
	Complete Series 1 Set (366):	35.00
	Complete Series 2 Set (355):	35.00
	Common Player:	.10
	Series 1 & 2 Pack (10):	1.50
	Series 1 & 2 Box (36):	35.00
	Series 2 Jumbo Box:	45.00

White Topps "throw-back" logo.

Series 1 (1:8852): Values Undetermined
Series 2 (1:4487): Values Undetermined

1a	Alex Rodriguez (Red Topps)	1.00
2	Dan Wilson	.10
3	Jimmy Rollins	.25
4	Jermaine Dye	.10
5	Steve Karsay	.10
6	Timoniel Perez	.10
7	Jose Vidro	.10
8	Jose Vidro	.10
9	Eddie Guardado	.10
10a	Mark Prior (Red Topps)	.50
11a	Curt Schilling (Red Topps)	.40
12	Dennis Cook	.10
13	Andruw Jones	.40
14	David Segui	.10
15	Trot Nixon	.10
16	Antonio Alfonseca	.10
17	Magglio Ordonez	.20
18	Jason LaRue	.10
19	Danys Baez	.10
20a	Todd Helton (Red Topps)	.40
21	Denny Neagle	.10
22	Dave Mlicki	.10
23	Roberto Hernandez	.10
24	Odalis Perez	.10
25	Nick Neugebauer	.10
26	David Ortiz	.10
27	Andres Galarraga	.15
28	Edgardo Alfonzo	.10
29	Chad Bradford	.10
30a	Jason Giambi (Red Topps)	.40
31	Brian Giles	.25
32	Deivi Cruz	.10
33	Robb Nen	.10
34	Jeff Nelson	.10
35	Edgar Renteria	.10
36	Aubrey Huff	.10
37	Brandon Duckworth	.10
38	Juan Gonzalez	.40
39	Sidney Ponson	.10
40	Eric Hinske	.10
41	Kevin Appier	.10
42	Danny Bautista	.10
43	Javier Lopez	.10
44	Jeff Conine	.10
45	Carlos Baerga	.10
46	Ugueth Urbina	.10
47	Mark Buehrle	.10
48	Aaron Boone	.10
49	Chuck Finley	.10
50a	Sammy Sosa (Red Topps)	1.00
51	Jose Jimenez	.10
52	Chris Truby	.10
53	Luis Castillo	.10

#	Player	Value
54	Orlando Merced	.10
55	Brian Jordan	.10
56	Eric Young	.10
57	Bobby Kielty	.10
58	Luis Rivas	.10
59	Brad Wilkerson	.10
60	Roberto Alomar	.40
61a	Roger Clemens (Red Topps)	1.00
62	Scott Hatteberg	.10
63	Andy Ashby	.10
64	Mike Williams	.10
65	Ron Gant	.10
66	Benito Santiago	.10
67	Bret Boone	.10
68	Matt Morris	.10
69	Troy Glaus	.40
70	Austin Kearns	.25
71	Jim Thome	.40
72	Rickey Henderson	.40
73a	Luis Gonzalez (Red Topps)	.20
74	Brad Fullmer	.10
75	Benny Agbayani	.10
76	Randy Wolf	.10
77a	Miguel Tejada (Red Topps)	.25
78	Jimmy Anderson	.10
79	Ramon Martinez	.10
80a	Ivan Rodriguez (Red Topps)	.40
81	John Flaherty	.10
82	Shannon Stewart	.10
83	Orlando Palmeiro	.10
84	Rafael Furcal	.10
85	Kenny Rogers	.10
86	Bud Smith	.10
87	Mo Vaughn	.15
88	Jose Cruz Jr.	.10
89	Mike Matheny	.10
90a	Alfonso Soriano (Red Topps)	.50
91	Orlando Cabrera	.10
92	Jeffrey Hammonds	.10
93	Hideo Nomo	.25
94	Carlos Febles	.10
95	Billy Wagner	.10
96	Alex Gonzalez	.10
97	Todd Zeile	.10
98	Omar Vizquel	.20
99	Jose Rijo	.10
100a	Ichiro Suzuki (Red Topps)	1.00
101	Steve Cox	.10
102	Hideki Irabu	.10
103	Roy Halladay	.10
104	David Eckstein	.10
105	Greg Maddux	.75
106	Chris Richard	.10
107	Travis Driskill	.10
108	Fred McGriff	.15
109	Frank Thomas	.50
110	Shawn Green	.10
111	Ruben Quevedo	.10
112	Jacque Jones	.10
113	Tomokazu Ohka	.10
114	Joe McEwing	.10
115	Ramiro Mendoza	.10
116	Mark Mulder	.20
117	Mike Lieberthal	.10
118	Jack Wilson	.10
119	Randall Simon	.10
120	Bernie Williams	.40
121	Marvin Benard	.10
122	Jamie Moyer	.10
123	Andy Benes	.10
124	Tino Martinez	.10
125	Esteban Yan	.10
126	Gabe Kapler	.10
127	Jason Isringhausen	.10
128	Chris Carpenter	.10
129	Mike Cameron	.10
130a	Gary Sheffield (Red Topps)	.25
131	Geronimo Gil	.10
132	Brian Daubach	.10
133	Corey Patterson	.10
134	Aaron Rowand	.10
135	Chris Reitsma	.10
136	Bob Wickman	.10
137	Paul Shuey	.10
138	Jason Jennings	.10
139	Brandon Inge	.10
140	Larry Walker	.20
141	Ramon Santiago	.10
142	Hansel Izquierdo	.10
143	Jose Vizcaino	.10
144	Mark Quinn	.10
145	Michael Tucker	.10
146	Darren Dreifort	.10
147	Mark Loretta	.10
148	Corey Koskie	.10
149	Tony Armas Jr.	.10
150a	Kazuhisa Ishii (Red Topps)	.10
151	Al Leiter	.10
152	Steve Trachsel	.10
153	Mike Stanton	.10
154	David Justice	.15
155	Marlon Anderson	.10
156	Jason Kendall	.10
157	Brian Lawrence	.10
158	J.T. Snow Jr.	.10
159	Edgar Martinez	.10
160a	Pat Burrell (Red Topps)	.25
161	Kerry Robinson	.10
162	Greg Vaughn	.10
163	Carl Everett	.10
164	Vernon Wells	.10
165	Jose Mesa	.10
166	Troy Percival	.10
167	Erubiel Durazo	.10
168	Jason Marquis	.10
169	Jerry Hairston Jr.	.10
170a	Vladimir Guerrero (Red Topps)	.50
171	Byung-Hyun Kim	.10
172	Marcus Giles	.10
173	Johnny Damon	.10
174	Jon Lieber	.10
175	Ray Durham	.10
176	Sean Casey	.10
177a	Adam Dunn (Red Topps)	.40
178	Juan Pierre	.10
179	Damion Easley	.10
180a	Barry Zito (Red Topps)	.25
181	Abraham Nunez	.10
182	Pokey Reese	.10
183	Jeff Kent	.20
184	Russ Ortiz	.10
185	Ruben Sierra	.10
186	Brent Abernathy	.10
187	Ismael Valdes	.10
188	Darrin Fletcher	.10
189	Craig Counsell	.10
190	David Wells	.10
191	Ramon Hernandez	.10
192	Adam Kennedy	.10
193	Tony Womack	.10
194	Wes Helms	.10
195	Tony Batista	.10
196	Rolando Arrojo	.10
197	Matt Clement	.10
198	Sandy Alomar	.10
199	Scott Sullivan	.10
200a	Albert Pujols (Red Topps)	1.00
201	Kirk Rueter	.10
202	Phil Nevin	.10
203	Kip Wells	.10
204	Ron Coomer	.10
205	Jeromy Burnitz	.10
206	Kyle Lohse	.10
207	Paul Bako	.10
208	Paul LoDuca	.10
209	Carlos Beltran	.10
210	Roy Oswalt	.25
211	Mike Lowell	.10
212	Robert Fick	.10
213	Todd Jones	.10
214	C.C. Sabathia	.10
215	Danny Graves	.10
216	Todd Hundley	.10
217	Tim Wakefield	.10
218	Dustin Hermanson	.10
219	Kevin Millwood	.10
220	Jorge Posada	.25
221	Bobby Jones	.10
222	Carlos Guillen	.10
223	Fernando Vina	.10
224	Ryan Rupe	.10
225	Kelvim Escobar	.10
226	Ramon Ortiz	.10
227	Junior Spivey	.10
228	Juan Cruz	.10
229	Melvin Mora	.10
230a	Lance Berkman (Red Topps)	.25
231	Brent Butler	.10
232	Matt Anderson	.10
233	Derrek Lee	.10
234	Matt Lawton	.10
235	Chuck Knoblauch	.10
236	Eric Gagne	.10
237	Alex Sanchez	.10
238	Denny Hocking	.10
239	Rick Reed	.10
240	Rey Ordonez	.10
241	Orlando Hernandez	.10
242	Robert Person	.10
243	Sean Burroughs	.10
244	Jeff Cirillo	.10
245	Mike Lamb	.10
246	Jose Valentin	.10
247	Ellis Burks	.10
248	Shawn Chacon	.10
249	Josh Beckett	.10
250a	Nomar Garciaparra (Red Topps)	1.00
251	Craig Biggio	.20
252	Joe Randa	.10
253	Mark Grudzielanek	.10
254	Glendon Rusch	.10
255	Michael Barrett	.10
256	Tyler Houston	.10
257	Ryan Dempster	.10
258	Wade Miller	.10
259	Adrian Beltre	.20
260	Vicente Padilla	.10
261	Kazuhiro Sasaki	.10
262	Mike Scioscia	.10
263	Bobby Cox	.10
264	Mike Hargrove	.10
265	Grady Little	.10
266	Alex Gonzalez	.10
267	Jerry Manuel	.10
268	Bob Boone	.10
269	Joel Skinner	.10
270	Clint Hurdle	.10
271	Luis Pujols	.10
272	Bob Brenly	.10
273	Jeff Torborg	.10
274	Jimy Williams	.10
275	Tony Pena	.10
276	Jim Tracy	.10
277	Jerry Royster	.10
278	Ron Gardenhire	.10
279	Frank Robinson	.10
280	Bobby Valentine	.10
281	Joe Torre	.10
282	Art Howe	.10
283	Larry Bowa	.10
284	Lloyd McClendon	.10
285	Bruce Bochy	.10
286	Dusty Baker	.10
287	Lou Pinella	.10
288	Tony LaRussa	.10
289	Hal McRae	.10
290	Jerry Narron	.10
291	Carlos Tosca	.10
292	Chris Duncan RC	2.00
293	Franklin Gutierrez RC	1.00
294	Adam LaRoche	.10
295	Manuel Ramirez RC	.10
296	Il Kim RC	.10
297	Wayne Lydon RC	.20
298	Daryl Clark RC	.25
299	Sean Pierce	.10
300a	Andy Marte RC (Red Topps)	1.00
301	Matt Peterson RC	.25
302	Gonzalo Lopez RC	.25
303	Bernie Castro RC	.10
304	Cliff Lee	.10
305	Jason Perry RC	.50
306	Jaime Bubela RC	.10
307	Alexis Rios	.10
308	Brendan Harris RC	.25
309	Ramon Martinez	.25
310	Terry Tiffee RC	.40
311	Kevin Youkilis RC	1.00
312	Ruddy Lugo RC	.20
313	C.J. Wilson	.10
314	Mike McNutt RC	.10
315	Jeff Clark RC	.25
316	Mark Malaska RC	.10
317	Doug Waechter RC	.25
318	Derell McCall RC	.10
319	Scott Tyler	.10
320	Craig Brazell RC	.40
321a	Walter Young (Red Topps)	.10
322a	Marlon Byrd, Jorge Padilla (Red Topps)	.10
323	Chris Snelling, Shin-Soo Choo	.10
324a	Hank Blalock, Mark Teixeira (Red Topps)	.10
325	Josh Hamilton, Carl Crawford	.20
326	Orlando Hudson, Josh Phelps	.10
327	Jack Cust, Rene Reyes	.10
328	Angel Berroa, Alexis Gomez	.10
329	Michael Cuddyer, Michael Restovich	.10
330	Juan Rivera, Marcus Thames	.10
331	Brandon Puffer, Jung Bong	.10
332	Mike Cameron, Shawn Green	.10
333	Team Shot	.10
334	Jason Giambi	.25
335	Derek Lowe	.10
336	Manny Ramirez, Mike Sweeney, Bernie Williams	.25
338	Alfonso Soriano, Alex Rodriguez, Derek Jeter	.50
339	Alex Rodriguez, Jim Thome, Rafael Palmeiro	.10
340	Magglio Ordonez, Alex Rodriguez, Miguel Tejada	.40
341	Pedro Martinez, Derek Lowe, Barry Zito	.25
342	Pedro Martinez, Roger Clemens, Mike Mussina	.25
343	Larry Walker, Vladimir Guerrero, Todd Helton	.25
344	Sammy Sosa, Albert Pujols, Shawn Green	.40
345	Sammy Sosa, Lance Berkman, Shawn Green	.40
346	Lance Berkman, Albert Pujols, Pat Burrell	.10
347	Randy Johnson, Greg Maddux, Tom Glavine	.25
348	Randy Johnson, Curt Schilling, Kerry Wood	.25
349	AL Division Series	.10
350	AL & NL Division Series	.20
351	AL & NL Division Series	.20
352	NL Division Series	.10
353	AL Championship Series	.10
354	Postseason Highlight	.10
355	NL Championship Series	.10
356	Jason Giambi	.25
357	Alfonso Soriano	.50
358	Alex Rodriguez	.75
359	Eric Chavez	.10
360	Torii Hunter	.10
361	Bernie Williams	.20
362	Garret Anderson	.10
363	Jorge Posada	.20
364	Derek Lowe	.10
365	Barry Zito	.20
366	Manny Ramirez	.25
367	Mike Scioscia	.10
368a	Francisco Rodriguez (Red Topps)	.10
370a	Chipper Jones (Red Topps)	.50
371	Chris Singleton	.10
372	Cliff Floyd	.10
373	Bobby Hill	.10
374	Antonio Osuna	.10
375	Barry Larkin	.25
376	Charles Nagy	.10
377	Denny Stark	.10
378	Dean Palmer	.10
379	Eric Owens	.10
380a	Randy Johnson (Red Topps)	.50
381	Jeff Suppan	.10
382	Eric Karros	.10
383	Luis Vizcaino	.10
384	Johan Santana	.10
385	Javier Vazquez	.10
386	John Thomson	.10
387a	Nick Johnson (Red Topps)	.10
388	Mark Ellis	.10
389	Doug Glanville	.10
390a	Ken Griffey Jr. (Red Topps)	.75
391	Bubba Trammell	.10
392	Livan Hernandez	.10
393	Desi Relaford	.10
394	Eli Marrero	.10
395	Jared Sandberg	.10
396a	Barry Bonds (Red Topps)	1.50
397	Esteban Loaiza	.10
398	Aaron Sele	.10
399	Geoff Blum	.10
400a	Derek Jeter (Red Topps)	1.50
401	Eric Byrnes	.10
402	Mike Timlin	.10
403	Mark Kotsay	.10
404	Rich Aurilia	.10
405	Joel Pineiro	.10
406	Chuck Finley	.10
407	Bengie Molina	.10
408	Steve Finley	.10
409	Julio Franco	.10
410	Marty Cordova	.10
411	Shea Hillenbrand	.10
412	Mark Bellhorn	.10
413	Jon Garland	.10
414	Reggie Taylor	.10
415	Milton Bradley	.10
416	Carlos Pena	.10
417	Andy Fox	.10
418	Brad Ausmus	.10
419	Brent Mayne	.10
420	Paul Quantrill	.10
421a	Carlos Delgado (Red Topps)	.20
422	Kevin Mench	.10
423	Joe Kennedy	.10
424	Mike Crudale	.10
425	Mark McLemore	.10
426	Bill Mueller	.10
427	Robert Mackowiak	.10
428	Ricky Ledee	.10
429	Ted Lilly	.10
430	Sterling Hitchcock	.10
431	Scott Strickland	.10
432	Damion Easley	.10
433a	Torii Hunter (Red Topps)	.25
434	Brad Radke	.10
435	Geoff Jenkins	.10
436	Paul Byrd	.10
437	Morgan Ensberg	.10
438	Mike Maroth	.10
439	Mike Hampton	.10
440	Adam Hyzdu	.10
441	Vance Wilson	.10
442	Todd Ritchie	.10
443	Flash Gordon	.10
444	John Burkett	.10
445	Rodrigo Lopez	.10
446	Tim Spooneybarger	.10
447	Quinton McCracken	.10
448	Tim Salmon	.20
449	Jarrod Washburn	.10
450a	Pedro Martinez (Red Topps)	.50
451	Dustan Mohr	.10
452	Julio Lugo	.10
453	Scott Stewart	.10
454	Armando Benitez	.10
455	Raul Mondesi	.20
456	Robin Ventura	.20
457	Bobby Abreu	.20
458	Josh Fogg	.10
459	Ryan Klesko	.20
460	Tsuyoshi Shinjo	.10
461a	Jim Edmonds (Red Topps)	.25
462	Cliff Politte	.10
463	Chan Ho Park	.10
464	John Mabry	.10
465	Woody Williams	.10
466	Jason Michaels	.10
467	Scott Schoeneweis	.10
468	Brian Anderson	.10
469	Brett Tomko	.10
470	Scott Erickson	.10
471	Tony Clark	.10
472	Danny Wright	.10
473	Jason Schmidt	.10
474	Scott Williamson	.10
475	Einar Diaz	.10
476	Jay Payton	.10
477	Juan Acevedo	.10
478	Ben Grieve	.10
479	Raul Ibanez	.10
480	Richie Sexson	.25
481	Rick Reed	.10
482	Pedro Astacio	.10
483	Adam Piatt	.10
484	Bud Smith	.10
485	Tomas Perez	.10
486	Adam Eaton	.10
487	Rafael Palmeiro	.25
488	Jason Tyner	.10
489a	Scott Rolen (Red Topps)	.50
490	Randy Winn	.10
491	Ryan Jensen	.10
492	Trevor Hoffman	.10
493	Craig Wilson	.10
494	Jeremy Giambi	.10
495	Daryle Ward	.10
496	Shane Spencer	.10
497	Andy Pettitte	.25
498	John Franco	.10
499	Masato Yoshii	.10
500a	Mike Piazza (Red Topps)	1.00
501	Cristian Guzman	.10
502	Jose Hernandez	.10
503	Octavio Dotel	.10
504	Brad Penny	.10
505	Jose Ortiz	.10
506	Ryan Dempster	.10
507	Joe Crede	.10
508	Chad Hermansen	.10
509	Gary Matthews Jr.	.10
510	Matt Franco	.10
511	Ben Weber	.10
512	Dave Berg	.10
513	Michael Young	.10
514	Frank Catalanotto	.10
515a	Darin Erstad (Red Topps)	.25
516	Matt Williams	.10
517	B.J. Surhoff	.10
518	Kerry Ligtenberg	.10
519	Mike Bordick	.10
520	Arthur Rhodes	.10
521	Joe Girardi	.10
522	D'Angelo Jimenez	.10
523	Paul Konerko	.10
524	Jose Macias	.10
525	Joe Mays	.10
526	Marquis Grissom	.10
527	Neifi Perez	.10
528	Preston Wilson	.10
529	Jeff Weaver	.10
530a	Eric Chavez (Red Topps)	.25
531	Placido Polanco	.10
532	Ray Lankford	.10
533	James Baldwin	.10
534	Toby Hall	.10
535	Brendan Donnelly	.10
536	Benji Gil	.10
537	Damian Moss	.10
538	Jorge Julio	.10
539	Matt Clement	.10
540	Brian Moehler	.10
541	Lee Stevens	.10
542	Jimmy Haynes	.10
543	Kevin Millar	.10
544	Dave Roberts	.10
545	J.C. Romero	.10
546	Bartolo Colon	.10
547	Roger Cedeno	.10
548	Mariano Rivera	.20
549	Billy Koch	.10
550a	Manny Ramirez (Red Topps)	.50
551	Travis Lee	.10
552	Oliver Perez	.10
553	Tim Worrell	.10
554	Rafael Soriano	.10
555	Damian Miller	.10
556	John Smoltz	.10
557	Willis Roberts	.10
558a	Tim Hudson (Red Topps)	.25
559	Moises Alou	.20
560	Gary Glover	.10
561	Corky Miller	.10
562	Ben Broussard	.10
563	Gabe Kapler	.10
564	Chris Woodward	.10
565	Paul Wilson	.10
566	Todd Hollandsworth	.10
567	So Taguchi	.10
568	John Olerud	.10
569	Reggie Sanders	.10
570	Jake Peavy	.10
571	Kris Benson	.10
572	Todd Pratt	.10
573	Ray Durham	.10
574	David Wells	.10
575	Chris Widger	.10
576	Shawn Wooten	.10
577	Tom Glavine	.25
578	Antonio Alfonseca	.10
579	Keith Foulke	.10
580	Shawn Estes	.10
581	Travis Fryman	.10
582	Dmitri Young	.10
583	A.J. Burnett	.10
584	Richard Hidalgo	.10
585a	Mike Sweeney (Red Topps)	.10
586	Alex Cora	.10
587	Matt Stairs	.10
588	Doug Mientkiewicz	.10
589	Fernando Tatis	.10
590	David Weathers	.10
591	Cory Lidle	.10
592	Dan Plesac	.10
593a	Jeff Bagwell (Red Topps)	.50
594	Steve Sparks	.10
595	Sandy Alomar Jr.	.10
596	John Lackey	.10
597	Rick Helling	.10
598	Mark DeRosa	.10
599	Carlos Lee	.10
600a	Garret Anderson (Red Topps)	.20
601	Vinny Castilla	.10
602	Ryan Drese	.10
603	LaTroy Hawkins	.10
604	David Bell	.10
605	Freddy Garcia	.10
606	Miguel Cairo	.10
607	Scott Spiezio	.10
608	Mike Remlinger	.10
609	Tony Graffanino	.10
610	Russell Branyan	.10
611	Chris Magruder	.10
612	Jose Contreras RC	.75
613	Carl Pavano	.10
614	Kevin Brown	.10
615	Tyler Houston	.10
616	A.J. Pierzynski	.10
617	Tony Fiore	.10
618	Peter Bergeron	.10
619	Rondell White	.10
620	Brett Myers	.10
621	Kevin Young	.10
622	Kenny Lofton	.10
623	Ben Davis	.10
624	J.D. Drew	.10
625	Chris Gomez	.10
626	Karim Garcia	.10
627	Ricky Gutierrez	.10
628	Mark Redman	.10
629	Juan Encarnacion	.10
630	Anaheim Angels	.25
631	Arizona Diamondbacks	.10
632	Atlanta Braves	.25
633	Baltimore Orioles	.10
634	Boston Red Sox	.25
635	Chicago Cubs	.10
636	Chicago White Sox	.10
637	Cincinnati Reds	.10
638	Cleveland Indians	.10
639	Colorado Rockies	.10
640	Detroit Tigers	.10
641	Florida Marlins	.10
642	Houston Astros	.10
643	Kansas City Royals	.10
644	Los Angeles Dodgers	.10
645	Milwaukee Brewers	.10
646	Minnesota Twins	.10
647	Montreal Expos	.10
648	New York Mets	.10
649	New York Yankees	.50
650	Oakland Athletics	.10
651	Philadelphia Phillies	.10
652	Pittsburgh Pirates	.10
653	San Diego Padres	.10
654	San Francisco Giants	.10
655	Seattle Mariners	.10
656	St. Louis Cardinals	.10
657	Tampa Bay Devil Rays	.10
658	Texas Rangers	.10
659	Toronto Blue Jays	.10
660	Bryan Bullington RC	1.00
661	Jeremy Guthrie	.10
662	Joey Gomes	.25
663	Evel Bastida-Martinez RC	.40
664	Brian Wright RC	.10
665	B.J. Upton	.10
666	Jeff Francis	.10
667	Drew Meyer	.10
668	Jeremy Hermida	.10
669	Khalil Greene	.75
670	Darrell Rasner	.10
671	Cole Hamels	.50
672	James Loney	.10
673	Sergio Santos	.10
674	Jason Pridie	.10
675	Brandon Phillips, Victor Martinez	.10
676	Hee Seop Choi, Nic Jackson	.10
677	Dontrelle Willis, Jason Stokes	.10
678	Chad Tracy, Lyle Overbay	.10
679	Joe Borchard, Corwin Malone	.10
680	Joe Mauer, Justin Morneau	.25
681	Drew Henson, Brandon Claussen	.10
682	Chase Utley, Gavin Floyd	.25

683	Taggert Bozied, Xavier Nady	.25
684	Aaron Heilman, Jose Reyes	.25
685	Kenny Rogers	.10
686	Bengie Molina	.10
687	John Olerud	.10
688	Bret Boone	.10
689	Eric Chavez	.15
690	Alex Rodriguez	.75
691	Darin Erstad	.15
692	Ichiro Suzuki	.15
693	Torii Hunter	.15
694	Greg Maddux	.40
695	Brad Ausmus	.10
696	Todd Helton	.20
697	Fernando Vina	.10
698	Scott Rolen	.25
699	Edgar Renteria	.10
700	Andruw Jones	.20
701	Larry Walker	.10
702	Jim Edmonds	.10
703	Barry Zito	.10
704	Randy Johnson	.40
705	Miguel Tejada	.15
706	Barry Bonds	.75
707	Eric Hinske	.10
708	Jason Jennings	.10
709	Todd Helton	.20
710	Jeff Kent	.10
711	Edgar Renteria	.10
712	Scott Rolen	.25
713	Barry Bonds	.75
714	Sammy Sosa	.50
715	Vladimir Guerrero	.40
716	Mike Piazza	.75
717	Curt Schilling	.20
718	Randy Johnson	.40
719	Bobby Cox	.10
720	World Series Card	.10
721	World Series Card	.10

Black
Stars: 10-20X
Production 52 Sets

Gold

Stars: 3-6X
Production 2,003 Sets

Autographs
		NM/M
	Common Autograph:	8.00
HB	Hank Blalock	20.00
MB	Mark Buehrle	20.00
EC	Eric Chavez	25.00
DE	Darin Erstad	15.00
OH	Orlando Hudson	10.00
AK	Austin Kearns	15.00
JL	Jason Lane	10.00
PL	Paul LoDuca	12.00
JDM	J.D. Martin	8.00
JM	Joe Mauer	40.00
EM	Eric Milton	10.00
NN	Nick Neugebauer	10.00
MP	Mark Prior	40.00
SR	Scott Rolen	50.00
BS	Ben Sheets	15.00
MTE	Mark Teixeira	20.00
MTH	Marcus Thames	8.00

Autographs Series 2
		NM/M
	Common Autograph:	8.00
JB	Josh Beckett	30.00
LB	Lance Berkman	40.00
CE	Clint Everts	8.00
CF	Cliff Floyd	20.00
BH	Brad Hawpe	8.00
EH	Eric Hinske	10.00
TH	Torii Hunter	20.00
AK	Austin Kearns	15.00
PK	Paul Konerko	20.00
PL	Paul LoDuca	15.00
MO	Magglio Ordonez	20.00
JPH	Josh Phelps	10.00
AP	Albert Pujols	120.00
MT	Miguel Tejada	30.00
BU	B.J. Upton	25.00
JV	Jose Vidro	10.00
DW	Dontrelle Willis	25.00
BZ	Barry Zito	15.00

All-Stars
	NM/M
Complete Set (20):	20.00

Topps All-Stars

	Common Player:	.50
	Inserted 1:15	
TAS1	Alfonso Soriano	1.50
TAS2	Barry Bonds	4.00
TAS3	Ichiro Suzuki	2.00
TAS4	Alex Rodriguez	3.00
TAS5	Miguel Tejada	.75
TAS6	Nomar Garciaparra	2.50
TAS7	Jason Giambi	2.00
TAS8	Manny Ramirez	1.50
TAS9	Derek Jeter	4.00
TAS10	Garret Anderson	.50
TAS11	Barry Zito	.50
TAS12	Sammy Sosa	2.00
TAS13	Vladimir Guerrero	1.50
TAS14	Vladimir Guerrero	1.50
TAS15	Mike Piazza	2.50
TAS16	Shawn Green	.50
TAS17	Luis Gonzalez	.50
TAS18	Todd Helton	.75
TAS19	Torii Hunter	.75
TAS20	Curt Schilling	.75

Blue Backs

		NM/M
	Complete Set (40):	50.00
	Common Player:	.75
	Inserted 1:12	
BB1	Albert Pujols	2.00
BB2	Barry Bonds	5.00
BB3	Ichiro Suzuki	3.00
BB4	Sammy Sosa	2.50
BB5	Kazuhisa Ishii	.75
BB6	Alex Rodriguez	4.00
BB7	Derek Jeter	5.00
BB8	Vladimir Guerrero	2.00
BB9	Ken Griffey Jr.	2.50
BB10	Jason Giambi	2.50
BB11	Todd Helton	1.00
BB12	Mike Piazza	3.00
BB13	Nomar Garciaparra	3.00
BB14	Chipper Jones	2.50
BB15	Ivan Rodriguez	1.00
BB16	Luis Gonzalez	.75
BB17	Pat Burrell	1.00
BB18	Mark Prior	1.50
BB19	Adam Dunn	1.50
BB20	Jeff Bagwell	1.50
BB21	Austin Kearns	1.00
BB22	Alfonso Soriano	2.00
BB23	Jim Thome	1.50
BB24	Bernie Williams	1.00
BB25	Pedro J. Martinez	2.00
BB26	Lance Berkman	1.00
BB27	Randy Johnson	2.00
BB28	Rafael Palmeiro	1.00
BB29	Richie Sexson	.75
BB30	Troy Glaus	1.50
BB31	Shawn Green	.75
BB32	Larry Walker	.75
BB33	Eric Hinske	.75
BB34	Andruw Jones	1.50
BB35	Carlos Delgado	.75
BB36	Curt Schilling	1.50
BB37	Greg Maddux	2.50
BB38	Jimmy Rollins	.75
BB39	Eric Chavez	1.00
BB40	Scott Rolen	1.00

Draft Picks
		NM/M
	Complete Set (10):	30.00

1-5 issued in retail sets
6-10 issued in holiday sets
1	Brandon Wood	10.00
2	Ryan Wagner	5.00
3	Sean Rodriguez	3.00
4	Chris Lubanski	5.00
5	Chad Billingsley	3.00
6	Javi Herrera	3.00
7	Brian McFall	3.00
8	Nicholas Markakis	5.00
9	Adam Miller	5.00
10	Daric Barton	5.00

Flashback
		NM/M
	Complete Set (14):	50.00
	Common Player:	2.00
	HTA Exclusive	
GB	George Brett	6.00
LD	Lenny Dykstra	3.00
HK	Harmon Killebrew	6.00
BM	Bill Madlock	2.00
EM	Eddie Mathews	4.00
DM	Dale Murphy	5.00
JP	Jim Palmer	3.00
MP	Mike Piazza	6.00
RR	Robin Roberts	3.00
AR	Al Rosen	2.00
NR	Nolan Ryan	10.00
TS	Tom Seaver	5.00
WS	Warren Spahn	4.00
CY	Carl Yastrzemski	6.00

Futures Game

Flashback photos of alumni of the All-Star Futures Game are featured on this set of cards given away at the 2003 event July 13 in connection with All-Star Weekend in Chicago. The design follows the basic Topps format for 2003 and includes a special Futures Game logo.
		NM/M
	Complete Set (6):	5.00
	Common Player:	.50
1	Alfonso Soriano	2.00
2	Pat Burrell	1.00
3	Adam Dunn	1.00
4	Barry Zito	.75
5	Mark Buehrle	.50
6	Rafael Furcal	.75

Hit Parade

		NM/M
	Complete Set (30):	30.00
	Common Player:	.50
	Inserted 1:12	
HP1	Barry Bonds	4.00
HP2	Sammy Sosa	2.50
HP3	Rafael Palmeiro	1.00
HP4	Fred McGriff	.75
HP5	Ken Griffey Jr.	2.50
HP6	Juan Gonzalez	1.00
HP7	Andres Galarraga	.50
HP8	Jeff Bagwell	1.50
HP9	Frank Thomas	1.50
HP10	Matt Williams	.50
HP11	Barry Bonds	4.00
HP12	Rafael Palmeiro	1.00
HP13	Fred McGriff	.75
HP14	Andres Galarraga	.50
HP15	Ken Griffey Jr.	2.50
HP16	Sammy Sosa	2.50
HP17	Jeff Bagwell	1.50
HP18	Juan Gonzalez	1.00
HP19	Frank Thomas	1.50
HP20	Matt Williams	.50
HP21	Rickey Henderson	1.00
HP22	Rafael Palmeiro	1.00
HP23	Roberto Alomar	1.00
HP24	Barry Bonds	4.00
HP25	Mark Grace	1.00
HP26	Fred McGriff	.75
HP27	Julio Franco	.50
HP28	Craig Biggio	.50
HP29	Andres Galarraga	.50
HP30	Barry Larkin	.50

Hobby Masters

		NM/M
	Complete Set (20):	40.00
	Common Player:	1.00
	Inserted 1:18	
HM1	Ichiro Suzuki	4.00
HM2	Kazuhisa Ishii	1.00
HM3	Derek Jeter	6.00
HM4	Barry Bonds	5.00
HM5	Sammy Sosa	3.00
HM6	Alex Rodriguez	5.00
HM7	Mike Piazza	4.00
HM8	Chipper Jones	2.00
HM9	Vladimir Guerrero	2.00
HM10	Nomar Garciaparra	2.00
HM11	Todd Helton	1.00
HM12	Jason Giambi	2.00
HM13	Ken Griffey Jr.	3.00
HM14	Albert Pujols	2.00
HM15	Ivan Rodriguez	1.00
HM16	Mark Prior	1.50
HM17	Adam Dunn	1.50
HM18	Randy Johnson	2.00
HM19	Pedro J. Martinez	2.00
HM20	Alfonso Soriano	3.00

Own The Game

		NM/M
	Complete Set (30):	30.00
	Common Player:	.50
	Inserted 1:12	
OG1	Ichiro Suzuki	3.00
OG2	Barry Bonds	4.00
OG3	Todd Helton	.75
OG4	Larry Walker	.75
OG5	Mike Sweeney	.50
OG6	Sammy Sosa	2.50
OG7	Lance Berkman	.50
OG8	Alex Rodriguez	4.00
OG9	Jim Thome	1.25
OG10	Shawn Green	1.00
OG11	Troy Glaus	1.00
OG12	Richie Sexson	.50
OG13	Paul Konerko	.50
OG14	Jason Giambi	2.50
OG15	Chipper Jones	2.50
OG16	Torii Hunter	.50
OG17	Albert Pujols	1.50
OG18	Jose Vidro	.50
OG19	Alfonso Soriano	2.00
OG20	Luis Castillo	.50
OG21	Mike Lowell	.50
OG22	Garret Anderson	.50
OG23	Jimmy Rollins	.50
OG24	Curt Schilling	1.00
OG25	Kazuhisa Ishii	.50
OG26	Randy Johnson	1.50
OG27	Tom Glavine	.75
OG28	Roger Clemens	2.50
OG29	Pedro J. Martinez	1.50
OG30	Derek Lowe	.50

Prime Cuts Autograph
	NM/M
Production 50 Sets	
EC	Eric Chavez	100.00
LB	Lance Berkman	120.00
AJ	Andruw Jones	100.00
CJ	Chipper Jones	150.00
MO	Magglio Ordonez	120.00
MT	Miguel Tejada	120.00

Prime Cuts Pine Tar Series
		NM/M
Pine Tar Series		
Production 200 Sets		
Trademark Series:		1-1.5X
Production 100 Sets		
Prime Cuts Series:		1.5-2X
Production 50 Sets		
RA	Roberto Alomar	20.00
LB	Lance Berkman	15.00
EC	Eric Chavez	20.00
AD	Adam Dunn	25.00
DE	Darin Erstad	15.00
NG	Nomar Garciaparra	40.00
JG	Juan Gonzalez	15.00
TH	Todd Helton	25.00
AJ	Andruw Jones	20.00
CJ	Chipper Jones	30.00
RP	Rafael Palmeiro	20.00
MP	Mike Piazza	30.00
AP	Albert Pujols	40.00
AR	Alex Rodriguez	25.00
IR	Ivan Rodriguez	25.00
SR	Scott Rolen	20.00
AS	Alfonso Soriano	25.00
MT	Miguel Tejada	15.00
FT	Frank Thomas	25.00
MV	Mo Vaughn	10.00
BW	Bernie Williams	25.00

Prime Cuts Pine Tar Series 2
		NM/M
Pine Tar Series:		
Production 200		
RA	Roberto Alomar	20.00
LB	Lance Berkman	15.00
HB	Hank Blalock	25.00
BBO	Barry Bonds	40.00
EC	Eric Chavez	20.00
CD	Carlos Delgado	10.00
AD	Adam Dunn	25.00
NG	Nomar Garciaparra	30.00
LG	Luis Gonzalez	8.00
TG	Tony Gwynn	25.00
RH	Rickey Henderson	25.00
RJ	Randy Johnson	25.00
EM	Edgar Martinez	20.00
TM	Tino Martinez	15.00
MO	Magglio Ordonez	10.00
RP	Rafael Palmeiro	15.00
JP	Jorge Posada	15.00
AP	Albert Pujols	40.00
MP	Mark Prior	25.00
AR	Alex Rodriguez	25.00
AS	Alfonso Soriano	25.00
Trademark Series:		1-1.5X
Production 100		
Prime Cuts:		1.5-2.5X
Production 50		

2003 Topps Record Breakers

		NM/M
	Complete Set (50):	40.00
	Common Player:	.50
	Inserted 1:6	
JB	Jeff Bagwell	1.50
LBE	Lance Berkman	1.00
BB	Barry Bonds	5.00
GB	George Brett	2.50
LB	Lou Brock	.50
RCA	Rod Carew	.50
LC	Luis Castillo	.50
RC	Roger Clemens	2.50
CD	Carlos Delgado	.50
CF	Cliff Floyd	.50
GF	George Foster	.50
AG	Andres Galarraga	.50
JG	Jason Giambi	2.50
BG	Bob Gibson	1.00
TG	Troy Glaus	1.00
JGO	Juan Gonzalez	1.00
LGO	Luis Gonzalez	.50
SG	Shawn Green	.75
HG	Hank Greenberg	1.00
KG	Ken Griffey Jr.	3.00
VG	Vladimir Guerrero	1.50
RG	Ron Guidry	.50
TH	Todd Helton	1.00
RH	Rickey Henderson	.75
FJ	Fergie Jenkins	.50
RJ	Randy Johnson	1.50
CJ	Chipper Jones	3.00
HK	Harmon Killebrew	1.00
CK	Chuck Klein	.50
JM	Juan Marichal	1.00
PM	Pedro J. Martinez	1.50
EM	Eddie Mathews	1.00
DM	Don Mattingly	4.00
FM	Fred McGriff	.50
JO	John Olerud	.50
RP	Rafael Palmeiro	1.00
MP	Mike Piazza	3.00
FR	Frank Robinson	.50
AR	Alex Rodriguez	4.00
NR	Nolan Ryan	6.00
MSC	Mike Schmidt	3.00
CS	Curt Schilling	1.00
TS	Tom Seaver	1.00
RS	Richie Sexson	.50
GS	Gary Sheffield	.50
SS	Sammy Sosa	3.00
MS	Mike Sweeney	.50
HW	Hack Wilson	.50
PW	Preston Wilson	.50
RY	Robin Yount	1.00

Series 2
		NM/M
	Complete Set (50):	40.00
	Common Player:	.50
	Inserted 1:6	
RA	Roberto Alomar	1.00
GA	Garret Anderson	.75
LA	Luis Aparicio	.50
JB	Jeff Bagwell	1.50
LB	Lance Berkman	1.00
CB	Craig Biggio	.75
WB	Wade Boggs	.75
BB	Barry Bonds	5.00
GB	George Brett	2.50
LBR	Lou Brock	.75
JD	Johnny Damon	.50
CD	Carlos Delgado	.50
LD	Lenny Dykstra	.50
DE	Darin Erstad	.50
BF	Bob Feller	.75
GF	George Foster	.50
NG	Nomar Garciaparra	3.00
LG	Luis Gonzalez	.50
DG	Dwight Gooden	.50
SG	Shawn Green	.75
KG	Ken Griffey Jr.	2.50
VG	Vladimir Guerrero	1.50
TG	Tony Gwynn	1.00
TH	Todd Helton	1.00
RH	Rickey Henderson	1.00
RJ	Randy Johnson	1.50
JK	Jeff Kent	.50
TK	Ted Kluszewski	.50
GM	Greg Maddux	2.50
JM	Juan Marichal	1.00
EM	Edgar Martinez	.50
WM	Willie Mays	4.00
JME	Jose Mesa	.50
PM	Paul Molitor	1.00
JP	Jim Palmer	.75
TR	Tim Raines	.50
MR	Manny Ramirez	1.50
JR	Jim Rice	.50
FR	Frank Robinson	1.00
AR	Alex Rodriguez	4.00
TS	Tom Seaver	2.00
RS	Richie Sexson	.75
JS	John Smoltz	.75
SS	Sammy Sosa	2.50
WS	Willie Stargell	1.00
IS	Ichiro Suzuki	2.50
FT	Frank Thomas	1.50
JT	Jim Thome	1.50
LW	Larry Walker	.50
RY	Robin Yount	2.00

Autographs
		NM/M
	Common Autograph:	20.00
CF	Cliff Floyd	20.00
LG	Luis Gonzalez	30.00
FJ	Fergie Jenkins	25.00
CJ	Chipper Jones	75.00
HK	Harmon Killebrew	60.00
RP	Rafael Palmeiro	60.00
MS	Mike Schmidt	100.00
RS	Richie Sexson	30.00
MSW	Mike Sweeney	30.00
RY	Robin Yount	75.00

Autographs Series 2
		NM/M
	Common Autograph:	25.00
	Inserted 1:2,218	
LA	Luis Aparicio	40.00
LB	Lance Berkman	40.00
LBR	Lou Brock	40.00
GF	George Foster	25.00
JM	Juan Marichal	40.00
DM	Don Mattingly	125.00
WM	Willie Mays	150.00

Relics
	NM/M
Common Player:	6.00

51 2Bs in 1962
Cincinnati Reds' Doubles Season Leader
Frank Robinson

		NM/M
JB	Jeff Bagwell/Jsy	8.00
LB	Lance Berkman/Bat	10.00
GB	George Brett/Bat	25.00
LC	Luis Castillo/Bat	5.00
CD	Carlos Delgado/Jsy	8.00
LGO	Luis Gonzalez/Jsy	6.00
SG	Shawn Green/Jsy	
HG	Hank Greenberg/Bat	30.00
TH	Todd Helton/Jsy	10.00
RH	Rickey Henderson/Bat	15.00
CJ	Chipper Jones/Jsy	12.00
PM	Pedro Martinez/Jsy	10.00
DM	Don Mattingly/Bat	35.00
MP	Mike Piazza/Bat	15.00
FR	Frank Robinson/Bat	12.00
AR	Alex Rodriguez/Jsy	15.00
NR	Nolan Ryan/Jsy	35.00
MS	Mike Sweeney/Bat	8.00
HW	Hack Wilson/Bat	50.00
RY	Robin Yount/Jsy	15.00

Relics Series 2

		NM/M
Common Player:		5.00
WB	Wade Boggs/Bat	5.00
GB	George Brett/Bat	25.00
CD	Carlos Delgado/Jsy	6.00
DE	Darin Erstad/Bat	
LG	Luis Gonzalez/Jsy	5.00
TH	Todd Helton/Bat	8.00
RH	Rogers Hornsby/Bat	35.00
TK	Ted Kluszewski/Bat	15.00
EM	Edgar Martinez/Bat	12.00
JR	Jim Rice/Jsy	8.00
FR	Frank Robinson/Bat	12.00
AR	Alex Rodriguez/Jsy	15.00
NRA	Nolan Ryan/Jsy	30.00
RS	Richie Sexson/Jsy	
FT	Frank Thomas/Bat	10.00
RY	Robin Yount	15.00

Red Backs

RAFAEL PALMEIRO

		NM/M
Complete Set (40):		50.00
Common Player:		.50
Inserted 1:12		
TRB1	Nomar Garciaparra	3.00
TRB2	Ichiro Suzuki	2.50
TRB3	Alex Rodriguez	4.00
TRB4	Sammy Sosa	2.50
TRB5	Barry Bonds	5.00
TRB6	Vladimir Guerrero	1.50
TRB7	Derek Jeter	5.00
TRB8	Miguel Tejada	1.00
TRB9	Alfonso Soriano	2.00
TRB10	Manny Ramirez	1.50
TRB11	Adam Dunn	1.50
TRB12	Jason Giambi	2.50
TRB13	Mike Piazza	3.00
TRB14	Scott Rolen	1.50
TRB15	Shawn Green	.75
TRB16	Randy Johnson	1.00
TRB17	Todd Helton	1.00
TRB18	Garret Anderson	.50
TRB19	Curt Schilling	1.00
TRB20	Albert Pujols	2.00
TRB21	Chipper Jones	2.50
TRB22	Luis Gonzalez	.50
TRB23	Mark Prior	1.50
TRB24	Jim Thome	1.50
TRB25	Ivan Rodriguez	1.00
TRB26	Torii Hunter	1.00
TRB27	Lance Berkman	1.00
TRB28	Troy Glaus	1.50
TRB29	Andruw Jones	1.00
TRB30	Barry Zito	.75
TRB31	Jeff Bagwell	1.50
TRB32	Magglio Ordonez	.75
TRB33	Pat Burrell	1.50
TRB34	Mike Sweeney	.50
TRB35	Rafael Palmeiro	1.00
TRB36	Larry Walker	.50
TRB37	Carlos Delgado	.50
TRB38	Brian Giles	.50
TRB39	Pedro J. Martinez	1.50
TRB40	Greg Maddux	2.50

Nolan Ryan No-Hitters

		NM/M
Complete Set (7):		45.00
Common Ryan (1-7):		8.00
RB-NR1–NR7	Nolan Ryan	8.00

Nolan Ryan Record Breakers Autographs

		NM/M
Inserted 1:1,894		
HTA Exclusive		
NR	Nolan Ryan	200.00
NRA	Nolan Ryan	200.00
NRR	Nolan Ryan	200.00

Stadium Seat Relics

		NM/M
Common Player:		15.00
Inserted 1:37 Series 2 HTA		
JB	Johnny Bench	30.00
DC	Dave Concepcion	20.00
AD	Adam Dunn	20.00
KG	Ken Griffey Jr.	25.00
AK	Austin Kearns	20.00
BL	Barry Larkin	25.00
JM	Joe Morgan	15.00
PO	Paul O'Neill	15.00
TP	Tony Perez	20.00
TS	Tom Seaver	25.00

Team Topps Legends Autographs

WILLIE MAYS
SAN FRANCISCO GIANTS

		NM/M
Common Player:		
VB	Vida Blue	20.00
BF	Bob Feller	25.00
WM	Willie Mays	125.00
GM	Gil McDougald	12.00
RR	Robin Roberts	25.00
BT	Bobby Thomson	20.00
LT	Luis Tiant	8.00
CY	Carl Yastrzemski	50.00

Team Topps Legends Autographs Series 2

Common Player:

Turn Back The Clock Autographs

		NM/M
Common Player:		
LD	Lenny Dykstra	15.00
BM	Bill Madlock	10.00
DM	Dale Murphy	40.00
JP	Jim Palmer	20.00

2003 Topps All-Time Fan Favorites

CECIL COOPER
1st BASE
BREWERS

		NM/M
Complete Set (150):		30.00
Common Player:		.25
Pack (6):		4.00
Box (24):		75.00
1	Willie Mays	3.00
2	Whitey Ford	1.00
3	Stan Musial	2.50
4	Paul Blair	.25
5	Harold Reynolds	.25
6	Bob Friend	.25
7	Rod Carew	.75
8	Kirk Gibson	.25
9	Graig Nettles	.25
10	Ozzie Smith	1.00
11	Tony Perez	.25
12	Tim Wallach	.25
13	Bert Campaneris	.25
14	Cory Snyder	.25
15	Dave Parker	.25
16	Darrell Evans	.25
17	Joe Pepitone	.25
18	Don Sutton	.25
19	Dale Murphy	1.00
20	George Brett	2.50
21	Carlton Fisk	.25
22	Bob Watson	.25
23	Wally Joyner	.25
24	Paul Molitor	1.00
25	Keith Hernandez	.25
26	Jerry Koosman	.25
27	George Bell	.25
28	Boog Powell	.25
29	Bruce Sutter	.75
30	Ernie Banks	1.50
31	Steve Lyons	.25
32	Earl Weaver	.25
33	Dave Stieb	.25
34	Alan Trammell	.25
35	Bret Saberhagen	.25
36	J.R. Richard	.25
37	Mickey Rivers	.25
38	Juan Marichal	.75
39	Gaylord Perry	.25
40	Don Mattingly	3.00
41	Bobby Grich	.25
42	Steve Sax	.25
43	Sparky Anderson	.25
44	Luis Aparicio	.25
45	Fergie Jenkins	.50
46	Jim Palmer	.75
47	Howard Johnson	.25
48	Dwight Evans	.25
49	Bill Buckner	.25
50	Cal Ripken Jr.	4.00
51	Jose Cruz	.25
52	Tony Oliva	.25
53	Bobby Richardson	.25
54	Luis Tiant	.25
55	Warren Spahn	1.00
56	Phil Rizzuto	.25
57	Eric Davis	.25
58	Vida Blue	.25
59	Steve Balboni	.25
60	Mike Schmidt	2.50
61	Ken Griffey Sr.	.25
62	Jim Abbott	.25
63	Whitey Herzog	.25
64	Rich "Goose" Gossage	.25
65	Tony Armas	.25
66	Bill "Moose" Skowron	.25
67	Don Newcombe	.25
68	Bill Madlock	.25
69	Lance Parrish	.25
70	Reggie Jackson	1.50
71	Willie Wilson	.25
72	Terry Pendleton	.25
73	Jimmy Piersall	.25
74	George Foster	.25
75	Bob Horner	.25
76	Chris Sabo	.25
77	Fred Lynn	.25
78	Jim Rice	.25
79	Maury Wills	.25
80	Yogi Berra	1.50
81	Johnny Sain	.25
82	Tom Lasorda	.50
83	Bill Mazeroski	.25
84	John Kruk	.25
85	Bob Feller	.75
86	Frank Robinson	.75
87	Red Schoendienst	.25
88	Gary Carter	.50
89	Andre Dawson	.25
90	Tim McCarver	.25
91	Robin Yount	1.00
92	Phil Niekro	.25
93	Joe Morgan	.25
94	Darren Daulton	.25
95	Bobby Thomson	.25
96	Alvin Davis	.25
97	Robin Roberts	.25
98	Kirby Puckett	1.50
99	Jack Clark	.25
100	Hank Aaron	3.00
101	Orlando Cepeda	.25
102	Vern Law	.25
103	Cecil Cooper	.25
104	Don Larsen	.50
105	Mario Mendoza	.25
106	Tony Gwynn	1.50
107	Ernie Harwell	.25
108a	Monte Irvin (No facsimile autograph.)	.75
108b	Monte Irvin (W/ facsimile autograph.)	1.50
109	Tommy John	.25
110	Rollie Fingers	.75
111	Johnny Podres	.25
112	Jeff Reardon	.25
113	Buddy Bell	.25
114	Dwight Gooden	.50
115	Garry Templeton	.25
116	Johnny Bench	2.00
117	Joe Rudi	.25
118	Ron Guidry	.50
119	Vince Coleman	.25
120	Al Kaline	2.00
121	Carl Yastrzemski	1.50
122	Hank Bauer	.25
123	Mark Fidrych	.25
124	Paul O'Neill	.50
125	Ron Cey	.25
126	Willie McGee	.25
127	Harmon Killebrew	1.50
128	Dave Concepcion	.25
129	Harold Baines	.25
130	Lou Brock	.50
131	Lee Smith	.25
132	Willie McCovey	.75
133	Steve Garvey	.25
134	Kent Tekulve	.25
135	Tom Seaver	1.50
136	Bo Jackson	1.00
137	Walt Weiss	.25
138	Brook Jacoby	.25
139	Dennis Eckersley	.50
140	Duke Snider	1.00
141	Lenny Dykstra	.25
142	Greg Luzinski	.25
143	Jim Bunning	.25
144	Jose Canseco	.75
145	Ron Santo	.25
146	Bert Blyleven	.25
147	Wade Boggs	.75
148	Brooks Robinson	1.00
149	Ray Knight	.25
150	Nolan Ryan	4.00

Refractors

ROYALS
George Brett
3rd Base
GEORGE BRETT

Cards (1-150):	3-6X
Production 299 Sets	

Autographs

ROYALS
SS-2B
BUDDY BIANCALANA

		NM/M
Common Autograph:		8.00
SP's Production 50		
HA	Hank Aaron/SP	250.00
JA	Jim Abbott	10.00
SA	Sparky Anderson/SP	30.00
LA	Luis Aparicio	10.00
TA	Tony Armas	10.00
HBA	Harold Baines	15.00
SB	Steve Balboni	8.00
EB	Ernie Banks/SP	120.00
HB	Hank Bauer	35.00
BBE	Buddy Bell	15.00
GB	George Bell	10.00
JBE	Johnny Bench/SP	100.00
YB	Yogi Berra/SP	100.00
BBI	Buddy Biancalana	8.00
PB	Paul Blair	10.00
VB	Vida Blue	15.00
BB	Bert Blyleven	15.00
WB	Wade Boggs/SP	75.00
GBR	George Brett/SP	250.00
LB	Lou Brock/SP	60.00
BBU	Bill Buckner	10.00
JB	Jim Bunning/SP	75.00
BC	Bert Campaneris	10.00
JOS	Jose Canseco	60.00
RCA	Rod Carew/SP	75.00
GC	Gary Carter/SP	40.00
JCA	Joe Carter/SP	35.00
OC	Orlando Cepeda/SP	60.00
RCE	Ron Cey	10.00
JC	Jack Clark	15.00
VC	Vince Coleman	10.00
DC	Dave Concepcion/SP	35.00
CC	Cecil Cooper	10.00
JCR	Jose Cruz	10.00
RDA	Ron Darling	10.00
DD	Darren Daulton	15.00
AD	Alvin Davis	8.00
ED	Eric Davis	15.00
ADA	Andre Dawson/SP	50.00
DDE	Doug DeCinces	10.00
RD	Rob Dibble	15.00
LDU	Leon Durham	10.00
LD	Lenny Dykstra	15.00
DEC	Dennis Eckersley/SP	60.00
DE	Darrell Evans	10.00
DEV	Dwight Evans/SP	40.00
BF	Bob Feller	15.00
MF	Mark Fidrych	10.00
RF	Rollie Fingers/SP	40.00
CF	Carlton Fisk/SP	60.00
WF	Whitey Ford/SP	100.00
GF	George Foster	10.00
BFR	Bob Friend	10.00
SG	Steve Garvey	20.00
KGI	Kirk Gibson/SP	75.00
DG	Dwight Gooden/SP	30.00
RG	Rich "Goose" Gossage/SP	30.00
BGR	Bobby Grich	10.00
KG	Ken Griffey Sr./SP	30.00
RGU	Ron Guidry	15.00
TG	Tony Gwynn/SP	100.00
EH	Ernie Harwell	40.00
KH	Keith Hernandez/SP	60.00
WHE	Willie Hernandez	10.00
TH	Tom Herr	10.00
WH	Whitey Herzog	20.00
BH	Bob Horner	8.00
MI	Monte Irvin/SP	40.00
BJ	Bo Jackson/SP	100.00
RJ	Reggie Jackson/SP	100.00
BJA	Brook Jacoby	8.00
FJ	Fergie Jenkins	15.00
TJ	Tommy John	15.00
HJ	Howard Johnson	10.00
WJ	Wally Joyner	10.00
AK	Al Kaline/SP	75.00
HK	Harmon Killebrew/SP	80.00
RK	Ralph Kiner/SP	65.00
RKI	Ron Kittle	10.00
RY	Ray Knight	10.00
JK	Jerry Koosman	20.00
JKR	John Kruk/SP	60.00
CL	Carney Lansford	15.00
DL	Don Larsen	15.00
TL	Tom Lasorda/SP	40.00
VL	Vern Law	15.00
BL	Bill Lee	10.00
CLE	Chet Lemon	10.00
GL	Greg Luzinski	15.00
FL	Fred Lynn/SP	25.00
SL	Steve Lyons	10.00
BMA	Bill Madlock	10.00
JMA	Juan Marichal/SP	75.00
DON	Don Mattingly/SP	150.00
WM	Willie Mays/SP	150.00
BMZ	Bill Mazeroski/SP	50.00
TM	Tim McCarver/SP	10.00
WMC	Willie McCovey/SP	60.00
MCG	Willie McGee/SP	60.00
TMC	Tug McGraw	20.00
MM	Mario Mendoza	10.00
KM	Kevin Mitchell	10.00
PM	Paul Molitor/SP	60.00
JMO	John Montefusco	10.00
JM	Joe Morgan/SP	30.00
DM	Dale Murphy/SP	60.00
SM	Stan Musial/SP	120.00
GN	Graig Nettles	15.00
DN	Don Newcombe/SP	40.00
PN	Phil Niekro/SP	40.00
AO	Al Oliver	10.00
PO	Paul O'Neill/SP	75.00
MP	Mike Pagliarulo	10.00
JP	Jim Palmer/SP	60.00
DP	Dave Parker/SP	40.00
LP	Lance Parrish	10.00
TP	Terry Pendleton	15.00
JPE	Joe Pepitone	10.00
TPE	Tony Perez/SP	65.00
GP	Gaylord Perry	25.00
BP	Boog Powell	10.00
KP	Kirby Puckett/SP	65.00
JRE	Jeff Reardon	10.00
HR	Harold Reynolds/SP	40.00
JRI	Jim Rice/SP	45.00
JR	J.R. Richard	10.00
CR	Cal Ripken Jr./SP	225.00
MR	Mickey Rivers	10.00
PR	Phil Rizzuto/SP	75.00
RR	Robin Roberts	25.00
BRO	Brooks Robinson/SP	100.00
FR	Frank Robinson/SP	75.00
JRU	Joe Rudi	10.00
NR	Nolan Ryan/SP	200.00
BSA	Bret Saberhagen/SP	40.00
CS	Chris Sabo	8.00
RSA	Ron Santo	25.00
SS	Steve Sax	8.00
MS	Mike Schmidt/SP	150.00
RS	Red Schoendienst	15.00
TSE	Tom Seaver/SP	100.00
KS	Kevin Seitzer	10.00
BS	Bill "Moose" Skowron	15.00
LS	Lee Smith	10.00
OS	Ozzie Smith/SP	100.00
DSN	Duke Snider/SP	60.00
CN	Cory Snyder	15.00
WS	Warren Spahn	40.00
CSP	Chris Speier	10.00
DS	Dave Stieb	15.00
BSU	Bruce Sutter	35.00
DSU	Don Sutton/SP	40.00
KT	Kent Tekulve	10.00
GT	Garry Templeton	10.00
BT	Bobby Thomson/SP	25.00
LT	Luis Tiant/SP	40.00
AT	Alan Trammell	20.00
TW	Tim Wallach	10.00
BW	Bob Watson	10.00
EW	Earl Weaver	10.00
WW	Walt Weiss	8.00
MW	Maury Wills	10.00
WWI	Willie Wilson/SP	20.00
CY	Carl Yastrzemski/SP	150.00
SY	Steve Yeager	10.00
RYO	Robin Yount/SP	100.00

Best Seat Relics

BEST SEAT IN THE HOUSE

		NM/M
Common Card:		20.00
BS1	Jim Palmer, Frank Robinson, Brooks Robinson	25.00
BS2	Wally Joyner, Rod Carew, Bobby Grich	20.00
BS3	Phil Garner, Willie Stargell, Dave Parker, Kent Tekulve	20.00
BS4	Rollie Fingers, Robin Yount, Paul Molitor	25.00
BS5	Phil Niekro, Dale Murphy, Bob Horner	20.00

Relics

		NM/M
Common Player:		8.00
HBA	Harold Baines/Bat	12.00
GBR	George Brett/Jsy	25.00
JOS	Jose Canseco/Bat	12.00
RCA	Rod Carew/Bat	10.00
GC	Gary Carter/Bat	8.00
NC	Norm Cash/Jsy	25.00
VC	Vince Coleman/Bat	8.00
JCR	Jose Cruz/Bat	6.00
RDA	Ron Darling/Jsy	8.00
ADA	Andre Dawson/Bat	8.00
LD	Lenny Dykstra/Bat	10.00
DEC	Dennis Eckersley/Jsy	10.00
CF	Curt Flood/Bat	10.00
GF	George Foster/Bat	8.00
BFR	Bob Friend/Jsy	6.00
SG	Steve Garvey/Bat	6.00
KGI	Kirk Gibson/Bat	8.00
KH	Keith Hernandez/Bat	12.00
WHE	Willie Hernandez/Bat	8.00
BH	Bob Horner/Bat	6.00
BJ	Bo Jackson/Bat	20.00
WJ	Wally Joyner/Bat	8.00
GL	Greg Luzinski/Bat	6.00
FL	Fred Lynn/Bat	8.00
DON	Don Mattingly/Bat	30.00
MCG	Willie McGee/Bat	15.00
TMC	Tug McGraw/Jsy	10.00
KM	Kevin Mitchell/Bat	8.00
JM	Joe Morgan/Bat	15.00
DM	Dale Murphy/Bat	15.00
PO	Paul O'Neill/Bat	8.00
DP	Dave Parker/Bat	6.00
LP	Lance Parrish/Bat	12.00
KP	Kirby Puckett/Bat	15.00
HR	Harold Reynolds/Bat	6.00
JRI	Jim Rice/Bat	8.00
BR	Bobby Richardson/Bat	15.00
JRU	Joe Rudi/Bat	6.00
CS	Chris Sabo/Bat	8.00
MS	Mike Schmidt/Bat	25.00
WS	Willie Stargell/Bat	12.00
AT	Alan Trammell/Bat	15.00
MW	Maury Wills/Bat	6.00

ABBREVIATIONS

SP - Short Print

Team Topps Legend Autograph

	NM/M
Common Autograph:	10.00
Paul Blair	10.00
Lou Brock	30.00
Jim Bunning	15.00
Gary Carter	30.00
Rich "Goose" Gossage	15.00
Al Kaline	50.00
Willie Mays	120.00
Joe Morgan	30.00
Stan Musial	75.00
Graig Nettles	15.00
Johnny Sain	15.00
Mike Schmidt	75.00

2003 Topps Bazooka

JEFF BAGWELL 1B

	NM/M
Complete Set (280):	40.00
Common Player:	.15
Pack (8):	2.00
Box (24):	40.00

Card #7 has 31 variations.

1	Luis Castillo	.15
2	Randy Winn	.15
3	Orlando Hudson	.15
4	Fernando Vina	.15
5	Pat Burrell	.25
6	Brad Wilkerson	.15
7	Bazooka Joe	.25
8	Javy Lopez	.25
9	Juan Pierre	.15
10	Hideo Nomo	.40
11	Barry Larkin	.25
12	Alfonso Soriano	.75
13	Rodrigo Lopez	.15
14	Mark Ellis	.15
15	Tim Salmon	.25
16	Garret Anderson	.25
17	Aaron Boone	.15
18	Jason Kendall	.15
19	Hee Seop Choi	.15
20	Jorge Posada	.40
21	Sammy Sosa	1.50
22	Mark Prior	.75
23	Mark Teixeira	.50
24	Manny Ramirez	.50
25	Jim Thome	.75
26	A.J. Pierzynski	.15
27	Scott Rolen	.75
28	Austin Kearns	.25
29	Bret Boone	.15
30	Ken Griffey Jr.	1.00
31	Greg Maddux	1.00
32	Derek Lowe	.15
33	David Wells	.15
34	A.J. Burnett	.15
35	Randall Simon	.15
36	Nick Johnson	.15
37	Junior Spivey	.15
38	Eric Gagne	.40
39	Darin Erstad	.25
40	Marty Cordova	.15
41	Brett Myers	.15
42	Mo Vaughn	.15
43	Randy Wolf	.15
44	Vicente Padilla	.15
45	Elmer Dessens	.15
46	Jason Simontacchi	.15
47	John Mabry	.15
48	Torii Hunter	.25
49	Lyle Overbay	.15
50	Kirk Saarloos	.15
51	Bernie Williams	.50
52	Wade Miller	.15
53	Bobby Abreu	.25
54	Wilson Betemit	.15
55	Edwin Almonte	.15
56	Jarrod Washburn	.15
57	Drew Henson	.25
58	Tony Batista	.15
59	Juan Rivera	.15
60	Larry Walker	.25
61	Brandon Phillips	.15
62	Franklyn German	.15
63	Victor Martinez	.25
64	Moises Alou	.25
65	Nomar Garciaparra	1.00
66	Willie Harris	.15
67	Sean Casey	.25
68	Omar Vizquel	.25
69	Robert Fick	.15
70	Curt Schilling	.50
71	Adam Kennedy	.15
72	Scott Hairston	.15
73	Jimmy Journell	.15
74	Rafael Furcal	.25
75	Barry Zito	.25
76	Ed Rogers	.15
77	Cliff Floyd	.15
78	Matt Clement	.15
79	Mike Lowell	.25
80	Randy Johnson	.75
81	Craig Biggio	.25
82	Carlos Beltran	.50
83	Paul LoDuca	.15
84	Jose Vidro	.15
85	Gary Sheffield	.40
86	Jacque Jones	.15
87	Corey Hart	.15
88	Roberto Alomar	.40
89	Robin Ventura	.25
90	Pedro Martinez	.75
91	Scott Hatteberg	.15
92	Marlon Byrd	.15
93	Pokey Reese	.15
94	Sean Burroughs	.15
95	Magglio Ordonez	.25
96	Tsuyoshi Shinjo	.15
97	John Olerud	.15
98	Edgar Renteria	.15
99	Ben Grieve	.15
100	Mariano Rivera	.25
101	Ivan Rodriguez	.50
102	Josh Phelps	.15
103	Nobuaki Yoshida RC	.40
104	Roy Halladay	.25
105	Mark Buehrle	.15
106	Chan Ho Park	.15
107	Joe Kennedy	.15
108	Shin-Soo Choo	.15
109	Ryan Jensen	.15
110	Todd Helton	.25
111	Chris Duncan RC	1.00
112	Taggert Bozied	.15
113	Sean Burnett	.15
114	Mike Lieberthal	.15
115	Josh Beckett	.25
116	Andy Pettitte	.40
117	Jose Reyes	.25
118	Bartolo Colon	.15
119	Justin Morneau	.25
120	Lance Berkman	.25
121	Mike Wodnicki RC	.40
122	Craig Brazell RC	.50
123	Troy Glaus	.40
124	John Smoltz	.25
125	Mike Sweeney	.15
126	Jay Gibbons	.15
127	Kerry Wood	.75
128	Ellis Burks	.15
129	Carlos Pena	.15
130	Shawn Green	.25
131	Jason Stokes	.15
132	Raul Ibanez	.15
133	Francisco Rodriguez	.25
134	Adrian Beltre	.25
135	Richie Sexson	.40
136	Paul Byrd	.15
137	Bobby Kielty	.15
138	Dewon Brazelton	.15
139	Jeremy Griffiths	.15
140	Vladimir Guerrero	.75
141	Jake Peavy	.15
142	Bryan Bullington RC	1.00
143	Orlando Cabrera	.15
144	Scott Erickson	.15
145	Doug Mientkiewicz	.15
146	Derrek Lee	.25
147	Daryl Clark RC	.15
148	Trevor Hoffman	.15
149	Gabe Gross	.15
150	Roger Clemens	1.50
151	Khalil Greene	1.00
152	Cory Doyne RC	.40
153	Brandon Roberson RC	.40
154	Josh Fogg	.15
155	Eric Chavez	.25
156	Kris Benson	.15
157	Billy Koch	.15
158	Jermaine Dye	.15
159	Kip Bouknight RC	.15
160	Brian Giles	.25
161	Justin Huber	.15
162	Mike Restovich	.15
163	Brandon Webb RC	.75
164	Odalis Perez	.15
165	Phil Nevin	.15
166	Dontrelle Willis	.25
167	Aaron Heilman	.15
168	Dustin Moseley RC	.15
169	Rylan Reed RC	.40
170	Miguel Tejada	.40
171	Nic Jackson	.15
172	Anthony Webster RC	.40
173	Jorge Julio	.15
174	Kevin Millwood	.25
175	Brian Jordan	.15
176	Terry Tiffee RC	.40
177	Dallas McPherson	.15
178	Freddy Garcia	.15
179	Jamie Moyer	.15
180	Rafael Palmeiro	.25
181	Mike O'Keefe RC	.40
182	Kevin Youkilis RC	.15
183	Kip Wells	.15
184	Joe Mauer	.25
185	Edgar Martinez	.25
186	Jaime Bubela RC	.40
187	Jose Hernandez	.15
188	Josh Hamilton	.15
189	Matt Diaz RC	.40
190	Chipper Jones	.75
191	Kevin Mench	.15
192	Joey Gomes	.15
193	Shannon Stewart	.15
194	Damian Miller	.15
195	Mike Piazza	1.00
196	Damian Moss	.15
197	Mike Fontenot	.15
198	Shea Hillenbrand	.15
199	Evel Bastida-Martinez RC	.40
200	Jason Giambi	.40
201	Aron Weston RC	.40
202	Frank Thomas	.50
203	Carlos Lee	.15
204	C.C. Sabathia	.15
205	Jim Edmonds	.25
206	Jemel Spearman RC	.40
207	Jason Jennings	.15
208	Jeremy Bonderman	1.00
209	Preston Wilson	.15
210	Eric Hinske	.15
211	Will Smith	.15
212	Matthew Hagen RC	.15
213	Joe Randa	.15
214	James Loney	.15
215	Carlos Delgado	.25
216	Kris Kroski RC	.50
217	Cristian Guzman	.15
218	Tomokazu Ohka	.15
219	Al Leiter	.15
220	Adam Dunn	.50
221	Raul Mondesi	.25
222	Donald Hood RC	.40
223	Mark Mulder	.25
224	Mike Williams	.15
225	Ryan Klesko	.25
226	Rich Aurilia	.15
227	Chris Snelling	.15
228	Gary Schneidmiller RC	.15
229	Ichiro Suzuki	1.50
230	Luis Gonzalez	.25
231	Rocco Baldelli	.15
232	Callix Crabbe RC	.40
233	Adrian Gonzalez	.15
234	Corey Koskie	.15
235	Tom Glavine	.15
236	Kevin Beavers RC	.40
237	Frank Catalanotto	.15
238	Kevin Cash	.15
239	Nick Trzesniak RC	.50
240	Paul Konerko	.15
241	Jose Cruz Jr.	.15
242	Hank Blalock	.50
243	J.D. Drew	.15
244	Kazuhiro Sasaki	.15
245	Jeff Bagwell	.50
246	Jason Schmidt	.25
247	Xavier Nady	.15
248	Aramis Ramirez	.40
249	Jimmy Rollins	.20
250	Alex Rodriguez	1.50
251	Terrence Long	.15
252	Derek Jeter	2.00
253	Edgardo Alfonzo	.15
254	Toby Hall	.15
255	Kazuhisa Ishii	.15
256	Brad Nelson	.15
257	Kevin Brown	.25
258	Roy Oswalt	.25
259	Mike Cameron	.15
260	Juan Gonzalez	.40
261	Dmitri Young	.15
262	Jose Jimenez	.15
263	Wily Mo Pena	.25
264	Joe Borchard	.15
265	Mike Mussina	.50
266	Fred McGriff	.25
267	Johnny Damon	.25
268	Joel Pineiro	.15
269	Andruw Jones	.50
270	Tim Hudson	.25
271	Chad Tracy	.15
272	Brad Fullmer	.15
273	Boof Bonser	.15
274	Clint Nageotte	.15
275	Jeff Kent	.25
276	Tino Martinez	.15
277	Matt Morris	.15
278	Jonny Gomes	.15
279	Benito Santiago	.15
280	Albert Pujols	1.50

Silver

ROBERTO ALOMAR 2B

	NM/M
Stars:	1-3X
Inserted 1:1	

Blasts

	NM/M
Common Player:	4.00
Refractors:	3-4X
Production 25 Sets	
RA	Roberto Alomar	6.00
LB	Lance Berkman	6.00
WB	Wilson Betemit	4.00
JD	Johnny Damon	6.00
CD	Carlos Delgado	6.00
JDD	J.D. Drew	8.00
DE	Darin Erstad	4.00
AG	Andres Galarraga	4.00
LG	Luis Gonzalez	4.00
SG	Shawn Green	6.00
TG	Tony Gwynn	8.00
RH	Rickey Henderson	10.00
DH	Drew Henson	4.00
NJ	Nick Johnson	4.00
CJ	Chipper Jones	10.00
RK	Ryan Klesko	4.00
PL	Paul LoDuca	4.00
EM	Edgar Martinez	8.00
TM	Tino Martinez	4.00
RM	Raul Mondesi	4.00
RP	Rafael Palmeiro	6.00
MP	Mike Piazza	12.00
JP	Jorge Posada	8.00
ANR	Aramis Ramirez	4.00
MR	Manny Ramirez	8.00
AR	Alex Rodriguez	12.00
IR	Ivan Rodriguez	8.00
GS	Gary Sheffield	6.00
TS	Tsuyoshi Shinjo	4.00
AS	Alfonso Soriano	10.00
MS	Mike Sweeney	4.00
RV	Robin Ventura	4.00
BW	Bernie Williams	10.00

Comics

	NM/M
Complete Set (12):	4.00
Common Player:	.25
Inserted 1:4	
	Roger Clemens	.40
	Nomar Garciaparra	.60
	Jason Giambi	.40
	Derek Jeter	.75
	Randy Johnson	.30
	Chipper Jones	.40
	Mike Piazza	.50
	Albert Pujols	.30
	Alex Rodriguez	.60
	Alfonso Soriano	.40
	Sammy Sosa	.40
	Ichiro Suzuki	.50

Piece of Americana

	NM/M
Common Player:	5.00

Mini

DMITRI YOUNG 1B

Stars:	1-3X
Inserted 1:1	

PIECE OF AMERICANA

CURT SCHILLING

Refractors:	3-4X
Production 25 Sets	
JB	Jeff Bagwell	10.00
CB	Craig Biggio	5.00
BB	Bret Boone	5.00
DB	Dewon Brazelton	5.00
CD	Carlos Delgado	5.00
AD	Adam Dunn	10.00
JE	Jim Edmonds	6.00
RF	Rafael Furcal	5.00
NG	Nomar Garciaparra	15.00
SG	Shawn Green	5.00
CG	Cristian Guzman	5.00
TG	Tony Gwynn	10.00
THA	Toby Hall	5.00
TH	Todd Helton	6.00
AH	Aubrey Huff	5.00
AJ	Andruw Jones	5.00
CJ	Chipper Jones	10.00
JK	Jeff Kent	5.00
AL	Al Leiter	5.00
PL	Paul LoDuca	5.00
MM	Mike Mussina	8.00
MO	Magglio Ordonez	5.00
RP	Rafael Palmeiro	6.00
MP	Mike Piazza	12.00
PA	Albert Pujols	10.00
IR	Ivan Rodriguez	5.00
CS	Curt Schilling	6.00
FT	Frank Thomas	6.00
LW	Larry Walker	5.00
PW	Preston Wilson	5.00

Stand-Ups

JIM THOME PHILADELPHIA PHILLIES' FIRST BASE

	NM/M
Complete Set (25):	20.00
Common Player:	.40
Inserted 1:8	
1	Albert Pujols	2.50
2	Alfonso Soriano	1.00
3	Ichiro Suzuki	2.00
4	Sammy Sosa	2.00
5	Randy Johnson	1.00
6	Torii Hunter	.50
7	Vladimir Guerrero	1.00
8	Nomar Garciaparra	2.00
9	Alex Rodriguez	3.00
10	Troy Glaus	.50
11	Greg Maddux	1.50
12	Derek Jeter	3.00
13	Lance Berkman	.40
14	Larry Walker	.40
15	Adam Dunn	.50
16	Shawn Green	.50
17	Curt Schilling	.75
18	Todd Helton	.75
19	Pedro Martinez	1.00
20	Pat Burrell	.50
21	Miguel Tejada	.50
22	Manny Ramirez	1.00
23	Mike Piazza	1.50
24	Chipper Jones	1.00
25	Jason Giambi	1.00

4-On-1 Stickers

	NM/M
Complete Set (55):	10.00

	Common Sticker:	.20
	Inserted 1:4	
1	Mark Prior, Roy Oswalt, Jarrod Washburn, Barry Zito	.30
2	Troy Glaus, Shea Hillenbrand, Eric Chavez, Eric Hinske	.30
3	Orlando Hudson, Alfonso Soriano, Roberto Alomar, Jose Vidro	.40
4	Nomar Garciaparra, Derek Jeter, Miguel Tejada, Alex Rodriguez	.75
5	Jason Giambi, Jim Thome, Todd Helton, Rafael Palmeiro	.40
6	Mike Williams, Trevor Hoffman, Billy Koch, John Smoltz	.20
7	Jorge Posada, Mike Piazza, A.J. Pierzynski, Ivan Rodriguez	.50
8	Vladimir Guerrero, Jim Edmonds, Manny Ramirez, Brad Wilkerson	.40
9	Shawn Green, Sammy Sosa, Torii Hunter, Larry Walker	.40
10	Bernie Williams, Ken Griffey Jr., Ichiro Suzuki, Adam Dunn	.50
11	John Olerud, Mike Lieberthal, Terrence Long, Drew Henson	.20
12	Edgar Martinez, Bret Boone, Mo Vaughn, Robert Fisk	.40
13	Randy Johnson, Roger Clemens, Pedro Martinez, Greg Maddux	.40
14	Curt Schilling, Tim Hudson, Tom Glavine, Kerry Wood	.20
15	Paul Konerko, Mike Sweeney, Cristian Guzman, Scott Rolen	.20
16	Josh Phelps, Brandon Phillips, Hee Seop Choi, Hank Blalock	.20
17	Benito Santiago, Barry Larkin, Gary Sheffield, Carlos Delgado	.20
18	Juan Rivera, Jose Reyes, Sean Burroughs, Carlos Pena	.20
19	Tony Batista, Tim Salmon, Jeff Bagwell, Raul Ibanez	.25
20	Edgardo Alfonzo, Nic Jackson, Luis Castillo, Damian Miller	.20
21	David Wells, Ryan Klesko, Phil Nevin, Jeff Kent	.20
22	Derek Lowe, Vicente Padilla, Kevin Millwood, Joel Pineiro	.20
23	Fernando Vina, Darin Erstad, Jimmy Rollins, Doug Mientkiewicz	.20
24	Joe Mauer, Justin Huber, Jason Stokes, Chad Tracy	.20
25	Austin Kearns, Junior Spivey, Brett Myers, Victor Martinez	.25
26	Khalil Greene, Gabe Gross, Kevin Cash, James Loney	.20
27	Albert Pujols, Mark Buehrle, Chipper Jones, Lance Berkman	.40
28	Adam Kennedy, Craig Biggio, Johnny Damon, Randy Winn	.20
29	Brian Giles, J.D. Drew, Marlon Byrd, Joe Borchard	.20
30	Al Leiter, Mike Mussina, Bartolo Colon, Freddy Garcia	.20
31	Jason Kendall, Richie Sexson, Mike Lowell, Paul LoDuca	.20
32	Pat Burrell, Garret Anderson, Cliff Floyd, Andruw Jones	.25
33	Xavier Nady, Bobby Abreu, Taggert Bozied, Adrian Beltre	.20
34	Rocco Baldelli, Dontrelle Willis, Chris Snelling, Mark Teixeira	.20

35 Willie Harris, Nick Johnson, Jason Jennings, Kazuhisa Ishii .20
36 Mark Mulder, Sean Burnett, Paul Byrd, Josh Beckett .20
37 Corey Koskie, Aramis Ramirez, Tino Martinez, Moises Alou .20
38 Jose Cruz Jr., Roy Halliday, Dewon Brazelton, Jonny Gomes .20
39 Odalis Perez, Kevin Brown, Matt Clement, Randy Wolf .20
40 Eric Gagne, Jose Jimenez, Franklyn German, Edwin Almonte .20
41 Luis Gonzalez, Shannon Stewart, Brian Jordan, Juan Gonzalez .25
42 Toby Hall, Joe Kennedy, Javier Lopez, Damian Moss .20
43 Magglio Ordonez, Carlos Lee, Randall Simon, Dmitri Young .20
44 Sean Casey, Aaron Boone, Jacque Jones, Michael Restovich .20
45 Adrian Gonzalez, Corey Hart, Fred McGriff, Frank Thomas .25
46 C.C. Sabathia, Omar Vizquel, Andy Pettitte, Robin Ventura .20
47 Jason Schmidt, Ellis Burks, Joe Randa, Tsuyoshi Shinjo .20
48 Mike Cameron, Pokey Reese, Jermaine Dye, Preston Wilson .20
49 Chan Ho Park, Kazuhisa Sasaki, Tomokazu Ohka, Hideo Nomo .20
50 Jason Simontacchi, Kip Wells, Matt Morris, Rodrigo Lopez .20
51 Dallas McPherson, Josh Hamilton, Jeremy Bonderman, Aaron Heilman .20
52 Nobuaki Yoshida, Chris Duncan, Craig Brazell, Bryan Bullington .20
53 Daryl Clark, Brandon Webb, Dustin Moseley, Mike O'Keefe .20
54 Kevin Youkilis, Jaime Bubela, Matt Diaz, Joey Gomes .20
55 Kris Kroski, Donald Hood, Gary Schneidmiller, Callix Crabbe .20

Chicago Cubs Reprints

For a third year the Cubs contracted with Topps to provide a series of reprint cards for use as give-aways at special games throughout the season. Each reprint features a Wrigley Field logo on front and is sequentially numbered to 20,000 in a strip of gold foil on back. Each card was distributed in a cello wrapper with the date of the promotion and names of the sponsor(s).

NM/M
Complete Set (6): 10.00
Common Player: 2.00
(1) Glenn Beckert 2.00
(2) Hee Seop Choi 2.00
(3) Bobby Hill 2.00
(4) Bill Madlock 2.00
(5) Ron Santo 4.00
(6) Steve Stone 2.00

2003 Topps Chrome

NM/M
Complete Set (440): 160.00
Common Player: .25
Series 1 & 2 Hobby Pack (4): 2.50
Hobby Box (24): 50.00
1 Alex Rodriguez 4.00
2 Eddie Guardado .25
3 Curt Schilling 1.50
4 Andruw Jones 1.00
5 Magglio Ordonez .75
6 Todd Helton 1.00
7 Odalis Perez .25
8 Edgardo Alfonzo .25
9 Eric Hinske .25
10 Danny Bautista .25
11 Sammy Sosa 2.50
12 Roberto Alomar 1.00
13 Roger Clemens 3.00
14 Austin Kearns 1.00
15 Luis Gonzalez .50
16 Mo Vaughn .50
17 Alfonso Soriano 1.50
18 Orlando Cabrera .25
19 Hideo Nomo .75
20 Omar Vizquel .25
21 Greg Maddux 2.50
22 Fred McGriff .50
23 Frank Thomas 1.25
24 Shawn Green .75
25 Jacque Jones .25
26 Bernie Williams 1.00
27 Corey Patterson .75
28 Cesar Izturis .25
29 Larry Walker .75
30 Darren Dreifort .25
31 Al Leiter .25
32 Jason Marquis .25
33 Sean Casey .25
34 Craig Counsell .25
35 Albert Pujols 3.00
36 Kyle Lohse .25
37 Paul LoDuca .25
38 Roy Oswalt .50
39 Danny Graves .25
40 Kevin Millwood .25
41 Lance Berkman 1.00
42 Denny Hocking .25
43 Jose Valentin .25
44 Josh Beckett .75
45 Nomar Garciaparra 3.00
46 Craig Biggio .50
47 Omar Daal .25
48 Jimmy Rollins .25
49 Jermaine Dye .25
50 Edgar Renteria .50
51 Brandon Duckworth .25
52 Luis Castillo .25
53 Andy Ashby .25
54 Mike Williams .25
55 Benito Santiago .25
56 Bret Boone .25
57 Randy Wolf .25
58 Ivan Rodriguez 1.50
59 Shannon Stewart .25
60 Jose Cruz Jr. .25
61 Billy Wagner .25
62 Alex Gonzalez .25
63 Ichiro Suzuki 3.00
64 Joe McEwing .25
65 Mark Mulder .50
66 Mike Cameron .25
67 Corey Koskie .25
68 Marlon Anderson .25
69 Jason Kendall .25
70 J.T. Snow Jr. .25
71 Edgar Martinez .50
72 Vernon Wells .25
73 Vladimir Guerrero 2.00
74 Adam Dunn 1.50
75 Barry Zito .50
76 Jeff Kent .50
77 Russ Ortiz .25
78 Phil Nevin .25
79 Carlos Beltran 1.00
80 Mike Lowell .50
81 Bob Wickman .25
82 Junior Spivey .25
83 Melvin Mora .25
84 Derrek Lee .50
85 Chuck Knoblauch .25
86 Eric Gagne .75
87 Orlando Hernandez .50
88 Robert Person .25
89 Elmer Dessens .25
90 Wade Miller .25
91 Adrian Beltre .50
92 Kazuhiro Sasaki .25
93 Timoniel Perez .25
94 Jose Vidro .25
95 Geronimo Gil .25
96 Trot Nixon .25
97 Denny Neagle .25
98 Roberto Hernandez .25
99 David Ortiz 1.50
100 Robb Nen .25
101 Sidney Ponson .25
102 Kevin Appier .25
103 Javier Lopez .50
104 Jeff Conine .25
105 Mark Buehrle .25
106 Jason Simontacchi .25
107 Jose Jimenez .25
108 Brian Jordan .25
109 Brad Wilkerson .25
110 Scott Hatteberg .25
111 Matt Morris .50
112 Miguel Tejada .75
113 Rafael Furcal .50
114 Steve Cox .25
115 Roy Halladay .25
116 David Eckstein .25
117 Tomokazu Ohka .25
118 Jack Wilson .25
119 Randall Simon .25
120 Jamie Moyer .25
121 Andy Benes .25
122 Tino Martinez .50
123 Esteban Yan .25
124 Jason Isringhausen .25
125 Chris Carpenter .25
126 Aaron Rowand .25
127 Brandon Inge .25
128 Jose Vizcaino .25
129 Jose Mesa .25
130 Troy Percival .25
131 Jon Lieber .25
132 Brian Giles .50
133 Aaron Boone .25
134 Bobby Higginson .25
135 Luis Rivas .25
136 Troy Glaus 1.00
137 Jim Thome 1.50
138 Ramon Martinez .25
139 Jay Gibbons .25
140 Mike Lieberthal .25
141 Juan Uribe .25
142 Gary Sheffield .75
143 Ramon Santiago .25
144 Ben Sheets .50
145 Tony Armas Jr. .25
146 Kazuhisa Ishii .25
147 Erubiel Durazo .25
148 Jerry Hairston Jr. .25
149 Byung-Hyun Kim .25
150 Marcus Giles .25
151 Johnny Damon .75
152 Terrence Long .25
153 Juan Pierre .25
154 Aramis Ramirez .75
155 Brent Abernathy .25
156 Ismael Valdes .25
157 Mike Mussina 1.00
158 Ramon Hernandez .25
159 Adam Kennedy .25
160 Tony Womack .25
161 Tony Batista .25
162 Kip Wells .25
163 Jeromy Burnitz .25
164 Todd Hundley .25
165 Tim Wakefield .25
166 Derek Lowe .25
167 Jorge Posada .75
168 Ramon Ortiz .25
169 Brent Butler .25
170 Shane Halter .25
171 Matt Lawton .25
172 Alex Sanchez .25
173 Eric Milton .25
174 Vicente Padilla .25
175 Steve Karsay .25
176 Mark Prior 1.50
177 Kerry Wood 1.50
178 Jason LaRue .25
179 Danys Baez .25
180 Nick Neugebauer .25
181 Andres Galarraga .25
182 Jason Giambi 1.00
183 Aubrey Huff .25
184 Juan Gonzalez 1.00
185 Ugueth Urbina .25
186 Rickey Henderson .75
187 Brad Fullmer .25
188 Todd Zeile .25
189 Jason Jennings .25
190 Vladimir Nunez .25
191 David Justice .50
192 Brian Lawrence .25
193 Pat Burrell .50
194 Pokey Reese .25
195 Robert Fick .25
196 C.C. Sabathia .25
197 Fernando Vina .25
198 Sean Burroughs .25
199 Ellis Burks .25
200 Joe Randa .25
201 Chris Duncan RC 8.00
202 Franklin Gutierrez RC 1.00
203 Adam LaRoche .25
204 Manuel Ramirez RC 1.00
205 Il Kim RC 1.00
206 Daryl Clark RC 1.00
207 Sean Pierce .25
208 Andy Marte RC 5.00
209 Bernie Castro RC 1.00
210 Jason Perry RC 1.00
211 Jaime Bubela RC 1.00
212 Alexis Rios .25
213 Brendan Harris RC .25
214 Ramon A. Martinez RC .25
215 Terry Tiffee RC .25
216 Kevin Youkilis RC 4.00
217 Derell McCall RC 1.00
218 Scott Tyler 1.00
219 Craig Brazell RC 2.50
220 Walter Young 1.00
221 Francisco Rodriguez .40
222 Chipper Jones 2.00
223 Chris Singleton .25
224 Cliff Floyd .25
225 Bobby Hill .25
226 Antonio Osuna .25
227 Barry Larkin .50
228 Dean Palmer .25
229 Eric Owens .25
230 Randy Johnson 1.50
231 Jeff Suppan .25
232 Eric Karros .25
233 Johan Santana .25
234 Javier Vazquez .25
235 John Thomson .25
236 Nick Johnson .25
237 Mark Ellis .25
238 Doug Glanville .25
239 Ken Griffey Jr. 2.50
240 Bubba Trammell .25
241 Livan Hernandez .25
242 Desi Relaford .25
243 Eli Marrero .25
244 Jared Sandberg .25
245 Barry Bonds 4.00
246 Aaron Sele .25
247 Derek Jeter 5.00
248 Eric Byrnes .25
249 Rich Aurilia .25
250 Joel Pineiro .25
251 Chuck Finley .25
252 Bengie Molina .25
253 Steve Finley .25
254 Marty Cordova .25
255 Shea Hillenbrand .25
256 Milton Bradley .25
257 Carlos Pena .25
258 Brad Ausmus .25
259 Carlos Delgado .75
260 Kevin Mench .25
261 Joe Kennedy .25
262 Mark McLemore .25
263 Bill Mueller .25
264 Ricky Ledee .25
265 Ted Lilly .25
266 Sterling Hitchcock .25
267 Scott Strickland .25
268 Damion Easley .25
269 Torii Hunter .50
270 Brad Radke .25
271 Geoff Jenkins .25
272 Paul Byrd .25
273 Morgan Ensberg .25
274 Mike Hampton .25
275 Flash Gordon .25
276 John Burkett .25
277 Rodrigo Lopez .25
278 Tim Spooneybarger .25
279 Quinton McCracken .25
280 Tim Salmon .50
281 Jarrod Washburn .25
282 Pedro J. Martinez 1.50
283 Julio Lugo .25
284 Armando Benitez .25
285 Raul Mondesi .50
286 Robin Ventura .25
287 Bobby Abreu .25
288 Josh Fogg .25
289 Ryan Klesko .50
290 Tsuyoshi Shinjo .25
291 Jim Edmonds .75
292 Chan Ho Park .25
293 John Mabry .25
294 Woody Williams .25
295 Scott Schoeneweis .25
296 Brian Anderson .25
297 Brett Tomko .25
298 Scott Erickson .25
299 Tony Clark .25
300 Danny Wright .25
301 Jason Schmidt .25
302 Scott Williamson .25
303 Einar Diaz .25
304 Jay Payton .25
305 Juan Acevedo .25
306 Ben Grieve .25
307 Raul Ibanez .25
308 Richie Sexson .75
309 Rick Reed .25
310 Pedro Astacio .25
311 Bud Smith .25
312 Tomas Perez .25
313 Adam Eaton .25
314 Rafael Palmeiro 1.50
315 Jason Tyner .25
316 Scott Rolen 2.00
317 Randy Winn .25
318 Ryan Jensen .25
319 Trevor Hoffman .25
320 Craig Wilson .25
321 Jeremy Giambi .25
322 Andy Pettitte .50
323 John Franco .25
324 Felipe Lopez .25
325 Mike Piazza 3.00
326 Cristian Guzman .25
327 Jose Hernandez .25
328 Octavio Dotel .25
329 Brad Penny .25
330 Charles Johnson .25
331 Ryan Dempster .25
332 Joe Crede .25
333 Chad Hermansen .25
334 Gary Matthews Jr. .25
335 Frank Catalanotto .25
336 Darin Erstad .50
337 Matt Williams .25
338 B.J. Surhoff .25
339 Kerry Ligtenberg .25
340 Mike Bordick .25
341 Joe Girardi .25
342 D'Angelo Jimenez .25
343 Paul Konerko .25
344 Joe Mays .25
345 Marquis Grissom .25
346 Neifi Perez .25
347 Preston Wilson .25
348 Jeff Weaver .50
349 Eric Chavez .50
350 Placido Polanco .25
351 Ray Lankford .25
352 James Baldwin .25
353 Toby Hall .25
354 Benji Gil .25
355 Damian Moss .25
356 Jorge Julio .25
357 Matt Clement .25
358 Lee Stevens .25
359 Dave Roberts .25
360 J.C. Romero .25
361 Bartolo Colon .25
362 Roger Cedeno .25
363 Mariano Rivera .50
364 Billy Koch .25
365 Manny Ramirez 1.50
366 Travis Lee .25
367 Oliver Perez .25
368 Rafael Soriano .25
369 Damian Miller .25
370 John Smoltz .50
371 Willis Roberts .25
372 Tim Hudson .50
373 Moises Alou .50
374 Corky Miller .25
375 Ben Broussard .25
376 Gabe Kapler .25
377 Chris Woodward .25
378 Todd Hollandsworth .25
379 So Taguchi .25
380 John Olerud .50
381 Reggie Sanders .25
382 Jake Peavy .25
383 Kris Benson .25
384 Ray Durham .25
385 David Wells .25
386 Tom Glavine .75
387 Antonio Alfonseca .25
388 Keith Foulke .25
389 Shawn Estes .25
390 Mark Grace .50
391 Dmitri Young .25
392 A.J. Burnett .25
393 Richard Hidalgo .25
394 Mike Sweeney .25
395 Doug Mientkiewicz .25
396 Cory Lidle .25
397 Jeff Bagwell 1.50
398 Steve Sparks .25
399 Sandy Alomar Jr. .25
400 John Lackey .25
401 Rick Helling .25
402 Carlos Lee .25
403 Garret Anderson .50
404 Vinny Castilla .25
405 David Bell .25
406 Freddy Garcia .25
407 Scott Spiezio .25
408 Russell Branyan .25
409 Jose Contreras RC 3.00
410 Kevin Brown .50
411 Tyler Houston .25
412 A.J. Pierzynski .25
413 Peter Bergeron .25
414 Brett Myers .25
415 Kenny Lofton .25
416 Ben Davis .25
417 J.D. Drew .50
418 Ricky Gutierrez .25
419 Mark Redman .25
420 Juan Encarnacion .25
421 Bryan Bullington RC 4.00
422 Jeremy Guthrie .25
423 Joey Gomes .50
424 Evel Bastida-Martinez RC 1.50
425 Brian Wright RC 1.00
426 B.J. Upton 1.00
427 Jeff Francis .25
428 Jeremy Hermida .25
429 Khalil Greene 3.00
430 Darrell Rasner .25
431 Brandon Phillips, Victor Martinez .75
432 Hee Seop Choi, Nic Jackson .75
433 Dontrelle Willis, Jason Stokes 1.00
434 Chad Tracy, Lyle Overbay .25
435 Joe Borchard, Corwin Malone .25
436 Joe Mauer, Justin Morneau 1.00
437 Drew Henson, Brandon Claussen .50
438 Chase Utley, Gavin Floyd .50
439 Taggert Bozied, Xavier Nady .25
440 Aaron Heilman, Jose Reyes 1.50

Refractors

Stars: 1-2X
Production 699 Sets
Gold Refractors: 1.5-3X
Production 449 Sets
Black Refractors: 3-5X
Production 199 Sets

Uncirculated X-Fractors

Stars: 5-10X
Inserted 1:Hobby Box
Production 50 Sets

Blue Backs Relics

NM/M
Common Player: 6.00
Bat Relics Inserted 1:236
RA Roberto Alomar/Bat 10.00
JBA Jeff Bagwell/Jsy 10.00
JB Josh Beckett/Jsy 10.00
LB Lance Berkman/Bat 8.00
EC Eric Chavez/Jsy 6.00
AD Adam Dunn/Jsy 15.00
NG Nomar Garciaparra/Jsy 15.00
SG Shawn Green/Jsy 8.00
NJ Nick Johnson/Bat 8.00
PK Paul Konerko/Bat 8.00
MO Magglio Ordonez/Jsy 8.00
MP Mike Piazza/Jsy 15.00
AP Albert Pujols/Jsy 15.00
AR Alex Rodriguez/Bat 15.00
JR Jimmy Rollins/Jsy 6.00
TS Tsuyoshi Shinjo/Bat 8.00
AS Alfonso Soriano/Bat 10.00
FT Frank Thomas/Jsy 8.00
BW Bernie Williams/Bat 10.00
KW Kerry Wood/Jsy 8.00

Record Breakers Relics Series 2

NM/M
Common Player: 5.00
JB Jeff Bagwell 8.00

BB	Barry Bonds	20.00
BB2	Barry Bonds	20.00
BB3	Barry Bonds	20.00
JC	Jose Canseco	10.00
RC	Rod Carew	8.00
RC2	Rod Carew	8.00
DLE	Dennis Eckersley	8.00
DE	Darin Erstad	5.00
LG	Luis Gonzalez	5.00
RH	Rickey Henderson	15.00
RJ	Randy Johnson	8.00
DM	Don Mattingly	30.00
PM	Paul Molitor	15.00
MR	Manny Ramirez	15.00
HR	Harold Reynolds	5.00
AR	Alex Rodriguez	15.00
TS	Tom Seaver	20.00
JS	John Smoltz	8.00
SS	Sammy Sosa	15.00

Red Backs Relics

		NM/M
Common Player:		5.00
Inserted 1:49		
RA	Roberto Alomar	8.00
GA	Garret Anderson	8.00
JB	Jeff Bagwell	8.00
PB	Pat Burrell	5.00
AD	Adam Dunn	8.00
NG	Nomar Garciaparra	12.00
TH	Todd Helton	8.00
TKH	Torii Hunter	8.00
RJ	Randy Johnson	8.00
AJ	Andruw Jones	8.00
CJ	Chipper Jones	10.00
PM	Pedro J. Martinez	10.00
MP	Mike Piazza	10.00
AP	Albert Pujols	15.00
MR	Manny Ramirez	8.00
AR	Alex Rodriguez	10.00
SR	Scott Rolen	8.00
CS	Curt Schilling	8.00
AS	Alfonso Soriano	10.00
MS	Mike Sweeney	5.00

2003 Topps eTopps

Topps continued its on-line card program with a third annual eTopps edition in 2003. Initial Player Offerings were again made for only one week with allocations having to made for some cards in high demand. The number of each card actually sold in shown parenthetically. After the IPO, cards could be bought and sold within portfolios, or physically delivered (for a fee) for more traditional venues. The 2-1/2" x 3-1/2" cards are printed on metallic foil with vertical portrait and action photos on front. Horizontal backs have another portrait photo, a 2002 recap and 2003 "prospectus," and a few biographical bits and stats. The listings here include the initial offering price and the number of cards sold during the open or-

Values shown are for cards that have not been authenticated and/or graded by an independent certification company. Because the standards and reputations of such companies vary widely, prices listed here cannot be correlated to values for "slabbed" cards.

dering period. Values shown are for cards in a virtual portfolio, rather than "in hand." Taking physical possession of a card from an eTopps portfolio costs about $6 apiece.

		NM/M
Complete Set (122):		275.00
Common Player:		1.50
1	Troy Glaus ($6.50 / 1,454)	1.50
2	Manny Ramirez ($6.50 / 1,970)	1.50
3	Magglio Ordonez ($6.50 / 1,007)	3.00
4	Jim Thome ($6.50 / 3,393)	1.50
5	Torii Hunter ($6.50 / 2,027)	1.50
6	Jason Giambi ($9.50 / 2,065)	1.50
7	Tim Hudson ($6.50 / 1,690)	1.50
8	Ichiro ($6.50 / 3,465)	2.50
9	Aubrey Huff ($6.50 / 3,234)	1.50
10	Alex Rodriguez ($9.50 / 2,847)	4.00
11	Francisco Rodriguez ($6.50 / 3,627)	1.50
12	Joe Borchard ($4 / 3,000)	1.50
13	Mark Teixeira ($9.50 / 5,000)	5.00
14	Marlon Byrd ($6.50 / 1,822)	1.50
15	Carlos Delgado ($6.50 / 2,500)	1.50
16	Tom Glavine ($6.50 / 2,407)	1.50
17	Curt Schilling ($6.50 / 1,333)	1.50
18	Mark Prior ($9.50 / 4,000)	1.50
19	Ken Griffey Jr. ($6.50 / 1,238)	4.00
20	Todd Helton ($6.50 / 2,315)	1.50
21	Jeff Bagwell ($6.50 / 1,678)	1.75
22	Shawn Green ($6.50 / 1,162)	1.50
23	Vladimir Guerrero ($9.50 / 2,523)	1.75
24	Roberto Alomar ($6.50 / 1,394)	1.50
25	Brian Giles ($6.50 / 1,500)	2.00
26	Barry Bonds ($9.50 / 4,000)	9.00
27	Albert Pujols ($9.50 / 3,000)	5.00
28	Nomar Garciaparra ($9.50 / 2,177)	1.50
29	Alfonso Soriano ($9.50 / 3,500)	1.50
30	Barry Zito ($6.50 / 2,500)	2.00
31	Edgar Martinez ($6.50 / 2,732)	3.00
32	Ivan Rodriguez ($6.50 / 1,436)	1.50
33	Greg Maddux ($6.50 / 2,004)	2.00
34	Sammy Sosa ($9.50 / 1,425)	2.00
35	Austin Kearns ($6.50 / 3,000)	1.50
36	Craig Biggio ($6.50 / 1,317)	1.75
37	Mike Piazza ($6.50 / 1,355)	2.25
38	Andruw Jones ($6.50 / 1,589)	2.75
39	Jeff Kent ($6.50 / 1,685)	1.50
40	Roy Oswalt ($6.50 / 2,108)	2.75
41	Miguel Tejada ($6.50 / 2,630)	1.75
42	Derek Jeter ($9.50 / 3,054)	3.75
43	Pedro Martinez ($9.50 / 1,754)	1.50
44	Jarrod Washburn ($6.50 / 1,196)	2.00
45	Randy Johnson ($9.50 / 1,117)	5.25
46	Bernie Williams ($6.50 / 1,750)	1.50
47	Chipper Jones ($6.50 / 1,443)	1.75
48	Gary Sheffield ($6.50 / 1,500)	1.75
49	Larry Walker ($6.50 / 1,001)	3.50
50	Lance Berkman ($6.50 / 1,107)	2.50
51	Garret Anderson ($6.50 / 2,647)	1.50
52	Jason Schmidt ($6.50 / 1,840)	3.25
53	Rodrigo Lopez ($4 / 1,500)	2.50
54	Oliver Perez ($4 / 1,996)	3.50
55	Derek Lowe ($6.50 / 1,434)	1.50
56	Vicente Padilla ($6.50 / 995)	3.50
57	Paul Konerko ($6.50 / 1,151)	3.00
58	Bartolo Colon ($6.50 / 2,028)	1.50
59	Omar Vizquel ($4.00 / 3,413)	2.00
60	Adam Dunn ($6.50 / 1,812)	1.50
61	Carlos Pena ($4 / 1,402)	1.50
62	Richie Sexson ($6.50 / 1,380)	2.25
63	Paul Byrd ($4 / 2,000)	1.50
64	Eric Gagne ($6.50 / 2,929)	1.50
65	Brad Radke ($4 / 827)	4.50
66	A.J. Burnett ($6.50 / 1,009)	11.50
67	Brandon Phillips ($4 / 4,000)	1.50
68	Mike Hampton ($6.50 / 763)	9.00
69	Tim Salmon ($6.50 / 1,548)	1.50
70	Roger Clemens ($9.50 / 3,000)	2.75
71	Jake Peavy ($4 / 2,500)	3.75
72	Pat Burrell ($6.50 / 1,168)	2.75
73	Ben Sheets ($4 / 1,500)	8.00
74	Fred McGriff ($6.50 / 1,323)	1.75
75	John Smoltz ($6.50 / 3,161)	5.00
76	Josh Phelps ($6.50 / 2,500)	1.50
77	John Olerud ($6.50 / 1,620)	3.00
78	Eric Chavez ($4 / 2,054)	1.50
79	Jeff Weaver ($4 / 1,877)	1.50
80	Scott Rolen ($6.50 / 2,000)	2.00
81	Carl Crawford ($6.50 / 1,518)	3.00
82	Rafael Palmeiro ($6.50 / 1,500)	1.50
83	Roy Halladay ($6.50 / 2,500)	2.50
84	Josh Beckett ($6.50 / 1,130)	4.50
85	Jorge Posada ($6.50 / 2,171)	1.50
86	Mark Mulder ($6.50 / 2,000)	1.50
87	Eric Milton ($4 / 1,758)	1.50
88	Angel Berroa ($6.50 / 1,614)	1.50
89	Jason Lane ($4 / 1,952)	1.50
90	Kerry Wood ($6.50 / 2,000)	1.50
91	Brad Wilkerson ($4 / 2,944)	1.50
92	Orlando Hudson ($4 / 2,500)	2.50
93	Mike Mussina ($6.50 / 2,000)	1.50
94	Hee Seop Choi ($6.50 / 3,000)	1.50
95	Chris Snelling ($6.50 / 2,879)	1.50
96	Tomo Ohka ($4 / 1,975)	1.50
97	Andy Pettitte ($4 / 2,367)	1.50
98	Drew Henson ($4 / 3,000)	1.50
99	Chin-Feng Chen ($4 / 2,500)	1.50
100	Jason Jennings ($6.50 / 1,761)	1.50
101	Hideki Matsui ($9 / 8,000)	2.00
102	Jose Contreras ($9.50 / 6,000)	1.50
103	Rocco Baldelli ($6.50 / 5,000)	2.25
104	Jeremy Bonderman ($6.50 / 3,000)	3.50
105	Jesse Foppert ($6.50 / 3,500)	5.00
106	Randy Wolf ($6.50 / 1,874)	1.50
107	Kevin Millwood ($6.50 / 3,000)	1.50
108	Eric Byrnes ($6.50 / 2,500)	1.50
109	Edgar Renteria ($6.50 / 2,015)	1.50
110	Jose Reyes ($6.50 / 5,000)	4.00
111	Dontrelle Willis ($6.50 / 5,000)	3.00
112	Mike Lowell ($6.50 / 2,500)	1.50
113	Jerome Williams ($6.50 / 3,000)	3.00
114	Esteban Loaiza ($6.50 / 2,364)	1.50
115	Gil Meche ($6.50 / 2,000)	1.75
116	Ty Wigginton ($4 / 2,000)	1.50
118	Brett Myers ($6.50 / 2,115)	1.50
119	Miguel Cabrera ($6.50 / 2,610)	13.50
120	Brandon Webb ($6.50 / 3,000)	1.50
121	Aaron Heilman ($6.50 / 1,229)	2.00
122	Rich Harden ($6.50 / 5,000)	2.75
123	Morgan Ensberg ($6.50 / 1,329)	2.75

All-Star Most Valuable Player

This card was offered for $5 in the weeks after the All-Star Game, with production set at 4,000.

		NM/M
1	All-Star MVP (Garret Anderson)	1.50

All-Star Top Vote Getters

This card was offered for $5 in the weeks preceding the All-Star Game, with no limit set on production. The players appearing on the card were announced after the voting.

		NM/M
1	Ichiro Suzuki, Albert Pujols/3,938	4.00

Classics

Topps continued its eTopps Classics line-up in 2003 with 20 cards of former greats. Numbering and format were contiguous with the 2002 issue. Like regular eTopps cards, Classics could only be ordered during a one-week Initial Player Offering period. Cards were issued in a quantity of up to 4,000 each at $12.50. The number of cards actually sold is shown parenthetically. Fronts have a color or colorized action photo, backs have a picture of one of that player's Topps cards, along with career notes, stats, etc. Values shown are for cards in a virtual portfolio, rather than "in hand." Taking physical possession of a card from an eTopps portfolio costs about $6 apiece.

		NM/M
Complete Set (20):		210.00
Common Player:		9.00
21	Gary Carter/908	9.00
22	Eddie Murray/930	12.00
23	Luis Aparicio/778	17.50
24	Lou Brock/1,135	9.00
25	George Brett/1,128	17.50
26	Bob Feller/962	10.00
27	Carlton Fisk/890	10.00
28	Willie McCovey/915	11.00
29	Willie Stargell/843	14.00
30	Roberto Clemente/1,664	20.00
31	Lou Gehrig/3,049	9.00
32	Johnny Bench/1,144	20.00
33	Walter Johnson/888	11.00
34	Christy Mathewson/868	9.00
35	Rogers Hornsby/826	12.00
36	Lefty Grove/885	9.50
37	Josh Gibson/1,133	9.00
38	Mel Ott/917	9.00
39	Nap Lajoie/886	9.00
40	Yogi Berra/1,281	9.00

Events

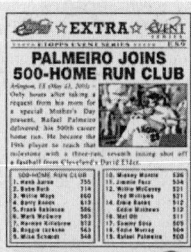

Highlights of the 2003 season were commemorated by Topps with the issue of special eTopps cards. Like the regular-issue eTopps cards, the cards were only available directly from Topps on-line. Up to 5,000 of each card were possible with an initial order price of $8 each. Only the baseball related Events cards are listed here, along with the number of cards actually sold during the one-week ordering window. Values shown represent cards in a virtual portfolio rather than "in hand." To physically take possession of a card in a portfolio costs about $7 apiece.

		NM/M
ES9	Rafael Palmeiro/1,633 (Joins 500-HR Club)	2.00
ES10	Roger Clemens/3,418 (Records 300 W's & 4000 K's)	5.00
ES11	Barry Bonds/2,649 (Establishes 500-500 Club)	6.00
ES13	Carlos Delgado/630 (Smashes 4 Home Runs)	8.00

FanFest Promos

Attendees visiting Topps' booth at the All-Star FanFest could obtain a pair of eTopps promo cards. Fronts are identical to the issued versions except for the appearance of an All-Star Game logo. Backs have an offer of $5 off an initial eTopps order.

	NM/M
Luis Aparicio (Classic)	2.00
Mark Buehrle	2.00

2003 Topps Gallery

	NM/M
Complete Set (200):	60.00

Common Player:		.25
SP's Inserted 1:20		
Pack (5):		2.50
Box (20):		45.00
1	Jason Giambi	.50
1	Jason Giambi/SP/ Drk Blue Jsy	2.00
2	Miguel Tejada	.50
3	Mike Lieberthal	.25
4	Jason Kendall	.40
5	Robb Nen	.25
6	Freddy Garcia	.25
7	Scott Rolen	.75
8	David Wells	.25
9	Rafael Palmeiro	.75
10	Garret Anderson	.50
11	Curt Schilling	.75
12	Greg Maddux	1.00
13	Rodrigo Lopez	.25
14	Nomar Garciaparra	1.50
14	N.Garciaparra/SP/ Navy Elbow Pad	4.00
15	Kerry Wood	.75
16	Frank Thomas	.75
17	Ken Griffey Jr.	1.00
18	Jim Thome	.75
19	Todd Helton	.75
20	Lance Berkman	.50
21	Robert Fick	.25
22	Kevin Brown	.40
23	Richie Sexson	.50
24	Eddie Guardado	.25
25	Vladimir Guerrero	1.00
26	Mike Piazza	1.50
27	Bernie Williams	.50
28	Eric Chavez	.40
29	Jimmy Rollins	.25
30	Ichiro Suzuki	1.50
30	Ichiro Suzuki/SP/ Black Long Shirt	3.00
31	J.D. Drew	.25
32	Nick Johnson	.25
33	Shannon Stewart	.25
34	Tim Salmon	.40
35	Andruw Jones	.75
36	Jay Gibbons	.25
37	Johnny Damon	.50
38	Fred McGriff	.40
39	Carlos Lee	.25
40	Adam Dunn	.75
40	Adam Dunn/SP/ Red Sleeves & Helmet	1.50
41	Jason Jennings	.25
42	Mike Lowell	.40
43	Mike Sweeney	.25
44	Shawn Green	.50
45	Doug Mientkiewicz	.25
46	Bartolo Colon	.25
47	Edgardo Alfonzo	.25
48	Roger Clemens	2.00
49	Randy Wolf	.25
50	Alex Rodriguez	2.00
50	Alex Rodriguez/SP/ Red Undershirt	4.00
51	Vernon Wells	.40
52	Kenny Lofton	.40
53	Mariano Rivera	.25
54	Brian Jordan	.25
55	Roberto Alomar	.50
56	Carlos Pena	.40
57	Moises Alou	.40
58	John Smoltz	.40
59	Adam Kennedy	.25
60	Randy Johnson	1.00
61	Mark Buehrle	.25
62	C.C. Sabathia	.40
63	Craig Biggio	.40
64	Eric Karros	.25
65	Jose Vidro	.25
66	Tim Hudson	.40
67	Trevor Hoffman	.25
68	Bret Boone	.25
69	Carl Crawford	.25
70	Derek Jeter	2.50
71	Troy Percival	.25
72	Gary Sheffield	.50
73	Rickey Henderson	.50
74	Paul Konerko	.40
75	Larry Walker	.40
76	Pat Burrell	.50
77	Brian Giles	.40
78	Jeff Kent	.40
79	Kazuhiro Sasaki	.25
80	Chipper Jones	1.00
81	Darin Erstad	.40
82	Sean Casey	.40
83	Luis Gonzalez	.40
84	Roy Oswalt	.25
85	Dustan Mohr	.25
86	Al Leiter	.25
87	Mike Mussina	.50
88	Vicente Padilla	.25
89	Rich Aurilia	.25
90	Albert Pujols	2.00
91	John Olerud	.40
92	Ivan Rodriguez	.75
93	Eric Hinske	.25
94	Phil Nevin	.25
95	Barry Zito	.50
96	Armando Benitez	.25
97	Torii Hunter	.50

ABBREVIATIONS

SP - Short Print

98	Paul LoDuca	.25
99	Preston Wilson	.40
100	Sammy Sosa	1.50
100	Sammy Sosa/SP/ No Shin Guard	4.00
101	Jarrod Washburn	.25
102	Steve Finley	.25
103	Cliff Floyd	.25
104	Mark Prior	1.00
105	Austin Kearns	.50
106	Jeff Bagwell	.75
107	A.J. Pierzynski	.25
108	Pedro J. Martinez	1.00
109	Orlando Cabrera	.25
110	Raul Mondesi	.25
111	Russ Ortiz	.25
112	Ruben Sierra	.25
113	Tino Martinez	.25
114	Manny Ramirez	.75
115	Troy Glaus	.50
116	Magglio Ordonez	.50
117	Omar Vizquel	.40
118	Carlos Beltran	.40
119	Jose Hernandez	.25
120	Javier Vazquez	.25
121	Jorge Posada	.50
122	Aramis Ramirez	.40
123	Jason Schmidt	.40
124	Jamie Moyer	.25
125	Jim Edmonds	.50
126	Aubrey Huff	.25
127	Carlos Delgado	.50
128	Junior Spivey	.25
129	Tom Glavine	.50
130	Marty Cordova	.25
131	Derek Lowe	.25
132	Ellis Burks	.25
133	Barry Bonds	2.50
134	Josh Beckett	.25
135	Raul Ibanez	.25
136	Kazuhisa Ishii	.25
137	Geoff Jenkins	.25
138	Eric Milton	.25
139	Mo Vaughn	.40
140	Mark Mulder	.40
141	Bobby Abreu	.40
142	Ryan Klesko	.40
143	Tsuyoshi Shinjo	.25
144	Jose Mesa	.25
145	Shea Hillenbrand	.25
146	Edgar Renteria	.25
147	Juan Gonzalez	.50
148	Edgar Martinez	.25
149	Matt Morris	.25
150	Alfonso Soriano	1.00
150	Alfonso Soriano/SP/ No Elbow Pad	2.50
151	Bryan Bullington **RC**	2.50
151	Bryan Bullington/SP/ Red Background **RC**	6.00
152	Andy Marte **RC**	3.00
152	Andy Marte/SP/ No Necklace **RC**	4.00
153	Brendan Harris **RC**	1.00
154	Juan Camacho **RC**	1.00
155	Byron Gettis **RC**	1.00
156	Daryl Clark **RC**	1.00
157	J.D. Durbin **RC**	1.00
158	Craig Brazell **RC**	1.50
158	Craig Brazell/SP/ Black Jersey **RC**	3.00
159	Jason Kubel **RC**	1.00
160	Brandon Roberson **RC**	1.00
161	Jose Contreras **RC**	2.00
162	Hanley Ramirez **RC**	3.00
163	Jaime Bubela **RC**	1.00
164	Chris Duncan **RC**	8.00
165	Tyler Johnson **RC**	1.00
166	Adam LaRoche	.25
167	Walter Young	.25
168	Ryan Kibler	.25
169	Tommy Whiteman **RC**	.25
170	Trey Hodges	.25
171	Francisco Rodriguez	.25
172	Jason Arnold	.25
173	Brett Myers	.25
174	Rocco Baldelli	.50
175	Adrian Gonzalez	.25
176	Dontrelle Willis	1.00
177	Kris Honel	.25
178	Marlon Byrd	.25
179	Aaron Heilman	.25
180	Casey Kotchman	.25
181	Miguel Cabrera	.25
182	Hee Seop Choi	.50
183	Drew Henson	.25
184	Jose Reyes	.50
185	Michael Cuddyer	.25
186	Brandon Phillips	.25
187	Victor Martinez	.25
188	Joe Mauer	.50
189	Hank Blalock	.75
190	Mark Teixeira	.25
191	Willie Mays	2.00
192	George Brett	2.00
193	Tony Gwynn	2.00
194	Carl Yastrzemski	1.00
195	Nolan Ryan	3.00
196	Reggie Jackson	.75
197	Mike Schmidt	1.50
198	Cal Ripken Jr.	3.00
199	Don Mattingly	2.00
200	Tom Seaver	.75

Rainbow Refractors

Stars (1-200): 2-3X
Inserted 1:1
Rookies (151-165): 1X
Inserted 1:1

Currency Collection

		NM/M
Common Player:		4.00
Inserted 1:Box		
BA	Bobby Abreu	6.00
HC	Hee Seop Choi	6.00
BC	Bartolo Colon	6.00
LG	Luis Gonzalez	6.00
VG	Vladimir Guerrero	12.00
KI	Kazuhisa Ishii	4.00
AJ	Andruw Jones	8.00
RL	Rodrigo Lopez	6.00
PM	Pedro J. Martinez	10.00
RM	Raul Mondesi	4.00
MO	Magglio Ordonez	8.00
VP	Vicente Padilla	6.00
RP	Rafael Palmeiro	6.00
AP	Albert Pujols	20.00
MR	Manny Ramirez	8.00
ER	Edgar Renteria	6.00
JR	Jose Reyes	8.00
MRI	Mariano Rivera	10.00
FR	Francisco Rodriguez	4.00
KS	Kazuhiro Sasaki	4.00
AS	Alfonso Soriano	8.00
SS	Sammy Sosa	15.00
IS	Ichiro Suzuki	15.00
OV	Omar Vizquel	10.00
LW	Larry Walker	5.00

Heritage

		NM/M
Complete Set (25):		75.00
Common Player:		1.50
Inserted 1:10		
WB	Wade Boggs	1.50
GB	George Brett	8.00
JC	Jose Canseco	1.50
RC	Roger Clemens	6.00
AD	Adam Dunn	2.00
NG	Nomar Garciaparra	5.00
TG	Tom Glavine	1.50
SG	Shawn Green	1.50
TGW	Tony Gwynn	3.00
RH	Rickey Henderson	2.00
DJ	Derek Jeter	8.00
RJ	Randy Johnson	3.00
HK	Harmon Killebrew	4.00
KR	Jerry Koosman, Nolan Ryan	10.00
WM	Willie Mays	8.00
HN	Hideo Nomo	2.00
KP	Kirby Puckett	3.00
IR	Ivan Rodriguez	2.00
DS	Duke Snider	2.00
AS	Alfonso Soriano	3.00
IS	Ichiro Suzuki	5.00
MT	Miguel Tejada	1.50
JT	Jim Thome	2.00
BW	Bernie Williams	2.00
CY	Carl Yastrzemski	3.00

Heritage Relics

		NM/M
Common Player:		5.00
WB	Wade Boggs	5.00
GB	George Brett	20.00
JC	Jose Canseco	8.00
RC	Roger Clemens	15.00
SG	Shawn Green	5.00
TG	Tony Gwynn	10.00
RH	Rickey Henderson	10.00
HK	Harmon Killebrew	25.00
HN	Hideo Nomo	5.00
KP	Kirby Puckett	15.00

Heritage Autographed Relics

		NM/M
Inserted 1:3,260		
WB	Wade Boggs	70.00
KP	Kirby Puckett/25	80.00

Originals Relics

		NM/M
Common Player:		5.00
RA	Roberto Alomar	6.00
MA	Moises Alou	5.00
LB	Lance Berkman	5.00
BB	Bret Boone	5.00
AD	Adam Dunn	5.00
NG	Nomar Garciaparra	12.00
LG	Luis Gonzalez	5.00
SG	Shawn Green	5.00
TG	Tony Gwynn	8.00
TH	Todd Helton	8.00
RH	Rickey Henderson	8.00
DH	Drew Henson	5.00
THU	Torii Hunter	6.00
AJ	Andruw Jones	6.00
CJ	Chipper Jones	8.00
JM	Joe Mauer	10.00
MO	Magglio Ordonez	5.00
RP	Rafael Palmeiro	5.00
MP	Mike Piazza	10.00
AP	Albert Pujols	15.00
MR	Manny Ramirez	8.00
AR	Alex Rodriguez	10.00
IR	Ivan Rodriguez	8.00
GS	Gary Sheffield	6.00
AS	Alfonso Soriano	6.00
MT	Miguel Tejada	5.00
FT	Frank Thomas	8.00
JT	Jim Thome	8.00
BW	Bernie Williams	8.00
CY	Carl Yastrzemski	20.00

2003 Topps Gallery HOF Edition

		NM/M
Complete Set (74):		35.00
Common Player:		.40
SP Variations:		2-4X
Inserted 1:1		
Pack (5):		4.00
Box (20):		70.00
1	Willie Mays	2.00
2	Al Kaline	1.50
3	Hank Aaron	2.00
4	Carl Yastrzemski	1.00
5	Luis Aparicio	.40
6	Sam Crawford	.40
7	Tom Lasorda	.40
8	John McGraw	.40
9	Edd Roush	.40
10	Reggie Jackson	1.00
11	Jim "Catfish" Hunter	.40
12	Roberto Clemente	2.00
13	Ralph Kiner	.40
14	Frankie Frisch	.40
15	Nolan Ryan	4.00
16	Brooks Robinson	1.00
17	Phil Niekro	.40
18	Joe Cronin	.40
19	Joe Tinker	.40
20	Johnny Bench	1.50
21	Harry Heilmann	.40
22	Ernie Harwell	.40
23	Warren Spahn	1.00
24	George Kelly	.40
25	Phil Rizzuto	1.00
26	Robin Roberts	.40
27	Ozzie Smith	1.00
28	Jim Palmer	.40
29	Duke Snider	1.00
30	Bob Feller	.40
31	Buck Leonard	.40
32	Kirby Puckett	1.00
33	Monte Irvin	.40
34	Chuck Klein	.40
35	Willie Stargell	.75
36	Juan Marichal	.40
37	Lou Brock	.40
38	Bucky Harris	.40
39	Bobby Doerr	.40
40	Lee MacPhail	.40
41	Heinie Manush	.40
42	George Brett	1.50
43	Harmon Killebrew	1.50
44	Whitey Ford	1.00
45	Eddie Mathews	1.50
46	Gaylord Perry	.40
47	Red Schoendienst	.40
48	Earl Weaver	.40
49	Joe Morgan	.40
50	Mike Schmidt	2.00
51	Willie McCovey	.40
52	Stan Musial	2.00
53	Don Sutton	.40
54	Hank Greenberg	.40
55	Robin Yount	1.00
56	Tom Seaver	1.00
57	Tony Perez	.40
58	George Sisler	.40
59	Jim Bottomley	.40
60	Yogi Berra	1.50
61	Fred Lindstrom	.40
62	Napoleon Lajoie	.40
63	Frank Robinson	1.00
64	Carlton Fisk	.40
65	Orlando Cepeda	.40
66	Fergie Jenkins	.40
67	Ernie Banks	1.50
68	Bill Mazeroski	.40
69	Jim Bunning	.40
70	Rollie Fingers	.40
71	Jimmie Foxx	1.50
72	Rod Carew	.40
73	Sparky Anderson	.40
74	George Kell	.40

Refractors

	NM/M
Cards (1-74):	2-4X
Inserted 1:1	
SP Refractors:	4-8X
Inserted 1:Box	

Accent Mark Autograph

		NM/M
Common Player:		
Refractors:		1-2X
Production 25 Sets		
YB	Yogi Berra	65.00
BD	Bobby Doerr	40.00
LM	Lee MacPhail	40.00
RR	Robin Roberts	40.00
RS	Red Schoendienst	30.00
WS	Warren Spahn	30.00

ARTifact Relics

		NM/M
Common Player:		6.00
Refractors:		1.5-3X
Production 25 Sets		
HA	Hank Aaron/Bat	25.00
SA	Sparky Anderson/Jsy	8.00
LA	Luis Aparicio/Bat	15.00
EB	Ernie Banks/Jsy	30.00
JBE	Johnny Bench/Bat	12.00
JB	Jim Bottomley/Bat	15.00
GB	George Brett/Jsy	25.00
RCA	Rod Carew/Jsy	10.00
OC	Orlando Cepeda/Bat	8.00
TC	Ty Cobb/Bat	80.00
EC	Eddie Collins/Bat	12.00
SC	Sam Crawford/Bat	20.00
BD	Bobby Doerr/Jsy	15.00
CF	Carlton Fisk/Bat	8.00
FF	Frankie Frisch/Bat	15.00
LG	Lou Gehrig/Bat	125.00
HG	Hank Greenberg/Bat	25.00
BH	Bucky Harris/Bat	12.00
HH	Harry Heilmann/Bat	20.00
RJ	Reggie Jackson/Bat	10.00
AK	Al Kaline/Bat	15.00
GK	George Kelly/Bat	20.00
HK	Harmon Killebrew/ Jsy	25.00
CK	Chuck Klein/Bat	15.00
TLA	Tom Lasorda/Jsy	15.00
HM	Heinie Manush/Bat	15.00
EM	Eddie Mathews/Jsy	30.00
WM	Willie Mays/Jsy	45.00
WMC	Willie McCovey/Bat	8.00
JM	Joe Morgan/Bat	8.00
SM	Stan Musial/Bat	20.00
PN	Phil Niekro/Jsy	6.00
JP	Jim Palmer/Bat	20.00
TP	Tony Perez/Bat	8.00
GP	Gaylord Perry/Jsy	8.00
KP	Kirby Puckett/Bat	12.00
BRO	Brooks Robinson/ Bat	20.00
FR	Frank Robinson/Bat	10.00
JR	Jackie Robinson/Bat	35.00
ER	Edd Roush/Bat	20.00
BR	Babe Ruth/Bat	140.00
NR	Nolan Ryan/Bat	40.00
MS	Mike Schmidt/Jsy	25.00
TS	Tom Seaver/Bat	25.00
GS	George Sisler/Bat	12.00
OS	Ozzie Smith/Bat	15.00
DS	Duke Snider/Bat	12.00
WS	Willie Stargell/Jsy	10.00
DSU	Don Sutton/Bat	8.00
JT	Joe Tinker/Bat	20.00
HW	Honus Wagner/Bat	140.00
PW	Paul Waner/Bat	25.00
HWI	Hoyt Wilhelm/Jsy	8.00
CY	Carl Yastrzemski/Bat	20.00
RY	Robin Yount/Bat	10.00

ARTifact Autograph Relics

		NM/M
Common Player:		30.00
Refractors:		1-1.5X
Production 25 Sets		
OC	Orlando Cepeda	30.00
BD	Bobby Doerr	45.00
AK	Al Kaline	75.00
HK	Harmon Killebrew	75.00
JM	Joe Morgan	40.00
JP	Jim Palmer	50.00
BRO	Brooks Robinson	60.00
MS	Mike Schmidt	225.00
RS	Red Schoendienst	30.00
DS	Duke Snider	50.00
RY	Robin Yount	125.00

Currency Connection

		NM/M
Common Player:		12.00
1:Box		
EB	Ernie Banks	20.00
OC	Orlando Cepeda	15.00
TC	Ty Cobb	40.00
BF	Bob Feller	25.00
LG	Lou Gehrig	35.00
HG	Hank Greenberg	20.00
WM	Willie Mays	20.00
WMA	Willie Mays	20.00
WMC	Willie McCovey	12.00
SM	Stan Musial	30.00
JR	Jackie Robinson	25.00
BR	Babe Ruth	60.00

Patch Relics

		NM/M
Common Player:		40.00
Production 25 Sets		
GB	George Brett	125.00
CH	Jim "Catfish" Hunter	40.00
FJ	Fergie Jenkins	40.00
HK	Harmon Killebrew	80.00
TL	Tom Lasorda	40.00
EM	Eddie Matthews	80.00
WM	Willie McCovey	40.00
JP	Jim Palmer	40.00
NR	Nolan Ryan	125.00
MS	Mike Schmidt	125.00
OS	Ozzie Smith	75.00
CY	Carl Yastrzemski	80.00
RY	Robin Yount	85.00

Team Topps Legends Autographs

	NM/M
Common Player:	
Vern Law	20.00
Johnny Sain	30.00

2003 Topps Heritage

		NM/M
Complete Set (430):		350.00
Common Player:		.40
Common High # SP (364-430):		4.00
Pack (8):		5.00
Box (24):		100.00
1	Alex Rodriguez	3.00

Base Set

#	Player	Price
1	Alex Rodriguez/Black/SP	10.00
2	Jose Cruz Jr.	.40
3	Ichiro Suzuki/SP	10.00
4	Rich Aurilia	.40
5	Trevor Hoffman	.40
6	Brian Giles	.75
6	Brian Giles/Old Logo/SP	5.00
7	Albert Pujols	2.00
7	Albert Pujols/Black/SP	10.00
8	Vicente Padilla	.40
9	Bobby Crosby	.40
10	Derek Jeter	4.00
10	Derek Jeter/Old Logo/SP	15.00
11	Pat Burrell	.50
11	Pat Burrell/Old Logo/SP	5.00
12	Armando Benitez	.40
13	Javier Vazquez	.40
14	Justin Morneau	.75
15	Doug Mientkiewicz	.40
16	Kevin Brown	.40
17	Alexis Gomez	.40
18	Lance Berkman	.75
18	Lance Berkman/Black/SP	5.00
19	Adrian Gonzalez	.50
20	Todd Helton	.75
20	Todd Helton/Black/SP	6.00
21	Carlos Pena	.40
22	Matt Lawton	.40
23	Elmer Dessens	.40
24	Hee Seop Choi	.40
25	Chris Duncan/SP RC	12.00
26	Ugueth Urbina	.40
27	Rodrigo Lopez	.40
27	Rodrigo Lopez/Old Logo/SP	4.00
28	Damian Moss	.40
29	Steve Finley	.40
30	Sammy Sosa	1.50
30	Sammy Sosa/Old Logo/SP	6.00
31	Kevin Cash	.40
32	Kenny Rogers	.40
33	Ben Grieve	.40
34	Jason Simontacchi	.40
35	Shin-Soo Choo	.40
36	Freddy Garcia	.40
37	Jesse Foppert	.40
38	Tony LaRussa	.40
39	Mark Kotsay	.40
40	Barry Zito	.75
41	Josh Fogg	.40
42	Marlon Byrd	.40
43	Marcus Thames	.40
44	Al Leiter	.50
45	Michael Barrett	.40
46	Jake Peavy	.75
47	Dustan Mohr	.40
48	Alex Sanchez	.40
49	Chin-Feng Chen	.40
50	Kazuhisa Ishii	.40
50	Kazuhisa Ishii/Black/SP	5.00
51	Carlos Beltran	.75
52	Franklin Gutierrez RC	1.50
53	Miguel Cabrera	1.00
54	Roger Clemens	2.50
55	Juan Cruz	.40
56	Jason Young	.40
57	Alex Herrera	.40
58	Aaron Boone	.40
59	Mark Buehrle	.50
60	Larry Walker	.75
61	Morgan Ensberg	.40
62	Barry Larkin	.75
63	Joe Borchard	.40
64	Jason Dubois	.40
65	Juan Acevedo	.40
66	Jay Gibbons	.40
67	Vinny Castilla	.40
68	Jeff Mathis	.40
69	Curt Schilling	1.00
70	Garret Anderson	.50
71	Josh Phelps	.40
72	Chan Ho Park	.40
73	Edgar Renteria	.50
74	Kazuhiro Sasaki	.40
75	Lloyd McClendon	.40
76	Jon Lieber	.40
77	Rolando Viera	.40
78	Jeff Conine	.40
79	Kevin Millwood	.40
80	Randy Johnson	1.50
80	Randy Johnson/Black/SP	8.00
81	Troy Percival	.40
82	Cliff Floyd	.40
83	Tony Graffanino	.40
84	Austin Kearns	.50
85	Manuel Ramirez/SP RC	5.00
86	Jim Tracy	.40
87	Rondell White	.40
88	Trot Nixon	.40
89	Carlos Lee	.50
90	Mike Lowell	.50
91	Raul Ibanez	.40
92	Ricardo Rodriguez	.40
93	Ben Sheets	.40
94	Jason Perry/SP RC	4.00
95	Mark Teixeira	.75
96	Brad Fullmer	.40
97	Casey Kotchman	.40
98	Craig Counsell	.40
99	Jason Marquis	.40
100	Nomar Garciaparra	2.00
100	Nomar Garciaparra/Old Logo/SP	10.00
101	Ed Rogers	.40
102	Wilson Betemit	.40
103	Wayne Lydon RC	1.00
104	Jack Cust	.40
105	Derrek Lee	.75
106	Jim Kavourias	.40
107	Joe Randa	.40
108	Taylor Buchholz	.40
109	Gabe Kapler	.40
110	Preston Wilson	.40
111	Craig Biggio	.50
112	Paul LoDuca	.40
113	Eddie Guardado	.40
114	Andres Galarraga	.40
115	Edgardo Alfonzo	.40
116	Robin Ventura	.40
117	Jeremy Giambi	.40
118	Ray Durham	.40
119	Mariano Rivera	.50
120	Jimmy Rollins	.50
121	Dennis Tankersley	.40
122	Jason Schmidt	.50
123	Bret Boone	.50
124	Josh Hamilton	.50
125	Scott Rolen	.75
126	Steve Cox	.40
127	Larry Bowa	.40
128	Adam LaRoche/SP	5.00
129	Ryan Klesko	.40
130	Tim Hudson	.40
131	Brandon Claussen	.40
132	Craig Brazell/SP RC	4.00
133	Grady Little	.40
134	Jarrod Washburn	.40
135	Lyle Overbay	.40
136	John Burkett	.40
137	Daryl Clark RC	.40
138	Kirk Rueter	.40
139	Joe Mauer,	2.00
139	Joe Mauer,/Jake Mauer	1.00
139	Joe Mauer,/Jake Mauer/Black/SP	8.00
140	Troy Glaus	.75
141	Trey Hodges/SP	4.00
142	Dallas McPherson	.40
143	Art Howe	.40
144	Jesus Cota	.40
145	J.R. House	.40
146	Reggie Sanders	.40
147	Clint Nageotte	.40
148	Jim Edmonds	.50
149	Carl Crawford	.50
150	Mike Piazza	2.00
150	Mike Piazza/Black/SP	10.00
151	Seung Jun Song	.40
152	Roberto Hernandez	.40
153	Marquis Grissom	.40
154	Billy Wagner	.40
155	Josh Beckett	.50
156	Randall Simon	.40
156	Randall Simon/Old Logo/SP	4.00
157	Ben Broussard	.40
158	Russell Branyan	.40
159	Frank Thomas	1.00
160	Alex Escobar	.40
161	Mark Bellhorn	.40
162	Melvin Mora	.40
163	Andruw Jones	.75
164	Danny Bautista	.40
165	Ramon Ortiz	.40
166	Wily Mo Pena	.40
167	Jose Jimenez	.40
168	Mark Redman	.40
169	Angel Berroa	.40
170	Andy Marte/SP RC	15.00
171	Juan Gonzalez	.75
172	Fernando Vina	.40
173	Joel Pineiro	.40
174	Boof Bonser	.40
175	Bernie Castro/SP RC	4.00
176	Bobby Cox	.40
177	Jeff Kent	.50
178	Oliver Perez	.40
179	Chase Utley	1.00
180	Mark Mulder	.40
181	Bobby Abreu	.50
182	Ramiro Mendoza	.40
183	Aaron Heilman	.40
184	A.J. Pierzynski	.40
185	Eric Gagne	.75
186	Kirk Saarloos	.40
187	Ron Gardenhire	.40
188	Dmitri Young	.40
189	Todd Zeile	.40
190	Jim Thome	1.00
190	Jim Thome/Old Logo/SP	8.00
191	Cliff Lee	.40
192	Matt Morris	.40
193	Robert Fick	.40
194	C.C. Sabathia	.40
195	Alexis Rios	.40
196	D'Angelo Jimenez	.40
197	Edgar Martinez	.40
198	Robb Nen	.40
199	Taggert Bozied	.40
200	Vladimir Guerrero/SP	8.00
201	Mark Loretta	.40
202	Brendan Harris RC	.75
203	Mike Hargrove	.40
204	Vernon Wells	.40
205	Hank Blalock	.75
206	Mike Cameron	.40
207	Tony Batista	.40
208	Matt Williams	.40
209	Tony Womack	.40
210	Ramon A. Martinez RC	.40
211	Aaron Sele	.40
212	Mark Grace	.75
213	Joe Crede	.40
214	Ryan Dempster	.40
215	Omar Vizquel	.40
216	Juan Pierre	.40
217	Denny Bautista	.40
218	Chuck Knoblauch	.40
219	Eric Karros	.40
220	Victor Diaz	.40
221	Jacque Jones	.40
222	Jose Vidro	.40
223	Joe McEwing	.40
224	Nick Johnson	.40
225	Eric Chavez	.50
226	Jose Mesa	.40
227	Aramis Ramirez	.75
228	John Lackey	.40
229	David Bell	.40
230	John Olerud	.50
231	Tino Martinez	.40
232	Randy Winn	.40
233	Todd Hollandsworth	.40
234	Ruddy Lugo RC	.75
235	Carlos Delgado	.75
236	Chris Narveson	.40
237	Tim Salmon	.75
238	Orlando Palmeiro	.40
239	Jeff Clark/SP RC	4.00
240	Byung-Hyun Kim	.40
241	Mike Remlinger	.40
242	Johnny Damon	1.00
243	Corey Patterson	.40
244	Paul Konerko	.75
245	Danny Graves	.40
246	Ellis Burks	.40
247	Gavin Floyd	.40
248	Jaime Bubela RC	.75
249	Sean Burroughs	.40
250	Alex Rodriguez/SP	10.00
251	Gabe Gross	.40
252	Rafael Palmeiro	.75
253	Dewon Brazelton	.40
254	Jimmy Journell	.40
255	Rafael Soriano	.40
256	Jerome Williams	.40
257	Xavier Nady	.40
258	Mike Williams	.40
259	Randy Wolf	.40
260	Miguel Tejada	.75
260	Miguel Tejada/Black/SP	5.00
261	Juan Rivera	.40
262	Rey Ordonez	.40
263	Bartolo Colon	.40
264	Eric Milton	.40
265	Jeffrey Hammonds	.40
266	Odalis Perez	.40
267	Mike Sweeney	.40
268	Richard Hidalgo	.40
269	Alex Gonzalez	.40
270	Aaron Cook	.40
271	Earl Snyder	.40
272	Todd Walker	.40
273	Aaron Rowand	.40
274	Matt Clement	.40
275	Anastacio Martinez	.40
276	Mike Bordick	.40
277	John Smoltz	.50
278	Scott Hairston	.40
279	David Eckstein	.40
280	Shannon Stewart	.40
281	Carl Everett	.40
282	Aubrey Huff	.40
283	Mike Mussina	.75
284	Ruben Sierra	.40
285	Russ Ortiz	.40
286	Brian Lawrence	.40
287	Kip Wells	.40
288	Placido Polanco	.40
289	Ted Lilly	.40
290	Andy Pettitte	.50
291	John Buck	.40
292	Orlando Cabrera	.40
293	Cristian Guzman	.40
294	Ruben Quevedo	.40
295	Cesar Izturis	.40
296	Ryan Ludwick	.40
297	Roy Oswalt	.75
298	Jason Stokes	.40
299	Mike Hampton	.40
300	Pedro Martinez	1.50
301	Nic Jackson	.40
302	Magglio Ordonez	.50
302	Magglio Ordonez/Old Logo/SP	5.00
303	Manny Ramirez	1.00
304	Jorge Julio	.40
305	Javy Lopez	.50
306	Roy Halladay	.50
307	Kevin Mench	.40
308	Jason Isringhausen	.40
309	Carlos Guillen	.40
310	Tsuyoshi Shinjo	.40
311	Phil Nevin	.40
312	Pokey Reese	.40
313	Jorge Padilla	.40
314	Jermaine Dye	.40
315	David Wells	.40
316	Mo Vaughn	.40
317	Bernie Williams	.75
318	Michael Restovich	.40
319	Jose Hernandez	.40
320	Richie Sexson	.75
321	Daryle Ward	.40
322	Luis Castillo	.40
323	Rene Reyes	.40
324	Victor Martinez	.40
325	Adam Dunn	.75
325	Adam Dunn/Old Logo/SP	6.00
326	Corwin Malone	.40
327	Kerry Wood	.50
328	Rickey Henderson	.75
329	Marty Cordova	.40
330	Greg Maddux	2.00
331	Miguel Batista	.40
332	Chris Bootcheck	.40
333	Carlos Baerga	.40
334	Antonio Alfonseca	.40
335	Shane Halter	.40
336	Juan Encarnacion	.40
337	Flash Gordon	.40
338	Hideo Nomo	.75
339	Torii Hunter	.75
340	Alfonso Soriano	1.00
340	Alfonso Soriano/Black/SP	6.00
341	Roberto Alomar	.75
342	David Justice	.50
343	Mike Lieberthal	.40
344	Jeff Weaver	.40
345	Timoniel Perez	.40
346	Travis Lee	.40
347	Sean Casey	.40
348	Willie Harris	.40
349	Derek Lowe	.40
350	Tom Glavine	.75
351	Eric Hinske	.40
352	Rocco Baldelli	.40
353	J.D. Drew	.60
354	Jamie Moyer	.40
355	Todd Linden	.40
356	Benito Santiago	.40
357	Brad Baker	.40
358	Alex Gonzalez	.40
359	Brandon Duckworth	.40
360	John Rheinecker	.40
361	Orlando Hernandez	.40
362	Pedro Astacio	.40
363	Brad Wilkerson	.40
364	David Ortiz	8.00
365	Geoff Jenkins	4.00
366	Brian Jordan	4.00
367	Paul Byrd	4.00
368	Jason Lane	4.00
369	Jeff Bagwell	6.00
370	Bobby Higginson	4.00
371	Juan Uribe	4.00
372	Lee Stevens	4.00
373	Jimmy Haynes	4.00
374	Jose Valentin	4.00
375	Ken Griffey Jr.	10.00
376	Shea Hillenbrand	4.00
377	Gary Matthews Jr.	4.00
378	Gary Sheffield	5.00
379	Rick Helling	4.00
380	Junior Spivey	4.00
381	Francisco Rodriguez	4.00
382	Chipper Jones	6.00
383	Orlando Hudson	4.00
384	Ivan Rodriguez	4.00
385	Chris Snelling	4.00
386	Kenny Lofton	4.00
387	Eric Cyr	4.00
388	Jason Kendall	4.00
389	Marlon Anderson	4.00
390	Billy Koch	4.00
391	Shelly Duncan	4.00
392	Jose Reyes	6.00
393	Fernando Tatis	4.00
394	Michael Cuddyer	4.00
395	Mark Prior	6.00
396	Dontrelle Willis	4.00
397	Jay Payton	4.00
398	Brandon Phillips	4.00
399	Dustin Moseley RC	4.00
400	Jason Giambi	5.00
401	John Mabry	4.00
402	Ron Gant	4.00
403	J.T. Snow	4.00
404	Jeff Cirillo	4.00
405	Darin Erstad	4.00
406	Luis Gonzalez	4.00
407	Marcus Giles	4.00
408	Brian Daubach	4.00
409	Moises Alou	4.00
410	Raul Mondesi	4.00
411	Adrian Beltre	4.00
412	A.J. Burnett	4.00
413	Jason Jennings	4.00
414	Edwin Almonte	4.00
415	Fred McGriff	4.00
416	Tim Raines Jr.	4.00
417	Rafael Furcal	4.00
418	Erubiel Durazo	4.00
419	Drew Henson	4.00
420	Kevin Appier	4.00
421	Chad Tracy	4.00
422	Adam Wainwright	4.00
423	Choo Freeman	4.00
424	Sandy Alomar Jr.	4.00
425	Corey Koskie	4.00
426	Jeromy Burnitz	4.00
427	Jorge Posada	4.00
428	Jason Arnold	4.00
429	Brett Myers	4.00
430	Shawn Green	4.00

Pirates — RANDALL SIMON, 1b-of Pittsburgh Pirates

Chrome

	Price
NM/M	
Common Player:	1.00

Production 1,954 Sets
Refractors: 1.5-2X
Production 554 Sets

#	Player	Price
THC1	Alex Rodriguez	8.00
THC2	Ichiro Suzuki	8.00
THC3	Brian Giles	4.00
THC4	Albert Pujols	4.00
THC5	Derek Jeter	10.00
THC6	Pat Burrell	3.00
THC7	Lance Berkman	2.00
THC8	Todd Helton	2.00
THC9	Chris Duncan	20.00
THC10	Rodrigo Lopez	1.00
THC11	Sammy Sosa	5.00
THC12	Barry Zito	2.00
THC13	Marlon Byrd	1.00
THC14	Al Leiter	1.00
THC15	Kazuhisa Ishii	1.50
THC16	Franklin Gutierrez	1.00
THC17	Roger Clemens	5.00
THC18	Mark Buehrle	1.00
THC19	Larry Walker	1.00
THC20	Curt Schilling	2.50
THC21	Garret Anderson	1.50
THC22	Randy Johnson	1.00
THC23	Cliff Floyd	1.00
THC24	Austin Kearns	2.00
THC25	Manuel Ramirez	2.00
THC26	Raul Ibanez	1.00
THC27	Jason Perry	1.00
THC28	Mark Teixeira	2.00
THC29	Nomar Garciaparra	6.00
THC30	Wayne Lydon	1.00
THC31	Preston Wilson	1.00
THC32	Paul LoDuca	1.00
THC33	Edgardo Alfonzo	1.00
THC34	Jeremy Giambi	1.00
THC35	Mariano Rivera	1.50
THC36	Jimmy Rollins	1.00
THC37	Bret Boone	1.00
THC38	Scott Rolen	2.00
THC39	Adam LaRoche	1.50
THC40	Tim Hudson	1.50
THC41	Craig Brazell	1.00
THC42	Daryl Clark	1.00
THC43	Joe Mauer,/Jake Mauer	3.00
THC44	Troy Glaus	2.50
THC45	Sean Pierce	1.00
THC46	Carl Crawford	2.00
THC47	Mike Piazza	6.00
THC48	Josh Beckett	1.00
THC49	Randall Simon	1.00
THC50	Frank Thomas	2.50
THC51	Andruw Jones	2.00
THC52	Andy Marte	4.00
THC53	Bernie Castro	1.00
THC54	Jim Thome	3.00
THC55	Alexis Rios	1.00
THC56	Vladimir Guerrero	4.00
THC57	Walter Young	1.00
THC58	Hank Blalock	1.50
THC59	Ramon A. Martinez	1.00
THC60	Jacque Jones	1.00
THC61	Nick Johnson	1.00
THC62	Ruddy Lugo	1.00
THC63	Carlos Delgado	1.00
THC64	Jeff Clark	1.00
THC65	Johnny Damon	1.00
THC66	Jaime Bubela	1.00
THC67	Alex Rodriguez	8.00
THC68	Rafael Palmeiro	2.00
THC69	Miguel Tejada	2.00
THC70	Bartolo Colon	1.00
THC71	Mike Sweeney	1.00
THC72	John Smoltz	1.50
THC73	Shannon Stewart	1.00
THC74	Mike Mussina	2.00
THC75	Roy Oswalt	1.50
THC76	Pedro Martinez	4.00
THC77	Magglio Ordonez	3.00
THC78	Manny Ramirez	3.00
THC79	David Wells	1.50
THC80	Richie Sexson	1.50
THC81	Adam Dunn	2.50
THC82	Greg Maddux	5.00
THC83	Alfonso Soriano	5.00
THC84	Roberto Alomar	2.00
THC85	Derek Lowe	1.00
THC86	Tom Glavine	2.00
THC87	Jeff Bagwell	2.50
THC88	Ken Griffey Jr.	6.00
THC89	Shea Hillenbrand	1.00
THC90	Gary Sheffield	1.50
THC91	Chipper Jones	4.00
THC92	Orlando Hudson	1.00
THC93	Jose Cruz Jr.	1.00
THC94	Mark Prior	2.50
THC95	Jason Giambi	5.00
THC96	Luis Gonzalez	1.50
THC97	Drew Henson	1.50
THC98	Cristian Guzman	1.00
THC99	Shawn Green	1.50
THC100	Jose Vidro	1.00

Clubhouse Collection Autographed

No Pricing
Production 25 Sets

Clubhouse Collection Relics

	Player	NM/M
	Common Player:	10.00
EB	Ernie Banks	25.00
AD	Adam Dunn	15.00
JG	Jim Gilliam	12.00
SG	Shawn Green	10.00
CJ	Chipper Jones	15.00
AK	Al Kaline	25.00
EM	Eddie Mathews	20.00
WM	Willie Mays	40.00
AP	Albert Pujols	15.00
AR	Alex Rodriguez	15.00
DS	Duke Snider	25.00
KW	Kerry Wood	10.00

Clubhouse Collection Dual Relics

NM/M
Production 54 Sets

		NM/M
SG	Duke Snider, Shawn Green	80.00
BW	Ernie Banks, Kerry Wood	80.00
MJ	Eddie Mathews, Chipper Jones	100.00

Flashbacks

		NM/M
	Complete Set (10):	12.00
	Common Player:	.75
	Inserted 1:12	
F1	Willie Mays	3.00
F2	Yogi Berra	2.00
F3	Ted Kluszewski	.75
F4	Stan Musial	3.00
F5	Hank Aaron	3.00
F6	Duke Snider	1.50
F7	Richie Ashburn	.75
F8	Robin Roberts	.75
F9	Mickey Vernon	.75
F10	Don Larsen	.75

Flashbacks Autographs

Production 25:

Grandstand Glory

		NM/M
	Common Player:	10.00
RA	Richie Ashburn	15.00
EB	Ernie Banks	20.00
YB	Yogi Berra	20.00
DG	Dick Groat	12.00
AK	Al Kaline	15.00
TK	Ted Kluszewski	12.00
EM	Eddie Mathews	12.00

		NM/M
WM	Willie Mays	35.00
AP	Andy Pafko	10.00
PR	Phil Rizzuto	15.00
HS	Hank Sauer	10.00
DS	Duke Snider	15.00
WS	Warren Spahn	15.00

New Age Performers

Complete Set (15): 20.00
Common Player: .75
Inserted 1:15

NA1	Mike Piazza	3.00
NA2	Ichiro Suzuki	3.00
NA3	Derek Jeter	4.00
NA4	Alex Rodriguez	3.00
NA5	Sammy Sosa	2.00
NA6	Jason Giambi	1.00
NA7	Vladimir Guerrero	1.50
NA8	Albert Pujols	1.50
NA9	Todd Helton	.75
NA10	Nomar Garciaparra	2.50
NA11	Randy Johnson	1.50
NA12	Jim Thome	1.00
NA13	Andruw Jones	.75
NA14	Miguel Tejada	.75
NA15	Alfonso Soriano	1.50

Real One Autographs

Common Autograph: 15.00
Inserted 1:188
Special Editions (Red Ink): 1.5-2X
Production 54

HA	Hank Aaron	250.00
EB	Ernie Banks	150.00
MB	Matt Batts	25.00
HB	Hank Bauer	40.00
LB	Lance Berkman	50.00
YB	Yogi Berra	80.00
MBL	Mike Blyzka	25.00
JC	Jose Cruz Jr.	15.00
RF	Roy Face	40.00
WF	Whitey Ford	60.00
DG	Dick Groat	40.00
GH	Gene Hermanski	25.00
CH	Cal Hogue	25.00
MI	Monte Irvin	50.00
LJ	Larry Jansen	30.00
AK	Al Kaline	80.00
CK	Charlie Kress	25.00
DK	Dick Kryhoski	25.00
TL	Tom Lasorda	70.00
VL	Vern Law	30.00
DL	Don Lenhardt	25.00
DLU	Don Lund	25.00
EM	Eddie Mayo	25.00
WM	Willie Mays	200.00
MM	Mickey Micelotta	25.00
RM	Ray Murray	25.00
AP	Andy Pafko	60.00
PP	Paul Penson	30.00
JPO	Johnny Podres	40.00
JP	Joe Presko	25.00
PR	Phil Rizzuto	50.00
PRO	Preacher Roe	50.00
JR	Jimmy Rollins	25.00
BR	Bob Ross	25.00
JS	Johnny Sain	40.00
MS	Mike Sandlock	25.00
CS	Carl Scheib	25.00
BSH	Bobby Shantz	40.00
BS	Bill "Moose" Skowron	40.00
DS	Duke Snider	80.00
BT	Bob Talbot	25.00
JV	Jose Vidro	15.00
BWE	Bill Werle	25.00
LW	Leroy Wheat	25.00
JW	Jim Willis	25.00

Real One Special Edition Autographs

Production 54 Sets

RO-MB	Matt Batts	50.00
RO-HB	Hank Bauer	75.00
RO-MBL	Mike Blyzka	40.00
RO-RF	Roy Face	60.00
RO-WF	Whitey Ford	120.00
RO-DG	Dick Groat	60.00
RO-MI	Monte Irvin	80.00
RO-LJ	Larry Jansen	35.00
RO-CK	Charlie Kress	60.00
RO-TL	Tom Lasorda	65.00
RO-VL	Vern Law	40.00
RO-DL	Don Lenhardt	75.00
RO-EM	Eddie Mayo	45.00
RO-MM	Mickey Micelotta	45.00
RO-RM	Ray Murray	45.00
RO-PP	Paul Penson	40.00
RO-JPO	Johnny Podres	70.00
RO-JP	Joe Presko	50.00
RO-PR	Phil Rizzuto	75.00
RO-PRO	Preacher Roe	80.00
RO-BR	Bob Ross	40.00
RO-JS	Johnny Sain	65.00
RO-MS	Mike Sandlock	35.00
RO-CS	Carl Scheib	35.00
RO-BSH	Bobby Shantz	60.00
RO-BS	Bill "Moose" Skowron	80.00
RO-BT	Bob Talbot	50.00
RO-BWE	Bill Werle	60.00
RO-LW	Leroy Wheat	50.00
RO-JW	Jim Willis	60.00

Team Legends Autographs

Common Autograph: 35.00

	Luis Aparicio	35.00
	Jim Bunning	35.00
	Al Kaline	70.00
	Don Larsen	40.00
	Duke Snider	70.00

Then and Now

Complete Set (10): 12.00
Common Card: .75
Inserted 1:15

TN1	Ted Kluszewski, Alex Rodriguez	3.00
TN2	Ted Kluszewski, Alex Rodriguez	3.00
TN3	Robin Roberts, Randy Johnson	1.00
TN4	Don Mueller, Alfonso Soriano	1.50
TN5	Stan Musial, Garret Anderson	2.00
TN6	Minnie Minoso, Johnny Damon	.75
TN7	Robin Roberts, Randy Johnson	1.00
TN8	Duke Snider, Alex Rodriguez	3.00
TN9	Robin Roberts, Randy Johnson	1.00
TN10	Johnny Antonelli, Pedro Martinez	1.00

2003 Topps Opening Day

Complete Set (165): 30.00
Common Player: .10
Pack (6): 1.00
Box (36): 30.00

1	Alex Rodriguez	1.00
2	Jarrod Washburn	.10
3	Kevin Brown	.10
4	Chipper Jones	.75
5	Ken Griffey Jr.	.75
6	Shea Hillenbrand	.10
7	Moises Alou	.20
8	Carlos Lee	.10
9	Marty Cordova	.10
10	Derek Jeter	1.50
11	Dmitri Young	.10
12	Barry Bonds	1.50
13	Jeff Bagwell	.40
14	Paul Byrd	.10
15	Carlos Delgado	.20
16	Richie Sexson	.10
17	Torii Hunter	.20
18	Bartolo Colon	.10
19	Robin Ventura	.10
20	Mike Piazza	1.00
21	Tim Hudson	.20
22	Brett Myers	.10
23	Ryan Klesko	.20
24	Tsuyoshi Shinjo	.10
25	Cliff Floyd	.10
26	Scott Rolen	.50
27	Randy Winn	.10
28	Rafael Palmeiro	.25
29	Carlos Pena	.10
30	Randy Johnson	.50
31	Jimmy Rollins	.10
32	Jermaine Dye	.10
33	Jose Vidro	.10
34	Jorge Julio	.10
35	Mark Prior	.50
36	Curt Schilling	.40
37	A.J. Pierzynski	.10
38	Andruw Jones	.50
39	Kerry Wood	.50
40	Todd Helton	.40
41	Magglio Ordonez	.20
42	Darin Erstad	.20
43	Barry Larkin	.20
44	Edgardo Alfonzo	.10
45	Jason Giambi	.25
46	Eric Chavez	.20
47	Brian Giles	.20
48	Raul Ibanez	.10
49	Edgar Renteria	.20
50	Sammy Sosa	.75
51	Bobby Hill	.10
52	A.J. Burnett	.10
53	Juan Gonzalez	.25
54	Eric Hinske	.10
55	Roberto Alomar	.25
56	Javier Lopez	.10
57	Mark Buehrle	.10
58	Garret Anderson	.10
59	Mike Hampton	.10
60	Rich Aurilia	.10
61	Brian Jordan	.10
62	Brad Wilkerson	.10
63	Geoff Jenkins	.10
64	Brad Radke	.10
65	Roger Clemens	1.00
66	Scott Hatteberg	.10
67	Mike Williams	.10
68	Steve Finley	.10
69	Benito Santiago	.20
70	John Smoltz	.20
71	Bret Boone	.10
72	Matt Morris	.10
73	Manny Ramirez	.50
74	Troy Glaus	.25
75	Austin Kearns	.25
76	Jim Thome	.50
77	Luis Gonzalez	.20
78	Freddy Garcia	.10
79	Randy Wolf	.10
80	Miguel Tejada	.25
81	Paul Konerko	.25
82	Ivan Rodriguez	.25
83	Shannon Stewart	.10
84	Rafael Furcal	.10
85	Cristian Guzman	.10
86	Mo Vaughn	.10
87	Jose Cruz Jr.	.10
88	Alfonso Soriano	.50
89	Orlando Cabrera	.10
90	Ichiro Suzuki	1.00
91	Omar Vizquel	.20
92	Hideo Nomo	.25
93	Roy Halladay	.10
94	Mike Sweeney	.10
95	Greg Maddux	.75
96	David Eckstein	.10
97	Jay Gibbons	.10
98	Andy Pettitte	.25
99	Frank Thomas	.40
100	Shawn Green	.25
101	Jacque Jones	.10
102	Pedro J. Martinez	.50
103	Mark Mulder	.20
104	Rodrigo Lopez	.10
105	Bernie Williams	.25
106	Aaron Boone	.10
107	Mike Lieberthal	.10
108	Jim Edmonds	.20
109	Tino Martinez	.20
110	Gary Sheffield	.25
111	Mike Cameron	.10
112	Jason Jennings	.10
113	Larry Walker	.20
114	Corey Koskie	.10
115	Kazuhisa Ishii	.10
116	Jose Hernandez	.10
117	Al Leiter	.10
118	David Justice	.20
119	Jason Kendall	.10
120	Edgar Martinez	.20
121	Pat Burrell	.25
122	Vladimir Guerrero	.40
123	Juan Rivera	.10
124	Byung-Hyun Kim	.10
125	Adam Dunn	.40
126	Tim Salmon	.20
127	Terrence Long	.10
128	Johnny Damon	.25
129	Aramis Ramirez	.10
130	Barry Zito	.20
131	Mike Lowell	.10
132	Adam Kennedy	.10
133	J.D. Drew	.20
134	Tony Batista	.10
135	Albert Pujols	1.50
136	Doug Mientkiewicz	.10
137	Phil Nevin	.10
138	Paul LoDuca	.10
139	Roy Oswalt	.20
140	Jeff Kent	.20
141	Robert Fick	.10
142	Aubrey Huff	.10
143	C.C. Sabathia	.20
144	Tim Wakefield	.10
145	Derek Lowe	.10
146	Kevin Millwood	.10
147	Jorge Posada	.25
148	Fernando Vina	.10
149	Junior Spivey	.10
150	Lance Berkman	.25
151	Eric Gagne	.25
152	Mariano Rivera	.20
153	Alex Sanchez	.10
154	Ellis Burks	.10
155	Josh Beckett	.10
156	Nomar Garciaparra	1.00
157	Craig Biggio	.20
158	Adrian Beltre	.25
159	Vicente Padilla	.10
160	Mike Cameron/HL	.10
161	Shawn Green/HL	.20
162	A's Team Shot/HL	.10
163	Jason Giambi/HL	.20
164	Derek Lowe/HL	.10
165	Checklist	.10

Stickers

Stars: .5-1.5X
Inserted 1:1

2003 Topps Pristine

Complete Set (190):
Common Player: 1.00
Common Rookie: 1.00
Common Uncommon RC: 2.50
Production 1,499
Common Rare RC: 5.00
Production 499
Pack (8): 30.00
Box (5): 140.00

1	Pedro J. Martinez	2.50
2	Derek Jeter	6.00
3	Alex Rodriguez	6.00
4	Miguel Tejada	1.00
5	Nomar Garciaparra	2.50
6	Austin Kearns	1.50
7	Jose Vidro	1.00
8	Bret Boone	1.00
9	Scott Rolen	2.00
10	Mike Sweeney	1.00
11	Jason Schmidt	1.00
12	Alfonso Soriano	2.50
13	Tim Hudson	1.50
14	A.J. Pierzynski	1.00
15	Lance Berkman	2.00
16	Frank Thomas	2.00
17	Gary Sheffield	1.50
18	Jarrod Washburn	1.00
19	Hideo Nomo	1.50
20	Barry Zito	1.50
21	Kevin Millwood	1.50
22	Matt Morris	1.00
23	Carl Crawford	2.00
24	Carlos Delgado	2.00
25	Mike Piazza	3.00
26	Brad Radke	1.00
27	Richie Sexson	1.50
28	Kevin Brown	1.00
29	Carlos Beltran	2.00
30	Curt Schilling	2.00
31	Chipper Jones	3.00
32	Paul Konerko	1.50
33	Larry Walker	1.50
34	Jeff Bagwell	2.00
35	Jason Giambi	1.50
36	Mark Mulder	1.50
37	Vicente Padilla	1.00
38	Kris Benson	1.00
39	Bernie Williams	1.50
40	Jim Thome	2.00
41	Roger Clemens	5.00
42	Roberto Alomar	1.50
43	Torii Hunter	1.50
44	Bobby Abreu	1.50
45	Jeff Kent	1.50
46	Roy Oswalt	1.50
47	Bartolo Colon	1.00
48	Greg Maddux	4.00
49	Tom Glavine	1.50
50	Sammy Sosa	3.00
51	Ichiro Suzuki	4.00
52	Mark Prior	1.50
53	Manny Ramirez	2.00
54	Andruw Jones	1.50
55	Randy Johnson	3.00
56	Garret Anderson	1.50
57	Roy Halladay	1.00
58	Rafael Palmeiro	2.00
59	Rocco Baldelli	1.50
60	Albert Pujols	6.00
61	Edgar Renteria	1.00
62	John Olerud	1.00
63	Rich Aurilia	1.00
64	Ryan Klesko	1.00
65	Brian Giles	1.50
66	Eric Chavez	1.50
67	Jorge Posada	1.50
68	Cliff Floyd	1.00
69	Vladimir Guerrero	2.00
70	Cristian Guzman	1.00
71	Raul Ibanez	1.00
72	Paul LoDuca	1.00
73	A.J. Burnett	1.00
74	Ken Griffey Jr.	4.00
75	Mark Buehrle	1.50
76	Moises Alou	1.50
77	Adam Dunn	2.00
78	Tony Batista	1.00
79	Troy Glaus	1.50
80	Luis Gonzalez	1.50
81	Shea Hillenbrand	1.00
82	Kerry Wood	1.50
83	Magglio Ordonez	1.00
84	Omar Vizquel	1.00
85	Bobby Higginson	1.00
86	Mike Lowell	1.00
87	Runelvys Hernandez	1.00
88	Shawn Green	1.50
89	Erubiel Durazo	1.00
90	Pat Burrell	1.50
91	Todd Helton	2.00
92	Jim Edmonds	1.50
93	Aubrey Huff	1.00
94	Eric Hinske	1.00
95	Barry Bonds	6.00
96	Willie Mays	5.00
97	Bo Jackson	2.00
98	Carl Yastrzemski	2.00
99	Don Mattingly	5.00
100	Gary Carter	1.50
101	Jose Contreras/C RC	1.00
102	Jose Contreras/U RC	4.00
103	Jose Contreras/R RC	8.00
104	Dan Haren/C	
105	Dan Haren/U	4.00
106	Dan Haren/R	8.00
107	Michel Hernandez/C RC	1.00
108	Michel Hernandez/U RC	2.50
109	Michel Hernandez/R RC	5.00
110	Bobby Basham/C RC	1.00
111	Bobby Basham/U RC	2.50
112	Bobby Basham/R RC	5.00
113	Bryan Bullington/C RC	1.50
114	Bryan Bullington/U RC	2.50
115	Bryan Bullington/R RC	5.00
116	Bernie Castro/C RC	1.00
117	Bernie Castro/U RC	2.50
118	Bernie Castro/R RC	5.00
119	Chien-Ming Wang/C RC	25.00
120	Chien-Ming Wang/U RC	30.00
121	Chien-Ming Wang/R RC	40.00
122	Eric Crozier/C RC	1.00
123	Eric Crozier/U RC	2.50
124	Eric Crozier/R RC	5.00
125	Michael Garciaparra/C	1.00
126	Michael Garciaparra/U	2.50
127	Michael Garciaparra/R	5.00
128	Joey Gomes/C	1.00
129	Joey Gomes/U	2.50
130	Joey Gomes/R	5.00
131	Wilfredo Ledezma/C RC	1.00
132	Wilfredo Ledezma/U RC	2.50
133	Wilfredo Ledezma/R RC	5.00
134	Branden Florence/C RC	1.00
135	Branden Florence/U RC	2.50
136	Branden Florence/R RC	5.00
137	Jeremy Bonderman/C	6.00
138	Jeremy Bonderman/U	10.00
139	Jeremy Bonderman/R	15.00
140	Travis Ishikawa/C RC	1.00
141	Travis Ishikawa/U RC	2.50
142	Travis Ishikawa/R RC	5.00
143	Ben Francisco/C RC	1.00
144	Ben Francisco/U RC	2.50
145	Ben Francisco/R RC	5.00
146	Jason Kubel/C RC	4.00
147	Jason Kubel/U RC	6.00
148	Jason Kubel/R RC	10.00
149	Tyler Martin/C RC	1.00
150	Tyler Martin/U RC	2.50
151	Tyler Martin/R RC	5.00
152	Jason Perry/C	1.50
153	Jason Perry/U	2.50
154	Jason Perry/R	5.00
155	Ryan Shealy/C RC	4.00
156	Ryan Shealy/U RC	5.00
157	Ryan Shealy/R RC	10.00
158	Hanley Ramirez/C RC	12.00
159	Hanley Ramirez/U RC	15.00
160	Hanley Ramirez/R RC	25.00
161	Rajai Davis/C RC	
162	Rajai Davis/U RC	2.50
163	Rajai Davis/R RC	5.00
164	Gary Schneidmiller/C RC	1.00
165	Gary Schneidmiller/U RC	2.50
166	Gary Schneidmiller/R RC	5.00
167	Haj Turay/C RC	1.00
168	Haj Turay/U RC	2.50
169	Haj Turay/R RC	5.00
170	Kevin Youkilis/C RC	4.00
171	Kevin Youkilis/U RC	8.00
172	Kevin Youkilis/R RC	15.00
173	Shane Bazzell/C RC	1.00
174	Shane Bazzell/U RC	2.50
175	Shane Bazzell/R RC	5.00
176	Elizardo Ramirez/C RC	1.50
177	Elizardo Ramirez/U RC	3.00
178	Elizardo Ramirez/R RC	5.00
179	Robinson Cano/C RC	25.00
180	Robinson Cano/U RC	30.00
181	Robinson Cano/R RC	35.00
182	Nook Logan/C RC	1.00
183	Nook Logan/U RC	2.50
184	Nook Logan/R RC	5.00
185	Dustin McGowan/C RC	1.00
186	Dustin McGowan/U RC	3.00
187	Dustin McGowan/R RC	5.00
188	Ryan Howard/C	40.00
189	Ryan Howard/U	40.00
190	Ryan Howard/R	65.00

Plates

No pricing due to scarcity.
Four plates per player.

Refractors

Veterans (1-100): 4-6X
Production 99
Common RC's: .75-1.5X
Production 1,599
Uncommon RC's: 1-2X
Production 499
Rare RC's: 1.5-3X
Production 99
Veteran Gold Refrac.(1-100):4-8X
Rookie Golds (101-190): 2-4X
Production 69 Sets

Bomb Squad

Common Player: 4.00
Refractors: No Pricing
Production 25 Sets

MO1	Moises Alou	4.00
MO2	Moises Alou	4.00
GA1	Garret Anderson	5.00
GA2	Garret Anderson	5.00
JRB	Jeff Bagwell	6.00
JB	Johnny Bench	10.00
LB1	Lance Berkman	5.00
LB2	Lance Berkman	5.00
HB	Hank Blalock	5.00
BB	Barry Bonds	15.00
GB1	George Brett	12.00
GB2	George Brett	12.00
GC	Gary Carter	5.00
EC1	Eric Chavez	4.00
EC2	Eric Chavez	4.00
CC	Carl Crawford	4.00
AD	Adam Dunn	6.00
DE1	Darin Erstad	4.00
DE2	Darin Erstad	4.00
CF	Cliff Floyd	4.00
NG1	Nomar Garciaparra	10.00
NG2	Nomar Garciaparra	10.00
JG	Jason Giambi	6.00
TG1	Troy Glaus	5.00
TG2	Troy Glaus	5.00
JAG	Juan Gonzalez	6.00
LG	Luis Gonzalez	4.00
SG	Shawn Green	5.00
VG1	Vladimir Guerrero	8.00
VG2	Vladimir Guerrero	8.00
TH	Todd Helton	6.00
RH	Rickey Henderson	10.00
AJ	Andruw Jones	6.00
CJ	Chipper Jones	8.00

Code	Player	Price
JK	Jeff Kent	4.00
MO	Magglio Ordonez	4.00
RP	Rafael Palmeiro	15.00
MP	Mike Piazza	10.00
AP1	Albert Pujols	15.00
AP2	Albert Pujols	15.00
MR	Manny Ramirez	6.00
AR1	Alex Rodriguez	10.00
AR2	Alex Rodriguez	10.00
TS	Tim Salmon	4.00
MS1	Mike Schmidt	12.00
MS2	Mike Schmidt	12.00
GS	Gary Sheffield	5.00
AS	Alfonso Soriano	8.00
SS1	Sammy Sosa	12.00
SS2	Sammy Sosa	10.00
MT	Miguel Tejada	4.00
FT	Frank Thomas	6.00
JT	Jim Thome	10.00

Borders

NM/M
Common Player: 4.00
Inserted 1:9
Refractors: No Pricing
Production 25 Sets

Code	Player	Price
CC	Chin-Feng Chen	40.00
VG	Vladimir Guerrero	8.00
CG	Cristian Guzman	4.00
KI	Kazuhisa Ishii	4.00
AJ	Andruw Jones	6.00
PM	Pedro J. Martinez	8.00
MO	Magglio Ordonez	4.00
AP	Albert Pujols	15.00
MR	Manny Ramirez	6.00
IR	Ivan Rodriguez	6.00
TS	Tsuyoshi Shinjo	4.00
AS	Alfonso Soriano	8.00
SS	Sammy Sosa	10.00
MT	Miguel Tejada	4.00
BW	Bernie Williams	6.00

Corners

NM/M
Common Duo: 6.00
Inserted 1:12
Refractors: No Pricing
Production 25 Sets

Code	Players	Price
CD	Eric Chavez, Erubiel Durazo	6.00
VG	Robin Ventura, Jason Giambi	10.00
WG	Matt Williams, Mark Grace	8.00
RM	Scott Rolen, Tino Martinez	10.00
BM	Adrian Beltre, Fred McGriff	6.00
GS	Troy Glaus, Scott Spiezio	8.00
KM	Corey Koskie, Doug Mientkiewicz	6.00
BT	David Bell, Jim Thome	10.00
BK	Sean Burroughs, Ryan Klesko	6.00
AS	Edgardo Alfonzo, J.T. Snow	6.00
TP	Mark Teixeira, Rafael Palmeiro	10.00

Factor

NM/M
Common Player: 4.00
Inserted 1:9
Refractors: No Pricing
Production 25 Sets

Code	Player	Price
LB	Lance Berkman	4.00
AD	Adam Dunn	6.00
DE	Darin Erstad	10.00
NG	Nomar Garciaparra	10.00
JG	Jason Giambi	6.00
TG	Troy Glaus	5.00
VG	Vladimir Guerrero	8.00
TH	Todd Helton	6.00
TKH	Torii Hunter	5.00

Code	Player	Price
MO	Magglio Ordonez	4.00
MP	Mike Piazza	10.00
MR	Manny Ramirez	6.00
AR	Alex Rodriguez	10.00
AS	Alfonso Soriano	8.00
SS	Sammy Sosa	10.00

Mini

NM/M
Common Player: 1.00

Code	Player	Price
RB	Rocco Baldelli	1.50
BWB	Bobby Basham	1.00
JB	Jeremy Bonderman	4.00
BB	Barry Bonds	6.00
BPB	Bryan Bullington	3.00
RJC	Robinson Cano	20.00
BC	Bernie Castro	1.00
EC	Eric Chavez	1.00
RC	Roger Clemens	5.00
JC	Jose Contreras	2.00
ELC	Eric Crozier	1.00
RD	Rajai Davis	1.00
NG	Nomar Garciaparra	5.00
JG	Jason Giambi	2.00
BG	Brian Giles	1.50
VG	Vladimir Guerrero	3.00
DH	Dan Haren	2.00
MH	Michel Hernandez	1.00
RH	Ryan Howard	60.00
DJ	Derek Jeter	6.00
AK	Austin Kearns	2.00
JK	Jeff Kent	1.50
JJK	Jason Kubel	4.00
WL	Wilfredo Ledezma	1.00
NL	Nook Logan	1.00
TM	Tyler Martin	1.00
DM	Dustin McGowan	1.00
MO	Magglio Ordonez	1.00
MJP	Mike Piazza	4.00
MP	Mark Prior	6.00
ER	Elizardo Ramirez	1.00
AR	Alex Rodriguez	6.00
RS	Ryan Shealy	3.00
AS	Alfonso Soriano	3.00
SS	Sammy Sosa	4.00
IS	Ichiro Suzuki	3.00
MT	Miguel Tejada	1.50
JT	Jim Thome	2.00
CW	Chien-Ming Wang	40.00
KY	Kevin Youkilis	6.00

Mini Autograph

NM/M
Production 100

Code	Player	Price
RC	Roger Clemens	125.00

Personal Endorsements

NM/M
Common Autograph: 6.00
Golds: No Pricing
Production 25 Sets

Code	Player	Price
AB	Andrew Brown	6.00
RYC	Ryan Church	10.00
DE	David Eckstein	10.00
LF	Lew Ford	10.00
JG	Jay Gibbons	10.00
RJH	Rich Harden	25.00
KH	Ken Harvey	6.00
PK	Paul Konerko	20.00
ML	Mike Lowell	10.00
VM	Victor Martinez	20.00
BM	Brett Myers	10.00
JP	Josh Phelps	8.00
SR	Scott Rolen	25.00
FS	Felix Sanchez	6.00
KS	Kelly Shoppach	15.00
MS	Mike Sweeney	10.00
FV	Fernando Vina	6.00

Primary Elements

NM/M
Many not priced due to scarcity.
Production 50 Sets
Refractors: No Pricing
Production 10

Code	Player	Price
BRB	Bret Boone	15.00
NG	Nomar Garciaparra	35.00
LG	Luis Gonzalez	10.00
SG	Shawn Green	10.00
TH	Todd Helton	20.00
TKH	Torii Hunter	20.00
KI	Kazuhisa Ishii	10.00
AJ	Andruw Jones	15.00
CJ	Chipper Jones	20.00

Code	Player	Price
PM	Pedro J. Martinez	20.00
MO	Magglio Ordonez	10.00
RP	Rafael Palmeiro	15.00
MP	Mike Piazza	25.00
AR	Alex Rodriguez	50.00
MT	Miguel Tejada	15.00
BZ	Barry Zito	15.00

Solo Bonds

NM/M
Common Bonds: 20.00
Refractors: No Pricing
Production 25

Code	Player	Price
GG	Barry Bonds	20.00
HR	Barry Bonds	20.00
BB	Barry Bonds	20.00
MVP	Barry Bonds	20.00

Double Bonds

NM/M
Common Duo: 25.00
Refractors: No Pricing
Production 25

Code	Players	Price
BJ	Barry Bonds, Randy Johnson	50.00
BT	Miguel Tejada, Barry Bonds	25.00
BM	Willie Mays, Barry Bonds	75.00
BR	Alex Rodriguez, Barry Bonds	35.00

2003 Topps Retired Signature Edition

NM/M
Complete Set (110): 100.00
Common Player: .50
Pack (5): 30.00
Box (5): 120.00

#	Player	Price
1	Willie Mays	4.00
2	Tony Perez	1.00
3	Tom Seaver	2.00
4	Johnny Bench	4.00
5	Rod Carew	1.50
6	Red Schoendienst	.50
7	Phil Rizzuto	1.00
8	Ozzie Smith	2.50
9	Maury Wills	.50
10	Hank Aaron	4.00
11	Jim Palmer	1.00
12	Jose Cruz	.50
13	Dave Parker	.50
14	Don Sutton	.75
15	Brooks Robinson	2.00
16	Bo Jackson	.75
17	Andre Dawson	.75
18	Fergie Jenkins	.75
19	George Foster	.50
20	George Brett	5.00
21	Jerry Koosman	.50
22	John Kruk	.50
23	Kent Tekulve	.50
24	Lee Smith	.50
25	Nolan Ryan	6.00
26	Paul O'Neill	.50
27	Rich "Goose" Gossage	.50
28	Ron Santo	.50
29	Tom Lasorda	.75
30	Tony Gwynn	2.00
31	Vida Blue	.50
32	Whitey Herzog	.50
33	Willie McGee	.50
34	Bill Mazeroski	.50
35	Al Kaline	3.00
36	Bobby Richardson	.50
37	Carlton Fisk	1.00
38	Darrell Evans	.50
39	Dave Concepcion	.50
40	Cal Ripken Jr.	5.00
41	Dwight Evans	.50
42	Earl Weaver	.50
43	Fred Lynn	.50
44	Greg Luzinski	.50
45	Duke Snider	1.50
46	Hank Bauer	.50
47	Jim Rice	.50
48	Johnny Sain	.50
49	Lenny Dykstra	.50
50	Mike Schmidt	4.00
51	Orlando Cepeda	.50
52	Ralph Kiner	.75
53	Robin Roberts	.50
54	Ron Guidry	.50
55	Steve Garvey	.50
56	Tony Oliva	.75
57	Whitey Ford	1.00
58	Willie McCovey	1.00
59	Phil Niekro	.50
60	Stan Musial	3.00
61	Rollie Fingers	1.00
62	Robin Yount	2.00
63	Alan Trammell	1.00
64	Bill Buckner	.50
65	Bob Feller	1.00
66	Bruce Sutter	.75
67	Dale Murphy	1.00
68	Dennis Eckersley	1.00
69	Don Newcombe	.50
70	Don Mattingly	5.00
71	Dwight Gooden	.50
72	Frank Robinson	1.50
73	Gary Carter	1.00
74	Graig Nettles	.50
75	Harmon Killebrew	2.00
76	Jim Bunning	.50
77	Joe Morgan	1.00
78	Joe Rudi	.50
79	Jose Canseco	1.00
80	Ernie Banks	3.00
81	Luis Aparicio	.50
82	Luis Tiant	.50
83	Mark Fidrych	.50
84	Kirk Gibson	.50
85	Lou Brock	1.00
86	Juan Marichal	1.00
87	Monte Irvin	1.00
88	Paul Molitor	1.00
89	Tommy John	.50
90	Warren Spahn	1.50
91	Wade Boggs	1.00
92	Reggie Jackson	2.00
93	Kirby Puckett	3.00
94	Boog Powell	.50
95	Carl Yastrzemski	2.00
96	Bobby Thomson	.50
97	Bill "Moose" Skowron	.50
98	Bill Madlock	.50
99	Sparky Anderson	.50
100	Yogi Berra	2.00
101	Bobby Doerr	.50
102	Gaylord Perry	.50
103	George Kell	.50
104	Harold Reynolds	.50
105	Joe Carter	.50
106	Johnny Podres	.50
107	Ron Cey	.50
108	Tim McCarver	.50
109	Tug McGraw	.50
110	Don Larsen	1.00

Black

NM/M
Cards (1-110): 2-4X
Production 99 Sets

Autographs

NM/M
Common Autograph: 10.00
Inserted 1:1
Refractors: 1-2.5X
Production 25 Sets

Code	Player	Price
HA	Hank Aaron/30	300.00
JA	Jim Abbott	20.00
SA	Sparky Anderson	20.00
LA	Luis Aparicio	12.00
HB	Harold Baines	10.00
EB	Ernie Banks/24	175.00
HBA	Hank Bauer	20.00
JBE	Johnny Bench	65.00
YB	Yogi Berra/25	150.00
VB	Vida Blue	15.00
BB	Bert Blyleven	10.00
WB	Wade Boggs/77	125.00
GB	George Brett/25	180.00
LB	Lou Brock/76	120.00
BBU	Bill Buckner	10.00
JB	Jim Bunning/76	100.00
JCA	Jose Canseco	40.00
RCA	Rod Carew	60.00
GC	Gary Carter/77	100.00
JC	Joe Carter	25.00
OC	Orlando Cepeda/75	180.00
RCE	Ron Cey	10.00
JCR	Jose Cruz	10.00
AD	Andre Dawson	20.00
BD	Bobby Doerr	20.00
LD	Lenny Dykstra	20.00
DEC	Dennis Eckersley	65.00
DE	Darrell Evans	10.00
DEV	Dwight Evans/78	80.00
BF	Bob Feller	80.00
MF	Mark Fidrych	20.00
RF	Rollie Fingers	25.00
CF	Carlton Fisk	65.00
WF	Whitey Ford	65.00
GF	George Foster	10.00
SG	Steve Garvey	15.00
KG	Kirk Gibson	40.00
DG	Dwight Gooden	30.00
RG	Rich "Goose" Gossage	15.00
BGR	Bobby Grich	15.00
KGR	Ken Griffey Sr.	25.00
RGU	Ron Guidry	35.00
TG	Tony Gwynn/25	165.00
WH	Whitey Herzog	15.00
BH	Bob Horner	10.00
MI	Monte Irvin	60.00
BJ	Bo Jackson	75.00
RJ	Reggie Jackson	100.00
FJ	Fergie Jenkins	20.00
TJ	Tommy John	25.00
AK	Al Kaline	75.00
GK	George Kell	30.00
HK	Harmon Killebrew/76	150.00
RK	Ralph Kiner	125.00
JK	Jerry Koosman	25.00
JKR	John Kruk	35.00
DL	Don Larsen	15.00
TL	Tom Lasorda/76	100.00
GL	Greg Luzinski	15.00
FL	Fred Lynn	20.00
BM	Bill Madlock	10.00
JMA	Juan Marichal	35.00
DON	Don Mattingly/81	175.00
BMA	Bill Mazeroski	15.00
TM	Tim McCarver	25.00
WMC	Willie McCovey	50.00
WMG	Willie McGee	25.00
TMC	Tug McGraw	50.00
PM	Paul Molitor	75.00
JM	Joe Morgan	35.00
DM	Dale Murphy	40.00
SM	Stan Musial/28	185.00
PN	Phil Niekro	15.00
GN	Graig Nettles	10.00
DN	Don Newcombe	15.00
TO	Tony Oliva	25.00
PO	Paul O'Neill	50.00
JP	Jim Palmer	50.00
DP	Dave Parker	20.00
LP	Lance Parrish	10.00
TP	Terry Pendleton	10.00
TP	Tony Perez	40.00
GP	Gaylord Perry	10.00
JPI	Jimmy Piersall	10.00
JPO	Johnny Podres	10.00
BP	Boog Powell	10.00
HR	Harold Reynolds	20.00
JR	Jim Rice	30.00
BR	Bobby Richardson	10.00
CR	Cal Ripken Jr./25	340.00
PR	Phil Rizzuto/70	140.00
RR	Robin Roberts	25.00
BRO	Brooks Robinson/75	140.00
FR	Frank Robinson	60.00
JRU	Joe Rudi	10.00
NR	Nolan Ryan/77	200.00
BSA	Bret Saberhagen	25.00
RSA	Ron Santo	20.00
MS	Mike Schmidt/83	200.00
RS	Red Schoendienst/83	100.00
TS	Tom Seaver	65.00
BS	Bill "Moose" Skowron	10.00
LS	Lee Smith	15.00
OS	Ozzie Smith	65.00
DSN	Duke Snider/75	100.00
WS	Warren Spahn	50.00
DS	Dave Stieb	15.00
BSU	Bruce Sutter	35.00
DSU	Don Sutton	20.00
KT	Kent Tekulve	20.00
BT	Bobby Thomson	10.00
LT	Luis Tiant	10.00
AT	Alan Trammell	20.00
BW	Bob Watson	10.00
EW	Earl Weaver	12.00
MW	Maury Wills	10.00
CY	Carl Yastrzemski	
RY	Robin Yount/25	150.00

2003 Topps Total

NM/M
Complete Set (990): 125.00

Common Player: .10
Pack (10): 1.00
Box (36): 25.00

#	Player	Price
1	Brent Abernathy	.10
2	Bobby Hill	.10
3	Victor Martinez	.10
4	Chip Ambres	.10
5	Matt Anderson	.10
6	Ricardo Aramboles	.10
7	Carlos Pena	.10
8	Aaron Guiel	.10
9	Luke Allen	.10
10	Francisco Rodriguez	.20
11	Jason Marquis	.10
12	Edwin Almonte	.10
13	Grant Balfour	.10
14	Adam Piatt	.10
15	Andy Phillips	.10
16	Adrian Beltre	.10
17	Brandon Backe	.10
18	Dave Berg	.10
19	Brett Myers	.10
20	Brian Meadows	.10
21	Chin-Feng Chen	.25
22	Blake Williams	.10
23	Josh Bard	.10
24	Josh Beckett	.10
25	Kip Bouknight RC	.20
26	Matt Childers	.10
27	Adam Everett	.10
28	Mike Bordick	.10
29	Antonio Alfonseca	.10
30	Doug Creek	.10
31	J.D. Drew	.20
32	Milton Bradley	.10
33	David Wells	.10
34	Vance Wilson	.10
35	Jeff Fassero	.10
36	Sandy Alomar	.10
37	Ryan Vogelsong	.10
38	Roger Clemens	1.25
39	Juan Gonzalez	.40
40	Dustin Hermanson	.10
41	Andy Ashby	.10
42	Adam Hyzdu	.10
43	Ben Broussard	.10
44	Ryan Klesko	.10
45	Chris Buglovsky	.10
46	Bud Smith	.10
47	Aaron Boone	.10
48	Cliff Floyd	.10
49	Alex Cora	.10
50	Curt Schilling	.40
51	Michael Cuddyer	.10
52	Mike Venafro	.10
53	Carlos Gullien	.10
54	Angel Berroa	.10
55	Eli Marrero	.10
56	A.J. Burnett	.10
57	Oliver Perez	.10
58	Matt Morris	.25
59	Valerio De Los Santos	.10
60	Austin Kearns	.50
61	Darren Dreifort	.10
62	Jason Standridge	.10
63	Carlos Silva	.10
64	Moises Alou	.10
65	Jason Anderson	.10
66	Russell Branyan	.10
67	B.J. Ryan	.10
68	Cory Aldridge	.10
69	Ellis Burks	.10
70	Troy Glaus	.50
71	Kelly Wunsch	.10
72	Brad Wilkerson	.10
73	Jayson Durocher	.10
74	Tony Fiore	.10
75	Brian Giles	.25
76	Billy Wagner	.10
77	Neifi Perez	.10
78	Jose Valverde	.10
79	Brent Butler	.10
80	Mario Ramos	.10
81	Kerry Robinson	.10
82	Brent Mayne	.10
83	Sean Casey	.10
84	Danys Baez	.25
85	Chase Utley	.25
86	Jared Sandberg	.10
87	Terrence Long	.10
88	Kevin Walker	.10
89	Royce Clayton	.10
90	Shea Hillenbrand	.10
91	Brad Lidge	.10
92	Shawn Chacon	.10
93	Kevin Frederick	.10
94	Chris Snelling	.10
95	Omar Vizquel	.20
96	Joe Borchard	.10
97	Matt Belisle	.10
98	Steve Smyth	.10
99	Raul Mondesi	.20
100	Chipper Jones	1.00
101	Victor Alvarez	.10
102	J.M. Gold	.10
103	Willis Roberts	.10
104	Eddie Guardado	.10
105	Brad Voyles	.10
106	Bronson Arroyo	.10
107	Juan Castro	.10
108	Dan Pleasac	.10
109	Ramon Castro	.10
110	Tim Salmon	.25
111	Damion Easley	.10
112	J.D. Closser	.10
113	Mark Buehrle	.10
114	Steve Karsay	.10
115	Cristian Guerrero	.10

No.	Player	Val	No.	Player	Val	No.	Player	Val	No.	Player	Val	No.	Player	Val	No.	Player	Val
116	Brad Ausmus	.10	233	Scott Schoeneweis	.10	351	Ichiro Suzuki	1.00	469	Bubba Trammell	.10	587	Kyle Snyder	.10	705	Steve Finley	.10
117	Cristian Guzman	.10	234	Corey Hart	.10	352	Brandon Inge	.10	470	Scott Sullivan	.10	588	Paul Quantrill	.10	706	Sean Smith	.10
118	Dan Wilson	.10	235	Brett Tomko	.10	353	Jack Wilson	.10	471	Mike Mussina	.40	589	Trot Nixon	.10	707	Jeremy Giambi	.10
119	Jake Westbrook	.10	236	Shane Bazzell RC	.20	354	John Ennis	.10	472	Ramon Ortiz	.10	590	J.T. Snow	.10	708	Scott Hodges	.10
120	Manny Ramirez	.50	237	Tim Hummel	.10	355	Jamal Strong	.10	473	Lyle Overbay	.10	591	Kevin Young	.10	709	Vicente Padilla	.10
121	Jason Giambi	.75	238	Al Reyes	.10	356	Jason Jennings	.10	474	Mike Lowell	.10	592	Tomokazu Ohka	.10	710	Bert Snow	.10
122	Bob Wickman	.10	239	Daryle Ward	.10	357	Jeff Kent	.20	475	Greg Vaughn	.10	593	Brian Boehringer	.10	711	Aaron Rowand	.10
123	Aaron Cook	.10	240	Ismael Valdes	.10	358	Scott Chiasson	.10	476	Larry Bigbie	.10	594	Danny Patterson	.10	712	Dennis Tankersley	.10
124	Alfredo Amezaga	.10	241	Brian Fuentes	.10	359	Jeremy Griffiths	.10	477	Rey Sanchez	.10	595	Jeff Tam	.10	713	Rick Bauer	.10
125	Corey Thurman	.10	242	Cesar Izturis	.10	360	Paul Konerko	.10	478	Magglio Ordonez	.25	596	Anastacio Martinez	.10	714	Tim Olson RC	.25
126	Brandon Puffer	.10	243	Mark Bellhorn	.10	361	Jeff Austin	.10	479	Rondell White	.10	597	Rod Barajas	.10	715	Jeff Urban	.10
127	Hee Seop Choi	.25	244	Geoff Jenkins	.10	362	Todd Van Poppel	.10	480	Jay Witasick	.10	598	Octavio Dotel	.10	716	Steve Sparks	.10
128	Javier Vazquez	.10	245	Derek Jeter	2.00	363	Sun-Woo Kim	.10	481	Jimmy Rollins	.25	599	Jason Tyner	.10	717	Glendon Rusch	.10
129	Carlos Valderrama	.10	246	Anderson Machado	.10	364	Jerry Hairston	.10	482	Mike Maroth	.10	600	Gary Sheffield	.40	718	Ricky Stone	.10
130	Jerome Williams	.10	247	Dave Roberts	.10	365	Tony Torcato	.10	483	Mark Quinn	.10	601	Ruben Quevedo	.10	719	Benji Gil	.10
131	Wilson Betemit	.10	248	Jaime Cerda	.10	366	Arthur Rhodes	.10	484	Nick Neugebauer	.10	602	Jay Payton	.10	720	Pete Walker	.10
132	Bruce Chen	.10	249	Woody Williams	.10	367	Jose Jimenez	.10	485	Victor Zambrano	.10	603	Mo Vaughn	.10	721	Tim Worrell	.10
133	Esteban Yan	.10	250	Vernon Wells	.20	368	Matt LeCroy	.10	486	Travis Lee	.10	604	Pat Burrell	.40	722	Michael Tejera	.10
134	Brandon Berger	.10	251	Jon Lieber	.10	369	Curtis Lesanic	.10	487	Bobby Bradley	.10	605	Fernando Vina	.10	723	David Kelton	.10
135	Bill Hall	.10	252	Franklyn German	.10	370	Ramon Vasquez	.10	488	Marcus Giles	.10	606	Wes Anderson	.10	724	Britt Reames	.10
136	LaTroy Hawkins	.10	253	David Segui	.10	371	Joe Randa	.10	489	Steve Trachsel	.10	607	Alex Gonzalez	.10	725	John Stephens	.10
137	Nate Cornejo	.10	254	Freddy Garcia	.10	372	John Franco	.10	490	Derek Lowe	.10	608	Ted Lilly	.10	726	Mark McLemore	.10
138	Jim Mecir	.10	255	James Baldwin	.10	373	Charles Johnson	.10	491	Hideo Nomo	.25	609	Nick Punto	.10	727	Jeff Zimmerman	.10
139	Joe Crede	.10	256	Tony Alvarez	.10	374	Craig Wilson	.10	492	Brad Hawpe	.10	610	Ryan Madson	.10	728	Checklist	.10
140	Andres Galarraga	.10	257	Walter Young	.10	375	Michael Young	.10	493	Jesus Medrano	.10	611	Odalis Perez	.10	729	Andres Torres	.10
141	Dave Williams	.10	258	Alex Herrera	.10	376	Mark Ellis	.10	494	Rick Ankiel	.10	612	Chris Woodward	.10	730	Checklist	.10
142	Joey Eischen	.10	259	Robert Fick	.10	377	Joe Mauer	.25	495	Pasqual Coco	.10	613	John Olerud	.25	731	Johan Santana	.10
143	Mike Timlin	.10	260	Rob Bell	.10	378	Checklist	.10	496	Michael Barrett	.10	614	Brad Cresse	.10	732	Dane Sardinha	.10
144	Jose Cruz Jr.	.10	261	Ross Gload	.10	379	Jason Kendall	.10	497	Joe Beimel	.10	615	Chad Zerbe	.10	733	Rodrigo Rosario	.10
145	Wes Helms	.10	262	Dee Brown	.10	380	Checklist	.10	498	Marty Cordova	.10	616	Brad Penny	.10	734	Frank Thomas	.50
146	Brian Roberts	.10	263	Mike Bacsik	.10	381	Alex Gonzalez	.10	499	Aaron Sele	.10	617	Barry Larkin	.40	735	Tom Glavine	.25
147	Bret Prinz	.10	264	Corey Patterson	.10	382	Flash Gordon	.10	500	Sammy Sosa	1.00	618	Brandon Duckworth	.10	736	Doug Mirabelli	.10
148	Brian Hunter	.10	265	Marvin Bernard	.10	383	John Buck	.10	501	Ivan Rodriguez	.40	619	Brad Radke	.10	737	Juan Uribe	.10
149	Chad Hermansen	.10	266	Eddie Rogers	.10	384	Shigetoshi Hasegawa	.10	502	Keith Osik	.10	620	Giovanni Carrara	.10	738	Ryan Anderson	.10
150	Andruw Jones	.40	267	Elio Serrano	.10	385	Scott Stewart	.10	503	Hank Blalock	.25	621	Juan Pierre	.10	739	Sean Burroughs	.10
151	Kurt Ainsworth	.10	268	D'Angelo Jimenez	.10	386	Luke Hudson	.10	504	Craig Monroe	.10	622	Rick Reed	.10	740	Eric Chavez	.10
152	Clifford Bartosh	.10	269	Adam Johnson	.10	387	Todd Jones	.10	505	Junior Spivey	.10	623	Omar Daal	.10	741	Enrique Wilson	.10
153	Kyle Lohse	.10	270	Gregg Zaun	.10	388	Fred McGriff	.25	506	Edgardo Alfonzo	.10	624	Jose Hernandez	.10	742	Elmer Dessens	.10
154	Brian Jordan	.10	271	Nick Johnson	.10	389	Mike Sweeney	.10	507	Alex Graman	.10	625	Greg Maddux	1.00	743	Marlon Byrd	.10
155	Coco Crisp	.10	272	Geoff Goetz	.10	390	Marlon Anderson	.10	508	J.J. Davis	.10	626	Henry Mateo	.10	744	Brendan Donnelly	.10
156	Tomas Perez	.10	273	Ryan Drese	.10	391	Terry Adams	.10	509	Roger Cedeno	.10	627	Kip Wells	.10	745	Gary Bennett	.10
157	Keith Foulke	.10	274	Eric DuBose	.10	392	Mark DeRosa	.10	510	Joe Roa	.10	628	Kevin Cash	.10	746	Roy Oswalt	.10
158	Chris Carpenter	.10	275	Barry Zito	.25	393	Doug Mientkiewicz	.10	511	Wily Mo Pena	.10	629	Mark Redman	.10	747	Andy Van Hekken	.10
159	Mike Remlinger	.10	276	Mike Crudale	.10	394	Miguel Cairo	.10	512	Eric Munson	.10	630	Luis Gonzalez	.25	748	Jesus Colome	.10
160	Dewon Brazelton	.10	277	Paul Byrd	.10	395	Jamie Moyer	.10	513	Arnie Munoz RC	.10	631	Jason Conti	.10	749	Erick Almonte	.10
161	Brook Fordyce	.10	278	Eric Gagne	.10	396	Josh Towers	.10	514	Miguel Asencio	.10	632	Ricardo Rincon	.10	750	Frank Catalanotto	.10
162	Rusty Greer	.10	279	Aramis Ramirez	.10	397	Matt Clement	.10	515	Andy Pettitte	.25	633	Mike Bynum	.10	751	Matt Herges	.10
163	Scott Downs	.10	280	Ray Durham	.10	398	Bengie Molina	.10	516	Jim Edmonds	.25	634	Mike Redmond	.10	752	Carlos Delgado	.40
164	Jason Dubois	.10	281	Tony Graffanino	.10	399	Marcus Thames	.10	517	Jeff DaVanon	.10	635	Chance Capel	.10	753	Ryan Franklin	.10
165	David Coggin	.10	282	Jeremy Guthrie	.10	400	Nick Bierbrodt	.10	518	Aaron Myette	.10	636	Chris Widger	.10	754	Wilken Ruan	.10
166	Jose Hernandez	.10	283	Erik Bedard	.10	401	Tim Kalita	.10	519	C.C. Sabathia	.10	637	Michael Restovich	.10	755	Kelvim Escobar	.10
167	Carlos Hernandez	.10	284	Vince Faison	.10	402	Corwin Malone	.10	520	Gerardo Garcia	.10	638	Mark Grudzielanek	.10	756	Tim Drew	.10
168	Matt Williams	.10	285	Bobby Kielty	.10	403	Jesse Orosco	.10	521	Brian Schneider	.10	639	Brandon Larson	.10	757	Jarrod Washburn	.10
169	Rheal Cormier	.10	286	Francis Beltran	.10	404	Brandon Phillips	.10	522	Wes Obermueller	.10	640	Luis De Los Santos	.10	758	Runelvys Hernandez	.10
170	Duaner Sanchez	.10	287	Alexis Gomez	.10	405	Eric Cyr	.10	523	John Mabry	.10	641	Javy Lopez	.20	759	Cory Vance	.10
171	Craig Counsell	.10	288	Vladimir Guerrero	.75	406	Jason Michaels	.10	524	Casey Fossum	.10	642	Rene Reyes	.10	760	Doug Glanville	.10
172	Edgar Martinez	.20	289	Kevin Appier	.10	407	Julio Lugo	.10	525	Toby Hall	.10	643	Orlando Merced	.10	761	Ryan Rupe	.10
173	Zack Greinke	.10	290	Gil Meche	.10	408	Gabe Kapler	.10	526	Denny Neagle	.10	644	Jason Phillips	.10	762	Jermaine Dye	.10
174	Pedro Feliz	.10	291	Marquis Grissom	.10	409	Mark Mulder	.25	527	Willie Bloomquist	.10	645	Luis Ugueto	.10	763	Mike Cameron	.10
175	Randy Choate	.10	292	John Burkett	.10	410	Adam Eaton	.10	528	A.J. Pierzynski	.10	646	Ron Calloway	.10	764	Scott Erickson	.10
176	Jon Garland	.10	293	Vinny Castilla	.10	411	Ken Harvey	.10	529	Bartolo Colon	.10	647	Josh Paul	.10	765	Richie Sexson	.25
177	Keith Ginter	.10	294	Tyler Walker	.10	412	Jolbert Cabrera	.10	530	Chad Harville	.10	648	Todd Greene	.10	766	Jose Vidro	.10
178	Carlos Febles	.10	295	Shane Halter	.10	413	Eric Milton	.10	531	Blaine Neal	.10	649	Joe Giradi	.10	767	Brian West	.10
179	Gregor Blanco RC	.10	296	Geronimo Gil	.10	414	Josh Hall RC	.20	532	Luis Terrero Jr.	.10	650	Todd Ritchie	.10	768	Shawn Estes	.10
180	Jack Cust	.10	297	Eric Hinske	.10	415	Bob File	.10	533	Reggie Taylor	.10	651	Lou Merloni	.10	769	Brian Tallet	.10
181	Koyie Hill	.10	298	Adam Dunn	.50	416	Brett Evert	.10	534	Melvin Mora	.10	652	Shawn Wooten	.10	770	Larry Walker	.25
182	Ricky Gutierrez	.10	299	Mike Kinkade	.10	417	Ron Chiavacci	.10	535	Tino Martinez	.10	653	David Riske	.10	771	Josh Hamilton	.10
183	Ben Grieve	.10	300	Mark Prior	.50	418	Jorge De La Rosa	.10	536	Peter Bergeron	.10	654	Luis Rivas	.10	772	Orlando Hudson	.10
184	Livan Hernandez	.10	301	Corey Koskie	.10	419	Quinton McCracken	.10	537	Jorge Padilla	.10	655	Roy Halladay	.10	773	Justin Morneau	.20
185	Jason Isringhausen	.10	302	David Dellucci	.10	420	Luther Hackman	.10	538	Oscar Villarreal RC	.20	656	Travis Driskill	.10	774	Ryan Bukvich	.10
186	Gookie Dawkins	.10	303	Todd Helton	.40	421	Gary Knotts	.10	539	David Weathers	.10	657	Ricky Ledee	.10	775	Mike Gonzalez	.10
187	Roberto Alomar	.40	304	Greg Miller	.10	422	Kevin Brown	.20	540	Mike Lamb	.10	658	Tony Perez	.10	776	Tsuyoshi Shinjo	.10
188	Eric Junge	.10	305	Delvin James	.10	423	Jeff Cirillo	.10	541	Greg Norton	.10	659	Fernando Rodney	.10	777	Matt Mantei	.10
189	Carlos Beltran	.10	306	Humberto Cota	.10	424	Damaso Marte	.10	542	Michael Tucker	.10	660	Trevor Hoffman	.10	778	Jimmy Journell	.10
190	Denny Hocking	.10	307	Aaron Harang	.10	425	Chan Ho Park	.10	543	Ben Kozlowski	.10	661	Pat Hentgen	.10	779	Brian Lawrence	.10
191	Jason Schmidt	.10	308	Jeremy Hill	.10	426	Nathan Haynes	.10	544	Alex Sanchez	.10	662	Bret Boone	.10	780	Mike Lieberthal	.10
192	Cory Lidle	.10	309	Billy Koch	.10	427	Matt Lawton	.10	545	Trey Lunsford	.10	663	Ryan Jensen	.10	781	Scott Mullen	.10
193	Robert Mackowiak	.10	310	Brandon Claussen	.10	428	Mike Stanton	.10	546	Abraham Nunez	.10	664	Ricardo Rodriguez	.10	782	Zach Day	.10
194	Charlton Jimerson RC	.10	311	Matt Ginter	.10	429	Bernie Williams	.40	547	Mike Lincoln	.10	665	Jeremy Lambert	.10	783	John Thomson	.10
195	Darin Erstad	.25	312	Jason Lane	.10	430	Kevin Jarvis	.10	548	Orlando Hernandez	.10	666	Troy Percival	.10	784	Ben Sheets	.10
196	Jason Davis	.10	313	Ben Weber	.10	431	Joe McEwing	.10	549	Kevin Mench	.10	667	Jon Rauch	.10	785	Damon Minor	.10
197	Luis Castillo	.10	314	Alan Benes	.10	432	Mark Kotsay	.10	550	Garret Anderson	.25	668	Mariano Rivera	.25	786	Jose Valentin	.10
198	Juan Encarnacion	.10	315	Oscar Herinquez	.10	433	Juan Cruz	.10	551	Kyle Farnsworth	.10	669	Jason LaRue	.10	787	Armando Benitez	.10
199	Jeffrey Hammonds	.10	316	Danny Graves	.10	434	Russ Ortiz	.10	552	Kevin Olsen	.10	670	J.C. Romero	.10	788	Jamie Walker	.10
199		.10	317	Jason Johnson	.10	435	Jeff Nelson	.10	553	Joel Pineiro	.10	671	Cody Ross	.10	789	Preston Wilson	.10
200	Nomar Garciaparra	1.50	318	Jason Grimsley	.10	436	Alan Embree	.10	554	Jorge Julio	.10	672	Eric Byrnes	.10	790	Josh Wilson	.10
201	Ryan Christianson	.10	319	Steve Kline	.10	437	Miguel Tejada	.25	555	Jose Mesa	.10	673	Paul LoDuca	.10	791	Phil Nevin	.10
202	Willie Banks	.10	320	Johnny Damon	.10	438	Kirk Saarloos	.10	556	Jorge Posada	.40	674	Brad Fullmer	.10	792	Roberto Hernandez	.10
203	Damian Moss	.10	321	Jay Gibbons	.10	439	Cliff Lee	.10	557	Jose Ortiz	.10	675	Cliff Politte	.10	793	Mike Williams	.10
204	Chris Richard	.10	322	J.J. Putz	.10	440	Ryan Ludwick	.10	558	Mike Tonis	.10	676	Justin Miller	.10	794	Jake Peavy	.10
205	Todd Hundley	.10	323	Stephen Randolph RC	.10	441	Derrek Lee	.10	559	Gabe White	.10	677	Nic Jackson	.10	795	Paul Shuey	.10
206	Paul Bako	.10	324	Bobby Higginson	.10	442	Bobby Abreu	.20	560	Rafael Furcal	.10	678	Kris Benson	.10	796	Chad Bradford	.10
207	Adam Kennedy	.10	325	Kazuhisa Ishii	.10	443	Dustan Mohr	.10	561	Matt Franco	.10	679	Carl Sadler	.10	797	Bobby Jenks	.10
208	Scott Hatteberg	.10	326	Carlos Lee	.10	444	Nook Logan RC	.25	562	Trey Hodges	.10	680	Joe Nathan	.10	798	Sean Douglass	.10
209	Andy Pratt	.10	327	J.R. House	.10	445	Seth McClung	.10	563	Esteban German	.10	681	Julio Santana	.10	799	Damian Miller	.10
210	Ken Griffey Jr.	1.00	328	Mark Loretta	.10	446	Miguel Olivo	.10	564	Josh Fogg	.10	682	Wade Miller	.10	800	Mark Wohlers	.10
211	Chris George	.10	329	Mike Matheny	.10	447	Henry Blanco	.10	565	Fernando Tatis	.10	683	Josh Pearce	.10	801	Ty Wigginton	.10
212	Lance Niekro	.10	330	Ben Diggins	.10	448	Seung Jun Song	.10	566	Alex Cintron	.10	684	Tony Armas	.10	802	Alfonso Soriano	1.00
213	Greg Colbrunn	.10	331	Seth Etherton	.10	449	Kris Wilson	.10	567	Grant Roberts	.10	685	Al Leiter	.10	803	Randy Johnson	.75
214	Herbert Perry	.10	332	Eli Whiteside RC	.20	450	Xavier Nady	.10	568	Gene Stechschulte	.10	686	Raul Ibanez	.10	804	Placido Polanco	.10
215	Cody Ransom	.10	333	Juan Rivera	.10	451	Corky Miller	.10	569	Rafael Palmeiro	.25	687	Danny Bautista	.10	805	Drew Henson	.10
216	Craig Biggio	.25	334	Jeff Conine	.10	452	Jim Thome	.50	570	Mike Hampton	.10	688	Travis Hafner	.10	806	Tony Womack	.10
217	Miguel Batista	.10	335	John McDonald	.10	453	George Lombard	.10	571	Ben Davis	.10	689	Rylan Reed RC	.10	807	Pokey Reese	.10
218	Alex Escobar	.10	336	Erik Hiljus	.10	454	Rey Ordonez	.10	572	Dean Palmer	.10	690	Pedro J. Martinez	.75	808	Albert Pujols	.75
219	Willie Harris	.10	337	David Eckstein	.10	455	Deivis Santos	.10	573	Jerrod Riggan	.10	691	Ramon Santiago	.10	809	Shane Reynolds	.10
220	Scott Strickland	.10	338	Jeff Bagwell	.50	456	Mike Myers	.10	574	Nate Frese	.10	692	Felipe Lopez	.10	810	Mike Rivera	.10
221	Felix Rodriguez	.10	339	Matt Holliday	.10	457	Edgar Renteria	.10	575	Josh Phelps	.10	693	David Ross	.10	811	John Lackey	.10
222	Torii Hunter	.25	340	Jeff Liefer	.10	458	Braden Looper	.10	576	Freddie Bynum	.10	694	Chone Figgins	.10	812	Brian Wright RC	.20
223	Tyler Houston	.10	341	Greg Myers	.10	459	Guillermo Mota	.10	577	Morgan Ensberg	.10	695	Antonio Osuna	.10	813	Eric Good	.10
224	Darrell May	.10	342	Scott Sauerbeck	.10	460	Scott Rolen	.50	578	Juan Rincon	.10	696	Jay Powell	.10	814	Dernell Stenson	.10
225	Benito Santiago	.10	343	Omar Infante	.10	461	Lance Berkman	.10	579	Kazuhiro Sasaki	.10	697	Roy Smith	.10	815	Kirk Rueter	.10
226	Ryan Dempster	.10	344	Ryan Langerhans	.10	462	Jeff Heaverlo	.10	580	Yorvit Torrealba	.10	698	Alexis Rios	.10	816	Todd Zeile	.10
227	Andy Fox	.10	345	Abraham Nunez	.10	463	Ramon Hernandez	.10	581	Tim Wakefield	.10	699	Tanyon Sturtze	.10	817	Brad Thomas	.10
228	Jung Bong	.10	346	Mike MacDougal	.10	464	Jason Simontacchi	.10	582	Sterling Hitchcock	.10	700	Turk Wendell	.10	818	Shawn Sedlacek	.10
229	Jose Macias	.10	347	Travis Phelps	.10	465	So Taguchi	.10	583	Craig Paquette	.10	701	Richard Hidalgo	.10	819	Garrett Stephenson	.10
230	Shannon Stewart	.10	348	Dan Reichert	.10	466	Dave Veres	.10	584	Kevin Millwood	.25	702	Joe Mays	.10	820	Mark Teixeira	.25
231	Buddy Groom	.10	349	Alex Rodriguez	1.50	467	Shane Loux	.10	585	Damian Rolls	.10	703	Jorge Sosa	.10	821	Tim Hudson	.25
232	Eric Valent	.10	350	Bobby Seay	.10	468	Rodrigo Lopez	.10	586	Brad Baisley	.10	704	Eric Karros	.10	822	Mike Koplove	.10

No.	Player	Value		No.	Player	Value
823	Chris Reitsma	.10		940	Clay Hensley RC	.50
824	Rafael Soriano	.10		941	David Pahucki RC	.20
825	Ugueth Urbina	.10		942	Wilton Reynolds RC	.20
826	Matt White	.10		943	Michael Hinckley RC	.20
827	Colin Young	.10		944	Josh Willingham RC	.20
828	Pat Strange	.10		945	Pete LaForest RC	.20
829	Juan Pena	.10		946	Pete Smart	.10
830	Joe Thurston	.10		947	Jay Stizman	.10
831	Shawn Green	.25		948	Mark Malaska RC	.20
832	Pedro Astacio	.10		949	Mike Gallo RC	.20
833	Danny Wright	.10		950	Tyler Martin RC	.20
834	Weston O'Brien RC	.20		951	Shane Victorino	.10
835	Luis Lopez	.10		952	Ryan Howard	30.00
836	Randall Simon	.10		953	Daryl Clark RC	.20
837	Jaret Wright	.10		954	Dayton Buller	.10
838	Jayson Werth	.10		955	Carlos Zambrano	.10
839	Endy Chavez	.10		956	Chris Booker	.10
840	Checklist	.10		957	Brandon Watson RC	.20
841	Chad Paronto	.10		958	Matt DeMarco RC	.20
842	Randy Winn	.10		959	Doug Waechter RC	.75
843	Sidney Ponson	.10		960	Callix Crabbe RC	.20
844	Robin Ventura	.10		961	Jairo Garcia RC	.20
845	Rich Aurilia	.10		962	Jason Perry RC	.20
846	Joaquin Benoit	.10		963	Eric Riggs RC	.20
847	Barry Bonds	2.00		964	Travis Ishikawa RC	.40
848	Carl Crawford	.10		965	Jorge Piedra RC	.20
849	Jeromy Burnitz	.10		966	Manuel Ramirez RC	.20
850	Orlando Cabrera	.10		967	Tyler Johnson RC	.20
851	Luis Vizcaino	.10		968	Jaime Bubela RC	.20
852	Randy Wolf	.10		969	Haj Turay RC	.20
853	Benny Agbayani	.10		970	Tyson Graham RC	.20
854	Jeremy Affeldt	.10		971	David DeJesus RC	.20
855	Einar Diaz	.10		972	Franklin Gutierrez RC	.20
856	Carl Everett	.10		973	Craig Brazell RC	1.00
857	Wiki Gonzalez	.10		974	Keith Stamler RC	.20
858	Steve Belcher	.10		975	Jemel Spearman RC	.20
859	Travis Harper	.10		976	Kade Johnson RC	.10
860	Mike Piazza	1.25		977	Nick Trzesniak RC	.20
861	Will Ohman	.10		978	Bill Simon RC	.20
862	Eric Young	.10		979	Matthew Hagen RC	.20
863	Jason Grabowski	.10		980	Kris Kroski RC	.20
864	Rett Johnson RC	.20		981	Prentice Redman RC	.50
865	Aubrey Huff	.10		982	Kevin Randel RC	.20
866	John Smoltz	.10		983	Thomari Stori-Harden	.10
867	Mickey Callaway	.10		984	Brian Shackelford RC	.20
868	Joe Kennedy	.10		985	Mike Adams RC	.20
869	Tim Redding	.10		986	Brian McCann RC	5.00
870	Colby Lewis	.10		987	Mike McNutt RC	.20
871	Salomon Torres	.10		988	Aron Weston RC	.20
872	Marco Scutaro	.10		989	Dustin Moseley RC	.20
873	Tony Batista	.10		990	Bryan Bullington RC	1.50
874	Dmitri Young	.10				
875	Scott Williamson	.10				
876	Scott Spezio	.10				
877	John Webb	.10				
878	Jose Acevedo	.10				
879	Kevin Orie	.10				
880	Jacque Jones	.10				
881	Ben Francisco RC	.25				
882	Bobby Basham RC	.25				
883	Corey Shafer RC	.20				
884	J.D. Durbin RC	.20				
885	Chien-Ming Wang RC	2.50				
886	Adam Stern	.10				
887	Wayne Lydon RC	.20				
888	Derell McCall RC	.20				
889	Jon Nelson RC	.20				
890	Willie Eyre RC	.20				
891	Ramon A. Martinez RC	.20				
892	Adrian Myers RC	.20				
893	Jamie Athas RC	.20				
894	Ismael Castro RC	.20				
895	David Martinez	.10				
896	Terry Tiffee RC	.20				
897	Nathan Panther RC	.25				
898	Kyle Roat RC	.20				
899	Kason Gabbard RC	.20				
900	Hanley Ramirez RC	1.50				
901	Bryan Grace RC	.20				
902	B.J. Barns RC	.50				
903	Greg Bruso RC	.15				
904	Mike Neu RC	.15				
905	Dustin Yount RC	.50				
906	Shane Victorino RC	.20				
907	Brian Burgamy RC	.20				
908	Beau Kemp RC	.20				
909	Eny Cabreja RC	.50				
910	Dexter Cooper RC	.20				
911	Chris Colton RC	.20				
912	David Cash RC	.20				
913	Bernie Castro RC	.20				
914	Luis Hodge RC	.20				
915	Jeff Clark RC	.20				
916	Jason Kubel RC	1.00				
917	T.J. Bohn RC	.20				
918	Luke Steidlmayer RC	.20				
919	Natthew Petterson	.10				
920	Darrell Rasner	.10				
921	Scott Tyler	.10				
922	Gary Schneidmiller RC	.20				
923	Kerry Wood	.40				
924	Ryan Cameron RC	.20				
925	Wilfredo Rodriguez	.20				
926	Rajai Davis RC	.20				
927	Evel Bastida-Martinez RC	.20				
928	Chris Duncan RC	2.00				
929	David Pember RC	.20				
930	Branden Florence RC	.20				
931	Eric Eckenstahler	.20				
932	Hong-Chih Kuo RC	1.00				
933	Il Kim RC	.20				
934	Michael Garciaparra	.50				
935	Tommy Whiteman RC	.20				
936	Gary Harris RC	.20				
937	Derry Hammond	.10				
938	Joey Gomes	.20				
939	Donald Hood RC	.20				

Silver

Jim Thome

Stars (1-990): 1-2X
Inserted 1:1

Award Winners

Complete Set (30): 20.00
Common Player: .50
Inserted 1:12

No.	Player	Value
AW1	Barry Zito	.75
AW2	Randy Johnson	1.50
AW3	Miguel Tejada	.75
AW4	Barry Bonds	3.00
AW5	Sammy Sosa	2.00
AW6	Barry Bonds	3.00
AW7	Mike Piazza	2.50
AW8	Todd Helton	.75
AW9	Jeff Kent	.50
AW10	Edgar Renteria	.50
AW11	Scott Rolen	.75
AW12	Vladimir Guerrero	1.00
AW13	Mike Hampton	.50
AW14	Jason Giambi	1.50
AW15	Alfonso Soriano	1.50
AW16	Alex Rodriguez	3.00
AW17	Eric Chavez	.50
AW18	Jorge Posada	.50
AW19	Bernie Williams	.75
AW20	Magglio Ordonez	.50
AW21	Garret Anderson	.50
AW22	Manny Ramirez	1.00
AW23	Jason Jennings	.50
AW24	Eric Hinske	.50
AW25	Billy Koch	.50
AW26	John Smoltz	.50
AW27	Alex Rodriguez	3.00
AW28	Barry Bonds	3.00
AW29	Tony LaRussa	.50
AW30	Mike Scioscia	.50

Total Production

NM/M
Complete Set (10): 10.00
Common Player: .40
Inserted 1:18

No.	Player	Value
TP1	Barry Bonds	2.50
TP2	Manny Ramirez	.75
TP3	Albert Pujols	1.00
TP4	Jason Giambi	1.00
TP5	Magglio Ordonez	.40
TP6	Mike Piazza	1.50
TP7	Todd Helton	.75
TP8	Miguel Tejada	.50
TP9	Sammy Sosa	1.50
TP10	Alex Rodriguez	2.50

Total Signatures

NM/M
Common Autograph:
Inserted 1:176

	Player	Value
MB	Marlon Byrd	10.00
EM	Eli Marrero	8.00
BP	Brandon Phillips	10.00
MT	Marcus Thames	8.00
TT	Tony Torcato	8.00

Total Topps

JOSE VIDRO Montreal Expos

NM/M
Complete Set (50): 25.00
Common Player: .25
Inserted 1:7

No.	Player	Value
TT1	Ichiro Suzuki	1.50
TT2	Alex Rodriguez	2.50
TT3	Barry Bonds	2.50
TT4	Jason Giambi	1.00
TT5	Troy Glaus	.75
TT6	Greg Maddux	1.50
TT7	Albert Pujols	1.00
TT8	Randy Johnson	1.00
TT9	Chipper Jones	1.50
TT10	Magglio Ordonez	.25
TT11	Jim Thome	.75
TT12	Jeff Kent	.40
TT13	Curt Schilling	.50
TT14	Alfonso Soriano	.50
TT15	Rafael Palmeiro	.50
TT16	Carlos Delgado	.50
TT17	Torii Hunter	.50
TT18	Pat Burrell	.50
TT19	Adam Dunn	.75
TT20	Roberto Alomar	.50
TT21	Eric Chavez	.40
TT22	Derek Jeter	3.00
TT23	Nomar Garciaparra	2.00
TT24	Lance Berkman	.40
TT25	Jim Edmonds	.50
TT26	Todd Helton	.75
TT27	Sammy Sosa	1.50
TT28	Phil Nevin	.25
TT29	Andruw Jones	.40
TT30	Barry Zito	.50
TT31	Richie Sexson	.40
TT32	Ken Griffey Jr.	1.50
TT33	Gary Sheffield	.40
TT34	Shawn Green	.40
TT35	Mike Sweeney	.40
TT36	Mike Lowell	.25
TT37	Larry Walker	.40
TT38	Manny Ramirez	.75
TT39	Miguel Tejada	.40
TT40	Mike Piazza	2.00
TT41	Scott Rolen	.75
TT42	Brian Giles	.40
TT43	Garret Anderson	.40
TT44	Vladimir Guerrero	.75
TT45	Bartolo Colon	.25
TT46	Jorge Posada	.40
TT47	Ivan Rodriguez	.50
TT48	Ryan Klesko	.25
TT49	Jose Vidro	.25
TT50	Pedro J. Martinez	.75

2003 Topps Traded & Rookies

NM/M
Complete Set (275): 50.00
Common Player: .15
Pack (8 + 2 Chrome):
Box (24): 40.00
Chrome Cards: 2-4X

No.	Player	Value		No.	Player	Value		No.	Player	Value
T1	Juan Pierre	.15		T70	Jeremy Fikac	.15		T187	Thomari Story-Harden RC	
T2	Mark Grudzielanek	.15		T71	Jeff Kent	.25		T188	Dusty Brown RC	.25
T3	Tanyon Sturtze	.15		T72	Andres Galarraga	.25		T189	Rob Hammock RC	.25
T4	Greg Vaughn	.15		T73	Rickey Henderson	.50		T190	Jorge Padilla RC	.25
T5	Greg Myers	.15		T74	Royce Clayton	.15		T191	Chris De La Cruz RC	.25
T6	Randall Simon	.15		T75	Troy O'Leary	.15		T192	Eli Whiteside RC	.25
T7	Todd Hundley	.15		T76	Ron Coomer	.15		T193	Jason Kubel RC	1.0
T8	Marlon Anderson	.15		T77	Greg Colbrunn	.15		T194	Jon Schuerholz RC	.25
T9	Jeff Reboulet	.15		T78	Wes Helms	.15		T195	Stephen Randolph RC	.25
T10	Alex Sanchez	.15		T79	Kevin Millwood	.25		T196	Andy Sisco	.75
T11	Mike Rivera	.15		T80	Damion Easley	.15		T197	Sean Smith	.15
T12	Todd Walker	.15		T81	Bobby Kielty	.15		T198	Jon-Mark Sprowl RC	.75
T13	Ray King	.15		T82	Keith Osik	.15		T199	Matt Kata RC	.40
T14	Shawn Estes	.15		T83	Ramiro Mendoza	.15		T200	Robinson Cano RC	6.00
T15	Gary Mathews Jr.	.15		T84	Shea Hillenbrand	.15		T201	Nook Logan RC	.25
T16	Jaret Wright	.15		T85	Shannon Stewart	.15		T202	Ben Francisco RC	.25
T17	Edgardo Alfonzo	.15		T86	Eddie Perez	.15		T203	Arnie Munoz RC	.15
T18	Omar Daal	.15		T87	Ugueth Urbina	.15		T204	Eric Chavez	.15
T19	Ryan Rupe	.15		T88	Orlando Palmeiro	.15		T205	Eric Riggs RC	.25
T20	Tony Clark	.15		T89	Graeme Lloyd	.15		T206	Beau Kemp RC	.25
T21	Damon Minor	.15		T90	John Vander Wal	.15		T207	Travis Wong RC	.25
T22	Mike Stanton	.15		T91	Gary Bennett	.15		T208	Dustin Yount RC	.50
T23	Ramon Martinez	.15		T92	Shane Reynolds	.15		T209	Brian McCann	4.00
T24	Armando Rios	.15		T93	Steve Parris	.15		T210	Wilton Reynolds RC	.25
T25	Johnny Estrada	.15		T94	Julio Lugo	.15		T211	Matt Bruback RC	.50
T26	Joe Girardi	.15		T95	John Halama	.15		T212	Andrew Brown RC	.25
T27	Ivan Rodriguez	.75		T96	Carlos Baerga	.15		T213	Edgar Gonzalez RC	.25
T28	Robert Fick	.15		T97	Jim Parque	.15		T214	Eider Torres RC	.25
T29	Rick White	.15		T98	Mike Williams	.15		T215	Aquilino Lopez RC	.50
T30	Robert Person	.15		T99	Fred McGriff	.25		T216	Bobby Basham RC	.50
T31	Alan Benes	.15		T100	Kenny Rogers	.15		T217	Tim Olson RC	.25
T32	Chris Carpenter	.40		T101	Matt Herges	.15		T218	Nathan Panther RC	.50
T33	Chris Widger	.15		T102	Jay Bell	.15		T219	Bryan Grace RC	.25
T34	Travis Hafner	.40		T103	Esteban Yan	.15		T220	Dusty Gomon RC	.25
T35	Mike Venafro	.15		T104	Eric Owens	.15		T221	Wilfredo Ledezma RC	.25
T36	Jon Lieber	.15		T105	Aaron Fultz	.15		T222	Josh Willingham RC	.75
T37	Orlando Hernandez	.15		T106	Rey Sanchez	.15		T223	David Cash RC	.25
T38	Aaron Myette	.15		T107	Jim Thome	.75		T224	Oscar Villarreal RC	.25
T39	Paul Bako	.15		T108	Aaron Boone	.15		T225	Jeff Duncan RC	.25
T40	Erubiel Durazo	.15		T109	Raul Mondesi	.25		T226	Kade Johnson RC	.25
T41	Mark Guthrie	.15		T110	Kenny Lofton	.25		T227	Luke Steidlmayer RC	.25
T42	Steve Avery	.15		T111	Jose Guillen	.15		T228	Brandon Watson RC	.50
T43	Damian Jackson	.15		T112	Aramis Ramirez	.40		T229	Jose Morales	.15
T44	Rey Ordonez	.15		T113	Sidney Ponson	.15		T230	Mike Gallo RC	.25
T45	John Flaherty	.15		T114	Scott Williamson	.15		T231	Tyler Adamczyk RC	.25
T46	Byung-Hyun Kim	.15		T115	Robin Ventura	.15		T232	Adam Stern	.15
T47	Tom Goodwin	.15		T116	Dusty Baker	.15		T233	Brennan King RC	.25
T48	Elmer Dessens	.15		T117	Felipe Alou	.15		T234	Dan Haren	.75
T49	Al Martin	.15		T118	Buck Showalter	.15		T235	Michel Hernandez RC	.25
T50	Gene Kingsale	.15		T119	Jack McKeon	.15		T236	Ben Fritz	.15
T51	Lenny Harris	.15		T120	Art Howe	.15		T237	Clay Hensley RC	.50
T52	David Ortiz	.75		T121	Bobby Crosby	.40		T238	Tyler Johnson RC	.25
T53	John Rocker	.15		T122	Adrian Gonzalez	.25		T239	Pete LaForest RC	.25
T54	Mike DiFelice	.15		T123	Kevin Cash	.15		T240	Tyler Martin RC	.25
T55	Nick Bierbrodt	.15		T124	Shin-Soo Choo	.25		T241	J.D. Durbin RC	.50
T56	Todd Zeile	.15		T125	Chin-Feng Chen	.25		T242	Shane Victorino RC	.25
T57	Roberto Hernandez	.15		T126	Miguel Cabrera	.75		T243	Rajai Davis RC	.50
T58	Albie Lopez	.15		T127	Jason Young	.15		T244	Ismael Castro RC	.25
T59	Roberto Alomar	.15		T128	Alex Herrera	.15		T245	Chien-Ming Wang RC	4.00
T60	Russ Ortiz	.15		T129	Jason Dubois	.15		T246	Travis Ishikawa RC	.40
T61	Brian Daubach	.15		T130	Jeff Mathis	.15		T247	Corey Shafer RC	.50
T62	Carl Everett	.15		T131	Casey Kotchman	.15		T248	Gary Schneidmiller RC	.25
T63	Jeromy Burnitz	.15		T132	Ed Rogers	.15		T249	David Pember RC	.25
T64	Mark Bellhorn	.15		T133	Wilson Betemit	.15		T250	Keith Stamler RC	.25
T65	Ruben Sierra	.15		T134	Jim Kavourias	.15		T251	Tyson Graham RC	.25
T66	Mike Fetters	.15		T135	Taylor Buchholz	.15		T252	Ryan Cameron RC	.25
T67	Armando Benitez	.15		T136	Adam LaRoche	.15		T253	Eric Eckenstahler	.15
T68	Delvi Cruz	.15		T137	Dallas McPherson	.40		T254	Matthew Peterson RC	.25
T69	Jose Cruz Jr.	.15		T138	Jesus Cota	.15		T255	Dustin McGowan RC	.50
				T139	Clint Nageotte	.15		T256	Prentice Redman RC	.40
				T140	Boof Bonser	.15		T257	Haj Turay RC	.25
				T141	Walter Young	.15		T258	Carlos Guzman RC	.25
				T142	Joe Crede	.25		T259	Matt DeMarco RC	.25
				T143	Denny Bautista	.15		T260	Derek Michaelis RC	.25
				T144	Victor Diaz	.15		T261	Brian Burgamy RC	.25
				T145	Chris Narveson	.15		T262	Jay Sitzman RC	.25
				T146	Gabe Gross	.15		T263	Chris Fallon RC	.25
				T147	Jimmy Journell	.15		T264	Mike Adams RC	.25
				T148	Rafael Soriano	.15		T265	Clint Barmes RC	.75
				T149	Jerome Williams	.15		T266	Eric Reed RC	.50
				T150	Aaron Cook	.15		T267	Willie Eyre RC	.25
				T151	Anastacio Martinez	.15		T268	Carlos Duran RC	.40
				T152	Scott Hairston	.15		T269	Nick Trzesniak RC	.25
				T153	John Buck	.15		T270	Ferdin Tejeda RC	.25
				T154	Ryan Ludwick	.15		T271	Michael Garciaparra	.25
				T155	Chris Bootcheck	.15		T272	Michael Hinckley RC	.75
				T156	John Rheinecker	.15		T273	Branden Florence RC	.25
				T157	Jason Lane	.15		T274	Trent Oeltjen RC	.40
				T158	Shelley Duncan	.15		T275	Mike Neu RC	.25
				T159	Adam Wainwright	.15				
				T160	Jason Arnold	.15				
				T161	Jonny Gomes	.15				
				T162	James Loney	.25				
				T163	Mike Fontenot	.15				
				T164	Khalil Greene	1.00				
				T165	Sean Burnett	.15				
				T166	David Martinez	.15				
				T167	Felix Pie RC	3.00				
				T168	Joe Valentine RC	.50				
				T169	Brandon Webb RC	1.50				
				T170	Matt Diaz RC	.25				
				T171	Lew Ford RC	.75				
				T172	Jeremy Griffiths	.15				
				T173	Matt Hensley RC	.50				
				T174	Charlie Manning RC	.15				
				T175	Elizardo Ramirez RC	.25				
				T176	Greg Aquino RC	.25				
				T177	Felix Sanchez RC	.50				
				T178	Kelly Shoppach RC	.25				
				T179	Bubba Nelson RC	.25				
				T180	Mike O'Keefe RC	.25				
				T181	Hanley Ramirez RC	3.00				
				T182	Todd Wellemeyer RC	.50				
				T183	Dustin Moseley RC	.15				
				T184	Eric Crozier RC	.50				
				T185	Ryan Shealy RC	1.00				
				T186	Jeremy Bonderman	2.00				

Chrome Refractor

SHANNON STEWART OF

Stars: 4-8X
Rookies: 2-4X
Inserted 1:12

KL	Kenny Lofton	10.00
FL	Felipe Lopez	6.00
FM	Fred McGriff	5.00
KM	Kevin Millar	5.00
RO	Rey Ordonez	4.00
JP	Juan Pierre	5.00
SH	Tsuyoshi Shinjo	4.00
SS	Shane Spencer	4.00
JT	Jim Thome	10.00
BT	Bubba Trammell	4.00
RW	Rondell White	4.00
PW	Preston Wilson	4.00
TZ	Todd Zeile	6.00

Stars: 5-10X
Rookies: 1-2.5X
Production 2003 Sets

Future Phenoms
NM/M

	Common Player:	4.00
RB	Rocco Baldelli	6.00
WB	Wilson Betemit	4.00
HB	Hank Blalock	6.00
WPB	Willie Bloomquist	15.00
MB	Marlon Byrd	4.00
CC	Chin-Feng Chen	20.00
CDC	Carl Crawford	6.00
TH	Travis Hafner	6.00
TAH	Trey Hodges	4.00
JM	Justin Morneau	10.00
BP	Brandon Phillips	4.00
MR	Michael Restovich	4.00
CS	Chris Snelling	4.00
MT	Mark Teixeira	8.00
JT	Joe Thurston	4.00

Hall of Fame

NM/M

	Common Player:	8.00
GC	Gary Carter	8.00
EM	Eddie Murray	15.00

Hall of Fame Dual
NM/M

	Complete Set (1):	
CM	Gary Carter, Eddie Murray	25.00

Signature Moves
NM/M

	Common Player:	8.00
EA	Erick Almonte	8.00
DB	David Bell	10.00
JB	Joe Borchard	8.00
BC	Bartolo Colon	12.00
JC	Jose Cruz Jr.	8.00
JJC	Jack Cust	10.00
RF	Robert Fick	8.00
CF	Cliff Floyd	15.00
JF	Jesse Foppert	10.00
JG	Joey Gomes	8.00
KG	Khalil Greene	25.00
JL	James Loney	20.00
VM	Victor Martinez	20.00
FP	Felix Pie	60.00
ER	Elizardo Ramirez	12.00
JR	Jose Reyes	40.00
JS	Jason Stokes	15.00
MT	Mark Teixeira	25.00
BU	B.J. Upton	25.00
WY	Walter Young	10.00

Tools of the Trade
NM/M

	Common Player:	4.00
EA	Edgardo Alfonzo	4.00
DB	David Bell	4.00
JC	Jose Cruz Jr.	4.00
ED	Erubiel Durazo	4.00
RD	Ray Durham	4.00
RF	Robert Fick	4.00
CF	Cliff Floyd	4.00
AG	Andres Galarraga	5.00
JG	Jeremy Giambi	4.00
TG	Tom Glavine	6.00
EK	Eric Karros	5.00
JK	Jeff Kent	5.00

Tools of the Trade Dual
NM/M

	Common Player:	10.00
KM	Kevin Millwood	10.00
IR	Ivan Rodriguez	15.00
JT	Jim Thome	15.00

2003 Topps Tribute

Complete Set (110):	300.00
Common Player:	1.00
Common Auto. (101-110):	35.00
Pack (5):	35.00
Box (6):	160.00

1	Jim Thome	2.50
2	Edgardo Alfonzo	1.00
3	Edgar Martinez	1.50
4	Scott Rolen	2.50
5	Eric Hinske	1.00
6	Mark Mulder	1.50
7	Jason Giambi	2.50
8	Bernie Williams	2.00
9	Cliff Floyd	1.00
10	Ichiro Suzuki	5.00
11	Pat Burrell	1.50
12	Garret Anderson	1.50
13	Gary Sheffield	1.50
14	Johnny Damon	3.00
15	Kerry Wood	1.50
16	Bartolo Colon	1.00
17	Adam Dunn	2.00
18	Omar Vizquel	1.50
19	Todd Helton	2.00
20	Nomar Garciaparra	4.00
21	A.J. Burnett	1.00
22	Craig Biggio	1.50
23	Carlos Beltran	2.50
24	Kazuhisa Ishii	1.00
25	Vladimir Guerrero	2.50
26	Roberto Alomar	2.00
27	Roger Clemens	6.00
28	Tim Hudson	2.00
29	Brian Giles	1.50
30	Barry Bonds	8.00
31	Jim Edmonds	1.50
32	Rafael Palmeiro	2.00
33	Francisco Rodriguez	1.00
34	Andruw Jones	2.00
35	Shea Hillenbrand	1.00
36	Moises Alou	1.50
37	Luis Gonzalez	1.00
38	Darin Erstad	1.00
39	John Smoltz	1.50
40	Derek Jeter	8.00
41	Aubrey Huff	1.50
42	Eric Chavez	1.50
43	Doug Mientkiewicz	1.00
44	Lance Berkman	2.00
45	Josh Beckett	1.50
46	Austin Kearns	1.50
47	Frank Thomas	2.50
48	Pedro J. Martinez	3.00
49	Tim Salmon	1.50
50	Alex Rodriguez	8.00
51	Ryan Klesko	1.00
52	Tom Glavine	1.50
53	Shawn Green	1.50
54	Jeff Kent	1.50
55	Carlos Pena	1.00
56	Paul Konerko	1.50
57	Troy Glaus	2.00
58	Manny Ramirez	2.50
59	Jason Jennings	1.00
60	Randy Johnson	3.00
61	Ivan Rodriguez	2.00
62	Roy Oswalt	1.50
63	Kevin Brown	1.50
64	Jose Vidro	1.00
65	Jorge Posada	1.50
66	Mike Piazza	5.00
67	Bret Boone	1.50
68	Carlos Delgado	2.00
69	Jimmy Rollins	2.00
70	Alfonso Soriano	3.00
71	Greg Maddux	5.00
72	Mark Prior	2.00
73	Jeff Bagwell	2.50
74	Richie Sexson	2.00
75	Sammy Sosa	4.00
76	Curt Schilling	2.00
77	Mike Sweeney	1.00
78	Torii Hunter	1.50
79	Larry Walker	1.50
80	Miguel Tejada	1.50
81	Rich Aurilia	1.00
82	Bobby Abreu	1.50
83	Phil Nevin	1.00
84	Rodrigo Lopez	1.00
85	Chipper Jones	3.00
86	Ken Griffey Jr.	5.00
87	Mike Lowell	1.00
88	Magglio Ordonez	1.50
89	Barry Zito	1.50
90	Albert Pujols	8.00
91	Corey Shafer RC	2.00
92	Dan Haren	4.00
93	Jeremy Bonderman	6.00
94	Branden Florence RC	2.00
95	Evel Bastida-Martinez RC	2.00
96	Brian Wright RC	2.00
97	Elizardo Ramirez RC	2.00
98	Michael Garciaparra RC	3.00
99	Clay Hensley RC	2.00
100	Bobby Basham RC	4.00
101	Jose Contreras RC	20.00
102	Bryan Bullington RC	15.00
103	Joey Gomes	10.00
104	Craig Brazell RC	15.00
105	Andy Marte RC	60.00
106	Hanley Ramirez RC	70.00
107	Ryan Shealy RC	30.00
108	Daryl Clark RC	10.00
109	Tyler Johnson RC	15.00
110	Ben Francisco RC	10.00

Gold Proof

Cards (1-100): No Pricing
Production 25
Autos. (101-110) are 1 of 1.

Red Proof

Stars (1-100): 2-4X
Production 225
Autos. (101-110): 1-2.5X
Production 50

Matching Marks Dual Relics
NM/M

	Common Duo:	10.00
	Premiere Proofs:	1.5X
	Production 50	
PH	Rafael Palmeiro, Rickey Henderson	15.00
GR	Nomar Garciaparra, Alex Rodriguez	25.00
AP	Roberto Alomar, Rafael Palmeiro	15.00
MP	Fred McGriff, Rafael Palmeiro	10.00
HR	Rickey Henderson, Manny Ramirez	15.00
RP	Manny Ramirez, Mike Piazza	20.00
BG	Jeff Bagwell, Juan Gonzalez	10.00
BP	Barry Bonds, Rafael Palmeiro	35.00
SB	Sammy Sosa, Jeff Bagwell	20.00
SG	Alfonso Soriano, Vladimir Guerrero	15.00
PS	Rafael Palmeiro, Sammy Sosa	20.00
MG	Fred McGriff, Juan Gonzalez	10.00
PA	Rafael Palmeiro, Roberto Alomar	15.00

Memorable Materials

NM/M

	Common Player:	8.00
	Premiere Proofs:	1.5X
	Production 50	
BB	Barry Bonds	30.00
JG	Jason Giambi	8.00
JG2	Jason Giambi	8.00
TG	Troy Glaus	8.00
LG	Luis Gonzalez	8.00
SG	Shawn Green	8.00
VG	Vladimir Guerrero	10.00
RH	Rickey Henderson	10.00
TH	Torii Hunter	8.00
AJ	Andruw Jones	8.00
GM	Greg Maddux	15.00
AP	Albert Pujols	20.00
CR	Cal Ripken Jr.	45.00
AR	Alex Rodriguez	10.00
AS	Alfonso Soriano	10.00
SS	Sammy Sosa	15.00
SS2	Sammy Sosa	15.00
MT	Miguel Tejada	8.00
KW	Kerry Wood	8.00

Milestone Materials

NM/M

	Common Player:	8.00
	Premiere Proofs:	1.5X
	Production 50	
RA	Roberto Alomar	10.00
JB1	Jeff Bagwell	10.00
JB2	Jeff Bagwell	10.00
BB1	Barry Bonds	25.00
BB2	Barry Bonds	25.00
BB3	Barry Bonds	25.00
BB4	Barry Bonds	25.00
BB5	Barry Bonds	25.00
NG	Nomar Garciaparra	20.00
JG1	Juan Gonzalez	10.00
JG2	Juan Gonzalez	10.00
VG	Vladimir Guerrero	10.00
TH	Todd Helton	10.00
RH1	Rickey Henderson	10.00
RH2	Rickey Henderson	10.00
RH3	Rickey Henderson	10.00
RH4	Rickey Henderson	10.00
RH5	Rickey Henderson	10.00
CJ	Chipper Jones	12.00
FM1	Fred McGriff	8.00
FM2	Fred McGriff	8.00
FM3	Fred McGriff	8.00
RP1	Rafael Palmeiro	10.00
RP2	Rafael Palmeiro	10.00
RP3	Rafael Palmeiro	10.00
RP4	Rafael Palmeiro	10.00
MP1	Mike Piazza	15.00
MP2	Mike Piazza	15.00
MR1	Manny Ramirez	10.00
MR2	Manny Ramirez	10.00
AR	Alex Rodriguez	15.00
SS1	Sammy Sosa	15.00
SS2	Sammy Sosa	15.00
SS3	Sammy Sosa	15.00
FT	Frank Thomas	12.00

Modern Marks Autographs
NM/M

	Common Autograph:	10.00
	Premiere Proofs:	1.5X
	Production 50	
LB	Lance Berkman	20.00
RC	Roger Clemens	120.00
CF	Cliff Floyd	10.00
EH	Eric Hinske	10.00
TH	Torii Hunter	10.00
PK	Paul Konerko	15.00
PL	Paul LoDuca	15.00
MO	Magglio Ordonez	20.00

Perennial All-Stars Relics

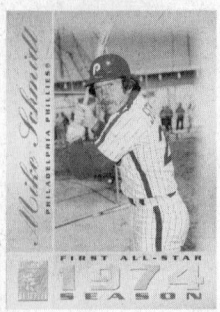

NM/M

	Common Player:	8.00
	Premiere Proofs:	1.5X
	Production 50	
RA	Roberto Alomar	10.00
CB	Craig Biggio	8.00
BB	Barry Bonds	25.00
RC	Roger Clemens	20.00
RH	Rickey Henderson	15.00
CJ	Chipper Jones	10.00
GM	Greg Maddux	15.00
EM	Edgar Martinez	15.00
PM	Pedro J. Martinez	15.00
MM	Mike Mussina	10.00
MP	Mike Piazza	20.00
MR	Manny Ramirez	10.00
AR	Alex Rodriguez	15.00
IR	Ivan Rodriguez	8.00
BS	Benito Santiago	8.00
CS	Curt Schilling	8.00
GS	Gary Sheffield	8.00
JS	John Smoltz	8.00
SS	Sammy Sosa	20.00
FT	Frank Thomas	10.00
LW	Larry Walker	10.00
BW	Bernie Williams	10.00

Performance Tribute Doubles

NM/M

	Common Duo:	10.00
	Premiere Proofs:	1.5X
	Production 50	
ZJ	Barry Zito, Randy Johnson	15.00
SA	Alfonso Soriano, Roberto Alomar	15.00
RR	Cal Ripken Jr., Alex Rodriguez	60.00
RT	Alex Rodriguez, Miguel Tejada	15.00
GG	Luis Gonzalez, Troy Glaus	10.00
PW	Albert Pujols, Kerry Wood	25.00
RG	Alex Rodriguez, Nomar Garciaparra	30.00
BJ	Barry Bonds, Chipper Jones	25.00
SG	Sammy Sosa, Juan Gonzalez	15.00
PS	Mike Piazza, Benito Santiago	15.00
PR	Mike Piazza, Ivan Rodriguez	15.00
MM	Pedro J. Martinez, Greg Maddux	15.00
CM	Roger Clemens, Greg Maddux	35.00
JP	Chipper Jones, Mike Piazza	20.00

Performance Tribute Triples

NM/M

	Common Trio:	20.00
	Premiere Proofs:	1.5X
	Production 50	
SMP	Sammy Sosa, Rafael Palmeiro, Fred McGriff	25.00
CMJ	Roger Clemens, Greg Maddux, Randy Johnson	30.00
RHP	Manny Ramirez, Mike Piazza, Rickey Henderson	30.00
STB	Sammy Sosa, Frank Thomas, Jeff Bagwell	20.00
BMP	Barry Bonds, Fred McGriff, Rafael Palmeiro	30.00

Solo Bonds
NM/M

	Premiere Proof:	1.5X
	Production 50	
SB	Barry Bonds	25.00

Double Bonds
NM/M

	Premiere Proof:	1.5X
	Production 50	
BT-DB	Barry Bonds	40.00

Triple Bonds
NM/M

	Premiere Proof:	1.5X
	Production 50	
TB	Barry Bonds	60.00

Team Tribute Doubles
NM/M

	Common Duo:	10.00
	Premiere Proofs:	1.5X
	Production 50	
MS	Greg Maddux, John Smoltz	35.00
IN	Kazuhisa Ishii, Hideo Nomo	25.00
WH	Larry Walker, Todd Helton	10.00
BB	Craig Biggio, Jeff Bagwell	15.00
RP	Alex Rodriguez, Rafael Palmeiro	15.00
GR	Nomar Garciaparra, Manny Ramirez	20.00

Team Tribute Triples

NM/M

	Common Trio:	15.00
	Premiere Proofs:	1.5X
	Production 50	
JSJ	Andruw Jones, Gary Sheffield, Chipper Jones	30.00
GRM	Nomar Garciaparra, Manny Ramirez, Pedro J. Martinez	40.00
ASP	Moises Alou, Sammy Sosa, Corey Patterson	30.00
TOK	Frank Thomas, Magglio Ordonez, Paul Konerko	20.00
BBB	Craig Biggio, Lance Berkman, Jeff Bagwell	20.00
MHM	Joe Mauer, Torii Hunter, Doug Mientkiewicz	25.00
SGV	Alfonso Soriano, Jason Giambi, Robin Ventura	25.00
CTM	Eric Chavez, Miguel Tejada, Mark Mulder	25.00
HZM	Tim Hudson, Barry Zito, Mark Mulder	25.00
TBB	Jim Thome, Marlon Byrd, Pat Burrell	25.00
MOB	Edgar Martinez, John Olerud, Bret Boone	20.00
PER	Albert Pujols, Jim Edmonds, Scott Rolen	40.00
RGP	Alex Rodriguez, Juan Gonzalez, Rafael Palmeiro	25.00
RBT	Alex Rodriguez, Hank Blalock, Mark Teixeira	25.00

Tribute to the Stars
NM/M

	Common Player:	10.00
	Premiere Proofs:	1.5X
	Production 50	
RA	Roberto Alomar	15.00
GA	Garret Anderson	15.00
LB	Lance Berkman	10.00
BB	Barry Bonds	50.00
PB	Pat Burrell	15.00

Code	Player	NM/M
EC	Eric Chavez	15.00
AD	Adam Dunn	15.00
NG	Nomar Garciaparra	40.00
TG	Troy Glaus	15.00
VG	Vladimir Guerrero	15.00
TH	Todd Helton	15.00
RH	Rickey Henderson	15.00
THU	Torii Hunter	10.00
AJ	Andruw Jones	10.00
CJ	Chipper Jones	15.00
GM	Greg Maddux	20.00
RP	Rafael Palmeiro	10.00
MP	Mike Piazza	20.00
AP	Albert Pujols	40.00
AR	Alex Rodriguez	30.00
AS	Alfonso Soriano	15.00
SS	Sammy Sosa	25.00
FT	Frank Thomas	15.00
JT	Jim Thome	15.00
LW	Larry Walker	10.00

Tribute to the Stars Patchworks

NM/M
Common Player: 25.00
Production 50 Sets

Code	Player	Price
JB	Jeff Bagwell	35.00
BB	Barry Bonds	80.00
NG	Nomar Garciaparra	50.00
LG	Luis Gonzalez	25.00
SG	Shawn Green	25.00
TH	Todd Helton	35.00
THU	Torii Hunter	25.00
RJ	Randy Johnson	40.00
CJ	Chipper Jones	35.00
GM	Greg Maddux	50.00
PM	Pedro J. Martinez	40.00
RP	Rafael Palmeiro	30.00
AP	Albert Pujols	80.00
MR	Manny Ramirez	35.00
AR	Alex Rodriguez	50.00
AR2	Alex Rodriguez	40.00
CS	Curt Schilling	25.00
SS	Sammy Sosa	40.00
FT	Frank Thomas	35.00
KW	Kerry Wood	30.00

40/40 Club

NM/M
Première Proof: 1.5X
Production 50

Code	Player	Price
CBR	Jose Canseco, Barry Bonds, Alex Rodriguez	85.00

600 HR Club Relic

NM/M
Premiere Proofs: 1.5X
Production 50
Gold: No Pricing
Production One Set

Code	Player	Price
HA-600	Hank Aaron	35.00
BB-600	Barry Bonds	30.00
WM-600	Willie Mays	45.00
BR-600	Babe Ruth	125.00

600 HR Club Double Relic

NM/M
Premiere Proofs: 1.5X
Production 50

Code	Player	Price
BA-600	Barry Bonds, Hank Aaron	80.00
BA-600	Barry Bonds, Willie Mays	80.00
BA-600	Barry Bonds, Babe Ruth	200.00

600 HR Club Quad Relic

NM/M
Premiere Proof: 1X
Production 25

Code	Player	Price
BA-600	Hank Aaron, Babe Ruth, Willie Mays, Barry Bonds	625.00

All-Star Edition

NM/M
Complete Set (50): 50.00
Common Player: 1.00
Pack (5): 40.00
Box (6): 200.00

#	Player	Price
1	Willie Mays	8.00
2	Don Mattingly	8.00
3	Hoyt Wilhelm	1.00
4	Hank Aaron	8.00
5	Hank Greenberg	1.00
6	Johnny Bench	5.00
7	Duke Snider	3.00
8	Carl Yastrzemski	3.00
9	Jim Palmer	1.00
10	Roberto Clemente	8.00
11	Mike Schmidt	8.00
12	Joe Cronin	1.00
13	Lou Brock	1.00
14	Orlando Cepeda	1.00
15	Bill Mazeroski	1.00
16	Whitey Ford	3.00
17	Rod Carew	1.00
18	Joe Morgan	1.00
19	Luis Aparicio	1.00
20	Nolan Ryan	10.00
21	Bobby Doerr	1.00
22	Dale Murphy	2.00
23	Bob Feller	1.00
24	Paul Molitor	2.00
25	Tom Seaver	3.00
26	Ozzie Smith	1.00
27	Stan Musial	6.00
28	Willie McCovey	1.00
29	Gary Carter	1.00
30	Reggie Jackson	3.00
31	Gaylord Perry	1.00
32	George Brett	8.00
33	Rocky Colavito	1.00
34	Wade Boggs	2.00
35	Cal Ripken Jr.	8.00
36	Carlton Fisk	1.00
37	Al Kaline	3.00
38	Kirby Puckett	4.00
39	Phil Rizzuto	2.00
40	Willie Stargell	1.00
41	Harmon Killebrew	3.00
42	Red Schoendienst	1.00
43	Tony Gwynn	3.00
44	Ralph Kiner	1.00
45	Yogi Berra	4.00
46	Jim "Catfish" Hunter	1.00
47	Frank Robinson	2.00
48	Ernie Banks	4.00
49	Warren Spahn	2.00
50	Brooks Robinson	3.00

All-Star Edition Premier Proof

Cards (1-50): 4-8X
Numbered to last two digits of 1st All-Star Year.

All-Star Edition All-Star Signing

NM/M
Common Autograph: 40.00
Premier Proofs: 1.5-2X
Production 25 Sets

Code	Player	Price
LB	Lou Brock	50.00
GC	Gary Carter	40.00
OC	Orlando Cepeda	40.00
AD	Andre Dawson	40.00
TG	Tony Gwynn	80.00
AK	Al Kaline	75.00
DMA	Don Mattingly	125.00
DM	Dale Murphy	75.00
JP	Jim Palmer	40.00
MS	Mike Schmidt	100.00
DSN	Duke Snider	45.00

A-S Edition Memorable Match-up Relic

NM/M
Common Card: 50.00
Production 150 Sets
Premier Proofs: 1.5-2X
Production 25 Sets

Code	Players	Price
YB	Carl Yastrzemski, Johnny Bench	70.00
BS	George Brett, Mike Schmidt	120.00
MJ	Willie Mays, Reggie Jackson	65.00
BF	Johnny Bench, Carlton Fisk	50.00
CM	Gary Carter, Don Mattingly	85.00
KA	Harmon Killebrew, Hank Aaron	125.00
BG	Wade Boggs, Tony Gwynn	60.00
PG	Kirby Puckett, Tony Gwynn	60.00
YBR	Carl Yastrzemski, Lou Brock	60.00

All-Star Edition Perennial Patch Relics

NM/M
Common Player: 40.00
Production 30 Sets

Code	Player	Price
WB	Wade Boggs	75.00
GB	George Brett	220.00
GC	Gary Carter	40.00
TG	Tony Gwynn	125.00
HK	Harmon Killebrew	90.00
WM	Willie McCovey	40.00
JM	Joe Morgan	40.00
DMU	Dale Murphy	120.00
CR	Cal Ripken Jr.	225.00
NR	Nolan Ryan/Rangers	200.00
NRA	Nolan Ryan/Astros	200.00
MS	Mike Schmidt	200.00
OS	Ozzie Smith	120.00
WS	Willie Stargell	75.00
CY	Carl Yastrzemski	190.00

All-Star Edition Tribute Relics

NM/M
Common Player: 10.00
Inserted 1:1

Code	Player	Price
HA	Hank Aaron	35.00
LA	Luis Aparicio	10.00
EB	Ernie Banks	20.00
JBE	Johnny Bench	20.00
YB	Yogi Berra	40.00
WB	Wade Boggs	15.00
GB	George Brett	20.00
LB	Lou Brock/bat	30.00
LBU	Lou Brock/Jsy	15.00
RCA	Roy Campanella	20.00
ROD	Rod Carew	15.00
GC	Gary Carter	10.00
OC	Orlando Cepeda	12.00
RC	Roberto Clemente	60.00
TC	Ty Cobb	100.00
JCR	Joe Cronin	15.00
AD	Andre Dawson	10.00
DD	Dizzy Dean	40.00
BD	Bobby Doerr	10.00
BF	Bob Feller	15.00
CF	Carlton Fisk	15.00
WF	Whitey Ford	30.00
JF	Jimmie Foxx	15.00
LG	Lou Gehrig	125.00
HG	Hank Greenberg	40.00
TG	Tony Gwynn	20.00
RH	Rogers Hornsby	20.00
CH	Jim "Catfish" Hunter	20.00
RJ	Reggie Jackson	15.00
AK	Al Kaline	25.00
HK	Harmon Killebrew	20.00
NL	Napoleon Lajoie	60.00
EM	Eddie Mathews	15.00
DMA	Don Mattingly	30.00
WM	Willie Mays	40.00
BM	Bill Mazeroski	20.00
WMC	Willie McCovey	18.00
JMI	Johnny Mize	30.00
PM.	Paul Molitor	15.00
JMO	Joe Morgan	30.00
TM	Thurman Munson	30.00
DM	Dale Murphy	50.00
SM	Stan Musial	30.00
DN	Don Newcombe	10.00
MO	Mel Ott	30.00
JP	Jim Palmer	20.00
KP	Kirby Puckett	20.00
CRB	Cal Ripken Jr.	40.00
PR	Phil Rizzuto	15.00
BRO	Brooks Robinson	15.00
FR	Frank Robinson	10.00
JR	Jackie Robinson	40.00
BR	Babe Ruth	140.00
NR	Nolan Ryan/Rangers	40.00
NRA	Nolan Ryan/Astros	40.00
MS	Mike Schmidt	20.00
RS	Red Schoendienst	15.00
TSE	Tom Seaver	25.00
OS	Ozzie Smith	15.00
DSN	Duke Snider	20.00
TS	Tris Speaker	75.00
WST	Willie Stargell	20.00
HW	Honus Wagner	125.00
WHI	Hoyt Wilhelm	10.00
CY	Carl Yastrzemski	30.00

All-Star Edition 1st Class Cuts

NM/M
Production One Set

Code	Player	Price
FC-TC	Ty Cobb (3/03 auction)	7,600
FC-JR	Jackie Robinson (3/03 auction)	3,500
FC-BR	Babe Ruth (6/04 auction)	7,300

World Series

NM/M
Complete Set (150): 150.00
Common Player: 1.00
Pack (5): 50.00
Box (6): 260.00

#	Player	Price
1	Willie Mays	8.00
2	Gary Carter	1.50
3	Yogi Berra	1.50
4	Dennis Eckersley	1.50
5	Willie McCovey	1.50
6	Willie Stargell	1.00
7	Mike Schmidt	8.00
8	Robin Yount	1.00
9	Bucky Harris	1.00
10	Carl Yastrzemski	4.00
11	Lenny Dykstra	1.00
12	Boog Powell	1.00
13	Bill Lee	1.00
14	Lou Brock	1.50
15	Bob Friend	1.00
16	Hank Greenberg	1.50
17	Maury Wills	1.00
18	Tommy Lasorda	1.00
19	Bill "Moose" Skowron	1.00
20	Frank Robinson	2.00
21	Rollie Fingers	1.00
22	Doug DeCinces	1.00
23	Eric Davis	1.00
24	Johnny Podres	1.00
25	Darrell Evans	1.00
26	Ron Cey	1.00
27	Ray Knight	1.00
28	Don Larsen	1.00
29	Harold Baines	1.00
30	Brooks Robinson	4.00
31	Wade Boggs	2.00
32	Joe Morgan	1.00
33	Kirk Gibson	1.00
34	Tommy John	1.00
35	Monte Irvin	2.00
36	Rich "Goose" Gossage	1.00
37	Tug McGraw	1.00
38	Walt Weiss	1.00
39	Bill Madlock	1.00
40	Juan Marichal	2.00
41	Willie McGee	1.00
42	Joe Cronin	1.00
43	Paul Blair	1.00
44	Norm Cash	1.00
45	Ken Griffey Sr.	1.00
46	Bret Saberhagen	1.00
47	Don Sutton	1.00
48	Kirby Puckett	4.00
49	Keith Hernandez	1.00
50	George Brett	8.00
51	Bobby Richardson	1.00
52	Jose Canseco	2.00
53	Greg Luzinski	1.00
54	Bill Mazeroski	1.00
55	Red Schoendienst	1.00
56	Graig Nettles	1.00
57	Jerry Koosman	1.00
58	Tony Perez	1.00
59	Jim Rice	1.00
60	Duke Snider	4.00
61	David Justice	1.00
62	Johnny Sain	1.00
63	Chuck Klein	1.00
64	Sparky Anderson	1.00
65	Alan Trammell	2.00
66	Willie Wilson	1.00
67	Hoyt Wilhelm	1.00
68	Joe Pepitone	1.00
69	Darren Daulton	1.00
70	Tom Seaver	4.00
71	Jim "Catfish" Hunter	1.00
72	Tim McCarver	1.00
73	Dave Parker	1.00
74	Earl Weaver	1.00
75	Ted Kluszewski	1.00
76	John Kruk	1.00
77	Dwight Evans	1.00
78	Ron Darling	1.00
79	Tony Oliva	1.00
80	Johnny Bench	5.00
81	Sam Crawford	1.00
82	Steve Yeager	1.00
83	Paul Molitor	2.00
84	Bert Campaneris	1.00
85	Mickey Rivers	1.00
86	Vince Coleman	1.00
87	Kent Tekulve	1.00
88	Dwight Gooden	1.00
89	Whitey Herzog	1.00
90	Whitey Ford	4.00
91	Warren Spahn	3.00
92	Fred Lynn	1.00
93	Joe Tinker	1.00
94	Bill Buckner	1.00
95	Bob Feller	2.00
96	Hank Bauer	1.00
97	Joe Rudi	1.00
98	Steve Sax	1.00
99	Bruce Sutter	1.50
100	Nolan Ryan	10.00
101	Bobby Thomson	1.00
102	Bob Watson	1.00
103	Vida Blue	1.00
104	Robin Roberts	1.00
105	Orlando Cepeda	2.00
106	Jim Bottomley	1.00
107	Heinie Manush	1.00
108	Jim Gilliam	1.00
109	Dave Concepcion	1.00
110	Al Kaline	5.00
111	Howard Johnson	1.00
112	Phil Rizzuto	2.00
113	Steve Garvey	1.00
114	George Foster	1.00
115	Carlton Fisk	2.00
116	Don Newcombe	1.00
117	Lance Parrish	1.00
118	Reggie Jackson	4.00
119	Luis Aparicio	1.00
120	Jim Palmer	1.50
121	Ron Guidry	1.00
122	Frankie Frisch	1.00
123	Chet Lemon	1.00
124	Cecil Cooper	1.00
125	Harmon Killebrew	4.00
126	Luis Tiant	1.00
127	John McGraw	1.00
128	Paul O'Neill	1.00
129	Jack Clark	1.00
130	Stan Musial	6.00
131	Mike Schmidt	1.00
132	Kirby Puckett	2.00
133	Carlton Fisk	1.50
134	Bill Mazeroski	1.00
135	Johnny Podres	1.00
136	Robin Yount	1.00
137	David Justice	1.00
138	Bobby Thomson	1.00
139	Joe Carter	1.00
140	Reggie Jackson	1.50
141	Kirk Gibson	1.00
142	Whitey Ford	1.50
143	Don Larsen	1.00
144	Duke Snider	1.50
145	Carl Yastrzemski	1.50
146	Johnny Bench	2.00
147	Lou Brock	1.00
148	Ted Kluszewski	1.00
149	Jim Palmer	1.00
150	Willie Mays	5.00

World Series Gold

Golds (1-150): 4-8X
Production 100 Sets

World Series Tribute Relic

NM/M
Common Player: 10.00
Production 425 unless noted.
Golds: No Pricing
Production 25

Code	Player	Price
HA	Hank Aaron/50	60.00
HB	Hank Bauer/50	30.00
JBE	Johnny Bench	25.00
YB	Yogi Berra	20.00
WB	Wade Boggs	15.00
JB	Jim Bottomley/50	30.00
GB	George Brett	25.00
LB	Lou Brock	15.00
JC	Jose Canseco	10.00
NC	Norm Cash/50	25.00
OC	Orlando Cepeda/50	30.00
RC	Roberto Clemente/50	120.00
TC	Ty Cobb	120.00
SC	Sam Crawford/50	50.00
CF	Carlton Fisk	40.00
JF	Jimmie Foxx/50	80.00
FF	Frankie Frisch	15.00
LG	Lou Gehrig	185.00
HG	Hank Greenberg/50	60.00
TG	Tony Gwynn	25.00
BH	Bucky Harris	10.00
RH	Rogers Hornsby	35.00
CH	Jim "Catfish" Hunter	15.00
RJ	Reggie Jackson	25.00
HK	Harmon Killebrew	25.00
CK	Chuck Klein	10.00
TK	Ted Kluszewski	15.00
HM	Heinie Manush/50	35.00
JM	Juan Marichal	25.00
RM	Roger Maris/50	75.00
BMA	Billy Martin	15.00
WM	Willie Mays	50.00
BM	Bill Mazeroski	15.00
WMC	Willie McCovey	15.00
TM	Thurman Munson	30.00
SM	Stan Musial	30.00
KP	Kirby Puckett	20.00
CR	Cal Ripken Jr.	35.00
FR	Frank Robinson	15.00
JR	Jackie Robinson	40.00
ER	Edd Roush/50	15.00
BR	Babe Ruth	140.00
MS	Mike Schmidt	25.00
RS	Red Schoendienst	15.00
TS	Tom Seaver	15.00
OS	Ozzie Smith	20.00
TSP	Tris Speaker	90.00
WS	Willie Stargell/50	25.00
BT	Bobby Thomson	15.00
JT	Joe Tinker	30.00
HW	Honus Wagner/50	150.00
CY	Carl Yastrzemski	30.00
RY	Robin Yount	20.00

World Series Autographed Relic

NM/M
Inserted 1:55
Golds: No Pricing
Production 25 Sets

Code	Player	Price
LB	Lou Brock	40.00
JC	Jose Canseco	40.00
CF	Carlton Fisk	120.00
HK	Harmon Killebrew	75.00
WM	Willie Mays	275.00
BM	Bill Mazeroski	60.00
MS	Mike Schmidt	100.00
BT	Bobby Thomson	40.00

World Series Cut Signature Relic

No pricing due to scarcity.
Production One Set

World Series Fan Fare Relic

NM/M
Common Player: 10.00
Inserted 1:Box

Code	Player	Price
HB	Hank Bauer	10.00
YB	Yogi Berra	20.00
WF	Whitey Ford	15.00
DJ	David Justice	10.00
DL	Don Larsen	15.00
BM	Billy Martin	10.00
DN	Don Newcombe	10.00

1457 · Relic

PO	Paul O'Neill	15.00
JP	Johnny Podres	15.00
PR	Phil Rizzuto	15.00
MS	Bill "Moose" Skowron	10.00
DS	Duke Snider	15.00

World Series Memorabilia Match-Up Relic

NM/M
Common Player:
Varying quantities produced

GF	Hank Greenberg, Frankie Frisch/34	90.00
GK	Hank Greenberg, Chuck Klein/35	90.00
PR	Phil Rizzuto, Willie Mays/51	150.00
FS	Whitey Ford, Duke Snider/53	75.00
AS	Luis Aparicio, Duke Snider/59	35.00
MF	Bill Mazeroski, Whitey Ford/60	50.00
KB	Al Kaline, Lou Brock/68	75.00
RS	Frank Robinson, Tom Seaver/69	40.00
RBE	Brooks Robinson, Johnny Bench/70	55.00
AM	Sparky Anderson, Billy Martin/76	25.00
SP	Willie Stargell, Jim Palmer/79	40.00
SB	Mike Schmidt, George Brett/80	80.00
SY	Ozzie Smith, Robin Yount/82	50.00
SRI	Mike Schmidt, Cal Ripken Jr./83	120.00
TG	Alan Trammell, Tony Gwynn/84	50.00
WB	Mookie Wilson, Bill Buckner/86	40.00
EG	Dennis Eckersley, Kirk Gibson/88	35.00

World Series Pastime Patches Relics

No pricing due to scarcity.
Production 15 Sets

World Series Series Signatures

NM/M
Common Autograph: 25.00
Golds: No Pricing
Production 25

SA	Sparky Anderson	25.00
JC	Joe Carter	25.00
WF	Whitey Ford	60.00
SG	Steve Garvey	25.00
KG	Kirk Gibson	30.00
DJ	David Justice	40.00
AK	Al Kaline	50.00
DN	Don Newcombe	40.00
JP	Jim Palmer	30.00
BR	Brooks Robinson	75.00
MS	Bill "Moose" Skowron	25.00
AT	Alan Trammell	25.00
EW	Earl Weaver	25.00
MW	Maury Wills	25.00
MWI	Mookie Wilson	30.00

World Series Team Tribute Relic

NM/M
Common Card: 15.00
Production 275 unless noted.

	Carl Yastrzemski, Fred Lynn, Carlton Fisk	50.00
OSD	Paul O'Neill, Chris Sabo, Eric Davis	25.00
FPG	George Foster, Tony Perez, Ken Griffey Jr.	25.00
CPM	Dave Concepcion, Tony Perez, Joe Morgan	50.00
KCA	Al Kaline, Norm Cash	40.00
TA	Alan Trammell, Sparky Anderson	15.00
GT	Kirk Gibson, Alan Trammell	25.00
SB	Bret Saberhagen, George Brett	40.00
CYG	Ron Cey, Steve Yeager, Steve Garvey	30.00
YM	Robin Yount, Paul Molitor	40.00
SRK	Tom Seaver, Nolan Ryan, Jerry Koosman	50.00
HCD	Keith Hernandez, Gary Carter, Lenny Dykstra	30.00
GB	Lou Gehrig, Babe Ruth/25	500.00
EC	Dennis Eckersley, Jose Canseco	25.00
HJ	Jim "Catfish" Hunter, Reggie Jackson	30.00
SPM	Willie Stargell, Dave Parker, Bill Madlock	30.00
CM	Orlando Cepeda, Juan Marichal	30.00
MM	Willie Mays, Willie McCovey	50.00
SMC	Ozzie Smith, Willie McGee, Vince Coleman	40.00

World Series Tribute Singles

NM/M
Common Player: 8.00
Premiere Proofs: 1.5X
Production 50

TG	Troy Glaus	8.00
MR	Mariano Rivera	10.00

World Series Tribute Doubles

NM/M
Common Duo: 10.00
Premiere Proofs: 1.5X
Production 50

PP	Jorge Posada, Andy Pettitte	15.00
WO	Bernie Williams, Paul O'Neill	15.00
LP	John Lackey, Troy Percival	10.00
SJ	Curt Schilling, Randy Johnson	15.00
BG	Barry Bonds, Troy Glaus	35.00
WG	Bernie Williams, Luis Gonzalez	10.00
PC	Mike Piazza, Roger Clemens	35.00

World Series Tribute Triples

NM/M
Common Trio: 15.00
Premiere Proofs: 1.5X
Production 50

LGP	John Lackey, Troy Glaus, Troy Percival	15.00
EGS	Darin Erstad, Troy Glaus, Tim Salmon	15.00

2003 Topps 205

NM/M
Complete Set (335): 150.00
Common Player: .20
SP's inserted 1:5
25 variations in base set and minis
Mini-Cards(316-335):
Exclusive Mini Cards
Price for minis (316-335) are Polar Bear
Series 1 or 2 Pack (8): 4.00
Series 1 or 2 Box (20): 65.00

#	Player	Price
1	Barry Bonds	2.50
1	Barry Bonds/Variation	3.00
2	Bret Boone	.40
3	Albert Pujols	2.00
3	Albert Pujols/Variation	2.00
4	Carl Crawford	.20
5	Bartolo Colon	.20
6	Cliff Floyd	.20
7	John Olerud	.40
8	Jason Giambi	.50
8	Jason Giambi/Variation	.75
9	Edgardo Alfonzo	.20
10	Ivan Rodriguez	.50
11	Jim Edmonds	.50
12	Mike Piazza	1.50
12	Mike Piazza/Variation	1.50
13	Greg Maddux	1.50
14	Jose Vidro	.20
15	Vladimir Guerrero	.75
15	Vladimir Guerrero/Variation	1.00
16	Bernie Williams	.50
17	Roger Clemens	2.00
18	Miguel Tejada	.50
18	Miguel Tejada/Variation	.75
19	Carlos Delgado	.40
20	Alfonso Soriano	.75
20	Alfonso Soriano/Variation	.75
21	Bobby Cox	.20
22	Mike Scioscia	.20
23	John Smoltz	.40
24	Luis Gonzalez	.40
25	Shawn Green	.40
26	Raul Ibanez	.20
27	Andruw Jones	.50
28	Josh Beckett	.40
29	Derek Lowe	.20
30	Todd Helton	.75
31	Barry Larkin	.40
32	Jason Jennings	.20
33	Darin Erstad	.40
34	Magglio Ordonez	.40
35	Mike Sweeney	.20
36	Kazuhisa Ishii	.20
37	Ron Gardenhire	.20
38	Tim Hudson	.40
39	Tim Salmon	.50
40	Pat Burrell	.40
40	Pat Burrell/Variation	.50
41	Manny Ramirez	.75
42	Nick Johnson	.40
43	Tom Glavine	.40
44	Mark Mulder	.20
45	Brian Jordan	.20
46	Rafael Palmeiro	.50
47	Vernon Wells	.40
48	Bob Brenly	.20
49	C.C. Sabathia	.40
50	Alex Rodriguez	2.50
50	Alex Rodriguez/Variation	2.50
51	Sammy Sosa	1.50
51	Sammy Sosa/Variation	2.00
52	Paul Konerko	.40
53	Craig Biggio	.40
54	Moises Alou	.40
55	Johnny Damon	.40
56	Torii Hunter	.40
57	Omar Vizquel	.40
58	Orlando Hernandez	.20
59	Barry Zito	.40
60	Lance Berkman	.50
61	Carlos Beltran	.50
62	Edgar Renteria	.40
63	Ben Sheets	.40
64	Doug Mientkiewicz	.20
65	Troy Glaus	.50
66	Preston Wilson	.20
67	Kerry Wood	.75
68	Frank Thomas	.75
69	Jimmy Rollins	.40
70	Brian Giles	.40
71	Bobby Higginson	.20
72	Larry Walker	.40
73	Randy Johnson	1.00
74	Tony LaRussa	.20
75	Derek Jeter	3.00
75	Derek Jeter/Variation	3.00
76	Bobby Abreu	.40
77	Adam Dunn	.75
77	Adam Dunn/Variation	.75
78	Ryan Klesko	.20
79	Francisco Rodriguez	.40
80	Scott Rolen	.75
81	Roberto Alomar	.50
82	Joe Torre	.50
83	Jim Thome	.75
84	Kevin Millwood	.40
85	J.T. Snow	.20
86	Trevor Hoffman	.20
87	Jay Gibbons	.20
88	Mark Prior	1.00
88	Mark Prior/Variation	1.50
89	Rich Aurilia	.20
90	Chipper Jones	1.00
91	Richie Sexson	.50
92	Gary Sheffield	.50
93	Pedro J. Martinez	1.00
94	Rodrigo Lopez	.20
95	Al Leiter	.20
96	Jorge Posada	.20
97	Luis Castillo	.20
98	Aubrey Huff	.20
99	A.J. Pierzynski	.20
100	Ichiro Suzuki	2.00
100	Ichiro Suzuki/Variation	2.00
101	Eric Chavez	.40
102	Brett Myers	.20
103	Jason Kendall	.40
104	Jeff Kent	.40
105	Eric Hinske	.20
106	Jacque Jones	.20
107	Phil Nevin	.20
108	Roy Oswalt	.40
109	Curt Schilling	.75
110	Nomar Garciaparra	2.00
110	Nomar Garciaparra/Variation	2.00
111	Garret Anderson	.40
112	Eric Gagne	.40
113	Javier Vazquez	.40
114	Jeff Bagwell	.75
115	Mike Lowell	.40
116	Carlos Pena	.20
117	Ken Griffey Jr.	1.50
118	Tony Batista	.20
119	Edgar Martinez	.20
120	Austin Kearns	.50
121	Jason Stokes	.50
122	Jose Reyes	.50
123	Rocco Baldelli	.40
124	Joe Borchard	.20
125	Joe Mauer	.40
126	Gavin Floyd	.20
127	Mark Teixeira	.50
128	Jeremy Guthrie	.20
129	B.J. Upton	.40
130	Khalil Greene	2.00
131	Hanley Ramirez RC	3.00
132	Andy Marte RC	3.00
133	J.D. Durbin RC	1.00
134	Jason Kubel RC	2.00
135	Craig Brazell RC	.75
136	Bryan Bullington RC	1.00
137	Jose Contreras RC	1.00
138	Brian Burgamy RC	.75
139	Evel Bastida-Martinez RC	.50
140	Joey Gomes	1.00
141	Ismael Castro RC	.75
142	Travis Wong RC	.75
143	Michael Garciaparra	.50
144	Arnaldo Munoz RC	.20
145	Louis Sockalexis	2.00
146	Dick Hoblitzell	1.00
147	George "Peaches" Graham	.50
148	Hal Chase	.50
149	John McGraw	1.00
150	Bobby Wallace	.50
151	Dave Shean	.20
152	Dick Hoblitzell/SP	3.00
153	Hal Chase	.20
154	George Wiltse	.20
155	George Brett	2.00
156	Willie Mays	3.00
157	Honus Wagner/SP	4.00
158	Nolan Ryan	1.00
159	Reggie Jackson	1.00
160	Mike Schmidt	1.50
161	Josh Barfield	.40
162	Grady Sizemore	.40
163	Justin Morneau	.40
164	Laynce Nix	.20
165	Zack Greinke	.50
166	Victor Martinez	.50
167	Jeff Mathis	.20
168	Casey Kotchman	.20
169	Gabe Gross	.20
170	Edwin Jackson RC	1.50
171	Delmon Young/SP RC	10.00
172	Eric Duncan/SP	2.00
173	Brian Snyder/SP	1.00
174	Chris Lubanski/SP RC	4.00
175	Ryan Harvey/SP RC	5.00
176	Nicholas Markakis/SP RC	6.00
177	Chad Billingsley/SP RC	3.00
178	Elizardo Ramirez	.20
179	Ben Francisco	.20
180	Franklin Gutierrez/SP RC	.20
181	Aaron Hill/SP	2.00
182	Kevin Correia	.20
183	Kelly Shoppach/SP RC	.75
184	Felix Pie/SP RC	5.00
185	Adam Loewen/SP RC	5.00
186	Danny Garcia	.20
187	Rickie Weeks/SP RC	8.00
188	Robby Hammock/SP	2.00
189	Ryan Wagner/SP RC	2.00
190	Matt Kata/SP	1.50
191	Bo Hart/SP RC	.20
192	Brandon Webb/SP RC	3.00
193	Bengie Molina	.20
194	Junior Spivey	.20
195	Gary Sheffield	.50
196	Jason Johnson	.20
197	David Ortiz	.75
198	Roberto Alomar	.50
199	Wily Mo Pena	.20
200	Sammy Sosa	2.00
201	Jay Payton	.20
202	Dmitri Young	.20
203	Derek Lee	.40
204	Jeff Bagwell	.75
204	Jeff Bagwell/Variation	.75
205	Runelvys Hernandez	.20
206	Kevin Brown	.40
207	Wes Helms	.20
208	Eddie Guardado	.20
209	Orlando Cabrera	.20
210	Alfonso Soriano	.75
211	Ty Wigginton	.20
212	Rich Harden	.40
212	Rich Harden/Variation	.50
213	Mike Lieberthal	.20
214	Brian Giles	.40
215	Jason Schmidt	.40
216	Jamie Moyer	.20
217	Matt Morris	.20
218	Victor Zambrano	.20
219	Roy Halladay	.50
220	Mike Hampton	.20
221	Kevin Millar	.20
222	Hideo Nomo	.50
223	Milton Bradley	.20
224	Jose Guillen	.20
225	Derek Jeter	3.00
226	Rondell White	.20
227	Hank Blalock	.50
227	Hank Blalock/Variation	.50
228	Shigetoshi Hasegawa	.20
229	Mike Mussina	.50
230	Cristian Guzman	.20
231	Todd Helton	.75
231	Todd Helton/Variation	.75
232	Kenny Lofton	.40
233	Carl Everett	.20
234	Shea Hillenbrand	.20
235	Brad Fullmer	.20
236	Bernie Williams	.50
237	Vicente Padilla	.20
238	Tim Worrell	.20
239	Juan Gonzalez	.40
240	Ichiro Suzuki	2.00
241	Aaron Boone	.20
242	Shannon Stewart	.20
243	Barry Zito	.40
243	Barry Zito/Variation	.40
244	Reggie Sanders	.20
245	Scott Podsednik	.40
246	Miguel Cabrera	.75
247	Angel Berroa	.20
248	Carlos Zambrano	.20
249	Marlon Byrd	.20
250	Mark Prior	1.00
251	Esteban Loaiza	.20
252	David Eckstein	.20
253	Alex Cintron	.20
254	Melvin Mora	.20
255	Russ Ortiz	.20
256	Carlos Lee	.20
257	Tino Martinez	.20
258	Randy Wolf	.20
259	Jason Phillips	.20
260	Vladimir Guerrero	1.00
261	Brad Wilkerson	.20
262	Ivan Rodriguez	.75
263	Matt Lawton	.20
264	Adam Dunn	.50
265	Joe Borowski	.20
266	Jody Gerut	.20
267	Alex Rodriguez	2.50
268	Brendan Donnelly	.20
269	Randy Johnson	.40
269	Randy Johnson/Variation	1.00
270	Nomar Garciaparra	2.50
271	Javy Lopez	.50
272	Travis Hafner	.20
273	Juan Pierre	.20
274	Morgan Ensberg	.20
275	Albert Pujols	2.00
276	Jason LaRue	.20
277	Paul LoDuca	.20
278	Andy Pettitte	.50
279	Mike Piazza	1.50
280	Jim Thome	1.00
280	Jim Thome/Variation	1.00
281	Marquis Grissom	.20
282	Woody Williams	.20
283	Curt Schilling	.75
283	Curt Schilling/Variation	.75
284	Chipper Jones	1.00
284	Chipper Jones/Variation	1.00
285	Deivi Cruz	.20
286	Johnny Damon	.50
287	Chin-Hui Tsao	.20
288	Alex Gonzalez	.20
289	Billy Wagner	.40
290	Jason Giambi	.50
291	Keith Foulke	.20
292	Jerome Williams	.20
293	Livan Hernandez	.20
294	Aaron Guiel	.20
295	Randall Simon	.20
296	Byung-Hyun Kim	.20
297	Jorge Julio	.20
298	Miguel Batista	.20
299	Rafael Furcal	.40
300	Dontrelle Willis/SP	1.00
300	Dontrelle Willis/Variation	1.00
301	Alex Sanchez	.20
302	Shawn Chacon	.20
303	Matt Clement	.20
304	Luis Matos	.20
305	Steve Finley	.20
306	Marcus Giles	.40
307	David Wells	.20
308	Jeromy Burnitz	.20
309	Mike MacDougal	.20
310	Mariano Rivera	.40
311	Adrian Beltre	.40
312	Mark Loretta	.20
313	Ugueth Urbina	.20
314	Bill Mueller	.20
315	Johan Santana	.50
316	Willie Mays	2.00
317	Delmon Young	4.00
318	Rickie Weeks	4.00
319	Ryan Wagner	.50
320	Brandon Webb	.50
321	Chris Lubanski	1.00
322	Ryan Harvey	3.00
323	Nicholas Markakis	1.00
324	Chad Billingsley	1.00
325	Aaron Hill	.40
326	Brian Snyder	.40
327	Eric Duncan	.40
328	Sammy Sosa	1.50
329	Alfonso Soriano	1.00
330	Ichiro Suzuki	2.00
331	Alex Rodriguez	2.00
332	Nomar Garciaparra	2.00
333	Albert Pujols	2.00
334	Jim Thome	1.00
335	Dontrelle Willis	.50

Mini Parallel

GLAUS ANAHEIM AMER.

Polar Bear:	1-2X
Sovereign:	1-2X
Sovereign Green:	2-3X
American Beauty:	1-2X
Amer. Beauty Purple:	3-5X
Cycle:	1-2X
Cycle Purple:	3-5X
Drum:	2-4X
Honest:	1-2X
Honest Purple:	3-5X
Piedmont:	1-2X
Piedmont Purple:	3-5X
Sweet Caporal:	1-2X
Sweet Caporal Purple:	3-5X
Bazooka:	No Pricing
Production 5 Sets	
Brooklyn:	1.5-4X
Brooklyn: Varies for common, rare & Unc.	

T-205 Autographs

NM/M
Common Autograph: 12.00

LB	Lance Berkman	25.00
MB	Marlon Byrd	10.00
CF	Cliff Floyd	15.00
TH	Torii Hunter	15.00
PL	Paul LoDuca	15.00
MO	Magglio Ordonez	20.00
JR	Jose Reyes	30.00
SR	Scott Rolen	40.00
MS	Mike Sweeney	20.00

ABBREVIATIONS

SP - Short Print

Series 2

HA	Hank Aaron/50	280.00
LC	Luis Castillo	10.00
ED	Eric Duncan	20.00
RH	Rich Harden	25.00
FP	Felix Pie	40.00
RWA	Ryan Wagner	15.00
JW	Jerome Williams	20.00
DW	Dontrelle Willis	25.00

T-205 Relics

	NM/M
Common Player:	4.00
RA	Roberto Alomar/Bat	6.00
GA	Garret Anderson/Jsy	5.00
JB	Jeff Bagwell/Jsy	6.00
LB	Lance Berkman/Bat	8.00
BB	Barry Bonds	25.00
AB	A.J. Burnett/Jsy	4.00
LC	Luis Castillo/Jsy	4.00
EC	Eric Chavez/Bat	5.00
JD	Johnny Damon/Bat	6.00
AD	Adam Dunn/Bat	8.00
RF	Rafael Furcal/Bat	6.00
EG	Eric Gagne/Jsy	8.00
NG	Nomar Garciaparra/Jsy	15.00
BG	Brian Giles/Bat	5.00
LG	Luis Gonzalez/Jsy	4.00
TH	Todd Helton/Jsy	10.00
KI	Kazuhisa Ishii/Jsy	6.00
JJ	Jason Jennings/Jsy	4.00
NJ	Nick Johnson/Bat	4.00
RJ	Randy Johnson/Bat	8.00
JK	Jeff Kent/Bat	4.00
AL	Al Leiter/Jsy	4.00
KL	Kenny Lofton/Jsy	4.00
DL	Derek Lowe/Jsy	4.00
GM	Greg Maddux/Jsy	15.00
PM	Pedro Martinez/Jsy	10.00
MO	Magglio Ordonez/Jsy	4.00
RO	Roy Oswalt/Jsy	4.00
RP	Rafael Palmeiro/Jsy	6.00
TP	Troy Percival/Jsy	4.00
MP	Mike Piazza/Bat	10.00
AP	Albert Pujols/Jsy	20.00
MR	Manny Ramirez/Bat	8.00
AR	Alex Rodriguez/Bat	10.00
SR	Scott Rolen/Bat	15.00
CS	Curt Schilling/Jsy	6.00
JS	John Smoltz/Jsy	4.00
AS	Alfonso Soriano/Jsy	10.00
MS	Mike Sweeney/Bat	4.00
JT	Jim Thome/Bat	12.00
MV	Mo Vaughn/Jsy	4.00
BW	Bernie Williams/Bat	10.00
BZ	Barry Zito/Jsy	4.00

Series 2

RA	Roberto Alomar	4.00
JB	Jeff Bagwell	6.00
RBB	Rocco Baldelli/Bat	8.00
RB	Rocco Baldelli/Jsy	8.00
CB	Craig Biggio	4.00
HB	Hank Blalock	6.00
WB	Wade Boggs	15.00
BB	Bret Boone	10.00
GB	George Brett	25.00
KB	Kevin Brown	4.00
SB	Sean Burroughs	4.00
MC	Mike Cameron	4.00
JC	Jose Canseco	8.00
GC	Gary Carter	6.00
RC	Roger Clemens	15.00
CD	Carlos Delgado	6.00
BD	Brandon Duckworth	4.00
JE	Jim Edmonds	6.00
DE	Darin Erstad	4.00
RF	Rafael Furcal	4.00
NG	Nomar Garciaparra	10.00
JG	Jason Giambi	6.00
JGI	Jeremy Giambi	4.00
BG	Brian Giles	4.00
TG	Troy Glaus	6.00
JGO	Juan Gonzalez	6.00
LG	Luis Gonzalez	4.00
MG	Mark Grace	10.00
MGR	Marquis Grissom	4.00
VG	Vladimir Guerrero	8.00
CG	Cristian Guzman	4.00
RH	Rickey Henderson	8.00
RJ	Randy Johnson	10.00
AJ	Andruw Jones	6.00
CJB	Chipper Jones	8.00
KL	Kenny Lofton	4.00
GM	Greg Maddux	10.00
EM	Edgar Martinez	4.00
PM	Pedro J. Martinez	8.00

TM	Tino Martinez	6.00
FM	Fred McGriff	6.00
MM	Mark Mulder	4.00
EMU	Eddie Murray	25.00
JO	John Olerud	4.00
PO	Paul O'Neill	4.00
RP	Rafael Palmeiro	8.00
CP	Corey Patterson	10.00
BP	Brad Penny	4.00
MP	Mike Piazza	10.00
JP	Jorge Posada	15.00
APB	Albert Pujols/bat	20.00
AP	Albert Pujols/Jsy	20.00
ARA	Aramis Ramirez	6.00
FR	Frank Robinson	15.00
AR	Alex Rodriguez	10.00
IR	Ivan Rodriguez	8.00
SR	Scott Rolen	8.00
NR	Nolan Ryan	40.00
CS	Curt Schilling	6.00
MS	Mike Schmidt	25.00
GS	Gary Sheffield	6.00
TS	Tsuyoshi Shinjo	4.00
AS	Alfonso Soriano	8.00
SS	Sammy Sosa	15.00
SST	Shannon Stewart	4.00
MT	Mark Teixeira	6.00
MTE	Miguel Tejada	6.00
FT	Frank Thomas	8.00
RV	Robin Ventura	4.00
LW	Larry Walker	4.00
VW	Vernon Wells	8.00
BW	Bernie Williams	6.00
DW	Dontrelle Willis	8.00

Team Topps Legends Autographs

	NM/M
Common Player:	
	Stan Musial	65.00
	Jim Palmer	20.00
	Gaylord Perry	10.00
	Robin Yount	75.00

Triple Folder

	NM/M
Complete Set (100):	60.00
Common Card:	.25
Inserted 1:1	
Series 1 Brooklyn Variation: 4-8X	
Inserted 1:72	
Series 2 Brooklyn Variation: 2-4X	
Inserted 1:29	
TF1	Barry Bonds, Jason LaRue	1.50
TF2	Alfonso Soriano, Derek Jeter	1.50
TF3	Alex Rodriguez, Miguel Tejada	1.50
TF4	Nomar Garciaparra, Derek Jeter	2.00
TF5	Omar Vizquel, Alex Rodriguez	1.50
TF6	Paul Konerko, Omar Vizquel	.25
TF7	Paul Konerko, Magglio Ordonez	.25
TF8	Doug Mientkiewicz, Darin Erstad	.25
TF9	Jason Kendall, Jimmy Rollins	.25
TF10	Shawn Green, Roberto Alomar	.25
TF11	Derek Jeter, Roberto Alomar	1.50
TF12	Bobby Abreu, Luis Castillo	.25
TF13	Randy Johnson, Ivan Rodriguez	.75
TF14	Mike Piazza, Kerry Wood	1.00
TF15	Roger Clemens, Jorge Posada	1.00
TF16	Ichiro Suzuki, Ryan Klesko	1.00
TF17	Alfonso Soriano, Chipper Jones	1.00
TF18	Barry Bonds, Nick Johnson	1.50
TF19	Chipper Jones, Andruw Jones	.75
TF20	Bobby Abreu, Paul Konerko	.25
TF21	Rafael Palmeiro, Alex Rodriguez	1.50
TF22	Eric Hinske, Carlos Delgado	.25
TF23	Nomar Garciaparra, Jay Gibbons	1.00
TF24	Mike Piazza, Luis Gonzalez	1.00
TF25	J.T. Snow, Vladimir Guerrero	.50

TF26	Jason Giambi, Bernie Williams	.75
TF27	Mark Mulder, Miguel Tejada, Richie Sexson	.25
TF28	Doug Mientkiewicz, Jimmy Rollins	.25
TF29	Eric Chavez, Derek Jeter	2.00
TF30	Alfonso Soriano, Bret Boone	1.00
TF31	Chipper Jones, Mike Piazza	1.00
TF32	Ichiro Suzuki, Bret Boone	1.00
TF33	Bobby Abreu, Mike Piazza	1.00
TF34	Jimmy Rollins, Pat Burrell	.25
TF35	Ichiro Suzuki, Miguel Tejada	1.00
TF36	Jason LaRue, Barry Bonds	1.50
TF37	Derek Jeter, Alfonso Soriano	1.50
TF38	Miguel Tejada, Alex Rodriguez	1.50
TF39	Derek Jeter, Nomar Garciaparra	2.00
TF40	Alex Rodriguez, Omar Vizquel	1.50
TF41	Curt Schilling, Randy Johnson	.75
TF42	Jorge Posada, Roger Clemens	1.50
TF43	Ryan Klesko, Ichiro Suzuki	1.00
TF44	Nick Johnson, Barry Bonds	1.50
TF45	Alex Rodriguez, Rafael Palmeiro	1.50
TF46	Vladimir Guerrero, J.T. Snow	.50
TF47	Derek Jeter, Eric Chavez	2.00
TF48	Bret Boone, Ichiro Suzuki	1.00
TF49	Mike Piazza, Bobby Abreu	1.00
TF50	Miguel Tejada, Ichiro Suzuki	1.00
TF51	Juan Pierre, Jim Thome	.50
TF52	Kevin Millwood, Jim Thome	.50
TF53	Hank Blalock, Jorge Posada	.40
TF54	Deivi Cruz, Hank Blalock	.25
TF55	Rafael Furcal, Ty Wigginton	.25
TF56	Jim Thome, Nomar Garciaparra	1.50
TF57	Craig Biggio, Jason Giambi	.75
TF58	Aaron Boone, Jason Giambi	.75
TF59	Jason Giambi, Bernie Williams	.75
TF60	Cristian Guzman, Jody Gerut	.25
TF61	Todd Helton, Jose Reyes	.50
TF62	Derek Jeter, Hank Blalock	2.00
TF63	Mike Piazza, Jimmy Rollins	1.00
TF64	Bernie Williams, Derek Jeter	2.00
TF65	Andruw Jones, Rafael Furcal	.50
TF66	Mike Piazza, Andruw Jones	1.00
TF67	Mike Piazza, Cliff Floyd	1.00
TF68	Jason Kendall, Albert Pujols	1.50
TF69	Nomar Garciaparra, Manny Ramirez	1.50
TF70	Jorge Posada, Alex Rodriguez	1.50
TF71	Derek Jeter, Alex Rodriguez	2.00
TF72	Mike Sweeney, Alex Rodriguez	1.50
TF73	Marquis Grissom, Ivan Rodriguez	.50
TF74	Jason Phillips, Gary Sheffield	.40
TF75	Chipper Jones, Gary Sheffield	1.00
TF76	Junior Spivey, Gary Sheffield	.40
TF77	Al Leiter, Ichiro Suzuki	.75
TF78	Jose Vidro, Jim Thome	.75
TF79	Jimmy Rollins, Paul LoDuca	.25
TF80	Alex Rodriguez, Rafael Palmeiro	1.50
TF81	Albert Pujols, Jim Edmonds	1.50
TF82	Eric Chavez, Mike Sweeney	.25
TF83	Cristian Guzman, Jimmy Rollins	.25
TF84	Alfonso Soriano, Bernie Williams	.50
TF85	Ichiro Suzuki, Derek Jeter	2.00
TF86	Jimmy Rollins, Derek Lee	.25

TF87	Shawn Green, Paul LoDuca	.25
TF88	Carlos Delgado, Jorge Posada	.50
TF89	Dmitri Young, C.C. Sabathia	.25
TF90	Dontrelle Willis, Shawn Chacon	.25
TF91	Edgar Martinez, Alex Rodriguez	1.50
TF92	Edgar Martinez, Carlos Delgado	.50
TF93	Edgar Martinez, Esteban Loaiza	.25
TF94	Roy Halladay, C.C. Sabathia	.25
TF95	Ichiro Suzuki, Albert Pujols	1.50
TF96	Ichiro Suzuki, Shigetoshi Hasegawa	1.00
TF97	Geoff Jenkins, Aaron Boone	.25
TF98	Nomar Garciaparra, Alfonso Soriano	1.50
TF99	Jorge Posada, Alfonso Soriano	.75
TF100	Vernon Wells, Garret Anderson	.25

Triple Folder Autographs

	NM/M
Inserted 1:355	
RH	Rich Harden	40.00
RW	Ryan Wagner	40.00
JW	Jerome Williams	35.00
DW	Dontrelle Willis	40.00

World Series Lineup

Inserted 1:27,440
No Pricing

2004 Topps Pre-Production

	NM/M
Complete Set (3):	4.00
Common Player:	1.00
PP1	Jason Giambi	3.00
PP2	Curt Schilling	1.50
PP3	Jimmy Rollins	1.00

2004 Topps

	NM/M
Complete Set (732):	60.00
Complete Team Factory Set (737):	75.00
Complete Factory Set (742):	75.00
Common Player:	.15
Pack (10):	2.00
Box (36):	55.00
Jumbo Box (12):	65.00
1	Jim Thome	.40
2	Aramis Ramirez	.25
3	Mark Kotsay	.15
4	Edgardo Alfonzo	.15
5	Ben Davis	.15
6	Mike Matheny	.15
7	Marlon Anderson	.15
8	Chan Ho Park	.15
9	Ichiro Suzuki	.75
10	Kevin Millwood	.25
11	Bengie Molina	.15
12	Tom Glavine	.25
13	Junior Spivey	.15

14	Marcus Giles	.15
15	David Segui	.15
16	Kevin Millar	.15
17	Corey Patterson	.15
18	Aaron Rowand	.15
19	Derek Jeter	1.00
20	Jason LaRue	.15
21	Chris Hammond	.15
22	Jay Payton	.15
23	Bobby Higginson	.15
24	Lance Berkman	.15
25	Juan Pierre	.15
26	Brent Mayne	.15
27	Fred McGriff	.25
28	Richie Sexson	.25
29	Tim Hudson	.15
30	Mike Piazza	.50
31	Brad Radke	.15
32	Jeff Weaver	.15
33	Ramon Hernandez	.15
34	David Bell	.15
35	Craig Wilson	.15
36	Jake Peavy	.15
37	Tim Worrell	.15
38	Gil Meche	.15
39	Albert Pujols	1.00
40	Michael Young	.15
41	Josh Phelps	.15
42	Brendan Donnelly	.15
43	Steve Finley	.15
44	John Smoltz	.15
45	Jay Gibbons	.15
46	Trot Nixon	.15
47	Carl Pavano	.15
48	Frank Thomas	.40
49	Mark Prior	1.00
50	Danny Graves	.15
51	Milton Bradley	.15
52	Jose Jimenez	.15
53	Shane Halter	.15
54	Mike Lowell	.15
55	Geoff Blum	.15
56	Michael Tucker	.15
57	Paul LoDuca	.15
58	Vicente Padilla	.15
59	Jacque Jones	.15
60	Fernando Tatis	.15
61	Ty Wigginton	.15
62	Pedro Astacio	.15
63	Andy Pettitte	.25
64	Terrence Long	.15
65	Cliff Floyd	.15
66	Mariano Rivera	.25
67	Mike Williams	.15
68	Marlon Byrd	.15
69	Mark Mulder	.25
70	Damian Moss	.15
71	Carlos Guillen	.15
72	Fernando Vina	.15
73	Lance Carter	.15
74	Hank Blalock	.25
75	Jimmy Rollins	.15
76	Kevin Appier	.15
77	Javy Lopez	.25
78	Jerry Hairston Jr.	.15
79	Andruw Jones	.40
80	Rodrigo Lopez	.15
81	Johnny Damon	.25
82	Hee Seop Choi	.15
83	Miguel Olivo	.15
84	Scott Sullivan	.15
85	Matt Lawton	.15
86	Juan Uribe	.15
87	Steve Sparks	.15
88	Tim Spooneybarger	.15
89	Jose Vidro	.15
90	Luis Rivas	.15
91	Hideo Nomo	.25
92	Javier Vazquez	.15
93	Al Leiter	.15
94	Darren Dreifort	.15
95	Mike DeJean	.15
96	Zach Day	.15
97	Jorge Posada	.25
98	John Halama	.15
99	Alex Rodriguez	1.00
100	Orlando Palmeiro	.15
101	Dave Berg	.15
102	Brad Fullmer	.15
103	Mike Hampton	.15
104	Willis Roberts	.15
105	Ramiro Mendoza	.15
106	Juan Cruz	.15
107	Esteban Loaiza	.15
108	Aaron Boone	.15
109	Todd Helton	.40
110	Braden Looper	.15
111	Octavio Dotel	.15
112	Mike MacDougal	.15
113	Cesar Izturis	.15
114	Johan Santana	.25
115	Jose Contreras	.25
116	Placido Polanco	.15
117	Kenny Lofton	.15
118	Adam Eaton	.15
119	Vernon Wells	.25
120	Ben Grieve	.15
121	Randy Winn	.15
122	Ismael Valdes	.15
123	Eric Owens	.15
124	Curt Schilling	.25
125	Russ Ortiz	.15
126	Mark Buehrle	.15
127	Danys Baez	.15
128	Dmitri Young	.15
129	Kazuhisa Ishii	.15
130	A.J. Pierzynski	.15
131	Michael Barrett	.15

133	Joe McEwing	.15
134	Robin Ventura	.15
135	Tom Wilson	.15
136	Carlos Zambrano	.15
137	Brett Tomko	.15
138	Jeff Nelson	.15
139	Jarrod Washburn	.15
140	Greg Maddux	.50
141	Craig Counsell	.15
142	Reggie Taylor	.15
143	Omar Vizquel	.25
144	Alex Gonzalez	.15
145	Billy Wagner	.15
146	Brian Jordan	.15
147	Wes Helms	.15
148	Kyle Lohse	.15
149	Timoniel Perez	.15
150	Jason Giambi	.50
151	Erubiel Durazo	.15
152	Mike Lieberthal	.15
153	Jason Kendall	.15
154	Xavier Nady	.15
155	Kirk Rueter	.15
156	Mike Cameron	.15
157	Miguel Cairo	.15
158	Woody Williams	.15
159	Toby Hall	.15
160	Bernie Williams	.40
161	Darin Erstad	.25
162	Matt Mantei	.15
163	Geronimo Gil	.15
164	Bill Mueller	.15
165	Damian Miller	.15
166	Tony Graffanino	.15
167	Sean Casey	.15
168	Brandon Phillips	.15
169	Mike Remlinger	.15
170	Adam Dunn	.25
171	Carlos Lee	.15
172	Juan Encarnacion	.15
173	Angel Berroa	.15
174	Desi Relaford	.15
175	Paul Quantrill	.15
176	Ben Sheets	.15
177	Eddie Guardado	.15
178	Rocky Biddle	.15
179	Mike Stanton	.15
180	Eric Chavez	.25
181	Jason Michaels	.15
182	Terry Adams	.15
183	Kip Wells	.15
184	Brian Lawrence	.15
185	Bret Boone	.25
186	Tino Martinez	.15
187	Aubrey Huff	.15
188	Kevin Mench	.15
189	Tim Salmon	.25
190	Carlos Delgado	.40
191	John Lackey	.15
192	Oscar Villarreal	.15
193	Sidney Ponson	.15
194	Derek Lowe	.15
195	Mark Grudzielanek	.15
196	Flash Gordon	.15
197	Matt Clement	.15
198	Scott Williamson	.15
199	Brandon Inge	.15
200	Nomar Garciaparra	1.00
201	Antonio Osuna	.15
202	Jose Mesa	.15
203	Randall Simon	.15
204	Jack Wilson	.15
205	Ray Durham	.15
206	Freddy Garcia	.15
207	J.D. Drew	.15
208	Einar Diaz	.15
209	Roy Halladay	.25
210	David Eckstein	.15
211	Jason Marquis	.15
212	Jorge Julio	.15
213	Tim Wakefield	.15
214	Moises Alou	.25
215	Bartolo Colon	.25
216	Jimmy Haynes	.15
217	Preston Wilson	.15
218	Luis Castillo	.15
219	Richard Hidalgo	.15
220	Manny Ramirez	.40
221	Mike Mussina	.25
222	Randy Wolf	.15
223	Kris Benson	.15
224	Ryan Klesko	.15
225	Rich Aurilia	.15
226	Kelvim Escobar	.15
227	Francisco Cordero	.15
228	Kazuhiro Sasaki	.15
229	Danny Bautista	.15
230	Rafael Furcal	.15
231	Travis Driskill	.15
232	Kyle Farnsworth	.15
233	Jose Valentin	.15
234	Felipe Lopez	.15
235	C.C. Sabathia	.15
236	Brad Penny	.15
237	Brad Ausmus	.15
238	Raul Ibanez	.15
239	Adrian Beltre	.25
240	Rocco Baldelli	.25
241	Orlando Hudson	.15
242	Dave Roberts	.15
243	Doug Mientkiewicz	.15
244	Brad Wilkerson	.15
245	Scott Strickland	.15
246	Sterling Hitchcock	.15
247	Chad Bradford	.15
248	Gary Bennett	.15
249	Jose Cruz Jr.	.25
250	Jeff Kent	.25

459 Ramon Santiago .15

...hka .15
...catalanotto .15
...an Guzman .15
...ando Cabrera .15
Mike Scioscia .15
Bob Brenly .15
Bobby Cox .15
270 Mike Hargrove .15
271 Grady Little .15
272 Dusty Baker .15
273 Jerry Manuel .15
274 Bob Boone .15
275 Eric Wedge .15
276 Clint Hurdle .15
277 Alan Trammell .15
278 Jack McKeon .15
279 Jimy Williams .15
280 Tony Pena .15
281 Jim Tracy .15
282 Ned Yost .15
283 Ron Gardenhire .15
284 Frank Robinson .25
285 Art Howe .15
286 Joe Torre .25
287 Ken Macha .15
288 Larry Bowa .15
289 Lloyd McClendon .15
290 Bruce Bochy .15
291 Felipe Alou .15
292 Bob Melvin .15
293 Tony LaRussa .15
294 Lou Piniella .15
295 Buck Showalter .15
296 Carlos Tosca .15
297 Anthony Acevedo **RC** .25
298 Anthony Lerew **RC** .75
299 Blake Hawksworth **RC** .50
300 Brayan Pena **RC** .50
301 Casey Myers **RC** .50
302 Craig Ansman **RC** .50
303 David Murphy .40
304 David Crouthers .15
305 Dioner Navarro **RC** .40
306 Donald Levinski .15
307 Jesse Roman **RC** .40
308 Sung Ki Jung **RC** .25
309 Jon Knott **RC** .15
310 Josh Labandeira **RC** .25
311 Kenny Perez **RC** .25
312 Khalid Ballouli **RC** .25
313 Kyle Davies **RC** .40
314 Marcus McBeth **RC** .40
315 Matt Creighton **RC** .40
316 Chris O'Riordan **RC** .50
317 Mike Gosling .15
318 Nic Ungs **RC** .40
319 Omar Falcon **RC** .40
320 Rodney Choy Foo **RC** .40
321 Tim Frend **RC** .50
322 Todd Self **RC** .50
323 Tydus Meadows **RC** .40
324 Yadier Molina **RC** .50
325 Zachary Duke **RC** 2.00
326 Zach Miner **RC** 1.00
327 Bernie Castro, Khalil Greene .15
328 Ryan Madson, Elizardo Ramirez .15
329 Rich Harden, Bobby Crosby .15
330 Zack Greinke, Jimmy Gobble .15
331 Bobby Jenks, Casey Kotchman .15
332 Sammy Sosa .50
333 Kevin Millwood .25
334 Rafael Palmeiro .25
335 Roger Clemens .75
336 Eric Gagne .15
337 Bill Mueller, Manny Ramirez, Derek Jeter .50
338 Vernon Wells, Ichiro Suzuki, Michael Young .40
339 Alex Rodriguez, Frank Thomas, Carlos Delgado .50
340 Carlos Delgado, Alex Rodriguez, Bret Boone .50
341 Pedro Martinez, Tim Hudson, Esteban Loaiza .25
342 Esteban Loaiza, Pedro Martinez, Roy Halladay .25
343 Albert Pujols, Todd Helton, Edgar Renteria .50
344 Albert Pujols, Todd Helton, Juan Pierre .50
345 Jim Thome, Richie Sexson, Javy Lopez .25
346 Preston Wilson, Gary Sheffield, Jim Thome .25

347 Jason Schmidt, Kevin Brown, Mark Prior .50
348 Kerry Wood, Mark Prior, Javier Vazquez .50
349 AL Division Series .15
350 NL Division Series .15
351 NL Championship Series .15
352 AL Championship Series .25
353 AL & NL Division Series .15
354 AL Championship Series .15
355 World Series Highlights .25
356 Carlos Delgado .25
357 Bret Boone .15
358 Alex Rodriguez .50
359 Bill Mueller .15
360 Vernon Wells .15
361 Garret Anderson .15
362 Magglio Ordonez .25
363 Jorge Posada .15
364 Roy Halladay .15
365 Andy Pettitte .15
366 Frank Thomas .25
367 Jody Gerut .15
368 Sammy Sosa .75
369 Joe Crede .15
370 Gary Sheffield .25
371 Coco Crisp .15
372 Torii Hunter .25
373 Derrek Lee .15
374 Adam Everett .15
375 Miguel Tejada .25
376 Jeremy Affeldt .15
377 Robin Ventura .15
378 Scott Podsednik .40
379 Matthew LeCroy .15
380 Vladimir Guerrero .40
381 Tony Clark .15
382 Jeff Nelson .15
383 Chris Singleton .15
384 Bobby Abreu .25
385 Josh Fogg .15
386 Trevor Hoffman .15
387 Jesse Foppert .15
388 Edgar Martinez .25
389 Edgar Renteria .25
390 Chipper Jones .50
391 Eric Munson .15
392 Dewon Brazelton .15
393 John Thomson .15
394 Chris Woodward .15
395 Aaron Sele .15
396 Elmer Dessens .15
397 Johnny Estrada .15
398 Damian Moss .15
399 Gabe Kapler .15
400 Dontrelle Willis .40
401 Troy Glaus .25
402 Raul Mondesi .20
403 Shane Reynolds .15
404 Kurt Ainsworth .15
405 Pedro J. Martinez .50
406 Eric Karros .15
407 Billy Koch .15
408 Scott Schoeneweis .15
409 Paul Wilson .15
410 Mike Sweeney .15
411 Jason Bay .15
412 Mark Redman .15
413 Jason Jennings .15
414 Rondell White .25
415 Todd Hundley .15
416 Shannon Stewart .15
417 Jae Weong Seo .15
418 Livan Hernandez .15
419 Mark Ellis .15
420 Pat Burrell .25
421 Mark Loretta .15
422 Robb Nen .15
423 Joel Pineiro .15
424 Jason Simontacchi .15
425 Sterling Hitchcock .15
426 Rey Ordonez .15
427 Greg Myers .15
428 Shane Spencer .15
429 Carlos Baerga .15
430 Garret Anderson .25
431 Horacio Ramirez .15
432 Brian Roberts .15
433 Damian Jackson .15
434 Doug Glanville .15
435 Brian Daubach .15
436 Alex Escobar .15
437 Alex Sanchez .15
438 Jeff Bagwell .40
439 Darrell May .15
440 Shawn Green .25
441 Geoff Jenkins .25
442 Endy Chavez .15
443 Nick Johnson .15
444 Jose Guillen .15
445 Tomas Perez .15
446 Phil Nevin .15
447 Jason Schmidt .25
448 Julio Mateo .15
449 So Taguchi .15
450 Randy Johnson .40
451 Paul Byrd .15
452 Chone Figgins .15
453 Larry Bigbie .15
454 Scott Williamson .15
455 Ramon Martinez .15
456 Roberto Alomar .25
457 Ryan Dempster .15
458 Ryan Ludwick .15

459 Ramon Santiago .15
460 Jeff Conine .15
461 Brad Lidge .15
462 Ken Harvey .15
463 Guillermo Mota .15
464 Rick Reed .15
465 Joey Eischen .15
466 Wade Miller .15
467 Steve Karsay .15
468 Chase Utley .15
469 Matt Stairs .15
470 Yorvit Torrealba .15
471 Joe Kennedy .15
472 Reed Johnson .15
473 Victor Zambrano .15
474 Jeff DaVanon .15
475 Luis Gonzalez .25
476 Rod Barajas .15
477 Ray King .15
478 Jack Cust .15
479 Omar Daal .15
480 Todd Walker .15
481 Shawn Estes .15
482 Chris Reitsma .15
483 Jake Westbrook .15
484 Jeremy Bonderman .15
485 A.J. Burnett .15
486 Roy Oswalt .25
487 Kevin Brown .25
488 Eric Milton .15
489 Claudio Vargas .15
490 Roger Cedeno .15
491 David Wells .15
492 Scott Hatteberg .15
493 Ricky Ledee .15
494 Eric Young .15
495 Armando Benitez .15
496 Dan Haren .15
497 Carl Crawford .25
498 Laynce Nix .15
499 Eric Hinske .15
500 Ivan Rodriguez .40
501 Scot Shields .15
502 Brandon Webb .15
503 Mark DeRosa .15
504 Jhonny Peralta .15
505 Adam Kennedy .15
506 Tony Batista .15
507 Jeff Suppan .15
508 Kenny Lofton .25
509 Scott Sullivan .15
510 Ken Griffey Jr. .60
511 Billy Traber .15
512 Larry Walker .25
513 Mike Maroth .15
514 Todd Hollandsworth .15
515 Kirk Saarloos .15
516 Carlos Beltran .25
517 Andy Ashby .15
518 Jose Macias .15
519 Karim Garcia .15
520 Jose Reyes .40
521 Brandon Duckworth .15
522 Brian Giles .25
523 J.T. Snow Jr. .15
524 Jamie Moyer .15
525 Jason Isringhausen .15
526 Julio Lugo .15
527 Mark Teixeira .25
528 Cory Lidle .15
529 Lyle Overbay .15
530 Troy Percival .15
531 Robby Hammock .15
532 Robert Fick .15
533 Jason Johnson .15
534 Brandon Lyon .15
535 Antonio Alfonseca .15
536 Tom Goodwin .15
537 Paul Konerko .25
538 D'Angelo Jimenez .15
539 Ben Broussard .15
540 Magglio Ordonez .25
541 Ellis Burks .15
542 Carlos Pena .15
543 Chad Fox .15
544 Jeriome Robertson .15
545 Travis Hafner .15
546 Joe Randa .15
547 Wil Cordero .15
548 Brady Clark .15
549 Ruben Sierra .15
550 Barry Zito .25
551 Brett Myers .15
552 Oliver Perez .15
553 Trey Hodges .15
554 Benito Santiago .15
555 David Ross .15
556 Ramon Vazquez .15
557 Joe Nathan .15
558 Dan Wilson .15
559 Garrett Stephenson .15
560 Jim Edmonds .25
561 Shawn Wooten .15
562 Matt Kata .15
563 Vinny Castilla .15
564 Marty Cordova .15
565 Aramis Ramirez .15
566 Carl Everett .15
567 Ryan Freel .15
568 Jason Davis .15
569 Mark Bellhorn .15
570 Craig Monroe .15
571 Ugueth Urbina .15
572 Tim Redding .15
573 Kevin Appier .15
574 Jeromy Burnitz .15
575 Miguel Cabrera .40
576 Orlando Hernandez .15

577 Casey Blake .15
578 Aaron Boone .15
579 Jermaine Dye .15
580 Jerome Williams .15
581 John Olerud .15
582 Scott Rolen .40
583 Bobby Kielty .15
584 Travis Lee .15
585 Jeff Cirillo .15
586 Scott Spiezio .15
587 Stephen Randolph .15
588 Melvin Mora .15
589 Mike Timlin .15
590 Kerry Wood .50
591 Tony Womack .15
592 Jody Gerut .15
593 Franklyn German .15
594 Morgan Ensberg .15
595 Odalis Perez .15
596 Michael Cuddyer .15
597 Jon Lieber .15
598 Mike Williams .15
599 Jose Hernandez .15
600 Alfonso Soriano .50
601 Marquis Grissom .15
602 Matt Morris .25
603 Damian Rolls .15
604 Juan Gonzalez .25
605 Aquilino Lopez .15
606 Jose Valverde .15
607 Scott Sauerbeck .15
608 Joe Borowski .15
609 Josh Bard .15
610 Austin Kearns .25
611 Chin-Hui Tsao .15
612 Wilfredo Ledezma .15
613 Aaron Guiel .15
614 LaTroy Hawkins .15
615 Tony Armas Jr. .15
616 Steve Trachsel .15
617 Ted Lilly .15
618 Todd Pratt .15
619 Sean Burroughs .15
620 Rafael Palmeiro .40
621 Jeremi Gonzalez .15
622 Quinton McCracken .15
623 David Ortiz .25
624 Randall Simon .15
625 Wily Mo Pena .15
626 Nate Cornejo .15
627 Brian Anderson .15
628 Corey Koskie .15
629 Keith Foulke .15
630 Rheal Cormier .15
631 Sidney Ponson .15
632 Gary Matthews Jr. .15
633 Herbert Perry .15
634 Shea Hillenbrand .15
635 Craig Biggio .25
636 Barry Larkin .25
637 Orlando Merced .15
638 Anaheim Angels .15
639 Arizona Diamondbacks .15
640 Atlanta Braves .15
641 Baltimore Orioles .15
642 Boston Red Sox .25
643 Chicago Cubs .40
644 Chicago White Sox .15
645 Cincinnati Reds .15
646 Cleveland Indians .15
647 Colorado Rockies .15
648 Detroit Tigers .15
649 Florida Marlins .15
650 Houston Astros .15
651 Kansas City Royals .15
652 Los Angeles Dodgers .15
653 Milwaukee Brewers .15
654 Minnesota Twins .15
655 Montreal Expos .15
656 New York Mets .15
657 New York Yankees .50
658 Oakland Athletics .15
659 Philadelphia Phillies .15
660 Pittsburgh Pirates .15
661 San Diego Padres .15
662 San Francisco Giants .15
663 Seattle Mariners .15
664 St. Louis Cardinals .15
665 Tampa Bay Devil Rays .15
666 Texas Rangers .15
667 Toronto Blue Jays .15
668 Kyle Sleeth .15
669 Bradley Sullivan .15
670 Carlos Quentin .50
671 Conor Jackson 1.00
672 Jeffrey Allison .15
673 Matthew Moses .25
674 Tim Stauffer .15
675 Estee Harris **RC** .25
676 David Aardsma .15
677 Omar Quintanilla .25
678 Aaron Hill .15
679 Tony Richie .15
680 Lastings Milledge 3.00
681 Brad Snyder .15
682 Jason Hirsh .50
683 Logan Kensing **RC** .40
684 Chris Lubanski .15
685 Ryan Harvey .15
686 Ryan Wagner .15
687 Rickie Weeks .50
688 Jeremy Guthrie .15
689 Edwin Jackson, Greg Miller .15
690 Neal Cotts, Jeremy Reed .15

691 Nicholas Markakis, Adam Loewen .15
692 Delmon Young, B.J. Upton .75
693 Nomar Garciaparra, Alfonso Soriano .50
694 Ichiro Suzuki, Albert Pujols .50
695 Jim Thome, Mike Schmidt .40
696 Mike Mussina .25
697 Bengie Molina .15
698 John Olerud .15
699 Bret Boone .15
700 Eric Chavez .25
701 Alex Rodriguez .75
702 Mike Cameron .15
703 Ichiro Suzuki .75
704 Torii Hunter .25
705 Mike Hampton .15
706 Mike Matheny .15
707 Derrek Lee .15
708 Luis Castillo .15
709 Scott Rolen .40
710 Edgar Renteria .25
711 Andruw Jones .25
712 Jose Cruz Jr. .15
713 Jim Edmonds .15
714 Roy Halladay .25
715 Eric Gagne .25
716 Alex Rodriguez .75
717 Angel Berroa .15
718 Dontrelle Willis .25
719 Todd Helton .25
720 Marcus Giles .15
721 Edgar Renteria .15
722 Scott Rolen .40
723 Albert Pujols .75
724 Gary Sheffield .25
725 Javy Lopez .25
726 Eric Gagne .15
727 Randy Wolf .15
728 Bobby Cox .15
729 Scott Podsednik .40
730 World Series Game 4 .15
731 World Series Game 5 .15
732 World Series Game 6 .15
733 World Series MVP .25

Black
Black (1-733): 15-30X
Production 53 Sets

Gold

Stars (1-733): 5-10X
Production 2,004 Sets

1st Edition
NM/M
Stars: 3-5X
HTA Exclusive
1st Edition Pack (10): 3.00
1st Edition Box (20): 55.00

All-Stars

NM/M
Complete Set (20): 20.00
Common Player: .50
Inserted 1:16
TAS1 Jason Giambi 1.50
TAS2 Ichiro Suzuki 2.50
TAS3 Alex Rodriguez 3.00
TAS4 Albert Pujols 3.00
TAS5 Alfonso Soriano 1.50
TAS6 Nomar Garciaparra 2.50
TAS7 Andruw Jones 1.00
TAS8 Carlos Delgado .75
TAS9 Gary Sheffield .75
TAS10 Jorge Posada .75
TAS11 Magglio Ordonez .75
TAS12 Kerry Wood 1.50
TAS13 Garret Anderson .75
TAS14 Bret Boone .75
TAS15 Hank Blalock .75
TAS16 Mike Lowell .50
TAS17 Todd Helton 1.00
TAS18 Vernon Wells .50
TAS19 Roger Clemens 3.00
TAS20 Scott Rolen 1.50

All-Star Patch Relics

No Pricing
Inserted 1:7,698

All-Star Stitches

NM/M
Common Player: 5.00
Inserted 1:137
GA Garret Anderson 6.00
HB Hank Blalock 5.00
AB Aaron Boone 5.00
BD Brendan Donnelly 5.00
CE Carl Everett 5.00
KF Keith Foulke 5.00
RF Rafael Furcal 8.00
EGA Eric Gagne 8.00
NG Nomar Garciaparra 15.00
TG Troy Glaus 8.00
EG Eddie Guardado 5.00
SH Shigetoshi Hasegawa 5.00
TH Todd Helton 8.00
RH Ramon Hernandez 8.00
AJ Andruw Jones 8.00
EL Esteban Loaiza 5.00
PL Paul LoDuca 5.00
JL Javy Lopez 8.00
ML Mike Lowell 5.00
EM Edgar Martinez 5.00
MMO Melvin Mora 5.00
JM Jamie Moyer 5.00
MM Mark Mulder 5.00
RO Russ Ortiz 6.00
JP Jorge Posada 6.00
ER Edgar Renteria 5.00
AR Alex Rodriguez 15.00
SR Scott Rolen 10.00
JS Jason Schmidt 6.00
JV Jose Vidro 5.00
BW Billy Wagner 5.00
VW Vernon Wells 6.00
RWH Rondell White 5.00
WW Woody Williams 6.00
PW Preston Wilson 6.00
RW Randy Wolf 5.00
KW Kerry Wood 8.00

Autographs
NM/M
Common Player:
JB Josh Beckett 50.00
HB Hank Blalock 20.00
CF Cliff Floyd 8.00
JG Jay Gibbons 15.00
KG Khalil Greene 10.00
EH Eric Hinske 10.00
TH Torii Hunter 25.00
AK Austin Kearns 25.00
PK Paul Konerko 15.00
PL Paul LoDuca 10.00
ML Mike Lowell 20.00
VM Victor Martinez 20.00
MO Magglio Ordonez 15.00
JP Josh Phelps 8.00
MP Mark Prior 40.00
ER Elizardo Ramirez 8.00
BS Benito Santiago 15.00
MS Mike Sweeney 20.00
MT Mark Teixeira 25.00
BU B.J. Upton 20.00
JV Jose Vidro 8.00
Series 2
GA Garret Anderson 35.00
LB Lance Berkman 35.00
AB Aaron Boone 35.00
BB Bobby Brownlie 30.00
MC Miguel Cabrera 40.00
ZG Zack Greinke 20.00
AH Aubrey Huff 20.00
DM Dustin McGowan 15.00
SP Scott Podsednik 25.00
JP Jorge Posada 8.00
IR Ivan Rodriguez 45.00
SR Scott Rolen 30.00
DW Dontrelle Willis 30.00

Derby Digs
NM/M
Common Player: 8.00
Inserted 1:585

GA	Garret Anderson	8.00
BB	Bret Boone	8.00
CD	Carlos Delgado	8.00
JE	Jim Edmonds	8.00
JG	Jason Giambi	15.00
AP	Albert Pujols	25.00
RS	Richie Sexson	8.00

Fall Classic Covers

		NM/M
Complete Set (99):		125.00
Common Card:		2.00
Inserted 1:12		
FC1903	1903 World Series	2.00
FC1905	1905 World Series	2.00
FC1906	1906 World Series	2.00
FC1907	1907 World Series	2.00
FC1908	1908 World Series	2.00
FC1909	1909 World Series	2.00
FC1910	1910 World Series	2.00
FC1911	1911 World Series	2.00
FC1912	1912 World Series	2.00
FC1913	1913 World Series	2.00
FC1914	1914 World Series	2.00
FC1915	1915 World Series	2.00
FC1916	1916 World Series	2.00
FC1917	1917 World Series	2.00
FC1918	1918 World Series	2.00
FC1919	1919 World Series	2.00
FC1920	1920 World Series	2.00
FC1921	1921 World Series	2.00
FC1922	1922 World Series	2.00
FC1923	1923 World Series	2.00
FC1924	1924 World Series	2.00
FC1925	1925 World Series	2.00
FC1926	1926 World Series	2.00
FC1927	1927 World Series	2.00
FC1928	1928 World Series	2.00
FC1929	1929 World Series	2.00
FC1930	1930 World Series	2.00
FC1931	1931 World Series	2.00
FC1932	1932 World Series	2.00
FC1933	1933 World Series	2.00
FC1934	1934 World Series	2.00
FC1935	1935 World Series	2.00
FC1936	1936 World Series	2.00
FC1937	1937 World Series	2.00
FC1938	1938 World Series	2.00
FC1939	1939 World Series	2.00
FC1940	1940 World Series	2.00
FC1941	1941 World Series	2.00
FC1942	1942 World Series	2.00
FC1943	1943 World Series	2.00
FC1944	1944 World Series	2.00
FC1945	1945 World Series	2.00
FC1946	1946 World Series	2.00
FC1947	1947 World Series	2.00
FC1948	1948 World Series	2.00
FC1949	1949 World Series	2.00
FC1950	1950 World Series	2.00
FC1951	1951 World Series	2.00
FC1952	1952 World Series	2.00
FC1953	1953 World Series	2.00
FC1954	1954 World Series	2.00
FC1955	1955 World Series	2.00
FC1956	1956 World Series	2.00
FC1957	1957 World Series	2.00
FC1958	1958 World Series	2.00
FC1959	1959 World Series	2.00
FC1960	1960 World Series	2.00
FC1961	1961 World Series	2.00
FC1962	1962 World Series	2.00
FC1963	1963 World Series	2.00
FC1964	1964 World Series	2.00
FC1965	1965 World Series	2.00
FC1966	1966 World Series	2.00
FC1967	1967 World Series	2.00
FC1968	1968 World Series	2.00
FC1969	1969 World Series	2.00
FC1970	1970 World Series	2.00
FC1971	1971 World Series	2.00
FC1972	1972 World Series	2.00
FC1973	1973 World Series	2.00
FC1974	1974 World Series	2.00
FC1975	1975 World Series	2.00
FC1976	1976 World Series	2.00
FC1977	1977 World Series	2.00
FC1978	1978 World Series	2.00
FC1979	1979 World Series	2.00
FC1980	1980 World Series	2.00
FC1981	1981 World Series	2.00
FC1982	1982 World Series	2.00
FC1983	1983 World Series	2.00
FC1984	1984 World Series	2.00
FC1985	1985 World Series	2.00
FC1986	1986 World Series	2.00

FC1987	1987 World Series	2.00
FC1988	1988 World Series	2.00
FC1989	1989 World Series	2.00
FC1990	1990 World Series	2.00
FC1991	1991 World Series	2.00
FC1992	1992 World Series	2.00
FC1993	1993 World Series	2.00
FC1995	1995 World Series	2.00
FC1996	1996 World Series	2.00
FC1997	1997 World Series	2.00
FC1998	1998 World Series	2.00
FC1999	1999 World Series	2.00
FC2000	2000 World Series	2.00
FC2001	2001 World Series	2.00
FC2002	2002 World Series	2.00
FC2003	2003 World Series	2.00

Hit Parade

Rafael Palmeiro

		NM/M
Complete Set (30):		20.00
Common Player:		.50
Inserted 1:7		
HP1	Sammy Sosa	3.00
HP2	Rafael Palmeiro	1.00
HP3	Fred McGriff	.50
HP4	Ken Griffey Jr.	2.00
HP5	Juan Gonzalez	1.00
HP6	Frank Thomas	1.00
HP7	Andres Galarraga	1.00
HP8	Jim Thome	1.50
HP9	Jeff Bagwell	1.00
HP10	Mike Piazza	2.00
HP11	Rafael Palmeiro	1.00
HP12	Sammy Sosa	3.00
HP13	Fred McGriff	.50
HP14	Andres Galarraga	.50
HP15	Juan Gonzalez	1.00
HP16	Frank Thomas	1.00
HP17	Jeff Bagwell	1.00
HP18	Ken Griffey Jr.	2.00
HP19	Ruben Sierra	.50
HP20	Ellis Burks	.50
HP21	Rafael Palmeiro	1.00
HP22	Roberto Alomar	.75
HP23	Julio Franco	.50
HP24	Andres Galarraga	.50
HP25	Fred McGriff	.50
HP26	Craig Biggio	.75
HP27	Barry Larkin	.75
HP28	Edgar Martinez	.50
HP29	Ellis Burks	.50
HP30	Sammy Sosa	3.00

Hobby Masters

ALFONSO SORIANO

HOBBY Masters

		NM/M
Complete Set (20):		40.00
Common Player:		.75
Inserted 1:12		
HM1	Albert Pujols	3.00
HM2	Mark Prior	4.00
HM3	Alex Rodriguez	4.00
HM4	Nomar Garciaparra	3.00
HM5	Barry Bonds	4.00
HM6	Sammy Sosa	3.00
HM7	Alfonso Soriano	2.00
HM8	Ichiro Suzuki	2.50
HM9	Derek Jeter	4.00
HM10	Jim Thome	1.50
HM11	Jason Giambi	1.50
HM12	Mike Piazza	2.50
HM13	Barry Zito	1.00
HM14	Randy Johnson	2.00
HM15	Adam Dunn	1.00
HM16	Vladimir Guerrero	2.00
HM17	Gary Sheffield	.75
HM18	Carlos Delgado	1.00
HM19	Chipper Jones	2.50
HM20	Dontrelle Willis	1.00

Own the Game

GARRET ANDERSON

		NM/M
Complete Set (30):		25.00
Common Player:		.50
Inserted 1:18		
OG1	Jim Thome	1.50
OG2	Albert Pujols	3.00
OG3	Alex Rodriguez	3.00
OG4	Barry Bonds	4.00
OG5	Ichiro Suzuki	2.00
OG6	Derek Jeter	3.00
OG7	Nomar Garciaparra	3.00
OG8	Alfonso Soriano	1.50
OG9	Gary Sheffield	.75
OG10	Jason Giambi	1.00
OG11	Todd Helton	1.00
OG12	Garret Anderson	.50
OG13	Carlos Delgado	1.00
OG14	Manny Ramirez	1.00
OG15	Richie Sexson	.75
OG16	Vernon Wells	.50
OG17	Preston Wilson	.50
OG18	Frank Thomas	1.50
OG19	Shawn Green	.75
OG20	Rafael Furcal	.50
OG21	Juan Pierre	.50
OG22	Javy Lopez	.50
OG23	Edgar Renteria	.50
OG24	Mark Prior	3.00
OG25	Pedro J. Martinez	1.50
OG26	Kerry Wood	1.00
OG27	Curt Schilling	.75
OG28	Roy Halladay	.50
OG29	Eric Gagne	.50
OG30	Brandon Webb	.50

Series Seats Relics

		NM/M
Common Player:		10.00
Inserted 1:316		
LA	Luis Aparicio	15.00
BF	Bob Feller	12.00
RJ	Reggie Jackson	20.00
AK	Al Kaline	20.00
HK	Harmon Killebrew	25.00
WM	Willie Mays	25.00
BM	Bill Mazeroski	20.00
PM	Paul Molitor	20.00
JP	Jim Palmer	15.00
LP	Lou Piniella	10.00
BP	Boog Powell	10.00
BR	Brooks Robinson	15.00
FR	Frank Robinson	15.00
WS	Warren Spahn	15.00
RY	Robin Yount	20.00

Series Stitches Relics

SERIES STITCHES

		NM/M
Common Player:		10.00
JBE	Josh Beckett	10.00
JB	Johnny Bench	25.00
GB	George Brett	30.00
JCA	Jose Canseco	15.00
GC	Gary Carter	12.00
JC	Joe Carter	10.00
RC	Roger Clemens	20.00
LD	Lenny Dykstra	15.00
SG	Steve Garvey	10.00
KG	Kirk Gibson	10.00
DG	Dwight Gooden	15.00
RJA	Reggie Jackson	20.00
RJ	Randy Johnson	10.00
CJ	Chipper Jones	15.00
DJ	David Justice	15.00
HK	Harmon Killebrew	30.00
WM	Willie Mays	50.00
PO	Paul O'Neill	20.00
KP	Kirby Puckett	25.00
FR	Frank Robinson	20.00
MS	Mike Schmidt	30.00
TS	Tom Seaver	25.00
AS	Alfonso Soriano	15.00
RY	Robin Yount	20.00

Team Topps Legends Autographs

		NM/M
Inserted 1:766		
SG	Steve Garvey	15.00
BP	Boog Powell	10.00

World Series Highlights

WORLD SERIES HIGHLIGHTS

KIRBY PUCKETT HITS WORLD SERIES GAME-WINNING HOME RUN

		NM/M
Complete Set (30):		35.00
Common Player:		1.00
Inserted 1:18		
LB	Lou Brock	1.00
CF	Carlton Fisk	1.50
KG	Kirk Gibson	1.00
RJ	Reggie Jackson	2.00
DL	Don Larsen	1.00
MM	Willie Mays	4.00
BM	Bill Mazeroski	1.00
SM	Stan Musial	3.00
JP	Jim Palmer	1.00
KP	Kirby Puckett	2.00
BR	Brooks Robinson	1.00
MS	Mike Schmidt	4.00
TS	Tom Seaver	2.00
CY	Carl Yastrzemski	2.00
RY	Robin Yount	2.00
Series 2		
DB	Dusty Baker	1.00
JB	Johnny Bench	2.50
JCA	Jose Canseco	1.50
JC	Joe Carter	1.00
WF	Whitey Ford	2.00
LG	Luis Gonzalez	1.00
AJ	Andruw Jones	1.50
DJ	David Justice	1.00
AK	Al Kaline	2.00
WM	Willie McCovey	1.00
JP	Johnny Podres	1.00
FR	Frank Robinson	1.50
OS	Ozzie Smith	2.00
DS	Duke Snider	1.50
BT	Bobby Thomson	1.00

World Series Highlights Autographs

		NM/M
Common Player:		
LB	Lou Brock	30.00
CF	Carlton Fisk	50.00
KG	Kirk Gibson	30.00
DL	Don Larsen	25.00
BM	Bill Mazeroski	30.00
JP	Jim Palmer	25.00
BR	Brooks Robinson	40.00
MS	Mike Schmidt	65.00
RY	Robin Yount	50.00
Series 2		
DB	Dusty Baker	20.00
JB	Johnny Bench	50.00
WF	Whitey Ford	35.00
RJ	Reggie Jackson	40.00
DJ	David Justice	30.00
AK	Al Kaline	40.00
SM	Stan Musial	75.00
JP	Johnny Podres	15.00
DS	Duke Snider	35.00
BT	Bobby Thomson	20.00

2004 Topps All-Time Fan Favorites

CATCHER EXPOS — GARY CARTER

		NM/M
Complete Set (150):		35.00
Common Player:		.25
Pack (6):		4.00
Box (24):		80.00
1	Willie Mays	2.50
2	Bob Gibson	.75
3	Dave Steib	.25

4	Tim McCarver	.25
5	Reggie Jackson	.75
6	John Candelaria	.25
7	Lenny Dykstra	.25
8	Tony Oliva	.50
9	Frank Viola	.25
10	Don Mattingly	2.50
11	Garry Maddox	.25
12	Randy Jones	.25
13	Joe Carter	.25
14	Orlando Cepeda	.50
15	Bob Sheppard	.25
16	Bobby Grich	.25
17	George Scott	.25
18	Mickey Rivers	.25
19	Ron Santo	.25
20	Mike Schmidt	2.00
21	Luis Aparicio	.25
22	Cesar Geronimo	.25
23	Jack Morris	.25
24	Jeffrey Loria	.25
25	George Brett	2.00
26	Paul O'Neill	.50
27	Reggie Smith	.25
28	Robin Yount	1.00
29	Andre Dawson	.50
30	Whitey Ford	.75
31	Ralph Kiner	.50
32	Will Clark	.50
33	Keith Hernandez	.25
34	Tony Fernandez	.25
35	Willie McGee	.25
36	Harmon Killebrew	.75
37	Dave Kingman	.25
38	Kirk Gibson	.25
39	Terry Steinbach	.25
40	Frank Robinson	.75
41	Chet Lemon	.25
42	Mike Cuellar	.25
43	Darrell Evans	.25
44	Don Kessinger	.25
45	Dave Concepcion	.25
46	Sparky Anderson	.25
47	Bret Saberhagen	.25
48	Brett Butler	.25
49	Kent Hrbek	.25
50	Hank Aaron	2.50
51	Rudolph Giuliani	.25
52	Clete Boyer	.25
53	Mookie Wilson	.25
54	Dave Stewart	.25
55	Gary Matthews	.25
56	Roy Face	.25
57	Vida Blue	.25
58	Jimmy Key	.25
59	Al Hrabosky	.25
60	Al Kaline	.75
61	Mike Scott	.25
62	Jack McDowell	.25
63	Reggie Jackson	.75
64	Earl Weaver	.25
65	Ernie Harwell	.25
66	David Justice	.25
67	Wilbur Wood	.25
68	Mike Boddicker	.25
69	Don Zimmer	.25
70	Jim Palmer	.50
71	Doug DeCinces	.25
72	Ryne Sandberg	1.00
73	Don Newcombe	.25
74	Denny Martinez	.25
75	Carl Yastrzemski	1.50
76	Bake McBride	.25
77	Andy Van Slyke	.25
78	Bruce Sutter	.50
79	Bobby Valentine	.25
80	Johnny Bench	1.50
81	Orel Hershiser	.25
82	Danny Tartabull	.25
83	Lou Whitaker	.25
84	Alan Trammell	.25
85	Sam McDowell	.25
86	Ray Knight	.25
87	Fernando Valenzuela	.25
88	Ben Oglivie	.25
89	Billy Beane	.25
90	Yogi Berra	1.00
91	Jose Canseco	.25
92	Bobby Bonilla	.25
93	Darren Daulton	.25
94	Harold Reynolds	.25
95	Lou Brock	.50
96	Pete Incaviglia	.25
97	Eric Gregg	.25
98	Devon White	.25
99	Kelly Gruber	.25
100	Nolan Ryan	3.00
101	Carlton Fisk	.50
102	George Foster	.25
103	Dennis Eckersley	.25
104	Rick Sutcliffe	.25
105	Cal Ripken Jr.	3.00
106	Norm Cash	.25
107	Charlie Hough	.25
108	Paul Molitor	.75
109	Maury Wills	.25
110	Tom Seaver	1.00
111	Brooks Robinson	.75
112	Jim Rice	.25
113	Dwight Gooden	.25
114	Harold Baines	.25
115	Tim Raines	.25
116	Roy Smalley	.25
117	Richie Allen	.25
118	Ron Swoboda	.25
119	Ron Guidry	.25
120	Duke Snider	.75
121	Ferguson Jenkins	.50

122	Mark Fidrych	.25
123	Buddy Bell	.25
124	Bo Jackson	.50
125	Stan Musial	2.00
126	Jesse Barfield	.25
127	Tony Gwynn	1.25
128	Phil Garner	.25
129	Dale Murphy	.50
130	Wade Boggs	.75
131	Sid Fernandez	.25
132	Monte Irvin	.25
133	Peter Ueberroth	.25
134	Gary Gaetti	.25
135	Gorman Thomas	.25
136	Davey Lopes	.25
137	Sy Berger	.25
138	Buck O'Neil	.25
139	Herb Score	.25
140	Rod Carew	.75
141	Joe Buck	.25
142	Willie Horton	.25
143	Hal McRae	.25
144	Rollie Fingers	.25
145	Tom Brunansky	.25
146	Fay Vincent	.25
147	Gary Carter	.50
148	Bobby Richardson	.25
149	Steve Garvey	.25
150	Don Larsen	.50

Refractor

KELLY GRUBER — Blue Jays

Cards (1-150):	3-6X
Production 299 Sets	

Autographs

NOLAN RYAN P — ANGELS

		NM/M
Common Autograph:		10.00
Inserted 2:Box		
SP's Noted		
HA	Hank Aaron/50	350.00
RA	Richie Allen	15.00
SA	Sparky Anderson/100	20.00
LA	Luis Aparicio/100	40.00
HB	Harold Baines/100	20.00
JB	Jesse Barfield	10.00
BB	Billy Beane/100	25.00
BBE	Buddy Bell	20.00
JBE	Johnny Bench/100	150.00
SB	Sy Berger	50.00
YB	Yogi Berra/100	90.00
VB	Vida Blue	15.00
MB	Mike Boddicker	15.00
WB	Wade Boggs/50	100.00
BMB	Bobby Bonilla	20.00
GB	George Brett/50	100.00
LB	Lou Brock/100	60.00
TB	Tom Brunansky	25.00
JB	Joe Buck/100	30.00
JCA	Jose Canseco/100	65.00
RC	Rod Carew/100	60.00
GC	Gary Carter/50	60.00
JC	Joe Carter/100	45.00
OC	Orlando Cepeda/100	65.00
DC	Dave Concepcion/100	40.00
DD	Darren Daulton	40.00
AD	Andre Dawson/100	40.00
LD	Lenny Dykstra/100	20.00
DEC	Dennis Eckersley/100	40.00
DE	Darrell Evans	10.00
SF	Sid Fernandez/100	15.00
TF	Tony Fernandez	15.00
MF	Mark Fidrych/100	40.00
RF	Rollie Fingers/100	40.00
WF	Whitey Ford/100	100.00
GF	George Foster	10.00

Best Seat In The House

BEST SEAT IN THE HOUSE

		NM/M
	Common Card:	15.00
BS1	Tom Seaver, Johnny Bench, George Foster	15.00
BS2	Frank Robinson, Jim Palmer, Brooks Robinson	15.00
BS3	Dave Parker, Bill Madlock, Bill Mazeroski	15.00
BS4	Kent Hrbek, Rod Carew, Harmon Killebrew	30.00

Relics

		NM/M
	Common Player:	5.00
WB	Wade Boggs	10.00
GB	George Brett	15.00
LB	Lou Brock	10.00

	...00	
	...00	
		25.00
		25.00
		30.00
		10.00
	...gh	15.00
	...ky	15.00
	...aviglia	20.00
	...e Irvin/100	25.00
	...Jackson/50	100.00
	...Reggie Jackson	80.00
	Ferguson Jenkins	15.00
	Randy Jones	10.00
DJ	David Justice	25.00
AK	Al Kaline/50	100.00
DKE	Don Kessinger	15.00
JK	Jimmy Key/50	45.00
HK	Harmon Killebrew/100	85.00
RK	Ralph Kiner	40.00
DK	Dave Kingman	40.00
RKN	Ray Knight/100	40.00
DLA	Don Larsen	15.00
CL	Chet Lemon	15.00
DL	Davey Lopes	10.00
GM	Gary Mathews	10.00
DON	Don Mattingly/50	125.00
WM	Willie Mays/50	225.00
TM	Tim McCarver	40.00
JM	Jack McDowell	25.00
SM	Sam McDowell/100	50.00
WMC	Willie McGee/100	15.00
PM	Paul Molitor/50	85.00
JMO	Jack Morris	10.00
DM	Dale Murphy/50	75.00
SM	Stan Musial/100	100.00
BO	Buck O'Neil	30.00
PO	Paul O'Neill/50	60.00
BO	Ben Oglivie	30.00
TO	Tony Oliva	30.00
JP	Jim Palmer/50	100.00
TR	Tim Raines	25.00
HR	Harold Reynolds/100	30.00
JR	Jim Rice/100	40.00
BR	Bobby Richardson	15.00
CR	Cal Ripken Jr./50	200.00
MR	Mickey Rivers	10.00
BRO	Brooks Robinson/50	100.00
FR	Frank Robinson/100	80.00
NR	Nolan Ryan	175.00
BS	Bret Saberhagen/100	45.00
RYN	Ryne Sandberg/100	100.00
RS	Ron Santo	30.00
MS	Mike Schmidt/50	100.00
GS	George Scott	15.00
MSC	Mike Scott	10.00
TSE	Tom Seaver/50	100.00
DSN	Duke Snider/100	75.00
DS	Dave Stewart	10.00
DST	Dave Stieb	25.00
RSU	Rick Sutcliffe/100	40.00
BSU	Bruce Sutter	35.00
RSW	Ron Swoboda	15.00
AT	Alan Trammell/100	60.00
PU	Peter Ueberroth/100	60.00
BV	Bobby Valentine/100	50.00
AV	Andy Van Slyke/100	65.00
FVI	Fay Vincent/100	50.00
EW	Earl Weaver	50.00
MW	Maury Wills	10.00
MWI	Mookie Wilson	10.00
WW	Wilbur Wood	15.00
CY	Carl Yastrzemski/50	100.00
RY	Robin Yount/50	100.00
DZ	Don Zimmer	30.00

(Second column — letter-coded relics)

JC	Jose Canseco/Jsy	8.00
JCB	Jose Canseco/Bat	8.00
GC	Gary Carter	8.00
DE	Dennis Eckersley	5.00
CF	Carlton Fisk	10.00
GF	George Foster	5.00
KG	Kirk Gibson	5.00
KH	Keith Hernandez	8.00
RJ	Reggie Jackson	10.00
DJ	David Justice	5.00
HK	Harmon Killebrew	20.00
WM	Willie Mays	30.00
JM	Joe Morgan	5.00
GN	Graig Nettles	8.00
JP	Jim Palmer	8.00
DP	Dave Parker	5.00
KP	Kirby Puckett	10.00
HR	Harold Reynolds	5.00
JR	Jim Rice	5.00
BR	Brooks Robinson	12.00
FRB	Frank Robinson/Bat	8.00
FR	Frank Robinson/Jsy	8.00
NR	Nolan Ryan	25.00
BS	Bret Saberhagen	5.00
MS	Mike Schmidt	15.00
DS	Darryl Strawberry	8.00
EW	Earl Weaver	8.00
MW	Maury Wills	5.00
CY	Carl Yastrzemski	20.00

2004 Topps Bazooka

		NM/M
	Complete Set (300):	40.00
	Common Player:	.15
	Variations (30): Same Price	
	Pack (8):	2.00
	Box (24):	40.00
1	Bobby Abreu	.25
2	Jesse Foppert	.15
3	Shea Hillenbrand	.15
4	Jose Lima	.15
5	Manny Ramirez	.50
6	Denny Neagle	.15
7	Frank Thomas	.50
8	A.J. Burnett	.15
9	Carl Everett	.15
10	Scott Podsednik	.25
11	Travis Lee	.15
12	Mike Mussina	.40
13	Runelvys Hernandez	.15
14	Shannon Stewart	.15
15	Miguel Cabrera	.40
16	Edgardo Alfonzo	.15
17	Victor Zambrano	.15
18	Rafael Furcal	.25
19	Eric Hinske	.15
20	Paul LoDuca	.15
21	Phil Nevin	.15
22	Aramis Ramirez	.15
23	Jim Thome	.75
24	Jeromy Burnitz	.15
25	Mark Prior	1.50
26	Ramon Hernandez	.15
27	Cliff Lee	.15
28	Greg Myers	.15
29	Robert Fick	.15
30	Mike Sweeney	.15
31	Carlos Zambrano	.15
32	Roberto Alomar	.40
33	Orlando Cabrera	.25
34	Orlando Hudson	.15
35	Nomar Garciaparra	1.50
36	Esteban Loaiza	.15
37	Laynce Nix	.15
38	Joe Randa	.15
39	Juan Uribe	.15
40	Pat Burrell	.40
41	Steve Finley	.15
42	Livan Hernandez	.15
43	Al Leiter	.15
44	Brett Myers	.15
45	Jody Gerut	.15
46	Mark Teixeira	.40
47	Barry Zito	.40
48	Moises Alou	.25
49	Mike Cameron	.15
50	Albert Pujols	1.50
51	Tim Hudson	.25
52	Kenny Lofton	.25
53	Trot Nixon	.15
54	Tim Redding	.15
55	Marlon Byrd	.15
56	Javier Vazquez	.25
57	Sean Burroughs	.15
58	Cliff Floyd	.15
59	Juan Rivera	.15
60	Mike Lieberthal	.15
61	Xavier Nady	.15
62	Brad Radke	.15
63	Miguel Tejada	.40
64	Ichiro Suzuki	1.00
65	Garret Anderson	.25
66	Sean Casey	.15
67	Jason Giambi	.75
68	Aubrey Huff	.15
69	Javy Lopez	.25
70	Hideo Nomo	.25
71	Mark Redman	.15
72	Jose Vidro	.15
73	Rich Aurilia	.15
74	Luis Castillo	.15
75	Jay Gibbons	.15
76	Torii Hunter	.25
77	Derek Lowe	.15
78	Wes Obermueller	.15
79	Edgar Renteria	.15
80	Jeff Bagwell	.50
81	Fernando Vina	.15
82	Frank Catalanotto	.15
83	Marcus Giles	.15
84	Raul Ibanez	.15
85	Mike Lowell	.25
86	Tomokazu Ohka	.15
87	Jose Reyes	.25
88	Omar Vizquel	.25
89	Shawn Chacon	.15
90	Rocco Baldelli	.25
91	Brian Giles	.25
92	Kazuhisa Ishii	.15
93	Greg Maddux	1.00
94	John Olerud	.25
95	Eric Chavez	.25
96	Doug Waechter	.15
97	Tony Batista	.15
98	Jeriome Robertson	.15
99	Troy Glaus	.25
100	Eric Gagne	.25
101	Pedro J. Martinez	.75
102	Magglio Ordonez	.25
103	Alex Rodriguez	2.00
104	Jason Bay	.15
105	Larry Walker	.25
106	Matt Clement	.15
107	Tom Glavine	.25
108	Geoff Jenkins	.25
109	Victor Martinez	.15
110	David Ortiz	.15
111	Ivan Rodriguez	.40
112	Jarrod Washburn	.15
113	Josh Beckett	.25
114	Bartolo Colon	.25
115	Juan Gonzalez	.40
116	Derek Jeter	2.00
117	Edgar Martinez	.25
118	Ramon Ortiz	.15
119	Scott Rolen	.75
120	Brandon Webb	.15
121	Carlos Beltran	.25
122	Jose Contreras	.25
123	Luis Gonzalez	.25
124	Jason Johnson	.15
125	Luis Matos	.15
126	Russ Ortiz	.15
127	Damian Rolls	.15
128	David Wells	.15
129	Adrian Beltre	.15
130	Shawn Green	.25
131	Nate Cornejo	.15
132	Nick Johnson	.15
133	Joe Mays	.15
134	Roy Oswalt	.25
135	C.C. Sabathia	.15
136	Vernon Wells	.25
137	Kris Benson	.15
138	Carl Crawford	.25
139	Ken Griffey Jr.	1.00
140	Randy Johnson	.75
141	Fred McGriff	.25
142	Vicente Padilla	.15
143	Tim Salmon	.25
144	Kip Wells	.15
145	Lance Berkman	.25
146	Jose Cruz Jr.	.15
147	Marquis Grissom	.15
148	Jacque Jones	.15
149	Gil Meche	.15
150	Vladimir Guerrero	.75
151	Reggie Sanders	.15
152	Ty Wigginton	.15
153	Angel Berroa	.15
154	Johnny Damon	.25
155	Rafael Palmeiro	.50
156	Chipper Jones	.75
157	Kevin Millar	.15
158	Corey Patterson	.25
159	Johan Santana	.15
160	Bernie Williams	.40
161	Craig Biggio	.25
162	Carlos Delgado	.50
163	Aaron Guiel	.15
164	Wade Miller	.15
165	Andruw Jones	.50
166	Jay Payton	.15
167	Benito Santiago	.15
168	Woody Williams	.15
169	Casey Blake	.15
170	Adam Dunn	.40
171	Jose Guillen	.15
172	Brian Jordan	.15
173	Kevin Millwood	.25
174	Carlos Pena	.15
175	Curt Schilling	.50
176	Jerome Williams	.15
177	Hank Blalock	.25
178	Erubiel Durazo	.15
179	Cristian Guzman	.15
180	Austin Kearns	.40
181	Raul Mondesi	.15
182	Andy Pettitte	.25
183	Jason Schmidt	.15
184	Jeremy Bonderman	.15
185	Dontrelle Willis	.25
186	Ray Durham	.15
187	Jerry Hairston Jr.	.15
188	Jason Kendall	.15
189	Melvin Mora	.15
190	Jeff Kent	.25
191	Jae Weong Seo	.15
192	Jack Wilson	.15
193	Cesar Izturis	.15
194	Jermaine Dye	.15
195	Roy Halladay	.15
196	Jason Phillips	.15
197	Matt Morris	.15
198	Mike Piazza	1.00
199	Richie Sexson	.40
200	Alfonso Soriano	.75
201	Mark Mulder	.15
202	David Eckstein	.15
203	Mike Hampton	.15
204	Ryan Klesko	.15
205	Damian Moss	.15
206	Juan Pierre	.15
207	Ben Sheets	.15
208	Randy Winn	.15
209	Bret Boone	.25
210	Jim Edmonds	.25
211	Rich Harden	.15
212	Paul Konerko	.15
213	Jamie Moyer	.15
214	A.J. Pierzynski	.15
215	Gary Sheffield	.25
216	Randy Wolf	.15
217	Kevin Brown	.25
218	Morgan Ensberg	.15
219	Bo Hart	.15
220	Bill Mueller	.15
221	Corey Koskie	.15
222	Joel Pineiro	.15
223	Preston Wilson	.15
224	Aaron Boone	.15
225	Kerry Wood	.50
226	Darin Erstad	.25
227	Wes Helms	.15
228	Brian Lawrence	.15
229	Mark Buehrle	.15
230	Sammy Sosa	1.25
231	Sidney Ponson	.15
232	Dmitri Young	.15
233	Ellis Burks	.15
234	Kelvim Escobar	.15
235	Todd Helton	.25
236	Matt Lawton	.15
237	Eric Munson	.15
238	Jorge Posada	.50
239	Junior Spivey	.15
240	Michael Young	.15
241	Ramon Nivar	.15
242	Edwin Jackson	.15
243	Felix Pie	.15
244	Ryan Wagner	.15
245	Grady Sizemore	.25
246	Bobby Jenks	.15
247	Chad Billingsley	.15
248	Casey Kotchman	.15
249	Bobby Crosby	.15
250	Khalil Greene	.15
251	Danny Garcia	.15
252	Nicholas Markakis	.15
253	Bernie Castro	.15
254	Aaron Hill	.15
255	Josh Barfield	.15
256	Ryan Wagner	.15
257	Ryan Harvey	.15
258	Jimmy Gobble	.15
259	Ryan Madson	.15
260	Zack Greinke	.15
261	Rene Reyes	.15
262	Eric Duncan	.15
263	Chris Lubanski	.15
264	Jeff Mathis	.15
265	Rickie Weeks	.15
266	Justin Morneau	.25
267	Brian Snyder	.15
268	Neal Cotts	.15
269	Joe Borchard	.15
270	Larry Bigbie	.15
271	Marcus McBeth RC	.40
272	Tydus Meadows RC	.15
273	Zach Miner RC	.50
274	Anthony Lerew RC	.40
275	Yadier Molina RC	.40
276	Jon Knott RC	.40
277	Matthew Moses	.40
278	Sung Jung RC	.40
279	Mike Gosling	.15
280	David Murphy	.15
281	Tim Frend RC	.40
282	Casey Myers RC	.40
283	Brayan Pena RC	.40
284	Omar Falcon RC	.40
285	Blake Hawksworth RC	.40
286	Jesse Roman RC	.40
287	Kyle Davies RC	.40
288	Matt Creighton RC	.40
289	Rodney Choy Foo RC	.40
290	Kyle Sleeth	.40
291	Carlos Quentin	.50
292	Khalid Ballouli RC	.15
293	Tim Stauffer	.15
294	Craig Ansman RC	.40
295	Dioner Navarro RC	.40
296	Josh Labandeira RC	.40
297	Jeff Allison	.15
298	Anthony Acevedo RC	.40
299	Brad Sullivan	.15
300	Conor Jackson	.50

Red
Cards (1-300): 1-2X
Inserted 1:1

Mini
Stars (1-300): 1-2X
Inserted 1:1

Adventures

		NM/M
	Common Player:	4.00
EA	Edgardo Alfonzo	4.00
JB	Jeff Bagwell	8.00
LB	Lance Berkman	6.00
CB	Craig Biggio	4.00
KB	Kevin Brown	4.00
PB	Pat Burrell	6.00
MB	Marlon Byrd	4.00
SC	Sean Casey	4.00
LC	Luis Castillo	4.00
EC	Eric Chavez	5.00
AD1	Adam Dunn	6.00
AD2	Adam Dunn	6.00
CE	Carl Everett	4.00
CF	Cliff Floyd	4.00
NG	Nomar Garciaparra	10.00
JG	Jason Giambi	8.00
JDG	Jeremy Giambi	4.00
TEG	Troy Glaus	5.00
TG	Tom Glavine	5.00
LG	Luis Gonzalez	4.00
SG	Shawn Green	5.00
BG	Ben Grieve	4.00
VG	Vladimir Guerrero	8.00
CG	Cristian Guzman	4.00
TH	Toby Hall	4.00
TAH1	Tim Hudson	4.00
TAH2	Tim Hudson	4.00
GJ	Geoff Jenkins	4.00
RJ	Randy Johnson	8.00
AJ	Andruw Jones	6.00
CJ	Chipper Jones	8.00
JK	Jason Kendall	4.00
PK	Paul Konerko	4.00
PL	Paul LoDuca	4.00
ML	Mike Lowell	4.00
GM	Greg Maddux	8.00
KM	Kevin Millwood	6.00
MM	Mark Mulder	5.00
MCM	Mike Mussina	6.00
HN	Hideo Nomo	8.00
JO	John Olerud	4.00
RP1	Rafael Palmeiro	6.00
RP2	Rafael Palmeiro	6.00
BP	Brad Penny	4.00
MP1	Mike Piazza	10.00
MP2	Mike Piazza	10.00
AP	Albert Pujols	15.00
MR	Manny Ramirez	8.00
AR1	Alex Rodriguez	10.00
AR2	Alex Rodriguez	10.00
TJS	Tim Salmon	5.00
CS	Curt Schilling	8.00
AS	Alfonso Soriano	6.00
MT	Miguel Tejada	6.00
JT	Jim Thome	8.00
LW	Larry Walker	4.00
JW	Jarrod Washburn	4.00
BW	Bernie Williams	6.00
DW	Dontrelle Willis	6.00
PW	Preston Wilson	4.00

KW	Kerry Wood	6.00
BZ	Barry Zito	6.00

Blasts

		NM/M
	Common Player:	4.00
RA	Roberto Alomar	6.00
MA	Moises Alou	4.00
RSA	Rich Aurilia	4.00
JB	Jeff Bagwell	8.00
RB	Rocco Baldelli	4.00
TB	Tony Batista	4.00
CIB	Carlos Beltran	4.00
LB	Lance Berkman	5.00
CB	Craig Biggio	6.00
HB	Hank Blalock	6.00
BB	Bret Boone	5.00
JNB	Jeromy Burnitz	4.00
SB	Sean Burroughs	4.00
CC	Carl Crawford	4.00
AD	Adam Dunn	6.00
CE	Carl Everett	4.00
BF	Brad Fullmer	4.00
RF	Rafael Furcal	5.00
AJG	Andres Galarraga	4.00
NG	Nomar Garciaparra	12.00
JG	Jason Giambi	8.00
TG	Troy Glaus	5.00
AG	Adrian Gonzalez	4.00
JAG	Juan Gonzalez	6.00
LG	Luis Gonzalez	4.00
SG	Shawn Green	4.00
MG	Marquis Grissom	4.00
VG	Vladimir Guerrero	8.00
CG	Cristian Guzman	4.00
NH	Nathan Haynes	4.00
TKH	Todd Helton	6.00
AH	Aubrey Huff	4.00
TH	Torii Hunter	4.00
CJ	Chipper Jones	8.00
PK	Paul Konerko	4.00
ML	Matt Lawton	4.00
CL	Carlos Lee	4.00
PL	Paul LoDuca	4.00
EM	Edgar Martinez	4.00
TM	Tino Martinez	4.00
FM	Fred McGriff	5.00
DM	Doug Mientkiewicz	4.00
JO	John Olerud	4.00
MO	Magglio Ordonez	4.00
RP	Rafael Palmeiro	8.00
CP	Corey Patterson	4.00
MP	Mike Piazza	10.00
JP	Jorge Posada	6.00
AP	Albert Pujols	15.00
ANR	Aramis Ramirez	4.00
MR	Manny Ramirez	8.00
JR	Juan Rivera	4.00
AR	Alex Rodriguez	10.00
IR	Ivan Rodriguez	6.00
SR	Scott Rolen	8.00
TJS	Tim Salmon	4.00
GS	Gary Sheffield	5.00
RS	Ruben Sierra	4.00
AS	Alfonso Soriano	4.00
SS	Shannon Stewart	5.00
ST	So Taguchi	5.00
MCT	Mark Teixeira	5.00
MT	Miguel Tejada	8.00
FT	Frank Thomas	8.00
MAT	Michael Tucker	4.00
MV	Mo Vaughn	4.00
OV	Omar Vizquel	4.00
LW	Larry Walker	5.00
VW	Vernon Wells	5.00
RW	Rondell White	6.00
BW	Bernie Williams	6.00

Comics

		NM/M
	Complete Set (24):	6.00
	Common Player:	.25
	Inserted 1:4	
BC1	Garret Anderson	.25
BC2	Jeff Bagwell	.50
BC3	Hank Blalock	.25
BC4	Roy Halladay	.25
BC5	Dontrelle Willis	.25
BC6	Roger Clemens	.25
BC7	Carlos Delgado	.40
BC8	Rafael Furcal	.25
BC9	Eric Gagne	.25
BC10	Nomar Garciaparra	.75
BC11	Derek Jeter	.75
BC12	Esteban Loaiza	.25
BC13	Kevin Millwood	.25

BC14	Bill Mueller	.25
BC15	Rafael Palmeiro	.40
BC16	Albert Pujols	.75
BC17	Jose Reyes	.25
BC18	Alex Rodriguez	.75
BC19	Alfonso Soriano	.40
BC20	Sammy Sosa	.50
BC21	Ichiro Suzuki	.50
BC22	Frank Thomas	.40
BC23	Brad Wilkerson	.25
BC24	Houston Astros	.25

One-Liners

BAZOOKA ONE-LINERS
"RUN EVERYTHING OUT AND BE IN BY TWELVE."
RED SCHOENDIENST   ST. LOUIS CARDINALS

		NM/M
	Common Player:	5.00
DA	Dick Allen	8.00
JB	Johnny Bench	10.00
BB	Bert Blyleven	5.00
WB1	Wade Boggs	6.00
WB2	Wade Boggs	6.00
GB	George Brett	20.00
BC	Bert Campaneris	5.00
RC	Rod Carew	8.00
GC	Gary Carter	5.00
JCA	Joe Carter	5.00
OC	Orlando Cepeda	5.00
RD	Ron Darling	5.00
AD	Andre Dawson	8.00
DE	Dennis Eckersley	10.00
KG1	Kirk Gibson	5.00
KG2	Kirk Gibson	5.00
DW	Dwight Gooden	5.00
KH	Keith Hernandez	5.00
RJ	Reggie Jackson	10.00
DJ1	David Justice	8.00
DJ2	David Justice	8.00
HK	Harmon Killebrew	20.00
JK	Jerry Koosman	5.00
BM	Bill Madlock	5.00
WM	Willie Mays	30.00
WMC	Willie McGee	8.00
TM	Tug McGraw	8.00
JM	Joe Morgan	8.00
DM	Dale Murphy	15.00
EM	Eddie Murray	10.00
PN	Phil Niekro	5.00
DP	Dave Parker	5.00
GP	Gaylord Perry	5.00
KP1	Kirby Puckett	10.00
KP2	Kirby Puckett	10.00
FR	Frank Robinson	10.00
NR	Nolan Ryan	15.00
BS	Bret Saberhagen	5.00
RSA	Ron Santo	10.00
MS	Mike Schmidt	15.00
RS	Red Schoendienst	5.00
TS	Tom Seaver	8.00
WS	Willie Stargell	8.00
CY	Carl Yastrzemski	15.00
RY	Robin Yount	10.00

Stand-Ups

VERNON WELLS   TORONTO BLUE JAYS   OUTFIELD

		NM/M
	Complete Set (25):	20.00
	Common Player:	.50
	Inserted 1:8	
1	Jose Reyes	.50
2	Jim Thome	1.00
3	Roy Halladay	.50
4	Jason Giambi	1.00
5	Dontrelle Willis	1.00
6	Mike Piazza	1.50
7	Chipper Jones	1.00
8	Mark Prior	2.00
9	Todd Helton	.75
10	Miguel Cabrera	.75
11	Derek Jeter	3.00
12	Nomar Garciaparra	2.00
13	Alex Rodriguez	3.00
14	Miguel Tejada	.75
15	Carlos Delgado	.75
16	Pedro J. Martinez	1.00
17	Sammy Sosa	2.00
18	Ichiro Suzuki	1.50
19	Vladimir Guerrero	1.00
20	Alfonso Soriano	1.00

21	Eric Chavez	.50
22	Albert Pujols	2.50
23	Ivan Rodriguez	.75
24	Vernon Wells	.50
25	Eric Gagne	.50

Tattoos

		NM/M
	Complete Set (55):	8.00
	Common Player:	.15
	Inserted 1:4	
JB	Jeff Bagwell	.25
BAZ	Bazooka Logo	.15
LB	Lance Berkman	.15
CB	Craig Biggio	.15
KB	Kevin Brown	.15
PB	Pat Burrell	.15
MB	Marlon Byrd	.15
SC	Sean Casey	.15
LC	Luis Castillo	.15
EC	Eric Chavez	.15
AD	Adam Dunn	.15
CF	Cliff Floyd	.15
NG	Nomar Garciaparra	.75
JG	Jason Giambi	.40
TFG	Troy Glaus	.15
TG	Tom Glavine	.15
LG	Luis Gonzalez	.15
SG	Shawn Green	.15
VG	Vladimir Guerrero	.40
CG	Cristian Guzman	.15
TH	Toby Hall	.15
TAH	Tim Hudson	.15
GJ	Geoff Jenkins	.15
RJ	Randy Johnson	.40
AJ	Andruw Jones	.25
CJ	Chipper Jones	.40
JK	Jason Kendall	.15
PK	Paul Konerko	.15
PL	Paul LoDuca	.15
ML	Mike Lowell	.15
GM	Greg Maddux	.50
KM	Kevin Millwood	.15
MM	Mark Mulder	.15
MCM	Mike Mussina	.15
HN	Hideo Nomo	.15
JO	John Olerud	.15
RP	Rafael Palmeiro	.25
BP	Brad Penny	.15
MP	Mike Piazza	.50
AP	Albert Pujols	1.00
MR	Manny Ramirez	.25
AR	Alex Rodriguez	1.00
TJS	Tim Salmon	.25
CS	Curt Schilling	.25
AS	Alfonso Soriano	.40
MT	Miguel Tejada	.40
JT	Jim Thome	.40
TOP	Topps Logo	.15
LW	Larry Walker	.15
JW	Jarrod Washburn	.15
BW	Bernie Williams	.15
DW	Dontrelle Willis	.15
PW	Preston Wilson	.15
KW	Kerry Wood	.25
BZ	Barry Zito	.25

4-on-1 Stickers

		NM/M
	Complete Set (40):	8.00
	Common Player:	.20
	Inserted 1:4	
1	Rich Harden, Dontrelle Willis, Jerome Williams, Brandon Webb	.20
2	Eric Duncan, Derek Jeter, Alfonso Soriano, Jason Giambi	.75
3	Grady Sizemore, Rocco Baldelli, Ichiro Suzuki, Vladimir Guerrero	.50
4	Roy Halladay, Pedro J. Martinez, Curt Schilling, Brett Myers	.40
5	Alex Rodriguez, Angel Berroa, Jose Reyes, Khalil Greene	.75
6	Kerry Wood, Adam Dunn, Jeff Kent, Scott Rolen	.40
7	Miguel Cabrera, Scott Podsednik, Bo Hart, Mark Teixeira	.20
8	Rickie Weeks, Josh Barfield, Albert Pujols, Vernon Wells	.50
9	Torii Hunter, Garret Anderson, Bobby Abreu, Ken Griffey Jr.	.40
10	Jay Gibbons, Chipper Jones, Mike Piazza, Mike Sweeney	.40
11	David Ortiz, Nick Johnson, Carlos Delgado, Frank Thomas	.40
12	Todd Helton, Jose Vidro, Mike Lowell, Miguel Tejada	.40
13	Randy Wolf, Mark Mulder, Johan Santana, Randy Johnson	.40
14	Bret Boone, Aubrey Huff, Eric Chavez, Javy Lopez	.15
15	Jason Schmidt, Roy Oswalt, Joel Pineiro, Mark Prior	.50
16	Kevin Millwood, Andy Pettitte, Matt Morris, Tim Hudson	.20
17	Javier Vazquez, Esteban Loaiza, Orlando Cabrera, Roberto Alomar	.20
18	Al Leiter, David Wells, Mike Hampton, Jarrod Washburn	.20
19	Paul LoDuca, Mike Lieberthal, Brian Giles, Andruw Jones	.20
20	Maggio Ordonez, Corey Patterson, Aaron Boone, Jeff Bagwell	.40
21	Troy Glaus, Edgar Martinez, Manny Ramirez, Raul Ibanez	.30
22	Sammy Sosa, Barry Zito, Bartolo Colon, Austin Kearns	.50
23	Jim Edmonds, Gary Sheffield, Preston Wilson, Shawn Green	.20
24	Bernie Williams, Juan Pierre, Josh Beckett, Mike Mussina	.20
25	Ramon Hernandez, Jason Kendall, Jason Phillips, A.J. Pierzynski	.20
26	Pat Burrell, Laynce Nix, Mike Cameron, Cliff Floyd	.20
27	Eric Gagne, Carl Crawford, Jose Guillen, Steve Finley	.20
28	Ellis Burks, Livan Hernandez, Derek Lowe, Kazuhisa Ishii	.20
29	Jorge Posada, Jeff Mathis, Victor Martinez, Ivan Rodriguez	.20
30	Jim Thome, Marcus Giles, Nomar Garciaparra, Hank Blalock	.50
31	Edgar Renteria, Bobby Crosby, Neal Cotts, Russ Ortiz	.20
32	Zack Greinke, Cristian Guzman, Cesar Izturis, Kevin Brown	.20
33	Bobby Jenks, Ramon Nivar, Richie Sexson, Ryan Klesko	.20
34	Omar Vizquel, Carlos Pena, Rafael Furcal, Gil Meche	.20
35	Kenny Lofton, Tim Salmon, Marquis Grissom, Craig Biggio	.20
36	Kyle Davies, Anthony Lerew, Brayan Pena, Sung Jung	.20
37	Rodney Choy Foo, Craig Ansman, David Murphy, Matthew Moses	.20
38	Carlos Quentin, Dioner Navarro, Marcus McBeth, Josh Labandeira	.20
39	Kyle Sleeth, Conor Jackson, Brad Sullivan, Jeff Allison	.20
40	Yadier Molina, Jon Knott, Blake Hawksworth, Tim Stauffer	.20

Chicago Cubs Reprints

For a fourth year the Cubs contracted with Topps to provide a series of reprint cards for use as give-aways at special games throughout the season. Each reprint features a Wrigley Field logo on front and is sequentially numbered to 20,000 in a strip of gold foil on back. Each card was distributed in a cello wrapper with the date of the promotion and names of the sponsor(s).

		NM/M
	Complete Set (2):	5.00
	Common Player:	2.00
(1)	Shawon Dunston	2.00
(2)	Mark Prior	2.00

2004 Topps Chrome

		NM/M
	Complete Set (466):	
	Common Player:	.25
	Common Rookie Auto. (221-246):	10.00
	Inserted 1:21	
	Series 1 Pack (4):	3.50
	Series 1 Box (20):	50.00
	Series 2 Pack (4):	3.50
	Series 2 Box (20):	50.00
1	Jim Thome	1.00
2	Reggie Sanders	.25
3	Mark Kotsay	.25
4	Edgardo Alfonzo	.25
5	Tim Wakefield	.25
6	Moises Alou	.50
7	Jorge Julio	.25
8	Bartolo Colon	.50
9	Chan Ho Park	.25
10	Ichiro Suzuki	3.00
11	Kevin Millwood	.50
12	Preston Wilson	.40
13	Tom Glavine	.75
14	Junior Spivey	.25
15	Marcus Giles	.40
16	David Segui	.25
17	Kevin Millar	.25
18	Corey Patterson	.40
19	Aaron Rowand	.25
20	Derek Jeter	4.00
21	Luis Castillo	.25
22	Manny Ramirez	1.50
23	Jay Payton	.25
24	Bobby Higginson	.25
25	Lance Berkman	.75
26	Juan Pierre	.25
27	Mike Mussina	1.00
28	Fred McGriff	.50
29	Richie Sexson	.75
30	Tim Hudson	.25
31	Mike Piazza	2.00
32	Brad Radke	.25
33	Jeff Weaver	.25
34	Ramon Hernandez	.25
35	David Bell	.25
36	Randy Wolf	.25
37	Jake Peavy	.50
38	Tim Worrell	.25
39	Gil Meche	.25
40	Albert Pujols	4.00
41	Michael Young	.25
42	Josh Phelps	.25
43	Brendan Donnelly	.25
44	Steve Finley	.25
45	John Smoltz	.50
46	Jay Gibbons	.25
47	Trot Nixon	.25
48	Carl Pavano	.25
49	Frank Thomas	1.00
50	Mark Prior	1.00
51	Danny Graves	.25
52	Milton Bradley	.25
53	Kris Benson	.25
54	Ryan Klesko	.25
55	Mike Lowell	.25
56	Geoff Blum	.25
57	Michael Tucker	.25
58	Paul LoDuca	.25
59	Vicente Padilla	.25
60	Jacque Jones	.25
61	Fernando Tatis	.25
62	Ty Wigginton	.25
63	Rich Aurilia	.25
64	Andy Pettitte	.25
65	Terrence Long	.25
66	Cliff Floyd	.25
67	Mariano Rivera	.50
68	Kelvim Escobar	.25
69	Marlon Byrd	.25
70	Mark Mulder	.50
71	Francisco Cordero	.25
72	Carlos Guillen	.25
73	Fernando Vina	.25
74	Lance Carter	.25
75	Hank Blalock	.75
76	Jimmy Rollins	.25
77	Francisco Rodriguez	.25
78	Javy Lopez	.25
79	Jerry Hairston Jr.	.25
80	Andruw Jones	.75
81	Rodrigo Lopez	.25
82	Johnny Damon	1.00
83	Hee Seop Choi	.25
84	Kazuhiro Sasaki	.25
85	Danny Bautista	.25
86	Matt Lawton	.25
87	Juan Uribe	.25
88	Rafael Furcal	.25
89	Kyle Farnsworth	.25
90	Jose Vidro	.25
91	Luis Rivas	.25
92	Hideo Nomo	.75
93	Javier Vazquez	.50
94	Al Leiter	.40
95	Jose Valentin	.25
96	Alex Cintron	.25
97	Zach Day	.25
98	Jorge Posada	.75
99	C.C. Sabathia	.25
100	Alex Rodriguez	3.00
101	Brad Penny	.25
102	Brad Ausmus	.25
103	Raul Ibanez	.25
104	Mike Hampton	.25
105	Adrian Beltre	.50
106	Ramiro Mendoza	.25
107	Rocco Baldelli	.75
108	Esteban Loaiza	.25
109	Russell Branyan	.25
110	Todd Helton	1.00
111	Braden Looper	.25
112	Octavio Dotel	.25
113	Mike MacDougal	.25
114	Cesar Izturis	.25
115	Johan Santana	1.00
116	Jose Contreras	.50
117	Placido Polanco	.25
118	Jason Phillips	.25
119	Orlando Hudson	.25
120	Vernon Wells	.25
121	Ben Grieve	.25
122	Dave Roberts	.25
123	Ismael Valdes	.25
124	Eric Owens	.25
125	Curt Schilling	1.00
126	Russ Ortiz	.25
127	Mark Buehrle	.50
128	Doug Mientkiewicz	.25
129	Dmitri Young	.25
130	Kazuhisa Ishii	.25
131	A.J. Pierzynski	.25
132	Brad Wilkerson	.25
133	Joe McEwing	.25
134	Alex Cora	.25
135	Jose Cruz Jr.	.25
136	Carlos Zambrano	.50
137	Jeff Kent	.25
138	Shigetoshi Hasegawa	.25
139	Jarrod Washburn	.25
140	Greg Maddux	2.00
141	Josh Beckett	.75
142	Miguel Batista	.25
143	Omar Vizquel	.40
144	Alex Gonzalez	.25
145	Billy Wagner	.25
146	Brian Jordan	.25
147	Wes Helms	.25
148	Deivi Cruz	.25
149	Alex Gonzalez	.25
150	Jason Giambi	1.00
151	Erubiel Durazo	.25
152	Mike Lieberthal	.25
153	Jason Kendall	.25
154	Xavier Nady	.25
155	Kirk Rueter	.25
156	Mike Cameron	.25
157	Miguel Cairo	.25
158	Woody Williams	.25
159	Toby Hall	.25
160	Bernie Williams	.75
161	Darin Erstad	.50
162	Matt Mantei	.25
163	Shawn Chaco.	
164	Bill Mueller	
165	Damian Miller	
166	Tony Graffanino	
167	Sean Casey	
168	Brandon Phillips	
169	Runelvys Hernande.	
170	Adam Dunn	
171	Carlos Lee	
172	Juan Encarnacion	
173	Angel Berroa	
174	Desi Relaford	
175	Joe Mays	
176	Ben Sheets	.5.
177	Eddie Guardado	.25
178	Rocky Biddle	.25
179	Eric Gagne	.50
180	Eric Chavez	.50
181	Jason Michaels	.25
182	Dustan Mohr	.25
183	Kip Wells	.25
184	Brian Lawrence	.25
185	Bret Boone	.25
186	Tino Martinez	.40
187	Aubrey Huff	.25
188	Kevin Mench	.25
189	Tim Salmon	.50
190	Carlos Delgado	1.00
191	John Lackey	.25
192	Eric Byrnes	.25
193	Luis Matos	.25
194	Derek Lowe	.50
195	Mark Grudzielanek	.25
196	Flash Gordon	.25
197	Matt Clement	.25
198	Byung-Hyun Kim	.25
199	Brandon Inge	.25
200	Nomar Garciaparra	1.50
201	Frank Catalanotto	.25
202	Cristian Guzman	.25
203	Bo Hart	.25
204	Jack Wilson	.25
205	Ray Durham	.25
206	Freddy Garcia	.25
207	J.D. Drew	.50
208	Orlando Cabrera	.25
209	Roy Halladay	.50
210	David Eckstein	.25
211	Omar Falcon RC	2.00
212	Todd Self RC	2.00
213	David Murphy	3.00
214	Dioner Navarro RC	4.00
215	Marcus McBeth RC	3.00
216	Chris O'Riordan RC	3.00
217	Rodney Choy Foo RC	2.00
218	Tim Frend RC	3.00
219	Yadier Molina RC	6.00
220	Zachary Duke RC	4.00
221	Anthony Lerew/ Auto. RC	15.00
222	Blake Hawksworth/ Auto. RC	15.00
223	Brayan Pena/ Auto. RC	10.00
224	Craig Ansman/ Auto. RC	10.00
225	Jon Knott/Auto. RC	10.00
226	Josh Labandeira/ Auto. RC	10.00
227	Khalid Ballouli/ Auto. RC	10.00
228	Kyle Davies/Auto. RC	25.00
229	Matt Creighton/ Auto.	15.00
230	Mike Gosling/Auto.	15.00
231	Nic Ungs/Auto. RC	10.00
232	Zach Miner/Auto. RC	20.00
233	Donald Levinski/ Auto.	10.00
234	Bradley Sullivan	15.00
235	Carlos Quentin	40.00
236	Conor Jackson	40.00
237	Estee Harris RC	15.00
238	Jeffrey Allison	10.00
239	Kyle Sleeth	20.00
240	Matthew Moses	15.00
241	Tim Stauffer	15.00
242	Brad Snyder	10.00
243	Jason Hirsh	20.00
244	Lastings Milledge	50.00
245	Logan Kensing RC	15.00
246	Kory Casto	10.00
247	David Aardsma	1.50
248	Omar Quintanilla	2.00
249	Ervin Santana RC	4.00
250	Merkin Valdez RC	2.00
251	Vito Chiaravalloti RC	3.00
252	Travis Blackley RC	3.00
253	Chris Shelton RC	4.00
254	Rudy Guillen RC	3.00
255	Bobby Brownlie RC	3.00
256	Paul Maholm RC	4.00
257	Roger Clemens	3.00
258	Laynce Nix	.25
259	Eric Hinske	.25
260	Ivan Rodriguez	1.00
261	Brandon Webb	.50
262	Jhonny Peralta	.25
263	Adam Kennedy	.25
264	Tony Batista	.25
265	Jeff Suppan	.25
266	Kenny Lofton	.50
267	Scott Sullivan	.25
268	Ken Griffey Jr.	2.00
269	Billy Traber	.25
270	Larry Walker	.50
271	Todd Hollandsworth	.25
272	Carlos Beltran	1.00

.25
.75
.25
.50
...lock .25
...son .25
... Lyon .25
...o Alfonseca .25
... Goodwin .25
...aul Konerko .50
D'Angelo Jimenez .25
Ben Broussard .25
Magglio Ordonez .25
294 Carlos Pena .25
295 Chad Fox .25
296 Jeriome Robertson .25
297 Travis Hafner .50
298 Joe Randa .25
299 Brady Clark .25
300 Barry Zito .75
301 Ruben Sierra .25
302 Brett Myers .25
303 Oliver Perez .25
304 Benito Santiago .25
305 David Ross .25
306 Joe Nathan .25
307 Jim Edmonds .50
308 Matt Kata .25
309 Vinny Castilla .25
310 Marty Cordova .25
311 Aramis Ramirez .50
312 Carl Everett .25
313 Ryan Freel .25
314 Mark Bellhorn .25
315 Ugueth Urbina .25
316 Tim Redding .25
317 Jeromy Burnitz .25
318 Miguel Cabrera 1.00
319 Orlando Hernandez .25
320 Casey Blake .25
321 Aaron Boone .25
322 Jermaine Dye .25
323 Jerome Williams .25
324 John Olerud .50
325 Scott Rolen 1.00
326 Bobby Kielty .25
327 Travis Lee .25
328 Jeff Cirillo .25
329 Scott Spiezio .25
330 Melvin Mora .25
331 Mike Timlin .25
332 Kerry Wood .50
333 Tony Womack .25
334 Jody Gerut .25
335 Morgan Ensberg .25
336 Odalis Perez .25
337 Michael Cuddyer .25
338 Jose Hernandez .25
339 LaTroy Hawkins .25
340 Marquis Grissom .25
341 Matt Morris .50
342 Juan Gonzalez .75
343 Jose Valverde .25
344 Joe Borowski .25
345 Josh Bard .25
346 Austin Kearns .50
347 Chin-Hui Tsao .25
348 Wilfredo Ledezma .25
349 Aaron Guiel .25
350 Alfonso Soriano 1.00
351 Ted Lilly .25
352 Sean Burroughs .25
353 Rafael Palmeiro .75
354 Quinton McCracken .25
355 David Ortiz 1.00
356 Randall Simon .25
357 Wily Mo Pena .25
358 Brian Anderson .25
359 Corey Koskie .25
360 Keith Foulke .25
361 Sidney Ponson .25
362 Gary Matthews Jr. .25
363 Herbert Perry .25
364 Shea Hillenbrand .25
365 Craig Biggio .50
366 Barry Larkin .50
367 Orlando Merced .25
368 Sammy Sosa 1.50
369 Joe Crede .50
370 Gary Sheffield .75
371 Coco Crisp .25
372 Torii Hunter .50
373 Derrek Lee .75
374 Adam Everett .25
375 Miguel Tejada .75
376 Jeremy Affeldt .25
377 Robin Ventura .25
378 Scott Podsednik .75
379 Matthew LeCroy .25
380 Vladimir Guerrero 1.50
381 Steve Karsay .25
382 Jeff Nelson .25
383 Chase Utley .75
384 Bobby Abreu .50
385 Josh Fogg .25
386 Trevor Hoffman .25
387 Matt Stairs .25
388 Edgar Martinez .50
389 Edgar Renteria .50
390 Chipper Jones 1.50

Eric Munson .25
Rewon Brazelton .25
John Thomson .25
Chris Woodward .25
395 Joe Kennedy .25
396 Reed Johnson .25
397 Johnny Estrada .25
398 Damian Moss .25
399 Victor Zambrano .25
400 Dontrelle Willis .50
401 Troy Glaus .75
402 Raul Mondesi .25
403 Jeff DaVanon .25
404 Kurt Ainsworth .25
405 Pedro J. Martinez 1.50
406 Eric Karros .25
407 Billy Koch .25
408 Luis Gonzalez .50
409 Jack Cust .25
410 Mike Sweeney .25
411 Jason Bay .75
412 Mark Redman .25
413 Jason Jennings .25
414 Rondell White .50
415 Todd Hundley .25
416 Shannon Stewart .25
417 Jae Weong Seo .25
418 Livan Hernandez .25
419 Mark Ellis .25
420 Pat Burrell .50
421 Mark Loretta .25
422 Robb Nen .25
423 Joel Pineiro .25
424 Todd Walker .25
425 Jeremy Bonderman .50
426 A.J. Burnett .25
427 Greg Myers .25
428 Roy Oswalt .50
429 Carlos Baerga .25
430 Garret Anderson .50
431 Horacio Ramirez .25
432 Brian Roberts .25
433 Kevin Brown .50
434 Eric Milton .25
435 Brian Daubach .25
436 Alex Escobar .25
437 Alex Sanchez .25
438 Jeff Bagwell 1.00
439 Claudio Vargas .25
440 Shawn Green .50
441 Geoff Jenkins .25
442 David Wells .25
443 Nick Johnson .25
444 Jose Guillen .25
445 Scott Hatteberg .25
446 Phil Nevin .25
447 Jason Schmidt .50
448 Ricky Ledee .25
449 So Taguchi .25
450 Randy Johnson .75
451 Eric Young .25
452 Chone Figgins .25
453 Larry Bigbie .25
454 Scott Williamson .25
455 Ramon Martinez .25
456 Roberto Alomar .50
457 Ryan Dempster .25
458 Ryan Ludwick .25
459 Ramon Santiago .25
460 Jeff Conine .25
461 Brad Lidge .25
462 Ken Harvey .25
463 Guillermo Mota .25
464 Rick Reed .25
465 Armando Benitez .25
466 Wade Miller .25

Refractors

Cards (1-220, 247-466): 1-2X
Inserted 1:4
Rookie Auto. (221-246): 1.5-2X
Production 100
Gold Refractor (1-220): 1-2X
Inserted 1:5
Rookie Gold Refractor (221-246): 2-3X
Production 50
Black Refractor (1-220): 2-4X
Inserted 1:10
Rookie Black Refractor: No Pricing
Production 25

Fashionably Great

NM/M
Common Player: 5.00
Inserted 1:Box
JB Jeff Bagwell 10.00
CB Craig Biggio .25
HB Hank Blalock 8.00
JBO Joe Borchard 5.00
KB Kevin Brown .25
EC Eric Chavez 6.00
CD Carlos Delgado 6.00
AD Adam Dunn 6.00
FG Freddy Garcia 5.00
CF Cliff Floyd 5.00

NG Nomar Garciaparra 10.00
TH Trevor Hoffman 5.00
TH Tim Hudson 6.00
AJ Andruw Jones 6.00
CJ Chipper Jones 8.00
DL Derek Lowe 6.00
PM Pedro J. Martinez 8.00
FM Fred McGriff 8.00
MM Mark Mulder 6.00
BM Brett Myers 5.00
JO John Olerud 4.00
RP Rafael Palmeiro 8.00
WP Wily Mo Pena 5.00
MP Mike Piazza 10.00
AP Albert Pujols 15.00
MR Manny Ramirez 8.00
JR Juan Rivera 4.00
AR Alex Rodriguez 12.00
IR Ivan Rodriguez 8.00
CS Curt Schilling 6.00
JS John Smoltz 6.00
SS Sammy Sosa 12.00
MS Mike Sweeney 5.00
FT Frank Thomas 10.00
JV Jose Vidro 6.00
BW Billy Wagner 6.00
VW Vernon Wells 5.00

Handle With Care

No pricing due to scarcity.
Production 5 Sets

Town Heroes

NM/M
Common Player: 5.00
LB Lance Berkman 5.00
EC Eric Chavez 5.00
NG Nomar Garciaparra 12.00
JG Jason Giambi 8.00
RH Rich Harden 5.00
TH Tim Hudson 6.00
CJ Chipper Jones 8.00
MM Mark Mulder 6.00
HN Hideo Nomo 8.00
RP Rafael Palmeiro 8.00
MP Mark Prior 8.00
AP Albert Pujols 15.00
MR Manny Ramirez 8.00
JR Jose Reyes 8.00
AR Alex Rodriguez 10.00
SS Sammy Sosa 15.00
SST Shannon Stewart 5.00
MT Miguel Tejada 6.00
FT Frank Thomas 8.00
KW Kerry Wood 10.00
BZ Barry Zito 8.00

2004 Topps Clubhouse Collection Relics

NM/M
Common Player: 4.00
2 Relics Per Pack
Pack (2): 18.00
Box (10): 140.00
HA Hank Aaron/113 50.00
BA Bobby Abreu 6.00
RA Roberto Alomar 6.00
EA Edgardo Alfonzo/286 4.00
TA Tony Armas Jr. 4.00
JB Jeff Bagwell 8.00
RB Rocco Baldelli 6.00
TB Tony Batista 4.00
HB Hank Bauer 10.00
JPB Josh Beckett/195 6.00
JBE Johnny Bench 10.00
AB Armando Benitez 4.00
LB Lance Berkman 6.00
YB Yogi Berra 10.00
HBL Hank Blalock 8.00
WB Wade Boggs/250 6.00
BB Bret Boone 4.00
GB George Brett 12.00
KB Kevin Brown 6.00
JBU Jeromy Burnitz 4.00

PB Pat Burrell 6.00
MB Marlon Byrd 4.00
MC Miguel Cabrera 8.00
GC Gary Carter/221 8.00
JCA Joe Carter/259 6.00
RLC Roger Cedeno 4.00
OC Orlando Cepeda 8.00
RCE Ron Cey 6.00
EC Eric Chavez 8.00
CFC Chin-Feng Chen 8.00
JC Jeff Cirillo 4.00
WC Will Clark 8.00
RC Roberto Clemente 75.00
DC Dave Concepcion 8.00
CCR Carl Crawford 8.00
CD Carlos Delgado/200 6.00
AD Adam Dunn 8.00
DE Dennis Eckersley 10.00
CE Carl Everett 4.00
SF Steve Finley 4.00
CFL Cliff Floyd 4.00
WF Whitey Ford/296 15.00
BF Brad Fullmer/200 4.00
JF Jonathan Fulton 6.00
RF Rafael Furcal 4.00
EG Eric Gagne 8.00
NG Nomar Garciaparra 12.00
JG Jason Giambi 8.00
TGL Troy Glaus 6.00
TG Tom Glavine 8.00
AG Adrian Gonzalez 4.00
LG Luis Gonzalez 6.00
JGO Juan Gonzalez 8.00
MG Mark Grace 8.00
SG Shawn Green 4.00
KG Ken Griffey Jr./200 15.00
MDG Marquis Grissom 4.00
VG Vladimir Guerrero 8.00
CG Cristian Guzman 4.00
TGW Tony Gwynn 10.00
MH Mickey Hall 4.00
EH Estee Harris/206 4.00
THE Todd Helton 8.00
RHE Rickey Henderson 10.00
RH Ramon Hernandez 4.00
OH Orel Hershiser 8.00
JH James Houser/182 8.00
OHU Orlando Hudson 8.00
TH Tim Hudson 6.00
THU Torii Hunter 6.00
KI Kazuhisa Ishii 4.00
RJ Reggie Jackson 10.00
DJ Derek Jeter 20.00
AJ Andruw Jones 6.00
CJ Chipper Jones 8.00
AK Al Kaline 15.00
JKE Jeff Kent/200 4.00
PK Paul Konerko 6.00
BL Barry Larkin/200 10.00
AL Al Leiter 4.00
SL Steve Lerud 4.00
EL Esteban Loaiza 4.00
PL Paul LoDuca 4.00
JL Javy Lopez 4.00
DL Derek Lowe/200 4.00
CL Chris Lubanski/209 8.00
GM Greg Maddux 15.00
EMA Edgar Martinez/200 8.00
PM Pedro Martinez/200 10.00
TM Tino Martinez 6.00
EM Eddie Mathews/174 25.00
WM Willie Mays 60.00
FM Fred McGriff 6.00
KM Kevin Millwood 4.00
MM Mark Mulder 6.00
EMU Eddie Murray 12.00
BM Brett Myers 4.00
HN Hideo Nomo/207 8.00
JO John Olerud 6.00
MO Magglio Ordonez 8.00
RP Rafael Palmeiro/200 10.00
CP Chan Ho Park 4.00
DP Dave Parker/292 10.00
CPA Corey Patterson/267 8.00
WP Wily Mo Pena 4.00
TPE Troy Percival 4.00
TP Tony Perez 10.00
MP Mike Piazza 10.00
JP Jorge Posada/264 8.00
AP Albert Pujols 15.00
ARA Aramis Ramirez 8.00
MR Manny Ramirez/207 8.00
JRE Jose Reyes 6.00
CR Cal Ripken Jr. 20.00
FR Frank Robinson 8.00
JR Jackie Robinson/262 50.00
AR Alex Rodriguez 10.00
IR Ivan Rodriguez 8.00
SR Scott Rolen 10.00
JRO Jimmy Rollins 8.00
NR Nolan Ryan 20.00
CS C.C. Sabathia 4.00
TS Tim Salmon 8.00
RSA Ryne Sandberg 15.00
JS Jay Sborz 6.00
CSC Curt Schilling 8.00
MS Mike Schmidt 15.00
RS Richie Sexson/200 6.00
GS Gary Sheffield 8.00
RSI Ruben Sierra 10.00
OS Ozzie Smith 15.00
JSM John Smoltz 8.00
DS Duke Snider 15.00
AS Alfonso Soriano 6.00
SS Sammy Sosa 12.00
WS Willie Stargell/200 10.00
CST Casey Stengel/217 10.00

MSW Mike Sweeney 4.00
MTE Miguel Tejada 6.00
MT Mark Teixeira 6.00
FT Frank Thomas 8.00
JT Jim Thome 8.00
FV Fernando Valenzuela 8.00
JVI Jose Vidro 4.00
BWA Billy Wagner 4.00
LW Larry Walker 4.00
VW Vernon Wells/200 4.00
BW Bernie Williams 6.00
PW Preston Wilson 4.00
JV Javier Vazquez 6.00
CY Carl Yastrzemski 15.00
RY Robin Yount 12.00
BZ Barry Zito/230 6.00

Black

Black: 2-3X
Production 25 Sets

Copper

Copper: .75-1.5X
Production 99 Sets

Red

Red: No Pricing
Production One Set

All-Star Appeal Ball

No Pricing
Production 10 Sets

Collectible All-Star Appeal Ball Autograph

NM/M
Production 30 Sets
GA Garret Anderson 30.00
HB Hank Blalock 35.00
JP Jorge Posada 50.00

All-Star Appeal Base

NM/M
Common Player: 5.00
Production 65 Sets
On Deck Circle: 1X
Production 90 Sets
GA Garret Anderson 8.00
HB Hank Blalock 8.00
BB Bret Boone 5.00
CD Carlos Delgado 6.00
JE Jim Edmonds 6.00
RF Rafael Furcal 6.00
NG Nomar Garciaparra 15.00
JG Jason Giambi 8.00
TG Troy Glaus 6.00
LG Luis Gonzalez 6.00
TH Todd Helton 6.00
AJ Andruw Jones 6.00
JL Javy Lopez 6.00
ML Mike Lowell 6.00
EM Edgar Martinez 6.00
MO Magglio Ordonez 8.00
JP Jorge Posada 8.00
AP Albert Pujols 25.00
ER Edgar Renteria 6.00
AR Alex Rodriguez 15.00
SR Scott Rolen 10.00
RS Richie Sexson 6.00
GS Gary Sheffield 8.00
AS Alfonso Soriano 10.00
VW Vernon Wells 6.00
PW Preston Wilson 5.00

Collectible All-Star Appeal Base Autograph

NM/M
Production 50 Sets
GA Garret Anderson 25.00
JP Jorge Posada 35.00
GS Gary Sheffield 25.00

Collectible All-Star Appeal On Deck Circle

NM/M
Common Player:

Production 90 Sets

GA Garret Anderson 8.00
HB Hank Blalock 8.00
AB Aaron Boone 5.00
BB Bret Boone 5.00
LC Luis Castillo 5.00
CD Carlos Delgado 6.00
JE Jim Edmonds 6.00
CE Carl Everett 5.00
RF Rafael Furcal 6.00
NG Nomar Garciaparra 15.00
JG Jason Giambi 8.00
TG Troy Glaus 6.00
LG Luis Gonzalez 6.00
TH Todd Helton 8.00
AJ Andruw Jones 8.00
PL Paul LoDuca 5.00
JL Javy Lopez 6.00
ML Mike Lowell 6.00
EM Edgar Martinez 6.00
MM Melvin Mora 5.00
MO Magglio Ordonez 8.00
JP Jorge Posada 8.00
AP Albert Pujols 20.00
ER Edgar Renteria 8.00
AR Alex Rodriguez 15.00
SR Scott Rolen 10.00
RS Richie Sexson 6.00
GS Gary Sheffield 8.00
AS Alfonso Soriano 10.00
JV Jose Vidro 5.00
VW Vernon Wells 6.00
RW Rondell White 5.00
PW Preston Wilson 5.00

Collectible All-Star Appeal On Deck Autograph

NM/M
Quantity produced listed
GA Garret Anderson/320 15.00
HB Hank Blalock/920 15.00
JP Jorge Posada/420 30.00
GS Gary Sheffield/170 25.00

Career Legends Relics

NM/M
Common Player:
BR1 Babe Ruth/60 175.00
BR2 Babe Ruth/171 150.00
BR3 Babe Ruth/45 200.00
EB1 Ernie Banks/143 15.00
EB3 Ernie Banks/47 20.00
EB6 Ernie Banks/15 15.00
LG1 Lou Gehrig/49 125.00
LG2 Lou Gehrig/184 100.00
LG3 Lou Gehrig/52 125.00
TC3 Ty Cobb/47 120.00
WM1 Willie Mays/52 70.00
WM2 Willie Mays/141 60.00

DoublePlay Relics

NM/M
Production 75 Sets
CLE Omar Vizquel, Brandon Phillips, Travis Hafner 10.00
NYM Ty Wigginton, Jose Reyes, Mike Piazza 25.00
NYY Derek Jeter, Alex Rodriguez, Jason Giambi 50.00
PHI Jimmy Rollins, David Bell, Jim Thome 20.00
SDP Khalil Greene, Sean Burroughs, Phil Nevin 10.00

Frozen Ropes Relics

NM/M
Common Player: 5.00
Production 50 Sets
BA Bobby Abreu 8.00
JB Jeff Bagwell 10.00
RB Rocco Baldelli 8.00
JBE Johnny Bench 20.00
LB Lance Berkman 5.00
CB Craig Biggio 6.00
HB Hank Blalock 10.00
WB Wade Boggs 8.00
GC Gary Carter 8.00
EC Eric Chavez 8.00

ADA	Andre Dawson	8.00
AD	Adam Dunn	10.00
CE	Carl Everett	5.00
RF	Rafael Furcal	5.00
JG	Jason Giambi	8.00
LG	Luis Gonzalez	5.00
SG	Shawn Green	5.00
VG	Vladimir Guerrero	15.00
TH	Todd Helton	10.00
AH	Aubrey Huff	5.00
CJ	Chipper Jones	15.00
PK	Paul Konerko	5.00
EM	Edgar Martinez	8.00
DM	Don Mattingly	40.00
DMU	Dale Murphy	12.00
MO	Magglio Ordonez	8.00
RP	Rafael Palmeiro	10.00
MP	Mike Piazza	15.00
KP	Kirby Puckett	15.00
AP	Albert Pujols	25.00
MR	Manny Ramirez	10.00
JR	Jose Reyes	8.00
BR	Brooks Robinson	15.00
AR	Alex Rodriguez	15.00
IR	Ivan Rodriguez	10.00
RS	Ryne Sandberg	40.00
MS	Mike Schmidt	40.00
GS	Gary Sheffield	6.00
OS	Ozzie Smith	25.00
DS	Duke Snider	15.00
AS	Alfonso Soriano	10.00
SS	Sammy Sosa	15.00
MT	Miguel Tejada	8.00
JT	Jim Thome	10.00
BW	Bernie Williams	8.00
PW	Preston Wilson	5.00
CY	Carl Yastrzemski	20.00

Collectible Heart of the Line-Up Relics

NM/M

Production 100 unless noted.

ARI	Steve Finley, Richie Sexson, Luis Gonzalez	10.00
CHC	Sammy Sosa, Moises Alou, Aramis Ramirez	35.00
CHW	Magglio Ordonez, Frank Thomas, Carlos Lee/78	20.00
CIN	Ken Griffey Jr., Austin Kearns, Adam Dunn	25.00
COL	Todd Helton, Larry Walker, Preston Wilson	15.00
NYY	Alex Rodriguez, Jason Giambi, Gary Sheffield	35.00
PHI	Jim Thome, Pat Burrell, Bobby Abreu	20.00
SEA	Edgar Martinez, Bret Boone, John Olerud	10.00
STL	Albert Pujols, Jim Edmonds, Scott Rolen	40.00
TEX	Alfonso Soriano, Mark Teixeira, Hank Blalock	20.00
TOR	Vernon Wells, Carlos Delgado, Eric Hinske	10.00

Patch Place Relics

No Pricing
Production 25 or less.

Power Pieces Relics

NM/M

Quantity produced listed

CD	Carlos Delgado/25	10.00
THU	Torii Hunter/48	8.00
AJ	Andruw Jones/25	10.00
PM	Pedro Martinez/45	10.00
WM	Willie Mays/24	85.00
BM	Brett Myers/39	5.00
BP	Brad Penny/31	5.00
MP	Mike Piazza/31	40.00
NR	Nolan Ryan/34	50.00
CS	Curt Schilling/38	8.00
BZ	Barry Zito/75	6.00

2004 Topps Cracker Jack

NM/M

Complete Set with SP's (250):		160.00
Common Player:		.25
Common SP:		2.00
SP's inserted 1:3		
Pack (8):		3.00
Box (24):		60.00
1	Jose Reyes/SP	2.00
1	Edgar Renteria	.25
2	Albert Pujols	2.00
3	Albert Pujols/SP/Swinging	6.00
4	Garret Anderson	.50
5	Bobby Abreu	.40
6	Andruw Jones	.75
7	Jeff Kent	.40

PUJOLS, St. Louis - Nationals

8	Magglio Ordonez	.50
9	Kris Benson	.25
10	Luis Gonzalez	.40
11	Corey Patterson	.25
12	Connie Mack	.25
13	Vernon Wells/SP	2.00
14	Jim Edmonds	.50
15	Bret Boone	.25
16	Travis Lee	.25
17	Alex Rodriguez/SP	6.00
No #	Alex Rodriguez	2.00
18	Erubiel Durazo	.25
19	Brett Myers	.25
20	Scott Rolen/SP	3.00
21	Paul LoDuca	.25
22	Geoff Jenkins	.50
23	Charles Comiskey	.25
24	Cliff Floyd	.25
25	Jim Thome	.75
25	Jim Thome/SP/Fielding	3.00
26	Russ Ortiz	.25
27	Bill Mueller	.25
28	Kenny Lofton	.40
29	Jay Gibbons	.40
30	Ken Griffey Jr.	1.50
31	Jeff Bagwell	.75
32	Jose Lima	.25
33	Brad Radke	.25
34	Ramon Hernandez	.25
35	Brian Giles/SP	2.00
36	Jeremy Bonderman	.25
37	Jerome Williams	.25
38	Rafael Palmeiro	.50
39	Scott Podsednik	.75
40	Rafael Furcal	.40
41	Roy Oswalt	.40
42	Orlando Hudson	.25
43	Todd Helton	.75
44	Kerry Wood	1.00
45	Tom Glavine	.40
46	David Eckstein	.25
47	Trot Nixon	.25
48	Preston Wilson	.25
50	Eric Gagne/SP	3.00
51	Ichiro Suzuki/SP	5.00
52	Juan Gonzalez	.75
53	Torii Hunter	.50
54	Bartolo Colon	.40
55	Dick Hoblitzell	.25
56	Al Leiter	.25
57	Johnny Damon	.40
58	Larry Walker	.40
59	Brian Jordan	.25
60	Richie Sexson/SP	3.00
61	Orlando Cabrera	.25
62	Jason Phillips	.25
63	Phil Nevin	.25
64	John Olerud	.40
65	Miguel Tejada	.50
66	Nap Lajoie	.50
67	C.C. Sabathia	.25
68	Ty Wigginton	.25
69	Troy Glaus	.50
70	Mike Piazza	1.50
71	Craig Biggio	.40
72	Cristian Guzman	.25
73	Dmitri Young	.25
74	Roger Clemens	2.00
75	Runelvys Hernandez	.25
76	Nomar Garciaparra	2.00
77	Mark Mulder	.40
78	Derek Lowe	.25
79	Paul Konerko	.25
80	Sammy Sosa/SP	5.00
81	Vladimir Guerrero	1.00
82	Xavier Nady	.25
83	Joel Pineiro	.25
84	Chipper Jones	1.50
85	Manny Ramirez	.75
86	Burt Shotton	.25
87	Raul Ibanez/SP	2.00
88	Eric Chavez	.50
89	Frank Catalanotto	.25
90	Dontrelle Willis	.50
91	Roy Halladay	.50
92	Jermaine Dye	.25
93	Jason Kendall	.25
94	Jacque Jones	.25
95	Gary Sheffield	.50
95	Gary Sheffield/SP/Yanks	3.00
96	Mike Lieberthal	.25
97	Adam Dunn	.50
98	Carl Crawford	.50
99	Reggie Sanders	.25
100	Mark Prior/SP	6.00
101	Luis Matos	.25

102	Barry Zito	.50
103	Randy Johnson	1.00
104	Kevin Brown	.50
105	Pat Burrell	.50
106	Steve Finley	.25
107	Moises Alou	.25
108	David Ortiz/SP	3.00
109	Austin Kearns/SP	2.00
110	Carlos Beltran	.50
111	Shawn Green	.40
112	Javier Vazquez	.50
113	Hideo Nomo	.50
114	Kazuhisa Ishii	.25
115	Corey Koskie	.25
116	Kevin Millwood	.25
117	Randy Wolf	.40
118	Darin Erstad	.25
119	Fernando Vina	.25
120	Pedro J. Martinez	1.00
121	Melvin Mora	.25
122	Carl Everett	.25
123	Matt Morris	.40
124	Greg Maddux	1.50
125	Jason Schmidt	.25
126	Mark Teixeira/SP	3.00
127	Randy Winn	.25
128	Rich Aurilia	.25
129	Vicente Padilla	.25
130	Tim Hudson	.50
131	Marlon Byrd	.25
132	Jae Weong Seo	.25
133	Branch Rickey	.25
134	A.J. Pierzynski	.25
135	Ryan Klesko	.40
136	Eric Hinske	.25
137	Mike Cameron	.25
138	Roberto Alomar	.50
139	Jarrod Washburn	.25
140	Curt Schilling	.75
140	Curt Schilling/SP/Red Sox	3.00
141	Omar Vizquel	.25
142	Mike Sweeney	.25
143	Wade Miller	.25
144	Jose Vidro	.25
145	Rich Harden/SP	2.00
146	Eric Munson	.25
147	Lance Berkman	.50
148	Mark Buehrle	.25
149	Carlos Delgado	.75
150	Sean Burroughs	.25
151	Kevin Millar	.25
152	Frank Thomas	.75
153	Adrian Beltre	.25
154	Shannon Stewart	.25
155	Johan Santana	.25
156	Edgardo Alfonzo	.25
157	Jose Cruz Jr.	.25
158	Sidney Ponson	.25
159	Edgar Martinez	.50
160	Jamie Moyer	.25
161	Tony Batista	.25
162	Wes Helms	.25
163	Brandon Webb/SP	2.00
164	Gil Meche	.25
165	Marcus Giles/SP	2.00
166	Angel Berroa/SP	2.00
167	Rocco Baldelli/SP	3.00
168	Michael Young	.25
169	Esteban Loaiza	.25
170	Casey Blake	.25
171	Jody Gerut	.25
172	Bo Hart/SP	.25
173	Kelvim Escobar	.25
174	Aaron Guiel	.25
175	Javy Lopez/SP	3.00
176	Aubrey Huff	.25
177	Hank Blalock	.50
178	Edwin Jackson	.25
178	Edwin Jackson/SP/#104	2.00
179	Delmon Young/SP	2.00
180	Bobby Jenks	.25
181	Felix Pie	.25
181	Felix Pie/SP/#80	2.00
182	Jeremy Reed/SP	2.00
183	Aaron Hill	.25
184	Casey Kotchman/SP	2.00
185	Grady Sizemore	.50
186	Joe Mauer/SP	3.00
187	Ryan Harvey	.25
188	Neal Cotts	.25
189	Victor Martinez	.25
190	Rene Reyes	.25
191	Eric Duncan	.25
192	B.J. Upton/SP	2.00
193	Khalil Greene/SP	2.00
194	Bobby Crosby	.25
195	Rickie Weeks/SP	3.00
196	Zack Greinke/SP	2.00
197	Laynce Nix	.25
198	Vito Chiaravalloti/SP RC	2.00
199	Estee Harris RC	.25
200	Jon Knott/SP RC	.25
201	Dioner Navarro RC	.75
201	Dioner Navarro/SP/#236	2.00
202	Craig Ansman RC	.50
203	Travis Blackley RC	.25
204	Yadier Molina RC	.50

SP - Short Print

205	Rodney Choy Foo RC	.50
206	Kyle Sleeth/SP	5.00
207	Jeff Allison	1.00
208	Josh Labandeira RC	.50
209	Lastings Milledge/SP	10.00
210	Rudy Guillen/SP RC	3.00
211	Blake Hawksworth/SP RC	
212	David Aardsma	.50
213	Shawn Hill RC	.50
214	Erick Aybar/SP RC	3.00
215	Ervin Santana RC	1.00
216	Tim Stauffer/SP	1.00
217	Merkin Valdez RC	.25
218	Jack McKeon	.25
219	Derek Lee	.50
220	Josh Beckett/SP	3.00
221	Luis Castillo	.50
222	Mike Lowell	.50
223	Juan Pierre	.40
224	Ivan Rodriguez	.75
224	Ivan Rodriguez/SP/Tigers	3.00
225	A.J. Burnett	.25
226	Miguel Cabrera/SP	4.00
227	Jeffrey Loria	.25
228	Joe Torre	.25
229	Jason Giambi	.75
229	Jason Giambi/SP/Fielding	3.00
230	Aaron Boone	.25
231	Jose Contreras	.25
232	Derek Jeter/SP	6.00
233	Nick Johnson	.25
234	Mike Mussina	.75
235	Andy Pettitte	.50
236	Jorge Posada/SP	3.00
237	Alfonso Soriano	.75
238	Bernie Williams	.50

Mini

BIGGIO, Houston - Nationals

Mini:		1-2X
Mini SP:		1X
Inserted 1:Pack		
Mini SP's Inserted 1:20		
SP's are same as in base set.		

Mini Autograph

NM/M

Common Autograph:		
Inserted 1:258		
95	Gary Sheffield/50	40.00
112	Javier Vazquez	15.00
163	Brandon Webb	15.00
165	Marcus Giles	12.00
221	Luis Castillo	8.00
226	Miguel Cabrera	35.00

Mini Blue

Mini Blue:		3-6X
Mini Blue SP:		1-2X
Inserted 1:10		
Mini Blue SP's Inserted 1:60		
SP's are same as in base set.		

Mini White

No Pricing
Production One Set

Sticker

Stickers:		1X
SP Stickers:		.5X
Inserted 1:Surprise Pack		
SP's Inserted 1:10 Surprise Packs		

Secret Surprise Signatures

NM/M

Common Autograph:		8.00
CF	Cliff Floyd	15.00
BG	Brian Giles	15.00
AH	Aubrey Huff	15.00
ML	Mike Lamb	8.00
DM	Dustin McGowan	20.00
FP	Felix Pie	20.00
SP	Scott Podsednik	20.00
SR	Scott Rolen	30.00
MV	Merkin Valdez	15.00
JW	Jerome Williams	20.00
DW	Dontrelle Willis	30.00

Take Me Out to/Ballgame Relics

NM/M

Common Player:		5.00

AUTHENTIC GAME-USED BAT — HANK BLALOCK, Texas - Rangers

BA	Bobby Abreu	5.00
MA	Moises Alou	6.00
GA	Garret Anderson	8.00
JB	Jeff Bagwell	8.00
RB	Rocco Baldelli	8.00
LB	Lance Berkman	5.00
AB	Angel Berroa	5.00
CB	Craig Biggio	5.00
HB	Hank Blalock	5.00
BB1	Bret Boone/Bat	5.00
BB2	Bret Boone/Jsy	5.00
PB	Pat Burrell	6.00
MC	Miguel Cabrera	8.00
EC	Eric Chavez	5.00
AD	Adam Dunn	5.00
JE	Jim Edmonds	8.00
RF	Rafael Furcal	6.00
NG	Nomar Garciaparra/Bat	10.00
NG	Nomar Garciaparra/Jsy	10.00
JG	Jason Giambi	8.00
MG	Marcus Giles	5.00
TG	Troy Glaus	8.00
LG	Luis Gonzalez	5.00
SG	Shawn Green/Bat	6.00
SG	Shawn Green/Jsy	6.00
TH	Todd Helton	6.00
TKH	Torii Hunter	6.00
CJ	Chipper Jones	8.00
PL	Paul LoDuca	5.00
JL	Javy Lopez/Bat	6.00
JL	Javy Lopez/Jsy	6.00
MP	Mike Piazza	8.00
AP	Albert Pujols/Bat	15.00
AP	Albert Pujols/Jsy	15.00
MR	Manny Ramirez	8.00
JR	Jose Reyes	6.00
AR	Alex Rodriguez/Bat/Yanks	15.00
AR	Alex Rodriguez/Jsy	10.00
IR	Ivan Rodriguez	8.00
JRO	Jimmy Rollins	5.00
AS	Alfonso Soriano/Bat	8.00
AS	Alfonso Soriano/Jsy	8.00
SS	Sammy Sosa/Bat	10.00
SS	Sammy Sosa/Jsy	10.00
MS	Mike Sweeney	5.00
MT	Mark Teixeira	6.00
MT	Miguel Tejada	6.00
JT	Jim Thome	8.00
LW	Larry Walker	5.00
VW	Vernon Wells	5.00
KW	Kerry Wood	5.00
MY	Michael Young	5.00

Jack 1,2,3 Strikes You're Out Relics

NM/M

Common Player:		4.00
JB	Josh Beckett	8.00
KB	Kevin Brown	5.00
EG	Eric Gagne	8.00
RH	Rich Harden	4.00
RJ	Randy Johnson	8.00
DL	Derek Lowe	6.00
PM	Pedro J. Martinez	8.00
KM	Kevin Millwood	6.00
MAM	Mark Mulder	5.00
MM	Mike Mussina	15.00
BM	Brett Myers	4.00
HN	Hideo Nomo	5.00
CCS	C.C. Sabathia	5.00
CS	Curt Schilling	15.00
JS	John Smoltz	6.00
BW	Billy Wagner	4.00
KW	Kerry Wood	10.00
BZ	Barry Zito	6.00

2004 Topps eTopps

Topps continued its on-line card program for a fourth year in 2004. Initial Player Offerings

($4.50-7.50 per card) were again made for one week, with allocations having to be made for some cards in high demand. The number of each card actually sold is shown parenthetically. After the IPO, cards could be bought and sold within portfolios, or physically delivered (for a fee) for more traditional venues. The 2-1/2" x 3-1/2" cards' fronts have an action photo at top and a strip of fading portrait photos below. Backs repeat the portrait photo, have a 2003 recap and 2004 "prospectus," and a few biographical bits and stats. New for 2004 was a subset of team cards picturing several stars. A total of 119 cards was issued, skip-numbered between 1-133. Values shown are for cards in a virtual portfolio, rather than "in hand." Taking physical possession of a card from an eTopps portfolio costs about $6 apiece.

NM/M

Complete Set (119):		175.00
Common Player:		1.50
1	Andy Pettitte/1,991	1.50
2	Jason Giambi/1,565	1.50
3	Kevin Youkilis/2,171	1.50
4	Casey Blake/1,420	1.50
5	Ryan Ludwick/1,321	1.50
6	Craig Wilson/1,544	1.50
7	Curt Schilling/2,216	1.50
8	Mark Prior/3,750	1.50
9	Casey Kotchman/2,006	1.75
10	Scott Podsednik/2,500	1.75
11	Carlos Guillen/1,541	1.50
12	Clint Nageotte/1,526)	1.50
13	Melvin Mora/1,432	1.50
14	Ivan Rodriguez/2,104	1.75
15	Travis Hafner/2,500	3.00
16	Mike Piazza/2,500	1.50
17	Brian Giles/1,267	2.00
18	Derek Jeter/2,708	5.75
19	Edwin Jackson/3,655	1.50
20	Chipper Jones/2,158	1.50
21	Jody Gerut/1,436	1.50
22	Carlos Lee/1,562	2.00
23	Jason Schmidt/1,659	1.75
25	Ichiro/2,228)	1.75
27	Corey Patterson/2,500	1.50
30	Kerry Wood/1,824	1.50
31	Jim Thome/1,908	1.50
32	Hideki Matsui/2,500	2.00
33	Rocco Baldelli/2,500	1.50
34	Jose Reyes/1,739)	1.50
35	Dontrelle Willis/3,750	1.50
36	Miguel Cabrera/3,750	2.00
37	Brandon Webb/2,072	1.50
38	Rich Harden/1,823)	2.75
40	Vladimir Guerrero/1,913	1.50
41	Hank Blalock/3,303	1.50
42	Kazuo Matsui/5,000	1.50
43	Joe Mauer/4,888	3.00
44	Keith Foulke/1,896	1.50
45	Josh Beckett/3,178	1.50
46	Jamie Moyer/1,573	1.50
47	Victor Martinez/2,500	2.25
49	Derek Lee/1,920	1.50
51	Roger Clemens/3,750	2.25
52	David Ortiz/1,655	2.25
53	Jason Bay/2,336	4.75
54	Erubiel Durazo/1,577	1.50
55	Gary Sheffield/1,639	1.50
56	Jeff Kent/2,036	1.50
57	Ken Harvey/1,621	1.50
58	Jason Varitek/2,698	1.50
59	Jeromy Burnitz/2,148	1.50
60	Nomar Garciaparra/2,074	1.50
61	Javy Lopez/3,204)	1.50
62	Eric Gagne/2,279)	1.50
63	Khalil Greene/3,456)	3.00
64	Carlos Zambrano/3,492	1.50
65	Lyle Overbay/2,789	1.50
68	Laynce Nix/1,760	1.50
69	Manny Ramirez/1,909	1.75
70	Alfonso Soriano/1,820	1.50
71	Mike Lieberthal/1,479	1.50
72	Juan Pierre/2,500	1.50
73	Frank Thomas/1,835	1.50
74	Sean Casey/1,851	1.50
75	Albert Pujols/3,750	4.25
76	Bill Mueller/1,977	1.75
78	Randy Johnson/2,725	1.50
79	Carlos Beltran/2,500	1.50
80	Pedro Martinez/1,726	1.50
81	Lew Ford/1,932	1.50
82	Javier Vazquez/1,936	1.50
83	Kevin Brown/2,635	1.50
84	Johnny Estrada/1,590	1.50
85	Ken Griffey Jr./2,396	2.75
87	Jorge Posada/2,176	1.50
89	Bobby Crosby/3,498	2.50
90	Sammy Sosa/3,248	1.50

91	Shingo Takatsu/1,678	1.50
92	Akinori Otsuka/1,544	1.50
93	Michael Young/2,004	3.25
94	Aaron Miles/1,608	1.50
95	Miguel Tejada/1,548	1.50
96	Chad Tracy/2,534	2.50
99	Todd Helton/1,998	1.50
100	Alex Rodriguez/5,000	2.50
101	Bartolo Colon/1,973	1.50
102	Philadelphia Phillies/2,500	1.50
103	Seattle Mariners/2,500	1.50
104	Atlanta Braves/2,500	1.50
105	Chicago White Sox/2,458	1.50
106	Pittsburgh Pirates/2,500	1.50
107	St. Louis Cardinals/2,500	1.75
108	Houston Astros/2,500	1.50
109	Toronto Blue Jays/2,500	1.50
110	Arizona Diamondbacks/1,818	8.00
111	New York Mets/2,570	1.50
112	Minnesota Twins/2,500	1.50
113	Baltimore Orioles/2,750	1.50
114	Cleveland Indians/2,219	1.50
115	Boston Red Sox/3,750	5.25
116	Tampa Bay Devil Rays/2,191	1.50
117	Chicago Cubs/3,750	1.50
118	Texas Rangers/2,500	1.50
119	Cincinnati Reds/2,500	1.50
120	Anaheim Angels/2,500	1.50
121	Colorado Rockies/2,500	1.50
122	K.C. Royals/2,120	1.50
123	Florida Marlins/2,500	1.50
124	Oakland A's/2,375	1.50
125	L.A. Dodgers/2,155	1.50
126	Milwaukee Brewers/2,500	1.50
127	S.F. Giants/2,500	1.50
128	Montreal Expos/2,500	1.50
129	San Diego Padres/2,500	1.50
130	New York Yankees/3,750	1.50
131	Detroit Tigers/2,750	1.50
132	Matt Holliday/2,425	2.00
133	Zack Greinke/3,750	2.25

Classics

Topps continued its eTopps Classics line-up in 2004 with 20 cards of former greats. Numbering and format were contiguous with earlier issues. Like regular eTopps cards, Classics could only be ordered during a one-week Initial Player Offering period. Cards were issued in a quantity of 1,200 each at $9.50. The number of cards actually sold is shown parenthetically. Fronts have a color or colorized action photo, backs have a picture of one of that player's Topps cards, along with career notes, stats, etc. Values shown are for cards in a virtual portfolio, rather than "in hand." Taking physical possession of a card from an eTopps portfolio costs about $6 apiece.

		NM/M
	Complete Set(20):	175.00
	Common Player:	8.00
41	Orlando Cepeda/806	10.00
42	Wade Boggs/908	10.00
43	Al Kaline/962	9.00
44	Jim Palmer/768	20.00
45	Ozzie Smith/1,161	8.00
46	Rod Carew/908	8.00
47	Paul Molitor/850	8.00
48	Hank Aaron/1,250	25.00
49	Robin Yount/1,002	8.00
50	Hank Greenberg/769	15.00
51	Robin Roberts/807	10.00
52	Casey Stengel/898	8.00
53	Cy Young/1,200	9.00
54	Thurman Munson/1,250	9.00
55	Roy Campanella/984	8.00
56	Satchel Paige/1,222	8.00
57	Tris Speaker/795	11.00
58	Jimmie Foxx/952	9.00
59	Dizzy Dean/967	9.00
60	"Cool Papa" Bell/988	8.00

Econ

A four-card set honoring local athletes was issued in conjunction with the 25th National Sports Collectors Convention and the 2nd Topps Econ in Cleveland in late July. Only one baseball player was included. Persons purchasing VIP admission packs at the show received a version of the card without the eTopps authenticity sticker on back.

		NM/M
1	Bob Lemon ($5.25 / 978)	3.25
1	Bob Lemon (Unstickered show version.)	2.00

Events Series

A RIVALRY CONTINUED...

A RIVALRY REBORN!

Values shown are for cards in a virtual portfolio rather than "in hand." Each card originally sold for $4.50. Quantity actually issued is shown parenthetically.

		NM/M
	Complete Set (12):	25.00
	Common Card:	1.50
1	Alex Rodriguez, Curt Schilling/1,500	2.50
2	Albert Pujols, Carlos Beltran/1,298	2.00
3	Hideki Matsui, Mariano Rivera/1,294	1.50
4	Carlos Beltran/1,427	1.50
5	Jeff Kent, David Ortiz/1,126	1.50
6	Jim Edmonds/983	6.00
7	Derek Lowe, Johnny Damon/2,116	1.50
8	Scott Rolen, Albert Pujols/1,119	3.00
9	Mark Bellhorn, Curt Schilling/1,173	1.50
10	Pedro Martinez/1,250	1.50
11	Derek Lowe/2,565	2.00
12	Manny Ramirez/1,500	2.00

2004 Topps Heritage

		NM/M
	Complete Set (475):	400.00

	Common Player:	.40
	Common SP (398-475):	4.00
	Variations & SP's Inserted 1:2	
	Pack (8):	5.00
	Box (24):	100.00
1	Jim Thome	1.50
1	Jim Thome/SP/Hitting	8.00
2	Nomar Garciaparra/SP	10.00
3	Aramis Ramirez	.40
4	Rafael Palmeiro/SP	6.00
5	Danny Graves	.40
6	Casey Blake	.40
7	Juan Uribe	.40
8	Dmitri Young	.40
8	Dmitri Young/SP/Old Logo	4.00
9	Billy Wagner	.40
10	Jason Giambi	.75
10	Jason Giambi/SP/Batting Stance	6.00
11	Carlos Beltran	1.00
12	Chad Hermansen	.40
13	B.J. Upton	.75
14	Dustan Mohr	.40
15	Endy Chavez	.40
16	Cliff Floyd	.40
17	Bernie Williams	.75
18	Eric Chavez	.50
19	Chase Utley	.75
20	Randy Johnson	1.50
21	Vernon Wells	.50
22	Juan Gonzalez	.75
23	Joe Kennedy	.40
24	Bengie Molina	.40
25	Carlos Lee	.40
26	Horacio Ramirez	.40
27	Anthony Acevedo RC	1.00
28	Sammy Sosa/SP	10.00
29	Jon Garland	.40
30	Adam Dunn	1.00
30	Adam Dunn/SP/Hitting	6.00
31	Aaron Rowand	.40
32	Jody Gerut	.40
33	Chin-Hui Tsao	.40
34	Alex Sanchez	.40
35	A.J. Burnett	.40
36	Brad Ausmus	.40
37	Blake Hawksworth RC	1.50
38	Francisco Rodriguez	.40
39	Alex Cintron	.40
40	Chipper Jones	1.50
40	Chipper Jones/SP/Fielding	6.00
41	Deivi Cruz	.40
42	Bill Mueller	.40
43	Joe Borowski	.40
44	Jimmy Haynes	.40
45	Mark Loretta	.40
46	Jerome Williams	.40
47	Gary Sheffield/SP	6.00
48	Richard Hidalgo	.40
49	Jason Kendall	.40
49	Jason Kendall/SP/Old Logo	4.00
50	Ichiro Suzuki/SP	8.00
51	Jim Edmonds	.75
52	Frank Catalanotto	.40
53	Jose Contreras	.40
54	Mo Vaughn	.40
55	Brendan Donnelly	.40
56	Luis Gonzalez	.50
57	Robert Fick	.40
58	Laynce Nix	.40
59	Johnny Damon	.75
60	Magglio Ordonez	.50
60	Magglio Ordonez/SP/Hitting	6.00
61	Matt Clement	.40
62	Ryan Ludwick	.40
63	Luis Castillo	.40
64	David Crouthers	.40
65	Dave Berg	.40
66	Kyle Davies RC	3.00
67	Tim Salmon	.50
68	Marcus Giles	.40
69	Marty Cordova	.40
70	Todd Helton	1.00
70	Todd Helton/SP/Purple Jersey	6.00
71	Jeff Kent	.50
72	Michael Tucker	.40
73	Cesar Izturis	.40
74	Paul Quantrill	.40
75	Conor Jackson	3.00
76	Placido Polanco	.40
77	Adam Eaton	.40
78	Ramon Hernandez	.40
79	Edgardo Alfonzo	.40
80	Dioner Navarro RC	1.00
81	Woody Williams	.40
82	Rey Ordonez	.40
83	Randy Winn	.40
84	Casey Myers RC	1.00
85	Rodney Choy Foo RC	2.00
85	Rodney Choy Foo/SP/Old Logo	6.00
86	Ray Durham	.40
87	Sean Burroughs	.40
88	Tim Frend RC	3.00
89	Shigetoshi Hasegawa	.40
90	Jeff Allison	.40
91	Orlando Hudson	.40
92	Matt Creighton/SP RC	6.00
93	Tim Worrell	.40
94	Kris Benson	.40
95	Mike Lieberthal	.40
96	David Wells	.40
97	Jason Phillips	.40
98	Bobby Cox	.40
99	Johan Santana	.75
100	Alex Rodriguez	3.00
100	Alex Rodriguez/SP/Throwing	10.00
101	John Vander Wal	.40
102	Orlando Cabrera	.50
103	Hideo Nomo	.75
104	Todd Walker	.40
105	Jason Johnson	.40
106	Matt Mantei	.40
107	Jarrod Washburn	.40
108	Preston Wilson	.40
109	Carl Pavano	.40
110	Geoff Blum	.40
111	Eric Gagne	.50
112	Geoff Jenkins	.50
113	Joe Torre	.50
114	Jon Knott RC	1.50
115	Hank Blalock	.75
116	John Olerud	.50
117	Pat Burrell	.75
117	Pat Burrell/Old Logo	5.00
118	Aaron Boone	.40
119	Zach Day	.40
120	Frank Thomas	1.00
120	Frank Thomas/Old Logo	6.00
121	Kyle Farnsworth	.40
122	Derek Lowe	.50
123	Zach Miner/SP RC	6.00
124	Matt Moses/SP	8.00
125	Jesse Roman RC	1.50
126	Josh Phelps	.40
127	Nic Ungs RC	1.50
128	Dan Haren	.40
129	Kirk Rueter	.40
130	Jack McKeon	.40
131	Keith Foulke	.40
132	Garrett Stephenson	.40
133	Wes Helms	.40
134	Raul Ibanez	.50
135	Morgan Ensberg	.40
136	Jay Payton	.40
137	Billy Koch	.40
138	Mark Grudzielanek	.40
139	Rodrigo Lopez	.40
140	Corey Patterson	.40
141	Troy Percival	.40
142	Shea Hillenbrand	.40
143	Brad Fullmer	.40
144	Ricky Nolasco	1.50
145	Mark Teixeira	.75
146	Tydus Meadows RC	1.50
147	Toby Hall	.40
148	Orlando Palmeiro	.40
149	Khalid Ballouli RC	1.50
150	Grady Little	.40
151	David Eckstein	.50
152	Kenny Perez RC	1.50
153	Ben Grieve	.40
154	Ismael Valdes	.40
155	Bret Boone	.50
156	Jesse Foppert	.40
157	Vicente Padilla	.40
158	Bobby Abreu	.50
159	Scott Hatteberg	.40
160	Carlos Quentin	4.00
161	Anthony Lerew RC	1.50
162	Lance Carter	.40
163	Robb Nen	.40
164	Zachary Duke/SP RC	15.00
165	Xavier Nady	.40
166	Kip Wells	.40
167	Kevin Millwood	.75
168	Jon Lieber	.40
169	Jose Reyes	.50
170	Eric Byrnes	.40
171	Paul Konerko	.40
172	Chris Lubanski	.40
173	Jae Weong Seo	.40
174	Corey Koskie	.40
175	Tim Stauffer	.40
176	John Lackey	.40
177	Danny Bautista	.40
178	Shane Reynolds	.40
179	Jorge Julio	.40
180	Manny Ramirez	1.00
180	Manny Ramirez/SP/Old Logo	6.00
181	Alex Gonzalez	.40
182	Moises Alou	.75
182	Moises Alou/SP/Old Logo	6.00
183	Mark Buehrle	.40
184	Carlos Guillen	.40
185	Nate Cornejo	.40
186	Billy Traber	.40
187	Jason Jennings	.40
188	Eric Munson	.40
189	Braden Looper	.40
190	Juan Encarnacion	.40
191	Dusty Baker	.40
192	Travis Lee	.40
193	Miguel Cairo	.40
194	Rich Aurilia/SP	5.00
195	Flash Gordon	.40
196	Freddy Garcia	.40
197	Brian Lawrence	.40
198	Jorge Posada/SP	8.00
199	Javier Vazquez	.40
200	Albert Pujols	3.00
200	Albert Pujols/SP/Old Logo	12.00
201	Victor Zambrano	.40
202	Eli Marrero	.40
203	Joel Pineiro	.40
204	Rondell White	.50
205	Craig Ansman RC	2.00
206	Michael Young	.40
207	Carlos Baerga	.40
208	Andruw Jones	1.00
209	Jerry Hairston Jr.	.40
210	Shawn Green/SP	6.00
211	Ron Gardenhire	.40
212	Darin Erstad	.50
213	Brandon Webb	.50
213	Brandon Webb/SP/Glove In Air	6.00
214	Greg Maddux	2.00
215	Reed Johnson	.40
216	John Thomson	.40
217	Tino Martinez	.40
218	Mike Cameron	.40
219	Edgar Martinez	.40
220	Eric Young	.40
221	Reggie Sanders	.40
222	Randy Wolf	.40
223	Erubiel Durazo	.40
224	Mike Mussina	.75
225	Tom Glavine	.75
226	Troy Glaus	.40
227	Oscar Villarreal	.40
228	David Segui	.40
229	Jeff Suppan	.40
230	Kenny Lofton	.50
231	Esteban Loaiza	.40
232	Felipe Lopez	.40
233	Matt Lawton	.40
234	Mark Bellhorn	.40
235	Wilfredo Ledezma	.40
236	Todd Hollandsworth	.40
237	Octavio Dotel	.40
238	Darren Dreifort	.40
239	Paul LoDuca	.40
240	Richie Sexson	.75
241	Doug Mientkiewicz	.40
242	Luis Rivas	.40
243	Claudio Vargas	.40
244	Mark Ellis	.40
245	Brett Myers	.40
246	Jake Peavy	.40
247	Marquis Grissom	.40
248	Armando Benitez	.40
249	Ryan Franklin	.40
250	Alfonso Soriano	1.50
250	Alfonso Soriano/SP/Fielding	6.00
251	Tim Hudson	.75
252	Shannon Stewart	.40
253	A.J. Pierzynski	.40
254	Runelvys Hernandez	.40
255	Roy Oswalt	.50
256	Shawn Chacon	.40
257	Tony Graffanino	.40
258	Tim Wakefield	.40
259	Damian Miller	.40
260	Joe Crede	.40
261	Jason LaRue	.40
262	Jose Jimenez	.40
263	Juan Pierre	.40
264	Wade Miller	.40
265	Odalis Perez	.40
266	Eddie Guardado	.40
267	Rocky Biddle	.40
268	Jeff Nelson	.40
269	Terrence Long	.40
270	Ramon Ortiz	.40
271	Raul Mondesi	.50
272	Ugueth Urbina	.40
273	Jeromy Burnitz	.40
274	Brad Radke	.40
275	Jose Vidro	.40
276	Bobby Jenks	.40
277	Ty Wigginton	.40
278	Jose Guillen	.40
279	Delmon Young	.75
280	Brian Giles	.40
281	Jason Schmidt	.50
282	Nicholas Markakis	.40
283	Felipe Alou	.40
284	Carl Crawford	.40
285	Neifi Perez	.40
286	Miguel Tejada	.75
287	Victor Martinez	.40
288	Adam Kennedy	.40
289	Kerry Ligtenberg	.40
290	Scott Williamson	.40
291	Tony Womack	.40
292	Travis Hafner	.40
293	Bobby Crosby	.40
294	Chad Billingsley	.40
295	Russ Ortiz	.40
296	John Burkett	.40
297	Carlos Zambrano	.40
298	Randall Simon	.40
299	Juan Castro	.40
300	Mike Lowell	.40
301	Fred McGriff	.50
302	Glendon Rusch	.40
303	Sung Ki Jung RC	.40
304	Rocco Baldelli	.75
305	Fernando Vina	.40
306	Gil Meche	.40
307	Jose Cruz Jr.	.40
308	Bernie Castro	.40
309	Scott Spiezio	.40
310	Paul Byrd	.40
311	Jay Gibbons	.50
311	Jay Gibbons/SP/Old Logo	6.00
312	Trot Nixon	.40
313	Chris O'Riordan RC	1.50
314	Julio Lugo	.40
315	Ben Davis	.40
316	Mike Williams	.40
317	Trevor Hoffman	.40
318	Andy Pettitte	.75
319	Orlando Hernandez	.40
320	Juan Rivera	.40
321	Elizardo Ramirez	.40
322	Junior Spivey	.40
323	Tony Batista	.40
324	Mike Remlinger	.40
325	Alex Gonzalez	.40
326	Aaron Hill	.40
327	Steve Finley	.40
328	Vinny Castilla	.40
329	Eric Duncan	.40
330	Mike Gosling	.40
331	Eric Hinske	.40
332	Scott Rolen	1.50
333	Benito Santiago	.40
334	Jimmy Gobble	.40
335	Bobby Higginson	.40
336	Kelvim Escobar	.40
337	Mike DeJean	.40
338	Sidney Ponson	.40
339	Todd Self RC	1.50
340	Jeff Cirillo	.40
341	Jimmy Rollins	.50
342	Barry Zito	.75
342	Barry Zito/SP/Green Jersey	6.00
343	Felix Pie	.40
344	Matt Morris	.40
345	Kazuhiro Sasaki	.40
346	Jack Wilson	.40
347	Nick Johnson	.40
348	Wil Cordero	.40
349	Ryan Madson	.40
350	Torii Hunter	.75
351	Andy Ashby	.40
352	Aubrey Huff	.40
353	Brad Lidge	.40
354	Derrek Lee	.40
355	Yadier Molina RC	2.00
356	Paul Wilson	.40
357	Omar Vizquel	.50
358	Rene Reyes	.40
359	Marlon Anderson	.40
360	Bobby Kielty	.40
361	Ryan Wagner	.40
361	Ryan Wagner/SP/Old Logo	5.00
362	Justin Morneau	.50
363	Shane Spencer	.40
364	David Bell	.40
365	Matt Stairs	.40
366	Joe Borchard	.40
367	Mark Redman	.40
368	Dave Roberts	.40
369	Desi Relaford	.40
370	Rich Harden	.40
371	Fernando Tatis	.40
372	Eric Karros	.40
373	Eric Milton	.40
374	Mike Sweeney	.40
375	Brian Daubach	.40
376	Brian Snyder	.40
377	Chris Reitsma	.40
378	Kyle Lohse	.40
379	Livan Hernandez	.40
380	Robin Ventura	.40
381	Jacque Jones	.40
382	Danny Kolb	.40
383	Casey Kotchman	.40
384	Cristian Guzman	.40
385	Josh Beckett	1.00
386	Khalil Greene	.40
387	Greg Myers	.40
388	Francisco Cordero	.40
389	Donald Levinski	.40
390	Roy Halladay	.75
391	J.D. Drew	.40
392	Jamie Moyer	.40
393	Ken Macha	.40
394	Jeff DaVanon	.40
395	Matt Kata	.40
396	Jack Cust	.40
397	Mike Timlin	.40
398	Zack Greinke	4.00
399	Byung-Hyun Kim	4.00
400	Kazuhisa Ishii	4.00
401	Brayan Pena RC	4.00
402	Garret Anderson	6.00
403	Kyle Sleeth	4.00
404	Javy Lopez	5.00
405	Damian Moss	4.00
406	David Ortiz	4.00
407	Pedro J. Martinez	8.00
408	Hee Seop Choi	4.00
409	Carl Everett	4.00
410	Dontrelle Willis	5.00
411	Ryan Harvey	4.00
412	Russell Branyan	5.00
413	Milton Bradley	4.00
414	Marcus McBeth RC	4.00
415	Carlos Pena	4.00
416	Ivan Rodriguez	6.00
417	Craig Biggio	5.00
418	Angel Berroa	4.00
419	Brian Jordan	4.00
420	Scott Podsednik	6.00
421	Omar Falcon RC	4.00

ABBREVIATIONS

SP - Short Print

422	Joe Mays	4.00
423	Brad Wilkerson	4.00
424	Al Leiter	4.00
425	Derek Jeter	15.00
426	Mark Mulder	5.00
427	Marlon Byrd	4.00
428	David Murphy	6.00
429	Phil Nevin	4.00
430	J.T. Snow Jr.	4.00
431	Brad Sullivan	6.00
432	Bo Hart	6.00
433	Josh Labandeira RC	5.00
434	Chan Ho Park	6.00
435	Carlos Delgado	6.00
436	Curt Schilling	6.00
437	John Smoltz	5.00
438	Luis Matos	5.00
439	Mark Prior	10.00
440	Roberto Alomar	6.00
441	Coco Crisp	4.00
442	Austin Kearns	5.00
443	Larry Walker	5.00
444	Neal Cotts	4.00
445	Jeff Bagwell	6.00
446	Adrian Beltre	4.00
447	Grady Sizemore	5.00
448	Keith Ginter	4.00
449	Vladimir Guerrero	8.00
450	Lyle Overbay	4.00
451	Rafael Furcal	5.00
452	Melvin Mora	4.00
453	Kerry Wood	8.00
454	Jose Valentin	4.00
455	Ken Griffey Jr.	8.00
456	Brandon Phillips	4.00
457	Miguel Cabrera	8.00
458	Edwin Jackson	5.00
459	Eric Owens	4.00
460	Miguel Batista	4.00
461	Mike Hampton	4.00
462	Kevin Millar	4.00
463	Bartolo Colon	5.00
464	Sean Casey	4.00
465	C.C. Sabathia	4.00
466	Rickie Weeks	8.00
467	Brad Penny	4.00
468	Mike MacDougal	4.00
469	Kevin Brown	6.00
470	Lance Berkman	5.00
471	Ben Sheets	5.00
472	Mariano Rivera	5.00
473	Mike Piazza	8.00
474	Ryan Klesko	5.00
475	Edgar Renteria	5.00

Chrome

Complete Set (110):
Common Player: 1.00
Production 1,955 Sets
Refractor: 1.5-2X
Production 555 Sets
Black Refractor: 2-4X
Production 55 Sets

THC1	Sammy Sosa	8.00
THC2	Nomar Garciaparra	8.00
THC3	Ichiro Suzuki	6.00
THC4	Rafael Palmeiro	3.00
THC5	Carlos Delgado	2.50
THC6	Troy Glaus	2.00
THC7	Jay Gibbons	1.50
THC8	Frank Thomas	3.00
THC9	Pat Burrell	2.00
THC10	Albert Pujols	8.00
THC11	Brandon Webb	1.50
THC12	Chipper Jones	4.00
THC13	Magglio Ordonez	2.00
THC14	Adam Dunn	2.00
THC15	Todd Helton	2.50
THC16	Jason Giambi	3.00
THC17	Alfonso Soriano	3.00
THC18	Barry Zito	2.00
THC19	Jim Thome	3.00
THC20	Alex Rodriguez	8.00
THC21	Hee Seop Choi	1.00
THC22	Pedro J. Martinez	3.00
THC23	Kerry Wood	3.00
THC24	Bartolo Colon	1.50
THC25	Austin Kearns	1.50
THC26	Ken Griffey Jr.	5.00
THC27	Coco Crisp	1.00
THC28	Larry Walker	1.50
THC29	Ivan Rodriguez	2.50
THC30	Dontrelle Willis	2.00
THC31	Miguel Cabrera	2.50
THC32	Jeff Bagwell	2.50
THC33	Lance Berkman	1.50
THC34	Shawn Green	1.50
THC35	Kevin Brown	1.50
THC36	Vladimir Guerrero	3.00
THC37	Mike Piazza	5.00
THC38	Derek Jeter	10.00
THC39	John Smoltz	1.50
THC40	Mark Prior	8.00
THC41	Gary Sheffield	2.00
THC42	Curt Schilling	2.00
THC43	Randy Johnson	3.00
THC44	Luis Gonzalez	1.50
THC45	Andruw Jones	2.50
THC46	Greg Maddux	5.00
THC47	Tony Batista	1.00
THC48	Esteban Loaiza	1.00
THC49	Chin-Hui Tsao	1.00
THC50	Mike Lowell	1.50
THC51	Jeff Kent	1.50
THC52	Richie Sexson	2.00
THC53	Torii Hunter	2.00
THC54	Jose Vidro	1.00
THC55	Jose Reyes	3.00
THC56	Jimmy Rollins	1.50
THC57	Bret Boone	1.50
THC58	Rocco Baldelli	2.00
THC59	Hank Blalock	2.00
THC60	Rickie Weeks	2.00
THC61	Rodney Choy Foo	1.00
THC62	Zach Miner	3.00
THC63	Brayan Pena	1.00
THC64	David Murphy	1.00
THC65	Matt Creighton	1.00
THC66	Kyle Sleeth	1.00
THC67	Matthew Moses	1.00
THC68	Josh Labandeira	1.00
THC69	Grady Sizemore	2.00
THC70	Edwin Jackson	1.00
THC71	Marcus McBeth	1.00
THC72	Bradley Sullivan	1.00
THC73	Zachary Duke	25.00
THC74	Omar Falcon	1.00
THC75	Conor Jackson	2.00
THC76	Carlos Quentin	4.00
THC77	Craig Ansman	1.00
THC78	Mike Gosling	1.00
THC79	Kyle Davies	1.00
THC80	Anthony Lerew	1.00
THC81	Sung Jung	1.00
THC82	David Crouthers	1.00
THC83	Kenny Perez	1.00
THC84	Jeffrey Allison	1.00
THC85	Nic Ungs	1.00
THC86	Donald Levinski	1.00
THC87	Anthony Acevedo	1.00
THC88	Todd Self	1.00
THC89	Tim Frend	1.00
THC90	Tydus Meadows	1.00
THC91	Khalid Ballouli	1.00
THC92	Dioner Navarro	1.00
THC93	Casey Myers	1.00
THC94	Jon Knott	1.00
THC95	Tim Stauffer	1.00
THC96	Ricky Nolasco	2.00
THC97	Blake Hawksworth	1.00
THC98	Jesse Roman	1.00
THC99	Yadier Molina	1.00
THC100	Chris O'Riordan	1.00
THC101	Cliff Floyd	1.00
THC102	Nick Johnson	1.00
THC103	Edgar Martinez	1.50
THC104	Brett Myers	1.00
THC105	Francisco Rodriguez	1.00
THC106	Scott Rolen	3.00
THC107	Mark Teixeira	2.00
THC108	Miguel Tejada	2.00
THC109	Vernon Wells	1.50
THC110	Jerome Williams	1.00

Clubhouse Collection

NM/M
Common Player: 5.00

BA	Bobby Abreu	6.00
RB	Rocco Baldelli	12.00
LB	Lance Berkman	6.00
YB	Yogi Berra	35.00
HB	Hank Blalock	8.00
BB	Bret Boone	6.00
KB	Kevin Brown	6.00
EC	Eric Chavez	5.00
RC	Roger Clemens	15.00
JD	Johnny Damon	10.00
AD	Adam Dunn	6.00
RF	Rafael Furcal	6.00
EG	Eric Gagne	8.00
NG	Nomar Garciaparra	15.00
JG	Jason Giambi	8.00
MG	Marcus Giles	8.00
TG	Troy Glaus	6.00
LG	Luis Gonzalez	5.00
SG	Shawn Green	6.00
TH	Tim Hudson	6.00
THU	Torii Hunter	8.00
KI	Kazuhisa Ishii	6.00
RJ	Randy Johnson	10.00
AJ	Andruw Jones	6.00
CJ	Chipper Jones	8.00
AK	Al Kaline	25.00
HK	Harmon Killebrew	30.00
PL	Paul LoDuca	5.00
JL	Javy Lopez	6.00
GM	Greg Maddux	20.00
PM	Pedro J. Martinez	10.00
WM	Willie Mays	100.00
FM	Fred McGriff	6.00
MM	Mark Mulder	5.00
SM	Stan Musial	40.00
BM	Brett Myers	5.00
AP	Albert Pujols	15.00
MR	Manny Ramirez	8.00
JRE	Jose Reyes	8.00
AR	Alex Rodriguez	10.00
IR	Ivan Rodriguez	6.00
SRB	Scott Rolen/Bat	8.00
SR	Scott Rolen/Jsy	8.00
JR	Jimmy Rollins	6.00
CS	C.C. Sabathia	5.00
GS	Gary Sheffield	8.00
JS	John Smoltz	8.00
DS	Duke Snider	30.00
AS	Alfonso Soriano	10.00
SS	Sammy Sosa	15.00
MS	Mike Sweeney	5.00
MTE	Mark Teixeira	10.00
MT	Miguel Tejada/Jsy	8.00
MTB	Miguel Tejada/Bat	8.00
JT	Jim Thome	10.00
VW	Vernon Wells	6.00
KW	Kerry Wood	10.00
BZ	Barry Zito	6.00

Clubhouse Collection Autograph

NM/M
Inserted 15,186
Production 25 Sets
WM Willie Mays 400.00

Clubhouse Collection - Dual

NM/M
Production 55 Sets
BC Yogi Berra, Roger Clemens 160.00
GS Shawn Green, Duke Snider 150.00

Doubleheader

NM/M
Complete Set (30): 50.00
Common Player: .75
Inserted 1:Box

1	Alex Rodriguez	5.00
2	Nomar Garciaparra	4.00
3	Ichiro Suzuki	4.00
4	Albert Pujols	4.00
5	Sammy Sosa	4.00
6	Derek Jeter	6.00
7	Jim Thome	2.00
8	Adam Dunn	1.00
9	Jason Giambi	2.00
10	Ivan Rodriguez	1.50
11	Todd Helton	1.50
12	Luis Gonzalez	.75
13	Jeff Bagwell	1.50
14	Lance Berkman	1.00
15	Alfonso Soriano	2.00
16	Dontrelle Willis	1.50
17	Mark Prior	4.00
18	Vladimir Guerrero	2.00
19	Mike Piazza	3.00
20	Roger Clemens	4.00
21	Randy Johnson	2.00
22	Curt Schilling	1.50
23	Gary Sheffield	1.00
24	Pedro J. Martinez	1.50
25	Carlos Delgado	1.50
26	Jimmy Rollins	.75
27	Andruw Jones	1.50
28	Chipper Jones	3.00
29	Rocco Baldelli	1.00
30	Hank Blalock	1.00

Flashbacks

AUGUST 19, 1955: ROBIN ROBERTS WINS 20 GAMES FOR 6TH SEASON IN A ROW

NM/M
Complete Set (10): 8.00
Common Player: .50
Inserted 1:12

F1	Duke Snider	1.50
F2	Johnny Podres	.50
F3	Don Newcombe	.50
F4	Al Kaline	1.50
F5	Willie Mays	4.00
F6	Stan Musial	3.00
F7	Harmon Killebrew	2.00
F8	Herb Score	.50
F9	Whitey Ford	1.00
F10	Robin Roberts	.50

Flashbacks Autograph

NM/M
Inserted 1:30,373

Grandstand Glory

NM/M
Common Player: 20.00

YB	Yogi Berra	20.00
AK	Al Kaline	30.00
HK	Harmon Killebrew	30.00
SM	Stan Musial	35.00
WS	Warren Spahn	20.00

New Age Performers

NM/M
Complete Set (15): 15.00
Common Player: .75
Inserted 1:5

NAP1	Jason Giambi	1.50
NAP2	Ichiro Suzuki	2.50
NAP3	Alex Rodriguez	3.00
NAP4	Alfonso Soriano	1.50
NAP5	Albert Pujols	3.00
NAP6	Nomar Garciaparra	3.00
NAP7	Mark Prior	3.00
NAP8	Derek Jeter	4.00
NAP9	Sammy Sosa	2.50
NAP10	Carlos Delgado	1.50
NAP11	Jim Thome	1.50
NAP12	Todd Helton	1.00
NAP13	Gary Sheffield	.75
NAP14	Vladimir Guerrero	1.50
NAP15	Josh Beckett	3.00

Real One Autograph

NM/M
Common Autograph: 30.00
Inserted 1:230
Red Autograph: 1.5-2X
Production 55

GA	Gair Allie	50.00
EB	Ernie Banks	100.00
YB	Yogi Berra	100.00
BB	Bob Borkowski	40.00
BC	Billy Consolo	55.00
CF	Cliff Floyd	30.00
BG	Bill Glynn	45.00
JG	Johnny Gray	45.00
AH	Aubrey Huff	30.00
AK	Al Kaline	100.00
HK	Harmon Killebrew	90.00
TK	Thornton Kipper	45.00
BK	Bob Kline	45.00
SK	Steve Kraly	60.00
LL	Lou Limmer	45.00
ML	Mike Lowell	40.00
WM	Willie Mays	185.00
BM	Bob Milliken	45.00
SM	Stan Musial	140.00
DN	Don Newcombe	65.00
MO	Magglio Ordonez	35.00
JP	Jim Pearce	45.00
HP	Harry Perkowski	45.00
DP	Duane Pillette	40.00
JPO	Johnny Podres	45.00
SR	Scott Rolen	45.00
FS	Frank Smith	45.00
DS	Duke Snider	85.00
VT	"Jake" Thies	45.00
HV	Harold Valentine	45.00
DW	Dontrelle Willis	50.00
BW	Bill Wilson	40.00
TW	Tom Wright	45.00

Team Topps Legends

NM/M
Inserted 1:505
Davey Johnson 12.00
Joe Rudi 15.00

Then And Now

NM/M
Complete Set (6): 8.00
Common Player: 1.00
Inserted 1:15

TN1	Willie Mays, Jim Thome	4.00
TN2	Al Kaline, Albert Pujols	4.00
TN3	Duke Snider, Carlos Delgado	1.50
TN4	Robin Roberts, Roy Halladay	1.00
TN5	Don Newcombe, Johan Santana	1.00
TN6	Herb Score, Kerry Wood	1.50

National Trading Card Day

As part of its participation in NTCD on April 3, Topps issued a 12-card foil pack with four baseball player cards, two football and three each basketball and hockey, plus a header. Only the baseball players are listed here. Fronts have action photos, gold-foil highlights and a NTCD logo. Backs have recent stats, a photo portrait and biographical data.

NM/M
Unopened Pack: 3.00
Common Player: .25

1	Rocco Baldelli	.35
2	Mark Prior	.50
3	Dontrelle Willis	.50
4	Jason Giambi	.25

2004 Topps Opening Day

NM/M
Complete Set (165): 25.00
Common Player: .10
Pack (6): 1.00
Box (36): 30.00

1	Jim Thome	.50
2	Edgardo Alfonzo	.10
3	Marlon Anderson	.10
4	Ichiro Suzuki	.50
5	Frank Thomas	.40
6	Tom Glavine	.25
7	Bo Hart	.10
8	Marcus Giles	.10
9	Kevin Millar	.10
10	Derek Jeter	1.50
11	Corey Patterson	.10
12	Jay Payton	.10
13	Lance Berkman	.20
14	Juan Pierre	.10
15	Mike Piazza	.75
16	Richie Sexson	.40
17	Tim Hudson	.25
18	Fred McGriff	.20
19	Brad Radke	.10
20	John Smoltz	.10
21	Jay Gibbons	.10
22	Michael Young	.10
23	Steve Finley	.10
24	Ramon Hernandez	.10
25	Albert Pujols	1.25
26	Trot Nixon	.10
27	Kevin Millwood	.10
28	Mark Prior	1.00
29	Mike Lowell	.20
30	Paul LoDuca	.10
31	Jacque Jones	.10
32	Ty Wigginton	.10
33	Cliff Floyd	.10
34	Marlon Byrd	.10
35	Mark Mulder	.20
36	Johnny Damon	.20
37	Jimmy Rollins	.25
38	Javy Lopez	.25
39	Andruw Jones	.40
40	Hank Blalock	.25
41	Hee Seop Choi	.10
42	Jose Vidro	.10
43	Hideo Nomo	.25
44	Javier Vazquez	.10
45	Jorge Posada	.25
46	Al Leiter	.10
47	Orlando Cabrera	.10
48	Mike Hampton	.10
49	Esteban Loaiza	.10
50	Todd Helton	.40
51	Jose Contreras	.20
52	Jason L. Phillips	.10
53	Vernon Wells	.20
54	Randy Winn	.10
55	Curt Schilling	.40
56	Mark Buehrle	.10
57	Dmitri Young	.10
58	Kazuhisa Ishii	.10
59	A.J. Pierzynski	.10
60	Greg Maddux	.75
61	Jarrod Washburn	.10
62	Omar Vizquel	.10
63	Alex Gonzalez	.10
64	Sean Casey	.10
65	Eric Chavez	.10
66	Mike Lieberthal	.10
67	Jason Kendall	.10
68	Mike Cameron	.10
69	Woody Williams	.10
70	Nomar Garciaparra	1.00
71	Bernie Williams	.25
72	Darin Erstad	.20
73	Bill Mueller	.10
74	Damian Miller	.10
75	Jason Giambi	.50
76	Adam Dunn	.25
77	Carlos Lee	.10
78	Angel Berroa	.10
79	Erubiel Durazo	.10
80	Bret Boone	.20
81	Aubrey Huff	.10
82	Carlos Delgado	.40
83	Toby Hall	.10
84	Roy Halladay	.25
85	Preston Wilson	.10
86	Bartolo Colon	.20
87	Moises Alou	.20
88	Luis Castillo	.10
89	Manny Ramirez	.40
90	Garret Anderson	.20
91	Ryan Klesko	.25
92	Rich Aurilia	.10
93	Rafael Furcal	.20
94	Rocco Baldelli	.40
95	Eric Gagne	.20
96	Jeff Kent	.20
97	Josh Beckett	.40
98	Alex Gonzalez	.10
99	Jose Cruz Jr.	.20
100	Alex Rodriguez	1.25
101	Troy Glaus	.25
102	Carlos Beltran	.20

103	Luis Gonzalez	.20
104	A.J. Burnett	.10
105	Gary Sheffield	.25
106	Benito Santiago	.10
107	Tony Batista	.10
108	David Ortiz	.20
109	Shannon Stewart	.10
110	Jim Edmonds	.25
111	Kenny Lofton	.20
112	Paul Konerko	.10
113	Rafael Palmeiro	.40
114	Pat Burrell	.25
115	Barry Zito	.25
116	Edgar Martinez	.20
117	Austin Kearns	.25
118	Geoff Jenkins	.25
119	Mike Mussina	.25
120	Alfonso Soriano	.50
121	Shea Hillenbrand	.10
122	Ivan Rodriguez	.40
123	Kerry Wood	.40
124	Scott Rolen	.50
125	Jeff Bagwell	.40
126	Roberto Alomar	.25
127	Carl Crawford	.40
128	Mike Sweeney	.10
129	Melvin Mora	.10
130	Larry Walker	.20
131	Matt Morris	.10
132	Shawn Green	.20
133	Scott Podsednik	.25
134	Phil Nevin	.10
135	Dontrelle Willis	.25
136	Torii Hunter	.25
137	Carl Everett	.10
138	Pedro J. Martinez	.50
139	Roy Oswalt	.25
140	Vladimir Guerrero	.50
141	Chipper Jones	.75
142	Jose Reyes	.25
143	Sammy Sosa	1.00
144	Nick Johnson	.10
145	Miguel Tejada	.25
146	Bobby Abreu	.20
147	Magglio Ordonez	.25
148	Sean Burroughs	.10
149	Jody Gerut	.10
150	Jermaine Dye	.10
151	Craig Biggio	.20
152	Randy Johnson	.50
153	Jeff Conine	.10
154	Edgar Renteria	.20
155	Mark Teixeira	.25
156	Eric Hinske	.10
157	Kevin Brown	.20
158	Ken Griffey Jr.	.75
159	Brandon Webb	.10
160	Brian Giles	.20
161	Jason Schmidt	.20
162	Aramis Ramirez	.10
163	Aaron Boone	.10
164	Miguel Cabrera	.40
165	Checklist	.10

Autograph

		NM/M
	Common Autograph:	10.00
	Inserted 1:629	
JD	Jeff Duncan	20.00
RH	Rich Harden	20.00
AT	Andres Torres	10.00
RW	Ryan Wagner	25.00
DW	Dontrelle Willis	30.00

Originals Signature Edition

		NM/M
	Common Autograph:	10.00
	Pack (4):	45.00
	Box (6):	220.00
	Second number reflects quantity produced	
JA1	Jim Abbott 88 TR/339	20.00
SA5	Sparky Anderson 83 MG/67	15.00
SA6	Sparky Anderson 84 MG/97	15.00
SA7	Sparky Anderson 85 MG/73	15.00
LA9	Luis Aparicio 69/49	20.00
LA12	Luis Aparicio 72/15	30.00
HB2	Harold Baines 82/31	25.00
HB3	Harold Baines 83/19	30.00
HB5	Harold Baines 85/97	15.00
HB6	Harold Baines 86/93	15.00
HB7	Harold Baines 87/115	15.00
JB2	Jesse Barfield 83/45	15.00
JB4	Jesse Barfield 85/60	15.00
JB5	Jesse Barfield 86/37	15.00
JB6	Jesse Barfield 87/180	10.00
KB2	Kevin Bass 84/71	10.00
KB3	Kevin Bass 85/30	10.00
KB4	Kevin Bass 86/44	10.00
KB5	Kevin Bass 87/74	10.00
KB6	Kevin Bass 90 TR/35	10.00
BB5	Buddy Bell 79/135	15.00
BB8	Buddy Bell 82/34	15.00
BB9	Buddy Bell 83/83	10.00
BB10	Buddy Bell 84/22	15.00
BB12	Buddy Bell 86/32	15.00
GB2	George Bell 84/67	10.00
GB3	George Bell 85/32	15.00
GB4	George Bell 86/46	15.00
GB5	George Bell 87/204	10.00
JBE2	Johnny Bench 79/14	125.00
JBE5	Johnny Bench 82/16	125.00
YB10	Yogi Berra 85 MG/27	100.00
VB5	Vida Blue 79/21	20.00
VB7	Vida Blue 81/227	10.00
VB8	Vida Blue 82/53	15.00
VB9	Vida Blue 83/45	15.00
BBL4	Bert Blyleven 79/45	25.00
BBL6	Bert Blyleven 81/29	25.00
BBL8	Bert Blyleven 83/41	20.00
BBL10	Bert Blyleven 85/40	20.00
BBL11	Bert Blyleven 86/62	20.00
BBL12	Bert Blyleven 87/54	20.00
MB2	Mike Boddicker 84/56	15.00
MB3	Mike Boddicker 85/139	10.00
MB4	Mike Boddicker 86/66	10.00
MB5	Mike Boddicker 87/88	10.00
WB2	Wade Boggs 84/20	75.00
WB3	Wade Boggs 85/25	75.00
WB5	Wade Boggs 87/45	60.00
LB4	Lou Brock 70/20	50.00
LB13	Lou Brock 79/27	50.00
TB2	Tom Brunansky 83/27	15.00
TB3	Tom Brunansky 84/62	15.00
TB5	Tom Brunansky 86/28	15.00
TB6	Tom Brunansky 87/193	10.00
BU8	Bill Buckner 81/39	20.00
BU9	Bill Buckner 82/38	20.00
BU10	Bill Buckner 83/47	15.00
BU11	Bill Buckner 84/31	20.00
BU12	Bill Buckner 84 TR/24	20.00
BU13	Bill Buckner 85/80	15.00
BU14	Bill Buckner 86/63	15.00
BC5	Bert Campaneris 79/107	10.00
BC7	Bert Campaneris 84/28	15.00
JC2	John Candelaria 79/77	20.00
JC4	John Candelaria 81/19	30.00
JC5	John Candelaria 82/42	25.00
JC6	John Candelaria 83/77	20.00
JC8	John Candelaria 85/61	20.00
JC9	John Candelaria 86/36	20.00
JCA2	Jose Canseco 87/99	60.00
RC4	Rod Carew 79/29	60.00
RC6	Rod Carew 81/21	75.00
RC7	Rod Carew 82/18	75.00
GC3	Gary Carter 79/21	40.00
GC4	Gary Carter 80/24	40.00
GC5	Gary Carter 81/22	40.00
JCR2	Joe Carter 86/24	50.00
JCR3	Joe Carter 87/23	50.00
RCE3	Ron Cey 79/55	15.00
RCE6	Ron Cey 82/34	15.00
RCE7	Ron Cey 83/87	15.00
RCE8	Ron Cey 83 TR/68	15.00
RCE11	Ron Cey 86/43	15.00
VC2	Vince Coleman 87/299	15.00
VC3	Vince Coleman 88/34	20.00
VC4	Vince Coleman 91 TR/32	25.00
DC6	Dave Concepcion 80/21	40.00
DC8	Dave Concepcion 82/43	30.00
DC9	Dave Concepcion 83/34	30.00
DC10	Dave Concepcion 84/24	40.00
DC11	Dave Concepcion 85/41	30.00
DC12	Dave Concepcion 86/69	25.00
JCU8	Jose Cruz Sr. 82/28	15.00
JCU9	Jose Cruz Sr. 83/102	10.00
JCU10	Jose Cruz Sr. 84/67	15.00
JCU11	Jose Cruz Sr. 85/68	10.00
JCU12	Jose Cruz Sr. 86/31	15.00
RD3	Ron Darling 87/224	15.00
DD2	Darren Daulton 87/269	10.00
DD4	Darren Daulton 92/32	15.00
DD5	Darren Daulton 94/17	20.00
DD6	Darren Daulton 96/22	20.00
ED3	Eric Davis 87/336	15.00
AD3	Andre Dawson 80/27	25.00
AD4	Andre Dawson 81/37	20.00
AD5	Andre Dawson 82/55	20.00
AD6	Andre Dawson 83/47	20.00
AD7	Andre Dawson 84/25	25.00
AD8	Andre Dawson 85/22	25.00
AD9	Andre Dawson 86/24	25.00
DDE2	Doug DeCinces 79/38	20.00
DDE3	Doug DeCinces 80/24	20.00
DDE4	Doug DeCinces 81/24	20.00
DDE5	Doug DeCinces 82/42	20.00
DDE6	Doug DeCinces 83/75	15.00
DDE7	Doug DeCinces 84/19	20.00
DDE8	Doug DeCinces 85/54	15.00
DDE9	Doug DeCinces 86/74	15.00
BD6	Bucky Dent 82/49	15.00
BD7	Bucky Dent 83/92	15.00
BD8	Bucky Dent 84/63	15.00
RDI2	Rob Dibble 90/31	25.00
RDI3	Rob Dibble 91/62	20.00
RDI4	Rob Dibble 92/56	20.00
RDI6	Rob Dibble 93/47	15.00
RDI7	Rob Dibble 94/37	15.00
LD2	Leon Durham 82/51	10.00
LD3	Leon Durham 83/52	10.00
LD4	Leon Durham 84/151	10.00
LD7	Leon Durham 87/87	10.00
LDY2	Lenny Dykstra 87/200	15.00
LDY3	Lenny Dykstra 88/30	25.00
LDY4	Lenny Dykstra 89/17	30.00
DE3	Dennis Eckersley 79/44	40.00
DE4	Dennis Eckersley 80/40	40.00
DEV5	Darrell Evans 79/19	20.00
DEV7	Darrell Evans 81/15	20.00
DEV8	Darrell Evans 82/25	20.00
DEV9	Darrell Evans 83/63	15.00
DEV10	Darrell Evans 84/81	10.00
DEV11	Darrell Evans 85/48	15.00
DEV12	Darrell Evans 86/82	10.00
SF2	Sid Fernandez 86/18	30.00
SF3	Sid Fernandez 87/211	15.00
SF4	Sid Fernandez 93/20	25.00
TF2	Tony Fernandez 86/41	15.00
TF3	Tony Fernandez 87/228	10.00
MF3	Mark Fidrych 79/74	25.00
MF4	Mark Fidrych 80/16	40.00
CF2	Cecil Fielder 87/208	30.00
CF3	Cecil Fielder 88/26	50.00
CF4	Cecil Fielder 89/16	50.00
RF3	Rollie Fingers 79/52	20.00
RF4	Rollie Fingers 80/15	40.00
RF5	Rollie Fingers 81/18	40.00
CFI3	Carlton Fisk 79/24	60.00
CFI4	Carlton Fisk 80/32	40.00
CFI6	Carlton Fisk 82/18	40.00
GF6	George Foster 79/20	20.00
GF10	George Foster 83/39	15.00
GF11	George Foster 84/112	20.00
GF12	George Foster 85/76	10.00
GF13	George Foster 86/64	10.00
SG4	Steve Garvey 79/26	30.00
SG7	Steve Garvey 82/122	15.00
SG9	Steve Garvey 84/32	20.00
SG10	Steve Garvey 85/129	15.00
CG3	Cesar Geronimo 79/28	15.00
CG5	Cesar Geronimo 81/21	15.00
CG6	Cesar Geronimo 82/52	10.00
CG7	Cesar Geronimo 83/67	10.00
CG8	Cesar Geronimo 84/70	10.00
KGI2	Kirk Gibson 82/35	20.00
KGI3	Kirk Gibson 83/35	20.00
KGI5	Kirk Gibson 85/44	20.00
KGI6	Kirk Gibson 86/44	20.00
KGI7	Kirk Gibson 87/65	20.00
DG3	Dwight Gooden 87/52	30.00
RG7	Rich "Goose" Gossage 81/21	20.00
RG8	Rich "Goose" Gossage 82/30	20.00
RG9	Rich "Goose" Gossage 83/34	20.00
RG10	Rich "Goose" Gossage 84/90	15.00
RG12	Rich "Goose" Gossage 86/30	15.00
BG2	Bobby Grich 79/29	20.00
BG3	Bobby Grich 80/70	15.00
BG5	Bobby Grich 82/45	15.00
BG6	Bobby Grich 83/85	10.00
BG7	Bobby Grich 84/57	15.00
BG8	Bobby Grich 85/36	15.00
KG5	Ken Griffey Sr. 80/15	30.00
KG7	Ken Griffey Sr. 82/18	30.00
KG8	Ken Griffey Sr. 83/70	15.00
KG9	Ken Griffey Sr. 84/64	15.00
KG10	Ken Griffey Sr. 85/32	20.00
KG11	Ken Griffey Sr. 86 TR/32	20.00
KGU2	Kelly Gruber 88/77	10.00
KGU3	Kelly Gruber 89/44	10.00
KGU4	Kelly Gruber 90/86	10.00
KGU5	Kelly Gruber 91/52	10.00
KGU6	Kelly Gruber 92/55	10.00
KGU7	Kelly Gruber 93/26	15.00
RGU4	Ron Guidry 80/22	40.00
RGU5	Ron Guidry 81/104	20.00
RGU6	Ron Guidry 82/73	40.00
RGU7	Ron Guidry 83/46	40.00
RGU8	Ron Guidry 84/40	40.00
RGU9	Ron Guidry 85/50	40.00
TG2	Tony Gwynn 84/95	60.00
KH3	Keith Hernandez 80/38	50.00
KH4	Keith Hernandez 81/19	50.00
KH5	Keith Hernandez 82/156	20.00
KH6	Keith Hernandez 83/17	50.00
TH2	Tom Herr 81/22	15.00
TH3	Tom Herr 82/42	15.00
TH4	Tom Herr 83/80	10.00
TH5	Tom Herr 84/30	15.00
TH6	Tom Herr 85/17	15.00
TH7	Tom Herr 86/28	15.00
TH8	Tom Herr 87/134	10.00
OH2	Orel Hershiser 86/23	40.00
OH3	Orel Hershiser 87/218	20.00
WH4	Whitey Herzog 83 MG/63	10.00
WH5	Whitey Herzog 84 MG/85	10.00
WH6	Whitey Herzog 85 MG/75	10.00
WH7	Whitey Herzog 86 MG/66	10.00
WH8	Whitey Herzog 87 MG/29	15.00
WH9	Whitey Herzog 88 MG/35	15.00
BH5	Bob Horner 83/69	15.00
BH6	Bob Horner 84/63	15.00
BH8	Bob Horner 86/118	15.00
BH9	Bob Horner 87/38	15.00
CH2	Charlie Hough 83/19	20.00
CH3	Charlie Hough 84/50	10.00
CH4	Charlie Hough 85/57	10.00
CH5	Charlie Hough 86/66	10.00
CH6	Charlie Hough 87/46	10.00
CH7	Charlie Hough 88/19	20.00
CH8	Charlie Hough 91 TR/70	10.00
CH9	Charlie Hough 92/25	15.00
AH6	Al Hrabosky 78/20	20.00
AH7	Al Hrabosky 79/40	15.00
AH8	Al Hrabosky 80/61	10.00
AH9	Al Hrabosky 81/38	15.00
AH10	Al Hrabosky 82/62	10.00
AH11	Al Hrabosky 89 Sr./20	20.00
BJ2	Bo Jackson 87/100	60.00
RJ8	Reggie Jackson 82/21	75.00
RJ11	Reggie Jackson 85/17	75.00
RJ12	Reggie Jackson 86/17	75.00
BJA2	Brook Jacoby 86/133	10.00
BJA3	Brook Jacoby 87/191	10.00
FJ7	Fergie Jenkins 78/17	40.00
FJ10	Fergie Jenkins 80/37	30.00
FJ11	Fergie Jenkins 81/32	30.00
FJ12	Fergie Jenkins 82/65	20.00
FJ13	Fergie Jenkins 83/22	30.00
FJ14	Fergie Jenkins 84/42	30.00
WJ2	Wally Joyner 87/335	15.00
DJ3	David Justice 93/32	20.00
AK10	Al Kaline 67/18	120.00
AK16	Al Kaline 73/25	140.00
JK2	Jimmy Key 86/21	20.00
JK3	Jimmy Key 87/263	10.00
JK5	Jimmy Key 92/37	20.00
DK4	Dave Kingman 81/25	30.00
DK6	Dave Kingman 83/32	30.00
DK7	Dave Kingman 85/26	30.00
RK2	Ron Kittle 85/86	10.00
RK3	Ron Kittle 86/15	15.00
RK4	Ron Kittle 87/201	15.00
RKN5	Ray Knight 82/25	20.00
RKN6	Ray Knight 83/36	20.00
RKN7	Ray Knight 84/26	20.00
RKN8	Ray Knight 85/68	15.00
RKN9	Ray Knight 86/80	15.00
RKN10	Ray Knight 87 TR/90	15.00
JKR2	John Kruk 87/214	15.00
JKR3	John Kruk 92/22	35.00
CL3	Carney Lansford 81/184	10.00
CL5	Carney Lansford 83/40	15.00
CL6	Carney Lansford 85/35	15.00
CL7	Carney Lansford 86/76	10.00
CLE3	Chet Lemon 79/24	20.00
CLE6	Chet Lemon 82/23	20.00
CLE7	Chet Lemon 83/35	15.00
CLE8	Chet Lemon 84/42	15.00
CLE9	Chet Lemon 85/32	15.00
CLE10	Chet Lemon 86/136	10.00
CLE11	Chet Lemon 87/27	20.00
JL2	Jim Leyritz 91/38	10.00
JL3	Jim Leyritz 93/49	10.00
JL4	Jim Leyritz 94/16	20.00
JL6	Jim Leyritz 97/62	10.00
JL7	Jim Leyritz 98/20	20.00
JL8	Jim Leyritz 99/124	10.00
JL9	Jim Leyritz 00/40	10.00
DL4	Davey Lopes 79/71	10.00
DL5	Davey Lopes 80/19	15.00
DL7	Davey Lopes 82/17	15.00
DL8	Davey Lopes 83/65	10.00
DL10	Davey Lopes 85/20	10.00
DL11	Davey Lopes 86/40	10.00
DL12	Davey Lopes 01 MG/67	10.00
DL13	Davey Lopes 02 MG/19	15.00
GL7	Greg Luzinski 80/21	30.00
GL9	Greg Luzinski 82/34	20.00
GL10	Greg Luzinski 83/75	10.00
GL11	Greg Luzinski 84/85	10.00
GL12	Greg Luzinski 85/92	10.00
BM7	Bill Madlock 82/26	15.00
BM8	Bill Madlock 83/55	15.00
BM9	Bill Madlock 84/69	15.00
BM10	Bill Madlock 85/60	15.00
BM11	Bill Madlock 86/63	15.00
BM12	Bill Madlock 87/42	15.00
GM3	Gary Matthews Sr. 83/20	15.00
GM4	Gary Matthews Sr. 84/43	10.00
GM5	Gary Matthews Sr. 85/39	10.00
GM6	Gary Matthews Sr. 86/38	10.00
GM7	Gary Matthews Sr. 87/82	15.00
GM8	Gary Matthews Sr. 88/30	15.00
DM3	Don Mattingly 87/84	100.00
WM9	Willie Mays 72/25	300.00
TM5	Tim McCarver 79/22	20.00
JM2	Jack McDowell 89/36	20.00
JM3	Jack McDowell 90 TR/61	15.00
JM4	Jack McDowell 91/33	20.00
JM5	Jack McDowell 92/38	20.00
JM6	Jack McDowell 93/27	20.00
JM9	Jack McDowell 96/15	25.00
JM10	Jack McDowell 97/27	20.00
WMC3	Willie McGee 84/66	25.00
WMC4	Willie McGee 86/24	40.00
WMC5	Willie McGee 87/117	25.00
PM1	Paul Molitor 79/15	60.00
PM2	Paul Molitor 80/26	50.00
PM4	Paul Molitor 82/32	50.00
JMO9	Joe Morgan 81/16	100.00
JMO10	Joe Morgan 82/18	40.00
JMO11	Joe Morgan 83/49	25.00
JMO14	Joe Morgan 85/40	25.00
DMU2	Dale Murphy 79/38	50.00
DMU6	Dale Murphy 84/29	40.00
DMU8	Dale Murphy 86/25	50.00
DMU9	Dale Murphy 87/91	25.00
SM5	Stan Musial 62/16	150.00
AO6	Al Oliver 79/42	15.00
AO8	Al Oliver 81/54	15.00
AO9	Al Oliver 82/45	15.00
AO10	Al Oliver 83/50	15.00
AO11	Al Oliver 84/51	15.00
AO12	Al Oliver 85/46	15.00
AO13	Al Oliver 86/44	15.00
PO2	Paul O'Neill 89/24	50.00
PO3	Paul O'Neill 90/18	50.00
PO4	Paul O'Neill 91/24	50.00
PO5	Paul O'Neill 97/33	40.00
JP3	Jim Palmer 80/33	30.00
JP4	Jim Palmer 81/23	30.00
JP5	Jim Palmer 82/24	30.00
DP6	Dave Parker 82/73	20.00
DP7	Dave Parker 83/30	30.00
DP9	Dave Parker 85/45	25.00
DP10	Dave Parker 86/29	30.00
BP9	Boog Powell 73/17	50.00
BP11	Boog Powell 75/19	40.00
TR2	Tim Raines 82/43	20.00
TR3	Tim Raines 83/26	25.00
TR5	Tim Raines 85/43	20.00
TR6	Tim Raines 86/21	15.00
TR7	Tim Raines 87/211	15.00
HR2	Harold Reynolds 87/255	10.00
JR7	Jim Rice 81/123	20.00
JR8	Jim Rice 82/24	35.00
JR9	Jim Rice 83/71	25.00
CR4	Cal Ripken Jr. 86/74	120.00
MR2	Mickey Rivers 79/35	15.00
MR5	Mickey Rivers 82/49	15.00
MR6	Mickey Rivers 83/79	10.00
MR7	Mickey Rivers 84/91	10.00
MR8	Mickey Rivers 85/34	15.00
BR11	Brooks Robinson 74/20	75.00
BR13	Brooks Robinson 76/17	75.00
JRU9	Joe Rudi 79/24	15.00
JRU10	Joe Rudi 80/45	15.00
JRU11	Joe Rudi 82/26	15.00
JRU12	Joe Rudi 83/75	10.00
NR5	Nolan Ryan 83/23	200.00
NR6	Nolan Ryan 84/20	200.00
NR8	Nolan Ryan 86/20	200.00
BS2	Bret Saberhagen 86/23	25.00
BS3	Bret Saberhagen 87/230	15.00
RS2	Ryne Sandberg 84/37	100.00
RS5	Ryne Sandberg 87/32	100.00
SS2	Steve Sax 83/34	15.00
SS4	Steve Sax 85/30	15.00
SS5	Steve Sax 86/45	15.00
SS6	Steve Sax 87/215	10.00
MS2	Mike Schmidt 80/100	60.00
MSC3	Mike Scott 82/32	15.00
MSC4	Mike Scott 83/55	15.00
MSC5	Mike Scott 84/68	15.00
MSC6	Mike Scott 86/73	10.00
MSC7	Mike Scott 87/36	15.00
MSC8	Mike Scott 88/21	15.00
TS2	Tom Seaver 79/44	85.00
TS4	Tom Seaver 81/16	100.00
TS5	Tom Seaver 82/25	100.00
KS2	Kevin Seitzer 88/88	10.00
KS3	Kevin Seitzer 89/39	10.00
KS4	Kevin Seitzer 90/18	15.00
KS5	Kevin Seitzer 91/39	10.00
KS6	Kevin Seitzer 92/49	10.00
KS9	Kevin Seitzer 93/38	10.00
KS10	Kevin Seitzer 94/22	15.00
KS13	Kevin Seitzer 97/24	15.00
LS5	Lee Smith 86/29	25.00
LS6	Lee Smith 87/237	15.00
LS7	Lee Smith 88/27	25.00
OS2	Ozzie Smith 81/28	60.00
OS3	Ozzie Smith 82/33	60.00
OS5	Ozzie Smith 84/19	75.00
OS6	Ozzie Smith 85/16	75.00
RM8	Reggie Smith 79/15	25.00
RM9	Reggie Smith 80/16	25.00
RM10	Reggie Smith 81/14	25.00
RM11	Reggie Smith 82/32	15.00
RM12	Reggie Smith 83/48	15.00
DS8	Duke Snider 64/18	150.00
CS2	Cory Snyder 87/291	10.00
CS3	Cory Snyder 91/39	15.00
DSW2	Dave Stewart 83/41	15.00
DSW3	Dave Stewart 84/60	15.00
DSW4	Dave Stewart 85/24	15.00
DSW5	Dave Stewart 86/53	15.00
DSW6	Dave Stewart 87/171	10.00
DSE2	Dave Stieb 81/21	35.00
DSE3	Dave Stieb 82/34	30.00
DSE4	Dave Stieb 83/70	35.00
DSE5	Dave Stieb 84/55	35.00
DSE6	Dave Stieb 85/55	25.00
DSE7	Dave Stieb 86/69	25.00
DSE8	Dave Stieb 87/75	25.00
DSR2	Darryl Strawberry 85/32	25.00
DSR3	Darryl Strawberry 86/24	25.00
DSR4	Darryl Strawberry 87/183	20.00
DSR5	Darryl Strawberry 87 AS/110	20.00

RU3	Rick Sutcliffe 82/53	20.00
RU4	Rick Sutcliffe 83/43	20.00
RU5	Rick Sutcliffe 84/33	20.00
RU6	Rick Sutcliffe 85/82	20.00
RU8	Rick Sutcliffe 87/19	25.00
BSU6	Bruce Sutter 82/111	20.00
BSU7	Bruce Sutter 83/45	25.00
BSU8	Bruce Sutter 84/24	30.00
BSU9	Bruce Sutter 85/19	35.00
BSU10	Bruce Sutter 86/78	20.00
BSU11	Bruce Sutter 87/36	25.00
KT5	Kent Tekulve 81/17	20.00
KT6	Kent Tekulve 82/36	15.00
KT7	Kent Tekulve 83/52	15.00
KT8	Kent Tekulve 84/71	15.00
KT9	Kent Tekulve 85/43	15.00
KT10	Kent Tekulve 86/57	15.00
KT11	Kent Tekulve 87/32	15.00
KT12	Kent Tekulve 87/20	15.00
LT2	Luis Tiant 68/16	40.00
LT11	Luis Tiant 79/22	30.00
LT12	Luis Tiant 80/23	30.00
LT13	Luis Tiant 81/20	30.00
LT14	Luis Tiant 82/51	15.00
LT15	Luis Tiant 83/58	15.00
AT2	Alan Trammell 80/17	30.00
AT3	Alan Trammell 81/26	30.00
AT4	Alan Trammell 82/40	30.00
AT5	Alan Trammell 83/21	30.00
AT6	Alan Trammell 84/57	30.00
AT7	Alan Trammell 85/39	30.00
AT8	Alan Trammell 86/23	30.00
AT9	Alan Trammell 87/15	30.00
AV2	Andy Van Slyke 85/35	35.00
AV3	Andy Van Slyke 86/37	35.00
AV4	Andy Van Slyke 87/178	25.00
AV5	Andy Van Slyke 87 TR/130	
FV3	Frank Viola 85/25	25.00
FV4	Frank Viola 86/99	15.00
FV5	Frank Viola 87/209	15.00
TW2	Tim Wallach 83/49	15.00
TW4	Tim Wallach 85/46	15.00
TW5	Tim Wallach 86/44	15.00
TW6	Tim Wallach 87/197	10.00
BW3	Bob Watson 79/77	10.00
BW6	Bob Watson 82/23	20.00
BW7	Bob Watson 83/93	10.00
BW8	Bob Watson 84/64	10.00
BW9	Bob Watson 85/68	10.00
EW4	Earl Weaver 78 MG/52	15.00
EW5	Earl Weaver 83 MG/38	20.00
EW7	Earl Weaver 86 MG/107	15.00
EW8	Earl Weaver 87 MG/175	10.00
WW2	Walt Weiss 89/34	10.00
WW3	Walt Weiss 91/30	10.00
WW4	Walt Weiss 92/71	10.00
WW7	Walt Weiss 97/49	10.00
WW10	Walt Weiss 99/40	10.00
WW11	Walt Weiss 01/51	10.00
MW2	Mookie Wilson 82/20	20.00
MW3	Mookie Wilson 83/41	15.00
MW5	Mookie Wilson 85/51	15.00
MW6	Mookie Wilson 86/47	15.00
MW7	Mookie Wilson 87/67	15.00
CY4	Carl Yastrzemski 80/60	100.00
CY5	Carl Yastrzemski 81/35	120.00
SY5	Steve Yeager 79/23	25.00
SY9	Steve Yeager 83/80	10.00
SY12	Steve Yeager 86/47	15.00
SY13	Steve Yeager 86 TR/100	
RY5	Robin Yount 80/18	100.00
RY6	Robin Yount 81/23	100.00
RY9	Robin Yount 84/15	125.00
RY11	Robin Yount 86/21	100.00

2004 Topps Pristine

NM/M
Complete Set (190):
Common Player: 1.00
Common Rookie: 1.50
Common Uncommon RC: 3.00
Production 999
Common Rare RC: 6.00
Production 499
Pack (8): 35.00
Box (5): 140.00

1	Jim Thome	2.00
2	Ryan Klesko	1.00
3	Ichiro Suzuki	4.00
4	Rocco Baldelli	1.00
5	Vernon Wells	1.00
6	Javier Vazquez	1.00
7	Billy Wagner	1.00
8	Jose Reyes	1.00
9	Lance Berkman	1.00
10	Alex Rodriguez	6.00
11	Pat Burrell	1.00
12	Mark Mulder	1.00
13	Mike Piazza	3.00
14	Miguel Cabrera	2.00
15	Larry Walker	1.00
16	Carlos Lee	1.00
17	Mark Prior	2.00
18	Pedro J. Martinez	2.00
19	Melvin Mora	1.00
20	Sammy Sosa	4.00
21	Bartolo Colon	1.00
22	Luis Gonzalez	1.00
23	Marcus Giles	1.00
24	Ken Griffey Jr.	3.00
25	Ivan Rodriguez	1.50
26	Carlos Beltran	1.50
27	Geoff Jenkins	1.00
28	Nick Johnson	1.00
29	Gary Sheffield	1.50
30	Alfonso Soriano	2.00
31	Scott Rolen	2.00
32	Garret Anderson	1.00
33	Richie Sexson	1.00
34	Curt Schilling	1.50
35	Greg Maddux	3.00
36	Adam Dunn	1.50
37	Preston Wilson	1.00
38	Josh Beckett	1.50
39	Roy Oswalt	1.00
40	Derek Jeter	6.00
41	Jason Kendall	1.00
42	Bret Boone	1.00
43	Torii Hunter	1.00
44	Roy Halladay	1.00
45	Edgar Renteria	1.00
46	Troy Glaus	1.00
47	Chipper Jones	2.00
48	Manny Ramirez	1.50
49	C.C. Sabathia	1.00
50	Albert Pujols	5.00
51	Randy Wolf	1.00
52	Eric Chavez	1.00
53	Kevin Brown	1.00
54	Cliff Floyd	1.00
55	Jeff Bagwell	1.50
56	Frank Thomas	1.50
57	David Ortiz	1.50
58	Rafael Palmeiro	1.00
59	Randy Johnson	2.00
60	Vladimir Guerrero	2.00
61	Carlos Delgado	1.00
62	Hank Blalock	1.50
63	Jim Edmonds	1.00
64	Jason Schmidt	1.00
65	Mike Lieberthal	1.00
66	Tim Hudson	1.00
67	Jorge Posada	1.00
68	Jose Vidro	1.00
69	Eric Gagne	1.00
70	Roger Clemens	5.00
71	Mike Lowell	1.00
72	Dontrelle Willis	1.00
73	Austin Kearns	1.00
74	Kerry Wood	2.00
75	Miguel Tejada	1.50
76	Bobby Abreu	1.00
77	Edgar Martinez	1.00
78	Joe Mauer	1.00
79	Mike Sweeney	1.00
80	Jason Giambi	1.00
81	Mark Teixeira	1.00
82	Aubrey Huff	1.00
83	Brian Giles	1.00
84	Barry Zito	1.00
85	Mike Mussina	1.50
86	Brandon Webb	1.00
87	Andruw Jones	1.50
88	Javy Lopez	1.00
89	Bill Mueller	1.00
90	Scott Podsednik	1.00
91	Moises Alou	1.00
92	Esteban Loaiza	1.00
93	Magglio Ordonez	1.00
94	Jeff Kent	1.00
95	Todd Helton	1.50
96	Juan Pierre	1.00
97	Jody Gerut	1.00
98	Angel Berroa	1.00
99	Shawn Green	1.00
100	Nomar Garciaparra	3.00
101	David Aardsma/C	1.50
102	David Aardsma/U	4.00
103	David Aardsma/R	8.00
104	Erick Aybar/C RC	5.00
105	Erick Aybar/U RC	10.00
106	Erick Aybar/R RC	15.00
107	Chad Bentz/C RC	1.50
108	Chad Bentz/U RC	3.00
109	Chad Bentz/R RC	6.00
110	Travis Blackley/C RC	1.50
111	Travis Blackley/U RC	3.00
112	Travis Blackley/R RC	6.00
113	Bobby Brownlie/C RC	4.00
114	Bobby Brownlie/U RC	8.00
115	Bobby Brownlie/R RC	10.00
116	Alberto Callaspo/C RC	1.50
117	Alberto Callaspo/U RC	3.00
118	Alberto Callaspo/R RC	6.00
119	Kazuo Matsui/C RC	5.00
120	Kazuo Matsui/U RC	8.00
121	Kazuo Matsui/R RC	12.00
122	Jesse Crain/C	3.00
123	Jesse Crain/U	5.00
124	Jesse Crain/R	8.00
125	Howard Kendrick/C RC	25.00
126	Howard Kendrick/U RC	30.00
127	Howard Kendrick/R RC	40.00
128	Blake Hawksworth/C RC	1.50
129	Blake Hawksworth/U RC	3.00
130	Blake Hawksworth/R RC	6.00
131	Conor Jackson/C	6.00
132	Conor Jackson/U	8.00
133	Conor Jackson/R	12.00
134	Paul Maholm/C RC	1.50
135	Paul Maholm/U RC	3.00
136	Paul Maholm/R RC	6.00
137	Lastings Milledge/C	8.00
138	Lastings Milledge/U	15.00
139	Lastings Milledge/R	20.00
140	Matt Moses/C	4.00
141	Matt Moses/U	6.00
142	Matt Moses/R	10.00
143	David Murphy/C	1.50
144	David Murphy/U	3.00
145	David Murphy/R	6.00
146	Dioner Navarro/C RC	5.00
147	Dioner Navarro/U RC	8.00
148	Dioner Navarro/R RC	12.00
149	Dustin Nippert/C RC	1.50
150	Dustin Nippert/U RC	3.00
151	Dustin Nippert/R RC	6.00
152	Vito Chiaravalotti/C RC	3.00
153	Vito Chiaravalotti/U RC	6.00
154	Vito Chiaravalotti/R RC	8.00
155	Akinori Otsuka/C RC	3.00
156	Akinori Otsuka/U RC	5.00
157	Akinori Otsuka/R RC	8.00
158	Casey Daigle/C RC	1.50
159	Casey Daigle/U RC	3.00
160	Casey Daigle/R RC	6.00
161	Carlos Quentin/C	5.00
162	Carlos Quentin/U	10.00
163	Carlos Quentin/R	15.00
164	Omar Quintanilla/C	4.00
165	Omar Quintanilla/U	8.00
166	Omar Quintanilla/R	12.00
167	Chris Saenz/C RC	1.50
168	Chris Saenz/U RC	3.00
169	Chris Saenz/R RC	6.00
170	Ervin Santana/C RC	1.50
171	Ervin Santana/U RC	3.00
172	Ervin Santana/R RC	6.00
173	Chris Shelton/C RC	4.00
174	Chris Shelton/U RC	8.00
175	Chris Shelton/R RC	12.00
176	Kyle Sleeth/C	1.50
177	Kyle Sleeth/U	3.00
178	Kyle Sleeth/R	6.00
179	Brad Snyder/C	4.00
180	Brad Snyder/U	8.00
181	Brad Snyder/R	12.00
182	Tim Stauffer/C	4.00
183	Tim Stauffer/U	8.00
184	Tim Stauffer/R	12.00
185	Shingo Takatsu/C RC	4.00
186	Shingo Takatsu/U RC	8.00
187	Shingo Takatsu/R RC	12.00
188	Merkin Valdez/C RC	1.50
189	Merkin Valdez/U RC	3.00
190	Merkin Valdez/R RC	6.00

Refractors

Veterans (1-100): 4-8X
Production 49
Common RC's: .75-1.5X
Production 999
UnCommon RC's: 1-2X
Production 399
Rare RC's: 1.5-3X
Production 49

Gold Refractors

Veterans (1-100): 4-8X
Common RC's: 4-8X
Uncommon RC's: 3-5X

Rare RC's: 1.5-3X
Production 41 Sets

Fantasy Favorite Relics

NM/M
Common Player: 4.00
Refractor: 2-4X
Production 25 Sets

MA	Moises Alou	6.00
JB	Jeff Bagwell	6.00
RB	Rocco Baldelli	6.00
AB	Angel Berroa	4.00
BB	Bret Boone	4.00
JD	Johnny Damon	8.00
CD	Carlos Delgado	4.00
RF	Rafael Furcal	4.00
RFJ	Rafael Furcal	4.00
EG	Eric Gagne	10.00
NG	Nomar Garciaparra	8.00
SG	Shawn Green	4.00
MG	Mark Grudzielanek	4.00
VG	Vladimir Guerrero	8.00
THE	Todd Helton	8.00
TH	Tim Hudson	6.00
DJ	Derek Jeter	20.00
AJ	Andruw Jones	6.00
CJ	Chipper Jones	8.00
CK	Corey Koskie	4.00
KL	Kenny Lofton	4.00
PM	Pedro J. Martinez	8.00
MPI	Mike Piazza	10.00
MP	Mark Prior	8.00
AP	Albert Pujols	15.00
AR	Alex Rodriguez	12.00
JR	Jimmy Rollins	4.00
MT	Mark Teixeira	4.00
FT	Frank Thomas	8.00
JT	Jim Thome	8.00
JV	Jose Vidro	4.00
LW	Larry Walker	4.00
BW	Brandon Webb	4.00
PW	Preston Wilson	4.00
KW	Kerry Wood	8.00

Going, Going, Gone! Relics

NM/M
Common Player: 4.00
Refractor: 2-4X
Production 25 Sets

LB	Lance Berkman	4.00
BB	Bret Boone	4.00
AD	Adam Dunn	8.00
JG	Juan Gonzalez	6.00
LG	Luis Gonzalez	4.00
VG	Vladimir Guerrero	8.00
TH	Todd Helton	8.00
CJ	Chipper Jones	8.00
JJ	Jacque Jones	4.00
JK	Jeff Kent	4.00
RK	Ryan Klesko	4.00
MO	Magglio Ordonez	4.00
DO	David Ortiz	10.00
MP	Mike Piazza	10.00
AP	Albert Pujols	15.00
MR	Manny Ramirez	8.00
AR	Alex Rodriguez	12.00
SR	Scott Rolen	8.00
AS	Alfonso Soriano	8.00
SS	Sammy Sosa	8.00
FT	Frank Thomas	8.00
JT	Jim Thome	10.00
VW	Vernon Wells	4.00

Key Acquisitions Relics

NM/M
Common Player: 4.00
Inserted 1:8
Refractors: 2-4X
Production 25 Sets

HC	Hee Seop Choi	4.00
JG	Juan Gonzalez	6.00
VG	Vladimir Guerrero	8.00
JL	Javy Lopez	6.00
AR	Alex Rodriguez	12.00
IR	Ivan Rodriguez	8.00
GS	Gary Sheffield	6.00
AS	Alfonso Soriano	8.00

Mini

NM/M
Common Player: 2.00
Inserted 1:5

DA	David Aardsma	5.00
EA	Erick Aybar	4.00
VC	Vito Chiaravalotti	4.00
NG	Nomar Garciaparra	4.00
JG	Jason Giambi	2.00
VG	Vladimir Guerrero	8.00
BH	Blake Hawksworth	4.00
CJA	Conor Jackson	8.00
DJ	Derek Jeter	6.00
CJ	Chipper Jones	8.00
HK	Howard Kendrick	10.00
KM	Kazuo Matsui	8.00
LM	Lastings Milledge	8.00
MM	Matt Moses	6.00
DM	David Murphy	4.00
DN	Dioner Navarro	10.00
AO	Akinori Otsuka	3.00
MPI	Mike Piazza	4.00
MP	Mark Prior	3.00
AP	Albert Pujols	6.00
AR	Alex Rodriguez	6.00
KS	Kyle Sleeth	4.00
SS	Sammy Sosa	4.00
TS	Tim Stauffer	4.00
IS	Ichiro Suzuki	5.00
ST	Shingo Takatsu	4.00
JT	Jim Thome	4.00
MV	Merkin Valdez	3.00
DW	Dontrelle Willis	3.00
KW	Kerry Wood	4.00

Mini Relics

NM/M
Common Player: 5.00
Inserted 1:51

JB	Jeff Bagwell	20.00
EG	Eric Gagne	15.00
NG	Nomar Garciaparra	12.00
CJ	Chipper Jones	12.00
PM	Pedro J. Martinez	12.00
MPI	Mike Piazza	12.00
MP	Mark Prior	10.00
AP	Albert Pujols	25.00
PW	Preston Wilson	5.00
KW	Kerry Wood	10.00

Patch Place Relics

NM/M
Common Player: 10.00
Refractor: No Pricing
Production 10 Sets

JB	Jeff Bagwell	20.00
RB	Rocco Baldelli	12.00
JBE	Josh Beckett	15.00
BB	Bret Boone	10.00
LC	Luis Castillo	10.00
CC	Chin-Feng Chen	40.00
CD	Carlos Delgado	10.00
AD	Adam Dunn	15.00
RF	Rafael Furcal	10.00
EG	Eric Gagne	15.00
NG	Nomar Garciaparra	40.00
LG	Luis Gonzalez	10.00
SG	Shawn Green	10.00
THE	Todd Helton	15.00
TH	Tim Hudson	10.00
RJ	Randy Johnson	15.00
AJ	Andruw Jones	10.00
CJ	Chipper Jones	15.00
AK	Austin Kearns	10.00
PL	Paul LoDuca	10.00
ML	Mike Lowell	10.00
PM	Pedro J. Martinez	20.00
MPI	Mike Piazza	35.00
MP	Mark Prior	15.00
AP	Albert Pujols	40.00
JR	Jose Reyes	15.00
JS	John Smoltz	15.00
SS	Sammy Sosa	20.00
FT	Frank Thomas	20.00
DW	Dontrelle Willis	10.00
PW	Preston Wilson	10.00
KW	Kerry Wood	20.00
BZ	Barry Zito	15.00

Personal Endorsements

NM/M
Common Autograph: 6.00
Golds: 1.5-3X
Production 25 Sets

DA	David Aardsma	15.00
GA	Garret Anderson	10.00
LB	Lance Berkman	20.00
HB	Hank Blalock	20.00
MC	Miguel Cabrera	30.00
VC	Vito Chiaravalotti	10.00
BC	Bobby Crosby	25.00
JF	Jennie Finch	120.00
MG	Marcus Giles	10.00
VG	Vladimir Guerrero	50.00
EH	Estee Harris	8.00
AH	Aubrey Huff	8.00
CJ	Conor Jackson	20.00
CL	Chris Lubanski	8.00
JM	Joe Mauer	35.00
WM	Willie Mays	200.00
DM	Dustin McGowan	6.00
BM	Brett Myers	10.00
SP	Scott Podsednik	10.00
JP	Jorge Posada	40.00
AR	Alex Rodriguez	150.00
IR	Ivan Rodriguez	40.00
ES	Ervin Santana	8.00
GS	Gary Sheffield	40.00
GS	Grady Sizemore	25.00
JV	Javier Vazquez	15.00
BW	Brandon Webb	6.00
DY	Delmon Young	15.00

Two of a Kind Autograph

Production 13

1, 2, 3 Triple Relics

NM/M
Inserted 1:171
Refractor: 1.5-2X
Production 25 Sets

NYY	Kenny Lofton, Derek Jeter, Alex Rodriguez	50.00
CHC	Mark Grudzielanek, Alex Gonzalez, Sammy Sosa	40.00
BOS	Johnny Damon, Bill Mueller, Nomar Garciaparra	40.00

2004 Topps Retired Signature Edition

NM/M
Complete Set (110): 125.00
Common Player: 1.00
Pack (5): 35.00
Box (5): 140.00

1	Willie Mays	6.00
2	Tony Gwynn	3.00
3	Dale Murphy	2.00
4	Lenny Dykstra	2.00
5	Johnny Bench	4.00
6	Bill Buckner	2.00
7	Ferguson Jenkins	1.50
8	George Brett	4.00
9	Ralph Kiner	2.00
10	Ernie Banks	4.00
11	Hal McRae	1.00
12	Lou Brock	2.00
13	Keith Hernandez	2.00

#	Player	Price
14	Jose Canseco	2.00
15	Whitey Ford	2.50
16	Dave Kingman	1.00
17	Tim Raines	1.00
18	Paul O'Neill	1.50
19	Lou Whitaker	1.00
20	Mike Schmidt	5.00
21	Wally Joyner	1.00
22	Kirk Gibson	1.00
23	Ryne Sandberg	5.00
24	Luis Tiant	1.00
25	Al Kaline	4.00
26	Brooks Robinson	3.00
27	Don Zimmer	1.00
28	Nolan Ryan	6.00
29	Maury Wills	1.00
30	Stan Musial	4.00
31	Garry Maddox	1.00
32	Tom Brunansky	1.00
33	Don Mattingly	1.00
34	Earl Weaver	1.00
35	Bobby Grich	1.00
36	Orlando Cepeda	1.50
37	Alan Trammell	1.50
38	Al Hrabosky	1.00
39	Davey Lopes	1.00
40	Rod Carew	2.00
41	Robin Yount	4.00
42	Dwight Gooden	1.00
43	Andre Dawson	1.50
44	Hank Aaron	6.00
45	Norm Cash	1.00
46	Reggie Jackson	2.50
47	Jim Rice	1.00
48	Carlton Fisk	2.00
49	Dave Parker	1.00
50	Cal Ripken Jr.	6.00
51	Roy Face	1.00
52	Bob Gibson	2.50
53	Jimmy Key	1.00
54	Al Oliver	1.00
55	Don Larsen	1.50
56	Tom Seaver	3.00
57	Tony Armas	1.00
58	Dave Stieb	1.00
59	Will Clark	2.00
60	Duke Snider	2.50
61	Cesar Geronimo	1.00
62	Ron Kittle	1.00
63	Ron Santo	2.00
64	Mickey Rivers	1.00
65	Jimmy Piersall	1.00
66	Ron Swoboda	1.00
67	Kent Hrbek	1.00
68	Dennis Eckersley	2.00
69	Greg Luzinski	1.00
70	Harmon Killebrew	3.00
71	Ron Guidry	1.00
72	Steve Garvey	1.00
73	Andy Van Slyke	1.00
74	Rich "Goose" Gossage	1.00
75	Ozzie Smith	3.00
76	Richie Allen	1.00
77	Vida Blue	1.00
78	Tony Oliva	1.00
79	Darryl Strawberry	1.00
80	Frank Robinson	2.00
81	Bruce Sutter	1.50
82	Dave Concepcion	1.00
83	Darrell Evans	1.00
84	Jack Morris	1.00
85	Bo Jackson	2.00
86	Orel Hershiser	1.00
87	Rob Dibble	1.00
88	Wade Boggs	2.00
89	Fernando Valenzuela	1.00
90	Jim Palmer	2.00
91	George Foster	1.00
92	Mike Scott	1.00
93	Paul Molitor	2.50
94	Gary Carter	1.00
95	Bobby Richardson	1.00
96	Rollie Fingers	1.00
97	Tim McCarver	1.00
98	John Candelaria	1.00
99	Dave Winfield	2.00
100	Yogi Berra	3.00
101	Bill Madlock	1.00
102	Jack McDowell	1.00
103	Luis Aparicio	1.00
104	Graig Nettles	1.00
105	Dave Stewart	1.00
106	Darren Daulton	1.00
107	Gary Gaetti	1.00
108	Tony Fernandez	1.00
109	Buddy Bell	1.00
110	Carl Yastrzemski	4.00

Black

Black (1-110): 4-6X
Production 99 Sets

Chrome Autographs

NM/M
Common Autograph: 10.00
Inserted 1:1
Refractor: 2-4X
SP Refractor: .75-2X
Production 25 Sets

ABBREVIATIONS

SP - Short Print

Code	Player	Price
HA	Hank Aaron/SP/50	300.00
TA	Tony Armas	10.00
EB	Ernie Banks/SP/50	180.00
BBE	Buddy Bell	12.00
JB	Johnny Bench/SP/75	80.00
YB	Yogi Berra/SP/75	80.00
VB	Vida Blue	10.00
WB	Wade Boggs	40.00
TB	Tom Brunansky	10.00
BB	Bill Buckner	12.00
JC	John Candelaria	20.00
JCA	Jose Canseco	35.00
RC	Rod Carew	35.00
GC	Gary Carter	20.00
OC	Orlando Cepeda	15.00
DD	Darren Daulton	10.00
BD	Bucky Dent	10.00
RD	Rob Dibble	12.00
DEC	Dennis Eckersley	30.00
DE	Darrell Evans	15.00
RF	Roy Face	15.00
TF	Tony Fernandez	10.00
WF	Whitey Ford/SP/75	90.00
RF	Rollie Fingers	15.00
CF	Carlton Fisk	40.00
GF	George Foster	12.00
CG	Cesar Geronimo	25.00
BG	Bob Gibson/SP/75	75.00
KG	Kirk Gibson	20.00
DG	Dwight Gooden/SP/75	40.00
GG	Rich "Goose" Gossage	15.00
BGR	Bobby Grich	10.00
TG	Tony Gwynn/SP/75	75.00
OH	Orel Hershiser	25.00
AH	Al Hrabosky	10.00
FJ	Ferguson Jenkins	15.00
WJ	Wally Joyner	10.00
JK	Jimmy Key	10.00
RK	Ralph Kiner	50.00
RKI	Ron Kittle	10.00
DL	Davey Lopes	10.00
GL	Greg Luzinski	15.00
BM	Bill Madlock	10.00
DM	Don Mattingly/SP/75	100.00
JM	Jack McDowell	10.00
PM	Paul Molitor	50.00
DM	Dale Murphy	25.00
SM	Stan Musial/SP/50	160.00
GN	Graig Nettles	12.00
TO	Tony Oliva	20.00
AO	Al Oliver	12.00
PO	Paul O'Neill	40.00
DP	Dave Parker	20.00
JP	Jimmy Piersall	15.00
BR	Bobby Richardson	15.00
CR	Cal Ripken Jr./SP/25	275.00
BRO	Brooks Robinson/SP/75	90.00
FR	Frank Robinson	30.00
NR	Nolan Ryan/SP/25	75.00
RSA	Ryne Sandberg	75.00
RS	Ron Santo	20.00
MS	Mike Schmidt/SP/75	150.00
TS	Tom Seaver/SP/75	75.00
OS	Ozzie Smith/SP/75	90.00
DSN	Duke Snider/SP/50	90.00
DST	Dave Stieb	12.00
DS	Darryl Strawberry	30.00
BS	Bruce Sutter	15.00
RS	Ron Swoboda	10.00
LT	Luis Tiant	15.00
AT	Alan Trammell	20.00
EW	Earl Weaver	10.00
MW	Maury Wills	10.00
CY	Carl Yastrzemski/SP/25	180.00
RY	Robin Yount/SP/50	125.00
DZ	Don Zimmer	20.00

Chrome Co-Signers

No Pricing
Production 25 Sets

2004 Topps Total

NM/M
Complete Set (880): 100.00
Common Player: .10
Pack (10): 1.00
Box (36): 30.00

#	Player	Price
1	Kevin Brown	.25
2	Mike Mordecai	.10
3	Seung Jun Song	.10
4	Mike Maroth	.10
5	Mike Lieberthal	.10
6	Billy Koch	.10
7	Mike Stanton	.10
8	Brad Penny	.10
9	Brooks Kieschnick	.10
10	Carlos Delgado	.40
11	Brady Clark	.10
12	Ramon Martinez	.10
13	Dan Wilson	.10
14	Guillermo Mota	.10
15	Trevor Hoffman	.10
16	Tony Batista	.10
17	Rusty Greer	.10
18	David Weathers	.10
19	Horacio Ramirez	.10
20	Aubrey Huff	.10
21	Casey Blake	.10
22	Ryan Bukvich	.10
23	Garrett Atkins	.10
24	Jose Contreras	.10
25	Chipper Jones	.75
26	Neifi Perez	.10
27	Scott Linebrink	.10
28	Matt Kinney	.10
29	Michael Restovich	.10
30	Scott Rolen	.75
31	John Franco	.10
32	Toby Hall	.10
33	Wily Mo Pena	.10
34	Dennis Tankersley	.10
35	Robb Nen	.10
36	Jose Valverde	.10
37	Chin-Feng Chen	.10
38	Gary Knotts	.10
39	Scott Elarton	.10
40	Bret Boone	.25
41	Josh Phelps	.10
42	Jason Larue	.10
43	Tim Redding	.10
44	Greg Myers	.10
45	Darin Erstad	.25
46	Kip Wells	.10
47	Matt Ford	.10
48	Jerome Williams	.10
49	Brian Meadows	.10
50	Albert Pujols	1.50
51	Kirk Saarloos	.10
52	Scott Eyre	.10
53	John Flaherty	.10
54	Rafael Soriano	.10
55	Shea Hillenbrand	.10
56	Kyle Farnsworth	.10
57	Nate Cornejo	.10
58	Kerry Robinson	.10
59	Yan Vogelsong	.10
60	Ryan Klesko	.20
61	Luke Hudson	.10
62	Justin Morneau	.20
63	Frank Catalanotto	.10
64	Derrick Turnbow	.10
65	Marcus Giles	.10
66	Mark Mulder	.25
67	Matt Anderson	.10
68	Mike Matheny	.10
69	Brian Lawrence	.10
70	Bobby Abreu	.10
71	Damian Moss	.10
72	Richard Hidalgo	.10
73	Mark Kotsay	.10
74	Mike Cameron	.10
75	Troy Glaus	.40
76	Matt Holliday	.10
77	Byung-Hyun Kim	.10
78	Aaron Sele	.10
79	Danny Graves	.10
80	Barry Zito	.10
81	Matt LeCroy	.10
82	Jason Isringhausen	.10
83	Colby Lewis	.10
84	Franklyn German	.10
85	Luis Matos	.10
86	Mike Timlin	.10
87	Miguel Batista	.10
88	John McDonald	.10
89	Joey Eischen	.10
90	Mike Mussina	.50
91	Jack Wilson	.20
92	Aaron Cook	.10
93	John Parrish	.10
94	Jose Valentin	.10
95	Johnny Damon	.20
96	Pat Burrell	.25
97	Brendan Donnelly	.10
98	Lance Carter	.10
99	Omar Daal	.10
100	Ichiro Suzuki	1.00
101	Robin Ventura	.10
102	Brian Shouse	.10
103	Kevin Jarvis	.10
104	Jason Young	.10
105	Moises Alou	.25
106	Wes Obermueller	.10
107	David Segui	.10
108	Mike MacDougal	.10
109	John Buck	.10
110	Gary Sheffield	.25
111	Yorvit Torrealba	.10
112	Matt Kata	.10
113	David Bell	.10
114	Juan Gonzalez	.40
115	Kelvim Escobar	.10
116	Ruben Sierra	.10
117	Todd Wellemeyer	.10
118	Jamie Walker	.10
119	Will Cunnane	.10
120	Cliff Floyd	.10
121	Aramis Ramirez	.40
122	Damaso Marte	.10
123	Juan Castro	.10
124	Chris Woodward	.10
125	Andruw Jones	.50
126	Ben Weber	.10
127	Dee Brown	.10
128	Steve Reed	.10
129	Gabe Kapler	.10
130	Miguel Cabrera	.75
131	Billy McMillon	.10
132	Julio Mateo	.10
133	Preston Wilson	.10
134	Tony Clark	.10
135	Carlos Lee	.20
136	Carlos Baerga	.10
137	Mike Crudale	.10
138	David Ross	.10
139	Josh Fogg	.10
140	Dmitri Young	.10
141	Cliff Lee	.10
142	Mike Lowell	.25
143	Jason Lane	.10
144	Pedro Feliz	.10
145	Ken Griffey Jr.	1.00
146	Dustin Hermanson	.10
147	Scott Hodges	.10
148	Aquilino Lopez	.10
149	Wes Helms	.10
150	Jason Giambi	.50
151	Erasmo Ramirez	.10
152	Sean Burroughs	.10
153	J.T. Snow	.10
154	Eddie Guardado	.10
155	C.C. Sabathia	.10
156	Kyle Lohse	.10
157	Roberto Hernandez	.10
158	Jason Simontacchi	.10
159	Tim Spooneybarger	.10
160	Alfonso Soriano	.50
161	Mike Gonzalez	.10
162	Alex Cora	.10
163	Kevin Gryboski	.10
164	Steve Cox	.10
165	Luis Castillo	.10
166	Odalis Perez	.10
167	Alex Sanchez	.10
168	Robert Mackowiak	.10
169	Francisco Rodriguez	.10
170	Roy Oswalt	.25
171	Omar Infante	.10
172	Ryan Jensen	.10
173	Ben Broussard	.10
174	Mark Hendrickson	.10
175	Manny Ramirez	.50
176	Rob Bell	.10
177	Adam Everett	.10
178	Chris George	.10
179	Ricky Gutierrez	.10
180	Eric Gagne	.40
181	Scott Schoeneweis	.10
182	Kris Benson	.10
183	Amaury Telemaco	.10
184	John Riedling	.10
185	Juan Pierre	.10
186	Ramon Ortiz	.10
187	Luis Rivas	.10
188	Larry Bigbie	.10
189	Robby Hammock	.10
190	Geoff Jenkins	.20
191	Chad Cordero	.10
192	Mark Ellis	.10
193	Mark Loretta	.10
194	Ryan Drese	.10
195	Lance Berkman	.10
196	Kevin Appier	.10
197	Enrique Calero (Kiko)	.10
198	Mickey Callaway	.10
199	Chase Utley	.25
200	Nomar Garciaparra	1.00
201	Kevin Cash	.10
202	Ramiro Mendoza	.10
203	Shane Reynolds	.10
204	Chris Spurling	.10
205	Aaron Guiel	.10
206	Mark Derosa	.10
207	Adam Kennedy	.10
208	Andy Pettitte	.25
209	Rafael Palmeiro	.50
210	Luis Gonzalez	.25
211	Ryan Franklin	.10
212	Bob Wickman	.10
213	Ron Calloway	.10
214	Jae Weong Seo	.10
215	Kazuhisa Ishii	.10
216	Sterling Hitchcock	.10
217	Jimmy Gobble	.10
218	Chad Moeller	.10
219	Jake Peavy	.10
220	John Smoltz	.25
221	Erick Almonte	.10
222	David Wells	.10
223	Brad Lidge	.10
224	Carlos Zambrano	.25
225	Kerry Wood	.75
226	Alex Cintron	.10
227	Javier Lopez	.25
228	Jeremy Griffiths	.10
229	Jon Garland	.10
230	Curt Schilling	.50
231	Alex Gonzalez	.10
232	Jay Gibbons	.10
233	Damian Jackson	.10
234	Jeriome Robertson	.10
235	Johan Santana	.10
236	Jose Guillen	.10
237	Jeff Connie	.10
238	Matt Roney	.10
239	Desi Relaford	.10
240	Frank Thomas	.50
241	Danny Patterson	.10
242	Kevin Mench	.10
243	Mike Redmond	.10
244	Jeff Suppan	.10
245	Carl Everett	.10
246	Jack Cressend	.10
247	Matt Mantei	.10
248	Enrique Wilson	.10
249	Craig Counsell	.10
250	Mark Prior	1.50
251	Jared Sandberg	.10
252	Scott Strickland	.10
253	Lew Ford	.10
254	Hee Seop Choi	.10
255	Jason Phillips	.10
256	Jason Jennings	.10
257	Todd Pratt	.10
258	Matt Herges	.10
259	Kerry Ligtenberg	.10
260	Austin Kearns	.25
261	Jay Witasick	.10
262	Tony Armas Jr.	.10
263	Tom Martin	.10
264	Oliver Perez	.10
265	Jorge Posada	.40
266	Joe Beimel	.10
267	Ben Hendrickson	.10
268	Reggie Sanders	.10
269	Julio Lugo	.10
270	Josh Beckett	.40
271	Kyle Snyder	.10
272	Felipe Lopez	.10
273	Kevin Millar	.10
274	Travis Hafner	.20
275	Magglio Ordonez	.25
276	Marlon Byrd	.10
277	Scott Spiezio	.10
278	Mark Corey	.10
279	Tim Salmon	.25
280	Alex Gonzalez	.10
281	Marquis Grissom	.10
282	Miguel Olivo	.10
283	Orlando Hudson	.10
284	Rondell White	.20
285	Jermaine Dye	.10
286	Paul Shuey	.10
287	Brandon Inge	.10
288	B.J. Surhoff	.10
289	Edgar Gonzalez	.10
290	Angel Berroa	.10
291	Claudio Vargas	.10
292	Cesar Izturis	.10
293	Brandon Phillips	.10
294	Jeff Duncan	.10
295	Randy Wolf	.10
296	Barry Larkin	.25
297	Felix Rodriguez	.10
298	Robb Quinlan	.10
299	Brian Jordan	.10
300	Dontrelle Willis	.25
301	Doug Davis	.10
302	Ricky Stone	.10
303	Travis Harper	.10
304	Jaret Wright	.10
305	Edgardo Alfonzo	.10
306	Quinton McCracken	.10
307	Jason Bay	.10
308	Joe Randa	.10
309	Steve Sparks	.10
310	Roy Halladay	.25
311	Antonio Alfonseca	.10
312	Michael Cuddyer	.10
313	John Patterson	.10
314	Chris Widger	.10
315	Shigetoshi Hasegawa	.10
316	Tim Wakefield	.10
317	Scott Hatteberg	.10
318	Mike Remlinger	.10
319	Jose Vizcaino	.10
320	Rocco Baldelli	.25
321	David Riske	.10
322	Steve Karsay	.10
323	Peter Bergeron	.10
324	Jeff Weaver	.10
325	Larry Walker	.25
326	Jack Cust	.10
327	Bo Hart	.10
328	Rod Beck	.10
329	Jose Acevedo	.10
330	Hank Blalock	.40
331	Flash Gordon	.10
332	Brian Fuentes	.10
333	Tomas Perez	.10
334	Lenny Harris	.10
335	Matt Morris	.25
336	Jeremi Gonzalez	.10
337	David Eckstein	.10
338	Aaron Rowand	.10
339	Rick Bauer	.10
340	Jim Edmonds	.25
341	Joe Borowski	.10
342	Eric Dubose	.10
343	D'Angelo Jimenez	.10
344	Tomokazu Ohka	.10
345	Victor Zambrano	.10
346	Joe McEwing	.10
347	Jorge Sosa	.10
348	Keith Ginter	.10
349	A.J. Pierzynski	.10
350	Mike Sweeney	.10
351	Shawn Chacon	.10
352	Matt Clement	.25
353	Vance Wilson	.10
354	Benito Santiago	.10
355	Eric Hinske	.10
356	Vladimir Guerrero	.75
357	Kenny Rogers	.10
358	Aaron Boone	.10
359	Jay Powell	.10
360	Phil Nevin	.10
361	Willie Harris	.10
362	Ty Wigginton	.10
363	Chad Fox	.10
364	Junior Spivey	.10
365	Brandon Webb	.10
366	Brett Myers	.10
367	Alexis Gomez	.10
368	Dave Roberts	.10
369	LaTroy Hawkins	.10
370	Kevin Millwood	.25
371	Brian Schneider	.10
372	Blaine Neal	.10
373	Jeromy Burnitz	.10
374	Ted Lilly	.10
375	Shawn Green	.25
376	Carlos Pena	.10
377	Gil Meche	.10
378	Jeff Bagwell	.50
379	Alex Escobar	.10
380	Erubiel Durazo	.10
381	Cristian Guzman	.10
382	Rocky Biddle	.10
383	Craig Wilson	.10
384	Rey Sanchez	.10
385	Russ Ortiz	.10
386	Freddy Garcia	.10
387	Luis Vizcaino	.10
388	David Ortiz	.40
389	Jose Molina	.10
390	Edgar Martinez	.25
391	Nate Bump	.10
392	Brent Mayne	.10
393	Ray King	.10
394	Paul Wilson	.10
395	Melvin Mora	.10
396	Morgan Ensberg	.10
397	Ramon Hernandez	.10
398	Juan Rincon	.10
399	Ron Mahay	.10
400	Jeff Kent	.25
401	Cal Eldred	.10
402	Mike Difelice	.10
403	Valerio De Los Santos	.10
404	Steve Finley	.25
405	Trot Nixon	.25
406	Kevin Walker	.10
407	John Vander Wal	.10
408	Ray Durham	.10
409	Aaron Heilman	.10
410	Edgar Renteria	.25
411	Mike Hampton	.10
412	Kirk Rueter	.10
413	Jim Mecir	.10
414	Brian Roberts	.10
415	Paul Konerko	.10
416	Reed Johnson	.10
417	Roger Clemens	1.50
418	Coco Crisp	.10
419	Carlos Hernandez	.10
420	Scott Podsednik	.40
421	Miguel Cairo	.10
422	Abraham Nunez	.10
423	Endy Chavez	.10
424	Eric Munson	.10
425	Torii Hunter	.25
426	Ben Howard	.10
427	Chris Gomez	.10
428	Francisco Cordero	.10
429	Jeffrey Hammonds	.10
430	Shannon Stewart	.10
431	Einar Diaz	.10
432	Eric Byrnes	.10
433	Marty Cordova	.10
434	Matt Ginter	.10
435	Victor Martinez	.10
436	Geronimo Gil	.10
437	Grant Balfour	.10
438	Ramon Vazquez	.10
439	Jose Cruz	.10
440	Orlando Cabrera	.10
441	Joe Kennedy	.10
442	Scott Williamson	.10
443	Troy Percival	.10
444	Derrek Lee	.25
445	Runelvys Hernandez	.10
446	Mark Grudzielanek	.10
447	Trey Hodges	.10
448	Jimmy Haynes	.10
449	Eric Milton	.10
450	Todd Helton	.50
451	Gregg Zaun	.10
452	Woody Williams	.10
453	Todd Walker	.10
454	Gary Matthews	.10
455	Fernando Vina	.10
456	Omar Vizquel	.10
457	Roberto Alomar	.40
458	Bill Hall	.10
459	Juan Rivera	.10
460	Tom Glavine	.40
461	Ramon Castro	.10
462	Cory Vance	.10
463	Dan Miceli	.10
464	Lyle Overbay	.10
465	Craig Biggio	.25
466	Ricky Ledee	.10
467	Michael Barrett	.10
468	Jason Anderson	.10
469	Matt Stairs	.10
470	Jarrod Washburn	.10
471	Todd Hundley	.10
472	Grant Roberts	.10
473	Randy Winn	.10
474	Pat Hentgen	.10

#	Player	Price
475	Jose Vidro	.10
476	Tony Torcato	.10
477	Jeremy Affeldt	.10
478	Carlos Guillen	.10
479	Paul Quantrill	.10
480	Rafael Furcal	.10
481	Adam Melhuse	.10
482	Jerry Hairston	.10
483	Adam Bernero	.10
484	Terrence Long	.10
485	Paul Lo Duca	.10
486	Corey Koskie	.10
487	John Lackey	.10
488	Chad Zerbe	.10
489	Vinny Castilla	.10
490	Corey Patterson	.20
491	John Olerud	.20
492	Josh Bard	.10
493	Darren Dreifort	.10
494	Jason Standridge	.10
495	Ben Sheets	.25
496	Jose Castillo	.10
497	Jay Payton	.10
498	Rob Bowen	.10
499	Bobby Higginson	.10
500	Alex Rodriguez	1.50
501	Octavio Dotel	.10
502	Rheal Cormier	.10
503	Felix Heredia	.10
504	Dan Wright	.10
505	Michael Young	.10
506	Wilfredo Ledezma	.10
507	Sun-Woo Kim	.10
508	Michael Tejera	.10
509	Herbert Perry	.10
510	Esteban Loaiza	.10
511	Alan Embree	.10
512	Ben Davis	.10
513	Greg Colbrunn	.10
514	Josh Hall	.10
515	Raul Ibanez	.10
516	Jayson Werth	.10
517	Corky Miller	.10
518	Jason Marquis	.10
519	Roger Cedeno	.10
520	Adam Dunn	.50
521	Paul Byrd	.10
522	Sandy Alomar	.10
523	Salomon Torres	.10
524	John Halama	.10
525	Mike Piazza	1.00
526	Buddy Groom	.10
527	Adrian Beltre	.25
528	Chad Harville	.10
529	Javier Vazquez	.20
530	Jody Gerut	.10
531	Elmer Dessens	.10
532	B.J. Ryan	.10
533	Chad Durbin	.10
534	Doug Mirabelli	.10
535	Bernie Williams	.40
536	Jeff Davanon	.10
537	Dave Berg	.10
538	Geoff Blum	.10
539	John Thomson	.10
540	Jeremy Bonderman	.10
541	Jeff Zimmerman	.10
542	Derek Lowe	.10
543	Scot Shields	.10
544	Michael Tucker	.10
545	Tim Hudson	.40
546	Ryan Ludwick	.10
547	Rick Reed	.10
548	Placido Polanco	.10
549	Tony Graffanino	.10
550	Garret Anderson	.40
551	Timoniel Perez	.10
552	Jesus Colome	.10
553	R.A. Dickey	.10
554	Tim Worrell	.10
555	Jason Kendall	.10
556	Tom Goodwin	.10
557	Joaquin Benoit	.10
558	Stephen Randolph	.10
559	Miguel Tejada	.40
560	A.J. Burnett	.10
561	Ben Diggins	.10
562	Juan Cruz	.10
563	Zach Day	.10
564	Antonio Perez	.10
565	Jason Schmidt	.25
566	Armando Benitez	.10
567	Denny Neagle	.10
568	Eric Eckenstahler	.10
569	Chan Ho Park	.10
570	Carlos Beltran	.40
571	Brett Tomko	.10
572	Henry Mateo	.10
573	Ken Harvey	.10
574	Matt Lawton	.10
575	Mariano Rivera	.25
576	Darrell May	.10
577	Jamie Moyer	.10
578	Paul Bako	.10
579	Cory Lidle	.10
580	Jacque Jones	.10
581	Jolbert Cabrera	.10
582	Jason Grimsley	.10
583	Danny Kolb	.10
584	Billy Wagner	.10
585	Rich Aurilia	.10
586	Vicente Padilla	.10
587	Oscar Villarreal	.10
588	Rene Reyes	.10
589	Jon Lieber	.10
590	Nick Johnson	.10
591	Bobby Crosby	.10
592	Steve Trachsel	.10

#	Player	Price
593	Brian Boehringer	.10
594	Juan Uribe	.10
595	Bartolo Colon	.20
596	Bobby Hill	.10
597	Andy Van Hekken	.10
598	Carl Pavano	.10
599	Kurt Ainsworth	.10
600	Derek Jeter	2.00
601	Doug Mientkiewicz	.10
602	Orlando Palmeiro	.10
603	J.C. Romero	.10
604	Scott Sullivan	.10
605	Brad Radke	.10
606	Fernando Rodney	.10
607	Jim Brower	.10
608	Josh Towers	.10
609	Brad Fullmer	.10
610	Jose Reyes	.25
611	Ryan Wagner	.10
612	Joe Mays	.10
613	Jung Bong	.10
614	Curtis Leskanic	.10
615	Al Leiter	.10
616	Wade Miller	.10
617	Keith Foulke	.10
618	Casey Fossum	.10
619	Craig Monroe	.10
620	Hideo Nomo	.25
621	Bob File	.10
622	Steve Kline	.10
623	Bobby Kielty	.10
624	Dewon Brazelton	.10
625	Eric Chavez	.25
626	Chris Carpenter	.10
627	Trever Miller	.10
628	Jason Davis	.10
629	Jose Jimenez	.10
630	Vernon Wells	.25
631	Kenny Lofton	.25
632	Chad Bradford	.10
633	Brad Wilkerson	.10
634	Pokey Reese	.10
635	Richie Sexson	.40
636	Chin-Hui Tsao	.10
637	Eli Marrero	.10
638	Chris Reitsma	.10
639	Daryle Ward	.10
640	Mark Teixeira	.25
641	Corwin Malone	.10
642	Adam Eaton	.10
643	Jimmy Rollins	.25
644	Brian Anderson	.10
645	Bill Mueller	.10
646	Jake Westbrook	.10
647	Bengie Molina	.10
648	Jorge Julio	.10
649	Billy Traber	.10
650	Randy Johnson	.75
651	Javy Lopez	.25
652	Doug Glanville	.10
653	Jeff Cirillo	.10
654	Tino Martinez	.10
655	Mark Buehrle	.10
656	Jason Michaels	.10
657	Damian Rolls	.10
658	Rosman Garcia	.10
659	Scott Hairston	.10
660	Carl Crawford	.25
661	Livan Hernandez	.10
662	Danny Bautista	.10
663	Brad Ausmus	.10
664	Juan Acevedo	.10
665	Sean Casey	.10
666	Pedro Martinez	.75
667	Milton Bradley	.10
668	Braden Looper	.10
669	Paul Abbott	.10
670	Joel Pinero	.10
671	Luis Terrero	.10
672	Rodrigo Lopez	.10
673	Joe Crede	.10
674	Mike Koplove	.10
675	Brian Giles	.25
676	Jeff Nelson	.10
677	Russell Branyan	.10
678	Mike DeJean	.10
679	Brian Daubach	.10
680	Ellis Burks	.10
681	Ryan Dempster	.10
682	Cliff Politte	.10
683	Brian Reith	.10
684	Scott Stewart	.10
685	Allan Simpson	.10
686	Shawn Estes	.10
687	Jason Johnson	.10
688	Wil Cordero	.10
689	Kelly Stinnett	.10
690	Jose Lima	.10
691	Gary Bennett	.10
692	T.J. Tucker	.10
693	Shane Spencer	.10
694	Chris Hammond	.10
695	Chris Singleton	.10
696	Xavier Nady	.10
697	Cody Ransom	.10
698	Ron Villone	.10
699	Brook Fordyce	.10
700	Sammy Sosa	1.50
701	Terry Adams	.10
702	Ricardo Rincon	.10
703	Tike Redman	.10
704	Chris Stynes	.10
705	Mark Redman	.10
706	Juan Encarnacion	.10
707	Jhonny Peralta	.10
708	Denny Hocking	.10
709	Ivan Rodriguez	.50
710	Jose Hernandez	.10

#	Player	Price
711	Brandon Duckworth	.10
712	Dave Burba	.10
713	Joe Nathan	.10
714	Dan Smith	.10
715	Karim Garcia	.10
716	Arthur Rhodes	.10
717	Shawn Wooten	.10
718	Ramon Santiago	.10
719	Luis Ugueto	.10
720	Danys Baez	.10
721	Alfredo Amezaga	.10
722	Sidney Ponson	.10
723	Joe Mauer	.50
724	Jesse Foppert	.10
725	Todd Greene	.10
726	Dan Haren	.10
727	Brandon Larson	.10
728	Bobby Jenks	.10
729	Grady Sizemore	.25
730	Ben Grieve	.10
731	Khalil Greene	.10
732	Chad Gaudin	.10
733	Johnny Estrada	.10
734	Joe Valentine	.10
735	Tim Raines	.10
736	Brandon Claussen	.10
737	Sam Marsonek	.10
738	Delmon Young	.10
739	David Dellucci	.10
740	Sergio Mitre	.10
741	Nick Neugebauer	.10
742	Laynce Nix	.10
743	Joe Thurston	.10
744	Ryan Langerhans	.10
745	Pete LaForest	.10
746	Arnie Munoz	.10
747	Rickie Weeks	.25
748	Neal Cotts	.10
749	Jonny Gomes	.10
750	Jim Thome	.75
751	Jon Rauch	.10
752	Edwin Jackson	.10
753	Ryan Madson	.10
754	Chad Tracy	.10
755	Eddie Perez	.10
756	Joe Borchard	.10
757	Jeremy Guthrie	.10
758	Jose Mesa	.10
759	Doug Waechter	.10
760	J.D. Drew	.25
761	Adam LaRoche	.10
762	Rich Harden	.10
763	Justin Speier	.10
764	Todd Zeile	.10
765	Turk Wendell	.10
766	Mark Bellhorn	.10
767	Mike Jackson	.10
768	Chone Figgins	.10
769	Mike Neu	.10
770	Greg Maddux	.10
771	Frank Brooks	.10
772	Alec Zumwalt RC	.25
773	Glendon Rusch	.10
774	Dustan Mohr	.10
775	Shane Halter	.10
776	Tom Wilson	.10
777	So Taguchi	.10
778	Eric Karros	.10
779	Ramon Nivar	.10
780	Marlon Anderson	.10
781	Brayan Pena RC	.10
782	Chris O'Riordan	.10
783	Dioner Navarro RC	1.50
784	Alberto Callaspo RC	.50
785	Hector Gimenez RC	.25
786	Yadier Molina RC	.40
787	Kevin Richardson	.25
788	Brian Pilkington	.10
789	Adam Greenberg	.10
790	Ervin Santana RC	1.00
791	Brent Colamarino	.75
792	Ben Himes	.25
793	Todd Self RC	.25
794	Brad Vericker	.25
795	Donald Kelly RC	.25
796	Brock Jacobsen	.25
797	Brock Peterson	.25
798	Carlos Sosa	.50
799	Chad Chop	.10
800	Matt Moses	1.00
801	Chris Aquila RC	.25
802	David Murphy	.25
803	Don Sutton RC	1.00
804	Jereme Milons	.10
805	Jon Coutlangus	.10
806	Greg Thissen	.10
807	Jose Capellan RC	1.00
808	Chad Santos RC	.10
809	Wardell Starling RC	.10
810	Kevin Kouzmanoff	2.00
811	Kevin Davidson	.40
812	Michael Mooney	.10
813	Rodney Choy Foo	.10
814	Reid Gorecki	.10
815	Rudy Guillen RC	1.00
816	Harvey Garcia	.10
817	Warner Madrigal RC	.50
818	Kenny Perez	.10
819	Joaquin Arias RC	.10
820	Benji Dequin	.10
821	Lastings Milledge	2.00
822	Blake Hawksworth RC	.10
823	Estee Harris RC	.50
824	Bobby Brownlie	.10
825	Wanell Severino RC	.10
826	Bobby Madritsch	.10
827	Travis Hanson	.40
828	Brandon Medders RC	.40

#	Player	Price
829	Kevin Howard RC	.50
830	Brian Steffek	.10
831	Terry Jones	.10
832	Anthony Acevedo	.40
833	Kory Casto	.10
834	Brooks Conrad	.10
835	Juan Gutierrez RC	.50
836	Charlie Zink RC	.10
837	David Aardsma	.40
838	Carl Loadenthal	.10
839	Donald Levinski	.10
840	Dustin Nippert RC	.75
841	Calvin Hayes	.10
842	Felix Hernandez RC	5.00
843	Tyler Davidson	.10
844	George Sherrill RC	.10
845	Craig Ansman RC	.10
846	Jeffrey Allison	.10
847	Tommy Murphy RC	.10
848	Jerome Gamble RC	.40
849	Jesse English RC	.10
850	Alex Romero RC	.10
851	Joel Zumaya RC	2.00
852	Carlos Quentin	2.00
853	Jose Valdez	.10
854	J.J. Furmaniak RC	.25
855	Juan Cedeno RC	.10
856	Kyle Sleeth	1.00
857	Josh Labandeira RC	.25
858	Lee Gwaltney	.10
859	Lincoln Holdzkom RC	.25
860	Ivan Ochoa	.10
861	Luke Anderson	.10
862	Conor Jackson	1.00
863	Matt Capps RC	.75
864	Merkin Valdez RC	.75
865	Paul Bacot	.50
866	Erick Aybar RC	1.00
867	Scott Proctor RC	1.00
868	Tim Stauffer	.50
869	Matt Creighton RC	.10
870	Zach Miner RC	1.00
871	Danny Gonzalez RC	.10
872	Tom Farmer	.10
873	John Santor	.10
874	Logan Kensing RC	.25
875	Vito Chiaravalloti RC	.50
876	Checklist	.10
877	Checklist	.10
878	Checklist	.10
879	Checklist	.10
880	Checklist	.10

Silver

NM/M
Stars: 2-3X
Inserted 1:1

I Press Plates

No Pricing
Production one for each color.

Autograph

TOTAL SIGNATURES

NM/M
Inserted 1:414 8.00
GB	Grant Balfour	8.00
LB	Larry Bigbie	10.00
BC	Brandon Claussen	8.00
TH	Toby Hall	8.00
JJ	Jimmy Journell	8.00

Total Award Winners

NM/M
Complete Set (30): 20.00
Common Player: .50
Inserted 1:12

AW1	Roy Halladay	.50
AW2	Eric Gagne	.50
AW3	Alex Rodriguez	3.00
AW4	Albert Pujols	3.00
AW5	Alex Rodriguez	3.00
AW6	Jorge Posada	.50
AW7	Javy Lopez	.50
AW8	Carlos Delgado	.50
AW9	Todd Helton	.75
AW10	Bret Boone	.50
AW11	Jose Vidro	.50
AW12	Bill Mueller	.50
AW13	Mike Lowell	.50
AW14	Alex Rodriguez	3.00
AW15	Edgar Renteria	.50
AW16	Garret Anderson	.50
AW17	Albert Pujols	3.00
AW18	Manny Ramirez	1.00
AW19	Vernon Wells	.50
AW20	Gary Sheffield	.50
AW21	Edgar Martinez	.50
AW22	Mike Hampton	.50
AW23	Angel Berroa	.50
AW24	Dontrelle Willis	.50
AW25	Keith Foulke	.50
AW26	Eric Gagne	.50
AW27	Alex Rodriguez	3.00
AW28	Albert Pujols	3.00
AW29	Tony Pena	.50
AW30	Jack McKeon	.50

Total Production

NM/M
Complete Set (10): 10.00
Common Player: .50
Inserted 1:18

TP1	Alex Rodriguez	3.00
TP2	Albert Pujols	3.00
TP3	Sammy Sosa	2.50
TP4	Carlos Delgado	.50
TP5	Gary Sheffield	.50
TP6	Manny Ramirez	1.00
TP7	Jim Thome	1.00
TP8	Todd Helton	.75
TP9	Garret Anderson	.50
TP10	Nomar Garciaparra	2.00

Total Topps

NM/M
Complete Set (50): 25.00
Common Player: .50
Inserted 1:7

TT1	Derek Jeter	3.00
TT2	Jose Reyes	.50
TT3	Miguel Tejada	.50
TT4	Larry Walker	.50
TT5	Frank Thomas	.75
TT6	Carlos Delgado	.50
TT7	Vernon Wells	.50
TT8	Jeff Bagwell	.75
TT9	Jason Giambi	.75
TT10	Mike Lowell	.50
TT11	Shannon Stewart	.50
TT12	Mike Piazza	1.50
TT13	Todd Helton	.50
TT14	Austin Kearns	.50
TT15	Jim Edmonds	.50
TT16	Jose Vidro	.50
TT17	Andruw Jones	.50
TT18	Gary Sheffield	.50
TT19	Eric Chavez	.50
TT20	Magglio Ordonez	.50
TT21	Geoff Jenkins	.50
TT22	Ken Griffey Jr.	1.50
TT23	Jeff Kent	.50
TT24	Jorge Posada	.50
TT25	Albert Pujols	2.00
TT26	Javy Lopez	.50
TT27	Alfonso Soriano	1.00
TT28	Brian Giles	.50
TT29	Mike Sweeney	.50
TT30	Miguel Cabrera	1.00
TT31	Luis Gonzalez	.50
TT32	Scott Rolen	1.00
TT33	Jim Thome	1.00
TT34	Garret Anderson	.75
TT35	Vladimir Guerrero	1.00
TT36	Shawn Green	.50
TT37	Hank Blalock	.75
TT38	Marcus Giles	.50
TT39	Torii Hunter	.50
TT40	Sammy Sosa	2.00
TT41	Nomar Garciaparra	2.00
TT42	Bobby Abreu	.50
TT43	Richie Sexson	.50
TT44	Manny Ramirez	.75
TT45	Troy Glaus	.75
TT46	Preston Wilson	.50
TT47	Ivan Rodriguez	.75
TT48	Ichiro Suzuki	1.50
TT49	Chipper Jones	.75
TT50	Alex Rodriguez	3.00

2004 Topps Traded & Rookies

NM/M
Complete Set (220): 50.00
Common Player: .10
Chrome Cards: 2-4X
Pack (10): 4.00
Box (24): 85.00

T1	Pokey Reese	.10
T2	Tony Womack	.10
T3	Michael Barrett	.10
T4	Juan Uribe	.10
T5	J.D. Drew	.25
T6	Marlon Anderson	.10
T7	Carlos Guillen	.10
T8	Royce Clayton	.10
T9	Fernando Vina	.10
T10	Milton Bradley	.10
T11	Eddie Perez	.10
T12	Ben Grieve	.10
T13	Brian Jordan	.10
T14	Tony Graffanino	.10
T15	Billy Wagner	.10
T16	Terrence Long	.10
T17	Casey Fossum	.10
T18	Denny Hocking	.10
T19	Reggie Sanders	.10
T20	Javy Lopez	.25
T21	Jay Payton	.10
T22	Cliff Politte	.10
T23	Eddie Guardado	.10
T24	Andy Pettitte	.50
T25	Richie Sexson	.40
T26	Ronnie Belliard	.10
T27	Michael Tucker	.10
T28	Brad Fullmer	.10
T29	Orlando Palmeiro	.10
T30	Bartolo Colon	.25
T31	Larry Walker	.40
T32	Mark Kotsay	.10
T33	Jason Marquis	.10
T34	Dustan Mohr	.10
T35	Javier Vazquez	.25
T36	Nomar Garciaparra	1.50
T37	Tino Martinez	.25
T38	Hee Seop Choi	.10
T39	Damian Miller	.10
T40	Jose Lima	.10
T41	Todd Zeile	.10
T42	Raul Ibanez	.10
T43	Danys Baez	.10
T44	Tony Clark	.10
T45	Greg Maddux	1.00
T46	Craig Counsell	.10
T47	Orlando Cabrera	.25
T48	Jose Cruz Jr.	.10
T49	Kris Benson	.10
T50	Alex Rodriguez	2.00
T51	Steve Finley	.10
T52	Ramon Hernandez	.10
T53	Esteban Loaiza	.10
T54	Ugueth Urbina	.10
T55	Jeff Weaver	.10
T56	Flash Gordon	.10
T57	Jose Contreras	.10
T58	Paul LoDuca	.10
T59	Junior Spivey	.10
T60	Curt Schilling	1.00
T61	Brad Penny	.10
T62	Braden Looper	.10
T63	Miguel Cairo	.10

No	Player	Price
T64	Juan Encarnacion	.10
T65	Miguel Batista	.10
T66	Terry Francona	.10
T67	Lee Mazzilli	.10
T68	Al Pedrique	.10
T69	Ozzie Guillen	.10
T70	Phil Garner	.10
T71	Matt Bush RC	1.50
T72	Homer Bailey RC	5.00
T73	Greg Golson RC	2.00
T74	Kyle Waldrop RC	1.00
T75	Richie Robnett RC	1.00
T76	Jay Rainville RC	1.50
T77	Bill Bray RC	.50
T78	Phillip Hughes RC	10.00
T79	Scott Elbert RC	.50
T80	Josh Fields RC	2.00
T81	Justin Orenduff RC	.75
T82	Dan Putnam RC	.75
T83	Chris Nelson RC	2.50
T84	Blake DeWitt RC	2.00
T85	J.P. Howell RC	1.00
T86	Huston Street RC	2.00
T87	Kurt Suzuki RC	1.50
T88	Erick San Pedro RC	.50
T89	Matt Tuiasosopo RC	1.50
T90	Matt Macri RC	1.00
T91	Chad Tracy	.20
T92	Scott Hairston	.20
T93	Jonny Gomes	.20
T94	Chin-Feng Chen	.20
T95	Chien-Ming Wang	.20
T96	Dustin McGowan	.20
T97	Chris Burke	.20
T98	Denny Bautista	.20
T99	Preston Larrison	.20
T100	Kevin Youkilis	.40
T101	John Maine	.20
T102	Guillermo Quiroz	.20
T103	David Krynzel	.20
T104	David Kelton	.20
T105	Edwin Encarnacion	.20
T106	Chad Gaudin	.20
T107	Sergio Mitre	.20
T108	Laynce Nix	.20
T109	David Parrish	.20
T110	Brandon Claussen	.20
T111	Frank Francisco RC	.25
T112	Brian Dallimore RC	.25
T113	Jim Crowell RC	.25
T114	Andres Blanco RC	.50
T115	Eduardo Villacis RC	.50
T116	Kazuhito Tadano RC	.50
T117	Aarom Baldiris RC	.25
T118	Justin Germano RC	.25
T119	Joey Gathright RC	1.00
T120	Franklyn Gracesqui RC	.25
T121	Chin-Lung Hu RC	.50
T122	Scott Olsen RC	1.00
T123	Tyler Davidson RC	.25
T124	Fausto Carmona RC	.50
T125	Tim Hutting RC	.25
T126	Ryan Meaux RC	.25
T127	Jon Connolly RC	.75
T128	Hector Made RC	.75
T129	Jamie Brown RC	.25
T130	Paul McAnulty RC	.50
T131	Chris Saenz RC	.25
T132	Marland Williams RC	.25
T133	Mike Huggins RC	.25
T134	Jesse Crain	.50
T135	Chad Bentz RC	.50
T136	Kazuo Matsui RC	.75
T137	Paul Maholm RC	.75
T138	Brock Jacobsen RC	.25
T139	Casey Daigle RC	.25
T140	Nyjer Morgan RC	.50
T141	Tom Mastny RC	.50
T142	Kody Kirkland RC	.50
T143	Jose Capellan RC	.50
T144	Felix Hernandez RC	6.00
T145	Shawn Hill RC	.25
T146	Danny Gonzalez RC	.25
T147	Scott Dohmann RC	.25
T148	Tommy Murphy RC	.50
T149	Akinori Otsuka RC	.50
T150	Miguel Perez RC	.50
T151	Mike Rouse RC	.25
T152	Ramon Ramirez RC	.50
T153	Luke Hughes RC	.25
T154	Howard Kendrick RC	8.00
T155	Ryan Budde RC	.25
T156	Charlie Zink RC	.50
T157	Warner Madrigal RC	.50
T158	Jason Szuminski RC	.25
T159	Chad Chop RC	.25
T160	Shingo Takatsu RC	.50
T161	Matt Lemanczyk RC	.25
T162	Wardell Starling RC	.50
T163	Nick Gorneault RC	.25
T164	Scott Proctor RC	.50
T165	Brooks Conrad RC	.25
T166	Hector Gimenez RC	.50
T167	Kevin Howard RC	.50
T168	Vince Perkins RC	.25
T169	Brock Peterson RC	.25
T170	Chris Shelton RC	1.00
T171	Erick Aybar RC	1.00
T172	Paul Bacot RC	.25
T173	Matt Capps RC	.25
T174	Kory Casto RC	.25
T175	Juan Cedeno RC	.25
T176	Vito Chiaravallotti RC	.25
T177	Alec Zumwalt RC	.25
T178	J.J. Furmaniak RC	.50
T179	Lee Gwaltney RC	.25
T180	Donald Kelly RC	.25
T181	Benji DeQuin RC	.25
T182	Brant Colamarino RC	.75
T183	Juan Gutierrez RC	.50
T184	Carl Loadenthal RC	.50
T185	Ricky Nolasco RC	1.25
T186	Jeff Salazar RC	1.00
T187	Rob Tejeda RC	.50
T188	Alex Romero RC	.25
T189	Yoann Torrealba RC	.25
T190	Carlos Sosa RC	.25
T191	Tim Bittner RC	.50
T192	Chris Aguila RC	.25
T193	Jason Frasor RC	.25
T194	Reid Gorecki RC	.25
T195	Dustin Nippert RC	.50
T196	Javier Guzman RC	.25
T197	Harvey Garcia RC	.50
T198	Ivan Ochoa RC	.25
T199	Dave Wallace RC	.25
T200	Joel Zumaya RC	2.50
T201	Casey Kotzke RC	.25
T202	Lincoln Holdzkom RC	.25
T203	Chad Santos RC	.25
T204	Brian Pilkington RC	.25
T205	Terry Jones RC	.25
T206	Jerome Gamble RC	.25
T207	Brad Eldred RC	.50
T208	David Pauley RC	1.00
T209	Kevin Davidson RC	.25
T210	Damaso Espino RC	.25
T211	Tom Farmer RC	.50
T212	Michael Mooney RC	.25
T213	James Tomlin RC	.25
T214	Greg Thissen RC	.25
T215	Calvin Hayes RC	.25
T216	Fernando Cortez RC	.25
T217	Sergio Silva RC	.25
T218	Jon DeVries RC	.25
T219	Don Sutton RC	1.00
T220	Leo Nunez RC	.25
T221	Barry Bonds HTA Redemption	5.00

Gold
Stars: 5-10X
Rookies: 2-3X
Production 2,004 Sets

Blue Refractor
No Pricing
Production One Set

Chrome Refractor
Stars: 4-8X
Rookies: 2-4X
Inserted 1:12

X-Fractor
No Pricing
Production 20 Sets

Printing Plates
No pricing due to scarcity.

Dual Transactions Relic
NM/M
Common Player:
Inserted 1:562

	Player	Price
RP	Rafael Palmeiro	15.00
AR	Alex Rodriguez	15.00
CS	Curt Schilling	15.00

Future Phenoms
NM/M
Common Player: 5.00

	Player	Price
KC	Kevin Cash	5.00
BC	Bobby Crosby	10.00
ED	Eric Duncan	5.00
AG	Adrian Gonzalez	8.00
NG	Nick Green	5.00
JH	J.J. Hardy	5.00
EJ	Edwin Jackson	5.00
MM	Mark Malaska	5.00
VM	Victor Martinez	8.00
KM	Kazuo Matsui	5.00
LM	Lastings Milledge	15.00
JM	Justin Morneau	10.00
DN	Dioner Navarro	5.00
RN	Ramon Nivar	5.00
BU	B.J. Upton	12.00
JW	Jayson Werth	10.00
DY	Delmon Young	10.00

Hall of Fame Relic
NM/M
Common Player:

	Player	Price
DE	Dennis Eckersley	10.00
PM	Paul Molitor	15.00

Hall of Fame Dual Relic
NM/M
Inserted 1:3,388

	Player	Price
ME	Paul Molitor, Dennis Eckersley	30.00

Signature Cuts
No Pricing
Production One Set

Signature Moves
NM/M
Common Autograph: 10.00

	Player	Price
MB	Milton Bradley	15.00
MK	Mark Kotsay	10.00
EM	Eli Marrero	10.00
MN	Mike Neu	10.00
AR	Alex Rodriguez	160.00
JV	Javier Vazquez	15.00
FV	Fernando Vina	10.00
AW	Adam Wainwright	35.00

Transactions Relics

NM/M
Common Player: 5.00
Inserted 1:106

	Player	Price
RA	Roberto Alomar	8.00
JB	Jeromy Burnitz	5.00
HC	Hee Seop Choi	5.00
RC	Roger Clemens	15.00
CE	Carl Everett	5.00
JG	Juan Gonzalez	8.00
VG	Vladimir Guerrero	10.00
BJ	Brian Jordan	5.00
KL	Kenny Lofton	5.00
JL	Javy Lopez	5.00
RP	Rafael Palmeiro	8.00
AP	Andy Pettitte	8.00
AR	Alex Rodriguez	25.00
IR	Ivan Rodriguez	10.00
RS	Reggie Sanders	5.00
RLS	Richie Sexson	5.00
GS	Gary Sheffield	10.00
MT	Miguel Tejada	8.00
RW	Rondell White	5.00

2004 Topps Tribute HOF

NM/M
Complete Set (80): 120.00
Common Player: 2.00
Pack (5): 50.00
Box (6): 260.00

No	Player	Price
1	Willie Mays	8.00
2	Richie Ashburn	2.00
3	Babe Ruth	10.00
4	Lou Gehrig	8.00
5	Carl Yastrzemski	5.00
6	Fergie Jenkins	2.00
7	Cool Papa Bell	3.00
8	Johnny Bench	4.00
9	Satchel Paige	4.00
10	Ty Cobb	6.00
11	Robin Roberts	2.00
12	Eddie Mathews	3.00
13	Tom Seaver	5.00
14	Kirby Puckett	3.00
15	Stan Musial	5.00
16	Ralph Kiner	2.00
17	Reggie Jackson	3.00
18	Walter Johnson	4.00
19	Phil Niekro	2.00
20	Mike Schmidt	6.00
21	Brooks Robinson	3.00
22	Jimmie Foxx	4.00
23	Nellie Fox	2.00
24	Joe Morgan	2.00
25	Cy Young	3.00
26	Hank Greenberg	3.00
27	Josh Gibson	3.00
28	Robin Yount	2.00
29	Hoyt Wilhelm	2.00
30	Yogi Berra	4.00
31	Rollie Fingers	2.00
32	Gaylord Perry	2.00
33	Ozzie Smith	4.00
34	Jim Palmer	2.00
35	Harmon Killebrew	3.00
36	Bob Feller	3.00
37	Chuck Klein	2.00
38	Mordecai Brown	2.00
39	Napoleon Lajoie	2.00
40	Al Kaline	3.00
41	Paul Molitor	3.00
42	Jackie Robinson	5.00
43	Mel Ott	3.00
44	Hank Aaron	5.00
45	Rod Carew	2.00
46	Rogers Hornsby	3.00
47	Bob Gibson	3.00
48	Juan Marichal	2.00
49	Bill Mazeroski	2.00
50	Roberto Clemente	8.00
51	Willie McCovey	2.00
52	Red Schoendienst	2.00
53	Nolan Ryan	8.00
54	Dennis Eckersley	2.00
55	Monte Irvin	2.00
56	George Kell	2.00
57	Gary Carter	2.00
58	Tony Perez	2.00
59	Carlton Fisk	2.00
60	Duke Snider	3.00
61	Bobby Doerr	2.00
62	John McGraw	2.00
63	George Sisler	2.00
64	Orlando Cepeda	2.00
65	Earl Weaver	2.00
66	Roy Campanella	3.00
67	Tris Speaker	3.00
68	Sparky Anderson	2.00
69	Willie Stargell	2.00
70	Honus Wagner	3.00
71	Lou Brock	2.00
72	Whitey Ford	2.00
73	George Brett	8.00
74	Luis Aparicio	2.00
75	Ernie Banks	4.00
76	Jim Bunning	2.00
77	Warren Spahn	3.00
78	Jim "Catfish" Hunter	2.00
79	Pee Wee Reese	2.00
80	Frank Robinson	2.00

Gold
Gold Print Run 61-99: 2-3X
Gold p/r 36-60: 2-4X
#' to last 2 digits of HOF induction yr.

Cooperstown Classmates Dual Cut Sig
No Pricing
Production One Set

Cooperstown Classmates Dual Reli
NM/M
Common Duo: 20.00
Gold: .75-1.5X
Production 25

	Players	Price
ME	Paul Molitor, Dennis Eckersley/75	35.00
KK	Chuck Klein, Al Kaline/75	35.00
RB	Nolan Ryan, George Brett/50	60.00
MP	Joe Morgan, Jim Palmer/75	20.00
SK	Duke Snider, Al Kaline/50	60.00
PC	Gaylord Perry, Rod Carew/50	30.00
BY	Johnny Bench, Carl Yastrzemski/75	50.00
CR	Orlando Cepeda, Nolan Ryan/75	60.00
MR	Juan Marichal, Brooks Robinson/50	35.00

Cooperstown Cut Signatures

NM/M
No Pricing
Production One Set

	Player	Price
JF	Jimmie Foxx (10/05 auction)	1,940
MO	Mel Ott (8/05 auction)	2,025

Cut Signatures

Dual Cut Signatures
No Pricing
Production One Set

Hall of Fame Patches Relics
NM/M
Common Player: 20.00
Gold: .75-1.5X
Production 1-25
No pricing for production 15 or less.

	Player	Price
GB	George Brett/50	40.00
RC	Rod Carew/100	25.00
DE	Dennis Eckersley/50	25.00
RJ	Reggie Jackson/50	25.00
FR	Frank Robinson/39	25.00
NR	Nolan Ryan/100	50.00
MS	Mike Schmidt/100	40.00
MS2	Mike Schmidt/100	40.00
RY	Robin Yount/35	40.00

Tribute Relics

NM/M
Common Player: 10.00
Golds: 1-3X
Production 25 Sets

	Player	Price
HA	Hank Aaron/Bat	30.00
JB	Johnny Bench/Jsy/250	15.00
JB2	Johnny Bench/Jsy	10.00
GB	George Brett/Jsy	15.00
GBB	George Brett/Bat	15.00
LBB	Lou Brock/Bat	10.00
GC	Gary Carter/Jsy/200	10.00
GCU	Gary Carter/Jsy	10.00
OC	Orlando Cepeda/Bat/100	20.00
RC	Roberto Clemente/Bat	50.00
TC	Ty Cobb/Jsy/20	275.00
TCB	Ty Cobb/Bat	75.00
CF	Carlton Fisk/Wall/300	60.00
WF	Whitey Ford/Jsy/50	60.00
JF	Jimmie Foxx/Bat/25	100.00
LG	Lou Gehrig/Bat/52	300.00
BG	Bob Gibson/Jsy	15.00
HG	Hank Greenberg/Bat	20.00
RH	Rogers Hornsby/Bat	40.00
RJ	Reggie Jackson/Jsy/110	15.00
RJB	Reggie Jackson/Bat/200	10.00
AK	Al Kaline/Jsy/125	20.00
AKB	Al Kaline/Bat	15.00
HK	Harmon Killebrew/Bat/135	30.00
CK	Chuck Klein/Bat/107	20.00
JMA	Juan Marichal/Jsy/125	10.00
WM1	Willie Mays/Glv/110	150.00
WM2	Willie Mays/Bat	30.00
WM3	Willie Mays/Jsy	30.00
WM4	Willie Mays/Jsy	30.00
WM5	Willie Mays/Jsy	30.00
PM	Paul Molitor/Jsy	10.00
PMB	Paul Molitor/Bat	10.00
JM	Joe Morgan/Bat	10.00
SM	Stan Musial/Jsy	10.00
MO	Mel Ott/Bat/25	100.00
JP	Jim Palmer/Jsy	10.00
JP2	Jim Palmer/Jsy	10.00
KP	Kirby Puckett/Jsy/175	15.00
KPB	Kirby Puckett/Bat	10.00
BRO	Brooks Robinson/Jsy	10.00
FR	Frank Robinson/Jsy	10.00
FRA	Frank Robinson/Jsy	10.00
FRB	Frank Robinson/Bat	10.00
JR	Jackie Robinson/Bat	25.00
BR	Babe Ruth/Bat/163	150.00
NR	Nolan Ryan/Jsy	25.00
NRA	Nolan Ryan/Jsy/425	25.00
NRJ	Nolan Ryan/Jsy	25.00
MS	Mike Schmidt/Jsy/50	30.00
MSB	Mike Schmidt/Bat	15.00
TS	Tom Seaver/Jsy	10.00
GS	George Sisler/Bat/455	25.00
OS	Ozzie Smith/Bat	15.00
DS	Duke Snider/Bat	10.00
TSP	Tris Speaker/Bat/85	120.00
HW	Honus Wagner/Bat/118	120.00
EW	Earl Weaver/Jsy/25	20.00
CY	Carl Yastrzemski/Wall/300	30.00
CYU	Carl Yastrzemski/Jsy	15.00
RY	Robin Yount/Jsy/50	25.00

Tribute Relic Autographs
NM/M
Common Player: 40.00
Gold: No Pricing
Production 5 Sets

	Player	Price
AKB	Al Kaline/95	60.00
BRO	Brooks Robinson/95	50.00
NRJ	Nolan Ryan/95	140.00
EW	Earl Weaver/55	40.00
CYU	Carl Yastrzemski/95	85.00

World Champions Boston Red Sox

NM/M
Complete Boxed Set (56): 25.00
Common Player: .25

No	Player	Price
1	Bronson Arroyo	.25
2	Alan Embree	.25
3	Keith Foulke	.25
4	Curt Leskanic	.25
5	Derek Lowe	.50
6	Pedro Martinez	2.00
7	Ramiro Mendoza	.25
8	Mike Myers	.25
9	Curt Schilling	2.00
10	Mike Timlin	.25
11	Tim Wakefield	.25
12	Scott Williamson	.25
13	Doug Mirabelli	.25
14	Mark Bellhorn	.25
15	Orlando Cabrera	.50
16	Ricky Gutierrez	.25
17	Doug Mientkiewicz	.25
18	Kevin Millar	.50
19	Bill Mueller	.25
20	Pokey Reese	.25
21	Kevin Youkilis	.25
22	Johnny Damon	1.50
23	Gabe Kapler	.25
24	David McCarty	.25
25	Trot Nixon	.25
26	Manny Ramirez	2.00
27	Dave Roberts	.25
28	Ellis Burks	.25
29	David Ortiz	2.00
30	Terry Francona	.25
31	Red Sox Team Card	.50
32	Curt Schilling (Season Highlights)	1.00
33	Kevin Millar (Season Highlights)	.25
34	Manny Ramirez (Season Highlights)	1.00
35	Orlando Cabrera (Season Highlights)	.25
36	Manny Ramirez (Season Highlights)	1.00
37	Red Sox All-Stars (Season Highlights)	.25
38	Pokey Reese (Season Highlights)	.25
39	Bill Mueller (Season Highlights)	.25
40	Curt Schilling (Postseason Highlights)	1.00
41	Pedro Martinez (Postseason Highlights)	1.00
42	David Ortiz (Postseason Highlights)	1.00
43	Kevin Millar (Postseason Highlights)	.25
44	Johnny Damon (Postseason Highlights)	1.00
45	Bill Mueller (Postseason Highlights)	.25
46	David Ortiz (Postseason Highlights)	1.00
47	Keith Foulke (Postseason Highlights)	.25
48	Curt Schilling (Postseason Highlights)	1.00
49	Game 7 Celebration	.50
50	David Ortiz (Postseason Highlights)	1.00
51	Mark Bellhorn (Postseason Highlights)	.25
52	Curt Schilling (Postseason Highlights)	1.00
53	Pedro Martinez (Postseason Highlights)	1.00
54	Red Sox Win World Series	1.00

55	Manny Ramirez (Postseason Highlights)	1.00

World Champions Boston Red Sox Team Card

		NM/M
Inserted 1:Set		
	Red Sox Team Card	1.00

Poland Spring N.Y. Yankees

PITCHER GOOSE GOSSAGE

This cello-wrapped stadium give-away set was sponsored by the team's bottled water concessionaire. Fronts have poses or action photos with team and sponsor logos in opposite corners. Backs have a close-up repeat of part of the front photo, along with personal data, lifetime stats and logos.

		NM/M
Complete Set (5):		10.00
Common Player:		2.00
1	Goose Gossage	2.00
2	Ron Guidry	2.00
3	Don Mattingly	6.00
4	Don Larsen	2.00
--	Sponsor's Card	.05

2005 Topps

		NM/M
Complete Set (732):		75.00
Factory Set (742):		80.00
Factory Set (737):		80.00
Common Player:		.10
Pack (10):		2.00
Box (36):		60.00
1	Alex Rodriguez	1.50
2	Placido Polanco	.10
3	Torii Hunter	.25
4	Lyle Overbay	.10
5	Johnny Damon	.40
6	Johnny Estrada	.10
7	Francisco Rodriguez	.10
8	Jason LaRue	.10
9	Jason LaRue	.10
10	Sammy Sosa	1.00
11	Randy Wolf	.10
12	Jason Bay	.10
13	Tom Glavine	.25
14	Michael Tucker	.10

15	Brian Giles	.20
16	Dan Wilson	.10
17	Jim Edmonds	.40
18	Danys Baez	.10
19	Roy Halladay	.20
20	Hank Blalock	.50
21	Darin Erstad	.20
22	Robby Hammock	.10
23	Mike Hampton	.10
24	Mark Bellhorn	.10
25	Jim Thome	.50
26	Scott Schoeneweis	.10
27	Jody Gerut	.10
28	Vinny Castilla	.10
29	Luis Castillo	.10
30	Ivan Rodriguez	.50
31	Craig Biggio	.20
32	Joe Randa	.10
33	Dave Roberts	.10
34	Scott Podsednik	.10
35	Cliff Floyd	.10
36	Livan Hernandez	.10
37	Eric Byrnes	.10
38	Ricky Ledee	.10
39	Jack Wilson	.10
40	Gary Sheffield	.40
41	Chan Ho Park	.10
42	Carl Crawford	.10
43	Miguel Batista	.10
44	David Bell	.10
45	Jeff DaVanon	.10
46	Brandon Webb	.10
47	Bronson Arroyo	.10
48	Melvin Mora	.10
49	David Ortiz	.50
50	Andruw Jones	.40
51	Chone Figgins	.10
52	Danny Graves	.10
53	Preston Wilson	.10
54	Jeremy Bonderman	.10
55	Chad Fox	.10
56	Dan Miceli	.10
57	Jimmy Gobble	.10
58	Darren Dreifort	.10
59	Matt LeCroy	.10
60	Jose Vidro	.10
61	Al Leiter	.10
62	Javier Vazquez	.10
63	Erubiel Durazo	.10
64	Doug Glanville	.10
65	Scot Shields	.10
66	Edgardo Alfonzo	.10
67	Ryan Franklin	.10
68	Francisco Cordero	.10
69	Brett Myers	.10
70	Curt Schilling	.50
71	Matt Kata	.10
72	Mark DeRosa	.10
73	Rodrigo Lopez	.10
74	Tim Wakefield	.10
75	Frank Thomas	.75
76	Jimmy Rollins	.25
77	Barry Zito	.25
78	Hideo Nomo	.25
79	Brad Wilkerson	.10
80	Adam Dunn	.50
81	Billy Traber	.10
82	Fernando Vina	.10
83	Nate Robertson	.10
84	Brad Ausmus	.10
85	Mike Sweeney	.10
86	Kip Wells	.10
87	Doug Mientkiewicz	.10
88	Zach Day	.10
89	Tony Clark	.10
90	Bret Boone	.10
91	Mark Loretta	.10
92	Jerome Williams	.10
93	Randy Winn	.10
94	Marlon Anderson	.10
95	Aubrey Huff	.10
96	Kevin Mench	.10
97	Frank Catalanotto	.10
98	Flash Gordon	.10
99	Scott Hatteberg	.10
100	Albert Pujols	1.50
101	Jose Molina, Bengie Molina	.10
102	Oscar Villarreal	.10
103	Jay Gibbons	.10
104	Byung-Hyun Kim	.10
105	Joe Borowski	.10
106	Mark Grudzielanek	.10
107	Mark Buehrle	.10
108	Paul Wilson	.10
109	Ronnie Belliard	.10
110	Larry Walker	.40
111	Tim Redding	.10
112	Hee Seop Choi	.10
113	Darrell May	.10
114	Jose Hernandez	.10
115	Ben Sheets	.25
116	Johan Santana	.40
117	Billy Wagner	.20
118	Mariano Rivera	.25
119	Steve Trachsel	.10
120	Akinori Otsuka	.10
121	Bobby Kielty	.10
122	Felix Rodriguez	.10
123	Raul Ibanez	.10
124	Mike Matheny	.10
125	Vernon Wells	.10
126	Jason Isringhausen	.10
127	Jose Guillen	.10
128	Danny Bautista	.10
129	Marcus Giles	.10
130	Javy Lopez	.25
131	Kevin Millar	.10

132	Kyle Farnsworth	.10
133	Carl Pavano	.10
134	D'Angelo Jimenez	.10
135	Casey Blake	.10
136	Matt Holliday	.10
137	Bobby Higginson	.10
138	Ramon Castro	.10
139	Alex Gonzalez	.10
140	Jeff Kent	.20
141	Aaron Guiel	.10
142	Shawn Green	.25
143	Bill Hall	.10
144	Shannon Stewart	.10
145	Juan Rivera	.10
146	Ty Wigginton	.10
147	Mike Mussina	.50
148	Eric Chavez	.25
149	Randall Simon	.10
150	Vladimir Guerrero	.75
151	Alex Cintron	.10
152	Horacio Ramirez	.10
153	Sidney Ponson	.10
154	Trot Nixon	.10
155	Greg Maddux	1.00
156	Esteban Loaiza	.10
157	Ryan Freel	.10
158	Matt Lawton	.10
159	Shawn Chacon	.10
160	Josh Beckett	.25
161	Ken Harvey	.10
162	Juan Cruz	.10
163	Juan Encarnacion	.10
164	Wes Helms	.10
165	Brad Radke	.10
166	Claudio Vargas	.10
167	Mike Cameron	.10
168	Jose Contreras	.10
169	Bobby Crosby	.10
170	Mike Lieberthal	.10
171	Robert Mackowiak	.10
172	Sean Burroughs	.10
173	J.T. Snow Jr.	.10
174	Paul Konerko	.10
175	Luis Gonzalez	.10
176	John Lackey	.10
177	Antonio Alfonseca	.10
178	Brian Roberts	.10
179	Bill Mueller	.10
180	Carlos Lee	.10
181	Corey Patterson	.10
182	Sean Casey	.25
183	Cliff Lee	.10
184	Jason Jennings	.10
185	Dmitri Young	.10
186	Brad Penny	.10
187	Andy Pettitte	.25
188	Juan Gonzalez	.25
189	Paul LoDuca	.10
190	Jason Phillips	.10
191	Rocky Biddle	.10
192	Lew Ford	.10
193	Mark Mulder	.10
194	Bobby Abreu	.25
195	Jason Kendall	.10
196	Terrence Long	.10
197	A.J. Pierzynski	.10
198	Eddie Guardado	.10
199	So Taguchi	.10
200	Jason Giambi	.25
201	Tony Batista	.10
202	Kyle Lohse	.10
203	Trevor Hoffman	.10
204	Tike Redman	.10
205	Neifi Perez	.10
206	Gil Meche	.10
207	Chris Carpenter	.10
208	Josh Phelps	.10
209	Eric Young	.10
210	Doug Waechter	.10
211	Jarrod Washburn	.10
212	Chad Tracy	.10
213	John Smoltz	.25
214	Jorge Julio	.10
215	Alex Gonzalez	.10
216	Shingo Takatsu	.10
217	Jose Acevedo	.10
218	Jason Davis	.10
219	Shawn Estes	.10
220	Lance Berkman	.25
221	Carlos Guillen	.10
222	Jeremy Affeldt	.10
223	Cesar Izturis	.10
224	Scott Sullivan	.10
225	Kazuo Matsui	.25
226	Josh Fogg	.10
227	Jason Schmidt	.25
228	Jason Marquis	.10
229	Scott Spiezio	.10
230	Miguel Tejada	.40
231	Bartolo Colon	.10
232	Jose Valverde	.10
233	Derrek Lee	.25
234	Scott Williamson	.10
235	Joe Crede	.10
236	Cory Lidle	.10
237	Mike MacDougal	.10
238	Eric Gagne	.25
239	Alex Sanchez	.10
240	Miguel Cabrera	.75
241	Luis Rivas	.10
242	Adam Everett	.10
243	Jason Johnson	.10
244	Travis Hafner	.25
245	Jose Valentin	.10
246	Stephen Randolph	.10
247	Rafael Furcal	.25
248	Adam Kennedy	.10
249	Luis Matos	.10

250	Mark Prior	.75
251	Angel Berroa	.10
252	Phil Nevin	.10
253	Oliver Perez	.10
254	Orlando Hudson	.10
255	Victor Zambrano	.10
256	Khalil Greene	.25
257	Tim Worrell	.10
258	Carlos Zambrano	.10
259	Elmer Dessens	.10
260	Gerald Laird	.10
261	Jose Cruz Jr.	.10
262	Michael Barrett	.10
263	Michael Young (Uncorrected error - Photo is Rod Barajas)	
264	Toby Hall	.10
265	Woody Williams	.10
266	Rich Harden	.10
267	Mike Scioscia	.10
268	Al Pedrique	.10
269	Bobby Cox	.10
270	Lee Mazzilli	.10
271	Terry Francona	.10
272	Dusty Baker	.10
273	Ozzie Guillen	.10
274	Dave Miley	.10
275	Eric Wedge	.10
276	Clint Hurdle	.10
277	Alan Trammell	.10
278	Jack McKeon	.10
279	Phil Garner	.10
280	Tony Pena	.10
281	Jim Tracy	.10
282	Ned Yost	.10
283	Ron Gardenhire	.10
284	Frank Robinson	.25
285	Art Howe	.10
286	Joe Torre	.25
287	Ken Macha	.10
288	Larry Bowa	.10
289	Lloyd McClendon	.10
290	Bruce Bochy	.10
291	Felipe Alou	.10
292	Bob Melvin	.10
293	Tony LaRussa	.10
294	Lou Piniella	.10
295	Buck Showalter	.10
296	Carlos Tosca	.10
297	Steven Doetsch RC	.10
298	Melky Cabrera RC	1.00
299	Luis Ramirez RC	.10
300	Chris Seddon RC	.10
301	Nate Schierholtz	.10
302	Ian Kinsler RC	2.00
303	Brandon Moss RC	1.50
304	Chadd Blasko RC	.10
305	Jeremy West RC	1.00
306	Sean Marshall RC	.75
307	Matt DeSalvo RC	.10
308	Ryan Sweeney RC	1.50
309	Matt Lindstrom RC	.10
310	Ryan Goleski RC	.50
311	Brett Harper RC	.25
312	Chris Roberson RC	.10
313	Andre Ethier RC	1.50
314	Chris Denorfia RC	.10
315	Ian Bladergroen RC	.75
316	Darren Fenster RC	.10
317	Kevin West RC	.10
318	Chaz Lytle RC	.50
319	James Jurries RC	.10
320	Matt Rogelstad RC	.10
321	Wade Robinson RC	.10
322	Jake Dittler	.10
323	Edgar Huerta RC	.10
324	Kole Strayhorn	.10
325	Jose Vaquedano RC	.10
326	Elvys Quezada RC	.10
327	John Maine, Val Majewski	.10
328	Rickie Weeks, J.J. Hardy	.10
329	Gabe Gross, Guillermo Quiroz	.10
330	David Wright, Craig Brazell	1.50
331	Dallas McPherson, Jeff Mathis	.10
332	Randy Johnson, Randy Johnson	.10
333	Ichiro Suzuki, Ichiro Suzuki	.10
334	Ken Griffey Jr., Greg Maddux	.10
335	Ichiro Suzuki, Melvin Mora, Vladimir Guerrero	.10
336	Ichiro Suzuki, Michael Young, Vladimir Guerrero	.10
337	Ichiro Suzuki, Melvin Mora, Vladimir Guerrero	.10
338	Ichiro Suzuki, Michael Young, Vladimir Guerrero	.10
339	Manny Ramirez, Paul Konerko, David Ortiz	.10
340	Miguel Tejada, David Ortiz, Manny Ramirez	.10
341	Johan Santana, Curt Schilling, Jake Westbrook	.10
342	Johan Santana, Pedro J. Martinez, Curt Schilling	.10
343	Todd Helton, Mark Loretta, Adrian Beltre	.10
344	Juan Pierre, Mark Loretta, Jack Wilson	.10
345	Adrian Beltre, Adam Dunn, Albert Pujols	.10
346	Vinny Castilla, Scott Rolen, Albert Pujols	.10

347	Jake Peavy, Randy Johnson, Ben Sheets	.10
348	Randy Johnson, Ben Sheets, Jason Schmidt	.10
349	Postseason Highlight	.10
350	Postseason Highlight	.10
351	Postseason Highlight	.10
352	Postseason Highlight	.10
353	Postseason Highlight	.10
354	Postseason Highlight	.10
355	Postseason Highlight	.10
356	Paul Konerko	.10
357	Alfonso Soriano	.10
358	Miguel Tejada	.10
359	Melvin Mora	.10
360	Vladimir Guerrero	.10
361	Ichiro Suzuki	.10
362	Manny Ramirez	.10
363	Ivan Rodriguez	.10
364	Johan Santana	.10
365	Paul Konerko	.10
366	David Ortiz	.10
367	Bobby Crosby	.10
368	Sox Celebration WS4	1.50
369	Garret Anderson	.25
370	Randy Johnson	.75
371	Charles Thomas	.10
372	Rafael Palmeiro	.40
373	Kevin Youkilis	.10
374	Freddy Garcia	.10
375	Magglio Ordonez	.10
376	Aaron Harang	.10
377	Grady Sizemore	.25
378	Chin-Hui Tsao	.10
379	Eric Munson	.10
380	Juan Pierre	.10
381	Brad Lidge	.10
382	Brian Anderson	.10
383	Alex Cora	.10
384	Brady Clark	.10
385	Todd Helton	.40
386	Chad Cordero	.10
387	Kris Benson	.10
388	Brad Halsey	.10
389	Jermaine Dye	.10
390	Manny Ramirez	.50
391	Daryle Ward	.10
392	Adam Eaton	.10
393	Brett Tomko	.10
394	Bucky Jacobsen	.10
395	Dontrelle Willis	.40
396	B.J. Upton	.25
397	Rocco Baldelli	.10
398	Ted Lilly	.10
399	Ryan Drese	.10
400	Ichiro Suzuki	1.25
401	Brendan Donnelly	.10
402	Brandon Lyon	.10
403	Nick Green	.10
404	Jerry Hairston Jr.	.10
405	Mike Lowell	.10
406	Kerry Wood	.50
407	Carl Everett	.10
408	Hideki Matsui	1.25
409	Omar Vizquel	.25
410	Joe Kennedy	.10
411	Carlos Pena	.10
412	Armando Benitez	.10
413	Carlos Beltran	.50
414	Kevin Appier	.10
415	Jeff Weaver	.10
416	Chad Moeller	.10
417	Joe Mays	.10
418	Terrmel Sledge	.10
419	Richard Hidalgo	.10
420	Kenny Lofton	.10
421	Justin Duchscherer	.10
422	Eric Milton	.10
423	Jose Mesa	.10
424	Ramon Hernandez	.10
425	Jose Reyes	.25
426	Joel Pineiro	.10
427	Matt Morris	.10
428	John Halama	.10
429	Gary Matthews Jr.	.10
430	Ryan Madson	.10
431	Mark Kotsay	.10
432	Carlos Delgado	.25
433	Casey Kotchman	.10
434	Greg Aquino	.10
435	Eli Marrero	.10
436	David Newhan	.10
437	Mike Timlin	.10
438	LaTroy Hawkins	.10
439	Jose Contreras	.10
440	Ken Griffey Jr.	1.00
441	C.C. Sabathia	.10
442	Brandon Inge	.10
443	Peter Munro	.10
444	John Buck	.10
445	Hee Seop Choi	.10
446	Chris Capuano	.10
447	Jesse Crain	.10
448	Geoff Jenkins	.10
449	Brian Schneider	.10
450	Mike Piazza	1.00
451	Jorge Posada	.40
452	Nick Swisher	.10
453	Kevin Millwood	.25
454	Mike Gonzalez	.10
455	Jake Peavy	.25
456	Dustin Hermanson	.10
457	Jeremy Reed	.10
458	Julian Tavarez	.10
459	Geoff Blum	.10
460	Alfonso Soriano	.50

461	Alexis Rios	.10
462	David Eckstein	.10
463	Shea Hillenbrand	.10
464	Russ Ortiz	.10
465	Kurt Ainsworth	.10
466	Orlando Cabrera	.10
467	Carlos Silva	.10
468	Ross Gload	.10
469	Josh Phelps	.10
470	Marquis Grissom	.10
471	Mike Maroth	.10
472	Guillermo Mota	.10
473	Chris Burke	.10
474	David DeJesus	.10
475	Jose Lima	.10
476	Cristian Guzman	.10
477	Nick Johnson	.10
478	Victor Zambrano	.10
479	Rod Barajas	.10
480	Damian Miller	.10
481	Chase Utley	.25
482	Todd Pratt	.10
483	Sean Burnett	.10
484	David Wells	.10
485	Dustan Mohr	.10
486	Bobby Madritsch	.10
487	Ray King	.10
488	Reed Johnson	.10
489	R.A. Dickey	.10
490	Scott Kazmir	.25
491	Tony Womack	.10
492	Tomas Perez	.10
493	Esteban Loaiza	.10
494	Tomokazu Ohka	.10
495	Mike Lamb	.10
496	Ramon Ortiz	.10
497	Richie Sexson	.40
498	J.D. Drew	.25
499	David Segui	.10
500	Barry Bonds	2.00
501	Aramis Ramirez	.10
502	Wily Mo Pena	.10
503	Jeromy Burnitz	.10
504	Craig Monroe	.10
505	Nomar Garciaparra	1.00
506	Brandon Backe	.10
507	Marcus Thames	.10
508	Derek Lowe	.10
509	Doug Davis	.10
510	Joe Mauer	.25
511	Endy Chavez	.10
512	Bernie Williams	.25
513	Mark Redman	.10
514	Jason Michaels	.10
515	Craig Wilson	.10
516	Ryan Klesko	.10
517	Ray Durham	.10
518	Jose Lopez	.10
519	Jeff Suppan	.10
520	Julio Lugo	.10
521	Mike Wood	.10
522	David Bush	.10
523	Juan Rincon	.10
524	Paul Quantrill	.10
525	Marlon Byrd	.10
526	Roy Oswalt	.25
527	Rondell White	.10
528	Troy Glaus	.25
529	Scott Hairston	.10
530	Chipper Jones	.75
531	Daniel Cabrera	.10
532	Doug Mientkiewicz	.10
533	Glendon Rusch	.10
534	Jon Garland	.10
535	Austin Kearns	.10
536	Jake Westbrook	.10
537	Aaron Miles	.10
538	Omar Infante	.10
539	Paul LoDuca	.10
540	Morgan Ensberg	.10
541	Tony Graffanino	.10
542	Milton Bradley	.25
543	Keith Ginter	.10
544	Justin Morneau	.40
545	Tony Armas Jr.	.10
546	Mike Stanton	.10
547	Kevin Brown	.10
548	Marco Scutaro	.10
549	Tim Hudson	.25
550	Pat Burrell	.25
551	Ty Wigginton	.10
552	Jeff Cirillo	.10
553	Jim Brower	.10
554	Jamie Moyer	.10
555	Larry Walker	.25
556	Dewon Brazelton	.10
557	Brian Jordan	.10
558	Josh Towers	.10
559	Shigetoshi Hasegawa	.10
560	Octavio Dotel	.10
561	Travis Lee	.10
562	Michael Cuddyer	.10
563	Junior Spivey	.10
564	Zack Greinke	.10
565	Roger Clemens	1.50
566	Chris Shelton	.10
567	Ugueth Urbina	.10
568	Rafael Betancourt	.10
569	Willie Harris	.10
570	Todd Hollandsworth	.10
571	Keith Foulke	.10
572	Larry Bigbie	.10
573	Paul Byrd	.10
574	Troy Percival	.10
575	Pedro Martinez	.75
576	Matt Clement	.10
577	Ryan Wagner	.10
578	Jeff Francis	.10

579	Jeff Conine	.10
580	Wade Miller	.10
581	Matt Stairs	.10
582	Gavin Floyd	.10
583	Kazuhisa Ishii	.10
584	Victor Santos	.10
585	Jacque Jones	.10
586	Sunny Kim	.10
587	Dan Kolb	.10
588	Cory Lidle	.10
589	Jose Castillo	.10
590	Alex Gonzalez	.10
591	Kirk Rueter	.10
592	Jolbert Cabrera	.10
593	Erik Bedard	.10
594	Ben Grieve	.10
595	Ricky Ledee	.10
596	Mark Hendrickson	.10
597	Laynce Nix	.10
598	Jason Frasor	.10
599	Kevin Gregg	.10
600	Derek Jeter	1.50
601	Luis Terrero	.10
602	Jaret Wright	.10
603	Edwin Jackson	.10
604	Dave Roberts	.10
605	Moises Alou	.25
606	Aaron Rowand	.10
607	Kazuhito Tadano	.10
608	Luis Gonzalez	.10
609	A.J. Burnett	.25
610	Jeff Bagwell	.40
611	Brad Penny	.10
612	Craig Counsell	.10
613	Corey Koskie	.10
614	Mark Ellis	.10
615	Felix Rodriguez	.10
616	Jay Payton	.10
617	Hector Luna	.10
618	Miguel Olivo	.10
619	Rob Bell	.10
620	Scott Rolen	.50
621	Ricardo Rodriguez	.10
622	Eric Hinske	.10
623	Tim Salmon	.10
624	Adam LaRoche	.10
625	B.J. Ryan	.10
626	Roberto Alomar	.25
627	Steve Finley	.10
628	Joe Nathan	.10
629	Scott Linebrink	.10
630	Vicente Padilla	.10
631	Raul Mondesi	.10
632	Yadier Molina	.10
633	Tino Martinez	.10
634	Mark Teixeira	.25
635	Kelvim Escobar	.10
636	Pedro Felix	.10
637	Rich Aurilia	.10
638	Los Angeles Angels of Anaheim	.10
639	Arizona Diamondbacks	.10
640	Atlanta Braves	.10
641	Baltimore Orioles	.10
642	Boston Red Sox	.10
643	Chicago Cubs	.10
644	Chicago White Sox	.10
645	Cincinnati Reds	.10
646	Cleveland Indians	.10
647	Colorado Rockies	.10
648	Detroit Tigers	.10
649	Florida Marlins	.10
650	Houston Astros	.10
651	Kansas City Royals	.10
652	Los Angeles Dodgers	.10
653	Milwaukee Brewers	.10
654	Minnesota Twins	.10
655	Montreal Expos	.10
656	New York Mets	.10
657	New York Yankees	.10
658	Oakland Athletics	.10
659	Philadelphia Phillies	.10
660	Pittsburgh Pirates	.10
661	San Diego Padres	.10
662	San Francisco Giants	.10
663	Seattle Mariners	.10
664	St. Louis Cardinals	.10
665	Tampa Bay Devil Rays	.10
666	Texas Rangers	.10
667	Toronto Blue Jays	.10
668	Billy Butler RC	.50
669	Wes Swackhamer RC	.25
670	Matt Campbell RC	.25
671	Ryan Webb RC	.50
672	Glen Perkins RC	.25
673	Michael Rogers RC	.50
674	Kevin Melillo RC	.25
675	Erik Cordier RC	.50
676	Landon Powell RC	.50
677	Justin Verlander RC	1.00
678	Eric Nielsen RC	.25
679	Alexander Smit RC	.25
680	Ryan Garko RC	.50
681	Bobby Livingston RC	.25
682	Jeff Niemann RC	.50
683	Wladimir Balentien RC	.50
684	Chip Cannon RC	.50
685	Yorman Bazardo RC	.25
686	Michael Bourn	.10
687	Andy LaRoche RC	2.00
688	Felix Hernandez, Justin Leone	.50
689	Ryan Howard, Cole Hamels	.75
690	Matt Cain, Merkin Valdez	.25
691	Andy Marte, Jeff Francoeur	.10

692	Chad Billingsley, Joel Guzman	.10
693	Jerry Hairston Jr., Scott Hairston	.10
694	Miguel Tejada, Lance Berkman	.25
695	Kenny Rogers	.10
696	Ivan Rodriguez	.25
697	Darin Erstad	.10
698	Bret Boone	.10
699	Eric Chavez	.10
700	Derek Jeter	1.00
701	Vernon Wells	.10
702	Ichiro Suzuki	.75
703	Torii Hunter	.10
704	Greg Maddux	.50
705	Mike Matheny	.10
706	Todd Helton	.25
707	Luis Castillo	.10
708	Scott Rolen	.40
709	Cesar Izturis	.10
710	Jim Edmonds	.25
711	Andruw Jones	.25
712	Steve Finley	.10
713	Johan Santana	.40
714	Roger Clemens	1.00
715	Vladimir Guerrero	.40
716	Barry Bonds	1.50
717	Bobby Crosby	.10
718	Jason Bay	.10
719	Albert Pujols	1.00
720	Mark Loretta	.10
721	Edgar Renteria	.10
722	Scott Rolen	.40
723	J.D. Drew	.10
724	Jim Edmonds	.25
725	Johnny Estrada	.10
726	Jason Schmidt	.10
727	Chris Carpenter	.10
728	Eric Gagne	.10
729	Jason Bay	.10
730	Bobby Cox	.10
731	Game 1	.50
732	Game 2	.50
733	Game 3	.50
734	Game 4	.50

Black

1st Edition:	20-50X
Production 54 Sets	

Gold

Stars:	5-10X
Production 2,005 Sets	

1st Edition

	NM/M
Stars:	3-5X
HTA Exclusive	
1st Edition Pack (10):	4.00
1st Edition Box (20):	65.00

All-Stars

		NM/M
Complete Set (15):		20.00
Common Player:		
Inserted 1:9		
TAS1	Todd Helton	.75
TAS2	Albert Pujols	3.00
TAS3	Vladimir Guerrero	1.00
TAS4	Ichiro Suzuki	2.00
TAS5	Randy Johnson	1.00
TAS6	Manny Ramirez	1.00
TAS7	Sammy Sosa	2.00
TAS8	Alfonso Soriano	1.00
TAS9	Jim Thome	1.00
TAS10	Barry Bonds	3.00
TAS11	Roger Clemens	3.00
TAS12	Mike Piazza	1.50
TAS13	Derek Jeter	3.00
TAS14	Alex Rodriguez	2.50
TAS15	Carlos Beltran	1.00

All-Star Patches

No Pricing
Production 25 Sets

All-Star Stitches Relics

		NM/M
Common Player:		5.00
Inserted 1:96		
BA	Bobby Abreu	8.00
MA	Moises Alou	10.00
RB	Ronnie Belliard	5.00

CB	Carlos Beltran	10.00
LB	Lance Berkman	10.00
HB	Hank Blalock	10.00
MC	Miguel Cabrera	10.00
CC	Carl Crawford	5.00
JE	Johnny Estrada	8.00
EG	Eric Gagne	10.00
JG	Jason Giambi	10.00
TG	Tom Glavine	10.00
FG	Flash Gordon	5.00
VG	Vladimir Guerrero	10.00
KH	Ken Harvey	5.00
TH	Todd Helton	10.00
JK	Jeff Kent	8.00
DK	Danny Kolb	8.00
BL	Barry Larkin	8.00
MLA	Matt Lawton	5.00
TL	Ted Lilly	5.00
EL	Esteban Loaiza	5.00
PL	Paul LoDuca	8.00
MLO	Mark Loretta	8.00
ML	Mike Lowell	8.00
VM	Victor Martinez	8.00
MM	Mark Mulder	8.00
JN	Joe Nathan	8.00
DO	David Ortiz	20.00
CP	Carl Pavano	8.00
MP	Mike Piazza	12.00
AP	Albert Pujols	25.00
MR	Manny Ramirez	8.00
ER	Edgar Renteria	8.00
MRI	Mariano Rivera	10.00
FR	Francisco Rodriguez	10.00
IR	Ivan Rodriguez	10.00
SR	Scott Rolen	12.00
CS	C.C. Sabathia	8.00
BS	Ben Sheets	10.00
GS	Gary Sheffield	10.00
AS	Alfonso Soriano	10.00
SS	Sammy Sosa	15.00
MT	Miguel Tejada	10.00
JT	Jim Thome	12.00
JW	Jack Wilson	10.00
MY	Michael Young	15.00
CZ	Carlos Zambrano	10.00

Autographs

		NM/M
Common Autograph:		
CB	Carlos Beltran	75.00
MC	Miguel Cabrera	40.00
JC	Jose Capellan	30.00
EC	Eric Chavez	25.00
DD	David DeJesus	20.00
ZG	Zack Greinke	25.00
CK	Casey Kotchman	20.00
JMA	John Maine	25.00
DM	Dallas McPherson	25.00
ARI	Alexis Rios	25.00
AR	Alex Rodriguez	160.00
CT	Chad Tracy	20.00
VW	Vernon Wells	25.00
DW	David Wright	80.00
Series 2		
JB	Jason Bay	25.00
CB	Carlos Beltran	60.00
MB	Milton Bradley	25.00
BB	Billy Butler	40.00
MC	Matt Campbell	15.00
EC	Eric Chavez	20.00
ECO	Erik Cordier	15.00
CC	Carl Crawford	15.00
EG	Eric Gagne	50.00
FH	Felix Hernandez	25.00
SK	Scott Kazmir	25.00
ML	Mark Loretta	15.00
GP	Glen Perkins	15.00
LP	Landon Powell	20.00
AR2	Alex Rodriguez/150	250.00
IR	Ivan Rodriguez	50.00
MR	Michael Rogers	35.00
JS	Johan Santana	50.00
TS	Termel Sledge	15.00
CW	Craig Wilson	10.00

Bonds MVP

	NM/M
Production 25-500	
BBI2	Barry Bonds/50	40.00
BBI3	Barry Bonds/100	30.00
BBI4	Barry Bonds/200	25.00
BBI5	Barry Bonds/300	20.00
BBI6	Barry Bonds/400	15.00
BBI7	Barry Bonds/500	15.00

Bonds MVP Autographs

No Pricing

Bonds MVP Relics

		NM/M
Production 25-500		
BBR3	Barry Bonds/100	50.00
BBR4	Barry Bonds/200	40.00
BBR5	Barry Bonds/300	40.00

BBR6	Barry Bonds/400	25.00
BBR7	Barry Bonds/500	25.00

Barry Bonds Home Run Highlights

	NM/M
Complete Set (330):	
Common Bonds:	1.50
Inserted 1:4	
BB1-330 Barry Bonds	1.50

Celebrity Threads Relics

		NM/M
Common Player:		8.00
Inserted 1:562		
CC	Cesar Cedeno	8.00
CF	Cecil Fielder	15.00
RF	Rollie Fingers	12.00
GG	Rich "Goose" Gossage	10.00
HR	Harold Reynolds	8.00
MS	Mike Scott	8.00
OS	Ozzie Smith	25.00
DW	Dave Winfield	15.00

Dem Bums

		NM/M
Complete Set (13):		40.00
Common Player:		4.00
Inserted 1:12		
WA	Walter Alston	4.00
BB	Bob Borkowski	4.00
RC	Roy Campanella	6.00
RCR	Roger Craig	4.00
CF	Carl Furillo	4.00
JG	Jim Gilliam	4.00
DH	Don Hoak	4.00
JH	Jim Hughes	4.00
RM	Russ Meyer	4.00
JR	Jackie Robinson	8.00
ER	Ed Roebuck	4.00
GS	George Shuba	4.00
KS	Karl Spooner	4.00

Dem Bums Cuts

No Pricing
Production One Set

Dem Bums Autographs

		NM/M
Common Autograph:		30.00
Common Player:		30.00
CE	Carl Erskine	30.00
CL	Clem Labine	50.00
JP	Johnny Podres	30.00
DS	Duke Snider	50.00
DZ	Don Zimmer	50.00

Derby Digs Relics

		NM/M
Common Player:		15.00
Production 100 Sets		
LB	Lance Berkman	15.00
HB	Hank Blalock	20.00
DO	David Ortiz	35.00
SS	Sammy Sosa	40.00
MT	Miguel Tejada	15.00
JT	Jim Thome	25.00
Series 2		
Production 10 Sets		

Grudge Match

	NM/M
Complete Set (10):	
Common Duo:	1.00
Inserted 1:24	
GM1	Jorge Posada, Pedro J. Martinez	2.00
GM2	Mike Piazza, Roger Clemens	3.00

GM3	Mariano Rivera, Luis Gonzalez	1.00
GM4	Carlos Zambrano, Jim Edmonds	1.00
GM5	Aaron Boone, Tim Wakefield	1.00
GM6	Manny Ramirez, Roger Clemens	3.00
GM7	Michael Tucker, Eric Gagne	1.00
GM8	Ivan Rodriguez, J.T. Snow	1.00
GM9	Alex Rodriguez, Bronson Arroyo	3.00
GM10	Corky Miller, Sammy Sosa	2.50

Hit Parade

		NM/M
Complete Set (30):		25.00
Common Player:		.50
Inserted 1:12		
HR1	Barry Bonds	4.00
HR2	Sammy Sosa	2.50
HR3	Rafael Palmeiro	1.00
HR4	Ken Griffey Jr.	2.00
HR5	Jeff Bagwell	1.00
HR6	Frank Thomas	1.00
HR7	Juan Gonzalez	.75
HR8	Jim Thome	1.00
HR9	Gary Sheffield	1.00
HR10	Manny Ramirez	1.50
RBI1	Barry Bonds	4.00
RBI2	Rafael Palmeiro	1.00
RBI3	Sammy Sosa	2.50
RBI4	Jeff Bagwell	1.00
RBI5	Ken Griffey Jr.	2.00
RBI6	Frank Thomas	1.00
RBI7	Juan Gonzalez	.75
RBI8	Gary Sheffield	1.00
RBI9	Ruben Sierra	.50
RBI10	Manny Ramirez	1.50
HIT1	Rafael Palmeiro	1.00
HIT2	Barry Bonds	4.00
HIT3	Roberto Alomar	.75
HIT4	Craig Biggio	.50
HIT5	Julio Franco	.50
HIT6	Steve Finley	.50
HIT7	Jeff Bagwell	1.00
HIT8	B.J. Surhoff	.50
HIT9	Marquis Grissom	.50
HIT10	Sammy Sosa	2.50

Hobby Masters

		NM/M
Complete Set (20):		25.00
Common Player:		.75
Inserted 1:18		
HM1	Alex Rodriguez	4.00
HM2	Sammy Sosa	2.50
HM3	Ichiro Suzuki	3.00
HM4	Albert Pujols	4.00
HM5	Derek Jeter	4.00
HM6	Jim Thome	1.50
HM7	Vladimir Guerrero	1.50
HM8	Nomar Garciaparra	1.50
HM9	Mike Piazza	2.00
HM10	Jason Giambi	.75
HM11	Hank Blalock	1.00
HM12	Alfonso Soriano	1.50
HM13	Dontrelle Willis	.75
HM14	Chipper Jones	1.50
HM15	Mark Prior	1.50
HM16	Todd Helton	1.50
HM17	Randy Johnson	1.50
HM18	Hank Blalock	1.00
HM19	Ken Griffey Jr.	2.00
HM20	Roger Clemens	3.00

Midsummer Covers Relics

No Pricing
Production 10 Sets
Series 2
Production 10 Sets

National Convention

A latter-day attempt to recreate the "missing" four cards from its original high-number series, these cards were available only as a cello-wrapped set to purchasers of the VIP Attendee package at the 2005 National Sports Collectors Convention in Chicago. Cards are in the original 3-3/4" x 2-5/8" format.

		NM/M
Complete Set (4):		20.00
Common Player:		3.00
175	Stan Musial	9.00
186	Whitey Ford	6.00
203	Bob Feller	5.00
209	Herb Score	3.00

1955 Luis Aparicio

This original format (3-3/4" x 2-5/8") card was only available at the Chicago White Sox booth during the 2005 National Sports Collectors Convention in Chicago.

		NM/M
NAT1	Luis Aparicio	7.50

On-Deck Relics

		NM/M
Inserted 1:1,493		
CB	Carlos Beltran	15.00
HB	Hank Blalock	12.00
TH	Todd Helton	12.00
AP	Albert Pujols	30.00
AR	Alex Rodriguez	25.00
IR	Ivan Rodriguez	15.00
SR	Scott Rolen	15.00
AS	Alfonso Soriano	15.00
SS	Sammy Sosa	25.00
JT	Jim Thome	15.00

Own The Game

		NM/M
Complete Set (30):		15.00
Common Player:		.50
Inserted 1:12		
OG1	Ichiro Suzuki	3.00
OG2	Todd Helton	1.00
OG3	Adrian Beltre	1.00
OG4	Albert Pujols	4.00
OG5	Adam Dunn	1.00
OG6	Jim Thome	1.50
OG7	Miguel Tejada	.75
OG8	David Ortiz	1.50
OG9	Manny Ramirez	1.50
OG10	Scott Rolen	1.50
OG11	Gary Sheffield	.75
OG12	Vladimir Guerrero	1.50
OG13	Jim Edmonds	.75
OG14	Ivan Rodriguez	1.00
OG15	Lance Berkman	.50
OG16	Michael Young	.50
OG17	Juan Pierre	.50
OG18	Craig Biggio	.50
OG19	Johnny Damon	.75
OG20	Jimmy Rollins	.50
OG21	Scott Podsednik	.50
OG22	Bobby Abreu	.50
OG23	Lyle Overbay	.50
OG24	Carl Crawford	.50
OG25	Mark Loretta	.50
OG26	Vinny Castilla	.50
OG27	Curt Schilling	1.00
OG28	Johan Santana	.75
OG29	Randy Johnson	1.50
OG30	Pedro J. Martinez	1.50

Power Brokers Cut Signatures

Complete Set (51):
Common Player:

Spokesman

	NM/M
Complete Set (4):	10.00
Common Player:	3.00
Inserted 1:24	
ARI1-4 Alex Rodriguez	3.00

Spokesman Autographs

	NM/M
Production 1-200	
ARA3 Alex Rodriguez/100	200.00
ARA4 Alex Rodriguez/200	180.00

Spokesman Relic

	NM/M
Inserted 1:5,627	
AR Alex Rodriguez	50.00

Spokesman Relics

	NM/M
Production 1-800	
ARR2 Alex Rodriguez/50	30.00
ARR3 Alex Rodriguez/300	20.00
ARR4 Alex Rodriguez/800	20.00

Spokesman Relic Autographs

13 Sets

Touch'em All Relics

Common Player:
Production 50 Sets
Series 2
Production 50 Sets

World Champion Red Sox Relics

		NM/M
Common Player:		
OC	Orlando Cabrera	20.00
OC2	Orlando Cabrera	20.00
JD	Johnny Damon	25.00
JD2	Johnny Damon	25.00
DL	Derek Lowe	20.00
PM	Pedro Martinez	20.00
DMI	Doug Mientkiewicz	15.00
KM	Kevin Millar	20.00
BM	Bill Mueller	15.00
BM2	Bill Mueller	15.00
TN	Trot Nixon	20.00
DO	David Ortiz	20.00
DO2	David Ortiz	20.00
MR	Manny Ramirez	25.00
MR2	Manny Ramirez	25.00
MR3	Manny Ramirez	25.00
PR	Pokey Reese	15.00
DR	Dave Roberts	15.00
CS	Curt Schilling	25.00
KY	Kevin Youkilis	15.00

World Treasures

No Pricing
Production One Set

World Treasures - Dual

No Pricing
Production One Set

1955 World Series Cut Signatures

Complete Set (21):
Common Player:

1955 World Series Dual Cut Signatures

Complete Set (3):
Common Player:
Production One Set

2005 Topps All-Time Fan Favorites

LOU BROCK — OUTFIELD

		NM/M
Complete Set (142):		40.00
Common Player:		.25
Pack (6):		5.00
Box (24):		110.00
1	Andy Van Slyke	.25
2	Bill Freehan	.25
3	Bo Jackson	.75
4	Mark Grace	.50
5	Chuck Knoblauch	.25
6	Candy Maldonado	.25
7	David Cone	.25
8	Don Mattingly	1.50
9	Darryl Strawberry	.25
10	Dick Williams	.25
11	Frank Robinson	.75
12	Glenn Hubbard	.25
13	Jim Abbott	.25
14	Jeff Brantley	.25
15	John Elway	2.00
16	Jim Leyland	.25
17	Jesse Orosco	.25
18	Joe Pepitone	.25
19	J.R. Richard	.25
20	Jerome Walton	.25
21	Kevin Maas	.25
22	Lou Brock	.50
23	Lou Whitaker	.25
24	Carl Erskine	.25
25	John Candelaria	.25
26	Mike Norris	.25
27	Nolan Ryan	2.00
28	Pedro Guerrero	.25
29	Roger Craig	.25
30	Ron Gant	.25
31	Sid Bream	.25
32	Sid Fernandez	.25
33	Tony LaRussa	.25
34	Tom Seaver	.75
35	Yogi Berra	.75
36	Andre Dawson	.75
37	Al Kaline	.75
38	Brett Butler	.25
39	Bob Gibson	.75
40	Bill Mazeroski	.25
41	Matty Alou	.25
42	Chet Lemon	.25
43	Cal Ripken Jr.	2.00
44	Dusty Baker	.25
45	Dwight Gooden	.25
46	Dave Winfield	.50
47	Ernie Banks	1.00
48	Gary Carter	.50
49	Howard Johnson	.25
50	Mike Schmidt	1.50
51	Matt Williams	.25
52	Ozzie Smith	1.00
53	Atlee Hammaker	.25
54	Cleon Jones	.25
55	Dave Johnson	.25
56	Denny McLain	.25
57	Don Zimmer	.25
58	Gregg Jefferies	.25
59	Jay Buhner	.25
60	Johnny Bench	.75
61	George Brett	1.50
62	Dale Murphy	.50
63	Bob Welch	.25
64	Paul O'Neill	.25
65	Mark Lemke	.25
66	Kevin McReynolds	.25
67	Jesus Alou	.25
68	Joe Pignatano	.25
69	Jim Lonborg	.25
70	Jerry Grote	.25
71	Joaquin Andujar	.25
72	Gary Gaetti	.25
73	Edgar Martinez	.25
74	Ron Darling	.25
75	Duke Snider	.75
76	Dave Magadan	.25
77	Doug Drabek	.25
78	Carl Yastrzemski	1.00
79	Mitch Williams	.25
80	Marvin Miller	.25
81	Michael Kay	.25
82	Lonnie Smith	.25
83	John Wetteland	.25
84	Johnny Podres	.25
85	Joe Morgan	.75
86	Juan Marichal	.50
87	Jeffrey Leonard	.25
88	Bob Feller	.50
89	Brooks Robinson	.75
90	Clem Labine	.25
91	Barry Lyons	.25
92	Harmon Killebrew	.75
93	Jim Frey	.25
94	John Kruk	.25
95	Ed Kranepool	.25
96	Jose Oquendo	.25
97	Johnny Pesky	.25
98	John Tudor	.25
99	Keith Hernandez	.25
100	Monte Irvin	.50
101	Marty Barrett	.25
102	Oscar Gamble	.25
103	Hank Bauer	.25
104	Ron Blomberg	.25
105	Rod Carew	.75
106	Rick Dempsey	.25
107	Walt Jocketty	.25
108	Tom Kelly	.25
109	Steve Carlton	.50
110	Rick Monday	.25
111	Rob Dibble	.25
112	Shawon Dunston	.25
113	Tony Gwynn	.75
114	Tom Niedenfuer	.25
115	Bob Dernier	.25
116	Anthony Young	.25
117	Reggie Jackson	.75
118	Steve Garvey	.25
119	Tim Raines	.25
120	Whitey Ford	.75
121	Rafael Santana	.25
122	Scott Brosius	.25
123	Stan Musial	1.50
124	Ron Santo	.25
125	Wade Boggs	.75
126	Jose Canseco	.50
127	Brady Anderson	.25
128	Vida Blue	.25
129	Charlie Hough	.25
130	Jim Kaat	.25
131	Zane Smith	.25
132	Bob Boone	.25
133	Travis Fryman	.25
134	Harold Baines	.25
135	Orlando Cepeda	.25
136	Mike Cuellar	.25
137	Tito Fuentes	.25
138	Daryl Boston	.25
139	Jim Leyritz	.25
140	Bill "Moose" Skowron	.25
141	Theo Epstein	.25
142	Barry Bonds	3.00

Refractor

Stars (1-142):	3-5X
Production 299 Sets	

Gold Refractor

No Pricing
Production 25 Sets

Printing Plates

No Pricing
Production one set per color (4):

Autographs

		NM/M
Common Autograph:		15.00
Rainbow:		No Pricing
Production 10 Sets		
JA	Jim Abbott	30.00
JAN	Joaquin Andujar	20.00
DB	Dusty Baker	25.00
MB	Marty Barrett	15.00
JBE	Dr. Jim Beckett/SP/90	100.00
JB	Johnny Bench/SP/40	125.00
YB	Yogi Berra/SP/90	125.00
RB	Ron Blomberg	15.00
JBR	Jeff Brantley	20.00
SB	Sid Bream	20.00
GB	George Brett/SP/40	250.00
SBR	Scott Brosius/SP/90	85.00
JBU	Jay Buhner	20.00
BB	Brett Butler	20.00
SC	Steve Carlton/SP/90	60.00
GC	Gary Carter	25.00
DC	David Cone	25.00
RCR	Roger Craig	25.00
RD	Rick Dempsey	15.00
DD	Doug Drabek	20.00
SD	Shawon Dunston	20.00
JE	John Elway/SP/40	250.00
BFE	Bob Feller	85.00
SF	Sid Fernandez	20.00
WF	Whitey Ford/SP/90	150.00
BF	Bill Freehan	20.00
GG	Gary Gaetti	15.00
OG	Oscar Gamble	15.00
RG	Ron Gant/SP/90	50.00
SG	Steve Garvey	50.00
BG	Bob Gibson/SP/90	100.00
DG	Dwight Gooden	40.00
JG	Jerry Grote	15.00
TG	Tony Gwynn/SP/90	125.00
AH	Atlee Hammaker	15.00
GH	Glenn Hubbard	20.00
MI	Monte Irvin	50.00
BJ	Bo Jackson	70.00
RJ	Reggie Jackson/SP/90	100.00
GJ	Gregg Jefferies	40.00
WJ	Walt Jocketty/SP/90	60.00
DJ	Dave Johnson	20.00
HJ	Howard Johnson	20.00
CJ	Cleon Jones	35.00
AK	Al Kaline	60.00
TK	Tom Kelly	25.00
HK	Harmon Killebrew	85.00
CK	Chuck Knoblauch	25.00
JK	John Kruk	30.00
CL	Clem Labine	40.00
TL	Tony LaRussa	30.00
MLE	Mark Lemke	15.00
CLE	Chet Lemon	15.00
JLE	Jim Leyland	20.00
JLO	Jim Lonborg	25.00
BL	Barry Lyons	15.00
KM	Kevin Maas	15.00
DMA	Dave Magadan	20.00
CM	Candy Maldonado	15.00
JMA	Juan Marichal/SP/90	140.00
EM	Edgar Martinez	30.00
DM	Don Mattingly	140.00
BM	Bill Mazeroski	75.00
DMC	Denny McLain	30.00
KMC	Kevin McReynolds	15.00
MM	Marvin Miller/SP/90	80.00
RM	Rick Monday	15.00
DMU	Dale Murphy	25.00
SM	Stan Musial/SP/40	150.00
TN	Tom Niedenfuer	15.00
MNO	Mike Norris	15.00
PO	Paul O'Neill	60.00
JO	Jesse Orosco	25.00
JOQ	Jose Oquendo	15.00
JPE	Joe Pepitone	25.00
JPY	Johnny Pesky	65.00
JP	Joe Pignatano	30.00
TR	Tim Raines	25.00
JR	J.R. Richard	15.00
CR	Cal Ripken Jr./SP/90	200.00
BR	Brooks Robinson/SP/90	125.00
FR	Frank Robinson	100.00
NR	Nolan Ryan/SP/40	140.00
RS	Rafael Santana	20.00
RSA	Ron Santo/SP/90	75.00
MS	Mike Schmidt/SP/40	160.00
LS	Lonnie Smith	15.00
DSN	Duke Snider/SP/40	60.00
DS	Darryl Strawberry	25.00
JT	John Tudor	35.00
AV	Andy Van Slyke	15.00
JW	Jerome Walton	15.00
BW	Bob Welch	30.00
JWE	John Wetteland	25.00
LW	Lou Whitaker/SP/90	60.00
DWI	Dick Williams/SP/90	75.00
MW	Matt Williams	25.00
MWI	Mitch Williams	25.00
DW	Dave Winfield/SP/90	125.00
CY	Carl Yastrzemski/SP/90	125.00
AY	Anthony Young	15.00
DZ	Don Zimmer/SP/40	50.00

Best Seat in House

	NM/M
Production 125 unless noted.	
Rainbow:	No Pricing
Production 25 Sets	
MFBJ Don Mattingly, Whitey Ford, Yogi Berra, Reggie Jackson/50	50.00
RRRD Brooks Robinson, Rick Dempsey, Frank Robinson, Cal Ripken Jr.	25.00
RR Brooks Robinson, Cal Ripken Jr.	25.00
CR Cal Ripken Jr., Frank Robinson	25.00
JD Dave Johnson, Rick Dempsey	10.00
KMLW Al Kaline, Lou Whitaker, Chet Lemon, Denny McLain	20.00

Fan Favorite Relics

		NM/M
Inserted 1:Box		
Rainbow:		No Pricing
Production 25 Sets		
WB	Wade Boggs/200	8.00
JCC	Jose Canseco/350	8.00
RC	Rod Carew/200	5.00
GC	Gary Carter/350	5.00
JC	Joe Carter/350	5.00
VC	Vince Coleman/200	5.00
ED	Eric Davis/350	5.00
AD	Andre Dawson/350	5.00
BD	Bucky Dent/200	5.00
LD	Lenny Dykstra/200	5.00
CF	Cecil Fielder/200	5.00
TG	Tony Gwynn/200	15.00
KH	Keith Hernandez/200	5.00
BJ	Bo Jackson/200	12.00
RJ	Reggie Jackson/350	10.00
WJ	Wally Joyner/200	5.00
WM	Willie McGee/350	5.00
DM	Dale Murphy/200	10.00
SM	Stan Musial/50	20.00
PO	Paul O'Neill/200	5.00
JR	Jim Rice/200	5.00
BR	Brooks Robinson/350	10.00
NR	Nolan Ryan/135	5.00
DS	Darryl Strawberry/350	5.00
BS	Bruce Sutter/350	7.50
MW	Mookie Wilson/135	5.00
CY	Carl Yastrzemski/50	25.00

League Leaders Tr-Signers

Production 50 Sets

Originals Relics

		NM/M
Production 50 Sets		
Actual vintage cards used.		
WB	Wade Boggs/Bat	15.00
RC	Rod Carew/Bat	20.00
GC	Gary Carter/Bat	10.00
AD	Andre Dawson/Bat	15.00
TG	Tony Gwynn/Jsy	20.00
BJ	Bo Jackson/Jsy	15.00
RJ	Reggie Jackson/Bat	20.00
DM	Dale Murphy/Bat	15.00
JR	Jim Rice/Bat	15.00
NR	Nolan Ryan/Jsy	35.00

Rookie Dual Autograph

		NM/M
Production 50 Sets		
SC	Tom Seaver, Rod Carew	160.00

2005 Topps Bazooka

ALEX RODRIGUEZ — NEW YORK YANKEES

		NM/M
Complete Set (220):		35.00
Common Player:		.15
Common (191-220):		.25
Pack (8):		2.50
Box (24):		50.00
1	Eric Gagne	.40
2	Aramis Ramirez	.40
3	Hank Blalock	.50
4	Jason Kendall	.15
5	Jeromy Burnitz	.15
6	Jose Guillen	.15
7	Tom Glavine	.40
8	Adrian Beltre	.25
9	Jason Bay	.25
10	Mark Teixeira	.40
11	Moises Alou	.25
12	Ronnie Belliard	.15
13	Aaron Guiel	.15
14	Vladimir Guerrero	.75
15	Scott Podsednik	.15
16	Alfonso Soriano	.75
17	Craig Wilson	.15
18	Jose Reyes	.25
19	Mark Prior	.75
20	Preston Wilson	.15
21	Shawn Green	.15
22	Troy Glaus	.25
23	Dmitri Young	.15
24	Garret Anderson	.25
25	Kazuo Matsui	.25
26	Kerry Wood	.25
27	Michael Young	.15
28	Oliver Perez	.15
29	Bartolo Colon	.15
30	Richie Sexson	.40
31	Brad Penny	.15
32	Carlos Guillen	.15
33	Carlos Zambrano	.25
34	David Wright	.50
35	Al Leiter	.15
36	Jack Wilson	.15
37	Ryan Drese	.15
38	Darin Erstad	.15
39	Derek Lee	.25
40	Ivan Rodriguez	.50
41	Kenny Rogers	.15
42	Mike Piazza	1.00
43	Phil Nevin	.15
44	Geoff Jenkins	.15
45	Jorge Posada	.40
46	Khalil Greene	.40
47	Randy Johnson	.75
48	Rondell White	.15
49	Sammy Sosa	1.25
50	Vernon Wells	.15
51	Ben Sheets	.40
52	Brian Giles	.15
53	Carlos Delgado	.40
54	Derek Jeter	2.00
55	Jeremy Bonderman	.15
56	Magglio Ordonez	.25
57	Chad Tracy	.15
58	Kevin Brown	.15
59	Luis Castillo	.15
60	Lyle Overbay	.15
61	Mark Buehrle	.15
62	Mark Loretta	.15
63	Orlando Hudson	.15
64	Adam Dunn	.50
65	Frank Thomas	.50
66	Jake Peavy	.25
67	Jason Giambi	.40
68	Joe Mauer	.25
69	Marcus Giles	.15
70	Mike Lowell	.25
71	Roy Halladay	.15
72	Aaron Rowand	.15
73	Alex Rodriguez	1.50
74	Brian Lawrence	.15
75	Gabe Gross	.15
76	Johnny Estrada	.15
77	Justin Morneau	.40
78	Miguel Cabrera	.40
79	Alex Rios	.15
80	Gary Sheffield	.40
81	Jason Schmidt	.25
82	Juan Pierre	.15
83	Paul Konerko	.15
84	Jermaine Dye	.15
85	Rafael Furcal	.15
86	Torii Hunter	.25
87	A.J. Pierzynski	.15
88	Carl Pavano	.15
89	Carlos Lee	.25
90	J.D. Drew	.25
91	Javier Vazquez	.15
92	Lew Ford	.15
93	Ted Lilly	.15
94	Austin Kearns	.15
95	Chipper Jones	.75
96	Erubiel Durazo	.15
97	Johan Santana	.50
98	Josh Beckett	.25
99	Mariano Rivera	.25
100	Mark Mulder	.25
101	Andruw Jones	.25
102	Barry Zito	.25
103	Bret Boone	.15
104	Paul LoDuca	.15
105	Shannon Stewart	.15
106	Wily Mo Pena	.25
107	Dontrelle Willis	.25
108	Eric Chavez	.15
109	Jamie Moyer	.15
110	Joe Nathan	.15
111	Sidney Ponson	.15
112	John Smoltz	.25
113	Ichiro Suzuki	1.50
114	Javy Lopez	.15
115	Victor Martinez	.25
116	Ken Griffey Jr.	1.00
117	Lance Berkman	.25
118	Scott Hatteberg	.15
119	Jim Edmonds	.25
120	Kazuhisa Ishii	.15
121	Miguel Tejada	.40
122	Roger Clemens	2.00
123	Ryan Freel	.15
124	Albert Pujols	2.00
125	Hideo Nomo	.25
126	Mark Kotsay	.15
127	Melvin Mora	.15
128	Roy Oswalt	.15
129	Sean Casey	.25
130	Casey Blake	.15
131	Edgar Renteria	.25
132	Jeff Kent	.25
133	Rafael Palmeiro	.50
134	Tim Hudson	.25
135	Tony Batista	.15
136	Andy Pettitte	.25
137	Brian Roberts	.15
138	Jose Vidro	.15
139	Omar Vizquel	.15
140	Rich Harden	.25
141	Scott Rolen	.75
142	Carlos Beltran	.50
143	Chris Carpenter	.15
144	Manny Ramirez	.75
145	Nick Johnson	.15
146	Pat Burrell	.15
147	C.C. Sabathia	.15
148	Johnny Damon	.25
149	Juan Rivera	.15
150	Ken Harvey	.15
151	Kevin Millwood	.15
152	Larry Walker	.50
153	Aubrey Huff	.15
154	Curt Schilling	.75
155	Jake Westbrook	.15
156	Randy Wolf	.15

ABBREVIATIONS

SP - Short Print

157	Zach Day	.15
158	Zack Greinke	.15
159	Brad Wilkerson	.15
160	Carl Crawford	.15
161	Jim Thome	.75
162	Mike Sweeney	.15
163	Pedro J. Martinez	.75
164	Travis Hafner	.15
165	Bobby Abreu	.25
166	Cliff Floyd	.15
167	David DeJesus	.15
168	David Ortiz	.75
169	Rocco Baldelli	.15
170	Todd Helton	.50
171	Dallas McPherson	.50
172	Kevin Youkilis	.15
173	Val Majewski	.15
174	Grady Sizemore	.25
175	Joey Gathright	.15
176	Rickie Weeks	.25
177	Jason Kubel	.25
178	Robinson Cano	.25
179	Nick Swisher	.25
180	Ryan Howard	.50
181	Tim Stauffer	.15
182	Merkin Valdez	.15
183	B.J. Upton	.25
184	Scott Kazmir	.40
185	Chris Burke	.25
186	Felix Hernandez	.25
187	Freddy Guzman	.15
188	Josh Labandeira	.15
189	Willy Taveras	.15
190	Casey Kotchman	.25
191	Steven Doetsch RC	.25
192	Melky Cabrera RC	.75
193	Luis Ramirez RC	.25
194	Chris Seddon RC	.40
195	Chad Orvella RC	.50
196	Ian Kinsler RC	1.50
197	Brandon Moss RC	1.00
198	Chadd Blasko RC	.25
199	Jeremy West RC	.75
200	Sean Marshall RC	.25
201	Matt DeSalvo RC	.25
202	Ryan Sweeney RC	1.50
203	Matt Lindstrom RC	.50
204	Ryan Goleski RC	.40
205	Brett Harper RC	.25
206	Chris Roberson RC	.25
207	Andre Ethier RC	1.00
208	Chris Denorfia RC	.25
209	Darren Fenster RC	.25
210	Elvys Quezada RC	.25
211	Kevin West RC	.50
212	Chaz Lytle RC	.25
213	James Jurries RC	.25
214	Matt Rogelstad RC	.25
215	Wade Robinson RC	.25
216	Ian Bladergroen RC	.75
217	Jake Dittler	.25
218	Nate McLouth RC	.40
219	Kole Strayhorn RC	.25
220	Jose Vaquedano RC	.25

Gold Chunks

Golds: 1-2X
Inserted 1:1

Minis

Mini: 1-2x
Inserted 1:1

Blasts

NM/M
Common Bat: 4.00

RA	Roberto Alomar	6.00
RB	Ron Belliard	4.00
AB	Angel Berroa	4.00
CB	Craig Biggio	8.00
HB	Hank Blalock	4.00
JB	Jeromy Burnitz	4.00
SB	Sean Burroughs	4.00
MC	Miguel Cabrera	10.00
VC	Vinny Castilla	4.00
TC	Tony Clark	4.00
JC	Jeff Conine	4.00
JCJ	Jose Cruz Jr.	4.00
AD	Adam Dunn	4.00
ME	Morgan Ensberg	4.00
DE	Darin Erstad	4.00
CE	Carl Everett	4.00
CF	Chone Figgins	4.00
JF	Julio Franco	4.00
NG	Nomar Garciaparra	8.00
AGO	Adrian Gonzalez	4.00
AG	Alex Gonzalez	4.00
LG	Luis Gonzalez	4.00
VG	Vladimir Guerrero	8.00
CGU	Carlos Guillen	4.00
CG	Cristian Guzman	4.00
TH	Todd Helton	6.00
LH	Livan Hernandez	4.00
RH	Richard Hidalgo	4.00
JK	Jeff Kent	4.00
PK	Paul Konerko	4.00
DL	Derrek Lee	4.00
ML	Mike Lowell	4.00
PM	Pedro Martinez	6.00
TM	Tino Martinez	4.00
VM	Victor Martinez	6.00
KM	Kazuo Matsui	8.00
MO	Magglio Ordonez	4.00
DO	David Ortiz	10.00
ARA	Aramis Ramirez	4.00
MR	Manny Ramirez	6.00
AR	Alex Rodriguez	20.00
CS	Curt Schilling	6.00
GS	Gary Sheffield	4.00
RS	Ruben Sierra	4.00
MT	Miguel Tejada	6.00
BU	B.J. Upton	10.00
JV	Jose Valentin	4.00
JVI	Jose Vidro	4.00
LW	Larry Walker	6.00
JW	Jayson Werth	4.00
PW	Preston Wilson	4.00
DW	David Wright	10.00
MY	Michael Young	4.00

Comics

NM/M
Complete Set (24): 8.00
Common Player: .25
Inserted 1:4

1	Randy Johnson	.50
2	Gary Sheffield	.25
3	Ken Griffey Jr.	.75
4	Alex Rodriguez	.75
5	Vladimir Guerrero	.50
6	David Bell	.25
7	Carlos Pena	.25
8	Eric Gagne	.25
9	Jim Thome	.50
10	Cleveland Indians	.50
11	Greg Maddux	.50
12	Miguel Tejada	.25
13	Ichiro Suzuki	.75
14	Mariano Rivera	.25
15	Juan Pierre	.25
16	Carl Crawford	.25
17	Mike Mussina	.25
18	Vladimir Guerrero	.50
19	Oliver Perez	.25
20	Ichiro Suzuki	.75
21	Johan Santana	.25
22	Kevin Brown	.25
23	Mike Piazza	.50
24	Randy Johnson	.50

Fun Facts Relics

NM/M
Common Relic: 4.00

HB	Harold Baines	4.00
WB	Wade Boggs	6.00
GB	George Brett	12.00
JC	Jose Canseco	8.00
RC	Rod Carew	12.00
GC	Gary Carter	4.00
DD	Darren Daulton	4.00
DE	Darrell Evans	4.00
CF	Cecil Fielder	8.00
KG	Ken Griffey Sr.	4.00
WH	Willie Horton	4.00
WJ	Wally Joyner	4.00
DJ	David Justice	4.00
DJ2	David Justice	4.00
RK	Ron Kittle	4.00
JL	Jim Leyritz	4.00
DP	Dave Parker	4.00
HR	Harold Reynolds	4.00
MR	Mickey Rivers	4.00
MS	Mike Schmidt	10.00
OS	Ozzie Smith	20.00
CS	Cory Snyder	4.00
DS	Darryl Strawberry	4.00
WW	Walt Weiss	4.00

Moments Relics

NM/M
Common Relic: 6.00
MB Matt Bush 8.00

RH	Ramon Hernandez	6.00
TL	Terrence Long	6.00
MM	Mark Mulder	6.00
MP	Mike Piazza	12.00
JP	Jorge Posada	8.00
AP	Albert Pujols	25.00
AR	Alex Rodriguez	12.00
IR	Ivan Rodriguez	8.00
KR	Kenny Rogers	6.00
AS	Alfonso Soriano	6.00
MT	Mark Teixeira	6.00
FT	Frank Thomas	6.00

Tatoos

NM/M
Common Player: .25
Inserted 1:4

1	Alex Rodriguez	.50
2	Randy Johnson	.50
3	Jim Thome	.25
4	Pedro Martinez	.50
5	Roger Clemens	.50
6	Troy Glaus	.25
7	Todd Helton	.25
8	Albert Pujols	.50
9	Sammy Sosa	.50
10	David Wright	.50
11	Mike Piazza	.50
12	Gary Sheffield	.25
13	David Ortiz	.50
14	Hank Blalock	.25
15	Miguel Tejada	.25
16	Dontrelle Willis	.25
17	Ivan Rodriguez	.25
18	Nomar Garciaparra	.50
19	Alfonso Soriano	.25
20	Adrian Beltre	.25
21	Torii Hunter	.25
22	Brian Giles	.25
23	Chipper Jones	.50
24	Carlos Beltran	.50
25	Manny Ramirez	.50

4-on-1 Stickers

NM/M
Common Sticker: .50
Inserted 1:3 Hobby

1	Alex Rodriguez, Hank Blalock, Scott Rolen, Mike Lowell	1.50
2	Jorge Posada, Ivan Rodriguez, Joe Mauer, Johnny Estrada	.75
3	Ichiro Suzuki, Carlos Beltran, Jim Edmonds, Brian Giles	1.50
4	Jim Thome, Mark Teixeira, Paul Konerko, Lyle Overbay	1.00
5	Jose Reyes, Mark Loretta, Jose Vidro, Luis Castillo	.50
6	Miguel Tejada, Derek Jeter, Michael Young, Edgar Renteria	2.00
7	Roy Oswalt, Rich Harden, Johan Santana, Mark Prior	1.00
8	Mariano Rivera, Eric Gagne, Joe Nathan, John Smoltz	.50
9	Larry Walker, Carl Crawford, Preston Wilson, Garret Anderson	.50
10	Wily Mo Pena, Mark Kotsay, Alex Rios, Geoff Jenkins	.50
11	Victor Martinez, David Wright, Justin Morneau, Jason Bay	.75
12	Carlos Lee, Andruw Jones, Ronnie Belliard, Eric Chavez	.50
13	Vladimir Guerrero, Vernon Wells, Miguel Cabrera, Adrian Beltre	.50
14	David Ortiz, Marcus Giles, Jeff Kent, Bobby Abreu	1.00
15	Juan Pierre, Torii Hunter, J.D. Drew, Austin Kearns	.50
16	Bartolo Colon, Manny Ramirez, Ken Griffey Jr., Dontrelle Willis	1.50
17	Andy Pettitte, Tim Hudson, Curt Schilling, Randy Johnson	1.50
18	Jamie Moyer, Zach Day, Al Leiter, Oliver Perez	.50
19	Kazuo Matsui, Roger Clemens, Khalil Greene, Javier Vazquez	2.00
20	Pedro Martinez, Rocco Baldelli, Mike Piazza, Melvin Mora	1.50
21	Hideo Nomo, Kazuhisa Ishii, Ken Harvey, Mike Sweeney	.50
22	Casey Blake, Ryan Freel, Bret Boone, Javy Lopez	.50
23	Craig Wilson, Shawn Green, Aramis Ramirez, Darin Erstad	.50
24	Troy Glaus, Lance Berkman, Scott Podsednik, Adam Dunn	.50
25	Albert Pujols, Gary Sheffield, Chipper Jones, Magglio Ordonez	2.00
26	Johnny Damon, Carlos Zambrano, Jason Schmidt, Ted Lilly	1.00
27	Sidney Ponson, Chris Carpenter, C.C. Sabathia, Kevin Millwood	.50
28	Carl Pavano, Mark Mulder, Rafael Furcal, Jack Wilson	.50
29	Jeremy Bonderman, Jake Westbrook, Zack Greinke, Tom Glavine	.50
30	Omar Vizquel, Carlos Guillen, Roy Halladay, Ben Sheets	.50
31	Kerry Wood, Kevin Brown, Moises Alou, Travis Hafner	.75
32	Nick Johnson, Erubiel Durazo, Alfonso Soriano, Jason Giambi	.75
33	Chad Tracy, Richie Sexson, Aubrey Huff, Brian Roberts	.50
34	Todd Helton, Dmitri Young, Jeromy Burnitz, Jose Guillen	.75
35	Juan Rivera, Shannon Stewart, Sammy Sosa, Cliff Floyd	1.00
36	Pat Burrell, Gabe Gross, Aaron Guiel, Paul LoDuca	.50
37	A.J. Pierzynski, Orlando Hudson, David DeJesus, Brian Lawrence	.50
38	Josh Beckett, Barry Zito, Mark Buehrle, Randy Wolf	1.50
39	Brad Penny, Jake Peavy, Rondell White, Brad Wilkerson	.50
40	Ryan Drese, Kenny Rogers, Jermaine Dye, Lew Ford	.50
41	Aaron Rowand, Jason Kendall, Tony Batista, Derrek Lee	.50
42	Phil Nevin, Sean Casey, Rafael Palmeiro, Frank Thomas	.75
43	Scott Hatteberg, Josh Labandeira, Jason Kubel, Nick Swisher	.50
44	Freddy Guzman, Tim Stauffer, Merkin Valdez, Felix Hernandez	.50
45	Willy Taveras, Grady Sizemore, Joey Gathright, Carlos Delgado	.50
46	Scott Kazmir, Rickie Weeks, Dallas McPherson, Kevin Youkilis	1.00
47	Val Majewski, Casey Kotchman, Ryan Howard, Chris Burke	.50
48	Robinson Cano, B.J. Upton, Jake Dittler, Ian Bladergroen	1.00
49	Brett Harper, James Jurries, Jeremy West, Matt Rogelstad	1.00
50	Darren Fenster, Nate Schierholtz, Brandon Moss, Ryan Sweeney	2.00
51	Chris Roberson, Steven Doetsch, Andre Ethier, Kevin West	.50
52	Melky Cabrera, Ryan Goleski, Chris Denorfia, Chaz Lytle	1.00
53	Luis Ramirez, Matt DeSalvo, Sean Marshall, Jose Vaquedano	.50
54	Chris Seddon, Chadd Blasko, Elvys Quezada, Wade Robinson	.50
55	Nate McLouth, Matt Lindstrom, Kole Strayhorn, Ian Kinsler	2.50

Chicago White Sox World Series Commemorative

NM/M
Complete Boxed Set (56):
Common Card: .25

1	Mark Buehrle	.50
2	A.J. Pierzynski	.50
3	Juan Uribe	.50
4	Tadahito Iguchi	.50
5	Paul Konerko	.75
6	Frank Thomas	2.50
7	Jermaine Dye	.50
8	Aaron Rowand	.50
9	Timo Perez	.50
10	Jose Contreras	.50
11	Carl Everett	.50
12	Pablo Ozuna	.50
13	Geoff Blum	.50
14	Cliff Politte	.50
15	Freddy Garcia	.50
16	Bobby Jenks	.50
17	Dustin Hermanson	.50
18	Neal Cotts	.50
19	Chris Widger	.50
20	Jon Garland	.50
21	Luis Vizcaino	.50
22	Damaso Marte	.50
23	Scott Podsednik	.75
24	Willie Harris	.50
25	Orlando Hernandez	.50
26	Joe Crede	.50
27	Ross Gload	.50
28	Brian Anderson	.50
29	Brandon McCarthy	.50
30	Ozzie Guillen	.50
31	Team Photo	.50
32	Buehrle Pitches 6+	.25
33	Sox Win 99 Games	.25
34	Buehrle Named Starter	.25
35	Podsednik Steals 59	.25
36	Konerko Tops 40 HRs	.25
37	Pierzynski Hits 2 of 5	.25
38	Chicago Socks Boston	.25
39	Sox Sweep Sox	.25
40	Pierzynski Safe	.25
41	Paul Hits Bunyanesque Homer	.25
42	It's a South Side Series	.25
43	Sox Starters Win Four (Buehrle)	.25
44	Sox Starters Win Four (Garland)	.25
45	Sox Starters Win Four (Garcia)	.25
46	Sox Starters Win Four (Contreras)	.25
47	World Series Game 1 (Crede, Jenks)	.25
48	World Series Game 2 (Konerko, Podsednik)	.25
49	World Series Game 3 (Blum)	.25
50	World Series Game 4 (Garcia, Uribe)	.25
51	World Series Game 4 (Garcia, Uribe)	.25
52	Astros Get Swept	.25
53	World Series Games 1, 4 (Podsednik, Dye, Iguchi)	.25
54	ALCS MVP (Konerko)	.25
55	World Series MVP (Dye)	.25
---	Team Composite Box Topper (4-5/8" x 3-1/4")	4.00

2005 Topps Chrome

NM/M
Complete Set (472):
Common Player: .25
Common Rookie Auto.
(221-252): 10.00
Inserted 1:20
Hobby Pack (4): 3.00
Hobby Box (20): 50.00

1	Alex Rodriguez	2.50
2	Placido Polanco	.25
3	Torii Hunter	.50
4	Lyle Overbay	.25
5	Johnny Damon	.75
6	Johnny Estrada	.25
7	Rich Harden	.25
8	Francisco Rodriguez	.25
9	Jarrod Washburn	.25
10	Sammy Sosa	1.00
11	Randy Wolf	.25
12	Jason Bay	.50
13	Tom Glavine	.25
14	Michael Tucker	.25
15	Brian Giles	.25
16	Chad Tracy	.25
17	Jim Edmonds	.50
18	John Smoltz	.50
19	Roy Halladay	.50
20	Hank Blalock	.75
21	Darin Erstad	.50
22	Todd Walker	.25
23	Mike Hampton	.25
24	Mark Bellhorn	.25
25	Jim Thome	1.00
26	Shingo Takatsu	.25
27	Jody Gerut	.25
28	Vinny Castilla	.25
29	Luis Castillo	.25
30	Ivan Rodriguez	.75
31	Craig Biggio	.50
32	Joe Randa	.25
33	Adrian Beltre	.50
34	Scott Podsednik	.50
35	Cliff Floyd	.25
36	Livan Hernandez	.25
37	Eric Byrnes	.25
38	Jose Acevedo	.25
39	Jack Wilson	.25
40	Gary Sheffield	.75
41	Chan Ho Park	.25
42	Carl Crawford	.25
43	Shawn Estes	.25
44	David Bell	.25
45	Jeff DaVanon	.25
46	Brandon Webb	.50
47	Lance Berkman	.50
48	Melvin Mora	.25
49	David Ortiz	1.00
50	Andruw Jones	.50
51	Chone Figgins	.25
52	Danny Graves	.25
53	Preston Wilson	.25
54	Jeremy Bonderman	.25
55	Carlos Guillen	.25
56	Cesar Izturis	.25
57	Kazuo Matsui	.50
58	Jason Schmidt	.25
59	Jason Marquis	.25
60	Jose Vidro	.25
61	Al Leiter	.40
62	Javier Vazquez	.25
63	Erubiel Durazo	.25
64	Scott Spiezio	.25
65	Scot Shields	.25
66	Edgardo Alfonzo	.25
67	Miguel Tejada	.50
68	Francisco Cordero	.25
69	Brett Myers	.25
70	Curt Schilling	1.00
71	Matt Kata	.25
72	Bartolo Colon	.25
73	Rodrigo Lopez	.25
74	Tim Wakefield	.25
75	Frank Thomas	.75
76	Jimmy Rollins	.25
77	Barry Zito	.50

#	Player	Price
78	Hideo Nomo	.50
79	Brad Wilkerson	.25
80	Adam Dunn	.75
81	Derrek Lee	.50
82	Joe Crede	.25
83	Nate Robertson	.25
84	John Thomson	.25
85	Mike Sweeney	.25
86	Kip Wells	.25
87	Eric Gagne	.50
88	David Wells	.25
89	Alex Sanchez	.25
90	Bret Boone	.25
91	Mark Loretta	.25
92	Miguel Cabrera	1.00
93	Randy Winn	.25
94	Adam Everett	.25
95	Aubrey Huff	.25
96	Kevin Mench	.25
97	Frank Catalanotto	.25
98	Flash Gordon	.25
99	Scott Hatteberg	.25
100	Albert Pujols	3.00
101	Jose Molina	.25
	Bengie Molina	.25
102	Jason Johnson	.25
103	Jay Gibbons	.25
104	Byung-Hyun Kim	.25
105	Joe Borowski	.25
106	Mark Grudzielanek	.25
107	Mark Buehrle	.25
108	Paul Wilson	.25
109	Ronnie Belliard	.25
110	Reggie Sanders	.25
111	Tim Redding	.25
112	Brian Lawrence	.25
113	Travis Hafner	.40
114	Jose Hernandez	.25
115	Ben Sheets	.50
116	Johan Santana	.75
117	Billy Wagner	.40
118	Mariano Rivera	.50
119	Steve Trachsel	.25
120	Akinori Otsuka	.25
121	Jose Valentin	.25
122	Orlando Hernandez	.25
123	Raul Ibanez	.25
124	Mike Matheny	.25
125	Vernon Wells	.25
126	Jason Isringhausen	.25
127	Jose Guillen	.25
128	Danny Bautista	.25
129	Marcus Giles	.25
130	Javy Lopez	.40
131	Kevin Millar	.25
132	Kyle Farnsworth	.25
133	Carl Pavano	.25
134	Rafael Furcal	.25
135	Casey Blake	.25
136	Matt Holliday	.25
137	Bobby Higginson	.25
138	Adam Kennedy	.25
139	Alex Gonzalez	.25
140	Jeff Kent	.40
141	Aaron Guiel	.25
142	Shawn Green	.40
143	Bill Hall	.25
144	Shannon Stewart	.25
145	Juan Rivera	.25
146	Coco Crisp	.25
147	Mike Mussina	.50
148	Eric Chavez	.50
149	Jon Lieber	.25
150	Vladimir Guerrero	1.00
151	Alex Cintron	.25
152	Luis Matos	.25
153	Sidney Ponson	.25
154	Trot Nixon	.25
155	Greg Maddux	2.00
156	Edgar Renteria	.50
157	Ryan Freel	.25
158	Matt Lawton	.25
159	Mark Prior	1.00
160	Josh Beckett	.25
161	Ken Harvey	.25
162	Angel Berroa	.25
163	Juan Encarnacion	.25
164	Wes Helms	.25
165	Brad Radke	.25
166	Phil Nevin	.25
167	Mike Cameron	.25
168	Billy Koch	.25
169	Bobby Crosby	.50
170	Mike Lieberthal	.25
171	Robert Mackowiak	.25
172	Sean Burroughs	.25
173	J.T. Snow Jr.	.25
174	Paul Konerko	.40
175	Luis Gonzalez	.25
176	John Lackey	.25
177	Oliver Perez	.25
178	Brian Roberts	.25
179	Bill Mueller	.25
180	Carlos Lee	.25
181	Corey Patterson	.50
182	Sean Casey	.40
183	Cliff Lee	.25
184	Jason Jennings	.25
185	Dmitri Young	.25
186	Juan Uribe	.25
187	Andy Pettitte	.50
188	Juan Gonzalez	.50
189	Orlando Hudson	.25
190	Jason Phillips	.25
191	Braden Looper	.25
192	Lew Ford	.25
193	Mark Mulder	.40
194	Bobby Abreu	.40
195	Jason Kendall	.25
196	Khalil Greene	.50
197	A.J. Pierzynski	.25
198	Tim Worrell	.25
199	So Taguchi	.25
200	Jason Giambi	.50
201	Tony Batista	.25
202	Carlos Zambrano	.50
203	Trevor Hoffman	.25
204	Odalis Perez	.25
205	Jose Cruz Jr.	.25
206	Michael Barrett	.25
207	Chris Carpenter	.25
208	Michael Young	.25
209	Toby Hall	.25
210	Woody Williams	.25
211	Chris Denorfia RC	1.00
212	Darren Fenster RC	1.00
213	Elvys Quezada RC	2.00
214	Ian Kinsler RC	6.00
215	Matt Lindstrom RC	2.00
216	Ryan Goleski RC	2.00
217	Ryan Sweeney RC	1.00
218	Sean Marshall RC	1.00
219	Steven Doetsch RC	2.00
220	Wade Robinson RC	3.00
221	Andre Ethier RC	80.00
222	Brandon Moss RC	25.00
223	Chadd Blasko RC	10.00
224	Chris Roberson RC	10.00
225	Chris Seddon RC	15.00
226	Ian Bladergroen RC	20.00
227	Jake Dittler RC	5.00
228	Jose Vaquedano RC	15.00
229	Jeremy West RC	35.00
230	Kole Strayhorn RC	10.00
231	Kevin West RC	15.00
232	Luis Ramirez RC	10.00
233	Melky Cabrera RC	50.00
234	Nate Schierholtz RC	15.00
235	Billy Butler RC	60.00
236	Brandon Szymanski RC	20.00
237	Chad Orvella RC	25.00
238	Chip Cannon RC	30.00
239	Eric Nielsen RC	15.00
240	Erik Cordier RC	25.00
241	Glen Perkins RC	20.00
242	Justin Verlander RC	60.00
243	Kevin Melillo RC	25.00
244	Landon Powell RC	20.00
245	Matt Campbell RC	35.00
246	Michael Rogers RC	15.00
247	Nate McLouth RC	25.00
248	Scott Mathieson RC	25.00
249	Shane Costa RC	15.00
250	Tony Giarratano RC	25.00
251	Tyler Pelland RC	20.00
252	Wes Swackhamer RC	20.00
253	Garret Anderson	.50
254	Randy Johnson	1.00
255	Charles Thomas	.25
256	Rafael Palmeiro	.75
257	Kevin Youkilis	.25
258	Freddy Garcia	.25
259	Magglio Ordonez	.25
260	Aaron Harang	.25
261	Grady Sizemore	.50
262	Chin-Hui Tsao	.25
263	Eric Munson	.25
264	Juan Pierre	.25
265	Brad Lidge	.25
266	Brian Anderson	.25
267	Todd Helton	.75
268	Chad Cordero	.25
269	Kris Benson	.25
270	Brad Halsey	.25
271	Jermaine Dye	.25
272	Manny Ramirez	1.00
273	Adam Eaton	.25
274	Brett Tomko	.25
275	Bucky Jacobsen	.25
276	Dontrelle Willis	.50
277	B.J. Upton	.25
278	Rocco Baldelli	.25
279	Ryan Drese	.25
280	Ichiro Suzuki	2.50
281	Brandon Lyon	.25
282	Nick Green	.25
283	Jerry Hairston	.25
284	Mike Lowell	.25
285	Kerry Wood	1.00
286	Omar Vizquel	.25
287	Carlos Beltran	.50
288	Carlos Pena	.25
289	Jeff Weaver	.25
290	Chad Moeller	.25
291	Joe Mays	.25
292	Terrmel Sledge	.25
293	Richard Hidalgo	.25
294	Justin Duchscherer	.25
295	Eric Milton	.25
296	Ramon Hernandez	.25
297	Jose Reyes	.50
298	Joel Pineiro	.25
299	Matt Morris	.25
300	John Halama	.25
301	Gary Matthews	.25
302	Ryan Madson	.25
303	Mark Kotsay	.25
304	Carlos Delgado	.50
305	Casey Kotchman	.25
306	Greg Aquino	.25
307	LaTroy Hawkins	.25
308	Jose Contreras	.25
309	Ken Griffey Jr.	2.00
310	C.C. Sabathia	.25
311	Brandon Inge	.25
312	John Buck	.25
313	Hee Seop Choi	.25
314	Chris Capuano	.25
315	Jesse Crain	.25
316	Geoff Jenkins	.25
317	Mike Piazza	2.00
318	Jorge Posada	.50
319	Nick Swisher	.25
320	Kevin Millwood	.25
321	Mike Gonzalez	.25
322	Jake Peavy	.25
323	Dustin Hermanson	.25
324	Jeremy Reed	.25
325	Alfonso Soriano	1.00
326	Alexis Rios	.25
327	David Eckstein	.25
328	Shea Hillenbrand	.25
329	Russ Ortiz	.25
330	Kurt Ainsworth	.25
331	Orlando Cabrera	.25
332	Carlos Silva	.25
333	Ross Gload	.25
334	Josh Phelps	.25
335	Mike Maroth	.25
336	Guillermo Mota	.25
337	Chris Burke	.25
338	David DeJesus	.25
339	Jose Lima	.25
340	Cristian Guzman	.25
341	Nick Johnson	.25
342	Victor Zambrano	.25
343	Rod Barajas	.25
344	Damian Miller	.25
345	Chase Utley	.50
346	Sean Burnett	.25
347	David Wells	.25
348	Dustan Mohr	.25
349	Bobby Madritsch	.25
350	Reed Johnson	.25
351	R.A. Dickey	.25
352	Scott Kazmir	.25
353	Tony Womack	.25
354	Thomas Perez	.25
355	Esteban Loaiza	.25
356	Tomokazu Ohka	.25
357	Ramon Ortiz	.25
358	Richie Sexson	.40
359	J.D. Drew	.40
360	Barry Bonds	4.00
361	Aramis Ramirez	.50
362	Wily Mo Pena	.25
363	Jeromy Burnitz	.25
364	Nomar Garciaparra	2.00
365	Brandon Backe	.25
366	Derek Lowe	.25
367	Doug Davis	.25
368	Joe Mauer	.75
369	Endy Chavez	.25
370	Bernie Williams	.50
371	Jason Michaels	.25
372	Craig Wilson	.25
373	Ryan Klesko	.25
374	Ray Durham	.25
375	Jose Lopez	.25
376	Jeff Suppan	.25
377	David Bush	.25
378	Marlon Byrd	.25
379	Roy Oswalt	.40
380	Rondell White	.25
381	Troy Glaus	.50
382	Scott Hairston	.25
383	Chipper Jones	1.00
384	Daniel Cabrera	.25
385	Jon Garland	.25
386	Austin Kearns	.25
387	Jake Westbrook	.25
388	Aaron Miles	.25
389	Omar Infante	.25
390	Paul LoDuca	.25
391	Morgan Ensberg	.25
392	Tony Graffanino	.25
393	Milton Bradley	.25
394	Keith Ginter	.25
395	Justin Morneau	.75
396	Tony Armas Jr.	.25
397	Kevin Brown	.25
398	Marco Scutaro	.25
399	Tim Hudson	.50
400	Pat Burrell	.40
401	Jeff Cirillo	.25
402	Larry Walker	.50
403	Dewon Brazelton	.25
404	Shigetoshi Hasegawa	.25
405	Octavio Dotel	.25
406	Michael Cuddyer	.25
407	Junior Spivey	.25
408	Zack Greinke	.25
409	Roger Clemens	3.00
410	Chris Shelton	.25
411	Ugueth Urbina	.25
412	Rafael Betancourt	.25
413	Willie Harris	.25
414	Keith Foulke	.25
415	Larry Bigbie	.25
416	Paul Byrd	.25
417	Troy Percival	.25
418	Pedro J. Martinez	1.00
419	Matt Clement	.25
420	Ryan Wagner	.25
421	Jeff Francis	.25
422	Jeff Conine	.25
423	Wade Miller	.25
424	Gavin Floyd	.25
425	Kazuhisa Ishii	.25
426	Victor Santos	.25
427	Jacque Jones	.25
428	Hideki Matsui	2.00
429	Cory Lidle	.25
430	Jose Castillo	.25
431	Alex Gonzalez	.25
432	Kirk Rueter	.25
433	Jolbert Cabrera	.25
434	Erik Bedard	.25
435	Ricky Ledee	.25
436	Mark Hendrickson	.25
437	Laynce Nix	.25
438	Jason Frasor	.25
439	Kevin Gregg	.25
440	Derek Jeter	3.00
441	Jaret Wright	.25
442	Edwin Jackson	.25
443	Moises Alou	.50
444	Aaron Rowand	.25
445	Kazuhito Tadano	.25
446	Luis Gonzalez	.40
447	A.J. Burnett	.40
448	Jeff Bagwell	.50
449	Brad Penny	.25
450	Corey Koskie	.25
451	Mark Ellis	.25
452	Hector Luna	.25
453	Miguel Olivo	.25
454	Scott Rolen	1.00
455	Ricardo Rodriguez	.25
456	Eric Hinske	.25
457	Tim Salmon	.25
458	Adam LaRoche	.25
459	B.J. Ryan	.25
460	Steve Finley	.25
461	Joe Nathan	.25
462	Vicente Padilla	.25
463	Yadier Molina	.25
464	Tino Martinez	.25
465	Mark Teixeira	.50
466	Kelvim Escobar	.25
467	Pedro Feliz	.25
468	Ryan Garko RC	4.00
469	Bobby Livingston RC	2.00
470	Yorman Bazardo RC	2.00
471	Michael Bourn RC	2.00
472	Andy LaRoche RC	10.00

Refractor

Cards (1-220): 2-3X
Inserted 1:6
Rookie Auto. (221-234): 1-1.5X
Production 500

Black Refractor

Cards (1-220): 3-5X
Production 225
Rookie Auto. (221-234): 1.5-3X
Production 200

Gold Refractor

No Pricing
Production One Set

X-Fractor

Cards (1-220): 5-10X
Rookie Auto.
(221-234): No Pricing
Production 25 Sets

Printing Plates

No Pricing
Production one set per color.

A-Rod Throwbacks

	NM/M
Common A-Rod:	3.00
ARI1 Alex Rodriguez	3.00

ARI2 Alex Rodriguez	3.00
ARI3 Alex Rodriguez	3.00
ARI4 Alex Rodriguez	3.00

Chrome The Game Relics

		NM/M
Common Player:		5.00
Inserted 1:Box		
JB	Jeff Bagwell	8.00
WB	Wade Boggs	6.00
TH	Torii Hunter	5.00
MPI	Mike Piazza	8.00
JP	Jorge Posada	6.00
MP	Mark Prior	5.00
AR	Alex Rodriguez	15.00
JS	John Smoltz	8.00
AS	Alfonso Soriano	8.00
SS	Sammy Sosa	5.00
MY	Michael Young	10.00

Chrome The Game Patch Relics

		NM/M
Common Player:		10.00
JB	Jeff Bagwell	15.00
JBE	Josh Beckett	10.00
LB	Lance Berkman	10.00
BB	Bret Boone	10.00
AD1	Adam Dunn	15.00
AD2	Adam Dunn	15.00
TG	Troy Glaus	10.00
TH	Todd Helton	15.00
KI	Kazuhisa Ishii	10.00
CJ	Chipper Jones	20.00
PL	Paul LoDuca	10.00
ML	Mike Lowell	10.00
PM	Pedro Martinez	20.00
HN	Hideo Nomo	10.00
MO	Magglio Ordonez	10.00
MPI	Mike Piazza	20.00
AP	Albert Pujols	25.00
AR	Alex Rodriguez	25.00
CS	C.C. Sabathia	10.00
SS	Sammy Sosa	20.00
MT	Mark Teixeira	15.00
FT	Frank Thomas	15.00
DW	Dontrelle Willis	10.00
KW	Kerry Wood	20.00

Dem Bums Autographs

		NM/M
Inserted 1:1,816		
CE	Carl Erskine	50.00
DS	Duke Snider	85.00

2005 Topps Cracker Jack

	NM/M
Complete Set (240):	
Common Player:	.25
Common SP:	3.00
Inserted 1:3	

		Price
	Pack (8):	4.00
	Box (20):	70.00
1	David Wright/SP	8.00
2	Rafael Furcal	.25
3	Alex Rodriguez/SP	1.50
4	Alex Rodriguez/SP/ Fielding	5.00
4	Victor Martinez/SP	3.00
5	Ken Griffey Jr.	1.50
6	Bobby Crosby/SP	3.00
7	Ivan Rodriguez	.50
8	Darin Erstad	.25
9	Javy Lopez	.25
10	Brian Giles	.25
11	Aaron Rowand/SP	3.00
12	Joe Torre	.25
13	Zack Greinke/SP	3.00
14	Shannon Stewart	.25
15	Jack Wilson	.25
16	Jose Vidro	.25
17	Josh Beckett	.40
---	Josh Beckett (No number.)	4.00
19	Barry Zito	.40
20	Bret Boone	.25
21	Greg Maddux	1.00
22	Carl Crawford/SP	3.00
23	Mark Teixeira	.50
24	Jason Schmidt	.40
25	Kazuhisa Ishii	.25
26	Mike Piazza	1.00
27	Daniel Cabrera/SP	3.00
28	Mike Lieberthal	.25
29	Gil Meche	.25
30	Phil Nevin	.25
31	Adrian Beltre/SP	3.00
32	Chipper Jones/SP	4.00
33	Zach Day	.25
34	Ben Sheets	.40
35	Carlos Zambrano	.25
36	Melvin Mora	.25
37	Joe Mauer	.75
38	Ken Harvey	.25
39	Bernie Williams	.40
40	Mike Maroth	.40
41	Eric Chavez	.25
42	Matt Lawton/SP	3.00
43	Ray Durham	.25
44	Vernon Wells	.25
45	Mike Lowell	.25
46	Jim Thome	.50
47	Joel Pineiro	.25
48	Lance Berkman	.40
49	Ryan Klesko	.25
50	Adam Dunn	.50
51	Vladimir Guerrero	.75
52	Eric Gagne/SP	4.00
53	Richie Sexson	.40
54	Javier Vazquez	.25
55	Roy Oswalt	.40
56	Carlos Delgado	.25
57	John Buck/SP	3.00
58	Kenny Rogers	.25
59	Sidney Ponson	.25
60	Vicente Padilla	.25
60	Mark Prior/SP	4.00
61	Mark Prior/SP/Portrait	4.00
62	A.J. Pierzynski	.25
63	Aubrey Huff	.25
64	Shea Hillenbrand	.25
65	Carlos Guillen	.25
66	Lyle Overbay	.25
67	Al Leiter	.25
68	Eric Hinske	.25
69	Laynce Nix	.25
70	Scott Hairston	.25
71	Roger Clemens	2.00
72	Cesar Izturis/SP	3.00
73	Shawn Green	.25
74	Marcus Giles	.25
75	Rafael Palmeiro	.50
75	Melky Cabrera/SP	3.00
76	Gary Sheffield/SP	4.00
77	Juan Pierre	.25
78	Pat Burrell	.40
79	Sean Burroughs	.25
80	Frank Thomas	.50
81	Andruw Jones	.40
82	C.C. Sabathia	.25
83	Jeff Bagwell	.50
84	Tom Glavine	.25
85	Craig Wilson/SP	3.00
85	Johan Santana	.75
85	Johan Santana/SP/ Portrait	4.00
86	Raul Ibanez	.25
87	Sean Casey	.25
88	Bucky Jacobsen	.25
89	B.J. Upton	.25
90	Bobby Abreu	.40
91	Geoff Jenkins	.25
92	Troy Glaus	.25
93	Dontrelle Willis	.40
94	Jose Lima	.25
95	Rocco Baldelli	.25
96	Aramis Ramirez	.25
97	Paul LoDuca	.25
98	Torii Hunter	.40
99	Jay Payton	.25
100	Carlos Beltran	.50
101	Jaret Wright	.25

Abbreviations

SP - Short Print

102	Jason Bay	.40
103	Cliff Floyd	.25
104	Mike Sweeney	.25
105	Sammy Sosa	1.50
106	Khalil Greene/SP	4.00
107	David DeJesus	.25
108	Jermaine Dye	.25
109	Miguel Cabrera	.75
110	Miguel Tejada/SP	5.00
111	Johnny Estrada/SP	3.00
112	Ronnie Belliard/SP	3.00
113	Austin Kearns	.25
114	Erubiel Durazo	.25
115	Preston Wilson	.25
116	Hideo Nomo	.40
117	Dmitri Young	.25
118	Jon Lieber	.25
119	Derrek Lee	.25
120	Todd Helton	.50
121	Omar Vizquel	.25
122	Wily Mo Pena	.40
123	J.D. Drew	.40
124	Matt Holliday	.25
125	Ichiro Suzuki	1.50
126	Mark Buehrle/SP	3.00
127	Eric Munson	.25
128	Jeff Kent	.25
129	Kerry Wood	.75
130	Mariano Rivera	.50
131	Nick Johnson	.25
132	Randy Winn	.25
133	Phil Garner	.25
134	Jose Reyes	.50
135	Michael Young/SP	3.00
135	Ian Kinsler/SP	5.00
136	Jose Contreras	.25
137	Oliver Perez	.25
138	Roy Halladay	.40
139	Kevin Millwood	.25
140	Jorge Posada	.40
141	Mike Cameron	.25
142	Edgardo Alfonzo	.25
143	Chris Shelton	.25
144	Luis Castillo	.25
145	Alfonso Soriano	.75
146	Ryan Drese/SP	3.00
147	Mark Mulder	.40
148	Jason Giambi	.25
149	Travis Hafner	.25
150	Randy Johnson	.75
151	Paul Konerko/SP	3.00
152	Mike Mussina	.50
153	Brad Wilkerson	.25
154	Tim Hudson	.40
155	Garret Anderson	.25
156	Chase Utley/SP	3.00
157	Jamie Moyer	.25
158	Scott Kazmir	.40
159	Brett Myers	.25
160	Kazuo Matsui	.25
161	Orlando Hudson	.25
162	Luis Gonzalez	.25
163	Kevin Youkilis	.25
164	Jason Kendall/SP	.25
164	Landon Powell/SP	3.00
165	Hank Blalock	.50
166	Mark Loretta/SP	3.00
167	Miguel Cairo	.25
168	Corey Patterson	.25
169	Carlos Zambrano	.25
170	Magglio Ordonez	.25
171	J.T. Snow	.25
172	Randy Wolf	.25
173	Rich Harden	.40
174	Bartolo Colon	.25
175	Derek Jeter	2.00
176	Casey Kotchman/SP	3.00
177	Val Majewski	.25
178	Grady Sizemore	.50
179	Rickie Weeks	.25
180	Robinson Cano	.75
181	Nick Swisher/SP	3.00
182	Ryan Howard	1.50
183	John Van Benschoten	.25
184	Delmon Young	.50
185	Aaron Hill	.25
186	Chris Burke/SP	3.00
187	Merkin Valdez	.25
188	Jeremy Reed	.25
189	Conor Jackson	.25
190	Melky Cabrera	.25
191	Joey Gathright/SP	3.00
192	Gavin Floyd	.25
193	Joe Blanton	.25
194	Jason Kubel	.25
195	Jeff Francis	.25
196	Angel Guzman/SP	3.00
197	Dallas McPherson	.25
198	Melky Cabrera RC	1.50
199	Jake Dittler	.25
200	Elvys Quezada RC	.25
201	Ian Kinsler/SP RC	5.00
202	Nate McLouth RC	.50
203	Chris Seddon RC	.75
204	Chad Orvella RC	.25
205	Ian Bladergroen RC	1.00
206	James Jurries/SP RC	4.00
207	Landon Powell RC	.75
208	Eric Nielsen RC	.50
209	Chris Roberson RC	.50
210	Andre Ethier RC	2.00
211	Chris Denorfia/SP RC	4.00
212	Darren Fenster RC	.50
213	Jeremy West RC	1.00
214	Sean Marshall RC	.50
215	Ryan Sweeney RC	.25
216	Steven Doetsch/SP RC	3.00
217	Kevin Melillo RC	.50

218	Chip Cannon RC	1.00
219	Tony LaRussa	.25
220	Chris Carpenter	.25
221	Edgar Renteria/SP/Red Sox	3.00
221	Edgar Renteria/SP/Cardinals	3.00
222	Albert Pujols	2.00
223	Jim Edmonds	.40
224	Jason Marquis	.25
225	Scott Rolen/SP	4.00
226	Larry Walker/SP	4.00
227	Matt Morris	.25
228	Mike Matheny	3.00
228	Mike Matheny/SP/Cardinals	3.00
229	Jeromy Burnitz	.25
230	Terry Francona	.25
231	Johnny Damon/SP	4.00
232	Keith Foulke	.25
233	Trot Nixon	.25
234	Manny Ramirez	.75
235	David Ortiz/SP	.25
236	Pedro Martinez/SP/Mets	4.00
236	Pedro J. Martinez/SP/Red Sox	4.00
237	Curt Schilling	.75
238	Kevin Millar	.25
239	Bill Mueller	.25
240	Mark Bellhorn	.25
	Josh Beckett/SP	3.00

Mini Blue
Stars:	8-15X
SP's:	4-6X

Production 50 Sets

Mini Grey
No Pricing
Production 25 Sets

Mini Red
Stars:	1-2X
Inserted 1:1	
SP's:	.75-1.5X
Inserted 1:20	

Mini Stickers
Stars:	1-2X
Inserted 1:1	
SP's:	.75-1.5X
Inserted 1:20	

Mini White
No Pricing
Production One Set

Autographs
NM/M
Production 50 Sets
Bonds Production 25
CB	Carlos Beltran	80.00
EG	Eric Gagne	40.00
AR	Alex Rodriguez	250.00
JS	Johan Santana	60.00

Secret Surprise Autographs
NM/M
GA	Garret Anderson	20.00
EC	Eric Chavez	20.00
EG	Eric Gagne	30.00
AG	Angel Guzman	8.00
SK	Scott Kazmir	25.00
MK	Mark Kotsay/100	15.00
ML	Mark Loretta/100	30.00
DM	Dallas McPherson/100	35.00
KM	Kevin Millar	20.00
MM	Melvin Mora	15.00
CN	Chris Nelson	12.00
RR	Richie Robnett	12.00
CS	C.C. Sabathia	15.00
JS	Johan Santana	50.00
CT	Curtis Thigpen	20.00
CW	Craig Wilson	12.00
DW	David Wright	50.00

Take Me Out To/Ballgame Relics

Inserted 1:16
JB	Jeff Bagwell	6.00
RB	Ronnie Belliard	4.00
CB	Carlos Beltran	8.00
AB	Adrian Beltre	6.00
LB1	Lance Berkman	6.00
LB2	Lance Berkman	4.00
AB1	Angel Berroa	4.00
AB2	Angel Berroa	4.00
CBI	Craig Biggio	6.00

HB1	Hank Blalock	8.00
HB2	Hank Blalock	8.00
HB3	Hank Blalock	8.00
SB	Sean Burroughs	4.00
MC	Miguel Cabrera	8.00
VC	Vinny Castilla	4.00
EC1	Eric Chavez	6.00
EC2	Eric Chavez	6.00
BC	Bobby Cox	6.00
CC	Coco Crisp	4.00
BCR	Bobby Crosby	4.00
AD	Adam Dunn	8.00
JE1	Jim Edmonds	6.00
JE2	Jim Edmonds	6.00
DE	Darin Erstad	4.00
JE	Johnny Estrada	4.00
RF	Rafael Furcal	4.00
JG	Jody Gerut	4.00
JGI	Jay Gibbons	4.00
MG	Marcus Giles	4.00
TG	Troy Glaus	4.00
LG	Luis Gonzalez	4.00
NG	Nick Green	4.00
SG	Shawn Green	4.00
VG	Vladimir Guerrero	10.00
JGU	Jose Guillen	6.00
CG	Cristian Guzman	4.00
TH	Todd Helton	8.00
THU	Torii Hunter	6.00
JJ	Jacque Jones	4.00
JK	Jason Kendall	4.00
BK	Bobby Kielty	4.00
RK	Ryan Klesko	4.00
PK	Paul Konerko	4.00
MK	Mark Kotsay	4.00
AL	Adam LaRoche	4.00
VM	Victor Martinez	6.00
KME	Kevin Mench	4.00
DM	Doug Mientkiewicz	4.00
KM	Kevin Millar	10.00
MM	Melvin Mora	4.00
PN	Phil Nevin	4.00
LN	Laynce Nix	4.00
MO	Magglio Ordonez	4.00
DO	David Ortiz	10.00
RP	Rafael Palmeiro	6.00
CP	Corey Patterson	4.00
MP	Mike Piazza	12.00
JP1	Jorge Posada	8.00
JP2	Jorge Posada	8.00
AP	Albert Pujols	20.00
MR	Manny Ramirez	10.00
JR	Jeremy Reed	4.00
MRE	Mike Restovich	4.00
AR	Alex Rodriguez	15.00
ARA	Aramis Ramirez	6.00
IR1	Ivan Rodriguez	8.00
IR2	Ivan Rodriguez	8.00
RS	Reggie Sanders	4.00
BS	Benito Santiago	4.00
GS	Gary Sheffield	8.00
AS	Alfonso Soriano	8.00
MT1	Mark Teixeira	8.00
MT2	Mark Teixeira	8.00
MT3	Mark Teixeira	8.00
MTE1	Miguel Tejada	8.00
MTE2	Miguel Tejada	8.00
CT	Charles Thomas	4.00
JT	Jim Thome	8.00
JTO	Joe Torre	10.00
OV	Omar Vizquel	6.00
BW	Bernie Williams	8.00
DW	Dontrelle Willis	8.00
MY	Michael Young	4.00

1,2,3 Strikes You're Out Relics
NM/M
Inserted 1:204
JB	Josh Beckett	8.00
RD	Ryan Drese	5.00
RO	Russ Ortiz	5.00
BR	Brad Radke	8.00
CS	Curt Schilling	15.00
JW	Jaret Wright	8.00

Alex Rodrguez Promos

Complete Set (3):	12.00
Common Card:	4.00
1 of 100:	2X
1 of 50:	3X
AR1 Alex Rodriguez/Follow-through	4.00
AR2 Alex Rodriguez/Throwing	4.00
AR3 Alex Rodriguez/Btg	4.00

2005 Topps eTopps

Topps continued its on-line card program for a fifth year in 2005. Initial Player Offerings (about $5-7 per card) were again made for one week, with allocations having to be made for some cards in high demand. The number of each card actually sold is shown parenthetically. After the IPO, cards could be bought and sold within portfolios, or physically delivered for a fee. The 2-1/2" x 3-1/2" cards' fronts have an action photo at top and a portrait photo below. Backs repeat the portrait photo, have a 2004 recap and 2005 "prospectus," and a few biographical bits and stats. A total of 111 cards was issued, skip-numbered between 1-220. Values shown are for cards in a virtual portfolio, rather than "in hand."

NM/M
Complete Set (111):		325.00
Common Player:		1.50
1	Los Angeles Angels of Anaheim/1,018	1.50
2	Arizona Diamondbacks/1,000	1.50
3	Atlanta Braves/1,275	2.00
4	Baltimore Orioles/1,189	1.50
5	Boston Red Sox/2,538	1.50
6	Chicago Cubs/1,300	1.50
7	Chicago White Sox/1,199	2.75
8	Cincinnati Reds/770	1.50
9	Cleveland Indians/974	1.50
10	Colorado Rockies/736	1.50
11	Detroit Tigers/832	1.50
12	Florida Marlins/863	1.50
13	Houston Astros/1,227	2.00
14	Kansas City Royals/807	1.50
15	Los Angeles Dodgers/1,000	1.50
16	Milwaukee Brewers/728	1.50
17	Minnesota Twins/888	1.50
18	New York Mets/1,300	1.50
19	New York Yankees/2,600	1.75
20	Oakland Athletics/739	1.75
21	Philadelphia Phillies/890	1.50
22	Pittsburgh Pirates/776	2.00
23	San Diego Padres/818	1.50
24	San Francisco Giants/1,051	2.50
25	Seattle Mariners/800	1.50
26	St. Louis Cardinals/1,300	2.00
27	Tampa Bay Devil Rays/688	1.75
28	Texas Rangers/705	1.50
29	Toronto Blue Jays/701	1.50
30	Washington Nationals/1,300	2.00
31	Adrian Beltre/1,298	1.75
33	Albert Pujols/2,600	5.50
34	Alex Rodriguez/2,259	4.00
35	Alexis Rios/1,158	1.50
36	Alfonso Soriano/793	1.50
40	Carlos Beltran/1,630	1.75
42	Carl Crawford/820	3.00
43	Carlos Guillen/920	2.00
44	Chipper Jones/927	3.25
45	Carl Pavano/826	2.00
46	Curt Schilling/1,288	1.50
47	Derek Jeter/2,000	3.50
48	David Ortiz/981	3.50
49	David Wright/2,956	8.00
50	David Wells/851	5.00
51	Eric Gagne/688	1.50
53	Gary Sheffield/857	3.25
54	Hank Blalock/814	3.75
55	Hideki Matsui/1,200	2.00
56	Ichiro Suzuki/2,223	2.00
57	Ivan Rodriguez/773	4.25
61	Johan Santana/2,600	7.25
63	Jim Thome/750	6.50
64	Ken Griffey Jr./1,200	3.50
67	Kerry Wood/756	2.00
68	Livan Hernandez/1,200	1.50
69	Miguel Cabrera/1,200	4.00
71	Mark Prior/1,337	1.75
72	Mike Piazza/1,057	2.50
73	Manny Ramirez/1,200	2.00
74	Miguel Tejada/944	2.75
75	Mark Teixeira/1,037	4.00
79	Pedro Martinez/1,163	1.75
80	Roger Clemens/1,667	3.00
82	Randy Johnson/2,196	1.75
86	Sammy Sosa/1,200	1.50
89	Todd Helton/785	3.50
91	Vladimir Guerrero/1,036	2.50
95	Dallas McPherson/2,350	2.25
99	Andy Marte/2,000	5.25
115	Grady Sizemore/1,200	4.00
133	David DeJesus/680	9.00
148	J.J. Hardy/1,523	2.50
149	Justin Morneau/1,664	3.75
152	Chien-Ming Wang/1,200	4.00
153	Dioner Navarro/939	3.25
156	Gavin Floyd/1,485	2.00
165	David Aardsma/889	2.00
167	B.J. Upton/1,910	3.00
174	Scott Kazmir/1,760	4.25
175	Adrian Gonzalez/938	6.25
181	Brendan Harris/977	2.00
185	Tim Hudson/859	2.25
186	Mark Mulder/860	2.50
188	Jeff Bagwell/823	2.75
189	Troy Glaus/824	2.75
191	Jim Edmonds/874	4.00
193	Johnny Damon/1,415	2.00
195	Billy Wagner/939	2.25
196	Dmitri Young/778	2.75
198	David Eckstein/874	5.00
199	Tadahito Iguchi/1,200	2.50
202	Jason Bartlett/913	2.50
202	Joe Blanton/1,097	2.75
203	Huston Street/1,200	7.75
204	Clint Barmes/2,000	3.25
207	Brian Roberts/1,200	2.25
208	John Garland/1,200	2.25
209	Robinson Cano/1,200	11.00
210	Zach Duke/2,000	6.75
211a	Rickie Weeks/1,675	4.50
211b	Brad Eldred/849	5.00
212a	Jeff Francoeur/2,000	9.50
212b	Felix Hernandez/2,000	12.75
213	Jonathan Papelbon/1,500	9.00
214	Conor Jackson/1,278	3.25
215	Dan Johnson/1,000	3.25
216	Prince Fielder/2,000	9.25
217	Jeremy Hermida/1,400	4.00
219	Melky Cabrera/1,000	3.50
220	Ryan Howard/2,000	6.00

Classics

Topps continued its eTopps Classics line-up in 2005 with five cards of former greats. Numbering and format were contiguous with earlier issues. Like regular eTopps cards, Classics could only be ordered during a one-week Initial Player Offering period. Cards were issued in a quantity of up to 2,000 each at $9.50. The number of cards actually sold is shown parenthetically. Fronts have a color photo, backs have a picture of one of that player's Topps cards, along with career notes, stats, etc. Values shown are for cards in a virtual portfolio, rather than "in hand."

NM/M
Complete Set (5):		45.00
Common Player:		6.00
61	Roger Maris/2,000	9.00
62	Ryne Sandberg/1,000	9.00
63	Don Mattingly/1,000	15.00
64	Ernie Banks/1,657	6.00
65	Mark Fidrych/976	6.00

Classic Events

Great moments of late 20th Century baseball history are captured in this series. Each card has a front photo depicting the event, with a write-up on back. Cards were issued in quantities of up to nearly 1,200 each (actual number issued is shown parenthetically) at an issue price of $9.50. Values shown are for cards in "virtual portfolios" rather than "in hand."

NM/M
Complete Set (20):		145.00
Common Player:		4.00
1	Bobby Thomson/819	5.00
2	Don Larsen/713	4.50
3	Bill Mazeroski/731	7.00
4	Bucky Dent/713	5.50
5	George Brett/1,000	6.75
6	Dwight Gooden/555	11.50
7	Bob Gibson/728	7.25
8	1989 World Series/1,000	4.00
9	Kirk Gibson/714	10.00
10	Reggie Jackson/979	10.00
11	Carlton Fisk/861	5.00
12	Mookie Wilson/577	9.00
13	Yogi Berra/1,000	4.00
14	Cal Ripken Jr./1,000	16.00
15	Denny McLain/576	12.50
16	Josh Gibson/728	5.75
17	Barry Bonds/1,000	16.50
18	Joe Carter/557	7.75
19	Nolan Ryan/1,000	7.75
20	Rickey Henderson/748	8.50

Events Series

Values shown are for cards in a virtual portfolio rather than "in hand." Each card originally sold for $4.50. Quantity actually issued is shown parenthetically.

NM/M
Complete Set (21):		50.00
Common Card:		1.50
1	NL Transactions/862	1.50
2	AL Transactions/977	1.50
3	Opening Day Hideki Matsui, Randy Johnson/1,000	1.50
4	David Ortiz/1,000	3.00
5	Lucky #7 David Wright/1,000	2.50
6	Alex Rodriguez/1,000	5.50
7	Derek Lee/1,000	1.00
8	Alex Rodriguez/1,000	6.50
9	Nationals Win 10 Nick Johnson, Livan Hernandez/678	3.50
10	Bob Abreu/800	2.00
11	Miguel Tejada/642	2.00
12	Rafael Palmeiro/1,000	1.50
13	Greg Maddux/1,000	6.00
14	Houston Astros Andy Pettitte, Roger Clemens/650	2.75
15	Tony LaRussa/550	4.00
16	Jeremy Hermida/760	2.50
17	Houston Marathon Chris Burke, Roger Clemens/1,000	1.75

18 Complete Series
Jose Contreras,
Mark Buehrle/840 1.50
19 Houston Astros/579 3.00
20 Chicago White Sox/
1,000 2.50
21 Jermaine Dye/746 2.00

2005 Topps Gallery

	NM/M
Complete Set (195):	175.00
Common Player:	.25
Common SP (151-195):	1.00
Inserted 1:1	
Variations 1:40	
Pack (5):	6.00
Box (20):	100.00

1 Alex Rodriguez 2.50
1 Alex Rodriguez/SP/
Black Bat Glove 8.00
2 Eric Chavez .50
3 Mike Piazza 1.50
4 Bret Boone .25
5 Albert Pujols 3.00
6 Vernon Wells .25
7 Andruw Jones .50
8 Miguel Tejada .50
9 Johnny Damon .75
10 Nomar Garciaparra 2.00
11 Pat Burrell .40
12 Bartolo Colon .25
13 Johnny Estrada .25
14 Luis Gonzalez .40
15 Jay Gibbons .25
16 Curt Schilling 1.00
17 Aramis Ramirez .50
18 Frank Thomas .75
19 Adam Dunn .75
20 Sammy Sosa 2.00
21 Matt Lawton .25
22 Preston Wilson .25
23 Carlos Pena .25
24 Josh Beckett .50
25 Carlos Beltran .75
26 Juan Gonzalez .50
27 Adrian Beltre .50
28 Lyle Overbay .25
29 Justin Morneau .50
30 Derek Jeter 3.00
31 Barry Zito .40
32 Bobby Abreu .50
33 Jason Bay .25
34 Jose Reyes .50
35 Nick Johnson .25
36 Lew Ford .25
37 Scott Podsednik .25
38 Rocco Baldelli .40
39 Eric Hinske .25
40 Ichiro Suzuki 2.50
40 Ichiro Suzuki/SP/
Writing On Wall 8.00
41 Larry Walker .50
42 Mark Teixeira .50
43 Khalil Greene .50
44 Edgardo Alfonzo .25
45 Javier Vazquez .25
46 Cliff Floyd .25
47 Geoff Jenkins .25
48 Ken Griffey Jr. 2.00
49 Vinny Castilla .25
50 Mark Prior 1.00
51 Jose Guillen .25
52 J.D. Drew .50
53 Rafael Palmeiro .75
54 Kevin Youkilis .25
55 Derrek Lee .50
56 Freddy Garcia .25
57 Wily Mo Pena .25
58 C.C. Sabathia .25
59 Craig Biggio .40
60 Ivan Rodriguez .75
61 Angel Berroa .25
62 Ben Sheets .50
63 Johan Santana .75
64 Al Leiter .40
65 Bernie Williams .50
66 Bobby Crosby .50
67 Jack Wilson .25
68 A.J. Pierzynski .25
69 Jimmy Rollins .50
70 Jason Giambi .50
71 Tom Glavine .50
72 Kevin Brown .25
73 B.J. Upton .50
74 Edgar Renteria .25
75 Alfonso Soriano 1.00

76 Mike Lieberthal .25
77 Kazuo Matsui .25
78 Phil Nevin .25
79 Shawn Green .40
80 Miguel Cabrera 1.00
81 Todd Helton .75
82 Magglio Ordonez .40
83 Manny Ramirez 1.00
84 Bill Mueller .25
85 Troy Glaus .50
86 Richie Sexson .50
87 Javy Lopez .40
88 David Ortiz 1.00
89 Greg Maddux 1.50
90 Vladimir Guerrero 1.00
91 Jeromy Burnitz .25
92 Jeff Kent .40
93 Travis Hafner .40
94 Mark Buehrle .25
95 Paul LoDuca .25
96 Roy Oswalt .40
97 Torii Hunter .40
98 Gary Sheffield .75
99 Erubiel Durazo .25
100 Jim Thome 1.00
100 Jim Thome/SP/
Kid's Shirt Is Red 6.00
101 Ken Harvey .25
102 Shannon Stewart .25
103 Dmitri Young .25
104 Kevin Millar .25
105 Kerry Wood 1.00
106 Paul Konerko .40
107 Ronnie Belliard .40
108 Mike Lowell .40
109 Hee Seop Choi .25
110 Joe Mauer .50
111 David Wright .50
112 Jorge Posada .50
113 Tim Hudson .50
114 Brian Giles .25
115 Jason Schmidt .50
116 Aubrey Huff .25
117 Hank Blalock .75
118 Jim Edmonds .50
119 Raul Ibanez .25
120 Carlos Delgado .50
121 Craig Wilson .40
122 Ryan Klesko .25
123 Mark Mulder .25
124 Jose Vidro .25
125 Mike Sweeney .25
126 Lance Berkman .50
127 Juan Pierre .25
128 Austin Kearns .25
129 Moises Alou .25
130 Garret Anderson .50
131 Pedro J. Martinez 1.00
132 Melvin Mora .25
133 Marcus Giles .25
134 Corey Patterson .50
135 Carlos Lee .40
136 Sean Casey .40
137 Jody Gerut .25
138 Jose Valentin .25
139 Aaron Miles .25
140 Randy Johnson 1.00
141 Carlos Guillen .25
142 Dontrelle Willis .50
143 Jeff Bagwell .75
144 Jason Kendall .25
145 Mark Loretta .25
146 Scott Rolen 1.00
147 Carl Crawford .25
148 Michael Young .25
149 Jermaine Dye .25
150 Chipper Jones .50
151 Melky Cabrera RC 3.00
152 Chris Seddon RC 4.00
153 Nate Schierholtz 4.00
154 Ian Kinsler RC 5.00
154 Ian Kinsler/SP/
Gold Background 15.00
155 Brandon Moss RC 4.00
155 Brandon Moss/SP/
Red Hat 10.00
156 Chadd Blasko RC 2.00
157 Jeremy West RC 2.00
157 Jeremy West/SP/
Navy Blue Jersey 6.00
158 Sean Marshall RC 2.00
159 Ryan Sweeney 4.00
160 Matt Lindstrom RC 2.00
161 Ryan Goleski RC 4.00
162 Brett Harper RC 2.00
163 Chris Roberson RC 3.00
164 Andre Ethier 8.00
165 Ian Bladergroen RC 2.00
165 Ian Bladergroen/SP/
Swinging 6.00
166 James Jurries RC 2.00
167 Billy Butler RC 6.00
167 Billy Butler/SP/
Black Jersey 15.00
168 Michael Rogers RC 3.00
168 Michael Rogers/SP/
Baseball In Hand 8.00
169 Tyler Clippard RC 15.00
170 Luis Ramirez RC 3.00
171 Casey Kotchman 2.00
172 Chris Burke 2.00
173 Dallas McPherson 1.00
174 Edwin Jackson 1.00
175 Felix Hernandez 4.00
176 Gavin Floyd 1.00
177 Guillermo Quiroz 1.00
178 Jason Kubel 1.00
179 Jeff Mathis 1.00

180 Rickie Weeks 1.00
181 Ryan Howard 3.00
182 Franklin Gutierrez 1.00
183 Jeremy Reed 5.00
184 Carlos Quentin 5.00
185 Jeff Francis 5.00
186 Nolan Ryan 6.00
187 Hank Aaron 4.00
187 Hank Aaron/SP/
Red 755 15.00
188 Duke Snider 4.00
189 Mike Schmidt 5.00
190 Ernie Banks 5.00
191 Frank Robinson 3.00
192 Harmon Killebrew 3.00
193 Al Kaline 3.00
194 Rod Carew 3.00
195 Johnny Bench 4.00

Artist's Proof

JP Jim Palmer 2.00
AP Albert Pujols 8.00
BR Brooks Robinson 3.00
FR Frank Robinson 2.00
RR Frank Robinson,
Brooks Robinson 3.00
RJ Alex Rodriguez,
Derek Jeter 8.00
IR Ivan Rodriguez 8.00
NR Nolan Ryan 8.00
CS Curt Schilling 5.00
MS Mike Schmidt 5.00
TS Jim Thome,
Mike Schmidt 5.00
OS Ozzie Smith 3.00
DSN Duke Snider 3.00
DS Darryl Strawberry 2.00
DW Dontrelle Willis 2.00

Stars (1-150): 2-4X
SP's (151-195): 1-2X
Inserted 1:1

Murray Olderman Sketches
No Pricing
Production One Set

Printing Plates
No Pricing
Production one for each color.

Gallo's Gallery Sketches

HANK BLALOCK • TEXAS RANGERS

	NM/M
Complete Set (20):	50.00
Common Player:	1.50
Inserted 1:15	

HA Hank Aaron 6.00
HB Hank Blalock 1.50
NG Nomar Garciaparra 4.00
VG Vladimir Guerrero 4.00
TH Todd Helton 1.50
DJ Derek Jeter 6.00
RJ Randy Johnson 2.00
CJ Chipper Jones 2.00
MPI Mike Piazza 4.00
MP Mark Prior 2.00
AP Albert Pujols 6.00
AR Alex Rodriguez 5.00
IR Ivan Rodriguez 1.50
NR Nolan Ryan 6.00
MS Mike Schmidt 5.00
AS Alfonso Soriano 2.00
SS Sammy Sosa 4.00
IS Ichiro Suzuki 4.00
MT Miguel Tejada 1.50
JT Jim Thome 2.00

Heritage Insert

	NM/M
Complete Set (25):	65.00
Common Player:	2.00
Inserted 1:15	

EB Ernie Banks 4.00
CB Carlos Beltran 3.00
JB Johnny Bench 4.00
HB Hank Blalock 2.00
GB George Brett 6.00
JC Jose Canseco 2.00
BG Bob Gibson 3.00
AK Al Kaline 3.00
DM Don Mattingly 6.00
RP Rafael Palmeiro 3.00

JOHNNY BENCH Catcher — REDS

IR Ivan Rodriguez 8.00
AS Alfonso Soriano 8.00
SS Sammy Sosa 10.00
MT Mark Teixeira 4.00
MTE Miguel Tejada 6.00
FT Frank Thomas 6.00
BU B.J. Upton 4.00
BW Bernie Williams 6.00
DW Dontrelle Willis 4.00
KW Kerry Wood 8.00
MY Michael Young 4.00

Penmanship Autographs

	NM/M
Common Autograph:	10.00

JB Jason Bartlett 10.00
TB Taylor Buchholz 10.00
EC Eric Chavez 15.00
FH Felix Hernandez 30.00
AH Aubrey Huff 15.00
JJ Justin Jones 15.00
DM Dallas McPherson 25.00
AR Alex Rodriguez 250.00
VW Vernon Wells 10.00

2005 Topps Heritage Relics

	NM/M
Common Player:	5.00
Inserted 1:40	

GB George Brett 12.00
JC Jose Canseco 8.00
DM Don Mattingly 15.00
AP Albert Pujols 15.00
AR Alex Rodriguez 15.00
IR Ivan Rodriguez 8.00
NR Nolan Ryan 20.00
OS Ozzie Smith 8.00
DS Darryl Strawberry 5.00
DW Dontrelle Willis 5.00

Heritage Relic Autographs

	NM/M
Production 25 Sets	

DM Don Mattingly 75.00
AR Alex Rodriguez 300.00
NR Nolan Ryan 150.00

Originals Relics

FRANK THOMAS

	NM/M
Common Player:	4.00
Inserted 1:10	

JB Jeff Bagwell 8.00
RB Rocco Baldelli 4.00
JBE Josh Beckett 4.00
LB Lance Berkman 4.00
AB Angel Berroa 4.00
HB Hank Blalock 8.00
HBB Hank Blalock 4.00
MC Miguel Cabrera 8.00
JD Johnny Damon 4.00
RD Ryan Drese 4.00
JG Jason Giambi 6.00
MG Marcus Giles 4.00
VG Vladimir Guerrero 8.00
RH Rich Harden 4.00
TH Todd Helton 8.00
CJ Chipper Jones 8.00
JL Javy Lopez 8.00
ML Mike Lowell 4.00
PM Pedro J. Martinez 8.00
KM Kazuo Matsui 6.00
LN Laynce Nix 4.00
DO David Ortiz 8.00
MP Mike Piazza 8.00
MPB Mike Piazza 8.00
MPR Mark Prior 8.00
AP Albert Pujols 15.00
MR Manny Ramirez 8.00
JR Jose Reyes 6.00
AR Alex Rodriguez 12.00

2005 Topps Heritage

DALLAS McPHERSON

	NM/M
Complete Set (475):	400.00
Common Player:	.40
Common SP (398-475):	4.00
SP's & Variations Inserted 1:2	
Pack (8):	5.00
Box (24):	100.00

1 Will Harridge .40
2 Warren Giles .40
3 Alfonso Soriano 1.00
3 Alfonso Soriano/
SP/Running 5.00
4 Mark Mulder .75
5 Todd Helton/SP 5.00
6 Jason Bay .40
6 Jason Bay/SP/
1956 Pirates Uni. 5.00
7 Ichiro Suzuki 2.50
7 ichiro Suzuki/SP/
Squatting On-Deck 8.00
8 Jim Tracy .40
9 Gavin Floyd .40
10 John Smoltz .75
11 Chicago Cubs .50
12 Darin Erstad .40
13 Chad Tracy .40
14 Charles Thomas .40
15 Miguel Tejada .75
16 Andre Ethier 6.00
17 Jeff Francis .40
18 Derrek Lee .50
19 Juan Uribe .40
20 Jim Edmonds/SP 5.00
21 Kenny Lofton .40
22 Brad Ausmus .40
23 Jon Garland .40
24 Edwin Jackson .40
25 Joe Mauer .75
26 Wes Helms .40
27 Brian Schneider .40
28 Kazuo Matsui .40
29 Tom Gordon .40
30 Hideo Nomo/SP 1.00
31 Albert Pujols/SP 15.00
31 Albert Pujols/SP/
1956 Cards Uni. 15.00
32 Carl Crawford .40
33 Vladimir Guerrero/SP .40
34 Nick Green .40
35 Jay Gibbons .40
36 Kevin Youkilis .40
37 Billy Wagner .40
38 Terrence Long .40
39 Kevin Mench .40
40 Garret Anderson .40
41 Reed Johnson .40
42 Reggie Sanders .40
43 Kirk Rueter .40
44 Jay Payton .40
45 Tike Redman .40
46 Mike Lieberthal .40
47 Damian Miller .40
48 Zach Day .40
49 Juan Rincon .40
50 Jim Thome 1.00
50 Jim Thome/SP/
Fielding 6.00

51 Jose Guillen .40
52 Richie Sexson .75
53 Juan Cruz .40
54 Byung-Hyun Kim .40
55 Carlos Zambrano .50
56 Carlos Lee .40
57 Adam Dunn .75
58 David Riske .40
59 Carlos Guillen .40
60 Larry Bowa .40
61 Barry Bonds 4.00
62 Chris Woodward .40
63 Matt DeSalvo RC 1.00
64 Brian Stavisky RC 1.00
65 Scot Shields .40
66 J.D. Drew .50
67 Erik Bedard .40
68 Scott Williamson .40
69 Mark Prior 1.00
69 Mark Prior/SP/
1956 Cubs Uni. 6.00
69   6.00
70 Ken Griffey Jr. 2.00
71 Kazuhito Tadano .40
72 Philadelphia Phillies .40
73 Jeremy Reed .40
74 Ricardo Rodriguez .40
75 Carlos Delgado .50
76 Eric Milton .40
77 Miguel Olivo .40
78 Edgardo Alfonzo .40
78 Edgardo Alfonzo/
SP/1956 Giants Uni. 4.00
79 Kazuhisa Ishii/SP 4.00
80 Jason Giambi .75
81 Cliff Floyd .40
82 Torii Hunter .50
82 Torii Hunter/SP/
1956 Senators Uni. 4.00
83 Odalis Perez .40
84 Scott Podsednik .40
85 Cleveland Indians .40
86 Jeff Suppan .40
87 Ray Durham .40
88 Tyler Clippard RC 10.00
89 Ryan Howard 2.00
90 Cincinnati Reds .40
91 Bengie Molina .40
92 Danny Bautista .40
93 Eli Marrero .40
94 Larry Bigbie .40
95 Atlanta Braves .40
96 Merkin Valdez .40
97 Rocco Baldelli .40
98 Woody Williams .40
99 Jason Frasor .40
100 Baltimore Orioles .40
101 Ivan Rodriguez/SP 6.00
102 Joe Kennedy .40
103 Mike Lowell .50
104 Armando Benitez .40
105 Craig Biggio .50
106 David DeJesus .40
107 Adrian Beltre .75
108 Phil Nevin .40
109 Cristian Guzman .40
110 Jorge Posada/SP 6.00
111 Boston Red Sox .75
112 Jeff Mathis .40
113 Bartolo Colon .40
114 Alex Cintron .40
115 Russ Ortiz .40
116 Doug Mientkiewicz .40
117 Placido Polanco .40
118 Magglio Ordonez .40
118 Magglio Ordonez/SP/
1956 White Sox Uni. 4.00
119 Chris Seddon RC 1.00
120 Bobby Abreu .50
121 Pittsburgh Pirates .40
122 Dallas McPherson .75
123 Rodrigo Lopez .40
124 Mark Bellhorn .40
125 Nomar Garciaparra 2.00
125 Nomar Garciaparra/SP/
1956 Cubs Uni. 8.00
126 Sean Casey .40
127 Ronnie Belliard .40
128 Tom Goodwin .40
129 Preston Wilson .40
130 Andruw Jones/SP 5.00
131 Roberto Alomar .75
132 John Buck .40
133 Jason LaRue .40
134 St. Louis Cardinals .75
135 Alex Rodriguez/SP 10.00
135 Alex Rodriguez/SP/
Fielding 10.00
136 Nate Robertson .40
137 Juan Pierre .40
138 Morgan Ensberg .40
139 Vinny Castilla .40
140 Jake Dittler 1.00
141 Chan Ho Park .40
142 Felix Hernandez 2.50
143 Jason Isringhausen .40
144 Dustan Mohr .40
145 Khalil Greene .75
146 Minnesota Twins .40
147 Vicente Padilla .40
148 Oliver Perez .40
149 Brian Giles .40
150 Shawn Green .40
151 Matt Lawton .40
152 Casey Blake .40
153 Frank Thomas .75
154 Orlando Hernandez .40
155 Eric Chavez .50

#	Player	Price
155	Eric Chavez/SP/ 1956 Kansas City Uni.	4.00
156	Chase Utley	.75
157	John Olerud	.40
158	Adam Eaton	.40
159	Josh Fogg	.40
160	Michael Tucker	.40
161	Kevin Brown	.40
162	Bobby Crosby	.50
163	Jason Schmidt	.50
164	Shannon Stewart	.40
165	Tony Womack	.40
166	Los Angeles Dodgers	.40
167	Franklin Gutierrez	.40
168	Ted Lilly	.40
169	Mark Teixeira	.40
170	Matt Morris	.40
171	Bucky Jacobsen	.40
172	Steven Doetsch RC	1.00
173	Jeff Weaver	.40
174	Tony Graffanino	.40
175	Jeff Bagwell	.75
176	Carl Pavano	.40
177	Junior Spivey	.40
178	Carlos Silva	.40
179	Tim Redding	.40
180	Brett Myers	.40
181	Mike Mussina	.75
182	Richard Hidalgo	.40
183	Nick Johnson	.40
184	Lew Ford	.40
185	Barry Zito	.50
186	Jimmy Rollins	.50
187	Jack Wilson	.40
188	Chicago White Sox	.40
189	Guillermo Quiroz	.40
190	Mark Hendrickson	.40
191	Jeremy Bonderman	.40
192	Jason Jennings	.40
193	Paul LoDuca	.40
194	A.J. Burnett	.40
195	Ken Harvey	.40
196	Geoff Jenkins	.40
197	Joe Mays	.40
198	Jose Vidro	.40
199	David Wright	.75
200	Randy Johnson	1.00
201	Jeff DeVanon	.40
202	Paul Byrd	.40
203	David Ortiz	1.00
204	Kyle Farnsworth	.40
205	Keith Foulke	.40
206	Joe Crede	.40
207	Austin Kearns	.40
208	Jody Gerut	.40
209	Shawn Chacon	.40
210	Carlos Pena	.40
211	Luis Castillo	.40
212	Chris Denorfia RC	1.00
213	Detroit Tigers	.40
214	Aubrey Huff	.40
215	Brad Fullmer	.40
216	Frank Catalanotto	.40
217	Raul Ibanez	.40
218	Ryan Klesko	.40
219	Octavio Dotel	.40
220	Robert Mackowiak	.40
221	Scott Hatteberg	.40
222	Pat Burrell	.40
223	Bernie Williams	.50
224	Kris Benson	.40
225	Eric Gagne	.40
226	San Francisco Giants	.40
227	Roy Oswalt	.40
228	Josh Beckett	.50
229	Lee Mazzilli	.40
230	Rickie Weeks	.50
231	Troy Glaus	.50
232	Chone Figgins	.40
233	John Thomson	.40
234	Trot Nixon	.40
235	Brad Penny	.40
236	Oakland Athletics	.40
237	Miguel Batista	.40
238	Ryan Drese	.40
239	Aaron Miles	.40
240	Randy Wolf	.40
241	Brian Lawrence	.40
242	A.J. Pierzynski	.40
243	Jamie Moyer	.40
244	Chris Carpenter	.40
245	So Taguchi	.40
246	Rob Bell	.40
247	Francisco Cordero	.40
248	Tom Glavine	.50
249	Jermaine Dye	.40
250	Cliff Lee	.40
251	New York Yankees	.75
252	Vernon Wells	.40
253	R.A. Dickey	.40
254	Larry Walker	.50
255	Randy Winn	.40
256	Pedro Feliz	.40
257	Mark Loretta	.40
258	Tim Worrell	.40
259	Kip Wells	.40
260	Cesar Izturis/SP	4.00
261	Carlos Beltran	.40
261	Carlos Beltran/SP/Btg	6.00
262	Juan Encarnacion	.40
263	Luis Gonzalez	.40
264	Grady Sizemore	.75
265	Paul Wilson	.40
266	Mark Buehrle	.40
267	Todd Hollandsworth	.40
268	Orlando Cabrera	.50
269	Sidney Ponson	.40
270	Mike Hampton	.40
271	Luis Gonzalez	.50
272	Brendan Donnelly	.40
273	Chipper Jones	1.00
273	Chipper Jones/SP/ Blue Background	6.00
274	Brandon Webb	.40
275	Marty Cordova	.40
276	Greg Maddux	2.00
277	Jose Contreras	.40
278	Aaron Harang	.40
279	Coco Crisp	.40
280	Bobby Higginson	.40
281	Guillermo Mota	.40
282	Andy Pettitte	.50
283	Jeremy West RC	3.00
284	Craig Brazell	.40
285	Eric Hinske	.40
286	Hank Blalock	.75
286	Hank Blalock/SP/ Fielding	6.00
287	B.J. Upton	.75
288	Jason Marquis	.40
289	Matt Herges	.40
290	Ramon Hernandez	.40
291	Marlon Byrd	.40
292	Ryan Sweeney/SP	8.00
293	Esteban Loaiza	.40
294	Al Leiter	.50
295	Alex Gonzalez	.40
296	Johan Santana	.75
296	Johan Santana/SP/ 1956 Senators Uni.	6.00
297	Milton Bradley	.40
298	Mike Sweeney	.40
299	Wade Miller	.40
300	Sammy Sosa	2.00
300	Sammy Sosa/SP/ Blue Background	8.00
301	Wily Mo Pena	.40
302	Tim Wakefield	.40
303	Rafael Palmeiro	.75
304	Rafael Furcal	.40
305	David Eckstein	.40
306	David Segui	.40
307	Kevin Millar	.40
308	Matt Clement	.40
309	Wade Robinson RC	1.00
310	Brad Radke	.40
311	Steve Finley	.40
312	Lance Berkman	.50
312	Lance Berkman/ SP/Fielding	5.00
313	Joe Randa	.40
314	Miguel Cabrera	1.00
315	Billy Koch	.40
316	Alex Sanchez	.40
317	Chin-Hui Tsao	.40
318	Omar Vizquel	.40
319	Ryan Freel	.40
320	LaTroy Hawkins	.40
321	Aaron Rowand	.40
322	Paul Konerko	.40
323	Joe Borowski	.40
324	Jarrod Washburn	.40
325	Jaret Wright	.40
326	Johnny Damon	.75
327	Corey Patterson	.50
328	Travis Hafner	.40
329	Shingo Takatsu	.40
330	Dmitri Young	.40
331	Matt Holliday	.40
332	Jeff Kent	.50
333	Desi Relaford	.40
334	Jose Hernandez	.40
335	Lyle Overbay	.40
336	Jacque Jones	.40
337	Terrmel Sledge	.40
338	Victor Zambrano	.40
339	Gary Sheffield	.75
340	Brad Wilkerson	.40
341	Ian Kinsler RC	5.00
342	Jesse Crain	.40
343	Orlando Hudson	.40
344	Laynce Nix	.40
345	Jose Cruz Jr.	.40
346	Edgar Renteria	.50
347	Eddie Guardado	.40
348	Jerome Williams	.40
349	Trevor Hoffman	.40
350	Mike Piazza	1.50
351	Jason Kendall	.40
352	Kevin Millwood	.40
353	Tim Hudson	.50
353	Tim Hudson/SP/ 1956 Braves Uni.	5.00
354	Paul Quantrill	.40
355	Jon Lieber	.40
356	Braden Looper	.40
357	Chad Cordero	.40
358	Joe Nathan	.40
359	Doug Davis	.40
360	Ian Bladergroen RC	1.00
361	Val Majewski	.40
362	Francisco Rodriguez	.40
363	Kelvim Escobar	.40
364	Marcus Giles	.40
365	Darren Fenster RC	1.00
366	David Bell	.40
367	Shea Hillenbrand	.40
368	Manny Ramirez	1.00
369	Ben Broussard	.40
370	Luis Ramirez RC	1.00
371	Dustin Hermanson	.40
372	Akinori Otsuka	.40
373	Chadd Blasko RC	1.00
374	Delmon Young	.75
375	Michael Young	.40
376	Bret Boone	.40
377	Jake Peavy	.40
378	Matt Lindstrom RC	1.00
379	Sean Burroughs	.40
380	Rich Harden	.40
381	Chris Roberson RC	1.00
382	John Lackey	.40
383	Johnny Estrada	.40
384	Matt Rogelstad RC	1.00
385	Toby Hall	.40
386	Adam LaRoche	.40
387	Bill Hall	.40
388	Tim Salmon	.50
389	Curt Schilling	1.00
389	Curt Schilling/SP/ Looking In	6.00
390	Michael Barrett	.40
391	Jose Acevedo	.40
392	Nate Schierholtz	1.00
393	J.T. Snow Jr.	.40
394	Mark Redman	.40
395	Ryan Madson	.40
396	Kevin West RC	1.00
397	Ramon Ortiz	.40
398	Derek Lowe	4.00
399	Kerry Wood	6.00
400	Derek Jeter	15.00
401	Livan Hernandez	4.00
402	Casey Kotchman	4.00
403	Chaz Lytle RC	6.00
404	Alexis Rios	4.00
405	Scott Spiezio	4.00
406	Craig Wilson	4.00
407	Felix Rodriguez	4.00
408	D'Angelo Jimenez	4.00
409	Rondell White	4.00
410	Shawn Estes	4.00
411	Troy Percival	4.00
412	Melvin Mora	4.00
413	Aramis Ramirez	6.00
414	Carl Everett	4.00
415	Elvys Quezada RC	6.00
416	Ben Sheets	4.00
417	Matt Stairs	4.00
418	Adam Everett	4.00
419	Jason Johnson	4.00
420	Billy Butler RC	15.00
421	Justin Morneau	6.00
422	Jose Reyes	6.00
423	Mariano Rivera	5.00
424	Jose Vaquedano RC	6.00
425	Gabe Gross	5.00
426	Scott Rolen	6.00
427	Ty Wigginton	4.00
428	James Jurries RC	6.00
429	Pedro J. Martinez	6.00
430	Mark Grudzielanek	4.00
431	Josh Phelps	4.00
432	Ryan Goleski RC	5.00
433	Mike Matheny	4.00
434	Bobby Kielty	4.00
435	Tony Batista	4.00
436	Corey Koskie	4.00
437	Brad Lidge	4.00
438	Dontrelle Willis	5.00
439	Angel Berroa	4.00
440	Jason Kubel	4.00
441	Roy Halladay	5.00
442	Brian Roberts	4.00
443	Bill Mueller	4.00
444	Adam Kennedy	4.00
445	Brandon Moss RC	5.00
446	Sean Burnett	4.00
447	Eric Byrnes	4.00
448	Matt Campbell RC	5.00
449	Ryan Webb RC	6.00
450	Jose Valentin	4.00
451	Jake Westbrook	4.00
452	Glen Perkins RC	6.00
453	Alex Gonzalez	4.00
454	Jeromy Burnitz	4.00
455	Zack Greinke	5.00
456	Sean Marshall RC	6.00
457	Erubiel Durazo	4.00
458	Michael Cuddyer	4.00
459	Hee Seop Choi	4.00
460	Melky Cabrera RC	8.00
461	Jerry Hairston Jr.	4.00
462	Moises Alou	4.00
463	Michael Rogers RC	6.00
464	Javy Lopez	4.00
465	Freddy Garcia	4.00
466	Brett Harper RC	5.00
467	Juan Gonzalez	5.00
468	Kevin Melillo RC	5.00
469	Todd Walker	4.00
470	C.C. Sabathia	5.00
471	Kole Strayhorn	5.00
472	Mark Kotsay	4.00
473	Javier Vazquez	4.00
474	Mike Cameron	4.00
475	Wes Swackhamer RC	6.00

Chrome Parallel

NM/M
Complete Set (110):
Common Player: 1.00
Production 1,956 Sets

Refractors: 1.5-2X
Production 556 Sets
Black Refractor: 3-5X
Production 56 Sets

#	Player	Price
THC1	Will Harridge	2.00
THC2	Warren Giles	2.00
THC3	Alex Rodriguez	10.00
THC4	Alfonso Soriano	5.00
THC5	Barry Bonds	12.00
THC6	Todd Helton	3.00
THC7	Kazuo Matsui	2.00
THC8	Garret Anderson	1.50
THC9	Mark Prior	5.00
THC10	Jim Thome	4.00
THC11	Jason Giambi	2.00
THC12	Ivan Rodriguez	4.00
THC13	Mike Lowell	1.00
THC14	Vladimir Guerrero	5.00
THC15	Adrian Beltre	2.00
THC16	Andruw Jones	2.00
THC17	Jose Vidro	1.00
THC18	Josh Beckett	1.50
THC19	Mike Sweeney	1.00
THC20	Sammy Sosa	6.00
THC21	Scott Rolen	5.00
THC22	Javy Lopez	1.50
THC23	Albert Pujols	12.00
THC24	Adam Dunn	3.00
THC25	Ken Griffey Jr.	6.00
THC26	Torii Hunter	1.50
THC27	Jorge Posada	2.00
THC28	Magglio Ordonez	1.00
THC29	Shawn Green	1.50
THC30	Frank Thomas	3.00
THC31	Barry Zito	1.50
THC32	David Ortiz	5.00
THC33	Pat Burrell	1.50
THC34	Luis Gonzalez	1.50
THC35	Chipper Jones	5.00
THC36	Hank Blalock	3.00
THC37	Rafael Palmeiro	3.00
THC38	Lance Berkman	2.00
THC39	Miguel Cabrera	5.00
THC40	Paul Konerko	1.00
THC41	Jeff Kent	1.50
THC42	Gary Sheffield	3.00
THC43	Mike Piazza	6.00
THC44	Bret Boone	1.00
THC45	Kerry Wood	5.00
THC46	Derek Jeter	12.00
THC47	Pedro J. Martinez	5.00
THC48	Jason Bay	2.00
THC49	Ichiro Suzuki	8.00
THC50	Miguel Tejada	3.00
THC51	Richie Sexson	2.00
THC52	Jeff Bagwell	3.00
THC53	Lew Ford	1.00
THC54	Randy Johnson	5.00
THC55	Carlos Beltran	3.00
THC56	Greg Maddux	6.00
THC57	Lyle Overbay	1.00
THC58	Michael Young	1.00
THC59	Curt Schilling	5.00
THC60	Jose Reyes	3.00
THC61	Dontrelle Willis	1.50
THC62	Nomar Garciaparra	6.00
THC63	Paul LoDuca	1.00
THC64	Larry Walker	2.00
THC65	Andre Ethier	8.00
THC66	Matt DeSalvo	2.00
THC67	Brian Stavisky	2.00
THC68	Tyler Clippard	20.00
THC69	Chris Seddon	3.00
THC70	Steven Doetsch	3.00
THC71	Chris Denorfia	2.00
THC72	Jeremy West	4.00
THC73	Ryan Sweeney	5.00
THC74	Ian Kinsler	10.00
THC75	Ian Bladergroen	4.00
THC76	Darren Fenster	4.00
THC77	Luis Ramirez	2.00
THC78	Chadd Blasko	2.00
THC79	Matt Lindstrom	2.00
THC80	Chris Roberson	3.00
THC81	Matt Rogelstad	3.00
THC82	Nate Schierholtz	4.00
THC83	Kevin West	4.00
THC84	Chaz Lytle	4.00
THC85	Elvys Quezada	4.00
THC86	Billy Butler	15.00
THC87	Jose Vaquedano	4.00
THC88	James Jurries	4.00
THC89	Ryan Goleski	4.00
THC90	Brandon Moss	4.00
THC91	Matt Campbell	4.00
THC92	Ryan Webb	5.00
THC93	Glen Perkins	4.00
THC94	Sean Marshall	4.00
THC95	Melky Cabrera	4.00
THC96	Michael Rogers	4.00
THC97	Brett Harper	4.00
THC98	Kevin Melillo	4.00
THC99	Kole Strayhorn	4.00
THC100	Wes Swackhamer	4.00
THC101	Rickie Weeks	2.00
THC102	Delmon Young	4.00
THC103	Kazuhito Tadano	1.00
THC104	Kazuhisa Ishii	1.00
THC105	David Wright	4.00
THC106	Eric Gagne	3.00
THC107	So Taguchi	1.00
THC108	B.J. Upton	4.00
THC109	Shingo Takatsu	1.00
THC110	Akinori Otsuka	1.00

Clubhouse Collection Relics

NM/M
Common Player: 5.00

	Player	Price
LA	Luis Aparicio	8.00
EB	Ernie Banks	15.00
LB	Lance Berkman	8.00
MC	Miguel Cabrera	8.00
AK	Al Kaline	15.00
AP	Albert Pujols	20.00
MR	Manny Ramirez	8.00
AR	Alex Rodriguez	15.00
RS	Red Schoendienst	8.00
GS	Gary Sheffield	8.00
AS	Alfonso Soriano	8.00
MT	Miguel Tejada	8.00
BW	Bernie Williams	5.00
DW	Dontrelle Willis	5.00

Clubhouse Collection Dual Relics

NM/M
Production 56 Sets

	Player	Price
MP	Stan Musial, Albert Pujols	85.00
KR	Al Kaline, Ivan Rodriguez	65.00
BG	Ernie Banks, Nomar Garciaparra	85.00

Clubhouse Collection Relic Autograph

NM/M
Production 25 Sets

	Player	Price
LA	Luis Aparicio	165.00
EB	Ernie Banks	200.00
AK	Al Kaline	200.00
HK	Harmon Killebrew	200.00
RS	Red Schoendienst	165.00

Flashbacks

NM/M
Complete Set (10): 8.00
Common Player: .50
Inserted 1:12

	Player	Price
HA	Hank Aaron	4.00
LA	Luis Aparicio	.50
EB	Ernie Banks	2.00
BF	Bob Feller	.50
AK	Al Kaline	1.50
DL	Don Larsen	.50
SM	Stan Musial	2.00
FR	Frank Robinson	.50
HS	Herb Score	.50
DS	Duke Snider	1.00

Flashbacks Autographs

NM/M
Common Player:
Production 25 Sets

	Player	Price
LA	Luis Aparicio	125.00
EB	Ernie Banks	200.00
BF	Bob Feller	165.00
AK	Al Kaline	165.00
DL	Don Larsen	175.00
SM	Stan Musial	200.00
FR	Frank Robinson	200.00
HS	Herb Score	150.00

Flashbacks Relics

NM/M
Common Player: 8.00
Inserted 1:96

	Player	Price
HA	Hank Aaron	15.00
LA	Luis Aparicio	8.00
EB	Ernie Banks	15.00
BF	Bob Feller	10.00
AK	Al Kaline	15.00
DL	Don Larsen	8.00
SM	Stan Musial	15.00
FR	Frank Robinson	10.00
HS	Herb Score	8.00
DS	Duke Snider	10.00

Flashbacks Relic Autographs

NM/M
Production 25 Sets

	Player	Price
LA	Luis Aparicio	150.00
EB	Ernie Banks	200.00
BF	Bob Feller	175.00
AK	Al Kaline	175.00
DL	Don Larsen	175.00
SM	Stan Musial	200.00
FR	Frank Robinson	200.00
HS	Herb Score	150.00

New Age Performers

NM/M
Complete Set (15): 15.00
Common Player: 1.00
Inserted 1:15

	Player	Price
NAP1	Alfonso Soriano	1.50
NAP2	Alex Rodriguez	1.50
NAP3	Ichiro Suzuki	3.00
NAP4	Albert Pujols	3.00
NAP5	Vladimir Guerrero	1.50
NAP6	Jim Thome	1.50
NAP7	Derek Jeter	4.00
NAP8	Sammy Sosa	2.50
NAP9	Ivan Rodriguez	1.50
NAP10	Manny Ramirez	1.50
NAP11	Todd Helton	1.50
NAP12	David Ortiz	1.50
NAP13	Gary Sheffield	1.50
NAP14	Nomar Garciaparra	2.00
NAP15	Randy Johnson	1.50

Real One Autographs

NM/M
Production 200 Sets

Red Ink:	1.5-2X	
Production 56 Sets		
HA	Hank Aaron	250.00
JA	Joe Astroth	50.00
EB	Ernie Banks	125.00
YB	Yogi Berra	100.00
JB	Jim Brady	50.00
CD	Chuck Diering	50.00
BF	Bob Feller	70.00
JG	Jim Greengrass	50.00
MI	Monte Irvin	60.00
SJ	Spook Jacobs	50.00
FM	Fred Marsh	50.00
JM	Jake Martin	50.00
RM	Rudy Minarcin	50.00
PM	Paul Minner	50.00
BN	Bob Nelson	50.00
LP	Laurin Pepper	40.00
LPO	Leroy Powell	60.00
JSA	Jose Santiago	50.00
JS	Johnny Schmitz	50.00
DS	Duke Snider	85.00
AS	Art Swanson	50.00
BT	Bill Tremel	50.00
WW	Wally Westlake	50.00

Then and Now

NM/M

Complete Set (10):		8.00
Common Duo:		.50
Inserted 1:15		
TN1	Hank Aaron, Ichiro Suzuki	4.00
TN2	Don Newcombe, Curt Schilling	1.50
TN3	Robin Roberts, Livan Hernandez	.50
TN4	Bob Friend, Livan Hernandez	.50
TN5	Herb Score, Randy Johnson	1.50
TN6	Whitey Ford, Jake Peavy	1.00
TN7	Jimmy Piersall, Lyle Overbay	.50
TN8	Clem Labine, Mariano Rivera	.75
TN9	Bill Bruton, Carl Crawford	.50
TN10	Eddie Yost, Bobby Abreu	.50

2005 Topps Opening Day

NM/M

Complete Set (165):		30.00
Common Player:		.15
Pack (6):		1.00
Box (36):		30.00
1	Alex Rodriguez	1.50
2	Placido Polanco	.15
3	Torii Hunter	.25
4	Lyle Overbay	.15
5	Johnny Damon	.50
6	Mike Cameron	.15
7	Ichiro Suzuki	1.50
8	Francisco Rodriguez	.15
9	Bobby Crosby	.15
10	Sammy Sosa	1.25
11	Randy Wolf	.15
12	Jason Bay	.25
13	Mike Lieberthal	.15
14	Paul Konerko	.15
15	Brian Giles	.15
16	Luis Gonzalez	.25
17	Jim Edmonds	.40
18	Carlos Lee	.25
19	Corey Patterson	.40
20	Hank Blalock	.50
21	Sean Casey	.25
22	Dmitri Young	.25
23	Mark Mulder	.25
24	Bobby Abreu	.25
25	Jim Thome	.50
26	Jason Kendall	.15
27	Jason Giambi	.15
28	Vinny Castilla	.15
29	Tony Batista	.15
30	Ivan Rodriguez	.50
31	Craig Biggio	.25
32	Chris Carpenter	.15
33	Adrian Beltre	.40
34	Scott Podsednik	.15
35	Cliff Floyd	.15
36	Chad Tracy	.15
37	John Smoltz	.25
38	Shingo Takatsu	.15
39	Jack Wilson	.15
40	Gary Sheffield	.50
41	Lance Berkman	.25
42	Carl Crawford	.25
43	Carlos Guillen	.15
44	David Bell	.15
45	Kazuo Matsui	.15
46	Jason Schmidt	.15
47	Jason Marquis	.15

48	Melvin Mora	.15
49	David Ortiz	.50
50	Andruw Jones	.40
51	Miguel Tejada	.50
52	Bartolo Colon	.15
53	Derrek Lee	.25
54	Eric Gagne	.25
55	Miguel Cabrera	.75
56	Travis Hafner	.15
57	Jose Valentin	.15
58	Mark Prior	.75
59	Phil Nevin	.15
60	Jose Vidro	.15
61	Khalil Greene	.25
62	Carlos Zambrano	.40
63	Erubiel Durazo	.15
64	Michael Young	.15
65	Woody Williams	.15
66	Edgardo Alfonzo	.15
67	Troy Glaus	.40
68	Garret Anderson	.25
69	Richie Sexson	.40
70	Curt Schilling	.75
71	Randy Johnson	.75
72	Chipper Jones	.75
73	J.D. Drew	.25
74	Russ Ortiz	.15
75	Frank Thomas	.50
76	Jimmy Rollins	.25
77	Barry Zito	.25
78	Rafael Palmeiro	.50
79	Brad Wilkerson	.15
80	Adam Dunn	.15
81	Doug Mientkiewicz	.15
82	Manny Ramirez	.75
83	Pedro J. Martinez	.25
84	Moises Alou	.25
85	Mike Sweeney	.15
86	Boston Red Sox WC	1.00
87	Matt Clement	.15
88	Nomar Garciaparra	1.00
89	Magglio Ordonez	.15
90	Bret Boone	.15
91	Mark Loretta	.15
92	Jose Contreras	.15
93	Randy Winn	.15
94	Austin Kearns	.15
95	Ken Griffey Jr.	1.25
96	Jake Westbrook	.15
97	Kazuhito Tadano	.15
98	C.C. Sabathia	.15
99	Todd Helton	.50
100	Albert Pujols	2.00
101	Jose Molina	.15
102	Aaron Miles	.15
103	Mike Lowell	.25
104	Paul LoDuca	.15
105	Juan Pierre	.15
106	Dontrelle Willis	.25
107	Jeff Bagwell	.40
108	Carlos Beltran	.25
109	Ronnie Belliard	.15
110	Roy Oswalt	.25
111	Zack Greinke	.15
112	Steve Finley	.15
113	Kazuhisa Ishii	.15
114	Justin Morneau	.40
115	Ben Sheets	.25
116	Johan Santana	.50
117	Billy Wagner	.15
118	Mariano Rivera	.40
119	Corey Koskie	.15
120	Akinori Otsuka	.15
121	Joe Mauer	.40
122	Jacque Jones	.15
123	Joe Nathan	.15
124	Nick Johnson	.15
125	Vernon Wells	.15
126	Mike Piazza	1.00
127	Jose Guillen	.15
128	Jose Reyes	.25
129	Marcus Giles	.25
130	Javy Lopez	.25
131	Kevin Millar	.15
132	Jorge Posada	.40
133	Carl Pavano	.25
134	Bernie Williams	.25
135	Kerry Wood	.75
136	Matt Holiday	.25
137	Kevin Brown	.15
138	Derek Jeter	2.00
139	Barry Bonds	2.00
140	Jeff Kent	.25
141	Mark Kotsay	.15
142	Shawn Green	.25
143	Tim Hudson	.25
144	Shannon Stewart	.15
145	Pat Burrell	.25
146	Gavin Floyd	.15
147	Mike Mussina	.50
148	Eric Chavez	.25
149	Jon Lieber	.15
150	Vladimir Guerrero	.75
151	Vicente Padilla	.15
152	Ryan Klesko	.15
153	Jake Peavy	.25
154	Scott Rolen	.75
155	Greg Maddux	1.00
156	Edgar Renteria	.25
157	Larry Walker	.25
158	Scott Kazmir	.25
159	B.J. Upton	.25
160	Mark Teixeira	.50
161	Ken Harvey	.15
162	Alfonso Soriano	.40
163	Carlos Delgado	.40
164	Alexis Rios	.15
165	Checklist	.15

Day Autographs

NM/M

Complete Set (6):		
Common Player:		
CC	Chad Cordero	10.00
FH	Felix Hernandez	25.00
AH	Aaron Hill	8.00
PM	Paul Maholm	8.00
OQ	Omar Quintanilla	15.00
AW	Anthony Whittington	8.00

MLB Game Worn Jersey Collection

NM/M

Target Retail Exclusive		
37	Vladimir Guerrero	8.00
38	Albert Pujols	15.00
39	Torii Hunter	4.00
40	Alfonso Soriano	6.00
41	Bobby Abreu	4.00
42	Moises Alou	6.00
43	Sean Burroughs	4.00
44	Shannon Stewart	4.00
45	Troy Glaus	6.00
46	Fernando Vina	4.00
47	Dan Wilson	4.00
48	Paul Konerko	4.00
49	Jimmy Rollins	6.00
50	Livan Hernandez	4.00
51	Sean Casey	4.00
52	Paul LoDuca	4.00
53	Richie Sexson	6.00
54	Aubrey Huff	4.00

2005 Topps Pack Wars

NM/M

Complete Set (175):		40.00
Common Player:		.25
Pack (7):		20.00
Box (7):		120.00
1	Alex Rodriguez	3.00
2	Eric Chavez	.40
3	Jimmy Rollins	.40
4	Jason Bay	.40
5	Nomar Garciaparra	2.00
6	Melvin Mora	.25
7	Bobby Abreu	.50
8	Bartolo Colon	.25
9	Orlando Cabrera	1.00
10	Albert Pujols	3.00
11	Barry Zito	.40
12	Vernon Wells	.40
13	J.D. Drew	.40
14	Darin Erstad	.40
15	Manny Ramirez	1.00
16	Derrek Lee	.40
17	Juan Uribe	.25
18	Wily Mo Pena	.25
19	Jeromy Burnitz	.25
20	Dontrelle Willis	.40
21	Craig Biggio	.40
22	Cesar Izturis	.25
23	Geoff Jenkins	.25
24	Joe Mauer	.50
25	Derek Jeter	3.00
26	David Wright	1.00
27	Jose Vidro	.25
28	Bobby Crosby	.25
29	Khalil Greene	.50
30	Ichiro Suzuki	2.00
31	Reggie Sanders	.25
32	A.J. Pierzynski	.25
33	Corey Patterson	.40
34	Frank Thomas	.75
35	Craig Wilson	.25
36	Carl Crawford	.25
37	Michael Young	.25
38	Mark Kotsay	.25
39	Javier Vazquez	.25
40	Kazuo Matsui	.25
41	Lew Ford	.25
42	Corey Koskie	.25
43	Larry Walker	.50
44	Mike Lowell	.40
45	Todd Helton	.75
46	Travis Hafner	.25
47	Sean Casey	.25
48	Ken Griffey Jr.	1.50
49	Milton Bradley	.25
50	Ivan Rodriguez	.75
51	Carlos Lee	.25
52	Aramis Ramirez	.50
53	Curt Schilling	1.00
54	Russ Ortiz	.25

55	Randy Johnson	1.00
56	Preston Wilson	.25
57	Jay Gibbons	.25
58	Mike Lieberthal	.25
59	Johnny Damon	.75
60	Mark Prior	1.00
61	Freddy Garcia	.25
62	Casey Blake	.25
63	Chipper Jones	1.00
64	Carlos Guillen	.25
65	Juan Pierre	.25
66	Tom Glavine	.50
67	Alex Sanchez	.25
68	Tony Batista	.25
69	Paul LoDuca	.25
70	Hank Blalock	.75
71	Pedro Feliz	.25
72	Jim Edmonds	.50
73	Phil Nevin	.25
74	Rocco Baldelli	.25
75	Alfonso Soriano	1.00
76	David Bell	.25
77	Eric Hinske	.25
78	Jose Guillen	.25
79	Marcus Giles	.25
80	Rafael Palmeiro	.75
81	Jeff Bagwell	.75
82	Kerry Wood	1.00
83	Johan Santana	.75
84	Troy Glaus	.75
85	Andruw Jones	.50
86	Barry Bonds	3.00
87	Jermaine Dye	.25
88	Carlos Zambrano	.50
89	Aaron Rowand	.25
90	Garret Anderson	.40
91	Ryan Klesko	.25
92	Paul Konerko	.25
93	Jeff Kent	.25
94	Richie Sexson	.50
95	Lyle Overbay	.25
96	Torii Hunter	.40
97	Mike Cameron	.25
98	Eric Byrnes	.25
99	Jason Kendall	.25
100	Vladimir Guerrero	1.00
101	Johnny Estrada	.25
102	Mark Bellhorn	.25
103	Moises Alou	.40
104	Ronnie Belliard	.25
105	Adam Dunn	.75
106	Dmitri Young	.25
107	Luis Castillo	.25
108	Carlos Beltran	.75
109	Steve Finley	.25
110	Shannon Stewart	.25
111	Al Leiter	.25
112	Bernie Williams	.50
113	Roy Oswalt	.40
114	Sean Burroughs	.25
115	Randy Winn	.25
116	Tony Womack	.25
117	Jim Thome	1.00
118	Aubrey Huff	.25
119	Bret Boone	.25
120	Carlos Delgado	.40
121	Jason Schmidt	.25
122	Rafael Furcal	.25
123	Miguel Tejada	.75
124	Bill Mueller	.25
125	Pedro Martinez	1.00
126	Michael Barrett	.25
127	Jody Gerut	.25
128	Vinny Castilla	.25
129	Rondell White	.25
130	Magglio Ordonez	.25
131	Lance Berkman	.25
132	Alex Gonzalez	.25
133	Mike Sweeney	.25
134	Ben Sheets	.50
135	Jacque Jones	.25
136	Brad Wilkerson	.25
137	Cliff Floyd	.25
138	Kevin Brown	.25
139	Scott Hatteberg	.25
140	Gary Sheffield	.50
141	Justin Morneau	.50
142	Scott Podsednik	.25
143	Shawn Green	.25
144	David Ortiz	1.00
145	Josh Beckett	.50
146	Tim Hudson	.50
147	Matt Lawton	.25
148	Mark Buehrle	.25
149	Todd Walker	.25
150	Jason Giambi	.50
151	Brian Giles	.25
152	Erubiel Durazo	.25
153	Jack Wilson	.25
154	Jose Reyes	.50
155	Scott Rolen	1.00
156	Raul Ibanez	.25
157	Mark Teixeira	.50
158	Luis Gonzalez	.25
159	Javy Lopez	.25
160	Greg Maddux	1.50
161	Kevin Millar	.25
162	Jose Valentin	.25
163	C.C. Sabathia	.25
164	Carlos Pena	.25
165	Miguel Cabrera	1.00
166	Adrian Beltre	.50
167	Sammy Sosa	.75
168	Nick Johnson	.25
169	Jorge Posada	.75
170	Mike Piazza	1.50
171	Mark Mulder	.50
172	Mark Loretta	.25

173	Edgardo Alfonzo	.25
174	Edgar Renteria	.50
175	Pat Burrell	.25

Autographs

NM/M

Common Autograph:		15.00
CB	Carlos Beltran	30.00
HB	Hank Blalock	20.00
AB	Aaron Boone	20.00
MC	Miguel Cabrera	25.00
EC	Eric Chavez	15.00
JE	Johnny Estrada	15.00
ZG	Zack Greinke	15.00
VM	Victor Martinez	15.00
CS	C.C. Sabathia	15.00
VW	Vernon Wells	10.00
MY	Michael Young	15.00

Collector Chips

NM/M

Common Player:		8.00
Inserted 1:Box		
Blue:		No Pricing
Production 25 Sets		
Red:		No Pricing
Production 10 Sets		
2	Ichiro Suzuki	30.00
3	Jim Thome	20.00
4	Albert Pujols	30.00
5	Vladimir Guerrero	15.00
6	Derek Jeter	30.00
7	Sammy Sosa	20.00
9	Ivan Rodriguez	10.00
11	Nomar Garciaparra	20.00
12	Ken Griffey Jr.	20.00
13	Mark Prior	10.00
14	Todd Helton	10.00
15	Mike Piazza	20.00
16	Jorge Posada	10.00
17	Chipper Jones	10.00
18	Randy Johnson	15.00
19	Gary Sheffield	8.00
20	Mike Schmidt	25.00
21	Ernie Banks	20.00
22	Frank Robinson	20.00
23	Reggie Jackson	20.00
24	George Brett	25.00
25	Nolan Ryan	30.00

Cut Signatures

No Pricing

Relics

NM/M

Common Player:		8.00
RC	Roger Clemens	12.00
NG	Nomar Garciaparra	8.00
VG	Vladimir Guerrero	10.00
TH	Todd Helton	8.00
THB	Todd Helton	8.00
CJ	Chipper Jones	8.00
CJB	Chipper Jones	8.00
GM	Greg Maddux	10.00
PM	Pedro Martinez	8.00
MR	Manny Ramirez	10.00
MRB	Manny Ramirez	10.00
AR	Alex Rodriguez	15.00
IR	Ivan Rodriguez	8.00
SR	Scott Rolen	10.00
GS	Gary Sheffield	8.00
AS	Alfonso Soriano	8.00
SS	Sammy Sosa	10.00
FT	Frank Thomas	8.00
JT	Jim Thome	8.00

Relic Autographs

NM/M

Common Autograph:		15.00
Production 200 Sets		
CB	Carlos Beltran	40.00
HB	Hank Blalock	25.00
MC	Miguel Cabrera	30.00
EC	Eric Chavez	20.00
JE	Johnny Estrada	15.00
VM	Victor Martinez	15.00
MY	Michael Young	20.00

2005 Topps Pristine

NM/M

Common 1-100		.75

Common Rookie (101-130):		1.00
Common (131-180):		3.00
Production 500		
Common (181-205):		10.00
Production 100		
Common (206-210):		
Production 49		
Pack (8):		30.00
Box (5):		125.00
1	Alex Rodriguez	3.00
2	Jake Peavy	.75
3	Bobby Crosby	.75
4	J.D. Drew	.75
5	Scott Rolen	1.50
6	Bobby Abreu	.75
7	Ken Griffey Jr.	2.50
8	Jeremy Bonderman	.75
9	Mike Sweeney	.75
10	Mark Prior	1.50
11	Tim Hudson	.75
12	Clint Barmes	.75
13	Jeff Bagwell	1.00
14	Andruw Jones	1.50
15	Carlos Delgado	.75
16	Rocco Baldelli	.75
17	Adam Dunn	1.50
18	Greg Maddux	2.00
19	Torii Hunter	.75
20	Miguel Tejada	1.50
21	Lyle Overbay	.75
22	Craig Wilson	.75
23	Scott Kazmir	.75
24	Alex Rios	.75
25	Ichiro Suzuki	3.00
26	Jorge Posada	.75
27	Jose Reyes	.75
28	Hank Blalock	.75
29	Troy Glaus	1.00
30	Todd Helton	1.50
31	Javy Lopez	.75
32	Barry Zito	.75
33	Jimmy Rollins	1.00
34	Mark Loretta	.75
35	Richie Sexson	.75
36	Nick Johnson	.75
37	Ivan Rodriguez	.75
38	Jeff Kent	.75
39	Jake Westbrook	.75
40	Carlos Beltran	1.00
41	Rich Harden	.75
42	Joe Mauer	1.00
43	Luis Gonzalez	.75
44	Frank Thomas	1.00
45	Michael Young	.75
46	Jason Schmidt	.75
47	Eric Chavez	.75
48	Vinny Castilla	.75
49	John Smoltz	1.00
50	Barry Bonds	4.00
51	Jim Edmonds	1.00
52	Edgar Renteria	.75
53	Jose Vidro	.75
54	Chipper Jones	1.50
55	Curt Schilling	1.50
56	Victor Martinez	.75
57	Josh Beckett	.75
58	Derrek Lee	1.50
59	Shawn Green	.75
60	Roger Clemens	4.00
61	Orlando Cabrera	.75
62	Mike Piazza	2.00
63	Gary Sheffield	1.00
64	Carl Crawford	.75
65	Johan Santana	1.50
66	Oliver Perez	.75
67	Manny Ramirez	1.50
68	Paul Konerko	1.00
69	Preston Wilson	.75
70	Sammy Sosa	2.00
71	Eric Gagne	.75
72	Geoff Jenkins	.75
73	Magglio Ordonez	.75
74	Kerry Wood	1.00
75	Albert Pujols	4.00
76	Roy Halladay	1.00
77	Aubrey Huff	.75
78	Nomar Garciaparra	1.50
79	Brian Roberts	.75
80	Randy Johnson	1.50
81	Pat Burrell	.75
82	Brian Giles	.75
83	Mike Mussina	1.00
84	Mark Teixeira	1.00
85	Pedro Martinez	1.50
86	Jason Bay	.75
87	Mark Buehrle	.75
88	Rafael Furcal	.75
89	Juan Pierre	.75
90	Jim Thome	1.00
91	Ben Sheets	1.00
92	Alfonso Soriano	1.50
93	Adrian Beltre	.75
94	Miguel Cabrera	1.50
95	Derek Jeter	4.00
96	Vernon Wells	.75
97	Lance Berkman	1.00
98	Hideki Matsui	2.50
99	David Ortiz	1.50
100	Vladimir Guerrero	1.50
101	Justin Verlander **RC**	3.00
102	Billy Butler **RC**	8.00
103	Wladimir Balentien **RC**	2.00
104	Jeremy West **RC**	2.00
105	Philip Humber **RC**	3.00
106	Tyler Pelland **RC**	1.00
107	Andy LaRoche **RC**	5.00
108	Hernan Iribarren **RC**	1.00
109	Luke Scott **RC**	1.00

#	Player	Price
110	Landon Powell RC	1.00
111	Alexander Smit RC	1.00
112	Ryan Garko RC	1.00
113	Bear Bay RC	1.00
114	Ian Bladergroen RC	1.00
115	Manny Parra RC	1.00
116	Andy Sides RC	1.00
117	Travis Chick RC	1.00
118	Stefan Bailie RC	1.00
119	Chuck Tiffany RC	2.00
120	Buck Coats RC	1.00
121	Jeff Niemann RC	2.00
122	Jake Postlewait RC	1.00
123	Matt Campbell RC	1.00
124	Kevin Melillo RC	2.00
125	Mike Morse RC	3.00
126	Anthony Reyes RC	6.00
127	Casey McGehee RC	1.00
128	Cody Haerther RC	1.00
129	Brandon McCarthy RC	4.00
130	Glen Perkins RC	1.00
131	Moises Alou	1.00
132	Nomar Garciaparra	6.00
133	Scott Rolen	6.00
134	Miguel Tejada	4.00
135	Alex Rodriguez	10.00
136	Michael Young	3.00
137	Tim Hudson	5.00
138	Troy Glaus	3.00
139	Eric Chavez	3.00
140	David Ortiz	10.00
141	Andruw Jones	5.00
142	Richie Sexson	5.00
143	Jim Thome	5.00
144	Javy Lopez	3.00
145	Lance Berkman	3.00
146	Gary Sheffield	5.00
147	Dontrelle Willis	4.00
148	Curt Schilling	5.00
149	Jorge Posada	5.00
150	Vladimir Guerrero	8.00
151	Adam Dunn	5.00
152	Ryan Drese	3.00
153	Hank Blalock	3.00
154	Kerry Wood	4.00
155	Alfonso Soriano	5.00
156	Aramis Ramirez	4.00
157	Mark Mulder	4.00
158	Paul Konerko	4.00
159	Jim Edmonds	6.00
160	Roger Clemens	10.00
161	Mariano Rivera	6.00
162	Rafael Palmeiro	6.00
163	Mark Teixeira	6.00
164	Eric Gagne	3.00
165	Sammy Sosa	8.00
166	Brett Myers	3.00
167	Kazuhisa Ishii	3.00
168	Ken Harvey	3.00
169	Johnny Estrada	3.00
170	Todd Helton	5.00
171	Rich Harden	3.00
172	Johnny Damon	6.00
173	Manny Ramirez	6.00
174	Benito Santiago	3.00
175	Albert Pujols	15.00
176	Chipper Jones	.75
177	Miguel Cabrera	8.00
178	Jeff Bagwell	5.00
179	Ivan Rodriguez	5.00
180	Mike Piazza	8.00
181	Chip Cannon RC	15.00
182	Erik Cordier RC	15.00
183	Billy Butler RC	40.00
184	C.J. Smith RC	10.00
185	Alfonso Soriano	25.00
186	Bobby Livingston RC	15.00
187	Wladimir Balentien RC	25.00
188	Mike Morse RC	30.00
189	Wes Swackhamer RC	30.00
190	Justin Verlander RC	50.00
191	Jake Postlewait RC	15.00
192	Michael Rogers RC	20.00
193	Matt Campbell RC	20.00
194	Eric Nielsen RC	15.00
195	Gary Sheffield	30.00
196	Glen Perkins RC	30.00
197	Kevin Melillo RC	30.00
198	Chad Orvella RC	10.00
199	Jeff Niemann RC	25.00
200	Alex Rodriguez	180.00
201	Brian Stavisky RC	15.00
202	Brian Miller RC	15.00
203	Landon Powell RC	25.00
204	Philip Humber RC	30.00
205	Mariano Rivera	100.00
206	Curt Schilling	50.00
207	Nolan Ryan	150.00

Red
Red (1-130): 2-4X
Production 66
Red (131-210): No Pricing
Production 3 Sets

Uncirculated Bronze
Bronze (1-130): 1.5-3X
Production 375
Bronze (131-180): 1-1.5X
Production 100
Bronze (181-205): No Pricing
Production 18
Bronze (206-210): No Pricing
Production 10

Doubles Act Autographs
No Pricing
Production 5 Sets

Fielder's Choice
No Pricing
Production 9 Sets

In The Name Patch
No Pricing
One card for each letter.

Personal Endorsements
NM/M
Common
Production 497 Sets
Uncirculated: No Pricing
Production 3 Sets

MB	Milton Bradley	10.00
BB	Billy Butler	25.00
LC	Lance Cormier	5.00
SE	Scott Elbert	8.00
JF	Josh Fields	5.00
LH	Livan Hernandez	12.00
JPH	J.P. Howell	8.00
PH	Philip Humber	10.00
ZJ	Zach Jackson	8.00
BJ	Blake Johnson	8.00
BL	Bobby Livingston	8.00
CO	Chad Orvella	8.00
GP	Glen Perkins	15.00
LP	Landon Powell	8.00
MR	Mike Rodriguez	8.00
MRO	Mark Rogers	8.00
TS	Terrmel Sledge	8.00
CJS	C.J. Smith	5.00
JS	Jeremy Sowers	10.00
JV	Justin Verlander	20.00

Uncommon
Production 247 Sets

JB	Jason Bay	25.00
AB	Aaron Boone	10.00
MB	Matt Bush	15.00
BB	Billy Butler	25.00
CC	Chip Cannon	8.00
CE	Carl Erskine	10.00
HK	Harmon Killebrew	25.00
BL	Bobby Livingston	8.00
ML	Mark Loretta	8.00
DO	David Ortiz	40.00
CW	Craig Wilson	10.00
DW	David Wright	60.00
DZ	Don Zimmer	15.00

Rare
Production 97 Sets

GA	Garret Anderson	15.00
EB	Ernie Banks	50.00
SM	Stan Musial	50.00
MR	Mariano Rivera	100.00
TS	Tom Seaver	30.00
AS	Alfonso Soriano	25.00

Scarce
Production 22 Sets

Personal Pieces

NM/M
Common
Production 425
Uncirculated: No Pricing
Production 3 Sets

JB	Jeff Bagwell	5.00
RB	Ronnie Belliard	3.00
AB	Adrian Beltre	3.00
LB	Lance Berkman	5.00
HB	Hank Blalock	5.00
EC	Eric Chavez	3.00
RC	Roger Clemens	12.00
BC	Bobby Crosby	5.00
JDD	J.D. Drew	5.00
AD	Adam Dunn	5.00
JE	Jim Edmonds	5.00
JES	Johnny Estrada	3.00
JG	Jason Giambi	3.00
JGI	Jay Gibbons	3.00
SG	Shawn Green	3.00
VG	Vladimir Guerrero	5.00
CG	Cristian Guzman	3.00
THA	Travis Hafner	5.00
TH	Todd Helton	5.00
THU	Tim Hudson	5.00
AJ	Andruw Jones	5.00
CJ	Chipper Jones	8.00
JL	Javy Lopez	3.00
ML	Mark Loretta	3.00
MLO	Mike Lowell	4.00
PM	Pedro Martinez	8.00
VM	Victor Martinez	3.00
KM	Kevin Millar	3.00
MM	Mark Mulder	3.00
BM	Brett Myers	3.00
LN	Laynce Nix	3.00
MP	Mike Piazza	8.00
MPR	Mark Prior	5.00
AP	Albert Pujols	15.00
BR	Brad Radke	3.00
MR	Manny Ramirez	8.00
ER	Edgar Renteria	3.00
MRI	Mariano Rivera	3.00
SR	Scott Rolen	5.00
CS	Curt Schilling	6.00
GS	Gary Sheffield	5.00
AS	Alfonso Soriano	5.00
MTE	Mark Teixeira	5.00
MT	Miguel Tejada	5.00
FT	Frank Thomas	8.00
JT	Jim Thome	5.00
BJU	B.J. Upton	3.00
BW	Bernie Williams	5.00
KW	Kerry Wood	5.00
BZ	Barry Zito	3.00

Uncommon
Production 200

CB	Carlos Beltran	5.00
AB	Adrian Beltre	3.00
MC	Miguel Cabrera	5.00
RC	Roger Clemens	12.00
JE	Jim Edmonds	3.00
EG	Eric Gagne	3.00
TG	Troy Glaus	5.00
TH	Torii Hunter	3.00
AJ	Andruw Jones	5.00
CJ	Chipper Jones	8.00
MM	Mark Mulder	5.00
MO	Magglio Ordonez	8.00
DO	David Ortiz	8.00
MP	Mike Piazza	8.00
JP	Jorge Posada	5.00
AP	Albert Pujols	15.00
MR	Manny Ramirez	8.00
MRI	Mariano Rivera	5.00
AR	Alex Rodriguez	15.00
IR	Ivan Rodriguez	5.00
SR	Scott Rolen	5.00
CS	Curt Schilling	6.00
AS	Alfonso Soriano	5.00
SS	Sammy Sosa	8.00
JT	Jim Thome	5.00

Rare

CB	Carlos Beltran	10.00
BB	Barry Bonds	40.00
RC	Roger Clemens	20.00
JD	Johnny Damon	12.00
EG	Eric Gagne	10.00
VG	Vladimir Guerrero	10.00
TH	Todd Helton	10.00
PM	Pedro Martinez	10.00
AP	Albert Pujols	25.00
AR	Alex Rodriguez	25.00

Scarce

Power Core
No Pricing
Production 3-10
Power Stick: No Pricing
Production One Set

Printing Plates
No Pricing
Production one set for each color.

Selective Swatch
No Pricing
Production One Set

Legends

NM/M
Complete Set (140):
Common Player: 1.00
Common SP (101-125): 2.00
Production 1,999
Common SP (126-135): 3.00
Production 999
Common SP (136-140): 4.00
Production 499
Pack (8): 30.00
Box (8): 120.00

1	Vida Blue	1.00
2	Bert Blyleven	1.00
3	Joe Carter	1.00
4	Bill Buckner	1.00
5	Luis Aparicio	1.00
6	Ernie Banks	2.50
7	Wade Boggs	2.00
8	George Brett	4.00
9	Lou Brock	2.00
10	Rod Carew	2.00
11	Gary Carter	1.00
12	Andre Dawson	1.00
13	Dennis Eckersley	1.00
14	Rollie Fingers	1.00
15	Steve Garvey	1.00
16	Dwight Gooden	1.00
17	Rich "Goose" Gossage	1.00
18	Ron Guidry	1.00
19	Keith Hernandez	1.00
20	Charlie Hough	1.00
21	Bo Jackson	2.50
22	Monte Irvin	2.00
23	Reggie Jackson	2.00
24	Ferguson Jenkins	1.00
25	Ralph Kiner	1.00
26	Juan Marichal	1.00
27	Stan Musial	4.00
28	Tony Oliva	1.00
29	Jim Palmer	1.50
30	Dave Parker	1.00
31	Gaylord Perry	1.00
32	Jimmy Piersall	1.00
33	Johnny Podres	1.00
34	Brooks Robinson	2.00
35	Frank Robinson	2.00
36	Nolan Ryan	5.00
37	Tom Seaver	3.00
38	Ozzie Smith	3.00
39	Duke Snider	3.00
40	Bobby Thomson	1.00
41	Carl Yastrzemski	3.00
42	Maury Wills	1.00
43	Robin Yount	3.00
44	Matt Williams	1.00
45	Orel Hershiser	1.00
46	Tim McCarver	1.00
47	Don Newcombe	1.00
48	Paul O'Neill	1.00
49	Al Kaline	2.00
50	Harmon Killebrew	2.00
51	Dave Kingman	1.00
52	Ken Griffey	1.00
53	George Foster	1.00
54	Mark Fidrych	1.00
55	Orlando Cepeda	1.00
56	Don Larsen	1.00
57	Bill Madlock	1.00
58	Dale Murphy	1.50
59	Graig Nettles	1.00
60	Phil Niekro	1.00
61	Al Oliver	1.00
62	Harold Reynolds	1.00
63	Bobby Richardson	1.00
64	Mike Scott	1.00
65	Dave Stewart	1.00
66	Rick Sutcliffe	1.00
67	Bruce Sutter	1.50
68	Luis Tiant	1.00
69	Bob Watson	1.00
70	Walt Weiss	1.00
71	Don Zimmer	1.00
72	Tommy John	1.00
73	Ray Knight	1.00
74	Jack Morris	1.00
75	Mickey Rivers	1.00
76	Lee Smith	1.00
77	Darryl Strawberry	1.00
78	David Justice	1.00
79	Wally Joyner	1.00
80	Jimmy Key	1.00
81	John Kruk	1.00
82	Greg Luzinski	1.00
83	Mookie Wilson	1.00
84	Wilbur Wood	1.00
85	Tim Raines	1.00
86	Jim Rice	1.00
87	Tony Armas	1.00
88	Harold Baines	1.00
89	Bucky Dent	1.00
90	Darrell Evans	1.00
91	Cecil Fielder	1.00
92	Jose Cruz	1.00
93	Dave Concepcion	1.00
94	Ron Cey	1.00
95	Davey Lopes	1.00
96	Boog Powell	1.00
97	Buddy Bell	1.00
98	George Bell	1.00
99	Bert Campaneris	1.00
100	Chet Lemon	1.00
101	Bo Jackson	4.00
102	Will Clark	2.00
103	Cecil Fielder	2.00
104	Ron Cey	2.00
105	Tony Gwynn	5.00
106	Orel Hershiser	2.00
107	Jimmy Key	2.00
108	Paul Molitor	3.00
109	Pete Incaviglia	2.00
110	Wally Joyner	2.00
111	Dave Kingman	2.00
112	Ron Guidry	2.00
113	Ron Darling	2.00
114	Mookie Wilson	2.00
115	Reggie Jackson	3.00
116	Walt Weiss	2.00
117	Joe Carter	2.00
118	Cory Snyder	2.00
119	Dave Winfield	3.00
120	Terry Steinbach	2.00
121	Matt Williams	2.00
122	Ozzie Smith	5.00
123	Jack McDowell	2.00
124	Bob Horner	2.00
125	Don Kessinger	2.00
126	Minnie Minoso	3.00
127	Cecil Kaiser	3.00
128	Buck O'Neil	3.00
129	Monte Irvin	4.00
130	Jim Gilliam	3.00
131	Josh Gibson	4.00
132	Ernie Banks	6.00
133	Don Newcombe	3.00
134	Red Moore	3.00
135	Willie Pope	3.00
136	Gary Carter	4.00
137	Bo Jackson	6.00
138	George Brett	8.00
139	Joe Carter	4.00
140	Nolan Ryan	8.00

Legends Refractor
Refractor (1-100): 1-1.5X
Production 549
Refractor (101-125): 1.5-2X
Production 199
Refractor (126-135): 1.5-2.5X
Production 99
Refractor (136-140): No Pricing
Production 25

Legends Refractors Gold Die-Cut
Gold (1-100): 3-4X
Gold (101-135): 1-2.5X
Gold (136-140): 1-1.5X
Production 65 Sets

Legends SuperFractor
No Pricing
Production One Set

Legends Printing Plates
No Pricing
One set produced per color.

Legends Leading Indicators

LEADING INDICATORS — TOTAL BASES LEADER – 1978 — JIM RICE — RED SOX
NM/M
Common Player: 4.00
Refractor: No Pricing
Production one or 25.

WB	Wade Boggs	10.00
RC	Rod Carew	8.00
AD	Andre Dawson	6.00
BF	Bob Feller	10.00
CF	Cecil Fielder	8.00
GF	George Foster	4.00
TG	Tony Gwynn	8.00
AK	Al Kaline	12.00
DK	Dave Kingman	4.00
RM	Roger Maris	35.00
DM	Don Mattingly	15.00
DBM	Dale Murphy	10.00
TO	Tony Oliva	6.00
PO	Paul O'Neill	10.00
DP	Dave Parker	4.00
GP	Gaylord Perry	4.00
TR	Tim Raines	4.00
TR2	Tim Raines	6.00
JR	Jim Rice	4.00
NR	Nolan Ryan	20.00
MS	Mike Scott	4.00
TS	Tom Seaver	10.00
DS	Darryl Strawberry	6.00
MW	Maury Wills	10.00
CY	Carl Yastrzemski	15.00

Legends Personal Endorsements

NM/M
Common Autograph: 10.00
Gold: No Pricing
Production 25 Sets

JA	Jim Abbott	15.00
LA	Luis Aparicio	15.00
BB	Bert Blyleven	15.00
GB	George Brett	50.00
GC	Gary Carter	15.00
RD	Ron Darling	15.00
AD	Andre Dawson	15.00
DE	Dennis Eckersley	15.00
DWE	Darrell Evans	15.00
CF	Carlton Fisk	25.00
GF	George Foster	10.00
GG	Rich "Goose" Gossage	10.00
BG	Bobby Grich	10.00
KH	Keith Hernandez	12.00
BJ	Bo Jackson	60.00
RJ	Reggie Jackson	50.00
AK	Al Kaline	40.00
DL	Don Larsen	15.00
JM	Jack McDowell	10.00
SM	Stan Musial	50.00
GN	Graig Nettles	15.00
JO	Jesse Orosco	10.00
JP	Jim Palmer	15.00
JAP	Jimmy Piersall	15.00
CR	Cal Ripken Jr.	125.00
BR	Brooks Robinson	30.00
NR	Nolan Ryan	90.00
DS	Duke Snider	40.00
EW	Earl Weaver	15.00
CY	Carl Yastrzemski	50.00
RY	Robin Yount	50.00

Legends Title Threads

1964 WORLD SERIES CHAMPION — CARDINALS TITLE THREADS — TIM McCARVER
NM/M
Common Player: 4.00
Refractors: No Pricing
Production 25 Sets

WB	Wade Boggs	10.00
GC	Gary Carter	6.00
JC	Joe Carter	6.00
OC	Orlando Cepeda	8.00
BD	Bucky Dent	6.00
LD	Lenny Dykstra	6.00
RF	Rollie Fingers	8.00
GF	George Foster	4.00
CS	Cesar Geronimo	6.00
GG	Rich "Goose" Gossage	6.00
KG	Ken Griffey Sr.	8.00
OH	Orel Hershiser	8.00
WH	Willie Horton	10.00
MI	Monte Irvin	12.00
DJ	David Justice	6.00
JK	Jimmy Key	6.00
EK	Ed Kranepool	6.00
TM	Tim McCarver	6.00
GN	Graig Nettles	8.00
PO	Paul O'Neill	10.00
JP	Jim Palmer	8.00
DS	Darryl Strawberry	6.00
MW	Mookie Wilson	4.00

Legends Valuable Performances

MOST VALUABLE PLAYER — KEITH HERNANDEZ MVP 1979 — CARDINALS
NM/M
Common Player: 4.00
Refractor: No Pricing
Production one or 25.

YB	Yogi Berra	15.00
JC	Jose Canseco	10.00
AD	Andre Dawson	6.00
DE	Dennis Eckersley	8.00
CF	Cecil Fielder	8.00
SG	Steve Garvey	6.00
KH	Keith Hernandez	4.00
RJ	Reggie Jackson	10.00
HK	Harmon Killebrew	12.00
DBM	Don Mattingly	15.00
JM	Joe Morgan	6.00
DM	Dave Murphy	10.00
SM	Stan Musial	15.00
DP	Dave Parker	4.00
JR	Jim Rice	8.00
CR	Cal Ripken Jr.	25.00
FR	Frank Robinson	8.00
MS	Mike Schmidt	15.00
CY	Carl Yastrzemski	15.00
RY	Robin Yount	15.00

2005 Topps Retired Signature Edition

NM/M
Complete Set (110): 150.00
Common Player: 1.00
Pack (5): 30.00
Box (5): 125.00

1	Josh Gibson	1.00
2	Andre Dawson	1.00
3	Al Kaline	2.00
4	Andy Van Slyke	1.00
5	Brett Butler	1.00
6	Bob Gibson	1.50
7	Bo Jackson	2.00
8	Carlton Fisk	1.00
9	Chuck Knoblauch	1.00
10	Cal Ripken Jr.	6.00
11	Carl Yastrzemski	3.00
12	Tom Niedenfuer	1.00
13	Dennis Eckersley	1.00
14	Darryl Strawberry	1.00
15	Dwight Gooden	1.00
16	Davey Johnson	1.00
17	Don Mattingly	3.00
18	Dave Winfield	1.50
19	Don Zimmer	1.00
20	Ernie Banks	2.00
21	George Brett	3.00
22	Gary Carter	1.00
23	Gregg Jefferies	1.00
24	Harold Baines	1.00
25	Ryne Sandberg	2.00
26	Howard Johnson	1.00
27	Jim Abbott	1.00
28	Johnny Bench	2.00
29	Jay Buhner	1.00
30	Johnny Podres	1.00
31	Jose Canseco	1.50
32	Keith Hernandez	1.00
33	Lou Brock	1.00
34	Lou Whitaker	1.00
35	Mark Fidrych	1.00
36	Orlando Cepeda	1.00
37	Ozzie Smith	2.00
38	Paul O'Neill	1.00
39	Reggie Jackson	1.50
40	Sid Fernandez	1.00
41	Tony Gwynn	2.00
42	Tim Raines	1.00
43	Tom Seaver	1.50
44	Vida Blue	1.00
45	Brady Anderson	1.00
46	Bob Brenly	1.00
47	Bob Feller	1.50
48	Bill Mazeroski	1.00
49	Brooks Robinson	1.50
50	Harmon Killebrew	1.50
51	Bob Welch	1.00
52	Carl Erskine	1.00
53	Dale Murphy	1.00
54	Denny McLain	1.00
55	Dave Magadan	1.00
56	Duke Snider	1.50
57	Ed Kranepool	1.00
58	Frank Robinson	1.50
59	Jesus Alou	1.00
60	Joe Girardi	1.00
61	John Kruk	1.00
62	Jim Leyland	1.00
63	Juan Marichal	1.00
64	Johnny Pesky	1.00
65	Jesse Orosco	1.00
66	Ken Singleton	1.00
67	Matty Alou	1.00
68	Monte Irvin	1.00
69	Matt Williams	1.00
70	Pedro Guerrero	1.00
71	Ron Blomberg	1.00
72	Rod Carew	1.50
73	Rafael Santana	1.00
74	Ralph Kiner	1.00
75	Wade Boggs	1.50
76	Roger Craig	1.00
77	Robin Yount	2.00
78	Steve Carlton	1.00
79	Shawon Dunston	1.00
80	Steve Garvey	1.00
81	Stan Musial	3.00
82	Travis Fryman	1.00
83	Tito Fuentes	1.00
84	Mike Cuellar	1.00
85	Roberto Clemente	4.00
86	Whitey Ford	1.50
87	Yogi Berra	2.00
88	Atlee Hammaker	1.00
89	Bill Freehan	1.00
90	Brian Cashman	1.00
91	Bobby Richardson	1.00
92	Bob Boone	1.00
93	Charlie Hough	1.00
94	Glenn Hubbard	1.00
95	Grady Little	1.00
96	Jimmy Piersall	1.00
97	Jim Frey	1.00
98	Jerry Grote	1.00
99	Jim Leyritz	1.00
100	Nolan Ryan	5.00
101	Jim Kaat	1.00
102	Joe Pepitone	1.00
103	J.R. Richard	1.00
104	John Candelaria	1.00
105	Bill "Moose" Skowron	1.00
106	Rick Cerone	1.00
107	Ron Santo	1.00
108	Rick Dempsey	1.00
109	Roy White	1.00
110	Tippy Martinez	1.00

Black
Black (1-110): 4-6X
Production 54 Sets

Gold

Gold (1-110): 2-4X
Production 500 Sets

Holographic
No Pricing
Production One Set

Autographs

NM/M
Common Autograph: 10.00

JAA	Jim Abbott	20.00
JA	Jesus Alou	15.00
MA	Matty Alou	15.00
BA	Brady Anderson	15.00
HB	Harold Baines	15.00
EB	Ernie Banks	150.00
JB	Johnny Bench	200.00
YB	Yogi Berra	200.00
RB	Ron Blomberg	15.00
DLB	Daryl Boston	10.00
BEB	Bob Brenly	10.00
GB	George Brett	150.00
LB	Lou Brock	25.00
JCB	Jay Buhner	25.00
BB	Brett Butler	20.00
JRC	John Candelaria	15.00
JC	Jose Canseco	50.00
RCC	Rod Carew	30.00
SC	Steve Carlton	35.00
GC	Gary Carter	20.00
BC	Brian Cashman	85.00
OC	Orlando Cepeda	15.00
RC	Rick Cerone	15.00
RLC	Roger Craig	15.00
MC	Mike Cuellar	15.00
RD	Ron Darling	15.00
AD	Andre Dawson	25.00
RRD	Rick Dempsey	15.00
BD	Bob Dernier	20.00
SD	Shawon Dunston	35.00
CE	Carl Erskine	30.00
BF	Bob Feller	30.00
SF	Sid Fernandez	30.00
CF	Carlton Fisk	30.00
BAF	Bill Freehan	10.00
JF	Jim Frey	15.00
TDF	Travis Fryman	15.00
TF	Tito Fuentes	15.00
REG	Ron Gant	25.00
SG	Steve Garvey	20.00
BG	Bob Gibson	150.00
DG	Dwight Gooden	20.00
JG	Jerry Grote	20.00
PG	Pedro Guerrero	15.00
TG	Tony Gwynn	100.00
AH	Atlee Hammaker	10.00
TH	Toby Harrah	15.00
KH	Keith Hernandez	20.00
CH	Charlie Hough	10.00
GH	Glenn Hubbard	10.00
MI	Monte Irvin	50.00
BJ	Bo Jackson	100.00
RJ	Reggie Jackson	150.00
GJ	Gregg Jefferies	20.00
HJ	Howard Johnson	25.00
JLK	Jim Kaat	15.00
AK	Al Kaline	40.00
HK	Harmon Killebrew	100.00
RK	Ralph Kiner	35.00
EK	Ed Kranepool	15.00
JK	John Kruk	20.00
TL	Tony LaRussa	15.00
JL	Jim Leyland	15.00
JJL	Jim Leyritz	15.00
GL	Grady Little	15.00
JRL	Jim Lonborg	15.00
DJM	Dave Magadan	15.00
JM	Juan Marichal	25.00
TM	Tippy Martinez	10.00
DM	Don Mattingly	140.00
BM	Bill Mazeroski	45.00
DDM	Denny McLain	20.00
DBM	Dale Murphy	30.00
TN	Tom Niedenfuer	15.00
PO	Paul O'Neill	40.00
JO	Jesse Orosco	10.00
JP	Joe Pepitone	15.00
JMP	Johnny Pesky	25.00
JAP	Jimmy Piersall	20.00
JJP	Johnny Podres	50.00
TR	Tim Raines	25.00
JR	J.R. Richard	20.00
BCR	Bobby Richardson	20.00
CR	Cal Ripken Jr.	180.00
BR	Brooks Robinson	80.00
FR	Frank Robinson	80.00
NR	Nolan Ryan	250.00
RS	Ryne Sandberg	90.00
RFS	Rafael Santana	10.00
RES	Ron Santo	30.00
TS	Tom Seaver	100.00
MS	Bill "Moose" Skowron	15.00
OS	Ozzie Smith	125.00
ZS	Zane Smith	10.00
DS	Duke Snider	60.00
DES	Darryl Strawberry	50.00
BW	Bob Welch	15.00
LW	Lou Whitaker	35.00
RW	Roy White	15.00
MW	Matt Williams	30.00
DW	Dave Winfield	50.00
CY	Carl Yastrzemski	120.00
AY	Anthony Young	10.00
RY	Robin Yount	125.00
DZ	Don Zimmer	30.00

Co-Signers
NM/M
Some not priced.

BS	Wade Boggs, Ryne Sandberg/49	140.00
BF	Johnny Bench, Carlton Fisk/49	125.00
GF	Bob Gibson, Whitey Ford/49	100.00

2005 Topps Rookie Cup

NM/M
Complete Set (160): 35.00
Common Player (1-150): .15
Common Rookie Auto. (151-160): 8.00
Inserted 1:62
Pack (7): 4.00
Box (24): 75.00

1	Pat Corrales	.15
2	Ron Santo	.25
3	Joe Torre	.25
4	Boog Powell	.15
5	Tom Tresh	.15
6	Jonny Gomes	.15
7	Rico Carty	.15
8	Bert Campaneris	.15
9	Tony Oliva	.25
10	Ron Swoboda	.15
11	Tony Perez	.40
12	Joe Morgan	.40
13	Davey Johnson	.15
14	Cleon Jones	.15
15	Tom Seaver	.50
16	Rod Carew	.50
17	Rick Monday	.15
18	Johnny Bench	.75
19	Bobby Cox	.15
20	Jerry Koosman	.15
21	Al Oliver	.25
22	Lou Piniella	.25
23	Larry Bowa	.25
24	Chris Chambliss	.15
25	Bill Buckner	.15
26	Don Baylor	.15
27	Buddy Bell	.15
28	Carlton Fisk	.50
29	Gary Mathews	.15
30	Davey Lopes	.15
31	Bob Boone	.15
32	Bill Madlock	.15
33	Claudell Washington	.15
34	Jim Rice	.15
35	Gary Carter	.15
36	Willie Randolph	.15
37	Chet Lemon	.15
38	Andre Dawson	.15
39	Eddie Murray	.50
40	Paul Molitor	.50
41	Ozzie Smith	1.00
42	Jeffrey Leonard	.15
43	Lonnie Smith	.15
44	Mookie Wilson	.15
45	Tim Wallach	.15
46	Tim Raines	.25
47	Fernando Valenzuela	.15
48	Cal Ripken Jr.	2.00
49	Ryne Sandberg	1.00
50	Willie McGee	.15
51	Darryl Strawberry	.15
52	Julio Franco	.15
53	Brook Jacoby	.15
54	Dwight Gooden	.15
55	Roger McDowell	.15
56	Ozzie Guillen	.15
57	Vince Coleman	.15
58	Pete Incaviglia	.15
59	Wally Joyner	.15
60	Jose Canseco	.50
61	Cory Snyder	.15
62	Devon White	.15
63	Walt Weiss	.15
64	Mark Grace	.40
65	Ron Gant	.15
66	Chris Sabo	.15
67	Jay Buhner	.15
68	Gary Sheffield	.40
69	Gregg Jefferies	.15
70	Ken Griffey Jr.	1.50
71	Tom Gordon	.15
72	Jim Abbott	.15
73	David Justice	.25
74	Larry Walker	.15
75	Sandy Alomar	.15
76	Chuck Knoblauch	.15
77	Jeff Bagwell	.50
78	Luis Gonzalez	.25
79	Ivan Rodriguez	.50
80	Eric Karros	.15
81	Jeff Kent	.15
82	Kenny Lofton	.15
83	Moises Alou	.25
84	Reggie Sanders	.15
85	Jeff Conine	.15
86	J.T. Snow	.15
87	Tim Salmon	.25
88	Mike Piazza	1.00
89	Manny Ramirez	.75
90	Ryan Klesko	.15
91	Javy Lopez	.15
92	Chipper Jones	.75
93	Ray Durham	.15
94	Garret Anderson	.15
95	Shawn Green	.15
96	Hideo Nomo	.25
97	Jermaine Dye	.15
98	Tony Clark	.15
99	Joe Randa	.15
100	Derek Jeter	2.00
101	Jason Kendall	.15
102	Billy Wagner	.15
103	Andruw Jones	.50
104	Dmitri Young	.15
105	Scott Rolen	.25
106	Nomar Garciaparra	.75
107	Jose Cruz Jr.	.15
108	Scott Hatteberg	.15
109	Mark Kotsay	.15
110	Todd Helton	.50
111	Miguel Cairo	.15
112	Magglio Ordonez	.25
113	Kerry Wood	.15
114	Preston Wilson	.15
115	Alex Gonzalez	.15
116	Carlos Beltran	.50
117	Rafael Furcal	.25
118	Pat Burrell	.25
119	Adam Kennedy	.15
120	Terrence Long	.15
121	Jay Payton	.15
122	Bengie Molina	.15
123	Albert Pujols	2.00
124	Craig Wilson	.15
125	Alfonso Soriano	.50
126	Jimmy Rollins	.25
127	Adam Dunn	.50
128	Ichiro Suzuki	1.50
129	Roy Oswalt	.15
130	C.C. Sabathia	.15
131	Brad Wilkerson	.15
132	Nick Johnson	.15
133	Eric Hinske	.15
134	Austin Kearns	.15
135	Dontrelle Willis	.40
136	Mark Teixeira	.25
137	Rocco Baldelli	.15
138	Scott Podsednik	.15
139	Brandon Webb	.25
140	Jason Bay	.15
141	Adam LaRoche	.15
142	Khalil Greene	.25
143	Joe Mauer	.50
144	Matt Holliday	.15
145	Chad Tracy	.15
146	Garrett Atkins	.15
147	Tadahito Iguchi	1.00
148	Russ Adams	.15
149	Huston Street	.15
150	Dan Johnson	.15
151	J. Brent Cox RC	15.00
152	John Drennen RC	30.00
153	Ryan Tucker RC	8.00
154	Yunel Escobar RC	25.00
155	Jacob Marceaux RC	10.00
156	Mark Pawelek RC	8.00
157	Brandon Snyder RC	25.00
158	Wade Townsend RC	8.00
159	Troy Tulowitzki RC	50.00
160	Kevin Whelan RC	12.00

Blue
Blue (1-150): 3-6X
Blue (151-160): 1-2X
Production 50 Sets

Gold
No Pricing
Production One Set

Green
Green (1-150): 2-4X
Production 199
Green (151-160): 1-2X
Production 99

Orange
Orange (1-150): 1.5-3X
Production 399
Orange (151-160): 1X
Production 299

Red
Red (1-150): 1-2X
Production 499
Red (151-160): 1X
Production 399

Silver
No Pricing
Production One Set

Yellow
Yellow (1-150): 2-3X
Production 299
Yellow (151-160): 1X
Production 199

Printing Plates
No Pricing
Production one set per color.

Autographs
NM/M
Common Autograph:
Silver: No Pricing
Production Five Sets
Gold: No Pricing
Production One Set

JBA	Jason Bay	20.00
JB	Johnny Bench	65.00
AD	Andre Dawson	15.00
JD	Jermaine Dye	8.00
RF	Rafael Furcal	12.00
MG	Mark Grace	25.00
DRJ	Dan Johnson	15.00
DJ	Davey Johnson	8.00
AJ	Andruw Jones	40.00
CJ	Chipper Jones	35.00
DJ	David Justice	20.00
EK	Eric Karros	8.00
MK	Mark Kotsay	8.00
CK	Chuck Knoblauch	20.00
RM	Roger McDowell	8.00
PM	Paul Molitor	50.00
BP	Boog Powell	15.00
MR	Manny Ramirez	50.00
JR	Jim Rice	30.00
RSA	Ron Santo	25.00
TS	Tom Seaver	50.00
GS	Gary Sheffield	25.00
DS	Darryl Strawberry	15.00
RS	Ron Swoboda	10.00
JT	Joe Torre	25.00
BW	Brad Wilkerson	8.00
DW	Dontrelle Willis	20.00

Dual Autographs
NM/M
Inserted 1:118

GS	Mark Grace, Ron Santo	80.00
BW	Jason Bay, Dontrelle Willis	50.00
WD	Brad Wilkerson, Andre Dawson	50.00
CS	J. Brent Cox, Tom Seaver	40.00
RTW	Ryan Tucker, Dontrelle Willis	20.00
EF	Yunel Escobar, Rafael Furcal	20.00
MM	Jacob Marceaux, Roger McDowell	20.00
SP	Brandon Snyder, Boog Powell	25.00
TS	Wade Townsend, Tom Seaver	50.00
TW	Troy Tulowitzki, Walt Weiss	30.00
WM	Kevin Whelan, Roger McDowell	15.00

Reprints
NM/M
Complete Set (150): 60.00
Common Player: .25
Reprints: 1-2X Base Card
2 Per Hobby Pack
1 Per Retail Pack
Chrome: No Pricing
Production 25 Sets
Refractor: No Pricing
15 Sets
Chrome Gold: No Pricing
Production One Set

1	Pat Corrales/66	.25
2	Ron Santo/61	.50
3	Joe Torre/62	.75
4	Boog Powell/63	.25
5	Tom Tresh/63	.25
6	Jonny Gomes/06	.25
7	Rico Carty/65	.25
8	Bert Campaneris/65	.25
9	Tony Oliva/65	.50
10	Ron Swoboda/66	.25
11	Tony Perez/66	.75
12	Joe Morgan/66	.75
13	Davey Johnson/67	.25
14	Cleon Jones/67	.25
15	Tom Seaver/68	1.00
16	Rod Carew/68	.75
17	Rick Monday/68	.25
18	Johnny Bench/69	1.50
19	Bobby Cox/69	.25
20	Jerry Koosman/69	.25
21	Al Oliver/70	.50
22	Lou Piniella/70	.40
23	Larry Bowa/71	.40
24	Chris Chambliss/72	.25
25	Bill Buckner/72	.25
26	Don Baylor/73	.25
27	Buddy Bell/73	.25
28	Carlton Fisk/73	.75
29	Gary Mathews/74	.25
30	Davey Lopes/74	.25
31	Bob Boone/74	.25
32	Bill Madlock 75	.25
33	Claudell Washington/75	.25
34	Jim Rice/76	.40
35	Gary Carter/76	.25
36	Willie Randolph/77	.25
37	Chet Lemon/77	.25
38	Andre Dawson/ 78	.40
39	Eddie Murray/78	.75
40	Paul Molitor/78	.75
41	Ozzie Smith/79	1.50
43	Jeffrey Leonard/80	.25
44	Lonnie Smith/81	.25
45	Tim Wallach/82	.25
46	Tim Raines/82	.40
47	Fernando Valenzuela/82	.25
48	Cal Ripken Jr./83	3.00
49	Ryne Sandberg/84	1.50
50	Willie McGee/83	.25
51	Darryl Strawberry/84	.25
52	Julio Franco/84	.25
53	Brook Jacoby/85	.25
54	Dwight Gooden/85	.25
55	Roger McDowell/86	.25
56	Ozzie Guillen/86	.25
57	Vince Coleman/86	.25
58	Pete Incaviglia/87	.25
59	Wally Joyner/87	.25
60	Jose Canseco/87	.75
61	Cory Snyder/87	.25
62	Devon White/88	.25
63	Walt Weiss/89	.25
64	Mark Grace/89	.50
65	Ron Gant/89	.25
66	Chris Sabo/89	.25
67	Jay Buhner/89	.25
68	Gary Sheffield/90	.50
69	Gregg Jefferies/90	.25
70	Ken Griffey Jr./90	2.00
71	Tom Gordon/90	.25
72	Jim Abbott/90	.25
73	David Justice/91	.40
74	Larry Walker/91	.40
75	Sandy Alomar Jr./91	.25
76	Chuck Knoblauch/92	.25
77	Jeff Bagwell/92	.50
78	Luis Gonzalez/92	.25
79	Ivan Rodriguez/92	.50
80	Eric Karros/93	.25
81	Jeff Kent/93	.25
82	Kenny Lofton/93	.25
83	Moises Alou/93	.25
84	Reggie Sanders/93	.25
85	Jeff Conine/94	.25
86	J.T. Snow/94	.25
87	Tim Salmon/94	.25
88	Mike Piazza/94	1.50
89	Manny Ramirez/95	.75
90	Ryan Klesko/95	.25
91	Javy Lopez/95	.25
92	Chipper Jones/96	1.00
93	Ray Durham/96	.25
94	Garret Anderson/96	.25
95	Shawn Green/96	.25
96	Hideo Nomo/96	.40

#	Player	Price
97	Jermaine Dye/97	.25
98	Tony Clark/97	.25
99	Joe Randa/97	.25
100	Derek Jeter/97	3.00
101	Jason Kendall/97	.25
102	Billy Wagner/97	.25
103	Andruw Jones/98	.75
104	Dmitri Young/98	.25
105	Scott Rolen/98	.75
106	Nomar Garciaparra/98	.75
107	Jose Cruz Jr./98	.25
108	Scott Hatteberg/98	.25
109	Mark Kotsay/99	.25
110	Todd Helton/99	.50
111	Miguel Cairo/99	.25
112	Magglio Ordonez/99	.25
113	Kerry Wood/99	.40
114	Preston Wilson/00	.25
115	Alex Gonzalez/00	.25
116	Carlos Beltran/00	.50
117	Rafael Furcal/01	.25
118	Pat Burrell/01	.25
119	Adam Kennedy/01	.25
120	Terrence Long/01	.25
121	Jay Payton/01	.25
122	Bengie Molina/01	.25
123	Albert Pujols/01	3.00
124	Craig Wilson/02	.25
125	Alfonso Soriano/02	.50
126	Jimmy Rollins/02	.50
127	Adam Dunn/02	.75
128	Ichiro Suzuki/02	2.00
129	Roy Oswalt/02	.40
130	C.C. Sabathia/02	.25
131	Brad Wilkerson/03	.25
132	Nick Johnson/03	.25
133	Eric Hinske/03	.25
134	Austin Kearns/03	.25
135	Dontrelle Willis/04	.75
136	Mark Teixeira/04	.75
137	Rocco Baldelli/04	.25
138	Scott Podsednik/04	.25
139	Brandon Webb/04	.25
140	Jason Bay/05	.25
141	Adam LaRoche/05	.25
142	Khalil Greene/05	.25
143	Joe Mauer/05	.50
144	Matt Holliday/05	.25
145	Chad Tracy/05	.25
146	Garrett Atkins/06	.25
147	Tadahito Iguchi/06	1.50
148	Russ Adams/06	.25
149	Huston Street/06	.25
150	Dan Johnson/06	.25

Original Relics

No Pricing
Production 1-10

2005 Topps Total

Barry Bonds

		NM/M
	Complete Set (770):	120.00
	Common Player:	.15
	Pack (10):	1.00
	Box (36):	35.00
1	Rafael Furcal	.15
2	Tony Clark	.15
3	Hideki Matsui	1.25
4	Zach Day	.15
5	Garret Anderson	.40
6	B.J. Surhoff	.15
7	Trevor Hoffman	.15
8	Kenny Lofton	.15
9	Ross Gload	.15
10	Jorge Cantu	.15
11	Joel Pineiro	.15
12	Alex Cintron	.15
13	Mike Matheny	.15
14	Rod Barajas	.15
15	Ray Durham	.15
16	Danys Baez	.15
17	Brian Schneider	.15
18	Tike Redman	.15
19	Ricardo Rodriguez	.15
20	Mike Sweeney	.15
21	Greg Myers	.15
22	Chone Figgins	.15
23	Brian Lawrence	.15
24	Joe Nathan	.15
25	Placido Polanco	.15
26	Yadier Molina	.15
27	Gary Bennett	.15
28	Yorvit Torrealba	.15
29	Javier Valentin	.15
30	Jason Giambi	.25
31	Brandon Claussen	.15

#	Player	Price
32	Miguel Olivo	.15
33	Josh Bard	.15
34	Ramon Hernandez	.15
35	Geoff Jenkins	.15
36	Bobby Kielty	.15
37	Luis A. Gonzalez	.15
38	Benito Santiago	.15
39	Brandon Inge	.15
40	Mark Prior	.50
41	Mike Lieberthal	.15
42	Toby Hall	.15
43	Brad Ausmus	.15
44	Damian Miller	.15
45	Mark Kotsay	.15
46	John Buck	.15
47	Oliver Perez	.25
48	Matt Morris	.25
49	Raul Chavez	.15
50	Randy Johnson	.50
51	David Bush	.15
52	Jose Macias	.15
53	Paul Wilson	.15
54	Wilfredo Ledezma	.15
55	J.D. Drew	.25
56	Pedro Martinez	.50
57	Josh Towers	.15
58	Jamie Moyer	.15
59	Scott Elarton	.15
60	Ken Griffey Jr.	1.00
61	Steve Trachsel	.15
62	Bubba Crosby	.15
63	Michael Barrett	.15
64	Odalis Perez	.15
65	B.J. Upton	.25
66	Eric Bruntlett	.15
67	Carlos Zambrano	.15
68	Brandon League	.15
69	Carlos Silva	.15
70	Lyle Overbay	.25
71	Runelvys Hernandez	.15
72	Brad Penny	.15
73	Ty Wigginton	.15
74	Orlando Hudson	.15
75	Roy Oswalt	.25
76	Jason LaRue	.15
77	Ismael Valdez	.15
78	Calvin Pickering	.15
79	Bill Hall	.15
80	Carl Crawford	.25
81	Tomas Perez	.15
82	Joe Kennedy	.15
83	Chris Woodward	.15
84	Jason Lane	.15
85	Steve Finley	.15
86	Jeff Francis	.15
87	Felipe Lopez	.15
88	Chan Ho Park	.15
89	Joe Crede	.15
90	Jose Vidro	.15
91	Casey Kotchman	.25
92	Brandon Backe	.15
93	Mike Hampton	.15
94	Ryan Dempster	.15
95	Wily Mo Pena	.25
96	Matt Holliday	.15
97	A.J. Pierzynski	.15
98	Jason Jennings	.15
99	Eli Marrero	.15
100	Carlos Beltran	.40
101	Scott Kazmir	.25
102	Kenny Rogers	.15
103	Roy Halladay	.25
104	Alex Cora	.15
105	Richie Sexson	.25
106	Ben Sheets	.25
107	Bartolo Colon	.25
108	Eddie Perez	.15
109	Vicente Padilla	.15
110	Sammy Sosa	1.00
111	Mark Ellis	.15
112	Woody Williams	.15
113	Todd Greene	.15
114	Nook Logan	.15
115	Francisco Rodriguez	.25
116	Miguel Batista	.15
117	Livan Hernandez	.15
118	Chris Aguila	.15
119	Coco Crisp	.15
120	Jose Reyes	.25
121	Ricky Ledee	.15
122	Brad Radke	.15
123	Carlos Guillen	.15
124	Paul Bako	.15
125	Tom Glavine	.25
126	Chad Moeller	.15
127	Mark Buehrle	.15
128	Casey Blake	.15
129	Juan Rivera	.15
130	Preston Wilson	.15
131	Nate Robertson	.15
132	Julio Franco	.15
133	Derek Lowe	.15
134	Rob Bell	.15
135	Javy Lopez	.25
136	Javier Vazquez	.15
137	Desi Relaford	.15
138	Danny Graves	.15
139	Josh Fogg	.15
140	Bobby Crosby	.25
141	Ramon Castro	.15
142	Jerry Hairston Jr.	.15
143	Morgan Ensberg	.15
144	Brandon Webb	.25
145	Jack Wilson	.15
146	Bill Mueller	.15
147	Troy Glaus	.25
148	Armando Benitez	.15
149	Adam LaRoche	.15

#	Player	Price
150	Hank Blalock	.40
151	Ryan Franklin	.15
152	Kevin Millwood	.15
153	Jason Marquis	.15
154	Dewon Brazelton	.15
155	Al Leiter	.15
156	Garrett Atkins	.15
157	Todd Walker	.15
158	Kris Benson	.15
159	Eric Milton	.15
160	Bret Boone	.15
161	Matthew LeCroy	.15
162	Chris Widger	.15
163	Ruben Gotay	.15
164	Craig Monroe	.15
165	Travis Hafner	.25
166	Vance Wilson	.15
167	Jason Grabowski	.15
168	Tim Salmon	.25
169	Henry Blanco	.15
170	Josh Beckett	.25
171	Jake Westbrook	.15
172	Paul LoDuca	.15
173	Julio Lugo	.15
174	Juan Cruz	.15
175	Mark Mulder	.25
176	Juan Castro	.15
177	Damion Easley	.15
178	LaTroy Hawkins	.15
179	Jon Lieber	.15
180	Vernon Wells	.25
181	Jeff DaVanon	.15
182	Dustan Mohr	.15
183	Ryan Freel	.15
184	Doug Davis	.15
185	Sean Casey	.25
186	Robb Quinlan	.15
187	J.D. Closser	.15
188	Tim Wakefield	.15
189	Brian Jordan	.15
190	Adam Dunn	.40
191	Antonio Perez	.15
192	Brett Tomko	.15
193	John Flaherty	.15
194	Michael Cuddyer	.15
195	Ronnie Belliard	.15
196	Tony Womack	.15
197	Jason Johnson	.15
198	Victor Santos	.15
199	Dan Haren	.15
200	Derek Jeter	1.50
201	Brian Anderson	.15
202	Carlos Pena	.15
203	Jaret Wright	.15
204	Paul Byrd	.15
205	Shannon Stewart	.15
206	Chris Carpenter	.15
207	Matt Stairs	.15
208	Brad Hawpe	.15
209	Bobby Higginson	.15
210	Torii Hunter	.25
211	Shawn Green	.25
212	Todd Hollandsworth	.15
213	Scott Erickson	.15
214	C.C. Sabathia	.15
215	Mike Mussina	.40
216	Jason Kendall	.15
217	Todd Pratt	.15
218	Danny Kolb	.15
219	Tony Armas	.15
220	Edgar Renteria	.25
221	Dave Roberts	.15
222	Luis Rivas	.15
223	Adam Everett	.15
224	Jeff Cirillo	.15
225	Orlando Hernandez	.15
226	Ken Harvey	.15
227	Corey Patterson	.25
228	Humberto Cota	.15
229	A.J. Burnett	.25
230	Roger Clemens	1.50
231	Joe Randa	.15
232	David Dellucci	.15
233	Troy Percival	.15
234	Dustin Hermanson	.15
235	Eric Gagne	.25
236	Terry Tiffee	.15
237	Tony Graffanino	.15
238	Jayson Werth	.15
239	Michael Sweeney	.15
240	Chipper Jones	.75
241	Aramis Ramirez	.40
242	Frank Catalanotto	.15
243	Mike Maroth	.15
244	Kelvim Escobar	.15
245	Bobby Abreu	.25
246	Kyle Lohse	.15
247	Jason Isringhausen	.15
248	Jose Lima	.15
249	Adrian Gonzalez	.15
250	Alex Rodriguez	1.50
251	Ramon Ortiz	.15
252	Frank Menechino	.15
253	Keith Ginter	.15
254	Kip Wells	.15
255	Dmitri Young	.15
256	Craig Biggio	.25
257	Ramon E. Martinez	.15
258	Jason Bartlett	.15
259	Brad Lidge	.15
260	Brian Giles	.25
261	Luis Terrero	.15
262	Miguel Ojeda	.15
263	Rich Harden	.25
264	Jacque Jones	.15
265	Marcus Giles	.25
266	Carlos Zambrano	.25
267	Michael Tucker	.15

#	Player	Price
268	Wes Obermueller	.15
269	Peter Orr	.50
270	Jim Thome	.50
271	Omar Vizquel	.25
272	Jose Valentin	.15
273	Juan Uribe	.15
274	Doug Mirabelli	.15
275	Jeff Kent	.25
276	Brad Wilkerson	.15
277	Chris Burke	.15
278	Endy Chavez	.15
279	Richard Hidalgo	.15
280	John Smoltz	.25
281	Jarrod Washburn	.15
282	Larry Bigbie	.15
283	Edgardo Alfonzo	.15
284	Cliff Lee	.15
285	Carlos Lee	.25
286	Olmedo Saenz	.15
287	Tomokazu Ohka	.15
288	Ruben Sierra	.15
289	Nick Swisher	.25
290	Frank Thomas	.40
291	Aaron Cook	.15
292	Cody McKay	.15
293	Hee Seop Choi	.15
294	Carl Pavano	.25
295	Scott Rolen	.50
296	Matt Kata	.15
297	Terrence Long	.15
298	Jimmy Gobble	.15
299	Jason Repko	.15
300	Manny Ramirez	.50
301	Dan Wilson	.15
302	Jhonny Peralta	.15
303	John Mabry	.15
304	Adam Melhuse	.15
305	Kerry Wood	.50
306	Ryan Langerhans	.15
307	Antonio Alfonseca	.15
308	Marco Scutaro	.15
309	Jamey Carroll	.15
310	Lance Berkman	.25
311	Willie Harris	.15
312	Phil Nevin	.15
313	Gregg Zaun	.15
314	Michael Ryan	.15
315	Zack Greinke	.15
316	Ted Lilly	.15
317	David Eckstein	.15
318	Tony Torcato	.15
319	Robert Mackowiak	.15
320	Mark Teixeira	.40
321	Jason Phillips	.15
322	Jeremy Reed	.15
323	Bengie Molina	.15
324	Terrmel Sledge	.15
325	Justin Morneau	.40
326	Sandy Alomar Jr.	.15
327	Jon Garland	.15
328	Jay Payton	.15
329	Jason Bay	.25
330	Tino Martinez	.25
331	Jeff Conine	.15
332	Shawn Chacon	.15
333	Angel Berroa	.15
334	Reggie Sanders	.15
335	Kevin Brown	.15
336	Brady Clark	.15
337	Casey Fossum	.15
338	Raul Ibanez	.15
339	Derrek Lee	.40
340	Victor Martinez	.25
341	Kazuhisa Ishii	.15
342	Royce Clayton	.15
343	Trot Nixon	.15
344	Eric Young	.15
345	Aubrey Huff	.15
346	Brett Myers	.25
347	Joey Gathright	.15
348	Mark Grudzielanek	.15
349	Scott Spiezio	.15
350	Eric Chavez	.25
351	Einar Diaz	.15
352	Dallas McPherson	.15
353	John Thomson	.15
354	Neifi Perez	.15
355	Larry Walker	.25
356	Billy Wagner	.15
357	Mike Cameron	.15
358	Jimmy Rollins	.25
359	Kevin Mench	.15
360	Joe Mauer	.25
361	Jose Molina	.15
362	Joe Borchard	.15
363	Kevin Cash	.15
364	Jay Gibbons	.15
365	Khalil Greene	.25
366	Justin Leone	.15
367	Eddie Guardado	.15
368	Mike Lamb	.15
369	Matt Riley	.15
370	Luis Gonzalez	.25
371	Alfredo Amezaga	.15
372	J.J. Hardy	.15
373	Hector Luna	.15
374	Greg Aquino	.15
375	Jim Edmonds	.25
376	Joe Blanton	.15
377	Russell Branyan	.15
378	J.T. Snow	.15
379	Magglio Ordonez	.25
380	Rafael Palmeiro	.40
381	Andruw Jones	.25
382	David DeJesus	.15
383	Marquis Grissom	.15
384	Bobby Hill	.15
385	Kazuo Matsui	.15

#	Player	Price
386	Mark Loretta	.15
387	Chris Shelton	.15
388	Johnny Estrada	.15
389	Adam Hyzdu	.15
390	Nomar Garciaparra	1.00
391	Mark Teahen	.15
392	Chris Capuano	.15
393	Ben Broussard	.15
394	Daniel Cabrera	.15
395	Jeremy Bonderman	.25
396	Darin Erstad	.15
397	Alex S. Gonzalez	.15
398	Kevin Millar	.15
399	Freddy Garcia	.15
400	Alfonso Soriano	.50
401	Koyie Hill	.15
402	Omar Infante	.15
403	Alex Gonzalez	.15
404	Pat Burrell	.25
405	Wes Helms	.15
406	Junior Spivey	.15
407	Joe Mays	.15
408	Jason Stanford	.15
409	Gil Meche	.15
410	Tim Hudson	.25
411	Chase Utley	.25
412	Matt Clement	.15
413	Nick Green	.15
414	Jose Vizcaino	.15
415	Ryan Klesko	.15
416	Vinny Castilla	.15
417	Brian Roberts	.40
418	Geronimo Gil	.15
419	Gary Matthews	.15
420	Jeff Weaver	.15
421	Jerome Williams	.15
422	Andy Pettitte	.40
423	Randy Wolf	.15
424	D'Angelo Jimenez	.15
425	Moises Alou	.25
426	Eric Byrnes	.15
427	Mark Redman	.15
428	Jermaine Dye	.15
429	Cory Lidle	.15
430	Jason Schmidt	.25
431	Jason W. Smith	.15
432	Jose Castillo	.15
433	Pokey Reese	.15
434	Matt Lawton	.15
435	Jose Guillen	.25
436	Craig Counsell	.15
437	Jose Hernandez	.15
438	Braden Looper	.15
439	Scott Hatteberg	.15
440	Gary Sheffield	.40
441	Gabe Gross	.15
442	Chris Gomez	.15
443	Dontrelle Willis	.40
444	Jamey Wright	.15
445	Rocco Baldelli	.15
446	Bernie Williams	.25
447	Sean Burroughs	.15
448	Willie Bloomquist	.15
449	Luis Castillo	.15
450	Mike Piazza	1.00
451	Ryan Drese	.15
452	Pedro Feliz	.15
453	Horacio Ramirez	.15
454	Luis Matos	.15
455	Craig Wilson	.15
456	Russ Ortiz	.15
457	Xavier Nady	.15
458	Hideo Nomo	.25
459	Miguel Cairo	.15
460	Mike Lowell	.25
461	Corky Miller	.15
462	Bobby Madritsch	.15
463	Jose Contreras	.15
464	Johnny Damon	.75
465	Miguel Cabrera	.50
466	Eric Hinske	.15
467	Marlon Byrd	.15
468	Aaron Miles	.15
469	Ramon Vazquez	.15
470	Michael Young	.25
471	Alex Sanchez	.15
472	Shea Hillenbrand	.15
473	Jeff Bagwell	.40
474	Erik Bedard	.15
475	Jake Peavy	.40
476	Jody Gerut	.15
477	Randy Winn	.15
478	Kevin Youkilis	.15
479	Eric Dubose	.15
480	David Wright	.75
481	Wilson Valdez	.15
482	Cliff Floyd	.15
483	Jose Mesa	.25
484	Doug Mientkiewicz	.15
485	Jorge Posada	.40
486	Sidney Ponson	.15
487	David Krynzel	.15
488	Octavio Dotel	.15
489	Matt Treanor	.15
490	Johan Santana	.40
491	John Patterson	.15
492	So Taguchi	.15
493	Carl Everett	.15
494	Jason Dubois	.15
495	Albert Pujols	1.50
496	Kirk Rueter	.15
497	Geoff Blum	.15
498	Juan Encarnacion	.15
499	Mark Hendrickson	.15
500	Barry Bonds	2.00
501	Cesar Izturis	.15
502	David Wells	.15
503	Jorge Julio	.15

#	Player	Price
504	Cristian Guzman	.15
505	Juan Pierre	.15
506	Adam Eaton	.15
507	Nick Johnson	.15
508	Mike Redmond	.15
509	Daryle Ward	.15
510	Adrian Beltre	.15
511	Laynce Nix	.15
512	Reed Johnson	.15
513	Jeremy Affeldt	.15
514	R.A. Dickey	.15
515	Alex Rios	.15
516	Orlando Palmeiro	.15
517	Mark Belhorn	.15
518	Adam Kennedy	.15
519	Curtis Granderson	.15
520	Todd Helton	.40
521	Aaron Boone	.15
522	Milton Bradley	.25
523	Timoniel Perez	.15
524	Jeff Suppan	.15
525	Austin Kearns	.15
526	Charles Thomas	.15
527	Bronson Arroyo	.15
528	Roger Cedeno	.15
529	Russ Adams	.15
530	Barry Zito	.25
531	Bob Wickman	.15
532	Deivi Cruz	.15
533	Mariano Rivera	.40
534	J.J. Davis	.15
535	Greg Maddux	1.00
536	Ryan Vogelsong	.15
537	Josh Phelps	.15
538	Scott Hairston	.15
539	Vladimir Guerrero	.75
540	Ivan Rodriguez	.50
541	David Newhan	.15
542	David Bell	.15
543	Lew Ford	.15
544	Grady Sizemore	.25
545	David Ortiz	.75
546	Jose Cruz Jr.	.15
547	Aaron Rowand	.15
548	Marcus Thames	.15
549	Scott Podsednik	.15
550	Ichiro Suzuki	1.25
551	Eduardo Perez	.15
552	Chris Snyder	.15
553	Corey Koskie	.15
554	Miguel Tejada	.50
555	Orlando Cabrera	.25
556	Rondell White	.15
557	Wade Miller	.15
558	Rodrigo Lopez	.15
559	Chad Tracy	.15
560	Paul Konerko	.25
561	Wil Cordero	.15
562	John McDonald	.15
563	Jason Ellison	.15
564	Jason Michaels	.15
565	Melvin Mora	.25
566	Ryan Church	.15
567	Ryan Ludwick	.15
568	Erubiel Durazo	.15
569	Noah Lowry	.15
570	Curt Schilling	.50
571	Esteban Loaiza	.15
572	Freddy Sanchez	.15
573	Rich Aurilia	.15
574	Travis Lee	.15
575	Dennis Tankersley, Chris George	.15
576	Jason Christiansen, Kevin Correia	.15
577	Ryan Bukvich, Randy Williams	.15
578	Terry Agams, Gavin Floyd	.15
579	Seth Etherton, Dan Meyer	.15
580	Justin Lehr, Derrick Turnbow	.15
581	Mike Gosling, Brad Halsey	.15
582	Jim Mecir, Logan Kensing	.15
583	Brad Hennessy, Jeff Fassero	.15
584	Jason Grilli, John Adkins	.15
585	Jesse Crain, Juan Rincon	.15
586	Jaime Cerda, Nate Field	.15
587	Bartolome Fortunato, Jae Weong Seo	.15
588	Frank Brooks, Yhency Brazoban	.15
589	Jamie Walker, Ugueth Urbina	.15
590	Bret Prinz, Scott Proctor	.15
591	Bob Howry, Jason Davis	.15
592	Amaury Telemaco, Tim Worrell	.15
593	Jose Acevedo, Kent Mercker	.15
594	Chris Hammond, Scott Linebrink	.15
595	Fernando Nieve, John Franco	.15
596	Mike Lincoln, Randy Flores	.15
597	Joe Borowski, Kyle Farnsworth	.15
598	Jesus Colome, Lance Carter	.15

599 Abe Alvarez, Lenny DiNardo .15
600 Chad Bradford, Kiko Calero .15
601 David Aardsma, Jim Brower .15
602 Geoff Geary, Ryan Madson .15
603 Ben Howard, Nate Bump .15
604 Chin-Hui Tsao, Jason Young .15
605 Aaron Harang, Ryan Wagner .15
606 Rick Bauer, Steve Kline .15
607 Lance Cormier, Randy Choate .15
608 Jon Leicester, Todd Wellemeyer .15
609 Jason Frasor, Vinnie Chulk .15
610 Brian Fuentes, Scott Dohmann .15
611 Matt Ginter, Tyler Yates .15
612 Cory Stewart, Salomon Torres .15
613 Cal Eldred, Mike Myers .15
614 Carlos Almanzar, Doug Brocail .15
615 George Sherrill, J.J. Putz .15
616 Bruce Chen, Matt Riley .15
617 Ben Weber, David Weathers .15
618 Dennys Reyes, Rudy Seanez .15
619 Ricardo Rincon, Tim Harikkala .15
620 D.J. Carrasco, Shawn Camp .15
621 Allan Simpson, Javier Lopez .15
622 Glendon Rusch, Mike Remlinger .15
623 Kevin Gryboski, Roman Colon .15
624 Chris Reitsma, Tom Martin .15
625 Chad Qualls, Dan Wheeler .15
626 Brooks Kieschnick, Matt Wise .15
627 Justin Speier, Kerry Ligtenberg .15
628 Francisco Cordero, Frank Francisco .15
629 Matt Thornton, Rafael Soriano .15
630 Mike Stanton, Steve Karsay .15
631 Mike MacDougal, Scott Sullivan .15
632 Brian Bruney, Oscar Villarreal .15
633 Jeff Bennett, Mike Adams .15
634 Dave Borkowski, Eddy Rodriguez .15
635 David Riske, Rafael Betancourt .15
636 Gary Glover, Jorge De La Rosa .15
637 Justin Wayne, Matt Perisho .15
638 Jeff Bajenaru, Luis Vizcaino .15
639 Erasmo Ramirez, Ron Mahay .15
640 John Grabow, Mike Gonzalez .15
641 J.C. Romero, Matt Guerrier .15
642 Brandon Duckworth, Tim Redding .15
643 Franklin Nunez, Travis Harper .15
644 Matt Herges, Tyler Walker .15
645 Elmer Dessens, Wilson Alvarez .15
646 Anastacio Martinez, Mark Malaska .15
647 Gary Knotts, Roberto Novoa .15
648 Jairo Garcia, Justin Duchscherer .15
649 Aaron Rakers, Todd Williams .15
650 Paul Quantrill, Tom Gordon .15
651 Brandon Lyon, Shawn Estes .15
652 Gustavo Chacin, Justin Miller .15
653 John Lackey, Scot Shields .15
654 Bobby Seay, Jorge Sosa .15
655 Chad Cordero, Luis Ayala .15
656 Julio Mateo, Ron Villone .15
657 Byung-Hyun Kim, Matt Mantei .15
658 Cliff Politte, Damaso Marte .15
659 Joe Valentine, Luke Hudson .15

660 John Riedling, Todd Jones .15
661 Aaron Heilman, Heath Bell .15
662 Akinori Otsuka, Blaine Neal .15
663 Joe Horgan, Joey Eischen .15
664 Grant Balfour, J.D. Durbin .15
665 Alan Embree, Mike Timlin .15
666 Keith Foulke .15
667 Aaron Fultz, Rheal Cormier .15
668 Kevin Gregg, Scott Dunn .15
669 Franklyn German, Steve Coyler .15
670 Scott Eyre, Wayne Franklin .15
671 Brian Meadows, Mike Johnston .15
672 Guillermo Mota, Tim Spooneybarger .15
673 B.J. Ryan, Jason Grimsley .15
674 Neal Cotts, Shingo Takatsu .15
675 Felix Heredia, Mike DeJean .15
676 Brian Shackelford, Josh Hancock .15
677 Jon Rauch, T.J. Tucker .15
678 Brian Shouse, Nick Regilio .15
679 Julian Tavarez, Ray King .15
680 Mike Wuertz, Stephen Randolph .15
681 Gabe White, Jorge Vasquez .15
682 Jose Valverde, Mike Koplove .15
683 Arthur Rhodes, Scott Sauerbeck .15
684 Felix Rodriguez, Tanyon Sturtze .15
685 Duaner Sanchez, Giovanni Carrara .15
686 Chad Harville, Mike Gallo .15
687 Dave Williams, Sean Burnett .15
688 Scott Atchison, Shigetoshi Hasegawa .15
689 Claudio Vargas, Francis Beltran .15
690 Brendan Donnelly, Esteban Yan .15
691 Ervin Santana, Jeff Mathis .15
692 Bill Bray, Clint Everts .15
693 Jason Kubel, Trevor Plouffe .15
694 Andy Marte, Jake Stevens .15
695 Aaron Hill, Chad Gaudin .15
696 Carlos Quentin, Jesus Cota .15
697 Chris Young, Thomas Diamond .15
698 Dan Johnson, Omar Quintanilla .15
699 John Maine, Val Majewski .15
700 James Houser, Jonny Gomes .15
701 David Murphy, Hanley Ramirez .15
702 Chris Lambert, Rick Ankiel .15
703 Angel Guzman, Felix Pie .15
704 Merkin Valdez, Nate Schierholtz .15
705 Arnie Munoz, Gio Gonzalez .15
706 Felix Hernandez, Travis Blackley .15
707 Edwin Encarnacion, Tony Blanco .15
708 Justin Germano, Tim Stauffer .15
709 Jeremy Guthrie, Jeremy Sowers .15
710 Jorge Cortes, Tom Gorzelanny .15
711 Logan Kensing, Taylor Tankersley .15
712 Neil Walker, Paul Maholm .15
713 Carlos Hernandez, Willy Taveras .50
714 Greg Golson, Ryan Howard 1.00
715 Blake DeWitt, Edwin Jackson .15
716 Dan Putnam, Huston Street .15
717 Mark Rogers, Rickie Weeks .25
718 Phillip Hughes, Robinson Cano .40
719 Jay Rainville, Kyle Waldrop .15
720 Craig Brazell, Yusmeiro Petit .15

721 Baltazar Lopez RC, Matt Brown RC .25
722 Brett Price RC, Jerry Owens RC .50
723 Dan Uggla RC, Kyle Nichols RC 2.00
724 Francisco Rosario RC, Jayce Tingler RC .25
725 Eulogio de la Cruz RC, Tony Giarratano RC .25
726 Matt Campbell RC, Shane Costa RC .25
727 Bill McCarthy RC, Martin Prado RC .25
728 Edinson Volquez RC, Ian Kinsler RC 3.00
729 Lorenzo Scott RC, Luis Ramirez RC .15
730 Chris Seddon RC, Elliot Johnson RC .75
731 Chris Dickerson RC, Thomas Pauly RC .15
732 Jason Motte RC, Stuart Pomeranz RC .25
733 Jose Vaquedano RC, Stefan Bailie RC .25
734 D.J. Houlton RC, Wade Robinson RC .25
735 Matt DeSalvo RC, Melky Cabrera RC .50
736 Brian Stavisky RC, Landon Powell RC .25
737 Scott Mathieson RC, Scott Mitchinson RC .50
738 Bear Bay RC, Sean Marshall RC .50
739 Brandon McCarthy RC, Pedro Lopez RC 1.50
740 Alexander Smit RC, Jair Jurrjens RC .25
741 Matt Rogelstad RC, Ryan Feierabend RC .25
742 Adam Boeve RC, Nate McLouth RC .25
743 Kevin Melillo RC, Michael Rogers RC .25
744 Heath Totten RC, Matthew Kemp RC 2.00
745 Trevor Hutchinson RC, Yorman Bazardo RC .15
746 Jesse Gutierrez RC, Tyler Pelland RC .25
747 Jeremy West RC, Willy Mota RC .25
748 Ryan Garko RC, Ryan Goleski RC .25
749 Bryan Triplett RC, Jared Gothreaux RC .25
750 Glen Perkins RC, Kevin West RC .25
751 Michael Esposito RC, Zachary Parker RC .25
752 Brian Miller RC, Ryan Sweeney RC .25
753 Buck Coats RC, Casey McGehee RC .25
754 Nate Cabrera RC, Zachary Cline RC .15
755 Bobby Livingston RC, Mike Morse RC .25
756 Brendan Ryan RC, Wes Swackhamer RC .25
757 John Hudgins RC, Nick Masset RC .25
758 George Kottaras RC, Peeter Ramos RC .25
759 Elvys Quezada RC, T.J. Beam RC .25
760 Dana Eveland RC, Travis Hinton RC .25
761 Chris Vines RC, James Jurries RC .25
762 Humberto Sanchez RC, Justin Verlander RC 2.00
763 Ian Bladergroen RC, Shawn Bowman RC .50
764 J.B. Thurmond RC, Pat Misch RC .25
765 Christian Colonel RC, Neil Wilson RC .25
766 Checklist 1 .15
767 Checklist 2 .15
768 Checklist 3 .15
769 Checklist 4 .15
770 Checklist 5 .15

Silver
Stars: 1-3X
Inserted 1:1

Press Plates
NM/M
Common Card Front P. Plate: 25.00
Common Card Back P. Plate: 15.00
Stars not priced
Production one set per color (4):

Award Winners
NM/M
Complete Set (30): 15.00
Common Player: .25
Inserted 1:10
AW1 Barry Bonds 2.00
AW2 Vladimir Guerrero .75

DAVID ORTIZ — TOTAL AWARD WINNER

AW3 Roger Clemens 2.00
AW4 Johan Santana .75
AW5 Jason Bay .25
AW6 Bobby Crosby .25
AW7 Eric Gagne .40
AW8 Mariano Rivera .50
AW9 Albert Pujols 2.00
AW10 Mark Teixeira .50
AW11 Mark Loretta .25
AW12 Alfonso Soriano .75
AW13 Jack Wilson .25
AW14 Miguel Tejada .25
AW15 Adrian Beltre .40
AW16 Melvin Mora .25
AW17 Barry Bonds 2.00
AW18 Jim Edmonds .50
AW19 Bobby Abreu .40
AW20 Manny Ramirez .75
AW21 Gary Sheffield .50
AW22 Vladimir Guerrero .75
AW23 Johnny Estrada .25
AW24 Victor Martinez .25
AW25 Ivan Rodriguez .50
AW26 Livan Hernandez .25
AW27 David Ortiz .75
AW28 Bobby Cox .25
AW29 Buck Showalter .25
AW30 Barry Bonds 2.00

Domination
NM/M
Complete Set (30): 15.00
Common Player: .25
Inserted 1:10
40 Mark Prior .75
50 Randy Johnson .75
56 Pedro Martinez .75
60 Ken Griffey Jr. 1.00
100 Carlos Beltran .50
110 Sammy Sosa 1.50
147 Troy Glaus .50
150 Hank Blalock .50
180 Vernon Wells .25
190 Adam Dunn .50
200 Derek Jeter 2.00
230 Roger Clemens 2.00
250 Alex Rodriguez 1.50
260 Brian Giles .25
270 Jim Thome .75
290 Frank Thomas .50
300 Manny Ramirez .75
345 Aubrey Huff .25
350 Eric Chavez .25
400 Alfonso Soriano .75
465 Miguel Cabrera .50
490 Johan Santana .50
495 Albert Pujols 2.00
500 Barry Bonds 2.00
510 Todd Helton .50
520 Vladimir Guerrero .75
540 Ivan Rodriguez .50
545 David Ortiz .75
554 Miguel Tejada .50

Domination Autograph
Production 10

Production

Total Production — Barry Bonds

NM/M
Complete Set (10): 8.00
Common Player: .40
Inserted 1:15
AB Adrian Beltre .40
BB Barry Bonds 2.00

VG Vladimir Guerrero .75
TH Todd Helton .50
AP Albert Pujols 2.00
MR Manny Ramirez .75
AR Alex Rodriguez 1.50
AS Alfonso Soriano .50
MT Miguel Tejada .50
JT Jim Thome .75

Signatures
NM/M
Common Autograph: 8.00
BB Brian Bruney 8.00
RC Robinson Cano 35.00
JG Joey Gathright 10.00
ZG Zack Greinke 12.00
BM Brett Myers 12.00
TT Terry Tiffee 15.00
DW David Wright 50.00

Team Checklists

Total Team Set — GIANTS

NM/M
Complete Set (30): 8.00
Common Player: .15
3 Miguel Tejada .15
6 Frank Thomas .50
8 Victor Martinez .25
9 Todd Helton .50
10 Ivan Rodriguez .50
11 Miguel Cabrera .50
12 Roger Clemens 1.00
13 Zack Greinke .50
14 Vladimir Guerrero .50
16 Ben Sheets .25
17 Johan Santana .25
18 Carlos Beltran .50
19 Alex Rodriguez 1.00
20 Eric Chavez .25
21 Jim Thome .50
22 Jason Bay .25
23 Brian Giles .25
24 Barry Bonds 1.50
25 Ichiro Suzuki 1.00
26 Albert Pujols 1.00
27 Carl Crawford .25
28 Alfonso Soriano .50
29 Roy Halladay .25
30 Jose Vidro .15
7 Adam Dunn .50
5 Kerry Wood .50
5 Luis Gonzalez .25
2 John Smoltz .25
4 David Ortiz .50
15 Eric Gagne .25

Total Topps

TOTAL TOPPS — Alfonso Soriano

NM/M
Complete Set (20): 12.00
Common Player: .25
Inserted 1:15
CB Carlos Beltran .25
AB Adrian Beltre .40
BB Barry Bonds 2.00
EC Eric Chavez .25
RC Roger Clemens 2.00
VG Vladimir Guerrero .75
TH Todd Helton .50
DJ Derek Jeter 2.00
RJ Randy Johnson .75
GM Greg Maddux 1.00
MP Mike Piazza 1.00
AP Albert Pujols 2.00
MR Manny Ramirez 1.50
AR Alex Rodriguez 1.50
IR Ivan Rodriguez .50
JS Johan Santana .50
AS Alfonso Soriano .75
SS Sammy Sosa 1.50
MT Miguel Tejada .50
JT Jim Thome .50

Pepcid Phillies

Kenny Lofton

This special version of Topps Total cards was an August 6 stadium giveaway on Phillies Alumni Night. Except for the numbering on the backs, most cards are identical to the regular Topps Total versions. A sponsor's card was included in the cello wrapped pack.

NM/M
Complete Set (22): 10:00
Common Player: .50
1 Jason Michaels .50
2 Ryan Howard, Greg Golson 1.00
3 Tim Worrell, Pedro Liriano .50
4 Geoff Geary, Ryan Madson .50
5 Rheal Cormier, Aaron Fultz .50
6 Kenny Lofton 1.00
7 Pat Burrell 1.00
8 Bobby Abreu .75
9 Chase Utley .75
10 Jim Thome 1.00
11 Jimmy Rollins 1.00
12 Tomas Perez .50
13 David Bell .50
14 Todd Pratt .50
15 Mike Lieberthal .50
16 Billy Wagner .50
17 Cory Lidle .50
18 Brett Myers .50
19 Vicente Padilla .50
20 Randy Wolf .50
21 Jon Lieber .50
--- Pepcid Sponsor's Card .50

2005 Topps Turkey Red

NM/M
Complete Set (315):
Common Player: .25
Common SP: 4.00
Inserted 1:4
Pack (8): 5.00
Box (24): 100.00
1 Barry Bonds/ Grey Uni./SP 15.00
1 Barry Bonds .25
2 Michael Young .25
3 Jim Edmonds .50
4 Cliff Floyd .25
5 Roger Clemens/ Blue Sky/SP 12.00
5 Roger Clemens/ Yellow Sky/SP 12.00
6 Hal Chase .25
7 Shannon Stewart .25
8 Fred Clarke .25
9 Travis Hafner .50
10 Sammy Sosa/ w/Name/SP 6.00
10 Sammy Sosa/ w/o Name/SP 6.00
11 Jermaine Dye .25
12 Lyle Overbay .25

ABBREVIATIONS
SP - Short Print

13	Oliver Perez	.25
14	Red Dooin	.25
15	Kid Elberfeld	.25
16	Mike Piazza/ Blue Uni./SP	6.00
16	Mike Piazza Pinstripe	1.50
17	Bret Boone	.25
18	Hughie Jennings	.25
19	Jeff Francis	.25
20	Manny Ramirez/SP	6.00
21	Russ Ortiz	.25
22	Carlos Zambrano	.50
23	Luis Castillo	.25
24	David DeJesus	.25
25	Carlos Beltran/SP	5.00
26	Doug Davis	.25
27	Bobby Abreu	.50
28	Rich Harden/SP	4.00
29	Brian Giles	.25
30	Richie Sexson/SP	4.00
31	Nick Johnson	.25
32	Roy Halladay	.50
33	Andy Pettitte	.50
34	Miguel Cabrera	1.00
35	Jeff Kent	.25
36	Chone Figgins	.25
37	Carlos Lee	.50
38	Greg Maddux	2.00
39	Preston Wilson	.25
40	Chipper Jones	1.00
41	Coco Crisp	.25
42	Adam Dunn	.75
43	Miguel Tejada CL	.50
44	Gary Sheffield CL	.50
45	Javy Lopez CL	.50
46	Scott Rolen CL	.50
47	Todd Helton CL	.50
48	Roger Clemens CL	1.00
49	Jimmy Rollins CL	.40
50	Ichiro Suzuki CL	1.00
51	Cliff Floyd CL	.25
52	Johan Santana CL	.50
53	Mark Teixeira	.75
54	Chris Carpenter	.25
55	Roy Oswalt/SP	4.00
56	Casey Kotchman	.25
57	Torii Hunter	.25
58	Jose Reyes	.50
59	Wily Mo Pena/SP	4.00
60	Magglio Ordonez/SP	4.00
61	Aaron Miles	.25
62	Dallas McPherson	.25
63	Javy Lopez	.25
64	Luis Gonzalez	.25
65	David Ortiz	1.00
66	Jorge Posada	.50
67	Xavier Nady	.25
68	Larry Walker	.50
69	Mark Loretta	.25
70	Jim Thome/SP	5.00
71	Livan Hernandez	.25
72	Garrett Atkins	.25
73	Milton Bradley	.25
74	B.J. Upton	.25
75	Ichiro Suzuki/ w/Name/SP	8.00
75	Ichiro Suzuki/ w/o Name/SP	8.00
76	Aramis Ramirez	.25
77	Eric Milton	.25
78	Troy Glaus/SP	4.00
79	David Newhan	.25
80	Delmon Young	.50
81	Justin Morneau	.40
82	Ramon Ortiz	.25
83	Eric Chavez/Blue Sky	.25
83	Eric Chavez/ Purple Sky/SP	4.00
84	Sean Burroughs	.25
85	Scott Rolen/SP	6.00
86	Rocco Baldelli	.25
87	Joe Mauer/SP	5.00
88	Tony Womack	.25
89	Ken Griffey Jr.	2.00
90	Alfonso Soriano/SP	6.00
91	Paul Konerko	.25
92	Guillermo Mota	.25
93	Lance Berkman	.50
94	Mark Buehrle	.25
95	Matt Clement	.25
96	Melvin Mora	.25
97	Khalil Greene	.25
98	David Wright	1.50
99	Jack Wilson	.25
100	Alex Rodriguez/ w/Bat/SP	10.00
100	Alex Rodriguez/ w/Glv/SP	10.00
101	Joe Nathan	.25
102	Adrian Beltre/ Grey Uni./SP	4.00
102	Adrian Beltre/ White Uni.	.25
103	Mike Sweeney	.25
104	Brad Lidge	.25
105	Shawn Green	.25
106	Miguel Tejada/SP	5.00
107	Derrek Lee	.75
108	Eric Hinske	.25
109	Eric Byrnes	.25
110	Hideki Matsui/SP	8.00
111	Tom Glavine	.50
112	Jimmy Rollins	.40
113	Ryan Drese	.25
114	Josh Beckett	.25
115	Curt Schilling/SP	6.00
116	Jeremy Bonderman	.25
117	Hideki Matsui	.25
118	Chase Utley	.50
119	Troy Percival	.25

120	Vladimir Guerrero/ w/Bat/SP	6.00
120	Vladimir Guerrero/ w/Glv/SP	6.00
121	Gary Sheffield	.50
122	Jeromy Burnitz	.25
123	Javier Vazquez	.25
124	Kevin Millar	.25
125	Randy Johnson/ Blue Sky	1.00
125	Randy Johnson/ Purple Sky/SP	5.00
126	Pat Burrell	.25
127	Jason Schmidt	.25
128	Jose Vidro	.25
129	Kip Wells	.25
130	Ivan Rodriguez/w/Cap	.75
130	Ivan Rodriguez/ w/Helmet/SP	6.00
131	C.C. Sabathia	.25
132	Carlos Delgado/SP	4.00
133	Bartolo Colon	.25
134	Andruw Jones	.50
135	Kerry Wood	.50
136	Sidney Ponson	.25
137	Eric Gagne	.25
138	Rickie Weeks	.50
139	Mariano Rivera	.25
140	Bobby Crosby	.25
141	Jamie Moyer	.25
142	Corey Koskie	.25
143	John Smoltz	.50
145	Frank Thomas	.75
146	Cristian Guzman	.25
147	Paul LoDuca	.25
148	Geoff Jenkins	.25
149	Nick Swisher	.25
149	Jason Bay/SP	4.00
150	Albert Pujols/SP	10.00
151	Edwin Jackson	.25
152	Carl Crawford	.25
153	Mark Mulder	.50
154	Rafael Palmeiro	.75
155	Pedro Martinez/SP	6.00
156	Jake Westbrook	.25
157	Sean Casey	.25
158	Aaron Rowand	.25
159	J.D. Drew	.25
160	Johan Santana/ Glove on Knee/SP	5.00
160	Johan Santana/ Throwing/SP	5.00
161	Gavin Floyd	.25
162	Vernon Wells	.25
163	Aubrey Huff	.25
164	Jeff Bagwell	.50
165	David Wells	.25
166	Brad Penny	.25
167	Austin Kearns	.25
168	Mike Mussina	.50
169	Randy Wolf	.25
170	Tim Hudson/SP	4.00
171	Casey Blake	.25
172	Edgar Renteria	.50
173	Ben Sheets	.50
174	Kevin Brown	.25
175	Nomar Garciaparra/SP	8.00
176	Armando Benitez	.25
177	Jody Gerut	.25
178	Craig Biggio	.50
179	Omar Vizquel	.25
180	Jake Peavy	.50
181	Gustavo Chacin/SP	4.00
182	Johnny Damon	.75
183	Mike Lieberthal	.25
184	Felix Hernandez/SP	10.00
185	Zach Day/SP	4.00
186	Matt Cain	.25
187	Erubiel Durazo	.25
188	Zack Greinke	.25
189	Matt Morris	.25
190	Billy Wagner	.25
191	Al Leiter	.25
192	Miguel Olivo	.25
193	Jose Capellan/SP	4.00
194	Adam Eaton	.25
195	Steven White/SP	4.00
196	Joe Randa	.25
197	Richard Hidalgo	.25
198	Orlando Cabrera	.25
199	Joel Guzman/SP	6.00
200	Garret Anderson	.50
201	Endy Chavez	.25
202	Andy Marte	.25
203	Jose Guillen	.25
204	Victor Martinez	.25
205	Johnny Estrada	.25
206	Damian Miller	.25
207	Ken Harvey	.25
208	Ronnie Belliard	.25
209	Chan Ho Park	.25
210	Laynce Nix	.25
211	Lew Ford	.25
212	Moises Alou	.50
213	Kris Benson	.25
214	Mike Gonzalez/SP	4.00
215	Chris Burke	.25
216	Juan Pierre	.25
217	Phil Nevin	.25
218	Jerry Hairston Jr.	.25
219	Jeremy Reed	.25
220	Scott Kazmir/SP	4.00
221	Mike Maroth	.25
222	Alex Rios	.25
223	Esteban Loaiza	.25
224	Terrmel Sledge	.25
225	Mark Prior/ Blue Sky/SP	5.00
225	Mark Prior/ Yellow Sky/SP	5.00
226	Hank Blalock	.50

227	Craig Wilson	.25
228	Cesar Izturis	.25
229	Dmitri Young	.25
230	Derek Jeter/ Blue Sky/SP	15.00
230	Derek Jeter/ Purple Sky/SP	15.00
231	Mark Kotsay	.25
232	Darin Erstad	.25
233	Brandon Backe/SP	4.00
234	Mike Lowell	.25
235	Scott Podsednik	.25
236	Michael Barrett	.25
237	Chad Tracy	.25
238	David Dellucci	.25
239	Brady Clark	.25
240	Jorge Cantu	.25
241	Wilfredo Ledezma	.25
242	Morgan Ensberg	.25
243	Omar Infante	.25
244	Corey Patterson	.25
245	Matt Holliday	.25
246	Vinny Castilla	.25
247	Jason Bartlett	.25
248	Noah Lowry	.25
249	Huston Street	.25
250	Russell Branyan	.25
251	Juan Uribe	.25
252	Larry Bigbie	.25
253	Grady Sizemore	.50
254	Pedro Feliz	.25
255	Brad Wilkerson	.25
256	Brandon Inge	.25
257	Dewon Brazelton	.25
258	Rodrigo Lopez	.25
259	Jacque Jones	.25
260	Jason Giambi	.50
261	Clint Barmes	.25
262	Willy Taveras	.25
263	Marcus Giles	.25
264	Joe Blanton	.25
265	John Thomson	.25
266	Steve Finley/SP	4.00
267	Kevin Millwood	.25
268	David Eckstein	.25
269	Barry Zito	.50
270	Todd Helton/ Purple Sky/SP	5.00
270	Todd Helton/ Yellow Sky/SP	5.00
271	Landon Powell RC	1.00
272	Justin Verlander RC	3.00
273	Wes Swackhamer RC	1.00
274	Wladimir Balentien RC	2.00
275	Philip Humber RC	1.00
276	Kevin Melillo RC	2.00
277	Billy Butler RC	5.00
278	Michael Rogers RC	1.00
279	Bobby Livingston RC	1.00
280	Glen Perkins RC	1.00
281	Michael Bourn RC	1.00
282	Tyler Pelland RC	1.00
283	Jeremy West RC	2.00
284	Brandon McCarthy RC	4.00
285	Ian Kinsler RC	3.00
286	Chris Roberson RC	1.00
287	Melky Cabrera RC	2.00
288	Ryan Sweeney RC	1.00
289	Chip Cannon RC	1.50
290	Andy LaRoche RC	5.00
291	Chuck Tiffany RC	1.00
292	Ian Bladergroen RC	1.00
293	Bear Bay RC	1.00
294	Hernan Iribarren RC	1.00
295	Stuart Pomeranz RC	1.00
296	Luke Scott RC	1.00
297	Chuck James RC	2.00
298	Kennard Bibbs RC	1.00
299	Steve Bondurant	1.50
300	Tom Oldham RC	1.00
301	Nolan Ryan	3.00
302	Reggie Jackson	1.00
303	Tom Seaver	1.50
304	Al Kaline	1.50
305	Cal Ripken Jr.	4.00
306	Josh Gibson	1.50
307	Frank Robinson	1.00
308	Duke Snider	1.00
309	Wade Boggs	1.50
310	Tony Gwynn	2.00
311	Carl Yastrzemski	2.00
312	Ryne Sandberg	2.00
313	Gary Carter	1.00
314	Brooks Robinson	1.50
315	Ernie Banks	1.50

Red

Stars (1-315):	1-2X
SP's:	.5-1X

White

Stars (1-315):	2-3X
SP's:	1-1.5X
Inserted 1:4	

Black

Stars (1-315):	3-5X
SP's:	1.5-2X
Inserted 1:20	

Gold

Stars (1-315):	5-10X
SP's:	3-5X
Production 50 Sets	

Suede

No Pricing
Production One Set

Autographs

		NM/M
MB	Matt Bush	25.00
CC	Carl Crawford	25.00
SE	Scott Elbert	20.00
JF	Josh Fields	15.00
EG	Eric Gagne	35.00
JG	Jody Gerut	15.00
JPH	J.P. Howell	15.00
ZJ	Zach Jackson	12.00
JJ	Jason Jaramillo	12.00
BJ	Blake Johnson	15.00
CN	Chris Nelson	10.00
DO	David Ortiz	50.00
ZP	Zachary Parker	12.00
DP	Dustin Pedroia	20.00
MR	Mariano Rivera	60.00
MRO	Mike Rodriguez	10.00
GS	Gary Sheffield	40.00
AS	Alfonso Soriano	40.00
JS	Jeremy Sowers	20.00

B-18 Blanket Boxloaders

		NM/M
	Common Blanket	8.00
	Barry Bonds	20.00
	Roger Clemens	20.00
	Todd Helton	8.00
	Derek Jeter	20.00
	Alex Rodriguez	15.00
	Curt Schilling	12.00
	Alfonso Soriano	8.00
	Ichiro Suzuki	15.00

Cabinet Boxloaders

		NM/M
Inserted 1:Box		
BB	Barry Bonds	25.00
GB	George W. Bush	10.00
RJ	Randy Johnson	12.00
MP	Mike Piazza	12.00
AP	Albert Pujols	20.00
MR	Manny Ramirez	12.00
AR	Alex Rodriguez	20.00
SR	Scott Rolen	10.00
JS	Johan Santana	12.00
SS	Sammy Sosa	15.00
WT	William H. Taft	10.00
MT	Miguel Tejada	10.00
JT	Jim Thome	10.00
GW	George Washington	25.00

Cabinet Autograph Relics

		NM/M
Production 5-450		
MB	Matt Bush/450	25.00
CC	Carl Crawford/450	25.00
JG	Jody Gerut/450	20.00
MK	Mark Kotsay/450	30.00
BM	Brett Myers/150	40.00
DO	David Ortiz/100	100.00
MR	Mariano Rivera/25	90.00
AR	Alex Rodriguez/25	400.00
GS	Gary Sheffield/100	100.00
AS	Alfonso Soriano/75	75.00

Relics

		NM/M
	Common Player:	4.00
JB	Jeff Bagwell	6.00

CB	Carlos Beltran	6.00
AB	Adrian Beltre	6.00
HB	Hank Blalock	6.00
BB	Barry Bonds	20.00
MC	Miguel Cabrera	8.00
RC	Roger Clemens	15.00
RC2	Roger Clemens	15.00
JD	Johnny Damon	10.00
JD2	Johnny Damon	10.00
VG	Vladimir Guerrero	8.00
TH	Todd Helton	6.00
CJ	Chipper Jones	8.00
ML	Mike Lowell	6.00
MM	Mark Mulder	4.00
MO	Magglio Ordonez	4.00
DO	David Ortiz	8.00
RP	Rafael Palmeiro	8.00
MP	Mike Piazza	8.00
MPR	Mark Prior	6.00
AP	Albert Pujols	15.00
MR	Manny Ramirez	8.00
AR	Alex Rodriguez	12.00
AR2	Alex Rodriguez	12.00
CS	Curt Schilling	8.00
GS	Gary Sheffield	6.00
AS	Alfonso Soriano	8.00
SS	Sammy Sosa	10.00
MTE	Mark Teixeira	6.00
MT	Miguel Tejada	8.00
JT	Jim Thome	6.00
LW	Larry Walker	4.00

2005 Topps Update

		NM/M
Complete Set (330):		35.00
Complete Factory Set (330):		40.00
Common Player:		.10
Pack (10):		2.00
Box (36):		60.00
1	Sammy Sosa	1.00
2	Jeff Francoeur	.25
3	Tony Clark	.10
4	Michael Tucker	.10
5	Mike Matheny	.10
6	Eric Young	.10
7	Jose Valentin	.10
8	Matt Lawton	.10
9	Juan Rivera	.10
10	Shawn Green	.25
11	Aaron Boone	.10
12	Woody Williams	.10
13	Brad Wilkerson	.10
14	Anthony Reyes RC	1.50
15	Russ Adams	.10
16	Gustavo Chacin	.10
17	Mike Restovich	.10
18	Humberto Quintero	.10
19	Matt Ginter	.10
20	Scott Podsednik	.25
21	Byung-Hyun Kim	.10
22	Orlando Hernandez	.10
23	Mark Grudzielanek	.10
24	Jody Gerut	.10
25	Adrian Beltre	.25
26	Scott Schoeneweis	.10
27	Marlon Anderson	.10
28	Jason Vargas	.10
29	Claudio Vargas	.10
30	Jason Kendall	.10
31	Aaron Small	.10
32	Juan Cruz	.10
33	Placido Polanco	.10
34	Jorge Sosa	.10
35	John Olerud	.10
36	Ryan Langerhans	.10
37	Randy Winn	.10
38	Zachary Duke	.25
39	Garrett Atkins	.10
40	Al Leiter	.10
41	Shawn Chacon	.10
42	Mark DeRosa	.10
43	Miguel Ojeda	.10
44	A.J. Pierzynski	.10
45	Carlos Lee	.10
46	LaTroy Hawkins	.10
47	Nick Green	.10

48	Shawn Estes	.10
49	Eli Marrero	.10
50	Jeff Kent	.10
51	Joe Randa	.10
52	Jose Hernandez	.10
53	Joe Blanton	.10
54	Huston Street	.10
55	Marlon Byrd	.10
56	Alex Sanchez	.10
57	Livan Hernandez	.10
58	Chris Young	.10
59	Brad Eldred	.10
60	Terrence Long	.10
61	Phil Nevin	.10
62	Kyle Farnsworth	.10
63	Jon Lieber	.10
64	Antonio Alfonseca	.10
65	Tony Graffanino	.10
66	Tadahito Iguchi RC	1.00
67	Brad Thompson	.10
68	Jose Vidro	.10
69	Jason Phillips	.10
70	Carl Pavano	.10
71	Pokey Reese	.10
72	Jerome Williams	.10
73	Kazuhisa Ishii	.10
74	Zach Day	.10
75	Edgar Renteria	.25
76	Mike Myers	.10
77	Jeff Cirillo	.10
78	Endy Chavez	.10
79	Jose Guillen	.10
80	Ugueth Urbina	.10
81	Vinny Castilla	.10
82	Javier Vazquez	.10
83	Willy Taveras	.10
84	Mark Mulder	.25
85	Mike Hargrove	.10
86	Buddy Bell	.10
87	Charlie Manuel	.10
88	Willie Randolph	.10
89	Bob Melvin	.10
90	Chris Lambert	.10
91	Homer Bailey	.20
92	Ervin Santana	.10
93	Bill Bray	.10
94	Thomas Diamond	.10
95	Trevor Plouffe	.10
96	James Houser	.10
97	Jake Stevens	.10
98	Anthony Whittington	.10
99	Phillip Hughes	.10
100	Greg Golson	.10
101	Paul Maholm	.10
102	Carlos Quentin	.10
103	Dan Johnson	.10
104	Mark Rogers	.10
105	Neil Walker	.10
106	Omar Quintanilla	.10
107	Blake DeWitt	.10
108	Taylor Tankersley	.10
109	David Murphy	.10
110	Felix Hernandez	.50
111	Craig Biggio	.10
112	Greg Maddux	.50
113	Bobby Abreu	.10
114	Alex Rodriguez	.75
115	Trevor Hoffman	.10
116	A.J. Pierzynski, Tadahito Iguchi	.25
117	Reggie Sanders	.10
118	Bengie Molina, Ervin Santana	.10
119	Chris Burke, Lance Berkman, Adam LaRoche	.10
120	Garret Anderson	.25
121	A.J. Pierzynski	.10
122	Paul Konerko	.25
123	Joe Crede	.10
124	Mark Buehrle, Jon Garland	.10
125	Freddy Garcia, Jose Contreras	.10
126	Reggie Sanders	.10
127	Roy Oswalt	.10
128	Roger Clemens	.75
129	Albert Pujols	.75
130	Roy Oswalt	.10
131	Joe Crede, Bobby Jenks	.10
132	Paul Konerko, Scott Podsednik	.25
133	Geoff Blum	.10
134	White Sox Sweep	.10
135	Alex Rodriguez, David Ortiz, Manny Ramirez	.50
136	Michael Young, Alex Rodriguez, Vladimir Guerrero	.50
137	David Ortiz, Mark Teixeira, Manny Ramirez	.25
138	Bartolo Colon, Jon Garland, Cliff Lee	
139	Kevin Millwood, Johan Santana, Mark Buehrle	
140	Johan Santana, Randy Johnson, John Lackey	.25
141	Andruw Jones, Derrek Lee, Albert Pujols	
142	Derek Lee, Albert Pujols, Miguel Cabrera	.50
143	Andruw Jones, Albert Pujols, Pat Burrell	.50

#	Player	Price
144	Dontrelle Willis, Chris Carpenter, Roy Oswalt	.25
145	Roger Clemens, Andy Pettitte, Dontrelle Willis	.50
146	Jake Peavy, Chris Carpenter, Pedro Martinez	.25
147	Mark Teixeira	.25
148	Brian Roberts	.10
149	Michael Young	.10
150	Alex Rodriguez	1.00
151	Johnny Damon	.25
152	Vladimir Guerrero	.25
153	Manny Ramirez	.25
154	David Ortiz	.25
155	Mariano Rivera	.25
156	Joe Nathan	.10
157	Albert Pujols	1.00
158	Jeff Kent	.10
159	Felipe Lopez	.10
160	Morgan Ensberg	.10
161	Miguel Cabrera	.25
162	Ken Griffey Jr.	.50
163	Andruw Jones	.25
164	Paul LoDuca	.10
165	Chad Cordero	.10
166	Ken Griffey Jr.	.50
167	Jason Giambi	.10
168	Willy Taveras	.10
169	Huston Street	.10
170	Chris Carpenter	.10
171	Bartolo Colon	.10
172	Bobby Cox	.10
173	Ozzie Guillen	.10
174	Andruw Jones	.25
175	Johnny Damon	.25
176	Alex Rodriguez	1.00
177	David Ortiz	.25
178	Manny Ramirez	.25
179	Miguel Tejada	.25
180	Vladimir Guerrero	.25
181	Mark Teixeira	.25
182	Ivan Rodriguez	.25
183	Brian Roberts	.10
184	Mark Buehrle	.10
185	Bobby Abreu	.25
186	Carlos Beltran	.25
187	Albert Pujols	1.00
188	Derrek Lee	.25
189	Jim Edmonds	.25
190	Aramis Ramirez	.10
191	Mike Piazza	.50
192	Jeff Kent	.10
193	David Eckstein	.10
194	Chris Carpenter	.10
195	Bobby Abreu	.25
196	Ivan Rodriguez	.25
197	Carlos Lee	.10
198	David Ortiz	.25
199	Hee Seop Choi	.10
200	Andruw Jones	.25
201	Mark Teixeira	.25
202	Jason Bay	.10
203	Hanley Ramirez	.10
204	Shin-Soo Choo	.10
205	Justin Huber	.10
206	Nelson Cruz RC	.50
207	Edwin Encarnacion	.10
208	Miguel Montero RC	.50
209	William Bergolla	.10
210	Luis Montanez	.10
211	Francisco Liriano	.50
212	Kevin Thompson	.10
213	B.J. Upton	.10
214	Conor Jackson	.10
215	Delmon Young	.25
216	Andy LaRoche	.50
217	Ryan Garko	.10
218	Josh Barfield	.10
219	Chris Young	.10
220	Justin Verlander	.25
221	Drew Anderson RC	.25
222	Luis Hernandez RC	.25
223	Jim Burt RC	.25
224	Mike Morse RC	.25
225	Elliot Johnson RC	.50
226	C.J. Smith RC	.25
227	Casey McGehee RC	.25
228	Brian Miller RC	.15
229	Chris Vines RC	.40
230	D.J. Houlton RC	.25
231	Chuck Tiffany RC	.25
232	Humberto Sanchez RC	.75
233	Baltazar Lopez RC	.25
234	Russell Martin RC	.50
235	Dana Eveland RC	.25
236	Johan Silva RC	.25
237	Adam Harben RC	1.00
238	Brian Bannister RC	.25
239	Adam Boeve RC	.25
240	Tom Oldham RC	.25
241	Cody Haerther RC	.25
242	Dan Santin RC	.25
243	Daniel Haigwood RC	.25
244	Craig Tatum RC	.25
245	Martin Prado RC	.25
246	Errol Simonitsch RC	.40
247	Lorenzo Scott RC	.25
248	Hayden Penn RC	.40
249	Heath Totten RC	.25
250	Nick Masset RC	.25
251	Pedro Lopez RC	.25
252	Benjamin Harrison	.25
253	Michael Spidale RC	.25
254	Jeremy Harts RC	.25
255	Danny Zell RC	.40
256	Kevin Collins RC	.15
257	Tony Arnerich RC	.15
258	Matt Albers RC	.50
259	Ricky Barrett RC	.25
260	Hernan Iribarren RC	.40
261	Sean Tracey RC	.25
262	Jerry Owens RC	.40
263	Steve Nelson RC	.25
264	Brandon McCarthy RC	1.00
265	David Shepard RC	.25
266	Steve Bondurant RC	.25
267	Billy Sadler	.15
268	Ryan Feierabend RC	.25
269	Stuart Pomeranz RC	.40
270	Shaun Marcum	.25
271	Erik Schindelwolf RC	.25
272	Stefan Bailie RC	.15
273	Mike Esposito RC	.25
274	Buck Coats RC	.40
275	Andy Sides RC	.25
276	Micah Schnurstein RC	.40
277	Jesse Gutierrez RC	.25
278	Jake Postlewait RC	.25
279	Willy Mota RC	.50
280	Ryan Speier RC	.25
281	Frank Mata RC	.25
282	Jair Jurrjens RC	.50
283	Nick Touchstone RC	.25
284	Matthew Kemp RC	1.50
285	Vinny Rottino RC	.40
286	J.B. Thurmond RC	.25
287	Kelvin Pichardo RC	.25
288	Scott Mitchinson RC	.25
289	Darwinson Salazar RC	.25
290	George Kottaras RC	.50
291	Ken Durost RC	.40
292	Jonathan Sanchez RC	.25
293	Brandon Moorhead RC	.25
294	Kennard Bibbs RC	.25
295	David Gassner RC	.40
296	Micah Furtado RC	.25
297	Ismael Ramirez RC	.25
298	Carlos Gonzalez RC	1.50
299	Brandon Sing RC	.25
300	Jason Motte RC	.25
301	Chuck James RC	1.00
302	Andy Santana RC	.25
303	Manny Parra RC	.40
304	Chris Young RC	1.00
305	Juan Senreiso RC	.25
306	Franklin Morales RC	.50
307	Jared Gothreaux RC	.15
308	Jayce Tingler RC	.25
309	Matt Brown RC	.25
310	Frank Diaz RC	.40
311	Stephen Drew RC	2.00
312	Jered Weaver RC	4.00
313	Ryan Braun RC	1.50
314	John Mayberry Jr. RC	.75
315	Aaron Thompson RC	.25
316	Cesar Carrillo RC	.50
317	Jacoby Ellsbury RC	1.00
318	Matt Garza RC	5.00
319	Cliff Pennington RC	.75
320	Colby Rasmus RC	1.50
321	Chris Volstad RC	1.00
322	Ricky Romero RC	.50
323	Ryan Zimmerman RC	3.00
324	C.J. Henry RC	.75
325	Jay Bruce RC	2.00
326	Beau Jones RC	.50
327	Mark McCormick RC	.50
328	Eli Iorg RC	.50
329	Andrew McCutchen RC	1.00
330	Mike Costanzo RC	.50

Blue
No Pricing
Production One Set

Gold
Gold Rookies:	2-4X
Gold Stars:	4-8X
Production 2,005 Sets	

All-Star Patches
NM/M

	Player	Price
	Common Player:	15.00
BA	Bobby Abreu/65	15.00
MA	Moises Alou/65	20.00
JB	Jason Bay/60	20.00
CB	Carlos Beltran/60	25.00
MB	Mark Buehrle/60	20.00
MC	Miguel Cabrera/70	30.00
CC	Chris Carpenter/70	20.00
MCL	Matt Clement/70	15.00
BC	Bartolo Colon/60	15.00
CCO	Chad Cordero/65	15.00
JD	Johnny Damon/60	25.00
DE	David Eckstein/65	20.00
JE	Jim Edmonds/50	20.00
ME	Morgan Ensberg/60	15.00
JG	Jon Garland/70	20.00
LG	Luis Gonzalez/70	15.00
LH	Livan Hernandez/65	15.00
JI	Jason Isringhausen/65	15.00
AJ	Andruw Jones/70	25.00
JK	Jeff Kent/65	20.00
PK	Paul Konerko/70	20.00
CL	Carlos Lee/65	20.00
DL	Derrek Lee/65	20.00
BL	Brad Lidge/65	15.00
FL	Felipe Lopez/35	20.00
MM	Melvin Mora/30	20.00
JN	Joe Nathan/65	15.00
DO	David Ortiz/70	25.00
RO	Roy Oswalt/60	20.00
JP	Jake Peavy/60	20.00
MP	Mike Piazza/50	30.00
SP	Scott Podsednik/65	20.00
AP	Albert Pujols/35	50.00
ARA	Aramis Ramirez/60	20.00
MR	Manny Ramirez/65	25.00
MRI	Mariano Rivera/65	30.00
AR	Alex Rodriguez/50	30.00
KR	Kenny Rogers/50	15.00
JS	Johan Santana/60	30.00
GS	Gary Sheffield/50	25.00
JSM	John Smoltz/65	30.00
IS	Ichiro Suzuki/50	40.00
MTE	Mark Teixeira/60	20.00
MT	Miguel Tejada/60	20.00
BW	Billy Wagner/50	15.00
DW	Dontrelle Willis/60	20.00
MY	Michael Young/50	20.00

All-Star Stitches
NM/M

	Player	Price
	Common Player:	4.00
BA	Bobby Abreu B	4.00
MA	Moises Alou C	6.00
JB	Jason Bay C	4.00
CB	Carlos Beltran D	6.00
MB	Mark Buehrle B	4.00
MC	Miguel Cabrera E	8.00
CC	Chris Carpenter E	4.00
LC	Luis Castillo B	4.00
MCL	Matt Clement B	4.00
BC	Bartolo Colon D	4.00
CCO	Chad Cordero D	4.00
JD	Johnny Damon B	8.00
DE	David Eckstein B	4.00
JE	Jim Edmonds A	6.00
ME	Morgan Ensberg B	4.00
JG	Jon Garland E	4.00
LG	Luis Gonzalez C	4.00
LH	Livan Hernandez E	4.00
JI	Jason Isringhausen E	4.00
AJ	Andruw Jones C	6.00
JK	Jeff Kent C	4.00
PK	Paul Konerko A	4.00
CL	Carlos Lee E	4.00
DL	Derrek Lee F	6.00
BL	Brad Lidge D	4.00
FL	Felipe Lopez B	4.00
MM	Melvin Mora B	4.00
JN	Joe Nathan D	4.00
DO	David Ortiz E	8.00
RO	Roy Oswalt A	4.00
JP	Jake Peavy D	4.00
MP	Mike Piazza E	8.00
SP	Scott Podsednik A	4.00
AP	Albert Pujols E	20.00
ARA	Aramis Ramirez E	4.00
MR	Manny Ramirez E	8.00
MRI	Mariano Rivera E	8.00
BR	Brian Roberts C	4.00
AR	Alex Rodriguez D	15.00
IR	Ivan Rodriguez A	4.00
KR	Kenny Rogers A	4.00
JS	Johan Santana C	6.00
GS	Gary Sheffield D	6.00
JSM	John Smoltz D	6.00
IS	Ichiro Suzuki A	20.00
MTE	Mark Teixeira C	6.00
MT	Miguel Tejada B	6.00
BW	Billy Wagner C	4.00
DW	Dontrelle Willis F	6.00
MY	Michael Young A	4.00

Derby Digs Jersey
NM/M

	Player	Price
BA	Bobby Abreu	25.00
JB	Jason Bay	15.00
AJ	Andruw Jones	25.00
CL	Carlos Lee	10.00
DO	David Ortiz	25.00
IR	Ivan Rodriguez	25.00
MT	Mark Teixeira	25.00

Hall of Fame Bat
NM/M

	Player	Price
WB	Wade Boggs A	10.00
RS	Ryne Sandberg B	15.00

Hall of Fame Dual Bat
NM/M
Production 200 Sets

	Player	Price
BS	Wade Boggs, Ryne Sandberg	25.00

Legendary Sacks
NM/M
Production 300 Sets

	Player	Price
JA	Jim Abbott	6.00
AD	Andre Dawson	6.00
MF	Mark Fidrych	6.00
RF	Rollie Fingers	6.00
BJ	Bo Jackson	8.00
HR	Harold Reynolds	4.00
OS	Ozzie Smith	8.00
LW	Lou Whitaker	4.00
DW	Dave Winfield	8.00

Midsummer Covers
NM/M
Production 150 Sets

	Player	Price
CB	Carlos Beltran	15.00
RC	Roger Clemens	25.00
VG	Vladimir Guerrero	15.00
DL	Derrek Lee	15.00
AP	Albert Pujols	40.00
BR	Brian Roberts	10.00
AR	Alex Rodriguez	30.00
IS	Ichiro Suzuki	50.00
MT	Miguel Tejada	15.00
DW	Dontrelle Willis	10.00

Printing Plates
No Pricing
Production one set per color.

Signature Moves
NM/M
Production 15-475 Sets
Red Foil: No Pricing
Production 25 Sets

	Player	Price
MA	Matt Albers/475	15.00
TC	Travis Chick/475	8.00
TG	Troy Glaus/275	20.00
TH	Tim Hudson/275	25.00
KI	Kazuhisa Ishii/275	15.00
GK	George Kottaras/475	15.00
BL	Bobby Livingston/475	10.00
MM	Mark Mulder/275	25.00
GP	Glen Perkins/275	15.00
JP	Jake Postlewait/275	15.00
HS	Humberto Sanchez	30.00
BS	Benito Santiago	15.00
RS	Richie Sexson/275	25.00
CJS	C.J. Smith/475	15.00
JV	Justin Verlander/275	35.00
TW	Tony Womack	15.00

Touch Em All Base
NM/M
Production 1,000 Sets

	Player	Price
VG	Vladimir Guerrero	8.00
DL	Derrek Lee	8.00
DO	David Ortiz	10.00
AP	Albert Pujols	20.00
MR	Manny Ramirez	10.00
AR	Alex Rodriguez	10.00
IR	Ivan Rodriguez	8.00
GS	Gary Sheffield	6.00
IS	Ichiro Suzuki	20.00
MT	Miguel Tejada	10.00

Washington Nationals Inaugural Lineup
NM/M
Inserted 1:10
Ball Relics: No Pricing
Production Five Sets

	Player	Price
VC	Vinny Castilla	.50
JG	Jose Guillen	1.00
CG	Cristian Guzman	.50
LH	Livan Hernandez	.50
NJ	Nick Johnson	.50
BS	Brian Schneider	.50
TS	Terrmel Sledge	.50
JV	Jose Vidro	.50
BW	Brad Wilkerson	.50
TEAM	Team Photo	1.00

2005 Topps Chrome Update
NM/M

Complete Set (237):	
Common Player:	.25
Common Rookie (106-215):	.50
Common RK Auto. (221-237):	10.00
Pack (4):	4.00
Box (20):	70.00

#	Player	Price
UH1	Sammy Sosa	1.00
UH2	Jeff Francoeur	.50
UH3	Tony Clark	.25
UH4	Michael Tucker	.25
UH5	Mike Matheny	.25
UH6	Eric Young	.25
UH7	Jose Valentin	.25
UH8	Matt Lawton	.25
UH9	Juan Rivera	.25
UH10	Shawn Green	.25
UH11	Aaron Boone	.25
UH12	Woody Williams	.25
UH13	Brad Wilkerson	.25
UH14	Anthony Reyes	5.00
UH15	Gustavo Chacin	.25
UH16	Mike Restovich	.25
UH17	Humberto Quintero	.25
UH18	Matt Ginter	.25
UH19	Scott Podsednik	.25
UH20	Byung-Hyun Kim	.25
UH21	Orlando Hernandez	.25
UH22	Mark Grudzielanek	.25
UH23	Jody Gerut	.25
UH24	Adrian Beltre	.50
UH25	Scott Schoeneweis	.25
UH26	Marlon Anderson	.25
UH27	Jason Vargas	.25
UH28	Claudio Vargas	.25
UH29	Jason Kendall	.25
UH30	Aaron Small	.25
UH31	Juan Cruz	.25
UH32	Placido Polanco	.25
UH33	Jorge Sosa	.25
UH34	John Olerud	.25
UH35	Ryan Langerhans	.25
UH36	Randy Winn	.25
UH37	Zachary Duke	.50
UH38	Garrett Atkins	.25
UH39	Al Leiter	.25
UH40	Shawn Chacon	.25
UH41	Mark DeRosa	.25
UH42	Miguel Ojeda	.25
UH43	A.J. Pierzynski	.25
UH44	Carlos Lee	.25
UH45	LaTroy Hawkins	.25
UH46	Nick Green	.25
UH47	Shawn Estes	.25
UH48	Eli Marrero	.25
UH49	Jeff Kent	.25
UH50	Joe Randa	.25
UH51	Jose Hernandez	.25
UH52	Joe Blanton	.25
UH53	Huston Street	.25
UH54	Marlon Byrd	.25
UH55	Alex Sanchez	.25
UH56	Livan Hernandez	.25
UH57	Chris Young	.25
UH58	Brad Eldred	.25
UH59	Terrence Long	.25
UH60	Phil Nevin	.25
UH61	Kyle Farnsworth	.25
UH62	Jon Lieber	.25
UH63	Antonio Alfonseca	.25
UH64	Tony Graffanino	.25
UH65	Tadahito Iguchi	1.00
UH66	Brad Thompson	.25
UH67	Jose Vidro	.25
UH68	Jason Phillips	.25
UH69	Carl Pavano	.25
UH70	Pokey Reese	.25
UH71	Jerome Williams	.25
UH72	Kazuhisa Ishii	.25
UH73	Felix Hernandez	.50
UH74	Edgar Renteria	.25
UH75	Mike Myers	.25
UH76	Jeff Cirillo	.25
UH77	Endy Chavez	.25
UH78	Jose Guillen	.25
UH79	Ugueth Urbina	.25
UH80	Zach Day	.25
UH81	Javier Vazquez	.25
UH82	Willy Taveras	.25
UH83	Mark Mulder	.25
UH84	Vinny Castilla	.25
UH85	Russ Adams	.25
UH86	Homer Bailey	.25
UH87	Ervin Santana	.25
UH88	Bill Bray	.25
UH89	Thomas Diamond	.25
UH90	Trevor Plouffe	.25
UH91	James Houser	.25
UH92	Jake Stevens	.25
UH93	Anthony Whittington	.25
UH94	Phillip Hughes	.25
UH95	Greg Golson	.25
UH96	Paul Maholm	.25
UH97	Carlos Quentin	.25
UH98	Dan Johnson	.25
UH99	Mark Rogers	.25
UH100	Neil Walker	.25
UH101	Omar Quintanilla	.25
UH102	Blake DeWitt	.25
UH103	Taylor Tankersley	.25
UH104	David Murphy	.25
UH105	Chris Lambert	.25
UH106	Drew Anderson RC	.50
UH107	Luis Hernandez RC	.50
UH108	Jim Burt RC	.50
UH109	Mike Morse RC	.50
UH110	Elliot Johnson RC	2.00
UH111	C.J. Smith RC	.50
UH112	Casey McGehee RC	.50
UH113	Brian Miller RC	.50
UH114	Chris Vines RC	.50
UH115	D.J. Houlton RC	.50
UH116	Chuck Tiffany RC	2.00
UH117	Humberto Sanchez RC	3.00
UH118	Baltazar Lopez RC	.50
UH119	Russell Martin RC	2.00
UH120	Dana Eveland RC	2.00
UH121	Johan Silva RC	.50
UH122	Adam Harben RC	1.00
UH123	Brian Bannister RC	.50
UH124	Adam Boeve RC	.75
UH125	Tom Oldham RC	.50
UH126	Cody Haerther RC	1.50
UH127	Dan Santin RC	.50
UH128	Daniel Haigwood RC	1.00
UH129	Craig Tatum RC	.50
UH130	Martin Prado RC	.50
UH131	Errol Simonitsch RC	.50
UH132	Lorenzo Scott RC	.50
UH133	Hayden Penn RC	1.00
UH134	Heath Totten RC	.50
UH135	Nick Masset RC	.50
UH136	Pedro Lopez RC	.50
UH137	Benjamin Harrison RC	.50
UH138	Michael Spidale RC	.50
UH139	Jeremy Harts RC	.50
UH140	Danny Zell RC	.50
UH141	Kevin Collins RC	.50
UH142	Tony Arnerich RC	.50
UH143	Matt Albers RC	1.50
UH144	Ricky Barrett RC	.50
UH145	Hernan Iribarren RC	.75
UH146	Sean Tracey RC	.50
UH147	Jerry Owens RC	1.00
UH148	Steve Nelson RC	.50
UH149	Brandon McCarthy RC	2.00
UH150	David Shepard RC	.75
UH151	Steve Bondurant RC	.75
UH152	Billy Sadler RC	.75
UH153	Ryan Feierabend RC	.75
UH154	Stuart Pomeranz RC	.75
UH155	Shawn Marcum RC	.50
UH156	Erik Schindewolf RC	.50
UH157	Stefan Bailie RC	.60
UH158	Mike Esposito RC	.75
UH159	Buck Coats RC	.75
UH160	Andy Sides RC	.50
UH161	Micah Schnurstein RC	.75
UH162	Jesse Gutierrez RC	.50
UH163	Jake Postlewait RC	.50
UH164	Willy Mota RC	.50
UH165	Ryan Speier RC	.50
UH166	Frank Mata RC	.50
UH167	Jair Jurrjens RC	1.00
UH168	Nick Touchstone RC	.50
UH169	Matthew Kemp RC	10.00
UH170	Vinny Rottino RC	.50
UH171	J.B. Thurmond RC	.50
UH172	Kelvin Pichardo RC	.50
UH173	Scott Mitchinson RC	.50
UH174	Darwinson Salazar RC	.50
UH175	George Kottaras RC	1.00
UH176	Ken Durost RC	.75
UH177	Jonathan Sanchez RC	2.00
UH178	Brandon Moorhead RC	.75
UH179	Kennard Bibbs RC	.75
UH180	David Gassner RC	.50
UH181	Micah Furtado RC	.50
UH182	Ismael Ramirez RC	.50
UH183	Carlos Gonzalez RC	5.00
UH184	Brandon Sing RC	.50
UH185	Jason Motte RC	.50
UH186	Chuck James RC	4.00
UH187	Andy Santana RC	.50
UH188	Manny Parra RC	1.00
UH189	Chris Young RC	5.00
UH190	Juan Senreiso RC	.50
UH191	Franklin Morales RC	2.50
UH192	Jared Gothreaux RC	.50
UH193	Jayce Tingler RC	.50
UH194	Matt Brown RC	.50
UH195	Frank Diaz RC	1.50
UH196	Stephen Drew RC	10.00
UH197	Jered Weaver RC	15.00
UH198	Ryan Braun RC	9.00
UH199	John Mayberry Jr. RC	2.50
UH200	Aaron Thompson RC	2.00
UH201	Ben Copeland RC	4.00
UH202	Jacoby Ellsbury RC	4.00
UH203	Garrett Olson RC	1.50
UH204	Cliff Pennington RC	2.00
UH205	Colby Rasmus RC	5.00
UH206	Chris Volstad RC	3.00
UH207	Ricky Romero RC	2.00
UH208	Ryan Zimmerman RC	10.00
UH209	C.J. Henry RC	2.00
UH210	Nick Cruz RC	1.00
UH211	Josh Wall RC	.50
UH212	Nick Webber RC	.50
UH213	Paul Kelly RC	1.00
UH214	Kyle Winters RC	1.50
UH215	Mitch Boggs RC	.75
UH216	Craig Biggio RC	.50
UH217	Greg Maddux RC	1.00
UH218	Bobby Abreu	.25
UH219	Alex Rodriguez	2.00
UH220	Trevor Hoffman	.25
UH221	Trevor Bell RC	20.00
UH222	Jay Bruce RC	60.00
UH223	Travis Buck RC	30.00
UH224	Cesar Carrillo RC	20.00
UH225	Mike Costanzo RC	20.00
UH226	Brent Cox RC	15.00
UH227	Matt Garza RC	40.00
UH228	Josh Geer RC	20.00
UH229	Tyler Greene RC	20.00
UH230	Eli Iorg RC	20.00
UH231	Craig Italiano RC	15.00
UH232	Beau Jones RC	20.00
UH233	Mark McCormick RC	15.00
UH234	Andrew McCutchen RC	50.00
UH235	Micah Owings RC	15.00
UH236	Cesar Ramos RC	15.00
UH237	Chaz Roe RC	15.00

Refractor
Stars (1-105):	2-3X
Rookies (106-215):	1-2X
Inserted 1:5	
Refractor Auto. (221-237):	1-1.5X
Production 500	

Black Refractor
Black (1-105):	2-4X
Black (106-215):	2-3X
Production 250	
Black Auto. (221-237):	1-2.5X
Production 200	

Gold SuperFractor
No Pricing
Production One Set

Red X-Fractor

Red (1-105):	4-8X
Red (106-215):	6-12X
Production 65	
Red Auto. (221-237):	No Pricing
Production 25	

Barry Bonds Home Run History

	NM/M
Complete Set (15):	40.00
Common Bonds:	3.00
Inserted 1:12	
Refractor:	1-2X
Inserted 1:71	
Black Refractor:	2-3X
Production 200 Sets	
Red X-Fractor:	4-6X
Production 25 Sets	
Gold Super:	No Pricing
Production One Set	
BB1 Barry Bonds	3.00
BB25 Barry Bonds	3.00
BB50 Barry Bonds	3.00
BB75 Barry Bonds	3.00
BB100 Barry Bonds	3.00
BB125 Barry Bonds	3.00
BB150 Barry Bonds	3.00
BB175 Barry Bonds	3.00
BB200 Barry Bonds	3.00
BB225 Barry Bonds	3.00
BB250 Barry Bonds	3.00
BB275 Barry Bonds	3.00
BB300 Barry Bonds	3.00
BB325 Barry Bonds	3.00
BB350 Barry Bonds	3.00

Printing Plates
No Pricing
Production one set per color.

Washington Nationals Commemorative Set

	NM/M
Complete Boxed Set (55):	20.00
Common Player:	.50
1 Nationals Logo	.50
2 Jose Vidro	.75
3 Joe Horgan	.50
4 Danny Rueckel	.50
5 Wil Cordero	.50
6 Cristian Guzman	.75
7 Alex Escobar	.50
8 Tony Armas Jr.	.50
9 Zach Day	.50
10 Jamey Carroll	.50
11 Nick Johnson	.75
12 John Patterson	.50
13 Josh Karp	.50
14 Brendan Harris	.50
15 Gary Bennett	.50
16 Terrmel Sledge	.50
17 Tomo Ohka	.50
18 Chad Cordero	.50
19 Luis Ayala	.50
20 Tony Blanco	.50
21 Endy Chavez	.75
22 George Arias	.50
23 Chad Durbin	.50
24 Phil Hiatt	.50
25 Henry Mateo	.50
26 Livan Hernandez	.50
27 Larry Broadway	.60
28 T.J. Tucker	.50
29 J.J. Davis	.50
30 Brian Schneider	.50
31 Vinny Castilla	.50
32 Michael Hinckley	.50
33 Brandon Watson	.50
34 Claudio Vargas	.50
35 Ryan Church	.50
36 Jose Guillen	.65

37 Gary Majewski	.50
38 Jon Rauch	.50
39 Brad Wilkerson	.50
40 Francis Beltran	.50
41 Esteban Loaiza	.50
42 Carlos Baerga	.50
43 Sunny Kim	.50
44 Ian Desmond	.50
45 Jeffrey Hammonds	.50
46 Hector Carrasco	.50
47 Drew McMillan	.50
48 Jared Sandberg	.50
49 Frank Robinson	1.00
50 RFK Stadium	.50
51 Senators Become Twins in 1961	.50
52 Senators Move to Texas in 1972	.50
53 Nationals Top Orioles	.50
54 First Moves (Vinny Castilla, Jose Guillen)	.50
55 First Moves (Cristian Guzman, Esteban Loaiza)	.50

Emerald Nuts S.F. Giants

The first 20,000 fans at the August 28 game at SBC Park received this foil-wrapped team set. High-gloss fronts are bordered in black with gold-foil highlights. Backs have a portrait photo, stats and career highlights. Cards are numbered with GTS prefix.

	NM/M
Complete Set (31):	7.50
Common Player:	.25
1 Barry Bonds	3.00
2 Armando Benitez	.25
3 Edgardo Alfonzo	.25
4 Kirk Rueter	.25
5 Ray Durham	.25
6 Michael Tucker	.25
7 Noah Lowry	.25
8 Jason Christiansen	.25
9 J.T. Snow	.35
10 Jason Schmidt	.35
11 Pedro Feliz	.25
12 Brett Tomko	.25
13 Jeff Fassero	.25
14 Mike Matheny	.25
15 Omar Vizquel	.25
16 Lance Niekro	.25
17 Scott Eyre	.25
18 Jesse Foppert	.25
19 Deivi Cruz	.25
20 Moises Alou	.35
21 Scott Munter	.25
22 Todd Linden	.25
23 Marquis Grissom	.25
24 Jason Ellison	.25
25 Tyler Walker	.25
26 LaTroy Hawkins	.25
27 Yorvit Torrealba	.25
28 Felipe Alou	.35
29 Coaches (Joe Lefebvre, Luis Pujols, Gene Glynn)	.25
30 Coaches (Dave Righetti, Ron Wotus, Mark Gardner)	.25
--- Checklist	.25

Poland Spring Yankees Legends
Stadium giveaway July 30.

	NM/M
Complete Set (5):	6.00
Common Player:	2.00
1 Paul O'Neill	2.00
2 Hank Bauer	2.00
3 Bill "Moose" Skowron	2.00
4 Graig Nettles	2.00
-- Sponsor's Card	.10

2006 Topps

	NM/M
Complete Set (659):	60.00
Complete Hobby Set (664):	75.00
Complete Holiday Set (659):	75.00

Complete Cardinals Set (664):	75.00
Complete Cubs Set (664):	75.00
Complete Pirates Set (664):	75.00
Complete Red Sox Set (664):	75.00
Complete Yankees Set (664):	75.00
Common Player:	.10
Pack (10):	2.00
Box (36):	60.00
Jumbo Pack (35):	6.00
Jumbo Box (12):	60.00
1 Alex Rodriguez	1.50
2 Jose Valentin	.10
3 Garrett Atkins	.10
4 Scott Hatteberg	.10
5 Carl Crawford	.25
6 Armando Benitez	.10
7 Mickey Mantle	5.00
8 Mike Morse	.10
9 Damian Miller	.10
10 Clint Barmes	.10
11 Michael Barrett	.10
12 Coco Crisp	.10
13 Tadahito Iguchi	.25
14 Chris Snyder	.10
15 Brian Roberts	.10
16 David Wright	1.00
17 Victor Santos	.10
18 Trevor Hoffman	.10
19 Jeremy Reed	.10
20 Bobby Abreu	.25
21 Lance Berkman	.25
22 Zach Day	.10
23 Jonny Gomes	.10
24 Jason Marquis	.10
25 Chipper Jones	.50
26 Scott Hairston	.10
27 Ryan Dempster	.10
28 Brandon Inge	.10
29 Aaron Harang	.10
30 Jon Garland	.10
31 Pokey Reese	.10
32 Mike MacDougal	.10
33 Mike Lieberthal	.10
34 Cesar Izturis	.10
35 Brad Wilkerson	.10
36 Jeff Suppan	.10
37 Adam Everett	.10
38 Bengie Molina	.10
39 Rickie Weeks	.25
40 Jorge Posada	.25
41 Rheal Cormier	.10
42 Reed Johnson	.10
43 Laynce Nix	.10
44 Carl Everett	.10
45 Greg Maddux	1.00
46 Jeff Francis	.10
47 Felipe Lopez	.10
48 Dan Johnson	.10
49 Humberto Cota	.10
50 Manny Ramirez	.50
51 Juan Uribe	.10
52 Jaret Wright	.10
53 Tomokazu Ohka	.10
54 Mike Matheny	.10
55 Joe Mauer	.25
56 Jarrod Washburn	.10
57 Randy Winn	.10
58 Pedro Feliz	.10
59 Kenny Rogers	.10
60 Rocco Baldelli	.10
61 Eric Hinske	.10
62 Damaso Marte	.10
63 Desi Relaford	.10
64 Juan Encarnacion	.10
65 Nomar Garciaparra	.50
66 Shawn Estes	.10
67 Brian Jordan	.10
68 Steve Kline	.10
69 Braden Looper	.10
70 Carlos Lee	.10
71 Tom Glavine	.25
72 Craig Biggio	.25
73 Steve Finley	.10
74 David Newhan	.10
75 Eric Gagne	.20
76 Tony Graffanino	.10
77 Dallas McPherson	.10
78 Nick Punto	.10
79 Mark Kotsay	.10
80 Kerry Wood	.25
81 Kyle Farnsworth	.10
82 Huston Street	.20
83 Endy Chavez	.10
84 So Taguchi	.10
85 Hank Blalock	.25

86 Brad Radke	.10
87 Chien-Ming Wang	.50
88 B.J. Surhoff	.10
89 Glendon Rusch	.10
90 Mark Buehrle	.25
91 Rafael Betancourt	.10
92 Lance Cormier	.10
93 Alex Gonzalez	.10
94 Matt Stairs	.10
95 Andy Pettitte	.25
96 Jesse Crain	.10
97 Kenny Lofton	.10
98 Geoff Blum	.10
99 Mark Redman	.10
100 Barry Bonds	1.50
101 Chad Orvella	.10
102 Xavier Nady	.10
103 Junior Spivey	.10
104 Bernie Williams	.25
105 Victor Martinez	.25
106 Nook Logan	.10
107 Mark Teahen	.10
108 Mike Lamb	.10
109 Jayson Werth	.10
110 Mariano Rivera	.25
111 Erubiel Durazo	.10
112 Ryan Vogelsong	.10
113 Bobby Madritsch	.10
114 Travis Lee	.10
115 Adam Dunn	.40
116 David Riske	.10
117 Troy Percival	.10
118 Chad Tracy	.20
119 Andy Marte	.20
120 Edgar Renteria	.20
121 Jason Giambi	.25
122 Justin Morneau	.40
123 J.T. Snow	.10
124 Danys Baez	.10
125 Carlos Delgado	.25
126 John Buck	.10
127 Shannon Stewart	.10
128 Mike Cameron	.10
129 Joe McEwing	.10
130 Richie Sexson	.10
131 Rod Barajas	.10
132 Russ Adams	.10
133 J.D. Closser	.10
134 Ramon Ortiz	.10
135 Josh Beckett	.25
136 Ryan Freel	.10
137 Victor Zambrano	.10
138 Ronnie Belliard	.10
139 Jason Michaels	.10
140 Brian Giles	.20
141 Randy Wolf	.10
142 Robinson Cano	.40
143 Joe Blanton	.10
144 Esteban Loaiza	.10
145 Troy Glaus	.25
146 Matt Clement	.10
147 Geoff Jenkins	.10
148 John Thomson	.10
149 A.J. Pierzynski	.10
150 Pedro Martinez	.50
151 Roger Clemens	1.50
152 Jack Wilson	.10
153 Ray King	.10
154 Ryan Church	.10
155 Paul LoDuca	.10
156 Dan Wheeler	.10
157 Carlos Zambrano	.25
158 Mike Timlin	.10
159 Brandon Claussen	.10
160 Travis Hafner	.25
161 Chris Shelton	.10
162 Rafael Furcal	.25
163 Flash Gordon	.10
164 Noah Lowry	.10
165 Larry Walker	.25
166 Dave Roberts	.10
167 Scott Schoeneweis	.10
168 Julian Tavarez	.10
169 Jhonny Peralta	.25
170 Vernon Wells	.25
171 Jorge Cantu	.20
172 Todd Greene	.10
173 Willy Taveras	.10
174 Corey Patterson	.10
175 Ivan Rodriguez	.40
176 Bobby Kielty	.10
177 Jose Reyes	.25
178 Barry Zito	.25
179 Deivi Cruz	.10
180 Mark Teixeira	.50
181 Chone Figgins	.10
182 Aaron Rowand	.10
183 Tim Wakefield	.10
184 Mike Maroth	.10
185 Johnny Damon	.50
186 Vicente Padilla	.10
187 Ryan Klesko	.10
188 Gary Matthews	.10
189 Jose Mesa	.10
190 Nick Johnson	.10
191 Freddy Garcia	.10
192 Larry Bigbie	.10
193 Chris Ray	.10
194 Torii Hunter	.25
195 Mike Sweeney	.10
196 Brad Penny	.10
197 Jason Frasor	.10
198 Kevin Mench	.10
199 Adam Kennedy	.10
200 Albert Pujols	1.50
201 Jody Gerut	.10
202 Luis Gonzalez	.10
203 Zack Greinke	.10

204 Miguel Cairo	.10
205 Jimmy Rollins	.25
206 Edgardo Alfonzo	.10
207 Billy Wagner	.10
208 B.J. Ryan	.10
209 Orlando Hudson	.10
210 Preston Wilson	.10
211 Melvin Mora	.10
212 Bill Mueller	.10
213 Javy Lopez	.10
214 Wilson Betemit	.10
215 Garret Anderson	.10
217 Russell Branyan	.10
217 Jeff Weaver	.10
218 Doug Mientkiewicz	.10
219 Mark Ellis	.10
220 Jason Bay	.25
221 Adam LaRoche	.10
222 C.C. Sabathia	.10
223 Humberto Quintero	.10
224 Bartolo Colon	.20
225 Ichiro Suzuki	1.00
226 Brett Tomko	.10
227 Corey Koskie	.10
228 David Eckstein	.10
229 Cristian Guzman	.10
230 Jeff Kent	.25
231 Chris Capuano	.10
232 Rodrigo Lopez	.10
233 Jason Phillips	.10
234 Luis Rivas	.10
235 Cliff Floyd	.10
236 Gil Meche	.10
237 Adam Eaton	.10
238 Matt Morris	.25
239 Kyle Davies	.10
240 David Wells	.10
241 John Smoltz	.25
242 Felix Hernandez	.50
243 Kenny Rogers	.10
244 Mark Teixeira	.25
245 Orlando Hudson	.10
246 Derek Jeter	1.00
247 Eric Chavez	.20
248 Torii Hunter	.10
249 Vernon Wells	.10
250 Ichiro Suzuki	.50
251 Greg Maddux	.50
252 Mike Matheny	.10
253 Derrek Lee	.25
254 Luis Castillo	.10
255 Omar Vizquel	.10
256 Mike Lowell	.10
257 Andruw Jones	.25
258 Jim Edmonds	.20
259 Bobby Abreu	.20
260 Bartolo Colon	.10
261 Chris Carpenter	.10
262 Alex Rodriguez	1.00
263 Albert Pujols	1.00
264 Huston Street	.10
265 Ryan Howard	.50
266 Bob Melvin	.10
267 Bobby Cox	.10
268 Baltimore Orioles	.10
269 Boston Red Sox	.25
270 Chicago White Sox	.25
271 Dusty Baker	.10
272 Jerry Narron	.10
273 Cleveland Indians	.10
274 Clint Hurdle	.10
275 Detroit Tigers	.10
276 Jack McKeon	.10
277 Phil Garner	.10
278 Kansas City Royals	.10
279 Jim Tracy	.10
280 Angels	.10
281 Milwaukee Brewers	.10
282 Minnesota Twins	.10
283 Willie Randolph	.10
284 New York Yankees	.50
285 Oakland Athletics	.10
286 Charlie Manuel	.10
287 Pete Mackanin	.10
288 Bruce Bochy	.10
289 Felipe Alou	.10
290 Seattle Mariners	.10
291 Tony LaRussa	.10
292 Tampa Bay Devil Rays	.10
293 Texas Rangers	.10
294 Toronto Blue Jays	.10
295 Frank Robinson	.25
296 Anderson Hernandez (RC)	
297b Alex Gordon (Cut-out card.)	80.00
298 Jason Botts (RC)	.10
299 Jeff Mathis (RC)	.10
300 Ryan Garko (RC)	.10
301 Charlton Jimerson (RC)	.10
302 Chris Denorfia (RC)	.10
303 Anthony Reyes (RC)	.10
304 Bryan Bullington (RC)	.10
305 Chuck James (RC)	.10
306 Danny Sandoval RC	.25
307 Walter Young (RC)	.10
308 Fausto Carmona (RC)	.10
309 Francisco Liriano (RC)	1.00
310 Hong-Chih Kuo (RC)	.10
311 Joe Saunders (RC)	.10
312 John Koronka (RC)	.10
313 Robert Andino RC	.25
314 Shaun Marcum (RC)	.10
315 Tom Gorzelanny (RC)	.10
316 Craig Breslow RC	.25
317 Chris Demaria RC	.50
318 Brayan Pena (RC)	.10
319 Rich Hill (RC)	.25

320 Rick Short RC	.25
321 C.J. Wilson (RC)	.10
322 Marshall McDougall (RC)	.10
323 Darrell Rasner (RC)	.10
324 Brandon Watson (RC)	.10
325 Paul McAnulty (RC)	.10
326 Derek Jeter, Alex Rodriguez	.50
327 Miguel Tejada, Melvin Mora	.25
328 Marcus Giles, Chipper Jones	.25
329 Manny Ramirez, David Ortiz	.25
330 Michael Barrett, Greg Maddux	.25
331 Matt Holliday	.10
332 Orlando Cabrera	.10
333 Ryan Langerhans	.10
334 Lew Ford	.10
335 Mark Prior	.40
336 Ted Lilly	.10
337 Michael Young	.10
338 Livan Hernandez	.10
339 Yadier Molina	.10
340 Eric Chavez	.10
341 Miguel Batista	.10
342 Bruce Chen	.10
343 Sean Casey	.10
344 Doug Davis	.10
345 Andruw Jones	.40
346 Hideki Matsui	1.00
347 Joe Randa	.10
348 Reggie Sanders	.10
349 Jason Jennings	.10
350 Joe Nathan	.10
351 Jose Lopez	.10
352 John Lackey	.10
353 Claudio Vargas	.10
354 Grady Sizemore	.25
355 Jonathan Papelbon (RC)	3.00
356 Luis Matos	.10
357 Orlando Hernandez	.10
358 Jamie Moyer	.10
359 Chase Utley	.25
360 Moises Alou	.10
361 Chad Cordero	.10
362 Brian McCann	.25
363 Jermaine Dye	.10
364 Ryan Madson	.10
365 Aramis Ramirez	.25
366 Matt Treanor	.10
367 Ray Durham	.10
368 Khalil Greene	.10
369 Mike Hampton	.10
370 Mike Mussina	.25
371 Brad Hawpe	.10
372 Marlon Byrd	.10
373 Woody Williams	.10
374 Victor Diaz	.10
375 Brady Clark	.10
376 Luis Gonzalez	.10
377 Raul Ibanez	.10
378 Tony Clark	.10
379 Shawn Chacon	.10
380 Marcus Giles	.10
381 Odalis Perez	.10
382 Steve Trachsel	.10
383 Russ Ortiz	.10
384 Toby Hall	.10
385 Bill Hall	.10
386 Luke Hudson	.10
387 Ken Griffey Jr.	1.00
388 Tim Hudson	.10
389 Brian Moehler	.10
390 Jake Peavy	.25
391 Casey Blake	.10
392 Sidney Ponson	.10
393 Brian Schneider	.10
394 J.J. Hardy	.10
395 Austin Kearns	.25
396 Pat Burrell	.25
397 Jason Vargas	.10
398 Ryan Howard	.75
399 Joe Crede	.10
400 Vladimir Guerrero	.50
401 Roy Halladay	.25
402 David Dellucci	.10
403 Brandon Webb	.10
404 Marlon Anderson	.10
405 Miguel Tejada	.25
406 Ryan Doumit	.10
407 Kevin Youkilis	.25
408 Jon Lieber	.10
409 Edwin Encarnacion	.10
410 Miguel Cabrera	.50
411 A.J. Burnett	.10
412 David Bell	.10
413 Gregg Zaun	.10
414 Lance Niekro	.10
415 Shawn Green	.10
416 Roberto Hernandez	.10
417 Jay Gibbons	.10
418 Johnny Estrada	.10
419 Omar Vizquel	.10
420 Gary Sheffield	.25
421 Brad Halsey	.10
422 Aaron Cook	.10
423 David Ortiz	.50
424 Tony Womack	.10
425 Joe Kennedy	.10
426 Dustin McGowan	.10
427 Carl Pavano	.10
428 Nick Green	.10
429 Francisco Cordero	.10
430 Octavio Dotel	.10

#	Player	Price
431	Julio Franco	.10
432	Brett Myers	.10
433	Casey Kotchman	.10
434	Frank Catalanotto	.10
435	Paul Konerko	.25
436	Keith Foulke	.10
437	Juan Rivera	.10
438	Todd Pratt	.10
439	Ben Broussard	.10
440	Scott Kazmir	.25
441	Rich Aurilia	.10
442	Craig Monroe	.10
443	Danny Kolb	.10
444	Curtis Granderson	.20
445	Jeff Francoeur	.20
446	Dustin Hermanson	.10
447	Jacque Jones	.10
448	Bobby Crosby	.10
449	Jason LaRue	.10
450	Derrek Lee	.40
451	Curt Schilling	.50
452	Jake Westbrook	.10
453	Daniel Cabrera	.10
454	Bobby Jenks	.10
455	Dontrelle Willis	.25
456	Brad Lidge	.10
457	Shea Hillenbrand	.10
458	Luis Castillo	.10
459	Mark Hendrickson	.10
460	Randy Johnson	.50
461	Placido Polanco	.10
462	Aaron Boone	.10
463	Todd Walker	.10
464	Nick Swisher	.10
465	Joel Piniero	.10
466	Jay Payton	.10
467	Cliff Lee	.10
468	Johan Santana	.50
469	Josh Willingham (RC)	.10
470	Jeremy Bonderman	.10
471	Runelvys Hernandez	.10
472	Duaner Sanchez	.10
473	Jason Lane	.10
474	Trot Nixon	.10
475	Ramon Hernandez	.10
476	Mike Lowell	.10
477	Chan Ho Park	.10
478	Doug Waechter	.10
479	Carlos Silva	.10
480	Jose Contreras	.10
481	Vinny Castilla	.10
482	Chris Reitsma	.10
483	Jose Guillen	.10
484	Aaron Hill	.10
485	Kevin Millwood	.10
486	Wily Mo Pena	.10
487	Rich Harden	.10
488	Chris Carpenter	.25
489	Jason Bartlett	.10
490	Magglio Ordonez	.20
491	John Rodriguez	.10
492	Bob Wickman	.10
493	Eddie Guardado	.10
494	Kip Wells	.10
495	Adrian Beltre	.20
496	Jose Capellan (RC)	.10
497	Scott Podsednik	.20
498	Brad Thompson	.10
499	Aaron Heilman	.10
500	Derek Jeter	1.50
501	Emil Brown	.10
502	Morgan Ensberg	.20
503	Nate Bump	.10
504	Phil Nevin	.10
505	Jason Schmidt	.20
506	Michael Cuddyer	.10
507	John Patterson	.10
508	Danny Haren	.10
509	Freddy Sanchez	.10
510	J.D. Drew	.25
511	Dmitri Young	.10
512	Eric Milton	.10
513	Ervin Santana	.10
514	Mark Loretta	.10
515	Mark Grudzielanek	.10
516	Derrick Turnbow	.10
517	Danny Bautista	.10
518	Lyle Overbay	.10
519	Julio Lugo	.10
520	Carlos Beltran	.40
521	Jose Cruz Jr.	.10
522	Jason Isringhausen	.10
523	Bronson Arroyo	.10
524	Ben Sheets	.20
525	Zachary Duke	.10
526	Ryan Wagner	.10
527	Jose Vidro	.10
528	Doug Mirabelli	.10
529	Kris Benson	.10
530	Carlos Guillen	.10
531	Juan Pierre	.10
532	Scot Shields	.10
533	Scott Hatteberg	.10
534	Tim Stauffer	.10
535	Jim Edmonds	.25
536	Scott Eyre	.10
537	Ben Johnson (RC)	.10
538	Mark Mulder	.25
539	Juan Rincon	.10
540	Gustavo Chacin	.10
541	Oliver Perez	.10
542	Chris Young	.10
543	Edinson Volquez	.10
544	Mark Bellhorn	.10
545	Kelvim Escobar	.10
546	Andrew Sisco	.10
547	Derek Lowe	.10
548	Sean Burroughs	.10
549	Erik Bedard	.10
550	Alfonso Soriano	.40
551	Matt Murton	.10
552	Eric Byrnes	.10
553	Chris Duffy	.10
554	Kazuo Matsui	.10
555	Scott Rolen	.40
556	Robert Mackowiak	.10
557	Chris Burke	.10
558	Jeromy Burnitz	.10
559	Jerry Hairston Jr.	.10
560	Jim Thome	.40
561	Miguel Olivo	.10
562	Jose Castillo	.10
563	Brad Ausmus	.10
564	Yorvit Torrealba	.10
565	David DeJesus	.10
566	Paul Byrd	.10
567	Brandon Backe	.10
568	Aubrey Huff	.10
569	Mike Jacobs (RC)	.10
570	Todd Helton	.40
571	Angel Berroa	.10
572	Todd Jones	.10
573	Jeff Bagwell	.25
574	Darin Erstad	.10
575	Roy Oswalt	.25
576	Rondell White	.10
577	Alex Rios	.10
578	Wes Helms	.10
579	Javier Vazquez	.10
580	Frank Thomas	.40
581	Brian Fuentes	.10
582	Francisco Rodriguez	.10
583	Craig Counsell	.10
584	Jorge Sosa	.10
585	Mike Piazza	.50
586	Mike Scioscia	.10
587	Joe Torre	.25
588	Ken Macha	.10
589	John Gibbons	.10
590	Joe Maddon	.10
591	Eric Wedge	.10
592	Mike Hargrove	.10
593	Sam Perlozzo	.10
594	Buck Showalter	.10
595	Terry Francona	.10
596	Buddy Bell	.10
597	Jim Leyland	.10
598	Ron Gardenhire	.10
599	Ozzie Guillen	.10
600	Ned Yost	.10
601	Atlanta Braves	.10
602	Philadelphia Phillies	.10
603	New York Mets	.10
604	Washington Nationals	.10
605	Florida Marlins	.10
606	Houston Astros	.10
607	Chicago Cubs	.25
608	St. Louis Cardinals	.25
609	Pittsburgh Pirates	.10
610	Cincinnati Reds	.10
611	Colorado Rockies	.10
612	Los Angeles Dodgers	.25
613	San Francisco Giants	.10
614	San Diego Padres	.10
615	Arizona Diamondbacks	.10
616	Kenji Johjima RC	2.00
617	Ryan Zimmerman (RC)	2.00
618	Craig Hansen RC	1.50
619	Joey Devine RC	.25
620	Hanley Ramirez (RC)	.50
621	Scott Olsen (RC)	.25
622	Jason Bergmann RC	.10
623	Geovany Soto (RC)	.10
624	J.J. Furmaniak (RC)	.10
625	Jeremy Accardo RC	.10
626	Mark Woodyard (RC)	.10
627	Matt Capps (RC)	.10
628	Tim Corcoran RC	.25
629	Ryan Jorgensen RC	.10
630	Ronny Paulino (RC)	.10
631	Dan Uggla (RC)	.50
632	Ian Kinsler (RC)	.25
633	Josh Barfield (RC)	.25
634	Reggie Abercrombie (RC)	.25
635	Joel Zumaya (RC)	1.00
636	Matt Cain (RC)	.25
637	Conor Jackson (RC)	.10
638	Bryan Anderson (RC)	.10
639	Prince Fielder (RC)	.25
640	Jeremy Hermida (RC)	.10
641	Justin Verlander (RC)	1.00
642	Brian Bannister (RC)	.10
643	Willie Eyre (RC)	.10
644	Ricky Nolasco (RC)	.10
645	Paul Maholm (RC)	.10
646	Johnny Damon, Ken Griffey Jr.	.25
647	Rondell White, Lew Ford	.10
648	Orlando Hernandez, Orlando Hudson	
649	Adam Dunn, Pat Burrell	.10
650	Mike Lieberthal, Jose Reyes	.10
651	Kazuo Matsui, Hank Blalock	.10
652	Michael Young, Prince Fielder, Rickie Weeks	.25
653	Travis Lee, Rocco Baldelli	.10
654		
655	Derrick Lee, Aramis Ramirez	.25
656	Grady Sizemore, Aaron Boone	.25
657	Luis Gonzalez, Shawn Green, Koyie Hill	.10
658	Ivan Rodriguez, Carlos Guillen	.10
659	Alex Rodriguez, Gary Sheffield	.25
660	Ervin Santana, Francisco Rodriguez	.10

Gold

Stars: 5-10X
Production 2,006 Sets

Black

Stars: 15-25X
Production 55 Sets
HTA Exclusive

Platinum

No Pricing
Production One Set

AFLAC

		NM/M
	Common Player:	15.00
BB	Blake Beavan	40.00
BK	Brett Krill	25.00
CC	Christian Colon	40.00
CR	Cameron Rupp	25.00
DB	Drake Britton	15.00
DD	Derek Dietrich	25.00
DM	D.J. LeMahieu	25.00
DR	Danny Rams	25.00
ED	Evan Danieli	30.00
EG	Erik Goeddel	30.00
FF	Freddie Freeman	25.00
GP	Greg Peavey	30.00
HM	Hunter Morris	15.00
JG	Jon Gilmore	15.00
JH	Jason Heyward	25.00
JL	Joe Leftridge	20.00
JS	Josh Smoker	15.00
JT	John Tolisano	25.00
JV	Josh Vitters	25.00
KB	Kyle Blair	15.00
KK	Kevin Keyes	15.00
MB	Madison Bumgarner	50.00
MH	Matt Harvey	60.00
MM	Michael Main	40.00
NN	Nick Noonan	15.00
NR	Neil Ramirez	25.00
PD	Paul Demny	15.00
RP	Rick Porcello	25.00
RS	Robert Stock	50.00
SB	Steven Brooks	25.00
SS	Sequoyah Stonecipher	75.00
TA	Tim Alderson	15.00
YG	Yasmani Grandal	25.00

Autographs

		NM/M
	Common Player:	
WB	Wade Boggs/250	40.00
JB	Jason Botts	10.00
MB	Milton Bradley	20.00
CB	Craig Breslow	10.00
FC	Fausto Carmona	15.00
BC	Brian Cashman/100	175.00
EC	Eric Chavez/200	60.00
LC	Lance Cormier	25.00
NC	Nelson Cruz	8.00
DD	Doug DeVore	8.00
TE	Theo Epstein	120.00
RG	Ryan Garko	20.00
AG	Alex Gordon	240.00
CG	Carlos Guillen	25.00
LH	Livan Hernandez	10.00
RH	Rich Hill	30.00
CJ	Chuck James	25.00
JJ	Josh Johnson	15.00
AL	Anthony Lerew	10.00
FL	Francisco Liriano	30.00
JM	Jeff Mathis	25.00
GN	Graig Nettles	25.00
SO	Scott Olsen	15.00
TO	Tim Olson	8.00
DO	David Ortiz/100	65.00
HR	Horacio Ramirez	12.00
DR	Darrell Rasner	10.00
ARE	Anthony Reyes	35.00
CR	Cal Ripken Jr./100	200.00
AR	Alex Rodriguez/100	450.00
RS	Ryne Sandberg/100	140.00
GS	Gary Sheffield/200	60.00
TS	Terrmel Sledge	20.00
BW	Brad Wilkerson	20.00
DW	Dave Winfield/100	150.00
MY	Michael Young	25.00

Series 2

GA	Garrett Atkins	20.00
CB	Clint Barmes	15.00
JB	Jose Bautista	15.00
BB	Barry Bonds/120	400.00
RC	Robinson Cano	50.00
GC	Gary Carter/250	40.00
BC	Brandon Claussen	10.00
DD	Doug Drabek/250	20.00
JF	Jeff Francis	20.00
DJ	Dan Johnson	15.00
AJ	Andruw Jones/50	50.00
SK	Scott Kazmir	30.00
DL	Derrek Lee/250	50.00
BM	Brandon McCarthy	15.00
CO	Chad Orvella	15.00
JP	Jonathan Papelbon	60.00
WP	Wily Mo Pena/250	30.00
BR	Brian Roberts/250	30.00
DSN	Duke Snider/250	60.00
DS	Darryl Strawberry/250	25.00
CV	Claudio Vargas	15.00
RZ	Ryan Zimmerman	60.00

Bonds Home Run History

	NM/M
Complete Set (48):	35.00
Common Bonds:	1.00
Inserted 1:4	
BB661-708 Barry Bonds	1.00

Declaration of Independence Cuts

No Pricing
Production One Set

Factory Set Rookie Bonus

NM/M

1-5 issued in retail factory sets.
6-10 issued in hobby factory sets.
11-20 issued in holidayfactory sets.

1	Nicholas Markakis	5.00
2	Kelly Shoppach	3.00
3	Jordan Tata	3.00
4	Ruddy Lugo	3.00
5	Josh Wilson	3.00
6	Fernando Nieve	3.00
7	Sendy Rleal	3.00
8	Jason Kubel	3.00
9	James Loney	5.00
10	Fabio Castro	3.00
11	Jonathan Broxton	3.00
12	Eliezer Alfonzo	3.00
13	Jason Hirsh	3.00
14	Rajai Davis	3.00
15	Henry Owens	5.00
16	Kevin Frandsen	3.00
17	Matt Garza	5.00
18	Chris Duncan	3.00
19	Chris Coste	3.00
20	Jeff Karstens	5.00

Factory Set Team Bonus

NM/M

Issued in specified factory team sets.

BRS1	Jonathan Papelbon	10.00
BRS2	Manny Ramirez	5.00
BRS3	David Ortiz	5.00
BRS4	Josh Beckett	3.00
BRS5	Curt Schilling	4.00
CC1	Sean Marshall	3.00
CC2	Freddie Bynum	3.00
CC3	Derrek Lee	4.00
CC4	Juan Pierre	3.00
CC5	Carlos Zambrano	3.00
NYY1	Wilbert Nieves	3.00
NYY2	Alex Rodriguez	6.00
NYY3	Derek Jeter	8.00
NYY4	Mariano Rivera	5.00
NYY5	Randy Johnson	5.00
PP1	Matt Capps	3.00
PP2	Paul Maholm	3.00
PP3	Nate McLouth	3.00
PP4	John Van Benschoten	3.00
PP5	Jason Bay	3.00
SLC1	Adam Wainwright	4.00
SLC2	Skip Schumaker	3.00
SLC3	Albert Pujols	10.00
SLC4	Jim Edmonds	3.00
SLC5	Scott Rolen	5.00

eTopps Classics

Topps continued its eTopps Classics line-up in 2006 with cards of former greats. The format was the same as earlier issues. Like regular eTopps cards, Classics could only be ordered during a one-week Initial Player Offering period. Cards were issued in a quantity of up to 3,000 each at $9.50-12.50. The number of cards actually sold is shown parenthetically. Fronts have a color or colorized action photo, backs have a picture of one of that player's Topps cards, along with career notes, stats, etc. Values shown are for cards in a virtual portfolio, rather than "in hand." Taking physical possession of a card from an eTopps portfolio costs about $6 apiece.

Complete Set (xx):
Common Player:

Hit Parade

		NM/M
	Common Player:	.50
RB11	Barry Bonds	3.00
RB12	Ken Griffey Jr.	2.00
RB13	Jeff Bagwell	.75
RB14	Gary Sheffield	.75
RB15	Frank Thomas	.75
RB16	Manny Ramirez	1.00
RB17	Ruben Sierra	.50
RB18	Jeff Kent	.50
RB19	Luis Gonzalez	.50
RBI10	Alex Rodriguez	3.00
HR1	Barry Bonds	3.00
HR2	Ken Griffey Jr.	2.00
HR3	Jeff Bagwell	.75
HR4	Gary Sheffield	.75
HR5	Frank Thomas	.75
HR6	Manny Ramirez	1.00
HR7	Jim Thome	1.00
HR8	Alex Rodriguez	3.00
HR9	Mike Piazza	1.00
HR10	Carlos Delgado	.75
HT1	Craig Biggio	.50
HT2	Barry Bonds	3.00
HT3	Julio Franco	.50
HT4	Steve Finley	.50
HT5	Gary Sheffield	.75
HT6	Jeff Bagwell	.75
HT7	Ken Griffey Jr.	2.00
HT8	Omar Vizquel	.50
HT9	Marquis Grissom	.50
HT10	Bernie Williams	.50

Hobby Masters

		NM/M
	Complete Set (20):	20.00
	Common Player:	.75
	Inserted 1:18	
HM1	Derrek Lee	1.00
HM2	Albert Pujols	4.00
HM3	Nomar Garciaparra	1.00
HM4	Alfonso Soriano	.75
HM5	Derek Jeter	4.00
HM6	Miguel Tejada	1.00
HM7	Alex Rodriguez	4.00
HM8	Jim Edmonds	.75
HM9	Mark Prior	1.00
HM10	Roger Clemens	4.00
HM11	Randy Johnson	1.50
HM12	Manny Ramirez	1.50
HM13	Curt Schilling	1.50
HM14	Vladimir Guerrero	1.50
HM15	Barry Bonds	4.00
HM16	Ichiro Suzuki	1.50
HM17	Pedro Martinez	1.50
HM18	Carlos Beltran	1.50
HM19	David Ortiz	1.50
HM20	Andruw Jones	1.00

King of England Cut Signature

Production One

The Mantle Collection

	NM/M
Complete Set (10):	65.00
Common Mantle:	8.00
Inserted 1:36	
Black:	No Pricing
Production 7 Sets	
MM2005 Mickey Mantle	8.00
MM2004 Mickey Mantle	8.00
MM2003 Mickey Mantle	8.00
MM2002 Mickey Mantle	8.00
MM2001 Mickey Mantle	8.00
MM2000 Mickey Mantle	8.00
MM1999 Mickey Mantle	8.00
MM1998 Mickey Mantle	8.00
MM1997 Mickey Mantle	8.00
MM1996 Mickey Mantle	8.00

The Mantle Collection Relics

	NM/M
Production 77-167	
Gold:	
Black:	No Pricing
Production 7 Sets	
MM2005 Mickey Mantle/167	160.00
MM2004 Mickey Mantle/157	160.00
MM2003 Mickey Mantle/147	160.00
MM2002 Mickey Mantle/137	160.00
MM2001 Mickey Mantle/127	200.00
MM2000 Mickey Mantle/117	200.00
MM1999 Mickey Mantle/107	200.00
MM1998 Mickey Mantle/97	200.00
MM1997 Mickey Mantle/87	200.00
MM1996 Mickey Mantle/77	200.00

The Mantle Collection Gold

	NM/M
Varying quantities produced	65.00
MM2005 Mickey Mantle/977	30.00
MM2004 Mickey Mantle/877	30.00
MM2003 Mickey Mantle/777	40.00
MM2002 Mickey Mantle/677	40.00
MM2001 Mickey Mantle/577	50.00
MM2000 Mickey Mantle/477	50.00
MM1999 Mickey Mantle/377	50.00
MM1998 Mickey Mantle/277	60.00
MM1997 Mickey Mantle/177	100.00
MM1996 Mickey Mantle/77	150.00

Mantle Homerun History

		NM/M
	Inserted 1:4	
MHR1	Mickey Mantle	2.00
	Common Mantle:	2.00
MHR2-101	Mickey Mantle	2.00

Mantle Homerun History Relic

Inserted 1:4,540
Series 2
Production 7 Sets

Mantle Homerun History Cut Signature

Production One

2006 Topps Opening Day

NM/M

Common Team:		.50
WI	Chicago White Sox	2.00
MN	New York Mets	2.00
RR	Texas Rangers	.50
BP	Milwaukee Brewers	.50
RC	Cincinnati Reds	1.00
PC	Philadelphia Phillies	1.00
OD	Baltimore Orioles	1.00
RD	Colorado Rockies	.50
DB	Los Angeles Dodgers	2.00
RT	Kansas City Royals	.50
MA	Seattle Mariners	1.00
AM	Houston Astros	1.00
PG	San Diego Padres	1.00
AY	Oakland Athletics	2.00
JT	Toronto Blue Jays	1.00

Day Relics
NM/M

Common Team:		25.00
WI	Chicago White Sox	40.00
MN	New York Mets	40.00
RR	Texas Rangers	30.00
BP	Milwaukee Brewers	25.00
RC	Cincinnati Reds	30.00
PC	Philadelphia Phillies	40.00
OD	Baltimore Orioles	25.00
RD	Colorado Rockies	25.00
DB	Los Angeles Dodgers	40.00
RT	Kansas City Royals	25.00
MA	Seattle Mariners	30.00
AM	Houston Astros	30.00
PG	San Diego Padres	40.00
AY	Oakland Athletics	40.00
JT	Toronto Blue Jays	30.00

Own the Game
NM/M

Complete Set (30): 20.00
Common Player: .75
Inserted 1:12

OG1	Derrek Lee	1.00
OG2	Michael Young	.75
OG3	Albert Pujols	3.00
OG4	Roger Clemens	3.00
OG5	Andy Pettitte	.75
OG6	Dontrelle Willis	.75
OG7	Michael Young	.75
OG8	Ichiro Suzuki	2.00
OG9	Derek Jeter	3.00
OG10	Andruw Jones	1.00
OG11	Alex Rodriguez	3.00
OG12	David Ortiz	1.00
OG13	David Ortiz	1.00
OG14	Manny Ramirez	1.00
OG15	Mark Teixeira	1.00
OG16	Albert Pujols	3.00
OG17	Alex Rodriguez	3.00
OG18	Derek Jeter	3.00
OG19	Chad Cordero	.50
OG20	Francisco Rodriguez	.50
OG21	Mariano Rivera	.75
OG22	Chone Figgins	.50
OG23	Jose Reyes	.50
OG24	Scott Podsednik	.50
OG25	Jake Peavy	.50
OG26	Johan Santana	1.00
OG27	Pedro Martinez	.75
OG28	Dontrelle Willis	.75
OG29	Chris Carpenter	.50
OG30	Bartolo Colon	.50

Signers of the Constitution
NM/M

Common Signer: 1.50
Inserted 1:8

AB	Abraham Baldwin	1.50
RB	Richard Bassett	1.50
GB	Gunning Bedford Jr.	1.50
JB	John Blair	1.50
WB	William Blount	1.50
DB	David Brearly	1.50
JBR	Jacob Broom	1.50
PB	Pierce Butler	1.50
DC	Daniel Carroll	1.50
GC	George Clymer	1.50
JD	Jonathan Dayton	1.50
JDI	John Dickinson	1.50
WF	William Few	1.50
TF	Thomas Fitzsimons	1.50
BF	Benjamin Franklin	4.00
NG	Nicholas Gilman	1.50
NGO	Nathaniel Gorham	1.50
AH	Alexander Hamilton	3.00
JI	Jared Ingersoll	1.50
DJ	Daniel of St. Thomas Jenifer	1.50
WJ	William Samuel Johnson	1.50
RK	Rufus King	1.50
JL	John Langdon	1.50
WL	William Livingston	1.50
JM	James Madison	2.00
JMC	James McHenry	1.50
TM	Thomas Mifflin	1.50
GM	Gouverneur Morris	1.50
RM	Robert Morris	1.50
WP	William Paterson	1.50
CCP	Charles Cotesworth Pinckney	1.50
CP	Charles Pinckney	1.50
GR	George Read	1.50
JR	John Rutledge	1.50
RS	Roger Sherman	1.50
RDS	Richard Dobbs Spaight	1.50
GW	George Washington	4.00
HW	Hugh Williamson	1.50
JW	James Wilson	1.50

Signers of the Declaration of Independence
NM/M

Complete Set (56): 80.00
Common Signer: 1.50
Inserted 1:4

JA	John Adams	3.00
SA	Samuel Adams	3.00
JB	Josiah Bartlett	1.50
CB	Carter Braxton	1.50
CC	Charles Carroll	1.50
SC	Samuel Chase	1.50
AC	Abraham Clark	1.50
GC	George Clymer	1.50
WE	William Ellery	1.50
WF	William Floyd	1.50
BF	Benjamin Franklin	4.00
EG	Elbridge Gerry	1.50
BG	Button Gwinnett	1.50
LH	Lyman Hall	1.50
JH	John Hancock	3.00
BH	Benjamin Harrison	1.50
JHA	John Hart	1.50
JHE	Joseph Hewes	1.50
TH	Thomas Heyward Jr.	1.50
WH	William Hooper	1.50
SH	Stephen Hopkins	1.50
FH	Francis Hopkinson	1.50
SHU	Samuel Huntington	1.50
TJ	Thomas Jefferson	1.50
FLL	Francis Lightfoot Lee	1.50
RHL	Richard Henry Lee	1.50
FL	Francis Lewis	1.50
PL	Philip Livingston	1.50
TL	Thomas Lynch Jr.	1.50
TM	Thomas McKean	1.50
AM	Arthur Middleton	1.50
LM	Lewis Morris	1.50
RM	Robert Morris	1.50
JM	John Morton	1.50
TN	Thomas Nelson Jr.	1.50
WP	William Paca	1.50
RTP	Robert Treat Paine	1.50
JP	John Penn	1.50
GRE	George Read	1.50
CR	Caesar Rodney	1.50
GR	George Ross	1.50
BR	Benjamin Rush	1.50
ER	Edward Rutledge	1.50
RS	Roger Sherman	1.50
JS	James Smith	1.50
RST	Richard Stockton	1.50
TS	Thomas Stone	1.50
GT	George Taylor	1.50
MT	Matthew Thornton	1.50
GW	George Walton	1.50
WW	William Whipple	1.50
WWI	William Williams	1.50
JW	James Wilson	1.50
JWI	John Witherspoon	1.50
OW	Oliver Wolcott	1.50
GWY	George Wythe	1.50

2006 Topps Stars

NM/M

Common Player:		.75
BB	Barry Bonds	3.00
MC	Miguel Cabrera	2.00
RC	Roger Clemens	3.00
VG	Vladimir Guerrero	1.00
TH	Todd Helton	.75
DJ	Derek Jeter	3.00
PM	Pedro Martinez	1.00
HM	Hideki Matsui	2.00
DO	David Ortiz	1.00
AP	Albert Pujols	3.00
MR	Manny Ramirez	1.00
AR	Alex Rodriguez	3.00
AS	Alfonso Soriano	.75
IS	Ichiro Suzuki	2.00
MT	Miguel Tejada	.75

Rookie of the Week
NM/M

Issued one per week via HTA shops.

1	Mickey Mantle	10.00
2	Barry Bonds	3.00
3	Roger Clemens	3.00
4	Ernie Banks	2.00
5	Nolan Ryan	5.00
6	Albert Pujols	4.00
7	Roberto Clemente	5.00
8	Frank Robinson	1.50
9	Brooks Robinson	1.50
10	Harmon Killebrew	1.50
11	Reggie Jackson	1.50
12	George Brett	3.00
13	Ichiro Suzuki	3.00
14	Cal Ripken Jr.	6.00
15	Tom Seaver	1.50
16	Johnny Bench	1.50
17	Mike Schmidt	2.00
18	Derek Jeter	5.00
19	Bob Gibson	1.50
20	Ozzie Smith	2.00
21	Rickey Henderson	1.50
22	Tony Gwynn	1.50
23	Wade Boggs	1.50
24	Ryne Sandberg	3.00
25	Mickey Mantle	10.00

Trading Places

NM/M

Common Player:		.50
MB	Milton Bradley	.50
CC	Coco Crisp	.50
JD	Johnny Damon	1.00
CD	Carlos Delgado	.75
JDN	Juan Encarnacion	.50
RF	Rafael Furcal	.50
NG	Nomar Garciaparra	1.00
TG	Troy Glaus	.50
RH	Ramon Hernandez	.50
KL	Kenny Lofton	.50
BM	Bill Mueller	.50
CP	Corey Patterson	.50
MJP	Mike Piazza	1.00
JP	Juan Pierre	.50
ER	Edgar Renteria	.50
AS	Alfonso Soriano	.75
FT	Frank Thomas	.75
JT	Jim Thome	1.00
BW	Brad Wilkerson	.50
PW	Preston Wilson	.50

Trading Places Autographs
NM/M

Autographed Relics: No Pricing
Production 25 Sets

JE	Johnny Estrada	10.00
KJ	Kenji Johjima	140.00
PL	Paul LoDuca	20.00
ML	Mike Lowell	25.00
BR	B.J. Ryan	30.00
TS	Terrmel Sledge	10.00
BW	Billy Wagner	30.00

Trading Places Autographed Relics

No Pricing
Production 25 Sets

Trading Places Relics
NM/M

Common Player:		4.00
MB	Milton Bradley	4.00
CC	Coco Crisp	6.00
JD	Johnny Damon	15.00
JE	Johnny Estrada	6.00
NG	Nomar Garciaparra	15.00
RH	Ramon Hernandez	4.00
KJ	Kenji Johjima	15.00
PL	Paul LoDuca	6.00
KL	Kenny Lofton	6.00
ML	Mike Lowell	10.00
BM	Bill Mueller	4.00
CP	Corey Patterson	8.00
JP	Juan Pierre	6.00
ER	Edgar Renteria	6.00
BR	B.J. Ryan	4.00
TS	Terrmel Sledge	4.00
AS	Alfonso Soriano	8.00
FT	Frank Thomas	8.00
JT	Jim Thome	10.00
BW	Billy Wagner	6.00
BW	Brad Wilkerson	4.00
PW	Preston Wilson	4.00

Walmart Cards

NM/M

Complete Set (18): 25.00
Common Player: .50

WM1	Stan Musial	2.00
WM2	Ted Williams	3.00
WM3	Yogi Berra	2.00
WM5	Mickey Mantle	10.00
WM6	Mickey Mantle	10.00
WM7	Alex Rodriguez	3.00
WM9	Gary Carter	.50
WM10	Roy Oswalt	.50
WM13	Carlos Lee	.50
WM14	Johan Santana	1.00
WM15	Roberto Clemente	3.00
WM16	Carl Yastrzemski	1.50
WM21	Chipper Jones	1.00
WM22	Ichiro Suzuki	2.00
WM23	Bobby Abreu	.50
WM24	Tom Seaver	1.00
WM25	Alfonso Soriano	.75
WM26	Andruw Jones	1.00
WM28	Adam Dunn	.75
WM30	Mark Teixeira	1.00
WM31	Albert Pujols	3.00
WM32	Cal Ripken Jr.	4.00
WM33	Ryne Sandberg	2.00
WM34	Don Mattingly	2.00
WM35	Roger Clemens	3.00
WM36	Jose Reyes	.50
WM38	Derek Lee	1.00
WM39	Miguel Cabrera	1.00
WM41	Barry Bonds	3.00
WM42	Barry Bonds	3.00
WM44	Livan Hernandez	.50
WM45	Derek Jeter	3.00
WM46	David Ortiz	1.00
WM48	Ivan Rodriguez	.75
WM52	Alex Rodriguez	3.00
WM53	Vladimir Guerrero	1.00

World Series Relics
NM/M

Common Player:		.50
MB	Mark Buehrle/ Glv/100	200.00
JC	Joe Crede	35.00
JD	Jermaine Dye	20.00
CEB	Carl Everett	15.00
CEU	Carl Everett/Uni./100	90.00
JG	Jon Garland	20.00
WH	Willie Harris	10.00
TI	Tadahito Iguchi	25.00
BJ	Bobby Jenks/ Glv/100	275.00
PKB	Paul Konerko	15.00
PKU	Paul Konerko	15.00
TP	Timoniel Perez	15.00
AP	A.J. Pierzynski	20.00
SP	Scott Podsednik	25.00
AR	Aaron Rowand	25.00
FT	Frank Thomas	20.00
JU	Juan Uribe	20.00

2K6 Promo Cards
NM/M

Complete Set (11): 10.00
Common Player: .75
Inserted 1:18

1	Derek Jeter	3.00
2	Andruw Jones	1.00
3	Miguel Cabrera	1.00
4	Derek Lee	1.00
5	Mariano Rivera	.75
6	Ivan Rodriguez	.75
7	Vladimir Guerrero	1.00
8	Albert Pujols	3.00
9	Alex Rodriguez	3.00
10	Alfonso Soriano	.75
11	Dontrelle Willis	.75

2006 Topps Allen & Ginter

NM/M

Complete Set (350):
Common Player: .25
Common SP: .50
SP's Inserted 1:2
Pack (7): 9.00

Box (24):		200.00
1	Albert Pujols	3.00
2	Aubrey Huff	.25
3	Mark Teixeira	.75
4	Vernon Wells	.50
5	Ken Griffey Jr./SP	4.00
6	Nick Swisher	.25
7	Jose Reyes	.50
8	David Wright	2.00
9	Vladimir Guerrero	1.00
10	Andruw Jones	.25
11	Ramon Hernandez	.25
12	Miguel Tejada	.75
13	Juan Pierre	.25
14	Jim Thome	.75
15	Austin Kearns/SP	.50
16	Jhonny Peralta	.25
17	Clint Barmes	.25
18	Angel Berroa	.25
19	Nomar Garciaparra	1.00
20	Joe Nathan	.25
21	Brandon Webb	.25
22	Chad Tracy	.25
23	Derek Jeter	3.00
24	Conor Jackson (RC)	.50
25	Jason Giambi/SP	.50
26	Johnny Estrada	.25
27	Luis Gonzalez	.40
28	Javier Vazquez	.25
29	Orlando Hudson	.25
30	Shawn Green	.40
31	Mark Buehrle	.25
32	Wily Mo Pena	.25
33	C.C. Sabathia	.25
34	Ronnie Belliard	.25
35	Travis Hafner/SP	1.00
36	Mike Jacobs (RC)	.25
37	Roy Oswalt	.50
38	Zack Greinke	.25
39	J.D. Drew	.40
40	Jeff Kent	.40
41	Ben Sheets	.25
42	Luis Castillo	.25
43	Carlos Delgado	.75
44	Cliff Floyd	.25
45	Danny Haren/SP	.25
46	Bobby Abreu	.50
47	Jeromy Burnitz	.25
48	Khalil Greene	.25
49	Moises Alou	.50
50	Alex Rodriguez/SP	5.00
51	Ervin Santana/SP	.25
52	Bartolo Colon/SP	.25
53	John Smoltz/SP	1.00
54	David Ortiz/SP	2.00
55	Hideki Matsui/SP	3.00
56	Jermaine Dye/SP	.50
57	Victor Martinez/SP	.50
58	Willy Taveras/SP	.50
59	Brady Clark/SP	.50
60	Justin Morneau	.50
61	Xavier Nady	.25
62	Rich Harden	.25
63	Jack Wilson	.25
64	Brian Giles	.25
65	Jon Lieber/SP	.50
66	Dan Johnson	.25
67	Billy Wagner	.25
68	Rickie Weeks	.40
69	Chris Ray (RC)	.25
70	Chris Shelton	.25
71	Dmitri Young	.25
72	Ivan Rodriguez	.75
73	Jeremy Bonderman	.25
74	Justin Verlander (RC)	1.00
75	Randy Johnson	1.00
76	Magglio Ordonez	.25
77	Brandon Inge	.25
78	Placido Polanco	.25
79	Ryan Howard	1.00
80	Jason Bay	.50
81	Sean Casey	.25
82	Jeremy Hermida (RC)	.50
83	Mike Cameron	.25
84	Trevor Hoffman	.25
85	Mike Matheny/SP	.25
86	Steve Finley	.25
87	Adam Everett	.25
88	Jason Isringhausen	.25
89	Jonny Gomes	.25
90	Barry Zito	.25
91	Bobby Crosby	.25
92	Eric Chavez	.25
93	Frank Thomas	.75
94	Huston Street	.50
95	Jorge Posada	.50
96	Casey Kotchman	.25
97	Darin Erstad	.25
98	Chipper Jones	1.00
99	Jeff Francoeur	.40
100	Barry Bonds	3.00
101	Alfonso Soriano	1.00
102	Brandon Claussen	.25
103	Aaron Boone	.25
104	Roger Clemens	3.00
105	Andy Pettitte/SP	.75
106	Nick Johnson	.25
107	Tom Gordon	.25
108	Orlando Hernandez	.25
109	Francisco Rodriguez	.25
110	Orlando Cabrera	.25
111	Edgar Renteria	.40
112	Tim Hudson	.50
113	Coco Crisp	.25
114	Matt Clement	.25
115	Greg Maddux/SP	3.00
116	Paul Konerko	.50
117	Felipe Lopez	.25
118	Garrett Atkins	.25
119	Akinori Otsuka	.25
120	Craig Biggio	.50
121	Danys Baez	.25
122	Brad Penny	.25
123	Eric Gagne	.25
124	Lew Ford	.25
125	Mariano Rivera/SP	1.00
126	Carlos Beltran	.75
127	Pedro Martinez	.75
128	Todd Helton	.75
129	Aaron Rowand	.25
130	Mike Lieberthal	.25
131	Oliver Perez	.25
132	Ryan Klesko	.25
133	Randy Winn	.25
134	Yuniesky Betancourt	.50
135	David Eckstein/SP	.50
136	Chad Orvella	.50
137	Toby Hall	.50
138	Hank Blalock	.50
139	B.J. Ryan	.50
140	Roy Halladay	.50
141	Livan Hernandez	.25
142	John Patterson	.25
143	Bengie Molina	.25
144	Brad Wilkerson	.25
145	Jorge Cantu/SP	.50
146	Mark Mulder	.50
147	Felix Hernandez	.50
148	Paul LoDuca	.25
149	Prince Fielder (RC)	4.00
150	Johnny Damon/SP	2.00
151	Ryan Langerhans/SP	.50
152	Kris Benson/SP	.50
153	Curt Schilling/SP	2.00
154	Manny Ramirez/SP	2.00
155	Robinson Cano/SP	1.50
156	Derek Lee/SP	1.50
157	A.J. Pierzynski/SP	.50
158	Adam Dunn/SP	1.00
159	Cliff Lee/SP	.50
160	Grady Sizemore	.50
161	Jeff Francis	.25
162	Dontrelle Willis	.25
163	Brad Ausmus	.25
164	Preston Wilson	.25
165	Derek Lowe/SP	.50
166	Chris Capuano	.25
167	Joe Mauer	.50
168	Torii Hunter	.40
169	Chase Utley	.25
170	Zachary Duke	.25
171	Jason Schmidt	.40
172	Adrian Beltre	.25
173	Eddie Guardado	.25
174	Richie Sexson	.50
175	Miguel Cabrera/SP	2.00
176	Julio Lugo	.25
177	Francisco Cordero	.25
178	Kevin Millwood	.25
179	A.J. Burnett	.25
180	Jose Guillen	.25
181	Larry Bigbie	.25
182	Raul Ibanez	.25
183	Jake Peavy	.50
184	Pat Burrell	.50
185	Tom Glavine/SP	.75
186	J.J. Hardy	.25
187	Emil Brown	.25
188	Lance Berkman	.50
189	Marcus Giles	.25
190	Scott Podsednik	.25
191	Chone Figgins	.25
192	Melvin Mora	.25
193	Mark Loretta	.25
194	Carlos Zambrano	.40
195	Chien-Ming Wang	.50
196	Mark Prior	.50
197	Bobby Jenks	.25
198	Brian Fuentes	.25
199	Garret Anderson	.25
200	Ichiro Suzuki	2.00
201	Brian Roberts	.25
202	Jason Kendall	.25
203	Milton Bradley	.25
204	Jimmy Rollins	.50
205	Brett Myers/SP	.50
206	Joe Randa	.25
207	Mike Piazza	1.00
208	Matt Morris	.25

ABBREVIATIONS

SP - Short Print

209	Omar Vizquel	.25
210	Jeremy Reed	.25
211	Chris Carpenter	.50
212	Jim Edmonds	.50
213	Scott Kazmir	.50
214	Travis Lee	.25
215	Michael Young/SP	.75
216	Rod Barajas	.25
217	Gustavo Chacin	.25
218	Lyle Overbay	.25
219	Troy Glaus	.50
220	Chad Cordero	.25
221	Jose Vidro	.25
222	Scott Rolen	.75
223	Carl Crawford	.50
224	Rocco Baldelli	.25
225	Mike Mussina	.50
226	Kelvim Escobar	.25
227	Corey Patterson	.25
228	Javy Lopez	.25
229	Jonathan Papelbon/ SP (RC)	5.00
230	Aramis Ramirez	.50
231	Tadahito Iguchi	.50
232	Morgan Ensberg	.25
233	Mark Grudzielanek	.25
234	Mike Sweeney	.25
235	Shawn Chacon/SP	.50
236	Nick Punto	.25
237	Geoff Jenkins	.25
238	Carlos Lee	.50
239	David DeJesus	.25
240	Brad Lidge	.25
241	Bob Wickman	.25
242	Jon Garland	.25
243	Kerry Wood	.50
244	Bronson Arroyo	.25
245	Matt Holliday/SP	.50
246	Josh Beckett	.50
247	Johan Santana	.75
248	Rafael Furcal	.25
249	Shannon Stewart	.25
250	Gary Sheffield	.25
251	Josh Barfield (RC)	.50
252	Kenji Johjima RC	2.00
253	Ian Kinsler (RC)	.50
254	Brian Anderson (RC)	.50
255	Matt Cain (RC)	1.00
256	Josh Willingham/ SP (RC)	.50
257	John Koronka (RC)	.50
258	Chris Duffy (RC)	.50
259	Brian McCann (RC)	.50
260	Hanley Ramirez (RC)	1.00
261	Hong-Chih Kuo (RC)	.50
262	Francisco Liriano (RC)	5.00
263	Anderson Hernandez (RC)	.50
264	Ryan Zimmerman (RC)	4.00
265	Brian Bannister/ SP (RC)	.50
266	Nolan Ryan	2.00
267	Frank Robinson	1.00
268	Roberto Clemente	3.00
269	Hank Greenberg	.50
270	Napoleon Lajoie	.50
271	Lloyd Waner	.25
272	Paul Waner	.25
273	Frankie Frisch	.25
274	Bill "Moose" Skowron	.25
275	Mickey Mantle	6.00
276	Brooks Robinson	1.00
277	Carl Yastrzemski	1.00
278	Johnny Pesky	.25
279	Stan Musial	1.50
280	Bill Mazeroski	.50
281	Harmon Killebrew	.75
282	Monte Irvin	.50
283	Bob Gibson	1.00
284	Ted Williams	2.00
285	Yogi Berra/SP	2.00
286	Ernie Banks	1.00
287	Bobby Doerr	.25
288	Josh Gibson	.50
289	Bob Feller	.25
290	Cal Ripken Jr.	3.00
291	Bobby Cox	.25
292	Terry Francona	.25
293	Dusty Baker	.25
294	Ozzie Guillen	.25
295	Jim Leyland	.50
296	Willie Randolph	.25
297	Joe Torre	.50
298	Felipe Alou	.25
299	Tony LaRussa	.25
300	Frank Robinson	.50
301	Mike Tyson	2.00
302	Duke Paoa Kahanamoku	.25
303	Jennie Finch	2.00
304	Brandi Chastain	.25
305	Danica Patrick/SP	10.00
306	Wendy Guey	.25
307	Hulk Hogan	.25
308	Carl Lewis	.25
309	John Wooden	.25
310	Randy Couture	.25
311	Andy Irons	.25
312	Takeru Kobayashi	.25
313	Leon/Spinks	.25
314	Jim Thorpe	1.00
315	Jerry Bailey/SP	.50
316	Adrian C. Anson	.25
317	John M. Ward	.25
318	Mike Kelly	.25
319	Cpt. Jack Glasscock	.25
320	Aaron Hill	.25

321	Derrick Turnbow	.25
322	Nicholas Markakis	.25
323	Brad Hawpe	.25
324	Kevin Mench	.25
325	John Lackey/SP	.50
326	Chester A. Arthur	.25
327	Ulysses S. Grant	.50
328	Abraham Lincoln	1.00
329	Grover Cleveland	.25
330	Benjamin Harrison	.25
331	Theodore Roosevelt	.25
332	Rutherford B. Hayes	.25
333	Chancellor Otto Von Bismarck	.25
334	Kaiser Wilhelm II	.25
335	Queen Victoria/SP	.50
336	Pope Leo XIII	.50
337	Thomas Edison	.50
338	Orville Wright	.50
339	Wilbur Wright	.50
340	Nathaniel Hawthorne	.25
341	Herman Melville	.25
342	Stonewall Jackson	.50
343	Robert E. Lee	.50
344	Andrew Carnegie	.25
345	John Rockefeller/SP	.50
346	Bob Fitzsimmons	.25
347	Billy the Kid	.25
348	Buffalo Bill	.25
349	Jesse James	.25
350	Statue of Liberty	.25

Mini

Bronson Arroyo.
BROOKLYN   NEW YORK

Mini:	2-4X
SP's:	1-2X
Mini SP's Inserted 1:13	
Mini (351-375):	No Pricing
#'s 351-375 Inserted In Rip Cards	
Allen & Ginter Back:	3-6X
Inserted 1:5	
A & G Back SP's:	2-3X
Inserted 1:65	
Bazooka Mini:	No Pricing
Production 25 Sets	
Black Mini:	5-10X
Inserted 1:10	
Black SP:	3-5X
Inserted 1:130	
Wood:	No Pricing
Production One Set	

Printing Plates
No Pricing
Production one set per color.

Relics

JAKE PEAVY.

		NM/M
Common Player:		4.00
CBA	Clint Barmes	4.00
CB	Carlos Beltran	10.00
BB	Barry Bonds	20.00
MB	Mark Buehrle	8.00
GWB	George W. Bush	300.00
MC	Miguel Cabrera	10.00
RC	Robinson Cano	20.00
JC	Jorge Cantu	6.00
EC	Eric Chavez	6.00
BC	Bobby Crosby	4.00
CD	Carlos Delgado	8.00
ZD	Zachary Duke	8.00

JDY	Jermaine Dye	8.00
JF	Jeff Francoeur	15.00
JG	Jonny Gomes	6.00
VG	Vladimir Guerrero	10.00
TH	Travis Hafner	10.00
FH	Felix Hernandez	8.00
MH	Matt Holliday	6.00
RH	Ryan Howard	30.00
JFK	John F. Kennedy	375.00
PK	Paul Konerko	10.00
HCK	Hong-Chih Kuo	20.00
RL	Ryan Langerhans	8.00
MM	Mickey Mantle	125.00
PM	Pedro Martinez	10.00
VM	Victor Martinez	8.00
HM	Hideki Matsui	15.00
BM	Brandon McCarthy	4.00
DO	David Ortiz	15.00
Ro	Roy Oswalt	6.00
JP	Jake Peavy	6.00
APE	Andy Pettitte	6.00
MPZ	Mike Piazza	10.00
MP	Mark Prior	8.00
AP	Albert Pujols	20.00
MR	Manny Ramirez	10.00
AR	Alex Rodriguez	20.00
JS	Johan Santana	10.00
GS	Curt Schilling	10.00
GS	Gary Sheffield	8.00
HS	Huston Street	6.00
NS	Nick Swisher	8.00
WT	Willy Taveras	6.00
MT	Miguel Tejada	10.00
FT	Frank Thomas	8.00
JT	Jim Thome	10.00
CU	Chase Utley	15.00
CMW	Chien-Ming Wang	50.00
DWI	Dontrelle Willis	8.00
DW	David Wright	15.00

Autographs
NM/M
Cards are not serial numbered.

JB	Jerry Bailey/200	80.00
JBA	Josh Barfield	20.00
CB	Clint Barmes	15.00
BB	Barry Bonds/25	500.00
MC	Miguel Cabrera/100	150.00
RC	Robinson Cano	60.00
BC	Brandi Chastain/200	75.00
EC	Eric Chavez	15.00
RA	Randy Couture	80.00
BF	Bob Feller	75.00
PF	Prince Fielder	50.00
JF	Jennie Finch/200	140.00
LF	Lew Ford	10.00
JG	Jonny Gomes	15.00
VG	Vladimir Guerrero/ 50	200.00
WG	Wendy Guey	30.00
TG	Tony Gwynn/50	250.00
TH	Travis Hafner	30.00
HH	Hulk Hogan/200	200.00
RH	Ryan Howard	150.00
AI	Andy Irons/200	40.00
KJ	Kenji Johjima/50	275.00
SK	Scott Kazmir	30.00
TK	Takeru Kobayashi/ 200	125.00
DL	Derek Lee	50.00
CL	Carl Lewis/200	120.00
FL	Francisco Liriano	50.00
VM	Victor Martinez	25.00
SM	Stan Musial/50	375.00
DP	Danica Patrick/100	500.00
WMP	Wily Mo Pena	20.00
CR	Cal Ripken Jr./50	300.00
AR	Alex Rodriguez/50	400.00
BJR	B.J. Ryan	15.00
NR	Nolan Ryan/50	350.00
ES	Ervin Santana	15.00
JS	Johan Santana/100	125.00
GS	Gary Sheffield/50	140.00
OS	Ozzie Smith/75	200.00
LS	Leon Spinks/200	75.00
HS	Huston Street	40.00
MT	Mike Tyson/200	275.00
CU	Chase Utley	75.00
BW	Billy Wagner	25.00
CMW	Chien-Ming Wang/100	400.00
DWI	Dontrelle Willis/100	40.00
JW	John Wooden/200	200.00
DW	David Wright	140.00
CY	Carl Yastrzemski/50	320.00
MY	Michael Young	35.00
RZ	Ryan Zimmerman	60.00

Dick Perez Sketches
NM/M

Common Player:		.25
Inserted 1:1		
Originals:		No Pricing
Production One Set		
ARI	Shawn Green	.50
ATL	Andruw Jones	.50
BAL	Miguel Tejada	.50
BOS	David Ortiz	.50
CHC	Derek Lee	.50
CHW	Paul Konerko	.50
CIN	Ken Griffey Jr.	1.00
CLE	Travis Hafner	.50
COL	Todd Helton	.50
DET	Ivan Rodriguez	.50
FLA	Miguel Cabrera	.75

HOU	Lance Berkman	.25
KC	Mike Sweeney	.25
LAA	Vladimir Guerrero	.75
LAD	Rafael Furcal	.25
MIL	Carlos Lee	.25
MIN	Johan Santana	.50
NYM	David Wright	1.00
NYY	Alex Rodriguez	2.00
OAK	Huston Street	.25
PHI	Bobby Abreu	.25
PIT	Jason Bay	.50
SDP	Jake Peavy	.50
SEA	Ichiro Suzuki	1.50
SFG	Barry Bonds	2.00
STL	Albert Pujols	2.00
TAM	Aubrey Huff	.25
TEX	Mark Teixeira	.25
TOR	Vernon Wells	.25
WAS	Alfonso Soriano	.75

Postcards

NM/M
Inserted 1:2 Hobby Boxes

BB	Barry Bonds	4.00
JG	Josh Gibson	2.00
KG	Ken Griffey Jr.	3.00
VG	Vladimir Guerrero	2.00
DJ	Derek Jeter	3.00
MM	Mickey Mantle	10.00
DO	David Ortiz	2.00
AP	Albert Pujols	4.00
MR	Manny Ramirez	2.00
CR	Cal Ripken Jr.	6.00
AR	Alex Rodriguez	4.00
I	Ichiro Suzuki	3.00
MT	Miguel Tejada	1.50
TW	Ted Williams	4.00
DW	David Wright	3.00

Personalized Postcards
One Set Produced

Allen & Ginter N43
NM/M
Inserted 1:2 Hobby Boxes

1	Alex Rodriguez	4.00
2	Barry Bonds	4.00
3	Albert Pujols	4.00
4	Josh Gibson	2.00
5	Nolan Ryan	4.00
6	Ichiro Suzuki	3.00
7	Mickey Mantle	10.00
8	Ted Williams	4.00
9	David Wright	4.00
10	Ken Griffey Jr.	3.00
11	Mark Teixeira	1.50
12	Adrian C. Anson	2.00
13	Mike Tyson	3.00
14	Kenji Johjima	2.00
15	Ryan Zimmerman	2.00

Allen & Ginter N43 Autographs
Production 10 Sets

Allen & Ginter N43 Relics
NM/M
Production 50 Sets

AP	Albert Pujols	100.00
JG	Josh Gibson	250.00

Rip Card
All prices for unripped cards.
1-4: Production 10 Sets
5-9: Production 15 Sets
10-19: Production 25 Sets
20-50: Production 99 Sets

TRAVIS HAFNER

RIP20	Kenji Johjima	100.00
RIP21	Cap Anson	100.00
RIP22	Ryan Zimmerman	100.00
RIP23	Andruw Jones	100.00
RIP24	Barry Bonds	150.00
RIP25	Cal Ripken Jr.	150.00
RIP26	David Ortiz	100.00
RIP27	Hideki Matsui	150.00
RIP28	Ken Griffey Jr.	100.00
RIP29	Manny Ramirez	100.00
RIP30	Mickey Mantle	200.00
RIP31	Alex Rodriguez	150.00
RIP32	Miguel Cabrera	150.00
RIP33	Miguel Tejada	100.00
RIP34	Pedro Martinez	100.00
RIP35	Albert Pujols	150.00
RIP36	Alex Rodriguez	150.00
RIP37	Alex Rodriguez, Derek Jeter	150.00
RIP38	Barry Bonds	150.00
RIP39	Derek Jeter	180.00
RIP40	Ichiro Suzuki	150.00
RIP41	Ichiro Suzuki, Hideki Matsui	150.00
RIP42	Josh Gibson	150.00
RIP43	Mickey Mantle	200.00
RIP44	Jonathan Papelbon	100.00
RIP45	Mickey Mantle, Ted Williams	200.00
RIP46	Albert Pujols	150.00
RIP47	Roberto Clemente	150.00
RIP48	Roger Clemens	150.00
RIP49	Ted Williams	150.00
RIP50	Vladimir Guerrero	100.00

2006 Topps Bazooka

JOHNNY DAMON

		NM/M
Complete Set (220):		30.00
Common Player:		.10
Pack (8):		2.50
Box (24):		50.00
1	Josh Gibson	.50
2	Scott Podsednik	.10
3	Sammy Sosa	.75
4	Ivan Rodriguez	.40
5	Derek Jeter	1.50
6	Manny Ramirez	.50
7	Nook Logan	.10
8	Adam Dunn	.40
9	Travis Hafner	.25
10	Felix Hernandez	.40
11	Larry Bigbie	.10
12	Magglio Ordonez	.25
13	Josh Beckett	.25
14	Mike Sweeney	.10
15	Mickey Mantle	2.00
16	Grady Sizemore	.25
17	Brian Fuentes	.10
18	Wily Mo Pena	.10
19	Morgan Ensberg	.10
20	Tim Hudson	.25
21	Justin Verlander (RC)	.40
22	Jermaine Dye	.10
23	Miguel Cabrera	.50
24	Greg Maddux	1.00
25	Jason Giambi	.25
26	Ben Sheets	.25
27	Brad Radke	.10
28	Torii Hunter	.25
29	Mike Piazza	.75
30	Jason Kendall	.10
31	Pat Burrell	.10
32	Khalil Greene	.10
33	Brian Roberts	.25
34	C.C. Sabathia	.10
35	Mike Mussina	.40
36	Bob Wickman	.10
37	Dmitri Young	.10
38	Dontrelle Willis	.25
39	David DeJesus	.10
40	J.D. Drew	.25
41	Chad Tracy	.10
42	Joe Mauer	.25
43	Melvin Mora	.10
44	Carlos Zambrano	.25
45	Mariano Rivera	.25
46	Coco Crisp	.10
47	Derek Lee	.50

48	Cliff Floyd	.10
49	Willy Taveras	.10
50	Albert Pujols	1.50
51	Aaron Boone	.10
52	Mark Mulder	.25
53	Brad Wilkerson	.10
54	Hank Blalock	.25
55	Hideki Matsui	1.00
56	Victor Martinez	.25
57	Jeremy Bonderman	.10
58	Felipe Lopez	.10
59	Paul LoDuca	.10
60	Derek Lowe	.10
61	Luis Gonzalez	.10
62	Paul Konerko	.25
63	Miguel Tejada	.40
64	Jeromy Burnitz	.10
65	Orlando Hernandez	.10
66	Curt Schilling	.50
67	Joe Nathan	.10
68	Jose Reyes	.25
69	David Wright	.75
70	Eric Chavez	.25
71	Rich Harden	.25
72	A.J. Pierzynski	.10
73	Trevor Hoffman	.25
74	Adrian Beltre	.25
75	Alex Rodriguez	1.50
76	Larry Walker	.25
77	Jorge Cantu	.10
78	Mark Teixeira	.40
79	Jeff Bagwell	.40
80	Jeff Francoeur	.25
81	Ichiro Suzuki	1.00
82	Jhonny Peralta	.10
83	Todd Helton	.40
84	Brad Penny	.10
85	Shawn Chacon	.10
86	Billy Wagner	.25
87	Jason Schmidt	.25
88	Austin Kearns	.10
89	Chris Carpenter	.25
90	Chipper Jones	.50
91	Shawn Green	.10
92	A.J. Burnett	.10
93	Joe Crede	.10
94	Mark Prior	.40
95	Andy Pettitte	.25
96	Edgar Renteria	.25
97	Roy Halladay	.25
98	Eric Milton	.10
99	Craig Biggio	.25
100	Barry Bonds	1.50
101	Troy Glaus	.25
102	Aaron Rowand	.10
103	Aramis Ramirez	.25
104	Nomar Garciaparra	.50
105	Randy Johnson	.25
106	David Ortiz	.50
107	Vinny Castilla	.10
108	Carl Crawford	.25
109	Zachary Duke	.25
110	Barry Zito	.25
111	Darin Erstad	.10
112	Chris Capuano	.10
113	Javy Lopez	.10
114	Lew Ford	.10
115	Robinson Cano	.25
116	Ronnie Belliard	.10
117	Placido Polanco	.10
118	Rickie Weeks	.25
119	Brad Lidge	.10
120	Andruw Jones	.40
121	Nick Swisher	.25
122	Bartolo Colon	.10
123	Juan Pierre	.10
124	Johan Santana	.50
125	Jorge Posada	.25
126	Jeff Francis	.10
127	Matt Holliday	.25
128	Carlos Delgado	.25
129	Zack Greinke	.10
130	Lyle Overbay	.10
131	Conor Jackson (RC)	.25
132	Mark Buehrle	.25
133	Chone Figgins	.10
134	Pedro Martinez	.50
135	Roger Clemens	1.50
136	Raul Ibanez	.10
137	Jim Edmonds	.25
138	Michael Young	.25
139	Preston Wilson	.10
140	Rafael Furcal	.10
141	Bobby Abreu	.25
142	Tadahito Iguchi	.10
143	B.J. Ryan	.10
144	Francisco Rodriguez	.25
145	J.T. Snow	.10
146	Aubrey Huff	.10
147	Mike Morse	.10
148	Jason Bay	.25
149	Roy Oswalt	.25
150	Carlos Beltran	.40
151	Carlos Lee	.25
152	Emil Brown	.10
153	Craig Monroe	.10
154	Kris Benson	.10
155	Gary Sheffield	.40
156	Jake Peavy	.25
157	David Eckstein	.10
158	Tom Glavine	.25
159	Jeff Kent	.25
160	Livan Hernandez	.10
161	Orlando Hudson	.10
162	Randy Winn	.10
163	Jimmy Rollins	.25
164	Luis Castillo	.10
165	Nick Johnson	.10

166	Johnny Damon	.50
167	Eric Gagne	.25
168	Geoff Jenkins	.10
169	Mike Cameron	.10
170	Marcus Giles	.10
171	Huston Street	.25
172	Moises Alou	.10
173	Scott Rolen	.50
174	Jose Vidro	.10
175	Alfonso Soriano	.40
176	Toby Hall	.10
177	Orlando Cabrera	.10
178	Brian Giles	.10
179	Erubiel Durazo	.10
180	Matt Morris	.10
181	Jack Wilson	.10
182	Brady Clark	.10
183	Shannon Stewart	.10
184	Kerry Wood	.25
185	Carl Pavano	.10
186	Chase Utley	.25
187	Omar Vizquel	.10
188	Vladimir Guerrero	.50
189	Richie Sexson	.25
190	John Smoltz	.25
191	Garret Anderson	.10
192	Jon Garland	.10
193	Julio Lugo	.10
194	Rocco Baldelli	.10
195	Jaret Wright	.10
196	Matt Clement	.10
197	Vernon Wells	.10
198	Sean Casey	.10
199	Lance Berkman	.25
200	Justin Morneau	.20
201	Shaun Marcum (RC)	.20
202	Chuck James (RC)	.20
203	Hong-Chih Kuo (RC)	.20
204	Darrell Rasner (RC)	.20
205	Anthony Reyes (RC)	.25
206	Francisco Liriano (RC)	.50
207	Joe Saunders (RC)	.20
208	Fausto Carmona (RC)	.20
209	Charlton Jimerson (RC)	.20
210	Bryan Bullington (RC)	.20
211	Tom Gorzelanny (RC)	.20
212	Anderson Hernandez (RC)	.20
213	Ryan Garko (RC)	.20
214	John Koronka (RC)	.20
215	Chris Denorfia (RC)	.20
216	Jeff Mathis (RC)	.20
217	Jose Bautista (RC)	.20
218	Danny Sandoval RC	.20
219	Robert Andino RC	.20
220	Justin Huber (RC)	.20

Gold
Stars: 1-2X
Inserted 1:1

Autographs
		NM/M
BM	Brandon McCarthy	12.00
KM	Kevin Millar	20.00
MM	Mike Morse	15.00
VZ	Victor Zambrano	15.00

Bazooka Basics
		NM/M
BA	Bobby Abreu	4.00
LB	Lance Berkman	6.00
CB	Craig Biggio	4.00
HB	Hank Blalock	4.00
SB	Sean Burroughs	4.00
MC	Miguel Cabrera	8.00
JD	Johnny Damon	8.00
CD	Carlos Delgado	4.00
EG	Eric Gagne	4.00
MG	Marcus Giles	4.00
MH	Matt Holliday	4.00
TH	Tim Hudson	6.00
AJ	Andruw Jones	6.00
CJ	Chipper Jones	8.00
ML	Mike Lowell	4.00
PM	Pedro Martinez	10.00
MM	Mark Mulder	4.00
MMU	Mike Mussina	6.00
AP	Albert Pujols	15.00
MR	Manny Ramirez	4.00
JR	Jose Reyes	6.00
BR	Brian Roberts	4.00
CS	Curt Schilling	4.00
MT	Mark Teixeira	6.00
BW	Bernie Williams	6.00
DW	Dontrelle Willis	6.00

Bazooka Blasts
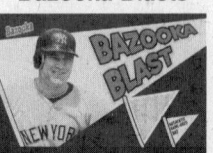

		NM/M
BA	Bobby Abreu	4.00
MA	Moises Alou	4.00
JB	Jason Bay	8.00
CB	Carlos Beltran	6.00
HB	Hank Blalock	4.00
BB	Barry Bonds	20.00

CC	Coco Crisp	4.00
JD	Johnny Damon	8.00
JD	J.D. Drew	4.00
AD	Adam Dunn	6.00
CF	Cliff Floyd	4.00
TG	Troy Glaus	4.00
VG	Vladimir Guerrero	6.00
GJ	Geoff Jenkins	4.00
AJ	Andruw Jones	6.00
CJ	Chipper Jones	6.00
PK	Paul Konerko	6.00
DL	Derrek Lee	6.00
PL	Paul LoDuca	4.00
ML	Mark Loretta	4.00
MM	Mickey Mantle/100	175.00
VM	Victor Martinez	4.00
TN	Trot Nixon	4.00
DO	David Ortiz	8.00
CP	Corey Patterson	4.00
MP	Mike Piazza	8.00
AR	Aramis Ramirez	6.00
AR	Alex Rodriguez	15.00
GS	Gary Sheffield	6.00
SS	Sammy Sosa	8.00
MT	Miguel Tejada	8.00
JT	Jim Thome	6.00
PW	Preston Wilson	4.00
DW	David Wright	10.00

Bazooka Rewind

		NM/M
CB	Clint Barmes	4.00
WB	William Bergolla	4.00
LB	Lance Berkman	6.00
CBI	Craig Biggio	6.00
JB	Jason Botts	4.00
PB	Pat Burrell	4.00
RC	Robinson Cano	15.00
SC	Shin-Soo Choo	4.00
CC	Carl Crawford	6.00
NC	Nelson Cruz	6.00
JDA	Johnny Damon	8.00
JD	Jermaine Dye	4.00
CE	Carl Everett	4.00
RG	Ryan Garko	4.00
JG	Jon Garland	4.00
MG	Mark Grudzielanek	4.00
JG	Jose Guillen	4.00
CG	Cristian Guzman	4.00
JH	Justin Huber	4.00
MJ	Mike Jacobs	8.00
NJ	Nick Johnson	4.00
AJ	Andruw Jones	6.00
AK	Adam Kennedy	4.00
PK	Paul Konerko	6.00
AML	Adam LaRoche	4.00
CL	Carlos Lee	4.00
FL	Francisco Liriano	8.00
LM	Luis Montanez	4.00
MM	Miguel Montero	4.00
AP	A.J. Pierzynski	6.00
SP	Scott Podsednik	6.00
HR	Hanley Ramirez	4.00
MR	Manny Ramirez	8.00
ER	Edgar Renteria	4.00
BR	Brian Roberts	4.00
AR	Alex Rodriguez	15.00
JR	Jimmy Rollins	4.00
AR	Aaron Rowand	4.00
TS	Terrmel Sledge	4.00
WT	Willy Taveras	4.00
FT	Frank Thomas	6.00
KT	Kevin Thompson	4.00
CU	Chase Utley	6.00
JV	Justin Verlander	6.00
RW	Rickie Weeks	6.00
DW	Dontrelle Willis	6.00
CY	Chris Young	4.00

Comics

		NM/M
Complete Set (24):		10.00
Common Player:		.25
Inserted 1:4		
1	Greg Maddux	1.00
2	Alex Rodriguez	1.00

3	Trevor Hoffman	.25
4	Rafael Palmeiro	.50
5	Roy Oswalt	.25
6	Bobby Abreu	.25
7	Miguel Tejada	.50
8	Vladimir Guerrero	.50
9	Mark Teixeira	.25
10	Zachary Duke	.25
11	Xavier Nady	.25
12	Alex Rodriguez	1.00
13	Jeremy Hermida	.25
14	Craig Biggio	.25
15	Manny Ramirez	.50
16	Texas Rangers	.25
17	Oakland A's	.25
18	Alex Rodriguez	1.00
19	Jason Giambi	.50
20	Aaron Small	.25
21	Jimmy Rollins	.25
22	Roger Clemens	1.00
23	White Sox/Mariners	.50
24	Andruw Jones	.50

Fortune
Stars: 1-2X
Inserted 1:1

Mickey Mantle Oversized Reprint
		NM/M
1952	Mickey Mantle	40.00
1953	Mickey Mantle	30.00
1956	Mickey Mantle	25.00
1957	Mickey Mantle	25.00
1958	Mickey Mantle	25.00
1959	Mickey Mantle	25.00
1960	Mickey Mantle	25.00
1961	Mickey Mantle	25.00
1962	Mickey Mantle	25.00
1963	Mickey Mantle	20.00
1964	Mickey Mantle	25.00
1965	Mickey Mantle	25.00
1966	Mickey Mantle	25.00
1967	Mickey Mantle	25.00
1968	Mickey Mantle	25.00
1969	Mickey Mantle	25.00

Stamps

		NM/M
Complete Set (30):		15.00
Common Player:		.50
Inserted 1:3 Hobby		
1	Bobby Abreu	.50
2	Lance Berkman	.50
3	Hank Blalock	.50
4	Barry Bonds	2.00
5	Mark Buehrle	.50
6	Miguel Cabrera	1.00
7	Jim Edmonds	.50
8	Morgan Ensberg	.50
9	Jeff Francoeur	.50
10	Roy Halladay	.50
11	Tim Hudson	.50
12	Derek Jeter	2.00
13	Andruw Jones	.75
14	Chipper Jones	1.00
15	Derek Lee	.75
16	Mickey Mantle	3.00
17	Victor Martinez	.50
18	Justin Morneau	.50
19	Manny Ramirez	1.00
20	Brian Roberts	.50
21	Alex Rodriguez	2.00
22	Ivan Rodriguez	.50
23	Johan Santana	.50
24	Alfonso Soriano	.50
25	Huston Street	.50
26	Ichiro Suzuki	1.00
27	Mark Teixeira	.50
28	Miguel Tejada	.50
29	Rickie Weeks	.50
30	Dontrelle Willis	.50

4-on-1 Stickers
		NM/M
1	Josh Gibson, Mickey Mantle, Alex Rodriguez, Barry Bonds	2.00
2	Jason Giambi, David Ortiz, Carlos Delgado, Jeff Bagwell	.75
3	Vernon Wells, Shannon Stewart, Carl Crawford, Torii Hunter	.50
4	Jason Kendall, Javy Lopez, Joe Mauer, Jorge Posada	.50
5	Roger Clemens, Andy Pettitte, Mike Mussina, Orlando Hernandez	1.00
6	Ivan Rodriguez, Rafael Palmeiro, Alfonso Soriano, Hank Blalock	.50
7	Pedro Martinez, Curt Schilling, Matt Clement, Derek Lowe	.75
8	J.D. Drew, Andruw Jones, Gary Sheffield, Vladimir Guerrero	.50
9	Tim Hudson, Greg Maddux, Tom Glavine, John Smoltz	.75
10	Justin Morneau, Albert Pujols, Mark Teixeira, Derek Lee	1.00
11	B.J. Ryan, Bob Wickman, Mariano Rivera, Trevor Hoffman	.50
12	Mike Morse, Mike Cameron, Mike Piazza, Mike Sweeney	.75
13	Michael Young, Jimmy Rollins, David Eckstein, Orlando Cabrera	.50
14	A.J. Burnett, A.J. Pierzynski, C.C. Sabathia, J.T. Snow	.50
15	Hideki Matsui, Ichiro Suzuki, Tadahito Iguchi, Chase Utley	1.00
16	Barry Zito, Zachary Duke, Zack Greinke, Jeff Francis	.50
17	Mark Buehrle, Mark Mulder, Mark Prior, Marcus Giles	.75
18	Sammy Sosa, Manny Ramirez, Bobby Abreu, Wily Mo Pena	.75
19	Scott Podsednik, Preston Wilson, Juan Pierre, Carlos Beltran	.50
20	Francisco Rodriguez, Billy Wagner, Huston Street, Joe Nathan	.50
21	Melvin Mora, Morgan Ensberg, Scott Rolen, Eric Chavez	.50
22	Garret Anderson, Jim Edmonds, Johnny Damon, Moises Alou	.50
23	Derek Jeter, Edgar Renteria, Miguel Tejada, Julio Lugo	1.00
24	Felix Hernandez, Dontrelle Willis, Rich Harden, Brian Fuentes	.50
25	Bartolo Colon, Jason Schmidt, Jeremy Bonderman, Carlos Zambrano	.50
26	Randy Johnson, Johan Santana, Roy Halladay, Chris Carpenter	.75
27	Roy Oswalt, Shawn Chacon, Kris Benson, Josh Beckett	.50
28	Jose Reyes, Felipe Lopez, Rafael Furcal, Jhonny Peralta	.50
29	Justin Verlander, Kerry Wood, Livan Hernandez, Matt Morris	.50
30	Khalil Greene, Nomar Garciaparra, Omar Vizquel, Jack Wilson	.50
31	Pat Burrell, Rocco Baldelli, Shawn Green, Jason Bay	.50
32	Brad Lidge, Brad Penny, Brad Radke, Brian Roberts	.50
33	Jeff Francoeur, Willy Taveras, Rickie Weeks, Robinson Cano	.50
34	Geoff Jenkins, Lance Berkman, Larry Bigbie, Matt Holliday	.50
35	Paul LoDuca, Toby Hall, Victor Martinez, Carlos Lee	.50
36	Aramis Ramirez, Chipper Jones, David Wright, Troy Glaus	.75
37	Randy Winn, Brad Wilkerson, Craig Monroe, Aaron Rowand	.50
38	Aaron Boone, Adrian Beltre, Vinny Castilla, Chone Figgins	.50
39	Larry Walker, Cliff Floyd, Luis Gonzalez, Adam Dunn	.50
40	Ronnie Belliard, Jeff Kent, Jorge Cantu, Placido Polanco	.50
41	Craig Biggio, Jose Vidro, Luis Castillo, Orlando Hudson	.50
42	Grady Sizemore, Lew Ford, Nick Swisher, Brian Giles	.50
43	David DeJesus, Emil Brown, Coco Crisp, Jeromy Burnitz	.50
44	Eric Gagne, Eric Milton, Jake Peavy, Jaret Wright	.50
45	Aubrey Huff, Austin Kearns, Brady Clark, Nook Logan	.50
46	Ben Sheets, Carl Pavano, Chris Capuano, Jon Garland	.50
47	Darin Erstad, Dmitri Young, Erubiel Durazo, Travis Hafner	.50
48	Magglio Ordonez, Miguel Cabrera, Jermaine Dye, Conor Jackson	.50
49	Richie Sexson, Sean Casey, Chad Tracy, Lyle Overbay	.50
50	Nick Johnson, Paul Konerko, Raul Ibanez, Todd Helton	.50
51	Shaun Marcum, Chuck James, Hong-Chih Kuo, Darrell Rasner	.50
52	Anthony Reyes, Francisco Liriano, Joe Saunders, Fausto Carmona	.50
53	Charlton Jimerson, Bryan Bullington, Tom Gorzelanny, Anderson Hernandez	.50
54	Ryan Garko, John Koronka, Chris Denorfia, Jeff Mathis	.50
55	Jose Bautista, Danny Sandoval, Robert Andino, Alex Gordon	.50

2006 Topps Chrome

		NM/M
Complete Set (354):		
Common Player:		.25
Common Auto. (331-354):		10.00
Pack (4):		3.50
Box (24):		70.00
1	Alex Rodriguez	3.00
2	Garrett Atkins	.25
3	Carl Crawford	.50
4	Clint Barmes	.25
5	Tadahito Iguchi	.50
6	Brian Roberts	.40
7	Mickey Mantle	8.00
8	David Wright	2.00
9	Jeremy Reed	.25
10	Bobby Abreu	.50
11	Lance Berkman	.50
12	Jonny Gomes	.25
13	Jason Marquis	.25
14	Chipper Jones	1.00

15	Jon Garland	.25
16	Brad Wilkerson	.25
17	Rickie Weeks	.50
18	Jorge Posada	.50
19	Greg Maddux	2.00
20	Jeff Francis	.25
21	Felipe Lopez	.25
22	Dan Johnson	.25
23	Manny Ramirez	1.00
24	Joe Mauer	.75
25	Randy Winn	.25
26	Pedro Feliz	.25
27	Kenny Rogers	.25
28	Rocco Baldelli	.25
29	Nomar Garciaparra	1.00
30	Carlos Lee	.50
31	Tom Glavine	.50
32	Craig Biggio	.40
33	Steve Finley	.25
34	Eric Gagne	.40
35	Dallas McPherson	.25
36	Mark Kotsay	.25
37	Kerry Wood	.25
38	Huston Street	.25
39	Hank Blalock	.50
40	Brad Radke	.25
41	Chien-Ming Wang	.75
42	Mark Buehrle	.40
43	Andy Pettitte	.50
44	Bernie Williams	.50
45	Victor Martinez	.50
46	Darin Erstad	.40
47	Gustavo Chacin	.25
48	Carlos Guillen	.25
49	Lyle Overbay	.25
50	Barry Bonds	3.00
51	Nook Logan	.25
52	Mark Teahen	.25
53	Mike Lamb	.25
54	Jayson Werth	.25
55	Mariano Rivera	.50
56	Julio Lugo	.25
57	Adam Dunn	.75
58	Troy Percival	.25
59	Chad Tracy	.25
60	Edgar Renteria	.50
61	Jason Giambi	.75
62	Justin Morneau	.75
63	Carlos Delgado	.75
64	John Buck	.25
65	Shannon Stewart	.25
66	Mike Cameron	.25
67	Richie Sexson	.50
68	Russ Adams	.25
69	Josh Beckett	.50
70	Ryan Freel	.25
71	Victor Zambrano	.25
72	Ronnie Belliard	.25
73	Brian Giles	.40
74	Randy Wolf	.25
75	Robinson Cano	.75
76	Joe Blanton	.25
77	Esteban Loaiza	.25
78	Troy Glaus	.50
79	Matt Clement	.25
80	Geoff Jenkins	.25
81	Roy Oswalt	.50
82	A.J. Pierzynski	.25
83	Pedro Martinez	1.00
84	Roger Clemens	3.00
85	Jack Wilson	.25
86	Mike Piazza	1.00
87	Paul LoDuca	.25
88	Jeff Bagwell	.50
89	Carlos Zambrano	.50
90	Brandon Claussen	.25
91	Travis Hafner	.50
92	Chris Shelton	.25
93	Rafael Furcal	.40
94	Frank Thomas	.75
95	Noah Lowry	.25
96	Jhonny Peralta	.25
97	Vernon Wells	.50
98	Jorge Cantu	.25
99	Willy Taveras	.25
100	Ivan Rodriguez	.75
101	Jose Reyes	.75
102	Barry Zito	.50
103	Mark Teixeira	.75
104	Chone Figgins	.50
105	Todd Helton	.75
106	Tim Wakefield	.25
107	Mike Maroth	.25
108	Johnny Damon	1.00
109	David DeJesus	.25
110	Ryan Klesko	.25
111	Nick Johnson	.25
112	Freddy Garcia	.25
113	Torii Hunter	.50
114	Mike Sweeney	.25
115	Scott Rolen	1.00
116	Jim Thome	.75
117	Adam Kennedy	.25
118	Albert Pujols	3.00
119	Kazuo Matsui	.25
120	Zack Greinke	.25
121	Jimmy Rollins	.25
122	Edgar Alfonzo	.25
123	Billy Wagner	.25
124	B.J. Ryan	.25
125	Orlando Hudson	.25
126	Preston Wilson	.25
127	Melvin Mora	.25
128	Alfonso Soriano	.75
129	Javy Lopez	.25
130	Wilson Betemit	.25
131	Garret Anderson	.25
132	Jason Bay	

#	Player	
133	Adam LaRoche	.25
134	C.C. Sabathia	.25
135	Bartolo Colon	.25
136	Ichiro Suzuki	2.00
137	Jim Edmonds	.50
138	David Eckstein	.25
139	Cristian Guzman	.25
140	Jeff Kent	.40
141	Chris Capuano	.25
142	Cliff Floyd	.25
143	Zachary Duke	.25
144	Matt Morris	.25
145	Jose Vidro	.25
146	David Wells	.25
147	John Smoltz	.50
148	Felix Hernandez	.50
149	Orlando Cabrera	.25
150	Mark Prior	.50
151	Ted Lilly	.25
152	Michael Young	.25
153	Livan Hernandez	.25
154	Yadier Molina	.25
155	Eric Chavez	.25
156	Miguel Batista	.25
157	Ben Sheets	.40
158	Oliver Perez	.25
159	Doug Davis	.25
160	Andruw Jones	.75
161	Hideki Matsui	1.50
162	Reggie Sanders	.25
163	Joe Nathan	.25
164	John Lackey	.25
165	Matt Murton	.25
166	Grady Sizemore	.75
167	Brad Thompson	.25
168	Kevin Millwood	.25
169	Orlando Hernandez	.25
170	Mark Mulder	.25
171	Chase Utley	.75
172	Moises Alou	.50
173	Wily Mo Pena	.25
174	Brian McCann	.25
175	Jermaine Dye	.25
176	Ryan Madson	.25
177	Aramis Ramirez	.50
178	Khalil Greene	.25
179	Mike Hampton	.25
180	Mike Mussina	.50
181	Rich Harden	.25
182	Woody Williams	.25
183	Chris Carpenter	.50
184	Brady Clark	.25
185	Luis Gonzalez	.25
186	Raul Ibanez	.25
187	Magglio Ordonez	.25
188	Adrian Beltre	.25
189	Marcus Giles	.25
190	Odalis Perez	.25
191	Derek Jeter	3.00
192	Jason Schmidt	.50
193	Toby Hall	.25
194	Danny Haren	.25
195	Tim Hudson	.50
196	Jake Peavy	.50
197	Casey Blake	.25
198	J.D. Drew	.25
199	Ervin Santana	.25
200	J.J. Hardy	.25
201	Austin Kearns	.25
202	Pat Burrell	.25
203	Jason Vargas	.25
204	Ryan Howard	1.50
205	Joe Crede	.25
206	Vladimir Guerrero	1.00
207	Roy Halladay	.50
208	David Dellucci	.25
209	Brandon Webb	.25
210	Ryan Church	.25
211	Miguel Tejada	.75
212	Mark Loretta	.25
213	Kevin Youkilis	.50
214	Jon Lieber	.25
215	Miguel Cabrera	1.00
216	A.J. Burnett	.25
217	David Bell	.25
218	Eric Byrnes	.25
219	Lance Niekro	.25
220	Shawn Green	.25
221	Ken Griffey Jr.	2.00
222	Johnny Estrada	.25
223	Omar Vizquel	.25
224	Gary Sheffield	.50
225	Brad Halsey	.25
226	Aaron Cook	.25
227	David Ortiz	1.00
228	Scott Kazmir	.50
229	Dustin McGowan	.25
230	Gregg Zaun	.25
231	Carlos Beltran	.75
232	Bob Wickman	.25
233	Brett Myers	.25
234	Casey Kotchman	.25
235	Jeff Francoeur	.25
236	Paul Konerko	.50
237	Juan Rivera	.25
238	Bobby Crosby	.25
239	Derek Lee	.75
240	Curt Schilling	1.00
241	Jake Westbrook	.25
242	Dontrelle Willis	.25
243	Brad Lidge	.25
244	Randy Johnson	1.00
245	Nick Swisher	.50
246	Johan Santana	.75
247	Jeremy Bonderman	.25
248	Ramon Hernandez	.25
249	Mike Lowell	.25
250	Javier Vazquez	.25
251	Jose Contreras	.25
252	Aubrey Huff	.25
253	Kenny Rogers	.25
254	Mark Teixeira	.50
255	Orlando Hudson	.25
256	Derek Jeter	2.00
257	Eric Chavez	.25
258	Torii Hunter	.25
259	Vernon Wells	.25
260	Ichiro Suzuki	1.00
261	Greg Maddux	1.00
262	Mike Matheny	.25
263	Derek Lee	.50
264	Luis Castillo	.25
265	Omar Vizquel	.25
266	Mike Lowell	.25
267	Andruw Jones	.50
268	Jim Edmonds	.25
269	Bobby Abreu	.25
270	Bartolo Colon	.25
271	Chris Carpenter	.25
272	Alex Rodriguez	2.00
273	Albert Pujols	2.00
274	Huston Street	.25
275	Ryan Howard	.75
276	Chris Denorfia (RC)	.50
277	John Van Benschoten (RC)	.50
278	Russell Martin (RC)	.50
279	Fausto Carmona (RC)	.50
280	Freddie Bynum (RC)	.50
281	Kelly Shoppach (RC)	.50
282	Chris Demaria RC	.50
283	Jordan Tata RC	.50
284	Ryan Zimmerman (RC)	6.00
285	Kenji Johjima RC	5.00
285	Kenji Johjima/ Auto. RC	90.00
286	Ruddy Lugo (RC)	.50
287	Tommy Murphy (RC)	.50
288	Bobby Livingston RC	.50
289	Anderson Hernandez RC	.50
290	Brian Slocum (RC)	.50
291	Sendy Rleal RC	.50
292	Ryan Spilborghs (RC)	.50
293	Brandon Fahey RC	1.00
294	Jason Kubel (RC)	.50
295	James Loney (RC)	.50
296	Jeremy Accardo RC	.50
297	Fabio Castro RC	.50
298	Matt Capps (RC)	.75
299	Casey Janssen RC	1.00
300	Martin Prado (RC)	1.00
301	Ronny Paulino (RC)	1.00
302	Josh Barfield (RC)	.50
303	Joel Zumaya (RC)	2.50
304	Matt Cain (RC)	1.00
305	Conor Jackson (RC)	.50
306	Brian Anderson (RC)	.50
307	Prince Fielder (RC)	4.00
308	Jeremy Hermida (RC)	.75
309	Justin Verlander (RC)	4.00
310	Brian Bannister (RC)	.50
311	Josh Willingham (RC)	.50
312	John Rheinecker (RC)	.50
313	Nicholas Markakis (RC)	.75
314	Jonathan Papelbon (RC)	8.00
315	Mike Jacobs (RC)	.50
316	Jose Capellan (RC)	.50
317	Michael Napoli RC	4.00
318	Ricky Nolasco (RC)	.50
319	Ben Johnson (RC)	.50
320	Paul Maholm (RC)	.50
321	Drew Meyer (RC)	.50
322	Jeff Mathis (RC)	.50
323	Fernando Nieve (RC)	.50
324	John Koronka (RC)	.50
325	Wilbert Nieves (RC)	.50
326	Nate McLouth (RC)	1.00
327	Howard Kendrick (RC)	4.00
328	Sean Marshall (RC)	1.50
329	Brandon Watson (RC)	.50
330	Skip Schumaker (RC)	.50
331	Ryan Garko (RC)	15.00
332	Jason Bergman (RC)	15.00
333	Chuck James (RC)	15.00
334	Adam Wainwright (RC)	30.00
335	Daniel Ortmeier (RC)	10.00
336	Francisco Liriano (RC)	40.00
337	Craig Breslow RC	15.00
338	Darrell Rasner (RC)	15.00
339	Jason Botts (RC)	15.00
340	Ian Kinsler (RC)	30.00
341	Joey Devine RC	15.00
342	Miguel Perez (RC)	10.00
343	Scott Olsen (RC)	15.00
344	Tyler Johnson (RC)	15.00
345	Anthony Lerew (RC)	10.00
346	Nelson Cruz (RC)	15.00
347	Willie Eyre (RC)	15.00
348	Josh Johnson (RC)	20.00
349	Shawn Marcum (RC)	15.00
350	Dustin Nippert (RC)	15.00
351	Josh Wilson (RC)	10.00
352	Hanley Ramirez (RC)	20.00
353	Reggie Abercrombie (RC)	15.00
354	Dan Uggla (RC)	30.00

Refractors
Cards (1-330): 2-3X
Inserted 1:4

Rookie Auto. (331-354): 1-1.5X
Production 500

Gold Super-Fractor
No Pricing
Production One Set

Black Refractors
Cards (1-330): 3-5X
Production 549
Rookie Auto. (331-354): 1.5-2X
Production 200

Blue Refractors
Cards (1-330): 2-4X
Inserted 1:8

Red Refractors
Cards (1-330): 4-8X
Production 90
Rookie Auto.
(331-354): No Pricing
Production 25

X-Fractor
Cards (1-330): 2-4X
Inserted 1:6 Retail

Bonds Home Run History

NM/M
Common Bonds: 2.00
Inserted 1:6
Refractors: 2-4X
Production 500 Sets
Black Refractor: 3-5X
Production 200 Sets
Red Refractor: 10-20X
Production 25 Sets

BBC375	Barry Bonds	2.00
BBC400	Barry Bonds	2.00
BBC425	Barry Bonds	2.00
BBC450	Barry Bonds	2.00
BBC475	Barry Bonds	2.00
BBC500	Barry Bonds	2.00
BBC525	Barry Bonds	2.00
BBC550	Barry Bonds	2.00
BBC575	Barry Bonds	2.00
BBC600	Barry Bonds	2.00
BBC625	Barry Bonds	2.00
BBC650	Barry Bonds	2.00
BBC675	Barry Bonds	2.00
BBC700	Barry Bonds	2.00

Mantle Home Run History

NM/M
Common Mantle: 3.00
Inserted 1:6
Refractor: 2-4X
Production 500 Sets
Black Refractor: 3-5X
Production 200 Sets
Red Refractor: 15-20X
Production 25 Sets

MHRC1	Mickey Mantle	3.00
MHRC7	Mickey Mantle	3.00
MHRC10	Mickey Mantle	3.00
MHRC20	Mickey Mantle	3.00
MHRC30	Mickey Mantle	3.00
MHRC40	Mickey Mantle	3.00
MHRC40	Mickey Mantle	3.00
MHRC50	Mickey Mantle	3.00
MHRC60	Mickey Mantle	3.00
MHRC70	Mickey Mantle	3.00
MHRC80	Mickey Mantle	3.00
MHRC90	Mickey Mantle	3.00
MHRC100	Mickey Mantle	3.00
MHRC110	Mickey Mantle	3.00

Signers of the Constitution
NM/M
Common Signer: 1.50
Inserted 1:7
Refractors: 1-2X
Inserted 1:11

AB	Abraham Baldwin	1.50
RB	Richard Bassett	1.50
GB	Gunning Bedford Jr.	1.50
JB	John Blair	1.50
WB	William Blount	1.50
DB	David Brearly	1.50
JBR	Jacob Broom	1.50
PB	Pierce Butler	1.50
DC	Daniel Carroll	1.50
GC	George Clymer	1.50
JD	Jonathan Dayton	1.50
JDI	John Dickinson	1.50
WF	William Few	1.50
TF	Thomas Fitzsimons	1.50
BF	Benjamin Franklin	4.00
NG	Nicholas Gilman	1.50
NGO	Nathaniel Gorham	1.50
AH	Alexander Hamilton	3.00
JI	Jared Ingersoll	1.50
DJ	Daniel of St. Thomas Jenifer	1.50
WJ	William Samuel Johnson	1.50
RK	Rufus King	1.50
JL	John Langdon	1.50
WL	William Livingston	1.50
JM	James Madison	2.00
JMC	James McHenry	1.50
TM	Thomas Mifflin	1.50
GM	Gouverneur Morris	1.50
RM	Robert Morris	1.50
WP	William Paterson	1.50
CCP	Charles Cotesworth Pinckney	1.50
CP	Charles Pinckney	1.50
GR	George Read	1.50
JR	John Rutledge	1.50
RS	Roger Sherman	1.50
RDS	Richard Dobbs Spaight	1.50
GW	George Washington	4.00
HW	Hugh Williamson	1.50
JW	James Wilson	1.50

Signers of Declaration/Independence

NM/M
Common Signer: 1.50
Inserted 1:5
Refractors: 1-2X
Inserted 1:9

JA	John Adams	2.00
SA	Samuel Adams	1.50
JB	Josiah Bartlett	1.50
CB	Carter Braxton	1.50
CC	Charles Carroll	1.50
SC	Samuel Chase	1.50
AC	Abraham Clark	1.50
GC	George Clymer	1.50
WE	William Ellery	1.50
WF	William Floyd	1.50
BF	Benjamin Franklin	4.00
EG	Elbridge Gerry	1.50
BG	Button Gwinnett	1.50
LH	Lyman Hall	1.50
JH	John Hancock	3.00
BH	Benjamin Harrison	1.50
JHA	John Hart	1.50
JHE	Joseph Hewes	1.50
TH	Thomas Heyward Jr.	1.50
WH	William Hooper	1.50
SH	Stephen Hopkins	1.50
FH	Francis Hopkinson	1.50
SHU	Samuel Huntington	1.50
TJ	Thomas Jefferson	4.00
FL	Francis Lewis	1.50
FLL	Francis Lightfoot Lee	1.50
RHL	Richard Henry Lee	1.50
PL	Philip Livingston	1.50
TL	Thomas Lynch Jr.	1.50
TM	Thomas McKean	1.50
AM	Arthur Middleton	1.50
LM	Lewis Morris	1.50
RM	Robert Morris	1.50
JM	John Morton	1.50
TN	Thomas Nelson Jr.	1.50
WP	William Paca	1.50
RTP	Robert Treat Paine	1.50
JP	John Penn	1.50
GRE	George Read	1.50
CR	Caesar Rodney	1.50
GR	George Ross	1.50
BR	Benjamin Rush	1.50
ER	Edward Rutledge	1.50
RS	Roger Sherman	1.50
JS	James Smith	1.50
RST	Richard Stockton	1.50
TS	Thomas Stone	1.50
GT	George Taylor	1.50
MT	Matthew Thornton	1.50
GW	George Walton	1.50
WW	William Whipple	1.50
WWI	William Williams	1.50
JW	James Wilson	1.50
JWI	John Witherspoon	1.50
OW	Oliver Wolcott	1.50
GWY	George Wythe	1.50

Printing Plates
No Pricing
Production one set per color.

2006 Topps Co-Signers

NM/M
Complete Set (120):
Common Player (1-100): .25
Common Auto. (101-120): 10.00
Pack (6): 12.00
Box (12): 135.00
Note: Each parallel has 3 versions.

1	Albert Pujols	3.00
2	Roger Clemens	3.00
3	Paul Konerko	.25
4	Jeff Francoeur	.25
5	Miguel Tejada	.75
6	Curt Schilling	1.00
7	Mickey Mantle	4.00
8	Miguel Cabrera	1.00
9	Derek Lee	1.00
10	Jeff Kent	.50
11	Gary Sheffield	.50
12	Rich Harden	.25
13	Scott Rolen	.75
14	David Wright	1.50
15	Troy Glaus	.50
16	Torii Hunter	.25
17	Nolan Ryan	.75
18	Alfonso Soriano	.50
19	Hank Blalock	.25
20	Chase Utley	.50
21	Ryan Howard	.75
22	Robinson Cano	1.00
23	Derek Jeter	3.00
24	Huston Street	.50
25	Jason Giambi	.50
26	Rafael Furcal	.25
27	Rickie Weeks	.50
28	Ivan Rodriguez	.50
29	Travis Hafner	.50
30	Greg Maddux	2.00
31	Andruw Jones	.75
32	Andy Pettitte	.50
33	Scott Podsednik	.25
34	Francisco Rodriguez	.25
35	Josh Beckett	.25
36	Lance Berkman	.50
37	Roy Oswalt	.50
38	Pedro Martinez	1.00
39	Jimmy Rollins	.50
40	Johan Santana	.75
41	Randy Johnson	1.00
42	Mariano Rivera	.50
43	Nick Johnson	.25
44	Josh Gibson	.50
45	Shawn Green	.25
46	Adrian Beltre	.25
47	Johnny Damon	1.00
48	Joe Mauer	.50
49	Todd Helton	.50
50	Alex Rodriguez	2.50
51	Jake Peavy	.50
52	David Ortiz	1.00
53	Mark Buehrle	.50
54	Eric Gagne	.25
55	Hideki Matsui	1.50
56	Bobby Abreu	.50
57	Victor Martinez	.50
58	Brian Roberts	.25
59	Chipper Jones	1.00
60	Carlos Beltran	.50
61	Tim Hudson	.50
62	Carlos Lee	.50
63	Barry Zito	.50
64	Moises Alou	.50
65	Mark Teixeira	.75
66	Lyle Overbay	.25
67	Kerry Wood	.50
68	B.J. Ryan	.25
69	Jim Edmonds	.50
70	Carlos Delgado	.50
71	Magglio Ordonez	.25
72	Juan Pierre	.25
73	Manny Ramirez	1.00
74	Dontrelle Willis	.50
75	Ichiro Suzuki	2.00
76	Nomar Garciaparra	1.00
77	Zachary Duke	.25
78	Chris Carpenter	.50
79	A.J. Burnett	.25
80	Scott Kazmir	.50
81	Carl Crawford	.50
82	Mark Prior	.50
83	Adam Dunn	.75
84	Justin Morneau	.50
85	Morgan Ensberg	.25
86	Pat Burrell	.25
87	Paul LoDuca	.25
88	Jason Bay	.50
89	Aubrey Huff	.25
90	Kevin Millwood	.25
91	Vernon Wells	.25
92	Javy Lopez	.25
93	Michael Young	.25
94	Felix Hernandez	.25
95	Ken Griffey Jr.	2.00
96	Bartolo Colon	.25
97	Billy Wagner	.25
98	Vladimir Guerrero	1.00
99	Jose Reyes	.75
100	Barry Bonds	3.00
101	Anthony LeRew (RC)	15.00
102	Ryan Zimmerman/ 440 (RC)	60.00
103	Craig Hansen/250 RC	50.00
104	Francisco Liriano (RC)	35.00
105	Jason Botts (RC)	10.00
106	Josh Johnson (RC)	15.00
107	Hanley Ramirez (RC)	25.00
108	Adam Wainwright (RC)	20.00
109	Kenji Johjima/ 200 RC	150.00
110	Daniel Ortmeier (RC)	10.00
111	Darrell Rasner (RC)	15.00
112	Chuck James (RC)	15.00
113	Nelson Cruz (RC)	15.00
114	Hong-Chih Kuo (RC)	15.00
115	Ryan Garko (RC)	15.00
116	R. Abercrombie (RC)	15.00
117	Ian Kinsler (RC)	30.00
118	Joel Zumaya (RC)	25.00
119	Willie Eyre (RC)	15.00
120	Dan Uggla (RC)	15.00

Bronze
Bronze (1-100): 2-3X
Production 150 Sets

Blue
Blue (1-100): 2-3X
Production 125 Sets

Gold
Gold (1-100): 2-3X
Production 115 Sets

Silver - Bronze
Silver/Bronze (1-100): 2-3X
Production 125 Sets

Silver - Blue
Silver/Blue (1-100): 2-3X
Production 75 Sets

Silver - Gold
Silver/Gold (1-100): 3-4X
Production 50 Sets

Hyper Silver - Bronze
Hyper Silver/Bronze (1-100): 2-3X
Production 75 Sets

Hyper Silver - Blue
Hyper Silver/Blue: No Pricing
Production 10 Sets

Hyper Silver - Gold
Hyper Silver/Gold: No Pricing
Production 5 Sets

Silver - Red
Silver/Red (1-100): 2-3X
Production 100 Sets

Hyper Silver - Red
Hyper Silver/Red: No Pricing
Production 25 Sets

Dual Autographs
NM/M

CS2	David Wright, Alex Rodriguez/25	275.00
CS3	Victor Martinez, Kenji Johjima/25	75.00
CS4	Kenji Johjima, Felix Hernandez/18	200.00
CS5	David Ortiz, Manny Ramirez/25	150.00
CS6	Nolan Ryan, Roger Clemens/25	350.00
CS7	David Ortiz, Albert Pujols/25	350.00
CS8	Chipper Jones, Dale Murphy/25	100.00
CS11	Stan Musial, Albert Pujols/20	500.00
CS15	Prince Fielder, Ryan Zimmerman	100.00
CS16	Cal Ripken Jr., Ozzie Smith/25	275.00
CS18	Don Larsen, Yogi Berra/25	200.00

CS19 Mike Schmidt, Brooks Robinson/25 125.00
CS20 Ryan Zimmerman, Wade Boggs/25 75.00
CS22 Ryan Howard, Derrek Lee/75 100.00
CS23 Jeff Mathis, Chris Snyder 15.00
CS25 Ray Knight, Keith Hernandez/100 30.00
CS26 Mike Schmidt, Chase Utley/25 100.00
CS27 Billy Wagner, Paul LoDuca/50 70.00
CS28 Tony Gwynn, Wade Boggs/25 140.00
CS30 Dwight Gooden, Darryl Strawberry/50 40.00
CS31 Ryan Howard, Huston Street 70.00
CS32 Mariano Rivera, Huston Street/25 140.00
CS33 Prince Fielder, Ryan Howard/50 100.00
CS34 Robinson Cano, Chase Utley/75 60.00
CS36 David Justice, Chipper Jones/25 80.00
CS37 Jose Reyes, David Wright/50 180.00
CS38 Jeff Mathis, Ryan Garko 15.00
CS39 Brandon McCarthy, Pedro Lopez 15.00
CS40 David Justice, Dale Murphy/100 60.00
CS42 Joe Mauer, Francisco Liriano 75.00
CS44 Ryan Zimmerman, David Wright/100 125.00
CS45 Rick Rhoden, Dave Parker/100 50.00
CS46 Jonathan Papelbon, Craig Breslow 50.00
CS48 Dan Johnson, Prince Fielder/100 40.00
CS49 Victor Martinez, Ryan Garko 20.00
CS50 Ben Hendrickson, Anthony Reyes 20.00
CS51 Nelson Cruz, Prince Fielder/100 50.00
CS52 Jonathan Papelbon, Anthony Reyes 50.00
CS53 Ben Hendrickson, Rich Hill 20.00
CS54 Shin-Soo Choo, Kenji Johjima/25 85.00
CS55 Francisco Liriano, Johan Santana/100 100.00
CS56 Brandon McCarthy, Zachary Duke 20.00
CS57 Josh Johnson, Scott Olsen 15.00
CS58 Tommy John, Bob Welch 20.00
CS59 Roy White, Joe Pepitone 30.00
CS60 Cecil Fielder, Prince Fielder 70.00
CS62 Conor Jackson, Ryan Howard 60.00
CS63 Dontrelle Willis, Zachary Duke/50 30.00
CS64 Mariano Rivera, Billy Wagner/25 150.00
CS65 Hong-Chih Kuo, Shin-Soo Choo 30.00
CS66 Jim Leyritz, Cecil Fielder 50.00
CS67 Scott Kazmir, Francisco Liriano 50.00
CS68 Scott Kazmir, Roy Oswalt/50 60.00
CS69 Chuck James, Anthony LeRew 20.00
CS70 Cecil Fielder, Ryan Howard 60.00
CS71 Chien-Ming Wang, Hong-Chih Kuo/25 200.00
CS72 Shin-Soo Choo, Chien-Ming Wang/50 150.00
CS73 Nelson Cruz, Jason Botts 20.00
CS74 Francisco Liriano, Ervin Santana 30.00
CS75 Adam Wainwright, Anthony Reyes 30.00
CS76 Ervin Santana, Scott Kazmir 35.00
CS77 Robinson Cano, Gary Sheffield 60.00
CS78 David Wright, Miguel Cabrera/50 120.00
CS79 Dan Johnson, Conor Jackson 20.00
CS80 Frank Tanana, Mickey Tettleton 15.00
CS81 Andruw Jones, Chipper Jones 100.00
CS82 Morgan Ensberg, Roy Oswalt 30.00
CS83 Michael Young, Ozzie Smith 50.00
CS84 Grady Sizemore, Nick Swisher 40.00
CS85 Garrett Atkins, Clint Barmes 20.00

Dual Cut Signatures
No Pricing

Solo Sigs
NM/M
CB Clint Barmes 10.00
CBR Craig Breslow 10.00
RC Robinson Cano 50.00
GC Gustavo Chacin 15.00
SSC Shin-Soo Choo 15.00
JC Jack Clark 10.00
ZD Zachary Duke 20.00
CF Cecil Fielder 25.00
PF Prince Fielder/250 50.00
RHI Rich Hill 35.00
RH Ryan Howard/100 75.00
DJ Dan Johnson/250 10.00
CJ Chipper Jones/25 80.00
AK Al Kaline/100 50.00
SK Scott Kazmir 20.00
DL Don Larsen 20.00
DLE Derrek Lee/50 40.00
VM Victor Martinez/50 25.00
JM Jeff Mathis 10.00
DM Don Mattingly/50 140.00
JMA Joe Mauer/75 40.00
CM Craig Monroe 10.00
SO Scott Olsen 15.00
DO David Ortiz/25 50.00
JP Jonathan Papelbon 60.00
ARE Anthony Reyes 20.00
RR Rick Rhoden 15.00
CR Cal Ripken Jr./20 250.00
AR Alex Rodriguez/20 160.00
NR Nolan Ryan/20 125.00
ES Ervin Santana/250 10.00
JS Johan Santana/50 40.00
CS Chris Snyder 8.00
DS Darryl Strawberry 20.00
HS Huston Street/250 25.00
DWI Dontrelle Willis 25.00
DW David Wright/75 125.00

2006 Topps Heritage

NM/M
Complete Set (485):
Common Player: .40
Common SP: 4.00
Pack (8): 5.00
Box (24): 100.00
1 David Ortiz/SP 8.00
2 Mike Piazza/SP 8.00
3 Daryle Ward .40
4 Rafael Furcal .40
5 Derek Lowe .40
6 Eric Chavez .75
7 Juan Uribe .40
8 C.C. Sabathia .40
9 Sean Casey .40
10 Barry Bonds/SP 15.00
11 Gary Sheffield .40
12 Ted Lilly .40
13 Lew Ford .40
14 Tom Gordon .40
15 Curt Schilling .40
16 Jason Kendall .40
17 Frank Catalanotto .40
18 Pedro Martinez/SP 8.00
19 David Dellucci .40
20 Andruw Jones 1.00
20 Andruw Jones w/Seats/SP 6.00
21 Brad Halsey .40
22 Vernon Wells .40
23 Derek Jeter 4.00
23 Derek Jeter Blue Letter/SP 15.00
24 Todd Helton 1.00
25 Randy Johnson/SP 8.00
26 Jay Gibbons .40
27 Joe Mays .40
28 Paul Konerko .75
29 Lyle Overbay .40
30 Jorge Posada .75
31 Brandon Webb .40
32 Marcus Giles .40
33 J.T. Snow .40
34 Todd Walker .40
35 Wily Mo Pena/SP 5.00
36 Carlos Delgado .75
37 David Wright 2.00
38 Shea Hillenbrand .40
39 Daniel Cabrera .40
40 Trevor Hoffman .40
41 Matt Morris .40
42 Mariano Rivera .75
43 Jeff Bagwell 1.00
44 J.D. Drew .40
45 Carl Pavano .40
46 Placido Polanco .40
47 Adrian Beltre .75
48 J.D. Closser .40
49 Paul LoDuca .40
50 Scott Rolen 1.00
51 Bernie Williams .75
52 Jose Guillen .40
53 Aubrey Huff .40
54 Greg Maddux 2.50
55 Derrek Lee/SP 8.00
56 Hideki Matsui 2.50
57 Jose Bautista .40
58 Kyle Farnsworth .40
59 Nate Robertson .40
60 Sammy Sosa 1.50
61 Javier Vazquez .40
62 Jeff Mathis (RC) .40
63 Mark Buehrle .75
64 Orlando Hernandez .40
65 Brandon Claussen .40
66 Miguel Batista .40
67 Eddie Guardado .40
68 Alex Gonzalez .40
69 Kris Benson .40
70 Bobby Abreu/SP 6.00
71 Vinny Castilla .40
72 Ben Broussard .40
73 Travis Hafner 1.00
74 Dmitri Young .40
75 Alex S. Gonzalez .40
76 Jason Bay/SP 6.00
77 Charlton Jimerson .40
78 Ryan Garko (RC) .50
79 Lance Berkman .75
80 Tim Hudson .75
80 Tim Hudson Blue Letter/SP 5.00
81 Guillermo Mota .40
82 Chris Young .40
83 Brad Lidge .40
84 A.J. Pierzynski .40
85 Maicer Izturis .40
86 Vladimir Guerrero 1.50
87 J.J. Hardy .40
88 Cesar Izturis .40
89 Mark Ellis .40
90 Chipper Jones 1.50
91 Chris Snelling/SP 4.00
92 Jose Reyes .75
93 Mike Lieberthal .40
94 Octavio Dotel .40
95 Alex Rodriguez/ Fielding/SP 10.00
95 Alex Rodriguez/ with Bat/SP 10.00
96 Brett Myers .40
97 New York Yankees 1.00
98 Ryan Klesko .40
99 Brian Jordan/SP 4.00
100 William Harridge, Warren Giles .40
101 Adam Eaton .40
102 Aaron Boone .40
103 Alex Rios .40
104 Andy Pettitte .75
105 Barry Zito .75
106 Bengie Molina/SP 4.00
107 Austin Kearns .50
108 Adam Everett .40
109 A.J. Burnett .40
110 Mark Prior 1.00
111 Russ Ortiz .40
112 Adam Dunn 1.00
113 Byung-Hyun Kim .40
114 Atlanta Braves .50
115 Carlos Silva .40
116 Chad Cordero .40
117 Chone Figgins .40
118 Chris Reitsma .40
119 Coco Crisp .40
120 David DeJesus .40
121 Chris Snyder .40
122 Brad Eldred .40
123 Humberto Cota/SP 5.00
124 Erubiel Durazo .40
125 Josh Beckett .75
126 Kenny Lofton .40
127 Joe Nathan/SP 5.00
128 Bryan Bullington .40
129 Jim Thome 1.00
130 Shawn Green .75
131 LaTroy Hawkins .40
132 Mark Kotsay .40
133 Matt Lawton .40
134 Luis Castillo .40
135 Michael Barrett .40
136 Preston Wilson .40
137 Orlando Cabrera .40
138 Chuck James (RC) .40
139 Raul Ibanez .40
140 Frank Thomas 1.00
141 Orlando Hudson .40
142 Scott Kazmir .40
143 Steve Finley .40
144 Danny Sandoval RC 1.00
145 Javy Lopez .40
146 Tony Giarratano .40
147 Terrence Long .40
148 Victor Martinez .40
149 Toby Hall .40
150 Fausto Carmona (RC) .40
151 Tim Wakefield .40
152 Troy Percival .40
153 Chris Denorfia (RC) .40
154 Junior Spivey .40
155 Desi Relaford .40
156 Francisco Liriano (RC) .75
157 Corey Koskie .40
158 Chris Carpenter .40
159 Robert Andino RC 1.00
160 Cliff Floyd .40
161 Pittsburgh Pirates .40
162 Anderson Hernandez (RC) .40
163 Mike Maroth .40
164 Aaron Rowand .40
165 Albert Pujols 4.00
165 Albert Pujols/ Red Shirt/SP 15.00
166 David Bell .40
167 Angel Berroa .40
168 B.J. Ryan .40
169 Bartolo Colon .40
170 Hong-Chih Kuo .40
171 Cincinnati Reds .40
172 Bill Mueller .40
173 John Koronka (RC) .40
174 Billy Wagner .40
175 Zack Greinke .40
176 Rick Short RC 1.00
177 Yadier Molina .40
178 Willy Taveras .40
179 Wes Helms .40
180 Wade Miller .40
181 Luis Gonzalez .40
182 Carlos Zambrano .40
183 Chicago Cubs .50
184 Victor Santos .40
185 Tyler Walker .40
186 Bobby Crosby .40
187 Trot Nixon .40
188 Nick Johnson .40
189 Nick Swisher .40
190 Brian Roberts .40
191 Nomar Garciaparra 1.50
192 Oliver Perez .40
193 Ramon Hernandez .40
194 Randy Winn .40
195 Ryan Church .40
196 Ryan Wagner .40
197 Todd Hollandsworth .40
198 Detroit Tigers .40
199 Tino Martinez .40
200 Roger Clemens 4.00
200 Roger Clemens/ Red Shirt/SP 12.00
201 Shawn Estes .40
202 Justin Morneau .75
203 Jeff Francis .40
204 Oakland Athletics .40
205 Jeff Francoeur .40
206 C.J. Wilson .40
207 Francisco Rodriguez .40
208 Edgardo Alfonzo .40
209 David Eckstein .40
210 Cory Lidle .40
211 Chase Utley .75
212 Rocco Baldelli .40
212 Rocco Baldelli/ Blue Letter/SP 5.00
213 So Taguchi .40
214 Philadelphia Phillies .40
215 Brad Hawpe .40
216 Walter Young .40
217 Tom Gorzelanny (RC) .40
218 Shaun Marcum (RC) .40
219 Ryan Howard 2.00
220 Damian Jackson .40
221 Craig Counsell .40
222 Damian Miller .40
223 Derrick Turnbow .40
224 Hank Blalock .75
225 Brayan Pena .40
226 Grady Sizemore 1.00
227 Ivan Rodriguez 1.00
228 Jason Isringhausen .40
229 Brian Fuentes .40
230 Jason Phillips .40
231 Jason Schmidt .75
232 Javier Valentin .40
233 Jeff Kent .75
234 John Buck .40
235 Mike Matheny .40
236 Jorge Cantu .40
237 Jose Castillo .40
238 Kenny Rogers .40
239 Kerry Wood .75
240 Kevin Mench .40
241 Tim Stauffer .40
242 Eric Milton .40
243 St. Louis Cardinals .75
244 Shawn Chacon .40
245 Mike Jacobs (RC) .40
246 Ryan Dempster .40
247 Todd Jones .40
248 Tom Glavine .75
249 Tony Graffanino .40
250 Ichiro Suzuki 2.50
251 Baltimore Orioles .50
252 Brad Radke .40
253 Brad Wilkerson .40
254 Carlos Lee .40
255 Alex Gordon .40
255 Alex Gordon Cut-Out 125.00
256 Gustavo Chacin .40
257 Jermaine Dye .40
258 Jose Mesa .40
259 Julio Lugo .40
260 Mark Redman .40
261 Brandon Watson (RC) .40
262 Pedro Feliz .40
263 Esteban Loaiza .40
264 Anthony Reyes .40
265 Jose Contreras/SP 6.00
266 Tadahito Iguchi/SP 8.00
267 Mark Loretta/SP 6.00
268 Ray Durham/SP 4.00
269 Neifi Perez/SP .40
270 Washington Nationals .40
271 Troy Glaus/SP 6.00
272 Matt Holliday/SP 4.00
273 Kevin Millwood/SP 5.00
274 Jon Lieber/SP 4.00
275 Cleveland Indians .40
276 Jeremy Reed/SP 4.00
277 Garrett Atkins/SP 4.00
278 Geoff Jenkins/SP 4.00
279 Joey Gathright/SP 4.00
280 Ben Sheets/SP 6.00
281 Melvin Mora/SP 4.00
282 Jonathan Papelbon/ SP (RC) 10.00
283 John Smoltz/SP 5.00
284 Jake Peavy/SP 5.00
285 Felix Hernandez/SP 6.00
286 Alfonso Soriano/SP 6.00
287 Bronson Arroyo/SP 4.00
288 Adam LaRoche/SP 5.00
289 Aramis Ramirez/SP 4.00
290 Brad Hennessey/SP 4.00
291 Conor Jackson/ SP (RC)
292 Rod Barajas/SP 4.00
293 Chris Young/SP 4.00
294 Jeremy Bonderman/ SP 4.00
295 Jack Wilson/SP 4.00
296 Jay Payton/SP 4.00
297 Danys Baez/SP 4.00
298 Jose Lima/SP 4.00
299 Luis A. Gonzalez/SP 4.00
300 Mike Sweeney/SP 4.00
301 Nelson Cruz/SP (RC) 6.00
302 Eric Gagne/SP 5.00
303 Juan Castro/SP 4.00
304 Joe Mauer/SP 6.00
305 Richie Sexson/SP 5.00
306 Roy Oswalt/SP 5.00
307 Rickie Weeks/SP 5.00
308 Pat Borders/SP 4.00
309 Mike Morse/SP 4.00
310 Matt Stairs/SP 4.00
311 Chad Tracy/SP 4.00
312 Matt Cain/SP (RC) 6.00
313 Mark Mulder/SP 4.00
314 Mark Grudzielanek/SP 4.00
315 Johnny Damon/SP 8.00
316 Casey Kotchman/SP 4.00
317 San Francisco Giants .40
318 Chris Burke/SP 4.00
319 Carl Crawford/SP 4.00
320 Edgar Renteria/SP 5.00
321 Chan Ho Park/SP 4.00
322 Boston Red Sox 4.00
323 Robinson Cano/SP 8.00
324 Los Angeles Dodgers .40
325 Miguel Tejada/ w/Bat/SP 6.00
325 Miguel Tejada/ Hand Up/SP 6.00
326 Jimmy Rollins/SP 5.00
327 Juan Pierre/SP 4.00
328 Dan Johnson/SP 4.00
329 Chicago White Sox .40
330 Pat Burrell/SP 5.00
331 Ramon Ortiz/SP 4.00
332 Rondell White/SP 4.00
333 David Wells/SP 4.00
334 Michael Young/SP 6.00
335 Mike Mussina/SP 6.00
336 Moises Alou/SP 5.00
337 Scott Podsednik/SP 5.00
338 Rich Harden/SP 6.00
339 Mark Teahen/SP 4.00
340 Jacque Jones/SP 4.00
341 Jason Giambi/SP 6.00
342 Bill Hall/SP 4.00
343 Jon Garland/SP 4.00
344 Dontrelle Willis/SP 6.00
345 Danny Haren/SP 4.00
346 Brian Giles/SP 4.00
347 Brad Penny/SP 4.00
348 Brandon McCarthy/SP 6.00
349 Chien-Ming Wang/SP 7.00
350 Torii Hunter/ Blue Letter/SP 5.00
350 Torii Hunter/ Red/Blue Letter/SP 5.00
351 Yhency Brazoban/SP 4.00
352 Rodrigo Lopez/SP 4.00
353 Paul McAnulty .40
354 Francisco Cordero .40
355 Brandon Inge .40
356 Jason Lane .40
357 Brian Schneider .40
358 Dustin Hermanson .40
359 Eric Hinske .40
360 Jarrod Washburn .40
361 Jayson Werth .40
362 Craig Breslow RC 1.00
363 Jeff Weaver .40
364 Jeromy Burnitz .40
365 Jhonny Peralta .75
366 Joe Crede .40
367 Johan Santana 1.50
368 Jose Valentin .40
369 Keith Foulke .40
370 Larry Bigbie .40
371 Manny Ramirez 1.50
372 Jim Edmonds .75
373 Horacio Ramirez .40
374 Garret Anderson .75
375 Felipe Lopez .75
376 Eric Byrnes .40
377 Darin Erstad .75
378 Carlos Zambrano .75
379 Craig Biggio .75
380 Darrell Rasner (RC) .40
381 Dave Roberts .40
382 Hanley Ramirez (RC) .40
383 Geoff Blum .40
384 Joel Pineiro .40
385 Kip Wells .40
386 Kelvim Escobar .40
387 John Patterson .40
388 Jody Gerut .40
389 Marshall McDougall .40
390 Mike MacDougal .40
391 Orlando Palmeiro .40
392 Rich Aurilia .40
393 Ronnie Belliard .40
394 Rich Hill .50
395 Scott Hatteberg .40
396 Ryan Langerhans .40
397 Richard Hidalgo .40
398 Omar Vizquel .40
399 Mike Lowell .40
400 Astros' Aces SP 8.00
401 Mike Cameron .40
402 Matt Clement .40
403 Miguel Cabrera 1.50
404 Milton Bradley .40
405 Laynce Nix .40
406 Robert Mackowiak .40
407 White Sox Power Hitters SP 10.00
408 Mark Teixeira 1.00
409 Brady Clark .40
410 Johnny Estrada .40
411 Juan Encarnacion .40
412 Morgan Ensberg .40
413 Nook Logan .40
414 Phil Nevin .40
415 Reggie Sanders .40
416 Roy Halladay .75
417 Livan Hernandez .40
418 Jose Vidro .40
419 Shannon Stewart .40
420 Brian Bruney .40
421 Royce Clayton .40
422 Chris Demaria RC 1.50
423 Eduardo Perez .40
424 Jeff Suppan .40
425 Jaret Wright .40
426 Joe Randa .40
427 Bobby Kielty .40
428 Jason Ellison .40
429 Gregg Zaun .40
430 Runelvys Hernandez .40
431 Joe McEwing .40
432 Jason LaRue .40
433 Aaron Miles .40
434 Adam Kennedy .40
435 Ambiorix Burgos .40
436 Armando Benitez .40
437 Brad Ausmus .40
438 Brandon Backe .40
439 Brian Anderson (RC) .40
440 Bruce Chen .40
441 Carlos Guillen .40
442 Casey Blake .40
443 Chris Capuano .40
444 Chris Duffy .40
445 Chris Ray .40
446 Clint Barmes .40
447 Andrew Sisco .40
448 Dallas McPherson .40
449 Tanyon Sturtze .40
450 Carlos Beltran 1.50
451 Jason Vargas .40
452 Ervin Santana .40
453 Jason Marquis .40
454 Juan Rivera .40
455 Jake Westbrook .40
456 Jason Johnson .40
457 Joe Blanton .40
458 Kevin Millar .40
459 Jon Thomson .40
460 J.P. Howell .40
461 Justin Verlander (RC) .40
462 Kelly Johnson .40
463 Kyle Davies .40
464 Lance Niekro .40
465 Magglio Ordonez .40
466 Melky Cabrera .40
467 Nick Punto .40
468 Paul Byrd .40
469 Randy Wolf .40
470 Ruben Gotay .40
471 Ryan Madson .40
472 Victor Diaz .40
473 Xavier Nady .40
474 Zachary Duke .40
475 Huston Street .75
475 Huston Street/ Blue Letter/SP 6.00
476 Brad Thompson .40
477 Jonny Gomes .40
478 B.J. Upton .40
479 Jamey Carroll .40
480 Mike Hampton .40
481 Tony Clark .40
482 Antonio Alfonseca .40
483 Justin Duchscherer .40
484 Mike Timlin .40
485 Joe Saunders .40

Chrome

		NM/M
Common Player:		2.00
Production 1,957 Sets		
Refractor:		1.5-2X
Production 557 Sets		
Black Refractor:		3-6X
Production 57 Sets		
1	Rafael Furcal	2.00
2	C.C. Sabathia	2.00
3	Sean Casey	2.00
4	Gary Sheffield	3.00
5	William Harridge, Warren Giles	2.00
6	Curt Schilling	3.00
7	Jay Gibbons	2.00
8	Paul Konerko	3.00
9	Lyle Overbay	2.00
10	Jorge Posada	3.00
11	Todd Walker	2.00
12	Carlos Delgado	3.00
13	David Wright	6.00
14	Matt Morris	2.00
15	Mariano Rivera	3.00
16	Jeff Bagwell	3.00
17	Carl Pavano	2.00
18	Adrian Beltre	3.00
19	Scott Rolen	4.00
20	Aubrey Huff	2.00
21	Hideki Matsui	6.00
22	Andruw Jones	3.00
23	Sammy Sosa	4.00
24	Mark Buehrle	3.00
25	Orlando Hernandez	2.00
26	Travis Hafner	3.00
27	Vladimir Guerrero	4.00
28	Chipper Jones	4.00
29	Jose Reyes	3.00
30	Roger Clemens	8.00
31	Aaron Boone	2.00
32	Andy Pettitte	3.00
33	David DeJesus	2.00
34	Shawn Green	2.00
35	Luis Castillo	2.00
36	Frank Thomas	3.00
37	Javy Lopez	2.00
38	Victor Martinez	2.00
39	Tim Wakefield	2.00
40	Cliff Floyd	2.00
41	Bartolo Colon	2.00
42	Billy Wagner	2.00
43	Dmitri Young	2.00
44	Mark Prior	3.00
45	Nick Johnson	2.00
46	Brian Roberts	2.00
47	Nomar Garciaparra	4.00
48	Jorge Cantu	2.00
49	Jeff Francoeur	3.00
50	Barry Bonds	10.00
51	Francisco Rodriguez	2.00
52	Rocco Baldelli	2.00
53	Ryan Howard	5.00
54	Hank Blalock	2.00
55	Ivan Rodriguez	3.00
56	Jason Schmidt	2.00
57	Jeff Kent	2.00
58	Jose Castillo	2.00
59	Kerry Wood	3.00
60	Chase Utley	2.00
61	Shawn Chacon	2.00
62	Tom Glavine	2.00
63	Ichiro Suzuki	6.00
64	Carlos Lee	2.00
65	Jeff Weaver	2.00
66	Jeromy Burnitz	2.00
67	Jhonny Peralta	2.00
68	Johan Santana	3.00
69	Keith Foulke	2.00
70	Manny Ramirez	4.00
71	Jim Edmonds	3.00
72	Garret Anderson	2.00
73	Felipe Lopez	2.00
74	Craig Biggio	2.00
75	Ryan Langerhans	2.00
76	Mike Cameron	2.00
77	Matt Clement	2.00
78	Miguel Cabrera	3.00
79	Mark Teixeira	3.00
80	Johnny Estrada	2.00
81	Nook Logan	2.00
82	Livan Hernandez	2.00
83	Roy Halladay	3.00
84	Jose Vidro	2.00
85	Shannon Stewart	2.00
86	Brian Bruney	2.00
87	Jaret Wright	2.00
88	Gregg Zaun	2.00

89	Jason LaRue	2.00
90	Adam Kennedy	2.00
91	Armando Benitez	2.00
92	Chris Ray	2.00
93	Clint Barmes	2.00
94	Ervin Santana	2.00
95	Justin Verlander	2.00
96	Magglio Ordonez	2.00
97	Todd Helton	3.00
98	Zachary Duke	2.00
99	Huston Street	2.00
100	Alex Rodriguez	8.00
101	Mike Hampton	2.00
102	Tony Clark	2.00
104	Barry Zito	2.00
105	Anderson Hernandez	2.00
106	B.J. Upton	2.00
107	Albert Pujols	10.00
108	Tim Hudson	3.00
109	Derek Jeter	10.00
110	Greg Maddux	6.00

Clubhouse Collection Relic Autograph

		NM/M
Production 25 Sets		
CCA-3	Brooks Robinson	125.00
CCA-4	Al Kaline	200.00
CCA-5	Stan Musial	250.00

Real One Autographs

		NM/M
Production 200 Sets		
Red Ink:		1.5-2X
Production 57 Sets		
EB	Ernie Banks	120.00
YB	Yogi Berra	120.00
TB	Tommy Byrne	50.00
BC	Bob Chakales	50.00
JAC	Jack Collum	40.00
JCR	Jack Crimian	50.00
JD	Jack Dittmer	60.00
WF	Whitey Ford	120.00
DK	Don Kaiser	40.00
NK	Nellie King	50.00
LK	Lou Kretlow	50.00
PL	Paul LaPalme	50.00
JM	Joe Margoneri	60.00
WM	Windy McCall	40.00
MP	Mel Parnell	60.00
JP	Jim Pyburn	50.00
DR	Dusty Rhodes	50.00
FR	Frank Robinson	120.00
JSM	Jim Small	50.00
SM	Stan Musial	160.00
RN	Ron Negray	40.00
EOB	Eddie O'Brien	50.00
KO	Karl Olson	50.00
EO	Ernie Oravetz	50.00
JRM	John (Red) Murff	50.00
DS	Duke Snider	140.00
JSN	Jerry Snyder	60.00
CT	Charles Thompson	50.00
BW	Bob Wiesler	60.00

Clubhouse Collection Relics

		NM/M
Common Player:		4.00
CB	Clint Barmes	6.00
BB	Barry Bonds	25.00
MC	Miguel Cabrera	8.00
RC	Robinson Cano	15.00
EC	Eric Chavez	4.00
SC	Shin-Soo Choo	4.00
CC	Carl Crawford	4.00
JD	Johnny Damon	6.00
JD2	Johnny Damon	6.00
AD	Adam Dunn	6.00
JE	Jim Edmonds	6.00
ME	Morgan Ensberg	4.00
JF	Jeff Francis	4.00
EG	Eric Gagne	4.00
KG	Khalil Greene	4.00
VG	Vladimir Guerrero	8.00
MH	Matt Holliday	4.00
TI	Tadahito Iguchi	10.00
CJ	Conor Jackson	4.00
AJ	Andruw Jones	6.00
AK	Al Kaline	20.00
DL	Derrek Lee	8.00
MM	Mickey Mantle	200.00
PM	Pedro Martinez	8.00
BM	Bill Mazeroski	30.00
MMU	Mark Mulder	4.00
SM	Stan Musial	35.00
DO	David Ortiz	10.00
JP	Jake Peavy	4.00
MP	Mike Piazza	8.00
AP	Albert Pujols	20.00
MR	Manny Ramirez	8.00
MR2	Manny Ramirez	8.00

BR	Brian Roberts	4.00
BR2	Brian Roberts	4.00
BRO	Brooks Robinson	30.00
FR	Frank Robinson	20.00
AR	Alex Rodriguez	20.00
AR2	Alex Rodriguez	20.00
JS	Johan Santana	6.00
CS	Curt Schilling	8.00
GS	Gary Sheffield	6.00
AS	Alfonso Soriano	6.00
MTE	Mark Teixeira	6.00
MT	Miguel Tejada	6.00
RW	Rickie Weeks	6.00
DWI	Dontrelle Willis	6.00
DW	David Wright	10.00

Clubhouse Collection Dual Relics

		NM/M
Production 57 Sets		
BR	Brooks Robinson, Brian Roberts	75.00
MR	Mickey Mantle, Alex Rodriguez	250.00
MP	Stan Musial, Albert Pujols	150.00

Flashbacks Autographs

No Pricing
Production 25 Sets

Flashbacks Relics

		NM/M
EB	Ernie Banks	15.00
YB	Yogi Berra	20.00
WF	Whitey Ford	20.00
AK	Al Kaline	15.00
MM	Mickey Mantle	40.00
BM	Bill Mazeroski	10.00
SM	Stan Musial	50.00
BRI	Bobby Richardson	15.00
BR	Brooks Robinson	10.00
FR	Frank Robinson	10.00

Flashbacks Relic Autographs

No Pricing
Production 25 Sets

Flashbacks

		NM/M
Complete Set (10):		10.00
Common Player:		.50
Inserted 1:12		
EB	Ernie Banks	1.50
YB	Yogi Berra	1.50
WF	Whitey Ford	1.00
AK	Al Kaline	1.50
MM	Mickey Mantle	5.00
BM	Bill Mazeroski	.50
SM	Stan Musial	1.50
BRI	Bobby Richardson	.50
BR	Brooks Robinson	1.00
FR	Frank Robinson	1.00

New Age Performers

		NM/M
Complete Set (15):		20.00
Common Player:		1.00
Inserted 1:15		
BB	Barry Bonds	4.00
MC	Miguel Cabrera	1.50
RC	Roger Clemens	2.00
VG	Vladimir Guerrero	1.50
CL	Carlos Lee	1.00
DL	Derrek Lee	1.50
PM	Pedro Martinez	1.50
DO	David Ortiz	1.50
GM	Mark Prior	1.00
AP	Albert Pujols	2.00
MR	Manny Ramirez	1.50
AR	Alex Rodriguez	4.00
GS	Gary Sheffield	1.00
IS	Ichiro Suzuki	2.50
MT	Mark Teixeira	1.50

Real One Cut Signatures

Production One Set

Clubhouse Collection Cut Signature Relic

Production One Set

Then and Now

		NM/M
Complete Set (10):		20.00
Common Duo:		1.00
Inserted 1:15		
TN1	Mickey Mantle, Alex Rodriguez	6.00
TN2	Ted Williams, Michael Young	3.00
TN3	Mickey Mantle, Jason Giambi	6.00
TN4	Luis Aparicio, Chone Figgins	1.00
TN5	Ted Williams, Alex Rodriguez	4.00
TN6	Stan Musial, Derrek Lee	2.00
TN7	Stan Musial, Derrek Lee	2.00
TN8	Red Schoendienst, Derrek Lee	1.50
TN9	Johnny Podres, Roger Clemens	4.00
TN10	Clem Labine, Chad Cordero	1.00

2006 Topps Opening Day

		NM/M
Complete Set (165):		25.00
Common Player:		.10
Pack (6):		1.00
Box (36):		30.00
1	Alex Rodriguez	1.50
2	Jhonny Peralta	.20
3	Garrett Atkins	.10
4	Vernon Wells	.25
5	Carl Crawford	.25
6	Josh Beckett	.25
7	Mickey Mantle	3.00
8	Willy Taveras	.10
9	Ivan Rodriguez	.40
10	Clint Barmes	.10
11	Jose Reyes	.25
12	Travis Hafner	.40
13	Tadahito Iguchi	.25
14	Barry Zito	.25
15	Brian Roberts	.25
16	David Wright	1.00
17	Mark Teixeira	.50
18	Roy Halladay	.25
19	Scott Rolen	.40
20	Bobby Abreu	.25
21	Lance Berkman	.25
22	Moises Alou	.20
23	Chone Figgins	.10
24	Aaron Rowand	.10
25	Chipper Jones	.50
26	Johnny Damon	.50
27	Matt Clement	.10
28	Nick Johnson	.10
29	Freddy Garcia	.10
30	Jon Garland	.10
31	Torii Hunter	.20
32	Mike Sweeney	.20
33	Mike Lieberthal	.10
34	Rafael Furcal	.20
35	Brad Wilkerson	.10
36	Brad Penny	.10
37	Jorge Cantu	.10
38	Paul Konerko	.25
39	Rickie Weeks	.25
40	Jorge Posada	.25
41	Albert Pujols	1.50
42	Zack Greinke	.10
43	Jimmy Rollins	.25
44	Mark Prior	.40
45	Greg Maddux	1.00
46	Jeff Francis	.10
47	Felipe Lopez	.10
48	Dan Johnson	.10
49	B.J. Ryan	.10
50	Manny Ramirez	.50
51	Melvin Mora	.10
52	Javy Lopez	.10
53	Garret Anderson	.20
54	Jason Bay	.25
55	Joe Mauer	.25
56	C.C. Sabathia	.10
57	Bartolo Colon	.10

58	Ichiro Suzuki	1.00
59	Andruw Jones	.50
60	Rocco Baldelli	.10
61	Jeff Kent	.25
62	Cliff Floyd	.10
63	John Smoltz	.25
64	Shawn Green	.20
65	Nomar Garciaparra	.50
66	Miguel Cabrera	.50
67	Vladimir Guerrero	.50
68	Gary Sheffield	.25
69	Jake Peavy	.25
70	Carlos Lee	.20
71	Tom Glavine	.25
72	Craig Biggio	.25
73	Steve Finley	.10
74	Adrian Beltre	.10
75	Eric Gagne	.10
76	Aubrey Huff	.10
77	Livan Hernandez	.10
78	Scott Podsednik	.10
79	Todd Helton	.40
80	Kerry Wood	.25
81	Randy Johnson	.50
82	Huston Street	.50
83	Pedro Martinez	.50
84	Roger Clemens	1.50
85	Hank Blalock	.20
86	Carlos Beltran	.40
87	Chien-Ming Wang	.25
88	Rich Harden	.25
89	Mike Mussina	.25
90	Mark Buehrle	.25
91	Michael Young	.20
92	Mark Mulder	.20
93	Khalil Greene	.10
94	Johan Santana	.25
95	Andy Pettitte	.25
96	Derek Jeter	1.50
97	Jack Wilson	.10
98	Ben Sheets	.25
99	Miguel Tejada	.40
100	Barry Bonds	1.50
101	Dontrelle Willis	.50
102	Curt Schilling	.50
103	Jose Contreras	.10
104	Jeremy Bonderman	.10
105	David Ortiz	.50
106	Lyle Overbay	.10
107	Robinson Cano	.25
108	Tim Hudson	.25
109	Paul LoDuca	.10
110	Mariano Rivera	.25
111	Derrek Lee	.50
112	Wily Mo Pena	.10
113	Morgan Ensberg	.20
114	Roy Oswalt	.20
115	Adam Dunn	.40
116	Hideki Matsui	1.00
117	Pat Burrell	.25
118	Jason Schmidt	.20
119	Alfonso Soriano	.40
120	Aramis Ramirez	.25
121	Jason Giambi	.25
122	Orlando Hernandez	.10
123	Magglio Ordonez	.10
124	Troy Glaus	.25
125	Carlos Delgado	.25
126	Kevin Millwood	.20
127	Shannon Stewart	.10
128	Luis Castillo	.10
129	Jim Edmonds	.25
130	Richie Sexson	.25
131	Dmitri Young	.10
132	Russ Adams	.10
133	Nick Swisher	.10
134	Jermaine Dye	.10
135	Anderson Hernandez (RC)	.10
136	Justin Huber (RC)	.10
137	Jason Botts (RC)	.10
138	Jeff Mathis (RC)	.10
139	Ryan Garko (RC)	.10
140	Charlton Jimerson (RC)	.10
141	Chris Denorfia (RC)	.10
142	Anthony Reyes (RC)	.10
143	Bryan Bullington (RC)	.10
144	Chuck James (RC)	.10
145	Danny Sandoval RC	.25
146	Walter Young (RC)	.10
147	Fausto Carmona (RC)	.25
148	Francisco Liriano (RC)	.25
149	Hong-Chih Kuo (RC)	.10
150	Joe Saunders (RC)	.10
151	John Koronka (RC)	.10
152	Robert Andino RC	.10
153	Shaun Marcum (RC)	.10
154	Tom Gorzelanny (RC)	.10
155	Craig Breslow RC	.25
156	Chris Demaria RC	.50
157	Brayan Pena (RC)	.25
158	Rich Hill (RC)	.25
159	Rick Short RC	.25
160	Darrell Rasner (RC)	.10
161	C.J. Wilson (RC)	.10
162	Brandon Watson (RC)	.10
163	Paul McAnulty (RC)	.10
164	Marshall McDougall (RC)	.10
165	Checklist	.10

Red Foil

		NM/M
Red:		2-3X
Production 2,006 Sets		

Printing Plates

No Pricing
Production one set per color.

Autographs

		NM/M
BE	Brad Eldred	15.00
JE	Johnny Estrada	20.00
TH	Toby Hall	10.00
MK	Mark Kotsay	10.00
EM	Eli Marrero	10.00
VZ	Victor Zambrano	10.00

SI For Kids

		NM/M
1	Vladimir Guerrero	.50
2	Marcus Giles	.15
3	Michael Young	.15
4	Derek Jeter	1.50
5	Barry Bonds	1.50
6	Ivan Rodriguez	.40
7	Miguel Cabrera	.50
8	Jim Edmonds	.25
9	Jack Wilson	.15
10	Khalil Greene	.15
11	Miguel Tejada	.40
12	Eric Chavez	.25
13	Shannon Stewart	.15
14	Julio Lugo	.15
15	Andruw Jones	.50
16	Nick Johnson, Randy Johnson	.50
17	Tadahito Iguchi, Ivan Rodriguez	.25
18	Roy Oswalt, Jose Reyes	.25
19	Manny Ramirez, Ronnie Belliard	.50
20	Todd Helton, Khalil Greene	.25
21	David Ortiz, Dontrelle Willis	.50
22	Ichiro Suzuki, Johnny Damon	.75
23	Craig Biggio, Jack Wilson	.15
24	Brian Roberts, Richie Sexson	.25
25	Chipper Jones, Marcus Giles	.50

2006 Topps Sterling

		NM/M
Common Player:		10.00
Production 250 Sets		
Box (Five Cards):		300.00
1	Barry Bonds	10.00
2	Barry Bonds	10.00
3	Barry Bonds	10.00
4	Barry Bonds	10.00
5	Barry Bonds	10.00
6	Barry Bonds	10.00
7	Barry Bonds	10.00
8	Barry Bonds	10.00
9	Barry Bonds	10.00
10	Barry Bonds	10.00
11	Barry Bonds	10.00
12	Barry Bonds	10.00
13	Barry Bonds	10.00
14	Barry Bonds	10.00
15	Barry Bonds	10.00
16	Barry Bonds	10.00
17	Barry Bonds	10.00
18	Barry Bonds	10.00
19	Barry Bonds	10.00
20	Mickey Mantle	25.00
21	Mickey Mantle	25.00
22	Mickey Mantle	25.00
23	Mickey Mantle	25.00
24	Mickey Mantle	25.00
25	Mickey Mantle	25.00
26	Mickey Mantle	25.00
27	Mickey Mantle	25.00
28	Mickey Mantle	25.00
29	Mickey Mantle	25.00
30	Mickey Mantle	25.00
31	Mickey Mantle	25.00
32	Mickey Mantle	25.00
33	Mickey Mantle	25.00
34	Mickey Mantle	25.00
35	Mickey Mantle	25.00
36	Mickey Mantle	25.00
37	Mickey Mantle	25.00
38	Mickey Mantle	25.00
39	Mickey Mantle	25.00
40	Josh Gibson	30.00
41	Josh Gibson	30.00
42	Josh Gibson	30.00
43	Josh Gibson	30.00

No.	Name	Price		No.	Name	Price
44	Rickey Henderson	10.00		162	Carl Yastrzemski	15.00
45	Rickey Henderson	10.00		163	Carl Yastrzemski	15.00
46	Rickey Henderson	10.00		164	Carl Yastrzemski	15.00
47	Rickey Henderson	10.00		165	Carl Yastrzemski	15.00
48	Rickey Henderson	10.00		166	Carl Yastrzemski	15.00
49	Rickey Henderson	10.00		167	Carl Yastrzemski	15.00
50	Rickey Henderson	10.00		168	Carl Yastrzemski	15.00
51	Rickey Henderson	10.00		169	Carl Yastrzemski	15.00
52	Rickey Henderson	10.00		170	Carl Yastrzemski	15.00
53	Rickey Henderson	10.00		171	Carl Yastrzemski	15.00
54	Ted Williams	15.00		172	Carl Yastrzemski	15.00
55	Ted Williams	15.00		173	Carl Yastrzemski	15.00
56	Ted Williams	15.00		174	Carl Yastrzemski	15.00
57	Ted Williams	15.00		175	Carl Yastrzemski	15.00
58	Ted Williams	15.00		176	Tony Gwynn	15.00
59	Ted Williams	15.00		177	Tony Gwynn	15.00
60	Ted Williams	15.00		178	Tony Gwynn	15.00
61	Ted Williams	15.00		179	Tony Gwynn	15.00
62	Ted Williams	15.00		180	Tony Gwynn	15.00
63	Roberto Clemente	25.00		181	Tony Gwynn	15.00
64	Roberto Clemente	25.00		182	Tony Gwynn	15.00
65	Roberto Clemente	25.00		183	Tony Gwynn	15.00
66	Roberto Clemente	25.00		184	Tony Gwynn	15.00
67	Roberto Clemente	25.00		185	Tony Gwynn	15.00
68	Nolan Ryan	20.00		186	Ryne Sandberg	15.00
69	Nolan Ryan	20.00		187	Ryne Sandberg	15.00
70	Nolan Ryan	20.00		188	Ryne Sandberg	15.00
71	Nolan Ryan	20.00		189	Ryne Sandberg	15.00
72	Nolan Ryan	20.00		190	Ryne Sandberg	15.00
73	Nolan Ryan	20.00		191	Ozzie Smith	15.00
74	Nolan Ryan	20.00		192	Ozzie Smith	15.00
75	Nolan Ryan	20.00		193	Ozzie Smith	15.00
76	Nolan Ryan	20.00		194	Ozzie Smith	15.00
77	Nolan Ryan	20.00		195	Ozzie Smith	15.00
78	Cal Ripken Jr.	20.00		196	Ozzie Smith	15.00
79	Cal Ripken Jr.	20.00		197	Ozzie Smith	15.00
80	Cal Ripken Jr.	20.00		198	Ozzie Smith	15.00
81	Cal Ripken Jr.	20.00		199	Ozzie Smith	15.00
82	Cal Ripken Jr.	20.00		200	Ozzie Smith	15.00
83	Cal Ripken Jr.	20.00				
84	Cal Ripken Jr.	20.00				
85	Cal Ripken Jr.	20.00				
86	Cal Ripken Jr.	20.00				
87	Cal Ripken Jr.	20.00				
88	Cal Ripken Jr.	20.00				
89	Cal Ripken Jr.	20.00				
90	Cal Ripken Jr.	20.00				
91	Cal Ripken Jr.	20.00				
92	Cal Ripken Jr.	20.00				
93	Cal Ripken Jr.	20.00				
94	Cal Ripken Jr.	20.00				
95	Cal Ripken Jr.	20.00				
96	Cal Ripken Jr.	20.00				
97	Stan Musial	15.00				
98	Stan Musial	15.00				
99	Stan Musial	15.00				
100	Stan Musial	15.00				
101	Stan Musial	15.00				
102	Reggie Jackson	15.00				
103	Reggie Jackson	15.00				
104	Reggie Jackson	15.00				
105	Reggie Jackson	15.00				
106	Reggie Jackson	15.00				
107	Johnny Bench	15.00				
108	Johnny Bench	15.00				
109	Johnny Bench	15.00				
110	Johnny Bench	15.00				
111	Johnny Bench	15.00				
112	George Brett	15.00				
113	George Brett	15.00				
114	George Brett	15.00				
115	George Brett	15.00				
116	George Brett	15.00				
117	George Brett	15.00				
118	George Brett	15.00				
119	George Brett	15.00				
120	George Brett	15.00				
121	George Brett	15.00				
122	Don Mattingly	15.00				
123	Don Mattingly	15.00				
124	Don Mattingly	15.00				
125	Don Mattingly	15.00				
126	Don Mattingly	15.00				
127	Don Mattingly	15.00				
128	Don Mattingly	15.00				
129	Don Mattingly	15.00				
130	Don Mattingly	15.00				
131	Don Mattingly	15.00				
132	Roger Maris	20.00				
133	Roger Maris	20.00				
134	Roger Maris	20.00				
135	Roger Maris	20.00				
136	Roger Maris	20.00				
137	Rod Carew	10.00				
138	Rod Carew	10.00				
139	Rod Carew	10.00				
140	Rod Carew	10.00				
141	Rod Carew	10.00				
142	Rod Carew	10.00				
143	Rod Carew	10.00				
144	Rod Carew	10.00				
145	Rod Carew	10.00				
146	Rod Carew	10.00				
147	Yogi Berra	15.00				
148	Yogi Berra	15.00				
149	Yogi Berra	15.00				
150	Yogi Berra	15.00				
151	Yogi Berra	15.00				
152	Mike Schmidt	15.00				
153	Mike Schmidt	15.00				
154	Mike Schmidt	15.00				
155	Mike Schmidt	15.00				
156	Mike Schmidt	15.00				
157	Carl Yastrzemski	15.00				
158	Carl Yastrzemski	15.00				
159	Carl Yastrzemski	15.00				
160	Carl Yastrzemski	15.00				
161	Carl Yastrzemski	15.00				

Baseball Cut Signatures

NM/M

Code	Name	Price
SA	Sparky Anderson	40.00
LA	Luis Aparicio	40.00
LB	Lou Brock	50.00
RC	Rod Carew	50.00
SC	Steve Carlton	50.00
GC	Gary Carter	40.00
OC	Orlando Cepeda	35.00
DE	Dennis Eckersley	40.00
BF	Bob Feller	40.00
RF	Rollie Fingers	40.00
CF	Carlton Fisk	60.00
BG	Bob Gibson	50.00
MI	Monte Irvin	40.00
AK	Al Kaline	60.00
GK	George Kell	40.00
HK	Harmon Killebrew	70.00
RK	Ralph Kiner	50.00
JM	Juan Marichal	40.00
JMO	Joe Morgan	50.00
PN	Phil Niekro	40.00
JP	Jim Palmer	40.00
TP	Tony Perez	40.00
GP	Gaylord Perry	40.00
RR	Robin Roberts	40.00
BR	Brooks Robinson	60.00
FR	Frank Robinson	60.00
RS	Ryne Sandberg	80.00
MS	Mike Schmidt	75.00
RSH	Red Schoendienst	60.00
DS	Duke Snider	75.00
EW	Earl Weaver	30.00
RY	Robin Yount	70.00

Career Stats Relics

No Pricing
Production 10 Sets
Prime: No Pricing
Production One Set
Sterling Silver: No Pricing
Production One Set

Career Stats Relics Autographs

Production 10 Sets
Prime: No Pricing
Production One Set
Sterling Silver: No Pricing
Production One Set

Cut from the Same Cloth Signatures

Production 1-5

Cut Signatures

NM/M

No.	Name	Price
46	Elmer Valo	80.00
53	Carl Furillo	100.00
61	Hal Newhouser	60.00
64	Dick Sisler	65.00
65	Frank Shea	75.00
66	Monty Stratton	80.00
67	Lloyd Waner	150.00
68	Sal Maglie	70.00
69	Waite Hoyt	80.00
70	Warren Spahn	100.00
72	A.B. Chandler	60.00
73	Al Barlick	75.00
74	Bill Dickey	100.00
75	Bill Terry	80.00
76	Billy Herman	75.00
77	Bob Lemon	60.00
78	Buck Leonard	80.00
79	Charles Gehringer	100.00
81	Earl Averill	60.00
82	Hoyt Wilhelm	80.00
83	Jim "Catfish" Hunter	100.00
84	Joe Sewell	80.00
85	Judy Johnson	80.00
86	Carl Hubbell	85.00
87	Lou Boudreau	65.00
88	Luke Appling	80.00
89	Ray Dandridge	75.00
90	Rick Ferrell	60.00
91	Stan Coveleski	75.00
92	Willie Stargell	120.00

Framed Burgundy

Burgundy (1-200): 3-5X
Production 10 Sets

Framed Silver

No Pricing
Production One Set

Framed White

White (1-200): 1-1.5X
Production 50 Sets

Five Relics

Production 10 Sets
Prime: No Pricing
Production 10 Sets
Sterling Silver: No Pricing
Production One Set

Five Relics Autographs

Production 10 Sets
Prime: No Pricing
Production 10 Sets
Sterling Silver: No Pricing
Production One Set

Josh Gibson Bat Barrel

Production One

Jumbo Jersey

Production 10 Sets
Prime: No Pricing
Production One Set
Patch: No Pricing
Production 10 Sets
Sterling Silver: No Pricing
Production One Set

Moments Relics

NM/M

Production 10 Sets
Prime: No Pricing
Production One Set

Code	Name	Price
BB	Barry Bonds HR 1	75.00
BB	Barry Bonds HR 2	75.00
BB	Barry Bonds HR 3	75.00
BB	Barry Bonds HR 4	75.00
BB	Barry Bonds HR 5	75.00
BB	Barry Bonds HR 6	75.00
BB	Barry Bonds HR 7	75.00
BB	Barry Bonds HR 8	75.00
BB	Barry Bonds HR 9	75.00
BB	Barry Bonds HR 1	75.00
BB	Barry Bonds HR 2	75.00
BB	Barry Bonds HR 3	75.00
BB	Barry Bonds HR 4	75.00
BB	Barry Bonds HR 5	75.00
BB	Barry Bonds HR 6	75.00
BB	Barry Bonds HR 7	75.00
BB	Barry Bonds HR 8	75.00
BB	Barry Bonds HR 1	75.00
BB	Barry Bonds HR 2	75.00
BB	Barry Bonds HR 3	75.00
BB	Barry Bonds HR 4	75.00
BB	Barry Bonds HR 5	75.00
BB	Barry Bonds HR 6	75.00
BB	Barry Bonds HR 7	75.00
BB	Barry Bonds HR 8	75.00
BB	Barry Bonds HR 1	75.00
BB	Barry Bonds HR 2	75.00
BB	Barry Bonds HR 3	75.00
BB	Barry Bonds HR 4	75.00
BB	Barry Bonds HR 5	75.00
BB	Barry Bonds HR 6	75.00
BB	Barry Bonds HR 7	75.00
BB	Barry Bonds HR 8	75.00
BB	Barry Bonds	75.00
BB	Barry Bonds 1993	75.00
BB	Barry Bonds 1994	75.00
BB	Barry Bonds 1995	75.00
BB	Barry Bonds 1996	75.00
BB	Barry Bonds 1997	75.00
BB	Barry Bonds 1998	75.00
BB	Barry Bonds 1999	75.00
BB	Barry Bonds 1993	75.00
BB	Barry Bonds 2001	75.00
BB	Barry Bonds 2002	75.00
BB	Barry Bonds 2003	75.00
BB	Barry Bonds 2004	75.00
BB	Barry Bonds 1993	75.00
BB	Barry Bonds 1994	75.00
BB	Barry Bonds 1995	75.00
BB	Barry Bonds 1996	75.00
BB	Barry Bonds 1997	75.00
BB	Barry Bonds 1998	75.00
BB	Barry Bonds 2000	75.00
BB	Barry Bonds 2001	75.00
BB	Barry Bonds 2002	75.00
BB	Barry Bonds 2003	75.00
BB	Barry Bonds 2004	75.00
BB	Barry Bonds 2002	75.00
BB	Barry Bonds 1993	75.00
BB	Barry Bonds 1994	75.00
BB	Barry Bonds 1996	75.00
BB	Barry Bonds 1997	75.00
BB	Barry Bonds 2000	75.00
BB	Barry Bonds 2001	75.00
BB	Barry Bonds 2002	75.00
BB	Barry Bonds 2003	75.00
BB	Barry Bonds 2004	75.00
BB	Barry Bonds 1993	75.00
BB	Barry Bonds 2001	75.00
BB	Barry Bonds 2002	75.00
BB	Barry Bonds 2003	75.00
BB	Barry Bonds 2004	75.00

Code	Name	Price
MM	Mickey Mantle WS HR 1	350.00
MM	Mickey Mantle WS HR 2	350.00
MM	Mickey Mantle WS HR 3	350.00
MM	Mickey Mantle WS HR 4	350.00
MM	Mickey Mantle WS HR 5	350.00
MM	Mickey Mantle WS HR 6	350.00
MM	Mickey Mantle WS HR 7	350.00
MM	Mickey Mantle WS HR 8	350.00
MM	Mickey Mantle WS HR 9	350.00
MM	Mickey Mantle WS HR 10	350.00
MM	Mickey Mantle WS HR 11	350.00
MM	Mickey Mantle WS HR 12	350.00
MM	Mickey Mantle WS HR 13	350.00
MM	Mickey Mantle WS HR 14	350.00
MM	Mickey Mantle WS HR 15	350.00
MM	Mickey Mantle WS HR 16	350.00
MM	Mickey Mantle WS HR 17	350.00
MM	Mickey Mantle WS HR 18	350.00
MM	Mickey Mantle 1952	350.00
MM	Mickey Mantle 1956	350.00
MM	Mickey Mantle 1957	350.00
MM	Mickey Mantle 1962	350.00
MM	Mickey Mantle 1953	350.00
MM	Mickey Mantle 1954	350.00
MM	Mickey Mantle 1955	350.00
MM	Mickey Mantle 1958	350.00
MM	Mickey Mantle 1959	350.00
MM	Mickey Mantle 1960	350.00
MM	Mickey Mantle 1961	350.00
MM	Mickey Mantle 1963	350.00
MM	Mickey Mantle 1964	350.00
MM	Mickey Mantle 1965	350.00
MM	Mickey Mantle 1967	350.00
MM	Mickey Mantle 1968	350.00
MM	Mickey Mantle HR 1	350.00
MM	Mickey Mantle HR 7	350.00
MM	Mickey Mantle HR 2	350.00
MM	Mickey Mantle HR 3	350.00
MM	Mickey Mantle HR 4	350.00
MM	Mickey Mantle HR 5	350.00
MM	Mickey Mantle HR 6	350.00
MM	Mickey Mantle HR 8	350.00
MM	Mickey Mantle HR 9	350.00
MM	Mickey Mantle HR 10	350.00
MM	Mickey Mantle HR 11	350.00
MM	Mickey Mantle HR 12	350.00
MM	Mickey Mantle HR 13	350.00
MM	Mickey Mantle HR 14	350.00
MM	Mickey Mantle HR 15	350.00
MM	Mickey Mantle HR 16	350.00
MM	Mickey Mantle HR 17	350.00
MM	Mickey Mantle HR 18	350.00
MM	Mickey Mantle HR 19	350.00
MM	Mickey Mantle HR 20	350.00
MM	Mickey Mantle HR 25	350.00
MM	Mickey Mantle HR 21	350.00
MM	Mickey Mantle HR 22	350.00
MM	Mickey Mantle HR 23	350.00
MM	Mickey Mantle HR 24	350.00
MM	Mickey Mantle HR 26	350.00
MM	Mickey Mantle HR 27	350.00
MM	Mickey Mantle HR 28	350.00
MM	Mickey Mantle HR 29	350.00
MM	Mickey Mantle HR 30	350.00
MM	Mickey Mantle HR 31	350.00

Code	Name	Price
MM	Mickey Mantle HR 32	350.00
MM	Mickey Mantle HR 33	350.00
MM	Mickey Mantle HR 34	350.00
MM	Mickey Mantle HR 35	350.00
MM	Mickey Mantle HR 36	350.00
MM	Mickey Mantle HR 37	350.00
MM	Mickey Mantle HR 38	350.00
MM	Mickey Mantle HR 39	350.00
MM	Mickey Mantle HR 40	350.00
MM	Mickey Mantle HR 50	350.00
MM	Mickey Mantle HR 60	350.00
MM	Mickey Mantle HR 41	350.00
MM	Mickey Mantle HR 42	350.00
MM	Mickey Mantle HR 43	350.00
MM	Mickey Mantle HR 44	350.00
MM	Mickey Mantle HR 45	350.00
MM	Mickey Mantle HR 46	350.00
MM	Mickey Mantle HR 47	350.00
MM	Mickey Mantle HR 48	350.00
MM	Mickey Mantle HR 49	350.00
MM	Mickey Mantle HR 51	350.00
MM	Mickey Mantle HR 52	350.00
MM	Mickey Mantle HR 53	350.00
MM	Mickey Mantle HR 54	350.00
MM	Mickey Mantle HR 55	350.00
MM	Mickey Mantle HR 56	350.00
MM	Mickey Mantle HR 57	350.00
MM	Mickey Mantle HR 58	350.00
MM	Mickey Mantle HR 59	350.00
MM	Mickey Mantle HR 75	350.00
MM	Mickey Mantle HR 61	350.00
MM	Mickey Mantle HR 62	350.00
MM	Mickey Mantle HR 63	350.00
MM	Mickey Mantle HR 64	350.00
MM	Mickey Mantle HR 65	350.00
MM	Mickey Mantle HR 66	350.00
MM	Mickey Mantle HR 67	350.00
MM	Mickey Mantle HR 68	350.00
MM	Mickey Mantle HR 69	350.00
MM	Mickey Mantle HR 70	350.00
MM	Mickey Mantle HR 71	350.00
MM	Mickey Mantle HR 72	350.00
MM	Mickey Mantle HR 73	350.00
MM	Mickey Mantle HR 74	350.00
MM	Mickey Mantle HR 76	350.00
MM	Mickey Mantle HR 77	350.00
MM	Mickey Mantle HR 78	350.00
MM	Mickey Mantle HR 79	350.00
MM	Mickey Mantle HR 80	350.00
MM	Mickey Mantle HR 90	350.00
MM	Mickey Mantle HR 81	350.00
MM	Mickey Mantle HR 82	350.00
MM	Mickey Mantle HR 83	350.00
MM	Mickey Mantle HR 84	350.00
MM	Mickey Mantle HR 85	350.00
MM	Mickey Mantle HR 86	350.00
MM	Mickey Mantle HR 87	350.00
MM	Mickey Mantle HR 88	350.00
MM	Mickey Mantle HR 89	350.00

Code	Name	Price
MM	Mickey Mantle HR 91	350.00
MM	Mickey Mantle HR 92	350.00
MM	Mickey Mantle HR 93	350.00
MM	Mickey Mantle HR 94	350.00
MM	Mickey Mantle HR 95	350.00
MM	Mickey Mantle HR 96	350.00
MM	Mickey Mantle HR 97	350.00
MM	Mickey Mantle HR 98	350.00
MM	Mickey Mantle HR 99	350.00
MM	Mickey Mantle HR 100	350.00
JG	Josh Gibson	500.00
JG	Josh Gibson	500.00
JG	Josh Gibson	500.00
JG	Josh Gibson	500.00
JG	Josh Gibson	500.00
JG	Josh Gibson	500.00
RH	Rickey Henderson 1980	60.00
RH	Rickey Henderson 1981	60.00
RH	Rickey Henderson 1982	60.00
RH	Rickey Henderson 1983	60.00
RH	Rickey Henderson 1984	60.00
RH	Rickey Henderson 1990	60.00
RH	Rickey Henderson 1998	60.00
RH	Rickey Henderson 1989	60.00
RH	Rickey Henderson 1991	60.00
RH	Rickey Henderson 1985	60.00
RH	Rickey Henderson 1986	60.00
RH	Rickey Henderson 1987	60.00
RH	Rickey Henderson 1980	60.00
RH	Rickey Henderson 1983	60.00
RH	Rickey Henderson 1990	60.00
RH	Rickey Henderson 1982	60.00
RH	Rickey Henderson 1984	60.00
RH	Rickey Henderson 1991	60.00
RH	Rickey Henderson 1985	60.00
RH	Rickey Henderson 1986	60.00
RH	Rickey Henderson 1987	60.00
RH	Rickey Henderson 1988	60.00
RH	Rickey Henderson 1981	60.00
RH	Rickey Henderson 1990	60.00
RH	Rickey Henderson 1989	60.00
RH	Rickey Henderson 1986	60.00
RH	Rickey Henderson 1988	60.00
RH	Rickey Henderson 1981	60.00
RH	Rickey Henderson 1990	60.00
RH	Rickey Henderson 1989	60.00
RH	Rickey Henderson 1986	60.00
RH	Rickey Henderson 1985	60.00
RH	Rickey Henderson 1983	60.00
RH	Rickey Henderson 1998	60.00
RH	Rickey Henderson 1982	60.00
RH	Rickey Henderson 1989	60.00
RH	Rickey Henderson 1990	60.00
RH	Rickey Henderson 1981	60.00
RH	Rickey Henderson 1985	60.00
TW	Ted Williams 0.406	150.00
TW	Ted Williams 0.5	150.00
TW	Ted Williams 0.308	150.00
TW	Ted Williams 0.341	150.00
TW	Ted Williams 0.421	150.00
TW	Ted Williams 0.436	150.00
TW	Ted Williams 0.42	150.00
TW	Ted Williams 0.405	150.00
TW	Ted Williams 0.397	150.00
TW	Ted Williams 0.4	150.00
TW	Ted Williams 0.414	150.00
TW	Ted Williams 0.409	150.00
TW	Ted Williams 0.411	150.00
TW	Ted Williams 0.399	150.00
TW	Ted Williams 0.404	150.00
TW	Ted Williams HR 1	150.00
TW	Ted Williams HR 20	150.00
TW	Ted Williams HR 36	150.00
TW	Ted Williams HR 1	150.00
TW	Ted Williams HR 10	150.00

Code	Description	Price
TW	Ted Williams HR 20	150.00
TW	Ted Williams HR 30	150.00
TW	Ted Williams HR 32	150.00
RC	Roberto Clemente HIT 1	200.00
RC	Roberto Clemente HIT 2	200.00
RC	Roberto Clemente HIT 3	200.00
RC	Roberto Clemente HIT 4	200.00
RC	Roberto Clemente HIT 5	200.00
RC	Roberto Clemente HIT 6	200.00
RC	Roberto Clemente HIT 7	200.00
RC	Roberto Clemente HIT 8	200.00
RC	Roberto Clemente HIT 9	200.00
RC	Roberto Clemente HIT 10	200.00
RC	Roberto Clemente HIT 11	200.00
RC	Roberto Clemente HIT 12	200.00
RC	Roberto Clemente HIT 21	200.00
RC	Roberto Clemente HIT 13	200.00
RC	Roberto Clemente HIT 14	200.00
RC	Roberto Clemente HIT 15	200.00
RC	Roberto Clemente HIT 16	200.00
RC	Roberto Clemente HIT 17	200.00
RC	Roberto Clemente HIT 18	200.00
RC	Roberto Clemente HIT 19	200.00
RC	Roberto Clemente HIT 20	200.00
RC	Roberto Clemente 1966	200.00
RC	Roberto Clemente 1971	200.00
RC	Roberto Clemente 1972	200.00
RC	Roberto Clemente 1961	200.00
RC	Roberto Clemente 1962	200.00
RC	Roberto Clemente 1963	200.00
RC	Roberto Clemente 1964	200.00
RC	Roberto Clemente 1965	200.00
RC	Roberto Clemente 1967	200.00
RC	Roberto Clemente 1968	200.00
RC	Roberto Clemente 1969	200.00
RC	Roberto Clemente 1970	200.00
NR	Nolan Ryan SO 1	100.00
NR	Nolan Ryan SO 50	100.00
NR	Nolan Ryan SO 100	100.00
NR	Nolan Ryan SO 200	100.00
NR	Nolan Ryan SO 10	100.00
NR	Nolan Ryan SO 20	100.00
NR	Nolan Ryan SO 30	100.00
NR	Nolan Ryan SO 40	100.00
NR	Nolan Ryan SO 60	100.00
NR	Nolan Ryan SO 70	100.00
NR	Nolan Ryan SO 80	100.00
NR	Nolan Ryan SO 90	100.00
NR	Nolan Ryan SO 125	100.00
NR	Nolan Ryan SO 150	100.00
NR	Nolan Ryan SO 175	100.00
NR	Nolan Ryan SO 225	100.00
NR	Nolan Ryan SO 300	100.00
NR	Nolan Ryan SO 350	100.00
NR	Nolan Ryan SO 380	100.00
NR	Nolan Ryan SO 382	100.00
NR	Nolan Ryan SO 383	100.00
NR	Nolan Ryan SO 250	100.00
NR	Nolan Ryan SO 275	100.00
NR	Nolan Ryan SO 310	100.00
NR	Nolan Ryan SO 320	100.00
NR	Nolan Ryan SO 330	100.00
NR	Nolan Ryan SO 340	100.00
NR	Nolan Ryan SO 360	100.00
NR	Nolan Ryan SO 370	100.00
NR	Nolan Ryan SO 375	100.00
NR	Nolan Ryan NO HIT 1	100.00
NR	Nolan Ryan NO HIT 2	100.00
NR	Nolan Ryan NO HIT 3	100.00
NR	Nolan Ryan NO HIT 4	100.00
NR	Nolan Ryan NO HIT 5	100.00
NR	Nolan Ryan NO HIT 6	100.00
NR	Nolan Ryan NO HIT 7	100.00
CR	Cal Ripken Jr. 1983	100.00
CR	Cal Ripken Jr. 1985	100.00
CR	Cal Ripken Jr. 1987	100.00
CR	Cal Ripken Jr. 1989	100.00
CR	Cal Ripken Jr. 1991	100.00
CR	Cal Ripken Jr. 1993	100.00
CR	Cal Ripken Jr. 1995	100.00
CR	Cal Ripken Jr. 1997	100.00
CR	Cal Ripken Jr. 1999	100.00
CR	Cal Ripken Jr. 2001	100.00
CR	Cal Ripken Jr. 1984	100.00
CR	Cal Ripken Jr. 1986	100.00
CR	Cal Ripken Jr. 1988	100.00
CR	Cal Ripken Jr. 1990	100.00
CR	Cal Ripken Jr. 1992	100.00
CR	Cal Ripken Jr. 1994	100.00
CR	Cal Ripken Jr. 1996	100.00
CR	Cal Ripken Jr. 1998	100.00
CR	Cal Ripken Jr. 2000	100.00
CR	Cal Ripken Jr. 1984	100.00
CR	Cal Ripken Jr. 1986	100.00
CR	Cal Ripken Jr. 1991	100.00
CR	Cal Ripken Jr. 1994	100.00
CR	Cal Ripken Jr. 1983	100.00
CR	Cal Ripken Jr. 1985	100.00
CR	Cal Ripken Jr. 1989	100.00
CR	Cal Ripken Jr. 1993	100.00
CR	Cal Ripken Jr. HIT 1	100.00
CR	Cal Ripken Jr. 1000	100.00
CR	Cal Ripken Jr. 1500	100.00
CR	Cal Ripken Jr. 2000	100.00
CR	Cal Ripken Jr. 2500	100.00
CR	Cal Ripken Jr. 2900	100.00
CR	Cal Ripken Jr. 3000	100.00
CR	Cal Ripken Jr. 3184	100.00
CR	Cal Ripken Jr. 100	100.00
CR	Cal Ripken Jr. 200	100.00
CR	Cal Ripken Jr. 300	100.00
CR	Cal Ripken Jr. 400	100.00
CR	Cal Ripken Jr. 500	100.00
CR	Cal Ripken Jr. 2100	100.00
CR	Cal Ripken Jr. 2200	100.00
CR	Cal Ripken Jr. 2300	100.00
CR	Cal Ripken Jr. 2400	100.00
CR	Cal Ripken Jr. 2600	100.00
CR	Cal Ripken Jr. 2700	100.00
CR	Cal Ripken Jr. 2800	100.00
CR	Cal Ripken Jr. HR 1	100.00
CR	HR 100	100.00
CR	HR 200	100.00
CR	Cal Ripken Jr. HR 300	100.00
CR	Cal Ripken Jr. HR 400	100.00
CR	Cal Ripken Jr. HR 431	100.00
CR	Cal Ripken Jr. HR 10	100.00
CR	Cal Ripken Jr. HR 25	100.00
CR	Cal Ripken Jr. HR 50	100.00
CR	Cal Ripken Jr. HR 75	100.00
CR	Cal Ripken Jr. HR 125	100.00
CR	Cal Ripken Jr. HR 150	100.00
CR	Cal Ripken Jr. HR 175	100.00
CR	Cal Ripken Jr. HR 225	100.00
CR	Cal Ripken Jr. HR 250	100.00
CR	Cal Ripken Jr. HR 275	100.00
CR	Cal Ripken Jr. HR 325	100.00
CR	Cal Ripken Jr. HR 350	100.00
CR	Cal Ripken Jr. HR 375	100.00
CR	Cal Ripken Jr. HR 425	100.00
CR	Cal Ripken Jr. GM 1	100.00
CR	Cal Ripken Jr. 500	100.00
CR	Cal Ripken Jr. 1000	100.00
CR	Cal Ripken Jr. 2000	100.00
CR	Cal Ripken Jr. 2130	100.00
CR	Cal Ripken Jr. 2131	100.00
CR	Cal Ripken Jr. 2632	100.00
CR	Cal Ripken Jr. 100	100.00
CR	Cal Ripken Jr. 200	100.00
CR	Cal Ripken Jr. 300	100.00
CR	Cal Ripken Jr. 400	100.00
CR	Cal Ripken Jr. 600	100.00
CR	Cal Ripken Jr. 700	100.00
CR	Cal Ripken Jr. 800	100.00
CR	Cal Ripken Jr. 900	100.00
CR	Cal Ripken Jr. 1250	100.00
CR	Cal Ripken Jr. 1500	100.00
CR	Cal Ripken Jr. 1750	100.00
CR	Cal Ripken Jr. 2500	100.00
CR	Cal Ripken Jr. 2600	100.00
SM	Stan Musial 1943	75.00
SM	Stan Musial 1946	75.00
SM	Stan Musial 1948	75.00
SM	Stan Musial 1950	75.00
SM	Stan Musial 1952	75.00
SM	Stan Musial 1942	75.00
SM	Stan Musial 1944	75.00
SM	Stan Musial 1947	75.00
SM	Stan Musial 1949	75.00
SM	Stan Musial 1951	75.00
SM	Stan Musial 1954	75.00
SM	Stan Musial 1956	75.00
SM	Stan Musial 1958	75.00
SM	Stan Musial 1962	75.00
SM	Stan Musial 1953	75.00
SM	Stan Musial 1955	75.00
SM	Stan Musial 1957	75.00
SM	Stan Musial 1959	75.00
SM	Stan Musial 1961	75.00
RJ	Reggie Jackson HR 1	60.00
RJ	Reggie Jackson HR 100	60.00
RJ	Reggie Jackson HR 200	60.00
RJ	Reggie Jackson HR 250	60.00
RJ	Reggie Jackson HR 300	60.00
RJ	Reggie Jackson HR 350	60.00
RJ	Reggie Jackson HR 400	60.00
RJ	Reggie Jackson HR 450	60.00
RJ	Reggie Jackson HR 550	60.00
RJ	Reggie Jackson HR 25	60.00
RJ	Reggie Jackson HR 50	60.00
RJ	Reggie Jackson HR 75	60.00
RJ	Reggie Jackson HR 150	60.00
JB	Johnny Bench 1968	65.00
JB	Johnny Bench 1969	65.00
JB	Johnny Bench 1971	65.00
JB	Johnny Bench 1973	65.00
JB	Johnny Bench 1975	65.00
JB	Johnny Bench 1976	65.00
GB	George Brett HIT 1	60.00
GB	George Brett HIT 3	60.00
GB	George Brett HIT 5	60.00
GB	George Brett HIT 7	60.00
GB	George Brett HIT 10	60.00
GB	George Brett HIT 12	60.00
GB	George Brett HIT 15	60.00
GB	George Brett HIT 16	60.00
GB	George Brett HIT 17	60.00
GB	George Brett HIT 18	60.00
GB	George Brett HIT 2	60.00
GB	George Brett HIT 4	60.00
GB	George Brett HIT 6	60.00
GB	George Brett HIT 8	60.00
GB	George Brett HIT 9	60.00
GB	George Brett HIT 11	60.00
GB	George Brett HIT 13	60.00
GB	George Brett HIT 14	60.00
GB	George Brett 1976	60.00
GB	George Brett 1980	60.00
GB	George Brett 1990	60.00
GB	George Brett 1976	60.00
GB	George Brett 1977	60.00
GB	George Brett 1979	60.00
GB	George Brett 1981	60.00
GB	George Brett 1983	60.00
GB	George Brett 1985	60.00
GB	George Brett 1988	60.00
GB	George Brett 1978	60.00
GB	George Brett 1980	60.00
GB	George Brett 1982	60.00
GB	George Brett 1984	60.00
GB	George Brett 1986	60.00
GB	George Brett 1980	60.00
GB	George Brett 1985	60.00
GB	George Brett 1988	60.00
RM	Roger Maris HR 1	125.00
RM	Roger Maris HR 2	125.00
RM	Roger Maris HR 5	125.00
RM	Roger Maris HR 9	125.00
RM	Roger Maris HR 10	125.00
RM	Roger Maris HR 15	125.00
RM	Roger Maris HR 3	125.00
RM	Roger Maris HR 4	125.00
RM	Roger Maris HR 6	125.00
RM	Roger Maris HR 7	125.00
RM	Roger Maris HR 8	125.00
RM	Roger Maris HR 11	125.00
RM	Roger Maris HR 12	125.00
RM	Roger Maris HR 13	125.00
RM	Roger Maris HR 14	125.00
RM	Roger Maris HR 20	125.00
RM	Roger Maris HR 25	125.00
RM	Roger Maris HR 30	125.00
RM	Roger Maris HR 16	125.00
RM	Roger Maris HR 17	125.00
RM	Roger Maris HR 18	125.00
RM	Roger Maris HR 19	125.00
RM	Roger Maris HR 21	125.00
RM	Roger Maris HR 22	125.00
RM	Roger Maris HR 23	125.00
RM	Roger Maris HR 24	125.00
RM	Roger Maris HR 26	125.00
RM	Roger Maris HR 27	125.00
RM	Roger Maris HR 28	125.00
RM	Roger Maris HR 29	125.00
YB	Yogi Berra 1951	75.00
YB	Yogi Berra 1951	75.00
YB	Yogi Berra 1954	75.00
YB	Yogi Berra 1955	75.00
MS	Mike Schmidt HR 1	50.00
MS	Mike Schmidt HR 2	50.00
MS	Mike Schmidt HR 3	50.00
MS	Mike Schmidt HR 4	50.00
CY	Carl Yastrzemski HR 1	60.00
CY	Carl Yastrzemski HR 5	60.00
CY	Carl Yastrzemski HR 10	60.00
CY	Carl Yastrzemski HR 15	60.00
CY	Carl Yastrzemski HR 2	60.00
CY	Carl Yastrzemski HR 3	60.00
CY	Carl Yastrzemski HR 4	60.00
CY	Carl Yastrzemski HR 6	60.00
CY	Carl Yastrzemski HR 7	60.00
CY	Carl Yastrzemski HR 8	60.00
CY	Carl Yastrzemski HR 9	60.00
CY	Carl Yastrzemski HR 11	60.00
CY	Carl Yastrzemski HR 12	60.00
CY	Carl Yastrzemski HR 13	60.00
CY	Carl Yastrzemski HR 14	60.00
CY	Carl Yastrzemski HR 20	60.00
CY	Carl Yastrzemski HR 25	60.00
CY	Carl Yastrzemski HR 30	60.00
CY	Carl Yastrzemski HR 16	60.00
CY	Carl Yastrzemski HR 17	60.00
CY	Carl Yastrzemski HR 18	60.00
CY	Carl Yastrzemski HR 19	60.00
CY	Carl Yastrzemski HR 21	60.00
CY	Carl Yastrzemski HR 22	60.00
CY	Carl Yastrzemski HR 23	60.00
CY	Carl Yastrzemski HR 24	60.00
CY	Carl Yastrzemski HR 26	60.00
CY	Carl Yastrzemski HR 27	60.00
CY	Carl Yastrzemski HR 28	60.00
CY	Carl Yastrzemski HR 29	60.00
CY	Carl Yastrzemski HR 35	60.00
CY	Carl Yastrzemski HR 40	60.00
CY	Carl Yastrzemski HR 44	60.00
CY	Carl Yastrzemski HR 31	60.00
CY	Carl Yastrzemski HR 32	60.00
CY	Carl Yastrzemski HR 33	60.00
CY	Carl Yastrzemski HR 34	60.00
CY	Carl Yastrzemski HR 36	60.00
CY	Carl Yastrzemski HR 37	60.00
CY	Carl Yastrzemski HR 38	60.00
CY	Carl Yastrzemski HR 39	60.00
CY	Carl Yastrzemski HR 41	60.00
CY	Carl Yastrzemski HR 42	60.00
CY	Carl Yastrzemski HR 43	60.00
CY	Carl Yastrzemski 1961	60.00
CY	Carl Yastrzemski 1964	60.00
CY	Carl Yastrzemski 1966	60.00
CY	Carl Yastrzemski 1967	60.00
CY	Carl Yastrzemski 1970	60.00
CY	Carl Yastrzemski 1972	60.00
CY	Carl Yastrzemski 1962	60.00
CY	Carl Yastrzemski 1963	60.00
CY	Carl Yastrzemski 1965	60.00
CY	Carl Yastrzemski 1968	60.00
CY	Carl Yastrzemski 1969	60.00
CY	Carl Yastrzemski 1971	60.00
CY	Carl Yastrzemski 1973	60.00
CY	Carl Yastrzemski 1975	60.00
CY	Carl Yastrzemski 1977	60.00
CY	Carl Yastrzemski 1980	60.00
CY	Carl Yastrzemski 1983	60.00
CY	Carl Yastrzemski 1974	60.00
CY	Carl Yastrzemski 1976	60.00
CY	Carl Yastrzemski 1978	60.00
CY	Carl Yastrzemski 1979	60.00
CY	Carl Yastrzemski 1981	60.00
CY	Carl Yastrzemski 1982	60.00
CY	Carl Yastrzemski 1963	60.00
CY	Carl Yastrzemski 1965	60.00
CY	Carl Yastrzemski 1966	60.00
CY	Carl Yastrzemski 1967	60.00
CY	Carl Yastrzemski 1968	60.00
CY	Carl Yastrzemski 1969	60.00
CY	Carl Yastrzemski 1970	60.00
CY	Carl Yastrzemski 1971	60.00
CY	Carl Yastrzemski 1972	60.00
CY	Carl Yastrzemski 1973	60.00
CY	Carl Yastrzemski 1974	60.00
CY	Carl Yastrzemski 1975	60.00
CY	Carl Yastrzemski 1976	60.00
CY	Carl Yastrzemski 1977	60.00
CY	Carl Yastrzemski 1978	60.00
CY	Carl Yastrzemski 1979	60.00
TG	Tony Gwynn 1984	60.00
TG	Tony Gwynn 1987	60.00
TG	Tony Gwynn 1988	60.00
TG	Tony Gwynn 1989	60.00
TG	Tony Gwynn 1994	60.00
TG	Tony Gwynn 1995	60.00
TG	Tony Gwynn 1996	60.00
TG	Tony Gwynn 1997	60.00
RS	Ryne Sandberg 1984	70.00
RS	Ryne Sandberg 1988	70.00
RS	Ryne Sandberg 1990	70.00
RS	Ryne Sandberg 1992	70.00
RS	Ryne Sandberg 1983	70.00
RS	Ryne Sandberg 1985	70.00
RS	Ryne Sandberg 1987	70.00
RS	Ryne Sandberg 1989	70.00

Moments Relics Autographs

NM/M

Production 10 Sets
Prime: No Pricing
Production One Set

Code	Description	Price
RH	Rickey Henderson 1980	125.00
RH	Rickey Henderson 1981	125.00
RH	Rickey Henderson 1982	125.00
RH	Rickey Henderson 1983	125.00
RH	Rickey Henderson 1984	125.00
RH	Rickey Henderson 1990	125.00
RH	Rickey Henderson 1998	125.00
RH	Rickey Henderson 1985	125.00
RH	Rickey Henderson 1986	125.00
RH	Rickey Henderson 1987	125.00
RH	Rickey Henderson 1980	125.00
RH	Rickey Henderson 1983	125.00
RH	Rickey Henderson 1990	125.00
RH	Rickey Henderson 1985	125.00
RH	Rickey Henderson 1986	125.00
RH	Rickey Henderson 1987	125.00
RH	Rickey Henderson 1981	125.00
RH	Rickey Henderson 1990	125.00
RH	Rickey Henderson 1986	125.00
RH	Rickey Henderson 1983	125.00
RH	Rickey Henderson 1998	125.00
RH	Rickey Henderson 1990	125.00
NR	Nolan Ryan SO 1	300.00
NR	Nolan Ryan SO 50	300.00
NR	Nolan Ryan SO 200	300.00
NR	Nolan Ryan SO 300	300.00
NR	Nolan Ryan SO 350	300.00
NR	Nolan Ryan SO 380	300.00
NR	Nolan Ryan SO 382	300.00
NR	Nolan Ryan SO 383	300.00
NR	Nolan Ryan NO HIT 1	300.00
NR	Nolan Ryan NO HIT 2	300.00
NR	Nolan Ryan NO HIT 3	300.00
NR	Nolan Ryan NO HIT 4	300.00
NR	Nolan Ryan NO HIT 5	300.00
NR	Nolan Ryan NO HIT 6	300.00
NR	Nolan Ryan NO HIT 7	300.00
CR	Cal Ripken Jr. 1983	300.00
CR	Cal Ripken Jr. 1985	300.00
CR	Cal Ripken Jr. 1987	300.00
CR	Cal Ripken Jr. 1989	300.00
CR	Cal Ripken Jr. 1991	300.00
CR	Cal Ripken Jr. 1993	300.00
CR	Cal Ripken Jr. 1995	300.00
CR	Cal Ripken Jr. 1997	300.00
CR	Cal Ripken Jr. 1999	300.00
CR	Cal Ripken Jr. 2001	300.00
CR	Cal Ripken Jr. 1984	300.00
CR	Cal Ripken Jr. 1986	300.00
CR	Cal Ripken Jr. 1991	300.00
CR	Cal Ripken Jr. 1994	300.00
CR	Cal Ripken Jr. HIT 1	300.00
CR	Cal Ripken Jr. 1000	300.00
CR	Cal Ripken Jr. 1500	300.00
CR	Cal Ripken Jr. 2000	300.00
CR	Cal Ripken Jr. 2500	300.00
CR	Cal Ripken Jr. 2900	300.00
CR	Cal Ripken Jr. 3000	300.00
CR	Cal Ripken Jr. 3184	300.00
CR	Cal Ripken Jr. HR 1	300.00
CR	Cal Ripken Jr. HR 100	300.00
CR	Cal Ripken Jr. HR 200	300.00
CR	Cal Ripken Jr. HR 300	300.00
CR	Cal Ripken Jr. HR 400	300.00
CR	Cal Ripken Jr. HR 431	300.00
CR	Cal Ripken Jr. GM 1	300.00
CR	Cal Ripken Jr. 500	300.00
CR	Cal Ripken Jr. 1000	300.00
CR	Cal Ripken Jr. 2000	300.00
CR	Cal Ripken Jr. 2130	300.00
CR	Cal Ripken Jr. 2131	300.00
CR	Cal Ripken Jr. 2632	300.00
SM	Stan Musial 1941	150.00
SM	Stan Musial 1943	150.00
SM	Stan Musial 1946	150.00
SM	Stan Musial 1948	150.00
SM	Stan Musial 1950	150.00
SM	Stan Musial 1952	150.00
SM	Stan Musial 1954	150.00
SM	Stan Musial 1956	150.00
SM	Stan Musial 1958	150.00
SM	Stan Musial 1960	150.00
SM	Stan Musial 1962	150.00
SM	Stan Musial 1963	150.00
RJ	Reggie Jackson HR 1	150.00
RJ	Reggie Jackson HR 100	150.00
RJ	Reggie Jackson HR 200	150.00
RJ	Reggie Jackson HR 250	150.00
RJ	Reggie Jackson HR 300	150.00
RJ	Reggie Jackson HR 350	150.00
RJ	Reggie Jackson HR 400	150.00
RJ	Reggie Jackson HR 450	150.00
RJ	Reggie Jackson HR 500	150.00
RJ	Reggie Jackson HR 550	150.00
RJ	Reggie Jackson HR 563	150.00
RJ	Reggie Jackson WSHR 1	150.00
RJ	Reggie Jackson WSHR 2	150.00
RJ	Reggie Jackson WS HR 3	150.00
RJ	Reggie Jackson 500 HR	150.00
JB	Johnny Bench 1968	150.00
JB	Johnny Bench 1969	150.00
JB	Johnny Bench 1970	150.00
JB	Johnny Bench 1971	150.00
JB	Johnny Bench 1972	150.00
JB	Johnny Bench 1973	150.00
JB	Johnny Bench 1974	150.00
JB	Johnny Bench 1975	150.00
JB	Johnny Bench 1976	150.00
JB	Johnny Bench 1977	150.00
JB	Johnny Bench 1975	150.00
JB	Johnny Bench 1976	150.00
GB	George Brett HIT 3	150.00
GB	George Brett HIT 5	150.00
GB	George Brett HIT 7	150.00
GB	George Brett HIT 10	150.00
GB	George Brett HIT 12	150.00
GB	George Brett HIT 15	150.00
GB	George Brett HIT 16	150.00
GB	George Brett HIT 17	150.00

Code	Player	Price
GB	George Brett HIT 18	150.00
GB	George Brett 1976	150.00
GB	George Brett 1980	150.00
GB	George Brett 1990	150.00
GB	George Brett 1976	150.00
GB	George Brett 1977	150.00
GB	George Brett 1979	150.00
GB	George Brett 1981	150.00
GB	George Brett 1983	150.00
GB	George Brett 1985	150.00
GB	George Brett 1988	150.00
DM	Don Mattingly GS 1	140.00
DM	Don Mattingly GS 2	140.00
DM	Don Mattingly GS 3	140.00
DM	Don Mattingly GS 4	140.00
DM	Don Mattingly GS 5	140.00
DM	Don Mattingly GS 6	140.00
DM	Don Mattingly HR 1	140.00
DM	Don Mattingly HR 2	140.00
DM	Don Mattingly HR 3	140.00
DM	Don Mattingly HR 4	140.00
DM	Don Mattingly HR 5	140.00
DM	Don Mattingly HR 6	140.00
DM	Don Mattingly HR 7	140.00
DM	Don Mattingly HR 8	140.00
DM	Don Mattingly HR 9	140.00
DM	Don Mattingly 1985	140.00
DM	Don Mattingly 1986	140.00
DM	Don Mattingly 1987	140.00
DM	Don Mattingly 1988	140.00
DM	Don Mattingly 1989	140.00
DM	Don Mattingly 1991	140.00
DM	Don Mattingly 1992	140.00
DM	Don Mattingly 1993	140.00
DM	Don Mattingly 1994	140.00
DM	Don Mattingly 1984	140.00
DM	Don Mattingly 1985	140.00
DM	Don Mattingly 1986	140.00
DM	Don Mattingly 1987	140.00
DM	Don Mattingly 1988	140.00
DM	Don Mattingly 1989	140.00
DM	Don Mattingly HR 1	140.00
DM	Don Mattingly HR 2	140.00
DM	Don Mattingly HR 3	140.00
DM	Don Mattingly HR 4	140.00
DM	Don Mattingly HR 5	140.00
DM	Don Mattingly HR 6	140.00
DM	Don Mattingly HR 7	140.00
DM	Don Mattingly HR 8	140.00
DM	Don Mattingly HR 9	140.00
RC	Rod Carew 1967	80.00
RC	Rod Carew 1968	80.00
RC	Rod Carew 1969	80.00
RC	Rod Carew 1970	80.00
RC	Rod Carew 1971	80.00
RC	Rod Carew 1972	80.00
RC	Rod Carew 1973	80.00
RC	Rod Carew 1974	80.00
RC	Rod Carew 1975	80.00
RC	Rod Carew 1976	80.00
RC	Rod Carew 1977	80.00
RC	Rod Carew 1978	80.00
RC	Rod Carew 1979	80.00
RC	Rod Carew 1980	80.00
RC	Rod Carew 1981	80.00
RC	Rod Carew 1982	80.00
RC	Rod Carew 1983	80.00
RC	Rod Carew 1984	80.00
RC	Rod Carew SH 1	80.00
RC	Rod Carew SH 2	80.00
RC	Rod Carew SH 3	80.00
RC	Rod Carew SH 4	80.00
RC	Rod Carew SH 5	80.00
RC	Rod Carew SH 6	80.00
RC	Rod Carew SH 7	80.00
RC	Rod Carew 100	80.00
RC	Rod Carew 200	80.00
RC	Rod Carew 300	80.00
RC	Rod Carew 400	80.00
RC	Rod Carew 500	80.00
RC	Rod Carew 600	80.00
RC	Rod Carew 700	80.00
RC	Rod Carew 800	80.00
RC	Rod Carew 900	80.00
RC	Rod Carew 1969	80.00
RC	Rod Carew 1972	80.00
RC	Rod Carew 1973	80.00
RC	Rod Carew 1974	80.00
RC	Rod Carew 1975	80.00
RC	Rod Carew 1977	80.00
RC	Rod Carew 1978	80.00
YB	Yogi Berra 1947	160.00
YB	Yogi Berra 1949	160.00
YB	Yogi Berra 1950	160.00
YB	Yogi Berra 1951	160.00
YB	Yogi Berra 1952	160.00
YB	Yogi Berra 1953	160.00
YB	Yogi Berra 1956	160.00
YB	Yogi Berra 1958	160.00
YB	Yogi Berra 1961	160.00
YB	Yogi Berra 1962	160.00
YB	Yogi Berra 1948	160.00
YB	Yogi Berra 1949	160.00
YB	Yogi Berra 1950	160.00
YB	Yogi Berra 1951	160.00
YB	Yogi Berra 1952	160.00
YB	Yogi Berra 1953	160.00
YB	Yogi Berra 1954	160.00
YB	Yogi Berra 1955	160.00
YB	Yogi Berra 1956	160.00
YB	Yogi Berra 1957	160.00
YB	Yogi Berra 1958	160.00
YB	Yogi Berra 1959	160.00
YB	Yogi Berra 1960	160.00
YB	Yogi Berra 1961	160.00
YB	Yogi Berra 1962	160.00
MS	Mike Schmidt HR 1	140.00
MS	Mike Schmidt HR 2	140.00

Code	Player	Price
MS	Mike Schmidt HR 3	140.00
MS	Mike Schmidt HR 4	140.00
MS	Mike Schmidt HIT 1	140.00
MS	Mike Schmidt HIT 2	140.00
MS	Mike Schmidt HIT 3	140.00
MS	Mike Schmidt HIT 4	140.00
MS	Mike Schmidt HIT 5	140.00
MS	Mike Schmidt HIT 6	140.00
MS	Mike Schmidt HIT 7	140.00
MS	Mike Schmidt HIT 8	140.00
MS	Mike Schmidt RUN 1	140.00
MS	Mike Schmidt RUN 2	140.00
MS	Mike Schmidt RUN 3	140.00
MS	Mike Schmidt RUN 4	140.00
MS	Mike Schmidt RUN 5	140.00
CY	Carl Yastrzemski HR 1	125.00
CY	Carl Yastrzemski HR 5	125.00
CY	Carl Yastrzemski HR 10	125.00
CY	Carl Yastrzemski HR 15	125.00
CY	Carl Yastrzemski HR 20	125.00
CY	Carl Yastrzemski HR 25	125.00
CY	Carl Yastrzemski HR 30	125.00
CY	Carl Yastrzemski HR 35	125.00
CY	Carl Yastrzemski HR 40	125.00
CY	Carl Yastrzemski HR 44	125.00
CY	Carl Yastrzemski 1961	125.00
CY	Carl Yastrzemski 1964	125.00
CY	Carl Yastrzemski 1966	125.00
CY	Carl Yastrzemski 1967	125.00
CY	Carl Yastrzemski 1970	125.00
CY	Carl Yastrzemski 1972	125.00
CY	Carl Yastrzemski 1973	125.00
CY	Carl Yastrzemski 1975	125.00
CY	Carl Yastrzemski 1977	125.00
CY	Carl Yastrzemski 1980	125.00
CY	Carl Yastrzemski 1963	125.00
CY	Carl Yastrzemski 1965	125.00
CY	Carl Yastrzemski 1966	125.00
CY	Carl Yastrzemski 1967	125.00
CY	Carl Yastrzemski 1968	125.00
CY	Carl Yastrzemski 1969	125.00
CY	Carl Yastrzemski 1970	125.00
CY	Carl Yastrzemski 1971	125.00
CY	Carl Yastrzemski 1972	125.00
CY	Carl Yastrzemski 1973	125.00
CY	Carl Yastrzemski 1974	125.00
CY	Carl Yastrzemski 1975	125.00
CY	Carl Yastrzemski 1976	125.00
CY	Carl Yastrzemski 1977	125.00
CY	Carl Yastrzemski 1978	125.00
CY	Carl Yastrzemski 1979	125.00
CY	Carl Yastrzemski 1982	125.00
CY	Carl Yastrzemski 1983	125.00
TG	Tony Gwynn 1983	120.00
TG	Tony Gwynn 1984	120.00
TG	Tony Gwynn 1985	120.00
TG	Tony Gwynn 1986	120.00
TG	Tony Gwynn 1987	120.00
TG	Tony Gwynn 1988	120.00
TG	Tony Gwynn 1989	120.00
TG	Tony Gwynn 1990	120.00
TG	Tony Gwynn 1991	120.00
TG	Tony Gwynn 1992	120.00
TG	Tony Gwynn 1993	120.00
TG	Tony Gwynn 1994	120.00
TG	Tony Gwynn 1995	120.00
TG	Tony Gwynn 1996	120.00
TG	Tony Gwynn 1997	120.00
TG	Tony Gwynn 1998	120.00
TG	Tony Gwynn 1999	120.00

Code	Player	Price
TG	Tony Gwynn 2000	120.00
TG	Tony Gwynn 2001	120.00
TG	Tony Gwynn 1984	120.00
TG	Tony Gwynn 1987	120.00
TG	Tony Gwynn 1988	120.00
VG	Tony Gwynn 1989	120.00
TG	Tony Gwynn 1994	120.00
TG	Tony Gwynn 1995	120.00
TG	Tony Gwynn 1996	120.00
TG	Tony Gwynn 1997	120.00
TG	Tony Gwynn 1984	120.00
TG	Tony Gwynn 1985	120.00
TG	Tony Gwynn 1986	120.00
TG	Tony Gwynn 1987	120.00
TG	Tony Gwynn 1989	120.00
TG	Tony Gwynn 1990	120.00
TG	Tony Gwynn 1991	120.00
TG	Tony Gwynn 1992	120.00
TG	Tony Gwynn 1993	120.00
TG	Tony Gwynn 1994	120.00
TG	Tony Gwynn 1995	120.00
TG	Tony Gwynn 1996	120.00
TG	Tony Gwynn 1997	120.00
TG	Tony Gwynn 1998	120.00
TG	Tony Gwynn 1999	120.00
TG	Tony Gwynn 1984	120.00
TG	Tony Gwynn 1986	120.00
TG	Tony Gwynn 1987	120.00
TG	Tony Gwynn 1989	120.00
TG	Tony Gwynn 1994	120.00
TG	Tony Gwynn 1995	120.00
TG	Tony Gwynn 1997	120.00
RS	Ryne Sandberg 1984	150.00
RS	Ryne Sandberg 1985	150.00
RS	Ryne Sandberg 1988	150.00
RS	Ryne Sandberg 1989	150.00
RS	Ryne Sandberg 1990	150.00
RS	Ryne Sandberg 1991	150.00
RS	Ryne Sandberg 1992	150.00
RS	Ryne Sandberg 1983	150.00
RS	Ryne Sandberg 1984	150.00
RS	Ryne Sandberg 1985	150.00
RS	Ryne Sandberg 1986	150.00
RS	Ryne Sandberg 1987	150.00
RS	Ryne Sandberg 1988	150.00
RS	Ryne Sandberg 1989	150.00
RS	Ryne Sandberg 1990	150.00
RS	Ryne Sandberg 1991	150.00
OS	Ozzie Smith 1980	100.00
OS	Ozzie Smith 1981	100.00
OS	Ozzie Smith 1982	100.00
OS	Ozzie Smith 1983	100.00
OS	Ozzie Smith 1984	100.00
OS	Ozzie Smith 1985	100.00
OS	Ozzie Smith 1986	100.00
OS	Ozzie Smith 1987	100.00
OS	Ozzie Smith 1988	100.00
OS	Ozzie Smith 1989	100.00
OS	Ozzie Smith 1990	100.00
OS	Ozzie Smith 1991	100.00
OS	Ozzie Smith 1992	100.00
OS	Ozzie Smith 2B 1	100.00
OS	Ozzie Smith 2B 2	100.00
OS	Ozzie Smith 2B 3	100.00
OS	Ozzie Smith 2B 4	100.00
OS	Ozzie Smith 2B 5	100.00
OS	Ozzie Smith 2B 6	100.00
OS	Ozzie Smith 2B 7	100.00
OS	Ozzie Smith 2B 8	100.00
OS	Ozzie Smith 2B 9	100.00
OS	Ozzie Smith 2B 10	100.00
OS	Ozzie Smith 2B 11	100.00
OS	Ozzie Smith 2B 12	100.00
OS	Ozzie Smith 2B 13	100.00
OS	Ozzie Smith 2B 14	100.00
OS	Ozzie Smith 2B 15	100.00
OS	Ozzie Smith 2B 16	100.00
OS	Ozzie Smith 2B 17	100.00
OS	Ozzie Smith 2B 18	100.00
OS	Ozzie Smith 2B 19	100.00
OS	Ozzie Smith 2B 20	100.00
OS	Ozzie Smith 2B 21	100.00
OS	Ozzie Smith 2B 22	100.00
OS	Ozzie Smith 2B 23	100.00
OS	Ozzie Smith 2B 24	100.00
OS	Ozzie Smith 2B 25	100.00
OS	Ozzie Smith 2B 26	100.00
OS	Ozzie Smith 2B 27	100.00
OS	Ozzie Smith 2B 28	100.00
OS	Ozzie Smith 2B 29	100.00
OS	Ozzie Smith 2B 30	100.00
OS	Ozzie Smith 2B 31	100.00
OS	Ozzie Smith 2B 32	100.00
OS	Ozzie Smith 2B 33	100.00
OS	Ozzie Smith 2B 34	100.00
OS	Ozzie Smith 2B 35	100.00
OS	Ozzie Smith 2B 36	100.00
OS	Ozzie Smith 2B 37	100.00
OS	Ozzie Smith 2B 38	100.00
OS	Ozzie Smith 2B 39	100.00
OS	Ozzie Smith 2B 40	100.00

Moments Relics Cut Signatures

Production 10 Sets
Prime: No Pricing
Production One Set

Quad Relics

Production 10 Sets
Prime: No Pricing
Production 10 Sets
Sterling Silver: No Pricing
Production One Set

Quad Relics Autographs

Production 10 Sets
Prime: No Pricing
Production 10 Sets
Sterling Silver: No Pricing
Production One Set

Season Stats Relics

Production 10 Sets
Prime: No Pricing
Production One Set
Sterling Silver: No Pricing
Production One Set

Season Stats Relics Autographs

Production 10 Sets
Prime: No Pricing
Production One Set
Sterling Silver: No Pricing
Production One Set

Six Relics

Production 10 Sets
Prime: No Pricing
Production 10 Sets
Sterling Silver: No Pricing
Production One Set

Six Relics Autographs

Production 10 Sets
Prime: No Pricing
Production 10 Sets
Sterling Silver: No Pricing
Production One Set

Triple Relics Autographs

Production 10 Sets
Prime: No Pricing
Production 10 Sets
Sterling Silver: No Pricing
Production One Set

Triple Threads

	NM/M
Complete Set (120):	
Common (1-100):	.50
Common (101-120):	
Production 225	
Pack (6):	140.00
Box (2):	270.00
1 Hideki Matsui	3.00
2 Josh Gibson	2.00
3 Roger Clemens	4.00
4 Paul Konerko	1.00
5 Brooks Robinson	1.00
6 Stan Musial	2.00
7 Dontrelle Willis	.75
8 Yogi Berra	1.50
9 John Smoltz	.75
10 Brian Roberts	.75
11 Gary Sheffield	.75
12 Wade Boggs	1.00
13 Alex Rodriguez	4.00
14 Ernie Banks	2.00
15 Ichiro Suzuki	3.00
16 Whitey Ford	1.00
17 Vladimir Guerrero	1.50
18 Tadahito Iguchi	.50
19 Robin Yount	1.50
20 Jason Schmidt	.50
21 Roberto Clemente	3.00
22 Andruw Jones	1.00
23 Don Mattingly	2.00
24 Joe Mauer	.50
25 Barry Bonds	4.00
26 Johnny Damon	1.50
27 Chris Carpenter	.75
28 Garret Anderson	.50
29 Scott Rolen	1.50
30 Tim Hudson	.75
31 Dave Winfield	.75
32 Steve Carlton	.75
33 Miguel Tejada	1.00
34 Nolan Ryan	3.00
35 Mark Buehrle	.75
36 Travis Hafner	.75
37 Rickie Weeks	.75
38 Sammy Sosa	1.50
39 Carlos Beltran	1.00
40 Todd Helton	1.00
41 Tom Seaver	1.50
42 Ted Williams	3.00
43 Alfonso Soriano	1.00
44 Reggie Jackson	1.00
45 Pedro Martinez	1.50
46 Randy Johnson	1.50
47 Ted Williams	3.00
48 Torii Hunter	.50
49 Manny Ramirez	1.50
50 George Brett	3.00
51 Chipper Jones	1.50
52 Nomar Garciaparra	1.50
53 Richie Sexson	.75
54 David Ortiz	1.50
55 Derek Jeter	4.00
56 Mickey Mantle	8.00
57 Michael Young	.75
58 Aramis Ramirez	.75
59 Bartolo Colon	.50
60 Troy Glaus	.75
61 Carlos Delgado	.75
62 Mike Sweeney	.50
63 Jorge Cantu	.50
64 Mike Mussina	.75
65 Hank Blalock	.75
66 Frank Robinson	1.50
67 Carl Yastrzemski	2.00
68 Adam Dunn	1.00
69 Eric Chavez	.75
70 Curt Schilling	1.50
71 Jeff Francoeur	.50
72 C.C. Sabathia	.50
73 Roy Oswalt	.50
74 Carlos Lee	.50
75 Barry Zito	.75
76 Derek Lee	1.00
77 Greg Maddux	3.00
78 Ivan Rodriguez	.75
79 Jeff Kent	.75
80 Gary Carter	.75
81 Jose Reyes	.75
82 Johan Santana	1.50
83 Magglio Ordonez	.50
84 Mark Prior	1.00
85 Johnny Bench	2.00
86 Vernon Wells	.75
87 Mark Mulder	.75
88 Cal Ripken Jr.	6.00
89 Mark Teixeira	1.00
90 Miguel Cabrera	1.50
91 Duke Snider	1.00
92 Jason Giambi	1.00
93 Albert Pujols	4.00
94 Carl Crawford	.75
95 Jim Edmonds	.75
96 Jose Contreras	.50
97 Victor Martinez	.50
98 Jeremy Bonderman	.50
99 Lance Berkman	.75
100 Rocco Baldelli	.50
101 Zachary Duke	25.00
102 Felix Hernandez	40.00
103 Dan Johnson	15.00
104 Brandon McCarthy	25.00
105 Huston Street	30.00
106 Robinson Cano	60.00
107 Jason Bay	25.00
108 Ryan Howard	100.00
109 Ervin Santana	20.00
110 Rich Harden	20.00
111 Aaron Hill	15.00
112 David Wright	80.00
113 Rich Hill (RC)	40.00
114 Nelson Cruz (RC)	20.00
115 Francisco Liriano (RC)	65.00
116 Hong-Chih Kuo (RC)	125.00
117 Ryan Garko (RC)	25.00
118 Craig Hansen RC	50.00
119 Shin-Soo Choo (RC)	25.00
120 Darrell Rasner (RC)	20.00

Sepia Tone

Sepia (1-100):	3-4X
Production 150	
Sepia (101-120):	1X
Production 125	

Emerald

Emerald (1-100):	4-6X
Production 99	
Emerald (101-120):	1X
Production 75	

Gold

Gold (1-100):	5-10X
Gold (101-120):	1-1.5X
Production 50 Sets	

Sapphire

Sapphire (1-100):	8-15X
Sapphire (101-120):	1-2X
Production 25 Sets	

Platinum

Platinum: No Pricing
Production One Set

Printing Plates

No Pricing
Production one set per color.

Heroes

	NM/M
Inserted 1:Pack	
Die-Cut:	2-3X
Production 50 Sets	

Autograph: No Pricing
Production 3 Sets

Code	Player	Price
MM1	Mickey Mantle	8.00
MM2	Mickey Mantle	8.00
MM3	Mickey Mantle	8.00
MM4	Mickey Mantle	8.00
MM5	Mickey Mantle	8.00
MM6	Mickey Mantle	8.00
MM7	Mickey Mantle	8.00
MM8	Mickey Mantle	8.00
MM9	Mickey Mantle	8.00
MM10	Mickey Mantle	8.00
TW1	Ted Williams	5.00
TW2	Ted Williams	5.00
TW3	Ted Williams	5.00
TW4	Ted Williams	5.00
TW5	Ted Williams	5.00
TW1	Ted Williams	5.00
TW2	Ted Williams	5.00
TW3	Ted Williams	5.00
TW4	Ted Williams	5.00
TW5	Ted Williams	5.00
FR1	Frank Robinson	4.00
FR2	Frank Robinson	4.00
FR3	Frank Robinson	4.00
FR4	Frank Robinson	4.00
FR5	Frank Robinson	4.00
FR6	Frank Robinson	4.00
FR7	Frank Robinson	4.00
FR8	Frank Robinson	4.00
FR9	Frank Robinson	4.00
FR10	Frank Robinson	4.00
CY1	Carl Yastrzemski	4.00
CY2	Carl Yastrzemski	4.00
CY3	Carl Yastrzemski	4.00
CY4	Carl Yastrzemski	4.00
CY5	Carl Yastrzemski	4.00
CY6	Carl Yastrzemski	4.00
CY7	Carl Yastrzemski	4.00
CY8	Carl Yastrzemski	4.00
CY9	Carl Yastrzemski	4.00
CY10	Carl Yastrzemski	4.00

Heroes Co-Signer Autographs

No Pricing
Production 3 Sets

Heroes Quad Signers

Production One Card

Heroes Cut Signatures

Production One Set

Triple Signed Hides

Production One Set

Triple Relic

	NM/M
Common Player:	
Production 18 Sets	
Gold:	No Pricing
Production 9 Sets	
Platinum:	No Pricing
Production 3 Sets	
1 Adam Dunn	30.00
2 Adam Dunn	30.00
3 Adrian Beltre	20.00
4 Adrian Beltre	20.00
5 Al Kaline	35.00
6 Al Kaline	35.00
7 Al Kaline	35.00
8 Joe Torre	25.00
9 Albert Pujols	90.00
10 Alex Rodriguez	100.00
11 Ichiro Suzuki	125.00
12 Alex Rodriguez	100.00
13 Alex Rodriguez	100.00
14 Alex Rodriguez	100.00
15 Alex Rodriguez	100.00
16 Alex Rodriguez	100.00
17 Alex Rodriguez	100.00
18 Alfonso Soriano	25.00
19 Dwight Gooden	25.00
20 Barry Bonds	100.00
21 Alfonso Soriano	25.00
22 Ozzie Smith	50.00
23 Andruw Jones	50.00
24 Andruw Jones	50.00
25 Andy Pettitte	30.00
26 Andy Pettitte	30.00
27 Aramis Ramirez	25.00
28 B.J. Upton	25.00
29 Barry Bonds	100.00
30 Vladimir Guerrero	35.00
31 Barry Bonds	100.00
32 Barry Bonds	100.00
33 Barry Bonds	100.00
34 Barry Bonds	100.00
35 Barry Bonds	100.00
36 Barry Bonds	100.00
37 Eric Chavez	25.00
38 Barry Zito	25.00
39 Ben Sheets	25.00
40 Bill Mazeroski	40.00
41 Bob Feller	30.00
42 Bobby Abreu	25.00
43 Bobby Cox	25.00
44 Bobby Doerr	20.00
45 Brad Lidge	20.00
46 Brian Giles	20.00

No.	Player	Price
47	Brian Roberts	25.00
48	Michael Young	20.00
49	Cal Ripken Jr.	100.00
50	Cal Ripken Jr.	100.00
51	Carl Yastrzemski	50.00
52	Carl Yastrzemski	50.00
53	Carl Yastrzemski	50.00
54	Carlos Beltran	30.00
55	Carlos Beltran	30.00
56	Carlos Delgado	30.00
57	Carlton Fisk	40.00
58	Carlton Fisk	40.00
59	Carlton Fisk	40.00
60	Chipper Jones	50.00
61	Chipper Jones	50.00
62	Chipper Jones	50.00
63	Chris Carpenter	25.00
64	Craig Biggio	30.00
65	Craig Biggio	30.00
66	Curt Schilling	35.00
67	Curt Schilling	35.00
68	Curt Schilling	35.00
69	Curt Schilling	35.00
70	Sammy Sosa	50.00
71	Darryl Strawberry	25.00
72	Darryl Strawberry	25.00
73	Alex Rodriguez	100.00
74	Dave Winfield	30.00
75	Dave Winfield	30.00
76	Jorge Posada	30.00
77	David Ortiz	35.00
78	David Ortiz	35.00
79	Derek Lee	30.00
80	Don Mattingly	40.00
81	Don Mattingly	40.00
82	Don Mattingly	40.00
83	Dontrelle Willis	25.00
84	Dontrelle Willis	25.00
85	Duke Snider	35.00
86	Dwight Gooden	25.00
87	Cal Ripken Jr.	100.00
88	David Ortiz	35.00
89	Ernie Banks	40.00
90	Ernie Banks	40.00
91	Ernie Banks	40.00
92	Frank Robinson	35.00
93	Frank Robinson	35.00
94	Frankie Frisch	30.00
95	Gary Carter	25.00
96	Mickey Mantle	200.00
97	Gary Sheffield	35.00
98	George Brett	50.00
99	George Brett	50.00
100	Greg Maddux	50.00
101	Hank Blalock	25.00
102	Hank Greenberg	65.00
103	Hank Greenberg	65.00
104	Hideki Matsui	80.00
105	Hideki Matsui	80.00
106	Hideki Matsui	80.00
107	Ichiro Suzuki	125.00
108	Johnny Bench	40.00
109	Ichiro Suzuki	125.00
110	Ivan Rodriguez	30.00
111	Ivan Rodriguez	30.00
112	Ivan Rodriguez	30.00
113	Ivan Rodriguez	30.00
114	Jake Peavy	20.00
115	Javy Lopez	20.00
116	Jeff Bagwell	35.00
117	Jim Edmonds	25.00
118	Jim Thome	30.00
119	Joe Mauer	20.00
120	Alex Rodriguez	100.00
121	Johan Santana	30.00
122	Johan Santana	30.00
123	Sean Burroughs	15.00
124	Johnny Bench	40.00
125	Johnny Damon	30.00
126	Jon Garland	20.00
127	Jon Garland	20.00
128	Jorge Posada	30.00
129	Manny Ramirez	30.00
130	Jose Canseco	25.00
131	Jose Reyes	25.00
132	Juan Marichal	25.00
133	Kerry Wood	25.00
134	Kerry Wood	25.00
135	Albert Pujols	90.00
136	Lance Berkman	30.00
137	Lloyd Waner	75.00
138	Lloyd Waner	75.00
139	Lou Brock	25.00
140	Miguel Tejada	25.00
141	Manny Ramirez	30.00
142	Mariano Rivera	35.00
143	Mariano Rivera	35.00
144	Mark Buehrle	30.00
145	Mark Mulder	25.00
146	Mark Mulder	25.00
147	Mark Prior	30.00
148	Mark Teixeira	20.00
149	Michael Young	20.00
150	Dale Murphy	35.00
151	Barry Zito	25.00
152	Mickey Mantle	200.00
153	Mickey Mantle	200.00
154	Mickey Mantle	200.00
155	Mickey Mantle	200.00
156	Miguel Cabrera	30.00
157	Miguel Tejada	25.00
158	Vladimir Guerrero	35.00
159	Miguel Tejada	25.00
160	Miguel Tejada	25.00
161	Mike Mussina	25.00
162	Mike Mussina	25.00
163	Mike Piazza	60.00
164	Gary Sheffield	35.00
165	Mike Piazza	60.00
166	Mike Schmidt	40.00
167	Mike Schmidt	40.00
168	Mike Schmidt	40.00
169	Monte Irvin	30.00
170	Morgan Ensberg	25.00
171	Lance Berkman	30.00
172	Nolan Ryan	65.00
173	Nolan Ryan	65.00
174	Nolan Ryan	65.00
175	Albert Pujols	90.00
176	Dave Winfield	30.00
177	Ozzie Smith	40.00
178	Pat Burrell	30.00
179	Paul Konerko	20.00
180	Paul Konerko	20.00
181	Paul Konerko	20.00
182	Paul Molitor	30.00
183	Pedro Martinez	35.00
184	Pedro Martinez	35.00
185	Pedro Martinez	35.00
186	Randy Johnson	35.00
187	Randy Johnson	35.00
188	Reggie Jackson	40.00
189	Reggie Jackson	40.00
190	Rickey Henderson	40.00
191	Rickey Henderson	40.00
192	Rickey Henderson	40.00
193	Rickey Henderson	40.00
194	Rickie Weeks	25.00
195	Rickie Weeks	25.00
196	Roberto Clemente	125.00
197	Roberto Clemente	125.00
198	Robin Yount	40.00
199	Rod Carew	30.00
200	Roger Clemens	60.00
201	Roger Clemens	60.00
202	Roger Clemens	60.00
203	Roger Clemens	60.00
204	Roger Clemens	60.00
205	Roger Clemens	60.00
206	Roy Halladay	25.00
207	Roy Oswalt	25.00
208	Roy Oswalt	25.00
209	Ryne Sandberg	60.00
210	Ryne Sandberg	60.00
211	Nolan Ryan	65.00
212	Sammy Sosa	60.00
213	Sammy Sosa	60.00
214	Sammy Sosa	60.00
215	Sammy Sosa	60.00
216	Scott Rolen	40.00
217	Scott Rolen	40.00
218	Orlando Cepeda	25.00
219	Stan Musial	50.00
220	Steve Carlton	25.00
221	Steve Carlton	25.00
222	Steve Carlton	25.00
223	Steve Garvey	20.00
224	Tadahito Iguchi	30.00
225	Ted Williams	80.00
226	Ted Williams	80.00
227	Tim Hudson	20.00
228	Tim Hudson	20.00
229	Todd Helton	25.00
230	Todd Helton	25.00
231	Todd Helton	25.00
232	Tom Seaver	40.00
233	Tony Gwynn	40.00
234	Tony Gwynn	40.00
235	Tony Gwynn	40.00
236	Torii Hunter	20.00
237	Torii Hunter	20.00
238	Travis Hafner	35.00
239	Mike Piazza	60.00
240	Albert Pujols	90.00
241	Wade Boggs	40.00
242	Willie Stargell	40.00
243	Willie Stargell	40.00
244	Willie Stargell	40.00
245	Willy Taveras	25.00

Triple Relic Combo

NM/M

Production 18 Sets
Gold: No Pricing
Production 9 Sets
Platinum: No Pricing
Production 3 Sets

No.	Players	Price
1	Albert Pujols, Alex Rodriguez, Barry Bonds	100.00
2	Alex Rodriguez, Barry Bonds, Albert Pujols	100.00
3	Albert Pujols, Alex Rodriguez, Manny Ramirez	100.00
4	Albert Pujols, Barry Bonds, Ted Williams	125.00
5	Alex Rodriguez, Barry Bonds, Chipper Jones	75.00
6	Alex Rodriguez, Roberto Clemente, Barry Bonds	125.00
7	Alex Rodriguez, Vladimir Guerrero, Ichiro Suzuki	80.00
8	Alex Rodriguez, Stan Musial, Ted Williams	120.00
9	Andruw Jones, Alfonso Soriano, Vladimir Guerrero	40.00
10	Barry Bonds, Ichiro Suzuki, Roberto Clemente	150.00
11	Barry Bonds, Lloyd Waner, Roberto Clemente	160.00
12	Barry Bonds, Manny Ramirez, Andruw Jones	60.00
13	Barry Bonds, Manny Ramirez, Ted Williams	100.00
14	Barry Bonds, Roberto Clemente, Willie Stargell	125.00
15	Carl Yastrzemski, Paul Molitor, Manny Ramirez	40.00
16	Don Mattingly, Paul Molitor, Manny Ramirez	40.00
17	Don Mattingly, Rod Carew, Tony Gwynn	70.00
18	Gary Sheffield, Vladimir Guerrero, Ivan Rodriguez	30.00
19	Hank Greenberg, Stan Musial, Ted Williams	125.00
20	Ichiro Suzuki, Chipper Jones, Barry Bonds	80.00
21	Ichiro Suzuki, Ted Williams, Roberto Clemente	150.00
22	Joe Morgan, Paul Molitor, Gary Carter	35.00
23	Manny Ramirez, Vladimir Guerrero, Roberto Clemente	90.00
24	Mike Piazza, Paul Molitor, Rickey Henderson	40.00
26	Paul Molitor, Andruw Jones, Robin Yount	40.00
27	Paul Molitor, Andruw Jones, Alfonso Soriano	35.00
28	Reggie Jackson, Vladimir Guerrero, Andruw Jones	35.00
29	Rickey Henderson, Wade Boggs, Tony Gwynn	60.00
31	Stan Musial, Ted Williams, Tony Gwynn	70.00
32	Ted Williams, Ichiro Suzuki, Wade Boggs	140.00
33	Albert Pujols, Ted Williams, Mickey Mantle	250.00
34	Andruw Jones, George Brett, Chipper Jones	60.00
35	Greg Maddux, Nolan Ryan, Steve Carlton	60.00
36	Greg Maddux, Steve Carlton, Tom Seaver	50.00
37	Nolan Ryan, Steve Carlton, Tom Seaver	50.00
38	Nolan Ryan, Tom Seaver, Roger Clemens	60.00
39	Roger Clemens, Nolan Ryan, Tom Seaver	60.00
40	Barry Bonds, Rickey Henderson, Tony Gwynn	60.00
41	Cal Ripken Jr., Carl Yastrzemski, Paul Molitor	85.00
42	Cal Ripken Jr., George Brett, Roberto Clemente	100.00
43	Cal Ripken Jr., George Brett, Tony Gwynn	85.00
44	Cal Ripken Jr., Paul Molitor, Rickey Henderson	85.00
45	Cal Ripken Jr., Paul Molitor, Tony Gwynn	80.00
46	George Brett, Cal Ripken Jr., Rod Carew	80.00
47	George Brett, Cal Ripken Jr., Rod Carew	80.00
48	George Brett, Robin Yount, Rod Carew	50.00
49	George Brett, Tony Gwynn, Wade Boggs	60.00
50	George Brett, Tony Gwynn, Wade Boggs	60.00
51	Paul Molitor, Robin Yount, Wade Boggs	40.00
52	Paul Waner, Rickey Henderson, Stan Musial	60.00
53	Paul Waner, Rickey Henderson, Wade Boggs	50.00
54	Paul Waner, Rod Carew, Wade Boggs	50.00
55	Rickey Henderson, Stan Musial, Wade Boggs	50.00
56	Roberto Clemente, Robin Yount, Rod Carew	80.00
57	Roberto Clemente, Robin Yount, Rod Carew	90.00
58	Roberto Clemente, Robin Yount, Tony Gwynn	90.00
59	Rod Carew, Stan Musial, Tony Gwynn	90.00
60	Stan Musial, Tony Gwynn, Wade Boggs	50.00
61	Wade Boggs	30.00
62	Barry Bonds, Mickey Mantle, Frank Robinson	140.00
63	Barry Bonds, Ted Williams, Mickey Mantle	160.00
64	Barry Bonds, Frank Robinson, Reggie Jackson	70.00
65	Barry Bonds, Frank Robinson, Harmon Killebrew	60.00
66	Frank Robinson, Barry Bonds, Mike Schmidt	60.00
67	Frank Robinson, Harmon Killebrew, Mickey Mantle	150.00
68	Josh Gibson, Barry Bonds, Mickey Mantle	200.00
69	Josh Gibson, Barry Bonds, Ted Williams	150.00
70	Mike Schmidt, Harmon Killebrew, Reggie Jackson	75.00
71	Dave Winfield, Vladimir Guerrero, Reggie Jackson	50.00
72	Rod Carew, Reggie Jackson, Vladimir Guerrero	30.00
73	Andruw Jones, Chipper Jones, Jeff Francoeur	30.00
74	Bobby Cox, Andruw Jones, Chipper Jones	75.00
75	Chipper Jones, Greg Maddux, Andruw Jones	50.00
76	Brian Roberts, Sammy Sosa, Miguel Tejada	40.00
77	Brooks Robinson, Cal Ripken Jr., Jim Palmer	65.00
78	Brooks Robinson, Jim Palmer, Frank Robinson	40.00
79	Cal Ripken Jr., Brooks Robinson, Miguel Tejada	50.00
80	Cal Ripken Jr., Frank Robinson, Sammy Sosa	80.00
81	Frank Robinson, Reggie Jackson, Brooks Robinson	75.00
82	Jim Palmer, Frank Robinson, Reggie Jackson	60.00
83	Jim Palmer, Reggie Jackson, Sammy Sosa	50.00
84	Jim Palmer, Sammy Sosa, Miguel Tejada	40.00
85	Miguel Tejada, Brian Roberts, Cal Ripken Jr.	80.00
86	Reggie Jackson, Frank Robinson, Sammy Sosa	50.00
87	Bobby Doerr, Carl Yastrzemski, Ted Williams	80.00
88	Carl Yastrzemski, David Ortiz, Manny Ramirez	60.00
89	Carl Yastrzemski, Ted Williams, David Ortiz	80.00
90	Carl Yastrzemski, Ted Williams, Manny Ramirez	80.00
91	Curt Schilling, David Ortiz, Johnny Damon	40.00
92	Curt Schilling, David Ortiz, Manny Ramirez	40.00
93	Curt Schilling, Manny Ramirez, Johnny Damon	40.00
94	David Ortiz, Johnny Damon, Manny Ramirez	50.00
95	Johnny Damon, Manny Ramirez, Ted Williams	60.00
96	Manny Ramirez, David Ortiz, Pedro Martinez	40.00
97	Manny Ramirez, Ted Williams, David Ortiz	60.00
98	Pedro Martinez, Roger Clemens, Manny Ramirez	50.00
99	Greg Maddux, Randy Johnson, Roger Clemens	50.00
100	Johan Santana, Pedro Martinez, Roger Clemens	60.00
101	Roger Clemens	50.00
102	Roger Clemens	50.00
103	Randy Johnson, Curt Schilling, Roger Clemens	75.00
104	Derrek Lee, Aramis Ramirez, Mark Prior	35.00
105	Derrek Lee, Ryne Sandberg, Sammy Sosa	65.00
106	Ernie Banks, Ryne Sandberg, Derrek Lee	60.00
107	Ernie Banks, Ryne Sandberg,	
108	Greg Maddux, Ryne Sandberg, Ernie Banks	75.00
109	Mark Prior, Kerry Wood, Greg Maddux	60.00
110	Sammy Sosa, Ernie Banks, Derrek Lee	60.00
111	Frank Robinson, Joe Morgan, Johnny Bench	40.00
112	Johnny Bench, Frank Robinson, Tom Seaver	50.00
113	Johnny Bench, Tom Seaver, Joe Morgan	50.00
114	Jermaine Dye, Scott Podsednik, Tadahito Iguchi	40.00
115	Jim Thome, Paul Konerko, Tadahito Iguchi	60.00
116	Jon Garland, Scott Podsednik, Mark Buehrle	25.00
117	Jon Garland, Tadahito Iguchi, Mark Buehrle	30.00
118	Paul Konerko, Sammy Sosa, Carlton Fisk	40.00
119	Paul Konerko, Tadahito Iguchi, Jermaine Dye	40.00
120	Al Kaline, Ivan Rodriguez, Hank Greenberg	60.00
121	Greg Maddux, Johan Santana, Roger Clemens	60.00
122	Juan Marichal, Nolan Ryan, Roger Clemens	80.00
123	Nolan Ryan, Randy Johnson, Whitey Ford	60.00
124	Cal Ripken Jr., Ozzie Smith, Mike Schmidt	60.00
125	Mike Schmidt, Cal Ripken Jr., Ozzie Smith	60.00
126	Al Kaline, Frank Robinson, Paul Waner	50.00
127	Al Kaline, Harmon Killebrew, Frank Robinson	75.00
128	Al Kaline, Mickey Mantle, Reggie Jackson	125.00
129	Al Kaline, Reggie Jackson, Stan Musial	60.00
130	Al Kaline, Robin Yount, Paul Waner	40.00
131	Barry Bonds, Chipper Jones, Manny Ramirez	65.00
132	Bob Feller, Juan Marichal, Nolan Ryan	60.00
133	Bob Feller, Whitey Ford, Steve Carlton	40.00
134	Bobby Doerr, Ted Williams, Wade Boggs	80.00
135	Brooks Robinson, Ozzie Smith, Ryne Sandberg	50.00
136	Carl Yastrzemski, George Brett, Paul Molitor	50.00
137	Carlton Fisk, Carl Yastrzemski, Wade Boggs	75.00
138	Joe Morgan, George Brett, Mike Schmidt	50.00
139	Yogi Berra, Carlton Fisk, Gary Carter	50.00
140	Andy Pettitte, Nolan Ryan, Brad Lidge	50.00
141	Andy Pettitte, Nolan Ryan, Randy Johnson	50.00
142	Andy Pettitte, Nolan Ryan, Roger Clemens	60.00
143	Andy Pettitte, Randy Johnson, Brad Lidge	30.00
144	Andy Pettitte, Roy Oswalt, Roger Clemens	50.00
145	Brad Lidge, Roy Oswalt, Andy Pettitte	35.00
146	Craig Biggio, Jeff Bagwell, Lance Berkman	40.00
147	Nolan Ryan, Roger Clemens, Randy Johnson	80.00
148	Roger Clemens, Brad Lidge, Andy Pettitte	50.00
149	Roger Clemens, Randy Johnson, Andy Pettitte	50.00
150	Ichiro Suzuki, Hideki Matsui	160.00
151	Ichiro Suzuki, Hideki Matsui, Kazuo Matsui	140.00
152	Ichiro Suzuki, Tadahito Iguchi, Hideki Matsui	150.00
153	Eric Gagne, Mike Piazza, Duke Snider	100.00
154	Gary Sheffield, Rickie Weeks, Paul Molitor	40.00
155	Paul Molitor, Gary Sheffield, Robin Yount	35.00
156	Robin Yount, Paul Molitor, Rickie Weeks	40.00
157	Harmon Killebrew, Rod Carew, Johan Santana	40.00
158	Harmon Killebrew, Torii Hunter, Rod Carew	40.00
159	Johan Santana, Joe Mauer, Torii Hunter	35.00
160	Paul Molitor, Rod Carew, Harmon Killebrew	40.00
161	Albert Pujols, Ichiro Suzuki, Barry Bonds	180.00
162	Alex Rodriguez, Barry Bonds, George Brett	60.00
163	Alex Rodriguez, Barry Bonds, Mickey Mantle	150.00
164	Ichiro Suzuki, Mickey Mantle	180.00
165	Alex Rodriguez, Reggie Jackson, Yogi Berra	50.00
166	Alex Rodriguez, Ted Williams, Mickey Mantle	200.00
167	Alex Rodriguez, Yogi Berra, Don Mattingly	60.00
168	Alex Rodriguez, Barry Bonds, Don Mattingly	70.00
169	Barry Bonds, Cal Ripken Jr., Miguel Tejada	60.00
170	Barry Bonds, Harmon Killebrew, Reggie Jackson	70.00
171	Barry Bonds, Roberto Clemente, Willie Stargell	120.00
172	Barry Bonds, Alex Rodriguez, Albert Pujols	100.00
173	Barry Bonds, Cal Ripken Jr., Mickey Mantle	200.00
174	Barry Bonds, Josh Gibson, Albert Pujols	120.00
175	Barry Bonds, Vladimir Guerrero, Ichiro Suzuki	75.00
176	Brooks Robinson, George Brett, Mike Schmidt	60.00
177	Barry Bonds, Ichiro Suzuki, Cal Ripken Jr.	120.00
178	Cal Ripken Jr., Don Mattingly, George Brett	90.00
179	Cal Ripken Jr., George Brett, Don Mattingly	90.00
180	Cal Ripken Jr., Mike Schmidt, Don Mattingly	100.00
181	Cal Ripken Jr., Roger Clemens, Don Mattingly	125.00
182	Chipper Jones, Dale Murphy, Don Mattingly	75.00
183	Don Mattingly, Mickey Mantle, Reggie Jackson	150.00
184	George Brett, Johnny Bench, Mike Schmidt	60.00
185	George Brett, Johnny Bench, Mike Schmidt	60.00
186	Ichiro Suzuki, Barry Bonds, Mickey Mantle	180.00
187	Ivan Rodriguez, Vladimir Guerrero, Miguel Tejada	35.00
188	Ivan Rodriguez, Yogi Berra, Johnny Bench	50.00

#	Players	Price
189	Ivan Rodriguez, Yogi Berra, Johnny Bench	50.00
190	Johnny Bench, Mike Piazza, Yogi Berra	50.00
191	Mickey Mantle, Barry Bonds, Ted Williams	200.00
192	Mickey Mantle, Ichiro Suzuki, Roberto Clemente	200.00
193	Mickey Mantle, Roberto Clemente, Stan Musial	200.00
194	Mickey Mantle, Ted Williams, Roberto Clemente	220.00
195	Mickey Mantle, Vladimir Guerrero, Roberto Clemente	200.00
196	Miguel Tejada, Reggie Jackson, Rickey Henderson	40.00
197	Reggie Jackson, Alex Rodriguez, Yogi Berra	50.00
198	Roberto Clemente, Mickey Mantle, Barry Bonds	180.00
199	Buck O'Neil, Josh Gibson, Monte Irvin	100.00
200	Carlos Beltran, Carlos Delgado, David Wright	60.00
201	Carlos Beltran, Carlos Delgado, Jose Reyes	50.00
202	Carlos Beltran, David Wright, Pedro Martinez	60.00
203	Darryl Strawberry, Dwight Gooden, Gary Carter	30.00
204	David Wright, Carlos Beltran, Mike Piazza	60.00
205	David Wright, Mike Piazza, Jose Reyes	75.00
206	Jose Reyes, Kazuo Matsui, David Wright	40.00
207	Alex Rodriguez, Don Mattingly, Mickey Mantle	180.00
208	Alex Rodriguez, Hideki Matsui, Joe Torre	80.00
209	Alex Rodriguez, Hideki Matsui, Mickey Mantle	200.00
210	Don Mattingly, Mickey Mantle, Roger Clemens	200.00
211	Hideki Matsui, Gary Sheffield, Alex Rodriguez	50.00
212	Hideki Matsui, Gary Sheffield, Jorge Posada	50.00
213	Jorge Posada, Roger Clemens, Mike Mussina	75.00
214	Mickey Mantle, Whitey Ford, Yogi Berra	200.00
215	Mike Mussina, Whitey Ford, Roger Clemens	65.00
216	Roger Clemens, Mickey Mantle, Alex Rodriguez	200.00
217	Wade Boggs, Joe Torre, Alfonso Soriano	30.00
218	Barry Zito, Mark Mulder, Tim Hudson	25.00
219	Jose Canseco, Reggie Jackson, Rickey Henderson	40.00
220	Mark Mulder, Miguel Tejada, Tim Hudson	40.00
221	Bobby Abreu, Pat Burrell, Jim Thome	40.00
222	Curt Schilling, Mike Schmidt, Steve Carlton	
223	Mike Schmidt, Pat Burrell, Scott Rolen	50.00
224	Barry Bonds, Roberto Clemente, Josh Gibson	150.00
225	Paul Waner, Roberto Clemente, Lloyd Waner	150.00
226	Willie Stargell, Bill Mazeroski, Roberto Clemente	140.00
227	Albert Pujols, Carlos Beltran, Dontrelle Willis	60.00
228	Albert Pujols, Dontrelle Willis, Ichiro Suzuki	90.00
229	Cal Ripken Jr., Albert Pujols, Orlando Cepeda	90.00
230	Cal Ripken Jr., Carlton Fisk, Tom Seaver	80.00
231	Cal Ripken Jr., Rod Carew, Carlton Fisk	75.00
232	Cal Ripken Jr., Rod Carew, Carlton Fisk	75.00
233	Jeff Bagwell, Albert Pujols, Mike Piazza	100.00
234	Mike Piazza, Jeff Bagwell, Scott Rolen	80.00
235	Rickey Henderson, Steve Garvey, Tony Gwynn	50.00
236	Adrian Beltre, Ichiro Suzuki, Alex Rodriguez	80.00
237	Ichiro Suzuki, Alex Rodriguez, Randy Johnson	100.00
238	Barry Bonds, Juan Marichal, Orlando Cepeda	75.00
239	Juan Marichal, Monte Irvin, Orlando Cepeda	40.00
240	Orlando Cepeda, Monte Irvin, Barry Bonds	60.00
241	Albert Pujols, Frankie Frisch, Stan Musial	120.00
242	Albert Pujols, Mark Mulder, Scott Rolen	75.00
243	Scott Rolen, Jim Edmonds, Albert Pujols	75.00
244	Stan Musial, Ozzie Smith, Albert Pujols	120.00
245	Alex Rodriguez, Ivan Rodriguez, Alfonso Soriano	50.00
246	Alex Rodriguez, Mark Teixeira, Alfonso Soriano	50.00
247	Alex Rodriguez, Nolan Ryan, Alfonso Soriano	60.00
248	Alfonso Soriano, Hank Blalock, Mark Teixeira	30.00
249	Alfonso Soriano, Hank Blalock, Michael Young	25.00
250	Mark Teixeira, Alfonso Soriano, Michael Young	30.00

Triple Relic Autograph

	NM/M
Production 18 Sets	
Gold:	No Pricing
Production 9 Sets	
Platinum:	No Pricing
Production 3 Sets	
1 Albert Pujols	475.00
2 Albert Pujols	475.00
3 Albert Pujols	475.00
4 Alex Rodriguez	275.00
5 Alex Rodriguez	275.00
6 Alex Rodriguez	275.00
7 Derek Lee	60.00
8 Barry Bonds	400.00
9 Ben Sheets	400.00
10 Ben Sheets	400.00
11 Brad Lidge	35.00
12 Brad Lidge	35.00
13 Cal Ripken Jr.	220.00
14 Cal Ripken Jr.	220.00
15 Cal Ripken Jr.	220.00
16 Carl Yastrzemski	100.00
17 Carl Yastrzemski	100.00
18 Carl Yastrzemski	100.00
19 Chase Utley	65.00
20 Chase Utley	65.00
21 Chien-Ming Wang	750.00
22 Chien-Ming Wang	400.00
23 Chien-Ming Wang	400.00
24 Chien-Ming Wang	400.00
25 Chris Carpenter	100.00
26 Chris Carpenter	100.00
27 Clint Barmes	25.00
28 Clint Barmes	25.00
29 Conor Jackson	30.00
30 Conor Jackson	30.00
31 David Ortiz	125.00
32 Don Mattingly	140.00
33 Don Mattingly	140.00
34 Don Mattingly	140.00
35 Duke Snider	75.00
36 Duke Snider	75.00
37 Ernie Banks	120.00
38 Frank Robinson	65.00
39 Frank Robinson	65.00
40 Frank Robinson	65.00
41 Garrett Atkins	35.00
42 Garrett Atkins	35.00
43 Derek Lee	60.00
44 Derek Lee	60.00
45 Derek Lee	60.00
46 J.J. Hardy	40.00
47 J.J. Hardy	40.00
48 Jake Peavy	40.00
49 Jake Peavy	40.00
50 Jeff Francis	30.00
51 Jeff Francis	30.00
52 Joe Mauer	50.00
53 Joe Mauer	50.00
54 Joey Devine	25.00
55 Joey Devine	25.00
56 Johan Santana	60.00
57 Johan Santana	60.00
58 Johan Santana	60.00
59 Johan Santana	60.00
60 Johnny Bench	80.00
61 Johnny Bench	80.00
62 Johnny Bench	80.00
63 Johnny Damon	80.00
64 Jonny Gomes	40.00
65 Jonny Gomes	40.00
66 Jose Reyes	50.00
67 Jose Reyes	50.00
68 Justin Morneau	40.00
69 Justin Morneau	40.00
70 Lou Brock	60.00
71 Lou Brock	60.00
72 Lou Brock	60.00
73 Lou Brock	60.00
74 Manny Ramirez	100.00
75 Mariano Rivera	150.00
76 Mark Prior	50.00
77 Miguel Cabrera	70.00
78 Miguel Cabrera	70.00
79 Miguel Cabrera	70.00
80 Miguel Cabrera	70.00
81 Mike Schmidt	100.00
82 Mike Schmidt	100.00
83 Mike Schmidt	100.00
84 Morgan Ensberg	35.00
85 Morgan Ensberg	35.00
86 Nick Swisher	60.00
87 Nick Swisher	60.00
88 Nolan Ryan	150.00
89 Nolan Ryan	150.00
90 Nolan Ryan	150.00
91 Zachary Duke	30.00
92 Zachary Duke	30.00
93 Ozzie Smith	80.00
94 Ozzie Smith	80.00
95 Ozzie Smith	80.00
96 Pedro Martinez	125.00
97 Robin Yount	75.00
98 Robin Yount	75.00
99 Robin Yount	75.00
100 Rod Carew	50.00
101 Rod Carew	50.00
102 Rod Carew	50.00
103 Rod Carew	50.00
104 Roger Clemens	180.00
105 Roger Clemens	180.00
106 Ryan Langerhans	40.00
107 Ryan Langerhans	40.00
108 Ryne Sandberg	100.00
109 Ryne Sandberg	100.00
110 Ryne Sandberg	100.00
111 Scott Kazmir	50.00
112 Scott Kazmir	50.00
113 Stan Musial	100.00
114 Stan Musial	100.00
115 Stan Musial	100.00
116 Steve Carlton	50.00
117 Steve Carlton	50.00
118 Steve Carlton	50.00
119 Steve Garvey	50.00
120 Steve Garvey	50.00
121 Tony Gwynn	100.00
122 Tony Gwynn	100.00
123 Tony Gwynn	100.00
124 Travis Hafner	50.00
125 Travis Hafner	50.00
126 Victor Martinez	50.00
127 Victor Martinez	50.00
128 Wade Boggs	60.00
129 Wade Boggs	60.00
130 Wade Boggs	60.00

Triple Relic Combos Autograph

	NM/M
Production 18 Sets	
Gold:	No Pricing
Production 9 Sets	
Platinum:	No Pricing
Production 3 Sets	
1 Albert Pujols, Barry Bonds, Alex Rodriguez	1,000
2 Felix Hernandez, Alex Rodriguez, Shin-Soo Choo	150.00
3 Nolan Ryan, Roger Clemens, Felix Hernandez	300.00
4 Johnny Damon, Alex Rodriguez, Robinson Cano	300.00
5 Manny Ramirez, Carl Yastrzemski, David Ortiz	250.00
6 Michael Young, Cal Ripken Jr., Ozzie Smith	300.00
7 Brian Roberts, Cal Ripken Jr., Frank Robinson	250.00
8 Stan Musial, Ozzie Smith, Lou Brock	180.00
9 Ozzie Smith, Stan Musial, Lou Brock	180.00
10 Tony Gwynn, Stan Musial, Rod Carew	180.00
11 Brooks Robinson, Cal Ripken Jr., Brian Roberts	200.00
12 Rod Carew, Robin Yount, Paul Molitor	120.00
13 Derek Lee, Ryne Sandberg, Mark Prior	180.00
14 Chien-Ming Wang, Steve Carlton, Dontrelle Willis	275.00
15 Brad Lidge, Mariano Rivera, Huston Street	180.00
16 Morgan Ensberg, Wade Boggs, David Wright	120.00
17 Ben Sheets, Steve Carlton, Felix Hernandez	80.00
18 Victor Martinez, Johnny Bench, Joe Mauer	125.00
19 David Wright, Mike Schmidt, Aaron Hill	160.00
20 Chase Utley, Mike Schmidt, Ryan Howard	200.00
21 Felix Hernandez, Steve Carlton, Brandon McCarthy	75.00
22 David Wright, Miguel Cabrera, Jason Bay	140.00
23 Robinson Cano, Don Mattingly, Chien-Ming Wang	350.00
24 Justin Morneau, Don Mattingly, Travis Hafner	100.00
25 Steve Garvey, Don Mattingly, Dan Johnson	100.00
26 Travis Hafner, Miguel Cabrera, Jason Bay	100.00
27 Ben Sheets, Johan Santana, Jake Peavy	75.00
28 Ervin Santana, Johan Santana, Ben Sheets	70.00
29 Chris Carpenter, Johan Santana, Rich Harden	120.00
30 Zachary Duke, Johan Santana, Brandon McCarthy	75.00

2006 Topps Turkey Red

	NM/M
Complete Set (316-630):	
Common Player:	.25
Common SP:	4.00
Inserted 1:4	
Pack (8):	4.50
Box (24):	90.00
316 Alex Rodriguez	3.00
316 Alex Rodriguez/Rangers/SP	8.00
316 Alex Rodriguez/M's/SP	8.00
317 Jeff Francoeur/SP	4.00
318 Shawn Green	.25
319 Daniel Cabrera	.25
320 Craig Biggio	.50
321 Jeremy Bonderman	.40
322 Mark Kotsay	.25
323 Cliff Floyd	.25
324 Jimmy Rollins	.40
325 Magglio Ordonez	.25
325 Magglio Ordonez/W. Sox/SP	4.00
326 C.C. Sabathia	.25
327 Oliver Perez	.25
328 Orlando Hudson	.25
329 Chris Ray	.25
330 Manny Ramirez	1.00
331 Paul Konerko	.50
332 Joe Mauer/SP	5.00
333 Jorge Posada	.50
334 Mark Ellis	.25
335 A.J. Burnett	.25
336 Mike Sweeney	.25
337 Shannon Stewart	.25
338 Jake Peavy/SP	4.00
339 Carlos Delgado/Mets/SP	5.00
339 Carlos Delgado/B. Jays/SP	5.00
340 Brian Roberts	.25
341 Dontrelle Willis	.50
342 Aaron Rowand	.25
343 Richie Sexson	.50
343 Richie Sexson/Brewers/SP	4.00
344 Chris Carpenter	.75
345 Carlos Zambrano	.40
346 Nomar Garciaparra	1.00
347 Carlos Lee	.40
348 Preston Wilson	.25
348 Preston Wilson/Marlins/SP	4.00
349 Mariano Rivera	.50
350 Ichiro Suzuki/SP	8.00
351 Mike Piazza	1.00
351 Mike Piazza Mets/SP	4.00
352 Jason Schmidt	.25
353 Jeff Weaver	.25
354 Rocco Baldelli	.25
355 Adam Dunn	.75
356 Jeromy Burnitz	.25
357 Chris Shelton/SP	4.00
358 Chone Figgins/SP	4.00
359 Javier Vazquez	.25
360 Chipper Jones	1.00
361 Frank Thomas	1.00
362 Mark Loretta	.25
363 Hideki Matsui	2.00
364 J.J. Hardy/SP	4.00
365 Todd Helton	.75
366 Reggie Sanders	.25
367 Jay Gibbons	.25
368 Johnny Estrada	.25
369 Grady Sizemore	.75
370 Jim Thome	1.00
371 Ivan Rodriguez	.75
372 Jason Bay	.75
373 Carl Crawford	.50
374 Adrian Beltre	.25
375 Derrek Lee/SP	6.00
376 Miguel Olivo	.25
377 Roy Oswalt	.50
378 Coco Crisp	.25
379 Moises Alou	.40
380 Kevin Millwood	.25
381 Mark Grudzielanek	.25
382 Justin Morneau	.25
383 Austin Kearns	.40
384 Brad Penny	.50
385 Troy Glaus	.50
386 Cliff Lee	.25
387 Armando Benitez	.25
388 Clint Barmes	.25
389 Orlando Cabrera	.25
390 Jim Edmonds/SP	4.00
391 Jermaine Dye	.25
392 Morgan Ensberg/SP	4.00
393 Paul LoDuca	.25
394 Eric Chavez	.25
395 Greg Maddux/SP	8.00
396 Jack Wilson	.25
397 Omar Vizquel	.25
398 Joe Nathan	.25
399 Bobby Abreu	.50
400 Barry Bonds/SP	8.00
401 Gary Sheffield	.50
402 John Patterson	.25
403 J.D. Drew	.25
404 Bruce Chen	.25
405 Johnny Damon	1.00
406 Aubrey Huff	.25
407 Mark Mulder	.40
408 Jamie Moyer	.25
409 Carlos Guillen	.25
410 Andruw Jones/SP	5.00
411 Jhonny Peralta/SP	4.00
412 Doug Davis	.25
413 Aaron Miles	.25
414 Jon Lieber	.25
415 Aaron Hill	.25
416 Josh Beckett/SP	4.00
417 Bobby Crosby	.25
418 Noah Lowry/SP	4.00
419 Sidney Ponson	.25
420 Luis Castillo	.25
421 Brad Wilkerson	.25
422 Felix Hernandez/SP	4.00
423 Vinny Castilla	.25
424 Tom Glavine	.50
425 Vladimir Guerrero	1.00
426 Javy Lopez	.25
427 Ronnie Belliard	.25
428 Dmitri Young	.25
429 Johan Santana	1.00
430 David Ortiz/Red Sox/SP	5.00
430 David Ortiz/Twins/SP	5.00
431 Ben Sheets	.25
432 Matt Holliday	.25
433 Brian McCann	.50
434 Joe Blanton	.25
435 Sean Casey	.25
436 Brad Lidge	.25
437 Chad Tracy	.25
438 Brett Myers	.25
439 Matt Morris	.25
440 Brian Giles	.25
441 Zachary Duke	.25
442 Jose Lopez	.25
443 Kris Benson	.25
444 Jose Reyes/SP	5.00
445 Travis Hafner	.75
446 Orlando Hernandez	.25
447 Edgar Renteria	.40
448 Scott Podsednik	.25
449 Nick Swisher/SP	4.00
450 Derek Jeter	8.00
451 Scott Kazmir	.50
452 Hank Blalock	.50
453 Jake Westbrook	.25
454 Miguel Cabrera	1.00
455 Ken Griffey Jr.	2.00
455 Ken Griffey Jr./M's/SP	8.00
456 Rafael Furcal	.50
457 Lance Berkman	.50
458 Aramis Ramirez	.50
459 Xavier Nady	.25
459 Xavier Nady/Padres/SP	4.00
460 Randy Johnson	1.00
460 Randy Johnson/Astros/SP	6.00
461 Khalil Greene	.25
462 Bartolo Colon	.25
463 Mike Lowell	.25
464 David DeJesus	.25
465 Ryan Howard/SP	8.00
466 Tim Salmon/SP	4.00
467 Mark Buehrle/SP	4.00
468 Curtis Granderson	.25
469 Kerry Wood	.50
470 Miguel Tejada	.75
471 Geoff Jenkins	.25
472 Jeremy Reed	.25
473 David Eckstein	.25
474 Lyle Overbay	.25
475 Michael Young	.25
476 Nick Johnson/Nats/SP	4.00
476 Nick Johnson/Yanks/SP	4.00
477 Carlos Beltran	1.00
478 Huston Street	.25
479 Brandon Webb	.25
480 Phil Nevin	.25
481 Ryan Madson/SP	4.00
482 Jason Giambi	1.00
483 Angel Berroa	.25
484 Casey Blake	.25
485 Pat Burrell	.50
486 B.J. Ryan	.25
487 Torii Hunter	.25
488 Garret Anderson	.25
489 Chase Utley/SP	6.00
490 Matt Murton	.25
491 Rich Harden	.25
492 Garrett Atkins	.25
493 Tadahito Iguchi/SP	5.00
494 Jarrod Washburn	.25
495 Carl Everett	.25
496 Kameron Loe	.25
497 Jorge Cantu/SP	4.00
498 Chris Young	.25
499 Marcus Giles	.25
500 Albert Pujols	3.00
501 Alfonso Soriano/Nats/SP	5.00
501 Alfonso Soriano/Yanks/SP	5.00
502 Randy Winn	.25
503 Roy Halladay	.50
504 Victor Martinez	.25
505 Pedro Martinez	1.00
506 Rickie Weeks	.40
507 Dan Johnson	.25
508 Tim Hudson	.25
508 Tim Hudson A's/SP	4.00
509 Mark Prior	.75
510 Melvin Mora	.25
511 Matt Clement	.25
512 Brandon Inge	.25
513 Mike Mussina	.75
514 Mike Cameron	.25
515 Barry Zito	.50
516 Luis Gonzalez	.25
517 Jose Castillo	.25
518 Andy Pettitte	.50
519 Wily Mo Pena	.25
520 Billy Wagner	.25
521 Ervin Santana/SP	4.00
522 Juan Pierre	.25
523 Danny Haren	.25
524 Adrian Gonzalez/SP	4.00
525 Robinson Cano	.75
526 Jeff Kent	.40
527 Cory Sullivan	.25
528 Joe Crede/SP	4.00
529 John Smoltz	.50
530 David Wright	2.00
531 Chad Cordero	.25
532 Scott Rolen/SP	5.00
533 Edwin Jackson	.25
534 Doug Mientkiewicz	.25
535 Mark Teixeira/SP	5.00
536 Kelvim Escobar	.25
537 Alex Rios	.25
538 Jose Vidro	.25
539 Alex Gonzalez	.25
540 Yadier Molina	.25
541 Ronny Cedeno/SP	4.00
542 Mark Hendrickson	.25
543 Russ Adams	.25
544 Chris Capuano	.25
545 Raul Ibanez	.25
546 Vicente Padilla	.25
547 Chris Duffy	.25
548 Bengie Molina	.25
549 Chien-Ming Wang	.75
550 Curt Schilling	.25
551 Craig Wilson	.25
552 Mike Lieberthal	.25
553 Kazuo Matsui	.25
554 Jeff Francis	.25
555 Brady Clark	.25
556 Willy Taveras	.25
557 Mike Maroth	.25
558 Bernie Williams	.50
559 Edwin Encarnacion	.25
560 Vernon Wells	.25
561 Livan Hernandez/Nats	.25

561 Livan Hernandez/ Giants/SP 4.00
562 Kenny Rogers .25
563 Steve Finley .25
564 Trot Nixon .25
565 Jonny Gomes/SP 4.00
566 Brandon Phillips .25
567 Shawn Chacon .25
568 David Bush .25
569 Jose Guillen .25
570 Gustavo Chacin .25
571 A. Rod Safe at the Plate CL 1.00
572 Pujols At Bat CL 1.00
573 Bonds On Deck CL 1.00
574 Breaking Up Two CL .25
575 Conference On The Mound CL 1.00
576 Touch Em All CL .50
577 Avoiding The Runner CL .25
578 Bunting The Runner Over CL .25
579 In The Hole CL .50
580 Jeter Steals Third CL 1.00
581 Nolan Ryan 2.00
582 Cal Ripken Jr. 3.00
583 Carl Yastrzemski 1.00
584 Duke Snider 1.00
585 Tom Seaver 1.00
586 Mickey Mantle 5.00
587 Jim Palmer .50
588 Gary Carter .25
589 Stan Musial 1.50
590 Luis Aparicio .25
591 Prince Fielder (RC) 4.00
592 Conor Jackson (RC) .50
593 Jeremy Hermida (RC) 1.00
594 Jeff Mathis (RC) .50
595 Alay Soler RC 1.00
596 Ryan Spilborghs (RC) .50
597 Chuck James (RC) 1.00
598 Josh Barfield (RC) 1.00
599 Ian Kinsler (RC) .50
600 Val Majewski (RC) .50
601 Brian Slocum (RC) .50
602 Matthew Kemp (RC) 2.00
603 Nate McLouth (RC) .50
604 Sean Marshall (RC) .50
605 Brian Bannister (RC) .50
606 Ryan Zimmerman (RC) 4.00
607 Kendry Morales (RC) 1.00
608 Jonathan Papelbon (RC) 4.00
609 Matt Cain (RC) 1.00
610 Anderson Hernandez (RC) .50
611 Jose Capellan (RC) .50
612 Lastings Milledge (RC) 2.00
613 Francisco Liriano (RC) 4.00
614 Hanley Ramirez (RC) 2.00
615 Bryan Anderson (RC) .50
616 Reggie Abercrombie (RC) .50
617 Erick Aybar (RC) .50
618 James Loney (RC) 1.00
619 Joel Zumaya (RC) .50
620 Travis Ishikawa (RC) .50
621 Jason Kubel (RC) .50
622 Drew Meyer (RC) .50
623 Kenji Johjima RC 4.00
624 Fausto Carmona (RC) .50
625 Nicholas Markakis (RC) .50
626 John Rheinecker (RC) .50
627 Melky Cabrera (RC) .50
628 Mike Pelfrey RC 5.00
629 Dan Uggla (RC) 1.00
630 Justin Verlander (RC) 4.00

White
Stars (316-630): 2-3X
SP's: 1X
Inserted 1:4

Red
Stars (316-630): 1-2X
SP's: .5-1X

Black

Stars (316-630): 3-5X
SP's: 1.5-2X
Inserted 1:20

Gold
Stars (316-630): 5-10X

SP's: 3-5X
Inserted 1:60

Suede
No Pricing
Production One Set

Autographs
NM/M
Common Auto.: 8.00
Suede: No Pricing
Production One Set
GA Garrett Atkins 15.00
JB Josh Barfield 20.00
CB Clint Barmes 15.00
MC Miguel Cabrera 50.00
RC Robinson Cano 80.00
JG Jonny Gomes 25.00
RH Ryan Howard 100.00
CJA Conor Jackson 15.00
KJ Kenji Johjima 90.00
DJ Dan Johnson 15.00
CJ Chipper Jones 75.00
DL Derrek Lee 40.00
PL Paul LoDuca 25.00
BM Brian McCann 30.00
BMC Brandon McCarthy/ Exch. 15.00
MM Mike Morse 10.00
RO Roy Oswalt 25.00
AR Alex Rodriguez 250.00
JS Johan Santana/Exch. 65.00
HS Huston Street/Exch. 25.00
NS Nick Swisher/Exch. 20.00
CV Claudio Vargas/Exch. 8.00
DW David Wright 85.00

Autographs Black
NM/M
Production 15 or 99.
GA Garrett Atkins/99 15.00
JB Josh Barfield/99 20.00
CB Clint Barmes/99 15.00
CJA Conor Jackson/99 20.00
DJ Dan Johnson/99 15.00
BM Brian McCann/99 40.00
BMC Brandon McCarthy/ 99 Exch 15.00
MM Mike Morse/99 30.00
NS Nick Swisher/ 99 Exch 20.00
CV Claudio Vargas/ 99 Exch 15.00

Autographs Gold
NM/M
Production 5 or 25.
JB Josh Barfield/25 40.00
BM Brian McCann/25 75.00
MM Mike Morse/25 30.00
NS Nick Swisher/25 Exch 30.00

Autographs Red
NM/M
Production 50 or 475.
GA Garrett Atkins/475 15.00
JB Josh Barfield/475 15.00
CB Clint Barmes/475 15.00
MC Miguel Cabrera/475 60.00
RC Robinson Cano/50 100.00
JG Jonny Gomes/50 30.00
RH Ryan Howard/50 125.00
CJA Conor Jackson/475 15.00
KJ Kenji Johjima/50 100.00
DJ Dan Johnson/475 15.00
CJ Chipper Jones/50 100.00
DL Derrek Lee/50 40.00
PL Paul LoDuca/50 30.00
BM Brian McCann/475 30.00
BMC Brandon McCarthy/ 475 Exch 15.00
MM Mike Morse/475 10.00
RO Roy Oswalt/50 30.00
AR Alex Rodriguez/50 250.00
JS Johan Santana/ 50 Exch 75.00
HS Huston Street/ 50 Exch 30.00
NS Nick Swisher/ 475 Exch 20.00
CV Claudio Vargas/ 475 Exch 8.00
DW David Wright/50 100.00

Autographs White
NM/M
Production 25 or 100
GA Garrett Atkins/200 15.00
JB Josh Barfield/200 20.00
CB Clint Barmes/200 15.00
CJA Conor Jackson/200 15.00
DJ Dan Johnson/200 15.00
BM Brian McCann/ 200 Exch 15.00
BMC Brandon McCarthy/ 200 Exch 15.00
MM Mike Morse/200 15.00
NS Nick Swisher/ 200 Exch 20.00
CV Claudio Vargas/ 200 Exch 10.00

B-18 Blankets
NM/M
Inserted 1:2 Boxes

Original B-18 Blanket: No Pricing
Inserted 1:159 Boxes
BB1 Barry Bonds/White 15.00
BB2 Barry Bonds/Red 15.00
VG1 Vladimir Guerrero/ White 10.00
VG2 Vladimir Guerrero/ Green 10.00
KJ1 Kenji Johjima/White 10.00
KJ2 Kenji Johjima/Green 10.00
DL1 Derrek Lee/White 10.00
DL2 Derrek Lee/Red 10.00
MM1 Mickey Mantle/White 25.00
MM2 Mickey Mantle/Blue 25.00
HM1 Hideki Matsui/White 10.00
HM2 Hideki Matsui/Blue 10.00
DO1 David Ortiz/White 10.00
DO2 David Ortiz/Orange 10.00
MR1 Manny Ramirez/ White 10.00
MR2 Manny Ramirez/ Orange 10.00
AR1 Alex Rodriguez/White 15.00
AR2 Alex Rodriguez/Blue 15.00
IS1 Ichiro Suzuki/White 10.00
IS2 Ichiro Suzuki/Green 10.00

Cabinet
NM/M
Common Player:
Inserted 1:2 Boxes
Cabinet Original: No Pricing
Inserted 1:4,340 Boxes
Suede: No Pricing
Inserted 1:634 Boxes
JB Josh Barfield 10.00
JBE Josh Beckett 10.00
BB Barry Bonds 25.00
JC Jorge Cantu 10.00
CCA Chris Carpenter 10.00
GC Gary Carter 10.00
CC Carl Crawford 10.00
JD Johnny Damon 20.00
CD Carlos Delgado 10.00
PF Prince Fielder 20.00
JF Jeff Francoeur 15.00
NG Nomar Garciaparra 15.00
TG Troy Glaus 10.00
JG Jonny Gomes 10.00
KG Ken Griffey Jr. 20.00
RH Ryan Howard 20.00
DJ Derek Jeter 30.00
NJ Nick Johnson 10.00
RJ Randy Johnson 20.00
AJ Andruw Jones 15.00
DL Derrek Lee 10.00
FL Francisco Liriano 10.00
MM Mickey Mantle 50.00
NM Nicholas Markakis 10.00
PM Pedro Martinez 15.00
HM Hideki Matsui 15.00
DO David Ortiz 20.00
JPA Jonathan Papelbon 25.00
JP Jake Peavy 10.00
MP Mike Piazza 15.00
AP Albert Pujols 30.00
AR Alex Rodriguez 25.00
IR Ivan Rodriguez 10.00
JR Jimmy Rollins 15.00
NR Nolan Ryan 25.00
JS Johan Santana 15.00
DS Duke Snider 20.00
AS Alfonso Soriano 15.00
IS Ichiro Suzuki 20.00
JT Jim Thome 15.00
DW David Wright 15.00
CY Carl Yastrzemski 25.00

Cabinet Autograph Relics
No Pricing
Inserted 1:86 Boxes
Suede: No Pricing
Production One Set

Cabinet Autograph Relics Dual
No Pricing
Inserted 1:1,368 Boxes
Suede: No Pricing
Production One Set

Relics
NM/M
Common Player: 4.00
Red: 1-1.5X
Production 150 Sets
White: 1.5-2X
Production 99 Sets
Black: 2-3X
Production 50 Sets
Gold: 2-4X
Production 25 Sets
Suede: No Pricing
Production One Set
CBA Clint Barmes 6.00
CB Carlos Beltran 8.00
LB Lance Berkman 6.00
HB Hank Blalock 4.00
MC Miguel Cabrera 8.00
RC Robinson Cano 15.00
CC Chris Carpenter 8.00
EC Eric Chavez 6.00
JC Jose Contreras 6.00
JD Johnny Damon 15.00
CD Carlos Delgado 6.00
JE Jim Edmonds 6.00
ME Morgan Ensberg 4.00
JF Jeff Francoeur 8.00
JG Jon Garland 4.00
VG Vladimir Guerrero 8.00
RHA Roy Halladay 6.00
RIH Rich Harden 6.00
JH Jeremy Hermida 6.00
RH Ryan Howard 25.00
TH Torii Hunter 6.00
CJ Andruw Jones 6.00
CJ Chipper Jones 8.00
PK Paul Konerko 8.00
DL Derrek Lee 6.00
BL Brad Lidge 6.00
PL Paul LoDuca 4.00
PM Pedro Martinez 10.00
HM Hideki Matsui 15.00
JM Joe Mauer 10.00
MM Mike Mussina 10.00
DO David Ortiz 15.00
RO Roy Oswalt 6.00
APE Andy Pettitte 6.00
MP Mike Piazza 10.00
AP Albert Pujols 20.00
MR Manny Ramirez 10.00
JR Jose Reyes 8.00
MRI Mariano Rivera 15.00
BR Brian Roberts 6.00
AR Alex Rodriguez 15.00
JS Johan Santana 10.00
IS Ichiro Suzuki 25.00
MT Mark Teixeira 8.00
BW Bernie Williams 8.00
DWI Dontrelle Willis 6.00
DW David Wright 15.00

2006 Topps Updates & Highlights

NM/M
Complete Factory Set (333): 40.00
Complete Set (330): 30.00
Common Player: .10
UH1 Austin Kearns .20
UH2 Adam Eaton .10
UH3 Juan Encarnacion .10
UH4 Jarrod Washburn .10
UH5 Alex Gonzalez .10
UH6 Toby Hall .10
UH7 Preston Wilson .10
UH8 Ramon Ortiz .10
UH9 Jason Michaels .10
UH10 Jeff Weaver .10
UH11 Russell Branyan .10
UH12 Brett Tomko .10
UH13 Doug Mientkiewicz .10
UH14 David Wells .10
UH15 Corey Koskie .10
UH16 Russ Ortiz .10
UH17 Carlos Pena .10
UH18 Mark Hendrickson .10
UH19 Julian Tavarez .10
UH20 Jeff Conine .10
UH21 Dioner Navarro .10
UH22 Bob Wickman .10
UH23 Felipe Lopez .10
UH24 Eddie Guardado .10
UH25 David Dellucci .10
UH26 Ryan Wagner .10
UH27 Nick Green .10
UH28 Gary Majewski .10
UH29 Shea Hillenbrand .10
UH30 Jae Weong Seo .10
UH31 Royce Clayton .10
UH32 David Riske .10
UH33 Joey Gathright .10
UH34 Robinson Tejeda .10
UH35 Edwin Jackson .10
UH36 Aubrey Huff .10
UH37 Akinori Otsuka .10
UH38 Juan Castro .10
UH39 Zach Day .10
UH40 Jeremy Accardo .10
UH41 Shawn Green .10
UH42 Kazuo Matsui .10
UH43 J.J. Putz .10
UH44 David Ross .10
UH45 Scott Williamson .10
UH46 Joe Borchard .10
UH47 Elmer Dessens .10
UH48 Odalis Perez .10
UH49 Kelly Shoppach .10
UH50 Brandon Phillips .10
UH51 Guillermo Mota .10

UH52 Alex Cintron .10
UH53 Denny Bautista .10
UH54 Josh Bard .10
UH55 Julio Lugo .10
UH56 Doug Mirabelli .10
UH57 Kip Wells .10
UH58 Adrian Gonzalez .10
UH59 Shawn Chacon .10
UH60 Marcus Thames .10
UH61 Craig Wilson .10
UH62 Cory Sullivan .10
UH63 Ben Broussard .10
UH64 Todd Walker .10
UH65 Greg Maddux 1.00
UH66 Xavier Nady .10
UH67 Oliver Perez .10
UH68 Sean Casey .10
UH69 Kyle Lohse .10
UH70 Carlos Lee .20
UH71 Rheal Cormier .10
UH72 Ronnie Belliard .10
UH73 Cory Lidle .10
UH74 David Bell .10
UH75 Wilson Betemit .10
UH76 Danys Baez .10
UH77 Mike Stanton .10
UH78 Kevin Mench .10
UH79 Sandy Alomar .10
UH80 Cesar Izturis .10
UH81 Jeremy Affeldt .10
UH82 Matt Stairs .10
UH83 Hector Luna .10
UH84 Tony Graffanino .10
UH85 J.P. Howell .10
UH86 Bengie Molina .10
UH87 Maicer Izturis .10
UH88 Marco Scutaro .10
UH89 Daryle Ward .10
UH90 Sal Fasano .10
UH91 Oscar Villarreal .10
UH92 Gabe Gross .10
UH93 Phil Nevin .10
UH94 Damon Hollins .10
UH95 Juan Cruz .10
UH96 Marlon Anderson .10
UH97 Jason Davis .10
UH98 Ryan Shealy .10
UH99 Francisco Cordero .10
UH100 Bobby Abreu .25
UH101 Roberto Hernandez .10
UH102 Gary Bennett .10
UH103 Aaron Sele .10
UH104 Nook Logan .10
UH105 Alfredo Amezaga .10
UH106 Chris Woodward .10
UH107 Kevin Jarvis .10
UH108 B.J. Upton .10
UH109 Alan Embree .10
UH110 Milton Bradley .10
UH111 Peter Orr .10
UH112 Jeff Cirillo .10
UH113 Corey Patterson .10
UH114 Josh Paul .10
UH115 Fernando Rodney .10
UH116 Jerry Hairston .10
UH117 Scott Proctor .10
UH118 Ambiorix Burgos .10
UH119 Jose Bautista .10
UH120 Livan Hernandez .10
UH121 John McDonald .10
UH122 Ronny Cedeno .10
UH123 Nate Robertson .10
UH124 Jamey Carroll .10
UH125 Alex Escobar .10
UH126 Endy Chavez .10
UH127 Jorge Julio .10
UH128 Kenny Lofton .10
UH129 Matt Diaz .10
UH130 David Bush .10
UH131 Jose Molina .10
UH132 Mike MacDougal .10
UH133 Benjamin Zobrist (RC) .25
UH134 Shane Komine RC .25
UH135 Casey Janssen RC .50
UH136 Kevin Frandsen (RC) .25
UH137 John Rheinecker (RC) .25
UH138 Matthew Kemp (RC) .75
UH139 Scott Mathieson (RC) .25
UH140 Jered Weaver (RC) .75
UH141 Joel Guzman (RC) .25
UH142 Anibal Sanchez (RC) .50
UH143 Melky Cabrera (RC) .50
UH144 Howie Kendrick (RC) .50
UH145 Cole Hamels (RC) 1.00
UH146 Willy Aybar (RC) .25
UH147 James Shields RC .50
UH148 Kevin Thompson (RC) .25
UH149 Jon Lester (RC) 1.00
UH150 Stephen Drew (RC) .75
UH151 Andre Ethier (RC) .50
UH152 Jordan Tata RC .25
UH153 Michael Napoli RC .50
UH154 Kason Gabbard (RC) .25
UH155 Lastings Milledge (RC) .50
UH156 Erick Aybar (RC) .50
UH157 Fausto Carmona (RC) .25
UH158 Russell Martin (RC) .50
UH159 David Pauley (RC) .25
UH160 Andy Marte (RC) .25
UH161 Carlos Quentin (RC) .25
UH162 Franklin Gutierrez (RC) .25
UH163 Taylor Buchholz (RC) .25
UH164 Josh Johnson (RC) .25
UH165 Chad Billingsley (RC) .50
UH166 Kendry Morales (RC) .25

UH167 Adam Loewen (RC) .25
UH168 Yusmeiro Petit (RC) .10
UH169 Matt Albers (RC) .25
UH170 John Maine (RC) .10
UH171 Alex Rodriguez .75
UH172 Mike Piazza .40
UH173 Cory Sullivan .10
UH174 Anibal Sanchez .10
UH175 Trevor Hoffman .10
UH176 Barry Bonds .75
UH177 Derek Jeter .75
UH178 Jose Reyes .25
UH179 Manny Ramirez .25
UH180 Vladimir Guerrero .25
UH181 Mariano Rivera .25
UH182 Postseason Highlights .25
UH183 Postseason Highlights .25
UH184 Postseason Highlights .25
UH185 Postseason Highlights .25
UH186 Postseason Highlights .25
UH187 Postseason Highlights .25
UH188 Postseason Highlights .25
UH189 Postseason Highlights .25
UH190 Postseason Highlights .25
UH191 Postseason Highlights .25
UH192 Postseason Highlights .25
UH193 Postseason Highlights .25
UH194 Postseason Highlights .25
UH195 Postseason Highlights .25
UH196 Postseason Highlights .25
UH197 Postseason Highlights .25
UH198 Postseason Highlights .25
UH199 Postseason Highlights .25
UH200 Postseason Highlights .25
UH201 Postseason Highlights .25
UH202 David Ortiz, Jermaine Dye, Travis Hafner .25
UH203 Joe Mauer, Derek Jeter, Robinson Cano .50
UH204 David Ortiz, Justin Morneau, Raul Ibanez .25
UH205 Carl Crawford, Chone Figgins, Ichiro Suzuki .50
UH206 Johan Santana, Chien-Ming Wang, Jon Garland .50
UH207 Johan Santana, Roy Halladay, C.C. Sabathia .25
UH208 Johan Santana, Jeremy Bonderman, John Lackey .25
UH209 Francisco Rodriguez, Bobby Jenks, B.J. Ryan .10
UH210 Ryan Howard, Albert Pujols, Alfonso Soriano 1.00
UH211 Freddy Sanchez, Miguel Cabrera, Albert Pujols .50
UH212 Ryan Howard, Albert Pujols, Lance Berkman 1.00
UH213 Jose Reyes, Juan Pierre, Hanley Ramirez .25
UH214 Derek Lowe, Brandon Webb, Carlos Zambrano .10
UH215 Roy Oswalt, Chris Carpenter, Brandon Webb .10
UH216 Aaron Harang, Jake Peavy, John Smoltz .10
UH217 Trevor Hoffman, Billy Wagner, Joe Borowski .10
UH218 Ichiro Suzuki .50
UH219 Derek Jeter .75
UH220 Alex Rodriguez .75
UH221 David Ortiz .25
UH222 Vladimir Guerrero .25
UH223 Ivan Rodriguez .25
UH224 Vernon Wells .10
UH225 Mark Loretta .10
UH226 Kenny Rogers .25
UH227 Alfonso Soriano .25
UH228 Carlos Beltran .25
UH229 Albert Pujols .75
UH230 Jason Bay .25
UH231 Edgar Renteria .10
UH232 David Wright .50
UH233 Chase Utley .25
UH234 Paul LoDuca .10
UH235 Brad Penny .10
UH236 Derrick Turnbow .10
UH237 Mark Redman .10
UH238 Francisco Liriano .10
UH239 A.J. Pierzynski .10
UH240 Grady Sizemore .25
UH241 Jose Contreras .10
UH242 Jermaine Dye .25
UH243 Jason Schmidt .10
UH244 Nomar Garciaparra .25
UH245 Scott Kazmir .10
UH246 Johan Santana .25
UH247 Chris Capuano .10
UH248 Magglio Ordonez .25
UH249 Gary Matthews .10
UH250 Carlos Lee .25
UH251 David Eckstein .10
UH252 Michael Young .25
UH253 Matt Holliday .25
UH254 Lance Berkman .25

UH255 Scott Rolen .25
UH256 Bronson Arroyo .10
UH257 Barry Zito .10
UH258 Brian McCann .10
UH259 Jose Lopez .10
UH260 Chris Carpenter .25
UH261 Roy Halladay .10
UH262 Jim Thome .25
UH263 Dan Uggla .10
UH264 Mariano Rivera .25
UH265 Roy Oswalt .20
UH266 Tom Gordon .10
UH267 Troy Glaus .10
UH268 Bobby Jenks .10
UH269 Freddy Sanchez .10
UH270 Paul Konerko .25
UH271 Joe Mauer .25
UH272 B.J. Ryan .10
UH273 Ryan Howard .75
UH274 Brian Fuentes .10
UH275 Miguel Cabrera .25
UH276 Brandon Webb .10
UH277 Mark Buehrle .10
UH278 Trevor Hoffman .10
UH279 Jonathan Papelbon .25
UH280 Andruw Jones .25
UH281 Miguel Tejada .20
UH282 Carlos Zambrano .20
UH283 Ryan Howard .75
UH284 David Wright .50
UH285 Miguel Cabrera .25
UH286 David Ortiz .25
UH287 Jermaine Dye .10
UH288 Miguel Tejada .25
UH289 Lance Berkman .10
UH290 Troy Glaus .10
UH291 David Wright, Tom Glavine .25
UH292 Ryan Howard, Tom Gordon .50
UH293 Miguel Cabrera, Dontrelle Willis .25
UH294 Andruw Jones, John Smoltz .25
UH295 Alfonso Soriano .10
UH296 Albert Pujols, Chris Carpenter .50
UH297 Adam Dunn, Bronson Arroyo .10
UH298 Lance Berkman, Roy Oswalt .25
UH299 Chris Capuano, Prince Fielder .25
UH300 Freddy Sanchez, Jason Bay .10
UH301 Carlos Zambrano, Juan Pierre .10
UH302 Adrian Gonzalez, Trevor Hoffman .10
UH303 Derek Lowe, Rafael Furcal .10
UH304 Omar Vizquel, Jason Schmidt .10
UH305 Brandon Webb, Chad Tracy .10
UH306 Matt Holliday, Garrett Atkins .10
UH307 Alex Rodriguez, Chien-Ming Wang .50
UH308 Curt Schilling, David Ortiz .25
UH309 Roy Halladay, Vernon Wells .10
UH310 Miguel Tejada, Erik Bedard .10
UH311 Carl Crawford, Scott Kazmir .10
UH312 Jeremy Bonderman, Magglio Ordonez .10
UH313 Justin Morneau, Johan Santana .10
UH314 Jon Garland, Jermaine Dye .10
UH315 Travis Hafner, C.C. Sabathia .10
UH316 Emil Brown, Mark Grudzielanek .10
UH317 Frank Thomas, Barry Zito .25
UH318 Jered Weaver, Vladimir Guerrero .25
UH319 Michael Young, Gary Matthews .10
UH320 Ichiro Suzuki, J.J. Putz .25
UH321 Derek Jeter, Robinson Cano .50
UH232 Mark Mulder, Chris Carpenter .25
UH323 Trevor Schmidt, Jason Schmidt .10
UH324 David Wright, Paul LoDuca .25
UH325 Lance Berkman, Roy Oswalt .25
UH326 Derek Jeter, Jose Reyes .25
UH327 David Wright, Cliff Floyd .25
UH328 Johan Santana, Francisco Liriano .25
UH329 Stephen Drew, J.D. Drew .25
UH330 Jeff Weaver .25

Black
Black: 15-25X
Production 55 Sets

Gold

Gold: 5-10X
Production 2,006 Sets

First Edition
1st Edition: 4-6X
Inserted 1:Hobby Box

Platinum
Production One Set

All-Star Autographs
No Pricing
Production 25 Sets

All-Star Stitches

Common Player: 4.00
Inserted 1:43
Patch: No Pricing
Production 10 Sets
BA Bronson Arroyo 8.00
JB Jason Bay 15.00
CB Carlos Beltran 10.00
LB Lance Berkman 10.00
MB Mark Buehrle 8.00
MC Miguel Cabrera 10.00
RC Robinson Cano 10.00
CFC Chris Capuano 4.00
CC Chris Carpenter 10.00
JC Jose Contreras 8.00
JD Jermaine Dye 6.00
DE David Eckstein 20.00
BF Brian Fuentes 4.00
TEG Troy Glaus 6.00
TMG Tom Glavine 6.00
TG Tom Gordon 4.00
VG Vladimir Guerrero 8.00
RH Roy Halladay 6.00
TH Trevor Hoffman 6.00
MH Matt Holliday 6.00
RJH Ryan Howard 25.00
BJ Bobby Jenks 4.00
AJ Andruw Jones 10.00
SK Scott Kazmir 6.00
PK Paul Konerko 6.00
CL Carlos Lee 8.00
PL Paul LoDuca 6.00
JL Jose Lopez 6.00
ML Mark Loretta 6.00
GM Gary Matthews 6.00
JM Joe Mauer 8.00
BM Brian McCann 15.00
MO Magglio Ordonez 8.00
DO David Ortiz 15.00
RO Roy Oswalt 6.00
JP Jonathan Papelbon 20.00
BP Brad Penny 4.00
AJP A.J. Pierzynski 4.00
AP Albert Pujols 25.00
MAR Mark Redman 4.00
ER Edgar Renteria 4.00
JR Jose Reyes 15.00
MR Mariano Rivera 10.00
AR Alex Rodriguez 15.00
IR Ivan Rodriguez 8.00
KR Kenny Rogers 4.00
SR Scott Rolen 8.00
BR B.J. Ryan 4.00
FS Freddy Sanchez 6.00
JS Johan Santana 10.00
JDS Jason Schmidt 6.00
GS Grady Sizemore 10.00
AS Alfonso Soriano 8.00

MT Miguel Tejada 8.00
JT Jim Thome 10.00
DT Derrick Turnbow 6.00
DU Dan Uggla 10.00
CU Chase Utley 10.00
BW Brandon Webb 10.00
VW Vernon Wells 8.00
DW David Wright 20.00
MY Michael Young 6.00
CZ Carlos Zambrano 8.00

All-Star Patches
No Pricing
Production 10 Sets

Barry Bonds HR History

Common Bonds HR History: 1.00
Inserted 1:6
Autographs: No Pricing
Production 5 Sets
BB709-734 Barry Bonds 1.00

Barry Bonds 715

NM/M
Inserted 1:36
715-BB Barry Bonds 3.00

Barry Bonds 715 Relic
NM/M
Production 715
Barry Bonds 35.00

Chrome RC Box Topper
NM/M
Production 599
Inserted one per box.
Refractors: 2-4X
Production 25 Sets
CRC1 Aaron Zobrist 3.00
CRC2 Shane Komine 3.00
CRC3 Casey Janssen 3.00
CRC4 Kevin Frandsen 5.00
CRC5 John Rheinecker 3.00
CRC6 Matthew Kemp 8.00
CRC7 Scott Mathieson 5.00
CRC8 Jered Weaver 8.00
CRC9 Joel Guzman 5.00
CRC10 Anibal Sanchez 5.00
CRC11 Melky Cabrera 5.00
CRC12 Howie Kendrick 5.00
CRC13 Cole Hamels 6.00
CRC14 Willy Aybar 3.00
CRC15 James Shields 3.00
CRC16 Kevin Thompson 3.00
CRC17 Jon Lester 10.00
CRC18 Stephen Drew 8.00
CRC19 Andre Ethier 8.00
CRC20 Jordan Tata 3.00
CRC21 Michael Napoli 5.00
CRC22 Kason Gabbard 5.00
CRC23 Lastings Milledge 5.00
CRC24 Erick Aybar 3.00
CRC25 Fausto Carmona 5.00
CRC26 Russell Martin 5.00
CRC27 David Pauley 5.00
CRC28 Andy Marte 5.00
CRC29 Carlos Quentin 5.00
CRC30 Franklin Gutierrez 5.00
CRC31 Taylor Buchholz 5.00
CRC32 Josh Johnson 5.00
CRC33 Chad Billingsley 8.00
CRC34 Kendry Morales 3.00
CRC35 Adam Loewen 5.00
CRC36 Yusmeiro Petit 3.00
CRC37 Matt Albers 5.00
CRC38 John Maine 5.00
CRC39 Josh Willingham 5.00
CRC40 Taylor Tankersley 5.00
CRC41 Pat Neshek 40.00
CRC42 Francisco Rosario 3.00
CRC43 Matt Smith 5.00
CRC44 Jonathan Sanchez 3.00
CRC45 Chris Demaria 3.00
CRC46 Manuel Corpas 5.00
CRC47 Kevin Reese 3.00
CRC48 Brent Clevlen 3.00
CRC49 Anderson Hernandez 3.00
CRC50 Chris Roberson 5.00

Derby Digs Relics
NM/M
Inserted 1:4,200
JD Jermaine Dye 25.00
TG Troy Glaus 25.00

Mickey Mantle HR History

NM/M
Common Mantle (102-201): 2.00
Inserted 1:4

Mickey Mantle HR History Relics
NM/M
Common Mantle: 140.00
Production 7 Sets

Midsummer Covers
No Pricing
Production 10 Sets

Rookie Debut

NM/M
Common Player: 1.00
Inserted 1:4
RD1 Joel Zumaya 2.00
RD2 Ian Kinsler 2.00
RD3 Kenji Johjima 3.00
RD4 Josh Barfield 1.00
RD5 Nicholas Markakis 2.00
RD6 Dan Uggla 2.00
RD7 Eric Reed 1.00
RD8 Carlos Martinez 1.00
RD9 Angel Pagan 1.50
RD10 Jason Childers 1.00
RD11 Ruddy Lugo 1.00
RD12 James Loney 2.50
RD13 Fernando Nieve 1.00
RD14 Reggie Abercrombie 1.00
RD15 Boone Logan 1.00
RD16 Brian Bannister 1.00
RD17 Ricky Nolasco 1.50
RD18 Willie Eyre 1.00
RD19 Fabio Castro 1.00
RD20 Jordan Tata 1.00
RD21 Taylor Buchholz 1.50
RD22 Scott Marshall 1.50
RD23 John Rheinecker 1.00
RD24 Casey Janssen 1.00
RD25 Russell Martin 1.50
RD26 Yusmeiro Petit 1.50
RD27 Kendry Morales 1.50
RD28 Alay Soler 1.00
RD29 Jered Weaver 3.00
RD30 Matthew Kemp 2.00
RD31 Enrique Gonzalez 1.00
RD32 Lastings Milledge 1.00
RD33 James Shields 1.00
RD34 David Pauley 1.00
RD35 Zach Jackson 1.00
RD36 Zach Miner 1.00
RD37 Jon Lester 3.00
RD38 Chad Billingsley 2.00
RD39 Scott Thorman 1.00
RD40 Anibal Sanchez 2.00
RD41 Mike Thompson 1.00
RD42 T.J. Beam 1.00
RD43 Stephen Drew 3.00
RD44 Joe Saunders 1.00
RD45 Carlos Quentin 1.50

Rookie Debut Autographs
NM/M
Common Autograph: 15.00
RA Reggie Abercrombie 15.00
MA Matt Albers 20.00
FC Fausto Carmona 15.00
FF Emiliano Fruto 20.00
IK Ian Kinsler 20.00

JL Jon Lester 35.00
BL Bobby Livingston 15.00
AL Adam Loewen 40.00
MN Michael Napoli 25.00
RN Ricky Nolasco 20.00
YP Yusmeiro Petit 15.00
MP Martin Prado 30.00
JS Jeremy Sowers 25.00
ST Scott Thorman 20.00

Signature Moves
NM/M
Common Autograph:
AH Aubrey Huff 20.00
JL Julio Lugo 20.00
BP Brandon Phillips 20.00
BW Brad Wilkerson 10.00
CW Craig Wilson 15.00

Touch 'Em All Relics
NM/M
Inserted 1:610
CB Carlos Beltran 20.00
RH Ryan Howard 30.00
JM Joe Mauer 20.00
DO David Ortiz 20.00
AP Albert Pujols 30.00
AR Alex Rodriguez 25.00
IS Ichiro Suzuki 25.00
MT Miguel Tejada 10.00
DW David Wright 25.00
MY Michael Young 8.00

1952 Edition

NM/M
Complete Set (312):
Common Player: .25
Common SP (276-312): 5.00
Common 52 Logo Variation: 4.00
Inserted 1:5
Pack (8): 4.50
Box (20): 80.00
1 Howie Kendrick (RC) 1.50
2 Enrique Gonzalez (RC) .25
3 Chuck James (RC) .75
4 Chris Britton RC .25
5 David Pauley (RC) .50
6 Angel Pagan (RC) .50
7 Pat Neshek RC 6.00
8 Walter Young (RC) .25
9 Chris Denorfia (RC) .25
10 Rafael Perez RC .50
11 Ryan Spilborghs (RC) .50
12 Jon Huber RC .50
13 Jordan Tata RC .25
14 Eric Reed RC .25
15 Norris Hopper RC .75
16 Scott Olsen RC .25
17 Fernando Nieve RC .25
18 Chris Booker RC .25
19 Chad Billingsley (RC) .75
20 Carlos Villanueva RC .75
21 Craig Hansen RC 2.00
22 David Gassner (RC) .25
23 Mike Pelfrey RC 4.00
24 Matt Smith (RC) 1.00
25 Chris Roberson (RC) .50
26 John Van Benschoten (RC) .25
27 Kevin Frandsen (RC) .25
28 Les Walrond (RC) .25
29 James Shields RC .50
30 Russell Martin RC .50
31 Benjamin Zobrist (RC) .25
32 John Rheinecker (RC) .25
33 Francisco Rosario (RC) .25
34 Santiago Ramirez (RC) .25
35 Michael Napoli (RC) 1.50
36 Tony Pena (RC) .50
37 Jeff Karstens RC 1.00
52 logo/SP RC 5.00
38 Phil Stockman (RC) .25
39 Kurt Birkins (RC) 1.00
40 Dustin Pedroia (RC) .50
41 Buck Coats (RC) .25
42 Jim Johnson (RC) 1.00
43 Angel Guzman (RC) .25
44 Kelly Shoppach (RC) .25
45 Josh Wilson (RC) .25
46 Jack Hannahan (RC) .75
47 Ricky Nolasco (RC) .25
48 T.J. Bohn (RC) .25
49 Joel Zumaya (RC) 1.00
50 Philip Barzilla RC .75

51 Justin Huber (RC) .25
52 Willy Aybar (RC) .25
52 Willy Aybar .25
52 logo/SP (RC) 4.00
53 Tony Gwynn Jr. (RC) .50
54 Chris Barnwell RC .75
55 Henry Owens RC .75
56 Jeff Bajenaru (RC) .50
57 Jonah Bayliss RC .50
58 Joshua Sharpless RC .50
59 Eliezer Alfonzo RC .50
60 Bobby Livingston (RC) .25
61 John Gall RC .50
62 Ruddy Lugo (RC) .25
63 Fabio Castro RC .50
64 Casey Janssen RC .75
65 Mike O'Connor RC .50
66 Kendry Morales (RC) .50
67 James Hoey RC .75
68 Dustin Moseley (RC) .25
69 Peter Moylan RC .25
70 Manny Delcarmen (RC) .50
71 Rich Hill (RC) .40
72 Boone Logan RC .25
73 Cody Ross (RC) .50
74 Fausto Carmona (RC) .75
75 Ramon Ramirez (RC) .50
76 Zach Miner (RC) .50
77 Hanley Ramirez (RC) .50
78 Josh Johnson (RC) .25
79 Taylor Buchholz (RC) .25
80 Joe Nelson (RC) .25
81 Hong-Chih Kuo (RC) .25
82 Chris Mabeus (RC) .25
83 Willie Eyre (RC) .25
84 John Maine (RC) .25
85 Yurendell DeCaster (RC) .25
86 Mike Thompson RC .50
87 Brian Wilson RC .50
88 Matt Cain RC .50
88 Matt Cain 52 logo/SP (RC) 8.00
89 Josh Rupe RC .25
90 Tyler Johnson RC .25
91 Jason Childers (RC) .50
92 Wes Littleton (RC) .25
93 Ty Taubenheim RC .50
94 Saul Rivera (RC) .50
95 Reggie Willits RC .50
96 Carlos Quentin (RC) .50
97 Macay McBride (RC) .25
98 Brandon Fahey RC .50
99 Sean Marshall (RC) .50
100 Sean Tracey (RC) .25
101 Brian Slocum (RC) .25
102 Choo Freeman (RC) .25
103 Brent Clevlen (RC) .25
104 Josh Willingham (RC) .25
105 Chris Resop RC .50
106 Chris Sampson RC 1.50
107 James Loney (RC) .50
107 James Loney .50
52 logo/SP (RC) 8.00
108 Matthew Kemp (RC) .50
109 Jason Kubel (RC) .50
110 Brian Bannister (RC) 4.00
111 Kevin Thompson (RC) .25
112 Jeremy Brown (RC) .25
113 Brian Sanches (RC) .25
114 Nate McLouth (RC) .25
115 Ben Johnson (RC) .25
116 Jonathan Sanchez (RC) .25
117 Mark Lowe (RC) .25
118 Skip Schumaker (RC) .25
119 Jason Hammel (RC) .50
120 Drew Meyer (RC) .50
121 Melvin Dorta RC .50
122 Jeff Mathis (RC) .50
123 Davis Romero (RC) .50
124 Joey Devine RC .50
125 Sendy Rleal RC .50
126 Freddie Bynum (RC) .25
127 Bryan Anderson (RC) .50
128 Jeremy Sowers (RC) .25
129 Ryan Shealy (RC) .25
130 Reggie Abercrombie (RC) .25
131 Matt Albers (RC) .25
132 Lastings Milledge (RC) .50
133 Robert Andino RC .50
134 Chris Demaria RC .50
135 Boof Bonser (RC) .25
136 Alay Soler (RC) .50
137 Wilbert Nieves (RC) .25
138 Mike Rouse (RC) .50
139 Carlos Ruiz (RC) .25
140 Matt Capps (RC) .50
141 Travis Ishikawa (RC) .50
142 Josh Kinney RC 1.50
143 Josh Rupe (RC) .25
144 Shaun Marcum (RC) .25
145 Jason Bergmann (RC) .25
146 Tommy Murphy (RC) .25
147 Martin Prado (RC) .25
148 Val Majewski (RC) .25
149 Ian Kinsler (RC) .25
150 Joe Winkelsas (RC) .25
151 Agustin Montero (RC) .25
152 Joe Inglett (RC) 1.00
153 Manuel Corpas RC .50
154 Yusmeiro Petit (RC) .25
155 Mark Woodyard (RC) .25
156 Jeff Fulchino RC .50
157 Stephen Andrade (RC) .25
158 Tim Hamulack (RC) .25
159 Colter Bean (RC) .25

160	Anderson Hernandez (RC)	.25
161	Kevin Reese (RC)	.25
162	Jasorf Windsor (RC)	.25
163	Paul Maholm (RC)	.25
163	Paul Maholm 52 logo/SP (RC)	4.00
164	Jeremy Accardo RC	.50
165	Joel Guzman (RC)	.25
166	Erick Aybar (RC)	.25
167	Scott Thorman (RC)	.25
168	Adam Loewen (RC)	.25
169	Carlos Marmol RC	.50
170	Bill Bray (RC)	.25
171	Edward Mujica RC	.25
172	Jeremy Hermida (RC)	.50
173	Taylor Tankersley (RC)	.25
174	Bobby Keppel (RC)	.25
175	Chris Young (RC)	.50
176	Josh Rabe RC	2.00
177	T.J. Beam (RC)	.25
178	Shane Komine	1.00
178	Shane Komine 52 logo/SP	6.00
179	Scott Mathieson (RC)	.25
180	Josh Barfield (RC)	.25
181	Justin Knoedler (RC)	.25
182	Emiliano Fruto RC	.50
183	Adam Wainwright (RC)	.25
184	Nick Masset (RC)	.25
185	Ryan Roberts RC	.50
186	Brandon Watson (RC)	.25
187	Chris Bootcheck (RC)	.25
188	Daniel Ortmeier (RC)	.25
189	Kevin Barry (RC)	.25
190	Cory Morris RC	.50
191	Kason Gabbard (RC)	.25
192	Tom Mastny (RC)	.25
193	David Aardsma (RC)	.25
194	Anthony Reyes (RC)	.25
195	Mike Jacobs (RC)	.25
196	Conor Jackson (RC)	.25
197	Kenji Johjima RC	3.00
198	Jack Taschner (RC)	.25
199	Renyel Pinto (RC)	.25
200	Chad Santos (RC)	.25
201	Aaron Rakers (RC)	.25
202	Franklin Gutierrez (RC)	.25
203	Chris Coste RC	2.00
204	Chris Iannetta RC	.50
205	Michael Vento (RC)	.25
206	Ryan O'Malley RC	1.00
207	Jason Botts (RC)	.25
208	John Hattig Jr. (RC)	.25
209	Brandon Harper RC	.50
210	Ryan Theriot (RC)	1.00
211	Travis Hughes (RC)	.25
212	Paul Hoover (RC)	.25
213	Brayan Pena (RC)	.25
214	Craig Breslow RC	.75
215	Eude Brito (RC)	.25
216	Melky Cabrera (RC)	.50
216	Melky Cabrera 52 logo/SP (RC)	8.00
217	Jonathan Broxton (RC)	5.00
217	Jonathan Broxton 52 logo/SP (RC)	8.00
218	Bryan Corey (RC)	.25
219	Ron Flores RC	.50
220	Andrew Brown (RC)	.25
221	Jaime Bubela (RC)	.25
222	Jason Bulger (RC)	.25
223	Alberto Callaspo (RC)	.25
224	Jose Capellan (RC)	.25
225	Cole Hamels (RC)	.50
225	Cole Hamels 52 logo/SP (RC)	6.00
226	Bernie Castro (RC)	.25
227	Shin-Soo Choo (RC)	.25
228	Doug Clark (RC)	.25
229	Roy Corcoran RC	.50
230	Tim Corcoran (RC)	.75
231	Nelson Cruz (RC)	.25
232	Rajai Davis (RC)	.25
233	Chris Duncan (RC)	.25
233	Chris Duncan 52 logo/SP (RC)	5.00
234	Scott Dunn (RC)	.25
235	Mike Esposito (RC)	.25
236	Scott Feldman RC	.50
237	Luis Figueroa RC	.50
238	Bartolome Fortunato (RC)	.25
239	Alejandro Freire RC	.50
240	J.J. Furmaniak RC	.50
241	Nicholas Markakis (RC)	.50
242	Matt Garza (RC)	1.00
243	Justin Germano (RC)	.25
244	Alexis Gomez (RC)	.25
245	Tom Gorzelanny (RC)	.25
246	Dan Uggla (RC)	.25
247	Jeremy Guthrie (RC)	.25
248	Stephen Drew (RC)	1.00
249	Brendan Harris (RC)	.25
250	Jeff Harris RC	.50
251	Corey Hart (RC)	.25
252	Chris Heintz RC	.25
253	Prince Fielder (RC)	1.00
254	Francisco Liriano (RC)	.50
255	Jason Hirsh (RC)	.25
256	J.R. House (RC)	.25
257	Zach Jackson (RC)	.25
258	Charlton Jimerson (RC)	.25
259	Greg Jones (RC)	.25
260	Mitch Jones (RC)	.25
261	Ryan Jorgensen RC	.50
262	Logan Kensing (RC)	.25

263	John Koronka (RC)	.25
264	Anthony Lerew (RC)	.25
265	Anibal Sanchez (RC)	.25
266	Juan Mateo RC	.50
267	Paul McAnulty (RC)	.25
268	Dustin McGowan (RC)	.25
269	Marty McLeary (RC)	.25
270	Ryan Zimmerman (RC)	2.00
271	Dustin Nippert (RC)	.25
272	Eric O'Flaherty RC	.50
273	Ronny Paulino (RC)	.25
274	Tony Pena (RC)	.25
275	Hayden Penn (RC)	.25
276	Miguel Perez (RC)	5.00
277	Paul Phillips (RC)	5.00
278	Omar Quintanilla (RC)	5.00
279	Guillermo Quiroz (RC)	5.00
280	Darrell Rasner (RC)	5.00
281	Kenny Ray (RC)	5.00
282	Royce Ring (RC)	5.00
283	Brian Rogers (RC)	5.00
284	Ed Rogers (RC)	5.00
285	Danny Sandoval RC	10.00
286	Joe Saunders (RC)	5.00
287	Chris Schroder RC	5.00
288	Mike Smith (RC)	5.00
289	Travis Smith (RC)	5.00
290	Geovany Soto (RC)	5.00
291	Brian Sweeney (RC)	5.00
292	Jon Switzer (RC)	5.00
293	Joe Thurston (RC)	5.00
294	Jermaine Van Buren (RC)	5.00
295	Ryan Garko (RC)	5.00
296	Cla Meredith (RC)	5.00
297	Luke Scott (RC)	5.00
298	Andy Marte (RC)	5.00
299	Jered Weaver (RC)	10.00
300	Freddy Guzman (RC)	5.00
301	Jonathan Papelbon (RC)	10.00
302	John-Ford Griffin (RC)	5.00
303	Jon Lester (RC)	15.00
304	Shawn Hill (RC)	5.00
305	Brian Myrow (RC)	10.00
306	Anderson Garcia RC	8.00
307	Andre Ethier (RC)	10.00
308	Ben Hendrickson (RC)	5.00
309	Alejandro Machado (RC)	5.00
310	Justin Verlander (RC)	15.00
311	Mickey Mantle/Blue	40.00
311	Mickey Mantle/Black	20.00
311	Mickey Mantle/Green	20.00
311	Mickey Mantle/Orange	20.00
311	Mickey Mantle Red	20.00
311	Mickey Mantle/Yellow	20.00
312	Steve Stemle RC	5.00

Chrome

		NM/M
	Common Player:	1.50
	Production 1,952 Sets	
	Refractor:	2-3X
	Production 552 Sets	
	Gold Refractor:	4-6X
	Production 52 Sets	
1	Howie Kendrick	4.00
2	David Pauley	1.50
3	Chris Denorfia	1.50
4	Jordan Tata	2.00
5	Fernando Nieve	1.50
6	Craig Hansen	1.50
7	Mickey Mantle	25.00
8	James Shields	2.00
9	Francisco Rosario	1.50
10	Jeff Karstens	3.00
11	Buck Coats	2.00
12	Josh Wilson	1.50
13	Joel Zumaya	4.00
14	Tony Gwynn Jr.	4.00
15	Jonah Bayliss	1.50
16	John Gall	1.50
17	Mike O'Connor	2.00
18	Peter Moylan	1.50
19	Cody Ross	1.50
20	Hanley Ramirez	3.00
21	Hong-Chih Kuo	3.00
22	Yurendell DeCaster	1.50
23	Sean Green	1.50
24	Ty Taubenheim	1.50
25	Macay McBride	1.50
26	Brian Slocum	1.50

27	Chris Resop	2.00
28	Jason Kubel	1.50
29	Brian Sanches	1.50
30	Mark Lowe	1.50
31	Melvin Dorta	1.50
32	Sendy Rleal	1.50
33	Ryan Shealy	1.50
34	Robert Andino	1.50
35	Wilbert Nieves	1.50
36	Travis Ishikawa	1.50
37	Jason Bergmann	1.50
38	Ian Kinsler	3.00
39	Manuel Corpas	1.50
40	Stephen Andrade	1.50
41	Kevin Reese	1.50
42	Joel Guzman	1.50
43	Carlos Marmol	2.00
44	Taylor Tankersley	1.50
45	T.J. Beam	1.50
46	Justin Knoedler	1.50
47	Ryan Roberts	1.50
48	Kevin Barry	1.50
49	David Aardsma	1.50
50	Kenji Johjima	5.00
51	Aaron Rakers	1.50
52	Michael Vento	1.50
53	Brandon Harper	1.50
54	Brayan Pena	1.50
55	Jonathan Broxton	2.00
56	Jaime Bubela	1.50
57	Cole Hamels	6.00
58	Roy Corcoran	1.50
59	Chris Duncan	4.00
60	Luis Figueroa	1.50
61	Kendry Morales	3.00
62	Tom Gorzelanny	1.50
63	Brendan Harris	1.50
64	Anibal Sanchez	3.00
65	Zach Jackson	1.50
66	Ryan Jorgensen	1.50
67	Josh Johnson	2.00
68	Marty McLeary	2.00
69	Ronny Paulino	1.50
70	Tyler Johnson	1.50
2	Reggie Abercrombie	1.50
72	Nicholas Markakis	6.00
73	J.J. Furmaniak	1.50
74	Prince Fielder	4.00
75	Enrique Gonzalez	1.50
76	Angel Pagan	1.50
77	Rafael Perez	2.00
78	Eric Reed	1.50
79	Chris Booker	1.50
80	David Gassner	1.50
81	John Van Benschoten	1.50
82	Russell Martin	2.00
83	Santiago Ramirez	1.50
84	Phil Stockman	1.50
85	Jim Johnson	3.00
86	Jack Hannahan	1.50
87	Philip Barzilla	1.50
88	Chris Barnwell	1.50
89	Joshua Sharpless	1.50
90	Chris Roberson	2.00

Debut Flashbacks

		NM/M
	Common Player:	2.00
	Chrome:	1.5-2X
	Production 1,952 Sets	
	Refractor:	2-3X
	Production 552 Sets	
	Gold Refractor:	4-6X
	Production 52 Sets	
1	Dontrelle Willis	2.00
2	Carlos Beltran	3.00
3	Albert Pujols	8.00
4	Ichiro Suzuki	5.00
5	Mike Piazza	3.00
6	Nomar Garciaparra	3.00
7	Scott Rolen	3.00
8	Mariano Rivera	3.00
9	David Ortiz	4.00
10	Johnny Damon	4.00
11	Tom Glavine	3.00
12	David Wright	5.00
13	Greg Maddux	5.00
14	Manny Ramirez	4.00
15	Alex Rodriguez	6.00
16	Roger Clemens	6.00
17	Alfonso Soriano	3.00
18	Frank Thomas	3.00
19	Chipper Jones	3.00
20	Ivan Rodriguez	3.00

Dynamic Duos

		NM/M
	Common Duo:	1.00
	Inserted 1:4	
1	Stephen Drew, Carlos Quentin	2.00
2	Jonathan Papelbon, Jon Lester	3.00
3	Joel Zumaya, Justin Verlander	4.00

DYNAMIC DUOS
ANDRE ETHIER   RUSSELL MARTIN

4	Dan Uggla, Hanley Ramirez	1.50
5	Jonathan Broxton, Chad Billingsley	1.00
6	Francisco Liriano, Matt Garza	1.50
7	Lastings Milledge, John Maine	1.50
8	Chris Coste, Cole Hamels	2.00
9	Michael Napoli, Howie Kendrick	1.50
10	Joe Inglett, Andy Marte	1.00
11	Jeremy Hermida, Josh Willingham	1.00
12	Matthew Kemp, James Loney	1.50
13	Andre Ethier, Russell Martin	1.50
14	Melky Cabrera, Jeff Karstens	1.50
15	Ricky Nolasco, Scott Olsen, Josh Johnson, Anibal Sanchez	1.50

Autograph

		NM/M
	Common Auto.:	10.00
	Red Ink:	2-3X
	Production 52 Sets	
RA	Reggie Abercrombie	15.00
MA	Matt Albers	10.00
BA	Brian Anderson	15.00
EA	Erick Aybar	15.00
BPB	Brian Bannister	15.00
TJB	T.J. Bohn	15.00
BB	Boof Bonser	25.00
WB	Bill Bray	20.00
MC	Melky Cabrera	45.00
MTC	Matt Cain	40.00
FC	Fabio Castro	20.00
BC	Buck Coats	10.00
YD	Yurendell DeCaster	10.00
SD	Stephen Drew	35.00
KF	Kevin Frandsen	10.00
EF	Emiliano Fruto	10.00
MG	Matt Garza	25.00
EG	Enrique Gonzalez	10.00
FG	Franklin Gutierrez	15.00
AG	Angel Guzman	15.00
JG	Joel Guzman	15.00
CI	Chris Iannetta	20.00
CHJ	Chuck James	20.00
JWK	Jeff Karstens	30.00
MK	Matthew Kemp	20.00
HK	Howie Kendrick	30.00
JK	Josh Kinney	20.00
HCK	Hong-Chih Kuo	40.00
AL	Anthony Lerew	15.00
CM	Chris Mabeus	10.00
TM	Tom Mastny	15.00
SM	Scott Mathieson	15.00
JM	Jeff Mathis	15.00
KM	Kendry Morales	15.00
EM	Edward Mujica	10.00
MN	Michael Napoli	15.00
RO	Ryan O'Malley	20.00
AP	Angel Pagan	10.00
JP	Jonathan Papelbon	40.00
YP	Yusmeiro Petit	15.00
AS	Anibal Sanchez	20.00
JFS	Joe Saunders	15.00
JS	Joshua Sharpless	15.00
BS	Brian Slocum	10.00
DU	Dan Uggla	15.00
JVB	John Van Benschoten	10.00

JV	Justin Verlander	50.00
JW	Jered Weaver	40.00
RZ	Ryan Zimmerman	60.00
BZ	Benjamin Zobrist	10.00
JZ	Joel Zumaya	50.00

Ticket to Stardom Relics

No Pricing
Production 10 Sets

2007 Topps

		NM/M
	Complete Set (330):	75.00
	Common Player:	.10
	Hobby Pack (10):	3.00
	Hobby Box (36):	100.00
	Jumbo Pack (50):	15.00
	Jumbo Box (10):	140.00
	Rack Pack (22):	5.00
	Rack Box (24):	100.00
1	John Lackey	.10
2	Nick Swisher	.25
3	Brad Lidge	.10
4	Bengie Molina	.10
5	Bobby Abreu	.25
6	Edgar Renteria	.25
7	Mickey Mantle	5.00
8	Preston Wilson	.10
9	Ryan Dempster	.10
10	C.C. Sabathia	.25
11	Julio Lugo	.10
12	J.D. Drew	.25
13	Miguel Batista	.10
14	Eliezer Alfonzo	.10
15	Andrew Miller RC	3.00
16	Yuniesky Betancourt	.10
17	Saul Rivera	.10
18	Orlando Hernandez	.10
19	Alfredo Amezaga	.10
20	Delmon Young (RC)	.50
21	Javy Lopez	.10
22	Corey Patterson	.10
23	Josh Bard	.10
24	Tom Gordon	.10
25	Gary Matthews	.10
26	Jason Jennings	.10
27	Joey Gathright	.10
28	Brandon Inge	.10
29	Pat Neshek	.10
30	Bronson Arroyo	.10
31	Jay Payton	.10
32	Andy Pettitte	.25
33	Ervin Santana	.25
34	Paul Konerko	.25
35	Joel Zumaya	.25
36	Gregg Zaun	.10
37	Tony Gwynn	.50
38	Adam LaRoche	.25
39	Jim Edmonds	.25
40	Derek Jeter	25.00
41	Rich Hill	.10
42	Livan Hernandez	.10
43	Aubrey Huff	.10
44	Todd Greene	.10
45	Andre Ethier	.25
46	Jeremy Sowers	.10
47	Ben Broussard	.10
48	Darren Oliver	.10
49	Nook Logan	.10
50	Miguel Cabrera	.50
51	Carlos Lee	.25
52	Jose Castillo	.10
53	Mike Piazza	.75
54	Daniel Cabrera	.10
55	Cole Hamels	.40
56	Mark Loretta	.10
57	Brian Fuentes	.10
58	Todd Coffey	.10
59	Brent Clevlen	.10
60	John Smoltz	.25
61	Ross Gload	.10
62	Dan Wheeler	.10
63	Scott Proctor	.10
64	Bobby Kielty	.10
65	Dan Uggla	.25
66	Lyle Overbay	.10
67	Geoff Jenkins	.10
68	Michael Barrett	.10
69	Casey Fossum	.10
70	Ivan Rodriguez	.40
71	Jose Lopez	.10
72	Jake Westbrook	.10
73	Moises Alou	.25
74	Jose Valverde	.10
75	Jered Weaver	.25
76	Lastings Milledge	.25
77	Austin Kearns	.10
78	Adam Loewen	.10
79	Josh Barfield	.10
80	Johan Santana	.40
81	Ian Kinsler	.25
82	Ian Snell	.10
83	Mike Lowell	.10
84	Elizardo Ramirez	.10
85	Scott Rolen	.40

86	Shannon Stewart	.10
87	Alexis Gomez	.10
88	Jimmy Gobble	.10
89	Jamey Carroll	.10
90	Chipper Jones	.50
91	Carlos Silva	.10
92	Joe Crede	.25
93	Michael Napoli	.10
94	Willy Travis	.10
95	Rafael Furcal	.25
96	Phil Nevin	.10
97	David Bush	.10
98	Marcus Giles	.10
99	Joe Blanton	.10
100	Dontrelle Willis	.25
101	Scott Kazmir	.25
102	Jeff Kent	.25
103	Pedro Feliz	.10
104	Johnny Estrada	.10
105	Travis Hafner	.25
106	Ryan Garko	.10
107	Rafael Soriano	.10
108	Wes Helms	.10
109	Billy Wagner	.10
110	Aaron Rowand	.10
111	Felipe Lopez	.10
112	Jeff Conine	.10
113	Nicholas Markakis	.25
114	John Koronka	.10
115	B.J. Ryan	.10
116	Tim Wakefield	.25
117	David Ross	.10
118	Emil Brown	.10
119	Michael Cuddyer	.10
120	Jason Giambi	.40
121	Alex Cintron	.10
122	Luke Scott	.10
123	Chone Figgins	.10
124	Huston Street	.25
125	Carlos Delgado	.40
126	Daryle Ward	.10
127	Chris Duncan	.10
128	Damian Miller	.10
129	Aramis Ramirez	.25
130	Albert Pujols	1.50
131	Chris Snyder	.10
132	Ray Durham	.10
133	Franklin Gutierrez	.10
134	Mike Jacobs	.10
135	Troy Tulowitzki (RC)	.75
136	Jon Rauch	.10
137	Jay Gibbons	.10
138	Adrian Gonzalez	.25
139	Randy Wolf	.10
140	Freddy Sanchez	.10
141	Rich Aurilia	.10
142	Trot Nixon	.10
143	Vicente Padilla	.10
144	Jack Wilson	.10
145	Jake Peavy	.25
146	Luke Hudson	.10
147	Javier Vazquez	.10
148	Scott Podsednik	.10
149	Ivan Rodriguez, Magglio Ordonez	.25
150	Todd Helton	.40
151	Kendry Morales	.10
152	Adam Everett	.10
153	Bob Wickman	.10
154	Bill Hall	.25
155	Jeremy Bonderman	.25
156	Ryan Theriot	.10
157	Rocco Baldelli	.25
158	Noah Lowry	.10
159	Jason Michaels	.10
160	Justin Verlander	.50
161	Eduardo Perez	.10
162	Chris Ray	.10
163	Dave Roberts	.10
164	Zachary Duke	.10
165	Mark Buehrle	.10
166	Hank Blalock	.10
167	Royce Clayton	.10
168	Mark Teahen	.10
169	Todd Jones	.10
170	Chien-Ming Wang	.50
171	Nick Punto	.10
172	Morgan Ensberg	.10
173	Robert Mackowiak	.10
174	Frank Catalanotto	.10
175	Matt Murton	.10
176	Alfonso Soriano, Carlos Beltran	.40
177	Francisco Cordero	.10
178	Jason Marquis	.10
179	Joe Nathan	.10
180	Roy Halladay	.25
181	Melvin Mora	.10
182	Ramon Ortiz	.10
183	Jose Valentin	.10
184	Gil Meche	.10
185	B.J. Upton	.25
186	Grady Sizemore	.40
187	Matt Cain	.10
188	Eric Byrnes	.10
189	Carl Crawford	.25
190	J.J. Putz	.10
191	Cla Meredith	.10
192	Matt Capps	.10
193	Rod Barajas	.10
194	Edwin Encarnacion	.10
195	James Loney	.10
196	Johnny Damon	.50
197	Freddy Garcia	.10
198	Mike Redmond	.10
199	Ryan Shealy	.10
200	Carlos Beltran	.40
201	Chuck James	.10

202	Mark Ellis	.10
203	Brad Ausmus	.10
204	Juan Rivera	.10
205	Cory Sullivan	.10
206	Ben Sheets	.25
207	Mark Mulder	.10
208	Carlos Quentin	.10
209	Jonathan Broxton	.10
210	Kazuo Matsui	.10
211	Armando Benitez	.10
212	Richie Sexson	.40
213	Josh Johnson	.10
214	Brian Schneider	.10
215	Craig Monroe	.10
216	Chris Duffy	.10
217	Chris Coste	.10
218	Clay Hensley	.10
219	Chris Gomez	.10
220	Hideki Matsui	.75
221	Robinson Tejeda	.10
222	Scott Hatteberg	.10
223	Jeff Francis	.10
224	Matt Thornton	.10
225	Robinson Cano	.40
226	New York Yankees	1.00
227	Oakland A's	.25
228	St. Louis Cardinals	.50
229	Minnesota Twins	.25
230	Barry Zito	.25
231	Baltimore Orioles	.25
232	Seattle Mariners	.25
233	Houston Astros	.25
234	Florida Marlins	.25
235	Reed Johnson	.25
236	Toronto Blue Jays	.25
237	Cincinnati Reds	.25
238	Philadelphia Phillies	.25
239	Anaheim Angels	.25
240	Chris Carpenter	.25
241	Atlanta Braves	.25
242	Washington Nationals	.25
243	Joe Torre	.50
244	Tampa Bay Devil Rays	.25
245	Chad Tracey	.10
246	Mike Hargrove	.10
247	Mike Scioscia	.10
248	Ron Gardenhire	.10
249	Tony LaRussa	.10
250	Anibal Sanchez	.10
251	Charlie Manuel	.10
252	John Gibbons	.10
253	Ken Macha	.10
254	Jerry Narron	.10
255	Brad Penny	.10
256	Bobby Cox	.10
257	Bob Melvin	.10
258	Mike Hargrove	.10
259	Phil Garner	.10
260	David Wright	1.00
261	Vinny Rottino (RC)	.25
262	Ryan Braun RC	1.00
263	Kevin Kouzmanoff (RC)	.25
264	David Murphy (RC)	.25
265	Jimmy Rollins	.25
266	Joe Maddon	.10
267	Grady Little	.10
268	Ryan Sweeney (RC)	.25
269	Fred Lewis (RC)	.25
270	Alfonso Soriano	.50
271	Delwyn Young (RC)	.25
272	Jeff Salazar (RC)	.25
273	Miguel Montero (RC)	.25
274	Shawn Riggans (RC)	.25
275	Greg Maddux	1.00
276	Brian Stokes (RC)	.25
277	Philip Humber (RC)	.25
278	Scott Moore (RC)	.25
279	Adam Lind (RC)	.25
280	Curt Schilling	.50
281	Chris Narveson (RC)	.50
282	Oswaldo Navarro RC	.50
283	Drew Anderson (RC)	.25
284	Jerry Owens (RC)	.25
285	Randy Johnson	.50
286	Joaquin Arias (RC)	.25
287	Jose Garcia (RC)	.25
288	Shane Youman RC	.25
289	Brian Burres (RC)	.25
290	Matt Holliday	.25
291	Ryan Feierabend (RC)	.25
292	Josh Fields (RC)	.25
293	Glen Perkins (RC)	.25
294	Mike Rabelo RC	.50
295	Jorge Posada	.25
296	Ubaldo Jimenez (RC)	.25
297	Brad Ausmus	.10
298	Eric Chavez	.25
299	Orlando Hudson	.10
300	Vladimir Guerrero	.50
301	Derek Jeter	1.00
302	Scott Rolen	.25
303	Mark Grudzielanek	.10
304	Kenny Rogers	.10
305	Frank Thomas	.25
306	Mike Cameron	.10
307	Torii Hunter	.25
308	Albert Pujols	1.00
309	Mark Teixeira	.25
310	Jonathan Papelbon	.50
311	Greg Maddux	.50
312	Carlos Beltran	.25
313	Ichiro Suzuki	.75
314	Andruw Jones	.25
315	Manny Ramirez	.50
316	Vernon Wells	.25
317	Omar Vizquel	.10
318	Ivan Rodriguez	.25
319	Brandon Webb	.25
320	Magglio Ordonez	.25
321	Johan Santana	.25
322	Ryan Howard	1.00
323	Justin Morneau	.25
324	Hanley Ramirez	.25
325	Joe Mauer	.25
326	Justin Verlander	.25
327	Derek Jeter, Bobby Abreu	.50
328	Carlos Delgado, David Wright	.50
329	Yadier Molina, Albert Pujols	.50
330	Ryan Howard	.50

Copper
Copper (1-330): 25-50X
Production 56 Sets

Gold
Gold: 8-15X
Production 2,007 Sets

Platinum
No Pricing
Production One Set

1st Edition
1st Edition: 5-10X
Hobby Exclusive 1:36

Own The Game
NM/M
Common Player: .50
Inserted 1:6

1	Ryan Howard	2.50
2	David Ortiz	1.00
3	Alfonso Soriano	1.00
4	Albert Pujols	3.00
5	Lance Berkman	.75
6	Jermaine Dye	.50
7	Travis Hafner	.75
8	Jim Thome	1.00
9	Carlos Beltran	1.00
10	Adam Dunn	.75
11	Ryan Howard	2.50
12	David Ortiz	1.00
13	Albert Pujols	3.00
14	Lance Berkman	.75
15	Justin Morneau	.75
16	Andruw Jones	1.00
17	Jermaine Dye	.50
18	Travis Hafner	.75
19	Alex Rodriguez	3.00
20	David Wright	2.00
21	Johan Santana	1.00
22	Chris Carpenter	.75
23	Brandon Webb	.50
24	Roy Oswalt	.75
25	Josh Johnson	.50

Hobby Masters
NM/M
Common Player: .50
Inserted 1:6

1	David Wright	3.00
2	Albert Pujols	4.00
3	David Ortiz	1.50
4	Ryan Howard	3.00
5	Alfonso Soriano	1.50
6	Delmon Young	1.50
7	Jered Weaver	1.50
8	Derek Jeter	4.00
9	Freddy Sanchez	.50
10	Alex Rodriguez	3.00
11	Johan Santana	1.50
12	Ichiro Suzuki	2.50
13	Andruw Jones	1.50
14	Vladimir Guerrero	1.50
15	Miguel Cabrera	1.50
16	Todd Helton	1.00
17	Manny Ramirez	1.50
18	Carlos Beltran	1.50
19	Justin Morneau	1.00
20	Francisco Liriano	1.00

Josh Gibson HR History
NM/M
Common Gibson: 1.00
Inserted 1:9

A-Rod Road to 500
NM/M
Complete Set (25): 80.00
Common A-Rod: 4.00

Generation Now
NM/M
All Ryan Howard's: 2.00
All Chase Utley's: 1.00
All C. Ming Wang's: 3.00
All Mike Napoli's: .50
All Justin Morneau's: 1.00
All David Wright's: 2.00
All Jered Weaver's: 1.00
All Andre Ethier's: 1.00

Generation Now Autographs
Production One Set

The Mickey Mantle Story
NM/M
Complete Set (15): 40.00
Common Mantle: 3.00

Mickey Mantle Home Run History
NM/M
Common Mantle HR History: 2.00
Inserted 1:9 Hobby

Mickey Mantle Home Run History Relics
No Pricing
Production 7 Sets

1952 Mickey Mantle Reprint Relic
Production 52

Unlock the Mick
NM/M
Complete Set (5):
Common Mantle: 2.00
Inserted 1:18
1-5 Mickey Mantle 2.00

A-Rod Road to 500 Autographs
Production One Set

2006 Highlights Autographs

NM/M
Some not priced yet

JH	John Hattig Jr.	8.00
AM	Andrew Miller	50.00
AS	Anibal Sanchez	15.00
MN	Michael Napoli	10.00
JL	James Loney	20.00
MH	Matt Holliday	15.00
TT	Troy Tulowitzki	20.00
HR	Hanley Ramirez	20.00
JF	Josh Fields	15.00
CQ	Carlos Quentin	15.00
MG	Matt Garza	15.00
JM	John Maine	25.00
TH	Travis Hafner	25.00
KM	Kevin Mench	15.00
CU	Chase Utley	50.00
DW	David Wright	75.00
JM	Justin Morneau	25.00
JS	Johan Santana	60.00
MC	Miguel Cabrera	35.00
DY	Delmon Young	30.00
DWW	Dontrelle Willis	20.00
CW	Chien-Ming Wang	225.00
JS	John Smoltz	50.00
AS	Alfonso Soriano	100.00
DO	David Ortiz	100.00
RH	Ryan Howard	150.00
AR	Alex Rodriguez	250.00

World Champion Relics
NM/M
Common Player: 40.00

1	Jeff Weaver	60.00
2	Chris Duncan	60.00
3	Chris Carpenter	75.00
4	Yadier Molina	40.00
5	Albert Pujols	150.00
6	Jim Edmonds	65.00
7	Ronnie Belliard	40.00
8	So Taguchi	80.00
9	Juan Encarnacion	50.00
10	Scott Rolen	75.00
11	Anthony Reyes	60.00
12	Preston Wilson	50.00
13	Jeff Suppan	60.00
14	Adam Wainwright	150.00
15	David Eckstein	100.00

2006 Highlights Relics
NM/M
Common Player: 5.00

AP	Albert Pujols	25.00
AR	Alex Rodriguez	20.00
AS	Alfonso Soriano	15.00
BM	Brian McCann	15.00
CB	Carlos Beltran	10.00
CD	Carlos Delgado	8.00
CQ	Carlos Quentin	10.00
CB	Craig Biggio	10.00
CS	Curt Schilling	10.00
DO	David Ortiz	10.00
DW	Dontrelle Willis	8.00
ER	Edgar Renteria	5.00
FT	Frank Thomas	10.00
GS	Gary Sheffield	8.00
IS	Ichiro Suzuki	25.00
IR	Ivan Rodriguez	10.00
JB	Jason Bay	10.00
JPM	Joe Mauer	20.00
JAS	Johan Santana	20.00
JS	John Smoltz	10.00
JR	Jose Reyes	15.00
JM	Justin Morneau	15.00
MO	Magglio Ordonez	5.00
MAR	Manny Ramirez	10.00
MR	Mariano Rivera	15.00
MT	Miguel Tejada	8.00
PK	Paul Konerko	10.00
RC	Robinson Cano	20.00
RO	Roy Oswalt	8.00
RH	Ryan Howard	25.00
SK	Scott Kazmir	8.00
SR	Scott Rolen	10.00
TG	Tom Glavine	5.00
TG	Troy Glaus	5.00
VW	Vernon Wells	8.00

In The Name
Production One Set

2007 Topps Heritage
NM/M
Complete Set (495):
Common Player: .40
Common SP: 5.00
Inserted 1:2
Common Variation: 5.00
Inserted 1:6
Pack (8): 3.00
Box (24): 65.00

1	David Ortiz	1.50
2	Roger Clemens	3.00
2	Roger Clemens/Yellow Team Name/SP	15.00
3	David Wells	.40
4	Ronny Paulino/SP	5.00
5	Derek Jeter/SP	20.00
6	Felix Hernandez	2.00
7	Todd Helton	1.00
8	David Eckstein	.40
8	David Eckstein/ Yellow Name/SP	5.00
9	Craig Wilson	.40
10	John Smoltz	.40
11	Robert Mackowiak	.40
11	Robert Mackowiak/ Yellow Team Name/SP	5.00
12	Scott Hatteberg	.40
13	Wilfredo Ledezma/SP	5.00
13	Wilfredo Ledezma/Yellow Team Name/SP	5.00
14	Bobby Abreu/SP	8.00
15	Austin Kearns	.40
16	Wilson Betemit	.40
17	Darren Oliver	.40
18	Josh Beckett	.40
19	San Francisco Giants	.40
20	Robinson Cano	1.00
20	Robinson Cano/Yellow Team Name/SP	8.00
21	Matt Cain	1.00
22	Jason Kendall/SP	5.00
23	Mark Kotsay/SP	5.00
23	Mark Kotsay/ Yellow Name/SP	5.00
24	Yadier Molina	.40
24	Yadier Molina/ Yellow Name/SP	5.00
25	Brad Penny	.40
26	Adrian Gonzalez	.40
27	Danny Haren	.40
28	Brian Giles	.40
29	Jose Lopez	.40
30	Ichiro Suzuki	2.50
30	Ichiro Suzuki/ Yellow Name/SP	10.00
31	Beltran Perez/SP (RC)	5.00
32	Brad Hawpe/SP	5.00
33	Jim Thome	1.50
33	Jim Thome/Yellow Team Name/SP	5.00
34	Mark DeRosa	.40
35	Woody Williams	.40
35	Woody Williams/Yellow Team Name/SP	5.00
36	Luis Gonzalez	.40
37	Billy Sadler (RC)	1.00
38	Dave Roberts	.40
39	Mitch Maier (RC)	1.00
40	Francisco Cordero/SP	5.00
41	Anthony Reyes/SP	8.00
42	Russell Martin	.40
43	Scott Proctor	.40
44	Washington Nationals	.40
45	Shane Victorino	.40
46	Joel Zumaya	1.00
46	Joel Zumaya/ Yellow Name/SP	5.00
47	Delmon Young (RC)	1.00
48	Alex Rios	5.00
49	Willy Taveras/SP	5.00
50	Mark Buehrle/SP	5.00
50	Mark Buehrle/Yellow Team Name/SP	5.00
51	Livan Hernandez	.40
52	Jason Bay	1.00
52	Jason Bay/Yellow Team Name/SP	5.00
53	Jose Valentin	.40
53	Jose Valentin/ Yellow Name/SP	5.00
54	Kevin Reese	.40
55	Felipe Lopez	.40
56	Ryan Sweeney (RC)	1.00
57	Kelvim Escobar	.40
57	Kelvim Escobar/ Yellow Name/SP	5.00
58	Nick Swisher/SP	5.00
58	Nick Swisher/Yellow Team Name/SP	8.00
59	Kevin Millwood/SP	.40
60	Preston Wilson	.40
60	Preston Wilson/ Yellow Name/SP	5.00
61	Mariano Rivera	.75
61	Mariano Rivera/ Yellow Name/SP	8.00
62	Josh Barfield	.40
63	Ryan Freel	.40
64	Tim Hudson	.75
64	Chris Narveson (RC)	1.00
65	Chris Narveson/ Yellow Name/SP	5.00
66	Matt Murton	.40
67	Melvin Mora/SP	5.00
68	Jason Jennings/SP	5.00
69	Emil Brown	.40
70	Magglio Ordonez	.40
70	Magglio Ordonez/ Yellow Name/SP	5.00
71	Los Angeles Dodgers	.40
72	Huston Street	.40
73	David Ross	.40
74	Juan Uribe	.40
75	Scott Podsednik	.40
76	Cole Hamels/SP	8.00
76	Cole Hamels/Yellow Team Name/SP	8.00
77	Rafael Furcal/SP	5.00
77	Rafael Furcal/ Yellow Team Name/SP	5.00
78	Ryan Theriot	.40
78	Ryan Theriot/ Yellow Name/SP	5.00
79	Corey Patterson	.40
79	Corey Patterson/Yellow Team Name/SP	5.00
80	Jered Weaver	.40
81	Stephen Drew	.75
81	Stephen Drew/Yellow Team Name/SP	8.00
82	Adam Kennedy	.40
83	Tony Gwynn Jr.	.40
84	Erik Bedard	.40
85	Omar Vizquel/SP	5.00
85	Omar Vizquel/Yellow Team Name/SP	5.00
86	Fred Lewis/SP (RC)	5.00
87	Brad Radke	.40
88	Shawn Chacon/ Yellow Name/SP	5.00
88	Frank Catalanotto	.40
89	Orlando Hudson	.40
90	Pat Burrell	.40
91	David DeJesus	.40
92	David Wright	2.50
92	David Wright/ Yellow Name/SP	10.00
93	Conor Jackson	.40
94	Xavier Nady/SP	5.00
95	Bill Hall/SP	8.00
96	Andre Ethier	.75
97	Jeff Suppan	.40
97	Jeff Suppan/ Yellow Name/SP	5.00
98	Ryan Zimmerman	.75
98	Ryan Zimmerman/ Yellow Name/SP	8.00
99	Yuniesky Betancourt	.40
100	Jose Contreras	5.00
100	Jose Contreras/Yellow Team Name/SP	5.00
101	Miguel Cairo	.40
101	Miguel Cairo/ Yellow Name/SP	5.00
102	Brian Roberts	.40
103	Carl Crawford/SP	8.00
104	Mike Lamb/SP	5.00
105	Mark Ellis	.40
106	Scott Rolen	1.50
107	Garrett Atkins	.40
108	Hanley Ramirez	.75
108	Hanley Ramirez/Yellow Team Name/SP	5.00
109	Trot Nixon	.40
110	Edgar Renteria	.40
111	Jeff Francis	.40
112	Marcus Thames/SP	5.00
113	Brian Burres/SP (RC)	5.00
114	Brian Schneider	.40
115	Jeremy Bonderman	.75
116	Ryan Madson	.40
117	Gerald Laird	.40
118	Roy Halladay	.75
119	Victor Martinez	.40
120	Greg Maddux	2.50
121	Jay Payton/SP	5.00
122	Jacque Jones/SP	5.00
123	Juan Lara RC	1.00
124	Derrick Turnbow	.40
125	Adam Everett	.40
126	Michael Cuddyer	.40
127	Gil Meche	.40
128	Willy Aybar	.40
129	Jerry Owens RC	1.00
130	Manny Ramirez/SP	10.00
131	Howie Kendrick/SP	8.00
132	Byung-Hyun Kim	.40
133	Kevin Kouzmanoff (RC)	1.00
134	Philadelphia Phillies	.40
135	Joe Blanton	.40
136	Ray Durham	.40
137	Luke Hudson	.40
138	Eric Byrnes	.40
139	Ryan Braun/SP RC	8.00
140	Johnny Damon/SP	10.00
141	Ambiorix Burgos	.40
142	Hideki Matsui	.40
143	Josh Johnson	.40
144	Miguel Cabrera	.40
146	Delwyn Young (RC)	1.00
147	Chuck James	.40
148	Morgan Ensberg	.40
149	Jose Vidro/SP	5.00
150	Alex Rodriguez/SP	15.00
151	Carlos Maldonado (RC)	1.00
152	Jason Schmidt	.40
153	Alex Escobar	.40
154	Chris Gomez	.40
155	Endy Chavez	.40
156	Kris Benson	.40
157	Bronson Arroyo	.40
158	Cleveland Indians/SP	8.00
159	Chris Ray/SP	5.00
160	Richie Sexson	.40
161	Huston Street	.40
162	Kevin Youkilis	.40
163	Armando Benitez	.40
164	Vinny Rottino (RC)	1.00
165	Garret Anderson	.40
166	Todd Greene	.40
167	Brian Stokes/SP (RC)	.40
168	Albert Pujols/SP	20.00
169	Todd Coffey	.40
170	Jason Michaels	.40
171	David Dellucci	.40
172	Eric Milton	.40
173	Austin Kearns	.40
174	Kansas City Royals	.40
175	Andy Cannizaro RC	2.00
176	David Weathers/SP	5.00
177	Jermaine Dye/SP	5.00
178	Wily Mo Pena	.40
179	Chris Burke	.40
180	Jeff Weaver	.40
181	Juan Encarnacion	.40
182	Jeremy Hermida	.40
183	Tim Wakefield	.40
184	Rich Hill	.40
185	Aaron Hill/SP	5.00
186	Scot Shields/SP	5.00
187	Randy Johnson	.40
188	Dan Johnson	.40
189	Sean Marshall	.40
190	Marcus Giles	.40
191	Jonathan Broxton	.40
192	Mike Piazza	.40
193	Carlos Quentin	.40
194	Derek Lowe/SP	5.00
195	Russell Branyan/SP	5.00
196	Jason Marquis	.40
197	Khalil Greene	.40
198	Ryan Dempster	.40
199	Ronnie Belliard	.40
200	Josh Fogg	.40
201	Carlos Lee	.40
202	Chris Denorfia	.40
203	Kendry Morales/SP	5.00
204	Rafael Soriano/SP	5.00
205	Brandon Phillips	.40
206	Andrew Miller RC	5.00
207	John Koronka	.40
208	Luis Castillo	.40
209	Angel Guzman	.40
210	Jim Edmonds	.40
211	Patrick Misch/SP	1.00
212	Ty Wigginton/SP	5.00
213	Brandon Inge/SP	5.00
214	Royce Clayton	.40
215	Ben Broussard	.40
216	St. Louis Cardinals	.40
217	Mark Mulder	.40
218	Kenji Johjima	.40
219	Joe Crede	.40
220	Danny Haren	.40
221	Josh Fields/SP (RC)	8.00
222	Pat Neshek/SP	10.00
223	Reed Johnson	.40
224	Mike Mussina	.40
225	Randy Winn	.40
226	Brian Rogers (RC)	.40
227	Juan Rivera	.40
228	Shawn Green	.40

ABBREVIATIONS
SP - Short Print

#	Player	Price
229	Mike Napoli	.40
230	Chase Utley/SP	10.00
231	John Nelson/SP (RC)	10.00
232	Casey Blake	.40
233	Lyle Overbay	.40
234	Adam LaRoche	.40
235	Jeff Weaver	.40
236	Johnny Estrada	.40
237	James Shields	.40
238	Jose Castillo	.40
239	Doug Davis/SP	5.00
240	Jason Giambi/SP	8.00
241	Mike Gonzalez	.40
242	Scott Downs	.40
243	Joe Inglett	.40
244	Matthew Kemp	.40
245	Ted Lilly	.40
246	New York Yankees	.40
247	Jamey Carroll	.40
248	Adam Wainwright/SP	8.00
249	Matt Thornton/SP	5.00
250	Alfonso Soriano	.40
251	Tom Gordon	.40
252	Dennis Sarfate (RC)	.40
253	Zachary Duke	.40
254	Hank Blalock	.40
255	Johan Santana	.40
256	Chicago White Sox	.40
257	Aaron Cook/SP	5.00
258	Cliff Lee/SP	5.00
259	Miguel Tejada	.40
260	Mike Lowell	.40
261	Ian Snell	.40
262	Jason Tyner	.40
263	Troy Tulowitzki (RC)	.40
264	Ervin Santana	.40
265	Jon Lester	.40
266	Andy Pettitte/SP	8.00
267	A.J. Pierzynski/SP	5.00
268	Rich Aurilia	.40
269	Phil Nevin	.40
270	Tom Glavine	.40
271	Chris Coste	.40
272	Moises Alou	.40
273	J.D. Drew	.40
274	Abraham Nunez	.40
275	Jorge Posada/SP	8.00
276	Jeff Conine/SP	5.00
277	Chad Cordero	.40
278	Nick Johnson	.40
279	Kevin Millar	.40
280	Mark Grudzielanek	.40
281	Chris Stewart RC	1.00
282	Nate Robertson	.40
283	Drew Anderson (RC)	1.00
284	Doug Mientkiewicz/SP	5.00
285	Ken Griffey Jr./SP	10.00
286	Cory Sullivan	.40
287	Chris Carpenter	.40
288	Gary Matthews	.40
289	Justin Verlander, Jeff Weaver	.40
290	Vicente Padilla	.40
291	Chris Roberson	.40
292	Chris Young	.40
293	Ryan Garko/SP	5.00
294	Miguel Batista/SP	.40
295	B.J. Upton	.40
296	Justin Verlander	.40
297	Benjamin Zobrist	.40
298	Ben Sheets	.40
299	Eric Chavez	.40
300	William Harridge, Warren Giles	.40
301	Placido Polanco	.40
302	Angel Sanchez/SP RC	5.00
303	Freddy Sanchez/SP	5.00
304	Magglio Ordonez, Carlos Guillen	.40
305	A.J. Burnett	.40
306	Juan Perez RC	1.00
307	Chris Britton	.40
308	Jon Garland	.40
309	Pedro Feliz	.40
310	Ryan Howard	.40
311	Aaron Harang/SP	5.00
312	Boston Red Sox/SP	8.00
313	Chad Billingsley	.40
314	Bobby Cox, Chipper Jones	.40
315	Johan Santana	.40
316	Juan Pierre	.40
317	Luke Scott	.40
318	Javier Valentin	.40
319	Mark Loretta	.40
320	Kenny Lofton/SP	5.00
321	Vladimir Guerrero/SP, Ivan Rodriguez/SP	8.00
322	Josh Willingham	.40
323	Lance Berkman	.40
324	Anibal Sanchez	.40
325	Maicer Izturis	.40
326	Brett Myers	.40
327	Chicago Cubs	.40
328	Francisco Liriano	.40
329	Craig Monroe/SP	5.00
330	Paul LoDuca/SP	5.00
331	Steve Trachsel	.40
332	Bernie Williams	.40
333	Carlos Guillen	.40
334	Johan Santana, Francisco Liriano	.40
335	David Bush	.40
336	Carlos Beltran	.40
337	Jason Isringhausen	.40
338	Todd Walker/SP	5.00
339	Jarrod Washburn/SP	5.00
340	Brandon Webb	.40
341	Pittsburgh Pirates	.40
342	Derrick Turnbow	.40
343	Chad Santos	.40
344	Brad Lidge	.40
345	Brad Ausmus	.40
346	Carlos Delgado	.40
347	Boone Logan/SP	5.00
348	Jimmy Rollins/SP	8.00
349	Orlando Hernandez	.40
350	Gary Sheffield	.40
351	Albert Pujols, Yadier Molina, Jim Edmonds, Chris Duncan	.40
352	Jake Peavy	.40
353	Jason Varitek	.40
354	Freddy Garcia	.40
355	Matt Diaz	.40
356	Bernie Castro/SP	5.00
357	Eric Stults/SP RC	5.00
358	John Lackey	.40
359	Bobby Jenks	.40
360	Mark Teixeira	.40
361	Jonathan Papelbon	.40
362	Paul Konerko	.40
363	Erik Bedard	.40
364	Eliezer Alfonzo	.40
365	Fernando Rodney/SP	5.00
366	Chris Duncan/SP	8.00
367	Jose Diaz RC	1.00
368	Travis Hafner	.40
369	Matt Capps	.40
370	Ivan Rodriguez	.40
371	David Murphy (RC)	1.00
372	Carlos Zambrano	.40
373	Chris Iannetta	.40
374	Jose Mesa/SP	5.00
375	Michael Young/SP	8.00
376	Bill Bray	.40
377	Milwaukee Brewers	.40
378	Robert Mackowiak	.40
379	Barry Zito	.40
380	Clay Hensley	.40
381	J.J. Putz	.40
382	C.C. Sabathia	.40
383	Eduardo Perez/SP	5.00
384	Scott Moore/SP (RC)	8.00
385	Scott Olsen	.40
386	Ryan Howard, Chase Utley, Aaron Rowand	.40
388	Mike Rouse	.40
389	Alexis Gomez	.40
390	Brian McCann	.40
391	Ryan Shealy	.40
392	Shane Youman/SP RC	8.00
393	Melky Cabrera/SP	8.00
394	Jeremy Sowers	.40
395	Casey Janssen	.40
396	Miguel Perez	.40
397	Detroit Tigers	.40
398	Reggie Abercrombie	.40
399	Ricky Nolasco	.40
400	Tadahito Iguchi	.40
401	Jose Reyes/SP	10.00
402	Juan Encarnacion/SP	5.00
403	Brandon Harper	.40
404	Torii Hunter	.40
405	Dan Uggla	.40
406	Orlando Cabrera	.40
407	Jose Capellan	.40
408	Baltimore Orioles	.40
409	Frank Thomas	.40
410	Francisco Rodriguez/SP	5.00
411	Ian Kinsler/SP	5.00
412	Billy Wagner	.40
413	Andy Marte	.40
414	Mike Jacobs	.40
415	Raul Ibanez	.40
416	Jhonny Peralta	.40
417	Chris Young	.40
418	Albert Pujols, Craig Monroe	.40
419	Scott Kazmir/SP	5.00
420	Norris Hopper/SP	8.00
421	Chris Capuano	.40
422	Troy Glaus	.40
423	Roy Oswalt	.40
424	Grady Sizemore	.40
425	Chone Figgins	.40
426	Chad Tracy	.40
427	Brian Fuentes	.40
428	Cincinnati Reds/SP	8.00
429	Ramon Hernandez/SP	5.00
430	Mike Cameron	.40
431	Dontrelle Willis	.40
432	Joshua Sharpless	.40
433	Adrian Beltre	.40
434	Curtis Granderson	.40
435	B.J. Ryan	.40
436	Ryan Howard, David Wright	.40
437	Vernon Wells/SP	8.00
438	Vladimir Guerrero/SP	8.00
439	Jake Westbrook	.40
440	Chipper Jones	.40
441	James Loney	.40
442	St. Louis Cardinals	.40
443	Oswaldo Navarro	.40
444	Joe Mauer	.40
445	Miguel Montero	.40
446	Franklin Gutierrez/SP	5.00
447	Mark Redman/SP	5.00
448	Mike Rabelo RC	.40
449	Philip Humber	.40
450	Justin Morneau	.40
451	Hector Gimenez	.40
452	Matt Holliday	.40
453	Akinori Otsuka	.40
454	Prince Fielder	.40
455	Chien-Ming Wang/SP	10.00
456	Shawn Riggans/SP	8.00
457	John Maine	.40
458	Adam Lind (RC)	1.00
459	Ubaldo Jimenez	.40
460	Drew Anderson	.40
461	Cla Meredith	.40
462	Joaquin Arias	.40
463	Kenny Rogers	.40
464	Jose Garcia/SP	5.00
465	Pedro Martinez/SP	8.00
466	Jeff Salazar	.40
467	Glen Perkins	.40
468	Travis Ishikawa	.40
469	Joe Borowski	.40
470	Jeremy Brown	.40
471	Andre Ethier	.40
472	Taylor Tankersley	.40
473	Lastings Milledge/SP	8.00
474	Brian Sanchez/SP	8.00
475	Ozzie Guillen, Phil Garner	.40
476	Albert Pujols	.40
477	David Ortiz	.40
478	Chase Utley	.40
479	Mark Loretta	.40
480	David Wright	.40
481	Alex Rodriguez	.40
482	Edgar Renteria/SP	5.00
483	Derek Jeter/SP	20.00
484	Alfonso Soriano	.40
485	Vladimir Guerrero	.40
486	Carlos Beltran	.40
487	Vernon Wells	.40
488	Jason Bay	.40
489	Ichiro Suzuki	.40
490	Paul LoDuca	.40
491	Ivan Rodriguez/SP	8.00
492	Brad Penny/SP	5.00
493	Roy Halladay	.40
494	Brian Fuentes	.40
495	Kenny Rogers	.40

Chrome

NM/M

Common Player: 2.00
Production 1,958 Sets
Refractors: 1.5-2X
Production 558 Sets
Black Refractors: 3-6X
Production 58 Sets

#	Player	Price
1	David Ortiz	6.00
2	John Smoltz	3.00
3	Brian Giles	2.00
4	Billy Sadler	4.00
5	Joel Zumaya	4.00
6	Felipe Lopez	3.00
7	Tim Hudson	3.00
8	David Ross	2.00
9	Adam Kennedy	2.00
10	David DeJesus	2.00
11	David DeJesus	2.00
12	Jose Contreras	2.00
13	Trot Nixon	2.00
14	Roy Halladay	2.00
15	Gil Meche	2.00
16	Ray Durham	2.00
17	Delwyn Young	2.00
18	Endy Chavez	2.00
19	Vinny Rottino	3.00
20	Austin Kearns	3.00
21	Jeremy Hermida	3.00
22	Jonathan Broxton	4.00
23	Josh Fogg	2.00
24	Angel Guzman	4.00
25	Kenji Johjima	4.00
26	Juan Rivera	2.00
27	Johnny Estrada	2.00
28	Ted Lilly	2.00
29	Hank Blalock	3.00
30	Troy Tulowitzki	4.00
31	Moises Alou	2.00
32	Chris Stewart	2.00
33	Vicente Padilla	2.00
34	Eric Chavez	3.00
35	Jon Garland	2.00
36	Luke Scott	3.00
37	Brett Myers	5.00
38	David Bush	2.00
39	Brad Lidge	2.00
40	Jason Varitek	4.00
41	Paul Konerko	4.00
42	David Murphy	2.00
43	Clay Hensley	2.00
44	Alexis Gomez	2.00
45	Reggie Abercrombie	2.00
46	Jose Capellan	2.00
47	Jhonny Peralta	3.00
48	Chone Figgins	3.00
49	Curtis Granderson	4.00
50	Oswaldo Navarro	3.00
51	Matt Holliday	4.00
52	Cla Meredith	2.00
53	Jeremy Brown	3.00
54	Mark Loretta	2.00
55	Jason Bay	4.00
56	Roger Clemens	8.00
57	Robert Mackowiak	2.00
58	Robinson Cano	6.00
59	Jose Lopez	3.00
60	Dave Roberts	2.00
61	Delmon Young	6.00
62	Ryan Sweeney	4.00
63	Chris Narveson	3.00
64	Juan Uribe	2.00
65	Tony Gwynn Jr.	2.00
66	David Wright	8.00
67	Miguel Cairo	2.00
68	Edgar Renteria	2.00
69	Victor Martinez	3.00
70	Willy Aybar	2.00
71	Luke Hudson	2.00
72	Chuck James	3.00
73	Kris Benson	2.00
74	Garret Anderson	2.00
75	Tim Wakefield	2.00
76	Mike Piazza	6.00
77	Carlos Lee	4.00
78	Jim Edmonds	4.00
79	Joe Crede	4.00
80	Shawn Green	3.00
81	James Shields	2.00
82	Johan Santana	8.00
83	Ervin Santana	2.00
84	J.D. Drew	4.00
85	Nate Robertson	3.00
86	Chris Roberson	2.00
87	Pedro Feliz	2.00
88	Javier Valentin	2.00
89	Carlos Beltran	5.00
90	Brad Ausmus	2.00
91	Freddy Garcia	2.00
92	Erik Bedard	4.00
93	Carlos Zambrano	4.00
94	J.J. Putz	2.00
95	Brian McCann	2.00
96	Ricky Nolasco	2.00
97	Chris Young	4.00
98	J.J. Putz	2.00
99	Brian McCann	2.00
100	Ricky Nolasco	2.00
101	Chris Young	4.00
102	Chad Tracy	2.00
103	B.J. Ryan	2.00
104	Joe Mauer	5.00
105	Akinori Otsuka	2.00
106	Akinori Otsuka	2.00
107	Joaquin Arias	2.00
108	Andre Ethier	4.00
109	David Wright	10.00
110	Ichiro Suzuki	8.00

1958 A.L. Home Run Champion

NM/M

Common Mantle: 3.00
Inserted 1:6

1-42	Mickey Mantle	3.00

New Age Performers

NM/M

Common Player: 1.00
Inserted 1:15

	Player	Price
RH	Ryan Howard	3.00
AR	Alex Rodriguez	3.00
AS	Alfonso Soriano	2.00
DO	David Ortiz	2.00
TH	Trevor Hoffman	1.00
DJ	Derek Jeter	4.00
AAS	Anibal Sanchez	1.00
RC	Roger Clemens	3.00
JS	Johan Santana	2.00
AP	Albert Pujols	4.00
CJ	Chipper Jones	2.00
FT	Frank Thomas	2.00
IR	Ivan Rodriguez	1.50
IS	Ichiro Suzuki	3.00
CB	Craig Biggio	1.00

Then and Now

NM/M

Common Player: 1.00
Inserted 1:15

	Player	Price
RH	Ryan Howard	3.00
DO	David Ortiz	2.00
JM	Joe Mauer	1.50
JR	Jose Reyes	2.00
JS	Johan Santana	2.00
AH	Aaron Harang	1.00
IS	Ichiro Suzuki	2.00
TH	Travis Hafner	1.50
FR	Francisco Rodriguez	1.00
CW	Chien-Ming Wang	2.00

Flashbacks

NM/M

Common Player: 1.00
Inserted 1:12

	Player	Price
SM	Stan Musial	2.00
AK	Al Kaline	2.00
BR	Brooks Robinson	2.00
RS	Red Schoendienst	1.00
LA	Luis Aparicio	1.00
WS	Warren Spahn	1.00
HS	Hank Sauer	1.00
LB	Lew Burdette	1.00
EY	Eddie Yost	1.00
JB	Jim Bunning	1.00

Real One Autographs

NM/M

Common Autograph:
Red Ink: 1.5-2X
Production 58 Sets

	Player	Price
AK	Al Kaline	150.00
BH	Bob Henrich	60.00
BM	Bobby Morgan	70.00
BP	Buddy Pritchard	65.00
BR	Brooks Robinson	100.00
BT	Bill Taylor	50.00
BW	Bill Wight	50.00
CH	Chuck Harmon	60.00
CJD	Jim Derrington	65.00
CR	Charley Rabe	60.00
DM	Dave Melton	60.00
DS	Duke Snider	100.00
DW	David Wright	140.00
DWW	Dontrelle Willis	50.00
DY	Delmon Young	60.00
DZ	Don Zimmer	50.00
EM	Ed Mayer	60.00
GK	George Kell	75.00
HP	Harding Peterson	60.00
JC	Joe Caffie	60.00
JD	Joe Durham	70.00
JL	Joe Lonnett	50.00
JM	Justin Morneau	60.00
JP	Johnny Podres	60.00
LA	Luis Aparicio	80.00
LM	Lloyd Merritt	60.00
LS	Lou Sleater	60.00
MB	Milt Bolling	60.00
MEB	Mack Burk	60.00
OH	Orlando Hudson	40.00
PS	Paul Smith	60.00
RC	Ray Crone	60.00
RH	Ryan Howard	250.00
RS	Red Schoendienst	85.00
SP	Stan Palys	60.00
TT	Tim Thompson	50.00

Flashback Autograph

No Pricing
Production 25 Sets

1958 Cut Signatures

Production One Set

A-Rod Road to 500

NM/M

Common A-Rod: 3.00
Inserted 1:24
Autograph: No Pricing
Production One Set

51-75	Alex Rodriguez	3.00

Clubhouse Collection

NM/M

Common Player: 8.00

	Player	Price
SM	Stan Musial	30.00
DS	Duke Snider	20.00
FR	Frank Robinson	20.00
BR	Brooks Robinson	15.00
YB	Yogi Berra	25.00
AK	Al Kaline	20.00
AW	Adam Wainwright	15.00
AJP	Albert Pujols	20.00
AR	Alex Rodriguez	20.00
ALR	Anthony Reyes	10.00
BU	B.J. Upton	8.00
BZ	Barry Zito	8.00
BS	Ben Sheets	10.00
BW	Billy Wagner	8.00
BR	Brian Roberts	10.00
CU	Chase Utley	15.00
CJ	Chipper Jones	15.00
CC	Chris Carpenter	15.00
CD	Chris Duncan	10.00
CJ	Conor Jackson	10.00
DE	David Eckstein	20.00
DO	David Ortiz	15.00
DW	David Wright	30.00
DY	Delmon Young	10.00
DWW	Dontrelle Willis	8.00
DM	Doug Mientkiewicz	8.00
ER	Edgar Renteria	8.00
EC	Eric Chavez	8.00
ES	Ervin Santana	8.00
FL	Francisco Liriano	10.00
GS	Gary Sheffield	10.00
HB	Hank Blalock	8.00
IR	Ivan Rodriguez	10.00
JS	Jeff Suppan	10.00
JW	Jeff Weaver	8.00
JR	Jimmy Rollins	10.00
JD	Johnny Damon	15.00
JRP	Jorge Posada	15.00
JBR	Jose Reyes	20.00
JV	Jose Vidro	8.00
JP	Juan Pierre	8.00
JM	Justin Morneau	15.00
LB	Lance Berkman	10.00
LG	Luis Gonzalez	8.00
MO	Magglio Ordonez	8.00
MR	Manny Ramirez	10.00
MK	Mark Kotsay	8.00
MT	Mark Teixeira	10.00
MM	Melvin Mora	8.00
MC	Miguel Cabrera	10.00
MOT	Miguel Tejada	8.00
MP	Mike Piazza	15.00
MA	Moises Alou	8.00
NS	Nick Swisher	10.00
OV	Omar Vizquel	8.00
PB	Pat Burrell	10.00
PP	Placido Polanco	8.00
RF	Rafael Furcal	8.00
RS	Rafael Furcal	8.00
RB	Ronnie Belliard	8.00
RH	Ryan Howard	30.00
TH	Todd Helton	10.00
TKH	Torii Hunter	10.00
VM	Victor Martinez	8.00
YM	Yadier Molina	15.00

Clubhouse Collection Dual Relic

NM/M

Production 58 Sets

	Player	Price
MP	Stan Musial, Albert Pujols	180.00
KR	Al Kaline, Ivan Rodriguez	80.00

Flashbacks Relics

NM/M

Common Player: 20.00

	Player	Price
SM	Stan Musial	30.00
AK	Al Kaline	25.00
BR	Brooks Robinson	25.00
RS	Red Schoendienst	20.00
WS	Warren Spahn	25.00
LB	Lew Burdette	25.00
EY	Eddie Yost	20.00
JB	Jim Bunning	20.00

Dual Flashbacks

Production 10 Sets

Clubhouse Collection Relic Autograph

Production 25 Sets

Flashbacks Relic Autograph

Production 25 Sets

Felt Team Emblem

NM/M

Inserted 1:Box

Team	Price
Los Angeles Dodgers	3.00
Washington Senators	3.00
San Francisco Giants	3.00
Boston Red Sox	3.00
Cincinnati Redlegs	3.00
Pittsburgh Pirates	3.00
Milwaukee Braves	3.00
Chicago Cubs	5.00
Baltimore Orioles	5.00
New York Yankees	5.00
Cleveland Indians	3.00
St. Louis Cardinals	5.00
Kansas City Athletics	3.00
Detroit Tigers	3.00
Chicago White Sox	3.00
Philadelphia Phillies	3.00

2007 Topps Opening Day

NM/M

Complete Set (220): 35.00
Common Player: .15
Pack (6): 1.25
Box (36): 40.00

#	Player	Price
1	Bobby Abreu	.25
2	Mike Piazza	.75
3	Jake Westbrook	.15
4	Zachary Duke	.15
5	David Wright	1.00
6	Adrian Gonzalez	.25
7	Mickey Mantle	3.00
8	Bill Hall	.15
9	Robinson Cano	.25
10	Dontrelle Willis	.25
11	J.D. Drew	.25
12	Paul Konerko	.25
13	Austin Kearns	.15
14	Mike Lowell	.15
15	Magglio Ordonez	.15
16	Rafael Furcal	.25
17	Matt Cain	.15
18	Craig Monroe	.15
19	Matt Holliday	.25
20	Edgar Renteria	.25
21	Mark Buehrle	.15
22	Carlos Quentin	.15
23	C.C. Sabathia	.25
24	Nicholas Markakis	.25
25	Chipper Jones	.50
26	Jason Giambi	.25
27	Barry Zito	.25
28	Jake Peavy	.25
29	Hank Blalock	.25
30	Johnny Damon	.50
31	Chad Tracy	.15
32	Nick Swisher	.25
33	Willy Taveras	.15
34	Chuck James	.15
35	Carlos Delgado	.40
36	Livan Hernandez	.15
37	Freddy Garcia	.15
38	Bronson Arroyo	.15
39	Jack Wilson	.15
40	Dan Uggla	.15
41	Chris Carpenter	.50
42	Jorge Posada	.40
43	Joe Mauer	.40
44	Corey Patterson	.15
45	Chien-Ming Wang	.50
46	Derek Jeter	1.50
47	Carlos Beltran	.25
48	Jim Edmonds	.25
49	Jeremy Sowers	.15
50	Randy Johnson	.50

51	Jered Weaver	.25
52	Josh Barfield	.15
53	Scott Rolen	.40
54	Ryan Shealy	.15
55	Freddy Sanchez	.15
56	Javier Vazquez	.15
57	Jeremy Bonderman	.25
58	Miguel Cabrera	.50
59	Kazuo Matsui	.15
60	Curt Schilling	.50
61	Alfonso Soriano	.50
62	Orlando Hernandez	.15
63	Joe Blanton	.15
64	Aramis Ramirez	.25
65	Ben Sheets	.25
66	Jimmy Rollins	.25
67	Mark Loretta	.15
68	Cole Hamels	.25
69	Albert Pujols	1.50
70	Moises Alou	.25
71	Mark Teahen	.15
72	Roy Halladay	.25
73	Cory Sullivan	.15
74	Frank Thomas	.50
75	Ryan Howard	1.50
76	Rocco Baldelli	.25
77	Manny Ramirez	.50
78	Ray Durham	.15
79	Gary Sheffield	.40
80	Jay Gibbons	.15
81	Todd Helton	.40
82	Gary Matthews	.15
83	Brandon Inge	.15
84	Jonathan Papelbon	.40
85	John Smoltz	.25
86	Chone Figgins	.15
87	Hideki Matsui	.75
88	Carlos Lee	.25
89	Jose Reyes	.75
90	Lyle Overbay	.25
91	Johan Santana	.50
92	Ian Kinsler	.15
93	Scott Kazmir	.25
94	Hanley Ramirez	.40
95	Greg Maddux	1.00
96	Johnny Estrada	.15
97	B.J. Upton	.25
98	Francisco Liriano	.25
99	Chase Utley	.50
100	Preston Wilson	.15
101	Marcus Giles	.15
102	Jeff Kent	.25
103	Grady Sizemore	.50
104	Ken Griffey Jr.	1.00
105	Garret Anderson	.15
106	Brian McCann	.25
107	Jon Garland	.15
108	Troy Glaus	.25
109	Brandon Webb	.25
110	Jason Schmidt	.25
111	Ramon Hernandez	.15
112	Justin Morneau	.50
113	Mike Cameron	.15
114	Andruw Jones	.40
115	Russell Martin	.15
116	Vernon Wells	.25
117	Orlando Hudson	.15
118	Derek Lowe	.15
119	Alex Rodriguez	1.50
120	Chad Billingsley	.15
121	Kenji Johjima	.15
122	Nick Johnson	.15
123	Danny Haren	.25
124	Mark Teixeira	.40
125	Jeff Francoeur	.25
126	Ted Lilly	.15
127	Jhonny Peralta	.15
128	Aaron Harang	.15
129	Ryan Zimmerman	.25
130	Jermaine Dye	.25
131	Orlando Cabrera	.25
132	Juan Pierre	.25
133	Brian Giles	.25
134	Jason Bay	.25
135	David Ortiz	.50
136	Chris Capuano	.15
137	Carlos Zambrano	.25
138	Luis Gonzalez	.15
139	Jeff Weaver	.15
140	Lance Berkman	.25
141	Raul Ibanez	.15
142	Jim Thome	.40
143	Jose Contreras	.15
144	David Eckstein	.15
145	Adam Dunn	.40
146	Alex Rios	.25
147	Garrett Atkins	.25
148	A.J. Burnett	.25
149	Jeremy Hermida	.15
150	Conor Jackson	.15
151	Adrian Beltre	.25
152	Torii Hunter	.25
153	Andrew Miller **RC**	3.00
154	Ichiro Suzuki	1.00
155	Mark Redman	.15
156	Paul LoDuca	.15
157	Xavier Nady	.15
158	Stephen Drew	.25
159	Eric Chavez	.25
160	Pedro Martinez	.50
161	Derek Lee	.40
162	David DeJesus	.15
163	Troy Tulowitzki **(RC)**	.25
164	Vinny Rottino **(RC)**	.25
165	Philip Humber **(RC)**	.25
166	Jerry Owens **(RC)**	.25
167	Ubaldo Jimenez **(RC)**	.25
168	Michael Young	.25

169	Ryan Braun **RC**	.25
170	Kevin Kouzmanoff **(RC)**	.25
171	Oswaldo Navarro **RC**	.25
172	Miguel Montero **(RC)**	.25
173	Roy Oswalt	.25
174	Shane Youman **RC**	.25
175	Josh Fields **(RC)**	.25
176	Adam Lind **(RC)**	.25
177	Miguel Tejada	.40
178	Delwyn Young **(RC)**	.25
179	Scott Moore **(RC)**	.25
180	Fred Lewis **(RC)**	.25
181	Glen Perkins **(RC)**	.25
182	Vladimir Guerrero	.50
183	Drew Anderson **(RC)**	.25
184	Jeff Salazar **(RC)**	.25
185	Tom Gordon	.15
186	The Bird	.15
187	Justin Verlander	.40
188	Delmon Young **(RC)**	.50
189	Homer	.15
190	Wally the Green Monster	.15
191	Southpaw	.15
192	Dinger	.15
193	Carl Crawford	.15
194	Slider	.15
195	Gapper	.15
196	Paws	.15
197	Billy the Marlin	.15
198	Ivan Rodriguez	.15
199	Slugger	.15
200	Junction Jack	.15
201	Bernie the Brewer	.15
202	Travis Hafner	.40
203	Stomper	.15
204	Mr. Met	.15
205	The Moose	.15
206	Phillie Phanatic	.15
207	Prince Fielder	.40
208	Julio Lugo	.15
209	Pirate Parrot	.15
210	Joel Zumaya	.25
211	Swinging Friar	.15
212	Jay Payton	.15
213	Lou Seal	.15
214	Fredbird	.15
215	Screech	.15
216	TC Bear	.15
217	Andre Ethier	.15
218	Ervin Santana	.15
219	Melvin Mora	.15
220	Checklist	.15

A-Rod Road to 500

		NM/M
Common A-Rod (76-100):		4.00

A-Rod Road to 500 Autograph

	NM/M
Production One set	4.00

1984 Toronto Blue Jays Fire Safety

TONY FERNANDEZ
1
infielder

This 35-card set was issued in conjuction with the Toronto Sun newspaper and various Ontario area fire departments. The cards feature full-color action photos on the fronts, along with the player name, number and position. Rather than the customary wide white border on front, the Blue Jays fire safety set features bright blue borders. The card backs include brief player biographies and a fire safety tip. The 2-1/2" x 3-1/2" cards were distributed five at a time at two-week intervals during the summer of 1984.

		NM/M
Complete Set (35):		6.00
Common Player:		.25
1	Tony Fernandez	.30
3	Jimy Williams	.25
4	Alfredo Griffin	.25
5	Rance Mulliniks	.25
6	Bobby Cox	.50
7	Damaso Garcia	.25
8	John Sullivan	.25

9	Rick Leach	.25
10	Dave Collins	.25
11	George Bell	.40
12	Ernie Whitt	.25
13	Buck Martinez	.25
15	Lloyd Moseby	.25
16	Garth Iorg	.25
17	Kelly Gruber	.25
18	Jim Clancy	.25
23	Mitch Webster	.25
24	Willie Aikens	.25
25	Roy Lee Jackson	.25
26	Willie Upshaw	.25
27	Jimmy Key	.50
29	Jesse Barfield	.25
31	Jim Acker	.25
33	Doyle Alexander	.25
34	Stan Clarke	.25
35	Bryan Clark	.25
37	Dave Stieb	.40
38	Jim Gott	.25
41	Al Widmar	.25
42	Billy Smith	.25
43	Cito Gaston	.25
44	Cliff Johnson	.25
48	Luis Leal	.25
53	Dennis Lamp	.25
---	Team Logo/Checklist	.25

1985 Toronto Blue Jays Fire Safety

JESSE BARFIELD
29
outfielder

The Toronto Blue Jays issued a 35-card fire safety set for the second year in a row in 1985. Cards feature players, coaches, manager, checklist and team picture. The full-color photos are on the card fronts with a blue border. The backs feature player stats and a safety tip. The cards measure 2-1/2" x 3-1/2" and were distributed throughout the Province of Ontario, Canada.

		NM/M
Complete Set (36):		5.00
Common Player:		.25
1	Tony Fernandez	.30
3	Jimy Williams	.25
4	Manny Lee	.25
5	Rance Mulliniks	.25
6	Bobby Cox	.40
7	Damaso Garcia	.25
8	John Sullivan	.25
11	George Bell	.30
12	Ernie Whitt	.25
13	Buck Martinez	.25
15	Lloyd Moseby	.25
16	Garth Iorg	.25
17	Kelly Gruber	.25
18	Jim Clancy	.25
22	Jimmy Key	.35
23	Mitch Webster	.25
24	Willie Aikens	.25
25	Len Matuszek	.25
26	Willie Upshaw	.25
28	Lou Thornton	.25
29	Jesse Barfield	.25
30	Ron Musselman	.25
31	Jim Acker	.25
33	Doyle Alexander	.25
36	Bill Caudill	.25
37	Dave Stieb	.30
41	Al Widmar	.25
42	Billy Smith	.25
43	Cito Gaston	.25
44	Jeff Burroughs	.25
46	Gary Lavelle	.25
48	Luis Leal	.25
50	Tom Henke	.30
53	Dennis Lamp	.25
---	Team Logo/Checklist	.25
---	Team Photo/Schedule	.25

1986 Toronto Blue Jays Fire Safety

This was the third consecutive year the Toronto Blue Jays issued a fire safety set of 36 baseball cards. The cards were given out at many fire stations in Ontario, Canada. The cards are printed in full

LLOYD MOSEBY
15
outfielder

color and include players and other personnel. The set was co-sponsored by the local fire departments, Bubble Yum and the Toronto Star. The cards measure 2-1/2" x 3-1/2".

		NM/M
Complete Set (36):		6.00
Common Player:		.25
1	Tony Fernandez	.30
3	Jimy Williams	.25
5	Rance Mulliniks	.25
7	Damaso Garcia	.25
8	John Sullivan	.25
9	Rick Leach	.25
11	George Bell	.30
12	Ernie Whitt	.25
13	Buck Martinez	.25
15	Lloyd Moseby	.25
16	Garth Iorg	.25
17	Kelly Gruber	.25
18	Jim Clancy	.25
22	Jimmy Key	.30
23	Cecil Fielder	2.00
24	John McLaren	.25
25	Steve Davis	.25
26	Willie Upshaw	.25
29	Jesse Barfield	.25
31	Jim Acker	.25
33	Doyle Alexander	.25
36	Bill Caudill	.25
37	Dave Stieb	.30
38	Mark Eichhorn	.25
39	Don Gordon	.25
41	Al Widmar	.25
42	Billy Smith	.25
43	Cito Gaston	.25
44	Cliff Johnson	.25
46	Gary Lavelle	.25
49	Tom Filer	.25
50	Tom Henke	.25
54	Dennis Lamp	.25
55	Jeff Hearron	.25
---	Team Photo	.25
---	10th Anniversary Logo Card	.25

1987 Toronto Blue Jays Fire Safety

JESSE BARFIELD
29
outfielder

For the fourth consecutive year, the Toronto Blue Jays issued a fire safety set of 36 cards. As in 1986, the set was sponsored by the local fire departments and governing agencies, Bubble Yum and the Toronto Star. The card fronts feature a full-color photo surrounded by a white border. The backs carry a fire safety tip and logos of all sponsors, plus player personal data and statistics. Produced on thin stock, cards in the set are the standard 2-1/2" x 3-1/2" size.

		NM/M
Complete Set (36):		6.00
Common Player:		.25
1	Tony Fernandez	.30
3	Jimy Williams	.25
5	Rance Mulliniks	.25
8	John Sullivan	.25
9	Rick Leach	.25

10	Mike Sharperson	.25
11	George Bell	.30
12	Ernie Whitt	.25
15	Lloyd Moseby	.25
16	Garth Iorg	.25
17	Kelly Gruber	.25
18	Jim Clancy	.25
19	Fred McGriff	2.00
22	Jimmy Key	.30
23	Cecil Fielder	.50
24	John McLaren	.25
26	Willie Upshaw	.25
29	Jesse Barfield	.25
31	Duane Ward	.25
32	Joe Johnson	.25
35	Jeff Musselman	.25
37	Dave Stieb	.30
38	Mark Eichhorn	.25
40	Rob Ducey	.25
41	Al Widmar	.25
42	Billy Smith	.25
43	Cito Gaston	.25
46	Jose Nunez	.25
47	Gary Lavelle	.25
48	Matt Stark	.25
49	Craig McMurtry	.25
50	Tom Henke	.25
54	Jeff Hearron	.25
55	John Cerutti	.25
---	Logo/Won-Loss Record	.25
---	Team Photo/Checklist	.25

1988 Toronto Blue Jays Fire Safety

PAT BORDERS
catcher

This 36-card set features action photos on 3-1/2" x 5" cards with white borders. Card numbers (player's uniform #) appear lower-left; team logo lower-right; player's name and position are printed bottom-center. Card backs are blue on white and include personal and career info, 1987 and career stats, sponsor logos and a fire safety tip. The set includes 34 player cards, a team photo checklist card and a team logo card with a year-by-year won/loss record. The set was sponsored by the Ontario Fire Chief Association, Ontario's Solicitor General, The Toronto Star and Bubble Yum and was distributed free as part of a community service project. At least some of the cards have been seen in a blank-back version, apparently used to answer fans autograph requests.

		NM/M
Complete Set (36):		5.00
Common Player:		.25
1	Tony Fernandez	.30
2	Nelson Liriano	.25
3	Jimy Williams	.25
4	Manny Lee	.25
5	Rance Mulliniks	.25
6	Silvestre Campusano	.25
7	John McLaren	.25
8	John Sullivan	.25
9	Rick Leach	.25
10	Pat Borders	.30
11	George Bell	.30
12	Ernie Whitt	.25
13	Jeff Musselman	.25
15	Lloyd Moseby	.25
16	Todd Stottlemyre	.75
17	Kelly Gruber	.25
18	Jim Clancy	.25
19	Fred McGriff	.75
21	Juan Beniquez	.25
22	Jimmy Key	.30
23	Cecil Fielder	.50
29	Jesse Barfield	.25
31	Duane Ward	.25
36	David Wells	1.00
37	Dave Stieb	.30
38	Mark Eichhorn	.25
40	Rob Ducey	.25
41	Al Widmar	.25
42	Billy Smith	.25
43	Cito Gaston	.25

46	Mike Flanagan	.25
50	Tom Henke	.25
55	John Cerutti	.25
57	Winston Llenas	.25
---	Team photo	.25
---	Team logo	.25

1989 Toronto Blue Jays Fire Safety

37 **DAVE STIEB**
Pitcher

The 1989 Blue Jays safety set consists of 36 standard-size cards co-sponsored by the Ontario Association of Fire Chiefs, Oh Henry! candy bars and A&P supermarkets. Card fronts feature color photos with the player's uniform number in large type in the upper left corner. His name and position are to the right above the photo. The Blue Jays "On the Move" logo is centered at the bottom. The backs of the cards include fire safety messages.

		NM/M
Complete Set (36):		6.00
Common Player:		.25
1	Tony Fernandez	.30
2	Nelson Liriano	.25
3	Jimy Williams	.25
4	Manny Lee	.25
5	Rance Mulliniks	.25
6	Silvestre Campusano	.25
7	John McLaren	.25
8	John Sullivan	.25
9	Bob Brenly	.25
10	Pat Borders	.25
11	George Bell	.30
12	Ernie Whitt	.25
13	Jeff Musselman	.25
15	Lloyd Moseby	.25
16	Greg Myers	.25
17	Kelly Gruber	.25
18	Tom Lawless	.25
19	Fred McGriff	.50
22	Jimmy Key	.30
25	Mike Squires	.25
26	Sal Butera	.25
29	Jesse Barfield	.25
30	Todd Stottlemyre	.35
31	Duane Ward	.25
36	David Wells	.50
37	Dave Stieb	.30
40	Rob Ducey	.25
41	Al Widman	.25
43	Cito Gaston	.25
44	Frank Wills	.25
46	Jose Nunez	.25
46	Mike Flanagan	.25
50	Tom Henke	.25
55	John Cerutti	.25
---	Team photo	.25
---	Team logo	.25

1990 Toronto Blue Jays Fire Safety

FRED McGRIFF
Infielder
19

This 35-card set was co-sponsored by the Ontario Association of Fire Chiefs, The Ministry of the Solicitor General, A & P/Dominion, Oh Henry, and the Toronto Blue Jays.

The card fronts feature full-color photos on white stock and display a special Blue Jays fan club logo in the upper left corner. The flip sides feature biographical information, statistics, and a fire fact. The cards are checklisted here by uniform number.

		NM/M
Complete Set (35):		6.00
Common Player:		.25
1	Tony Fernandez	.30
2	Nelson Liriano	.25
3	Mookie Wilson	.25
4	Manny Lee	.25
5	Rance Mulliniks	.25
7	John McLaren	.25
8	John Sullivan	.25
9	John Olerud	2.00
10	Pat Borders	.25
11	George Bell	.30
15	Gene Tenace	.25
18	Tom Lawless	.25
19	Fred McGriff	.50
21	Greg Myers	.25
22	Jimmy Key	.30
23	Alex Sanchez	.25
24	Glenallen Hill	.25
25	Mike Squires	.25
26	Ozzie Virgil	.25
27	Willie Blair	.25
28	Al Leiter	.30
30	Todd Stottlemyre	.25
31	Duane Ward	.25
34	Jim Acker	.25
36	David Wells	.50
37	Dave Steib	.30
39	Paul Kilgus	.25
42	Galen Cisco	.25
43	Cito Gaston	.25
44	Frank Wills	.25
47	Junior Felix	.25
50	Tom Henke	.25
55	John Cerutti	.25
---	Skydome/checklist	.25
---	Logo/schedule	.25

1991 Toronto Blue Jays Fire Safety

29 JOE CARTER Outfielder

The Blue Jays played host to the 1991 All-Star Game and the team's annual fire safety set prominently featured that honor. A headercard with the Jays All-Star logo was included in the set and each card carried the logo in full color on the front. The 2-1/2" x 3-1/2" cards have a color action photo at top which bleeds off the top and sides. Beneath the photo is a white border with the player's name, position and uniform number. Backs are printed in black-and-white and have a few biographical notes, 1990 and career stats, a Fire Fact safety message and logos of the cards' sponsors.

		NM/M
Complete Set (36):		6.00
Common Player:		.25
3	Mookie Wilson	.25
4	Manuel Lee	.25
5	Rance Mulliniks	.25
6	Mike Squires	.25
7	Rich Hacker	.25
8	John Sullivan	.25
9	John Olerud	.50
10	Pat Borders	.25
12	Roberto Alomar	3.00
13	Kenny Williams	.25
17	Pat Tabler	.25
18	Gene Tenace	.25
20	Rob Ducey	.25
21	Greg Myers	.25
22	Jimmy Key	.30
23	Mark Whiten	.25
24	Glenallen Hill	.25
25	Devon White	.35

28	Al Leiter	.30
29	Joe Carter	.50
30	Todd Stottlemyre	.25
31	Duane Ward	.25
34	Jim Acker	.25
35	Denis Boucher	.25
36	David Wells	.45
37	Dave Steib	.30
42	Galen Cisco	.25
43	Cito Gaston	.25
44	Frank Wills	.25
46	Ken Dayley	.25
50	Tom Henke	.25
56	Hector Torres	.25
88	Rene Gonzales	.25
---	BJ Birdy/Mascot	.25
---	All-Star Season Header/Checklist Card	.25

1992 Toronto Blue Jays Fire Safety

10 PAT BORDERS CATCHER

Hidden amid the myriad sponsors' logos on the backs of these cards is a fire safety message. The 2-1/2" x 3-1/2" cards are printed on thin cardboard and feature color player photos on front, along with a red, white and blue "Toronto Blue Jays Fanatic" logo. Fronts also carry uniform numbers, by which the set is checklisted here. Backs are printed in black-and-white with a few biographical details, 1991 and career stats.

		NM/M
Complete Set (36):		8.00
Common Player:		.25
1	Eddie Zosky	.25
2	Manuel Lee	.25
3	Bob Bailor	.25
4	Alfredo Griffin	.25
5	Rance Mulliniks	.25
7	Rich Hacker	.25
8	John Sullivan	.25
9	John Olerud	.50
10	Pat Borders	.25
12	Roberto Alomar	1.00
14	Derek Bell	.25
15	Pat Tabler	.25
17	Kelly Gruber	.25
18	Gene Tenace	.25
20	Rob Ducey	.25
21	Greg Myers	.25
22	Jimmy Key	.35
23	Candy Maldonado	.25
24	Turner Ward	.25
25	Devon White	.30
29	Joe Carter	.30
30	Todd Stottlemyre	.30
31	Duane Ward	.25
32	Dave Winfield	1.50
36	David Wells	.45
37	Dave Steib	.30
39	Larry Hisle	.25
40	Mike Timlin	.25
42	Galen Cisco	.25
43	Cito Gaston	.25
46	Bob MacDonald	.25
46	Ken Dayley	.25
47	Jack Morris	.25
50	Tom Henke	.25
66	Juan Guzman	.25
---	Checklist	.25

1993 Toronto Blue Jays Fire Safety

The Blue Jays produced a fire safety set for the 10th year in a row in 1993. In the first year of offering the item as a boxed set, the cards feature a full-bleed color photo on the front, with the player's name printed in white over a blue stripe across the top of the card. The Blue Jay's 1992 World Champi-

Todd Stottlemyre

ons logo appears in the upper left corner. Cards are checklisted here by uniform number.

		NM/M
Complete Set (36):		6.00
Common Player:		.25
1	Eddie Zosky	.25
2	Luis Sojo	.25
3	Bob Bailor	.25
4	Alfredo Griffin	.25
5	Domingo Martinez	.25
7	Rich Hacker	.25
8	John Sullivan	.25
9	John Olerud	.40
10	Pat Borders	.25
11	Darnell Coles	.25
12	Roberto Alomar	.75
14	Darrin Jackson	.25
16	Tom Quinlin	.25
18	Gene Tenace	.25
19	Paul Molitor	1.50
22	Dick Schofield	.25
24	Turner Ward	.25
25	Devon White	.30
27	Randy Knorr	.25
28	Al Leiter	.30
29	Joe Carter	.25
30	Todd Stottlemyre	.30
31	Duane Ward	.25
33	Ed Sprague	.25
34	Dave Stewart	.25
39	Larry Hisle	.25
40	Mike Timlin	.25
41	Pat Hentgen	.25
42	Galen Cisco	.25
43	Cito Gaston	.25
46	Ken Davley	.25
47	Jack Morris	.25
48	Mark Eichhorn	.25
50	Danny Cox	.25
66	Juan Guzman	.25
---	World's Champion Trophy/Checklist	.25

2002 Toronto Blue Jays Team Issue

#8 JOE LAWRENCE INFIELDER

This boxed set was a stadium giveaway. It features current players, coaches and a handful of "alumni." Backs have Major League stats, biographical data and either 2001 highlights or a short biography.

		NM/M
Complete Set (34):		10.00
Common Player:		.35
2	Dave Berg	.35
4	Chris Woodward	.35
5	Joe Lawrence	.35
7	Felipe Lopez	.35
9	Darrin Fletcher	.35
10	Vernon Wells	.50
11	Eric Hinske	.50
14	Carlos Tosca	.35
15	Tom Wilson	.35
19	Cliff Politte	.35
20	Ken Huckaby	.35
21	Esteban Loaiza	.35
23	Jose Cruz Jr.	.35
24	Shannon Stewart	.35
25a	Carlos Delgado	.50
25b	Devon White	.35
26	Cris Carpenter	.35
29	Scott Eyre	.35

32	Roy Halladay	.45
35	Corey Thurman	.35
39	Steve Parris	.35
40	Scott Cassidy	.35
41	Pete Walker	.35
43	Cito Gaston	.35
44	Luke Prokopec	.35
45	Kelvim Escobar	.35
47a	Jack Morris	.35
47b	Gil Patterson	.35
49	Felix Heredia	.35
50	Tom Henke	.35
52	Bruce Walton	.35
53	John Gibbons	.35
55	Brian Butterfield	.35
56	Mike Barnett	.35

1987 Toys "R" Us

JOHN CERUTTI · P.

Marked as a collectors' edition set and titled "Baseball Rookies," the 1987 Toys "R" Us issue was produced by Topps for the toy store chain. The set is comprised of 33 glossy-coated cards, each measuring 2-1/2" x 3-1/2". The card fronts are very colorful, employing nine different colors including deep black borders. The backs, printed in blue and orange, contain career highlights and composite minor and major league statistics. The set was distributed in a specially designed box and sold for $1.99 in retail outlets.

		NM/M
Complete Set (33):		15.00
Common Player:		.10
1	Andy Allanson	.10
2	Paul Assenmacher	.10
3	Scott Bailes	.10
4	Barry Bonds	12.50
5	Jose Canseco	.50
6	John Cerutti	.10
7	Will Clark	.10
8	Kal Daniels	.10
9	Jim Deshaies	.10
11	Mark Eichhorn	.10
11	Ed Hearn	.10
12	Pete Incaviglia	.10
13	Bo Jackson	.50
14	Wally Joyner	.10
15	Charlie Kerfeld	.10
16	Eric King	.10
17	John Kruk	.10
18	Barry Larkin	.10
19	Mike LaValliere	.10
20	Greg Mathews	.10
21	Kevin Mitchell	.10
22	Dan Plesac	.10
23	Bruce Ruffin	.10
24	Ruben Sierra	.10
25	Cory Snyder	.10
26	Kurt Stillwell	.10
27	Dale Sveum	.10
28	Danny Tartabull	.10
29	Andres Thomas	.10
30	Robby Thompson	.10
31	Jim Traber	.10
32	Mitch Williams	.10
33	Todd Worrell	.10

1988 Toys "R" Us Rookies

This 33-card boxed edition was produced by Topps for exclusive distribution at Toys "R" Us stores. The glossy standard-size cards spotlight rookies in both close-ups and action photos on a bright blue background inlaid with yellow. The Toys "R" Us logo frames the top left corner, above a curving white banner that reads "Topps 1988 Collectors' Edition Rookies." A black Topps logo hugs the upper right-hand edge of the photo.

LUIS POLONIA · CF

The player name, red-lettered on a tube of yellow, frames the bottom. Card backs are horizontal, blue and pink on a bright pink background and include the player name, personal information and career highlights and stats.

		NM/M
Complete Set (33):		3.00
Common Player:		.10
1	Todd Benzinger	.10
2	Bob Brower	.10
3	Jerry Browne	.10
4	DeWayne Buice	.10
5	Ellis Burks	.10
6	Ken Caminiti	.10
7	Casey Candaele	.10
8	Dave Cone	.10
9	Kelly Downs	.10
10	Mike Dunne	.10
11	Ken Gerhart	.10
12	Mike Greenwell	.10
13	Mike Henneman	.10
14	Sam Horn	.10
15	Joe Magrane	.10
16	Fred Manrique	.10
17	John Marzano	.10
18	Fred McGriff	.10
19	Mark McGwire	2.50
20	Jeff Musselman	.10
21	Randy Myers	.10
22	Matt Nokes	.10
23	Al Pedrique	.10
24	Luis Polonia	.10
25	Billy Ripken	.10
26	Benny Santiago	.10
27	Kevin Seitzer	.10
28	John Smiley	.10
29	Mike Stanley	.10
30	Terry Steinbach	.10
31	B.J. Surhoff	.10
32	Bobby Thigpen	.10
33	Devon White	.10

1989 Toys "R" Us Rookies

MARK GRACE · 1B

This glossy set of 33 top rookies was produced by Topps for the Toys "R" Us chain and was sold in a special box. Each player's name and position appear below the full-color photo, while the Toys "R" Us logo and "Topps 1989 Collector's Edition" appear along the top. Major and minor league stats are on the back. The set is numbered alphabetically.

		NM/M
Complete Set (33):		3.00
Common Player:		.10
1	Roberto Alomar	.50
2	Brady Anderson	.10
3	Tim Belcher	.10
4	Damon Berryhill	.10
5	Jay Buhner	.10
6	Sherman Corbett	.10
7	Kevin Elster	.10
8	Cecil Espy	.10
9	Dave Gallagher	.10
10	Ron Gant	.10

11	Paul Gibson	.10
12	Mark Grace	.50
13	Bryan Harvey	.10
14	Darrin Jackson	.10
15	Gregg Jefferies	.10
16	Ron Jones	.10
17	Ricky Jordan	.10
18	Roberto Kelly	.10
19	Al Leiter	.10
20	Jack McDowell	.10
21	Melido Perez	.10
22	Jeff Pico	.10
23	Jody Reed	.10
24	Chris Sabo	.10
25	Nelson Santovenia	.10
26	Mackey Sasser	.10
27	Mike Schooler	.10
28	Gary Sheffield	1.50
29	Pete Smith	.10
30	Pete Stanicek	.10
31	Jeff Treadway	.10
32	Walt Weiss	.10
33	Dave West	.10

1990 Toys "R" Us Rookies

JOEY BELLE · OF

This 33-card set marks the fourth straight year that Topps has produced a set to be sold exclusively at Toys "R" Us stores. The card fronts contain full-color photos of 1989 rookies. The flip sides are horizontal and provide both minor and major league totals. The complete set is packaged in a special box which features a checklist on the back.

		NM/M
Complete Set (33):		3.00
Common Player:		.10
1	Jim Abbott	.10
2	Eric Anthony	.10
3	Joey Belle	.50
4	Andy Benes	.10
5	Greg Briley	.10
6	Kevin Brown	.10
7	Mark Carreon	.10
8	Mike Devereaux	.10
9	Junior Felix	.10
10	Mark Gardner	.10
11	Bob Geren	.10
12	Tom Gordon	.10
13	Ken Griffey Jr.	2.50
14	Pete Harnisch	.10
15	Ken Hill	.10
16	Gregg Jefferies	.10
17	Derek Lilliquist	.10
18	Carlos Martinez	.10
19	Ramon Martinez	.10
20	Bob Milacki	.10
21	Gregg Olson	.10
22	Kenny Rogers	.10
23	Alex Sanchez	.10
24	Gary Sheffield	.10
25	Dwight Smith	.10
26	Billy Spiers	.10
27	Greg Vaughn	.10
28	Robin Ventura	.10
29	Jerome Walton	.10
30	Dave West	.10
31	John Wetteland	.10
32	Craig Worthington	.10
33	Todd Zeile	.10

1991 Toys "R" Us Rookies

Produced by Topps, this 33-card set features baseball's top young players. The cards are styled much like past Toys "R" Us issues featuring glossy photos. The backs are printed horizontally and include player information and statistics. This set is the fifth of its kind produced by Topps for Toys "R" Us.

		NM/M
Complete Set (33):		3.00
Common Player:		.10
1	Sandy Alomar, Jr.	.10

2	Kevin Appier	.10
3	Steve Avery	.10
4	Carlos Baerga	.10
5	Alex Cole	.10
6	Pat Combs	.10
7	Delino DeShields	.10
8	Travis Fryman	.10
9	Marquis Grissom	.10
10	Mike Harkey	.10
11	Glenallen Hill	.10
12	Jeff Huson	.10
13	Felix Jose	.10
14	Dave Justice	.50
15	Dana Kiecker	.10
16	Kevin Maas	.10
17	Ben McDonald	.10
18	Brian McRae	.10
19	Kent Mercker	.10
20	Hal Morris	.10
21	Chris Nabholz	.10
22	Tim Naehring	.10
23	Jose Offerman	.10
24	John Olerud	.25
25	Scott Radinsky	.10
26	Bill Sampen	.10
27	Frank Thomas	1.50
28	Randy Tomlin	.10
29	Greg Vaughn	.10
30	Robin Ventura	.10
31	Larry Walker	.50
32	Wally Whitehurst	.10
33	Todd Zeile	.10

1993 Toys "R" Us Topps Stadium Club

Featuring subsets labeled "Young Stars," "Future Stars" and "Rookie Stars," this 100-card set was sold in a plastic replica of a Toys "R" Us store, packaged with a dozen "Master Photos." Similar to regular 1993 Topps Stadium Club cards, the Toys "R" Us version features full-bleed photos on front, highlighted with goil-foil and a color Toys "R" Us logo in one of the upper corners. Backs have a background of a cloud-filled blue sky and green grass. A small player photo is at upper-right. Back information offers a few personal details, 1992 and career stats and a few career highlights. At bottom are the logos of all involved parties. The cards are UV-coated front and back. Each card is designated on the front as "Rookie Star," "Young Star" or "Future Star" in gold foil.

	NM/M
Unopened Set (100+12):	10.00
Complete Set (100):	6.00
Common Player:	.05
1 Ken Griffey Jr.	1.50
2 Chad Curtis	.05
3 Mike Bordick	.05
4 Ryan Klesko	.05
5 Pat Listach	.05
6 Jim Bullinger	.05

7	Tim Laker	.05
8	Mike Devereaux	.05
9	Kevin Young	.05
10	John Valentin	.05
11	Pat Mahomes	.05
12	Todd Hundley	.05
13	Roberto Alomar	.25
14	David Justice	.05
15	Mike Perez	.05
16	Royce Clayton	.05
17	Ryan Thompson	.05
18	Dave Hollins	.05
19	Brien Taylor	.05
20	Melvin Nieves	.05
21	Rheal Cormier	.05
22	Mike Piazza	1.50
23	Larry Walker	.05
24	Tim Wakefield	.05
25	Tim Costo	.05
26	Pedro Munoz	.05
27	Reggie Sanders	.05
28	Arthur Rhodes	.05
29	Scott Cooper	.05
30	Marquis Grissom	.05
31	Dave Nilsson	.05
32	John Patterson	.05
33	Ivan Rodriguez	.50
34	Andy Stankiewicz	.05
35	Bret Boone	.05
36	Gerald Williams	.05
37	Mike Mussina	.45
38	Henry Rodriguez	.05
39	Chuck Knoblauch	.05
40	Bob Wickman	.05
41	Donovan Osborne	.05
42	Mike Timlin	.05
43	Damion Easley	.05
44	Pedro Astacio	.05
45	David Segui	.05
46	Willie Greene	.05
47	Mike Trombley	.05
48	Bernie Williams	.05
49	Eric Anthony	.05
50	Tim Naehring	.05
51	Carlos Baerga	.05
52	Brady Anderson	.05
53	Mo Vaughn	.05
54	Willie Banks	.05
55	Mark Wohlers	.05
56	Jeff Bagwell	.75
57	Frank Seminara	.05
58	Robin Ventura	.05
59	Alan Embree	.05
60	Rey Sanchez	.05
61	Delino DeShields	.05
62	Todd Van Poppel	.05
63	Eric Karros	.05
64	Gary Sheffield	.35
65	Dan Wilson	.05
66	Frank Thomas	.75
67	Tim Salmon	.05
68	Dan Smith	.05
69	Kenny Lofton	.05
70	Carlos Garcia	.05
71	Scott Livingstone	.05
72	Sam Militello	.05
73	Juan Guzman	.05
74	Greg Colbrunn	.05
75	David Hulse	.05
76	Rusty Meacham	.05
77	Dave Fleming	.05
78	Rene Arocha	.05
79	Derrick May	.05
80	Cal Eldred	.05
81	Bernard Gilkey	.05
82	Deion Sanders	.05
83	Reggie Jefferson	.05
84	Jeff Kent	.05
85	Juan Gonzalez	.35
86	Bill Ashley	.05
87	Travis Fryman	.05
88	Roberto Hernandez	.05
89	Hipolito Pichardo	.05
90	Wil Cordero	.05
91	John Jaha	.05
92	Javy Lopez	.05
93	Derek Bell	.05
94	Jeff Juden	.05
95	Steve Avery	.05
96	Moises Alou	.05
97	Brian Jordan	.05
98	Brian Williams	.05
99	Bob Zupcic	.05
100	Ray Lankford	.05

Master Photos

Each boxed set of Toys "R" Us Stadium Club cards comes with a set of 12 Master Photos. Similar to the regular 1993 S.C. Master Photos, they feature at center a larger 2-3/4" x 3-3/4"), uncropped version of the photo used on the Toys "R" Us card. A gold holographic box on the photo delineates the dimensions of the regular card, while another separates the photo from the 5" by 7" white background. Topps, Toys "R" Us, and Master Photo logos appear at the top of the card. Blank white backs have a few logos and copyrights printed in black.

		NM/M
Complete Set (12):		4.00
Common Player:		.25
(1)	Willie Greene	.25
(2)	Frank Thomas	1.00
(3)	Chuck Knoblauch	.25
(4)	Marquis Grissom	.25
(5)	Scott Livingstone	.25
(6)	Ken Griffey Jr.	2.00
(7)	Carlos Baerga	.25
(8)	Ivan Rodriguez	.75
(9)	Moises Alou	.25
(10)	Sam Militello	.25
(11)	Eric Anthony	.25
(12)	Gary Sheffield	.50

Ty Cobb

This special gold-foil bordered card was available exclusively at TRU stores as part of a package of 65 plastic sheets sold by Megacards. The card is in the design of the contemporary Conlon Collection issue from Megacards and features on its front the classic photo of Cobb sliding into base. On the back, Conlon describes how he came to take the photo.

	NM/M
Ty Cobb	4.00

1992 Triple Play Previews

To introduce its base-brand Triple Play set in 1992, Donruss issued these preview cards. The format and photos on the previews are exactly like the issued versions; backs, however, differ in the numbering "X of 8" and the appearance of the word "PREVIEW" between the MLBPA and MLB logos at bottom.

	NM/M
Complete Set (8):	25.00
Common Player:	1.00
1 Ken Griffey Jr.	9.00
2 Darryl Strawberry	1.00
3 Andy Van Slyke (Little Hotshots)	1.00
4 Don Mattingly	7.50
5 Awesome Action (Gary Carter, Steve Finley)	1.00
6 Frank Thomas	5.00
7 Kirby Puckett	6.00
8 Fun at the Ballpark	1.00

1992 Triple Play

This set was released only in wax pack form. Cards feature red borders. Boyhood photos, mascots and ballparks are among the featured cards. This set was designed to give collectors an alternative product to the high-end card sets. The cards are standard size.

		NM/M
Complete Set (264):		6.00
Common Player:		.05
Wax Pack (12):		.40
Wax Box (36):		7.50
1	SkyDome	.05
2	Tom Foley	.05
3	Scott Erickson	.05
4	Matt Williams	.05
5	Dave Valle	.05
6	Andy Van Slyke (Little Hotshot)	.05
7	Tom Glavine	.25
8	Kevin Appier	.05
9	Pedro Guerrero	.05
10	Terry Steinbach	.05
11	Terry Mulholland	.05
12	Mike Boddicker	.05
13	Gregg Olson	.05
14	Tim Burke	.05
15	Candy Maldonado	.05
16	Orlando Merced	.05
17	Robin Ventura	.05
18	Eric Anthony	.05
19	Greg Maddux	.60
20	Erik Hanson	.05
21	Bob Ojeda	.05
22	Nolan Ryan	1.00
23	Dave Righetti	.05
24	Reggie Jefferson	.05
25	Jody Reed	.05
26	Awesome Action (Steve Finley, Gary Carter)	.10
27	Chili Davis	.05
28	Hector Villanueva	.05
29	Cecil Fielder	.05
30	Hal Morris	.05
31	Barry Larkin	.05
32	Bobby Thigpen	.05
33	Andy Benes	.05
34	Harold Baines	.05
35	David Cone	.05
36	Mark Langston	.05
37	Bryan Harvey	.05
38	John Kruk	.05
39	Scott Sanderson	.05
40	Lonnie Smith	.05
41	Awesome Action (Rex Hudler)	.05
42	George Bell	.05
43	Steve Finley	.05
44	Mickey Tettleton	.05
45	Robby Thompson	.05
46	Pat Kelly	.05
47	Marquis Grissom	.05
48	Tony Pena	.05
49	Alex Cole	.05
50	Steve Buechele	.05
51	Ivan Rodriguez	.45
52	John Smiley	.05
53	Gary Sheffield	.25
54	Greg Olson	.05
55	Ramon Martinez	.05
56	B.J. Surhoff	.05
57	Bruce Hurst	.05
58	Todd Stottlemyre	.05
59	Brett Butler	.05
60	Glenn Davis	.05
61	Awesome Action (Glenn Braggs, Kirt Manwaring)	.05
62	Lee Smith	.05
63	Rickey Henderson	.45
64	Fun at the Ballpark (David Cone, Jeff Innis, John Franco)	.05
65	Rick Aguilera	.05
66	Kevin Elster	.05
67	Dwight Evans	.05
68	Andujar Cedeno	.05
69	Brian McRae	.05
70	Benito Santiago	.05
71	Randy Johnson	.45
72	Roberto Kelly	.05
73	Awesome Action (Juan Samuel)	.05
74	Alex Fernandez	.05
75	Felix Jose	.05
76	Brian Harper	.05
77	Scott Sanderson (Little Hotshot)	.05
78	Ken Caminiti	.05
79	Mo Vaughn	.05
80	Roger McDowell	.05
81	Robin Yount	.45
82	Dave Magadan	.05
83	Julio Franco	.05
84	Roberto Alomar	.25
85	Steve Avery	.05
86	Travis Fryman	.05
87	Fred McGriff	.05
88	Dave Stewart	.05
89	Larry Walker	.05
90	Chris Sabo	.05
91	Chuck Finley	.05
92	Dennis Martinez	.05
93	Jeff Johnson	.05
94	Len Dykstra	.05
95	Mark Whiten	.05
96	Wade Taylor	.05
97	Lance Dickson	.05
98	Kevin Tapani	.05
99	Awesome Action (Luis Polonia, Tony Phillips)	.05
100	Milt Cuyler	.05
101	Willie McGee	.05
102	Awesome Action (Tony Fernandez, Ryne Sandberg)	.15
103	Albert Belle	.05
104	Todd Hundley	.05
105	Ben McDonald	.05
106	Doug Drabek	.05
107	Tim Raines	.05
108	Joe Carter	.05
109	Reggie Sanders	.05
110	John Olerud	.05
111	Darren Lewis	.05
112	Juan Gonzalez	.25
113	Awesome Action (Andre Dawson)	.05
114	Mark Grace	.05
115	George Brett	.65
116	Barry Bonds	1.00
117	Lou Whitaker	.05
118	Jose Oquendo	.05
119	Lee Stevens	.05
120	Phil Plantier	.05
121	Awesome Action (Devon White, Matt Merullo)	.05
122	Greg Vaughn	.05
123	Royce Clayton	.05
124	Bob Welch	.05
125	Juan Samuel	.05
126	Ron Gant	.05
127	Edgar Martinez	.05
128	Andy Ashby	.05
129	Jack McDowell	.05
130	Awesome Action (Dave Henderson, Jerry Browne)	.05
131	Leo Gomez	.05
132	Checklist 1-88	.05
133	Phillie Phanatic	.05
134	Bret Barberie	.05
135	Kent Hrbek	.05
136	Hall of Fame	.05
137	Omar Vizquel	.05
138	The Famous Chicken	.05
139	Terry Pendleton	.05
140	Jim Eisenreich	.05
141	Todd Zeile	.05
142	Todd Van Poppel	.05
143	Darren Daulton	.05
144	Mike Macfarlane	.05
145	Luis Mercedes	.05
146	Trevor Wilson	.05
147	Dave Steib	.05
148	Andy Van Slyke	.05
149	Carlton Fisk	.45
150	Craig Biggio	.05
151	Joe Girardi	.05
152	Ken Griffey Jr.	.65
153	Jose Offerman	.05
154	Bobby Witt	.05
155	Will Clark	.05
156	Steve Olin	.05
157	Greg Harris	.05
158	Dale Murphy (Little Hotshot)	.05
159	Don Mattingly	.65
160	Shawon Dunston	.05
161	Bill Gullickson	.05
162	Paul O'Neill	.05
163	Norm Charlton	.05
164	Bo Jackson	.10
165	Tony Fernandez	.05
166	Dave Henderson	.05
167	Dwight Gooden	.05
168	Junior Felix	.05
169	Lance Parrish	.05
170	Pat Combs	.05
171	Chuck Knoblauch	.05
172	John Smoltz	.05
173	Wrigley Field	.05
174	Andre Dawson	.25
175	Pete Harnisch	.05
176	Alan Trammell	.05
177	Kirk Dressendorfer	.05
178	Matt Nokes	.05
179	Wil Cordero	.05
180	Scott Cooper	.05
181	Glenallen Hill	.05
182	John Franco	.05
183	Rafael Palmeiro	.40
184	Jay Bell	.05
185	Bill Wegman	.05
186	Deion Sanders	.05
187	Darryl Strawberry	.05
188	Jaime Navarro	.05
189	Darren Jackson	.05
190	Eddie Zosky	.05
191	Mike Scioscia	.05
192	Chito Martinez	.05
193	Awesome Action (Pat Kelly, Ron Tingley)	.05
194	Ray Lankford	.05
195	Dennis Eckersley	.35
196	Awesome Action (Ivan Calderon, Mike Maddux)	.05
197	Shane Mack	.05
198	Checklist 89-176	.05
199	Cal Ripken, Jr.	1.00
200	Jeff Bagwell	.45
201	David Howard	.05
202	Kirby Puckett	.60
203	Harold Reynolds	.05
204	Jim Abbott	.05
205	Mark Lewis	.05
206	Frank Thomas	.45
207	Rex Hudler	.05
208	Vince Coleman	.05
209	Delino DeShields	.05
210	Luis Gonzalez	.05
211	Wade Boggs	.60
212	Orel Hershiser	.05
213	Cal Eldred	.05
214	Jose Canseco	.25
215	Jose Guzman	.05
216	Roger Clemens	.65
217	Dave Justice	.05
218	Tony Phillips	.05
219	Tony Gwynn	.60
220	Mitch Williams	.05
221	Bill Sampen	.05
222	Billy Hatcher	.05
223	Gary Gaetti	.05
224	Tim Wallach	.05
225	Kevin Maas	.05
226	Kevin Brown	.05
227	Sandy Alomar	.05
228	John Habyan	.05
229	Ryne Sandberg	.60
230	Greg Gagne	.05
231	Autographs (Mark McGwire)	.40
232	Mike LaValliere	.05
233	Mark Gubicza	.05
234	Lance Parrish (Little Hotshot)	.05
235	Carlos Baerga	.05
236	Howard Johnson	.05
237	Mike Mussina	.25
238	Ruben Sierra	.05
239	Lance Johnson	.05
240	Devon White	.05
241	Dan Wilson	.05
242	Kelly Gruber	.05
243	Brett Butler (Little Hotshot)	.05
244	Ozzie Smith	.60
245	Chuck McElroy	.05
246	Shawn Boskie	.05
247	Mark Davis	.05
248	Bill Landrum	.05
249	Frank Tanana	.05
250	Darryl Hamilton	.05
251	Gary DiSarcina	.05
252	Mike Greenwell	.05
253	Cal Ripken, Jr. (Little Hotshot)	.35
254	Paul Molitor	.45
255	Tim Teufel	.05
256	Chris Hoiles	.05
257	Rob Dibble	.05
258	Sid Bream	.05
259	Chito Martinez	.05
260	Dale Murphy	.15
261	Greg Hibbard	.05
262	Mark McGwire	.75
263	Oriole Park	.05
264	Checklist 177-264	.05

Gallery of Stars

Two levels of scarcity are represented in this insert issue.

Cards #1-6 (all cards have a GS prefix to the card number) feature in their new uniforms players who changed teams for 1993. Those inserts were found in the standard Triple Play foil packs and are somewhat more common than cards #7-12, which were found only in jumbo packs and which feature a better selection of established stars and rookies. All of the inserts feature the artwork of Dick Perez, with player portraits set against a colorful background. Silver-foil accents highlight the front design. Backs are red with a white "tombstone" containing a career summary.

	NM/M
Complete Set (12):	4.00
Common Player:	.15
1 Bobby Bonilla	.15
2 Wally Joyner	.15
3 Jack Morris	.15
4 Steve Sax	.15
5 Danny Tartabull	.15
6 Frank Viola	.15
7 Jeff Bagwell	.60
8 Ken Griffey Jr.	1.00
9 David Justice	.15
10 Ryan Klesko	.15
11 Cal Ripken, Jr.	1.50
12 Frank Thomas	.75

1993 Triple Play Promos

This set was given to dealers to preview the 1993 Donruss Triple Play issue. Cards are virtually identical to the regular-issue cards except for a large promotional sample notation printed on back.

	NM/M
Complete Set (12):	100.00
Common Player:	5.00
1 Ken Griffey Jr.	25.00
2 Roberto Alomar	6.00
3 Cal Ripken, Jr.	40.00
4 Eric Karros	5.00
5 Cecil Fielder	5.00
6 Gary Sheffield	7.50
7 Darren Daulton	5.00
8 Andy Van Slyke	5.00
9 Dennis Eckersley	10.00
10 Ryne Sandberg	25.00
11 Mark Grace	
(Little Hotshots)	5.00
12 Awesome Action #1	
(Luis Polonia,	
David Segui)	5.00

1993 Triple Play

MARK LEMKE 28

For the second year, Leaf-Donruss used the "Triple Play" brand name for its base-level card set aimed at the younger collector. The 264-card set was available in several types of retail packaging and included a number of special subsets, such as childhood photos (labeled LH - Little Hotshots - in the checklist) and insert sets. Checklist card #264 incorrectly shows card #129, Joe Robbie Stadium, as #259. There is a second card, "Equipment," which also bears #129. An "Action Baseball" scratch-off game card was included in each foil pack.

	NM/M
Complete Set (264):	10.00
Common Player:	.05
Wax Pack (12):	.60
Wax Box (36):	15.00

1	Ken Griffey Jr.	.50
2	Roberto Alomar	.10
3	Cal Ripken, Jr.	.75
4	Eric Karros	.05
5	Cecil Fielder	.05
6	Gary Sheffield	.15
7	Darren Daulton	.05
8	Andy Van Slyke	.05
9	Dennis Eckersley	.20
10	Ryne Sandberg	.35
11	Mark Grace	
	(Little Hotshots)	.05
12	Awesome Action #1	
	(Luis Polonia,	
	David Segui)	.05
13	Mike Mussina	.15
14	Vince Coleman	.05
15	Rafael Belliard	.05
16	Ivan Rodriguez	.20
17	Eddie Taubensee	.05
18	Cal Eldred	.05
19	Rick Wilkins	.05
20	Edgar Martinez	.05
21	Brian McRae	.05
22	Darren Holmes	.05
23	Mark Whiten	.05
24	Todd Zeile	.05
25	Scott Cooper	.05
26	Frank Thomas	.25
27	Wil Cordero	.05
28	Juan Guzman	.05
29	Pedro Astacio	.05
30	Steve Avery	.05
31	Barry Larkin	.05
32	President Clinton	2.00
33	Scott Erickson	.05
34	Mike Devereaux	.05
35	Tino Martinez	.05
36	Brent Mayne	.05
37	Tim Salmon	.05
38	Dave Hollins	.05
39	Royce Clayton	.05
40	Shawon Dunston	.05
41	Eddie Murray	.25
42	Larry Walker	.05
43	Jeff Bagwell	.25
44	Milt Cuyler	.05
45	Mike Bordick	.05
46	Mike Greenwell	.05
47	Steve Sax	.05
48	Chuck Knoblauch	.05
49	Charles Nagy	.05
50	Tim Wakefield	.05
51	Tony Gwynn	.35
52	Rob Dibble	.05
53	Mickey Morandini	.05
54	Steve Hosey	.05
55	Mike Piazza	.50
56	Bill Wegman	.05
57	Kevin Maas	.05
58	Gary DiSarcina	.05
59	Travis Fryman	.05
60	Ruben Sierra	.05
61	Awesome Action #2	
	(Ken Caminiti)	.05
62	Brian Jordan	.05
63	Scott Chiamparino	.05
64	Awesome Action #3	
	(Mike Bordick,	
	George Brett)	.05
65	Carlos Garcia	.05
66	Checklist 1-66	.05
67	John Smoltz	.05
68	Awesome Action #4	
	(Mark McGwire,	
	Brian Harper)	.20
69	Kurt Stillwell	.05
70	Chad Curtis	.05
71	Rafael Palmeiro	.20
72	Kevin Young	.05
73	Glenn Davis	.05
74	Dennis Martinez	.05
75	Sam Militello	.05
76	Mike Morgan	.05
77	Frank Thomas	
	(Little Hotshots)	.20
78	Staying Fit (Bip Roberts,	
	Mike Devereaux)	.05
79	Steve Buechele	.05
80	Carlos Baerga	.05
81	Robby Thompson	.05
82	Kirk McCaskill	.05
83	Lee Smith	.05
84	Gary Scott	.05
85	Tony Pena	.05
86	Howard Johnson	.05
87	Mark McGwire	.60
88	Bip Roberts	.05
89	Devon White	.05
90	John Franco	.05
91	Tom Browning	.05
92	Mickey Tettleton	.05
93	Jeff Conine	.05
94	Albert Belle	.05
95	Fred McGriff	.05
96	Nolan Ryan	.75
97	Paul Molitor	
	(Little Hotshots)	.10
98	Juan Bell	.05
99	Dave Fleming	.05
100	Craig Biggio	.05
101a	Andy Stankiewicz	
	(White name on front.)	.05
101b	Andy Stankiewicz	
	(Red name on front.)	.25
102	Delino DeShields	.05
103	Damion Easley	.05
104	Kevin McReynolds	.05

105	David Nied	.05
106	Rick Sutcliffe	.05
107	Will Clark	.05
108	Tim Raines	.05
109	Eric Anthony	.05
110	Mike LaValliere	.05
111	Dean Palmer	.05
112	Eric Davis	.05
113	Damon Berryhill	.05
114	Felix Jose	.05
115	Ozzie Guillen	.05
116	Pat Listach	.05
117	Tom Glavine	.15
118	Roger Clemens	.40
119	Dave Henderson	.05
120	Don Mattingly	.40
121	Orel Hershiser	.05
122	Ozzie Smith	.35
123	Joe Carter	.05
124	Bret Saberhagen	.05
125	Mitch Williams	.05
126	Jerald Clark	.05
127	Mile High Stadium	.05
128	Kent Hrbek	.05
129a	Equipment (Curt Schilling,	
	Mark Whiten)	.05
129b	Joe Robbie Stadium	.05
130	Gregg Jefferies	.05
131	John Orton	.05
132	Checklist 67-132	.05
133	Bret Boone	.05
134	Pat Borders	.05
135	Gregg Olson	.05
136	Brett Butler	.05
137	Rob Deer	.05
138	Darrin Jackson	.05
139	John Kruk	.05
140	Jay Bell	.05
141	Bobby Witt	.05
142	New Cubs (Dan Plesac,	
	Randy Myers,	
	Jose Guzman)	.05
143	Wade Boggs	
	(Little Hotshots)	.15
144	Awesome Action #5	
	(Kenny Lofton)	.05
145	Ben McDonald	.05
146	Dwight Gooden	.05
147	Terry Pendleton	.05
148	Julio Franco	.05
149	Ken Caminiti	.05
150	Greg Vaughn	.05
151	Sammy Sosa	.35
152	David Valle	.05
153	Wally Joyner	.05
154	Dante Bichette	.05
155	Mark Lewis	.05
156	Bob Tewksbury	.05
157	Billy Hatcher	.05
158	Jack McDowell	.05
159	Marquis Grissom	.05
160	Jack Morris	.05
161	Ramon Martinez	.05
162	Deion Sanders	.05
163	Tim Belcher	.05
164	Mascots	.05
165	Scott Leius	.05
166	Brady Anderson	.05
167	Randy Johnson	.25
168	Mark Gubicza	.05
169	Chuck Finley	.05
170	Terry Mulholland	.05
171	Matt Williams	.05
172	Dwight Smith	.05
173	Bobby Bonilla	.05
174	Ken Hill	.05
175	Doug Jones	.05
176	Tony Phillips	.05
177	Terry Steinbach	.05
178	Frank Viola	.05
179	Robin Ventura	.05
180	Shane Mack	.05
181	Kenny Lofton	.05
182	Jeff King	.05
183	Tim Teufel	.05
184	Chris Sabo	.05
185	Lenny Dykstra	.05
186	Trevor Wilson	.05
187	Darryl Strawberry	.05
188	Robin Yount	.25
189	Bob Wickman	.05
190	Luis Polonia	.05
191	Alan Trammell	.05
192	Bob Welch	.05
193	Awesome Action #6	.05
194	Tom Pagnozzi	.05
195	Bret Barberie	.05
196	Awesome Action #7	
	(Mike Scioscia)	.05
197	Randy Tomlin	.05
198	Checklist 133-198	.05
199	Ron Gant	.05
200	Awesome Action #8	
	(Roberto Alomar)	.05
201	Andy Benes	.05
202	Pepper	.05
203	Steve Finley	.05
204	Steve Olin	.05
205	Chris Hoiles	.05
206	John Wetteland	.05
207	Danny Tartabull	.05
208	Bernard Gilkey	.05
209	Tom Glavine	
	(Little Hotshots)	.05
210	Benito Santiago	.05
211	Mark Grace	.05
212	Glenallen Hill	.05
213	Jeff Brantley	.05

214	George Brett	.40
215	Mark Lemke	.05
216	Ron Karkovice	.05
217	Tom Brunansky	.05
218	Todd Hundley	.05
219	Rickey Henderson	.25
220	Joe Oliver	.05
221	Juan Gonzalez	.15
222	John Olerud	.05
223	Hal Morris	.05
224	Lou Whitaker	.05
225	Bryan Harvey	.05
226	Mike Gallego	.05
227	Willie McGee	.05
228	Jose Oquendo	.05
229	Darren Daulton	
	(Little Hotshots)	.05
230	Curt Schilling	.10
231	Jay Buhner	.05
232	New Astros (Doug Drabek,	
	Greg Swindell)	.05
233	Jaime Navarro	.05
234	Kevin Appier	.05
235	Mark Langston	.05
236	Jeff Montgomery	.05
237	Joe Girardi	.05
238	Ed Sprague	.05
239	Dan Walters	.05
240	Kevin Tapani	.05
241	Pete Harnisch	.05
242	Al Martin	.05
243	Jose Canseco	.15
244	Moises Alou	.05
245	Mark McGwire	
	(Little Hotshots)	.25
246	Luis Rivera	.05
247	George Bell	.05
248	B.J. Surhoff	.05
249	Dave Justice	.05
250	Brian Harper	.05
251	Sandy Alomar, Jr.	.05
252	Kevin Brown	.05
253	New Dodgers	
	(Tim Wallach, Jody Reed,	
	Todd Worrell)	.05
254	Ray Lankford	.05
255	Derek Bell	.05
256	Joe Grahe	.05
257	Charlie Hayes	.05
258	New Yankees	
	(Wade Boggs,	
	Jim Abbott)	.25
259	Joe Robbie Stadium	.05
260	Kirby Puckett	.35
261	Fun at the Ballpark	
	(Jay Bell,	
	Vince Coleman)	.05
262	Bill Swift	.05
263	Fun at the Ballpark	
	(Roger McDowell)	.05
264	Checklist 199-264	.05

Gallery

Gallery of Stars

Benito Santiago

The Gallery of Stars cards were found as random inserts in Triple Play jumbo packs. The cards feature Dick Perez painted representations of the players.

	NM/M
Complete Set (10):	7.00
Common Player:	.50
1 Barry Bonds	3.00
2 Andre Dawson	.65
3 Wade Boggs	1.50
4 Greg Maddux	1.50
5 Dave Winfield	1.00
6 Paul Molitor	1.00
7 Jim Abbott	.50
8 J.T. Snow	.50
9 Benito Santiago	.50
10 David Nied	.50

Action Baseball

TRIPLE ACTION BASEBALL

VERSUS

These game folders were inserted in each 1993 Triple Play foil pack. Because collation of the folders was very bad, few collectors bothered to save them. Measuring 2-1/2" x 5", fronts have an action photo of an unnamed player. Printed over the bottom of the photo are two full-color team logos, with a white "Versus" between. Inside the folder is a baseball diamond diagram, a three-inning scoreboard, rules for playing the game and 32 scratch-off squares for playing. Backs have a number designating the folder as "of 30."

	NM/M
Complete Set (30):	3.00
Common Player:	.10
1 Andy Van Slyke	.10
2 Bobby Bonilla	.10
3 Ozzie Smith	.30
4 Ryne Sandberg	.30
5 Darren Daulton	.10
6 Larry Walker	.10
7 Eric Karros	.10
8 Barry Larkin	.10
9 Deion Sanders	.10
10 Gary Sheffield	.20

League Leaders

NATIONAL LEAGUE

LEAGUE LEADERS

These "double-headed" cards feature one player on each side. The six cards were random inserts in Triple Play retail packs.

	NM/M
Complete Set (6):	7.00
Common Player:	.50
1 Barry Bonds,	
	Dennis Eckersley	3.50
2 Greg Maddux,	
	Dennis Eckersley	2.00
3 Eric Karros, Pat Listach	.50
4 Fred McGriff,	
	Juan Gonzalez	.75
5 Darren Daulton,	
	Cecil Fielder	.50
6 Gary Sheffield,	
	Edgar Martinez	.65

Nicknames

Popular nicknames of 10 of the game's top stars are featured in silver foil on this insert set found in Triple Play foil packs.

	NM/M
Complete Set (10):	10.00
Common Player:	.75
1 Frank Thomas	
	(Big Hurt)	1.25

11	Will Clark	.10
12	Jeff Bagwell	.25
13	Roberto Alomar	.15
14	Roger Clemens	.35
15	Cecil Fielder	.10
16	Robin Yount	.25
17	Cal Ripken, Jr.	.10
18	Carlos Baerga	.10
19	Don Mattingly	.35
20	Kirby Puckett	.30
21	Frank Thomas	.25
22	Juan Gonzalez	.15
23	Mark McGwire	.45
24	Ken Griffey Jr.	.40
25	Wally Joyner	.10
26	Chad Curtis	.10
27	Batting Glove	.10
28	Juan Guzman	.10
29	Dave Justice	.10
30	Joe Carter	.10

RYNO

Ryne Sandberg

2	Roger Clemens	
	(Rocket)	2.00
3	Ryne Sandberg (Ryno)	1.50
4	Will Clark (Thrill)	.75
5	Ken Griffey Jr. (Junior)	3.00
6	Dwight Gooden (Doc)	.75
7	Nolan Ryan (Express)	4.00
8	Deion Sanders	
	(Prime Time)	.75
9	Ozzie Smith (Wizard)	1.50
10	Fred McGriff	
	(Crime Dog)	.75

1994 Triple Play Promos

PIAZZA

This set was given to dealers to preview the 1994 Donruss Triple Play issue. Cards are virtually identical to the regular-issue cards except for a large black "Promotional Sample" printed diagonally in black on both front and back. Cards are numbered as "X of 10" on the promos.

	NM/M
Complete Set (10):	9.00
Common Player:	.50
1 Juan Gonzalez	.60
2 Frank Thomas	.85
3 Barry Bonds	3.00
4 Ken Griffey Jr.	1.50
5 Paul Molitor	.75
6 Mike Piazza	1.50
7 Tim Salmon	.50
8 Lenny Dykstra	.50
9 Don Mattingly	1.25
10 Greg Maddux	1.00

1994 Triple Play

Triple Play cards returned for a third year in 1994, this time with a borderless design. According to company officials, production was less than 1994 Donruss Series I baseball, which was roughly 17,500 20-box cases. In the regular-issue 300-card set, 10 players from each team were featured, along with a 17-card Rookie Review subset and several insert sets.

		NM/M
Complete Set (300):		7.50
Common Player:		.05
Wax Pack (12):		.50
Wax Box (36):		12.00
1	Mike Bordick	.05
2	Dennis Eckersley	.35
3	Brent Gates	.05
4	Rickey Henderson	.40
5	Mark McGwire	.65
6	Troy Neel	.05
7	Craig Paquette	.05
8	Ruben Sierra	.05
9	Terry Steinbach	.05
10	Bobby Witt	.05
11	Chad Curtis	.05
12	Chili Davis	.05
13	Gary DiSarcina	.05
14	Damion Easley	.05
15	Chuck Finley	.05
16	Joe Grahe	.05
17	Mark Langston	.05
18	Eduardo Perez	.05
19	Tim Salmon	.05
20	J.T. Snow	.05
21	Jeff Bagwell	.40
22	Craig Biggio	.05
23	Ken Caminiti	.05
24	Andujar Cedeno	.05
25	Doug Drabek	.05
26	Steve Finley	.05
27	Luis Gonzalez	.05
28	Pete Harnisch	.05
29	Darryl Kile	.05
30	Mitch Williams	.05
31	Roberto Alomar	.20
32	Joe Carter	.05
33	Juan Guzman	.05
34	Pat Hentgen	.05
35	Paul Molitor	.40
36	John Olerud	.05
37	Ed Sprague	.05
38	Dave Stewart	.05
39	Duane Ward	.05
40	Devon White	.05
41	Steve Avery	.05
42	Jeff Blauser	.05
43	Ron Gant	.05
44	Tom Glavine	.20
45	Dave Justice	.05
46	Greg Maddux	.45
47	Fred McGriff	.05
48	Terry Pendleton	.05
49	Deion Sanders	.05
50	John Smoltz	.05
51	Ricky Bones	.05
52	Cal Eldred	.05
53	Darryl Hamilton	.05
54	John Jaha	.05
55	Pat Listach	.05
56	Jaime Navarro	.05
57	Dave Nilsson	.05
58	B.J. Surhoff	.05
59	Greg Vaughn	.05
60	Robin Yount	.40
61	Bernard Gilkey	.05
62	Gregg Jefferies	.05
63	Brian Jordan	.05
64	Ray Lankford	.05
65	Tom Pagnozzi	.05
66	Ozzie Smith	.45
67	Bob Tewksbury	.05
68	Allen Watson	.50
69	Mark Whiten	.05
70	Todd Zeile	.05
71	Steve Buechele	.05
72	Mark Grace	.05
73	Jose Guzman	.05
74	Derrick May	.05
75	Mike Morgan	.05
76	Randy Myers	.05
77	Ryne Sandberg	.45
78	Sammy Sosa	.50
79	Jose Vizcaino	.05
80	Rick Wilkins	.05
81	Pedro Astacio	.05
82	Brett Butler	.05
83	Delino DeShields	.05
84	Orel Hershiser	.05
85	Eric Karros	.05
86	Ramon Martinez	.05
87	Jose Offerman	.05
88	Mike Piazza	.50
89	Darryl Strawberry	.05
90	Tim Wallach	.05
91	Moises Alou	.05
92	Wil Cordero	.05
93	Jeff Fassero	.05
94	Darrin Fletcher	.05
95	Marquis Grissom	.05
96	Ken Hill	.05
97	Mike Lansing	.05
98	Kirk Rueter	.05
99	Larry Walker	.05
100	John Wetteland	.05
101	Rod Beck	.05
102	Barry Bonds	.75
103	John Burkett	.05
104	Royce Clayton	.05
105	Darren Lewis	.05
106	Kirt Manwaring	.05
107	Willie McGee	.05
108	Bill Swift	.05

109	Robby Thompson	.05
110	Matt Williams	.05
111	Sandy Alomar Jr.	.05
112	Carlos Baerga	.05
113	Albert Belle	.05
114	Wayne Kirby	.05
115	Kenny Lofton	.05
116	Jose Mesa	.05
117	Eddie Murray	.40
118	Charles Nagy	.05
119	Paul Sorrento	.05
120	Jim Thome	.35
121	Rich Amaral	.05
122	Eric Anthony	.05
123	Mike Blowers	.05
124	Chris Bosio	.05
125	Jay Buhner	.05
126	Dave Fleming	.05
127	Ken Griffey Jr.	.50
128	Randy Johnson	.40
129	Edgar Martinez	.05
130	Tino Martinez	.05
131	Bret Barberie	.05
132	Ryan Bowen	.05
133	Chuck Carr	.05
134	Jeff Conine	.05
135	Orestes Destrade	.05
136	Chris Hammond	.05
137	Bryan Harvey	.05
138	Dave Magadan	.05
139	Benito Santiago	.05
140	Gary Sheffield	.30
141	Bobby Bonilla	.05
142	Jeromy Burnitz	.05
143	Dwight Gooden	.05
144	Todd Hundley	.05
145	Bobby Jones	.05
146	Jeff Kent	.05
147	Joe Orsulak	.05
148	Bret Saberhagen	.05
149	Pete Schourek	.05
150	Ryan Thompson	.05
151	Brady Anderson	.05
152	Harold Baines	.05
153	Mike Devereaux	.05
154	Chris Hoiles	.05
155	Ben McDonald	.05
156	Mark McLemore	.05
157	Mike Mussina	.25
158	Rafael Palmeiro	.40
159	Cal Ripken, Jr.	.75
160	Chris Sabo	.05
161	Brad Ausmus	.05
162	Derek Bell	.05
163	Andy Benes	.05
164	Doug Brocail	.05
165	Archi Cianfrocco	.05
166	Ricky Gutierrez	.05
167	Tony Gwynn	.45
168	Gene Harris	.05
169	Pedro Martinez	.40
170	Phil Plantier	.05
171	Darren Daulton	.05
172	Mariano Duncan	.05
173	Len Dykstra	.05
174	Tommy Greene	.05
175	Dave Hollins	.05
176	Danny Jackson	.05
177	John Kruk	.05
178	Terry Mulholland	.05
179	Curt Schilling	.20
180	Kevin Stocker	.05
181	Jay Bell	.05
182	Steve Cooke	.05
183	Carlos Garcia	.05
184	Joel Johnston	.05
185	Jeff King	.05
186	Al Martin	.05
187	Orlando Merced	.05
188	Don Slaught	.05
189	Andy Van Slyke	.05
190	Kevin Young	.05
191	Kevin Brown	.05
192	Jose Canseco	.25
193	Will Clark	.05
194	Juan Gonzalez	.20
195	Tom Henke	.05
196	David Hulse	.05
197	Dean Palmer	.05
198	Roger Pavlik	.05
199	Ivan Rodriguez	.35
200	Kevin Rogers	.05
201	Roger Clemens	.45
202	Scott Cooper	.05
203	Andre Dawson	.20
204	Mike Greenwell	.05
205	Billy Hatcher	.05
206	Jeff Russell	.05
207	Aaron Sele	.05
208	John Valentin	.05
209	Mo Vaughn	.05
210	Frank Viola	.05
211	Rob Dibble	.05
212	Willie Greene	.05
213	Roberto Kelly	.05
214	Barry Larkin	.05
215	Kevin Mitchell	.05
216	Hal Morris	.05
217	Joe Oliver	.05
218	Jose Rijo	.05
219	Reggie Sanders	.05
220	John Smiley	.05
221	Dante Bichette	.05
222	Ellis Burks	.05
223	Andres Galarraga	.05
224	Joe Girardi	.05
225	Charlie Hayes	.05
226	Darren Holmes	.05

227	Howard Johnson	.05
228	Roberto Mejia	.05
229	David Nied	.05
230	Armando Reynoso	.05
231	Kevin Appier	.05
232	David Cone	.05
233	Greg Gagne	.05
234	Tom Gordon	.05
235	Felix Jose	.05
236	Wally Joyner	.05
237	Jose Lind	.05
238	Brian McRae	.05
239	Mike MacFarlane	.05
240	Jeff Montgomery	.05
241	Eric Davis	.05
242	John Doherty	.05
243	Cecil Fielder	.05
244	Travis Fryman	.05
245	Bill Gullickson	.05
246	Mike Henneman	.05
247	Tony Phillips	.05
248	Mickey Tettleton	.05
249	Alan Trammell	.05
250	Lou Whitaker	.05
251	Rick Aguilera	.05
252	Scott Erickson	.05
253	Kent Hrbek	.05
254	Chuck Knoblauch	.05
255	Shane Mack	.05
256	Dave McCarty	.05
257	Pat Meares	.05
258	Kirby Puckett	.45
259	Kevin Tapani	.05
260	Dave Winfield	.40
261	Wilson Alvarez	.05
262	Jason Bere	.05
263	Alex Fernandez	.05
264	Ozzie Guillen	.05
265	Roberto Hernandez	.05
266	Lance Johnson	.05
267	Jack McDowell	.05
268	Tim Raines	.05
269	Frank Thomas	.40
270	Robin Ventura	.05
271	Jim Abbott	.05
272	Wade Boggs	.45
273	Mike Gallego	.05
274	Pat Kelly	.05
275	Jimmy Key	.05
276	Don Mattingly	.50
277	Paul O'Neill	.05
278	Mike Stanley	.05
279	Danny Tartabull	.05
280	Bernie Williams	.05
281	Chipper Jones	.45
282	Ryan Klesko	.05
283	Javier Lopez	.05
284	Jeffrey Hammonds	.05
285	Jeff McNeely	.05
286	Manny Ramirez	.40
287	Billy Ashley	.05
288	Raul Mondesi	.05
289	Cliff Floyd	.05
290	Rondell White	.05
291	Steve Karsay	.05
292	Midre Cummings	.05
293	Salomon Torres	.05
294	J.R. Phillips	.05
295	Marc Newfield	.05
296	Carlos Delgado	.30
297	Butch Huskey	.05
298	Checklist (Frank Thomas)	.05
299	Checklist (Barry Bonds)	.05
300	Checklist (Juan Gonzalez)	.05

Bomb Squad

Ten of the top major league home run hitters are included in this insert set. Fronts feature sepia-toned player photos within a wide brown frame. Gold foil enhances the typography. Backs have a white background with representations of vintage airplanes. A bar chart at left gives the player's home run totals by year. A small color portrait photo is at upper-right. Below are a few words about his homer history.

		NM/M
Complete Set (10):		5.00

Common Player:		.25
1	Frank Thomas	1.00
2	Cecil Fielder	.25
3	Juan Gonzalez	.45
4	Barry Bonds	2.50
5	Dave Justice	.25
6	Fred McGriff	.25
7	Ron Gant	.25
8	Ken Griffey Jr.	1.50
9	Albert Belle	.25
10	Matt Williams	.25

Medalists

Statistical performance over the 1992-93 seasons was used to rank the players appearing in the Medalists insert set. Horizontal format cards have photos of the first, second and third place winners in appropriate boxes of gold, silver and bronze foil. "Medalists," the "medals" and "Triple Play 94" are embossed on the front. Backs have color action photos of each player along with team logos and a few stats.

		NM/M
Complete Set (15):		10.00
Common Player:		.50
1	A.L. Catchers (Chris Hoiles, Mickey Tettleton, Brian Harper)	.50
2	N.L. Catchers (Darren Daulton, Rick Wilkins, Kirt Manwaring)	.50
3	A.L. First Basemen (Frank Thomas, Rafael Palmeiro, John Olerud)	1.00
4	N.L. First Basemen (Mark Grace, Fred McGriff, Jeff Bagwell)	1.00
5	A.L. Second Basemen (Roberto Alomar, Carlos Baerga, Lou Whitaker)	.50
6	N.L. Second Basemen (Ryne Sandberg, Craig Biggio, Robby Thompson)	1.25
7	A.L. Shortstops (Tony Fernandez, Cal Ripken, Jr., Alan Trammell)	2.00
8	N.L. Shortstops (Barry Larkin, Jay Bell, Jeff Blauser)	.50
9	A.L. Third Basemen (Robin Ventura, Travis Fryman, Wade Boggs)	1.25
10	N.L. Third Basemen (Terry Pendleton, Dave Hollins, Gary Sheffield)	.50
11	A.L. Outfielders (Ken Griffey Jr., Kirby Puckett, Albert Belle)	1.50
12	N.L. Outfielders (Barry Bonds, Andy Van Slyke, Len Dykstra)	2.00
13	A.L. Starters (Jack McDowell, Kevin Brown, Randy Johnson)	.60
14	N.L. Starters (Greg Maddux, Jose Rijo, Billy Swift)	1.25
15	Designated Hitters (Paul Molitor, Dave Winfield, Harold Baines)	.60

Nicknames

Eight of baseball's most colorful team nicknames are featured in this insert set. Fronts feature a background photo representative of the nickname, with a player photo is superimposed over that. Backs have another player photo and a history of the team's nickname.

		NM/M
Complete Set (8):		10.00
Common Player:		.75
1	Cecil Fielder	.75

2	Ryne Sandberg	1.50
3	Gary Sheffield	.90
4	Joe Carter	.75
5	John Olerud	.75
6	Cal Ripken, Jr.	3.00
7	Mark McGwire	2.50
8	Gregg Jefferies	.75

1990 Tropicana Team Mets

In 1990, Tropicana orange juice took over as sponsor of the junior Mets fan club. One of the membership perks was a nine-card sheet. Action photos were surrounded by team-color stripes of blue and orange and a white outer border. Backs have Team Mets and Tropicana logos, 1989 highlights and stats, career numbers and personal data. Individual cards measure 2-1/2" x 3-1/2", though they are not often sold other than as an original 7-1/2" x 10-1/2" sheet. Cards are checklisted here on the basis of uniform numbers found on the cards' fronts.

		NM/M
Complete Set (9):		4.00
Common Player:		.50
9	Gregg Jefferies	.50
16	Dwight Gooden	.50
18	Darryl Strawberry	.50
20	Howard Johnson	.50
21	Kevin Elster	.50
25	Keith Miller	.50
29	Frank Viola	.50
44	David Cone	.50
50	Sid Fernandez	.50

1991 Tropicana Team Mets

This nine-card sheet was a perk for members of the junior Mets fan club - Team Mets. Sponsored by Tropicana fruit juices for the second straight year, the 2-1/2" x 3-1/2" individual cards on the 7-1/2" x 10-1/2" sheet feature color action photos of the players, surrounded by team-color blue and orange stripes and an outer white border. Backs have 1990 highlights and stats, career stats and biographical details, along with the Team Mets and Tropicana logos. Cards are checklisted here according to the uniform numbers found on the front.

		NM/M
Complete Set (9):		4.00
Common Player:		.50
2	Mackey Sasser	.50
9	Gregg Jefferies	.50
10	Dave Magadan	.50
16	Dwight Gooden	.50
20	Howard Johnson	.50
22	Kevin McReynolds	.50
29	Frank Viola	.50
31	John Franco	.50
44	David Cone	.50

1983 True Value White Sox

Issued by the White Sox and True Value hardware stores, these 2-5/8" x 4-1/8" cards are among the scarcer early 1980s regional sets. The issue was originally scheduled as part of a promotion in which cards were given out at special Tuesday night games. The idea was sound, but rainouts forced the cancellation of some games so those scheduled cards were never given out. They were, however, smuggled out to hobby channels making it possible, although not easy, to assemble complete sets. The cards feature a large color photo with a wide white border. A team logo is at lower-left while the player's name, position and uniform number are in the lower-right. Backs feature a True Value ad along with statistics. The three cards which were never given out through the normal channels are considered scarcer than the others. They are Marc Hill, Harold Baines and Salome Barojas.

		NM/M
Complete Set (23):		12.00
Common Player:		.25
1	Scott Fletcher	.25
2	Harold Baines	3.50
5	Vance Law	.25
7	Marc Hill	2.00
10	Tony LaRussa	.40
11	Rudy Law	.25
14	Tony Bernazard	.25
17	Jerry Hairston Sr.	.25
19	Greg Luzinski	.25
24	Floyd Bannister	.25
25	Mike Squires	.25
30	Salome Barojas	2.00
31	LaMarr Hoyt	.25
34	Richard Dotson	.25
36	Jerry Koosman	.25
40	Britt Burns	.25
41	Dick Tidrow	.25
42	Ron Kittle	.25
44	Tom Paciorek	.25
45	Kevin Hickey	.25
53	Dennis Lamp	.25
67	Jim Kern	.25
72	Carlton Fisk	1.50

1984 True Value White Sox

True Value hardware stores and the White Sox gave

CARLTON FISK
Catcher 72

the Tuesday night baseball card promotion at Comiskey Park another try in 1984. The cards measure 2-5/8" x 4-1/8". In addition to the players, there are cards for manager Tony LaRussa, the coaching staff, and former Sox greats Luis Aparicio and Minnie Minoso. Card design is very similar to the 1983 cards. As the cards were given out two at a time, it was very difficult to acquire a complete set. Additionally, as numbers available vary because of attendance, some cards are scarcer than others.

		NM/M
Complete Set (30):		25.00
Common Player:		.50
1	Scott Fletcher	.50
3	Harold Baines	1.00
5	Vance Law	.50
7	Marc Hill	.50
8	Dave Stegman	.50
10	Tony LaRussa	1.00
11	Rudy Law	.50
16	Julio Cruz	.50
17	Jerry Hairston Sr.	.50
19	Greg Luzinski	.50
20	Jerry Dybzinski	.50
24	Floyd Bannister	.50
25	Mike Squires	.50
27	Ron Reed	.50
29	Greg Walker	.50
30	Salome Barojas	.50
31	LaMarr Hoyt	.50
32	Tim Hulett	.50
34	Richard Dotson	.50
40	Britt Burns	.50
41	Tom Seaver	5.00
42	Ron Kittle	.50
44	Tom Paciorek	.50
50	Juan Agosto	.50
59	Tom Brennan	.50
72	Carlton Fisk	3.00
---	Minnie Minoso	3.00
---	Luis Aparicio	3.00
---	Nancy Faust/Organist	1.00
---	The Coaching Staff (Ed Brinkman, Dave Duncan, Art Kusnyer, Tony LaRussa, Jim Leyland, Dave Nelson, Joe Nossek)	.50

1986 True Value

		NM/M

A 30-card set of 2-1/2" x 3-1/2" cards was available in three-card folders at True Value hardware stores with a purchase of $5 or more. Fronts feature a portrait flanked by stars with balls and bats at the bottom. The player's ID and a Major League Players Association logo are at bottom. Team insignia have been removed from the uniforms. Backs feature some personal information and brief 1985 statistics. Along with the player cards, the folders contained a sweepstakes card offering trips to post-season games and other prizes.

		NM/M
Complete Panel Set (10):		6.00
Complete Singles Set (30):		5.00
Common Player:		.05
	Panel (1)	.50

U

1991 Ultra

GEORGE BELL CUBS OUTFIELD

This 400-card set was originally going to be called the Elite set, but Fleer chose to use the Ultra label. The card fronts feature gray borders surrounding full-color action photos. The backs feature three player photos and statistics. Hot Prospects and Great Performers are among the special cards featured within the set.

		NM/M
Complete Set (400):		12.00
Common Player:		.05
Wax Pack (14):		.50
Wax Box (36):		9.00

1	Pedro Guerrero	.05
2	Steve Garvey	.10
3	Eddie Murray	.05
	Panel (2)	1.25
4	Pete Rose	.60
5	Don Mattingly	.50
6	Fernando Valenzuela	.50
	Panel (3)	.50
7	Jim Rice	.15
8	Kirk Gibson	.05
9	Ozzie Smith	.35
	Panel (4)	.75
10	Dale Murphy	.15
11	Robin Yount	.25
12	Tom Seaver	.25
	Panel (5)	.75
13	Reggie Jackson	.35
14	Ryne Sandberg	.35
15	Bruce Sutter	.25
	Panel (6)	.75
16	Gary Carter	.25
17	George Brett	.50
18	Rick Sutcliffe	.05
	Panel (7)	.25
19	Dave Steib	.05
20	Buddy Bell	.05
21	Alvin Davis	.05
	Panel (8)	1.00
22	Cal Ripken Jr.	.75
23	Bill Madlock	.05
24	Kent Hrbek	.05
	Panel (9)	1.00
25	Lou Whitaker	.05
26	Nolan Ryan	.75
27	Dwayne Murphy	.05
	Panel (10)	1.00
28	Mike Schmidt	.50
29	Andre Dawson	.15
30	Wade Boggs	.35

1986 True Value singles list:

1	Steve Avery	.05
2	Jeff Blauser	.05
3	Francisco Cabrera	.05
4	Ron Gant	.25
5	Tom Glavine	.25
6	Tommy Gregg	.05
7	Dave Justice	.05
8	Oddibe McDowell	.05
9	Greg Olson	.05
10	Terry Pendleton	.05
11	Lonnie Smith	.05
12	John Smoltz	.05
13	Jeff Treadway	.05
14	Glenn Davis	.05
15	Mike Devereaux	.05
16	Leo Gomez	.05
17	Chris Hoiles	.05
18	Dave Johnson	.05
19	Ben McDonald	.05
20	Randy Milligan	.05
21	Gregg Olson	.05
22	Joe Orsulak	.05
23	Bill Ripken	.05
24	Cal Ripken, Jr.	1.50
25	David Segui	.05
26	Craig Worthington	.05
27	Wade Boggs	.60
28	Tom Bolton	.05
29	Tom Brunansky	.05

30	Ellis Burks	.05
31	Roger Clemens	.65
32	Mike Greenwell	.05
33	Greg Harris	.05
34	Daryl Irvine	.05
35	Mike Marshall	.05
36	Tim Naehring	.05
37	Tony Pena	.05
38	Phil Plantier RC	.05
39	Carlos Quintana	.05
40	Jeff Reardon	.05
41	Jody Reed	.05
42	Luis Rivera	.05
43	Jim Abbott	.05
44	Chuck Finley	.05
45	Bryan Harvey	.05
46	Donnie Hill	.05
47	Jack Howell	.05
48	Wally Joyner	.05
49	Mark Langston	.05
50	Kirk McCaskill	.05
51	Lance Parrish	.05
52	Dick Schofield	.05
53	Lee Stevens	.05
54	Dave Winfield	.50
55	George Bell	.55
56	Damon Berryhill	.05
57	Mike Bielecki	.05
58	Andre Dawson	.25
59	Shawon Dunston	.05
60	Joe Girardi	.05
61	Mark Grace	.05
62	Mike Harkey	.05
63	Les Lancaster	.05
64	Greg Maddux	.60
65	Derrick May	.05
66	Ryne Sandberg	.60
67	Luis Salazar	.05
68	Dwight Smith	.05
69	Hector Villanueva	.05
70	Jerome Walton	.05
71	Mitch Williams	.05
72	Carlton Fisk	.50
73	Scott Fletcher	.05
74	Ozzie Guillen	.05
75	Greg Hibbard	.05
76	Lance Johnson	.05
77	Steve Lyons	.05
78	Jack McDowell	.05
79	Dan Pasqua	.05
80	Melido Perez	.05
81	Tim Raines	.05
82	Sammy Sosa	.60
83	Cory Snyder	.05
84	Bobby Thigpen	.05
85	Frank Thomas	.50
86	Robin Ventura	.05
87	Todd Benzinger	.05
88	Glenn Braggs	.05
89	Tom Browning	.05
90	Norm Charlton	.05
91	Eric Davis	.05
92	Rob Dibble	.05
93	Bill Doran	.05
94	Mariano Duncan	.05
95	Billy Hatcher	.05
96	Barry Larkin	.05
97	Randy Myers	.05
98	Hal Morris	.05
99	Joe Oliver	.05
100	Paul O'Neill	.05
101a	Jeff Reed	.05
101b	Beau Allred (Should be #104.)	.05
102	Jose Rijo	.05
103a	Chris Sabo	.05
103b	Carlos Baerga (Should be #106.)	.05
105	Sandy Alomar, Jr.	.05
106	Albert Belle	.05
107	Jerry Browne	.05
108	Tom Candiotti	.05
109	Alex Cole	.05
110	John Farrell	.05
111a	Chris James	.05
111b	Chris James (Should be #114.)	.05
112	Felix Fermin	.05
113	Brook Jacoby	.05
114	Doug Jones	.05
116a	Steve Olin	.05
116b	Mitch Webster (Should be #119.)	.05
117	Greg Swindell	.05
118	Turner Ward	.05
119	Dave Bergman	.05
120	Cecil Fielder	.65
121	Travis Fryman	.05
122	Mike Henneman	.05
123	Lloyd Moseby	.05
124	Dan Petry	.05
125	Tony Phillips	.05
126	Mark Salas	.05
127	Frank Tanana	.05
128	Alan Trammell	.05
129	Lou Whitaker	.05
130	Eric Anthony	.05
131	Craig Biggio	.05
132	Ken Caminiti	.05
133	Casey Candaele	.05
134	Andujar Cedeno	.05
135	Mark Davidson	.05
136	Jim Deshaies	.05
137	Mark Portugal	.05
138	Rafael Ramirez	.05
139	Mike Scott	.05
140	Eric Yelding	.05
141	Gerald Young	.05
142	Jose Appier	.05
143	Kevin Appier	.05

144	George Brett	.65
145	Jeff Conine RC	.40
146	Jim Eisenreich	.05
147	Tom Gordon	.05
148	Mark Gubicza	.05
149	Bo Jackson	.10
150	Brent Mayne	.05
151	Mike Macfarlane	.05
152	Brian McRae RC	.10
153	Jeff Montgomery	.05
154	Bret Saberhagen	.05
155	Kevin Seitzer	.05
156	Terry Shumpert	.05
157	Kurt Stillwell	.05
158	Danny Tartabull	.05
159	Tim Belcher	.05
160	Kal Daniels	.05
161	Alfredo Griffin	.05
162	Lenny Harris	.05
163	Jay Howell	.05
164	Ramon Martinez	.05
165	Mike Morgan	.05
166	Eddie Murray	.50
167	Jose Offerman	.05
168	Juan Samuel	.05
169	Mike Scioscia	.05
170	Mike Sharperson	.05
171	Darryl Strawberry	.05
172	Greg Brock	.05
173	Chuck Crim	.05
174	Jim Gantner	.05
175	Ted Higuera	.05
176	Mark Knudson	.05
177	Tim McIntosh	.05
178	Paul Molitor	.50
179	Dan Plesac	.05
180	Gary Sheffield	.35
181	Bill Spiers	.05
182	B.J. Surhoff	.05
183	Greg Vaughn	.05
184	Robin Yount	.50
185	Rick Aguilera	.05
186	Greg Gagne	.05
187	Dan Gladden	.05
188	Brian Harper	.05
189	Kent Hrbek	.05
190	Gene Larkin	.05
191	Shane Mack	.05
192	Pedro Munoz	.05
193	Al Newman	.05
194	Junior Ortiz	.05
195	Kirby Puckett	.60
196	Kevin Tapani	.05
197	Dennis Boyd	.05
198	Tim Burke	.05
199	Ivan Calderon	.05
200	Delino DeShields	.05
201	Mike Fitzgerald	.05
202	Steve Frey	.05
203	Andres Galarraga	.05
204	Marquis Grissom	.05
205	Dave Martinez	.05
206	Dennis Martinez	.05
207	Junior Noboa	.05
208	Spike Owen	.05
209	Scott Ruskin	.05
210	Tim Wallach	.05
211	Daryl Boston	.05
212	Vince Coleman	.05
213	David Cone	.05
214	Ron Darling	.05
215	Kevin Elster	.05
216	Sid Fernandez	.05
217	John Franco	.05
218	Dwight Gooden	.05
219	Tom Herr	.05
220	Todd Hundley	.05
221	Gregg Jefferies	.05
222	Howard Johnson	.05
223	Dave Magadan	.05
224	Kevin McReynolds	.05
225	Keith Miller	.05
226	Mackey Sasser	.05
227	Frank Viola	.05
228	Jesse Barfield	.05
229	Greg Cadaret	.05
230	Alvaro Espinoza	.05
231	Bob Geren	.05
232	Lee Guetterman	.05
233	Mel Hall	.05
234	Andy Hawkins	.05
235	Roberto Kelly	.05
236	Tim Leary	.05
237	Jim Leyritz	.05
238	Kevin Maas	.05
239	Don Mattingly	.65
240	Hensley Meulens	.05
241	Eric Plunk	.05
242	Steve Sax	.05
243	Todd Burns	.05
244	Jose Canseco	.35
245	Dennis Eckersley	.40
246	Mike Gallego	.05
247	Dave Henderson	.05
248	Rickey Henderson	.50
249	Rick Honeycutt	.05
250	Carney Lansford	.05
251	Mark McGwire	1.00
252	Mike Moore	.05
253	Terry Steinbach	.05
254	Dave Stewart	.05
255	Walt Weiss	.05
256	Bob Welch	.05
257	Curt Young	.05
258	Wes Chamberlain	.05
259	Pat Combs	.05
260	Darren Daulton	.05
261	Jose DeJesus	.05

262	Len Dykstra	.05
263	Charlie Hayes	.05
264	Von Hayes	.05
265	Ken Howell	.05
266	John Kruk	.05
267	Roger McDowell	.05
268	Mickey Morandini	.05
269	Terry Mulholland	.05
270	Dale Murphy	.15
271	Randy Ready	.05
272	Dickie Thon	.05
273	Stan Belinda	.05
274	Jay Bell	.05
275	Barry Bonds	1.50
276	Bobby Bonilla	.05
277	Doug Drabek	.05
278	Carlos Garcia RC	.05
279	Neal Heaton	.05
280	Jeff King	.05
281	Bill Landrum	.05
282	Mike LaValliere	.05
283	Jose Lind	.05
284	Orlando Merced RC	.10
285	Gary Redus	.05
286	Don Slaught	.05
287	Andy Van Slyke	.05
288	Jose DeLeon	.05
289	Pedro Guerrero	.05
290	Ray Lankford	.05
291	Joe Magrane	.05
292	Jose Oquendo	.05
293	Tom Pagnozzi	.05
294	Bryn Smith	.05
295	Lee Smith	.05
296	Ozzie Smith	.60
297	Milt Thompson	.05
298	Craig Wilson RC	.05
299	Todd Zeile	.05
300	Shawn Abner	.05
301	Andy Benes	.05
302	Paul Faries	.05
303	Tony Gwynn	.60
304	Greg Harris	.05
305	Thomas Howard	.05
306	Bruce Hurst	.05
307	Craig Lefferts	.05
308	Fred McGriff	.05
309	Dennis Rasmussen	.05
310	Bip Roberts	.05
311	Benito Santiago	.05
312	Garry Templeton	.05
313	Ed Whitson	.05
314	Dave Anderson	.05
315	Kevin Bass	.05
316	Jeff Brantley	.05
317	John Burkett	.05
318	Will Clark	.05
319	Steve Decker	.05
320	Scott Garrelts	.05
321	Terry Kennedy	.05
322	Mark Leonard	.05
323	Darren Lewis	.05
324	Greg Litton	.05
325	Willie McGee	.05
326	Kevin Mitchell	.05
327	Don Robinson	.05
328	Andres Santana	.05
329	Robby Thompson	.05
330	Jose Uribe	.05
331	Matt Williams	.05
332	Scott Bradley	.05
333	Henry Cotto	.05
334	Alvin Davis	.05
335	Ken Griffey Sr.	.05
336	Ken Griffey Jr.	.75
337	Erik Hanson	.05
338	Brian Holman	.05
339	Randy Johnson	.50
340	Edgar Martinez	.05
341	Tino Martinez	.05
342	Pete O'Brien	.05
343	Harold Reynolds	.05
344	David Valle	.05
345	Omar Vizquel	.05
346	Brad Arnsberg	.05
347	Kevin Brown	.05
348	Julio Franco	.05
349	Jeff Huson	.05
350	Rafael Palmeiro	.40
351	Geno Petralli	.05
352	Gary Pettis	.05
353	Kenny Rogers	.05
354	Jeff Russell	.05
355	Nolan Ryan	1.50
356	Ruben Sierra	.25
357	Bobby Witt	.05
358	Roberto Alomar	.15
359	Pat Borders	.05
360	Joe Carter	.05
361	Kelly Gruber	.05
362	Tom Henke	.05
363	Glenallen Hill	.05
364	Jimmy Key	.05
365	Manny Lee	.05
366	Rance Mulliniks	.05
367	John Olerud	.05
368	Dave Stieb	.05
369	Duane Ward	.05
370	David Wells	.05
371	Mark Whiten	.05
372	Mookie Wilson	.05
373	Willie Banks	.05
374	Steve Carter	.05
375	Scott Chiamparino	.05
376	Steve Chitren	.05
377	Darrin Fletcher	.05
378	Rich Garces	.05
379	Reggie Jefferson	.05

380	Eric Karros RC	.50
381	Pat Kelly	.05
382	Chuck Knoblauch	.05
383	Denny Neagle	.05
384	Dan Opperman	.05
385	John Ramos	.05
386	Henry Rodriguez RC	.05
387	Mo Vaughn	.05
388	Gerald Williams	.05
389	Mike York	.05
390	Eddie Zosky	.05
391	Barry Bonds (Great Performer)	.75
392	Cecil Fielder (Great Performer)	.05
393	Rickey Henderson (Great Performer)	.25
394	Dave Justice (Great Performer)	.05
395	Nolan Ryan (Great Performer)	.75
396	Bobby Thigpen (Great Performer)	.05
397	Checklist	.05
398	Checklist	.05
399	Checklist	.05
400	Checklist	.05

Gold

BO JACKSON
KANSAS CITY ROYALS • OUTFIELD

A pair of action photos flanking and below a portrait in a home plate frame at top-center are featured on these cards. Background is a graduated gold coloring. The Fleer Ultra Team logo is in the upper-left corner. Backs have narrative career information. The Puckett and Sandberg cards feature incorrect historical information on the backs.

		NM/M
Complete Set (10):		5.00
Common Player:		.15
1	Barry Bonds	2.50
2	Will Clark	.15
3	Doug Drabek	.15
4	Ken Griffey Jr.	1.50
5	Rickey Henderson	.75
6	Bo Jackson	.25
7	Ramon Martinez	.15
8	Kirby Puckett	1.00
9	Chris Sabo	.15
10	Ryne Sandberg	1.00

Update

RICK WILKINS CUBS CATCHER

This 120-card set was produced as a supplement to the premier Fleer Ultra set. Cards feature the same style as the regular Fleer Ultra cards. The cards were sold only as complete sets in full color, shrinkwrapped boxes.

		NM/M
Complete Set (120):		15.00
Common Player:		.05
1	Dwight Evans	.05
2	Chito Martinez	.05
3	Bob Melvin	.05
4	Mike Mussina RC	3.00
5	Jack Clark	.05
6	Dana Kiecker	.05

#	Player	Price
7	Steve Lyons	.05
8	Gary Gaetti	.05
9	Dave Gallagher	.05
10	Dave Parker	.05
11	Luis Polonia	.05
12	Luis Sojo	.05
13	Wilson Alvarez	.05
14	Alex Fernandez	.05
15	Craig Grebeck	.05
16	Ron Karkovice	.05
17	Warren Newson	.05
18	Scott Radinsky	.05
19	Glenallen Hill	.05
20	Charles Nagy	.05
21	Mark Whiten	.05
22	Milt Cuyler	.20
23	Paul Gibson	.05
24	Mickey Tettleton	.05
25	Todd Benzinger	.05
26	Storm Davis	.05
27	Kirk Gibson	.05
28	Bill Pecota	.05
29	Gary Thurman	.05
30	Darryl Hamilton	.05
31	Jaime Navarro	.05
32	Willie Randolph	.05
33	Bill Wegman	.05
34	Randy Bush	.05
35	Chili Davis	.05
36	Scott Erickson	.05
37	Chuck Knoblauch	.05
38	Scott Leius	.05
39	Jack Morris	.05
40	John Habyan	.05
41	Pat Kelly	.05
42	Matt Nokes	.05
43	Scott Sanderson	.05
44	Bernie Williams	.05
45	Harold Baines	.05
46	Brook Jacoby	.05
47	Ernest Riles	.05
48	Willie Wilson	.05
49	Jay Buhner	.05
50	Rich DeLucia	.05
51	Mike Jackson	.05
52	Bill Krueger	.05
53	Bill Swift	.05
54	Brian Downing	.05
55	Juan Gonzalez	.75
56	Dean Palmer	.05
57	Kevin Reimer	.05
58	Ivan Rodriguez **RC**	6.00
59	Tom Candiotti	.05
60	Juan Guzman	.05
61	Bob MacDonald	.05
62	Greg Myers	.05
63	Ed Sprague	.05
64	Devon White	.05
65	Rafael Belliard	.05
66	Juan Berenguer	.05
67	Brian Hunter	.05
68	Kent Mercker	.05
69	Otis Nixon	.05
70	Danny Jackson	.05
71	Chuck McElroy	.05
72	Gary Scott	.05
73	Heathcliff Slocumb	.05
74	Chico Walker	.05
75	Rick Wilkins	.05
76	Chris Hammond	.05
77	Luis Quinones	.05
78	Herm Winningham	.05
79	Jeff Bagwell **RC**	6.00
80	Jim Corsi	.05
81	Steve Finley	.05
82	Luis Gonzalez **RC**	1.00
83	Pete Harnisch	.05
84	Darryl Kile	.05
85	Brett Butler	.05
86	Gary Carter	1.00
87	Tim Crews	.05
88	Orel Hershiser	.05
89	Bob Ojeda	.05
90	Bret Barberie	.05
91	Barry Jones	.05
92	Gilberto Reyes	.05
93	Larry Walker	.05
94	Hubie Brooks	.05
95	Tim Burke	.05
96	Rick Cerone	.05
97	Jeff Innis	.05
98	Wally Backman	.05
99	Tommy Greene	.05
100	Ricky Jordan	.05
101	Mitch Williams	.05
102	John Smiley	.05
103	Randy Tomlin	.05
104	Gary Varsho	.05
105	Cris Carpenter	.05
106	Ken Hill	.05
107	Felix Jose	.05
108	Omar Oliveras **RC**	.05
109	Gerald Perry	.05
110	Jerald Clark	.05
111	Tony Fernandez	.05
112	Darrin Jackson	.05
113	Mike Maddux	.05
114	Tim Teufel	.05
115	Bud Black	.05
116	Kelly Downs	.05
117	Mike Felder	.05
118	Willie McGee	.05
119	Trevor Wilson	.05
120	Checklist	.05

1992 Ultra Pre-Production Samples

These cards were produced and distributed to hobby dealers to give them a preview of Ultra's second-year offering. Cards are virtually identical to the issued versions except for a white oval on back which has a "1992 / PRE-PRODUCTION / SAMPLE" notice printed in black. Each card (except the Gwynn) can also be found in a version with no card number on back; they are worth a small premium over the numbered promos. Two strips were issued, each with a different Gwynn card.

	NM/M
Uncut Strip:	25.00
Complete Set (6):	25.00
Common Player:	1.00
118 Todd Van Poppel	1.00
180 Rey Sanchez	1.00
271 Ozzie Smith	7.50
288 Royce Clayton	1.00
6/25 Roger Clemens (Award Winners)	10.00
2/10 Tony Gwynn (Commemorative Series)	7.50
7/10 Tony Gwynn (Commemorative Series)	7.50

1992 Ultra

Fleer released its second annual Ultra set in 1992. Card fronts feature full-color action photos with a marble accent at the card bottom. The flip sides are horizontal with two additional player photos. Many insert sets were randomly included in foil packs as premiums. These included rookie, All-Star and award winners, among others. A two-card Tony Gwynn send-away set was also available through an offer from Fleer. For $1 and 10 Ultra wrappers, collectors could receive the Gwynn cards. The set is numbered by team; cards #1-300 comprise Series I, cards #301-600 are Series II.

	NM/M
Complete Set (600):	12.00
Common Player:	.05
Ser. 1 or 2 Pack (14):	.60
Ser. 1 or 2 Box (36):	12.50
Tony Gwynn Auto.	60.00
1 Glenn Davis	.05
2 Mike Devereaux	.05
3 Dwight Evans	.05
4 Leo Gomez	.05

#	Player	Price
5	Chris Hoiles	.05
6	Sam Horn	.05
7	Chito Martinez	.05
8	Randy Milligan	.05
9	Mike Mussina	.30
10	Billy Ripken	.05
11	Cal Ripken, Jr.	1.00
12	Tom Brunansky	.05
13	Ellis Burks	.05
14	Jack Clark	.05
15	Roger Clemens	.60
16	Mike Greenwell	.05
17	Joe Hesketh	.05
18	Tony Pena	.05
19	Carlos Quintana	.05
20	Jeff Reardon	.05
21	Jody Reed	.05
22	Luis Rivera	.05
23	Mo Vaughn	.05
24	Gary DiSarcina	.05
25	Chuck Finley	.05
26	Gary Gaetti	.05
27	Bryan Harvey	.05
28	Lance Parrish	.05
29	Luis Polonia	.05
30	Dick Schofield	.05
31	Luis Sojo	.05
32	Wilson Alvarez	.05
33	Carlton Fisk	.40
34	Craig Grebeck	.05
35	Ozzie Guillen	.05
36	Greg Hibbard	.05
37	Charlie Hough	.05
38	Lance Johnson	.05
39	Ron Karkovice	.05
40	Jack McDowell	.05
41	Donn Pall	.05
42	Melido Perez	.05
43	Tim Raines	.05
44	Frank Thomas	.40
45	Sandy Alomar, Jr.	.05
46	Carlos Baerga	.05
47	Albert Belle	.05
48	Jerry Browne	.05
49	Felix Fermin	.05
50	Reggie Jefferson	.05
51	Mark Lewis	.05
52	Carlos Martinez	.05
53	Steve Olin	.05
54	Jim Thome	.35
55	Mark Whiten	.05
56	Dave Bergman	.05
57	Milt Cuyler	.05
58	Rob Deer	.05
59	Cecil Fielder	.05
60	Travis Fryman	.05
61	Scott Livingstone	.05
62	Tony Phillips	.05
63	Mickey Tettleton	.05
64	Alan Trammell	.05
65	Lou Whitaker	.05
66	Kevin Appier	.05
67	Mike Boddicker	.05
68	George Brett	.60
69	Jim Eisenreich	.05
70	Mark Gubicza	.05
71	David Howard	.05
72	Joel Johnston	.05
73	Mike Macfarlane	.05
74	Brent Mayne	.05
75	Brian McRae	.05
76	Jeff Montgomery	.05
77	Terry Shumpert	.05
78	Don August	.05
79	Dante Bichette	.05
80	Ted Higuera	.05
81	Paul Molitor	.40
82	Jamie Navarro	.05
83	Gary Sheffield	.30
84	Bill Spiers	.05
85	B.J. Surhoff	.05
86	Greg Vaughn	.05
87	Robin Yount	.40
88	Rick Aguilera	.05
89	Chili Davis	.05
90	Scott Erickson	.05
91	Brian Harper	.05
92	Kent Hrbek	.05
93	Chuck Knoblauch	.05
94	Scott Leius	.05
95	Shane Mack	.05
96	Mike Pagliarulo	.05
97	Kirby Puckett	.50
98	Kevin Tapani	.05
99	Jesse Barfield	.05
100	Alvaro Espinoza	.05
101	Mel Hall	.05
102	Pat Kelly	.05
103	Roberto Kelly	.05
104	Kevin Maas	.05
105	Don Mattingly	.60
106	Hensley Meulens	.05
107	Matt Nokes	.05
108	Steve Sax	.05
109	Harold Baines	.05
110	Jose Canseco	.30
111	Ron Darling	.05
112	Mike Gallego	.05
113	Dave Henderson	.05
114	Rickey Henderson	.40
115	Mark McGwire	.75
116	Terry Steinbach	.05
117	Dave Stewart	.05
118	Todd Van Poppel	.05
119	Bob Welch	.05
120	Greg Briley	.05
121	Jay Buhner	.05
122	Rich DeLucia	.05
123	Ken Griffey Jr.	.65
124	Erik Hanson	.05
125	Randy Johnson	.40
126	Edgar Martinez	.05
127	Tino Martinez	.05
128	Pete O'Brien	.05
129	Harold Reynolds	.05
130	Dave Valle	.05
131	Julio Franco	.05
132	Juan Gonzalez	.20
133	Jeff Huson	.05
134	Mike Jeffcoat	.05
135	Terry Mathews	.05
136	Rafael Palmeiro	.35
137	Dean Palmer	.05
138	Geno Petralli	.05
139	Ivan Rodriguez	.35
140	Jeff Russell	.05
141	Nolan Ryan	1.00
142	Ruben Sierra	.05
143	Roberto Alomar	.15
144	Pat Borders	.05
145	Joe Carter	.05
146	Kelly Gruber	.05
147	Jimmy Key	.05
148	Manny Lee	.05
149	Rance Mulliniks	.05
150	Greg Myers	.05
151	John Olerud	.05
152	Dave Stieb	.05
153	Todd Stottlemyre	.05
154	Duane Ward	.05
155	Devon White	.05
156	Eddie Zosky	.05
157	Steve Avery	.05
158	Rafael Belliard	.05
159	Jeff Blauser	.05
160	Sid Bream	.05
161	Ron Gant	.05
162	Tom Glavine	.25
163	Brian Hunter	.05
164	Dave Justice	.05
165	Mark Lemke	.05
166	Greg Olson	.05
167	Terry Pendleton	.05
168	Lonnie Smith	.05
169	John Smoltz	.05
170	Mike Stanton	.05
171	Jeff Treadway	.05
172	Paul Assenmacher	.05
173	George Bell	.05
174	Shawon Dunston	.05
175	Mark Grace	.05
176	Danny Jackson	.05
177	Les Lancaster	.05
178	Greg Maddux	.50
179	Luis Salazar	.05
180	Rey Sanchez	.05
181	Ryne Sandberg	.50
182	Jose Vizcaino	.05
183	Chico Walker	.05
184	Jerome Walton	.05
185	Glenn Braggs	.05
186	Tom Browning	.05
187	Rob Dibble	.05
188	Bill Doran	.05
189	Chris Hammond	.05
190	Billy Hatcher	.05
191	Barry Larkin	.05
192	Hal Morris	.05
193	Joe Oliver	.05
194	Paul O'Neill	.05
195	Jeff Reed	.05
196	Jose Rijo	.05
197	Chris Sabo	.05
198	Jeff Bagwell	.40
199	Craig Biggio	.05
200	Ken Caminiti	.05
201	Andujar Cedeno	.05
202	Steve Finley	.05
203	Luis Gonzalez	.05
204	Pete Harnisch	.05
205	Xavier Hernandez	.05
206	Darryl Kile	.05
207	Al Osuna	.05
208	Curt Schilling	.25
209	Brett Butler	.05
210	Kal Daniels	.05
211	Lenny Harris	.05
212	Stan Javier	.05
213	Ramon Martinez	.05
214	Roger McDowell	.05
215	Jose Offerman	.05
216	Juan Samuel	.05
217	Mike Scioscia	.05
218	Mike Sharperson	.05
219	Darryl Strawberry	.05
220	Delino DeShields	.05
221	Tom Foley	.05
222	Steve Frey	.05
223	Dennis Martinez	.05
224	Spike Owen	.05
225	Gilberto Reyes	.05
226	Tim Wallach	.05
227	Daryl Boston	.05
228	Tim Burke	.05
229	Vince Coleman	.05
230	David Cone	.05
231	Kevin Elster	.05
232	Dwight Gooden	.05
233	Todd Hundley	.05
234	Jeff Innis	.05
235	Howard Johnson	.05
236	Dave Magadan	.05
237	Mackey Sasser	.05
238	Anthony Young	.05
239	Wes Chamberlain	.05
240	Darren Daulton	.05
241	Len Dykstra	.05
242	Tommy Greene	.05
243	Charlie Hayes	.05
244	Dave Hollins	.05
245	Ricky Jordan	.05
246	John Kruk	.05
247	Mickey Morandini	.05
248	Terry Mulholland	.05
249	Dale Murphy	.25
250	Jay Bell	.05
251	Barry Bonds	1.00
252	Steve Buechele	.05
253	Doug Drabek	.05
254	Mike LaValliere	.05
255	Jose Lind	.05
256	Lloyd McClendon	.05
257	Orlando Merced	.05
258	Don Slaught	.05
259	John Smiley	.05
260	Zane Smith	.05
261	Randy Tomlin	.05
262	Andy Van Slyke	.05
263	Pedro Guerrero	.05
264	Felix Jose	.05
265	Ray Lankford	.05
266	Omar Olivares	.05
267	Jose Oquendo	.05
268	Tom Pagnozzi	.05
269	Bryn Smith	.05
270	Lee Smith	.05
271	Ozzie Smith	.50
272	Milt Thompson	.05
273	Todd Zeile	.05
274	Andy Benes	.05
275	Jerald Clark	.05
276	Tony Fernandez	.05
277	Tony Gwynn	.50
278	Greg Harris	.05
279	Thomas Howard	.05
280	Bruce Hurst	.05
281	Mike Maddux	.05
282	Fred McGriff	.05
283	Benito Santiago	.05
284	Kevin Bass	.05
285	Jeff Brantley	.05
286	John Burkett	.05
287	Will Clark	.05
288	Royce Clayton	.05
289	Steve Decker	.05
290	Kelly Downs	.05
291	Mike Felder	.05
292	Darren Lewis	.05
293	Kirt Manwaring	.05
294	Willie McGee	.05
295	Robby Thompson	.05
296	Matt Williams	.05
297	Trevor Wilson	.05
298	Checklist 1-108 (Sandy Alomar, Jr.)	.05
299	Checklist 109-208 (Rey Sanchez)	.05
300	Checklist 209-300 (Nolan Ryan)	.25
301	Brady Anderson	.05
302	Todd Frohwirth	.05
303	Ben McDonald	.05
304	Mark McLemore	.05
305	Jose Mesa	.05
306	Bob Milacki	.05
307	Gregg Olson	.05
308	David Segui	.05
309	Rick Sutcliffe	.05
310	Jeff Tackett	.05
311	Wade Boggs	.50
312	Scott Cooper	.05
313	John Flaherty	.05
314	Wayne Housie	.05
315	Peter Hoy	.05
316	John Marzano	.05
317	Tim Naehring	.05
318	Phil Plantier	.05
319	Frank Viola	.05
320	Matt Young	.05
321	Jim Abbott	.05
322	Hubie Brooks	.05
323	Chad Curtis **RC**	.25
324	Alvin Davis	.05
325	Junior Felix	.05
326	Von Hayes	.05
327	Mark Langston	.05
328	Scott Lewis	.05
329	Don Robinson	.05
330	Bobby Rose	.05
331	Lee Stevens	.05
332	George Bell	.05
333	Esteban Beltre	.05
334	Joey Cora	.05
335	Alex Fernandez	.05
336	Roberto Hernandez	.05
337	Mike Huff	.05
338	Kirk McCaskill	.05
339	Dan Pasqua	.05
340	Scott Radinsky	.05
341	Steve Sax	.05
342	Bobby Thigpen	.05
343	Robin Ventura	.05
344	Jack Armstrong	.05
345	Alex Cole	.05
346	Dennis Cook	.05
347	Glenallen Hill	.05
348	Thomas Howard	.05
349	Brook Jacoby	.05
350	Kenny Lofton	.05
351	Charles Nagy	.05
352	Rod Nichols	.05
353	Junior Ortiz	.05
354	Dave Otto	.05
355	Tony Perezchica	.05
356	Scott Scudder	.05
357	Paul Sorrento	.05
358	Skeeter Barnes	.05
359	Mark Carreon	.05
360	John Doherty	.05
361	Dan Gladden	.05
362	Bill Gullickson	.05
363	Shawn Hare	.05
364	Mike Henneman	.05
365	Chad Kreuter	.05
366	Mark Leiter	.05
367	Mike Munoz	.05
368	Kevin Ritz	.05
369	Mark Davis	.05
370	Tom Gordon	.05
371	Chris Gwynn	.05
372	Gregg Jefferies	.05
373	Wally Joyner	.05
374	Kevin McReynolds	.05
375	Keith Miller	.05
376	Rico Rossy	.05
377	Curtis Wilkerson	.05
378	Ricky Bones	.05
379	Chris Bosio	.05
380	Cal Eldred	.05
381	Scott Fletcher	.05
382	Jim Gantner	.05
383	Darryl Hamilton	.05
384	Doug Henry	.05
385	Pat Listach **RC**	.05
386	Tim McIntosh	.05
387	Edwin Nunez	.05
388	Dan Plesac	.05
389	Kevin Seitzer	.05
390	Franklin Stubbs	.05
391	William Suero	.05
392	Bill Wegman	.05
393	Willie Banks	.05
394	Jarvis Brown	.05
395	Greg Gagne	.05
396	Mark Guthrie	.05
397	Bill Krueger	.05
398	Pat Mahomes **RC**	.05
399	Pedro Munoz	.05
400	John Smiley	.05
401	Gary Wayne	.05
402	Lenny Webster	.05
403	Carl Willis	.05
404	Greg Cadaret	.05
405	Steve Farr	.05
406	Mike Gallego	.05
407	Charlie Hayes	.05
408	Steve Howe	.05
409	Dion James	.05
410	Jeff Johnson	.05
411	Tim Leary	.05
412	Jim Leyritz	.05
413	Melido Perez	.05
414	Scott Sanderson	.05
415	Andy Stankiewicz	.05
416	Mike Stanley	.05
417	Danny Tartabull	.05
418	Lance Blankenship	.05
419	Mike Bordick	.05
420	Scott Brosius **RC**	.05
421	Dennis Eckersley	.35
422	Scott Hemond	.05
423	Carney Lansford	.05
424	Henry Mercedes	.05
425	Mike Moore	.05
426	Gene Nelson	.05
427	Randy Ready	.05
428	Bruce Walton	.05
429	Willie Wilson	.05
430	Rich Amaral	.05
431	Dave Cochrane	.05
432	Henry Cotto	.05
433	Calvin Jones	.05
434	Kevin Mitchell	.05
435	Clay Parker	.05
436	Omar Vizquel	.05
437	Floyd Bannister	.05
438	Kevin Brown	.05
439	John Cangelosi	.05
440	Brian Downing	.05
441	Monty Fariss	.05
442	Jose Guzman	.05
443	Donald Harris	.05
444	Kevin Reimer	.05
445	Kenny Rogers	.05
446	Wayne Rosenthal	.05
447	Dickie Thon	.05
448	Derek Bell	.05
449	Juan Guzman	.05
450	Tom Henke	.05
451	Candy Maldonado	.05
452	Jack Morris	.05
453	David Wells	.05
454	Dave Winfield	.40
455	Juan Berenguer	.05
456	Damon Berryhill	.05
457	Mike Bielecki	.05
458	Marvin Freeman	.05
459	Charlie Leibrandt	.05
460	Kent Mercker	.05
461	Otis Nixon	.05
462	Alejandro Pena	.05
463	Ben Rivera	.05
464	Deion Sanders	.10
465	Mark Wohlers	.05
466	Shawn Boskie	.05
467	Frank Castillo	.05
468	Andre Dawson	.05
469	Joe Girardi	.05
470	Chuck McElroy	.05
471	Mike Morgan	.05
472	Ken Patterson	.05
473	Bob Scanlan	.05

474	Gary Scott	.05
475	Dave Smith	.05
476	Sammy Sosa	.50
477	Hector Villanueva	.05
478	Scott Bankhead	.05
479	Tim Belcher	.05
480	Freddie Benavides	.05
481	Jacob Brumfield	.05
482	Norm Charlton	.05
483	Dwayne Henry	.05
484	Dave Martinez	.05
485	Bip Roberts	.05
486	Reggie Sanders	.05
487	Greg Swindell	.05
488	Ryan Bowen	.05
489	Casey Candaele	.05
490	Juan Guerrero	.05
491	Pete Incaviglia	.05
492	Jeff Juden	.05
493	Rob Murphy	.05
494	Mark Portugal	.05
495	Rafael Ramirez	.05
496	Scott Servais	.05
497	Ed Taubensee	.05
498	Brian Williams	.05
499	Todd Benzinger	.05
500	John Candelaria	.05
501	Tom Candiotti	.05
502	Tim Crews	.05
503	Eric Davis	.05
504	Jim Gott	.05
505	Dave Hansen	.05
506	Carlos Hernandez	.05
507	Orel Hershiser	.05
508	Eric Karros	.05
509	Bob Ojeda	.05
510	Steve Wilson	.05
511	Moises Alou	.05
512	Bret Barberie	.05
513	Ivan Calderon	.05
514	Gary Carter	.40
515	Archi Cianfrocco	.05
516	Jeff Fassero	.05
517	Darrin Fletcher	.05
518	Marquis Grissom	.05
519	Chris Haney	.05
520	Ken Hill	.05
521	Chris Nabholz	.05
522	Bill Sampen	.05
523	John VanderWal	.05
524	David Wainhouse	.05
525	Larry Walker	.05
526	John Wetteland	.05
527	Bobby Bonilla	.05
528	Sid Fernandez	.05
529	John Franco	.05
530	Dave Gallagher	.05
531	Paul Gibson	.05
532	Eddie Murray	.40
533	Junior Noboa	.05
534	Charlie O'Brien	.05
535	Bill Pecota	.05
536	Willie Randolph	.05
537	Bret Saberhagen	.05
538	Dick Schofield	.05
539	Pete Schourek	.05
540	Ruben Amaro	.05
541	Andy Ashby	.05
542	Kim Batiste	.05
543	Cliff Brantley	.05
544	Mariano Duncan	.05
545	Jeff Grotewold	.05
546	Barry Jones	.05
547	Julio Peguero	.05
548	Curt Schilling	.25
549	Mitch Williams	.05
550	Stan Belinda	.05
551	Scott Bullett	.05
552	Cecil Espy	.05
553	Jeff King	.05
554	Roger Mason	.05
555	Paul Miller	.05
556	Denny Neagle	.05
557	Vocente Palacios	.05
558	Bob Patterson	.05
559	Tom Prince	.05
560	Gary Redus	.05
561	Gary Varsho	.05
562	Juan Agosto	.05
563	Cris Carpenter	.05
564	Mark Clark **RC**	.05
565	Jose DeLeon	.05
566	Rich Gedman	.05
567	Bernard Gilkey	.10
568	Rex Hudler	.05
569	Tim Jones	.05
570	Donovan Osborne	.05
571	Mike Perez	.05
572	Gerald Perry	.05
573	Bob Tewksbury	.05
574	Todd Worrell	.05
575	Dave Eiland	.05
576	Jeremy Hernandez	.05
577	Craig Lefferts	.05
578	Jose Melendez	.05
579	Randy Myers	.05
580	Gary Pettis	.05
581	Rich Rodriguez	.05
582	Gary Sheffield	.30
583	Craig Shipley	.05
584	Kurt Stillwell	.05
585	Tim Teufel	.05
586	Rod Beck **RC**	.05
587	Dave Burba	.05
588	Craig Colbert	.05
589	Bryan Hickerson	.05
590	Mike Jackson	.05
591	Mark Leonard	.05

592	Jim McNamara	.05
593	John Patterson	.05
594	Dave Righetti	.05
595	Cory Snyder	.05
596	Bill Swift	.05
597	Ted Wood	.05
598	Checklist 301-403 (Scott Sanderson)	
599	Checklist 404-498 (Junior Ortiz)	.05
600	Checklist 499-600 (Mike Morgan)	.05

All-Rookies

The 10 promising rookies in this set could be found on special cards inserted in Ultra Series 2 foil packs.

		NM/M
Complete Set (10):		2.00
Common Player:		.25
1	Eric Karros	.35
2	Andy Stankiewicz	.25
3	Gary DiSarcina	.25
4	Archi Cianfrocco	.25
5	Jim McNamara	.25
6	Chad Curtis	.25
7	Kenny Lofton	.35
8	Reggie Sanders	.25
9	Pat Mahomes	.25
10	Donovan Osborne	.25

All-Stars

An All-Star team from each league, with two pitchers, could be assembled by collecting these inserts from Ultra Series 2 foil packs.

		NM/M
Complete Set (20):		7.50
Common Player:		.15
1	Mark McGwire	1.25
2	Roberto Alomar	.30
3	Cal Ripken, Jr.	1.50
4	Wade Boggs	.75
5	Mickey Tettleton	.15
6	Ken Griffey Jr.	1.00
7	Roberto Kelly	.15
8	Kirby Puckett	.75
9	Frank Thomas	.65
10	Jack McDowell	.15
11	Will Clark	.15
12	Ryne Sandberg	.75
13	Barry Larkin	.15
14	Gary Sheffield	.35
15	Tom Pagnozzi	.15
16	Barry Bonds	1.50
17	Deion Sanders	.15
18	Darryl Strawberry	.15
19	David Cone	.15
20	Tom Glavine	.15

Award Winners

The 25 cards in this insert issue were randomly packaged with Series 1 Ultra. One of the Cal Ripken cards (#21) can be found with a photo made from a reversed negative, as well as with the proper orientation. Neither version carries a premium.

CAL RIPKEN, JR.

		NM/M
Complete Set (26):		10.00
Common Player:		.20
1	Jack Morris	.20
2	Chuck Knoblauch	.20
3	Jeff Bagwell	.75
4	Terry Pendleton	.20
5	Cal Ripken, Jr.	2.00
6	Roger Clemens	1.25
7	Tom Glavine	.35
8	Tom Pagnozzi	.20
9	Ozzie Smith	1.00
10	Andy Van Slyke	.20
11	Barry Bonds	2.00
12	Tony Gwynn	1.00
13	Matt Williams	.20
14	Will Clark	.20
15	Robin Ventura	.20
16	Mark Langston	.20
17	Devon White	.20
18	Don Mattingly	1.25
19	Don Mattingly	1.25
20	Roberto Alomar	.40
21a	Cal Ripken, Jr. (Reversed negative.)	2.00
21b	Cal Ripken, Jr. (Correct)	2.00
22	Ken Griffey Jr.	1.50
23	Kirby Puckett	1.00
24	Greg Maddux	1.00
25	Ryne Sandberg	1.00

Tony Gwynn

TONY GWYNN

This 12-card subset of Ultra's spokesman features 10 cards which were available as inserts in Series I foil packs, plus two cards labeled "Special No. 1" and "Special No. 2" which could only be obtained in a send-away offer. Some 2,000 of these cards carry a "certified" Gwynn autograph. Not part of the issue, but similar in format were a pair of extra Tony Gwynn cards. One pictures him with Fleer CEO Paul Mullan, the other shows him with the poster child for Casa de Amparo, a children's shelter in San Diego County.

		NM/M
Complete Set (12):		9.00
Common Card:		.75
Certified Autograph Card:		60.00
1	Tony Gwynn/Fielding	.75
2	Tony Gwynn/Btg	.75
3	Tony Gwynn/Fielding	.75
4	Tony Gwynn/Btg	.75
5	Tony Gwynn/ Base-Running	.75
6	Tony Gwynn (awards)	.75
7	Tony Gwynn/Bunting	.75
8	Tony Gwynn/Btg	.75
9	Tony Gwynn/Running	.75
10	Tony Gwynn/Btg	.75
1	Tony Gwynn	2.00
2	Tony Gwynn/Fielding	2.00
---	Tony Gwynn, Paul Mullan	3.00
---	Tony Gwynn (Casa de Amparo)	7.50

1993 Ultra

The first series of 300 cards retains Fleer's successful fea-

DENNIS ECKERSLEY
ATHLETICS • P

tures from 1992, including additional gold foil stamping, UV coating, and team color-coded marbled bars on the fronts. The backs feature a stylized ballpark background, which creates a 3-D effect, stats and portrait and an action photo. Dennis Eckersley is featured in a limited-edition "Career Highlights" set and personally autographed more than 2,000 of his cards, to be randomly inserted into both series' packs. A 10-card Home Run Kings subset and 25-card Ultra Awards Winners subset were also randomly inserted in packs. Ultra Rookies cards are included in both series. Ultra's second series has three limited-edition subsets: Ultra All-Stars, Ultra All-Rookie Team, and Strikeout Kings, plus cards featuring Colorado Rockies and Florida Marlins players.

		NM/M
Complete Set (650):		15.00
Common Player:		.05
Series 1 or 2 Pack (14):		.75
Series 1 or 2 Wax Box (36):		15.00
1	Steve Avery	.05
2	Rafael Belliard	.05
3	Damon Berryhill	.05
4	Sid Bream	.05
5	Ron Gant	.05
6	Tom Glavine	.20
7	Ryan Klesko	.05
8	Mark Lemke	.05
9	Javier Lopez	.05
10	Greg Olson	.05
11	Terry Pendleton	.05
12	Deion Sanders	.05
13	Mike Stanton	.05
14	Paul Assenmacher	.05
15	Steve Buechele	.05
16	Frank Castillo	.05
17	Shawon Dunston	.05
18	Mark Grace	.05
19	Derrick May	.05
20	Chuck McElroy	.05
21	Mike Morgan	.05
22	Bob Scanlan	.05
23	Dwight Smith	.05
24	Sammy Sosa	.60
25	Rick Wilkins	.05
26	Tim Belcher	.05
27	Jeff Branson	.05
28	Bill Doran	.05
29	Chris Hammond	.05
30	Barry Larkin	.05
31	Hal Morris	.05
32	Joe Oliver	.05
33	Jose Rijo	.05
34	Bip Roberts	.05
35	Chris Sabo	.05
36	Reggie Sanders	.05
37	Craig Biggio	.05
38	Ken Caminiti	.05
39	Steve Finley	.05
40	Luis Gonzalez	.05
41	Juan Guerrero	.05
42	Pete Harnisch	.05
43	Xavier Hernandez	.05
44	Doug Jones	.05
45	Al Osuna	.05
46	Eddie Taubensee	.05
47	Scooter Tucker	.05
48	Brian Williams	.05
49	Pedro Astacio	.05
50	Rafael Bournigal	.05
51	Brett Butler	.05
52	Tom Candiotti	.05
53	Eric Davis	.05
54	Lenny Harris	.05
55	Orel Hershiser	.05
56	Eric Karros	.05
57	Pedro Martinez	.50
58	Roger McDowell	.05
59	Jose Offerman	.05
60	Mike Piazza	.75
61	Moises Alou	.05
62	Kent Bottenfield	.05
63	Archi Cianfrocco	.05

64	Greg Colbrunn	.05
65	Wil Cordero	.05
66	Delino DeShields	.05
67	Darrin Fletcher	.05
68	Ken Hill	.05
69	Chris Nabholz	.05
70	Mel Rojas	.05
71	Larry Walker	.05
72	Sid Fernandez	.05
73	John Franco	.05
74	Dave Gallagher	.05
75	Todd Hundley	.05
76	Howard Johnson	.05
77	Jeff Kent	.05
78	Eddie Murray	.50
79	Bret Saberhagen	.05
80	Chico Walker	.05
81	Anthony Young	.05
82	Kyle Abbott	.05
83	Ruben Amaro Jr.	.05
84	Juan Bell	.05
85	Wes Chamberlain	.05
86	Darren Daulton	.05
87	Mariano Duncan	.05
88	Dave Hollins	.05
89	Ricky Jordan	.05
90	John Kruk	.05
91	Mickey Morandini	.05
92	Terry Mulholland	.05
93	Ben Rivera	.05
94	Mike Williams	.05
95	Stan Belinda	.05
96	Jay Bell	.05
97	Jeff King	.05
98	Mike LaValliere	.05
99	Lloyd McClendon	.05
100	Orlando Merced	.05
101	Zane Smith	.05
102	Randy Tomlin	.05
103	Andy Van Slyke	.05
104	Tim Wakefield	.05
105	John Wehner	.05
106	Bernard Gilkey	.05
107	Brian Jordan	.05
108	Ray Lankford	.05
109	Donovan Osborne	.05
110	Tom Pagnozzi	.05
111	Mike Perez	.05
112	Lee Smith	.05
113	Ozzie Smith	.60
114	Bob Tewksbury	.05
115	Todd Zeile	.05
116	Andy Benes	.05
117	Greg Harris	.05
118	Darrin Jackson	.05
119	Fred McGriff	.05
120	Rich Rodriguez	.05
121	Frank Seminara	.05
122	Gary Sheffield	.35
123	Craig Shipley	.05
124	Kurt Stillwell	.05
125	Dan Walters	.05
126	Rod Beck	.05
127	Mike Benjamin	.05
128	Jeff Brantley	.05
129	John Burkett	.05
130	Will Clark	.05
131	Royce Clayton	.05
132	Steve Hosey	.05
133	Mike Jackson	.05
134	Darren Lewis	.05
135	Kirt Manwaring	.05
136	Bill Swift	.05
137	Robby Thompson	.05
138	Brady Anderson	.05
139	Glenn Davis	.05
140	Leo Gomez	.05
141	Chito Martinez	.05
142	Ben McDonald	.05
143	Alan Mills	.05
144	Mike Mussina	.30
145	Gregg Olson	.05
146	David Segui	.05
147	Jeff Tackett	.05
148	Jack Clark	.05
149	Scott Cooper	.05
150	Danny Darwin	.05
151	John Dopson	.05
152	Mike Greenwell	.05
153	Tim Naehring	.05
154	Tony Pena	.05
155	Paul Quantrill	.05
156	Mo Vaughn	.05
157	Frank Viola	.05
158	Bob Zupcic	.05
159	Chad Curtis	.05
160	Gary DiSarcina	.05
161	Damion Easley	.05
162	Chuck Finley	.05
163	Tim Fortugno	.05
164	Rene Gonzales	.05
165	Joe Grahe	.05
166	Mark Langston	.05
167	John Orton	.05
168	Luis Polonia	.05
169	Julio Valera	.05
170	Wilson Alvarez	.05
171	George Bell	.05
172	Joey Cora	.05
173	Alex Fernandez	.05
174	Lance Johnson	.05
175	Ron Karkovice	.05
176	Jack McDowell	.05
177	Scott Radinsky	.05
178	Tim Raines	.05
179	Steve Sax	.05
180	Bobby Thigpen	.05
181	Frank Thomas	.50

182	Sandy Alomar Jr.	.05
183	Carlos Baerga	.05
184	Felix Fermin	.05
185	Thomas Howard	.05
186	Mark Lewis	.05
187	Derek Lilliquist	.05
188	Carlos Martinez	.05
189	Charles Nagy	.05
190	Scott Scudder	.05
191	Paul Sorrento	.05
192	Jim Thome	.40
193	Mark Whiten	.05
194	Milt Cuyler	.05
195	Rob Deer	.05
196	John Doherty	.05
197	Travis Fryman	.05
198	Dan Gladden	.05
199	Mike Henneman	.05
200	John Kiely	.05
201	Chad Kreuter	.05
202	Scott Livingstone	.05
203	Tony Phillips	.05
204	Alan Trammell	.05
205	Mike Boddicker	.05
206	George Brett	.65
207	Tom Gordon	.05
208	Mark Gubicza	.05
209	Gregg Jefferies	.05
210	Wally Joyner	.05
211	Kevin Koslofski	.05
212	Brent Mayne	.05
213	Brian McRae	.05
214	Kevin McReynolds	.05
215	Rusty Meacham	.05
216	Steve Shifflett	.05
217	James Austin	.05
218	Cal Eldred	.05
219	Darryl Hamilton	.05
220	Doug Henry	.05
221	John Jaha	.05
222	Dave Nilsson	.05
223	Jesse Orosco	.05
224	B.J. Surhoff	.05
225	Greg Vaughn	.05
226	Bill Wegman	.05
227	Robin Yount	.50
228	Rick Aguilera	.05
229	J.T. Bruett	.05
230	Scott Erickson	.05
231	Kent Hrbek	.05
232	Terry Jorgensen	.05
233	Scott Leius	.05
234	Pat Mahomes	.05
235	Pedro Munoz	.05
236	Kirby Puckett	.60
237	Kevin Tapani	.05
238	Lenny Webster	.05
239	Carl Willis	.05
240	Mike Gallego	.05
241	John Habyan	.05
242	Pat Kelly	.05
243	Kevin Maas	.05
244	Don Mattingly	.65
245	Hensley Meulens	.05
246	Sam Militello	.05
247	Matt Nokes	.05
248	Melido Perez	.05
249	Andy Stankiewicz	.05
250	Randy Velarde	.05
251	Bob Wickman	.05
252	Bernie Williams	.05
253	Lance Blankenship	.05
254	Mike Bordick	.05
255	Jerry Browne	.05
256	Ron Darling	.05
257a	Dennis Eckersley	.40
257b	Dennis Eckersley (Wt. 195; no "MLBPA" on back - unmarked sample card.)	1.50
257c	Dennis Eckersley (Wt. 195; no "Printed in USA" on back - unmarked sample card.)	1.50
258	Rickey Henderson	.50
259	Vince Horsman	.05
260	Troy Neel	.05
261	Jeff Parrett	.05
262	Terry Steinbach	.05
263	Bob Welch	.05
264	Bobby Witt	.05
265	Rich Amaral	.05
266	Bret Boone	.05
267	Jay Buhner	.05
268	Dave Fleming	.05
269	Randy Johnson	.50
270	Edgar Martinez	.05
271	Mike Schooler	.05
272	Russ Swan	.05
273	Dave Valle	.05
274	Omar Vizquel	.05
275	Kerry Woodson	.05
276	Kevin Brown	.05
277	Julio Franco	.05
278	Jeff Frye	.05
279	Juan Gonzalez	.25
280	Jeff Huson	.05
281	Rafael Palmeiro	.40
282	Dean Palmer	.05
283	Roger Pavlik	.05
284	Ivan Rodriguez	.40
285	Kenny Rogers	.05
286	Derek Bell	.05
287	Pat Borders	.05
288	Joe Carter	.05
289	Bob MacDonald	.05
290	Jack Morris	.05
291	John Olerud	.05

#	Player	
292	Ed Sprague	.05
293	Todd Stottlemyre	.05
294	Mike Timlin	.05
295	Duane Ward	.05
296	David Wells	.05
297	Devon White	.05
298	Checklist (Ray Lankford)	.05
299	Checklist (Bobby Witt)	.05
300	Checklist (Mike Piazza)	.40
301	Steve Bedrosian	.05
302	Jeff Blauser	.05
303	Francisco Cabrera	.05
304	Marvin Freeman	.05
305	Brian Hunter	.05
306	Dave Justice	.05
307	Greg Maddux	.60
308	Greg McMichael RC	.05
309	Kent Mercker	.05
310	Otis Nixon	.05
311	Pete Smith	.05
312	John Smoltz	.05
313	Jose Guzman	.05
314	Mike Harkey	.05
315	Greg Hibbard	.05
316	Candy Maldonado	.05
317	Randy Myers	.05
318	Dan Plesac	.05
319	Rey Sanchez	.05
320	Ryne Sandberg	.60
321	Tommy Shields RC	.05
322	Jose Vizcaino	.05
323	Matt Walbeck RC	.05
324	Willie Wilson	.05
325	Tom Browning	.05
326	Tim Costo	.05
327	Rob Dibble	.05
328	Steve Foster	.05
329	Roberto Kelly	.05
330	Randy Milligan	.05
331	Kevin Mitchell	.05
332	Tim Pugh RC	.05
333	Jeff Reardon	.05
334	John Roper RC	.05
335	Juan Samuel	.05
336	John Smiley	.05
337	San Wilson	.05
338	Scott Aldred	.05
339	Andy Ashby	.05
340	Freddie Benavides	.05
341	Dante Bichette	.05
342	Willie Blair	.05
343	Daryl Boston	.05
344	Vinny Castilla	.05
345	Jerald Clark	.05
346	Alex Cole	.05
347	Andres Galarraga	.05
348	Joe Girardi	.05
349	Ryan Hawblitzel RC	.05
350	Charlie Hayes	.05
351	Butch Henry	.05
352	Darren Holmes	.05
353	Dale Murphy	.20
354	David Nied	.05
355	Jeff Parrett	.05
356	Steve Reed RC	.05
357	Bruce Ruffin	.05
358	Danny Sheaffer RC	.05
359	Bryn Smith	.05
360	Jim Tatum RC	.05
361	Eric Young	.05
362	Gerald Young	.05
363	Luis Aquino	.05
364	Alex Arias RC	.05
365	Jack Armstrong	.05
366	Bret Barberie	.05
367	Ryan Bowen	.05
368	Greg Briley	.05
369	Cris Carpenter	.05
370	Chuck Carr	.25
371	Jeff Conine RC	.05
372	Steve Decker	.05
373	Orestes Destrade	.05
374	Monty Fariss	.05
375	Junior Felix	.05
376	Chris Hammond	.05
377	Bryan Harvey	.05
378	Trevor Hoffman RC	.05
379	Charlie Hough	.05
380	Joe Klink	.05
381	Richie Lewis RC	.05
382	Dave Magadan	.05
383	Bob McClure	.05
384	Scott Pose RC	.05
385	Rich Renteria RC	.05
386	Benito Santiago	.05
387	Walt Weiss	.05
388	Nigel Wilson	.05
389	Eric Anthony	.05
390	Jeff Bagwell	.50
391	Andujar Cedeno	.05
392	Doug Drabek	.05
393	Darryl Kile	.05
394	Mark Portugal	.05
395	Karl Rhodes	.05
396	Scott Servais	.05
397	Greg Swindell	.05
398	Tom Goodwin	.05
399	Kevin Gross	.05
400	Carlos Hernandez	.05
401	Ramon Martinez	.05
402	Raul Mondesi	.50
403	Jody Reed	.05
404	Mike Sharperson	.05
405	Cory Snyder	.05
406	Darryl Strawberry	.05
407	Rick Trlicek RC	.05
408	Tim Wallach	.05
409	Todd Worrell	.05
410	Tavo Alvarez	.05
411	Sean Berry RC	.05
412	Frank Bolick RC	.05
413	Cliff Floyd	.05
414	Mike Gardiner	.05
415	Marquis Grissom	.05
416	Tim Laker RC	.05
417	Mike Lansing RC	.10
418	Dennis Martinez	.05
419	John Vander Wal	.05
420	John Wetteland	.05
421	Rondell White	.05
422	Bobby Bonilla	.05
423	Jeromy Burnitz	.05
424	Vince Burnitz RC	.05
425	Mike Draper RC	.05
426	Tony Fernandez	.05
427	Dwight Gooden	.05
428	Jeff Innis	.05
429	Bobby Jones	.05
430	Mike Maddux	.05
431	Charlie O'Brien	.05
432	Joe Orsulak	.05
433	Pete Schourek	.05
434	Frank Tanana	.05
435	Ryan Thompson RC	.05
436	Kim Batiste	.05
437	Mark Davis	.05
438	Jose DeLeon	.05
439	Len Dykstra	.05
440	Jim Eisenreich	.05
441	Tommy Greene	.05
442	Pete Incaviglia	.05
443	Danny Jackson	.05
444	Todd Pratt RC	.05
445	Curt Schilling	.20
446	Milt Thompson	.05
447	David West	.05
448	Mitch Williams	.05
449	Steve Cooke	.05
450	Carlos Garcia	.05
451	Al Martin	.05
452	Blas Minor RC	.05
453	Dennis Moeller	.05
454	Denny Neagle	.05
455	Don Slaught	.05
456	Lonnie Smith	.05
457	Paul Wagner	.05
458	Bob Walk	.05
459	Kevin Young	.05
460	Rene Arocha RC	.05
461	Brian Barber	.05
462	Rheal Cormier	.05
463	Gregg Jefferies	.05
464	Joe Magrane	.05
465	Omar Olivares	.05
466	Geronimo Pena	.05
467	Allen Watson	.05
468	Mark Whiten	.05
469	Derek Bell	.05
470	Phil Clark	.05
471	Pat Gomez RC	.05
472	Tony Gwynn	.60
473	Jeremy Hernandez	.05
474	Bruce Hurst	.05
475	Phil Plantier	.05
476	Scott Sanders RC	.05
477	Tim Scott RC	.05
478	Darrell Sherman RC	.05
479	Guillermo Velasquez	.05
480	Tim Worrell RC	.05
481	Todd Benzinger	.05
482	Bud Black	.05
483	Barry Bonds	1.50
484	Dave Burba	.05
485	Bryan Hickerson	.05
486	Dave Martinez	.05
487	Willie McGee	.05
488	Jeff Reed	.05
489	Kevin Rogers	.05
490	Matt Williams	.05
491	Trevor Wilson	.05
492	Harold Baines	.05
493	Mike Devereaux	.05
494	Todd Frohwirth	.05
495	Chris Hoiles	.05
496	Luis Mercedes	.05
497	Sherman Obando RC	.05
498	Brad Pennington RC	.05
499	Harold Reynolds	.05
500	Arthur Rhodes	.05
501	Cal Ripken, Jr.	1.50
502	Rick Sutcliffe	.05
503	Fernando Valenzuela	.05
504	Mark Williamson	.05
505	Scott Bankhead	.05
506	Greg Blosser	.05
507	Ivan Calderon	.05
508	Roger Clemens	.65
509	Andre Dawson	.25
510	Scott Fletcher	.05
511	Greg Harris	.05
512	Billy Hatcher	.05
513	Bob Melvin	.05
514	Carlos Quintana	.05
515	Luis Rivera	.05
516	Jeff Russell	.05
517	Ken Ryan RC	.05
518	Chili Davis	.05
519	Jim Edmonds RC	1.50
520	Gary Gaetti	.05
521	Torey Lovullo RC	.05
522	Tony Percival RC	.05
523	Tim Salmon	.05
524	Scott Sanderson	.05
525	J.T. Snow RC	.75
526	Jerome Walton	.05
527	Jason Bere	.05
528	Rod Bolton RC	.05
529	Ellis Burks	.05
530	Carlton Fisk	.50
531	Craig Grebeck	.05
532	Ozzie Guillen	.05
533	Roberto Hernandez	.05
534	Bo Jackson	.10
535	Kirk McCaskill	.05
536	Dave Stieb	.05
537	Robin Ventura	.05
538	Albert Belle	.05
539	Mike Bielecki	.05
540	Glenallen Hill	.05
541	Reggie Jefferson	.05
542	Kenny Lofton	.05
543	Jeff Mutis RC	.05
544	Junior Ortiz	.05
545	Manny Ramirez	.50
546	Jeff Treadway	.05
547	Kevin Wickander	.05
548	Cecil Fielder	.05
549	Kirk Gibson	.05
550	Greg Gohr RC	.05
551	David Haas	.05
552	Bill Krueger	.05
553	Mike Moore	.05
554	Mickey Tettleton	.05
555	Lou Whitaker	.05
556	Kevin Appier	.05
557	Billy Brewer RC	.05
558	David Cone	.05
559	Greg Gagne	.05
560	Mark Gardner	.05
561	Phil Hiatt	.05
562	Felix Jose	.05
563	Jose Lind	.05
564	Mike Macfarlane	.05
565	Keith Miller	.05
566	Jeff Montgomery	.05
567	Hipolito Pechardo	.05
568	Ricky Bones	.05
569	Tom Brunansky	.05
570	Joe Kmak RC	.05
571	Pat Listach	.05
572	Graeme Lloyd RC	.05
573	Carlos Maldonado RC	.05
574	Josias Manzanillo	.05
575	Matt Mieske	.05
576	Kevin Reimer	.05
577	Bill Spiers	.05
578	Dickie Thon	.05
579	Willie Banks	.05
580	Jim Deshaies	.05
581	Mark Guthrie	.05
582	Brian Harper	.05
583	Chuck Knoblauch	.05
584	Gene Larkin	.05
585	Shane Mack	.05
586	David McCarty	.05
587	Mike Pagliarulo	.05
588	Mike Trombley	.05
589	Dave Winfield	.50
590	Jim Abbott	.05
591	Wade Boggs	.60
592	Russ Davis RC	.05
593	Steve Farr	.05
594	Steve Howe	.05
595	Mike Humphreys RC	.05
596	Jimmy Key	.05
597	Jim Leyritz	.05
598	Bobby Munoz RC	.05
599	Paul O'Neill	.05
600	Spike Owen	.05
601	Mike Stanley	.05
602	Danny Tartabull	.05
603	Scott Brosius	.05
604	Storm Davis	.05
605	Eric Fox	.05
606	Goose Gossage	.05
607	Scott Hammond	.05
608	Dave Henderson	.05
609	Mark McGwire	1.00
610	Mike Mohler RC	.05
611	Edwin Nunez	.05
612	Kevin Seitzer	.05
613	Ruben Sierra	.05
614	Chris Bosio	.05
615	Norm Charlton	.05
616	Jim Converse RC	.05
617	John Cummings RC	.05
618	Mike Felder	.05
619	Ken Griffey Jr.	.75
620	Mike Hampton	.05
621	Erik Hanson	.05
622	Bill Haselman	.05
623	Tino Martinez	.05
624	Lee Tinsley	.05
625	Fernando Vina RC	.05
626	David Wainhouse RC	.05
627	Jose Canseco	.30
628	Benji Gil	.05
629	Tom Henke	.05
630	David Hulse RC	.05
631	Manuel Lee	.05
632	Craig Lefferts	.05
633	Robb Nen RC	.05
634	Gary Redus	.05
635	Bill Ripken	.05
636	Nolan Ryan	1.50
637	Dan Smith	.05
638	Matt Whiteside RC	.05
639	Roberto Alomar	.25
640	Juan Guzman	.05
641	Pat Hentgen	.05
642	Darrin Jackson	.05
643	Randy Knorr	.05
644	Domingo Martinez RC	.05
645	Paul Molitor	.50
646	Dick Schofield	.05
647	Dave Stewart	.05
648	Checklist (Rey Sanchez)	.05
649	Checklist (Jeremy Hernandez)	.05
650	Checklist (Junior Ortiz)	.05

All-Rookies

These insert cards are foil stamped on both sides and were randomly inserted into Series 2 packs. The cards have black fronts, with six different colors of type. The player's uniform number and position are located in the upper-right corner. The player's name and Ultra logo are gold-foil stamped. Backs have a black background with a player photo and career summary.

		NM/M
Complete Set (10):		4.00
Common Player:		.25
1	Rene Arocha	.25
2	Jeff Conine	.25
3	Phil Hiatt	.25
4	Mike Lansing	.25
5	Al Martin	.25
6	David Nied	.25
7	Mike Piazza	3.00
8	Tim Salmon	.50
9	J.T. Snow	.45
10	Kevin Young	.25

All-Stars

This 20-card set features 10 of the top players from each league. Cards were randomly inserted into Series II packs and are foil stamped on both sides.

		NM/M
Complete Set (20):		17.50
Common Player:		.25
1	Darren Daulton	.25
2	Will Clark	.35
3	Ryne Sandberg	1.50
4	Barry Larkin	.25
5	Gary Sheffield	.40
6	Barry Bonds	3.00
7	Ray Lankford	.25
8	Larry Walker	.25
9	Greg Maddux	1.50
10	Lee Smith	.25
11	Ivan Rodriguez	.75
12	Mark McGwire	2.50
13	Carlos Baerga	.25
14	Cal Ripken, Jr.	3.00
15	Edgar Martinez	.25
16	Juan Gonzalez	1.00
17	Ken Griffey Jr.	2.00
18	Kirby Puckett	1.50
19	Frank Thomas	1.25
20	Mike Mussina	.65

Award Winners

This insert set features 18 Top Glove players (nine from each league), two rookies of the year; three MVPs (both leagues and World Series), both Cy

Young Award winners and one Player of the Year. All cards are UV coated and foil stamped on both sides and were found in Series I packs. Two formats are seen. Cards #1-18 are horizontal with player portrait and action photos on a marbled black background. Gold-foil graphics identify the player. Cards #19-25 are vertical with a black background that has "Fleer Ultra Award Winners" splashed around in trendy colors. The Ultra logo, player's name and his award are spelled out in gold foil. Horizontally arranged backs share many of their respective front elements, and have a summary of the season's performance which led to the award. There is a close-up player photo, as well.

		NM/M
Complete Set (25):		12.00
Common Player:		.25
1	Greg Maddux	.75
2	Tom Pagnozzi	.25
3	Mark Grace	.25
4	Jose Lind	.25
5	Terry Pendleton	.25
6	Ozzie Smith	.75
7	Barry Bonds	2.00
8	Andy Van Slyke	.25
9	Larry Walker	.25
10	Mark Langston	.25
11	Ivan Rodriguez	.60
12	Don Mattingly	.75
13	Roberto Alomar	.35
14	Robin Ventura	.25
15	Cal Ripken, Jr.	2.00
16	Ken Griffey Jr.	1.00
17	Kirby Puckett	.75
18	Devon White	.25
19	Pat Listach	.25
20	Eric Karros	.25
21	Pat Borders	.25
22	Greg Maddux	.75
23	Dennis Eckersley	.60
24	Barry Bonds	2.00
25	Gary Sheffield	.45

Career Highlights Promo Sheet

To introduce its "Career Highlights" insert cards in Fleer and Fleer Ultra, the company distributed this promo sheet picturing one card each from the Tom Glavine and Dennis Eckersley sets, overprinted with a gray "PROMOTIONAL SAMPLE" across front and back. A third panel on the sheet provides details of the mail-in offer through which additional cards from the sets could be ordered. The sheet measures 7-1/2"x3-1/2".

	NM/M
Three-Panel Strip:	2.50

Dennis Eckersley Career Highlights

This limited-edition subset chronicles Dennis Eckersley's illustrious career. Cards, which are UV coated and silver foil-stamped on both sides, were randomly inserted into both series' packs. Eckersley autographed more than 2,000 of the cards, which were also randomly inserted into packs. By sending in 10 Fleer Ultra wrappers plus $1, collectors could receive two additional Eckersley cards which were not avail-

able in regular packs. Card fronts have a color action photo, the background of which has been colorized into shades of purple. A black marble strip at bottom has the city name and years he was with the team in silver foil. A large black marble box in one corner has the "Dennis Eckersley Career Highlights" logo in silver foil. On back, a purple box is dropped out of a color photo, and silver-foil typography describes some phrase of Eck's career.

		NM/M
Complete Set (12):		6.00
Common Card:		.50
Autographed Card:		35.00
1	"Perfection" (A's 1987-92)	.50
2	"The Kid" (Indians 1975-77)	.50
3	"The Warrior" (Indians 1975-77)	.50
4	"Beantown Blazer" (Red Sox 1978-84)	.50
5	"Eckspeak" (Red Sox 1978-84)	.50
6	"Down to Earth" (Red Sox 1978-84)	.50
7	"Wrigley Bound" (Cubs 1984-86)	.50
8	"No Relief" (A's 1987-92)	.50
9	"In Control" (A's 1987-92)	.50
10	"Simply the Best" (A's 1987-92)	.50
11	"Reign of Perfection" (A's 1987-92)	.50
12	"Leaving His Mark" (A's 1987-92)	.50

Commemorative

Photos of Fleer's CEO and the company's spokesman, 1992 Cy Young/MVP winner Dennis Eckersley are superimposed on a background of Oakland-Alameda Country Stadium on this promo card. The back gives details of the forthcoming 1993 Fleer Ultra issue.

	NM/M
Dennis Eckersley, Paul Mullan	5.00

Home Run Kings

This insert set features top home run kings. Cards, which are UV coated and have gold foil stamping on both sides, were inserts in Series I packs.

		NM/M
Complete Set (10):		8.00
Common Player:		.50
1	Juan Gonzalez	.65
2	Mark McGwire	.50
3	Cecil Fielder	.50

		NM/M
4	Fred McGriff	.50
5	Albert Belle	.50
6	Barry Bonds	2.50
7	Joe Carter	.50
8	Gary Sheffield	.65
9	Darren Daulton	.50
10	Dave Hollins	.50

Performers

An Ultra Performers set of Fleer Ultra baseball cards was offered directly to collectors in 1993. The set, available only by mail, was limited to 150,000 sets. The cards featured gold-foil stamping and UV coating on each side and a six-photo design, including five on the front of the card. Each card was identified on the back by set serial number jet-printed in black in a strip at bottom.

		NM/M
Complete Set (10):		5.00
Common Player:		.25
1	Barry Bonds	2.50
2	Juan Gonzalez	.30
3	Ken Griffey Jr.	1.00
4	Eric Karros	.25
5	Pat Listach	.25
6	Greg Maddux	.75
7	David Nied	.25
8	Gary Sheffield	.40
9	J.T. Snow	.25
10	Frank Thomas	.65

Strikeout Kings

Five of baseball's top strikeout pitchers are featured in this second-series Ultra insert set. Cards are UV coated and foil stamped on both sides. Each card front has a picture of a pitcher winding up to throw. A baseball is in the background, with the pitcher in the forefront.

		NM/M
Complete Set (5):		7.50
Common Player:		.25
1	Roger Clemens	2.50
2	Juan Guzman	.25
3	Randy Johnson	1.25

4	Nolan Ryan	5.00
5	John Smoltz	.50

1994 Ultra

Issued in two series of 300 cards each, Ultra for 1994 represented a new highwater mark in production values for a mid-priced brand. Each side of the basic cards is UV coated and gold-foil embossed. Fronts feature full-bleed action photos. At bottom the player name, team, position and Fleer Ultra logo appear in gold foil above a gold-foil strip. Some rookie cards are specially designated with a large gold "ROOKIE" above the Ultra logo. Backs feature a basic background that is team color coordinated. Three more player action photos are featured on the back, along with a team logo and a modicum of stats and personal data. There is a gold stripe along the left edge and the player's name and card number appear in gold in the lower-left corner. The set features seven types of insert cards, packaged one per pack.

		NM/M
Complete Set (600):		15.00
Common Player:		.05
Series 1 or 2 Pack (14):		.50
Series 1 or 2 Wax Box (36):		15.00
1	Jeffrey Hammonds	.05
2	Chris Hoiles	.05
3	Ben McDonald	.05
4	Mark McLemore	.05
5	Alan Mills	.05
6	Jamie Moyer	.05
7	Brad Pennington	.05
8	Jim Poole	.05
9	Cal Ripken, Jr.	1.50
10	Jack Voigt	.05
11	Roger Clemens	.65
12	Danny Darwin	.05
13	Andre Dawson	.25
14	Scott Fletcher	.05
15	Greg Harris	.05
16	Billy Hatcher	.05
17	Jeff Russell	.05
18	Aaron Sele	.05
19	Mo Vaughn	.25
20	Mike Butcher	.05
21	Rod Correia	.05
22	Steve Frey	.05
23	Phil Leftwich RC	.05
24	Torey Lovullo	.05
25	Ken Patterson	.05
26	Eduardo Perez	.05
27	Tim Salmon	.25
28	J.T. Snow	.05
29	Chris Turner	.05
30	Wilson Alvarez	.05
31	Jason Bere	.05
32	Joey Cora	.05
33	Alex Fernandez	.05
34	Roberto Hernandez	.05
35	Lance Johnson	.05
36	Ron Karkovice	.05
37	Kirk McCaskill	.05
38	Jeff Schwarz	.05
39	Frank Thomas	.50
40	Sandy Alomar Jr.	.05
41	Albert Belle	.25
42	Felix Fermin	.05
43	Wayne Kirby	.05
44	Tom Kramer	.05
45	Kenny Lofton	.25
46	Jose Mesa	.05
47	Eric Plunk	.05
48	Paul Sorrento	.05
49	Jim Thome	.35
50	Bill Wertz	.05
51	John Doherty	.05
52	Cecil Fielder	.05
53	Travis Fryman	.25
54	Chris Gomez	.05
55	Mike Henneman	.05
56	Chad Kreuter	.05
57	Bob MacDonald	.05
58	Mike Moore	.05
59	Tony Phillips	.05
60	Lou Whitaker	.05
61	Kevin Appier	.05
62	Greg Gagne	.05
63	Chris Gwynn	.05
64	Bob Hamelin	.05
65	Chris Haney	.05
66	Phil Hiatt	.05
67	Felix Jose	.05
68	Jose Lind	.05
69	Mike Macfarlane	.05
70	Jeff Montgomery	.05
71	Hipolito Pichardo	.05
72	Juan Bell	.05
73	Cal Eldred	.05
74	Darryl Hamilton	.05
75	Doug Henry	.05
76	Mike Ignasiak	.05
77	John Jaha	.05
78	Graeme Lloyd	.05
79	Angel Miranda	.05
80	Dave Nilsson	.05
81	Troy O'Leary	.05
82	Kevin Reimer	.05
83	Willie Banks	.05
84	Larry Casian	.05
85	Scott Erickson	.05
86	Eddie Guardado	.05
87	Kent Hrbek	.05
88	Terry Jorgensen	.05
89	Chuck Knoblauch	.05
90	Pat Meares	.05
91	Mike Trombley	.05
92	Dave Winfield	.50
93	Wade Boggs	.60
94	Scott Kamieniecki	.05
95	Pat Kelly	.05
96	Jimmy Key	.05
97	Jim Leyritz	.05
98	Bobby Munoz	.05
99	Paul O'Neill	.05
100	Melido Perez	.05
101	Mike Stanley	.05
102	Danny Tartabull	.05
103	Bernie Williams	.05
104	Kurt Abbott RC	.05
105	Mike Bordick	.05
106	Ron Darling	.05
107	Brent Gates	.05
108	Miguel Jimenez	.05
109	Steve Karsay	.05
110	Scott Lydy	.05
111	Mark McGwire	1.00
112	Troy Neel	.05
113	Craig Paquette	.05
114	Bob Welch	.05
115	Bobby Witt	.05
116	Rich Amaral	.05
117	Mike Blowers	.05
118	Jay Buhner	.05
119	Dave Fleming	.05
120	Ken Griffey Jr.	.75
121	Tino Martinez	.05
122	Marc Newfield	.05
123	Ted Power	.05
124	Mackey Sasser	.05
125	Omar Vizquel	.05
126	Kevin Brown	.05
127	Juan Gonzalez	.25
128	Tom Henke	.05
129	David Hulse	.05
130	Dean Palmer	.05
131	Roger Pavlik	.05
132	Ivan Rodriguez	.40
133	Kenny Rogers	.05
134	Doug Strange	.05
135	Pat Borders	.05
136	Joe Carter	.05
137	Darnell Coles	.05
138	Pat Hentgen	.05
139	Al Leiter	.05
140	Paul Molitor	.50
141	John Olerud	.05
142	Ed Sprague	.05
143	Dave Stewart	.05
144	Mike Timlin	.05
145	Duane Ward	.05
146	Devon White	.05
147	Steve Avery	.05
148	Steve Bedrosian	.05
149	Damon Berryhill	.05
150	Jeff Blauser	.05
151	Tom Glavine	.05
152	Chipper Jones	.60
153	Mark Lemke	.05
154	Fred McGriff	.05
155	Greg McMichael	.05
156	Deion Sanders	.05
157	John Smoltz	.05
158	Mark Wohlers	.05
159	Jose Bautista	.05
160	Steve Buechele	.05
161	Mike Harkey	.05
162	Greg Hibbard	.05
163	Chuck McElroy	.05
164	Mike Morgan	.05
165	Kevin Roberson	.05
166	Ryne Sandberg	.60
167	Jose Vizcaino	.05
168	Rick Wilkins	.05
169	Willie Wilson	.05
170	Willie Greene	.05
171	Roberto Kelly	.05
172	Larry Luebbers	.05
173	Kevin Mitchell	.05
174	Joe Oliver	.05
175	John Roper	.05
176	Johnny Ruffin	.05
177	Reggie Sanders	.05
178	John Smiley	.05
179	Jerry Spradlin	.05
180	Freddie Benavides	.05
181	Dante Bichette	.05
182	Willie Blair	.05
183	Kent Bottenfield	.05
184	Jerald Clark	.05
185	Joe Girardi	.05
186	Roberto Mejia	.05
187	Steve Reed	.05
188	Armando Reynoso	.05
189	Bruce Ruffin	.05
190	Eric Young	.05
191	Luis Aquino	.05
192	Bret Barberie	.05
193	Ryan Bowen	.05
194	Chuck Carr	.05
195	Orestes Destrade	.05
196	Richie Lewis	.05
197	Dave Magadan	.05
198	Bob Natal	.05
199	Gary Sheffield	.30
200	Matt Turner	.05
201	Darrell Whitmore	.05
202	Eric Anthony	.05
203	Jeff Bagwell	.50
204	Andujar Cedeno	.05
205	Luis Gonzalez	.05
206	Xavier Hernandez	.05
207	Doug Jones	.05
208	Darryl Kile	.05
209	Scott Servais	.05
210	Greg Swindell	.05
211	Brian Williams	.05
212	Pedro Astacio	.05
213	Brett Butler	.05
214	Omar Daal	.05
215	Jim Gott	.05
216	Raul Mondesi	.05
217	Jose Offerman	.05
218	Mike Piazza	.75
219	Cory Snyder	.05
220	Tim Wallach	.05
221	Todd Worrell	.05
222	Moises Alou	.05
223	Sean Berry	.05
224	Wil Cordero	.05
225	Jeff Fassero	.05
226	Darrin Fletcher	.05
227	Cliff Floyd	.05
228	Marquis Grissom	.05
229	Ken Hill	.05
230	Mike Lansing	.05
231	Kirk Rueter	.05
232	John Wetteland	.05
233	Rondell White	.05
234	Tim Bogar	.05
235	Jeromy Burnitz	.05
236	Dwight Gooden	.05
237	Todd Hundley	.05
238	Jeff Kent	.05
239	Josias Manzanillo	.05
240	Joe Orsulak	.05
241	Ryan Thompson	.05
242	Kim Batiste	.05
243	Darren Daulton	.05
243a	Darren Daulton/OPS	1.00
244	Tommy Greene	.05
245	Dave Hollins	.05
246	Pete Incaviglia	.05
247	Danny Jackson	.05
248	Ricky Jordan	.05
249	John Kruk	.05
249a	John Kruk/OPS	1.00
250	Mickey Morandini	.05
251	Terry Mulholland	.05
252	Ben Rivera	.05
253	Kevin Stocker	.05
254	Jay Bell	.05
255	Steve Cooke	.05
256	Jeff King	.05
257	Al Martin	.05
258	Danny Miceli	.05
259	Blas Minor	.05
260	Don Slaught	.05
261	Paul Wagner	.05
262	Tim Wakefield	.05
263	Kevin Young	.05
264	Rene Arocha	.05
265	Richard Batchelor RC	.05
266	Gregg Jefferies	.05
267	Brian Jordan	.05
268	Jose Oquendo	.05
269	Donovan Osborne	.05
270	Erik Pappas	.05
271	Mike Perez	.05
272	Bob Tewksbury	.05
273	Mark Whiten	.05
274	Todd Zeile	.05
275	Andy Ashby	.05
276	Brad Ausmus	.05
277	Phil Clark	.05
278	Jeff Gardner	.05
279	Ricky Gutierrez	.05
280	Tony Gwynn	.60
281	Tim Mauser	.05
282	Scott Sanders	.05
283	Frank Seminara	.05
284	Wally Whitehurst	.05
285	Rod Beck	.05
286	Barry Bonds	1.50
287	Dave Burba	.05
288	Mark Carreon	.05
289	Royce Clayton	.05
290	Mike Jackson	.05
291	Darren Lewis	.05
292	Kirt Manwaring	.05
293	Dave Martinez	.05
294	Billy Swift	.05
295	Salomon Torres	.05
296	Matt Williams	.05
297	Checklist 1-103 (Joe Orsulak)	.05
298	Checklist 104-201 (Pete Incaviglia)	.05
299	Checklist 202-300 (Todd Hundley)	.05
300	Checklist - Inserts (John Doherty)	.05
301	Brady Anderson	.05
302	Harold Baines	.05
303	Damon Buford	.05
304	Mike Devereaux	.05
305	Sid Fernandez	.05
306	Rick Krivda	.05
307	Mike Mussina	.30
308	Rafael Palmeiro	.40
309	Arthur Rhodes	.05
310	Chris Sabo	.05
311	Lee Smith	.05
312	Gregg Zaun RC	.05
313	Scott Cooper	.05
314	Mike Greenwell	.05
315	Tim Naehring	.05
316	Otis Nixon	.05
317	Paul Quantrill	.05
318	John Valentin	.05
319	Dave Valle	.05
320	Frank Viola	.05
321	Brian Anderson RC	.10
322	Garret Anderson	.05
323	Chad Curtis	.05
324	Chili Davis	.05
325	Gary DiSarcina	.05
326	Damion Easley	.05
327	Jim Edmonds	.05
328	Chuck Finley	.05
329	Joe Grahe	.05
330	Bo Jackson	.10
331	Mark Langston	.05
332	Harold Reynolds	.05
333	James Baldwin	.05
334	Ray Durham RC	.50
335	Julio Franco	.05
336	Craig Grebeck	.05
337	Ozzie Guillen	.05
338	Joe Hall	.05
339	Darrin Jackson	.05
340	Jack McDowell	.05
341	Tim Raines	.05
342	Robin Ventura	.05
343	Carlos Baerga	.05
344	Derek Lilliquist	.05
345	Dennis Martinez	.05
346	Jack Morris	.05
347	Eddie Murray	.50
348	Chris Nabholz	.05
349	Charles Nagy	.05
350	Chad Ogea	.05
351	Manny Ramirez	.50
352	Omar Vizquel	.05
353	Tim Belcher	.05
354	Eric Davis	.05
355	Kirk Gibson	.05
356	Rick Greene	.05
357	Mickey Tettleton	.05
358	Alan Trammell	.05
359	David Wells	.05
360	Stan Belinda	.05
361	Vince Coleman	.05
362	David Cone	.05
363	Gary Gaetti	.05
364	Tom Gordon	.05
365	Dave Henderson	.05
366	Wally Joyner	.05
367	Brent Mayne	.05
368	Brian McRae	.05
369	Michael Tucker	.05
370	Ricky Bones	.05
371	Brian Harper	.05
372	Tyrone Hill	.05
373	Mark Kiefer	.05
374	Pat Listach	.05
375	Mike Matheny RC	.10
376	Jose Mercedes RC	.05
377	Jody Reed	.05
378	Kevin Seitzer	.05
379	B.J. Surhoff	.05
380	Greg Vaughn	.05
381	Turner Ward	.05
382	Wes Weger	.05
383	Bill Wegman	.05
384	Rick Aguilera	.05
385	Rich Becker	.05
386	Alex Cole	.05
387	Steve Dunn	.05
388	Keith Garagozzo RC	.05
389	LaTroy Hawkins RC	.05
390	Shane Mack	.05
391	David McCarty	.05
392	Pedro Munoz	.05
393	Derek Parks RC	.05
394	Kirby Puckett	.60
395	Kevin Tapani	.05
396	Matt Walbeck	.05
397	Jim Abbott	.05
398	Mike Gallego	.05
399	Xavier Hernandez	.05
400	Don Mattingly	.65
401	Terry Mulholland	.05
402	Matt Nokes	.05
403	Luis Polonia	.05
404	Bob Wickman	.05
405	Mark Acre	.05
406	Fausto Cruz RC	.05
407	Dennis Eckersley	.45
408	Rickey Henderson	.50
409	Stan Javier	.05
410	Carlos Reyes RC	.05
411	Ruben Sierra	.05
412	Terry Steinbach	.05
413	Bill Taylor	.05
414	Todd Van Poppel	.05
415	Eric Anthony	.05
416	Bobby Ayala	.05
417	Chris Bosio	.05
418	Tim Davis	.05
419	Randy Johnson	.50
420	Kevin King	.05
421	Anthony Manahan RC	.05
422	Edgar Martinez	.05
423	Keith Mitchell	.05
424	Roger Salkeld	.05
425	Mac Suzuki RC	.05
426	Dan Wilson	.05
427	Duff Brumley RC	.05
428	Jose Canseco	.30
429	Will Clark	.05
430	Steve Dreyer	.05
431	Rick Helling	.05
432	Chris James	.05
433	Matt Whiteside	.05
434	Roberto Alomar	.20
435	Scott Brow	.05
436	Domingo Cedeno RC	.05
437	Carlos Delgado	.35
438	Juan Guzman	.05
439	Paul Spoljaric	.05
440	Todd Stottlemyre	.05
441	Woody Williams	.05
442	Dave Justice	.05
443	Mike Kelly	.05
444	Ryan Klesko	.05
445	Javier Lopez	.05
446	Greg Maddux	.60
447	Kent Mercker	.05
448	Charlie O'Brien	.05
449	Terry Pendleton	.05
450	Mike Stanton	.05
451	Tony Tarasco	.05
452	Terrell Wade RC	.05
453	Willie Banks	.05
454	Shawon Dunston	.05
455	Mark Grace	.05
456	Jose Guzman	.05
457	Jose Hernandez	.05
458	Glenallen Hill	.05
459	Blaise Isley	.05
460	Brooks Kieschnick RC	.05
461	Derrick May	.05
462	Randy Myers	.05
463	Karl Rhodes	.05
464	Sammy Sosa	.60
465	Steve Trachsel RC	.10
466	Anthony Young	.05
467	Eddie Zambrano RC	.05
468	Bret Boone	.05
469	Tom Browning	.05
470	Hector Carrasco RC	.05
471	Rob Dibble	.05
472	Erik Hanson	.05
473	Thomas Howard	.05
474	Barry Larkin	.05
475	Hal Morris	.05
476	Jose Rijo	.05
477	John Burke	.05
478	Ellis Burks	.05
479	Marvin Freeman	.05
480	Andres Galarraga	.05
481	Greg Harris	.05
482	Charlie Hayes	.05
483	Darren Holmes	.05
484	Howard Johnson	.05
485	Marcus Moore RC	.05
486	David Nied	.05
487	Mark Thompson	.05
488	Walt Weiss	.05
489	Kurt Abbott	.05
490	Matias Carrillo	.05
491	Jeff Conine	.05
492	Chris Hammond	.05
493	Bryan Harvey	.05
494	Charlie Hough	.05
495	Yorkis Perez RC	.05
496	Pat Rapp	.05
497	Benito Santiago	.05
498	David Weathers	.05
499	Craig Biggio	.05
500	Ken Caminiti	.05
501	Doug Drabek	.05
502	Tony Eusebio RC	.10
503	Steve Finley	.05
504	Pete Harnisch	.05
505	Brian Hunter	.05
506	Domingo Jean	.05
507	Todd Jones	.05
508	Orlando Miller	.05
509	James Mouton	.05
510	Roberto Petagine	.05
511	Shane Reynolds	.05
512	Mitch Williams	.05
513	Billy Ashley	.05
514	Tom Candiotti	.05
515	Delino DeShields	.05
516	Kevin Gross	.05
517	Orel Hershiser	.05
518	Eric Karros	.05
519	Ramon Martinez	.05
520	Chan Ho Park RC	.75
521	Henry Rodriguez	.05
522	Joey Eischen	.05
523	Rod Henderson	.05

524	Pedro Martinez	.50
525	Mel Rojas	.05
526	Larry Walker	.05
527	Gabe White RC	.10
528	Bobby Bonilla	.05
529	Jonathan Hurst	.05
530	Bobby Jones	.05
531	Kevin McReynolds	.05
532	Bill Pulsipher	.05
533	Bret Saberhagen	.05
534	David Segui	.05
535	Pete Smith	.05
536	Kelly Stinnett RC	.05
537	Dave Telgheder	.05
538	Quilvio Veras RC	.05
539	Jose Vizcaino	.05
540	Pete Walker	.05
541	Ricky Bottalico	.05
542	Wes Chamberlain	.05
543	Mariano Duncan	.05
544	Len Dykstra	.05
545	Jim Eisenreich	.05
546	Phil Geisler RC	.05
547	Wayne Gomes RC	.10
548	Doug Jones	.05
549	Jeff Juden	.05
550	Mike Lieberthal	.05
551	Tony Longmire RC	.05
552	Tom Marsh	.05
553	Bobby Munoz	.05
554	Curt Schilling	.15
555	Carlos Garcia	.05
556	Ravelo Manzanillo RC	.05
557	Orlando Merced	.05
558	Will Pennyfeather RC	.05
559	Zane Smith	.05
560	Andy Van Slyke	.05
561	Rick White	.05
562	Luis Alicea	.05
563	Brian Barber RC	.05
564	Clint Davis RC	.05
565	Bernard Gilkey	.05
566	Ray Lankford	.05
567	Tom Pagnozzi	.05
568	Ozzie Smith	.60
569	Rick Sutcliffe	.05
570	Allen Watson	.05
571	Dmitri Young	.05
572	Derek Bell	.05
573	Andy Benes	.05
574	Archi Cianfrocco	.05
575	Joey Hamilton	.05
576	Gene Harris	.05
577	Trevor Hoffman	.05
578	Tim Hyers RC	.05
579	Brian Johnson RC	.05
580	Keith Lockhart RC	.05
581	Pedro Martinez	.05
582	Ray McDavid	.05
583	Phil Plantier	.05
584	Bip Roberts	.05
585	Dave Staton	.05
586	Todd Benzinger	.05
587	John Burkett	.05
588	Bryan Hickerson	.05
589	Willie McGee	.05
590	John Patterson	.05
591	Mark Portugal	.05
592	Kevin Rogers	.05
593	Joe Rosselli RC	.05
594	Steve Soderstrom RC	.05
595	Robby Thompson	.05
596	125th Anniversary card	.05
597	Checklist	.05
598	Checklist	.05
599	Checklist	.05
600	Checklist	.05

All-Rookie Team

A stylized sunrise landscape is the background for this insert set featuring top rookies and inserted into Ultra Series II packs at the rate of about one per 10. Backs repeat the motif with an action photo. Both sides are gold-foil enhanced and UV-coated.

		NM/M
Complete Set (10):		4.00
Common Player:		.35
1	Kurt Abbott	.35
2	Carlos Delgado	3.00
3	Cliff Floyd	.35
4	Jeffrey Hammonds	.35

5	Ryan Klesko	.35
6	Javier Lopez	.35
7	Raul Mondesi	.35
8	James Mouton	.35
9	Chan Ho Park	.50
10	Dave Staton	.35

All-Rookie Team Supers

This super-size (3-1/2" x 5-1/2") version of the Fleer Ultra II insert set featuring top rookies was included one per case of hobby packaging. Cards are identical to the smaller version. Both sides are gold-foil enhanced and UV-coated.

		NM/M
Complete Set (10):		5.00
Common Player:		.50
1	Kurt Abbott	.50
2	Carlos Delgado	3.00
3	Cliff Floyd	.50
4	Jeffrey Hammonds	.50
5	Ryan Klesko	.50
6	Javier Lopez	.50
7	Raul Mondesi	.50
8	James Mouton	.50
9	Chan Ho Park	.75
10	Dave Staton	.50

All-Stars

Fleer's opinion of the top 20 players in 1994 are featured in this most common of the Series II Ultra insert sets. Silver-foil highlights enhance the chase cards, found, according to stated odds, once per three packs, on average. National Leaguers have purple backgrounds front and back, American Leaguers have red.

		NM/M
Complete Set (20):		5.00
Common Player:		.15
1	Chris Hoiles	.15
2	Frank Thomas	.35
3	Roberto Alomar	.20
4	Cal Ripken, Jr.	1.00
5	Robin Ventura	.15
6	Albert Belle	.15
7	Juan Gonzalez	.20
8	Ken Griffey Jr.	.50
9	John Olerud	.15
10	Jack McDowell	.15
11	Mike Piazza	.50
12	Fred McGriff	.15
13	Ryne Sandberg	.40
14	Jay Bell	.15
15	Matt Williams	.15
16	Barry Bonds	1.00
17	Len Dykstra	.15
18	Dave Justice	.15
19	Tom Glavine	.20
20	Greg Maddux	.40

Award Winners

The most common of the Fleer Ultra insert sets for 1994 is the 25-card "Award Win-

ners." Horizontal format cards feature front and back background with a gold-embossed look. A player action photo appears on the front. A gold-foil seal on the front has a symbolic player representation flanked by the pictured player's name and award. A gold Fleer Ultra logo is at top. Backs have a player portrait photo and a write-up about the award. The name of the award and the player's name appear in gold foil at the top. Stated odds of finding an Award Winners card were one in three packs.

		NM/M
Complete Set (25):		5.00
Common Player:		.10
1	Ivan Rodriguez	.25
2	Don Mattingly	.45
3	Roberto Alomar	.20
4	Robin Ventura	.10
5	Omar Vizquel	.10
6	Ken Griffey Jr.	.50
7	Kenny Lofton	.10
8	Devon White	.10
9	Mark Langston	.10
10	Kirt Manwaring	.10
11	Mark Grace	.10
12	Robby Thompson	.10
13	Matt Williams	.10
14	Jay Bell	.10
15	Barry Bonds	.60
16	Marquis Grissom	.10
17	Larry Walker	.10
18	Greg Maddux	.40
19	Frank Thomas	.35
20	Barry Bonds	.60
21	Paul Molitor	.35
22	Jack McDowell	.10
23	Greg Maddux	.40
24	Tim Salmon	.10
25	Mike Piazza	.50

Career Achievement Awards

The outstanding careers of five of baseball's top veteran stars are recognized in this chase set, inserted on average once every 21 packs of Ultra Series II. The gold-highlighted horizontal fronts combine a current color photo with a background single-tint photo from the player's earlier days. Backs flip-flop the photo use, with the current photo in the background and the earlier photo in full color in the foreground. The gold Ultra Career Achievement Award seal is repeated on back, as well.

		NM/M
Complete Set (5):		4.00
Common Player:		.50
1	Joe Carter	.50
2	Paul Molitor	.75
3	Cal Ripken, Jr.	2.00
4	Ryne Sandberg	1.00
5	Dave Winfield	.75

Firemen

Ten of the major leagues' leading relief pitchers are featured in this Ultra insert set. Cards have an action photo of the player superimposed over a background photo of a fire truck. A shield at top, in gold foil, has a smoke-eater's helmet, stylized flames and proclaims

the player an "Ultra Fireman." Backs are horizontal in format and feature the pumper's control panel in the background photo. A color player portrait photo appears on one side, with a description of his relief role and successes in a whitened box. Fireman cards are found, on average, once per 11 packs, according to stated odds.

		NM/M
Complete Set (10):		2.00
Common Player:		.25
1	Jeff Montgomery	.25
2	Duane Ward	.25
3	Tom Henke	.25
4	Roberto Hernandez	.25
5	Dennis Eckersley	1.25
6	Randy Myers	.25
7	Rod Beck	.25
8	Bryan Harvey	.25
9	John Wetteland	.25
10	Mitch Williams	.25

Hitting Machines

A heavy metal background of gears and iron-letter logo is featured in this insert set honoring the game's top hitters. The cards turn up about once in every five packs of Ultra Series II. Both front and back are highlighted in silver foil.

		NM/M
Complete Set (10):		4.00
Common Player:		.15
1	Roberto Alomar	.25
2	Carlos Baerga	.15
3	Barry Bonds	2.00
4	Andres Galarraga	.15
5	Juan Gonzalez	.25
6	Tony Gwynn	.50
7	Paul Molitor	.40
8	John Olerud	.15
9	Mike Piazza	.75
10	Frank Thomas	.40

Home Run Kings

One of two high-end insert sets in '94 Ultra is the 12-card "Home Run Kings" found exclusively in 14-card foil packs, on an average of once per 36-pack box. Featuring the technology Fleer calls "etched metallization," the cards have a black background with a red and blue foil representation of a batter. An action photo of a player tak-

ing a mighty cut or starting his home-run trot is featured. A large gold-foil "Home Run King" crown-and-shield device are in an upper corner, while the Ultra logo and player name are in gold foil at bottom. Backs have a white background with the red and blue batter symbol. The player's name appears in gold foil at the top, along with a portrait photo and a summary of his home run prowess.

		NM/M
Complete Set (12):		15.00
Common Player:		.75
1	Juan Gonzalez	1.00
2	Ken Griffey Jr.	2.50
3	Frank Thomas	2.00
4	Albert Belle	.75
5	Rafael Palmeiro	1.50
6	Joe Carter	.75
7	Barry Bonds	4.00
8	Dave Justice	.75
9	Matt Williams	.75
10	Fred McGriff	.75
11	Ron Gant	.75
12	Mike Piazza	2.50

League Leaders

Arguably the least attractive of the '94 Ultra inserts are the "League Leaders." Fronts feature a full-bleed action photo on which the bottom has been recolored to a team hue giving the effect of teal, purple and magenta miasmas rising from the turf. An Ultra logo appears in gold foil in an upper corner, with the player's name in gold foil at about the dividing line between the natural color and colorized portions of the photo. A large "League Leader" appears in the bottom half of the photo, with the category led printed in the lower-left. Backs repeat the team color at top, fading to white at the bottom. In gold foil are "League Leader" and the category. A portrait photo appears at bottom. Several paragraphs detail the league leading performance of the previous season.

		NM/M
Complete Set (10):		3.00
Common Player:		.25
1	John Olerud	.25
2	Rafael Palmeiro	1.00
3	Kenny Lofton	.25
4	Jack McDowell	.25
5	Randy Johnson	1.50
6	Andres Galarraga	.25
7	Len Dykstra	.25
8	Chuck Carr	.25
9	Tom Glavine	.35
10	Jose Rijo	.25

On-Base Leaders

One of the lesser-known, but most valuable, stats - on-base percentage - is featured in this subset found exclusively in 17-card packs, at the rate of about one per 37 packs. The fronts feature color photos against a stat-filled printed-foil background.

		NM/M
Complete Set (12):		25.00
Common Player:		1.50
1	Roberto Alomar	2.00
2	Barry Bonds	6.50
3	Len Dykstra	1.50
4	Andres Galarraga	1.50
5	Mark Grace	1.50
6	Ken Griffey Jr.	5.00
7	Gregg Jefferies	1.50
8	Orlando Merced	1.50
9	Paul Molitor	3.50
10	John Olerud	1.50
11	Tony Phillips	1.50
12	Frank Thomas	3.50

Phillies Finest

As a tribute to two of Fleer's home-team heroes, the Philadelphia-based card company created an Ultra insert set featuring 12 cards each of "Phillies Finest," John Kruk and Darren Daulton. Twenty of the cards were issued as Series 1 and 2 inserts, about one in every eight packs, while four were available only by a mail-in offer. Fronts feature action photos with large block letters popping out of the background. The Ultra logo and player name appear in gold foil. Backs have portrait photos and career summaries, with the player's name and card number in gold foil. Daulton and Kruk each autographed 1,000 of the inserts. Stated odds of finding the autographed cards were one in 11,000 packs. Values listed are per-card.

		NM/M
Complete Set (24):		4.00
Common Player:		.25
Autographed Daulton:		45.00
Autographed Kruk:		30.00
1-5	Darren Daulton	.25
6-10	John Kruk	.25
11-15	Darren Daulton	.25
16-20	John Kruk	.25
9a	John Kruk/OPS	1.50
1M, 3M	Darren Daulton	.75
2M, 4M	John Kruk	.75

RBI Kings

Exclusive to the 19-card jumbo packs of Fleer Ultra are a series of 12 "RBI Kings" insert cards, found, according to stated odds, one per 36 packs. The horizontal-format card front uses Fleer's "etched metallized" technology to produce a sepia-toned background action photo, in front of which is a color player photo. An Ultra logo appears in gold foil in an upper corner while a fancy shield-and-scroll "RBI

King" logo and the player's name are in gold at the bottom. Backs repeat the basic front motif and include a color player portrait photo, his name in gold foil and a paragraph justifying his selection as an RBI King.

		NM/M
Complete Set (12):		16.00
Common Player:		1.00
1	Albert Belle	1.00
2	Frank Thomas	2.50
3	Joe Carter	1.00
4	Juan Gonzalez	1.25
5	Cecil Fielder	1.00
6	Carlos Baerga	1.00
7	Barry Bonds	5.00
8	David Justice	1.00
9	Ron Gant	1.00
10	Mike Piazza	3.50
11	Matt Williams	1.00
12	Darren Daulton	1.00

Rising Stars

An outer space background printed on metallic foil sets this chase set apart from most of the rest of the Ultra Series II inserts. The silver-foil enhanced cards of projected superstars of tomorrow are found on average once every 37 packs.

		NM/M
Complete Set (12):		15.00
Common Player:		1.00
1	Carlos Baerga	1.00
2	Jeff Bagwell	5.00
3	Albert Belle	1.00
4	Cliff Floyd	1.00
5	Travis Fryman	1.00
6	Marquis Grissom	1.00
7	Kenny Lofton	1.00
8	John Olerud	1.00
9	Mike Piazza	7.50
10	Kirk Rueter	1.00
11	Tim Salmon	1.00
12	Aaron Sele	1.00

Second Year Standouts

Approximately once every 11 packs, the Ultra insert find is a "Second Year Standout" card. Ten of the game's sophomore stars are featured. Fronts feature a pair of action photos against a team-color background. Gold-foil highlights are the Ultra logo, the player's name and a "Second Year Standout" shield. The shield and player name are repeated in gold foil on the back, as is the team color background. There is a player portrait photo at bottom and a summary of the player's 1993 season.

		NM/M
Complete Set (10):		5.00
Common Player:		.25
1	Jason Bere	.25

2	Brent Gates	.25
3	Jeffrey Hammonds	.25
4	Tim Salmon	.50
5	Aaron Sele	.25
6	Chuck Carr	.25
7	Jeff Conine	.25
8	Greg McMichael	.25
9	Mike Piazza	4.00
10	Kevin Stocker	.25

Strikeout Kings

A gold-foil "Strikeout Kings" crown-and-shield logo is featured on the front of this chase set. Cards are found on average once per seven packs. Each of the cards features the K-king in sequential action photos. Backs have a larger action photo with a large version of the Strikeout King shield in the background.

		NM/M
Complete Set (5):		2.00
Common Player:		.25
1	Randy Johnson	.75
2	Mark Langston	.25
3	Greg Maddux	1.00
4	Jose Rijo	.25
5	John Smoltz	.25

1995 Ultra

A clean design enhanced with three different colors of metallic foil graphics is featured on the basic cards of 1995 Fleer Ultra. Two series of 250 cards each were issued with cards arranged alphabetically within team, also sequenced alphabetically. Fronts have a gold-foil Ultra logo in an upper corner, with the player's name and team logo in a team-color coded foil at bottom. There are no other graphic elements on the borderless photos. Backs have a large photo rendered in a single color, again team-coded. A postage-stamp sized color photo in one corner is flanked by a few vital stats in silver foil. Career and '94 stats are printed at bottom, enhanced by the foil color from the front. Cards were issued in 12-card retail and hobby packs at $1.99 and jumbo pre-priced ($2.69) magazine packs. Each pack contains one of the several insert series from the appropriate series.

		NM/M
Complete Set (450):		10.00
Common Player:		.05
Gold Medallion:		2X
Series 1 or 2 Pack (12):		.50
Series 1 or 2 Wax Box (36):		12.50
1	Brady Anderson	.05
2	Sid Fernandez	.05
3	Jeffrey Hammonds	.05
4	Chris Hoiles	.05

5	Ben McDonald	.05
6	Mike Mussina	.35
7	Rafael Palmeiro	.65
8	Jack Voigt	.05
9	Wes Chamberlain	.05
10	Roger Clemens	1.00
11	Chris Howard	.05
12	Tim Naehring	.05
13	Otis Nixon	.05
14	Rich Rowland	.05
15	Ken Ryan	.05
16	John Valentin	.05
17	Mo Vaughn	.05
18	Brian Anderson	.05
19	Chili Davis	.05
20	Damion Easley	.05
21	Jim Edmonds	.05
22	Mark Langston	.05
23	Tim Salmon	.05
24	J.T. Snow	.05
25	Chris Turner	.05
26	Wilson Alvarez	.05
27	Joey Cora	.05
28	Alex Fernandez	.05
29	Roberto Hernandez	.05
30	Lance Johnson	.05
31	Ron Karkovice	.05
32	Kirk McCaskill	.05
33	Tim Raines	.05
34	Frank Thomas	.75
35	Sandy Alomar	.05
36	Albert Belle	.05
37	Mark Clark	.05
38	Kenny Lofton	.05
39	Eddie Murray	.75
40	Eric Plunk	.05
41	Manny Ramirez	.75
42	Jim Thome	.60
43	Omar Vizquel	.05
44	Danny Bautista	.05
45	Junior Felix	.05
46	Cecil Fielder	.05
47	Chris Gomez	.05
48	Chad Kreuter	.05
49	Mike Moore	.05
50	Tony Phillips	.05
51	Alan Trammell	.05
52	David Wells	.05
53	Kevin Appier	.05
54	Billy Brewer	.05
55	David Cone	.05
56	Greg Gagne	.05
57	Bob Hamelin	.05
58	Jose Lind	.05
59	Brent Mayne	.05
60	Brian McRae	.05
61	Terry Shumpert	.05
62	Ricky Bones	.05
63	Mike Fetters	.05
64	Darryl Hamilton	.05
65	John Jaha	.05
66	Graeme Lloyd	.05
67	Matt Mieske	.05
68	Kevin Seitzer	.05
69	Jose Valentin	.05
70	Turner Ward	.05
71	Rick Aguilera	.05
72	Rich Becker	.05
73	Alex Cole	.05
74	Scott Leius	.05
75	Pat Meares	.05
76	Kirby Puckett	1.00
77	Dave Stevens	.05
78	Kevin Tapani	.05
79	Matt Walbeck	.05
80	Wade Boggs	1.00
81	Scott Kamieniecki	.05
82	Pat Kelly	.05
83	Jimmy Key	.05
84	Paul O'Neill	.05
85	Luis Polonia	.05
86	Mike Stanley	.05
87	Danny Tartabull	.05
88	Bob Wickman	.05
89	Mark Acre	.05
90	Geronimo Berroa	.05
91	Mike Bordick	.05
92	Ron Darling	.05
93	Stan Javier	.05
94	Mark McGwire	1.50
95	Troy Neel	.05
96	Ruben Sierra	.05
97	Terry Steinbach	.05
98	Eric Anthony	.05
99	Chris Bosio	.05
100	Dave Fleming	.05
101	Ken Griffey Jr.	1.25
102	Reggie Jefferson	.05
103	Randy Johnson	.75
104	Edgar Martinez	.05
105	Bill Risley	.05
106	Dan Wilson	.05
107	Cris Carpenter	.05
108	Will Clark	.05
109	Juan Gonzalez	.40
110	Rusty Greer	.05
111	David Hulse	.05
112	Roger Pavlik	.05
113	Ivan Rodriguez	.75
114	Doug Strange	.05
115	Matt Whiteside	.05
116	Roberto Alomar	.20
117	Brad Cornett	.05
118	Carlos Delgado	.45
119	Alex Gonzalez	.05
120	Darren Hall	.05
121	Pat Hentgen	.05
122	Paul Molitor	.75

123	Ed Sprague	.05
124	Devon White	.05
125	Tom Glavine	.25
126	Dave Justice	.05
127	Roberto Kelly	.05
128	Mark Lemke	.05
129	Greg Maddux	1.00
130	Charles Johnson	.05
131	Kent Mercker	.05
132	Charlie O'Brien	.05
133	John Smoltz	.05
134	Willie Banks	.05
135	Steve Buechele	.05
136	Kevin Foster	.05
137	Glenallen Hill	.05
138	Ray Sanchez	.05
139	Sammy Sosa	1.00
140	Steve Trachsel	.05
141	Rick Wilkins	.05
142	Jeff Brantley	.05
143	Hector Carrasco	.05
144	Kevin Jarvis	.05
145	Barry Larkin	.05
146	Chuck McElroy	.05
147	Jose Rijo	.05
148	Johnny Ruffin	.05
149	Deion Sanders	.05
150	Eddie Taubensee	.05
151	Dante Bichette	.05
152	Ellis Burks	.05
153	Joe Girardi	.05
154	Charlie Hayes	.05
155	Mike Kingery	.05
156	Steve Reed	.05
157	Kevin Ritz	.05
158	Bruce Ruffin	.05
159	Eric Young	.05
160	Kurt Abbott	.05
161	Chuck Carr	.05
162	Chris Hammond	.05
163	Bryan Harvey	.05
164	Terry Mathews	.05
165	Yorkis Perez	.05
166	Pat Rapp	.05
167	Gary Sheffield	.40
168	Dave Weathers	.05
169	Jeff Bagwell	.75
170	Ken Caminiti	.05
171	Doug Drabek	.05
172	Steve Finley	.05
173	John Hudek	.05
174	Todd Jones	.05
175	James Mouton	.05
176	Shane Reynolds	.05
177	Scott Servais	.05
178	Tom Candiotti	.05
179	Omar Daal	.05
180	Darren Dreifort	.05
181	Eric Karros	.05
182	Ramon Martinez	.05
183	Raul Mondesi	.05
184	Henry Rodriguez	.05
185	Todd Worrell	.05
186	Moises Alou	.05
187	Sean Berry	.05
188	Wil Cordero	.05
189	Jeff Fassero	.05
190	Darrin Fletcher	.05
191	Butch Henry	.05
192	Ken Hill	.05
193	Mel Rojas	.05
194	John Wetteland	.05
195	Bobby Bonilla	.05
196	Rico Brogna	.05
197	Bobby Jones	.05
198	Jeff Kent	.05
199	Josias Manzanillo	.05
200	Kelly Stinnett	.05
201	Ryan Thompson	.05
202	Jose Vizcaino	.05
203	Lenny Dykstra	.05
204	Jim Eisenreich	.05
205	Dave Hollins	.05
206	Mike Lieberthal	.05
207	Mickey Morandini	.05
208	Bobby Munoz	.05
209	Curt Schilling	.20
210	Heathcliff Slocumb	.05
211	David West	.05
212	Dave Clark	.05
213	Steve Cooke	.05
214	Midre Cummings	.05
215	Carlos Garcia	.05
216	Jeff King	.05
217	Jon Lieber	.05
218	Orlando Merced	.05
219	Don Slaught	.05
220	Rick White	.05
221	Rene Arocha	.05
222	Bernard Gilkey	.05
223	Brian Jordan	.05
224	Tom Pagnozzi	.05
225	Vicente Palacios	.05
226	Geronimo Pena	.05
227	Ozzie Smith	1.00
228	Allen Watson	.05
229	Mark Whiten	.05
230	Brad Ausmus	.05
231	Derek Bell	.05
232	Andy Benes	.05
233	Tony Gwynn	1.00
234	Joey Hamilton	.05
235	Luis Lopez	.05
236	Pedro A. Martinez	.05
237	Scott Sanders	.05
238	Eddie Williams	.05
239	Rod Beck	.05
240	Dave Burba	.05

241	Darren Lewis	.05
242	Kirt Manwaring	.05
243	Mark Portugal	.05
244	Darryl Strawberry	.05
245	Robby Thompson	.05
246	William Van Landingham	.05
247	Matt Williams	.05
248	Checklist	.05
249	Checklist	.05
250	Checklist	.05
251	Harold Baines	.05
252	Bret Barberie	.05
253	Armando Benitez	.05
254	Mike Devereaux	.05
255	Leo Gomez	.05
256	Jamie Moyer	.05
257	Arthur Rhodes	.05
258	Cal Ripken Jr.	2.00
259	Luis Alicea	.05
260	Jose Canseco	.45
261	Scott Cooper	.05
262	Andre Dawson	.25
263	Mike Greenwell	.05
264	Aaron Sele	.05
265	Garret Anderson	.05
266	Chad Curtis	.05
267	Gary DiSarcina	.05
268	Chuck Finley	.05
269	Rex Hudler	.05
270	Andrew Lorraine	.05
271	Spike Owen	.05
272	Lee Smith	.05
273	Jason Bere	.05
274	Ozzie Guillen	.05
275	Norberto Martin	.05
276	Scott Ruffcorn	.05
277	Robin Ventura	.05
278	Carlos Baerga	.05
279	Jason Grimsley	.05
280	Dennis Martinez	.05
281	Charles Nagy	.05
282	Paul Sorrento	.05
283	Dave Winfield	.75
284	John Doherty	.05
285	Travis Fryman	.05
286	Kirk Gibson	.05
287	Lou Whitaker	.05
288	Gary Gaetti	.05
289	Tom Gordon	.05
290	Mark Gubicza	.05
291	Wally Joyner	.05
292	Mike Macfarlane	.05
293	Jeff Montgomery	.05
294	Jeff Cirillo	.05
295	Cal Eldred	.05
296	Pat Listach	.05
297	Jose Mercedes	.05
298	Dave Nilsson	.05
299	Duane Singleton	.05
300	Greg Vaughn	.05
301	Scott Erickson	.05
302	Denny Hocking	.05
303	Chuck Knoblauch	.05
304	Pat Mahomes	.05
305	Pedro Munoz	.05
306	Erik Schullstrom	.05
307	Jim Abbott	.05
308	Tony Fernandez	.05
309	Sterling Hitchcock	.05
310	Jim Leyritz	.05
311	Don Mattingly	1.00
312	Jack McDowell	.05
313	Melido Perez	.05
314	Bernie Williams	.05
315	Scott Brosius	.05
316	Dennis Eckersley	.65
317	Brent Gates	.05
318	Rickey Henderson	.75
319	Steve Karsay	.05
320	Steve Ontiveros	.05
321	Bill Taylor	.05
322	Todd Van Poppel	.05
323	Bob Welch	.05
324	Bobby Ayala	.05
325	Mike Blowers	.05
326	Jay Buhner	.05
327	Felix Fermin	.05
328	Tino Martinez	.05
329	Marc Newfield	.05
330	Greg Pirkl	.05
331	Alex Rodriguez	1.50
332	Kevin Brown	.05
333	John Burkett	.05
334	Jeff Frye	.05
335	Kevin Gross	.05
336	Dean Palmer	.05
337	Joe Carter	.05
338	Shawn Green	.35
339	Juan Guzman	.05
340	Mike Huff	.05
341	Al Leiter	.05
342	John Olerud	.05
343	Dave Stewart	.05
344	Todd Stottlemyre	.05
345	Steve Avery	.05
346	Jeff Blauser	.05
347	Chipper Jones	1.00
348	Mike Kelly	.05
349	Ryan Klesko	.05
350	Javier Lopez	.05
351	Fred McGriff	.05
352	Jose Oliva	.05
353	Terry Pendleton	.05
354	Mike Stanton	.05
355	Tony Tarasco	.05
356	Mark Wohlers	.05
357	Jim Bullinger	.05

358	Shawon Dunston	.05
359	Mark Grace	.05
360	Derrick May	.05
361	Randy Myers	.05
362	Karl Rhodes	.05
363	Bret Boone	.05
364	Brian Dorsett	.05
365	Ron Gant	.05
366	Brian R. Hunter	.05
367	Hal Morris	.05
368	Jack Morris	.05
369	John Roper	.05
370	Reggie Sanders	.05
371	Pete Schourek	.05
372	John Smiley	.05
373	Marvin Freeman	.05
374	Andres Galarraga	.05
375	Mike Munoz	.05
376	David Nied	.05
377	Walt Weiss	.05
378	Greg Colbrunn	.05
379	Jeff Conine	.05
380	Charles Johnson	.05
381	Kurt Miller	.05
382	Robb Nen	.05
383	Benito Santiago	.05
384	Craig Biggio	.05
385	Tony Eusebio	.05
386	Luis Gonzalez	.05
387	Brian L. Hunter	.05
388	Darryl Kile	.05
389	Orlando Miller	.05
390	Phil Plantier	.05
391	Greg Swindell	.05
392	Billy Ashley	.05
393	Pedro Astacio	.05
394	Brett Butler	.05
395	Delino DeShields	.05
396	Orel Hershiser	.05
397	Garey Ingram	.05
398	Chan Ho Park	.05
399	Mike Piazza	1.25
400	Ismael Valdes	.05
401	Tim Wallach	.05
402	Cliff Floyd	.05
403	Marquis Grissom	.05
404	Mike Lansing	.05
405	Pedro Martinez	.75
406	Kirk Rueter	.05
407	Tim Scott	.05
408	Jeff Shaw	.05
409	Larry Walker	.05
410	Rondell White	.05
411	John Franco	.05
412	Todd Hundley	.05
413	Jason Jacome	.05
414	Joe Orsulak	.05
415	Bret Saberhagen	.05
416	David Segui	.05
417	Darren Daulton	.05
418	Mariano Duncan	.05
419	Tommy Greene	.05
420	Gregg Jefferies	.05
421	John Kruk	.05
422	Kevin Stocker	.05
423	Jay Bell	.05
424	Al Martin	.05
425	Denny Neagle	.05
426	Zane Smith	.05
427	Andy Van Slyke	.05
428	Paul Wagner	.05
429	Tom Henke	.05
430	Danny Jackson	.05
431	Ray Lankford	.05
432	John Mabry	.05
433	Bob Tewksbury	.05
434	Todd Zeile	.05
435	Andy Ashby	.05
436	Andujar Cedeno	.05
437	Donnie Elliott	.05
438	Bryce Florie	.05
439	Trevor Hoffman	.05
440	Melvin Nieves	.05
441	Bip Roberts	.05
442	Barry Bonds	2.00
443	Royce Clayton	.05
444	Mike Jackson	.05
445	John Patterson	.05
446	J.R. Phillips	.05
447	Bill Swift	.05
448	Checklist	.05
449	Checklist	.05
450	Checklist	.05

Gold Medallion

Less than 10 percent of the production run of Fleer Ultra

(regular and insert sets) was produced in a special parallel Gold Medallion edition. On these special cards an embossed round gold seal replaces the Fleer Ultra logo in the upper corner. One Gold Medallion card was inserted into each Ultra foil pack.

	NM/M
Complete Set (450):	60.00
Common Player:	.25
Stars/Rookies:	2X

All-Rookies

Enlarged pieces of the central color action photo, set on a white background, make up the front design on these inserts. The player's name, card title and Ultra logo are printed in silver foil. Horizontal backs have another color photo, which is also repeated in single-color fashion. A career summary is printed over the larger photo. The All-Rookie inserts are found only in 12-card packs, at the rate of about one per four packs.

	NM/M
Complete Set (10):	2.25
Common Player:	.15
Gold Medallion:	2X
1 Cliff Floyd	.15
2 Chris Gomez	.15
3 Rusty Greer	.15
4 Bob Hamelin	.15
5 Joey Hamilton	.15
6 John Hudek	.15
7 Ryan Klesko	.15
8 Raul Mondesi	.15
9 Manny Ramirez	2.00
10 Steve Trachsel	.15

All-Stars

Twenty of the top players in the majors were chosen as Ultra All-Stars in this Series II chase set. Fronts have a color player photo at left. At right is a second photo, printed in only one color. A large "ALL-STAR" is at bottom, with the player's name above and team below in silver foil. An Ultra logo is at left. Backs have another color photo, with a '94 season summary printed in a black panel at right. These cards were found one per five packs, on average.

	NM/M
Complete Set (20):	7.50
Common Player:	.15
Gold Medallion:	2X
1 Moises Alou	.15
2 Albert Belle	.15
3 Craig Biggio	.15
4 Wade Boggs	.60

---

5 Barry Bonds	1.50
6 David Cone	.15
7 Ken Griffey Jr.	.75
8 Tony Gwynn	.60
9 Chuck Knoblauch	.15
10 Barry Larkin	.15
11 Kenny Lofton	.15
12 Greg Maddux	.60
13 Fred McGriff	.15
14 Paul O'Neill	.15
15 Mike Piazza	.75
16 Kirby Puckett	.60
17 Cal Ripken Jr.	1.50
18 Ivan Rodriguez	.45
19 Frank Thomas	.50
20 Matt Williams	.15

Award Winners

Various official and unofficial award winners from the 1994 season are featured in this Series I insert set. Horizontal cards have a color player photo on the right side, with a single-color, vertically compressed action photo at left. The player's award is printed in a white strip at top, while his name and team logo, along with the Ultra logo, are at bottom. All front typography is in gold foil. Backs repeat the compressed photo at left, combined with another color photo at right. A season summary is printed over the photo at left. The Award Winners inserts were common to all types of packaging, found at the rate of about one per four packs.

	NM/M
Complete Set (25):	6.00
Common Player:	.10
Gold Medallion:	2X
1 Ivan Rodriguez	.30
2 Don Mattingly	.65
3 Roberto Alomar	.20
4 Wade Boggs	.60
5 Omar Vizquel	.10
6 Ken Griffey Jr.	.75
7 Kenny Lofton	.10
8 Devon White	.10
9 Mark Langston	.10
10 Tom Pagnozzi	.10
11 Jeff Bagwell	.45
12 Craig Biggio	.10
13 Matt Williams	.10
14 Barry Larkin	.10
15 Barry Bonds	1.00
16 Marquis Grissom	.10
17 Darren Lewis	.10
18 Greg Maddux	.60
19 Frank Thomas	.45
20 Jeff Bagwell	.45
21 David Cone	.10
22 Greg Maddux	.60
23 Bob Hamelin	.10
24 Raul Mondesi	.10
25 Moises Alou	.10

Golden Prospects

A hobby-pack exclusive, found at the rate of one per eight packs on average in Series I. Fronts feature a player photo at right, with three horizontally and vertically compressed versions of the same photo at right. The photo's background has been rendered in a single color. All typography - Ultra logo, card title, name and team - is in gold foil. Backs are also horizontal and have a color player photo and career summary.

	NM/M
Complete Set (10):	5.00
Common Player:	.10
Gold Medallion:	2X

---

1 James Baldwin	.10
2 Alan Benes	.10
3 Armando Benitez	.10
4 Ray Durham	.10
5 LaTroy Hawkins	.10
6 Brian Hunter	.10
7 Derek Jeter	3.00
8 Charles Johnson	.10
9 Alex Rodriguez	2.00
10 Michael Tucker	.10

Gold Medallion Rookies Mail-in

This set of 20 was available only by mailing in 10 Fleer Ultra wrappers plus $5.95. A reported 100,000 sets were produced. The cards are in the same format as the regular-issue Fleer Ultra. Each card has a team logo, player name and "ROOKIE" notation in gold foil at bottom, and the round Gold Medallion seal in an upper-corner of the borderless game-action photo front. Backs have two more action photos, a large one in one-color and a small one in full-color. Much of the typography on back is rendered in gold foil. Card numbers have an M prefix.

	NM/M
Complete Set (20):	3.00
Common Player:	.10
M-1 Manny Alexander	.10
M-2 Edgardo Alfonzo	.10
M-3 Jason Bates	.10
M-4 Andres Berumen	.10
M-5 Darren Bragg	.10
M-6 Jamie Brewington	.10
M-7 Jason Christiansen	.10
M-8 Brad Clontz	.10
M-9 Marty Cordova	.10
M-10 Johnny Damon	1.50
M-11 Vaughn Eshelman	.10
M-12 Chad Fonville	.10
M-13 Curtis Goodwin	.10
M-14 Tyler Green	.10
M-15 Bob Higginson	.10
M-16 Jason Isringhausen	.10
M-17 Hideo Nomo	1.50
M-18 Jon Nunnally	.10
M-19 Carlos Perez	.10
M-20 Julian Tavarez	.10

Hitting Machines

Various mechanical devices and dynamics make up the letters of "HITTING MACHINE" behind the color player action photo in this insert set. Both of those elements, along with the gold-foil player name, team and Ultra logo are in UV-coated contrast to the matte-finish gray background. Backs are also horizontal in format and feature a portrait photo at right, against a gray-streaked background. A career summary is printed at right. The Hitting Machines series is found only in Series II Ultra retail packs, at the rate of one card per eight packs, on average.

	NM/M
Complete Set (10):	6.00
Common Player:	.40

Home Run Kings

Retail packaging of Fleer Ultra Series I was the hiding place for this sluggers' chase set. An average of one out of eight packs yielded a Home Run King insert. Fronts have a photo of the player's home run cut, while large letters "H," "R" and "K" are stacked vertically down one side. All front typography is in gold foil. Backs have another batting photo and a couple of sentences of recent career slugging prowess.

	NM/M
Complete Set (10):	7.50
Common Player:	.25
Gold Medallion:	2X
1 Ken Griffey Jr.	2.00
2 Frank Thomas	.75
3 Albert Belle	.25
4 Jose Canseco	.50
5 Cecil Fielder	.25
6 Matt Williams	.25
7 Jeff Bagwell	.75
8 Barry Bonds	3.00
9 Fred McGriff	.25
10 Andres Galarraga	.25

League Leaders

Top performers in major statistical categories are featured in this Series I insert. Cards were seeded in all types of Ultra packaging at the rate of about one card per three packs. Cards have a horizontal orientation with a color player action photo printed over a black logo of the appropriate league. American Leaguers' cards have a light brown overall background color, National Leaguers have dark green. The player's name, team and Ultra logos, and box with his league-leading category are printed in silver foil. The background from the front is carried onto the back, where a color portrait photo is at left, and a '94 season summary printed at right.

	NM/M
Complete Set (10):	2.50
Common Player:	.15
Gold Medallion:	2X
1 Paul O'Neill	.15
2 Kenny Lofton	.15
3 Jimmy Key	.15
4 Randy Johnson	.50
5 Lee Smith	.15
6 Tony Gwynn	.75
7 Craig Biggio	.15
8 Greg Maddux	.75
9 Andy Benes	.15
10 John Franco	.15

Gold Medallion:	2X
1 Jeff Bagwell	.65
2 Albert Belle	.25
3 Dante Bichette	.25
4 Barry Bonds	2.50
5 Jose Canseco	.50
6 Ken Griffey Jr.	1.00
7 Tony Gwynn	.75
8 Fred McGriff	.25
9 Mike Piazza	1.00
10 Frank Thomas	.65

On-Base Leaders

Numerous smaller versions in several sizes of the central action photo against a graduated color background from the front design of this Series II insert set. The player name, card title and Ultra logo are printed in gold foil down one side. Backs have a horizontal player photo with a large team logo at top, a smaller version at bottom and a 1994 season summary. One out of eight (on average) pre-priced packs yielded an On-Base Leaders insert.

	NM/M
Complete Set (10):	15.00
Common Player:	1.00
Gold Medallion:	2X
1 Jeff Bagwell	2.00
2 Albert Belle	1.00
3 Craig Biggio	1.00
4 Wade Boggs	2.50
5 Barry Bonds	6.00
6 Will Clark	1.00
7 Tony Gwynn	2.50
8 Dave Justice	1.00
9 Paul O'Neill	1.00
10 Frank Thomas	2.00

Power Plus

The scarcest of the Series I Ultra inserts are the Power Plus cards, printed on 100 percent etched foil and inserted at the rate of less than one per box. Fronts have a player action photo overprinted on a background of "POWER PLUS" logos in various metallic colors. A team logo and player name are at bottom in gold foil, as is the Ultra logo at top. Backs are conventionally printed and have a player photo on one side and season summary on the other.

	NM/M
Complete Set (6):	7.50
Common Player:	.50
Gold Medallion:	2X
1 Albert Belle	.50
2 Ken Griffey Jr.	2.00
3 Frank Thomas	1.00
4 Jeff Bagwell	1.00
5 Barry Bonds	4.00
6 Matt Williams	.50

RBI Kings

A bright aura surrounds the central player action photo on these cards, separating the player image from an indistinct colored background. At center is a large gold-foil "RBI KING" with the player's name above and team below. Backs

---

have a similar design with a white box at bottom covering the player's RBI abilities. This set is found only in Series I jumbo packs, at an average rate of one per eight packs.

	NM/M
Complete Set (10):	12.00
Common Player:	.50
Gold Medallion:	2X
1 Kirby Puckett	3.00
2 Joe Carter	.50
3 Albert Belle	.50
4 Frank Thomas	2.00
5 Julio Franco	.50
6 Jeff Bagwell	2.00
7 Matt Williams	.50
8 Dante Bichette	.50
9 Fred McGriff	.50
10 Mike Piazza	4.00

Rising Stars

The top of the line among Series II chase cards is this set printed on 100 percent etched foil and seeded at the rate of less than one per box, on average. Horizontal-format cards have two player photos on a background of multi-colored rays. The Ultra logo, card title, player name and team are printed in gold foil. Backs repeat the colored rays, have another player photo and a career summary.

	NM/M
Complete Set (9):	7.00
Common Player:	.50
Gold Medallion:	2X
1 Moises Alou	.50
2 Jeff Bagwell	1.50
3 Albert Belle	.65
4 Juan Gonzalez	1.50
5 Chuck Knoblauch	.50
6 Kenny Lofton	.50
7 Raul Mondesi	.50
8 Mike Piazza	2.50
9 Frank Thomas	1.50

Second Year Standouts

Fifteen of the game's sophomore stars are featured in this Series I insert set. Horizontal-format cards have player action photos front and back set against a background of orange and yellow rays. Besides the player name, card title and Ultra logo in gold-foil, the front features a pair of leafed branches flanking a team logo, all in embossed gold-foil. Backs have a career summary. The series was seeded at the average rate of one per six packs.

	NM/M
Complete Set (15):	3.50

Common Player:	.15
Gold Medallion:	2X
1 Cliff Floyd	.15
2 Chris Gomez	.15
3 Rusty Greer	.15
4 Darren Hall	.15
5 Bob Hamelin	.15
6 Joey Hamilton	.15
7 Jeffrey Hammonds	.15
8 John Hudek	.15
9 Ryan Klesko	.15
10 Raul Mondesi	.15
11 Manny Ramirez	3.00
12 Bill Risley	.15
13 Steve Trachsel	.15
14 William Van Landingham	.15
15 Rondell White	.15

Strikeout Kings

A purple background with several types of concentric and overlapping circular designs in white are the background of this Series II chase set. An action color photo of the K-King is at center, while down one side are stacked photos of the grips used for various pitches. The player name, card title and Ultra logo are in silver foil. Backs have a portrait photo and career summary with purple circles behind and a black background. Stated odds of finding a Strikeout King card are one in five packs, on average.

	NM/M
Complete Set (6):	3.00
Common Player:	.10
Gold Medallion:	2X
1 Andy Benes	.10
2 Roger Clemens	1.50
3 Randy Johnson	.75
4 Greg Maddux	1.00
5 Pedro Martinez	.75
6 Jose Rijo	.10

1996 Ultra Promotional Samples

A six-page glossy folder which was die-cut to hold three sample cards introduced Fleer's Ultra line for 1996. The fronts of all three cards are similar in format to the issued versions, but only the back of the basic-card sample replicates the issued version. Backs of the chase card samples contained product information.

	NM/M
Complete Set (8):	7.50
Common Player:	1.00
(1) Ken Griffey Jr. (Basic card.)	1.50

(2) Matt Williams (Basic card.)	1.00
(3) Barry Bonds (HR King)	2.50
(4) Frank Thomas (HR King)	1.25
(5) Roberto Alomar (Prime Leather)	1.00
(6) Cal Ripken Jr. (Prime Leather)	2.50
2 Tony Gwynn (Season Crown)	1.50
4 Kenny Lofton (Season Crown)	1.00

1996 Ultra

A 40 percent thicker cardboard stock and silver-foil highlights are featured in this year's edition. Fronts are very basic with a borderless action photo and silver-foil graphics. Backs feature a three-photo montage along with 1995 and career stats. The set was released in two 300-card series; each card is also reprinted as part of a limited-edition Gold Medallion parallel set. One Gold Medallion card is found in every pack. Each series has eight insert sets. Series 1 inserts are RBI Kings, Home Run Kings, Fresh Foundations, Diamond Producers, Power Plus, Season Crowns, Golden Prospects and Prime Leather. Series 2 inserts are Call to the Hall, Golden Prospects, Hitting Machines, On-Base Leaders, RESPECT, Rawhide, Rising Stars and Thunderclap. Checklist cards were also randomly inserted into packs from both series.

	NM/M
Complete Set (600):	22.50
Common Player:	.05
Gold Medallions:	2X
Series 1 or 2 Pack (12):	1.25
Series 1 or 2 Wax Box (24):	20.00
1 Manny Alexander	.05
2 Brady Anderson	.05
3 Bobby Bonilla	.05
4 Scott Erickson	.05
5 Curtis Goodwin	.05
6 Chris Hoiles	.05
7 Doug Jones	.05
8 Jeff Manto	.05
9 Mike Mussina	.35
10 Rafael Palmeiro	.25
11 Cal Ripken Jr.	1.50
12 Rick Aguilera	.05
13 Luis Alicea	.05
14 Stan Belinda	.05
15 Jose Canseco	.40
16 Roger Clemens	.85
17 Mike Greenwell	.05
18 Mike Macfarlane	.05
19 Tim Naehring	.05
20 Troy O'Leary	.05
21 John Valentin	.05
22 Mo Vaughn	.25
23 Tim Wakefield	.05
24 Brian Anderson	.05
25 Garret Anderson	.05
26 Chili Davis	.05
27 Gary DiSarcina	.05
28 Jim Edmonds	.25
29 Jorge Fabregas	.05
30 Chuck Finley	.05
31 Mark Langston	.05
32 Troy Percival	.05
33 Tim Salmon	.25
34 Lee Smith	.05
35 Wilson Alvarez	.05
36 Ray Durham	.05
37 Alex Fernandez	.05
38 Ozzie Guillen	.05
39 Roberto Hernandez	.05
40 Lance Johnson	.05
41 Ron Karkovice	.05

42 Lyle Mouton	.05
43 Tim Raines	.05
44 Frank Thomas	.60
45 Carlos Baerga	.05
46 Albert Belle	.25
47 Orel Hershiser	.05
48 Kenny Lofton	.05
49 Dennis Martinez	.05
50 Jose Mesa	.05
51 Eddie Murray	.60
52 Chad Ogea	.05
53 Manny Ramirez	.60
54 Jim Thome	.50
55 Omar Vizquel	.05
56 Dave Winfield	.60
57 Chad Curtis	.05
58 Cecil Fielder	.05
59 John Flaherty	.05
60 Travis Fryman	.05
61 Chris Gomez	.05
62 Bob Higginson	.05
63 Felipe Lira	.05
64 Brian Maxcy	.05
65 Alan Trammell	.05
66 Lou Whitaker	.05
67 Kevin Appier	.05
68 Gary Gaetti	.05
69 Tom Goodwin	.05
70 Tom Gordon	.05
71 Jason Jacome	.05
72 Wally Joyner	.05
73 Brent Mayne	.05
74 Jeff Montgomery	.05
75 Jon Nunnally	.05
76 Joe Vitiello	.05
77 Ricky Bones	.05
78 Jeff Cirillo	.05
79 Mike Fetters	.05
80 Darryl Hamilton	.05
81 David Hulse	.05
82 Dave Nilsson	.05
83 Kevin Seitzer	.05
84 Steve Sparks	.05
85 B.J. Surhoff	.05
86 Jose Valentin	.05
87 Greg Vaughn	.05
88 Marty Cordova	.05
89 Chuck Knoblauch	.05
90 Pat Meares	.05
91 Pedro Munoz	.05
92 Kirby Puckett	.75
93 Brad Radke	.05
94 Scott Stahoviak	.05
95 Dave Stevens	.05
96 Mike Trombley	.05
97 Matt Walbeck	.05
98 Wade Boggs	.75
99 Russ Davis	.05
100 Jim Leyritz	.05
101 Don Mattingly	.85
102 Jack McDowell	.05
103 Paul O'Neill	.05
104 Andy Pettitte	.30
105 Mariano Rivera	.15
106 Ruben Sierra	.05
107 Darryl Strawberry	.05
108 John Wetteland	.05
109 Bernie Williams	.05
110 Geronimo Berroa	.05
111 Scott Brosius	.05
112 Dennis Eckersley	.50
113 Brent Gates	.05
114 Rickey Henderson	.60
115 Mark McGwire	1.25
116 Ariel Prieto	.05
117 Terry Steinbach	.05
118 Todd Stottlemyre	.05
119 Todd Van Poppel	.05
120 Steve Wojciechowski	.05
121 Rich Amaral	.05
122 Bobby Ayala	.05
123 Mike Blowers	.05
124 Chris Bosio	.05
125 Joey Cora	.05
126 Ken Griffey Jr.	1.00
127 Randy Johnson	.60
128 Edgar Martinez	.05
129 Tino Martinez	.05
130 Alex Rodriguez	1.25
131 Dan Wilson	.05
132 Will Clark	.05
133 Jeff Frye	.05
134 Benji Gil	.05
135 Juan Gonzalez	.30
136 Rusty Greer	.05
137 Mark McLemore	.05
138 Roger Pavlik	.05
139 Ivan Rodriguez	.50
140 Kenny Rogers	.05
141 Mickey Tettleton	.05
142 Roberto Alomar	.20
143 Joe Carter	.05
144 Tony Castillo	.05
145 Alex Gonzalez	.05
146 Shawn Green	.35
147 Pat Hentgen	.05
148 Sandy Martinez RC	.05
149 Paul Molitor	.60
150 John Olerud	.05
151 Ed Sprague	.05
152 Jeff Blauser	.05
153 Brad Clontz	.05
154 Tom Glavine	.30
155 Marquis Grissom	.05
156 Chipper Jones	.75
157 David Justice	.05
158 Ryan Klesko	.05
159 Javier Lopez	.05

160 Greg Maddux	.75
161 John Smoltz	.05
162 Mark Wohlers	.05
163 Jim Bullinger	.05
164 Frank Castillo	.05
165 Shawon Dunston	.05
166 Kevin Foster	.05
167 Luis Gonzalez	.05
168 Mark Grace	.05
169 Rey Sanchez	.05
170 Scott Servais	.05
171 Sammy Sosa	.75
172 Ozzie Timmons	.05
173 Steve Trachsel	.05
174 Bret Boone	.05
175 Jeff Branson	.05
176 Jeff Brantley	.05
177 Dave Burba	.05
178 Ron Gant	.05
179 Barry Larkin	.05
180 Darren Lewis	.05
181 Mark Portugal	.05
182 Reggie Sanders	.05
183 Pete Schourek	.05
184 John Smiley	.05
185 Jason Bates	.05
186 Dante Bichette	.05
187 Ellis Burks	.05
188 Vinny Castilla	.05
189 Andres Galarraga	.05
190 Darren Holmes	.05
191 Armando Reynoso	.05
192 Kevin Ritz	.05
193 Bill Swift	.05
194 Larry Walker	.05
195 Kurt Abbott	.05
196 John Burkett	.05
197 Greg Colbrunn	.05
198 Jeff Conine	.05
199 Andre Dawson	.25
200 Chris Hammond	.05
201 Charles Johnson	.05
202 Robb Nen	.05
203 Terry Pendleton	.05
204 Quilvio Veras	.05
205 Jeff Bagwell	.60
206 Derek Bell	.05
207 Doug Drabek	.05
208 Tony Eusebio	.05
209 Mike Hampton	.05
210 Brian Hunter	.05
211 Todd Jones	.05
212 Orlando Miller	.05
213 James Mouton	.05
214 Shane Reynolds	.05
215 Dave Veres	.05
216 Billy Ashley	.05
217 Brett Butler	.05
218 Chad Fonville	.05
219 Todd Hollandsworth	.05
220 Eric Karros	.05
221 Ramon Martinez	.05
222 Raul Mondesi	.05
223 Hideo Nomo	.30
224 Mike Piazza	1.00
225 Kevin Tapani	.05
226 Ismael Valdes	.05
227 Todd Worrell	.05
228 Moises Alou	.05
229 Wil Cordero	.05
230 Jeff Fassero	.05
231 Darrin Fletcher	.05
232 Mike Lansing	.05
233 Pedro Martinez	.60
234 Carlos Perez	.05
235 Mel Rojas	.05
236 David Segui	.05
237 Tony Tarasco	.05
238 Rondell White	.05
239 Edgardo Alfonzo	.05
240 Rico Brogna	.05
241 Carl Everett	.05
242 Todd Hundley	.05
243 Butch Huskey	.05
244 Jason Isringhausen	.05
245 Bobby Jones	.05
246 Jeff Kent	.05
247 Bill Pulsipher	.05
248 Jose Vizcaino	.05
249 Ricky Bottalico	.05
250 Darren Daulton	.05
251 Jim Eisenreich	.05
252 Tyler Green	.05
253 Charlie Hayes	.05
254 Gregg Jefferies	.05
255 Tony Longmire	.05
256 Michael Mimbs	.05
257 Mickey Morandini	.05
258 Paul Quantrill	.05
259 Heathcliff Slocumb	.05
260 Jay Bell	.05
261 Jacob Brumfield	.05
262 Angelo Encarnacion RC	.05
263 John Ericks	.05
264 Mark Johnson	.05
265 Esteban Loaiza	.05
266 Al Martin	.05
267 Orlando Merced	.05
268 Dan Miceli	.05
269 Denny Neagle	.05
270 Brian Barber	.05
271 Scott Cooper	.05
272 Tripp Cromer	.05
273 Bernard Gilkey	.05
274 Tom Henke	.05
275 Brian Jordan	.05
276 John Mabry	.05
277 Tom Pagnozzi	.05

278 Mark Petkovsek RC	.05
279 Ozzie Smith	.75
280 Andy Ashby	.05
281 Brad Ausmus	.05
282 Ken Caminiti	.05
283 Glenn Dishman	.05
284 Tony Gwynn	.75
285 Joey Hamilton	.05
286 Trevor Hoffman	.05
287 Phil Plantier	.05
288 Jody Reed	.05
289 Eddie Williams	.05
290 Barry Bonds	1.50
291 Jamie Brewington	.05
292 Mark Carreon	.05
293 Royce Clayton	.05
294 Glenallen Hill	.05
295 Mark Leiter	.05
296 Kirt Manwaring	.05
297 J.R. Phillips	.05
298 Deion Sanders	.05
299 William Van Landingham	.05
300 Matt Williams	.05
301 Roberto Alomar	.20
302 Armando Benitez	.05
303 Mike Devereaux	.05
304 Jeffrey Hammonds	.05
305 Jimmy Haynes	.05
306 Scott McClain RC	.05
307 Kent Mercker	.05
308 Randy Myers	.05
309 B.J. Surhoff	.05
310 Tony Tarasco	.05
311 David Wells	.05
312 Wil Cordero	.05
313 Alex Delgado	.05
314 Tom Gordon	.05
315 Dwayne Hosey	.05
316 Jose Malave	.05
317 Kevin Mitchell	.05
318 Jamie Moyer	.05
319 Aaron Sele	.05
320 Heathcliff Slocumb	.05
321 Mike Stanley	.05
322 Jeff Suppan	.05
323 Jim Abbott	.05
324 George Arias	.05
325 Todd Greene	.05
326 Bryan Harvey	.05
327 J.T. Snow	.05
328 Randy Velarde	.05
329 Tim Wallach	.05
330 Harold Baines	.05
331 Jason Bere	.05
332 Darren Lewis	.05
333 Norberto Martin	.05
334 Tony Phillips	.05
335 Bill Simas	.05
336 Chris Snopek	.05
337 Kevin Tapani	.05
338 Danny Tartabull	.05
339 Robin Ventura	.05
340 Sandy Alomar	.05
341 Julio Franco	.05
342 Jack McDowell	.05
343 Charles Nagy	.05
344 Julian Tavarez	.05
345 Kimera Bartee	.05
346 Greg Keagle	.05
347 Mark Lewis	.05
348 Jose Lima	.05
349 Melvin Nieves	.05
350 Mark Parent	.05
351 Eddie Williams	.05
352 Johnny Damon	.30
353 Sal Fasano	.05
354 Mark Gubicza	.05
355 Bob Hamelin	.05
356 Chris Haney	.05
357 Keith Lockhart	.05
358 Mike Macfarlane	.05
359 Jose Offerman	.05
360 Bip Roberts	.05
361 Michael Tucker	.05
362 Chuck Carr	.05
363 Bobby Hughes	.05
364 John Jaha	.05
365 Mark Loretta	.05
366 Mike Matheny	.05
367 Ben McDonald	.05
368 Matt Mieske	.05
369 Angel Miranda	.05
370 Fernando Vina	.05
371 Rick Aguilera	.05
372 Rich Becker	.05
373 LaTroy Hawkins	.05
374 Dave Hollins	.05
375 Roberto Kelly	.05
376 Matt Lawton RC	.25
377 Paul Molitor	.60
378 Dan Naulty RC	.05
379 Rich Robertson	.05
380 Frank Rodriguez	.05
381 David Cone	.05
382 Mariano Duncan	.05
383 Andy Fox RC	.05
384 Joe Girardi	.05
385 Dwight Gooden	.05
386 Derek Jeter	1.50
387 Pat Kelly	.05
388 Jimmy Key	.05
389 Matt Luke RC	.05
390 Tino Martinez	.05
391 Jeff Nelson	.05
392 Melido Perez	.05
393 Tim Raines	.05
394 Ruben Rivera	.05

395 Kenny Rogers	.05
396 Tony Batista RC	.25
397 Allen Battle	.05
398 Mike Bordick	.05
399 Steve Cox	.05
400 Jason Giambi	.40
401 Doug Johns	.05
402 Pedro Munoz	.05
403 Phil Plantier	.05
404 Scott Spiezio	.05
405 George Williams	.05
406 Ernie Young	.05
407 Darren Bragg	.05
408 Jay Buhner	.05
409 Norm Charlton	.05
410 Russ Davis	.05
411 Sterling Hitchcock	.05
412 Edwin Hurtado	.05
413 Raul Ibanez RC	.05
414 Mike Jackson	.05
415 Luis Sojo	.05
416 Paul Sorrento	.05
417 Bob Wolcott	.05
418 Damon Buford	.05
419 Kevin Gross	.05
420 Darryl Hamilton	.05
421 Mike Henneman	.05
422 Ken Hill	.05
423 Dean Palmer	.05
424 Bobby Witt	.05
425 Tilson Brito	.05
426 Giovanni Carrara	.05
427 Domingo Cedeno	.05
428 Felipe Crespo	.05
429 Carlos Delgado	.40
430 Juan Guzman	.05
431 Erik Hanson	.05
432 Marty Janzen RC	.05
433 Otis Nixon	.05
434 Robert Perez	.05
435 Paul Quantrill	.05
436 Bill Risley	.05
437 Steve Avery	.05
438 Jermaine Dye	.05
439 Mark Lemke	.05
440 Marty Malloy RC	.05
441 Fred McGriff	.05
442 Greg McMichael	.05
443 Wonderful Monds	.05
444 Eddie Perez	.05
445 Jason Schmidt	.05
446 Terrell Wade	.05
447 Terry Adams	.05
448 Scott Bullett	.05
449 Robin Jennings RC	.05
450 Doug Jones	.05
451 Brooks Kieschnick	.05
452 Dave Magadan	.05
453 Jason Maxwell RC	.05
454 Brian McRae	.05
455 Rodney Myers	.05
456 Jaime Navarro	.05
457 Ryne Sandberg	.75
458 Vince Coleman	.05
459 Eric Davis	.05
460 Steve Gibralter	.05
461 Thomas Howard	.05
462 Mike Kelly	.05
463 Hal Morris	.05
464 Eric Owens	.05
465 Jose Rijo	.05
466 Chris Sabo	.05
467 Eddie Taubensee	.05
468 Trenidad Hubbard	.05
469 Curt Leskanic	.05
470 Quinton McCracken	.05
471 Jayhawk Owens	.05
472 Steve Reed	.05
473 Bryan Rekar	.05
474 Bruce Ruffin	.05
475 Bret Saberhagen	.05
476 Walt Weiss	.05
477 Eric Young	.05
478 Kevin Brown	.05
479 Al Leiter	.05
480 Pat Rapp	.05
481 Gary Sheffield	.35
482 Devon White	.05
483 Bob Abreu	.05
484 Sean Berry	.05
485 Craig Biggio	.05
486 Jim Dougherty	.05
487 Richard Hidalgo	.05
488 Darryl Kile	.05
489 Derrick May	.05
490 Greg Swindell	.05
491 Rick Wilkins	.05
492 Mike Blowers	.05
493 Tom Candiotti	.05
494 Roger Cedeno	.05
495 Delino DeShields	.05
496 Greg Gagne	.05
497 Karim Garcia	.10
498 Wilton Guerrero RC	.05
499 Chan Ho Park	.05
500 Israel Alcantara	.05
501 Shane Andrews	.05
502 Yamil Benitez	.05
503 Cliff Floyd	.05
504 Mark Grudzielanek	.05
505 Ryan McGuire	.05
506 Sherman Obando	.05
507 Jose Paniagua	.05
508 Henry Rodriguez	.05
509 Kirk Rueter	.05
510 Juan Acevedo	.05
511 John Franco	.05
512 Bernard Gilkey	.05

513	Lance Johnson	.05
514	Rey Ordonez	.05
515	Robert Person	.05
516	Paul Wilson	.05
517	Toby Borland	.05
518	David Doster RC	.05
519	Lenny Dykstra	.05
520	Sid Fernandez	.05
521	Mike Grace RC	.05
522	Rich Hunter RC	.05
523	Benito Santiago	.05
524	Gene Schall	.05
525	Curt Schilling	.15
526	Kevin Sefcik RC	.05
527	Lee Tinsley	.05
528	David West	.05
529	Mark Whiten	.05
530	Todd Zeile	.05
531	Carlos Garcia	.05
532	Charlie Hayes	.05
533	Jason Kendall	.05
534	Jeff King	.05
535	Mike Kingery	.05
536	Nelson Liriano	.05
537	Dan Plesac	.05
538	Paul Wagner	.05
539	Luis Alicea	.05
540	David Bell	.05
541	Alan Benes	.05
542	Andy Benes	.05
543	Mike Busby RC	.05
544	Royce Clayton	.05
545	Dennis Eckersley	.50
546	Gary Gaetti	.05
547	Ron Gant	.05
548	Aaron Holbert	.05
549	Ray Lankford	.05
550	T.J. Mathews	.05
551	Willie McGee	.05
552	Miguel Mejia RC	.05
553	Todd Stottlemyre	.05
554	Sean Bergman	.05
555	Willie Blair	.05
556	Andujar Cedeno	.05
557	Steve Finley	.05
558	Rickey Henderson	.60
559	Wally Joyner	.05
560	Scott Livingstone	.05
561	Marc Newfield	.05
562	Bob Tewksbury	.05
563	Fernando Valenzuela	.05
564	Rod Beck	.05
565	Doug Creek	.05
566	Shawon Dunston	.05
567	Osvaldo Fernandez RC	.20
568	Stan Javier	.05
569	Marcus Jensen	.05
570	Steve Scarsone	.05
571	Robby Thompson	.05
572	Allen Watson	.05
573	Roberto Alomar (Ultra Stars)	.10
574	Jeff Bagwell (Ultra Stars)	.30
575	Albert Belle (Ultra Stars)	.05
576	Wade Boggs (Ultra Stars)	.40
577	Barry Bonds (Ultra Stars)	.75
578	Juan Gonzalez (Ultra Stars)	.15
579	Ken Griffey Jr. (Ultra Stars)	.50
580	Tony Gwynn (Ultra Stars)	.40
581	Randy Johnson (Ultra Stars)	.30
582	Chipper Jones (Ultra Stars)	.40
583	Barry Larkin (Ultra Stars)	.05
584	Kenny Lofton (Ultra Stars)	.05
585	Greg Maddux (Ultra Stars)	.40
586	Raul Mondesi (Ultra Stars)	.05
587	Mike Piazza (Ultra Stars)	.50
588	Cal Ripken Jr. (Ultra Stars)	.75
589	Tim Salmon (Ultra Stars)	.05
590	Frank Thomas (Ultra Stars)	.35
591	Mo Vaughn (Ultra Stars)	.05
592	Matt Williams (Ultra Stars)	.05
593	Marty Cordova (Raw Power)	.05
594	Jim Edmonds (Raw Power)	.05
595	Cliff Floyd (Raw Power)	.05
596	Chipper Jones (Raw Power)	.40
597	Ryan Klesko (Raw Power)	.05
598	Raul Mondesi (Raw Power)	.05
599	Manny Ramirez (Raw Power)	.30
600	Ruben Rivera (Raw Power)	.05

Gold Medallion

Limited to less than 10 percent of the regular edition's pro-

duction, the Gold Medallion parallel set replaces the front photo's background with gold foil featuring a large embossed Fleer Ultra Gold Medallion seal at center. One Gold Medallion card is found in each foil pack.

	NM/M
Complete Set (600):	75.00
Common Player:	.25

Call to the Hall

Ten probable future Hall of Famers are featured on these cards, which use classic style original illustrations of the players. The cards were seeded one per every 24 Series 2 packs.

		NM/M
Complete Set (10):		10.00
Common Player:		1.00
Gold Medallion Edition:		2X
1	Barry Bonds	3.00
2	Ken Griffey Jr.	2.00
3	Tony Gwynn	1.25
4	Rickey Henderson	1.00
5	Greg Maddux	1.25
6	Eddie Murray	1.00
7	Cal Ripken Jr.	3.00
8	Ryne Sandberg	1.25
9	Ozzie Smith	1.25
10	Frank Thomas	1.00

Checklists

Fleer Ultra featured 10 checklist cards that were inserted every four packs. These cards featured a superstar player on the front and, throughout the set, a full checklist of all cards in the 1996 Ultra set on the back.

		NM/M
Complete Set (20):		9.00
Common Player:		.15
Gold Medallions:		2X
1	Jeff Bagwell	.50
2	Barry Bonds	1.00
3	Juan Gonzalez	.25
4	Ken Griffey Jr.	.65
5	Chipper Jones	.60
6	Mike Piazza	.65
7	Manny Ramirez	.50

8	Cal Ripken Jr.	1.00
9	Frank Thomas	.50
10	Matt Williams	.15
1	Albert Belle	.15
2	Cecil Fielder	.15
3	Ken Griffey Jr.	.65
4	Tony Gwynn	.60
5	Derek Jeter	1.00
6	Jason Kendall	.15
7	Ryan Klesko	.15
8	Greg Maddux	.60
9	Cal Ripken Jr.	1.00
10	Frank Thomas	.50

Diamond Dust

This card commemorates Cal Ripken's history-making 1995 record of playing in 2,131 consecutive regular-season games. Horizontal in format, the front has a color action photo of Ripken on a simulated leather background. Back has a photo of Ripken on the night he set the new record. Sandwiched between front and back is a dime-sized plastic capsule of dirt certified, according to the facsimile autograph of the team's head groundskeeper, to have been used on the infield at Oriole Park in Camden Yards during the 1995 season. Two versions of the card were made. A hand-numbered version limited to 2,131 was offered direct to dealers for $39.99. An unnumbered version was available to collectors as a wrapper redemption for $24.99.

	NM/M
Cal Ripken Jr. (Numbered)	40.00
Cal Ripken Jr. (Unnumbered)	20.00

Diamond Producers

A horizontal layout and two versions of the same photo printed on holographic foil are featured in this insert set. Stated odds of finding a Diamond Producers card are one per every 20 Series I packs.

		NM/M
Complete Set (12):		15.00
Common Player:		.50
Gold Medallions:		2X
1	Albert Belle	.50
2	Barry Bonds	3.00
3	Ken Griffey Jr.	2.00
4	Tony Gwynn	1.50
5	Greg Maddux	1.50
6	Hideo Nomo	.75
7	Mike Piazza	2.00
8	Kirby Puckett	1.50
9	Cal Ripken Jr.	3.00
10	Frank Thomas	1.25
11	Mo Vaughn	.50
12	Matt Williams	.50

Fresh Foundations

Rising stars who can carry their teams' fortunes into the next century are featured in this foil-printed insert set, found on average of one card per every three Series I foil packs.

		NM/M
Complete Set (10):		2.00
Common Player:		.15
Gold Medallions:		2X
1	Garret Anderson	.15
2	Marty Cordova	.15
3	Jim Edmonds	.15

4	Brian Hunter	.15
5	Chipper Jones	.50
6	Ryan Klesko	.15
7	Raul Mondesi	.15
8	Hideo Nomo	.25
9	Manny Ramirez	.40
10	Rondell White	.15

Golden Prospects, Series 1

A hobby-pack-only insert, these horizontal format cards have rainbow foil ballpark backgrounds and feature 1996's rookie crop. They are found on average of one per every five Series I packs.

		NM/M
Complete Set (10):		7.00
Common Player:		.25
Gold Medallions:		2X
1	Yamil Benitez	.25
2	Alberto Castillo	.25
3	Roger Cedeno	.25
4	Johnny Damon	1.00
5	Micah Franklin	.25
6	Jason Giambi	1.00
7	Jose Herrera	.25
8	Derek Jeter	5.00
9	Kevin Jordan	.25
10	Ruben Rivera	.25

Golden Prospects, Series 2

The Golden Prospects insert series continued with 15 more young stars found exclusively in Series 2 hobby packs, though in much lower numbers than the Series 1 inserts.

		NM/M
Complete Set (15):		10.00
Common Player:		1.00
Gold Medallions:		2X
1	Bob Abreu	1.50
2	Israel Alcantara	1.00
3	Tony Batista	1.00
4	Mike Cameron	1.00
5	Steve Cox	1.00
6	Jermaine Dye	1.00
7	Wilton Guerrero	1.00
8	Richard Hidalgo	1.00
9	Raul Ibanez	1.00
10	Marty Janzen	1.00
11	Robin Jennings	1.00
12	Jason Maxwell	1.00
13	Scott McClain	1.00
14	Wonderful Monds	1.00
15	Chris Singleton	1.00

Hitting Machines

These die-cut 1996 Fleer Ultra Series II insert cards

---

showcase the heaviest hitters on cards featuring a machine-gear design. The cards were seeded one per every 288 Series II packs.

		NM/M
Complete Set (10):		35.00
Common Player:		2.00
Gold Medallion:		2X
1	Albert Belle	2.00
2	Barry Bonds	12.00
3	Juan Gonzalez	2.50
4	Ken Griffey Jr.	6.00
5	Edgar Martinez	2.00
6	Rafael Palmeiro	3.00
7	Mike Piazza	6.00
8	Tim Salmon	2.00
9	Frank Thomas	4.00
10	Matt Williams	2.00

Home Run Kings Exchange Cards

Printed on cardboard, these super-scarce inserts are found at the rate of only one per 75 packs. Because of quality control problems, the cards were initially released as exchange cards, with instructions on back for a mail-in redemption offer for the actual wooden card. The redemption period expired Dec. 1, 1996.

		NM/M
Complete Set (12):		20.00
Common Player:		.75
1	Albert Belle	.75
2	Dante Bichette	.75
3	Barry Bonds	5.00
4	Jose Canseco	1.50
5	Juan Gonzalez	1.25
6	Ken Griffey Jr.	3.00
7	Mark McGwire	4.00
8	Manny Ramirez	2.50
9	Tim Salmon	.75
10	Frank Thomas	2.50
11	Mo Vaughn	.75
12	Matt Williams	.75

Home Run Kings

Printed on a thin wood veneer, these super-scarce inserts are seeded one per every 75 Series 1 packs. Because of quality control problems, the cards were initially released as exchange cards, with instructions on back for a mail-in redemption offer for the actual wooden card.

	NM/M
Complete Set (12):	50.00

Common Player:	2.50
Gold Medallions:	2X
1	Albert Belle	2.50
2	Dante Bichette	2.50
3	Barry Bonds	12.50
4	Jose Canseco	5.00
5	Juan Gonzalez	3.00
6	Ken Griffey Jr.	9.00
7	Mark McGwire	10.00
8	Manny Ramirez	6.50
9	Tim Salmon	2.50
10	Frank Thomas	6.50
11	Mo Vaughn	2.50
12	Matt Williams	2.50

On-Base Leaders

These 1996 Fleer Ultra Series II inserts feature 10 of the game's top on-base leaders. The cards were seeded one per every four packs.

		NM/M
Complete Set (10):		4.50
Common Player:		.25
Gold Medallions:		2X
1	Wade Boggs	.75
2	Barry Bonds	2.00
3	Tony Gwynn	.75
4	Rickey Henderson	.60
5	Chuck Knoblauch	.25
6	Edgar Martinez	.25
7	Mike Piazza	1.00
8	Tim Salmon	.25
9	Frank Thomas	.60
10	Jim Thome	.50

Power Plus

Etched-foil backgrounds, multiple player photos and a horizontal format are featured in this chase set. Stated odds of finding one of the dozen Power Plus cards are one per every 10 Series I packs.

		NM/M
Complete Set (12):		10.00
Common Player:		.40
Gold Medallions:		2X
1	Jeff Bagwell	1.25
2	Barry Bonds	3.00
3	Ken Griffey Jr.	2.00
4	Raul Mondesi	.40
5	Rafael Palmeiro	1.00
6	Mike Piazza	2.00
7	Manny Ramirez	1.25
8	Tim Salmon	.40
9	Reggie Sanders	.40
10	Frank Thomas	1.25
11	Larry Walker	.40
12	Matt Williams	.40

Prime Leather

An embossed leather-feel background is featured on these cards of top fielders, seeded one per every eight Series I packs, on average.

	NM/M
Complete Set (18):	17.50
Common Player:	.50
Gold Medallions:	2X

1 Ivan Rodriguez 1.50
2 Will Clark .50
3 Roberto Alomar .65
4 Cal Ripken Jr. 4.00
5 Wade Boggs 2.00
6 Ken Griffey Jr. 2.50
7 Kenny Lofton .50
8 Kirby Puckett 2.00
9 Tim Salmon .65
10 Mike Piazza 2.50
11 Mark Grace .50
12 Craig Biggio .50
13 Barry Larkin .50
14 Matt Williams .50
15 Barry Bonds 4.00
16 Tony Gwynn 2.00
17 Brian McRae .50
18 Raul Mondesi .50

Rawhide

Ten top fielders are featured on these 1996 Fleer Ultra Series II inserts. The cards were seeded one per every eight packs.

	NM/M
Complete Set (10):	10.00
Common Player:	.45
Gold Medallion:	2X

1 Roberto Alomar .65
2 Barry Bonds 3.00
3 Mark Grace .45
4 Ken Griffey Jr. 1.50
5 Kenny Lofton .45
6 Greg Maddux 1.00
7 Raul Mondesi .45
8 Mike Piazza 1.50
9 Cal Ripken Jr. 3.00
10 Matt Williams .45

RBI Kings

Retail packs are the exclusive provenance of this 10-card set of top RBI men. Stated odds of finding an RBI King card are one per every five Series I packs.

	NM/M
Complete Set (10):	4.00
Common Player:	.10
Gold Medallions:	2X

1 Derek Bell .10
2 Albert Belle .10
3 Dante Bichette .10
4 Barry Bonds 2.00
5 Jim Edmonds .15
6 Manny Ramirez 1.00
7 Reggie Sanders .10
8 Sammy Sosa 1.50
9 Frank Thomas 1.00
10 Mo Vaughn .10

R-E-S-P-E-C-T

These cards feature 10 players held in high esteem by their major league peers. The cards were seeded one per every 18 1996 Ultra Series II packs.

	NM/M
Complete Set (10):	20.00
Common Player:	.50
Gold Medallion:	2X

1 Joe Carter .50
2 Ken Griffey Jr. 3.00
3 Tony Gwynn 2.50
4 Greg Maddux 2.50
5 Eddie Murray 2.00
6 Kirby Puckett 2.50
7 Cal Ripken Jr. 5.00
8 Ryne Sandberg 2.50
9 Frank Thomas 2.00
10 Mo Vaughn .50

Rising Stars

Ten of baseball's best young players are spotlighted on these 1996 Fleer Ultra Series II inserts. Cards were seeded one per every four packs.

	NM/M
Complete Set (10):	4.00
Common Player:	.20
Gold Medallion:	2X

1 Garret Anderson .20
2 Marty Cordova .20
3 Jim Edmonds .35
4 Cliff Floyd .20
5 Brian Hunter .20
6 Chipper Jones 2.00
7 Ryan Klesko .20
8 Hideo Nomo .65
9 Manny Ramirez 1.25
10 Rondell White .20

Season Crowns

Large coats-of-arms printed on "Ultra Crystal" clear plastic are the background for player action photos in this insert set. Odds of one per every 10 Series II packs were stated.

	NM/M
Complete Set (10):	12.50
Common Player:	.75
Gold Medallions:	2X

1 Barry Bonds 4.00
2 Tony Gwynn 2.00
3 Randy Johnson 1.25
4 Kenny Lofton .75
5 Greg Maddux 2.00
6 Edgar Martinez .75
7 Hideo Nomo 1.00
8 Cal Ripken Jr. 4.00
9 Frank Thomas 1.25
10 Tim Wakefield .75

Thunderclap

The active career home run leaders are featured in this retail-exclusive Ultra insert set. Seeded only one per 72 packs, the Thunderclap cards have action photos on front with simulated lightning in the background and other graphic highlights rendered in holographic foil. Backs have a large portrait photo and career summary. Each of these scarce retail inserts can also be found in an even more elusive Gold Medallion version.

	NM/M
Complete Set (20):	45.00
Common Player:	1.00
Gold Medallion:	2X

1 Albert Belle 1.00
2 Barry Bonds 7.50
3 Bobby Bonilla 1.00
4 Jose Canseco 1.50
5 Joe Carter 1.00
6 Will Clark 1.00
7 Andre Dawson 1.50
8 Cecil Fielder 1.00
9 Andres Galarraga 1.00
10 Juan Gonzalez 1.50
11 Ken Griffey Jr. 5.00
12 Fred McGriff 1.00
13 Mark McGwire 6.00
14 Eddie Murray 2.50
15 Rafael Palmeiro 2.00
16 Kirby Puckett 4.00
17 Cal Ripken Jr. 7.50
18 Ryne Sandberg 4.00
19 Frank Thomas 2.50
20 Matt Williams 1.00

1997 Ultra Promo Strip

To introduce the concept of its new non-parallel parallel set, Fleer issued this three-card promo strip picturing regular (left), Gold Medallion (center) and Platinum Medallion (right) Cal Ripken, Jr., cards. Fronts have a "PROMOTIONAL SAMPLE," overprint in foil to match the cards' graphic highlights (silver, gold and prismatic). Backs, which have stats only through the 1995 season, have the same overprint in red.

	NM/M
Three-card Strip:	10.00

1997 Ultra

Ultra was issued in a 300-card Series 1 and 252-card Series 2, each with two parallel editions, Gold and Platinum, which feature "G" and "P" prefixes on the card number, respectively. Cards were issued in 10-card packs. Player names and the Ultra logo are in silver holographic foil. Backs contains complete year-by-year statistics, plus two photos of the player. This also marked the first time that the Gold and Platinum parallel sets displayed a different photo than the base cards. Inserts in Ultra included: Rookie Reflections, Double Trouble, Checklists, Season Crowns, RBI Kings, Power Plus, Fielder's Choice, Diamond Producers, HR Kings, and Baseball Rules.

	NM/M
Complete Set (553):	80.00
Common Player:	.05
Gold Medallion:	3X
Platinum Medallion:	25X
Series 1 Wax Pack (10):	1.25
Series 1 Wax Box (24):	20.00
Series 2 Wax Pack (10):	5.00
Series 2 Wax Box (24):	90.00

1 Roberto Alomar .25
2 Brady Anderson .05
3 Rocky Coppinger .05
4 Jeffrey Hammonds .05
5 Chris Hoiles .05
6 Eddie Murray .75
7 Mike Mussina .45
8 Jimmy Myers .05
9 Randy Myers .05
10 Arthur Rhodes .05
11 Cal Ripken Jr. 2.50
12 Jose Canseco .50
13 Roger Clemens 1.25
14 Tom Gordon .05
15 Jose Malave .05
16 Tim Naehring .05
17 Troy O'Leary .05
18 Bill Selby .05
19 Heathcliff Slocumb .05
20 Mike Stanley .05
21 Mo Vaughn .05
22 Garret Anderson .05
23 George Arias .05
24 Chili Davis .05
25 Jim Edmonds .25
26 Darin Erstad .25
27 Chuck Finley .05
28 Todd Greene .05
29 Troy Percival .05
30 Tim Salmon .05
31 Jeff Schmidt .05
32 Randy Velarde .05
33 Shad Williams .05
34 Wilson Alvarez .05
35 Harold Baines .05
36 James Baldwin .05
37 Mike Cameron .05
38 Ray Durham .05
39 Ozzie Guillen .05
40 Roberto Hernandez .05
41 Darren Lewis .05
42 Jose Munoz .05
43 Tony Phillips .05
44 Frank Thomas .75
45 Sandy Alomar Jr. .05
46 Albert Belle .05
47 Mark Carreon .05
48 Julio Franco .05
49 Orel Hershiser .05
50 Kenny Lofton .05
51 Jack McDowell .05
52 Jose Mesa .05
53 Charles Nagy .05
54 Manny Ramirez .75
55 Julian Tavarez .05
56 Omar Vizquel .05
57 Raul Casanova .05
58 Tony Clark .05
59 Travis Fryman .05
60 Bob Higginson .05
61 Melvin Nieves .05
62 Curtis Pride .05
63 Justin Thompson .05
64 Alan Trammell .05
65 Kevin Appier .05
66 Johnny Damon .35
67 Keith Lockhart .05
68 Jeff Montgomery .05
69 Jose Offerman .05
70 Bip Roberts .05
71 Jose Rosado .05
72 Chris Stynes .05
73 Mike Sweeney .05
74 Jeff Cirillo .05
75 Jeff D'Amico .05
76 John Jaha .05
77 Scott Karl .05
78 Mike Matheny .05
79 Ben McDonald .05
80 Matt Mieske .05
81 Marc Newfield .05
82 Dave Nilsson .05
83 Jose Valentin .05
84 Fernando Vina .05
85 Rick Aguilera .05
86 Marty Cordova .05
87 Chuck Knoblauch .05
88 Matt Lawton .05
89 Pat Meares .05
90 Paul Molitor .75
91 Greg Myers .05
92 Dan Naulty .05
93 Kirby Puckett 1.00
94 Frank Rodriguez .05
95 Wade Boggs 1.00
96 Cecil Fielder .05
97 Joe Girardi .05
98 Dwight Gooden .05
99 Derek Jeter 2.50
100 Tino Martinez .05
101 Ramiro Mendoza RC .05
102 Andy Pettitte .20
103 Mariano Rivera .15
104 Ruben Rivera .05
105 Kenny Rogers .05
106 Darryl Strawberry .05
107 Bernie Williams .05
108 Tony Batista .05
109 Geronimo Berroa .05
110 Bobby Chouinard .05
111 Brent Gates .05
112 Jason Giambi .05
113 Damon Mashore RC .05
114 Mark McGwire 2.00
115 Scott Spiezio .05
116 John Wasdin .05
117 Steve Wojciechowski .05
118 Ernie Young .05
119 Norm Charlton .05
120 Joey Cora .05
121 Ken Griffey Jr. 1.50
122 Sterling Hitchcock .05
123 Raul Ibanez .05
124 Randy Johnson .75
125 Edgar Martinez .05
126 Alex Rodriguez 2.00
127 Matt Wagner .05
128 Bob Wells .05
129 Dan Wilson .05
130 Will Clark .05
131 Kevin Elster .05
132 Juan Gonzalez .40
133 Rusty Greer .05
134 Darryl Hamilton .05
135 Mike Henneman .05
136 Ken Hill .05
137 Mark McLemore .05
138 Dean Palmer .05
139 Roger Pavlik .05
140 Ivan Rodriguez .65
141 Joe Carter .05
142 Carlos Delgado .50
143 Alex Gonzalez .05
144 Juan Guzman .05
145 Pat Hentgen .05
146 Marty Janzen .05
147 Otis Nixon .05
148 Charlie O'Brien .05
149 John Olerud .05
150 Robert Perez .05
151 Jermaine Dye .05
152 Tom Glavine .30
153 Andruw Jones .75
154 Chipper Jones 1.00
155 Ryan Klesko .05
156 Javier Lopez .05
157 Greg Maddux 1.00
158 Fred McGriff .05
159 Wonderful Monds .05
160 John Smoltz .05
161 Terrell Wade .05
162 Mark Wohlers .05
163 Brant Brown .05
164 Mark Grace .05
165 Tyler Houston .05
166 Robin Jennings .05
167 Jason Maxwell .05
168 Ryne Sandberg .05
169 Sammy Sosa 1.00
170 Amaury Telemaco .05
171 Steve Trachsel .05
172 Pedro Valdes RC .05
173 Tim Belk .05
174 Bret Boone .05
175 Jeff Brantley .05
176 Eric Davis .05
177 Barry Larkin .05
178 Chad Mottola .05
179 Mark Portugal .05
180 Reggie Sanders .05
181 John Smiley .05
182 Eddie Taubensee .05
183 Dante Bichette .05
184 Ellis Burks .05
185 Andres Galarraga .05
186 Curt Leskanic .05
187 Quinton McCracken .05
188 Jeff Reed .05
189 Kevin Ritz .05
190 Walt Weiss .05
191 Jamey Wright .05
192 Eric Young .05
193 Kevin Brown .05
194 Luis Castillo .05
195 Jeff Conine .05
196 Andre Dawson .25
197 Charles Johnson .05
198 Al Leiter .05
199 Ralph Milliard .05
200 Robb Nen .05
201 Edgar Renteria .05
202 Gary Sheffield .40
203 Bob Abreu .10
204 Jeff Bagwell .75
205 Derek Bell .05
206 Sean Berry .05
207 Richard Hidalgo .05
208 Todd Jones .05
209 Darryl Kile .05
210 Orlando Miller .05
211 Shane Reynolds .05
212 Billy Wagner .05
213 Donne Wall .05
214 Roger Cedeno .05
215 Greg Gagne .05
216 Karim Garcia .10
217 Wilton Guerrero .05
218 Todd Hollandsworth .05
219 Ramon Martinez .05
220 Raul Mondesi .05
221 Hideo Nomo .40
222 Chan Ho Park .05
223 Mike Piazza 1.50
224 Ismael Valdes .05
225 Moises Alou .05
226 Derek Aucoin .05
227 Yamil Benitez .05
228 Jeff Fassero .05
229 Darrin Fletcher .05
230 Mark Grudzielanek .05
231 Barry Manuel .05
232 Pedro Martinez .75
233 Henry Rodriguez .05
234 Ugueth Urbina .05
235 Rondell White .05
236 Carlos Baerga .05
237 John Franco .05
238 Bernard Gilkey .05
239 Todd Hundley .05
240 Butch Huskey .05
241 Jason Isringhausen .05
242 Lance Johnson .05
243 Bobby Jones .05
244 Alex Ochoa .05
245 Rey Ordonez .05
246 Paul Wilson .05
247 Ron Blazier .05
248 David Doster .05
249 Jim Eisenreich .05
250 Mike Grace .05
251 Mike Lieberthal .05
252 Wendell Magee .05
253 Mickey Morandini .05
254 Ricky Otero .05
255 Scott Rolen .60
256 Curt Schilling .20
257 Todd Zeile .05
258 Jermaine Allensworth .05
259 Trey Beamon .05
260 Carlos Garcia .05
261 Mark Johnson .05
262 Jason Kendall .05
263 Jeff King .05
264 Al Martin .05
265 Denny Neagle .05
266 Matt Ruebel .05
267 Marc Wilkins RC .05
268 Alan Benes .05
269 Dennis Eckersley .65
270 Ron Gant .05
271 Aaron Holbert .05
272 Brian Jordan .05
273 Ray Lankford .05
274 John Mabry .05
275 T.J. Mathews .05
276 Ozzie Smith 1.00
277 Todd Stottlemyre .05
278 Mark Sweeney .05
279 Andy Ashby .05
280 Steve Finley .05
281 John Flaherty .05
282 Chris Gomez .05
283 Tony Gwynn 1.00
284 Joey Hamilton .05
285 Rickey Henderson .75
286 Trevor Hoffman .05
287 Jason Thompson .05
288 Fernando Valenzuela .05
289 Greg Vaughn .05
290 Barry Bonds 2.50
291 Jay Canizaro .05
292 Jacob Cruz .05
293 Shawon Dunston .05
294 Shawn Estes .05
295 Mark Gardner .05
296 Marcus Jensen .05
297 Bill Mueller RC .35
298 Chris Singleton .05
299 Allen Watson .05
300 Matt Williams .05
301 Rod Beck .05
302 Jay Bell .05
303 Shawon Dunston .05
304 Reggie Jefferson .05
305 Darren Oliver .05
306 Benito Santiago .05
307 Gerald Williams .05
308 Damon Buford .05
309 Jeromy Burnitz .05
310 Sterling Hitchcock .05
311 Dave Hollins .05
312 Mel Rojas .05
313 Robin Ventura .05
314 David Wells .05
315 Cal Eldred .05
316 Gary Gaetti .05
317 John Hudek .05
318 Brian Johnson .05
319 Denny Neagle .05
320 Larry Walker .05
321 Russ Davis .05
322 Delino DeShields .05

No.	Player	Price
323	Charlie Hayes	.05
324	Jermaine Dye	.05
325	John Ericks	.05
326	Jeff Fassero	.05
327	Nomar Garciaparra	1.00
328	Willie Greene	.05
329	Greg McMichael	.05
330	Damion Easley	.05
331	Ricky Bones	.05
332	John Burkett	.05
333	Royce Clayton	.05
334	Greg Colbrunn	.05
335	Tony Eusebio	.05
336	Gregg Jefferies	.05
337	Wally Joyner	.05
338	Jim Leyritz	.05
339	Paul O'Neill	.05
340	Bruce Ruffin	.05
341	Michael Tucker	.05
342	Andy Benes	.05
343	Craig Biggio	.05
344	Rex Hudler	.05
345	Brad Radke	.05
346	Deion Sanders	.05
347	Moises Alou	.05
348	Brad Ausmus	.05
349	Armando Benitez	.05
350	Mark Gubicza	.05
351	Terry Steinbach	.05
352	Mark Whiten	.05
353	Ricky Bottalico	.05
354	Brian Giles RC	.75
355	Eric Karros	.05
356	Jimmy Key	.05
357	Carlos Perez	.05
358	Alex Fernandez	.05
359	J.T. Snow	.05
360	Bobby Bonilla	.05
361	Scott Brosius	.05
362	Greg Swindell	.05
363	Jose Vizcaino	.05
364	Matt Williams	.05
365	Darren Daulton	.05
366	Shane Andrews	.05
367	Jim Eisenreich	.05
368	Ariel Prieto	.05
369	Bob Tewksbury	.05
370	Mike Bordick	.05
371	Rheal Cormier	.05
372	Cliff Floyd	.05
373	David Justice	.05
374	John Wetteland	.05
375	Mike Blowers	.05
376	Jose Canseco	.50
377	Roger Clemens	1.25
378	Kevin Mitchell	.05
379	Todd Zeile	.05
380	Jim Thome	.60
381	Turk Wendell	.05
382	Rico Brogna	.05
383	Eric Davis	.05
384	Mike Lansing	.05
385	Devon White	.05
386	Marquis Grissom	.05
387	Todd Worrell	.05
388	Jeff Kent	.05
389	Mickey Tettleton	.05
390	Steve Avery	.05
391	David Cone	.05
392	Scott Cooper	.05
393	Lee Stevens	.05
394	Kevin Elster	.05
395	Tom Goodwin	.05
396	Shawn Green	.25
397	Pete Harnisch	.05
398	Eddie Murray	.75
399	Joe Randa	.05
400	Scott Sanders	.05
401	John Valentin	.05
402	Todd Jones	.05
403	Terry Adams	.05
404	Brian Hunter	.05
405	Pat Listach	.05
406	Kenny Lofton	.05
407	Hal Morris	.05
408	Ed Sprague	.05
409	Rich Becker	.05
410	Edgardo Alfonzo	.05
411	Albert Belle	.05
412	Jeff King	.05
413	Kirt Manwaring	.05
414	Jason Schmidt	.05
415	Allen Watson	.05
416	Lee Tinsley	.05
417	Brett Butler	.05
418	Carlos Garcia	.05
419	Mark Lemke	.05
420	Jaime Navarro	.05
421	David Segui	.05
422	Ruben Sierra	.05
423	B.J. Surhoff	.05
424	Julian Tavarez	.05
425	Billy Taylor	.05
426	Ken Caminiti	.05
427	Chuck Carr	.05
428	Benji Gil	.05
429	Terry Mulholland	.05
430	Mike Stanton	.05
431	Wil Cordero	.05
432	Chili Davis	.05
433	Mariano Duncan	.05
434	Orlando Merced	.05
435	Kent Mercker	.05
436	John Olerud	.05
437	Quilvio Veras	.05
438	Mike Fetters	.05
439	Glenallen Hill	.05
440	Bill Swift	.05
441	Tim Wakefield	.05
442	Pedro Astacio	.05
443	Vinny Castilla	.05
444	Doug Drabek	.05
445	Alan Embree	.05
446	Lee Smith	.05
447	Darryl Hamilton	.05
448	Brian McRae	.05
449	Mike Timlin	.05
450	Bob Wickman	.05
451	Jason Dickson	.05
452	Chad Curtis	.05
453	Mark Leiter	.05
454	Damon Berryhill	.05
455	Kevin Orie	.05
456	Dave Burba	.05
457	Chris Holt	.05
458	Ricky Ledee RC	.10
459	Mike Devereaux	.05
460	Pokey Reese	.05
461	Tim Raines	.05
462	Ryan Jones	.05
463	Shane Mack	.05
464	Darren Dreifort	.05
465	Mark Parent	.05
466	Mark Portugal	.05
467	Dante Powell	.05
468	Craig Grebeck	.05
469	Ron Villone	.05
470	Dmitri Young	.05
471	Shannon Stewart	.05
472	Rick Helling	.05
473	Bill Haselman	.05
474	Albie Lopez	.05
475	Glendon Rusch	.05
476	Derrick May	.05
477	Chad Ogea	.05
478	Kirk Reuter	.05
479	Chris Hammond	.05
480	Russ Johnson	.05
481	James Mouton	.05
482	Mike Macfarlane	.05
483	Scott Ruffcorn	.05
484	Jeff Frye	.05
485	Richie Sexson	.05
486	Emil Brown RC	.05
487	Desi Wilson	.05
488	Brent Gates	.05
489	Tony Graffanino	.05
490	Dan Miceli	.05
491	Orlando Cabrera RC	.65
492	Tony Womack RC	.20
493	Jerome Walton	.05
494	Mark Thompson	.05
495	Jose Guillen	.05
496	Willie Blair	.05
497	T.J. Staton RC	.05
498	Scott Kamieniecki	.05
499	Vince Coleman	.05
500	Jeff Abbott	.05
501	Chris Widger	.05
502	Kevin Tapani	.05
503	Carlos Castillo RC	.05
504	Luis Gonzalez	.05
505	Tim Belcher	.05
506	Armando Reynoso	.05
507	Jamie Moyer	.05
508	Randall Simon RC	.05
509	Vladimir Guerrero	.75
510	Wady Almonte RC	.05
511	Dustin Hermanson	.05
512	Deivi Cruz RC	.05
513	Luis Alicea	.05
514	Felix Heredia RC	.15
515	Don Slaught	.05
516	Shigetosi Hasegawa	.05
517	Matt Walbeck	.05
518	David Arias RC (Last name actually Ortiz.)	65.00
519	Brady Raggio RC	.05
520	Rudy Pemberton	.05
521	Wayne Kirby	.05
522	Calvin Maduro	.05
523	Mark Lewis	.05
524	Mike Jackson	.05
525	Sid Fernandez	.05
526	Mike Bielecki	.05
527	Bubba Trammell RC	.05
528	Brent Brede RC	.05
529	Matt Morris	.05
530	Joe Borowski	.05
531	Orlando Miller	.05
532	Jim Bullinger	.05
533	Robert Person	.05
534	Doug Glanville	.05
535	Terry Pendleton	.05
536	Jorge Posada	.05
537	Marc Sagmoen RC	.05
538	Fernando Tatis RC	.20
539	Aaron Sele	.05
540	Brian Banks	.05
541	Derrek Lee	.50
542	John Wasdin	.05
543	Justin Towle RC	.05
544	Pat Cline	.05
545	Dave Magadan	.05
546	Jeff Blauser	.05
547	Phil Nevin	.05
548	Todd Walker	.25
549	Elieser Marrero	.05
550	Bartolo Colon	.05
551	Jose Cruz Jr. RC	.50
552	Todd Dunwoody	.05
553	Hideki Irabu RC	.25

Gold Medallion Edition

A new concept in parallel editions was debuted by Ultra in Series I. While sharing the card numbers with regular-issue Ultra cards, the Gold Medallion Edition features a "G" prefix to the card number and gold-foil highlights on front. Unlike past parallels, however, the '97 Ultra Gold Medallion and Platinum Medallion inserts share a photograph which is entirely different from the regular Ultra base cards. Gold Medallion Edition cards are identified as such in the lower-right corner and were inserted at a rate of one per pack.

	NM/M
Complete Set (553):	100.00
Common Player:	.25
Stars/Rookies:	3X

Platinum Medallion Edition

A new concept in parallel editions was debuted by Ultra in Series I. While sharing the card numbers with regular-issue Ultra cards, the Platinum Medallion Edition features a "P" prefix to the card number and holographic-foil highlights on front. Unlike past parallels, however, the '97 Ultra Gold Medallion and Platinum Medallion inserts share a photograph which is entirely different from the regular Ultra base cards are identified as such in the lower-right corner and were inserted at a rate of one per 100 packs.

	NM/M
Common Player:	2.00
Stars/Rookies:	25X

Baseball Rules!

Baseball Rules was a 10-card insert that was found only in retail packs at a rate of one per 36 packs. The cards are die-cut with a player in front of a mound of baseballs with embossed seams on the front, while each card back explains a baseball term or rule.

		NM/M
Complete Set (10):		45.00
Common Player:		.50
1	Barry Bonds	10.00
2	Ken Griffey Jr.	6.00
3	Derek Jeter	10.00
4	Chipper Jones	5.00
5	Greg Maddux	5.00
6	Mark McGwire	7.50
7	Troy Percival	.50
8	Mike Piazza	6.00
9	Cal Ripken Jr.	10.00
10	Frank Thomas	4.00

Checklists

There are 10 Checklist cards in each series of Ultra baseball covering all regular-issue cards and inserts. The front of the card features a superstar, while the back contains a portion of the set checklist. The cards have the player's name and "CHECKLIST" in bold, all caps across the bottom in silver foil.

		NM/M
Complete Set (20):		5.00
Common Player:		.05
1	Dante Bichette	.05
2	Barry Bonds	.75
3	Ken Griffey Jr.	.35
4	Greg Maddux	.25
5	Mark McGwire	.50
6	Mike Piazza	.35
7	Cal Ripken Jr.	.75
8	John Smoltz	.05
9	Sammy Sosa	.25
10	Frank Thomas	.20
1	Andruw Jones	.20
2	Ken Griffey Jr.	.35
3	Frank Thomas	.20
4	Alex Rodriguez	.60
5	Cal Ripken Jr.	.75
6	Mike Piazza	.35
7	Greg Maddux	.25
8	Chipper Jones	.25
9	Derek Jeter	.75
10	Juan Gonzalez	.10

Diamond Producers

Printed on textured, uniform-like matterial, this 12-card insert contains some of the most consistent producers in baseball. Horizontal backs are conventionally printed with another color player photo on a pin-striped background and a few words about him. This was the most difficult insert Ultra foil-pack insert, with a ratio of one per 288.

		NM/M
Complete Set (12):		110.00
Common Player:		2.50
1	Jeff Bagwell	7.00
2	Barry Bonds	20.00
3	Ken Griffey Jr.	12.50
4	Chipper Jones	10.00
5	Kenny Lofton	2.50
6	Greg Maddux	10.00
7	Mark McGwire	15.00
8	Mike Piazza	12.50
9	Cal Ripken Jr.	20.00
10	Alex Rodriguez	15.00
11	Frank Thomas	7.50
12	Matt Williams	2.50

Double Trouble

Double Trouble is a 20-card, team color coded set pairing two stars from the same team on a horizontal front. These inserts were found every four packs.

		NM/M
Complete Set (20):		10.00
Common Player:		.15
1	Roberto Alomar, Cal Ripken Jr.	1.50
2	Mo Vaughn, Jose Canseco	.40
3	Jim Edmonds, Tim Salmon	.15
4	Harold Baines, Frank Thomas	.50
5	Albert Belle, Kenny Lofton	.15
6	Chuck Knoblauch, Marty Cordova	.15
7	Andy Pettitte, Derek Jeter	1.50
8	Jason Giambi, Mark McGwire	1.00
9	Ken Griffey Jr., Alex Rodriguez	1.00
10	Juan Gonzalez, Will Clark	.30
11	Greg Maddux, Chipper Jones	.60
12	Mark Grace, Sammy Sosa	.60
13	Dante Bichette, Andres Galarraga	.15
14	Jeff Bagwell, Derek Bell	.50
15	Hideo Nomo, Mike Piazza	.75
16	Henry Rodriguez, Moises Alou	.15
17	Rey Ordonez, Alex Ochoa	.15
18	Ray Lankford, Ron Gant	.15
19	Tony Gwynn, Rickey Henderson	.60
20	Barry Bonds, Matt Williams	1.50

Fame Game

This eight-card hobby-exclusive insert showcases players who have displayed Hall of Fame potential. The player photo on front and Fame Game logo are embossed and highlighted in gold and silver foil. Backs have a color portrait photo and a few words about the player. Cards were inserted 1:8 packs.

	NM/M
Complete Set (8):	20.00

	Player	Price
Common Player:		.35
1	Ken Griffey Jr.	1.75
2	Frank Thomas	1.00
3	Alex Rodriguez	2.00
4	Cal Ripken Jr.	3.00
5	Mike Piazza	1.75
6	Greg Maddux	1.25
7	Derek Jeter	3.00
8	Jeff Bagwell	1.00
9	Juan Gonzalez	.50
10	Albert Belle	.35
11	Tony Gwynn	1.25
12	Mark McGwire	2.00
13	Andy Pettitte	.45
14	Kenny Lofton	.35
15	Roberto Alomar	.40
16	Ryne Sandberg	1.25
17	Barry Bonds	3.00
18	Eddie Murray	1.00

Fielder's Choice

Fielder's Choice highlights 18 of the top defensive players in baseball. Fronts of the horizontal cards have a leather look and feel and are highlighted in gold foil. Backs are conventionally printed with another player photo and some words about his fielding ability. Fielder's Choice inserts were found every 144 packs.

		NM/M
Complete Set (18):		80.00
Common Player:		1.00
1	Roberto Alomar	1.50
2	Jeff Bagwell	6.00
3	Wade Boggs	7.50
4	Barry Bonds	15.00
5	Mark Grace	1.00
6	Ken Griffey Jr.	10.00
7	Marquis Grissom	1.00
8	Charles Johnson	1.00
9	Chuck Knoblauch	1.00
10	Barry Larkin	1.00
11	Kenny Lofton	1.00
12	Greg Maddux	7.50
13	Raul Mondesi	1.00
14	Rey Ordonez	1.00
15	Cal Ripken Jr.	15.00
16	Alex Rodriguez	12.50
17	Ivan Rodriguez	5.00
18	Matt Williams	1.00

Golden Prospects

This 10-card set was exclusive to hobby shop packs and highlighted the top young players in baseball. Action photos on front and portraits on back are set on a sepia background. Cards were inserted 1:4 packs.

		NM/M
Complete Set (10):		3.00
Common Player:		.25
1	Andruw Jones	1.50
2	Vladimir Guerrero	1.50
3	Todd Walker	.25
4	Karim Garcia	.25
5	Kevin Orie	.25
6	Brian Giles	.25
7	Jason Dickson	.25
8	Jose Guillen	.25
9	Ruben Rivera	.25
10	Derek Lee	1.00

Hitting Machines

This 36-card insert was only found in hobby packs and showcases the game's top hitters. Cards were inserted at a ratio of 1:36 packs.

		NM/M
Complete Set (18):		60.00
Common Player:		1.00
1	Andruw Jones	3.00
2	Ken Griffey Jr.	5.00
3	Frank Thomas	3.00
4	Alex Rodriguez	6.50
5	Cal Ripken Jr.	9.00
6	Mike Piazza	5.00
7	Derek Jeter	9.00
8	Albert Belle	1.00
9	Tony Gwynn	4.00
10	Jeff Bagwell	3.00
11	Mark McGwire	6.50
12	Kenny Lofton	1.00
13	Manny Ramirez	3.00
14	Roberto Alomar	1.25
15	Ryne Sandberg	4.00
16	Eddie Murray	3.00
17	Sammy Sosa	4.00
18	Ken Caminiti	1.00

HR Kings

HR Kings are printed on clear plastic with transparent refractive holofoil crowns and other objects in the plastic. Backs contain a white silhouette of the player with career summary and logos within the figure. Stated odds of finding an HR King card were one per 36 packs.

		NM/M
Complete Set (12):		30.00
Common Player:		1.00
1	Albert Belle	1.00
2	Barry Bonds	7.50
3	Juan Gonzalez	1.50
4	Ken Griffey Jr.	4.50
5	Todd Hundley	1.00
6	Ryan Klesko	1.00
7	Mark McGwire	6.00
8	Mike Piazza	4.50
9	Sammy Sosa	3.50
10	Frank Thomas	2.50
11	Mo Vaughn	1.00
12	Matt Williams	1.00

Leather Shop

Similar in design to the Power Plus insert in Series I, this 12-card insert salutes the game's top sluggers and was found only in hobby packs. Cards were inserted at a ratio of 1:8 packs. Front design features gold holographic foil graphics. Backs have another photo and a description of the player's skills.

		NM/M
Complete Set (12):		6.50
Common Player:		.25
1	Ken Griffey Jr.	.75
2	Frank Thomas	.50
3	Alex Rodriguez	1.00
4	Cal Ripken Jr.	1.50
5	Mike Piazza	.75
6	Chipper Jones	.65
7	Albert Belle	.25

Baseball's best fielders are honored in this 12-card hobby-exclusive insert. Cards were inserted at a ratio of 1:6 packs and feature an embossed grain-like finish on the fronts.

		NM/M
Complete Set (12):		9.00
Common Player:		.25
1	Ken Griffey Jr.	1.25
2	Alex Rodriguez	1.50
3	Cal Ripken Jr.	2.00
4	Derek Jeter	2.00
5	Juan Gonzalez	.45
6	Tony Gwynn	1.00
7	Jeff Bagwell	.75
8	Roberto Alomar	.40
9	Ryne Sandberg	1.00
10	Ken Caminiti	.25
11	Kenny Lofton	.25
12	John Smoltz	.25

Power Plus Series 1

Series 1 Power Plus is a 12-card insert utilizing silver rainbow holofoil in the background, with the featured player in the foreground. Backs have another action photo and the player's credentials. The insert captures power hitters that also excel in other areas of the game. Power Plus inserts can be found every 24 packs.

		NM/M
Complete Set (12):		15.00
Common Player:		.50
1	Jeff Bagwell	.75
2	Barry Bonds	3.00
3	Juan Gonzalez	.60
4	Ken Griffey Jr.	1.50
5	Chipper Jones	1.00
6	Mark McGwire	2.00
7	Mike Piazza	1.50
8	Cal Ripken Jr.	3.00
9	Alex Rodriguez	2.00
10	Sammy Sosa	1.00
11	Frank Thomas	.75
12	Matt Williams	.50

Power Plus Series 2

		NM/M
Complete Set (12):		30.00
Common Player:		1.00
1	Albert Belle	1.00
2	Barry Bonds	7.50
3	Juan Gonzalez	1.50
4	Ken Griffey Jr.	4.50
5	Todd Hundley	1.00
6	Ryan Klesko	1.00
7	Mark McGwire	6.00
8	Mike Piazza	4.50
9	Sammy Sosa	3.50
10	Frank Thomas	2.50
11	Mo Vaughn	1.00
12	Matt Williams	1.00

8	Juan Gonzalez	.35
9	Jeff Bagwell	.50
10	Mark McGwire	1.00
11	Mo Vaughn	.25
12	Barry Bonds	1.50

RBI Kings

Ten different players are featured in RBI Kings, which contain a metallic paisley background, with an English shield of armor and latin words in the background. RBI Kings were inserted every 18 packs of Series I.

		NM/M
Complete Set (10):		12.50
Common Player:		.75
1	Jeff Bagwell	1.50
2	Albert Belle	.75
3	Dante Bichette	.75
4	Barry Bonds	4.00
5	Jay Buhner	.75
6	Juan Gonzalez	1.00
7	Ken Griffey Jr.	2.50
8	Sammy Sosa	2.00
9	Frank Thomas	1.50
10	Mo Vaughn	.75

Rookie Reflections

Rookie Reflections features 10 of the 1996 season's top first-year players. Cards are inserted every four packs. Front features an action photo on a black-and-silver starburst pattern. Horizontal backs have another photo and a career summary of the prospect.

		NM/M
Complete Set (10):		3.50
Common Player:		.25
1	James Baldwin	.25
2	Jermaine Dye	.25
3	Darin Erstad	.40
4	Todd Hollandsworth	.25
5	Derek Jeter	3.00
6	Jason Kendall	.25
7	Alex Ochoa	.25
8	Rey Ordonez	.25
9	Edgar Renteria	.25
10	Scott Rolen	.50

Season Crowns

		NM/M
Complete Set (10):		20.00
Common Player:		.75
1	Barry Bonds	5.00
2	Mo Vaughn	.75
3	Mark McGwire	4.00
4	Jeff Bagwell	1.50
5	Juan Gonzalez	1.00
6	Alex Rodriguez	4.00
7	Chipper Jones	2.50
8	Ken Griffey Jr.	3.00
9	Mike Piazza	3.00
10	Frank Thomas	2.00

Top 30

This 30-card insert was found only in retail store packs

Season Crowns were found at a rate of one per eight packs of Ultra I Baseball. This etched, silver-foil insert contained 12 statistical leaders and award winners from the 1996 season.

		NM/M
Complete Set (12):		10.00
Common Player:		.50
1	Albert Belle	.50
2	Dante Bichette	.50
3	Barry Bonds	3.00
4	Kenny Lofton	.50
5	Edgar Martinez	.50
6	Mark McGwire	2.00
7	Andy Pettitte	.50
8	Mike Piazza	1.50
9	Alex Rodriguez	2.00
10	John Smoltz	.50
11	Sammy Sosa	1.25
12	Frank Thomas	1.00

Starring Role

Another hobby-exclusive insert, these 12 cards salute baseball's clutch performers and were found 1:288 packs.

		NM/M
Complete Set (12):		175.00
Common Player:		7.50
1	Andruw Jones	12.00
2	Ken Griffey Jr.	20.00
3	Frank Thomas	12.00
4	Alex Rodriguez	25.00
5	Cal Ripken Jr.	30.00
6	Mike Piazza	20.00
7	Greg Maddux	15.00
8	Chipper Jones	15.00
9	Derek Jeter	30.00
10	Juan Gonzalez	9.00
11	Albert Belle	7.50
12	Tony Gwynn	15.00

Thunderclap

This 10-card hobby-exclusive insert showcases hitters who strike fear in opposing pitchers. Cards were inserted 1:18 packs. Fronts are highlighted by streaks of gold prismatic foil lightning in a stormy sky. Backs have another player photo and a few words about him.

		NM/M
Complete Set (10):		20.00
Common Player:		.75
1	Barry Bonds	5.00
2	Mo Vaughn	.75
3	Mark McGwire	4.00
4	Jeff Bagwell	1.50
5	Juan Gonzalez	1.00
6	Alex Rodriguez	4.00
7	Chipper Jones	2.50
8	Ken Griffey Jr.	4.00
9	Mike Piazza	3.00
10	Frank Thomas	2.00

---

and salutes the 30 most collectible players in the game. Cards were inserted one per pack. A Top 30 Gold Medallion parallel set, die-cut around the top, was also produced and inserted 1:18 packs.

		NM/M
Complete Set (30):		12.00
Common Player:		.20
Gold Medallions:		6X
1	Andruw Jones	.75
2	Ken Griffey Jr.	1.25
3	Frank Thomas	.75
4	Alex Rodriguez	1.50
5	Cal Ripken Jr.	2.00
6	Mike Piazza	1.25
7	Greg Maddux	1.00
8	Chipper Jones	1.00
9	Derek Jeter	2.00
10	Juan Gonzalez	.40
11	Albert Belle	.20
12	Tony Gwynn	1.00
13	Jeff Bagwell	.75
14	Mark McGwire	1.50
15	Andy Pettitte	.30
16	Mo Vaughn	.20
17	Kenny Lofton	.20
18	Manny Ramirez	.75
19	Roberto Alomar	.40
20	Ryne Sandberg	1.00
21	Hideo Nomo	.40
22	Barry Bonds	2.00
23	Eddie Murray	.75
24	Ken Caminiti	.20
25	John Smoltz	.20
26	Pat Hentgen	.20
27	Todd Hollandsworth	.20
28	Matt Williams	.20
29	Bernie Williams	.20
30	Brady Anderson	.20

FanFest Larry Doby

In the same basic style as its regular-issue Ultra baseball series of 1997, Fleer issued a special Larry Doby card in conjunction with the All-Star FanFest in Cleveland, recognizing Doby's 50th anniversary of breaking the American League color barrier. The card has a black-and-white batting pose of Doby on front with his name, team and Fleer Ultra logo in red-shaded silver holographic foil. A color All-Star Game logo also appears on front. Backs have a red duotone photo of Doby fielding, his career stats and a few words about his career.

	NM/M
Larry Doby	4.00

1998 Ultra

Ultra was released in two series with a total of 501 cards: 250 in Series 1 and 251 in Series 2. Ten-card packs carried an SRP of $2.59. There were three parallel sets: Gold Medallion,

---

Platinum Medallion and Masterpieces. Series 1 has 210 regular cards, 25 Prospects (seeded 1:4 packs), 10 Season's Crowns (1:12) and five Checklists (1:8). Series 2 has 202 regular cards, 25 Pizzazz (1:4), 20 New Horizons and three checklists. Series 2 also added a Mike Piazza N.Y. Mets card as #501, inserted every 20 packs. Inserts in Series 1 include: Big Shots, Double Trouble, Kid Gloves, Back to the Future, Artistic Talents, Fall Classics, Power Plus, Prime Leather, Diamond Producers, Diamond Ink and Million Dollar Moments. Series 2 included: Notables, Rocket to Stardom, Millennium Men, Win Now, Ticket Studs, Diamond Immortals, Diamond Ink, Top 30 and 750 sequentially numbered Alex Rodriguez autographed promo cards.

		NM/M
Complete Set (501):		75.00
Common Player:		.05
Alex Rodriguez Auto. (750):		50.00
Pack (10):		1.25
Wax Box (24):		20.00
1	Ken Griffey Jr.	1.25
2	Matt Morris	.05
3	Roger Clemens	1.00
4	Matt Williams	.05
5	Roberto Hernandez	.05
6	Rondell White	.05
7	Tim Salmon	.05
8	Brad Radke	.05
9	Brett Butler	.05
10	Carl Everett	.05
11	Chili Davis	.05
12	Chuck Finley	.05
13	Darryl Kile	.05
14	Deivi Cruz	.05
15	Gary Gaetti	.05
16	Matt Stairs	.05
17	Pat Meares	.05
18	Will Cunnane	.05
19	Steve Woodard RC	.15
20	Andy Ashby	.05
21	Bobby Higginson	.05
22	Brian Jordan	.05
23	Craig Biggio	.25
24	Jim Edmonds	.05
25	Ryan McGuire	.05
26	Scott Hatteberg	.05
27	Willie Greene	.05
28	Albert Belle	.05
29	Ellis Burks	.05
30	Hideo Nomo	.40
31	Jeff Bagwell	.75
32	Kevin Brown	.05
33	Nomar Garciaparra	1.00
34	Pedro Martinez	.75
35	Raul Mondesi	.05
36	Ricky Bottalico	.05
37	Shawn Estes	.05
38	Shawon Dunston	.05
39	Terry Steinbach	.05
40	Tom Glavine	.25
41	Todd Dunwoody	.05
42	Deion Sanders	.05
43	Gary Sheffield	.45
44	Mike Lansing	.05
45	Mike Lieberthal	.05
46	Paul Sorrento	.05
47	Paul O'Neill	.05
48	Tom Goodwin	.05
49	Andruw Jones	.75
50	Barry Bonds	2.00
51	Bernie Williams	.05
52	Jeremi Gonzalez	.05
53	Mike Piazza	1.25
54	Russ Davis	.05
55	Vinny Castilla	.05
56	Rod Beck	.05
57	Andres Galarraga	.05
58	Ben McDonald	.05
59	Billy Wagner	.05
60	Charles Johnson	.05
61	Fred McGriff	.05
62	Dean Palmer	.05

No.	Player	Price
63	Frank Thomas	.75
64	Ismael Valdes	.05
65	Mark Bellhorn	.05
66	Jeff King	.05
67	John Wetteland	.05
68	Mark Grace	.05
69	Mark Kotsay	.05
70	Scott Rolen	.60
71	Todd Hundley	.05
72	Todd Worrell	.05
73	Wilson Alvarez	.05
74	Bobby Jones	.05
75	Jose Canseco	.05
76	Kevin Appier	.05
77	Neifi Perez	.05
78	Paul Molitor	.75
79	Quilvio Veras	.05
80	Randy Johnson	.75
81	Glendon Rusch	.05
82	Curt Schilling	.15
83	Alex Rodriguez	1.50
84	Rey Ordonez	.05
85	Jeff Juden	.05
86	Mike Cameron	.05
87	Ryan Klesko	.05
88	Trevor Hoffman	.05
89	Chuck Knoblauch	.05
90	Larry Walker	.05
91	Mark McLemore	.05
92	B.J. Surhoff	.05
93	Darren Daulton	.05
94	Ray Durham	.05
95	Sammy Sosa	1.00
96	Eric Young	.05
97	Gerald Williams	.05
98	Javy Lopez	.05
99	John Smiley	.05
100	Juan Gonzalez	.40
101	Shawn Green	.30
102	Charles Nagy	.05
103	David Justice	.05
104	Joey Hamilton	.05
105	Pat Hentgen	.05
106	Raul Casanova	.05
107	Tony Phillips	.05
108	Tony Gwynn	1.00
109	Will Clark	.05
110	Jason Giambi	.50
111	Jay Bell	.05
112	Johnny Damon	.30
113	Alan Benes	.05
114	Jeff Suppan	.05
115	Kevin Polcovich RC	.05
116	Shigetosi Hasegawa	.05
117	Steve Finley	.05
118	Tony Clark	.05
119	David Cone	.05
120	Jose Guillen	.05
121	Kevin Millwood RC	1.00
122	Greg Maddux	1.00
123	Dave Nilsson	.05
124	Hideki Irabu	.05
125	Jason Kendall	.05
126	Jim Thome	.60
127	Delino DeShields	.05
128	Edgar Renteria	.05
129	Edgardo Alfonzo	.05
130	J.T. Snow	.05
131	Jeff Abbott	.05
132	Jeffrey Hammonds	.05
133	Rich Loiselle	.05
134	Vladimir Guerrero	.75
135	Jay Buhner	.05
136	Jeff Cirillo	.05
137	Jeromy Burnitz	.05
138	Mickey Morandini	.05
139	Tino Martinez	.05
140	Jeff Shaw	.05
141	Rafael Palmeiro	.65
142	Bobby Bonilla	.05
143	Cal Ripken Jr.	2.00
144	Chad Fox RC	.05
145	Dante Bichette	.05
146	Dennis Eckersley	.65
147	Mariano Rivera	.15
148	Mo Vaughn	.05
149	Reggie Sanders	.05
150	Derek Jeter	2.00
151	Rusty Greer	.05
152	Brady Anderson	.05
153	Brett Tomko	.05
154	Jaime Navarro	.05
155	Kevin Orie	.05
156	Roberto Alomar	.20
157	Edgar Martinez	.05
158	John Olerud	.05
159	John Smoltz	.05
160	Ryne Sandberg	1.00
161	Billy Taylor	.05
162	Chris Holt	.05
163	Damion Easley	.05
164	Darin Erstad	.25
165	Joe Carter	.05
166	Kelvim Escobar	.05
167	Ken Caminiti	.05
168	Pokey Reese	.05
169	Ray Lankford	.05
170	Livan Hernandez	.05
171	Steve Kline	.05
172	Tom Gordon	.05
173	Travis Fryman	.05
174	Al Martin	.05
175	Andy Pettitte	.25
176	Jeff Kent	.05
177	Jimmy Key	.05
178	Mark Grudzielanek	.05
179	Tony Saunders	.05
180	Barry Larkin	.05
181	Bubba Trammell	.05
182	Carlos Delgado	.50
183	Carlos Baerga	.05
184	Derek Bell	.05
185	Henry Rodriguez	.05
186	Jason Dickson	.05
187	Ron Gant	.05
188	Tony Womack	.05
189	Justin Thompson	.05
190	Fernando Tatis	.05
191	Mark Wohlers	.05
192	Takashi Kashiwada	.05
193	Garret Anderson	.05
194	Jose Cruz, Jr.	.50
195	Ricardo Rincon	.05
196	Tim Naehring	.05
197	Moises Alou	.05
198	Eric Karros	.05
199	John Jaha	.05
200	Marty Cordova	.05
201	Travis Lee	.10
202	Mark Davis	.05
203	Vladimir Nunez	.05
204	Stanton Cameron	.05
205	Mike Stoner RC	.05
206	Rolando Arrojo RC	.40
207	Rick White	.05
208	Luis Polonia	.05
209	Greg Blosser	.05
210	Cesar Devarez	.05
211	Jeff Bagwell (Season Crown)	1.00
212	Barry Bonds (Season Crown)	3.00
213	Roger Clemens (Season Crown)	1.75
214	Nomar Garciaparra (Season Crown)	1.50
215	Ken Griffey Jr. (Season Crown)	2.00
216	Tony Gwynn (Season Crown)	1.50
217	Randy Johnson (Season Crown)	1.00
218	Mark McGwire (Season Crown)	3.00
219	Scott Rolen (Season Crown)	.75
220	Frank Thomas (Season Crown)	1.25
221	Matt Perisho (Prospect)	.25
222	Wes Helms (Prospect)	.25
223	David Dellucci RC (Prospect)	.25
224	Todd Helton (Prospect)	1.00
225	Brian Rose (Prospect)	.25
226	Aaron Boone (Prospect)	.25
227	Keith Foulke (Prospect)	.25
228	Homer Bush (Prospect)	.25
229	Shannon Stewart (Prospect)	.25
230	Richard Hidalgo (Prospect)	.25
231	Russ Johnson (Prospect)	.25
232	Henry Blanco RC (Prospect)	.25
233	Paul Konerko (Prospect)	.35
234	Antone Williamson (Prospect)	.25
235	Shane Bowers RC (Prospect)	.25
236	Jose Vidro (Prospect)	.25
237	Derek Wallace (Prospect)	.25
238	Ricky Ledee (Prospect)	.25
239	Ben Grieve (Prospect)	.25
240	Lou Collier (Prospect)	.25
241	Derrek Lee (Prospect)	.65
242	Ruben Rivera (Prospect)	.25
243	Jorge Velandia (Prospect)	.25
244	Andrew Vessel (Prospect)	.25
245	Chris Carpenter (Prospect)	.25
246	Checklist (Ken Griffey Jr.)	.65
247	Checklist (Andruw Jones)	.50
248	Checklist (Alex Rodriguez)	.75
249	Checklist (Frank Thomas)	.60
250	Checklist (Cal Ripken Jr.)	1.00
251	Carlos Perez	.05
252	Larry Sutton	.05
253	Brad Rigby	.05
254	Wally Joyner	.05
255	Todd Stottlemyre	.05
256	Nerio Rodriguez	.05
257	Jeff Frye	.05
258	Pedro Astacio	.05
259	Cal Eldred	.05
260	Chili Davis	.05
261	Freddy Garcia	.05
262	Bobby Witt	.05
263	Michael Coleman	.05
264	Mike Caruso	.05
265	Mike Lansing	.05
266	Dennis Reyes	.05
267	F.P. Santangelo	.05
268	Darryl Hamilton	.05
269	Mike Fetters	.05
270	Charlie Hayes	.05
271	Royce Clayton	.05
272	Doug Drabek	.05
273	James Baldwin	.05
274	Brian Hunter	.05
275	Chan Ho Park	.05
276	John Franco	.05
277	David Wells	.05
278	Eli Marrero	.05
279	Kerry Wood	.40
280	Donnie Sadler	.05
281	Scott Winchester RC	.05
282	Hal Morris	.05
283	Brad Fullmer	.05
284	Bernard Gilkey	.05
285	Ramiro Mendoza	.05
286	Kevin Brown	.05
287	David Segui	.05
288	Willie McGee	.05
289	Darren Oliver	.05
290	Antonio Alfonseca	.05
291	Eric Davis	.05
292	Mickey Morandini	.05
293	Frank Catalanotto RC	.20
294	Derrek Lee	.50
295	Todd Zeile	.05
296	Chuck Knoblauch	.05
297	Wilson Delgado	.05
298	Raul Ibanez	.05
299	Orel Hershiser	.05
300	Ozzie Guillen	.05
301	Aaron Sele	.05
302	Joe Carter	.05
303	Darryl Kile	.05
304	Shane Reynolds	.05
305	Todd Dunn	.05
306	Bob Abreu	.10
307	Doug Strange	.05
308	Jose Canseco	.50
309	Lance Johnson	.05
310	Harold Baines	.05
311	Todd Pratt	.05
312	Greg Colbrunn	.05
313	Masato Yoshii RC	.25
314	Felix Heredia	.05
315	Dennis Martinez	.05
316	Geronimo Berroa	.05
317	Darren Lewis	.05
318	Billy Ripken	.05
319	Enrique Wilson	.05
320	Alex Ochoa	.05
321	Doug Glanville	.05
322	Mike Stanley	.05
323	Gerald Williams	.05
324	Pedro Martinez	.75
325	Jaret Wright	.05
326	Terry Pendleton	.05
327	LaTroy Hawkins	.05
328	Emil Brown	.05
329	Walt Weiss	.05
330	Omar Vizquel	.05
331	Carl Everett	.05
332	Fernando Vina	.05
333	Mike Blowers	.05
334	Dwight Gooden	.05
335	Mark Lewis	.05
336	Jim Leyritz	.05
337	Kenny Lofton	.05
338	John Halama RC	.05
339	Jose Valentin	.05
340	Desi Relaford	.05
341	Dante Powell	.05
342	Ed Sprague	.05
343	Reggie Jefferson	.05
344	Mike Hampton	.05
345	Marquis Grissom	.05
346	Heathcliff Slocumb	.05
347	Francisco Cordova	.05
348	Ken Cloude	.05
349	Benito Santiago	.05
350	Denny Neagle	.05
351	Sean Casey	.15
352	Robb Nen	.05
353	Orlando Merced	.05
354	Adrian Brown	.05
355	Gregg Jefferies	.05
356	Otis Nixon	.05
357	Michael Tucker	.05
358	Eric Milton	.05
359	Travis Fryman	.05
360	Gary DiSarcina	.05
361	Mario Valdez	.05
362	Craig Counsell	.05
363	Jose Offerman	.05
364	Tony Fernandez	.05
365	Jason McDonald	.05
366	Sterling Hitchcock	.05
367	Donovan Osborne	.05
368	Troy Percival	.05
369	Henry Rodriguez	.05
370	Dmitri Young	.05
371	Jay Powell	.05
372	Jeff Conine	.05
373	Orlando Cabrera	.10
374	Butch Huskey	.05
375	Mike Lowell RC	.50
376	Kevin Young	.05
377	Jamie Moyer	.05
378	Jeff D'Amico	.05
379	Scott Erickson	.05
380	Magglio Ordonez RC	1.50
381	Melvin Nieves	.05
382	Ramon Martinez	.05
383	A.J. Hinch	.05
384	Jeff Brantley	.05
385	Kevin Elster	.05
386	Allen Watson	.05
387	Moises Alou	.05
388	Jeff Blauser	.05
389	Pete Harnisch	.05
390	Shane Andrews	.05
391	Rico Brogna	.05
392	Stan Javier	.05
393	David Howard	.05
394	Darryl Strawberry	.05
395	Kent Mercker	.05
396	Juan Encarnacion	.05
397	Sandy Alomar	.05
398	Al Leiter	.05
399	Tony Graffanino	.05
400	Terry Adams	.05
401	Bruce Aven	.05
402	Derrick Gibson	.05
403	Jose Cabrera	.05
404	Rich Becker	.05
405	David Ortiz	.50
406	Brian McRae	.05
407	Bobby Estalella	.05
408	Bill Mueller	.05
409	Dennis Eckersley	.65
410	Sandy Martinez	.05
411	Jose Vizcaino	.05
412	Jermaine Allensworth	.05
413	Miguel Tejada	.20
414	Turner Ward	.05
415	Glenallen Hill	.05
416	Lee Stevens	.05
417	Cecil Fielder	.05
418	Ruben Sierra	.05
419	Jon Nunnally	.05
420	Rod Myers	.05
421	Dustin Hermanson	.05
422	James Mouton	.05
423	Dan Wilson	.05
424	Roberto Kelly	.05
425	Antonio Osuna	.05
426	Jacob Cruz	.05
427	Brent Mayne	.05
428	Matt Karchner	.05
429	Damian Jackson	.05
430	Roger Cedeno	.05
431	Rickey Henderson	.75
432	Joe Randa	.05
433	Greg Vaughn	.05
434	Andres Galarraga	.05
435	Rod Beck	.05
436	Curtis Goodwin	.05
437	Brad Ausmus	.05
438	Bob Hamelin	.05
439	Todd Walker	.05
440	Scott Brosius	.05
441	Lenny Dykstra	.05
442	Abraham Nunez	.05
443	Brian Johnson	.05
444	Randy Myers	.05
445	Bret Boone	.15
446	Oscar Henriquez	.05
447	Mike Sweeney	.05
448	Kenny Rogers	.05
449	Mark Langston	.05
450	Luis Gonzalez	.05
451	John Burkett	.05
452	Bip Roberts	.05
453	Travis Lee (New Horizons)	.15
454	Felix Rodriguez (New Horizons)	.05
455	Andy Benes (New Horizons)	.05
456	Willie Blair (New Horizons)	.05
457	Brian Anderson (New Horizons)	.05
458	Jay Bell (New Horizons)	.05
459	Matt Williams (New Horizons)	.05
460	Devon White (New Horizons)	.05
461	Karim Garcia (New Horizons)	.10
462	Jorge Fabregas (New Horizons)	.05
463	Wilson Alvarez (New Horizons)	.05
464	Roberto Hernandez (New Horizons)	.05
465	Tony Saunders (New Horizons)	.05
466	Rolando Arrojo RC (New Horizons)	.35
467	Wade Boggs (New Horizons)	1.00
468	Fred McGriff (New Horizons)	.05
469	Paul Sorrento (New Horizons)	.05
470	Kevin Stocker (New Horizons)	.05
471	Bubba Trammell (New Horizons)	.05
472	Quinton McCracken (New Horizons)	.05
473	Checklist (Ken Griffey Jr.)	.65
474	Checklist (Cal Ripken Jr.)	1.00
475	Checklist (Frank Thomas)	.60
476	Ken Griffey Jr. (Pizzazz)	1.75
477	Cal Ripken Jr. (Pizzazz)	3.00
478	Frank Thomas (Pizzazz)	1.25
479	Alex Rodriguez (Pizzazz)	2.00
480	Nomar Garciaparra (Pizzazz)	1.50
481	Derek Jeter (Pizzazz)	3.00
482	Andruw Jones (Pizzazz)	1.00
483	Chipper Jones (Pizzazz)	1.50
484	Greg Maddux (Pizzazz)	1.50
485	Mike Piazza (Pizzazz)	1.75
486	Juan Gonzalez (Pizzazz)	.50
487	Jose Cruz (Pizzazz)	.50
488	Jaret Wright (Pizzazz)	.50
489	Hideo Nomo (Pizzazz)	.60
490	Scott Rolen (Pizzazz)	.65
491	Tony Gwynn (Pizzazz)	1.50
492	Roger Clemens (Pizzazz)	1.60
493	Darin Erstad (Pizzazz)	.50
494	Mark McGwire (Pizzazz)	2.00
495	Jeff Bagwell (Pizzazz)	1.00
496	Mo Vaughn (Pizzazz)	.50
497	Albert Belle (Pizzazz)	.50
498	Kenny Lofton (Pizzazz)	.50
499	Ben Grieve (Pizzazz)	.50
500	Barry Bonds (Pizzazz)	2.50
501	Mike Piazza (Mets)	1.50

	NM/M
Common Player:	5.00
Stars/RC's:	25X
Checklists:	25X
Season Crowns:	8X
Prospects:	8X
Pizzazz:	8X

Masterpiece

This top of the line parallel to '98 Ultra consists of a 1 of 1 version of each regular card.

	NM/M
Common Player:	50.00

Artistic Talents

This 18-card insert featured top players in the game on a canvas-like surface with the insert name in silver holographic letters across the top. The backs are done in black and white and numbered with an "AT" suffix.

		NM/M
Complete Set (18):		12.00
Common Player:		.40
Inserted 1:8		
1	Ken Griffey Jr.	1.00
2	Andruw Jones	.60
3	Alex Rodriguez	1.25
4	Frank Thomas	.60
5	Cal Ripken Jr.	1.50
6	Derek Jeter	1.50
7	Chipper Jones	.75
8	Greg Maddux	.75
9	Mike Piazza	1.00
10	Albert Belle	.40
11	Darin Erstad	.50
12	Juan Gonzalez	.50
13	Jeff Bagwell	.60
14	Tony Gwynn	.75
15	Mark McGwire	1.25
16	Scott Rolen	.50
17	Barry Bonds	1.50
18	Kenny Lofton	.40

Gold Medallion

This parallel to the Ultra set is found seeded on a one per pack ratio. Cards are similar to the regular-issue Ultra except for a gold presentation of the embossed player name on front and a shower of gold specks in the photo background. Backs have a "G" suffix to the card number and a "GOLD MEDALLION EDITION" notation at bottom. The short-printed subset cards from the regular Ultra edition are not short-printed in Gold Medallion.

	NM/M
Common Player:	.25
Stars/RC's:	2X
Checklists:	2X
Season Crowns:	1X
Prospects:	1X
Pizzazz:	1X

Platinum Medallion

Insertion odds on this super-scarce insert set are not given but each card is produced and serially numbered in an edition of only 100 (Series 1) or 98 (Series 2). Fronts are similar to regular Ultra cards except the photo is black-and-white and the name is rendered in silver prismatic foil. Backs are in color with the serial number printed in silver foil at bottom. Series 2 checklist cards #473-475 were not printed in Platinum, and the short-prints from the regular issue are not short-printed in this parallel edition.

Back to the Future

This 15-card insert was printed in a horizontal format with a baseball field background. Cards were numbered with a "BF" suffix.

		NM/M
Complete Set (15):		4.00
Common Player:		.10
Inserted 1:6		
1	Andruw Jones	.50
2	Alex Rodriguez	1.00
3	Derek Jeter	1.50
4	Darin Erstad	.25
5	Mike Cameron	.05

		NM/M
6	Scott Rolen	.35
7	Nomar Garciaparra	.75
8	Hideki Irabu	.10
9	Jose Cruz, Jr.	.10
10	Vladimir Guerrero	.50
11	Mark Kotsay	.10
12	Tony Womack	.10
13	Jason Dickson	.10
14	Jose Guillen	.10
15	Tony Clark	.10

Big Shots

Big Shots is a 15-card insert displaying some of the top home run hitters in baseball. A generic stadium is pictured across the bottom with the insert name running up the left side. Cards are numbered with a "BS" suffix and inserted one per four Series 1 packs.

		NM/M
Complete Set (15):		4.00
Common Player:		.10
Inserted 1:4		
1	Ken Griffey Jr.	.75
2	Frank Thomas	.35
3	Chipper Jones	.50
4	Albert Belle	.10
5	Juan Gonzalez	.25
6	Jeff Bagwell	.35
7	Mark McGwire	1.00
8	Barry Bonds	1.50
9	Manny Ramirez	.35
10	Mo Vaughn	.10
11	Matt Williams	.10
12	Jim Thome	.30
13	Tino Martinez	.10
14	Mike Piazza	.75
15	Tony Clark	.10

Diamond Immortals

This Series 2 insert showcases 15 top players on an intricate silver holographic foil design. Cards are numbered with a "DI" suffix.

		NM/M
Complete Set (15):		330.00
Common Player:		7.50
Inserted 1:288		
1	Ken Griffey Jr.	30.00
2	Frank Thomas	12.50
3	Alex Rodriguez	40.00
4	Cal Ripken Jr.	50.00
5	Mike Piazza	30.00
6	Mark McGwire	40.00
7	Greg Maddux	20.00
8	Andruw Jones	12.50
9	Chipper Jones	20.00
10	Derek Jeter	50.00
11	Tony Gwynn	20.00
12	Juan Gonzalez	9.00
13	Jose Cruz	7.50
14	Roger Clemens	25.00
15	Barry Bonds	50.00

Diamond Producers

This 15-card insert captures players on a prismatic silver design, with a wood back-

drop and a black felt frame around the border. Cards were seeded one per 288 Series 1 packs and numbered with a "DP" suffix.

		NM/M
Complete Set (15):		180.00
Common Player:		7.50
Inserted 1:288		
1	Ken Griffey Jr.	30.00
2	Andruw Jones	12.50
3	Alex Rodriguez	40.00
4	Frank Thomas	12.50
5	Cal Ripken Jr.	50.00
6	Derek Jeter	50.00
7	Chipper Jones	20.00
8	Greg Maddux	20.00
9	Mike Piazza	30.00
10	Juan Gonzalez	9.00
11	Jeff Bagwell	12.50
12	Tony Gwynn	20.00
13	Mark McGwire	40.00
14	Barry Bonds	50.00
15	Jose Cruz, Jr.	7.50

Double Trouble

Double Trouble includes 20 cards and pairs teammates on a horizontal format with the team's logo and the insert name featured in a silver holographic circle in the middle. These are numbered with a "DT" suffix and exclusive to Series 1 packs.

		NM/M
Complete Set (20):		12.00
Common Player:		.15
Inserted 1:4		
1	Ken Griffey Jr., Alex Rodriguez	1.25
2	Vladimir Guerrero, Pedro Martinez	.60
3	Andruw Jones, Kenny Lofton	.60
4	Chipper Jones, Greg Maddux	.65
5	Derek Jeter, Tino Martinez	1.50
6	Frank Thomas, Albert Belle	.60
7	Cal Ripken Jr., Roberto Alomar	1.50
8	Mike Piazza, Hideo Nomo	1.00
9	Darin Erstad, Jason Dickson	.15
10	Juan Gonzalez, Ivan Rodriguez	.25
11	Jeff Bagwell, Darryl Kile	.60
12	Tony Gwynn, Steve Finley	.65
13	Mark McGwire, Ray Lankford	1.00
14	Barry Bonds, Jeff Kent	1.50
15	Andy Pettitte, Bernie Williams	.25
16	Mo Vaughn, Nomar Garciaparra	.65
17	Matt Williams, Jim Thome	.15
18	Hideki Irabu, Mariano Rivera	.25
19	Roger Clemens, Jose Cruz, Jr.	.75
20	Manny Ramirez, David Justice	.60

Fall Classics

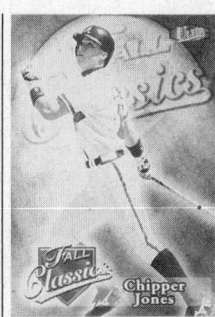

This Series 1 insert pictures 15 stars on a green holographic background. They are numbered with a "FC" suffix.

		NM/M
Complete Set (15):		35.00
Common Player:		1.00
Inserted 1:18		
1	Ken Griffey Jr.	3.00
2	Andruw Jones	1.50
3	Alex Rodriguez	4.00
4	Frank Thomas	1.50
5	Cal Ripken Jr.	5.00
6	Derek Jeter	5.00
7	Chipper Jones	2.00
8	Greg Maddux	2.00
9	Mike Piazza	4.00
10	Albert Belle	1.00
11	Juan Gonzalez	1.00
12	Jeff Bagwell	1.50
13	Tony Gwynn	2.00
14	Mark McGwire	3.00
15	Barry Bonds	5.00

Kid Gloves

Kid Gloves features top fielders on an embossed glove background. Exclusive to Series 1 packs, they are numbered with a "KG" suffix.

		NM/M
Complete Set (12):		9.00
Common Player:		.25
Inserted 1:8		
1	Andruw Jones	.75
2	Alex Rodriguez	2.00
3	Derek Jeter	3.00
4	Chipper Jones	1.00
5	Darin Erstad	.35
6	Todd Walker	.25
7	Scott Rolen	.65
8	Nomar Garciaparra	1.00
9	Jose Cruz, Jr.	.25
10	Charles Johnson	.25
11	Rey Ordonez	.25
12	Vladimir Guerrero	.75

Millennium Men

Millenium Men is a hobby-only insert exclusive to Series 2 packs. The tri-fold cards feature an embossed wax seal design and can be unfolded to reveal another shot of the player, team logo and statistics. They are numbered with a "MM" suffix.

	NM/M
Complete Set (15):	30.00

		.75
Common Player:		
Inserted 1:35		
1	Jose Cruz	.75
2	Ken Griffey Jr.	3.50
3	Cal Ripken Jr.	6.00
4	Derek Jeter	6.00
5	Andruw Jones	2.00
6	Alex Rodriguez	4.50
7	Chipper Jones	2.50
8	Scott Rolen	1.00
9	Nomar Garciaparra	2.50
10	Frank Thomas	2.00
11	Mike Piazza	3.50
12	Greg Maddux	2.50
13	Juan Gonzalez	1.00
14	Ben Grieve	.75
15	Jaret Wright	.75

Notables

This insert pictures a player on a holographic background with either an American League or National League logo in the background. Notables were seeded in Series 2 packs and numbered with a "N" suffix.

		NM/M
Complete Set (20):		13.50
Common Player:		.20
Inserted 1:4		
1	Frank Thomas	.50
2	Ken Griffey Jr.	1.25
3	Edgar Renteria	.20
4	Albert Belle	.20
5	Juan Gonzalez	.30
6	Jeff Bagwell	.50
7	Mark McGwire	1.50
8	Barry Bonds	2.25
9	Scott Rolen	.40
10	Mo Vaughn	.20
11	Andruw Jones	.50
12	Chipper Jones	.75
13	Tino Martinez	.20
14	Mike Piazza	1.25
15	Tony Clark	.20
16	Jose Cruz	.20
17	Nomar Garciaparra	.75
18	Cal Ripken Jr.	2.25
19	Alex Rodriguez	1.50
20	Derek Jeter	2.25

Power Plus

This insert is exclusive to Series 1 packs. Cards picture the player on an embossed blue background featuring plus signs. These are numbered with a "PP" suffix.

		NM/M
Complete Set (10):		16.00
Common Player:		1.00
Inserted 1:36		
1	Ken Griffey Jr.	4.00
2	Andruw Jones	2.00
3	Alex Rodriguez	3.00
4	Frank Thomas	2.00
5	Mike Piazza	3.00
6	Albert Belle	1.00
7	Juan Gonzalez	1.25
8	Jeff Bagwell	2.00
9	Barry Bonds	5.00
10	Jose Cruz, Jr.	1.00

Prime Leather

This insert features top fielders on a leather-like card stock, with a large baseball in the background. Cards are seeded in Series 1 packs and numbered with a "PL" suffix.

		NM/M
Complete Set (18):		135.00
Common Player:		2.00
Inserted 1:144		
1	Ken Griffey Jr.	12.50
2	Andruw Jones	7.50
3	Alex Rodriguez	15.00
4	Frank Thomas	7.50
5	Cal Ripken Jr.	20.00
6	Derek Jeter	20.00
7	Chipper Jones	10.00
8	Greg Maddux	10.00
9	Mike Piazza	12.50
10	Albert Belle	2.00
11	Darin Erstad	3.00
12	Juan Gonzalez	3.00
13	Jeff Bagwell	7.50
14	Tony Gwynn	10.00
15	Roberto Alomar	2.50
16	Barry Bonds	20.00
17	Kenny Lofton	2.00
18	Jose Cruz, Jr.	2.00

Rocket to Stardom

This insert set is exclusive to Series 2 packs. Cards are in black-and-white and are die-cut, embossed and numbered with an "RS" suffix.

		NM/M
Complete Set (15):		15.00
Common Player:		.75
Inserted 1:20		
1	Ben Grieve	.75
2	Magglio Ordonez	4.00
3	Travis Lee	1.00
4	Carl Pavano	.75
5	Brian Rose	.75
6	Brad Fullmer	.75
7	Michael Coleman	.75
8	Juan Encarnacion	.75
9	Karim Garcia	1.00
10	Todd Helton	7.50
11	Richard Hildalgo	.75
12	Paul Konerko	1.50
13	Rod Myers	.75
14	Jaret Wright	.75
15	Miguel Tejada	1.50

Ticket Studs

Fifteen players are featured on fold-out ticket-like cards in Ticket Studs. The cards arrive folded across the middle and open to reveal a full-length shot of the player with prismatic team color stripes over a white background that has section, seat and row numbers. Cards were inserted in Series 2 packs and are numbered with a "TS" suffix.

		NM/M
Complete Set (15):		150.00
Common Player:		2.50

Inserted 1:144		
1	Travis Lee	3.00
2	Tony Gwynn	12.00
3	Scott Rolen	6.00
4	Nomar Garciaparra	12.00
5	Mike Piazza	15.00
6	Mark McGwire	17.50
7	Ken Griffey Jr.	15.00
8	Juan Gonzalez	5.00
9	Jose Cruz	2.50
10	Frank Thomas	9.00
11	Derek Jeter	20.00
12	Chipper Jones	12.00
13	Cal Ripken Jr.	20.00
14	Andruw Jones	9.00
15	Alex Rodriguez	17.50

Top 30

Top 30 is a retail-only insert found only in Series 2.

		NM/M
Complete Set (30):		20.00
Common Player:		.15
Inserted 1:1 R		
1	Barry Bonds	2.00
2	Ivan Rodriguez	.65
3	Kenny Lofton	.15
4	Albert Belle	.15
5	Mo Vaughn	.15
6	Jeff Bagwell	.75
7	Mark McGwire	1.50
8	Darin Erstad	.35
9	Roger Clemens	1.00
10	Tony Gwynn	1.00
11	Scott Rolen	.45
12	Hideo Nomo	.35
13	Juan Gonzalez	.35
14	Mike Piazza	1.25
15	Greg Maddux	1.00
16	Chipper Jones	1.00
17	Andruw Jones	.75
18	Derek Jeter	2.00
19	Nomar Garciaparra	1.00
20	Alex Rodriguez	1.50
21	Frank Thomas	.75
22	Cal Ripken Jr.	2.00
23	Ken Griffey Jr.	1.25
24	Jose Cruz Jr.	.15
25	Jaret Wright	.15

26	Travis Lee	.30
27	Wade Boggs	1.00
28	Chuck Knoblauch	.15
29	Joe Carter	.15
30	Ben Grieve	.15

Win Now

This Series 2 insert has top players printed on plastic card stock, with a color shot of the player on the left side and a close-up shot on the right with black lines through it. Cards are numbered with a "WN" suffix.

		NM/M
Complete Set (20):		100.00
Common Player:		2.50
Inserted 1:72		
1	Alex Rodriguez	10.00
2	Andruw Jones	4.00
3	Cal Ripken Jr.	12.50
4	Chipper Jones	5.00
5	Darin Erstad	3.00
6	Derek Jeter	12.50
7	Frank Thomas	4.00
8	Greg Maddux	5.00
9	Hideo Nomo	3.00
10	Jeff Bagwell	4.00
11	Jose Cruz	2.50
12	Juan Gonzalez	3.00
13	Ken Griffey Jr.	7.50
14	Mark McGwire	10.00
15	Mike Piazza	7.50
16	Mo Vaughn	2.50
17	Nomar Garciaparra	5.00
18	Roger Clemens	6.00
19	Scott Rolen	3.00
20	Tony Gwynn	5.00

1999 Ultra Sample Sheet

This six-card sheet was issued to introduce potential customers to '99 Ultra's base cards. The sheet measures 7-1/2" x 7". Cards are virtually identical to the issued version, except for the diagonal black-and-white "PROMOTIONAL SAMPLE" overprint on front and back.

	NM/M
Complete Sheet:	5.00

1999 Ultra

Base cards feature the full career stats by year in 15 categories and career highlights.

There are short-printed subsets including Season Crowns (216-225) found 1:8 packs and Prospects (226-250) found 1:4 packs. Card fronts feature full bleed photography, and metallic foil stamping. There are three parallel versions Gold Medallion seeded 1 per pack with Prospects 1:40 and Season Crowns 1:80. Platinum Medallions are numbered to 99 with Prospects numbered to 65 and Season Crowns numbered to 50 sets. One of One Masterpiece parallels also exist. Packs consist of 10 cards with a S.R.P. of $2.69.

	NM/M
Complete Set (250):	35.00
Common Player:	.05
Common Season Crown:	.25
Inserted 1:8	
Common Prospect:	.25
Inserted 1:4	
Gold Medallion (1-215):	2X
Inserted 1:1	
Gold Medall. Prospect:	4X
Inserted 1:40	
Gold Medall. Season Crown:	3X
Inserted 1:80	
Platinums (1-215):	25X
Production 99 Sets	
Platinum Prospects:	6X
Production 65 Sets	
Platinum Season Crowns:	20X
Production 50 Sets	
Pack (10):	1.50
Wax Box (24):	25.00
1	Greg Maddux	1.00
2	Greg Vaughn	.05
3	John Wetteland	.05
4	Tino Martinez	.05
5	Todd Walker	.05
6	Troy O'Leary	.05
7	Barry Larkin	.05
8	Mike Lansing	.05
9	Delino DeShields	.05
10	Brett Tomko	.05
11	Carlos Perez	.05
12	Mark Langston	.05
13	Jamie Moyer	.05
14	Jose Guillen	.05
15	Bartolo Colon	.05
16	Brady Anderson	.05
17	Walt Weiss	.05
18	Shane Reynolds	.05
19	David Segui	.05
20	Vladimir Guerrero	.75
21	Freddy Garcia	.05
22	Carl Everett	.05
23	Jose Cruz Jr.	.05
24	David Ortiz	.40
25	Andruw Jones	.75
26	Darren Lewis	.05
27	Ray Lankford	.05
28	Wally Joyner	.05
29	Charles Johnson	.05
30	Derek Jeter	2.00
31	Sean Casey	.10
32	Bobby Bonilla	.05
33	Todd Zelle	.05
34	Todd Helton	.65
35	David Wells	.05
36	Darin Erstad	.30
37	Ivan Rodriguez	.65
38	Antonio Osuna	.05
39	Mickey Morandini	.05
40	Rusty Greer	.05
41	Rod Beck	.05
42	Larry Sutton	.05
43	Edgar Renteria	.05
44	Otis Nixon	.05
45	Eli Marrero	.05
46	Reggie Jefferson	.05
47	Trevor Hoffman	.05
48	Andres Galarraga	.05
49	Scott Brosius	.05
50	Vinny Castilla	.05
51	Bret Boone	.05
52	Masato Yoshii	.05
53	Matt Williams	.05
54	Robin Ventura	.05
55	Jay Powell	.05
56	Dean Palmer	.05
57	Eric Milton	.05
58	Willie McGee	.05
59	Tony Gwynn	1.00
60	Tom Gordon	.05
61	Dante Bichette	.05
62	Jaret Wright	.05
63	Devon White	.05
64	Frank Thomas	.75
65	Mike Piazza	1.25
66	Jose Offerman	.05
67	Pat Meares	.05
68	Brian Meadows	.05
69	Nomar Garciaparra	1.00
70	Mark McGwire	1.50
71	Tony Graffanino	.05
72	Ken Griffey Jr.	1.25
73	Ken Caminiti	.05
74	Todd Jones	.05
75	A.J. Hinch	.05
76	Marquis Grissom	.05

77	Jay Buhner	.05
78	Albert Belle	.05
79	Brian Anderson	.05
80	Quinton McCracken	.05
81	Omar Vizquel	.05
82	Todd Stottlemyre	.05
83	Cal Ripken Jr.	2.00
84	Magglio Ordonez	.30
85	John Olerud	.05
86	Hal Morris	.05
87	Derrek Lee	.40
88	Doug Glanville	.05
89	Marty Cordova	.05
90	Kevin Brown	.05
91	Kevin Young	.05
92	Rico Brogna	.05
93	Wilson Alvarez	.05
94	Bob Wickman	.05
95	Jim Thome	.50
96	Mike Mussina	.35
97	Al Leiter	.05
98	Travis Lee	.10
99	Jeff King	.05
100	Kerry Wood	.40
101	Cliff Floyd	.05
102	Jose Valentin	.05
103	Manny Ramirez	.75
104	Butch Huskey	.05
105	Scott Erickson	.05
106	Ray Durham	.05
107	Johnny Damon	.30
108	Craig Counsell	.05
109	Rolando Arrojo	.05
110	Bob Abreu	.05
111	Tony Womack	.05
112	Mike Stanley	.05
113	Kenny Lofton	.05
114	Eric Davis	.05
115	Jeff Conine	.05
116	Carlos Baerga	.05
117	Rondell White	.05
118	Billy Wagner	.05
119	Ed Sprague	.05
120	Jason Schmidt	.05
121	Edgar Martinez	.05
122	Travis Fryman	.05
123	Armando Benitez	.05
124	Matt Stairs	.05
125	Roberto Hernandez	.05
126	Jay Bell	.05
127	Justin Thompson	.05
128	John Jaha	.05
129	Mike Caruso	.05
130	Miguel Tejada	.20
131	Geoff Jenkins	.05
132	Wade Boggs	1.00
133	Andy Benes	.05
134	Aaron Sele	.05
135	Bret Saberhagen	.05
136	Mariano Rivera	.15
137	Neifi Perez	.05
138	Paul Konerko	.15
139	Barry Bonds	2.00
140	Garret Anderson	.05
141	Bernie Williams	.05
142	Gary Sheffield	.40
143	Rafael Palmeiro	.65
144	Orel Hershiser	.05
145	Craig Biggio	.05
146	Dmitri Young	.05
147	Damion Easley	.05
148	Henry Rodriguez	.05
149	Brad Radke	.05
150	Pedro Martinez	.75
151	Mike Lieberthal	.05
152	Jim Leyritz	.05
153	Chuck Knoblauch	.05
154	Darryl Kile	.05
155	Brian Jordan	.05
156	Chipper Jones	1.00
157	Pete Harnisch	.05
158	Moises Alou	.05
159	Ismael Valdes	.05
160	Stan Javier	.05
161	Mark Grace	.05
162	Jason Giambi	.40
163	Chuck Finley	.05
164	Juan Encarnacion	.05
165	Chan Ho Park	.05
166	Randy Johnson	.75
167	J.T. Snow	.05
168	Tim Salmon	.05
169	Brian Hunter	.05
170	Rickey Henderson	.75
171	Cal Eldred	.05
172	Curt Schilling	.25
173	Alex Rodriguez	1.50
174	Dustin Hermanson	.05
175	Mike Hampton	.05
176	Shawn Green	.30
177	Roberto Alomar	.20
178	Sandy Alomar Jr.	.05
179	Larry Walker	.05
180	Mo Vaughn	.05
181	Raul Mondesi	.05
182	Hideki Irabu	.05
183	Jim Edmonds	.05
184	Shawn Estes	.05
185	Tony Clark	.05
186	Dan Wilson	.05
187	Michael Tucker	.05
188	Jeff Shaw	.05
189	Mark Grudzielanek	.05
190	Roger Clemens	1.00
191	Juan Gonzalez	.40
192	Sammy Sosa	1.00
193	Troy Percival	.05
194	Robb Nen	.05

195	Bill Mueller	.05
196	Ben Grieve	.05
197	Luis Gonzalez	.05
198	Will Clark	.05
199	Jeff Cirillo	.05
200	Scott Rolen	.50
201	Reggie Sanders	.05
202	Fred McGriff	.05
203	Denny Neagle	.05
204	Brad Fullmer	.05
205	Royce Clayton	.05
206	Jose Canseco	.50
207	Jeff Bagwell	.75
208	Hideo Nomo	.40
209	Karim Garcia	.15
210	Kenny Rogers	.05
211	Checklist (Kerry Wood)	.25
212	Checklist (Alex Rodriguez)	.75
213	Checklist (Cal Ripken Jr.)	1.00
214	Checklist (Frank Thomas)	.50
215	Checklist (Ken Griffey Jr.)	.65
216	Alex Rodriguez (Season Crowns)	1.00
217	Greg Maddux (Season Crowns)	.50
218	Juan Gonzalez (Season Crowns)	.20
219	Ken Griffey Jr. (Season Crowns)	.75
220	Kerry Wood (Season Crowns)	.25
221	Mark McGwire (Season Crowns)	1.00
222	Mike Piazza (Season Crowns)	.75
223	Rickey Henderson (Season Crowns)	.40
224	Sammy Sosa (Season Crowns)	.50
225	Travis Lee (Season Crowns)	.25
226	Gabe Alvarez (Prospects)	.25
227	Matt Anderson (Prospects)	.25
228	Adrian Beltre (Prospects)	.35
229	Orlando Cabrera (Prospects)	.35
230	Orlando Hernandez (Prospects)	.25
231	Aramis Ramirez (Prospects)	.25
232	Troy Glaus (Prospects)	1.00
233	Gabe Kapler (Prospects)	.25
234	Jeremy Giambi (Prospects)	.25
235	Derrick Gibson (Prospects)	.25
236	Carlton Loewer (Prospects)	.25
237	Mike Frank (Prospects)	.25
238	Carlos Guillen (Prospects)	.25
239	Alex Gonzalez (Prospects)	.25
240	Enrique Wilson (Prospects)	.25
241	J.D. Drew (Prospects)	.75
242	Bruce Chen (Prospects)	.25
243	Ryan Minor (Prospects)	.25
244	Preston Wilson (Prospects)	.35
245	Josh Booty (Prospects)	.25
246	Luis Ordaz (Prospects)	.25
247	George Lombard (Prospects)	.25
248	Matt Clement (Prospects)	.25
249	Eric Chavez (Prospects)	.35
250	Corey Koskie (Prospects)	.30

Gold Medallion

The basic cards (#1-215) in this parallel set are found one per pack, while the short-printed versions are seen one per 40 packs (Prospects) or one per 80 packs (Season Crowns). Sharing the photos and format of the regular-issue cards, these inserts have a gold-foil background on front. On back, "GOLD MEDALLION EDITION" is printed in gold foil.

		NM/M
Common Player (1-215):		.25
Stars/RC's:		2X
Season Crowns (216-225):		4X
Prospects (226-250):		3X

Platinum Medallion

The basic cards (#1-215) in this parallel set are found in an individually serial numbered edition of 99. The short-printed cards were released in editions of 65 (Prospects) and 50 (Season Crowns). Sharing the photos and format of the regular-issue cards, these inserts have a silver-foil background on front. On back, "PLATINUM MEDALLION" is printed in silver foil along with the serial number.

		NM/M
Common Player (1-215):		5.00
Stars/RC's:		25X
Season Crowns (216-225):		20X
Prospects (226-250):		6X

Masterpiece

This top of the line parallel to '99 Ultra consists of a 1 of 1 version of each regular card.

	NM/M
Common Player:	50.00

Book On

This set features insider scouting reports on the game's best players, utilizing embossing and gold foil stamping.

		NM/M
Complete Set (20):		13.50
Common Player:		.25
Inserted 1:6		
1	Kerry Wood	.35
2	Ken Griffey Jr.	1.00
3	Frank Thomas	.65
4	Albert Belle	.25
5	Juan Gonzalez	.65
6	Jeff Bagwell	.65
7	Mark McGwire	1.25
8	Barry Bonds	1.50
9	Andruw Jones	.65
10	Mo Vaughn	.25
11	Scott Rolen	.40
12	Travis Lee	.25
13	Tony Gwynn	.75
14	Greg Maddux	.75
15	Mike Piazza	1.00
16	Chipper Jones	.75
17	Nomar Garciaparra	.75
18	Cal Ripken Jr.	1.50
19	Derek Jeter	1.50
20	Alex Rodriguez	1.25

Damage Inc.

This insert set has a business card design, for players who mean business.

		NM/M
Complete Set (15):		50.00
Common Player:		1.00
Inserted 1:72		
1	Alex Rodriguez	5.00
2	Greg Maddux	3.50
3	Cal Ripken Jr.	7.50
4	Chipper Jones	3.50
5	Derek Jeter	7.50
6	Frank Thomas	2.50
7	Juan Gonzalez	1.50
8	Ken Griffey Jr.	4.00
9	Kerry Wood	1.25
10	Mark McGwire	5.00
11	Mike Piazza	4.00
12	Nomar Garciaparra	3.50
13	Scott Rolen	1.50
14	Tony Gwynn	3.50
15	Travis Lee	1.00

Diamond Producers

This die-cut set uses full-foil plastic with custom embossing.

		NM/M
Complete Set (10):		140.00
Common Player:		6.00
Inserted 1:288		
1	Ken Griffey Jr.	17.50
2	Frank Thomas	12.00
3	Alex Rodriguez	20.00
4	Cal Ripken Jr.	25.00
5	Mike Piazza	17.50
6	Mark McGwire	20.00
7	Greg Maddux	15.00
8	Kerry Wood	6.00
9	Chipper Jones	15.00
10	Derek Jeter	25.00

RBI Kings

Found exclusively in retail packs, this set showcases baseball's top run producers.

		NM/M
Complete Set (30):		12.00
Common Player:		.15
Inserted 1:1 R		
1	Rafael Palmeiro	.40
2	Mo Vaughn	.15
3	Ivan Rodriguez	.40
4	Barry Bonds	1.25
5	Albert Belle	.25
6	Jeff Bagwell	.45
7	Mark McGwire	1.00
8	Darin Erstad	.25
9	Manny Ramirez	.45
10	Chipper Jones	.60

11	Jim Thome	.40
12	Scott Rolen	.35
13	Tony Gwynn	.60
14	Juan Gonzalez	.25
15	Mike Piazza	.75
16	Sammy Sosa	.60
17	Andruw Jones	.45
18	Derek Jeter	1.25
19	Nomar Garciaparra	.60
20	Alex Rodriguez	1.00
21	Frank Thomas	.45
22	Cal Ripken Jr.	1.25
23	Ken Griffey Jr.	.75
24	Travis Lee	.25
25	Paul O'Neill	.15
26	Greg Vaughn	.15
27	Andres Galarraga	.15
28	Tino Martinez	.15
29	Jose Canseco	.30
30	Ben Grieve	.15

Thunderclap

This set highlights the top hitters in the game. Card fronts feature a lightning bolt in the background.

		NM/M
Complete Set (15):		35.00
Common Player:		.75
Inserted 1:36		
1	Alex Rodriguez	4.00
2	Andruw Jones	1.50
3	Cal Ripken Jr.	6.00
4	Chipper Jones	2.50
5	Darin Erstad	.75
6	Derek Jeter	6.00
7	Frank Thomas	1.50
8	Jeff Bagwell	1.50
9	Juan Gonzalez	.75
10	Ken Griffey Jr.	3.00
11	Mark McGwire	4.00
12	Mike Piazza	3.00
13	Travis Lee	.75
14	Nomar Garciaparra	2.50
15	Scott Rolen	1.00

World Premiere

This set highlights rookies who made debuts in 1998.

		NM/M
Complete Set (15):		8.00
Common Player:		.50
Inserted 1:18		
1	Gabe Alvarez	.50
2	Kerry Wood	1.50
3	Orlando Hernandez	.60
4	Mike Caruso	.50
5	Matt Anderson	.50
6	Randall Simon	.50
7	Adrian Beltre	.65
8	Scott Elarton	.50
9	Karim Garcia	.60
10	Mike Frank	.50
11	Richard Hidalgo	.50
12	Paul Konerko	.60
13	Travis Lee	.65
14	J.D. Drew	1.50
15	Miguel Tejada	.75

2000 Ultra Sample

Product spokesman Alex Rodriguez is featured on the promo card for 2000 Ultra.

Virtually identical in format to the issued version, the card has a "PROMOTIONAL SAMPLE" overprint diagonally on front and back.

		NM/M
1	Alex Rodriguez	2.00

2000 Ultra

The 300-card base set features a borderless design with silver holographic foil stamping on the card front. Card backs have an action image along with complete year-by-year statistics. The base set includes a 50-card short-printed Prospects (1:4) subset. A Masterpiece one-of-one parallel was produced.

		NM/M
Complete Set (300):		35.00
Common Player:		.10
Common Player (251-300):		.50
Inserted 1:4		
Pack (10):		2.00
Wax Box (24):		35.00
1	Alex Rodriguez	1.50
2	Shawn Green	.25
3	Magglio Ordonez	.25
4	Tony Gwynn	.75
5	Joe McEwing	.10
6	Jose Rosado	.10
7	Sammy Sosa	1.00
8	Gary Sheffield	.25
9	Mickey Morandini	.10
10	Mo Vaughn	.15
11	Todd Hollandsworth	.10
12	Tom Gordon	.10
13	Charles Johnson	.10
14	Derek Bell	.10
15	Kevin Young	.10
16	Jay Buhner	.15
17	J.T. Snow	.10
18	Jay Bell	.10
19	John Rocker	.10
20	Ivan Rodriguez	.40
21	Pokey Reese	.10
22	Paul O'Neill	.20
23	Ronnie Belliard	.10
24	Ryan Rupe	.10
25	Travis Fryman	.20
26	Trot Nixon	.10
27	Wally Joyner	.10
28	Andy Pettitte	.25
29	Dan Wilson	.10
30	Orlando Hernandez	.20
31	Dmitri Young	.10
32	Edgar Renteria	.10
33	Eric Karros	.20
34	Fernando Seguignol	.10
35	Jason Kendall	.20
36	Jeff Shaw	.10
37	Matt Lawton	.20
38	Robin Ventura	.20
39	Scott Williamson	.10
40	Ben Grieve	.20
41	Billy Wagner	.10
42	Javy Lopez	.20
43	Joe Randa	.10
44	Neifi Perez	.10
45	David Justice	.20
46	Ray Durham	.10
47	Dustin Hermanson	.10
48	Andres Galarraga	.20
49	Brad Fullmer	.10
50	Nomar Garciaparra	1.50
51	David Cone	.15
52	David Nilsson	.10
53	David Wells	.10
54	Miguel Tejada	.25
55	Ismael Valdes	.10
56	Jose Lima	.10
57	Juan Encarnacion	.10
58	Fred McGriff	.20
59	Kenny Rogers	.10
60	Vladimir Guerrero	.75
61	Benito Santiago	.10
62	Chris Singleton	.10
63	Carlos Lee	.10
64	Sean Casey	.20
65	Tom Goodwin	.10
66	Todd Hundley	.10
67	Ellis Burks	.10
68	Tim Hudson	.25
69	Matt Stairs	.10
70	Chipper Jones	1.00
71	Craig Biggio	.25
72	Brian Rose	.10
73	Carlos Delgado	.40
74	Eddie Taubensee	.10
75	John Smoltz	.20
76	Ken Caminiti	.15
77	Rafael Palmeiro	.40
78	Sidney Ponson	.10
79	Todd Helton	.50
80	Juan Gonzalez	.50
81	Bruce Aven	.10
82	Desi Relaford	.10
83	Johnny Damon	.20
84	Albert Belle	.15
85	Mark McGwire	1.50
86	Rico Brogna	.10
87	Tom Glavine	.20
88	Harold Baines	.10
89	Chad Allen	.10
90	Barry Bonds	2.00
91	Mark Grace	.25
92	Paul Byrd	.10
93	Roberto Alomar	.40
94	Roberto Hernandez	.10
95	Steve Finley	.10
96	Bret Boone	.20
97	Charles Nagy	.10
98	Eric Chavez	.25
99	Jamie Moyer	.10
100	Ken Griffey Jr.	1.00
101	J.D. Drew	.20
102	Todd Stottlemyre	.10
103	Tony Fernandez	.10
104	Jeromy Burnitz	.10
105	Jeremy Giambi	.10
106	Livan Hernandez	.10
107	Marlon Anderson	.10
108	Troy Glaus	.50
109	Troy O'Leary	.10
110	Scott Rolen	.50
111	Bernard Gilkey	.10
112	Brady Anderson	.15
113	Chuck Knoblauch	.15
114	Jeff Weaver	.10
115	B.J. Surhoff	.10
116	Alex Gonzalez	.10
117	Vinny Castilla	.10
118	Tim Salmon	.20
119	Brian Jordan	.10
120	Corey Koskie	.10
121	Dean Palmer	.10
122	Gabe Kapler	.20
123	Jim Edmonds	.25
124	John Jaha	.10
125	Mark Grudzielanek	.10
126	Mike Bordick	.10
127	Mike Lieberthal	.10
128	Pete Harnisch	.10
129	Russ Ortiz	.10
130	Kevin Brown	.20
131	Troy Percival	.10
132	Alex Gonzalez	.10
133	Bartolo Colon	.10
134	John Valentin	.10
135	Jose Hernandez	.10
136	Marquis Grissom	.10
137	Wade Boggs	.25
138	Dante Bichette	.10
139	Bobby Higginson	.10
140	Frank Thomas	.50
141	Geoff Jenkins	.10
142	Jason Giambi	.50
143	Jeff Cirillo	.10
144	Sandy Alomar Jr.	.10
145	Luis Gonzalez	.20
146	Preston Wilson	.10
147	Carlos Beltran	.10
148	Greg Vaughn	.10
149	Carlos Febles	.10
150	Jose Canseco	.40
151	Kris Benson	.10
152	Chuck Finley	.10
153	Michael Barrett	.10
154	Rey Ordonez	.10
155	Adrian Beltre	.20
156	Andruw Jones	.50
157	Barry Larkin	.25
158	Brian Giles	.20
159	Carl Everett	.20
160	Manny Ramirez	.50
161	Daryl Kile	.10
162	Edgar Martinez	.15
163	Jeff Kent	.20
164	Matt Williams	.20
165	Mike Piazza	1.00
166	Pedro J. Martinez	.75
167	Ray Lankford	.10
168	Roger Cedeno	.10
169	Ron Coomer	.10
170	Cal Ripken Jr.	2.00
171	Jose Offerman	.10
172	Kenny Lofton	.20
173	Kent Bottenfield	.10
174	Kevin Millwood	.20
175	Omar Daal	.10
176	Orlando Cabrera	.20
177	Pat Hentgen	.10
178	Tino Martinez	.20
179	Tony Clark	.10
180	Roger Clemens	1.25
181	Brad Radke	.10
182	Darin Erstad	.10
183	Jose Jimenez	.10
184	Jim Thome	.50
185	John Wetteland	.10
186	Justin Thompson	.10
187	John Hamala	.10
188	Lee Stevens	.10
189	Miguel Cairo	.10
190	Mike Mussina	.40
191	Raul Mondesi	.15
192	Armando Rios	.10
193	Trevor Hoffman	.10
194	Tony Batista	.10
195	Will Clark	.40
196	Brad Ausmus	.10
197	Chili Davis	.10
198	Cliff Floyd	.10
199	Curt Schilling	.25
200	Derek Jeter	2.00
201	Henry Rodriguez	.10
202	Jose Cruz Jr.	.10
203	Omar Vizquel	.10
204	Randy Johnson	.75
205	Reggie Sanders	.10
206	Al Leiter	.10
207	Damion Easley	.10
208	David Bell	.10
209	Fernando Tatis	.10
210	Kerry Wood	.25
211	Kevin Appier	.10
212	Mariano Rivera	.20
213	Mike Caruso	.10
214	Moises Alou	.20
215	Randy Winn	.10
216	Roy Halladay	.20
217	Shannon Stewart	.10
218	Todd Walker	.10
219	Jim Parque	.10
220	Travis Lee	.10
221	Andy Ashby	.10
222	Ed Sprague	.10
223	Larry Walker	.20
224	Rick Helling	.10
225	Rusty Greer	.10
226	Todd Zeile	.10
227	Freddy Garcia	.15
228	Hideo Nomo	.40
229	Marty Cordova	.10
230	Greg Maddux	1.00
231	Rondell White	.20
232	Paul Konerko	.15
233	Warren Morris	.10
234	Bernie Williams	.40
235	Bobby Abreu	.20
236	John Olerud	.25
237	Doug Glanville	.10
238	Eric Young	.10
239	Robb Nen	.10
240	Jeff Bagwell	.50
241	Sterling Hitchcock	.10
242	Todd Greene	.10
243	Bill Mueller	.10
244	Rickey Henderson	.25
245	Chan Ho Park	.20
246	Jason Schmidt	.10
247	Jeff Zimmerman	.10
248	Jermaine Dye	.10
249	Randall Simon	.10
250	Richie Sexson	.40
251	Micah Bowie	.50
252	Joe Nathan	.50
253	Chris Woodward	.50
254	Lance Berkman	.75
255	Ruben Mateo	.50
256	Russell Branyan	.50
257	Randy Wolf	.75
258	A.J. Burnett	.75
259	Mark Quinn	.50
260	Buddy Carlyle	.50
261	Ben Davis	.50
262	Yamid Haad	.50
263	Mike Colangelo	.50
264	Rick Ankiel	.75
265	Jacque Jones	.50
266	Kelly Dransfeldt	.50
267	Matt Riley	.50
268	Adam Kennedy	.50
269	Octavio Dotel	.50
270	Francisco Cordero	.50
271	Wilton Veras	.50
272	Calvin Pickering	.50
273	Alex Sanchez	.50
274	Tony Armas Jr.	.50
275	Pat Burrell	1.00
276	Chad Meyers	.50
277	Ben Petrick	.50
278	Ramon Hernandez	.50
279	Ed Yarnall	.50
280	Erubiel Durazo	.50
281	Vernon Wells	1.00
282	Gary Matthews	.50
283	Kip Wells	.50
284	Peter Bergeron	.50
285	Travis Dawkins	.50
286	Jorge Toca	.50
287	Cole Liniak	.50
288	Chad Hermansen	.50
289	Eric Gagne	.50
290	Chad Hutchinson	.50
291	Eric Munson	.50
292	Wiki Gonzalez	.50
293	Alfonso Soriano	1.50
294	Trent Durrington	.50
295	Ben Molina	.50
296	Aaron Myette	.50
297	Willi Mo Pena	.75
298	Kevin Barker	.50
299	Geoff Blum	.50
300	Josh Beckett	.75

Gold Medallion

A parallel to the 300-card base set these have gold foil stamping over a metallic gold background. Cards 1-250 are seeded one per pack, Prospects 251-300 are seeded 1:24 packs. Card backs are numbered with a "G" suffix.

Stars:	2X
Inserted 1:1	
Prospects (251-300):	2-4X
Inserted 1:24	

Platinum Medallion

Platinum Medallion are a parallel to the 300-card base set and are die-cut like the Gold Medallion parallel inserts. Card fronts are stamped with silver foil over a metallic silver background. Card backs are serially numbered with cards 1-250 limited to 50 sets and Prospects limited to 25 numbered sets. Card backs are numbered with a "P" suffix.

Stars:	15-30X
Production 50 Sets	
Prospects (251-300):	4-8X
Production 25 Sets	

Masterpiece Edition

Masterpiece Edition is a 1 of 1 parallel to the 300-card base set and are "tombstone" die-cut like the Gold and Platinum Medallion inserts. Card fronts are stamped with purple foil over a white purple background. Card backs are overprinted with "The only 1 of 1 Masterpiece."

Club 3000

This three-card set is die-cut around the number 3,000 and commemorates 3,000 hit club members Wade Boggs, Tony Gwynn and Carl Yastrzemski. These were seeded 1:24 packs.

		NM/M
Common Player:		3.00
Inserted 1:24		
	Wade Boggs	2.00
	Tony Gwynn	3.00
	Carl Yastrzemski	3.00

Club 3000 Memorabilia

Each featured player has a total of four different memorabilia based inserts: hat; jersey; bat/jersey and bat/hat/jersey.

	NM/M
Wade Boggs/Bat/250	20.00
Wade Boggs/Hat/100	40.00
Wade Boggs/Jsy/440	20.00
Wade Boggs/	
Bat, Jsy/100	40.00
Wade Boggs/	
Bat, Hat, Jsy/25	150.00
Tony Gwynn/Bat/260	40.00
Tony Gwynn/Hat/115	60.00
Tony Gwynn/Jsy/450	25.00
Tony Gwynn/	
Bat, Jsy/100	65.00
Tony Gwynn/	
Bat, Hat, Jsy/25	375.00
Carl Yastrzemski/	
Bat/250	40.00
Carl Yastrzemski/	
Hat/100	60.00
Carl Yastrzemski/	
Jsy/440	25.00
Carl Yastrzemski/	
Bat, Jsy/100	75.00
Carl Yastrzemski/	
Bat, Hat, Jsy/25	300.00

Crunch Time

This 15-card insert set is printed on suede stock with gold foil stamping. These were seeded 1:72 packs and numbered with a "CT" suffix on the card back.

		NM/M
Complete Set (15):		50.00
Common Player:		2.00
Inserted 1:72		
1	Nomar Garciaparra	8.00
2	Ken Griffey Jr.	5.00
3	Mark McGwire	8.00
4	Alex Rodriguez	8.00
5	Derek Jeter	8.00
6	Sammy Sosa	6.00
7	Mike Piazza	5.00
8	Cal Ripken Jr.	10.00
9	Frank Thomas	3.00

		NM/M
10	Juan Gonzalez	3.00
11	J.D. Drew	2.00
12	Greg Maddux	5.00
13	Tony Gwynn	3.00
14	Vladimir Guerrero	3.00
15	Ben Grieve	2.00

Diamond Mine

GREG MADDUX

These were printed on a silver foil card front with Diamond Mine stamped in the background of the player image. These were inserted 1:6 packs and numbered with a "DM" suffix on the card back.

		NM/M
Complete Set (15):		20.00
Common Player:		1.00
Inserted 1:6		
1	Greg Maddux	1.50
2	Mark McGwire	2.00
3	Ken Griffey Jr.	1.50
4	Cal Ripken Jr.	3.00
5	Nomar Garciaparra	2.50
6	Mike Piazza	2.00
7	Alex Rodriguez	2.50
8	Frank Thomas	2.00
9	Juan Gonzalez	2.00
10	Derek Jeter	2.50
11	Tony Gwynn	1.00
12	Chipper Jones	1.50
13	Sammy Sosa	2.00
14	Roger Clemens	1.50
15	Vladimir Guerrero	1.00

Feel the Game

Alex Rodriguez

These memorabilia based inserts have a piece of game worn jersey or batting glove embedded into the card front.

	NM/M
Common Player:	5.00
Roberto Alomar	10.00
J.D. Drew	5.00
Tony Gwynn/SP	40.00
Randy Johnson	20.00
Greg Maddux	20.00
Edgar Martinez	10.00
Pedro Martinez	20.00
Kevin Millwood	10.00
Cal Ripken Jr.	40.00
Alex Rodriguez	25.00
Scott Rolen	10.00
Curt Schilling	10.00
Chipper Jones	20.00
Frank Thomas/SP	40.00
Robin Ventura	5.00

Fresh Ink

These autographed cards have the words "Fresh Ink" printed continually in the back-

ground image of the player. The signature is in a designated blank box intended for the autograph. Production numbers vary from player to player and are listed in parentheses after the player name.

		NM/M
Common Player:		5.00
1	Bobby Abreu/400	10.00
2	Chad Allen/1,000	5.00
3	Marlon Anderson/1,000	5.00
4	Glen Barker/1,000	5.00
5	Michael Barrett/1,000	5.00
6	Carlos Beltran/1,000	15.00
7	Adrian Beltre/1,000	8.00
8	Wade Boggs/250	40.00
9	Barry Bonds/250	150.00
10	Peter Bergeron/1,000	5.00
11	Pat Burrell/500	20.00
12	Roger Cedeno/500	5.00
13	Eric Chavez/750	10.00
14	Bruce Chen/600	5.00
15	Johnny Damon/750	8.00
16	Ben Davis/1,000	5.00
17	Carlos Delgado/300	10.00
18	Einar Diaz/1,000	5.00
19	Octavio Dotel/1,000	6.00
20	J.D. Drew/600	8.00
21	Scott Elarton/1,000	5.00
22	Freddy Garcia/500	8.00
23	Jeremy Giambi/1,000	5.00
24	Troy Glaus/500	20.00
25	Shawn Green/350	30.00
26	Tony Gwynn (250)	50.00
27	Richard Hidalgo/500	8.00
28	Bobby Higginson/1,000	6.00
29	Tim Hudson/1,000	10.00
30	Norm Hutchins/1,000	5.00
31	Derek Jeter/95	200.00
32	Randy Johnson/150	10.00
33	Gabe Kapler/750	8.00
34	Jason Kendall/400	8.00
35	Paul Konerko/500	8.00
36	Matt Lawton/1,000	6.00
37	Carlos Lee/1,000	5.00
38	Jose Macias/1,000	5.00
39	Greg Maddux/250	65.00
40	Ruben Mateo/250	8.00
41	Kevin Millwood/500	10.00
42	Warren Morris/1,000	5.00
43	Eric Munson/1,000	6.00
44	Heath Murray/1,000	5.00
45	Joe Nathan/1,000	5.00
46	Magglio Ordonez/350	10.00
47	Angel Pena/1,000	5.00
48	Cal Ripken Jr./350	125.00
49	Alex Rodriguez/350	80.00
50	Scott Rolen/350	35.00
51	Ryan Rupe/1,000	5.00
52	Curt Schilling/375	25.00
53	Randall Simon/1,000	5.00
54	Alfonso Soriano/1,000	60.00
55	Shannon Stewart/300	5.00
56	Miguel Tejada/1,000	25.00
57	Frank Thomas/150	60.00
58	Jeff Weaver/1,000	6.00
59	Randy Wolf/1,000	8.00
60	Ed Yarnall/1,000	5.00
61	Kevin Young/1,000	5.00
62	Tony Gwynn, Wade Boggs, Nolan Ryan/100	450.00
63	Rick Ankiel/500	5.00

Swing King

Printed on a clear, plastic stock this 10-card set features the top hitters in the game. Card fronts also utilize silver foil stamping. These were seeded 1:24 packs and are numbered on the card back with a "SK" suffix.

Abbreviations

SP - Short Print

		NM/M
Complete Set (10):		20.00
Common Player:		1.00
Inserted 1:24		
1	Cal Ripken Jr.	4.00
2	Nomar Garciaparra	3.00
3	Frank Thomas	1.00
4	Tony Gwynn	1.50
5	Ken Griffey Jr.	2.00
6	Chipper Jones	2.00
7	Mark McGwire	3.00
8	Sammy Sosa	2.50
9	Derek Jeter	3.00
10	Alex Rodriguez	3.00

Ultra Talented

ULTRA TALENTED

MIKE PIAZZA

Available exclusively in hobby packs these were printed on a holofoil background with gold foil stamping. Each card is serially numbered to 100 and are numbered on the card back with a "UT" suffix.

		NM/M
Common Player:		5.00
Production 100 Sets		
1	Sammy Sosa	15.00
2	Derek Jeter	20.00
3	Alex Rodriguez	20.00
4	Mike Piazza	15.00
5	Ken Griffey Jr.	15.00
6	Nomar Garciaparra	20.00
7	Mark McGwire	20.00
8	Cal Ripken Jr.	25.00
9	Frank Thomas	8.00
10	J.D. Drew	5.00

World Premiere

This insert set highlights ten young potential stars on a die-cut, silver foil etched design. These were inserted 1:12 packs and are numbered with a "WP" suffix on the card back.

		NM/M
Complete Set (10):		5.00
Common Player:		.50
Inserted 1:12		
1	Ruben Mateo	.50
2	Lance Berkman	1.00
3	Octavio Dotel	.50
4	Ben Davis	.50
5	Warren Morris	.50
6	Carlos Beltran	.75
7	Rick Ankiel	.50
8	Adam Kennedy	.50
9	Tim Hudson	1.00
10	Jorge Toca	.50

2001 Ultra

	NM/M
Complete Set (275):	65.00
Common Player:	.15
Common Prospect (251-275):	1.00
Inserted 1:4	
Pack (10):	3.00
Box (24):	55.00
1 Pedro Martinez	.75
2 Derek Jeter	2.00
3 Cal Ripken Jr.	2.00
4 Alex Rodriguez	1.50
5 Vladimir Guerrero	.75

BRIAN JORDAN

6	Troy Glaus	.40
7	Sammy Sosa	1.25
8	Mike Piazza	1.00
9	Tony Gwynn	.75
10	Tim Hudson	.25
11	John Flaherty	.15
12	Jeff Cirillo	.15
13	Ellis Burks	.15
14	Carlos Lee	.15
15	Carlos Beltran	.25
16	Ruben Rivera	.15
17	Richard Hidalgo	.15
18	Omar Vizquel	.15
19	Michael Barrett	.15
20	Jose Canseco	.40
21	Jason Giambi	.50
22	Greg Maddux	1.00
23	Charles Johnson	.15
24	Sandy Alomar	.15
25	Rick Ankiel	.25
26	Richie Sexson	.40
27	Matt Williams	.25
28	Joe Girardi	.15
29	Jason Kendall	.25
30	Brad Fullmer	.15
31	Alex Gonzalez	.15
32	Rick Helling	.15
33	Mike Mussina	.50
34	Joe Randa	.15
35	J.T. Snow	.15
36	Edgardo Alfonzo	.15
37	Dante Bichette	.15
38	Brad Ausmus	.15
39	Bobby Abreu	.25
40	Warren Morris	.15
41	Tony Womack	.15
42	Russell Branyan	.15
43	Mike Lowell	.15
44	Mark Grace	.40
45	Jeromy Burnitz	.15
46	J.D. Drew	.25
47	David Justice	.25
48	Alex Gonzalez	.15
49	Tino Martinez	.25
50	Raul Mondesi	.25
51	Rafael Furcal	.25
52	Marquis Grissom	.15
53	Kevin Young	.15
54	Jon Lieber	.15
55	Henry Rodriguez	.15
56	Dave Burba	.15
57	Shannon Stewart	.15
58	Preston Wilson	.15
59	Paul O'Neill	.25
60	Jimmy Haynes	.15
61	Darryl Kile	.15
62	Bret Boone	.25
63	Bartolo Colon	.25
64	Andres Galarraga	.25
65	Trot Nixon	.15
66	Steve Finley	.15
67	Shawn Green	.30
68	Robert Person	.15
69	Kenny Rogers	.15
70	Bobby Higginson	.15
71	Barry Larkin	.30
72	Al Martin	.15
73	Tom Glavine	.40
74	Rondell White	.15
75	Ray Lankford	.15
76	Moises Alou	.25
77	Matt Clement	.15
78	Geoff Jenkins	.25
79	David Wells	.15
80	Chuck Finley	.15
81	Andy Pettitte	.25
82	Travis Fryman	.15
83	Ron Coomer	.15
84	Mark McGwire	1.50
85	Kerry Wood	.50
86	Jorge Posada	.40
87	Jeff Bagwell	.50
88	Andruw Jones	.50
89	Ryan Klesko	.25
90	Mariano Rivera	.25
91	Lance Berkman	.25
92	Kenny Lofton	.25
93	Jacque Jones	.15
94	Eric Young	.15
95	Edgar Renteria	.15
96	Chipper Jones	1.00
97	Todd Helton	.50
98	Shawn Estes	.15
99	Mark Mulder	.25
100	Lee Stevens	.15
101	Jermaine Dye	.25
102	Greg Vaughn	.15
103	Chris Singleton	.15

104	Brady Anderson	.15
105	Terrence Long	.15
106	Quilvio Veras	.15
107	Magglio Ordonez	.40
108	Johnny Damon	.25
109	Jeffrey Hammonds	.15
110	Fred McGriff	.25
111	Carl Pavano	.15
112	Bobby Estalella	.15
113	Todd Hundley	.15
114	Scott Rolen	.75
115	Robin Ventura	.25
116	Pokey Reese	.15
117	Luis Gonzalez	.25
118	Jose Offerman	.15
119	Edgar Martinez	.25
120	Dean Palmer	.15
121	David Segui	.15
122	Troy O'Leary	.15
123	Tony Batista	.15
124	Todd Zeile	.15
125	Randy Johnson	.75
126	Luis Castillo	.15
127	Kris Benson	.15
128	John Olerud	.25
129	Eric Karros	.25
130	Eddie Taubensee	.15
131	Neifi Perez	.15
132	Matt Stairs	.15
133	Luis Alicea	.15
134	Jeff Kent	.25
135	Javier Vazquez	.15
136	Garret Anderson	.25
137	Frank Thomas	.50
138	Carlos Febles	.15
139	Albert Belle	.25
140	Tony Clark	.15
141	Pat Burrell	.50
142	Mike Sweeney	.15
143	Jay Buhner	.15
144	Gabe Kapler	.15
145	Derek Bell	.15
146	B.J. Surhoff	.15
147	Adam Kennedy	.15
148	Aaron Boone	.15
149	Todd Stottlemyre	.15
150	Roberto Alomar	.40
151	Orlando Hernandez	.25
152	Jason Varitek	.15
153	Gary Sheffield	.40
154	Cliff Floyd	.15
155	Chad Hermansen	.15
156	Carlos Delgado	.50
157	Aaron Sele	.15
158	Sean Casey	.15
159	Ruben Mateo	.15
160	Mike Bordick	.15
161	Mike Cameron	.15
162	Doug Glanville	.15
163	Damion Easley	.15
164	Carl Everett	.15
165	Bengie Molina	.15
166	Adrian Beltre	.25
167	Tom Goodwin	.15
168	Rickey Henderson	.40
169	Mo Vaughn	.25
170	Mike Lieberthal	.15
171	Ken Griffey Jr.	1.00
172	Juan Gonzalez	.50
173	Ivan Rodriguez	.50
174	Al Leiter	.15
175	Vinny Castilla	.15
176	Peter Bergeron	.15
177	Pedro Astacio	.15
178	Paul Konerko	.15
179	Mitch Meluskey	.15
180	Kevin Millwood	.25
181	Ben Grieve	.25
182	Barry Bonds	2.00
183	Rusty Greer	.15
184	Miguel Tejada	.40
185	Mark Quinn	.15
186	Larry Walker	.25
187	Jose Valentin	.15
188	Jose Vidro	.15
189	Delino DeShields	.15
190	Darin Erstad	.25
191	Bill Mueller	.15
192	Ray Durham	.15
193	Ken Caminiti	.15
194	Jim Thome	.75
195	Javy Lopez	.25
196	Fernando Vina	.15
197	Eric Chavez	.25
198	Eric Owens	.15
199	Brad Radke	.15
200	Travis Lee	.15
201	Tim Salmon	.25
202	Rafael Palmeiro	.25
203	Nomar Garciaparra	1.50
204	Mike Hampton	.25
205	Kevin Brown	.25
206	Juan Encarnacion	.15
207	Danny Graves	.15
208	Carlos Guillen	.15
209	Phil Nevin	.15
210	Matt Lawton	.15
211	Manny Ramirez	.50
212	James Baldwin	.15
213	Fernando Tatis	.15
214	Craig Biggio	.25
215	Brian Jordan	.15
216	Bernie Williams	.50
217	Ryan Dempster	.15
218	Roger Clemens	1.50
219	Jose Cruz Jr.	.15
220	John Valentin	.15
221	Dmitri Young	.15

222	Curt Schilling	.40
223	Jim Edmonds	.30
224	Chan Ho Park	.15
225	Brian Giles	.25
226	Jimmy Anderson	.15
227	Adam Piatt	.15
228	Kenny Kelly	.15
229	Randy Choate	.15
230	Eric Cammack	.15
231	Yovanny Lara	.15
232	Wayne Franklin	.15
233	Cameron Cairncross	.15
234	J.C. Romero	.15
235	Geraldo Guzman	.15
236	Morgan Burkhart	.15
237	Pascual Coco	.15
238	John Parrish	.15
239	Keith McDonald	.15
240	Carlos Casimiro	.15
241	Daniel Garibay	.15
242	Sang-Hoon Lee	.15
243	Hector Ortiz	.15
244	Jeff Sparks	.15
245	Jason Boyd	.15
246	Mark Buehrle	.15
247	Adam Melhuse	.15
248	Kane Davis	.15
249	Mike Darr	.15
250	Vicente Padilla	.15
251	Barry Zito (Prospects)	4.00
252	Tim Drew (Prospects)	1.00
253	Luis Matos (Prospects)	2.00
254	Alex Cabrera (Prospects)	1.00
255	Jon Garland (Prospects)	1.00
256	Milton Bradley (Prospects)	1.50
257	Juan Pierre (Prospects)	2.00
258	Ismael Villegas (Prospects)	1.00
259	Eric Munson (Prospects)	1.00
260	Tomas De La Rosa (Prospects)	1.00
261	Chris Richard (Prospects)	1.00
262	Jason Tyner (Prospects)	1.00
263	B.J. Waszgis (Prospects)	1.00
264	Jason Marquis (Prospects)	1.00
265	Dusty Allen (Prospects)	1.00
266	Corey Patterson (Prospects)	2.00
267	Eric Byrnes (Prospects)	2.00
268	Xavier Nady (Prospects)	2.00
269	George Lombard (Prospects)	1.00
270	Timoniel Perez (Prospects)	1.00
271	Gary Matthews Jr. (Prospects)	1.00
272	Chad Durbin (Prospects)	1.00
273	Tony Armas Jr. (Prospects)	2.00
274	Francisco Cordero (Prospects)	1.00
275	Alfonso Soriano (Prospects)	5.00

Gold Medallion

TONY ARMAS, JR.

Stars (1-250):	1-2X
Inserted 1:1	
Prospects (251-275):	1-2X
Inserted 1:24	

Platinum Medallion

Stars (1-250):	15-25X
Production 50 Sets	

Prospects (251-275): 5-10X
Production 25 Sets

Autographics

		NM/M
Common Player:		5.00
Inserted 1:48		
Silvers:		1-1.5X
Production 250 Sets		
1	Roberto Alomar	25.00
2	Jimmy Anderson	5.00
3	Lance Berkman	15.00
4	Barry Bonds	150.00
5	Roosevelt Brown	5.00
6	Jeromy Burnitz	5.00
7	Pat Burrell	10.00
8	Alex Cabrera	5.00
9	Eric Chavez	10.00
10	Joe Crede	5.00
11	Johnny Damon	30.00
12	Carlos Delgado	10.00
13	Adam Dunn	20.00
14	Jim Edmonds	15.00
15	Chad Green	5.00
16	Dustin Hermanson	5.00
17	Randy Johnson	50.00
18	Corey Lee	5.00
19	Derrek Lee	25.00
20	Terrence Long	5.00
21	Julio Lugo	5.00
22	Edgar Martinez	20.00
23	Justin Miller	5.00
24	Russ Ortiz	5.00
25	Pablo Ozuna	5.00
26	Adam Piatt	5.00
27	Mark Redman	5.00
28	Richie Sexson	15.00
29	Gary Sheffield	15.00
30	Alfonso Soriano	25.00
31	Jose Vidro	8.00
32	Vernon Wells	10.00
33	Preston Wilson	10.00
34	Jamey Wright	5.00
35	Julio Zuleta	5.00

Decade of Dominance

		NM/M
Complete Set (15):		15.00
Common Player:		.50
Inserted 1:8		
1	Barry Bonds	3.00
2	Mark McGwire	2.00
3	Sammy Sosa	2.00
4	Ken Griffey Jr.	1.50
5	Cal Ripken Jr.	3.00
6	Tony Gwynn	1.00
7	Albert Belle	.50
8	Frank Thomas	1.00
9	Randy Johnson	1.00
10	Juan Gonzalez	.75
11	Greg Maddux	1.50
12	Craig Biggio	.50
13	Edgar Martinez	.50
14	Roger Clemens	2.00
15	Andres Galarraga	.50

Fall Classics

		NM/M
Complete Set (37):		150.00
Common Player:		2.00
Inserted 1:20		
1	Jackie Robinson	8.00
2	Enos Slaughter	2.00
3	Mariano Rivera	2.00
4	Hank Bauer	2.00
5	Cal Ripken Jr.	12.00
6	Babe Ruth	15.00
7	Thurman Munson	5.00
8	Tom Glavine	3.00
9	Fred Lynn	2.00
10	Johnny Bench	6.00
11	Tony Lazzeri	2.00
12	Al Kaline	5.00
13	Reggie Jackson	5.00
14	Derek Jeter	10.00
15	Willie Stargell	3.00
16	Roy Campanella	4.00
17	Phil Rizzuto	4.00
18	Roberto Clemente	12.00
19	Carlton Fisk	4.00
20	Duke Snider	4.00
21	Ted Williams	12.00
22	Bill Skowron	2.00
23	Bucky Dent	2.00
24	Mike Schmidt	8.00
25	Lou Brock	3.00
26	Whitey Ford	5.00
27	Brooks Robinson	4.00
28	Roberto Alomar	4.00
29	Yogi Berra	5.00
30	Joe Carter	2.00
31	Bill Mazeroski	2.00
32	Bob Gibson	3.00
33	Hank Greenberg	4.00
34	Andruw Jones	4.00
35	Bernie Williams	3.00
36	Don Larsen	3.00
37	Billy Martin	3.00

Fall Classics Memorabilia

		NM/M
Common Player:		10.00
Inserted 1:288		
1	Jackie Robinson/Pants	80.00
2	Enos Slaughter/Bat	15.00
3	Mariano Rivera/Jsy	15.00
4	Hank Bauer/Bat	10.00
5	Cal Ripken Jr./Jsy	40.00
6	Thurman Munson/Bat	25.00
7	Tom Glavine/Jsy	15.00
8	Fred Lynn/Bat	10.00
9	Babe Ruth/Bat	200.00
10	Tony Lazzeri/Bat	10.00
11	Al Kaline/Jsy	20.00
12	Reggie Jackson/Jsy	20.00
13	Derek Jeter/Jsy	40.00
14	Willie Stargell/Bat	15.00
15	Roy Campanella/Bat	50.00
16	Phil Rizzuto/Bat	20.00
17	Roberto Clemente/Bat	120.00
18	Carlton Fisk/Jsy	20.00
19	Duke Snider/Bat	25.00
20	Ted Williams/Bat	120.00
21	Bill Skowron/Bat	10.00
22	Bucky Dent/Bat	10.00
23	Mike Schmidt/Jsy	40.00
24	Lou Brock/Jsy	15.00
25	Brooks Robinson/Bat	20.00
26	Johnny Bench/Jsy	25.00

Fall Classics Memorabilia Autographs

No pricing due to scarcity.

Feel the Game

		NM/M
Common Player:		5.00
Inserted 1:48		
Golds:		2X
Production 50 Sets		
1	Moises Alou	5.00
2	Brady Anderson	5.00
3	Adrian Beltre	5.00
4	Carlos Delgado	8.00
5	J.D. Drew	5.00
6	Jermaine Dye	5.00
7	Jason Giambi	8.00
8	Richard Hidalgo	5.00
9	Chipper Jones	10.00
10	Eric Karros	5.00
11	Raul Mondesi	5.00
12	Chan Ho Park	5.00
13	Ivan Rodriguez	8.00
14	Matt Stairs	5.00
15	Frank Thomas	8.00
16	Jose Vidro	5.00
17	Matt Williams	5.00
18	Preston Wilson	5.00

Power Plus

		NM/M
Complete Set (10):		15.00
Common Player:		1.00
Inserted 1:24		
1	Vladimir Guerrero	1.50
2	Mark McGwire	3.00
3	Mike Piazza	2.00
4	Derek Jeter	4.00
5	Chipper Jones	2.00
6	Carlos Delgado	1.00
7	Sammy Sosa	2.00
8	Ken Griffey Jr.	2.00
9	Nomar Garciaparra	2.50
10	Alex Rodriguez	3.00

Season Pass

Complete Set (6):
Common Player:

The Greatest Hits of ...

		NM/M
Complete Set (10):		10.00
Common Player:		.50
Inserted 1:12		
1	Mark McGwire	2.00
2	Alex Rodriguez	2.00
3	Ken Griffey Jr.	1.50
4	Ivan Rodriguez	.75
5	Cal Ripken Jr.	3.00
6	Todd Helton	.75
7	Derek Jeter	3.00
8	Pedro Martinez	1.00
9	Tony Gwynn	1.00
10	Jim Edmonds	.50

Tomorrow's Legends

		NM/M
Complete Set (15):		10.00
Common Player:		.25
Inserted 1:4		
1	Rick Ankiel	.25
2	J.D. Drew	.40
3	Carlos Delgado	.75
4	Todd Helton	.75

Alex Rodriguez/Seattle Mariners

5	Andruw Jones	.75
6	Troy Glaus	.75
7	Jermaine Dye	.25
8	Vladimir Guerrero	1.00
9	Brian Giles	.15
10	Scott Rolen	.75
11	Darin Erstad	.40
12	Derek Jeter	3.00
13	Alex Rodriguez	3.00
14	Pat Burrell	.50
15	Nomar Garciaparra	2.00

2002 Ultra

		NM/M
Complete Set (285):		100.00
Common Player:		.15
Common SP (201-285):		.50
Inserted 1:4		
Pack (10):		2.00
Box (24):		40.00
1	Jeff Bagwell	.50
2	Derek Jeter	2.00
3	Alex Rodriguez	1.50
4	Eric Chavez	.40
5	Tsuyoshi Shinjo	.15
6	Chris Stynes	.15
7	Ivan Rodriguez	.50
8	Cal Ripken Jr.	2.00
9	Freddy Garcia	.15
10	Chipper Jones	.75
11	Hideo Nomo	.25
12	Rafael Furcal	.25
13	Preston Wilson	.15
14	Jimmy Rollins	.15
15	Cristian Guzman	.15
16	Garret Anderson	.15
17	Todd Helton	.50
18	Moises Alou	.15
19	Tony Gwynn	.75
20	Jorge Posada	.40
21	Sean Casey	.15
22	Kazuhiro Sasaki	.15
23	Ray Lankford	.15
24	Manny Ramirez	.50
25	Barry Bonds	2.00
26	Fred McGriff	.25
27	Vladimir Guerrero	.75
28	Jermaine Dye	.25
29	Adrian Beltre	.25
30	Ken Griffey Jr.	1.00
31	Ramon Hernandez	.15
32	Kerry Wood	.75
33	Greg Maddux	1.00
34	Rondell White	.15
35	Mike Mussina	.50
36	Jim Edmonds	.40
37	Scott Rolen	.25
38	Mike Lowell	.25
39	Al Leiter	.15
40	Tony Clark	.15
41	Joe Mays	.15
42	Mo Vaughn	.25
43	Geoff Jenkins	.25
44	Curt Schilling	.25
45	Pedro Martinez	.75
46	Andy Pettitte	.40
47	Tim Salmon	.25
48	Carl Everett	.15
49	Lance Berkman	.25
50	Troy Glaus	.40
51	Ichiro Suzuki	1.00
52	Alfonso Soriano	.75
53	Tomo Ohka	.15
54	Dean Palmer	.15
55	Kevin Brown	.15
56	Albert Pujols	1.50
57	Homer Bush	.15
58	Tim Hudson	.40
59	Frank Thomas	.50
60	Joe Randa	.15
61	Chan Ho Park	.15
62	Bobby Higginson	.15
63	Bartolo Colon	.15
64	Aramis Ramirez	.40
65	Jeff Cirillo	.15
66	Roberto Alomar	.50
67	Mark Kotsay	.15
68	Mike Cameron	.15
69	Mike Hampton	.15
70	Trot Nixon	.15
71	Juan Gonzalez	.50
72	Damian Rolls	.15
73	Brad Fullmer	.15
74	David Ortiz	.15
75	Brandon Inge	.15
76	Orlando Hernandez	.15
77	Matt Stairs	.15
78	Jay Gibbons	.15
79	Greg Vaughn	.15
80	Brady Anderson	.15
81	Jim Thome	.75
82	Ben Sheets	.40
83	Rafael Palmeiro	.50
84	Edgar Renteria	.25
85	Doug Mientkiewicz	.15
86	Raul Mondesi	.15
87	Shane Reynolds	.15
88	Steve Finley	.15
89	Jose Cruz Jr.	.15
90	Edgardo Alfonzo	.15
91	Jose Valentin	.15
92	Mark McGwire	2.00
93	Mark Grace	.40
94	Mike Lieberthal	.15
95	Barry Larkin	.25
96	Chuck Knoblauch	.15
97	Deivi Cruz	.15
98	Jeromy Burnitz	.15
99	Shannon Stewart	.15
100	David Wells	.15
101	Brook Fordyce	.15
102	Rusty Greer	.15
103	Andruw Jones	.50
104	Jason Kendall	.15
105	Nomar Garciaparra	1.25
106	Shawn Green	.25
107	Craig Biggio	.25
108	Masato Yoshii	.15
109	Ben Petrick	.15
110	Gary Sheffield	.40
111	Travis Lee	.15
112	Matt Williams	.25
113	Billy Wagner	.15
114	Robin Ventura	.15
115	Jerry Hairston Jr.	.15
116	Paul LoDuca	.15
117	Darin Erstad	.25
118	Ruben Sierra	.15
119	Ricky Gutierrez	.15
120	Bret Boone	.25
121	John Rocker	.15
122	Roger Clemens	1.50
123	Eric Karros	.15
124	J.D. Drew	.25
125	Carlos Delgado	.40
126	Jeffrey Hammonds	.15
127	Jeff Kent	.25
128	David Justice	.25
129	Cliff Floyd	.15
130	Omar Vizquel	.25
131	Matt Morris	.25
132	Rich Aurilia	.25
133	Larry Walker	.25
134	Miguel Tejada	.25
135	Eric Young	.15
136	Aaron Sele	.15
137	Eric Milton	.15
138	Travis Fryman	.15
139	Magglio Ordonez	.25
140	Sammy Sosa	1.50
141	Pokey Reese	.15
142	Adam Eaton	.15
143	Adam Kennedy	.15
144	Mike Piazza	1.00
145	Larry Barnes	.15
146	Darryl Kile	.15
147	Tom Glavine	.25
148	Ryan Klesko	.15
149	Jose Vidro	.15
150	Joe Kennedy	.15
151	Bernie Williams	.40
152	C.C. Sabathia	.15
153	Alex Ochoa	.15
154	A.J. Pierzynski	.15
155	Johnny Damon	.25
156	Omar Daal	.15
157	A.J. Burnett	.15
158	Eric Munson	.15
159	Fernando Vina	.15
160	Chris Singleton	.15
161	Juan Pierre	.15
162	John Olerud	.15
163	Randy Johnson	.75
164	Paul Konerko	.25
165	Tino Martinez	.25
166	Richard Hidalgo	.15
167	Luis Gonzalez	.25
168	Ben Grieve	.15
169	Matt Lawton	.15
170	Gabe Kapler	.25
171	Mariano Rivera	.25
172	Kenny Lofton	.25
173	Brian Jordan	.15
174	Brian Giles	.15
175	Mark Quinn	.15
176	Neifi Perez	.15
177	Ellis Burks	.15
178	Bobby Abreu	.40
179	Jeff Weaver	.15
180	Andres Galarraga	.25
181	Javy Lopez	.25
182	Todd Walker	.15
183	Fernando Tatis	.15
184	Charles Johnson	.15
185	Pat Burrell	.40
186	Jay Bell	.15
187	Aaron Boone	.15
188	Jason Giambi	.50
189	Jay Payton	.15
190	Carlos Lee	.15
191	Phil Nevin	.15
192	Mike Sweeney	.15
193	J.T. Snow	.15
194	Dmitri Young	.15
195	Richie Sexson	.40
196	Derrek Lee	.25
197	Corey Koskie	.15
198	Edgar Martinez	.25
199	Wade Miller	.15
200	Tony Batista	.15
201	John Olerud	.50
202	Bret Boone	.50
203	Cal Ripken Jr.	3.00
204	Alex Rodriguez	2.50
205	Ichiro Suzuki	2.00
206	Manny Ramirez	.75
207	Juan Gonzalez	.75
208	Ivan Rodriguez	.75
209	Roger Clemens	2.00
210	Edgar Martinez	.50
211	Todd Helton	.75
212	Jeff Kent	.50
213	Chipper Jones	1.00
214	Rich Aurilia	.50
215	Barry Bonds	3.00
216	Sammy Sosa	2.00
217	Luis Gonzalez	.75
218	Mike Piazza	2.00
219	Randy Johnson	1.00
220	Larry Walker	.50
221	Todd Helton, Juan Uribe	.50
222	Pat Burrell, Eric Valent	.50
223	Edgar Martinez, Ichiro Suzuki	2.00
224	Ben Grieve, Jason Tyner	.50
225	Mark Quinn, Dee Brown	.50
226	Cal Ripken Jr., Brian Roberts	3.00
227	Cliff Floyd, Abraham Nunez	.50
228	Jeff Bagwell, Adam Everett	.75
229	Mark McGwire, Albert Pujols	3.00
230	Doug Mientkiewicz, Luis Rivas	.50
231	Juan Gonzalez, Danny Peoples	.75
232	Kevin Brown, Luke Prokopec	
233	Richie Sexson, Ben Sheets	.50
234	Jason Giambi, Jason Hart	.75
235	Barry Bonds, Carlos Valderrama	3.00
236	Tony Gwynn, Cesar Crespo	1.00
237	Ken Griffey Jr., Adam Dunn	1.50
238	Frank Thomas, Joe Crede	.75
239	Derek Jeter, Drew Henson	3.00
240	Chipper Jones, Wilson Betemit	1.00
241	Luis Gonzalez, Junior Spivey	.50
242	Bobby Higginson, Andres Torres	.50
243	Carlos Delgado, Vernon Wells	.50
244	Sammy Sosa, Corey Patterson	2.00
245	Nomar Garciaparra, Shea Hillenbrand	2.00
246	Alex Rodriguez, Jason Romano	2.50
247	Troy Glaus, David Eckstein	.75
248	Mike Piazza, Alex Escobar	2.00
249	Brian Giles, Jack Wilson	.50
250	Vladimir Guerrero, Scott Hodges	1.00
251	Bud Smith	1.00
252	Juan Diaz	1.00
253	Wilkin Ruan	1.00
254	Chris Spurling RC	1.00
255	Toby Hall	1.00
256	Jason Jennings	1.00
257	George Perez	1.00
258	D'Angelo Jimenez	1.00
259	Jose Acevedo	1.00
260	Josue Perez	1.00
261	Brian Rogers	1.00
262	Carlos Maldonado	1.00
263	Travis Phelps	1.00
264	Rob Mackowiak	1.50
265	Ryan Drese	1.00
266	Carlos Garcia	1.00
267	Alexis Gomez	1.00

268	Jeremy Affeldt	1.00
269	Scott Podsednik	3.00
270	Adam Johnson	1.00
271	Pedro Santana	1.00
272	Les Walrond	1.00
273	Jackson Melian	1.00
274	Carlos Hernandez	1.00
275	Mark Nussbeck RC	1.00
276	Cory Aldridge	1.00
277	Troy Mattes	1.00
278	Brent Abernathy	1.00
279	J.J. Davis	1.00
280	Brandon Duckworth	1.00
281	Kyle Lohse	1.00
282	Justin Kaye	1.00
283	Cody Ransom	1.00
284	Dave Williams	1.00
285	Luis Lopez	1.00

Gold Medallion

Stars (1-200): 2-3X
Inserted 1:1
Stars (201-250): 2-4X
Inserted 1:24
Prospects (251-285): 4-8X
Production 100

Fall Classic

		NM/M
	Complete Set (39):	180.00
	Common Player:	2.50
	Inserted 1:20	
1FC	Ty Cobb	10.00
2FC	Lou Gehrig	15.00
3FC	Babe Ruth	15.00
4FC	Stan Musial	8.00
5FC	Ted Williams	12.00
6FC	Dizzy Dean	6.00
7FC	Mickey Cochrane	2.50
8FC	Jimmie Foxx	8.00
9FC	Mel Ott	9.00
10FC	Rogers Hornsby	6.00
11FC	Hank Aaron	10.00
12FC	Clete Boyer	2.50
13FC	George Brett	10.00
14FC	Bob Gibson	5.00
15FC	Carlton Fisk	4.00
16FC	Johnny Bench	8.00
17FC	Rusty Staub	2.50
18FC	Willie McCovey	2.50
19FC	Paul Molitor	5.00
20FC	Jim Palmer	4.00
21FC	Frank Robinson	5.00
22FC	Derek Jeter	10.00
23FC	Earl Weaver	2.50
24FC	Lefty Grove	2.50
25FC	Tony Perez	2.50
26FC	Reggie Jackson	5.00
27FC	Sparky Anderson	2.50
28FC	Casey Stengel	2.50
29FC	Roy Campanella	6.00
30FC	Roberto Clemente	10.00
31FC	Don Drysdale	6.00
32FC	Joe Morgan	4.00
33FC	Eddie Murray	5.00
34FC	Nolan Ryan	15.00
35FC	Tom Seaver	8.00
36FC	Bill Mazeroski	2.50
37FC	Jackie Robinson	8.00
38FC	Kirk Gibson	2.50
39FC	Robin Yount	8.00

Fall Classic Autographs

		NM/M
	Common Autograph:	10.00
	Inserted 1:240	
1	Sparky Anderson	15.00
2	Johnny Bench/SP	40.00
3	George Brett/SP	80.00
4	Carlton Fisk	25.00
5	Bob Gibson	25.00
6	Kirk Gibson	15.00
7	Reggie Jackson/SP	40.00
8	Bill Mazeroski	20.00
10	Willie McCovey/SP	30.00
11	Joe Morgan	15.00
12	Eddie Murray/SP	40.00
14	Jim Palmer	15.00
15	Tony Perez	15.00
16	Frank Robinson	20.00
17	Nolan Ryan/SP	175.00
18	Tom Seaver/SP	30.00
19	Earl Weaver	15.00
20	Robin Yount/SP	50.00

Fall Classic Game-Used

Twenty-six players or managers who have had a role in World Series history are included in this insert series found at the announced rate of about one per 113 packs. Some players' cards can be found with more than one type of game-used memorabilia in varying rates of production (some with as few as 21 pieces reported by the manufacturer and shown here). Players are checklisted alphabetically.

	NM/M
Inserted 1:113	
Sparky Anderson/Pants	5.00
Johnny Bench/Jsy	5.00
Johnny Bench/Pants	10.00
George Brett/Bat	15.00
George Brett/Blue Jersey/65	45.00
George Brett/White Jersey	15.00
Roy Campanella/Bat/21	225.00
Carlton Fisk/Bat/42	35.00
Carlton Fisk/Jsy	15.00
Jimmie Foxx/Bat	35.00
Bob Gibson/Jsy	10.00
Kirk Gibson/Bat	5.00
Reggie Jackson/Bat	10.00
Reggie Jackson/Jsy/73	20.00
Derek Jeter/Pants	30.00
Willie McCovey/Jsy	5.00
Paul Molitor/Bat	10.00
Paul Molitor/Jsy	10.00
Joe Morgan/Bat	8.00
Joe Morgan/Jsy	5.00
Eddie Murray/Bat	10.00
Eddie Murray/Jsy/91	35.00
Jim Palmer/Gray Jersey/85	20.00
Jim Palmer/White Jersey	5.00
Tony Perez/Bat	8.00
Frank Robinson/Bat/40	25.00
Jackie Robinson/Jsy	50.00
Babe Ruth/Bat/44	200.00
Nolan Ryan/Pants	30.00
Tom Seaver/Jsy	10.00
Earl Weaver/Jsy	5.00
Ted Williams/Bat/30	200.00
Ted Williams/Jsy	75.00
Robin Yount/Bat	10.00
Robin Yount/Gray Jersey	10.00
Robin Yount/White Jersey/30	30.00

Glove Works

		NM/M
	Complete Set (15):	25.00
	Common Player:	1.00
	Inserted 1:20	
1GW	Andruw Jones	1.50
2GW	Derek Jeter	6.00
3GW	Cal Ripken Jr.	8.00
4GW	Larry Walker	1.00
5GW	Chipper Jones	2.00

ABBREVIATIONS
SP - Short Print

6GW	Barry Bonds	6.00
7GW	Scott Rolen	2.00
8GW	Jim Edmonds	1.00
9GW	Robin Ventura	1.00
10GW	Darin Erstad	1.00
11GW	Barry Larkin	1.00
12GW	Raul Mondesi	1.50
13GW	Mark Grace	1.50
14GW	Bernie Williams	1.50
15GW	Ivan Rodriguez	1.50

Glove Works Game Worn

	NM/M
Common Player:	10.00
Production 450 Sets	
Platinum (25 Sets) randomly inserted.	
Derek Jeter	35.00
Cal Ripken Jr.	50.00
Barry Bonds	40.00
Robin Ventura	10.00
Barry Larkin/SP	15.00
Raul Mondesi	10.00
Ivan Rodriguez	15.00

Hitting Machine

		NM/M
	Complete Set (25):	60.00
	Common Player:	1.00
	Inserted 1:20	
1HM	Frank Thomas	2.00
2HM	Derek Jeter	8.00
3HM	Vladimir Guerrero	3.00
4HM	Jim Edmonds	1.50
5HM	Mike Piazza	5.00
6HM	Ivan Rodriguez	2.00
7HM	Chipper Jones	3.00
8HM	Tony Gwynn	3.00
9HM	Manny Ramirez	2.00
10HM	Andruw Jones	2.00
11HM	Carlos Delgado	1.50
12HM	Bernie Williams	1.50
13HM	Larry Walker	1.00
14HM	Juan Gonzalez	1.50
15HM	Ichiro Suzuki	5.00
16HM	Albert Pujols	6.00
17HM	Barry Bonds	8.00
18HM	Cal Ripken Jr.	8.00
19HM	Edgar Martinez	1.00
20HM	Luis Gonzalez	1.00
21HM	Moises Alou	1.50
22HM	Roberto Alomar	2.00
23HM	Todd Helton	2.00
24HM	Rafael Palmeiro	2.00
25HM	Bobby Abreu	1.50

Hitting Machine Game Worn

	NM/M
Common Player:	8.00
Inserted 1:81	
Platinum (25 Sets) randomly inserted.	
Frank Thomas	15.00
Derek Jeter	25.00
Jim Edmonds	15.00
Mike Piazza	15.00
Ivan Rodriguez	15.00
Chipper Jones	15.00
Tony Gwynn	15.00
Manny Ramirez	10.00
Andruw Jones	10.00
Carlos Delgado	10.00
Bernie Williams	10.00
Larry Walker	8.00
Juan Gonzalez	10.00
Albert Pujols	30.00
Barry Bonds	25.00
Cal Ripken Jr.	40.00
Edgar Martinez	10.00
Luis Gonzalez	8.00
Moises Alou	10.00
Roberto Alomar	15.00
Todd Helton	15.00
Rafael Palmeiro	10.00
Bobby Abreu	10.00

On the Road Game-Used

	NM/M
Common Player:	10.00
Inserted 1:93	
Platinum (25 Sets) randomly inserted.	
Derek Jeter	30.00
Ivan Rodriguez	10.00
Carlos Delgado	8.00
Larry Walker	8.00
Roberto Alomar	15.00
Tony Gwynn	15.00
Greg Maddux	20.00
Barry Bonds	30.00
Todd Helton	15.00
Kazuhiro Sasaki	10.00
Jeff Bagwell	15.00
Omar Vizquel	8.00
Chan Ho Park	10.00
Tom Glavine	10.00

Rising Stars

		NM/M
	Complete Set (15):	15.00
	Common Player:	.50
	Inserted 1:12	
1RS	Ichiro Suzuki	2.50
2RS	Derek Jeter	4.00
3RS	Albert Pujols	3.00
4RS	Jimmy Rollins	1.00
5RS	Adam Dunn	1.00
6RS	Sean Casey	1.00
7RS	Kerry Wood	2.00
8RS	Tsuyoshi Shinjo	.50
9RS	Shea Hillenbrand	.50
10RS	Pat Burrell	1.00
11RS	Ben Sheets	1.00
12RS	Alfonso Soriano	1.50
13RS	J.D. Drew	1.00
14RS	Kazuhiro Sasaki	.50
15RS	Corey Patterson	.75

Rising Stars Game Worn

	NM/M
Common Player:	20.00
Production 100 Sets	
Platinum (25 Sets) randomly seeded.	
Derek Jeter	75.00
Albert Pujols	50.00
Tsuyoshi Shinjo	25.00
Alfonso Soriano	25.00
J.D. Drew	25.00
Kazuhiro Sasaki	20.00

2003 Ultra

		NM/M
	Complete Set (250):	75.00
	Common Player:	.15
	Common SP (201-250):	.50
	Inserted 1:4	
	Hobby Pack (10):	2.00
	Hobby Box (24):	35.00
1	Barry Bonds	2.00
2	Derek Jeter	2.50
3	Ichiro Suzuki	1.50
4	Mike Lowell	.15
5	Hideo Nomo	.50
6	Javier Vazquez	.15
7	Jeremy Giambi	.15
8	Jamie Moyer	.15
9	Rafael Palmeiro	.40
10	Magglio Ordonez	.25
11	Trot Nixon	.15
12	Luis Castillo	.15
13	Paul Byrd	.15
14	Adam Kennedy	.15
15	Trevor Hoffman	.15
16	Matt Morris	.15
17	Nomar Garciaparra	1.50
18	Matt Lawton	.15
19	Carlos Beltran	.15
20	Jason Giambi	1.25
21	Brian Giles	.25
22	Jim Edmonds	.25
23	Garret Anderson	.25
24	Tony Batista	.15
25	Aaron Boone	.15
26	Mike Hampton	.15
27	Billy Wagner	.15
28	Kazuhisa Ishii	.15
29	Al Leiter	.25
30	Pat Burrell	.40
31	Jeff Kent	.25
32	Randy Johnson	.75
33	Ray Durham	.15
34	Josh Beckett	.15
35	Cristian Guzman	.15
36	Roger Clemens	1.25
37	Freddy Garcia	.15
38	Roy Halladay	.15
39	David Eckstein	.15
40	Jerry Hairston Jr.	.15
41	Barry Larkin	.25
42	Larry Walker	.25
43	Craig Biggio	.25
44	Edgardo Alfonzo	.15
45	Marlon Byrd	.15
46	J.T. Snow	.15
47	Juan Gonzalez	.50
48	Ramon Ortiz	.15
49	Jay Gibbons	.15
50	Adam Dunn	.60
51	Juan Pierre	.15
52	Jeff Bagwell	.50
53	Kevin Brown	.15
54	Pedro Astacio	.15
55	Mike Lieberthal	.15
56	Johnny Damon	.25
57	Tim Salmon	.25
58	Mike Bordick	.15
59	Ken Griffey Jr.	1.50
60	Jason Jennings	.15
61	Lance Berkman	.50
62	Jeromy Burnitz	.15
63	Jimmy Rollins	.25
64	Tsuyoshi Shinjo	.15
65	Alex Rodriguez	2.00
66	Greg Maddux	1.25
67	Mark Prior	.40
68	Mike Maroth	.15
69	Geoff Jenkins	.15
70	Tony Armas Jr.	.15
71	Jermaine Dye	.15
72	Albert Pujols	.75
73	Shannon Stewart	.15
74	Troy Glaus	.60
75	Brook Fordyce	.15
76	Juan Encarnacion	.15
77	Todd Hollandsworth	.15
78	Roy Oswalt	.25
79	Paul LoDuca	.15
80	Mike Piazza	1.50
81	Bobby Abreu	.15
82	Sean Burroughs	.15
83	Randy Winn	.15
84	Curt Schilling	.50
85	Chris Singleton	.15
86	Sean Casey	.25
87	Todd Zeile	.15
88	Richard Hidalgo	.15
89	Roberto Alomar	.25
90	Tim Hudson	.25
91	Ryan Klesko	.15
92	Greg Vaughn	.15
93	Tony Womack	.15
94	Fred McGriff	.25
95	Tom Glavine	.40
96	Todd Walker	.15
97	Travis Fryman	.15
98	Shane Reynolds	.15
99	Shawn Green	.25
100	Mo Vaughn	.25
101	Adam Piatt	.15
102	Deivi Cruz	.15
103	Steve Cox	.15
104	Luis Gonzalez	.25
105	Russell Branyan	.15
106	Daryle Ward	.15
107	Mariano Rivera	.25
108	Phil Nevin	.15
109	Ben Grieve	.15
110	Moises Alou	.15
111	Omar Vizquel	.25
112	Joe Randa	.15
113	Jorge Posada	.40
114	Mark Kotsay	.15
115	Ryan Rupe	.15
116	Javy Lopez	.15
117	Corey Patterson	.15
118	Bobby Higginson	.15
119	Jose Vidro	.15
120	Barry Zito	.25
121	Matt Morris	.15
122	Gary Sheffield	.25
123	Kerry Wood	.25
124	Brandon Inge	.15
125	Jose Hernandez	.15
126	Michael Barrett	.15
127	Edgar Renteria	.15
128	Junior Spivey	.15
129	Jose Valentin	.15
130	Derrek Lee	.15
131	A.J. Pierzynski	.15
132	Mike Mussina	.50
133	Mike Mussina	.50
134	Bret Boone	.15
135	Chan Ho Park	.15
136	Steve Finley	.15
137	Mark Buehrle	.15
138	A.J. Burnett	.15
139	Ben Sheets	.15
140	David Ortiz	.15
141	Nick Johnson	.15
142	Randall Simon	.15
143	Carlos Delgado	.40
144	Darin Erstad	.25
145	Shea Hillenbrand	.15
146	Todd Helton	.40
147	Preston Wilson	.15
148	Eric Gagne	.15
149	Vladimir Guerrero	.75
150	Brandon Duckworth	.15
151	Rich Aurilia	.15
152	Ivan Rodriguez	.50
153	Andruw Jones	.50
154	Carlos Lee	.15
155	Robert Fick	.15
156	Jacque Jones	.15
157	Bernie Williams	.25
158	John Olerud	.25
159	Eric Hinske	.15
160	Matt Clement	.15
161	Dmitri Young	.15
162	Torii Hunter	.15
163	Carlos Pena	.15
164	Mike Cameron	.15
165	Raul Mondesi	.15
166	Pedro J. Martinez	.75
167	Bob Wickman	.15
168	Mike Sweeney	.15
169	David Wells	.15
170	Jason Kendall	.15
171	Tino Martinez	.15
172	Matt Williams	.15
173	Frank Thomas	.60
174	Cliff Floyd	.15
175	Corey Koskie	.15
176	Orlando Hernandez	.15
177	Edgar Martinez	.15
178	Richie Sexson	.25
179	Manny Ramirez	.60
180	Jim Thome	.50
181	Andy Pettitte	.40
182	Aramis Ramirez	.15
183	J.D. Drew	.25
184	Brian Jordan	.15
185	Sammy Sosa	1.25
186	Jeff Weaver	.15
187	Jeffrey Hammonds	.15
188	Eric Milton	.15
189	Eric Chavez	.25
190	Kazuhiro Sasaki	.15
191	Jose Cruz Jr.	.15
192	Derek Lowe	.15
193	C.C. Sabathia	.15
194	Adrian Beltre	.15
195	Alfonso Soriano	1.00
196	Jack Wilson	.15
197	Fernando Vina	.15
198	Chipper Jones	1.25
199	Paul Konerko	.15
200	Rusty Greer	.15
201	Jason Giambi	2.00
202	Alfonso Soriano	2.00
203	Shea Hillenbrand	.50
204	Alex Rodriguez	3.00
205	Jorge Posada	.60
206	Ichiro Suzuki	3.00
207	Manny Ramirez	1.00
208	Torii Hunter	.75
209	Todd Helton	.75
210	Roberto Alomar	.75
211	Scott Rolen	.75
212	Jimmy Rollins	.75
213	Mike Piazza	3.00
214	Barry Bonds	3.00
215	Sammy Sosa	2.00
216	Vladimir Guerrero	1.50
217	Lance Berkman	.75
218	Derek Jeter	4.00
219	Nomar Garciaparra	.75
220	Luis Gonzalez	.75
221	Kazuhisa Ishii	1.00
222	Satoru Komiyama	.50
223	So Taguchi	.50
224	Jorge Padilla	.50
225	Ben Howard	.50
226	Jason Simontacchi	.50
227	Barry Wesson	.50
228	Howie Clark	.50
229	Aaron Guiel	.50
230	Oliver Perez	.75
231	David Ross	.50
232	Julius Matos	.50
233	Chris Snelling	.50
234	Rodrigo Lopez	.50
235	Wilbert Nieves	.50
236	Brendan Donnelly	.50
237	Aaron Cook	.50
238	Anderson Machado	.50
239	Corey Thurman	.50
240	Tyler Yates	.50
241	Coco Crisp	4.00
242	Andy Van Hekken	1.50
243	Jim Rushford	2.00
244	Jerome Robertson	1.00
245	Shane Nance	.50
246	Kevin Cash	.50
247	Kirk Saarloos	1.50
248	Josh Bard	2.00
249	David Pember RC	1.00
250	Freddy Sanchez	.15

Gold Medallion

Stars (1-200): 2-3X
Inserted 1:1
Stars (201-220): 3-4X
Inserted 1:24
Rookies (221-250): 1-3X
Inserted 1:24

Back 2 Back

NM/M
Complete Set (17): 60.00
Common Player: 2.00
Production 1,000 Sets

1B2B	Derek Jeter	10.00
2B2B	Barry Bonds	8.00
3B2B	Mike Piazza	6.00
4B2B	Alex Rodriguez	8.00
5B2B	Todd Helton	2.00
6B2B	Edgar Martinez	2.00
7B2B	Chipper Jones	5.00
8B2B	Shawn Green	2.00
9B2B	Chan Ho Park	2.00
10B2B	Preston Wilson	2.00
11B2B	Manny Ramirez	3.00
12B2B	Aramis Ramirez	2.00
13B2B	Pedro J. Martinez	4.00
14B2B	Ivan Rodriguez	2.00
15B2B	Ichiro Suzuki	6.00
16B2B	Sammy Sosa	5.00
17B2B	Jason Giambi	5.00

Back 2 Back Memorabilia

NM/M
Common Player: 5.00
Production 500 Sets
Golds: 1.5-3X
Production 50 Sets

Derek Jeter	25.00
Barry Bonds/Bat	20.00
Mike Piazza/Jsy	12.00
Alex Rodriguez/Jsy	12.00
Todd Helton/Jsy	8.00
Edgar Martinez/Jsy	6.00
Chipper Jones/Jsy	15.00
Shawn Green/Jsy	6.00
Chan Ho Park/Bat	6.00
Preston Wilson/Jsy	5.00
Manny Ramirez/Jsy	5.00
Aramis Ramirez/Jsy	5.00
Pedro Martinez/Jsy	10.00
Ivan Rodriguez/Jsy	8.00
Ichiro Suzuki/Base	15.00
Sammy Sosa/Base	10.00
Jason Giambi/Base	8.00

Double Up

NM/M
Complete Set (16): 30.00
Common Player: 1.00
Inserted 1:8

1DU	Derek Jeter, Mike Piazza	4.00
2DU	Alex Rodriguez, Rafael Palmeiro	3.00
3DU	Chipper Jones, Andruw Jones	2.00
4DU	Derek Jeter, Alex Rodriguez	4.00
5DU	Nomar Garciaparra, Derek Jeter	4.00
6DU	Barry Bonds, Jason Giambi	3.00
7DU	Ichiro Suzuki, Hideo Nomo	3.00
8DU	Randy Johnson, Curt Schilling	1.00
9DU	Pedro J. Martinez, Nomar Garciaparra	2.50
10DU	Roger Clemens, Kevin Brown	2.00
11DU	Nomar Garciaparra, Manny Ramirez	2.50
12DU	Kazuhiro Sasaki, Hideo Nomo	1.00
13DU	Mike Piazza, Ivan Rodriguez	3.00
14DU	Ichiro Suzuki, Ken Griffey Jr.	3.00
15DU	Barry Bonds, Sammy Sosa	3.00
16DU	Alfonso Soriano, Roberto Alomar	2.00

Double Up Memorabilia

NM/M
Common Card: 15.00
Production 100 Sets

Derek Jeter, Mike Piazza	50.00
Alex Rodriguez, Rafael Palmeiro	25.00
Chipper Jones, Andruw Jones	15.00
Derek Jeter, Alex Rodriguez	50.00
Nomar Garciaparra, Derek Jeter	50.00
Barry Bonds, Jason Giambi	30.00
Ichiro Suzuki, Hideo Nomo	80.00
Randy Johnson, Curt Schilling	20.00
Pedro J. Martinez, Nomar Garciaparra	30.00
Roger Clemens, Kevin Brown	25.00
Nomar Garciaparra, Manny Ramirez	25.00
Kazuhiro Sasaki, Hideo Nomo	50.00
Mike Piazza, Ivan Rodriguez	25.00
Ichiro Suzuki, Ken Griffey Jr.	50.00
Barry Bonds, Sammy Sosa	40.00
Alfonso Soriano, Roberto Alomar	25.00

Moonshots

NM/M
Complete Set (20): 30.00
Common Player: .75
Inserted 1:12

1M	Mike Piazza	4.00
2M	Alex Rodriguez	4.00
3M	Manny Ramirez	1.50
4M	Ivan Rodriguez	1.00
5M	Luis Gonzalez	.75
6M	Shawn Green	.75
7M	Barry Bonds	5.00
8M	Jason Giambi	3.00
9M	Nomar Garciaparra	3.00
10M	Edgar Martinez	.75
11M	Mo Vaughn	.75
12M	Chipper Jones	3.00
13M	Todd Helton	1.00
14M	Raul Mondesi	.75
15M	Preston Wilson	.75
16M	Rafael Palmeiro	1.00
17M	Jim Edmonds	.75
18M	Bernie Williams	1.00
19M	Vladimir Guerrero	2.00
20M	Alfonso Soriano	2.00

Moonshots Memorabilia

NM/M
Common Player: 4.00
Inserted 1:20

Mike Piazza/Jsy	12.00
Alex Rodriguez/Jsy	12.00
Manny Ramirez/Jsy	5.00
Ivan Rodriguez/Jsy	5.00
Luis Gonzalez/Jsy	4.00
Shawn Green/Jsy	4.00
Barry Bonds/Jsy	12.00
Jason Giambi/Base	8.00
Nomar Garciaparra/Jsy	12.00
Edgar Martinez/Jsy	5.00
Mo Vaughn/Jsy	4.00
Chipper Jones/Jsy	6.00
Todd Helton/Jsy	6.00
Raul Mondesi/Jsy	5.00
Preston Wilson/Jsy	5.00
Rafael Palmeiro/Jsy	5.00
Jim Edmonds/Jsy	6.00
Bernie Williams/Jsy	6.00
Vladimir Guerrero/Base	5.00
Alfonso Soriano/Jsy	8.00

Photo Effex

Vladimir Guerrero
Montreal Expos™

NM/M
Complete Set (20): 45.00
Common Player: 1.00
Inserted 1:12
Golds: 6-12X
Production 25 Sets

1PE	Derek Jeter	6.00
2PE	Barry Bonds	5.00
3PE	Sammy Sosa	3.00
4PE	Troy Glaus	1.50
5PE	Albert Pujols	2.00
6PE	Alex Rodriguez	5.00
7PE	Ichiro Suzuki	4.00
8PE	Greg Maddux	3.00
9PE	Nomar Garciaparra	4.00
10PE	Jeff Bagwell	1.50
11PE	Chipper Jones	3.00
12PE	Mike Piazza	4.00
13PE	Randy Johnson	2.00
14PE	Vladimir Guerrero	2.00
15PE	Alfonso Soriano	3.00
16PE	Lance Berkman	1.00
17PE	Todd Helton	1.00
18PE	Mike Lowell	1.00
19PE	Carlos Delgado	1.00
20PE	Jason Giambi	3.00

When it was a Game

NM/M
Complete Set (40): 125.00
Common Player: 2.00
Inserted 1:20

1WG	Derek Jeter	10.00
2WG	Barry Bonds	8.00
3WG	Luis Aparicio	2.00
4WG	Richie Ashburn	2.00
5WG	Ernie Banks	5.00
6WG	Enos Slaughter	2.00
7WG	Yogi Berra	5.00
8WG	Lou Boudreau	2.00
9WG	Lou Brock	4.00
10WG	Jim Bunning	2.00
11WG	Rod Carew	4.00
12WG	Orlando Cepeda	2.00
13WG	Larry Doby	2.00
14WG	Bobby Doerr	2.00
15WG	Bob Feller	3.00
16WG	Brooks Robinson	5.00
17WG	Rollie Fingers	2.00
18WG	Whitey Ford	3.00
19WG	Bob Gibson	4.00
20WG	Jim "Catfish" Hunter	3.00
21WG	Nolan Ryan	15.00
22WG	Reggie Jackson	5.00
23WG	Fergie Jenkins	3.00
24WG	Al Kaline	6.00
25WG	Mike Schmidt	8.00
26WG	Harmon Killebrew	8.00
27WG	Ralph Kiner	4.00
28WG	Willie Stargell	4.00
29WG	Billy Williams	2.00
30WG	Tom Seaver	5.00
31WG	Juan Marichal	4.00
32WG	Eddie Mathews	6.00
33WG	Willie McCovey	4.00
34WG	Joe Morgan	4.00
35WG	Stan Musial	8.00
36WG	Robin Roberts	4.00
37WG	Robin Yount	8.00
38WG	Jim Palmer	3.00
39WG	Phil Rizzuto	4.00
40WG	Pee Wee Reese	4.00

When it was a Game Autograph

No Pricing

When it was a Game Memorabilia

NM/M
Common Player:
Varying quantities produced

Derek Jeter/Jsy/200	35.00
Barry Bonds/Bat/200	25.00
Yogi Berra/100	35.00
Larry Doby/Bat/150	20.00
Catfish Hunter/Jsy	8.00
Reggie Jackson/Bat	12.00
Tom Seaver/Jsy	15.00
Juan Marichal/Jsy	8.00
Eddie Mathews/Bat	25.00
Willie McCovey/Jsy/150	15.00
Joe Morgan/Jsy	10.00
Jim Palmer/Jsy/300	10.00

All-Vet Phillies Team

At the Phillies September 28 final game at Veterans Stadium, this cello-wrapped set of the greatest players to appear for the home team in that era was issued as a stadium give away. Fronts have gold-foil highlights on borderless game-action photos. Backs have personal data, full or partial major league stats and an assortment of licensor and sponsor logos.

NM/M
Complete Set (13): 6.00
Common Player: .50

1	Steve Carlton	1.00
2	Darren Daulton	.50
3	John Kruk	.50
4	Juan Samuel	.50
5	Mike Schmidt	2.00
6	Larry Bowa	.50
7	Greg Luzinski	.50
8	Garry Maddox	.50
9	Bobby Abreu	.50
10	Tug McGraw	.50
11	Curt Schilling	.75
12	Dallas Green	.50
---	Header Card	.05

2004 Ultra

NM/M
Complete Set (220): 45.00
Common Player: .15
Common All-Rookie (201-220): .50
Common Player (221-295): .25
Minor Stars (221-295): .40
Unlisted Stars (221-295): .60
Common Player (296-382): .15
Inserted 2:1
Common Player (383-395): 15.00

Production 500 Sets
Pack (8): 3.00
Box (24): 60.00

1	Magglio Ordonez	.40
2	Bobby Abreu	.25
3	Eric Munson	.15
4	Eric Byrnes	.15
5	Bartolo Colon	.25
6	Juan Encarnacion	.15
7	Jody Gerut	.15
8	Eddie Guardado	.15
9	Shea Hillenbrand	.15
10	Andruw Jones	.50
11	Carlos Lee	.25
12	Pedro J. Martinez	.75
13	Barry Larkin	.25
14	Angel Berroa	.15
15	Edgar Martinez	.25
16	Sidney Ponson	.15
17	Mariano Rivera	.25
18	Richie Sexson	.40
19	Frank Thomas	.60
20	Jerome Williams	.15
21	Barry Zito	.25
22	Roberto Alomar	.50
23	Rocky Biddle	.15
24	Orlando Cabrera	.25
25	Placido Polanco	.15
26	Morgan Ensberg	.15
27	Jason Giambi	.75
28	Jim Thome	.75
29	Vladimir Guerrero	.75
30	Tim Hudson	.25
31	Jacque Jones	.15
32	Derrek Lee	.25
33	Rafael Palmeiro	.40
34	Mike Mussina	.40
35	Corey Patterson	.15
36	Mike Cameron	.15
37	Ivan Rodriguez	.50
38	Ben Sheets	.15
39	Woody Williams	.15
40	Ichiro Suzuki	1.00
41	Moises Alou	.25
42	Craig Biggio	.25
43	Jorge Posada	.40
44	Craig Monroe	.15
45	Darin Erstad	.25
46	Jay Gibbons	.15
47	Aaron Guiel	.15
48	Travis Lee	.15
49	Jorge Julio	.15
50	Torii Hunter	.25
51	Luis Matos	.15
52	Brett Myers	.15
53	Sean Casey	.15
54	Mark Prior	1.50
55	Alex Rodriguez	1.50
56	Gary Sheffield	.40
57	Jason Varitek	.25
58	Dontrelle Willis	.40
59	Garret Anderson	.25
60	Casey Blake	.15
61	Jay Payton	.15
62	Carl Crawford	.25
63	Carl Everett	.15
64	Marcus Giles	.15
65	Jose Guillen	.15
66	Eric Karros	.15
67	Mike Lieberthal	.15
68	Hideki Matsui	3.00
69	Xavier Nady	.15
70	Hank Blalock	.40
71	Albert Pujols	1.50
72	Jose Cruz Jr.	.15
73	Randall Simon	.15
74	Javier Vazquez	.15
75	Preston Wilson	.15
76	Danys Baez	.15
77	Alex Cintron	.15
78	Jake Peavy	.15
79	Scott Rolen	.50
80	Robert Fick	.15
81	Brian Giles	.25
82	Roy Halladay	.25
83	Kazuhisa Ishii	.15
84	Austin Kearns	.40
85	Paul LoDuca	.25
86	Darrell May	.15
87	Phil Nevin	.15
88	Carlos Pena	.15
89	Manny Ramirez	.50
90	C.C. Sabathia	.25
91	John Smoltz	.25
92	Jose Vidro	.15
93	Randy Wolf	.15
94	Jeff Bagwell	.50
95	Barry Bonds	2.00
96	Frank Catalanotto	.15
97	Zach Day	.15
98	David Ortiz	.15
99	Troy Glaus	.40
100	Bo Hart	.15
101	Geoff Jenkins	.25
102	Jason Kendall	.15
103	Esteban Loiaza	.15
104	Doug Mientkiewicz	.15
105	Trot Nixon	.15
106	Troy Percival	.15
107	Aramis Ramirez	.15
108	Alex Sanchez	.15
109	Alfonso Soriano	.75
110	Omar Vizquel	.25
111	Kerry Wood	.50
112	Rocco Baldelli	.15
113	Bret Boone	.25
114	Shawn Chacon	.15
115	Carlos Delgado	.50
116	Shawn Green	.40
117	Tim Worrell	.15
118	Tom Glavine	.25
119	Shigetoshi Hasegawa	.15
120	Derek Jeter	2.00
121	Jeff Kent	.25
122	Braden Looper	.15
123	Kevin Millwood	.25
124	Hideo Nomo	.40
125	Jason Phillips	.15
126	Tim Redding	.15
127	Reggie Sanders	.15
128	Sammy Sosa	1.25
129	Billy Wagner	.25
130	Miguel Batista	.15
131	Milton Bradley	.15
132	Eric Chavez	.25
133	J.D. Drew	.15
134	Keith Foulke	.15
135	Luis Gonzalez	.25
136	LaTroy Hawkins	.15
137	Randy Johnson	.75
138	Byung-Hyun Kim	.15
139	Javy Lopez	.25
140	Melvin Mora	.15
141	Aubrey Huff	.15
142	Mike Piazza	1.00
143	Mark Redman	.15
144	Kazuhiro Sasaki	.15
145	Shannon Stewart	.15
146	Larry Walker	.25
147	Dmitri Young	.15
148	Josh Beckett	.50
149	Jae Weong Seo	.15
150	Hee Seop Choi	.15
151	Adam Dunn	.40
152	Rafael Furcal	.25
153	Juan Gonzalez	.50
154	Todd Helton	.50
155	Carlos Zambrano	.15
156	Ryan Klesko	.25
157	Mike Lowell	.25
158	Jamie Moyer	.15
159	Russ Ortiz	.15
160	Juan Pierre	.25
161	Edgar Renteria	.15
162	Curt Schilling	.40
163	Mike Sweeney	.15
164	Brandon Webb	.15
165	Michael Young	.25
166	Carlos Beltran	.25
167	Sean Burroughs	.15
168	Luis Castillo	.15
169	David Eckstein	.15
170	Eric Gagne	.25
171	Chipper Jones	1.00
172	Livan Hernandez	.15
173	Nick Johnson	.15
174	Corey Koskie	.15
175	Jason Schmidt	.15
176	Bill Mueller	.15
177	Steve Finley	.15
178	A.J. Pierzynski	.15
179	Rene Reyes	.15
180	Jason Johnson	.15
181	Mark Teixeira	.25
182	Kip Wells	.15
183	Mike MacDougal	.15
184	Lance Berkman	.25
185	Victor Zambrano	.15
186	Roger Clemens	1.50
187	Jim Edmonds	.25
188	Nomar Garciaparra	1.50
189	Ken Griffey Jr.	1.00
190	Richard Hidalgo	.15
191	Cliff Floyd	.15
192	Greg Maddux	1.00
193	Mark Mulder	.25
194	Roy Oswalt	.25
195	Marlon Byrd	.15
196	Jose Reyes	.25
197	Kevin Brown	.25
198	Miguel Tejada	.25
199	Vernon Wells	.25
200	Joel Pineiro	.15
201	Rickie Weeks	5.00
202	Chad Gaudin	1.50
203	Ryan Wagner	1.50
204	Chris Bootcheck	.50
205	Koyie Hill	.50
206	Jeff Duncan	1.00
207	Rich Harden	1.00
208	Edwin Jackson	.50
209	Robby Hammock	.50
210	Khalil Greene	.50
211	Chien-Ming Wang	.50
212	Prentice Redman	.50
213	Todd Wellemeyer	.50

#	Player	Price
214	Clint Barmes	1.00
215	Matt Kata	.50
216	Jon Leicester	.50
217	Jeremy Guthrie	.50
218	Chin-Hui Tsao	1.50
219	Dan Haren	5.00
220	Delmon Young	4.00
221	Vladimir Guerrero	1.00
222	Andy Pettitte	.60
223	Gary Sheffield	.60
224	Javier Vazquez	.25
225	Alex Rodriguez	2.50
226	Billy Wagner	.25
227	Miguel Tejada	.60
228	Greg Maddux	1.50
229	Ivan Rodriguez	.60
230	Roger Clemens	2.50
231	Alfonso Soriano	1.00
232	Miguel Cabrera	.75
233	Javy Lopez	.40
234	David Wells	.25
235	Eric Milton	.25
236	Armando Benitez	.25
237	Mike Cameron	.25
238	J.D. Drew	.40
239	Carlos Beltran	.60
240	Bartolo Colon	.40
241	Jose Guillen	.40
242	Kevin Brown	.40
243	Carlos Guillen	.25
244	Kenny Lofton	.25
245	Pokey Reese	.25
246	Rafael Palmeiro	.75
247	Nomar Garciaparra	2.50
248	Hee Seop Choi	.25
249	Juan Uribe	.25
250	Nick Johnson	.25
251	Scott Podsednik	.25
252	Richie Sexson	.60
253	Keith Foulke	.25
254	Jaret Wright	.25
255	Johnny Estrada	.25
256	Michael Barrett	.25
257	Bernie Williams	.60
258	Octavio Dotel	.25
259	Jeromy Burnitz	.25
260	Kevin Youkilis	.25
261	Derrek Lee	.40
262	Jack Wilson	.25
263	Craig Wilson	.25
264	Richard Hidalgo	.25
265	Royce Clayton	.25
266	Curt Schilling	.60
267	Joe Mauer	.75
268	Bobby Crosby	.25
269	Zack Greinke	.25
270	Victor Martinez	.25
271	Pedro Feliz	.25
272	Tony Batista	.25
273	Casey Kotchman	.25
274	Freddy Garcia	.25
275	Adam Everett	.25
276	Alexis Rios	.25
277	Lew Ford	.25
278	Adam LaRoche	.25
279	Lyle Overbay	.25
280	Juan Gonzalez	.40
281	A.J. Pierzynski	.25
282	Scott Hairston	.25
283	Danny Bautista	.25
284	Brad Penny	.25
285	Paul Konerko	.25
286	Matt Lawton	.25
287	Carl Pavano	.25
288	Pat Burrell	.40
289	Kenny Rogers	.25
290	Laynce Nix	.25
291	Johnny Damon	.40
292	Paul Wilson	.25
293	Vinny Castilla	.25
294	Aaron Miles	.25
295	Ken Harvey	.25
296	Onil Joseph RC	2.00
297	Kazuhito Tadano RC	3.00
298	Jeff Bennett RC	2.00
299	Chad Bentz RC	2.00
300	Akinori Otsuka RC	2.00
301	Jon Knott RC	2.00
302	Ian Snell RC	3.00
303	Fernando Nieve RC	2.00
304	Mike Rouse RC	2.00
305	Dennis Sarfate RC	2.00
306	Josh Labandeira RC	3.00
307	Chris Oxspring RC	2.00
308	Alfredo Simon RC	2.00
309	Rusty Tucker RC	2.00
310	Lincoln Holdzkom RC	2.00
311	Justin Leone RC	2.00
312	Jorge Sequea RC	2.00
313	Brian Dallimore RC	2.00
314	Tim Bittner RC	2.00
315	Ronny Cedeno RC	2.00
316	Justin Hampson RC	2.00
317	Ryan Wing RC	2.00
318	Mariano Gomez RC	2.00
319	Carlos Vasquez RC	2.00
320	Casey Daigle RC	2.00
321	Renyel Pinto RC	2.00
322	Chris Shelton RC	4.00
323	Mike Gosling RC	2.00
324	Aarom Baldiris RC	2.00
325	Ramon Ramirez RC	2.00
326	Roberto Novoa RC	2.00
327	Sean Henn RC	2.00
328	Nick Regilio RC	2.00
329	David Crouthers RC	2.00
330	Greg Dobbs RC	2.00
331	Angel Chavez RC	2.00
332	Luis A. Gonzalez RC	2.00
333	Justin Knoedler RC	2.00
334	Jason Frasor RC	2.00
335	Jerry Gil RC	2.00
336	Carlos Hines RC	2.00
337	Ivan Ochoa RC	3.00
338	Jose Capellan RC	2.00
339	Hector Gimenez RC	2.00
340	Shawn Hill RC	3.00
341	Freddy Guzman RC	2.00
342	Scott Proctor RC	2.00
343	Frank Francisco RC	2.00
344	Brandon Medders RC	2.00
345	Andy Green RC	2.00
346	Eddy Rodriguez RC	2.00
347	Tim Hamulack RC	2.00
348	Mike Wuertz RC	2.00
349	Arnie Munoz RC	2.00
350	Enemencio Pacheco RC	2.00
351	Dusty Bergman RC	2.00
352	Charles Thomas RC	5.00
353	William Bergolla RC	2.00
354	Ramon Castro RC	2.00
355	Justin Lehr RC	2.00
356	Lino Urdaneta RC	2.00
357	Donnie Kelly RC	2.00
358	Kevin Cave RC	2.00
359	Franklyn Gracesqui RC	2.00
360	Chris Aguila RC	2.00
361	Jorge Vasquez RC	2.00
362	Andres Blanco RC	2.00
363	Orlando Rodriguez RC	2.00
364	Colby Miller RC	2.00
365	Shawn Camp RC	2.00
366	Jake Woods RC	2.00
367	George Sherrill RC	2.00
368	Justin Huisman RC	2.00
369	Jimmy Serrano RC	3.00
370	Mike Johnston RC	3.00
371	Ryan Meaux RC	2.00
372	Scott Dohmann RC	2.00
373	Brad Halsey RC	5.00
374	Joey Gathright RC	5.00
375	Yadier Molina RC	3.00
376	Travis Blackley RC	2.00
377	Steve Andrade RC	2.00
378	Phil Stockman RC	2.00
379	Roman Colon RC	2.00
380	Jesse Crain RC	2.00
381	Edwardo Sierra RC	2.00
382	Justin Germano RC	2.00
383	Kazuo Matsui RC	30.00
384	Shingo Takatsu RC	20.00
385	John Gall RC	15.00
386	Chris Saenz RC	15.00
387	Merkin Valdez RC	20.00
388	Jamie Brown RC	15.00
389	Jason Bartlett RC	20.00
390	David Aardsma RC	30.00
391	Scott Kazmir RC	30.00
392	David Wright RC	40.00
393	Dioner Navarro RC	25.00
394	B.J. Upton RC	25.00
395	Gavin Floyd RC	30.00

Gold Medallion

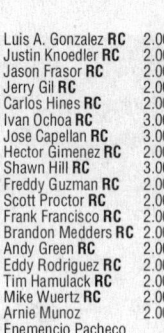

Cards (1-200):	2-3X
Inserted 1:1	
All-Rookies (201-220):	3-4X
Inserted 1:8	
Cards (221-295):	.75-1.5X
Inserted 1:1	
Cards (296-382):	.75-1.25X
Cards (383-395):	.25-.75X
Inserted 1:4	

Platinum Medallion

Cards (1-200):	8-15X
All-Rookies (201-220):	5-10X
Production 66 Sets	
Cards (221-295):	4-8X
Cards (296-382):	2-4X
Production 100 Sets	
Cards (383-395):	No Pricing
Production 13 Sets	

Diamond Producers

NM/M

Complete Set (10):	60.00
Common Player:	4.00
Inserted 1:144	
1DP Greg Maddux	8.00
2DP Dontrelle Willis	4.00

3DP Jim Thome	5.00
4DP Alfonso Soriano	4.00
5DP Alex Rodriguez	10.00
6DP Sammy Sosa	10.00
7DP Nomar Garciaparra	10.00
8DP Derek Jeter	15.00
9DP Adam Dunn	4.00
10DP Mark Prior	8.00

Diamond Producers Memorabilia

NM/M

Production 1,000 Sets

Dontrelle Willis	15.00
Alfonso Soriano	10.00
Alex Rodriguez	10.00
Sammy Sosa	10.00
Nomar Garciaparra	15.00
Mark Prior	10.00

Diamond Producers UltraSwatch

NM/M

Numbered to Jersey #.

Dontrelle Willis/35	25.00

Hitting Machines

NM/M

Common Player:	3.00
Inserted 1:12	
Die-Cut:	1-2X
1HM Albert Pujols	6.00
2HM Ken Griffey Jr.	5.00
3HM Vladimir Guerrero	3.50
4HM Mike Piazza	4.00
5HM Ichiro Suzuki	5.00
6HM Miguel Cabrera	3.00
7HM Hideki Matsui	6.00
8HM Nomar Garciaparra	6.00
9HM Derek Jeter	8.00
10HM Chipper Jones	4.00

Hitting Machines Game-Used Silver

NM/M

Common Player:	8.00
Inserted 1:74	
Gold:	1-3X
Production 50 Sets	
Platinum:	No Pricing
Production 10 Sets	
JB Jeff Bagwell	10.00
MC Miguel Cabrera	10.00
AD Adam Dunn	8.00
VG Vladimir Guerrero	10.00
TH Todd Helton	10.00
CJ Chipper Jones	12.00
HM Hideki Matsui	20.00
MP Mike Piazza	12.00
AP Albert Pujols	12.00
FT Frank Thomas	10.00

HR Kings

NM/M

Complete Set (10):	35.00
Inserted 1:96	
Golds:	2-3X
Production 50 Sets	
1HK Barry Bonds	8.00
2HK Albert Pujols	6.00
3HK Jason Giambi	3.00
4HK Jeff Bagwell	2.00
5HK Ken Griffey Jr.	4.00
6HK Alex Rodriguez	6.00
7HK Sammy Sosa	5.00
8HK Alfonso Soriano	3.00
9HK Chipper Jones	4.00
10HK Mike Piazza	4.00

Legendary 13 Memorabilia

Numbered to 13 each
Each player's jersey swatch on each card.
Masterpiece 1/1 auto. by named player.
Inserted 1:192 Series 2 Hobby

Legendary 13 Memorabilia Autographs

NM/M

Numbered to five each.
Masterpiece 1/1
Numbered with "L13A-" prefix.
Limited pricing due to scarcity.

TW Ted Williams	900.00

Legendary 13 Memorabilia Gold

Numbered to uniform #
Jersey, patch or bat swatch on each.
Masterpiece: 1/1
No pricing due to scarcity.

Legendary 13 Dual Memorabilia Autographs

NM/M

Numbered to 3 each
Masterpiece 1/1
No pricing due to scarcity.

Legendary 13 Dual Memorabilia Gold

Numbered to 22 each
Jersey, patch or bat swatches on each.
Platinum numbered to 10 each.
Masterpiece 1/1
Numbered with "L13D-" prefix.
No pricing due to scarcity.

Performers

NM/M

Complete Set (15):	12.00
Common Player:	.50
Inserted 1:6	
1UP Ichiro Suzuki	1.50
2UP Albert Pujols	2.00
3UP Barry Bonds	3.00
4UP Hideki Matsui	2.00
5UP Randy Johnson	1.00
6UP Jason Giambi	1.00
7UP Pedro J. Martinez	1.00
8UP Hank Blalock	.50
9UP Chipper Jones	1.50
10UP Mike Piazza	1.50
11UP Derek Jeter	3.00
12UP Vladimir Guerrero	1.00
13UP Barry Zito	.75
14UP Rocco Baldelli	.50
15UP Hideo Nomo	.75

Performers Memorabilia

NM/M

Common Player:	6.00
Production 500 Sets	
Albert Pujols	15.00
Barry Bonds/base	15.00
Randy Johnson	8.00
Jason Giambi	8.00
Pedro J. Martinez	10.00
Hank Blalock	6.00
Chipper Jones	10.00
Mike Piazza	10.00
Derek Jeter	15.00
Vladimir Guerrero	8.00
Rocco Baldelli	10.00
Hideo Nomo	15.00

Performers UltraSwatch

NM/M

Numbered to Jersey #.

Randy Johnson/51	15.00
Pedro Martinez/45	15.00
Mike Piazza/31	25.00
Vladimir Guerrero/27	20.00

RBI Kings

NM/M

Complete Set (10):	15.00
Inserted 1:32	
Golds:	3-4X
Production 50 Sets	
1RK Hideki Matsui	4.00
2RK Albert Pujols	4.00
3RK Todd Helton	1.50
4RK Jim Thome	1.50
5RK Carlos Delgado	1.50
6RK Alex Rodriguez	4.00
7RK Barry Bonds	5.00
8RK Manny Ramirez	1.50
9RK Vladimir Guerrero	1.50
10RK Nomar Garciaparra	4.00

Season Crowns Autograph

NM/M

Common Player:	15.00
Production 150 Sets	
Golds:	No Pricing
Production 25 Sets	
Rocco Baldelli	35.00
Hank Blalock	15.00
Bo Hart	30.00
Aubrey Huff	15.00
Chipper Jones	60.00
Austin Kearns	15.00
Mike Lowell	15.00
Corey Patterson	20.00
Carlos Pena	15.00
Jose Reyes	30.00
Scott Rolen	20.00
Miguel Tejada	25.00
Brandon Webb	15.00
Rickie Weeks	50.00
Dontrelle Willis	35.00

Season Crowns Memorabilia

NM/M

Common Player:	4.00
Production 399 Sets	
Golds:	1-2X
Production 99 Sets	
Platinums:	No Pricing
Production 25 Sets	
Adam Dunn	6.00
Carlos Pena	4.00
Torii Hunter	8.00
Gary Sheffield	8.00
Sean Casey	4.00
Lance Berkman	6.00
Tom Glavine	6.00
Sean Burroughs	4.00
Shawn Green	6.00
Jason Kendall	4.00
Vladimir Guerrero	10.00
Todd Helton	8.00
Tim Hudson	8.00
Troy Glaus	6.00
Larry Walker	4.00
Carlos Beltran	6.00
Hideo Nomo	4.00
Kazuhiro Sasaki	4.00
Mike Piazza	10.00
Scott Rolen	6.00
Carlos Delgado	6.00
Andruw Jones	8.00
Alfonso Soriano	10.00
Angel Berroa	4.00
Brandon Webb	8.00
Jason Giambi	8.00
Pedro J. Martinez	10.00
Manny Ramirez	8.00
Alex Rodriguez	10.00
Derek Jeter	15.00
Mark Mulder	6.00
Greg Maddux	10.00
Sammy Sosa	15.00
Jim Thome	10.00
Hank Blalock	6.00
Roberto Alomar	4.00
Omar Vizquel	5.00
Austin Kearns	4.00
Jeff Bagwell	8.00
Frank Thomas	8.00
Randy Johnson	8.00
Rocco Baldelli	12.00
Albert Pujols	15.00
Jose Reyes	8.00
Dontrelle Willis	12.00
Hideki Matsui/Base	20.00
Barry Bonds/Base	15.00
Ichiro Suzuki/Base	15.00
Chipper Jones	10.00
Roger Clemens	15.00

Strikeout Kings

NM/M

Complete Set (10):	10.00
Common Player:	.75
Inserted 1:24	
Golds:	3-5X
Production 50 Sets	
1KK Randy Johnson	1.50
2KK Pedro J. Martinez	1.50
3KK Curt Schilling	1.00
4KK Roger Clemens	3.00
5KK Mike Mussina	1.00
6KK Roy Halladay	.75
7KK Kerry Wood	1.00
8KK Dontrelle Willis	1.00
9KK Greg Maddux	2.00
10KK Mark Prior	2.00

Turn Back the Clock

NM/M

Common Player:	1.50
Inserted 1:6	
1 Roger Clemens	5.00
2 Alex Rodriguez	5.00
3 Randy Johnson	2.00
4 Pedro Martinez	2.00
5 Alfonso Soriano	2.00
6 Curt Schilling	1.50
7 Miguel Tejada	1.50
8 Scott Rolen	1.50
9 Jim Thome	2.00
10 Manny Ramirez	2.00
11 Vladimir Guerrero	2.00
12 Tom Glavine	1.50
13 Andy Pettitte	1.50
14 Ivan Rodriguez	1.50
15 Jason Giambi	2.00

16	Rafael Palmeiro	2.00
17	Greg Maddux	3.00
18	Hideo Nomo	1.50
19	Mike Mussina	1.50
20	Sammy Sosa	4.00

Turn Back the Clock Game-Used Copper

		NM/M
Common Player:		8.00
Production 399 Sets		
Silver:		.75-1.5X
Production 199 Sets		
Gold:		1-2X
Platinum Patch:		2-5X
Production 29 Sets		
RC	Roger Clemens	12.00
JG	Jason Giambi	10.00
TG	Tom Glavine	8.00
VG	Vladimir Guerrero	10.00
RJ	Randy Johnson	10.00
GM	Greg Maddux	12.00
PR	Pedro Martinez	10.00
MM	Mike Mussina	8.00
HM	Hideo Nomo	10.00
RP	Rafael Palmeiro	10.00
AP	Andy Pettitte	8.00
MR	Manny Ramirez	10.00
IR	Ivan Rodriguez	10.00
SR	Scott Rolen	10.00
CS	Curt Schilling	8.00
AS	Alfonso Soriano	10.00
SS	Sammy Sosa	12.00
MT	Miguel Tejada	8.00
JT	Jim Thome	10.00

3 Kings

	NM/M
Production 33 Sets	
Mike Piazza, Roger Clemens, Alex Rodriguez	70.00
Albert Pujols, Mark Prior, Todd Helton	50.00
Alfonso Soriano, Dontrelle Willis, Albert Pujols	60.00
P. Martinez, Sammy Sosa, Albert Pujols	70.00
Randy Johnson, Albert Pujols, Todd Helton	50.00
Dontrelle Willis, Chipper Jones, Albert Pujols	60.00
Dontrelle Willis, Jeff Bagwell, Jim Thome	40.00
Greg Maddux, Jason Giambi, Manny Ramirez	50.00

2005 Ultra

		NM/M
Common Player (1-200):		.15
Minor Stars (1-200):		.25
Unlisted Stars (1-200):		.50
Common Player (201-220):		2.00
Minor Stars (201-220):		3.00
Inserted 1:4		
Pack (8):		3.50
Box (24):		75.00
1	Andy Pettitte	.40
2	Jose Cruz	.15
3	Cliff Floyd	.25
4	Paul Konerko	.25
5	Joe Mauer	.75
6	Scott Spiezio	.15
7	Ben Sheets	.25
8	Kerry Wood	.50
9	Carl Pavano	.15
10	Matt Morris	.15
11	Kazuo Matsui	.75
12	Ivan Rodriguez	.40
13	Victor Martinez	.15
14	Justin Morneau	.25
15	Adam Everett	.15
16	Carl Crawford	.25
17	David Ortiz	.25
18	Jason Giambi	.75
19	Derrek Lee	.25
20	Magglio Ordonez	.25
21	Bobby Abreu	.25

22	Milton Bradley	.15
23	Jeff Bagwell	.50
24	Jim Edmonds	.25
25	Garret Anderson	.25
26	Jacque Jones	.15
27	Ted Lilly	.15
28	Greg Maddux	1.00
29	Jermaine Dye	.15
30	Bill Mueller	.15
31	Roy Oswalt	.25
32	Tony Womack	.15
33	Andruw Jones	.50
34	Tom Glavine	.25
35	Mariano Rivera	.25
36	Sean Casey	.15
37	Edgardo Alfonzo	.15
38	Brad Penny	.15
39	Johan Santana	.15
40	Mark Teixeira	.25
41	Manny Ramirez	.50
42	Gary Sheffield	.40
43	Matt Lawton	.15
44	Troy Percival	.15
45	Rocco Baldelli	.40
46	Doug Mientkiewicz	.15
47	Corey Patterson	.15
48	Austin Kearns	.15
49	Edgar Martinez	.25
50	Brad Radke	.15
51	Barry Larkin	.25
52	Chone Figgins	.15
53	Alexis Rios	.15
54	Alex Rodriguez	1.50
55	Vinny Castilla	.15
56	Javier Vazquez	.15
57	Javy Lopez	.15
58	Mike Cameron	.15
59	Brian Giles	.25
60	Dontrelle Willis	.25
61	Rafael Furcal	.15
62	Trot Nixon	.15
63	Mark Mulder	.25
64	Josh Beckett	.50
65	J.D. Drew	.25
66	Brandon Webb	.15
67	Wade Miller	.15
68	Lyle Overbay	.15
69	Pedro J. Martinez	.75
70	Rich Harden	.15
71	Al Leiter	.15
72	Adam Eaton	.15
73	Mike Sweeney	.15
74	Steve Finley	.15
75	Kris Benson	.15
76	Jim Thome	.75
77	Juan Pierre	.15
78	Bartolo Colon	.25
79	Carlos Delgado	.50
80	Jack Wilson	.15
81	Ken Harvey	.15
82	Nomar Garciaparra	1.50
83	Paul LoDuca	.15
84	Cesar Izturis	.15
85	Adrian Beltre	.15
86	Brian Roberts	.15
87	David Eckstein	.15
88	Jimmy Rollins	.15
89	Roger Clemens	1.00
90	Randy Johnson	.75
91	Orlando Hudson	.15
92	Tim Hudson	.25
93	Dmitri Young	.15
94	Chipper Jones	1.00
95	John Smoltz	.25
96	Billy Wagner	.15
97	Hideo Nomo	.25
98	Sammy Sosa	1.25
99	Darin Erstad	.25
100	Todd Helton	.50
101	Aubrey Huff	.15
102	Alfonso Soriano	.75
103	Jose Vidro	.15
104	Carlos Lee	.15
105	Corey Koskie	.15
106	Bret Boone	.15
107	Torii Hunter	.40
108	Aramis Ramirez	.15
109	Chase Utley	.15
110	Reggie Sanders	.15
111	Livan Hernandez	.15
112	Jeromy Burnitz	.15
113	Carlos Zambrano	.25
114	Hank Blalock	.40
115	Sidney Ponson	.15
116	Zack Greinke	.15
117	Trevor Hoffman	.15
118	Jeff Kent	.25
119	Richie Sexson	.40
120	Melvin Mora	.15
121	Eric Chavez	.25
122	Miguel Cabrera	.50
123	Ryan Freel	.15
124	Russ Ortiz	.15
125	Craig Wilson	.15
126	Craig Biggio	.25
127	Curt Schilling	.40
128	Kazuhisa Ishii	.15
129	Marquis Grissom	.15
130	Bernie Williams	.40
131	Travis Hafner	.15
132	Hee Seop Choi	.15
133	Scott Rolen	.15
134	Tony Batista	.15
135	Frank Thomas	.15
136	Jason Varitek	.50
137	Ichiro Suzuki	1.25
138	Junior Spivey	.15
139	Adam Dunn	.40

140	Jorge Posada	.40
141	Edgar Renteria	.15
142	Hideki Matsui	1.50
143	Carlos Guillen	.15
144	Jody Gerut	.15
145	Wily Mo Pena	.15
146	Derek Jeter	2.00
147	C.C. Sabathia	.15
148	Geoff Jenkins	.25
149	Albert Pujols	1.50
150	Eric Munson	.15
151	Moises Alou	.25
152	Jerry Hairston	.15
153	Ray Durham	.15
154	Mike Piazza	1.00
155	Omar Vizquel	.25
156	A.J. Pierzynski	.15
157	Michael Young	.25
158	Jason Bay	.15
159	Mark Loretta	.15
160	Shawn Green	.25
161	Luis Gonzalez	.25
162	Johnny Damon	.25
163	Eric Milton	.15
164	Mike Lowell	.15
165	Jose Guillen	.15
166	Eric Hinske	.15
167	Jason Kendall	.25
168	Carlos Beltran	.40
169	Johnny Estrada	.15
170	Scott Hatteberg	.15
171	Laynce Nix	.15
172	Eric Gagne	.25
173	Richard Hidalgo	.15
174	Bobby Crosby	.15
175	Woody Williams	.15
176	Justin Leone	.15
177	Orlando Cabrera	.15
178	Mark Prior	1.50
179	Jorge Julio	.15
180	Jamie Moyer	.15
181	Jose Reyes	.40
182	Ken Griffey Jr.	1.00
183	Mike Lieberthal	.15
184	Kenny Rogers	.15
185	Mike Mussina	.40
186	Preston Wilson	.15
187	Khalil Greene	.50
188	Angel Berroa	.15
189	Miguel Tejada	.40
190	Freddy Garcia	.15
191	Pat Burrell	.25
192	Luis Castillo	.15
193	Vladimir Guerrero	.75
194	Roy Halladay	.25
195	Barry Zito	.40
196	Lance Berkman	.25
197	Rafael Palmeiro	.50
198	Nate Robertson	.15
199	Jason Schmidt	.25
200	Scott Podsednik	.15
201	Casey Kotchman	3.00
202	Scott Kazmir	4.00
203	Bucky Jacobsen	4.00
204	Jeff Keppinger	3.00
205	David Bush	2.00
206	Gavin Floyd	5.00
207	David Wright	8.00
208	B.J. Upton	3.00
209	David Aardsma	2.00
210	Jason Bartlett	3.00
211	Dioner Navarro	2.00
212	Jason Kubel	3.00
213	Ryan Howard	8.00
214	Charles Thomas RC	2.00
215	Freddy Guzman	2.00
216	Brad Halsey	3.00
217	Joey Gathright	2.00
218	Jeff Francis	2.00
219	Terry Tiffee	2.00
220	Nick Swisher	5.00

Gold

	NM/M
Cards 1-200:	1-3X
Inserted 1:1	
Cards 201-220:	.5-1X
Inserted 1:8	

Platinum

	NM/M
Cards 1-200:	5-8X
Cards 201-220:	3-5X
Production 50 Sets	

Follow the Leader

	NM/M
Common Player:	1.50

	NM/M
Inserted 1:6	
Copper Game-Used:	3-5X
Inserted 1:72 (Hobby Only)	
Red Game-Used:	2-4X
Inserted 1:48 (Retail Only)	
Gold Game-Used:	4-6X
Production 250 Sets	
Platinum Game-Used:	5-8X
Production 99 Sets	
Ultra Game-Used:	
Numbered 26-51:	5-10X
Numbered 25 or less:	No Pricing
Production to player's jersey number.	
1	Roger Clemens	3.00
2	Albert Pujols	3.00
3	Sammy Sosa	2.50
4	Manny Ramirez	1.50
5	Vladimir Guerrero	2.00
6	Ivan Rodriguez	1.50
7	Mike Piazza	2.00
8	Scott Rolen	1.50
9	Ichiro Suzuki	2.50
10	Randy Johnson	2.00
11	Mark Prior	2.00
12	Jim Thome	2.00
13	Greg Maddux	2.50
14	Pedro J. Martinez	2.00
15	Miguel Cabrera	1.50

HR Kings

	NM/M
Common Player:	2.50
Inserted 1:96	
Ultra Kings Gold:	1-3X
Production 50 Sets	
1	Jim Thome	4.00
2	David Ortiz	3.00
3	Adam Dunn	3.00
4	Albert Pujols	8.00
5	Manny Ramirez	3.50
6	Vladimir Guerrero	4.00
7	Miguel Tejada	3.00
8	Rafael Palmeiro	3.50
9	Mark Teixeira	2.50
10	Sammy Sosa	6.00
11	Frank Thomas	3.50
12	Pat Burrell	2.50
13	Adrian Beltre	2.50
14	Miguel Cabrera	3.50
15	Gary Sheffield	3.00

RBI Kings

	NM/M
Common Player:	2.50
Inserted 1:32	
Ultra Kings Gold:	2-4X
Production 50 Sets	
1	Sean Casey	2.50
2	Ivan Rodriguez	2.50
3	Mike Piazza	4.00
4	Todd Helton	3.00
5	Scott Rolen	3.50
6	Hideki Matsui	6.00
7	Gary Sheffield	2.50
8	Alfonso Soriano	3.50
9	Bobby Abreu	2.50
10	Lance Berkman	2.50
11	Miguel Tejada	2.50
12	Travis Hafner	2.50
13	Hank Blalock	2.50
14	Jeff Bagwell	3.00
15	Chipper Jones	4.00

Season Crown Autographs Copper

	NM/M
Common Player:	20.00
Stated Production 199 Sets	
All 199 cards not released for some players.	
31	Roy Oswalt/50	25.00
80	Jack Wilson/199	20.00
125	Craig Wilson/130	20.00
157	Michael Young/150	20.00

Season Crown Autographs Gold

	NM/M
Common Player:	20.00
Stated Production 99 Sets	
All 99 cards not released	
for some players.	
21	Roy Oswalt/99	20.00
50	Brad Radke/89	20.00
51	Barry Larkin/99	20.00
62	Trot Nixon/37	25.00
70	Rich Harden/41	20.00
80	Jack Wilson/99	20.00
88	Jimmy Rollins/45	25.00
121	Eric Chavez/69	20.00
125	Craig Wilson/99	20.00
157	Michael Young/99	20.00
200	Scott Podsednik/99	20.00

Season Crown Autographs Platinum

	NM/M
Common Player:	25.00
Stated Production 50 Sets	
All 50 cards not released for some players.	
Masterpiece:	No Pricing
Production One Set	
20	Magglio Ordonez/50	25.00
25	Garret Anderson/50	25.00
31	Roy Oswalt/50	25.00
40	Mark Teixeira/50	30.00
50	Brad Radke/50	25.00
51	Barry Larkin/50	30.00
62	Trot Nixon/50	25.00
70	Rich Harden/50	25.00
80	Jack Wilson/50	25.00
87	David Eckstein/45	25.00
88	Jimmy Rollins/50	25.00
96	Billy Wagner/50	30.00
116	Zack Greinke/49	25.00
121	Eric Chavez/50	25.00
125	Craig Wilson/50	25.00
157	Michael Young/50	25.00
161	Luis Gonzalez/50	25.00
185	Mike Mussina/50	30.00
195	Barry Zito/50	25.00
199	Jason Schmidt/50	25.00
200	Scott Podsednik/50	25.00
201	Casey Kotchman/50	25.00

Season Crowns Copper Game-Used

	NM/M
Common Player:	5.00
Production 399 Sets	
Gold:	.75-1.5X
Production 99 Sets	
Platinum:	No Pricing
Production 25 Sets	
1	Andy Pettitte/Jsy	8.00
2	Cliff Floyd/Jsy	5.00
7	Ben Sheets/Jsy	8.00
8	Kerry Wood/Jsy	8.00
11	Kazuo Matsui/Bat	15.00
13	Victor Martinez/Jsy	8.00
17	David Carr/Jsy	8.00
20	Magglio Ordonez/Jsy	5.00
21	Bobby Abreu/Bat	5.00
24	Jim Edmonds/Jsy	5.00
31	Roy Oswalt/Jsy	8.00
33	Andruw Jones/Jsy	8.00
34	Tom Glavine/Bat	5.00
36	Sean Casey/Jsy	5.00
37	Edgardo Alfonzo/Bat	5.00
41	Manny Ramirez/Bat	8.00
42	Gary Sheffield/Bat	8.00
45	Rocco Baldelli/Jsy	8.00
48	Austin Kearns/Jsy	5.00
49	Edgar Martinez/Jsy	8.00
60	Dontrelle Willis/Jsy	8.00
65	J.D. Drew/Jsy	5.00
70	Rich Harden/Jsy	5.00
71	Al Leiter/Jsy	5.00
80	Jack Wilson/Bat	5.00
93	Dmitri Young/Bat	5.00
94	Chipper Jones/Bat	10.00
97	Hideo Nomo/Jsy	8.00
98	Sammy Sosa/Bat	12.00
100	Todd Helton/Bat	8.00
102	Alfonso Soriano/Bat	8.00
107	Torii Hunter/Jsy	8.00
114	Hank Blalock/Bat	8.00
119	Richie Sexson/Jsy	5.00
121	Eric Chavez/Jsy	5.00
130	Bernie Williams/Bat	8.00
135	Frank Thomas/Bat	8.00
139	Adam Dunn/Bat	8.00
142	Hideki Matsui/Bat	15.00
144	Jody Gerut/Bat	5.00
154	Mike Piazza/Bat	10.00
158	Jason Bay/Bat	8.00
162	Johnny Damon/Jsy	10.00
168	Carlos Beltran/Bat	8.00
173	Richard Hidalgo/Jsy	5.00
181	Jose Reyes/Bat	6.00
187	Khalil Greene/Jsy	15.00
191	Pat Burrell/Bat	8.00
193	Vladimir Guerrero/Bat	8.00
197	Rafael Palmeiro/Jsy	8.00

Strikeout Kings

	NM/M
Common Player:	2.50
Inserted 1:24	
Ultra Kings Gold:	2-4X
Production 50 Sets	
1	Pedro J. Martinez	3.50
2	Randy Johnson	3.50
3	Mark Mulder	2.50
4	Barry Zito	2.50
5	Roger Clemens	6.00
6	Mark Prior	2.50
7	Ben Sheets	2.50
8	Curt Schilling	2.50
9	Billy Wagner	2.50
10	Eric Gagne	2.50
11	Josh Beckett	3.00
12	Kerry Wood	3.00
13	Jason Schmidt	2.50
14	Roy Halladay	2.50
15	Greg Maddux	4.00

Ultra Kings Game-Used Gold

	NM/M
Common Player:	8.00
Production 150 Sets	
Ultra Swatch	
Numbered 51-75:	.75-1.5X
Numbered 26-50:	1-2X
Numbered 25 or less:	No Pricing
Production to player's jersey number.	
Platinum:	No Pricing
Production 25 Sets	
1	Pedro J. Martinez	12.00
2	Randy Johnson	12.00
3	Mark Mulder	8.00
4	Barry Zito	8.00
5	Roger Clemens	25.00
6	Mark Prior	20.00
7	Ben Sheets	8.00
8	Curt Schilling	8.00
9	Billy Wagner	8.00
10	Eric Gagne	8.00
11	Josh Beckett	10.00
12	Kerry Wood	10.00
13	Jason Schmidt	8.00
14	Roy Halladay	8.00
15	Greg Maddux	15.00
16	Sean Casey	8.00
17	Ivan Rodriguez	8.00
18	Mike Piazza	15.00
19	Todd Helton	10.00
20	Scott Rolen	12.00
21	Hideki Matsui	30.00
22	Gary Sheffield	8.00
23	Alfonso Soriano	12.00
24	Bobby Abreu	8.00
25	Lance Berkman	8.00
26	Miguel Tejada	8.00
27	Travis Hafner	8.00
28	Hank Blalock	8.00
29	Jeff Bagwell	10.00
30	Chipper Jones	15.00
31	Jim Thome	12.00
32	David Ortiz	8.00
33	Adam Dunn	8.00
34	Albert Pujols	25.00
35	Manny Ramirez	10.00
36	Vladimir Guerrero	12.00
37	Miguel Tejada	8.00
38	Rafael Palmeiro	10.00
39	Mark Teixeira	8.00
40	Sammy Sosa	20.00
41	Frank Thomas	10.00
42	Pat Burrell	8.00
43	Adrian Beltre	8.00
44	Miguel Cabrera	10.00
45	Gary Sheffield	8.00

Ultra 3 Kings Triple Swatch

	NM/M
Common Card:	40.00
Production 33 Sets	
1	Greg Maddux, Mark Prior, Kerry Wood	75.00
2	Mark Teixeira, Hank Blalock, Alfonso Soriano	40.00
3	Jeff Bagwell, Roger Clemens, Lance Berkman	60.00

4	Jim Thome, Pat Burrell, Billy Wagner	40.00
5	Gary Sheffield, Hideki Matsui, Mike Piazza	75.00
6	Scott Rolen, Chipper Jones, Adrian Beltre	40.00
7	Albert Pujols, Adam Dunn, Miguel Cabrera	50.00
8	Curt Schilling, Pedro J. Martinez, Manny Ramirez	60.00
9	Randy Johnson, Greg Maddux, Pedro J. Martinez	50.00
10	Josh Beckett, Miguel Cabrera, Ivan Rodriguez	40.00

2006 Ultra

	NM/M
Complete Set (251):	60.00
Common Player:	.15
Common SP (201-250):	.50
Inserted 1:4	
Pack (8):	3.00
Box (24):	65.00

1	Vladimir Guerrero	.75
2	Bartolo Colon	.15
3	Francisco Rodriguez	.15
4	Darin Erstad	.15
5	Chone Figgins	.15
6	Bengie Molina	.15
7	Roger Clemens	2.00
8	Lance Berkman	.25
9	Morgan Ensberg	.15
10	Roy Oswalt	.25
11	Andy Pettitte	.25
12	Craig Biggio	.25
13	Eric Chavez	.25
14	Barry Zito	.25
15	Huston Street	.15
16	Bobby Crosby	.15
17	Nick Swisher	.25
18	Rich Harden	.15
19	Vernon Wells	.25
20	Roy Halladay	.25
21	Alex Rios	.15
22	Orlando Hudson	.15
23	Shea Hillenbrand	.15
24	Gustavo Chacin	.15
25	Chipper Jones	.75
26	Andruw Jones	.50
27	Jeff Francoeur	.15
28	John Smoltz	.25
29	Tim Hudson	.25
30	Marcus Giles	.15
31	Carlos Lee	.25
32	Ben Sheets	.25
33	Rickie Weeks	.25
34	Chris Capuano	.15
35	Geoff Jenkins	.15
36	Brady Clark	.15
37	Albert Pujols	2.00
38	Jim Edmonds	.25
39	Chris Carpenter	.25
40	Mark Mulder	.25
41	Yadier Molina	.15
42	Scott Rolen	.75
43	Derek Lee	.50
44	Mark Prior	.50
45	Aramis Ramirez	.25
46	Carlos Zambrano	.25
47	Greg Maddux	1.50
48	Nomar Garciaparra	.75
49	Jonny Gomes	.25
50	Carl Crawford	.25
51	Scott Kazmir	.25
52	Jorge Cantu	.15
53	Julio Lugo	.15
54	Aubrey Huff	.15
55	Luis Gonzalez	.15
56	Brandon Webb	.25
57	Troy Glaus	.25
58	Shawn Green	.25
59	Craig Counsell	.15
60	Conor Jackson (RC)	.25
61	Jeff Kent	.25
62	Eric Gagne	.15
63	J.D. Drew	.25
64	Milton Bradley	.15
65	Jeff Weaver	.15
66	Cesar Izturis	.15
67	Jason Schmidt	.25
68	Moises Alou	.15
69	Pedro Feliz	.15

70	Randy Winn	.15
71	Omar Vizquel	.15
72	Noah Lowry	.15
73	Travis Hafner	.40
74	Victor Martinez	.25
75	C.C. Sabathia	.15
76	Grady Sizemore	.40
77	Coco Crisp	.15
78	Cliff Lee	.15
79	Raul Ibanez	.15
80	Ichiro Suzuki	1.00
81	Richie Sexson	.25
82	Felix Hernandez	.25
83	Adrian Beltre	.15
84	Jamie Moyer	.15
85	Miguel Cabrera	.75
86	A.J. Burnett	.15
87	Juan Pierre	.15
88	Carlos Delgado	.50
89	Dontrelle Willis	.25
90	Juan Encarnacion	.15
91	Carlos Beltran	.50
92	Jose Reyes	.50
93	David Wright	.75
94	Tom Glavine	.25
95	Mike Piazza	.75
96	Pedro Martinez	.75
97	Ryan Zimmerman (RC)	.15
98	Nick Johnson	.15
99	Jose Vidro	.15
100	Jose Guillen	.15
101	Livan Hernandez	.15
102	John Patterson	.15
103	Miguel Tejada	.25
104	Melvin Mora	.15
105	Brian Roberts	.15
106	Erik Bedard	.15
107	Javy Lopez	.15
108	Rodrigo Lopez	.15
109	Jake Peavy	.25
110	Mike Cameron	.15
111	Mark Loretta	.15
112	Brian Giles	.25
113	Trevor Hoffman	.15
114	Ramon Hernandez	.15
115	Bobby Abreu	.25
116	Chase Utley	.40
117	Pat Burrell	.25
118	Jimmy Rollins	.40
119	Ryan Howard	.75
120	Billy Wagner	.15
121	Jason Bay	.40
122	Oliver Perez	.15
123	Jack Wilson	.15
124	Zachary Duke	.15
125	Robert Mackowiak	.15
126	Freddy Sanchez	.15
127	Mark Teixeira	.50
128	Michael Young	.25
129	Alfonso Soriano	.50
130	Hank Blalock	.25
131	Kenny Rogers	.15
132	Kevin Mench	.15
133	Manny Ramirez	.75
134	Josh Beckett	.25
135	David Ortiz	.75
136	Johnny Damon	.75
137	Edgar Renteria	.15
138	Curt Schilling	.75
139	Ken Griffey Jr.	1.50
140	Adam Dunn	.50
141	Felipe Lopez	.15
142	Wily Mo Pena	.15
143	Aaron Harang	.15
144	Sean Casey	.15
145	Todd Helton	.50
146	Garrett Atkins	.15
147	Matt Holliday	.15
148	Jeff Francis	.15
149	Clint Barmes	.15
150	Luis Gonzalez	.15
151	Mike Sweeney	.15
152	Zack Greinke	.15
153	Angel Berroa	.15
154	Emil Brown	.15
155	David DeJesus	.15
156	Ivan Rodriguez	.50
157	Jeremy Bonderman	.15
158	Brandon Inge	.15
159	Craig Monroe	.15
160	Chris Shelton	.15
161	Dmitri Young	.15
162	Johan Santana	.50
163	Joe Mauer	.50
164	Torii Hunter	.25
165	Shannon Stewart	.15
166	Scott Baker	.15
167	Brad Radke	.15
168	Jon Garland	.15
169	Tadahito Iguchi	.15
170	Paul Konerko	.25
171	Scott Podsednik	.15
172	Mark Buehrle	.25
173	Joe Crede	.15
174	Derek Jeter	2.00
175	Alex Rodriguez	1.50
176	Hideki Matsui	1.00
177	Randy Johnson	.75
178	Gary Sheffield	.40
179	Mariano Rivera	.25
180	Jason Giambi	.40
181	Joey Devine RC	.50
182	Alejandro Freire RC	.50
183	Craig Hansen RC	2.00
184	Robert Andino RC	.50
185	Ryan Jorgensen RC	.50
186	Chris Demaria RC	.50
187	Jonah Bayliss RC	.50

188	Ryan Theriot (RC)	.25
189	Steve Stemle RC	.50
190	Brian Myrow RC	.50
191	Chris Heintz RC	.50
192	Ron Flores RC	.50
193	Danny Sandoval RC	.50
194	Craig Breslow RC	1.00
195	Jeremy Accardo RC	.50
196	Jeff Harris RC	.50
197	Tim Corcoran RC	.50
198	Scott Feldman RC	.50
199	Robinson Cano	.50
200	Jason Bergmann RC	3.00
201	Ken Griffey Jr.	4.00
202	Frank Thomas	1.00
203	Chipper Jones	2.00
204	Tony Clark	.50
205	Mike Lieberthal	.50
206	Manny Ramirez	2.00
207	Phil Nevin	.50
208	Derek Jeter	6.00
209	Preston Wilson	.50
210	Billy Wagner	.50
211	Alex Rodriguez	6.00
212	Trot Nixon	1.00
213	Jaret Wright	.50
214	Nomar Garciaparra	2.00
215	Paul Konerko	1.00
216	Paul Wilson	.50
217	Dustin Hermanson	.50
218	Todd Walker	.50
219	Matt Morris	.50
220	Darin Erstad	.50
221	Todd Helton	1.50
222	Geoff Jenkins	.50
223	Eric Chavez	1.00
224	Kris Benson	.50
225	Jon Garland	.50
226	Troy Glaus	1.00
227	Vernon Wells	1.00
228	Michael Cuddyer	.50
229	Justin Verlander (RC)	2.00
230	Pat Burrell	2.00
231	Mark Mulder	1.00
232	Corey Patterson	1.00
233	J.D. Drew	1.00
234	Austin Kearns	1.00
235	Felipe Lopez	.50
236	Sean Burroughs	.50
237	Ben Sheets	.50
238	Brett Myers	.50
239	Josh Beckett	1.00
240	Barry Zito	1.00
241	Adrian Gonzalez	.50
242	Rocco Baldelli	.50
243	Chris Burke	.50
244	Joe Mauer	2.00
245	Mark Prior	1.00
246	Mark Teixeira	2.00
247	Khalil Greene	.50
248	Zack Greinke	.50
249	Prince Fielder (RC)	4.00
250	Rickie Weeks	1.00
251	Kenji Johjima RC	20.00

Gold

Gold (1-200):	2-3X
Inserted 1:1	
Gold (201-251):	2-3X
Inserted 1:13	

AUTOGRAPHics
No Pricing

Diamond Producers

	NM/M
Complete Set (25):	
Common Player:	
DP1 Derek Jeter	3.00
DP2 Chipper Jones	1.00
DP3 Jim Edmonds	.75
DP4 Ken Griffey Jr.	2.00
DP5 David Ortiz	1.00
DP6 Manny Ramirez	1.00
DP7 Mark Teixeira	.75
DP8 Alex Rodriguez	3.00
DP9 Jeff Kent	.50
DP10 Albert Pujols	3.00
DP11 Todd Helton	.75
DP12 Miguel Cabrera	1.00
DP13 Hideki Matsui	2.00
DP14 Derek Lee	.75
DP15 Vladimir Guerrero	1.00
DP16 Miguel Tejada	.75
DP17 Jorge Cantu	.50
DP18 Travis Hafner	.50
DP19 Pat Burrell	.50
DP20 Bobby Abreu	.50
DP21 David Wright	2.00
DP22 Jason Bay	.75
DP23 Adam Dunn	.75
DP24 Eric Chavez	.50
DP25 Paul Konerko	.50

Feel the Game

	NM/M
Common Player:	4.00
BA Bobby Abreu	6.00
JB Josh Beckett	6.00
CB Carlos Beltran	8.00
AB Adrian Beltre	6.00
EC Eric Chavez	4.00
MC Matt Clement/SP	8.00
CD Carlos Delgado	6.00
BG Brian Giles	4.00
TG Troy Glaus	6.00
SG Shawn Green	4.00
KG Ken Griffey Jr.	20.00
VG Vladimir Guerrero	8.00
FH Felix Hernandez	8.00
DJ Derek Jeter	20.00
RJ Randy Johnson/SP	10.00
AJ Andruw Jones	8.00
CJ Chipper Jones	8.00
GM Greg Maddux	10.00
MO Magglio Ordonez	4.00
MP Mike Piazza	10.00
AP Albert Pujols	20.00
MR Manny Ramirez	8.00
JR Jose Reyes/SP	8.00
IR Ivan Rodriguez	6.00
RS Richie Sexson	6.00
AS Alfonso Soriano	8.00
MT Miguel Tejada	6.00
FT Frank Thomas/SP	6.00
PW Preston Wilson	4.00
DW David Wright	15.00

Home Run Kings

	NM/M
Complete Set (15):	10.00
Common Player:	.50
HRK1 Albert Pujols	3.00
HRK2 Ken Griffey Jr.	2.00
HRK3 Andruw Jones	1.00
HRK4 Alex Rodriguez	3.00
HRK5 David Ortiz	1.00
HRK6 Manny Ramirez	1.00
HRK7 Derek Lee	.75
HRK8 Mark Teixeira	.75
HRK9 Adam Dunn	.75
HRK10 Paul Konerko	.50
HRK11 Richie Sexson	.50
HRK12 Alfonso Soriano	.75
HRK13 Vladimir Guerrero	1.00
HRK14 Gary Sheffield	.75
HRK15 Mike Piazza	1.00

Midsummer Classic Kings

	NM/M
Complete Set (10):	10.00
Common Player:	.50
MCK1 Ken Griffey Jr.	2.00
MCK2 Mike Piazza	1.00
MCK3 Derek Jeter	3.00
MCK4 Roger Clemens	3.00
MCK5 Randy Johnson	1.00
MCK6 Miguel Tejada	.75
MCK7 Alfonso Soriano	.75
MCK8 Garret Anderson	.50
MCK9 Pedro Martinez	1.00
MCK10 Ivan Rodriguez	.75

RBI Kings

	NM/M
Complete Set (20):	15.00
Common Player:	.50

RBI1	Ken Griffey Jr.	2.00
RBI2	David Ortiz	1.00
RBI3	Manny Ramirez	1.00
RBI4	Mark Teixeira	.75
RBI5	Alex Rodriguez	3.00
RBI6	Andruw Jones	1.00
RBI7	Jeff Bagwell	.75
RBI8	Gary Sheffield	.75
RBI9	Richie Sexson	.50
RBI10	Jeff Kent	.50
RBI11	Albert Pujols	3.00
RBI12	Todd Helton	.75
RBI13	Miguel Cabrera	1.00
RBI14	Hideki Matsui	2.00
RBI15	Carlos Delgado	.75
RBI16	Carlos Lee	.75
RBI17	Derek Lee	.75
RBI18	Vladimir Guerrero	1.00
RBI19	Luis Gonzalez	.50
RBI20	Mike Piazza	1.00

Strikeout Kings

	NM/M
Complete Set (10):	8.00
Common Player:	.50
SOK1 Roger Clemens	3.00
SOK2 Johan Santana	1.00
SOK3 Jake Peavy	.50
SOK4 Randy Johnson	1.00
SOK5 Curt Schilling	1.00
SOK6 Chris Carpenter	.75
SOK7 Pedro Martinez	1.00
SOK8 Mark Prior	1.00
SOK9 Carlos Zambrano	.50
SOK10 John Smoltz	.50

Fine Fabrics

	NM/M
BA Bobby Abreu	6.00
JB Josh Beckett	6.00
CB Carlos Beltran	8.00
AB Adrian Beltre	6.00
HB Hank Blalock	6.00
SB Sean Burroughs	4.00
EC Eric Chavez	4.00
RC Roger Clemens/SP	15.00
MC Matt Clement	4.00
BC Bobby Crosby	4.00
CD Carlos Delgado	6.00
JD J.D. Drew	4.00
AD Adam Dunn	8.00
SF Steve Finley	4.00
JG Jason Giambi	10.00
BG Brian Giles	4.00
TG Troy Glaus	6.00
SG Shawn Green	4.00
KH Khalil Greene/SP	8.00
KG Ken Griffey Jr.	20.00
VG Vladimir Guerrero	8.00
TH Travis Hafner	8.00
FH Felix Hernandez	8.00
RH Ramon Hernandez	4.00
RY Ryan Howard	15.00
DJ Derek Jeter	20.00
RJ Randy Johnson/SP	10.00
AJ Andruw Jones	8.00
CJ Chipper Jones	8.00
JK Jeff Kent	8.00
RK Ryan Klesko	4.00
DL Derek Lee	8.00
GM Greg Maddux	10.00
MO Magglio Ordonez	4.00
DO David Ortiz	8.00
CP Corey Patterson	6.00
MP Mike Piazza	10.00
JP Jorge Posada	8.00
AP Albert Pujols	20.00
MR Manny Ramirez	10.00

JR	Jose Reyes	8.00
BR	Brian Roberts	6.00
IR	Ivan Rodriguez	6.00
SR	Scott Rolen	10.00
RS	Richie Sexson	6.00
JS	John Smoltz	8.00
AS	Alfonso Soriano	8.00
SS	Sammy Sosa	10.00
HS	Huston Street	4.00
TX	Mark Teixeira	8.00
MT	Miguel Tejada	8.00
FT	Frank Thomas	8.00
CU	Chase Utley	15.00
VW	Vernon Wells	6.00
BW	Bernie Williams	6.00
WI	Dontrelle Willis	6.00
PW	Preston Wilson	4.00
KW	Kerry Wood	6.00
DW	David Wright	15.00
BZ	Barry Zito	6.00

Rising Stars

	NM/M
Complete Set (10):	10.00
Common Player:	.50
URS1 Ryan Howard	3.00
URS2 Huston Street	.50
URS3 Jeff Francoeur	.75
URS4 Felix Hernandez	1.50
URS5 Chase Utley	2.00
URS6 Robinson Cano	1.00
URS7 Zachary Duke	.50
URS8 Scott Kazmir	1.00
URS9 Willy Taveras	.50
URS10 Tadahito Iguchi	1.00

1989 Upper Deck Promos

In 1988, Upper Deck produced a two-card test set to be distributed as samples for the 1989 set; 18,000 of each card were produced. The cards were distributed to dealers at the 1988 National Sports Collectors Convention. Two other variations of the promo cards exist. Both variations involve differences in where the hologram was placed. Fewer than 5,000 of one of the hologram variations exist, while less than 1,000 of the third variation exist. Joyner and Buice were selected for the promo cards because of a reported investment interest in Upper Deck; they were later required to sell their interest in the card company due to their active-player status.

	NM/M
Complete Set A (2):	5.00
Complete Set B (2):	9.00
Complete Set C (2):	15.00
1a DeWayne Buice (1/2" x 3/16" hologram at bottom)	2.00
1b DeWayne Buice (Hologram extends to bottom edge.)	3.00
1c DeWayne Buice (Hologram at top.)	5.00
700a Wally Joyner (1/2" x 3/16" hologram at bottom)	2.50

ABBREVIATIONS
SP - Short Print

		NM/M
700b	Wally Joyner (Hologram extends to bottom edge.)	6.00
700c	Wally Joyner (Hologram at top.)	10.00

1989 Upper Deck Show Samples

Tommy John

At the Nov. 26-27, 1988 Anaheim card show, Upper Deck distributed samples of its forthcoming premiere set. While card fronts are nearly identical to the same players' issued versions (except they lack the position indicator at topright), the backs are blank, also lacking the hologram. All cards in this sample distribution are from the range of card numbers between 206-250, in five contiguous groups of five, with gaps of five between them. The samples are listed here in alphabetical order. Uncut sheets of the samples were reported to be widely available at the show.

	NM/M
Complete Set (25):	90.00
Common Player:	3.00
Uncut Sheet (25):	100.00
Mike Aldrete	3.00
Andy Allanson	3.00
Scott Bailes	3.00
Phil Bradley	3.00
Scott Bradley	3.00
Jay Buhner	3.00
Brett Butler	3.00
John Candelaria	3.00
Bruce Fields	3.00
Von Hayes	3.00
Rickey Henderson	15.00
Steve Jeltz	3.00
Tommy John	4.50
Ron Kittle	3.00
Bob Melvin	3.00
Lance Parrish	3.00
Willie Randolph	4.50
Harold Reynolds	3.00
Rafael Santana	3.00
Rod Scurry	3.00
Chris Speier	3.00
Greg Swindell	3.00
Kent Tekulve	3.00
Matt Williams	3.00
Paul Zuvella	3.00

1989 Upper Deck

Dale Murphy

This premiere "Collector's Choice" issue from Upper Deck contains 700 cards (2-1/2" x 3-1/2") with full-color photos on both sides. The first 26 cards feature Star Rookies. The set also includes 26 special portrait cards with team checklist backs and seven numerical checklist cards. Major 1988 award winners (Cy Young, Rookie of Year, MVP) are honored on 10 cards in the set, in addition to their in-

dividual player cards. There are also special cards for the Most Valuable Players in both League Championship series and the World Series. The card fronts feature player photos framed by a white border. A vertical brown and green artist's rendition of the runner's lane that leads from home plate to first base is found along the right margin. Backs carry full-color action poses that fill the card back, except for a compact (yet complete) stats chart. A high-number series, cards 701-800, featuring rookies and traded players, was released in mid-season in foil packs mixed within the complete set, in boxed complete sets and in high number set boxes.

		NM/M
	Unopened Fact. Set (800):	80.00
	Complete Set (800):	45.00
	Complete Low Set (700):	40.00
	Complete High Set (100):	5.00
	Common Player:	.05
	Low Foil Pack (15):	4.00
	Low Foil Box (36):	100.00
	High Foil Pack (15):	2.00
	High Foil Box (36):	60.00
1	Ken Griffey Jr. RC	40.00
2	Luis Medina RC	.05
3	Tony Chance RC	.05
4	Dave Otto RC	.05
5	Sandy Alomar, Jr. RC	1.00
6	Rolando Roomes RC	.05
7	David West RC	.05
8	Cris Carpenter RC	.05
9	Gregg Jefferies	.25
10	Doug Dascenzo RC	.05
11	Ron Jones RC	.05
12	Luis de los Santos RC	.05
13a	Gary Sheffield RC ("SS" upside-down)	8.00
13b	Gary Sheffield RC ("SS" correct)	8.00
14	Mike Harkey RC	.05
15	Lance Blankenship RC	.05
16	William Brennan RC	.05
17	John Smoltz	.05
18	Ramon Martinez RC	.25
19	Mark Lemke RC	.05
20	Juan Bell RC	.05
21	Rey Palacios RC	.05
22	Felix Jose RC	.05
23	Van Snider RC	.05
24	Dante Bichette RC	.75
25	Randy Johnson RC	15.00
26	Carlos Quintana RC	.05
27	Star Rookie Checklist 1-26	.05
28	Mike Schooler RC	.05
29	Randy St. Claire	.05
30	Jerald Clark RC	.05
31	Kevin Gross	.05
32	Dan Firova RC	.05
33	Jeff Calhoun	.05
34	Tommy Hinzo	.05
35	Ricky Jordan RC	.05
36	Larry Parrish	.05
37	Bret Saberhagen	.05
38	Mike Smithson	.05
39	Dave Dravecky	.05
40	Ed Romero	.05
41	Jeff Musselman	.05
42	Ed Hearn	.05
43	Rance Mulliniks	.05
44	Jim Eisenreich	.05
45	Sil Campusano RC	.05
46	Mike Krukow	.05
47	Paul Gibson RC	.05
48	Mike LaCoss	.05
49	Larry Herndon	.05
50	Scott Garrelts	.05
51	Dwayne Henry	.05
52	Jim Acker	.05
53	Steve Sax	.05
54	Pete O'Brien	.05
55	Paul Runge	.05
56	Rick Rhoden	.05
57	John Dopson RC	.05
58	Casey Candaele	.05
59	Dave Righetti	.05
60	Joe Hesketh	.05
61	Frank DiPino	.05
62	Tim Laudner	.05
63	Jamie Moyer	.05
64	Fred Toliver	.05
65	Mitch Webster	.05
66	John Tudor	.05
67	John Cangelosi	.05
68	Mike Devereaux	.05
69	Brian Fisher	.05
70	Mike Marshall	.05
71	Zane Smith	.05
72a	Brian Holton (Ball not visible on card front, photo actually Shawn Hillegas.)	.75
72b	Brian Holton (Ball visible, correct photo.)	.05
73	Jose Guzman	.05

74	Rick Mahler	.05
75	John Shelby	.05
76	Jim Deshaies	.05
77	Bobby Meacham	.05
78	Bryn Smith	.05
79	Joaquin Andujar	.05
80	Richard Dotson	.05
81	Charlie Lea	.05
82	Calvin Schiraldi	.05
83	Les Straker	.05
84	Les Lancaster	.05
85	Allan Anderson	.05
86	Junior Ortiz	.05
87	Jesse Orosco	.05
88	Felix Fermin	.05
89	Dave Anderson	.05
90	Rafael Belliard	.05
91	Franklin Stubbs	.05
92	Cecil Espy	.05
93	Albert Hall	.05
94	Tim Leary	.05
95	Mitch Williams	.05
96	Tracy Jones	.05
97	Danny Darwin	.05
98	Gary Ward	.05
99	Neal Heaton	.05
100	Jim Pankovits	.05
101	Bill Doran	.05
102	Tim Wallach	.05
103	Joe Magrane	.05
104	Ozzie Virgil	.05
105	Alvin Davis	.05
106	Tom Brookens	.05
107	Shawon Dunston	.05
108	Tracy Woodson	.05
109	Nelson Liriano	.05
110	Devon White	.05
111	Steve Balboni	.05
112	Buddy Bell	.05
113	German Jimenez RC	.05
114	Ken Dayley	.05
115	Andres Galarraga	.05
116	Mike Scioscia	.05
117	Gary Pettis	.05
118	Ernie Whitt	.05
119	Bob Boone	.05
120	Ryne Sandberg	1.50
121	Bruce Benedict	.05
122	Hubie Brooks	.05
123	Mike Moore	.05
124	Wallace Johnson	.05
125	Bob Horner	.05
126	Chili Davis	.05
127	Manny Trillo	.05
128	Chet Lemon	.05
129	John Cerutti	.05
130	Orel Hershiser	.05
131	Terry Pendleton	.05
132	Jeff Blauser	.05
133	Mike Fitzgerald	.05
134	Henry Cotto	.05
135	Gerald Young	.05
136	Luis Salazar	.05
137	Alejandro Pena	.05
138	Jack Howell	.05
139	Tony Fernandez	.05
140	Mark Grace	.05
141	Ken Caminiti	.05
142	Mike Jackson	.05
143	Larry McWilliams	.05
144	Andres Thomas	.05
145	Nolan Ryan	2.00
146	Mike Davis	.05
147	DeWayne Buice	.05
148	Jody Davis	.05
149	Jesse Barfield	.05
150	Matt Nokes	.05
151	Jerry Reuss	.05
152	Rick Cerone	.05
153	Storm Davis	.05
154	Marvell Wynne	.05
155	Will Clark	.05
156	Luis Aguayo	.05
157	Willie Upshaw	.05
158	Randy Bush	.05
159	Ron Darling	.05
160	Kal Daniels	.05
161	Spike Owen	.05
162	Luis Polonia	.05
163	Kevin Mitchell	.05
164	Dave Gallagher RC	.05
165	Benito Santiago	.05
166	Greg Gagne	.05
167	Ken Phelps	.05
168	Sid Fernandez	.05
169	Bo Diaz	.05
170	Cory Snyder	.05
171	Eric Show	.05
172	Robby Thompson	.05
173	Marty Barrett	.05
174	Dave Henderson	.05
175	Ozzie Guillen	.05
176	Barry Lyons	.05
177	Kelvin Torve RC	.05
178	Don Slaught	.05
179	Steve Lombardozzi	.05
180	Chris Sabo RC	.05
181	Jose Uribe	.05
182	Shane Mack	.05
183	Ron Karkovice	.05
184	Todd Benzinger	.05
185	Dave Stewart	.05
186	Julio Franco	.05
187	Ron Robinson	.05
188	Wally Backman	.05
189	Randy Velarde	.05
190	Joe Carter	.05
191	Bob Welch	.05

192	Kelly Paris	.05
193	Chris Brown	.05
194	Rick Reuschel	.05
195	Roger Clemens	1.60
196	Dave Concepcion	.05
197	Al Newman	.05
198	Brook Jacoby	.05
199	Mookie Wilson	.05
200	Don Mattingly	1.60
201	Dick Schofield	.05
202	Mark Gubicza	.05
203	Gary Gaetti	.05
204	Dan Pasqua	.05
205	Andre Dawson	.35
206	Chris Speier	.05
207	Kent Tekulve	.05
208	Rod Scurry	.05
209	Scott Bailes	.05
210	Rickey Henderson	1.00
211	Harold Baines	.05
212	Tony Armas	.05
213	Kent Hrbek	.05
214	Darrin Jackson	.05
215	George Brett	1.60
216	Rafael Santana	.05
217	Andy Allanson	.05
218	Brett Butler	.05
219	Steve Jeltz	.05
220	Jay Buhner	.05
221	Bo Jackson	.15
222	Angel Salazar	.05
223	Kirk McCaskill	.05
224	Steve Lyons	.05
225	Bert Blyleven	.05
226	Scott Bradley	.05
227	Bob Melvin	.05
228	Ron Kittle	.05
229	Phil Bradley	.05
230	Tommy John	.05
231	Greg Walker	.05
232	Juan Berenguer	.05
233	Pat Tabler	.05
234	Terry Clark RC	.05
235	Rafael Palmeiro	.75
236	Paul Zuvella	.05
237	Willie Randolph	.05
238	Bruce Fields	.05
239	Mike Aldrete	.05
240	Lance Parrish	.05
241	Greg Maddux	1.50
242	John Moses	.05
243	Melido Perez	.05
244	Willie Wilson	.05
245	Mark McLemore	.05
246	Von Hayes	.05
247	Matt Williams	.05
248	John Candelaria	.05
249	Harold Reynolds	.05
250	Greg Swindell	.05
251	Juan Agosto	.05
252	Mike Felder	.05
253	Vince Coleman	.05
254	Larry Sheets	.05
255	George Bell	.05
256	Terry Steinbach	.05
257	Jack Armstrong RC	.05
258	Dickie Thon	.05
259	Ray Knight	.05
260	Darryl Strawberry	.05
261	Doug Sisk	.05
262	Alex Trevino	.05
263	Jeff Leonard	.05
264	Tom Henke	.05
265	Ozzie Smith	1.50
266	Dave Bergman	.05
267	Tony Phillips	.05
268	Mark Davis	.05
269	Kevin Elster	.05
270	Barry Larkin	.05
271	Manny Lee	.05
272	Tom Brunansky	.05
273	Craig Biggio	.05
274	Jim Gantner	.05
275	Eddie Murray	1.00
276	Jeff Reed	.05
277	Tim Teufel	.05
278	Rick Honeycutt	.05
279	Guillermo Hernandez	.05
280	John Kruk	.05
281	Luis Alicea RC	.15
282	Jim Clancy	.05
283	Billy Ripken	.05
284	Craig Reynolds	.05
285	Robin Yount	1.00
286	Jimmy Jones	.05
287	Ron Oester	.05
288	Terry Leach	.05
289	Dennis Eckersley	.75
290	Alan Trammell	.05
291	Jimmy Key	.05
292	Chris Bosio	.05
293	Jose DeLeon	.05
294	Jim Traber	.05
295	Mike Scott	.05
296	Roger McDowell	.05
297	Garry Templeton	.05
298	Doyle Alexander	.05
299	Nick Esasky	.05
300	Mark McGwire	1.75
301	Darryl Hamilton RC	.05
302	Dave Smith	.05
303	Rick Sutcliffe	.05
304	Dave Stapleton	.05
305	Alan Ashby	.05
306	Pedro Guerrero	.05
307	Ron Guidry	.05
308	Steve Farr	.05
309	Curt Ford	.05

310	Claudell Washington	.05
311	Tom Prince	.05
312	Chad Kreuter RC	.15
313	Ken Oberkfell	.05
314	Jerry Browne	.05
315	R.J. Reynolds	.05
316	Scott Bankhead	.05
317	Milt Thompson	.05
318	Mario Diaz	.05
319	Bruce Ruffin	.05
320	Dave Valle	.05
321a	Gary Varsho RC (Batting righty on card back, photo actually Mike Bielecki.)	1.00
321b	Gary Varsho RC (Batting lefty on card back, correct photo.)	.05
322	Paul Mirabella	.05
323	Chuck Jackson	.05
324	Drew Hall	.05
325	Don August	.05
326	Israel Sanchez RC	.05
327	Denny Walling	.05
328	Joel Skinner	.05
329	Danny Tartabull	.05
330	Tony Pena	.05
331	Jim Sundberg	.05
332	Jeff Robinson	.05
333	Odibbe McDowell	.05
334	Jose Lind	.05
335	Paul Kilgus	.05
336	Juan Samuel	.05
337	Mike Campbell	.05
338	Mike Maddux	.05
339	Darnell Coles	.05
340	Bob Dernier	.05
341	Rafael Ramirez	.05
342	Scott Sanderson	.05
343	B.J. Surhoff	.05
344	Billy Hatcher	.05
345	Pat Perry	.05
346	Jack Clark	.05
347	Gary Thurman	.05
348	Timmy Jones RC	.05
349	Dave Winfield	1.00
350	Frank White	.05
351	Dave Collins	.05
352	Jack Morris	.05
353	Eric Plunk	.05
354	Leon Durham	.05
355	Ivan DeJesus	.05
356	Brian Holman RC	.05
357a	Dale Murphy (Reversed negative.)	17.50
357b	Dale Murphy (Corrected)	.25
358	Mark Portugal	.05
359	Andy McGaffigan	.05
360	Tom Glavine	.25
361	Keith Moreland	.05
362	Todd Stottlemyre	.05
363	Dave Leiper	.05
364	Cecil Fielder	.05
365	Carmelo Martinez	.05
366	Dwight Evans	.05
367	Kevin McReynolds	.05
368	Rich Gedman	.05
369	Len Dykstra	.05
370	Jody Reed	.05
371	Jose Canseco	.60
372	Rob Murphy	.05
373	Mike Henneman	.05
374	Walt Weiss	.05
375	Rob Dibble RC	.05
376	Kirby Puckett	1.50
377	Denny Martinez	.05
378	Ron Gant	.05
379	Brian Harper	.05
380	Nelson Santovenia RC	.05
381	Lloyd Moseby	.05
382	Lance McCullers	.05
383	Dave Stieb	.05
384	Tony Gwynn	1.50
385	Mike Flanagan	.05
386	Bob Ojeda	.05
387	Bruce Hurst	.05
388	Dave Magadan	.05
389	Wade Boggs	1.50
390	Gary Carter	1.00
391	Frank Tanana	.05
392	Curt Young	.05
393	Jeff Treadway	.05
394	Darrell Evans	.05
395	Glenn Hubbard	.05
396	Chuck Cary	.05
397	Frank Viola	.05
398	Jeff Parrett	.05
399	Terry Blocker RC	.05
400	Dan Gladden	.05
401	Louie Meadows RC	.05
402	Tim Raines	.05
403	Joey Meyer	.05
404	Larry Andersen	.05
405	Rex Hudler	.05
406	Mike Schmidt	1.60
407	John Franco	.05
408	Brady Anderson	.05
409	Don Carman	.05
410	Eric Davis	.05
411	Bob Stanley	.05
412	Pete Smith	.05
413	Jim Rice	.25
414	Bruce Sutter	.75
415	Oil Can Boyd	.05
416	Ruben Sierra	.05
417	Mike LaValliere	.05
418	Steve Buechele	.05
419	Gary Redus	.05

420	Scott Fletcher	.05
421	Dale Sveum	.05
422	Bob Knepper	.05
423	Luis Rivera	.05
424	Ted Higuera	.05
425	Kevin Bass	.05
426	Ken Gerhart	.05
427	Shane Rawley	.05
428	Paul O'Neill	.05
429	Joe Orsulak	.05
430	Jackie Gutierrez	.05
431	Gerald Perry	.05
432	Mike Greenwell	.05
433	Jerry Royster	.05
434	Ellis Burks	.05
435	Ed Olwine	.05
436	Dave Rucker	.05
437	Charlie Hough	.05
438	Bob Walk	.05
439	Bob Brower	.05
440	Barry Bonds	2.00
441	Tom Foley	.05
442	Rob Deer	.05
443	Glenn Davis	.05
444	Dave Martinez	.05
445	Bill Wegman	.05
446	Lloyd McClendon	.05
447	Dave Schmidt	.05
448	Darren Daulton	.05
449	Frank Williams	.05
450	Don Aase	.05
451	Lou Whitaker	.05
452	Goose Gossage	.05
453	Ed Whitson	.05
454	Jim Walewander	.05
455	Damon Berryhill	.05
456	Tim Burke	.05
457	Barry Jones	.05
458	Joel Youngblood	.05
459	Floyd Youmans	.05
460	Mark Salas	.05
461	Jeff Russell	.05
462	Darrell Miller	.05
463	Jeff Kunkel	.05
464	Sherman Corbett RC	.05
465	Curtis Wilkerson	.05
466	Bud Black	.05
467	Cal Ripken, Jr.	2.00
468	John Farrell	.05
469	Terry Kennedy	.05
470	Tom Candiotti	.05
471	Roberto Alomar	.20
472	Jeff Robinson	.05
473	Vance Law	.05
474	Randy Ready	.05
475	Walt Terrell	.05
476	Kelly Downs	.05
477	Johnny Paredes RC	.05
478	Shawn Hillegas	.05
479	Bob Brenly	.05
480	Otis Nixon	.05
481	Johnny Ray	.05
482	Geno Petralli	.05
483	Stu Cliburn	.05
484	Pete Incaviglia	.05
485	Brian Downing	.05
486	Jeff Stone	.05
487	Carmen Castillo	.05
488	Tom Niedenfuer	.05
489	Jay Bell	.05
490	Rick Schu	.05
491	Jeff Pico RC	.05
492	Mark Parent RC	.05
493	Eric King	.05
494	Al Nipper	.05
495	Andy Hawkins	.05
496	Daryl Boston	.05
497	Ernie Riles	.05
498	Pascual Perez	.05
499	Bill Long	.05
500	Kirt Manwaring	.05
501	Chuck Crim	.05
502	Candy Maldonado	.05
503	Dennis Lamp	.05
504	Glenn Braggs	.05
505	Joe Price	.05
506	Ken Williams	.05
507	Bill Pecota	.05
508	Rey Quinones	.05
509	Jeff Bittiger RC	.05
510	Kevin Seitzer	.05
511	Steve Bedrosian	.05
512	Todd Worrell	.05
513	Chris James	.05
514	Jose Oquendo	.05
515	David Palmer	.05
516	John Smiley	.05
517	Dave Clark	.05
518	Mike Dunne	.05
519	Ron Washington	.05
520	Bob Kipper	.05
521	Lee Smith	.05
522	Juan Castillo	.05
523	Don Robinson	.05
524	Kevin Romine	.05
525	Paul Molitor	1.00
526	Mark Langston	.05
527	Donnie Hill	.05
528	Larry Owen	.05
529	Jerry Reed	.05
530	Jack McDowell	.05
531	Greg Mathews	.05
532	John Russell	.05
533	Dan Quisenberry	.05
534	Greg Gross	.05
535	Danny Cox	.05
536	Terry Francona	.05
537	Andy Van Slyke	.05

538	Mel Hall	.05
539	Jim Gott	.05
540	Doug Jones	.05
541	Criag Lefferts	.05
542	Mike Boddicker	.05
543	Greg Brock	.05
544	Atlee Hammaker	.05
545	Tom Bolton	.05
546	Mike Macfarlane RC	.25
547	Rich Renteria RC	.05
548	John Davis	.05
549	Floyd Bannister	.05
550	Mickey Brantley	.05
551	Duane Ward	.05
552	Dan Petry	.05
553	Mickey Tettleton	.05
554	Rick Leach	.05
555	Mike Witt	.05
556	Sid Bream	.05
557	Bobby Witt	.05
558	Tommy Herr	.05
559	Randy Milligan	.05
560	Jose Cecena RC	.05
561	Mackey Sasser	.05
562	Carney Lansford	.05
563	Rick Aguilera	.05
564	Ron Hassey	.05
565	Dwight Gooden	.05
566	Paul Assenmacher	.05
567	Neil Allen	.05
568	Jim Morrison	.05
569	Mike Pagliarulo	.05
570	Ted Simmons	.05
571	Mark Thurmond	.05
572	Fred McGriff	.05
573	Wally Joyner	.05
574	Jose Bautista RC	.05
575	Kelly Gruber	.05
576	Cecilio Guante	.05
577	Mark Davidson	.05
578	Bobby Bonilla	.05
579	Mike Stanley	.05
580	Gene Larkin	.05
581	Stan Javier	.05
582	Howard Johnson	.05
583a	Mike Gallego (Photo on card back reversed.)	.75
583b	Mike Gallego (Correct photo.)	.05
584	David Cone	.05
585	Doug Jennings RC	.05
586	Charlie Hudson	.05
587	Dion James	.05
588	Al Leiter	.05
589	Charlie Puleo	.05
590	Roberto Kelly	.05
591	Thad Bosley	.05
592	Pete Stanicek	.05
593	Pat Borders RC	.25
594	Bryan Harvey RC	.05
595	Jeff Ballard	.05
596	Jeff Reardon	.05
597	Doug Drabek	.05
598	Edwin Correa	.05
599	Keith Atherton	.05
600	Dave LaPoint	.05
601	Don Baylor	.05
602	Tom Pagnozzi	.05
603	Tim Flannery	.05
604	Gene Walter	.05
605	Dave Parker	.05
606	Mike Diaz	.05
607	Chris Gwynn	.05
608	Odell Jones	.05
609	Carlton Fisk	1.00
610	Jay Howell	.05
611	Tim Crews	.05
612	Keith Hernandez	.05
613	Willie Fraser	.05
614	Jim Eppard	.05
615	Jeff Hamilton	.05
616	Kurt Stillwell	.05
617	Tom Browning	.05
618	Jeff Montgomery	.05
619	Jose Rijo	.05
620	Jamie Quirk	.05
621	Willie McGee	.05
622	Mark Grant	.05
623	Bill Swift	.05
624	Orlando Mercado	.05
625	John Costello RC	.05
626	Jose Gonzalez	.05
627a	Bill Schroeder (Putting on shin guards on card back, photo actually Ronn Reynolds.)	.75
627b	Bill Schroeder (Arms crossed on card back, correct photo.)	.05
628a	Fred Manrique (Throwing on card back, photo actually Ozzie Guillen.)	.75
628b	Fred Manrique (Batting on card back, correct photo.)	.05
629	Ricky Horton	.05
630	Dan Plesac	.05
631	Alfredo Griffin	.05
632	Chuck Finley	.05
633	Kirk Gibson	.05
634	Randy Myers	.05
635	Greg Minton	.05
636	Herm Winningham	.05
637	Charlie Leibrandt	.05
638	Tim Birtsas	.05
639	Bill Buckner	.05
640	Danny Jackson	.05
641	Greg Booker	.05
642	Jim Presley	.05
643	Gene Nelson	.05
644	Rod Booker	.05
645	Dennis Rasmussen	.05
646	Juan Nieves	.05
647	Bobby Thigpen	.05
648	Tim Belcher	.05
649	Mike Young	.05
650	Ivan Calderon	.05
651	Oswaldo Peraza RC	.05
652a	Pat Sheridan (No position on front.)	8.00
652b	Pat Sheridan (Position on front.)	.05
653	Mike Morgan	.05
654	Mike Heath	.05
655	Jay Tibbs	.05
656	Fernando Valenzuela	.05
657	Lee Mazzilli	.05
658	Frank Viola	.05
659	Jose Canseco	.60
660	Walt Weiss	.05
661	Orel Hershiser	.05
662	Kirk Gibson	.05
663	Chris Sabo	.05
664	Dennis Eckersley	.75
665	Orel Hershiser	.05
666	Kirk Gibson	.05
667	Orel Hershiser	.05
668	Wally Joyner/TC	.05
669	Nolan Ryan/TC	1.00
670	Jose Canseco/TC	.30
671	Fred McGriff/TC	.05
672	Dale Murphy/TC	.20
673	Paul Molitor/TC	.50
674	Ozzie Smith/TC	.75
675	Ryne Sandberg/TC	.40
676	Kirk Gibson/TC	.05
677	Andres Galarraga/TC	.05
678	Will Clark/TC	.05
679	Cory Snyder/TC	.05
680	Alvin Davis/TC	.05
681	Darryl Strawberry/TC	.05
682	Cal Ripken, Jr./TC	1.00
683	Tony Gwynn/TC	.40
684	Mike Schmidt/TC	.85
685	Andy Van Slyke/TC	.05
686	Ruben Sierra/TC	.05
687	Wade Boggs/TC	.40
688	Eric Davis/TC	.05
689	George Brett/TC	.85
690	Alan Trammell/TC	.05
691	Frank Viola/TC	.05
692	Harold Baines/TC	.05
693	Don Mattingly/TC	.85
694	Checklist 1-100	.05
695	Checklist 101-200	.05
696	Checklist 201-300	.05
697	Checklist 301-400	.05
698	Checklist 401-500	.05
699	Checklist 501-600	.05
700	Checklist 601-700	.05
701	Checklist 701-800	.05
702	Jessie Barfield	.05
703	Walt Terrell	.05
704	Dickie Thon	.05
705	Al Leiter	.05
706	Dave LaPoint	.05
707	Charlie Hayes RC	.05
708	Andy Hawkins	.05
709	Mickey Hatcher	.05
710	Lance McCullers	.05
711	Ron Kittle	.05
712	Bert Blyleven	.05
713	Rick Dempsey	.05
714	Ken Williams	.05
715	Steve Rosenberg RC	.05
716	Joe Skalski RC	.05
717	Spike Owen	.05
718	Todd Burns	.05
719	Kevin Gross	.05
720	Tommy Herr	.05
721	Rob Ducey	.05
722	Gary Green RC	.05
723	Gregg Olson RC	.10
724	Greg Harris RC	.05
725	Craig Worthington RC	.05
726	Tom Howard RC	.05
727	Dale Mohorcic	.05
728	Rich Yett	.05
729	Mel Hall	.05
730	Floyd Youmans	.05
731	Lonnie Smith	.05
732	Wally Backman	.05
733	Trevor Wilson	.05
734	Jose Alvarez	.05
735	Bob Milacki RC	.05
736	Tom Gordon RC	.50
737	Wally Whitehurst RC	.05
738	Mike Aldrete	.05
739	Keith Miller	.05
740	Randy Milligan	.05
741	Jeff Parrett	.05
742	Steve Finley RC	.75
743	Junior Felix RC	.25
744	Pete Harnisch RC	.25
745	Bill Spiers RC	.05
746	Hensley Meulens RC	.05
747	Juan Bell	.05
748	Steve Sax	.05
749	Phil Bradley	.05
750	Rey Quinones	.05
751	Tommy Gregg RC	.05
752	Kevin Brown RC	.25
753	Derek Lilliquist RC	.05
754	Todd Zeile RC	.75
755	Jim Abbott RC	.05
756	Ozzie Canseco RC	.05
757	Nick Esasky	.05
758	Mike Moore	.05
759	Rob Murphy	.05
760	Rick Mahler	.05
761	Fred Lynn	.05
762	Kevin Blankenship RC	.05
763	Eddie Murray	1.00
764	Steve Searcy RC	.05
765	Jerome Walton RC	.05
766	Erik Hanson RC	.05
767	Bob Boone	.05
768	Edgar Martinez RC	.05
769	Jose DeJesus RC	.05
770	Greg Briley RC	.05
771	Steve Peters RC	.05
772	Rafael Palmeiro	.75
773	Jack Clark	.05
774	Nolan Ryan	2.00
775	Lance Parrish	.05
776	Joe Girardi RC	.30
777	Willie Randolph	.05
778	Mitch Williams	.05
779	Dennis Cook RC	.05
780	Dwight Smith RC	.05
781	Lenny Harris RC	.10
782	Torey Lovullo RC	.05
783	Norm Charlton RC	.15
784	Chris Brown	.05
785	Todd Benzinger	.05
786	Shane Rawley	.05
787	Omar Vizquel RC	2.00
788	LaVel Freeman RC	.05
789	Jeffrey Leonard	.05
790	Eddie Williams RC	.05
791	Jamie Moyer	.05
792	Bruce Hurst	.05
793	Julio Franco	.05
794	Claudell Washington	.05
795	Jody Davis	.05
796	Oddibe McDowell	.05
797	Paul Kilgus	.05
798	Tracy Jones	.05
799	Steve Wilson RC	.05
800	Pete O'Brien	.05

1990 Upper Deck

Tom Gordon

Following the success of its first issue, Upper Deck released another 800-card set in 1990. The cards feature full-color photos on both sides in the standard 2-1/2" x 3-1/2" format. The artwork of Vernon Wells Sr. is featured on the front of all team checklist cards. The 1990 set also introduces two new Wells illustrations - a tribute to Mike Schmidt upon his retirement and one commemorating Nolan Ryan's 5,000 career strikeouts. The cards are similar in design to the 1989 issue. The high-number series (701-800) was released as a boxed set, in factory sets and in foil packs at mid-season. Cards #101-199 can be found either with or without the copyright line on back; no premium attaches to either.

NM/M

Unopened Factory Set (800):		20.00
Complete Set (800):		15.00
Complete Low Set (700):		12.00
Complete High Set (100):		5.00
Common Player:		.05
Low or High Foil Pack (15):		.50
Low or High Foil Box (36):		12.00
1	Star Rookie Checklist	.05
2	Randy Nosek RC	.05
3	Tom Drees RC	.05
4	Curt Young	.05
5	Angels checklist (Devon White)	.05
6	Luis Salazar	.05
7	Phillies checklist (Von Hayes)	.05
8	Jose Bautista	.05
9	Marquis Grissom RC	.50
10	Dodgers checklist (Orel Hershiser)	.05
11	Rick Aguilera	.05

12	Padres checklist (Benito Santiago)	.05
13	Deion Sanders	.10
15	Marvell Wynne	.05
16	Pirates checklist (Bobby Bonilla)	.05
17	Sammy Sosa RC	5.00
18	Yankees checklist (Steve Sax)	.05
19	Jack Howell	.05
20	Mike Schmidt Retires (Mike Schmidt)	.75
21	Robin Ventura	.05
22	Brian Meyer RC	.05
23	Blaine Beatty RC	.05
24	Mariners checklist (Ken Griffey Jr.)	.50
25	Greg Vaughn	.05
26	Xavier Hernandez RC	.05
27	Jason Grimsley RC	.05
28	Eric Anthony RC	.05
29	Expos checklist (Tim Raines)	.05
30	David Wells	.05
31	Hal Morris RC	.05
32	Royals checklist (Bo Jackson)	.10
33	Kelly Mann RC	.05
34	Nolan Ryan 5000 Strikeouts (Nolan Ryan)	1.00
35	Scott Service RC	.05
36	Athletics checklist (Mark McGwire)	.50
37	Tino Martinez	.05
38	Chili Davis	.05
39	Scott Sanderson	.05
40	Giants checklist (Kevin Mitchell)	.05
41	Tigers checklist (Lou Whitaker)	.05
42	Scott Coolbaugh RC	.05
43	Jose Cano RC	.05
44	Jose Vizcaino RC	.10
45	Bob Hamelin RC	.05
46	Jose Offerman RC	.15
47	Kevin Blankenship	.05
48	Twins checklist (Kirby Puckett)	.40
49	Tommy Greene RC	.05
50	N.L. Top Vote Getter (Will Clark)	.05
51	Rob Nelson RC	.05
52	Chris Hammond RC	.15
53	Indians checklist (Joe Carter)	.05
54a	Ben McDonald RC (Orioles Logo)	1.00
54b	Ben McDonald RC (Star Rookie logo.)	.25
55	Andy Benes	.05
56	John Olerud RC	1.00
57	Red Sox checklist (Roger Clemens)	.45
58	Tony Armas	.05
59	George Canale RC	.05
60a	Orioles checklist Mickey Tettleton (#683 Jamie Weston)	1.00
60b	Orioles checklist Mickey Tettleton (#683 Mickey Weston)	.05
61	Mike Stanton RC	.05
62	Mets checklist (Dwight Gooden)	.05
63	Kent Mercker RC	.10
64	Francisco Cabrera RC	.05
65	Steve Avery RC	.05
66	Jose Canseco	.35
67	Matt Merullo RC	.05
68	Cardinals checklist (Vince Coleman)	.05
69	Ron Karkovice	.05
70	Kevin Maas RC	.05
71	Dennis Cook RC	.05
72	Juan Gonzalez RC	2.00
73	Cubs checklist (Andre Dawson)	.10
74	Dean Palmer RC	.05
75	A.L. Top Vote Getter (Bo Jackson)	.10
76	Rob Richie RC	.05
77	Bobby Rose RC	.05
78	Brian DuBois RC	.05
79	White Sox checklist (Ozzie Guillen)	.05
80	Gene Nelson	.05
81	Bob McClure	.05
82	Rangers checklist (Julio Franco)	.05
83	Greg Minton	.05
84	Braves checklist (John Smoltz)	.05
85	Willie Fraser	.05
86	Neal Heaton	.05
87	Kevin Tapani RC	.05
88	Astros checklist (Mike Scott)	.05
89a	Jim Gott (Incorrect photo.)	1.00
89b	Jim Gott (Correct photo.)	.05
90	Lance Johnson	.05
91	Brewers checklist (Robin Yount)	.35
92	Jeff Parrett	.05
93	Julio Machado RC	.05
94	Ron Jones	.05
95	Blue Jays checklist (George Bell)	.05
96	Jerry Reuss	.05
97	Brian Fisher	.05
98	Kevin Ritz RC	.05
99	Reds checklist (Barry Larkin)	.05
100	Checklist 1-100	.05
101	Gerald Perry	.05
102	Kevin Appier RC	.05
103	Julio Franco	.05
104	Craig Biggio	.05
105	Bo Jackson	.10
106	Junior Felix	.05
107	Mike Harkey RC	.05
108	Fred McGriff	.05
109	Rick Sutcliffe	.05
110	Pete O'Brien	.05
111	Kelly Gruber	.05
112	Pat Borders	.05
113	Dwight Evans	.05
114	Dwight Gooden	.05
115	Kevin Batiste RC	.05
116	Eric Davis	.05
117	Kevin Mitchell	.05
118	Ron Oester	.05
119	Brett Butler	.05
120	Danny Jackson	.05
121	Tommy Gregg	.05
122	Ken Caminiti	.05
123	Kevin Brown	.05
124	George Brett	.85
125	Mike Scott	.05
126	Cory Snyder	.05
127	George Bell	.05
128	Mark Grace	.05
129	Devon White	.05
130	Tony Fernandez	.05
131	Don Aase	.05
132	Rance Mulliniks	.05
133	Marty Barrett	.05
134	Nelson Liriano	.05
135	Mark Carreon RC	.05
136	Candy Maldonado	.05
137	Tim Birtsas	.05
138	Tom Brookens	.05
139	John Franco	.05
140	Mike LaCoss	.05
141	Jeff Treadway	.05
142	Pat Tabler	.05
143	Darrell Evans	.05
144	Rafael Ramirez	.05
145	Oddibe McDowell	.05
146	Brian Downing	.05
147	Curtis Wilkerson	.05
148	Ernie Whitt	.05
149	Bill Schroeder	.05
150	Domingo Ramos	.05
151	Rick Honeycutt	.05
152	Don Slaught	.05
153	Mitch Webster	.05
154	Tony Phillips	.05
155	Paul Kilgus	.05
156	Ken Griffey Jr.	1.50
157	Gary Sheffield	.35
158	Wally Backman	.05
159	B.J. Surhoff	.05
160	Louie Meadows	.05
161	Paul O'Neill	.05
162	Jeff McKnight RC	.05
163	Alvaro Espinoza RC	.05
164	Scott Scudder RC	.05
165	Jeff Reed	.05
166	Gregg Jefferies	.05
167	Barry Larkin	.05
168	Gary Carter	.60
169	Robby Thompson	.05
170	Rolando Roomes	.05
171	Mark McGwire	1.50
172	Steve Sax	.05
173	Mark Williamson	.05
174	Mitch Williams	.05
175	Brian Holton	.05
176	Rob Deer	.05
177	Tim Raines	.05
178	Mike Felder	.05
179	Harold Reynolds	.05
180	Terry Francona	.05
181	Chris Sabo	.05
182	Darryl Strawberry	.05
183	Willie Randolph	.05
184	Billy Ripken	.05
185	Mackey Sasser	.05
186	Todd Benzinger	.05
187	Kevin Elster	.05
188	Jose Uribe	.05
189	Tom Browning	.05
190	Keith Miller	.05
191	Don Mattingly	.85
192	Dave Parker	.05
193	Roberto Kelly	.05
194	Phil Bradley	.05
195	Ron Hassey	.05
196	Gerald Young	.05
197	Hubie Brooks	.05
198	Bill Doran	.05
199	Al Newman	.05
200	Checklist 101-200	.05
201	Terry Puhl	.05
202	Frank DiPino	.05
203	Jim Clancy	.05
204	Bob Ojeda	.05
205	Alex Trevino	.05
206	Dave Henderson	.05
207	Henry Cotto	.05
208	Rafael Belliard	.05
209	Stan Javier	.05
210	Jerry Reed	.05
211	Doug Dascenzo	.05
212	Andres Thomas	.05
213	Greg Maddux	.75
214	Mike Schooler	.05
215	Lonnie Smith	.05
216	Jose Rijo	.05
217	Greg Gagne	.05
218	Jim Gantner	.05
219	Allan Anderson	.05
220	Rick Mahler	.05
221	Jim Deshaies	.05
222	Keith Hernandez	.05
223	Vince Coleman	.05
224	David Cone	.05
225	Ozzie Smith	.75
226	Matt Nokes	.05
227	Barry Bonds	2.00
228	Felix Jose	.05
229	Dennis Powell	.05
230	Mike Gallego	.05
231	Shawon Dunston	.05
232	Ron Gant	.05
233	Omar Vizquel	.05
234	Derek Lilliquist	.05
235	Erik Hanson	.05
236	Kirby Puckett	.75
237	Bill Spiers	.05
238	Dan Gladden	.05
239	Bryan Clutterbuck RC	.05
240	John Moses	.05
241	Ron Darling	.05
242	Joe Magrane	.05
243	Dave Magadan	.05
244	Pedro Guerrero	.05
245	Glenn Davis	.05
246	Terry Steinbach	.05
247	Fred Lynn	.05
248	Gary Redus	.05
249	Kenny Williams	.05
250	Sid Bream	.05
251	Bob Welch	.05
252	Bill Buckner	.05
253	Carney Lansford	.05
254	Paul Molitor	.60
255	Jose DeJesus	.05
256	Orel Hershiser	.05
257	Tom Brunansky	.05
258	Mike Davis	.05
259	Jeff Ballard	.05
260	Scott Terry	.05
261	Sid Fernandez	.05
262	Mike Marshall	.05
263	Howard Johnson	.05
264	Kirk Gibson	.05
265	Kevin McReynolds	.05
266	Cal Ripken, Jr.	2.00
267	Ozzie Guillen	.05
268	Jim Traber	.05
269	Bobby Thigpen	.05
270	Joe Orsulak	.05
271	Bob Boone	.05
272	Dave Stewart	.05
273	Tim Wallach	.05
274	Luis Aquino	.05
275	Mike Moore	.05
276	Tony Pena	.05
277	Eddie Murray	.60
278	Milt Thompson	.05
279	Alejandro Pena	.05
280	Ken Dayley	.05
281	Carmen Castillo	.05
282	Tom Henke	.05
283	Mickey Hatcher	.05
284	Roy Smith RC	.05
285	Manny Lee	.05
286	Dan Pasqua	.05
287	Larry Sheets	.05
288	Garry Templeton	.05
289	Eddie Williams	.05
290	Brady Anderson	.05
291	Spike Owen	.05
292	Storm Davis	.05
293	Chris Bosio	.05
294	Jim Eisenreich	.05
295	Don August	.05
296	Jeff Hamilton	.05
297	Mickey Tettleton	.05
298	Mike Scioscia	.05
299	Kevin Hickey RC	.05
300	Checklist 201-300	.05
301	Shawn Abner	.05
302	Kevin Bass	.05
303	Bip Roberts RC	.05
304	Joe Girardi	.05
305	Danny Darwin	.05
306	Mike Heath	.05
307	Mike Macfarlane	.05
308	Ed Whitson	.05
309	Tracy Jones	.05
310	Scott Fletcher	.05
311	Darnell Coles	.05
312	Mike Brumley	.05
313	Bill Swift	.05
314	Charlie Hough	.05
315	Jim Presley	.05
316	Luis Polonia	.05
317	Mike Morgan	.05
318	Lee Guetterman	.05
319	Jose Oquendo	.05
320	Wayne Tolleson	.05
321	Jody Reed	.05
322	Damon Berryhill	.05
323	Roger Clemens	.85
324	Ryne Sandberg	.75
325	Benito Santiago	.05
326	Bret Saberhagen	.05
327	Lou Whitaker	.05

No.	Player	Price
328	Dave Gallagher	.05
329	Mike Pagliarulo	.05
330	Doyle Alexander	.05
331	Jeffrey Leonard	.05
332	Torey Lovullo	.05
333	Pete Incaviglia	.05
334	Rickey Henderson	.60
335	Rafael Palmeiro	.50
336	Ken Hill RC	.05
337	Dave Winfield	.60
338	Alfredo Griffin	.05
339	Andy Hawkins	.05
340	Ted Power	.05
341	Steve Wilson	.05
342	Jack Clark	.05
343	Ellis Burks	.05
344	Tony Gwynn	.75
345	Jerome Walton	.05
346	Roberto Alomar	.20
347	Carlos Martinez RC	.05
348	Chet Lemon	.05
349	Willie Wilson	.05
350	Greg Walker	.05
351	Tom Bolton	.05
352	German Gonzalez RC	.05
353	Harold Baines	.05
354	Mike Greenwell	.05
355	Ruben Sierra	.05
356	Andres Galarraga	.05
357	Andre Dawson	.25
358	Jeff Brantley	.05
359	Mike Bielecki	.05
360	Ken Oberkfell	.05
361	Kurt Stillwell	.05
362	Brian Holman	.05
363	Kevin Seitzer	.05
364	Alvin Davis	.05
365	Tom Gordon	.05
366	Bobby Bonilla	.05
367	Carlton Fisk	.60
368	Steve Carter RC	.05
369	Joel Skinner	.05
370	John Cangelosi	.05
371	Cecil Espy	.05
372	Gary Wayne RC	.05
373	Jim Rice	.20
374	Mike Dyer RC	.05
375	Joe Carter	.05
376	Dwight Smith	.05
377	John Wetteland RC	.15
378	Ernie Riles	.05
379	Otis Nixon	.05
380	Vance Law	.05
381	Dave Bergman	.05
382	Frank White	.05
383	Scott Bradley	.05
384	Israel Sanchez	.05
385	Gary Pettis	.05
386	Donn Pall RC	.05
387	John Smiley	.05
388	Tom Candiotti	.05
389	Junior Ortiz	.05
390	Steve Lyons	.05
391	Brian Harper	.05
392	Fred Manrique	.05
393	Lee Smith	.05
394	Jeff Kunkel	.05
395	Claudell Washington	.05
396	John Tudor	.05
397	Terry Kennedy	.05
398	Lloyd McClendon	.05
399	Craig Lefferts	.05
400	Checklist 301-400	.05
401	Keith Moreland	.05
402	Rich Gedman	.05
403	Jeff Robinson	.05
404	Randy Ready	.05
405	Rick Cerone	.05
406	Jeff Blauser	.05
407	Larry Andersen	.05
408	Joe Boever	.05
409	Felix Fermin	.05
410	Glenn Wilson	.05
411	Rex Hudler	.05
412	Mark Grant	.05
413	Dennis Martinez	.05
414	Darrin Jackson	.05
415	Mike Aldrete	.05
416	Roger McDowell	.05
417	Jeff Reardon	.05
418	Darren Daulton	.20
419	Tim Laudner	.05
420	Don Carman	.05
421	Lloyd Moseby	.05
422	Doug Drabek	.05
423	Lenny Harris	.05
424	Jose Lind	.05
425	Dave Johnson RC	.05
426	Jerry Browne	.05
427	Eric Yelding RC	.05
428	Brad Komminsk RC	.05
429	Jody Davis	.05
430	Mariano Duncan	.05
431	Mark Davis	.05
432	Nelson Santovenia	.05
433	Bruce Hurst	.05
434	Jeff Huson RC	.05
435	Chris James	.05
436	Mark Guthrie RC	.05
437	Charlie Hayes RC	.05
438	Shane Rawley	.05
439	Dickie Thon	.05
440	Juan Berenguer	.05
441	Kevin Romine	.05
442	Bill Landrum	.05
443	Todd Frohwirth	.05
444	Craig Worthington	.05
445	Fernando Valenzuela	.05
446	Albert Belle	.05
447	Ed Whited RC	.05
448	Dave Smith	.05
449	Dave Clark	.05
450	Juan Agosto	.05
451	Dave Valle	.05
452	Kent Hrbek	.05
453	Von Hayes	.05
454	Gary Gaetti	.05
455	Greg Briley	.05
456	Glenn Braggs	.05
457	Kirt Manwaring	.05
458	Mel Hall	.05
459	Brook Jacoby	.05
460	Pat Sheridan	.05
461	Rob Murphy	.05
462	Jimmy Key	.05
463	Nick Esasky	.05
464	Rob Ducey	.05
465	Carlos Quintana	.05
466	Larry Walker RC	1.00
467	Todd Worrell	.05
468	Kevin Gross	.05
469	Terry Pendleton	.05
470	Dave Martinez	.05
471	Gene Larkin	.05
472	Len Dykstra	.05
473	Barry Lyons	.05
474	Terry Mulholland RC	.05
475	Chip Hale RC	.05
476	Jesse Barfield	.05
477	Dan Plesac	.05
478a	Scott Garrelts (Photo actually Bill Bathe.)	1.00
478b	Scott Garrelts (Correct photo.)	.05
479	Dave Righetti	.05
480	Gus Polidor RC	.05
481	Mookie Wilson	.05
482	Luis Rivera	.05
483	Mike Flanagan	.05
484	Dennis "Oil Can" Boyd	.05
485	John Cerutti	.05
486	John Costello	.05
487	Pascual Perez	.05
488	Tommy Herr	.05
489	Tom Foley	.05
490	Curt Ford	.05
491	Steve Lake	.05
492	Tim Teufel	.05
493	Randy Bush	.05
494	Mike Jackson	.05
495	Steve Jeltz	.05
496	Paul Gibson	.05
497	Steve Balboni	.05
498	Bud Black	.05
499	Dale Sveum	.05
500	Checklist 401-500	.05
501	Timmy Jones	.05
502	Mark Portugal	.05
503	Ivan Calderon	.05
504	Rick Rhoden	.05
505	Willie McGee	.05
506	Kirk McCaskill	.05
507	Dave LaPoint	.05
508	Jay Howell	.05
509	Johnny Ray	.05
510	Dave Anderson	.05
511	Chuck Crim	.05
512	Joe Hesketh	.05
513	Dennis Eckersley	.40
514	Greg Brock	.05
515	Tim Burke RC	.05
516	Frank Tanana	.05
517	Jay Bell	.05
518	Guillermo Hernandez	.05
519	Randy Kramer RC	.05
520	Charles Hudson	.05
521	Jim Corsi RC	.05
522	Steve Rosenberg	.05
523	Cris Carpenter	.05
524	Matt Winters RC	.05
525	Melido Perez	.05
526	Chris Gwynn RC	.05
527	Bert Blyleven	.05
528	Chuck Cary RC	.05
529	Daryl Boston	.05
530	Dale Mohorcic	.05
531	Geronimo Berroa RC	.05
532	Edgar Martinez	.05
533	Dale Murphy	.20
534	Jay Buhner	.05
535	John Smoltz	.05
536	Andy Van Slyke	.05
537	Mike Henneman RC	.05
538	Miguel Garcia RC	.05
539	Frank Williams RC	.05
540	R.J. Reynolds	.05
541	Shawn Hillegas RC	.05
542	Walt Weiss	.05
543	Greg Hibbard RC	.05
544	Nolan Ryan	2.00
545	Todd Zeile	.05
546	Hensley Meulens	.05
547	Tim Belcher RC	.05
548	Mike Witt	.05
549	Greg Cadaret RC	.05
550	Franklin Stubbs	.05
551	Tony Castillo RC	.05
552	Jeff Robinson	.05
553	Steve Olin RC	.05
554	Alan Trammell	.05
555	Wade Boggs	.75
556	Will Clark	.05
557	Jeff King	.05
558	Mike Fitzgerald	.05
559	Ken Howell RC	.05
560	Bob Kipper	.05
561	Scott Bankhead RC	.05
562a	Jeff Innis RC (Photo actually David West.)	1.00
562b	Jeff Innis RC (Correct photo.)	.05
563	Randy Johnson	.60
564	Wally Whithurst RC	.05
565	Gene Harris RC	.05
566	Norm Charlton RC	.05
567	Robin Yount	.60
568	Joe Oliver RC	.05
569	Mark Parent	.05
570	John Farrell RC	.05
571	Tom Glavine	.20
572	Rod Nichols RC	.05
573	Jack Morris	.05
574	Greg Swindell RC	.05
575	Steve Searcy RC	.05
576	Ricky Jordan RC	.05
577	Matt Williams	.05
578	Mike LaValliere RC	.05
579	Bryn Smith	.05
580	Bruce Ruffin RC	.05
581	Randy Myers	.05
582	Rick Wrona RC	.05
583	Juan Samuel	.05
584	Les Lancaster RC	.05
585	Jeff Musselman	.05
586	Rob Dibble RC	.05
587	Eric Show	.05
588	Jesse Orosco	.05
589	Herm Winningham	.05
590	Andy Allanson	.05
591	Dion James	.05
592	Carmelo Martinez RC	.05
593	Luis Quinones RC	.05
594	Dennis Rasmussen RC	.05
595	Rich Yett	.05
596	Bob Walk RC	.05
597a	Andy McGaffigan (Player #48, photo actually Rich Thompson.)	.75
597b	Andy McGaffigan (Player #27, correct photo.)	.05
598	Billy Hatcher RC	.05
599	Bob Knepper	.05
600	Checklist 501-600	.05
601	Joey Cora RC	.05
602	Steve Finley RC	.20
603	Kal Daniels	.05
604	Gregg Olson	.05
605	Dave Steib	.05
606	Kenny Rogers RC	.05
607	Zane Smith	.05
608	Bob Geren RC	.05
609	Chad Kreuter	.05
610	Mike Smithson RC	.05
611	Jeff Wetherby RC	.05
612	Gary Mielke RC	.05
613	Pete Smith	.05
614	Jack Daugherty RC	.05
615	Lance McCullers	.05
616	Don Robinson	.05
617	Jose Guzman	.05
618	Steve Bedrosian RC	.05
619	Jamie Moyer	.05
620	Atlee Hammaker RC	.05
621	Rick Luecken RC	.05
622	Greg W. Harris RC	.05
623	Pete Harnisch	.05
624	Jerald Clark RC	.05
625	Jack McDowell	.05
626	Frank Viola	.05
627	Ted Higuera	.05
628	Marty Pevey RC	.05
629	Bill Wegman	.05
630	Eric Plunk RC	.05
631	Drew Hall	.05
632	Doug Jones RC	.05
633	Geno Petralli	.05
634	Jose Alvarez RC	.05
635	Bob Milacki	.05
636	Bobby Witt RC	.05
637	Trevor Wilson	.05
638	Jeff Russell RC	.05
639	Mike Krukow	.05
640	Rick Leach RC	.05
641	Dave Schmidt	.05
642	Terry Leach RC	.05
643	Calvin Schiraldi	.05
644	Bob Melvin RC	.05
645	Jim Abbott	.05
646	Jaime Navarro RC	.05
647	Mark Langston	.05
648	Juan Nieves RC	.05
649	Damaso Garcia	.05
650	Charlie O'Brien RC	.05
651	Eric King	.05
652	Mike Boddicker	.05
653	Duane Ward	.05
654	Bob Stanley	.05
655	Sandy Alomar, Jr.	.05
656	Danny Tartabull	.05
657	Randy McCament	.05
658	Charlie Leibrandt	.05
659	Dan Quisenberry	.05
660	Paul Assenmacher RC	.05
661	Walt Terrell	.05
662	Tim Leary	.05
663	Randy Milligan	.05
664	Bo Diaz RC	.05
665	Mark Lemke	.05
666	Jose Gonzalez RC	.10
667	Chuck Finley	.05
668	John Kruk	.60
669	Dick Schofield	.05
670	Tim Crews	.05
671	John Dopson	.05
672	John Orton RC	.05
673	Eric Hetzel RC	.05
674	Lance Parrish	.05
675	Ramon Martinez	.05
676	Mark Gubicza	.05
677	Greg Litton	.05
678	Greg Mathews	.05
679	Dave Dravecky	.05
680	Steve Farr	.05
681	Mike Devereaux	.05
682	Ken Griffey Sr.	.05
683a	Jamie Weston RC (First name incorrect.)	1.00
683b	Mickey Weston RC (Corrected)	.05
684	Jack Armstrong	.05
685	Steve Buechele	.05
686	Bryan Harvey	.05
687	Lance Blankenship	.05
688	Dante Bichette	.05
689	Todd Burns RC	.05
690	Dan Petry	.05
691	Kent Anderson RC	.05
692	Todd Stottlemyre	.05
693	Wally Joyner	.05
694	Mike Rochford RC	.05
695	Floyd Bannister	.05
696	Rick Reuschel	.05
697	Jose DeLeon RC	.05
698	Jeff Montgomery	.05
699	Kelly Downs	.05
700a	Checklist 601-700 (#683 Jamie Weston)	.05
700b	Checklist 601-700 (# 683 Mickey Weston)	.05
701	Jim Gott	.05
702	"Rookie Threats" (Delino DeShields, Larry Walker, Marquis Grissom)	.25
703	Alejandro Pena	.05
704	Willie Randolph	.05
705	Tim Leary	.05
706	Chuck McElroy RC	.05
707	Gerald Perry RC	.05
708	Tom Brunansky	.05
709	John Franco	.05
710	Mark Davis	.05
711	Dave Justice RC	1.50
712	Storm Davis	.05
713	Scott Ruskin RC	.05
714	Glenn Braggs	.05
715	Kevin Bearse RC	.05
716	Jose Nunez RC	.05
717	Tim Layana RC	.05
718	Greg Myers RC	.05
719	Pete O'Brien	.05
720	John Candelaria	.05
721	Craig Grebeck	.05
722	Shawn Boskie RC	.05
723	Jim Leyritz RC	.10
724	Bill Sampen RC	.05
725	Scott Radinsky RC	.05
726	Todd Hundley RC	.25
727	Scott Hemond RC	.05
728	Lenny Webster RC	.05
729	Jeff Reardon	.05
730	Mitch Webster	.05
731	Brian Bohanon RC	.05
732	Rick Parker RC	.05
733	Terry Shumpert RC	.05
734a	Nolan Ryan (300-win stripe on front)	1.50
734b	Nolan Ryan (No stripe.)	4.00
735	John Burkett	.05
736	Derrick May RC	.05
737	Carlos Baerga RC	.05
738	Greg Smith RC	.05
739	Joe Kraemer RC	.05
740	Scott Sanderson RC	.05
741	Hector Villanueva RC	.05
742	Mike Fetters RC	.05
743	Mark Gardner RC	.05
744	Mark Nokes RC	.05
745	Dave Winfield	.60
746	Delino DeShields RC	.15
747	Dann Howitt RC	.05
748	Tony Pena	.05
749	Oil Can Boyd	.05
750	Mike Benjamin RC	.05
751	Alex Cole RC	.05
752	Eric Gunderson RC	.05
753	Howard Farmer RC	.05
754	Joe Carter	.05
755	Ray Lankford RC	.05
756	Sandy Alomar, Jr.	.05
757	Alex Sanchez RC	.05
758	Nick Esasky	.05
759	Stan Belinda RC	.05
760	Jim Presley RC	.05
761	Gary DiSarcina RC	.05
762	Wayne Edwards RC	.05
763	Pat Combs RC	.05
764	Mickey Pina RC	.05
765	Wilson Alvarez RC	.05
766	Dave Parker	.05
767	Mike Blowers RC	.05
768	Tony Phillips	.05
769	Pascual Perez	.05
770	Gary Pettis	.05
771	Fred Lynn	.05
772	Mel Rojas RC	.10
773	David Segui RC	.05
774	Gary Carter	.60
775	Rafael Valdez RC	.05
776	Glenallen Hill RC	.05
777	Keith Hernandez	.05
778	Billy Hatcher	.05
779	Marty Clary RC	.05
780	Candy Maldonado RC	.05
781	Mike Marshall	.05
782	Billy Jo Robidoux RC	.05
783	Mark Langston	.05
784	Paul Sorrento RC	.05
785	Dave Hollins RC	.05
786	Cecil Fielder	.05
787	Matt Young	.05
788	Jeff Huson	.05
789	Lloyd Moseby	.05
790	Ron Kittle	.05
791	Hubie Brooks	.05
792	Craig Lefferts	.05
793	Kevin Bass	.05
794	Bryn Smith RC	.05
795	Juan Samuel	.05
796	Sam Horn	.05
797	Randy Myers	.05
798	Chris James RC	.05
799	Bill Gullickson	.05
800	Checklist 701-800	.05

1990 Upper Deck Baseball Heroes Reggie Jackson

This Baseball Heroes set is devoted to Reggie Jackson. The cards, numbered 1-9, are the first in a continuing series of cards issued in subsequent years. An unnumbered cover card that says "Baseball Heroes" was also issued. The Jackson cards were randomly inserted in high number foil packs only. Jackson also autographed 2,500 numbered cards, which were randomly included in high number packs.

		NM/M
	Complete Set (10):	5.00
	Common Player:	.05
	Autographed Card:	100.00
1	1969 Emerging Superstar (Reggie Jackson)	.50
2	1973 An MVP Year (Reggie Jackson)	.50
3	1977 "Mr. October" (Reggie Jackson)	.50
4	1978 Jackson vs. Welch (Reggie Jackson)	.50
5	1982 Under the Halo (Reggie Jackson)	.50
6	1984 500! (Reggie Jackson)	.50
7	1986 Moving Up the List (Reggie Jackson)	.50
8	1987 A Great Career Ends (Reggie Jackson)	.50
9	Heroes Checklist 1-9 (Reggie Jackson)	.50
----	Header Card	.50

1990 Upper Deck Black-Box Variations

It appears that card #702 in 1990 UD was originally intended to be Mike Witt, but that it was replaced by a "Rookie Threats" card picturing three Expos. At least a few examples of the Witt card, factory cancelled with a large black ink box on back, have made their way into the market, along with a #800 checklist card naming Witt as #702.

		NM/M
702	Mike Witt	450.00
800	Checklist 701-800	250.00

1991 Upper Deck

Shawn Abner

More than 110 rookies are included among the first 700 cards in the 1991 Upper Deck set. A 100-card high-number series was released in late summer. Cards feature top quality white stock and color photos on front and back. A nine-card "Baseball Heroes" bonus set honoring Nolan Ryan, is among the many insert specials in the '91 UD set. Others include a card of Chicago Bulls superstar Michael Jordan. Along with the Ryan bonus cards, 2,500 cards personally autographed and numbered by Ryan were randomly inserted. Upper Deck cards are packaged in tamper-proof foil packs. Each pack contains 15 cards and a 3-1/2" x 2-1/2" 3-D team logo hologram sticker.

		NM/M
	Unopened Factory Set (800):	13.50
	Complete Set (800):	10.00
	Complete Low Series (700):	9.00
	Complete High Series (100):	1.00
	Common Player:	.05
	Low or High Wax Pack (15):	.60
	Low or High Wax Box (36):	13.50
1	Star Rookie Checklist	.05
2	Phil Plantier RC	.05
3	D.J. Dozier RC	.05
4	Dave Hansen RC	.05
5	Mo Vaughn RC	.10
6	Leo Gomez RC	.05
7	Scott Aldred RC	.05
8	Scott Chiamparino RC	.05
9	Lance Dickson RC	.05
10	Sean Berry RC	.05
11	Bernie Williams RC	.25
12	Brian Barnes RC	.05
13	Narciso Elvira RC	.05
14	Mike Gardiner RC	.05
15	Greg Colbrunn RC	.05
16	Bernard Gilkey RC	.05
17	Mark Lewis RC	.05
18	Mickey Morandini RC	.05
19	Charles Nagy RC	.05
20	Geronimo Pena RC	.05
21	Henry Rodriguez RC	.05
22	Scott Cooper RC	.05
23	Andujar Cedeno RC	.05
24	Eric Karros RC	.25
25	Steve Decker RC	.05
26	Kevin Belcher RC	.05
27	Jeff Conine RC	.25
28	Oakland Athletics checklist (Dave Stewart)	.05
29	Chicago White Sox checklist (Carlton Fisk)	.20
30	Texas Rangers checklist (Rafael Palmeiro)	.20
31	California Angels checklist (Chuck Finley)	.05
32	Seattle Mariners checklist (Harold Reynolds)	.05
33	Kansas City Royals checklist (Bret Saberhagen)	.05
34	Minnesota Twins checklist (Gary Gaetti)	.05
35	Scott Leius	.05
36	Neal Heaton	.05
37	Terry Lee RC	.05
38	Gary Redus	.05
39	Barry Jones	.05

No.	Player	Value
40	Chuck Knoblauch	.05
41	Larry Andersen	.05
42	Darryl Hamilton	.05
43	Boston Red Sox checklist (Mike Greenwell)	.05
44	Toronto Blue Jays checklist (Kelly Gruber)	.05
45	Detroit Tigers checklist (Jack Morris)	.05
46	Cleveland Indians checklist (Sandy Alomar Jr.)	.05
47	Baltimore Orioles checklist (Gregg Olson)	.05
48	Milwaukee Brewers checklist (Dave Parker)	.05
49	New York Yankees checklist (Roberto Kelly)	.05
50	Top Prospect '91 checklist	.05
51	Kyle Abbott RC (Top Prospect)	.05
52	Jeff Juden RC (Top Prospect)	.05
53	Todd Van Poppel RC (Top Prospect)	.10
54	Steve Karsay RC (Top Prospect)	.10
55	Chipper Jones RC (Top Prospect)	2.00
56	Chris Johnson RC (Top Prospect)	.05
57	John Ericks RC (Top Prospect)	.05
58	Gary Scott RC (Top Prospect)	.05
59	Kiki Jones RC (Top Prospect)	.05
60	Wil Cordero RC (Top Prospect)	.05
61	Royce Clayton RC (Top Prospect)	.05
62	Tim Costo RC (Top Prospect)	.05
63	Roger Salkeld RC (Top Prospect)	.05
64	Brook Fordyce RC (Top Prospect)	.05
65	Mike Mussina RC (Top Prospect)	1.00
66	Dave Staton RC (Top Prospect)	.05
67	Mike Lieberthal RC (Top Prospect)	.50
68	Kurt Miller RC (Top Prospect)	.05
69	Dan Peltier RC (Top Prospect)	.05
70	Greg Blosser RC (Top Prospect)	.05
71	Reggie Sanders RC (Top Prospect)	.25
72	Brent Mayne RC (Top Prospect)	.05
73	Rico Brogna RC (Top Prospect)	.05
74	Willie Banks RC (Top Prospect)	.05
75	Len Brutcher RC (Top Prospect)	.05
76	Pat Kelly RC (Top Prospect)	.05
77	Cincinnati Reds checklist (Chris Sabo)	.05
78	Los Angeles Dodgers checklist (Ramon Martinez)	.05
79	San Francisco Giants checklist (Matt Williams)	.05
80	San Diego Padres checklist (Roberto Alomar)	.05
81	Houston Astros checklist (Glenn Davis)	.05
82	Atlanta Braves checklist (Ron Gant)	.05
83	"Fielder's Feat" (Cecil Fielder)	.05
84	Orlando Merced RC	.10
85	Domingo Ramos	.05
86	Tom Bolton	.05
87	Andres Santana	.05
88	John Dopson RC	.05
89	Kenny Williams	.05
90	Marty Barrett	.05
91	Tom Pagnozzi	.05
92	Carmelo Martinez	.05
93	"Save Master" (Bobby Thigpen)	.05
94	Pittsburgh Pirates checklist (Barry Bonds)	.05
95	New York Mets checklist (Gregg Jefferies)	.05
96	Montreal Expos checklist (Tim Wallach)	.05
97	Philadelphia Phillies checklist (Lenny Dykstra)	.05
98	St. Louis Cardinals checklist (Pedro Guerrero)	.05
99	Chicago Cubs checklist (Mark Grace)	.05
100	Checklist 1-100	.05
101	Kevin Elster	.05
102	Tom Brookens	.05
103	Mackey Sasser	.05
104	Felix Fermin RC	.05
105	Kevin McReynolds	.05
106	Dave Steib	.05
107	Jeffrey Leonard	.05
108	Dave Henderson	.05
109	Sid Bream	.05
110	Henry Cotto	.05
111	Shawon Dunston	.05
112	Mariano Duncan RC	.05
113	Joe Girardi	.05
114	Billy Hatcher	.05
115	Greg Maddux	.50
116	Jerry Browne	.05
117	Juan Samuel	.05
118	Steve Olin	.05
119	Alfredo Griffin	.05
120	Mitch Webster RC	.05
121	Joel Skinner	.05
122	Frank Viola	.05
123	Cory Snyder	.05
124	Howard Johnson	.05
125	Carlos Baerga	.50
126	Tony Fernandez	.05
127	Dave Stewart	.05
128	Jay Buhner	.05
129	Mike LaValliere	.05
130	Scott Bradley	.05
131	Tony Phillips	.05
132	Ryne Sandberg	.50
133	Paul O'Neill	.05
134	Mark Grace	.05
135	Chris Sabo	.05
136	Ramon Martinez	.05
137	Brook Jacoby	.05
138	Candy Maldonado	.05
139	Mike Scioscia	.05
140	Chris James	.05
141	Craig Worthington	.05
142	Manny Lee	.05
143	Tim Raines	.05
144	Sandy Alomar, Jr.	.05
145	John Olerud	.05
146	Ozzie Canseco RC	.05
147	Pat Borders	.05
148	Harold Reynolds	.05
149	Tom Henke	.05
150	R.J. Reynolds	.05
151	Mike Gallego	.05
152	Bobby Bonilla	.05
153	Terry Steinbach	.05
154	Barry Bonds	1.00
155	Jose Canseco	.30
156	Gregg Jefferies	.05
157	Matt Williams	.05
158	Craig Biggio	.05
159	Daryl Boston	.05
160	Ricky Jordan	.05
161	Stan Belinda	.05
162	Ozzie Smith	.50
163	Tom Brunansky	.05
164	Todd Zeile	.05
165	Mike Greenwell	.05
166	Kal Daniels	.05
167	Kent Hrbek	.05
168	Franklin Stubbs	.05
169	Dick Schofield	.05
170	Junior Ortiz	.05
171	Hector Villanueva RC	.05
172	Dennis Eckersley	.35
173	Mitch Williams	.05
174	Mark McGwire	.75
175	Fernando Valenzuela	.05
176	Gary Carter	.40
177	Dave Magadan	.05
178	Robby Thompson	.05
179	Bob Ojeda	.05
180	Ken Caminiti	.05
181	Don Slaught	.05
182	Luis Rivera	.05
183	Jay Bell	.05
184	Jody Reed	.05
185	Wally Backman	.05
186	Dave Martinez	.05
187	Luis Polonia	.05
188	Shane Mack	.05
189	Spike Owen	.05
190	Scott Bailes	.05
191	John Russell	.05
192	Walt Weiss	.05
193	Jose Oquendo	.05
194	Carney Lansford	.05
195	Jeff Huson	.05
196	Keith Miller	.05
197	Eric Yelding	.05
198	Ron Darling	.05
199	John Kruk	.05
200	Checklist 101-200	.05
201	John Shelby	.05
202	Bob Geren	.05
203	Lance McCullers	.05
204	Alvaro Espinoza	.05
205	Mark Salas	.05
206	Mike Pagliarulo	.05
207	Jose Uribe	.05
208	Jim Deshaies RC	.05
209	Ron Karkovice	.05
210	Rafael Ramirez	.05
211	Donnie Hill	.05
212	Brian Harper RC	.05
213	Jack Howell	.05
214	Wes Gardner	.05
215	Tim Burke	.05
216	Doug Jones RC	.05
217	Hubie Brooks	.05
218	Tom Candiotti	.05
219	Gerald Perry	.05
220	Jose DeLeon RC	.05
221	Wally Whitehurst	.05
222	Alan Mills RC	.05
223	Alan Trammell	.05
224	Dwight Gooden	.05
225	Travis Fryman	.05
226	Joe Carter	.05
227	Julio Franco	.05
228	Craig Lefferts	.05
229	Gary Pettis	.05
230	Dennis Rasmussen	.05
231a	Brian Downing (No position on front.)	2.00
231b	Brian Downing (DH on front)	.05
232	Carlos Quintana RC	.05
233	Gary Gaetti	.05
234	Mark Langston	.05
235	Tim Wallach	.05
236	Greg Swindell	.05
237	Eddie Murray	.40
238	Jeff Manto RC	.05
239	Lenny Harris	.05
240	Jesse Orosco	.05
241	Scott Lusader	.05
242	Sid Fernandez	.05
243	Jim Leyritz	.05
244	Cecil Fielder	.05
245	Darryl Strawberry	.05
246	Frank Thomas RC	.50
247	Kevin Mitchell	.05
248	Lance Johnson RC	.05
249	Rick Rueschel	.05
250	Mark Portugal	.05
251	Derek Lilliquist	.05
252	Brian Holman RC	.05
253	Rafael Valdez	.05
254	B.J. Surhoff	.05
255	Tony Gwynn	.50
256	Andy Van Slyke	.05
257	Todd Stottlemyre	.05
258	Jose Lind	.05
259	Greg Myers	.05
260	Jeff Ballard RC	.05
261	Bobby Thigpen	.05
262	Jimmy Kremers RC	.05
263	Robin Ventura	.05
264	John Smoltz	.05
265	Sammy Sosa	.50
266	Gary Sheffield	.30
267	Len Dykstra	.05
268	Bill Spiers	.05
269	Charlie Hayes	.05
270	Brett Butler	.05
271	Bip Roberts	.05
272	Rob Deer	.05
273	Fred Lynn	.05
274	Dave Parker	.05
275	Andy Benes	.05
276	Glenallen Hill RC	.05
277	Steve Howard RC	.05
278	Doug Drabek	.05
279	Joe Oliver	.05
280	Todd Benzinger	.05
281	Eric King	.05
282	Jim Presley	.05
283	Ken Patterson RC	.05
284	Jack Daugherty RC	.05
285	Ivan Calderon	.05
286	Edgar Diaz RC	.05
287	Kevin Bass	.05
288	Don Carman RC	.05
289	Greg Brock	.05
290	John Franco	.05
291	Joey Cora	.05
292	Bill Wegman	.05
293	Eric Show	.05
294	Scott Bankhead	.05
295	Garry Templeton	.05
296	Mickey Tettleton	.05
297	Luis Sojo	.05
298	Jose Rijo	.05
299	Dave Johnson	.05
300	Checklist 201-300	.05
301	Mark Grant	.05
302	Pete Harnisch	.05
303	Greg Olson	.05
304	Anthony Telford RC	.05
305	Lonnie Smith	.05
306	Chris Hoiles	.05
307	Bryn Smith	.05
308	Mike Devereaux	.05
309a	Milt Thompson ("86" in stats obscured by "bull's eye")	.50
309b	Milt Thompson ("86" visible)	.05
310	Bob Melvin	.05
311a	Luis Salazar (Circled dot over "i" in Luis on back.)	2.00
311b	Luis Salazar (Corrected)	.05
312	Ed Whitson RC	.05
313	Charlie Hough	.05
314	Dave Clark	.05
315	Eric Gunderson RC	.05
316	Dan Petry	.05
317	Dante Bichette	.05
318	Mike Heath	.05
319	Damon Berryhill	.05
320	Walt Terrell	.05
321	Scott Fletcher	.05
322	Dan Plesac	.05
323	Jack McDowell	.05
324	Paul Molitor	.40
325	Ozzie Guillen	.05
326	Gregg Olson	.05
327	Pedro Guerrero	.05
328	Bob Milacki RC	.05
329	John Tudor	.05
330	Steve Finley	.05
331	Jack Clark	.05
332	Jerome Walton	.05
333	Andy Hawkins	.05
334	Derrick May	.05
335	Roberto Alomar	.20
336	Jack Morris	.05
337	Dave Winfield	.40
338	Steve Searcy	.05
339	Chili Davis	.05
340	Larry Sheets	.05
341	Ted Higuera	.05
342	David Segui RC	.10
343	Greg Cadaret	.05
344	Robin Yount	.40
345	Nolan Ryan	1.00
346	Ray Lankford	.05
347	Cal Ripken, Jr.	1.00
348	Lee Smith	.05
349	Brady Anderson	.05
350	Frank DiPino	.05
351	Hal Morris	.05
352	Deion Sanders	.10
353	Barry Larkin	.05
354	Don Mattingly	.60
355	Eric Davis	.05
356	Jose Offerman	.05
357	Mel Rojas	.05
358	Rudy Seanez RC	.05
359	Oil Can Boyd	.05
360	Nelson Liriano	.05
361	Ron Gant	.05
362	Howard Farmer RC	.05
363	Dave Justice	.05
364	Delino DeShields	.05
365	Steve Avery	.05
366	David Cone	.05
367	Lou Whitaker	.05
368	Von Hayes	.05
369	Frank Tanana	.05
370	Tim Teufel	.05
371	Randy Myers	.05
372	Roberto Kelly	.05
373	Jack Armstrong	.05
374	Kelly Gruber	.05
375	Kevin Maas	.05
376	Randy Johnson	.40
377	David West	.05
378	Brent Knackert RC	.05
379	Rick Honeycutt	.05
380	Kevin Gross	.05
381	Tom Foley	.05
382	Jeff Blauser	.05
383	Scott Ruskin RC	.05
384	Andres Thomas RC	.05
385	Dennis Martinez	.05
386	Mike Henneman	.05
387	Felix Jose	.05
388	Alejandro Pena	.05
389	Chet Lemon	.05
390	Craig Wilson RC	.05
391	Chuck Crim	.05
392	Mel Hall	.05
393	Mark Knudson	.05
394	Norm Charlton	.05
395	Mike Felder	.05
396	Tim Layana RC	.05
397	Steve Frey RC	.05
398	Bill Doran	.05
399	Dion James	.05
400	Checklist 301-400	.05
401	Ron Hassey	.05
402	Don Robinson	.05
403	Gene Nelson	.05
404	Terry Kennedy	.05
405	Todd Burns	.05
406	Roger McDowell	.05
407	Bob Kipper	.05
408	Darren Daulton	.05
409	Chuck Cary	.05
410	Bruce Ruffin	.05
411	Juan Berenguer	.05
412	Gary Ward	.05
413	Al Newman	.05
414	Danny Jackson	.05
415	Greg Gagne	.05
416	Tom Herr	.05
417	Jeff Parrett	.05
418	Jeff Reardon	.05
419	Mark Lemke	.05
420	Charlie O'Brien RC	.05
421	Willie Randolph	.05
422	Steve Bedrosian	.05
423	Mike Moore	.05
424	Jeff Brantley RC	.05
425	Bob Welch	.05
426	Terry Mulholland	.05
427	Willie Blair RC	.05
428	Darrin Fletcher RC	.05
429	Mike Witt	.05
430	Joe Boever	.05
431	Tom Gordon	.05
432	Pedro Munoz RC	.05
433	Kevin Seitzer	.05
434	Kevin Tapani	.05
435	Bret Saberhagen	.05
436	Ellis Burks	.05
437	Chuck Finley	.05
438	Mike Boddicker	.05
439	Francisco Cabrera	.05
440	Todd Hundley	.05
441	Kelly Downs	.05
442	Dann Howitt RC	.05
443	Scott Garrelts	.05
444	Rickey Henderson	.40
445	Will Clark	.05
446	Ben McDonald	.05
447	Dale Murphy	.20
448	Dave Righetti	.05
449	Dickie Thon	.05
450	Ted Power	.05
451	Scott Coolbaugh	.05
452	Dwight Smith	.05
453	Pete Incaviglia	.05
454	Andre Dawson	.25
455	Ruben Sierra	.05
456	Andres Galarraga	.05
457	Alvin Davis	.05
458	Tony Castillo	.05
459	Pete O'Brien	.05
460	Charlie Leibrandt	.05
461	Vince Coleman	.05
462	Steve Sax	.05
463	Omar Oliveras RC	.05
464	Oscar Azocar RC	.05
465	Joe Magrane RC	.05
466	Karl Rhodes RC	.05
467	Benito Santiago	.05
468	Joe Klink RC	.05
469	Sil Campusano	.05
470	Mark Parent	.05
471	Shawn Boskie RC	.05
472	Kevin Brown	.05
473	Rick Sutcliffe	.05
474	Rafael Palmeiro	.35
475	Mike Harkey	.05
476	Jaime Navarro	.05
477	Marquis Grissom	.05
478	Marty Clary	.05
479	Greg Briley RC	.05
480	Tom Glavine	.05
481	Lee Guetterman	.05
482	Rex Hudler	.05
483	Dave LaPoint RC	.05
484	Terry Pendleton	.05
485	Jesse Barfield	.05
486	Jose DeJesus	.05
487	Paul Abbott RC	.05
488	Ken Howell	.05
489	Greg W. Harris	.05
490	Roy Smith	.05
491	Paul Assenmacher	.05
492	Geno Petralli	.05
493	Steve Wilson	.05
494	Kevin Reimer RC	.05
495	Bill Long	.05
496	Mike Jackson RC	.05
497	Oddibe McDowell	.05
498	Bill Swift	.05
499	Jeff Treadway	.05
500	Checklist 401-500	.05
501	Gene Larkin	.05
502	Bob Boone	.05
503	Allan Anderson	.05
504	Luis Aquino RC	.05
505	Mark Guthrie	.05
506	Joe Orsulak	.05
507	Dana Kiecker RC	.05
508	Dave Gallagher RC	.05
509	Greg A. Harris	.05
510	Mark Williamson	.05
511	Casey Candaele	.05
512	Mookie Wilson	.05
513	Dave Smith	.05
514	Chuck Carr RC	.05
515	Glenn Wilson	.05
516	Mike Fitzgerald RC	.05
517	Devon White	.05
518	Dave Hollins	.05
519	Mark Eichhorn	.05
520	Otis Nixon	.05
521	Terry Shumpert RC	.05
522	Scott Erickson RC	.15
523	Danny Tartabull	.05
524	Orel Hershiser	.05
525	George Brett	.60
526	Greg Vaughn	.05
527	Tim Naehring RC	.05
528	Curt Schilling RC	.25
529	Chris Bosio	.05
530	Sam Horn	.05
531	Mike Scott	.05
532	George Bell	.05
533	Eric Anthony	.05
534	Julio Valera RC	.05
535	Glenn Davis	.05
536	Larry Walker	.05
537	Pat Combs	.05
538	Chris Nabholz RC	.05
539	Kirk McCaskill	.05
540	Randy Ready	.05
541	Mark Gubicza	.05
542	Rick Aguilera	.05
543	Brian McRae RC	.05
544	Kirby Puckett	.50
545	Bo Jackson	.10
546	Wade Boggs	.50
547	Tim McIntosh RC	.05
548	Randy Milligan RC	.05
549	Dwight Evans	.05
550	Billy Ripken	.05
551	Erik Hanson	.05
552	Lance Parrish	.05
553	Tino Martinez	.05
554	Jim Abbott	.05
555	Ken Griffey Jr.	.65
556	Milt Cuyler RC	.05
557	Mark Leonard RC	.05
558	Jay Howell	.05
559	Lloyd Moseby	.05
560	Chris Gwynn	.05
561	Mark Whiten RC	.05
562	Harold Baines	.05
563	Junior Felix	.05
564	Darren Lewis	.05
565	Fred McGriff	.05
566	Kevin Appier	.05
567	Luis Gonzalez RC	1.00
568	Frank White	.05
569	Juan Agosto	.05
570	Mike Macfarlane	.05
571	Bert Blyleven	.05
572	Ken Griffey Sr.	.05
573	Lee Stevens	.05
574	Edgar Martinez	.05
575	Wally Joyner	.05
576	Tim Belcher	.05
577	John Burkett	.05
578	Mike Morgan	.05
579	Paul Gibson	.05
580	Jose Vizcaino	.05
581	Duane Ward	.05
582	Scott Sanderson	.05
583	David Wells	.05
584	Willie McGee	.05
585	John Cerutti	.05
586	Danny Darwin	.05
587	Kurt Stillwell	.05
588	Rich Gedman	.05
589	Mark Davis	.05
590	Bill Gullickson	.05
591	Matt Young	.05
592	Bryan Harvey RC	.05
593	Omar Vizquel	.05
594	Scott Lewis RC	.05
595	Dave Valle	.05
596	Tim Crews RC	.05
597	Mike Bielecki	.05
598	Mike Sharperson	.05
599	Dave Bergman	.05
600	Checklist 501-600	.05
601	Steve Lyons	.05
602	Bruce Hurst	.05
603	Donn Pall	.05
604	Jim Vatcher RC	.05
605	Dan Pasqua	.05
606	Kenny Rogers	.05
607	Jeff Schulz RC	.05
608	Brad Arnsberg RC	.05
609	Willie Wilson	.05
610	Jamie Moyer	.05
611	Ron Oester	.05
612	Dennis Cook RC	.05
613	Rick Mahler	.05
614	Bill Landrum	.05
615	Scott Scudder	.05
616	Tom Edens RC	.05
617	"1917 Revisited" (Chicago White Sox team photo.)	.05
618	Jim Gantner	.05
619	Darrel Akerfelds RC	.05
620	Ron Robinson	.05
621	Scott Radinsky	.05
622	Pete Smith	.05
623	Melido Perez	.05
624	Jerald Clark RC	.05
625	Carlos Martinez	.05
626	Wes Chamberlain RC	.05
627	Bobby Witt	.05
628	Ken Dayley RC	.05
629	Jim Barfield RC	.05
630	Bob Tewksbury	.05
631	Glenn Braggs	.05
632	Jim Neidlinger RC	.05
633	Tom Browning	.05
634	Kirk Gibson	.05
635	Rob Dibble	.05
636	"Stolen Base Leaders" (Lou Brock, Rickey Henderson)	.15
637	Jeff Montgomery	.05
638	Mike Schooler	.05
639	Storm Davis	.05
640	Rich Rodriguez RC	.05
641	Phil Bradley	.05
642	Kent Mercker	.05
643	Carlton Fisk	.40
644	Mike Bell	.05
645	Alex Fernandez RC	.05
646	Juan Gonzalez	.30
647	Ken Hill	.05
648	Jeff Russell	.05
649	Chuck Malone RC	.05
650	Steve Buechele	.05
651	Mike Benjamin	.05
652	Tony Pena	.05
653	Trevor Wilson	.05
654	Alex Cole	.05
655	Roger Clemens	.60
656	"The Bashing Years" (Mark McGwire)	.50
657	Joe Grahe RC	.05
658	Jim Eisenreich	.05
659	Dan Gladden	.05
660	Steve Farr RC	.05
661	Bill Sampen RC	.05
662	Dave Rohde RC	.05
663	Mark Gardner	.05
664	Mike Simms RC	.05
665	Moises Alou	.05
666	Mickey Hatcher	.05
667	Jimmy Key	.05
668	John Wetteland	.05
669	John Smiley	.05
670	Jim Acker	.05
671	Pascual Perez	.05
672	Reggie Harris RC	.05
673	Matt Nokes	.05
674	Rafael Novoa RC	.05
675	Hensley Meulens	.05
676	Jeff M. Robinson RC	.05
677	"Ground Breaking" (New Comiskey Park)	.15
678	Johnny Ray	.05
679	Greg Hibbard	.05

680	Paul Sorrento	.05
681	Mike Marshall	.05
682	Jim Clancy	.05
683	Rob Murphy	.05
684	Dave Schmidt RC	.05
685	Jeff Gray RC	.05
686	Mike Hartley RC	.05
687	Jeff King	.05
688	Stan Javier RC	.05
689	Bob Walk	.05
690	Jim Gott	.05
691	Mike LaCoss	.05
692	John Farrell	.05
693	Tim Leary	.05
694	Mike Walker RC	.05
695	Eric Plunk	.05
696	Mike Fetters	.05
697	Wayne Edwards	.05
698	Tim Drummond RC	.05
699	Willie Fraser	.05
700	Checklist 601-700	.05
701	Mike Heath	.05
702	"Rookie Threats" (Luis Gonzalez, Karl Rhodes, Jeff Bagwell)	.45
703	Jose Mesa	.05
704	Dave Smith RC	.05
705	Danny Darwin	.05
706	Rafael Belliard	.05
707	Rob Murphy	.05
708	Terry Pendleton	.05
709	Mike Pagliarulo	.05
710	Sid Bream	.05
711	Junior Felix	.05
712	Dante Bichette	.05
713	Kevin Gross	.05
714	Luis Sojo	.05
715	Bob Ojeda	.05
716	Julio Machado RC	.05
717	Steve Farr	.05
718	Franklin Stubbs	.05
719	Mike Boddicker	.05
720	Willie Randolph	.05
721	Willie McGee	.05
722	Chili Davis	.05
723	Danny Jackson	.05
724	Cory Snyder	.05
725	"MVP Lineup" (Andre Dawson, George Bell, Ryne Sandberg)	.20
726	Rob Deer	.05
727	Rich DeLucia RC	.05
728	Mike Perez RC	.05
729	Mickey Tettleton	.05
730	Mike Blowers	.05
731	Gary Gaetti	.05
732	Brett Butler	.05
733	Dave Parker	.05
734	Eddie Zosky RC	.05
735	Jack Clark	.05
736	Jack Morris	.05
737	Kirk Gibson	.05
738	Steve Bedrosian	.05
739	Candy Maldonado	.05
740	Matt Young	.05
741	Rich Garces RC	.05
742	George Bell	.05
743	Deion Sanders	.10
744	Bo Jackson	.10
745	Luis Mercedes RC	.05
746	Reggie Jefferson RC	.05
747	Pete Incaviglia	.05
748	Chris Hammond	.05
749	Mike Stanton	.05
750	Scott Sanderson	.05
751	Paul Faries RC	.05
752	Al Osuna RC	.05
753	Steve Chitren RC	.05
754	Tony Fernandez	.05
755	Jeff Bagwell RC	1.50
756	Kirk Dressendorfer RC	.05
757	Glenn Davis	.05
758	Gary Carter	.40
759	Zane Smith	.05
760	Vance Law	.05
761	Denis Boucher RC	.05
762	Turner Ward RC	.05
763	Roberto Alomar	.20
764	Albert Belle	.05
765	Joe Carter	.05
766	Pete Schourek RC	.05
767	Heathcliff Slocumb RC	.05
768	Vince Coleman	.05
769	Mitch Williams	.05
770	Brian Downing	.05
771	Dana Allison RC	.05
772	Pete Harnisch	.05
773	Tim Raines	.05
774	Darryl Kile RC	.05
775	Fred McGriff	.05
776	Dwight Evans	.05
777	Joe Slusarski	.05
778	Dave Righetti	.05
779	Jeff Hamilton	.05
780	Ernest Riles	.05
781	Ken Dayley	.05
782	Eric King	.05
783	Devon White	.05
784	Beau Allred RC	.05
785	Mike Timlin RC	.05
786	Ivan Calderon	.05
787	Hubie Brooks	.05
788	Juan Agosto RC	.05
789	Barry Jones	.05
790	Wally Backman	.05
791	Jim Presley	.05
792	Charlie Hough	.05
793	Larry Andersen	.05
794	Steve Finley	.05
795	Shawn Abner	.05
796	Jeff M. Robinson	.05
797	Joe Bitker RC	.05
798	Eric Show	.05
799	Bud Black	.05
800	Checklist 701-800	.05
SP1	Michael Jordan	3.00
SP2	"A Day to Remember" (Rickey Henderson, Nolan Ryan)	1.00
HH1	Hank Aaron (Hologram)	1.00

Baseball Heroes Hank Aaron

This set devoted to Hank Aaron is numbered 19-27 and includes an unnumbered "Baseball Heroes" cover card. The cards are found in foil and jumbo packs of Upper Deck high-number cards.

		NM/M
Complete Set (10):		4.00
Common Aaron:		.50
Autographed Card:		180.00
Aaron Header:		1.00
19	1954 Rookie Year	.50
20	1957 MVP	.50
21	1966 Move to Atlanta	.50
22	1970 3,000	.50
23	1974 715	.50
24	1975 Return to Milwaukee	.50
25	1976 755	.50
26	1982 Hall of Fame	.50
27	Checklist - Heroes 19-27	.50

Baseball Heroes Nolan Ryan

This set devoted to Nolan Ryan is numbered 10-18 and includes an unnumbered "Baseball Heroes" cover card. The cards are found in low-number foil and jumbo boxes. One out of every hundred of the autographed cards was specially inscribed "Strike Out King."

		NM/M
Complete Set (10):		3.00
Common Player:		.50
Ryan Header Card:		1.00
Autographed Card:		200.00
"Strike Out King" Auto.:		575.00
10	1968 Victory #1	.50
11	1973 A Career Year	.50
12	1975 Double Milestone	.50
13	1979 Back Home	.50
14	1981 All-Time Leader	.50
15	1989 5,000	.50
16	1990 The Sixth	.50
17	1990 ... and Still Counting	.50
18	Checklist - Heroes 10-18	.50

Heroes of Baseball

This four-card set features three members of Baseball's Hall of Fame: Harmon Killebrew, Gaylord Perry and Ferguson Jenkins. Each has a card for himself, plus there's a card which features all three players. The cards were found in specially-marked low number foil packs. Upper Deck also produced 3,000 autographed and numbered cards for each player.

		NM/M
Complete Set (4):		7.00
Common Card:		2.00
1	Harmon Killebrew	2.00
1a	Harmon Killebrew/ Auto.	10.00
2	Gaylord Perry	2.00
2a	Gaylord Perry/Auto.	10.00
3	Ferguson Jenkins	2.00
3a	Ferguson Jenkins/ Auto.	10.00
4	Gaylord Perry, Ferguson Jenkins, Harmon Killebrew	2.00

Silver Sluggers

Each year the "Silver Slugger" award is presented to the player at each position with the highest batting average in each league. Upper Deck produced special cards in honor of the 1990 season award winners. The cards were randomly inserted in jumbo packs of Upper Deck cards. The cards feature a "SS" designation along with the card number. The cards are designed like the regular issue Upper Deck cards from 1991, but feature a Silver Slugger bat along the left border of the card.

		NM/M
Complete Set (18):		5.00
Common Player:		.15
1	Julio Franco	.15
2	Alan Trammell	.15
3	Rickey Henderson	.75
4	Jose Canseco	.50
5	Barry Bonds	2.00
6	Eddie Murray	.75
7	Kelly Gruber	.15
8	Ryne Sandberg	1.00
9	Darryl Strawberry	.15
10	Ellis Burks	.15
11	Lance Parrish	.15
12	Cecil Fielder	.15
13	Matt Williams	.15
14	Dave Parker	.15
15	Bobby Bonilla	.15
16	Don Robinson	.15
17	Benito Santiago	.15
18	Barry Larkin	.15

Final Edition

Upper Deck surprised the hobby with the late-season release of this 100-card boxed set. The cards are numbered with an "F" designation. A special "Minor League Diamond Skills" subset (cards #1-21) features several top prospects. An All-Star subset (cards #79-

Oil Can Boyd

99) is also included in this set. The cards are styled like the regular 1991 Upper Deck issue Special team hologram cards are included with the set.

		NM/M
Complete Set (100):		9.00
Common Player:		.05
1	Ryan Klesko, Reggie Sanders (Minor League Diamond Skills Checklist)	.10
2	Pedro Martinez RC	5.00
3	Lance Dickson RC	.05
4	Royce Clayton	.05
5	Scott Bryant RC	.05
6	Dan Wilson RC	.05
7	Dmitri Young RC	.05
8	Ryan Klesko	.50
9	Tom Goodwin RC	.05
10	Rondell White RC	.25
11	Reggie Sanders	.05
12	Todd Van Poppel	.05
13	Arthur Rhodes RC	.05
14	Eddie Zosky	.05
15	Gerald Williams RC	.05
16	Robert Eenhoorn RC	.05
17	Jim Thome RC	3.00
18	Marc Newfield RC	.05
19	Kerwin Moore RC	.05
20	Jeff McNeely RC	.05
21	Frankie Rodriguez	.05
22	Andy Mota RC	.05
23	Chris Haney RC	.05
24	Kenny Lofton RC	.25
25	Dave Nilsson RC	.05
26	Derek Bell	.05
27	Frank Castillo RC	.05
28	Candy Maldonado	.05
29	Chuck McElroy	.05
30	Chito Martinez RC	.05
31	Steve Howe RC	.05
32	Freddie Benavides RC	.05
33	Scott Kamieniecki	.05
34	Denny Neagle RC	.05
35	Mike Humphreys RC	.05
36	Mike Remlinger RC	.05
37	Scott Coolbaugh	.05
38	Darren Lewis	.05
39	Thomas Howard RC	.05
40	John Candelaria	.05
41	Todd Benzinger	.05
42	Wilson Alvarez	.05
43	Patrick Lennon RC	.05
44	Rusty Meacham RC	.05
45	Ryan Bowen RC	.05
46	Rick Wilkins RC	.10
47	Ed Sprague RC	.05
48	Bob Scanlan RC	.05
49	Tom Candiotti	.05
50	Dennis Martinez (Perfecto)	.05
51	Oil Can Boyd	.05
52	Glenallen Hill	.05
53	Scott Livingstone RC	.05
54	Brian Hunter RC	.05
55	Ivan Rodriguez RC	1.50
56	Keith Mitchell RC	.05
57	Roger McDowell	.05
58	Otis Nixon	.05
59	Juan Bell RC	.05
60	Bill Krueger	.05
61	Chris Donnels RC	.05
62	Tommy Greene	.05
63	Doug Simons RC	.05
64	Andy Ashby RC	.15
65	Anthony Young RC	.05
66	Kevin Morton RC	.05
67	Bret Barberie RC	.05
68	Scott Servais RC	.05
69	Ron Darling	.05
70	Vicente Palacios	.05
71	Tim Burke RC	.05
72	Gerald Alexander RC	.05
73	Reggie Jefferson	.05
74	Dean Palmer	.05
75	Mark Whiten	.05
76	Randy Tomlin RC	.05
77	Mark Wohlers RC	.05
78	Brook Jacoby	.05
79	Ken Griffey Jr., Ryne Sandberg (All-Star Checklist)	.25
80	Jack Morris/AS	.05
81	Sandy Alomar, Jr./AS	.05
82	Cecil Fielder/AS	.05
83	Roberto Alomar/AS	.10
84	Wade Boggs/AS	.25
85	Cal Ripken, Jr./AS	.60
86	Rickey Henderson/AS	.15
87	Ken Griffey Jr./AS	.60
88	Dave Henderson/AS	.05
89	Danny Tartabull/AS	.05
90	Tom Glavine/AS	.10
91	Benito Santiago/AS	.05
92	Will Clark/AS	.05
93	Ryne Sandberg/AS	.05
94	Chris Sabo/AS	.05
95	Ozzie Smith/AS	.50
96	Ivan Calderon/AS	.05
97	Tony Gwynn/AS	.25
98	Andre Dawson/AS	.05
99	Bobby Bonilla/AS	.05
100	Checklist	.05

Comic Ball 2 Promos

Among the most sought-after promo cards in the promo-card mania that marked the 1991 National Sports Collectors Convention in Anaheim, Calif., was this set of Upper Deck preview cards for its Comic Ball 2 set. One card was given out each day of the National, from July 4-7, with the giveaway date noted in a banner at top. Fronts picture Reggie Jackson and Nolan Ryan with various Looney Tunes cartoon characters. Backs have information on the upcoming Comic Ball 2 issue against a cartoon puzzle background.

		NM/M
Complete Set (4):		6.00
Common Player:		1.00
7/4/91	Nolan Ryan (w/ Bugs Bunny, Daffy Duck)	2.50
7/5/91	Reggie Jackson (w/ Taz)	1.00
7/6/91	Nolan Ryan (w/ Speedy Gonzalez)	2.50
7/7/91	Reggie Jackson (w/ Sylvester, Elmer Fudd)	1.00

Comic Ball 2

Despite featuring two popular superstars on dozens of the cards, this 198-piece issue has found little favor with collectors. Most cards are arranged in 18-card sequences which tell a baseball-related cartoon tale starring Bugs Bunny, Daffy Duck, Wile E. Coyote and the rest of the Looney Tune characters. Actual-photo "guest appearances" by Nolan Ryan and Reggie Jackson highlight these presentations. There are also "Seventh Inning Stretch" cards featuring the ballplayers in scenes with the cartoon figures. When arranged in nine-pocket plastic sheets, card backs form a cartoon picture puzzle. Cards are typical Upper Deck quality

ABBREVIATIONS

AS - All-Star

with semi-gloss front and back surfaces and a circular hologram on the backs in the standard 2-1/2" x 3-1/2" format. Nine hologram stickers featuring Ryan and Jackson along with the cartoon characters were produced as random pack inserts. Because the cards are licensed by Major League Baseball, the players and cartoon critters are depicted in Major League uniforms.

	NM/M
Complete Set (198):	5.00
Common Card, Cartoon:	.05
Common Card, Ryan/Jackson:	.10
Hologram Sticker:	2.00
Wax Pack:	.50
Wax Box (36):	7.50

Comic Ball 2 Holograms

Nine silver-foil hologram stickers combine photos of Reggie Jackson and/or Nolan Ryan with various Warner Brothers cartoon stars and were issued as random pack inserts in Comic Ball 2. The 2-1/2" x 3-1/2" round-cornered stickers are blank-backed and unnumbered.

		NM/M
Complete Set (9):		17.50
Common Player:		3.00
(1)	Reggie Jackson (w/Daffy)	3.00
(2)	Reggie Jackson (w/Speedy)	3.00
(3)	Reggie Jackson (w/Sylvester)	3.00
(4)	Reggie Jackson (w/Taz)	3.00
(5)	Reggie Jackson, Nolan Ryan (w/Roadrunner & Wile)	3.00
(6)	Nolan Ryan (w/Bugs)	3.00
(7)	Nolan Ryan (w/Sylvester)	3.00
(8)	Nolan Ryan (w/?)	3.00
(9)	Nolan Ryan (w/?)	3.00

1992 Upper Deck

Upper Deck introduced a new look in 1992. The baseline style was no longer used. The cards feature full-color action photos on white stock, with the player's name and the Upper Deck logo along the top border. The team name is in the photo's bottom-right corner. Once again a 100-card high number series was released in late summer. Ted Williams autographed 2,500 Baseball Heroes cards which were randomly inserted into packs. Subsets featured in the 1992 issue include Star Rookies and Top Prospects. Cards originating from factory sets have gold-foil holograms on back, rather than silver.

	NM/M
Unopened Fact. Set (800):	20.00
Complete Set (800):	15.00
Common Player:	.05
Low or High Pack (15):	.50
Low or High Box (36):	12.50
Jumbo Pack (27):	1.00
Jumbo Box (20):	16.00
Bench/Morgan Auto.:	75.00
Ted Williams Auto.:	425.00

1 Star Rookie Checklist (Ryan Klesko, Jim Thome) .25
2 Royce Clayton (Star Rookie) .05
3 Brian Jordan RC (Star Rookie) .30
4 Dave Fleming RC (Star Rookie) .05
5 Jim Thome (Star Rookie) .40
6 Jeff Juden (Star Rookie) .05
7 Roberto Hernandez RC (Star Rookie) .15
8 Kyle Abbott RC (Star Rookie) .05
9 Chris George RC (Star Rookie) .05
10 Rob Maurer RC (Star Rookie) .05
11 Donald Harris RC (Star Rookie) .05
12 Ted Wood RC (Star Rookie) .05
13 Patrick Lennon RC (Star Rookie) .05
14 Willie Banks (Star Rookie) .05
15 Roger Salkeld RC (Star Rookie) .05
16 Wil Cordero (Star Rookie) .05
17 Arthur Rhodes RC (Star Rookie) .40
18 Pedro Martinez (Star Rookie) .40
19 Andy Ashby RC (Star Rookie) .10
20 Tom Goodwin (Star Rookie) .05
21 Braulio Castillo RC (Star Rookie) .05
22 Todd Van Poppel (Star Rookie) .05
23 Brian Williams RC (Star Rookie) .05
24 Ryan Klesko (Star Rookie) .05
25 Kenny Lofton (Star Rookie) .05
26 Derek Bell (Star Rookie) .05
27 Reggie Sanders (Star Rookie) .05
28 Dave Winfield (Winfield's 400th) .25
29 Atlanta Braves Checklist (Dave Justice) .05
30 Cincinnati Reds Checklist (Rob Dibble) .05
31 Houston Astros Checklist (Craig Biggio) .05
32 Los Angeles Dodgers Checklist (Eddie Murray) .20
33 San Diego Padres Checklist (Fred McGriff) .05
34 San Francisco Giants Checklist (Willie McGee) .05
35 Chicago Cubs Checklist (Shawon Dunston) .05
36 Montreal Expos Checklist (Delino DeShields) .05
37 New York Mets Checklist (Howard Johnson) .05
38 Philadelphia Phillies Checklist (John Kruk) .05
39 Pittsburgh Pirates Checklist (Doug Drabek) .05
40 St. Louis Cardinals Checklist (Todd Zeile) .05
41 Steve Avery (Playoff Perfection) .05
42 Jeremy Hernandez RC .05
43 Doug Henry RC .05
44 Chris Donnels RC .05
45 Mo Sanford RC .05
46 Scott Kamieniecki RC .10
47 Mark Lemke .05
48 Steve Farr .05
49 Francisco Oliveras .05
50 Ced Landrum RC .05
51 Top Prospect Checklist (Rondell White, Marc Newfield) .05
52 Eduardo Perez RC (Top Prospect) .10
53 Tom Nevers RC (Top Prospect) .05
54 David Zancanaro RC (Top Prospect) .05
55 Shawn Green RC (Top Prospect) 1.50
56 Mark Wohlers RC (Top Prospect) .05
57 Dave Nilsson (Top Prospect) .05
58 Dmitri Young (Top Prospect) .05
59 Ryan Hawblitzel RC (Top Prospect) .05
60 Raul Mondesi (Top Prospect) .05
61 Rondell White (Top Prospect) .05
62 Steve Hosey (Top Prospect) .05
63 Manny Ramirez RC (Top Prospect) 2.00
64 Marc Newfield (Top Prospect) .05
65 Jeromy Burnitz (Top Prospect) .05
66 Mark Smith RC (Top Prospect) .05
67 Joey Hamilton RC (Top Prospect) .10
68 Tyler Green RC (Top Prospect) .05
69 John Farrell RC (Top Prospect) .05
70 Kurt Miller RC (Top Prospect) .05
71 Jeff Plympton RC (Top Prospect) .05
72 Dan Wilson (Top Prospect) .05
73 Joe Vitiello RC (Top Prospect) .05
74 Rico Brogna (Top Prospect) .05
75 David McCarty RC (Top Prospect) .05
76 Bob Wickman RC (Top Prospect) .05
77 Carlos Rodriguez RC (Top Prospect) .05
78 Jim Abbott (Stay in School) .05
79 Bloodlines (Pedro Martinez, Ramon Martinez) .05
80 Bloodlines (Kevin Mitchell, Keith Mitchell) .05
81 Bloodlines (Sandy Jr. & Roberto Alomar, Sandy Jr. & Roberto Alomar) .10
82 Bloodlines (Cal Jr. & Billy Ripken, Cal Jr. & Billy Ripken) .40
83 Bloodlines (Tony & Chris Gwynn, Tony & Chris Gwynn) .20
84 Bloodlines (Dwight Gooden, Gary Sheffield) .15
85 Bloodlines (Ken, Sr.; Ken, Jr.; & Craig Griffey, Ken, Sr.; Ken, Jr.; & Craig Griffey) .30
86 California Angels Checklist (Jim Abbott) .05
87 Chicago White Sox Checklist (Frank Thomas) .05
88 Kansas City Royals Checklist (Danny Tartabull) .05
89 Minnesota Twins Checklist (Scott Erickson) .05
90 Oakland Athletics Checklist (Rickey Henderson) .25
91 Seattle Mariners Checklist (Edgar Martinez) .05
92 Texas Rangers Checklist (Nolan Ryan) .50
93 Baltimore Orioles Checklist (Ben McDonald) .05
94 Boston Red Sox Checklist (Ellis Burks) .05
95 Cleveland Indians Checklist (Greg Swindell) .05
96 Detroit Tigers Checklist (Cecil Fielder) .05
97 Milwaukee Brewers Checklist (Greg Vaughn) .05
98 New York Yankees Checklist (Kevin Maas) .05
99 Toronto Blue Jays Checklist (Dave Stieb) .05
100 Checklist 1-100 .05
101 Joe Oliver .05
102 Hector Villanueva .05
103 Ed Whitson .05
104 Danny Jackson .05
105 Chris Hammond .05
106 Ricky Jordan .05
107 Kevin Bass .05
108 Darrin Fletcher .05
109 Junior Ortiz .05
110 Tom Bolton .05
111 Jeff King .05
112 Dave Magadan .05
113 Mike LaValliere .05
114 Hubie Brooks .05
115 Jay Bell .05
116 David Wells .05
117 Jim Leyritz .05
118 Manuel Lee .05
119 Alvaro Espinoza .05
120 B.J. Surhoff .05
121 Hal Morris .05
122 Shawon Dunston .05
123 Chris Sabo .05
124 Andre Dawson .25
125 Eric Davis .05
126 Chili Davis .05
127 Dale Murphy .15
128 Kirk McCaskill .05
129 Terry Mulholland .05
130 Rick Aguilera .05
131 Vince Coleman .05
132 Andy Van Slyke .05
133 Gregg Jefferies .05
134 Barry Bonds 1.00
135 Dwight Gooden .05
136 Dave Stieb .05
137 Albert Belle .05
138 Teddy Higuera .05
139 Jesse Barfield .05
140 Pat Borders .05
141 Bip Roberts .05
142 Rob Dibble .05
143 Mark Grace .05
144 Barry Larkin .05
145 Ryne Sandberg .50
146 Scott Erickson .05
147 Luis Polonia .05
148 John Burkett .05
149 Luis Sojo .05
150 Dickie Thon .05
151 Walt Weiss .05
152 Mike Scioscia .05
153 Mark McGwire .75
154 Matt Williams .05
155 Rickey Henderson .40
156 Sandy Alomar, Jr. .05
157 Brian McRae .05
158 Harold Baines .05
159 Kevin Appier .05
160 Felix Fermin .05
161 Leo Gomez .05
162 Craig Biggio .05
163 Ben McDonald .05
164 Randy Johnson .40
165 Cal Ripken, Jr. 1.00
166 Frank Thomas .40
167 Delino DeShields .05
168 Greg Gagne .05
169 Ron Karkovice .05
170 Charlie Leibrandt .05
171 Dave Righetti .05
172 Dave Henderson .05
173 Steve Decker .05
174 Darryl Strawberry .05
175 Will Clark .05
176 Ruben Sierra .05
177 Ozzie Smith .50
178 Charles Nagy .05
179 Gary Pettis .05
180 Kirk Gibson .05
181 Randy Milligan .05
182 Dave Valle .05
183 Chris Hoiles .05
184 Tony Phillips .05
185 Brady Anderson .05
186 Scott Fletcher .05
187 Gene Larkin .05
188 Lance Johnson .05
189 Greg Olson .05
190 Melido Perez .05
191 Lenny Harris .05
192 Terry Kennedy .05
193 Mike Gallego .05
194 Willie McGee .05
195 Juan Samuel .05
196 Jeff Huson .05
197 Alex Cole .05
198 Ron Robinson .05
199 Joel Skinner .05
200 Checklist 101-200 .05
201 Kevin Reimer .05
202 Stan Belinda .05
203 Pat Tabler .05
204 Jose Guzman .05
205 Jose Lind .05
206 Spike Owen .05
207 Joe Orsulak .05
208 Charlie Hayes .05
209 Mike Devereaux .05
210 Mike Fitzgerald .05
211 Willie Randolph .05
212 Rod Nichols .05
213 Mike Boddicker .05
214 Bill Spiers .05
215 Steve Olin .05
216 David Howard RC .05
217 Gary Varsho .05
218 Mike Harkey .05
219 Luis Aquino .05
220 Chuck McElroy RC .05
221 Doug Drabek .05
222 Dave Winfield .40
223 Rafael Palmeiro .35
224 Joe Carter .25
225 Bobby Bonilla .05
226 Ivan Calderon .05
227 Gregg Olson .05
228 Tim Wallach .05
229 Terry Pendleton .05
230 Gilberto Reyes RC .05
231 Carlos Baerga .05
232 Greg Vaughn .05
233 Bret Saberhagen .05
234 Gary Sheffield .30
235 Mark Lewis .05
236 George Bell .05
237 Danny Tartabull .05
238 Willie Wilson .05
239 Doug Dascenzo .05
240 Bill Pecota .05
241 Julio Franco .05
242 Ed Sprague .05
243 Juan Gonzalez .20
244 Chuck Finley .05
245 Ivan Rodriguez .35
246 Len Dykstra .05
247 Deion Sanders .10
248 Dwight Evans .05
249 Larry Walker .05
250 Billy Ripken .05
251 Mickey Tettleton .05
252 Tony Pena .05
253 Benito Santiago .05
254 Kirby Puckett .50
255 Cecil Fielder .05
256 Howard Johnson .05
257 Andujar Cedeno .05
258 Jose Rijo .05
259 Al Osuna .05
260 Todd Hundley .05
261 Orel Hershiser .05
262 Ray Lankford .05
263 Robin Ventura .05
264 Felix Jose .05
265 Eddie Murray .40
266 Kevin Mitchell .05
267 Gary Carter .40
268 Mike Benjamin .05
269 Dick Schofield .05
270 Jose Uribe .05
271 Pete Incaviglia .05
272 Tony Fernandez .05
273 Alan Trammell .05
274 Tony Gwynn .50
275 Mike Greenwell .05
276 Jeff Bagwell .40
277 Frank Viola .05
278 Randy Myers .05
279 Ken Caminiti .05
280 Bill Doran .05
281 Dan Pasqua .05
282 Alfredo Griffin .05
283 Jose Oquendo .05
284 Kal Daniels .05
285 Bobby Thigpen .05
286 Robby Thompson .05
287 Mark Eichhorn .05
288 Mike Felder .05
289 Dave Gallagher .05
290 Dave Anderson .05
291 Mel Hall .05
292 Jerald Clark .05
293 Al Newman .05
294 Rob Deer .05
295 Matt Nokes .05
296 Jack Armstrong .05
297 Jim Deshaies .05
298 Jeff Innis .05
299 Jeff Reed .05
300 Checklist 201-300 .05
301 Lonnie Smith .05
302 Jimmy Key .05
303 Junior Felix .05
304 Mike Heath .05
305 Mark Langston .05
306 Greg W. Harris .05
307 Brett Butler .05
308 Luis Rivera RC .05
309 Bruce Ruffin .05
310 Paul Faries .05
311 Terry Leach .05
312 Scott Brosius RC .10
313 Scott Leius .05
314 Harold Reynolds .05
315 Jack Morris .05
316 David Segui .05
317 Bill Gullickson .05
318 Todd Frohwirth .05
319 Mark Leiter RC .05
320 Jeff M. Robinson .05
321 Gary Gaetti .05
322 John Smoltz .05
323 Andy Benes .05
324 Kelly Gruber .05
325 Jim Abbott .05
326 John Kruk .05
327 Kevin Seitzer .05
328 Darrin Jackson .05
329 Kurt Stillwell RC .05
330 Mike Maddux .05
331 Dennis Eckersley .35
332 Dan Gladden .05
333 Jose Canseco .30
334 Kent Hrbek .05
335 Ken Griffey Sr. .05
336 Greg Swindell .05
337 Trevor Wilson RC .05
338 Sam Horn .05
339 Mike Henneman .05
340 Jerry Browne .05
341 Glenn Braggs .05
342 Tom Glavine .20
343 Wally Joyner .05
344 Fred McGriff .20
345 Ron Gant .05
346 Ramon Martinez .05
347 Wes Chamberlain .05
348 Terry Shumpert .05
349 Tim Teufel .05
350 Wally Backman .05
351 Joe Girardi .05
352 Devon White .05
353 Greg Maddux .50
354 Ryan Bowen RC .05
355 Roberto Alomar .20
356 Don Mattingly .60
357 Pedro Guerrero .05
358 Steve Sax .05
359 Joey Cora .05
360 Jim Gantner .05
361 Brian Barnes RC .05
362 Kevin McReynolds .05
363 Bret Barberie .05
364 David Cone .05
365 Dennis Martinez .05
366 Brian Hunter RC .05
367 Edgar Martinez .05
368 Steve Finley .05
369 Greg Briley .05
370 Jeff Blauser .05
371 Todd Stottlemyre .05
372 Luis Gonzalez .05
373 Rick Wilkins .05
374 Darryl Kile RC .05
375 John Olerud .05
376 Lee Smith .05
377 Kevin Maas .05
378 Dante Bichette .05
379 Tom Pagnozzi .05
380 Mike Flanagan .05
381 Charlie O'Brien .05
382 Dave Martinez .05
383 Keith Miller .05
384 Scott Ruskin .05
385 Kevin Elster .05
386 Alvin Davis .05
387 Casey Candaele .05
388 Pete O'Brien .05
389 Jeff Treadway RC .05
390 Scott Bradley .05
391 Mookie Wilson .05
392 Jimmy Jones .05
393 Candy Maldonado .05
394 Eric Yelding .05
395 Tom Henke .05
396 Franklin Stubbs .05
397 Milt Thompson .05
398 Mark Carreon .05
399 Randy Velarde .05
400 Checklist 301-400 .05
401 Omar Vizquel .05
402 Joe Boever .05
403 Bill Krueger .05
404 Jody Reed .05
405 Mike Schooler RC .05
406 Jason Grimsley .05
407 Greg Myers .05
408 Randy Ready .05
409 Mike Timlin RC .15
410 Mitch Williams .05
411 Garry Templeton .05
412 Greg Cadaret .05
413 Donnie Hill .05
414 Wally Whitehurst .05
415 Scott Sanderson .05
416 Thomas Howard .05
417 Neal Heaton .05
418 Charlie Hough .05
419 Jack Howell .05
420 Greg Hibbard .05
421 Carlos Quintana .05
422 Kim Batiste RC .05
423 Paul Molitor .40
424 Ken Griffey Jr. .65
425 Phil Plantier .05
426 Denny Neagle .05
427 Von Hayes .05
428 Shane Mack .05
429 Darren Daulton .05
430 Dwayne Henry .05
431 Lance Parrish .05
432 Mike Humphreys RC .05
433 Tim Burke .05
434 Bryan Harvey .05
435 Pat Kelly .05
436 Ozzie Guillen .05
437 Bruce Hurst .05
438 Sammy Sosa .50
439 Dennis Rasmussen .05
440 Ken Patterson .05
441 Jay Buhner .05
442 Pat Combs .05
443 Wade Boggs .50
444 George Brett .60
445 Mo Vaughn .05
446 Chuck Knoblauch .05
447 Tom Candiotti .05
448 Mark Portugal .05
449 Mickey Morandini .05
450 Duane Ward .05
451 Otis Nixon .05
452 Bob Welch .05
453 Rusty Meacham .05
454 Keith Mitchell .05
455 Marquis Grissom .05
456 Robin Yount .40
457 Harvey Pulliam RC .05
458 Jose DeLeon RC .05
459 Mark Gubicza .05
460 Darryl Hamilton .05
461 Tom Browning .05
462 Monty Fariss .05
463 Jerome Walton .05
464 Paul O'Neill .05
465 Dean Palmer .05
466 Travis Fryman .05
467 John Smiley .05
468 Lloyd Moseby .05
469 John Wehner RC .05
470 Skeeter Barnes RC .05
471 Steve Chitren .05
472 Kent Mercker .05
473 Terry Steinbach .05
474 Andres Galarraga .05
475 Steve Avery .05
476 Tom Gordon .05
477 Cal Eldred .05
478 Omar Olivares RC .05
479 Julio Machado .05
480 Bob Milacki .05
481 Les Lancaster .05
482 John Candelaria .05
483 Brian Downing .05
484 Roger McDowell .05
485 Scott Scudder .05
486 Zane Smith .05
487 John Cerutti .05
488 Steve Buechele .05
489 Paul Gibson .05
490 Curtis Wilkerson .05
491 Marvin Freeman .05
492 Tom Foley .05
493 Juan Berenguer .05
494 Ernest Riles .05
495 Sid Bream .05
496 Chuck Crim .05
497 Mike Macfarlane .05
498 Dale Sveum .05
499 Storm Davis .05
500 Checklist 401-500 .05
501 Jeff Reardon .05
502 Shawn Abner .05
503 Tony Fossas .05
504 Cory Snyder .05
505 Matt Young .05
506 Allan Anderson RC .05
507 Mark Lee .05
508 Gene Nelson .05
509 Mike Pagliarulo .05
510 Rafael Belliard .05
511 Jay Howell .05
512 Bob Tewksbury .05
513 Mike Morgan .05
514 John Franco .05
515 Kevin Gross .05
516 Lou Whitaker .05
517 Orlando Merced .05
518 Todd Benzinger .05
519 Gary Redus .05
520 Walt Terrell .05
521 Jack Clark .05
522 Dave Parker .05
523 Tim Naehring .05
524 Mark Whiten .05
525 Ellis Burks .05
526 Frank Castillo RC .05
527 Brian Harper .05
528 Brook Jacoby .05
529 Rick Sutcliffe .05
530 Joe Klink .05
531 Terry Bross .05
532 Jose Offerman .05
533 Todd Zeile .05
534 Eric Karros .05
535 Anthony Young RC .05
536 Milt Cuyler .05
537 Randy Tomlin .05
538 Scott Livingstone RC .05
539 Jim Eisenreich .05
540 Don Slaught .05
541 Scott Cooper .05
542 Joe Grahe RC .05
543 Tom Brunansky .05
544 Eddie Zosky .05
545 Roger Clemens .60
546 Dave Justice .05
547 Dave Stewart .05
548 David West .05
549 Dave Smith .05
550 Dan Plesac .05
551 Alex Fernandez .05
552 Bernard Gilkey .05
553 Jack McDowell .05
554 Tino Martinez .05
555 Bo Jackson .10
556 Bernie Williams .05
557 Mark Gardner .05
558 Glenallen Hill .05
559 Oil Can Boyd .05
560 Chris James .05
561 Scott Servais RC .05
562 Rey Sanchez RC .05
563 Paul McClellan RC .05
564 Andy Mota RC .05
565 Darren Lewis .05
566 Jose Melendez RC .05
567 Tommy Greene .05
568 Rich Rodriguez .05
569 Heathcliff Slocumb RC .05
570 Joe Hesketh RC .05
571 Carlton Fisk .40
572 Erik Hanson .05
573 Wilson Alvarez .05
574 Rheal Cormier RC .05
575 Tim Raines .05
576 Bobby Witt .05
577 Roberto Kelly .05
578 Kevin Brown .05
579 Chris Nabholz .05
580 Jesse Orosco .05
581 Jeff Brantley .05
582 Rafael Ramirez .05
583 Kelly Downs .05
584 Mike Simms .05
585 Mike Remlinger RC .05

586	Dave Hollins		.05
587	Larry Andersen		.05
588	Mike Gardiner		.05
589	Craig Lefferts		.05
590	Paul Assenmacher RC		.05
591	Bryn Smith		.05
592	Donn Pall		.05
593	Mike Jackson		.05
594	Scott Radinsky		.05
595	Brian Holman		.05
596	Geronimo Pena		.05
597	Mike Jeffcoat		.05
598	Carlos Martinez RC		.05
599	Geno Petralli		.05
600	Checklist 501-600		.05
601	Jerry Don Gleaton		.05
602	Adam Peterson RC		.05
603	Craig Grebeck		.05
604	Mark Guthrie		.05
605	Frank Tanana		.05
606	Hensley Meulens RC		.05
607	Mark Davis		.05
608	Eric Plunk		.05
609	Mark Williamson		.05
610	Lee Guetterman RC		.05
611	Bobby Rose		.05
612	Bill Wegman		.05
613	Mike Hartley		.05
614	Chris Beasley RC		.05
615	Chris Bosio		.05
616	Henry Cotto		.05
617	Chico Walker RC		.05
618	Russ Swan RC		.05
619	Bob Walk		.05
620	Billy Swift		.05
621	Warren Newson RC		.05
622	Steve Bedrosian RC		.05
623	Ricky Bones RC		.05
624	Kevin Tapani		.05
625	Juan Guzman RC		.05
626	Jeff Johnson RC		.05
627	Jeff Montgomery		.05
628	Ken Hill		.05
629	Gary Thurman		.05
630	Steve Howe RC		.05
631	Jose DeJesus		.05
632	Bert Blyleven		.05
633	Jaime Navarro		.05
634	Lee Stevens RC		.05
635	Pete Harnisch		.05
636	Bill Landrum		.05
637	Rich DeLucia		.05
638	Luis Salazar RC		.05
639	Rob Murphy		.05
640	A.L. Diamond Skills Checklist (Rickey Henderson, Jose Canseco)		.05
641	Roger Clemens (Diamond Skills)		.40
642	Jim Abbott (Diamond Skills)		.05
643	Travis Fryman (Diamond Skills)		.05
644	Jesse Barfield (Diamond Skills)		.05
645	Cal Ripken, Jr. (Diamond Skills)		.50
646	Wade Boggs (Diamond Skills)		.35
647	Cecil Fielder (Diamond Skills)		.05
648	Rickey Henderson (Diamond Skills)		.20
649	Jose Canseco (Diamond Skills)		.15
650	Ken Griffey Jr. (Diamond Skills)		.45
651	Kenny Rogers		.05
652	Luis Mercedes RC		.05
653	Mike Stanton		.05
654	Glenn Davis		.05
655	Nolan Ryan		1.00
656	Reggie Jefferson		.05
657	Javier Ortiz RC		.05
658	Greg A. Harris		.05
659	Mariano Duncan		.05
660	Jeff Shaw		.05
661	Mike Moore		.05
662	Chris Haney RC		.05
663	Joe Slusarski RC		.05
664	Wayne Housie RC		.05
665	Carlos Garcia		.05
666	Bob Ojeda		.05
667	Bryan Hickerson RC		.05
668	Tim Belcher		.05
669	Ron Darling		.05
670	Rex Hudler RC		.05
671	Sid Fernandez		.05
672	Chito Martinez RC		.05
673	Pete Schourek RC		.05
674	Armando Reynoso RC		.05
675	Mike Mussina		.30
676	Kevin Morton RC		.05
677	Norm Charlton		.05
678	Danny Darwin		.05
679	Eric King		.05
680	Ted Power		.05
681	Barry Jones		.05
682	Carney Lansford		.05
683	Mel Rojas		.05
684	Rick Honeycutt		.05
685	Jeff Fassero RC		.05
686	Cris Carpenter RC		.05
687	Tim Crews		.05
688	Scott Terry		.05
689	Chris Gwynn		.05
690	Gerald Perry		.05
691	John Barfield		.05
692	Bob Melvin		.05
693	Juan Agosto		.05
694	Alejandro Pena RC		.05
695	Jeff Russell		.05
696	Carmelo Martinez		.05
697	Bud Black		.05
698	Dave Otto RC		.05
699	Billy Hatcher		.05
700	Checklist 601-700		.05
701	Clemente Nunez RC		.05
702	"Rookie Threats" (Donovan Osborne, Brian Jordan, Mark Clark)		.05
703	Mike Morgan		.05
704	Keith Miller		.05
705	Kurt Stillwell		.05
706	Damon Berryhill		.05
707	Von Hayes		.05
708	Rick Sutcliffe		.05
709	Hubie Brooks		.05
710	Ryan Turner RC		.05
711	N.L. Diamond Skills Checklist (Barry Bonds, Andy Van Slyke)		.30
712	Jose Rijo (Diamond Skills)		.05
713	Tom Glavine (Diamond Skills)		.05
714	Shawon Dunston (Diamond Skills)		.05
715	Andy Van Slyke (Diamond Skills)		.05
716	Ozzie Smith (Diamond Skills)		.35
717	Tony Gwynn (Diamond Skills)		.35
718	Will Clark (Diamond Skills)		.05
719	Marquis Grissom (Diamond Skills)		.05
720	Howard Johnson (Diamond Skills)		.05
721	Barry Bonds (Diamond Skills)		.50
722	Kirk McCaskill		.05
723	Sammy Sosa		.50
724	George Bell		.05
725	Gregg Jefferies		.05
726	Gary DiSarcina RC		.05
727	Mike Bordick		.05
728	Eddie Murray (400 Homes Run Club)		.20
729	Rene Gonzales		.05
730	Mike Bielecki		.05
731	Calvin Jones RC		.05
732	Jack Morris		.05
733	Frank Viola		.05
734	Dave Winfield		.40
735	Kevin Mitchell		.05
736	Billy Swift		.05
737	Dan Gladden		.05
738	Mike Jackson		.05
739	Mark Carreon		.05
740	Kirt Manwaring		.05
741	Randy Myers		.05
742	Kevin McReynolds		.05
743	Steve Sax		.05
744	Wally Joyner		.05
745	Gary Sheffield		.25
746	Danny Tartabull		.05
747	Julio Valera		.05
748	Denny Neagle		.05
749	Lance Blankenship		.05
750	Mike Gallego		.05
751	Bret Saberhagen		.05
752	Ruben Amaro RC		.05
753	Eddie Murray		.40
754	Kyle Abbott RC		.05
755	Bobby Bonilla		.05
756	Eric Davis		.05
757	Eddie Taubensee RC		.05
758	Andres Galarraga		.05
759	Pete Incaviglia		.05
760	Tom Candiotti		.05
761	Tim Belcher		.05
762	Ricky Bones		.05
763	Bip Roberts		.05
764	Pedro Munoz		.05
765	Greg Swindell		.05
766	Kenny Lofton		.05
767	Gary Carter		.40
768	Charlie Hayes		.05
769	Dickie Thon		.05
770	Diamond Debuts Checklist (Donovan Osborne)		.05
771	Bret Boone (Diamond Debuts)		.10
772	Archi Cianfrocco RC (Diamond Debuts)		.05
773	Mark Clark RC (Diamond Debuts)		.05
774	Chad Curtis RC (Diamond Debuts)		.20
775	Pat Listach RC (Diamond Debuts)		.05
776	Pat Mahomes RC (Diamond Debuts)		.05
777	Donovan Osborne RC (Diamond Debuts)		.05
778	John Patterson RC (Diamond Debuts)		.05
779	Andy Stankiewicz RC (Diamond Debuts)		.05
780	Turk Wendell RC (Diamond Debuts)		.10
781	Bill Krueger		.05
782	Rickey Henderson (Grand Theft)		.20
783	Kevin Seitzer		.05
784	Dave Martinez		.05
785	John Smiley		.05
786	Matt Stairs		.05
787	Scott Scudder		.05
788	John Wetteland		.05
789	Jack Armstrong		.05
790	Ken Hill		.05
791	Dick Schofield		.05
792	Mariano Duncan		.05
793	Bill Pecota		.05
794	Mike Kelly RC		.05
795	Willie Randolph		.05
796	Butch Henry RC		.05
797	Carlos Hernandez RC		.05
798	Doug Jones		.05
799	Melido Perez		.05
800	Checklist		.05
SP3	"Prime Time's Two" (Deion Sanders)		.25
SP4	"Mr. Baseball" (Tom Selleck, Frank Thomas)		2.00
HH2	Ted Williams (Hologram)		2.00

Baseball Heroes Bench/Morgan

This set is devoted to two of the vital cogs in Cincinnati's Big Red Machine: Hall of Famers Johnny Bench and Joe Morgan. Cards, numbered 37-45, were included in high number packs. An unnumbered cover card was also produced. Both players autographed 2,500 of card #45, the painting of the Reds duo by sports artist Vernon Wells.

		NM/M
Complete Set (10):		4.00
Common Card:		.50
Autographed Card:		65.00
---	Header Card	.75
37	1968 Rookie of the Year (Johnny Bench)	.75
38	1968-77 Ten Straight Gold Gloves (Johnny Bench)	.75
39	1970 & 1972 MVP (Johnny Bench)	.75
40	1965 Rookie Year (Joe Morgan)	.50
41	1975-76 Back-to-Back MVP (Joe Morgan)	.50
42	1980-83 The Golden Years (Joe Morgan)	.50
43	1972-79 Big Red Machine (Johnny Bench, Joe Morgan)	.60
44	1989 & 1990 Hall of Fame (Johnny Bench, Joe Morgan)	.60
45	Checklist - Heroes 37-45 (Johnny Bench, Joe Morgan)	.60

Bench-Morgan Box Bottoms

The eight Heroes of Baseball high-number cards featuring Johnny Bench and/or Joe Morgan were also issued in a box-bottom version measuring about 5" x 7". The blank-back box bottoms are listed here according to the corresponding number of the regular-size cards.

		NM/M
Complete Set (8):		7.00
Common Card:		1.00
(37)	1968 Rookie of the Year (Johnny Bench)	1.00
(38)	1968-77 Ten Straight Gold Gloves (Johnny Bench)	1.00
(39)	1970 & 1972 MVP (Johnny Bench)	1.00
(40)	1965 Rookie Year (Joe Morgan)	1.00
(41)	1975-76 Back-to-Back MVP (Joe Morgan)	1.00
(42)	1980-83 The Golden Years (Joe Morgan)	1.00
(43)	1972-79 Big Red Machine (Johnny Bench, Joe Morgan)	1.00
(44)	1989 & 1990 Hall of Fame (Johnny Bench, Joe Morgan)	1.00

Baseball Heroes Ted Williams

This Baseball Heroes set devoted to Ted Williams continues where previous efforts left off by numbering it from 28-36. An unnumbered "Baseball Heroes" cover card is also included. Cards were found in low-number foil and jumbo packs. Williams also autographed 2,500 cards, which were numbered and randomly inserted in low-number packs.

		NM/M
Complete Set (10):		3.00
Common Player:		.50
Autographed Card:		425.00
---	Header Card	.75
28	1939 Rookie Year (Ted Williams)	.50
29	1941 .406! (Ted Williams)	.50
30	1942 Triple Crown Year (Ted Williams)	.50
31	1946 & 1949 MVP (Ted Williams)	.50
32	1947 Second Triple Crown (Ted Williams)	.50
33	1950s Player of the Decade (Ted Williams)	.50
34	1960 500 Home Run Club (Ted Williams)	.50
35	1966 Hall of Fame (Ted Williams)	.50
36	Checklist - Heroes 28-36 (Ted Williams)	.50

Ted Williams Box Bottoms

Foil-pack boxes of low-number 1992 Upper Deck baseball featured on their bottom an oversize reproduction of the front of one of the Ted Williams "Baseball Heroes" insert cards. Eight different box-bottom cards were produced, measuring 5" x 7" and printed on a mottled orange background. The box-bottom cards are blank-backed and unnumbered. They are checklisted here according to the card numbers of the regular-size version.

		NM/M
Complete Set (8):		6.00
Common Player:		1.00
(28)	1939 - Rookie Year (Ted Williams)	1.00
(29)	1941 - .406 (Ted Williams)	1.00
(30)	1942 - Triple Crown Year (Ted Williams)	1.00
(31)	1946, 1949 - MVP (Ted Williams)	1.00
(32)	1947 - Second Triple Crown (Ted Williams)	1.00
(33)	1950s - Player of the Decade (Ted Williams)	1.00
(34)	1960 - 500 Hokme Run Club (Ted Williams)	1.00
(35)	1966 - Hall of Fame (Ted Williams)	1.00

College POY Holograms

This three-card hologram set features the College Player of the Year winners from 1989-91. Cards were randomly inserted in high number foil packs and have a CP prefix for numbering.

		NM/M
Complete Set (3):		.75
Common Player:		.25
1	David McCarty	.25
2	Mike Kelly	.25
3	Ben McDonald	.25

Hall of Fame Heroes

This set features three top players from the 1970s: Vida Blue, Lou Brock and Rollie Fingers. The cards continue from last year's set by using numbers H5-H8. The three players are each on one card; the fourth card features all three. They were found in low-number foil packs and specially-marked jumbo packs. Both types of packs could also contain autographed cards; each player signed 3,000 cards.

		NM/M
Complete Set (4):		2.50
Common Player:		.50
5	Vida Blue	.50
5a	Vida Blue/Auto.	20.00
6	Lou Brock	1.00
6a	Lou Brock/Auto.	35.00
7	Rollie Fingers	.50
7a	Rollie Fingers/Auto.	30.00
8	Vida Blue, Lou Brock, Rollie Fingers	1.00

Heroes Highlights

Special packaging of 1992 Upper Deck high numbers produced for sales to dealers at its Heroes of Baseball show series included these cards of former players as inserts. Cards have a Heroes Highlights banner including the player's name and the date of his career highlight beneath the photo. In a tombstone frame on back, the highlight is chronicled. Cards are

numbered alphabetically by player name, with the card number carrying an HI prefix.

		NM/M
Complete Set (10):		4.00
Common Player:		.45
1	Bobby Bonds	.45
2	Lou Brock	.45
3	Rollie Fingers	.45
4	Bob Gibson	.45
5	Reggie Jackson	.75
6	Gaylord Perry	.45
7	Robin Roberts	.45
8	Brooks Robinson	.45
9	Billy Williams	.45
10	Ted Williams	2.00

Home Run Heroes

This 26-card set features a top home run hitter from each major league team. The cards, numbered HR1-HR26, were found in low-number jumbo packs, one per pack.

		NM/M
Complete Set (26):		5.00
Common Player:		.15
1	Jose Canseco	.45
2	Cecil Fielder	.15
3	Howard Johnson	.15
4	Cal Ripken, Jr.	1.50
5	Matt Williams	.15
6	Joe Carter	.15
7	Ron Gant	.15
8	Frank Thomas	.75
9	Andre Dawson	.40
10	Fred McGriff	.15
11	Danny Tartabull	.15
12	Chili Davis	.15
13	Albert Belle	.15
14	Jack Clark	.15
15	Paul O'Neill	.15
16	Darryl Strawberry	.15
17	Dave Winfield	.75
18	Jay Buhner	.15
19	Juan Gonzalez	.25
20	Greg Vaughn	.15
21	Barry Bonds	1.50
22	Matt Nokes	.15
23	John Kruk	.15
24	Ivan Calderon	.15
25	Jeff Bagwell	.75
26	Todd Zeile	.15

Scouting Report

These cards were randomly inserted in Upper Deck high-number jumbo packs. The set is numbered SR1-SR25 and features 25 top prospects, including 1992 Rookies of the Year Pat Listach and Eric Karros. "Scouting Report" is written down the side on the front in silver lettering. The back features a clipboard which shows a photo, a player profile and a major league scouting report.

		NM/M
Complete Set (25):		2.00
Common Player:		.25
1	Andy Ashby	.25
2	Willie Banks	.25
3	Kim Batiste	.25
4	Derek Bell	.25
5	Archi Cianfrocco	.25
6	Royce Clayton	.25
7	Gary DiSarcina	.25
8	Dave Fleming	.25
9	Butch Henry	.25
10	Todd Hundley	.25
11	Brian Jordan	.25
12	Eric Karros	.25
13	Pat Listach	.25
14	Scott Livingstone	.25
15	Kenny Lofton	.25
16	Pat Mahomes	.25
17	Denny Neagle	.25
18	Dave Nilsson	.25
19	Donovan Osborne	.25
20	Reggie Sanders	.25
21	Andy Stankiewicz	.25
22	Jim Thome	1.50
23	Julio Valera	.25
24	Mark Wohlers	.25
25	Anthony Young	.25

Ted Williams' Best Hitters/Future

Twenty of the best hitters in baseball according to legend Ted Williams are featured in this special insert set from Upper Deck. The cards are styled much like the 1992 FanFest cards and showcase each chosen player. Each card is numbered with a "T" designation.

		NM/M
Complete Set (20):		3.00
Common Player:		.12
1	Wade Boggs	.50
2	Barry Bonds	1.00
3	Jose Canseco	.25
4	Will Clark	.10
5	Cecil Fielder	.10
6	Tony Gwynn	.50
7	Rickey Henderson	.40
8	Fred McGriff	.10
9	Kirby Puckett	.50
10	Ruben Sierra	.10
11	Roberto Alomar	.20
12	Jeff Bagwell	.40
13	Albert Belle	.10
14	Juan Gonzalez	.20
15	Ken Griffey Jr.	.75
16	Chris Hoiles	.10
17	Dave Justice	.10
18	Phil Plantier	.10
19	Frank Thomas	.40
20	Robin Ventura	.10

FanFest

This 54-card boxed set was made available through special offers at the 1992 National Sports Collectors Convention and at the 1992 All-Star FanFest in San Diego. Card fronts feature a glossy UV finish, silver-foil stamping and the All-Star FanFest logo. The card backs include a player profile. Both "Future Heroes" and past and

present "All-Star Heroes" are featured. The complete set was packaged in an attractive blue box with white pinstripes.

		NM/M
Complete Set (54):		6.00
Common Player:		.10
1	Steve Avery	.10
2	Ivan Rodriguez	.60
3	Jeff Bagwell	.75
4	Delino DeShields	.10
5	Royce Clayton	.10
6	Robin Ventura	.10
7	Phil Plantier	.10
8	Ray Lankford	.10
9	Juan Gonzalez	.40
10	Frank Thomas	.75
11	Roberto Alomar	.30
12	Sandy Alomar, Jr.	.10
13	Wade Boggs	1.25
14	Barry Bonds	2.50
15	Bobby Bonilla	.10
16	George Brett	1.50
17	Jose Canseco	.60
18	Will Clark	.10
19	Roger Clemens	1.50
20	Eric Davis	.10
21	Rob Dibble	.10
22	Cecil Fielder	.10
23	Dwight Gooden	.10
24	Ken Griffey Jr.	2.00
25	Tony Gwynn	1.25
26	Bryan Harvey	.10
27	Rickey Henderson	.75
28	Howard Johnson	.10
29	Wally Joyner	.10
30	Barry Larkin	.10
31	Don Mattingly	1.50
32	Mark McGwire	2.25
33	Dale Murphy	.30
34	Rafael Palmeiro	.60
35	Kirby Puckett	1.25
36	Cal Ripken, Jr.	2.50
37	Nolan Ryan	2.50
38	Chris Sabo	.10
39	Ryne Sandberg	1.25
40	Benito Santiago	.10
41	Ruben Sierra	.10
42	Ozzie Smith	1.25
43	Darryl Strawberry	.10
44	Robin Yount	.75
45	Rollie Fingers	.20
46	Reggie Jackson	1.25
47	Billy Williams	.20
48	Lou Brock	.20
49	Gaylord Perry	.20
50	Ted Williams	2.00
51	Brooks Robinson	.50
52	Bob Gibson	.20
53	Bobby Bonds	.10
54	Robin Roberts	.20

FanFest Gold

One out of every 60 sets of Upper Deck FanFest All-Stars was produced with gold-foil printing highlights rather than silver. The sets were randomly inserted into cases.

	NM/M
Complete Set (54):	30.00
Common Player:	.25

FanFest Ted Williams Super

This large-format (8-1/2" x 11") card is essentially an enlargement of Ted Williams' card issued with the FanFest All-Star Heroes boxed set by UD. The Williams super cards were distributed at the FanFest event and are serially numbered on back within an edition of 2,500.

Ted Williams   25.00

MVP Holograms

State of the art holography is presented in this 54-card plastic-cased set featuring a top pitcher and a top position player from each major league team, plus 1991 MVPs Terry Pendleton and Cal Ripken, Jr. The hologram on the front of each card feature a closeup and a field-action photo of the player; his name and position are in a strip at bottom. Full-color backs have a player photo on the right and career summary on the left. A custom album for the set was available via a mail offer for $10. Each set includes a numbered certificate of authenticity, verifying its position within a total issue of 216,000 sets.

		NM/M
Complete Set (54):		6.00
Common Player:		.10
1	A.L. Checklist (Cal Ripken, Jr.)	.40
2	N.L. Checkklist (Terry Pendleton)	.10
3	Jim Abbott	.10
4	Roberto Alomar	.25
5	Kevin Appier	.10
6	Steve Avery	.10
7	Jeff Bagwell	.40
8	Albert Belle	.10
9	Andy Benes	.10
10	Wade Boggs	.50
11	Barry Bonds	1.00
12	George Brett	.60
13	Ivan Calderon	.10
14	Jose Canseco	.30
15	Will Clark	.10
16	Roger Clemens	.60
17	David Cone	.10
18	Doug Drabek	.10
19	Dennis Eckersley	.35
20	Scott Erickson	.10
21	Cecil Fielder	.10
22	Ken Griffey Jr.	.75
23	Bill Gullickson	.10
24	Juan Guzman	.10
25	Pete Harnisch	.10
26	Howard Johnson	.10
27	Randy Johnson	.40
28	John Kruk	.10
29	Barry Larkin	.10
30	Greg Maddux	.50
31	Dennis Martinez	.10
32	Ramon Martinez	.10
33	Don Mattingly	.60
34	Jack McDowell	.10
35	Fred McGriff	.10
36	Paul Molitor	.40
37	Charles Nagy	.10
38	Gregg Olson	.10
39	Terry Pendleton	.10
40	Luis Polonia	.10
41	Kirby Puckett	.50
42	Dave Righetti	.10
43	Jose Rijo	.10
44	Cal Ripken, Jr.	1.00
45	Nolan Ryan	1.00
46	Ryne Sandberg	.50
47	Scott Sanderson	.10
48	Ruben Sierra	.10
49	Lee Smith	.10
50	Ozzie Smith	.50
51	Darryl Strawberry	.10
52	Frank Thomas	.40
53	Bill Wegman	.10
54	Mitch Williams	.10

Comic Ball 3

The third series of Comic Ball cards was issued in 1992 and was the second to combine photos of real ballplayers with Looney Tune cartoon characters in several cartoon strip-style series. Players featured in the set with Bugs, Taz and the gang were Jim Abbott and the Ken Griffeys, Sr. and Jr. Each of the 198 regular cards features a puzzle-piece back. A special album to house the set was sold separately. A series of holograms which also combined the players and cartoon figures was issued as pack inserts.

	NM/M
Complete Set (198):	6.00
Common Card:	.05
Hologram:	1.00

Comic Ball 3 Holograms

These blank-back holograms which combine player pictures with those of cartoon characters were issued as inserts in Comic Ball 3 foil packs.

		NM/M
Common Hologram:		.50
(1)	Jim Abbott (w/Tweety)	1.00
(2)	Jim Abbott (w/Taz)	1.00
(3)	Ken Griffey Jr. (w/Bugs)	2.00
(4)	Ken Griffey Jr. (w/Wile E. Coyote)	2.00
(5)	Chuck Jones/Artist (w/Bugs)	.50

1993 Upper Deck

Upper Deck introduced its 1993 set in a two-series format to adjust to expansion. Cards 1-420 make up the first series. Special subsets in Series 1 include rookies, teammates and community heroes. Fronts feature color player photos surrounded by a white border. Backs feature vertical photos, a change from the past, and more complete statistics than Upper Deck had in the past. The hologram appears in the lower-left corner on the card back. One out of 20 factory sets featured cards with gold, rather than silver, holograms.

	NM/M
Unopened Fact. Set (840):	30.00
Complete Set (840):	25.00
Common Player:	.05
Gold Hologram:	4X
Series 1 or 2 Pack (15):	.75
Series 1 or 2 Wax Box (36):	17.50
Jumbo Pack, USA (27):	1.50
Jumbo Box, USA (20):	17.50
Jumbo Pack, Canada (23):	2.00
Jumbo Box, Canada (20):	20.00
1	Tim Salmon (Checklist)	.05
2	Mike Piazza (Star Rookie)	1.25
3	Rene Arocha RC (Star Rookie)	.05
4	Willie Greene RC (Star Rookie)	.05
5	Manny Alexander RC (Star Rookie)	.05
6	Dan Wilson (Star Rookie)	.05
7	Dan Smith RC (Star Rookie)	.05
8	Kevin Rogers RC (Star Rookie)	.05
9	Nigel Wilson RC (Star Rookie)	.05
10	Joe Vitko RC (Star Rookie)	.05
11	Tim Costo RC (Star Rookie)	.05
12	Alan Embree RC (Star Rookie)	.05
13	Jim Tatum RC (Star Rookie)	.05
14	Cris Colon RC (Star Rookie)	.05
15	Steve Hosey RC (Star Rookie)	.05
16	Sterling Hitchcock RC (Star Rookie)	.15
17	Dave Mlicki RC (Star Rookie)	.05
18	Jessie Hollins RC (Star Rookie)	.05
19	Bobby J. Jones RC (Star Rookie)	.05
20	Kurt Miller RC (Star Rookie)	.05
21	Melvin Nieves RC (Star Rookie)	.05
22	Billy Ashley RC (Star Rookie)	.05
23	J.T. Snow RC (Star Rookie)	.50
24	Chipper Jones (Star Rookie)	.85
25	Tim Salmon (Star Rookie)	.25
26	Tim Pugh RC (Star Rookie)	.05
27	David Nied (Star Rookie)	.05
28	Mike Trombley RC (Star Rookie)	.05
29	Javier Lopez (Star Rookie)	.05
30	Community Heroes Checklist (Jim Abbott)	.05
31	Jim Abbott (Community Heroes)	.05
32	Dale Murphy (Community Heroes)	.10
33	Tony Pena (Community Heroes)	.05
34	Kirby Puckett (Community Heroes)	.40
35	Harold Reynolds (Community Heroes)	.05
36	Cal Ripken, Jr. (Community Heroes)	.65
37	Nolan Ryan (Community Heroes)	.65
38	Ryne Sandberg (Community Heroes)	.35
39	Dave Stewart (Community Heroes)	.05
40	Dave Winfield (Community Heroes)	.25
41	Teammates Checklist (Joe Carter, Mark McGwire)	.50
42	Blockbuster Trade (Joe Carter, Roberto Alomar)	.05
43	Brew Crew (Pat Listach, Robin Yount, Paul Molitor)	.15
44	Iron and Steal (Brady Anderson, Cal Ripken, Jr.)	.45
45	Youthful Tribe (Albert Belle, Sandy Alomar Jr., Jim Thome, Carlos Baerga, Kenny Lofton)	.25
46	Motown Mashers (Cecil Fielder, Mickey Tettleton)	.05
47	Yankee Pride (Roberto Kelly, Don Mattingly)	.45
48	Boston Cy Sox (Frank Viola, Roger Clemens)	.30
49	Bash Brothers (Ruben Sierra, Mark McGwire)	.50
50	Twin Titles (Kent Hrbek, Kirby Puckett)	.35
51	Southside Sluggers (Robin Ventura, Frank Thomas)	.35
52	Latin Stars (Jose Canseco, Ivan Rodriguez, Rafael Palmeiro, Juan Gonzalez)	.35
53	Lethal Lefties (Mark Langston, Jim Abbott, Chuck Finley)	.05
54	Royal Family (Gregg Jefferies, George Brett, Wally Joyner)	.35
55	Pacific Sox Exchange (Kevin Mitchell, Jay Buhner, Ken Griffey Jr.)	.40
56	George Brett	.85
57	Scott Cooper	.05
58	Mike Maddux	.05
59	Rusty Meacham RC	.05
60	Wil Cordero	.05
61	Tim Teufel	.05
62	Jeff Montgomery	.05
63	Scott Livingstone RC	.05
64	Doug Dascenzo	.05
65	Bret Boone	.05
66	Tim Wakefield RC	.10
67	Curt Schilling	.20
68	Frank Tanana	.05
69	Len Dykstra	.05
70	Derek Lilliquist	.05
71	Anthony Young RC	.05
72	Hipolito Pichardo RC	.05
73	Rod Beck RC	.05
74	Kent Hrbek	.05
75	Tom Glavine	.20
76	Kevin Brown	.05
77	Chuck Finley	.05
78	Bob Walk	.05
79	Rheal Cormier	.05
80	Rick Sutcliffe	.05
81	Harold Baines	.05
82	Lee Smith	.05
83	Geno Petralli	.05
84	Jose Oquendo	.05
85	Mark Gubicza	.05
86	Mickey Tettleton	.05
87	Bobby Witt	.05
88	Mark Lewis	.05
89	Kevin Appier	.05
90	Mike Stanton	.05
91	Rafael Belliard	.05
92	Kenny Rogers	.05
93	Randy Velarde	.05
94	Luis Sojo	.05
95	Mark Leiter	.05
96	Jody Reed	.05
97	Pete Harnisch	.05
98	Tom Candiotti	.05
99	Mark Portugal	.05
100	Dave Valle	.05
101	Shawon Dunston	.05
102	B.J. Surhoff	.05
103	Jay Bell	.05
104	Sid Bream	.05
105	Checklist 1-105 (Frank Thomas)	.35
106	Mike Morgan	.05
107	Bill Doran	.05
108	Lance Blankenship	.05
109	Mark Lemke	.05
110	Brian Harper	.05
111	Brady Anderson	.05
112	Bip Roberts	.05
113	Mitch Williams	.05
114	Craig Biggio	.05
115	Eddie Murray	.65
116	Matt Nokes	.05
117	Lance Parrish	.05
118	Bill Swift	.05
119	Jeff Innis	.05
120	Mike LaValliere	.05
121	Hal Morris	.05
122	Walt Weiss	.05
123	Ivan Rodriguez	.60
124	Andy Van Slyke	.05
125	Roberto Alomar	.20
126	Robby Thompson	.05
127	Sammy Sosa	.75
128	Mark Langston	.05
129	Jerry Browne	.05
130	Chuck McElroy	.05
131	Frank Viola	.05
132	Leo Gomez	.05
133	Ramon Martinez	.05
134	Don Mattingly	.85
135	Roger Clemens	.85
136	Rickey Henderson	.65
137	Darren Daulton	.05
138	Ken Hill	.05
139	Ozzie Guillen	.05
140	Jerald Clark	.05
141	Dave Fleming	.05
142	Delino DeShields	.05
143	Matt Williams	.05
144	Larry Walker	.05
145	Ruben Sierra	.05
146	Ozzie Smith	.75
147	Chris Sabo	.05
148	Carlos Hernandez RC	.05
149	Pat Borders	.05
150	Orlando Merced	.05
151	Royce Clayton	.05
152	Kurt Stillwell	.05
153	Dave Hollins	.05
154	Mike Greenwell	.05
155	Nolan Ryan	1.50
156	Felix Jose	.05
157	Junior Felix	.05
158	Derek Bell	.05
159	Steve Buechele	.05
160	John Burkett	.05
161	Pat Howell RC	.05
162	Milt Cuyler	.05
163	Terry Pendleton	.05
164	Jack Morris	.05

#	Player	Price
165	Tony Gwynn	.75
166	Deion Sanders	.10
167	Mike Devereaux	.05
168	Ron Darling	.05
169	Orel Hershiser	.05
170	Mike Jackson	.05
171	Doug Jones	.05
172	Dan Walters RC	.05
173	Darren Lewis	.05
174	Carlos Baerga	.05
175	Ryne Sandberg	.75
176	Gregg Jefferies	.05
177	John Jaha	.05
178	Luis Polonia	.05
179	Kirt Manwaring	.05
180	Mike Magnante	.05
181	Billy Ripken	.05
182	Mike Moore	.05
183	Eric Anthony	.05
184	Lenny Harris	.05
185	Tony Pena	.05
186	Mike Felder	.05
187	Greg Olson	.05
188	Rene Gonzales	.05
189	Mike Bordick	.05
190	Mel Rojas	.05
191	Todd Frohwirth	.05
192	Darryl Hamilton	.05
193	Mike Fetters	.05
194	Omar Olivares RC	.05
195	Tony Phillips	.05
196	Paul Sorrento	.05
197	Trevor Wilson	.05
198	Kevin Gross	.05
199	Ron Karkovice	.05
200	Brook Jacoby	.05
201	Mariano Duncan	.05
202	Dennis Cook	.05
203	Daryl Boston	.05
204	Mike Perez	.05
205	Manuel Lee	.05
206	Steve Olin	.05
207	Charlie Hough	.05
208	Scott Scudder	.05
209	Charlie O'Brien	.05
210	Checklist 106-210 (Barry Bonds)	.60
211	Jose Vizcaino	.05
212	Scott Leius	.05
213	Kevin Mitchell	.05
214	Brian Barnes	.05
215	Pat Kelly	.05
216	Chris Hammond	.05
217	Rob Deer	.05
218	Cory Snyder	.05
219	Gary Carter	.65
220	Danny Darwin	.05
221	Tom Gordon	.05
222	Gary Sheffield	.40
223	Joe Carter	.05
224	Jay Buhner	.05
225	Jose Offerman	.05
226	Jose Rijo	.05
227	Mark Whiten	.05
228	Randy Milligan	.05
229	Bud Black	.05
230	Gary DiSarcina	.05
231	Steve Finley	.05
232	Dennis Martinez	.05
233	Mike Mussina	.30
234	Joe Oliver	.05
235	Chad Curtis	.05
236	Shane Mack	.05
237	Jaime Navarro	.05
238	Brian McRae	.05
239	Chili Davis	.05
240	Jeff King	.05
241	Dean Palmer	.05
242	Danny Tartabull	.05
243	Charles Nagy	.05
244	Ray Lankford	.05
245	Barry Larkin	.05
246	Steve Avery	.05
247	John Kruk	.05
248	Derrick May	.05
249	Stan Javier	.05
250	Roger McDowell	.05
251	Dan Gladden	.05
252	Wally Joyner	.05
253	Pat Listach	.05
254	Chuck Knoblauch	.05
255	Sandy Alomar Jr.	.05
256	Jeff Bagwell	.65
257	Andy Stankiewicz	.05
258	Darrin Jackson	.05
259	Brett Butler	.05
260	Joe Orsulak	.05
261	Andy Benes	.05
262	Kenny Lofton	.05
263	Robin Ventura	.05
264	Ron Gant	.05
265	Ellis Burks	.05
266	Juan Guzman	.05
267	Wes Chamberlain	.05
268	John Smiley	.05
269	Franklin Stubbs	.05
270	Tom Browning	.05
271	Dennis Eckersley	.60
272	Carlton Fisk	.65
273	Lou Whitaker	.05
274	Phil Plantier	.05
275	Bobby Bonilla	.05
276	Ben McDonald	.05
277	Bob Zupcic	.05
278	Terry Steinbach	.05
279	Terry Mulholland	.05
280	Lance Johnson	.05
281	Willie McGee	.05
282	Bret Saberhagen	.05
283	Randy Myers	.05
284	Randy Tomlin	.05
285	Mickey Morandini	.05
286	Brian Williams	.05
287	Tino Martinez	.05
288	Jose Melendez	.05
289	Jeff Huson	.05
290	Joe Grahe	.05
291	Mel Hall	.05
292	Otis Nixon	.05
293	Todd Hundley	.05
294	Casey Candaele	.05
295	Kevin Seitzer	.05
296	Eddie Taubensee	.05
297	Moises Alou	.05
298	Scott Radinsky	.05
299	Thomas Howard	.05
300	Kyle Abbott	.05
301	Omar Vizquel	.05
302	Keith Miller	.05
303	Rick Aguilera	.05
304	Bruce Hurst	.05
305	Ken Caminiti	.05
306	Mike Pagliarulo	.05
307	Frank Seminara	.05
308	Andre Dawson	.30
309	Jose Lind	.05
310	Joe Boever	.05
311	Jeff Parrett RC	.05
312	Alan Mills	.05
313	Kevin Tapani	.05
314	Darryl Kile	.05
315	Checklist 211-315 (Will Clark)	.05
316	Mike Sharperson	.05
317	John Orton	.05
318	Bob Tewksbury	.05
319	Xavier Hernandez	.05
320	Paul Assenmacher	.05
321	John Franco	.05
322	Mike Timlin	.05
323	Jose Guzman	.05
324	Pedro Martinez	.65
325	Bill Spiers	.05
326	Melido Perez	.05
327	Mike Macfarlane	.05
328	Ricky Bones	.05
329	Scott Bankhead	.05
330	Rich Rodriguez	.05
331	Geronimo Pena	.05
332	Bernie Williams	.05
333	Paul Molitor	.65
334	Roger Mason	.05
335	David Cone	.05
336	Randy Johnson	.65
337	Pat Mahomes	.05
338	Erik Hanson	.05
339	Duane Ward	.05
340	Al Martin	.05
341	Pedro Munoz	.05
342	Greg Colbrunn	.05
343	Julio Valera	.05
344	John Olerud	.05
345	George Bell	.05
346	Devon White	.05
347	Donovan Osborne	.05
348	Mark Gardner	.05
349	Zane Smith	.05
350	Wilson Alvarez	.05
351	Kevin Koslofski RC	.05
352	Roberto Hernandez	.05
353	Glenn Davis	.05
354	Reggie Sanders	.05
355	Ken Griffey Jr.	1.00
355a	Ken Griffey Jr. (Promo, 1992-dated hologram on back.)	3.00
355b	Ken Griffey Jr. (8-1/2" x 11" limited edition of 1,000)	15.00
356	Marquis Grissom	.05
357	Jack McDowell	.05
358	Jimmy Key	.05
359	Stan Belinda	.05
360	Gerald Williams	.05
361	Sid Fernandez	.05
362	Alex Fernandez	.05
363	John Smoltz	.05
364	Travis Fryman	.05
365	Jose Canseco	.50
366	Dave Justice	.05
367	Pedro Astacio RC	.10
368	Tim Belcher	.05
369	Steve Sax	.05
370	Gary Gaetti	.05
371	Jeff Frye	.05
372	Bob Wickman	.05
373	Ryan Thompson RC	.05
374	David Hulse RC	.05
375	Cal Eldred	.05
376	Ryan Klesko	.05
377	Damion Easley RC	.10
378	John Kiely RC	.05
379	Jim Bullinger RC	.05
380	Brian Bohanon	.05
381	Rod Brewer	.05
382	Fernando Ramsey RC	.05
383	Sam Militello	.05
384	Arthur Rhodes	.05
385	Eric Karros	.05
386	Rico Brogna	.05
387	John Valentin RC	.10
388	Kerry Woodson RC	.05
389	Ben Rivera RC	.05
390	Matt Whiteside RC	.05
391	Henry Rodriguez	.05
392	John Wetteland	.05
393	Kent Mercker	.05
394	Bernard Gilkey	.05
395	Doug Henry	.05
396	Mo Vaughn	.05
397	Scott Erickson	.05
398	Bill Gullickson	.05
399	Mark Guthrie	.05
400	Dave Martinez	.05
401	Jeff Kent RC	.50
402	Chris Hoiles	.05
403	Mike Henneman	.05
404	Chris Nabholz	.05
405	Tom Pagnozzi	.05
406	Kelly Gruber	.05
407	Bob Welch	.05
408	Frank Castillo	.05
409	John Dopson	.05
410	Steve Farr	.05
411	Henry Cotto	.05
412	Bob Patterson	.05
413	Todd Stottlemyre	.05
414	Greg A. Harris	.05
415	Denny Neagle	.05
416	Bill Wegman	.05
417	Willie Wilson	.05
418	Terry Leach	.05
419	Willie Randolph	.05
420	Checklist 316-420 (Mark McGwire)	.65
421	Calvin Murray (Top Prospects Checklist)	.05
422	Pete Janicki RC (Top Prospect)	.05
423	Todd Jones RC (Top Prospect)	.05
424	Mike Neill (Top Prospect)	.05
425	Carlos Delgado (Top Prospect)	.40
426	Jose Oliva (Top Prospect)	.05
427	Tyrone Hill (Top Prospect)	.05
428	Dmitri Young (Top Prospect)	.05
429	Derek Wallace RC (Top Prospect)	.05
430	Michael Moore RC (Top Prospect)	.05
431	Cliff Floyd (Top Prospect)	.05
432	Calvin Murray (Top Prospect)	.05
433	Manny Ramirez (Top Prospect)	.75
434	Marc Newfield (Top Prospect)	.05
435	Charles Johnson (Top Prospect)	.05
436	Butch Huskey (Top Prospect)	.05
437	Brad Pennington (Top Prospect)	.05
438	Ray McDavid RC (Top Prospect)	.05
439	Chad McConnell (Top Prospect)	.05
440	Midre Cummings RC (Top Prospect)	.05
441	Benji Gil (Top Prospect)	.05
442	Frank Rodriguez (Top Prospect)	.05
443	Chad Mottola RC (Top Prospect)	.05
444	John Burke RC (Top Prospect)	.05
445	Michael Tucker (Top Prospect)	.05
446	Rick Greene (Top Prospect)	.05
447	Rich Becker (Top Prospect)	.05
448	Mike Robertson (Top Prospect)	.05
449	Derek Jeter RC (Top Prospect)	10.00
450	Checklist 451-470 Inside the Numbers (David McCarty, Ivan Rodriguez)	.05
451	Jim Abbott (Inside the Numbers)	.05
452	Jeff Bagwell (Inside the Numbers)	.40
453	Jason Bere (Inside the Numbers)	.05
454	Delino DeShields (Inside the Numbers)	.05
455	Travis Fryman (Inside the Numbers)	.05
456	Alex Gonzalez (Inside the Numbers)	.05
457	Phil Hiatt (Inside the Numbers)	.05
458	Dave Hollins (Inside the Numbers)	.05
459	Chipper Jones (Inside the Numbers)	.65
460	Dave Justice (Inside the Numbers)	.05
461	Ray Lankford (Inside the Numbers)	.05
462	David McCarty (Inside the Numbers)	.05
463	Mike Mussina (Inside the Numbers)	.15
464	Jose Offerman (Inside the Numbers)	.05
465	Dean Palmer (Inside the Numbers)	.05
466	Geronimo Pena (Inside the Numbers)	.05
467	Eduardo Perez (Inside the Numbers)	.05
468	Ivan Rodriguez (Inside the Numbers)	.25
469	Reggie Sanders (Inside the Numbers)	.05
470	Bernie Williams (Inside the Numbers)	.05
471	Checklist 472-485 Team Stars (Barry Bonds, Matt Williams, Will Clark)	.45
472	Strike Force (John Smoltz, Steve Avery, Greg Maddux, Tom Glavine)	.10
473	Red October (Jose Rijo, Rob Dibble, Roberto Kelly, Reggie Sanders, Barry Larkin)	.10
474	Four Corners (Gary Sheffield, Phil Plantier, Tony Gwynn, Fred McGriff)	.20
475	Shooting Stars (Doug Drabek, Craig Biggio, Jeff Bagwell)	.15
476	Giant Sticks (Will Clark, Barry Bonds, Matt Williams)	.40
477	Boyhood Friends (Darryl Strawberry, Eric Davis)	.05
478	Rock Solid (Dante Bichette, David Nied, Andres Galarraga)	.05
479	Inaugural Catch (Dave Magadan, Orestes Destrade, Bret Barbarie, Jeff Conine)	.05
480	Steel City Champions (Tim Wakefield, Andy Van Slyke, Jay Bell)	.05
481	"Les Grandes Etoiles" (Marquis Grissom, Delino DeShields, Dennis Martinez, Larry Walker)	.05
482	Runnin' Redbirds (Geronimo Pena, Ray Lankford, Ozzie Smith, Bernard Gilkey)	.10
483	Ivy Leaguers (Ryne Sandberg, Mark Grace, Randy Myers)	.15
484	Big Apple Power Switch (Eddie Murray, Bobby Bonilla, Howard Johnson)	.10
485	Hammers & Nails (John Kruk, Dave Hollins, Darren Daulton, Len Dykstra)	.05
486	Barry Bonds (Award Winners)	.60
487	Dennis Eckersley (Award Winners)	.30
488	Greg Maddux (Award Winners)	.40
489	Dennis Eckersley (Award Winners)	.30
490	Eric Karros (Award Winners)	.05
491	Pat Listach (Award Winners)	.05
492	Gary Sheffield (Award Winners)	.10
493	Mark McGwire (Award Winners)	.75
494	Gary Sheffield (Award Winners)	.10
495	Edgar Martinez (Award Winners)	.05
496	Fred McGriff (Award Winners)	.05
497	Juan Gonzalez (Award Winners)	.20
498	Darren Daulton (Award Winners)	.05
499	Cecil Fielder (Award Winners)	.05
500	Checklist 501-510 Diamond Debuts (Brent Gates)	.05
501	Tavo Alvarez (Diamond Debuts)	.05
502	Rod Bolton (Diamond Debuts)	.05
503	John Cummings RC (Diamond Debuts)	.05
504	Brent Gates (Diamond Debuts)	.05
505	Tyler Green (Diamond Debuts)	.05
506	Jose Martinez RC (Diamond Debuts)	.05
507	Troy Percival (Diamond Debuts)	.05
508	Kevin Stocker (Diamond Debuts)	.05
509	Matt Walbeck RC (Diamond Debuts)	.10
510	Rondell White (Diamond Debuts)	.05
511	Billy Ripken	.05
512	Mike Moore	.05
513	Jose Lind	.05
514	Chito Martinez	.05
515	Jose Guzman	.05
516	Kim Batiste	.05
517	Jeff Tackett	.05
518	Charlie Hough	.05
519	Marvin Freeman	.05
520	Carlos Martinez	.05
521	Eric Young	.05
522	Pete Incaviglia	.05
523	Scott Fletcher	.05
524	Orestes Destrade	.05
525	Checklist 421-525 (Ken Griffey Jr.)	.40
526	Ellis Burks	.05
527	Juan Samuel	.05
528	Dave Magadan	.05
529	Jeff Parrett	.05
530	Bill Krueger	.05
531	Frank Bolick	.05
532	Alan Trammell	.05
533	Walt Weiss	.05
534	David Cone	.05
535	Greg Maddux	.75
536	Kevin Young	.05
537	Dave Hansen	.05
538	Alex Cole	.05
539	Greg Hibbard	.05
540	Gene Larkin	.05
541	Jeff Reardon	.05
542	Felix Jose	.05
543	Jimmy Key	.05
544	Reggie Jefferson	.05
545	Gregg Jefferies	.05
546	Dave Stewart	.05
547	Tim Wallach	.05
548	Spike Owen	.05
549	Tommy Greene	.05
550	Fernando Valenzuela	.05
551	Rich Amaral	.05
552	Bret Barberie	.05
553	Edgar Martinez	.05
554	Jim Abbott	.05
555	Frank Thomas	.65
556	Wade Boggs	.75
557	Tom Henke	.05
558	Milt Thompson	.05
559	Lloyd McClendon	.05
560	Vinny Castilla	.05
561	Ricky Jordan	.05
562	Andujar Cedeno	.05
563	Greg Vaughn	.05
564	Cecil Fielder	.05
565	Kirby Puckett	.75
566	Mark McGwire	1.25
567	Barry Bonds	1.50
568	Jody Reed	.05
569	Todd Zeile	.05
570	Mark Carreon	.05
571	Joe Girardi	.05
572	Luis Gonzalez	.05
573	Mark Grace	.05
574	Rafael Palmeiro	.60
575	Darryl Strawberry	.05
576	Will Clark	.05
577	Fred McGriff	.05
578	Kevin Reimer	.05
579	Dave Righetti	.05
580	Juan Bell	.05
581	Jeff Brantley	.05
582	Brian Hunter	.05
583	Tim Naehring	.05
584	Glenallen Hill	.05
585	Cal Ripken, Jr.	1.50
586	Albert Belle	.05
587	Robin Yount	.65
588	Chris Bosio	.05
589	Pete Smith	.05
590	Chuck Carr	.05
591	Jeff Blauser	.05
592	Kevin McReynolds	.05
593	Andres Galarraga	.05
594	Kevin Maas	.05
595	Eric Davis	.05
596	Brian Jordan	.05
597	Tim Raines	.05
598	Rick Wilkins	.05
599	Steve Cooke	.05
600	Mike Gallego	.05
601	Mike Munoz	.05
602	Luis Rivera	.05
603	Junior Ortiz	.05
604	Brent Mayne	.05
605	Luis Alicea	.05
606	Damon Berryhill	.05
607	Dave Henderson	.05
608	Kirk McCaskill	.05
609	Jeff Fassero	.05
610	Mike Harkey	.05
611	Francisco Cabrera	.05
612	Rey Sanchez	.05
613	Scott Servais	.05
614	Darrin Fletcher	.05
615	Felix Fermin	.05
616	Kevin Seitzer	.05
617	Bob Scanlan	.05
618	Billy Hatcher	.05
619	John Vander Wal	.05
620	Joe Hesketh	.05
621	Hector Villanueva	.05
622	Randy Milligan	.05
623	Tony Tarasco RC	.05
624	Russ Swan	.05
625	Willie Wilson	.05
626	Frank Tanana	.05
627	Pete O'Brien	.05
628	Lenny Webster	.05
629	Mark Clark	.05
630	Checklist 526-630 (Roger Clemens)	.40
631	Alex Arias	.05
632	Chris Gwynn	.05
633	Tom Bolton	.05
634	Greg Briley	.05
635	Kent Bottenfield	.05
636	Kelly Downs	.05
637	Manuel Lee	.05
638	Al Leiter	.05
639	Jeff Gardner	.05
640	Mike Gardiner	.05
641	Mark Gardner	.05
642	Jeff Branson	.05
643	Paul Wagner	.05
644	Sean Berry	.05
645	Phil Hiatt	.05
646	Kevin Mitchell	.05
647	Charlie Hayes	.05
648	Jim Deshaies	.05
649	Dan Pasqua	.05
650	Mike Maddux	.05
651	Domingo Martinez RC	.05
652	Greg McMichael RC	.05
653	Eric Wedge RC	.05
654	Mark Whiten	.05
655	Bobby Kelly	.05
656	Julio Franco	.05
657	Gene Harris	.05
658	Pete Schourek	.05
659	Mike Bielecki	.05
660	Ricky Gutierrez	.05
661	Chris Hammond	.05
662	Tim Scott	.05
663	Norm Charlton	.05
664	Doug Drabek	.05
665	Dwight Gooden	.05
666	Jim Gott	.05
667	Randy Myers	.05
668	Darren Holmes	.05
669	Tim Spehr	.05
670	Bruce Ruffin	.05
671	Bobby Thigpen	.05
672	Tony Fernandez	.05
673	Darrin Jackson	.05
674	Gregg Olson	.05
675	Rob Dibble	.05
676	Howard Johnson	.05
677	Mike Lansing RC	.15
678	Charlie Leibrandt	.05
679	Kevin Bass	.05
680	Hubie Brooks	.05
681	Scott Brosius	.05
682	Randy Knorr	.05
683	Dante Bichette	.05
684	Bryan Harvey	.05
685	Greg Gohr	.05
686	Willie Banks	.05
687	Robb Nen	.05
688	Mike Scioscia	.05
689	John Farrell	.05
690	John Candelaria	.05
691	Damon Buford	.05
692	Todd Worrell	.05
693	Pat Hentgen	.05
694	John Smiley	.05
695	Greg Swindell	.05
696	Derek Bell	.05
697	Terry Jorgensen	.05
698	Jimmy Jones	.05
699	David Wells	.05
700	Dave Martinez	.05
701	Steve Bedrosian	.05
702	Jeff Russell	.05
703	Joe Magrane	.05
704	Matt Mieske	.05
705	Paul Molitor	.65
706	Dale Murphy	.15
707	Steve Howe	.05
708	Greg Gagne	.05
709	Dave Eiland	.05
710	David West	.05
711	Luis Aquino	.05
712	Joe Orsulak	.05
713	Eric Plunk	.05
714	Mike Felder	.05
715	Joe Klink	.05
716	Lonnie Smith	.05
717	Monty Fariss	.05
718	Craig Lefferts	.05
719	John Habyan	.05
720	Willie Blair	.05
721	Darnell Coles	.05
722	Mark Williamson	.05
723	Bryn Smith	.05
724	Greg W. Harris	.05
725	Graeme Lloyd RC	.05
726	Cris Carpenter	.05
727	Chico Walker	.05
728	Tracy Woodson	.05
729	Jose Uribe	.05
730	Stan Javier	.05
731	Jay Howell	.05
732	Freddie Benavides	.05
733	Jeff Reboulet	.05
734	Scott Sanderson	.05
735	Checklist 631-735 (Ryne Sandberg)	.20
736	Archi Cianfrocco	.05
737	Daryl Boston	.05
738	Craig Grebeck	.05
739	Doug Dascenzo	.05
740	Gerald Young	.05
741	Candy Maldonado	.05

742	Joey Cora	.05
743	Don Slaught	.05
744	Steve Decker	.05
745	Blas Minor	.05
746	Storm Davis	.05
747	Carlos Quintana	.05
748	Vince Coleman	.05
749	Todd Burns	.05
750	Steve Frey	.05
751	Ivan Calderon	.05
752	Steve Reed RC	.05
753	Danny Jackson	.05
754	Jeff Conine	.05
755	Juan Gonzalez	.35
756	Mike Kelly	.05
757	John Doherty	.05
758	Jack Armstrong	.05
759	John Wehner	.05
760	Scott Bankhead	.05
761	Jim Tatum	.05
762	Scott Pose RC	.05
763	Andy Ashby	.05
764	Ed Sprague	.05
765	Harold Baines	.05
766	Kirk Gibson	.05
767	Troy Neel	.05
768	Dick Schofield	.05
769	Dickie Thon	.05
770	Butch Henry	.05
771	Junior Felix	.05
772	Ken Ryan RC	.05
773	Trevor Hoffman	.05
774	Phil Plantier	.05
775	Bo Jackson	.10
776	Benito Santiago	.05
777	Andre Dawson	.25
778	Bryan Hickerson	.05
779	Dennis Moeller	.05
780	Ryan Bowen	.05
781	Eric Fox	.05
782	Joe Kmak	.05
783	Mike Hampton	.05
784	Darrell Sherman RC	.05
785	J.T. Snow	.05
786	Dave Winfield	.65
787	Jim Austin	.05
788	Craig Shipley	.05
789	Greg Myers	.05
790	Todd Benzinger	.05
791	Cory Snyder	.05
792	David Segui	.05
793	Armando Reynoso	.05
794	Chili Davis	.05
795	Dave Nilsson	.05
796	Paul O'Neill	.05
797	Jerald Clark	.05
798	Jose Mesa	.05
799	Brian Holman	.05
800	Jim Eisenreich	.05
801	Mark McLemore	.05
802	Luis Sojo	.05
803	Harold Reynolds	.05
804	Dan Plesac	.05
805	Dave Stieb	.05
806	Tom Brunansky	.05
807	Kelly Gruber	.05
808	Bob Ojeda	.05
809	Dave Burba	.05
810	Joe Boever	.05
811	Jeremy Hernandez	.05
812	Angels Checklist (Tim Salmon)	.05
813	Astros Checklist (Jeff Bagwell)	.35
814	Athletics Checklist (Mark McGwire)	.75
815	Blue Jays Checklist (Roberto Alomar)	.10
816	Braves Checklist (Steve Avery)	.05
817	Brewers Checklist (Pat Listach)	.05
818	Cardinals Checklist (Gregg Jefferies)	.05
819	Cubs Checklist (Sammy Sosa)	.40
820	Dodgers Checklist (Darryl Strawberry)	.05
821	Expos Checklist (Dennis Martinez)	.05
822	Giants Checklist (Robby Thompson)	.05
823	Indians Checklist (Albert Belle)	.05
824	Mariners Checklist (Randy Johnson)	.30
825	Marlins Checklist (Nigel Wilson)	.05
826	Mets Checklist (Bobby Bonilla)	.05
827	Orioles Checklist (Glenn Davis)	.05
828	Padres Checklist (Gary Sheffield)	.10
829	Phillies Checklist (Darren Daulton)	.05
830	Pirates Checklist (Jay Bell)	.05
831	Rangers Checklist (Juan Gonzalez)	.20
832	Red Sox Checklist (Andre Dawson)	.10
833	Reds Checklist (Hal Morris)	.05
834	Rockies Checklist (David Nied)	.05
835	Royals Checklist (Felix Jose)	.05

836	Tigers Checklist (Travis Fryman)	.05
837	Twins Checklist (Shane Mack)	.05
838	White Sox Checklist (Robin Ventura)	.05
839	Yankees Checklist (Danny Tartabull)	.05
840	Checklist 736-840 (Roberto Alomar)	.10
SP5	3,000 Hits (Robin Yount, George Brett)	.50
SP6	Nolan Ryan	1.50

Gold Holograms

Unlike 1992, when gold holograms were found on the back of every card originating in a factory set, in 1993 the use of gold holograms was limited to just one factory set per 20-set case, creating a scarce parallel version.

	NM/M
Complete Fact. Set (840):	200.00
Common Player:	.50

Baseball Heroes Reggie Jackson Supers

Upper Deck issued a large version of its 1990 Heroes Reggie Jackson cards that was available in retail outlets. Just as in the case of the regular issue Jackson insert cards, there are 10 cards (nine numbered and one unnumbered header card). The cards are 3-1/2" x 5" and identical to the smaller Heroes cards in every other respect. Each of the individual cards carries a sequential number out of a limit of 10,000. The cards were sold one to a package that also included two packs of 1993 Upper Deck cards for about $5.

	NM/M
Complete Set (10):	25.00
Common Card:	3.00
1	1969 Emerging Superstar (Reggie Jackson)	3.00
2	1973 An MVP Year (Reggie Jackson)	3.00
3	1977 "Mr. October" (Reggie Jackson)	3.00
4	1978 Jackson vs. Welch (Reggie Jackson)	3.00
5	1982 Under the Halo (Reggie Jackson)	3.00
6	1984 500! (Reggie Jackson)	3.00
7	1986 Moving Up the List (Reggie Jackson)	3.00
8	1987 A Great Career Ends (Reggie Jackson)	3.00
9	Heroes Checklist (Reggie Jackson)	3.00
---	Header Card	3.00

Baseball Heroes Willie Mays

This 10-card insert set includes eight individually-titled cards, an illustrated checklist and one header card. The set is a continuation of Upper Deck's previous Heroes efforts, honoring greats such as Hank Aaron, Nolan Ryan and Reggie Jackson, and is numbered 46-54. Cards were randomly inserted into Series 1 foil packs.

		NM/M
Complete Set (10):		4.00
Common Card:		.50
Header Card:		1.00
46	1951 Rookie-of-the-Year	.50
47	1954 The Catch	.50
48	1956-57 30-30 Club	.50
49	1961 Four-Homer Game	.50
50	1965 Most Valuable Player	.50
51	1969 600-Home Run Club	.50
52	1972 New York Homecoming	.50
53	1979 Hall of Fame	.50
54	Checklist - Heroes 46-54	.50

Clutch Performers

Reggie Jackson has selected the players who perform the best under pressure for this 20-card insert set. Cards were available only in Series II retail packs and use the prefix "R" for numbering. Fronts have a black bottom panel with "Clutch Performers" printed in dark gray. Jackson's facsimile autograph is overprinted in gold foil. On back, under a second player photo, is Jackson's picture and his assessment of the player. There are a few lines of stats to support the player's selection to this exclusive company.

		NM/M
Complete Set (20):		8.00
Common Player:		.25
1	Roberto Alomar	.30
2	Wade Boggs	1.00
3	Barry Bonds	2.50
4	Jose Canseco	.40
5	Joe Carter	.25
6	Will Clark	.25
7	Roger Clemens	1.25
8	Dennis Eckersley	.60
9	Cecil Fielder	.25
10	Juan Gonzalez	.60
11	Ken Griffey Jr.	2.00
12	Rickey Henderson	.75
13	Barry Larkin	.25
14	Don Mattingly	1.25
15	Fred McGriff	.25
16	Terry Pendleton	.25
17	Kirby Puckett	1.00
18	Ryne Sandberg	1.00
19	John Smoltz	.25
20	Frank Thomas	.75

Future Heroes

This insert set includes eight player cards, a checklist and an unnumbered header card. The cards are numbered 55-63 as a continuation of previous Heroes sets, but this one features more than one player; previous sets featured only one player. Card fronts have a Future Heroes logo and a facsimile autograph. The player's name is revealed using a peeled-back paper effect. Cards were randomly inserted in Series II foil packs.

	NM/M
Complete Set (10):	5.00
Common Player:	.50
Header Card:	.25
55	Roberto Alomar	.50
56	Barry Bonds	2.50
57	Roger Clemens	1.00
58	Juan Gonzalez	.50
59	Ken Griffey Jr.	1.50
60	Mark McGwire	2.00
61	Kirby Puckett	.85
62	Frank Thomas	.75
63	Checklist	.05

Highlights

These 20 insert cards commemorate highlights from the 1992 season. Cards, which were randomly inserted in Series II packs, have a '92 Season Highlights logo on the bottom, with the player's name inside a banner trailing from the logo. The date of the significant event is under the player's name. Card backs have the logo at the top and are numbered with an "HI" prefix. A headline describes what highlight occurred, while the text describes the event.

		NM/M
Complete Set (20):		20.00
Common Player:		.25
1	Roberto Alomar	.50
2	Steve Avery	.25
3	Harold Baines	.25
4	Damon Berryhill	.25
5	Barry Bonds	7.50
6	Bret Boone	.25
7	George Brett	4.00
8	Francisco Cabrera	.25
9	Ken Griffey Jr.	5.00
10	Rickey Henderson	2.00
11	Kenny Lofton	.25
12	Mickey Morandini	.25
13	Eddie Murray	2.00
14	David Nied	.25
15	Jeff Reardon	.25
16	Bip Roberts	.25
17	Nolan Ryan	7.50
18	Ed Sprague	.25
19	Dave Winfield	2.00
20	Robin Yount	2.00

Home Run Heroes

This 28-card insert set features the top home run hitters from each team for 1992.

Cards, inserted in Series I jumbo packs, are numbered with an "HR" prefix. The card fronts have "Home Run Heroes" printed vertically at the left edge and an embossed bat with the player's name and Upper Deck trademark at bottom. Backs have a purple or pink posterized photo and a few words about the player.

		NM/M
Complete Set (28):		7.50
Common Player:		.15
Header Card:		.25
1	Juan Gonzalez	.50
2	Mark McGwire	2.25
3	Cecil Fielder	.15
4	Fred McGriff	.15
5	Albert Belle	.15
6	Barry Bonds	2.50
7	Joe Carter	.15
8	Darren Daulton	.15
9	Ken Griffey Jr.	2.00
10	Dave Hollins	.15
11	Ryne Sandberg	1.00
12	George Bell	.15
13	Danny Tartabull	.15
14	Mike Devereaux	.15
15	Greg Vaughn	.15
16	Larry Walker	.15
17	Dave Justice	.15
18	Terry Pendleton	.15
19	Eric Karros	.15
20	Ray Lankford	.15
21	Matt Williams	.15
22	Eric Anthony	.15
23	Bobby Bonilla	.15
24	Kirby Puckett	1.00
25	Mike Macfarlane	.15
26	Tom Brunansky	.15
27	Paul O'Neill	.15
28	Gary Gaetti	.15

Looss Collection

Sports photographer Walter Iooss Jr. has captured 26 current players in this insert set featuring their candid portraits. Cards have full-bleed photos and gold foil stamping. Backs have biographical sketches and are numbered using a WI prefix. They are available in Series I retail packs.

		NM/M
Complete Set (27):		10.00
Common Player:		.25
Header Card:		.25
1	Tim Salmon	.25
2	Jeff Bagwell	.75
3	Mark McGwire	1.50
4	Roberto Alomar	.35
5	Steve Avery	.25
6	Paul Molitor	.75
7	Ozzie Smith	1.00
8	Mark Grace	.25
9	Eric Karros	.25
10	Delino DeShields	.25
11	Will Clark	.25
12	Albert Belle	.35
13	Ken Griffey Jr.	1.50
14	Howard Johnson	.25
15	Cal Ripken, Jr.	2.00
16	Fred McGriff	.25
17	Darren Daulton	.25
18	Andy Van Slyke	.25
19	Nolan Ryan	2.00
20	Wade Boggs	1.00
21	Barry Larkin	.25
22	George Brett	1.25
23	Cecil Fielder	.25
24	Kirby Puckett	1.00
25	Frank Thomas	.75
26	Don Mattingly	1.25

Looss Collection Supers

Upper Deck issued a series of 27 individually numbered oversized cards identical to the Iooss Collection inserts from the regular 1993 Upper Deck set. The cards are 3-1/2" x 5" and each is numbered on back to a limit of 10,000. The cards were available in retail outlets such as WalMart, packaged in blister packs with two foil packs of 1993 Upper Deck cards for around $5. Authetically autographed and numbered (on card fronts) of some players' cards were sold by Upper Deck Authenticated.

		NM/M
Complete Set (27):		20.00
Common Player:		.50
Header Card:		.25
1	Tim Salmon	.50
2	Jeff Bagwell	1.00
3	Mark McGwire	2.00
4	Roberto Alomar	.75
5	Steve Avery	.50
6	Paul Molitor	1.00
7	Ozzie Smith	1.25
8	Mark Grace	.50
9	Eric Karros	.50
10	Delino DeShields	.50
11	Will Clark	.50
12	Albert Belle	.50
13	Ken Griffey, Jr.	2.00
14	Howard Johnson	.50
15	Cal Ripken, Jr.	2.50
16	Fred McGriff	.50
17	Darren Daulton	.50
18	Andy Van Slyke	.50
19	Nolan Ryan	2.50
20	Wade Boggs	1.25
21	Barry Larkin	.50
22	George Brett	1.50
23	Cecil Fielder	.50
24	Kirby Puckett	1.25
25	Frank Thomas	1.00
26	Don Mattingly	1.50

On Deck

These UV-coated cards feature 25 of the game's top players. Each card has a full-bleed photo on the front and questions and answers on the back. Available only in Series II jumbo packs, the cards have a D prefix for numbering.

		NM/M
Complete Set (25):		10.00
Common Player:		.15
1	Jim Abbott	.15
2	Roberto Alomar	.35
3	Carlos Baerga	.15
4	Albert Belle	.15
5	Wade Boggs	1.00
6	George Brett	1.25
7	Jose Canseco	.45
8	Will Clark	.25
9	Roger Clemens	1.25
10	Dennis Eckersley	.65
11	Cecil Fielder	.15
12	Juan Gonzalez	.40
13	Ken Griffey Jr.	1.50
14	Tony Gwynn	1.00
15	Bo Jackson	.20
16	Chipper Jones	.75

17	Eric Karros	.15
18	Mark McGwire	2.00
19	Kirby Puckett	1.00
20	Nolan Ryan	2.50
21	Tim Salmon	.15
22	Ryne Sandberg	1.00
23	Darryl Strawberry	.15
24	Frank Thomas	.75
25	Andy Van Slyke	.15

Supers

A series of six 1993 Upper Deck cards and one from 1991 was re-issued in an 8-1/2" x 11" format, though the manner of distribution is unclear. The cards are virtually identical in design to the regularly issued versions, except for the size, the lack of a hologram on back, and a 1993 dated seal with an individual serial number. The Ryan card was issued in an edition of 5,000, the Karros and Finley cards were issued in an edition of 2,500; the others were limited to 1,000 each.

		NM/M
Complete Set (7):		24.00
Common Card:		3.00
6	Kirby Puckett (Triple Crown Contender)	4.50
10	Barry Bonds/SP	7.50
24	Eric Karros/1991	3.00
75	Tom Glavine/1993	3.00
77	Chuck Finley	3.00
155	Nolan Ryan	7.50
199	Roger Clemens/SP	5.00

Then And Now

This 18-card lithograph set features both Hall of Famers and current players. The cards feature a combination of four-color player photos and a holographic background. They were random inserts in both Series I and Series II packs. Numbering includes the prefix TN. A limited edition of 2,500 supersize 5" by 7" Mickey Mantle Then And Now cards was created for sale through Upper Deck Authenticated.

		NM/M
Complete Set (18):		30.00
Common Player:		.75
1	Wade Boggs	2.00
2	George Brett	2.50
3	Rickey Henderson	1.25
4	Cal Ripken, Jr.	4.00
5	Nolan Ryan	4.00
6	Ryne Sandberg	2.00
7	Ozzie Smith	2.00
8	Darryl Strawberry	.75
9	Dave Winfield	1.25
10	Dennis Eckersley	1.00
11	Tony Gwynn	2.00
12	Howard Johnson	.75
13	Don Mattingly	2.50
14	Eddie Murray	1.25
15	Robin Yount	1.25
16	Reggie Jackson	2.00
17	Mickey Mantle	6.00
17a	Mickey Mantle (5" x 7")	13.50
18	Willie Mays	3.00

Abbreviations

SP - Short Print

Triple Crown Contenders

These insert cards were available in 1993 Upper Deck Series I foil packs sold by hobby dealers. The set features 10 players who are candidates to win baseball's Triple Crown. Card fronts have a crown and the player's name at the bottom. Backs put that material at the top and explain why the player might lead the league in home runs, batting average and runs batted in.

		NM/M
Complete Set (10):		6.00
Common Player:		.25
1	Barry Bonds	1.50
2	Jose Canseco	.45
3	Will Clark	.25
4	Ken Griffey Jr.	1.25
5	Fred McGriff	.25
6	Kirby Puckett	.75
7	Cal Ripken, Jr.	1.50
8	Gary Sheffield	.35
9	Frank Thomas	.60
10	Larry Walker	.25

5th Anniversary

This 15-card insert set replicates 15 of Upper Deck's most popular cards from its first five years. Foil stamping and a fifth-anniversary logo appear on the cards, which are otherwise reproductions of the originals. The prefix A appears before each card number. The cards were available in Series II hobby packs only.

		NM/M
Complete Set (15):		7.00
Common Player:		.25
1	Ken Griffey Jr.	1.50
2	Gary Sheffield	.35
3	Roberto Alomar	.35
4	Jim Abbott	.25
5	Nolan Ryan	2.00
6	Juan Gonzalez	.35
7	Dave Justice	.25
8	Carlos Baerga	.25
9	Reggie Jackson	1.00
10	Eric Karros	.25
11	Chipper Jones	1.00
12	Ivan Rodriguez	.50
13	Pat Listach	.25
14	Frank Thomas	.90
15	Tim Salmon	.25

5th Anniversary Supers

This set of oversized (3-1/2" x 5") cards is simply an enlarged version of the Upper Deck 5th Anniversary subset that was inserted with the company's 1993 cards. There are 15 cards in the set, which are reprinted versions

Gary Sheffield

of some of the most popular cards in the last five years from Upper Deck. Each of the cards carries a number on the back out of an edition of 10,000. The cards were sold individually in blister packs at retail outlets along with two packs of 1993 Upper Deck.

		NM/M
Complete Set (15):		17.50
Common Player:		1.00
1	Ken Griffey Jr.	2.50
2	Gary Sheffield	1.25
3	Roberto Alomar	1.25
4	Jim Abbott	1.00
5	Nolan Ryan	3.00
6	Juan Gonzalez	1.25
7	David Justice	1.00
8	Carlos Baerga	1.00
9	Reggie Jackson	2.00
10	Eric Karros	1.00
11	Chipper Jones	2.00
12	Ivan Rodriguez	1.50
13	Pat Listach	1.00
14	Frank Thomas	1.75
15	Tim Salmon	1.00

Heroes of Baseball Previews

This four-card preview set was produced in conjunction with the All-Star FanFest in Baltimore to re-introduce the concept of T202-style "triplefolder" baseball cards. The preview set came in a specially decorated box. The 5-1/4" x 2-1/4" cards feature Ted Williams, Mickey Mantle and Reggie Jackson in various combinations of photos and artwork on each card. Backs are printed in red and gold and include an infield-shaped hologram. Written summaries of the players and their careers are featured. Cards have an "HOB" prefix to their number. A special offering of uncut 27" x 20" sheets containing eight complete sets of the preview cards is sold by UD Authenticated in a numbered edition of 2,000.

		NM/M
Complete Set (4):		5.00
Common Card:		1.00
Uncut UDA Sheet:		20.00
1	Triple Threat (Mickey Mantle, Ted Williams)	2.00
2	Changing of the Guard (Mickey Mantle, Reggie Jackson)	1.50
3	Night and Day (Reggie Jackson, Ted Williams)	1.00
4	Hall-of-Fame Trio (Reggie Jackson, Mickey Mantle, Ted Williams)	1.50

All-Time Heroes

This 1993 set pays homage to one of the classiest, turn-of-the-century card sets, the T202 Hassan Triple Folders. The All-Time Heroes cards are 2-1/4" x 5-1/4" and feature two side panels and a larger middle panel, which features an action shot of the player. A portrait of the player and the Baseball Assistance Team (BAT) logo flank the action photo. Card backs have a biography and career summary. A Classic Combinations subset of 35 cards features artwork or photographs of two or more great players together, plus individual photos on the side panels. Production was limited to 5,140 numbered cases of 12-card foil packs. Ten T202 reprints were also produced and were randomly inserted in the foil packs.

		NM/M
Complete Set (165):		35.00
Common Player:		.10
Wax Pack (12):		2.00
Wax Box (24):		30.00
1	Hank Aaron	2.00
2	Tommie Agee	.10
3	Bob Allison	.10
4	Matty Alou	.10
5	Sal Bando	.10
6	Hank Bauer	.15
7	Don Baylor	.10
8	Glenn Beckert	.10
9	Yogi Berra	.50
10	Buddy Biancalana	.10
11	Jack Billingham	.10
12	Joe Black	.10
13	Paul Blair	.10
14	Steve Blass	.10
15	Ray Boone	.10
16	Lou Boudreau	.10
17	Ken Brett	.10
18	Nellie Briles	.10
19	Bobby Brown	.10
20	Bill Buckner	.10
21	Don Buford	.10
22	Al Bumbry	.10
23	Lew Burdette	.10
24	Jeff Burroughs	.10
25	Johnny Callison	.10
26	Bert Campaneris	.10
27	Rico Carty	.10
28	Dave Cash	.10
29	Cesar Cedeno	.10
30	Frank Chance	.25
31	Joe Charboneau	.15
32	Ty Cobb	2.00
33	Jerry Coleman	.10
34	Cecil Cooper	.10
35	Frankie Crossetti	.10
36	Alvin Dark	.10
37	Tommy Davis	.10
38	Dizzy Dean	.25
39	Doug DeCinces	.10
40	Bucky Dent	.10
41	Larry Dierker	.10
42	Larry Doby	.20
43	Moe Drabowsky	.10
44	Dave Dravecky	.10
45	Del Ennis	.10
46	Carl Erskine	.10
47	Johnny Evers	.25
48	Elroy Face	.10
49	Rick Ferrell	.10
50	Mark Fidrych	.15
51	Curt Flood	.10
52	Whitey Ford	.50
53	George Foster	.10
54	Jimmie Foxx	.25
55	Jim Fregosi	.10
56	Phil Garner	.10
57	Ralph Garr	.10
58	Lou Gehrig	2.00
59	Bobby Grich	.10
60	Jerry Grote	.10
61	Harvey Haddix	.10
62	Toby Harrah	.10
63	Bud Harrelson	.10
64	Jim Hegan	.10
65	Gil Hodges	.25
66	Ken Holtzman	.10
67	Bob Horner	.10
68	Rogers Hornsby	.25
69	Carl Hubbell	.25
70	Ron Hunt	.10
71	Monte Irvin	.10
72a	Reggie Jackson (Regular issue, black printing on back.)	.50
72b	Reggie Jackson (Dealer promo, red printing on back.)	6.00
73	Larry Jansen	.10
74	Ferguson Jenkins	.10
75	Tommy John	.10
76	Cliff Johnson	.10
77	Davey Johnson	.10
78	Walter Johnson	.45
79	George Kell	.10
80	Don Kessinger	.10
81	Vern Law	.10
82	Dennis Leonard	.10
83	Johnny Logan	.10
84	Mickey Lolich	.10
85	Jim Lonborg	.10
86	Bill Madlock	.10
87	Mickey Mantle	4.00
88	Billy Martin	.25
89	Christy Mathewson	.45
90	Lee May	.10
91	Willie Mays	2.00
92	Bill Mazeroski	.25
93	Gil McDougald	.10
94	Sam McDowell	.10
95	Minnie Minoso	.10
96	Johnny Mize	.25
97	Rick Monday	.10
98	Wally Moon	.10
99	Manny Mota	.10
100	Bobby Murcer	.10
101	Ron Necciai	.10
102	Al Oliver	.10
103	Mel Ott	.15
104	Mel Parnell	.10
105	Jimmy Piersall	.10
106	Johnny Podres	.15
107	Bobby Richardson	.15
108	Robin Roberts	.15
109	Al Rosen	.10
110	Babe Ruth	3.00
111	Joe Sambito	.10
112	Manny Sanguillen	.10
113	Ron Santo	.10
114	Bill Skowron	.15
115	Enos Slaughter	.15
116	Warren Spahn	.20
117	Tris Speaker	.20
118	Frank Thomas	.10
119	Bobby Thomson	.10
120	Andre Thornton	.10
121	Marv Throneberry	.10
122	Luis Tiant	.10
123	Joe Tinker	.25
124	Honus Wagner	.50
125	Bill White	.10
126	Ted Williams	1.00
127	Earl Wilson	.10
128	Joe Wood	.10
129	Cy Young	.40
130	Richie Zisk	.10
131	Babe Ruth, Lou Gehrig	2.00
132	Ted Williams, Rogers Hornsby	1.00
133	Lou Gehrig, Babe Ruth	2.00
134	Babe Ruth, Mickey Mantle	3.00
135	Mickey Mantle, Reggie Jackson	1.00
136	Mel Ott, Carl Hubbell	
137	Mickey Mantle, Willie Mays	2.00
138	Cy Young, Walter Johnson	.25
139	Honus Wagner, Rogers Hornsby	.25
140	Mickey Mantle, Whitey Ford	2.00
141	Mickey Mantle, Billy Martin	2.00
142	Cy Young, Walter Johnson	.25
143	Christy Mathewson, Walter Johnson	.25
144	Warren Spahn, Christy Mathewson	.15
145	Honus Wagner, Ty Cobb	.50
146	Babe Ruth, Ty Cobb	1.00
147	Joe Tinker, Johnny Evers	.15
148	Johnny Evers, Frank Chance	.15
149	Hank Aaron, Babe Ruth	1.00
150	Willie Mays, Hank Aaron	1.00
151	Babe Ruth, Willie Mays	1.00
152	Babe Ruth, Whitey Ford	1.00
153	Larry Doby, Minnie Minoso	.25
154	Babe Ruth, Monte Irvin	.10
155	Joe Wood, Christy Mathewson	.15
156	Christy Mathewson, Cy Young	.25
157	Cy Young, Joe Wood	.15
158	Cy Young, Whitey Ford	.20
159	Cy Young, Ferguson Jenkins	.15
160	Ty Cobb, Rogers Hornsby	.45
161	Tris Speaker, Ted Williams	1.00
162	Rogers Hornsby, Ted Williams	1.00
163	Willie Mays, Monte Irvin	.50
164	Willie Mays, Bobby Thomson	.50
165	Reggie Jackson, Mickey Mantle	2.00

All-Time Heroes T202 Reprints

A series of 10 reprints of the classic 1912 Hassan "Tri-

plefolders" baseball cards on which the All-Time Heroes set was patterned were included as random inserts in the Upper Deck Old-Timers set. The reprints measure 5-1/4" x 2-1/4" (same as the originals). The Hassan cigarette ads on the backs of the originals have been replaced on the reprints by an Upper Deck hologram and the logos of the card company, B.A.T., Major League Baseball and the Cooperstown Collection. The Hassan cards are known as T202, their designation in the "American Card Catalog." The reprints are un-numbered and are checklisted here alphabetically in order of the player appearing on the left end of each card.

		NM/M
Complete Set (10):		10.00
Common Player:		.50
(1)	Art Devlin, Christy Mathewson	1.00
(2)	Hugh Jennings, Ty Cobb	2.00
(3)	John Kling, Cy Young	1.00
(4)	Jack Knight, Walter Johnson	.75
(5)	John McGraw, Hugh Jennings	.50
(6)	George Moriarty, Ty Cobb	2.00
(7)	Charley O'Leary, Ty Cobb	2.00
(8)	Charley O'Leary, Ty Cobb	2.00
(9)	Joe Tinker, rank Chance	1.00
(10)	Joe Wood, Tris Speaker	.50

Diamond Gallery

Utilizing something the company calls lithogram technology, Upper Deck produced a 36-card set that combines four-color photography and a holographic image. The set features one star from each of the 28 teams, along with a subset spotlighting top rookies from 1993 and cards saluting Nolan Ryan, Rickey Henderson and Ozzie Smith. The set comes in a specially-designed box, with a numbered checklist card. The set was limited to a total of 123,600.

		NM/M
Complete Set (36):		6.00
Common Player:		.10
1	Tim Salmon	.10
2	Jeff Bagwell	.30
3	Mark McGwire	.75
4	Roberto Alomar	.25
5	Terry Pendleton	.10
6	Robin Yount	.30
7	Ray Lankford	.10
8	Ryne Sandberg	.40
9	Darryl Strawberry	.10
10	Marquis Grissom	.10
11	Barry Bonds	1.00
12	Carlos Baerga	.10
13	Ken Griffey Jr.	.65
14	Benito Santiago	.10
15	Dwight Gooden	.10
16	Cal Ripken, Jr.	1.00
17	Tony Gwynn	.40
18	Dave Hollins	.10
19	Andy Van Slyke	.10
20	Juan Gonzalez	.25
21	Roger Clemens	.50
22	Barry Larkin	.30
23	Dave Nied	.10
24	George Brett	.50
25	Travis Fryman	.10
26	Kirby Puckett	.40
27	Frank Thomas	.30
28	Don Mattingly	.50
29	Rickey Henderson	.30

30	Nolan Ryan		1.00
31	Ozzie Smith		.40
32	Wil Cordero		.10
33	Phil Hiatt		.10
34	Mike Piazza		.65
35	J.T. Snow		.10
36	Kevin Young		.10

Fun Packs

Aimed at the younger audience, this product features 150 "regular" player cards and 75 specialty cards in a variety of subsets, plus two different types of insert cards. Basic player cards feature a photo (generally in action) on a background of purple, green and red, highlighted by yellow and orange stripes. On back is a white panel on red, yellow and orange blended stripes. In the panel is a cartoon, a trivia question and answer, brief biographical details, stats, and career summary. The basic player cards are arranged within the set alphabetically by team. The teams are also arranged alphabetically by nickname. Leading off each team's roster is a "Glow Stars" sticker, featuring a player photo against a parti-colored background. The area around the photo is die-cut to allow the picture to be separated from the background and stuck to a wall, where the white and green outlines glow in the dark. Cards #1-9 and designated "Stars of Tomorrow." Both front and back have a background of a star-studded purple sky. Cards #10-21 are "Hot Shots" - heat-sensitive cards. When touched the black textured ink surrounding the player photo turns clear, revealing a colored pattern beneath. The Hot Shot cards were available only via mail-in redemption. Cards #22-27 are "Kid Stars" and feature a childhood photo. Cards #28-37 are checklisted as "Upper Deck Heroes," though that designation does not appear on the cards. The subset is done in comic-book art style. Cards #216-220 are double-size (2-1/2"x7") "Fold-outs." The five checklist cards which conclude the set have player photos on front.

		NM/M
Complete Set (225):		15.00
Common Player:		.05
Wax Pack (6):		.50
Wax Box (36):		15.00
1	Wil Cordero	
	(Stars of Tomorrow)	.05
2	Brent Gates	
	(Stars of Tomorrow)	.05
3	Benji Gil	
	(Stars of Tomorrow)	.05
4	Phil Hiatt	
	(Stars of Tomorrow)	.05
5	David McCarty	
	(Stars of Tomorrow)	.05
	Mike Piazza	
	(Stars of Tomorrow)	1.50
7	Tim Salmon	
	(Stars of Tomorrow)	.05
8	J.T. Snow RC	
	(Stars of Tomorrow)	.05
9	Kevin Young	
	(Stars of Tomorrow)	.05
10	Roberto Alomar	
	(Hot Shots)	.65

11	Barry Bonds		
	(Hot Shots)		1.50
12	Jose Canseco		
	(Hot Shots)		.35
13	Will Clark (Hot Shots)		.10
14	Roger Clemens		
	(Hot Shots)		.75
15	Juan Gonzalez		
	(Hot Shots)		.25
16	Ken Griffey Jr.		
	(Hot Shots)		1.00
17	Mark McGwire		
	(Hot Shots)		1.25
18	Nolan Ryan		
	(Hot Shots)		1.50
19	Ryne Sandberg		
	(Hot Shots)		.65
20	Gary Sheffield		
	(Hot Shots)		.30
21	Frank Thomas		
	(Hot Shots)		.60
22	Roberto Alomar		
	(Kid Stars)		.10
23	Roger Clemens		
	(Kid Stars)		.45
24	Ken Griffey Jr.		
	(Kid Stars)		.50
25	Gary Sheffield		
	(Kid Stars)		.15
26	Nolan Ryan (Kid Stars)		.75
27	Frank Thomas		
	(Kid Stars)		.40
28	Reggie Jackson		
	(Heroes)		.45
29	Roger Clemens		
	(Heroes)		.45
30	Ken Griffey Jr. (Heroes)		.50
31	Bo Jackson (Heroes)		.10
32	Cal Ripken, Jr. (Heroes)		.75
33	Nolan Ryan (Heroes)		.75
34	Deion Sanders (Heroes)		.10
35	Ozzie Smith (Heroes)		.40
36	Frank Thomas (Heroes)		.35
37	Tim Salmon		
	(Glow Stars)		.05
38	Chili Davis		.05
39	Chuck Finley		.05
40	Mark Langston		.05
41	Luis Polonia		.05
42	Jeff Bagwell		
	(Glow Stars)		.30
43	Jeff Bagwell		.50
44	Craig Biggio		.05
45	Ken Caminiti		.05
46	Doug Drabek		.05
47	Steve Finley		.05
48	Mark McGwire		
	(Glow Stars)		.65
49	Dennis Eckersley		.45
50	Rickey Henderson		.50
51	Mark McGwire		1.25
52	Ruben Sierra		.05
53	Terry Steinbach		.05
54	Roberto Alomar		
	(Glow Stars)		.10
55	Roberto Alomar		.20
56	Joe Carter		.05
57	Juan Guzman		.05
58	Paul Molitor		.50
59	Jack Morris		.05
60	John Olerud		.05
61	Tom Glavine		
	(Glow Stars)		.10
62	Steve Avery		.05
63	Tom Glavine		.20
64	Dave Justice		.05
65	Greg Maddux		.65
66	Terry Pendleton		.05
67	Deion Sanders		.10
68	John Smoltz		.05
69	Robin Yount		
	(Glow Stars)		.30
70	Cal Eldred		.05
71	Pat Listach		.05
72	Greg Vaughn		.05
73	Robin Yount		.50
74	Ozzie Smith		
	(Glow Stars)		.45
75	Gregg Jefferies		.05
76	Ray Lankford		.05
77	Lee Smith		.05
78	Ozzie Smith		.65
79	Bob Tewksbury		.05
80	Ryne Sandberg		
	(Glow Stars)		.35
81	Mark Grace		.05
82	Mike Morgan		.05
83	Randy Myers		.05
84	Ryne Sandberg		.65
85	Sammy Sosa		.65
86	Eric Karros		
	(Glow Stars)		.05
87	Brett Butler		.05
88	Orel Hershiser		.05
89	Eric Karros		.05
90	Ramon Martinez		.05
91	Jose Offerman		.05
92	Darryl Strawberry		.05
93	Marquis Grissom		
	(Glow Stars)		.05
94	Delino DeShields		.05
95	Marquis Grissom		.05
96	Ken Hill		.05
97	Dennis Martinez		.05
98	Larry Walker		.05
99	Barry Bonds		
	(Glow Stars)		.65
100	Barry Bonds		1.50

101	Will Clark		.05
102	Bill Swift		.05
103	Robby Thompson		.05
104	Matt Williams		.05
105	Carlos Baerga		
	(Glow Stars)		.05
106	Sandy Alomar, Jr.		.05
107	Carlos Baerga		.05
108	Albert Belle		.05
109	Kenny Lofton		.05
110	Charles Nagy		.05
111	Ken Griffey Jr.		
	(Glow Stars)		.50
112	Jay Buhner		.05
113	Dave Fleming		.05
114	Ken Griffey Jr.		1.00
115	Randy Johnson		.50
116	Edgar Martinez		.05
117	Benito Santiago		
	(Glow Stars)		.05
118	Bret Barberie		.05
119	Jeff Conine		.05
120	Brian Harvey		.05
121	Benito Santiago		.05
122	Walt Weiss		.05
123	Dwight Gooden		
	(Glow Stars)		.05
124	Bobby Bonilla		.05
125	Tony Fernandez		.05
126	Dwight Gooden		.05
127	Howard Johnson		.05
128	Eddie Murray		.50
129	Bret Saberhagen		.05
130	Cal Ripken, Jr.		
	(Glow Stars)		.75
131	Brady Anderson		.05
132	Mike Devereaux		.05
133	Ben McDonald		.05
134	Mike Mussina		.30
135	Cal Ripken, Jr.		1.50
136	Fred McGriff		
	(Glow Stars)		.05
137	Andy Benes		.05
138	Tony Gwynn		.65
139	Fred McGriff		.05
140	Phil Plantier		.05
141	Gary Sheffield		.25
142	Darren Daulton		
	(Glow Stars)		.05
143	Darren Daulton		.05
144	Len Dykstra		.05
145	Dave Hollins		.05
146	John Kruk		.05
147	Mitch Williams		.05
148	Andy Van Slyke		
	(Glow Stars)		.05
149	Jay Bell		.05
150	Zane Smith		.05
151	Andy Van Slyke		.05
152	Tim Wakefield		.05
153	Juan Gonzalez		
	(Glow Stars)		.15
154	Kevin Brown		.05
155	Jose Canseco		.35
156	Juan Gonzalez		.25
157	Rafael Palmeiro		.40
158	Dean Palmer		.05
159	Ivan Rodriguez		.45
160	Nolan Ryan		1.50
161	Roger Clemens		
	(Glow Stars)		.05
162	Roger Clemens		.75
163	Andre Dawson		.25
164	Mike Greenwell		.05
165	Tony Pena		.05
166	Frank Viola		.05
167	Barry Larkin		
	(Glow Stars)		.05
168	Rob Dibble		.05
169	Roberto Kelly		.05
170	Barry Larkin		.05
171	Kevin Mitchell		.05
172	Bip Roberts		.05
173	Andres Galarraga		
	(Glow Stars)		.05
174	Dante Bichette		.05
175	Jerald Clark		.05
176	Andres Galarraga		.05
177	Charlie Hayes		.05
178	David Nied		.05
179	David Cone		
	(Glow Stars)		.05
180	Kevin Appler		.05
181	George Brett		.75
182	David Cone		.05
183	Felix Jose		.05
184	Wally Joyner		.05
185	Cecil Fielder		
	(Glow Stars)		.05
186	Cecil Fielder		.05
187	Travis Fryman		.05
188	Tony Phillips		.05
189	Mickey Tettleton		.05
190	Lou Whitaker		.05
191	Kirby Puckett		
	(Glow Stars)		.35
192	Scott Erickson		.05
193	Chuck Knoblauch		.05
194	Shane Mack		.05
195	Kirby Puckett		.65
196	Dave Winfield		.50
197	Frank Thomas		
	(Glow Stars)		.40
198	George Bell		.05
199	Bo Jackson		.10
200	Jack McDowell		.05
201	Tim Raines		.05
202	Frank Thomas		.05

203	Robin Ventura		.05
204	Jim Abbott		
	(Glow Stars)		.05
205	Jim Abbott		.05
206	Wade Boggs		.65
207	Jimmy Key		.05
208	Don Mattingly		.75
209	Danny Tartabull		.05
210	Brett Butler		
	(All-Star Advice)		.05
211	Tony Gwynn		
	(All-Star Advice)		.35
212	Rickey Henderson		
	(All-Star Advice)		.25
213	Ramon Martinez		
	(All-Star Advice)		.05
214	Nolan Ryan		
	(All-Star Advice)		.75
215	Ozzie Smith		
	(All-Star Advice)		.35
216	Marquis Grissom		
	(Fold-Out)		.05
217	Dean Palmer		
	(Fold-Out)		.05
218	Cal Ripken, Jr.		
	(Fold-Out)		.75
219	Deion Sanders		
	(Fold-Out)		.05
220	Darryl Strawberry		
	(Fold-Out)		.05
221	David McCarty		
	(Checklist)		.05
222	Barry Bonds		
	(Checklist)		.65
223	Juan Gonzalez		
	(Checklist)		.15
224	Ken Griffey Jr.		
	(Checklist)		.50
225	Frank Thomas		
	(Checklist)		.25
	Trade Upper Deck		
	("Hot Shots" redemption		
	card.)		.05

Fun Packs Mascot Madness

Upper Deck's high-tech lithogram process of combining color photos and holograms was used to create the five-card "Mascot Madness" inserts which were randomly found in Fun Packs. Backs have a description of the mascot and explain his role with the team.

		NM/M
Complete Set (5):		2.50
Common Card:		.50
1	Phillie Phanatic	.50
2	Pirate Parrot	.50
3	Fredbird	.50
4	BJ Birdy	.50
5	Youppi/Mascot	.50

Fun Packs All-Star Scratch-Off

Randomly inserted into Fun Packs was a series of nine "All-Star Scratch-Off" game cards. Fronts and backs have a star-studded blue background. Inside the folded, double-size (2-1/2" x 7") cards are American and National League line-ups which can be used to play a baseball game, the rules of which are explained on the card backs. On front are photos of two of the players in the line-up,

matched by position from each league. The inserts are numbered with an "AS" prefix.

		NM/M
Complete Set (9):		5.00
Common Player:		.25
1	Fred McGriff,	
	Frank Thomas	.45
2	Darren Daulton,	
	Ivan Rodriguez	.35
3	Mark McGwire,	
	Will Clark	1.25
4	Ryne Sandberg,	
	Roberto Alomar	.50
5	Robin Ventura,	
	Terry Pendleton	.25
6	Cal Ripken Jr.,	
	Ozzie Smith	1.50
7	Barry Bonds,	
	Juan Gonzalez	1.50
8	Marquis Grissom,	
	Ken Griffey Jr.	1.00
9	Tony Gwynn,	
	Kirby Puckett	.50

1994 Upper Deck

Upper Deck's 1994 offering was a typical presentation, combining high-quality regular-issue cards with innovative subsets and high-tech chase cards. Series 1, besides the standard player cards, features subsets including Star Rookies with metallic borders, "Fantasy Team" stars, Home Field Advantage cards showcasing National League stadiums, and, stars under the age of 25 in a subset titled, "The Future is Now." Regular-issue cards feature a color photo on front and a second, black-and-white version of the same photo at left in a vertically stretched format. The player's name, team and Upper Deck logo appear on front in copper foil. Backs have a color photo, stats and an infield-shaped hologram. Series 2 offered in addition to regular cards, subsets of American League Home Field Advantage cards, a group of "Classic Alumni" minor league players, a selection of "Diamond Debuts" cards and a group of "Top Prospects." Series 1 retail packaging contained a special Mickey Mantle/Ken Griffey, Jr. card that could be found bearing either one or both of the players' autographs in an edition of 1,000 each. Series 2 retail packs offered a chance to find an autographed version of Alex Rodriguez' Classic Alumni card.

		NM/M
Complete Set (550):		30.00
Complete Series 1 (280):		25.00
Complete Series 2 (270):		5.00
Common Player:		.05
Series 1 Hobby Pack (12):		2.50
Series 1 Hobby Box (36):		65.00
Series 1 Retail Pack (12):		2.00
Series 1 Retail Box (36):		40.00
Series 2 Hobby Pack (12):		.75
Series 2 Hobby Box (36):		20.00
Series 2 Retail Pack (12):		1.25
Series 2 Retail Box (36):		25.00
1	Brian Anderson RC	
	(Star Rookie)	.15
2	Shane Andrews	
	(Star Rookie)	.05
3	James Baldwin	
	(Star Rookie)	.05
4	Rich Becker	
	(Star Rookie)	.05

5	Greg Blosser		
	(Star Rookie)		.05
6	Ricky Bottalico RC		
	(Star Rookie)		.05
7	Midre Cummings		
	(Star Rookie)		.05
8	Carlos Delgado		
	(Star Rookie)		.50
9	Steve Dreyer RC		
	(Star Rookie)		.05
10	Joey Eischen RC		
	(Star Rookie)		.05
11	Carl Everett		
	(Star Rookie)		.05
12	Cliff Floyd (Star Rookie)		.05
13	Alex Gonzalez		
	(Star Rookie)		.05
14	Jeff Granger		
	(Star Rookie)		.05
15	Shawn Green		
	(Star Rookie)		.35
16	Brian Hunter		
	(Star Rookie)		.05
17	Butch Huskey		
	(Star Rookie)		.05
18	Mark Hutton		
	(Star Rookie)		.05
19	Michael Jordan RC		
	(Star Rookie)		5.00
20	Steve Karsay		
	(Star Rookie)		.05
21	Jeff McNeely		
	(Star Rookie)		.05
22	Marc Newfield		
	(Star Rookie)		.05
23	Manny Ramirez		
	(Star Rookie)		.60
24	Alex Rodriguez RC		
	(Star Rookie)		15.00
25	Scott Ruffcorn		
	(Star Rookie)		.05
26	Paul Spoljaric		
	(Star Rookie)		.05
27	Salomon Torres RC		
	(Star Rookie)		.05
28	Steve Trachsel		
	(Star Rookie)		.05
29	Chris Turner RC		
	(Star Rookie)		.05
30	Gabe White		
	(Star Rookie)		.05
31	Randy Johnson		
	(Fantasy Team)		.40
32	John Wetteland		
	(Fantasy Team)		.05
33	Mike Piazza		
	(Fantasy Team)		.65
34	Rafael Palmeiro		
	(Fantasy Team)		.35
35	Roberto Alomar		
	(Fantasy Team)		.10
36	Matt Williams		
	(Fantasy Team)		.05
37	Travis Fryman		
	(Fantasy Team)		.05
38	Barry Bonds		
	(Fantasy Team)		1.00
39	Marquis Grissom		
	(Fantasy Team)		.05
40	Albert Belle		
	(Fantasy Team)		.05
41	Steve Avery		
	(Future/Now)		.05
42	Jason Bere		
	(Future/Now)		.05
43	Alex Fernandez		
	(Future/Now)		.05
44	Mike Mussina		
	(Future/Now)		.15
45	Aaron Sele		
	(Future/Now)		.05
46	Rod Beck (Future/Now)		.05
47	Mike Piazza		
	(Future/Now)		.65
48	John Olerud		
	(Future/Now)		.05
49	Carlos Baerga		
	(Future/Now)		.05
50	Gary Sheffield		
	(Future/Now)		.20
51	Travis Fryman		
	(Future/Now)		.05
52	Juan Gonzalez		
	(Future/Now)		.20
53	Ken Griffey Jr.		
	(Future/Now)		.65
54	Tim Salmon		
	(Future/Now)		.05
55	Frank Thomas		
	(Future/Now)		.45
56	Tony Phillips		.05
57	Julio Franco		.05
58	Kevin Mitchell		.05
59	Raul Mondesi		.75
60	Rickey Henderson		.05
61	Jay Buhner		.05
62	Bill Swift		.05
63	Brady Anderson		.05
64	Ryan Klesko		.05
65	Darren Daulton		.05
66	Damion Easley		.05
67	Mark McGwire		1.50
68	John Roper		.05
69	Dave Telgheder		.05
70	Dave Nied		.05
71	Mo Vaughn		.05
72	Tyler Green		.05
73	Dave Magadan		.05

No.	Player	Price
74	Chili Davis	.05
75	Archi Cianfrocco	.05
76	Joe Girardi	.05
77	Chris Hoiles	.05
78	Ryan Bowen	.05
79	Greg Gagne	.05
80	Aaron Sele	.05
81	Dave Winfield	.75
82	Chad Curtis	.05
83	Andy Van Slyke	.05
84	Kevin Stocker	.05
85	Deion Sanders	.05
86	Bernie Williams	.05
87	John Smoltz	.05
88	Ruben Santana RC	.05
89	Dave Stewart	.05
90	Don Mattingly	1.00
91	Joe Carter	.05
92	Ryne Sandberg	.90
93	Chris Gomez	.05
94	Tino Martinez	.05
95	Terry Pendleton	.05
96	Andre Dawson	.25
97	Wil Cordero	.05
98	Kent Hrbek	.05
99	John Olerud	.05
100	Kirt Manwaring	.05
101	Tim Bogar	.05
102	Mike Mussina	.30
103	Nigel Wilson	.05
104	Ricky Gutierrez	.05
105	Roberto Mejia	.05
106	Tom Pagnozzi	.05
107	Mike Macfarlane	.05
108	Jose Bautista	.05
109	Luis Ortiz	.05
110	Brent Gates	.05
111	Tim Salmon	.05
112	Wade Boggs	.90
113	Tripp Cromer RC	.05
114	Denny Hocking	.05
115	Carlos Baerga	.05
116	J.R. Phillips RC	.05
117	Bo Jackson	.10
118	Lance Johnson	.05
119	Bobby Jones	.05
120	Bobby Witt	.05
121	Ron Karkovice	.05
122	Jose Vizcaino	.05
123	Danny Darwin	.05
124	Eduardo Perez	.05
125	Brian Looney	.05
126	Pat Hentgen	.05
127	Frank Viola	.05
128	Darren Holmes	.05
129	Wally Whitehurst	.05
130	Matt Walbeck	.05
131	Albert Belle	.05
132	Steve Cooke	.05
133	Kevin Appier	.05
134	Joe Oliver	.05
135	Benji Gil	.05
136	Steve Buechele	.05
137	Devon White	.05
138	Sterling Hitchcock	.05
139	Phil Leftwich RC	.05
140	Jose Canseco	.45
141	Rick Aguilera	.05
142	Rod Beck	.05
143	Jose Rijo	.05
144	Tom Glavine	.25
145	Phil Plantier	.05
146	Jason Bere	.05
147	Jamie Moyer	.05
148	Wes Chamberlain	.05
149	Glenallen Hill	.05
150	Mark Whiten	.05
151	Bret Barberie	.05
152	Chuck Knoblauch	.05
153	Trevor Hoffman	.05
154	Rick Wilkins	.05
155	Juan Gonzalez	.40
156	Ozzie Guillen	.05
157	Jim Eisenreich	.05
158	Pedro Astacio	.05
159	Joe Magrane	.05
160	Ryan Thompson	.05
161	Jose Lind	.05
162	Jeff Conine	.05
163	Todd Benzinger	.05
164	Roger Salkeld	.05
165	Gary DiSarcina	.05
166	Kevin Gross	.05
167	Charlie Hayes	.05
168	Tim Costo	.05
169	Wally Joyner	.05
170	Johnny Ruffin	.05
171	Kirk Rueter RC	.10
172	Len Dykstra	.05
173	Ken Hill	.05
174	Mike Bordick	.05
175	Billy Hall	.05
176	Rob Butler	.05
177	Jay Bell	.05
178	Jeff Kent	.05
179	David Wells	.05
180	Dean Palmer	.05
181	Mariano Duncan	.05
182	Orlando Merced	.05
183	Brett Butler	.05
184	Milt Thompson	.05
185	Chipper Jones	.90
186	Paul O'Neill	.05
187	Mike Greenwell	.05
188	Harold Baines	.05
189	Todd Stottlemyre	.05
190	Jeromy Burnitz	.05
191	Rene Arocha	.05
192	Jeff Fassero	.05
193	Robby Thompson	.05
194	Greg W. Harris	.05
195	Todd Van Poppel	.05
196	Jose Guzman	.05
197	Shane Mack	.05
198	Carlos Garcia	.05
199	Kevin Roberson	.05
200	David McCarty	.05
201	Alan Trammell	.05
202	Chuck Carr	.05
203	Tommy Greene	.05
204	Wilson Alvarez	.05
205	Dwight Gooden	.05
206	Tony Tarasco	.05
207	Darren Lewis	.05
208	Eric Karros	.05
209	Chris Hammond	.05
210	Jeffrey Hammonds	.05
211	Rich Amaral	.05
212	Danny Tartabull	.05
213	Jeff Russell	.05
214	Dave Staton	.05
215	Kenny Lofton	.05
216	Manuel Lee	.05
217	Brian Koelling	.05
218	Scott Lydy	.05
219	Tony Gwynn	.90
220	Cecil Fielder	.05
221	Royce Clayton	.05
222	Reggie Sanders	.05
223	Brian Jordan	.05
224	Ken Griffey Jr.	1.25
224a	Ken Griffey Jr./PC	3.00
225	Fred McGriff	.05
226	Felix Jose	.05
227	Brad Pennington	.05
228	Chris Bosio	.05
229	Mike Stanley	.05
230	Willie Greene	.05
231	Alex Fernandez	.05
232	Brad Ausmus	.05
233	Darrell Whitmore	.05
234	Marcus Moore	.05
235	Allen Watson	.05
236	Jose Offerman	.05
237	Rondell White	.05
238	Jeff King	.05
239	Luis Alicea	.05
240	Dan Wilson	.05
241	Ed Sprague	.05
242	Todd Hundley	.05
243	Al Martin	.05
244	Mike Lansing	.05
245	Ivan Rodriguez	.65
246	Dave Fleming	.05
247	John Doherty	.05
248	Mark McLemore	.05
249	Bob Hamelin	.05
250	Curtis Pride RC	.05
251	Zane Smith	.05
252	Eric Young	.05
253	Brian McRae	.05
254	Tim Raines	.05
255	Javier Lopez	.05
256	Melvin Nieves	.05
257	Randy Myers	.05
258	Willie McGee	.05
259	Jimmy Key	.05
260	Tom Candiotti	.05
261	Eric Davis	.05
262	Craig Paquette	.05
263	Robin Ventura	.05
264	Pat Kelly	.05
265	Gregg Jefferies	.05
266	Cory Snyder	.05
267	Dave Justice	.05
	(Home Field Advantage)	.05
268	Sammy Sosa	.05
	(Home Field Advantage)	.45
269	Barry Larkin	.05
	(Home Field Advantage)	.05
270	Andres Galarraga	.05
	(Home Field Advantage)	.20
271	Gary Sheffield	.05
	(Home Field Advantage)	.40
272	Jeff Bagwell	.05
	(Home Field Advantage)	.65
273	Mike Piazza	.05
	(Home Field Advantage)	.05
274	Larry Walker	.05
275	Bobby Bonilla	.05
	(Home Field Advantage)	.05
276	John Kruk	.05
	(Home Field Advantage)	.05
277	Jay Bell	.05
	(Home Field Advantage)	.05
278	Ozzie Smith	.05
	(Home Field Advantage)	.45
279	Tony Gwynn	.05
	(Home Field Advantage)	.45
280	Barry Bonds (Home Field Advantage)	1.00
281	Cal Ripken, Jr. (Home Field Advantage)	1.00
282	Mo Vaughn	.05
	(Home Field Advantage)	.40
283	Tim Salmon	.05
	(Home Field Advantage)	.05
284	Frank Thomas	.05
	(Home Field Advantage)	.40
285	Albert Belle	.05
	(Home Field Advantage)	.05
286	Cecil Fielder	.05
	(Home Field Advantage)	.05
287	Wally Joyner	.05
288	Greg Vaughn	.05
	(Home Field Advantage)	.05
289	Kirby Puckett	.05
	(Home Field Advantage)	.45
290	Don Mattingly	.05
	(Home Field Advantage)	.50
291	Terry Steinbach	.05
	(Home Field Advantage)	.05
292	Ken Griffey Jr.	.05
	(Home Field Advantage)	.90
293	Juan Gonzalez	.05
	(Home Field Advantage)	.20
294	Paul Molitor	.05
	(Home Field Advantage)	.40
295	Tavo Alvarez	.05
	(Classic Alumni)	.05
296	Matt Brunson	.05
	(Classic Alumni)	.05
297	Shawn Green	.05
	(Classic Alumni)	.20
298	Alex Rodriguez	.05
	(Classic Alumni)	2.00
299	Shannon Stewart	.05
	(Classic Alumni)	.05
300	Frank Thomas	.75
301	Mickey Tettleton	.05
302	Pedro Munoz	.05
303	Jose Valentin	.05
304	Orestes Destrade	.05
305	Pat Listach	.05
306	Scott Brosius	.05
307	Kurt Miller RC	.05
308	Rob Dibble	.05
309	Mike Blowers	.05
310	Jim Abbott	.05
311	Mike Jackson	.05
312	Craig Biggio	.05
313	Kurt Abbott RC	.05
314	Chuck Finley	.05
315	Andres Galarraga	.05
316	Mike Moore	.05
317	Doug Strange	.05
318	Pedro J. Martinez	.75
319	Kevin McReynolds	.05
320	Greg Maddux	.90
321	Mike Henneman	.05
322	Scott Leius	.05
323	John Franco	.05
324	Jeff Blauser	.05
325	Kirby Puckett	.90
326	Darryl Hamilton	.05
327	John Smiley	.05
328	Derrick May	.05
329	Jose Vizcaino	.05
330	Randy Johnson	.75
331	Jack Morris	.05
332	Graeme Lloyd	.05
333	Dave Valle	.05
334	Greg Myers	.05
335	John Wetteland	.05
336	Jim Gott	.05
337	Tim Naehring	.05
338	Mike Kelly	.05
339	Jeff Montgomery	.05
340	Rafael Palmeiro	.65
341	Eddie Murray	.75
342	Xavier Hernandez	.05
343	Bobby Munoz	.05
344	Bobby Bonilla	.05
345	Travis Fryman	.05
346	Steve Finley	.05
347	Chris Sabo	.05
348	Armando Reynoso	.05
349	Ramon Martinez	.05
350	Will Clark	.05
351	Moises Alou	.05
352	Jim Thome	.50
353	Bob Tewksbury	.05
354	Andujar Cedeno	.05
355	Orel Hershiser	.05
356	Mike Devereaux	.05
357	Mike Perez	.05
358	Dennis Martinez	.05
359	Dave Nilsson	.05
360	Ozzie Smith	.90
361	Eric Anthony	.05
362	Scott Sanders	.05
363	Paul Sorrento	.05
364	Tim Belcher	.05
365	Dennis Eckersley	.60
366	Mel Rojas	.05
367	Tom Henke	.05
368	Randy Tomlin	.05
369	B.J. Surhoff	.05
370	Larry Walker	.05
371	Joey Cora	.05
372	Mike Harkey	.05
373	John Valentin	.05
374	Doug Jones	.05
375	Dave Justice	.05
376	Vince Coleman	.05
377	David Hulse	.05
378	Kevin Seitzer	.05
379	Pete Harnisch	.05
380	Ruben Sierra	.05
381	Mark Lewis	.05
382	Bip Roberts	.05
383	Paul Wagner	.05
384	Stan Javier	.05
385	Barry Larkin	.05
386	Mark Portugal	.05
387	Roberto Kelly	.05
388	Andy Benes	.05
389	Felix Fermin	.05
390	Marquis Grissom	.05
391	Troy Neel	.05
392	Chad Kreuter	.05
393	Gregg Olson	.05
394	Charles Nagy	.05
395	Jack McDowell	.05
396	Luis Gonzalez	.05
397	Benito Santiago	.05
398	Chris James	.05
399	Terry Mulholland	.05
400	Barry Bonds	2.00
401	Joe Grahe	.05
402	Duane Ward	.05
403	John Burkett	.05
404	Scott Servais	.05
405	Bryan Harvey	.05
406	Bernard Gilkey	.05
407	Greg McMichael	.05
408	Tim Wallach	.05
409	Ken Caminiti	.05
410	John Kruk	.05
411	Darrin Jackson	.05
412	Mike Gallego	.05
413	David Cone	.05
414	Lou Whitaker	.05
415	Sandy Alomar Jr.	.05
416	Bill Wegman	.05
417	Pat Borders	.05
418	Roger Pavlik	.05
419	Pete Smith	.05
420	Steve Avery	.05
421	David Segui	.05
422	Rheal Cormier	.05
423	Harold Reynolds	.05
424	Edgar Martinez	.05
425	Cal Ripken, Jr.	2.00
426	Jaime Navarro	.05
427	Sean Berry	.05
428	Bret Saberhagen	.05
429	Bob Welch	.05
430	Juan Guzman	.05
431	Cal Eldred	.05
432	Dave Hollins	.05
433	Sid Fernandez	.05
434	Willie Banks	.05
435	Darryl Kile	.05
436	Henry Rodriguez	.05
437	Tony Fernandez	.05
438	Walt Weiss	.05
439	Kevin Tapani	.05
440	Mark Grace	.05
441	Brian Harper	.05
442	Kent Mercker	.05
443	Anthony Young	.05
444	Todd Zeile	.05
445	Greg Vaughn	.05
446	Ray Lankford	.05
447	David Weathers	.05
448	Bret Boone	.05
449	Charlie Hough	.05
450	Roger Clemens	1.00
451	Mike Morgan	.05
452	Doug Drabek	.05
453	Danny Jackson	.05
454	Dante Bichette	.05
455	Roberto Alomar	.20
456	Ben McDonald	.05
457	Kenny Rogers	.05
458	Bill Gullickson	.05
459	Darrin Fletcher	.05
460	Curt Schilling	.05
461	Billy Hatcher	.05
462	Howard Johnson	.05
463	Mickey Morandini	.05
464	Frank Castillo	.05
465	Delino DeShields	.05
466	Gary Gaetti	.05
467	Steve Farr	.05
468	Roberto Hernandez	.05
469	Jack Armstrong	.05
470	Paul Molitor	.75
471	Melido Perez	.05
472	Greg Hibbard	.05
473	Jody Reed	.05
474	Tom Gordon	.05
475	Gary Sheffield	.35
476	John Jaha	.05
477	Shawon Dunston	.05
478	Reggie Jefferson	.05
479	Don Slaught	.05
480	Jeff Bagwell	.75
481	Tim Pugh	.05
482	Kevin Young	.05
483	Ellis Burks	.05
484	Greg Swindell	.05
485	Mark Langston	.05
486	Omar Vizquel	.05
487	Kevin Brown	.05
488	Terry Steinbach	.05
489	Mark Lemke	.05
490	Matt Williams	.05
491	Pete Incaviglia	.05
492	Karl Rhodes	.05
493	Shawn Green	.30
494	Hal Morris	.05
495	Derek Bell	.05
496	Luis Polonia	.05
497	Otis Nixon	.05
498	Ron Darling	.05
499	Mitch Williams	.05
500	Mike Piazza	1.25
501	Pat Meares	.05
502	Scott Cooper	.05
503	Scott Erickson	.05
504	Jeff Juden	.05
505	Lee Smith	.05
506	Bobby Ayala	.05
507	Dave Henderson	.05
508	Erik Hanson	.05
509	Bob Wickman	.05
510	Sammy Sosa	.90
511	Hector Carrasco	.05
	(Diamond Debuts)	.05
512	Tim Davis	.05
	(Diamond Debuts)	.05
513	Joey Hamilton	.05
	(Diamond Debuts)	.05
514	Robert Eenhoorn	.05
	(Diamond Debuts)	.05
515	Jorge Fabregas	.05
	(Diamond Debuts)	.05
516	Tim Hyers	.05
	(Diamond Debuts)	.05
517	John Hudek	.05
	(Diamond Debuts)	.05
518	James Mouton RC	.05
	(Diamond Debuts)	.05
519	Herbert Perry	.05
	(Diamond Debuts)	.05
520	Chan Ho Park RC	.05
	(Diamond Debuts)	.75
521	Bill VanLandingham	.05
	(Diamond Debuts)	.05
522	Paul Shuey	.05
	(Top Prospects)	.05
523	Ryan Hancock RC	.05
	(Top Prospects)	.05
524	Billy Wagner RC	.05
	(Top Prospects)	.25
525	Jason Giambi	.05
	(Top Prospects)	.50
526	Jose Silva RC	.05
	(Top Prospects)	.05
527	Terrell Wade RC	.05
	(Top Prospects)	.05
528	Todd Dunn	.05
	(Top Prospects)	.05
529	Alan Benes RC	.05
	(Top Prospects)	.05
530	Brooks Kieschnick RC	.05
	(Top Prospects)	.05
531	Todd Hollandsworth	.05
	(Top Prospects)	.05
532	Brad Fullmer RC	.05
	(Top Prospects)	.15
533	Steve Soderstrom RC	.05
	(Top Prospects)	.05
534	Daron Kirkreit	.05
	(Top Prospects)	.05
535	Arquimedez Pozo RC	.05
	(Top Prospects)	.05
536	Charles Johnson	.05
	(Top Prospects)	.05
537	Preston Wilson	.05
	(Top Prospects)	.10
538	Alex Ochoa	.05
	(Top Prospects)	.05
539	Derek Lee RC	.05
	(Top Prospects)	3.00
540	Wayne Gomes RC	.05
	(Top Prospects)	.05
541	Jermaine Allensworth RC	.05
	(Top Prospects)	.05
542	Mike Bell RC	.05
	(Top Prospects)	.05
543	Trot Nixon RC	.05
	(Top Prospects)	1.25
544	Pokey Reese	.05
	(Top Prospects)	.05
545	Neifi Perez RC	.05
	(Top Prospects)	.05
546	Johnny Damon	.05
	(Top Prospects)	.30
547	Matt Brunson	.05
	(Top Prospects)	.05
548	LaTroy Hawkins RC	.05
	(Top Prospects)	.05
549	Eddie Pearson RC	.05
	(Top Prospects)	.05
550	Derek Jeter	.05
	(Top Prospects)	2.00

NM/M
Complete Set (550): 75.00
Common Player: .25
Stars: 1.5X

Baseball Heroes Mickey Mantle

Mickey Mantle Baseball Hero is a 10-card set that chronicles his career. The cards, which include an unnumbered header card, were randomly inserted into both hobby and retail packs of Series II Upper Deck Baseball. This set starts with his rookie season in 1951 and concludes with his induction into The Hall of Fame. It is numbered 64-72 and was the eighth in the continuing "Baseball Heroes" series, which began in 1990.

NM/M

No.	Card	Price
	Complete Set (10):	25.00
	Common Card:	3.00
64	1951 - The Early Years (Mickey Mantle)	3.00
65	1953 - Tape Measure Home Runs (Mickey Mantle)	3.00
66	1956 - Triple Crown Season (Mickey Mantle)	3.00
67	1957 - 2nd Consecutive MVP (Mickey Mantle)	3.00
68	1961 - Chases The Babe (Mickey Mantle)	3.00
69	1964 - Series Home Run Record (Mickey Mantle)	3.00
70	1967 - 500th Home Run (Mickey Mantle)	3.00
71	1974: Hall of Fame (Mickey Mantle)	3.00
72	Mickey Mantle/Portrait	3.00
----	Header Card (Mickey Mantle)	5.00

line next to the UD logo. Backs are identical to the regular cards. (Forty-five of the first series cards can be found with player names on back in either silver or copper.) Electric Diamond cards are found, on average, about every other pack.

Electric Diamond

Each of the regular-issue and subset cards from 1994 Upper Deck was also produced in a limited edition premium insert "Electric Diamond" version. Where the regular cards have the Upper Deck logo, player and team are in copper foil, the Electric Diamond version has those elements in a silver prismatic foil, along with an "Electric Diamond" identification

Diamond Collection

The premium chase cards in 1994 Upper Deck are a series of Diamond Collection cards issued in regional subsets. Ten cards are found unique to each of three geographic areas of distribution. Western region cards carry a "W" prefix to the card number, Central cards have a "C" prefix and Eastern cards have an "E" prefix. The region is also indicated in silver-foil printing on the front of the card, with a large "W," "C" or "E" in a compass design. The player's name and team are presented in a foil strip at bottom. A "Diamond Collection" logo is shown in embossed-look typography in the background. Diamond Collection cards are inserted only in hobby packs.

	NM/M
Complete Set (30):	40.00
Common Player:	.25
Complete Central (10):	18.00
1 Michael Jordan	10.00
2 Jeff Bagwell	2.00
3 Barry Larkin	.25
4 Kirby Puckett	2.50
5 Manny Ramirez	2.00
6 Ryne Sandberg	2.50
7 Ozzie Smith	2.50
8 Frank Thomas	2.00
9 Andy Van Slyke	.25
10 Robin Yount	2.00
Complete East (10):	11.00
1 Roberto Alomar	1.00
2 Roger Clemens	2.50
3 Len Dykstra	.25
4 Cecil Fielder	.25
5 Cliff Floyd	.25
6 Dwight Gooden	.25
7 Dave Justice	.25
8 Don Mattingly	2.50
9 Cal Ripken, Jr.	6.00
10 Gary Sheffield	.50
Complete West (10):	14.00
1 Barry Bonds	4.00
2 Andres Galarraga	.25
3 Juan Gonzalez	1.50
4 Ken Griffey Jr.	3.00
5 Tony Gwynn	2.00
6 Rickey Henderson	1.50
7 Bo Jackson	.50
8 Mark McGwire	4.00
9 Mike Piazza	4.00
10 Tim Salmon	.50

Jumbo Checklists

Each hobby foil box of 1994 Upper Deck cards contains one jumbo checklist card. Each of the 5" x 7" cards features Ken Griffey, Jr. There is a large color action photo along with a hologram of the player on front, highlighted by copper-foil printing. Backs have one of four checklists and are numbered with a "CL" prefix.

	NM/M
Complete Set (4):	4.00
Common Card:	1.00
1 Numerical Checklist (Ken Griffey Jr.)	1.00
2 Alphabetical Checklist (Ken Griffey Jr.)	1.00
3 Team Checklist (Ken Griffey Jr.)	1.00
4 Insert Checklist (Ken Griffey Jr.)	1.00

Mickey Mantle's Long Shots

Retail packaging was the exclusive venue for this insert set of contemporary long-ball sluggers. Horizontal fronts feature game-action photos with holographic foil rendering of the background. In one of the lower corners appears the logo "1994 Mickey Mantle's Long Shots". Backs have a color player photo at top, with a photo of Mantle beneath and a statement by him about the featured player. Previous season and career stats are included. Cards are numbered with an "MM" prefix. Besides the 20 current player cards there is a Mickey Mantle card and two trade cards which could be redeemed for complete insert card sets.

	NM/M
Complete Set (21):	20.00
Common Player:	.50
Electric Diamonds:	1X
(1) Mickey Mantle Trade Card (Silver): (Redeemable for 21-card Mantle Long Shots set.)	4.00
(2) Mickey Mantle Trade Card (Blue): (Redeemable for Electric Diamond version Mantle Long Shots set.)	4.00
1 Jeff Bagwell	1.50
2 Albert Belle	.50
3 Barry Bonds	4.00
4 Jose Canseco	.75
5 Joe Carter	.50
6 Carlos Delgado	.75
7 Cecil Fielder	.50
8 Cliff Floyd	.50
9 Juan Gonzalez	.75
10 Ken Griffey Jr.	2.50
11 David Justice	.50
12 Fred McGriff	.50
13 Mark McGwire	3.00
14 Dean Palmer	.50
15 Mike Piazza	2.50
16 Manny Ramirez	1.50
17 Tim Salmon	.50
18 Frank Thomas	1.50
19 Mo Vaughn	.50
20 Matt Williams	.50
21 Header (Mickey Mantle)	4.00

Mantle-Griffey Autographed Inserts

First series retail packs of '94 UD were the exclusive venue for a special card featuring spokesmen Ken Griffey Jr. and Mickey Mantle. The front has a painting of the two stars. On back are career highlights and a comparison of the players' first five seasons. A large numbered elliptical hologram on back authenticates the autographs. One thousand cards were issued with either or both signatures.

	NM/M
KG1 Ken Griffey Jr., Mickey Mantle (Griffey Autograph)	250.00
MM1 Ken Griffey Jr., Mickey Mantle (Mantle Autograph)	650.00
GM1 Ken Griffey Jr., Mickey Mantle (Both Autographs)	1,150

Next Generation

Next Generation linked 20 of the top current stars with all-time greats, using the HoloView card printing technology. Next Generation trade cards could be redeemed for a complete set matching the cards found in retail packs. This insert set was inserted at a rate of one per 20 packs, while the Trade Card was inserted one per case.

	NM/M
Complete Set (18):	100.00
Common Player:	1.50
1 Roberto Alomar	2.50

---

2 Carlos Delgado	4.00
3 Cliff Floyd	1.50
4 Alex Gonzalez	1.50
5 Juan Gonzalez	3.00
6 Ken Griffey Jr.	10.00
7 Jeffrey Hammonds	1.50
8 Michael Jordan	30.00
9 Dave Justice	1.50
10 Ryan Klesko	1.50
11 Javier Lopez	1.50
12 Raul Mondesi	1.50
13 Mike Piazza	10.00
14 Kirby Puckett	7.50
15 Manny Ramirez	6.50
16 Alex Rodriguez	30.00
17 Tim Salmon	1.50
18 Gary Sheffield	4.00

Alex Rodriguez Autograph

Available exclusively in Series 2 retail packaging was this special version of A-Rod's Classic Alumni card. The card is authentically signed in blue Sharpie and carries on its back an authentication hologram.

	NM/M
A298 Alex Rodriguez (Classic Alumni, Autographed)	300.00

SP Insert

Fifteen SP Preview cards were inserted into Series II packs of Upper Deck baseball. The cards were inserted with regional distribution and gave collectors a chance to see what the SP super-premium cards would look like. There were five cards available in the East, Central and West and were inserted at a rate of about one per 36 packs. Most of the preview inserts have different front and back photos than the regularly issued SPs, along with other differences in typography and graphics elements.

	NM/M
Complete Set (15):	60.00
Common Player:	.50
EASTERN REGION	
1 Roberto Alomar	1.00
2 Cliff Floyd	.50
3 Javier Lopez	.50
4 Don Mattingly	6.00
5 Cal Ripken Jr.	10.00
CENTRAL REGION	
1 Jeff Bagwell	3.00
2 Michael Jordan	10.00
3 Kirby Puckett	6.00
4 Manny Ramirez	3.00
5 Frank Thomas	4.00
WESTERN REGION	
1 Barry Bonds	10.00
2 Juan Gonzalez	1.50
3 Ken Griffey Jr.	5.00
4 Mike Piazza	5.00
5 Tim Salmon	.50

Ken Griffey Jr. 5th Anniversary Jumbo

The origins of this card are unknown. Besides producing 15-card sets of top players in a black-bordered 5th Anniversary

---

insert set in regular and 3-1/2" x 5-1/2" formats, UD issued an 8-1/2" x 11" 5th Anniversary card of Griffey. In virtually all respects except size, the jumbo card is identical to the others. It is, however, numbered as back from within an edition of 5,000.

	NM/M
Ken Griffey Jr.	20.00

All-Stars

Produced in commemoration of the 1994 All-Star Game, this boxed set features photography by Walter Iooss, Jr. on most cards, shown to its best advantage on a large 3-1/2" x 5" format. The front of each card has a foil seal of the Pittsburgh All-Star Game logo. On most sets, the seal is in green foil; every 40th set has the seals in gold. The left side of the card backs features a smaller version of the front photo and a few sentences about the player. Some cards feature a second, larger photo of the player on back, but most have a photo and write-up of a teammate. The last six cards in the set honor the 125th anniversary of professional baseball. An album to house the set was made available for $10 via a mail-in offer card in the set.

	NM/M
Complete Set (48):	9.00
Common Player:	.15
Gold:	4X
1 Ken Griffey Jr.	1.00
2 Ruben Sierra, Todd Van Poppel	.15
3 Bryan Harvey, Gary Sheffield	.35
4 Gregg Jefferies, Brian Jordan	.15
5 Ryne Sandberg	.75
6 Matt Williams, John Burkett	.15
7 Darren Daulton, John Kruk	.15
8 Don Mattingly, Wade Boggs	.75
9 Pat Listach, Greg Vaughn	.15
10 Tim Salmon, Eduardo Perez	.25
11 Fred McGriff, Tom Glavine	.25
12 Mo Vaughn, Andre Dawson	.35
13 Brian McRae, Kevin Appier	.15
14 Kirby Puckett, Kent Hrbek	.75
15 Cal Ripken, Jr.	2.00
16 Roberto Alomar, Paul Molitor	.65
17 Tony Gwynn, Phil Plantier	.75
18 Greg Maddux, Steve Avery	.75
19 Mike Mussina, Chris Hoiles	.50
20 Randy Johnson	.65
21 Roger Clemens, Aaron Sele	.75
22 Will Clark, Dean Palmer	.25
23 Cecil Fielder, Travis Fryman	.15
24 John Olerud, Joe Carter	.15
25 Juan Gonzalez	.65
26 Jose Rijo, Barry Larkin	.15
27 Andy Van Slyke, Jeff King	.15
28 Larry Walker, Marquis Grissom	.15
29 Kenny Lofton, Albert Belle	.25
30 Mark Grace, Sammy Sosa	1.00

---

31 Mike Piazza	1.00
32 Ramon Martinez, Orel Hershiser	.15
33 Dave Justice, Terry Pendleton	.15
34 Ivan Rodriguez, Jose Canseco	.50
35 Barry Bonds	2.00
36 Jeff Bagwell, Craig Biggio	.65
37 Jay Bell, Orlando Merced	.15
38 Jeff Kent, Dwight Gooden	.15
39 Andres Galarraga, Charlie Hayes	.15
40 Frank Thomas	.70
41 Bobby Bonilla	.15
42 Jack McDowell, Tim Raines	.15
43 1869 Red Stockings	.15
44 Ty Cobb	.50
45 Babe Ruth	1.50
46 Mickey Mantle	2.50
47 Reggie Jackson	.50
48 Ken Griffey Jr.	1.00
48a Ken Griffey Jr./PC	1.00

All-Time Heroes

The All-Time Heroes set provided collectors with both Ted Williams cards from Topps 1954 reprint set, from which they were absent due to a contractual obligation between Ted Williams and the Upper Deck Co. An agreement between Topps and Upper Deck allowed both Williams' cards to be offered in the All-Time Heroes set. There is also a 1954 Mickey Mantle inserted that has no number, but bears the same design as original 1954 Topps cards. The basic All-Time Heroes of Baseball set contains 225 cards. The cards were patterned after cards from the early 60's, with black borders across the top and bottom. Black-and-white photographs give the 2-1/2" x 3-1/2" cards a nostalgic appearance. All-Time Heroes also has autographed cards of Mantle, Brett, Jackson and Seaver, along with a Next in Line insert set and a parallel, bronze-foil 125th anniversary set. Cards #1-18 comprise an Off the Wire subset. Cards #101-125 are a Major League 125th Anniversary subset. Cards #151-177 are a Diamond Legends subset. Cards #208-224 are a subset titled Heroes of Baseball.

	NM/M
Complete Set (225):	20.00
Common Player:	.10
Wax Box:	65.00
1 Ted Williams/OTW	.75
2 Johnny Vander Meer/OTW	.10
3 Lou Brock/OTW	.10
4 Lou Gehrig/OTW	.75
5 Hank Aaron /OTW	.50
6 Tommie Agee/OTW	.10
7 Mickey Mantle/OTW	.75
8 Bill Mazeroski/OTW	.30
9 Reggie Jackson, Bud Harrelson/OTW	.20
10 Willie Mays, Mickey Mantle/OTW	1.25

---

11 Roy Campanella/OTW	.20
12 Harvey Haddix/OTW	.10
13 Jimmy Piersall/OTW	.10
14 Enos Slaughter/OTW	.10
15 Nolan Ryan /OTW	.75
16 Bobby Thomson/OTW	.10
17 Willie Mays/OTW	.50
18 Bucky Dent/OTW	.10
19 Joe Garagiola	.20
20 George Brett	.75
21 Cecil Cooper	.10
22 Ray Boone	.10
23 King Kelly	.10
24 Willie Mays	1.00
25 Napoleon Lajoie	.10
26 Gil McDougald	.10
27 Nelson Briles	.10
28 Bucky Dent	.10
29 Manny Sanguillen	.10
30 Ty Cobb	1.00
31 Jim Grant	.10
32 Del Ennis	.10
33 Ron Hunt	.10
34 Nolan Ryan	1.50
35 Christy Mathewson	.75
36 Robin Roberts	.10
37 Frank Crosetti	.10
38 Johnny Vander Meer	.10
39 Virgil Trucks	.10
40 Lou Gehrig	1.50
41 Luke Appling	.10
42 Rico Petrocelli	.10
43 Harry Walker	.10
44 Reggie Jackson	.65
44a Reggie Jackson/PC	4.00
45 Mel Ott	.10
46 Phil Cavaretta	.10
47 Larry Doby	.10
48 Johnny Mize	.10
49 Ralph Kiner	.10
50 Ted Williams	1.50
51 Bobby Thomson	.10
52 Joe Black	.10
53 Monte Irvin	.10
54 Bill Virdon	.10
55 Honus Wagner	1.00
56 Herb Score	.10
57 Jerry Coleman	.10
58 Jimmie Foxx	.30
59 Elroy Face	.10
60 Babe Ruth	2.00
61 Jimmy Piersall	.10
62 Ed Charles	.10
63 Johnny Podres	.10
64 Charlie Neal	.10
65 Bill White	.10
66 Bill Skowron	.10
67 Al Rosen	.10
68 Eddie Lopat	.10
69 Bud Harrelson	.10
70 Steve Carlton	.10
71 Vida Blue	.10
72 Don Newcombe	.10
73 Al Bumbry	.10
74 Bill Madlock	.10
(75) Checklist 1-75 (Hank Aaron)	.50
76 Bill Mazeroski	.50
77 Ron Cey	.10
78 Tommy John	.10
79 Lou Brock	.75
80 Walter Johnson	.75
81 Harvey Haddix	.10
82 Al Oliver	.10
83 Johnny Logan	.10
84 Dave Dravecky	.10
85 Tony Oliva	.10
86 Dave Kingman	.10
87 Luis Tiant	.10
88 Sal Bando	.10
89 Cesar Cedeno	.10
90 Warren Spahn	.10
91 Mickey Lolich	.10
92 Lew Burdette	.10
93 Hank Bauer	.10
94 Marv Throneberry	.10
95 Willie Stargell	.10
96 George Kell	.10
97 Fergie Jenkins	.10
98 Al Kaline	.10
99 Billy Martin	.10
100 Mickey Mantle	3.00
101 1869 - Red Stockings (125th)	.20
102 1892 King Kelly (125th)	.10
103 1901 Nap Lajoie (125th)	.10
104 1905 Christy Mathewson (125th)	.40
105 1910 Cy Young (125th)	.40
106 1915 Ty Cobb (125th)	.75
(107) Checklist 136-180 (Reggie Jackson)	.40
108 1924 Rogers Hornsby (125th)	.10
109 1926 Walter Johnson (125th)	.40
110 1927 Babe Ruth (125th)	1.00
111 1930 Hack Wilson (125th)	.10
112 1939 Lou Gehrig (125th)	.75
113 1941 Ted Williams (125th)	.75
113a 1941 Ted Williams (125th) (Autographed edition of 2,500)	250.00

ABBREVIATIONS

PC - Promo Card

114	1949 Yogi Berra (125th)	.30
115	1951 Bobby Thomson (125th)	.10
116	1953 Mickey Mantle (125th)	1.50
117	1954 Willie Mays (125th)	.50
118	1960 Bill Mazeroski (125th)	.30
119	1967 Bob Gibson (125th)	.10
120	1969 Miracle Mets (125th)	.50
121	1974 Hank Aaron (125th)	.50
122	1977 Reggie Jackson (125th)	.40
123	1980 George Brett (125th)	.20
124	1982 Steve Carlton (125th)	.10
125	1991 Nolan Ryan (125th)	.75
126	Frank Thomas	.10
127	Sam McDowell	.10
128	Jim Lonberg	.10
129	Bert Campaneris	.10
130	Bob Gibson	.10
131	Bobby Richardson	.10
132	Bobby Grich	.10
133	Billy Pierce	.10
134	Enos Slaughter	.10
(135)	Checklist 181-225 (Honus Wagner)	.50
136	Orlando Cepeda	.10
137	Rennie Stennett	.10
138	Gene Alley	.10
139	Manny Mota	.10
140	Rogers Hornsby	.10
141	Joe Charboneau	.20
142	Rick Farrell	.10
143	Toby Harrah	.10
144	Hank Aaron	1.00
145	Yogi Berra	.50
146	Whitey Ford	.50
147	Roy Campanella	.50
148	Graig Nettles	.10
149	Bobby Brown	.10
150	Checklist 76-150 (Willie Mays)	.50
151	Cy Young/DL	.40
152	Walter Johnson/DL	.40
153	Christy Mathewson/DL	.40
154	Warren Spahn/DL	.10
155	Steve Carlton/DL	.10
156	Bob Gibson/DL	.10
157	Whitey Ford/DL	.30
158	Yogi Berra/DL	.30
159	Roy Campanella/DL	.30
160	Lou Gehrig/DL	.75
161	Johnny Mize/DL	.10
162	Rogers Hornsby/DL	.10
163	Honus Wagner/DL	.50
164	Hank Aaron/DL	.50
165	Babe Ruth/DL	1.00
166	Willie Mays/DL	.50
167	Reggie Jackson/DL	.40
168	Mickey Mantle/DL	1.50
169	Jimmie Foxx/DL	.10
170	Ted Williams/DL	.75
171	Mel Ott/DL	.10
172	Willie Stargell/DL	.10
173	Al Kaline/DL	.10
174	Ty Cobb/DL	.75
175	Napoleon Lajoie/DL	.10
176	Lou Brock/DL	.10
177	Tom Seaver/DL	.10
178	Mark Fidrych	.20
179	Don Baylor	.10
180	Tom Seaver	.10
181	Jerry Grote	.10
182	George Foster	.10
183	Buddy Bell	.10
184	Ralph Garr	.10
185	Steve Garvey	.10
186	Joe Torre	.10
187	Carl Erskine	.10
188	Tommy Davis	.10
189	Bill Buckner	.10
190	Hack Wilson	.10
191	Steve Bass	.10
192	Ken Brett	.10
193	Lee May	.10
194	Bob Horner	.10
195	Boog Powell	.10
196	Darrell Evans	.10
197	Paul Blair	.10
198	Johnny Callison	.10
199	Jimmie Reese	.10
200	Cy Young	.75
201	Ron Santo	.10
202	Rico Carty	.10
203	Ron Necciai	.10
204	Lou Boudreau	.10
205	Minnie Minoso	.10
206	Eddie Yost	.10
207	Tommie Agee	.10
208	Dave Kingman (Heroes)	.10
209	Tony Oliva (Heroes)	.10
210	Reggie Jackson (Heroes)	.40
211	Paul Blair (Heroes)	.10
212	Fergie Jenkins (Heroes)	.10
213	Steve Garvey (Heroes)	.10
214	Bert Campaneris (Heroes)	.10
215	Orlando Cepeda (Heroes)	.10
216	Bill Madlock (Heroes)	.10
217	Rennie Stennett (Heroes)	.10
218	Frank Thomas (Heroes)	.10
219	Bob Gibson (Heroes)	.10
220	Lou Brock (Heroes)	.10
221	Rico Carty (Heroes)	.10
222	Mickey Mantle (Heroes)	1.50
223	Robin Roberts (Heroes)	.10
224	Manny Sanguillen (Heroes)	.10
225	Checklist 151-225 (Mickey Mantle)	1.50

All-Time Heroes 125th Anniversary

This parallel set was issued at the rate of one card per pack of Upper Deck All-Time Heroes cards. They are identical to the regular-issue version except for the presence on front of bronze-foil stamping which reads, "Major League Baseball / 125th Anniversary."

		NM/M
Complete Set (225):		40.00
Common Player:		.25
Stars:		2X
15	Nolan Ryan/OTW (Overprint at left.)	1.00
15	Nolan Ryan/OTW (Overprint at right.)	1.00

All-Time Heroes Autographs

Four players' autographed cards were randomly inserted into packs of All-Time Heroes at a reported rate of about 1:385. Seaver, Jackson and Mantle signed 1,000 each, Brett signed 2,000.

		NM/M
Complete Set (4):		650.00
Common Player:		45.00
(1)	Mickey Mantle	550.00
(2)	Reggie Jackson	40.00
(3)	George Brett	60.00
(4)	Tom Seaver	25.00

All-Time Heroes Next In Line

The Next in Line insert set includes 20 top minor leaguers. These cards were randomly inserted into every 39 packs with only 2,500 of each card produced.

		NM/M
Complete Set (20):		40.00
Common Player:		1.00
1	Mike Bell	1.00
2	Alan Benes	1.00
3	D.J. Boston	1.00
4	Johnny Damon	5.00

5	Brad Fullmer	1.00
6	LaTroy Hawkins	1.00
7	Derek Jeter	25.00
8	Daron Kirkreit	1.00
9	Trot Nixon	3.00
10	Alex Ochoa	1.00
11	Kirk Presley	1.00
12	Jose Silva	1.00
13	Terrell Wade	1.00
14	Billy Wagner	1.50
15	Glenn Williams	1.00
16	Preston Wilson	1.50
17	Wayne Gomes	1.00
18	Ben Grieve	1.00
19	Dustin Hermanson	1.00
20	Paul Wilson	1.00

All-Time Heroes 1954 Topps Archives

Two cards that were not included in the Topps 1954 Archives Set and one that wasn't even in the original 1954 set were randomly inserted into All-Time Heroes foil packs. Both Ted Williams cards, numbers 1 and 250, were left out of the Archives set because of contractual obligations of Williams with Upper Deck. In addition, a Mickey Mantle card with the original 1954 design was randomly inserted. Mantle was signed exclusively with Bowman in 1954 and 1955, and therefore, was not in either Topps set.

		NM/M
Complete Set (3):		150.00
1	Ted Williams	50.00
250	Ted Williams	50.00
259	Mickey Mantle	75.00

American Epic

Baseball, The American Epic traces the history of the game, highlighting players, personalities, events and stadiums that have contributed to the national pastime. The set was patterned after a 1994 18-hour TV documentary. This boxed set contains 80 cards. It explains the roots of the game and showcases some of baseball's great players and events. Each set contains a randomly inserted card of either Michael Jordan, Babe Ruth or Mickey Mantle. Cards from the regular set are in black-and-white, with the player name and the featured year running down the left side in white print. Card backs contain half color, depending on what "inning" the card is from, and half white. The color side tells a story, the white side gives statistics and highlights.

		NM/M
Complete Set (81):		12.50
Common Player:		.15
1	1880s - Our Game	.15
2	1845 - Alexander Cartwright	.15
3	1857 - Henry Chadwick	.15
4	1866 - The Fair Sex	.15
5	1869 - Harry Wright	.15
6	1876 - Albert Goodwill Spalding	.15
7	1883 - Cap Anson	.15
8	1884 - Moses Fleetwood Walker	.25
9	1886 - King Kelly	.15
10	1890 - John Montgomery Ward	.15
11	1909 - Ty Cobb	.75
12	1904 - John McGraw	.15
13	1904 - Rube Waddell	.15
14	1905 - Christy Mathewson	.25
15	1907 - Walter Johnson	.25
16	1908 - Alta Weiss	.15
17	1908 - Fred Merkle	.15
18	1908 - Take Me Out To The Ball Game	.15
19	1909 - John Henry Lloyd	.15
20	1909 - Honus Wagner	.40
21	1915 - Woodrow Wilson	.15
22	1910 - Napoleon Lajoie	.15
23	1911 - Addie Joss	.15
24	1912 - Joe Wood	.15
25	1912 - Royal Rooters	.15
26	1913 - Ebbets Field	.15
27	1914 - Johnny Evers	.15
28	1918 - World War II	.15
29	1919 - Joe Jackson	.75
30	1927 - Babe Ruth	1.50
31	1920 - Rube Foster	.15
32	1920 - Ray Chapman	.15
33	1921 - Kenesaw M. Landis	.15
34	1923 - Yankee Stadium	.15
35	1924 - Rogers Hornsby	.15
36	1923 - Warren G. Harding	.15
37	1925 - Lou Gehrig	.75
38	1926 - Grover C. Alexander	.15
39	1929 - House of David	.15
40	1933 - Satchel Paige	.40
41	1931 - Lefty Grove	.15
42	1932 - Jimmie Foxx	.15
43	1932 - Connie Mack	.15
44	1937 - Josh Gibson	.15
45	1934 - Dizzy Dean	.15
46	1934 - Carl Hubbell	.15
47	1937 - Franklin D. Roosevelt	.15
48	1938 - Bob Feller	.15
49	1939 - Cool Papa Bell	.15
50	1947 - Jackie Robinson	.75
51	1941 - Ted Williams	.15
52	1941 - Sym-Phony Band	.15
53	1944 - Annabel Lee	.15
54	1945 - Hank Greenberg	.15
55	1947 - Branch Rickey	.15
56	1948 - Harry S. Truman	.15
57	1953 - Casey Stengel	.15
58	1951 - Bobby Thomson	.15
59	1952 - Dwight D. Eisenhower	.15
60	1952 - Mario Cuomo	.15
61	1952 - Buck O'Neil	.15
62	1955 - Yogi Berra	.15
63	1956 - Mickey Mantle	2.00
64	1956 - Don Larsen	.15
65	1961 - John F. Kennedy	.15
66	1960 - Bill Mazeroski	.15
67	1961 - Roger Maris	.25
68	1966 - Frank Robinson	.15
69	1969 - Bob Gibson	.15
70	1970 - Tom Seaver	.15
71	1969 - Curt Flood	.15
72	1972 - Roberto Clemente	.75
73	1975 - Luis Tiant	.15
74	1975 - Marvin Miller	.15
75	1977 - Reggie Jackson	.15
76	1979 - Willie Stargell	.15
77	1985 - Pete Rose	.75
78	1994 - Bill Clinton	.15
79	1991 - Nolan Ryan	.75
80	1993 - George Brett	.25
---	Checklist	.08

American Epic Inserts

In addition to the regular 80-card set, each boxed set contains one special insert card, depending on where it was purchased. At retail locations, an additional Babe Ruth card was included. Michael Jordan was included in sets purchased through direct mail outlets. Mickey Mantle was featured in sets purchased from QVC (sets purchased from Upper Deck Authenticated included an autographed card of Mantle). The inserts are numbered BC1- BC3.

		NM/M
Complete Set (3):		6.00
Common Player:		2.00
1	Mickey Mantle	2.00
2	Michael Jordan	2.00
3	Babe Ruth	2.00

American Epic Little Debbie Mail-in

Fifteen of the cards from Upper Deck's "An American Epic" card set were chosen for use in a mail-in promotion with Little Debbie snack cakes. These cards are identical to the Epic versions except for the card numbers, which include an "LD" prefix. The back of card LD1 is a checklist for the set and includes a Little Debbie logo. Sets sold for about $4, with proofs of purchase.

		NM/M
Complete Set (15):		4.50
Common Player:		.25
1	Our Game/Checklist	.05
2	Alexander Cartwright	.25
3	King Kelly	.25
4	John McGraw	.25
5	Christy Mathewson	.40
6	Walter Johnson	.40
7	Ted Williams	.75
8	Annabel Lee	.25
9	Jackie Robinson	.50
10	Bobby Thomson	.25
11	Buck O'Neil	.25
12	Mickey Mantle	1.50
13	Bob Gibson	.25
14	Curt Flood	.25
15	Reggie Jackson	.40

Fun Packs

In its second year this product again offered a basic set of some 160 players, surrounded by several special subsets. The first nine cards feature Stars of Tomorrow. There is a group of 18 Stand Out cards on which the background can be folded to create a player figure. Profiles cards

feature playing tips from six young stars. A group of nine Headline Stars cards features two players on each which fold back to reveal a holographic photo. What's the Call cards offer game problems and cartoon caricatures of nine players. There are nine Fold Outs cards which open to reveal action photos. The subsets concluded with seven heat-activated Fun Cards on which the background temporarily appears when body heat is applied. Each five-card foil pack also includes a scratch-off game card; one for each major league team and one All-Star team for each league.

		NM/M
Complete Set (240):		35.00
Common Player:		.05
Wax Box:		15.00
1	Manny Ramirez (Stars of Tomorrow)	.75
2	Cliff Floyd (Stars of Tomorrow)	.05
3	Rondell White (Stars of Tomorrow)	.05
4	Carlos Delgado (Stars of Tomorrow)	.50
5	Chipper Jones (Stars of Tomorrow)	1.25
6	Javier Lopez (Stars of Tomorrow)	.05
7	Ryan Klesko (Stars of Tomorrow)	.05
8	Steve Karsay (Stars of Tomorrow)	.05
9	Rich Becker (Stars of Tomorrow)	.05
10	Gary Sheffield	.35
11	Jeffrey Hammonds	.05
12	Roberto Alomar	.20
13	Brent Gates	.05
14	Andres Galarraga	.05
15	Tim Salmon	.05
16	Dwight Gooden	.05
17	Mark Grace	.05
18	Andy Van Slyke	.05
19	Juan Gonzalez	.40
20	Mickey Tettleton	.05
21	Roger Clemens	1.25
22	Will Clark	.05
23	Dave Justice	.05
24	Ken Griffey Jr.	1.50
24a	Ken Griffey Jr./PC	1.50
25	Barry Bonds	2.50
26	Bill Swift	.05
27	Fred McGriff	.05
28	Randy Myers	.05
29	Joe Carter	.05
30	Nigel Wilson	.05
31	Mike Piazza	1.50
32	Dave Winfield	.75
33	Steve Avery	.05
34	Kirby Puckett	.90
35	Frank Thomas	.75
36	Aaron Sele	.05
37	Ricky Gutierrez	.05
38	Curt Schilling	.25
39	Mike Greenwell	.05
40	Andy Benes	.05
41	Kevin Brown	.05
42	Mo Vaughn	.05
43	Dennis Eckersley	.60
44	Ken Hill	.05
45	Cecil Fielder	.05
46	Bobby Jones	.05
47	Tom Glavine	.25
48	Wally Joyner	.05
49	Ellis Burks	.05
50	Jason Bere	.05
51	Randy Johnson	.75
52	Darryl Kile	.05
53	Jeff Montgomery	.05
54	Alex Fernandez	.05

ABBREVIATIONS
PC - Promo Card

55	Kevin Appier	.05
56	Brian McRae	.05
57	John Wetteland	.05
58	Bob Tewksbury	.05
59	Todd Van Poppel	.05
60	Ryne Sandberg	.90
61	Bret Barberie	.05
62	Phil Plantier	.05
63	Chris Hoiles	.05
64	Tony Phillips	.05
65	Salomon Torres	.05
66	Juan Guzman	.05
67	Paul O'Neill	.05
68	Dante Bichette	.05
69	Len Dykstra	.05
70	Ivan Rodriguez	.65
71	Dean Palmer	.05
72a	Brett Butler	.05
72b	Phil Hiatt (Checklisted as #172.)	.05
73	Rick Aguilera	.05
74	Robby Thompson	.05
75	Jim Abbott	.05
76	Al Martin	.05
77	Roberto Hernandez	.05
78	Jay Buhner	.05
79	Devon White	.05
80	Travis Fryman	.05
81	Jeromy Burnitz	.05
82	John Burkett	.05
83	Orlando Merced	.05
84	Jose Rijo	.05
85	Eddie Murray	.75
86	Howard Johnson	.05
87	Chuck Carr	.05
88	Pedro J. Martinez	.75
89	Charlie Hayes	.05
90	Matt Williams	.05
91	Steve Finley	.05
92	Pat Listach	.05
93	Sandy Alomar, Jr.	.05
94	Delino DeShields	.05
95	Rod Beck	.05
97	Todd Zeile (Checklisted as #96)	.05
98a	Darryl Hamilton	.05
98b	Duane Ward (Checklisted as #97)	.05
99	John Olerud	.05
100	Andre Dawson	.25
101	Ozzie Smith	.90
102	Rick Wilkins	.05
103	Alan Trammell	.05
104	Jeff Blauser	.05
105	Bret Boone	.05
106	J.T. Snow	.05
107	Kenny Lofton	.05
108	Cal Ripken, Jr.	2.50
109	Carlos Baerga	.05
110	Bip Roberts	.05
111	Barry Larkin	.05
112	Mark Langston	.05
113	Ozzie Guillen	.05
114	Chad Curtis	.05
115	Dave Hollins	.05
116	Reggie Sanders	.05
117	Jeff Conine	.05
118	Mark Whiten	.05
119	Tony Gwynn	.90
120	John Kruk	.05
121	Eduardo Perez	.05
122	Walt Weiss	.05
123	Don Mattingly	1.00
124	Rickey Henderson	.75
125	Mark McGwire	2.00
126	Wade Boggs	.90
127	Bobby Bonilla	.05
128	Jeff King	.05
129	Jack McDowell	.05
130	Albert Belle	.05
131	Greg Maddux	.90
132	Dennis Martinez	.05
133	Jose Canseco	.40
134	Bryan Harvey	.05
135	Dave Fleming	.05
136	Larry Walker	.05
137	Ken Caminiti	.05
138	Doug Drabek	.05
139	Ron Gant	.05
140	Darren Daulton	.05
141	Ruben Sierra	.05
142	Kirk Rueter	.05
143	Raul Mondesi	.05
144	Greg Vaughn	.05
145	Danny Tartabull	.05
146	Eric Karros	.05
147	Chuck Knoblauch	.05
148	Mike Mussina	.30
149	Brady Anderson	.05
150	Paul Molitor	.75
151	Bo Jackson	.10
152	Jeff Bagwell	.75
153	Gregg Jefferies	.05
154	Rafael Palmeiro	.65
155	Orel Hershiser	.05
156	Derek Bell	.05
157	Jeff Kent	.05
158	Craig Biggio	.05
159	Marquis Grissom	.05
160	Matt Mieske	.05
161	Jay Bell	.05
162	Sammy Sosa	.90
163	Robin Ventura	.05
164	Deion Sanders	.05
165	Jimmy Key	.05
166	Cal Eldred	.05
167	David McCarty	.05
168	Carlos Garcia	.05

169	Willie Greene	.05
170	Michael Jordan RC	2.50
171	Roberto Mejia	.05
173	Marc Newfield	.05
174	Kevin Stocker	.05
175	Randy Johnson (Standouts)	.40
176	Ivan Rodriguez (Standouts)	.30
177	Frank Thomas (Standouts)	.45
178	Roberto Alomar (Standouts)	.10
179	Travis Fryman (Standouts)	.05
180	Cal Ripken, Jr. (Standouts)	1.25
181	Juan Gonzalez (Standouts)	.30
182	Ken Griffey Jr. (Standouts)	.75
183	Albert Belle (Standouts)	.05
184	Greg Maddux (Standouts)	.50
185	Mike Piazza (Standouts)	.75
186	Fred McGriff (Standouts)	.05
187	Robby Thompson (Standouts)	.05
188	Matt Williams (Standouts)	.05
189	Jeff Blauser (Standouts)	.05
190	Barry Bonds (Standouts)	1.25
191	Len Dykstra (Standouts)	.05
192	Dave Justice (Standouts)	.05
193	Ken Griffey Jr. (Profiles)	.75
194	Barry Bonds (Profiles)	1.25
195	Frank Thomas (Profiles)	.45
196	Juan Gonzalez (Profiles)	.30
197	Randy Johnson (Profiles)	.40
198	Chuck Carr (Profiles)	.05
199	Barry Bonds, Juan Gonzalez (Headline Stars)	1.00
200	Ken Griffey Jr., Don Mattingly (Headline Stars)	.75
201	Roberto Alomar, Carlos Baerga (Headline Stars)	.10
202	Dave Winfield, Robin Yount (Headline Stars)	.40
203	Mike Piazza, Tim Salmon (Headline Stars)	.75
204	Albert Belle, Frank Thomas (Headline Stars)	.45
205	Cliff Floyd, Rondell White (Headline Stars)	.05
206	Kirby Puckett, Tony Gwynn (Headline Stars)	.50
207	Roger Clemens, Greg Maddux (Headline Stars)	.50
208	Mike Piazza (What's The Call)	.75
209	Jose Canseco (What's The Call)	.20
210	Frank Thomas (What's The Call)	.45
211	Roberto Alomar (What's The Call)	.10
212	Barry Bonds (What's The Call)	1.25
213	Rickey Henderson (What's The Call)	.40
214	John Kruk (What's The Call)	.05
215	Juan Gonzalez (What's The Call)	.40
216	Ken Griffey Jr. (What's The Call)	.75
217	Roberto Alomar (Foldouts)	.10
218	Craig Biggio (Foldouts)	.05
219	Cal Ripken, Jr. (Foldouts)	1.25
220	Mike Piazza (Foldouts)	.75
221	Brent Gates (Foldouts)	.05
222	Walt Weiss (Foldouts)	.05
223	Bobby Bonilla (Foldouts)	.05
224	Ken Griffey Jr. (Foldouts)	1.25
225	Barry Bonds (Foldouts)	1.25
226	Barry Bonds (Fun Cards)	1.25
227	Joe Carter (Fun Cards)	.05
228	Mike Greenwell (Fun Cards)	.05
229	Ken Griffey Jr. (Fun Cards)	.75
230	John Kruk (Fun Cards)	.05
231	Mike Piazza (Fun Cards)	.75
232	Kirby Puckett (Fun Cards)	.05
233	John Smoltz (Fun Cards)	.05
234	Rick Wilkins (Fun Cards)	.05

235	Checklist 1-40 (Ken Griffey Jr.)	.65
236	Checklist 41-80 (Frank Thomas)	.45
237	Checklist 81-120 (Barry Bonds)	1.00
238	Checklist 121-160 (Mike Piazza)	.65
239	Checklist 161-200 (Tim Salmon)	.05
240	Checklist 201-240 (Juan Gonzalez)	.35

Scratch-off Game Cards:

(1)	National League	.05
(2)	Atlanta Braves	.05
(3)	Chicago Cubs	.05
(4)	Cincinnati Reds	.05
(5)	Colorado Rockies	.05
(6)	Florida Marlins	.05
(7)	Houston Astros	.05
(8)	Los Angeles Dodgers	.05
(9)	Montreal Expos	.05
(10)	New York Mets	.05
(11)	Philadelphia Phillies	.05
(12)	Pittsburgh Pirates	.05
(13)	St. Louis Cardinals	.05
(14)	San Diego Padres	.05
(15)	San Francisco Giants	.05

GM "Baseball" Previews

This nine-card set is closely related to the 80-card issue subsequently released in conjunction with the public television series "Baseball" by Ken Burns. This preview issue, carrying the logo of General Motors (principal sponsor of the TV series), was issued in cello and foil packs and was available, generally with a test drive, at GM automobile dealerships. Card backs have some biographical and statistical highlights and a career summary.

		NM/M
Complete Set (9):		6.00
Common Player:		.50
1	Hank Aaron	1.25
2	Roberto Clemente	1.50
3	Ty Cobb	.50
4	Hank Greenberg	.50
5	Mickey Mantle	3.00
6	Satchel Paige	.50
7	Jackie Robinson	.75
8	Babe Ruth	2.00
9	Ted Williams	1.00

GTS Mickey Mantle Phone Cards

Upper Deck and Global Telecommunication Solutions combined to produce this set of phone cards paralleling the Mantle Heroes insert cards found in the regular UD issue. The phone cards were sold in two series of five cards each for $59.95 per series. Fronts of the 2-1/8" x 3-3/8" plastic cards feature black-and-white or color photos of Mantle, along with mention of a career highlight. Backs are printed in black and have instructions for use of the card. A card picturing the 1869 Cincinnati Red Stockings was included as a random insert in the first series of Mantle phone card sets.

		NM/M
Complete Set (10):		20.00
Common Card:		3.00
(1)	Mickey Mantle/Portrait	3.00
(2)	Mickey Mantle (1951: The Early Years)	3.00
(3)	Mickey Mantle (1953: Tape Measure Home Runs)	3.00
(4)	Mickey Mantle (1956: Triple Crown Season)	3.00
(5)	Mickey Mantle (1957: Second Consecutive MVP)	3.00
(6)	Mickey Mantle (1961: Chasing the Babe)	3.00
(7)	Mickey Mantle (1964: Series Home Run Record)	3.00
(8)	Mickey Mantle (1967: 500th Home Run)	3.00
(9)	Mickey Mantle (1974: Hall of Fame)	3.00
(10)	Mickey Mantle/Portrait	3.00
(11)	1869 Cincinnati Red Stockings	10.00

1995 Upper Deck

Issued in two series of 225 base cards each, with loads of subsets and inserts, the 1995 Upper Deck set was a strong collector favorite from the outset. Basic cards feature a borderless front photo with the player's name and UD logo in bronze foil. Backs have another large color photo, recent stats and career totals and appropriate logos, along with the infield-shaped hologram. Subsets in each series include Star Rookies and Top Prospects, each with special designs highlighting the game's young stars. Series I has a "'90s Midpoint Analysis" subset studying the decade's superstars, and Series II has another hot rookies' subset, Diamond Debuts. The set closes with a five-card "Final Tribute" subset summarizing the careers of five recently retired superstars. Retail and hobby versions were sold with each featuring some unique insert cards. Basic packaging of each type was the 12-card foil pack at $1.99, though several other configurations were also released.

		NM/M
Complete Set (450):		20.00
Common Player:		.05
Electric Diamond:		2X
Electric Diamond Golds:		8X
Series 1 or 2 Pack (12):		.85
Series 1 or 2 Wax Box (36):		20.00
1	Ruben Rivera (Top Prospect)	.05
2	Bill Pulsipher (Top Prospect)	.05
3	Ben Grieve (Top Prospect)	.05
4	Curtis Goodwin (Top Prospect)	.05
5	Damon Hollins (Top Prospect)	.05
6	Todd Greene (Top Prospect)	.05
7	Glenn Williams (Top Prospect)	.05
8	Bret Wagner (Top Prospect)	.05
9	Karim Garcia RC (Top Prospect)	.50
10	Nomar Garciaparra (Top Prospect)	1.00
11	Raul Casanova RC (Top Prospect)	.10
12	Matt Smith (Top Prospect)	.05
13	Paul Wilson (Top Prospect)	.05
14	Jason Isringhausen (Top Prospect)	.05
15	Reid Ryan (Top Prospect)	.05
16	Lee Smith	.05
17	Chili Davis	.05
18	Brian Anderson	.05
19	Gary DiSarcina	.05
20	Bo Jackson	.10
21	Chuck Finley	.05
22	Darryl Kile	.05
23	Shane Reynolds	.05
24	Tony Eusebio	.05
25	Craig Biggio	.05
26	Doug Drabek	.05
27	Brian L. Hunter	.05
28	James Mouton	.05
29	Geronimo Berroa	.05
30	Rickey Henderson	.75
31	Steve Karsay	.05
32	Steve Ontiveros	.05
33	Ernie Young	.05
34	Dennis Eckersley	.65
35	Mark McGwire	1.50
36	Dave Stewart	.05
37	Pat Hentgen	.05
38	Carlos Delgado	.45
39	Joe Carter	.05
40	Roberto Alomar	.20
41	John Olerud	.05
42	Devon White	.05
43	Roberto Kelly	.05
44	Jeff Blauser	.05
45	Fred McGriff	.05
46	Tom Glavine	.25
47	Mike Kelly	.05
48	Javy Lopez	.05
49	Greg Maddux	1.00
50	Matt Mieske	.05
51	Troy O'Leary	.05
52	Jeff Cirillo	.05
53	Cal Eldred	.05
54	Pat Listach	.05
55	Jose Valentin	.05
56	John Mabry	.05
57	Bob Tewksbury	.05
58	Brian Jordan	.05
59	Gregg Jefferies	.05
60	Ozzie Smith	1.00
61	Geronimo Pena	.05
62	Mark Whiten	.05
63	Rey Sanchez	.05
64	Willie Banks	.05
65	Mark Grace	.05
66	Randy Myers	.05
67	Steve Trachsel	.05
68	Derrick May	.05
69	Brett Butler	.05
70	Eric Karros	.05
71	Tim Wallach	.05
72	Delino DeShields	.05
73	Darren Dreifort	.05
74	Orel Hershiser	.05
75	Billy Ashley	.05
76	Sean Berry	.05
77	Ken Hill	.05
78	John Wetteland	.05
79	Moises Alou	.05
80	Cliff Floyd	.05
81	Marquis Grissom	.05
82	Larry Walker	.05
83	Rondell White	.05
84	William Van Landingham	.05
85	Matt Williams	.05
86	Rod Beck	.05
87	Darren Lewis	.05
88	Robby Thompson	.05
89	Darryl Strawberry	.05
90	Kenny Lofton	.05
91	Charles Nagy	.05
92	Sandy Alomar Jr.	.05
93	Mark Clark	.05
94	Dennis Martinez	.05
95	Dave Winfield	.75
96	Jim Thome	.60
97	Manny Ramirez	.75
98	Goose Gossage	.05
99	Tino Martinez	.05
100	Ken Griffey Jr.	1.25
100a	Ken Griffey Jr./OPS	2.00
101	Greg Maddux (Analysis: '90s Midpoint)	.50
102	Randy Johnson (Analysis: '90s Midpoint)	.40
103	Barry Bonds (Analysis: '90s Midpoint)	1.00
104	Juan Gonzalez (Analysis: '90s Midpoint)	.20
105	Frank Thomas (Analysis: '90s Midpoint)	.40
106	Matt Williams (Analysis: '90s Midpoint)	.05
107	Paul Molitor (Analysis: '90s Midpoint)	.40
108	Fred McGriff (Analysis: '90s Midpoint)	.05
109	Carlos Baerga (Analysis: '90s Midpoint)	.05
110	Ken Griffey Jr. (Analysis: '90s Midpoint)	.65
111	Reggie Jefferson	.05
112	Randy Johnson	.75
113	Marc Newfield	.05
114	Robb Nen	.05
115	Jeff Conine	.05
116	Kurt Abbott	.05
117	Charlie Hough	.05
118	Dave Weathers	.05
119	Juan Castillo	.05
120	Bret Saberhagen	.05
121	Rico Brogna	.05
122	John Franco	.05
123	Todd Hundley	.05
124	Jason Jacome	.05
125	Bobby Jones	.05
126	Bret Barberie	.05
127	Ben McDonald	.05
128	Harold Baines	.05
129	Jeffrey Hammonds	.05
130	Mike Mussina	.30
131	Chris Hoiles	.05
132	Brady Anderson	.05
133	Eddie Williams	.05
134	Andy Benes	.05
135	Tony Gwynn	1.00
136	Bip Roberts	.05
137	Joey Hamilton	.05
138	Luis Lopez	.05
139	Ray McDavid	.05
140	Lenny Dykstra	.05
141	Mariano Duncan	.05
142	Fernando Valenzuela	.05
143	Bobby Munoz	.05
144	Kevin Stocker	.05
145	John Kruk	.05
146	Jon Lieber	.05
147	Zane Smith	.05
148	Steve Cooke	.05
149	Andy Van Slyke	.05
150	Jay Bell	.05
151	Carlos Garcia	.05
152	John Dettmer	.05
153	Darren Oliver	.05
154	Dean Palmer	.05
155	Otis Nixon	.05
156	Rusty Greer	.05
157	Rick Helling	.05
158	Jose Canseco	.40
159	Roger Clemens	1.00
160	Andre Dawson	.25
161	Mo Vaughn	.05
162	Aaron Sele	.05
163	John Valentin	.05
164	Brian Hunter	.05
165	Bret Boone	.05
166	Hector Carrasco	.05
167	Pete Schourek	.05
168	Willie Greene	.05
169	Kevin Mitchell	.05
170	Deion Sanders	.05
171	John Roper	.05
172	Charlie Hayes	.05
173	David Nied	.05
174	Ellis Burks	.05
175	Dante Bichette	.05
176	Marvin Freeman	.05
177	Eric Young	.05
178	David Cone	.05
179	Greg Gagne	.05
180	Bob Hamelin	.05
181	Wally Joyner	.05
182	Jeff Montgomery	.05
183	Jose Lind	.05
184	Chris Gomez	.05
185	Travis Fryman	.05
186	Kirk Gibson	.05
187	Mike Moore	.05
188	Lou Whitaker	.05
189	Sean Bergman	.05
190	Shane Mack	.05
191	Rick Aguilera	.05
192	Denny Hocking	.05
193	Chuck Knoblauch	.05
194	Kevin Tapani	.05
195	Kent Hrbek	.05
196	Ozzie Guillen	.05
197	Wilson Alvarez	.05
198	Tim Raines	.05
199	Scott Ruffcorn	.05
200	Michael Jordan	2.00
201	Robin Ventura	.05
202	Jason Bere	.05
203	Darrin Jackson	.05
204	Russ Davis	.05
205	Jimmy Key	.05
206	Jack McDowell	.05
207	Jim Abbott	.05
208	Paul O'Neill	.05
209	Bernie Williams	.05
210	Don Mattingly	1.00

ABBREVIATIONS

OPS - Overprinted "Promotional Sample"

211	Orlando Miller (Star Rookie)	.05
212	Alex Gonzalez (Star Rookie)	.05
213	Terrell Wade (Star Rookie)	.05
214	Jose Oliva (Star Rookie)	.05
215	Alex Rodriguez (Star Rookie)	1.50
216	Garret Anderson (Star Rookie)	.05
217	Alan Benes (Star Rookie)	.05
218	Armando Benitez (Star Rookie)	.05
219	Dustin Hermanson (Star Rookie)	.05
220	Charles Johnson (Star Rookie)	.05
221	Julian Tavarez (Star Rookie)	.05
222	Jason Giambi (Star Rookie)	.50
223	LaTroy Hawkins (Star Rookie)	.05
224	Todd Hollandsworth (Star Rookie)	.05
225	Derek Jeter (Star Rookie)	2.00
226	Hideo Nomo RC (Star Rookie)	2.00
227	Tony Clark (Star Rookie)	.05
228	Roger Cedeno (Star Rookie)	.05
229	Scott Stahoviak (Star Rookie)	.05
230	Michael Tucker (Star Rookie)	.05
231	Joe Rosselli (Star Rookie)	.05
232	Antonio Osuna (Star Rookie)	.05
233	Bobby Higginson RC (Star Rookie)	.05
234	Mark Grudzielanek RC (Star Rookie)	.25
235	Ray Durham (Star Rookie)	.05
236	Frank Rodriguez (Star Rookie)	.05
237	Quilvio Veras (Star Rookie)	.05
238	Darren Bragg (Star Rookie)	.05
239	Ugueth Urbina (Star Rookie)	.05
240	Jason Bates (Star Rookie)	.05
241	David Bell (Diamond Debuts)	.05
242	Ron Villone (Diamond Debuts)	.05
243	Joe Randa (Diamond Debuts)	.05
244	Carlos Perez RC (Diamond Debuts)	.05
245	Brad Clontz (Diamond Debuts)	.05
246	Steve Rodriguez (Diamond Debuts)	.05
247	Joe Vitiello (Diamond Debuts)	.05
248	Ozzie Timmons (Diamond Debuts)	.05
249	Rudy Pemberton (Diamond Debuts)	.05
250	Marty Cordova (Diamond Debuts)	.05
251	Tony Graffanino (Top Prospect)	.05
252	Mark Johnson RC (Top Prospect)	.05
253	Tomas Perez RC (Top Prospect)	.05
254	Jimmy Hurst (Top Prospect)	.05
255	Edgardo Alfonzo (Top Prospect)	.05
256	Jose Malave (Top Prospect)	.05
257	Brad Radke RC (Top Prospect)	.30
258	Jon Nunnally (Top Prospect)	.05
259	Dilson Torres (Top Prospect)	.05
260	Esteban Loaiza (Top Prospect)	.05
261	Freddy Garcia RC (Top Prospect)	.05
262	Don Wengert (Top Prospect)	.05
263	Robert Person RC (Top Prospect)	.05
264	Tim Unroe RC (Top Prospect)	.05
265	Juan Acevedo (Top Prospect)	.05
266	Eduardo Perez	.05
267	Tony Phillips	.05
268	Jim Edmonds	.05
269	Jorge Fabregas	.05
270	Tim Salmon	.05
271	Mark Langston	.05
272	J.T. Snow	.05
273	Phil Plantier	.05
274	Derek Bell	.05
275	Jeff Bagwell	.75
276	Luis Gonzalez	.05
277	John Hudek	.05
278	Todd Stottlemyre	.05
279	Mark Acre	.05
280	Ruben Sierra	.05
281	Mike Bordick	.05
282	Ron Darling	.05
283	Brent Gates	.05
284	Todd Van Poppel	.05
285	Paul Molitor	.75
286	Ed Sprague	.05
287	Juan Guzman	.05
288	David Cone	.05
289	Shawn Green	.30
290	Marquis Grissom	.05
291	Kent Mercker	.05
292	Steve Avery	.05
293	Chipper Jones	1.00
294	John Smoltz	.05
295	Dave Justice	.05
296	Ryan Klesko	.05
297	Joe Oliver	.05
298	Ricky Bones	.05
299	John Jaha	.05
300	Greg Vaughn	.05
301	Dave Nilsson	.05
302	Kevin Seitzer	.05
303	Bernard Gilkey	.05
304	Allen Battle	.05
305	Ray Lankford	.05
306	Tom Pagnozzi	.05
307	Allen Watson	.05
308	Danny Jackson	.05
309	Ken Hill	.05
310	Todd Zeile	.05
311	Kevin Roberson	.05
312	Steve Buechele	.05
313	Rick Wilkins	.05
314	Kevin Foster	.05
315	Sammy Sosa	1.00
316	Howard Johnson	.05
317	Greg Hansell	.05
318	Pedro Astacio	.05
319	Rafael Bournigal	.05
320	Mike Piazza	1.25
321	Ramon Martinez	.05
322	Raul Mondesi	.05
323	Ismael Valdes	.05
324	Wil Cordero	.05
325	Tony Tarasco	.05
326	Roberto Kelly	.05
327	Jeff Fassero	.05
328	Mike Lansing	.05
329	Pedro J. Martinez	.75
330	Kirk Rueter	.05
331	Glenallen Hill	.05
332	Kirt Manwaring	.05
333	Royce Clayton	.05
334	J.R. Phillips	.05
335	Barry Bonds	2.00
336	Mark Portugal	.05
337	Terry Mulholland	.05
338	Omar Vizquel	.05
339	Carlos Baerga	.05
340	Albert Belle	.75
341	Eddie Murray	.75
342	Wayne Kirby	.05
343	Chad Ogea	.05
344	Tim Davis	.05
345	Jay Buhner	.05
346	Bobby Ayala	.05
347	Mike Blowers	.05
348	Dave Fleming	.05
349	Edgar Martinez	.05
350	Andre Dawson	.30
351	Darrell Whitmore	.05
352	Chuck Carr	.05
353	John Burkett	.05
354	Chris Hammond	.05
355	Gary Sheffield	.40
356	Pat Rapp	.05
357	Greg Colbrunn	.05
358	David Segui	.05
359	Jeff Kent	.05
360	Bobby Bonilla	.05
361	Pete Harnisch	.05
362	Ryan Thompson	.05
363	Jose Vizcaino	.05
364	Brett Butler	.05
365	Cal Ripken Jr.	2.00
366	Rafael Palmeiro	.65
367	Leo Gomez	.05
368	Andy Van Slyke	.05
369	Arthur Rhodes	.05
370	Ken Caminiti	.05
371	Steve Finley	.05
372	Melvin Nieves	.05
373	Andujar Cedeno	.05
374	Trevor Hoffman	.05
375	Fernando Valenzuela	.05
376	Ricky Bottalico	.05
377	Dave Hollins	.05
378	Charlie Hayes	.05
379	Tommy Greene	.05
380	Darren Daulton	.05
381	Curt Schilling	.05
382	Midre Cummings	.05
383	Al Martin	.05
384	Jeff King	.05
385	Orlando Merced	.05
386	Denny Neagle	.05
387	Don Slaught	.05
388	Dave Clark	.05
389	Kevin Gross	.05
390	Will Clark	.05
391	Ivan Rodriguez	.65
392	Benji Gil	.05
393	Jeff Frye	.05
394	Kenny Rogers	.05
395	Juan Gonzalez	.40
396	Mike Macfarlane	.05
397	Lee Tinsley	.05
398	Tim Naehring	.05
399	Tim Vanegmond	.05
400	Mike Greenwell	.05
401	Ken Ryan	.05
402	John Smiley	.05
403	Tim Pugh	.05
404	Reggie Sanders	.05
405	Barry Larkin	.05
406	Hal Morris	.05
407	Jose Rijo	.05
408	Lance Painter	.05
409	Joe Girardi	.05
410	Andres Galarraga	.05
411	Mike Kingery	.05
412	Roberto Mejia	.05
413	Walt Weiss	.05
414	Bill Swift	.05
415	Larry Walker	.05
416	Billy Brewer	.05
417	Pat Borders	.05
418	Tom Gordon	.05
419	Kevin Appier	.05
420	Gary Gaetti	.05
421	Greg Gohr	.05
422	Felipe Lira	.05
423	John Doherty	.05
424	Chad Curtis	.05
425	Cecil Fielder	.05
426	Alan Trammell	.05
427	David McCarty	.05
428	Scott Erickson	.05
429	Pat Mahomes	.05
430	Kirby Puckett	1.00
431	Dave Stevens	.05
432	Pedro Munoz	.05
433	Chris Sabo	.05
434	Alex Fernandez	.05
435	Frank Thomas	.75
436	Roberto Hernandez	.05
437	Lance Johnson	.05
438	Jim Abbott	.05
439	John Wetteland	.05
440	Melido Perez	.05
441	Tony Fernandez	.05
442	Pat Kelly	.05
443	Mike Stanley	.05
444	Danny Tartabull	.05
445	Wade Boggs	1.00
446	Robin Yount (Final Tribute)	.75
447	Ryne Sandberg (Final Tribute)	1.00
448	Nolan Ryan (Final Tribute)	2.00
449	George Brett (Final Tribute)	1.00
450	Mike Schmidt (Final Tribute)	1.00

David Justice — Atlanta Braves — OF

Diamond logo in the upper corner and the player's name at bottom are printed in gold foil, rather than the silver of the ED cards or the copper of the regular-issue UD cards.

	NM/M
Complete Set (450):	650.00
Common Player:	2.00
Stars/Rookies:	8X

Update Trade Cards

Inserted into Series 2 at the rate of about one per 11 packs was this five-card series of trade cards. Each card could be mailed in with $2 to receive nine cards from a special UD Update set picturing traded or free agent players in the uniforms of their new teams. The front of each trade card pictures one of the traded players in his old uniform against a red and blue background. Backs have instructions for redeeming the trade cards. The mail-in offer expired Feb. 1, 1996. Cards are numbered with a "TC" prefix.

		NM/M
Complete Set (5):		6.00
Common Player:		1.00
1	Orel Hershiser	1.00
2	Terry Pendleton	1.00
3	Benito Santiago	1.00
4	Kevin Brown	1.00
5	Gregg Jefferies	1.00

Electric Diamond

Tom Glavine — Atlanta Braves — P

Included as an insert at the rate of one per retail foil pack and two per jumbo pack, this set parallels the regular issue. The only differences are that the Electric Diamond cards utilize silver-foil highlights on front, compared to the copper foil on the regular cards. The Electric Diamond cards also include a home-plate shaped logo printed in silver foil in one of the upper corners.

	NM/M
Complete Set (1-450):	60.00
Common Player:	.25
Stars/Rookies:	2X

Electric Diamond Gold

A parallel set of a parallel set, the Electric Diamond Gold cards were found at an average rate of one per 36 retail packs. They differ from the standard ED inserts in that the home plate-shaped Electric

line. Update cards share the same format as the regular 1995 Upper Deck set.

		NM/M
Complete Set (45):		7.50
Common Player:		.25
451	Jim Abbott	.25
452	Danny Tartabull	.25
453	Ariel Prieto	.25
454	Scott Cooper	.25
455	Tom Henke	.25
456	Todd Zeile	.25
457	Brian McRae	.25
458	Luis Gonzalez	.25
459	Jaime Navarro	.25
460	Todd Worrell	.25
461	Roberto Kelly	.25
462	Chad Fonville	.25
463	Shane Andrews	.25
464	David Segui	.25
465	Deion Sanders	.50
466	Orel Hershiser	.25
467	Ken Hill	.25
468	Andy Benes	.25
469	Terry Pendleton	.25
470	Bobby Bonilla	.25
471	Scott Erickson	.25
472	Kevin Brown	.25
473	Glenn Dishman	.25
474	Phil Plantier	.25
475	Gregg Jefferies	.25
476	Tyler Green	.25
477	Heathcliff Slocumb	.25
478	Mark Whiten	.25
479	Mickey Tettleton	.25
480	Tim Wakefield	.25
481	Vaughn Eshelman	.25
482	Rick Aguilera	.25
483	Erik Hanson	.25
484	Willie McGee	.25
485	Troy O'Leary	.25
486	Benito Santiago	.25
487	Darren Lewis	.25
488	Dave Burba	.25
489	Ron Gant	.25
490	Bret Saberhagen	.25
491	Vinny Castilla	.25
492	Frank Rodriguez	.25
493	Andy Pettitte	5.00
494	Ruben Sierra	.25
495	David Cone	.25

Autograph Trade Cards

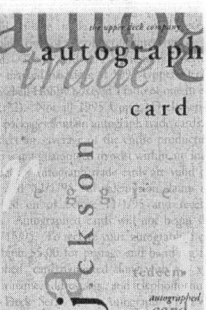

On the average of once every 72 packs (two boxes) of Series II hobby, a trade card good for an autographed player card could be found as an insert. The cards feature the player name, but no picture, on front, while the reverse has instructions for redeeming the card for a $5 fee. The autograph trade cards expired on Nov. 1, 1995.

		NM/M
Complete Set (5):		15.00
Common Player:		2.00
(1)	Roger Clemens	4.00
(2)	Reggie Jackson	3.00
(3)	Willie Mays	6.00
(4)	Raul Mondesi	2.00
(5)	Frank Robinson	3.00

Autograph Redemption Cards

These cards were sent to collectors who redeemed Autograph Trade cards found in Series II Upper Deck baseball. A certificate of authenticity with a holographic serial number matching that on the card back was issued with each card.

		NM/M
Complete Set (5):		220.00
Common Player:		15.00
AC1	Reggie Jackson	20.00
AC2	Willie Mays	100.00

Update

Orel Hershiser — Cleveland Indians — P

These cards depicting traded and free agent players in the uniforms of their new 1995 teams were available only by redeeming trade cards found in Series 2 packs. Each trade-in card was good for one nine-card segment of the Update series when sent with $2 prior to the Feb. 1, 1996 dead-

New York Yankees — OF

AC3	Frank Robinson	30.00
AC4	Roger Clemens	125.00
AC5	Raul Mondesi	10.00

Autographed Jumbos

By sending in quantities of foil wrappers from Upper Deck baseball cards, collectors could receive a jumbo 5" x 7" blow-up of a player's card. The offer was limited to 8,000 Roger Clemens cards (Series I) and 6,000 Alex Rodriguez cards (Series II). Each card bears a serial number hologram on back and comes with a matching Upper Deck Authenticated authenticity guarantee card.

		NM/M
Complete Set (2):		100.00
(1)	Roger Clemens	50.00
(2)	Alex Rodriguez	75.00

Award Winners Predictors (Hobby)

Candidates for 1995 MVP and Rookie of the Year in each league are featured in the interactive insert series called Predictors. Twenty potential award winners were released in each of Series 1 and 2 at the rate of one per 30 packs on average. Cards feature on front a player photo inside a diamond cutout on a rich looking black and marbled background. In gold foil are his name and team at top, and "PREDICTOR" and the category at bottom. Backs feature game rules and details for redeeming the card if the pictured player wins the specified award. Winners could trade in the card for a foil-enhanced set of Predictor cards. The trade-in offer expired at the end of 1995. Cards are numbered with a "H" prefix.

		NM/M
Complete Set (40):		50.00
Common Player:		.50
Winner Exchange Cards:		2X
1	Albert Belle	.50
2	Juan Gonzalez	1.50
3	Ken Griffey Jr.	3.00
4	Kirby Puckett	2.50
5	Frank Thomas	2.00
6	Jeff Bagwell	2.00

7	Barry Bonds	5.00
8	Mike Piazza	3.00
9	Matt Williams	.50
10	1995 MVP Long Shot (Winner)	.50
11	Armando Benitez	.50
12	Alex Gonzalez	.50
13	Shawn Green	1.50
14	Derek Jeter	5.00
15	Alex Rodriguez	4.00
16	Alan Benes	.50
17	Brian L. Hunter	.50
18	Charles Johnson	.50
19	Jose Oliva	.50
20	1995 ROY Long Shot	.50
21	Cal Ripken Jr.	5.00
22	Don Mattingly	2.75
23	Roberto Alomar	.75
24	Kenny Lofton	.50
25	Will Clark	.50
26	Mark McGwire	4.00
27	Greg Maddux	2.50
28	Fred McGriff	.50
29	Andres Galarraga	.50
30	Jose Canseco	1.50
31	Ray Durham	.50
32	Mark Grudzielanek	.50
33	Scott Ruffcorn	.50
34	Michael Tucker	.50
35	Garret Anderson	.50
36	Darren Bragg	.50
37	Quilvio Veras	.50
38	Hideo Nomo (Winner)	4.00
39	Chipper Jones	2.50
40	Marty Cordova (Winner)	1.50

Baseball Heroes Babe Ruth

In the 100th anniversary year of his birth, Babe Ruth was the featured star in Upper Deck continuing "Heroes" insert set. Ten cards, including an unnumbered header, were issued in Series 2 packs. The cards featured colorized photos printed on metallic foil on the front. Backs have stats and/or biographical data. On average, one Babe Ruth Heroes card is found per 34 packs.

		NM/M
Complete Set (10):		45.00
Common Card:		6.00
73	1914-18 Pitching Career (Babe Ruth)	6.00
74	1919 - Move to Outfield (Babe Ruth)	6.00
75	1920 - Renaissance Man (Babe Ruth)	6.00
76	1923 - House That Ruth Built (Babe Ruth)	6.00
77	1927 - 60-Homer Season (Babe Ruth)	6.00
78	1928 - Three-homer Game (Babe Ruth)	6.00
79	1932 - The Called Shot (Babe Ruth)	6.00
80	1930-35 - Milestones (Babe Ruth)	6.00
81	1935 - The Last Hurrah (Babe Ruth)	6.00
---	Header Card	7.50

Checklists

Upscale checklists for the 1995 UD set were part of the insert card program, seeded about one per 17 packs, on average. Horizontally formatted fronts are printed on metallic

foil and include a career highlight of the pictured player. Backs have the checklist data. Five checklists were issued in each of Series I and Series II.

		NM/M
Complete Set (10):		3.00
Common Player:		.25
1	Checklist 1-75 (Montreal Expos)	.25
2	Checklist 76-150 (Fred McGriff)	.25
3	Checklist 151-225 John Valentin (Unassisted triple play.)	.25
4	Special Edition Checklist (Greg Maddux)	.75
5	Special Edition Checklist 69-135 Kenny Rogers (perfect game)	.25
1	Checklist 226-300 (Cecil Fielder)	.25
2	Checklist 301-375 (Tony Gwynn)	.75
3	Checklist 376-450 (Greg Maddux)	.75
4	Special Edition Checklist 136-203 (Randy Johnson)	.50
5	Special Edition Checklist 204-270 (Mike Schmidt)	.75

League Leaders Predictors (Retail)

Candidates for the Triple Crown categories of league leaders in hits, home runs and RBIs are featured in this retail-only insert set, found at the average rate of one per 30 packs in both Series 1 and 2. If the player pictured on the card front won the category specified on his card, it could be redeemed for a special foil-enhanced version of the subset prior to the Dec. 31, 1995 deadline. Cards are numbered with a "R" prefix.

		NM/M
Complete Set (60):		65.00
Common Player:		.50
Winner Exchange Cards:		2X
1	Albert Belle (Winner)	1.50
2	Jose Canseco	1.50
3	Juan Gonzalez	1.00
4	Ken Griffey Jr.	3.00
5	Frank Thomas	2.00
6	Jeff Bagwell	2.00
7	Barry Bonds	5.00
8	Fred McGriff	.50
9	Matt Williams	.50
10	1995 Home Run Long Shot (Winner)	.50
11	Albert Belle (Winner)	1.50
12	Joe Carter	.50
13	Cecil Fielder	.50
14	Kirby Puckett	2.50
15	Frank Thomas	2.00
16	Jeff Bagwell	2.00
17	Barry Bonds	5.00
18	Mike Piazza	3.00
19	Matt Williams	.50
20	1995 RBI Long Shot (Winner)	.50
21	Wade Boggs	2.50
22	Kenny Lofton	.50
23	Paul Molitor	2.00
24	Paul O'Neill	.50
25	Frank Thomas	2.00
26	Jeff Bagwell	2.00
27	Tony Gwynn (Winner)	5.00
28	Gregg Jefferies	.50
29	Hal Morris	.50
30	1995 Batting Long Shot (Winner)	.50
31	Joe Carter	.50
32	Cecil Fielder	.50
33	Rafael Palmeiro	1.50
34	Larry Walker	.50
35	Manny Ramirez	2.00
36	Tim Salmon	.50
37	Mike Piazza	3.00
38	Andres Galarraga	.50
39	Dave Justice	.50
40	Gary Sheffield	1.50
41	Juan Gonzalez	1.00
42	Jose Canseco	1.50
43	Will Clark	.50
44	Rafael Palmeiro	1.50
45	Ken Griffey Jr.	3.00
46	Ruben Sierra	.50
47	Larry Walker	.50
48	Fred McGriff	.50
49	Dante Bichette (Winner)	.50
50	Darren Daulton	.50
51	Will Clark	.50
52	Ken Griffey Jr.	3.00
53	Don Mattingly	2.75
54	John Olerud	.50
55	Kirby Puckett	2.50
56	Raul Mondesi	.50
57	Moises Alou	.50
58	Bret Boone	.50
59	Albert Belle	.50
60	Mike Piazza	3.00

Steal of a Deal

A horizontal format with an action photo printed over a green foil background and a large bronze seal indicating how the player was acquired are featured in this 15-card insert set. The front has a terracotta border, which is carried over to the back. A large green box on back details the transaction and describes why it can be categorized as a "steal" for the player's new team. These top-of-the-line chase cards were seeded in both hobby and retail packs of Series I at the average rate of one per 34 packs. Cards are numbered with a "SD" prefix.

		NM/M
Complete Set (15):		25.00
Common Player:		1.00
1	Mike Piazza	6.00
2	Fred McGriff	1.00
3	Kenny Lofton	1.00
4	Jose Oliva	1.00
5	Jeff Bagwell	3.00
6	Roberto Alomar, Joe Carter	1.00
7	Steve Karsay	1.00
8	Ozzie Smith	4.00
9	Dennis Eckersley	2.00
10	Jose Canseco	1.50
11	Carlos Baerga	1.00
12	Cecil Fielder	1.00
13	Don Mattingly	5.00
14	Bret Boone	1.00
15	Michael Jordan	10.00

Special Edition

Printed on metallic foil on front, and inserted into hobby packs only at the rate of one per pack, this insert set is found in both Series 1 (#1-135) and Series 2 (#136-270). A silver stripe at top has the name of the issue and the issuer, while stacked black and silver bars at bottom have the player name, team and position. Backs are conventionally printed and have another color photo, career data and 1994 and lifetime stats.

		NM/M
Complete Set (270):		60.00
Common Player:		.10
Gold:		3X
1	Cliff Floyd	.10
2	Wil Cordero	.10
3	Pedro Martinez	1.50
4	Larry Walker	.10
5	Derek Jeter	4.00
6	Mike Stanley	.10
7	Melido Perez	.10
8	Jim Leyritz	.10
9	Danny Tartabull	.10
10	Wade Boggs	2.00
11	Ryan Klesko	.10
12	Steve Avery	.10
13	Damon Hollins	.10
14	Chipper Jones	2.00
15	Dave Justice	.10
16	Glenn Williams	.10
17	Jose Oliva	.10
18	Terrell Wade	.10
19	Alex Fernandez	.10
20	Frank Thomas	1.50
21	Ozzie Guillen	.10
22	Roberto Hernandez	.10
23	Albie Lopez	.10
24	Eddie Murray	1.50
25	Albert Belle	.10
26	Omar Vizquel	.10
27	Carlos Baerga	.10
28	Jose Rijo	.10
29	Hal Morris	.10
30	Reggie Sanders	.10
31	Jack Morris	.10
32	Raul Mondesi	.10
33	Karim Garcia	.15
34	Todd Hollandsworth	.10
35	Mike Piazza	2.50
36	Chan Ho Park	.10
37	Ramon Martinez	.10
38	Kenny Rogers	.10
39	Will Clark	.10
40	Juan Gonzalez	.75
41	Ivan Rodriguez	1.25
42	Orlando Miller	.10
43	John Hudek	.10
44	Luis Gonzalez	.10
45	Jeff Bagwell	1.50
46	Cal Ripken Jr.	4.00
47	Mike Oquist	.10
48	Armando Benitez	.10
49	Ben McDonald	.10
50	Rafael Palmeiro	1.25
51	Curtis Goodwin	.10
52	Vince Coleman	.10
53	Tom Gordon	.10
54	Mike Macfarlane	.10
55	Brian McRae	.10
56	Matt Smith	.10
57	David Segui	.10
58	Paul Wilson	.10
59	Bill Pulsipher	.10
60	Bobby Bonilla	.10
61	Jeff Kent	.10
62	Ryan Thompson	.10
63	Jason Isringhausen	.10
64	Ed Sprague	.10
65	Paul Molitor	1.50
66	Juan Guzman	.10
67	Alex Gonzalez	.10
68	Shawn Green	.50
69	Mark Portugal	.10
70	Barry Bonds	4.00
71	Robby Thompson	.10
72	Royce Clayton	.10
73	Ricky Bottalico	.10
74	Doug Jones	.10
75	Darren Daulton	.10
76	Gregg Jefferies	.10
77	Scott Cooper	.10
78	Nomar Garciaparra	2.00
79	Ken Ryan	.10
80	Mike Greenwell	.10
81	LaTroy Hawkins	.10
82	Rich Becker	.10
83	Scott Erickson	.10
84	Pedro Munoz	.10
85	Kirby Puckett	2.00
86	Orlando Merced	.10
87	Jeff King	.10
88	Midre Cummings	.10
89	Bernard Gilkey	.10
90	Ray Lankford	.10
91	Todd Zeile	.10
92	Alan Benes	.10
93	Bret Wagner	.10
94	Rene Arocha	.10
95	Cecil Fielder	.10
96	Alan Trammell	.10
97	Tony Phillips	.10
98	Junior Felix	.10
99	Brian Harper	.10
100	Greg Vaughn	.10
101	Ricky Bones	.10
102	Walt Weiss	.10
103	Lance Painter	.10
104	Roberto Mejia	.10
105	Andres Galarraga	.10
106	Todd Van Poppel	.10
107	Ben Grieve	.10
108	Brent Gates	.10
109	Jason Giambi	1.00
110	Ruben Sierra	.10
111	Terry Steinbach	.10
112	Chris Hammond	.10
113	Charles Johnson	.10

		NM/M
114	Jesus Tavarez	.10
115	Gary Sheffield	.40
116	Chuck Carr	.10
117	Bobby Ayala	.10
118	Randy Johnson	1.50
119	Edgar Martinez	.10
120	Alex Rodriguez	3.00
121	Kevin Foster	.10
122	Kevin Roberson	.10
123	Sammy Sosa	2.00
124	Steve Trachsel	.10
125	Eduardo Perez	.10
126	Tim Salmon	.10
127	Todd Greene	.10
128	Jorge Fabregas	.10
129	Mark Langston	.10
130	Mitch Williams	.10
131	Raul Casanova	.10
132	Mel Nieves	.10
133	Andy Benes	.10
134	Dustin Hermanson	.10
135	Trevor Hoffman	.10
136	Mark Grudzielanek	.10
137	Ugueth Urbina	.10
138	Moises Alou	.10
139	Rondell Kelly	.10
140	Rondell White	.10
141	Paul O'Neill	.10
142	Jimmy Key	.10
143	Jack McDowell	.10
144	Ruben Rivera	.10
145	Don Mattingly	2.25
146	John Wetteland	.10
147	Tom Glavine	.25
148	Marquis Grissom	.10
149	Javy Lopez	.10
150	Fred McGriff	.10
151	Greg Maddux	2.00
152	Chris Sabo	.10
153	Ray Durham	.10
154	Robin Ventura	.10
155	Jim Abbott	.10
156	Jimmy Hurst	.10
157	Tim Raines	.10
158	Dennis Martinez	.10
159	Kenny Lofton	.10
160	Dave Winfield	1.50
161	Manny Ramirez	.10
162	Jim Thome	1.00
163	Barry Larkin	.10
164	Bret Boone	.10
165	Deion Sanders	.10
166	Ron Gant	.10
167	Benito Santiago	.10
168	Hideo Nomo	.75
169	Billy Ashley	.10
170	Roger Cedeno	.10
171	Ismael Valdes	.10
172	Eric Karros	.10
173	Rusty Greer	.10
174	Rick Helling	.10
175	Nolan Ryan	4.00
176	Dean Palmer	.10
177	Phil Plantier	.10
178	Darryl Kile	.10
179	Derek Bell	.10
180	Doug Drabek	.10
181	Craig Biggio	.10
182	Kevin Brown	.10
183	Harold Baines	.10
184	Jeffrey Hammonds	.10
185	Chris Hoiles	.10
186	Mike Mussina	.50
187	Bob Hamelin	.10
188	Jeff Montgomery	.10
189	Michael Tucker	.10
190	George Brett	2.25
191	Edgardo Alfonzo	.10
192	Brett Butler	.10
193	Bobby Jones	.10
194	Todd Hundley	.10
195	Bret Saberhagen	.10
196	Pat Hentgen	.10
197	Roberto Alomar	.30
198	David Cone	.10
199	Carlos Delgado	1.00
200	Joe Carter	.10
201	William Van Landingham	.10
202	Rod Beck	.10
203	J.R. Phillips	.10
204	Darren Lewis	.10
205	Matt Williams	.10
206	Lenny Dykstra	.10
207	Dave Hollins	.10
208	Mike Schmidt	2.25
209	Charlie Hayes	.10
210	Mo Vaughn	.10
211	Jose Malave	.10
212	Roger Clemens	2.25
213	Jose Canseco	.75
214	Mark Whiten	.10
215	Marty Cordova	.10
216	Rick Aguilera	.10
217	Kevin Tapani	.10
218	Chuck Knoblauch	.10
219	Al Martin	.10
220	Jay Bell	.10
221	Carlos Garcia	.10
222	Freddy Garcia	.10
223	Jon Lieber	.10
224	Danny Jackson	.10
225	Ozzie Smith	2.00
226	Brian Jordan	.10
227	Ken Hill	.10
228	Scott Cooper	.10
229	Chad Curtis	.10
230	Lou Whitaker	.10

231	Kirk Gibson	.10
232	Travis Fryman	.10
233	Jose Valentin	.10
234	Dave Nilsson	.10
235	Cal Eldred	.10
236	Matt Mieske	.10
237	Bill Swift	.10
238	Marvin Freeman	.10
239	Jason Bates	.10
240	Larry Walker	.10
241	David Nied	.10
242	Dante Bichette	.10
243	Dennis Eckersley	1.25
244	Todd Stottlemyre	.10
245	Rickey Henderson	1.50
246	Geronimo Berroa	.10
247	Mark McGwire	3.00
248	Quilvio Veras	.10
249	Terry Pendleton	.10
250	Andre Dawson	.30
251	Jeff Conine	.10
252	Kurt Abbott	.10
253	Jay Buhner	.10
254	Darren Bragg	.10
255	Ken Griffey Jr.	2.50
256	Tino Martinez	.10
257	Mark Grace	.10
258	Ryne Sandberg	2.00
259	Randy Myers	.10
260	Howard Johnson	.10
261	Lee Smith	.10
262	J.T. Snow	.10
263	Chili Davis	.10
264	Chuck Finley	.10
265	Eddie Williams	.10
266	Joey Hamilton	.10
267	Ken Caminiti	.10
268	Andujar Cedeno	.10
269	Steve Finley	.10
270	Tony Gwynn	2.00

Special Edition Gold

An insert set within an insert set, gold-foil enhanced versions of the Special Edition cards were seeded into hobby packs at the rate of about one per box. The substitution of gold ink for silver is also carried over onto the background of the card back.

	NM/M
Complete Set (270):	350.00
Common Player:	1.50
Stars/Rookies:	3X

Cal Ripken Commemorative Jumbo

To commemorate Cal Ripken's 2,131st consecutive game, UD issued this 5" x 3" die-cut card. Five thousand of the cards were issued with silver foil highlights; 2,131 with gold trim. Each card is serially numbered in the lower-right corner on back.

	NM/M
Cal Ripken Jr. (Silver edition of 5,000.)	10.00
Cal Ripken Jr. (Gold edition of 2,131.)	13.50

Sports Drink Reggie Jackson

UD partnered with Energy Foods to produce "Upper Deck Authentic Sports Drink." Each

$2.99 six pack contained a cellowrapped Reggie Jackson card. The cards are 2-1/2" x 3-1/2" and have a color photo on front on which the team logos have been removed. Backs has a subdued photo of a player swinging a bat with a stadium scene in the background. A few career highlights are presented along with the sports drink logo and UD hologram. Each card could also be found in a version with a gold-foil facsimile autograph on front.

		NM/M
Complete Set (3):		5.00
Common Card:		2.00
Gold:		1-1.5X
1/3	Reggie Jackson/ Swinging Bat	2.00
2/3	Reggie Jackson/ Portrait	2.00
3/3	Reggie Jackson/ Batting follow-thru	2.00

Eagle Snacks Ballpark Legends

Nine Hall of Famers comprise this set which was produced by UD for the Eagle snack food company. Sets were available via mail-in redemption for proofs of purchase and $1. Fronts have sepia photos on which uniform logos have been removed. The Eagle Ballpark Legends is at upperleft, the UD logo is at lower-left, followed by the player name. Backs of the 2-1/2" x 3-1/2" cards have career summary and personal data. Autographed cards of Harmon Killebrew were random inserts.

		NM/M
Complete Set (9):		3.00
Common Player:		.25
1	Nolan Ryan	1.00
2	Reggie Jackson	.50
3	Tom Seaver	.50
4	Harmon Killebrew	.25
4a	Harmon Killebrew/ Auto.	20.00
5	Ted Williams	.75
6	Whitey Ford	.50
7	Al Kaline	.50
8	Willie Stargell	.25
9	Bob Gibson	.25

GTS Phone Cards

In conjunction with Global Telecommunications Service, Upper Deck issued a series of 15 phone cards described as being the first licensed by Major League Baseball and the Players Association. Measuring about 2-1/8" x 3-3/8" with round cor-

---

ners, the cards were printed on heavy plastic and utilized the basic format and photos from the players' 1994 Upper Deck baseball cards. Issue price, with phone time, was $12 each. Cards are numbered with a "MLB" prefix.

		NM/M
Complete Set (15):		21.00
Common Player:		1.00
01	Tony Gwynn	2.00
02	Fred McGriff	1.00
03	Frank Thomas	1.50
04	Ken Griffey Jr.	2.50
05	Cecil Fielder	1.00
06	Barry Bonds	3.00
07	Don Mattingly	2.25
08	Dave Justice	1.00
09	Roger Clemens	2.25
10	Cal Ripken Jr.	3.00
11	Roberto Alomar	1.25
12	Gary Sheffield	1.25
13	Jeff Bagwell	1.50
14	Kirby Puckett	2.00
15	Ozzie Smith	2.00

Metallic Impressions Michael Jordan

Michael Jordan's brief, highly publicized baseball career is chronicled in this metallic card set produced for UD by Metallic Impressions and sold in a special lithographed tin box. Each of the 2-5/8" x 3-9/16" cards has a gold-tone rolled edge. Fronts feature photos of Jordan in action. Backs have another photo and a career summary in a horizontal format. Cards are numbered with a "JT" prefix.

		NM/M
Complete Boxed Set (5):		7.50
Common Card:		1.50
1	Starting Out (Michael Jordan)	1.50
2	West to Arizona (Michael Jordan)	1.50
3	Hitting (Michael Jordan)	1.50
4	Baserunning (Michael Jordan)	1.50
5	Fielding (Michael Jordan)	1.50

Metallic Impressions Mickey Mantle

Sharing the card-front images with the UD phone cards of 1994, these metal cards trace the career of Mickey Mantle. Sold in an embossed metal box, the cards measure 2-5/8"

---

x 3-9/16" and have rolled goldtone metal borders. Fronts have black-and-white or color photos of Mantle. Backs have a career summary in a red box against a background of pinstriped flannel, along with a small color photo of Mantle. The issue was reportedly limited to 19,950 sets.

		NM/M
Complete Boxed Set (10):		17.50
Common Player:		3.00
1	The Commerce Comet (Mickey Mantle)	3.00
2	1951 - The Early Years (Mickey Mantle)	3.00
3	1953 - Tape-Measure Home Runs (Mickey Mantle)	3.00
4	1956 - Triple Crown Season (Mickey Mantle)	3.00
5	1957 - Second Consecutive MVP (Mickey Mantle)	3.00
6	1961 - Chasing the Babe (Mickey Mantle)	3.00
7	1964 - Series Home Run Record (Mickey Mantle)	3.00
8	1967 - 500th Home Run (Mickey Mantle)	3.00
9	1974 - Hall of Famer (Mickey Mantle)	3.00
10	Checklist (Mickey Mantle)	3.00

1996 Upper Deck Promo

To debut its 1996 issue, Upper Deck issued this sample card. It is identical in format to the regular-issue card, except that it is numbered 100 and overprinted diagonally on each side, "For Promotional Use Only."

		NM/M
100	Ken Griffey Jr.	2.00

1996 Upper Deck

Upper Deck Series 1 consists of 240 base cards. There are 187 regular player cards plus

---

subsets of Star Rookies, Young at Heart, Beat the Odds, Milestones, Post-season, checklists, and expansion logos. The issue was marketed in 10-card foil packs in hobby and retail versions. Series 1 insert sets are Blue Chip Prospects, Future Shock and Power Driven. Cal Ripken Jr. Collection cards are inserted in both series, as are Retail Predictor (home runs, batting average and RBIs) and Hobby Predictor (Player of the Month, Pitcher of the Month and rookie hits leaders) cards. Series 2 has 240 cards, including subsets for Star Rookies, Diamond Debuts, Strange But True, Managerial Salutes and Best of a Generation. Insert sets include Hot Commodities, Hideo Nomo Highlights, Run Producers and the Lovero Collection. Factory sets comprising both regular series and the Update series were issued in two serially numbered versions, a regular boxed set in an edition of 15,000 and a wooden boxed set numbered to 500.

		NM/M
Unopened Wood Box Set (510):		40.00
Unopened Fact. Set (510):		35.00
Complete Set (480):		20.00
Common Player:		.05
Wax Pack (10):		.75
Wax Box (32):		17.50
1	Cal Ripken Jr. (Milestones)	1.00
2	Eddie Murray (Milestones)	.40
3	Mark Wohlers	.05
4	Dave Justice	.05
5	Chipper Jones	1.00
6	Javier Lopez	.05
7	Mark Lemke	.05
8	Marquis Grissom	.05
9	Tom Glavine	.25
10	Greg Maddux	1.00
11	Manny Alexander	.05
12	Curtis Goodwin	.05
13	Scott Erickson	.05
14	Chris Hoiles	.05
15	Rafael Palmeiro	.65
16	Rick Krivda	.05
17	Jeff Manto	.05
18	Mo Vaughn	.05
19	Tim Wakefield	.05
20	Roger Clemens	1.00
21	Tim Naehring	.05
22	Troy O'Leary	.05
23	Mike Greenwell	.05
24	Stan Belinda	.05
25	John Valentin	.05
26	J.T. Snow	.05
27	Gary DiSarcina	.05
28	Mark Langston	.05
29	Brian Anderson	.05
30	Jim Edmonds	.05
31	Garret Anderson	.05
32	Orlando Palmeiro	.05
33	Brian McRae	.05
34	Kevin Foster	.05
35	Sammy Sosa	1.00
36	Todd Zeile	.05
37	Jim Bullinger	.05
38	Luis Gonzalez	.05
39	Lyle Mouton	.05
40	Ray Durham	.05
41	Ozzie Guillen	.05
42	Alex Fernandez	.05
43	Brian Keyser	.05
44	Robin Ventura	.05
45	Reggie Sanders	.05
46	Pete Schourek	.05
47	John Smiley	.05
48	Jeff Brantley	.05
49	Thomas Howard	.05
50	Bret Boone	.05
51	Kevin Jarvis	.05
52	Jeff Branson	.05
53	Carlos Baerga	.05
54	Jim Thome	.50
55	Manny Ramirez	.75
56	Omar Vizquel	.05
57	Jose Mesa	.05
58	Julian Tavarez	.05
59	Orel Hershiser	.05
60	Larry Walker	.05
61	Bret Saberhagen	.05
62	Vinny Castilla	.05
63	Eric Young	.05
64	Bryan Rekar	.05
65	Andres Galarraga	.05
66	Steve Reed	.05
67	Chad Curtis	.05
68	Bobby Higginson	.05
69	Phil Nevin	.05
70	Cecil Fielder	.05
71	Felipe Lira	.05
72	Chris Gomez	.05

		NM/M
73	Charles Johnson	.05
74	Quilvio Veras	.05
75	Jeff Conine	.05
76	John Burkett	.05
77	Greg Colbrunn	.05
78	Terry Pendleton	.05
79	Shane Reynolds	.05
80	Jeff Bagwell	.75
81	Orlando Miller	.05
82	Mike Hampton	.05
83	James Mouton	.05
84	Brian L. Hunter	.05
85	Derek Bell	.05
86	Kevin Appier	.05
87	Joe Vitiello	.05
88	Wally Joyner	.05
89	Michael Tucker	.05
90	Johnny Damon	.20
91	Jon Nunnally	.05
92	Jason Jacome	.05
93	Chan Ho Park	.05
94	Hideo Nomo	.40
95	Ismael Valdes	.05
96	Greg Gagne	.05
98	Diamondbacks-Devil Rays (Expansion Card)	.10
99	Raul Mondesi	.05
100	Dave Winfield (Young at Heart)	.75
101	Dennis Eckersley (Young at Heart)	.35
102	Andre Dawson (Young at Heart)	.15
103	Dennis Martinez (Young at Heart)	.05
104	Lance Parrish (Young at Heart)	.05
105	Eddie Murray (Young at Heart)	.40
106	Alan Trammell (Young at Heart)	.05
107	Lou Whitaker (Young at Heart)	.05
108	Ozzie Smith (Young at Heart)	.50
109	Paul Molitor (Young at Heart)	.40
110	Rickey Henderson (Young at Heart)	.40
111	Tim Raines (Young at Heart)	.05
112	Harold Baines (Young at Heart)	.05
113	Lee Smith (Young at Heart)	.05
114	Fernando Valenzuela (Young at Heart)	.05
115	Cal Ripken Jr. (Young at Heart)	1.00
116	Tony Gwynn (Young at Heart)	.50
117	Wade Boggs (Young at Heart)	.50
118	Todd Hollandsworth	.05
119	Dave Nilsson	.05
120	Jose Valentin RC	.05
121	Steve Sparks	.05
122	Chuck Carr	.05
123	John Jaha	.05
124	Scott Karl	.05
125	Chuck Knoblauch	.05
126	Brad Radke	.05
127	Pat Meares	.05
128	Ron Coomer	.05
129	Pedro Munoz	.05
130	Kirby Puckett	1.00
131	David Segui	.05
132	Mark Grudzielanek	.05
133	Mike Lansing	.05
134	Sean Berry	.05
135	Rondell White	.05
136	Pedro Martinez	.75
137	Carl Everett	.05
138	Dave Mlicki	.05
139	Bill Pulsipher	.05
140	Jason Isringhausen	.05
141	Rico Brogna	.05
142	Edgardo Alfonzo	.05
143	Jeff Kent	.05
144	Andy Pettitte	.25
145	Mike Piazza	.65
146	Cliff Floyd (Beat the Odds)	.05
147	Jason Isringhausen (Beat the Odds)	.05
148	Tim Wakefield (Beat the Odds)	.05
149	Chipper Jones (Beat the Odds)	.50
150	Hideo Nomo (Beat the Odds)	.20
151	Mark McGwire (Beat the Odds)	.75
152	Ron Gant (Beat the Odds)	.05
153	Gary Gaetti (Beat the Odds)	.05
154	Don Mattingly	1.00
155	Paul O'Neill	.05
156	Derek Jeter	2.00
157	Joe Girardi	.05
158	Ruben Sierra	.05
159	Jorge Posada	.05
160	Geronimo Berroa	.05
161	Steve Ontiveros	.05
162	George Williams	.05

		NM/M
163	Doug Johns	.05
164	Ariel Prieto	.05
165	Scott Brosius	.05
166	Mike Bordick	.05
167	Tyler Green	.05
168	Mickey Morandini	.05
169	Darren Daulton	.05
170	Gregg Jefferies	.05
171	Jim Eisenreich	.05
172	Heathcliff Slocumb	.05
173	Kevin Stocker	.05
174	Esteban Loaiza	.05
175	Jeff King	.05
176	Mark Johnson	.05
177	Denny Neagle	.05
178	Orlando Merced	.05
179	Carlos Garcia	.05
180	Brian Jordan	.05
181	Mike Morgan	.05
182	Mark Petkovsek	.05
183	Bernard Gilkey	.05
184	John Mabry	.05
185	Tom Henke	.05
186	Glenn Dishman	.05
187	Andy Ashby	.05
188	Bip Roberts	.05
189	Melvin Nieves	.05
190	Ken Caminiti	.05
191	Brad Ausmus	.05
192	Deion Sanders	.05
193	Jamie Brewington	.05
194	Glenallen Hill	.05
195	Barry Bonds	2.00
196	William Van Landingham	.05
197	Mark Carreon	.05
198	Royce Clayton	.05
199	Joey Cora	.05
200	Ken Griffey Jr.	1.25
201	Jay Buhner	.05
202	Alex Rodriguez	1.50
203	Norm Charlton	.05
204	Andy Benes	.05
205	Edgar Martinez	.05
206	Juan Gonzalez	.40
207	Will Clark	.05
208	Kevin Gross	.05
209	Roger Pavlik	.05
210	Ivan Rodriguez	.65
211	Rusty Greer	.05
212	Angel Martinez	.05
213	Tomas Perez	.05
214	Alex Gonzalez	.05
215	Joe Carter	.05
216	Shawn Green	.30
217	Edwin Hurtado	.05
218	Edgar Martinez, Tony Pena (Post Season Checklist)	.05
219	Chipper Jones, Barry Larkin (Post Season Checklist)	.05
220	Orel Hershiser (Post Season Checklist)	.05
221	Mike Devereaux (Post Season Checklist)	.05
222	Tom Glavine (Post Season Checklist)	.05
223	Karim Garcia (Star Rookies)	.10
224	Arquimedez Pozo (Star Rookies)	.05
225	Billy Wagner (Star Rookies)	.05
226	John Wasdin (Star Rookies)	.05
227	Jeff Suppan (Star Rookies)	.05
228	Steve Gibralter (Star Rookies)	.05
229	Jimmy Haynes (Star Rookies)	.05
230	Ruben Rivera (Star Rookies)	.05
231	Chris Snopek (Star Rookies)	.05
232	Alex Ochoa (Star Rookies)	.05
233	Shannon Stewart (Star Rookies)	.05
234	Quinton McCracken (Star Rookies)	.05
235	Trey Beamon (Star Rookies)	.05
236	Billy McMillon (Star Rookies)	.05
237	Steve Cox (Star Rookies)	.05
238	George Arias (Star Rookies)	.05
239	Yamil Benitez (Star Rookies)	.05
240	Todd Greene (Star Rookies)	.05
241	Jason Kendall (Star Rookies)	.05
242	Brooks Kieschnick (Star Rookies)	.05
243	Osvaldo Fernandez RC (Star Rookie)	.15
244	Livan Hernandez RC (Star Rookie)	.35
245	Rey Ordonez (Star Rookie)	.05
246	Mike Grace RC (Star Rookie)	.05
247	Jay Canizaro (Star Rookie)	.05

248	Bob Wolcott (Star Rookie)	.05
249	Jermaine Dye (Star Rookie)	.05
250	Jason Schmidt (Star Rookie)	.05
251	Mike Sweeney RC (Star Rookie)	1.00
252	Marcus Jensen (Star Rookie)	.05
253	Mendy Lopez (Star Rookie)	.05
254	Wilton Guerrero RC (Star Rookie)	.10
255	Paul Wilson (Star Rookie)	.05
256	Edgar Renteria (Star Rookie)	.05
257	Richard Hidalgo (Star Rookie)	.05
258	Bob Abreu (Star Rookie)	.10
259	Robert Smith RC (Diamond Debuts)	.05
260	Sal Fasano (Diamond Debuts)	.05
261	Enrique Wilson (Diamond Debuts)	.05
262	Rich Hunter RC (Diamond Debuts)	.05
263	Sergio Nunez (Diamond Debuts)	.05
264	Dan Serafini (Diamond Debuts)	.05
265	David Doster RC (Diamond Debuts)	.05
266	Ryan McGuire (Diamond Debuts)	.05
267	Scott Spiezio (Diamond Debuts)	.05
268	Rafael Orellano (Diamond Debuts)	.05
269	Steve Avery	.05
270	Fred McGriff	.05
271	John Smoltz	.05
272	Ryan Klesko	.05
273	Jeff Blauser	.05
274	Brad Clontz	.05
275	Roberto Alomar	.20
276	B.J. Surhoff	.05
277	Jeffrey Hammonds	.05
278	Brady Anderson	.05
279	Bobby Bonilla	.05
280	Cal Ripken Jr.	2.00
281	Mike Mussina	.30
282	Wil Cordero	.05
283	Mike Stanley	.05
284	Aaron Sele	.05
285	Jose Canseco	.40
286	Tom Gordon	.05
287	Heathcliff Slocumb	.05
288	Lee Smith	.05
289	Troy Percival	.05
290	Tim Salmon	.05
291	Chuck Finley	.05
292	Jim Abbott	.05
293	Chili Davis	.05
294	Steve Trachsel	.05
295	Mark Grace	.05
296	Rey Sanchez	.05
297	Scott Servais	.05
298	Jaime Navarro	.05
299	Frank Castillo	.05
300	Frank Thomas	.75
301	Jason Bere	.05
302	Danny Tartabull	.05
303	Darren Lewis	.05
304	Roberto Hernandez	.05
305	Tony Phillips	.05
306	Wilson Alvarez	.05
307	Jose Rijo	.05
308	Hal Morris	.05
309	Mark Portugal	.05
310	Barry Larkin	.05
311	Dave Burba	.05
312	Eddie Taubensee	.05
313	Sandy Alomar Jr.	.05
314	Dennis Martinez	.05
315	Albert Belle	.15
316	Eddie Murray	.75
317	Charles Nagy	.05
318	Chad Ogea	.05
319	Kenny Lofton	.05
320	Dante Bichette	.05
321	Armando Reynoso	.05
322	Walt Weiss	.05
323	Ellis Burks	.05
324	Kevin Ritz	.05
325	Bill Swift	.05
326	Jason Bates	.05
327	Tony Clark	.05
328	Travis Fryman	.05
329	Mark Parent	.05
330	Alan Trammell	.05
331	C.J. Nitkowski	.05
332	Jose Lima	.05
333	Phil Plantier	.05
334	Kurt Abbott	.05
335	Andre Dawson	.25
336	Chris Hammond	.05
337	Robb Nen	.05
338	Pat Rapp	.05
339	Al Leiter	.05
340	Gary Sheffield	.35
341	Todd Jones	.05
342	Doug Drabek	.05
343	Greg Swindell	.05
344	Tony Eusebio	.05

345	Craig Biggio	.05
346	Darryl Kile	.05
347	Mike Macfarlane	.05
348	Jeff Montgomery	.05
349	Chris Haney	.05
350	Bip Roberts	.05
351	Tom Goodwin	.05
352	Mark Gubicza	.05
353	Joe Randa	.05
354	Ramon Martinez	.05
355	Eric Karros	.05
356	Delino DeShields	.05
357	Brett Butler	.05
358	Todd Worrell	.05
359	Mike Blowers	.05
360	Mike Piazza	1.25
361	Ben McDonald	.05
362	Ricky Bones	.05
363	Greg Vaughn	.05
364	Matt Mieske	.05
365	Kevin Seitzer	.05
366	Jeff Cirillo	.05
367	LaTroy Hawkins	.05
368	Frank Rodriguez	.05
369	Rick Aguilera	.05
370	Roberto Alomar (Best of a Generation)	.15
371	Albert Belle (Best of a Generation)	.15
372	Wade Boggs (Best of a Generation)	.50
373	Barry Bonds (Best of a Generation)	1.00
374	Roger Clemens (Best of a Generation)	.65
375	Dennis Eckersley (Best of a Generation)	.35
376	Ken Griffey Jr. (Best of a Generation)	.65
377	Tony Gwynn (Best of a Generation)	.40
378	Rickey Henderson (Best of a Generation)	.40
379	Greg Maddux (Best of a Generation)	.50
380	Fred McGriff (Best of a Generation)	.05
381	Paul Molitor (Best of a Generation)	.40
382	Eddie Murray (Best of a Generation)	.40
383	Mike Piazza (Best of a Generation)	.65
384	Kirby Puckett (Best of a Generation)	.50
385	Cal Ripken Jr. (Best of a Generation)	1.00
386	Ozzie Smith (Best of a Generation)	.50
387	Frank Thomas (Best of a Generation)	.45
388	Matt Walbeck	.05
389	Dave Stevens	.05
390	Marty Cordova	.05
391	Darrin Fletcher	.05
392	Cliff Floyd	.05
393	Mel Rojas	.05
394	Shane Andrews	.05
395	Moises Alou	.05
396	Carlos Perez	.05
397	Jeff Fassero	.05
398	Bobby Jones	.05
399	Todd Hundley	.05
400	John Franco	.05
401	Jose Vizcaino	.05
402	Bernard Gilkey	.05
403	Pete Harnisch	.05
404	Pat Kelly	.05
405	David Cone	.05
406	Bernie Williams	.05
407	John Wetteland	.05
408	Scott Kamieniecki	.05
409	Tim Raines	.05
410	Wade Boggs	1.00
411	Terry Steinbach	.05
412	Jason Giambi	.40
413	Todd Van Poppel	.05
414	Pedro Munoz	.05
415	Eddie Murray-1990 (Strange But True)	.40
416	Dennis Eckersley-1990 (Strange But True)	.35
417	Bip Roberts-1992 (Strange But True)	.05
418	Glenallen Hill-1992 (Strange But True)	.05
419	John Hudek-1994 (Strange But True)	.05
420	Derek Bell-1995 (Strange But True)	.05
421	Larry Walker-1995 (Strange But True)	.05
422	Greg Maddux-1995 (Strange But True)	.50
423	Ken Caminiti-1995 (Strange But True)	.05
424	Brent Gates	.05
425	Mark McGwire	1.50
426	Mark Whiten	.05
427	Sid Fernandez	.05
428	Ricky Bottalico	.05
429	Mike Mimbs	.05
430	Lenny Dykstra	.05
431	Todd Zeile	.05
432	Benito Santiago	.05
433	Danny Miceli	.05
434	Al Martin	.05
435	Jay Bell	.05

436	Charlie Hayes	.05
437	Mike Kingery	.05
438	Paul Wagner	.05
439	Tom Pagnozzi	.05
440	Ozzie Smith	1.00
441	Ray Lankford	.05
442	Dennis Eckersley	.65
443	Ron Gant	.05
444	Alan Benes	.05
445	Rickey Henderson	.75
446	Jody Reed	.05
447	Trevor Hoffman	.05
448	Andujar Cedeno	.05
449	Steve Finley	.05
450	Tony Gwynn	1.00
451	Joey Hamilton	.05
452	Mark Leiter	.05
453	Rod Beck	.05
454	Kirt Manwaring	.05
455	Matt Williams	.05
456	Robby Thompson	.05
457	Shawon Dunston	.05
458	Russ Davis	.05
459	Paul Sorrento	.05
460	Randy Johnson	.75
461	Chris Bosio	.05
462	Luis Sojo	.05
463	Sterling Hitchcock	.05
464	Benji Gil	.05
465	Mickey Tettleton	.05
466	Mark McLemore	.05
467	Darryl Hamilton	.05
468	Ken Hill	.05
469	Dean Palmer	.05
470	Carlos Delgado	.40
471	Ed Sprague	.05
472	Otis Nixon	.05
473	Pat Hentgen	.05
474	Juan Guzman	.05
475	John Olerud	.05
476	Checklist (Buck Showalter)	.05
477	Checklist (Bobby Cox)	.05
478	Checklist (Tommy Lasorda)	.05
479	Checklist (Jim Leyland)	.05
480	Checklist (Sparky Anderson)	.05

Update

Available only via a mail-in wrapper redemption or in factory sets, this update set offers cards of players who changed teams after the base card set was issued, as well as a few rookies and others. Cards share the earlier issue's format and are numbered with a "U" suffix.

		NM/M
Complete Set (30):		8.00
Common Player:		.25
481	Randy Myers	.25
482	Kent Mercker	.25
483	David Wells	.35
484	Kevin Mitchell	.25
485	Randy Velarde	.25
486	Ryne Sandberg	4.00
487	Doug Jones	.25
488	Terry Adams	.25
489	Kevin Tapani	.25
490	Harold Baines	.25
491	Eric Davis	.25
492	Julio Franco	.25
493	Jack McDowell	.25
494	Devon White	.25
495	Kevin Brown	.35
496	Rick Wilkins	.25
497	Sean Berry	.25
498	Keith Lockhart	.25
499	Mark Loretta	.25
500	Paul Molitor	2.50
501	Roberto Kelly	.25
502	Lance Johnson	.25
503	Tino Martinez	.25
504	Kenny Rogers	.25
505	Todd Stottlemyre	.25
506	Gary Gaetti	.25
507	Royce Clayton	.25
508	Andy Benes	.25
509	Wally Joyner	.25
510	Erik Hanson	.25

A Cut Above

		NM/M

Blue Chip Prospects

Twenty top young stars who could make a major impact in the major leagues in upcoming seasons are featured in this insert set. Each card is highlighted with blue-foil printing and double die-cut technology, which includes a zig-zag pattern around the top and a die-cut around both bottom corners. The cards are found one per 20 packs in Series 1 foil packs. Cards are numbered with a "BC" prefix.

		NM/M
Complete Set (20):		50.00
Common Player:		1.00
1	Hideo Nomo	4.00
2	Johnny Damon	3.50
3	Jason Isringhausen	1.00
4	Bill Pulsipher	1.00
5	Marty Cordova	1.00
6	Michael Tucker	1.00
7	John Wasdin	1.00
8	Karim Garcia	1.50
9	Ruben Rivera	1.00
10	Chipper Jones	10.00
11	Billy Wagner	1.00
12	Brooks Kieschnick	1.00
13	Alex Ochoa	1.00
14	Roger Cedeno	1.00
15	Alex Rodriguez	15.00
16	Jason Schmidt	1.00
17	Derek Jeter	20.00
18	Brian L. Hunter	1.00
19	Garret Anderson	1.00
20	Manny Ramirez	7.50

Diamond Destiny

This late-season release is found exclusively in retail foil packs labeled "Upper Deck Tech." They are inserted at a rate of one per pack, sold with eight regular 1996 Upper Deck cards at a suggested retail of around $3. The cards have three versions of the same action photo; in color and black-and-white on front, and in black-and-white on back. A large team logo also appears on front and back. In the upper half of the card is a 1-3/16" diameter round color transparency portrait of the player. The basic version of this chase set had bronze foil highlights. Parallel silver and gold versions are found on average of one per 35 and one per 143 packs, respectively. Cards are numbered with a "DD" prefix.

		NM/M
Complete Set (Bronze):		35.00
Common Player (Bronze):		.30
Silver:		6X
Gold:		12X
1	Chipper Jones	1.50

2	Fred McGriff	.30
3	Ryan Klesko	.30
4	John Smoltz	.30
5	Greg Maddux	1.50
6	Cal Ripken Jr.	3.00
7	Roberto Alomar	.45
8	Eddie Murray	1.25
9	Brady Anderson	.30
10	Mo Vaughn	.30
11	Roger Clemens	1.75
12	Darin Erstad	.60
13	Sammy Sosa	1.50
14	Frank Thomas	1.25
15	Barry Larkin	.30
16	Albert Belle	.30
17	Manny Ramirez	1.25
18	Kenny Lofton	.30
19	Dante Bichette	.30
20	Gary Sheffield	.75
21	Jeff Bagwell	1.25
22	Hideo Nomo	.65
23	Mike Piazza	2.00
24	Kirby Puckett	1.50
25	Paul Molitor	1.25
26	Chuck Knoblauch	.30
27	Wade Boggs	1.50
28	Derek Jeter	3.00
29	Rey Ordonez	.30
30	Mark McGwire	2.50
31	Ozzie Smith	1.50
32	Tony Gwynn	1.50
33	Barry Bonds	.30
34	Matt Williams	.30
35	Ken Griffey Jr.	2.00
36	Jay Buhner	.30
37	Randy Johnson	1.25
38	Alex Rodriguez	2.00
39	Juan Gonzalez	.65
40	Joe Carter	.30

Future Stock

Future Stock inserts are found on average of one per six packs of Series 1, highlighting 20 young stars on a die-cut design. Each card has a blue border, vertical photo and silver-foil stamping on the front. Cards are numbered with a "FS" prefix.

		NM/M
Complete Set (20):		4.00
Common Player:		.25
1	George Arias	.25
2	Brian Barnes	.25
3	Trey Beamon	.25
4	Yamil Benitez	.25
5	Jamie Brewington	.25
6	Tony Clark	.25
7	Steve Cox	.25
8	Carlos Delgado	.75
9	Chad Fonville	.25
10	Steve Gibralter	.25
11	Curtis Goodwin	.25
12	Todd Greene	.25
13	Jimmy Haynes	.25
14	Quinton McCracken	.25
15	Billy McMillon	.25
16	Chan Ho Park	.25
17	Arquimedez Pozo	.25
18	Chris Snopek	.25
19	Shannon Stewart	.25
20	Jeff Suppan	.25

Gameface

This insert was exclusive to $1.50 Wal-Mart retail packs. Fronts have an action photo vignetted in white with a gold-foil Gameface logo. Backs have another photo and a few sentences about the player. One Gameface card was found in each pack.

		NM/M
Complete Set (10):		6.00
Common Player:		.15
1	Ken Griffey Jr.	1.00
2	Frank Thomas	.65
3	Barry Bonds	1.50
4	Albert Belle	.15
5	Cal Ripken Jr.	1.50
6	Mike Piazza	1.00
7	Chipper Jones	.75
8	Matt Williams	.15
9	Hideo Nomo	.40
10	Greg Maddux	.75

Hobby Predictor

These inserts depict 60 top players as possible winners in the categories of Player of the Month, Pitcher of the Month and Rookie Hits Leader. If the pictured player won that category any month of the season the card was redeemable for a 10-card set with a different look, action photos and printed on silver-foil stock. Hobby Predictor inserts are found on average once per dozen packs in both series. Winning cards are indicated by (W).

		NM/M
Complete Set (60):		35.00
Common Player:		.40
H1	Albert Belle	.40
H2	Kenny Lofton	.40
H3	Rafael Palmeiro	.65
H4	Ken Griffey Jr.	2.00
H5	Tim Salmon	.40
H6	Cal Ripken Jr.	3.00
H7	Mark McGwire/W	4.50
H8	Frank Thomas/W	1.25
H9	Mo Vaughn/W	.60
H10	Player of the Month Long Shot/W	.40
H11	Roger Clemens	1.75
H12	David Cone	.40
H13	Jose Mesa	.40
H14	Randy Johnson	.75
H15	Steve Finley	.40
H16	Mike Mussina	.50
H17	Kevin Appier	.40
H18	Kenny Rogers	.40
H19	Lee Smith	.40
H20	Pitcher of the Month Long Shot/W	.40
H21	George Arias	.40
H22	Jose Herrera	.40
H23	Tony Clark	.40
H24	Todd Greene	.40
H25	Derek Jeter/W	6.00
H26	Arquimedez Pozo	.40
H27	Matt Lawton	.40
H28	Shannon Stewart	.40
H29	Chris Snopek	.40
H30	Rookie Hits Long Shot	.40
H31	Jeff Bagwell/W	1.25
H32	Dante Bichette	.40
H33	Barry Bonds/W	6.00
H34	Tony Gwynn	1.50
H35	Chipper Jones	1.50
H36	Eric Karros	.40
H37	Barry Larkin	.40
H38	Mike Piazza	2.00
H39	Matt Williams	.40
H40	Player of the Month Long Shot/W	.40
H41	Osvaldo Fernandez	.40
H42	Tom Glavine	.60
H43	Jason Isringhausen	.40
H44	Greg Maddux	1.50
H45	Pedro Martinez	.75
H46	Hideo Nomo	.60
H47	Pete Schourek	.40
H48	Paul Wilson	.40

H49	Mark Wohlers	.40
H50	Pitcher of the Month	
	Long Shot	.40
H51	Bob Abreu	.40
H52	Trey Beamon	.40
H53	Yamil Benitez	.40
H54	Roger Cedeno/W	.60
H55	Todd Hollandsworth	.40
H56	Marvin Benard	.40
H57	Jason Kendall	.40
H58	Brooks Kieschnick	.40
H59	Rey Ordonez/W	.60
H60	Rookie Hits Long	
	Shot/W	.40

Hobby Predictor Redemption

Persons who redeemed winning cards from UD's interactive Predictor insert series received a 10-card set of the top players in various statistical categories. The redemption cards are similar in format to the Predictor cards, but have fronts printed on silver-foil. In place of the contest rules found on the backs of Predictor cards, the redemption cards have a career summary.

		NM/M
Complete Set (60):		45.00
Common Player:		.50
H1	Albert Belle	.50
H2	Kenny Lofton	.50
H3	Rafael Palmeiro	.75
H4	Ken Griffey Jr.	2.50
H5	Tim Salmon	.50
H6	Cal Ripken Jr.	4.00
H7	Mark McGwire	3.00
H8	Frank Thomas	1.00
H9	Mo Vaughn	.50
H10	Player of the Month	
	Long Shot	.50
H11	Roger Clemens	2.25
H12	David Cone	.50
H13	Jose Mesa	.50
H14	Randy Johnson	1.00
H15	Steve Finley	.50
H16	Mike Mussina	.65
H17	Kevin Appier	.50
H18	Kenny Rogers	.50
H19	Lee Smith	.50
H20	Pitcher of the Month	
	Long Shot	.50
H21	George Arias	.50
H22	Jose Herrera	.50
H23	Tony Clark	.50
H24	Todd Greene	.50
H25	Derek Jeter	4.00
H26	Arquimedez Pozo	.50
H27	Matt Lawton	.50
H28	Shannon Stewart	.50
H29	Chris Snopek	.50
H30	Rookie Hits Long Shot	.50
H31	Jeff Bagwell	1.00
H32	Dante Bichette	.50
H33	Barry Bonds	4.00
H34	Tony Gwynn	2.00
H35	Chipper Jones	2.00
H36	Eric Karros	.50
H37	Barry Larkin	.50
H38	Mike Piazza	2.50
H39	Matt Williams	.50
H40	Player of the Month	
	Long Shot	.50
H41	Osvaldo Fernandez	.50
H42	Tom Glavine	.65
H43	Jason Isringhausen	.50
H44	Greg Maddux	2.00
H45	Pedro Martinez	1.00
H46	Hideo Nomo	.65
H47	Pete Schourek	.50
H48	Paul Wilson	.50
H49	Mark Wohlers	.50
H50	Pitcher of the Month	
	Long Shot	.50
H51	Bob Abreu	.50
H52	Trey Beamon	.50
H53	Yamil Benitez	.50
H54	Roger Cedeno	.50
H55	Todd Hollandsworth	.50
H56	Marvin Benard	.50
H57	Jason Kendall	.50

Hot Commodities

These 20 die-cut cards were seeded one per every 37 1996 Upper Deck Series 2 packs. Cards are numbered with a "HC" prefix.

		NM/M
Complete Set (20):		30.00
Common Player:		.75
1	Ken Griffey Jr.	3.00
2	Hideo Nomo	1.50
3	Roberto Alomar	1.50
4	Paul Wilson	.75
5	Albert Belle	.75
6	Manny Ramirez	2.25
7	Kirby Puckett	2.50
8	Johnny Damon	2.00
9	Randy Johnson	2.25
10	Greg Maddux	2.50
11	Chipper Jones	2.50
12	Barry Bonds	5.00
13	Mo Vaughn	.75
14	Mike Piazza	3.00
15	Cal Ripken Jr.	5.00
16	Tim Salmon	.75
17	Sammy Sosa	2.50
18	Kenny Lofton	.75
19	Tony Gwynn	2.50
20	Frank Thomas	2.25

Lovero Collection

Every sixth pack of 1996 Upper Deck Series II has a V.J. Lovero insert card. This 20-card set features unique shots from Lovero, one of the most well-known photographers in the country. Some of the cards feature Randy Johnson wearing a conehead, Frank Thomas blowing a bubble while throwing the ball, and Jay Buhner and his child both chewing with a bat. Cards are numbered with a "VJ" prefix.

		NM/M
Complete Set (20):		17.50
Common Player:		.25
1	Rod Carew	1.00
2	Hideo Nomo	.50
3	Derek Jeter	3.00
4	Barry Bonds	3.00
5	Greg Maddux	1.50
6	Mark McGwire/W	
	(Will Clark.)	2.50
7	Jose Canseco	.25
8	Ken Caminiti	.25
9	Raul Mondesi	.25
10	Ken Griffey Jr.	2.50
11	Jay Buhner	.25
12	Randy Johnson	1.00
13	Roger Clemens	2.00
14	Brady Anderson	.25
15	Frank Thomas	1.00
16	Angels Outfielders	.25
17	Mike Piazza	2.50
18	Dante Bichette	.25
19	Tony Gwynn	1.50
20	Jim Abbott	.25

Nomo Highlights

The 1995 rookie season of Los Angeles Dodgers' pitcher Hideo Nomo is recapped in this five-card 1996 Upper Deck insert set. The cards were seeded

one per every 23 Series 2 packs. A 5" x 7" version of each card was also issued as a retail box insert. Values are the same as for small cards.

		NM/M
Complete Set (5):		3.00
Common Card:		.75
1-5	Hideo Nomo	.75

Power Driven

Twenty of the game's top power hitters are analyzed in depth by baseball writer Peter Gammons on these Series 1 insert cards. Found once per 36 packs, on average, the cards are printed on an embossed light F/X design. Cards are numbered with a "PD" prefix.

		NM/M
Complete Set (20):		24.00
Common Player:		.30
1	Albert Belle	.30
2	Barry Bonds	5.00
3	Jay Buhner	.30
4	Jose Canseco	.75
5	Cecil Fielder	.30
6	Juan Gonzalez	.75
7	Ken Griffey Jr.	3.00
8	Eric Karros	.30
9	Fred McGriff	.30
10	Mark McGwire	4.00
11	Rafael Palmeiro	1.25
12	Mike Piazza	3.00
13	Manny Ramirez	1.50
14	Tim Salmon	.30
15	Reggie Sanders	.30
16	Sammy Sosa	2.50
17	Frank Thomas	1.50
18	Mo Vaughn	.30
19	Larry Walker	.30
20	Matt Williams	.30

1996 Upper Deck Retail Predictor

Retail Predictor inserts feature 60 possible winners in the categories of monthly leader in home runs, batting average and RBIs. If the pictured player led a category in

any month, his card was redeemable for a 10-card set featuring action photos on silver foil. Retail Predictors are found on average once per 12 packs in each series. Winning cards are indicated by (W).

		NM/M
Complete Set (60):		40.00
Common Player:		.40
R1	Albert Belle/W	.60
R2	Jay Buhner/W	.60
R3	Juan Gonzalez	.50
R4	Ken Griffey Jr.	2.00
R5	Mark McGwire/W	4.00
R6	Rafael Palmeiro	.65
R7	Tim Salmon	.40
R8	Frank Thomas	1.00
R9	Mo Vaughn/W	.60
R10	Home Run Long	
	Shot/W	.40
R11	Albert Belle/W	.60
R12	Jay Buhner	.40
R13	Jim Edmonds	.40
R14	Cecil Fielder	.40
R15	Ken Griffey Jr.	2.00
R16	Edgar Martinez	.40
R17	Manny Ramirez	.75
R18	Frank Thomas	1.00
R19	Mo Vaughn/W	.60
R20	RBI Long Shot/W	.40
R21	Roberto Alomar/W	1.00
R22	Carlos Baerga	.40
R23	Wade Boggs	1.50
R24	Ken Griffey Jr.	2.00
R25	Chuck Knoblauch	.40
R26	Kenny Lofton	.40
R27	Edgar Martinez	.40
R28	Tim Salmon	.40
R29	Frank Thomas	1.00
R30	Batting Average Long	
	Shot/W	.40
R31	Dante Bichette	.40
R32	Barry Bonds/W	4.50
R33	Ron Gant	.40
R34	Chipper Jones	1.50
R35	Fred McGriff	.40
R36	Mike Piazza	2.00
R37	Sammy Sosa	1.50
R38	Larry Walker	.40
R39	Matt Williams	.40
R40	Home Run Long Shot	.40
R41	Jeff Bagwell/W	1.25
R42	Dante Bichette	.40
R43	Barry Bonds/W	4.50
R44	Jeff Conine	.40
R45	Andres Galarraga	.40
R46	Mike Piazza	2.00
R47	Reggie Sanders	.40
R48	Sammy Sosa	1.50
R49	Matt Williams	.40
R50	RBI Long Shot	.40
R51	Jeff Bagwell	.75
R52	Derek Bell	.40
R53	Dante Bichette	.40
R54	Craig Biggio	.40
R55	Barry Bonds	2.50
R56	Bret Boone	.40
R57	Tony Gwynn	1.50
R58	Barry Larkin	.40
R59	Mike Piazza/W	3.50
R60	AVG Long Shot	.40

Retail Predictor Redemption

Persons who redeemed winning cards from UD's interactive Predictor insert series received a 10-card set of the top players in various statistical categories. The redemption cards are similar in format to the Predictor cards, but have fronts printed on silver-foil. In place of the contest rules found on the backs of Predictor cards, the redemption cards have a career summary.

		NM/M
Complete Set (60):		25.00
Common Player:		.25
R1	Albert Belle	.25
R2	Jay Buhner	.25
R3	Juan Gonzalez	.35
R4	Ken Griffey Jr.	1.00
R5	Mark McGwire	1.50
R6	Rafael Palmeiro	.50
R7	Tim Salmon	.25
R8	Frank Thomas	.60
R9	Mo Vaughn	.25
R10	Home Run Long Shot	.25
R11	Albert Belle	.25
R12	Jay Buhner	.25
R13	Jim Edmonds	.25
R14	Cecil Fielder	.25
R15	Ken Griffey Jr.	1.00
R16	Edgar Martinez	.25
R17	Manny Ramirez	.60
R18	Frank Thomas	.60
R19	Mo Vaughn	.25
R20	RBI Long Shot	.25
R21	Roberto Alomar	.35
R22	Carlos Baerga	.25
R23	Wade Boggs	.75
R24	Ken Griffey Jr.	1.00
R25	Chuck Knoblauch	.25
R26	Kenny Lofton	.25
R27	Edgar Martinez	.25
R28	Tim Salmon	.25
R29	Frank Thomas	.60
R30	Batting Average	
	Long Shot	.25
R31	Dante Bichette	.25
R32	Barry Bonds	2.00
R33	Ron Gant	.25
R34	Chipper Jones	.75
R35	Fred McGriff	.25
R36	Mike Piazza	1.00
R37	Sammy Sosa	.75
R38	Larry Walker	.25
R39	Matt Williams	.25
R40	Home Run Long Shot	.25
R41	Jeff Bagwell	.60
R42	Dante Bichette	.25
R43	Barry Bonds	2.00
R44	Jeff Conine	.25
R45	Andres Galarraga	.25
R46	Mike Piazza	1.00
R47	Reggie Sanders	.25
R48	Sammy Sosa	.75
R49	Matt Williams	.25
R50	RBI Long Shot	.25
R51	Jeff Bagwell	.60
R52	Derek Bell	.25
R53	Dante Bichette	.25
R54	Craig Biggio	.25
R55	Barry Bonds	2.00
R56	Bret Boone	.25
R57	Tony Gwynn	.75
R58	Barry Larkin	.25
R59	Mike Piazza	1.00
R60	AVG Long Shot	.25

Cal Ripken Collection

Part of a cross-brand insert set, four cards are included as Series I inserts at the rate of one per 24 packs. Five cards are also included in Series II, one per every 23 packs. They chronicle Cal Ripken's career and highlights.

		NM/M
Complete Set (8):		12.50
Common Card:		2.00
Header:		2.00
5-8	Cal Ripken Jr.	2.00
13-17	Cal Ripken Jr.	2.00

Cal Ripken Collection Supers

The career of Cal Ripken Jr. to the point of his 2,131st consecutive major league game is chronicled in this boxed set of 3-1/2" x 5" cards. The tale is told in reverse order, with card #1 marking the record and #22 detailing Ripken's first major league experience. Fronts have photos of Ripken in various stages of his career and feature a gold-foil

facsimile autograph. Backs have a green and black background with a portrait of Ripken at top. At center are a few sentences about his career and a season's stats.

		NM/M
Complete Set (22):		10.00
Common Card:		.75
1	Cal Ripken Jr.	.75
	(w/Barry Bonds)	1.00
3-21	Cal Ripken Jr.	.75
22	Cal Ripken Jr.	
	(w/Eddie Murray)	.75

Run Producers

These double die-cut, embossed and color foil-stamped cards feature 20 of the game's top RBI men. The cards were seeded one per every 71 packs of 1996 Upper Deck Series II. Cards are numbered with a "RP" prefix.

		NM/M
Complete Set (20):		50.00
Common Player:		1.00
1	Albert Belle	1.00
2	Dante Bichette	1.00
3	Barry Bonds	10.00
4	Jay Buhner	1.00
5	Jose Canseco	2.00
6	Juan Gonzalez	1.50
7	Ken Griffey Jr.	6.00
8	Tony Gwynn	5.00
9	Kenny Lofton	1.00
10	Edgar Martinez	1.00
11	Fred McGriff	1.00
12	Mark McGwire	7.50
13	Rafael Palmeiro	2.50
14	Mike Piazza	6.00
15	Manny Ramirez	3.00
16	Tim Salmon	1.00
17	Sammy Sosa	5.00
18	Frank Thomas	3.00
19	Mo Vaughn	1.00
20	Matt Williams	1.00

All-Star Supers

The starting line-ups of the 1996 All-Star Game are featured in super-size (3-1/2" x 5") versions of their 1996 Upper Deck cards in this special boxed set sold at Wal-Mart late in the year for around $18. Other than a large silver-foil All-Star Game logo in the lower-left corner of each photo, these cards are identical to the regular-issue versions, right down to the silver- and bronze-foil highlights on front and the card numbers on back.

		NM/M
Complete Set (18):		7.50
Common Player:		.25
80	Jeff Bagwell	.75
195	Barry Bonds	2.00

200	Ken Griffey Jr.	1.25
271	John Smoltz	.25
275	Roberto Alomar	.45
280	Cal Ripken Jr.	2.00
300	Frank Thomas	.75
310	Barry Larkin	.25
313	Sandy Alomar Jr.	.25
315	Albert Belle	.25
317	Charles Nagy	.25
319	Kenny Lofton	.25
320	Dante Bichette	.25
345	Craig Biggio	.25
360	Mike Piazza	1.25
410	Wade Boggs	1.00
450	Tony Gwynn	1.00
455	Matt Williams	.25

Ken Griffey Jr. All-Star

Junior's seventh All-Star team selection was marked with the issue of this special jumbo (3-1/2" x 5") card. The front has an action photo with the 1996 All-Star Game logo and is highlighted in silver foil, including a reproduction of his autograph. The top is die-cut. On back is a portrait photo with Griffey's All-Star history overprinted, and a serial number from within an edition of 2,500. The card was an exclusive to a TV shopping network.

	NM/M
Ken Griffey Jr.	12.00

Ken Griffey Jr. 22kt Gold

This standard-size card has a gold-foil facsimile autograph on front and is serially numbered on back from within an edition of 5,000. A certificate of authenticity accompanied the card when sold new.

	NM/M
Ken Griffey Jr.	7.50

National Heroes

Two baseball stars are included in this series of collec-

tor issues believed to have been a TV shop-at-home exclusive. Measuring 3-1/2" x 5", the cards are die-cut into a torn ticket shape. Fronts have color action photos on a gold-foil background. Two versions of each card were issued, an edition of 5,000 unsigned cards and an autographed edition serially numbered on front to a limit of 250.

		NM/M
Complete Set (2):		20.00
Complete Set, Autographed (2):		190.00
(1)	Ken Griffey Jr.	7.50
(1a)	Ken Griffey Jr./Auto.	90.00
(2)	Cal Ripken Jr.	10.00
(2a)	Cal Ripken Jr./Auto.	100.00

Hideo Nomo R.O.Y.

The Japanese pitcher's 1995 Rookie of the Year season was commemorated with this large-format (3-1/2" x 5"), die-cut card sold only via TV shopping programs. The card has an action photo of Nomo on front and is highlighted in gold foil, including a replica of his autograph. On back is an action photo, major league career summary and stats and a serial number from within an edition of 5,000 pieces.

	NM/M
Hideo Nomo	15.00

Meet the Stars

These 7" x 5" cards were issued in conjunction with UD's "Meet the Stars" promotion.

		NM/M
Complete Set (2):		12.00
(1)	Dynamic Debut/1989 (Ken Griffey Jr.)	5.00
(2)	Magic Memories/1995 (Ken Griffey Jr.)	5.00

Statistics Leaders Supers

National League and American League winners of important statistical categories, along with major award winners for the 1996 season are featured in this boxed set

of large-format (3-1/2" x 5") cards. Besides the size, these cards differ from the regular-issue 1996 UD cards of the same players only in the addition of a silver-foil award shield on front and the card number on back. Players with multiple awards have identical cards. The set was sold only at retail outlets with a suggested price of about $20.

		NM/M
Complete Set (23):		4.00
Common Player:		.15
1	Alex Rodriguez (AL Batting)	1.50
2	Tony Gwynn (NL Batting)	.60
3	Mark McGwire (AL HR)	1.50
4	Andres Galarraga (NL HR)	.15
5	Albert Belle (AL RBI)	.15
6	Andres Galarraga (NL RBI)	.15
7	Kenny Lofton (AL steals)	.15
8	Eric Young (NL Steals)	.15
9	Andy Pettitte (AL Wins)	.25
10	John Smoltz (NL Wins)	.15
11	Roger Clemens (AL K's)	.75
12	John Smoltz (NL Ks)	.15
13	Juan Guzman (AL ERA)	.15
14	Kevin Brown (NL ERA)	.15
15	John Wetteland (AL saves)	.15
16	Jeff Brantley (NL Saves)	.15
17	Todd Worrell (NL Saves)	.15
18	Derek Jeter (AL ROY)	2.00
19	Todd Hollandsworth (NL ROY)	.15
20	Juan Gonzalez (AL MVP)	.30
21	Ken Caminiti (NL MVP)	.15
22	Pat Hentgen (AL CY)	.15
23	John Smoltz (NL CY)	.15

1997 Upper Deck

The 520-card set was issued in two series in 12-card packs. Base card fronts feature a game-action shot with the player's name near the bottom edge above a bronze-foil, wood-grain stripe. A team logo is in the lower-left corner in silver foil. Each card front has the date of the game pictured with a brief description. Backs contain more detailed game highlight descriptions and statistics, along with a small action shot in the upper-left quadrant. Series 1 subsets are: Jackie Robinson Tribute (1-9), Strike Force (65-72), Defensive Gems (136-153), Global Impact (181-207), Season Highlights Checklist (214-222) and Star Rookies (223-240). A 30-card update to Series 1 was released early in the season featuring 1996 postseason highlights and star rookies. Those card faces have red or purple borders and are numbered 241 to 270. Second series subsets include Star Rookie (271-288), Season Highlights (316-324), Capture the Flag (370-387), the short-printed (about one per seven packs) Griffey Hot List (415-424), and Diamond Debuts (469-483). A second update set of 30 was released near the end of the 1997 season, numbered

521-550 and featuring traded players and rookies. Both of the update sets were available only via a mail-in redemption offer.

		NM/M
Complete Set (550):		75.00
Complete Series 1 Set (240):		35.00
Complete Update Set (241-270):		5.00
Complete Series 2 Set (271-520):		35.00
Complete Update Set (521-550):		7.50
Common Player:		.05
Series 1 or 2 Pack (12):		1.50
Series 1 or 2 Wax Box (28):		25.00
1	Jackie Robinson	.50
2	Jackie Robinson	.50
3	Jackie Robinson	.50
4	Jackie Robinson	.50
5	Jackie Robinson	.50
6	Jackie Robinson	.50
7	Jackie Robinson	.50
8	Jackie Robinson	.50
9	Jackie Robinson	.50
10	Chipper Jones	1.00
11	Marquis Grissom	.05
12	Jermaine Dye	.05
13	Mark Lemke	.05
14	Terrell Wade	.05
15	Fred McGriff	.20
16	Tom Glavine	.20
17	Mark Wohlers	.05
18	Randy Myers	.05
19	Roberto Alomar	.25
20	Cal Ripken Jr.	2.00
21	Rafael Palmeiro	.65
22	Mike Mussina	.30
23	Brady Anderson	.05
24	Jose Canseco	.50
25	Mo Vaughn	.50
26	Roger Clemens	1.00
27	Tim Naehring	.05
28	Jeff Suppan	.05
29	Troy Percival	.05
30	Sammy Sosa	1.00
31	Amaury Telemaco	.05
32	Rey Sanchez	.05
33	Scott Servais	.05
34	Steve Trachsel	.05
35	Mark Grace	.05
36	Wilson Alvarez	.05
37	Harold Baines	.05
38	Tony Phillips	.05
39	James Baldwin	.05
40	Frank Thomas (Wrong Ken Griffey Jr.'s vital data.)	.85
41	Lyle Mouton	.05
42	Chris Snopek	.05
43	Hal Morris	.05
44	Eric Davis	.05
45	Barry Larkin	.05
46	Reggie Sanders	.05
47	Pete Schourek	.05
48	Lee Smith	.05
49	Charles Nagy	.05
50	Albert Belle	.05
51	Julio Franco	.05
52	Kenny Lofton	.05
53	Orel Hershiser	.05
54	Omar Vizquel	.05
55	Eric Young	.05
56	Curtis Leskanic	.05
57	Quinton McCracken	.05
58	Kevin Ritz	.05
59	Walt Weiss	.05
60	Dante Bichette	.05
61	Marc Lewis	.05
62	Tony Clark	.05
63	Travis Fryman	.05
64	John Smoltz	.05
65	Greg Maddux (Strike Force)	.50
66	Tom Glavine (Strike Force)	.10
67	Mike Mussina (Strike Force)	.15
68	Andy Pettitte (Strike Force)	.15
69	Mariano Rivera (Strike Force)	.10
70	Hideo Nomo (Strike Force)	.20
71	Kevin Brown (Strike Force)	.05
72	Randy Johnson (Strike Force)	.40
73	Felipe Lira	.05
74	Kimera Bartee	.05
75	Alan Trammell	.05
76	Kevin Brown	.05
77	Edgar Renteria	.05
78	Al Leiter	.05
79	Charles Johnson	.05
80	Andre Dawson	.05
81	Billy Wagner	.05
82	Donne Wall	.05
83	Jeff Bagwell	.75
84	Keith Lockhart	.05
85	Jeff Montgomery	.05
86	Tom Goodwin	.05
87	Tim Belcher	.05
88	Mike Macfarlane	.05

89	Joe Randa	.05
90	Brett Butler	.05
91	Todd Worrell	.05
92	Todd Hollandsworth	.05
93	Ismael Valdes	.05
94	Hideo Nomo	.40
95	Mike Piazza	1.25
96	Jeff Cirillo	.05
97	Ricky Bones	.05
98	Fernando Vina	.05
99	Ben McDonald	.05
100	John Jaha	.05
101	Mark Loretta	.05
102	Paul Molitor	.75
103	Rick Aguilera	.05
104	Marty Cordova	.05
105	Kirby Puckett	1.00
106	Dan Naulty	.05
107	Frank Rodriguez	.05
108	Shane Andrews	.05
109	Henry Rodriguez	.05
110	Mark Grudzielanek	.05
111	Pedro Martinez	.75
112	Ugueth Urbina	.05
113	David Segui	.05
114	Rey Ordonez	.05
115	Bernard Gilkey	.05
116	Butch Huskey	.05
117	Paul Wilson	.05
118	Alex Ochoa	.05
119	John Franco	.05
120	Dwight Gooden	.05
121	Ruben Rivera	.05
122	Andy Pettitte	.20
123	Tino Martinez	.05
124	Bernie Williams	.05
125	Wade Boggs	1.00
126	Paul O'Neill	.05
127	Scott Brosius	.05
128	Ernie Young	.05
129	Doug Johns	.05
130	Geronimo Berroa	.05
131	Jason Giambi	.50
132	John Wasdin	.05
133	Jim Eisenreich	.05
134	Ricky Otero	.05
135	Ricky Bottalico	.05
136	Mark Langston (Defensive Gems)	.05
137	Greg Maddux (Defensive Gems)	.50
138	Ivan Rodriguez (Defensive Gems)	.35
139	Charles Johnson (Defensive Gems)	.05
140	J.T. Snow (Defensive Gems)	.05
141	Mark Grace (Defensive Gems)	.05
142	Roberto Alomar (Defensive Gems)	.15
143	Craig Biggio (Defensive Gems)	.05
144	Ken Caminiti (Defensive Gems)	.05
145	Matt Williams (Defensive Gems)	.05
146	Omar Vizquel (Defensive Gems)	.05
147	Cal Ripken Jr. (Defensive Gems)	1.00
148	Ozzie Smith (Defensive Gems)	.40
149	Rey Ordonez (Defensive Gems)	.05
150	Ken Griffey Jr. (Defensive Gems)	.65
151	Devon White (Defensive Gems)	.05
152	Barry Bonds (Defensive Gems)	1.00
153	Kenny Lofton (Defensive Gems)	.05
154	Mickey Morandini	.05
155	Gregg Jefferies	.05
156	Curt Schilling	.20
157	Jason Kendall	.05
158	Francisco Cordova	.05
159	Dennis Eckersley	.65
160	Ron Gant	.05
161	Ozzie Smith	1.00
162	Brian Jordan	.05
163	John Mabry	.05
164	Andy Ashby	.05
165	Steve Finley	.05
166	Fernando Valenzuela	.05
167	Archi Cianfrocco	.05
168	Wally Joyner	.05
169	Greg Vaughn	.05
170	Barry Bonds	2.00
171	William Van Landingham	.05
172	Marvin Benard	.05
173	Rich Aurilia	.05
174	Jay Canizaro	.05
175	Ken Griffey Jr.	1.25
176	Bob Wells	.05
177	Jay Buhner	.05
178	Sterling Hitchcock	.05
179	Edgar Martinez	.05
180	Rusty Greer	.05
181	Dave Nilsson (Global Impact)	.05
182	Larry Walker (Global Impact)	.05
183	Edgar Renteria (Global Impact)	.05

184	Rey Ordonez (Global Impact)	.05
185	Rafael Palmeiro (Global Impact)	.35
186	Osvaldo Fernandez (Global Impact)	.05
187	Raul Mondesi (Global Impact)	.40
188	Manny Ramirez (Global Impact)	.40
189	Sammy Sosa (Global Impact)	.50
190	Robert Eenhoorn (Global Impact)	.05
191	Devon White (Global Impact)	.05
192	Hideo Nomo (Global Impact)	.20
193	Mac Suzuki (Global Impact)	.05
194	Chan Ho Park (Global Impact)	.05
195	Fernando Valenzuela (Global Impact)	.05
196	Andruw Jones (Global Impact)	.40
197	Vinny Castilla (Global Impact)	.05
198	Dennis Martinez (Global Impact)	.05
199	Ruben Rivera (Global Impact)	.05
200	Juan Gonzalez (Global Impact)	.20
201	Roberto Alomar (Global Impact)	.30
202	Edgar Martinez (Global Impact)	.05
203	Ivan Rodriguez (Global Impact)	.35
204	Carlos Delgado (Global Impact)	.20
205	Andres Galarraga (Global Impact)	.05
206	Ozzie Guillen (Global Impact)	.05
207	Midre Cummings (Global Impact)	.05
208	Roger Pavlik	.05
209	Darren Oliver	.05
210	Dean Palmer	.05
211	Ivan Rodriguez	.65
212	Otis Nixon	.05
213	Pat Hentgen	.05
214	Ozzie Smith, Andre Dawson, Kirby Puckett CL (Season Highlights)	.10
215	Barry Bonds, Gary Sheffield, Brady Anderson (Checklist/Season Highlights)	.25
216	Ken Caminiti (Checklist/Season Highlights)	.05
217	John Smoltz (Checklist/Season Highlights)	.05
218	Eric Young (Checklist/Season Highlights)	.05
219	Juan Gonzalez (Checklist/Season Highlights)	.10
220	Eddie Murray (Checklist/Season Highlights)	.15
221	Tommy Lasorda (Checklist/Season Highlights)	.05
222	Paul Molitor (Checklist/Season Highlights)	.15
223	Luis Castillo	.05
224	Justin Thompson	.05
225	Rocky Coppinger	.05
226	Jermaine Allensworth	.05
227	Jeff D'Amico	.05
228	Jamey Wright	.05
229	Scott Rolen	.60
230	Darin Erstad	.05
231	Marty Janzen	.05
232	Jacob Cruz	.05
233	Raul Ibanez	.05
234	Nomar Garciaparra	1.00
235	Todd Walker	.05
236	Brian Giles RC	.75
237	Matt Beech	.05
238	Mike Cameron	.05
239	Jose Paniagua	.05
240	Andruw Jones	.75
241	Brant Brown (Star Rookies)	.25
242	Robin Jennings (Star Rookies)	.25
243	Willie Adams (Star Rookies)	.25
244	Ken Caminiti (Division Series)	.25
245	Brian Jordan (Division Series)	.25
246	Chipper Jones (Division Series)	2.50
247	Juan Gonzalez (Division Series)	1.00
248	Bernie Williams (Division Series)	.25

249 Roberto Alomar (Division Series) .30
250 Bernie Williams (Post-Season) .25
251 David Wells (Post-Season) .25
252 Cecil Fielder (Post-Season) .25
253 Darryl Strawberry (Post-Season) .25
254 Andy Pettitte (Post-Season) .40
255 Javier Lopez (Post-Season) .25
256 Gary Gaetti (Post-Season) .25
257 Ron Gant (Post-Season) .25
258 Brian Jordan (Post-Season) .25
259 John Smoltz (Post-Season) .25
260 Greg Maddux (Post-Season) 2.50
261 Tom Glavine (Post-Season) .45
262 Chipper Jones (World Series) 2.50
263 Greg Maddux (World Series) 2.50
264 David Cone (World Series) .25
265 Jim Leyritz (World Series) .25
266 Andy Pettitte (World Series) .40
267 John Wetteland (World Series) .25
268 Dario Veras RC (Star Rookie) .25
269 Neifi Perez (Star Rookie) .25
270 Bill Mueller (Star Rookie) .25
271 Vladimir Guerrero (Star Rookie) .75
272 Dmitri Young (Star Rookie) .05
273 Nerio Rodriguez RC (Star Rookie) .05
274 Kevin Orie (Star Rookie) .05
275 Felipe Crespo (Star Rookie) .05
276 Danny Graves (Star Rookie) .05
277 Roderick Myers (Star Rookie) .05
278 Felix Heredia RC (Star Rookie) .25
279 Ralph Milliard (Star Rookie) .05
280 Greg Norton (Star Rookie) .05
281 Derek Wallace (Star Rookie) .05
282 Trot Nixon (Star Rookie) .10
283 Bobby Chouinard (Star Rookie) .05
284 Jay Witasick (Star Rookie) .05
285 Travis Miller (Star Rookie) .05
286 Brian Bevil (Star Rookie) .05
287 Bobby Estalella (Star Rookie) .05
288 Steve Soderstrom (Star Rookie) .05
289 Mark Langston .05
290 Tim Salmon .05
291 Jim Edmonds .05
292 Garret Anderson .05
293 George Arias .05
294 Gary DiSarcina .05
295 Chuck Finley .05
296 Todd Greene .05
297 Randy Velarde .05
298 David Justice .05
299 Ryan Klesko .05
300 John Smoltz .05
301 Javier Lopez .05
302 Greg Maddux 1.00
303 Denny Neagle .05
304 B.J. Surhoff .05
305 Chris Hoiles .05
306 Eric Davis .05
307 Scott Erickson .05
308 Mike Bordick .05
309 John Valentin .05
310 Heathcliff Slocumb .05
311 Tom Gordon .05
312 Mike Stanley .05
313 Reggie Jefferson .05
314 Darren Bragg .05
315 Troy O'Leary .05
316 John Mabry (Season Highlight) .05
317 Mark Whiten (Season Highlight) .05
318 Edgar Martinez (Season Highlight) .05
319 Alex Rodriguez (Season Highlight) .75
320 Mark McGwire (Season Highlight) .75
321 Hideo Nomo (Season Highlight) .20

322 Todd Hundley (Season Highlight) .05
323 Barry Bonds (Season Highlight) 1.00
324 Andruw Jones (Season Highlight) .40
325 Ryne Sandberg 1.00
326 Brian McRae .05
327 Frank Castillo .05
328 Shawon Dunston .05
329 Ray Durham .05
330 Robin Ventura .05
331 Ozzie Guillen .05
332 Roberto Hernandez .05
333 Albert Belle .25
334 Dave Martinez .05
335 Willie Greene .05
336 Jeff Brantley .05
337 Kevin Jarvis .05
338 John Smiley .05
339 Eddie Taubensee .05
340 Bret Boone .05
341 Kevin Seitzer .05
342 Jack McDowell .05
343 Sandy Alomar Jr. .05
344 Chad Curtis .05
345 Manny Ramirez .75
346 Chad Ogea .05
347 Jim Thome .05
348 Mark Thompson .05
349 Ellis Burks .05
350 Andres Galarraga .05
351 Vinny Castilla .05
352 Kirt Manwaring .05
353 Larry Walker .05
354 Omar Olivares .05
355 Bobby Higginson .05
356 Melvin Nieves .05
357 Brian Johnson .05
358 Devon White .05
359 Jeff Conine .05
360 Gary Sheffield .35
361 Robb Nen .05
362 Mike Hampton .05
363 Bob Abreu .10
364 Luis Gonzalez .05
365 Derek Bell .05
366 Sean Berry .05
367 Craig Biggio .05
368 Darryl Kile .05
369 Shane Reynolds .05
370 Jeff Bagwell (Capture the Flag) .40
371 Ron Gant (Capture the Flag) .05
372 Andy Benes (Capture the Flag) .05
373 Gary Gaetti (Capture the Flag) .05
374a Ramon Martinez (Capture the Flag)(Gold back.) .05
374b Ramon Martinez (Capture the Flag)(White back.) .05
375 Raul Mondesi (Capture the Flag) .05
376a Steve Finley (Capture the Flag)(Gold back.) .05
376b Steve Finley (Capture the Flag)(White back.) .05
377 Ken Caminiti (Capture the Flag) .05
378 Tony Gwynn (Capture the Flag) .40
379 Dario Veras (Capture the Flag) .05
380 Andy Pettitte (Capture the Flag) .10
381 Ruben Rivera (Capture the Flag) .05
382 David Cone (Capture the Flag) .05
383 Roberto Alomar (Capture the Flag) .20
384 Edgar Martinez (Capture the Flag) .05
385 Ken Griffey Jr. (Capture the Flag) .65
386 Mark McGwire (Capture the Flag) .75
387 Rusty Greer (Capture the Flag) .05
388 Jose Rosado .05
389 Kevin Appier .25
390 Johnny Damon .05
391 Jose Offerman .05
392 Michael Tucker .05
393 Craig Paquette .05
394 Bip Roberts .05
395 Ramon Martinez .05
396 Greg Gagne .05
397 Chan Ho Park .05
398 Karim Garcia .10
399 Wilton Guerrero .05
400 Eric Karros .05
401 Raul Mondesi .05
402 Matt Mieske .05
403 Mike Fetters .05
404 Dave Nilsson .05
405 Jose Valentin .05
406 Scott Karl .05
407 Marc Newfield .05
408 Cal Eldred .05
409 Rich Becker .05
410 Terry Steinbach .05
411 Chuck Knoblauch .05
412 Pat Meares .05
413 Brad Radke .05

415a Kirby Puckett (should be #414) 1.00
415b Andruw Jones (Griffey Hot List) 1.50
416 Chipper Jones (Griffey Hot List) 2.00
417 Mo Vaughn (Griffey Hot List) .50
418 Frank Thomas (Griffey Hot List) 1.50
419 Albert Belle (Griffey Hot List) .50
420 Mark McGwire (Griffey Hot List) 3.00
421 Derek Jeter (Griffey Hot List) 4.50
422 Alex Rodriguez (Griffey Hot List) 3.00
423 Juan Gonzalez (Griffey Hot List) .75
424 Ken Griffey Jr. (Griffey Hot List) 2.50
425 Rondell White .05
426 Darrin Fletcher .05
427 Cliff Floyd .05
428 Mike Lansing .05
429 F.P. Santangelo .05
430 Todd Hundley .05
431 Mark Clark .05
432 Pete Harnisch .05
433 Jason Isringhausen .05
434 Bobby Jones .05
435 Lance Johnson .05
436 Carlos Baerga .05
437 Mariano Duncan .05
438 David Cone .05
439 Mariano Rivera .15
440 Derek Jeter 2.00
441 Joe Girardi .05
442 Charlie Hayes .05
443 Tim Raines .05
444 Darryl Strawberry .05
445 Cecil Fielder .05
446 Ariel Prieto .05
447 Tony Batista .05
448 Brent Gates .05
449 Scott Spiezio .05
450 Mark McGwire 1.50
451 Don Wengert .05
452 Mike Lieberthal .05
453 Lenny Dykstra .05
454 Rex Hudler .05
455 Darren Daulton .05
456 Kevin Stocker .05
457 Trey Beamon .05
458 Midre Cummings .05
459 Mark Johnson .05
460 Al Martin .05
461 Kevin Elster .05
462 Jon Lieber .05
463 Jason Schmidt .05
464 Paul Wagner .05
465 Andy Benes .05
466 Alan Benes .05
467 Royce Clayton .05
468 Gary Gaetti .05
469 Curt Lyons (Diamond Debuts) .05
470 Eugene Kingsale (Diamond Debuts) .05
471 Damian Jackson (Diamond Debuts) .05
472 Wendell Magee (Diamond Dubuts) .05
473 Kevin L. Brown (Diamond Debuts) .05
474 Raul Casanova (Diamond Debuts) .05
475 Ramiro Mendoza RC (Diamond Debuts) .25
476 Todd Dunn (Diamond Debuts) .05
477 Chad Mottola (Diamond Debuts) .05
478 Andy Larkin (Diamond Debuts) .05
479 Jaime Bluma (Diamond Debuts) .05
480 Mac Suzuki (Diamond Debuts) .05
481 Brian Banks (Diamond Debuts) .05
482 Desi Wilson (Diamond Debuts) .05
483 Einar Diaz (Diamond Debuts) .05
484 Tom Pagnozzi .05
485 Ray Lankford .05
486 Todd Stottlemyre .05
487 Donovan Osborne .05
488 Trevor Hoffman .05
489 Chris Gomez .05
490 Ken Caminiti .05
491 John Flaherty .05
492 Tony Gwynn 1.00
493 Joey Hamilton .05
494 Rickey Henderson .75
495 Glenallen Hill .05
496 Rod Beck .05
497 Osvaldo Fernandez .05
498 Rick Wilkins .05
499 Joey Cora .05
500 Alex Rodriguez 1.50
501 Randy Johnson .75
502 Paul Sorrento .05
503 Dan Wilson .05
504 Jamie Moyer .05
505 Will Clark .05

506 Mickey Tettleton .05
507 John Burkett .05
508 Ken Hill .05
509 Mark McLemore .05
510 Juan Gonzalez .40
511 Bobby Witt .05
512 Carlos Delgado .40
513 Alex Gonzalez .25
514 Shawn Green .25
515 Joe Carter .05
516 Juan Guzman .05
517 Charlie O'Brien .05
518 Ed Sprague .05
519 Mike Timlin .05
520 Roger Clemens 1.00
521 Eddie Murray 2.00
522 Jason Dickson .25
523 Jim Leyritz .25
524 Michael Tucker .25
525 Kenny Lofton .25
526 Jimmy Key .25
527 Mel Rojas .25
528 Deion Sanders .25
529 Bartolo Colon .25
530 Matt Williams .25
531 Marquis Grissom .25
532 David Justice .25
533 Bubba Trammell RC .35
534 Moises Alou .25
535 Bobby Bonilla .25
536 Alex Fernandez .25
537 Jay Bell .25
538 Chili Davis .25
539 Jeff King .25
540 Todd Zeile .25
541 John Olerud .25
542 Jose Guillen .25
543 Derek Lee 1.00
544 Dante Powell .25
545 J.T. Snow .25
546 Jeff Kent .25
547 Jose Cruz Jr. RC .75
548 John Wetteland .25
549 Orlando Merced .25
550 Hideki Irabu RC .50

Amazing Greats

The 20-card, regular-sized insert set was included every 138 packs of 1997 Upper Deck baseball. The cards include real wood with two player shots imaged on the card front. The team logo appears in the upper right corner of the horizontal card. The cards are numbered with the "AG" prefix.

		NM/M
Complete Set (20):		140.00
Common Player:		2.50
1	Ken Griffey Jr.	12.50
2	Roberto Alomar	3.00
3	Alex Rodriguez	15.00
4	Paul Molitor	7.50
5	Chipper Jones	10.00
6	Tony Gwynn	10.00
7	Kenny Lofton	2.50
8	Albert Belle	2.50
9	Matt Williams	2.50
10	Frank Thomas	7.50
11	Greg Maddux	10.00
12	Sammy Sosa	10.00
13	Kirby Puckett	10.00
14	Jeff Bagwell	7.50
15	Cal Ripken Jr.	20.00
16	Manny Ramirez	7.50
17	Barry Bonds	20.00
18	Mo Vaughn	2.50
19	Eddie Murray	7.50
20	Mike Piazza	12.50

Blue Chip Prospects

This 20-card insert was found in packs of Series II and features a die-cut design. Cards appear to have a photo slide attached to them featuring a portrait shot of the promising youngster depicted on the card. A total of 500 of each card were produced. Cards are numbered with a "BC" prefix.

		NM/M
Common Player:		6.00
Production 500 Sets		
1	Andruw Jones	25.00
2	Derek Jeter	60.00
3	Scott Rolen	15.00
4	Manny Ramirez	25.00
5	Todd Walker	6.00
6	Rocky Coppinger	6.00
7	Nomar Garciaparra	30.00
8	Darin Erstad	7.50
9	Jermaine Dye	6.00
10	Vladimir Guerrero	25.00
11	Edgar Renteria	6.00
12	Bob Abreu	7.50
13	Karim Garcia	6.00
14	Jeff D'Amico	6.00
15	Chipper Jones	30.00
16	Todd Hollandsworth	6.00
17	Andy Pettitte	9.00
18	Ruben Rivera	6.00
19	Jason Kendall	6.00
20	Alex Rodriguez	40.00

Game Jersey

The three-card, regular-sized set was inserted every 800 packs of Upper Deck Series I. The cards contained a square of the player's game-used jersey, and carried a "GJ" card number prefix.

		NM/M
Complete Set (3):		160.00
Common Player:		15.00
GJ1	Ken Griffey Jr.	135.00
GJ2	Tony Gwynn	25.00
GJ3	Rey Ordonez	15.00

Hot Commodities

This 20-card insert from Series II features a flame pattern behind the image of the player depicted on the front of the card. Odds of finding a card were 1:13 packs. Cards are numbered with a "HC" prefix.

		NM/M
Complete Set (20):		20.00
Common Player:		.30
1	Alex Rodriguez	2.00
2	Andruw Jones	1.00
3	Derek Jeter	2.50
4	Frank Thomas	1.00
5	Ken Griffey Jr.	1.50
6	Chipper Jones	1.25
7	Juan Gonzalez	.50
8	Cal Ripken Jr.	2.50
9	John Smoltz	.30
10	Mark McGwire	2.00
11	Barry Bonds	2.50
12	Albert Belle	.30
13	Mike Piazza	1.50
14	Manny Ramirez	1.00
15	Mo Vaughn	.30
16	Tony Gwynn	1.25
17	Vladimir Guerrero	1.00
18	Hideo Nomo	.50
19	Greg Maddux	1.25
20	Kirby Puckett	1.25

Long Distance Connection

This 20-card insert from Series II features the top home run hitters in the game. Odds of finding a card were 1:35 packs. Cards are numbered with a "LD" prefix.

		NM/M
Complete Set (20):		32.50
Common Player:		.60
1	Mark McGwire	4.00
2	Brady Anderson	.60
3	Ken Griffey Jr.	3.00
4	Albert Belle	.60
5	Juan Gonzalez	1.25
6	Andres Galarraga	.60
7	Jay Buhner	.60
8	Mo Vaughn	.60
9	Barry Bonds	5.00
10	Gary Sheffield	1.25
11	Todd Hundley	.60
12	Frank Thomas	2.00
13	Sammy Sosa	2.50
14	Rafael Palmeiro	1.75
15	Alex Rodriguez	4.00
16	Mike Piazza	3.00
17	Ken Caminiti	.60
18	Chipper Jones	2.50
19	Manny Ramirez	2.00
20	Andruw Jones	2.00

Memorable Moments

This issue was a one per pack insert in special Series 1 and 2 Collector's Choice six-card retail packs. In standard 2-1/2" x 3-1/2", the cards are die-cut at top and bottom in a wave pattern. Fronts, highlighted in matte bronze foil, have action photos and a career highlight. Backs have another photo and a more complete explanation of the Memorable Moment.

		NM/M
Complete Set (20):		20.00
Common Player:		.50
1	Andruw Jones	.75
2	Chipper Jones	1.00
3	Cal Ripken Jr.	2.50
4	Frank Thomas	.75
5	Manny Ramirez	.75
6	Mike Piazza	1.50
7	Mark McGwire	2.00
8	Barry Bonds	2.50
9	Ken Griffey Jr.	1.50
10	Alex Rodriguez	2.00
1	Ken Griffey Jr.	1.50
2	Albert Belle	.50
3	Derek Jeter	2.50
4	Greg Maddux	1.00
5	Tony Gwynn	1.00
6	Ryne Sandberg	1.00
7	Juan Gonzalez	.60
8	Roger Clemens	1.25
9	Jose Cruz Jr.	.50
10	Mo Vaughn	.50

Power Package

The 20-card, regular-sized, die-cut set was inserted every 23 packs of 1997 Upper Deck baseball. The player's name is printed in gold foil along the top border of the card face, which also features Light F/X. The die-cut cards have a silver-foil border and team-color frame with a "Power Package" logo in gold foil centered on the bottom border. The card backs have a short highlight in a brown box bordered by team colors and are numbered with the "PP" prefix.

		NM/M
Complete Set (20):		30.00
Common Player:		1.00
1	Ken Griffey Jr.	3.50
2	Joe Carter	1.00
3	Rafael Palmeiro	1.75
4	Jay Buhner	1.00
5	Sammy Sosa	3.00
6	Fred McGriff	1.00
7	Jeff Bagwell	2.00
8	Albert Belle	1.00
9	Matt Williams	1.00
10	Mark McGwire	4.00
11	Gary Sheffield	1.25
12	Tim Salmon	1.00
13	Ryan Klesko	1.00
14	Manny Ramirez	2.00
15	Mike Piazza	3.50
16	Barry Bonds	5.00
17	Mo Vaughn	1.00
18	Jose Canseco	1.25
19	Juan Gonzalez	1.25
20	Frank Thomas	2.00

Power Package Jumbos

Unlike the regular Power Package inserts found in Series 1 packs, these jumbo versions are not die-cut. The 5" x 7" jumbos are found one per retail foil box of Series 1. Cards are numbered with a "PP" prefix.

		NM/M
Complete Set (20):		30.00
Common Player:		1.00
1	Ken Griffey Jr.	3.50
2	Joe Carter	1.00
3	Rafael Palmeiro	1.75
4	Jay Buhner	1.00
5	Sammy Sosa	3.00
6	Fred McGriff	1.00
7	Jeff Bagwell	2.00
8	Albert Belle	1.00
9	Matt Williams	1.00
10	Mark McGwire	4.00
11	Gary Sheffield	1.25
12	Tim Salmon	1.00
13	Ryan Klesko	1.00
14	Manny Ramirez	2.00
15	Mike Piazza	3.50
16	Barry Bonds	5.00
17	Mo Vaughn	1.00
18	Jose Canseco	1.25
19	Juan Gonzalez	1.25
20	Frank Thomas	2.00

Predictor

A new concept in interactive cards was UD's Series II Predictor inserts. Each player's card has four scratch-off baseball bats at the top-right. Under each bat is printed a specific accomplishment - hit for cycle, CG shutout, etc. - If the player attained that goal during the '97 season, and if the collector had scratched off the correct bat among the four, the Predictor card could be redeemed (with $2) for a premium TV cel card of the player. Thus if the player made one of his goals, the collector had a 25 percent chance of choosing the right bat. Two goals gave a 50 percent chance, etc. The Predictor cards have color action photos of the players at the left end of the horizontal format. The background at left and bottom is a red scorecard motif. Behind the bats is a black-and-white stadium scene. Backs repeat the red scorecard design with contest rules printed in white. A (W) in the checklist here indicates the player won one or more of his goals making his cards eligible for redemption. The redemption period ended Nov. 22, 1997. Values shown are for unscratched cards.

		NM/M
Complete Set (30):		15.00
Common Player:		.10
Values for unscratched cards.		
1	Andruw Jones	.40
2	Chipper Jones	.50
3	Greg Maddux/W	1.00
4	Fred McGriff/W	.25
5	John Smoltz/W	.25
6	Brady Anderson/W	.25
7	Cal Ripken Jr./W	2.00
8	Mo Vaughn/W	.25
9	Sammy Sosa	.50
10	Albert Belle/W	.25
11	Frank Thomas	.40
12	Kenny Lofton/W	.25
13	Jim Thome	.30
14	Dante Bichette/W	.25
15	Andres Galarraga	.10
16	Gary Sheffield	.25
17	Hideo Nomo/W	.40
18	Mike Piazza/W	1.25
19	Derek Jeter/W	2.00
20	Bernie Williams	.10
21	Mark McGwire/W	1.50
22	Ken Caminiti/W	.25
23	Tony Gwynn/W	1.00
24	Barry Bonds/W	2.00
25	Jay Buhner/W	.25
26	Ken Griffey Jr./W	1.25
27	Alex Rodriguez/W	1.50
28	Juan Gonzalez/W	.40
29	Dean Palmer/W	.25
30	Roger Clemens/W	1.00

Predictor Prize Cards

Persons who redeemed winning Predictor scratch-off cards prior to the Nov. 22, 1997 deadline received a premium version of that player's card. A $2 per card handling fee was charged. The Predictor prize cards are in a format similar to the scratch-off cards, with a red background on front and back depicting the motif of a baseball score card. The prize cards are print-

ed on plastic in 3-1/2" x 2-1/2" format. Fronts have a player portrait photo at left. At right is a large semi-circular mirrored window with an action photo visible when held to the light. Backs have a few stats, copyright data, logos, etc., with a reverse image in the window. Card fronts were covered with a sheet of peel-off protection plastic. The prize cards are numbered on back with a "P" prefix.

		NM/M
Complete Set (22):		35.00
Common Player:		.60
3	Greg Maddux	2.50
4	Fred McGriff	.60
5	John Smoltz	.60
6	Brady Anderson	.60
7	Cal Ripken Jr.	5.00
8	Mo Vaughn	.60
11	Frank Thomas	1.75
12	Kenny Lofton	.60
14	Dante Bichette	.60
17	Hideo Nomo	1.00
18	Mike Piazza	3.00
19	Derek Jeter	5.00
21	Mark McGwire	4.00
22	Ken Caminiti	.60
23	Tony Gwynn	2.50
24	Barry Bonds	5.00
25	Jay Buhner	.60
26	Ken Griffey Jr.	3.00
27	Alex Rodriguez	4.00
28	Juan Gonzalez	1.00
29	Dean Palmer	.60
30	Roger Clemens	2.75

Rock Solid Foundation

The 20-card, regular-sized set was inserted every seven packs of 1997 Upper Deck baseball. The card fronts feature rainbow foil with the player's name in silver foil along the top border. The team logo appears in gold foil in the lower right corner with "Rock Solid Foundation" also printed in gold foil over a marbled background. The card backs have the same marbled background with a close-up shot on the upper half. A short text is also included and the cards are numbered with the "RS" prefix.

		NM/M
Complete Set (20):		7.50
Common Player:		.15
1	Alex Rodriguez	1.50
2	Rey Ordonez	.15
3	Derek Jeter	2.00
4	Darin Erstad	.35
5	Chipper Jones	1.25
6	Johnny Damon	.35
7	Ryan Klesko	.15
8	Charles Johnson	.15
9	Andy Pettitte	.30
10	Manny Ramirez	.75
11	Ivan Rodriguez	.65
12	Jason Kendall	.15
13	Rondell White	.15
14	Alex Ochoa	.15
15	Javy Lopez	.15
16	Pedro Martinez	.75
17	Carlos Delgado	.50
18	Paul Wilson	.15
19	Alan Benes	.15
20	Raul Mondesi	.15

Run Producers

A 24-card insert found in Series II, Run Producers salutes the top offensive players in the game. Cards were inserted 1:69 packs. Die-cut into a

shield shape, the cards have an action photo in a home-plate shaped center section and several colors of foil highlights. Backs have recent stats and career highlights. Cards are numbered with a "RP" prefix.

		NM/M
Complete Set (24):		45.00
Common Player:		.50
1	Ken Griffey Jr.	5.00
2	Barry Bonds	7.50
3	Albert Belle	.50
4	Mark McGwire	6.00
5	Frank Thomas	3.00
6	Juan Gonzalez	1.50
7	Brady Anderson	.50
8	Andres Galarraga	.50
9	Rafael Palmeiro	2.50
10	Alex Rodriguez	6.00
11	Jay Buhner	.50
12	Gary Sheffield	1.50
13	Sammy Sosa	4.00
14	Dante Bichette	.50
15	Mike Piazza	5.00
16	Manny Ramirez	3.00
17	Kenny Lofton	.50
18	Mo Vaughn	.50
19	Tim Salmon	.50
20	Chipper Jones	4.00
21	Jim Thome	2.00
22	Ken Caminiti	.50
23	Jeff Bagwell	3.00
24	Paul Molitor	3.00

Star Attractions

These die-cut cards were inserted one per pack of retail "Memorabila Madness" Collector's Choice (#11-20) and Upper Deck (#1-10) cards. Fronts have action photos, backs have portrait photos. A gold version of the inserts was exclusive to retail packaging.

		NM/M
Complete Set (20):		30.00
Common Player:		.30
Gold:		1.5X
1	Ken Griffey Jr.	3.00
2	Barry Bonds	5.00
3	Jeff Bagwell	2.00
4	Nomar Garciaparra	2.50
5	Tony Gwynn	2.50
6	Roger Clemens	2.75
7	Chipper Jones	2.50
8	Tino Martinez	.30
9	Albert Belle	.30
10	Kenny Lofton	.30
11	Alex Rodriguez	4.00
12	Mark McGwire	4.00
13	Cal Ripken Jr.	5.00
14	Larry Walker	.30
15	Mike Piazza	3.00
16	Frank Thomas	2.00
17	Juan Gonzalez	.65
18	Greg Maddux	2.50
19	Jose Cruz Jr.	.30
20	Mo Vaughn	.30

Ticket to Stardom

The 20-card, regular-sized, die-cut set was inserted every 34 packs of 1997 Upper

Deck baseball. Card fronts have a gold-foil border on three sides with a portrait and action photo. Half of the player's league emblem appears on either the left or right border of the horizontal cards, as two cards can be placed together to form a "ticket." The card backs feature an in-depth text with the same headshot as the card front and are numbered with the "TS" prefix.

		NM/M
Complete Set (20):		35.00
Common Player:		.75
1	Chipper Jones	5.00
2	Jermaine Dye	.75
3	Rey Ordonez	.75
4	Alex Ochoa	.75
5	Derek Jeter	7.50
6	Ruben Rivera	.75
7	Billy Wagner	.75
8	Jason Kendall	.75
9	Darin Erstad	1.00
10	Alex Rodriguez	6.00
12	Bob Abreu	.75
12	Richard Hidalgo	.75
13	Karim Garcia	.75
14	Andruw Jones	4.00
15	Carlos Delgado	1.50
16	Rocky Coppinger	.75
17	Jeff D'Amico	.75
18	Johnny Damon	.75
19	John Wasdin	.75
20	Manny Ramirez	4.00

Ticket to Stardom Retail

Double-size "full ticket" versions of Upper Deck's Series 1 Ticket to Stardom inserts were produced as an incentive for collectors to buy a boxed three-pack of Collector's Choice cards in a special retail-only packaging. Unlike the insert Ticket cards which feature only one player and measure 3-1/2" x 2-1/2", the retail version measures 5" x 2-1/2" and features two players. The basic format of the retail cards follows the inserts, with gold-foil background, a vignetted player portrait at one end with an action photo toward center and a league logo at center. Arrangement of graphics on the retail ticket prevent unscrupulous persons from cutting them in half and passing them off as the more valuable insert cards. Backs repeat the player portrait photo and present a career summary. Cards are numbered in the upper-left corner. Seven players were dropped from the original Ticket checklist and replaced in the retail issue with new faces. Cards are numbered with a "TS" prefix.

		NM/M
Complete Set (10):		24.00
Common Player:		1.50
1	Chipper Jones, Andruw Jones	4.00
2	Rey Ordonez, Kevin Orie	1.50
3	Derek Jeter, Nomar Garciaparra	6.00
4	Billy Wagner, Jason Kendall	1.50
5	Darin Erstad, Alex Rodriguez	5.00
6	Bob Abreu, Jose Guillen	1.50
7	Wilton Guerrero, Vladimir Guerrero	3.00
8	Carlos Delgado, Rocky Coppinger	2.00
9	Jason Dickson, Johnny Damon	2.00
10	Bartolo Colon, Manny Ramirez	3.00

Ken Griffey Jr. Highlight Reel

Using its trademarked Diamond Vision technology to provide action scenes on these 5" x 3-1/2" plastic cards. Each card has two scenes which go into action as the angle of vision is changed. Cards were sold in retail outlets in plastic blister packs at a suggested $9.99 price.

		NM/M
Complete Set (5):		12.50
Common Card:		3.00
1	Record Setter (Ken Griffey Jr.)	3.00
2	Long Distance Connection (Ken Griffey Jr.)	3.00
3	Home Run Derby (Ken Griffey Jr.)	3.00
4	Swing for the Ages (Ken Griffey Jr.)	3.00
5	Postseason Power (Ken Griffey Jr.)	3.00

Tony Gwynn Commemorative

Tony Gwynn's record-tying eighth batting title in 1997 is commemorated on this 3-1/2" x 4-7/8" card marketed by UD Authenticated. The card has a batting pose on front with a die-cut background of bats citing the year and average of each of his batting titles. The back has three color photos and is numbered within an edition of 2,500.

	NM/M
Tony Gwynn	7.50

Home Team Heroes

These large-format cards were issued both as a 12-card boxed set (original price about $20) and as a blister-pack insert to enhance the sales of special Collector's Choice team sets at Wal-Mart. Each $4.99 pack contains a 14-card team set and a Home Team Heroes card of one of 12 teams, plus a random assortment of Collector's Choice cards. The Heroes cards are 5" x 3-1/2" with a die-cut pattern at top. Fronts are rendered in team colors with two player action photos superimposed on a background of the players' home ballpark. The ballpark scene is executed in etched silver foil and there are silver-foil graphics around the card front. Backs are conventionally printed with small photos and a few sentences about each player.

	NM/M
Complete Set (12):	10.00
Common Player:	.50

		NM/M
1	Alex Rodriguez, Ken Griffey Jr.	2.00
2	Bernie Williams, Derek Jeter	2.50
3	Bernard Gilkey, Randy Hundley	.50
4	Hideo Nomo, Mike Piazza	1.50
5	Andruw Jones, Chipper Jones	1.00
6	John Smoltz, Greg Maddux	1.00
7	Mike Mussina, Cal Ripken Jr.	2.50
8	Andres Galarraga, Dante Bichette	.50
9	Juan Gonzalez, Ivan Rodriguez	.65
10	Albert Belle, Frank Thomas	.75
11	Jim Thome, Manny Ramirez	.75
12	Ken Caminiti, Tony Gwynn	1.00

Jackie Robinson Jumbos

The nine Jackie Robinson commemorative cards which lead off the '97 Upper Deck set were also issued in a large-format (3-1/2" x 5") version as a complete boxed set. The jumbos are printed in sepia tones on gold-foil backgrounds and, like the standard-size cards, are highlighted with silver-foil graphics on front. Backs are also identical to the regular cards. Complete sets only were sold in a gold-foil stamped box with the 50th anniversary logo.

		NM/M
Complete Set (10):		13.50
Common Player:		2.00
1	The Beginnings (Jackie Robinson)	2.00
2	Breaking the Barrier (Jackie Robinson)	2.00
3	The MVP Season (Jackie Robinson)	2.00
4	The '51 Season (Jackie Robinson)	2.00
5	The '52 and '53 Seasons (Jackie Robinson)	2.00
6	The '54 Season (Jackie Robinson)	2.00
7	The '55 Season (Jackie Robinson)	2.00
8	The '56 Season (Jackie Robinson)	2.00
9	The Hall of Fame (Jackie Robinson)	2.00
--	Checklist	.10

Jackie Robinson Tribute

This retail exclusive card commemorates the 50th anniversary of Robinson's major league debut. The 5" x 3-1/2" card has a tombstone contour top edge and a sepia photo on

front of Robinson at bat. Also on front are 50th anniversary and UD logos and a large gold-foil facsimile autograph. Back has a photo of Robinson sliding into home plate, his career stats and a serial number from within an edition of 5,000.

	NM/M
Jackie Robinson	3.50

1997 Upper Deck UD3

Released in April, this 60-card set is broken down into three different 20-card subsets, each utilizing a different print technology. There are 20 PRO-motion cards (Light F/X cards featuring a special foil stock), 20 Future Impact cards (Cel-Chrome cards that feature a 3-D image on transparent chromium), and 20 Homerun Heroes (Electric Wood cards printed on an embossed wood/paper stock.) Cards were sold in three-card packs (with one sub-set card per pack) for $3.99 each. Inserts include Superb Signatures, Generation Next and Marquee Attraction.

		NM/M
Complete Set (60):		30.00
Common Player:		.15
Pack (3):		1.50
Wax Box (24):		30.00
1	Mark McGwire	2.50
2	Brady Anderson	.15
3	Ken Griffey Jr.	2.00
4	Albert Belle	.15
5	Andres Galarraga	.15
6	Juan Gonzalez	.40
7	Jay Buhner	.15
8	Mo Vaughn	.15
9	Barry Bonds	3.00
10	Gary Sheffield	.40
11	Todd Hundley	.15
12	Ellis Burks	.15
13	Ken Caminiti	.15
14	Vinny Castilla	.15
15	Sammy Sosa	1.50
16	Frank Thomas	.75
17	Rafael Palmeiro	.65
18	Mike Piazza	2.00
19	Matt Williams	.15
20	Eddie Murray	.75
21	Roger Clemens	1.75
22	Tim Salmon	.15
23	Robin Ventura	.15
24	Ron Gant	.15
25	Cal Ripken Jr.	3.00
26	Bernie Williams	.15
27	Hideo Nomo	.75
28	Ivan Rodriguez	.65
29	John Smoltz	.15
30	Paul Molitor	.75
31	Greg Maddux	1.50
32	Raul Mondesi	.15
33	Roberto Alomar	.25
34	Barry Larkin	.15
35	Tony Gwynn	1.50
36	Jim Thome	.60
37	Kenny Lofton	.15
38	Jeff Bagwell	.75
39	Ozzie Smith	1.50
40	Kirby Puckett	1.50
41	Andruw Jones	.75
42	Vladimir Guerrero	.75
43	Edgar Renteria	.15
44	Luis Castillo	.15
45	Darin Erstad	.30
46	Nomar Garciaparra	1.50
47	Todd Greene	.15
48	Jason Kendall	.15
49	Rey Ordonez	.15
50	Alex Rodriguez	2.50
51	Manny Ramirez	.75
52	Todd Walker	.15
53	Ruben Rivera	.15
54	Andy Pettitte	.30
55	Derek Jeter	3.00
56	Todd Hollandsworth	.15
57	Rocky Coppinger	.15
58	Scott Rolen	.60
59	Jermaine Dye	.15
60	Chipper Jones	1.50

Generation Next

A 20-card insert saluting the game's up-and-coming

stars with two different photos of the player on each card front. Odds of finding these cards were 1:11 packs. Cards are numbered with a "GN" prefix.

		NM/M
Complete Set (20):		35.00
Common Player:		1.00
1	Alex Rodriguez	5.00
2	Vladimir Guerrero	2.50
3	Luis Castillo	1.00
4	Rey Ordonez	1.00
5	Andruw Jones	2.50
6	Darin Erstad	1.25
7	Edgar Renteria	1.00
8	Jason Kendall	1.00
9	Jermaine Dye	1.00
10	Chipper Jones	3.00
11	Rocky Coppinger	1.00
12	Andy Pettitte	1.25
13	Todd Greene	1.00
14	Todd Hollandsworth	1.00
15	Derek Jeter	6.00
16	Ruben Rivera	1.00
17	Todd Walker	1.00
18	Nomar Garciaparra	3.00
19	Scott Rolen	2.00
20	Manny Ramirez	2.50

Marquee Attraction

The game's top names are featured in this insert set, inserted 1:144 packs. Cards featured a peel-off protector that would expose a holographic image on the card fronts. Cards are numbered with a "MA" prefix.

		NM/M
Complete Set (10):		40.00
Common Player:		1.25
1	Ken Griffey Jr.	6.00
2	Mark McGwire	7.50
3	Juan Gonzalez	1.75
4	Barry Bonds	9.00
5	Frank Thomas	2.50
6	Albert Belle	1.25
7	Mike Piazza	6.00
8	Cal Ripken Jr.	9.00
9	Mo Vaughn	1.25
10	Alex Rodriguez	7.50

Superb Signatures

Autographed cards of Ken Griffey Jr., Ken Caminiti, Vladimir Guerrero, and Derek Jeter were inserted 1:1,500 packs.

		NM/M
Complete Set (4):		450.00
Common Autograph:		15.00
1	Ken Caminiti	45.00
2	Ken Griffey Jr.	150.00
3	Vladimir Guerrero	50.00
4	Derek Jeter	225.00

Pepsi Mariners Insert

Though unmarked as such, this set was sponsored by Pepsi with single cards inserted into 12-packs of soda in the Northwest. Format of the cards is similar to UD's regular 1996 issue, with borderless color photos on front

and back. At bottom-front is a Mariners-blue foil area with the player identification. Backs differ from the regular '96 UD cards in the use of a "M" prefix to the card number.

		NM/M
Complete Set (19):		12.00
Common Player:		.25
1	Joey Cora	.25
2	Ken Griffey Jr.	5.00
3	Jay Buhner	.50
4	Alex Rodriguez	6.00
5	Norm Charlton	.25
6	Edgar Martinez	.50
7	Paul Sorrento	.25
8	Randy Johnson	2.00
9	Rich Amaral	.25
10	Russ Davis	.25
11	Bob Wolcott	.25
12	Jamie Moyer	.25
13	Bob Wells	.25
14	Makoto Suzuki	.25
15	Dan Wilson	.25
16	Tim Davis	.25
17	Bobby Ayala	.25
18	Salomon Torres	.25
19	Raul Ibanez	.25

Pepsi Mariners SGA

This team set, sponsored by Pepsi, was a stadium giveaway to the first 20,000 fans attending the July 12 game at the Kingdome. Format of the cards is similar to UD's regular 1996 issue, with borderless color photos on front and back. At bottom-front is a Mariners-blue foil area with the player identification. Backs differ from the regular '96 UD cards in the use of a "P" prefix to the card number and the inclusion of a Pepsi logo at lower-left.

		NM/M
Complete Set (21):		12.00
Common Player:		.25
1	Joey Cora	.25
2	Ken Griffey Jr.	5.00
3	Jay Buhner	.50
4	Alex Rodriguez	6.00
5	Norm Charlton	.25
6	Edgar Martinez	.50
7	Paul Sorrento	.25
8	Randy Johnson	2.00
9	Rich Amaral	.25
10	Russ Davis	.25
11	Greg McCarthy	.25
12	Jamie Moyer	.25
13	Jeff Fassero	.25
14	Scott Sanders	.25
15	Dan Wilson	.25
16	Mike Blowers	.25
17	Bobby Ayala	.25
18	Brent Gates	.25
19	John Marzano	.25
20	Lou Piniella	.25
---	Pepsi Header Card/ Coupon	.05

Shimano

Tony Gwynn

Two ballplayers are included with four professional fishermen in this set produced by Upper Deck as a premium with the purchase of Shimano fishing reels. Fronts have pictures of the fishermen displaying their trophy. Backs have a portrait photo, baseball and fishing stats and data.

		NM/M
Complete Set (19):		12.00
Common Player:		.25
5	Jay Buhner	3.00
6	Tony Gwynn	30.00

1998 Upper Deck

Upper Deck Baseball was released in three series. Series 1 consists of 270 base cards, with five subsets. Inserts included A Piece of the Action, Amazing Greats, National Pride, Ken Griffey Jr.'s Home Run Chronicles and 10th Anniversary Preview. The 270-card Series 2 also has five subsets. Inserts include Prime Nine, Ken Griffey Jr.'s Home Run Chronicles, Tape Measure Titans, Blue Chip Prospects, Clearly Dominant and A Piece of the Action. The third series, Upper Deck Rookie Edition, has a 210-card base set. Cards #601-630, the Eminent Prestige subset, are short-printed, about one per four packs. Mike Piazza's card in Series 3 can be found depicting him either as a Marlin or a Met. Insert sets were Ken Griffey Jr. Game Jersey, Game Jersey Rookie Cards, Unparalleled, Destination Stardom, All-Star Credentials and Retrospectives.

		NM/M
Complete Set (750):		100.00
Complete Series 1 Set (270):		25.00
Complete Series 2 Set (270):		25.00
Complete Series 3 Set (210):		75.00
Common Emminent Prestige (601-630):		.25
Common Player:		.05
Series 1 or 2 Pack (12):		1.50
Series 3 Pack (10):		1.50
Series 1 or 2 Wax Box (24):		35.00
Series 3 Wax Box (24):		35.00
1	Tino Martinez (History in the Making)	.05
2	Jimmy Key (History in the Making)	.05
3	Jay Buhner (History in the Making)	.05
4	Mark Gardner (History in the Making)	.05
5	Greg Maddux (History in the Making)	.25

6	Pedro Martinez (History in the Making)	.20
7	Hideo Nomo, Shigetoshi Hasegawa (History in the Making)	.25
8	Sammy Sosa (History in the Making)	.35
9	Mark McGwire (Griffey Hot List)	.50
10	Ken Griffey Jr. (Griffey Hot List)	.45
11	Larry Walker (Griffey Hot List)	.05
12	Tino Martinez (Griffey Hot List)	.05
13	Mike Piazza (Griffey Hot List)	.40
14	Jose Cruz, Jr. (Griffey Hot List)	.05
15	Tony Gwynn (Griffey Hot List)	.25
16	Greg Maddux (Griffey Hot List)	.25
17	Roger Clemens (Griffey Hot List)	.35
18	Alex Rodriguez (Griffey Hot List)	.50
19	Shigetosi Hasegawa	.05
20	Eddie Murray	.50
21	Jason Dickson	.05
22	Darin Erstad	.25
23	Chuck Finley	.05
24	Dave Hollins	.05
25	Garret Anderson	.05
26	Michael Tucker	.05
27	Kenny Lofton	.05
28	Javier Lopez	.05
29	Fred McGriff	.05
30	Greg Maddux	.65
31	Jeff Blauser	.05
32	John Smoltz	.05
33	Mark Wohlers	.05
34	Scott Erickson	.05
35	Jimmy Key	.05
36	Harold Baines	.05
37	Randy Myers	.05
38	B.J. Surhoff	.05
39	Eric Davis	.05
40	Rafael Palmeiro	.35
41	Jeffrey Hammonds	.05
42	Mo Vaughn	.05
43	Tom Gordon	.05
44	Tim Naehring	.05
45	Darren Bragg	.05
46	Aaron Sele	.05
47	Troy O'Leary	.05
48	John Valentin	.05
49	Doug Glanville	.05
50	Ryne Sandberg	.65
51	Steve Trachsel	.05
52	Mark Grace	.05
53	Kevin Foster	.05
54	Kevin Tapani	.05
55	Kevin Orie	.05
56	Lyle Mouton	.05
57	Ray Durham	.05
58	Jaime Navarro	.05
59	Mike Cameron	.05
60	Albert Belle	.05
61	Doug Drabek	.05
62	Chris Snopek	.05
63	Eddie Taubensee	.05
64	Terry Pendleton	.05
65	Barry Larkin	.05
66	Willie Greene	.05
67	Deion Sanders	.05
68	Pokey Reese	.05
69	Jeff Shaw	.05
70	Jim Thome	.35
71	Orel Hershiser	.05
72	Omar Vizquel	.05
73	Brian Giles	.05
74	David Justice	.05
75	Bartolo Colon	.05
76	Sandy Alomar Jr.	.05
77	Neifi Perez	.05
78	Eric Young	.05
79	Vinny Castilla	.05
80	Dante Bichette	.05
81	Quinton McCracken	.05
82	Jamey Wright	.05
83	John Thomson	.05
84	Damion Easley	.05
85	Justin Thompson	.05
86	Willie Blair	.05
87	Raul Casanova	.05
88	Bobby Higginson	.05
89	Bubba Trammell	.05
90	Tony Clark	.05
91	Livan Hernandez	.05
92	Charles Johnson	.05
93	Edgar Renteria	.05
94	Alex Fernandez	.05
95	Gary Sheffield	.30
96	Moises Alou	.05
97	Tony Saunders	.05
98	Robb Nen	.05
99	Darryl Kile	.05
100	Craig Biggio	.05
101	Chris Holt	.05
102	Bob Abreu	.10
103	Luis Gonzalez	.05
104	Billy Wagner	.05
105	Brad Ausmus	.05
106	Chili Davis	.05
107	Tim Belcher	.05
108	Dean Palmer	.05
109	Jeff King	.05

No.	Player	Price
110	Jose Rosado	.05
111	Mike Macfarlane	.05
112	Jay Bell	.05
113	Todd Worrell	.05
114	Chan Ho Park	.05
115	Raul Mondesi	.05
116	Brett Butler	.05
117	Greg Gagne	.05
118	Hideo Nomo	.25
119	Todd Zeile	.05
120	Eric Karros	.05
121	Cal Eldred	.05
122	Jeff D'Amico	.05
123	Antone Williamson	.05
124	Doug Jones	.05
125	Dave Nilsson	.05
126	Gerald Williams	.05
127	Fernando Vina	.05
128	Ron Coomer	.05
129	Matt Lawton	.05
130	Paul Molitor	.50
131	Todd Walker	.05
132	Rick Aguilera	.05
133	Brad Radke	.05
134	Bob Tewksbury	.05
135	Vladimir Guerrero	.50
136	Tony Gwynn (Define The Game)	.25
137	Roger Clemens (Define The Game)	.35
138	Dennis Eckersley (Define The Game)	.15
139	Brady Anderson (Define The Game)	.05
140	Ken Griffey Jr. (Define The Game)	.40
141	Derek Jeter (Define The Game)	.75
142	Ken Caminiti (Define The Game)	.05
143	Frank Thomas (Define The Game)	.20
144	Barry Bonds (Define The Game)	.75
145	Cal Ripken Jr. (Define The Game)	.75
146	Alex Rodriguez (Define The Game)	.50
147	Greg Maddux (Define The Game)	.25
148	Kenny Lofton (Define The Game)	.05
149	Mike Piazza (Define The Game)	.40
150	Mark McGwire (Define The Game)	.50
151	Andruw Jones (Define The Game)	.20
152	Rusty Greer (Define The Game)	.05
153	F.P. Santangelo (Define The Game)	.05
154	Mike Lansing	.05
155	Lee Smith	.05
156	Carlos Perez	.05
157	Pedro Martinez	.50
158	Ryan McGuire	.05
159	F.P. Santangelo	.05
160	Rondell White	.05
161	Takashi Kashiwada RC	.05
162	Butch Huskey	.05
163	Edgardo Alfonzo	.05
164	John Franco	.05
165	Todd Hundley	.05
166	Rey Ordonez	.05
167	Armando Reynoso	.05
168	John Olerud	.05
169	Bernie Williams	.05
170	Andy Pettitte	.15
171	Wade Boggs	.65
172	Paul O'Neill	.05
173	Cecil Fielder	.05
174	Charlie Hayes	.05
175	David Cone	.05
176	Hideki Irabu	.05
177	Mark Bellhorn	.05
178	Steve Karsay	.05
179	Damon Mashore	.05
180	Jason McDonald	.05
181	Scott Spiezio	.05
182	Ariel Prieto	.05
183	Jason Giambi	.30
184	Wendell Magee	.05
185	Rico Brogna	.05
186	Garrett Stephenson	.05
187	Wayne Gomes	.05
188	Ricky Bottalico	.05
189	Mickey Morandini	.05
190	Mike Lieberthal	.05
191	Kevin Polcovich RC	.05
192	Francisco Cordova	.05
193	Kevin Young	.05
194	Jon Lieber	.05
195	Kevin Elster	.05
196	Tony Womack	.05
197	Lou Collier	.05
198	Mike Defelice RC	.05
199	Gary Gaetti	.05
200	Dennis Eckersley	.40
201	Alan Benes	.05
202	Willie McGee	.05
203	Ron Gant	.05
204	Fernando Valenzuela	.05
205	Mark McGwire	1.00
206	Archi Cianfrocco	.05
207	Andy Ashby	.05
208	Steve Finley	.05
209	Quilvio Veras	.05
210	Ken Caminiti	.05
211	Rickey Henderson	.50
212	Joey Hamilton	.05
213	Derrek Lee	.30
214	Bill Mueller	.05
215	Shawn Estes	.05
216	J.T. Snow	.05
217	Mark Gardner	.05
218	Terry Mulholland	.05
219	Dante Powell	.05
220	Jeff Kent	.05
221	Jamie Moyer	.05
222	Joey Cora	.05
223	Jeff Fassero	.05
224	Dennis Martinez	.05
225	Ken Griffey Jr.	.75
226	Edgar Martinez	.05
227	Russ Davis	.05
228	Dan Wilson	.05
229	Will Clark	.05
230	Ivan Rodriguez	.40
231	Benji Gil	.05
232	Lee Stevens	.05
233	Mickey Tettleton	.05
234	Julio Santana	.05
235	Rusty Greer	.05
236	Bobby Witt	.05
237	Ed Sprague	.05
238	Pat Hentgen	.05
239	Kevin Escobar	.05
240	Joe Carter	.05
241	Carlos Delgado	.25
242	Shannon Stewart	.05
243	Benito Santiago	.05
244	Tino Martinez (Season Highlights)	.05
245	Ken Griffey Jr. (Season Highlights)	.40
246	Kevin Brown (Season Highlights)	.05
247	Ryne Sandberg (Season Highlights)	.35
248	Mo Vaughn (Season Highlights)	.05
249	Darryl Hamilton (Season Highlights)	.05
250	Randy Johnson (Season Highlights)	.20
251	Steve Finley (Season Highlights)	.05
252	Bobby Higginson (Season Highlights)	.05
253	Brett Tomko (Star Rookie)	.05
254	Mark Kotsay (Star Rookie)	.05
255	Jose Guillen (Star Rookie)	.05
256	Elieser Marrero (Star Rookie)	.05
257	Dennis Reyes (Star Rookie)	.05
258	Richie Sexson (Star Rookie)	.05
259	Pat Cline (Star Rookie)	.05
260	Todd Helton (Star Rookie)	.50
261	Juan Melo (Star Rookie)	.05
262	Matt Morris (Star Rookie)	.05
263	Jeremi Gonzalez (Star Rookie)	.05
264	Jeff Abbott (Star Rookie)	.05
265	Aaron Boone (Star Rookie)	.05
266	Todd Dunwoody (Star Rookie)	.05
267	Jaret Wright (Star Rookie)	.05
268	Derrick Gibson (Star Rookie)	.05
269	Mario Valdez (Star Rookie)	.05
270	Fernando Tatis (Star Rookie)	.05
271	Craig Counsell (Star Rookie)	.05
272	Brad Rigby (Star Rookie)	.05
273	Danny Clyburn (Star Rookie)	.05
274	Brian Rose (Star Rookie)	.05
275	Miguel Tejada (Star Rookie)	.15
276	Jason Varitek (Star Rookie)	.05
277	David Dellucci RC (Star Rookie)	.15
278	Michael Coleman (Star Rookie)	.05
279	Adam Riggs (Star Rookie)	.05
280	Ben Grieve (Star Rookie)	.05
281	Brad Fullmer (Star Rookie)	.05
282	Ken Cloude (Star Rookie)	.05
283	Tom Evans (Star Rookie)	.05
284	Kevin Millwood RC (Star Rookie)	.75
285	Paul Konerko (Star Rookie)	.15
286	Juan Encarnacion (Star Rookie)	.05
287	Chris Carpenter (Star Rookie)	.05
288	Tom Fordham (Star Rookie)	.05
289	Gary DiSarcina	.05
290	Tim Salmon	.05
291	Troy Percival	.05
292	Todd Greene	.05
293	Ken Hill	.05
294	Dennis Springer	.05
295	Jim Edmonds	.05
296	Allen Watson	.05
297	Brian Anderson	.05
298	Keith Lockhart	.05
299	Tom Glavine	.20
300	Chipper Jones	.65
301	Randall Simon	.05
302	Mark Lemke	.05
303	Ryan Klesko	.05
304	Denny Neagle	.05
305	Andruw Jones	.50
306	Mike Mussina	.30
307	Brady Anderson	.05
308	Chris Hoiles	.05
309	Mike Bordick	.05
310	Cal Ripken Jr.	1.50
311	Geronimo Berroa	.05
312	Armando Benitez	.05
313	Roberto Alomar	.25
314	Tim Wakefield	.05
315	Reggie Jefferson	.05
316	Jeff Frye	.05
317	Scott Hatteberg	.05
318	Steve Avery	.05
319	Robinson Checo	.05
320	Nomar Garciaparra	.65
321	Lance Johnson	.05
322	Tyler Houston	.05
323	Mark Clark	.05
324	Terry Adams	.05
325	Sammy Sosa	.65
326	Scott Servais	.05
327	Manny Alexander	.05
328	Norberto Martin	.05
329	Scott Eyre RC	.05
330	Frank Thomas	.50
331	Robin Ventura	.05
332	Matt Karchner	.05
333	Keith Foulke	.05
334	James Baldwin	.05
335	Chris Stynes	.05
336	Bret Boone	.05
337	Jon Nunnally	.05
338	Dave Burba	.05
339	Eduardo Perez	.05
340	Reggie Sanders	.05
341	Mike Remlinger	.05
342	Pat Watkins	.05
343	Chad Ogea	.05
344	John Smiley	.05
345	Kenny Lofton	.05
346	Jose Mesa	.05
347	Charles Nagy	.05
348	Bruce Aven	.05
349	Enrique Wilson	.05
350	Manny Ramirez	.50
351	Jerry DiPoto	.05
352	Ellis Burks	.05
353	Kirt Manwaring	.05
354	Vinny Castilla	.05
355	Larry Walker	.05
356	Kevin Ritz	.05
357	Pedro Astacio	.05
358	Scott Sanders	.05
359	Deivi Cruz	.05
360	Brian L. Hunter	.05
361	Pedro Martinez (History in the Making)	.20
362	Tom Glavine (History in the Making)	.05
363	Willie McGee (History in the Making)	.05
364	J.T. Snow (History in the Making)	.05
365	Rusty Greer (History in the Making)	.05
366	Mike Grace (History in the Making)	.05
367	Tony Clark (History in the Making)	.05
368	Ben Grieve (History in the Making)	.05
369	Gary Sheffield (History in the Making)	.10
370	Joe Oliver	.05
371	Todd Jones	.05
372	Frank Catalanotto RC	.05
373	Brian Moehler	.05
374	Cliff Floyd	.05
375	Bobby Bonilla	.05
376	Al Leiter	.05
377	Josh Booty	.05
378	Darren Daulton	.05
379	Jay Powell	.05
380	Felix Heredia	.05
381	Jim Eisenreich	.05
382	Richard Hidalgo	.05
383	Mike Hampton	.05
384	Shane Reynolds	.05
385	Jeff Bagwell	.50
386	Derek Bell	.05
387	Ricky Gutierrez	.05
388	Bill Spiers	.05
389	Jose Offerman	.05
390	Johnny Damon	.25
391	Jermaine Dye	.05
392	Jeff Montgomery	.05
393	Glendon Rusch	.05
394	Mike Sweeney	.05
395	Kevin Appier	.05
396	Joe Vitiello	.05
397	Ramon Martinez	.05
398	Darren Dreifort	.05
399	Wilton Guerrero	.05
400	Mike Piazza	.75
401	Eddie Murray	.50
402	Ismael Valdes	.05
403	Todd Hollandsworth	.05
404	Mark Loretta	.05
405	Jeromy Burnitz	.05
406	Jeff Cirillo	.05
407	Scott Karl	.05
408	Mike Matheny	.05
409	Jose Valentin	.05
410	John Jaha	.05
411	Terry Steinbach	.05
412	Torii Hunter	.05
413	Pat Meares	.05
414	Marty Cordova	.05
415	Jaret Wright (Postseason Headliners)	.05
416	Mike Mussina (Postseason Headliners)	.10
417	John Smoltz (Postseason Headliners)	.05
418	Devon White (Postseason Headliners)	.05
419	Denny Neagle (Postseason Headliners)	.05
420	Livan Hernandez (Postseason Headliners)	.05
421	Kevin Brown (Postseason Headliners)	.05
422	Marquis Grissom (Postseason Headliners)	.05
423	Mike Mussina (Postseason Headliners)	.10
424	Eric Davis (Postseason Headliners)	.05
425	Tony Fernandez (Postseason Headliners)	.05
426	Moises Alou (Postseason Headliners)	.05
427	Sandy Alomar Jr. (Postseason Headliners)	.05
428	Gary Sheffield (Postseason Headliners)	.10
429	Jaret Wright (Postseason Headliners)	.05
430	Livan Hernandez (Postseason Headliners)	.05
431	Chad Ogea (Postseason Headliners)	.05
432	Edgar Renteria (Postseason Headliners)	.05
433	LaTroy Hawkins	.05
434	Rich Robertson	.05
435	Chuck Knoblauch	.05
436	Jose Vidro	.05
437	Dustin Hermanson	.05
438	Jim Bullinger	.05
439	Orlando Cabrera (Star Rookie)	.10
440	Vladimir Guerrero	.50
441	Ugueth Urbina	.05
442	Brian McRae	.05
443	Matt Franco	.05
444	Bobby Jones	.05
445	Bernard Gilkey	.05
446	Dave Mlicki	.05
447	Brian Bohanon	.05
448	Mel Rojas	.05
449	Tim Raines	.05
450	Derek Jeter	1.50
451	Roger Clemens (Upper Echelon)	.35
452	Nomar Garciaparra (Upper Echelon)	.35
453	Mike Piazza (Upper Echelon)	.40
454	Mark McGwire (Upper Echelon)	.50
455	Ken Griffey Jr. (Upper Echelon)	.40
456	Larry Walker (Upper Echelon)	.05
457	Alex Rodriguez (Upper Echelon)	.50
458	Tony Gwynn (Upper Echelon)	.25
459	Frank Thomas (Upper Echelon)	.20
460	Tino Martinez (Upper Echelon)	.05
461	Chad Curtis	.05
462	Ramiro Mendoza	.05
463	Joe Girardi	.05
464	David Wells	.05
465	Mariano Rivera	.15
466	Willie Adams	.05
467	George Williams	.05
468	Dave Telgheder	.05
469	Dave Magadan	.05
470	Matt Stairs	.05
471	Billy Taylor	.05
472	Jimmy Haynes	.05
473	Gregg Jefferies	.05
474	Midre Cummings	.05
475	Curt Schilling	.15
476	Mike Grace	.05
477	Mark Leiter	.05
478	Matt Beech	.05
479	Scott Rolen	.35
480	Jason Kendall	.05
481	Esteban Loaiza	.05
482	Jermaine Allensworth	.05
483	Mark Smith	.05
484	Jason Schmidt	.05
485	Jose Guillen	.05
486	Al Martin	.05
487	Delino DeShields	.05
488	Todd Stottlemyre	.05
489	Brian Jordan	.05
490	Ray Lankford	.05
491	Matt Morris	.05
492	Royce Clayton	.05
493	John Mabry	.05
494	Wally Joyner	.05
495	Trevor Hoffman	.05
496	Chris Gomez	.05
497	Sterling Hitchcock	.05
498	Pete Smith	.05
499	Greg Vaughn	.05
500	Tony Gwynn	.65
501	Will Cunnane	.05
502	Darryl Hamilton	.05
503	Brian Johnson	.05
504	Kirk Rueter	.05
505	Barry Bonds	1.50
506	Osvaldo Fernandez	.05
507	Stan Javier	.05
508	Julian Tavarez	.05
509	Rich Aurilia	.05
510	Alex Rodriguez	1.00
511	David Segui	.05
512	Rich Amaral	.05
513	Raul Ibanez	.05
514	Jay Buhner	.05
515	Randy Johnson	.50
516	Heathcliff Slocumb	.05
517	Tony Saunders	.05
518	Kevin Elster	.05
519	John Burkett	.05
520	Juan Gonzalez	.25
521	John Wetteland	.05
522	Domingo Cedeno	.05
523	Darren Oliver	.05
524	Roger Pavlik	.05
525	Jose Cruz Jr.	.05
526	Woody Williams	.05
527	Alex Gonzalez	.05
528	Robert Person	.05
529	Juan Guzman	.05
530	Roger Clemens	.70
531	Shawn Green	.20
532	Cordova, Ricon, Smith (Season Highlights)	.05
533	Nomar Garciaparra (Season Highlights)	.35
534	Roger Clemens (Season Highlights)	.35
535	Mark McGwire (Season Highlights)	.50
536	Larry Walker (Season Highlights)	.05
537	Mike Piazza (Season Highlights)	.40
538	Curt Schilling (Season Highlights)	.05
539	Tony Gwynn (Season Highlights)	.25
540	Ken Griffey Jr. (Season Highlights)	.40
541	Carl Pavano (Star Rookies)	.05
542	Shane Monahan (Star Rookies)	.05
543	Gabe Kapler RC (Star Rookies)	.25
544	Eric Milton (Star Rookies)	.05
545	Gary Matthews Jr. RC (Star Rookies)	.05
546	Mike Kinkade RC (Star Rookies)	.25
547	Ryan Christenson RC (Star Rookies)	.10
548	Corey Koskie RC (Star Rookies)	.25
549	Norm Hutchins (Star Rookies)	.05
550	Russell Branyan (Star Rookies)	.05
551	Masato Yoshii RC (Star Rookies)	.25
552	Jesus Sanchez RC (Star Rookies)	.05
553	Anthony Sanders (Star Rookies)	.05
554	Edwin Diaz (Star Rookies)	.05
555	Gabe Alvarez (Star Rookies)	.05
556	Carlos Lee RC (Star Rookies)	.25
557	Mike Darr (Star Rookies)	.05
558	Kerry Wood (Star Rookies)	.20
559	Carlos Guillen (Star Rookies)	.05
560	Sean Casey (Star Rookies)	.15
561	Manny Aybar RC (Star Rookies)	.05
562	Octavio Dotel (Star Rookies)	.05
563	Jarrod Washburn (Star Rookies)	.05
564	Mark L. Johnson (Star Rookies)	.05
565	Ramon Hernandez (Star Rookies)	.05
566	Rich Butler RC (Star Rookies)	.05
567	Mike Caruso (Star Rookies)	.05
568	Cliff Politte (Star Rookies)	.05
569	Scott Elarton (Star Rookies)	.05
570	Magglio Ordonez RC (Star Rookies)	1.50
571	Adam Butler RC (Star Rookies)	.05
572	Marlon Anderson (Star Rookies)	.05
573	Julio Ramirez RC (Star Rookies)	.05
574	Darron Ingram RC (Star Rookies)	.05
575	Bruce Chen (Star Rookies)	.05
576	Steve Woodard RC (Star Rookies)	.05
577	Hiram Bocachica (Star Rookies)	.05
578	Kevin Witt (Star Rookies)	.05
579	Javier Vazquez (Star Rookies)	.10
580	Alex Gonzalez (Star Rookies)	.05
581	Brian Powell (Star Rookies)	.05
582	Wes Helms (Star Rookies)	.05
583	Ron Wright (Star Rookies)	.05
584	Rafael Medina (Star Rookies)	.05
585	Daryle Ward (Star Rookies)	.05
586	Geoff Jenkins (Star Rookies)	.25
587	Preston Wilson (Star Rookies)	.05
588	Jim Chamblee RC (Star Rookies)	.05
589	Mike Lowell RC (Star Rookies)	.25
590	A.J. Hinch (Star Rookies)	.05
591	Francisco Cordero RC (Star Rookies)	.10
592	Rolando Arrojo RC (Star Rookies)	.25
593	Braden Looper (Star Rookies)	.05
594	Sidney Ponson (Star Rookies)	.05
595	Matt Clement (Star Rookies)	.05
596	Carlton Loewer (Star Rookies)	.05
597	Brian Meadows (Star Rookies)	.05
598	Danny Klassen (Star Rookies)	.05
599	Larry Sutton (Star Rookies)	.05
600	Travis Lee (Star Rookies)	.15
601	Randy Johnson (Eminent Prestige)	1.50
602	Greg Maddux (Eminent Prestige)	2.00
603	Roger Clemens (Eminent Prestige)	2.25
604	Jaret Wright (Eminent Prestige)	.25
605	Mike Piazza (Eminent Prestige)	2.50
606	Tino Martinez (Eminent Prestige)	.25
607	Frank Thomas (Eminent Prestige)	1.50
608	Mo Vaughn (Eminent Prestige)	.25
609	Todd Helton (Eminent Prestige)	1.00
610	Mark McGwire (Eminent Prestige)	3.00
611	Jeff Bagwell (Eminent Prestige)	1.50
612	Travis Lee (Eminent Prestige)	.40
613	Scott Rolen (Eminent Prestige)	1.00
614	Cal Ripken Jr. (Eminent Prestige)	4.00
615	Chipper Jones (Eminent Prestige)	2.00
616	Nomar Garciaparra (Eminent Prestige)	2.00
617	Alex Rodriguez (Eminent Prestige)	3.00
618	Derek Jeter (Eminent Prestige)	4.00
619	Tony Gwynn (Eminent Prestige)	2.00
620	Ken Griffey Jr. (Eminent Prestige)	2.50
621	Kenny Lofton (Eminent Prestige)	.25

622	Juan Gonzalez (Eminent Prestige)	.75
623	Jose Cruz Jr. (Eminent Prestige)	.25
624	Larry Walker (Eminent Prestige)	.25
625	Barry Bonds (Eminent Prestige)	4.00
626	Ben Grieve (Eminent Prestige)	.25
627	Andruw Jones (Eminent Prestige)	1.50
628	Vladimir Guerrero (Eminent Prestige)	1.50
629	Paul Konerko (Eminent Prestige)	.50
630	Paul Molitor (Eminent Prestige)	1.50
631	Cecil Fielder	.05
632	Jack McDowell	.05
633	Mike James	.05
634	Brian Anderson	.05
635	Jay Bell	.05
636	Devon White	.05
637	Andy Stankiewicz	.05
638	Tony Batista	.05
639	Omar Daal	.05
640	Matt Williams	.05
641	Brent Brede	.05
642	Jorge Fabregas	.05
643	Karim Garcia	.10
644	Felix Rodriguez	.05
645	Andy Benes	.05
646	Willie Blair	.05
647	Jeff Suppan	.05
648	Yamil Benitez	.05
649	Walt Weiss	.05
650	Andres Galarraga	.05
651	Doug Drabek	.05
652	Ozzie Guillen	.05
653	Joe Carter	.05
654	Dennis Eckersley	.40
655	Pedro Martinez	.50
656	Jim Leyritz	.05
657	Henry Rodriguez	.05
658	Rod Beck	.05
659	Mickey Morandini	.05
660	Jeff Blauser	.05
661	Ruben Sierra	.05
662	Mike Sirotka	.05
663	Pete Harnisch	.05
664	Damian Jackson	.05
665	Dmitri Young	.05
666	Steve Cooke	.05
667	Geronimo Berroa	.05
668	Shawon Dunston	.05
669	Mike Jackson	.05
670	Travis Fryman	.05
671	Dwight Gooden	.05
672	Paul Assenmacher	.05
673	Eric Plunk	.05
674	Mike Lansing	.05
675	Darryl Kile	.05
676	Luis Gonzalez	.05
677	Frank Castillo	.05
678	Joe Randa	.05
679	Bip Roberts	.05
680	Derrek Lee	.30
681a	Mike Piazza/Marlins	2.00
681b	Mike Piazza/Mets	1.00
682	Sean Berry	.05
683	Ramon Garcia	.05
684	Carl Everett	.05
685	Moises Alou	.05
686	Hal Morris	.05
687	Jeff Conine	.05
688	Gary Sheffield	.25
689	Jose Vizcaino	.05
690	Charles Johnson	.05
691	Bobby Bonilla	.05
692	Marquis Grissom	.05
693	Alex Ochoa	.05
694	Mike Morgan	.05
695	Orlando Merced	.05
696	David Ortiz	.30
697	Brent Gates	.05
698	Otis Nixon	.05
699	Trey Moore	.05
700	Derrick May	.05
701	Rich Becker	.05
702	Al Leiter	.05
703	Chili Davis	.05
704	Scott Brosius	.05
705	Chuck Knoblauch	.05
706	Kenny Rogers	.05
707	Mike Blowers	.05
708	Mike Fetters	.05
709	Tom Candiotti	.05
710	Rickey Henderson	.50
711	Bob Abreu	.05
712	Mark Lewis	.05
713	Doug Glanville	.05
714	Desi Relaford	.05
715	Kent Mercker	.05
716	J. Kevin Brown	.05
717	James Mouton	.05
718	Mark Langston	.05
719	Greg Myers	.05
720	Orel Hershiser	.05
721	Charlie Hayes	.05
722	Robb Nen	.05
723	Glenallen Hill	.05
724	Tony Saunders	.05
725	Wade Boggs	.65
726	Kevin Stocker	.05
727	Wilson Alvarez	.05
728	Albie Lopez	.05
729	Dave Martinez	.05
730	Fred McGriff	.05
731	Quinton McCracken	.05
732	Bryan Rekar	.05
733	Paul Sorrento	.05
734	Roberto Hernandez	.05
735	Bubba Trammell	.05
736	Miguel Cairo	.05
737	John Flaherty	.05
738	Terrell Wade	.05
739	Roberto Kelly	.05
740	Mark Mclemore (McLemore)	.05
741	Danny Patterson	.05
742	Aaron Sele	.05
743	Tony Fernandez	.05
744	Randy Myers	.05
745	Jose Canseco	.30
746	Darrin Fletcher	.05
747	Mike Stanley	.05
748	Marquis Grissom (Season Highlights)	.05
749	Fred McGriff (Season Highlights)	.05
750	Travis Lee (Season Highlights)	.05

Amazing Greats

The 30-card Amazing Greats insert is printed on acetate. The cards are labeled "One of 2,000." A die-cut parallel was sequentially numbered to 250. Amazing Greats was an insert in Upper Deck Series One packs. Cards carry an "AG" prefix.

		NM/M
	Complete Set (30):	75.00
	Common Player:	.60
	Die-Cuts (250):	8X
1	Ken Griffey Jr.	5.00
2	Derek Jeter	7.50
3	Alex Rodriguez	6.00
4	Paul Molitor	3.00
5	Jeff Bagwell	3.00
6	Larry Walker	.60
7	Kenny Lofton	.60
8	Cal Ripken Jr.	7.50
9	Juan Gonzalez	1.50
10	Chipper Jones	4.00
11	Greg Maddux	4.00
12	Roberto Alomar	1.25
13	Mike Piazza	5.00
14	Andres Galarraga	.60
15	Barry Bonds	7.50
16	Andy Pettitte	1.25
17	Nomar Garciaparra	4.00
18	Hideki Irabu	.60
19	Tony Gwynn	4.00
20	Frank Thomas	3.00
21	Roger Clemens	4.50
22	Sammy Sosa	5.00
23	Jose Cruz, Jr.	.60
24	Manny Ramirez	3.00
25	Mark McGwire	6.00
26	Randy Johnson	3.00
27	Mo Vaughn	.60
28	Gary Sheffield	1.50
29	Andruw Jones	3.00
30	Albert Belle	.60

A Piece of the Action

A Piece of the Action was inserted in Series 1, 2 and 3 packs. Series 1 featured 10 cards: five with a piece of game-used jersey and five with a piece of game-used bat. Series 2 offered a piece of game-used bat and jersey on four cards. Series 3 inserts featured a piece of jersey only. The cards were inserted one per 2,500 packs in Series 1 and 2; the insertion rate in Series 3 was not revealed.

		NM/M
	Complete Set (14):	250.00
	Common Player:	5.00
	Inserted 1:2,500	
(1)	Jay Buhner/Bat	25.00
(2)	Tony Gwynn/Bat	25.00
(3)	Tony Gwynn/Jsy	25.00
(4)	Todd Hollandsworth/Bat	5.00
(5)	Todd Hollandsworth/Jsy	5.00
(6)	Greg Maddux/Jsy	40.00
(7)	Alex Rodriguez/Bat	40.00
(8)	Alex Rodriguez/Jsy	40.00
(9)	Gary Sheffield/Bat	15.00
(10)	Gary Sheffield/Jsy	15.00
RA	Roberto Alomar	35.00
JB	Jay Buhner	10.00
AJ	Andruw Jones	40.00
GS	Gary Sheffield	15.00

Blue Chip Prospects

Inserted in Series 2 packs, these inserts are printed on die-cut acetate. The cards are sequentially numbered to 2,000. They carry a "BC" prefix.

		NM/M
	Complete Set (30):	75.00
	Common Player:	2.00
1	Nomar Garciaparra	8.00
2	Scott Rolen	5.00
3	Jason Dickson	2.00
4	Darin Erstad	3.00
5	Brad Fullmer	2.00
6	Jaret Wright	2.00
7	Justin Thompson	2.00
8	Matt Morris	2.00
9	Fernando Tatis	2.00
10	Alex Rodriguez	12.00
11	Todd Helton	6.50
12	Andy Pettitte	2.50
13	Jose Cruz Jr.	2.00
14	Mark Kotsay	2.00
15	Derek Jeter	15.00
16	Paul Konerko	3.00
17	Todd Dunwoody	2.00
18	Vladimir Guerrero	5.00
19	Miguel Tejada	5.00
20	Chipper Jones	8.00
21	Kevin Orie	2.00
22	Juan Encarnacion	2.00
23	Brian Rose	2.00
24	Andruw Jones	6.00
25	Livan Hernandez	2.00
26	Brian Giles	2.00
27	Brett Tomko	2.00
28	Jose Guillen	2.00
29	Aaron Boone	2.00
30	Ben Grieve	2.00

Clearly Dominant

Clearly Dominant was an insert in Series 2. Printed on Light F/X plastic stock, the 30-card set is sequentially numbered to 250. They carry a "CD" prefix.

		NM/M
	Complete Set (30):	300.00
	Common Player:	3.00
	Production 250 Sets	
1	Mark McGwire	25.00
2	Derek Jeter	30.00
3	Alex Rodriguez	25.00
4	Paul Molitor	12.00
5	Jeff Bagwell	12.00
6	Ivan Rodriguez	10.00
7	Kenny Lofton	3.00
8	Cal Ripken Jr.	30.00
9	Albert Belle	3.00
10	Chipper Jones	15.00
11	Gary Sheffield	5.00
12	Roberto Alomar	4.00
13	Mo Vaughn	3.00
14	Andres Galarraga	3.00
15	Nomar Garciaparra	4.00
16	Randy Johnson	12.00
17	Mike Mussina	6.00
18	Greg Maddux	15.00
19	Tony Gwynn	15.00
20	Frank Thomas	12.00
21	Roger Clemens	17.50
22	Dennis Eckersley	10.00
23	Juan Gonzalez	6.00
24	Tino Martinez	3.00
25	Andruw Jones	12.00
26	Larry Walker	3.00
27	Ken Caminiti	3.00
28	Mike Piazza	20.00
29	Barry Bonds	30.00
30	Ken Griffey Jr.	20.00

Ken Griffey Jr.'s HR Chronicles

Griffey's Home Run Chronicles was inserted in both Series 1 and 2 packs. Series 1 had cards spotlighting one of Junior's first 30 home runs of the 1997 season. Series 2 had 26 cards highlighting the rest of his 1997 home run output. In both series, the cards were inserted one per nine packs. Cards are numbered "XX of 56" and printed on silver-metallic foil on front.

	NM/M
Complete Set (56):	45.00
Common Card:	1.00
Inserted 1:9	

National Pride

National Pride is a 42-card insert printed on die-cut rainbow foil. The set honors the nationality of the player with their country's flag in the background. The cards were inserted one per 24 packs. Cards are numbered with a "NP" prefix.

		NM/M
	Complete Set (42):	65.00
	Common Player:	.75
1	Dave Nilsson	.75
2	Larry Walker	.75
3	Edgar Renteria	.75
4	Jose Canseco	1.25
5	Rey Ordonez	.75
6	Rafael Palmeiro	2.50
7	Livan Hernandez	.75
8	Andruw Jones	3.00
9	Manny Ramirez	3.00
10	Sammy Sosa	4.00
11	Raul Mondesi	.75
12	Moises Alou	.75
13	Pedro Martinez	3.00
14	Vladimir Guerrero	3.00
15	Chili Davis	.75
16	Hideo Nomo	1.50
17	Hideki Irabu	.75
18	Shigetosi Hasegawa	.75
19	Takashi Kashiwada	.75
20	Chan Ho Park	.75
21	Fernando Valenzuela	.75
22	Vinny Castilla	.75
23	Armando Reynoso	.75
24	Karim Garcia	1.00
25	Marvin Benard	.75
26	Mariano Rivera	1.00
27	Juan Gonzalez	1.50
28	Roberto Alomar	1.00
29	Ivan Rodriguez	2.50
30	Carlos Delgado	1.00
31	Bernie Williams	.75
32	Edgar Martinez	.75
33	Frank Thomas	3.00
34	Barry Bonds	7.50
35	Mike Piazza	5.00
36	Chipper Jones	4.00
37	Cal Ripken Jr.	7.50
38	Alex Rodriguez	5.00
39	Ken Griffey Jr.	5.00
40	Andres Galarraga	.75
41	Omar Vizquel	.75
42	Ozzie Guillen	.75

Prime Nine

Nine of the most popular players are featured in this insert set. The cards are printed on silver-foil stock and inserted 1:5 in Series 2 packs.

		NM/M
	Complete Set (60):	50.00
	Common Griffey:	1.00
	Common Piazza:	1.25
	Common Thomas:	.60
	Common McGwire:	1.25
	Common Ripken:	1.75
	Common Gonzalez:	.50
	Common Gwynn:	.70
	Common Bonds:	1.75
	Common Maddux:	.70
	Inserted 1:5	
PN1	Ken Griffey Jr./1989-1992	1.00
PN2	Ken Griffey Jr./1993	1.00
PN3	Ken Griffey Jr./1994	1.00
PN4	Ken Griffey Jr./1995	1.00
PN5	Ken Griffey Jr./1996	1.00
PN6	Ken Griffey Jr./1997	1.00
PN7	Ken Griffey Jr./1997	1.00
PN8	Mike Piazza/1991	1.00
PN9	Mike Piazza/1992	1.00
PN10	Mike Piazza/1993	1.00
PN11	Mike Piazza/1994	1.00
PN12	Mike Piazza/1995	1.00
PN13	Mike Piazza/1996	1.00
PN14	Mike Piazza/1997	1.00
PN15	Frank Thomas/1991	.60
PN16	Frank Thomas/1992	.60
PN17	Frank Thomas/1993	.60
PN18	Frank Thomas/1994	.60
PN19	Frank Thomas/1995	.60
PN20	Frank Thomas/1996	.60
PN21	Frank Thomas/1997	.60
PN22	Mark McGwire/1987	1.25
PN23	Mark McGwire/1988-1990	1.25
PN24	Mark McGwire/1992	1.25
PN25	Mark McGwire/1995-1996	1.25
PN26	Mark McGwire/1997	1.25
PN27	Mark McGwire/1997	1.25
PN28	Mark McGwire/1997	1.25
PN29	Cal Ripken Jr./1982	1.75
PN30	Cal Ripken Jr./1983	1.75
PN31	Cal Ripken Jr./1989	1.75
PN32	Cal Ripken Jr./1991	1.75
PN33	Cal Ripken Jr./1995	1.75
PN34	Cal Ripken Jr./1996	1.75
PN35	Cal Ripken Jr./1997	1.75
PN36	Juan Gonzalez/1992	.50
PN37	Juan Gonzalez/1993	.50
PN38	Juan Gonzalez/1994	.50
PN39	Juan Gonzalez/1995	.50
PN40	Juan Gonzalez/1996	.50
PN41	Juan Gonzalez/1996	.50
PN42	Juan Gonzalez/1997	.50
PN43	Tony Gwynn/1984	.75
PN44	Tony Gwynn/1987-1989	.75
PN45	Tony Gwynn/1990-1993	.75
PN46	Tony Gwynn/1994	.75
PN47	Tony Gwynn/1995	.75
PN48	Tony Gwynn/1997	.75
PN49	Tony Gwynn/1997	.75
PN50	Barry Bonds/1986-1992	1.75
PN51	Barry Bonds/1990-1993	1.75
PN52	Barry Bonds/1993	1.75
PN53	Barry Bonds/1994	1.75
PN54	Barry Bonds/1996	1.75
PN55	Barry Bonds/1997	1.75
PN56	Greg Maddux/1992	.75
PN57	Greg Maddux/1993-1994	.75
PN58	Greg Maddux/1995	.75
PN59	Greg Maddux/1996	.75
PN60	Greg Maddux/1997	.75

Tape Measure Titans

Tape Measure Titans is a 30-card insert seeded 1:23 in Series 2. The set honors the game's top home run hitters. A parallel gold version was also created with each card serially numbered to 2,667 on front.

		NM/M
	Complete Set (30):	45.00
	Common Player:	.40
	Inserted 1:23	
	Gold:	1.5X
1	Mark McGwire	5.00
2	Andres Galarraga	.40
3	Jeff Bagwell	2.00
4	Larry Walker	.40
5	Frank Thomas	2.50
6	Rafael Palmeiro	1.50
7	Nomar Garciaparra	.40
8	Mo Vaughn	.40
9	Albert Belle	.60
10	Ken Griffey Jr.	4.00
11	Manny Ramirez	2.00
12	Jim Thome	.40
13	Tony Clark	.40
14	Juan Gonzalez	2.00
15	Mike Piazza	4.00
16	Jose Canseco	1.00
17	Jay Buhner	.40
18	Alex Rodriguez	5.00
19	Jose Cruz Jr.	.40
20	Tino Martinez	.40
21	Carlos Delgado	.75
22	Andruw Jones	2.00
23	Chipper Jones	3.00
24	Fred McGriff	.40
25	Matt Williams	.40
26	Sammy Sosa	4.00
27	Vinny Castilla	.40
28	Tim Salmon	.60
29	Ken Caminiti	.40
30	Barry Bonds	6.00

10th Anniversary Preview

10th Anniversary Preview is a 60-card set. The foil cards have the same design as the 1989 Upper Deck base cards. The set was inserted one per five packs. Retail versions have the words "PREVIEW EDITION" stamped vertically in gold foil at left. While scarcer than the hobby version, they do not command a premium.

	NM/M
Complete Set (60):	45.00
Common Player:	.30

		NM/M
1	Greg Maddux	2.00
2	Mike Mussina	.50
3	Roger Clemens	2.25
4	Hideo Nomo	.75
5	David Cone	.30
6	Tom Glavine	.45
7	Andy Pettitte	.60
8	Jimmy Key	.30
9	Randy Johnson	1.50
10	Dennis Eckersley	1.00
11	Lee Smith	.30
12	John Franco	.30
13	Randy Myers	.30
14	Mike Piazza	2.50
15	Ivan Rodriguez	1.25
16	Todd Hundley	.30
17	Sandy Alomar Jr.	.30
18	Frank Thomas	1.50
19	Rafael Palmeiro	1.25
20	Mark McGwire	3.00
21	Mo Vaughn	.30
22	Fred McGriff	.30
23	Andres Galarraga	.30
24	Mark Grace	.30
25	Jeff Bagwell	1.50
26	Roberto Alomar	.45
27	Chuck Knoblauch	.30
28	Ryne Sandberg	2.00
29	Eric Young	.30
30	Craig Biggio	.30
31	Carlos Baerga	.30
32	Robin Ventura	.30
33	Matt Williams	.30
34	Wade Boggs	2.00
35	Dean Palmer	.30
36	Chipper Jones	2.00
37	Vinny Castilla	.30
38	Ken Caminiti	.30
39	Omar Vizquel	.30
40	Cal Ripken Jr.	3.50
41	Derek Jeter	3.50
42	Alex Rodriguez	3.00
43	Barry Larkin	.30
44	Mark Grudzielanek	.30
45	Albert Belle	.30
46	Manny Ramirez	1.50
47	Jose Canseco	.75
48	Ken Griffey Jr.	2.50
49	Juan Gonzalez	.75
50	Kenny Lofton	.30
51	Sammy Sosa	2.00
52	Larry Walker	.30
53	Gary Sheffield	.60
54	Rickey Henderson	1.50
55	Tony Gwynn	2.00
56	Barry Bonds	3.50
57	Paul Molitor	1.50
58	Edgar Martinez	.30
59	Chili Davis	.30
60	Eddie Murray	1.50

Jumbos

For $3 and 10 foil-pack wrappers, collectors could receive this set of large-format (3-1/2" x 5") cards in a mail-in redemption. The cards are identical to the standard-size versions.

		NM/M
Complete Set (15):		6.00
Common Player:		.25
27	Kenny Lofton	.25
30	Greg Maddux	.75
40	Rafael Palmeiro	.50
50	Ryne Sandberg	.75
60	Albert Belle	.25
65	Barry Larkin	.25
67	Deion Sanders	.25
95	Gary Sheffield	.40
130	Paul Molitor	.60
135	Vladimir Guerrero	.60
176	Hideki Irabu	.25
205	Mark McGwire	2.00
211	Rickey Henderson	.60
225	Ken Griffey Jr.	1.50
230	Ivan Rodriguez	.50

5x7 Inserts

Each box of specially marked Series 2 retail packs contains one of these oversize (5" x 7") versions of UD cards. Besides being four times the

size of the regular cards, the jumbo versions do not have the metallic-foil highlights on front nor the hologram on back.

		NM/M
Complete Set (10):		30.00
Common Player:		1.00
310	Cal Ripken Jr.	6.00
320	Nomar Garciaparra	3.00
330	Frank Thomas	2.50
355	Larry Walker	1.00
385	Jeff Bagwell	2.50
400	Mike Piazza	4.00
450	Derek Jeter	6.00
500	Tony Gwynn	3.00
510	Alex Rodriguez	5.00
530	Roger Clemens	3.50

Richie Ashburn Tribute

As part of the company's participation at SportsFest in May 1998, the company issued a tribute card for Phillies Hall of Famer and broadcasting great Richie Ashburn. The card front features a color action photo, part of which is repeated on the back along with Ashburn's career stats and highlights.

		NM/M
1	Richie Ashburn	4.00

Ken Griffey Most Memorable Home Runs

This retail-exclusive boxed set features 11 large-format (3-1/2" x 5") cards depicting Junior's key home runs. The cards have brushed gold-foil graphic highlights on front and a large photo with details of the memorable home run on back. Each card in the set also exists in an autographed and numbered edition of 10 which were randomly inserted. The set was originally sold with a 4" x 6" lucite card holder for about $12.

		NM/M
Complete Set (11):		7.50
Common Card:		1.00
Autographed Card:		225.00
1	Ken Griffey Jr. (First ML HR)	1.00

		NM/M
2	Ken Griffey Jr. (Father-son HRs)	1.00
3	Ken Griffey Jr. (1992 All-Star HR)	1.00
4	Ken Griffey Jr. (HR in eight straight)	1.00
5	Ken Griffey Jr. (32 HR in June 1994)	1.00
6	Ken Griffey Jr. (Game-winning HR)	1.00
7	Ken Griffey Jr. (5th Division Series HR)	1.00
8	Ken Griffey Jr. (April record)	1.00
9	Ken Griffey Jr. (50th HR in 1997)	1.00
10	Ken Griffey Jr. (56th in 1997)	1.00
11	Ken Griffey Jr. (300th)	1.00

Mark McGwire's Chase for 62

This boxed set chronicles the Cardinal slugger's quest for the single-season home run record. Sold only as a boxed set of 30 cards in standard 2-1/2" x 3-1/2" format, plus a 3-1/2" x 5" card picturing home runs No. 61 and 62, these sets were offered only on a television home shopping show (individually serial numbered red box) and in selected retail stores (unnumbered yellow box). The cards in each version are identical. Issue price was about $20. Card fronts have color poses or action photos at right; at left is a monochrome portrait photo in red. Backs repeat the large front photo, also in red monochrome, and have a few words about a McGwire homer or other highlight. Each card has a silver-foil UD logo on front and a diamond-shaped hologram on back.

		NM/M
Complete Boxed Set:		7.50
Common Card:		.50
1-30	Mark McGwire	.50
---	Mark McGwire (3-1/2" x 5" HR #61/62)	3.00

Mark McGwire - Sept. 8, 1998

This is one of many special issues from Upper Deck commemorating McGwire's record-breaking 1998 season. Most such cards were produced for retail-only sales, or for home shopping television shows. This blank-back, round-cornered card is 5" x 3" and has flicker-action scenes of Big Mac's home run swing and his salute to the crowd following his historic blast.

		NM/M
	Mark McGwire	6.00

Mark McGwire 70/62 Home Runs

This 3-1/2" x 5" die-cut card was one of many special issues from UD commemorating McG-

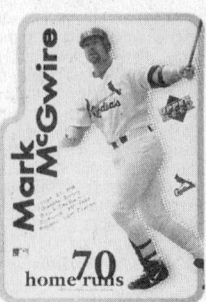

wire's record-breaking season in 1998. This card is highlighted on front with red foil and has a photo of the player with details of his 70th HR. On back in similar format is another photo and details of his 62nd home run, along with a serial number from within the edition of 17,000.

		NM/M
	Mark McGwire	4.00

PowerDeck Audio Card

A late-1990s reinvention of the "talking" baseball card, this was the first application of UD's "PowerDeck" technology to the trading card field. Specially marked hobby boxes of '98 UD baseball could contain one of three Ken Griffey, Jr., audio cards. The cards are standard 2-1/2" x 3-1/2" and were made to be inserted into a "dummy" plastic disc which could then be played in any audio CD, offering comments from Griffey, trivia, and career highlights. Insertion rate of each of the Griffey cards varies and is detailed in the listings.

		NM/M
Complete Set (3):		45.00
Common Card:		2.00
(1)	Ken Griffey Jr./Blue Jsy (1:46 Packs)	3.00
(2)	Ken Griffey Jr./Blue Jsy (1:500 Packs)	12.00
(3)	Ken Griffey Jr./White Jsy (1:2,400 Packs)	35.00

Rookie Edition Preview

		NM/M
Complete Set (10):		5.00
Common Player:		.50
1	Nomar Garciaparra	2.00
2	Scott Rolen	1.00
3	Mark Kotsay	.50
4	Todd Helton	1.50
5	Paul Konerko	.60
6	Juan Encarnacion	.50
7	Brad Fullmer	.50
8	Miguel Tejada	.65
9	Richard Hidalgo	.50
10	Ben Grieve	.50

Rookie Edition A Piece of the Action

A Piece of the Action consists of five Game Jersey cards. Three rookie Game Jersey cards were sequentially numbered to 200, while a Ken Griffey Jr. Game Jersey card

was numbered to 300. Griffey also signed and hand-numbered 24 Game Jersey cards.

		NM/M
Common Card:		15.00
KG	Ken Griffey Jr./300	100.00
KGS	Ken Griffey Jr./24 (Signed)	300.00
BG	Ben Grieve/200	15.00
JC	Jose Cruz Jr./200	15.00
TL	Travis Lee/200	15.00

Rookie Edition All-Star Credentials

All-Star Credentials is a 30-card insert seeded 1:9. It features the game's top players.

		NM/M
Complete Set (30):		25.00
Common Player:		.25
Inserted 1:9		
AS1	Ken Griffey Jr.	1.50
AS2	Travis Lee	.40
AS3	Ben Grieve	.25
AS4	Jose Cruz Jr.	.25
AS5	Andruw Jones	.75
AS6	Craig Biggio	.25
AS7	Hideo Nomo	.40
AS8	Cal Ripken Jr.	2.50
AS9	Jaret Wright	.25
AS10	Mark McGwire	2.00
AS11	Derek Jeter	2.50
AS12	Scott Rolen	.60
AS13	Jeff Bagwell	.75
AS14	Manny Ramirez	.75
AS15	Alex Rodriguez	2.00
AS16	Chipper Jones	1.00
AS17	Larry Walker	.25
AS18	Barry Bonds	2.50
AS19	Tony Gwynn	1.00
AS20	Mike Piazza	1.50
AS21	Roger Clemens	1.25
AS22	Greg Maddux	1.00
AS23	Jim Thome	.60
AS24	Tino Martinez	.25
AS25	Nomar Garciaparra	1.00
AS26	Juan Gonzalez	.40
AS27	Kenny Lofton	.25
AS28	Randy Johnson	.75
AS29	Todd Helton	.65
AS30	Frank Thomas	.75

Rookie Edition Destination Stardom

This 60-card insert features top young players. Fronts are printed on a foil background. The insertion

rate was one card per five packs. Cards have a "DS" prefix to the card number.

		NM/M
Complete Set (60):		40.00
Common Player:		.50
Inserted 1:5		
1	Travis Lee	.75
2	Nomar Garciaparra	3.50
3	Alex Gonzalez	.50
4	Richard Hidalgo	.50
5	Jaret Wright	.50
6	Mike Kinkade	.50
7	Matt Morris	.50
8	Gary Mathews Jr.	.50
9	Brett Tomko	.50
10	Todd Helton	2.00
11	Scott Elarton	.50
12	Scott Rolen	1.50
13	Jose Cruz Jr.	.50
14	Jarrod Washburn	.50
15	Sean Casey	.50
16	Magglio Ordonez	2.00
17	Gabe Alvarez	.50
18	Todd Dunwoody	.50
19	Kevin Witt	.50
20	Ben Grieve	.50
21	Daryle Ward	.50
22	Matt Clement	.50
23	Carlton Loewer	.50
24	Javier Vazquez	.50
25	Paul Konerko	.60
26	Preston Wilson	.60
27	Wes Helms	.50
28	Derek Jeter	5.00
29	Corey Koskie	.50
30	Russell Branyan	.50
31	Vladimir Guerrero	2.50
32	Ryan Christenson	.50
33	Carlos Lee	.60
34	David Dellucci	.50
35	Bruce Chen	.50
36	Ricky Ledee	.50
37	Ron Wright	.50
38	Derek Lee	1.50
39	Miguel Tejada	.75
40	Brad Fullmer	.50
41	Rich Butler	.50
42	Chris Carpenter	.50
43	Alex Rodriguez	4.00
44	Darron Ingram	.50
45	Kerry Wood	1.50
46	Jason Varitek	.50
47	Ramon Hernandez	.50
48	Aaron Boone	.50
49	Juan Encarnacion	.50
50	A.J. Hinch	.50
51	Mike Lowell	.60
52	Fernando Tatis	.50
53	Jose Guillen	.50
54	Mike Caruso	.50
55	Carl Pavano	.50
56	Chris Clemons	.50
57	Mark L. Johnson	.50
58	Ken Cloude	.50
59	Rolando Arrojo	.50
60	Mark Kotsay	.50

Rookie Edition Eminent Prestige 5x7

This 4X super-size (5" x 7") version is a partial parallel of the Rookie Edition Eminent Prestige subset. It was available only in specially marked retail packaging.

		NM/M
Complete Set (10):		25.00
Common Player:		2.00
605	Mike Piazza	3.50
607	Frank Thomas	2.50
610	Mark McGwire	4.00
611	Jeff Bagwell	2.50
612	Travis Lee	2.00
614	Cal Ripken Jr.	5.00
616	Nomar Garciaparra	3.00
617	Alex Rodriguez	4.00
619	Tony Gwynn	3.00
620	Ken Griffey Jr.	3.50

Rookie Edition Retrospectives

Retrospectives is a 30-card insert seeded 1:24. The cards offer a look back at the careers of baseball's top stars.

		NM/M
Complete Set (30):		55.00
Common Player:		.50
Inserted 1:24		
1	Dennis Eckersley	2.50
2	Rickey Henderson	3.00
3	Harold Baines	.50
4	Cal Ripken Jr.	7.50
5	Tony Gwynn	4.00
6	Wade Boggs	4.00
7	Orel Hershiser	.50
8	Joe Carter	.50
9	Roger Clemens	4.50
10	Barry Bonds	7.50
11	Mark McGwire	6.00
12	Greg Maddux	4.00
13	Fred McGriff	.50
14	Rafael Palmeiro	3.00
15	Craig Biggio	.50
16	Brady Anderson	.50
17	Randy Johnson	3.00
18	Gary Sheffield	1.00
19	Albert Belle	.50
20	Ken Griffey Jr.	5.00
21	Juan Gonzalez	1.50
22	Larry Walker	.50
23	Tino Martinez	.50
24	Frank Thomas	3.00
25	Jeff Bagwell	3.00
26	Kenny Lofton	.50
27	Mo Vaughn	.50
28	Mike Piazza	5.00
29	Alex Rodriguez	6.00
30	Chipper Jones	4.00

Rookie Edition Unparalleled

Unparalleled is a 20-card, hobby-only insert. The set consists of holo-pattern foil-stamped cards. They were inserted one per 72 packs.

		NM/M
Complete Set (20):		75.00
Common Player:		1.00
Inserted 1:72		
1	Ken Griffey Jr.	6.00
2	Travis Lee	1.50
3	Ben Grieve	1.00
4	Jose Cruz Jr.	1.00
5	Nomar Garciaparra	5.00
6	Hideo Nomo	1.75
7	Kenny Lofton	1.00
8	Cal Ripken Jr.	10.00
9	Roger Clemens	5.50
10	Mike Piazza	6.00
11	Jeff Bagwell	3.50
12	Chipper Jones	5.00
13	Greg Maddux	5.00
14	Randy Johnson	3.50
15	Alex Rodriguez	7.50
16	Barry Bonds	10.00
17	Frank Thomas	3.50
18	Juan Gonzalez	1.75
19	Tony Gwynn	5.00
20	Mark McGwire	7.50

1998 Upper Deck Special F/X

Special F/X is a retail-only product. The 150-card set consists of 125 regular cards, the 15-card Star Rookies subset and a 10-card subset called Ken Griffey Jr.'s Hot List. The base cards are printed on 20-point stock. The only insert is Power Zone which has four levels: Level One, Level Two - Octoberbest, Level Three - Power Driven and Level Four - Superstar Xcitement.

		NM/M
Complete Set (150):		30.00
Common Player:		.05
1	Ken Griffey Jr.	
	(Griffey Hot List)	1.00
2	Mark McGwire	
	(Griffey Hot List)	1.25
3	Alex Rodriguez	
	(Griffey Hot List)	2.50
4	Larry Walker	
	(Griffey Hot List)	.05
5	Tino Martinez	
	(Griffey Hot List)	.05
6	Mike Piazza	
	(Griffey Hot List)	2.50
7	Jose Cruz Jr.	
	(Griffey Hot List)	.05
8	Greg Maddux	
	(Griffey Hot List)	.75
9	Tony Gwynn	
	(Griffey Hot List)	.75
10	Roger Clemens	
	(Griffey Hot List)	1.75
11	Jason Dickson	.05
12	Darin Erstad	.25
13	Chuck Finley	.05
14	Dave Hollins	.05
15	Garret Anderson	.05
16	Michael Tucker	.05
17	Javier Lopez	.05
18	John Smoltz	.05
19	Mark Wohlers	.05
20	Greg Maddux	1.50
21	Scott Erickson	.05
22	Jimmy Key	.05
23	B.J. Surhoff	.05
24	Eric Davis	.05
25	Rafael Palmeiro	.75
26	Tim Naehring	.05
27	Darren Bragg	.05
28	Troy O'Leary	.05
29	John Valentin	.05
30	Mo Vaughn	.05
31	Mark Grace	.05
32	Kevin Foster	.05
33	Kevin Tapani	.05
34	Kevin Orie	.05
35	Albert Belle	.05
36	Ray Durham	.05
37	Jaime Navarro	.05
38	Mike Cameron	.05
39	Eddie Taubensee	.05
40	Barry Larkin	.05
41	Willie Greene	.05
42	Jeff Shaw	.05
43	Omar Vizquel	.05
44	Brian Giles	.05
45	Jim Thome	.60
46	David Justice	.05
47	Sandy Alomar Jr.	.05
48	Neifi Perez	.05
49	Dante Bichette	.05
50	Vinny Castilla	.05
51	John Thomson	.05
52	Damion Easley	.05
53	Justin Thompson	.05
54	Bobby Higginson	.05
55	Tony Clark	.05
56	Charles Johnson	.05
57	Edgar Renteria	.05
58	Alex Fernandez	.05
59	Gary Sheffield	.50
60	Livan Hernandez	.05
61	Craig Biggio	.05
62	Chris Holt	.05
63	Billy Wagner	.05
64	Brad Ausmus	.05
65	Dean Palmer	.05
66	Tim Belcher	.05
67	Jeff King	.05
68	Jose Rosado	.05
69	Chan Ho Park	.05
70	Raul Mondesi	.05
71	Hideo Nomo	.50
72	Todd Zeile	.05
73	Eric Karros	.05
74	Cal Eldred	.05
75	Jeff D'Amico	.05
76	Doug Jones	.05
77	Dave Nilsson	.05
78	Todd Walker	.05
79	Rick Aguilera	.05
80	Paul Molitor	1.00
81	Brad Radke	.05
82	Vladimir Guerrero	1.00
83	Carlos Perez	.05
84	F.P. Santangelo	.05
85	Rondell White	.05
86	Butch Huskey	.05
87	Edgardo Alfonzo	.05
88	John Franco	.05
89	John Olerud	.05
90	Todd Hundley	.05
91	Bernie Williams	.05
92	Andy Pettitte	.30
93	Paul O'Neill	.05
94	David Cone	.05
95	Jason Giambi	.50
96	Damon Mashore	.05
97	Scott Spiezio	.05
98	Ariel Prieto	.05
99	Rico Brogna	.05
100	Mike Lieberthal	.05
101	Garrett Stephenson	.05
102	Ricky Bottalico	.05
103	Kevin Polcovich	.05
104	Jon Lieber	.05
105	Kevin Young	.05
106	Tony Womack	.05
107	Gary Gaetti	.05
108	Alan Benes	.05
109	Willie McGee	.05
110	Mark McGwire	2.50
111	Ron Gant	.05
112	Andy Ashby	.05
113	Steve Finley	.05
114	Quilvio Veras	.05
115	Ken Caminiti	.05
116	Joey Hamilton	.05
117	Bill Mueller	.05
118	Mark Gardner	.05
119	Shawn Estes	.05
120	J.T. Snow	.05
121	Dante Powell	.05
122	Jeff Kent	.05
123	Jamie Moyer	.05
124	Joey Cora	.05
125	Ken Griffey Jr.	2.00
126	Jeff Fassero	.05
127	Edgar Martinez	.05
128	Will Clark	.05
129	Lee Stevens	.05
130	Ivan Rodriguez	.75
131	Rusty Greer	.05
132	Ed Sprague	.05
133	Pat Hentgen	.05
134	Shannon Stewart	.05
135	Carlos Delgado	.40
136	Brett Tomko	
	(Star Rookie)	.05
137	Jose Guillen	
	(Star Rookie)	.05
138	Elieser Marrero	
	(Star Rookie)	.05
139	Dennis Reyes	
	(Star Rookie)	.05
140	Mark Kotsay	
	(Star Rookie)	.05
141	Richie Sexson	
	(Star Rookie)	.05
142	Todd Helton	
	(Star Rookie)	.75
143	Jeremi Gonzalez	
	(Star Rookie)	.05
144	Jeff Abbott	
	(Star Rookie)	.05
145	Matt Morris	
	(Star Rookie)	.05
146	Aaron Boone	
	(Star Rookie)	.05
147	Todd Dunwoody	
	(Star Rookie)	.05
148	Mario Valdez	
	(Star Rookie)	.05
149	Fernando Tatis	
	(Star Rookie)	.05
150	Jaret Wright	
	(Star Rookie)	.05

OctoberBest

OctoberBest is Level Two of the Power Zone insert. This 20-card insert is die-cut and printed on silver foil. Inserted one per 34 packs, the set features the postseason exploits of 20 players from Power Zone Level One.

		NM/M
Complete Set (15):		40.00
Common Player:		1.00
Inserted 1:34		
PZ1	Frank Thomas	3.00
PZ2	Juan Gonzalez	1.50
PZ3	Mike Piazza	5.00
PZ4	Mark McGwire	6.00
PZ5	Jeff Bagwell	3.00
PZ6	Barry Bonds	7.50
PZ7	Ken Griffey Jr.	5.00
PZ8	John Smoltz	1.00
PZ9	Andruw Jones	3.00
PZ10	Greg Maddux	4.00
PZ11	Sandy Alomar Jr.	1.00
PZ12	Roberto Alomar	1.25
PZ13	Chipper Jones	4.00
PZ14	Kenny Lofton	1.00
PZ15	Tom Glavine	1.25

Power Driven

Power Driven is Level Three of the Power Zone insert. Inserted 1:69, the set features the top 10 power hitters from Power Zone Level Two. The cards feature gold Light F/X technology.

		NM/M
Complete Set (10):		40.00
Common Player:		1.50
Inserted 1:69		
PZ1	Frank Thomas	4.50
PZ2	Juan Gonzalez	2.50
PZ3	Mike Piazza	6.00
PZ4	Larry Walker	1.50
PZ5	Mark McGwire	7.50
PZ6	Jeff Bagwell	4.50
PZ7	Mo Vaughn	1.50
PZ8	Barry Bonds	10.00
PZ9	Tino Martinez	1.50
PZ10	Ken Griffey Jr.	6.00

Power Zone

Power Zone Level One is seeded one per seven packs. The cards are printed using silver Light F/X technology.

		NM/M
Complete Set (20):		40.00
Common Player:		.50
Inserted 1:7		
PZ1	Jose Cruz Jr.	.50
PZ2	Frank Thomas	2.50
PZ3	Juan Gonzalez	1.25
PZ4	Mike Piazza	4.50
PZ5	Mark McGwire	4.50
PZ6	Barry Bonds	6.00
PZ7	Greg Maddux	3.00
PZ8	Alex Rodriguez	4.50
PZ9	Nomar Garciaparra	3.00
PZ10	Ken Griffey Jr.	3.50
PZ11	John Smoltz	.50
PZ12	Andruw Jones	2.50
PZ13	Sandy Alomar Jr.	.50
PZ14	Roberto Alomar	1.00
PZ15	Chipper Jones	3.00
PZ16	Kenny Lofton	.50
PZ17	Larry Walker	.50
PZ18	Jeff Bagwell	2.50
PZ19	Mo Vaughn	.50
PZ20	Tom Glavine	.50

Superstar Xcitement

Printed on Light F/X gold foil, this 10-card set features the same players as the Power

Driven insert. This set is Power Zone Level Four and is sequentially numbered to 250.

		NM/M
Complete Set (10):		275.00
Common Player:		10.00
Production 250 Sets		
PZ1	Jose Cruz Jr.	10.00
PZ2	Frank Thomas	25.00
PZ3	Juan Gonzalez	10.00
PZ4	Mike Piazza	40.00
PZ5	Mark McGwire	45.00
PZ6	Barry Bonds	50.00
PZ7	Greg Maddux	35.00
PZ8	Alex Rodriguez	45.00
PZ9	Nomar Garciaparra	35.00
PZ10	Ken Griffey Jr.	40.00

1998 Upper Deck UD 3

The 270-card base set of UD 3 is actually three levels of the same 90 players. Light FX cards comprise #1-90. The first 30 cards are Future Impact players. Cards #31-60 are Power Corps and cards #61-90 are The Establishment. Cards #91-180 repeat the three subsets in Embossed technology while the final 90 cards repeat the basic sequence in Rainbow technology. Because each subset at each level is seeded at a different rate, few collectors bother to try to understand the relative scarcities and the issue is largely ignored. The insertion ratio for each tier is shown in the checklist. UD 3 was offered in three-card packs at an SRP of $3.99.

	NM/M
Complete Set (270):	200.00
Common Future Impact	
(1-30):	.50
Inserted 1:12	
Die-Cuts (2,000 Sets):	1X
Common Power Corps	
(31-60):	.25
Inserted 1:1	
Die-Cuts (2,000 Sets):	3X
Common Establishment	
(61-90):	.25
Inserted 1:7	
Die-Cuts (2,000 Sets):	2X
Common Future Impact Embossed	
(91-120):	.25
Inserted 1:6	
Die-Cuts (1,000 Sets):	3X
Common Power Corps Embossed	
(121-150):	.25
Inserted 1:4	
Die-Cuts (1,000 Sets):	6X
Common Establishment	
Embossed (151-180):	.25
Inserted 1:1	
Die-Cuts (1,000 Sets):	12X
Common Future Impact Rainbow	
(181-210):	.25
Inserted 1:1	
Die-Cuts (100 Sets):	15X
Common Power Corps Rainbow	
(211-5240):	.25
Inserted 1:12	
Die-Cuts (100 Sets):	8X
Common Establishment Rainbow	
(241-270):	.75
Inserted 1:24	
Die-Cuts (100 Sets):	5X
Pack (3):	1.00
Wax Box (24):	20.00

1	Travis Lee	.50
2	A.J. Hinch	.50
3	Mike Caruso	.50
4	Miguel Tejada	.75
5	Brad Fullmer	.50
6	Eric Milton	.50
7	Mark Kotsay	.50
8	Darin Erstad	.75
9	Magglio Ordonez	1.00
10	Ben Grieve	.50
11	Brett Tomko	.50
12	Mike Kinkade RC	.75
13	Rolando Arrojo	.50
14	Todd Helton	1.00
15	Scott Rolen	1.00
16	Bruce Chen	.50
17	Daryle Ward	.50
18	Jaret Wright	.50
19	Sean Casey	.65
20	Paul Konerko	.65
21	Kerry Wood	1.00
22	Russell Branyan	.50
23	Gabe Alvarez	.50
24	Juan Encarnacion	.50
25	Andruw Jones	1.50
26	Vladimir Guerrero	1.50
27	Eli Marrero	.50
28	Matt Clement	.50
29	Gary Matthews Jr.	.50
30	Derrek Lee	1.50
31	Ken Caminiti	.25
32	Gary Sheffield	.50
33	Jay Buhner	.25
34	Ryan Klesko	.25
35	Nomar Garciaparra	.75
36	Vinny Castilla	.25
37	Tony Clark	.25
38	Sammy Sosa	.75
39	Tino Martinez	.25
40	Mike Piazza	1.00
41	Manny Ramirez	.65
42	Larry Walker	.25
43	Jose Cruz Jr.	.25
44	Matt Williams	.25
45	Frank Thomas	.65
46	Jim Edmonds	.25
47	Raul Mondesi	.25
48	Alex Rodriguez	1.50
49	Albert Belle	.25
50	Mark McGwire	1.50
51	Tim Salmon	.25
52	Andres Galarraga	.25
53	Jeff Bagwell	.65
54	Jim Thome	.25
55	Barry Bonds	2.50
56	Carlos Delgado	.40
57	Mo Vaughn	.25
58	Chipper Jones	.75
59	Juan Gonzalez	.40
60	Ken Griffey Jr.	1.00
61	David Cone	.25
62	Hideo Nomo	.75
63	Edgar Martinez	.25
64	Fred McGriff	.25
65	Cal Ripken Jr.	4.00
66	Todd Hundley	.25
67	Barry Larkin	.25
68	Dennis Eckersley	.25
69	Randy Johnson	1.50
70	Paul Molitor	1.50
71	Eric Karros	.25
72	Rafael Palmeiro	1.00
73	Chuck Knoblauch	.25
74	Ivan Rodriguez	1.25
75	Greg Maddux	2.00
76	Dante Bichette	.25
77	Brady Anderson	.25
78	Craig Biggio	.25
79	Derek Jeter	4.00
80	Roger Clemens	2.25
81	Roberto Alomar	.40
82	Wade Boggs	2.00
83	Charles Johnson	.25
84	Mark Grace	.25
85	Kenny Lofton	.25
86	Mike Mussina	1.00
87	Pedro Martinez	1.50
88	Curt Schilling	.50
89	Bernie Williams	.25
90	Tony Gwynn	2.00
91	Travis Lee	.40
92	A.J. Hinch	.25
93	Mike Caruso	.25
94	Miguel Tejada	.40
95	Brad Fullmer	.25
96	Eric Milton	.25
97	Mark Kotsay	.25
98	Darin Erstad	1.00
99	Magglio Ordonez	1.00
100	Ben Grieve	.25
101	Brett Tomko	.25
102	Mike Kinkade RC	.40
103	Rolando Arrojo	.25
104	Todd Helton	1.00
105	Scott Rolen	1.00
106	Bruce Chen	.25
107	Daryle Ward	.25
108	Jaret Wright	.25
109	Sean Casey	.25
110	Paul Konerko	.25
111	Kerry Wood	1.00
112	Russell Branyan	.25
113	Gabe Alvarez	.25
114	Juan Encarnacion	.25
115	Andruw Jones	1.50
116	Vladimir Guerrero	1.50
117	Eli Marrero	.25
118	Matt Clement	.25

119	Gary Matthews Jr.	.25	
120	Derrek Lee	1.00	
121	Ken Caminiti	.25	
122	Gary Sheffield	.50	
123	Jay Buhner	.25	
124	Ryan Klesko	.25	
125	Nomar Garciaparra	1.50	
126	Vinny Castilla	.25	
127	Tony Clark	.25	
128	Sammy Sosa	1.50	
129	Tino Martinez	.25	
130	Mike Piazza	2.00	
131	Manny Ramirez	1.00	
132	Larry Walker	.25	
133	Jose Cruz Jr.	.25	
134	Matt Williams	.25	
135	Frank Thomas	1.00	
136	Jim Edmonds	.25	
137	Raul Mondesi	.25	
138	Alex Rodriguez	3.00	
139	Albert Belle	.25	
140	Mark McGwire	3.00	
141	Tim Salmon	.25	
142	Andres Galarraga	.25	
143	Jeff Bagwell	1.00	
144	Jim Thome	.75	
145	Barry Bonds	5.00	
146	Carlos Delgado	.50	
147	Mo Vaughn	.50	
148	Chipper Jones	1.50	
149	Juan Gonzalez	.50	
150	Ken Griffey Jr.	2.00	
151	David Cone	.25	
152	Hideo Nomo	.40	
153	Edgar Martinez	.25	
154	Fred McGriff	.25	
155	Cal Ripken Jr.	2.00	
156	Todd Hundley	.25	
157	Barry Larkin	.25	
158	Dennis Eckersley	.65	
159	Randy Johnson	.75	
160	Paul Molitor	.75	
161	Eric Karros	.25	
162	Rafael Palmeiro	.65	
163	Chuck Knoblauch	.25	
164	Ivan Rodriguez	.65	
165	Greg Maddux	1.00	
166	Dante Bichette	.25	
167	Brady Anderson	.25	
168	Craig Biggio	.25	
169	Derek Jeter	2.00	
170	Roger Clemens	1.25	
171	Roberto Alomar	.30	
172	Wade Boggs	1.00	
173	Charles Johnson	.25	
174	Mark Grace	.25	
175	Kenny Lofton	.25	
176	Mike Mussina	.40	
177	Pedro Martinez	.40	
178	Curt Schilling	.40	
179	Bernie Williams	.25	
180	Tony Gwynn	1.00	
181	Travis Lee	.40	
182	A.J. Hinch	.25	
183	Mike Caruso	.25	
184	Miguel Tejada	.40	
185	Brad Fullmer	.25	
186	Eric Milton	.25	
187	Mark Kotsay	.25	
188	Darin Erstad	.25	
189	Magglio Ordonez	1.25	
190	Ben Grieve	.25	
191	Brett Tomko	.25	
192	Mike Kinkade RC	.40	
193	Rolando Arrojo	.25	
194	Todd Helton	.65	
195	Scott Rolen	.60	
196	Bruce Chen	.25	
197	Daryle Ward	.25	
198	Jaret Wright	.25	
199	Sean Casey	.40	
200	Paul Konerko	.40	
201	Kerry Wood	.60	
202	Russell Branyan	.25	
203	Gabe Alvarez	.25	
204	Juan Encarnacion	.25	
205	Andruw Jones	1.50	
206	Vladimir Guerrero	1.50	
207	Eli Marrero	.25	
208	Matt Clement	.25	
209	Gary Matthews Jr.	.25	
210	Derrek Lee	1.00	
211	Ken Caminiti	.50	
212	Gary Sheffield	1.00	
213	Jay Buhner	.50	
214	Ryan Klesko	.50	
215	Nomar Garciaparra	3.00	
216	Vinny Castilla	.50	
217	Tony Clark	.50	
218	Sammy Sosa	3.00	
219	Tino Martinez	.50	
220	Mike Piazza	4.00	
221	Manny Ramirez	2.00	
222	Larry Walker	.50	
223	Jose Cruz Jr.	.50	
224	Matt Williams	.50	
225	Frank Thomas	2.00	
226	Jim Edmonds	.50	
227	Raul Mondesi	.50	
228	Alex Rodriguez	6.00	
229	Albert Belle	.50	
230	Mark McGwire	6.00	
231	Tim Salmon	.50	
232	Andres Galarraga	.50	
233	Jeff Bagwell	2.00	
234	Jim Thome	1.50	
235	Barry Bonds	9.00	
236	Carlos Delgado	.75	
237	Mo Vaughn	.50	
238	Chipper Jones	3.00	
239	Juan Gonzalez	1.00	
240	Ken Griffey Jr.	4.00	
241	David Cone	.75	
242	Hideo Nomo	1.50	
243	Edgar Martinez	.75	
244	Fred McGriff	.75	
245	Cal Ripken Jr.	12.00	
246	Todd Hundley	.75	
247	Barry Larkin	.75	
248	Dennis Eckersley	3.00	
249	Randy Johnson	4.50	
250	Paul Molitor	4.50	
251	Eric Karros	.75	
252	Rafael Palmeiro	3.50	
253	Chuck Knoblauch	.75	
254	Ivan Rodriguez	4.00	
255	Greg Maddux	6.00	
256	Dante Bichette	.75	
257	Brady Anderson	.75	
258	Craig Biggio	.75	
259	Derek Jeter	12.00	
260	Roger Clemens	6.50	
261	Roberto Alomar	1.25	
262	Wade Boggs	6.00	
263	Charles Johnson	.75	
264	Mark Grace	.75	
265	Kenny Lofton	.75	
266	Mike Mussina	1.25	
267	Pedro Martinez	4.50	
268	Curt Schilling	1.50	
269	Bernie Williams	1.50	
270	Tony Gwynn	6.00	

Die-Cut

Die-cut versions of all 270 cards in UD 3 were available in three sequentially numbered tiers. Light FX were numbered to 2,000 sets; Embossed cards were numbered to 1,000 and Rainbow cards were numbered to 100.

Light FX Die-Cuts (2,000 Each)
Future Impact (1-30): .75X
Power Corps (31-60): 3X
Establishment (61-90): 2X
Embossed Die-Cuts (1,000 Each)
Future Impact (91-120): 1X
Power Corps (121-150): 3X
Establishment (151-180): 6X
Rainbow Die-Cuts (100 Each)
Future Impact (181-210): 20X
Power Corps (211-240): 4X
Establishment (241-270): 12X

Power Corps Jumbos

Ten of the Power Corps cards from UD 3 were selected to be reproduced in jumbo 4X (5" x 7") format as box-toppers for special retail packaging of UD 3.

		NM/M
Complete Set (10):		60.00
Common Player:		2.50
35	Ken Griffey Jr.	7.50
38	Sammy Sosa	6.00
40	Mike Piazza	7.50
45	Frank Thomas	5.00
48	Alex Rodriguez	10.00
50	Mark McGwire	10.00
55	Barry Bonds	12.50
58	Chipper Jones	6.00
59	Juan Gonzalez	2.50
60	Ken Griffey Jr.	7.50

1998 UD Retro

The 129-card set is comprised of 99 regular player cards and 30 Futurama subset cards. Card fronts have a white border encasing the player photo. Retro is packaged in a lunchbox featuring one of six players. Each lunchbox contains 24 six-card packs.

	NM/M
Complete Set (129):	15.00

Common Player:		.05	
Pack (6):		2.25	
Lunchbox (24):		40.00	
1	Jim Edmonds	.05	
2	Darin Erstad	.25	
3	Tim Salmon	.05	
4	Jay Bell	.05	
5	Matt Williams	.05	
6	Andres Galarraga	.05	
7	Andruw Jones	.60	
8	Chipper Jones	.75	
9	Greg Maddux	.75	
10	Rafael Palmeiro	.05	
11	Cal Ripken Jr.	2.00	
12	Brooks Robinson	.15	
13	Nomar Garciaparra	.75	
14	Pedro Martinez	.60	
15	Mo Vaughn	.50	
16	Ernie Banks	.50	
17	Mark Grace	.05	
18	Gary Matthews	.05	
19	Sammy Sosa	.75	
20	Albert Belle	.05	
21	Carlton Fisk	.15	
22	Frank Thomas	.60	
23	Ken Griffey Sr.	.05	
24	Paul Konerko	.15	
25	Barry Larkin	.15	
26	Sean Casey	.10	
27	Tony Perez	.05	
28	Bob Feller	.15	
29	Kenny Lofton	.05	
30	Manny Ramirez	.60	
31	Jim Thome	.45	
32	Omar Vizquel	.05	
33	Dante Bichette	.05	
34	Larry Walker	.05	
35	Tony Clark	.05	
36	Damion Easley	.05	
37	Cliff Floyd	.05	
38	Livan Hernandez	.05	
39	Jeff Bagwell	.60	
40	Craig Biggio	.05	
41	Al Kaline	.15	
42	Johnny Damon	.20	
43	Dean Palmer	.05	
44	Charles Johnson	.05	
45	Eric Karros	.05	
46	Gaylord Perry	.05	
47	Raul Mondesi	.05	
48	Gary Sheffield	.30	
49	Eddie Mathews	.15	
50	Warren Spahn	.15	
51	Jeromy Burnitz	.05	
52	Jeff Cirillo	.05	
53	Marquis Grissom	.05	
54	Paul Molitor	.60	
55	Kirby Puckett	.75	
56	Brad Radke	.05	
57	Todd Walker	.05	
58	Vladimir Guerrero	.60	
59	Brad Fullmer	.05	
60	Rondell White	.05	
61	Bobby Jones	.05	
62	Hideo Nomo	.30	
63	Mike Piazza	1.00	
64	Tom Seaver	.15	
65	Frank J. Thomas	.05	
66	Yogi Berra	.50	
67	Derek Jeter	2.00	
68	Tino Martinez	.05	
69	Paul O'Neill	.05	
70	Andy Pettitte	.20	
71	Rollie Fingers	.05	
72	Rickey Henderson	.60	
73	Matt Stairs	.05	
74	Scott Rolen	.25	
75	Curt Schilling	.05	
76	Jose Guillen	.05	
77	Jason Kendall	.05	
78	Lou Brock	.10	
79	Bob Gibson	.10	
80	Ray Lankford	.05	
81	Mark McGwire	1.50	
82	Kevin Brown	.05	
83	Ken Caminiti	.05	
84	Tony Gwynn	.75	
85	Greg Vaughn	.05	
86	Barry Bonds	2.00	
87	Willie Stargell	.10	
88	Willie McCovey	.10	
89	Ken Griffey Jr.	1.00	
90	Randy Johnson	.60	
91	Alex Rodriguez	1.50	
92	Quinton McCracken	.05	
93	Fred McGriff	.05	
94	Juan Gonzalez	.30	
95	Ivan Rodriguez	.50	
97	Nolan Ryan	1.50	
98	Jose Canseco	.45	
99	Roger Clemens	.90	
100	Jose Cruz Jr.	.05	
101	Justin Baughman RC	.05	
102	David Dellucci RC (Futurama)	.15	
103	Travis Lee (Futurama)	.15	
104	Troy Glaus RC (Futurama)	1.00	
105	Kerry Wood (Futurama)	.40	
106	Mike Caruso (Futurama)	.05	
107	Jim Parque RC (Futurama)	.10	
108	Brett Tomko (Futurama)	.05	
109	Russell Branyan (Futurama)	.05	
110	Jaret Wright (Futurama)	.05	
111	Todd Helton (Futurama)	.60	
112	Gabe Alvarez (Futurama)	.05	
113	Matt Anderson RC (Futurama)	.10	
114	Alex Gonzalez (Futurama)	.05	
115	Mark Kotsay (Futurama)	.10	
116	Derrek Lee (Futurama)	.50	
117	Richard Hidalgo (Futurama)	.05	
118	Adrian Beltre (Futurama)	.10	
119	Geoff Jenkins (Futurama)	.05	
120	Eric Milton (Futurama)	.05	
121	Brad Fullmer (Futurama)	.05	
122	Vladimir Guerrero (Futurama)	.60	
123	Carl Pavano (Futurama)	.05	
124	Orlando Hernandez RC (Futurama)	.25	
125	Ben Grieve (Futurama)	.05	
126	A.J. Hinch (Futurama)	.05	
127	Matt Clement (Futurama)	.05	
128	Gary Matthews Jr. RC (Futurama)	.05	
129	Aramis Ramirez (Futurama)	.05	
130	Rolando Arrojo (Futurama)	.05	

Big Boppers

The game's heavy hitters are the focus of this insert set. Cards have a color action photo on a sepia background. Each card is individually serial numbered in red foil in the upper-right, within an edition of 500. Backs repeat part of the front photo, in sepia only, and have recent stats and hitting highlights. Cards are numbered with a "B" prefix.

		NM/M
Complete Set (30):		80.00
Common Player:		1.00
Production 500 Sets		
B1	Darin Erstad	1.50
B2	Rafael Palmeiro	3.00
B3	Cal Ripken Jr.	10.00
B4	Nomar Garciaparra	5.00
B5	Mo Vaughn	1.00
B6	Frank Thomas	4.00
B7	Albert Belle	1.00
B8	Jim Thome	2.50
B9	Manny Ramirez	4.00
B10	Tony Clark	1.00
B11	Tino Martinez	1.00
B12	Ben Grieve	1.00
B13	Ken Griffey Jr.	6.00
B14	Alex Rodriguez	7.50
B15	Jay Buhner	1.00
B16	Juan Gonzalez	2.00
B17	Jose Cruz Jr.	1.00
B18	Jose Canseco	2.50
B19	Travis Lee	1.50
B20	Chipper Jones	5.00
B21	Andres Galarraga	1.00
B22	Andruw Jones	4.00
B23	Sammy Sosa	5.00
B24	Vinny Castilla	1.00
B25	Larry Walker	1.00
B26	Jeff Bagwell	4.00
B27	Gary Sheffield	2.00
B28	Mike Piazza	6.00
B29	Mark McGwire	7.50
B30	Barry Bonds	10.00

Groovy Kind of Glove

This 30-card set showcases baseball's top defensive players on a psychadelic, wavy and colorful background. They were inserted 1:7 packs.

		NM/M
Complete Set (30):		50.00
Common Player:		.60
Inserted 1:7		
G1	Roberto Alomar	1.00
G2	Cal Ripken Jr.	7.50
G3	Nomar Garciaparra	3.50
G4	Frank Thomas	2.25
G5	Robin Ventura	.60
G6	Omar Vizquel	.60
G7	Kenny Lofton	.60
G8	Ben Grieve	.60
G9	Alex Rodriguez	6.00
G10	Ken Griffey Jr.	5.00
G11	Ivan Rodriguez	1.50
G12	Travis Lee	.75
G13	Matt Williams	.60
G14	Greg Maddux	3.50
G15	Andres Galarraga	.60
G16	Andruw Jones	2.25
G17	Kerry Wood	1.25
G18	Mark Grace	.60
G19	Craig Biggio	.60
G20	Charles Johnson	.60
G21	Raul Mondesi	.60
G22	Mike Piazza	5.00
G23	Rey Ordonez	.60
G24	Derek Jeter	7.50
G25	Scott Rolen	1.25
G26	Mark McGwire	6.00
G27	Ken Caminiti	.60
G28	Tony Gwynn	3.50
G29	J.T. Snow	.60
G30	Barry Bonds	7.50

Legendary Cut

This insert features an actual Babe Ruth cut signature and is limited to a total of three cards.

		NM/M
LC	Babe Ruth (3 issued; 1/04 auction)	9,500

New Frontier

This set spotlights 30 of baseball's top young prospects and is limited to 1,000 sequentially numbered sets.

		NM/M
Complete Set (30):		45.00
Common Player:		1.00
Production 1,000 Sets		
NF1	Justin Baughman	1.00
NF2	David Dellucci	1.00
NF3	Travis Lee	1.50
NF4	Troy Glaus	6.00
NF5	Mike Caruso	1.00
NF6	Jim Parque	1.00
NF7	Kerry Wood	2.00
NF8	Brett Tomko	1.00
NF9	Russell Branyan	1.00
NF10	Jaret Wright	1.00
NF11	Todd Helton	5.00
NF12	Gabe Alvarez	1.00
NF13	Matt Anderson	1.00
NF14	Alex Gonzalez	1.00
NF15	Mark Kotsay	1.00
NF16	Derrek Lee	3.00
NF17	Richard Hidalgo	1.00
NF18	Adrian Beltre	2.00
NF19	Geoff Jenkins	1.00
NF20	Eric Milton	1.00
NF21	Brad Fullmer	1.00
NF22	Vladimir Guerrero	6.00
NF23	Carl Pavano	1.00
NF24	Orlando Hernandez	1.25
NF25	Ben Grieve	1.00
NF26	A.J. Hinch	1.00
NF27	Matt Clement	1.00
NF28	Gary Matthews	1.00
NF29	Aramis Ramirez	1.00
NF30	Rolando Arrojo	1.00

Quantum Leap

This 30-card insert set highlights the technological advancements of Upper Deck products on a horizontal format. A total of 50 serially numbered sets were produced.

		NM/M
Common Player:		15.00
Production 50 Sets		
Q1	Darin Erstad	20.00
Q2	Cal Ripken Jr.	100.00
Q3	Nomar Garciaparra	50.00
Q4	Frank Thomas	40.00
Q5	Kenny Lofton	15.00
Q6	Ben Grieve	15.00
Q7	Ken Griffey Jr.	60.00
Q8	Alex Rodriguez	75.00
Q9	Juan Gonzalez	20.00
Q10	Jose Cruz Jr.	15.00
Q11	Roger Clemens	55.00
Q12	Travis Lee	15.00
Q13	Chipper Jones	50.00
Q14	Greg Maddux	50.00
Q15	Kerry Wood	20.00
Q16	Jeff Bagwell	40.00
Q17	Mike Piazza	60.00
Q18	Scott Rolen	30.00
Q19	Mark McGwire	75.00
Q20	Tony Gwynn	50.00
Q21	Larry Walker	15.00
Q22	Derek Jeter	100.00
Q23	Sammy Sosa	50.00
Q24	Barry Bonds	100.00
Q25	Mo Vaughn	15.00
Q26	Roberto Alomar	20.00
Q27	Todd Helton	30.00
Q28	Ivan Rodriguez	30.00
Q29	Vladimir Guerrero	40.00
Q30	Albert Belle	15.00

Sign of the Times

This retro-style autographed 31-card set features both retired legends and current players. They were inserted 1:36 packs.

		NM/M
Common Autograph:		7.50
Inserted 1:36		
EB	Ernie Banks/300	30.00
YB	Yogi Berra/150	45.00
RB	Russell Branyan/750	7.50
LB	Lou Brock/300	15.00
JC	Jose Cruz Jr./300	7.50
RF	Rollie Fingers/600	7.50
BF	Bob Feller/600	17.50
CF	Carlton Fisk/600	25.00
BGi	Bob Gibson/300	25.00
BGr	Ben Grieve/300	7.50
KGj	Ken Griffey Jr./100	185.00
KGs	Ken Griffey Sr./600	7.50
TG	Tony Gwynn/200	35.00
AK	Al Kaline/600	17.50
PK	Paul Konerko/750	7.50
TLe	Travis Lee/300	7.50

EM	Eddie Mathews/600	25.00
GMj	Gary Matthews Jr./750	7.50
GMs	Gary Matthews/600	7.50
WM	Willie McCovey/600	25.00
TP	Tony Perez/600	17.50
GP	Gaylord Perry/1,000	7.50
KP	Kirby Puckett/450	50.00
BR	Brooks Robinson/300	17.50
SR	Scott Rolen/300	10.00
NR	Nolan Ryan/500	100.00
TS	Tom Seaver/300	30.00
WS	Warren Spahn/600	25.00
WiS	Willie Stargell/600	25.00
FT	Frank Thomas/600	7.50
KW	Kerry Wood/200	30.00

Time Capsule

Another retro-styled card that featured current stars who were destined to earn a place in baseball history. They were inserted 1:2 packs.

		NM/M
Complete Set (50):		35.00
Common Player:		.25
Inserted 1:2		
TC1	Mike Mussina	.50
TC2	Rafael Palmeiro	.65
TC3	Cal Ripken Jr.	3.00
TC4	Nomar Garciaparra	1.50
TC5	Pedro Martinez	1.00
TC6	Mo Vaughn	.25
TC7	Albert Belle	.25
TC8	Frank Thomas	1.00
TC9	David Justice	.25
TC10	Kenny Lofton	.25
TC11	Manny Ramirez	1.00
TC12	Jim Thome	.60
TC13	Derek Jeter	3.00
TC14	Tino Martinez	.25
TC15	Ben Grieve	.25
TC16	Rickey Henderson	.25
TC17	Ken Griffey Jr.	2.00
TC18	Randy Johnson	1.00
TC19	Alex Rodriguez	2.50
TC20	Wade Boggs	1.50
TC21	Fred McGriff	.25
TC22	Juan Gonzalez	.50
TC23	Ivan Rodriguez	.75
TC24	Nolan Ryan	2.50
TC25	Jose Canseco	.50
TC26	Roger Clemens	1.75
TC27	Jose Cruz Jr.	.25
TC28	Travis Lee	.40
TC29	Matt Williams	.25
TC30	Andres Galarraga	.25
TC31	Andruw Jones	1.00
TC32	Chipper Jones	1.50
TC33	Greg Maddux	1.50
TC34	Kerry Wood	.50
TC35	Barry Larkin	.25
TC36	Dante Bichette	.25
TC37	Larry Walker	.25
TC38	Livan Hernandez	.25
TC39	Jeff Bagwell	1.00
TC40	Craig Biggio	.25
TC41	Charles Johnson	.25
TC42	Gary Sheffield	.50
TC43	Marquis Grissom	.25
TC44	Mike Piazza	2.00
TC45	Scott Rolen	.65
TC46	Curt Schilling	.40
TC47	Mark McGwire	2.50
TC48	Ken Caminiti	.25
TC49	Tony Gwynn	1.50
TC50	Barry Bonds	1.00

Lunchbox

Lunchboxes were the form of packaging for UD Retro. Six different players are featured with each lunchbox containing 24 six-card packs, with a SRP of $4.99.

		NM/M
Complete Set (6):		40.00
Common Lunchbox:		4.00
	Nomar Garciaparra	6.00
	Ken Griffey Jr.	7.50

Chipper Jones	6.00
Travis Lee	4.00
Mark McGwire	10.00
Cal Ripken Jr.	12.00

1999 Upper Deck

Released in two series, base card fronts feature a textured silver border along the left and right sides. The player name and Upper Deck logo also are stamped in silver foil. Backs have a small photo, with stats and career highlights. Randomly seeded in packs are 100 Ken Griffey Jr. rookie cards that were bought back by Upper Deck from the hobby and autographed. Upper Deck also re-inserted one pack of '89 Upper Deck inside every hobby box. Ten-card hobby packs carry a S.R.P. of $2.99. Cards #256-265 were never produced.

		NM/M
Complete Set (525):		45.00
Complete Series 1 (255):		25.00
Complete Series 2 (270):		20.00
Common Player:		.05
Exclusive Stars/RC's:		15X
Production 100 each		
Pack (10):		1.50
Wax Box (24):		35.00
1	Troy Glaus (Star Rookies)	.60
2	Adrian Beltre (Star Rookies)	.25
3	Matt Anderson (Star Rookies)	.05
4	Eric Chavez (Star Rookies)	.15
5	Jin Cho (Star Rookies)	.05
6	Robert Smith RC	.05
7	George Lombard (Star Rookies)	.05
8	Mike Kinkade (Star Rookies)	.05
9	Seth Greisinger (Star Rookies)	.05
10	J.D. Drew (Star Rookies)	.50
11	Aramis Ramirez (Star Rookies)	.05
12	Carlos Guillen (Star Rookies)	.05
13	Justin Baughman (Star Rookies)	.05
14	Jim Parque (Star Rookies)	.05
15	Ryan Jackson (Star Rookies)	.05
16	Ramon Martinez (Star Rookies)	.05
17	Orlando Hernandez (Star Rookies)	.05
18	Jeremy Giambi (Star Rookies)	.05
19	Gary DiSarcina	.05
20	Darin Erstad	.25
21	Troy Glaus	.50
22	Chuck Finley	.05
23	Dave Hollins	.05
24	Troy Percival	.05
25	Tim Salmon	.05
26	Brian Anderson	.05
27	Jay Bell	.05
28	Andy Benes	.05
29	Brent Brede	.05
30	David Dellucci	.05
31	Karim Garcia	.10
32	Travis Lee	.20
33	Andres Galarraga	.05
34	Ryan Klesko	.05
35	Keith Lockhart	.05
36	Kevin Millwood	.05
37	Denny Neagle	.05
38	John Smoltz	.05
39	Michael Tucker	.05
40	Walt Weiss	.05
41	Dennis Martinez	.05
42	Javy Lopez	.05
43	Brady Anderson	.05
44	Harold Baines	.05
45	Mike Bordick	.05
46	Roberto Alomar	.20
47	Scott Erickson	.05
48	Mike Mussina	.30
49	Cal Ripken Jr.	2.00
50	Darren Bragg	.05
51	Dennis Eckersley	.50
52	Nomar Garciaparra	.75
53	Scott Hatteberg	.05
54	Troy O'Leary	.05
55	Bret Saberhagen	.05
56	John Valentin	.05
57	Rod Beck	.05
58	Jeff Blauser	.05
59	Brant Brown	.05
60	Mark Clark	.05
61	Mark Grace	.05
62	Kevin Tapani	.05
63	Henry Rodriguez	.05
64	Mike Cameron	.05
65	Mike Caruso	.05
66	Ray Durham	.05
67	Jaime Navarro	.05
68	Magglio Ordonez	.30
69	Mike Sirotka	.05
70	Sean Casey	.15
71	Barry Larkin	.05
72	Jon Nunnally	.05
73	Paul Konerko	.15
74	Chris Stynes	.05
75	Brett Tomko	.05
76	Dmitri Young	.05
77	Sandy Alomar	.05
78	Bartolo Colon	.05
79	Travis Fryman	.05
80	Brian Giles	.05
81	David Justice	.05
82	Omar Vizquel	.05
83	Jaret Wright	.05
84	Jim Thome	.40
85	Charles Nagy	.05
86	Pedro Astacio	.05
87	Todd Helton	.50
88	Darryl Kile	.05
89	Mike Lansing	.05
90	Neifi Perez	.05
91	John Thomson	.05
92	Larry Walker	.05
93	Tony Clark	.05
94	Deivi Cruz	.05
95	Damion Easley	.05
96	Brian L. Hunter	.05
97	Todd Jones	.05
98	Brian Moehler	.05
99	Gabe Alvarez	.05
100	Craig Counsell	.05
101	Cliff Floyd	.05
102	Livan Hernandez	.05
103	Andy Larkin	.05
104	Derrek Lee	.35
105	Brian Meadows	.05
106	Moises Alou	.05
107	Sean Berry	.05
108	Craig Biggio	.05
109	Ricky Gutierrez	.05
110	Mike Hampton	.05
111	Jose Lima	.05
112	Billy Wagner	.05
113	Hal Morris	.05
114	Johnny Damon	.30
115	Jeff King	.05
116	Jeff Montgomery	.05
117	Glendon Rusch	.05
118	Larry Sutton	.05
119	Bobby Bonilla	.05
120	Jim Eisenreich	.05
121	Eric Karros	.05
122	Matt Luke	.05
123	Ramon Martinez	.05
124	Gary Sheffield	.40
125	Eric Young	.05
126	Charles Johnson	.05
127	Jeff Cirillo	.05
128	Marquis Grissom	.05
129	Jeromy Burnitz	.05
130	Bob Wickman	.05
131	Scott Karl	.05
132	Mark Loretta	.05
133	Fernando Vina	.05
134	Matt Lawton	.05
135	Pat Meares	.05
136	Eric Milton	.05
137	Paul Molitor	.60
138	David Ortiz	.35
139	Todd Walker	.05
140	Shane Andrews	.05
141	Brad Fullmer	.05
142	Vladimir Guerrero	.60
143	Dustin Hermanson	.05
144	Ryan McGuire	.05
145	Ugueth Urbina	.05
146	John Franco	.05
147	Butch Huskey	.05
148	Bobby Jones	.05
149	John Olerud	.05
150	Rey Ordonez	.05
151	Mike Piazza	1.25
152	Hideo Nomo	.30
153	Masato Yoshii	.05
154	Derek Jeter	2.00
155	Chuck Knoblauch	.05
156	Paul O'Neill	.05
157	Andy Pettitte	.20
158	Mariano Rivera	.15
159	Darryl Strawberry	.05
160	David Wells	.05
161	Jorge Posada	.05
162	Ramiro Mendoza	.05
163	Miguel Tejada	.15
164	Ryan Christenson	.05
165	Rickey Henderson	.60
166	A.J. Hinch	.05
167	Ben Grieve	.05
168	Kenny Rogers	.05
169	Matt Stairs	.05
170	Bob Abreu	.05
171	Rico Brogna	.05
172	Doug Glanville	.05
173	Mike Grace	.05
174	Desi Relaford	.05
175	Scott Rolen	.40
176	Jose Guillen	.05
177	Francisco Cordova	.05
178	Al Martin	.05
179	Jason Schmidt	.05
180	Turner Ward	.05
181	Kevin Young	.05
182	Mark McGwire	1.50
183	Delino DeShields	.05
184	Eli Marrero	.05
185	Tom Lampkin	.05
186	Ray Lankford	.05
187	Willie McGee	.05
188	Matt Morris	.05
189	Andy Ashby	.05
190	Kevin Brown	.05
191	Ken Caminiti	.05
192	Trevor Hoffman	.05
193	Wally Joyner	.05
194	Greg Vaughn	.05
195	Danny Darwin	.05
196	Shawn Estes	.05
197	Orel Hershiser	.05
198	Jeff Kent	.05
199	Bill Mueller	.05
200	Robb Nen	.05
201	J.T. Snow	.05
202	Ken Cloude	.05
203	Russ Davis	.05
204	Jeff Fassero	.05
205	Ken Griffey Jr.	1.00
206	Shane Monahan	.05
207	David Segui	.05
208	Dan Wilson	.05
209	Wilson Alvarez	.05
210	Wade Boggs	.75
211	Miguel Cairo	.05
212	Bubba Trammell	.05
213	Quinton McCracken	.05
214	Paul Sorrento	.05
215	Kevin Stocker	.05
216	Will Clark	.05
217	Rusty Greer	.05
218	Rick Helling	.05
219	Mike McLemore	.05
220	Ivan Rodriguez	.50
221	John Wetteland	.05
222	Jose Canseco	.40
223	Roger Clemens	.85
224	Carlos Delgado	.25
225	Darrin Fletcher	.05
226	Alex Gonzalez	.05
227	Jose Cruz Jr.	.05
228	Shannon Stewart	.05
229	Rolando Arrojo (Foreign Focus)	.05
230	Livan Hernandez (Foreign Focus)	.05
231	Orlando Hernandez (Foreign Focus)	.05
232	Raul Mondesi (Foreign Focus)	.05
233	Moises Alou (Foreign Focus)	.05
234	Pedro Martinez (Foreign Focus)	.30
235	Sammy Sosa (Foreign Focus)	.50
236	Vladimir Guerrero (Foreign Focus)	.40
237	Bartolo Colon (Foreign Focus)	.05
238	Miguel Tejada (Foreign Focus)	.05
239	Ismael Valdes (Foreign Focus)	.05
240	Mariano Rivera (Foreign Focus)	.05
241	Jose Cruz Jr. (Foreign Focus)	.05
242	Juan Gonzalez (Foreign Focus)	.20
243	Ivan Rodriguez (Foreign Focus)	.15
244	Sandy Alomar (Foreign Focus)	.05
245	Roberto Alomar (Foreign Focus)	.10
246	Magglio Ordonez (Foreign Focus)	.05
247	Kerry Wood (Highlights Checklist)	.10
248	Mark McGwire (Highlights Checklist)	.75
249	David Wells (Highlights Checklist)	.05
250	Rolando Arrojo (Highlights Checklist)	.05
251	Ken Griffey Jr. (Highlights Checklist)	.65
252	Trevor Hoffman (Highlights Checklist)	.05
253	Travis Lee (Highlights Checklist)	.05
254	Roberto Alomar (Highlights Checklist)	.10
255	Sammy Sosa (Highlights Checklist)	.50
266	Pat Burrell RC (Star Rookie)	2.00
267	Shea Hillenbrand RC (Star Rookie)	.65
268	Robert Fick (Star Rookie)	.05
269	Roy Halladay (Star Rookie)	.05
270	Ruben Mateo (Star Rookie)	.05
271	Bruce Chen (Star Rookie)	.05
272	Angel Pena (Star Rookie)	.05
273	Michael Barrett (Star Rookie)	.05
274	Kevin Witt (Star Rookie)	.05
275	Damon Minor (Star Rookie)	.05
276	Ryan Minor (Star Rookie)	.05
277	A.J. Pierzynski (Star Rookie)	.05
278	A.J. Burnett RC (Star Rookie)	.50
279	Dermal Brown (Star Rookie)	.05
280	Joe Lawrence (Star Rookie)	.05
281	Derrick Gibson (Star Rookie)	.05
282	Carlos Febles (Star Rookie)	.05
283	Chris Haas (Star Rookie)	.05
284	Cesar King (Star Rookie)	.05
285	Calvin Pickering (Star Rookie)	.05
286	Mitch Meluskey (Star Rookie)	.05
287	Carlos Beltran (Star Rookie)	.50
288	Ron Belliard (Star Rookie)	.05
289	Jerry Hairston Jr. (Star Rookie)	.05
290	Fernando Seguignol (Star Rookie)	.05
291	Kris Benson (Star Rookie)	.05
292	Chad Hutchinson RC (Star Rookie)	.05
293	Jarrod Washburn	.05
294	Jason Dickson	.05
295	Mo Vaughn	.05
296	Garrett Anderson	.05
297	Jim Edmonds	.05
298	Ken Hill	.05
299	Shigetosi Hasegawa	.05
300	Todd Stottlemyre	.05
301	Randy Johnson	.60
302	Omar Daal	.05
303	Steve Finley	.05
304	Matt Williams	.05
305	Danny Klassen	.05
306	Tony Batista	.05
307	Brian Jordan	.05
308	Greg Maddux	.75
309	Chipper Jones	.75
310	Bret Boone	.05
311	Ozzie Guillen	.05
312	John Rocker	.05
313	Tom Glavine	.25
314	Andruw Jones	.60
315	Albert Belle	.05
316	Charles Johnson	.05
317	Will Clark	.05
318	B.J. Surhoff	.05
319	Delino DeShields	.05
320	Heathcliff Slocumb	.05
321	Sidney Ponson	.05
322	Juan Guzman	.05
323	Reggie Jefferson	.05
324	Mark Portugal	.05
325	Tim Wakefield	.05
326	Jason Varitek	.05
327	Jose Offerman	.05
328	Pedro Martinez	.60
329	Trot Nixon	.05
330	Kevin Young	.30
331	Sammy Sosa	.75
332	Glenallen Hill	.05
333	Gary Gaetti	.05
334	Mickey Morandini	.05
335	Benito Santiago	.05
336	Jeff Blauser	.05
337	Frank Thomas	.65
338	Paul Konerko	.15
339	Jaime Navarro	.05
340	Carlos Lee	.05
341	Brian Simmons	.05
342	Mark Buehrle	—
343	Jeff Abbot	.05
344	Steve Avery	.05
345	Mike Cameron	.05
346	Michael Tucker	.05
347	Greg Vaughn	.05
348	Hal Morris	.05
349	Pete Harnisch	.05
350	Denny Neagle	.05
351	Manny Ramirez	.60
352	Roberto Alomar	.20
353	Dwight Gooden	.05
354	Kenny Lofton	.05
355	Mike Jackson	.05
356	Charles Nagy	.05
357	Enrique Wilson	.05
358	Russ Branyan	.05
359	Richie Sexson	.05
360	Vinny Castilla	.05
361	Dante Bichette	.05
362	Kirt Manwaring	.05
363	Darryl Hamilton	.05
364	Jamey Wright	.05
365	Curt Leskanic	.05
366	Jeff Reed	.05
367	Bobby Higginson	.05
368	Justin Thompson	.05
369	Brad Ausmus	.05
370	Dean Palmer	.05
371	Gabe Kapler	.05
372	Juan Encarnacion	.05
373	Karim Garcia	.10
374	Alex Gonzalez	.05
375	Braden Looper	.05
376	Preston Wilson	.05
377	Todd Dunwoody	.05
378	Alex Fernandez	.05
379	Mark Kotsay	.05
380	Mark Mantei	.05
381	Ken Caminiti	.05
382	Scott Elarton	.05
383	Jeff Bagwell	.60
384	Derek Bell	.05
385	Ricky Gutierrez	.05
386	Richard Hildalgo	.05
387	Shane Reynolds	.05
388	Carl Everett	.05
389	Scott Service	.05
390	Jeff Suppan	.05
391	Joe Randa	.05
392	Kevin Appier	.05
393	Shane Halter	.05
394	Chad Kreuter	.05
395	Mike Sweeney	.05
396	Kevin Brown	.05
397	Devon White	.05
398	Todd Hollandsworth	.05
399	Todd Hundley	.05
400	Chan Ho Park	.05
401	Mark Grudzielanek	.05
402	Raul Mondesi	.05
403	Ismael Valdes	.05
404	Rafael Roque	.05
405	Sean Berry	.05
406	Kevin Barker	.05
407	Dave Nilsson	.05
408	Geoff Jenkins	.05
409	Jim Abbott	.05
410	Bobby Hughes	.05
411	Corey Koskie	.05
412	Rick Aguilera	.05
413	LaTroy Hawkins	.05
414	Ron Coomer	.05
415	Denny Hocking	.05
416	Marty Cordova	.05
417	Terry Steinbach	.05
418	Rondell White	.05
419	Wilton Guerrero	.05
420	Shane Andrews	.05
421	Orlando Cabrera	.05
422	Carl Pavano	.05
423	Jeff Vasquez	.05
424	Chris Widger	.05
425	Robin Ventura	.05
426	Rickey Henderson	.60
427	Al Leiter	.05
428	Bobby Jones	.05
429	Brian McRae	.05
430	Roger Cedeno	.05
431	Bobby Bonilla	.05
432	Edgardo Alfonzo	.05
433	Bernie Williams	.05
434	Ricky Ledee	.05
435	Chili Davis	.05
436	Tino Martinez	.05
437	Scott Brosius	.05
438	David Cone	.05
439	Joe Girardi	.05
440	Roger Clemens	.85
441	Chad Curtis	.05
442	Hideki Irabu	.05
443	Jason Giambi	.40
444	Scott Spezio	.05
445	Tony Phillips	.05
446	Ramon Hernandez	.05
447	Mike Macfarlane	.05
448	Tom Candiotti	.05
449	Billy Taylor	.05
450	Bobby Estella	.05
451	Curt Schilling	.25
452	Carlton Loewer	.05
453	Marlon Anderson	.05
454	Kevin Jordan	.05
455	Ron Gant	.05
456	Chad Ogea	.05
457	Abraham Nunez	.05
458	Jason Kendall	.05
459	Pat Meares	.05
460	Brant Brown	.05
461	Brian Giles	.05
462	Chad Hermansen	.05
463	Freddy Garcia	.05
464	Edgar Renteria	.05
465	Fernando Tatis	.05
466	Eric Davis	.05
467	Darren Bragg	.05
468	Donovan Osborne	.05
469	Manny Aybar	.05
470	Jose Jimenez	.05
471	Kent Mercker	.05
472	Reggie Sanders	.05

473	Ruben Rivera	.05
474	Tony Gwynn	.75
475	Jim Leyritz	.05
476	Chris Gomez	.05
477	Matt Clement	.05
478	Carlos Hernandez	.05
479	Sterling Hitchcock	.05
480	Ellis Burks	.05
481	Barry Bonds	2.00
482	Marvin Bernard	.05
483	Kirk Rueter	.05
484	F.P. Santangelo	.05
485	Stan Javier	.05
486	Jeff Kent	.05
487	Alex Rodriguez	1.50
488	Tom Lampkin	.05
489	Jose Mesa	.05
490	Jay Buhner	.05
491	Edgar Martinez	.05
492	Butch Huskey	.05
493	John Mabry	.05
494	Jamie Moyer	.05
495	Roberto Hernandez	.05
496	Tony Saunders	.05
497	Fred McGriff	.05
498	Dave Martinez	.05
499	Jose Canseco	.40
500	Rolando Arrojo	.05
501	Esteban Yan	.05
502	Juan Gonzalez	.30
503	Rafael Palmeiro	.50
504	Aaron Sele	.05
505	Royce Clayton	.05
506	Todd Zeile	.05
507	Tom Goodwin	.05
508	Lee Stevens	.05
509	Esteban Loaiza	.05
510	Joey Hamilton	.05
511	Homer Bush	.05
512	Willie Greene	.05
513	Shawn Green	.25
514	David Wells	.05
515	Kelvim Escobar	.05
516	Tony Fernandez	.05
517	Pat Hentgen	.05
518	Mark McGwire (Arms Race)	.75
519	Ken Griffey Jr. (Arms Race)	.65
520	Sammy Sosa (Arms Race)	.50
521	Juan Gonzalez (Arms Race)	.20
522	J.D. Drew (Arms Race)	.10
523	Chipper Jones (Arms Race)	.40
524	Alex Rodriguez (Arms Race)	.75
525	Mike Piazza (Arms Race)	.65
526	Nomar Garciaparra (Arms Race)	.50
527	Season Highlights Checklist (Mark McGwire)	.75
528	Season Highlights Checklist (Sammy Sosa)	.50
529	Season Highlights Checklist (Scott Brosius)	.05
530	Season Highlights Checklist (Cal Ripken Jr.)	1.00
531	Season Highlights Checklist (Barry Bonds)	1.00
532	Season Highlights Checklist (Roger Clemens)	.40
533	Season Highlights Checklist (Ken Griffey Jr.)	.65
534	Season Highlights Checklist (Alex Rodriguez)	.75
535	Season Highlights Checklist (Curt Schilling)	.05

Exclusives

Randomly inserted into hobby packs, this parallel issue is individually serial numbered on back from within an edition of 100 of each card. Besides the serial number, the inserts are readily apparent by the use of copper metallic foil graphic highlights on front. Series 1 Exclusive cards have the serial number on back in gold foil; Series 2 Exclusives have the number

---

ink-jetted in black. A green-foil parallel of the parallel was issued in quantities of just one card each for Series 1, and 10 cards each for Series 2.

	NM/M
Common Player:	3.00
Stars/Rookies:	15X
Greens (1-255):	Values Undetermined
Greens (266-535):	100X

Crowning Glory

These double-sided cards feature players who reached milestones during the '98 season. There are three cards in the set, with four different versions of each card. The regular version is seeded 1:23 packs. Doubles are numbered to 1,000, Triples numbered to 25 and Home Runs are limited to one each.

		NM/M
Complete Set (3):		22.50
Common Player:		3.00
Inserted 1:23		
Doubles (1,000 Sets):		2X
Triples (25 Sets):		8X
Home Runs (1 Set):		Values Undetermined
CG1	Roger Clemens, Kerry Wood	6.00
CG2	Mark McGwire, Barry Bonds	12.00
CG3	Ken Griffey Jr., Mark McGwire	7.50

Forte

This 30-card set features the top players in the game, highlighted by blue holofoil treatment. Numbers on card backs have an "F" prefix and are seeded 1:23 packs. There are also die-cut parallels to Forte: Double, Triple and Home Run. Doubles are sequentially numbered to 2,000 sets, Triples are limited to 100 numbered sets and Home Runs are limited to 10 numbered sets.

		NM/M
Complete Set (30):		50.00
Common Player:		.50
Inserted 1:23		
Doubles (2,000 Sets):		3X
Triples (100):		15X
Quadruples (10):		40X
1	Darin Erstad	1.50
2	Troy Glaus	1.50
3	Mo Vaughn	.50
4	Greg Maddux	2.50
5	Andres Galarraga	.50
6	Chipper Jones	2.50
7	Cal Ripken Jr.	5.00
8	Albert Belle	.50
9	Nomar Garciaparra	2.50
10	Sammy Sosa	2.50
11	Kerry Wood	1.00
12	Frank Thomas	2.00

13	Jim Thome	1.50
14	Jeff Bagwell	2.00
15	Vladimir Guerrero	2.00
16	Mike Piazza	3.00
17	Derek Jeter	5.00
18	Ben Grieve	.50
19	Eric Chavez	.50
20	Scott Rolen	1.50
21	Mark McGwire	4.00
22	J.D. Drew	1.00
23	Tony Gwynn	2.50
24	Barry Bonds	5.00
25	Alex Rodriguez	4.00
26	Ken Griffey Jr.	3.00
27	Ivan Rodriguez	1.50
28	Juan Gonzalez	1.00
29	Roger Clemens	2.75
30	Andruw Jones	2.00

Game Jersey

A piece of game-worn jersey is framed by a baseball diamond schematic. A round portrait photo appears at top-right, along with the player's uniform number. A small action photo is at bottom center. Backs have another round portrait photo and a statement of authenticity. Game Jersey cards bearing an H1 or H2 designation were hobby-only inserts at a rate of one per 288 packs in the appropriate series. Cards with an HR1 or HR2 notation were found in both hobby and retail packs at a rate of 1:2,500. Autographed versions of some cards were produced, with the edition number noted.

		NM/M
Common Player:		6.00
AB	Adrian Beltre/H1	10.00
EC	Eric Chavez/H2	6.00
JD	J.D. Drew/H2	10.00
JDs	J.D. Drew/ Auto./8/H2	150.00
DE	Darin Erstad/H1	10.00
BF	Brad Fullmer/H2	4.50
JG	Juan Gonzalez/HR1	15.00
BG	Ben Grieve/H1	6.00
KG	Ken Griffey Jr./H1	20.00
KGs	Ken Griffey Jr./ Auto./24/H1	150.00
JR	Ken Griffey Jr./HR2	20.00
JRs	Ken Griffey Jr./ Auto./24/HR2	150.00
TGw	Tony Gwynn/H1	15.00
TH	Todd Helton/H2	15.00
CJ	Charles Johnson/HR1	6.00
CJ	Chipper Jones/H2	15.00
TL	Travis Lee/H1	6.00
GM	Greg Maddux/HR2	15.00
MP	Mike Piazza/HR1	20.00
MR	Manny Ramirez/H2	10.00
AR	Alex Rodriguez/HR1	25.00
IR	Ivan Rodriguez/H1	7.50
NRa	Nolan Ryan/ Astros/H2	25.00
NRas	Nolan Ryan/H2/ Auto./34	450.00
NRb	Nolan Ryan/ Rangers/HR2	25.00
SS	Sammy Sosa/H2	20.00
BT	Bubba Trammell/H2	6.00
FT	Frank Thomas/HR2	15.00
KW	Kerry Wood/HR1	15.00
KWs	Kerry Wood/ Auto./34/HR1	150.00

Grand Slam Record Breakers

These cards were part of an unannounced multi-manufacturer (Fleer, Upper Deck, Topps, Pacific) insert program which was exclusive to Wal-Mart. Each company produced cards of Mark McGwire and Sammy Sosa, along with two other premier sluggers. Each company's cards share a "Power Elite" logo at top and "Home Run Heroes" logo vertically at right.

		NM/M
Complete Set (4):		5.00
Common Player:		1.00
5	Mark McGwire	2.00
6	Sammy Sosa	1.25
7	Ken Griffey Jr.	1.50
8	Frank Thomas	2.00

These gold-foil accented cards were inserts in a limited distribution retail packaging.

		NM/M
Complete Set (10):		7.50
Common Player:		.50
G1	Mark McGwire	1.50
G2	Sammy Sosa	1.50
G3	Ken Griffey Jr.	1.50
G4	Roger Clemens	1.00
G5	Kerry Wood	.75
G6	Cal Ripken Jr.	2.00
G7	Barry Bonds	2.00
G8	David Wells	.50
G9	Sammy Sosa	1.50
G10	Mark McGwire	1.50

Homerun Heroes

These gold-foil enhanced cards were inserted one per specially marked five-card foil pack, plus one as a topper in each tin can of this retail exclusive product. The first six players on the checklist were featured on the cans in which the cards were sold.

		NM/M
Complete Set (10):		10.00
Common Player:		.50
Complete Set Cans (6):		10.00
Common Player Can:		2.00
H1	Ken Griffey Jr.	1.25
H2	Mark McGwire	2.00
H3	Sammy Sosa	1.00
H4	Troy Glaus	.75
H5	Mike Piazza	2.00
H6	Chipper Jones	1.00
H7	Vladimir Guerrero	.75
H8	Frank Thomas	.75
H9	Juan Gonzalez	.50
H10	Alex Rodriguez	2.00
1	Ken Griffey Jr.	2.50
2	Mark McGwire	2.50
3	Sammy Sosa	2.00
4	Troy Glaus	1.50
5	Mike Piazza	2.50
6	Chipper Jones	2.00

Home Run Heroes

These cards were part of an unannounced multi-manufacturer (Fleer, Upper Deck, Topps, Pacific) insert program which was exclusive to Wal-Mart. Each company produced cards of Mark McGwire and Sammy Sosa, along with two other premier sluggers. Each company's cards share a "Power Elite" logo at top and "Home Run Heroes" logo vertically at right.

		NM/M
Complete Set (10):		10.00
Common Player:		.50
S1	Ken Griffey Jr.	1.50
S2	Mark McGwire	1.50
S3	Sammy Sosa	1.00
S4	Cal Ripken Jr.	2.00
S5	Nomar Garciaparra	1.00
S6	Alex Rodriguez	1.50
S7	Kerry Wood	.50
S8	Juan Gonzalez	.50
S9	Derek Jeter	2.00
S10	Greg Maddux	1.00

Piece of History 500 Club Babe Ruth

Limited to a reported 50 pieces and inserted into Series 2 Upper Deck packs, this card

---

Immaculate Perception

Done in a horizontal format, this 27-card set features baseball's most celebrated players. Card fronts are enhanced with copper and silver foil stamping, encasing the player's image. The cards are numbered with an I prefix and are seeded 1:23 packs. There are also three parallel versions: Doubles numbered to 1,000, Triples numbered to 25 and Home Runs which are limited to one.

		NM/M
Complete Set (27):		45.00
Common Player:		.25
Inserted 1:23		
Doubles (1,000 Sets):		1.5X
Triples (25):		8X
Home Runs (1):		Values Undetermined
I1	Jeff Bagwell	2.00
I2	Craig Biggio	.25
I3	Barry Bonds	5.00
I4	Roger Clemens	2.75
I5	Jose Cruz Jr.	.25
I6	Nomar Garciaparra	2.50
I7	Tony Clark	.25
I8	Ben Grieve	.25
I9	Ken Griffey Jr.	3.00
I10	Tony Gwynn	2.50
I11	Randy Johnson	2.00
I12	Chipper Jones	2.00
I13	Travis Lee	.40
I14	Kenny Lofton	.25
I15	Greg Maddux	2.50
I16	Mark McGwire	4.00
I17	Hideo Nomo	1.00
I18	Mike Piazza	3.00
I19	Manny Ramirez	2.00
I20	Cal Ripken Jr.	5.00
I21	Alex Rodriguez	4.00
I22	Scott Rolen	1.50
I23	Frank Thomas	2.00
I24	Kerry Wood	2.00
I25	Larry Walker	.25
I26	Vinny Castilla	.25
I27	Derek Jeter	5.00

Opening Season Superstars

These gold-foil enhanced cards were inserted one per specially marked five-card foil pack, in limited retail-exclusive distribution.

		NM/M
Complete Set (10):		10.00
Common Player:		.50
S1	Ken Griffey Jr.	1.50
S2	Mark McGwire	1.50
S3	Sammy Sosa	1.00
S4	Cal Ripken Jr.	2.00
S5	Nomar Garciaparra	1.00
S6	Alex Rodriguez	1.50
S7	Kerry Wood	.50
S8	Juan Gonzalez	.50
S9	Derek Jeter	2.00
S10	Greg Maddux	1.00

Piece of History 500 Club Babe Ruth

Limited to a reported 50 pieces and inserted into Series 2 Upper Deck packs, this card

---

differs from the Piece of History Ruth bat cards on the photos used and the 500 Club notation.

		NM/M
BR	Babe Ruth	4,000

Babe Ruth Piece of History Bat

Limited to approximately 400, this card has an imbedded chip of a bat from an actual game-used Louisville Slugger swung by the Bambino himself. A "signed" version of this card also exists, which incorporates a cut signature of Ruth along with a piece of his game-used bat; only three exist.

		NM/M
PH	Babe Ruth/Bat	900.00
PHLC	Babe Ruth/Legendary Cut Auto.	25,000

Textbook Excellence

This 30-card set features the game's most fundamentally sound performers. Card fronts have a photo of the featured player on a silver-foil-stamped grid background. Vertically at left is player identification on a brown background. These are seeded 1:23 packs. Three hobby-only parallels were also issued: Double, Triple and Home Run. Doubles are numbered to 2,000 sets, Triples are limited to 100 numbered sets and Home Runs are limited to 10 numbered sets. Cards are numbered with a "T" prefix.

		NM/M
Complete Set (30):		12.50
Common Player:		.25
Inserted 1:4		
Doubles (2,000 Sets):		1.5X
Triples (100):		5X
Quadruples (10):		40X
T1	Mo Vaughn	.25
T2	Greg Maddux	.75
T3	Chipper Jones	.75
T4	Andruw Jones	.60
T5	Cal Ripken Jr.	2.00
T6	Albert Belle	.25
T7	Roberto Alomar	.30
T8	Nomar Garciaparra	.75
T9	Kerry Wood	.30
T10	Sammy Sosa	.75
T11	Greg Vaughn	.25
T12	Jeff Bagwell	.60
T13	Kevin Brown	.25
T14	Vladimir Guerrero	.60
T15	Mike Piazza	.75
T16	Bernie Williams	.25
T17	Derek Jeter	2.00
T18	Ben Grieve	.25
T19	Eric Chavez	.25
T20	Scott Rolen	.50
T21	Mark McGwire	1.50
T22	David Wells	.25
T23	J.D. Drew	.50
T24	Tony Gwynn	.75
T25	Barry Bonds	2.00
T26	Alex Rodriguez	1.50
T27	Ken Griffey Jr.	1.00
T28	Juan Gonzalez	.30
T29	Ivan Rodriguez	.50
T30	Roger Clemens	.85

View to a Thrill

This 30-card set focuses on baseball's best overall athletes. There are two photos of the featured player on the card front, highlighted by silver foil and some embossing. These are inserted 1:7 packs. Numbered parallel sets were produced of: Doubles (2,000), Triples (100) and Quadruples (10).

	NM/M
Complete Set (30):	25.00
Common Player:	.35
Inserted 1:7	
Doubles (2,000 Sets):	1.5X
Triples (100):	4X
Quadruples (10):	30X
V1	Mo Vaughn	.35
V2	Darin Erstad	.40
V3	Travis Lee	.40
V4	Chipper Jones	1.50
V5	Greg Maddux	1.50
V6	Gabe Kapler	.35
V7	Cal Ripken Jr.	3.00
V8	Nomar Garciaparra	1.50
V9	Kerry Wood	.40
V10	Frank Thomas	1.00
V11	Manny Ramirez	1.00
V12	Larry Walker	.35
V13	Tony Clark	.35
V14	Jeff Bagwell	1.00
V15	Craig Biggio	.35
V16	Vladimir Guerrero	1.00
V17	Mike Piazza	2.00
V18	Bernie Williams	.35
V19	Derek Jeter	3.00
V20	Ben Grieve	.35
V21	Eric Chavez	.35
V22	Scott Rolen	.65
V23	Mark McGwire	2.50
V24	Tony Gwynn	1.50
V25	Barry Bonds	3.00
V26	Ken Griffey Jr.	2.00
V27	Alex Rodriguez	2.50
V28	J.D. Drew	.65
V29	Juan Gonzalez	.50
V30	Roger Clemens	1.75

Wonder Years

These inserts look like a throwback to the groovin' '70s, with brightly striped green and pink borders. "Wonder Years" is across the top of the front in yellow. Backs have the player's three best seasons' stats along with a mention of a milestone. The cards are numbered with a WY prefix and are seeded 1:7 packs. There are three parallel versions: Doubles numbered to 1,000, Triples numbered to 25 and Home Runs that are limited to one.

	NM/M
Complete Set (30):	30.00
Common Player:	.50
Inserted 1:7	
Doubles (2,000):	2.5X
Triples (50):	10X
Home Runs (1):	
Values Undetermined	
WY1	Kerry Wood	.75
WY2	Travis Lee	.65
WY3	Jeff Bagwell	1.50
WY4	Barry Bonds	4.00
WY5	Roger Clemens	2.25
WY6	Jose Cruz Jr.	.50
WY7	Andres Galarraga	.50
WY8	Nomar Garciaparra	2.00
WY9	Juan Gonzalez	.75
WY10	Ken Griffey Jr.	2.50
WY11	Tony Gwynn	2.00
WY12	Derek Jeter	4.00
WY13	Randy Johnson	1.50
WY14	Andruw Jones	1.50
WY15	Chipper Jones	2.00
WY16	Kenny Lofton	.50
WY17	Greg Maddux	2.00
WY18	Tino Martinez	.50
WY19	Mark McGwire	3.00
WY20	Paul Molitor	1.50
WY21	Mike Piazza	2.50
WY22	Manny Ramirez	1.50
WY23	Cal Ripken Jr.	4.00
WY24	Alex Rodriguez	3.00
WY25	Sammy Sosa	2.00
WY26	Frank Thomas	1.50
WY27	Mo Vaughn	.50
WY28	Larry Walker	.50
WY29	Scott Rolen	1.00
WY30	Ben Grieve	.50

10th Anniversary Team

This 30-card set commemorates Upper Deck's 10th Anniversary, as collectors selected their favorite players for this set. Regular versions are seeded 1:4 packs, Doubles numbered to 4,000, Triples numbered to 100 and Home Runs which are limited to one set.

	NM/M
Complete Set (30):	20.00
Common Player:	.15
Inserted 1:4	
Doubles (4,000 Sets):	2X
Triples (100):	6X
Home Runs (1):	
Values Undetermined	
X1	Mike Piazza	1.50
X2	Mark McGwire	2.00
X3	Roberto Alomar	.30
X4	Chipper Jones	1.00
X5	Cal Ripken Jr.	3.00
X6	Ken Griffey Jr.	1.50
X7	Barry Bonds	3.00
X8	Tony Gwynn	1.00
X9	Nolan Ryan	3.00
X10	Randy Johnson	.75
X11	Dennis Eckersley	.65
X12	Ivan Rodriguez	.65
X13	Frank Thomas	.75
X14	Craig Biggio	.15
X15	Wade Boggs	1.00
X16	Alex Rodriguez	2.00
X17	Albert Belle	.15
X18	Juan Gonzalez	.40
X19	Rickey Henderson	.75
X20	Greg Maddux	1.00
X21	Tom Glavine	.35
X22	Randy Myers	.15
X23	Sandy Alomar	.15
X24	Jeff Bagwell	.75
X25	Derek Jeter	3.00
X26	Matt Williams	.15
X27	Kenny Lofton	.15
X28	Sammy Sosa	1.00
X29	Larry Walker	.15
X30	Roger Clemens	1.25

Ken Griffey Jr. Supers

These large-format (5"x 7") reproductions of each of Junior's regular-issue UD cards from 1989-98 were issued as a Wal-Mart exclusive in Series 1 UD baseball. Autographed versions of the super-sized Griffey cards were also found in the boxes. The supers were also distributed at the July 1999 National Sports Collectors Convention as a wrapper-redemption premium at the card company's booth. Other than the lack of a hologram on back, the cards are identical 4X blowups of the issued cards.

	NM/M
Complete Set (10):	15.00
Common Player:	2.00
Autographed Card:	75.00
1	Ken Griffey Jr./1989	5.00
156	Ken Griffey Jr./1990	2.00
555	Ken Griffey Jr./1991	2.00
424	Ken Griffey Jr./1992	2.00
355	Ken Griffey Jr./1993	2.00
224	Ken Griffey Jr./1994	2.00
100	Ken Griffey Jr./1995	2.00
200	Ken Griffey Jr./1996	2.00
175	Ken Griffey Jr./1997	2.00
225	Ken Griffey Jr./1998	2.00

Ken Griffey Jr. 1989 Buyback Autograph

One hundred authentically autographed 1989 Ken Griffey Jr. Upper Deck rookie cards were seeded into Series 1 packs. UD bought the cards on the open market, had them autographed by Griffey and added a diamond-shaped authentication hologram on back

	NM/M
Ken Griffey Jr./100	1,250

1999 Upper Deck Black Diamond

This 120-card base set features metallic foil fronts, while card backs have the featured player's vital information along with a close-up photo. The Diamond Debut subset (91-120) are short-printed and seeded 1:4 packs.

	NM/M
Complete Set (120):	30.00
Common Player:	.10
Common Diamond Debut (91-120):	.25
Inserted 1:4	
Double Diamonds (3,000 Each):	3X
Double Diamond Debuts (2,500):	2X
Triple Diamonds (1,500):	6X
Triple Diamond Debuts (1,000):	3X
Pack (6):	2.00
Wax Box (30):	40.00
1	Darin Erstad	.25
2	Tim Salmon	.10
3	Jim Edmonds	.10
4	Matt Williams	.10
5	David Dellucci	.10
6	Jay Bell	.10
7	Andres Galarraga	.10
8	Chipper Jones	1.00
9	Greg Maddux	1.00
10	Andruw Jones	.75
11	Cal Ripken Jr.	2.50
12	Rafael Palmeiro	.65
13	Brady Anderson	.10
14	Mike Mussina	.40
15	Nomar Garciaparra	1.00
16	Mo Vaughn	.10
17	Pedro Martinez	.75
18	Sammy Sosa	1.00
19	Henry Rodriguez	.10
20	Frank Thomas	.75
21	Magglio Ordonez	.40
22	Albert Belle	.10
23	Paul Konerko	.20
24	Sean Casey	.10
25	Jim Thome	.60
26	Kenny Lofton	.10
27	Sandy Alomar Jr.	.10
28	Jaret Wright	.10
29	Larry Walker	.10
30	Todd Helton	.65
31	Vinny Castilla	.10
32	Tony Clark	.10
33	Damion Easley	.10
34	Mark Kotsay	.10
35	Derek Lee	.50
36	Moises Alou	.10
37	Jeff Bagwell	.75
38	Craig Biggio	.10
39	Randy Johnson	.75
40	Dean Palmer	.10
41	Johnny Damon	.35
42	Chan Ho Park	.10
43	Raul Mondesi	.10
44	Gary Sheffield	.40
45	Jeromy Burnitz	.10
46	Marquis Grissom	.10
47	Jeff Cirillo	.10
48	Paul Molitor	.75
49	Todd Walker	.10
50	Vladimir Guerrero	.75
51	Brad Fullmer	.10
52	Mike Piazza	1.50
53	Hideo Nomo	.40
54	Carlos Baerga	.10
55	John Olerud	.10
56	Derek Jeter	2.50
57	Hideki Irabu	.10
58	Tino Martinez	.10
59	Bernie Williams	.10
60	Miguel Tejada	.25
61	Ben Grieve	.10
62	Jason Giambi	.55
63	Scott Rolen	.60
64	Doug Glanville	.10
65	Desi Relaford	.10
66	Tony Womack	.10
67	Jason Kendall	.10
68	Jose Guillen	.10
69	Tony Gwynn	1.00
70	Ken Caminiti	.10
71	Greg Vaughn	.10
72	Kevin Brown	.10
73	Barry Bonds	2.50
74	J.T. Snow	.10
75	Jeff Kent	.10
76	Ken Griffey Jr.	1.50
77	Alex Rodriguez	2.00
78	Edgar Martinez	.10
79	Jay Buhner	.10
80	Mark McGwire	2.00
81	Delino DeShields	.10
82	Brian Jordan	.10
83	Quinton McCracken	.10
84	Fred McGriff	.10
85	Juan Gonzalez	.40
86	Ivan Rodriguez	.65
87	Will Clark	.10
88	Roger Clemens	1.25
89	Jose Cruz Jr.	.10
90	Babe Ruth	2.00
91	Troy Glaus (Diamond Debut)	1.00
92	Jarrod Washburn (Diamond Debut)	.25
93	Travis Lee (Diamond Debut)	.75
94	Bruce Chen (Diamond Debut)	.25
95	Mike Caruso (Diamond Debut)	.25
96	Jim Parque (Diamond Debut)	.25
97	Kerry Wood (Diamond Debut)	.50
98	Jeremy Giambi (Diamond Debut)	.25
99	Matt Anderson (Diamond Debut)	.25
100	Seth Greisinger (Diamond Debut)	.25
101	Gabe Alvarez (Diamond Debut)	.25
102	Rafael Medina (Diamond Debut)	.25
103	Daryle Ward (Diamond Debut)	.25
104	Alex Cora (Diamond Debut)	.25
105	Adrian Beltre (Diamond Debut)	.50
106	Geoff Jenkins (Diamond Debut)	.25
107	Eric Milton (Diamond Debut)	.25
108	Carl Pavano (Diamond Debut)	.25
109	Eric Chavez (Diamond Debut)	.50
110	Orlando Hernandez (Diamond Debut)	.25
111	A.J. Hinch (Diamond Debut)	.25
112	Carlton Loewer (Diamond Debut)	.25
113	Aramis Ramirez (Diamond Debut)	.25
114	Cliff Politte (Diamond Debut)	.25
115	Matt Clement (Diamond Debut)	.25
116	Alex Gonzalez (Diamond Debut)	.25
117	J.D. Drew (Diamond Debut)	.75
118	Shane Monahan (Diamond Debut)	.25
119	Rolando Arrojo (Diamond Debut)	.25
120	George Lombard (Diamond Debut)	.25

Black Diamond Double Diamond

Double Diamonds are the most common parallels to the Black Diamond base set. Cards feature a red metallic-foil background or highlights. Regular-player cards (#1-90) are serially numbered on back from within an edition of 3,000 each. Diamond Debut cards (#91-120) are individually numbered within an edition of 2,500 each.

	NM/M
Complete Set (120):	200.00
Common Player (1-90):	.25
Common Diamond Debut (91-120):	1.00
Stars (1-90):	3X
Diamond Debuts (91-120):	2X

Triple Diamond

Triple Diamonds

Triple Diamonds are the mid-level of scarcity among the parallel inserts to the Black Diamond base cards. They feature yellow metallic-foil backgrounds (1-90) and highlights (91-120). Regular-player cards are serially numbered on back from within an edition of 1,500 each. Diamond Debut cards are individually numbered within an edition of 1,000 each.

	NM/M
Common Player (1-90):	1.00
Common Diamond Debut (91-120):	1.50
Stars (1-90):	6X
Diamond Debuts (91-120):	3X

Quadruple Diamond

Quadruple Diamonds are the scarcest of the parallel inserts to the Black Diamond base cards. The regular player cards (#1-90) feature a green metallic-foil background and are serially numbered on back from within an edition of 150 each. Diamond Debut cards (#91-120) also feature green foil highlights on front and are individually numbered within an edition of 100 each. Quad Diamond cards of Sosa, Griffey and McGwire were limited to the number of home runs each hit the previous season.

	NM/M
Common Player (1-90):	4.00
Production 150 each.	
Common Diamond Debut (91-120):	6.00
Production 100 each.	
Stars (1-90):	25X
Diamond Debuts (91-120):	8X
18	Sammy Sosa/66	50.00
76	Ken Griffey Jr. /56	60.00
80	Mark McGwire/70	75.00

A Piece of History

This six-card set features green metallic foil fronts with a diamond-shaped piece of game-used bat from the featured player embedded on the card front. No insertion ratio was released.

	NM/M
Common Player:	5.00
JG	Juan Gonzalez	7.50
TG	Tony Gwynn	10.00
BW	Bernie Williams	5.00
MM	Mark McGwire	200.00
MV	Mo Vaughn	5.00
SS	Sammy Sosa	25.00

Diamond Dominance

This 30-card set features full-bleed metallic foil fronts and includes the top stars of the game along with Babe Ruth. Each card is numbered with a "D" prefix and is limited to 1,500 sequentially numbered sets.

		NM/M
Complete Set (30):		65.00
Common Player:		.50
Production 1,500 Sets		
D01	Kerry Wood	1.00
D02	Derek Jeter	6.00
D03	Alex Rodriguez	5.00
D04	Frank Thomas	2.00
D05	Jeff Bagwell	2.00
D06	Mo Vaughn	.50
D07	Ivan Rodriguez	1.50
D08	Cal Ripken Jr.	6.00
D09	Rolando Arrojo	.50
D10	Chipper Jones	3.00
D11	Kenny Lofton	.50
D12	Paul Konerko	.75
D13	Mike Piazza	4.00
D14	Ben Grieve	.50
D15	Nomar Garciaparra	3.00
D16	Travis Lee	.65
D17	Scott Rolen	1.00
D18	Juan Gonzalez	3.00
D19	Tony Gwynn	3.00
D20	Tony Clark	.50
D21	Roger Clemens	3.50
D22	Sammy Sosa	3.00
D23	Larry Walker	.50
D24	Ken Griffey Jr.	4.00
D25	Mark McGwire	6.00
D26	Barry Bonds	6.00
D27	Vladimir Guerrero	2.00
D28	Tino Martinez	.50
D29	Greg Maddux	3.00
D30	Babe Ruth	5.00

Mystery Numbers

The player's card number determines scarcity in this hobby-only insert set. The basic set has an action photo set against a silver-foil background of repeated numerals. Backs have a portrait photo and significant stat numbers from the 1998 season. Each base Mystery Numbers card is individually numbered within an edition of 100 cards times the card number within the 30-card set (i.e., card #24 has an edition of 2,400) for a total of 46,500 cards. An emerald version of the Mystery Numbers cards has a total issue of 465 cards, with cards issued to a limit of the player's card number multiplied by 1.

		NM/M
Complete Set (30):		100.00
Common Player:		.75
M1	Babe Ruth/100	25.00
M2	Ken Griffey Jr./200	12.50

M3	Kerry Wood/300	4.00
M4	Mark McGwire/400	12.50
M5	Alex Rodriguez/500	12.50
M6	Chipper Jones/600	6.00
M7	Nomar Garciaparra/700	6.00
M8	Derek Jeter/800	10.00
M9	Mike Piazza/900	6.00
M10	Roger Clemens/1,000	4.50
M11	Greg Maddux/1,100	4.00
M12	Scott Rolen/1,200	1.25
M13	Cal Ripken Jr./1,300	7.50
M14	Ben Grieve/1,400	.75
M15	Troy Glaus/1,500	3.00
M16	Sammy Sosa/1,600	4.50
M17	Darin Erstad/1,700	1.25
M18	Juan Gonzalez/1,800	1.25
M19	Pedro Martinez/1,900	1.50
M20	Larry Walker/2,000	.75
M21	Vladimir Guerrero/2,100	1.50
M22	Jeff Bagwell/2,200	1.50
M23	Jaret Wright/2,300	.75
M24	Travis Lee/2,400	.75
M25	Barry Bonds/2,500	6.00
M26	Orlando Hernandez/2,600	.75
M27	Frank Thomas/2,700	1.50
M28	Tony Gwynn/2,800	2.00
M29	Andres Galarraga/2,900	.75
M30	Craig Biggio/3,000	.75

Piece of History 500 Club

A veneer of lumber from one of Mr. October's war clubs is included in this special insert card. A facsimile autograph is also featured on front. A premium version with an authentic autograph serially numbered from within an edition of 44 (his uniform number) was also issued. Backs have a congratulatory authentication message from Upper Deck CEO Richard McWilliam.

	NM/M
Reggie Jackson	165.00
Reggie Jackson/Auto.	500.00

1999 Upper Deck Century Legends

The first 47 cards in the 131-card set are taken from The Sporting News' list of Baseball's 100 Greatest Players. Each card bears a Sporting News photo of the featured player and his ranking in silver and copper foil. The next 50 cards tout Upper Deck's rankings of the Top 50 contemporary players. Rounding out the base set are two subsets: 21st Century Phenoms and Century Memories. Because of contractual problems, cards #11, 25, 26 and 126 were never issued. A die-cut parallel version of each card, serially numbered to 100 each, was produced as the "Century Collection."

	NM/M
Complete Set (131):	20.00
Common Player:	.10
Century Collection:	20X
Production 100 Sets	
Pack (5):	3.00

		NM/M
Wax Box (24):		60.00
1	Babe Ruth (Top 50)	2.00
1	Babe Ruth (SAMPLE overprint on back)	2.00
2	Willie Mays (Top 50)	1.00
3	Ty Cobb (Top 50)	1.00
4	Walter Johnson (Top 50)	.40
5	Hank Aaron (Top 50)	1.00
6	Lou Gehrig (Top 50)	1.50
7	Christy Mathewson (Top 50)	.40
8	Ted Williams (Top 50)	1.25
9	Rogers Hornsby (Top 50)	.25
10	Stan Musial (Top 50)	.65
12	Grover Alexander (Top 50)	.25
13	Honus Wagner (Top 50)	.40
14	Cy Young (Top 50)	.40
15	Jimmie Foxx (Top 50)	.25
16	Johnny Bench (Top 50)	.50
17	Mickey Mantle (Top 50)	2.00
18	Josh Gibson (Top 50)	.40
19	Satchel Paige (Top 50)	.50
20	Roberto Clemente (Top 50)	1.50
21	Warren Spahn (Top 50)	.20
22	Frank Robinson (Top 50)	.20
23	Lefty Grove (Top 50)	.20
24	Eddie Collins (Top 50)	.10
27	Tris Speaker (Top 50)	.25
28	Mike Schmidt (Top 50)	.50
29	Napoleon LaJoie (Top 50)	.20
30	Steve Carlton (Top 50)	.25
31	Bob Gibson (Top 50)	.25
32	Tom Seaver (Top 50)	.25
33	George Sisler (Top 50)	.10
34	Barry Bonds (Top 50)	1.50
35	Joe Jackson (Top 50)	1.25
36	Bob Feller (Top 50)	.25
37	Hank Greenberg (Top 50)	.25
38	Ernie Banks (Top 50)	.40
39	Greg Maddux (Top 50)	.75
40	Yogi Berra (Top 50)	.40
41	Nolan Ryan (Top 50)	2.00
42	Mel Ott (Top 50)	.25
43	Al Simmons (Top 50)	.10
44	Jackie Robinson (Top 50)	1.25
45	Carl Hubbell (Top 50)	.25
46	Charley Gehringer (Top 50)	.10
47	Buck Leonard (Top 50)	.10
48	Reggie Jackson (Top 50)	.40
49	Tony Gwynn (Top 50)	.75
50	Roy Campanella (Top 50)	.40
51	Ken Griffey Jr. (Contemporaries)	1.00
52	Barry Bonds (Contemporaries)	1.50
53	Roger Clemens (Contemporaries)	.85
54	Tony Gwynn (Contemporaries)	.75
55	Cal Ripken Jr. (Contemporaries)	1.50
56	Greg Maddux (Contemporaries)	.75
57	Frank Thomas (Contemporaries)	.65
58	Mark McGwire (Contemporaries)	1.25
59	Mike Piazza (Contemporaries)	1.00
60	Wade Boggs (Contemporaries)	.75
61	Alex Rodriguez (Contemporaries)	1.25
62	Juan Gonzalez (Contemporaries)	.30
63	Mo Vaughn (Contemporaries)	.10
64	Albert Belle (Contemporaries)	.10
65	Sammy Sosa (Contemporaries)	.75
66	Nomar Garciaparra (Contemporaries)	.75
67	Derek Jeter (Contemporaries)	1.50
68	Kevin Brown (Contemporaries)	.10
69	Jose Canseco (Contemporaries)	.35
70	Randy Johnson (Contemporaries)	.60
71	Tom Glavine (Contemporaries)	.25
72	Barry Larkin (Contemporaries)	.10
73	Curt Schilling (Contemporaries)	.25
74	Moises Alou (Contemporaries)	.10
75	Fred McGriff (Contemporaries)	.10
76	Pedro Martinez (Contemporaries)	.65
77	Andres Galarraga (Contemporaries)	.10

78	Will Clark (Contemporaries)	.10
79	Larry Walker (Contemporaries)	.10
80	Ivan Rodriguez (Contemporaries)	.50
81	Chipper Jones (Contemporaries)	.75
82	Jeff Bagwell (Contemporaries)	.60
83	Craig Biggio (Contemporaries)	.10
84	Kerry Wood (Contemporaries)	.35
85	Roberto Alomar (Contemporaries)	.20
86	Vinny Castilla (Contemporaries)	.10
87	Kenny Lofton (Contemporaries)	.10
88	Rafael Palmeiro (Contemporaries)	.10
89	Manny Ramirez (Contemporaries)	.60
90	David Wells (Contemporaries)	.10
91	Mark Grace (Contemporaries)	.10
92	Bernie Williams (Contemporaries)	.10
93	David Cone (Contemporaries)	.10
94	John Olerud (Contemporaries)	.10
95	John Smoltz (Contemporaries)	.10
96	Tino Martinez (Contemporaries)	.10
97	Raul Mondesi (Contemporaries)	.10
98	Gary Sheffield (Contemporaries)	.35
99	Orel Hershiser (Contemporaries)	.10
100	Rickey Henderson (Contemporaries)	.65
101	J.D. Drew (21st Century Phenoms)	.50
102	Troy Glaus (21st Century Phenoms)	.50
103	Nomar Garciaparra (21st Century Phenoms)	.75
104	Scott Rolen (21st Century Phenoms)	.45
105	Ryan Minor (21st Century Phenoms)	.10
106	Travis Lee (21st Century Phenoms)	.20
107	Roy Halladay (21st Century Phenoms)	.10
108	Carlos Beltran (21st Century Phenoms)	.50
109	Alex Rodriguez (21st Century Phenoms)	1.25
110	Eric Chavez (21st Century Phenoms)	.20
111	Vladimir Guerrero (21st Century Phenoms)	.60
112	Ben Grieve (21st Century Phenoms)	.15
113	Kerry Wood (21st Century Phenoms)	.30
114	Alex Gonzalez (21st Century Phenoms)	.10
115	Darin Erstad (21st Century Phenoms)	.30
116	Derek Jeter (21st Century Phenoms)	1.50
117	Jaret Wright (21st Century Phenoms)	.10
118	Jose Cruz Jr. (21st Century Phenoms)	.10
119	Chipper Jones (21st Century Phenoms)	.75
120	Gabe Kapler (21st Century Phenoms)	.10
121	Satchel Paige (Century Memories)	.50
122	Willie Mays (Century Memories)	1.00
123	Roberto Clemente (Century Memories)	1.50
124	Lou Gehrig (Century Memories)	1.50
125	Mark McGwire (Century Memories)	1.25
127	Bob Gibson (Century Memories)	.25
128	Johnny Vander Meer (Century Memories)	.10
129	Walter Johnson (Century Memories)	.25
130	Ty Cobb (Century Memories)	.75
131	Don Larsen (Century Memories)	.20
132	Jackie Robinson (Century Memories)	1.00
133	Tom Seaver (Century Memories)	.25
134	Johnny Bench (Century Memories)	.35
135	Frank Robinson (Century Memories)	.25

All-Century Team

This 10-card set highlights Upper Deck's all-time all-star team. These were seeded 1:23 packs.

		NM/M
Complete Set (10):		30.00
Common Player:		2.50
Inserted 1:23		
1	Babe Ruth	7.50
2	Ty Cobb	3.50
3	Willie Mays	3.50
4	Lou Gehrig	6.00
5	Jackie Robinson	5.00
6	Mike Schmidt	2.50
7	Ernie Banks	2.50
8	Johnny Bench	2.50
9	Cy Young	2.50
10	Lineup Sheet	.25

Century Artifacts

A total of nine cards were inserted, redeemable for memorabilia from some of the top players of the century. Due to the limited nature of these one-of-one inserts and the fact that most or all were redeemed, no pricing is assigned. Each cut signature was framed with the player's Century Legends card.

Century MVPs

This collection selects 100 cards from Upper Deck's '99 MVP brand and adds a rainbow-foil shift to each card. These are limited to only one numbered set.

One Set Produced
Values Undetermined

Epic Milestones

This nine-card set showcases nine of the most impressive milestones established in major league history. Each card is numbered with an "EM" prefix and are seeded 1:12 packs. Because of a contractual dispute, card #1 was never issued.

		NM/M
Complete Set (9):		5.00
Common Player:		.25
Inserted 1:12		
2	Jackie Robinson	.75
3	Nolan Ryan	1.00
4	Mark McGwire	.75
5	Roger Clemens	.60
6	Sammy Sosa	.50
7	Cal Ripken Jr.	1.00
8	Rickey Henderson	.25
9	Hank Aaron	.75
10	Barry Bonds	1.00

Epic Signatures

This 30-card set features autographs from retired and current stars on a horizonal format. A player portrait appears over a ballpark background on front. The portrait is repeated on

back with a statement of authenticity. Cards are numbered with player initials. These autographed cards are seeded 1:24 packs. Exchange cards of Fisk, Bench, Berra and McCovey were originally inserted into packs and had to be mailed in for the autographed card. They are valued about 10 percent of the corresponding signed card.

		NM/M
Common Player:		10.00
Inserted 1:24		
EB	Ernie Banks	65.00
JB	Johnny Bench	40.00
YB	Yogi Berra	50.00
BB	Barry Bonds	180.00
SC	Steve Carlton	20.00
BD	Bucky Dent	10.00
BF	Bob Feller	15.00
CF	Carlton Fisk	25.00
BG	Bob Gibson	25.00
JG	Juan Gonzalez	20.00
Jr.	Ken Griffey Jr.	100.00
Sr.	Ken Griffey Sr.	10.00
VG	Vladimir Guerrero	30.00
TG	Tony Gwynn	40.00
RJ	Reggie Jackson	40.00
HK	Harmon Killebrew	30.00
DL	Don Larsen	15.00
GM	Greg Maddux	100.00
EMa	Eddie Mathews	80.00
BM	Bill Mazeroski	30.00
WMc	Willie McCovey	20.00
SM	Stan Musial	80.00
FR	Frank Robinson	30.00
AR	Alex Rodriguez	150.00
NR	Nolan Ryan	150.00
MS	Mike Schmidt	50.00
TS	Tom Seaver	40.00
WS	Warren Spahn	50.00
FT	Frank Thomas	50.00
BT	Bobby Thomson	10.00

Century Epic Signatures

This 32-card autographed set features signatures from retired and current stars. The cards have a horizontal format and have gold foil stamping. Each card is hand numbered to 100.

		NM/M
Common Player:		20.00
Production 100 Sets		
EB	Ernie Banks	85.00
JB	Johnny Bench	90.00
YB	Yogi Berra	75.00
BB	Barry Bonds	240.00
SC	Steve Carlton	50.00
BD	Bucky Dent	20.00
BF	Bob Feller	50.00
CF	Carlton Fisk	40.00
BG	Bob Gibson	60.00
JG	Juan Gonzalez	60.00
Jr.	Ken Griffey Jr.	165.00
Sr.	Ken Griffey Sr.	20.00
VG	Vladimir Guerrero	70.00
TG	Tony Gwynn	90.00
RJ	Reggie Jackson	60.00
HK	Harmon Killebrew	75.00
DL	Don Larsen	30.00
GM	Greg Maddux	150.00
EMa	Eddie Mathews	90.00
WM	Willie Mays	300.00
BM	Bill Mazeroski	25.00
WMc	Willie McCovey	50.00
SM	Stan Musial	100.00
FR	Frank Robinson	50.00
AR	Alex Rodriguez	200.00
NR	Nolan Ryan	200.00
MS	Mike Schmidt	125.00
TS	Tom Seaver	75.00
WS	Warren Spahn	80.00
FT	Frank Thomas	80.00
BT	Bobby Thomson	20.00
TW	Ted Williams	750.00

Jerseys of the Century

This nine-card set features a swatch of game-worn jersey from the featured current and retired player.

		NM/M
Common Player:		12.50
Inserted 1:418		
GB	George Brett	25.00
RC	Roger Clemens	25.00
TG	Tony Gwynn	20.00
GM	Greg Maddux	20.00
EM	Eddie Murray	15.00
NR	Nolan Ryan	90.00
MS	Mike Schmidt	25.00
OZ	Ozzie Smith	20.00
DW	Dave Winfield	15.00

Legendary Cuts

A total of nine of these one-fo-one inserts exist. These are actual "cut" signatures from some of baseball's all-time greats.

		NM/M
Values Undetermined		
CY	Cy Young	
	(11/00 auction)	1,850

Memorable Shots

This 10-card insert set focuses on the most memorable home runs launched during this century. The player's image is framed in an embossed foil, frame-like design. These are seeded 1:12 packs, each card back is numbered with an "HR" prefix.

		NM/M
Complete Set (10):		15.00
Common Player:		.50
Inserted 1:12		
1	Babe Ruth	5.00
2	Bobby Thomson	1.00
3	Kirk Gibson	.50
4	Carlton Fisk	.50
5	Bill Mazeroski	1.00
6	Bucky Dent	.50
7	Mark McGwire	2.00
8	Mickey Mantle	5.00
9	Joe Carter	.50
10	Mark McGwire	2.00

500 Club Piece History

This Jimmie Foxx insert has a piece of of a game-used Louisville Slugger once swung by Foxx, embedded into the card front. An estimated 350 cards of this one exist.

		NM/M
JF	Jimmie Foxx	125.00

1999 Upper Deck Challengers for 70

Celebrating Mark McGwire's record-setting season of 1998, and featuring those who would chase his single-season home run crown in 1999, Upper Deck issued this specialty product. The base set of 90 cards is fractured into subsets of Power Elite (#1-10), Power Corps (#11-40), Rookie Power (#41-45), and Home Run Highlights (#46-90). Several styles of inserts and numbered parallels were included in the 5-card foil packs. A parallel set with each card serially numbered to 600 was also issued, titled "Challengers Edition."

		NM/M
Complete Set (90):		15.00
Common Player:		.05
Challenger's Edition (600 Sets):		5X
Pack (5):		2.00
Wax Box (20):		25.00
1	Mark McGwire (Power Elite)	1.50
2	Sammy Sosa (Power Elite)	1.00
3	Ken Griffey Jr. (Power Elite)	1.25
4	Alex Rodriguez (Power Elite)	1.50
5	Albert Belle (Power Elite)	.05
6	Mo Vaughn (Power Elite)	.05
7	Mike Piazza (Power Elite)	1.25
8	Frank Thomas (Power Elite)	.75
9	Juan Gonzalez (Power Elite)	.35
10	Barry Bonds (Power Elite)	2.00
11	Rafael Palmeiro (Power Corps)	.60
12	Jose Canseco (Power Corps)	.50
13	Nomar Garciaparra (Power Corps)	1.00
14	Carlos Delgado (Power Corps)	.20
15	Brian Jordan (Power Corps)	.05
16	Vladimir Guerrero (Power Corps)	.65
17	Vinny Castilla (Power Corps)	.05
18	Chipper Jones (Power Corps)	1.00
19	Jeff Bagwell (Power Corps)	.65
20	Moises Alou (Power Corps)	.05
21	Tony Clark (Power Corps)	.05
22	Jim Thome (Power Corps)	.50
23	Tino Martinez (Power Corps)	.05
24	Greg Vaughn (Power Corps)	.05
25	Javy Lopez (Power Corps)	.05
26	Jeromy Burnitz (Power Corps)	.05
27	Cal Ripken Jr. (Power Corps)	2.00
28	Manny Ramirez (Power Corps)	.65
29	Darin Erstad (Power Corps)	.25
30	Ken Caminiti (Power Corps)	.05
31	Edgar Martinez (Power Corps)	.05
32	Ivan Rodriguez (Power Corps)	.60
33	Larry Walker (Power Corps)	.05
34	Todd Helton (Power Corps)	.60
35	Andruw Jones (Power Corps)	.65
36	Ray Lankford (Power Corps)	.05
37	Travis Lee (Power Corps)	.10
38	Raul Mondesi (Power Corps)	.05
39	Scott Rolen (Power Corps)	.50
40	Ben Grieve (Power Corps)	.05
41	J.D. Drew (Rookie Power)	.50
42	Troy Glaus (Rookie Power)	.60
43	Eric Chavez (Rookie Power)	.10
44	Gabe Kapler (Rookie Power)	.05
45	Michael Barrett (Rookie Power)	.05
46	Mark McGwire (HR Highlights)	.75
47	Jose Canseco (HR Highlights)	.25
48	Greg Vaughn (HR Highlights)	.05
49	Albert Belle (HR Highlights)	.05
50	Mark McGwire (HR Highlights)	.75
51	Vinny Castilla (HR Highlights)	.05
52	Vladimir Guerrero (HR Highlights)	.35
53	Andres Galarraga (HR Highlights)	.05
54	Rafael Palmeiro (HR Highlights)	.30
55	Juan Gonzalez (HR Highlights)	.20
56	Ken Griffey Jr. (HR Highlights)	.60
57	Barry Bonds (HR Highlights)	1.00
58	Mo Vaughn (HR Highlights)	.05
59	Nomar Garciaparra (HR Highlights)	.50
60	Tino Martinez (HR Highlights)	.05
61	Mark McGwire (HR Highlights)	.75
62	Mark McGwire (HR Highlights)	.75
63	Mark McGwire (HR Highlights)	.75
64	Mark McGwire (HR Highlights)	.75
65	Mark McGwire (HR Highlights)	.75
66	Sammy Sosa (HR Highlights)	.50
67	Mark McGwire (HR Highlights)	.75
68	Mark McGwire (HR Highlights)	.75
69	Mark McGwire (HR Highlights)	.75
70	Todd Helton (HR Highlights)	.75
71	Mark McGwire (HR Highlights)	.75
72	Scott Brosius (HR Highlights)	.05
73	Tony Gwynn (HR Highlights)	.40
74	Chipper Jones (HR Highlights)	.50
75	Jeff Bagwell (HR Highlights)	.35
76	Moises Alou (HR Highlights)	.05
77	Manny Ramirez (HR Highlights)	.35
78	Carlos Delgado (HR Highlights)	.05
79	Kerry Wood (HR Highlights)	.20
80	Ken Griffey Jr. (HR Highlights)	.60
81	Cal Ripken Jr. (HR Highlights)	1.00
82	Alex Rodriguez (HR Highlights)	.75
83	Barry Bonds (HR Highlights)	1.00
84	Ken Griffey Jr. (HR Highlights)	.60
85	Travis Lee (HR Highlights)	.15
86	George Lombard (HR Highlights)	.05
87	Michael Barrett (HR Highlights)	.05
88	Jeremy Giambi (HR Highlights)	.05
89	Troy Glaus (HR Highlights)	.30
90	J.D. Drew (HR Highlights)	.25

Challengers Insert

Found one per pack, this insert series identifies 30 top

contenders for the 1999 home run crown. Action photos on front are highlighted by red graphics and silver-foil. Backs repeat a detail of the front photo and present a capsule of the player's 1998 season. Cards have a "C" prefix to the number. A parallel edition, utilizing refractive foil details on front, is serially numbered within an edition of 70 each.

		NM/M
Complete Set (30):		9.00
Common Player:		.15
Parallel Edition (70 Sets):		15X
1	Mark McGwire	1.00
2	Sammy Sosa	.65
3	Ken Griffey Jr.	.75
4	Alex Rodriguez	1.00
5	Albert Belle	.15
6	Mo Vaughn	.15
7	Mike Piazza	.75
8	Frank Thomas	.50
9	Juan Gonzalez	.25
10	Barry Bonds	1.50
11	Rafael Palmeiro	.35
12	Nomar Garciaparra	.65
13	Vladimir Guerrero	.45
14	Vinny Castilla	.15
15	Chipper Jones	.60
16	Jeff Bagwell	.45
17	Moises Alou	.15
18	Tony Clark	.15
19	Jim Thome	.35
20	Tino Martinez	.15
21	Greg Vaughn	.15
22	Manny Ramirez	.45
23	Darin Erstad	.25
24	Ken Caminiti	.15
25	Ivan Rodriguez	.35
26	Andruw Jones	.45
27	Travis Lee	.25
28	Scott Rolen	.35
29	Ben Grieve	.15
30	J.D. Drew	.35

70 Longball Legends

Top home-run threats are featured in this insert series. The action photos on front are repeated in a diffused version on back, where they are joined by a second photo and a bar-graph of the player's home run production in recent seasons. Cards have an "L" prefix to the number. Stated odds of picking a Longball Legends card are one per 39 packs.

		NM/M
Complete Set (30):		20.00
Common Player:		.50
1	Ken Griffey Jr.	1.50
2	Mark McGwire	2.00
3	Sammy Sosa	1.00
4	Cal Ripken Jr.	2.50
5	Barry Bonds	2.50
6	Larry Walker	.50
7	Fred McGriff	.50
8	Alex Rodriguez	2.00

9	Frank Thomas	.75
10	Juan Gonzalez	.60
11	Jeff Bagwell	.75
12	Mo Vaughn	.50
13	Albert Belle	.50
14	Mike Piazza	1.50
15	Vladimir Guerrero	.75
16	Chipper Jones	1.00
17	Ken Caminiti	.50
18	Rafael Palmeiro	.65
19	Nomar Garciaparra	1.00
20	Jim Thome	.60
21	Edgar Martinez	.50
22	Ivan Rodriguez	.65
23	Andres Galarraga	.50
24	Scott Rolen	.60
25	Darin Erstad	.65
26	Moises Alou	.50
27	J.D. Drew	.65
28	Andruw Jones	.75
29	Manny Ramirez	.75
30	Tino Martinez	.50

70 Mark on History

The details of Mark McGwire's successful assault on the single-season home run record are captured in this 25-card insert set, found on average of one per five packs. Cards have action photos set against a split red-and-black background and are highlighted in red metallic foil. Backs have details of the home run featured on front, a quote from McGwire and another photo. Cards have an "M" prefix to the number. A parallel edition number to 70 was also issued.

		NM/M
Complete Set (25):		25.00
Common McGwire:		1.50
Parallel:		8X
01-25 Mark McGwire		1.50

70 Piece of History 500

A piece of game-used bat from 500-HR club member Harmon Killebrew is featured on these inserts. Only 350 cards were issued, along with three (his uniform number) authentically autographed versions. Backs have an action photo and a congratulatory authentication message from UD CEO Richard McWilliam.

		NM/M
Harmon Killebrew		120.00
Harmon Killebrew/ Auto.		450.00

70 Swinging/ Fences

Fifteen top sluggers are included in this insert set. The players' power swing is captured in a muted textured-look background. Back has a color portrait photo and an "S" prefix to the card number. Stated insertion rate is one per 19 packs.

		NM/M
Complete Set (15):		15.00
Common Player:		.50

1	Ken Griffey Jr.	1.50
2	Mark McGwire	2.00
3	Sammy Sosa	1.25
4	Alex Rodriguez	2.00
5	Nomar Garciaparra	1.25
6	J.D. Drew	.75
7	Vladimir Guerrero	1.00
8	Ben Grieve	.50
9	Chipper Jones	1.25
10	Gabe Kapler	.50
11	Travis Lee	.60
12	Todd Helton	.75
13	Juan Gonzalez	.60
14	Mike Piazza	1.50
15	Mo Vaughn	.50

70 Autographed Swinging

A total of 2,700 autographed versions of Swinging for the Fences inserts were featured in the Challengers for 70 issue. Only six of the 15 players' cards were included in this premium version.

		NM/M
Complete Set (6):		200.00
Common Player:		5.00
JR	Ken Griffey Jr.	95.00
VG	Vladimir Guerrero	25.00
TH	Todd Helton	15.00
GK	Gabe Kapler	5.00
TL	Travis Lee	7.50
AR	Alex Rodriguez	90.00

1999 Upper Deck UD Choice Previews

A month prior to the release of its new UD Choice brand baseball series, Upper Deck issued this 55-card Preview version. Sold in five-card cello packs for about 75 cents only at retail outlets, the cards are identical to the issued versions of the same players except for the appearance at top front of a gold foil-stamped "PREVIEW."

	NM/M
Complete Set (55):	16.00
Common Player:	.10

46 Tim Salmon .10
48 Chuck Finley .10
50 Matt Williams .10
52 Travis Lee .20
54 Andres Galarraga .10
56 Greg Maddux .75
58 Cal Ripken Jr. 1.50
60 Rafael Palmeiro .50
62 Nomar Garciaparra .75
64 Pedro Martinez .60
66 Kerry Wood .35
67 Sammy Sosa .75
70 Albert Belle .10
72 Frank Thomas .60
74 Pete Harnisch .10
76 Manny Ramirez .60
78 Travis Fryman .10
80 Kenny Lofton .10
82 Larry Walker .10
84 Gabe Alvarez .10
86 Damion Easley .10
88 Mark Kotsay .10
90 Jeff Bagwell .60
93 Craig Biggio .10
94 Larry Sutton .10
96 Johnny Damon .30
98 Gary Sheffield .35
100 Mark Grudzielanek .10
102 Jeff Cirillo .10
104 Mark Loretta .10
106 David Ortiz .40
108 Brad Fullmer .10
110 Vladimir Guerrero .60
112 Brian McRae .10
114 Rey Ordonez .10
115 Derek Jeter 1.50
118 Paul O'Neill .10
120 A.J. Hinch .10
122 Miguel Tejada .15
124 Scott Rolen .45
126 Bobby Abreu .10
128 Jason Kendall .10
130 Mark McGwire 1.25
132 Eli Marrero .10
136 Kevin Brown .10
137 Tony Gwynn .75
138 Bill Mueller .10
140 Barry Bonds 1.50
142 Ken Griffey Jr. 1.00
143 Alex Rodriguez 1.25
146 Rolando Arrojo .10
148 Quinton McCracken .10
150 Will Clark .10
152 Juan Gonzalez .30
154 Carlos Delgado .25

1999 Upper Deck UD Choice

The 155-card base set consists of 110 regular player cards and two subsets, 27 Star Rookies and 18 Cover Glory subset cards. Card fronts have a white border, with the Upper Deck UD Choice logo on the bottom right of the front. Card backs have complete year-by-year stats along with some vital information. Each pack contains 12 cards. A parallel version also exists, called Prime Choice Reserve and are numbered to 100.

	NM/M
Complete Set (155):	7.50
Common Player:	.03
Prime Choice Reserve Stars:	10X
Production 100 Sets	
Pack (12):	.50
Wax Box (36):	10.00

1 Gabe Kapler (Rookie Class) .25
2 Jin Ho Cho (Rookie Class) .05
3 Matt Anderson (Rookie Class) .05
4 Ricky Ledee (Rookie Class) .05
5 Bruce Chen (Rookie Class) .05
6 Alex Gonzalez (Rookie Class) .05
7 Ryan Minor (Rookie Class)
8 Michael Barrett (Rookie Class) .05
9 Carlos Beltran (Rookie Class) .50
10 Ramon Martinez (Rookie Class)
11 Dermal Brown (Rookie Class) .05
12 Robert Fick (Rookie Class) .05
13 Preston Wilson (Rookie Class) .05
14 Orlando Hernandez (Rookie Class) .05
15 Troy Glaus (Rookie Class) .65
16 Calvin Pickering (Rookie Class) .05
17 Corey Koskie (Rookie Class) .05
18 Fernando Seguignol (Rookie Class) .05
19 Carlos Guillen (Rookie Class) .05
20 Kevin Witt (Rookie Class) .05
21 Mike Kinkade (Rookie Class) .05
22 Eric Chavez (Rookie Class) .15
23 Mike Lowell (Rookie Class) .10
24 Adrian Beltre (Rookie Class) .10
25 George Lombard (Rookie Class) .05
26 Jeremy Giambi (Rookie Class) .05
27 J.D. Drew (Rookie Class) .40
28 Mark McGwire (Cover Glory) .60
29 Kerry Wood (Cover Glory) .15
30 David Wells (Cover Glory) .05
31 Juan Gonzalez (Cover Glory) .15
32 Randy Johnson (Cover Glory) .35
33 Derek Jeter (Cover Glory) .75
34 Tony Gwynn (Cover Glory) .45
35 Greg Maddux (Cover Glory) .45
36 Cal Ripken Jr. (Cover Glory) .75
37 Ken Griffey Jr. (Cover Glory) .50
38 Bartolo Colon (Cover Glory) .05
39 Troy Glaus (Cover Glory) .30
40 Ben Grieve (Cover Glory) .05
41 Roger Clemens (Cover Glory) .50
42 Chipper Jones (Cover Glory) .45
43 Scott Rolen (Cover Glory) .25
44 Nomar Garciaparra (Cover Glory) .45
45 Sammy Sosa (Cover Glory) .45
46 Tim Salmon .05
47 Darin Erstad .25
48 Chuck Finley .05
49 Garrett Anderson .05
50 Matt Williams .05
51 Jay Bell .05
52 Travis Lee .10
53 Andruw Jones .05
54 Andres Galarraga .05
55 Chipper Jones .75
56 Greg Maddux .75
57 Javy Lopez .05
58 Cal Ripken Jr. 1.50
59 Brady Anderson .05
60 Rafael Palmeiro .50
61 B.J. Surhoff .05
62 Nomar Garciaparra .75
63 Troy O'Leary .05
64 Pedro Martinez .65
65 Jason Varitek .05
66 Kerry Wood .75
67 Sammy Sosa .75
68 Mark Grace .05
69 Mickey Morandini .05
70 Albert Belle .05
71 Mike Caruso .05
72 Frank Thomas .65
73 Sean Casey .10
74 Pete Harnisch .05
75 Dmitri Young .05
76 Manny Ramirez .65
77 Omar Vizquel .05
78 Travis Fryman .05
79 Jim Thome .40
80 Kenny Lofton .05
81 Todd Helton .50
82 Larry Walker .05
83 Vinny Castilla .05
84 Gabe Alvarez .05
85 Tony Clark .05
86 Damion Easley .05
87 Livan Hernandez .05
88 Mark Kotsay .05
89 Cliff Floyd .05
90 Jeff Bagwell .65
91 Moises Alou .05
92 Randy Johnson .65
93 Craig Biggio .05
94 Larry Sutton .05
95 Dean Palmer .05
96 Johnny Damon .20
97 Charles Johnson .05
98 Gary Sheffield .25
99 Raul Mondesi .05
100 Mark Grudzielanek .05
101 Jeromy Burnitz .05
102 Jeff Cirillo .05
103 Jose Valentin .05
104 Mark Loretta .05
105 Todd Walker .05
106 David Ortiz .35
107 Brad Radke .05
108 Brad Fullmer .05
109 Rondell White .05
110 Vladimir Guerrero .65
111 Mike Piazza 1.00
112 Brian McRae .05
113 John Olerud .05
114 Rey Ordonez .05
115 Derek Jeter 1.50
116 Bernie Williams .05
117 David Wells .05
118 Paul O'Neill .05
119 Tino Martinez .05
120 A.J. Hinch .05
121 Jason Giambi .30
122 Miguel Tejada .10
123 Ben Grieve .05
124 Scott Rolen .50
125 Desi Relaford .05
126 Bobby Abreu .10
127 Jose Guillen .05
128 Jason Kendall .05
129 Aramis Ramirez .05
130 Mark McGwire 1.25
131 Ray Lankford .05
132 Eli Marrero .05
133 Wally Joyner .05
134 Greg Vaughn .05
135 Trevor Hoffman .05
136 Kevin Brown .05
137 Tony Gwynn .75
138 Bill Mueller .05
139 Ellis Burks .05
140 Barry Bonds 1.50
141 Robb Nen .05
142 Ken Griffey Jr. 1.00
143 Alex Rodriguez 1.25
144 Jay Buhner .05
145 Edgar Martinez .05
146 Rolando Arrojo .05
147 Robert Smith .05
148 Quinton McCracken .05
149 Ivan Rodriguez .50
150 Will Clark .05
151 Mark McLemore .05
152 Juan Gonzalez .35
153 Jose Cruz Jr. .05
154 Carlos Delgado .25
155 Roger Clemens .85

Prime Choice Reserve

Each card in the UD Choice set is also found in a parallel version with the words "Prime Choice Reserve" repeated in the background of the photo in refractive foil. On back, the parallels are individually serial numbered within an edition of 100 each.

	NM/M
Common Player:	2.50
Stars:	10X

All-Star Game '99

These super-size (3-1/2" x 5") versions of 1999 UD Choice cards were issued as a boxed set exclusively for retail outlet sales. The cards are in a format identical to the regular-issue UD Choice except for a large All-Star

Game logo in one of the upper corners. Fronts have game-action photos; backs have a small portrait, major league stats and career highlights. The set was sold in a green-foil enhanced box with a special card commemorating the 1999 game July 13 in Boston.

	NM/M
Complete Set (21):	12.50
Common Player:	.35

1 Kenny Lofton .35
2 Pedro Martinez .75
3 Nomar Garciaparra 1.00
4 Ken Griffey Jr. 1.25
5 Derek Jeter 2.00
6 Manny Ramirez .75
7 Ivan Rodriguez .65
8 Bernie Williams .35
9 Cal Ripken Jr. 2.00
10 Jim Thome .60
11 Mike Piazza 1.25
12 Jeff Bagwell .75
13 Craig Biggio .35
14 Mark McGwire 1.50
15 Matt Williams .05
16 Chipper Jones 1.00
17 Tony Gwynn 1.00
18 Sammy Sosa 1.00
19 Raul Mondesi .35
20 Larry Walker .35
--- Header Card .05

Mini Bobbing Head

Inserted 1:5 packs, some of the game's best players can be assembled into a miniature bobbing head figure by following the instructions on the card backs.

	NM/M
Complete Set (30):	15.00
Common Player:	.25
Inserted 1:5	

B1 Randy Johnson .50
B2 Troy Glaus .50
B3 Chipper Jones .65
B4 Cal Ripken Jr. 1.50
B5 Nomar Garciaparra .65
B6 Pedro Martinez .50
B7 Kerry Wood .35
B8 Sammy Sosa .65
B9 Frank Thomas .50
B10 Paul Konerko .35
B11 Omar Vizquel .25
B12 Kenny Lofton .25
B13 Gabe Kapler .25
B14 Adrian Beltre .35
B15 Orlando Hernandez .35
B16 Derek Jeter 1.50
B17 Mike Piazza .75
B18 Tino Martinez .25
B19 Ben Grieve .25
B20 Rickey Henderson .50
B21 Scott Rolen .40
B22 Aramis Ramirez .25
B23 Greg Vaughn .25
B24 Tony Gwynn .65
B25 Barry Bonds 1.50
B26 Alex Rodriguez 1.00
B27 Ken Griffey Jr. .75
B28 Mark McGwire 1.00
B29 J.D. Drew .45
B30 Juan Gonzalez .30

Piece of History 500 Club

A piece from an Eddie Murray game-used bat was incor-

porated into each of these cards, which are limited to 350.

	NM/M
EM Eddie Murray/350	150.00

StarQuest

This four-tiered 30-card set features four different colors for each of the levels. Singles are seeded one per pack and have blue foil etching, Doubles (1:8) have green foil etching, Triples (1:23) have red foil etching and Home Runs are limited to 100 numbered sets with gold foil etching.

	NM/M
Complete Set (30):	7.50
Common Player:	.10
Inserted 1:1	
Green (1:8):	1.5X
Red (1:23):	3X
Gold (100 Sets):	50X

SQ1 Ken Griffey Jr. .60
SQ2 Sammy Sosa .50
SQ3 Alex Rodriguez .75
SQ4 Derek Jeter 1.00
SQ5 Troy Glaus .35
SQ6 Mike Piazza .60
SQ7 Barry Bonds .50
SQ8 Tony Gwynn .50
SQ9 Juan Gonzalez .20
SQ10 Chipper Jones .50
SQ11 Greg Maddux .50
SQ12 Randy Johnson .40
SQ13 Roger Clemens .55
SQ14 Ben Grieve .10
SQ15 Nomar Garciaparra .50
SQ16 Travis Lee .15
SQ17 Frank Thomas .40
SQ18 Vladimir Guerrero .40
SQ19 Scott Rolen .30
SQ20 Ivan Rodriguez .35
SQ21 Cal Ripken Jr. 1.00
SQ22 Mark McGwire .75
SQ23 Jeff Bagwell .40
SQ24 Tony Clark .10
SQ25 Kerry Wood .25
SQ26 Kenny Lofton .10
SQ27 Adrian Beltre .15
SQ28 Larry Walker .10
SQ29 Curt Schilling .25
SQ30 Jim Thome .40

Yard Work

This 30-card set showcases the top power hitters in the game. The right side of the card is covered in bronze foil and stamped with Yard Work. They are numbered with a Y-prefix and seeded 1:13 packs.

	NM/M
Complete Set (30):	20.00
Common Player:	.35
Inserted 1:13	

Y1 Andres Galarraga .35
Y2 Chipper Jones 1.50
Y3 Rafael Palmeiro .35
Y4 Nomar Garciaparra 1.50
Y5 Sammy Sosa 1.50
Y6 Frank Thomas 1.00
Y7 J.D. Drew .75
Y8 Albert Belle .35
Y9 Jim Thome .60
Y10 Manny Ramirez 1.00
Y11 Larry Walker .35
Y12 Vinny Castilla .35
Y13 Tony Clark .35
Y14 Jeff Bagwell 1.00
Y15 Moises Alou .35
Y16 Dean Palmer .35
Y17 Gary Sheffield .50
Y18 Vladimir Guerrero 1.00
Y19 Mike Piazza 1.75
Y20 Tino Martinez .35
Y21 Ben Grieve .35
Y22 Greg Vaughn .35
Y23 Ken Caminiti .35
Y24 Barry Bonds 3.00
Y25 Ken Griffey Jr. 1.75
Y26 Alex Rodriguez 2.25
Y27 Mark McGwire 2.25
Y28 Juan Gonzalez .50
Y29 Jose Canseco .50
Y30 Jose Cruz Jr. .35

1999 Upper Deck Encore

Encore is a 180-card partial parallel of Upper Deck Series 1, utilizing a special holo-foil treatment on each card. The Encore set consists of 90 base cards and three short-printed subsets: 45 Star Rookies (1:4), 30 Homer Odyssey (1:6) and 15 Stroke of Genius (1:8).

	NM/M
Complete Set (180):	75.00
Common Player (1-90):	.05
Common Player (91-135):	.25
Inserted 1:4	
Common Player (136-165):	.35
Inserted 1:6	
Common Player (166-180):	.50
Inserted 1:8	
Gold (1-90):	10X
Gold (91-135):	1.5X
Gold (136-165):	3X
Gold (166-180):	4X
Production 125 Sets	
Pack (6):	1.50
Wax Box (24):	25.00

1 Darin Erstad .25
2 Mo Vaughn .25
3 Travis Lee .15
4 Randy Johnson .60
5 Matt Williams .05
6 John Smoltz .05
7 Greg Maddux .75
8 Chipper Jones .75
9 Tom Glavine .25
10 Andruw Jones .60
11 Cal Ripken Jr. 1.50
12 Mike Mussina .30
13 Albert Belle .05
14 Nomar Garciaparra .75
15 Jose Offerman .05
16 Pedro Martinez .60
17 Trot Nixon .10
18 Kerry Wood .40
19 Sammy Sosa .60
20 Frank Thomas .60
21 Paul Konerko .15
22 Sean Casey .15
23 Barry Larkin .05
24 Greg Vaughn .05
25 Travis Fryman .05
26 Jaret Wright .05
27 Jim Thome .45
28 Manny Ramirez .60
29 Roberto Alomar .25
30 Kenny Lofton .05
31 Todd Helton .60
32 Larry Walker .05
33 Vinny Castilla .05

34	Dante Bichette	.05
35	Tony Clark	.05
36	Dean Palmer	.05
37	Gabe Kapler	.05
38	Juan Encarnacion	.05
39	Alex Gonzalez	.05
40	Preston Wilson	.05
41	Mark Kotsay	.05
42	Moises Alou	.05
43	Craig Biggio	.05
44	Ken Caminiti	.05
45	Jeff Bagwell	.60
46	Johnny Damon	.30
47	Gary Sheffield	.25
48	Kevin Brown	.05
49	Raul Mondesi	.05
50	Jeff Cirillo	.05
51	Jeromy Burnitz	.05
52	Todd Walker	.05
53	Corey Koskie	.05
54	Brad Fullmer	.05
55	Vladimir Guerrero	.60
56	Mike Piazza	1.25
57	Robin Ventura	.05
58	Rickey Henderson	.60
59	Derek Jeter	1.50
60	Paul O'Neill	.05
61	Bernie Williams	.05
62	Tino Martinez	.05
63	Roger Clemens	.85
64	Ben Grieve	.05
65	Jason Giambi	.35
66	Bob Abreu	.10
67	Scott Rolen	.40
68	Curt Schilling	.25
69	Marlon Anderson	.05
70	Kevin Young	.05
71	Jason Kendall	.05
72	Brian Giles	.05
73	Mark McGwire	1.25
74	Fernando Tatis	.05
75	Eric Davis	.05
76	Trevor Hoffman	.05
77	Tony Gwynn	.75
78	Matt Clement	.05
79	Robb Nen	.05
80	Barry Bonds	1.50
81	Ken Griffey Jr.	1.00
82	Alex Rodriguez	1.25
83	Wade Boggs	.75
84	Fred McGriff	.05
85	Jose Canseco	.30
86	Ivan Rodriguez	.50
87	Juan Gonzalez	.30
88	Rafael Palmeiro	.50
89	Carlos Delgado	.25
90	David Wells	.05
91	Troy Glaus (Star Rookies)	1.00
92	Adrian Beltre (Star Rookies)	.50
93	Matt Anderson (Star Rookies)	.25
94	Eric Chavez (Star Rookies)	.40
95	Jeff Weaver RC (Star Rookies)	.50
96	Warren Morris (Star Rookies)	.25
97	George Lombard (Star Rookies)	.25
98	Mike Kinkade (Star Rookies)	.25
99	Kyle Farnsworth RC (Star Rookies)	.25
100	J.D. Drew (Star Rookies)	.50
101	Joe McEwing RC (Star Rookies)	.50
102	Carlos Guillen (Star Rookies)	.25
103	Kelly Dransfeldt RC (Star Rookies)	.25
104	Eric Munson RC (Star Rookies)	.50
105	Armando Rios (Star Rookies)	.25
106	Ramon Martinez (Star Rookies)	.25
107	Orlando Hernandez (Star Rookies)	.45
108	Jeremy Giambi (Star Rookies)	.25
109	Pat Burrell RC (Star Rookies)	2.50
110	Shea Hillenbrand RC (Star Rookies)	1.00
111	Billy Koch (Star Rookies)	.25
112	Roy Halladay (Star Rookies)	.35
113	Ruben Mateo (Star Rookies)	.25
114	Bruce Chen (Star Rookies)	.25
115	Angel Pena (Star Rookies)	.25
116	Michael Barrett (Star Rookies)	.25
117	Kevin Witt (Star Rookies)	.25
118	Damon Minor (Star Rookies)	.25
119	Ryan Minor (Star Rookies)	.25
120	A.J. Pierzynski (Star Rookies)	.25
121	A.J. Burnett RC (Star Rookies)	.50
122	Christian Guzman (Star Rookies)	.25
123	Joe Lawrence (Star Rookies)	.25
124	Derrick Gibson (Star Rookies)	.25
125	Carlos Febles (Star Rookies)	.25
126	Chris Haas (Star Rookies)	.25
127	Cesar King (Star Rookies)	.25
128	Calvin Pickering (Star Rookies)	.25
129	Mitch Meluskey (Star Rookies)	.25
130	Carlos Beltran (Star Rookies)	1.00
131	Ron Belliard (Star Rookies)	.25
132	Jerry Hairston Jr. (Star Rookies)	.25
133	Fernando Seguignol (Star Rookies)	.25
134	Kris Benson (Star Rookies)	.25
135	Chad Hutchinson RC (Star Rookies)	.25
136	Ken Griffey Jr. (Homer Odyssey)	1.50
137	Mark McGwire (Homer Odyssey)	2.00
138	Sammy Sosa (Homer Odyssey)	1.25
139	Albert Belle (Homer Odyssey)	.35
140	Mo Vaughn (Homer Odyssey)	.35
141	Alex Rodriguez (Homer Odyssey)	2.00
142	Manny Ramirez (Homer Odyssey)	.75
143	J.D. Drew (Homer Odyssey)	.50
144	Juan Gonzalez (Homer Odyssey)	.45
145	Vladimir Guerrero (Homer Odyssey)	.75
146	Fernando Tatis (Homer Odyssey)	.35
147	Mike Piazza (Homer Odyssey)	2.00
148	Barry Bonds (Homer Odyssey)	2.50
149	Ivan Rodriguez (Homer Odyssey)	.60
150	Jeff Bagwell (Homer Odyssey)	.75
151	Raul Mondesi (Homer Odyssey)	.35
152	Nomar Garciaparra (Homer Odyssey)	1.25
153	Jose Canseco (Homer Odyssey)	.50
154	Greg Vaughn (Homer Odyssey)	.35
155	Scott Rolen (Homer Odyssey)	.50
156	Vinny Castilla (Homer Odyssey)	.35
157	Troy Glaus (Homer Odyssey)	.65
158	Craig Biggio (Homer Odyssey)	.35
159	Tino Martinez (Homer Odyssey)	.35
160	Jim Thome (Homer Odyssey)	.60
161	Frank Thomas (Homer Odyssey)	1.00
162	Tony Clark (Homer Odyssey)	.35
163	Ben Grieve (Homer Odyssey)	.35
164	Matt Williams (Homer Odyssey)	.35
165	Derek Jeter (Homer Odyssey)	2.50
166	Ken Griffey Jr. (Strokes of Genius)	2.00
167	Tony Gwynn (Strokes of Genius)	1.50
168	Mike Piazza (Strokes of Genius)	2.00
169	Mark McGwire (Strokes of Genius)	2.50
170	Sammy Sosa (Strokes of Genius)	1.50
171	Juan Gonzalez (Strokes of Genius)	.50
172	Mo Vaughn (Strokes of Genius)	.50
173	Derek Jeter (Strokes of Genius)	3.00
174	Bernie Williams (Strokes of Genius)	.50
175	Ivan Rodriguez (Strokes of Genius)	.75
176	Barry Bonds (Strokes of Genius)	3.00
177	Scott Rolen (Strokes of Genius)	.75
178	Larry Walker (Strokes of Genius)	.50
179	Chipper Jones (Strokes of Genius)	1.50
180	Alex Rodriguez (Strokes of Genius)	2.50

FX Gold

This is a 180-card parallel to the base set featuring gold holo-foil treatment and limited to 125 sequentially numbered sets.

	NM/M
Common Player:	1.00
Gold (1-90):	10X
Gold (91-135):	1.5X
Gold (136-165):	3X
Gold (166-180):	4X

Batting Practice Caps

This 15-card set features actual swatch pieces of the highlighted players' batting practice cap embedded into each card. These are seeded 1:750 packs.

		NM/M
Complete Set (15):		85.00
Common Player:		4.00
Inserted 1:750		
CB	Carlos Beltran	8.00
BB	Barry Bonds	30.00
VC	Vinny Castilla	4.00
EC	Eric Chavez	6.00
TC	Tony Clark	4.00
JD	J.D. Drew	6.00
VG	Vladimir Guerrero	8.00
TG	Tony Gwynn	15.00
TH	Todd Helton	8.00
GK	Gabe Kapler	4.00
JK	Jason Kendall	4.00
DP	Dean Palmer	4.00
BH	Frank Thomas	8.00
GV	Greg Vaughn	4.00
TW	Todd Walker	4.00

Driving Forces

This 15-card set is highlighted by holo-foil treatment on the card fronts on a thick card stock. Baseball's top performers are featured in this set and are seeded 1:23 packs. A Gold parallel exists and is limited to 10 sets.

		NM/M
Complete Set (15):		30.00
Common Player:		1.00
Inserted 1:23		
Gold (10 Sets):		30X
D1	Ken Griffey Jr.	3.00
D2	Mark McGwire	4.00
D3	Sammy Sosa	2.50
D4	Albert Belle	1.00
D5	Alex Rodriguez	4.00
D6	Mo Vaughn	1.00
D7	Juan Gonzalez	1.00
D8	Jeff Bagwell	2.00
D9	Mike Piazza	3.00
D10	Frank Thomas	2.00
D11	Barry Bonds	5.00
D12	Vladimir Guerrero	2.50
D13	Chipper Jones	2.50
D14	Tony Gwynn	2.50
D15	J.D. Drew	1.50

McGwired!

This 10-card set salutes baseball's reigning single season home run king. These are seeded 1:23 packs. A gold parallel also is randomly seeded and is limited to 500 sequentially numbered sets. A small photo of the pitcher McGwire hit the historic home run off of is pictured as well.

		NM/M
Complete Set (10):		12.50
Common Card:		1.50
Inserted 1:23		
Parallel:		2X
Production 500 Sets		
1	Mark McGwire, Carl Pavano	1.50
2	Mark McGwire, Michael Morgan	1.50
3	Mark McGwire, Steve Trachsel	1.50
4	Mark McGwire,	2.50
5	Mark McGwire,	2.50
6	Mark McGwire, Scott Elarton	1.50
7	Mark McGwire, Jim Parque	1.50
8	Mark McGwire,	2.50
9	Mark McGwire, Rafael Roque	1.50
10	Mark McGwire, Jaret Wright	1.50

Pure Excitement

This 30-card set features Light F/X technology and includes the top players in baseball. These are seeded 1:7 packs.

		NM/M
Complete Set (30):		35.00
Common Player:		.50
Inserted 1:7		
1	Mo Vaughn	.50
2	Darin Erstad	.75
3	Travis Lee	.65
4	Chipper Jones	1.50
5	Greg Maddux	1.50
6	Gabe Kapler	.50
7	Cal Ripken Jr.	4.00
8	Nomar Garciaparra	1.50
9	Kerry Wood	.75
10	Frank Thomas	1.00
11	Manny Ramirez	.50
12	Larry Walker	.50
13	Tony Clark	.50
14	Jeff Bagwell	1.00
15	Craig Biggio	.50
16	Vladimir Guerrero	.50
17	Mike Piazza	2.00
18	Bernie Williams	.50
19	Derek Jeter	4.00
20	Ben Grieve	.60
21	Eric Chavez	.50
22	Scott Rolen	.75
23	Mark McGwire	3.00
24	Tony Gwynn	1.50
25	Barry Bonds	4.00
26	Ken Griffey Jr.	2.00
27	Alex Rodriguez	3.00
28	J.D. Drew	.75
29	Juan Gonzalez	.60
30	Roger Clemens	1.75

Rookie Encore

This 10-card set highlights the top rookie prospects in 1999, including J.D. Drew and Gabe Kapler. These are seeded 1:23 packs. A parallel version is also randomly seeded and limited to 500 sequentially numbered sets.

		NM/M
Complete Set (10):		17.50
Common Player:		1.00
Inserted 1:23		
FX Gold:		2X
Production 500 Sets		
1	J.D. Drew	2.00
2	Eric Chavez	1.00
3	Gabe Kapler	1.00
4	Bruce Chen	1.00
5	Carlos Beltran	3.00
6	Troy Glaus	5.00
7	Roy Halladay	1.00
8	Adrian Beltre	2.00
9	Michael Barrett	1.00
10	Pat Burrell	5.00

UD Authentics

This six-card autographed set features signatures of Griffey Jr. and Nomar Garciaparra. These are seeded 1:288 packs.

		NM/M
Complete Set (6):		130.00
Common Player:		5.00
Inserted 1:288		
MB	Michael Barrett	4.00
PB	Pat Burrell	10.00
JD	J.D. Drew	12.00
NG	Nomar Garciaparra	70.00
TG	Troy Glaus	12.00
JR	Ken Griffey Jr.	90.00

Upper Realm

This 15-card set focuses on the top stars of the game. Card fronts utilize holo-foil treatment, with the initials UR lightly foiled. Card backs are numbered with a "U" prefix and are seeded 1:11 packs.

		NM/M
Complete Set (15):		13.00
Common Player:		.30
Inserted 1:11		
1	Ken Griffey Jr.	1.25
2	Mark McGwire	1.50
3	Sammy Sosa	.75
4	Tony Gwynn	.75
5	Alex Rodriguez	1.50
6	Juan Gonzalez	.40
7	J.D. Drew	.50
8	Roger Clemens	.85
9	Greg Maddux	.75
10	Randy Johnson	.60
11	Mo Vaughn	.30
12	Derek Jeter	2.00
13	Vladimir Guerrero	.60
14	Cal Ripken Jr.	2.00
15	Nomar Garciaparra	.75

2K Countdown

This set recognizes the countdown to the next century with a salute to baseball's next century of superstars including Derek Jeter and Alex Rodriguez. These are done on a horizontal format and inserted 1:11 packs.

		NM/M
Complete Set (10):		16.00
Common Player:		.75
Inserted 1:11		
1	Ken Griffey Jr.	2.00
2	Derek Jeter	3.00
3	Mike Piazza	2.00
4	J.D. Drew	.75
5	Vladimir Guerrero	1.00
6	Chipper Jones	1.50
7	Alex Rodriguez	2.50
8	Nomar Garciaparra	1.50
9	Mark McGwire	2.50
10	Sammy Sosa	1.50

Ken Griffey Jr. Santa Hat Card

A swatch of red velvet, ostensibly from "a special holiday-worn Santa hat," is featured on this card given to customers and associates of UD. The standard-size card is highlighted in gold-foil front and back and features pictures of the spokesman in a Santa hat on each side, as well.

		NM/M
HH-1	Ken Griffey Jr.	40.00

1999 Upper Deck HoloGrFX Sample

Numbered 60, rather than 56 as in the regular-issue version, this card, which also bears a white "SAMPLE" notation on back, was issued to preview the new UD brand.

		NM/M
60	Ken Griffey Jr.	2.50

1999 Upper Deck HoloGrFX

HoloGrFX was distributed exclusively to retail and the base set is comprised of 60 base cards, each utilizing holographic technology. A parallel gold-enhanced AUsome version is found about once every eight packs.

		NM/M
Complete Set (60):		12.00
Common Player:		.10
AUsome:		1.5X
Inserted 1:8		
Pack (3):		1.00
Wax Box (36):		20.00
1	Mo Vaughn	.10
2	Troy Glaus	.60
3	Tim Salmon	.10
4	Randy Johnson	.65
5	Travis Lee	.25
6	Chipper Jones	.75
7	Greg Maddux	.75
8	Andruw Jones	.65
9	Tom Glavine	.25
10	Cal Ripken Jr.	1.50
11	Albert Belle	.10
12	Nomar Garciaparra	.75
13	Pedro J. Martinez	.65
14	Sammy Sosa	.75
15	Frank Thomas	.75
16	Greg Vaughn	.10
17	Kenny Lofton	.10
18	Jim Thome	.50
19	Manny Ramirez	.65
20	Todd Helton	.60
21	Larry Walker	.10
22	Tony Clark	.10
23	Juan Encarnacion	.10
24	Mark Kotsay	.10
25	Jeff Bagwell	.65
26	Craig Biggio	.10
27	Ken Caminiti	.10
28	Carlos Beltran	.50
29	Jeremy Giambi	.10
30	Raul Mondesi	.10
31	Kevin Brown	.10
32	Jeromy Burnitz	.10
33	Corey Koskie	.10
34	Todd Walker	.10
35	Vladimir Guerrero	.65
36	Mike Piazza	1.00
37	Robin Ventura	.10
38	Derek Jeter	1.50
39	Roger Clemens	.85
40	Bernie Williams	.10
41	Orlando Hernandez	.10
42	Ben Grieve	.10
43	Eric Chavez	.15
44	Scott Rolen	.45
45	Pat Burrell RC	1.50
46	Warren Morris	.10
47	Jason Kendall	.10
48	Mark McGwire	1.25
49	J.D. Drew	.50
50	Tony Gwynn	.75
51	Trevor Hoffman	.10
52	Barry Bonds	1.50
53	Ken Griffey Jr.	1.00
54	Alex Rodriguez	1.25
55	Jose Canseco	.35
56	Juan Gonzalez	.30
57	Ivan Rodriguez	.60
58	Rafael Palmeiro	.60
59	David Wells	.10
60	Carlos Delgado	.25

Future Fame

This six-card set focuses on players who are destined for Hall of Fame greatness. Card fronts feature a horizon-

tal format on a die-cut design. These are seeded 1:34 packs. A parallel Gold (AU) version is also randomly seeded in every 1:432 packs.

		NM/M
Complete Set (6):		15.00
Common Player:		2.50
Inserted 1:34		
Gold:		2X
Inserted 1:210		
1	Tony Gwynn	2.50
2	Cal Ripken Jr.	5.00
3	Mark McGwire	4.00
4	Ken Griffey Jr.	3.50
5	Greg Maddux	2.50
6	Roger Clemens	3.00

Launchers

This 15-card set highlights the top home run hitters on holographic patterned foil fronts, including McGwire and Sosa. These are seeded 1:3 packs. A Gold (AU) parallel version is also seeded 1:105 packs.

		NM/M
Complete Set (15):		20.00
Common Player:		.50
Inserted 1:3		
Gold:		2X
Inserted 1:105		
1	Mark McGwire	3.00
2	Ken Griffey Jr.	2.50
3	Sammy Sosa	2.00
4	J.D. Drew	.75
5	Mo Vaughn	.50
6	Juan Gonzalez	2.00
7	Mike Piazza	2.50
8	Alex Rodriguez	3.00
9	Chipper Jones	2.00
10	Nomar Garciaparra	2.00
11	Vladimir Guerrero	1.00
12	Albert Belle	.50
13	Barry Bonds	4.00
14	Frank Thomas	1.00
15	Jeff Bagwell	1.00

StarView

This nine-card set highlights the top players in the game on a rainbow foil, full bleed design. These are seeded 1:17 packs. A Gold parallel version is also randomly seeded 1:210 packs.

		NM/M
Complete Set (9):		25.00
Common Player:		2.50
Inserted 1:17		
Gold:		2X
Inserted 1:210		

1	Mark McGwire	5.00
2	Ken Griffey Jr.	4.00
3	Sammy Sosa	2.50
4	Nomar Garciaparra	2.50
5	Roger Clemens	3.00
6	Greg Maddux	2.50
7	Mike Piazza	4.00
8	Alex Rodriguez	5.00
9	Chipper Jones	2.50

UD Authentics

This autographed set is done on a horizontal format, with the player signature across the front of a shadow image of the featured player in the background.

		NM/M
Common Player:		4.00
Inserted 1:431		
CB	Carlos Beltran	25.00
BC	Bruce Chen	4.00
JD	J.D. Drew	12.00
AG	Alex Gonzalez	4.00
JR	Ken Griffey Jr.	80.00
CJ	Chipper Jones	50.00
GK	Gabe Kapler	6.00
MK	Mike Kinkade	4.00
CK	Corey Koskie	7.50
GL	George Lombard	4.00
RM	Ryan Minor	4.00
SM	Shane Monahan	4.00

500 Club Piece of History

This two card collection features game-used bat chips from bats swung by Willie McCovey and Eddie Mathews embedded into each card. 350 cards of each player exist. Each player also autographed these inserts to their respective jersey numbers: McCovey (44) and Mathews (41).

	NM/M
Eddie Mathews/350	150.00
Eddie Mathews/ Auto./41	550.00
Willie McCovey 350	120.00
Willie McCovey/ Auto./44	650.00

Hitter.Net Ted Williams

To promote Ted Williams' web site, UD issued this card to persons attending the 1999 All-Star Game July 13 at Fenway Park in Boston. Enclosed in a cellophane wrapper, the 2-1/2" x 3-1/2" card has a sepia photo of a young Williams superimposed on an aerial view of the ballpark. There is a facsimile autograph on front as well as the hitter.net logo. On back are var-

ious advertisements for the service, along with a photo of an autographed baseball.

		NM/M
9	Ted Williams	7.50

1999 UD Ionix

Ionix is a 90-card set that includes a 30-card "Techno" short-printed subset (1:4 packs). Four-card packs sold for $4.99. The first 60 cards of the set are included in a parallel set in which the photo from the back of the regular card was put on the front of a rainbow-foil Reciprocal card. These cards are sequentially numbered to 750. The Techno subset cards were also paralleled on a Reciprocal version sequentially numbered to 100. Due to an error, all Techno card numbers bear the "R" prefix intended for the Reciprocals; actual Reciprocal cards also bear a dot-matrix serial number on front.

		NM/M
Complete Set (90):		45.00
Common Player (1-60):		.25
Common Techno (61-90):		.50
Inserted 1:4		
Reciprocals (1-60):		3X
Production 750 Sets		
Techno Reciprocals (61-90):		1.5X
Production 100 Sets		
Pack (4):		2.00
Wax Box (20):		25.00
1	Troy Glaus	.60
2	Darin Erstad	.50
3	Travis Lee	.35
4	Matt Williams	.25
5	Chipper Jones	.75
6	Greg Maddux	.75
7	Andruw Jones	.65
8	Andres Galarraga	.25
9	Tom Glavine	.35
10	Cal Ripken Jr.	2.00
11	Ryan Minor	.25
12	Nomar Garciaparra	1.00
13	Mo Vaughn	.25
14	Pedro Martinez	.65
15	Sammy Sosa	.75
16	Kerry Wood	.50
17	Albert Belle	.25
18	Frank Thomas	.65
19	Sean Casey	.25
20	Kenny Lofton	.25
21	Manny Ramirez	.65
22	Jim Thome	.60
23	Bartolo Colon	.25
24	Jaret Wright	.25
25	Larry Walker	.25
26	Tony Clark	.25
27	Gabe Kapler	.25
28	Edgar Renteria	.25
29	Randy Johnson	.65
30	Craig Biggio	.65
31	Jeff Bagwell	.65
32	Moises Alou	.25
33	Johnny Damon	.50
34	Adrian Beltre	.35
35	Jeromy Burnitz	.25
36	Todd Walker	.25
37	Corey Koskie	.25
38	Vladimir Guerrero	.65
39	Mike Piazza	1.00
40	Hideo Nomo	.35
41	Derek Jeter	2.00
42	Tino Martinez	.25
43	Orlando Hernandez	.25
44	Ben Grieve	.25
45	Rickey Henderson	.65
46	Scott Rolen	.60
47	Curt Schilling	.35
48	Aramis Ramirez	.25
49	Tony Gwynn	.75
50	Kevin Brown	.25
51	Barry Bonds	2.00
52	Ken Griffey Jr.	1.00
53	Alex Rodriguez	1.50
54	Mark McGwire	1.50
55	J.D. Drew	.60
56	Rolando Arrojo	.25
57	Ivan Rodriguez	.60
58	Juan Gonzalez	.35
59	Roger Clemens	.85
60	Jose Cruz Jr.	.25
61	Travis Lee (Techno)	.65
62	Andres Galarraga (Techno)	.50
63	Andruw Jones (Techno)	1.50
64	Chipper Jones (Techno)	2.00
65	Greg Maddux (Techno)	2.00
66	Cal Ripken Jr. (Techno)	4.00
67	Nomar Garciaparra (Techno)	2.00
68	Mo Vaughn (Techno)	.50
69	Sammy Sosa (Techno)	2.00
70	Frank Thomas (Techno)	1.50
71	Kerry Wood (Techno)	.75
72	Kenny Lofton (Techno)	1.00
73	Manny Ramirez (Techno)	1.50
74	Larry Walker (Techno)	.50
75	Jeff Bagwell (Techno)	1.50
76	Randy Johnson (Techno)	1.50
77	Paul Molitor (Techno)	1.50
78	Derek Jeter (Techno)	4.00
79	Tino Martinez (Techno)	.50
80	Mike Piazza (Techno)	2.50
81	Ben Grieve (Techno)	.50
82	Scott Rolen (Techno)	.75
83	Mark McGwire (Techno)	3.00
84	Tony Gwynn (Techno)	2.00
85	Barry Bonds (Techno)	4.00
86	Ken Griffey Jr. (Techno)	2.50
87	Alex Rodriguez (Techno)	3.00
88	Juan Gonzalez (Techno)	.75
89	Roger Clemens (Techno)	2.25
90	J.D. Drew (Techno)	1.00
100	Ken Griffey Jr. (SAMPLE)	2.50

Reciprocal

Reciprocal is a parallel of the Ionix base set in which the front and back photos have been switched. Card numbers carry an "R" prefix. The first 60 Reciprocal parallels were produced in an edition of 750 each; the Techno subset Reciprocals (#61-90) are an edition of just 100 each.

Stars (1-60):	3X
Stars (61-90):	1.5X

Cyber

This insert set consisted of 25-cards of baseball's superstars and red-hot rookies. One card was inserted every 53 packs.

	NM/M
Complete Set (25):	125.00
Common Player:	2.00

C01	Ken Griffey Jr.	8.00
C02	Cal Ripken Jr.	12.50
C03	Frank Thomas	5.00
C04	Greg Maddux	6.50
C05	Mike Piazza	8.00
C06	Alex Rodriguez	10.00
C07	Chipper Jones	6.50
C08	Derek Jeter	12.50
C09	Mark McGwire	10.00
C10	Juan Gonzalez	2.50
C11	Kerry Wood	2.50
C12	Tony Gwynn	6.50
C13	Scott Rolen	4.00
C14	Nomar Garciaparra	6.50
C15	Roger Clemens	7.00
C16	Sammy Sosa	6.50
C17	Travis Lee	2.00
C18	Ben Grieve	2.00
C19	Jeff Bagwell	4.00
C20	Ivan Rodriguez	4.00
C21	Barry Bonds	12.50
C22	J.D. Drew	4.00
C23	Kenny Lofton	2.00
C24	Andruw Jones	5.00
C25	Vladimir Guerrero	5.00

HoloGrFX

This insert set consisted of 10-cards, and featured only the best players in the game. The cards in this set were holographically enhanced. These cards were rare with one card inserted every 1,500 packs.

	NM/M
Complete Set (10):	800.00
Common Player:	50.00
Inserted 1:1,500	
HG01	Ken Griffey Jr.	100.00
HG02	Cal Ripken Jr.	150.00
HG03	Frank Thomas	75.00
HG04	Greg Maddux	90.00
HG05	Mike Piazza	100.00
HG06	Alex Rodriguez	125.00
HG07	Chipper Jones	90.00
HG08	Derek Jeter	150.00
HG09	Mark McGwire	125.00
HG10	Juan Gonzalez	50.00

Hyper

This insert set featured the top players in baseball, and consisted of 20-cards. Hyper cards were inserted one per nine packs.

	NM/M
Complete Set (20):	37.00
Common Player:	.75
Inserted 1:9	
H01	Ken Griffey Jr.	3.00
H02	Cal Ripken Jr.	4.50
H03	Frank Thomas	1.50
H04	Greg Maddux	2.25
H05	Mike Piazza	3.00
H06	Alex Rodriguez	3.75
H07	Chipper Jones	2.25
H08	Derek Jeter	4.50
H09	Mark McGwire	3.75
H10	Juan Gonzalez	.75
H11	Kerry Wood	1.00
H12	Tony Gwynn	2.25
H13	Scott Rolen	1.00
H14	Nomar Garciaparra	2.25
H15	Roger Clemens	2.75

		NM/M
H16	Sammy Sosa	2.25
H17	Travis Lee	1.00
H18	Ben Grieve	.75
H19	Jeff Bagwell	1.50
H20	J.D. Drew	1.00

Nitro

Baseball's ten most collectible players are featured in this 10-card insert set. Each card features Ionix technology with rainbow foil and a unique color pattern. Nitro cards are inserted one per 18 packs.

		NM/M
Complete Set (10):		18.00
Common Player:		1.00
Inserted 1:18		
N01	Ken Griffey Jr.	2.50
N02	Cal Ripken Jr.	4.00
N03	Frank Thomas	1.50
N04	Greg Maddux	2.00
N05	Mike Piazza	2.50
N06	Alex Rodriguez	3.00
N07	Chipper Jones	2.00
N08	Derek Jeter	4.00
N09	Mark McGwire	3.00
N10	J.D. Drew	1.00

Warp Zone

This 15-card insert set contained a special holographic foil enhancement. Warp Zone cards were inserted one per 216 packs.

		NM/M
Complete Set (15):		195.00
Common Player:		6.00
Inserted 1:216		
WZ1	Ken Griffey Jr.	20.00
WZ2	Cal Ripken Jr.	30.00
WZ3	Frank Thomas	10.00
WZ4	Greg Maddux	15.00
WZ5	Mike Piazza	20.00
WZ6	Alex Rodriguez	25.00
WZ7	Chipper Jones	15.00
WZ8	Derek Jeter	30.00
WZ9	Mark McGwire	25.00
WZ10	Juan Gonzalez	6.00
WZ11	Kerry Wood	6.00
WZ12	Tony Gwynn	15.00
WZ13	Scott Rolen	6.00
WZ14	Nomar Garciaparra	15.00
WZ15	J.D. Drew	6.00

500 Club Piece of History

These cards feature an actual piece of game-used bat from one of Hall-of-Famer Frank Robinson's Louisville Sluggers. Approximately 350

---

were made. Robinson also autographed 20 of his Piece of History inserts.

		NM/M
FR	Frank Robinson/350	165.00
FRA	Frank Robinson/ Auto. 20	650.00

Mark McGwire Tribute Lunchbox

One of many special issues produced by Upper Deck in celebration of McGwire's short-lived season home run record, this 30-card set was sold in a metal lunchbox. Each 2-1/2" x 3-1/2" card has a large action photo on front and a small round portrait, along with the card title. The back has the same photos, with the large photo in a ghosted image as a background for the desciption of the highlight presented on the card.

		NM/M
Complete Boxed Set (30):		10.00
Common Card:		.50
1-30	Mark McGwire	.50

Mark McGwire 70 HR - A New Record

This is one of many special issues from Upper Deck commemorating McGwire's record-breaking 1998 season. Most such cards were produced for retail-only sales, or for home shopping television shows. This blank-back, round-cornered card is 3-1/2" x 2-1/2" and has a flicker-action scene of Big Mac's home run swing.

		NM/M
	Mark McGwire	4.00

Mark McGwire 500 Home Run Card Set

This TV-exclusive product depicts milestone home runs leading up to Big Mac's 500th career clout on Aug. 5, 1999. Sold in a shrink-wrapped decorative box, the basic design of the 2-1/2" x 3-1/2" cards has a central photo, usually an action shot, with a black pinstriped border at left and a red striped border at right. The word "MILESTONES" appears at the top of the picture. In a gray tab at left is a date or year, while his

---

name is in a matching black tab at right. A silver-foil UD logo is at bottom. Backs have a grainy red monochromatic background photo on which are overprinted the details of the pictured blast, along with appropriate logos. Some cards have a silver-foil home run number printed on front. A special card pictures his 1st and 500th career homers. Issue price was about $30.

		NM/M
Complete Boxed Set (30):		7.00
Common Card:		.35
1-30	Mark McGwire	.35

1999 Upper Deck MVP Samples

		NM/M
S3	Ken Griffey Jr.	2.00
S3	Ken Griffey Jr. (Silver signature.)	2.00

1999 Upper Deck MVP

Card fronts of the 220-card set feature silver foil stamping and a white border. Backs feature year-by-year statistics, a small photo of the featured player and a brief career note. MVP was distributed in 36-pack boxes, with a SRP of $1.59 for 10-card packs.

		NM/M
Complete Set (220):		10.00
Common Player:		.05
Silver Script:		1X
Inserted 1:2		
Gold Script:		10X
Production 100 Sets		
Super Script:		30X
Production 25 Sets		
Pack (10):		1.00
Wax Box (36):		20.00
1	Mo Vaughn	.05
2	Tim Belcher	.05
3	Jack McDowell	.05
4	Troy Glaus	.60
5	Darin Erstad	.40
6	Tim Salmon	.15
7	Jim Edmonds	.25
8	Randy Johnson	.60
9	Steve Finley	.05
10	Travis Lee	.15
11	Matt Williams	.05
12	Todd Stottlemyre	.05
13	Jay Bell	.05
14	David Dellucci	.05
15	Chipper Jones	.75
16	Andruw Jones	.60
17	Greg Maddux	.75
18	Tom Glavine	.25
19	Javy Lopez	.05
20	Brian Jordan	.05
21	George Lombard	.05
22	John Smoltz	.05
23	Cal Ripken Jr.	1.50
24	Charles Johnson	.05

25	Albert Belle	.15
26	Brady Anderson	.05
27	Mike Mussina	.35
28	Calvin Pickering	.05
29	Ryan Minor	.05
30	Jerry Hairston Jr.	.05
31	Nomar Garciaparra	1.00
32	Pedro Martinez	.60
33	Jason Varitek	.05
34	Troy O'Leary	.05
35	Donnie Sadler	.05
36	Mark Portugal	.05
37	John Valentin	.05
38	Kerry Wood	.35
39	Sammy Sosa	1.00
40	Mark Grace	.10
41	Henry Rodriguez	.05
42	Rod Beck	.05
43	Benito Santiago	.05
44	Kevin Tapani	.05
45	Frank Thomas	.60
46	Mike Caruso	.05
47	Magglio Ordonez	.40
48	Paul Konerko	.05
49	Ray Durham	.05
50	Jim Parque	.05
51	Carlos Lee	.05
52	Denny Neagle	.05
53	Pete Harnisch	.05
54	Michael Tucker	.05
55	Sean Casey	.15
56	Eddie Taubensee	.05
57	Barry Larkin	.05
58	Pokey Reese	.05
59	Sandy Alomar	.05
60	Roberto Alomar	.25
61	Bartolo Colon	.05
62	Kenny Lofton	.05
63	Omar Vizquel	.05
64	Travis Fryman	.05
65	Jim Thome	.05
66	Manny Ramirez	.60
67	Jaret Wright	.05
68	Darryl Kile	.05
69	Kirt Manwaring	.05
70	Vinny Castilla	.05
71	Todd Helton	.60
72	Dante Bichette	.05
73	Larry Walker	.05
74	Derrick Gibson	.05
75	Gabe Kapler	.05
76	Dean Palmer	.05
77	Matt Anderson	.05
78	Bobby Higginson	.05
79	Damion Easley	.05
80	Tony Clark	.05
81	Juan Encarnacion	.05
82	Livan Hernandez	.05
83	Alex Gonzalez	.05
84	Preston Wilson	.05
85	Derek Lee	.05
86	Mark Kotsay	.05
87	Todd Dunwoody	.05
88	Cliff Floyd	.05
89	Ken Caminiti	.05
90	Jeff Bagwell	.60
91	Moises Alou	.05
92	Craig Biggio	.05
93	Billy Wagner	.05
94	Richard Hidalgo	.05
95	Derek Bell	.05
96	Hipolito Pichardo	.05
97	Jeff King	.05
98	Carlos Beltran	.40
99	Jeremy Giambi	.05
100	Larry Sutton	.05
101	Johnny Damon	.20
102	Dee Brown	.05
103	Kevin Brown	.10
104	Chan Ho Park	.05
105	Raul Mondesi	.05
106	Eric Karros	.05
107	Adrian Beltre	.15
108	Devon White	.05
109	Gary Sheffield	.35
110	Sean Berry	.05
111	Alex Ochoa	.05
112	Marquis Grissom	.05
113	Fernando Vina	.05
114	Jeff Cirillo	.05
115	Geoff Jenkins	.05
116	Jeromy Burnitz	.05
117	Brad Radke	.05
118	Eric Milton	.05
119	A.J. Pierzynski	.05
120	Todd Walker	.05
121	David Ortiz	.05
122	Corey Koskie	.05
123	Vladimir Guerrero	.60
124	Rondell White	.05
125	Brad Fullmer	.05
126	Ugueth Urbina	.05
127	Dustin Hermanson	.05
128	Michael Barrett	.05
129	Fernando Seguignol	.05
130	Mike Piazza	1.00
131	Rickey Henderson	.60
132	Rey Ordonez	.05
133	John Olerud	.05
134	Robin Ventura	.05
135	Hideo Nomo	.60
136	Mike Kinkade	.05
137	Al Leiter	.05
138	Brian McRae	.05
139	Derek Jeter	1.50
140	Bernie Williams	.15
141	Paul O'Neill	.05
142	Scott Brosius	.05

143	Tino Martinez	.05
144	Roger Clemens	.85
145	Orlando Hernandez	.10
146	Mariano Rivera	.10
147	Ricky Ledee	.05
148	A.J. Hinch	.05
149	Ben Grieve	.10
150	Eric Chavez	.15
151	Miguel Tejada	.15
152	Matt Stairs	.05
153	Ryan Christenson	.05
154	Jason Giambi	.35
155	Curt Schilling	.25
156	Scott Rolen	.45
157	Pat Burrell RC	1.50
158	Doug Glanville	.05
159	Bobby Abreu	.05
160	Rico Brogna	.05
161	Ron Gant	.05
162	Jason Kendall	.05
163	Aramis Ramirez	.05
164	Jose Guillen	.05
165	Emil Brown	.05
166	Pat Meares	.05
167	Kevin Young	.05
168	Brian Giles	.05
169	Mark McGwire	1.25
170	J.D. Drew	.40
171	Edgar Renteria	.05
172	Fernando Tatis	.05
173	Matt Morris	.05
174	Eli Marrero	.05
175	Ray Lankford	.05
176	Tony Gwynn	.75
177	Sterling Hitchcock	.05
178	Ruben Rivera	.05
179	Wally Joyner	.05
180	Trevor Hoffman	.05
181	Jim Leyritz	.05
182	Carlos Hernandez	.05
183	Barry Bonds	1.50
184	Ellis Burks	.05
185	F.P. Santangelo	.05
186	J.T. Snow	.05
187	Ramon Martinez	.05
188	Jeff Kent	.05
189	Robb Nen	.05
190	Ken Griffey Jr.	1.00
191	Alex Rodriguez	1.25
192	Shane Monahan	.05
193	Carlos Guillen	.05
194	Edgar Martinez	.05
195	David Segui	.05
196	Jose Mesa	.05
197	Jose Canseco	.35
198	Rolando Arrojo	.05
199	Wade Boggs	.75
200	Fred McGriff	.05
201	Quinton McCracken	.05
202	Bobby Smith	.05
203	Bubba Trammell	.05
204	Juan Gonzalez	.60
205	Ivan Rodriguez	.45
206	Rafael Palmeiro	.45
207	Royce Clayton	.05
208	Rick Helling	.05
209	Todd Zeile	.05
210	Rusty Greer	.05
211	David Wells	.05
212	Roy Halladay	.05
213	Carlos Delgado	.25
214	Darrin Fletcher	.05
215	Shawn Green	.15
216	Kevin Witt	.05
217	Jose Cruz Jr.	.05
218	Checklist (Ken Griffey Jr.)	.45
219	Checklist (Sammy Sosa)	.45
220	Checklist (Mark McGwire)	.50

Scripts/Super Scripts

Three different parallels of the 220 base cards in MVP are inserted bearing a metallic-foil facsimile autograph on front. Silver Script cards are found about every other pack. Gold Script cards are hobby-only and serially numbered to 100 apiece. Also hobby-only are Super Script versions on which

---

the autograph is in holographic foil and the cards are numbered on the back to 25 apiece.

Silver Script:	1X
Gold Script:	10X
Super Script:	30X

All-Star Game

In conjunction with Fan-Fest held in Boston prior to the All-Star Game, UD issued a set of specially marked versions of its MVP issue. It was reported that 15,000 three-card packs were distributed at the show, with some cards reportedly short-printed. The cards have a format virtually identical to the regular-issue MVP cards, except for the presence on front of a bright silver-foil All-Star logo and an AS prefix to the card number on back.

		NM/M
Complete Set (30):		12.50
Common Player:		.25
1	Mo Vaughn	.25
2	Randy Johnson	.60
3	Chipper Jones	.75
4	Greg Maddux	.75
5	Cal Ripken Jr.	2.00
6	Albert Belle	.35
7	Nomar Garciaparra	1.00
8	Pedro Martinez	.60
9	Sammy Sosa	1.00
10	Frank Thomas	.60
11	Sean Casey	.35
12	Roberto Alomar	.30
13	Manny Ramirez	.60
14	Larry Walker	.25
15	Jeff Bagwell	.60
16	Craig Biggio	.25
17	Raul Mondesi	.25
18	Vladimir Guerrero	.60
19	Mike Piazza	1.00
20	Derek Jeter	2.00
21	Roger Clemens	.85
22	Scott Rolen	.40
23	Mark McGwire	1.50
24	Tony Gwynn	.75
25	Barry Bonds	2.00
26	Ken Griffey Jr.	1.00
27	Alex Rodriguez	1.50
28	Jose Canseco	.40
29	Juan Gonzalez	.60
30	Ivan Rodriguez	.50

Dynamics

This 15-card set features holofoil treatment on the card fronts with silver foil stamping. Card backs are numbered with a "D" prefix and are inserted 1:28 packs.

		NM/M
Complete Set (15):		17.50
Common Player:		.60
Inserted 1:28		
1	Ken Griffey Jr.	2.00
2	Alex Rodriguez	2.50
3	Nomar Garciaparra	2.00

4	Mike Piazza	2.00
5	Mark McGwire	2.25
6	Sammy Sosa	2.00
7	Chipper Jones	1.50
8	Mo Vaughn	.60
9	Tony Gwynn	1.50
10	Vladimir Guerrero	1.25
11	Derek Jeter	3.00
12	Jeff Bagwell	1.25
13	Cal Ripken Jr.	3.00
14	Juan Gonzalez	1.25
15	J.D. Drew	.90

Game-Used Souvenirs

This set has a piece of game-used bat from the featured player embedded into each card. These are found exclusively in hobby packs at a rate of 1:144 packs.

		NM/M
Complete Set (9):		75.00
Common Player:		5.00
Inserted 1:144		
JB	Jeff Bagwell	8.00
BB	Barry Bonds	20.00
JD	J.D. Drew	8.00
KGj	Ken Griffey Jr.	15.00
CJ	Chipper Jones	10.00
MP	Mike Piazza	15.00
CR	Cal Ripken Jr.	20.00
SR	Scott Rolen	5.00
MV	Mo Vaughn	5.00

Signed Game-Used Souvenirs

Ken Griffey Jr. and Chipper Jones both signed their Game Used Souvenir inserts to their jersey number, Griffey (24) and Jones (10). These were seeded exclusively in hobby packs.

		NM/M
KGj	Ken Griffey Jr.	300.00
CJ	Chipper Jones	200.00

Power Surge

This 15-card set features baseball's top home run hitters, utilizing rainbow-foil technology. Card backs are numbered with a "P" prefix and are seeded 1:9 packs.

		NM/M
Complete Set (15):		12.50
Common Player:		.50
Inserted 1:9		
1	Mark McGwire	1.50
2	Sammy Sosa	1.25
3	Ken Griffey Jr.	1.25
4	Alex Rodriguez	1.50
5	Juan Gonzalez	.75
6	Nomar Garciaparra	1.25
7	Vladimir Guerrero	.75
8	Chipper Jones	1.00
9	Albert Belle	.50
10	Frank Thomas	.75
11	Mike Piazza	1.25
12	Jeff Bagwell	.75
13	Manny Ramirez	.75
14	Mo Vaughn	.50
15	Barry Bonds	2.00

ProSign

This 30-card autographed set is randomly seeded exclusively in retail packs

at a rate of 1:216 packs. Card backs are numbered with the featured player's initials.

		NM/M
Common Autograph:		5.00
Inserted 1:216 R		
MA	Matt Anderson	5.00
CB	Carlos Beltran	15.00
RB	Russ Branyan	5.00
EC	Eric Chavez	10.00
BC	Bruce Chen	5.00
BF	Brad Fuller	5.00
NG	Nomar Garciaparra	80.00
JG	Jeremy Giambi	5.00
DG	Derrick Gibson	5.00
CG	Chris Gomez	5.00
AG	Alex Gonzalez	5.00
BG	Ben Grieve	5.00
JR	Ken Griffey Jr.	80.00
RH	Richard Hidalgo	5.00
SH	Shea Hillenbrand	10.00
CJ	Chipper Jones/SP	50.00
GK	Gabe Kapler	6.00
SK	Scott Karl	5.00
CK	Corey Koskie	7.50
RL	Ricky Ledee	5.00
ML	Mike Lincoln	5.00
GL	George Lombard	5.00
MLo	Mike Lowell	7.50
RM	Ryan Minor	5.00
SM	Shane Monahan	5.00
AN	Abraham Nunez	5.00
JP	Jim Parque	5.00
CP	Calvin Pickering	5.00
JRa	Jason Rakers	5.00
RR	Ruben Rivera	5.00
IR	Ivan Rodriguez/SP	50.00
KW	Kevin Witt	5.00

Scout's Choice

Utilizing Light F/X technology, this 15-card set highlights the top young prospects in the game. Card backs are numbered with an "SC" prefix and are seeded 1:9 packs.

		NM/M
Complete Set (15):		5.00
Common Player:		.25
Inserted 1:9		
1	J.D. Drew	.65
2	Ben Grieve	.35
3	Troy Glaus	1.50
4	Gabe Kapler	.25
5	Carlos Beltran	.45
6	Aramis Ramirez	.25
7	Pat Burrell	1.00
8	Kerry Wood	.65
9	Ryan Minor	.25
10	Todd Helton	1.00
11	Eric Chavez	.35
12	Russ Branyon	.25
13	Travis Lee	.35
14	Ruben Mateo	.25
15	Roy Halladay	.35

Super Tools

This 15-card insert set focuses on baseball's top stars and utilizes holo foil technology on the card fronts. Card backs are numbered with a "T" prefix and are seeded 1:14 packs.

	NM/M
Complete Set (15):	25.00

Common Player:		.50
Inserted 1:14		
1	Ken Griffey Jr.	2.50
2	Alex Rodriguez	3.00
3	Sammy Sosa	3.00
4	Vladimir Guerrero	1.50
5	Ben Grieve	.50
6	Mike Piazza	2.50
7	Kenny Lofton	.50
8	Barry Bonds	4.00
9	Darin Erstad	1.00
10	Nomar Garciaparra	2.00
11	Cal Ripken Jr.	4.00
12	J.D. Drew	1.00
13	Larry Walker	.50
14	Chipper Jones	2.00

Swing Time

This 12-card set focuses on top hitters in the game and points out three aspects why the featured player is such a successful hitter. Printed on a full foiled front these are seeded 1:6 packs. Cards are numbered with an "S" prefix.

		NM/M
Complete Set (12):		5.00
Common Player:		.35
Inserted 1:6		
1	Ken Griffey Jr.	.75
2	Mark McGwire	1.00
3	Sammy Sosa	.60
4	Tony Gwynn	.60
5	Alex Rodriguez	1.00
6	Nomar Garciaparra	.60
7	Barry Bonds	1.50
8	Frank Thomas	.45
9	Chipper Jones	.60
10	Ivan Rodriguez	.35
11	Mike Piazza	.75
12	Derek Jeter	.75

500 Club Piece of History

This insert has a piece of game-used bat once swung by Mike Schmidt embedded into each card. A total of 350 of this insert was produced. Schmidt also signed 20 of the inserts.

	NM/M
Mike Schmidt/350	160.00
Mike Schmidt/ Auto./20	1,250

1999 Upper Deck Ovation

Cards 1-60 in the base set have the look and feel of an actual baseball. A player photo is

in the foreground with a partial image of a baseball in the background on the card front. Cards 61-90 make up two subsets: World Premiere (61-80) is a 20-card collection consisting of 20 rookie prospects and Superstar Spotlight (81-90) is a 10-card lineup of baseball's biggest stars. Both subsets are short-printed, World Premiere are seeded 1:3.5 packs and Superstar Spotlight 1:6 packs. Five-card packs carry a S.R.P. of $3.99 per pack.

		NM/M
Complete Set (90):		20.00
Common Player:		.05
Common World Premiere:		.15
Inserted 1:3.5		
Common Superstar Spotlight:		.60
Inserted 1:6		
Pack (5):		2.00
Box (20):		30.00
1	Ken Griffey Jr.	1.50
2	Rondell White	.05
3	Tony Clark	.05
4	Barry Bonds	2.50
5	Larry Walker	.05
6	Greg Vaughn	.05
7	Mark Grace	.05
8	John Olerud	.05
9	Matt Williams	.05
10	Craig Biggio	.05
11	Quinton McCracken	.05
12	Kerry Wood	.35
13	Derek Jeter	2.50
14	Frank Thomas	.75
15	Tino Martinez	.05
16	Albert Belle	.05
17	Ben Grieve	.05
18	Cal Ripken Jr.	2.50
19	Johnny Damon	.30
20	Jose Cruz Jr.	.05
21	Barry Larkin	.05
22	Jason Giambi	.45
23	Sean Casey	.10
24	Scott Rolen	.60
25	Jim Thome	.45
26	Curt Schilling	.25
27	Moises Alou	.05
28	Alex Rodriguez	2.00
29	Mark Kotsay	.05
30	Darin Erstad	.25
31	Mike Mussina	.30
32	Todd Walker	.05
33	Nomar Garciaparra	1.00
34	Vladimir Guerrero	.75
35	Jeff Bagwell	.75
36	Mark McGwire	2.00
37	Travis Lee	.15
38	Dean Palmer	.05
39	Fred McGriff	.05
40	Sammy Sosa	1.00
41	Mike Piazza	1.50
42	Andres Galarraga	.05
43	Pedro Martinez	.75
44	Juan Gonzalez	.40
45	Greg Maddux	1.00
46	Jeromy Burnitz	.05
47	Roger Clemens	1.25
48	Vinny Castilla	.05
49	Kevin Brown	.05
50	Mo Vaughn	.05
51	Raul Mondesi	.05
52	Randy Johnson	.75
53	Ray Lankford	.05
54	Jaret Wright	.05
55	Tony Gwynn	1.00
56	Chipper Jones	1.00
57	Gary Sheffield	.40
58	Ivan Rodriguez	.65
59	Kenny Lofton	.05
60	Jason Kendall	.05
61	J.D. Drew (World Premiere)	.75
62	Gabe Kapler (World Premiere)	.15
63	Adrian Beltre (World Premiere)	.40
64	Carlos Beltran (World Premiere)	.50
65	Eric Chavez (World Premiere)	.35
66	Mike Lowell (World Premiere)	.25
67	Troy Glaus (World Premiere)	1.00
68	George Lombard (World Premiere)	.15
69	Alex Gonzalez (World Premiere)	.15
70	Mike Kinkade (World Premiere)	.15
71	Jeremy Giambi (World Premiere)	.15
72	Bruce Chen (World Premiere)	.15
73	Preston Wilson (World Premiere)	.25
74	Kevin Witt (World Premiere)	.15
75	Carlos Guillen (World Premiere)	.15
76	Ryan Minor (World Premiere)	.15
77	Corey Koskie (World Premiere)	.15
78	Robert Fick (World Premiere)	.15
79	Michael Barrett (World Premiere)	.15
80	Calvin Pickering (World Premiere)	.15
81	Ken Griffey Jr. (Superstar Spotlight)	1.00
82	Mark McGwire (Superstar Spotlight)	1.50
83	Cal Ripken Jr. (Superstar Spotlight)	2.00
84	Derek Jeter (Superstar Spotlight)	2.00
85	Chipper Jones (Superstar Spotlight)	.75
86	Nomar Garciapparra (Garciaparra) (Superstar Spotlight)	.75
87	Sammy Sosa (Superstar Spotlight)	.75
88	Juan Gonzalez (Superstar Spotlight)	.30
89	Mike Piazza (Superstar Spotlight)	1.00
90	Alex Rodriguez (Superstar Spotlight)	1.50

Standing Ovation

Stars (1-60):		3X
World Premiere (61-80):		1.5X
Superstar Spotlight (81-90):		2X
Production 500 Sets		

Curtain Calls

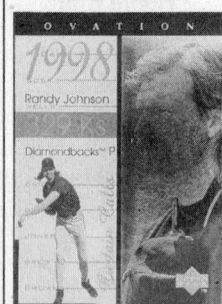

This 20-card set focuses on the most memorable accomplishments posted during the '98 season. Card fronts have two images of the player, one on the right half and a smaller image on the bottom left. Copper foil stamping is used to enhance the card front. These are numbered with a "R" prefix and are seeded 1:8 packs.

		NM/M
Complete Set (20):		20.00
Common Player:		.25
Inserted 1:8		
R1	Mark McGwire	2.00
R2	Sammy Sosa	1.00
R3	Ken Griffey Jr.	1.50
R4	Alex Rodriguez	2.00
R5	Roger Clemens	1.25
R6	Cal Ripken Jr.	2.50
R7	Barry Bonds	2.50
R8	Kerry Wood	.40
R9	Nomar Garciaparra	2.00
R10	Derek Jeter	2.50
R11	Juan Gonzalez	.50
R12	Greg Maddux	1.00
R13	Pedro Martinez	1.00
R14	David Wells	.25
R15	Moises Alou	.25
R16	Tony Gwynn	1.00
R17	Albert Belle	.25
R18	Mike Piazza	1.50
R19	Ivan Rodriguez	.65
R20	Randy Johnson	.75

Major Production

This 20-card set utilizes thermography technology to simulate the look and feel of home plate and highlights some of the game's most productive players. These are inserted 1:45 packs and are numbered with an "S" prefix.

		NM/M
Complete Set (20):		45.00
Common Player:		.75
Inserted 1:45		
S1	Mike Piazza	4.00
S2	Mark McGwire	5.00
S3	Chipper Jones	3.00
S4	Cal Ripken Jr.	6.00
S5	Ken Griffey Jr.	4.00
S6	Barry Bonds	6.00
S7	Tony Gwynn	3.00
S8	Randy Johnson	2.50
S9	Ivan Rodriguez	2.00
S10	Frank Thomas	2.50
S11	Alex Rodriguez	5.00
S12	Albert Belle	.75
S13	Juan Gonzalez	1.25
S14	Greg Maddux	3.00
S15	Jeff Bagwell	2.50
S16	Derek Jeter	6.00
S17	Matt Williams	.75
S18	Kenny Lofton	.75
S19	Sammy Sosa	3.00
S20	Roger Clemens	3.50

Piece of History

This 16-card set has actual pieces of game-used bat, from the featured player, imbedded into the card. These are inserted 1:247 packs. Ben Grieve autographed 25 versions of his Piece of History insert cards. Although there is no regular Piece of History Kerry Wood card, Upper Deck inserted 25 autographed Piece of History game-used baseball cards. These have a piece of one of Wood's game-hurled baseballs from the 1998 season.

		NM/M
Common Player:		5.00
Inserted 1:247		
BB	Barry Bonds	25.00
CJ	Chipper Jones	15.00
BW	Bernie Williams	5.00
KGj	Ken Griffey Jr.	20.00
NG	Nomar Garciaparra	15.00
JG	Juan Gonzalez	5.00
DJ	Derek Jeter	25.00
SS	Sammy Sosa	15.00
TG	Tony Gwynn	15.00

ABBREVIATIONS

SP - Short Print

AR	Alex Rodriguez	20.00
CR	Cal Ripken Jr.	25.00
BG	Ben Grieve	5.00
VG	Vladimir Guerrero	10.00
MP	Mike Piazza	20.00
BGAU	Ben Grieve/Auto./25	30.00
KWAU	Kerry Wood/Auto./25	50.00

ReMarkable

This three-tiered 15-card insert showcases Mark McGwire's historic '98 season. Cards #1-5 are Bronze and inserted 1:9 packs; cards #6-10 are Silver and inserted 1:25 packs; and cards #11-15 are Gold and inserted 1:99 packs.

	NM/M
Complete Set (15):	20.00
Common #1-5:	1.50
Inserted 1:9	
Common #6-10:	2.25
Inserted 1:25	
Common #11-15:	3.00
Inserted 1:99	
MM1 Mark McGwire	1.50
MM2 Mark McGwire	1.50
MM3 Mark McGwire	1.50
MM4 Mark McGwire	1.50
MM5 Mark McGwire	1.50
MM6 Mark McGwire	2.25
MM7 Mark McGwire	2.25
MM8 Mark McGwire	2.25
MM9 Mark McGwire	2.25
MM10 Mark McGwire	2.25
MM11 Mark McGwire	3.00
MM12 Mark McGwire	3.00
MM13 Mark McGwire	3.00
MM14 Mark McGwire	3.00
MM15 Mark McGwire	3.00

500 Club Piece of History

Each of these cards actually has a piece of game-used Louisville Slugger, once swung by Mickey Mantle, embedded. Approximately 350 cards exist. There is also one card with a cut signature of Mantle and a piece of his game-used bat on it.

	NM/M
MIC-P Mickey Mantle/350	600.00
Mickey Mantle/ Bat Auto.	8,000

1999 Upper Deck PowerDeck

This 25-card set is comprised of 25 digital PowerDeck interactive trading cards, complete with video and audio content. There is also a parallel "paper" version of the base set called Auxiliary Power. Each digital card includes 32 megabytes of information and is compatible with almost any internet ready computer. One PowerDeck digital card comes in every three-card pack.

	NM/M
Complete Set (25):	20.00
Common Player:	.50
Pack (3):	1.50
Wax Box (24):	20.00
1 Ken Griffey Jr.	2.00
2 Mark McGwire	2.50

3	Cal Ripken Jr.	3.00
4	Sammy Sosa	1.50
5	Derek Jeter	3.00
6	Mike Piazza	2.00
7	Nomar Garciaparra	1.50
8	Greg Maddux	1.50
9	Tony Gwynn	1.50
10	Roger Clemens	1.75
11	Scott Rolen	1.00
12	Alex Rodriguez	2.50
13	Manny Ramirez	1.25
14	Chipper Jones	1.50
15	Juan Gonzalez	.65
16	Ivan Rodriguez	1.00
17	Frank Thomas	1.25
18	Mo Vaughn	.50
19	Barry Bonds	3.00
20	Vladimir Guerrero	1.25
21	Jose Canseco	.65
22	Jeff Bagwell	1.25
23	Pedro Martinez	1.25
24	Gabe Kapler	.50
25	J.D. Drew	.75
---	Checklist	.10

Auxiliary Power

A "paper" parallel version of the 25-card digital set. These have a horizontal format with silver-foil graphics. Backs repeat the front portrait photo along with the player's past five years of statistics and a brief career highlight. Card numbers are prefixed with "AUX-."

	NM/M
Complete Set (25):	6.00
Common Player:	.10
1 Ken Griffey Jr.	.50
2 Mark McGwire	.60
3 Cal Ripken Jr.	.75
4 Sammy Sosa	.40
5 Derek Jeter	.75
6 Mike Piazza	.50
7 Nomar Garciaparra	.40
8 Greg Maddux	.40
9 Tony Gwynn	.40
10 Roger Clemens	.45
11 Scott Rolen	.25
12 Alex Rodriguez	.60
13 Manny Ramirez	.30
14 Chipper Jones	.40
15 Juan Gonzalez	.15
16 Ivan Rodriguez	.25
17 Frank Thomas	.30
18 Mo Vaughn	.10
19 Barry Bonds	.75
20 Vladimir Guerrero	.30
21 Jose Canseco	.20
22 Jeff Bagwell	.30
23 Pedro Martinez	.30
24 Gabe Kapler	.10
25 J.D. Drew	.25

Most Valuable Performances

This seven-card digital insert set consists of capturing true MVP performances from some of baseball's greatest players. These were seeded 1:287 packs.

	NM/M
Complete Set (7):	75.00
Common Player:	6.00
Inserted 1:287	
1 Sammy Sosa	10.00
2 Barry Bonds	20.00
3 Cal Ripken Jr.	20.00
4 Juan Gonzalez	6.00
5 Ken Griffey Jr.	12.50
6 Roger Clemens	10.00
7 Mark McGwire, Sammy Sosa	12.50

MVP Auxiliary

A "paper" parallel version of the digital set, these also were inserted 1:287 packs. They have

a horizontal format using silver holofoil and also have different photos from the digital version.

	NM/M
Complete Set (7):	60.00
Common Player:	4.00
Inserted 1:287	
1 Sammy Sosa	7.50
2 Barry Bonds	15.00
3 Cal Ripken Jr.	15.00
4 Juan Gonzalez	4.00
5 Ken Griffey Jr.	10.00
6 Roger Clemens	7.50
7 Mark McGwire, Sammy Sosa	12.50

Powerful Moments

This six-card digital interactive set has game-action footage pinpointing specific milestones in each of the featured players' careers. These were inserted 1:7 packs.

	NM/M
Complete Set (6):	10.00
Common Player:	1.00
Inserted 1:7	
1 Mark McGwire	2.00
2 Sammy Sosa	1.00
3 Cal Ripken Jr.	3.00
4 Ken Griffey Jr.	1.50
5 Derek Jeter	3.00
6 Alex Rodriguez	2.00

Powerful Moments Auxiliary

This "paper" parallel version of the digital set is also inserted 1:7 packs on a horizontal format. Different photos were used from the digital set.

	NM/M
Complete Set (6):	10.00
Common Player:	1.00
Inserted 1:7	
Gold (One each.):	
Values Undetermined	
1 Mark McGwire	2.00
2 Sammy Sosa	1.00
3 Cal Ripken Jr.	3.00
4 Ken Griffey Jr.	1.50
5 Derek Jeter	3.00
6 Alex Rodriguez	2.00

Time Capsule

Six MLB Rookies of the Year are honored in this digital set with the digital content going back to the rookie seasons of the featured players. These were seeded 1:23 packs.

	NM/M
Complete Set (6):	12.50
Common Player:	1.00
Inserted 1:23	
1 Ken Griffey Jr.	2.50
2 Mike Piazza	2.50
3 Mark McGwire	3.00
4 Derek Jeter	4.00
5 Jose Canseco	1.00
6 Nomar Garciaparra	2.00

Time Capsule- Auxiliary Power

This "paper' parallel set of the digital version utilizes a similar design as the digital in-

sert and uses different photos as well. Horizontal fronts have a thin vertical monochromatic portrait at left. At right is an action photos set on a metallized background. Backs repeat the front portrait and have a screen simulation along with stats and data. These were inserted 1:23 packs.

	NM/M
Complete Set (6):	15.00
Common Player:	1.00
Inserted 1:23	
Gold (one of each):	
Values Undetermined	
1 Ken Griffey Jr.	2.50
2 Mike Piazza	2.50
3 Mark McGwire	3.00
4 Derek Jeter	4.00
5 Jose Canseco	1.00
6 Nomar Garciaparra	2.00

A Season to Remember

This special box-topper CD insert presents audio-visual highlights of the 1999 season, featuring players like David Cone, Ken Griffey, Jr., Mark McGwire, Tony Gwynn, Wade Boggs, Sammy Sosa and Cal Ripken, Jr. McGwire is pictured on this CD hitting his 500th home run.

	NM/M
Mark McGwire	3.00

Athletes of the Century

Babe Ruth was baseball's representative in a four-sport set of CD "cards" produced by Upper Deck.

	NM/M
Babe Ruth	1.00

World Series Power Deck

This CD-ROM card titled "Season to Remember" was distributed at Yankee Stadium during Game 4 of the 1999 World Series and features highlights of the Yankees championship season.

	NM/M
Season to Remember (1999, Yankees)	12.00

1999 UD Retro

The 110-card base set is comprised of 88 current stars and 22 retired greats. Card fronts have a tan, speckled border while card backs have a year-by-year compilation of the player's stats along with a career note. Retro is packaged in lunchboxes, 24 packs to a box with an S.R.P. of $4.99 per six-card pack.

Complete Set (110):		15.00
Common Player:		.05
Gold:		12X
Production 250 Sets		
Platinum 1/1:		
Values Undetermined		
Wax Pack (6):		2.50
Lunchbox (24):		45.00
1	Mo Vaughn	.05
2	Troy Glaus	.65
3	Tim Salmon	.05
4	Randy Johnson	.75
5	Travis Lee	.15
6	Matt Williams	.05
7	Greg Maddux	.85
8	Chipper Jones	.85
9	Andruw Jones	.75
10	Tom Glavine	.25
11	Javy Lopez	.05
12	Albert Belle	.05
13	Cal Ripken Jr.	2.00
14	Brady Anderson	.05
15	Nomar Garciaparra	.85
16	Pedro J. Martinez	.85
17	Sammy Sosa	.85
18	Mark Grace	.05
19	Frank Thomas	.75
20	Ray Durham	.05
21	Sean Casey	.10
22	Greg Vaughn	.05
23	Barry Larkin	.05
24	Manny Ramirez	.75
25	Jim Thome	.05
26	Jaret Wright	.05
27	Kenny Lofton	.05
28	Larry Walker	.25
29	Todd Helton	.65
30	Vinny Castilla	.05
31	Tony Clark	.05
32	Juan Encarnacion	.05
33	Dean Palmer	.05
34	Mark Kotsay	.05
35	Alex Gonzalez	.05
36	Shane Reynolds	.05
37	Ken Caminiti	.05
38	Jeff Bagwell	.75
39	Craig Biggio	.05
40	Carlos Febles	.35
41	Carlos Beltran	.05
42	Jeremy Giambi	.05
43	Raul Mondesi	.05
44	Adrian Beltre	.10
45	Kevin Brown	.05
46	Jeromy Burnitz	.05
47	Jeff Cirillo	.05
48	Corey Koskie	.05
49	Todd Walker	.05
50	Vladimir Guerrero	.75
51	Michael Barrett	.05
52	Mike Piazza	1.00
53	Robin Ventura	.05
54	Edgardo Alfonzo	.05
55	Derek Jeter	2.00
56	Roger Clemens	.90
57	Tino Martinez	.05
58	Orlando Hernandez	.05
59	Chuck Knoblauch	.05
60	Bernie Williams	.05
61	Eric Chavez	.10
62	Ben Grieve	.05
63	Jason Giambi	.40
64	Scott Rolen	.60
65	Curt Schilling	.05
66	Bobby Abreu	.10
67	Jason Kendall	.05
68	Kevin Young	.05
69	Mark McGwire	1.50
70	J.D. Drew	.60
71	Eric Davis	.05
72	Tony Gwynn	.85
73	Trevor Hoffman	.05
74	Barry Bonds	2.00
75	Robb Nen	.05
76	Ken Griffey Jr.	1.00
77	Alex Rodriguez	1.50
78	Jay Buhner	.05
79	Carlos Guillen	.05
80	Jose Canseco	.40
81	Bobby Smith	.05
82	Juan Gonzalez	.40
83	Ivan Rodriguez	.65
84	Rafael Palmeiro	.65
85	Rick Helling	.05
86	Jose Cruz Jr.	.05
87	David Wells	.05
88	Carlos Delgado	.20
89	Nolan Ryan	1.50

90	George Brett	.90
91	Robin Yount	.50
92	Paul Molitor	.50
93	Dave Winfield	.50
94	Steve Garvey	.25
95	Ozzie Smith	.85
96	Ted Williams	1.50
97	Don Mattingly	.90
98	Mickey Mantle	2.50
99	Harmon Killebrew	.25
100	Rollie Fingers	.10
101	Kirk Gibson	.05
102	Bucky Dent	.05
103	Willie Mays	1.00
104	Babe Ruth	1.50
105	Gary Carter	.50
106	Reggie Jackson	.85
107	Frank Robinson	.25
108	Ernie Banks	.50
109	Eddie Murray	.50
110	Mike Schmidt	.90

Gold/Platinum

This is a 110-card parallel to the base set. Cards have a gold-tone front and are sequentially numbered to 250 sets. A one-of-one Platinum parallel to the base set also is randomly seeded.

	NM/M
Common Gold:	1.00
Gold Stars:	15X
Platinum 1/1:	
Values Undetermined	

Distant Replay

This 15-card set recounts the most memorable plays from the 1998 season. Card fronts have a black-and-white photo of the player and along the bottom of the photo a date of the memorable play and brief description are given. These are seeded 1:8 packs. A parallel version, Level 2, is also randomly seeded, limited to 100 sequentially numbered sets.

	NM/M
Complete Set (15):	30.00
Common Player:	1.00
Inserted 1:8	
Level 2:	6X
Production 100 Sets	
1 Ken Griffey Jr.	2.50
2 Mark McGwire	3.00
3 Cal Ripken Jr.	4.00
4 Greg Maddux	2.00
5 Nomar Garciaparra	2.00
6 Roger Clemens	2.25
7 Alex Rodriguez	3.00
8 Frank Thomas	1.50
9 Mike Piazza	2.50
10 Chipper Jones	2.00
11 Juan Gonzalez	1.00
12 Tony Gwynn	2.00
13 Barry Bonds	4.00
14 Ivan Rodriguez	1.00
15 Derek Jeter	4.00

INKredible

INKredible is an autographed insert set that consists

of both current players and retired stars. Card fronts have a small photo in the upper left portion of the featured player and a large signing area. These are seeded 1:23 packs.

		NM/M
Common Player:		4.00
Inserted 1:23		
CBe	Carlos Beltran	30.00
GB	George Brett/SP	80.00
PB	Pat Burrell	10.00
SC	Sean Casey	10.00
TC	Tony Clark	4.00
BD	Bucky Dent	8.00
DE	Darin Erstad	15.00
RF	Rollie Fingers	8.00
SG	Steve Garvey	10.00
KG	Kirk Gibson	10.00
RG	Rusty Greer	4.00
JR	Ken Griffey Jr.	80.00
TG	Tony Gwynn	30.00
CJ	Chipper Jones	30.00
GK	Gabe Kapler	5.00
HK	Harmon Killebrew	30.00
FL	Fred Lynn	10.00
DM	Don Mattingly	50.00
PM	Paul Molitor	20.00
EM	Eddie Murray/SP	50.00
PO	Paul O'Neill	15.00
AP	Angel Pena	4.00
MR	Manny Ramirez	30.00
IR	Ivan Rodriguez	25.00
NR	Nolan Ryan	150.00
OZ	Ozzie Smith	30.00
DWe	David Wells	15.00
BW	Bernie Williams	40.00
DW	Dave Winfield	20.00
RY	Robin Yount	35.00

INKredible Level 2

A parallel to INKredible autographed inserts, these are hand-numbered to the featured player's jersey number.

		NM/M
Common Player:		10.00
Limited to player's jersey #.		
CBe	Carlos Beltran/36	60.00
PB	Pat Burrell/76	80.00
SC	Sean Casey/21	40.00
TC	Tony Clark/17	20.00
BD	Bucky Dent/20	25.00
DE	Darin Erstad/17	50.00
RF	Rollie Fingers/34	25.00
KG	Kirk Gibson/23	30.00
RG	Rusty Greer/29	20.00
JR	Ken Griffey Jr./24	200.00
TG	Tony Gwynn/19	150.00
GK	Gabe Kapler/23	40.00
FL	Fred Lynn/19	30.00
DM	Don Mattingly/23	200.00
EM	Eddie Murray/33	90.00
PO	Paul O'Neill/21	50.00
AP	Angel Pena/36	10.00
MR	Manny Ramirez/24	80.00
NR	Nolan Ryan/34	400.00
DWe	David Wells/33	25.00
BW	Bernie William/51	60.00
DW	Dave Winfield/31	60.00
RY	Robin Yount/19	90.00

Old/New School

This 30-card insert set captures 15 Old School players and 15 New School players. Each card is sequentially numbered to 1,000. A parallel version is also randomly seeded and is limited to 50 sequentially numbered sets. Old School cards are basically black-and-white with color graphic highlights on front and back. New School cards have multiple computer-enhanced color photos and silver-foil highlights.

		NM/M
Complete Set (30):		35.00
Common Player:		.40
Production 1,000 Sets		
Level 2:		5X
Production 50 Sets		
1	Ken Griffey Jr.	2.50
2	Alex Rodriguez	3.00
3	Frank Thomas	1.50
4	Cal Ripken Jr.	4.00
5	Chipper Jones	2.00
6	Craig Biggio	.40
7	Greg Maddux	2.00
8	Jeff Bagwell	1.50
9	Juan Gonzalez	.75
10	Mark McGwire	3.00
11	Mike Piazza	2.50
12	Mo Vaughn	.40
13	Roger Clemens	2.25
14	Sammy Sosa	2.00
15	Tony Gwynn	2.00
16	Gabe Kapler	.40
17	J.D. Drew	1.00
18	Pat Burrell	1.00
19	Roy Halladay	.40
20	Jeff Weaver	.40
21	Troy Glaus	1.00
22	Vladimir Guerrero	1.50
23	Michael Barrett	.40
24	Carlos Beltran	.40
25	Scott Rolen	1.00
26	Nomar Garciaparra	2.00
27	Warren Morris	.40
28	Alex Gonzalez	.40
29	Kyle Farnsworth	.40
30	Derek Jeter	4.00

Piece of History 500 Club

Each one of these inserts features a piece of game-used bat swung by Ted Williams embedded into each card. A total of 350 of these were issued. Williams also autographed nine of the 500 Club Piece of History cards.

		NM/M
TW	Ted Williams/350	250.00

Throwback Attack

These inserts have a "Retro" look, borrowing heavily from 1959 Topps. Highlighting top players, the set features card fronts with a circular player photo on a bright orange background. At top in white is, "throwback attack." There is a white border. Backs have a ghosted image of the front photo and career highlights. Cards are numbered with a "T" prefix and are seeded 1:5 packs.

A parallel version is also randomly seeded and limited to 500 numbered sets.

		NM/M
Complete Set (15):		20.00
Common Player:		.50
Inserted 1:5		
Level 2:		3X
Production 500 Sets		
1	Ken Griffey Jr.	2.00
2	Mark McGwire	2.50
3	Sammy Sosa	1.25
4	Roger Clemens	1.50
5	J.D. Drew	.75
6	Alex Rodriguez	2.50
7	Greg Maddux	1.25
8	Mike Piazza	2.00
9	Juan Gonzalez	.50
10	Mo Vaughn	.50
11	Cal Ripken Jr.	3.00
12	Frank Thomas	1.00
13	Nomar Garciaparra	1.25
14	Vladimir Guerrero	1.00
15	Tony Gwynn	1.25

Lunchbox

Lunchboxes were the packaging for UD Retro. Each lunchbox contains 24 six-card packs and features 16 different current or retired baseball legends including Babe Ruth.

		NM/M
Complete Set (17):		140.00
Common Lunchbox:		7.50
1 dual-player per case		
	Roger Clemens	7.50
	Ken Griffey Jr.	7.50
	Mickey Mantle	10.00
	Mark McGwire	10.00
	Mike Piazza	7.50
	Alex Rodriguez	7.50
	Babe Ruth	10.00
	Sammy Sosa	7.50
	Ted Williams	10.00
	Ken Griffey Jr.,		
	Mark McGwire	12.50
	Ken Griffey Jr.,		
	Babe Ruth	12.50
	Ken Griffey Jr.,		
	Ted Williams	12.50
	Mickey Mantle,		
	Babe Ruth	15.00
	Mark McGwire,		
	Mickey Mantle	15.00
	Mark McGwire,		
	Babe Ruth	15.00
	Mark McGwire,		
	Ted Williams	15.00

1999 Upper Deck Ultimate Victory

The 180-card base set includes two 30-card shortprinted (1:4) subsets: McGwire Magic (151-180) and 1999 Rookie (121-150). The base cards have a silver foil border with the featured players' last five seasons of statistics along with a brief career highlight. There are two parallels randomly inserted: Victory Collection and Ultimate Collection. Victory Collection is seeded 1:12 packs with a holographic, prismatic look. Ultimate Collection has a gold holographic, prismatic look and are serially numbered "xxx/100" on the card front.

		NM/M
Complete Set (180):		125.00
Common Player:		.10
Common 99 Rookie		
(121-150):		.50
Common McGwire Magic		
(151-180):		1.00
Victory (1-120):		3.5X
Victory SP (121-180):		2X
Inserted 1:12		
Ultimate (1-120):		12X
Ultimate SP (121-180):		5X
Production 100 Sets		
Pack (5):		4.50
Wax Box (24):		75.00
1	Troy Glaus	.65
2	Tim Salmon	.10
3	Mo Vaughn	.10
4	Garret Anderson	.10
5	Darin Erstad	.30
6	Randy Johnson	.75
7	Matt Williams	.10
8	Travis Lee	.25
9	Jay Bell	.10
10	Steve Finley	.10
11	Luis Gonzalez	.10
12	Greg Maddux	1.00
13	Chipper Jones	1.00
14	Javy Lopez	.10
15	Tom Glavine	.35
16	John Smoltz	.10
17	Cal Ripken Jr.	3.00
18	Charles Johnson	.10
19	Albert Belle	.10
20	Mike Mussina	.40
21	Pedro Martinez	.75
22	Nomar Garciaparra	1.00
23	Jose Offerman	.10
24	Sammy Sosa	1.00
25	Mark Grace	.10
26	Kerry Wood	.35
27	Frank Thomas	.75
28	Ray Durham	.10
29	Paul Konerko	.20
30	Pete Harnisch	.10
31	Greg Vaughn	.10
32	Sean Casey	.20
33	Manny Ramirez	.75
34	Jim Thome	.65
35	Sandy Alomar	.10
36	Roberto Alomar	.30
37	Travis Fryman	.10
38	Kenny Lofton	.10
39	Omar Vizquel	.10
40	Larry Walker	.10
41	Todd Helton	.65
42	Vinny Castilla	.10
43	Tony Clark	.10
44	Juan Encarnacion	.10
45	Dean Palmer	.10
46	Damion Easley	.10
47	Mark Kotsay	.10
48	Cliff Floyd	.10
49	Jeff Bagwell	.75
50	Ken Caminiti	.10
51	Craig Biggio	.10
52	Moises Alou	.10
53	Johnny Damon	.35
54	Larry Sutton	.10
55	Kevin Brown	.10
56	Adrian Beltre	.25
57	Raul Mondesi	.10
58	Gary Sheffield	.50
59	Jeromy Burnitz	.10
60	Sean Berry	.10
61	Jeff Cirillo	.10
62	Brad Radke	.10
63	Todd Walker	.10
64	Matt Lawton	.10
65	Vladimir Guerrero	.75
66	Rondell White	.10
67	Dustin Hermanson	.10
68	Mike Piazza	2.00
69	Rickey Henderson	.75
70	Robin Ventura	.10
71	John Olerud	.10
72	Derek Jeter	3.00
73	Roger Clemens	1.25
74	Orlando Hernandez	.10
75	Paul O'Neill	.10
76	Bernie Williams	.10
77	Chuck Knoblauch	.10
78	Tino Martinez	.10
79	Jason Giambi	.50
80	Ben Grieve	.10
81	Matt Stairs	.10
82	Scott Rolen	.60
83	Ron Gant	.10
84	Bobby Abreu	.10
85	Curt Schilling	.35
86	Brian Giles	.10
87	Jason Kendall	.10
88	Kevin Young	.10
89	Mark McGwire	2.00
90	Fernando Tatis	.10
91	Ray Lankford	.10
92	Eric Davis	.10
93	Tony Gwynn	1.00
94	Reggie Sanders	.10
95	Wally Joyner	.10
96	Trevor Hoffman	.10
97	Robb Nen	.10
98	Barry Bonds	3.00
99	Jeff Kent	.10
100	J.T. Snow	.10
101	Ellis Burks	.10
102	Ken Griffey Jr.	1.50
103	Alex Rodriguez	2.00
104	Jay Buhner	.10
105	Edgar Martinez	.10
106	David Bell	.10
107	Bobby Smith	.10
108	Wade Boggs	1.00
109	Fred McGriff	.10
110	Rolando Arrojo	.10
111	Jose Canseco	.50
112	Ivan Rodriguez	.65
113	Juan Gonzalez	.40
114	Rafael Palmeiro	.65
115	Rusty Greer	.10
116	Todd Zeile	.10
117	Jose Cruz Jr.	.10
118	Carlos Delgado	.35
119	Shawn Green	.30
120	David Wells	.10
121	Eric Munson RC (99 Rookie)	2.50
122	Lance Berkman (99 Rookie)	1.00
123	Ed Yarnall (99 Rookie)	.50
124	Jacque Jones (99 Rookie)	1.00
125	Kyle Farnsworth (99 Rookie)	1.00
126	Ryan Rupe (99 Rookie)	1.00
127	Jeff Weaver RC (99 Rookie)	2.00
128	Gabe Kapler (99 Rookie)	.50
129	Alex Gonzalez (99 Rookie)	.50
130	Randy Wolf (99 Rookie)	1.00
131	Ben Davis (99 Rookie)	.50
132	Carlos Beltran (99 Rookie)	2.00
133	Jim Morris (99 Rookie)	2.00
134	Jeff Zimmerman (99 Rookie)	2.00
135	Bruce Aven (99 Rookie)	.50
136	Alfonso Soriano RC (99 Rookie)	50.00
137	Tim Hudson RC (99 Rookie)	15.00
138	Josh Beckett RC (99 Rookie)	30.00
139	Michael Barrett (99 Rookie)	.50
140	Eric Chavez (99 Rookie)	1.00
141	Pat Burrell RC (99 Rookie)	10.00
142	Kris Benson (99 Rookie)	1.00
143	J.D. Drew (99 Rookie)	2.00
144	Matt Clement (99 Rookie)	1.00
145	Rick Ankiel RC (99 Rookie)	4.00
146	Vernon Wells (99 Rookie)	1.00
147	Ruben Mateo (99 Rookie)	.50
148	Roy Halladay (99 Rookie)	1.00
149	Joe McEwing (99 Rookie)	.50
150	Freddy Garcia RC (99 Rookie)	8.00
151	Mark McGwire (McGwire Magic)	1.00
152	Mark McGwire (McGwire Magic)	1.00
153	Mark McGwire (McGwire Magic)	1.00
154	Mark McGwire (McGwire Magic)	1.00
155	Mark McGwire (McGwire Magic)	1.00
156	Mark McGwire (McGwire Magic)	1.00
157	Mark McGwire (McGwire Magic)	1.00
158	Mark McGwire (McGwire Magic)	1.00
159	Mark McGwire (McGwire Magic)	1.00
160	Mark McGwire (McGwire Magic)	1.00
161	Mark McGwire (McGwire Magic)	1.00
162	Mark McGwire (McGwire Magic)	1.00
163	Mark McGwire (McGwire Magic)	1.00
164	Mark McGwire (McGwire Magic)	1.00
165	Mark McGwire (McGwire Magic)	1.00
166	Mark McGwire (McGwire Magic)	1.00
167	Mark McGwire (McGwire Magic)	1.00
168	Mark McGwire (McGwire Magic)	1.00
169	Mark McGwire (McGwire Magic)	1.00
170	Mark McGwire (McGwire Magic)	1.00
171	Mark McGwire (McGwire Magic)	1.00
172	Mark McGwire (McGwire Magic)	1.00
173	Mark McGwire (McGwire Magic)	1.00
174	Mark McGwire (McGwire Magic)	1.00
175	Mark McGwire (McGwire Magic)	1.00
176	Mark McGwire (McGwire Magic)	1.00
177	Mark McGwire (McGwire Magic)	1.00
178	Mark McGwire (McGwire Magic)	1.00
179	Mark McGwire (McGwire Magic)	1.00
180	Mark McGwire (McGwire Magic)	1.00

Victory Collection

This parallel of the base set features a prismatic foil design on front. The cards are found on average of one per 12 packs. A 1-of-1 edition also exists, but is not priced here due to rarity and demand variability.

	NM/M
Common Player (1-120, 151-180):	1.00
Common Player (121-150):	5.00
Stars (1-120):	3.5X
Stars (121-150):	2X

Ultimate Collection

This parallel insert set is individually serial numbered on front from within an edition of 100 cards each. Card fronts have silver holographic prismatic foil background and a silver-foil serial number. Backs are identical to the regular-issue cards.

	NM/M
Common Player (1-120, 151-180):	2.00
Common Player (121-150):	12.00
Stars (1-120):	12X
Stars (121-150):	5X

Bleacher Reachers

This 11-card set focuses on the hitters who were vying for the 1999 home run title. They have a horizontal format with a holographic foil card front. Card backs have a small photo along with three-year statistical totals. They are numbered with a "BR" prefix and were inserted 1:23 packs.

		NM/M
Complete Set (11):		20.00
Common Player:		.75
Inserted 1:23		
1	Ken Griffey Jr.	2.50
2	Mark McGwire	3.00
3	Sammy Sosa	2.00
4	Barry Bonds	4.00
5	Nomar Garciaparra	2.00
6	Juan Gonzalez	.75
7	Jose Canseco	.75
8	Manny Ramirez	1.50
9	Mike Piazza	2.50
10	Jeff Bagwell	1.50
11	Alex Rodriguez	3.00

Fame-Used Memorabilia

This four-card set has a piece of game-used bat embedded into each card, from either George Brett, Robin Yount, Nolan Ryan or Orlando Cepeda. Approximately 350 bat cards of each player were produced.

		NM/M
Complete Set (4):		50.00
Common Player:		7.50
Production 350 Cards		
GB	George Brett	20.00
OC	Orlando Cepeda	7.50
NR	Nolan Ryan	25.00
RY	Robin Yount	10.00

Fame-Used Combo

This insert has a piece of game-used bat from each of the 1999 Hall of Fame inductees and is limited to 99 sequentially numbered singles.

	NM/M
Edition of 99:	
HOF	Nolan Ryan, George Brett, Robin Yount, Orlando Cepeda	250.00

Frozen Ropes

This 10-card set spotlights baseball's top hitters and are seeded 1:23 packs.

		NM/M
Complete Set (10):		15.00
Common Player:		.50
Inserted 1:23		
1	Ken Griffey Jr.	2.00
2	Mark McGwire	2.50
3	Sammy Sosa	1.50
4	Derek Jeter	3.00
5	Tony Gwynn	1.50
6	Nomar Garciaparra	1.50
7	Alex Rodriguez	2.50
8	Mike Piazza	2.00
9	Mo Vaughn	.50
10	Craig Biggio	.50

STATure

This 15-card set highlights players with outstanding statistical achievements. The featured stat for the player runs down the right side of the card. Fronts are printed on metallic foil with a textured pattern behind the player photo. Conventionally printed backs repeat the front design numbered with an "S" prefix. These were seeded 1:6 packs.

	NM/M
Complete Set (15):	9.00

Tribute 1999

This four-card set is devoted to 1999's Hall of Fame inductees. Card fronts have a horizontal format over a holographic foil design. Card backs have the featured players' year-by-year statistics and are numbered with a "T" prefix.

		NM/M
Complete Set (4):		5.00
Common Player:		1.00
Inserted 1:11		
1	Nolan Ryan	2.00
2	Robin Yount	1.50
3	George Brett	1.50
4	Orlando Cepeda	1.00

Ultimate Competitors

This 12-card set has a close-up photo, along with two miniature action photos in the foreground, all printed on silver foil. Backs repeat the front photos and have a few words about the player's competitive desire. These were seeded 1:23 packs and are numbered with a "U" prefix on the card back.

		NM/M
Complete Set (12):		20.00
Common Player:		.60
Inserted 1:23		
1	Ken Griffey Jr.	3.00
2	Roger Clemens	2.50
3	Scott Rolen	1.00
4	Greg Maddux	2.00
5	Mark McGwire	4.00
6	Derek Jeter	5.00
7	Randy Johnson	1.50
8	Cal Ripken Jr.	5.00
9	Craig Biggio	.50
10	Kevin Brown	.50

| 11 | Chipper Jones | 2.00 |
| 12 | Vladimir Guerrero | 1.50 |

Ultimate Hit Men

This insert set spotlights the eight candidates who competed for the 1999 batting titles. Inserted on the average of 1:23 packs they were numbered with an "H" prefix on the card back.

		NM/M
Complete Set (8):		15.00
Common Player:		1.00
Inserted 1:23		
1	Tony Gwynn	2.00
2	Cal Ripken Jr.	4.00
3	Wade Boggs	2.00
4	Larry Walker	1.00
5	Alex Rodriguez	3.00
6	Derek Jeter	4.00
7	Ivan Rodriguez	1.25
8	Ken Griffey Jr.	2.50

Victory

This 470-card base set is printed on 20-point stock and has a white border with UV coating. The set consists of a number of subsets including, 30-card Mark McGwire Magic, 30 team checklist cards, 50 '99 rookies, 15 Power Trip, 20 Rookie Flashback, 15 Big Play Makers and 10 History in the Making. Twelve-card packs had an SRP of $.99.

	NM/M
Complete Set (470):	30.00
Common Player:	.05
Pack (12):	.75
Wax Box (36):	20.00
1	Anaheim Angels (Team Checklist)	.05
2	Mark Harriger RC (99 Rookie)	.10
3	Mo Vaughn (Power Trip)	.05
4	Darin Erstad (Big Play Makers)	.10
5	Troy Glaus	.45
6	Tim Salmon	.05
7	Mo Vaughn	.25
8	Darin Erstad	.05
9	Garret Anderson	.05
10	Todd Greene	.05
11	Troy Percival	.05
12	Chuck Finley	.05
13	Jason Dickson	.05
14	Jim Edmonds	.05
15	Arizona Diamondbacks (Team Checklist)	.05
16	Randy Johnson	.50
17	Matt Williams	.15
18	Travis Lee	.15
19	Jay Bell	.05
20	Tony Womack	.05
21	Steve Finley	.05
22	Bernard Gilkey	.05
23	Tony Batista	.05
24	Todd Stottlemyre	.05
25	Omar Daal	.05
26	Atlanta Braves (Team Checklist)	.05
27	Bruce Chen (99 Rookie)	.05
28	George Lombard (99 Rookie)	.05
29	Chipper Jones (Power Trip)	.35
30	Chipper Jones (Big Play Makers)	.35
31	Greg Maddux	.65
32	Chipper Jones	.65
33	Javy Lopez	.05
34	Tom Glavine	.25
35	John Smoltz	.05
36	Andruw Jones	.50
37	Brian Jordan	.05
38	Walt Weiss	.05
39	Bret Boone	.05
40	Andres Galarraga	.05
41	Baltimore Orioles (Team Checklist)	.05
42	Ryan Minor (99 Rookie)	.05
43	Jerry Hairston Jr. (99 Rookie)	.05
44	Calvin Pickering (99 Rookie)	.05
45	Cal Ripken Jr. (History in the Making)	.75
46	Cal Ripken Jr.	1.50
47	Charles Johnson	.05
48	Albert Belle	.05
49	Delino DeShields	.05
50	Mike Mussina	.30
51	Scott Erickson	.05
52	Brady Anderson	.05
53	B.J. Surhoff	.05
54	Harold Baines	.05
55	Will Clark	.05
56	Boston Red Sox (Team Checklist)	.05
57	Shea Hillenbrand RC (99 Rookie)	.50
58	Trot Nixon (99 Rookie)	.05
59	Jin Ho Cho (99 Rookie)	.05
60	Nomar Garciaparra (Power Trip)	.35
61	Nomar Garciaparra (Big Play Makers)	.35
62	Pedro Martinez	.50
63	Nomar Garciaparra	.65
64	Jose Offerman	.05
65	Jason Varitek	.05
66	Darren Lewis	.05
67	Troy O'Leary	.05
68	Donnie Sadler	.05
69	John Valentin	.05
70	Tim Wakefield	.05
71	Bret Saberhagen	.05
72	Chicago Cubs (Team Checklist)	.05
73	Kyle Farnsworth RC (99 Rookie)	.10
74	Sammy Sosa (Power Trip)	.35
75	Sammy Sosa (Big Play Makers)	.35
76	Sammy Sosa (History in the Making)	.35
77	Kerry Wood (History in the Making)	.10
78	Sammy Sosa	.65
79	Mark Grace	.05
80	Kerry Wood	.05
81	Kevin Tapani	.05
82	Benito Santiago	.05
83	Gary Gaetti	.05
84	Mickey Morandini	.05
85	Glenallen Hill	.05
86	Henry Rodriguez	.05
87	Rod Beck	.05
88	Chicago White Sox (Team Checklist)	.05
89	Carlos Lee (99 Rookie)	.10
90	Mark Johnson (99 Rookie)	.05
91	Frank Thomas (Power Trip)	.30
92	Frank Thomas	.50
93	Jim Parque	.05
94	Mike Sirotka	.05
95	Mike Caruso	.05
96	Ray Durham	.05
97	Magglio Ordonez	.25
98	Paul Konerko	.15
99	Bob Howry	.05
100	Brian Simmons	.05
101	Jaime Navarro	.05
102	Cincinnati Reds (Team Checklist)	.05
103	Denny Neagle	.05
104	Pete Harnisch	.05
105	Greg Vaughn	.05
106	Brett Tomko	.05
107	Mike Cameron	.05
108	Sean Casey	.10
109	Aaron Boone	.05
110	Michael Tucker	.05
111	Dmitri Young	.05
112	Barry Larkin	.15
113	Cleveland Indians (Team Checklist)	.05
114	Russ Branyan (99 Rookie)	.05
115	Jim Thome (Power Trip)	.20
116	Manny Ramirez (Power Trip)	.25
117	Manny Ramirez	.50
118	Jim Thome	.40
119	David Justice	.05
120	Sandy Alomar	.05
121	Roberto Alomar	.20
122	Jaret Wright	.05
123	Bartolo Colon	.05
124	Travis Fryman	.05
125	Kenny Lofton	.05
126	Omar Vizquel	.05
127	Colorado Rockies (Team Checklist)	.05
128	Derrick Gibson (99 Rookie)	.05
129	Larry Walker (Big Play Makers)	.05
130	Larry Walker	.05
131	Dante Bichette	.05
132	Todd Helton	.45
133	Neifi Perez	.05
134	Vinny Castilla	.05
135	Darryl Kile	.05
136	Pedro Astacio	.05
137	Darryl Hamilton	.05
138	Mike Lansing	.05
139	Kirt Manwaring	.05
140	Detroit Tigers (Team Checklist)	.05
141	Jeff Weaver RC (99 Rookie)	.50
142	Gabe Kapler (99 Rookie)	.05
143	Tony Clark (Power Trip)	.05
144	Tony Clark	.05
145	Juan Encarnacion	.05
146	Dean Palmer	.05
147	Damion Easley	.05
148	Bobby Higginson	.05
149	Karim Garcia	.05
150	Justin Thompson	.05
151	Matt Anderson	.05
152	Willie Blair	.05
153	Brian Hunter	.05
154	Florida Marlins (Team Checklist)	.05
155	Alex Gonzalez (99 Rookie)	.05
156	Mark Kotsay	.05
157	Livan Hernandez	.05
158	Cliff Floyd	.05
159	Todd Dunwoody	.05
160	Alex Fernandez	.05
161	Mark Mantei	.05
162	Derrek Lee	.40
163	Kevin Orie	.05
164	Craig Counsell	.05
165	Rafael Medina	.05
166	Houston Astros (Team Checklist)	.05
167	Daryle Ward (99 Rookie)	.05
168	Mitch Meluskey (99 Rookie)	.05
169	Jeff Bagwell (Power Trip)	.25
170	Jeff Bagwell	.50
171	Ken Caminiti	.05
172	Craig Biggio	.05
173	Derek Bell	.05
174	Moises Alou	.05
175	Billy Wagner	.05
176	Shane Reynolds	.05
177	Carl Everett	.05
178	Scott Elarton	.05
179	Richard Hidalgo	.05
180	Kansas City Royals (Team Checklist)	.05
181	Carlos Beltran (99 Rookie)	.60
182	Carlos Febles (99 Rookie)	.05
183	Jeremy Giambi (99 Rookie)	.05
184	Johnny Damon	.30
185	Joe Randa	.05
186	Jeff King	.05
187	Hipolito Pichardo	.05
188	Kevin Appier	.05
189	Chad Kreuter	.05
190	Rey Sanchez	.05
191	Larry Sutton	.05
192	Jeff Montgomery	.05
193	Jermaine Dye	.05
194	Los Angeles Dodgers (Team Checklist)	.05
195	Adam Riggs (99 Rookie)	.05
196	Angel Pena (99 Rookie)	.05
197	Todd Hundley	.05
198	Kevin Brown	.05
199	Ismael Valdes	.05
200	Chan Ho Park	.05
201	Adrian Beltre	.15
202	Mark Grudzielanek	.05
203	Raul Mondesi	.05
204	Gary Sheffield	.35
205	Eric Karros	.05
206	Devon White	.05
207	Milwaukee Brewers (Team Checklist)	.05
208	Ron Belliard (99 Rookie)	.05
209	Rafael Roque (99 Rookie)	.05
210	Jeromy Burnitz	.05
211	Fernando Vina	.05
212	Scott Karl	.05
213	Jim Abbott	.05
214	Sean Berry	.05
215	Marquis Grissom	.05
216	Geoff Jenkins	.05
217	Jeff Cirillo	.05
218	Dave Nilsson	.05
219	Jose Valentin	.05
220	Minnesota Twins (Team Checklist)	.05
221	Corey Koskie (99 Rookie)	.05
222	Christian Guzman (99 Rookie)	.05
223	A.J. Pierzynski (99 Rookie)	.05
224	David Ortiz	.05
225	Brad Radke	.05
226	Todd Walker	.05
227	Matt Lawton	.05
228	Rick Aguilera	.05
229	Eric Milton	.05
230	Marty Cordova	.05
231	Torii Hunter	.05
232	Ron Coomer	.05
233	LaTroy Hawkins	.05
234	Montreal Expos (Team Checklist)	.05
235	Fernando Seguignol (99 Rookie)	.05
236	Michael Barrett (99 Rookie)	.05
237	Vladimir Guerrero (Big Play Makers)	.25
238	Vladimir Guerrero	.50
239	Brad Fullmer	.05
240	Rondell White	.05
241	Ugueth Urbina	.05
242	Dustin Hermanson	.05
243	Orlando Cabrerra	.05
244	Wilton Guerrero	.05
245	Carl Pavano	.05
246	Javier Vasquez	.05
247	Chris Widger	.05
248	New York Mets (Team Checklist)	.05
249	Mike Kinkade (99 Rookie)	.05
250	Octavio Dotel (99 Rookie)	.05
251	Mike Piazza (Power Trip)	.40
252	Mike Piazza	.75
253	Rickey Henderson	.50
254	Edgardo Alfonzo	.05
255	Robin Ventura	.05
256	Al Leiter	.05
257	Brian McRae	.05
258	Rey Ordonez	.05
259	Bobby Bonilla	.05
260	Orel Hershiser	.05
261	John Olerud	.05
262	New York Yankees (Team Checklist)	.05
263	Ricky Ledee (99 Rookie)	.05
264	Bernie Williams (Big Play Makers)	.05
265	Derek Jeter (Big Play Makers)	.75
266	Scott Brosius (History in the Making)	.05
267	Derek Jeter	1.50
268	Roger Clemens	.65
269	Orlando Hernandez	.05
270	Scott Brosius	.05
271	Paul O'Neill	.05
272	Bernie Williams	.05
273	Chuck Knoblauch	.05
274	Tino Martinez	.05
275	Mariano Rivera	.10
276	Jorge Posada	.05
277	Oakland Athletics (Team Checklist)	.05
278	Eric Chavez (99 Rookie)	.15
279	Ben Grieve (History in the Making)	.05
280	Jason Giambi	.30
281	John Jaha	.05
282	Miguel Tejada	.15
283	Ben Grieve	.05
284	Matt Stairs	.05
285	Ryan Christenson	.05
286	A.J. Hinch	.05
287	Kenny Rogers	.05
288	Tom Candiotti	.05
289	Scott Spezio	.05
290	Philadelphia Phillies (Team Checklist)	.05
291	Pat Burrell RC (99 Rookie)	1.50
292	Marlon Anderson (99 Rookie)	.05
293	Scott Rolen (Big Play Makers)	.20
294	Scott Rolen	.40
295	Doug Glanville	.05
296	Rico Brogna	.05
297	Ron Gant	.05
298	Bobby Abreu	.05
299	Desi Relaford	.05
300	Curt Schilling	.25
301	Chad Ogea	.05
302	Kevin Jordan	.05
303	Carlton Loewer	.05
304	Pittsburgh Pirates (Team Checklist)	.05
305	Kris Benson (99 Rookie)	.05
306	Brian Giles	.05
307	Jason Kendall	.05
308	Jose Guillen	.05
309	Pat Meares	.05

#	Player	Price
310	Brant Brown	.05
311	Kevin Young	.05
312	Ed Sprague	.05
313	Francisco Cordova	.05
314	Aramis Ramirez	.05
315	Freddy Garcia	.05
316	Saint Louis Cardinals (Team Checklist)	.05
317	J.D. Drew (99 Rookie)	.40
318	Chad Hutchinson RC (99 Rookie)	.05
319	Mark McGwire (Power Trip)	.50
320	J.D. Drew (Power Trip)	.20
321	Mark McGwire (Big Play Makers)	.50
322	Mark McGwire (History in the Making)	.50
323	Mark McGwire	1.00
324	Fernando Tatis	.05
325	Edgar Renteria	.05
326	Ray Lankford	.05
327	Willie McGee	.05
328	Ricky Bottalico	.05
329	Eli Marrero	.05
330	Matt Morris	.05
331	Eric Davis	.05
332	Darren Bragg	.05
333	Padres (Team Checklist)	.05
334	Matt Clement (99 Rookie)	.05
335	Ben Davis (99 Rookie)	.05
336	Gary Matthews Jr. (99 Rookie)	.05
337	Tony Gwynn (Big Play Makers)	.35
338	Tony Gwynn (History in the Making)	.35
339	Tony Gwynn	.65
340	Reggie Sanders	.05
341	Ruben Rivera	.05
342	Wally Joyner	.05
343	Sterling Hitchcock	.05
344	Carlos Hernandez	.05
345	Andy Ashby	.05
346	Trevor Hoffman	.05
347	Chris Gomez	.05
348	Jim Leyritz	.05
349	San Francisco Giants (Team Checklist)	.05
350	Armando Rios (99 Rookie)	.05
351	Barry Bonds (Power Trip)	.75
352	Barry Bonds (Big Play Makers)	.75
353	Barry Bonds (History in the Making)	.75
354	Robb Nen	.05
355	Bill Mueller	.05
356	Barry Bonds	1.50
357	Jeff Kent	.05
358	J.T. Snow	.05
359	Ellis Burks	.05
360	F.P. Santangelo	.05
361	Marvin Benard	.05
362	Stan Javier	.05
363	Shawn Estes	.05
364	Seattle Mariners (Team Checklist)	.05
365	Carlos Guillen (99 Rookie)	.05
366	Ken Griffey Jr. (Power Trip)	.40
367	Alex Rodriguez (Power Trip)	.50
368	Ken Griffey Jr. (Big Play Makers)	.40
369	Alex Rodriguez (Big Play Makers)	.50
370	Ken Griffey Jr. (History in the Making)	.40
371	Alex Rodriguez (History in the Making)	.50
372	Ken Griffey Jr.	.75
373	Alex Rodriguez	1.00
374	Jay Buhner	.05
375	Edgar Martinez	.05
376	Jeff Fassero	.05
377	David Bell	.05
378	David Segui	.05
379	Russ Davis	.05
380	Dan Wilson	.05
381	Jamie Moyer	.05
382	Tampa Bay Devil Rays (Team Checklist)	.05
383	Roberto Hernandez	.05
384	Bobby Smith	.05
385	Wade Boggs	.65
386	Fred McGriff	.05
387	Rolando Arrojo	.05
388	Jose Canseco	.35
389	Wilson Alvarez	.05
390	Kevin Stocker	.05
391	Miguel Cairo	.05
392	Quinton McCracken	.05
393	Texas Rangers (Team Checklist)	.05
394	Ruben Mateo (99 Rookie)	.05
395	Cesar King (99 Rookie)	.05
396	Juan Gonzalez (Power Trip)	.15
397	Juan Gonzalez (Big Play Makers)	.15
398	Ivan Rodriguez	.40
399	Juan Gonzalez	.25
400	Rafael Palmeiro	.40
401	Rick Helling	.05
402	Aaron Sele	.05
403	John Wetteland	.05
404	Rusty Greer	.05
405	Todd Zeile	.05
406	Royce Clayton	.05
407	Tom Goodwin	.05
408	Toronto Blue Jays (Team Checklist)	.05
409	Kevin Witt (99 Rookie)	.05
410	Roy Halladay (99 Rookie)	.05
411	Jose Cruz Jr.	.05
412	Carlos Delgado	.30
413	Willie Greene	.05
414	Shawn Green	.25
415	Homer Bush	.05
416	Shannon Stewart	.05
417	David Wells	.05
418	Kelvim Escobar	.05
419	Joey Hamilton	.05
420	Alex Gonzalez	.05
421	Mark McGwire (McGwire Magic)	.20
422	Mark McGwire (McGwire Magic)	.20
423	Mark McGwire (McGwire Magic)	.20
424	Mark McGwire (McGwire Magic)	.20
425	Mark McGwire (McGwire Magic)	.20
426	Mark McGwire (McGwire Magic)	.20
427	Mark McGwire (McGwire Magic)	.20
428	Mark McGwire (McGwire Magic)	.20
429	Mark McGwire (McGwire Magic)	.20
430	Mark McGwire (McGwire Magic)	.20
431	Mark McGwire (McGwire Magic)	.20
432	Mark McGwire (McGwire Magic)	.20
433	Mark McGwire (McGwire Magic)	.20
434	Mark McGwire (McGwire Magic)	.20
435	Mark McGwire (McGwire Magic)	.20
436	Mark McGwire (McGwire Magic)	.20
437	Mark McGwire (McGwire Magic)	.20
438	Mark McGwire (McGwire Magic)	.20
439	Mark McGwire (McGwire Magic)	.20
440	Mark McGwire (McGwire Magic)	.20
441	Mark McGwire (McGwire Magic)	.20
442	Mark McGwire (McGwire Magic)	.20
443	Mark McGwire (McGwire Magic)	.20
444	Mark McGwire (McGwire Magic)	.20
445	Mark McGwire (McGwire Magic)	.20
446	Mark McGwire (McGwire Magic)	.20
447	Mark McGwire (McGwire Magic)	.20
448	Mark McGwire (McGwire Magic)	.20
449	Mark McGwire (McGwire Magic)	.20
450	Mark McGwire (McGwire Magic)	.20
451	Chipper Jones '93 (Rookie Flashback)	.35
452	Cal Ripken Jr. '81 (Rookie Flashback)	.75
453	Roger Clemens '84 (Rookie Flashback)	.40
454	Wade Boggs '82 (Rookie Flashback)	.35
455	Greg Maddux '86 (Rookie Flashback)	.35
456	Frank Thomas '90 (Rookie Flashback)	.30
457	Jeff Bagwell '91 (Rookie Flashback)	.25
458	Mike Piazza '92 (Rookie Flashback)	.45
459	Randy Johnson '88 (Rookie Flashback)	.05
460	Mo Vaughn '91 (Rookie Flashback)	.05
461	Mark McGwire '86 (Rookie Flashback)	.50
462	Rickey Henderson '79 (Rookie Flashback)	.25
463	Barry Bonds '86 (Rookie Flashback)	.75
464	Tony Gwynn '82 (Rookie Flashback)	.35
465	Ken Griffey Jr. '89 (Rookie Flashback)	.45
466	Alex Rodriguez '94 (Rookie Flashback)	.50
467	Sammy Sosa '89 (Rookie Flashback)	.35
468	Juan Gonzalez '89 (Rookie Flashback)	.15
469	Kevin Brown '86 (Rookie Flashback)	.05
470	Fred McGriff '86 (Rookie Flashback)	.05

2000 Upper Deck

Released in two 270-card series the base cards feature full-bleed fronts with gold foil etching and stamping. Card backs have complete year-by-year statistics.

	NM/M
Complete Set (540):	40.00
Complete Series I (270):	20.00
Complete Series II (270):	20.00
Common Player:	.15
Silver Stars:	5-10X
Rookies:	2-4X
Hobby Pack (10):	3.00
Hobby Box (24):	55.00

#	Player	Price
1	Rick Ankiel (Star Rookie)	.20
2	Vernon Wells (Star Rookie)	.50
3	Ryan Anderson (Star Rookie)	.15
4	Ed Yarnall (Star Rookie)	.15
5	Brian McNichol (Star Rookie)	.15
6	Ben Petrick (Star Rookie)	.15
7	Kip Wells (Star Rookie)	.15
8	Eric Munson (Star Rookie)	.15
9	Matt Riley (Star Rookie)	.15
10	Peter Bergeron (Star Rookie)	.15
11	Eric Gagne (Star Rookie)	.25
12	Ramon Ortiz (Star Rookie)	.25
13	Josh Beckett (Star Rookie)	.50
14	Alfonso Soriano (Star Rookie)	1.50
15	Jorge Toca (Star Rookie)	.15
16	Buddy Carlyle (Star Rookie)	.15
17	Chad Hermansen (Star Rookie)	.15
18	Matt Perisho (Star Rookie)	.15
19	Tomokazu Ohka RC (Star Rookie)	.75
20	Jacque Jones (Star Rookie)	.15
21	Josh Paul (Star Rookie)	.15
22	Dermal Brown (Star Rookie)	.15
23	Adam Kennedy (Star Rookie)	.15
24	Chad Harville (Star Rookie)	.15
25	Calvin Murray (Star Rookie)	.15
26	Chad Meyers (Star Rookie)	.15
27	Brian Cooper (Star Rookie)	.15
28	Troy Glaus	.50
29	Ben Molina	.15
30	Troy Percival	.15
31	Ken Hill	.15
32	Chuck Finley	.15
33	Todd Greene	.15
34	Tim Salmon	.25
35	Gary DiSarcina	.15
36	Luis Gonzalez	.25
37	Tony Womack	.15
38	Omar Daal	.15
39	Randy Johnson	.50
40	Erubiel Durazo	.20
41	Jay Bell	.15
42	Steve Finley	.15
43	Travis Lee	.15
44	Greg Maddux	1.00
45	Bret Boone	.25
46	Brian Jordan	.15
47	Kevin Millwood	.25
48	Odalis Perez	.15
49	Javy Lopez	.25
50	John Smoltz	.25
51	Bruce Chen	.15
52	Albert Belle	.15
53	Jerry Hairston Jr.	.15
54	Will Clark	.40
55	Sidney Ponson	.15
56	Charles Johnson	.15
57	Cal Ripken Jr.	2.00
58	Ryan Minor	.15
59	Mike Mussina	.40
60	Tom Gordon	.15
61	Jose Offerman	.15
62	Trot Nixon	.15
63	Pedro Martinez	.75
64	John Valentin	.15
65	Jason Varitek	.15
66	Juan Pena	.15
67	Troy O'Leary	.15
68	Sammy Sosa	1.25
69	Henry Rodriguez	.15
70	Kyle Farnsworth	.15
71	Glenallen Hill	.15
72	Lance Johnson	.15
73	Mickey Morandini	.15
74	Jon Lieber	.15
75	Kevin Tapani	.15
76	Carlos Lee	.15
77	Ray Durham	.15
78	Jim Parque	.15
79	Bob Howry	.15
80	Magglio Ordonez	.25
81	Paul Konerko	.20
82	Mike Caruso	.15
83	Chris Singleton	.15
84	Sean Casey	.20
85	Barry Larkin	.25
86	Pokey Reese	.15
87	Eddie Taubensee	.15
88	Scott Williamson	.15
89	Jason LaRue	.15
90	Aaron Boone	.20
91	Jeffrey Hammonds	.15
92	Omar Vizquel	.20
93	Manny Ramirez	.20
94	Kenny Lofton	.20
95	Jaret Wright	.15
96	Einar Diaz	.15
97	Charles Nagy	.15
98	David Justice	.25
99	Richie Sexson	.25
100	Steve Karsay	.15
101	Todd Helton	.50
102	Dante Bichette	.15
103	Larry Walker	.25
104	Pedro Astacio	.15
105	Neifi Perez	.15
106	Brian Bohanon	.15
107	Edgard Clemente	.15
108	Dave Veres	.15
109	Gabe Kapler	.15
110	Juan Encarnacion	.15
111	Jeff Weaver	.15
112	Damion Easley	.15
113	Justin Thompson	.15
114	Brad Ausmus	.15
115	Frank Catalanotto	.15
116	Todd Jones	.15
117	Preston Wilson	.25
118	Cliff Floyd	.15
119	Mike Lowell	.15
120	Jorge Fabregas	.15
121	Alex Gonzalez	.15
122	Braden Looper	.15
123	Bruce Aven	.15
124	Richard Hidalgo	.15
125	Mitch Meluskey	.15
126	Jeff Bagwell	.50
127	Jose Lima	.15
128	Derek Bell	.15
129	Billy Wagner	.15
130	Shane Reynolds	.15
131	Moises Alou	.25
132	Carlos Beltran	.25
133	Carlos Febles	.15
134	Jermaine Dye	.15
135	Jeremy Giambi	.15
136	Joe Randa	.15
137	Jose Rosado	.15
138	Chad Kreuter	.15
139	Jose Vizcaino	.15
140	Adrian Beltre	.25
141	Kevin Brown	.25
142	Ismael Valdes	.15
143	Angel Pena	.15
144	Chan Ho Park	.15
145	Mark Grudzielanek	.15
146	Jeff Shaw	.15
147	Geoff Jenkins	.20
148	Jeromy Burnitz	.15
149	Hideo Nomo	.25
150	Ron Belliard	.15
151	Sean Berry	.15
152	Mark Loretta	.15
153	Steve Woodard	.15
154	Joe Mays	.15
155	Eric Milton	.15
156	Corey Koskie	.15
157	Ron Coomer	.15
158	Brad Radke	.15
159	Terry Steinbach	.15
160	Christian Guzman	.15
161	Vladimir Guerrero	.50
162	Wilton Guerrero	.15
163	Michael Barrett	.15
164	Chris Widger	.15
165	Fernando Seguignol	.15
166	Ugueth Urbina	.15
167	Dustin Hermanson	.15
168	Kenny Rogers	.15
169	Edgardo Alfonzo	.15
170	Orel Hershiser	.15
171	Robin Ventura	.20
172	Octavio Dotel	.15
173	Rickey Henderson	.25
174	Roger Cedeno	.15
175	John Olerud	.25
176	Derek Jeter	2.00
177	Tino Martinez	.25
178	Orlando Hernandez	.20
179	Chuck Knoblauch	.15
180	Bernie Williams	.40
181	Chili Davis	.15
182	David Cone	.15
183	Ricky Ledee	.15
184	Paul O'Neill	.15
185	Jason Giambi	.50
186	Eric Chavez	.25
187	Matt Stairs	.15
188	Miguel Tejada	.25
189	Olmedo Saenz	.15
190	Tim Hudson	.40
191	John Jaha	.15
192	Randy Velarde	.15
193	Rico Brogna	.15
194	Mike Lieberthal	.20
195	Marlon Anderson	.15
196	Bobby Abreu	.25
197	Ron Gant	.15
198	Randy Wolf	.15
199	Desi Relaford	.15
200	Doug Glanville	.15
201	Warren Morris	.15
202	Kris Benson	.15
203	Kevin Young	.15
204	Brian Giles	.25
205	Jason Schmidt	.15
206	Ed Sprague	.15
207	Francisco Cordova	.15
208	Mark McGwire	2.00
209	Jose Jimenez	.15
210	Fernando Tatis	.15
211	Kent Bottenfield	.15
212	Eli Marrero	.15
213	Edgar Renteria	.15
214	Joe McEwing	.15
215	J.D. Drew	.20
216	Tony Gwynn	.75
217	Gary Matthews Jr.	.15
218	Eric Owens	.15
219	Damian Jackson	.15
220	Reggie Sanders	.15
221	Trevor Hoffman	.15
222	Ben Davis	.15
223	Shawn Estes	.15
224	F.P. Santangelo	.15
225	Livan Hernandez	.15
226	Ellis Burks	.15
227	J.T. Snow	.15
228	Jeff Kent	.25
229	Robb Nen	.15
230	Marvin Benard	.15
231	Ken Griffey Jr.	1.00
232	John Halama	.15
233	Gil Meche	.15
234	David Bell	.15
235	Brian L. Hunter	.15
236	Jay Buhner	.25
237	Edgar Martinez	.25
238	Jose Mesa	.15
239	Wilson Alvarez	.15
240	Wade Boggs	.40
241	Fred McGriff	.25
242	Jose Canseco	.40
243	Kevin Stocker	.15
244	Roberto Hernandez	.15
245	Bubba Trammell	.15
246	John Flaherty	.15
247	Ivan Rodriguez	.40
248	Rusty Greer	.15
249	Rafael Palmeiro	.40
250	Jeff Zimmerman	.15
251	Royce Clayton	.15
252	Todd Zeile	.15
253	John Wetteland	.15
254	Ruben Mateo	.15
255	Kelvim Escobar	.15
256	David Wells	.15
257	Shawn Green	.40
258	Homer Bush	.15
259	Shannon Stewart	.15
260	Carlos Delgado	.25
261	Roy Halladay	.25
262	Fernando Tatis CL	.15
263	Jose Jimenez CL	.15
264	Tony Gwynn CL	.40
265	Wade Boggs CL	.15
266	Cal Ripken Jr. CL	1.00
267	David Cone CL	.15
268	Mark McGwire CL	.75
269	Pedro Martinez CL	.40
270	Nomar Garciaparra CL	.75
271	Nick Johnson (Star Rookie)	.40
272	Mark Quinn (Star Rookie)	.15
273	Roosevelt Brown (Star Rookie)	.15
274	Adam Everett (Star Rookie)	.15
275	Jason Marquis (Star Rookie)	.15
276	Kazuhiro Sasaki RC (Star Rookie)	1.50
277	Aaron Myette (Star Rookie)	.15
278	Danys Baez RC (Star Rookie)	.50
279	Travis Dawkins (Star Rookie)	.15
280	Mark Mulder (Star Rookie)	.25
281	Chris Haas (Star Rookie)	.15
282	Milton Bradley (Star Rookie)	.15
283	Brad Penny (Star Rookie)	.15
284	Rafael Furcal (Star Rookie)	.25
285	Luis Matos RC (Star Rookie)	1.00
286	Victor Santos (Star Rookie)	.15
287	Rico Washington RC (Star Rookie)	.15
288	Rob Bell (Star Rookie)	.15
289	Joe Crede (Star Rookie)	.15
290	Pablo Ozuna (Star Rookie)	.15
291	Wascar Serrano RC (Star Rookie)	.15
292	Sang-Hoon Lee RC (Star Rookie)	.25
293	Chris Wakeland (Star Rookie)	.15
294	Luis Rivera (Star Rookie)	.15
295	Mike Lamb RC (Star Rookie)	.20
296	Wily Pena (Star Rookie)	.20
297	Mike Meyers RC (Star Rookie)	.15
298	Mo Vaughn	.20
299	Darin Erstad	.25
300	Garret Anderson	.25
301	Tim Belcher	.15
302	Scott Spiezio	.15
303	Kent Bottenfield	.15
304	Orlando Palmeiro	.15
305	Jason Dickson	.15
306	Matt Williams	.20
307	Brian Anderson	.15
308	Hanley Frias	.15
309	Todd Stottlemyre	.15
310	Matt Mantei	.15
311	David Dellucci	.15
312	Armando Reynoso	.15
313	Bernard Gilkey	.15
314	Chipper Jones	1.00
315	Tom Glavine	.25
316	Quilvio Veras	.15
317	Andruw Jones	.50
318	Bobby Bonilla	.15
319	Reggie Sanders	.15
320	Andres Galarraga	.20
321	George Lombard	.15
322	John Rocker	.15
322	Wally Joyner	.15
324	B.J. Surhoff	.15
325	Scott Erickson	.15
326	Delino DeShields	.15
327	Jeff Conine	.15
328	Mike Timlin	.15
329	Brady Anderson	.15
330	Mike Bordick	.15
331	Harold Baines	.15
332	Nomar Garciaparra	1.50
333	Bret Saberhagen	.15
334	Ramon Martinez	.15
335	Donnie Sadler	.15
336	Wilton Veras	.15
337	Mike Stanley	.15
338	Brian Rose	.15
339	Carl Everett	.15
340	Tim Wakefield	.15
341	Mark Grace	.25
342	Kerry Wood	.30
343	Eric Young	.15
344	Jose Nieves	.15
345	Ismael Valdes	.15
346	Joe Girardi	.15
347	Damon Buford	.15
348	Ricky Gutierrez	.15
349	Frank Thomas	.50
350	Brian Simmons	.15
351	James Baldwin	.15
352	Brook Fordyce	.15
353	Jose Valentin	.15
354	Mike Sirotka	.15
355	Greg Norton	.15
356	Dante Bichette	.15
357	Deion Sanders	.15
358	Ken Griffey Jr.	1.00
359	Denny Neagle	.15
360	Dmitri Young	.15
361	Pete Harnisch	.15
362	Michael Tucker	.15
363	Roberto Alomar	.40
364	Dave Roberts	.15
365	Jim Thome	.50
366	Bartolo Colon	.15
367	Travis Fryman	.20
368	Chuck Finley	.15
369	Russell Branyan	.15
370	Alex Ramirez	.15
371	Jeff Cirillo	.15
372	Jeffrey Hammonds	.15
373	Scott Karl	.15
374	Brent Mayne	.15
375	Tom Goodwin	.15
376	Jose Jimenez	.15
377	Rolando Arrojo	.15
378	Terry Shumpert	.15
379	Juan Gonzalez	.50
380	Bobby Higginson	.15

381	Tony Clark	.15
382	Dave Mlicki	.15
383	Deivi Cruz	.15
384	Brian Moehler	.15
385	Dean Palmer	.15
386	Luis Castillo	.15
387	Mike Redmond	.15
388	Alex Fernandez	.15
389	Brant Brown	.15
390	Dave Berg	.15
391	A.J. Burnett	.15
392	Mark Kotsay	.15
393	Craig Biggio	.20
394	Daryle Ward	.15
395	Lance Berkman	.25
396	Roger Cedeno	.15
397	Scott Elarton	.15
398	Octavio Dotel	.15
399	Ken Caminiti	.15
400	Johnny Damon	.25
401	Mike Sweeney	.15
402	Jeff Suppan	.15
403	Rey Sanchez	.15
404	Blake Stein	.15
405	Ricky Bottalico	.15
406	Jay Witasick	.15
407	Shawn Green	.40
408	Orel Hershiser	.15
409	Gary Sheffield	.40
410	Todd Hollandsworth	.15
411	Terry Adams	.15
412	Todd Hundley	.15
413	Eric Karros	.15
414	F.P. Santangelo	.15
415	Alex Cora	.15
416	Marquis Grissom	.15
417	Henry Blanco	.15
418	Jose Hernandez	.15
419	Kyle Peterson	.15
420	John Snyder RC	.15
421	Bob Wickman	.15
422	Jamey Wright	.15
423	Chad Allen	.15
424	Todd Walker	.15
425	J.C. Romero RC	.15
426	Butch Huskey	.15
427	Jacque Jones	.15
428	Matt Lawton	.15
429	Rondell White	.25
430	Jose Vidro	.15
431	Hideki Irabu	.15
432	Javier Vazquez	.15
433	Lee Stevens	.15
434	Mike Thurman	.15
435	Geoff Blum	.15
436	Mike Hampton	.15
437	Mike Piazza	1.00
438	Al Leiter	.15
439	Derek Bell	.15
440	Armando Benitez	.15
441	Rey Ordonez	.15
442	Todd Zeile	.15
443	Roger Clemens	1.25
444	Ramiro Mendoza	.15
445	Andy Pettitte	.25
446	Scott Brosius	.15
447	Mariano Rivera	.25
448	Jim Leyritz	.15
449	Jorge Posada	.25
450	Omar Olivares	.15
451	Ben Grieve	.15
452	A.J. Hinch	.15
453	Gil Heredia	.15
454	Kevin Appier	.15
455	Ryan Christenson	.15
456	Ramon Hernandez	.15
457	Scott Rolen	.50
458	Alex Arias	.15
459	Andy Ashby	.15
460		
461	Robert Person	.15
462	Paul Byrd	.15
463	Curt Schilling	.25
464	Mike Jackson	.15
465	Jason Kendall	.25
466	Pat Meares	.15
467	Bruce Aven	.15
468	Todd Ritchie	.15
469	Wil Cordero	.15
470	Aramis Ramirez	.15
471	Andy Benes	.15
472	Ray Lankford	.15
473	Fernando Vina	.15
474a	Jim Edmonds	.25
474b	Kevin Jordan	
	(should be #460)	.15
475	Craig Paquette	.15
476	Pat Hentgen	.15
477	Darryl Kile	.15
478	Sterling Hitchcock	.15
479	Ruben Rivera	.15
480	Ryan Klesko	.15
481	Phil Nevin	.15
482	Woody Williams	.15
483	Carlos Hernandez	.15
484	Brian Meadows	.15
485	Bret Boone	.25
486	Barry Bonds	1.50
487	Russ Ortiz	.15
488	Bobby Estalella	.15
489	Rich Aurilia	.15
490	Bill Mueller	.15
491	Joe Nathan	.15
492	Russ Davis	.15
493	John Olerud	.15
494	Alex Rodriguez	1.50
495	Fred Garcia	.15
496	Carlos Guillen	.15

497	Aaron Sele	.15
498	Brett Tomko	.15
499	Jamie Moyer	.15
500	Mike Cameron	.15
501	Vinny Castilla	.15
502	Gerald Williams	.15
503	Mike DiFelice	.15
504	Ryan Rupe	.15
505	Greg Vaughn	.15
506	Miguel Cairo	.15
507	Juan Guzman RC	.15
508	Jose Guillen	.15
509	Gabe Kapler	.15
510	Rick Helling	.15
511	David Segui	.15
512	Doug Davis	.15
513	Justin Thompson	.15
514	Chad Curtis	.15
515	Tony Batista	.15
516	Billy Koch	.15
517	Raul Mondesi	.20
518	Joey Hamilton	.15
519	Darrin Fletcher	.15
520	Brad Fullmer	.15
521	Jose Cruz Jr.	.15
522	Kevin Witt	.15
523	Mark McGwire	
	(All-UD Team)	1.00
524	Roberto Alomar	
	(All-UD Team)	.25
525	Chipper Jones	
	(All-UD Team)	.50
526	Derek Jeter	
	(All-UD Team)	1.00
527	Ken Griffey Jr.	
	(All-UD Team)	.50
528	Sammy Sosa	
	(All-UD Team)	.75
529	Manny Ramirez	
	(All-UD Team)	.40
530	Ivan Rodriguez	
	(All-UD Team)	.25
531	Pedro J. Martinez	
	(All-UD Team)	.40
532	Mariano Rivera (Season Highlights Checklist)	.15
533	Sammy Sosa (Season Highlights Checklist)	.75
534	Cal Ripken Jr. (Season Highlights Checklist)	1.00
535	Vladimir Guerrero (Season Highlights Checklist)	.40
536	Tony Gwynn (Season Highlights Checklist)	.25
537	Mark McGwire (Season Highlights Checklist)	1.00
538	Bernie Williams (Season Highlights Checklist)	.25
539	Pedro J. Martinez (Season Highlights Checklist)	.40
540	Ken Griffey Jr. (Season Highlights Checklist)	.50

Exclusives

Labeled "UD Exclusives," these parallel sets were issued in two versions, silvers numbered to 100 each, and golds which were 1-of-1. Except for the appropriately colored foil highlights on front and dot-matrix serial number, the Exclusives are identical to the regular-issue cards. They were inserted exclusively into hobby packs. Because of their rarity and variable demand, the unique gold cards are not priced.

	NM/M
Common Silver Exclusive:	1.00
Silver Stars/Rookies:	8X

Cooperstown Calling

This insert set features players deemed by Upper Deck as future Hall of Famers. Card fronts feature silver holo-foil with gold foil stamping. Card backs are numbered with a "CC" prefix and are seeded 1:23 packs.

	NM/M
Complete Set (15):	25.00
Common Player:	.75
Inserted 1:23	
1 Roger Clemens	3.00
2 Cal Ripken Jr.	5.00
3 Ken Griffey Jr.	3.00
4 Mike Piazza	3.00
5 Tony Gwynn	2.00
6 Sammy Sosa	2.50
7 Jose Canseco	1.00
8 Larry Walker	.75
9 Barry Bonds	4.00
10 Greg Maddux	2.50
11 Derek Jeter	5.00
12 Mark McGwire	4.00
13 Randy Johnson	2.00
14 Frank Thomas	1.50
15 Jeff Bagwell	1.50

e-Card

Randomly inserted in series 2 packs, each e-card has an ID number stamped on the card front that can be entered on Upper Deck's website. Collectors then find out if that card "evolves" into a signature card, jersey card or a signed jersey card. They are seeded 1:9 packs and are numbered with an "E" prefix on the card back.

	NM/M
Complete Set (6):	10.00
Common Player:	1.00
Inserted 1:12	
1 Ken Griffey Jr.	2.00
2 Alex Rodriguez	3.00
3 Cal Ripken Jr.	3.00
4 Jeff Bagwell	1.00
5 Barry Bonds	3.00
6 Manny Ramirez	1.00

eVolve Jersey

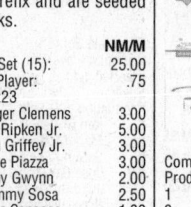

	NM/M
Common Player:	15.00
Production 300 Sets	
1 Ken Griffey Jr.	40.00
2 Alex Rodriguez	40.00
3 Cal Ripken Jr.	65.00
4 Jeff Bagwell	20.00
5 Barry Bonds	50.00
6 Manny Ramirez	20.00

eVolve Signed Jersey

	NM/M
Common Player:	80.00
Production 50 Sets	
1 Ken Griffey Jr.	150.00
2 Alex Rodriguez	150.00
3 Cal Ripken Jr.	200.00

4	Jeff Bagwell	60.00
5	Barry Bonds	150.00
6	Manny Ramirez	60.00

eVolve Signature

	NM/M
Common Player:	40.00
Production 200 Sets	
1 Ken Griffey Jr.	85.00
2 Alex Rodriguez	85.00
3 Cal Ripken Jr.	150.00
4 Jeff Bagwell	40.00
5 Barry Bonds	120.00
6 Manny Ramirez	40.00

Faces of the Game

Randomly inserted in Series 1 at a rate of 1:11 packs, card fronts feature a close-up photo of the featured player with bronze foil etching and stamping. Backs are numbered with an "F" prefix. Two parallel versions are available. Silvers are serially numbered to 100 and golds limited to one set.

	NM/M
Complete Set (20):	30.00
Common Player:	.75
Inserted 1:11	
Silver:	4-8X
Production 100 Sets	
1 Ken Griffey Jr.	2.50
2 Mark McGwire	3.00
3 Sammy Sosa	2.00
4 Alex Rodriguez	3.00
5 Manny Ramirez	1.00
6 Derek Jeter	4.00
7 Jeff Bagwell	1.00
8 Roger Clemens	2.00
9 Scott Rolen	.75
10 Tony Gwynn	1.50
11 Nomar Garciaparra	2.50
12 Randy Johnson	1.50
13 Greg Maddux	2.00
14 Mike Piazza	2.50
15 Frank Thomas	1.00
16 Cal Ripken Jr.	4.00
17 Ivan Rodriguez	.75
18 Mo Vaughn	.75
19 Chipper Jones	2.00
20 Sean Casey	.75

Five-Tool Talents

Randomly inserted in series 2 at a rate of 1:11 packs, this 15-card set spotlights players who have "five tools." Card fronts have silver holo-foil throughout with silver foil stamping. Card backs are numbered with an "FT" prefix.

	NM/M
Common Player:	10.00
AR Alex Rodriguez	30.00
TG Tony Gwynn	20.00
FT Frank Thomas	15.00
MW Matt Williams	10.00
JT Jim Thome	15.00
MV Mo Vaughn	10.00
TGI Tom Glavine	15.00
BG Ben Grieve	10.00

	NM/M
Complete Set (15):	15.00
Common Player:	.50
Inserted 1:11	
1 Vladimir Guerrero	1.50
2 Barry Bonds	3.00
3 Jason Kendall	.50
4 Derek Jeter	4.00
5 Ken Griffey Jr.	2.50
6 Andruw Jones	.75
7 Bernie Williams	.75
8 Jose Canseco	.75
9 Shawn Green	.50
10 Shawn Green	.50
11 Nomar Garciaparra	.75
12 Jeff Bagwell	1.00
13 Larry Walker	.75
14 Chipper Jones	1.00
15 Alex Rodriguez	3.00

Game Balls

These inserts feature a piece of game-used baseball embedded into the card from the featured player. Card backs are numbered with the featured player's initials and are found on the average of 1:287 series 2 packs.

	NM/M
Common Player:	10.00
JB Jeff Bagwell	10.00
RC Roger Clemens	30.00
KG Ken Griffey Jr.	25.00
VG Vladimir Guerrero	15.00
TG Tony Gwynn	25.00
DJ Derek Jeter	40.00
CJ Chipper Jones	20.00
GM Greg Maddux	20.00
MM Mark McGwire	50.00
AR Alex Rodriguez	30.00
BW Bernie Williams	10.00

Game Jersey

These have a piece of game-used jersey from the featured player embedded into the card. This regular version is found both in hobby and retail packs at a rate of 1:2,500 packs.

	NM/M
Common Player:	10.00
Inserted 1:2,500	
JC Jose Canseco	15.00
JG Juan Gonzalez	15.00
VG Vladimir Guerrero	20.00
TH Todd Helton	15.00
CJ Chipper Jones	25.00
GK Gabe Kapler	10.00
GM Greg Maddux	35.00
MR Manny Ramirez	20.00
CR Cal Ripken Jr.	60.00
GV Greg Vaughn	10.00

Game Jersey Series 2

These jersey inserts are found in both hobby and retail packs and are seeded 1:287 packs.

	NM/M
Common Player:	10.00
AR Alex Rodriguez	30.00
TG Tony Gwynn	20.00
FT Frank Thomas	15.00
MW Matt Williams	10.00
JT Jim Thome	15.00
MV Mo Vaughn	10.00
TGI Tom Glavine	15.00
BG Ben Grieve	10.00

TrG	Troy Glaus	15.00
RJ	Randy Johnson	20.00
KM	Kevin Millwood	10.00
KG	Ken Griffey Jr.	25.00
AB	Albert Belle	10.00
DC	David Cone	10.00
MH	Mike Hampton	10.00
EC	Eric Chavez	10.00
EM	Edgar Martinez	15.00
PW	Preston Wilson	10.00
RV	Robin Ventura	10.00

Game Jersey Hobby

These game-used memorabilia inserts were found exclusively in series 1 packs at a rate of 1:288.

	NM/M
Common Player:	10.00
Inserted 1:288	
JB Jeff Bagwell	15.00
TG Troy Glaus	15.00
CY Tom Glavine	10.00
Jr. Ken Griffey Jr.	25.00
DJ Derek Jeter	40.00
PM Pedro J. Martinez	20.00
MP Mike Piazza	30.00
AR Alex Rodriguez	30.00
FT Frank Thomas	15.00
LW Larry Walker	10.00

Game Jersey Autograph Hobby Series 2

Found exclusively in series 2 packs these autographed game-used memorabilia inserts are found only in hobby packs at a rate of 1:287.

	NM/M
Common Player:	30.00
H-KG Ken Griffey Jr.	100.00
H-CR Cal Ripken Jr.	150.00
H-DJ Derek Jeter	150.00
H-IR Ivan Rodriguez	40.00
H-AR Alex Rodriguez	100.00
H-MR Manny Ramirez	50.00
H-JC Jose Canseco	30.00
H-BB Barry Bonds	180.00
H-SR Scott Rolen	40.00
H-PO Paul O'Neill	40.00
H-JK Jason Kendall	30.00
H-VG Vladimir Guerrero	50.00
H-JB Jeff Bagwell	40.00

Game Jersey Patch

Inserted in Series 1 packs at a rate of 1:10,000, these memorabilia inserts have a piece of game-used uniform patch embedded. A 1-of-1 patch of each player was also issued, but cannot be priced due to rarity.

	NM/M
Common Player:	40.00
Inserted 1:10,000	
JB Jeff Bagwell	60.00
JC Jose Canseco	60.00
TG Troy Glaus	50.00
CY Tom Glavine	60.00
Jr. Ken Griffey Jr.	100.00
VG Vladimir Guerrero	100.00
TH Todd Helton	60.00
DJ Derek Jeter	150.00
CJ Chipper Jones	75.00
GK Gabe Kapler	40.00

		NM/M
GM	Greg Maddux	100.00
PM	Pedro J. Martinez	100.00
MP	Mike Piazza	100.00
MR	Manny Ramirez	80.00
CR	Cal Ripken Jr.	200.00
AR	Alex Rodriguez	125.00
FT	Frank Thomas	80.00
GV	Greg Vaughn	40.00
LW	Larry Walker	50.00

Game Jersey Patch Series 2

Inserted in Series 2 packs, these memorabilia inserts have a game-used uniform patch embedded and are seeded 1:7,500 packs. A limited one-of-one patch insert for each player is also randomly seeded and are not priced due to their limited nature.

		NM/M
Common Player:		50.00
JB	Jeff Bagwell	75.00
BB	Barry Bonds	200.00
JC	Jose Canseco	75.00
TGI	Troy Glaus	75.00
KG	Ken Griffey Jr.	125.00
VG	Vladimir Guerrero	100.00
TG	Tony Gwynn	100.00
DJ	Derek Jeter	150.00
RJ	Randy Johnson	100.00
AJ	Andruw Jones	80.00
CJ	Chipper Jones	100.00
GM	Greg Maddux	100.00
PM	Pedro Martinez	100.00
MR	Manny Ramirez	100.00
CR	Cal Ripken Jr.	200.00
SR	Scott Rolen	75.00
AR	Alex Rodriguez	150.00
IR	Ivan Rodriguez	90.00
FT	Frank Thomas	100.00
MV	Mo Vaughn	50.00
MW	Matt Williams	50.00

Hit Brigade

Fifteen of the game's top hitters are featured on a full foiled front with bronze foil stamping. Card backs are numbered with an "H" prefix and are found in series 1 packs at a rate of 1:8. Two parallels are randomly inserted: Silvers are serial numbered to 100 and Golds are limited to one set.

		NM/M
Complete Set (15):		15.00
Common Player:		.50
Inserted 1:8		
Silver:		5-10X
Production 100 Sets		
1	Ken Griffey Jr.	2.00
2	Tony Gwynn	1.00
3	Alex Rodriguez	2.50
4	Derek Jeter	3.00
5	Mike Piazza	2.00
6	Sammy Sosa	1.50
7	Juan Gonzalez	.75
8	Scott Rolen	.50
9	Nomar Garciaparra	2.50
10	Barry Bonds	2.50
11	Craig Biggio	.50
12	Chipper Jones	1.50
13	Frank Thomas	.75
14	Larry Walker	.50
15	Mark McGwire	2.50

Hot Properties

This set spotlights rookies and prospects who have a

---

bright future. Card fronts have a horizontal format on a holo-foiled stock with silver foil stamping. Card backs are numbered with an "HP" prefix and are found in series 2 packs at a rate of 1:11.

		NM/M
Complete Set (15):		10.00
Common Player:		.50
Inserted 1:11		
1	Carlos Beltran	1.00
2	Rick Ankiel	.50
3	Sean Casey	1.00
4	Preston Wilson	1.00
5	Vernon Wells	1.00
6	Pat Burrell	1.50
7	Eric Chavez	1.00
8	J.D. Drew	1.00
9	Alfonso Soriano	2.00
10	Gabe Kapler	1.00
11	Rafael Furcal	1.00
12	Ruben Mateo	.50
13	Corey Koskie	.75
14	Kip Wells	.50
15	Ramon Ortiz	.75

The People's Choice

This 15-card set is printed on a full holo-foiled front with gold foil stamping. Card backs are numbered with a "PC" prefix and are seeded 1:23 packs.

		NM/M
Complete Set (15):		20.00
Common Player:		.75
Inserted 1:23		
1	Mark McGwire	3.00
2	Nomar Garciaparra	3.00
3	Derek Jeter	3.00
4	Shawn Green	.75
5	Manny Ramirez	1.00
6	Pedro Martinez	1.50
7	Ivan Rodriguez	.75
8	Alex Rodriguez	3.00
9	Juan Gonzalez	1.00
10	Ken Griffey Jr.	2.00
11	Sammy Sosa	2.50
12	Jeff Bagwell	1.00
13	Chipper Jones	1.50
14	Cal Ripken Jr.	4.00
15	Mike Piazza	2.00

Pennant Driven

This 10-card horizontal set has a holo-foiled card front with silver foil stamping. Card backs are numbered with a "PD" prefix and are seeded 1:4 packs.

		NM/M
Complete Set (10):		8.00
Common Player:		.50
Inserted 1:4		
1	Derek Jeter	2.00
2	Roberto Alomar	.50
3	Chipper Jones	1.50
4	Jeff Bagwell	.75
5	Roger Clemens	1.00
6	Nomar Garciaparra	1.50
7	Manny Ramirez	.75
8	Mike Piazza	1.50
9	Ivan Rodriguez	.75
10	Randy Johnson	.75

Piece of History-500 Club

This card features a piece of a game-used Louisville Slugger

---

once swung by Aaron. Approximately 350 cards were produced. Also randomly inserted are 44 autographed versions.

		NM/M
755HR	Hank Aaron	275.00
HAAU	Hank Aaron/ Auto./44	900.00

Power Deck

Collectors need access to a CD-ROM in order to enjoy these interactive cards. Found exclusively in hobby packs cards 1-8 are seeded 1:23 packs and cards 9-11 are found 1:287 packs.

		NM/M
Complete Set (11):		60.00
Common Player:		2.50
Inserted 1:23		
1	Ken Griffey Jr.	5.00
2	Cal Ripken Jr.	7.50
3	Mark McGwire	6.00
4	Tony Gwynn	3.50
5	Roger Clemens	3.50
6	Alex Rodriguez	6.00
7	Sammy Sosa	3.50
8	Derek Jeter	7.50
9	Ken Griffey Jr.	25.00
10	Mark McGwire	30.00
11	Reggie Jackson	15.00

Power MARK

		NM/M
Complete Set (10):		25.00
Common McGwire:		3.00
Inserted 1:23		
Silver:		5-10X
Production 100 Sets		
1-10	Mark McGwire	3.00

Power Rally

This 15-card set highlights the top hitters and are

---

numbered with an "P" prefix on the card back. They are found 1:11 packs. Two parallel version are also seeded: Coppers are limited to 100 serial numbered sets and Golds are limited to one set.

		NM/M
Complete Set (15):		20.00
Common Player:		.75
Inserted 1:11		
Silver:		4-8X
Production 100 Sets		
1	Ken Griffey Jr.	2.50
2	Mark McGwire	3.00
3	Sammy Sosa	2.00
4	Jose Canseco	.75
5	Juan Gonzalez	1.00
6	Bernie Williams	.75
7	Jeff Bagwell	1.00
8	Chipper Jones	2.00
9	Vladimir Guerrero	1.50
10	Mo Vaughn	.75
11	Derek Jeter	4.00
12	Mike Piazza	2.50
13	Barry Bonds	3.00
14	Alex Rodriguez	3.00
15	Nomar Garciaparra	2.50

Prime Performers

This 10-card set has a horizontal format on a full holo foiled front, with silver foil etching and stamping. Card backs are numbered with a "PP" prefix and found 1:8 packs.

		NM/M
Complete Set (10):		10.00
Common Player:		.50
Inserted 1:8		
1	Manny Ramirez	.75
2	Pedro Martinez	1.00
3	Carlos Delgado	.50
4	Ken Griffey Jr.	2.00
5	Derek Jeter	3.00
6	Chipper Jones	1.50
7	Sean Casey	.50
8	Shawn Green	.50
9	Sammy Sosa	1.50
10	Alex Rodriguez	2.50

STATitude

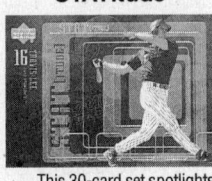

This 30-card set spotlights the most statistically dominant players on a horizontal format with silver foil stamping. Card backs are numbered with an "S" prefix and are inserted 1:4. Two parallel versions are randomly inserted: Coppers are limited to 100 serial numbered sets and Golds are limited to one set.

		NM/M
Complete Set (30):		25.00
Common Player:		.40
Inserted 1:4		
Silver:		5-10X
Production 100 Sets		
1	Mo Vaughn	.40
2	Matt Williams	.40
3	Travis Lee	.40
4	Chipper Jones	1.50
5	Greg Maddux	1.50
6	Gabe Kapler	.40
7	Cal Ripken Jr.	3.00
8	Nomar Garciaparra	2.00
9	Sammy Sosa	1.50
10	Frank Thomas	.75
11	Manny Ramirez	.75
12	Larry Walker	.50
13	Ivan Rodriguez	.50
14	Jeff Bagwell	.75
15	Craig Biggio	.50
16	Vladimir Guerrero	1.00
17	Mike Piazza	2.00
18	Bernie Williams	.50
19	Derek Jeter	3.00
20	Jose Canseco	.50
21	Eric Chavez	.50
22	Scott Rolen	.50

23	Mark McGwire	2.50
24	Tony Gwynn	1.00
25	Barry Bonds	2.50
26	Ken Griffey Jr.	2.00
27	Alex Rodriguez	2.50
28	J.D. Drew	.50
29	Juan Gonzalez	.50
30	Roger Clemens	1.50

2K Plus

This 12-card set showcases the talents of baseball's next millennium. They are numbered with an "2K" prefix on the card back and are seeded 1:23 packs. Two parallel versions are also randomly inserted: Coppers are limited to 100 serial numbered sets and Golds are limited on one set produced.

		NM/M
Complete Set (12):		15.00
Common Player:		.50
Inserted 1:23		
Silver:		5-10X
Production 100 Sets		
1	Ken Griffey Jr.	2.00
2	J.D. Drew	.50
3	Derek Jeter	3.00
4	Nomar Garciaparra	3.00
5	Pat Burrell	.75
6	Ruben Mateo	.50
7	Carlos Beltran	.50
8	Vladimir Guerrero	1.00
9	Scott Rolen	1.00
10	Chipper Jones	2.00
11	Alex Rodriguez	3.00
12	Magglio Ordonez	.75

3,000 Hit Club Series 1

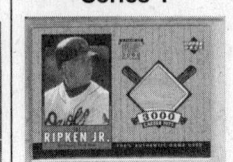

Game-used memorabilia from Orioles teammates Ripken and Murray were inserted in the cross-brand 3,000 Hit Club inserts in Series 1 UD.

		NM/M
CR-B	Cal Ripken Jr. Bat/350	25.00
CR-J	Cal Ripken Jr./ Jsy/350	25.00
CR-JB	Cal Ripken Jr./ Jsy/Bat/100	150.00
EM-B	Eddie Murray/ Bat/350	10.00
EM-J	Eddie Murray/ Jsy/350	8.00
EM-JB	Eddie Murray/ Jsy/Bat/100	60.00

3,000 Hit Club Series 2

This cross-brand series spotlights Hank Aaron. The series includes a Jersey card (350 produced), Bat card (350 produced), Jersey/Bat combo

---

(100 produced) and Autographed Jersey/Bat combo (44 produced).

		NM/M
HA-B	Hank Aaron/ Bat/350	50.00
HA-JB	Hank Aaron/ Bat/Jsy/100	100.00
HA-J	Hank Aaron/ Jsy/350	50.00
HA-JBS	Hank Aaron/ Auto. Bat/Jsy/44	700.00

Black Diamond

The base set consists of 120-cards, including a 30 card Diamond Debut (91-120) subset that are seeded 1:4 packs. Card fronts are full foiled with silver etching. Card backs have the player's past five years of statistics, a brief career note and small photo.

		NM/M
Complete Set (120):		25.00
Common Player:		.15
Common Diamond Debut:		.50
Pack (6):		1.50
Wax Box (24):		30.00
1	Darin Erstad	.25
2	Tim Salmon	.25
3	Mo Vaughn	.20
4	Matt Williams	.25
5	Travis Lee	.15
6	Randy Johnson	.75
7	Tom Glavine	.40
8	Chipper Jones	1.50
9	Greg Maddux	1.50
10	Andruw Jones	.50
11	Brian Jordan	.15
12	Cal Ripken Jr.	2.50
13	Albert Belle	.20
14	Mike Mussina	.50
15	Nomar Garciaparra	2.00
16	Troy O'Leary	.15
17	Pedro J. Martinez	1.00
18	Sammy Sosa	1.50
19	Henry Rodriguez	.15
20	Frank Thomas	.75
21	Magglio Ordonez	.40
22	Greg Vaughn	.15
23	Barry Larkin	.25
24	Sean Casey	.25
25	Jim Thome	.75
26	Kenny Lofton	.25
27	Roberto Alomar	.50
28	Manny Ramirez	.75
29	Larry Walker	.50
30	Todd Helton	.75
31	Gabe Kapler	.15
32	Tony Clark	.15
33	Dean Palmer	.15
34	Cliff Floyd	.15
35	Alex Gonzalez	.15
36	Moises Alou	.25
37	Jeff Bagwell	.75
38	Craig Biggio	.25
39	Richard Hidalgo	.15
40	Carlos Beltran	.25
41	Johnny Damon	.15
42	Adrian Beltre	.25
43	Gary Sheffield	.40
44	Kevin Brown	.25
45	Jeromy Burnitz	.15
46	Jeff Cirillo	.15
47	Joe Mays	.15
48	Todd Walker	.15
49	Vladimir Guerrero	.75
50	Michael Barrett	.15
51	Rickey Henderson	.40
52	Mike Piazza	1.50
53	Robin Ventura	.25
54	John Olerud	.25
55	Edgardo Alfonzo	.25
56	Derek Jeter	2.00
57	Orlando Hernandez	.25
58	Tino Martinez	.25
59	Bernie Williams	.25
60	Roger Clemens	1.50
61	Eric Chavez	.25
62	Ben Grieve	.15
63	Jason Giambi	1.00
64	Scott Rolen	.50
65	Bobby Abreu	.25

66	Curt Schilling	.40
67	Mike Lieberthal	.15
68	Warren Morris	.15
69	Brian Giles	.25
70	Eric Owens	.15
71	Tony Gwynn	1.00
72	Reggie Sanders	.15
73	Barry Bonds	2.00
74	J.T. Snow	.15
75	Jeff Kent	.25
76	Ken Griffey Jr.	1.50
77	Alex Rodriguez	2.00
78	Edgar Martinez	.15
79	Jay Buhner	.15
80	Mark McGwire	2.00
81	J.D. Drew	.25
82	Eric Davis	.15
83	Fernando Tatis	.15
84	Wade Boggs	.50
85	Fred McGriff	.25
86	Juan Gonzalez	.75
87	Ivan Rodriguez	.50
88	Rafael Palmeiro	.50
89	Shawn Green	.40
90	Carlos Delgado	.60
91	Pat Burrell (Diamond Debut)	1.00
92	Eric Munson (Diamond Debut)	.50
93	Jorge Toca (Diamond Debut)	.50
94	Rick Ankiel (Diamond Debut)	.50
95	Tony Armas Jr. (Diamond Debut)	.75
96	Byung-Hyun Kim (Diamond Debut)	.75
97	Alfonso Soriano (Diamond Debut)	3.00
98	Mark Quinn (Diamond Debut)	.50
99	Ryan Rupe (Diamond Debut)	.50
100	Adam Kennedy (Diamond Debut)	.50
101	Jeff Weaver (Diamond Debut)	.75
102	Ramon Ortiz (Diamond Debut)	.75
103	Eugene Kingsale (Diamond Debut)	.50
104	Josh Beckett (Diamond Debut)	1.00
105	Eric Gagne (Diamond Debut)	1.00
106	Peter Bergeron (Diamond Debut)	.50
107	Erubiel Durazo (Diamond Debut)	.75
108	Chad Meyers (Diamond Debut)	.50
109	Kip Wells (Diamond Debut)	.50
110	Chad Harville (Diamond Debut)	.50
111	Matt Riley (Diamond Debut)	.50
112	Ben Petrick (Diamond Debut)	.50
113	Ed Yarnall (Diamond Debut)	.50
114	Calvin Murray (Diamond Debut)	.50
115	Vernon Wells (Diamond Debut)	1.00
116	A.J. Burnett (Diamond Debut)	.75
117	Jacque Jones (Diamond Debut)	.75
118	Francisco Cordero (Diamond Debut)	.50
119	Tomokazu Ohka RC (Diamond Debut)	1.50
120	Julio Ramirez (Diamond Debut)	.50

Reciprocal Cut

A parallel to the 120-card base set, the die-cut design can be used to differentiate them from base cards. Card backs are also numbered with an "R" prefix. Cards 1-90 are found 1:7 packs and Diamond Debuts (91-120) are seeded 1:12 packs.

Stars (1-90): 2-5X

Diamond Debuts 1-1.5X
Diamond Debuts 1-90 inserted 1:7
Diamond Debuts Inserted 1:12

Final Cut

A parallel to the 120-card base set the die-cut design can be used to distinguish them from base cards, the card backs are also numbered with an "F" prefix. Each card is serial numbered within an edition of 100 sets.

Stars (1-90):	5-10X
Diamond Debuts:	2-4X
Production 100 Sets	

A Piece of History Single

These memorabilia inserts have a piece of game-used bat embedded into the card front and are seeded 1:179 packs.

		NM/M
Common Player:		8.00
Inserted 1:179		
AB	Albert Belle	8.00
BB	Barry Bonds	40.00
JC	Jose Canseco	10.00
DE	Darin Erstad	8.00
JR	Ken Griffey Jr.	25.00
VG	Vladimir Guerrero	15.00
TG	Tony Gwynn	20.00
TH	Todd Helton	20.00
DJ	Derek Jeter	40.00
AJ	Andruw Jones	10.00
CJ	Chipper Jones	20.00
TL	Travis Lee	8.00
RM	Raul Mondesi	8.00
MP	Mike Piazza	25.00
CAL	Cal Ripken Jr.	50.00
AR	Alex Rodriguez	25.00
IR	Ivan Rodriguez	10.00
SR	Scott Rolen	10.00
MV	Mo Vaughn	8.00

A Piece of History Double

These memorabilia inserts have two pieces of game-used bat embedded into the card front and are a parallel to the single set. They are inserted 1:1,079 packs.

		NM/M
Common Player:		10.00
Inserted 1:1079		
AB	Albert Belle	10.00
BB	Barry Bonds	75.00
JC	Jose Canseco	20.00
DE	Darin Erstad	15.00
JR	Ken Griffey Jr.	50.00
VG	Vladimir Guerrero	30.00
TG	Tony Gwynn	40.00
TH	Todd Helton	15.00
DJ	Derek Jeter	75.00
AJ	Andruw Jones	15.00
CJ	Chipper Jones	40.00
TL	Travis Lee	10.00
RM	Raul Mondesi	10.00
MP	Mike Piazza	50.00
CAL	Cal Ripken Jr.	80.00
AR	Alex Rodriguez	50.00
IR	Ivan Rodriguez	15.00
SR	Scott Rolen	15.00
MV	Mo Vaughn	10.00

Barrage

This 10-card set features a prismatic background with sil-

---

ver foil stamping. Card backs are numbered with a "B" prefix and are seeded 1:29 packs.

		NM/M
Complete Set (10):		15.00
Common Player:		1.00
Inserted 1:29		
1	Mark McGwire	3.00
2	Ken Griffey Jr.	2.00
3	Sammy Sosa	2.50
4	Jeff Bagwell	1.00
5	Juan Gonzalez	1.00
6	Alex Rodriguez	3.00
7	Manny Ramirez	1.00
8	Ivan Rodriguez	1.00
9	Chipper Jones	2.00
10	Mike Piazza	2.00

Constant Threat

A 10-card set spotlighting the top hitters in the game. Card backs are numbered with a "T" prefix and are seeded 1:29 packs.

		NM/M
Complete Set (10):		20.00
Common Player:		1.00
Inserted 1:29		
1	Ken Griffey Jr.	2.00
2	Vladimir Guerrero	1.00
3	Alex Rodriguez	3.00
4	Sammy Sosa	2.50
5	Juan Gonzalez	1.00
6	Derek Jeter	3.00
7	Nomar Garciaparra	3.00
8	Barry Bonds	4.00
9	Chipper Jones	2.00
10	Mike Piazza	2.00

Diamonation

This 10-card set has a holo-foil background with gold foil etching and stamping. Card backs are numbered with a "D" prefix and have an insertion ratio of 1:4 packs.

		NM/M
Complete Set (10):		6.00
Common Player:		.50
Inserted 1:4		
1	Ken Griffey Jr.	1.00
2	Randy Johnson	1.00
3	Mark McGwire	1.50
4	Manny Ramirez	.75
5	Scott Rolen	.75
6	Bernie Williams	.75
7	Roger Clemens	1.50
8	Mo Vaughn	.50
9	Frank Thomas	.75
10	Sean Casey	.50

Diamond Gallery

This 10-card set spotlights the featured player in a baseball diamond frame with a prismatic background. Gold foil etching and stamping is also used throughout. Card backs are numbered with a "G" prefix and are seeded 1:14 packs.

		NM/M
Complete Set (10):		20.00
Common Player:		1.50
Inserted 1:14		
1	Derek Jeter	3.00
2	Alex Rodriguez	3.00
3	Nomar Garciaparra	3.00
4	Cal Ripken Jr.	4.00
5	Sammy Sosa	2.50
6	Tony Gwynn	1.50
7	Mark McGwire	3.00
8	Roger Clemens	2.50
9	Greg Maddux	2.00
10	Pedro Martinez	1.50

DiamondMight

DiamondMight's have a horizontal format, utilizing holo-foil and gold foil stamping. Card backs are numbered with an "M" prefix and are seeded 1:14 packs.

		NM/M
Complete Set (10):		15.00
Common Player:		1.00
Inserted 1:14		
1	Ken Griffey Jr.	2.00
2	Mark McGwire	3.00
3	Sammy Sosa	2.50
4	Manny Ramirez	.60
5	Jeff Bagwell	1.00
6	Frank Thomas	1.00
7	Mike Piazza	2.00
8	Juan Gonzalez	1.00
9	Barry Bonds	4.00
10	Alex Rodriguez	3.00

Diamonds in the Rough

This 10-card set has a horizontal format utilizing holo-foil and gold foil stamping. Card backs are numbered with an "R" prefix and seeded 1:9 packs.

		NM/M
Complete Set (10):		8.00
Common Player:		.75
Inserted 1:9		
1	Pat Burrell	2.00
2	Eric Munson	.75
3	Alfonso Soriano	3.00
4	Ruben Mateo	.75
5	A.J. Burnett	1.00
6	Ben Davis	.75
7	Lance Berkman	1.50
8	Ed Yarnall	.75
9	Rick Ankiel	.75
10	Ryan Bradley	.75

---

500 Club Piece of History

These Reggie Jackson inserts are part of a cross brand insert series paying tribute to baseball's 500 home run club members. These have a piece of Jackson's game-used bat embedded. An autographed version signed to his jersey number (44) are also randomly inserted.

		NM/M
Reggie Jackson		165.00
Reggie Jackson Auto./44		500.00

Rookie Edition

		NM/M
Complete Set (154):		200.00
Common Player:		.15
Common Rookie Gem (91-120):		4.00
Production 1,000		
Rookie Jersey Gems (121-136): Inserted 1:24		
USA Authentics (137-154): Inserted 1:96		
Golds (1-90):		2-4X
Gold Gems (91-120):		1X
Gold Jerseys (121-136):		1-2X
Pack (6):		40.00
Box (24):		
1	Troy Glaus	.75
2	Mo Vaughn	.40
3	Darin Erstad	.40
4	Jason Giambi	.40
5	Tim Hudson	.25
6	Ben Grieve	.25
7	Eric Chavez	.25
8	Tony Batista	.15
9	Carlos Delgado	.60
10	David Wells	.15
11	Greg Vaughn	.15
12	Fred McGriff	.25
13	Manny Ramirez	.75
14	Roberto Alomar	.60
15	Jim Thome	.40
16	Alex Rodriguez	2.50
17	Edgar Martinez	.15
18	John Olerud	.20
19	Albert Belle	.40
20	Mike Mussina	.40
21	Cal Ripken Jr.	2.50
22	Ivan Rodriguez	.75
23	Rafael Palmeiro	.40
24	Pedro J. Martinez	.75
25	Nomar Garciaparra	2.00
26	Carl Everett	.15
27	Jermaine Dye	.15
28	Mike Sweeney	.15
29	Juan Gonzalez	.75
30	Bobby Higginson	.15
31	Dean Palmer	.15
32	Jacque Jones	.15
33	Eric Milton	.15
34	Matt Lawton	.15
35	Magglio Ordonez	.25
36	Paul Konerko	.15
37	Frank Thomas	1.00
38	Ray Durham	.15
39	Roger Clemens	1.00
40	Derek Jeter	2.50
41	Bernie Williams	.50
42	Jose Canseco	.40
43	Craig Biggio	.25
44	Richard Hidalgo	.15
45	Jeff Bagwell	.75
46	Greg Maddux	1.50
47	Chipper Jones	1.50
48	Rafael Furcal	.25
49	Andruw Jones	.50
50	Geoff Jenkins	.25
51	Jeromy Burnitz	.15
52	Mark McGwire	3.00

53	Rick Ankiel	.50
54	Jim Edmonds	.25
55	Kerry Wood	.25
56	Sammy Sosa	2.00
57	Matt Williams	.25
58	Randy Johnson	.75
59	Steve Finley	.15
60	Curt Schilling	.15
61	Kevin Brown	.15
62	Gary Sheffield	.30
63	Shawn Green	.30
64	Jose Vidro	.15
65	Vladimir Guerrero	1.00
66	Jeff Kent	.15
67	Barry Bonds	1.00
68	Ryan Dempster	.15
69	Cliff Floyd	.15
70	Preston Wilson	.15
71	Mike Piazza	2.00
72	Al Leiter	.15
73	Edgardo Alfonzo	.25
74	Derek Bell	.15
75	Ryan Klesko	.15
76	Tony Gwynn	1.00
77	Bobby Abreu	.15
78	Pat Burrell	.50
79	Scott Rolen	.50
80	Mike Lieberthal	.15
81	Jason Kendall	.15
82	Brian Giles	.25
83	Ken Griffey Jr.	2.00
84	Pokey Reese	.15
85	Dmitri Young	.15
86	Sean Casey	.15
87	Jeff Cirillo	.15
88	Todd Helton	.75
89	Jeffrey Hammonds	.15
90	Larry Walker	.30
91	Barry Zito RC	15.00
92	Keith Ginter RC	6.00
93	Dane Sardinha RC	4.00
94	Kenny Kelly RC	4.00
95	Ryan Kohlmeier RC	4.00
96	Leo Estrella RC	4.00
97	Danys Baez RC	4.00
98	Paul Rigdon RC	4.00
99	Mike Lamb RC	4.00
100	Aaron McNeal RC	4.00
101	Juan Pierre RC	6.00
102	Rico Washington RC	4.00
103	Luis Matos RC	8.00
104	Adam Bernero RC	4.00
105	Wascar Serrano RC	4.00
106	Chris Richard RC	4.00
107	Justin Miller RC	4.00
108	Julio Zuleta RC	4.00
109	Alex Cabrera RC	4.00
110	Gene Stechschulte RC	4.00
111	Tony Mota RC	4.00
112	Tomokazu Ohka RC	4.00
113	Geraldo Guzman RC	4.00
114	Scott Downs RC	4.00
115	Timoniel Perez RC	4.00
116	Chad Durbin RC	4.00
117	Sun-Woo Kim RC	4.00
118	Tomas de la Rosa RC	4.00
119	Javier Cardona RC	4.00
120	Kazuhiro Sasaki RC	6.00
121	Brad Cresse RC (Rookie Jersey Gems)	5.00
122	Matt Wheatland RC (Rookie Jersey Gems)	5.00
123	Joe Torres RC (Rookie Jersey Gems)	5.00
124	Dave Krynzel RC (Rookie Jersey Gems)	5.00
125	Ben Diggins RC (Rookie Jersey Gems)	8.00
126	Sean Burnett RC (Rookie Jersey Gems)	5.00
127	David Espinosa RC (Rookie Jersey Gems)	5.00
128	Scott Heard RC (Rookie Jersey Gems)	5.00
129	Daylan Holt RC (Rookie Jersey Gems)	5.00
130	Koyie Hill RC (Rookie Jersey Gems)	5.00
131	Mark Buehrle RC (Rookie Jersey Gems)	15.00
132	Xavier Nady RC (Rookie Jersey Gems)	8.00
133	Mike Tonis RC (Rookie Jersey Gems)	5.00
134	Matt Ginter RC (Rookie Jersey Gems)	5.00
135	Lorenzo Barcelo RC (Rookie Jersey Gems)	5.00
136	Cory Vance RC (Rookie Jersey Gems)	5.00
137	Sean Burroughs (USA Authentics)	8.00
138	Todd Williams (USA Authentics)	5.00
139	Brad Wilkerson RC (USA Authentics)	5.00
140	Ben Sheets RC (USA Authentics)	20.00
141	Kurt Ainsworth RC (USA Authentics)	8.00
142	Anthony Sanders (USA Authentics)	5.00
143	Ryan Franklin (USA Authentics)	5.00
144	Shane Heams RC (USA Authentics)	5.00
145	Roy Oswalt RC (USA Authentics)	20.00

#	Player	Price
146	Jon Rauch RC (USA Authentics)	5.00
147	Brent Abernathy RC (USA Authentics)	5.00
148	Ernie Young (USA Authentics)	5.00
149	Chris George (USA Authentics)	5.00
150	Gookie Dawkins (USA Authentics)	5.00
151	Adam Everett (USA Authentics)	5.00
152	John Cotton RC (USA Authentics)	5.00
153	Pat Borders (USA Authentics)	5.00
154	Doug Mientkiewicz (USA Authentics)	5.00

Rookie Edition Authentics

NM/M

Jeter Authentic Pinstripes

#	Player	Price
APJ	Derek Jeter/Jsy/1,000	35.00
APB	Derek Jeter/Bat/1,000	35.00
APC	Derek Jeter/Cap/200	70.00
APG	Derek Jeter/Glv/200	80.00

Rookie Edition Combos

NM/M

Random game-used inserts. 25 produced of each combo bat 100 produced of combo jersey

#	Player	Price
JDM	Derek Jeter, Joe DiMaggio, Mickey Mantle/Bat	925.00
JWO	Derek Jeter, Bernie Williams, Paul O'Neill/Jsy	150.00

Rookie Edition Diamonation

NM/M

Complete Set (9): 10.00
Common Player: .50
Inserted 1:12

#	Player	Price
1	Pedro J. Martinez	1.00
2	Derek Jeter	2.50
3	Jason Giambi	1.00
4	Todd Helton	.75
5	Nomar Garciaparra	2.50
6	Randy Johnson	1.00
7	Jeff Bagwell	.75
8	Cal Ripken Jr.	3.00
9	Ivan Rodriguez	1.00

Rookie Edition Diamond Gallery

NM/M

Complete Set (6): 10.00
Common Player: 1.00
Inserted 1:20

#	Player	Price
1	Sammy Sosa	2.00
2	Barry Bonds	3.00
3	Vladimir Guerrero	1.00
4	Cal Ripken Jr.	3.00
5	Mike Piazza	1.50
6	Mark McGwire	2.00

Rookie Edition Diamond Might

NM/M

Complete Set (9): 10.00

#	Player	Price
4	Gil Hodges	25.00
5	Carl Furillo	15.00
6	Don Newcombe	10.00
7	Sandy Koufax	50.00
8	Roy Campanella	25.00
9	Jim Gilliam	10.00
10	Don Drysdale	20.00
11	Sandy Amoros	10.00
12	Joe Black	10.00
13	Carl Erskine	10.00
14	Johnny Podres	10.00
15	Zack Wheat	10.00

Brooklyn Dodgers Master Collection Legends

The "Legends of Flatbush" are remembered in this series of memorabilia cards inserted into each Dodgers Master Collection. Each card's number has a "LOF" prefix.

NM/M

Complete Set (11): 800.00
Common Player: 20.00

#	Player	Price
1	Gil Hodges/Bat	35.00
2	Jackie Robinson/Bat	100.00
3	Pee Wee Reese/Bat	30.00
4	Jim Gilliam/Bat	20.00
5	Roy Campanella/Bat	50.00
6	Zack Wheat/Bat	20.00
7	Carl Furillo/Bat	40.00
8	Don Newcombe/Bat/Auto.	45.00
9	Duke Snider/Bat/Auto.	80.00
10	Don Drysdale/Jsy	40.00
11	Sandy Koufax/Jsy/Auto.	650.00

Brooklyn Dodgers Master Collection Mystery Pack

Each of the Master Collection sets included a sealed mystery pack containing a premium autograph/memorabilia card. Numbers produced are indicated where known.

NM/M

Values Undetermined

#	Player	Price
JR-BC	Jackie Robinson/Bat/5 (Cut sig.)	3,500
PW-BC	Pee Wee Reese/Bat/8 (Cut sig.)	325.00

2000 Upper Deck Gold Reserve

Gold Reserve is primarily a retail product that has virtually the same design as regular 2000 Upper Deck base cards. The set consists of 300-cards each with the Upper Deck logo and the featured player's last name stamped in gold foil. Above the player name "Gold Reserve" is stamped in gold foil.

The Fantastic Finds subset (268-297) are serial stamped within an edition of 2,500 for each of the subset cards.

NM/M

Complete Set (300): 75.00
Common Player: .15
Common 268-297: 3.00
Production 2,500 Sets
Pack (10): 2.00
Box (24): 40.00

#	Player	Price
1	Mo Vaughn	.20
2	Darin Erstad	.25
3	Garret Anderson	.25
4	Troy Glaus	.50
5	Troy Percival	.15
6	Kent Bottenfield	.15
7	Orlando Palmeiro	.15
8	Tim Salmon	.25
9	Jason Giambi	.75
10	Eric Chavez	.25
11	Matt Stairs	.15
12	Miguel Tejada	.40
13	Tim Hudson	.25
14	John Jaha	.15
15	Ben Grieve	.15
16	Kevin Appier	.15
17	David Wells	.15
18	Jose Cruz Jr.	.15
19	Homer Bush	.15
20	Shannon Stewart	.15
21	Carlos Delgado	.50
22	Roy Halladay	.25
23	Tony Batista	.15
24	Raul Mondesi	.25
25	Fred McGriff	.25
26	Jose Canseco	.40
27	Roberto Hernandez	.15
28	Vinny Castilla	.15
29	Gerald Williams	.15
30	Ryan Rupe	.15
31	Greg Vaughn	.15
32	Miguel Cairo	.15
33	Roberto Alomar	.40
34	Jim Thome	.50
35	Bartolo Colon	.15
36	Omar Vizquel	.25
37	Manny Ramirez	.50
38	Chuck Finley	.15
39	Travis Fryman	.25
40	Kenny Lofton	.25
41	Richie Sexson	.40
42	Charles Nagy	.15
43	John Halama	.15
44	David Bell	.15
45	Jay Buhner	.15
46	Edgar Martinez	.15
47	Alex Rodriguez	1.50
48	Fred Garcia	.15
49	Aaron Sele	.15
50	Jamie Moyer	.15
51	Mike Cameron	.15
52	Albert Belle	.20
53	Jerry Hairston Jr.	.15
54	Sidney Ponson	.15
55	Cal Ripken Jr.	2.00
56	Mike Mussina	.40
57	B.J. Surhoff	.15
58	Brady Anderson	.15
59	Mike Bordick	.15
60	Ivan Rodriguez	.40
61	Rusty Greer	.15
62	Rafael Palmeiro	.40
63	John Wetteland	.15
64	Ruben Mateo	.15
65	Gabe Kapler	.15
66	David Segui	.15
67	Justin Thompson	.15
68	Rick Helling	.15
69	Jose Offerman	.15
70	Trot Nixon	.15
71	Pedro Martinez	.75
72	Jason Varitek	.15
73	Troy O'Leary	.15
74	Nomar Garciaparra	1.50
75	Carl Everett	.15
76	Wilton Veras	.15
77	Tim Wakefield	.15
78	Ramon Martinez	.15
79	Johnny Damon	.25
80	Mike Sweeney	.15
81	Rey Sanchez	.15
82	Carlos Beltran	.25
83	Carlos Febles	.15
84	Jermaine Dye	.15
85	Joe Randa	.15
86	Jose Rosado	.15
87	Jeff Suppan	.15
88	Juan Encarnacion	.15
89	Damion Easley	.15
90	Brad Ausmus	.15
91	Todd Jones	.15
92	Juan Gonzalez	.50
93	Bobby Higginson	.15
94	Tony Clark	.15
95	Brian Moehler	.15
96	Dean Palmer	.15
97	Joe Mays	.15
98	Eric Milton	.15
99	Corey Koskie	.15
100	Ron Coomer	.15
101	Brad Radke	.15
102	Todd Walker	.15
103	Butch Huskey	.15
104	Jacque Jones	.15
105	Frank Thomas	.50
106	Mike Sirotka	.15
107	Carlos Lee	.15
108	Ray Durham	.15
109	Bob Howry	.15
110	Magglio Ordonez	.25
111	Paul Konerko	.15
112	Chris Singleton	.15
113	James Baldwin	.15
114	Derek Jeter	2.00
115	Tino Martinez	.25
116	Orlando Hernandez	.25
117	Chuck Knoblauch	.15
118	Bernie Williams	.50
119	David Cone	.25
120	Paul O'Neill	.25
121	Roger Clemens	1.25
122	Mariano Rivera	.25
123	Ricky Ledee	.15
124	Richard Hidalgo	.25
125	Jeff Bagwell	.50
126	Jose Lima	.15
127	Billy Wagner	.15
128	Shane Reynolds	.15
129	Moises Alou	.25
130	Craig Biggio	.25
131	Roger Cedeno	.15
132	Octavio Dotel	.15
133	Greg Maddux	1.00
134	Brian Jordan	.15
135	Kevin Millwood	.25
136	Javy Lopez	.25
137	Bruce Chen	.15
138	Chipper Jones	1.00
139	Tom Glavine	.40
140	Andruw Jones	.40
141	Andres Galarraga	.25
142	Reggie Sanders	.15
143	Geoff Jenkins	.25
144	Jeromy Burnitz	.15
145	Ron Belliard	.15
146	Mark Loretta	.15
147	Steve Woodard	.15
148	Marquis Grissom	.15
149	Bob Wickman	.15
150	Mark McGwire	1.50
151	Fernando Tatis	.15
152	Edgar Renteria	.15
153	J.D. Drew	.20
154	Ray Lankford	.15
155	Fernando Vina	.15
156	Pat Hentgen	.15
157	Jim Edmonds	.25
158	Mark Grace	.25
159	Kerry Wood	.40
160	Eric Young	.15
161	Ismael Valdes	.15
162	Sammy Sosa	1.25
163	Henry Rodriguez	.15
164	Kyle Farnsworth	.15
165	Glenallen Hill	.15
166	Jon Lieber	.15
167	Luis Gonzalez	.25
168	Tony Womack	.15
169	Omar Daal	.15
170	Randy Johnson	.75
171	Erubiel Durazo	.15
172	Jay Bell	.15
173	Steve Finley	.15
174	Travis Lee	.15
175	Matt Williams	.25
176	Matt Mantei	.15
177	Adrian Beltre	.25
178	Kevin Brown	.25
179	Chan Ho Park	.15
180	Mark Grudzielanek	.15
181	Jeff Shaw	.15
182	Shawn Green	.25
183	Gary Sheffield	.40
184	Todd Hundley	.15
185	Eric Karros	.25
186	Kevin Elster	.15
187	Vladimir Guerrero	.75
188	Michael Barrett	.15
189	Chris Widger	.15
190	Ugueth Urbina	.15
191	Dustin Hermanson	.15
192	Rondell White	.15
193	Jose Vidro	.15
194	Hideki Irabu	.15
195	Lee Stevens	.15
196	Livan Hernandez	.15
197	Ellis Burks	.15
198	J.T. Snow	.15
199	Jeff Kent	.25
200	Robb Nen	.15
201	Marvin Benard	.15
202	Barry Bonds	1.50
203	Russ Ortiz	.15
204	Rich Aurilia	.15
205	Joe Nathan	.15
206	Preston Wilson	.25
207	Cliff Floyd	.15
208	Mike Lowell	.15
209	Ryan Dempster	.15
210	Luis Castillo	.15
211	Alex Fernandez	.15
212	Mark Kotsay	.15
213	Brant Brown	.15
214	Edgardo Alfonzo	.15
215	Robin Ventura	.15
216	Rickey Henderson	.25
217	Mike Hampton	.15
218	Mike Piazza	1.00
219	Al Leiter	.15
220	Derek Bell	.15
221	Armando Benitez	.15
222	Rey Ordonez	.15
223	Todd Zeile	.15
224	Tony Gwynn	.75
225	Eric Owens	.15
226	Damian Jackson	.15
227	Trevor Hoffman	.15
228	Ben Davis	.15
229	Sterling Hitchcock	.15
230	Ruben Rivera	.15
231	Ryan Klesko	.15
232	Phil Nevin	.15
233	Mike Lieberthal	.15
234	Bobby Abreu	.25
235	Doug Glanville	.15
236	Rico Brogna	.15
237	Scott Rolen	.50
238	Andy Ashby	.15
239	Robert Person	.15
240	Curt Schilling	.25
241	Mike Jackson	.15
242	Warren Morris	.15
243	Kris Benson	.15
244	Kevin Young	.15
245	Brian Giles	.25
246	Jason Schmidt	.15
247	Jason Kendall	.25
248	Todd Ritchie	.15
249	Wil Cordero	.15
250	Aramis Ramirez	.15
251	Sean Casey	.25
252	Barry Larkin	.25
253	Pokey Reese	.15
254	Scott Williamson	.15
255	Aaron Boone	.25
256	Dante Bichette	.15
257	Ken Griffey Jr.	1.00
258	Denny Neagle	.15
259	Dmitri Young	.15
260	Todd Helton	.50
261	Larry Walker	.25
262	Pedro Astacio	.15
263	Neifi Perez	.15
264	Jeff Cirillo	.15
265	Jeffrey Hammonds	.15
266	Tom Goodwin	.15
267	Rolando Arrojo	.15
268	Rick Ankiel (Fantastic Finds)	3.00
269	Pat Burrell (Fantastic Finds)	4.00
270	Eric Munson (Fantastic Finds)	3.00
271	Rafael Furcal (Fantastic Finds)	3.00
272	Brad Penny (Fantastic Finds)	3.00
273	Adam Kennedy (Fantastic Finds)	3.00
274	Mike Lamb RC (Fantastic Finds)	3.00
275	Matt Riley (Fantastic Finds)	3.00
276	Eric Gagne (Fantastic Finds)	5.00
277	Kazuhiro Sasaki RC (Fantastic Finds)	3.00
278	Julio Lugo (Fantastic Finds)	3.00
279	Kip Wells (Fantastic Finds)	3.00
280	Danys Baez RC (Fantastic Finds)	3.00
281	Josh Beckett (Fantastic Finds)	4.00
282	Alfonso Soriano (Fantastic Finds)	4.00
283	Vernon Wells (Fantastic Finds)	4.00
284	Nick Johnson (Fantastic Finds)	3.00
285	Ramon Ortiz (Fantastic Finds)	3.00
286	Peter Bergeron (Fantastic Finds)	3.00
287	Wascar Serrano RC (Fantastic Finds)	3.00
288	Josh Paul (Fantastic Finds)	3.00
289	Mark Quinn (Fantastic Finds)	3.00
290	Jason Marquis (Fantastic Finds)	3.00
291	Rob Bell (Fantastic Finds)	3.00
292	Pablo Ozuna (Fantastic Finds)	3.00
293	Milton Bradley (Fantastic Finds)	3.00
294	Roosevelt Brown (Fantastic Finds)	3.00
295	Terrence Long (Fantastic Finds)	3.00
296	Chad Durbin RC (Fantastic Finds)	3.00
297	Matt LeCroy (Fantastic Finds)	3.00
298	Ken Griffey Jr. (Checklist)	.50
299	Mark McGwire (Checklist)	.75
300	Derek Jeter (Checklist)	1.00

Rookie Edition Diamond Skills

NM/M

Common Player: .50
Inserted 1:12

#	Player	Price
1	Mark McGwire	2.50
2	Mike Piazza	1.50
3	Frank Thomas	.75
4	Ken Griffey Jr.	1.50
5	Sammy Sosa	2.00
6	Alex Rodriguez	2.50
7	Carlos Delgado	.50
8	Vladimir Guerrero	1.00
9	Barry Bonds	3.00

NM/M

Complete Set (6): 8.00
Common Player: .75
Inserted 1:20

#	Player	Price
1	Alex Rodriguez	2.50
2	Chipper Jones	1.50
3	Ken Griffey Jr.	1.50
4	Pedro J. Martinez	1.00
5	Ivan Rodriguez	.75
6	Derek Jeter	2.50

Brooklyn Dodgers Master Collection

Following on the success of its Yankees Master Collection, UD produced a more limited edition set featuring the Brooklyn Dodgers. Only 250 numbered boxed sets were produced. Each set includes 15 base cards, 11 Legends of Flatbush memorabilia/autograph cards and a mystery pack containing a premium memorabilia/autograph card. The set concentrates on Dodgers of the 1950s, along with Zach Wheat. The set was issued in a laser-engraved wooden box.

NM/M

Complete Unopened Set: 1,250
Complete Opened Set: 800.00

Brooklyn Dodgers Master Collection Base Set

Portrait and action photos are combined in a horizontal format for the base cards in the Dodgers Masters Collection. Cards are numbered on back with a "BD" prefix.

NM/M

Complete Set (15): 230.00
Common Player: 10.00

#	Player	Price
1	Jackie Robinson	50.00
2	Duke Snider	25.00
3	Pee Wee Reese	25.00

Game-Used Ball

		NM/M
Common Player:		10.00
Inserted 1:480		
JB	Jeff Bagwell	25.00
BB	Barry Bonds	70.00
SC	Sean Casey	10.00
RC	Roger Clemens	35.00
NG	Nomar Garciaparra	40.00
SG	Shawn Green	10.00
KG	Ken Griffey Jr.	30.00
TG	Tony Gwynn	25.00
DJ	Derek Jeter	60.00
AJ	Andruw Jones	15.00
CJ	Chipper Jones	30.00
GM	Greg Maddux	30.00
MM	Mark McGwire	60.00
MP	Mike Piazza	30.00
MR	Manny Ramirez	15.00
IR	Ivan Rodriguez	15.00
SR	Scott Rolen	10.00
GS	Gary Sheffield	10.00
SS	Sammy Sosa	30.00
BW	Bernie Williams	10.00

Setting the Standard

This 15-card set spotlights the top hitters and are inserted 1:11 packs. Card fronts feature gold foil stamping and card backs are numbered with an "S" prefix.

		NM/M
Complete Set (15):		25.00
Common Player:		.50
Inserted 1:11		
1	Tony Gwynn	1.50
2	Manny Ramirez	1.00
3	Derek Jeter	3.00
4	Cal Ripken Jr.	4.00
5	Mo Vaughn	.50
6	Jose Canseco	.75
7	Barry Bonds	4.00
8	Nomar Garciaparra	3.00
9	Juan Gonzalez	1.00
10	Mark McGwire	3.00
11	Alex Rodriguez	3.00
12	Jeff Bagwell	1.00
13	Ken Griffey Jr.	2.00
14	Frank Thomas	3.00
15	Sammy Sosa	2.50

Solid Gold Gallery

This 12-card set features close-up shots of the featured player accentuated by gold foil stamping. Card backs are numbered with a "G" prefix, these were seeded 1:13 packs.

	NM/M
Complete Set (12):	20.00

		NM/M
Common Player:		1.00
Inserted 1:13		
1	Ken Griffey Jr.	2.00
2	Alex Rodriguez	3.00
3	Mike Piazza	2.00
4	Sammy Sosa	2.50
5	Derek Jeter	3.00
6	Jeff Bagwell	1.00
7	Mark McGwire	3.00
8	Cal Ripken Jr.	4.00
9	Pedro Martinez	1.50
10	Chipper Jones	2.00
11	Ivan Rodriguez	1.00
12	Vladimir Guerrero	1.00

UD Authentics

		NM/M
Inserted 1:480		
CB	Carlos Beltran	40.00
JC	Jose Canseco	35.00
SG	Shawn Green	20.00
TG	Tony Gwynn	30.00
CJ	Chipper Jones	60.00
MR	Manny Ramirez	25.00
CR	Cal Ripken Jr.	100.00
AR	Alex Rodriguez	80.00
IR	Ivan Rodriguez	20.00

UD Authentics Gold

Values Undetermined

24-Karat Gems

This 15-card set features gold foil stamping on the front and are numbered on the back with a "K" prefix. They are found on the average of 1:7 packs.

		NM/M
Complete Set (15):		12.00
Common Player:		.50
Inserted 1:7		
1	Pedro Martinez	1.50
2	Scott Rolen	1.00
3	Jason Giambi	1.50
4	Jeromy Burnitz	.50
5	Rafael Palmeiro	1.00
6	Rick Ankiel	.50
7	Carlos Beltran	.75
8	Derek Jeter	3.00
9	Jason Kendall	.50
10	Chipper Jones	2.00
11	Carlos Delgado	1.00
12	Alex Rodriguez	3.00
13	Randy Johnson	1.50
14	Tony Gwynn	1.50
15	Shawn Green	.75

3,000 Hit Club

This on-going cross brand insert series features Al Kaline. Each card features a piece of Kaline's game-used bat, he also signed six cards.

	NM/M
AK-B Al Kaline/Bat/400	20.00

2000 Upper Deck Hitter's Club

The 90-card base set includes only hitters and fea-

tures past and current stars. The base set consists of 50 regular cards, 25 Why 3K?, and 15 Hitting the Show subset cards. Card backs of the 50 regular cards have complete year-by-year statistics.

		NM/M
Complete Set (90):		20.00
Common Player:		.15
Pack (5):		1.50
Wax Box (24):		25.00
1	Mo Vaughn	.20
2	Troy Glaus	.40
3	Jeff Bagwell	.50
4	Craig Biggio	.25
5	Jason Giambi	.75
6	Eric Chavez	.25
7	Carlos Delgado	.50
8	Chipper Jones	1.00
9	Andruw Jones	.50
10	Andres Galarraga	.20
11	Jeromy Burnitz	.15
12	Mark McGwire	1.50
13	Mark Grace	.25
14	Sammy Sosa	1.25
15	Jose Canseco	.40
16	Vinny Castilla	.15
17	Matt Williams	.25
18	Gary Sheffield	.25
19	Shawn Green	.25
20	Vladimir Guerrero	.50
21	Barry Bonds	1.50
22	Manny Ramirez	.50
23	Roberto Alomar	.40
24	Jim Thome	.50
25	Ken Griffey Jr.	1.00
26	Alex Rodriguez	1.50
27	Edgar Martinez	.15
28	Preston Wilson	.25
29	Mike Piazza	1.00
30	Robin Ventura	.25
31	Albert Belle	.20
32	Cal Ripken Jr.	2.00
33	Tony Gwynn	.75
34	Scott Rolen	.50
35	Bob Abreu	.25
36	Brian Giles	.25
37	Ivan Rodriguez	.40
38	Rafael Palmeiro	.40
39	Nomar Garciaparra	1.50
40	Sean Casey	.20
41	Larry Walker	.25
42	Todd Helton	.25
43	Carlos Beltran	.25
44	Dean Palmer	.15
45	Juan Gonzalez	.50
46	Corey Koskie	.15
47	Frank Thomas	.50
48	Magglio Ordonez	.25
49	Derek Jeter	2.00
50	Bernie Williams	.40
51	Paul Waner (Why 3k?)	.25
52	Honus Wagner (Why 3k?)	.50
53	Tris Speaker (Why 3k?)	.25
54	Nap Lajoie (Why 3k?)	.25
55	Eddie Collins (Why 3k?)	.25
56	Roberto Clemente (Why 3k?)	1.00
57	Ty Cobb (Why 3k?)	1.50
58	Cap Anson (Why 3k?)	.50
59	Robin Yount (Why 3k?)	.50
60	Carl Yastrzemski (Why 3k?)	.50
61	Dave Winfield (Why 3k?)	.25
62	Stan Musial (Why 3k?)	1.00
63	Eddie Murray (Why 3k?)	.40
64	Paul Molitor (Why 3k?)	.25
65	Willie Mays (Why 3k?)	1.50
66	Al Kaline (Why 3k?)	.50
67	Tony Gwynn (Why 3k?)	.75
68	Rod Carew (Why 3k?)	.40
69	Lou Brock (Why 3k?)	.25
70	George Brett (Why 3k?)	.50
71	Wade Boggs (Why 3k?)	.25
72	Hank Aaron (Why 3k?)	1.50
73	Jorge Luis Toca (Hitting the Show)	.15
74	J.D. Drew (Hitting the Show)	.15
75	Pat Burrell (Hitting the Show)	.25
76	Vernon Wells (Hitting the Show)	.25
77	Julio Ramirez (Hitting the Show)	.15
78	Gabe Kapler (Hitting the Show)	.15
79	Erubiel Durazo (Hitting the Show)	.15
80	Lance Berkman (Hitting the Show)	.25
81	Peter Bergeron (Hitting the Show)	.15
82	Alfonso Soriano (Hitting the Show)	.75
83	Jacque Jones (Hitting the Show)	.15
84	Ben Petrick (Hitting the Show)	.15
85	Jerry Hairston Jr. (Hitting the Show)	.15
86	Kevin Witt (Hitting the Show)	.15
87	Dermal Brown (Hitting the Show)	.15
88	Chad Hermansen (Hitting the Show)	.15
89	Ruben Mateo (Hitting the Show)	.15
90	Checklist (Ken Griffey Jr.)	.50

Accolades

These inserts have a full foiled front with gold foil stamping. Card backs are numbered with an "A" prefix and are seeded 1:11 packs.

		NM/M
Complete Set (10):		12.00
Common Player:		.75
Inserted 1:11		
1	Robin Yount	1.00
2	Tony Gwynn	1.00
3	Sammy Sosa	2.00
4	Mike Piazza	1.50
5	Cal Ripken Jr.	3.00
6	Mark McGwire	2.50
7	Barry Bonds	2.50
8	Wade Boggs	.75
9	Ken Griffey Jr.	1.50
10	Willie Mays	2.00

Autographs

Former and current players are featured in this signature set, which are seeded 1:215 packs. Card backs are numbered with the featured player's initials.

		NM/M
Common Player:		15.00
Inserted 1:215		
HA	Hank Aaron #44	220.00
WB	Wade Boggs #12	30.00
GB	George Brett #5	80.00
Lou	Lou Brock #20	15.00
Rod	Rod Carew #29	15.00
TG	Tony Gwynn #19	40.00
Al	Al Kaline #6	30.00
WM	Willie Mays #24	150.00
PM	Paul Molitor #4	30.00
EM	Eddie Murray #33	30.00
Man	Stan Musial #6	75.00
Cal	Cal Ripken Jr. #8	150.00
DW	Dave Winfield #31	20.00
Yaz	Carl Yastrzemski #7	60.00
RY	Robin Yount #19	40.00

Epic Performances

This 10-card set (#EP2 was not issued) showcases some of baseball's top performances on a fully foiled card front with gold-foil stamping. Card backs are numbered with an "EP" prefix.

		NM/M
Complete Set (10):		12.00
Common Player:		1.00
Inserted 1:3		
1	Mark McGwire	2.50
3	Sammy Sosa	2.00
4	Ken Griffey Jr.	1.50
5	Carl Yastrzemski	1.00
6	Tony Gwynn	1.50
7	Nomar Garciaparra	2.50
8	Cal Ripken Jr.	3.00
9	George Brett	1.50
10	Hank Aaron	2.00
11	Wade Boggs	1.00

Eternals

These inserts were printed on a fully foiled front with "Eternals" printed a number of times in the background. The player name and Upper Deck logo are stamped in gold foil at bottom. Card backs are numbered with an "E" prefix.

		NM/M
Complete Set (10):		20.00
Common Player:		1.00
Inserted 1:23		
1	Cal Ripken Jr.	4.00
2	Mark McGwire	3.00
3	Ken Griffey Jr.	2.00
4	Nomar Garciaparra	3.00
5	Tony Gwynn	1.50
6	Derek Jeter	3.00
7	Jose Canseco	1.00
8	Mike Piazza	2.00
9	Alex Rodriguez	3.00
10	Barry Bonds	4.00

Generations of Excellence

This 10-card insert set features two players who are linked either by team or position. Gold-foil stamping is used throughout. Card backs are numbered with a "GE" prefix.

		NM/M
Complete Set (10):		15.00
Common Card:		1.00
Inserted 1:6		
1	Cal Ripken Jr., Eddie Murray	3.00
2	Vladimir Guerrero, Roberto Clemente	2.00
3	George Brett, Robin Yount	2.00
4	Barry Bonds, Willie Mays	3.00
5	Chipper Jones, Hank Aaron	2.00
6	Mark McGwire, Sammy Sosa	2.00
7	Tony Gwynn, Wade Boggs	1.00
8	Rickey Henderson, Lou Brock	1.00
9	Derek Jeter, Nomar Garciaparra	3.00
10	Alex Rodriguez, Ken Griffey Jr.	2.50

On Target

This 10-card set is printed on a full foiled front with silver foil stamping. Card backs are numbered with an "OT" prefix and are seeded 1:23 packs.

		NM/M
Complete Set (10):		12.00
Common Player:		.50
Inserted 1:23		
1	Nomar Garciaparra	3.00
2	Sean Casey	.50
3	Alex Rodriguez	3.00
4	Troy Glaus	1.00
5	Ivan Rodriguez	1.00
6	Chipper Jones	2.00
7	Manny Ramirez	1.00
8	Derek Jeter	3.00
9	Vladimir Guerrero	1.00
10	Scott Rolen	1.00

The Hitters' Club

These inserts are seeded 1:95 packs and are numbered on the back with an "HC" prefix.

		NM/M
Complete Set (10):		60.00
Common Player:		3.00
1	Rod Carew	5.00
2	Alex Rodriguez	15.00
3	Willie Mays	10.00
4	George Brett	10.00
5	Tony Gwynn	8.00
6	Stan Musial	8.00
7	Frank Thomas	5.00
8	Wade Boggs	3.00
9	Larry Walker	3.00
10	Nomar Garciaparra	15.00

3,000 Hit Club

Upper Deck's cross brand series pays tribute to players who have reached 3,000 hits. Hitter's Club features Wade Boggs and Tony Gwynn inserts with Bat, Bat and Cap and Autographed versions randomly inserted.

	NM/M
Common Player:	25.00

		NM/M
WB	Wade Boggs/Bat/350	25.00
WB	Wade Boggs/Bat & Cap/50	65.00
TG	Tony Gwynn/Bat/350	25.00
TG	Tony Gwynn/Bat & Cap/50	100.00
TG	Tony Gwynn AU/19	550.00
GB	Tony Gwynn, Wade Boggs/Bat/99	85.00

2000 Upper Deck HoloGrFX

The base set consists of 90-cards on a horizontal format. The cards have a holo-foil front utilizing HoloGrFX technology.

		NM/M
	Complete Set (90):	20.00
	Common Player:	.15
	Pack (4):	1.50
	Wax Box (32):	25.00
1	Mo Vaughn	.20
2	Troy Glaus	.50
3	Daryle Ward	.15
4	Jeff Bagwell	.50
5	Craig Biggio	.25
6	Jose Lima	.15
7	Jason Giambi	.75
8	Eric Chavez	.25
9	Tim Hudson	.25
10	Raul Mondesi	.50
11	Carlos Delgado	.50
12	David Wells	.15
13	Chipper Jones	1.00
14	Greg Maddux	1.00
15	Andruw Jones	.50
16	Brian Jordan	.15
17	Jeromy Burnitz	.15
18	Ron Belliard	.15
19	Mark McGwire	1.50
20	Fernando Tatis	.15
21	J.D. Drew	.25
22	Sammy Sosa	1.00
23	Mark Grace	.40
24	Greg Vaughn	.15
25	Jose Canseco	.40
26	Vinny Castilla	.15
27	Fred McGriff	.25
28	Matt Williams	.25
29	Randy Johnson	.75
30	Erubiel Durazo	.15
31	Shawn Green	.25
32	Gary Sheffield	.40
33	Kevin Brown	.25
34	Vladimir Guerrero	.50
35	Michael Barrett	.15
36	Russ Ortiz	.15
37	Barry Bonds	1.50
38	Jeff Kent	.25
39	Kenny Lofton	.25
40	Manny Ramirez	.50
41	Roberto Alomar	.40
42	Richie Sexson	.25
43	Edgar Martinez	.25
44	Alex Rodriguez	1.50
45	Fred Garcia	.15
46	Preston Wilson	.15
47	Alex Gonzalez	.15
48	Mike Hampton	.15
49	Mike Piazza	1.00
50	Robin Ventura	.15
51	Edgardo Alfonzo	.15
52	Albert Belle	.15
53	Cal Ripken Jr.	2.00
54	B.J. Surhoff	.15
55	Tony Gwynn	.75
56	Trevor Hoffman	.15
57	Mike Lieberthal	.15
58	Scott Rolen	.50
59	Bob Abreu	.25
60	Curt Schilling	.40
61	Jason Kendall	.25
62	Brian Giles	.25
63	Kris Benson	.15
64	Rafael Palmeiro	.40
65	Ivan Rodriguez	.50
66	Gabe Kapler	.40
67	Nomar Garciaparra	1.50
68	Pedro Martinez	.75
69	Troy O'Leary	.15
70	Barry Larkin	.25
71	Dante Bichette	.15
72	Sean Casey	.20
73	Ken Griffey Jr.	1.00
74	Jeff Cirillo	.15
75	Todd Helton	.50
76	Larry Walker	.25
77	Carlos Beltran	.25
78	Jermaine Dye	.15
79	Juan Gonzalez	.50
80	Juan Encarnacion	.15
81	Dean Palmer	.15
82	Corey Koskie	.15
83	Eric Milton	.15
84	Frank Thomas	.50
85	Magglio Ordonez	.25
86	Carlos Lee	.15
87	Derek Jeter	2.00
88	Tino Martinez	.25
89	Bernie Williams	.50
90	Roger Clemens	1.50

A Piece of the Series

This inserts have a piece of game-used base from a 1999 World Series game embedded. These were inserted at a rate of 1:215 packs.

		NM/M
	Common Player:	5.00
	Inserted 1:215	
1	Derek Jeter	40.00
2	Chipper Jones	20.00
3	Roger Clemens	30.00
4	Greg Maddux	30.00
5	Bernie Williams	10.00
6	Andruw Jones	10.00
7	Tino Martinez	8.00
8	Brian Jordan	5.00
9	Mariano Rivera	8.00
10	Paul O'Neill	8.00
11	Tom Glavine	10.00

A Piece of Series Autograph

This is an autographed parallel of the Piece of Series insert set that is limited to 25 sets.

		NM/M
	Common Player:	40.00
	Production 25 Sets	
PSA1	Derek Jeter	300.00
PSA2	Chipper Jones	125.00
PSA3	Roger Clemens	220.00
PSA4	Greg Maddux	220.00
PSA6	Andruw Jones	85.00
PSA7	Tino Martinez	65.00
PSA8	Brian Jordan	40.00
PSA11	Paul O'Neill	75.00
PSA12	Tom Glavine	100.00

Bomb Squad

This set highlights top home run hitters in a horizontal format with complete holo-foiled fronts. Card backs are numbered with a "BS" prefix.

		NM/M
	Complete Set (6):	15.00
	Common Player:	2.00
	Inserted 1:34	
1	Ken Griffey Jr.	2.00
2	Mark McGwire	3.00
3	Chipper Jones	2.00
4	Alex Rodriguez	3.00
5	Sammy Sosa	2.50
6	Barry Bonds	4.00

Future Fame

This six-card set has a horizontal format that is completely holo-foiled with silver foil stamping. Card backs are numbered with an "FF" prefix and seeded 1:34 packs.

		NM/M
	Complete Set (6):	10.00
	Common Player:	2.00
	Inserted 1:34	
1	Cal Ripken Jr.	4.00
2	Mark McGwire	3.00
3	Greg Maddux	2.00
4	Tony Gwynn	1.50
5	Ken Griffey Jr.	2.00
6	Roger Clemens	2.50

Longball Legacy

This 15-card set spotlights the top home run hitters on a horizontal format and completely holo-foiled. Card backs are numbered with an "LL" prefix and seeded 1:6 packs.

		NM/M
	Complete Set (15):	15.00
	Common Player:	.50
	Inserted 1:6	
1	Mike Piazza	2.00
2	Ivan Rodriguez	.75
3	Jeff Bagwell	1.00
4	Alex Rodriguez	3.00
5	Jose Canseco	.75
6	Mark McGwire	3.00
7	Scott Rolen	.75
8	Carlos Delgado	.75
9	Mo Vaughn	.50
10	Manny Ramirez	1.00
11	Matt Williams	.50
12	Sammy Sosa	2.50
13	Ken Griffey Jr.	2.00
14	Nomar Garciaparra	3.00
15	Larry Walker	.50

Stars of the System

This 10-card set features some of baseball's top prospects on a horizontal format. The fronts are completely holo-foiled with silver foil stamping. Card backs are numbered with an "SS" prefix and seeded 1:8 packs.

		NM/M
	Complete Set (10):	8.00
	Common Player:	.75
	Inserted 1:8	
1	Rick Ankiel	.75
2	Alfonso Soriano	2.00
3	Vernon Wells	1.00
4	Ben Petrick	.75
5	Francisco Cordero	.75
6	Matt Riley	.75
7	A.J. Burnett	1.00
8	Pat Burrell	1.50
9	Ed Yarnall	.75
10	Dermal Brown	.75

StarView

This eight-card set features top stars on a horizontal format. Card backs are numbered with an "SV" prefix and inserted 1:11 packs.

		NM/M
	Complete Set (8):	15.00
	Common Player:	2.00
	Inserted 1:11	
1	Ken Griffey Jr.	2.00
2	Nomar Garciaparra	3.00
3	Chipper Jones	2.00
4	Mark McGwire	3.00
5	Sammy Sosa	2.50
6	Derek Jeter	4.00
7	Mike Piazza	2.00
8	Alex Rodriguez	3.00

3,000 Hit Club

Upper Deck pays tribute to members of the 3,000 Hit Club with this cross-brand insert series. Robin Yount and George Brett are featured on a game-used bat card (350 produced), game-used jersey card (350 produced), a bat combo of both players (99 produced) and an autographed combo (10 produced).

		NM/M
	Common Card:	20.00
RY	Robin Yount/Bat/350	20.00
RYJ	Robin Yount/Jsy/350	20.00
GB	George Brett/Bat/350	35.00
GBJ	George Brett/Jsy/350	35.00
BY	George Brett, Robin Yount/Bat/99	120.00
BYJ	George Brett, Robin Yount/Jsy/99	120.00

2000 UD Ionix

The base set consists of 90 cards, including a 30-card Futuristics subset that were seeded 1:4 packs. A Reciprocal parallel to the base set are also randomly inserted. The cards can distinguished by a holo-foiled front and the number on the back has an "R" prefix. Reciprocals 1-60 are found 1:4 packs, while Futuristics Reciprocals are found on the average of 1:11 packs.

		NM/M
	Complete Set (90):	50.00
	Common Player:	.15
	Common Futuristic:	.50
	Inserted 1:4	
	Reciprocal (1-60)	1.5-2X
	Reciprocal (61-90)	1-1.5X
	Inserted 1:4	
	Future Recip. 1:11	
	Pack (4):	2.00
	Wax Box (24):	35.00
1	Mo Vaughn	.20
2	Troy Glaus	.75
3	Jeff Bagwell	.75
4	Craig Biggio	.15
5	Jose Lima	.15
6	Jason Giambi	1.00
7	Tim Hudson	.40
8	Shawn Green	.50
9	Carlos Delgado	.75
10	Chipper Jones	1.50
11	Andruw Jones	.75
12	Greg Maddux	1.50
13	Jeromy Burnitz	.15
14	Mark McGwire	2.00
15	J.D. Drew	.25
16	Sammy Sosa	2.00
17	Jose Canseco	.50
18	Fred McGriff	.40
19	Randy Johnson	.75
20	Matt Williams	.25
21	Kevin Brown	.40
22	Gary Sheffield	.40
23	Vladimir Guerrero	.75
24	Barry Bonds	2.50
25	Jim Thome	.75
26	Manny Ramirez	.75
27	Roberto Alomar	.50
28	Kenny Lofton	.25
29	Ken Griffey Jr.	1.50
30	Alex Rodriguez	2.50
31	Alex Gonzalez	.15
32	Preston Wilson	.15
33	Mike Piazza	1.50
34	Robin Ventura	.25
35	Cal Ripken Jr.	2.50
36	Albert Belle	.20
37	Tony Gwynn	1.00
38	Scott Rolen	.75
39	Curt Schilling	.50
40	Brian Giles	.25
41	Juan Gonzalez	.75
42	Ivan Rodriguez	.75
43	Rafael Palmeiro	.60
44	Pedro J. Martinez	.75
45	Nomar Garciaparra	2.00
46	Sean Casey	.25
47	Aaron Boone	.25
48	Barry Larkin	.40
49	Larry Walker	.25
50	Vinny Castilla	.20
51	Carlos Beltran	.25
52	Gabe Kapler	.15
53	Dean Palmer	.15
54	Eric Milton	.15
55	Corey Koskie	.15
56	Frank Thomas	.75
57	Magglio Ordonez	.40
58	Roger Clemens	2.00
59	Bernie Williams	.75
60	Derek Jeter	2.50
61	Josh Beckett (Futuristics)	1.50
62	Eric Munson (Futuristics)	1.00
63	Rick Ankiel (Futuristics)	1.00
64	Matt Riley (Futuristics)	1.00
65	Robert Ramsay (Futuristics)	1.00
66	Vernon Wells (Futuristics)	2.00
67	Eric Gagne (Futuristics)	1.50
68	Robert Fick (Futuristics)	1.50
69	Mark Quinn (Futuristics)	1.00
70	Kip Wells (Futuristics)	1.00
71	Peter Bergeron (Futuristics)	1.00
72	Ed Yarnall (Futuristics)	1.00
73	Jorge Luis Toca (Futuristics)	1.00
74	Alfonso Soriano (Futuristics)	4.00
75	Calvin Murray (Futuristics)	1.00
76	Ramon Ortiz (Futuristics)	1.50
77	Chad Meyers (Futuristics)	1.00
78	Jason LaRue (Futuristics)	1.00
79	Pat Burrell (Futuristics)	1.00
80	Chad Hermansen (Futuristics)	1.00
81	Lance Berkman (Futuristics)	1.50
82	Erubiel Durazo (Futuristics)	1.50
83	Juan Pena (Futuristics)	1.00
84	Adam Kennedy (Futuristics)	1.00
85	Ben Petrick (Futuristics)	1.00
86	Kevin Barker (Futuristics)	1.00
87	Bruce Chen (Futuristics)	1.00
88	Jerry Hairston Jr. (Futuristics)	1.00
89	A.J. Burnett (Futuristics)	1.00
90	Gary Matthews Jr. (Futuristics)	1.00

Atomic

This 15-card insert set has a horizontal format on a holo-foiled front. Card backs are numbered with an "A" prefix and are found 1:8 packs.

		NM/M
	Complete Set (15):	25.00
	Common Player:	1.00
	Inserted 1:8	
1	Pedro J. Martinez	1.50
2	Mark McGwire	3.00
3	Ken Griffey Jr.	2.00
4	Jeff Bagwell	1.00
5	Greg Maddux	2.00
6	Derek Jeter	3.00
7	Cal Ripken Jr.	4.00
8	Manny Ramirez	1.00
9	Randy Johnson	1.50
10	Nomar Garciaparra	3.00
11	Tony Gwynn	1.50
12	Bernie Williams	1.00
13	Mike Piazza	2.00
14	Roger Clemens	3.00
15	Alex Rodriguez	3.00

Awesome Powers

The title of this insert set is a takeoff on the Austin Powers movie that was popular at the time of this release. The cards have a holo-foil front with a "groovin'" '70s backdrop. Card backs are numbered with an "AP" prefix.

		NM/M
	Complete Set (15):	50.00
	Common Player:	1.00
	Inserted 1:23	
1	Ken Griffey Jr.	4.00
2	Mike Piazza	4.00
3	Carlos Delgado	2.00
4	Mark McGwire	6.00
5	Chipper Jones	4.00
6	Scott Rolen	2.00
7	Cal Ripken Jr.	8.00
8	Alex Rodriguez	6.00
9	Larry Walker	1.00
10	Sammy Sosa	5.00
11	Barry Bonds	6.00
12	Nomar Garciaparra	6.00
13	Jose Canseco	1.50
14	Manny Ramirez	2.00
15	Jeff Bagwell	2.00

BIOrhythm

This 15-card set has a holo-foil front and are seeded 1:11 packs. Card backs have a brief career note and are numbered with a "B" prefix.

		NM/M
	Complete Set (15):	25.00
	Common Player:	.50
	Inserted 1:11	
1	Randy Johnson	1.50
2	Derek Jeter	3.00
3	Sammy Sosa	2.50
4	Jose Lima	.50
5	Chipper Jones	2.00
6	Barry Bonds	4.00
7	Ken Griffey Jr.	2.00
8	Nomar Garciaparra	3.00
9	Frank Thomas	1.00
10	Pedro Martinez	1.50
11	Larry Walker	.50
12	Greg Maddux	2.00
13	Alex Rodriguez	3.00
14	Mark McGwire	3.00
15	Cal Ripken Jr.	4.00

Pyrotechnics

This 15-card set has a holo-foiled front with an insertion ratio of 1:72 packs. Card backs are numbered with a "P" prefix.

Shockwave section image

		NM/M
Complete Set (15):		125.00
Common Player:		5.00
Inserted 1:72		
1	Roger Clemens	12.00
2	Chipper Jones	10.00
3	Alex Rodriguez	15.00
4	Jeff Bagwell	5.00
5	Mark McGwire	15.00
6	Pedro Martinez	6.00
7	Manny Ramirez	5.00
8	Cal Ripken Jr.	20.00
9	Mike Piazza	10.00
10	Derek Jeter	15.00
11	Ken Griffey Jr.	15.00
12	Frank Thomas	5.00
13	Sammy Sosa	12.00
14	Nomar Garciaparra	15.00
15	Greg Maddux	10.00

Shockwave

Baseball's top hitters are spotlighted on a holo-foil front. They are found on the average of 1:4 packs and are numbered on the card back with an "S" prefix.

		NM/M
Complete Set (15):		15.00
Common Player:		.50
Inserted 1:4		
1	Mark McGwire	2.00
2	Sammy Sosa	1.00
3	Manny Ramirez	1.00
4	Ken Griffey Jr.	1.50
5	Vladimir Guerrero	1.00
6	Barry Bonds	2.50
7	Albert Belle	.50
8	Ivan Rodriguez	1.00
9	Chipper Jones	1.50
10	Mo Vaughn	.50
11	Jose Canseco	.75
12	Jeff Bagwell	1.00
13	Matt Williams	.50
14	Alex Rodriguez	2.50
15	Carlos Delgado	.75

UD Authentics

These autographed inserts have a horizontal format and are found on the average of 1:144 packs.

		NM/M
Common Player:		10.00
Inserted 1:144		
CBE	Carlos Beltran	30.00
AB	Adrian Beltre	15.00
PB	Pat Burrell	15.00
JC	Jose Canseco	25.00
SC	Sean Casey	15.00
BD	Ben Davis	10.00
SG	Shawn Green	15.00
JR	Ken Griffey Jr.	100.00
VG	Vladimir Guerrero	30.00

DJ	Derek Jeter	100.00
GK	Gabe Kapler	10.00
RM	Ruben Mateo	10.00
RB	Joe McEwing	10.00
MR	Manny Ramirez	35.00
SR	Scott Rolen	30.00
MW	Matt Williams	15.00

Warp Zone

This 15-card set has a holo-foiled front with an insertion ratio of 1:288 packs. Card backs are numbered with a "WZ" prefix.

		NM/M
Complete Set (15):		250.00
Common Player:		8.00
Inserted 1:288		
1	Cal Ripken Jr.	30.00
2	Barry Bonds	30.00
3	Ken Griffey Jr.	20.00
4	Nomar Garciaparra	25.00
5	Chipper Jones	20.00
6	Ivan Rodriguez	8.00
7	Greg Maddux	20.00
8	Derek Jeter	25.00
9	Mike Piazza	20.00
10	Sammy Sosa	20.00
11	Roger Clemens	20.00
12	Alex Rodriguez	25.00
13	Vladimir Guerrero	10.00
14	Pedro Martinez	10.00
15	Mark McGwire	25.00

3,000 Hit Club

Upper Deck's cross-brand insert series paying tribute to baseball's 3,000 Hit Club members spotlights Roberto Clemente in UD Ionix. Three versions were randomly inserted: A game-used bat card, bat/cut signature card and a cut signature card.

		NM/M
RC1	Roberto Clemente/Bat/350	125.00

2000 Upper Deck Legends

The 135-card base set consists of 90 regular player cards, 30 20th Century Legends (1:5) and 15 Generation Y2K (1:9). The base cards have a full foiled front with silver foil stamping. Card backs have complete year-by-year statistics.

		NM/M
Complete Set (135):		80.00

Common Player:		.15
Common Y2K:		.75
Inserted 1:9		
Common 20th Century Legend		1.00
Inserted 1:5		
Pack (7):		5.00
Box (24):		90.00
1	Darin Erstad	.25
2	Troy Glaus	.75
3	Mo Vaughn	.20
4	Craig Biggio	.25
5	Jeff Bagwell	.75
6	Reggie Jackson	1.00
7	Tim Hudson	.25
8	Jason Giambi	1.00
9	Hank Aaron	2.00
10	Greg Maddux	1.50
11	Chipper Jones	1.50
12	Andres Galarraga	.25
13	Robin Yount	.75
14	Jeromy Burnitz	.15
15	Paul Molitor	.50
16	David Wells	.15
17	Carlos Delgado	.75
18	Ernie Banks	.75
19	Sammy Sosa	2.00
20	Kerry Wood	.40
21	Stan Musial	.75
22	Bob Gibson	.50
23	Mark McGwire	2.00
24	Fernando Tatis	.15
25	Randy Johnson	1.00
26	Matt Williams	.40
27	Jackie Robinson	2.00
28	Sandy Koufax	1.50
29	Shawn Green	.40
30	Kevin Brown	.25
31	Gary Sheffield	.40
32	Greg Vaughn	.15
33	Jose Canseco	.50
34	Gary Carter	.75
35	Vladimir Guerrero	.75
36	Willie Mays	2.00
37	Barry Bonds	2.00
38	Jeff Kent	.25
39	Bob Feller	.40
40	Roberto Alomar	.75
41	Jim Thome	.75
42	Manny Ramirez	.75
43	Alex Rodriguez	2.00
44	Preston Wilson	.15
45	Tom Seaver	.50
46	Robin Ventura	.15
47	Mike Piazza	1.50
48	Mike Hampton	.15
49	Brooks Robinson	.75
50	Frank Robinson	.75
51	Cal Ripken Jr.	2.50
52	Albert Belle	.20
53	Eddie Murray	.40
54	Tony Gwynn	1.00
55	Roberto Clemente	1.50
56	Willie Stargell	.25
57	Brian Giles	.25
58	Jason Kendall	.25
59	Mike Schmidt	1.00
60	Bob Abreu	.25
61	Scott Rolen	.50
62	Curt Schilling	.40
63	Johnny Bench	1.00
64	Sean Casey	.15
65	Barry Larkin	.25
66	Ken Griffey Jr.	1.50
67	George Brett	1.50
68	Carlos Beltran	.15
69	Nolan Ryan	3.00
70	Ivan Rodriguez	.75
71	Rafael Palmeiro	.40
72	Larry Walker	.25
73	Todd Helton	.75
74	Jeff Cirillo	.15
75	Carl Everett	.15
76	Nomar Garciaparra	2.00
77	Pedro Martinez	1.00
78	Harmon Killebrew	.50
79	Corey Koskie	.15
80	Ty Cobb	2.00
81	Dean Palmer	.15
82	Juan Gonzalez	.75
83	Carlton Fisk	.15
84	Frank Thomas	.75
85	Magglio Ordonez	.25
86	Lou Gehrig	2.00
87	Babe Ruth	3.00
88	Derek Jeter	2.50
89	Roger Clemens	.75
90	Bernie Williams	.50
91	Rick Ankiel (Generation Y2K)	.75
92	Kip Wells (Generation Y2K)	.75
93	Pat Burrell (Generation Y2K)	1.50
94	Mark Quinn (Generation Y2K)	.75
95	Ruben Mateo (Generation Y2K)	.75
96	Adam Kennedy (Generation Y2K)	.75
97	Brad Penny (Generation Y2K)	.75
98	Kazuhiro Sasaki RC (Generation Y2K)	2.00
99	Peter Bergeron (Generation Y2K)	.75
100	Rafael Furcal (Generation Y2K)	1.00

101	Eric Munson (Generation Y2K)	.75
102	Nick Johnson (Generation Y2K)	1.00
103	Rob Bell (Generation Y2K)	.75
104	Vernon Wells (Generation Y2K)	1.00
105	Ben Petrick (Generation Y2K)	.75
106	Babe Ruth (20th Century Legends)	8.00
107	Mark McGwire (20th Century Legends)	5.00
108	Nolan Ryan (20th Century Legends)	5.00
109	Hank Aaron (20th Century Legends)	5.00
110	Barry Bonds (20th Century Legends)	6.00
111	Nomar Garciaparra (20th Century Legends)	5.00
112	Roger Clemens (20th Century Legends)	5.00
113	Johnny Bench (20th Century Legends)	2.50
114	Alex Rodriguez (20th Century Legends)	6.00
115	Cal Ripken Jr. (20th Century Legends)	8.00
116	Willie Mays (20th Century Legends)	6.00
117	Mike Piazza (20th Century Legends)	4.00
118	Reggie Jackson (20th Century Legends)	4.00
119	Tony Gwynn (20th Century Legends)	4.00
120	Cy Young (20th Century Legends)	2.00
121	George Brett (20th Century Legends)	4.00
122	Greg Maddux (20th Century Legends)	4.00
123	Yogi Berra (20th Century Legends)	2.00
124	Sammy Sosa (20th Century Legends)	5.00
125	Randy Johnson (20th Century Legends)	2.50
126	Bob Gibson (20th Century Legends)	2.00
127	Lou Gehrig (20th Century Legends)	6.00
128	Ken Griffey Jr. (20th Century Legends)	4.00
129	Derek Jeter (20th Century Legends)	6.00
130	Mike Schmidt (20th Century Legends)	3.00
131	Pedro Martinez (20th Century Legends)	2.50
132	Jackie Robinson (20th Century Legends)	5.00
133	Jose Canseco (20th Century Legends)	1.00
134	Ty Cobb (20th Century Legends)	5.00
135	Stan Musial (20th Century Legends)	3.00

Gold

Gold graphic enhancements are featured on this parallel edition. On back, a dot-matrix printed "1/1" attests to the status of these cards as unique specimens. Because only one of each card was produced, attaching values can be problematic. Values shown here represent specimens offered at auction shortly after the cards were issued.

		NM/M
Common Player:		75.00
10	Greg Maddux	340.00
13	Robin Yount	450.00
15	Paul Molitor	450.00
31	Gary Sheffield	175.00
36	Willie Mays	1,175
53	Eddie Murray	1,000
82	Juan Gonzalez	230.00
87	Babe Ruth	2,025
89	Roger Clemens	250.00
107	Mark McGwire (20th Century Legends)	1,580
119	Tony Gwynn (20th Century Legends)	190.00
126	Bob Gibson (20th Century Legends)	275.00
130	Mike Schmidt (20th Century Legends)	900.00

Commemorative Collection

A metallized photo background on front distinguishes these 1-of-100 inserts from their base-card parallels.

Backs have an ink-jetted serial number from within each card's edition of 100.

Stars (1-90):		4-8X
Y2K:		1-2X
20th Century Legends:		2-3X
Production 100 Sets		

Defining Moments

This 10-card set highlights the featured player's greatest baseball moment with a date stamped in gold foil on the front and a description of the moment on the back. Card backs are numbered with a "DM" prefix and seeded 1:12 packs.

		NM/M
Complete Set (10):		20.00
Common Player:		1.00
Inserted 1:12		
1	Reggie Jackson	1.50
2	Hank Aaron	3.00
3	Babe Ruth	4.00
4	Cal Ripken Jr.	4.00
5	Carlton Fisk	1.00
6	Ken Griffey Jr.	2.00
7	Nolan Ryan	4.00
8	Roger Clemens	2.50
9	Willie Mays	3.00
10	Mark McGwire	3.00

Eternal Glory

This six-card set has a full holo-foiled front with gold foil stamping. Card backs are numbered with an "EG" prefix and are inserted 1:24 packs.

		NM/M
Complete Set (7):		15.00
Common Player:		2.00
Inserted 1:24		
1	Nolan Ryan	4.00
2	Ken Griffey Jr.	2.00
3	Sammy Sosa	2.50
5	Derek Jeter	4.00
6	Willie Mays	3.00
7	Roger Clemens	3.00

Legendary Jerseys

This game-used memorabilia insert set has a swatch of

game-used jersey embedded and were inserted 1:48 packs.

		NM/M
Common Player:		8.00
Inserted 1:48		
HA	Hank Aaron	40.00
JB	Jeff Bagwell	10.00
JB	Johnny Bench	20.00
WB	Wade Boggs	10.00
BaB	Barry Bonds	40.00
BoB	Bobby Bonds	8.00
GB	George Brett	30.00
LB	Lou Brock	8.00
JC	Jose Canseco	10.00
RC	Roger Clemens	30.00
DC	Dave Concepcion	8.00
DD	Don Drysdale	25.00
RF	Rollie Fingers	8.00
LG	Lou Gehrig/Pants	250.00
BG	Bob Gibson/Pants	20.00
KG	Ken Griffey Jr.	35.00
TG	Tony Gwynn	20.00
RJ	Reggie Jackson	10.00
DJ	Derek Jeter	40.00
RaJ	Randy Johnson	20.00
CJ	Chipper Jones	20.00
SK	Sandy Koufax	250.00
SK	Sandy Koufax/Auto./32	1,200
GM	Greg Maddux	30.00
MM	Mickey Mantle	150.00
RM	Roger Maris/Pants	60.00
EM	Eddie Mathews	20.00
WM	Willie Mays/SP/29	675.00
BM	Bill Mazeroski	8.00
WMc	Willie McCovey	10.00
TM	Thurman Munson	30.00
DM	Dale Murphy	10.00
SM	Stan Musial/SP/28	650.00
JP	Jim Palmer	8.00
GP	Gaylord Perry	8.00
MR	Manny Ramirez	10.00
CR	Cal Ripken Jr.	40.00
BR	Brooks Robinson	20.00
FR	Frank Robinson	10.00
AR	Alex Rodriguez	35.00
NR	Nolan Ryan	40.00
MS	Mike Schmidt	25.00
TS	Tom Seaver	20.00
OS	Ozzie Smith	8.00
WS	Willie Stargell	8.00
FT	Frank Thomas	10.00
JT	Joe Torre	8.00
EW	Earl Weaver	8.00
MW	Matt Williams	8.00
MW	Maury Wills	8.00
DW	Dave Winfield	10.00

Legendary Signatures

These autographed inserts are signed in blue Sharpie on the bottom panel. A Gold parallel version is also randomly seeded which has gold-foil stamping and is individually numbered to 50.

		NM/M
Common Player:		8.00
Inserted 1:23		
Golds:		1-2X
Production 50 Sets		
HA	Hank Aaron/SP/94	275.00
JB	Johnny Bench	30.00
BB	Bobby Bonds	8.00
LB	Lou Brock	8.00
GB	George Brett	60.00
JC	Jose Canseco	20.00

ABBREVIATIONS

SP - Short Print

GC	Gary Carter	10.00
SC	Sean Casey	8.00
RC	Roger Clemens	80.00
DC	Dave Concepcion	8.00
AD	Andre Dawson	10.00
KG	Ken Griffey Jr.	85.00
VG	Vladimir Guerrero	30.00
TG	Tony Gwynn	40.00
RJ	Reggie Jackson	35.00
DJ	Derek Jeter/SP/61	400.00
RaJ	Randy Johnson	50.00
CJ	Chipper Jones	35.00
HK	Harmon Killebrew	25.00
FL	Fred Lynn	8.00
DM	Dale Murphy	15.00
SM	Stan Musial	50.00
PN	Phil Niekro	8.00
JP	Jim Palmer	10.00
MP	Mike Piazza	120.00
MR	Manny Ramirez/SP/141	60.00
CR	Cal Ripken Jr.	120.00
AR	Alex Rodriguez	85.00
IR	Ivan Rodriguez	25.00
NR	Nolan Ryan	85.00
MS	Mike Schmidt	50.00
TS	Tom Seaver	30.00
OS	Ozzie Smith	40.00
WS	Willie Stargell	60.00
FT	Frank Thomas	30.00
AT	Alan Trammell	10.00
BW	Matt Williams	8.00

Ones for the Ages

This seven-card set has a holo-foiled front with gold foil etching and stamping. The player image is in a classic picture framed design. Card backs are numbered with an "O" prefix and seeded 1:24 packs.

		NM/M
Complete Set (7):		15.00
Inserted 1:24		
01	Ty Cobb	2.50
02	Cal Ripken Jr.	4.00
03	Babe Ruth	4.00
04	Jackie Robinson	2.50
05	Mark McGwire	3.00
06	Alex Rodriguez	3.00
07	Mike Piazza	4.00

Reflections in Time

This 10-card horizontal insert set features two players, past and present, linked by significant events or statistics. Card fronts are completely holo-foiled with gold foil stamping. Card backs are numbered with an "R" prefix and inserted 1:12 packs.

		NM/M
Complete Set (10):		25.00
Common Player:		2.00
Inserted 1:12		
1	Ken Griffey Jr., Hank Aaron	3.00
2	Sammy Sosa, Roberto Clemente	3.00
3	Roger Clemens, Nolan Ryan	4.00
4	Ivan Rodriguez, Johnny Bench	2.00
5	Alex Rodriguez, Ernie Banks	3.00
6	Tony Gwynn, Stan Musial	2.00
7	Barry Bonds, Willie Mays	4.00

8	Cal Ripken Jr., Lou Gehrig	4.00
9	Chipper Jones, Mike Schmidt	2.50
10	Mark McGwire, Babe Ruth	4.00

UD Millennium Team

This nine-card set has a complete holo-foiled front with silver foil stamping. The set is Upper Deck's selections for the all-time 20th century team and are inserted 1:4 packs. Card backs are numbered with an "UD" prefix.

		NM/M
Complete Set (10):		15.00
Common Player:		1.50
Inserted 1:4		
1	Mark McGwire	2.00
2	Jackie Robinson	2.00
3	Mike Schmidt	1.50
4	Cal Ripken Jr.	3.00
5	Babe Ruth	3.00
6	Willie Mays	2.00
8	Johnny Bench	1.50
9	Nolan Ryan	3.00
10	Ken Griffey Jr.	1.50

3,000 Hit Club

Upper Deck's continuing series pays tribute to Carl Yastrzemski and Paul Molitor. The series includes 350 Bat cards, 350 Jersey cards, 100 Bat/Jersey combo cards and eight autographed Bat/Jersey combo cards from Yastrzemski and 350 Bat cards from Molitor.

		NM/M
CY	Carl Yastrzemski/Bat/350	30.00
CY	Carl Yastrzemski/Jsy/350	30.00
CY	Carl Yastrzemski/Bat/Jsy/100	80.00

2000 Upper Deck MVP

The base set consists of 220-cards with a white bordered design and bronze foil stamping. Card backs have a maximum of 10 year-by-year statistics.

		NM/M
Complete Set (220):		20.00

Common Player:		.10
Pack (10):		1.25
Wax Box (28):		25.00
1	Garret Anderson	.25
2	Mo Vaughn	.15
3	Tim Salmon	.20
4	Ramon Ortiz	.10
5	Darin Erstad	.20
6	Troy Glaus	.50
7	Troy Percival	.10
8	Jeff Bagwell	.50
9	Ken Caminiti	.10
10	Daryle Ward	.10
11	Craig Biggio	.25
12	Jose Lima	.10
13	Moises Alou	.20
14	Octavio Dotel	.10
15	Ben Grieve	.20
16	Jason Giambi	.50
17	Tim Hudson	.20
18	Eric Chavez	.20
19	Matt Stairs	.10
20	Miguel Tejada	.25
21	John Jaha	.10
22	Chipper Jones	1.00
23	Kevin Millwood	.20
24	Brian Jordan	.10
25	Andruw Jones	.25
26	Andres Galarraga	.20
27	Greg Maddux	1.00
28	Reggie Sanders	.10
29	Javy Lopez	.20
30	Jeromy Burnitz	.10
31	Kevin Barker	.10
32	Jose Hernandez	.10
33	Ron Belliard	.10
34	Henry Blanco	.10
35	Marquis Grissom	.10
36	Geoff Jenkins	.20
37	Carlos Delgado	.50
38	Raul Mondesi	.20
39	Roy Halladay	.20
40	Tony Batista	.10
41	David Wells	.10
42	Shannon Stewart	.10
43	Vernon Wells	.20
44	Sammy Sosa	1.00
45	Ismael Valdes	.10
46	Joe Girardi	.10
47	Mark Grace	.20
48	Henry Rodriguez	.10
49	Kerry Wood	.25
50	Eric Young	.10
51	Mark McGwire	2.00
52	Daryle Kile	.10
53	Fernando Vina	.10
54	Ray Lankford	.10
55	J.D. Drew	.20
56	Fernando Tatis	.10
57	Rick Ankiel	.10
58	Matt Williams	.20
59	Erubiel Durazo	.15
60	Tony Womack	.10
61	Jay Bell	.10
62	Randy Johnson	.75
63	Steve Finley	.10
64	Matt Mantei	.10
65	Luis Gonzalez	.20
66	Gary Sheffield	.25
67	Eric Gagne	.10
68	Adrian Beltre	.20
69	Mark Grudzielanek	.10
70	Kevin Brown	.20
71	Chan Ho Park	.10
72	Shawn Green	.40
73	Vinny Castilla	.15
74	Fred McGriff	.25
75	Wilson Alvarez	.10
76	Greg Vaughn	.10
77	Gerald Williams	.10
78	Ryan Rupe	.10
79	Jose Canseco	.25
80	Vladimir Guerrero	.50
81	Dustin Hermanson	.10
82	Michael Barrett	.20
83	Rondell White	.20
84	Tony Armas Jr.	.10
85	Wilton Guerrero	.10
86	Jose Vidro	.10
87	Barry Bonds	1.50
88	Russ Ortiz	.10
89	Ellis Burks	.10
90	Jeff Kent	.20
91	Russ Davis	.10
92	J.T. Snow	.10
93	Roberto Alomar	.40
94	Manny Ramirez	.50
95	Chuck Finley	.10
96	Kenny Lofton	.20
97	Jim Thome	.50
98	Bartolo Colon	.20
99	Omar Vizquel	.20
100	Richie Sexson	.25
101	Mike Cameron	.10
102	Brett Tomko	.10
103	Edgar Martinez	.20
104	Alex Rodriguez	1.50
105	John Olerud	.20
106	Fred Garcia	.10
107	Kazuhiro Sasaki RC	1.00
108	Preston Wilson	.10
109	Luis Castillo	.10
110	A.J. Burnett	.10
111	Mike Lowell	.10
112	Cliff Floyd	.10
113	Brad Penny	.10
114	Alex Gonzalez	.10
115	Mike Piazza	1.00

116	Derek Bell	.10
117	Edgardo Alfonzo	.20
118	Rickey Henderson	.20
119	Todd Zeile	.10
120	Mike Hampton	.10
121	Al Leiter	.20
122	Robin Ventura	.10
123	Cal Ripken Jr.	1.50
124	Mike Mussina	.40
125	B.J. Surhoff	.10
126	Jerry Hairston Jr.	.10
127	Brady Anderson	.10
128	Albert Belle	.10
129	Sidney Ponson	.10
130	Tony Gwynn	.75
131	Ryan Klesko	.10
132	Sterling Hitchcock	.10
133	Eric Owens	.10
134	Trevor Hoffman	.10
135	Al Martin	.10
136	Bret Boone	.25
137	Brian Giles	.25
138	Chad Hermansen	.10
139	Kevin Young	.10
140	Kris Benson	.10
141	Warren Morris	.10
142	Jason Kendall	.20
143	Wil Cordero	.10
144	Scott Rolen	.50
145	Curt Schilling	.40
146	Doug Glanville	.10
147	Mike Lieberthal	.10
148	Mike Jackson	.10
149	Rico Brogna	.10
150	Andy Ashby	.10
151	Bob Abreu	.20
152	Sean Casey	.20
153	Pete Harnisch	.10
154	Dante Bichette	.10
155	Pokey Reese	.10
156	Aaron Boone	.20
157	Ken Griffey Jr.	1.00
158	Barry Larkin	.25
159	Scott Williamson	.10
160	Carlos Beltran	.20
161	Jermaine Dye	.10
162	Jose Rosado	.10
163	Joe Randa	.10
164	Johnny Damon	.20
165	Mike Sweeney	.10
166	Mark Quinn	.10
167	Ivan Rodriguez	.40
168	Rusty Greer	.10
169	Ruben Mateo	.10
170	Doug Davis	.10
171	Gabe Kapler	.10
172	Justin Thompson	.10
173	Rafael Palmeiro	.40
174	Larry Walker	.20
175	Neifi Perez	.10
176	Rolando Arrojo	.10
177	Jeffrey Hammonds	.10
178	Todd Helton	.50
179	Pedro Astacio	.10
180	Jeff Cirillo	.10
181	Pedro Martinez	.75
182	Carl Everett	.10
183	Troy O'Leary	.10
184	Nomar Garciaparra	1.25
185	Jose Offerman	.10
186	Bret Saberhagen	.10
187	Trot Nixon	.10
188	Jason Varitek	.10
189	Todd Walker	.10
190	Eric Milton	.10
191	Chad Allen	.10
192	Jacque Jones	.10
193	Brad Radke	.10
194	Corey Koskie	.10
195	Joe Mays	.10
196	Juan Gonzalez	.50
197	Jeff Weaver	.10
198	Juan Encarnacion	.10
199	Deivi Cruz	.10
200	Damion Easley	.10
201	Tony Clark	.20
202	Dean Palmer	.10
203	Frank Thomas	.50
204	Carlos Lee	.20
205	Mike Sirotka	.10
206	Kip Wells	.10
207	Magglio Ordonez	.20
208	Paul Konerko	.20
209	Chris Singleton	.10
210	Derek Jeter	1.50
211	Tino Martinez	.25
212	Mariano Rivera	.20
213	Roger Clemens	.75
214	Nick Johnson	.25
215	Paul O'Neill	.20
216	Bernie Williams	.40
217	David Cone	.20
218	Checklist (Ken Griffey Jr.)	.50
219	Checklist (Sammy Sosa)	.50
220	Checklist (Mark McGwire)	.75

Silver

A parallel to the 220-card base set. These 1:2 pack inserts can be distinguished from the base cards by the silver foil

stamping and a silver foiled facsimile signature of the featured player on the card bottom.

Stars:		1-2X
Inserted 1:2		

Gold

A parallel to the base set, these can be distinguished from base cards with gold script stamping. Each card is also serial numbered on the card front within an edition of 50 sets.

Stars:		10-20X
Production 50 Sets		

Super

A parallel to the 220-card base set, these inserts can be distinguished from the base cards by the holo-foil stamping used on the Upper Deck logo and the featured player's facsimile signature on the card bottom. The card fronts are also serial numbered within an edition of 25 sets.

Stars:		15-30X
Production 25 Sets		

All-Star Game

		NM/M
Complete Set (30):		25.00
Common Player:		.25
AS1	Mo Vaughn	.25
AS2	Jeff Bagwell	.75
AS3	Jason Giambi	.75
AS4	Chipper Jones	1.50
AS5	Greg Maddux	1.00
AS6	Tony Batista	.25
AS7	Sammy Sosa	2.00
AS8	Mark McGwire	2.50
AS9	Randy Johnson	.75
AS10	Shawn Green	.75
AS11	Greg Vaughn	.25
AS12	Vladimir Guerrero	.75
AS13	Barry Bonds	2.50
AS14	Manny Ramirez	.75
AS15	Alex Rodriguez	2.50
AS16	Preston Wilson	.25
AS17	Mike Piazza	1.50
AS18	Cal Ripken Jr.	3.00
AS19	Tony Gwynn	1.00
AS20	Scott Rolen	.75
AS21	Ken Griffey Jr.	1.50
AS22	Carlos Beltran	.25
AS23	Ivan Rodriguez	.60
AS24	Larry Walker	.25
AS25	Nomar Garciaparra	2.00
AS26	Pedro Martinez	.75
AS27	Juan Gonzalez	.75
AS28	Frank Thomas	.75
AS29	Derek Jeter	2.50
AS30	Bernie Williams	.50

Drawing Power

This seven-card set has a holo-foil front with silver foil stamping. Card backs are numbered with a "DP" prefix.

		NM/M
Complete Set (7):		12.00
Common Player:		1.00
Inserted 1:28		
1	Mark McGwire	3.00
2	Ken Griffey Jr.	2.00
3	Mike Piazza	2.00
4	Chipper Jones	2.00
5	Nomar Garciaparra	3.00
6	Sammy Sosa	2.50
7	Jose Canseco	1.00

Game-Used Souvenirs

These memorabilia inserts feature a game-used piece of glove embedded and are found exclusively in hobby packs at a rate of 1:130 packs.

		NM/M
Common Glove:		8.00
Inserted 1:130		
RA	Roberto Alomar	15.00
JB	Jeff Bagwell	20.00
AB	Albert Belle	8.00
BB	Barry Bonds	65.00
JC	Jose Canseco	15.00
WC	Will Clark	20.00
AF	Alex Fernandez	8.00
JG	Jason Giambi	15.00
TGl	Troy Glaus	15.00
AG	Alex Gonzalez	8.00
BG	Ben Grieve	8.00
KG	Ken Griffey Jr.	40.00
VG	Vladimir Guerrero	15.00
TG	Tony Gwynn	30.00
AJ	Andruw Jones	15.00
CJ	Chipper Jones	30.00
KL	Kenny Lofton	8.00
RM	Raul Mondesi	8.00
PO	Paul O'Neill	10.00
RP	Rafael Palmeiro	15.00
MR	Manny Ramirez	15.00
CR	Cal Ripken Jr.	65.00
AR	Alex Rodriguez	40.00
IR	Ivan Rodriguez	15.00
NR	Nolan Ryan	65.00
TS	Tim Salmon	8.00
LW	Larry Walker	8.00
BW	Bernie Williams	15.00
MW	Matt Williams	8.00

Game-Used Souvenirs - Bats

These memorabilia inserts have a piece of game-used bat embedded and are seeded exclusively in hobby packs at a rate of 1:130 packs.

		NM/M
Common Bat:		8.00
Inserted 1:130		
BB	Barry Bonds	40.00

JC	Jose Canseco	8.00
KG	Ken Griffey Jr.	20.00
VG	Vladimir Guerrero	10.00
TG	Tony Gwynn	15.00
CJ	Chipper Jones	15.00
MR	Manny Ramirez	10.00
AR	Alex Rodriguez	20.00
IR	Ivan Rodriguez	8.00
BW	Bernie Williams	10.00

Game-Used Souvenirs - Bats Autograph

Production 25 Sets
Values Undetermined

Prolifics

This seven-card set features a full holo-foiled front with silver foil stamping and are seeded 1:28 packs. Card backs are numbered with a "P" prefix.

		NM/M
Complete Set (7):		10.00
Common Player:		.50
Inserted 1:28		
1	Manny Ramirez	1.00
2	Vladimir Guerrero	1.00
3	Derek Jeter	3.00
4	Pedro Martinez	1.50
5	Shawn Green	.50
6	Alex Rodriguez	3.00
7	Cal Ripken Jr.	4.00

ProSign

These autographed inserts are found exclusively in retail packs at a rate of 1:216.

		NM/M
Common Player:		5.00
Inserted 1:216 R		
RA	Rick Ankiel	5.00
MB	Michael Barrett	5.00
RB	Rob Bell	5.00
CB	Carlos Beltran	20.00
LB	Lance Berkman	15.00
RB	Rico Brogna	5.00
SC	Sean Casey	8.00
DD	Doug Davis	5.00
ED	Erubiel Durazo	8.00
RF	Robert Fick	5.00
NG	Nomar Garciaparra	65.00
AG	Alex Gonzalez	8.00
KG	Ken Griffey Jr.	60.00
TG	Tony Gwynn	40.00
TH	Tim Hudson	15.00
DJ	Derek Jeter	80.00
CJ	Chipper Jones	50.00
MM	Mike Meyers	5.00
EM	Eric Milton	8.00
JM	Jim Morris	5.00
WM	Warren Morris	5.00
TN	Trot Nixon	8.00
BP	Ben Petrick	5.00
AP	Adam Piatt	5.00
MP	Mike Piazza	60.00
MQ	Mark Quinn	5.00
MR	Manny Ramirez	25.00
RR	Rob Ramsay	5.00
MRe	Mike Redmond	5.00
MRi	Mariano Rivera	15.00
AR	Alex Rodriguez	65.00
MS	Mike Sweeney	8.00
BT	Bubba Trammell	8.00
JV	Jose Vidro	8.00
DW	Daryle Ward	8.00
KW	Kip Wells	8.00
SW	Scott Williamson	5.00
PW	Preston Wilson	8.00
KW	Kevin Witt	8.00
TW	Tony Womack	5.00
EY	Ed Yarnall	5.00
JZ	Jeff Zimmerman	5.00

Pure Grit

These 1:6 pack inserts have a full holo-foiled front with silver foil stamping. Card backs are numbered with a "G" prefix.

		NM/M
Complete Set (10):		10.00
Common Player:		.50
Inserted 1:6		
1	Derek Jeter	2.00
2	Kevin Brown	.50
3	Craig Biggio	.50
4	Ivan Rodriguez	.75
5	Scott Rolen	.75
6	Carlos Beltran	.50
7	Ken Griffey Jr.	1.50
8	Cal Ripken Jr.	2.50
9	Nomar Garciaparra	2.00
10	Randy Johnson	1.00

Scout's Choice

This ten-card set spotlights some of the best prospects in 2000. The inserts have a full holo-foiled front with silver foil stamping. Card backs are numbered with an "SC" prefix and are seeded 1:14 packs.

		NM/M
Complete Set (10):		8.00
Common Player:		.50
Inserted 1:14		
1	Rick Ankiel	.50
2	Vernon Wells	1.00
3	Pat Burrell	1.50
4	Travis Dawkins	.50
5	Eric Munson	.50
6	Nick Johnson	1.00
7	Dermal Brown	.50
8	Alfonso Soriano	2.00
9	Ben Petrick	.50
10	Adam Everett	.50

Second Season Standouts

This 10-card set has a full holo-foiled card front with silver foil stamping. Card backs are numbered with an "SS" prefix and inserted 1:6 packs.

	NM/M
Complete Set (10):	6.00

Common Player:		.25
Inserted 1:6		
1	Pedro Martinez	1.00
2	Mariano Rivera	.40
3	Orlando Hernandez	.25
4	Ken Caminiti	.25
5	Bernie Williams	.50
6	Jim Thome	.75
7	Nomar Garciaparra	2.00
8	Edgardo Alfonzo	.25
9	Derek Jeter	2.50
10	Kevin Millwood	.40

3,000 Hit Club

Upper Deck used this cross-brand insert series to salute the players who accomplished 3,000 hits in their career. Stan Musial is featured and offers a game-used memorabilia bat, jersey, jersey/bat combo and combo autograph versions.

		NM/M
Common Player:		
SM	Stan Musial/Jsy/350	30.00
SM	Stan Musial/Bat/350	30.00
SM	Stan Musial/Jsy/Bat/100	80.00

2000 UD N.Y. Yankees Master Collection

The most popular franchise in sports history was the subject of this Master Collection limited to 500 numbered sets. Issued in a serially-numbered mahogany box with pewter team-logo inlay, each set includes 25 cards honoring the Yankees' World Championships between 1923-1999. There is also a "Team of the Century" card set with 10 game-used bat cards and a special Gehrig commemorative. Each set also includes a Mystery Pack containing one of 14 autographed memorabilia cards. Retail price at time of issue was around $6,000. Because unopened sets may contain one of the better "Mystery Pack" cards, they maintain a significant premium.

	NM/M
Complete Boxed Set, Unopened:	3,250
Complete Boxed Set, Opened:	1,650
N.Y. Yankees Master Collection Wood Box	100.00

Mystery Cards

Each Master Collection set contains one foil-pack Mystery Card ranging from autographed player memorabilia-cards to cut signatures. The Gehrig, Mantle, Martin, Munson and Ruth cards are each uniquely numbered on back with the player's initials or initials plus "C" (for cut signature) as a prefix. The Berra, Ford, Jackson and Jeter cards are not "numbered," but are identified by player initials and type of memorabilia. The number issued of each card is shown in parentheses. Some cards remain unpriced due to rarity.

		NM/M
Unopened Mystery Pack:		600.00
BM	Billy Martin (bat-cut)(2) (8/05 auction)	615.00
BR	Babe Ruth (bat-cut)(3)	9,500
BR-C	Babe Ruth (cut)(3)	7,500
DJ-B	Derek Jeter/ Bat-Auto./100	450.00
DJ-J	Derek Jeter/ Jsy-Auto./100	500.00
LG-C	Lou Gehrig/Cut)	3,000
MM	Mickey Mantle/ bat-cut/7	4,000
RJ-B	Reggie Jackson/ Bat-Auto./100	400.00
WF-J	Whitey Ford/ Jsy-Auto./100	450.00
YB-B	Yogi Berra/ Bat-Auto./80	450.00

Team of the Century

An 11-player "Team of the Century" card set within the Yankees Master Collection features game-used bat cards from 10 of the players and a special Lou Gehrig commemorative card (Upper Deck could not get a Gehrig gamer to cut up for the cards). Each card carries an individual serial number from an edition of 500 each.

		NM/M
Complete Set (11):		1,575
Common Player:		56.00
ATY1	Babe Ruth	400.00
ATY2	Mickey Mantle	550.00
ATY3	Reggie Jackson	135.00
ATY4	Don Mattingly	135.00
ATY5	Billy Martin	90.00
ATY6	Graig Nettles	55.00
ATY7	Derek Jeter	110.00
ATY8	Yogi Berra	135.00
ATY9	Thurman Munson	145.00
ATY10	Whitey Ford	110.00
ATY11	Lou Gehrig	35.00

World Series Champions

Each of the Yankees' 25 World Series Championships between 1923-1999 is marked with one of these "base" cards in the Master Collection. Fronts of the 2-1/2" x 3-1/2" cards have black-and-white or color poses or action photos highlighted with holographic foil. Backs have a portrait photo, a World Series summary and the player's career and Series stats. Each card is serially numbered within an edition of 500.

		NM/M
Complete Set (25):		480.00
Common Player:		12.50
NYY1	Babe Ruth/1923	50.00
NYY2	Lou Gehrig/1927	35.00
NYY3	Tony Lazzeri/1928	12.50
NYY4	Babe Ruth/1932	50.00
NYY5	Lou Gehrig/1936	35.00
NYY6	Lefty Gomez/1937	25.00
NYY7	Bill Dickey/1938	25.00
NYY8	Bill Dickey/1939	25.00
NYY9	Tommy Henrich/1941	17.50
NYY10	Spud Chandler/1943	12.50
NYY11	Tommy Henrich/1947	17.50
NYY12	Phil Rizzuto/1949	25.00
NYY13	Whitey Ford/195)	25.00
NYY14	Yogi Berra/1951	30.00
NYY15	Casey Stengel/1952	17.50
NYY16	Billy Martin/1953	17.50
NYY17	Don Larsen/1956	22.00
NYY18	Elston Howard/1958	12.50
NYY19	Roger Maris/1961	30.00
NYY20	Mickey Mantle/1962	50.00
NYY21	Reggie Jackson/1977	30.00
NYY22	Bucky Dent/1978	15.00
NYY23	Derek Jeter/1996	25.00
NYY24	Derek Jeter/1998	25.00
NYY25	Derek Jeter/1999	25.00

Opening Day 2K

As part of a multi-manufacturer promotion, UD issued eight cards of an "Opening Day 2K" set. Packages containing some of the 32 cards in the issue were distributed by MLB teams early in the season. The cards were also available exclusively as inserts in Upper Deck Victory and Hitters Club packs sold at K-Mart stores early in the season. The Upper Deck OD2K cards have gold-foil graphic highlights on front. Backs have a monochromatic version of the front photo and are numbered with an "OD" prefix.

		NM/M
Complete Set (8):		6.00
Common Player:		.50
17	Ken Griffey Jr.	1.50
18	Sammy Sosa	1.00
19	Pedro Martinez	.75
20	Manny Ramirez	.65
21	Shawn Green	.65
22	Carlos Beltran	.40
23	Juan Gonzalez	.50
24	Jeromy Burnitz	.50

2000 Upper Deck Ovation

The base set consists of 90-cards, including a 20-card World Premiere subset and 10-card Superstar Spotlight subset. World Premiere's are

found 1:3 packs and Superstar Spotlight's 1:6 packs. Card fronts are embossed, intended to resemble the feel of a baseball and also has silver foil stamping.

		NM/M
Complete Set (90):		65.00
Common Player:		.25
Common World Prem. (61-80):		1.00
Inserted 1:3		
Common Super. Spot. (81-90):		1.50
Inserted 1:6		
Pack (5):		2.00
Wax Box (20):		30.00
1	Mo Vaughn	.25
2	Troy Glaus	.75
3	Jeff Bagwell	.75
4	Craig Biggio	.40
5	Mike Hampton	.25
6	Jason Giambi	.75
7	Tim Hudson	.40
8	Chipper Jones	1.50
9	Greg Maddux	1.50
10	Kevin Millwood	.40
11	Brian Jordan	.25
12	Jeromy Burnitz	.25
13	David Wells	.25
14	Carlos Delgado	.75
15	Sammy Sosa	2.50
16	Mark McGwire	3.00
17	Matt Williams	.25
18	Randy Johnson	.75
19	Erubiel Durazo	.40
20	Kevin Brown	.40
21	Shawn Green	.75
22	Gary Sheffield	.50
23	Jose Canseco	.50
24	Vladimir Guerrero	1.00
25	Barry Bonds	3.00
26	Manny Ramirez	.75
27	Roberto Alomar	.75
28	Richie Sexson	.40
29	Jim Thome	.75
30	Alex Rodriguez	2.50
31	Ken Griffey Jr.	1.50
32	Preston Wilson	.25
33	Mike Piazza	1.50
34	Al Leiter	.25
35	Robin Ventura	.25
36	Cal Ripken Jr.	3.00
37	Albert Belle	.25
38	Tony Gwynn	1.00
39	Brian Giles	.40
40	Jason Kendall	.25
41	Scott Rolen	.75
42	Bob Abreu	.40
43	Ken Griffey Jr.	1.50
44	Sean Casey	.25
45	Carlos Beltran	.40
46	Gabe Kapler	.25
47	Ivan Rodriguez	.75
48	Rafael Palmeiro	.50
49	Larry Walker	.40
50	Nomar Garciaparra	2.00
51	Pedro J. Martinez	1.00
52	Eric Milton	.25
53	Juan Gonzalez	.75
54	Tony Clark	.25
55	Frank Thomas	.75
56	Magglio Ordonez	.40
57	Roger Clemens	1.50
58	Derek Jeter	2.50
59	Bernie Williams	.50
60	Orlando Hernandez	.40
61	Rick Ankiel (World Premiere)	1.00
62	Josh Beckett (World Premiere)	1.50
63	Vernon Wells (World Premiere)	1.50
64	Alfonso Soriano (World Premiere)	3.00
65	Pat Burrell (World Premiere)	2.00
66	Eric Munson (World Premiere)	1.00
67	Chad Hutchinson (World Premiere)	1.00
68	Eric Gagne (World Premiere)	1.00
69	Peter Bergeron (World Premiere)	1.00

70	Ryan Anderson (Supposed to have been withdrawn, all known cards have embossed UD racing mark.)	300.00
71	A.J. Burnett (World Premiere)	1.00
72	Jorge Luis Toca (World Premiere)	1.00
73	Matt Riley (World Premiere)	1.00
74	Chad Hermansen (World Premiere)	1.00
75	Doug Davis (World Premiere)	1.00
76	Jim Morris (World Premiere)	1.00
77	Ben Petrick (World Premiere)	1.00
78	Mark Quinn (World Premiere)	1.00
79	Ed Yarnall (World Premiere)	1.00
80	Ramon Ortiz (World Premiere)	1.00
81	Ken Griffey Jr. (Superstar Spotlight)	3.00
82	Mark McGwire (Superstar Spotlight)	5.00
83	Derek Jeter (Superstar Spotlight)	5.00
84	Jeff Bagwell (Superstar Spotlight)	1.50
85	Nomar Garciaparra (Superstar Spotlight)	5.00
86	Sammy Sosa (Superstar Spotlight)	4.00
87	Mike Piazza (Superstar Spotlight)	3.00
88	Alex Rodriguez (Superstar Spotlight)	5.00
89	Cal Ripken Jr. (Superstar Spotlight)	6.00
90	Pedro Martinez (Superstar Spotlight)	2.00

Standing Ovation

A parallel to the 120-card base set, these are identical to the base cards besides the holographic silver stamping on the card front and the backs serially numbered to 50.

Stars (1-60):	8-15X
World Prem. (61-80):	2-3X
Super. Spot. (81-90):	3-5X
Production 50 Sets	

A Piece of History

These memorabilia inserts feature a piece of game-used bat embedded and are limited to 400 sets produced.

		NM/M
	Common Player:	5.00
	Production 400 Sets	
JB	Jeff Bagwell	10.00
CB	Carlos Beltran	10.00
SC	Sean Casey	5.00
KG	Ken Griffey Jr.	25.00
DJ	Derek Jeter	35.00
TG	Tony Gwynn	15.00
AJ	Andruw Jones	10.00
CJ	Chipper Jones	20.00
RP	Rafael Palmeiro	10.00
MP	Mike Piazza	20.00
MR	Manny Ramirez	10.00
CR	Cal Ripken Jr.	35.00
AR	Alex Rodriguez	25.00
SR	Scott Rolen	10.00
SS	Sammy Sosa	25.00
FT	Frank Thomas	10.00

A Piece of History - Signed

Values Undetermined

Center Stage

Ten of baseball's top performers are highlighted on a card that features gold foil stamping and etching. Card backs are numbered with an "CS" prefix and are seeded 1:9 packs. Two parallels to this insert set are randomly inserted: Golds are found 1:39 packs and Rainbows are seeded 1:99 packs.

		NM/M
	Complete Set (10):	20.00
	Common Player:	1.00
	Inserted 1:9	
	Gold:	2X
	Inserted 1:39	
	Rainbow:	3-4X
	Inserted 1:99	
1	Jeff Bagwell	1.00
2	Ken Griffey Jr.	2.00
3	Nomar Garciaparra	3.00
4	Mike Piazza	2.00
5	Mark McGwire	3.00
6	Alex Rodriguez	3.00
7	Cal Ripken Jr.	4.00
8	Derek Jeter	3.00
9	Chipper Jones	2.00
10	Sammy Sosa	2.50

Curtain Calls

This 20-card set features gold foil stamping and highlights some memorable playoff moments. Card backs are numbered with a "CC" prefix.

		NM/M
	Complete Set (20):	15.00
	Common Player:	.50
	Inserted 1:3	
1	David Cone	.50
2	Mark McGwire	2.00
3	Sammy Sosa	2.00
4	Eric Milton	.50
5	Bernie Williams	.75
6	Tony Gwynn	1.00
7	Nomar Garciaparra	2.00
8	Manny Ramirez	1.00
9	Wade Boggs	.50
10	Randy Johnson	1.00
11	Cal Ripken Jr.	3.00
12	Pedro J. Martinez	1.00
13	Alex Rodriguez	2.00
14	Fernando Tatis	.50
15	Vladimir Guerrero	1.00
16	Robin Ventura	.50
17	Larry Walker	.50
18	Carlos Beltran	.50
19	Jose Canseco	.75
20	Ken Griffey Jr.	1.50

Diamond Futures

This 10-card set highlights some of baseball's top prospects on a full foiled front

with silver foil stamping. Card backs are numbered with a "DM" prefix.

		NM/M
	Complete Set (10):	8.00
	Common Player:	.50
	Inserted 1:6	
1	J.D. Drew	.75
2	Alfonso Soriano	2.50
3	Preston Wilson	1.00
4	Erubiel Durazo	.75
5	Rick Ankiel	.50
6	Octavio Dotel	.50
7	A.J. Burnett	.50
8	Carlos Beltran	.75
9	Vernon Wells	1.00
10	Troy Glaus	2.00

Lead Performers

Upper Deck chose 10 players for this set who are thought of as leaders on and off the field. Card fronts have silver foil stamping and card backs are numbered with an "LP" prefix.

		NM/M
	Complete Set (10):	20.00
	Common Player:	1.00
	Inserted 1:19	
1	Mark McGwire	3.00
2	Derek Jeter	3.00
3	Vladimir Guerrero	1.00
4	Mike Piazza	2.00
5	Cal Ripken Jr.	4.00
6	Sammy Sosa	2.50
7	Jeff Bagwell	1.00
8	Nomar Garciaparra	3.00
9	Chipper Jones	2.00
10	Ken Griffey Jr.	2.00

Super Signatures

This two-card insert set features Ken Griffey Jr. and Mike Piazza. Spotlighting the autographs of Griffey and Piazza, Super Signatures is issued in three versions: Silver, numbered to 100; Gold, numbered to 50; and Rainbow, numbered to 10.

		NM/M
	Common Card:	
KG	Ken Griffey/Gold/50	180.00
KG	Ken Griffey/Silver/100	100.00
MP	Mike Piazza/Gold/50	180.00
MP	Mike Piazza/Silver/100	150.00

Superstar Theatre

This 20-card set is printed on a full foiled card front enhanced by silver foil stamping and etching. Card backs are numbered with an "ST" prefix.

		NM/M
	Complete Set (20):	20.00
	Common Player:	.50
	Inserted 1:19	
1	Ivan Rodriguez	1.00

2	Brian Giles	.50
3	Bernie Williams	1.00
4	Greg Maddux	2.00
5	Frank Thomas	1.00
6	Sean Casey	.50
7	Mo Vaughn	.50
8	Carlos Delgado	1.00
9	Tony Gwynn	1.50
10	Pedro Martinez	1.50
11	Scott Rolen	1.00
12	Mark McGwire	3.00
13	Manny Ramirez	1.00
14	Rafael Palmeiro	.75
15	Jose Canseco	.75
16	Randy Johnson	1.50
17	Gary Sheffield	.75
18	Larry Walker	.50
19	Barry Bonds	4.00
20	Roger Clemens	3.00

3,000 Hit Club

Upper Deck's cross brand insert series pays tribute to members of the elite 3,000 Hit Club. Ovation features Willie Mays in the series, which has four versions: Bat card, 300 produced; Jersey card, 350 produced; Bat/Jersey combo, 50 produced; and Bat/Jersey autograph, 24 produced.

		NM/M
1	Willie Mays/Jsy/350	40.00
2	Willie Mays/Bat/300	40.00
3	Willie Mays/Jsy/Bat/50	180.00
4	Willie Mays/Jsy/Bat/Auto./24	675.00

2000 Upper Deck PowerDeck

		NM/M
	Complete Set (12):	50.00
	Common Card:	3.00
	Pack (1):	4.00
	Box:	40.00
1	Sammy Sosa	6.00
2	Ken Griffey Jr.	6.00
3	Mark McGwire	8.00
4	Derek Jeter	6.00
5	Alex Rodriguez	8.00
6	Nomar Garciaparra	6.00
7	Mike Piazza	5.00
8	Cal Ripken Jr.	8.00
9	Ivan Rodriguez	3.00
10	Chipper Jones	5.00
11	Pedro Martinez	3.00
12	Manny Ramirez	3.00

Magical Moments

		NM/M
	Inserted 1:10 H	
KG	Ken Griffey Jr.	6.00
CR	Cal Ripken Jr.	10.00

Magical Moments Autograph

		NM/M
	Each signed 50 cards.	
KG	Ken Griffey Jr.	180.00
CR	Cal Ripken Jr.	275.00

Power Trio

		NM/M
	Complete Set (3):	15.00
	Common Player:	5.00
	Inserted 1:7	
PT1	Derek Jeter	6.00
PT2	Ken Griffey Jr.	5.00
PT3	Mark McGwire	6.00

2000 Upper Deck Pros and Prospects

The 132-card base set consists of 90 regular player cards, a 30-card Prospective Superstars subset and a 12-card Pro-Fame subset. Prospective Superstars are serially numbered to 1,350 and Pro-Fame are serially numbered to 1,000. Card fronts have a white-bordered design with silver foil stamping. Both subsets are serially numbered on the card front.

		NM/M
	Complete Set (132):	300.00
	Common Player (1-90):	.15
	Common (91-120):	5.00
	Production 1,350 Sets	
	Common (121-132):	4.00
	Production 1,000 Sets	
	Pack (5):	2.50
	Box (24):	40.00
1	Darin Erstad	.40
2	Troy Glaus	.75
3	Mo Vaughn	.20
4	Jason Giambi	.75
5	Tim Hudson	.75
6	Ben Grieve	.15
7	Eric Chavez	.25
8	Shannon Stewart	.15
9	Raul Mondesi	.25
10	Carlos Delgado	.75
12	Jose Canseco	.40
13	Fred McGriff	.25
14	Greg Vaughn	.15
15	Manny Ramirez	.75
16	Roberto Alomar	.50
17	Jim Thome	.75
18	Alex Rodriguez	2.50
19	Fred Garcia	.15
20	John Olerud	.25
21	Cal Ripken Jr.	2.50
22	Albert Belle	.20
23	Mike Mussina	.40
24	Ivan Rodriguez	.50
25	Rafael Palmeiro	.50
26	Ruben Mateo	.15
27	Gabe Kapler	.25
28	Pedro Martinez	1.00
29	Nomar Garciaparra	2.00
30	Carl Everett	.15
31	Carlos Beltran	.15
32	Jermaine Dye	.15
33	Johnny Damon	.25
34	Juan Gonzalez	.75
35	Juan Encarnacion	.15
36	Dean Palmer	.15
37	Jacque Jones	.15
38	Matt Lawton	.15
39	Frank Thomas	.75
40	Paul Konerko	.15
41	Magglio Ordonez	.25
42	Derek Jeter	2.00
43	Bernie Williams	.50
44	Mariano Rivera	.25
45	Roger Clemens	1.50
46	Jeff Bagwell	.75
47	Craig Biggio	.25
48	Richard Hidalgo	.15
49	Chipper Jones	1.50
50	Andres Galarraga	.25
51	Andruw Jones	.50
52	Greg Maddux	1.50
53	Jeromy Burnitz	.15
54	Geoff Jenkins	.15
55	Mark McGwire	2.00
56	Jim Edmonds	.25
57	Fernando Tatis	.15
58	J.D. Drew	.25
59	Sammy Sosa	2.00
60	Kerry Wood	.50

60	Randy Johnson	.75
61	Matt Williams	.25
62	Erubiel Durazo	.15
63	Shawn Green	.25
64	Kevin Brown	.25
65	Gary Sheffield	.25
66	Adrian Beltre	.25
67	Vladimir Guerrero	.75
68	Jose Vidro	.15
69	Barry Bonds	2.00
70	Jeff Kent	.25
71	Preston Wilson	.15
72	Ryan Dempster	.15
73	Mike Lowell	.15
74	Mike Piazza	1.50
75	Robin Ventura	.25
76	Edgardo Alfonzo	.15
77	Derek Bell	.15
78	Tony Gwynn	1.00
79	Matt Clement	.15
80	Scott Rolen	.75
81	Bobby Abreu	.25
82	Curt Schilling	.40
83	Brian Giles	.25
84	Jason Kendall	.25
85	Kris Benson	.15
86	Ken Griffey Jr.	1.50
87	Sean Casey	.25
88	Pokey Reese	.15
89	Larry Walker	.25
90	Todd Helton	.75
91	Rick Ankiel (Prospective Superstars)	5.00
92	Milton Bradley (Prospective Superstars)	5.00
93	Vernon Wells (Prospective Superstars)	6.00
94	Rafael Furcal (Prospective Superstars)	6.00
95	Kazuhiro Sasaki RC (Prospective Superstars)	8.00
96	Joe Torres RC (Prospective Superstars)	5.00
97	Adam Kennedy (Prospective Superstars)	5.00
98	Adam Piatt (Prospective Superstars)	5.00
99	Matt Wheatland RC (Prospective Superstars)	5.00
100	Alex Cabrera RC (Prospective Superstars)	5.00
101	Barry Zito RC (Prospective Superstars)	25.00
102	Mike Lamb RC (Prospective Superstars)	5.00
103	Scott Heard RC (Prospective Superstars)	5.00
104	Danys Baez RC (Prospective Superstars)	8.00
105	Matt Riley (Prospective Superstars)	5.00
106	Mark Mulder (Prospective Superstars)	6.00
107	Wilfredo Rodriguez RC (Prospective Superstars)	5.00
108	Luis Matos RC (Prospective Superstars)	5.00
109	Alfonso Soriano (Prospective Superstars)	8.00
110	Pat Burrell (Prospective Superstars)	6.00
111	Mike Tonis RC (Prospective Superstars)	5.00
112	Aaron McNeal RC (Prospective Superstars)	5.00
113	Dave Krynzel RC (Prospective Superstars)	8.00
114	Josh Beckett (Prospective Superstars)	5.00
115	Sean Burnett RC (Prospective Superstars)	8.00
116	Eric Munson (Prospective Superstars)	5.00
117	Scott Downs RC (Prospective Superstars)	5.00
118	Brian Tollberg RC (Prospective Superstars)	5.00
119	Nick Johnson (Prospective Superstars)	5.00
120	Leo Estrella RC (Prospective Superstars)	5.00
121	Ken Griffey Jr. (Pro Fame)	8.00
122	Frank Thomas (Pro Fame)	4.00
123	Cal Ripken Jr. (Pro Fame)	15.00
124	Ivan Rodriguez (Pro Fame)	4.00

125	Derek Jeter (Pro Fame)	12.00
126	Mark McGwire (Pro Fame)	12.00
127	Pedro Martinez (Pro Fame)	5.00
128	Chipper Jones (Pro Fame)	8.00
129	Sammy Sosa (Pro Fame)	10.00
130	Alex Rodriguez (Pro Fame)	10.00
131	Vladimir Guerrero (Pro Fame)	4.00
132	Jeff Bagwell (Pro Fame)	4.00

Future Forces

This 10-card set highlights top prospects on a card front featuring gold foil stamping and etching. Card backs are numbered with an "F" prefix.

		NM/M
Complete Set (10):		5.00
Common Player:		.50
Inserted 1:6		
1	Pat Burrell	2.00
2	Brad Penny	.50
3	Rick Ankiel	.50
4	Adam Kennedy	.50
5	Eric Munson	.50
6	Rafael Furcal	.75
7	Mark Mulder	.75
8	Vernon Wells	.75
9	Matt Riley	.50
10	Nick Johnson	.75

ProMotion

This 10-card set spotlights some of baseball's best all-around talents using gold foil stamping. Card backs are numbered with a "P" prefix and are seeded 1:6 packs.

		NM/M
Complete Set (10):		15.00
Common Player:		.75
Inserted 1:6		
1	Derek Jeter	3.00
2	Mike Piazza	1.50
3	Mark McGwire	2.50
4	Ivan Rodriguez	.75
5	Kerry Wood	.75
6	Nomar Garciaparra	2.00
7	Sammy Sosa	2.00
8	Alex Rodriguez	2.50
9	Ken Griffey Jr.	1.50
10	Vladimir Guerrero	1.00

Rare Breed

Baseball's top performers are spotlighted in this 12-card set on a full foiled silver front with gold foil stamping. Card backs are numbered with an "R" prefix and are inserted 1:12 packs.

	NM/M
Complete Set (12):	15.00
Common Player:	.50

design with gold foil stamping. Card backs are numbered with a "B" prefix.

		NM/M
Complete Set (10):		15.00
Common Player:		1.00
Inserted 1:12		
1	Sammy Sosa	2.50
2	Tony Gwynn	1.50
3	Pedro Martinez	1.50
4	Mark McGwire	3.00
5	Chipper Jones	2.00
6	Derek Jeter	3.00
7	Ken Griffey Jr.	2.00
8	Cal Ripken Jr.	4.00
9	Greg Maddux	2.00
10	Ivan Rodriguez	1.00

3,000 Hit Club

Upper Deck's continuing series features Lou Brock and Rod Carew. The series features 350 numbered bat cards, 350 numbered jersey cards and 100 numbered bat/jersey combos. Each player also signed the bat/jersey combos to their jersey number, as Brock signed 20 and Carew 29.

	NM/M
Lou Brock Bat/350	20.00
Lou Brock/Jsy/350	20.00
Lou Brock/ Bat/Jsy/100	40.00
Rod Carew/Bat/350	20.00
Rod Carew/Jsy/350	20.00
Rod Carew/ Bat/Jsy/100	40.00

2000 Upper Deck Rookie Update

		NM/M
Common Player:		.25
Common Rookie:		5.00
Pack (4):		4.50
Box (15):		50.00
SP Authentic Update		
(136-164) Production 1,700		
136	Barry Zito RC (Future Watch)	30.00
137	Aaron McNeal RC (Future Watch)	5.00
138	Teofilo Perez RC (Future Watch)	5.00
139	Sun-Woo Kim RC (Future Watch)	5.00
140	Xavier Nady RC (Future Watch)	15.00
141	Matt Wheatland RC (Future Watch)	5.00
142	Brent Abernathy RC (Future Watch)	5.00
143	Cory Vance RC (Future Watch)	5.00
144	Scott Heard RC (Future Watch)	5.00
145	Mike Meyers RC (Future Watch)	5.00
146	Ben Diggins RC (Future Watch)	5.00
147	Luis Matos RC (Future Watch)	8.00
148	Ben Sheets RC (Future Watch)	15.00
149	Kurt Ainsworth RC (Future Watch)	10.00
150	Dave Krynzel RC (Future Watch)	8.00
151	Alex Cabrera RC (Future Watch)	5.00
152	Mike Tonis RC (Future Watch)	5.00
153	Dane Sardinha RC (Future Watch)	5.00
154	Keith Ginter RC (Future Watch)	8.00
155	David Espinosa RC (Future Watch)	5.00
156	Joe Torres RC (Future Watch)	8.00
157	Daylan Holt RC (Future Watch)	5.00
158	Koyie Hill RC (Future Watch)	5.00
159	Brad Wilkerson RC (Future Watch)	10.00
160	Juan Pierre RC (Future Watch)	10.00
161	Matt Ginter RC (Future Watch)	8.00
162	Dane Artman RC (Future Watch)	5.00
163	Jon Rauch RC (Future Watch)	8.00
164	Sean Burnett RC (Future Watch)	8.00
166	Darin Erstad	.50
167	Ben Grieve	.25
168	David Wells	.25
169	Fred McGriff	.40
170	Bob Wickman	.25
171	Al Martin	.25
172	Melvin Mora	.25
173	Ricky Ledee	.25
174	Dante Bichette	.25
175	Mike Sweeney	.25
176	Bobby Higginson	.25
177	Matt Lawton	.25
178	Charles Johnson	.25
179	David Justice	.50
180	Richard Hidalgo	.40
181	B.J. Surhoff	.25
182	Richie Sexson	.50
183	Jim Edmonds	.50
184	Rondell White	.25
185	Curt Schilling	.50
186	Tom Goodwin	.25
187	Jose Vidro	.25
188	Ellis Burks	.25
189	Henry Rodriguez	.25
190	Mike Bordick	.25
191	Eric Owens	.25
192	Travis Lee	.25
193	Kevin Young	.25
194	Aaron Boone	.40
195	Todd Hollandsworth	.25
SPx Update		
(121-135, 182-196) 1,600		
(136-151) Production 1,500		
Common Autograph		10.00
121	Brad Wilkerson RC	12.00
122	Roy Oswalt RC	125.00
123	Wascar Serrano RC	5.00
124	Sean Burnett RC	10.00
125	Alex Cabrera RC	5.00
126	Timoniel Perez RC	5.00
127	Juan Pierre RC	10.00
128	Daylan Holt RC	5.00
129	Tomokazu Ohka RC	5.00
130	Kazuhiro Sasaki RC	10.00
131	Kurt Ainsworth RC	10.00
132	Brent Abernathy RC	5.00
133	Danys Baez RC	5.00
134	Brad Cresse RC	5.00
135	Ryan Franklin RC	5.00
136	Mike Lamb RC	10.00
137	David Espinosa RC	5.00
138	Matt Wheatland RC	5.00
139	Xavier Nady RC	45.00
140	Scott Heard RC	5.00
141	Pascual Coco RC	5.00
142	Justin Miller RC	5.00
143	Dave Krynzel RC	10.00
144	Dane Sardinha RC	5.00
145	Ben Sheets RC	80.00
146	Leo Estrella RC	10.00
147	Ben Diggins RC	10.00
148	Barry Zito RC	60.00
149	Joe Torres RC	10.00
150	Mike Meyers RC	10.00
151	Kris Wilson RC	10.00
152	Darin Erstad	.50
153	Richard Hidalgo	.40
154	Eric Chavez	.50
155	B.J. Surhoff	.25
156	Richie Sexson	.75
157	Raul Mondesi	.50
158	Rondell White	.50
159	Jim Edmonds	.75
160	Curt Schilling	.75
161	Tom Goodwin	.25
162	Fred McGriff	.50
163	Jose Vidro	.25
164	Ellis Burks	.25
165	David Segui	.25
166	Aaron Sele	.25
167	Henry Rodriguez	.25
168	Mike Bordick	.25
169	Mike Mussina	1.00
170	Ryan Klesko	.25
171	Kevin Young	.25
172	Travis Lee	.25
173	Aaron Boone	.50
174	Jermaine Dye	.25
175	Ricky Ledee	.25
176	Jeffrey Hammonds	.25
177	Carl Everett	.25
178	Matt Lawton	.25
179	Bobby Higginson	.25
180	Charles Johnson	.25
181	David Justice	.75
182	Joey Nation RC	4.00
183	Rico Washington RC	5.00
184	Luis Matos RC	15.00
185	Chris Wakeland	4.00
186	Sun-Woo Kim RC	4.00
187	Keith Ginter RC	5.00
188	Geraldo Guzman RC	4.00
189	Jay Spurgeon RC	4.00
190	Jace Brewer RC	4.00

191	Juan Guzman RC	4.00
192	Ross Gload RC	4.00
193	Paxton Crawford RC	4.00
194	Ryan Kohlmeier RC	4.00
195	Julio Zuleta RC	4.00
196	Matt Ginter RC	4.00
UD Pros & Prospects Update		
(133-162) Production 1,600		
133	Dane Artman RC	5.00
134	Juan Pierre RC	8.00
135	Jace Brewer RC	5.00
136	Sun-Woo Kim RC	6.00
137	Jon Rauch RC	6.00
138	Juan Guzman RC	5.00
139	Daylan Holt RC	5.00
140	Rico Washington RC	5.00
141	Ben Diggins RC	8.00
142	Mike Meyers RC	5.00
143	Chris Wakeland	5.00
144	Cory Vance RC	5.00
145	Keith Ginter RC	8.00
146	Koyie Hill RC	5.00
147	Julio Zuleta RC	5.00
148	Geraldo Guzman RC	5.00
149	Jay Spurgeon RC	5.00
150	Ross Gload RC	5.00
151	Ben Sheets RC	15.00
152	Josh Kalinowski RC	6.00
153	Kurt Ainsworth RC	5.00
154	Paxton Crawford RC	5.00
155	Xavier Nady RC	6.00
156	Brad Wilkerson RC	10.00
157	Kris Wilson RC	5.00
158	Paul Rigdon RC	5.00
159	Ryan Kohlmeier RC	5.00
160	Dane Sardinha RC	5.00
161	Javier Cardona RC	5.00
162	Brad Cresse RC	5.00
163	Ron Gant	.25
164	Mark Mulder	.50
165	David Wells	.25
166	Jason Tyner	.25
167	David Segui	.25
168	Al Martin	.25
169	Melvin Mora	.25
170	Ricky Ledee	.25
171	Rolando Arrojo	.25
172	Mike Sweeney	.25
173	Bobby Higginson	.25
174	Eric Milton	.25
175	Charles Johnson	.25
176	David Justice	.50
177	Moises Alou	.50
178	Andy Ashby	.25
179	Richie Sexson	.50
180	Will Clark	.75
181	Rondell White	.40
182	Curt Schilling	.75
183	Tom Goodwin	.25
184	Lee Stevens	.25
185	Ellis Burks	.25
186	Henry Rodriguez	.25
187	Mike Bordick	.25
188	Ryan Klesko	.50
189	Travis Lee	.25
190	Kevin Young	.25
191	Barry Larkin	.75
192	Jeff Cirillo	.25

Winning Materials

		NM/M
Common Card:		10.00
Inserted 1:15		
NG-PM	Nomar Garciaparra, Pedro Martinez	40.00
DJ-AR	Derek Jeter, Alex Rodriguez	40.00
DJ-NG	Derek Jeter, Nomar Garciaparra	40.00
MM-KG	Mark McGwire, Ken Griffey Jr.	40.00
MM-SS	Mark McGwire, Sammy Sosa	40.00
MM-RA	Mark McGwire, Rick Ankiel	30.00
KG-SS	Ken Griffey Jr., Sammy Sosa	25.00
RC-PM	Roger Clemens, Pedro Martinez	30.00
CR-TG	Cal Ripken Jr., Tony Gwynn	40.00
JC-BB	Jose Canseco, Barry Bonds	30.00
FT-MO	Frank Thomas, Magglio Ordonez	10.00
JB-CB	Jeff Bagwell, Craig Biggio	10.00
MP-RV	Mike Piazza, Robin Ventura	25.00
IR-RP	Ivan Rodriguez, Rafael Palmeiro	10.00
J-G-R	Derek Jeter, Nomar Garciaparra, Alex Rodriguez	75.00

G-S-R	Ken Griffey Jr., Sammy Sosa, Alex Rodriguez	40.00

Winning Materials Gold

		NM/M
Common Player:		5.00
JC	John Cotton	5.00
BS	Ben Sheets	15.00
SB	Sean Burroughs	8.00
MN	Mike Neill	8.00
DM	Doug Mientkiewicz	8.00
EY	Ernie Young	5.00
GD	Travis Dawkins, Mike Kinkade	5.00
BS	Sean Burroughs, Ben Sheets	15.00
AE	Brent Abernathy, Adam Everett	5.00
EY	Brad Wilkerson, Ernie Young	8.00

2000 Upper Deck Ultimate Victory

		NM/M
Complete Set (120):		200.00
Common Player:		.15
Common Ultimate Rookie (91-120):		4.00
Varying Production Levels		
Pack (5):		1.50
Box (24):		25.00
1	Mo Vaughn	.20
2	Darin Erstad	.40
3	Troy Glaus	.40
4	Adam Kennedy	.15
5	Jason Giambi	.25
6	Ben Grieve	.15
7	Terrence Long	.15
8	Tim Hudson	.25
9	David Wells	.15
10	Carlos Delgado	.25
11	Shannon Stewart	.15
12	Greg Vaughn	.15
13	Gerald Williams	.15
14	Manny Ramirez	.60
15	Roberto Alomar	.60
16	Jim Thome	.75
17	Edgar Martinez	.25
18	Alex Rodriguez	2.50
19	Matt Riley	.15
20	Cal Ripken Jr.	2.50
21	Mike Mussina	.20
22	Albert Belle	.20
23	Ivan Rodriguez	.75
24	Rafael Palmeiro	.50
25	Nomar Garciaparra	2.00
26	Pedro Martinez	1.00
27	Carl Everett	.15
28	Tomokazu Ohka RC	.25
29	Jermaine Dye	.15
30	Johnny Damon	.25
31	Dean Palmer	.15
32	Juan Gonzalez	.75
33	Eric Milton	.15
34	Matt Lawton	.15
35	Frank Thomas	.75
36	Paul Konerko	.15
37	Magglio Ordonez	.25
38	Jon Garland	.15
39	Derek Jeter	2.50
40	Roger Clemens	1.50
41	Bernie Williams	.50
42	Nick Johnson	.15
43	Julio Lugo	.15
44	Jeff Bagwell	.75
45	Richard Hidalgo	.15
46	Chipper Jones	1.50
47	Greg Maddux	1.50
48	Andruw Jones	.50
49	Andres Galarraga	.50
50	Rafael Furcal	.50
51	Jeromy Burnitz	.25
52	Geoff Jenkins	.25
53	Mark McGwire	2.00
54	Jim Edmonds	.15
55	Rick Ankiel	.15
56	Sammy Sosa	2.00
57	Julio Zuleta RC	.25
58	Kerry Wood	.40
59	Randy Johnson	.75
60	Matt Williams	.25
61	Steve Finley	.15
62	Gary Sheffield	.40
63	Kevin Brown	.25

Signed Game-Worn Jerseys

Each of these Game Jersey cards has a piece of jersey swatch and autograph from the featured player. A Level 2 "Gold" version is limited to the player's corresponding uniform number.

		NM/M
Common Player:		25.00
Inserted 1:96		
BB	Barry Bonds	200.00
JC	Jose Canseco	40.00
JD	J.D. Drew	25.00
TG	Tom Glavine	40.00
LG	Luis Gonzalez	25.00
KG	Ken Griffey Jr.	100.00
TG	Tony Gwynn	50.00
DJ	Derek Jeter/SP	350.00
RJ	Randy Johnson	80.00
CJ	Chipper Jones	50.00
KL	Kenny Lofton	25.00
CR	Cal Ripken Jr.	140.00
AR	Alex Rodriguez	120.00
IR	Ivan Rodriguez	40.00
SR	Scott Rolen	50.00
GS	Gary Sheffield	40.00
FT	Frank Thomas	40.00
MV	Mo Vaughn	25.00
RV	Robin Ventura	25.00
MW	Matt Williams	25.00
PW	Preston Wilson	25.00

The Best in the Bigs

This 10-card set spotlights baseball's best performers on a white bordered

(Continued in Inserted 1:12 list)

		NM/M
	Inserted 1:12	
1	Mark McGwire	3.00
2	Frank Thomas	1.00
3	Mike Piazza	2.00
4	Barry Bonds	4.00
5	Manny Ramirez	1.00
6	Ken Griffey Jr.	2.00
7	Nomar Garciaparra	3.00
8	Randy Johnson	1.50
9	Vladimir Guerrero	1.00
10	Jeff Bagwell	1.00
11	Rick Ankiel	.50
12	Alex Rodriguez	3.00

#	Player	Price
64	Shawn Green	.25
65	Milton Bradley	.15
66	Vladimir Guerrero	.75
67	Jose Vidro	.15
68	Barry Bonds	2.00
69	Jeff Kent	.25
70	Preston Wilson	.15
71	Mike Lowell	.15
72	Mike Piazza	2.00
73	Robin Ventura	.25
74	Edgardo Alfonzo	.15
75	Jay Payton	.15
76	Tony Gwynn	1.00
77	Adam Eaton	.15
78	Phil Nevin	.15
79	Scott Rolen	.75
80	Bob Abreu	.25
81	Pat Burrell	.25
82	Brian Giles	.25
83	Jason Kendall	.25
84	Kris Benson	.15
85	Gookie Dawkins	.15
86	Ken Griffey Jr.	1.50
87	Barry Larkin	.40
88	Larry Walker	.25
89	Todd Helton	.75
90	Ben Petrick	.15
91	Alex Cabrera 3,500 **RC** (Ultimate Rookie 2000)	4.00
92	Matt Wheatland 1,000 **RC** (Ultimate Rookie 2000)	4.00
93	Joe Torres 1,000 **RC** (Ultimate Rookie 2000)	4.00
94	Xavier Nady 1,000 **RC** (Ultimate Rookie 2000)	12.00
95	Kenny Kelly 3,500 **RC** (Ultimate Rookie 2000)	4.00
96	Matt Ginter 3,500 **RC** (Ultimate Rookie 2000)	4.00
97	Ben Diggins 1,000 **RC** (Ultimate Rookie 2000)	8.00
98	Danys Baez 3,500 **RC** (Ultimate Rookie 2000)	6.00
99	Daylan Holt 2,500 **RC** (Ultimate Rookie 2000)	4.00
100	Kazuhiro Sasaki 3,500 **RC** (Ultimate Rookie 2000)	5.00
101	Dane Artman 2,500 **RC** (Ultimate Rookie 2000)	4.00
102	Mike Tonis 1,000 **RC** (Ultimate Rookie 2000)	4.00
103	Timoniel Perez 2,500 **RC** (Ultimate Rookie 2000)	4.00
104	Barry Zito 2,500 **RC** (Ultimate Rookie 2000)	20.00
105	Koyie Hill 2,500 **RC** (Ultimate Rookie 2000)	4.00
106	Brad Wilkerson 2,500 **RC** (Ultimate Rookie 2000)	8.00
107	Juan Pierre 3,500 **RC** (Ultimate Rookie 2000)	8.00
108	Aaron McNeal 3,500 **RC** (Ultimate Rookie 2000)	4.00
109	Jay Spurgeon 3,500 **RC** (Ultimate Rookie 2000)	4.00
110	Sean Burnett 1,000 **RC** (Ultimate Rookie 2000)	8.00
111	Luis Matos 3,500 **RC** (Ultimate Rookie 2000)	8.00
112	Dave Krynzel 1,000 **RC** (Ultimate Rookie 2000)	6.00
113	Scott Heard 1,000 **RC** (Ultimate Rookie 2000)	4.00
114	Ben Sheets 2,500 **RC** (Ultimate Rookie 2000)	15.00
115	Dane Sardinha 1,000 **RC** (Ultimate Rookie 2000)	4.00
116	David Espinosa 1,000 **RC** (Ultimate Rookie 2000)	4.00
117	Leo Estrella 3,500 **RC** (Ultimate Rookie 2000)	4.00
118	Kurt Ainsworth 2,500 **RC** (Ultimate Rookie 2000)	4.00
119	Jon Rauch 2,500 **RC** (Ultimate Rookie 2000)	4.00
120	Ryan Franklin 2,500 (Ultimate Rookie 2000)	4.00

Collection

Parallel 25 Stars:	20-40X
Rookies (91-120):	2-4X
Production 25 Sets	
Parallel 100 Stars:	4-8X
Rookies (91-120):	1-2X
Production 100 Sets	
Parallel 250 Stars:	2-4X
Rookies (91-120):	1-2X
Production 250 Sets	

Diamond Dignitaries

		NM/M
Complete Set (10):		20.00
Common Player:		1.00
Inserted 1:23		
1	Ken Griffey Jr.	2.00
2	Nomar Garciaparra	3.00
3	Chipper Jones	2.00
4	Ivan Rodriguez	1.00
5	Mark McGwire	3.00
6	Cal Ripken Jr.	4.00
7	Vladimir Guerrero	1.00
8	Alex Rodriguez	3.00
9	Sammy Sosa	2.50
10	Derek Jeter	3.00

HOF Game Jersey

		NM/M
Common Card:		8.00
SA	Sparky Anderson	8.00
CF	Carlton Fisk	10.00
TP	Tony Perez	8.00

HOF Game Jersey Combo

		NM/M
UV-C	Sparky Anderson, Carlton Fisk, Tony Perez	40.00

Lasting Impressions

		NM/M
Complete Set (10):		15.00
Common Player:		1.00
Inserted 1:11		
1	Barry Bonds	3.00
2	Mike Piazza	2.00
3	Manny Ramirez	1.00
4	Pedro J. Martinez	1.50
5	Mark McGwire	2.00
6	Ken Griffey Jr.	2.00
7	Ivan Rodriguez	1.00
8	Jeff Bagwell	1.00
9	Randy Johnson	1.50
10	Alex Rodriguez	3.00

Starstruck

	NM/M
Complete Set (10):	20.00
Common Player:	1.00
Inserted 1:11	
1 Alex Rodriguez	3.00
2 Frank Thomas	1.00
3 Derek Jeter	3.00
4 Mark McGwire	3.00
5 Nomar Garciaparra	3.00
6 Chipper Jones	2.00
7 Cal Ripken Jr.	4.00
8 Sammy Sosa	2.00
9 Vladimir Guerrero	1.00
10 Ken Griffey Jr.	2.00

Victory

Victory offers no inserts just your standard 440-card base set that features a white bordered design, with two player images on the card front. The base set includes three subsets: Rookie 2000 (331-370); Big Play Makers (371-390) and JUNIOR Circuit (391-440).

	NM/M
Complete Set (440):	20.00
Complete Factory Set (466):	25.00
Common Player:	.10
Common Griffey (391-440):	.50
Common USA (441-466):	.40
Pack (12):	1.00
Wax Box (36):	25.00

#	Player	Price
1	Mo Vaughn	.15
2	Garret Anderson	.20
3	Tim Salmon	.20
4	Troy Percival	.10
5	Orlando Palmeiro	.10
6	Darin Erstad	.20
7	Ramon Ortiz	.10
8	Ben Molina	.10
9	Troy Glaus	.40
10	Jim Edmonds	.20
11	Mo Vaughn, Troy Percival	.15
12	Craig Biggio	.25
13	Roger Cedeno	.10
14	Shane Reynolds	.10
15	Jeff Bagwell	.50
16	Octavio Dotel	.10
17	Moises Alou	.20
18	Jose Lima	.10
19	Ken Caminiti	.15
20	Richard Hidalgo	.10
21	Billy Wagner	.10
22	Lance Berkman	.20
23	Jeff Bagwell, Jose Lima	.25
24	Jason Giambi	.50
25	Randy Velarde	.10
26	Miguel Tejada	.25
27	Matt Stairs	.10
28	A.J. Hinch	.10
29	Olmedo Saenz	.10
30	Ben Grieve	.10
31	Ryan Christenson	.10
32	Eric Chavez	.20
33	Tim Hudson	.20
34	John Jaha	.10
35	Jason Giambi, Matt Stairs	.25
36	Raul Mondesi	.20
37	Tony Batista	.10
38	David Wells	.10
39	Homer Bush	.10
40	Carlos Delgado	.40
41	Billy Koch	.10
42	Darrin Fletcher	.10
43	Tony Fernandez	.10
44	Shannon Stewart	.10
45	Roy Halladay	.20
46	Chris Carpenter	.10
47	Carlos Delgado, David Wells	.20
48	Chipper Jones	1.00
49	Greg Maddux	1.00
50	Andruw Jones	.40
51	Andres Galarraga	.20
52	Tom Glavine	.20
53	Brian Jordan	.10
54	John Smoltz	.15
55	John Rocker	.10
56	Javy Lopez	.15
57	Eddie Perez	.10
58	Kevin Millwood	.20
59	Chipper Jones, Greg Maddux	.50
60	Jeromy Burnitz	.10
61	Steve Woodard	.10
62	Ron Belliard	.10
63	Geoff Jenkins	.20
64	Bob Wickman	.10
65	Marquis Grissom	.10
66	Henry Blanco	.10
67	Mark Loretta	.10
68	Alex Ochoa	.10
69	Marquis Grissom, Jeromy Burnitz	.10
70	Mark McGwire	1.50
71	Edgar Renteria	.10
72	Dave Veres	.10
73	Eli Marrero	.10
74	Fernando Tatis	.10
75	J.D. Drew	.20
76	Ray Lankford	.10
77	Daryle Kile	.10
78	Kent Bottenfield	.10
79	Joe McEwing	.10
80	Mark McGwire, Ray Lankford	.75
81	Sammy Sosa	1.25
82	Jose Nieves	.10
83	Jon Lieber	.10
84	Henry Rodriguez	.10
85	Mark Grace	.20
86	Eric Young	.10
87	Kerry Wood	.25
88	Ismael Valdes	.10
89	Glenallen Hill	.10
90	Sammy Sosa, Mark Grace	.60
91	Greg Vaughn	.10
92	Fred McGriff	.20
93	Ryan Rupe	.10
94	Bubba Trammell	.10
95	Miguel Cairo	.10
96	Roberto Hernandez	.10
97	Jose Canseco	.40
98	Wilson Alvarez	.10
99	John Flaherty	.10
100	Vinny Castilla	.15
101	Jose Canseco, Roberto Hernandez	.25
102	Randy Johnson	.50
103	Matt Williams	.15
104	Matt Mantei	.10
105	Steve Finley	.10
106	Luis Gonzalez	.20
107	Travis Lee	.10
108	Omar Daal	.10
109	Jay Bell	.10
110	Erubiel Durazo	.10
111	Tony Womack	.10
112	Todd Stottlemyre	.10
113	Randy Johnson, Matt Williams	.25
114	Gary Sheffield	.25
115	Adrian Beltre	.25
116	Kevin Brown	.20
117	Todd Hundley	.10
118	Eric Karros	.20
119	Shawn Green	.40
120	Chan Ho Park	.20
121	Mark Grudzielanek	.10
122	Todd Hollandsworth	.10
123	Jeff Shaw	.10
124	Darren Dreifort	.10
125	Gary Sheffield, Kevin Brown	.15
126	Vladimir Guerrero	.50
127	Michael Barrett	.10
128	Dustin Hermanson	.10
129	Jose Vidro	.10
130	Chris Widger	.10
131	Mike Thurman	.10
132	Wilton Guerrero	.10
133	Brad Fullmer	.10
134	Rondell White	.20
135	Ugueth Urbina	.10
136	Vladimir Guerrero, Rondell White	.40
137	Barry Bonds	1.50
138	Russ Ortiz	.10
139	J.T. Snow	.10
140	Joe Nathan	.10
141	Rich Aurilia	.10
142	Jeff Kent	.20
143	Armando Rios	.10
144	Ellis Burks	.10
145	Robb Nen	.10
146	Marvin Benard	.10
147	Barry Bonds, Russ Ortiz	.75
148	Manny Ramirez	.50
149	Bartolo Colon	.10
150	Kenny Lofton	.10
151	Sandy Alomar Jr.	.10
152	Travis Fryman	.15
153	Omar Vizquel	.15
154	Roberto Alomar	.40
155	Richie Sexson	.25
156	David Justice	.20
157	Jim Thome	.50
158	Manny Ramirez, Roberto Alomar	.25
159	Ken Griffey Jr.	1.00
160	Edgar Martinez	.15
161	Fred Garcia	.10
162	Alex Rodriguez	1.50
163	John Halama	.10
164	Russ Davis	.10
165	David Bell	.10
166	Gil Meche	.10
167	Jamie Moyer	.10
168	John Olerud	.20
169	Ken Griffey Jr., Fred Garcia	.50
170	Preston Wilson	.20
171	Antonio Alfonseca	.10
172	A.J. Burnett	.10
173	Luis Castillo	.10
174	Mike Lowell	.10
175	Alex Fernandez	.10
176	Mike Redmond	.10
177	Alex Gonzalez	.10
178	Vladimir Nunez	.10
179	Mark Kotsay	.10
180	Preston Wilson, Luis Castillo	.10
181	Mike Piazza	1.00
182	Darryl Hamilton	.10
183	Al Leiter	.20
184	Robin Ventura	.20
185	Rickey Henderson	.20
186	Rey Ordonez	.10
187	Edgardo Alfonzo	.10
188	Derek Bell	.10
189	Mike Hampton	.10
190	Armando Benitez	.10
191	Mike Piazza, Rickey Henderson	.50
192	Cal Ripken Jr.	1.50
193	B.J. Surhoff	.10
194	Mike Mussina	.40
195	Albert Belle	.15
196	Jerry Hairston Jr.	.10
197	Will Clark	.20
198	Sidney Ponson	.10
199	Brady Anderson	.10
200	Scott Erickson	.10
201	Ryan Minor	.10
202	Cal Ripken Jr., Albert Belle	.75
203	Tony Gwynn	.75
204	Bret Boone	.20
205	Ryan Klesko	.10
206	Ben Davis	.10
207	Matt Clement	.10
208	Eric Owens	.10
209	Trevor Hoffman	.10
210	Sterling Hitchcock	.10
211	Phil Nevin	.10
212	Tony Gwynn, Trevor Hoffman	.40
213	Scott Rolen	.20
214	Bob Abreu	.50
215	Curt Schilling	.25
216	Rico Brogna	.10
217	Robert Person	.10
218	Doug Glanville	.10
219	Mike Lieberthal	.10
220	Andy Ashby	.10
221	Randy Wolf	.10
222	Bob Abreu, Curt Schilling	.20
223	Brian Giles	.20
224	Jason Kendall	.20
225	Kris Benson	.10
226	Warren Morris	.10
227	Kevin Young	.10
228	Al Martin	.10
229	Wil Cordero	.10
230	Bruce Aven	.10
231	Todd Ritchie	.10
232	Jason Kendall, Brian Giles	.10
233	Ivan Rodriguez	.50
234	Rusty Greer	.10
235	Ruben Mateo	.10
236	Justin Thompson	.10
237	Rafael Palmeiro	.25
238	Chad Curtis	.10
239	Royce Clayton	.10
240	Gabe Kapler	.10
241	Jeff Zimmerman	.10
242	John Wetteland	.10
243	Ivan Rodriguez, Rafael Palmeiro	.25
244	Nomar Garciaparra	1.25
245	Pedro Martinez	.75
246	Jose Offerman	.10
247	Jason Varitek	.10
248	Troy O'Leary	.10
249	John Valentin	.10
250	Trot Nixon	.10
251	Carl Everett	.10
252	Wilton Veras	.10
253	Bret Saberhagen	.10
254	Nomar Garciaparra, Pedro J. Martinez	.60
255	Sean Casey	.10
256	Barry Larkin	.25
257	Pokey Reese	.10
258	Pete Harnisch	.10
259	Aaron Boone	.20
260	Dante Bichette	.10
261	Scott Williamson	.10
262	Steve Parris	.10
263	Dmitri Young	.10
264	Mike Cameron	.10
265	Sean Casey, Scott Williamson	.10
266	Larry Walker	.25
267	Rolando Arrojo	.10
268	Pedro Astacio	.10
269	Todd Helton	.50
270	Jeff Cirillo	.10
271	Neifi Perez	.10
272	Brian Bohanon	.10
273	Jeffrey Hammonds	.10
274	Tom Goodwin	.10
275	Larry Walker, Todd Helton	.25
276	Carlos Beltran	.15
277	Jermaine Dye	.10
278	Mike Sweeney	.10
279	Joe Randa	.10
280	Jose Rosado	.10
281	Carlos Febles	.10
282	Jeff Suppan	.10
283	Johnny Damon	.20
284	Jeremy Giambi	.10
285	Mike Sweeney, Carlos Beltran	.10
286	Tony Clark	.10
287	Damion Easley	.10
288	Jeff Weaver	.10
289	Dean Palmer	.10
290	Juan Gonzalez	.50
291	Juan Encarnacion	.10
292	Todd Jones	.10
293	Karim Garcia	.10
294	Deivi Cruz	.10
295	Dean Palmer, Juan Encarnacion	.10
296	Corey Koskie	.10
297	Brad Radke	.10
298	Doug Mientkiewicz	.10
299	Ron Coomer	.10
300	Joe Mays	.10
301	Eric Milton	.10
302	Jacque Jones	.10
303	Chad Allen	.10
304	Cristian Guzman	.10
305	Jason Ryan	.10
306	Todd Walker	.10
307	Corey Koskie, Eric Milton	.10
308	Frank Thomas	.50
309	Paul Konerko	.10
310	Mike Sirotka	.10
311	Jim Parque	.10
312	Magglio Ordonez	.25
313	Bob Howry	.10
314	Carlos Lee	.10
315	Ray Durham	.10
316	Chris Singleton	.10
317	Brook Fordyce	.10
318	Frank Thomas, Magglio Ordonez	.25
319	Derek Jeter	1.50
320	Roger Clemens	1.00
321	Paul O'Neill	.20
322	Bernie Williams	.40
323	Mariano Rivera	.20
324	Tino Martinez	.20
325	David Cone	.10
326	Chuck Knoblauch	.10
327	Darryl Strawberry	.10
328	Orlando Hernandez	.10
329	Ricky Ledee	.10
330	Derek Jeter, Bernie Williams	.75
331	Pat Burrell (Rookie 2000)	.50
332	Alfonso Soriano (Rookie 2000)	.75
333	Josh Beckett (Rookie 2000)	.25
334	Matt Riley (Rookie 2000)	.15
335	Brian Cooper (Rookie 2000)	.10
336	Eric Munson (Rookie 2000)	.20
337	Vernon Wells (Rookie 2000)	.25
338	Juan Pena (Rookie 2000)	.10
339	Mark DeRosa (Rookie 2000)	.10
340	Kip Wells (Rookie 2000)	.10
341	Roosevelt Brown (Rookie 2000)	.10
342	Jason LaRue (Rookie 2000)	.10
343	Ben Petrick (Rookie 2000)	.10
344	Mark Quinn (Rookie 2000)	.10
345	Julio Ramirez (Rookie 2000)	.10
346	Rod Barajas (Rookie 2000)	.10
347	Robert Fick (Rookie 2000)	.10
348	David Newhan (Rookie 2000)	.10
349	Eric Gagne (Rookie 2000)	.15
350	Jorge Toca (Rookie 2000)	.10
351	Mitch Meluskey (Rookie 2000)	.10
352	Ed Yarnall (Rookie 2000)	.10
353	Chad Hermansen (Rookie 2000)	.10
354	Peter Bergeron (Rookie 2000)	.10
355	Dermal Brown (Rookie 2000)	.10
356	Adam Kennedy (Rookie 2000)	.10
357	Kevin Barker (Rookie 2000)	.10
358	Francisco Cordero (Rookie 2000)	.10
359	Travis Dawkins (Rookie 2000)	.10

360	Jeff Williams (Rookie 2000)	.10
361	Chad Hutchinson (Rookie 2000)	.10
362	D'Angelo Jimenez (Rookie 2000)	.10
363	Derrick Gibson (Rookie 2000)	.10
364	Calvin Murray (Rookie 2000)	.10
365	Doug Davis (Rookie 2000)	.10
366	Rob Ramsay RC (Rookie 2000)	.20
367	Mark Redman (Rookie 2000)	.10
368	Rick Ankiel (Rookie 2000)	.10
369	Domingo Guzman (Rookie 2000)	.10
370	Eugene Kingsale (Rookie 2000)	.10
371	Nomar Garciaparra (Big Play Makers)	.75
372	Ken Griffey Jr. (Big Play Makers)	.50
373	Randy Johnson (Big Play Makers)	.25
374	Jeff Bagwell (Big Play Makers)	.25
375	Ivan Rodriguez (Big Play Makers)	.25
376	Derek Jeter (Big Play Makers)	.75
377	Carlos Beltran (Big Play Makers)	.10
378	Vladimir Guerrero (Big Play Makers)	.40
379	Sammy Sosa (Big Play Makers)	.60
380	Barry Bonds (Big Play Makers)	.75
381	Pedro Martinez (Big Play Makers)	.40
382	Chipper Jones (Big Play Makers)	.50
383	Mo Vaughn (Big Play Makers)	.10
384	Mike Piazza (Big Play Makers)	.50
385	Alex Rodriguez (Big Play Makers)	.75
386	Manny Ramirez (Big Play Makers)	.25
387	Mark McGwire (Big Play Makers)	.75
388	Tony Gwynn (Big Play Makers)	.50
389	Sean Casey (Big Play Makers)	.10
390	Cal Ripken Jr. (Big Play Makers)	.75
391	Ken Griffey Jr.	.40
392	Ken Griffey Jr.	.40
393	Ken Griffey Jr.	.40
394	Ken Griffey Jr.	.40
395	Ken Griffey Jr.	.40
396	Ken Griffey Jr.	.40
397	Ken Griffey Jr.	.40
398	Ken Griffey Jr.	.40
399	Ken Griffey Jr.	.40
400	Ken Griffey Jr.	.40
401	Ken Griffey Jr.	.40
402	Ken Griffey Jr.	.40
403	Ken Griffey Jr.	.40
404	Ken Griffey Jr.	.40
405	Ken Griffey Jr.	.40
406	Ken Griffey Jr.	.40
407	Ken Griffey Jr.	.40
408	Ken Griffey Jr.	.40
409	Ken Griffey Jr.	.40
410	Ken Griffey Jr.	.40
411	Ken Griffey Jr.	.40
412	Ken Griffey Jr.	.40
413	Ken Griffey Jr.	.40
414	Ken Griffey Jr.	.40
415	Ken Griffey Jr.	.40
416	Ken Griffey Jr.	.40
417	Ken Griffey Jr.	.40
418	Ken Griffey Jr.	.40
419	Ken Griffey Jr.	.40
420	Ken Griffey Jr.	.40
421	Ken Griffey Jr.	.40
422	Ken Griffey Jr.	.40
423	Ken Griffey Jr.	.40
424	Ken Griffey Jr.	.40
425	Ken Griffey Jr.	.40
426	Ken Griffey Jr.	.40
427	Ken Griffey Jr.	.40
428	Ken Griffey Jr.	.40
429	Ken Griffey Jr.	.40
430	Ken Griffey Jr.	.40
431	Ken Griffey Jr.	.40
432	Ken Griffey Jr.	.40
433	Ken Griffey Jr.	.40
434	Ken Griffey Jr.	.40
435	Ken Griffey Jr.	.40
436	Ken Griffey Jr.	.40
437	Ken Griffey Jr.	.40
438	Ken Griffey Jr.	.40
439	Ken Griffey Jr.	.40
440	Ken Griffey Jr.	.40
441	Tommy Lasorda	.50
442	Sean Burroughs	.75
443	Rick Krivda	.40
444	Ben Sheets RC	1.50
445	Pat Borders	.40
446	Brent Abernathy RC	.75
447	Tim Young	.40
448	Adam Everett	.50
449	Anthony Sanders	.40
450	Ernie Young	.40
451	Brad Wilkerson RC	1.50
452	Kurt Ainsworth	1.00
453	Ryan Franklin	.40
454	Todd Williams	.40
455	Jon Rauch RC	.50
456	Roy Oswalt RC	5.00
457	Shane Heams	.50
458	Chris George	.50
459	Bobby Seay	.40
460	Mike Kinkade	.40
461	Marcus Jensen	.40
462	Travis Dawkins	.50
463	Doug Mientkiewicz	.40
464	John Cotton	.40
465	Mike Neill	.40
466	Team Photo USA	2.50

2000 Upper Deck Yankees Legends Sample

This promo card was issued to preview the Yankees Legends set. With silver-foil graphics on front, it is identical in design to the base cards in the regularly issued version. Back has a "SAMPLE" overprint across the stats.

		NM/M
NY7	Mickey Mantle	5.00

2000 Upper Deck Yankees Legends

		NM/M
	Complete Set (90):	17.50
	Common Player:	.15
	Pack (5):	6.00
	Box (24):	100.00
1	Babe Ruth	2.00
2	Mickey Mantle	2.00
3	Lou Gehrig	2.00
4	Joe DiMaggio	2.00
5	Yogi Berra	.75
6	Don Mattingly	1.00
7	Reggie Jackson	.75
8	Dave Winfield	.40
9	Bill Skowron	.15
10	Willie Randolph	.15
11	Phil Rizzuto	.50
12	Tony Kubek	.15
13	Thurman Munson	1.00
14	Roger Maris	1.00
15	Billy Martin	.40
16	Elston Howard	.15
17	Graig Nettles	.15
18	Whitey Ford	.50
19	Earl Combes	.15
20	Tony Lazzeri	.15
21	Bob Meusel	.15
22	Joe Gordon	.15
23	Jerry Coleman	.15
24	Joe Torre	.50
25	Bucky Dent	.15
26	Don Larsen	.40
27	Bobby Richardson	.15
28	Ron Guidry	.15
29	Bobby Murcer	.15
30	Tommy Henrich	.15
31	Hank Bauer	.15
32	Joe Pepitone	.15
33	Clete Boyer	.15
34	Chris Chambliss	.15
35	Tommy John	.15
36	Goose Gossage	.15
37	Red Ruffing	.15
38	Charlie Keller	.15
39	Billy Gardner	.15
40	Hector Lopez	.15
41	Cliff Johnson	.15
42	Oscar Gamble	.15
43	Allie Reynolds	.15
44	Mickey Rivers	.15
45	Bill Dickey	.40
46	Dave Righetti	.15
47	Mel Stottlemyre	.15
48	Waite Hoyt	.15
49	Lefty Gomez	.15
50	Wade Boggs	.50
51	Billy Martin (Magic Numbers)	.25
52	Babe Ruth (Magic Numbers)	1.00
53	Lou Gehrig (Magic Numbers)	1.00
54	Joe DiMaggio (Magic Numbers)	1.00
55	Mickey Mantle (Magic Numbers)	1.00
56	Yogi Berra (Magic Numbers)	.40
57	Bill Dickey (Magic Numbers)	.25
58	Roger Maris (Magic Numbers)	.50
59	Phil Rizzuto (Magic Numbers)	.25
60	Thurman Munson (Magic Numbers)	.50
61	Whitey Ford (Magic Numbers)	.25
62	Don Mattingly (Magic Numbers)	.50
63	Elston Howard (Magic Numbers)	.15
64	Casey Stengel (Magic Numbers)	.15
65	Reggie Jackson (Magic Numbers)	.50
66	Babe Ruth/1923 (The Championship Years)	1.00
67	Lou Gehrig/1927 (The Championship Years)	1.00
68	Tony Lazzeri/1928 (The Championship Years)	.15
69	Babe Ruth/1932 (The Championship Years)	1.00
70	Lou Gehrig/1936 (The Championship Years)	1.00
71	Lefty Gomez (1937 (The Championship Years)	.15
72	Bill Dickey (1938 (The Championship Years)	.25
73	Tommy Henrich (1939 (The Championship Years)	
74	Joe DiMaggio/1941 (The Championship Years)	1.00
75	Spud Chandler/1943 (The Championship Years)	.15
76	Tommy Henrich/1947 (The Championship Years)	.15
77	Phil Rizzuto/1949 (The Championship Years)	.25
78	Whitey Ford/1950 (The Championship Years)	.25
79	Yogi Berra/1951 (The Championship Years)	.40
80	Casey Stengel/1952 (The Championship Years)	.15
81	Billy Martin/1953 (The Championship Years)	.25
82	Don Larsen/1956 (The Championship Years)	.25
83	Elston Howard/1958 (The Championship Years)	.15
84	Roger Maris/1961 (The Championship Years)	.50
85	Mickey Mantle/1962 (The Championship Years)	1.00
86	Reggie Jackson/1977 (The Championship Years)	.50
87	Bucky Dent/1978 (The Championship Years)	.15
88	Wade Boggs/1996 (The Championship Years)	.25
89	Joe Torre/1998 (The Championship Years)	.25
90	Joe Torre/1999 (The Championship Years)	.25

DiMaggio Memorabilia

		NM/M
YLB-JD	Joe DiMaggio/Bat	125.00
YLG-JD	Joe DiMaggio/Gold Bat/56)	200.00
YLC-JD	Joe DiMaggio/Bat, Cut Sig./5)	650.00

Legendary Lumber

		NM/M
	Common Player:	7.00
	Inserted 1:23	
HB	Hank Bauer	8.00
YB	Yogi Berra	20.00
PB	Paul Blair	6.00
CB	Clete Boyer	6.00
CC	Chris Chambliss	6.00
JC	Joe Collins	6.00
BD	Bucky Dent	8.00
JD	Joe DiMaggio	140.00
OG	Oscar Gamble	6.00
BG	Billy Gardner	6.00
TH	Tommy Henrich	6.00
RH	Ralph Houk	8.00
EH	Elston Howard	8.00
RJ	Reggie Jackson	20.00
TJ	Tommy John	6.00
CJ	Cliff Johnson	6.00
CK	Charlie Keller	6.00
TK	Tony Kubek	8.00
HL	Hector Lopez	6.00
MM	Mickey Mantle	165.00
RM	Roger Maris	70.00
DM	Don Mattingly	45.00
TM	Thurman Munson	35.00
BM	Bobby Murcer	8.00
GN	Graig Nettles	10.00
JP	Joe Pepitone	6.00
WR	Willie Randolph	6.00
MR	Mickey Rivers	6.00
BR	Babe Ruth	185.00
MS	Moose Skowron	6.00
DW	Dave Winfield	15.00

Legendary Lumber/ Signture Cut

		NM/M
MM-LC	Mickey Mantle/7	4,000

Legendary Pinstripes

		NM/M
	Common Player:	20.00
	Inserted 1:144	
BD	Bucky Dent	20.00
WF	Whitey Ford	50.00
LG	Lou Gehrig	300.00
GG	Goose Gossage	20.00
RG	Ron Guidry	20.00
TH	Tommy Henrich	20.00
EH	Elston Howard	20.00
RJ	Reggie Jackson	40.00
HL	Hector Lopez	20.00
MM	Mickey Mantle	250.00
RM	Roger Maris	75.00
BM	Billy Martin	40.00
DM	Don Mattingly	60.00
TM	Thurman Munson	75.00
JP	Joe Pepitone	20.00
AR	Allie Reynolds	20.00
BR	Bobby Richardson	20.00
PR	Phil Rizzuto	40.00
DW	Dave Winfield	40.00

Autograph Legendary Pinstripe

	NM/M
Common Player:	30.00

BD	Bucky Dent	30.00
WF	Whitey Ford	60.00
GG	Goose Gossage	30.00
RG	Ron Guidry	35.00
TH	Tommy Henrich	30.00
GM	Gil MacDougald	30.00
DM	Don Mattingly	150.00
JP	Joe Pepitone	30.00
PR	Phil Rizzuto	60.00
DW	Dave Winfield	35.00

Monument Park

		NM/M
	Complete Set (6):	20.00
	Common Player:	1.50
	Inserted 1:23	
1	Lou Gehrig	6.00
2	Babe Ruth	6.00
3	Mickey Mantle	6.00
4	Joe DiMaggio	6.00
5	Thurman Munson	3.00
6	Elston Howard	1.50

Murderer's Row

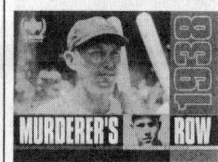

		NM/M
	Complete Set (10):	17.50
	Common Player:	1.50
	Inserted 1:11	
1	Tony Lazzeri	1.50
2	Babe Ruth	6.00
3	Bob Meusel	1.50
4	Lou Gehrig	6.00
5	Joe Dugan	1.50
6	Bill Dickey	1.50
7	Waite Hoyt	1.50
8	Red Ruffing	1.50
9	Earl Combes	1.50
10	Lefty Gomez	1.50

Pride of the Pinstripes

		NM/M
	Complete Set (6):	17.50
	Common Player:	2.50
	Inserted 1:23	
1	Babe Ruth	6.00
2	Mickey Mantle	6.00
3	Joe DiMaggio	5.00
4	Lou Gehrig	5.00
5	Reggie Jackson	2.50
6	Yogi Berra	2.50

The Golden Years

	NM/M
Complete Set (10):	20.00

	Common Player:	1.50
	Inserted 1:11	
1	Joe DiMaggio	6.00
2	Phil Rizzuto	2.50
3	Yogi Berra	3.00
4	Billy Martin	2.50
5	Whitey Ford	2.50
6	Roger Maris	5.00
7	Mickey Mantle	7.50
8	Elston Howard	1.50
9	Tommy Henrich	1.50
10	Joe Gordon	1.50

The New Dynasty

		NM/M
	Complete Set (10):	15.00
	Common Player:	1.50
	Inserted 1:11	
1	Reggie Jackson	3.50
2	Graig Nettles	1.50
3	Don Mattingly	6.50
4	Goose Gossage	1.50
5	Dave Winfield	3.00
6	Chris Chambliss	1.50
7	Thurman Munson	4.00
8	Willie Randolph	1.50
9	Ron Guidry	2.50
10	Bucky Dent	2.50

22kt Gold Ken Griffey Jr. Rookie Card

A 22-karat gold embossed card replicating in all important details the 1989 Upper Deck Ken Griffey Jr. rookie card was issued by UD. The card was accompanied by a commemorative collectors' sheet describing the original rookie card and the gold version. The gold card was offered to members of UD's Collectors Club for $24.

		NM/M
1	Ken Griffey Jr.	24.00

2001 Upper Deck

	NM/M
Complete Set (450):	125.00
Complete Series 1 (270):	25.00
Complete Series 2 (180):	100.00
Common Player:	.15
Series 1 Pack (10):	2.00
Series 1 Box (24):	35.00
Series 2 Pack (10):	6.00
Series 2 Box (24):	120.00

1	Jeff DaVanon (Star Rookie)	.25
2	Aubrey Huff (Star Rookie)	.25
3	Pascual Coco (Star Rookie)	.25
4	Barry Zito (Star Rookie)	.75

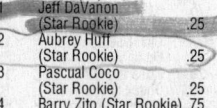

#	Player	Price
5	Augie Ojeda (Star Rookie)	.25
6	Chris Richard (Star Rookie)	.25
7	Josh Phelps (Star Rookie)	.25
8	Kevin Nicholson (Star Rookie)	.25
9	Juan Guzman (Star Rookie)	.25
10	Brandon Kolb (Star Rookie)	.25
11	Johan Santana (Star Rookie)	4.00
12	Josh Kalinowski (Star Rookie)	.25
13	Tike Redman (Star Rookie)	.25
14	Ivanon Coffie (Star Rookie)	.25
15	Chad Durbin (Star Rookie)	.25
16	Derrick Turnbow (Star Rookie)	.25
17	Scott Downs (Star Rookie)	.25
18	Jason Grilli (Star Rookie)	.25
19	Mark Buehrle (Star Rookie)	.25
20	Paxton Crawford (Star Rookie)	.25
21	Bronson Arroyo (Star Rookie)	.25
22	Tomas de la Rosa (Star Rookie)	.25
23	Paul Rigdon (Star Rookie)	.25
24	Rob Ramsay (Star Rookie)	.25
25	Damian Rolls (Star Rookie)	.25
26	Jason Conti (Star Rookie)	.25
27	John Parrish (Star Rookie)	.25
28	Geraldo Guzman (Star Rookie)	.25
29	Tony Mota (Star Rookie)	.25
30	Luis Rivas (Star Rookie)	.25
31	Brian Tollberg (Star Rookie)	.25
32	Adam Bernero (Star Rookie)	.25
33	Michael Cuddyer (Star Rookie)	.25
34	Josue Espada (Star Rookie)	.25
35	Joe Lawrence (Star Rookie)	.25
36	Chad Moeller (Star Rookie)	.25
37	Nick Bierbrodt (Star Rookie)	.25
38	Dewayne Wise (Star Rookie)	.25
39	Javier Cardona (Star Rookie)	.25
40	Hiram Bocachica (Star Rookie)	.25
41	Giuseppe Chiaramonte (Star Rookie)	.25
42	Alex Cabrera (Star Rookie)	.25
43	Jimmy Rollins (Star Rookie)	.40
44	Pat Flury RC (Star Rookie)	.25
45	Leo Estrella (Star Rookie)	.25
46	Darin Erstad	.40
47	Seth Etherton	.15
48	Troy Glaus	.25
49	Brian Cooper	.15
50	Tim Salmon	.25
51	Adam Kennedy	.15
52	Bengie Molina	.15
53	Jason Giambi	.50
54	Miguel Tejada	.40
55	Tim Hudson	.25
56	Eric Chavez	.25
57	Terrence Long	.15
58	Jason Isringhausen	.15
59	Ramon Hernandez	.15
60	Raul Mondesi	.25
61	David Wells	.15
62	Shannon Stewart	.15
63	Tony Batista	.15
64	Brad Fullmer	.15
65	Chris Carpenter	.15
66	Homer Bush	.15
67	Gerald Williams	.15
68	Miguel Cairo	.15
69	Ryan Rupe	.15
70	Greg Vaughn	.25
71	John Flaherty	.15
72	Dan Wheeler	.15
73	Fred McGriff	.25
74	Roberto Alomar	.40
75	Bartolo Colon	.25
76	Kenny Lofton	.25
77	David Segui	.15
78	Omar Vizquel	.25
79	Russ Branyan	.15
80	Chuck Finley	.15
81	Manny Ramirez	.50
82	Alex Rodriguez	1.50
83	John Halama	.15
84	Mike Cameron	.15
85	David Bell	.15
86	Jay Buhner	.15
87	Aaron Sele	.15
88	Rickey Henderson	.40
89	Brook Fordyce	.15
90	Cal Ripken Jr.	2.00
91	Mike Mussina	.40
92	Delino DeShields	.15
93	Melvin Mora	.15
94	Sidney Ponson	.15
95	Brady Anderson	.15
96	Ivan Rodriguez	.50
97	Ricky Ledee	.15
98	Rick Helling	.15
99	Ruben Mateo	.15
100	Luis Alicea	.15
101	John Wetteland	.15
102	Mike Lamb	.15
103	Carl Everett	.15
104	Troy O'Leary	.15
105	Wilton Veras	.15
106	Pedro Martinez	.75
107	Rolando Arrojo	.15
108	Scott Hatteberg	.15
109	Jason Varitek	.25
110	Jose Offerman	.15
111	Carlos Beltran	.25
112	Johnny Damon	.15
113	Mark Quinn	.15
114	Rey Sanchez	.15
115	Mac Suzuki	.15
116	Jermaine Dye	.25
117	Chris Fussell	.15
118	Jeff Weaver	.15
119	Dean Palmer	.15
120	Robert Fick	.15
121	Brian Moehler	.15
122	Damion Easley	.15
123	Juan Encarnacion	.15
124	Tony Clark	.15
125	Cristian Guzman	.15
126	Matt LeCroy	.15
127	Eric Milton	.15
128	Jay Canizaro	.15
129	David Ortiz	.15
130	Brad Radke	.15
131	Jacque Jones	.15
132	Magglio Ordonez	.25
133	Carlos Lee	.25
134	Mike Sirotka	.15
135	Ray Durham	.15
136	Paul Konerko	.25
137	Charles Johnson	.15
138	James Baldwin	.15
139	Jeff Abbott	.15
140	Roger Clemens	1.50
141	Derek Jeter	2.00
142	David Justice	.25
143	Ramiro Mendoza	.15
144	Chuck Knoblauch	.15
145	Orlando Hernandez	.25
146	Alfonso Soriano	.75
147	Jeff Bagwell	.50
148	Julio Lugo	.15
149	Mitch Meluskey	.15
150	Jose Lima	.15
151	Richard Hidalgo	.15
152	Moises Alou	.25
153	Scott Elarton	.15
154	Andruw Jones	.50
155	Quilvio Veras	.15
156	Greg Maddux	1.00
157	Brian Jordan	.15
158	Andres Galarraga	.20
159	Kevin Millwood	.25
160	Rafael Furcal	.25
161	Jeromy Burnitz	.15
162	Jimmy Haynes	.15
163	Mark Loretta	.15
164	Ron Belliard	.15
165	Richie Sexson	.40
166	Kevin Barker	.15
167	Jeff D'Amico	.15
168	Rick Ankiel	.15
169	Mark McGwire	1.50
170	J.D. Drew	.25
171	Eli Marrero	.15
172	Darryl Kile	.15
173	Edgar Renteria	.15
174	Will Clark	.40
175	Eric Young	.15
176	Mark Grace	.25
177	Jon Lieber	.15
178	Damon Buford	.15
179	Kerry Wood	.50
180	Rondell White	.15
181	Joe Girardi	.15
182	Curt Schilling	.40
183	Randy Johnson	.75
184	Steve Finley	.15
185	Kelly Stinnett	.15
186	Jay Bell	.15
187	Matt Mantei	.15
188	Luis Gonzalez	.25
189	Shawn Green	.25
190	Todd Hundley	.15
191	Chan Ho Park	.15
192	Adrian Beltre	.15
193	Mark Grudzielanek	.15
194	Gary Sheffield	.25
195	Tom Goodwin	.15
196	Lee Stevens	.15
197	Javier Vazquez	.15
198	Milton Bradley	.15
199	Vladimir Guerrero	.75
200	Carl Pavano	.15
201	Orlando Cabrera	.15
202	Tony Armas Jr.	.15
203	Jeff Kent	.25
204	Calvin Murray	.15
205	Ellis Burks	.15
206	Barry Bonds	2.00
207	Russ Ortiz	.15
208	Marvin Benard	.15
209	Joe Nathan	.15
210	Preston Wilson	.15
211	Cliff Floyd	.15
212	Mike Lowell	.15
213	Ryan Dempster	.15
214	Brad Penny	.15
215	Mike Redmond	.15
216	Luis Castillo	.15
217	Derek Bell	.15
218	Mike Hampton	.25
219	Todd Zeile	.15
220	Robin Ventura	.25
221	Mike Piazza	1.00
222	Al Leiter	.25
223	Edgardo Alfonzo	.15
224	Mike Bordick	.15
225	Phil Nevin	.15
226	Ryan Klesko	.25
227	Adam Eaton	.15
228	Eric Owens	.15
229	Tony Gwynn	.75
230	Matt Clement	.15
231	Wiki Gonzalez	.15
232	Robert Person	.15
233	Doug Glanville	.15
234	Scott Rolen	.50
235	Mike Lieberthal	.15
236	Randy Wolf	.15
237	Bobby Abreu	.25
238	Pat Burrell	.40
239	Bruce Chen	.15
240	Kevin Young	.15
241	Todd Ritchie	.15
242	Adrian Brown	.15
243	Chad Hermansen	.15
244	Warren Morris	.15
245	Kris Benson	.15
246	Jason Kendall	.25
247	Pokey Reese	.15
248	Rob Bell	.15
249	Ken Griffey Jr.	1.00
250	Sean Casey	.15
251	Aaron Boone	.15
252	Pete Harnisch	.15
253	Barry Larkin	.40
254	Dmitri Young	.15
255	Todd Hollandsworth	.15
256	Pedro Astacio	.15
257	Todd Helton	.50
258	Terry Shumpert	.15
259	Neifi Perez	.15
260	Jeffrey Hammonds	.15
261	Ben Petrick	.15
262	Mark McGwire	.75
263	Derek Jeter	1.00
264	Sammy Sosa	.75
265	Cal Ripken Jr.	1.00
266	Pedro J. Martinez	.40
267	Barry Bonds	1.00
268	Fred McGriff	.20
269	Randy Johnson	.40
270	Darin Erstad	.25
271	Ichiro Suzuki RC (Star Rookie)	15.00
272	Wilson Betemit RC (Star Rookie)	.50
273	Corey Patterson RC (Star Rookie)	.25
274	Sean Douglass RC (Star Rookie)	.25
275	Mike Penney RC (Star Rookie)	.25
276	Nate Teut RC (Star Rookie)	.25
277	Ricardo Rodriguez RC (Star Rookie)	.25
278	Brandon Duckworth RC (Star Rookie)	.50
279	Rafael Soriano RC (Star Rookie)	.75
280	Juan Diaz RC (Star Rookie)	.25
281	Horacio Ramirez RC (Star Rookie)	.75
282	Tsuyoshi Shinjo RC (Star Rookie)	.50
283	Keith Ginter (Star Rookie)	.15
284	Esix Snead RC (Star Rookie)	.15
285	Erick Almonte RC (Star Rookie)	.25
286	Travis Hafner RC (Star Rookie)	3.00
287	Jason Smith RC (Star Rookie)	.15
288	Jackson Melian RC (Star Rookie)	.25
289	Tyler Walker RC (Star Rookie)	.25
290	Jason Standridge RC (Star Rookie)	.25
291	Juan Uribe RC (Star Rookie)	.50
292	Adrian Hernandez RC (Star Rookie)	.25
293	Jason Michaels RC (Star Rookie)	.25
294	Jason Hart (Star Rookie)	.15
295	Albert Pujols RC (Star Rookie)	80.00
296	Morgan Ensberg RC (Star Rookie)	2.00
297	Brandon Inge (Star Rookie)	.25
298	Jesus Colome (Star Rookie)	.15
299	Kyle Kessel RC (Star Rookie)	.15
300	Timo Perez (Star Rookie)	.25
301	Mo Vaughn	.20
302	Ismael Valdes	.15
303	Glenallen Hill	.15
304	Garret Anderson	.40
305	Johnny Damon	.25
306	Jose Ortiz	.15
307	Mark Mulder	.25
308	Adam Piatt	.15
309	Gil Heredia	.15
310	Mike Sirotka	.15
311	Carlos Delgado	.50
312	Alex Gonzalez	.15
313	Jose Cruz Jr.	.15
314	Darrin Fletcher	.15
315	Ben Grieve	.15
316	Vinny Castilla	.15
317	Wilson Alvarez	.15
318	Brent Abernathy	.15
319	Ellis Burks	.15
320	Jim Thome	.75
321	Juan Gonzalez	.50
322	Ed Taubensee	.15
323	Travis Fryman	.15
324	John Olerud	.25
325	Edgar Martinez	.25
326	Fred Garcia	.15
327	Bret Boone	.15
328	Kazuhiro Sasaki	.25
329	Albert Belle	.25
330	Mike Bordick	.15
331	David Segui	.15
332	Pat Hentgen	.15
333	Alex Rodriguez	1.50
334	Andres Galarraga	.15
335	Gabe Kapler	.15
336	Ken Caminiti	.15
337	Rafael Palmeiro	.50
338	Manny Ramirez	.50
339	David Cone	.15
340	Nomar Garciaparra	1.50
341	Trot Nixon	.15
342	Derek Lowe	.15
343	Roberto Hernandez	.15
344	Mike Sweeney	.15
345	Carlos Febles	.15
346	Jeff Suppan	.15
347	Roger Cedeno	.15
348	Bobby Higginson	.15
349	Deivi Cruz	.15
350	Mitch Meluskey	.15
351	Matt Lawton	.15
352	Mark Redman	.15
353	Jay Canizaro	.15
354	Corey Koskie	.15
355	Matt Kinney	.15
356	Frank Thomas	.50
357	Sandy Alomar Jr.	.15
358	David Wells	.15
359	Jim Parque	.15
360	Chris Singleton	.15
361	Tino Martinez	.15
362	Paul O'Neill	.25
363	Mike Mussina	.40
364	Bernie Williams	.50
365	Andy Pettitte	.40
366	Mariano Rivera	.25
367	Brad Ausmus	.15
368	Craig Biggio	.25
369	Lance Berkman	.25
370	Shane Reynolds	.15
371	Chipper Jones	1.00
372	Tom Glavine	.40
373	B.J. Surhoff	.15
374	John Smoltz	.25
375	Rico Brogna	.15
376	Geoff Jenkins	.15
377	Jose Hernandez	.15
378	Tyler Houston	.15
379	Henry Blanco	.15
380	Jeffrey Hammonds	.15
381	Jim Edmonds	.25
382	Fernando Vina	.15
383	Andy Benes	.15
384	Ray Lankford	.15
385	Dustin Hermanson	.15
386	Todd Hundley	.15
387	Sammy Sosa	1.50
388	Tom Gordon	.15
389	Bill Mueller	.15
390	Ron Coomer	.15
391	Matt Stairs	.15
392	Mark Grace	.40
393	Matt Williams	.25
394	Todd Stottlemyre	.15
395	Tony Womack	.15
396	Erubiel Durazo	.15
397	Reggie Sanders	.15
398	Andy Ashby	.15
399	Eric Karros	.15
400	Kevin Brown	.25
401	Darren Dreifort	.15
402	Fernando Tatis	.15
403	Jose Vidro	.15
404	Peter Bergeron	.15
405	Geoff Blum	.15
406	J.T. Snow	.15
407	Livan Hernandez	.15
408	Robb Nen	.15
409	Bobby Estalella	.15
410	Rich Aurilia	.15
411	Eric Davis	.15
412	Charles Johnson	.15
413	Alex Gonzalez	.15
414	A.J. Burnett	.15
415	Antonio Alfonseca	.15
416	Derek Lee	.15
417	Jay Payton	.15
418	Kevin Appier	.15
419	Steve Trachsel	.15
420	Rey Ordonez	.15
421	Darryl Hamilton	.15
422	Ben Davis	.15
423	Damian Jackson	.15
424	Mark Kotsay	.15
425	Trevor Hoffman	.15
426	Travis Lee	.15
427	Omar Daal	.15
428	Paul Byrd	.15
429	Reggie Taylor	.15
430	Brian Giles	.25
431	Derek Bell	.15
432	Francisco Cordova	.15
433	Pat Meares	.15
434	Scott Williamson	.15
435	Jason LaRue	.15
436	Michael Tucker	.15
437	Wilton Guerrero	.15
438	Mike Hampton	.15
439	Ron Gant	.15
440	Jeff Cirillo	.15
441	Denny Neagle	.15
442	Larry Walker	.40
443	Juan Pierre	.15
444	Todd Walker	.15
445	Jason Giambi	.40
446	Jeff Kent	.15
447	Mariano Rivera	.15
448	Edgar Martinez	.15
449	Troy Glaus	.25
450	Alex Rodriguez	.75

1924 ALL-STAR GAME SALUTE

Inserted 1:288

HA	Hank Aaron/Bat	35.00
HA	Hank Aaron/Jsy	35.00
LA	Luis Aparicio/Jsy	10.00
JB	Johnny Bench/Bat	20.00
JB	Johnny Bench/Jsy	20.00
LB	Lou Brock/Bat	15.00
RC	Roberto Clemente/Jsy	125.00
RJ	Reggie Jackson/Jsy	20.00
TM	Thurman Munson/Jsy	35.00
BR	Brooks Robinson/Bat	20.00
FR	Frank Robinson/Jsy	15.00
TS	Tom Seaver/Jsy	20.00

Big League Beat

Ramirez helps Tribe turn back Bucs — Bases-Loaded Bomber — RBI Champion

		NM/M
Complete Set (20):		15.00
Common Player:		.50
Inserted 1:3		
1	Barry Bonds	2.00
2	Nomar Garciaparra	1.50
3	Mark McGwire	1.50
4	Roger Clemens	1.25
5	Chipper Jones	1.00
6	Jeff Bagwell	.50
7	Sammy Sosa	1.50
8	Cal Ripken Jr.	2.00
9	Randy Johnson	.75
10	Carlos Delgado	.50
11	Manny Ramirez	.50
12	Derek Jeter	2.00
13	Tony Gwynn	.75
14	Pedro J. Martinez	.75
15	Jose Canseco	.50
16	Frank Thomas	.75
17	Alex Rodriguez	1.50
18	Bernie Williams	.50
19	Greg Maddux	1.00
20	Rafael Palmeiro	.50

Exclusives

Silver Stars: 8-15X
Production 100 Sets
Gold Stars: 15-30X
Production 25 Sets

All-Star Heroes Base Cards

NM/M
Quantity produced listed

DJ	Derek Jeter/2000	20.00
MP	Mike Piazza/1996	10.00

All-Star Heroes Bat Cards

NM/M

	Common Player:	10.00
RoC	Roberto Clemente/1961	75.00
KG	Ken Griffey Jr./1992	20.00
TP	Tony Perez/1967	10.00
CR	Cal Ripken Jr./1991	40.00
AR	Alex Rodriguez/1998	20.00
BR	Babe Ruth/1933	175.00

All-Star Heroes Jersey Cards

NM/M

	Common Player:	10.00
RC	Roger Clemens/1986	20.00
JD	Joe DiMaggio/36	300.00
TG	Tony Gwynn/1994	10.00
RJ	Randy Johnson/1993	10.00
ASH-MM	Mickey Mantle/54	400.00
ASH-SS	Sammy Sosa/2000	20.00

All-Star Salute

NM/M
Common Player: 10.00

Big League Challenge Jerseys

NM/M
Common Player: 5.00
Inserted 1:288

BB	Barry Bonds	40.00
JC	Jose Canseco	8.00
JE	Jim Edmonds	8.00
TF	Steve Finley	5.00
TG	Troy Glaus	8.00
TH	Todd Helton	10.00
RH	Richard Hidalgo	5.00
RP	Rafael Palmeiro	10.00
MP	Mike Piazza	20.00
GS	Gary Sheffield	8.00
FT	Frank Thomas	10.00

Classic Midsummer Moments

NM/M
Complete Set (20): 25.00

		NM/M
Common Player:		.50
Inserted 1:12		
CM1	Joe DiMaggio/1936	3.00
CM2	Joe DiMaggio/1951	3.00
CM3	Mickey Mantle/1952	4.00
CM4	Mickey Mantle/1968	4.00
CM5	Roger Clemens/1986	2.50
CM6	Mark McGwire/1987	2.50
CM7	Cal Ripken Jr./1991	1.50
CM8	Ken Griffey Jr./1992	1.50
CM9	Randy Johnson/1993	1.00
CM10	Tony Gwynn/1994	1.00
CM11	Fred McGriff/1994	.50
CM12	Hideo Nomo/1995	.75
CM13	Jeff Conine/1995	.50
CM14	Mike Piazza/1996	1.50
CM15	Sandy Alomar Jr./1997	.50
CM16	Alex Rodriguez/1998	2.50
CM17	Roberto Alomar/1998	.75
CM18	Pedro Martinez/1999	1.00
CM19	Andres Galarraga/2000	.50
CM20	Derek Jeter/2000	2.50

Joe DiMaggio Bat Cards - Hawaii

Three special Joe DiMaggio bat-piece cards were created by Upper Deck for distribution at the 2001 Hawaii trade show. Most cards have a photo of the player on left-front with a small piece of game-used bat, either the "NY" logo or the surrounding area. These cards are numbered on back within an edition of 450 pieces. An even more limited card has both a bat piece and a cut-signature autograph on front, along with a small photo portrait. On back, these cards are numbered within an edition of just five.

		NM/M
KY-JD1	Joe DiMaggio/Bat Piece/Autograph	2,250
KY-JD2	Joe DiMaggio/Bat Piece	125.00

e-Card

		NM/M
Complete Set (6):		10.00
Common Player:		1.00
Inserted 1:12		
1	Andruw Jones	1.00
2	Alex Rodriguez	3.00
3	Frank Thomas	1.50
4	Todd Helton	1.00
5	Troy Glaus	1.00
6	Barry Bonds	4.00

eVolve Jersey

Because of the addition of Suzuki and Sosa cards after the initial checklist was promulgated by Upper Deck, and the possibility that cards on the initial list may have been deleted, the accuracy of this

list cannot be verified. Card numbers have an "EJ-" prefix. Production was reported as 300 of each card.

		NM/M
Common Player:		10.00
BB	Barry Bonds	60.00
TG	Troy Glaus	10.00
TH	Todd Helton	15.00
AJ	Andruw Jones	15.00
AR	Alex Rodriguez	30.00
SS	Sammy Sosa	40.00
IS	Ichiro Suzuki	65.00
FT	Frank Thomas	15.00

eVolve Jersey Autograph

Because of the addition of Suzuki and Sosa cards after the initial checklist was promulgated by Upper Deck, and the possibility that cards on the initial list cannot be verified. Cards have an "ESJ-" prefix. The edition is limited to 50 numbered cards each.

		NM/M
Common Player:		50.00
BB	Barry Bonds	180.00
TG	Troy Glaus	50.00
TH	Todd Helton	50.00
AJ	Andruw Jones	50.00
AR	Alex Rodriguez	120.00
SS	Sammy Sosa	180.00
IS	Ichiro Suzuki	300.00
FT	Frank Thomas	75.00

eVolve Signature

Because of the addition of Suzuki and Sosa cards after the initial checklist was promulgated by Upper Deck, and the possibility that cards on the initial list may have been deleted, the accuracy of this list cannot be verified. Cards have an "ES-" prefix to their number. Production was reported as 200 of each card.

		NM/M
Common Player:		35.00
BB	Barry Bonds	200.00
TG	Troy Glaus	35.00
TH	Todd Helton	35.00
AJ	Andruw Jones	35.00
AR	Alex Rodriguez	75.00
SS	Sammy Sosa	150.00
IS	Ichiro Suzuki	250.00
FT	Frank Thomas	40.00

2001 Upper Deck Game Jersey

		NM/M
Common Player:		8.00
Inserted 1:288		
KG	Ken Griffey Jr.	30.00
TG	Tony Gwynn	20.00
TH	Todd Helton	12.00
TiH	Tim Hudson	10.00
DJ	Derek Jeter	50.00
AJ	Andruw Jones	10.00
SK	Sandy Koufax	100.00
PO	Paul O'Neill	10.00
MR	Manny Ramirez	10.00
CR	Cal Ripken Jr.	60.00
AR	Alex Rodriguez	40.00
IR	Ivan Rodriguez	10.00
NRa	Nolan Ryan	65.00
NRr	Nolan Ryan	65.00
FT	Fernando Tatis	8.00
RV	Robin Ventura	8.00
BW	Bernie Williams	10.00
MW	Matt Williams	8.00

Autograph

	NM/M
Print Runs Listed	

		NM/M
Common Player:		10.00
KG	Ken Griffey/30	250.00
RA	Rick Ankiel/66	25.00
SK	Sandy Koufax/32	900.00
JP	Javy Lopez/8	110.00
NRa	Nolan Ryan/Mets/30	350.00
NRr	Nolan Ryan/Angels/30	350.00
RV	Robin Ventura/4	50.00
MW	Matt Williams/9	200.00

Autograph Series 2

		NM/M
Common Player:		30.00
Inserted 1:288 H		
JB	Johnny Bench	50.00
BB	Barry Bonds	200.00
JC	Jose Canseco	40.00
RC	Roger Clemens	125.00
TG	Troy Glaus	30.00
KG	Ken Griffey Jr.	100.00
AJ	Andruw Jones	40.00
CJ	Chipper Jones	50.00
CR	Cal Ripken Jr./SP	200.00
AR	Alex Rodriguez	100.00
IR	Ivan Rodriguez/SP	75.00
NR	Nolan Ryan	150.00
GS	Gary Sheffield	30.00
SS	Sammy Sosa/SP	150.00

Hobby Autograph

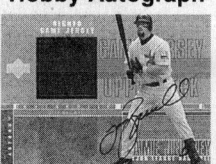

		NM/M
Common Player:		15.00
Inserted 1:288		
RA	Rick Ankiel	15.00
JB	Jeff Bagwell	40.00
BB	Barry Bonds	180.00
JC	Jose Canseco	50.00
SC	Sean Casey	25.00
JD	J.D. Drew	30.00
JG	Jason Giambi	30.00
SG	Shawn Green	30.00
KG	Ken Griffey Jr.	100.00
MH	Mike Hampton	20.00
RJ	Randy Johnson	75.00
JL	Javy Lopez	20.00
GM	Greg Maddux	125.00
RP	Rafael Palmeiro	40.00
AR	Alex Rodriguez	125.00
NRm	Nolan Ryan	125.00
NRa	Nolan Ryan	125.00
FT	Frank Thomas	50.00

Combo

		NM/M
		8.00
Production 50 Sets		
BB-KG	Barry Bonds, Ken Griffey Jr.	100.00
IR-RP	Ivan Rodriguez, Rafael Palmeiro	25.00
DJ-AR	Derek Jeter, Alex Rodriguez	100.00
MM-KG	Mickey Mantle, Ken Griffey Jr.	250.00
TG-CR	Tony Gwynn, Cal Ripken Jr.	100.00

Abbreviations

SP - Short Print

		NM/M
NR-AR	Nolan Ryan/Astros/Rangers	100.00
NR-MA	Nolan Ryan/Mets/Astros	100.00
RJ-GM	Randy Johnson, Greg Maddux	50.00
VG-MR	Vladimir Guerrero, Manny Ramirez	40.00
BB-JC	Barry Bonds, Jose Canseco	80.00
FT-JB	Frank Thomas, Jeff Bagwell	40.00
AJ-KG	Andruw Jones, Ken Griffey Jr.	60.00

Combo Autograph

Production 10 Sets
Values Undetermined

Patch

		NM/M
Common Player:		40.00
Production 25 Sets		
RA	Rick Ankiel	40.00
JB	Jeff Bagwell	60.00
BB	Barry Bonds	150.00
JC	Jose Canseco	50.00
JG	Jason Giambi	50.00
KG	Ken Griffey Jr.	75.00
TG	Tony Gwynn	75.00
DJ	Derek Jeter	125.00
RP	Rafael Palmeiro	60.00
CR	Cal Ripken Jr.	150.00
AR	Alex Rodriguez	100.00
IR	Ivan Rodriguez	60.00
NRa	Nolan Ryan	150.00
NRr	Nolan Ryan	150.00
FT	Frank Thomas	60.00

Patch Gold

		NM/M
Production 25 Sets		
BB	Barry Bonds	200.00
JC	Jose Canseco	100.00
JG	Jason Giambi	100.00
KG	Ken Griffey Jr.	150.00
TG	Tony Gwynn	100.00
DJ	Derek Jeter	200.00
CR	Cal Ripken Jr.	200.00
NRa	Nolan Ryan	200.00
NRr	Nolan Ryan	200.00
FT	Frank Thomas	90.00

Patch Autograph

		NM/M
Print Runs Listed		
RA	Rick Ankiel /66	65.00
KG	Ken Griffey Jr /30	600.00

2001 Upper Deck Game-Used Ball

		NM/M
Common Player:		10.00
Production 100 Sets		
RA	Rick Ankiel	10.00
JB	Jeff Bagwell	15.00
BB	Barry Bonds	50.00
JG	Jason Giambi	15.00
SG	Shawn Green	10.00
KG	Ken Griffey Jr.	35.00
ToG	Tony Gwynn	50.00
DJ	Derek Jeter	60.00
RJ	Randy Johnson	25.00
AJ	Andruw Jones	15.00
MM	Mark McGwire	50.00
AR	Alex Rodriguez	40.00
IR	Ivan Rodriguez	15.00
SS	Sammy Sosa	40.00

Series 2

		NM/M
Common Player:		5.00
Inserted 1:288		
JB	Jeff Bagwell	10.00
BB	Barry Bonds	30.00
RC	Roger Clemens	20.00
NG	Nomar Garciaparra	30.00
KG	Ken Griffey Jr.	20.00
VG	Vladimir Guerrero	10.00
DJ	Derek Jeter	30.00
AJ	Andruw Jones	10.00
CJ	Chipper Jones	8.00
JK	Jeff Kent	5.00
MM	Mark McGwire	40.00
MP	Mike Piazza	20.00
CR	Cal Ripken Jr.	25.00
MR	Mariano Rivera	8.00
AR	Alex Rodriguez	20.00
GS	Gary Sheffield	8.00
SS	Sammy Sosa	20.00
BW	Bernie Williams	10.00

Autographs

		NM/M
Production 25 Sets		
RA	Rick Ankiel	40.00
JB	Jeff Bagwell	60.00
BB	Barry Bonds	150.00
JG	Jason Giambi	75.00
KG	Ken Griffey Jr.	90.00
SG	Shawn Green	60.00
TH	Todd Helton	60.00
RJ	Randy Johnson	90.00
AR	Alex Rodriguez	80.00

Home Run Explosion

		NM/M
Complete Set (15):		20.00
Common Player:		.50
Inserted 1:12		
1	Mark McGwire	3.00
2	Chipper Jones	2.00
3	Jeff Bagwell	1.00
4	Carlos Delgado	1.00
5	Barry Bonds	4.00
6	Troy Glaus	1.00
7	Sammy Sosa	2.50
8	Alex Rodriguez	3.00
9	Mike Piazza	2.00
10	Vladimir Guerrero	1.50
11	Ken Griffey Jr.	2.00
12	Frank Thomas	1.00
13	Ivan Rodriguez	1.00
14	Jason Giambi	1.00
15	Carl Everett	.50

Home Run Derby Heroes

		NM/M
Complete Set (10):		25.00
Common Player:		1.00
Inserted 1:36		

		NM/M
HD1	Mark McGwire/1999	5.00
HD2	Sammy Sosa/2000	3.00
HD3	Frank Thomas/1996	2.00
HD4	Cal Ripken Jr./1991	5.00
HD5	Tino Martinez/1997	1.00
HD6	Ken Griffey Jr./1999	5.00
HD7	Barry Bonds/1996	5.00
HD8	Albert Belle/1995	1.00
HD9	Mark McGwire/1992	5.00
HD10	Juan Gonzalez/1993	2.00

Midseason Superstar Summit

		NM/M
Complete Set (15):		25.00
Common Player:		.75
Inserted 1:24		
MS1	Derek Jeter	5.00
MS2	Sammy Sosa	3.00
MS3	Jeff Bagwell	1.50
MS4	Tony Gwynn	1.50
MS5	Alex Rodriguez	4.00
MS6	Greg Maddux	2.50
MS7	Jason Giambi	1.50
MS8	Mark McGwire	4.00
MS9	Barry Bonds	5.00
MS10	Ken Griffey Jr.	3.00
MS11	Carlos Delgado	1.50
MS12	Troy Glaus	1.50
MS13	Todd Helton	1.50
MS14	Manny Ramirez	1.50
MS15	Jeff Kent	.75

Most Wanted

		NM/M
Complete Set (15):		20.00
Common Player:		.75
Inserted 1:14 Series 1		
MW1	Mark McGwire	2.50
MW2	Cal Ripken Jr.	3.00
MW3	Ivan Rodriguez	.75
MW4	Pedro Martinez	1.00
MW5	Sammy Sosa	2.00
MW6	Tony Gwynn	1.00
MW7	Vladimir Guerrero	1.00
MW8	Derek Jeter	3.00
MW9	Mike Piazza	1.50
MW10	Chipper Jones	1.50
MW11	Alex Rodriguez	2.50
MW12	Barry Bonds	3.00
MW13	Jeff Bagwell	.75
MW14	Frank Thomas	.75
MW15	Nomar Garciaparra	2.00

Rookie Roundup

		NM/M
Complete Set (10):		5.00
Common Player:		.50
Inserted 1:6		
1	Rick Ankiel	.50
2	Adam Kennedy	.50
3	Mike Lamb	.50
4	Adam Eaton	.50
5	Rafael Furcal	.75
6	Pat Burrell	1.50
7	Adam Piatt	.50
8	Eric Munson	.50
9	Brad Penny	.50
10	Mark Mulder	.75

Subway Series Heroes - Hawaii

These cards were created for the Kit Young Hawaii trade show and were distributed on

HAWAII XVI

a one-per-day basis and as a complete set in a special engraved plexiglass frame measuring 8-1/2" x 6-7/8". Cards have black-and-white portrait or action photos. On a photo of a 1956 World Series scoreboard is a genuine autograph. Backs have career highlights, an authentication message, logos and are numbered from within an edition of 450 of each card.

	NM/M
Complete Set in Frame:	110.00
Complete Card Set (4):	75.00
Common Player:	20.00
KY-SS1 Don Larsen	20.00
KY-SS2 Whitey Ford	35.00
KY-SS3 Johnny Podres	20.00
KY-SS4 Duke Snider	35.00

Subway Series Jersey Cards

	NM/M
Common Player:	5.00
Inserted 1:144	
SS-EA Edgardo Alfonzo	5.00
SS-RC Roger Clemens	40.00
SS-JF John Franco	5.00
SS-OH Orlando Hernandez	8.00
SS-AL Al Leiter	5.00
SS-PO Paul O'Neill	10.00
SS-JP Jay Payton	5.00
SS-TP Timo Perez	5.00
SS-AP Andy Pettitte	15.00
SS-BW Bernie Williams	15.00

Superstar Summit

	NM/M
Complete Set (15):	25.00
Common Player:	1.00
Inserted 1:12	
1 Derek Jeter	4.00
2 Randy Johnson	1.50
3 Barry Bonds	4.00
4 Frank Thomas	1.00
5 Cal Ripken Jr.	4.00
6 Pedro J. Martinez	1.50
7 Ivan Rodriguez	1.00
8 Mike Piazza	2.00
9 Mark McGwire	3.00
10 Manny Ramirez	1.00
11 Ken Griffey Jr.	2.00
12 Sammy Sosa	2.50
13 Alex Rodriguez	3.00
14 Chipper Jones	2.00
15 Nomar Garciaparra	2.50

The Franchise

	NM/M
Complete Set (10):	25.00
Common Player:	1.50
Inserted 1:36	
F1 Frank Thomas	1.50
F2 Mark McGwire	5.00
F3 Ken Griffey Jr.	3.00
F4 Manny Ramirez	1.50
F5 Alex Rodriguez	5.00
F6 Greg Maddux	3.00

F7 Sammy Sosa	4.00
F8 Derek Jeter	6.00
F9 Mike Piazza	3.00
F10 Vladimir Guerrero	2.00

The People's Choice

	NM/M
Complete Set (15):	35.00
Common Player:	1.50
Inserted 1:24	
PC1 Alex Rodriguez	5.00
PC2 Ken Griffey Jr.	3.00
PC3 Mark McGwire	5.00
PC4 Todd Helton	1.50
PC5 Manny Ramirez	1.50
PC6 Mike Piazza	3.00
PC7 Vladimir Guerrero	2.00
PC8 Randy Johnson	2.00
PC9 Cal Ripken Jr.	6.00
PC10 Andruw Jones	1.50
PC11 Sammy Sosa	4.00
PC12 Derek Jeter	6.00
PC13 Pedro Martinez	2.00
PC14 Frank Thomas	1.50
PC15 Nomar Garciaparra	4.00

UD Game-Worn Patch

	NM/M
Common Player:	40.00
P-JB Johnny Bench	120.00
P-BB Barry Bonds	150.00
P-KG Ken Griffey Jr.	100.00
P-CJ Chipper Jones	60.00
P-CR Cal Ripken Jr.	150.00
P-AR Alex Rodriguez	125.00
P-IR Ivan Rodriguez	60.00
P-NR Nolan Ryan	150.00
P-SS Sammy Sosa	100.00

Cincinnati Reds Team Set

MICHAEL TUCKER 34

This boxed set has 20 player cards in standard 2-1/2" x 3-1/2" format and a 3-1/2" x 5" checklist/team history card. Cards have borderless action photos on front with an Upper Deck Collectibles logo at top-left. At bottom are the team and player name, position and uniform number. Backs have a smaller version of the front photo, some biographical and career notes and 1999-2000 stats. Cards are numbered with a "CR" prefix.

	NM/M
Complete Set (21):	7.50
Common Player:	.50
1 Ken Griffey Jr.	3.00
2 Dmitri Young	.50
3 Michael Tucker	.50
4 Aaron Boone	.75
5 Barry Larkin	1.00
6 Pokey Reese	.50
7 Sean Casey	1.00
8 Jason LaRue	.50
9 Scott Williamson	.50
10 Pete Harnisch	.50

11 Danny Graves	.50
12 Rob Bell	.50
13 Gookie Dawkins	.50
14 Kelly Stinnett	.50
15 Leo Estrella	.50
16 Wilton Guerrero	.50
17 Elmer Dessens	.65
18 Seth Etherton	.65
19 Donnie Sadler	.50
20 Scott Sullivan	.50
21 Checklist	.50

2001 Upper Deck Decade

TIGERS
Al Kaline
Outfield

	NM/M
Complete Set (180):	25.00
Common Player:	.15
Pack (5):	1.50
Box (24):	30.00
1 Nolan Ryan	3.00
2 Don Baylor	.15
3 Bobby Grich	.15
4 Reggie Jackson	.50
5 Jim "Catfish" Hunter	.25
6 Gene Tenace	.15
7 Rollie Fingers	.25
8 Sal Bando	.15
9 Bert Campaneris	.15
10 John Mayberry	.15
11 Rico Carty	.15
12 Gaylord Perry	.25
13 Andre Thornton	.15
14 Buddy Bell	.15
15 Dennis Eckersley	.25
16 Ruppert Jones	.15
17 Brooks Robinson	.75
18 Tommy Davis	.15
19 Eddie Murray	.25
20 Boog Powell	.15
21 Al Oliver	.15
22 Jeff Burroughs	.15
23 Mike Hargrove	.15
24 Dwight Evans	.15
25 Fred Lynn	.15
26 Rico Petrocelli	.15
27 Carlton Fisk	.50
28 Luis Aparicio	.15
29 Amos Otis	.15
30 Hal McRae	.15
31 Jason Thompson	.15
32 Al Kaline	.75
33 Jim Perry	.15
34 Bert Blyleven	.15
35 Harmon Killebrew	1.00
36 Wilbur Wood	.15
37 Jim Kaat	.15
38 Ron Guidry	.15
39 Thurman Munson	1.00
40 Graig Nettles	.15
41 Bobby Murcer	.15
42 Chris Chambliss	.15
43 Roy White	.15
44 J.R. Richard	.15
45 Jose Cruz	.15
46 Hank Aaron	2.00
47 Phil Niekro	.15
48 Bob Horner	.15
49 Darryl Evans	.15
50 Gorman Thomas	.15
51 Don Money	.15
52 Robin Yount	.75
53 Joe Torre	.25
54 Tim McCarver	.15
55 Lou Brock	.40
56 Keith Hernandez	.15
57 Bill Madlock	.15
58 Ron Santo	.15
59 Billy Williams	.15
60 Ferguson Jenkins	.25
61 Steve Garvey	.15
62 Bill Russell	.15
63 Maury Wills	.25
64 Ron Cey	.15
65 Manny Mota	.15
66 Ron Fairly	.15
67 Steve Rogers	.15
68 Gary Carter	.15
69 Andre Dawson	.25
70 Bobby Bonds	.25
71 Jack Clark	.15
72 Willie McCovey	.15
73 Tom Seaver	1.00
74 Bud Harrelson	.15
75 Dave Kingman	.15
76 Jerry Koosman	.15
77 Jon Matlack	.15
78 Randy Jones	.15

79 Ozzie Smith	1.00
80 Garry Maddox	.15
81 Mike Schmidt	1.00
82 Greg Luzinski	.15
83 Tug McGraw	.15
84 Willie Stargell	.75
85 Dave Parker	.15
86 Roberto Clemente	2.00
87 Johnny Bench	1.50
88 Joe Morgan	.40
89 George Foster	.15
90 Ken Griffey Sr.	.15
91 Carlton Fisk 1972 (1970s Rookie Flashbacks)	.50
92 Andre Dawson 1977 (1970s Rookie Flashbacks)	.25
93 Fred Lynn 1975 (1970s Rookie Flashbacks)	.15
94 Eddie Murray 1977 (1970s Rookie Flashbacks)	.15
95 Bob Horner 1978 (1970s Rookie Flashbacks)	.15
96 Jon Matlack 1972 (1970s Rookie Flashbacks)	.15
97 Mike Hargrove 1974 (1970s Rookie Flashbacks)	.15
98 Robin Yount 1974 (1970s Rookie Flashbacks)	.50
99 Mike Schmidt 1972 (1970s Rookie Flashbacks)	.50
100 Gary Carter 1974 (1970s Rookie Flashbacks)	.15
101 Ozzie Smith 1978 (1970s Rookie Flashbacks)	.50
102 Paul Molitor 1978 (1970s Rookie Flashbacks)	.50
103 Dennis Eckersley 1975 (1970s Rookie Flashbacks)	.15
104 Dale Murphy 1976 (1970s Rookie Flashbacks)	.15
105 Bert Blyleven 1970 (1970s Rookie Flashbacks)	.15
106 Thurman Munson 1970 (1970s Rookie Flashbacks)	.75
107 Dave Parker 1973 (1970s Rookie Flashbacks)	.15
108 Jack Clark 1975 (1970s Rookie Flashbacks)	.15
109 Keith Hernandez 1974 (1970s Rookie Flashbacks)	.15
110 Ron Cey 1971 (1970s Rookie Flashbacks)	.15
111 Billy Williams 1970 (Decade Dateline)	.15
112 Tom Seaver 1970 (Decade Dateline)	.75
113 Reggie Jackson 1971 (Decade Dateline)	.75
114 Barry Bonds 1971 (Decade Dateline)	.15
115 Willie Stargell 1971 (Decade Dateline)	.40
116 Harmon Killebrew 1971 (Decade Dateline)	.50
117 Roberto Clemente 1972 (Decade Dateline)	1.00
118 Wilbur Wood 1972 (Decade Dateline)	.15
119 Billy Williams 1972 (Decade Dateline)	.15
120 Nolan Ryan 1973 (Decade Dateline)	1.50
121 Ron Blomberg 1973 (Decade Dateline)	.15
122 Hank Aaron 1974 (Decade Dateline)	1.00
123 Lou Brock 1974 (Decade Dateline)	.25
124 Al Kaline 1974 (Decade Dateline)	.40
125 Brooks Robinson 1975 (Decade Dateline)	.40
126 Bill Madlock 1975 (Decade Dateline)	.15
127 Rennie Stennett 1975 (Decade Dateline)	.15
128 Carlton Fisk 1975 (Decade Dateline)	.40
129 Chris Chambliss 1976 (Decade Dateline)	.15
130 Ruppert Jones 1977 (Decade Dateline)	.15
131 Ron Fairly 1977 (Decade Dateline)	.15
132 George Foster 1977 (Decade Dateline)	.15
133 Reggie Jackson 1977 (Decade Dateline)	.75
134 Ron Guidry 1978 (Decade Dateline)	.15
135 Gaylord Perry 1978 (Decade Dateline)	.15
136 Bucky Dent 1978 (Decade Dateline)	.15
137 Dave Kingman 1979 (Decade Dateline)	.15
138 Lou Brock 1979 (Decade Dateline)	.15
139 Thurman Munson 1979 (Decade Dateline)	.75
140 Willie Stargell 1979 (Decade Dateline)	.40

141 Johnny Bench 1970 NL MVP (1970s Award Winners)	.75
142 Boog Powell 1970 AL MVP (1970s Award Winners)	.15
143 Jim Perry 1970 AL CY (1970s Award Winners)	.15
144 Joe Torre 1971 NL MVP (1970s Award Winners)	.15
145 Chris Chambliss 1971 AL ROY (1970s Award Winners)	.15
146 Ferguson Jenkins 1971 NL CY (1970s Award Winners)	.15
147 Carlton Fisk 1972 AL ROY (1970s Award Winners)	.40
148 Gaylord Perry 1972 AL CY (1970s Award Winners)	.15
149 Johnny Bench 1972 NL MVP (1970s Award Winners)	.75
150 Reggie Jackson 1973 AL MVP (1970s Award Winners)	.75
151 Tom Seaver 1973 NL CY (1970s Award Winners)	.15
152 Thurman Munson 1973 AL GG (1970s Award Winners)	.75
153 Steve Garvey 1974 NL MVP (1970s Award Winners)	.15
154 Jim "Catfish" Hunter 1974 AL CY (1970s Award Winners)	.15
155 Mike Hargrove 1974 AL ROY (1970s Award Winners)	.15
156 Joe Morgan 1975 NL MVP (1970s Award Winners)	.15
157 Fred Lynn 1975 AL MVP & ROY (1970s Award Winners)	.15
158 Tom Seaver 1975 NL CY (1970s Award Winners)	.75
159 Thurman Munson 1976 AL MVP (1970s Award Winners)	.75
160 Randy Jones 1976 NL CY (1970s Award Winners)	.15
161 Joe Morgan 1976 NL ROY (1970s Award Winners)	.15
162 George Foster 1977 NL MVP (1970s Award Winners)	.15
163 Eddie Murray 1977 AL ROY (1970s Award Winners)	.25
164 Andre Dawson 1977 NL ROY (1970s Award Winners)	.25
165 Gaylord Perry 1978 NL CY (1970s Award Winners)	.15
166 Ron Guidry 1978 AL CY (1970s Award Winners)	.15
167 Dave Parker 1978 NL MVP (1970s Award Winners)	.15
168 Don Baylor 1979 AL MVP (1970s Award Winners)	.15
169 Bruce Sutter 1979 NL CY (1970s Award Winners)	.30
170 Willie Stargell 1979 NL co-MVP (1970s Award Winners)	.40
171 Brooks Robinson 1970 (1970s World Series Highlights)	.50
172 Roberto Clemente 1971 (1970s World Series Highlights)	1.00
173 Gene Tenace 1972 (1970s World Series Highlights)	.15
174 Reggie Jackson 1973 (1970s World Series Highlights)	.75
175 Rollie Fingers 1974 (1970s World Series Highlights)	.15
176 Carlton Fisk 1975 (1970s World Series Highlights)	.40
177 Johnny Bench 1976 (1970s World Series Highlights)	.75
178 Reggie Jackson 1977 (1970s World Series Highlights)	.75
179 Bucky Dent 1978 (1970s World Series Highlights)	.15
180 Willie Stargell 1979 (1970s World Series Highlights)	.40

Bellbottomed Bashers

	NM/M
Complete Set (10):	12.00
Common Player:	1.00

WILLIE McCOVEY • Giants

	NM/M
Inserted 1:14	
BB1 Reggie Jackson	2.00
BB2 Gorman Thomas	1.00
BB3 Willie McCovey	1.50
BB4 Willie Stargell	1.50
BB5 Mike Schmidt	3.00
BB6 George Foster	1.00
BB7 Johnny Bench	2.50
BB8 Dave Kingman	1.00
BB9 Graig Nettles	1.00
BB10 Steve Garvey	1.00

Decade Dynasties

	NM/M
Complete Set (10):	15.00
Common Player:	1.00
Inserted 1:14	
D1 Boog Powell	1.00
D2 Johnny Bench	3.00
D3 Willie Stargell	1.50
D4 Jim "Catfish" Hunter	1.00
D5 Steve Garvey	1.00
D6 Carlton Fisk	2.00
D7 Mike Schmidt	4.00
D8 Hal McRae	1.00
D9 Tom Seaver	3.00
D10 Reggie Jackson	2.50

Game-Used Bat

GAME-USED BAT
OZZIE SMITH • Padres

	NM/M
Common Player:	5.00
Inserted 1:24 H	
HA Hank Aaron	40.00
DB Don Baylor	5.00
BB Bobby Bonds	5.00
GC Gary Carter	8.00
JaC Jack Clark	5.00
RC Roberto Clemente/243	100.00
DC Dave Concepcion	5.00
JoC Jose Cruz	5.00
TD Tommy Davis	5.00
AD Andre Dawson	8.00
DaE Darryl Evans	5.00
DwE Dwight Evans	5.00
CF Carlton Fisk	10.00
GF George Foster	5.00
SG Steve Garvey	5.00
BG Bobby Grich	5.00
KG Ken Griffey Sr.	5.00
BH Bud Harrelson/290	5.00
KH Keith Hernandez/243	20.00
RH Ron Hunt	5.00
ReJ Reggie Jackson	15.00
RaJ Randy Jones	5.00
GL Greg Luzinski	5.00
FL Fred Lynn	5.00
GM Garry Maddox	5.00
BiM Bill Madlock	5.00
TiM Tim McCarver	5.00
TuM Tug McGraw/97	25.00
HM Hal McRae	5.00
RM Rick Monday	5.00
WM Willie Montanez	5.00
JM Joe Morgan	5.00
BoM Bobby Murcer	20.00
EM Eddie Murray	10.00
GN Graig Nettles/219	15.00
AO Al Oliver	5.00
DP Dave Parker	5.00
BP Boog Powell	5.00
WR Willie Randolph	5.00
BR Bill Russell	5.00
NR Nolan Ryan	50.00
RS Ron Santo	5.00
ToS Tom Seaver/121	20.00

OS	Ozzie Smith	15.00
RW	Roy White	5.00
MW	Maury Wills	5.00
DW	Dave Winfield	8.00

Game-Used Bat Combo

NM/M
Common Card: 20.00
Inserted 1:336

NYY	Reggie Jackson, Graig Nettles, Chris Chambliss, Roy White	40.00
LA	Steve Garvey, Ron Cey, Bill Russell, Rick Monday	25.00
NYM	Tom Seaver, Bud Harrelson, Ron Hunt, Tug McGraw	50.00
CIN	Johnny Bench, George Foster, Ken Griffey Sr., Joe Morgan	50.00
ROY	Andre Dawson, Fred Lynn, Carlton Fisk, Eddie Murray	40.00
MVPN	Johnny Bench, Steve Garvey, Willie Stargell, George Foster	50.00
BAT	Keith Hernandez, Bill Madlock, Fred Lynn, Dave Parker	20.00
GGA	Carlton Fisk, Graig Nettles, Bobby Grich, Fred Lynn	25.00
GGN	Johnny Bench, Roberto Clemente, Dave Concepcion, Garry Maddox	100.00
WS72	Reggie Jackson, Bert Campaneris, Dave Concepcion, Johnny Bench/97	80.00
WS73	Reggie Jackson, Bert Campaneris, Tom Seaver, Bud Harrelson	40.00
WS74	Reggie Jackson, Bert Campaneris, Steve Garvey, Ron Cey	40.00
WS75	Carlton Fisk, Fred Lynn, George Foster, Joe Morgan	40.00
WS76	Chris Chambliss, Graig Nettles, Johnny Bench, Ken Griffey Sr./97	80.00
WS77	Reggie Jackson, Graig Nettles, Steve Garvey, Ron Cey	40.00
WS78	Graig Nettles, Chris Chambliss, Bill Russell, Ron Cey/238	50.00
ASMV	Bill Madlock, Joe Morgan, Steve Garvey, Dave Parker	40.00
RY	Chris Chambliss, Reggie Jackson, Roy White, Hal McRae/238	40.00
RD	George Foster, Joe Morgan, Ron Cey, Bill Russell	25.00

Game-Used Jersey

NM/M
Common Player: 8.00
Inserted 1:168

HA	Hank Aaron	40.00
LA	Luis Aparicio	8.00
JB	Johnny Bench	20.00
RC	Roberto Clemente	100.00
WD	Willie Davis	8.00
RF	Rollie Fingers	8.00
CF	Carlton Fisk	10.00
RG	Ron Guidry	8.00
BH	Burt Hooton	8.00
CH	Jim "Catfish" Hunter	10.00
RJ	Reggie Jackson	15.00
JKa	Jim Kaat	8.00
JKo	Jerry Koosman	8.00
BM	Bill Madlock	8.00
JM	Jon Matlack	8.00
TM	Tug McGraw	8.00
BM	Bobby Murcer	15.00
JP	Jim Perry	8.00
LP	Lou Piniella	10.00
WR	Willie Randolph	8.00
NR	Nolan Ryan/50	75.00
TS	Tom Seaver	20.00
WS	Willie Stargell	10.00
MW	Maury Wills	8.00

Game-Used Jersey Autograph

NM/M
Common Autograph: 20.00
Inserted 1:168 H

HA	Hank Aaron/97	200.00
LA	Luis Aparicio	30.00
SB	Sal Bando	20.00
JB	Johnny Bench	70.00
RF	Rollie Fingers	25.00
CF	Carlton Fisk/243	40.00
KG	Ken Griffey Sr.	40.00
RG	Ron Guidry	30.00
BH	Burt Hooton	20.00
RJ	Reggie Jackson/291	65.00
JKa	Jim Kaat	25.00
JKo	Jerry Koosman	20.00
BM	Bill Madlock	20.00
TM	Tug McGraw	20.00
BM	Bobby Murcer	20.00
RP	Rico Petrocelli	25.00
NR	Nolan Ryan/291	125.00
MW	Maury Wills	20.00

Game-Used Patch

Inserted 1:7,500
No pricing due to scarcity.

The Arms Race

NM/M
Complete Set (10): 10.00
Common Player: .50
Inserted 1:14

AR1	Nolan Ryan	4.00
AR2	Ferguson Jenkins	1.00
AR3	Jim "Catfish" Hunter	1.00
AR4	Tom Seaver	2.00
AR5	Randy Jones	.15
AR6	J.R. Richard	.50
AR7	Rollie Fingers	1.00
AR8	Gaylord Perry	.75
AR9	Ron Guidry	.75
AR10	Phil Niekro	.75

70s Disco Era Dandies

NM/M
Complete Set (6): 5.00
Common Player: .50
Inserted 1:23

DE1	Mike Schmidt	2.00
DE2	Johnny Bench	1.00
DE3	Lou Brock	.50

DE4	Reggie Jackson	2.00
DE5	Willie Stargell	.50
DE6	Tom Seaver	1.00

70s Super Powers

NM/M
Complete Set (6): 12.00
Common Player: 1.50
Inserted 1:24

SP1	Reggie Jackson	3.00
SP2	Joe Morgan	1.50
SP3	Willie Stargell	2.00
SP4	Willie McCovey	1.50
SP5	Mike Schmidt	4.00
SP6	Nolan Ryan	5.00

2001 Upper Deck Evolution

NM/M
Complete Set (120): 125.00
Common Player: .15
Common SP (91-120): 3.00
Production 2,250
Pack (5): 2.00
Box (24): 40.00

1	Darin Erstad	.25
2	Troy Glaus	.50
3	Jason Giambi	.50
4	Tim Hudson	.40
5	Jermaine Dye	.15
6	Barry Zito	.40
7	Carlos Delgado	.50
8	Shannon Stewart	.15
9	Jose Cruz Jr.	.15
10	Greg Vaughn	.15
11	Juan Gonzalez	.50
12	Roberto Alomar	.50
13	Omar Vizquel	.25
14	Jim Thome	.50
15	Edgar Martinez	.25
16	John Olerud	.25
17	Kazuhiro Sasaki	.15
18	Cal Ripken Jr.	2.00
19	Alex Rodriguez	1.50
20	Ivan Rodriguez	.50
21	Rafael Palmeiro	.50
22	Pedro Martinez	.75
23	Nomar Garciaparra	1.50
24	Manny Ramirez	.50
25	Carl Everett	.15
26	Mark Quinn	.15
27	Mike Sweeney	.15
28	Neifi Perez	.15
29	Tony Clark	.15
30	Eric Milton	.15
31	Doug Mientkiewicz	.15
32	Corey Koskie	.15
33	Frank Thomas	.50
34	David Wells	.15
35	Magglio Ordonez	.40
36	Derek Jeter	2.00
37	Mike Mussina	.40
38	Bernie Williams	.50
39	Roger Clemens	1.50
40	David Justice	.25
41	Jeff Bagwell	.50
42	Richard Hidalgo	.25
43	Wade Miller	.15
44	Chipper Jones	1.00
45	Greg Maddux	1.00
46	Andruw Jones	.50
47	Rafael Furcal	.25
48	Geoff Jenkins	.25
49	Jeromy Burnitz	.15
50	Ben Sheets	.25
51	Richie Sexson	.40
52	Mark McGwire	1.50
53	Jim Edmonds	.40
54	Darryl Kile	.15
55	J.D. Drew	.25
56	Sammy Sosa	1.50
57	Kerry Wood	.25
58	Randy Johnson	.75
59	Luis Gonzalez	.25
60	Matt Williams	.25
61	Kevin Brown	.25
62	Gary Sheffield	.40
63	Shawn Green	.40
64	Chan Ho Park	.25
65	Vladimir Guerrero	.75
66	Jose Vidro	.15
67	Fernando Tatis	.15
68	Barry Bonds	2.00
69	Jeff Kent	.25
70	Russ Ortiz	.15
71	Preston Wilson	.15
72	Ryan Dempster	.15
73	Charles Johnson	.15
74	Mike Piazza	1.00
75	Edgardo Alfonzo	.25
76	Robin Ventura	.25
77	Jay Payton	.15
78	Tony Gwynn	.75
79	Phil Nevin	.15
80	Pat Burrell	.40
81	Scott Rolen	.50
82	Bob Abreu	.25
83	Brian Giles	.25
84	Jason Kendall	.25
85	Ken Griffey Jr.	1.00
86	Barry Larkin	.40
87	Sean Casey	.25
88	Todd Helton	.50
89	Larry Walker	.25
90	Mike Hampton	.15
91	Ichiro Suzuki RC	20.00
92	Albert Pujols RC	40.00
93	Wilson Betemit RC	3.00
94	Jay Gibbons RC	8.00
95	Juan Uribe RC	5.00
96	Morgan Ensberg RC	3.00
97	Christian Parker RC	3.00
98	Tsuyoshi Shinjo RC	4.00
99	Jack Wilson RC	3.00
100	Donaldo Mendez RC	3.00
101	Ryan Freel RC	4.00
102	Juan Diaz RC	3.00
103	Horacio Ramirez RC	8.00
104	Ricardo Rodriguez RC	3.00
105	Erick Almonte RC	3.00
106	Josh Towers RC	3.00
107	Adrian Hernandez RC	3.00
108	Brandon Duckworth RC	4.00
109	Travis Hafner RC	10.00
110	Martin Vargas RC	3.00
111	Kris Keller RC	3.00
112	Brian Lawrence RC	3.00
113	Esix Snead RC	3.00
114	Wilken Ruan RC	3.00
115	Jose Mieses RC	3.00
116	Johnny Estrada RC	8.00
117	Elpidio Guzman RC	3.00
118	Sean Douglass RC	3.00
119	Billy Sylvester RC	3.00
120	Bret Prinz RC	3.00

Autographed Bat/Jersey

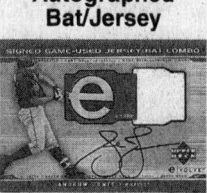

NM/M
Common Player: 25.00

RB	Russell Branyan	25.00
PB	Pat Burrell	40.00
CD	Carlos Delgado	40.00
JD	J.D. Drew	25.00
JaG	Jason Giambi	65.00
SG	Shawn Green	40.00
KG	Ken Griffey Jr.	100.00
AJ	Andruw Jones	50.00
CJ	Chipper Jones	60.00
JK	Jason Kendall	30.00
CR	Cal Ripken Jr.	150.00
AR	Alex Rodriguez	150.00
GS	Gary Sheffield	50.00
SS	Sammy Sosa	200.00
IS	Ichiro Suzuki	300.00

Game-Used Bat Cards

NM/M
Common Player: 5.00
Winners Evolve Into Bat/Jsy Auto.
Inserted 1:120

RB	Russell Branyan	5.00
PB	Pat Burrell	8.00
CD	Carlos Delgado	8.00
JD	J.D. Drew	5.00
JaG	Jason Giambi	8.00
KG	Ken Griffey Jr.	20.00
AJ	Andruw Jones	8.00
JK	Jason Kendall	5.00
AR	Alex Rodriguez	15.00
GS	Gary Sheffield	6.00

Game-Used Jersey Cards

NM/M
Common Player: 5.00
Inserted 1:120

RB	Russell Branyan	5.00
PB	Pat Burrell	8.00
JD	J.D. Drew	5.00
JaG	Jason Giambi	10.00
BG	Brian Giles	6.00
TG	Troy Glaus	8.00
SG	Shawn Green	6.00
KG	Ken Griffey Jr.	20.00
AJ	Andruw Jones	8.00
CJ	Chipper Jones	10.00
JK	Jason Kendall	5.00
CR	Cal Ripken Jr.	30.00
AR	Alex Rodriguez	15.00
GS	Gary Sheffield	8.00
SS	Sammy Sosa	15.00

Ichiro Suzuki All-Star Game

NM/M
Random Inserts

51B	Ichiro Suzuki/Bronze	8.00
51S	Ichiro Suzuki/Silver/2001	20.00
51G	Ichiro Suzuki/Gold/51	120.00

UD Classics

NM/M
Complete Set (15): 15.00
Common Player: .50
Prices for unscratched cards.
Winners Evolve Into Game Jersey.
Inserted 1:4

EC1	Ken Griffey Jr.	3.00
EC2	Gary Sheffield	.75
EC3	Randy Johnson	1.50
EC4	Sammy Sosa	3.00
EC5	Carlos Delgado	.50
EC6	Ichiro Suzuki	3.00
EC7	Andruw Jones	1.00
EC8	Chipper Jones	2.00
EC9	Kazuhiro Sasaki	.50
EC10	Shawn Green	.75
EC11	Alex Rodriguez	3.00
EC12	Brian Giles	.75
EC13	J.D. Drew	.50
EC14	Pat Burrell	1.00
EC15	Ivan Rodriguez	1.00

UD Classics Jersey

NM/M
Common Player: 1.00
Prices for unscratched cards.
Winners evolve into Game Jersey.

2001 Upper Deck Gold Glove

NM/M
Common Player: .25
Common SP (91-129): 4.00
Production 1,000
Common SP (130-135): 8.00
Production 500
Pack (4): 8.00
Box (20): 140.00

1	Troy Glaus	1.00
2	Darin Erstad	.50
3	Jason Giambi	1.00
4	Tim Hudson	.50
5	Jermaine Dye	.25
6	Raul Mondesi	.25
7	Carlos Delgado	1.00
8	Shannon Stewart	.25
9	Greg Vaughn	.25
10	Aubrey Huff	.25
11	Juan Gonzalez	1.00
12	Roberto Alomar	1.00
13	Omar Vizquel	.25
14	Jim Thome	1.00
15	John Olerud	.50
16	Edgar Martinez	.50
17	Kazuhiro Sasaki	.25
18	Aaron Sele	.25
19	Cal Ripken Jr.	4.00
20	Chris Richard	.25
21	Ivan Rodriguez	1.00
22	Rafael Palmeiro	.75
23	Alex Rodriguez	3.00
24	Pedro Martinez	1.50
25	Nomar Garciaparra	3.00
26	Manny Ramirez	1.00
27	Neifi Perez	.25
28	Mike Sweeney	.25
29	Bobby Higginson	.25
30	Dean Palmer	.25
31	Tony Clark	.25
32	Doug Mientkiewicz	.25
33	Brad Radke	.25
34	Joe Mays	.25
35	Frank Thomas	1.00
36	Magglio Ordonez	.50
37	Carlos Lee	.25
38	Bernie Williams	1.00
39	Mike Mussina	1.00
40	Derek Jeter	4.00
41	Roger Clemens	2.50
42	Craig Biggio	.40
43	Jeff Bagwell	1.00
44	Lance Berkman	.50
45	Andruw Jones	1.00
46	Greg Maddux	2.00
47	Chipper Jones	.25
48	Geoff Jenkins	.40
49	Ben Sheets	.25
50	Jeromy Burnitz	.25
51	Jim Edmonds	.25
52	Mark McGwire	3.00
53	Mike Matheny	.25
54	J.D. Drew	.25
55	Sammy Sosa	2.50
56	Kerry Wood	.75
57	Fred McGriff	.40
58	Randy Johnson	1.50
59	Steve Finley	.25
60	Mark Grace	.75
61	Matt Williams	.40
62	Luis Gonzalez	.40
63	Shawn Green	.40
64	Kevin Brown	.40
65	Gary Sheffield	.40
66	Vladimir Guerrero	1.25
67	Tony Armas Jr.	.25
68	Barry Bonds	4.00

69	J.T. Snow	.25
70	Jeff Kent	.25
71	Charles Johnson	.25
72	Preston Wilson	.25
73	Cliff Floyd	.25
74	Robin Ventura	.25
75	Mike Piazza	2.00
76	Edgardo Alfonzo	.25
77	Tony Gwynn	1.50
78	Ryan Klesko	.50
79	Scott Rolen	1.00
80	Mike Lieberthal	.25
81	Pat Burrell	.75
82	Jason Kendall	.25
83	Brian Giles	.50
84	Ken Griffey Jr.	2.50
85	Barry Larkin	.50
86	Pokey Reese	.25
87	Larry Walker	.40
88	Mike Hampton	.25
89	Juan Pierre	.25
90	Todd Helton	1.00
91	Mike Penney RC	4.00
92	Wilkin Ruan RC	4.00
93	Greg Miller RC	4.00
94	Johnny Estrada RC	8.00
95	Tsuyoshi Shinjo RC	4.00
96	Josh Towers RC	4.00
97	Horacio Ramirez RC	6.00
98	Ryan Freel RC	4.00
99	Morgan Ensberg RC	10.00
100	Adrian Hernandez RC	8.00
101	Juan Uribe RC	6.00
102	Jose Mieses RC	4.00
103	Jack Wilson RC	8.00
104	Cesar Crespo RC	4.00
105	Bud Smith RC	4.00
106	Erick Almonte RC	4.00
107	Elpidio Guzman RC	4.00
108	Brandon Duckworth RC	4.00
109	Juan Diaz RC	4.00
110	Kris Keller RC	4.00
111	Jason Michaels RC	4.00
112	Bret Prinz RC	4.00
113	Henry Mateo RC	4.00
114	Ricardo Rodriguez RC	4.00
115	Travis Hafner RC	20.00
116	Nate Teut RC	4.00
117	Alexis Gomez RC	4.00
118	Billy Sylvester RC	4.00
119	Adam Pettyjohn RC	4.00
120	Josh Fogg RC	4.00
121	Juan Cruz RC	4.00
122	Carlos Valderrama RC	4.00
123	Jay Gibbons RC	10.00
124	Donaldo Mendez RC	4.00
125	William Ortega RC	4.00
126	Sean Douglass RC	4.00
127	Christian Parker RC	4.00
128	Grant Balfour RC	4.00
129	Joe Kennedy RC	4.00
130	Albert Pujols RC	140.00
131	Wilson Betemit RC	10.00
132	Mark Teixeira RC	50.00
133	Mark Prior RC	30.00
134	Dewon Brazelton RC	10.00
135	Ichiro Suzuki RC	60.00

Limited

Stars (1-90):	4-8X
Rookies (91-135):	.75-1.5X
Production 100 Sets	

Finite

	NM/M
Common Player:	9.00

Batting Gloves

Stars (1-90):		15-25X
Rookies (91-135):		3-5X
Production 25 Sets		

		NM/M
Common Player:		5.00
Inserted 1:20		
BA	Bobby Abreu	8.00
BA	Brady Anderson	5.00
TB	Tony Batista	5.00
BB	Barry Bonds	30.00
MC	Marty Cordova	5.00
JC	Jose Cruz	5.00
RF	Rafael Furcal	8.00
AG	Andres Galarraga	5.00
JG	Juan Gonzalez	8.00
KGR	Ken Griffey Jr./Reds	20.00
KGM	Ken Griffey Jr.	20.00
CJ	Chipper Jones	10.00
EM	Edgar Martinez	5.00
PO	Paul O'Neill	5.00
RP	Rafael Palmeiro	10.00
NP	Neifi Perez	5.00
MR	Manny Ramirez	8.00
ARR	Alex Rodriguez/ Rangers	20.00
ARM	Alex Rodriguez/M's	20.00
HR	Henry Rodriguez	5.00
IR	Ivan Rodriguez	8.00
GS	Gary Sheffield	8.00
SS	Sammy Sosa	15.00
FT	Fernando Tatis	5.00
MT	Miguel Tejada	8.00

Fielder's Gloves

		NM/M
Common Player:		6.00
Inserted 1:60		
GA	Garret Anderson/100	15.00
CB	Craig Biggio	15.00
JBi	Johnny Blanchard	10.00
BB	Barry Bonds	50.00
KC	Ken Caminiti	10.00
RCa	Roy Campanella	60.00
GC	Gary Carter	10.00
RCe	Roger Cedeno	10.00
JD	Johnny Damon	15.00
LD	Leon Day/100	60.00
OD	Octavio Dotel	5.00
JE	Jim Edmonds	15.00
DE	Dock Ellis	10.00
AF	Alex Fernandez	6.00
CF	Cliff Floyd	10.00
NF	Nellie Fox	25.00
RF	Rafael Furcal	10.00
AG	Alex Gonzalez	6.00
BG	Ben Grieve	8.00
KG	Ken Griffey Jr.	30.00
MG	Marquis Grissom	8.00
LG	Lefty Grove	100.00
THe	Todd Helton	20.00
OH	Orlando Hernandez	8.00
THo	Todd Hollandsworth	8.00
HI	Hideki Irabu	8.00
JI	Jason Isringhausen	10.00
RJ	Reggie Jackson	20.00
CJ	Chipper Jones	25.00
JKa	Jim Kaat	10.00
JKe	Jason Kendall	10.00
RK	Ryan Klesko	8.00
HK	Harvey Kuenn	15.00
CL	Carlos Lee	8.00
KL	Kenny Lofton	10.00
JL	Javy Lopez	10.00
GL	Greg Luzinski	10.00
EM	Edgar Martinez	15.00
PM	Pedro Martinez	25.00
JO	John Olerud	10.00
PO	Paul O'Neill	15.00
RP	Rafael Palmeiro	15.00
CP	Chan Ho Park	10.00
MP	Mike Piazza	30.00
MR	Manny Ramirez	25.00
FR	Frank Robinson	15.00
AR	Alex Rodriguez	30.00
IR	Ivan Rodriguez	15.00
TS	Tim Salmon	8.00
AS	Aaron Sele	6.00
GS	Gary Sheffield	10.00
OS	Ozzie Smith	40.00
SS	Sammy Sosa	30.00
I	Ichiro Suzuki	250.00
FT	Frank Thomas	20.00
OV	Omar Vizquel	15.00
DW	Dave Winfield	20.00
MY	Masato Yoshii	10.00

Fielder's Gloves Autograph

		NM/M
Common Player:		5.00
Inserted 1:240		
JD	Johnny Damon	50.00
CF	Cliff Floyd	50.00
RF	Rafael Furcal	25.00
KG	Ken Griffey Jr./49	150.00
RJ	Reggie Jackson/68	60.00
JK	Jim Kaat	25.00
JK	Jason Kendall	20.00
RK	Ryan Klesko	20.00
KL	Kenny Lofton	20.00
JL	Javy Lopez	20.00
GL	Greg Luzinski	20.00
EM	Edgar Martinez	50.00
JO	John Olerud	25.00
PO	Paul O'Neill	50.00
FR	Frank Robinson	50.00
IR	Ivan Rodriguez	60.00
OS	Ozzie Smith	85.00
FT	Frank Thomas	60.00
DW	Dave Winfield	50.00

Game-Used Ball

		NM/M
Common Player:		5.00
Inserted 1:20		
GC	Ken Griffey Jr., Sean Casey	20.00
RR	Alex Rodriguez, Ivan Rodriguez	20.00
SW	Sammy Sosa, Rondell White	15.00
MP	Mark McGwire, Albert Pujols	75.00
RE	Manny Ramirez, Carl Everett	15.00
GE	Troy Glaus, Darin Erstad	8.00
GT	Jason Giambi, Miguel Tejada	10.00
IO	Ichiro Suzuki, John Olerud	40.00
RP	Ivan Rodriguez, Rafael Palmeiro	10.00
GV	Vladimir Guerrero, Jose Vidro	10.00
PS	Mike Piazza, Tsuyoshi Shinjo	20.00
JJ	Chipper Jones, Andruw Jones	15.00
RB	Scott Rolen, Pat Burrell	10.00
WF	Preston Wilson, Cliff Floyd	5.00
JF	Andruw Jones, Rafael Furcal	
BB	Jeff Bagwell, Lance Berkman	15.00
PE	Albert Pujols, Jim Edmonds	35.00
JB	Geoff Jenkins, Jeromy Burnitz	5.00
KG	Jason Kendall, Brian Giles	5.00
BK	Barry Bonds, Jeff Kent	25.00
NK	Phil Nevin, Ryan Klesko	
SG	Gary Sheffield, Shawn Green	8.00
GG	Luis Gonzalez, Mark Grace	10.00
HW	Todd Helton, Larry Walker	10.00
WP	Larry Walker, Juan Pierre	5.00
AG	Roberto Alomar, Juan Gonzalez	10.00
VM	Greg Vaughn, Fred McGriff	
RB	Cal Ripken Jr., Tony Batista	30.00
DM	Carlos Delgado, Raul Mondesi	8.00
MG	Doug Mientkiewicz, Cristian Guzman	5.00
TO	Frank Thomas, Magglio Ordonez	10.00
HC	Bobby Higginson, Tony Clark	
SB	Mike Sweeney, Carlos Beltran	5.00

MO	Edgar Martinez, John Olerud	8.00
EA	Darin Erstad, Garret Anderson	8.00
TC	Miguel Tejada, Eric Chavez	8.00
PR	Rafael Palmeiro, Alex Rodriguez	20.00
BA	Pat Burrell, Bobby Abreu	8.00
FJ	Cliff Floyd, Charles Johnson	5.00
VP	Robin Ventura, Mike Piazza	15.00
WS	Kerry Wood, Sammy Sosa	20.00
DP	J.D. Drew, Albert Pujols	40.00
BH	Lance Berkman, Richard Hidalgo	8.00
BS	Jeromy Burnitz, Richie Sexson	5.00
LG	Barry Larkin, Ken Griffey Jr.	20.00
GR	Brian Giles, Aramis Ramirez	5.00
JG	Randy Johnson, Luis Gonzalez	15.00
GB	Shawn Green, Adrian Beltre	8.00
KA	Jeff Kent, Rich Aurilia	5.00
GK	Tony Gwynn, Ryan Klesko	15.00
MJ	Greg Maddux, Chipper Jones	20.00
HH	Mike Hampton, Todd Helton	10.00
SV	Tsuyoshi Shinjo, Robin Ventura	5.00
GJ	Cristian Guzman, Jacque Jones	5.00
CJ	Roger Clemens, Derek Jeter	125.00

Jerseys

		NM/M
Common Player:		5.00
Inserted 1:20		
LA	Luis Aparicio	5.00
JB	Jeff Bagwell	8.00
BB	Barry Bonds	25.00
GC	Gary Carter	5.00
CC	Cesar Cedeno	5.00
DE	Darin Erstad	6.00
CF	Carlton Fisk	8.00
MG	Mark Grace	8.00
SG	Shawn Green	5.00
KG	Ken Griffey Jr.	20.00
RG	Ron Guidry	5.00
AJ	Andruw Jones	8.00
JK	Jim Kaat	5.00
GM	Greg Maddux	15.00
MM	Mickey Mantle	175.00
RM	Roger Maris	75.00
DM	Don Mattingly	30.00
TM	Thurman Munson	60.00
MM	Mike Mussina	10.00
RP	Rafael Palmeiro	10.00
BR	Bobby Richardson	8.00
CR	Cal Ripken Jr.	35.00
IR	Ivan Rodriguez	10.00
OS	Ozzie Smith	15.00
IS	Ichiro Suzuki	65.00
OV	Omar Vizquel	8.00
BW	Bernie Williams	8.00

2001 Upper Deck Hall of Famers

Complete Set (90):		25.00
Common Player:		.15
Hobby Pack (5):		4.00
Box (24):		80.00
1	Reggie Jackson	.75
2	Hank Aaron	1.50
3	Eddie Mathews	.40
4	Warren Spahn	.40
5	Robin Yount	.40
6	Lou Brock	.25
7	Dizzy Dean	.15
8	Bob Gibson	.25
9	Stan Musial	.75
10	Enos Slaughter	.15
11	Rogers Hornsby	.25
12	Ernie Banks	.50
13	Ferguson Jenkins	.15
14	Roy Campanella	.75
15	Pee Wee Reese	.25
16	Jackie Robinson	1.50
17	Juan Marichal	.15
18	Christy Mathewson	.15
19	Willie Mays	1.50
20	Hoyt Wilhelm	.15
21	Buck Leonard	.15
22	Bob Feller	.40
23	Cy Young	.40
24	Satchel Paige	.40
25	Tom Seaver	.40
26	Brooks Robinson	.40
27	Mike Schmidt	.75
28	Roberto Clemente	1.50
29	Ralph Kiner	.40
30	Willie Stargell	.50
31	Honus Wagner	.75
32	Josh Gibson	.40
33	Nolan Ryan	1.50
34	Carlton Fisk	.15
35	Jimmie Foxx	.75
36	Johnny Bench	.75
37	Joe Morgan	.40
38	George Brett	.75
39	Walter Johnson	.40
40	Cool Papa Bell	.15
41	Ty Cobb	1.00
42	Al Kaline	.15
43	Harmon Killebrew	.15
44	Luis Aparicio	.15
45	Yogi Berra	.75
46	Joe DiMaggio	1.50
47	Whitey Ford	.25
48	Lou Gehrig	2.00
49	Mickey Mantle	2.00
50	Babe Ruth	2.00
51	Josh Gibson (Origins of the Game)	.15
52	Honus Wagner (Origins of the Game)	.20
53	Hoyt Wilhelm (Origins of the Game)	.15
54	Cy Young (Origins of the Game)	.20
55	Walter Johnson (Origins of the Game)	.20
56	Satchel Paige (Origins of the Game)	.25
57	Rogers Hornsby (Origins of the Game)	.20
58	Christy Mathewson (Origins of the Game)	.15
59	Tris Speaker (Origins of the Game)	.20
60	Nap Lajoie (Origins of the Game)	.15
61	Mickey Mantle (The National Pastime)	1.00
62	Jackie Robinson (The National Pastime)	.75
63	Nolan Ryan (The National Pastime)	.75
64	Josh Gibson (The National Pastime)	.20
65	Yogi Berra (The National Pastime)	.40
66	Brooks Robinson (The National Pastime)	.20
67	Stan Musial (The National Pastime)	.40
68	Mike Schmidt (The National Pastime)	.40
69	Joe DiMaggio (The National Pastime)	1.00
70	Ernie Banks (The National Pastime)	.25
71	Willie Stargell (The National Pastime)	.25
72	Johnny Bench (The National Pastime)	.40
73	Willie Mays (The National Pastime)	.75
74	Satchel Paige (The National Pastime)	.25
75	Bob Gibson (The National Pastime)	.20
76	Harmon Killebrew (The National Pastime)	.15
77	Al Kaline (The National Pastime)	.15
78	Carlton Fisk (The National Pastime)	.15
79	Tom Seaver (The National Pastime)	.25
80	Reggie Jackson (The National Pastime)	.40
81	Bob Gibson (The Hall of Records)	.20
82	Nolan Ryan (The Hall of Records)	.75
83	Walter Johnson (The Hall of Records)	.20
84	Stan Musial (The Hall of Records)	.40
85	Josh Gibson (The Hall of Records)	.20
86	Cy Young (The Hall of Records)	.20
87	Joe DiMaggio (The Hall of Records)	1.00
88	Hoyt Wilhelm (The Hall of Records)	.15
89	Lou Brock (The Hall of Records)	.15
90	Mickey Mantle (The Hall of Records)	1.00

Cooperative Collectible Game Bat

		NM/M
Common Player:		5.00
Inserted 1:24		
HA	Hank Aaron	30.00
LA	Luis Aparicio	5.00
EB	Ernie Banks	15.00
JB	Johnny Bench	15.00
YB	Yogi Berra	10.00
JBo	Jim Bottomley	5.00
GB	George Brett	20.00
RC	Roy Campanella	30.00
OC	Orlando Cepeda	5.00
RC	Roberto Clemente/ SP/409	120.00
JD	Joe DiMaggio	100.00
CF	Carlton Fisk	10.00
RF	Rollie Fingers	5.00
JF	Jimmie Foxx	50.00
HG	Hank Greenberg	40.00
RH	Rogers Hornsby	100.00
RJ	Reggie Jackson	15.00
GK	George Kell	5.00
RK	Ralph Kiner	10.00
MM	Mickey Mantle	125.00
WM	Willie Mays	30.00
JM	Johnny Mize	10.00
JMo	Joe Morgan	5.00
MO	Mel Ott	50.00
JP	Jim Palmer/SP/372	50.00
TP	Tony Perez	5.00
BR	Brooks Robinson	10.00
FR	Frank Robinson	10.00
JR	Jackie Robinson/ SP/371	175.00
BR	Babe Ruth	200.00
NR	Nolan Ryan	50.00
RS	Red Schoendienst	5.00
ES	Enos Slaughter	5.00
DS	Duke Snider	10.00
WS	Willie Stargell	5.00
BW	Billy Williams	5.00
EW	Early Wynn	5.00
RY	Robin Yount	15.00

Cooperative Collectible Game Jersey

		NM/M
Common Player:		10.00
Inserted 1:168		
LA	Luis Aparicio	10.00
OC	Orlando Cepeda	10.00
RC	Roberto Clemente	100.00
JD	Joe DiMaggio	100.00
DD	Don Drysdale/ SP/49	200.00
LG	Lou Gehrig/SP/194	250.00
MM	Mickey Mantle/ SP/216	250.00
WM	Willie Mays	80.00
JM	Joe Morgan	10.00
TP	Tony Perez	5.00
PW	Pee Wee Reese	15.00
BR	Brooks Robinson	20.00
FR	Frank Robinson	10.00
NR	Nolan Ryan	30.00
TS	Tom Seaver	15.00
DS	Duke Snider/SP/267	50.00
WS	Willie Stargell	15.00
DSu	Don Sutton	10.00

Cooperative Collectible Jersey Autograph

		NM/M
Common Autograph:		40.00
Inserted 1:504		
LA	Luis Aparicio	40.00
OC	Orlando Cepeda	40.00
RJ	Reggie Jackson	75.00
EB	Ernie Banks	90.00
JM	Joe Morgan	40.00
TP	Tony Perez	40.00
GB	George Brett	125.00
BR	Brooks Robinson	80.00
FR	Frank Robinson	60.00
NR	Nolan Ryan	175.00
TS	Tom Seaver	75.00
DS	Duke Snider	65.00
WS	Willie Stargell	75.00
DSu	Don Sutton	40.00

Hall of Fame Gallery

		NM/M
Complete Set (15):		25.00
Common Player:		1.00
Inserted 1:6		
1	Reggie Jackson	1.50
2	Tom Seaver	1.50
3	Bob Gibson	1.50
4	Jackie Robinson	3.00
5	Joe DiMaggio	3.00
6	Ernie Banks	1.50
7	Mickey Mantle	4.00
8	Willie Mays	3.00
9	Cy Young	1.50
10	Nolan Ryan	4.00
11	Johnny Bench	1.50
12	Yogi Berra	1.50
13	Satchel Paige	1.00
14	George Brett	2.00
15	Stan Musial	2.00

Mantle Pinstripes Exclusive

		NM/M
Complete Set (56):		75.00
Common Mantle:		2.00
One Pack/Box		

Mantle Pinstripe Memorabilia

	NM/M
Print runs listed:	

MMB	Mickey Mantle/ Bat/100		100.00
MMCJ	Mickey Mantle, Joe DiMaggi/ Jsy/50		300.00
MMJ	Mickey Mantle/ Jsy/100		125.00

The Class of '36

		NM/M
Complete Set (5):		8.00
Common Player:		1.50
Inserted 1:17		
1	Ty Cobb	2.00
2	Babe Ruth	5.00
3	Christy Mathewson	1.50
4	Walter Johnson	1.50
5	Honus Wagner	1.50

The Endless Summer

		NM/M
Complete Set (11):		15.00
Common Player:		1.00
Inserted 1:8		
1	Mickey Mantle	4.00
2	Yogi Berra	1.00
3	Mike Schmidt	2.50
4	Jackie Robinson	2.50
5	Johnny Bench	1.50
6	Tom Seaver	1.50
7	Ernie Banks	1.50
8	Harmon Killebrew	1.00
9	Joe DiMaggio	3.00
10	Willie Mays	3.00
11	Brooks Robinson	1.00

20th Century Showcase

		NM/M
Complete Set (11):		15.00
Common Player:		1.00
Inserted 1:8		
1	Cy Young	1.00
2	Joe DiMaggio	3.00
3	Harmon Killebrew	1.00
4	Stan Musial	2.00
5	Mickey Mantle	4.00
6	Satchel Paige	1.00
7	Nolan Ryan	2.00
8	Bob Gibson	1.00
9	Ernie Banks	1.00
10	Mike Schmidt	2.00
11	Willie Mays	3.00

2001 Upper Deck Legends

		NM/M
Complete Set (90):		20.00
Common Player:		.20
Pack (5):		4.00
Box (24):		80.00
1	Darin Erstad	.40
2	Troy Glaus	.75

3	Nolan Ryan	3.00
4	Reggie Jackson	.50
5	Jim "Catfish" Hunter	.20
6	Jason Giambi	.50
7	Tim Hudson	.30
8	Miguel Tejada	.30
9	Carlos Delgado	.50
10	Shannon Stewart	.20
11	Greg Vaughn	.20
12	Larry Doby	.20
13	Jim Thome	.40
14	Juan Gonzalez	.75
15	Roberto Alomar	.50
16	Edgar Martinez	.20
17	John Olerud	.40
18	Eddie Murray	.40
19	Cal Ripken Jr.	2.50
20	Alex Rodriguez	2.00
21	Ivan Rodriguez	.75
22	Rafael Palmeiro	.40
23	Jimmie Foxx	.50
24	Cy Young	.50
25	Manny Ramirez	.75
26	Pedro Martinez	1.00
27	Nomar Garciaparra	2.00
28	George Brett	1.00
29	Mike Sweeney	.20
30	Jermaine Dye	.20
31	Ty Cobb	1.50
32	Dean Palmer	.20
33	Harmon Killebrew	.50
34	Matt Lawton	.20
35	Luis Aparicio	.20
36	Frank Thomas	.75
37	Magglio Ordonez	.20
38	David Wells	.20
39	Mickey Mantle	3.00
40	Joe DiMaggio	3.00
41	Roger Maris	.75
42	Babe Ruth	3.00
43	Derek Jeter	2.50
44	Roger Clemens	1.00
45	Bernie Williams	.50
46	Jeff Bagwell	.75
47	Richard Hidalgo	.40
48	Warren Spahn	.40
49	Greg Maddux	1.50
50	Chipper Jones	1.50
51	Andruw Jones	.50
52	Robin Yount	.50
53	Jeromy Burnitz	.20
54	Jeffrey Hammonds	.20
55	Ozzie Smith	.50
56	Stan Musial	1.00
57	Mark McGwire	2.50
58	Jim Edmonds	.30
59	Sammy Sosa	1.50
60	Ernie Banks	.50
61	Kerry Wood	.20
62	Randy Johnson	.75
63	Luis Gonzalez	.40
64	Don Drysdale	.50
65	Jackie Robinson	2.00
66	Gary Sheffield	.20
67	Kevin Brown	.20
68	Vladimir Guerrero	1.00
69	Willie Mays	1.50
70	Mel Ott	.20
71	Jeff Kent	.20
72	Barry Bonds	1.00
73	Preston Wilson	.20
74	Ryan Dempster	.20
75	Tom Seaver	.40
76	Mike Piazza	2.00
77	Robin Ventura	.20
78	Dave Winfield	.40
79	Tony Gwynn	1.00
80	Bob Abreu	.20
81	Scott Rolen	.40
82	Mike Schmidt	.75
83	Roberto Clemente	1.50
84	Brian Giles	.20
85	Ken Griffey Jr.	2.00
86	Frank Robinson	.40
87	Johnny Bench	.75
88	Todd Helton	.75
89	Larry Walker	.40
90	Mike Hampton	.20

Fiorentino Collection

		NM/M
Complete Set (14):		40.00
Common Player:		1.50
Inserted 1:12		
F1	Babe Ruth	6.00
F2	Satchel Paige	1.50
F3	Joe DiMaggio	5.00
F4	Willie Mays	4.00
F5	Ty Cobb	3.00
F6	Nolan Ryan	5.00
F7	Lou Gehrig	5.00
F8	Jackie Robinson	4.00
F9	Hank Aaron	4.00
F10	Roberto Clemente	4.00
F11	Stan Musial	3.00
F12	Johnny Bench	2.00
F13	Honus Wagner	1.50
F14	Reggie Jackson	1.50

Legendary Cuts

		NM/M
Most not priced due to scarcity.		
C-TC	Ty Cobb/3	3,150
C-BRu	Babe Ruth/7	6,000

Legendary Game Jerseys

		NM/M
Common Player:		5.00
Inserted 1:24		
HA	Hank Aaron	40.00
JB	Jeff Bagwell	8.00
EB	Ernie Banks	15.00
YB	Yogi Berra	10.00
BB	Barry Bonds	25.00
JC	Jose Canseco	10.00
RCI	Roger Clemens	20.00
RoC	Roberto Clemente/ 195	170.00
JD	Joe DiMaggio/245	175.00
KG	Ken Griffey Jr.	15.00
TG	Tony Gwynn	10.00
RJa	Reggie Jackson	10.00
RJo	Randy Johnson	10.00
CJ	Chipper Jones	10.00
GM	Greg Maddux	15.00
MM	Mickey Mantle/245	200.00
RM	Roger Maris/343	65.00
PM	Pedro Martinez	10.00
WM	Willie Mays	30.00
SM	Stan Musial/490	30.00
MP	Mike Piazza	20.00
MR	Manny Ramirez	8.00
CR	Cal Ripken Jr.	30.00
AR	Alex Rodriguez	20.00
IR	Ivan Rodriguez	8.00
NR	Nolan Ryan	50.00
KS	Kazuhiro Sasaki	5.00
TS	Tom Seaver	15.00
GS	Gary Sheffield	5.00
OS	Ozzie Smith	15.00
SS	Sammy Sosa	15.00
DW	Dave Winfield	15.00
RY	Robin Yount	12.00

Legendary Jerseys Autograph

		NM/M
Inserted 1:288		
EB	Ernie Banks	75.00

RC	Roger Clemens/211	100.00
KG	Ken Griffey Jr.	80.00
RJ	Reggie Jackson/224	60.00
SM	Stan Musial/266	100.00
AR	Alex Rodriguez	85.00
NR	Nolan Ryan	125.00
TS	Tom Seaver	60.00
OS	Ozzie Smith	60.00
SS	Sammy Sosa/91	175.00

Legendary Jerseys Gold

		NM/M
Common Player:		30.00
Production 25 Sets		
RCI	Roger Clemens	75.00
RoC	Roberto Clemente	180.00
KG	Ken Griffey Jr.	75.00
RJ	Reggie Jackson	40.00
WM	Willie Mays	120.00
AR	Alex Rodriguez	75.00
NR	Nolan Ryan	100.00
SS	Sammy Sosa	75.00
DW	Dave Winfield	30.00

Legendary Jerseys Gold Autograph

No pricing due to scarcity.
Production 25 Sets

Legendary Lumber

		NM/M
Common Player:		5.00
Inserted 1:24		
HA	Hank Aaron	30.00
LA	Luis Aparicio	5.00
EB	Ernie Banks/80	50.00
JB	Johnny Bench	15.00
BB	Barry Bonds	25.00
RCa	Roy Campanella/335	40.00
JC	Jose Canseco	8.00
RCI	Roger Clemens	20.00
RoC	Roberto Clemente/ 170	120.00
JD	Joe DiMaggio	85.00
JF	Jimmie Foxx/351	50.00
KG	Ken Griffey Jr.	15.00
TG	Tony Gwynn	10.00
RJ	Reggie Jackson	10.00
RJ	Randy Johnson	10.00
AJ	Andruw Jones	8.00
CJ	Chipper Jones	10.00
MM	Mickey Mantle	150.00
RM	Roger Maris	40.00
WM	Willie Mays	30.00

EM	Eddie Murray	8.00
MO	Mel Ott/355	40.00
MP	Mike Piazza	15.00
AP	Albert Pujols	45.00
MR	Manny Ramirez	8.00
FR	Frank Robinson	8.00
CR	Cal Ripken Jr.	40.00
AR	Alex Rodriguez	15.00
IR	Ivan Rodriguez	8.00
GS	Gary Sheffield	5.00
OS	Ozzie Smith	10.00
SS	Sammy Sosa	15.00

Legendary Lumber Autograph

		NM/M
Common Player:		25.00
Inserted 1:288		
LA	Luis Aparicio	25.00
EB	Ernie Banks	65.00
RC	Roger Clemens/227	100.00
KG	Ken Griffey Jr.	80.00
TG	Tony Gwynn	60.00
RJ	Reggie Jackson/211	60.00
EM	Eddie Murray	40.00
AR	Alex Rodriguez	100.00
SS	Sammy Sosa/66	240.00

Legendary Lumber Gold

		NM/M
Common Player:		25.00
Production 25 Sets		
RC	Roger Clemens	75.00
RC	Roberto Clemente	180.00
KG	Ken Griffey Jr.	75.00
RJ	Reggie Jackson	40.00
WM	Willie Mays	120.00
AR	Alex Rodriguez	75.00
GS	Gary Sheffield	25.00
SS	Sammy Sosa	75.00

Legendary Lumber Gold Autograph

No pricing due to scarcity.
Production 25 Sets

Reflections

		NM/M
Complete Set (10):		25.00
Common Card:		1.00
Inserted 1:18		
R1	Bernie Williams, Mickey Mantle	6.00
R2	Pedro Martinez, Cy Young	2.00
R3	Barry Bonds, Willie Mays	5.00
R4	Scott Rolen, Mike Schmidt	3.00
R5	Mark McGwire, Stan Musial	4.00
R6	Ken Griffey Jr., Frank Robinson	3.00
R7	Sammy Sosa, Andre Dawson	3.00
R8	Kevin Brown, Don Drysdale	1.50
R9	Jason Giambi, Reggie Jackson	1.50
R10	Tim Hudson, Jim "Catfish" Hunter	1.00

2001 Upper Deck Legends of New York

The greatest players, teams and events of 20th Century Major League baseball in New York City are featured in this specialty set. The 200-card base

DEM BUMS

GIL HODGES POWERS DODGERS TO PENNANT

set is comprised of a number of different subsets. The front of each card in the base set has an area of flocking in team colors.

		NM/M
Complete Set (200):		40.00
Common Player:		.20
Pack (5):		2.50
Box (24):		50.00
1	Billy Herman	.20
2	Carl Erskine	.20
3	Burleigh Grimes	.20
4	Don Newcombe	.20
5	Gil Hodges	.75
6	Pee Wee Reese	.75
7	Jackie Robinson	2.00
8	Duke Snider	1.00
9	Jim Gilliam	.20
10	Roy Campanella	1.50
11	Carl Furillo	.20
12	Casey Stengel	.75
13	Casey Stengel	.40
14	Billy Herman	.20
15	Jackie Robinson	1.00
16	Jackie Robinson	1.00
17	Gil Hodges	.40
18	Carl Furillo	.20
19	Roy Campanella	.40
20	Don Newcombe	.20
21	Duke Snider	.75
22	Casey Stengel	.40
23	Burleigh Grimes	.20
24	Pee Wee Reese	.50
25	Jackie Robinson	1.00
26	Jackie Robinson	1.00
27	Carl Erskine	.20
28	Roy Campanella	.75
29	Duke Snider	.75
30	Rube Marquard	.20
31	Ross Youngs	.20
32	Bobby Thomson	.20
33	Christy Mathewson	1.00
34	Carl Hubbell	.20
35	Hoyt Wilhelm	.20
36	Johnny Mize	.40
37	John McGraw	.20
38	Monte Irvin	.50
39	Travis Jackson	.20
40	Mel Ott	1.00
41	Dusty Rhodes	.20
42	Leo Durocher	.50
43	John McGraw	.20
44	Christy Mathewson	.50
45	The Polo Grounds	.20
46	Travis Jackson	.20
47	Mel Ott	.50
48	Johnny Mize	.20
49	Leo Durocher	.30
50	Bobby Thomson	.20
51	Monte Irvin	.30
52	Bobby Thomson	.20
53	Christy Mathewson	.50
54	Christy Mathewson	.50
55	Christy Mathewson	.50
56	John McGraw	.20
57	John McGraw	.20
58	John McGraw	.20
59	Travis Jackson	.20
60	Mel Ott	.50
61	Mel Ott	.50
62	Carl Hubbell	.20
63	Bobby Thomson	.20
64	Monte Irvin	.20
65	Al Weis	.20
66	Donn Clendenon	.20
67	Ed Kranepool	.20
68	Gary Carter	.20
69	Tommie Agee	.20
70	Jon Matlack	.20
71	Ken Boswell	.20
72	Len Dykstra	.20
73	Nolan Ryan	3.00
74	Ray Sadecki	.20
75	Ron Darling	.20
76	Ron Swoboda	.20
77	Dwight Gooden	.20
78	Tom Seaver	1.00
79	Wayne Garrett	.20
80	Casey Stengel	.50
81	Tom Seaver	.50
82	Tommie Agee	.20
83	Tom Seaver	.50
84	Yogi Berra	.50
85	Yogi Berra	.50
86	Tom Seaver	.50
87	Dwight Gooden	.20

88	Gary Carter	.20
89	Ron Darling	.20
90	Tommie Agee	.20
91	Tom Seaver	.50
92	Gary Carter	.20
93	Len Dykstra	.20
94	Babe Ruth	3.00
95	Bill Dickey	.20
96	Rich "Goose" Gossage	.20
97	Casey Stengel	.50
98	Jim "Catfish" Hunter	.75
99	Charlie Keller	.20
100	Chris Chambliss	.20
101	Don Larsen	.40
102	Dave Winfield	.75
103	Don Mattingly	2.00
104	Elston Howard	.20
105	Frankie Crosetti	.20
106	Hank Bauer	.20
107	Joe DiMaggio	3.00
108	Graig Nettles	.20
109	Lefty Gomez	.20
110	Phil Rizzuto	1.00
111	Lou Gehrig	2.00
112	Lou Piniella	.20
113	Mickey Mantle	3.00
114	Red Rolfe	.20
115	Reggie Jackson	1.00
116	Roger Maris	1.50
117	Ray White	.20
118	Thurman Munson	1.50
119	Tom Tresh	.20
120	Tommy Henrich	.20
121	Waite Hoyt	.20
122	Willie Randolph	.20
123	Whitey Ford	.75
124	Yogi Berra	.75
125	Babe Ruth	1.50
126	Babe Ruth	1.50
127	Lou Gehrig	1.25
128	Babe Ruth	1.50
129	Joe DiMaggio	1.50
130	Joe DiMaggio	1.50
131	Mickey Mantle	1.50
132	Roger Marris	.75
133	Mickey Mantle	1.50
134	Reggie Jackson	.75
135	Babe Ruth	1.50
136	Babe Ruth	1.50
137	Babe Ruth	1.50
138	Lefty Gomez	.20
139	Lou Gehrig	1.25
140	Lou Gehrig	1.25
141	Joe DiMaggio	1.50
142	Joe DiMaggio	1.50
143	Casey Stengel	.40
144	Mickey Mantle	1.50
145	Yogi Berra	.50
146	Mickey Mantle	1.50
147	Elston Howard	.40
148	Whitey Ford	.50
149	Reggie Jackson	.50
150	Reggie Jackson	.50
151	John McGraw, Babe Ruth	1.00
152	Babe Ruth, John McGraw	1.00
153	Lou Gehrig, Mel Ott	.75
154	Joe DiMaggio, Mel Ott	1.00
155	Joe DiMaggio, Billy Herman	1.00
156	Joe DiMaggio, Jackie Robinson	1.50
157	Mickey Mantle, Bobby Thomson	1.00
158	Yogi Berra, Pee Wee Reese	.75
159	Roy Campanella, Mickey Mantle	1.00
160	Don Larsen, Duke Snider	.50
161	Christy Mathewson	.75
162	Christy Mathewson	.50
163	Rube Marquard	.20
164	Christy Mathewson	.50
165	John McGraw	.20
166	Burleigh Grimes	.20
167	Babe Ruth	1.50
168	Burleigh Grimes	.20
169	Babe Ruth	1.50
170	John McGraw	.40
171	Lou Gehrig	1.25
172	Babe Ruth	1.50
173	Babe Ruth	1.50
174	Carl Hubbell	.20
175	Joe DiMaggio	1.50
176	Lou Gehrig	1.25
177	Leo Durocher	.40
178	Mel Ott	.50
179	Joe DiMaggio	1.50
180	Jackie Robinson	1.00
181	Babe Ruth	1.50
182	Bobby Thomson	.20
183	Joe DiMaggio	1.50
184	Mickey Mantle	1.50
185	Monte Irvin	.20
186	Roy Campanella	.50
187	Duke Snider	.50
188	Dusty Rhodes	.20
189	Yogi Berra	.50
190	Mickey Mantle	1.50
191	Mickey Mantle	1.50
192	Casey Stengel	.40
193	Tom Seaver	.50
194	Mickey Mantle	1.50
195	Tommie Agee	.20
196	Tom Seaver	.50
197	Chris Chambliss	.20

198	Reggie Jackson	.50
199	Reggie Jackson	.50
200	Gary Carter	.20

Bat Cards

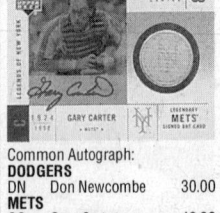

	NM/M
Common Player:	5.00
Inserted 1:24	

DODGERS
JG	Jim Gilliam	10.00
BH	Billy Herman	8.00
DN	Don Newcombe/67	40.00

GIANTS
BTh	Bobby Thomson	25.00

METS
KB	Ken Boswell	5.00
GC	Gary Carter	15.00
LD	Len Dykstra	5.00
WG	Wayne Garrett	8.00
EK	Ed Kranepool	10.00
JM	J.C. Martin	8.00
NR	Nolan Ryan	40.00
TS	Tom Seaver	20.00
RSw	Ron Swoboda	8.00
AW	Al Weis	5.00

YANKEES
HB	Hank Bauer	10.00
YB	Yogi Berra	15.00
CC	Chris Chambliss/130	15.00
BD	Bill Dickey	15.00
TH	Tommy Henrich	8.00
EH	Elston Howard	10.00
RJ	Reggie Jackson	15.00
CK	Charlie Keller	8.00
MM	Mickey Mantle/134	200.00
RM	Roger Maris/60	85.00
DM	Don Mattingly	30.00
TM	Thurman Munson	20.00
LP	Lou Piniella	8.00
MR	Mickey Rivers	5.00
BR	Babe Ruth/107	250.00
TT	Tom Tresh	10.00
DW	Dave Winfield	10.00

Bat Autographs

	NM/M
Common Autograph:	

DODGERS
DN	Don Newcombe	30.00

METS
GC	Gary Carter	40.00
DC	Donn Clendenon	30.00
NR	Nolan Ryan/129	200.00
TS	Tom Seaver/89	100.00

YANKEES
YB	Yogi Berra	75.00
CC	Chris Chambliss	30.00
RJ	Reggie Jackson/123	75.00
DM	Don Mattingly	100.00
MR	Mickey Rivers	25.00
RW	Roy White	25.00

Cut Signatures

	NM/M
Most not priced due to scarcity.	
LC-JD Joe DiMaggio (38 Issued)	1,000

Combination Signatures

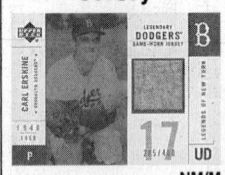

	NM/M
Common Card:	75.00
NP	Don Newcombe, Johnny Podres	85.00

Triple-Combination Signatures

	NM/M
Production 25 Sets	
S-NPE	Don Newcombe, Johnny Podres, Carl Erskine	175.00
S-WMN	Dave Winfield, Don Mattingly, Graig Nettles	175.00
S-RSS	Nolan Ryan, Tom Seaver, Ron Swoboda	450.00
S-LBP	Don Larsen, Yogi Berra, Joe Pepitone	125.00
S-GJG	Ron Guidry, Tommy John, Rich "Goose" Gossage	100.00
S-CND	Chris Chambliss, Graig Nettles, Bucky Dent	100.00
S-LRG	Sparky Lyle, Dave Righetti, Rich "Goose" Gossage	100.00

Dodgers Game Jersey

	NM/M
Common Player:	5.00
Gold Edition of 400:	1.25X
HB	Hank Behrman	5.00
CD	Chuck Dressen	5.00
CE	Carl Erskine	10.00
SJ	Spider Jurgenson	5.00
JR	Jackie Robinson/126	120.00

Giants Game Jersey

	NM/M
Complete Set (1):	
CM	Christy Mathewson/63	350.00

Mets Game Jersey

	NM/M
Common Player:	5.00
Gold Edition of 400:	1.25X
RD	Ron Darling	5.00
JM	Jon Matlack	5.00
RS	Ray Sadecki	5.00
TS	Tom Seaver	15.00
CS	Casey Stengel	8.00
JT	Joe Torre	5.00

WM	Dave Winfield, Don Mattingly	200.00
RS	Nolan Ryan, Tom Seaver	400.00
LB	Don Larsen, Yogi Berra	150.00
GJ	Ron Guidry, Tommy John	60.00
CN	Chris Chambliss, Graig Nettles	60.00
RD	Willie Randolph, Bucky Dent	60.00
RW	Mickey Rivers, Roy White	60.00
WJ	Dave Winfield, Reggie Jackson	150.00

Yankees Game Jersey

	NM/M
Common Player:	5.00
Gold Edition of 400:	1.25X
HB	Hank Bauer	8.00
FC	Frank Crosetti	10.00
TH	Tommy Henrich	10.00
EH	Elston Howard	10.00
CH	Jim "Catfish" Hunter	10.00
DM	Duke Maas	5.00
MM	Mickey Mantle/63.	250.00
LM	Lindy McDaniel	5.00
TM	Thurman Munson	30.00
GN	Graig Nettles	10.00
PN	Phil Niekro	10.00
JP	Joe Pepitone	8.00
WR	Willie Randolph	8.00
RR	Red Rolfe	5.00
BT	Bob Turley	8.00
DW	Dave Winfield	15.00

Signed Game Jersey

	NM/M
Common Autograph:	15.00

DODGERS
CE	Carl Erskine	50.00
JP	Johnny Podres/193	50.00

METS
GF	George Foster/196	30.00
NR	Nolan Ryan/47	200.00
CS	Craig Swan	30.00

YANKEES
YG	Yogi Berra/73	125.00
BD	Bucky Dent	30.00
RG	Rich Gossage/145	40.00
RG	Ron Guidry	50.00
TJ	Tommy John	30.00
DL	Don Larsen	60.00
HL	Hector Lopez/195	15.00
SL	Sparky Lyle	30.00
DM	Don Mattingly/72	125.00
PN	Phil Niekro/195	40.00
GN	Graig Nettles	30.00
JP	Joe Pepitone	30.00
WR	Willie Randolph	30.00

Ebbets Field G-U Base

	NM/M
Complete Set (1):	
JR	Jackie Robinson/100	50.00
JR	Jackie Robinson/Silver/50	60.00
JR	Jackie Robinson/Gold/25	75.00

Ebbets Field Seat

	NM/M
Complete Set (1):	
JR	Jackie Robinson	50.00

Shea Stadium G-U Base

	NM/M
Quantity produced listed	
TS	Tom Seaver/100	25.00

TS	Tom Seaver/Silver/50	40.00
TS	Tom Seaver/Gold/25	50.00

United We Stand

UNITED WE STAND

Images from the aftermath of the 9/11/01 terrorist attack on New York's World Trade Center are featured in this insert series found in the UD Legends of New York issue. Red, white and blue stars and stripes are the background on card backs for a message from Upper Deck concerning relief efforts.

	NM/M
Complete Set (15):	10.00
Common Card:	1.00
Inserted 1:12	
USA1-15 United We Stand	1.00

Yankee Stadium Seat

Complete Set (1):	

Los Angeles Dodgers Team Set

This boxed set has 20 player cards in standard 2-1/2" x 3-1/2" format and a 3-1/2" x 5" checklist. Cards have borderless action photos on front with an Upper Deck Collectibles logo at top-left. At bottom are the team and player name, position and uniform number. Backs have a smaller version of the front photo, some biographical and career notes and 1999-2000 stats. Cards are numbered with an "LA" prefix.

		NM/M
Complete Set (21):		10.00
Common Player:		.50
1	Gary Sheffield	1.00
2	Shawn Green	1.00
3	Kevin Brown	.50
4	Adrian Beltre	.50
5	Eric Karros	.50
6	Darren Dreifort	.50
7	Chan Ho Park	.50
8	Alex Cora	.50
9	Mark Grudzielanek	.50
10	Paul LoDuca	.75
11	Dave Hansen	.50
12	Tom Goodwin	.50
13	Ramon Martinez	.50
14	Luke Prokopec	.50
15	Chad Kreuter	.50
16	Jeff Shaw	.50

#	Player	Price
17	Eric Gagne	.75
18	Andy Ashby	.50
19	F.P. Santangelo	.50
20	Mike Fetters	.50
21	Checklist	.50

2001 Upper Deck MVP

NM/M

Complete Set (330):		35.00
Common Player:		.10
Pack (8):		1.50
Box (24):		30.00
1	Mo Vaughn	.10
2	Troy Percival	.10
3	Adam Kennedy	.10
4	Darin Erstad	.25
5	Tim Salmon	.10
6	Bengie Molina	.10
7	Troy Glaus	.40
8	Garret Anderson	.25
9	Ismael Valdes	.10
10	Glenallen Hill	.10
11	Tim Hudson	.25
12	Eric Chavez	.20
13	Johnny Damon	.10
14	Barry Zito	.40
15	Jason Giambi	.40
16	Terrence Long	.10
17	Jason Hart	.10
18	Jose Ortiz	.10
19	Miguel Tejada	.25
20	Jason Isringhausen	.10
21	Adam Piatt	.10
22	Jeremy Giambi	.10
23	Tony Batista	.10
24	Darrin Fletcher	.10
25	Mike Sirotka	.10
26	Carlos Delgado	.40
27	Billy Koch	.10
28	Shannon Stewart	.10
29	Raul Mondesi	.15
30	Brad Fullmer	.10
31	Jose Cruz Jr.	.10
32	Kelvim Escobar	.10
33	Greg Vaughn	.10
34	Aubrey Huff	.10
35	Gerald Williams	.10
36	Ben Grieve	.10
37	John Flaherty	.10
38	(John Flaherty)	
39	Fred McGriff	.15
40	Ryan Rupe	.10
41	Travis Harper	.10
42	Steve Cox	.10
43	Roberto Alomar	.40
44	Jim Thome	.50
45	Russell Branyan	.10
46	Bartolo Colon	.20
47	Omar Vizquel	.15
48	Travis Fryman	.15
49	Kenny Lofton	.10
50	Chuck Finley	.10
51	Ellis Burks	.10
52	Eddie Taubensee	.10
53	Juan Gonzalez	.40
54	Edgar Martinez	.20
55	Aaron Sele	.10
56	John Olerud	.20
57	Jay Buhner	.10
58	Mike Cameron	.10
59	John Halama	.10
60	Ichiro Suzuki RC	8.00
61	David Bell	.10
62	Freddy Garcia	.10
63	Carlos Guillen	.10
64	Bret Boone	.20
65	Al Martin	.10
66	Cal Ripken Jr.	1.50
67	Delino DeShields	.10
68	Chris Richard	.10
69	Sean Douglass RC	.25
70	Melvin Mora	.10
71	Luis Matos	.10
72	Sidney Ponson	.10
73	Mike Bordick	.10
74	Brady Anderson	.10
75	David Segui	.10
76	Jeff Conine	.10
77	Alex Rodriguez	1.25
78	Gabe Kapler	.10
79	Ivan Rodriguez	.40
80	Rick Helling	.10
81	Kenny Rogers	.10
82	Andres Galarraga	.15
83	Rusty Greer	.10
84	Justin Thompson	.10
85	Ken Caminiti	.10
86	Rafael Palmeiro	.40
87	Ruben Mateo	.10
88	Travis Hafner RC	1.00
89	Manny Ramirez	.40
90	Pedro Martinez	.50
91	Carl Everett	.10
92	Dante Bichette	.10
93	Derek Lowe	.10
94	Jason Varitek	.10
95	Nomar Garciaparra	1.25
96	David Cone	.10
97	Tomokazu Ohka	.10
98	Troy O'Leary	.10
99	Trot Nixon	.10
100	Jermaine Dye	.10
101	Joe Randa	.10
102	Jeff Suppan	.10
103	Roberto Hernandez	.10
104	Mike Sweeney	.10
105	Mac Suzuki	.10
106	Carlos Febles	.10
107	Jose Rosado	.10
108	Mark Quinn	.10
109	Carlos Beltran	.20
110	Dean Palmer	.10
111	Mitch Meluskey	.10
112	Bobby Higginson	.10
113	Brandon Inge	.10
114	Tony Clark	.10
115	Brian Moehler	.10
116	Juan Encarnacion	.10
117	Damion Easley	.10
118	Roger Cedeno	.10
119	Jeff Weaver	.10
120	Matt Lawton	.10
121	Jay Canizaro	.10
122	Eric Milton	.10
123	Corey Koskie	.10
124	Mark Redman	.10
125	Jacque Jones	.10
126	Brad Radke	.10
127	Cristian Guzman	.10
128	Joe Mays	.10
129	Denny Hocking	.10
130	Frank Thomas	.40
131	David Wells	.10
132	Ray Durham	.10
133	Paul Konerko	.10
134	Joe Crede	.10
135	Jim Parque	.10
136	Carlos Lee	.10
137	Magglio Ordonez	.10
138	Sandy Alomar Jr.	.10
139	Chris Singleton	.10
140	Jose Valentin	.10
141	Roger Clemens	1.00
142	Derek Jeter	1.50
143	Orlando Hernandez	.15
144	Tino Martinez	.10
145	Bernie Williams	.40
146	Jorge Posada	.20
147	Mariano Rivera	.20
148	David Justice	.20
149	Paul O'Neill	.10
150	Mike Mussina	.25
151	Christian Parker RC	.10
152	Andy Pettitte	.25
153	Alfonso Soriano	.50
154	Jeff Bagwell	.40
155	Morgan Ensberg RC	.50
156	Daryle Ward	.10
157	Craig Biggio	.20
158	Richard Hidalgo	.10
159	Shane Reynolds	.10
160	Scott Elarton	.10
161	Julio Lugo	.10
162	Moises Alou	.10
163	Lance Berkman	.20
164	Chipper Jones	.75
165	Greg Maddux	1.00
166	Javy Lopez	.15
167	Andruw Jones	.40
168	Rafael Furcal	.25
169	Brian Jordan	.10
170	Wes Helms	.10
171	Tom Glavine	.25
172	B.J. Surhoff	.10
173	John Smoltz	.10
174	Quilvio Veras	.10
175	Rico Brogna	.10
176	Jeromy Burnitz	.10
177	Jeff D'Amico	.10
178	Geoff Jenkins	.20
179	Henry Blanco	.10
180	Mark Loretta	.10
181	Richie Sexson	.25
182	Jimmy Haynes	.10
183	Jeffrey Hammonds	.10
184	Ron Belliard	.10
185	Tyler Houston	.10
186	Mark McGwire	1.00
187	Rick Ankiel	.10
188	Darryl Kile	.10
189	Jim Edmonds	.25
190	Mike Matheny	.10
191	Edgar Renteria	.10
192	Ray Lankford	.10
193	Garrett Stephenson	.10
194	J.D. Drew	.20
195	Fernando Vina	.10
196	Dustin Hermanson	.10
197	Sammy Sosa	1.00
198	Corey Patterson	.25
199	Jon Lieber	.10
200	Kerry Wood	.40
201	Todd Hundley	.10
202	Kevin Tapani	.10
203	Rondell White	.10
204	Eric Young	.10
205	Matt Stairs	.10
206	Bill Mueller	.10
207	Randy Johnson	.50
208	Mark Grace	.25
209	Jay Bell	.10
210	Curt Schilling	.25
211	Erubiel Durazo	.10
212	Luis Gonzalez	.20
213	Steve Finley	.10
214	Matt Williams	.20
215	Reggie Sanders	.10
216	Tony Womack	.10
217	Gary Sheffield	.25
218	Kevin Brown	.15
219	Adrian Beltre	.20
220	Shawn Green	.20
221	Darren Dreifort	.10
222	Chan Ho Park	.10
223	Eric Karros	.15
224	Alex Cora	.10
225	Mark Grudzielanek	.10
226	Andy Ashby	.10
227	Vladimir Guerrero	.75
228	Tony Armas Jr.	.10
229	Fernando Tatis	.10
230	Jose Vidro	.10
231	Javier Vazquez	.10
232	Lee Stevens	.10
233	Milton Bradley	.10
234	Carl Pavano	.10
235	Peter Bergeron	.10
236	Wilton Guerrero	.10
237	Ugueth Urbina	.10
238	Barry Bonds	1.50
239	Livan Hernandez	.10
240	Jeff Kent	.15
241	Pedro Feliz	.10
242	Bobby Estalella	.10
243	J.T. Snow	.10
244	Shawn Estes	.10
245	Robb Nen	.10
246	Rich Aurilia	.10
247	Russ Ortiz	.10
248	Preston Wilson	.10
249	Brad Penny	.10
250	Cliff Floyd	.10
251	A.J. Burnett	.10
252	Mike Lowell	.10
253	Luis Castillo	.10
254	Ryan Dempster	.10
255	Derrek Lee	.10
256	Charles Johnson	.10
257	Pablo Ozuna	.10
258	Antonio Alfonseca	.10
259	Mike Piazza	1.00
260	Robin Ventura	.10
261	Al Leiter	.15
262	Timoniel Perez	.10
263	Edgardo Alfonzo	.10
264	Jay Payton	.10
265	Tsuyoshi Shinjo RC	.75
266	Todd Zeile	.10
267	Armando Benitez	.10
268	Glendon Rusch	.10
269	Rey Ordonez	.10
270	Kevin Appier	.10
271	Tony Gwynn	.50
272	Phil Nevin	.10
273	Mark Kotsay	.10
274	Ryan Klesko	.20
275	Adam Eaton	.10
276	Mike Darr	.10
277	Damian Jackson	.10
278	Woody Williams	.10
279	Chris Gomez	.10
280	Trevor Hoffman	.10
281	Xavier Nady	.15
282	Scott Rolen	.40
283	Bruce Chen	.10
284	Pat Burrell	.30
285	Mike Lieberthal	.10
286	Brandon Duckworth RC	.40
287	Travis Lee	.10
288	Bobby Abreu	.10
289	Jimmy Rollins	.25
290	Robert Person	.10
291	Randy Wolf	.10
292	Jason Kendall	.10
293	Derek Bell	.10
294	Brian Giles	.25
295	Kris Benson	.10
296	John Vander Wal	.10
297	Todd Ritchie	.10
298	Warren Morris	.10
299	Kevin Young	.10
300	Francisco Cordova	.10
301	Aramis Ramirez	.10
302	Ken Griffey Jr.	1.00
303	Pete Harnisch	.10
304	Aaron Boone	.10
305	Sean Casey	.20
306	Jackson Melian RC	.10
307	Rob Bell	.10
308	Barry Larkin	.25
309	Dmitri Young	.10
310	Danny Graves	.10
311	Pokey Reese	.10
312	Leo Estrella	.10
313	Todd Helton	.25
314	Mike Hampton	.15
315	Juan Pierre	.10
316	Brent Mayne	.10
317	Larry Walker	.25
318	Denny Neagle	.10
319	Jeff Cirillo	.10
320	Pedro Astacio	.10
321	Todd Hollandsworth	.10
322	Neifi Perez	.10
323	Ron Gant	.10
324	Todd Walker	.10
325	Alex Rodriguez/CL	.50
326	Ken Griffey Jr./CL	.50
327	Mark McGwire/CL	.50
328	Pedro Martinez/CL	.30
329	Derek Jeter/CL	.75
330	Mike Piazza/CL	.40

Authentic Griffey

NM/M

Inserted 1:288		
AGS	Ken Griffey Jr./Auto.	125.00
AGJ	Ken Griffey Jr./Jsy	15.00
AGC	Ken Griffey Jr./Cap	40.00
AGB	Ken Griffey Jr./Bat	15.00
AGU	Ken Griffey Jr./Uni.	15.00
AGGS	Ken Griffey/Gold Auto./30	250.00
AGGJ	Ken Griffey/Gold Jsy/30	75.00
AGGC	Ken Griffey/Gold Cap/30	75.00
AGGB	Ken Griffey/Gold Bat/30	75.00
CGR	Ken Griffey Jr., Alex Rodriguez/100	35.00
CGS	Ken Griffey Jr., Sammy Sosa/100	35.00
CGT	Ken Griffey Jr., Frank Thomas/100	25.00

Drawing Power

NM/M

Complete Set (10):		10.00
Common Player:		.75
Inserted 1:12		
DP1	Mark McGwire	2.00
DP2	Vladimir Guerrero	1.00
DP3	Manny Ramirez	.75
DP4	Frank Thomas	.75
DP5	Ken Griffey Jr.	1.50
DP6	Alex Rodriguez	2.50
DP7	Mike Piazza	1.50
DP8	Derek Jeter	3.00
DP9	Sammy Sosa	2.00
DP10	Todd Helton	.75

Mantle Pinstripes Exclusive

NM/M

Complete Set (56):	75.00
Common Mantle:	2.00
One Pack/Box	

Mantle Pinstripes Exclusive Memorabilia

NM/M

Print Runs Listed

MMCJ3	Mickey Mantle, Ken Griffey Jr./50	200.00
MMJ3	Mickey Mantle/Jsy/100	125.00

Souvenirs Batting Gloves

NM/M

Common Player:		8.00
Inserted 1:96 H		20.00
BB	Barry Bonds	40.00
TrG	Troy Glaus	10.00
JG	Juan Gonzalez	10.00
KG	Ken Griffey Jr.	20.00
ToG	Tony Gwynn/200	30.00
CJ	Chipper Jones	15.00
JL	Javy Lopez	8.00
GM	Greg Maddux/95	60.00
EM	Edgar Martinez	8.00
FM	Fred McGriff	8.00
RP	Rafael Palmeiro	15.00
CR	Cal Ripken Jr.	50.00
AR	Alex Rodriguez	10.00
IR	Ivan Rodriguez	10.00
SS	Sammy Sosa	20.00
MT	Miguel Tejada	8.00
FT	Frank Thomas	10.00
MV	Mo Vaughn	8.00

Souvenirs Batting Gloves Autographs

NM/M

Production 25 Sets		
KG	Ken Griffey Jr.	150.00
ToG	Tony Gwynn	80.00
CR	Cal Ripken Jr.	250.00
AR	Alex Rodriguez	150.00
IR	Ivan Rodriguez	80.00
SS	Sammy Sosa	250.00
FT	Frank Thomas	80.00

Souvenirs Two-Player Bat Combo

NM/M

Common Combo:		10.00
Inserted 1:144		
TS	Frank Thomas, Sammy Sosa	25.00
RR	Alex Rodriguez, Ivan Rodriguez	25.00
TG	Jim Thome, Ken Griffey Jr.	25.00
GS	Ken Griffey Jr., Sammy Sosa	30.00
WA	Kerry Wood, Rick Ankiel	10.00
3K	Tony Gwynn, Cal Ripken Jr.	40.00
DV	Carlos Delgado, Jose Vidro	10.00
JJ	Andruw Jones, Chipper Jones	20.00
HR	Jose Canseco, Ken Griffey Jr.	20.00
JF	Chipper Jones, Rafael Furcal	15.00
OW	Paul O'Neill, Bernie Williams	10.00
TO	Frank Thomas, Magglio Ordonez	15.00
RM	Alex Rodriguez, Edgar Martinez	20.00
RP	Ivan Rodriguez, Rafael Palmeiro	15.00

Souvenirs Two-Player Bat Autograph

NM/M

Production 25 Sets		
RG	Alex Rodriguez, Ken Griffey Jr.	250.00
SG	Sammy Sosa, Ken Griffey Jr.	300.00
RR	Alex Rodriguez, Ivan Rodriguez	200.00
JG	Chipper Jones, Troy Glaus	125.00
TS	Frank Thomas, Sammy Sosa	275.00
GD	Jason Giambi, Carlos Delgado	75.00
3K	Cal Ripken Jr., Tony Gwynn	300.00
TG	Frank Thomas, Jason Giambi	85.00
HH	Todd Helton, Mike Hampton	60.00

Souvenirs Three Player Bat Combo

No pricing due to scarcity.
Production 25 Sets

Super Tools

NM/M

Complete Set (20):		20.00
Common Player:		.50
Inserted 1:6		
ST1	Ken Griffey Jr.	1.50
ST2	Carlos Delgado	.75
ST3	Alex Rodriguez	2.50
ST4	Troy Glaus	.75
ST5	Jeff Bagwell	.75
ST6	Ichiro Suzuki	3.00
ST7	Derek Jeter	3.00
ST8	Jim Edmonds	.50
ST9	Vladimir Guerrero	1.00
ST10	Jason Giambi	.75
ST11	Todd Helton	.75
ST12	Cal Ripken Jr.	3.00
ST13	Barry Bonds	3.00
ST14	Nomar Garciaparra	2.00
ST15	Randy Johnson	1.00
ST16	Jermaine Dye	.50
ST17	Andruw Jones	.75
ST18	Ivan Rodriguez	.75
ST19	Sammy Sosa	2.00
ST20	Pedro Martinez	1.00

2001 Upper Deck Ovation

NM/M

Complete Set (90):	150.00
Common Player:	.20
Common WP (61-90):	3.00
WP Production 2,000	
Pack (5):	5.00
Box (20):	80.00

1	Troy Glaus	.50
2	Darin Erstad	.40
3	Jason Giambi	.50
4	Tim Hudson	.40
5	Eric Chavez	.30
6	Carlos Delgado	.50
7	David Wells	.20
8	Greg Vaughn	.20
9	Omar Vizquel	.20
10	Jim Thome	.50
11	Roberto Alomar	.40
12	John Olerud	.30
13	Edgar Martinez	.20
14	Cal Ripken Jr.	2.00
15	Alex Rodriguez	1.50
16	Ivan Rodriguez	.50
17	Manny Ramirez	.50
18	Nomar Garciaparra	1.50
19	Pedro Martinez	.75
20	Jermaine Dye	.20
21	Juan Gonzalez	.50
22	Matt Lawton	.20
23	Frank Thomas	.50
24	Magglio Ordonez	.40
25	Bernie Williams	.40
26	Derek Jeter	2.00
27	Roger Clemens	1.50
28	Jeff Bagwell	.50
29	Richard Hidalgo	.20
30	Chipper Jones	1.00
31	Greg Maddux	1.00
32	Andruw Jones	.50
33	Jeromy Burnitz	.20
34	Mark McGwire	1.50
35	Jim Edmonds	.40
36	Sammy Sosa	1.50
37	Kerry Wood	.50
38	Randy Johnson	.75
39	Steve Finley	.20
40	Gary Sheffield	.40
41	Kevin Brown	.40
42	Shawn Green	.40
43	Vladimir Guerrero	.75
44	Jose Vidro	.20
45	Barry Bonds	2.00
46	Jeff Kent	.30
47	Preston Wilson	.20
48	Luis Castillo	.20
49	Mike Piazza	1.00
50	Edgardo Alfonzo	.20
51	Tony Gwynn	.75
52	Ryan Klesko	.30
53	Scott Rolen	.50
54	Bob Abreu	.30
55	Jason Kendall	.20
56	Brian Giles	.30
57	Ken Griffey Jr.	1.00
58	Barry Larkin	.40
59	Todd Helton	.50
60	Mike Hampton	.20
61	Corey Patterson (World Premiere)	3.00
62	Timoniel Perez (World Premiere)	3.00
63	Toby Hall (World Premiere)	3.00
64	Brandon Inge (World Premiere)	3.00
65	Joe Crede (World Premiere)	3.00
66	Xavier Nady (World Premiere)	3.00
67	Adam Pettyjohn RC (World Premiere)	3.00
68	Keith Ginter (World Premiere)	3.00
69	Brian Cole (World Premiere)	3.00
70	Tyler Walker RC (World Premiere)	3.00
71	Juan Uribe RC (World Premiere)	5.00
72	Alex Hernandez (World Premiere)	3.00
73	Leo Estrella (World Premiere)	3.00
74	Joey Nation (World Premiere)	3.00
75	Aubrey Huff (World Premiere)	3.00
76	Ichiro Suzuki RC (World Premiere)	75.00
77	Jay Spurgeon (World Premiere)	3.00
78	Sun-Woo Kim (World Premiere)	3.00
79	Pedro Feliz (World Premiere)	3.00
80	Pablo Ozuna (World Premiere)	3.00
81	Hiram Bocachica (World Premiere)	3.00
82	Brad Wilkerson (World Premiere)	3.00
83	Rocky Biddle (World Premiere)	3.00
84	Aaron McNeal (World Premiere)	3.00
85	Adam Bernero (World Premiere)	3.00
86	Danys Baez (World Premiere)	3.00
87	Dee Brown (World Premiere)	3.00
88	Jimmy Rollins (World Premiere)	4.00
89	Jason Hart (World Premiere)	3.00
90	Ross Gload (World Premiere)	3.00

A Piece of History

NM/M

Common Player: 5.00
Inserted 1:40

RA	Rick Ankiel	5.00
JB	Johnny Bench	15.00
BB	Barry Bonds	30.00
KB	Kevin Brown	5.00
JC	Jose Canseco	8.00
RC	Roger Clemens	15.00
DC	David Cone	5.00
CD	Carlos Delgado	8.00
JD	Joe DiMaggio	100.00
DD	Don Drysdale/SP	25.00
DE	Darin Erstad	5.00
RF	Rollie Fingers/SP	8.00
CF	Carlton Fisk	10.00
RF	Rafael Furcal	5.00
TrG	Troy Glaus	8.00
TG	Tom Glavine	8.00
SG	Shawn Green	5.00
KG	Ken Griffey Jr.	15.00
KGs	Ken Griffey Sr.	5.00
MH	Mike Hampton	5.00
RJ	Randy Johnson	10.00
AJ	Andruw Jones	8.00
CJ	Chipper Jones	10.00
GM	Greg Maddux	15.00
MM	Mickey Mantle	125.00
JP	Jim Palmer	10.00
CR	Cal Ripken Jr.	30.00
BR	Brooks Robinson	15.00
AR	Alex Rodriguez	15.00
IR	Ivan Rodriguez	8.00
NR	Nolan Ryan/SP	120.00
TS	Tom Seaver	10.00
GS	Gary Sheffield	5.00
OS	Ozzie Smith/SP	20.00
SS	Sammy Sosa	15.00
FT	Frank Thomas	8.00
BW	Bernie Williams	8.00
MW	Matt Williams	5.00
EW	Early Wynn	5.00

A Piece of History Autograph

Common Player: Values Undetermined

POH Combo Cards

Production 25 Sets
Values Undetermined

Curtain Calls

NM/M

Complete Set (10): 10.00
Common Player: .50
Inserted 1:7

1	Sammy Sosa	2.00
2	Darin Erstad	.50
3	Barry Bonds	2.50
4	Todd Helton	.75
5	Mike Piazza	1.50
6	Ken Griffey Jr.	1.50
7	Nomar Garciaparra	.75
8	Carlos Delgado	.75
9	Jason Giambi	.75
10	Alex Rodriguez	2.00

ABBREVIATIONS

SP - Short Print

DiMaggio Pinstripes Exclusive

NM/M

Complete Set (56): 60.00
Common DiMaggio: 1.50
One Pack/Box

DiMaggio Pinstripes Memorabilia

NM/M

Print Runs Listed: 150.00
JDB	Joe DiMaggio/Bat/100	75.00
JDCJ	Joe DiMaggio, Mickey Mantle/Jsy/50	300.00
JDJ	Joe DiMaggio/Jsy/100	100.00

Lead Performers

NM/M

Complete Set (11): 15.00
Common Player: 1.00
Inserted 1:12

1	Mark McGwire	3.00
2	Derek Jeter	4.00
3	Alex Rodriguez	3.00
4	Frank Thomas	1.00
5	Sammy Sosa	2.50
6	Mike Piazza	2.00
7	Vladimir Guerrero	1.50
8	Pedro Martinez	1.50
9	Carlos Delgado	1.00
10	Ken Griffey Jr.	2.00
11	Jeff Bagwell	1.00

Superstar Theatre

NM/M

Complete Set (11): 20.00
Common Player: 1.00
Inserted 1:12
1	Nomar Garciaparra	2.50

2	Ken Griffey Jr.	2.00
3	Frank Thomas	1.00
4	Derek Jeter	4.00
5	Mike Piazza	2.00
6	Sammy Sosa	2.50
7	Barry Bonds	4.00
8	Alex Rodriguez	3.00
9	Todd Helton	1.00
10	Mark McGwire	3.00
11	Jason Giambi	1.00

2001 Upper Deck Pros & Prospects

NM/M

Complete Set (141):
Common Player: .15
Common (91-135): 4.00
Production 1,250
Common (136-141): 8.00
Production 500
Pack (5): 6.00
Box (24): 120.00

1	Troy Glaus	.50
2	Darin Erstad	.40
3	Tim Hudson	.40
4	Jason Giambi	.50
5	Jermaine Dye	.15
6	Barry Zito	.40
7	Carlos Delgado	.50
8	Shannon Stewart	.15
9	Raul Mondesi	.15
10	Greg Vaughn	.15
11	Ben Grieve	.15
12	Roberto Alomar	.40
13	Juan Gonzalez	.50
14	Jim Thome	.50
15	C.C. Sabathia	.15
16	Edgar Martinez	.25
17	Kazuhiro Sasaki	.25
18	Aaron Sele	.15
19	John Olerud	.25
20	Cal Ripken Jr.	2.00
21	Rafael Palmeiro	.50
22	Ivan Rodriguez	.50
23	Alex Rodriguez	1.50
24	Manny Ramirez	.50
25	Pedro Martinez	.75
26	Carl Everett	.15
27	Nomar Garciaparra	1.50
28	Neifi Perez	.15
29	Mike Sweeney	.15
30	Bobby Higginson	.15
31	Tony Clark	.15
32	Doug Mientkiewicz	.15
33	Cristian Guzman	.15
34	Brad Radke	.15
35	Magglio Ordonez	.40
36	Carlos Lee	.15
37	Frank Thomas	.50
38	Roger Clemens	1.50
39	Bernie Williams	.40
40	Derek Jeter	2.00
41	Tino Martinez	.25
42	Wade Miller	.15
43	Jeff Bagwell	.50
44	Lance Berkman	.25
45	Richard Hidalgo	.15
46	Greg Maddux	1.00
47	Andruw Jones	.40
48	Chipper Jones	1.00
49	Rafael Furcal	.25
50	Jeromy Burnitz	.15
51	Geoff Jenkins	.25
52	Ben Sheets	.25
53	Mark McGwire	1.50
54	Jim Edmonds	.40
55	J.D. Drew	.25
56	Fred McGriff	.25
57	Sammy Sosa	1.50
58	Kerry Wood	.50
59	Randy Johnson	.75
60	Luis Gonzalez	.25
61	Curt Schilling	.40
62	Kevin Brown	.25
63	Shawn Green	.25
64	Gary Sheffield	.40
65	Vladimir Guerrero	.75
66	Jose Vidro	.15
67	Barry Bonds	2.00
68	Jeff Kent	.25
69	Rich Aurilia	.15
70	Preston Wilson	.15
71	Charles Johnson	.15
72	Cliff Floyd	.15
73	Mike Piazza	1.00
74	Al Leiter	.25
75	Matt Lawton	.15

76	Tony Gwynn	.75
77	Ryan Klesko	.25
78	Phil Nevin	.15
79	Scott Rolen	.50
80	Pat Burrell	.40
81	Jimmy Rollins	.25
82	Jason Kendall	.25
83	Brian Giles	.25
84	Aramis Ramirez	.15
85	Ken Griffey Jr.	1.00
86	Barry Larkin	.40
87	Sean Casey	.25
88	Larry Walker	.25
89	Todd Helton	.50
90	Mike Hampton	.15
91	Juan Cruz RC	4.00
92	Brian Lawrence RC	4.00
93	Brandon Lyon RC	4.00
94	Adrian Hernandez RC	4.00
95	Jose Mieses RC	4.00
96	Juan Uribe RC	4.00
97	Morgan Ensberg RC	12.00
98	Wilson Betemit RC	8.00
99	Ryan Freel RC	4.00
100	Jack Wilson RC	8.00
101	Cesar Crespo RC	4.00
102	Bret Prinz RC	4.00
103	Horacio Ramirez RC	8.00
104	Elpidio Guzman RC	4.00
105	Josh Towers RC	4.00
106	Brandon Duckworth RC	4.00
107	Esix Snead RC	4.00
108	Billy Sylvester RC	4.00
109	Alexis Gomez RC	4.00
110	Johnny Estrada RC	4.00
111	Joe Kennedy RC	4.00
112	Travis Hafner RC	25.00
113	Martin Vargas RC	4.00
114	Jay Gibbons RC	10.00
115	Andres Torres RC	4.00
116	Sean Douglass RC	4.00
117	Juan Diaz RC	4.00
118	Greg Miller RC	4.00
119	Carlos Valderrama RC	4.00
120	William Ortega RC	4.00
121	Josh Fogg RC	4.00
122	Wilken Ruan RC	4.00
123	Kris Keller RC	4.00
124	Erick Almonte RC	4.00
125	Ricardo Rodriguez RC	4.00
126	Grant Balfour RC	4.00
127	Nick Maness RC	4.00
128	Jeremy Owens RC	4.00
129	Doug Nickle RC	4.00
130	Bert Snow RC	4.00
131	Jason Smith RC	4.00
132	Henry Mateo RC	4.00
133	Mike Penney RC	4.00
134	Bud Smith RC	4.00
135	Junior Spivey RC	4.00
136	Ichiro Suzuki RC	90.00
137	Albert Pujols RC	180.00
138	Mark Teixeira RC	100.00
139	Dewon Brazelton RC	8.00
140	Mark Prior RC	30.00
141	Tsuyoshi Shinjo RC	8.00

Bats

NM/M

Common Card: 4.00
Inserted 1:24
Golds: 3-5X
Production 25 Sets
WI	Bernie Williams, Ichiro Suzuki	35.00
RG	Manny Ramirez, Juan Gonzalez	8.00
RP	Ivan Rodriguez, Mike Piazza	15.00
BT	Jeff Bagwell, Frank Thomas	8.00
GBo	Ken Griffey Jr., Barry Bonds	35.00
SG	Sammy Sosa, Luis Gonzalez	15.00
KA	Jeff Kent, Roberto Alomar	4.00
RF	Alex Rodriguez, Rafael Furcal	15.00
PT	Rafael Palmeiro, Jim Thome	10.00
JP	Chipper Jones, Albert Pujols	40.00
GBu	Shawn Green, Jeromy Burnitz	4.00
JL	Andruw Jones, Kenny Lofton	6.00
MJ	Greg Maddux, Randy Johnson	15.00

Legends Bats

NM/M

Common Card: 15.00
Inserted 1:216

	Gold:	3-5X
	Production 25 Sets	
RF	Manny Ramirez, Carlton Fisk	15.00
BY	Jeromy Burnitz, Robin Yount	15.00
WJ	Bernie Williams, Reggie Jackson	15.00
RG	Cal Ripken Jr., Tony Gwynn	50.00

Franchise Building Blocks

NM/M

Complete Set (30): 25.00
Common Player:
Inserted 1:6

F1	Darin Erstad, Elpidio Guzman	.50
F2	Jason Giambi, Jason Hart	1.00
F3	Carlos Delgado, Vernon Wells	.75
F4	Greg Vaughn, Aubrey Huff	.50
F5	Jim Thome, C.C. Sabathia	1.00
F6	Edgar Martinez, Ichiro Suzuki	3.00
F7	Cal Ripken Jr., Josh Towers	3.00
F8	Ivan Rodriguez, Carlos Pena	1.00
F9	Nomar Garciaparra, Dernell Stenson	2.00
F10	Mike Sweeney, Dee Brown	.50
F11	Bobby Higginson, Brandon Inge	.50
F12	Brad Radke, Adam Johnson	.50
F13	Frank Thomas, Joe Crede	1.00
F14	Derek Jeter, Nick Johnson	3.00
F15	Jeff Bagwell, Morgan Ensberg	1.00
F16	Chipper Jones, Wilson Betemit	1.50
F17	Jeromy Burnitz, Ben Sheets	.50
F18	Mark McGwire, Albert Pujols	3.00
F19	Sammy Sosa, Corey Patterson	2.00
F20	Luis Gonzalez, Jack Cust	.50
F21	Kevin Brown, Luke Prokopec	.50
F22	Vladimir Guerrero, Wilken Ruan	.50
F23	Barry Bonds, Carlos Valderrama	3.00
F24	Preston Wilson, Abraham Nunez	.50
F25	Mike Piazza, Alex Escobar	1.50
F26	Tony Gwynn, Xavier Nady	1.00
F27	Scott Rolen, Jimmy Rollins	1.00
F28	Jason Kendall, Jack Wilson	.50
F29	Ken Griffey Jr., Adam Dunn	1.50
F30	Todd Helton, Juan Uribe	1.00

Ichiro World Tour

NM/M

Complete Set (15): 25.00
Common Ichiro:

Inserted 1:12
WT1-15 Ichiro Suzuki 2.00

Specialty Jersey

		NM/M
Common Player:		4.00
Inserted 1:24		
Golds:		3-5X
Production 25 Sets		
RA	Roberto Alomar	6.00
BB	Barry Bonds	25.00
JE	Jim Edmonds	4.00
JG	Juan Gonzalez	6.00
SG	Shawn Green	4.00
TG	Tony Gwynn	10.00
RJ	Randy Johnson	10.00
CR	Cal Ripken Jr.	30.00
AR	Alex Rodriguez	15.00
SR	Scott Rolen	8.00
SS	Sammy Sosa	15.00
I	Ichiro	60.00
JT	Jim Thome	8.00
LW	Larry Walker	4.00

Then & Now Jersey

		NM/M
Common Player:		4.00
Inserted 1:24		
Golds:		3-5X
Production 25 Sets		
RA	Rick Ankiel	4.00
BB	Barry Bonds	30.00
KB	Kevin Brown	6.00
RC	Roger Clemens	20.00
JE	Jim Edmonds	6.00
FG	Freddy Garcia	4.00
JGi	Jason Giambi	8.00
JGo	Juan Gonzalez	8.00
KG	Ken Griffey Jr.	20.00
RJ	Randy Johnson	10.00
GM	Greg Maddux	20.00
PM	Pedro Martinez	10.00
XN	Xavier Nady	4.00
PN	Mike Piazza	15.00
MP	Mike Piazza	15.00
MR	Manny Ramirez	8.00
AR	Alex Rodriguez	15.00
CS	Curt Schilling	6.00
GS	Gary Sheffield	6.00
RV	Robin Ventura	4.00

Then & Now Combo Jersey

		NM/M
Complete Set (1):		
NR	Nolan Ryan	100.00

2001 Upper Deck Prospect Premieres

		NM/M
Complete Set (90):		100.00
Common Player:		.25
Common Auto. SP		
(91-102):		10.00
Auto. Production 1,000		
Pack (4):		12.00
Box (18):		180.00
1	Jeff Mathis RC	1.00
2	Jake Woods RC	.25
3	Dallas McPherson RC	3.00
4	Steven Shell RC	.25

5	Ryan Budde RC	.25
6	Kirk Saarloos RC	.40
7	Ryan Stegall RC	.25
8	Bobby Crosby RC	4.00
9	J.T. Stotts RC	.25
10	Neal Cotts RC	.75
11	Jeremy Bonderman RC	3.00
12	Brandon League RC	.40
13	Tyrell Godwin RC	.25
14	Gabe Gross RC	1.50
15	Chris Neylan RC	.25
16	Michael Rouse RC	.25
17	Macay McBride RC	.25
18	Josh Burrus RC	.25
19	Adam Stern RC	.25
20	Richard Lewis RC	.40
21	Cole Barthel RC	.50
22	Mike Jones RC	.25
23	J.J. Hardy RC	2.50
24	Brad Nelson RC	1.00
25	Justin Pope RC	.25
26	Dan Haren RC	.75
27	Andy Sisco RC	.25
28	Ryan Theriot RC	2.50
29	Ricky Nolasco RC	1.00
30	Jon Switzer RC	.25
31	Justin Wechsler RC	.25
32	Mike Gosling RC	.25
33	Scott Hairston RC	1.00
34	Brian Pilkington RC	.25
35	Kole Strayhorn RC	.25
36	David Taylor RC	.25
37	Donald Levinski RC	.25
38	Mike Hinckley RC	.50
39	Nick Long RC	.25
40	Brad Hennessey RC	.25
41	Noah Lowry RC	2.00
42	Josh Cram RC	.25
43	Jesse Foppert RC	.50
44	Julian Benavidez RC	.25
45	Daniel Denham RC	.25
46	Travis Foley RC	.40
47	Mike Conroy RC	.25
48	Jake Dittler RC	.25
49	Rene Rivera RC	.25
50	John Cole RC	.25
51	Lazaro Abreu RC	.25
52	David Wright RC	30.00
53	Aaron Heilman RC	.40
54	Lenny DiNardo RC	.25
55	Alhaji Turay RC	.40
56	Chris Smith RC	.25
57	Rommie Lewis RC	.25
58	Bryan Bass RC	.25
59	David Crouthers RC	.25
60	Josh Barfield RC	2.00
61	Jake Peavy RC	3.00
62	Ryan Howard RC	50.00
63	Gavin Floyd RC	1.50
64	Mike Floyd RC	.25
65	Stefan Bailie RC	.25
66	Jon DeVries RC	.25
67	Steve Kelly RC	.25
68	Alan Moye RC	.25
69	Justin Gillman RC	.25
70	Jayson Nix RC	1.00
71	John Draper RC	.25
72	Kenny Baugh RC	.25
73	Michael Woods RC	.25
74	Preston Larrison RC	.25
75	Matt Coenen RC	.25
76	Scott Tyler RC	.50
77	Jose Morales RC	.25
78	Corwin Malone RC	.50
79	Dennis Ulacia RC	.40
80	Andy Gonzalez RC	.25
81	Kris Honel RC	1.00
82	Wyatt Allen RC	.25
83	Ryan Wing RC	.25
84	Sean Henn RC	.25
85	John-Ford Griffin RC	.50
86	Bronson Sardinha RC	.75
87	Jon Skaggs RC	.25
88	Shelley Duncan RC	.50
89	Jason Arnold RC	.75
90	Aaron Rifkin RC	.50
91	Colt Griffin RC	15.00
92	J.D. Martin RC	10.00
93	Justin Wayne RC	20.00
94	John VanBenschotten RC	20.00
95	Chris Burke RC	20.00
96	Casey Kotchman RC	40.00
97	Michael Garciaparra RC	10.00
98	Jake Gautreau RC	10.00
99	Jerome Williams RC	20.00

100	Greg Nash RC	10.00
101	Joe Borchard RC	15.00
102	Mark Prior RC	90.00

Heroes of Baseball Bat

			NM/M
Common Player:			4.00
Inserted 1:18			
DB	Don Baylor		4.00
WB	Wade Boggs		8.00
BB	Bill Buckner		4.00
GC	Gary Carter		8.00
DE	Dwight Evans		4.00
SG	Steve Garvey		4.00
KiG	Kirk Gibson		4.00
KeG	Ken Griffey Sr.		4.00
RJ	Reggie Jackson		10.00
DL	Davey Lopes		4.00
FL	Fred Lynn		4.00
BM	Bill Madlock		4.00
TM	Tim McCarver		4.00
JM	Joe Morgan		4.00
MM	Manny Mota		4.00
EM	Eddie Murray		8.00
AO	Al Oliver		4.00
DP	Dave Parker		4.00
TP	Tony Perez		4.00
KP	Kirby Puckett		15.00
OS	Ozzie Smith		10.00
DW	Dave Winfield		8.00

HOB Bat Autograph

Production 25 Sets
Values Undetermined

HOB Dual Combo Jersey

			NM/M
Common Duo:			8.00
Inserted 1:144			
BH	Bryan Bass, J.J. Hardy		10.00
DG	Shelley Duncan, Tyrell Godwin		8.00
GS	Steve Garvey, Reggie Smith		10.00
HB	Aaron Heilman, Jeremy Bonderman		10.00
JJ	Michael Jordan, Michael Jordan		100.00
SG	Jon Switzer, Mike Gosling		8.00
WP	Dave Winfield, Kirby Puckett		20.00

HOB Dual Combo Jersey Autograph

Values Undetermined

HOB Triple Combo Jersey

	NM/M
Common Card:	8.00

Inserted 1:144		
BKH	Bobby Crosby, Michael Garciaparra, Bronson Sardinha	15.00
BBC	Chris Burke, Bryan Bass, Bubba Crosby	10.00
GGH	Jake Gautreau, Tyrell Godwin, Aaron Heilman	8.00
GMS	Colt Griffin, J.D. Martin, Jon Switzer	8.00
GKB	Gabe Gross, Casey Kotchman, Kenny Baugh	10.00
JMD	Michael Jordan, Mickey Mantle, Joe DiMaggio	350.00
JPW	Michael Jordan, Kirby Puckett, Dave Winfield	40.00
MMD	Roger Maris, Mickey Mantle, Joe DiMaggio	700.00
VPJ	John VanBenschotten, Mark Prior, Mike Jones	25.00

HOB Triple Combo Jersey Autograph

Values Undetermined

MJ Grandslam Bat

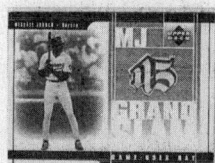

		NM/M
Common MJ:		25.00
MJ1	Michael Jordan	25.00
MJ2	Michael Jordan	25.00
MJ3	Michael Jordan	25.00
MJ4	Michael Jordan	25.00
MJ5	Michael Jordan/ White Sox	40.00

Tribute to 42

		NM/M
Inserted 1:750		
42-B	Jackie Robinson/Bat	40.00
42-J	Jackie Robinson/Jsy	60.00
42-C	Jackie Robinson/ Cut	500.00
42-B	Jackie Robinson/ Bat/42	100.00
42-J	Jackie Robinson/ Jsy/42	100.00

2001 UD Reserve

		NM/M
Complete Set (210):		
Common Player:		.15
Common SP (181-210):		3.00
Production 2,500		
Pack (5):		3.00
Box (24):		60.00
1	Darin Erstad	.25
2	Tim Salmon	.25
3	Bengie Molina	.15
4	Troy Glaus	.50

5	Glenallen Hill	.15
6	Garret Anderson	.25
7	Jason Giambi	.50
8	Johnny Damon	.25
9	Eric Chavez	.25
10	Tim Hudson	.25
11	Miguel Tejada	.25
12	Barry Zito	.25
13	Jose Ortiz	.15
14	Tony Batista	.15
15	Carlos Delgado	.50
16	Shannon Stewart	.15
17	Raul Mondesi	.15
18	Ben Grieve	.15
19	Aubrey Huff	.15
20	Greg Vaughn	.15
21	Fred McGriff	.25
22	Gerald Williams	.15
23	Bartolo Colon	.15
24	Roberto Alomar	.40
25	Jim Thome	.50
26	Omar Vizquel	.25
27	Juan Gonzalez	.50
28	Ellis Burks	.15
29	Edgar Martinez	.25
30	Aaron Sele	.15
31	Jay Buhner	.15
32	Mike Cameron	.15
33	Kazuhiro Sasaki	.15
34	John Olerud	.25
35	Cal Ripken Jr.	2.00
36	Brady Anderson	.15
37	Pat Hentgen	.15
38	Chris Richard	.15
39	Jerry Hairston Jr.	.15
40	Mike Bordick	.15
41	Ivan Rodriguez	.50
42	Rick Helling	.15
43	Rafael Palmeiro	.50
44	Alex Rodriguez	1.50
45	Andres Galarraga	.25
46	Rusty Greer	.15
47	Ruben Mateo	.15
48	Ken Caminiti	.15
49	Nomar Garciaparra	1.50
50	Pedro Martinez	.75
51	Manny Ramirez	.50
52	Carl Everett	.15
53	Dante Bichette	.15
54	Hideo Nomo	.40
55	Mike Sweeney	.15
56	Carlos Beltran	.25
57	Jeff Suppan	.15
58	Jermaine Dye	.15
59	Mark Quinn	.15
60	Joe Randa	.15
61	Bobby Higginson	.15
62	Tony Clark	.15
63	Brian Moehler	.15
64	Dean Palmer	.15
65	Brandon Inge	.15
66	Damion Easley	.15
67	Brad Radke	.15
68	Corey Koskie	.15
69	Cristian Guzman	.15
70	Eric Milton	.15
71	Jacque Jones	.15
72	Matt Lawton	.15
73	Frank Thomas	.50
74	David Wells	.15
75	Magglio Ordonez	.25
76	Paul Konerko	.15
77	Sandy Alomar Jr.	.15
78	Ray Durham	.15
79	Roger Clemens	1.50
80	Bernie Williams	.50
81	Derek Jeter	2.00
82	David Justice	.25
83	Paul O'Neill	.25
84	Mike Mussina	.40
85	Jorge Posada	.40
86	Jeff Bagwell	.50
87	Richard Hidalgo	.15
88	Craig Biggio	.25
89	Scott Elarton	.15
90	Moises Alou	.25
91	Greg Maddux	1.00
92	Rafael Furcal	.25
93	Andruw Jones	.50
94	Tom Glavine	.25
95	Chipper Jones	1.00
96	Javy Lopez	.25
97	Richie Sexson	.40
98	Jeromy Burnitz	.15
99	Jeff D'Amico	.15
100	Jeffrey Hammonds	.15
101	Geoff Jenkins	.25
102	Ben Sheets	.25
103	Mark McGwire	1.50
104	Rick Ankiel	.15
105	Darryl Kile	.15
106	Edgar Renteria	.15
107	Jim Edmonds	.25
108	J.D. Drew	.25
109	Sammy Sosa	1.50
110	Corey Patterson	.25
111	Kerry Wood	.50
112	Todd Hundley	.15
113	Rondell White	.15
114	Matt Stairs	.15
115	Randy Johnson	.75
116	Mark Grace	.40
117	Steve Finley	.25
118	Luis Gonzalez	.25
119	Matt Williams	.25
120	Curt Schilling	.40
121	Gary Sheffield	.40
122	Kevin Brown	.25

123	Shawn Green	.25
124	Eric Karros	.15
125	Chan Ho Park	.25
126	Adrian Beltre	.15
127	Vladimir Guerrero	.75
128	Fernando Tatis	.15
129	Lee Stevens	.15
130	Jose Vidro	.15
131	Peter Bergeron	.15
132	Michael Barrett	.15
133	Jeff Kent	.25
134	Russ Ortiz	.15
135	Barry Bonds	2.00
136	J.T. Snow	.15
137	Livan Hernandez	.15
138	Rich Aurilia	.15
139	Preston Wilson	.15
140	Mike Lowell	.15
141	Ryan Dempster	.15
142	Charles Johnson	.15
143	Matt Clement	.15
144	Luis Castillo	.15
145	Mike Piazza	1.00
146	Al Leiter	.15
147	Robin Ventura	.25
148	Jay Payton	.15
149	Todd Zeile	.15
150	Edgardo Alfonzo	.15
151	Tony Gwynn	.75
152	Ryan Klesko	.15
153	Phil Nevin	.15
154	Mark Kotsay	.15
155	Trevor Hoffman	.15
156	Damian Jackson	.15
157	Scott Rolen	.50
158	Mike Lieberthal	.15
159	Bruce Chen	.15
160	Bobby Abreu	.25
161	Pat Burrell	.40
162	Travis Lee	.15
163	Jason Kendall	.15
164	Derek Bell	.15
165	Kris Benson	.15
166	Kevin Young	.15
167	Brian Giles	.25
168	Pat Meares	.15
169	Sean Casey	.25
170	Pokey Reese	.15
171	Pete Harnisch	.15
172	Barry Larkin	.25
173	Ken Griffey Jr.	1.00
174	Dmitri Young	.15
175	Mike Hampton	.15
176	Todd Helton	.50
177	Jeff Cirillo	.15
178	Denny Neagle	.15
179	Larry Walker	.25
180	Todd Hollandsworth	.15
181	Ichiro Suzuki (Rookie Reserve)	35.00
182	Wilson Betemit RC (Rookie Reserve)	6.00
183	Adrian Hernandez RC (Rookie Reserve)	3.00
184	Travis Hafner RC (Rookie Reserve)	15.00
185	Sean Douglass RC (Rookie Reserve)	3.00
186	Juan Diaz RC (Rookie Reserve)	3.00
187	Horacio Ramirez RC (Rookie Reserve)	5.00
188	Morgan Ensberg RC (Rookie Reserve)	10.00
189	Brandon Duckworth RC (Rookie Reserve)	3.00
190	Jack Wilson RC (Rookie Reserve)	8.00
191	Erick Almonte RC (Rookie Reserve)	3.00
192	Ricardo Rodriguez RC (Rookie Reserve)	3.00
193	Elpidio Guzman RC (Rookie Reserve)	3.00
194	Juan Uribe RC (Rookie Reserve)	5.00
195	Ryan Freel RC (Rookie Reserve)	4.00
196	Christian Parker RC (Rookie Reserve)	3.00
197	Jackson Melian RC (Rookie Reserve)	3.00
198	Jose Mieses RC (Rookie Reserve)	3.00
199	Andres Torres RC (Rookie Reserve)	3.00
200	Jason Smith RC (Rookie Reserve)	3.00
201	Johnny Estrada RC (Rookie Reserve)	6.00
202	Cesar Crespo RC (Rookie Reserve)	3.00
203	Carlos Valderrama RC (Rookie Reserve)	3.00
204	Albert Pujols RC (Rookie Reserve)	100.00
205	Wilken Ruan RC (Rookie Reserve)	3.00
206	Josh Fogg RC (Rookie Reserve)	3.00
207	Bert Snow RC (Rookie Reserve)	3.00
208	Brian Lawrence RC (Rookie Reserve)	5.00
209	Esix Snead RC (Rookie Reserve)	3.00
210	Tsuyoshi Shinjo RC (Rookie Reserve)	4.00

Big Game Reserve

		NM/M
Complete Set (10):		15.00
Common Player:		1.00
Inserted 1:24		
BG1	Alex Rodriguez	3.00
BG2	Ken Griffey Jr.	2.00
BG3	Mark McGwire	3.00
BG4	Derek Jeter	4.00
BG5	Sammy Sosa	2.50
BG6	Pedro Martinez	1.50
BG7	Jason Giambi	1.00
BG8	Todd Helton	1.00
BG9	Carlos Delgado	1.00
BG10	Mike Piazza	2.00

G-U Reserve Base/Ball Duo

		NM/M
Inserted 1:240		
JR	Derek Jeter, Alex Rodriguez	50.00
JP	Derek Jeter, Mike Piazza	60.00
MP	Mark McGwire, Mike Piazza	100.00
MJ	Mark McGwire, Derek Jeter	100.00
RM	Alex Rodriguez, Mark McGwire	100.00
CR	Roger Clemens, Alex Rodriguez	40.00
ST	Sammy Sosa, Frank Thomas	40.00
GD	Vladimir Guerrero, Carlos Delgado	20.00
BH	Barry Bonds, Todd Helton	35.00
MG	Mark McGwire, Ken Griffey Jr.	40.00
GS	Ken Griffey Jr., Sammy Sosa	20.00
GJ	Ken Griffey Jr., Derek Jeter	35.00
JN	Chipper Jones, Nomar Garciaparra	20.00
NJ	Nomar Garciaparra, Derek Jeter	35.00
GR	Nomar Garciaparra, Alex Rodriguez	30.00

G-U Reserve Base/Ball Trio

		NM/M
Inserted 1:480		
JRG	Derek Jeter, Alex Rodriguez, Nomar Garciaparra	50.00
SGM	Sammy Sosa, Ken Griffey Jr., Mark McGwire	65.00
PRS	Mike Piazza, Alex Rodriguez, Sammy Sosa	40.00
GSG	Ken Griffey Jr., Sammy Sosa, Vladimir Guerrero	30.00
THM	Frank Thomas, Todd Helton, Mark McGwire	65.00
CMJ	Roger Clemens, Pedro Martinez, Derek Jeter	45.00
BSH	Barry Bonds, Gary Sheffield, Todd Helton	40.00

GPJ	Vladimir Guerrero, Mike Piazza, Chipper Jones	30.00
MJR	Mark McGwire, Derek Jeter, Alex Rodriguez	75.00
JGS	Derek Jeter, Ken Griffey Jr., Sammy Sosa	45.00

G-U Reserve Base/Ball Quad

		NM/M
Production 50 Sets		
SGRM	Sammy Sosa, Ken Griffey Jr., Alex Rodriguez, Mark McGwire	175.00
GPJG	Vladimir Guerrero, Mike Piazza, Chipper Jones, Nomar Garciaparra	65.00
THMJ	Frank Thomas, Todd Helton, Mark McGwire, Derek Jeter	90.00
GBJE	Ken Griffey Jr., Barry Bonds, Andruw Jones, Jim Edmonds	75.00
PMJR	Mike Piazza, Mark McGwire, Derek Jeter, Alex Rodriguez	150.00

Jerseys Duo

		NM/M
Common Duo:		15.00
Inserted 1:240		
HG	Tim Hudson, Jason Giambi	25.00
BK	Barry Bonds, Jeff Kent	40.00
JJ	Andruw Jones, Chipper Jones	25.00
GE	Troy Glaus, Darin Erstad	15.00
WO	David Wells, Magglio Ordonez	15.00
WE	Bernie Williams, Jim Edmonds	15.00
DG	Carlos Delgado, Jason Giambi	20.00
GK	Jason Giambi, Jeff Kent	20.00
JW	Randy Johnson, David Wells	25.00
JG	Chipper Jones, Troy Glaus	25.00
SB	Gary Sheffield, Barry Bonds	40.00
HE	Todd Helton, Darin Erstad	20.00
RB	Alex Rodriguez, Tony Batista	25.00
GW	Brian Giles, Bernie Williams	15.00
SG	Sammy Sosa, Troy Glaus	30.00

Jerseys Trio

		NM/M
Common Trio:		25.00
Inserted 1:480		
GHD	Jason Giambi, Todd Helton, Carlos Delgado	30.00
RSS	Alex Rodriguez, Sammy Sosa, Gary Sheffield	50.00
WEJ	Bernie Williams, Jim Edmonds, Andruw Jones	25.00
HJW	Tim Hudson, Randy Johnson, David Wells	30.00
SOD	Sammy Sosa, Magglio Ordonez, Carlos Delgado	40.00
GGR	Jason Giambi, Troy Glaus, Alex Rodriguez	40.00
BWD	Tony Batista, Bernie Williams, Carlos Delgado	25.00
BSH	Barry Bonds, Gary Sheffield, Todd Helton	50.00
WSH	David Wells, Sammy Sosa, Todd Helton	40.00
EKE	Darin Erstad, Jeff Kent, Jim Edmonds	25.00

Jerseys Quad

		NM/M
Common Quad:		25.00

		NM/M
Production 50 Sets		
DRGS	Carlos Delgado, Alex Rodriguez, Troy Glaus, Sammy Sosa	40.00
GWBG	Jason Giambi, Bernie Williams, Barry Bonds, Brian Giles	75.00
HKEJ	Todd Helton, Jeff Kent, Jim Edmonds, Chipper Jones	40.00
HKEJ	Gary Sheffield, Magglio Ordonez, Darin Erstad, Tony Batista	25.00
JRSB	Andruw Jones, Alex Rodriguez, Sammy Sosa, Barry Bonds	100.00

The New Order

		NM/M
Complete Set (10):		15.00
Common Player:		.75
Inserted 1:24		
NO1	Vladimir Guerrero	1.50
NO2	Andruw Jones	1.00
NO3	Corey Patterson	.75
NO4	Derek Jeter	4.00
NO5	Alex Rodriguez	3.00
NO6	Pat Burrell	.75
NO7	Ichiro Suzuki	5.00
NO8	Barry Zito	.75
NO9	Rafael Furcal	.75
NO10	Troy Glaus	1.00

UD Royalty

		NM/M
Complete Set (10):		15.00
Common Player:		1.00
Inserted 1:24		
R1	Ken Griffey Jr.	2.00
R2	Derek Jeter	4.00
R3	Alex Rodriguez	3.00
R4	Sammy Sosa	2.50
R5	Mark McGwire	3.00
R6	Mike Piazza	2.00
R7	Vladimir Guerrero	1.50
R8	Chipper Jones	2.00
R9	Frank Thomas	1.00
R10	Nomar Garciaparra	3.00

2001 Upper Deck Rookie Update

		NM/M
Common Player:		.25
Common Rookie:		
Pack (4):		17.00
Box (18):		260.00
Sweet Spot		
Common SP (121-150):		3.00
Production 1,500		
91	Garret Anderson	.50
92	Jermaine Dye	.25

Mark Grace

93	Shannon Stewart	.25
94	Ben Grieve	.25
95	Juan Gonzalez	.75
96	Bret Boone	.50
97	Tony Batista	.25
98	Rafael Palmeiro	1.00
99	Carl Everett	.25
100	Mike Sweeney	.25
101	Tony Clark	.25
102	Doug Mientkiewicz	.25
103	Jose Canseco	.50
104	Mike Mussina	.75
105	Lance Berkman	.50
106	Andruw Jones	.75
107	Geoff Jenkins	.40
108	Matt Morris	.25
109	Fred McGriff	.40
110	Luis Gonzalez	.50
111	Kevin Brown	.25
112	Tony Armas Jr.	.25
113	John Vander Wal	.25
114	Cliff Floyd	.25
115	Matt Lawton	.25
116	Phil Nevin	.25
117	Pat Burrell	.50
118	Aramis Ramirez	.25
119	Sean Casey	.40
120	Larry Walker	.25
121	Albert Pujols RC	200.00
122	Johnny Estrada RC	8.00
123	Wilson Betemit RC	3.00
124	Adrian Hernandez RC	3.00
125	Morgan Ensberg RC	15.00
126	Horacio Ramirez RC	6.00
127	Josh Towers RC	6.00
128	Juan Uribe RC	5.00
129	Wilken Ruan RC	3.00
130	Andres Torres RC	3.00
131	Brian Lawrence RC	4.00
132	Ryan Freel RC	4.00
133	Brandon Duckworth RC	4.00
134	Juan Diaz RC	3.00
135	Rafael Soriano RC	6.00
136	Ricardo Rodriguez RC	3.00
137	Bud Smith RC	3.00
138	Mark Teixeira RC	70.00
139	Mark Prior RC	25.00
140	Jackson Melian RC	3.00
141	Dewon Brazelton RC	3.00
142	Greg Miller RC	3.00
143	Billy Sylvester RC	3.00
144	Elpidio Guzman RC	3.00
145	Jack Wilson RC	8.00
146	Jose Mieses RC	3.00
147	Brandon Lyon RC	3.00
148	Tsuyoshi Shinjo RC	4.00
149	Juan Cruz RC	3.00
150	Jay Gibbons RC	8.00

SPx

Common (181-205):		3.00
Production 1,500		
Cards (206-210) Autographed		
151	Garret Anderson	.50
152	Jermaine Dye	.25
153	Shannon Stewart	.25
154	Toby Hall	.25
155	C.C. Sabathia	.40
156	Bret Boone	.50
157	Tony Batista	.25
158	Gabe Kapler	.25
159	Carl Everett	.25
160	Mike Sweeney	.25
161	Dean Palmer	.25
162	Doug Mientkiewicz	.25
163	Carlos Lee	.25
164	Mike Mussina	.75
165	Lance Berkman	.25
166	Ken Caminiti	.25
167	Ben Sheets	.40
168	Matt Morris	.25
169	Fred McGriff	.40
170	Curt Schilling	.50
171	Paul LoDuca	.25
172	Javier Vazquez	.25
173	Rich Aurilia	.25
174	A.J. Burnett	.25
175	Al Leiter	.40
176	Mark Kotsay	.25
177	Jimmy Rollins	.40
178	Aramis Ramirez	.25
179	Aaron Boone	.25
180	Jeff Cirillo	.25
181	Johnny Estrada RC	3.00
182	Dave Williams RC	3.00
183	Donaldo Mendez RC	3.00
184	Junior Spivey RC	8.00

185	Jay Gibbons RC	10.00
186	Kyle Lohse RC	8.00
187	Willie Harris RC	3.00
188	Juan Cruz RC	5.00
189	Joe Kennedy RC	3.00
190	Duaner Sanchez RC	3.00
191	Jorge Julio RC	5.00
192	Cesar Crespo RC	3.00
193	Casey Fossum RC	5.00
194	Brian Roberts RC	15.00
195	Troy Mattes RC	3.00
196	Rob Mackowiak RC	3.00
197	Tsuyoshi Shinjo RC	8.00
198	Nick Punto RC	3.00
199	Wilmy Caceres RC	3.00
200	Jeremy Affeldt RC	3.00
201	Bret Prinz RC	3.00
202	Delvin James RC	3.00
203	Luis Pineda RC	3.00
204	Matt White RC	3.00
205	Brandon Knight RC	3.00
206	Albert Pujols RC	900.00
207	Mark Teixeira RC	240.00
208	Mark Prior RC	125.00
209	Dewon Brazelton RC	10.00
210	Bud Smith RC	8.00

SP Authentic

Common (211-240):		4.00
Production 1,500		
181	Garrett Anderson	.50
182	Jermaine Dye	.25
183	Shannon Stewart	.25
184	Ben Grieve	.25
185	Ellis Burks	.25
186	John Olerud	.50
187	Tony Batista	.25
188	Ruben Sierra	.25
189	Carl Everett	.25
190	Neifi Perez	.25
191	Tony Clark	.25
192	Doug Mientkiewicz	.25
193	Carlos Lee	.25
194	Jorge Posada	.50
195	Lance Berkman	.50
196	Ken Caminiti	.25
197	Ben Sheets	.25
198	Matt Morris	.25
199	Fred McGriff	.40
200	Mark Grace	.50
201	Paul LoDuca	.25
202	Tony Armas, Jr.	.25
203	Andres Galarraga	.40
204	Cliff Floyd	.25
205	Matt Lawton	.25
206	Ryan Klesko	.40
207	Jimmy Rollins	.25
208	Aramis Ramirez	.25
209	Aaron Boone	.25
210	Jose Ortiz	.25
211	Mark Prior RC	60.00
212	Mark Teixeira RC	125.00
213	Bud Smith RC	4.00
214	Wilmy Caceres RC	4.00
215	Dave Williams RC	4.00
216	Delvin James RC	4.00
217	Endy Chavez RC	4.00
218	Doug Nickle RC	4.00
219	Bret Prinz RC	4.00
220	Troy Mattes RC	4.00
221	Duaner Sanchez RC	4.00
222	Dewon Brazelton RC	4.00
223	Brian Bowles RC	4.00
224	Donaldo Mendez RC	4.00
225	Jorge Julio RC	6.00
226	Matt White RC	4.00
227	Casey Fossum RC	6.00
228	Mike Rivera RC	4.00
229	Joe Kennedy RC	4.00
230	Kyle Lohse RC	6.00
231	Juan Cruz RC	6.00
232	Jeremy Affeldt RC	4.00
233	Brandon Lyon RC	4.00
234	Brian Roberts RC	15.00
235	Willie Harris RC	4.00
236	Pedro Santana RC	4.00
237	Rafael Soriano RC	6.00
238	Steve Green RC	4.00
239	Junior Spivey RC	6.00
240	Rob Mackowiak RC	4.00

Ichiro ROY

		NM/M
Complete Set (51):		35.00
Common Ichiro:		1.00
1-50	Ichiro Suzuki	1.00
51	Checklist (Ichiro Suzuki)	1.00

Ichiro ROY Game Jersey

	NM/M
Numbers 1-12 Production	
100	50.00
Numbers 13-17 Production	
50	75.00
Numbers 18-19 Production	
25	150.00
J-I1-12 Ichiro Suzuki	50.00
J-I13-17 Ichiro Suzuki	75.00
J-I18-19 Ichiro Suzuki	150.00

Ichiro ROY Game-Used Bat

	NM/M
Numbers 1-12 Production	
100	50.00
Numbers 13-17 Production	
50	75.00
Numbers 18-19 Production	
25	150.00
B-I1-12 Ichiro Suzuki	50.00
B-I13-17 Ichiro Suzuki	75.00
B-I18-19 Ichiro Suzuki	150.00

SP Chirography

		NM/M
Common Autograph:		15.00
Production 250		
Silver:		.75-1.5X
Production 100		
Gold:		No Pricing
Production 25 sets		
LB	Lance Berkman/100	10.00
KG	Ken Griffey Jr./250	90.00
TG	Tony Gwynn/250	30.00
TG	Tony Gwynn/100	40.00
MS	Doug Mientkiewicz/100	15.00
JP	Jorge Posada/250	25.00
JP	Jorge Posada/100	30.00
CR	Cal Ripken Jr.	100.00
MS	Mike Sweeney/100	15.00

SP Chirography - Ichiro

Available only as a redemption in UD Rookie Update. Three versions were produced, an unnumbered autographed card, a Silver parallel autograph numbered to 100 and a Gold autograph parallel numbered to 25.

	NM/M
Ichiro (Unnumbered)	300.00
Ichiro/Silver/100	500.00

USA Touch of Gold

		NM/M
Common Autograph:		8.00
Production 500 Sets		
BA	Brent Abernathy	8.00
KU	Kurt Ainsworth	10.00
PB	Pat Borders	8.00
SB	Sean Burroughs	12.00
JC	John Cotton	8.00
TD	Gookie Dawkins	8.00
AE	Adam Everett	8.00
RF	Ryan Franklin	8.00
CG	Chris George	8.00
SH	Shane Heams	8.00
MJ	Marcus Jensen	8.00
MK	Mike Kinkade	8.00
RK	Rick Krivda	8.00
DM	Doug Mientkiewicz	12.00
MN	Mike Neill	8.00
RO	Roy Oswalt	20.00
JR	Jon Rauch	8.00

AS	Anthony Sanders	8.00
BSe	Bobby Seay	8.00
BSh	Ben Sheets	12.00
BW	Brad Wilkerson	8.00
TW	Todd Williams	8.00
EY	Ernie Young	8.00
TY	Tim Young	8.00

Winning Materials 2-Player

	NM/M
Common Card:	10.00
Inserted 1:15	
BB-LG	Barry Bonds, Luis Gonzalez	25.00
JG-BB	Jason Giambi, Barry Bonds	25.00
IR-AR	Ivan Rodriguez, Alex Rodriguez	25.00
AP-JE	Albert Pujols, Jim Edmonds	35.00
GS-SG	Gary Sheffield, Shawn Green	15.00
MP-EA	Mike Piazza, Edgardo Alfonzo	20.00
LW-TH	Larry Walker, Todd Helton	15.00
MR-JG	Manny Ramirez, Juan Gonzalez	15.00
TG-CR	Tony Gwynn, Cal Ripken Jr.	40.00
SR-BA	Scott Rolen, Bobby Abreu	15.00
JB-CB	Jeff Bagwell, Craig Biggio	20.00
KG-SC	Ken Griffey Jr., Sean Casey	25.00
EM-JM	Eric Milton, Joe Mays	10.00
HN-MY	Hideo Nomo, Masato Yoshii	20.00
TS-HN	Tsuyoshi Shinjo, Hideo Nomo	15.00
CS-RJ	Curt Schilling, Randy Johnson	20.00
AS-KS	Aaron Sele, Kazuhiro Sasaki	10.00
PM-RJ	Pedro Martinez, Randy Johnson	15.00
BW-MR	Bernie Williams, Mariano Rivera	15.00
TG-X2	Tony Gwynn	15.00
CR-X2	Cal Ripken Jr.	40.00
JB-RY	Jeromy Burnitz, Robin Yount	15.00
CR-EM	Cal Ripken Jr., Eddie Murray	30.00
TG-DW	Tony Gwynn, Dave Winfield	15.00
FT-MO	Frank Thomas, Magglio Ordonez	15.00
PM-GM	Pedro Martinez, Greg Maddux	20.00
BW-RJ	Bernie Williams, Reggie Jackson	20.00
SS-EB	Sammy Sosa, Ernie Banks	30.00
CP-FV	Chan Ho Park, Fernando Valenzuela	10.00

Winning Materials 3-Player Jersey

	NM/M
Common Card:	10.00
Inserted 1:15	
KBA	Jeff Kent, Barry Bonds, Rich Aurilia	25.00
JAF	Chipper Jones, Andruw Jones, Rafael Furcal	15.00
GZH	Jason Giambi, Barry Zito, Tim Hudson	15.00
SKB	Gary Sheffield, Eric Karros, Kevin Brown	15.00
SSM	Aaron Sele, Ichiro Suzuki, Edgar Martinez	40.00
HDG	Todd Helton, Carlos Delgado, Jason Giambi	15.00
VRF	Omar Vizquel, Alex Rodriguez, Rafael Furcal	25.00
SYN	Kazuhiro Sasaki, Masato Yoshii, Hideo Nomo	20.00

BTD	Jeff Bagwell, Frank Thomas, Carlos Delgado	15.00
BGG	Barry Bonds, Luis Gonzalez, Ken Griffey Jr.	30.00
RPK	Ivan Rodriguez, Mike Piazza, Jason Kendall	20.00
PPV	Jay Payton, Mike Piazza, Robin Ventura	15.00
CHN	Roger Clemens, Tim Hudson, Hideo Nomo	20.00
PWO	Andy Pettitte, Bernie Williams, Paul O'Neill	20.00
TDK	Frank Thomas, Ray Durham, Paul Konerko	15.00
SJC	Curt Schilling, Randy Johnson, Roger Clemens	20.00
DEA	J.D. Drew, Jim Edmonds, Bobby Abreu	15.00
DOP	Carlos Delgado, Magglio Ordonez, Albert Pujols	35.00
TGA	Jim Thome, Juan Gonzalez, Roberto Alomar	15.00
GWS	Luis Gonzalez, Matt Williams, Curt Schilling	20.00
MGJ	Greg Maddux, Tom Glavine, Andruw Jones	20.00

2001 Upper Deck Sweet Spot

	NM/M
Complete Set (90):	300.00
Common Player:	.25
Common Sweet Beginnings:	5.00
(61-90) Production 1,000	
Pack (4):	15.00
Box (18):	250.00
1	Troy Glaus	.75
2	Darin Erstad	.50
3	Jason Giambi	.75
4	Tim Hudson	.50
5	Ben Grieve	.25
6	Carlos Delgado	.75
7	David Wells	.25
8	Greg Vaughn	.25
9	Roberto Alomar	.75
10	Jim Thome	.75
11	John Olerud	.50
12	Edgar Martinez	.40
13	Cal Ripken Jr.	3.00
14	Albert Belle	.25
15	Ivan Rodriguez	.75
16	Alex Rodriguez	2.50
17	Pedro Martinez	1.00
18	Nomar Garciaparra	2.00
19	Manny Ramirez	.75
20	Jermaine Dye	.25
21	Juan Gonzalez	.75
22	Dean Palmer	.25
23	Matt Lawton	.25
24	Eric Milton	.25
25	Frank Thomas	.75
26	Magglio Ordonez	.50
27	Derek Jeter	3.00
28	Bernie Williams	.75
29	Roger Clemens	2.00
30	Jeff Bagwell	.75
31	Richard Hidalgo	.25
32	Chipper Jones	1.50
33	Greg Maddux	1.50
34	Richie Sexson	.50
35	Jeromy Burnitz	.25
36	Mark McGwire	2.50
37	Jim Edmonds	.50
38	Sammy Sosa	2.00
39	Randy Johnson	1.00
40	Steve Finley	.25
41	Gary Sheffield	.50
42	Shawn Green	.50
43	Vladimir Guerrero	1.00
44	Jose Vidro	.25
45	Barry Bonds	3.00
46	Jeff Kent	.40
47	Preston Wilson	.25
48	Luis Castillo	.25
49	Mike Piazza	1.50
50	Edgardo Alfonzo	.25
51	Tony Gwynn	1.00

52	Ryan Klesko	.40
53	Scott Rolen	.75
54	Bob Abreu	.40
55	Jason Kendall	.40
56	Brian Giles	.40
57	Ken Griffey Jr.	1.50
58	Barry Larkin	.50
59	Todd Helton	.75
60	Mike Hampton	.25
61	Corey Patterson (Sweet Beginnings)	5.00
62	Ichiro Suzuki **RC** (Sweet Beginnings)	160.00
63	Jason Grilli (Sweet Beginnings)	5.00
64	Brian Cole (Sweet Beginnings)	5.00
65	Juan Pierre (Sweet Beginnings)	5.00
66	Matt Ginter (Sweet Beginnings)	5.00
67	Jimmy Rollins (Sweet Beginnings)	8.00
68	Jason Smith **RC** (Sweet Beginnings)	5.00
69	Israel Alcantara (Sweet Beginnings)	5.00
70	Adam Pettyjohn **RC** (Sweet Beginnings)	5.00
71	Luke Prokopec (Sweet Beginnings)	5.00
72	Barry Zito (Sweet Beginnings)	5.00
73	Keith Ginter (Sweet Beginnings)	5.00
74	Sun-Woo Kim (Sweet Beginnings)	5.00
75	Ross Gload (Sweet Beginnings)	5.00
76	Matt Wise (Sweet Beginnings)	5.00
77	Aubrey Huff (Sweet Beginnings)	5.00
78	Ryan Franklin (Sweet Beginnings)	5.00
79	Brandon Inge (Sweet Beginnings)	5.00
80	Wes Helms (Sweet Beginnings)	5.00
81	Junior Spivey **RC** (Sweet Beginnings)	8.00
82	Ryan Vogelsong (Sweet Beginnings)	5.00
83	John Parrish (Sweet Beginnings)	5.00
84	Joe Crede (Sweet Beginnings)	5.00
85	Damian Rolls (Sweet Beginnings)	5.00
86	Esix Snead **RC** (Sweet Beginnings)	5.00
87	Rocky Biddle (Sweet Beginnings)	5.00
88	Brady Clark (Sweet Beginnings)	5.00
89	Timoniel Perez (Sweet Beginnings)	5.00
90	Jay Spurgeon (Sweet Beginnings)	5.00

Big League Challenge

	NM/M
Complete Set (20):	20.00
Common Player:	.50
Inserted 1:6	
1	Mark McGwire	2.50
2	Richard Hidalgo	.50
3	Alex Rodriguez	2.50
4	Shawn Green	.75
5	Frank Thomas	1.00
6	Chipper Jones	1.50
7	Rafael Palmeiro	1.00
8	Troy Glaus	1.50
9	Mike Piazza	1.50
10	Andruw Jones	1.00
11	Todd Helton	1.00
12	Jason Giambi	1.00
13	Sammy Sosa	2.00
14	Carlos Delgado	1.00
15	Barry Bonds	3.00
16	Jose Canseco	.75
17	Jim Edmonds	.75
18	Manny Ramirez	1.00
19	Gary Sheffield	.75
20	Nomar Garciaparra	2.00

DiMaggio Pinstripes Exclusive

	NM/M
Complete Set (56):	60.00
Common DiMaggio:	1.50
Production: One Pack/Box	

DiMaggio Pinstripes Memorablila

	NM/M
Print Runs Listed:	150.00
JDB	Joe DiMaggio/ Bat/100	80.00
JDCJ	Joe DiMaggio, Lou Gehrig/Jsy/50	600.00
JDJ	Joe DiMaggio/ Jsy/100	100.00

Game Jerseys

	NM/M
Common Player:	8.00
Inserted 1:18	
BB	Barry Bonds	25.00
JC	Jose Canseco	8.00
RC	Roger Clemens	20.00
RC	Roberto Clemente	125.00
JD	Joe DiMaggio	80.00
KG	Ken Griffey Jr.	20.00
RJ	Randy Johnson	10.00
AJ	Andruw Jones	10.00
CJ	Chipper Jones	10.00
MM	Mickey Mantle	150.00
WM	Willie Mays	100.00
SM	Stan Musial	65.00
CR	Cal Ripken Jr.	40.00
AR	Alex Rodriguez	20.00
IR	Ivan Rodriguez	8.00
NR	Nolan Ryan	65.00
DS	Duke Snider	10.00
SS	Sammy Sosa	20.00
IS	Ichiro Suzuki	100.00
FT	Frank Thomas	10.00

S.S. Game-Used Bases Tier 1

	NM/M
Common Card:	5.00
BH	Barry Bonds, Todd Helton	25.00
MG	Mark McGwire, Ken Griffey Jr.	60.00
JG	Chipper Jones, Nomar Garciaparra	20.00
GD	Vladimir Guerrero, Carlos Delgado	8.00
ST	Sammy Sosa, Frank Thomas	20.00
SR	Gary Sheffield, Alex Rodriguez	15.00

GR	Tony Gwynn, Ivan Rodriguez	10.00
PJ	Mike Piazza, Derek Jeter	30.00
HG	Jeffrey Hammonds, Troy Glaus	5.00
JGi	Randy Johnson, Jason Giambi	8.00
BD	Jeff Bagwell, Jermaine Dye	8.00
RR	Scott Rolen, Cal Ripken Jr.	25.00
GR	Ken Griffey Jr., Manny Ramirez	15.00
RJ	Alex Rodriguez, Derek Jeter	40.00
MP	Mark McGwire, Timoniel Perez	35.00
CP	Roger Clemens, Mike Piazza	20.00

S.S. Game-Used Bases Tier 2

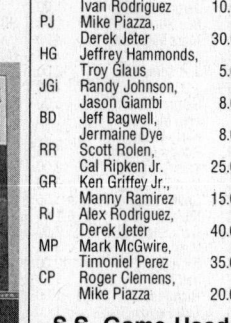

	NM/M
Common Card:	20.00
Production 50 Sets	
BHK	Barry Bonds, Todd Helton, Jeff Kent	75.00
MGE	Mark McGwire, Ken Griffey Jr., Bobby Edmonds	120.00
JGJ	Chipper Jones, Nomar Garciaparra, Andruw Jones	60.00
GDM	Vladimir Guerrero, Carlos Delgado, Raul Mondesi	20.00
STO	Sammy Sosa, Frank Thomas, Magglio Ordonez	50.00
SRM	Gary Sheffield, Alex Rodriguez, Edgar Martinez	50.00
GRP	Tony Gwynn, Ivan Rodriguez, Rafael Palmeiro	40.00
PJW	Mike Piazza, Derek Jeter, Bernie Williams	75.00
HGH	Jeffrey Hammonds, Troy Glaus, Todd Helton	20.00
JGC	Randy Johnson, Jason Giambi, Eric Chavez	25.00
BDH	Jeff Bagwell, Jermaine Dye, Richard Hidalgo	20.00
RRB	Scott Rolen, Cal Ripken Jr., Albert Belle	75.00
GRT	Ken Griffey Jr., Manny Ramirez, Jim Thome	50.00

Game-Used Bat

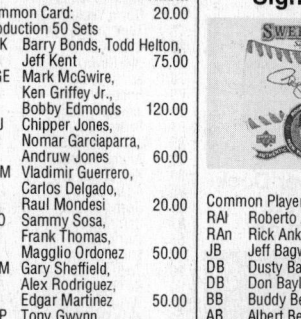

	NM/M
Common Player:	5.00
Inserted 1:18	
HA	Hank Aaron	60.00
RA	Rick Ankiel	5.00
BB	Barry Bonds	25.00
JC	Jose Canseco	8.00
TC	Ty Cobb	175.00
JD	Joe DiMaggio	80.00
KG	Ken Griffey Jr.	15.00
RJ	Reggie Jackson	10.00
AJ	Andruw Jones	10.00
MM	Mickey Mantle	140.00
WM	Willie Mays	75.00
SM	Stan Musial	50.00
CR	Cal Ripken Jr.	40.00
AR	Alex Rodriguez	20.00
IR	Ivan Rodriguez	8.00
NR	Nolan Ryan	65.00
GS	Gary Sheffield	8.00
SS	Sammy Sosa	20.00
FT	Frank Thomas	10.00

Players Party

	NM/M
Complete Set (10):	10.00
Common Player:	.75
Inserted 1:12	
1	Derek Jeter	3.00
2	Randy Johnson	1.00
3	Frank Thomas	1.00
4	Nomar Garciaparra	2.00
5	Ken Griffey Jr.	1.50
6	Carlos Delgado	.75
7	Mike Piazza	1.50

ABBREVIATIONS

SP - Short Print

8	Barry Bonds	3.00
9	Sammy Sosa	2.00
10	Pedro Martinez	1.00

Signatures

	NM/M
Common Player:	20.00
RAl	Roberto Alomar	40.00
RAn	Rick Ankiel	20.00
JB	Jeff Bagwell/SP/214	120.00
DB	Dusty Baker	20.00
DB	Don Baylor	20.00
BB	Buddy Bell	20.00
AB	Albert Belle	25.00
MB	Milton Bradley	20.00
PB	Pat Burrell	30.00
JC	Jose Canseco	60.00
CB	Chris Chambliss	20.00
RC	Roger Clemens	140.00
CD	Carlos Delgado	30.00
JD	Joe DiMaggio/ SP/150	600.00
DE	Darin Erstad	25.00
RF	Rafael Furcal	25.00
JG	Joe Garagiola	50.00
JG	Jason Giambi	50.00
TGl	Troy Glaus	40.00
SG	Shawn Green	20.00
KG	Ken Griffey/SP/100	350.00
TGw	Tony Gwynn	110.00
AH	Art Howe	20.00
TH	Tim Hudson	30.00
DJ	Davey Johnson	20.00
RJ	Randy Johnson	85.00
AJ	Andruw Jones	50.00
CJ	Chipper Jones	80.00
ML	Mike Lamb	20.00
TL	Tony LaRussa	20.00
DL	Davey Lopes	20.00
BM	Bill Madlock	20.00
MM	Mickey Mantle/ SP/10	3,500
WM	Willie Mays	200.00
HM	Hal McRae	20.00
SM	Stan Musial	120.00
PO	Paul O'Neill	50.00
LP	Lou Piniella	25.00
JR	Jim Rice	25.00
AR	Alex Rodriguez/ SP/154	200.00
IR	Ivan Rodriguez/ SP/150	100.00
BR	Babe Ruth/SP/1 (8/03 auction)	12,000
NR	Nolan Ryan	200.00
GS	Gary Sheffield	30.00
SS	Sammy Sosa/ SP/148	250.00
FT	Frank Thomas	60.00
AT	Alan Trammell	25.00
BV	Bobby Valentine	20.00
RV	Robin Ventura	20.00
MW	Matt Williams	25.00

Texas Rangers Team Set

This set was produced for sale by the team, retailing for about $15 at souvenir outlets. Standard-size cards have game-action photos on front. Backs repeat part of the photo and have personal data, stats and logos. Card numbers carry a "TR" prefix.

		NM/M
Complete Set (20):		15.00
Common Player:		.50
1	Alex Rodriguez	3.00
2	Rafael Palmeiro	1.50
3	Ivan Rodriguez	1.50
4	Andres Galarraga	.50
5	Ken Caminiti	.50
6	Ruben Mateo	.50
7	Rusty Greer	.50
8	Rick Helling	.50
9	Gabe Kapler	.50
10	Kenny Rogers	.50
11	Randy Velarde	.50
12	Doug Davis	.50
13	Bill Haselman	.50
14	Tim Crabtree	.50
15	Darren Oliver	.50
16	Jeff Zimmerman	.50
17	Ricky Ledee	.50
18	Mark Petkovsek	.50
19	Frank Catalanotto	.50
20	Nolan Ryan	5.00

2001 Upper Deck Ultimate Collection

	NM/M
Common Player:	1.00
Common SP (91-100):	5.00
Production 1,000	
Common SP (101-110):	5.00
Production 750	
Common (111-120):	20.00
Production 250	
Pack (4):	160.00
Box (4):	575.00
1	Troy Glaus	2.50
2	Darin Erstad	1.50
3	Jason Giambi	3.00
4	Barry Zito	2.00
5	Tim Hudson	2.00
6	Miguel Tejada	1.50
7	Carlos Delgado	2.50
8	Shannon Stewart	1.00
9	Greg Vaughn	1.00
10	Toby Hall	1.00
11	Roberto Alomar	2.00
12	Juan Gonzalez	2.50
13	Jim Thome	3.00
14	Edgar Martinez	1.50
15	Freddy Garcia	1.00
16	Bret Boone	1.50
17	Kazuhiro Sasaki	1.50
18	Cal Ripken Jr.	10.00
19	Tim Raines Jr.	1.00
20	Alex Rodriguez	8.00
21	Ivan Rodriguez	2.50
22	Rafael Palmeiro	2.50
23	Pedro Martinez	3.00
24	Nomar Garciaparra	6.00
25	Manny Ramirez	2.50
26	Hideo Nomo	2.00
27	Mike Sweeney	1.00
28	Carlos Beltran	1.50
29	Tony Clark	1.00
30	Dean Palmer	1.00
31	Doug Mientkiewicz	1.00
32	Cristian Guzman	1.00
33	Corey Koskie	1.00
34	Frank Thomas	3.00
35	Magglio Ordonez	1.50
36	Jose Canseco	2.00
37	Roger Clemens	6.00
38	Derek Jeter	10.00
39	Bernie Williams	2.00
40	Mike Mussina	2.00
41	Tino Martinez	1.00
42	Jeff Bagwell	2.50
43	Lance Berkman	2.00
44	Roy Oswalt	1.50
45	Chipper Jones	5.00
46	Greg Maddux	5.00
47	Andruw Jones	2.50
48	Tom Glavine	2.00
49	Richie Sexson	2.00
50	Jeromy Burnitz	1.00
51	Ben Sheets	1.00
52	Mark McGwire	8.00
53	Matt Morris	1.00
54	Jim Edmonds	2.00
55	J.D. Drew	1.50
56	Sammy Sosa	6.00
57	Fred McGriff	1.00
58	Kerry Wood	2.50
59	Randy Johnson	3.00
60	Luis Gonzalez	2.00
61	Curt Schilling	2.00
62	Shawn Green	1.50
63	Kevin Brown	1.50
64	Gary Sheffield	2.00
65	Vladimir Guerrero	3.00
66	Barry Bonds	10.00
67	Jeff Kent	1.50
68	Rich Aurilia	1.00
69	Cliff Floyd	1.00
70	Charles Johnson	1.00
71	Josh Beckett	2.00
72	Mike Piazza	5.00
73	Edgardo Alfonzo	1.00
74	Robin Ventura	1.00
75	Tony Gwynn	2.50
76	Ryan Klesko	1.50
77	Phil Nevin	1.00
78	Scott Rolen	2.50
79	Bobby Abreu	1.00
80	Jimmy Rollins	1.50
81	Brian Giles	1.50
82	Jason Kendall	1.00
83	Aramis Ramirez	1.00
84	Ken Griffey Jr.	6.00
85	Adam Dunn	1.50
86	Sean Casey	1.50
87	Barry Larkin	2.00
88	Larry Walker	1.50
89	Mike Hampton	1.50
90	Todd Helton	2.50
91	Ken Harvey	5.00
92	William Ortega RC	5.00
93	Juan Diaz RC	5.00
94	Greg Miller RC	5.00
95	Brandon Berger RC	5.00
96	Brandon Lyon RC	5.00
97	Jay Gibbons RC	20.00
98	Rob Mackowiak RC	5.00
99	Erick Almonte RC	5.00
100	Jason Middlebrook RC	5.00
101	Johnny Estrada RC	10.00
102	Juan Uribe RC	10.00
103	Travis Hafner RC	30.00
104	Morgan Ensberg RC	30.00
105	Mike Rivera RC	5.00
106	Josh Towers RC	5.00
107	Adrian Hernandez RC	5.00
108	Rafael Soriano RC	10.00
109	Jackson Melian RC	5.00
110	Wilken Ruan RC	5.00
111	Albert Pujols RC	375.00
112	Tsuyoshi Shinjo RC	15.00
113	Brandon Duckworth RC	20.00
114	Juan Cruz RC	20.00
115	Dewon Brazelton RC	20.00
116	Mark Prior/Auto. RC	240.00
117	Mark Teixeira/Auto. RC	450.00
118	Wilson Betemit/Auto. RC	25.00
119	Bud Smith/Auto. RC	25.00
120	Ichiro Suzuki/Auto. RC	750.00

Ichiro

	NM/M
Pricing not available for all Ichiro's.	
B-IA	Ichiro Suzuki/Bat Away	65.00
B-IH	Ichiro Suzuki/Bat Home	65.00
B-IS	Ichiro Suzuki/Bat/250	80.00
B-IG	Ichiro Suzuki/Bat/200	90.00
SB-I	Ichiro Suzuki/Bat/Auto./50	675.00
J-IA	Ichiro Suzuki/Jsy/Away	50.00
J-IH	Ichiro Suzuki/Jsy/Home	50.00
J-IS	Ichiro Suzuki/Jsy/250	75.00
J-IG	Ichiro Suzuki/Jsy/200	85.00
SJ-I	Ichiro Suzuki/Jsy/Auto./50	675.00
UB-I	Ichiro Suzuki/Base	25.00
UB-IC	Ichiro Suzuki/Base/150	80.00
UB-IS	Ichiro Suzuki/Base/50	100.00
BB-I	Ichiro Suzuki/Ball	60.00
BB-IC	Ichiro Suzuki/Ball/150	85.00
BB-IS	Ichiro Suzuki/Ball/50	100.00
SBB-I	Ichiro Suzuki/Ball/Auto./25	675.00
C-I	Ichiro Suzuki/Glv/75	180.00
BG-I	Ichiro Suzuki/Bat/Glv/75	180.00

Game Jersey

	NM/M
Common Player:	10.00
Inserted 1:2	
RA	Roberto Alomar	20.00
JB	Jeff Bagwell	20.00
BB	Barry Bonds	50.00
JC	Jose Canseco	15.00
RC	Roger Clemens	40.00
CD	Carlos Delgado	10.00
DE	Darin Erstad	10.00
JaG	Jason Giambi	20.00
JG	Juan Gonzalez	20.00
LG	Luis Gonzalez	10.00
SG	Shawn Green	10.00
KG	Ken Griffey Jr.	40.00
TG	Tony Gwynn	20.00
TH	Todd Helton	15.00
RJ	Randy Johnson	15.00
AJ	Andruw Jones	15.00
CJ	Chipper Jones	25.00
GM	Greg Maddux	40.00
MO	Magglio Ordonez	10.00
MP	Mike Piazza	30.00
AP	Albert Pujols	75.00
CR	Cal Ripken Jr.	75.00
AR	Alex Rodriguez	40.00
IR	Ivan Rodriguez	15.00
SR	Scott Rolen	10.00
GS	Gary Sheffield	10.00
SS	Sammy Sosa	40.00
FT	Frank Thomas	15.00
LW	Larry Walker	10.00
BW	Bernie Williams	10.00

Magic Numbers

	NM/M
Common Player:	10.00
Production 150	
Coppers #'d to 24 not priced.	
Silvers #'d to 20 not priced.	
Golds #'d to 15 not priced.	
RA	Roberto Alomar	20.00
JB	Jeff Bagwell	50.00
BB	Barry Bonds	50.00
JC	Jose Canseco	15.00
RC	Roger Clemens	50.00
CD	Carlos Delgado	15.00
DE	Darin Erstad	15.00
JaG	Jason Giambi	20.00
JG	Juan Gonzalez	20.00
LG	Luis Gonzalez	10.00
SG	Shawn Green	10.00
KG	Ken Griffey Jr.	40.00
TG	Tony Gwynn	20.00
TH	Todd Helton	15.00
RJ	Randy Johnson	15.00
AJ	Andruw Jones	15.00
CJ	Chipper Jones	25.00
GM	Greg Maddux	40.00
MO	Magglio Ordonez	10.00
MP	Mike Piazza	30.00
AP	Albert Pujols	75.00
CR	Cal Ripken Jr.	90.00
AR	Alex Rodriguez	40.00
IR	Ivan Rodriguez	15.00
SR	Scott Rolen	10.00
GS	Gary Sheffield	10.00
SS	Sammy Sosa	40.00
FT	Frank Thomas	15.00
LW	Larry Walker	10.00
BW	Bernie Williams	10.00

Ultimate Signatures

	NM/M
Common Autograph:	20.00

BB-IS	Ichiro Suzuki/Ball/50	100.00
SBB-I	Ichiro Suzuki/Ball/Auto./25	675.00
C-I	Ichiro Suzuki/Glv/75	180.00
BG-I	Ichiro Suzuki/Bat/Glv/75	180.00

Inserted 1:4		
Silvers #'d to 24 not priced.		
Golds #'d to 15 not priced.		
RA	Roberto Alomar	40.00
EB	Ernie Banks	50.00
BaB	Barry Bonds	200.00
RC	Roger Clemens	100.00
CD	Carlos Delgado	25.00
CF	Carlton Fisk	40.00
JaG	Jason Giambi	25.00
TGI	Tom Glavine	40.00
LG	Luis Gonzalez	25.00
KG	Ken Griffey Jr.	100.00
TG	Tony Gwynn	60.00
RK	Ryan Klesko	20.00
SK	Sandy Koufax	275.00
EM	Edgar Martinez	30.00
TP	Tony Perez	20.00
KP	Kirby Puckett	50.00
CR	Cal Ripken Jr.	125.00
AR	Alex Rodriguez	80.00
IR	Ivan Rodriguez	50.00
TS	Tom Seaver	40.00
GS	Gary Sheffield	30.00
DS	Duke Snider	35.00
SS	Sammy Sosa	120.00
FT	Frank Thomas	50.00
JT	Jim Thome	40.00
RY	Robin Yount	60.00

Victory

		NM/M
Complete Set (660):		50.00
Common Player:		.15
1	Troy Glaus	.50
2	Scott Spiezio	.15
3	Gary DiSarcina	.15
4	Darin Erstad	.20
5	Tim Salmon	.20
6	Troy Percival	.15
7	Ramon Ortiz	.15
8	Orlando Palmeiro	.15
9	Tim Belcher	.15
10	Mo Vaughn	.20
11	Bengie Molina	.15
12	Benji Gil	.15
13	Scott Schoeneweis	.15
14	Garret Anderson	.15
15	Matt Wise	.15
16	Adam Kennedy	.15
17	Jarrod Washburn	.15
18	Darin Erstad, Troy Percival	.15
19	Jason Giambi	.20
20	Tim Hudson	.20
21	Ramon Hernandez	.15
22	Eric Chavez	.15
23	Gil Heredia	.15
24	Jason Isringhausen	.15
25	Jeremy Giambi	.15
26	Miguel Tejada	.15
27	Barry Zito	.50
28	Terrence Long	.15
29	Ryan Christenson	.15
30	Mark Mulder	.15
31	Olmedo Saenz	.15
32	Adam Piatt	.15
33	Ben Grieve	.15
34	Omar Olivares	.15
35	John Jaha	.15
36	Jason Giambi, Tim Hudson	.15
37	Carlos Delgado	.40
38	Esteban Loaiza	.15
39	Brad Fullmer	.15
40	David Wells	.15
41	Chris Woodward	.15
42	Billy Koch	.15
43	Shannon Stewart	.15
44	Chris Carpenter	.15
45	Steve Parris	.15
46	Darrin Fletcher	.15
47	Joey Hamilton	.15
48	Jose Cruz Jr.	.15
49	Vernon Wells	.15
50	Raul Mondesi	.15
51	Kelvim Escobar	.15
52	Tony Batista	.15
53	Alex Gonzalez	.15
54	Carlos Delgado, David Wells	.20
55	Greg Vaughn	.15
56	Albie Lopez	.15
57	Randy Winn	.15
58	Ryan Rupe	.15
59	Steve Cox	.15
60	Vinny Castilla	.15

61	Jose Guillen	.15
62	Wilson Alvarez	.15
63	Bryan Rekar	.15
64	Gerald Williams	.15
65	Esteban Yan	.15
66	Felix Martinez	.15
67	Fred McGriff	.20
68	John Flaherty	.15
69	Jason Tyner	.15
70	Russ Johnson	.15
71	Roberto Hernandez	.15
72	Greg Vaughn, Albie Lopez	.15
73	Eddie Taubensee	.15
74	Bob Wickman	.15
75	Ellis Burks	.15
76	Kenny Lofton	.20
77	Einar Diaz	.15
78	Travis Fryman	.15
79	Omar Vizquel	.15
80	Jason Bere	.15
81	Bartolo Colon	.15
82	Jim Thome	.20
83	Roberto Alomar	.40
84	Chuck Finley	.15
85	Steve Woodard	.15
86	Russ Branyan	.15
87	Dave Burba	.15
88	Jaret Wright	.15
89	Jacob Cruz	.15
90	Steve Karsay	.15
91	Manny Ramirez, Bartolo Colon	.20
92	Raul Ibanez	.15
93	Freddy Garcia	.15
94	Edgar Martinez	.15
95	Jay Buhner	.15
96	Jamie Moyer	.15
97	John Olerud	.20
98	Aaron Sele	.15
99	Kazuhiro Sasaki	.20
100	Mike Cameron	.15
101	John Halama	.15
102	David Bell	.15
103	Gil Meche	.15
104	Carlos Guillen	.15
105	Mark McLemore	.15
106	Stan Javier	.15
107	Al Martin	.15
108	Dan Wilson	.15
109	Alex Rodriguez, Kazuhiro Sasaki	.50
110	Cal Ripken Jr.	1.50
111	Delino DeShields	.15
112	Sidney Ponson	.15
113	Albert Belle	.15
114	Jose Mercedes	.15
115	Scott Erickson	.15
116	Jerry Hairston Jr.	.15
117	Brook Fordyce	.15
118	Luis Matos	.15
119	Eugene Kingsale	.15
120	Jeff Conine	.15
121	Chris Richard	.15
122	Fernando Lunar	.15
123	John Parrish	.15
124	Brady Anderson	.15
125	Ryan Kohlmeier	.15
126	Melvin Mora	.15
127	Albert Belle, Jose Mercedes	.15
128	Ivan Rodriguez	.50
129	Justin Thompson	.15
130	Kenny Rogers	.15
131	Rafael Palmeiro	.30
132	Rusty Greer	.15
133	Gabe Kapler	.15
134	John Wetteland	.15
135	Mike Lamb	.15
136	Doug Davis	.15
137	Ruben Mateo	.15
138	Alex Rodriguez	1.25
139	Chad Curtis	.15
140	Rick Helling	.15
141	Ryan Glynn	.15
142	Andres Galarraga	.25
143	Ricky Ledee	.15
144	Frank Catalanotto	.15
145	Rafael Palmeiro, Rick Helling	.20
146	Pedro Martinez	.60
147	Wilton Veras	.15
148	Manny Ramirez	.50
149	Rolando Arrojo	.15
150	Nomar Garciaparra	1.00
151	Darren Lewis	.15
152	Troy O'Leary	.15
153	Tomokazu Ohka	.15
154	Carl Everett	.15
155	Jason Varitek	.15
156	Frank Castillo	.15
157	Pete Schourek	.15
158	Jose Offerman	.15
159	Derek Lowe	.15
160	John Valentin	.15
161	Dante Bichette	.15
162	Trot Nixon	.15
163	Nomar Garciaparra, Pedro Martinez	.25
164	Jermaine Dye	.15
165	Dave McCarty	.15
166	Jose Rosado	.15
167	Mike Sweeney	.15
168	Rey Sanchez	.15
169	Jeff Suppan	.15
170	Chad Durbin	.15
171	Carlos Beltran	.15
172	Brian Meadows	.15

173	Todd Dunwoody	.15
174	Johnny Damon	.15
175	Blake Stein	.15
176	Carlos Febles	.15
177	Joe Randa	.15
178	Makoto Suzuki	.15
179	Mark Quinn	.15
180	Gregg Zaun	.15
181	Mike Sweeney, Jeff Suppan	.15
182	Juan Gonzalez	.50
183	Dean Palmer	.15
184	Wendell Magee	.15
185	Todd Jones	.15
186	Bobby Higginson	.15
187	Brian Moehler	.15
188	Juan Encarnacion	.15
189	Tony Clark	.15
190	Rich Becker	.15
191	Roger Cedeno	.15
192	Mitch Meluskey	.15
193	Shane Halter	.15
194	Jeff Weaver	.15
195	Deivi Cruz	.15
196	Damion Easley	.15
197	Robert Fick	.15
198	Matt Anderson	.15
199	Bobby Higginson, Brian Moehler	.15
200	Brad Radke	.15
201	Mark Redman	.15
202	Corey Koskie	.15
203	Matt Lawton	.15
204	Eric Milton	.15
205	Chad Moeller	.15
206	Jacque Jones	.15
207	Matt Kinney	.15
208	Jay Canizaro	.15
209	Torii Hunter	.15
210	Ron Coomer	.15
211	Chad Allen	.15
212	Denny Hocking	.15
213	Cristian Guzman	.15
214	LaTroy Hawkins	.15
215	Joe Mays	.15
216	David Ortiz	.15
217	Matt Lawton, Eric Milton	.15
218	Frank Thomas	.60
219	Jose Valentin	.15
220	Mike Sirotka	.15
221	Kip Wells	.15
222	Magglio Ordonez	.25
223	Herbert Perry	.15
224	James Baldwin	.15
225	Jon Garland	.15
226	Sandy Alomar	.15
227	Chris Singleton	.15
228	Keith Foulke	.15
229	Paul Konerko	.15
230	Jim Parque	.15
231	Greg Norton	.15
232	Carlos Lee	.15
233	Cal Eldred	.15
234	Ray Durham	.15
235	Jeff Abbott	.15
236	Frank Thomas, Mike Sirotka	.25
237	Derek Jeter	1.50
238	Glenallen Hill	.15
239	Roger Clemens	1.00
240	Bernie Williams	.40
241	David Justice	.25
242	Luis Sojo	.15
243	Orlando Hernandez	.20
244	Mike Mussina	.20
245	Jorge Posada	.20
246	Andy Pettitte	.20
247	Paul O'Neill	.20
248	Scott Brosius	.15
249	Alfonso Soriano	.50
250	Mariano Rivera	.20
251	Chuck Knoblauch	.15
252	Ramiro Mendoza	.15
253	Tino Martinez	.15
254	David Cone	.15
255	Derek Jeter, Andy Pettitte	.40
256	Jeff Bagwell	.50
257	Lance Berkman	.20
258	Craig Biggio	.20
259	Scott Elarton	.15
260	Bill Spiers	.15
261	Moises Alou	.15
262	Billy Wagner	.15
263	Shane Reynolds	.15
264	Tony Eusebio	.15
265	Julio Lugo	.15
266	Jose Lima	.15
267	Octavio Dotel	.15
268	Brad Ausmus	.15
269	Daryle Ward	.15
270	Glen Barker	.15
271	Wade Miller	.15
272	Richard Hidalgo	.25
273	Chris Truby	.15
274	Jeff Bagwell, Scott Elarton	.15
275	Greg Maddux	.75
276	Chipper Jones	.75
277	Tom Glavine	.25
278	Brian Jordan	.15
279	Andruw Jones	.40
280	Kevin Millwood	.15
281	Rico Brogna	.15
282	George Lombard	.15
283	Reggie Sanders	.15
284	John Rocker	.15

#	Player	Price
285	Rafael Furcal	.25
286	John Smoltz	.15
287	Javy Lopez	.15
288	Walt Weiss	.15
289	Quilvio Veras	.15
290	Eddie Perez	.15
291	B.J. Surhoff	.15
292	Chipper Jones, Tom Glavine	.25
293	Jeromy Burnitz	.15
294	Charlie Hayes	.15
295	Jeff D'Amico	.15
296	Jose Hernandez	.15
297	Richie Sexson	.15
298	Tyler Houston	.15
299	Paul Rigdon	.15
300	Jamey Wright	.15
301	Mark Loretta	.15
302	Geoff Jenkins	.20
303	Luis Lopez	.15
304	John Snyder	.15
305	Henry Blanco	.15
306	Curtis Leskanic	.15
307	Ron Belliard	.15
308	Jimmy Haynes	.15
309	Marquis Grissom	.15
310	Geoff Jenkins, Jeff D'Amico	.15
311	Mark McGwire	1.00
312	Rick Ankiel	.20
313	Dave Veres	.15
314	Carlos Hernandez	.15
315	Jim Edmonds	.20
316	Andy Benes	.15
317	Garrett Stephenson	.15
318	Ray Lankford	.15
319	Dustin Hermanson	.15
320	Steve Kline	.15
321	Mike Matheny	.15
322	Edgar Renteria	.15
323	J.D. Drew	.15
324	Craig Paquette	.15
325	Darryl Kile	.15
326	Fernando Vina	.15
327	Eric Davis	.15
328	Placido Polanco	.15
329	Jim Edmonds, Darryl Kile	.15
330	Sammy Sosa	1.00
331	Rick Aguilera	.15
332	Willie Greene	.15
333	Kerry Wood	.20
334	Todd Hundley	.15
335	Rondell White	.20
336	Julio Zuleta	.15
337	Jon Lieber	.15
338	Joe Girardi	.15
339	Damon Buford	.15
340	Kevin Tapani	.15
341	Ricky Gutierrez	.15
342	Bill Mueller	.15
343	Ruben Quevedo	.15
344	Eric Young	.15
345	Gary Matthews Jr.	.15
346	Daniel Garibay	.15
347	Sammy Sosa, Jon Lieber	.30
348	Randy Johnson	.50
349	Matt Williams	.15
350	Kelly Stinnett	.15
351	Brian Anderson	.15
352	Steve Finley	.15
353	Curt Schilling	.15
354	Erubiel Durazo	.15
355	Todd Stottlemyre	.15
356	Mark Grace	.15
357	Luis Gonzalez	.20
358	Danny Bautista	.15
359	Matt Mantei	.15
360	Tony Womack	.15
361	Armando Reynoso	.15
362	Greg Colbrunn	.15
363	Jay Bell	.15
364	Byung-Hyun Kim	.15
365	Luis Gonzalez, Randy Johnson	.20
366	Gary Sheffield	.20
367	Eric Karros	.15
368	Jeff Shaw	.15
369	Jim Leyritz	.15
370	Kevin Brown	.20
371	Alex Cora	.15
372	Andy Ashby	.15
373	Eric Gagne	.15
374	Chan Ho Park	.15
375	Shawn Green	.20
376	Kevin Elster	.15
377	Mark Grudzielanek	.15
378	Darren Dreifort	.15
379	Dave Hansen	.15
380	Bruce Aven	.15
381	Adrian Beltre	.20
382	Tom Goodwin	.15
383	Gary Sheffield, Chan Ho Park	.15
384	Vladimir Guerrero	.60
385	Ugueth Urbina	.15
386	Michael Barrett	.15
387	Geoff Blum	.15
388	Fernando Tatis	.15
389	Carl Pavano	.15
390	Jose Vidro	.15
391	Orlando Cabrera	.15
392	Terry Jones	.15
393	Mike Thurman	.15
394	Lee Stevens	.15
395	Tony Armas Jr.	.15
396	Wilton Guerrero	.15
397	Peter Bergeron	.15
398	Milton Bradley	.15
399	Javier Vazquez	.15
400	Fernando Seguignol	.15
401	Vladimir Guerrero, Dustin Hermanson	.25
402	Barry Bonds	.60
403	Russ Ortiz	.15
404	Calvin Murray	.15
405	Armando Rios	.15
406	Livan Hernandez	.15
407	Jeff Kent	.20
408	Bobby Estalella	.15
409	Felipe Crespo	.15
410	Shawn Estes	.15
411	J.T. Snow	.15
412	Marvin Benard	.15
413	Joe Nathan	.15
414	Robb Nen	.15
415	Shawon Dunston	.15
416	Mark Gardner	.15
417	Kirk Rueter	.15
418	Rich Aurilia	.15
419	Doug Mirabelli	.15
420	Russ Davis	.15
421	Barry Bonds, Livan Hernandez	.30
422	Cliff Floyd	.15
423	Luis Castillo	.15
424	Antonio Alfonseca	.15
425	Preston Wilson	.15
426	Ryan Dempster	.15
427	Jesus Sanchez	.15
428	Derrek Lee	.15
429	Brad Penny	.15
430	Mark Kotsay	.15
431	Alex Fernandez	.15
432	Mike Lowell	.15
433	Chuck Smith	.15
434	Alex Gonzalez	.15
435	Dave Berg	.15
436	A.J. Burnett	.15
437	Charles Johnson	.15
438	Reid Cornelius	.15
439	Mike Redmond	.15
440	Preston Wilson, Ryan Dempster	.15
441	Mike Piazza	.75
442	Kevin Appier	.15
443	Jay Payton	.15
444	Steve Trachsel	.15
445	Al Leiter	.20
446	Joe McEwing	.15
447	Armando Benitez	.15
448	Edgardo Alfonzo	.15
449	Glendon Rusch	.15
450	Mike Bordick	.15
451	Lenny Harris	.15
452	Matt Franco	.15
453	Darryl Hamilton	.15
454	Bobby J. Jones	.15
455	Robin Ventura	.15
456	Todd Zeile	.15
457	John Franco	.15
458	Mike Piazza, Al Leiter	.40
459	Tony Gwynn	.75
460	John Mabry	.15
461	Trevor Hoffman	.15
462	Phil Nevin	.15
463	Ryan Klesko	.15
464	Wiki Gonzalez	.15
465	Matt Clement	.15
466	Alex Arias	.15
467	Woody Williams	.15
468	Ruben Rivera	.15
469	Sterling Hitchcock	.15
470	Ben Davis	.15
471	Bubba Trammell	.15
472	Jay Witasick	.15
473	Eric Owens	.15
474	Damian Jackson	.15
475	Adam Eaton	.15
476	Mike Darr	.15
477	Phil Nevin, Trevor Hoffman	.15
478	Scott Rolen	.25
479	Robert Person	.15
480	Mike Lieberthal	.15
481	Reggie Taylor	.15
482	Paul Byrd	.15
483	Bruce Chen	.15
484	Pat Burrell	.25
485	Kevin Jordan	.15
486	Bobby Abreu	.15
487	Randy Wolf	.15
488	Kevin Sefcik	.15
489	Brian Hunter	.15
490	Doug Glanville	.15
491	Kent Bottenfield	.15
492	Travis Lee	.15
493	Jeff Brantley	.15
494	Omar Daal	.15
495	Bobby Abreu, Randy Wolf	.15
496	Jason Kendall	.15
497	Adrian Brown	.15
498	Warren Morris	.15
499	Brian Giles	.20
500	Jimmy Anderson	.15
501	John Vander Wal	.15
502	Mike Williams	.15
503	Aramis Ramirez	.15
504	Pat Meares	.15
505	Jason Schmidt	.15
506	Todd Ritchie	.15
507	Abraham Nunez	.15
508	Jose Silva	.15
509	Francisco Cordova	.15
510	Kevin Young	.15
511	Derek Bell	.15
512	Kris Benson	.15
513	Brian Giles, Jose Silva	.15
514	Ken Griffey Jr.	1.00
515	Scott Williamson	.15
516	Dmitri Young	.15
517	Sean Casey	.20
518	Barry Larkin	.25
519	Juan Castro	.15
520	Danny Graves	.15
521	Aaron Boone	.15
522	Pokey Reese	.15
523	Elmer Dessens	.15
524	Michael Tucker	.15
525	Benito Santiago	.15
526	Pete Harnisch	.15
527	Alex Ochoa	.15
528	Gookie Dawkins	.15
529	Seth Etherton	.15
530	Rob Bell	.15
531	Ken Griffey Jr., Steve Parris	.50
532	Todd Helton	.50
533	Jose Jimenez	.15
534	Todd Walker	.15
535	Ron Gant	.15
536	Neifi Perez	.15
537	Butch Huskey	.15
538	Pedro Astacio	.15
539	Juan Pierre	.15
540	Jeff Cirillo	.15
541	Ben Petrick	.15
542	Brian Bohanon	.15
543	Larry Walker	.25
544	Masato Yoshii	.15
545	Denny Neagle	.15
546	Brent Mayne	.15
547	Mike Hampton	.20
548	Todd Hollandsworth	.15
549	Brian Rose	.15
550	Todd Helton, Pedro Astacio	.20
551	Jason Hart	.15
552	Joe Crede	.15
553	Timoniel Perez	.15
554	Brady Clark	.15
555	Adam Pettyjohn RC	.15
556	Jason Grilli	.15
557	Paxton Crawford	.15
558	Jay Spurgeon	.15
559	Hector Ortiz	.15
560	Vernon Wells	.15
561	Aubrey Huff	.15
562	Xavier Nady	.25
563	Billy McMillon	.15
564	Ichiro Suzuki RC	8.00
565	Tomas de la Rosa	.15
566	Matt Ginter	.15
567	Sun-Woo Kim	.15
568	Nick Johnson	.15
569	Pablo Ozuna	.15
570	Tike Redman	.15
571	Brian Cole	.15
572	Ross Gload	.15
573	Dee Brown	.15
574	Tony McKnight	.15
575	Allen Levrault	.15
576	Lesli Brea	.15
577	Adam Bernero	.15
578	Tom Davey	.15
579	Morgan Burkhart	.15
580	Britt Reames	.15
581	Dave Coggin	.15
582	Trey Moore	.15
583	Matt Kinney	.15
584	Pedro Feliz	.15
585	Brandon Inge	.15
586	Alex Hernandez	.15
587	Toby Hall	.15
588	Grant Roberts	.15
589	Brian Sikorski	.15
590	Aaron Myette	.15
591	Derek Jeter (Big Play Makers)	1.00
592	Ivan Rodriguez (Big Play Makers)	.40
593	Alex Rodriguez (Big Play Makers)	.75
594	Carlos Delgado (Big Play Makers)	.30
595	Mark McGwire (Big Play Makers)	.75
596	Troy Glaus (Big Play Makers)	.40
597	Sammy Sosa (Big Play Makers)	.75
598	Vladimir Guerrero (Big Play Makers)	.50
599	Manny Ramirez (Big Play Makers)	.40
600	Pedro J. Martinez (Big Play Makers)	.50
601	Chipper Jones (Big Play Makers)	.75
602	Jason Giambi (Big Play Makers)	.20
603	Frank Thomas (Big Play Makers)	.75
604	Ken Griffey Jr. (Big Play Makers)	.75
605	Nomar Garciaparra (Big Play Makers)	.75
606	Randy Johnson (Big Play Makers)	.40
607	Mike Piazza (Big Play Makers)	.75
608	Barry Bonds (Big Play Makers)	.50
609	Todd Helton (Big Play Makers)	.40
610	Jeff Bagwell (Big Play Makers)	.40
611	Ken Griffey Jr. (Victory's Best)	.75
612	Carlos Delgado (Victory's Best)	.40
613	Jeff Bagwell (Victory's Best)	.40
614	Jason Giambi (Victory's Best)	.20
615	Cal Ripken Jr. (Victory's Best)	1.00
616	Brian Giles (Victory's Best)	.15
617	Bernie Williams (Victory's Best)	.30
618	Greg Maddux (Victory's Best)	.75
619	Troy Glaus (Victory's Best)	.40
620	Greg Vaughn (Victory's Best)	.15
621	Sammy Sosa (Victory's Best)	.75
622	Pat Burrell (Victory's Best)	.20
623	Ivan Rodriguez (Victory's Best)	.40
624	Chipper Jones (Victory's Best)	.75
625	Barry Bonds (Victory's Best)	.50
626	Roger Clemens (Victory's Best)	.50
627	Jim Edmonds (Victory's Best)	.15
628	Nomar Garciaparra (Victory's Best)	.75
629	Frank Thomas (Victory's Best)	.50
630	Mike Piazza (Victory's Best)	.75
631	Randy Johnson (Victory's Best)	.40
632	Andruw Jones (Victory's Best)	.30
633	David Wells (Victory's Best)	.15
634	Manny Ramirez (Victory's Best)	.40
635	Preston Wilson (Victory's Best)	.15
636	Todd Helton (Victory's Best)	.40
637	Kerry Wood (Victory's Best)	.15
638	Albert Belle (Victory's Best)	.15
639	Juan Gonzalez (Victory's Best)	.40
640	Vladimir Guerrero (Victory's Best)	.50
641	Gary Sheffield (Victory's Best)	.15
642	Larry Walker (Victory's Best)	.15
643	Magglio Ordonez (Victory's Best)	.15
644	Jermaine Dye (Victory's Best)	.15
645	Scott Rolen (Victory's Best)	.20
646	Tony Gwynn (Victory's Best)	.50
647	Shawn Green (Victory's Best)	.15
648	Roberto Alomar (Victory's Best)	.30
649	Eric Milton (Victory's Best)	.15
650	Mark McGwire (Victory's Best)	.75
651	Tim Hudson (Victory's Best)	.15
652	Jose Canseco (Victory's Best)	.15
653	Tom Glavine (Victory's Best)	.20
654	Derek Jeter (Victory's Best)	1.00
655	Alex Rodriguez (Victory's Best)	.75
656	Darin Erstad (Victory's Best)	.15
657	Jason Kendall (Victory's Best)	.15
658	Pedro Martinez (Victory's Best)	.50
659	Richie Sexson (Victory's Best)	.15
660	Rafael Palmeiro (Victory's Best)	.20

2001 Upper Deck Vintage Sample

Styled shamelessly after the 1963 Topps set, this retro-look UD issue was previewed with a sample card. Virtually identical in format to the issued version, the promo has

stats on back only through 1999 and is overprinted with a large diagonal "SAMPLE."

NM/M
#	Player	Price
30	Ken Griffey Jr.	4.00

2001 Upper Deck Vintage

NM/M

Complete Set (400):	30.00
Common Player:	.10
Pack (10):	2.00
Box (24):	40.00

#	Player	Price
1	Darin Erstad	.25
2	Seth Etherton	.10
3	Troy Glaus	.50
4	Bengie Molina	.10
5	Mo Vaughn	.20
6	Tim Salmon	.25
7	Ramon Ortiz	.10
8	Adam Kennedy	.10
9	Garret Anderson	.25
10	Troy Percival	.10
11	2000 Angels Lineup	.10
12	Jason Giambi	.50
13	Tim Hudson	.25
14	Adam Piatt	.10
15	Miguel Tejada	.25
16	Mark Mulder	.25
17	Eric Chavez	.25
18	Ramon Hernandez	.10
19	Terrence Long	.10
20	Jason Isringhausen	.10
21	Barry Zito	.50
22	Ben Grieve	.15
23	2000 Athletics Lineup	.10
24	David Wells	.15
25	Raul Mondesi	.20
26	Darrin Fletcher	.10
27	Shannon Stewart	.10
28	Kelvim Escobar	.10
29	Tony Batista	.10
30	Carlos Delgado	.50
31	Brad Fullmer	.10
32	Billy Koch	.10
33	Jose Cruz Jr.	.10
34	2000 Blue Jays Lineup	.10
35	Greg Vaughn	.10
36	Roberto Hernandez	.10
37	Vinny Castilla	.10
38	Gerald Williams	.10
39	Aubrey Huff	.10
40	Bryan Rekar	.10
41	Albie Lopez	.10
42	Fred McGriff	.25
43	Miguel Cairo	.10
44	Ryan Rupe	.10
45	2000 Devil Rays Lineup	.10
46	Jim Thome	.50
47	Roberto Alomar	.50
48	Bartolo Colon	.25
49	Omar Vizquel	.20
50	Travis Fryman	.10
51	Manny Ramirez	.50
52	Dave Burba	.10
53	Chuck Finley	.10
54	Russ Branyan	.10
55	Kenny Lofton	.25
56	2000 Indians Lineup	.10
57	Alex Rodriguez	1.50
58	Jay Buhner	.10
59	Aaron Sele	.10
60	Kazuhiro Sasaki	.25
61	Edgar Martinez	.20
62	John Halama	.10
63	Mike Cameron	.10
64	Fred Garcia	.10
65	John Olerud	.20
66	Jamie Moyer	.10
67	Gil Meche	.10
68	2000 Mariners Lineup	.10
69	Cal Ripken Jr.	2.00
70	Sidney Ponson	.10
71	Chris Richard	.10
72	Jose Mercedes	.10
73	Albert Belle	.15
74	Mike Mussina	.50
75	Brady Anderson	.15
76	Delino DeShields	.10
77	Melvin Mora	.10
78	Luis Matos	.10
79	Brook Fordyce	.10
80	2000 Orioles Lineup	.10
81	Rafael Palmeiro	.50
82	Rick Helling	.10
83	Ruben Mateo	.10
84	Rusty Greer	.10
85	Ivan Rodriguez	.50
86	Doug Davis	.10
87	Gabe Kapler	.10
88	Mike Lamb	.10
89	Alex Rodriguez	1.50
90	Kenny Rogers	.10
91	2000 Rangers Lineup	.10
92	Nomar Garciaparra	1.50
93	Trot Nixon	.10
94	Tomokazu Ohka	.10
95	Pedro Martinez	.75
96	Dante Bichette	.10
97	Jason Varitek	.10
98	Rolando Arrojo	.10
99	Carl Everett	.10
100	Derek Lowe	.10
101	Troy O'Leary	.10
102	Tim Wakefield	.10
103	2000 Red Sox Lineup	.10
104	Mike Sweeney	.10
105	Carlos Febles	.10
106	Joe Randa	.10
107	Jeff Suppan	.10
108	Mac Suzuki	.10
109	Jermaine Dye	.10
110	Carlos Beltran	.10
111	Mark Quinn	.10
112	Johnny Damon	.20
113	2000 Royals Lineup	.10
114	Tony Clark	.10
115	Dean Palmer	.10
116	Brian Moehler	.10
117	Brad Ausmus	.10
118	Juan Gonzalez	.50
119	Juan Encarnacion	.10
120	Jeff Weaver	.10
121	Bobby Higginson	.10
122	Todd Jones	.10
123	Deivi Cruz	.10
124	2000 Tigers Lineup	.10
125	Corey Koskie	.10
126	Matt Lawton	.10
127	Mark Redman	.10
128	David Ortiz	.10
129	Jay Canizaro	.10
130	Eric Milton	.10
131	Jacque Jones	.10
132	J.C. Romero	.10
133	Ron Coomer	.10
134	Brad Radke	.10
135	2000 Twins Lineup	.10
136	Carlos Lee	.10
137	Frank Thomas	.75
138	Mike Sirotka	.10
139	Charles Johnson	.10
140	James Baldwin	.10
141	Magglio Ordonez	.25
142	Jon Garland	.10
143	Paul Konerko	.10
144	Ray Durham	.10
145	Keith Foulke	.10
146	Chris Singleton	.10
147	2000 White Sox Lineup	.10
148	Bernie Williams	.50
149	Orlando Hernandez	.15
150	David Justice	.25
151	Andy Pettitte	.25
152	Mariano Rivera	.25
153	Derek Jeter	2.00
154	Jorge Posada	.25
155	Jose Canseco	.50
156	Glenallen Hill	.10
157	Paul O'Neill	.25
158	Denny Neagle	.10
159	Chuck Knoblauch	.10
160	Roger Clemens	1.50
161	2000 Yankees Lineup	.10
162	Jeff Bagwell	.50
163	Moises Alou	.20
164	Lance Berkman	.40
165	Shane Reynolds	.10
166	Ken Caminiti	.10
167	Craig Biggio	.25
168	Jose Lima	.10
169	Octavio Dotel	.10
170	Richard Hidalgo	.20
171	Scott Elarton	.10
172	2000 Astros Lineup	.10
173	Rafael Furcal	.25
174	Greg Maddux	1.00
175	Quilvio Veras	.10
176	Chipper Jones	1.00
177	Andres Galarraga	.25
178	Brian Jordan	.10
179	Tom Glavine	.25
180	Kevin Millwood	.25
181	Javier Lopez	.25

#	Player	Price
182	B.J. Surhoff	.10
183	Andruw Jones	.50
184	Andy Ashby	.10
185	2000 Braves Lineup	.10
186	Richie Sexson	.40
187	Jeff D'Amico	.10
188	Ron Belliard	.10
189	Jeromy Burnitz	.10
190	Jimmy Haynes	.10
191	Marquis Grissom	.10
192	Jose Hernandez	.10
193	Geoff Jenkins	.20
194	Jamey Wright	.10
195	Mark Loretta	.10
196	2000 Brewers Lineup	.10
197	Rick Ankiel	.10
198	Mark McGwire	1.50
199	Fernando Vina	.10
200	David Renteria	.10
201	Darryl Kile	.10
202	Jim Edmonds	.25
203	Ray Lankford	.10
204	Garrett Stephenson	.10
205	Fernando Tatis	.10
206	Will Clark	.40
207	J.D. Drew	.15
208	2000 Cardinals Lineup	.10
209	Mark Grace	.25
210	Eric Young	.10
211	Sammy Sosa	1.50
212	Jon Lieber	.10
213	Joe Girardi	.10
214	Kevin Tapani	.10
215	Ricky Gutierrez	.10
216	Kerry Wood	.50
217	Rondell White	.20
218	Damon Buford	.10
219	2000 Cubs Lineup	.10
220	Luis Gonzalez	.25
221	Randy Johnson	.75
222	Jay Bell	.10
223	Erubiel Durazo	.10
224	Matt Williams	.25
225	Steve Finley	.10
226	Curt Schilling	.40
227	Todd Stottlemyre	.10
228	Tony Womack	.10
229	Brian Anderson	.10
230	2000 Diamondbacks Lineup	.10
231	Gary Sheffield	.40
232	Adrian Beltre	.25
233	Todd Hundley	.10
234	Chan Ho Park	.10
235	Shawn Green	.25
236	Kevin Brown	.25
237	Tom Goodwin	.10
238	Mark Grudzielanek	.10
239	Ismael Valdes	.10
240	Eric Karros	.10
241	2000 Dodgers Lineup	.10
242	Jose Vidro	.10
243	Javier Vazquez	.20
244	Orlando Cabrera	.10
245	Peter Bergeron	.10
246	Vladimir Guerrero	.75
247	Dustin Hermanson	.10
248	Tony Armas Jr.	.10
249	Lee Stevens	.10
250	Milton Bradley	.10
251	Carl Pavano	.10
252	2000 Expos Lineup	.10
253	Ellis Burks	.10
254	Robb Nen	.10
255	J.T. Snow	.10
256	Barry Bonds	2.00
257	Shawn Estes	.10
258	Jeff Kent	.20
259	Kirk Rueter	.10
260	Bill Mueller	.10
261	Livan Hernandez	.10
262	Rich Aurilia	.10
263	2000 Giants Lineup	.10
264	Ryan Dempster	.10
265	Cliff Floyd	.10
266	Mike Lowell	.10
267	A.J. Burnett	.10
268	Preston Wilson	.10
269	Luis Castillo	.10
270	Henry Rodriguez	.10
271	Antonio Alfonseca	.10
272	Derek Lee	.10
273	Mark Kotsay	.10
274	Brad Penny	.10
275	2000 Marlins Lineup	.10
276	Mike Piazza	1.00
277	Jay Payton	.10
278	Al Leiter	.15
279	Mike Bordick	.10
280	Armando Benitez	.10
281	Todd Zeile	.10
282	Mike Hampton	.20
283	Edgardo Alfonzo	.10
284	Derek Bell	.10
285	Robin Ventura	.20
286	2000 Mets Lineup	.10
287	Tony Gwynn	.75
288	Trevor Hoffman	.10
289	Ryan Klesko	.20
290	Phil Nevin	.10
291	Matt Clement	.10
292	Ben Davis	.10
293	Ruben Rivera	.10
294	Bret Boone	.25
295	Adam Eaton	.10
296	Eric Owens	.10
297	2000 Padres Lineup	.10
298	Bob Abreu	.20

#	Player	Price
299	Mike Lieberthal	.10
300	Robert Person	.10
301	Scott Rolen	.50
302	Randy Wolf	.10
303	Bruce Chen	.10
304	Travis Lee	.10
305	Kent Bottenfield	.10
306	Pat Burrell	.50
307	Doug Glanville	.10
308	2000 Phillies Lineup	.10
309	Brian Giles	.25
310	Todd Ritchie	.10
311	Warren Morris	.10
312	John Vander Wal	.10
313	Kris Benson	.10
314	Jason Kendall	.10
315	Kevin Young	.10
316	Francisco Cordova	.10
317	Jimmy Anderson	.10
318	2000 Pirates Lineup	.10
319	Ken Griffey Jr.	1.00
320	Pokey Reese	.10
321	Chris Stynes	.10
322	Barry Larkin	.40
323	Steve Parris	.10
324	Michael Tucker	.10
325	Dmitri Young	.10
326	Pete Harnisch	.10
327	Adam Graves	.10
328	Aaron Boone	.10
329	Sean Casey	.10
330	2000 Reds Lineup	.10
331	Todd Helton	.50
332	Pedro Astacio	.10
333	Larry Walker	.25
334	Ben Petrick	.10
335	Brian Bohanon	.10
336	Juan Pierre	.10
337	Jeffrey Hammonds	.10
338	Jeff Cirillo	.10
339	Todd Hollandsworth	.10
340	2000 Rockies Lineup	.10
341	Matt Wise, Keith Luuloa, Derrick Turnbow (Vintage Rookies)	.10
342	Jason Hart, Jose Ortiz, Mario Encarnacion (Vintage Rookies)	.10
343	Vernon Wells, Pascual Coco, Josh Phelps (Vintage Rookies)	.25
344	Travis Harper, Kenny Kelley, Toby Hall (Vintage Rookies)	.10
345	Danys Baez, Tim Drew, Martin Vargas RC (Vintage Rookies)	.10
346	Ichiro Suzuki RC, Ryan Franklin, Ryan Christianson (Vintage Rookies)	10.00
347	Jay Spurgeon, Lesli Brea, Carlos Casimiro (Vintage Rookies)	.10
348	B.J. Waszgis, Brian Sikorski, Joaquin Benoit (Vintage Rookies)	.10
349	Sun-Woo Kim, Paxton Crawford, Steve Lomasney (Vintage Rookies)	.10
350	Kris Wilson, Orber Moreno, Dee Brown (Vintage Rookies)	.10
351	Mark Johnson, Brandon Inge, Adam Bernero (Vintage Rookies)	.10
352	Danny Ardoin, Matt Kinney, Jason Ryan (Vintage Rookies)	.10
353	Rocky Biddle, Joe Crede, Aaron Myette (Vintage Rookies)	.10
354	Nick Johnson, D'Angelo Jimenez, Willi Mo Pena (Vintage Rookies)	.10
355	Tony McKnight, Aaron McNeal, Keith Ginter (Vintage Rookies)	.25
356	Mark DeRosa, Jason Marquis, Wes Helms (Vintage Rookies)	.10
357	Allen Levrault, Horacio Estrada, Santiago Perez (Vintage Rookies)	.10
358	Luis Saturria, Gene Stechschulte, Britt Reames (Vintage Rookies)	.10
359	Joey Nation, Corey Patterson, Cole Liniak (Vintage Rookies)	.25
360	Alex Cabrera, Geraldo Guzman, Nelson Figueroa (Vintage Rookies)	.10
361	Hiram Bocachica, Mike Judd, Luke Prokopec (Vintage Rookies)	.10
362	Tomas de la Rosa, Yohanny Valera, Talmadge Nunnari (Vintage Rookies)	.10

#	Player	Price
363	Ryan Vogelsong, Juan Melo, Chad Zerbe (Vintage Rookies)	.10
364	Jason Grilli, Pablo Ozuna, Ramon Castro (Vintage Rookies)	.10
365	Timoniel Perez, Grant Roberts, Brian Cole (Vintage Rookies)	.10
366	Tom Davey, Xavier Nady, Dave Maurer (Vintage Rookies)	.50
367	Jimmy Rollins, Mark Brownson, Reggie Taylor (Vintage Rookies)	.25
368	Alex Hernandez, Adam Hyzdu, Tike Redman (Vintage Rookies)	.10
369	Brady Clark, John Riedling, Mike Bell (Vintage Rookies)	.10
370	Giovanni Carrara, Josh Kalinowski, Elvis Pena (Vintage Rookies)	.10
371	Jim Edmonds (Postseason Scrapbook)	.10
372	Edgar Martinez (Postseason Scrapbook)	.10
373	Rickey Henderson (Postseason Scrapbook)	.10
374	Barry Zito (Postseason Scrapbook)	.25
375	Tino Martinez (Postseason Scrapbook)	.10
376	J.T. Snow (Postseason Scrapbook)	.10
377	Bobby Jones (Postseason Scrapbook)	.10
378	Alex Rodriguez (Postseason Scrapbook)	1.00
379	Mike Hampton (Postseason Scrapbook)	.10
380	Roger Clemens (Postseason Scrapbook)	.50
381	Jay Payton (Postseason Scrapbook)	.10
382	John Olerud (Postseason Scrapbook)	.10
383	David Justice (Postseason Scrapbook)	.25
384	Mike Hampton (Postseason Scrapbook)	.10
385	Yankees Celebrate (Postseason Scrapbook)	.75
386	Jose Vizcaino (Postseason Scrapbook)	.10
387	Roger Clemens (Postseason Scrapbook)	.75
388	Todd Zeile (Postseason Scrapbook)	.10
389	Derek Jeter (Postseason Scrapbook)	1.25
390	Yankees Celebrate (Postseason Scrapbook)	.50
391	Nomar Garciaparra - AL Batting (Big League Leaders)	.75
392	Todd Helton - NL Batting (Big League Leaders)	.25
393	Troy Glaus - AL HR (Big League Leaders)	.25
394	Sammy Sosa - NL HR (Big League Leaders)	.25
395	Edgar Martinez - AL RBI (Big League Leaders)	.10
396	Todd Helton - NL RBI (Big League Leaders)	.25
397	Pedro Martinez - AL ERA (Big League Leaders)	.40
398	Kevin Brown - NL ERA (Big League Leaders)	.10
399	David Wells, Tim Hudson - AL Wins (Big League Leaders)	.10
400	Tom Glavine - NL Wins (Big League Leaders)	.10

All-Star Tributes

	Complete Set (10):	20.00
	Common Player:	1.00
	Inserted 1:23	
1	Derek Jeter	4.00
2	Mike Piazza	2.00
3	Carlos Delgado	1.00
4	Pedro Martinez	1.50
5	Vladimir Guerrero	1.50
6	Mark McGwire	3.00
7	Alex Rodriguez	3.00
8	Barry Bonds	4.00

ALL-STAR TRIBUTES

9	Chipper Jones	2.00
10	Sammy Sosa	2.50

Fantasy Outfield Combo Jersey
NM/M

Production 25 Cards
FO-CJ Joe DiMaggio, Mickey Mantle, Ken Griffey Jr. 1,000

Glory Days

GLORY DAYS

JIM EDMONDS

		NM/M
	Complete Set (15):	15.00
	Common Player:	.50
	Inserted 1:15	
1	Jermaine Dye	.50
2	Chipper Jones	2.00
3	Todd Helton	1.00
4	Magglio Ordonez	.75
5	Tony Gwynn	1.50
6	Jim Edmonds	.75
7	Rafael Palmeiro	1.00
8	Barry Bonds	4.00
9	Carl Everett	.50
10	Mike Piazza	2.50
11	Brian Giles	.50
12	Tony Batista	.50
13	Jeff Bagwell	1.00
14	Ken Griffey Jr.	2.00
15	Troy Glaus	1.00

Mantle Pinstripes Exclusive
NM/M

Complete Set (56):	75.00
Common Mantle:	2.00
One Pack/Box	

Mantle Pinstripes Memorabilia
NM/M

Print Runs Listed:
MMB	Mickey Mantle/Bat/100	100.00
MMCJ	Mickey Mantle, Roger Maris/Jsy/50	300.00
MMJ	Mickey Mantle/Jsy/100	125.00

Matinee Idols

MATINEE Idols

CAL RIPKEN JR. BALTIMORE ORIOLES — THIRD BASE

	NM/M
Complete Set (20):	10.00
Common Player:	.50

Inserted 1:4		
1	Ken Griffey Jr.	1.00
2	Derek Jeter	2.00
3	Barry Bonds	2.00
4	Chipper Jones	1.00
5	Mike Piazza	1.00
6	Todd Helton	.50
7	Randy Johnson	.50
8	Alex Rodriguez	1.50
9	Sammy Sosa	1.50
10	Cal Ripken Jr.	2.00
11	Nomar Garciaparra	1.50
12	Carlos Delgado	.50
13	Jason Giambi	.50
14	Ivan Rodriguez	.50
15	Vladimir Guerrero	.75
16	Gary Sheffield	.50
17	Frank Thomas	.50
18	Jeff Bagwell	.50
19	Pedro Martinez	.75
20	Mark McGwire	1.50

Retro Rules

CARDINALS mark mcgwire • 1b
RETRO RULES

		NM/M
	Complete Set (15):	20.00
	Common Player:	.50
	Inserted 1:15	
1	Nomar Garciaparra	3.00
2	Frank Thomas	1.00
3	Jeff Bagwell	1.00
4	Sammy Sosa	2.50
5	Derek Jeter	4.00
6	David Wells	.50
7	Vladimir Guerrero	1.50
8	Jim Thome	1.00
9	Mark McGwire	3.00
10	Todd Helton	1.00
11	Tony Gwynn	1.50
12	Bernie Williams	1.50
13	Cal Ripken Jr.	4.00
14	Brian Giles	.75
15	Jason Giambi	1.00

Timeless Teams Bat

GENE TENACE
TIMELESS TEAMS

		NM/M
	Common Player:	8.00
	Inserted 1:72	
NYY-JD	Joe DiMaggio	150.00
NYY-TH	Tommy Henrich	8.00
NYY-CK	Charlie Keller	8.00
NYY-BD	Bill Dickey	20.00
BK-JR	Jackie Robinson	90.00
BK-RC	Roy Campanella	50.00
BK-GH	Gil Hodges	25.00
BK-DN	Don Newcombe	8.00
LA-SG	Steve Garvey	8.00
LA-RC	Ron Cey	8.00
LA-BR	Bill Russell	8.00
LA-DB	Dusty Baker	8.00
BA-BP	Boog Powell	8.00
BA-BR	Brooks Robinson	25.00
BA-FR	Frank Robinson	20.00
BA-MB	Mark Belanger	8.00
PI-RC	Roberto Clemente	100.00
PI-WS	Willie Stargell	20.00
PI-MS	Manny Sanguillen	8.00
PI-AO	Al Oliver	8.00
OA-RJ	Reggie Jackson	20.00
OA-SB	Sal Bando	8.00
OA-GT	Gene Tenace	8.00
OA-JR	Joe Rudi	8.00
CI2-JB	Johnny Bench	20.00
CI2-TP	Tony Perez	15.00
CI2-JM	Joe Morgan	8.00
CI2-KG	Ken Griffey Sr.	8.00
NYM-NR	Nolan Ryan	40.00
NYM-RS	Ron Swoboda	8.00
NYM-EK	Ed Kranepool	8.00
NYM-TA	Tommie Agee	8.00

Timeless Teams Combo Bat
NM/M

Common Card:	75.00

ROBERTO CLEMENTE WILLIE STARGELL MANNY SANGUILLEN AL OLIVER
TIMELESS TEAMS Vintage

Production 100 Sets
NYY41	Joe DiMaggio, Tommy Henrich, Bill Dickey, Charlie Keller	200.00
BKN55	Jackie Robinson, Roy Campanella, Gil Hodges, Don Newcombe	175.00
BAL70	Frank Robinson, Brooks Robinson, Mark Belanger, Boog Powell	120.00
LA81	Steve Garvey, Ron Cey, Dusty Baker, Bill Russell	75.00
PIT71	Roberto Clemente, Willie Stargell, Bill Mazeroski, Al Oliver	200.00
OAK72	Reggie Jackson, Sal Bando, Gene Tenace, Joe Rudi	80.00
CIN75	Johnny Bench, Tony Perez, Joe Morgan, Ken Griffey Sr.	120.00
NYM69	Nolan Ryan, Ron Swoboda, Ed Kranepool, Tommie Agee	200.00

Timeless Teams Jersey

MICKEY MANTLE
TIMELESS TEAMS

		NM/M
	Common Player:	15.00
	Inserted 1:288	
NYY-MM	Mickey Mantle	160.00
NYY-RM	Roger Maris	50.00
NYY-BR	Bobby Richardson	15.00
CI-DC	Dave Concepcion	15.00
CI-TP	Tony Perez	20.00
CI-KG	Ken Griffey Sr.	15.00
CI-JM	Joe Morgan	20.00

Timeless Teams Combo Jersey

MICKEY MANTLE ROGER MARIS BOBBY RICHARDSON
TIMELESS TEAMS Vintage

NM/M

Production 100 Sets
NYY61	Mickey Mantle, Roger Maris, Bobby Richardson	250.00
CIN75	Dave Concepcion, Tony Perez, Ken Griffey Sr.	120.00

Coca-Cola Cal Ripken, Jr. Tribute

To commemorate his final season Upper Deck produced for Coca-Cola a set of eight cards featuring highlights from the Iron Man's career. Cards #1-

4 were given away in a cello pack to fans at the September 21 and October 1 O's games at Camden Yards. Cards #5-8 were given away at games on September 22-23 and October 2-3. Also in each cello pack was a Coke coupon card. Fronts have borderless color photos with an UD logo and Ripken's name in gold foil. A special Ripken Tribute logo appears at lower-left. Backs repeat the front photo, have a large uniform number 8 in the background and present various sets of stats. The Coke logo appears among those on back.

	NM/M
Complete Set (8):	10.00
Common Card:	1.50
1 Cal Ripken, Jr. (Rookie of the Year)	1.50
2 Cal Ripken, Jr. (1991 AL MVP)	1.50
3 Cal Ripken, Jr. (1991 Gold Glove)	1.50
4 Cal Ripken, Jr. (The "Iron Man")	1.50
5 Cal Ripken, Jr. (400th HR)	1.50
6 Cal Ripken, Jr. (3,000 Hit)	1.50
7 Cal Ripken, Jr. (2001 All-Star MVP)	1.50
8 Cal Ripken, Jr. (Retirement Announcement)	1.50
Coupon Card	.25

Ritz-Oreo

In conjunction with its sponsorship of the 2001 All-Star Game in Seattle, Ritz-Oreo issued a pair of cards distributed in product packages. In standard 2-1/2" x 3-1/2" format, one card is bordered in red and pictures Griffey batting; a blue bordered card has a picture of him throwing. Backs have biographical data - "Height: 150 Oreos / Weight: 27,060 Ritz," recent stats, a quote and logos of all parties involved. The cards were also available with a pair of Fleer Derek Jeter cards in a mail-in offer.

	NM/M
Complete Set (2):	3.00
(1) Ken Griffey Jr./Btg	2.00
(2) Ken Griffey Jr./ Throwing	2.00

Twizzlers Big League Challenge

Each specially marked 16-oz. package of Twizzlers candy contained one card from this set. The 2-1/2" x 3-1/2" cards

have on front a photo from the Big League Challenge event, with UD and Twizzlers logos and the player's 2000 home run total. Backs repeat the Big League Challenge logo and have career highlights.

	NM/M
Complete Set (10):	7.50
Common Player:	.50
1 Jason Giambi	1.00
2 Carlos Delgado	.50
3 Troy Glaus	1.00
4 Jim Edmonds	.50
5 Richard Hidalgo	.50
6 Gary Sheffield	.50
7 Todd Helton	.75
8 Jose Canseco	.75
9 Frank Thomas	1.00
10 Barry Bonds	2.00

2002 Upper Deck

	NM/M
Complete Set (745):	150.00
Complete Series I (500):	100.00
Complete Series II (245):	50.00
Common Player:	.15
Series 1 Hobby Pack (8):	4.00
Series 1 Hobby Box (24):	75.00
Series 2 Hobby Pack (8):	1.25
Series 2 Hobby Box (24):	25.00
1 Mark Prior (Star Rookie)	4.00
2 Mark Teixeira (Star Rookie)	1.50
3 Brian Roberts (Star Rookie)	.25
4 Jason Romano (Star Rookie)	.25
5 Dennis Stark RC (Star Rookie)	.50
6 Oscar Salazar (Star Rookie)	.50
7 John Patterson (Star Rookie)	.25
8 Shane Loux (Star Rookie)	.25
9 Marcus Giles (Star Rookie)	.40
10 Juan Cruz (Star Rookie)	.25
11 Jorge Julio (Star Rookie)	.25
12 Adam Dunn (Star Rookie)	.50
13 Delvin James (Star Rookie)	.25
14 Jeremy Affeldt (Star Rookie)	.25
15 Tim Raines Jr. (Star Rookie)	.25
16 Luke Hudson (Star Rookie)	.25
17 Todd Sears (Star Rookie)	.25
18 George Perez (Star Rookie)	.25
19 Wilmy Caceres (Star Rookie)	.25
20 Abraham Nunez (Star Rookie)	.25
21 Mike Amrhein (Star Rookie)	.25
22 Carlos Hernandez (Star Rookie)	.25
23 Scott Hodges (Star Rookie)	.25
24 Brandon Knight (Star Rookie)	.25
25 Geoff Goetz (Star Rookie)	.25
26 Carlos Garcia (Star Rookie)	.25
27 Luis Pineda (Star Rookie)	.25
28 Chris Gissell (Star Rookie)	.25
29 Jae Weong (Star Rookie)	.25
30 Paul Phillips (Star Rookie)	.25
31 Cory Aldridge (Star Rookie)	.25
32 Aaron Cook RC (Star Rookie)	.50
33 Rendy Espina (Star Rookie)	.25
34 Jason Phillips (Star Rookie)	.25
35 Carlos Silva (Star Rookie)	.25
36 Ryan Mills (Star Rookie)	.25
37 Pedro Santana (Star Rookie)	.25
38 John Grabow (Star Rookie)	.25
39 Cody Ransom (Star Rookie)	.15
40 Orlando Woodlands (Star Rookie)	.25
41 Bud Smith (Star Rookie)	.25
42 Junior Guerrero (Star Rookie)	.25
43 David Brous (Star Rookie)	.25
44 Steve Green (Star Rookie)	.15
45 Brian Rogers (Star Rookie)	.15
46 Juan Figueroa (Star Rookie)	.15
47 Nick Punto (Star Rookie)	.15
48 Junior Herndon (Star Rookie)	.25
49 Justin Kaye (Star Rookie)	
50 Jason Karnuth (Star Rookie)	
51 Troy Glaus	.40
52 Bengie Molina	.15
53 Ramon Ortiz	.15
54 Adam Kennedy	.15
55 Jarrod Washburn	.15
56 Troy Percival	.15
57 David Eckstein	.15
58 Ben Weber	.15
59 Larry Barnes	.15
60 Ismael Valdes	.15
61 Benji Gil	.15
62 Scott Schoeneweis	.15
63 Pat Rapp	.15
64 Jason Giambi	.50
65 Mark Mulder	.25
66 Ron Gant	.15
67 Johnny Damon	.25
68 Adam Piatt	.15
69 Jermaine Dye	.25
70 Jason Hart	.15
71 Eric Chavez	.40
72 Jim Mecir	.15
73 Barry Zito	.40
74 Jason Isringhausen	.15
75 Jeremy Giambi	.15
76 Olmedo Saenz	.15
77 Terrence Long	.15
78 Ramon Hernandez	.15
79 Chris Carpenter	.15
80 Raul Mondesi	.15
81 Carlos Delgado	.50
82 Billy Koch	.15
83 Vernon Wells	.25
84 Darrin Fletcher	.15
85 Homer Bush	.15
86 Pasqual Coco	.15
87 Shannon Stewart	.15
88 Chris Woodward	.15
89 Joe Lawrence	.15
90 Esteban Loaiza	.15
91 Cesar Izturis	.15
92 Kelvim Escobar	.15
93 Greg Vaughn	.15
94 Brent Abernathy	.15
95 Tanyon Sturtze	.15
96 Steve Cox	.15
97 Aubrey Huff	.15
98 Jesus Colome	.15
99 Ben Grieve	.15
100 Esteban Yan	.15
101 Joe Kennedy	.15
102 Felix Martinez	.15
103 Nick Bierbrodt	.15
104 Damian Rolls	.15
105 Russ Johnson	.15
106 Toby Hall	.15
107 Roberto Alomar	.40
108 Bartolo Colon	.25
109 John Rocker	.15
110 Juan Gonzalez	.50
111 Einar Diaz	.15
112 Chuck Finley	.15
113 Kenny Lofton	.25
114 Danys Baez	.15
115 Travis Fryman	.25
116 C.C. Sabathia	.25
117 Paul Shuey	.15
118 Marty Cordova	.15
119 Ellis Burks	.15
120 Bob Wickman	.15
121 Edgar Martinez	.25
122 Freddy Garcia	.15
123 Ichiro Suzuki	1.50
124 John Olerud	.25
125 Gil Meche	.15
126 Dan Wilson	.15
127 Aaron Sele	.15
128 Kazuhiro Sasaki	.25
129 Mark McLemore	.15
130 Carlos Guillen	.15
131 Al Martin	.15
132 David Bell	.15
133 Jay Buhner	.15
134 Stan Javier	.15
135 Tony Batista	.15
136 Jason Johnson	.15
137 Brook Fordyce	.15
138 Mike Kinkade	.15
139 Willis Roberts	.15
140 David Segui	.15
141 Josh Towers	.15
142 Jeff Conine	.15
143 Chris Richard	.15
144 Pat Hentgen	.15
145 Melvin Mora	.15
146 Jerry Hairston Jr.	.15
147 Calvin Maduro	.15
148 Brady Anderson	.15
149 Alex Rodriguez	1.50
150 Kenny Rogers	.15
151 Chad Curtis	.15
152 Ricky Ledee	.15
153 Rafael Palmeiro	.50
154 Rob Bell	.15
155 Rick Helling	.15
156 Doug Davis	.15
157 Mike Lamb	.15
158 Gabe Kapler	.15
159 Jeff Zimmerman	.15
160 Bill Haselman	.15
161 Tim Crabtree	.15
162 Carlos Pena	.15
163 Nomar Garciaparra	1.00
164 Shea Hillenbrand	.15
165 Hideo Nomo	.40
166 Manny Ramirez	.50
167 Jose Offerman	.15
168 Scott Hatteberg	.15
169 Trot Nixon	.25
170 Darren Lewis	.15
171 Derek Lowe	.25
172 Troy O'Leary	.15
173 Tim Wakefield	.15
174 Chris Stynes	.15
175 John Valentin	.15
176 David Cone	.15
177 Neifi Perez	.15
178 Brent Mayne	.15
179 Dan Reichert	.15
180 A.J. Hinch	.15
181 Chris George	.15
182 Mike Sweeney	.15
183 Jeff Suppan	.15
184 Roberto Hernandez	.15
185 Joe Randa	.15
186 Paul Byrd	.15
187 Luis Ordaz	.15
188 Kris Wilson	.15
189 Dee Brown	.15
190 Tony Clark	.15
191 Matt Anderson	.15
192 Robert Fick	.15
193 Juan Encarnacion	.15
194 Dean Palmer	.15
195 Victor Santos	.15
196 Damion Easley	.15
197 Jose Lima	.15
198 Deivi Cruz	.15
199 Roger Cedeno	.15
200 Jose Macias	.15
201 Jeff Weaver	.15
202 Brandon Inge	.15
203 Brian Moehler	.15
204 Brad Radke	.15
205 Doug Mientkiewicz	.15
206 Cristian Guzman	.15
207 Corey Koskie	.15
208 LaTroy Hawkins	.15
209 J.C. Romero	.15
210 Chad Allen	.15
211 Torii Hunter	.25
212 Travis Miller	.15
213 Joe Mays	.15
214 Todd Jones	.15
215 David Ortiz	.40
216 Brian Buchanan	.15
217 A.J. Pierzynski	.15
218 Carlos Lee	.15
219 Gary Glover	.15
220 Jose Valentin	.15
221 Aaron Rowand	.15
222 Sandy Alomar Jr.	.15
223 Herbert Perry	.15
224 Jon Garland	.15
225 Mark Buehrle	.15
226 Chris Singleton	.15
227 Kip Wells	.15
228 Ray Durham	.15
229 Joe Crede	.15
230 Keith Foulke	.15
231 Royce Clayton	.15
232 Andy Pettitte	.40
233 Derek Jeter	2.00
234 Jorge Posada	.40
235 Roger Clemens	1.50
236 Paul O'Neill	.25
237 Nick Johnson	.15
238 Gerald Williams	.15
239 Mariano Rivera	.25
240 Alfonso Soriano	.50
241 Ramiro Mendoza	.15
242 Mike Mussina	.50
243 Luis Sojo	.15
244 Scott Brosius	.15
245 David Justice	.25
246 Wade Miller	.15
247 Brad Ausmus	.15
248 Jeff Bagwell	.50
249 Daryle Ward	.15
250 Shane Reynolds	.15
251 Chris Truby	.15
252 Billy Wagner	.15
253 Craig Biggio	.25
254 Moises Alou	.25
255 Vinny Castilla	.15
256 Tim Redding	.15
257 Roy Oswalt	.40
258 Julio Lugo	.15
259 Chipper Jones	.75
260 Greg Maddux	1.00
261 Ken Caminiti	.15
262 Kevin Millwood	.25
263 Keith Lockhart	.15
264 Rey Sanchez	.15
265 Jason Marquis	.15
266 Brian Jordan	.15
267 Steve Karsay	.15
268 Wes Helms	.15
269 B.J. Surhoff	.15
270 Wilson Betemit	.15
271 John Smoltz	.25
272 Rafael Furcal	.25
273 Jeromy Burnitz	.15
274 Jimmy Haynes	.15
275 Mark Loretta	.15
276 Jose Hernandez	.15
277 Paul Rigdon	.15
278 Alex Sanchez	.15
279 Chad Fox	.15
280 Devon White	.15
281 Tyler Houston	.15
282 Ronnie Belliard	.15
283 Luis Lopez	.15
284 Ben Sheets	.40
285 Curtis Leskanic	.15
286 Henry Blanco	.15
287 Mark McGwire	2.00
288 Edgar Renteria	.25
289 Matt Morris	.25
290 Gene Stechschulte	.15
291 Dustin Hermanson	.15
292 Eli Marrero	.15
293 Albert Pujols	1.50
294 Luis Saturria	.15
295 Bobby Bonilla	.15
296 Garrett Stephenson	.15
297 Jim Edmonds	.40
298 Rick Ankiel	.15
299 Placido Polanco	.15
300 Dave Veres	.15
301 Sammy Sosa	1.50
302 Eric Young	.15
303 Kerry Wood	.75
304 Jon Lieber	.15
305 Joe Girardi	.15
306 Fred McGriff	.25
307 Jeff Fassero	.15
308 Julio Zuleta	.15
309 Kevin Tapani	.15
310 Rondell White	.15
311 Julian Tavarez	.15
312 Tom Gordon	.15
313 Corey Patterson	.25
314 Bill Mueller	.15
315 Randy Johnson	.75
316 Chad Moeller	.15
317 Tony Womack	.15
318 Erubiel Durazo	.15
319 Luis Gonzalez	.25
320 Brian Anderson	.15
321 Reggie Sanders	.15
322 Greg Colbrunn	.15
323 Robert Ellis	.15
324 Jack Cust	.15
325 Bret Prinz	.15
326 Steve Finley	.15
327 Byung-Hyun Kim	.15
328 Albie Lopez	.15
329 Gary Sheffield	.40
330 Mark Grudzielanek	.15
331 Paul LoDuca	.15
332 Tom Goodwin	.15
333 Andy Ashby	.15
334 Hiram Bocachica	.15
335 Dave Hansen	.15
336 Kevin Brown	.25
337 Marquis Grissom	.15
338 Terry Adams	.15
339 Chan Ho Park	.15
340 Adrian Beltre	.25
341 Luke Prokopec	.15
342 Jeff Shaw	.15
343 Vladimir Guerrero	.75
344 Orlando Cabrera	.15
345 Tony Armas Jr.	.15
346 Michael Barrett	.15
347 Geoff Blum	.15
348 Ryan Minor	.15
349 Peter Bergeron	.15
350 Graeme Lloyd	.15
351 Jose Vidro	.15
352 Javier Vazquez	.15
353 Matt Blank	.15
354 Masato Yoshii	.15
355 Carl Pavano	.15
356 Barry Bonds	2.00
357 Shawon Dunston	.15
358 Livan Hernandez	.15
359 Felix Rodriguez	.15
360 Pedro Feliz	.15
361 Calvin Murray	.15
362 Robb Nen	.15
363 Marvin Benard	.15
364 Russ Ortiz	.15
365 Jason Schmidt	.25
366 Rich Aurilia	.15
367 John Vander Wal	.15
368 Benito Santiago	.15
369 Ryan Dempster	.15
370 Charles Johnson	.15
371 Alex Gonzalez	.15
372 Luis Castillo	.15
373 Mike Lowell	.25
374 Antonio Alfonseca	.15
375 A.J. Burnett	.15
376 Brad Penny	.15
377 Jason Grilli	.15
378 Derrek Lee	.25
379 Matt Clement	.15
380 Eric Owens	.15
381 Vladimir Nunez	.15
382 Cliff Floyd	.15
383 Mike Piazza	1.25
384 Lenny Harris	.15
385 Glendon Rusch	.15
386 Todd Zeile	.15
387 Al Leiter	.25
388 Armando Benitez	.15
389 Alex Escobar	.15
390 Kevin Appier	.15
391 Matt Lawton	.15
392 Bruce Chen	.15
393 John Franco	.15
394 Tsuyoshi Shinjo	.15
395 Rey Ordonez	.15
396 Joe McEwing	.15
397 Ryan Klesko	.15
398 Brian Lawrence	.15
399 Kevin Walker	.15
400 Phil Nevin	.15
401 Bubba Trammell	.15
402 Wiki Gonzalez	.15
403 D'Angelo Jimenez	.15
404 Rickey Henderson	.40
405 Mike Darr	.15
406 Trevor Hoffman	.15
407 Damian Jackson	.15
408 Santiago Perez	.15
409 Cesar Crespo	.15
410 Robert Person	.15
411 Travis Lee	.15
412 Scott Rolen	.75
413 Turk Wendell	.15
414 Randy Wolf	.15
415 Kevin Jordan	.15
416 Jose Mesa	.15
417 Mike Lieberthal	.15
418 Bobby Abreu	.25
419 Tomas Perez	.15
420 Doug Glanville	.15
421 Reggie Taylor	.15
422 Jimmy Rollins	.40
423 Brian Giles	.25
424 Rob Mackowiak	.15
425 Bronson Arroyo	.15
426 Kevin Young	.15
427 Jack Wilson	.15
428 Adam Brown	.15
429 Chad Hermansen	.15
430 Jimmy Anderson	.15
431 Aramis Ramirez	.25
432 Todd Ritchie	.15
433 Pat Meares	.15
434 Warren Morris	.15
435 Derek Bell	.15
436 Ken Griffey Jr.	1.00
437 Elmer Dessens	.15
438 Ruben Rivera	.15
439 Jason LaRue	.15
440 Sean Casey	.25
441 Pete Harnisch	.15
442 Danny Graves	.15
443 Aaron Boone	.15
444 Dmitri Young	.15
445 Brandon Larson	.15
446 Pokey Reese	.15
447 Todd Walker	.15
448 Juan Castro	.15
449 Todd Helton	.50
450 Ben Petrick	.15
451 Juan Pierre	.15
452 Jeff Cirillo	.15
453 Juan Uribe	.15
454 Brian Bohanon	.15
455 Terry Shumpert	.15
456 Mike Hampton	.15
457 Shawn Chacon	.15
458 Adam Melhuse	.15
459 Greg Norton	.15
460 Gabe White	.15
461 Ichiro Suzuki (World Stage)	1.50
462 Carlos Delgado (World Stage)	.40
463 Manny Ramirez (World Stage)	.50
464 Miguel Tejada (World Stage)	.25
465 Tsuyoshi Shinjo (World Stage)	.15
466 Bernie Williams (World Stage)	.40
467 Juan Gonzalez (World Stage)	.50
468 Andruw Jones (World Stage)	.40
469 Ivan Rodriguez (World Stage)	.50
470 Larry Walker (World Stage)	
471 Hideo Nomo (World Stage)	.25
472 Albert Pujols (World Stage)	1.00
473 Pedro Martinez (World Stage)	.75

474 Vladimir Guerrero (World Stage) .75
475 Tony Batista (World Stage) .15
476 Kazuhiro Sasaki (World Stage) .15
477 Richard Hidalgo (World Stage) .15
478 Carlos Lee (World Stage) .15
479 Roberto Alomar (World Stage) .40
480 Rafael Palmeiro (World Stage) .50
481 Ken Griffey Jr. (Griffey Gallery) .50
482 Ken Griffey Jr. (Griffey Gallery) .50
483 Ken Griffey Jr. (Griffey Gallery) .50
484 Ken Griffey Jr. (Griffey Gallery) .50
485 Ken Griffey Jr. (Griffey Gallery) .50
486 Ken Griffey Jr. (Griffey Gallery) .50
487 Ken Griffey Jr. (Griffey Gallery) .50
488 Ken Griffey Jr. (Griffey Gallery) .50
489 Ken Griffey Jr. (Griffey Gallery) .50
490 Ken Griffey Jr. (Griffey Gallery) .50
491 Barry Bonds (Season Highlights Checklist) .75
492 Hideo Nomo (Season Highlights Checklist) .15
493 Ichiro Suzuki (Season Highlights Checklist) .50
494 Cal Ripken Jr. (Season Highlights Checklist) .75
495 Tony Gwynn (Season Highlights Checklist) .40
496 Randy Johnson (Season Highlights Checklist) .40
497 A.J. Burnett (Season Highlights Checklist) .15
498 Rickey Henderson (Season Highlights Checklist) .15
499 Albert Pujols (Season Highlights Checklist) .75
500 Luis Gonzalez (Season Highlights Checklist) .25
501 Brandon Puffer RC .50
502 Rodrigo Rosario RC .50
503 Tom Shearn RC .50
504 Reed Johnson RC .50
505 Chris Baker RC .50
506 John Ennis RC .50
507 Luis Martinez RC .50
508 So Taguchi RC .75
509 Scotty Layfield RC .50
510 Francis Beltran RC .50
511 Brandon Backe RC .50
512 Doug DeVore RC .50
513 Jeremy Ward RC .50
514 Jose Vaverde RC .50
515 P.J. Bevis RC .50
516 Victor Alvarez RC .50
517 Kazuhisa Ishii RC 2.00
518 Jorge Nunez RC .50
519 Eric Good RC .50
520 Ron Calloway RC .50
521 Valentino Pasucci .25
522 Nelson Castro RC .50
523 Deivis Santos .25
524 Luis Ugueto RC .50
525 Matt Thornton .25
526 Hansel Izquierdo RC .75
527 Tyler Yates RC .50
528 Mark Corey RC .50
529 Jaime Cerda RC .50
530 Satoru Komiyama RC .50
531 Steve Bechler RC .50
532 Ben Howard RC .50
533 Anderson Machado RC .50
534 Jorge Padilla RC .50
535 Eric Junge RC .50
536 Adrian Burnside RC .50
537 Mike Gonzalez RC .50
538 Josh Hancock RC .50
539 Colin Young RC .50
540 Rene Reyes RC .50
541 Cam Esslinger RC .50
542 Tim Kalita RC .50
543 Kevin Frederick RC .50
544 Kyle Kane RC .50
545 Edwin Almonte RC .50
546 Aaron Sele .15
547 Garret Anderson .40
548 Darin Erstad .25
549 Brad Fullmer .15
550 Kevin Appier .15
551 Tim Salmon .25
552 David Justice .25
553 Billy Koch .15
554 Scott Hatteberg .15
555 Tim Hudson .25
556 Miguel Tejada .25
557 Carlos Pena .15
558 Mike Sirotka .15
559 Jose Cruz Jr. .15
560 Josh Phelps .15
561 Brandon Lyon .15
562 Luke Prokopec .15
563 Felipe Lopez .15
564 Jason Standridge .15
565 Chris Gomez .15
566 John Flaherty .15
567 Jason Tyner .15
568 Bobby Smith .15
569 Wilson Alvarez .15
570 Matt Lawton .15
571 Omar Vizquel .25
572 Jim Thome .75
573 Brady Anderson .15
574 Alex Escobar .15
575 Russell Branyan .15
576 Bret Boone .25
577 Ben Davis .15
578 Mike Cameron .15
579 Jamie Moyer .15
580 Ruben Sierra .15
581 Jeff Cirillo .15
582 Marty Cordova .15
583 Mike Bordick .15
584 Brian Roberts .15
585 Luis Matos .15
586 Geronimo Gil .15
587 Jay Gibbons .15
588 Carl Everett .15
589 Ivan Rodriguez .50
590 Chan Ho Park .25
591 Juan Gonzalez .50
592 Hank Blalock .40
593 Todd Van Poppel .15
594 Pedro J. Martinez .75
595 Jason Varitek .15
596 Tony Clark .15
597 Johnny Damon .25
598 Dustin Hermanson .15
599 John Burkett .15
600 Carlos Beltran .40
601 Mark Quinn .15
602 Chuck Knoblauch .15
603 Michael Tucker .15
604 Carlos Febles .15
605 Jose Rosado .15
606 Dmitri Young .15
607 Bobby Higginson .15
608 Craig Paquette .15
609 Mitch Meluskey .15
610 Wendell Magee .15
611 Mike Rivera .15
612 Jacque Jones .15
613 Luis Rivas .15
614 Eric Milton .15
615 Eddie Guardado .15
616 Matt LeCroy .15
617 Mike Jackson .15
618 Magglio Ordonez .25
619 Frank Thomas .50
620 Rocky Biddle .15
621 Paul Konerko .25
622 Todd Ritchie .15
623 Jon Rauch .15
624 John Vander Wal .15
625 Rondell White .15
626 Jason Grabbe .15
627 Robin Ventura .15
628 David Wells .15
629 Bernie Williams .50
630 Lance Berkman .15
631 Richard Hidalgo .15
632 Gregg Zaun .15
633 Jose Vizcaino .15
634 Octavio Dotel .15
635 Morgan Ensberg .15
636 Andruw Jones .50
637 Tom Glavine .40
638 Gary Sheffield .40
639 Vinny Castilla .25
640 Javy Lopez .25
641 Albie Lopez .15
642 Geoff Jenkins .25
643 Jeffrey Hammonds .15
644 Alex Ochoa .15
645 Richie Sexson .40
646 Eric Young .15
647 Glendon Rusch .15
648 Tino Martinez .25
649 Fernando Vina .15
650 J.D. Drew .25
651 Woody Williams .15
652 Darryl Kile .15
653 Jason Isringhausen .15
654 Moises Alou .25
655 Alex Gonzalez .15
656 Delino DeShields .15
657 Todd Hundley .15
658 Chris Stynes .15
659 Jason Bere .15
660 Curt Schilling .40
661 Craig Counsell .15
662 Mark Grace .25
663 Matt Williams .25
664 Jay Bell .15
665 Rick Helling .15
666 Shawn Green .40
667 Eric Karros .15
668 Hideo Nomo .40
669 Omar Daal .15
670 Brian Jordan .15
671 Cesar Izturis .15
672 Fernando Tatis .15
673 Lee Stevens .15
674 Tomokazu Ohka .15
675 Brian Schneider .15
676 Brad Wilkerson .15
677 Bruce Chen .15
678 Tsuyoshi Shinjo .15
679 Jeff Kent .25
680 Kirk Rueter .15
681 J.T. Snow .15
682 David Bell .15
683 Reggie Sanders .15
684 Preston Wilson .15
685 Vic Darensbourg .15
686 Josh Beckett .40
687 Pablo Ozuna .15
688 Mike Redmond .15
689 Scott Strickland .15
690 Mo Vaughn .25
691 Roberto Alomar .50
692 Edgardo Alfonzo .15
693 Shawn Estes .15
694 Roger Cedeno .15
695 Jeromy Burnitz .15
696 Ray Lankford .15
697 Mark Kotsay .15
698 Kevin Jarvis .15
699 Bobby Jones .15
700 Sean Burroughs .15
701 Ramon Vazquez .15
702 Pat Burrell .40
703 Marlon Byrd .15
704 Brandon Duckworth .15
705 Marlon Anderson .15
706 Vicente Padilla .15
707 Kip Wells .15
708 Jason Kendall .15
709 Pokey Reese .15
710 Pat Meares .15
711 Kris Benson .15
712 Armando Rios .15
713 Mike Williams .15
714 Barry Larkin .40
715 Adam Dunn .50
716 Juan Encarnacion .15
717 Scott Williamson .15
718 Wilton Guerrero .15
719 Chris Reitsma .15
720 Larry Walker .25
721 Denny Neagle .15
722 Todd Zeile .15
723 Jose Ortiz .15
724 Jason Jennings .15
725 Tony Eusebio .15
726 Ichiro Suzuki 1.00
727 Barry Bonds 1.50
728 Randy Johnson .50
729 Albert Pujols 1.00
730 Roger Clemens .50
731 Sammy Sosa .50
732 Alex Rodriguez .50
733 Chipper Jones .40
734 Rickey Henderson .15
735 Mariners Team Photo .15
736 Luis Gonzalez .25
737 Derek Jeter 1.50
738 Ichiro Suzuki .50
739 Barry Bonds 1.50
740 Curt Schilling .25
741 Shawn Green .25
742 Jason Giambi .50
743 Roberto Alomar .25
744 Larry Walker .15
745 Mark McGwire .75

AL Centennial Bats

NM/M
Inserted 1:144
JD Joe DiMaggio 125.00
MM Mickey Mantle 150.00
BR Babe Ruth 150.00

AL Centennial Jerseys

NM/M
Common Player: 10.00
Inserted 1:144
PM Pedro Martinez 10.00
CR Cal Ripken Jr. 40.00
AR Alex Rodriguez 15.00
IR Ivan Rodriguez 10.00
NR Nolan Ryan 40.00
FT Frank Thomas 10.00

AL Centennial G-U Jerseys Autograph

No Pricing
Production 25 Sets

All-Star Salute Game Jerseys

NM/M
Common Player: 10.00
Inserted 1:144
SA Sparky Anderson 10.00
LB Lou Boudreau 10.00
DE Dennis Eckersley 10.00
NF Nellie Fox 15.00
KG Ken Griffey Jr. 25.00
AR Alex Rodriguez 25.00
DS Don Sutton 10.00
IS Ichiro Suzuki 40.00

Big Fly Zone

NM/M
Complete Set (10): 15.00
Common Player: .50
Inserted 1:14
Z1 Mark McGwire 4.00
Z2 Ken Griffey Jr. 3.00
Z3 Manny Ramirez 1.00
Z4 Sammy Sosa 3.00
Z5 Todd Helton 1.00
Z6 Barry Bonds 4.00
Z7 Luis Gonzalez .50
Z8 Alex Rodriguez 4.00
Z9 Carlos Delgado 1.00
Z10 Chipper Jones 1.50

Breakout Performers

NM/M
Complete Set (10): 10.00
Common Player: .50
Inserted 1:14
BP1 Ichiro Suzuki 3.00
BP2 Albert Pujols 4.00
BP3 Doug Mientkiewicz .50
BP4 Lance Berkman 1.00
BP5 Tsuyoshi Shinjo .50
BP6 Ben Sheets 1.00
BP7 Jimmy Rollins .75
BP8 J.D. Drew .75
BP9 Bret Boone 1.00
BP10 Alfonso Soriano 1.00

Championship Caliber

NM/M
Complete Set (6): 10.00
Common Player: 1.00
Inserted 1:23
CC1 Derek Jeter 5.00
CC2 Roberto Alomar 1.00
CC3 Chipper Jones 2.00
CC4 Gary Sheffield 1.00
CC5 Roger Clemens 3.00
CC6 Greg Maddux 2.50

Championship Caliber Swatches

NM/M
Common Player: 8.00
Inserted 1:288
RA Roberto Alomar/SP 20.00
KB Kevin Brown/SP 10.00
CF Cliff Floyd 10.00
ChJ Charles Johnson 8.00
RJ Randy Johnson 10.00
CJo Chipper Jones/SP 25.00
BL Barry Larkin 10.00
GM Greg Maddux/SP 40.00
TM Tino Martinez 8.00
JO John Olerud 8.00
AP Andy Pettitte 10.00
JP Jorge Posada 10.00
CS Curt Schilling 10.00
BW Bernie Williams 10.00

Chasing History

NM/M
Complete Set (15): 12.00
Common Player: .50
CH1 Sammy Sosa 2.00
CH2 Ken Griffey Jr. 1.50
CH3 Roger Clemens 2.00
CH4 Barry Bonds 3.00
CH5 Rafael Palmeiro 1.00
CH6 Andres Galarraga .50
CH7 Juan Gonzalez 1.00
CH8 Roberto Alomar 1.00
CH9 Randy Johnson 1.00
CH10 Jeff Bagwell 1.00
CH11 Fred McGriff .50
CH12 Matt Williams .50
CH13 Greg Maddux 1.50
CH14 Robb Nen .50
CH15 Kenny Lofton .50

Combo Bat

NM/M
Inserted 1:288
CB-RG Alex Rodriguez, Ken Griffey Jr. 30.00
CB-DM Joe DiMaggio, Mickey Mantle 200.00

Combo Jersey

NM/M
Common Duo: 10.00
Inserted 1:288
RS Alex Rodriguez, Sammy Sosa 30.00
RM Nolan Ryan, Pedro Martinez 40.00
RC Nolan Ryan, Roger Clemens 50.00
BS Barry Bonds, Sammy Sosa 40.00
HK Shigetoshi Hasegawa, Byung-Hun Kim 10.00

First Timers Jerseys

NM/M
Common Player: 8.00
Inserted 1:288
RB Russell Branyan 8.00
OD Omar Daal 8.00
FG Freddy Garcia 8.00
ML Matt Lawton 8.00
JM Joe Mays 8.00
EM Eric Milton 8.00
CP Corey Patterson 10.00
AP Albert Pujols 50.00
SS Shannon Stewart 8.00

First Timers Jerseys Autograph

No Pricing
Production 25 Sets

Game Jerseys

NM/M
Common Player: 8.00
Production 350 Sets
Golds: .75-1.5X
Production 100
TB Tony Batista 8.00
AB Adrian Beltre 8.00
JC Jeff Cirillo 8.00
KG Ken Griffey Jr. 20.00
TH Tim Hudson 10.00
MP Mike Piazza 15.00
SR Scott Rolen 15.00
CS Curt Schilling 15.00
SS Sammy Sosa 25.00
FT Frank Thomas 12.00
PW Preston Wilson 8.00

Game Jersey Autograph

NM/M
Common Player: 20.00
Production 200 Sets
BB Barry Bonds 200.00
CD Carlos Delgado 25.00
RF Rafael Furcal 20.00
JGi Jason Giambi 35.00
KG Ken Griffey Jr. 125.00
AJ Andruw Jones 35.00
AP Albert Pujols 125.00
CR Cal Ripken Jr. 200.00
NR Nolan Ryan 140.00
GS Gary Sheffield 20.00
IS Ichiro Suzuki 300.00
PW Preston Wilson 20.00

Game-Used Base

NM/M
Common Player: 5.00
Inserted 1:288
BB Barry Bonds 20.00
RC Roger Clemens 20.00
CD Carlos Delgado 5.00
JG Jason Giambi 10.00
TG Troy Glaus 8.00
JG Juan Gonzalez 10.00
LG Luis Gonzalez 8.00
SG Shawn Green 5.00
KG Ken Griffey Jr. 15.00
DJ Derek Jeter 25.00
AJ Andruw Jones 8.00
CJ Chipper Jones 10.00
MM Mark McGwire 15.00
MP Mike Piazza 15.00
CR Cal Ripken Jr. 40.00
AR Alex Rodriguez 8.00
IR Ivan Rodriguez 8.00
KS Kazuhiro Sasaki 5.00
SS Sammy Sosa 20.00
IS Ichiro Suzuki 50.00

ABBREVIATIONS

SP - Short Print

Game-Used Base Autograph

Complete Set (1):
Production 25

Game-Used Base Combo

NM/M
Common Combo: 40.00
Inserted 1:288
RG Alex Rodriguez, Ken Griffey Jr. 40.00
MJ Mark McGwire, Derek Jeter 60.00

Game-Worn Gems

NM/M
Common Player: 5.00
Inserted 1:48
Golds: 1-2X
Production 100 Sets
RA Roberto Alomar 8.00
EC Eric Chavez 6.00
CD Carlos Delgado 8.00
DE Darin Erstad/SP 10.00
FG Freddy Garcia/SP 8.00
TG Tom Glavine 8.00
JG Juan Gonzalez 8.00
LG Luis Gonzalez/SP 10.00
MH Mike Hampton/SP 8.00
CJ Chipper Jones 8.00
JK Jason Kendall 5.00
RK Ryan Klesko/SP 8.00
GM Greg Maddux 15.00
EM Edgar Martinez 8.00
PM Pedro Martinez/SP 15.00
TM Tino Martinez 8.00
JM Joe Mays 5.00
EM Eric Milton 5.00
PN Phil Nevin 5.00
HN Hideo Nomo/SP 30.00
JO John Olerud/SP 8.00
RP Robert Person 8.00
CR Cal Ripken Jr. 40.00
IR Ivan Rodriguez 10.00
SR Scott Rolen 15.00
CS Curt Schilling 10.00
AS Aaron Sele 8.00
GS Gary Sheffield/SP 8.00
FT Frank Thomas 10.00
OV Omar Vizquel/SP 10.00
RY Robin Yount 15.00

Double Game-Worn Gems

NM/M
Common Card: 8.00
Production 450 Sets
Golds: 1-2X
Production 100 Sets
NK Phil Nevin, Ryan Klesko 8.00
VB Omar Vizquel, Russell Branyan 10.00
DH Jermaine Dye, Tim Hudson 10.00
TO Frank Thomas, Magglio Ordonez 15.00
MI Edgar Martinez, Ichiro Suzuki/150 80.00
GS Luis Gonzalez, Curt Schilling 15.00
AP Roberto Alomar, Mike Piazza 20.00
PL Robert Person, Mike Lieberthal 8.00
MM Kevin Millwood, Greg Maddux 20.00
KG Jason Kendall, Brian Giles 10.00
DF Carlos Delgado, Shannon Stewart 10.00
PN Chan Ho Park, Hideo Nomo 30.00

Global Swatch Jerseys

NM/M
Common Player: 5.00
Inserted 1:144
CD Carlos Delgado 8.00
SH Shigetoshi Hasegawa 5.00
BK Byung-Hun Kim 5.00

HN	Hideo Nomo	35.00
CP	Chan Ho Park	5.00
MR	Manny Ramirez	10.00
KS	Kazuhiro Sasaki	5.00
TS	Tsuyoshi Shinjo	5.00
IS	Ichiro Suzuki	50.00
MY	Masato Yoshii	5.00

Global Swatch Jerseys Autograph
No Pricing
Production 25 Sets

McGwire Memorabilia
NM/M
Common Card:

AM-J	Mark McGwire/Jsy/70	150.00
AM-B	Mark McGwire/Bat/70	150.00
MMc	Mark McGwire/500 HR Club Bat/350	300.00
MM-SS	Mark McGwire, Sammy Sosa/25 (Combo Jersey)	300.00
MM-KG	Mark McGwire, Ken Griffey Jr./25 (Combo Jersey)	300.00
MM-JG	Mark McGwire, Jason Giambi/25 (Combo Jersey)	250.00

Patch Numbers
Complete Set (3):
Common Player:

Return of the Ace

NM/M
Complete Set (15): 15.00
Common Player: 1.00
Inserted 1:11

RA1	Randy Johnson	2.00
RA2	Greg Maddux	3.00
RA3	Pedro Martinez	2.00
RA4	Freddy Garcia	1.00
RA5	Matt Morris	1.00
RA6	Mark Mulder	1.00
RA7	Wade Miller	1.00
RA8	Kevin Brown	1.00
RA9	Roger Clemens	4.00
RA10	Jon Lieber	1.00
RA11	C.C. Sabathia	1.00
RA12	Tim Hudson	1.50
RA13	Curt Schilling	2.00
RA14	Al Leiter	1.00
RA15	Mike Mussina	1.50

Sons of Summer Game Jerseys
NM/M
Common Player: 10.00
Inserted 1:288

RA	Roberto Alomar	10.00
JB	Jeff Bagwell	10.00
RC	Roger Clemens	15.00
JG	Juan Gonzalez	10.00
GM	Greg Maddux	15.00
PM	Pedro Martinez/SP	15.00
MP	Mike Piazza	15.00
AR	Alex Rodriguez	15.00

Superstar Summit

NM/M
Complete Set (6): 15.00
Common Player: 1.50
Inserted 1:23

SS1	Sammy Sosa	3.00
SS2	Alex Rodriguez	4.00
SS3	Mark McGwire	4.00
SS4	Barry Bonds	4.00
SS5	Mike Piazza	3.00
SS6	Ken Griffey Jr.	2.50

Superstar Summit II

NM/M
Complete Set (15): 25.00
Common Player: 1.00
Inserted 1:11

SS1	Alex Rodriguez	4.00
SS2	Jason Giambi	1.00
SS3	Vladimir Guerrero	1.50
SS4	Randy Johnson	1.50
SS5	Chipper Jones	1.50
SS6	Ichiro Suzuki	3.00
SS7	Sammy Sosa	2.50
SS8	Greg Maddux	2.00
SS9	Ken Griffey Jr.	2.50
SS10	Todd Helton	1.00
SS11	Barry Bonds	4.00
SS12	Derek Jeter	4.00
SS13	Mike Piazza	3.00
SS14	Ivan Rodriguez	1.00
SS15	Frank Thomas	1.00

The People's Choice Game Jerseys

NM/M
Common Player: 5.00
Inserted 1:24
Golds: 1-2X
Production 100 Sets

JBa	Jeff Bagwell	10.00
EB	Ellis Burks/SP	10.00
JBu	Jeromy Burnitz	5.00
OD	Omar Daal	5.00
CD	Carlos Delgado	8.00
RF	Rafael Furcal	6.00
AG	Andres Galarraga/SP	10.00
BG	Brian Giles	5.00
JG	Juan Gonzalez	10.00
KG	Ken Griffey Jr.	20.00
TG	Tony Gwynn	12.00
SH	Sterling Hitchcock	5.00
HI	Hideki Irabu	5.00
CJ	Charles Johnson	5.00
DL	Derek Lowe	8.00
GM	Greg Maddux	15.00
TM	Tino Martinez	10.00
JN	Jeff Nelson	5.00
RO	Rey Ordonez	5.00
RP	Rafael Palmeiro/SP	15.00
RP	Robert Person/SP	10.00
AP	Andy Pettitte	10.00
MP	Mike Piazza	15.00
TR	Tim Raines	5.00
MRa	Manny Ramirez	10.00
MRi	Mariano Rivera	8.00
AR	Alex Rodriguez	15.00
TS	Tim Salmon	6.00
CS	Curt Schilling	5.00
TSh	Tsuyoshi Shinjo	5.00
JS	J.T. Snow	5.00
SS	Sammy Sosa	20.00
MS	Mike Stanton	5.00
FT	Frank Thomas	10.00
RV	Robin Ventura	6.00
OV	Omar Vizquel	5.00
DW	David Wells	6.00
BW	Bernie Williams	8.00
MW	Matt Williams/SP	10.00

UD Patch Logo

NM/M
Common Player: 60.00
Inserted 1:2,500

Prices for Stripes & Numbers identical.

BB	Barry Bonds	125.00
JG	Jason Giambi	60.00
KG	Ken Griffey Jr.	100.00
PM	Pedro Martinez	80.00
CR	Cal Ripken Jr.	150.00
AR	Alex Rodriguez	125.00
SS	Sammy Sosa	100.00

UD Patch Numbers
Complete Set (7):
Common Player:

UD Patch Stripes

NM/M
Complete Set (7):
Common Player:

Patch Stripes Autograph
Complete Set (2):
Common Player:

Yankees Dynasty Combo Base
NM/M
Common Combo: 50.00

JW	Derek Jeter, Bernie Williams	60.00
CJ	Roger Clemens, Derek Jeter	75.00

Yankees Dynasty Jerseys
NM/M
Common Combo: 20.00
Inserted 1:288

PR	Andy Pettitte, Mariano Rivera	25.00
BT	Wade Boggs, Joe Torre	25.00
CP	Roger Clemens, Jorge Posada	50.00
DM	Joe DiMaggio, Mickey Mantle	300.00
RK	Willie Randolph, Chuck Knoblauch	20.00
BJ	Scott Brosius, David Justice	20.00
OM	Paul O'Neill, Tino Martinez	25.00
WO	Bernie Williams, Paul O'Neill	25.00
WG	David Wells, Dwight Gooden	25.00
GC	Joe Girardi, David Cone	25.00
KR	Chuck Knoblauch, Tim Raines	25.00

2001 All-Star HR Derby Jerseys
NM/M
Common Player: 10.00
Inserted 1:288

BrB	Bret Boone	10.00
JG	Jason Giambi	15.00
TH	Todd Helton	15.00
AR	Alex Rodriguez	20.00
SS	Sammy Sosa	25.00

2001's Greatest Hits

NM/M
Complete Set (10): 20.00
Common Player: 1.00
Inserted 1:14

GH1	Barry Bonds	4.00
GH2	Ichiro Suzuki	3.00
GH3	Albert Pujols	3.00
GH4	Mike Piazza	2.50
GH5	Alex Rodriguez	3.00
GH6	Mark McGwire	3.00
GH7	Manny Ramirez	1.00
GH8	Ken Griffey Jr.	2.00
GH9	Sammy Sosa	3.00
GH10	Derek Jeter	4.00

2002 UD Authentics

Kazuhisa Ishii
NM/M
Complete Set (200): 50.00
Common Player: .25
Reversed Negatives: 1-2.5X
Inserted 1:9
Pack (5): 2.50
Box (18): 35.00

1	Brad Fullmer	.25
2	Garret Anderson	.40
3	Darin Erstad	.25
4	Jarrod Washburn	.25
5	Troy Glaus	.40
6	Barry Zito	.40
7	David Justice	.40
8	Eric Chavez	.40
9	Tim Hudson	.25
10	Miguel Tejada	.40
11	Jermaine Dye	.25
12	Mark Mulder	.40
13	Carlos Delgado	.50
14	Jose Cruz Jr.	.25
15	Shannon Stewart	.25
16	Raul Mondesi	.25
17	Tanyon Sturtze	.25
18	Toby Hall	.25
19	Greg Vaughn	.25
20	Aubrey Huff	.25
21	Ben Grieve	.25
22	Brent Abernathy	.25
23	Jim Thome	.75
24	C.C. Sabathia	.25
25	Matt Lawton	.25
26	Omar Vizquel	.25
27	Ellis Burks	.25
28	Russ Branyan	.25
29	Bartolo Colon	.40
30	Ichiro Suzuki	1.50
31	John Olerud	.40
32	Freddy Garcia	.25
33	Mike Cameron	.25
34	Jeff Cirillo	.25
35	Kazuhiro Sasaki	.40
36	Edgar Martinez	.40
37	Bret Boone	.25
38	Jeff Conine	.25
39	Melvin Mora	.25
40	Jason Johnson	.25
41	Chris Richard	.25
42	Tony Batista	.25
43	Ivan Rodriguez	.50
44	Gabe Kapler	.25
45	Rafael Palmeiro	.50
46	Alex Rodriguez	1.50
47	Juan Gonzalez	.50
48	Carl Everett	.25
49	Nomar Garciaparra	1.50
50	Trot Nixon	.25
51	Manny Ramirez	.50
52	Pedro J. Martinez	.75
53	Johnny Damon	.40
54	Shea Hillenbrand	.25
55	Mike Sweeney	.25
56	Mark Quinn	.25
57	Joe Randa	.25
58	Carlos Beltran	.40
59	Chuck Knoblauch	.25
60	Robert Fick	.25
61	Jeff Weaver	.25
62	Bobby Higginson	.25
63	Dean Palmer	.25
64	Dmitri Young	.25
65	Corey Koskie	.25
66	Doug Mientkiewicz	.25
67	Joe Mays	.25
68	Torii Hunter	.40
69	Cristian Guzman	.25
70	Jacque Jones	.25
71	Magglio Ordonez	.25
72	Paul Konerko	.25
73	Carlos Lee	.25
74	Mark Buehrle	.25
75	Jose Canseco	.50
76	Frank Thomas	.50
77	Roger Clemens	1.50
78	Derek Jeter	2.00
79	Jason Giambi	.50
80	Rondell White	.25
81	Bernie Williams	.50
82	Jorge Posada	.50
83	Mike Mussina	.50
84	Alfonso Soriano	.75
85	Wade Miller	.25
86	Jeff Bagwell	.50
87	Craig Biggio	.40
88	Roy Oswalt	.40
89	Lance Berkman	.40
90	Daryle Ward	.25
91	Chipper Jones	.75
92	Greg Maddux	1.00
93	Marcus Giles	.25
94	Gary Sheffield	.50
95	Tom Glavine	.50
96	Andruw Jones	.50
97	Rafael Furcal	.25
98	Richie Sexson	.40
99	Ben Sheets	.40
100	Jose Hernandez	.25
101	Geoff Jenkins	.40
102	Jeffrey Hammonds	.25
103	Edgar Renteria	.40
104	Matt Morris	.40
105	Tino Martinez	.25
106	Jim Edmonds	.40
107	Albert Pujols	1.50
108	J.D. Drew	.40
109	Fernando Vina	.25
110	Darryl Kile	.25
111	Sammy Sosa	1.50
112	Fred McGriff	.40
113	Kerry Wood	.75
114	Moises Alou	.25
115	Jon Lieber	.25
116	Mark Grace	.50
117	Randy Johnson	.75
118	Curt Schilling	.50
119	Luis Gonzalez	.40
120	Steve Finley	.25
121	Matt Williams	.40
122	Shawn Green	.40
123	Kevin Brown	.40
124	Adrian Beltre	.40
125	Paul LoDuca	.25
126	Hideo Nomo	.50
127	Brian Jordan	.25
128	Vladimir Guerrero	.75
129	Javier Vazquez	.25
130	Jose Vidro	.25
131	Orlando Cabrera	.25
132	Jeff Kent	.40
133	Rich Aurilia	.25
134	Russ Ortiz	.25
135	Barry Bonds	2.00
136	Preston Wilson	.25
137	Ryan Dempster	.25
138	Cliff Floyd	.25
139	Josh Beckett	.40
140	Mike Lowell	.25
141	Mike Piazza	1.00
142	Roberto Alomar	.40
143	Al Leiter	.40
144	Edgardo Alfonzo	.25
145	Roger Cedeno	.25
146	Jeromy Burnitz	.25
147	Phil Nevin	.25
148	Mark Kotsay	.25
149	Ryan Klesko	.25
150	Trevor Hoffman	.25
151	Bobby Abreu	.40
152	Scott Rolen	.75
153	Jimmy Rollins	.40
154	Robert Person	.25
155	Pat Burrell	.40
156	Randy Wolf	.25
157	Brian Giles	.40
158	Aramis Ramirez	.50
159	Kris Benson	.25
160	Jason Kendall	.25
161	Ken Griffey Jr.	1.00
162	Sean Casey	.40
163	Adam Dunn	.50
164	Barry Larkin	.50
165	Todd Helton	.50
166	Mike Hampton	.25
167	Larry Walker	.40
168	Juan Pierre	.25
169	Juan Uribe	.25
170	So Taguchi RC	2.00
171	Brendan Donnelly RC	.50
172	Chris Baker RC	.50
173	John Ennis RC	.50
174	Francis Beltran RC	.75
175	Danny Wright RC	.50
176	Brandon Backe RC	.75
177	Mark Corey RC	.75
178	Kazuhisa Ishii RC	3.00
179	Ron Calloway RC	.50
180	Kevin Frederick RC	.50
181	Jaime Cerda RC	.75
182	Doug DeVore RC	.50
183	Brandon Puffer RC	.75
184	Andy Pratt RC	.50
185	Adrian Burnside RC	.50
186	Josh Hancock RC	.75
187	Jorge Nunez RC	.50
188	Tyler Yates RC	1.00
189	Kyle Kane RC	.75
190	Jose Valverde RC	.50
191	Matt Thornton RC	.50
192	Ben Howard RC	.50
193	Reed Johnson RC	1.50
194	Rene Reyes RC	.50
195	Jeremy Ward RC	.50
196	Steve Bechler RC	.50
197	Cam Esslinger RC	.50
198	Michael Crudale RC	.50
199	Todd Donovan RC	.50
200		

Retro UD Jerseys
NM/M
Common Player: 5.00
Inserted 1:16
Golds: 1-2X

Production 275 Sets
Reverse Neg.: 1-2X
Production 350 Sets

JB	Jeff Bagwell	15.00
KB	Kevin Brown	8.00
EC	Eric Chavez	8.00
RC	Roger Clemens/SP	25.00
CD	Carlos Delgado	8.00
JD	J.D. Drew	10.00
JE	Jim Edmonds	8.00
DE	Darin Erstad	5.00
RF	Rafael Furcal	5.00
JG	Jason Giambi	10.00
TG	Tom Glavine	10.00
LG	Luis Gonzalez	8.00
KG	Ken Griffey Jr.	20.00
TH	Todd Helton	12.00
RJ	Randy Johnson	12.00
AJ	Andruw Jones	8.00
CJ	Chipper Jones	15.00
GM	Greg Maddux	15.00
MP	Mike Piazza	15.00
MR	Manny Ramirez	10.00
AR	Alex Rodriguez	15.00
IR	Ivan Rodriguez	10.00
SS	Sammy Sosa/SP	20.00
MS	Mike Sweeney	5.00
FT	Frank Thomas	10.00
BW	Bernie Williams	10.00
BZ	Barry Zito	8.00

UD Heroes of Baseball

NM/M
Complete Set (30): 150.00
Ichiro: 8.00
Griffey Jr.: 6.00
Alex Rodriguez: 8.00
Production 1,989 Sets

HB-I1	Ichiro Suzuki	8.00
HB-I2	Ichiro Suzuki	8.00
HB-I3	Ichiro Suzuki	8.00
HB-I4	Ichiro Suzuki	8.00
HB-I5	Ichiro Suzuki	8.00
HB-I6	Ichiro Suzuki	8.00
HB-I7	Ichiro Suzuki	8.00
HB-I8	Ichiro Suzuki	8.00
HB-I9	Ichiro Suzuki	8.00
HB-I10	Ichiro Suzuki	8.00
HB-G1	Ken Griffey Jr.	6.00
HB-G2	Ken Griffey Jr.	6.00
HB-G3	Ken Griffey Jr.	6.00
HB-G4	Ken Griffey Jr.	6.00
HB-G5	Ken Griffey Jr.	6.00
HB-G6	Ken Griffey Jr.	6.00
HB-G7	Ken Griffey Jr.	6.00
HB-G8	Ken Griffey Jr.	6.00
HB-G9	Ken Griffey Jr.	6.00
HB-G10	Ken Griffey Jr.	6.00
HB-R1	Alex Rodriguez	8.00
HB-R2	Alex Rodriguez	8.00
HB-R3	Alex Rodriguez	8.00
HB-R4	Alex Rodriguez	8.00
HB-R5	Alex Rodriguez	8.00
HB-R6	Alex Rodriguez	8.00
HB-R7	Alex Rodriguez	8.00
HB-R8	Alex Rodriguez	8.00
HB-R9	Alex Rodriguez	8.00
HB-R10	Alex Rodriguez	8.00

Signed UD Heroes of Baseball
NM/M
Random Inserts:

G	Ken Griffey Jr./185	125.00
R	Alex Rodriguez/185	90.00
I	Ichiro Suzuki/125	400.00

Retro UD Star Rookie Jerseys

NM/M
Common Player: 5.00
Inserted 1:16
Golds: 1-2X

Production 275 Sets
CB	Craig Biggio	8.00
PB	Pat Burrell	8.00
BG	Brian Giles	5.00
JG	Juan Gonzalez	8.00
LG	Luis Gonzalez	8.00
SG	Shawn Green	8.00
KG	Ken Griffey Jr.	20.00
RJ	Randy Johnson	10.00
CJ	Chipper Jones	10.00
DJ	David Justice	5.00
RK	Ryan Klesko	5.00
KL	Kenny Lofton	5.00
PM	Pedro J. Martinez	15.00
HN	Hideo Nomo	15.00
JO	John Olerud	8.00
MO	Magglio Ordonez	8.00
RP	Robert Person	5.00
AP	Albert Pujols	20.00
MR	Manny Ramirez/SP	15.00
AR	Alex Rodriguez	20.00
IR	Ivan Rodriguez	10.00
KS	Kazuhiro Sasaki	8.00
GS	Gary Sheffield	8.00
SS	Sammy Sosa/SP	20.00
I	Ichiro Suzuki	40.00
JT	Jim Thome	12.00
LW	Larry Walker	5.00

Signed Retro UD Star Rookie Jerseys

NM/M
Production 40 Sets
KG	Ken Griffey Jr.	100.00
AR	Alex Rodriguez	150.00
JT	Jim Thome	75.00

Reverse Negative Retro UD Jerseys
Complete Set (29):
Common Player:

Stars of '89 Jerseys

NM/M
Common Player: 5.00
Inserted 1:16
RA	Roberto Alomar	8.00
KB	Kevin Brown	8.00
EB	Ellis Burks	5.00
JC	Jose Canseco	5.00
RC	Roger Clemens	15.00
DC	David Cone	5.00
AG	Andres Galarraga	5.00
TG	Tom Glavine	10.00
JG	Juan Gonzalez	10.00
MG	Mark Grace	5.00
KG	Ken Griffey Jr.	20.00
RH	Rickey Henderson	10.00
RJ	Randy Johnson	10.00
DJ	David Justice	5.00
BL	Barry Larkin/SP	15.00
AL	Al Leiter	5.00
GM	Greg Maddux	15.00
EM	Edgar Martinez	5.00
FM	Fred McGriff	5.00
JO	John Olerud	5.00
PO	Paul O'Neill	5.00
RP	Rafael Palmeiro	8.00
CS	Curt Schilling	8.00
GS	Gary Sheffield	8.00
SS	Sammy Sosa	15.00
RV	Robin Ventura	5.00
LW	Larry Walker	5.00
MW	Matt Williams	5.00

1989 Flashbacks

NM/M
Complete Set (12): 30.00
Common Player: 1.50
Production 4,225 Sets
F1	Ken Griffey Jr.	8.00
F2	Gary Sheffield	1.50
F3	Randy Johnson	3.00
F4	Roger Clemens	4.00
F5	Greg Maddux	3.00
F6	Mark Grace	2.00
F7	Barry Bonds	5.00
F8	Roberto Alomar	2.00
F9	Sammy Sosa	5.00
F10	Rafael Palmeiro	2.00
F11	Edgar Martinez	1.50
F12	Jose Canseco	2.00

2002 Upper Deck Ballpark Idols

NM/M
Complete Set (245): 125.00
Common Player: .15
Common (201-245): 3.00
Production 1,750
Pack (5): 2.00
Box (24 + Bobber): 50.00
1	Troy Glaus	.40
2	Kevin Appier	.15
3	Darin Erstad	.25
4	Garret Anderson	.25
5	Brad Fullmer	.15
6	Tim Salmon	.25
7	Eric Chavez	.25
8	Tim Hudson	.25
9	David Justice	.25
10	Barry Zito	.25
11	Miguel Tejada	.40
12	Mark Mulder	.40
13	Jermaine Dye	.15
14	Carlos Delgado	.40
15	Jose Cruz Jr.	.15
16	Brandon Lyon	.15
17	Shannon Stewart	.15
18	Eric Hinske	.25
19	Chris Carpenter	.15
20	Greg Vaughn	.15
21	Tanyon Sturtze	.15
22	Jason Tyner	.15
23	Toby Hall	.15
24	Ben Grieve	.15
25	Jim Thome	.75
26	Omar Vizquel	.25
27	Ricky Gutierrez	.15
28	C.C. Sabathia	.15
29	Ellis Burks	.15
30	Matt Lawton	.15
31	Milton Bradley	.15
32	Edgar Martinez	.25
33	Ichiro Suzuki	1.50
34	Bret Boone	.25
35	Freddy Garcia	.25
36	Mike Cameron	.15
37	John Olerud	.15
38	Kazuhiro Sasaki	.15
39	Jeff Cirillo	.15
40	Jeff Conine	.15
41	Marty Cordova	.15
42	Tony Batista	.15
43	Jerry Hairston Jr.	.15
44	Jason Johnson	.15
45	David Segui	.15
46	Alex Rodriguez	2.00
47	Rafael Palmeiro	.50
48	Carl Everett	.15
49	Chan Ho Park	.15
50	Ivan Rodriguez	.50
51	Juan Gonzalez	.50
52	Hank Blalock	.50
53	Manny Ramirez	.50
54	Pedro J. Martinez	.75
55	Tony Clark	.15
56	Nomar Garciaparra	1.25
57	Johnny Damon	.25
58	Trot Nixon	.15
59	Rickey Henderson	.50
60	Mike Sweeney	.15
61	Neifi Perez	.15
62	Joe Randa	.15
63	Carlos Beltran	.25
64	Chuck Knoblauch	.15
65	Michael Tucker	.15
66	Dean Palmer	.15
67	Bobby Higginson	.15
68	Dmitri Young	.15
69	Randall Simon	.15
70	Mitch Meluskey	.15
71	Damion Easley	.15
72	Joe Mays	.15
73	Doug Mientkiewicz	.15
74	Corey Koskie	.15
75	Brad Radke	.15
76	Cristian Guzman	.15
77	Torii Hunter	.25
78	Eric Milton	.15
79	Frank Thomas	.50
80	Paul Konerko	.25
81	Mark Buehrle	.15
82	Magglio Ordonez	.25
83	Carlos Lee	.15
84	Joe Crede	.15
85	Derek Jeter	2.00
86	Bernie Williams	.50
87	Mike Mussina	.50
88	Jorge Posada	.40
89	Roger Clemens	1.50
90	Jason Giambi	.50
91	Alfonso Soriano	.75
92	Rondell White	.15
93	Jeff Bagwell	.50
94	Lance Berkman	.40
95	Roy Oswalt	.25
96	Richard Hidalgo	.15
97	Wade Miller	.15
98	Craig Biggio	.25
99	Greg Maddux	1.00
100	Chipper Jones	.75
101	Gary Sheffield	.40
102	Rafael Furcal	.15
103	Andruw Jones	.50
104	Vinny Castilla	.15
105	Marcus Giles	.15
106	Tom Glavine	.40
107	Richie Sexson	.40
108	Geoff Jenkins	.15
109	Glendon Rusch	.15
110	Eric Young	.15
111	Ben Sheets	.25
112	Alex Sanchez	.15
113	Albert Pujols	1.50
114	J.D. Drew	.25
115	Matt Morris	.25
116	Jim Edmonds	.40
117	Tino Martinez	.15
118	Scott Rolen	.75
119	Edgar Renteria	.15
120	Sammy Sosa	1.50
121	Kerry Wood	.75
122	Moises Alou	.25
123	Jon Lieber	.15
124	Fred McGriff	.25
125	Juan Cruz	.15
126	Alex Gonzalez	.15
127	Corey Patterson	.25
128	Randy Johnson	.75
129	Luis Gonzalez	.25
130	Steve Finley	.15
131	Matt Williams	.15
132	Curt Schilling	.50
133	Mark Grace	.40
134	Craig Counsell	.15
135	Shawn Green	.25
136	Kevin Brown	.25
137	Hideo Nomo	.40
138	Paul LoDuca	.15
139	Brian Jordan	.15
140	Eric Karros	.15
141	Adrian Beltre	.15
142	Vladimir Guerrero	.75
143	Fernando Tatis	.15
144	Javier Vazquez	.15
145	Orlando Cabrera	.15
146	Tony Armas Jr.	.15
147	Jose Vidro	.15
148	Barry Bonds	2.00
149	Rich Aurilia	.15
150	Tsuyoshi Shinjo	.15
151	Jeff Kent	.25
152	Russ Ortiz	.15
153	Jason Schmidt	.15
154	Reggie Sanders	.15
155	Preston Wilson	.15
156	Luis Castillo	.15
157	Charles Johnson	.15
158	Josh Beckett	.40
159	Derrek Lee	.25
160	Mike Lowell	.15
161	Mike Piazza	1.00
162	Roberto Alomar	.40
163	Al Leiter	.15
164	Mo Vaughn	.25
165	Jeromy Burnitz	.15
166	Edgardo Alfonzo	.15
167	Roger Cedeno	.15
168	Ryan Klesko	.25
169	Brian Lawrence	.15
170	Sean Burroughs	.15
171	Phil Nevin	.15
172	Ramon Vazquez	.15
173	Mark Kotsay	.15
174	Marlon Anderson	.15
175	Mike Lieberthal	.15
176	Bobby Abreu	.25
177	Pat Burrell	.40
178	Robert Person	.15
179	Brandon Duckworth	.15
180	Jimmy Rollins	.25
181	Brian Giles	.25
182	Pokey Reese	.15
183	Kris Benson	.15
184	Aramis Ramirez	.25
185	Jason Kendall	.15
186	Kip Wells	.15
187	Ken Griffey Jr.	1.00
188	Adam Dunn	.50
189	Barry Larkin	.40
190	Sean Casey	.15
191	Austin Kearns	.25
192	Aaron Boone	.15
193	Todd Helton	.50
194	Juan Pierre	.15
195	Mike Hampton	.15
196	Jose Ortiz	.15
197	Larry Walker	.25
198	Juan Uribe	.15
199	Ichiro Suzuki (Checklist)	.75
200	Jason Giambi (Checklist)	.25
201	Franklyn German RC	3.00
202	Rodrigo Rosario RC	3.00
203	Brandon Puffer RC	3.00
204	Kirk Saarloos RC	3.00
205	Chris Baker RC	3.00
206	John Ennis RC	3.00
207	Luis Martinez RC	3.00
208	So Taguchi RC	6.00
209	Michael Crudale RC	3.00
210	Francis Beltran RC	3.00
211	Brandon Backe RC	3.00
212	Felix Escalona RC	3.00
213	Jose Valverde RC	4.00
214	Doug DeVore RC	3.00
215	Kazuhisa Ishii RC	6.00
216	Victor Alvarez RC	3.00
217	Ron Calloway RC	3.00
218	Eric Good RC	3.00
219	Jorge Nunez RC	3.00
220	Deivis Santos RC	3.00
221	Nelson Castro RC	3.00
222	Matt Thornton RC	3.00
223	Jason Simontacchi RC	3.00
224	Hansel Izquierdo RC	3.00
225	Tyler Yates RC	4.00
226	Jaime Cerda RC	3.00
227	Satoru Komiyama RC	3.00
228	Steve Bechler RC	3.00
229	Ben Howard RC	3.00
230	Todd Donovan RC	3.00
231	Jorge Padilla RC	3.00
232	Eric Junge RC	3.00
233	Anderson Machado RC	3.00
234	Adrian Burnside RC	3.00
235	Mike Gonzalez RC	3.00
236	Josh Hancock RC	3.00
237	Anastasio Martinez RC	3.00
238	Chris Booker RC	3.00
239	Rene Reyes RC	3.00
240	Cam Esslinger RC	3.00
241	Oliver Perez RC	10.00
242	Tim Kalita RC	3.00
243	Kevin Frederick RC	3.00
244	Mitch Wylie RC	3.00
245	Edwin Almonte RC	3.00

Bronze
Stars (1-200): 5-10X
SP's (201-245): .75-1.5X
Production 100 Sets

Gold
No pricing due to scarcity.
Production 25 Sets

Bobbers
NM/M
Inserted 1:Box
Roberto Alomar	10.00
Jeff Bagwell	15.00
Josh Beckett	10.00
Barry Bonds	30.00
Sean Burroughs	8.00
Roger Clemens	20.00
Joe DiMaggio/555/Away	40.00
Joe DiMaggio/361/Home	50.00
Nomar Garciaparra	20.00
Jason Giambi	10.00
Luis Gonzalez	8.00
Ken Griffey Jr.	20.00
Vladimir Guerrero	15.00
Kazuhisa Ishii	10.00
Derek Jeter/SP/Away	40.00
Randy Johnson/D'backs	15.00
Randy Johnson/Expos	15.00
Chipper Jones	15.00
Greg Maddux	20.00
Mickey Mantle/777/Away	50.00
Mickey Mantle/536/Home	60.00
Mark McGwire/Cards	35.00
Mike Piazza/Mets	20.00
Mark Prior	15.00
Albert Pujols	25.00
Alex Rodriguez	20.00
Ivan Rodriguez	10.00
Curt Schilling/D'backs	10.00
Sammy Sosa/Cubs/Away	25.00
Ichiro Suzuki/SP/Away	30.00
Frank Thomas	10.00
Jim Thome	15.00

ABBREVIATIONS
SP - Short Print

Bobbers Autograph
NM/M
Common Autograph
Inserted 1:14 Boxes
Josh Beckett	60.00

Bobbers Gold
NM/M
Amount produced listed.
Joe DiMaggio/56/Away	100.00
Joe DiMaggio/41/Home	125.00
Mickey Mantle/77/Away	140.00
Mickey Mantle/61/Home	125.00

Field Garb Jerseys
NM/M
Common Player: 4.00
Inserted 1:72
TB	Tony Batista	4.00
BG	Brian Giles	4.00
RJ	Randy Johnson	10.00
JK	Jeff Kent	4.00
TM	Tino Martinez	4.00
JO	John Olerud	4.00
AR	Alex Rodriguez	12.00
IR	Ivan Rodriguez	6.00
MS	Mike Sweeney	4.00
RV	Robin Ventura	4.00
LW	Larry Walker	4.00
BZ	Barry Zito	6.00

Figure Heads

NM/M
Complete Set (10): 20.00
Common Player: 1.00
Inserted 1:12
F1	Ichiro Suzuki	3.00
F2	Sammy Sosa	2.50
F3	Alex Rodriguez	4.00
F4	Jason Giambi	1.00
F5	Barry Bonds	4.00
F6	Chipper Jones	1.50
F7	Mike Piazza	2.00
F8	Derek Jeter	4.00
F9	Nomar Garciaparra	2.50
F10	Ken Griffey Jr.	2.50

Player's Club Jerseys
NM/M
Common Player: 6.00
Inserted 1:72
KB	Kevin Brown	6.00
DE	Darin Erstad	8.00
RF	Rafael Furcal	6.00
TH	Tim Hudson	6.00
AJ	Andruw Jones	8.00
JK	Jason Kendall	6.00
MM	Mark McGwire/SP	70.00
PN	Phil Nevin	6.00
HN	Hideo Nomo	20.00
MO	Magglio Ordonez	6.00
CS	Curt Schilling	6.00
IS	Ichiro Suzuki/SP	40.00
JT	Jim Thome	12.00

Playmakers 2002

NM/M
Complete Set (20): 25.00
Common Player: .75
Inserted 1:6
P1	Ken Griffey Jr.	2.00
P2	Alex Rodriguez	4.00
P3	Sammy Sosa	2.50
P4	Derek Jeter	4.00
P5	Mike Piazza	2.00
P6	Jason Giambi	2.00
P7	Barry Bonds	4.00
P8	Frank Thomas	1.00
P9	Randy Johnson	1.50
P10	Chipper Jones	1.50
P11	Jeff Bagwell	1.00
P12	Vladimir Guerrero	1.50
P13	Albert Pujols	2.00
P14	Nomar Garciaparra	2.50
P15	Ichiro Suzuki	3.00
P16	Troy Glaus	1.00
P17	Ivan Rodriguez	1.00
P18	Carlos Delgado	.75
P19	Greg Maddux	2.00
P20	Todd Helton	1.00

Uniform Sluggers
NM/M
Common Player: 5.00
Inserted 1:72
JB	Jeff Bagwell	8.00
JGi	Jason Giambi	8.00
JGo	Juan Gonzalez	8.00
SG	Shawn Green	5.00
KG	Ken Griffey Jr./SP	25.00
TH	Todd Helton	8.00
CJ	Chipper Jones	8.00
MM	Mickey Mantle/SP	100.00
MP	Mike Piazza	15.00
AR	Alex Rodriguez	12.00
BW	Bernie Williams	8.00

2002 Upper Deck Collectors Club

As one of the membership benefits of its Collector's Club, persons opting for the MLB option received an exclusive 20-card set. Typical UD quality with UV coating on front and back, silver-foil highlights on front and a hologram on back, the cards are standard 2-1/2" x 3-1/2". Fronts have game-action photos bordered in blue. Backs have a portrait photo, biographical data, career highlights and recent stats. Cards are numbered with an "MLB" prefix.

NM/M
Complete Set (20): 15.00
Common Player: .25
1	Alex Rodriguez	2.00
2	Barry Bonds	1.00
3	Ken Griffey Jr.	2.00
4	Sammy Sosa	.50
5	Jason Giambi	.50
6	Ichiro	3.00
7	Chipper Jones	1.50
8	Derek Jeter	1.50
9	Nomar Garciaparra	1.00
10	Greg Maddux	1.50
11	Mike Piazza	1.50
12	Frank Thomas	1.00
13	Albert Pujols	1.50
14	Randy Johnson	.50
15	Pedro Martinez	.50
16	Todd Helton	.25
17	Vladimir Guerrero	.60
18	Jeff Bagwell	.60
19	Roger Clemens	.75
20	Shawn Green	.50

Memorabilia

Besides the 20-card base set benefit of joining Upper Deck's Collectors Club, one of six game-used memorabilia cards was also included. The cards are horizontal in format with a color action photo on front. Backs have a statement of authenticity.

NM/M
Complete Set (6): 50.00
Common Player: 10.00
AR-B	Alex Rodriguez/Bat	10.00
AR-J	Alex Rodriguez/Jsy	10.00
JR-B	Ken Griffey Jr./Bat	10.00
JR-J	Ken Griffey Jr./Jsy	10.00
SS-B	Sammy Sosa/Bat	15.00
SS-J	Sammy Sosa/Jsy	15.00

2002 Upper Deck Diamond Connection

NM/M

Complete Set (550):	
Common Player:	.15
Common RK (91-200):	4.00
Production 1,500	
Common Jersey (201-270):	4.00
Production 775	
Common Jersey (271-320):	5.00
Production 200	
Common Jersey (321-353):	5.00
Production 150	
Common Jersey (354-368):	6.00
Production 100	
Common Bat (369-438):	5.00
Production 775	
Common Bat (439-488):	5.00
Production 200	
Common Bat (489-521):	5.00
Production 150	
Common Bat (522-536):	10.00
Production 100	
Pack (5):	4.00
Box (14):	50.00

No.	Player	Price
1	Troy Glaus	.40
2	Darin Erstad	.40
3	Barry Zito	.40
4	Eric Chavez	.40
5	Tim Hudson	.40
6	Miguel Tejada	.40
7	Carlos Delgado	.40
8	Shannon Stewart	.15
9	Greg Vaughn	.15
10	Jim Thome	.75
11	C.C. Sabathia	.15
12	Ichiro Suzuki	1.50
13	Edgar Martinez	.25
14	Bret Boone	.25
15	Freddy Garcia	.15
16	Jeff Conine	.15
17	Alex Rodriguez	2.00
18	Rafael Palmeiro	.50
19	Ivan Rodriguez	.50
20	Juan Gonzalez	.50
21	Pedro J. Martinez	.75
22	Nomar Garciaparra	1.50
23	Manny Ramirez	.50
24	Carlos Beltran	.25
25	Mike Sweeney	.15
26	Dmitri Young	.15
27	Bobby Higginson	.15
28	Corey Koskie	.15
29	Cristian Guzman	.15
30	Doug Mientkiewicz	.15
31	Torii Hunter	.25
32	Frank Thomas	.50
33	Mark Buehrle	.15
34	Carlos Lee	.15
35	Magglio Ordonez	.40
36	Roger Clemens	1.50
37	Bernie Williams	.50
38	Jason Giambi	.75
39	Derek Jeter	2.00
40	Mike Mussina	.50
41	Jeff Bagwell	.50
42	Richard Hidalgo	.15
43	Lance Berkman	.40
44	Roy Oswalt	.40
45	Chipper Jones	.75
46	Gary Sheffield	.40
47	Andruw Jones	.50
48	Greg Maddux	1.00
49	Geoff Jenkins	.15
50	Ben Sheets	.25
51	Richie Sexson	.40
52	Albert Pujols	1.50
53	Matt Morris	.25
54	J.D. Drew	.40
55	Tino Martinez	.25
56	Sammy Sosa	1.50
57	Kerry Wood	.75
58	Moises Alou	.25
59	Fred McGriff	.25
60	Randy Johnson	.75
61	Luis Gonzalez	.25
62	Curt Schilling	.50
63	Kevin Brown	.40
64	Shawn Green	.40
65	Paul LoDuca	.15
66	Vladimir Guerrero	.75
67	Jose Vidro	.25
68	Barry Bonds	2.00
69	Jeff Kent	.25
70	Rich Aurilia	.15
71	Preston Wilson	.15
72	Josh Beckett	.40
73	Cliff Floyd	.25
74	Mike Piazza	1.00
75	Mo Vaughn	.25
76	Roberto Alomar	.40
77	Jeromy Burnitz	.15
78	Phil Nevin	.15
79	Sean Burroughs	.15
80	Scott Rolen	.75
81	Bobby Abreu	.25
82	Pat Burrell	.40
83	Brian Giles	.40
84	Jason Kendall	.15
85	Ken Griffey Jr.	1.00
86	Adam Dunn	.50
87	Aaron Boone	.15
88	Larry Walker	.25
89	Todd Helton	.50
90	Mike Hampton	.15
91	Brandon Puffer RC	4.00
92	Rodrigo Rosario RC	4.00
93	Tom Shearn RC	4.00
94	Morgan Ensberg RC	4.00
95	Jason Lane	4.00
96	Franklyn German RC	4.00
97	Carlos Pena	4.00
98	Joe Orloski RC	4.00
99	Reed Johnson RC	6.00
100	Chris Baker RC	4.00
101	Corey Thurman RC	4.00
102	Gustavo Chacin RC	4.00
103	Eric Hinske	4.00
104	John Foster RC	4.00
105	John Ennis RC	4.00
106	Kevin Gryboski RC	4.00
107	Jung Bong RC	4.00
108	Travis Wilson RC	4.00
109	Luis Martinez RC	4.00
110	Brian Mallette RC	4.00
111	Takahito Nomura RC	4.00
112	Bill Hall RC	4.00
113	Jeff Deardorff RC	4.00
114	Cristian Guerrero RC	4.00
115	Scotty Layfield RC	4.00
116	Michael Crudale RC	4.00
117	So Taguchi RC	4.00
118	Jeremy Lambert RC	4.00
119	Jimmy Journell RC	4.00
120	Francis Beltran RC	4.00
121	Mark Prior	6.00
122	Ben Christensen RC	4.00
123	Jorge Sosa RC	4.00
124	Brandon Backe RC	4.00
125	Steve Kent RC	4.00
126	Felix Escalona RC	4.00
127	P.J. Bevis RC	4.00
128	Jose Valverde RC	4.00
129	Doug DeVore RC	4.00
130	Jeremy Ward RC	4.00
131	Mike Koplove	4.00
132	Luis Terrero RC	4.00
133	John Patterson	4.00
134	Victor Alvarez RC	4.00
135	Kirk Saarloos RC	4.00
136	Kazuhisa Ishii RC	8.00
137	Steve Colyer RC	4.00
138	Cesar Izturis RC	4.00
139	Ron Calloway RC	4.00
140	Eric Good RC	4.00
141	Jorge Nunez RC	4.00
142	Ron Chiavacci RC	4.00
143	Donnie Bridges RC	4.00
144	Nelson Castro RC	4.00
145	Deivis Santos RC	4.00
146	Kurt Ainsworth RC	4.00
147	Arturo McDowell RC	4.00
148	Allan Simpson RC	4.00
149	Matt Thornton RC	4.00
150	Luis Ugueto RC	4.00
151	J.J. Putz RC	4.00
152	Hansel Izquierdo RC	4.00
153	Oliver Perez RC	4.00
154	Jaime Cerda RC	4.00
155	Mark Corey RC	4.00
156	Tyler Yates RC	6.00
157	Satoru Komiyama RC	4.00
158	Adam Walker RC	4.00
159	Steve Bechler RC	6.00
160	Erik Bedard RC	4.00
161	Todd Donovan RC	4.00
162	Clifford Bartosh RC	4.00
163	Ben Howard RC	8.00
164	Andy Shibilo RC	4.00
165	Dennis Tankersley RC	4.00
166	Mike Bynum RC	4.00
167	Anderson Machado RC	4.00
168	Peter Zamora RC	5.00
169	Eric Junge RC	4.00
170	Elio Serrano RC	4.00
171	Jorge Padilla RC	4.00
172	Marlon Byrd RC	4.00
173	Adrian Burnside RC	4.00
174	Mike Gonzalez RC	4.00
175	J.R. House RC	4.00
176	Hank Blalock RC	6.00
177	Travis Hughes RC	4.00
178	Mark Teixeira RC	6.00
179	Josh Hancock RC	4.00
180	Anastacio Martinez RC	4.00
181	Jorge de la Rosa RC	4.00
182	Ben Broussard RC	4.00
183	Austin Kearns RC	4.00
184	Corky Miller RC	4.00
185	Colin Young RC	4.00
186	Cam Esslinger RC	4.00
187	Rene Reyes RC	4.00
188	Aaron Cook RC	4.00
189	Alexis Gomez	4.00
190	Nate Field RC	4.00
191	Miguel Asencio RC	4.00
192	Brandon Berger	4.00
193	Fernando Rodney	4.00
194	Andy Van Hekken	4.00
195	Kevin Frederick RC	4.00
196	Todd Sears	4.00
197	Edwin Almonte RC	4.00
198	Kyle Kane RC	4.00
199	Mitch Wylie RC	4.00
200	Mike Porzio	4.00
201	Darin Erstad	6.00
202	Tim Salmon	6.00
203	Jeff Bagwell	10.00
204	Lance Berkman	6.00
205	Eric Chavez	6.00
206	Tim Hudson	6.00
207	Carlos Delgado	6.00
208	Chipper Jones	10.00
209	Gary Sheffield	6.00
210	Greg Maddux	15.00
211	Tom Glavine	6.00
212	Mike Mussina	10.00
213	J.D. Drew	6.00
214	Rick Ankiel	4.00
215	Sammy Sosa	15.00
216	Mike Lieberthal	6.00
217	Fred McGriff	8.00
218	David Wells	4.00
219	Curt Schilling	10.00
220	Luis Gonzalez	8.00
221	Mark Grace	10.00
222	Kevin Brown	4.00
223	Hideo Nomo	20.00
224	Jose Vidro	4.00
225	Jeff Kent	4.00
226	Rich Aurilia	4.00
227	Kenny Lofton	4.00
228	C.C. Sabathia	4.00
229	Edgar Martinez	8.00
230	Freddy Garcia	6.00
231	Cliff Floyd	4.00
232	Preston Wilson	4.00
233	Mike Piazza	10.00
234	Roberto Alomar	8.00
235	Trevor Hoffman	4.00
236	Ryan Klesko	5.00
237	Sean Burroughs	4.00
238	Scott Rolen	10.00
239	Pat Burrell	8.00
240	Edgardo Alfonzo	4.00
241	Brian Giles	8.00
242	Jason Kendall	5.00
243	Alex Rodriguez	15.00
244	Juan Gonzalez	8.00
245*	Ken Griffey Jr.	12.00
246	Rafael Palmeiro	8.00
247	Ken Griffey Jr.	12.00
248	Adam Dunn	15.00
249	Barry Larkin	5.00
250	Manny Ramirez	10.00
251	Pedro Martinez	10.00
252	Todd Helton	8.00
253	Larry Walker	6.00
254	Randy Johnson	10.00
255	Mike Sweeney	4.00
256	Carlos Beltran	6.00
257	Dmitri Young	4.00
258	Joe Mays	4.00
259	Doug Mientkiewicz	4.00
260	Corey Koskie	4.00
261	Magglio Ordonez	8.00
262	Frank Thomas	8.00
263	Ray Durham	4.00
264	Jason Giambi	10.00
265	Bernie Williams	8.00
266	Roger Clemens	15.00
267	Mariano Rivera	6.00
268	Robin Ventura	4.00
269	Andy Pettitte	10.00
270	Jorge Posada	8.00
271	Mike Piazza	15.00
272	Alex Rodriguez	15.00
273	Ken Griffey Jr.	15.00
274	Jason Giambi	10.00
275	Frank Thomas	8.00
276	Greg Maddux	15.00
277	Sammy Sosa	15.00
278	Roger Clemens	15.00
279	Jeff Bagwell	10.00
280	Todd Helton	8.00
281	Ichiro Suzuki	40.00
282	Randy Johnson	10.00
283	Jim Thome	15.00
284	Ivan Rodriguez	8.00
285	Darin Erstad	6.00
286	Eric Chavez	8.00
287	Barry Zito	10.00
288	Carlos Delgado	8.00
289	Omar Vizquel	8.00
290	Edgar Martinez	8.00
291	Manny Ramirez	10.00
292	Mike Sweeney	6.00
293	Tom Glavine	6.00
294	Joe Mays	6.00
295	Eric Milton	6.00
296	Magglio Ordonez	8.00
297	Bernie Williams	8.00
298	Trevor Hoffman	6.00
299	Andruw Jones	8.00
300	Aubrey Huff	8.00
301	Jim Edmonds	8.00
302	Kerry Wood	10.00
303	Luis Gonzalez	8.00
304	Shawn Green	6.00
305	Jose Vidro	5.00
306	Jeff Kent	5.00
307	Edgardo Alfonzo	5.00
308	Preston Wilson	5.00
309	Roberto Alomar	10.00
310	Jeromy Burnitz	5.00
311	Phil Nevin	5.00
312	Ryan Klesko	5.00
313	Bobby Abreu	6.00
314	Scott Rolen	12.00
315	Kazuhiro Sasaki	5.00
316	Jason Kendall	5.00
317	Sean Casey	5.00
318	Larry Walker	5.00
319	Mike Hampton	5.00
320	Juan Gonzalez	8.00
321	Darin Erstad	8.00
322	Tim Hudson	8.00
323	Carlos Delgado	8.00
324	Greg Vaughn	5.00
325	Jim Thome	15.00
326	Ichiro Suzuki	40.00
327	Rafael Palmeiro	8.00
328	Alex Rodriguez	15.00
329	Juan Gonzalez	8.00
330	Manny Ramirez	10.00
331	Carlos Beltran	6.00
332	Eric Milton	5.00
333	Frank Thomas	8.00
334	Roger Clemens	15.00
335	Jason Giambi	10.00
336	Lance Berkman	8.00
337	Greg Maddux	15.00
338	Chipper Jones	10.00
339	Sean Casey	5.00
340	Jim Edmonds	8.00
341	Kerry Wood	10.00
342	Sammy Sosa	15.00
343	Luis Gonzalez	8.00
344	Shawn Green	6.00
345	Jeff Kent	6.00
346	Preston Wilson	5.00
347	Roberto Alomar	10.00
348	Phil Nevin	5.00
349	Scott Rolen	12.00
350	Mike Sweeney	5.00
351	Ken Griffey Jr.	15.00
352	Todd Helton	8.00
353	Larry Walker	5.00
354	Alex Rodriguez	15.00
355	Pedro J. Martinez	10.00
356	Frank Thomas	10.00
357	Jason Giambi	10.00
358	Bernie Williams	8.00
359	Jeff Bagwell	10.00
360	Chipper Jones	10.00
361	Sammy Sosa	20.00
362	Randy Johnson	10.00
363	Shawn Green	6.00
364	Mike Piazza	15.00
365	Ken Griffey Jr.	50.00
366	Ken Griffey Jr.	15.00
367	Larry Walker	8.00
368	Jim Edmonds	8.00
369	Darin Erstad	8.00
370	Tim Salmon	8.00
371	Mark Kotsay	5.00
372	Craig Biggio	8.00
373	Eric Chavez	10.00
374	David Justice	8.00
375	Carlos Delgado	8.00
376	Chipper Jones	15.00
377	Gary Sheffield	6.00
378	Greg Maddux	10.00
379	Eric Karros	5.00
380	Fred McGriff	8.00
381	J.D. Drew	8.00
382	Rick Ankiel	5.00
383	Sammy Sosa	15.00
384	Moises Alou	5.00
385	Ben Grieve	5.00
386	Greg Vaughn	5.00
387	Jay Payton	5.00
388	Luis Gonzalez	8.00
389	Ray Durham	5.00
390	Shawn Green	8.00
391	Hideo Nomo	20.00
392	Jose Vidro	5.00
393	Jeff Kent	5.00
394	Adrian Beltre	5.00
395	Jim Thome	15.00
396	Bobby Abreu	5.00
397	Edgar Martinez	10.00
398	Carl Everett	5.00
399	Luis Castillo	5.00
400	Preston Wilson	5.00
401	Jermaine Dye	8.00
402	Roberto Alomar	8.00
403	Todd Hundley	5.00
404	Ryan Klesko	5.00
405	Phil Nevin	5.00
406	Scott Rolen	10.00
407	Rafael Furcal	5.00
408	Miguel Tejada	8.00
409	Brian Giles	8.00
410	Jason Kendall	5.00
411	Alex Rodriguez	15.00
412	Juan Gonzalez	8.00
413	Ivan Rodriguez	8.00
414	Rafael Palmeiro	8.00
415	Ken Griffey Jr.	15.00
416	Edgardo Alfonzo	5.00
417	Barry Larkin	5.00
418	Manny Ramirez	8.00
419	Pedro J. Martinez	12.00
420	Todd Helton	8.00
421	Larry Walker	8.00
422	Garret Anderson	6.00
423	Mike Sweeney	5.00
424	Carlos Beltran	5.00
425	Javier Lopez	5.00
426	J.T. Snow	5.00
427	Doug Mientkiewicz	5.00
428	John Olerud	5.00
429	Magglio Ordonez	6.00
430	Frank Thomas	8.00
431	Kenny Lofton	5.00
432	Al Leiter	5.00
433	Bernie Williams	8.00
434	Roger Clemens	15.00
435	Tom Glavine	8.00
436	Robin Ventura	6.00
437	Chan Ho Park	5.00
438	Jorge Posada	8.00
439	Charles Johnson	5.00
440	Alex Rodriguez	20.00
441	Ken Griffey Jr.	15.00
442	Mark Kotsay	5.00
443	Frank Thomas	20.00
444	Greg Maddux	20.00
445	Sammy Sosa	20.00
446	Tom Glavine	10.00
447	Chipper Jones	15.00
448	Todd Helton	8.00
449	Jeff Cirillo	5.00
450	Steve Finley	5.00
451	Jim Thome	15.00
452	Ivan Rodriguez	8.00
453	Darin Erstad	8.00
454	Eric Chavez	8.00
455	Miguel Tejada	8.00
456	Carlos Delgado	8.00
457	Omar Vizquel	5.00
458	Edgar Martinez	10.00
459	Johnny Damon	8.00
460	Russell Branyan	5.00
461	Kenny Lofton	5.00
462	Jermaine Dye	5.00
463	Ellis Burks	5.00
464	Magglio Ordonez	8.00
465	Bernie Williams	10.00
466	Tim Salmon	5.00
467	Andruw Jones	5.00
468	Jeffrey Hammonds	5.00
469	Jim Edmonds	10.00
470	Kerry Wood	15.00
471	Luis Gonzalez	8.00
472	Shawn Green	8.00
473	Jose Vidro	5.00
474	Jeff Kent	5.00
475	Javier Lopez	6.00
476	Preston Wilson	5.00
477	Roberto Alomar	10.00
478	Robin Ventura	6.00
479	Phil Nevin	5.00
480	Ryan Klesko	8.00
481	Bobby Abreu	5.00
482	Scott Rolen	10.00
483	Brian Giles	5.00
484	Jason Kendall	5.00
485	Tsuyoshi Shinjo	5.00
486	Larry Walker	5.00
487	Mike Lieberthal	5.00
488	Juan Gonzalez	8.00
489	Darin Erstad	6.00
490	Tom Glavine	10.00
491	Carlos Delgado	6.00
492	Greg Vaughn	5.00
493	Jim Thome	15.00
494	Mark Grace	15.00
495	Rafael Palmeiro	8.00
496	Alex Rodriguez	20.00
497	Juan Gonzalez	10.00
498	Miguel Tejada	8.00
499	Carlos Beltran	5.00
500	Andruw Jones	8.00
501	Frank Thomas	10.00
502	Andres Galarraga	5.00
503	Gary Sheffield	8.00
504	Craig Biggio	5.00
505	Greg Maddux	20.00
506	Chipper Jones	15.00
507	Pat Burrell	10.00
508	Jim Edmonds	8.00
509	Kerry Wood	15.00
510	Sammy Sosa	20.00
511	Luis Gonzalez	8.00
512	Shawn Green	8.00
513	Edgardo Alfonzo	5.00
514	Preston Wilson	5.00
515	Roberto Alomar	8.00
516	Phil Nevin	5.00
517	Scott Rolen	15.00
518	Brian Giles	5.00
519	Jorge Posada	10.00
520	Todd Helton	12.00
521	Larry Walker	8.00
522	Alex Rodriguez	25.00
523	Pedro J. Martinez	20.00
524	Frank Thomas	12.00
525	Jason Giambi	15.00
526	Bernie Williams	15.00
527	J.D. Drew	10.00
528	Chipper Jones	20.00
529	Sammy Sosa	25.00
530	Randy Johnson	15.00
531	Shawn Green	8.00
532	Kevin Brown	8.00
533	Brian Giles	8.00
534	Ken Griffey Jr.	25.00
535	Larry Walker	8.00
536	Jim Edmonds	8.00
537	Sean Casey/Jsy/775	10.00
538	Ichiro Suzuki/Jsy/775	40.00
539	Pat Burrell/Jsy/200	10.00
540	Adam Dunn/Jsy/200	20.00
541	Lance Berkman/ Jsy/200	10.00
542	Cliff Floyd/Jsy/150	8.00
543	Roger Clemens/ Jsy/100	20.00
544	Kerry Wood/Bat/775	15.00
545	Andruw Jones/ Bat/775	8.00
546	Manny Ramirez/ Bat/200	10.00
547	Jorge Posada/ Bat/200	10.00
548	Fred McGriff/Bat/200	8.00
549	Mike Sweeney/ Bat/150	6.00
550	Todd Helton/Bat/100	12.00

Great Connections

NM/M

Production 50 Sets

GC-GR	Jason Giambi, Babe Ruth	350.00
GC-MD	Mickey Mantle, Joe DiMaggio	350.00
GC-MR	Mark McGwire, Babe Ruth	350.00
GC-MS	Mark McGwire, Sammy Sosa	200.00
GC-RR	Alex Rodriguez, Nolan Ryan	150.00
GC-IG	Ichiro Suzuki, Ken Griffey Jr.	150.00

Memorabilia Signatures Bat

NM/M

Varying quantities produced

JD	Joe DiMaggio/20	600.00
JG	Jason Giambi/49	60.00
KG	Ken Griffey Jr./49	150.00
MMc	Mark McGwire/49	300.00
JM	Joe Morgan/99	35.00
KP	Kirby Puckett/145	75.00
CR	Cal Ripken Jr/145	150.00
AR	Alex Rodriguez/145	100.00
NR	Nolan Ryan/99	150.00
SS	Sammy Sosa/99	150.00
IS	Ichiro Suzuki/99	250.00

Memorabilia Signatures Jersey

NM/M

Varying quantities produced

Gold:		.75-1X

Production 150

EB	Ernie Banks/150	80.00
JD	Joe DiMaggio/20	550.00
KG	Ken Griffey Jr./49	150.00
SK	Sandy Koufax/150	300.00
MMc	Mark McGwire/49	300.00
JM	Joe Morgan/99	35.00
CR	Cal Ripken Jr/145	150.00
AR	Alex Rodriguez/145	150.00
NR	Nolan Ryan/99	150.00
SS	Sammy Sosa/99	200.00
IS	Ichiro Suzuki/99	250.00

Employees Mark McGwire Jersey-Bat Card

To thank its employees for "dedication and commitment to excellence," UD created this special game-used jersey-bat card in an edition of 350 serially numbered pieces. The 3-1/2" x 2-1/2" horizontal cards have action and portrait photos of Big Mac on front. Near the center is a laser-cut Cardinals logo cut from a McGwire bat, superimposed on a swatch of jersey. The serial number is in gold foil below. Back has another portrait photo and a message from UD CEO Richard McWilliam.

	NM/M
UDC-MM Mark McGwire	165.00

2002 Upper Deck Honor Roll

		NM/M
Complete Set (100):		25.00
Common Player:		.15
Pack (5):		2.00
Box (24):		30.00
1	Randy Johnson	.50
2	Mike Piazza	.75
3	Albert Pujols	1.00
4	Roberto Alomar	.25
5	Chipper Jones	.50
6	Rich Aurilia	.15
7	Barry Bonds	1.00
8	Ken Griffey Jr.	.75
9	Sammy Sosa	.75
10	Roger Clemens	.75
11	Ivan Rodriguez	.40
12	Jason Giambi	.40
13	Bret Boone	.15
14	Troy Glaus	.25
15	Alex Rodriguez	.75
16	Manny Ramirez	.40
17	Bernie Williams	.40
18	Ichiro Suzuki	.75
19	Matt Thornton	.25
20	Chris Baker RC	.25
21	Tyler Yates RC	.50
22	Jorge Nunez RC	.50
23	Rene Reyes RC	.50
24	Ben Howard RC	.50
25	Ron Calloway RC	.40
26	Danny Wright	.15
27	Reed Johnson RC	.50
28	Randy Johnson	.25
29	Randy Johnson	.25
30	Randy Johnson	.25
31	Randy Johnson	.25
32	Mike Piazza	.50
33	Mike Piazza	.50
34	Mike Piazza	.50
35	Mike Piazza	.50
36	Albert Pujols	.75
37	Albert Pujols	.75
38	Albert Pujols	.75
39	Albert Pujols	.75
40	Roberto Alomar	.20
41	Roberto Alomar	.20
42	Roberto Alomar	.20
43	Roberto Alomar	.20
44	Chipper Jones	.50
45	Chipper Jones	.50
46	Chipper Jones	.50
47	Chipper Jones	.50
48	Rich Aurilia	.15
49	Rich Aurilia	.15
50	Rich Aurilia	.15
51	Rich Aurilia	.15
52	Barry Bonds	1.00
53	Barry Bonds	1.00
54	Barry Bonds	1.00
55	Barry Bonds	1.00
56	Ken Griffey Jr.	.75
57	Ken Griffey Jr.	.75
58	Ken Griffey Jr.	.75
59	Ken Griffey Jr.	.75
60	Sammy Sosa	.50
61	Sammy Sosa	.50
62	Sammy Sosa	.50
63	Sammy Sosa	.50
64	Roger Clemens	.75
65	Roger Clemens	.75
66	Roger Clemens	.75
67	Roger Clemens	.75
68	Ivan Rodriguez	.25
69	Ivan Rodriguez	.25
70	Ivan Rodriguez	.25
71	Ivan Rodriguez	.25
72	Jason Giambi	.25
73	Jason Giambi	.25
74	Jason Giambi	.25
75	Jason Giambi	.25
76	Bret Boone	.15
77	Bret Boone	.15
78	Bret Boone	.15
79	Bret Boone	.15
80	Troy Glaus	.20
81	Troy Glaus	.20
82	Troy Glaus	.20
83	Troy Glaus	.20
84	Alex Rodriguez	.75
85	Alex Rodriguez	.75
86	Alex Rodriguez	.75
87	Alex Rodriguez	.75
88	Manny Ramirez	.25
89	Manny Ramirez	.25
90	Manny Ramirez	.25
91	Manny Ramirez	.25
92	Bernie Williams	.20
93	Bernie Williams	.20
94	Bernie Williams	.20
95	Bernie Williams	.20
96	Ichiro Suzuki	1.00
97	Ichiro Suzuki	1.00
98	Ichiro Suzuki	1.00
99	Ichiro Suzuki	1.00
100	Checklist	
	(Original nine players.)	
	(Nine team names.)	.25

Silver

Stars:	4-8X
Production 100 Sets	

Batting Glove

		NM/M
Numbered to 250.		
BB	Bret Boone/89	20.00
JG	Jason Giambi	20.00
KG	Ken Griffey Jr.	40.00
AR	Alex Rodriguez	25.00
IR1	Ivan Rodriguez	20.00
IR2	Ivan Rodriguez	20.00
SS	Sammy Sosa	30.00
I	Ichiro Suzuki/46	150.00

Game Jersey

		NM/M
Common Player:		10.00
Inserted 1:90		
Golds:		2-3X
Production 99 Sets		
Each player has multiple versions.		
BB	Bret Boone/SP/45	10.00
RC	Roger Clemens	20.00
JG	Jason Giambi/SP	15.00
KG	Ken Griffey Jr.	25.00
CJ	Chipper Jones	15.00
AR	Alex Rodriguez	15.00
IR	Ivan Rodriguez	10.00
SS	Sammy Sosa/SP	25.00
I	Ichiro Suzuki/SP	40.00

Star Swatches Game Jersey

		NM/M
Common Player:		10.00
Inserted 1:90		
Golds:		2-5X
Production 24		
BB	Bret Boone/45	10.00
RC	Roger Clemens/29	40.00
JG	Jason Giambi	10.00
KG	Ken Griffey Jr./SP	25.00
CJ	Chipper Jones	15.00
AR	Alex Rodriguez	15.00
IR	Ivan Rodriguez	10.00

		NM/M
SS'	Sammy Sosa	20.00
I	Ichiro Suzuki/SP	40.00

Time Capsule Game Jersey

		NM/M
Common Player:		8.00
Inserted 1:90		
Golds:		2-3X
Production 99 Sets		
BB	Bret Boone	8.00
RC	Roger Clemens	20.00
JG	Jason Giambi/52	15.00
CJ	Chipper Jones	10.00
AR	Alex Rodriguez	15.00
IR	Ivan Rodriguez/SP	15.00
SS	Sammy Sosa	20.00
I	Ichiro Suzuki	40.00

Stitch of Nine Game Jersey

		NM/M
Common Player:		10.00
Inserted 1:90		
Golds:		2-5X
Production 24 Sets		
BB	Bret Boone/45	10.00
RC	Roger Clemens	20.00
JG	Jason Giambi/SP	10.00
KG	Ken Griffey Jr.	15.00
CJ	Chipper Jones	10.00
AR	Alex Rodriguez	15.00
IR	Ivan Rodriguez	10.00
SS	Sammy Sosa	20.00
I	Ichiro Suzuki/85	40.00

Game-Used Bat

		NM/M
Common Player:		10.00
Numbered to 99.		
Each player has multiple versions.		
BB	Bret Boone	10.00
RC	Roger Clemens	30.00
JG	Jason Giambi	15.00
KG	Ken Griffey Jr.	40.00
CJ	Chipper Jones	20.00
AR	Alex Rodriguez	20.00
IR	Ivan Rodriguez	15.00
SS	Sammy Sosa	30.00
I	Ichiro Suzuki	40.00

ABBREVIATIONS

SP - Short Print

2002 Upper Deck MVP

		NM/M
Complete Set (300):		20.00
Common Player:		.10
Pack (8):		1.50
Box (24):		25.00
1	Darin Erstad	.20
2	Ramon Ortiz	.10
3	Garret Anderson	.20
4	Jarrod Washburn	.10
5	Troy Glaus	.20
6	Brendan Donnelly RC	.10
7	Troy Percival	.10
8	Tim Salmon	.15
9	Aaron Sele	.10
10	Brad Fullmer	.10
11	Scott Hatteberg	.10
12	Barry Zito	.20
13	Tim Hudson	.20
14	Miguel Tejada	.25
15	Jermaine Dye	.10
16	Mark Mulder	.20
17	Eric Chavez	.15
18	Terrence Long	.10
19	Carlos Pena	.20
20	David Justice	.20
21	Jeremy Giambi	.10
22	Shannon Stewart	.10
23	Raul Mondesi	.15
24	Chris Carpenter	.10
25	Carlos Delgado	.20
26	Mike Sirotka	.10
27	Reed Johnson RC	.10
28	Darrin Fletcher	.10
29	Jose Cruz Jr.	.10
30	Vernon Wells	.20
31	Tanyon Sturtze	.10
32	Toby Hall	.10
33	Brent Abernathy	.10
34	Ben Grieve	.10
35	Joe Kennedy	.10
36	Dewon Brazelton	.10
37	Aubrey Huff	.10
38	Steve Cox	.10
39	Greg Vaughn	.10
40	Brady Anderson	.10
41	Chuck Finley	.10
42	Jim Thome	.40
43	Russell Branyan	.10
44	C.C. Sabathia	.20
45	Matt Lawton	.10
46	Omar Vizquel	.20
47	Bartolo Colon	.10
48	Alex Escobar	.10
49	Ellis Burks	.10
50	Bret Boone	.20
51	John Olerud	.20
52	Jeff Cirillo	.10
53	Ichiro Suzuki	1.00
54	Kazuhiro Sasaki	.20
55	Freddy Garcia	.10
56	Edgar Martinez	.15
57	Matt Thornton	.10
58	Mike Cameron	.10
59	Carlos Guillen	.10
60	Jeff Conine	.10
61	Tony Batista	.10
62	Jason Johnson	.10
63	Melvin Mora	.10
64	Brian Roberts	.10
65	Josh Towers	.10
66	Steve Bechler RC	.10
67	Jerry Hairston Jr.	.10
68	Chris Richard	.10
69	Alex Rodriguez	1.00
70	Chan Ho Park	.10
71	Ivan Rodriguez	.25
72	Jeff Zimmerman	.10
73	Mark Teixeira	.20
74	Gabe Kapler	.10
75	Frank Catalanotto	.10
76	Rafael Palmeiro	.25
77	Doug Davis	.10
78	Carl Everett	.10
79	Pedro J. Martinez	.40
80	Nomar Garciaparra	.75
81	Tony Clark	.10
82	Trot Nixon	.20
83	Manny Ramirez	.25
84	Josh Hancock RC	.10

85	Johnny Damon	.20
86	Jose Offerman	.10
87	Rich Garces	.10
88	Shea Hillenbrand	.20
89	Carlos Beltran	.20
90	Mike Sweeney	.10
91	Jeff Suppan	.10
92	Joe Randa	.10
93	Chuck Knoblauch	.10
94	Mark Quinn	.10
95	Neifi Perez	.10
96	Carlos Febles	.10
97	Miguel Asencio RC	.10
98	Michael Tucker	.10
99	Dean Palmer	.10
100	Jose Lima	.10
101	Craig Paquette	.10
102	Dmitri Young	.10
103	Bobby Higginson	.10
104	Jeff Weaver	.20
105	Matt Anderson	.10
106	Damion Easley	.10
107	Eric Milton	.10
108	Doug Mientkiewicz	.10
109	Cristian Guzman	.10
110	Brad Radke	.10
111	Torii Hunter	.20
112	Corey Koskie	.10
113	Joe Mays	.10
114	Jacque Jones	.10
115	David Ortiz	.20
116	Kevin Frederick RC	.10
117	Magglio Ordonez	.20
118	Ray Durham	.10
119	Mark Buehrle	.10
120	Jon Garland	.10
121	Paul Konerko	.10
122	Todd Ritchie	.10
123	Frank Thomas	.25
124	Edwin Almonte RC	.10
125	Carlos Lee	.10
126	Kenny Lofton	.15
127	Roger Clemens	.75
128	Derek Jeter	1.00
129	Jorge Posada	.20
130	Bernie Williams	.25
131	Mike Mussina	.25
132	Alfonso Soriano	.40
133	Robin Ventura	.15
134	John Vander Wal	.10
135	Jason Giambi	.25
136	Mariano Rivera	.20
137	Rondell White	.10
138	Jeff Bagwell	.25
139	Wade Miller	.10
140	Richard Hidalgo	.10
141	Julio Lugo	.10
142	Roy Oswalt	.20
143	Rodrigo Rosario RC	.10
144	Lance Berkman	.20
145	Craig Biggio	.20
146	Shane Reynolds	.10
147	John Smoltz	.20
148	Chipper Jones	.40
149	Gary Sheffield	.20
150	Rafael Furcal	.10
151	Greg Maddux	.50
152	Tom Glavine	.20
153	Andruw Jones	.25
154	John Ennis RC	.20
155	Vinny Castilla	.10
156	Marcus Giles	.10
157	Javy Lopez	.10
158	Richie Sexson	.20
159	Geoff Jenkins	.20
160	Jeffrey Hammonds	.10
161	Alex Ochoa	.10
162	Ben Sheets	.20
163	Jose Hernandez	.10
164	Eric Young	.10
165	Luis Montanez	.10
166	Albert Pujols	.75
167	Darryl Kile	.10
168	So Taguchi RC	.50
169	Jim Edmonds	.20
170	Fernando Vina	.10
171	Matt Morris	.10
172	J.D. Drew	.20
173	Bud Smith	.10
174	Edgar Renteria	.20
175	Placido Polanco	.10
176	Tino Martinez	.10
177	Sammy Sosa	.75
178	Moises Alou	.20
179	Kerry Wood	.40
180	Delino DeShields	.10
181	Alex Gonzalez	.10
182	Jon Lieber	.10
183	Fred McGriff	.15
184	Corey Patterson	.10
185	Mark Prior	.50
186	Tom Gordon	.10
187	Francis Beltran RC	.10
188	Randy Johnson	.40
189	Luis Gonzalez	.20
190	Matt Williams	.15
191	Mark Grace	.25
192	Curt Schilling	.25
193	Doug DeVore RC	.20
194	Erubiel Durazo	.10
195	Steve Finley	.15
196	Craig Counsell	.10
197	Shawn Green	.25
198	Kevin Brown	.10
199	Paul LoDuca	.10
200	Brian Jordan	.15
201	Andy Ashby	.10
202	Darren Dreifort	.10

203	Adrian Beltre	.15
204	Victor Alvarez RC	.10
205	Eric Karros	.10
206	Hideo Nomo	.25
207	Vladimir Guerrero	.40
208	Javier Vazquez	.10
209	Michael Barrett	.10
210	Jose Vidro	.10
211	Brad Wilkerson	.10
212	Tony Armas Jr.	.10
213	Eric Good RC	.10
214	Orlando Cabrera	.10
215	Lee Stevens	.10
216	Jeff Kent	.10
217	Rich Aurilia	.10
218	Robb Nen	.10
219	Calvin Murray	.10
220	Russ Ortiz	.10
221	Deivis Santos	.10
222	Marvin Benard	.10
223	Jason Schmidt	.10
224	Reggie Sanders	.10
225	Barry Bonds	1.00
226	Brad Penny	.10
227	Cliff Floyd	.10
228	Mike Lowell	.20
229	Derrek Lee	.10
230	Ryan Dempster	.10
231	Josh Beckett	.20
232	Hansel Izquierdo RC	.10
233	Preston Wilson	.10
234	A.J. Burnett	.10
235	Charles Johnson	.10
236	Mike Piazza	.50
237	Al Leiter	.20
238	Jay Payton	.10
239	Roger Cedeno	.10
240	Jeromy Burnitz	.10
241	Roberto Alomar	.20
242	Mo Vaughn	.20
243	Shawn Estes	.10
244	Armando Benitez	.10
245	Tyler Yates RC	.10
246	Phil Nevin	.10
247	D'Angelo Jimenez	.10
248	Ramon Vazquez	.10
249	Bubba Trammell	.10
250	Trevor Hoffman	.10
251	Ben Howard RC	.20
252	Mark Kotsay	.10
253	Ray Lankford	.10
254	Ryan Klesko	.10
255	Scott Rolen	.40
256	Robert Person	.10
257	Jimmy Rollins	.25
258	Pat Burrell	.20
259	Anderson Machado RC	.10
260	Randy Wolf	.10
261	Travis Lee	.10
262	Mike Lieberthal	.10
263	Doug Glanville	.10
264	Bobby Abreu	.10
265	Brian Giles	.15
266	Kris Benson	.10
267	Aramis Ramirez	.10
268	Kevin Young	.10
269	Jack Wilson	.10
270	Mike Williams	.10
271	Jimmy Anderson	.10
272	Jason Kendall	.10
273	Pokey Reese	.10
274	Robert Mackowiak	.10
275	Sean Casey	.20
276	Juan Encarnacion	.10
277	Austin Kearns	.20
278	Danny Graves	.10
279	Ken Griffey Jr.	.50
280	Barry Larkin	.20
281	Todd Walker	.10
282	Elmer Dessens	.10
283	Aaron Boone	.10
284	Adam Dunn	.40
285	Larry Walker	.15
286	Rene Reyes RC	.20
287	Juan Uribe	.10
288	Mike Hampton	.10
289	Todd Helton	.40
290	Juan Pierre	.10
291	Denny Neagle	.10
292	Jose Ortiz	.10
293	Todd Zeile	.10
294	Ben Petrick	.10
295	Checklist 1-50 (Ken Griffey Jr.)	.25
296	Checklist 51-100 (Derek Jeter)	.50
297	Checklist 101-150 (Sammy Sosa)	.30
298	Checklist 151-200 (Ichiro Suzuki)	.50
299	Checklist 201-250 (Barry Bonds)	.50
300	Checklist 251-300 (Alex Rodriguez)	.40

Silver

Stars:	5-10X
Production 100 Sets	

Gold

No Pricing	
Production 25 Sets	

Ichiro - A Season to Remember

	NM/M
Complete Set (10):	15.00
Ichiro's (1-10):	2.00
Inserted 1:10	
I1-10 Ichiro Suzuki	2.50

Ichiro - A Season to Remember Bat

No Pricing
Production 25

A Season to Remember Jersey

Complete Set (1):

Souvenirs Bats

		NM/M
	Common Player:	8.00
	Inserted 1:144	
RA	Roberto Alomar	20.00
CD	Carlos Delgado	8.00
BG	Brian Giles	8.00
LG	Luis Gonzalez	8.00
SG	Shawn Green	8.00
KG	Ken Griffey Jr.	25.00
TH	Todd Helton	15.00
DJ	David Justice	8.00
JK	Jeff Kent	8.00
RK	Ryan Klesko	8.00
GM	Greg Maddux	20.00
EM	Edgar Martinez	10.00
DM	Doug Mientkiewicz	8.00
MO	Magglio Ordonez	8.00
RP	Rafael Palmeiro/97	18.00
MP	Mike Piazza/97	25.00
AR	Alex Rodriguez	15.00
IR	Ivan Rodriguez	10.00
SR	Scott Rolen	10.00
GS	Gary Sheffield	8.00
SS	Sammy Sosa	20.00
MS	Mike Sweeney	8.00
FT	Frank Thomas/97	25.00
JT	Jim Thome	10.00
GV	Greg Vaughn	8.00
LW	Larry Walker	8.00
BW	Bernie Williams	10.00

Souvenirs Jerseys

		NM/M
	Common Player:	5.00
	Inserted 1:48	
RA	Roberto Alomar	10.00
GA	Garret Anderson	10.00
JB	Jeff Bagwell	10.00
AB	Adrian Beltre	8.00
JB	Jeromy Burnitz	5.00
RC	Roger Clemens	15.00
CD	Carlos Delgado	8.00
DE	Darin Erstad	8.00
RF	Rafael Furcal	5.00
JG	Juan Gonzalez	10.00
THo	Trevor Hoffman	5.00
THu	Tim Hudson	8.00
JK	Jeff Kent	8.00
PK	Paul Konerko/SP	10.00
MK	Mark Kotsay	5.00
KL	Kenny Lofton	8.00
EM	Edgar Martinez	10.00
JP	Jay Payton/SP	10.00
MP	Mike Piazza	15.00
AR	Alex Rodriguez	15.00
IR	Ivan Rodriguez	10.00
SR	Scott Rolen	10.00
TS	Tim Salmon	8.00
FT	Frank Thomas	15.00
JT	Jim Thome/SP	15.00
RV	Robin Ventura	5.00
OV	Omar Vizquel	5.00
PW	Preston Wilson	5.00
TZ	Todd Zeile	5.00

Souvenirs Bat/Jersey Combos

	NM/M
Common Card:	10.00
Inserted 1:144	
Gold:	No Pricing
Production 25 Sets	

EA	Edgardo Alfonzo	10.00
RA	Roberto Alomar	15.00
JB	Jeff Bagwell	20.00
AB	Adrian Beltre	15.00
CD	Carlos Delgado	15.00
DE	Darin Erstad	20.00
JG	Jason Giambi	20.00
BG	Brian Giles	15.00
LG	Luis Gonzalez	15.00
SG	Shawn Green	15.00
KG	Ken Griffey Jr.	40.00
TH	Todd Helton	20.00
RJ	Randy Johnson	25.00
CJ	Chipper Jones	20.00
JK	Jeff Kent	15.00
MO	Magglio Ordonez	15.00
RP	Rafael Palmeiro	20.00
MP	Mike Piazza	15.00
AR	Alex Rodriguez	25.00
IR	Ivan Rodriguez	15.00
SR	Scott Rolen	15.00
SS	Sammy Sosa	15.00
JT	Jim Thome	25.00
RV	Robin Ventura	10.00
OV	Omar Vizquel/97	20.00
BW	Bernie Williams/97	25.00
TZ	Todd Zeile	10.00

National Convention

A multi-sport set of 15 cards was specially produced as a give-away for attendees at the 2002 National Sports Collectors Convention in Chicago. VIP admissions received the complete set, regular showgoers received a three-card cello pack. The baseball cards follow the format of UD's regular 2002 issue and feature a distinguishing line of type on front and special numbering on back. Only the baseball players from the set are listed here.

		NM/M
	Complete Baseball Set (5):	10.00
	Common Player:	2.00
N1	Mark McGwire	3.00
N2	Sammy Sosa	3.00
N3	Jason Giambi	2.00
N4	Ichiro	3.00
N5	Ken Griffey Jr.	3.00

2002 Upper Deck Ovation

		NM/M
	Complete Set (120):	120.00
	Common Player:	.25
	Common (61-89, 120):	3.00
	Production 2,002	
	Pack (5):	1.50
	Box (24):	30.00
1	Troy Glaus	.40
2	David Justice	.40
3	Tim Hudson	.40
4	Jermaine Dye	.25
5	Carlos Delgado	.40
6	Greg Vaughn	.25
7	Jim Thome	.75
8	C.C. Sabathia	.25
9	Ichiro Suzuki	1.50
10	Edgar Martinez	.40
11	Chris Richard	.25
12	Rafael Palmeiro	.50
13	Alex Rodriguez	2.00
14	Ivan Rodriguez	.50
15	Nomar Garciaparra	1.50
16	Manny Ramirez	.75
17	Pedro J. Martinez	.50
18	Mike Sweeney	.25
19	Dmitri Young	.25
20	Doug Mientkiewicz	.25
21	Brad Radke	.25
22	Cristian Guzman	.25
23	Frank Thomas	.75
24	Magglio Ordonez	.40
25	Bernie Williams	.40
26	Derek Jeter	2.00
27	Jason Giambi	.50
28	Roger Clemens	1.50
29	Jeff Bagwell	.50
30	Lance Berkman	.40
31	Chipper Jones	.75
32	Gary Sheffield	.40
33	Greg Maddux	1.00
34	Richie Sexson	.25
35	Albert Pujols	1.50
36	Tino Martinez	.25
37	J.D. Drew	.40
38	Sammy Sosa	1.50
39	Moises Alou	.40
40	Randy Johnson	.75
41	Luis Gonzalez	.40
42	Shawn Green	.40
43	Kevin Brown	.25
44	Vladimir Guerrero	.75
45	Barry Bonds	2.00
46	Jeff Kent	.40
47	Cliff Floyd	.25
48	Josh Beckett	.50
49	Mike Piazza	1.00
50	Mo Vaughn	.25
51	Jeromy Burnitz	.25
52	Roberto Alomar	.40
53	Phil Nevin	.25
54	Scott Rolen	.75
55	Jimmy Rollins	.40
56	Brian Giles	.40
57	Ken Griffey Jr.	1.00
58	Sean Casey	.40
59	Larry Walker	.40
60	Todd Helton	.50
61	Rodrigo Rosario RC	5.00
62	Reed Johnson RC	8.00
63	John Ennis RC	3.00
64	Luis Martinez RC	3.00
65	So Taguchi RC	6.00
66	Brandon Backe RC	3.00
67	Doug DeVore RC	3.00
68	Victor Alvarez RC	3.00
69	Kazuhisa Ishii RC	8.00
70	Eric Good RC	3.00
71	Deivis Santos	3.00
72	Matt Thornton	3.00
73	Hansel Izquierdo RC	3.00
74	Tyler Yates RC	6.00
75	Jaime Cerda RC	3.00
76	Satoru Komiyama RC	3.00
77	Steve Bechler RC	3.00
78	Ben Howard RC	3.00
79	Jorge Padilla RC	3.00
80	Eric Junge RC	3.00
81	Anderson Machado RC	3.00
82	Adrian Burnside RC	3.00
83	Josh Hancock RC	3.00
84	Anastacio Martinez RC	3.00
85	Rene Reyes RC	3.00
86	Nate Field RC	3.00
87	Tim Kalita RC	3.00
88	Kevin Frederick RC	3.00
89	Edwin Almonte RC	3.00
90	Ichiro Suzuki	.75
91	Ichiro Suzuki	.75
92	Ichiro Suzuki	.75
93	Ichiro Suzuki	.75
94	Ichiro Suzuki	.75
95	Ken Griffey Jr.	.75
96	Ken Griffey Jr.	.75
97	Ken Griffey Jr.	.75
98	Ken Griffey Jr.	.75
99	Ken Griffey Jr.	.75
100	Jason Giambi	.40
101	Jason Giambi	.40
102	Jason Giambi	.40
103	Jason Giambi	.40
104	Jason Giambi	.40
105	Sammy Sosa	.75
106	Sammy Sosa	.75
107	Sammy Sosa	.75
108	Sammy Sosa	.75
109	Sammy Sosa	.75
110	Alex Rodriguez	.75
111	Alex Rodriguez	.75
112	Alex Rodriguez	.75
113	Alex Rodriguez	.75
114	Alex Rodriguez	.75
115	Mark McGwire	.75
116	Mark McGwire	.75
117	Mark McGwire	.75
118	Mark McGwire	.75
119	Mark McGwire	.75
120	Alex Rodriguez, Ken Griffey Jr., Mark McGwire, Sammy Sosa, Jason Giambi, Ichiro Suzuki	15.00

Silver

(1-60):	1-3X
(61-89, 120):	.5-1X
(90-119):	2-4X

Gold

(1-60) Print Run 25-50	8-15X
(1-60) P/R 51-75:	4-8X
(1-60) P/R 76-90:	3-5X

(61-120) 25 of each produced
Print runs based on stats.

Authentic McGwire

		NM/M
	Varying quantities produced	
AM-B	Mark McGwire/Bat/70	100.00
AM-BG	Mark McGwire/Bat/50	100.00
AM-J	Mark McGwire/Jsy/70	100.00
AM-JG	Mark McGwire/Jsy/50	100.00

Diamond Futures Jersey

		NM/M
	Common Player:	5.00
	Inserted 1:72	
	Golds production 25 no pricing.	
LB	Lance Berkman	8.00
RB	Russell Branyan	5.00
PB	Pat Burrell	8.00
FG	Freddy Garcia	5.00
TH	Tim Hudson	6.00
JK	Jason Kendall	8.00
JP	Jorge Posada	10.00
IR	Ivan Rodriguez	10.00
JR	Jimmy Rollins	5.00
KS	Kazuhiro Sasaki	5.00
JV	Jose Vidro	5.00
BZ	Barry Zito	5.00

Lead Performer Jersey

		NM/M
	Common Player:	5.00
	Inserted 1:72	
	Golds:	No Pricng
	Production 25 Sets	
JB	Jeff Bagwell	8.00
CD	Carlos Delgado	6.00
JGi	Jason Giambi	10.00
JG	Juan Gonzalez	8.00
LG	Luis Gonzalez	8.00
KG	Ken Griffey Jr./SP	20.00
MP	Mike Piazza	15.00
AR	Alex Rodriguez	15.00
IR	Ivan Rodriguez	8.00
SS	Sammy Sosa/SP	15.00
IS	Ichiro Suzuki	40.00
FT	Frank Thomas	8.00

Spokesman Spotlight

No Pricng
Production 25 Sets

Swatches Jersey

		NM/M
	Common Player:	5.00
	Inserted 1:72	
	Golds: 25 sets produced, no pricing.	
RA	Roberto Alomar/SP	20.00
EB	Ellis Burks	5.00
JB	Jeromy Burnitz	5.00
EC	Eric Chavez	6.00
CD	Carlos Delgado	6.00
DE	Darin Erstad	5.00
MG	Mark Grace	5.00
CJ	Chipper Jones	12.00
GM	Greg Maddux	15.00
PM	Pedro J. Martinez	10.00
AR	Alex Rodriguez	15.00
BW	Bernie Williams	10.00

2002 Upper Deck Piece of History

		NM/M
	Complete Set (132):	200.00
	Common Player:	.50
	Common SP (91-132):	5.00
	Production 625	
	Pack (5):	2.00
	Box (24):	40.00
1	Troy Glaus	.40
2	Darin Erstad	.25
3	Reggie Jackson	.50
4	Miguel Tejada	.40
5	Tim Hudson	.25
6	Jim "Catfish" Hunter	.40
7	Joe Carter	.15
8	Carlos Delgado	.40
9	Greg Vaughn	.15
10	Early Wynn	.15
11	Omar Vizquel	.15
12	Jim Thome	.75
13	Ichiro Suzuki	1.50
14	Edgar Martinez	.25
15	Freddy Garcia	.15
16	Cal Ripken Jr./SP	15.00
17	Jeff Conine	.15
18	Juan Gonzalez	.40
19	Nolan Ryan/SP	15.00
20	Alex Rodriguez/SP	10.00
21	Rafael Palmeiro	.50
22	Ivan Rodriguez	.50
23	Carlton Fisk	.25
24	Wade Boggs	.30
25	Pedro J. Martinez	.75
26	Nomar Garciaparra	1.50
27	Manny Ramirez	.50
28	Mike Sweeney	.15
29	Bobby Higginson	.15
30	Kirby Puckett	.75
31	Doug Mientkiewicz	.15
32	Corey Koskie	.15
33	Joe Mays	.15
34	Frank Thomas	.50
35	Magglio Ordonez	.40
36	Jason Giambi/SP	5.00
37	Derek Jeter/SP	10.00
38	Mickey Mantle/SP	15.00
39	Joe DiMaggio	2.00
40	Roger Maris	1.00
41	Roger Clemens	1.50
42	Bernie Williams	.50
43	Jeff Bagwell	.50
44	Lance Berkman	.25
45	Eddie Mathews	.40
46	Andruw Jones	.40
47	Phil Niekro	.15
48	Gary Sheffield	.25
49	Chipper Jones	.75
50	Greg Maddux	1.00
51	Robin Yount	.50
52	Richie Sexson	.25
53	Jim Edmonds	.25
54	J.D. Drew	.25
55	Albert Pujols	1.50
56	Andre Dawson	.25
57	Billy Williams	.15
58	Ernie Banks	.50
59	Sammy Sosa/SP	10.00
60	Randy Johnson	.75
61	Curt Schilling	.50
62	Luis Gonzalez	.25
63	Kirk Gibson	.15
64	Steve Garvey	.15
65	Sandy Koufax/SP	15.00
66	Shawn Green	.25
67	Hideo Nomo	.25
68	Kevin Brown	.15
69	Vladimir Guerrero	.75
70	Tim Raines	.15
71	Gaylord Perry	.15
72	Mel Ott	.25
73	Willie McCovey	.15
74	Barry Bonds/SP	10.00
75	Jeff Kent	.15
76	Cliff Floyd	.15
77	Dwight Gooden	.15
78	Tom Seaver	.15
79	Mike Piazza	1.00
80	Roberto Alomar	.50
81	Dave Winfield	.25
82	Tony Gwynn	.50
83	Scott Rolen	.75
84	Bill Mazeroski	.15
85	Willie Stargell	.25
86	Brian Giles	.25
87	Ken Griffey Jr./SP	10.00
88	Sean Casey	.25
89	Todd Helton	.50
90	Larry Walker	.25
91	Brendan Donnelly RC	5.00
92	Tom Shearn RC	5.00
93	Brandon Puffer RC	5.00
94	Corey Thurman RC	5.00
95	Reed Johnson RC	8.00
96	Gustavo Chacin RC	5.00
97	Chris Baker RC	5.00
98	John Ennis RC	5.00
99	So Taguchi RC	8.00
100	Michael Crudale RC	5.00
101	Francis Beltran RC	5.00
102	Jose Valverde RC	8.00
103	Doug DeVore RC	5.00
104	Jeremy Ward RC	5.00
105	P.J. Bevis RC	5.00
106	Steve Kent RC	5.00
107	Brandon Backe RC	5.00
108	Jorge Nunez RC	5.00
109	Kazuhisa Ishii RC	10.00
110	Ron Calloway RC	5.00
111	Valentino Pasucci RC	5.00
112	J.J. Putz RC	5.00
113	Matt Thornton RC	5.00
114	Allan Simpson RC	5.00
115	Jaime Cerda RC	5.00
116	Mark Corey RC	5.00
117	Tyler Yates RC	8.00
118	Steve Bechler RC	5.00
119	Ben Howard RC	5.00
120	Clifford Bartosh RC	5.00
121	Todd Donovan RC	5.00
122	Eric Junge RC	5.00
123	Adrian Burnside RC	5.00
124	Andy Pratt RC	5.00
125	Josh Hancock RC	5.00
126	Rene Reyes RC	5.00
127	Cam Esslinger RC	5.00
128	Colin Young RC	5.00
129	Kevin Frederick RC	5.00
130	Kyle Kane RC	5.00
131	Mitch Wylie RC	5.00
132	Danny Wright	5.00

Batting Champs

		NM/M
	Complete Set (10):	18.00
	Common Player:	1.50
	Inserted 1:30	
B1	Tony Gwynn	2.00
B2	Frank Thomas	2.00
B3	Billy Williams	1.50
B4	Edgar Martinez	1.50
B5	Bernie Williams	1.50
B6	Mickey Mantle	6.00
B7	Larry Walker	1.50
B8	Gary Sheffield	1.50
B9	Wade Boggs	1.50
B10	Alex Rodriguez	4.00

Batting Champ Jerseys

		NM/M
	Common Player:	8.00
	Inserted 1:96	
WB	Wade Boggs	10.00
AG	Andres Galarraga	5.00
TG	Tony Gwynn	15.00
MM	Mickey Mantle/50	200.00
EM	Edgar Martinez	10.00
JO	John Olerud	8.00
PO	Paul O'Neil	10.00
TR	Tim Raines	8.00
AR	Alex Rodriguez	15.00
GS	Gary Sheffield/SP	8.00
FT	Frank Thomas	10.00
LW	Larry Walker/SP	8.00
BeW	Bernie Williams	10.00

Batting Champ Jerseys Autograph

Complete Set (5):
Common Player:

ERA Leaders

		NM/M
	Complete Set (10):	18.00
	Common Player:	1.00
	Inserted 1:30	
E1	Greg Maddux	3.00
E2	Pedro J. Martinez	3.00
E3	Freddy Garcia	1.00
E4	Randy Johnson	2.00
E5	Tom Seaver	2.00
E6	Early Wynn	1.00
E7	Dwight Gooden	1.00
E8	Kevin Brown	1.00
E9	Roger Clemens	3.00
E10	Nolan Ryan	6.00

POH ERA Leaders Jerseys

		NM/M
Common Player:		8.00
Inserted 1:96		
KB	Kevin Brown	8.00
RC	Roger Clemens	15.00
FG	Freddy Garcia	8.00
DG	Dwight Gooden	8.00
CH	"Catfish" Hunter/SP	15.00
RJ	Randy Johnson	15.00
SK	Sandy Koufax/SP	100.00
GM	Greg Maddux	15.00
PM	Pedro Martinez	15.00
PN	Phil Niekro	8.00
NR	Nolan Ryan/SP	50.00
TS	Tom Seaver	15.00

ERA Leaders Jerseys Autographs

		NM/M
Production 24 Sets		
RC	Roger Clemens	200.00
SK	Sandy Koufax	750.00

History Hitting for the Cycle

		NM/M
Complete Set (20):		35.00
Common Player:		1.00
Inserted 1:15		
H1	Alex Rodriguez	4.00
H2	Andre Dawson	1.00
H3	Cal Ripken Jr.	6.00
H4	Carlton Fisk	1.50
H5	Dante Bichette	1.00
H6	Dave Winfield	1.50
H7	Eric Chavez	1.00
H8	Robin Yount	2.00
H9	Jason Kendall	1.00
H10	Jay Buhner	1.00
H11	Jeff Kent	1.00
H12	Joe DiMaggio	6.00
H13	John Olerud	1.00
H14	Kirby Puckett	3.00
H15	Luis Gonzalez	1.50
H16	Mark Grace	1.50
H17	Mickey Mantle	6.00
H18	Miguel Tejada	1.00
H19	Rondell White	1.00
H20	Todd Helton	2.00

Hitting for the Cycle Bats

		NM/M
Inserted 1:576		
DB	Dante Bichette	10.00
JB	Jay Buhner	10.00
EC	Eric Chavez	10.00
AD	Andre Dawson	10.00
CF	Carlton Fisk	25.00
LG	Luis Gonzalez	10.00
MM	Mickey Mantle/50	200.00
CR	Cal Ripken Jr./SP	75.00
AR	Alex Rodriguez	25.00
DW	Dave Winfield	15.00

Hitting for the Cycle Bats Authentic

No Pricing
Production 10 Sets

Tape Measure Heroes

		NM/M
Complete Set (30):		50.00
Common Player:		1.00

		NM/M
Inserted 1:10		
TM1	Joe Carter	1.00
TM2	Cal Ripken Jr.	6.00
TM3	Mike Piazza	4.00
TM4	Shawn Green	1.25
TM5	Mark McGwire	5.00
TM6	Reggie Jackson	1.50
TM7	Mickey Mantle	6.00
TM8	Manny Ramirez	2.00
TM9	Mo Vaughn	1.00
TM10	Jeff Bagwell	2.00
TM11	Sammy Sosa	3.00
TM12	Tony Gwynn	3.00
TM13	Bill Mazeroski	1.00
TM14	Jose Canseco	1.50
TM15	Brian Giles	1.00
TM16	Kirk Gibson	1.00
TM17	Kirby Puckett	3.00
TM18	Wade Boggs	1.50
TM19	Albert Pujols	3.00
TM20	David Justice	1.00
TM21	Steve Garvey	1.00
TM22	Luis Gonzalez	1.50
TM23	Derek Jeter	6.00
TM24	Robin Yount	2.00
TM25	Barry Bonds	4.00
TM26	Alex Rodriguez	4.00
TM27	Willie Stargell	1.50
TM28	Carlton Fisk	1.50
TM29	Carlos Delgado	1.50
TM30	Ken Griffey Jr.	5.00

Tape Measure Heroes Jerseys

		NM/M
Common Player:		5.00
Inserted 1:96		
JB	Jeff Bagwell	12.00
WB	Wade Boggs	15.00
JCa	Jose Canseco	10.00
JoC	Joe Carter	5.00
CD	Carlos Delgado	8.00
CF	Carlton Fisk	10.00
SGa	Steve Garvey	5.00
KGi	Kirk Gibson	8.00
BG	Brian Giles	5.00
SGr	Shawn Green	8.00
KGr	Ken Griffey Jr./90	40.00
MMa	Mickey Mantle/50	200.00
RM	Roger Maris/50	100.00
BM	Bill Mazeroski	10.00
MP	Mike Piazza	15.00
MR	Manny Ramirez	10.00
CR	Cal Ripken Jr.	30.00
AR	Alex Rodriguez	15.00
SS	Sammy Sosa	15.00
WS	Willie Stargell	15.00
RY	Robin Yount/SP	25.00

The MVP Club

		NM/M
Complete Set (14):		30.00
Common Player:		1.00
Inserted 1:22		
M1	Jason Giambi	2.00
M2	Sammy Sosa	3.00
M3	Cal Ripken Jr.	6.00
M4	Robin Yount	2.00
M5	Ken Griffey Jr.	5.00
M6	Kirk Gibson	1.00
M7	Mickey Mantle	6.00
M8	Barry Bonds	3.00
M9	Frank Thomas	2.00
M10	Reggie Jackson	2.00
M11	Jeff Bagwell	2.00
M12	Roger Clemens	3.00
M13	Steve Garvey	1.00
M14	Chipper Jones	3.00

MVP Club Jerseys

		NM/M
Common Player:		8.00
Inserted 1:96		
JB	Jeff Bagwell	10.00
RC	Roger Clemens	15.00
SG	Steve Garvey	8.00
JGi	Jason Giambi	10.00
KGi	Kirk Gibson	10.00
JGo	Juan Gonzalez	10.00
KGr	Ken Griffey Jr.	15.00
RJ	Reggie Jackson	15.00
CJ	Chipper Jones	15.00
JK	Jeff Kent	8.00
BL	Barry Larkin/SP	25.00
MM	Mickey Mantle/50	200.00

RM	Roger Maris/50	100.00
CR	Cal Ripken Jr.	35.00
IR	Ivan Rodriguez	10.00
SS	Sammy Sosa	15.00
FT	Frank Thomas	10.00
RY	Robin Yount/SP	25.00

MVP Club Jerseys Autograph

No Pricing
Production 10 Sets

The 500 Home Run Club

		NM/M
Complete Set (9):		25.00
Common Player:		1.50
Inserted 1:9		
HR1	Harmon Killebrew	3.00
HR2	Jimmie Foxx	3.00
HR3	Reggie Jackson	3.00
HR4	Mickey Mantle	8.00
HR5	Ernie Banks	3.00
HR6	Eddie Mathews	3.00
HR7	Mark McGwire	6.00
HR8	Willie McCovey	1.50
HR9	Mel Ott	3.00

POH 500 HR Club Jerseys

		NM/M
Inserted 1:336		
HA	Hank Aaron	40.00
EB	Ernie Banks/SP	40.00
JF	Jimmie Foxx	40.00
RJ	Reggie Jackson	25.00
MM	Mickey Mantle/50	200.00
EM	Eddie Mathews	40.00
WM	Willie McCovey	20.00
MO	Mel Ott	40.00

500 HR Club Jerseys Autograph

No Pricing
Production 10 Sets

300 Game Winners

		NM/M
Complete Set (6):		12.00
Common Player:		1.00
Inserted 1:50		
GW1	Nolan Ryan	6.00
GW2	Tom Seaver	3.00
GW3	Cy Young	3.00
GW4	Gaylord Perry	1.00
GW5	Early Wynn	1.00
GW6	Phil Niekro	1.00

300 Game Winners Jerseys

		NM/M
Common Player:		15.00
Inserted 1:576		
PN	Phil Niekro	10.00
GP	Gaylord Perry	10.00
NR	Nolan Ryan/SP	50.00
TS	Tom Seaver/SP	20.00

2002 Upper Deck Prospect Premieres

		NM/M
Complete Set (109)		
Common Player (1-60)		.40
Common (61-85)		5.00
Inserted 1:18		
Common (86-97)		10.00
Inserted 1:18		
Pack (4):		8.00
Box (18):		120.00
1	Josh Rupe RC	.40
2	Blair Johnson RC	.40
3	Jason Pridie RC	.75
4	Tim Gilhooly RC	.40
5	Kennard Jones RC	.40
6	Darrell Rasner RC	.40
7	Adam Donachie RC	.75
8	Josh Murray RC	.40
9	Brian Dopirak RC	1.00
10	Jason Cooper RC	.50
11	Zach Hammes RC	.40
12	Jon Lester RC	15.00
13	Kevin Jepsen RC	.40
14	Curtis Granderson RC	1.50
15	David Bush RC	.75
16	Joel Guzman RC	.50
17a	Matt Pender/Black RC (Photo is Curtis Granderson.)	.40
17b	Matt Pender/White (correct photo.)	2.00
18	Derick Grigsby RC	.40
19	Jeremy Reed RC	3.00
20	Jonathan Broxton RC	1.00
21	Jesse Crain RC	.40
22	Justin Jones RC	1.00
23	Brian Slocum RC	.50
24	Brian McCann RC	5.00
25	Francisco Liriano RC	8.00
26	Fred Lewis RC	.50
27	Steve Stanley RC	.40
28	Chris Snyder RC	.40
29	Daniel Cevette RC	.40
30	Kiel Fisher RC	.40
31	Brandon Wheeder RC	.40
32	Pat Osborn RC	.40
33	Taber Lee RC	.40
34	Dan Ortmeyer RC	.75
35	Josh Johnson RC	2.00
36	Val Majewski RC	.75
37	Larry Broadway RC	.50
38	Joey Gomes RC	1.00
39	Eric Thomas RC	.40
40	James Loney RC	4.00
41	Charlie Morton RC	.40
42	Mark McLemore RC	.40
43	Matt Craig RC	.40
44	Ryan Rodriguez RC	.40
45	Rich Hill RC	2.00
46	Bob Malek RC	.40
47	Justin Maureau RC	.40
48	Randy Braun RC	.40
49	Brian Grant RC	.50
50	Tyler Davidson RC	.50
51	Travis Hanson RC	.50
52	Kyle Boyer RC	.40
53	James Holcomb RC	.40
54	Ryan Williams RC	.40
55	Ben Crockett RC	.40
56	Adam Greenberg RC	.75
57	John Baker RC	.40
58	Matt Carson RC	.40
59	Jonathan George RC	.40
60	David Jensen RC	.40
61	Nick Swisher RC	15.00
62	Brent Cleven RC	8.00
63	Royce Ring RC	8.00
64	Mike Nixon RC	5.00
65	Ricky Barrett RC	5.00
66	Russ Adams RC	8.00
67	Joe Mauer RC	30.00
68	Jeff Francoeur RC	40.00
69	Joseph Blanton RC	10.00
70	Micah Schilling RC	8.00
71	John McCurdy RC	5.00
72	Sergio Santos RC	8.00
73	Josh Womack RC	5.00
74	Jared Doyle RC	5.00
75	Ben Fritz RC	5.00
76	Greg Miller RC	10.00
77	Luke Hagerty RC	8.00
78	Matt Whitney RC	10.00
79	Dan Meyer RC	5.00
80	Bill Murphy RC	5.00
81	Zach Segovia RC	8.00
82	Steve Obenchain RC	8.00
83	Matt Clanton RC	8.00
84	Mark Teahen RC	10.00
85	Kyle Pawelczyk RC	8.00
86	Khalil Greene/ Auto.	50.00
87	Joe Saunders/ Auto.	10.00
88	Jeremy Hermida/ Auto. RC	60.00
89	Drew Meyer/Auto. RC	10.00
90	Jeff Francis/Auto. RC	25.00
91	Scott Moore/ Auto.	10.00
92	Prince Fielder/ Auto. RC	125.00
93	Zack Greinke/ Auto. RC	40.00
94	Chris Gruler/Auto. RC	10.00
95	Scott Kazmir/ Auto.	100.00
96	B.J. Upton/Auto. RC	65.00
97	Clint Everts/Auto. RC	15.00

98	Cal Ripken Jr.	1.00
99	Cal Ripken Jr.	1.00
100	Mark McGwire	1.00
101	Mark McGwire	1.00
102	Mark McGwire	1.00
103	Mark McGwire	1.00
104	Mark McGwire	1.00
105	Joe DiMaggio	1.00
106	Joe DiMaggio	1.00
107	Joe DiMaggio	1.00
108	Joe DiMaggio	1.00
109	Joe DiMaggio	1.00

UD Heroes of Baseball

		NM/M
Complete Ripken Set (10):		15.00
Common Ripken:		2.00
Complete Morgan Set (10):		4.00
Common Morgan:		.50
Complete Stargell Set (10):		5.00
Common Stargell:		.50
Complete Seaver Set (10):		10.00
Common Seaver:		1.25
Complete Mantle Set (10):		15.00
Common Mantle:		2.00
Complete DiMaggio Set (10):		12.00
Common DiMaggio:		1.50
Complete Gwynn Set (10):		10.00
Common Gwynn:		1.25
Complete McGwire Set (10):		12.00
Common McGwire:		1.50
Complete Ozzie Smith (10):		8.00
Common Ozzie:		1.00
Sets include Headers		
Inserted 1:1		

Heroes of Baseball Quads

		NM/M
Common Quad:		10.00
Production 85 Sets		
1	Joe DiMaggio, Tony Gwynn	15.00
2	Joe DiMaggio, Tony Gwynn, Cal Ripken Jr.	20.00
3	Joe DiMaggio, Mickey Mantle, Willie Stargell	20.00
4	Tony Gwynn, Ozzie Smith, Willie Stargell	10.00
5	Tony Gwynn, Willie Stargell, Joe DiMaggio, Joe Morgan	15.00
6	Tony Gwynn, Willie Stargell, Cal Ripken Jr., Ozzie Smith	15.00
7	Mickey Mantle, Mark McGwire, Joe Morgan, Tom Seaver	20.00
8	Mickey Mantle, Tom Seaver	20.00
9	Mark McGwire, Joe Morgan	20.00
10	Mark McGwire, Cal Ripken Jr., Tony Gwynn, Joe DiMaggio	25.00
11	Mark McGwire, Tom Seaver, Joe Morgan, Ozzie Smith	15.00

12	Joe Morgan, Tony Gwynn	10.00
13	Joe Morgan, Joe DiMaggio, Mickey Mantle, Cal Ripken Jr.	25.00
14	Joe Morgan, Joe DiMaggio, Willie Stargell, Tony Gwynn	15.00
15	Ozzie Smith, Joe DiMaggio, Ozzie Smith, Willie Stargell	15.00
16	Ozzie Smith, Mark McGwire, Willie Stargell, Tony Gwynn	15.00
17	Ozzie Smith, Tom Seaver, Mark McGwire	15.00
18	Cal Ripken Jr., Mickey Mantle, Joe DiMaggio, Joe Morgan	20.00
19	Cal Ripken Jr., Mark McGwire, Cal Ripken Jr.	20.00
20	Tom Seaver, Joe DiMaggio, Tom Seaver, Joe DiMaggio	15.00
21	Tom Seaver, Joe Morgan, Ozzie Smith, Willie Stargell	10.00
22	Tom Seaver, Cal Ripken Jr., Mark McGwire, Mickey Mantle	20.00
23	Willie Stargell, Ozzie Smith	10.00
24	Willie Stargell, Ozzie Smith, Tom Seaver, Joe Morgan	10.00

Future Gems Quads

		NM/M
Common Card:		4.00
Inserted 1:Box		
1	David Bush, Matt Craig, Blair Johnson, Brian McCann	4.00
2	Jason Cooper, Jonathan George, Larry Broadway, Joel Guzman	4.00
3	Matt Craig, Josh Murray, Brian McCann, Jason Pridie	4.00
4	Jesse Crain, Brian Grant, Curtis Granderson, Joey Gomes	4.00
5	Tyler Davidson, Val Majewski, Kennard Jones, Daniel Cevette	4.00
6	Joe DiMaggio, Jon Lester, Mac, Mark McLemore	4.00
7	Jonathan George, Jeremy Reed, Adam Donachie, Matt Carson	4.00
8	Jonathan George, Eric Thomas, Joel Guzman, Kiel Fisher	4.00
9	Tim Gilhooly, Brandon Wheeder, Brian Slocum, Brian Dopirak	4.00
10	Brian Grant, Rich Hill, Joey Gomes, Joe DiMaggio	4.00
11	Derick Grigsby, Bob Malek, James Loney, Fred Lewis	4.00
12	Zach Hammes, James Holcomb, Cal Ripken Jr., Kennard Jones	4.00
13	Rich Hill, Mark McGwire, Brian Grant, Matt Carson	4.00
14	James Holcomb, David Jensen, Kennard Jones, Ryan Williams	4.00
15	David Jensen, Francisco Liriano, Ryan Williams, Travis Hanson	4.00

16	Blair Johnson, Jesse Crain, Adam Greenberg, Curtis Granderson	4.00
17	Jon Lester, Jonathan George, Adam Donachie, Mark McLemore	4.00
18	Francisco Liriano, Mark McGwire, Travis Hanson, Taber Lee	4.00
19	Val Majewski, Charlie Morton, Daniel Cevette, Joey Gomes	4.00
20	Bob Malek, Zach Hammes, Fred Lewis, Cal Ripken Jr.	4.00
21	Justin Maureau, Joe DiMaggio, Chris Snyder, Mark McGwire	4.00
22	Mark McGwire, Bob Malek, Joe DiMaggio, Kyle Boyer	4.00
23	Charlie Morton, David Bush, Joey Gomes, Blair Johnson	4.00
24	Josh Murray, Mark McGwire, Jason Pridie, Joe DiMaggio	4.00
25	Matt Pender, Mark McGwire, Mark McLemore, Ryan Rodriguez	4.00
26	Jason Pridie, Josh Murray, Matt Craig, Brian McCann	4.00
27	Jeremy Reed, Blair Johnson, Matt Carson, Adam Greenberg	4.00
28	Cal Ripken Jr., Jason Cooper, Matt Carson, Larry Broadway	4.00
29	Ryan Rodriguez, Eric Thomas, Pat Osborn, Randy Braun	4.00
30	Josh Rupe, Tyler Davidson, John Baker, Kennard Jones	4.00
31	Eric Thomas, Derick Grigsby, Randy Braun, James Loney	4.00
32	Eric Thomas, Matt Pender, Kiel Fisher, Mark McLemore	4.00
33	Brandon Wheeler, Rich Hill, Brian Dopirak, Brian Grant	4.00

2002 Upper Deck Rookie Debut

		NM/M
Common Player:		.10
Pack (5):		1.50
Box (24):		30.00
Honor Roll		
Common Honor Roll RK (131-190):		.25
Golds (131-190):		5-10X
Production 50		
101	Curt Schilling	.40
102	Geronimo Gil	.10
103	Cliff Floyd	.10
104	Derek Lowe	.10
105	Hee Seop Choi	.50
106	Mark Prior	.50
107	Joe Borchard	.10
108	Austin Kearns	.40
109	Adam Dunn	.50
110	Brandon Phillips	.10
111	Carlos Pena	.10
112	Andy Van Hekken	.10
113	Juan Encarnacion	.10
114	Lance Berkman	.25
115	Torii Hunter	.25
116	Bartolo Colon	.10
117	Raul Mondesi	.20
118	Alfonso Soriano	.75
119	Miguel Tejada	.40
120	Ray Durham	.25
121	Eric Chavez	.20
122	Brett Myers	.10

123	Marlon Byrd	.10
124	Sean Burroughs	.10
125	Kenny Lofton	.10
126	Scott Rolen	.50
127	Carl Crawford	.10
128	Josh Phelps	.10
129	Eric Hinske	.10
130	Orlando Hudson	.10
131	Barry Wesson	.40
132	Jose Valverde RC	.25
133	Kevin Gryboski RC	.25
134	Trey Hodges RC	.25
135	Howie Clark RC	.25
136	Josh Hancock RC	.25
137	Freddy Sanchez RC	.25
138	Francis Beltran RC	.10
139	Mike Mahoney	.10
140	Brian Tallet	.10
141	Jason Davis RC	.50
142	Carl Sadler RC	.25
143	Jason Beverlin RC	.25
144	Josh Bard RC	.25
145	Aaron Cook RC	.25
146	Eric Eckenstahler RC	.25
147	Tim Kalita RC	.25
148	Franklyn German RC	.25
149	Hansel Izquierdo RC	.25
150	Brandon Puffer RC	.25
151	Rodrigo Rosario RC	.25
152	Kirk Saarloos	.10
153	Jeriome Robertson RC	.25
154	Jeremy Hill RC	.25
155	Wes Obermueller RC	.25
156	Aaron Guiel RC	.25
157	Kazuhisa Ishii RC	1.00
158	David Ross	.10
159	Jayson Durocher RC	.25
160	Luis Martinez RC	.25
161	Shane Nance RC	.25
162	Eric Good RC	.25
163	Jamey Carroll RC	.25
164	Jaime Cerda RC	.25
165	Satoru Komiyama RC	.25
166	Adam Walker RC	.25
167	Nate Field RC	.25
168	Cody McKay RC	.25
169	Jose Flores RC	.25
170	Eric Junge RC	.25
171	Jorge Padilla RC	.25
172	Oliver Perez RC	1.00
173	Julius Matos RC	.25
174	Wilbert Nieves RC	.25
175	Clay Condrey RC	.25
176	Mike Crudale RC	.25
177	Jason Simontacchi RC	.50
178	So Taguchi RC	.50
179	Jose Rodriguez	.10
180	Jorge Sosa RC	.25
181	Felix Escalona RC	.25
182	Lance Carter RC	.25
183	Travis Hughes	.10
184	Reynaldo Garcia RC	.25
185	Mike Smith	.10
186	Corey Thurman RC	.25
187	Ken Huckaby RC	.25
188	Reed Johnson RC	.50
189	Kevin Cash RC	.25
190	Scott Wiggins RC	.25

Ovation

Common SP (151-180):		3.00
Production 2,002		
Golds (151-180):		2-4X
Production 50		
121	Curt Schilling	.50
122	Cliff Floyd	.15
123	Derek Lowe	.15
124	Hee Seop Choi	.25
125	Mark Prior	.75
126	Joe Borchard	.15
127	Austin Kearns	.50
128	Adam Dunn	.75
129	Jay Payton	.15
130	Carlos Pena	.15
131	Andy Van Hekken	.15
132	Andres Torres	.15
133	Ben Diggins	.15
134	Torii Hunter	.40
135	Bartolo Colon	.25
136	Raul Mondesi	.25
137	Alfonso Soriano	1.00
138	Miguel Tejada	.75
139	Ray Durham	.15
140	Eric Chavez	.40
141	Marlon Byrd	.15
142	Brett Myers	.15
143	Sean Burroughs	.15
144	Kenny Lofton	.15
145	Scott Rolen	.75
146	Carl Crawford	.15
147	Jayson Werth	.15
148	Josh Phelps	.15
149	Eric Hinske	.15
150	Orlando Hudson	.15
151	Jose Valverde RC	5.00
152	Trey Hodges RC	3.00
153	Joey Dawley RC	3.00
154	Travis Driskill RC	3.00
155	Howie Clark RC	3.00
156	Jorge De La Rosa RC	3.00
157	Freddy Sanchez RC	3.00
158	Earl Snyder RC	3.00
159	Cliff Lee RC	8.00
160	Josh Bard RC	3.00
161	Aaron Cook RC	3.00
162	Franklyn German RC	3.00
163	Brandon Puffer RC	3.00
164	Kirk Saarloos	3.00
165	Jeriome Robertson RC	3.00

166	Miguel Asencio RC	3.00
167	Shawn Sedlacek	3.00
168	Jayson Durocher RC	3.00
169	Shane Nance RC	3.00
170	Jamey Carroll RC	8.00
171	Oliver Perez RC	10.00
172	Wilbert Nieves	3.00
173	Clay Condrey RC	3.00
174	Chris Snelling RC	5.00
175	Mike Crudale RC	3.00
176	Jason Simontacchi RC	3.00
177	Felix Escalona RC	3.00
178	Lance Carter RC	3.00
179	Scott Wiggins RC	3.00
180	Kevin Cash RC	3.00

Victory

Common RK (606-660):		.10
551	John Lackey	.25
552	Francisco Rodriguez	.50
553	Cliff Floyd	.10
554	Derek Lowe	.10
555	Mark Bellhorn	.10
556	Matt Clement	.10
557	Hee Seop Choi	.25
558	Joe Borchard	.10
559	Ryan Dempster	.10
560	Russell Branyan	.10
561	Brandon Larson	.10
562	Coco Crisp	.10
563	Karim Garcia	.10
564	Brandon Phillips	.10
565	Jay Payton	.10
566	Gabe Kapler	.10
567	Carlos Pena	.10
568	George Lombard	.10
569	Andy Van Hekken	.10
570	Andres Torres	.10
571	Justin Wayne	.10
572	Juan Encarnacion	.10
573	Abraham Nunez	.10
574	Peter Munro	.10
575	Jason Lane	.10
576	Dave Roberts	.10
577	Eric Gagne	.10
578	Alex Sanchez	.10
579	Jim Rushford RC	.10
580	Ben Diggins	.10
581	Eddie Guardado	.10
582	Bartolo Colon	.20
583	Endy Chavez	.10
584	Raul Mondesi	.20
585	Jeff Weaver	.10
586	Marcus Thames	.10
587	Ted Lilly	.10
588	Ray Durham	.10
589	Jeremy Giambi	.10
590	Vicente Padilla	.10
591	Brett Myers	.10
592	Josh Fogg	.10
593	Tony Alvarez	.10
594	Jake Peavy	.10
595	Dennis Tankersley	.10
596	Sean Burroughs	.10
597	Kenny Lofton	.10
598	Scott Rolen	.50
599	Chuck Finley	.10
600	Carl Crawford	.10
601	Kevin Mench	.10
602	Juan Gonzalez	.50
603	Jayson Werth	.10
604	Eric Hinske	.10
605	Josh Phelps	.10
606	Jose Valverde RC	.20
607	John Ennis RC	.20
608	Trey Hodges RC	.20
609	Kevin Gryboski RC	.20
610	Travis Driskill RC	.20
611	Howie Clark RC	.20
612	Freddy Sanchez RC	.20
613	Josh Hancock RC	.20
614	Jorge De La Rosa RC	.20
615	Mike Mahoney	.10
616	Jason Davis RC	.20
617	Josh Bard RC	.20
618	Jason Beverlin RC	.20
619	Carl Sadler RC	.20
620	Earl Snyder RC	.50
621	Aaron Cook RC	.20
622	Eric Eckenstahler RC	.20
623	Franklyn German RC	.20
624	Kirk Saarloos	.50
625	Rodrigo Rosario RC	.20
626	Jeriome Robertson RC	.20
627	Brandon Puffer RC	.20
628	Miguel Asencio RC	.20
629	Aaron Guiel RC	.30
630	Ryan Bukvich RC	.20
631	Jeremy Hill RC	.20
632	Kazuhisa Ishii RC	.75
633	Jayson Durocher RC	.20
634	Shane Nance RC	.20
635	Eric Good RC	.20
636	Jamey Carroll RC	.50
637	Jaime Cerda RC	.20
638	Nate Field RC	.20
639	Cody McKay RC	.20
640	Jose Flores RC	.20
641	Jorge Padilla RC	.20
642	Anderson Machado RC	.20
643	Eric Junge RC	.20
644	Oliver Perez RC	.75
645	Julius Matos RC	.20
646	Ben Howard RC	.20
647	Julio Mateo RC	.20
648	Matt Thornton	.20
649	Chris Snelling RC	.50
650	Jason Simontacchi RC	.50
651	So Taguchi RC	.40

652	Mike Crudale RC	.20
653	Mike Coolbaugh	.10
654	Felix Escalona RC	.20
655	Jorge Sosa RC	.20
656	Lance Carter RC	.20
657	Reynaldo Garcia RC	.20
658	Kevin Cash RC	.40
659	Ken Huckaby RC	.20
660	Scott Wiggins RC	.20

Climbing the Ladder
Common Player:
Production 25 Sets, Not Priced

Elite Company
Common Player:
Production 25, Not Priced

Making Their Marks
Common Player:
Production 25 Sets, Not Priced

Solid Contact

		NM/M
Common Player:		4.00
Inserted 1:24		
BA	Bobby Abreu	4.00
EA	Edgardo Alfonzo	4.00
RA	Roberto Alomar	10.00
MA	Moises Alou	6.00
JC	Jose Cruz Jr.	6.00
CD	Carlos Delgado/SP	8.00
JE	Jim Edmonds	6.00
CE	Carl Everett	4.00
JG	Jason Giambi/50	15.00
BG	Brian Giles	6.00
KG	Ken Griffey Jr.	15.00
TH	Todd Helton	8.00
JK	Jason Kendall	4.00
BL	Barry Larkin	10.00
EM	Edgar Martinez	8.00
FM	Fred McGriff	8.00
DM	Doug Mientkiewicz	6.00
JO	John Olerud	6.00
MO	Magglio Ordonez	6.00
JP	Jorge Posada	10.00
AR	Alex Rodriguez	15.00
IR	Ivan Rodriguez	6.00
GS	Gary Sheffield	6.00
SS	Sammy Sosa	15.00
TA	Fernando Tatis	4.00
FT	Frank Thomas	8.00
JT	Jim Thome	12.00
OV	Omar Vizquel	6.00
BW	Bernie Williams	8.00
MW	Matt Williams	4.00

2002 Upper Deck Rookie Update

		NM/M
Common Player:		.25
Pack (5):		3.00
Box (15):		35.00
SP Authentic		
Common SP (201-230):		5.00
Production 1,999		
171	Erubiel Durazo	.25
172	Junior Spivey	.25
173	Geronimo Gil	.25
174	Cliff Floyd	.25
175	Brandon Larsen	.25
176	Aaron Boone	.25
177	Shawn Estes	.25
178	Austin Kearns	.75
179	Joe Borchard	.25
180	Russell Branyan	.25
181	Jay Payton	.25
182	Andres Torres	.25
183	Andy Van Hekken	.25
184	Alex Sanchez	.25
185	Endy Chavez	.25
186	Bartolo Colon	.25

187	Raul Mondesi	.40
188	Robin Ventura	.25
189	Mike Mussina	.75
190	Jorge Posada	.75
191	Ted Lilly	.25
192	Ray Durham	.25
193	Brett Myers	.25
194	Marlon Byrd	.25
195	Vicente Padilla	.25
196	Josh Fogg	.25
197	Kenny Lofton	.25
198	Scott Rolen	1.00
199	Jason Lane	.25
200	Josh Phelps	.25
201	Travis Driskill RC	5.00
202	Howie Clark RC	5.00
203	Mike Mahoney	5.00
204	Brian Tallet	5.00
205	Kirk Saarloos	5.00
206	Shawn Sedlacek	5.00
207	Aaron Guiel RC	5.00
208	Shawn Sedlacek	5.00
209	Jose Diaz	5.00
210	Jorge Nunez	5.00
211	Danny Mota	5.00
212	David Ross	5.00
213	Jayson Durocher RC	5.00
214	Shane Nance RC	5.00
215	Wilbert Nieves RC	5.00
216	Freddy Sanchez RC	5.00
217	Alex Pelaez	5.00
218	Jamey Carroll RC	5.00
219	J.J. Trujillo	5.00
220	Kevin Pickford	5.00
221	Clay Condrey RC	5.00
222	Chris Snelling RC	5.00
223	Cliff Lee RC	8.00
224	Jeremy Hill RC	5.00
225	Jose Rodriguez	5.00
226	Lance Carter RC	5.00
227	Ken Huckaby RC	5.00
228	Scott Wiggins RC	5.00
229	Corey Thurman RC	5.00
230	Kevin Cash RC	5.00

SPx

Common SPx Auto. (221-250):		10.00
Production 825		
191	Tom Glavine	.75
192	Cliff Floyd	.25
193	Mark Prior	1.50
194	Corey Patterson	.50
195	Paul Konerko	.50
196	Adam Dunn	1.00
197	Joe Borchard	.25
198	Carlos Pena	.25
199	Juan Encarnacion	.25
200	Luis Castillo	.25
201	Torii Hunter	.50
202	Hee Seop Choi	.50
203	Bartolo Colon	.40
204	Raul Mondesi	.25
205	Jeff Weaver	.25
206	Eric Munson	.25
207	Alfonso Soriano	1.00
208	Ray Durham	.25
209	Eric Chavez	.50
210	Brett Myers	.25
211	Jeremy Giambi	.25
212	Vicente Padilla	.25
213	Felipe Lopez	.25
214	Sean Burroughs	.25
215	Kenny Lofton	.25
216	Scott Rolen	1.00
217	Carl Crawford	.25
218	Juan Gonzalez	.75
219	Orlando Hudson	.25
220	Eric Hinske	.25
221	Adam Walker RC	10.00
222	Aaron Cook RC	10.00
223	Cam Esslinger RC	10.00
224	Kirk Saarloos	10.00
225	Jose Diaz	10.00
226	David Ross	10.00
227	Jayson Durocher RC	10.00
228	Brian Mallette	10.00
229	Aaron Guiel RC	10.00
230	Jorge Nunez	10.00
231	Satoru Komiyama RC	15.00
232	Tyler Yates RC	15.00
233	Peter Zamora RC	10.00
234	Mike Gonzalez RC	10.00
235	Oliver Perez RC	30.00
236	Julius Matos RC	10.00
237	Andy Shibilo	10.00
238	Jason Simontacchi RC	10.00
239	Ron Chiavacci RC	10.00
240	Deivis Santos	10.00
241	Travis Driskill RC	10.00
242	Jorge De La Rosa RC	10.00
243	Anastacio Martinez RC	10.00
244	Earl Snyder RC	10.00
245	Freddy Sanchez RC	10.00
246	Miguel Asencio RC	10.00
247	Juan Brito	10.00
248	Franklyn German RC	10.00
249	Chris Snelling RC	10.00
250	Ken Huckaby RC	10.00

Diamond Connection

Common SP (601-630):		4.00
Production 1,999		
571	Erubiel Durazo	.25
572	Geronimo Gil	.25
573	Shea Hillenbrand	.50
574	Cliff Floyd	.25
575	Corey Patterson	.50

576	Joe Borchard	.25
577	Austin Kearns	.75
578	Ryan Dempster	.25
579	Brandon Larsen	.25
580	Luis Castillo	.25
581	Juan Encarnacion	.25
582	Chin-Feng Chen	.25
583	Hideo Nomo	.75
584	Bartolo Colon	.40
585	Raul Mondesi	.40
586	Eric Munson	.25
587	Alfonso Soriano	1.00
588	Ted Lilly	.25
589	Ray Durham	.25
590	Brett Myers	.25
591	Brandon Phillips	.25
592	Kenny Lofton	.25
593	Scott Rolen	1.00
594	Jim Edmonds	.50
595	Carl Crawford	.25
596	Hank Blalock	.50
597	Kevin Mench	.25
598	Josh Phelps	.25
599	Orlando Hudson	.25
600	Eric Hinske	.25
601	Mike Mahoney	4.00
602	Jason Davis RC	8.00
603	Trey Hodges RC	4.00
604	Josh Bard RC	4.00
605	Jeriome Robertson RC	4.00
606	Jose Diaz	4.00
607	Jorge Nunez	4.00
608	Danny Mota	4.00
609	David Ross	4.00
610	Jayson Durocher RC	4.00
611	Freddy Sanchez RC	4.00
612	Julius Matos RC	4.00
613	Wilbert Nieves RC	4.00
614	Brian Kozlowski	4.00
615	Jason Simontacchi RC	4.00
616	Mike Coolbaugh	4.00
617	Travis Driskill RC	4.00
618	Howie Clark RC	4.00
619	Earl Snyder RC	6.00
620	Carl Sadler RC	4.00
621	Jason Beverlin RC	4.00
622	Terry Pearson	4.00
623	Eric Eckenstahler RC	4.00
624	Shawn Sedlacek	4.00
625	Aaron Guiel RC	5.00
626	Ryan Bukvich RC	4.00
627	Julio Mateo RC	4.00
628	Chris Snelling RC	6.00
629	Lance Carter RC	4.00
630	Scott Wiggins RC	4.00

Star Tributes

		NM/M
Common Player:		5.00
Inserted 1:15		
JB	Josh Beckett	8.00
LB	Lance Berkman	6.00
RC	Roger Clemens	15.00
CD	Carlos Delgado	5.00
JD	Joe DiMaggio/SP	75.00
AD	Adam Dunn	8.00
JG	Jason Giambi	10.00
TG	Tom Glavine	8.00
LG	Luis Gonzalez/SP	8.00
SG	Shawn Green	5.00
KG	Ken Griffey Jr.	12.00
KI	Kazuhisa Ishii	8.00
RJ	Randy Johnson	10.00
CJ	Chipper Jones	10.00
PM	Pedro J. Martinez	8.00
MM	Mark McGwire/SP	50.00
RP	Rafael Palmeiro	8.00
MPi	Mike Piazza	10.00
MPr	Mark Prior	5.00
AR	Alex Rodriguez	10.00
IR	Ivan Rodriguez	8.00
KS	Kazuhiro Sasaki	8.00
CS	Curt Schilling	8.00
TS	Tsuyoshi Shinjo	5.00
AS	Alfonso Soriano	10.00
SS	Sammy Sosa	12.00
MS	Mike Sweeney	5.00
FT	Frank Thomas	8.00

Signed Star Tributes

	NM/M
Production 50 Sets	
Copper & Silver:	No Pricing
Production 25	
Gold:	No Pricing
Production 5	
SS-MM Mark McGwire	350.00

USA Future Watch Swatches

	NM/M
Common Player:	5.00
Inserted 1:15	

Red:	1.5-2X	
Production 50		
Copper:	No Pricing	
Production 25		
Gold:	No Pricing	
Production 5		
AA	Abe Alvarez	5.00
MA	Michael Aubrey	10.00
KB	Kyle Bakker	8.00
CC	Chad Cordero	5.00
SC	Shane Costa	5.00
SF	Sam Fuld	8.00
AH	Aaron Hill	8.00
PH	Philip Humber	8.00
CJ	Conor Jackson	5.00
GJ	Grant Johnson	5.00
MJ	Mark Jurich	5.00
WL	Wes Littleton	8.00
EP	Eric Patterson	5.00
DP	Dustin Pedroia	5.00
LP	Landon Powell	5.00
CQ	Carlos Quentin	8.00
CS	Clint Sammons	5.00
KS	Kyle Sleeth	10.00
HS	Huston Street	5.00
BS	Brad Sullivan	8.00
RW	Rickie Weeks	15.00
BZ	Bob Zimmermann	5.00

2002 Upper Deck Sweet Spot

		NM/M
Complete Set (175):		
Common Player:		.25
Common (91-130):		4.00
Production 1,300		
Common Auto. (131-145):		15.00
Production 750 or 100		
Common Game Faces		
(146-175):		3.00
Inserted 1:24		
Parallel (146-175):		1.5X-3X
Production 100		
Pack (4):		8.00
Box (12):		90.00
1	Troy Glaus	.50
2	Darin Erstad	.50
3	Tim Hudson	.50
4	Eric Chavez	.50
5	Barry Zito	.50
6	Miguel Tejada	.50
7	Carlos Delgado	.50
8	Eric Hinske	.25
9	Ben Grieve	.25
10	Jim Thome	1.00
11	C.C. Sabathia	.25
12	Omar Vizquel	.40
13	Ichiro Suzuki	2.00
14	Edgar Martinez	.40
15	Bret Boone	.40
16	Freddy Garcia	.25
17	Tony Batista	.25
18	Geronimo Gil	.25
19	Alex Rodriguez	2.50
20	Rafael Palmeiro	.75
21	Ivan Rodriguez	.75
22	Hank Blalock	.50
23	Juan Gonzalez	.75
24	Nomar Garciaparra	2.00
25	Pedro J. Martinez	1.00
26	Manny Ramirez	1.00
27	Mike Sweeney	.25
28	Carlos Beltran	.50
29	Dmitri Young	.25
30	Torii Hunter	.50
31	Eric Milton	.25
32	Corey Koskie	.25
33	Frank Thomas	.75
34	Mark Buehrle	.25
35	Magglio Ordonez	.50
36	Roger Clemens	2.00
37	Derek Jeter	3.00
38	Jason Giambi	.75
39	Alfonso Soriano	1.00
40	Bernie Williams	.50
41	Jeff Bagwell	.75
42	Roy Oswalt	.50

43	Lance Berkman	.50
44	Greg Maddux	1.50
45	Chipper Jones	1.00
46	Gary Sheffield	.50
47	Andruw Jones	.75
48	Richie Sexson	.50
49	Ben Sheets	.50
50	Albert Pujols	2.00
51	Matt Morris	.25
52	J.D. Drew	.50
53	Sammy Sosa	2.00
54	Kerry Wood	1.00
55	Mark Prior	1.00
56	Moises Alou	.50
57	Corey Patterson	.50
58	Randy Johnson	1.00
59	Luis Gonzalez	.40
60	Curt Schilling	.75
61	Shawn Green	.50
62	Kevin Brown	.25
63	Paul LoDuca	.25
64	Adrian Beltre	.25
65	Vladimir Guerrero	1.00
66	Jose Vidro	.25
67	Javier Vazquez	.25
68	Barry Bonds	3.00
69	Jeff Kent	.40
70	Rich Aurilia	.25
71	Mike Lowell	.40
72	Josh Beckett	.50
73	Brad Penny	.25
74	Roberto Alomar	.50
75	Mike Piazza	1.50
76	Jeromy Burnitz	.25
77	Mo Vaughn	.25
78	Phil Nevin	.25
79	Sean Burroughs	.25
80	Jeremy Giambi	.25
81	Bobby Abreu	.50
82	Jimmy Rollins	.50
83	Pat Burrell	.50
84	Brian Giles	.50
85	Aramis Ramirez	.50
86	Ken Griffey Jr.	1.50
87	Adam Dunn	.75
88	Austin Kearns	.50
89	Todd Helton	.75
90	Larry Walker	.50
91	Earl Snyder RC	6.00
92	Jorge Padilla RC	4.00
93	Felix Escalona RC	4.00
94	John Foster RC	4.00
95	Brandon Puffer RC	4.00
96	Steve Bechler RC	4.00
97	Hansel Izquierdo RC	4.00
98	Chris Baker RC	4.00
99	Jeremy Ward RC	4.00
100	Kevin Frederick RC	4.00
101	Josh Hancock RC	4.00
102	Allan Simpson RC	4.00
103	Mitch Wylie RC	4.00
104	Mark Corey RC	4.00
105	Victor Alvarez RC	4.00
106	Todd Donovan RC	4.00
107	Nelson Castro RC	4.00
108	Chris Booker RC	4.00
109	Corey Thurman RC	4.00
110	Kirk Saarloos RC	4.00
111	Michael Crudale RC	4.00
112	Jason Simontacchi RC	4.00
113	Ron Calloway RC	4.00
114	Brandon Backe RC	4.00
115	Tom Shearn RC	4.00
116	Oliver Perez RC	6.00
117	Kyle Kane RC	4.00
118	Francis Beltran RC	4.00
119	So Taguchi RC	8.00
120	Doug DeVore RC	4.00
121	Juan Brito RC	4.00
122	Clifford Bartosh RC	4.00
123	Eric Junge RC	4.00
124	Joe Orloski RC	4.00
125	Scotty Layfield RC	4.00
126	Jorge Sosa RC	4.00
127	Satoru Komiyama RC	4.00
128	Edwin Almonte RC	4.00
129	Takahito Nomura RC	4.00
130	John Ennis RC	4.00
131	Kazuhisa Ishii RC Auto./100 RC	90.00
132	Ben Howard RC Auto./100 RC	20.00
133	Aaron Cook/ Auto./750 RC	15.00
134	Anderson Machado/ Auto./750 RC	15.00
135	Luis Ugueto/ Auto./750 RC	15.00
136	Tyler Yates/ Auto./750 RC	20.00
137	Rodrigo Rosario/ Auto./750 RC	15.00
138	Jaime Cerda/ Auto./750 RC	15.00
139	Luis Martinez/ Auto./750 RC	15.00
140	Rene Reyes/ Auto./750 RC	15.00
141	Eric Good/ Auto./750 RC	15.00
142	Matt Thornton/ Auto./100	25.00
143	Steve Kent/ Auto./750 RC	15.00
144	Jose Valverde/ Auto./750 RC	15.00
145	Adrian Burnside/ Auto./750 RC	15.00

146	Barry Bonds	15.00
147	Ken Griffey Jr.	10.00
148	Alex Rodriguez	12.00
149	Jason Giambi	4.00
150	Chipper Jones	5.00
151	Nomar Garciaparra	4.00
152	Mike Piazza	10.00
153	Sammy Sosa	10.00
154	Derek Jeter	15.00
155	Jeff Bagwell	4.00
156	Albert Pujols	10.00
157	Ichiro Suzuki	10.00
158	Randy Johnson	4.00
159	Frank Thomas	4.00
160	Greg Maddux	8.00
161	Jim Thome	5.00
162	Scott Rolen	4.00
163	Shawn Green	3.00
164	Vladimir Guerrero	6.00
165	Troy Glaus	4.00
166	Carlos Delgado	4.00
167	Luis Gonzalez	3.00
168	Roger Clemens	10.00
169	Todd Helton	4.00
170	Eric Chavez	4.00
171	Rafael Palmeiro	4.00
172	Pedro J. Martinez	4.00
173	Lance Berkman	3.00
174	Josh Beckett	4.00
175	Sean Burroughs	3.00

Bat Barrels

Common Player:	
100 Total Produced	

Legendary Signatures

		NM/M
Common Autograph:		20.00
Inserted 1:72		
LA	Luis Aparicio/485	25.00
RF	Rollie Fingers/866	20.00
SG	Steve Garvey/871	20.00
KH	Keith Hernandez/906	20.00
FJ	Ferguson Jenkins/ 857	20.00
AK	Al Kaline/835	40.00
SK	Sandy Koufax/485	200.00
FL	Fred Lynn/853	20.00
MM	Mark McGwire/90	575.00
PM	Paul Molitor/852	30.00
GP	Gaylord Perry/921	20.00
BP	Boog Powell/944	20.00
CR	Cal Ripken Jr./194	175.00
BR	Brooks Robinson	35.00
AT	Alan Trammell/843	25.00

Mark McGwire Priority Signing Redemption

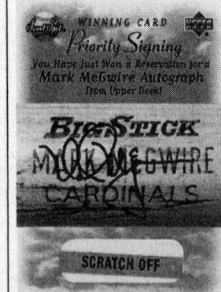

		NM/M
100 Produced		
MM	Mark McGwire	500.00

Signatures

		NM/M
Common Autograph:		25.00
Inserted 1:72		
LB	Lance Berkman/291	35.00
HB	Hank Blalock/291	40.00
BB	Barry Bonds/380	200.00
JB	Jeromy Burnitz/291	20.00
SB	Sean Burroughs/291	20.00
RC	Roger Clemens/194	150.00

CD	Carlos Delgado/291	25.00
AD	Adam Dunn/291	40.00
FG	Freddy Garcia/145	25.00
JG	Jason Giambi/291	40.00
BG	Brian Giles/291	25.00
TG	Tom Glavine/291	20.00
LG	Luis Gonzalez/291	20.00
KG	Ken Griffey Jr./291	125.00
AJ	Andruw Jones/291	20.00
RO	Roy Oswalt/291	20.00
MPr	Mark Prior/291	60.00
AR	Alex Rodriguez/ 291	160.00
SR	Scott Rolen/291	40.00
SS	Sammy Sosa/145	200.00
MS	Mike Sweeney/291	20.00
IS	Ichiro Suzuki/145	160.00
FT	Frank Thomas/291	60.00
JT	Jim Thome/291	20.00
BZ	Barry Zito/291	30.00

Sweet Swatches

		NM/M
Common Player:		5.00
Inserted 1:12		
JBa	Jeff Bagwell	8.00
JBe	Josh Beckett	6.00
SB	Sean Burroughs	5.00
EC	Eric Chavez	5.00
DE	Darin Erstad	5.00
JGi	Jason Giambi	8.00
BG	Brian Giles	5.00
JGo	Juan Gonzalez	6.00
LG	Luis Gonzalez	5.00
SG	Shawn Green	5.00
KG	Ken Griffey Jr.	15.00
KI	Kazuhisa Ishii	10.00
CJ	Chipper Jones	10.00
GM	Greg Maddux	12.00
PM	Pedro J. Martinez	10.00
MP	Mike Piazza	10.00
AR	Alex Rodriguez	15.00
IR	Ivan Rodriguez	8.00
SR	Scott Rolen	8.00
SS	Sammy Sosa	15.00
IS	Ichiro Suzuki	40.00
FT	Frank Thomas	15.00
OV	Omar Vizquel	5.00
BW	Bernie Williams	8.00

USA Jerseys

		NM/M
Common Player:		5.00
Inserted 1:12		
BA	Brent Abernathy	5.00
TB	Taggert Bozied	8.00
DB	Dewon Brazelton	5.00
AE	Adam Everett	5.00
DG	Danny Graves	5.00
JG	Jake Gautreau	5.00
JK	Josh Karp	5.00
AK	Adam Kennedy	8.00
JM	Joe Mauer	20.00
DM	Doug Mientkiewicz	6.00
EM	Eric Munson	5.00
XN	Xavier Nady	5.00
RO	Roy Oswalt	8.00
MP	Mark Prior	10.00
JR	Jon Rauch	5.00
MT	Mark Teixeira	8.00
JW	Justin Wayne	5.00

Classics

	NM/M
Complete Set (90):	40.00

Common Player:		.40
Pack (4):		20.00
Box (12):		200.00
1	Mickey Mantle	4.00
2	Joe DiMaggio	3.00
3	Babe Ruth	3.00
4	Ty Cobb	1.50
5	Nolan Ryan	3.00
6	Sandy Koufax	2.00
7	Cy Young	1.00
8	Roberto Clemente	2.00
9	Lefty Grove	.50
10	Lou Gehrig	2.50
11	Walter Johnson	1.00
12	Honus Wagner	1.00
13	Christy Mathewson	.75
14	Jackie Robinson	1.50
15	Joe Morgan	.50
16	Reggie Jackson	.75
17	Eddie Collins	.40
18	Cal Ripken Jr.	3.00
19	Hank Greenberg	.40
20	Harmon Killebrew	.75
21	Johnny Bench	1.00
22	Ernie Banks	.75
23	Willie McCovey	.40
24	Mel Ott	.40
25	Tom Seaver	1.00
26	Tony Gwynn	.75
27	Dave Winfield	.50
28	Willie Stargell	.40
29	Mark McGwire	2.00
30	Al Kaline	.75
31	Jimmie Foxx	.75
32	Satchel Paige	1.50
33	Eddie Murray	.40
34	Lou Boudreau	.40
35	"Shoeless" Joe Jackson	1.50
36	Luke Appling	.40
37	Ralph Kiner	.40
38	Robin Yount	.75
39	Paul Molitor	.75
40	Juan Marichal	.40
41	Brooks Robinson	.75
42	Wade Boggs	.50
43	Kirby Puckett	.75
44	Yogi Berra	.75
45	George Sisler	.40
46	Buck Leonard	.40
47	Billy Williams	.40
48	Duke Snider	.75
49	Don Drysdale	.60
50	Bill Mazeroski	.40
51	Tony Oliva	.40
52	Luis Aparicio	.40
53	Carlton Fisk	.40
54	Kirk Gibson	.40
55	Jim "Catfish" Hunter	.40
56	Joe Carter	.40
57	Gaylord Perry	.40
58	Don Mattingly	2.00
59	Eddie Mathews	1.25
60	Ferguson Jenkins	.40
61	Roy Campanella	1.00
62	Orlando Cepeda	.40
63	Tony Perez	.40
64	Dave Parker	.40
65	Richie Ashburn	.40
66	Andre Dawson	.40
67	Dwight Evans	.40
68	Rollie Fingers	.40
69	Dale Murphy	.40
70	Ron Santo	.40
71	Steve Garvey	.40
72	Monte Irvin	.40
73	Alan Trammell	.40
74	Ryne Sandberg	1.00
75	Gary Carter	.40
76	Fred Lynn	.40
77	Maury Wills	.40
78	Ozzie Smith	1.00
79	Bobby Bonds	.40
80	Mickey Cochrane	.60
81	Dizzy Dean	.60
82	Graig Nettles	.40
83	Keith Hernandez	.40
84	Boog Powell	.40
85	Jack Clark	.40
86	Dave Stewart	.40
87	Tommy Lasorda	.40
88	Dennis Eckersley	.40
89	Ken Griffey Sr.	.40
90	Bucky Dent	.40

Classics Bat Barrels

Values Undetermined due to scarcity.

Classics Game Jersey

		NM/M
Common Player:		5.00
Inserted 1:8		
WB	Wade Boggs	12.00
GC	Gary Carter	10.00
JC	Joe Carter	5.00
JD	Joe DiMaggio/53	180.00
RF	Rollie Fingers	5.00
SG	Steve Garvey	5.00
TG	Tony Gwynn	15.00
RJ	Reggie Jackson	15.00
SK	Sandy Koufax/SP	125.00
BM	Bill Madlock	5.00
MM	Mickey Mantle/53	250.00
JMa	Juan Marichal	10.00
DM	Don Mattingly	25.00
PM	Paul Molitor	15.00
EM	Eddie Murray	10.00
GN	Graig Nettles	8.00
DP	Dave Parker	5.00
CR	Cal Ripken Jr.	25.00
NR	Nolan Ryan	40.00
RS	Ryne Sandberg	15.00
TS	Tom Seaver	15.00
OS	Ozzie Smith	15.00
DSn	Duke Snider/53	80.00
WS	Willie Stargell	10.00
DSt	Dave Stewart	5.00
BW	Billy Williams	8.00
RY	Robin Yount	15.00

Classics Game Jersey Gold

The game-jersey cards in Sweet Spot Classics were paralleled in a special Gold Edition, with each player's swatch cards numbered within an edition of 25 each.

No Pricing
Production 25 Sets

Classics Game-Used Bats

		NM/M
Common Player:		5.00
Inserted 1:8		
JB	Johnny Bench	15.00
YB	Yogi Berra	15.00
WB	Wade Boggs	12.00
BBo	Bob Boone	5.00
BBu	Bill Buckner	5.00
GC	Gary Carter	10.00
RC	Roberto Clemente	50.00
BD	Bucky Dent	8.00
JD	Joe DiMaggio/40	180.00
DE	Dwight Evans	8.00
SG	Steve Garvey	8.00
HG	Hank Greenberg/SP	50.00
KG	Ken Griffey Sr.	8.00
TG	Tony Gwynn	15.00
RJ	Reggie Jackson	10.00
FJ	Ferguson Jenkins	10.00
AK	Al Kaline	15.00

FL	Fred Lynn	5.00
BM	Bill Madlock	5.00
DM	Don Mattingly	25.00
PM	Paul Molitor	15.00
TM	Thurman Munson	35.00
GN	Graig Nettles	8.00
DP	Dave Parker	5.00
KP	Kirby Puckett	15.00
CR	Cal Ripken Jr.	25.00
BR	Brooks Robinson	15.00
NR	Nolan Ryan	40.00
BW	Billy Williams	8.00
DW	Dave Winfield	10.00

Classics Game-Used Bats Gold

Each of the Game-Used Bats cards in Sweet Spot Classics can also be found in a Gold Edition, numbered to just 25 for each player.

		NM/M
	Common Player:	25.00
JB	Johnny Bench	100.00
YB	Yogi Berra	125.00
WB	Wade Boggs	100.00
BBo	Bob Boone	40.00
BBu	Bill Buckner	35.00
GC	Gary Carter	40.00
RC	Roberto Clemente	250.00
BD	Bucky Dent	25.00
JD	Joe DiMaggio	250.00
DE	Dwight Evans	25.00
SG	Steve Garvey	35.00
HG	Hank Greenberg	125.00
KG	Ken Griffey Sr.	25.00
TG	Tony Gwynn	125.00
RJ	Reggie Jackson	150.00
FJ	Ferguson Jenkins	45.00
AK	Al Kaline	75.00
FL	Fred Lynn	25.00
BM	Bill Madlock	25.00
DM	Don Mattingly	125.00
PM	Paul Molitor	40.00
TM	Thurman Munson	150.00
GN	Graig Nettles	25.00
DP	Dave Parker	25.00
KP	Kirby Puckett	125.00
CR	Cal Ripken Jr.	225.00
BR	Brooks Robinson	75.00
NR	Nolan Ryan	175.00
BW	Billy Williams	45.00
DW	Dave Winfield	45.00

Classics Sweet Spot Signatures

		NM/M
	Common Autograph:	20.00
	Inserted 1:24	
EB	Ernie Banks	60.00
JB	Johnny Bench	60.00
YB	Yogi Berra/100	150.00
AD	Andre Dawson/100	100.00
BD	Bucky Dent	20.00
DeE	Dennis Eckersley	40.00
RF	Rollie Fingers	25.00
CF	Carlton Fisk/100	125.00
SG	Steve Garvey	25.00
KG	Kirk Gibson/SP	50.00
KH	Keith Hernandez	30.00
RJ	Reggie Jackson/SP	100.00
FJ	Ferguson Jenkins	25.00
AK	Al Kaline	40.00
SK	Sandy Koufax/SP	250.00
TL	Tommy Lasorda	35.00
FL	Fred Lynn	25.00
DoM	Don Mattingly	100.00
BM	Bill Mazeroski	40.00
WM	Willie McCovey/SP	75.00
PM	Paul Molitor	40.00
JM	Joe Morgan	25.00
DaM	Dale Murphy	50.00
GP	Gaylord Perry	25.00
BP	Boog Powell	25.00
KP	Kirby Puckett	180.00
CR	Cal Ripken Jr.	180.00
BR	Brooks Robinson	50.00
NR	Nolan Ryan/74	300.00
TS	Tom Seaver	50.00
OS	Ozzie Smith/137	200.00
DaS	Dave Stewart	25.00
AT	Alan Trammell	30.00
DW	Dave Winfield/70	125.00

Classics Sweet Spot Signatures Gold

Each of the Sweet Spot Signatures autographed ball-panel cards was also made in a Gold Edition numbered to just 25 of each player.

No Pricing
Production 25 Sets

Classics Classic Signatures - Hawaii

As part of its participation in the Hawaii hobby trade conference in March 2002 Upper Deck foil-packed 400 specially marked pieces of its Classic Signatures insert card for distribution to retailers. The ultra-thick cards with an actual autographed piece of baseball displayed are overprinted "HAWAII XVII" in the lower-right corner. Numbers in parentheses are the reported production for that player.

		NM/M
	Common Player:	50.00
AD	Andre Dawson/10	200.00
AK	Al Kaline/25	80.00
AT	Alan Trammell/25	60.00
BD	Bucky Dent/25	50.00
BP	Boog Powell/25	60.00
BR	Brooks Robinson/25	150.00
CF	Carlton Fisk/10	200.00
CR	Cal Ripken Jr./10	600.00
DaM	Dale Murphy/10	400.00
DaS	Dave Stewart/25	50.00
DeE	Dennis Eckersley/25	75.00
EB	Ernie Banks/10	150.00
FJ	Ferguson Jenkins/25	50.00
FL	Fred Lynn/25	75.00
GP	Gaylord Perry/25	75.00
KH	Keith Hernandez/20	65.00
PM	Paul Molitor/25	75.00
RF	Rollie Fingers/25	60.00
SG	Steve Garvey/25	75.00
SK	Sandy Koufax/5	800.00

2002 Upper Deck UD-Plus

		NM/M
	Common Player:	2.00
	Production 1,125 Sets	
	1 two-card pack per Series 2 H pack	
	Comp. Set can be exchanged for Jsy cards.	
	Redemption Deadline 5-16-03	
UD1	Darin Erstad	3.00
UD2	Troy Glaus	3.00
UD3	Tim Hudson	2.00
UD4	Jermaine Dye	2.00
UD5	Barry Zito	2.00
UD6	Carlos Delgado	3.00
UD7	Shannon Stewart	2.00
UD8	Greg Vaughn	2.00
UD9	Jim Thome	5.00
UD10	C.C. Sabathia	2.00
UD11	Ichiro Suzuki	10.00
UD12	Edgar Martinez	2.00
UD13	Bret Boone	2.00
UD14	Freddy Garcia	2.00
UD15	Matt Thornton	2.00
UD16	Jeff Conine	2.00
UD17	Steve Bechler	2.00
UD18	Rafael Palmeiro	4.00
UD19	Juan Gonzalez	4.00
UD20	Alex Rodriguez	10.00
UD21	Ivan Rodriguez	4.00
UD22	Carl Everett	2.00
UD23	Manny Ramirez	4.00
UD24	Nomar Garciaparra	10.00
UD25	Pedro J. Martinez	4.00
UD26	Mike Sweeney	2.00
UD27	Chuck Knoblauch	2.00
UD28	Dmitri Young	2.00
UD29	Bobby Higginson	2.00
UD30	Dean Palmer	2.00
UD31	Doug Mientkiewicz	2.00
UD32	Corey Koskie	2.00
UD33	Brad Radke	2.00
UD34	Cristian Guzman	2.00
UD35	Frank Thomas	8.00
UD36	Magglio Ordonez	3.00
UD37	Carlos Lee	2.00
UD38	Roger Clemens	10.00
UD39	Bernie Williams	3.00
UD40	Derek Jeter	15.00
UD41	Jason Giambi	4.00
UD42	Mike Mussina	4.00
UD43	Jeff Bagwell	4.00
UD44	Lance Berkman	3.00
UD45	Wade Miller	2.00
UD46	Greg Maddux	8.00
UD47	Chipper Jones	5.00
UD48	Andruw Jones	4.00
UD49	Gary Sheffield	3.00
UD50	Richie Sexson	3.00
UD51	Albert Pujols	10.00
UD52	J.D. Drew	3.00
UD53	Matt Morris	3.00
UD54	Jim Edmonds	3.00
UD55	So Taguchi	2.00
UD56	Sammy Sosa	10.00
UD57	Fred McGriff	3.00
UD58	Kerry Wood	5.00
UD59	Moises Alou	3.00
UD60	Randy Johnson	7.00
UD61	Luis Gonzalez	3.00
UD62	Mark Grace	3.00
UD63	Curt Schilling	4.00
UD64	Matt Williams	2.00
UD65	Kevin Brown	3.00
UD66	Brian Jordan	2.00
UD67	Shawn Green	3.00
UD68	Hideo Nomo	3.00
UD69	Kazuhisa Ishii	4.00
UD70	Vladimir Guerrero	4.00
UD71	Jose Vidro	2.00
UD72	Eric Good	2.00
UD73	Barry Bonds	15.00
UD74	Jeff Kent	3.00
UD75	Rich Aurilia	2.00
UD76	Deivis Santos	2.00
UD77	Preston Wilson	2.00
UD78	Cliff Floyd	2.00
UD79	Josh Beckett	4.00
UD80	Hansel Izquierdo	2.00
UD81	Mike Piazza	10.00
UD82	Roberto Alomar	3.00
UD83	Mo Vaughn	3.00
UD84	Jeromy Burnitz	2.00
UD85	Phil Nevin	2.00
UD86	Ryan Klesko	2.00
UD87	Bobby Abreu	3.00
UD88	Scott Rolen	5.00
UD89	Jimmy Rollins	2.50
UD90	Jason Kendall	2.00
UD91	Brian Giles	3.00
UD92	Aramis Ramirez	3.00
UD93	Ken Griffey Jr.	10.00
UD94	Sean Casey	3.00
UD95	Barry Larkin	3.00
UD96	Adam Dunn	4.00
UD97	Todd Helton	4.00
UD98	Larry Walker	3.00
UD99	Mike Hampton	2.00
UD100	Rene Reyes	2.00

Memorabila Moments Jerseys

		NM/M
	Common DiMaggio (1-5):	125.00
	Common Mantle: (1-5):	200.00
MM-JD1	Joe DiMaggio	125.00
MM-JD2	Joe DiMaggio	125.00
MM-JD3	Joe DiMaggio	125.00
MM-JD4	Joe DiMaggio	125.00
MM-JD5	Joe DiMaggio	125.00
MM-MM1	Mickey Mantle/25 (Pants)	200.00
MM-MM2	Mickey Mantle	200.00
MM-MM3	Mickey Mantle	200.00
MM-MM4	Mickey Mantle	200.00
MM-MM5	Mickey Mantle	200.00

Milestone Game Jerseys

Complete Set (10):
Common Player:

Pinstripe Immortals

Complete Set (10):
Common Player:

2002 Upper Deck Ultimate Collection

		NM/M
	Complete Set (120):	
	Common Player (1-60):	2.00
	Production 799	
	Common Player (61-110, 114-120):	10.00
	Production 550	
	Common (111-113):	25.00
	Production 330	
	Pack (4):	100.00
	Box (4):	350.00
1	Troy Glaus	2.50
2	Luis Gonzalez	2.00
3	Curt Schilling	2.50
4	Randy Johnson	4.00
5	Andruw Jones	2.50
6	Greg Maddux	6.00
7	Chipper Jones	5.00
8	Gary Sheffield	2.00
9	Cal Ripken Jr.	12.00
10	Manny Ramirez	3.00
11	Pedro J. Martinez	4.00
12	Nomar Garciaparra	8.00
13	Sammy Sosa	5.00
14	Kerry Wood	4.00
15	Mark Prior	4.00
16	Magglio Ordonez	2.00
17	Frank Thomas	3.00
18	Adam Dunn	3.00
19	Ken Griffey Jr.	8.00
20	Jim Thome	4.00
21	Larry Walker	2.00
22	Todd Helton	3.00
23	Nolan Ryan	12.00
24	Jeff Bagwell	3.00
25	Roy Oswalt	2.00
26	Lance Berkman	2.00
27	Mike Sweeney	2.00
28	Shawn Green	2.00
29	Hideo Nomo	2.00
30	Torii Hunter	2.00
31	Vladimir Guerrero	5.00
32	Tom Seaver	4.00
33	Mike Piazza	8.00
34	Roberto Alomar	2.00
35	Derek Jeter	12.00
36	Alfonso Soriano	4.00
37	Jason Giambi	4.00
38	Roger Clemens	8.00
39	Mike Mussina	2.50
40	Bernie Williams	2.50
41	Joe DiMaggio	10.00
42	Mickey Mantle	15.00
43	Miguel Tejada	3.00
44	Eric Chavez	2.00
45	Barry Zito	2.00
46	Pat Burrell	2.00
47	Jason Kendall	2.00
48	Brian Giles	2.00
49	Barry Bonds	15.00
50	Ichiro Suzuki	10.00
51	Stan Musial	4.00
52	J.D. Drew	2.00
53	Scott Rolen	4.00
54	Albert Pujols	10.00
55	Mark McGwire	10.00
56	Alex Rodriguez	10.00
57	Ivan Rodriguez	3.00
58	Juan Gonzalez	2.50
59	Rafael Palmeiro	3.00
60	Carlos Delgado	2.50
61	Jose Valverde RC	10.00
62	Doug DeVore RC	10.00
63	John Ennis RC	10.00
64	Joey Dawley	10.00
65	Trey Hodges RC	10.00
66	Mike Mahoney	10.00
67	Aaron Cook RC	10.00
68	Rene Reyes RC	10.00
69	Mark Corey	10.00
70	Hansel Izquierdo RC	10.00
71	Brandon Puffer RC	10.00
72	Jeriome Robertson RC	10.00
73	Jose Diaz	10.00
74	David Ross	10.00
75	Jayson Durocher RC	10.00
76	Eric Good RC	10.00
77	Satoru Komiyama	10.00
78	Tyler Yates RC	10.00
79	Eric Junge RC	10.00
80	Anderson Machado RC	10.00
81	Adrian Burnside RC	10.00
82	Ben Howard RC	10.00
83	Clay Condrey RC	10.00
84	Nelson Castro RC	10.00
85	So Taguchi RC	15.00
86	Mike Crudale RC	10.00
87	Scotty Layfield RC	10.00
88	Steve Bechler RC	10.00
89	Travis Driskill RC	10.00
90	Howie Clark RC	10.00
91	Josh Hancock RC	10.00
92	Jorge De La Rosa RC	10.00
93	Anastacio Martinez RC	10.00
94	Brian Tallet RC	10.00
95	Carl Sadler RC	10.00
96	Cliff Lee RC	15.00
97	Josh Bard RC	10.00
98	Wes Obermueller RC	10.00
99	Juan Brito	10.00
100	Aaron Guiel RC	10.00
101	Jeremy Hill RC	10.00
102	Kevin Frederick RC	10.00
103	Nate Field RC	10.00
104	Julio Mateo RC	10.00
105	Chris Snelling RC	15.00
106	Felix Escalona RC	10.00
107	Reynaldo Garcia RC	10.00
108	Mike Smith RC	10.00
109	Ken Huckaby RC	10.00
110	Kevin Cash RC	10.00
111	Kazuhisa Ishii/ Auto. RC	40.00
112	Freddy Sanchez/ Auto. RC	25.00
113	Jason Simontacchi/ Auto. RC	25.00
114	Jorge Padilla/ Auto. RC	15.00
115	Kirk Saarloos/Auto.	15.00
116	Rodrigo Rosario/ Auto. RC	15.00
117	Oliver Perez/ Auto. RC	50.00
118	Miguel Asencio/ Auto. RC	15.00
119	Franklyn German/ Auto. RC	15.00
120	Jaime Cerda/ Auto. RC	15.00

Double Barrel

		NM/M
	Quantity produced listed	
DB-RI	Ivan Rodriguez, Alex Rodriguez/5	2,225
DB-RR	Cal Ripken Jr., Alex Rodriguez/9	1,625
DB-TO	Magglio Ordonez, Frank Thomas/4	950.00

Jerseys Tier 1

		NM/M
	Common Player:	10.00
	Production 99 Sets	
	Golds:	.75-1.5X
	Production 50 Sets	
RC	Roger Clemens	20.00
JD	Joe DiMaggio	100.00
AD	Adam Dunn	15.00
JG	Jason Giambi	15.00
KG	Ken Griffey Jr.	20.00
KI	Kazuhisa Ishii	15.00
RJ	Randy Johnson	15.00
AJ	Andruw Jones	15.00
CJ	Chipper Jones	15.00
MM	Mickey Mantle	125.00
PM	Pedro J. Martinez	15.00
MC	Mark McGwire	60.00
MP	Mike Piazza	15.00
PR	Mark Prior	15.00
MR	Manny Ramirez	15.00
CR	Cal Ripken Jr.	40.00
AR	Alex Rodriguez	15.00
IR	Ivan Rodriguez	15.00
AS	Alfonso Soriano	20.00
SS	Sammy Sosa	25.00
IS	Ichiro Suzuki	45.00

Jerseys Tier 2

		NM/M
	Same price as Tier 1	
	Production 99 Sets	
	Golds:	1.5-2X
	Production 25 Sets	
JF-RC	Roger Clemens	20.00
JF-JD	Joe DiMaggio	100.00
JF-AD	Adam Dunn	15.00
JF-JG	Jason Giambi	15.00
JF-KG	Ken Griffey Jr.	20.00
JF-KI	Kazuhisa Ishii	10.00
JF-RJ	Randy Johnson	15.00
JF-AJ	Andruw Jones	10.00
JF-CJ	Chipper Jones	15.00
JF-MM	Mickey Mantle	125.00
JF-PM	Pedro J. Martinez	15.00
JF-MC	Mark McGwire	60.00
JF-MP	Mike Piazza	15.00
JF-PR	Mark Prior	20.00
JF-MR	Manny Ramirez	15.00
JF-CR	Cal Ripken Jr.	40.00
JF-AR	Alex Rodriguez	15.00
JF-IR	Ivan Rodriguez	15.00
JF-AS	Alfonso Soriano	15.00
JF-SS	Sammy Sosa	25.00
JF-IS	Ichiro Suzuki	45.00

Jerseys Tier 3

		NM/M
	Common Player:	8.00
	Stars: .4-.6X Tier 1 price	
	Production 199 Sets	
JP-RC	Roger Clemens	15.00
JP-AD	Adam Dunn	10.00
JP-JG	Jason Giambi	10.00
JP-KG	Ken Griffey Jr.	15.00
JP-KI	Kazuhisa Ishii	8.00
JP-RJ	Randy Johnson	12.00
JP-AJ	Andruw Jones	10.00
JP-CJ	Chipper Jones	12.00
JP-MM	Mickey Mantle	75.00
JP-PM	Pedro J. Martinez	10.00
JP-MC	Mark McGwire	40.00
JP-MP	Mike Piazza	15.00
JP-PR	Mark Prior	10.00
JP-MR	Manny Ramirez	8.00
JP-CR	Cal Ripken Jr.	30.00
JP-AR	Alex Rodriguez	15.00
JP-IR	Ivan Rodriguez	10.00
JP-AS	Alfonso Soriano	12.00
JP-SS	Sammy Sosa	20.00
JP-IS	Ichiro Suzuki	30.00
JP-BW	Bernie Williams	8.00

Jerseys Tier 4

		NM/M
	Common Player:	8.00
	Stars: .4-.6X Tier 1 price	
	Production 199 Sets	
JR-RC	Roger Clemens	15.00
JR-AD	Adam Dunn	10.00
JR-JG	Jason Giambi	10.00
JR-KG	Ken Griffey Jr.	15.00
JR-KI	Kazuhisa Ishii	8.00
JR-RJ	Randy Johnson	10.00
JR-AJ	Andruw Jones	8.00
JR-CJ	Chipper Jones	10.00
JR-MM	Mickey Mantle	75.00
JR-PM	Pedro J. Martinez	10.00
JR-MC	Mark McGwire	40.00
JR-MP	Mike Piazza	15.00
JR-PR	Mark Prior	10.00
JR-MR	Manny Ramirez	8.00
JR-CR	Cal Ripken Jr.	15.00
JR-AR	Alex Rodriguez	15.00
JR-IR	Ivan Rodriguez	8.00
JR-AS	Alfonso Soriano	15.00
JR-SS	Sammy Sosa	20.00
JR-IS	Ichiro Suzuki	30.00
JR-BW	Bernie Williams	8.00

Mark McGwire Signing Redemption

		NM/M
Exchange Card 1:500 Packs:		
1-MM	Mark McGwire	600.00

Signatures Tier 1

		NM/M
Common Autograph:		20.00
Quantity produced listed		
Golds:		No Pricing
Production 25 Sets		
RA1	Roberto Alomar/155	45.00
LB1	Lance Berkman/179	25.00
PB1	Pat Burrell/95	25.00
RC1	Roger Clemens/320	80.00
CD1	Carlos Delgado/95	25.00
JD1	J.D. Drew/220	25.00
AD1	Adam Dunn/125	45.00
JG1	Jason Giambi/295	25.00
BG1	Brian Giles/220	20.00
LG1	Luis Gonzalez/199	25.00
KG1	Ken Griffey Jr./195	100.00
JK1	Jason Kendall/220	20.00
MP1	Mark Prior/160	60.00
CR1	Cal Ripken Jr./75	165.00
AR1	Alex Rodriguez/329	100.00
SR1	Scott Rolen/160	30.00
GS1	Gary Sheffield/95	20.00
JT1	Jim Thome/95	60.00
BZ1	Barry Zito/199	25.00

Signatures Tier 2

		NM/M
Quantity produced listed		
Golds:		No Pricing
Production 10 Sets		
JB2	Jeff Bagwell/51	55.00
LB2	Lance Berkman/85	40.00
JG2	Jason Giambi/50	60.00
LG2	Luis Gonzalez/70	25.00
KG2	Ken Griffey Jr./30	150.00
TG2	Tony Gwynn/51	75.00
TH2	Todd Helton/51	60.00
AJ2	Andruw Jones/51	50.00
MP2	Mark Prior/60	60.00
KP2	Kirby Puckett/75	60.00
AR2	Alex Rodriguez/75	100.00
SR2	Scott Rolen/60	50.00
DS2	Duke Snider/51	60.00
FT2	Frank Thomas/51	65.00
KW2	Kerry Wood/51	75.00
BZ2	Barry Zito/70	40.00

Signed Excellence

		NM/M
Quantity produced listed		
Golds: No Pricing		
Production One Set		
I1	Ichiro Suzuki/56	375.00
I2	Ichiro Suzuki/51	375.00
I5	Ichiro Suzuki/Btg	250.00

I6	Ichiro Suzuki/ Throwing	250.00
MM1	Mark McGwire/70	275.00
MM2	Mark McGwire/65	275.00
MM3	Mark McGwire/49	300.00
MM5	Mark McGwire/ Standing	220.00
MM6	Mark McGwire/ Waving	220.00
MM7	Mark McGwire/ Fielding	220.00
SS1	Sammy Sosa/66	175.00
SS2	Sammy Sosa/64	175.00
SS3	Sammy Sosa/54	175.00
SS5	Sammy Sosa/ Running	150.00
SS6	Sammy Sosa/ Holding Bat	150.00
SS7	Sammy Sosa/150	150.00

Signed Excellence Gold

Complete Set (5):	
Common Player:	

Patch

		NM/M
Common Player:		25.00
Production 100 Sets		
LG	Luis Gonzalez	25.00
SG	Shawn Green	25.00
TH	Todd Helton	40.00
KI	Kazuhisa Ishii	40.00
CJ	Chipper Jones	40.00
MM	Mark McGwire	125.00
MP	Mark Prior	30.00
IR	Ivan Rodriguez	40.00
SS	Sammy Sosa	65.00
IS	Ichiro Suzuki	150.00

Double Patches

	NM/M
Production 100 Sets	
Golds:	.75-1.5X
Production 50 Sets	

DE	J.D. Drew, Jim Edmonds	60.00
GC	Jason Giambi, Roger Clemens	80.00
IG	Ken Griffey Jr., Ichiro Suzuki	125.00
JS	Randy Johnson, Curt Schilling	60.00
MG	Tom Glavine, Greg Maddux	75.00
MS	Sammy Sosa, Mark McGwire	150.00
PA	Mike Piazza, Roberto Alomar	80.00
RG	Alex Rodriguez, Juan Gonzalez	80.00
RM	Manny Ramirez, Pedro J. Martinez	50.00

2002 Upper Deck Victory

		NM/M
Complete Set (550):		40.00
Common Player:		.10
Pack (10):		1.00
Box (36):		25.00
1	Troy Glaus	.30
2	Tim Salmon	.20
3	Troy Percival	.10
4	Darin Erstad	.25
5	Adam Kennedy	.10
6	Scott Spiezio	.10
7	Ramon Ortiz	.10
8	Ismael Valdes	.10
9	Jarrod Washburn	.10
10	Garret Anderson	.20
11	David Eckstein	.10
12	Mo Vaughn	.25
13	Benji Gil	.10
14	Bengie Molina	.10
15	Scott Schoeneweis	.10
16	Troy Glaus, Ramon Ortiz	.20
17	David Justice	.25
18	Jermaine Dye	.10
19	Eric Chavez	.25
20	Jeremy Giambi	.10
21	Terrence Long	.10
22	Miguel Tejada	.20
23	Johnny Damon	.10
24	Jason Hart	.10
25	Adam Piatt	.10
26	Billy Koch	.10
27	Ramon Hernandez	.10
28	Eric Byrnes	.10
29	Olmedo Saenz	.10
30	Barry Zito	.20
31	Tim Hudson	.25
32	Mark Mulder	.10
33	Jason Giambi, Mark Mulder	.25
34	Carlos Delgado	.40
35	Shannon Stewart	.10
36	Vernon Wells	.10
37	Homer Bush	.10
38	Brad Fullmer	.10
39	Jose Cruz	.10
40	Felipe Lopez	.10
41	Raul Mondesi	.20
42	Esteban Loaiza	.10
43	Darrin Fletcher	.10
44	Mike Sirotka	.10
45	Luke Prokopec	.10
46	Chris Carpenter	.10
47	Roy Halladay	.10
48	Kelvim Escobar	.10
49	Carlos Delgado, Billy Koch	.20
50	Nick Bierbrodt	.10
51	Greg Vaughn	.10
52	Ben Grieve	.10
53	Damian Rolls	.10
54	Russ Johnson	.10
55	Brent Abernathy	.10
56	Steve Cox	.10
57	Aubrey Huff	.10
58	Randy Winn	.10
59	Jason Tyner	.10
60	Tanyon Sturtze	.10
61	Joe Kennedy	.10
62	Jared Sandberg	.10
63	Esteban Yan	.10
64	Ryan Rupe	.10
65	Toby Hall	.10
66	Greg Vaughn, Tanyon Sturtze	.10
67	Matt Lawton	.10
68	Juan Gonzalez	.40
69	Jim Thome	.25
70	Einar Diaz	.10
71	Ellis Burks	.10
72	Kenny Lofton	.10
73	Omar Vizquel	.10
74	Russell Branyan	.10
75	Brady Anderson	.10
76	John Rocker	.10
77	Travis Fryman	.10
78	Wil Cordero	.10
79	Chuck Finley	.10
80	C.C. Sabathia	.10
81	Bartolo Colon	.10
82	Bob Wickman	.10
83	Roberto Alomar, C.C. Sabathia	.10
84	Ichiro Suzuki	1.50
85	Edgar Martinez	.10
86	Aaron Sele	.10
87	Carlos Guillen	.10
88	Bret Boone	.10
89	John Olerud	.20
90	Jamie Moyer	.10
91	Ben Davis	.10
92	Dan Wilson	.10
93	Jeff Cirillo	.10
94	John Halama	.10
95	Freddy Garcia	.10
96	Kazuhiro Sasaki	.10
97	Mike Cameron	.10
98	Paul Abbott	.10
99	Mark McLemore	.10
100	Ichiro Suzuki, Freddy Garcia	.50
101	Jeff Conine	.10
102	David Segui	.10
103	Marty Cordova	.10
104	Tony Batista	.10
105	Chris Richard	.10
106	Willis Roberts	.10
107	Melvin Mora	.10
108	Mike Bordick	.10
109	Jay Gibbons	.10
110	Mike Kinkade	.10
111	Brian Roberts	.10
112	Jerry Hairston Jr.	.10
113	Jason Johnson	.10
114	Josh Towers	.10
115	Calvin Maduro	.10
116	Sidney Ponson	.10
117	Jeff Conine, Jason Johnson	.10
118	Alex Rodriguez	1.00
119	Ivan Rodriguez	.40
120	Frank Catalanotto	.10
121	Mike Lamb	.10
122	Ruben Sierra	.10
123	Rusty Greer	.10
124	Rafael Palmeiro	.20
125	Gabe Kapler	.15
126	Aaron Myette	.10
127	Kenny Rogers	.10
128	Carl Everett	.10
129	Rick Helling	.10
130	Ricky Ledee	.10
131	Michael Young	.10
132	Doug Davis	.10
133	Jeff Zimmerman	.10
134	Alex Rodriguez, Rick Helling	.40
135	Manny Ramirez	.40
136	Nomar Garciaparra	1.00
137	Jason Varitek	.10
138	Dante Bichette	.10
139	Tony Clark	.10
140	Scott Hatteberg	.10
141	Trot Nixon	.10
142	Hideo Nomo	.25
143	Dustin Hermanson	.10
144	Chris Stynes	.10
145	Jose Offerman	.10
146	Pedro Martinez	.50
147	Shea Hillenbrand	.10
148	Tim Wakefield	.10
149	Troy O'Leary	.10
150	Ugueth Urbina	.10
151	Manny Ramirez, Hideo Nomo	.25
152	Carlos Beltran	.10
153	Dee Brown	.10
154	Mike Sweeney	.10
155	Luis Alicea	.10
156	Raul Ibanez	.10
157	Mark Quinn	.10
158	Joe Randa	.10
159	Roberto Hernandez	.10
160	Neifi Perez	.10
161	Carlos Febles	.10
162	Jeff Suppan	.10
163	Dave McCarty	.10
164	Blake Stein	.10
165	Chad Durbin	.10
166	Paul Byrd	.10
167	Carlos Beltran, Jeff Suppan	.10
168	Craig Paquette	.10
169	Dean Palmer	.10
170	Shane Halter	.10
171	Bobby Higginson	.10
172	Robert Fick	.10
173	Jose Macias	.10
174	Deivi Cruz	.10
175	Damion Easley	.10
176	Brandon Inge	.10
177	Mark Redman	.10
178	Dmitri Young	.10
179	Steve Sparks	.10
180	Jeff Weaver	.10
181	Victor Santos	.10
182	Jose Lima	.10
183	Matt Anderson	.10
184	Roger Cedeno, Steve Sparks	.10
185	Doug Mientkiewicz	.10
186	Cristian Guzman	.10
187	Torii Hunter	.10
188	Matt LeCroy	.10
189	Corey Koskie	.10
190	Jacque Jones	.10
191	Luis Rivas	.10
192	David Ortiz	.10
193	A.J. Pierzynski	.10
194	Brian Buchanan	.10
195	Joe Mays	.10
196	Brad Radke	.10
197	Denny Hocking	.10
198	Eric Milton	.10
199	LaTroy Hawkins	.10
200	Doug Mientkiewicz, Joe Mays	.10
201	Magglio Ordonez	.20
202	Jose Valentin	.10
203	Chris Singleton	.10
204	Aaron Rowand	.10
205	Paul Konerko	.10
206	Carlos Lee	.10
207	Ray Durham	.10
208	Keith Foulke	.10
209	Todd Ritchie	.10
210	Royce Clayton	.10
211	Jose Canseco	.10
212	Frank Thomas	.40
213	David Wells	.10
214	Mark Buehrle	.10
215	Jon Garland	.10
216	Magglio Ordonez, Mark Buehrle	.15
217	Derek Jeter	1.50
218	Bernie Williams	.30
219	Rondell White	.10
220	Jorge Posada	.20
221	Alfonso Soriano	.50
222	Ramiro Mendoza	.10
223	Jason Giambi	.75
224	John Vander Wal	.10
225	Steve Karsay	.10
226	Nick Johnson	.10
227	Mariano Rivera	.20
228	Orlando Hernandez	.10
229	Andy Pettitte	.20
230	Robin Ventura	.10
231	Roger Clemens	.60
232	Mike Mussina	.40
233	Derek Jeter, Roger Clemens	.50
234	Moises Alou	.20
235	Lance Berkman	.20
236	Craig Biggio	.20
237	Octavio Dotel	.10
238	Jeff Bagwell	.40
239	Richard Hidalgo	.10
240	Morgan Ensberg	.10
241	Julio Lugo	.10
242	Daryle Ward	.10
243	Roy Oswalt	.20
244	Billy Wagner	.10
245	Brad Ausmus	.10
246	Jose Vizcaino	.10
247	Wade Miller	.10
248	Shane Reynolds	.10
249	Jeff Bagwell, Wade Miller	.20
250	Chipper Jones	.75
251	Brian Jordan	.10
252	B.J. Surhoff	.10
253	Rafael Furcal	.10
254	Julio Franco	.10
255	Javy Lopez	.10
256	John Burkett	.10
257	Andruw Jones	.20
258	Marcus Giles	.10
259	Wes Helms	.10
260	Greg Maddux	.75
261	John Smoltz	.20
262	Tom Glavine	.20
263	Vinny Castilla	.10
264	Kevin Millwood	.10
265	Jason Marquis	.10
266	Chipper Jones, Greg Maddux	.40
267	Tyler Houston	.10
268	Mark Loretta	.10
269	Richie Sexson	.20
270	Jeromy Burnitz	.10
271	Jimmy Haynes	.10
272	Geoff Jenkins	.20
273	Ron Belliard	.10
274	Jose Hernandez	.10
275	Jeffrey Hammonds	.10
276	Curtis Leskanic	.10
277	Devon White	.10
278	Ben Sheets	.10
279	Henry Blanco	.10
280	Jamey Wright	.10
281	Allen Levrault	.10
282	Jeff D'Amico	.10
283	Richie Sexson, Jimmy Haynes	.10
284	Albert Pujols	.75
285	Jason Isringhausen	.10
286	J.D. Drew	.25
287	Placido Polanco	.10
288	Jim Edmonds	.20
289	Fernando Vina	.10
290	Edgar Renteria	.10
291	Mike Matheny	.10
292	Bud Smith	.10
293	Mike Defelice	.10
294	Woody Williams	.10
295	Eli Marrero	.10
296	Matt Morris	.10
297	Darryl Kile	.10
298	Kerry Robinson	.10
299	Luis Saturria	.10
300	Albert Pujols, Matt Morris	.40
301	Sammy Sosa	.75
302	Michael Tucker	.10
303	Bill Mueller	.10
304	Ricky Gutierrez	.10
305	Fred McGriff	.20
306	Eric Young	.10
307	Corey Patterson	.10
308	Alex Gonzalez	.10
309	Ron Coomer	.10
310	Kerry Wood	.20
311	Delino DeShields	.10
312	Jon Lieber	.10
313	Tom Gordon	.10
314	Todd Hundley	.10
315	Jason Bere	.10
316	Kevin Tapani	.10
317	Sammy Sosa, Jon Lieber	.40
318	Steve Finley	.10
319	Luis Gonzalez	.25
320	Mark Grace	.25
321	Craig Counsell	.10
322	Matt Williams	.20
323	Tony Womack	.10
324	Junior Spivey	.10
325	David Dellucci	.10
326	Jay Bell	.10
327	Curt Schilling	.25
328	Randy Johnson	.40
329	Danny Bautista	.10
330	Miguel Batista	.10
331	Erubiel Durazo	.10
332	Brian Anderson	.10
333	Byung-Hyun Kim	.10
334	Luis Gonzalez, Curt Schilling	.10
335	Paul LoDuca	.10
336	Gary Sheffield	.20
337	Shawn Green	.25
338	Adrian Beltre	.10
339	Darren Dreifort	.10
340	Mark Grudzielanek	.10
341	Eric Karros	.10
342	Cesar Izturis	.10
343	Tom Goodwin	.10
344	Marquis Grissom	.10
345	Kevin Brown	.20
346	James Baldwin	.10
347	Terry Adams	.10
348	Alex Cora	.10
349	Andy Ashby	.10
350	Chan Ho Park	.20
351	Shawn Green, Chan Ho Park	.20
352	Jose Vidro	.10
353	Vladimir Guerrero	.40
354	Orlando Cabrera	.10
355	Fernando Tatis	.10
356	Michael Barrett	.10
357	Lee Stevens	.10
358	Geoff Blum	.10
359	Brad Wilkerson	.10
360	Peter Bergeron	.10
361	Javier Vazquez	.10
362	Tony Armas Jr.	.10
363	Tomokazu Ohka	.10
364	Scott Strickland	.10
365	Vladimir Guerrero, Javier Vazquez	.20
366	Barry Bonds	.75
367	Rich Aurilia	.10
368	Jeff Kent	.10
369	Andres Galarraga	.20
370	Desi Relaford	.10
371	Shawon Dunston	.10
372	Benito Santiago	.10
373	Tsuyoshi Shinjo	.10
374	Calvin Murray	.10
375	Marvin Benard	.10
376	J.T. Snow	.10
377	Livan Hernandez	.10
378	Russ Ortiz	.10
379	Robb Nen	.10
380	Jason Schmidt	.10
381	Barry Bonds, Russ Ortiz	.30
382	Cliff Floyd	.10
383	Antonio Alfonseca	.10
384	Mike Redmond	.10
385	Mike Lowell	.10
386	Derek Lee	.10
387	Preston Wilson	.10
388	Luis Castillo	.10
389	Charles Johnson	.10
390	Eric Owens	.10
391	Alex Gonzalez	.10
392	Josh Beckett	.10
393	Brad Penny	.10
394	Ryan Dempster	.10
395	Matt Clement	.10
396	A.J. Burnett	.10
397	Cliff Floyd, Ryan Dempster	.10
398	Mike Piazza	1.00
399	Joe McEwing	.10
400	Todd Zeile	.10
401	Jay Payton	.10
402	Roger Cedeno	.10
403	Rey Ordonez	.10
404	Edgardo Alfonzo	.10
405	Roberto Alomar	.30
406	Glendon Rusch	.10
407	Timo Perez	.10
408	Al Leiter	.15
409	Lenny Harris	.10
410	Shawn Estes	.10
411	Armando Benitez	.10
412	Kevin Appier	.10
413	Bruce Chen	.10
414	Mike Piazza, Al Leiter	.40
415	Phil Nevin	.10
416	Ryan Klesko	.10
417	Mark Kotsay	.10
418	Ray Lankford	.10
419	Mike Darr	.10
420	D'Angelo Jimenez	.10
421	Bubba Trammell	.10
422	Adam Eaton	.10
423	Ramon Vazquez	.10
424	Cesar Crespo	.10
425	Trevor Hoffman	.10
426	Kevin Jarvis	.10
427	Wiki Gonzalez	.10
428	Damian Jackson	.10
429	Brian Lawrence	.10
430	Phil Nevin, Trevor Hoffman	.10
431	Scott Rolen	.25
432	Marlon Anderson	.10
433	Bobby Abreu	.10
434	Jimmy Rollins	.10
435	Doug Glanville	.10
436	Travis Lee	.10
437	Brandon Duckworth	.10
438	Pat Burrell	.25
439	Kevin Jordan	.10
440	Robert Person	.10
441	Johnny Estrada	.10
442	Randy Wolf	.10
443	Jose Mesa	.10
444	Mike Lieberthal	.10
445	Bobby Abreu, Robert Person	.10
446	Brian Giles	.20
447	Jason Kendall	.10
448	Aramis Ramirez	.10
449	Rob Mackowiak	.10
450	Abraham Nunez	.10
451	Pat Meares	.10
452	Craig Wilson	.10
453	Jack Wilson	.10
454	Gary Matthews Jr.	.10
455	Kevin Young	.10
456	Derek Bell	.10
457	Kip Wells	.10
458	Jimmy Anderson	.10
459	Kris Benson	.10
460	Brian Giles, Todd Ritchie	.10

461 Sean Casey .20
462 Wilton Guerrero .10
463 Jason LaRue .10
464 Juan Encarnacion .10
465 Todd Walker .10
466 Aaron Boone .10
467 Pete Harnisch .10
468 Ken Griffey Jr. 1.00
469 Adam Dunn .40
470 Barry Larkin .20
471 Kelly Stinnett .10
472 Pokey Reese .10
473 Brady Clark .10
474 Scott Williamson .10
475 Danny Graves .10
476 Ken Griffey Jr., Elmer Dessens .10
477 Larry Walker .25
478 Todd Helton .40
479 Juan Pierre .10
480 Juan Uribe .10
481 Mario Encarnacion .10
482 Jose Ortiz .10
483 Todd Hollandsworth .10
484 Alex Ochoa .10
485 Mike Hampton .10
486 Terry Shumpert .10
487 Denny Neagle .10
488 Jose Jimenez .10
489 Jason Jennings .10
490 Todd Helton, Mike Hampton .20
491 Tim Redding .10
492 Mark Teixeira 2.00
493 Alex Cintron .10
494 Tim Raines Jr. .10
495 Juan Cruz .20
496 Joe Crede .10
497 Steve Green .10
498 Mike Rivera .10
499 Mark Prior 1.00
500 Ken Harvey .10
501 Tim Spooneybarger .10
502 Adam Everett .10
503 Jason Standridge .10
504 Nick Neugebauer .10
505 Adam Johnson .10
506 Sean Douglass .10
507 Brandon Berger .10
508 Alex Escobar .10
509 Doug Nickle .10
510 Jason Middlebrook .10
511 Dewon Brazelton .10
512 Yorvit Torrealba .10
513 Henry Mateo .10
514 Dennis Tankersley .10
515 Marlon Byrd .75
516 Andy Barkett .10
517 Orlando Hudson .10
518 Josh Fogg .10
519 Ryan Drese .10
520 Mike MacDougal .10
521 Luis Pineda .10
522 Jack Cust .10
523 Kurt Ainsworth .10
524 Bart Miadich .10
525 Dernell Stenson .10
526 Carlos Zambrano .10
527 Austin Kearns .50
528 Larry Barnes .10
529 Mike Cuddyer .10
530 Carlos Pena .10
531 Derek Jeter 1.00
532 Ken Griffey Jr. .75
533 Manny Ramirez .25
534 Luis Gonzalez .20
535 Sammy Sosa .50
536 Roger Clemens .40
537 Phil Nevin .10
538 Mike Piazza .75
539 Alex Rodriguez .75
540 Jason Giambi .50
541 Randy Johnson .25
542 Albert Pujols .50
543 Jeff Bagwell .25
544 Shawn Green .15
545 Carlos Delgado .15
546 Pedro Martinez .25
547 Todd Helton .25
548 Roberto Alomar .20
549 Barry Bonds .40
550 Ichiro Suzuki 1.00

Gold

RANDY JOHNSON

Stars: 3-6X
Inserted 1:2

2002 Upper Deck Vintage

RED SOX
manny ramirez • outfield

NM/M
Complete Set (300): 30.00
Common Player: .10
Pack (10): 2.00
Box/24: 35.00

1 Darin Erstad .20
2 Mo Vaughn .20
3 Ramon Ortiz .10
4 Garret Anderson .25
5 Troy Glaus .40
6 Troy Percival .10
7 Tim Salmon .20
8 Wilmy Caceres, Elpidio Guzman .10
9 2001 Anaheim Angels .10
10 Jason Giambi .50
11 Mark Mulder .25
12 Jermaine Dye .10
13 Miguel Tejada .40
14 Tim Hudson .25
15 Eric Chavez .25
16 Barry Zito .25
17 Oscar Salazar, Juan Pena .10
18 2001 Oakland Athletics .10
19 Carlos Delgado .40
20 Raul Mondesi .15
21 Chris Carpenter .10
22 Jose Cruz Jr. .10
23 Alex Gonzalez .10
24 Brad Fullmer .10
25 Shannon Stewart .10
26 Brandon Lyon, Vernon Wells .10
27 2001 Toronto Blue Jays .10
28 Greg Vaughn .10
29 Toby Hall .10
30 Ben Grieve .10
31 Aubrey Huff .10
32 Tanyon Sturtze .10
33 Brent Abernathy .10
34 Dewon Brazelton, Delvin James .10
35 2001 Tampa Bay Devil Rays .10
36 Roberto Alomar .40
37 Juan Gonzalez .50
38 Bartolo Colon .25
39 C.C. Sabathia .10
40 Jim Thome .75
41 Omar Vizquel .20
42 Russell Branyan .10
43 Ryan Drese, Roy Smith .10
44 2001 Cleveland Indians .10
45 Edgar Martinez .20
46 Bret Boone .20
47 Freddy Garcia .10
48 John Olerud .25
49 Kazuhiro Sasaki .10
50 Ichiro Suzuki 1.50
51 Mike Cameron .10
52 Rafael Soriano, Dennis Stark .10
53 2001 Seattle Mariners .10
54 Tony Batista .10
55 Jeff Conine .10
56 Jason Johnson .10
57 Jay Gibbons .10
58 Chris Richard .10
59 Josh Towers .10
60 Jerry Hairston Jr. .10
61 Sean Douglass, Tim Raines Jr. .10
62 2001 Baltimore Orioles .10
63 Alex Rodriguez 1.50
64 Ruben Sierra .10
65 Ivan Rodriguez .50
66 Gabe Kapler .20
67 Rafael Palmeiro .50
68 Frank Catalanotto .10
69 Mark Teixeira, Carlos Pena .40
70 2001 Texas Rangers .10
71 Nomar Garciaparra 1.00
72 Pedro Martinez .75
73 Trot Nixon .10
74 Dante Bichette .10
75 Manny Ramirez .50
76 Carl Everett .10
77 Hideo Nomo .40
78 Dernell Stenson, Juan Diaz .10
79 2001 Boston Red Sox .10
80 Mike Sweeney .10
81 Carlos Febles .10

82 Dee Brown .10
83 Neifi Perez .10
84 Mark Quinn .10
85 Carlos Beltran .25
86 Joe Randa .10
87 Ken Harvey, Mike MacDougal .10
88 2001 Kansas City Royals .10
89 Dean Palmer .10
90 Jeff Weaver .10
91 Jose Lima .10
92 Tony Clark .10
93 Damion Easley .10
94 Bobby Higginson .10
95 Robert Fick .10
96 Pedro Santana, Mike Rivera .10
97 2001 Detroit Tigers .10
98 Doug Mientkiewicz .10
99 David Ortiz .25
100 Joe Mays .10
101 Corey Koskie .10
102 Eric Milton .10
103 Cristian Guzman .10
104 Brad Radke .10
105 Adam Johnson, Juan Rincon .10
106 2001 Minnesota Twins .10
107 Frank Thomas .50
108 Carlos Lee .10
109 Mark Buehrle .10
110 Jose Canseco .25
111 Magglio Ordonez .25
112 Jon Garland .10
113 Ray Durham .10
114 Joe Crede, Josh Fogg .10
115 2001 Chicago White Sox .10
116 Derek Jeter 2.00
117 Roger Clemens 1.50
118 Alfonso Soriano .75
119 Paul O'Neill .25
120 Jorge Posada .25
121 Bernie Williams .40
122 Mariano Rivera .25
123 Tino Martinez .20
124 Mike Mussina .50
125 Nick Johnson, Erick Almonte .10
126 2001 New York Yankees .10
127 Jeff Bagwell .50
128 Wade Miller .10
129 Lance Berkman .25
130 Moises Alou .25
131 Craig Biggio .25
132 Roy Oswalt .20
133 Richard Hidalgo .15
134 Morgan Ensberg, Tim Redding .10
135 2001 Houston Astros .10
136 Greg Maddux 1.00
137 Chipper Jones .75
138 Brian Jordan .10
139 Marcus Giles .10
140 Andruw Jones .40
141 Tom Glavine .40
142 Rafael Furcal .25
143 Wilson Betemit, Horacio Ramirez .10
144 2001 Atlanta Braves .10
145 Jeromy Burnitz .10
146 Ben Sheets .25
147 Geoff Jenkins .20
148 Devon White .10
149 Jimmy Haynes .10
150 Richie Sexson .40
151 Jose Hernandez .10
152 Jose Mieses, Alex Sanchez .10
153 2001 Milwaukee Brewers .10
154 Mark McGwire 2.00
155 Albert Pujols 1.50
156 Matt Morris .20
157 J.D. Drew .25
158 Jim Edmonds .25
159 Bud Smith .10
160 Darryl Kile .10
161 William Ortega, Luis Saturria .10
162 2001 St. Louis Cardinals .10
163 Sammy Sosa 1.00
164 Jon Lieber .10
165 Eric Young .10
166 Kerry Wood .75
167 Fred McGriff .25
168 Corey Patterson .25
169 Rondell White .10
170 Juan Cruz, Mark Prior 1.00
171 2001 Chicago Cubs .10
172 Luis Gonzalez .25
173 Randy Johnson .75
174 Matt Williams .20
175 Mark Grace .25
176 Steve Finley .10
177 Reggie Sanders .10
178 Curt Schilling .25
179 Alex Cintron, Jack Cust .10
180 2001 Arizona Diamondbacks .10
181 Gary Sheffield .25
182 Paul LoDuca .10
183 Chan Ho Park .10
184 Shawn Green .25
185 Eric Karros .15

186 Adrian Beltre .25
187 Kevin Brown .25
188 Ricardo Rodriguez, Carlos Garcia .10
189 2001 Los Angeles Dodgers .10
190 Vladimir Guerrero .75
191 Javier Vazquez .10
192 Jose Vidro .10
193 Fernando Tatis .10
194 Orlando Cabrera .10
195 Lee Stevens .10
196 Tony Armas Jr. .10
197 Donnie Bridges, Henry Mateo .10
198 2001 Montreal Expos .10
199 Barry Bonds 2.00
200 Rich Aurilia .10
201 Russ Ortiz .10
202 Jeff Kent .10
203 Jason Schmidt .25
204 John Vander Wal .10
205 Robb Nen .10
206 Yorvit Torrealba, Kurt Ainsworth .10
207 2001 San Francisco Giants .10
208 Preston Wilson .10
209 Brad Penny .10
210 Cliff Floyd .10
211 Luis Castillo .10
212 Ryan Dempster .10
213 Charles Johnson .10
214 A.J. Burnett .10
215 Abraham Nunez, Josh Beckett .20
216 2001 Florida Marlins .10
217 Mike Piazza 1.00
218 Al Leiter .20
219 Edgardo Alfonzo .10
220 Tsuyoshi Shinjo .10
221 Matt Lawton .10
222 Robin Ventura .15
223 Jay Payton .10
224 Alex Escobar, Jae Weong Seo .10
225 2001 New York Mets .10
226 Ryan Klesko .20
227 D'Angelo Jimenez .10
228 Trevor Hoffman .10
229 Phil Nevin .10
230 Mark Kotsay .10
231 Brian Lawrence .10
232 Bubba Trammell .10
233 Jason Middlebrook, Xavier Nady .10
234 2001 San Diego Padres .10
235 Scott Rolen .75
236 Jimmy Rollins .25
237 Mike Lieberthal .10
238 Bobby Abreu .25
239 Brandon Duckworth .10
240 Robert Person .10
241 Pat Burrell .20
242 Nick Punto, Carlos Silva .10
243 2001 Philadelphia Phillies .10
244 Brian Giles .20
245 Jack Wilson .10
246 Kris Benson .10
247 Jason Kendall .25
248 Aramis Ramirez .25
249 Todd Ritchie .10
250 Robert Mackowiak .10
251 John Grabow, Humberto Cota .10
252 2001 Pittsburgh Pirates .10
253 Ken Griffey Jr. 1.00
254 Barry Larkin .25
255 Sean Casey .25
256 Aaron Boone .10
257 Dmitri Young .10
258 Pokey Reese .10
259 Adam Dunn .50
260 David Espinosa, Dane Sardinha .10
261 2001 Cincinnati Reds .10
262 Todd Helton .50
263 Mike Hampton .20
264 Juan Pierre .10
265 Larry Walker .25
266 Juan Uribe .10
267 Jose Ortiz .10
268 Jeff Cirillo .10
269 Jason Jennings, Luke Hudson .10
270 2001 Colorado Rockies .10
271 Ichiro Suzuki, Jason Giambi, Roberto Alomar (League Leaders) .75
272 Larry Walker, Todd Helton, Moises Alou (League Leaders) .10
273 Alex Rodriguez, Jim Thome, Rafael Palmeiro (League Leaders) .75
274a Barry Bonds, Sammy Sosa, Juan Gonzalez (League Leaders) (no player names) 1.00
274b Barry Bonds, Sammy Sosa, Juan Gonzalez (League Leaders) (player names added) 3.00

275 Roger Clemens, Mark Mulder, Jamie Moyer (League Leaders) .50
276 Curt Schilling, Matt Morris, Randy Johnson (League Leaders) .10
277 Freddy Garcia, Mike Mussina, Joe Mays (League Leaders) .10
278 Randy Johnson, Curt Schilling, John Burkett (League Leaders) .10
279 Mariano Rivera, Kazuhiro Sasaki, Keith Foulke (League Leaders) .10
280 Robb Nen, Armando Benitez, Trevor Hoffman (League Leaders) .10
281 Jason Giambi .25
282 Jorge Posada .15
283 Jim Thome .25
284 Edgar Martinez .10
285 Andruw Jones .25
286 Chipper Jones .50
287 Matt Williams .15
288 Curt Schilling .10
289 Derek Jeter 1.00
290 Mike Mussina .10
291 Bret Boone .10
292 Alfonso Soriano .25
293 Randy Johnson .25
294 Tom Glavine .20
295 Curt Schilling .20
296 Randy Johnson .20
297 Derek Jeter 1.00
298 Tino Martinez .10
299 Curt Schilling .20
300 Luis Gonzalez .20

Day at the Park

DAY AT THE PARK
DEREK JETER • YANKEES

NM/M
Complete Set (6): 15.00
Inserted 1:23
DP1 Ichiro Suzuki 3.00
DP2 Derek Jeter 5.00
DP3 Alex Rodriguez 4.00
DP4 Mark McGwire 4.00
DP5 Barry Bonds 5.00
DP6 Sammy Sosa 3.00

Night-Gamers

NIGHT-GAMERS
troy · GLAUS

NM/M
Complete Set (12): 10.00
Common Player: .50
Inserted 1:11
NG1 Todd Helton .75
NG2 Manny Ramirez .75
NG3 Ivan Rodriguez .50
NG4 Albert Pujols 2.50
NG5 Greg Maddux 1.50
NG6 Carlos Delgado .50
NG7 Frank Thomas .75
NG8 Derek Jeter 3.00
NG9 Troy Glaus .50
NG10 Jeff Bagwell .75
NG11 Juan Gonzalez .75
NG12 Randy Johnson 1.00

Sandlot Stars

jason giambi · first base
SANDLOT STARS

NM/M
Complete Set (12): 15.00
Common Player: .75
Inserted 1:11

SS1 Ken Griffey Jr. 1.50
SS2 Derek Jeter 3.00
SS3 Ichiro Suzuki 2.00
SS4 Nomar Garciaparra 2.00
SS5 Sammy Sosa 2.00
SS6 Chipper Jones 1.00
SS7 Jason Giambi .75
SS8 Alex Rodriguez 2.50
SS9 Mark McGwire 2.50
SS10 Barry Bonds 3.00
SS11 Mike Piazza 2.00
SS12 Vladimir Guerrero 1.00

Special Collection Jerseys

NM/M
Common Player: 8.00
Inserted 1:144
StB Stan Bahnsen 8.00
SaB Sal Bando 10.00
BC Bert Campaneris 8.00
AD Andre Dawson 15.00
RF Rollie Fingers 15.00
MG Mark Grace 15.00
MH Mike Hegan 8.00
CH "Catfish" Hunter 15.00
RJ Reggie Jackson 15.00
FJ Ferguson Jenkins 15.00
PL Paul Linblad 8.00
JR Joe Rudi 10.00
RS Ryne Sandberg 50.00
SS Sammy Sosa 25.00
BW Billy Williams 10.00

Timeless Teams Bat

NM/M
Inserted 1:288
SEA Ichiro Suzuki, Edgar Martinez, John Olerud, Bret Boone 75.00
NYY Mariano Rivera, Bernie Williams, Paul O'Neill, Jorge Posada 40.00
ATL Tom Glavine, Greg Maddux, Chipper Jones, Andruw Jones 40.00
CLE Juan Gonzalez, Jim Thome, Roberto Alomar, Kenny Lofton 30.00
OAK Jose Canseco, Ricky Henderson, Dave Parker, Don Baylor 30.00
OF Mickey Mantle, Joe DiMaggio, Reggie Jackson, Babe Ruth 300.00
1B Willie McCovey, Frank Thomas, Hank Greenberg, Eddie Murray 30.00
OF Ken Griffey Jr., Barry Bonds, Ricky Henderson, Tony Gwynn 50.00

Timeless Teams Combos

TIMELESS TEAMS

NM/M
Inserted 1:288
NYY00 Roger Clemens, Mariano Rivera, Bernie Williams 40.00
ATL96 Greg Maddux, Chipper Jones, Andruw Jones 40.00
OAK74 Rollie Fingers, Jim "Catfish" Hunter, Reggie Jackson 40.00
HOF36 Ty Cobb, Babe Ruth, Honus Wagner/Pants 1,500

Timeless Teams Jerseys

NM/M
Common Player: 10.00
Inserted 1:144
JB Johnny Bench 20.00

DE	Dwight Evans	15.00
RF	Rollie Fingers	15.00
CH	"Catfish" Hunter	15.00
RJ	Reggie Jackson	15.00
AJ	Andruw Jones	15.00
CJ	Chipper Jones	15.00
FL	Fred Lynn	15.00
EMa	Edgar Martinez	15.00
WM	Willie McCovey	15.00
EMu	Eddie Murray	15.00
KS	Kazuhiro Sasaki	10.00

Vintage Aces Jerseys

NM/M

Common Player:		8.00
Inserted 1:144		
JD	John Denny	8.00
TH	Tim Hudson	10.00
FJ	Ferguson Jenkins	10.00
RJ	Randy Johnson	20.00
GM	Greg Maddux	25.00
JM	Juan Marichal	15.00
MMa	Mike Marshall	8.00
PM	Pedro Martinez	20.00
MMu	Mike Mussina	25.00
HN	Hideo Nomo	20.00
NR	Nolan Ryan	100.00
JS	Johnny Sain	20.00
MT	Mike Torrez	8.00

Vintage Signature Combos

NM/M

Production 100 Sets		
FB	Carlton Fisk,	
	Johnny Bench	100.00
JM	Reggie Jackson,	
	Willie McCovey	80.00
SD	Ryne Sandberg,	
	Andre Dawson	100.00
BR	Sal Bando, Joe Rudi	40.00
EL	Dwight Evans,	
	Fred Lynn	60.00
AT	Roberto Alomar,	
	Jim Thome	75.00
BB	Yogi Berra,	
	Johnny Bench	100.00
GR	Ken Griffey Jr.,	
	Alex Rodriguez	300.00
JO	Edgar Martinez,	
	John Olerud	60.00

2002 Upper Deck World Series Heroes

NM/M

Complete Set (180):		20.00
Common Player:		.15
Common RC (91-135):		1.50
Common (136-180):		1.00
Inserted 1:10		
Pack (5):		2.00
Box (24):		40.00
1	Jim "Catfish" Hunter	.15
2	Jimmie Foxx	.50
3	Mark McGwire	2.00
4	Rollie Fingers	.25
5	Rickey Henderson	.40
6	Joe Carter	.15
7	John Olerud	.15
8	Roberto Alomar	.50
9	Pat Hentgen	.15
10	Devon White	.15
11	Eddie Mathews	.50
12	Greg Maddux	1.00
13	Chipper Jones	.75
14	Tom Glavine	.25
15	Andruw Jones	.50
16	David Justice	.25
17	Fred McGriff	.25
18	Ryan Klesko	.15
19	John Smoltz	.25
20	Javy Lopez	.25
21	Marquis Grissom	.15
22	Robin Yount	.75
23	Ozzie Smith	.75
24	Frankie Frisch	.25
25	Stan Musial	1.00
26	Randy Johnson	.75
27	Luis Gonzalez	.25
28	Matt Williams	.15
29	Steve Finley	.15
30	Sandy Koufax	1.50

31	Duke Snider	.50
32	Kirk Gibson	.15
33	Steve Garvey	.15
34	Jackie Robinson	1.50
35	Don Drysdale	.50
36	Juan Marichal	.50
37	Mel Ott	.50
38	Orlando Cepeda	.15
39	Jim Thome	.75
40	Manny Ramirez	.50
41	Omar Vizquel	.15
42	Lou Boudreau	.15
43	Gary Sheffield	.25
44	Moises Alou	.25
45	Livan Hernandez	.15
46	Edgar Renteria	.25
47	Al Leiter	.15
48	Tom Seaver	.75
49	Gary Carter	.15
50	Mike Piazza	1.00
51	Nolan Ryan	2.00
52	Robin Ventura	.15
53	Mike Hampton	.15
54	Jesse Orosco	.15
55	Cal Ripken Jr.	2.00
56	Brooks Robinson	.75
57	Tony Gwynn	.75
58	Kevin Brown	.15
59	Curt Schilling	.50
60	Cy Young	.75
61	Honus Wagner	.75
62	Willie Stargell	.40
63	Wade Boggs	.40
64	Carlton Fisk	.40
65	Ken Griffey Sr.	.15
66	Joe Morgan	.15
67	Johnny Bench	1.00
68	Barry Larkin	.40
69	Jose Rijo	.15
70	Ty Cobb	1.50
71	Kirby Puckett	1.00
72	Chuck Knoblauch	.15
73	Harmon Killebrew	.50
74	Mickey Mantle	2.50
75	Joe DiMaggio	2.00
76	Don Larsen	.40
77	Thurman Munson	.75
78	Roger Maris	1.50
79	Phil Rizzuto	.50
80	Babe Ruth	2.50
81	Lou Gehrig	2.00
82	Billy Martin	.40
83	Derek Jeter	1.50
84	Roger Clemens	1.50
85	Tino Martinez	.15
86	Bernie Williams	.25
87	Mariano Rivera	.25
88	Andy Pettitte	.40
89	David Wells	.15
90	Jorge Posada	.15
91	Rodrigo Rosario RC	1.50
92	Brandon Puffer RC	1.50
93	Franklyn German RC	1.50
94	Reed Johnson RC	1.50
95	Chris Baker RC	1.50
96	John Ennis RC	1.50
97	Luis Martinez RC	1.50
98	Takaki Nomura RC	1.50
99	So Taguchi RC	4.00
100	Michael Crudale RC	1.50
101	Francis Beltran RC	1.50
102	Steve Kent RC	1.50
103	Jorge Sosa RC	1.50
104	Felix Escalona RC	1.50
105	Jose Valverde RC	1.50
106	Doug DeVore RC	1.50
107	Kazuhisa Ishii RC	4.00
108	Victor Alvarez RC	1.50
109	Eric Good RC	1.50
110	Jorge Nunez RC	1.50
111	Ron Calloway RC	1.50
112	Nelson Castro RC	1.50
113	Matt Thornton RC	1.50
114	Luis Ugueto RC	1.50
115	Hansel Izquierdo RC	1.50
116	Jaime Cerda RC	1.50
117	Mark Corey RC	1.50
118	Tyler Yates RC	2.50
119	Satoru Komiyama RC	1.50
120	Steve Bechler RC	1.50
121	Ben Howard RC	1.50
122	Anderson Machado RC	1.50
123	Jorge Padilla RC	1.50
124	Eric Junge RC	1.50
125	Adrian Burnside RC	1.50
126	Mike Gonzalez RC	1.50
127	Anastacio Martinez RC	1.50
128	Josh Hancock RC	1.50
129	Rene Reyes RC	1.50
130	Aaron Cook RC	1.50
131	Cam Esslinger RC	1.50
132	Juan Brito RC	1.50
133	Miguel Ascencio RC	1.50
134	Kevin Frederick RC	1.50
135	Edwin Almonte RC	1.50
136	Troy Glaus	1.00
137	Darin Erstad	1.00
138	Jeff Bagwell	1.50
139	Lance Berkman	1.50
140	Tim Hudson	1.25
141	Eric Chavez	1.25
142	Barry Zito	1.50
143	Carlos Delgado	1.00
144	Richie Sexson	1.50
145	Albert Pujols	4.00
146	Sammy Sosa	4.00
147	Kerry Wood	2.00
148	Greg Vaughn	1.00

149	Shawn Green	1.00
150	Vladimir Guerrero	2.50
151	Barry Bonds	6.00
152	C.C. Sabathia	1.00
153	Ichiro Suzuki	5.00
154	Freddy Garcia	1.00
155	Edgar Martinez	1.00
156	Josh Beckett	1.00
157	Cliff Floyd	1.00
158	Mo Vaughn	1.00
159	Jeromy Burnitz	1.00
160	Sean Burroughs	1.00
161	Phil Nevin	1.00
162	Scott Rolen	2.00
163	Brian Giles	1.25
164	Alex Rodriguez	5.00
165	Ivan Rodriguez	1.50
166	Juan Gonzalez	1.25
167	Rafael Palmeiro	1.50
168	Nomar Garciaparra	4.00
169	Pedro J. Martinez	2.00
170	Ken Griffey Jr.	4.00
171	Adam Dunn	1.50
172	Todd Helton	1.50
173	Mike Sweeney	1.00
174	Carlos Beltran	1.00
175	Dmitri Young	1.00
176	Doug Mientkiewicz	1.00
177	Torii Hunter	1.00
178	Frank Thomas	1.50
179	Magglio Ordonez	1.00
180	Jason Giambi	1.50

Base

NM/M

Complete Set (1):		
DJ	Derek Jeter	35.00

Bats

NM/M

Common Player:		15.00
Inserted 1:288		
JD	Joe DiMaggio/SP	100.00
MM	Mickey Mantle	125.00
KP	Kirby Puckett	25.00
ES	Enos Slaughter	15.00

Jerseys

NM/M

Common Player:		10.00
Inserted 1:288		
JC	Joe Carter	10.00
CF	Carlton Fisk	15.00
DL	Don Larsen	20.00
BM	Bill Mazeroski	15.00

Jerseys Autograph

No Pricing
Production 25 Sets

Match-Ups Memorabilia

NM/M

Common Card:		8.00
Inserted 1:24		
MU00	Mike Piazza,	
	Roger Clemens	15.00
MU00a	Andy Pettitte,	
	Mike Piazza	15.00
MU00b	Al Leiter,	
	Derek Jeter	10.00
MU00d	Edgardo Alfonzo,	
	Mariano Rivera	8.00
MU00e	John Franco,	
	Derek Jeter	10.00
MU00c	Robin Ventura,	
	Roger Clemens	8.00
MU01	Mariano Rivera,	
	Luis Gonzalez	8.00
MU01a	Paul O'Neill,	
	Curt Schilling	8.00
MU01b	Bernie Williams,	
	Randy Johnson	8.00
MU01c	David Justice,	
	Curt Schilling	8.00
MU01d	Randy Johnson,	
	Bernie Williams	8.00
MU01e	Curt Schilling,	
	Tino Martinez	8.00
MU01f	Roger Clemens,	
	Luis Gonzalez	15.00
MU01g	Paul O'Neill,	
	Byung-Hyun Kim	10.00
MU01h	Luis Gonzalez,	
	Mariano Rivera/97	12.00
MU03	Honus Wagner,	
	Cy Young	100.00
MU09	Ty Cobb, Honus	
	Wagner/SP	125.00
MU30	Jimmie Foxx	25.00
MU36	Joe DiMaggio,	
	Mel Ott/SP	80.00
MU49	Duke Snider,	
	Joe DiMaggio	25.00

MU53	Jackie Robinson,	
	Billy Martin	25.00
MU55	Mickey Mantle,	
	Jackie Robinson	110.00
MU56	Don Larsen,	
	Duke Snider	25.00
MU56a	Don Larsen,	
	Jackie Robinson	20.00
MU57	Eddie Mathews,	
	Yogi Berra	15.00
MU58	Yogi Berra,	
	Eddie Mathews	15.00
MU62	Roger Maris,	
	Juan Marichal	40.00
MU63	Sandy Koufax,	
	Mickey Mantle	100.00
MU66	Don Drysdale, Brooks	
	Robinson/SP	40.00
MU69	Nolan Ryan,	
	Brooks Robinson	50.00
MU72	Joe Morgan, Jim	
	"Catfish" Hunter	8.00
MU72a	Rollie Fingers,	
	Johnny Bench	10.00
MU73	Tom Seaver,	
	"Catfish" Hunter	15.00
MU74	Jim "Catfish" Hunter,	
	Steve Garvey	15.00
MU74a	Davey Lopes,	
	Jim "Catfish" Hunter	8.00
MU76	Ken Griffey Sr.,	
	Thurman Munson	12.00
MU76a	Thurman Munson,	
	Johnny Bench	20.00
MU77	Thurman Munson,	
	Steve Garvey	15.00
MU78	Thurman Munson,	
	Steve Garvey	12.00
MU78a	Bill Russell,	
	Thurman Munson	12.00
MU81	Steve Garvey,	
	Dave Winfield	8.00
MU82	Robin Yount,	
	Ozzie Smith	15.00
MU83	Cal Ripken Jr.,	
	Joe Morgan	25.00
MU84	Jack Morris,	
	Tony Gwynn	12.00
MU86	Jesse Orosco,	
	Roger Clemens	35.00
MU87	Ozzie Smith,	
	Kirby Puckett	15.00
MU88	Mark McGwire,	
	Kirk Gibson/SP	60.00
MU90	Barry Larkin,	
	Mark McGwire/SP	20.00
MU91	Tom Glavine,	
	Kirby Puckett	15.00
MU93	Joe Carter,	
	Curt Schilling	8.00
MU95	Dennis Martinez,	
	David Justice	8.00
MU96	Andruw Jones,	
	Andy Pettitte	8.00
MU96a	Tim Raines,	
	Tom Glavine	10.00
MU96b	Kenny Rogers,	
	Chipper Jones	8.00
MU95a	Kenny Lofton,	
	John Smoltz	8.00
MU97	Jim Thome,	
	Kevin Brown	10.00
MU98	Tony Gwynn,	
	Bernie Williams	10.00
MU98a	Trevor Hoffman,	
	Bernie Williams/SP	8.00
MU99	Jorge Posada,	
	Greg Maddux	15.00
MU99a	Greg Maddux,	
	Derek Jeter	15.00
MU99b	Paul O'Neill,	
	John Smoltz	8.00
MU99c	Chipper Jones,	
	Mariano Rivera	15.00

Patch Collection

NM/M

Common Patch:		15.00
Inserted 1:Hobby Box		
WS03	1903 World Series	25.00
WS05	1905 World Series	25.00
WS06	1906 World Series	20.00
WS07	1907 World Series	20.00
WS08	1908 World Series	25.00
WS09	1909 World Series	20.00
WS10	1910 World Series	20.00
WS11	1911 World Series	20.00
WS12	1912 World Series	30.00
WS13	1913 World Series	20.00

WS14	1914 World Series	25.00
WS15	1915 World Series	20.00
WS16	1916 World Series	25.00
WS17	1917 World Series	20.00
WS18	1918 World Series	30.00
WS19	1919 World Series	25.00
WS20	1920 World Series	15.00
WS21	1921 World Series	20.00
WS22	1922 World Series	20.00
WS23	1923 World Series	20.00
WS24	1924 World Series	20.00
WS25	1925 World Series	20.00
WS26	1926 World Series	20.00
WS27	1927 World Series	30.00
WS28	1928 World Series	20.00
WS29	1929 World Series	20.00
WS30	1930 World Series	20.00
WS31	1931 World Series	20.00
WS32	1932 World Series	20.00
WS33	1933 World Series	20.00
WS34	1934 World Series	20.00
WS35	1935 World Series	20.00
WS36	1936 World Series	20.00
WS37	1937 World Series	20.00
WS38	1938 World Series	20.00
WS39	1939 World Series	20.00
WS40	1940 World Series	20.00
WS41	1941 World Series	20.00
WS42	1942 World Series	20.00
WS43	1943 World Series	20.00
WS44	1944 World Series	30.00
WS45	1945 World Series	20.00
WS46	1946 World Series	25.00
WS47	1947 World Series	20.00
WS48	1948 World Series	30.00
WS49	1949 World Series	25.00
WS50	1950 World Series	25.00
WS51	1951 World Series	25.00
WS52	1952 World Series	20.00
WS53	1953 World Series	25.00
WS54	1954 World Series	15.00
WS55	1955 World Series	25.00
WS56	1956 World Series	25.00
WS57	1957 World Series	20.00
WS58	1958 World Series	20.00
WS59	1959 World Series	20.00
WS60	1960 World Series	20.00
WS61	1961 World Series	35.00
WS62	1962 World Series	20.00
WS63	1963 World Series	20.00
WS64	1964 World Series	20.00
WS65	1965 World Series	20.00
WS66	1966 World Series	20.00
WS67	1967 World Series	20.00
WS68	1968 World Series	20.00
WS69	1969 World Series	35.00
WS70	1970 World Series	20.00
WS71	1971 World Series	20.00
WS72	1972 World Series	20.00
WS73	1973 World Series	20.00
WS74	1974 World Series	20.00
WS75	1975 World Series	30.00
WS76	1976 World Series	20.00
WS77	1977 World Series	20.00
WS78	1978 World Series	20.00
WS79	1979 World Series	20.00
WS80	1980 World Series	20.00
WS81	1981 World Series	20.00
WS82	1982 World Series	25.00
WS83	1983 World Series	20.00
WS84	1984 World Series	20.00
WS85	1985 World Series	20.00
WS86	1986 World Series	20.00
WS87	1987 World Series	20.00
WS88	1988 World Series	20.00
WS89	1989 World Series	20.00
WS90	1990 World Series	20.00
WS91	1991 World Series	20.00
WS92	1992 World Series	20.00
WS93	1993 World Series	20.00
WS95	1995 World Series	20.00
WS96	1996 World Series	20.00
WS97	1997 World Series	20.00
WS98	1998 World Series	15.00
WS99	1999 World Series	20.00
WS01	2001 World Series	20.00

Patch Collection Autographs

NM/M

Inserted 1:336		
WS93	Joe Carter	40.00
WS99	Roger Clemens	100.00
WS74	Rollie Fingers	30.00
WS75	Carlton Fisk	60.00
WS81	Steve Garvey	35.00
WS65	Sandy Koufax	250.00
WS56	Don Larsen	60.00
WS89	Mark McGwire	275.00
WS76	Joe Morgan	40.00
WS91	Kirby Puckett	60.00
WS83	Cal Ripken Jr.	175.00
WS70	Brooks Robinson	80.00
WS69	Nolan Ryan	200.00
WS73	Tom Seaver	60.00
WS55	Duke Snider	75.00
WS82	Ozzie Smith	90.00

2002 Upper Deck 40-Man

NM/M

Complete Set (1182):		200.00
Common Player:		.15
Silvers:		1-3X
Inserted 1:4		

Rainbows: 5-10X
Production 40 Sets
Hobby Pack (10): 1.75
Hobby Box (24): 30.00

1	Darin Erstad	.40
2	Kevin Appier	.15
3	Scott Schoeneweis	.15
4	Bengie Molina	.15
5	Troy Glaus	.50
6	Adam Kennedy	.15
7	Aaron Sele	.15
8	Garret Anderson	.25
9	Ramon Ortiz	.15
10	Dennis Cook	.15
11	Scott Spiezio	.15
12	Orlando Palmeiro	.15
13	Troy Percival	.15
14	David Eckstein	.15
15	Jarrod Washburn	.40
16	Nathan Haynes	.15
17	Benji Gil	.15
18	Alfredo Amezega	.15
19	Ben Weber	.15
20	Al Levine	.15
21	Brad Fullmer	.15
22	Elpidio Guzman	.15
23	Tim Salmon	.25
24	Jose Nieves	.15
25	Shawn Wooten	.15
26	Lou Pote	.15
27	Mickey Callaway	.15
28	Steve Green	.15
29	John Lackey	.15
30	Mark Lukasiewicz	.15
31	Jorge Fabregas	.15
32	Jeff Da Vanon	.15
33	Elvin Nina	.15
34	Donne Wall	.15
35	Eric Chavez	.50
36	Jermaine Dye	.15
37	Scott Hatteberg	.15
38	Mark Mulder	.50
39	Ramon Hernandez	.15
40	Jim Mecir	.15
41	Barry Zito	.50
42	Greg Myers	.15
43	David Justice	.50
44	Mike Magnante	.15
45	Terrence Long	.15
46	Tim Hudson	.50
47	Olmedo Saenz	.15
48	Billy Koch	.15
49	Carlos Pena	.15
50	Mike Venafro	.15
51	Mark Ellis	.15
52	Randy Velarde	.15
53	Jeremy Giambi	.15
54	Mike Colagelo	.15
55	Mike Holtz	.15
56	Chad Bradford	.15
57	Miguel Tejada	.50
58	Mike Fyhrie	.15
59	Eric Hiljus	.15
60	Juan Pena	.15
61	Mario Valdez	.15
62	Franklyn German RC	.50
63	Carlos Delgado	.15
64	Orlando Hudson	.15
65	Chris Carpenter	.15
66	Kelvim Escobar	.15
67	Felipe Lopez	.15
68	Brandon Lyon	.15
69	Jose Cruz Jr.	.15
70	Luke Prokopec	.15
71	Darrin Fletcher	.15
72	Bob File	.15
73	Felix Heredia	.15
74	Mike Sirotka	.15
75	Shannon Stewart	.15
76	Joe Lawrence	.15
77	Chris Woodward	.15
78	Dan Plesac	.15
79	Pedro Borbon	.15
80	Roy Halladay	.40
81	Raul Mondesi	.15
82	Steve Parris	.15
83	Homer Bush	.15
84	Esteban Loaiza	.15
85	Vernon Wells	.25
86	Justin Miller	.15
87	Scott Eyre	.15
88	Dave Berg	.15
89	Gustavo Chacin RC	.15
90	Joe Orloski RC	.40
91	Corey Thurman RC	.15
92	Tom Wilson	.15
93	Eric Hinske	.50
94	Chris Baker RC	.15

No.	Player	Price
95	Reed Johnson RC	.40
96	Greg Vaughn	.15
97	Toby Hall	.15
98	Brent Abernathy	.15
99	Bobby Smith	.15
100	Tanyon Sturtze	.15
101	Chris Gomez	.15
102	Joe Kennedy	.15
103	Ben Grieve	.15
104	Aubrey Huff	.15
105	Jesus Colome	.15
106	Felix Escalona RC	.40
107	Paul Wilson	.15
108	Ryan Rupe	.15
109	Jason Tyner	.15
110	Esteban Yan	.15
111	Russ Johnson	.15
112	Randy Winn	.15
113	Wilson Alvarez	.15
114	Wilmy Caceres	.15
115	Steve Cox	.15
116	Dewon Brazelton	.15
117	Doug Creek	.15
118	Jason Conti	.15
119	John Flaherty	.15
120	Delvin James	.15
121	Steve Kent RC	.15
122	Kevin McGlinchy	.15
123	Travis Phelps	.15
124	Bobby Seay	.15
125	Travis Harper	.15
126	Victor Zambrano	.15
127	Jace Brewer	.15
128	Jason Smith	.15
129	Ramon Soler	.15
130	Brandon Backe RC	.50
131	Jorge Sosa RC	.25
132	Jim Thome	.75
133	Brady Anderson	.15
134	C.C. Sabathia	.15
135	Einar Diaz	.15
136	Ricky Gutierrez	.15
137	Danys Baez	.15
138	Bob Wickman	.15
139	Milton Bradley	.15
140	Bartolo Colon	.40
141	Jolbert Cabrera	.15
142	Eddie Taubensee	.15
143	Ellis Burks	.15
144	Omar Vizquel	.40
145	Eddie Perez	.15
146	Jaret Wright	.15
147	Chuck Finley	.15
148	Paul Shuey	.15
149	Travis Fryman	.15
150	Wil Cordero	.15
151	Ricardo Rincon	.15
152	Victor Martinez	.15
153	Charles Nagy	.15
154	Alex Escobar	.15
155	Russell Branyan	.15
156	Matt Lawton	.15
157	Ryan Drese	.15
158	Jerrod Riggan	.15
159	David Riske	.15
160	Jake Westbrook	.15
161	Mark Wohlers	.15
162	John McDonald	.15
163	Ichiro Suzuki	1.50
164	Freddy Garcia	.15
165	Edgar Martinez	.15
166	Ben Davis	.15
167	Shigetoshi Hasegawa	.15
168	Carlos Guillen	.15
169	Ruben Sierra	.15
170	Joel Pineiro	.15
171	Norm Charlton	.15
172	Bret Boone	.15
173	Jamie Moyer	.15
174	Jeff Nelson	.15
175	Kazuhiro Sasaki	.50
176	Jeff Cirillo	.15
177	Mark McLemore	.15
178	Paul Abbott	.15
179	Mike Cameron	.15
180	Dan Wilson	.15
181	John Olerud	.50
182	Arthur Rhodes	.15
183	Desi Relaford	.15
184	John Halama	.15
185	Antonio Perez	.15
186	Ryan Anderson	.15
187	James Baldwin	.15
188	Ryan Franklin	.15
189	Justin Kaye	.15
190	J.J. Putz RC	.40
191	Allan Simpson RC	.40
192	Matt Thornton	.15
193	Luis Ugueto RC	.40
194	Chris Richard	.15
195	Sidney Ponson	.15
196	Brook Fordyce	.15
197	Luis Matos	.15
198	Josh Towers	.15
199	David Segui	.15
200	Chris Brock	.15
201	Tony Batista	.15
202	Erik Bedard	.15
203	Marty Cordova	.15
204	Jerry Hairston Jr.	.15
205	Jason Johnson	.15
206	Buddy Groom	.15
207	Mike Bordick	.15
208	Melvin Mora	.15
209	Calvin Maduro	.15
210	Jeff Conine	.15
211	Luis Rivera	.15
212	Jay Gibbons	.15
213	B.J. Ryan	.15
214	Sean Douglass	.15
215	Rodrigo Lopez	.15
216	Rick Bauer	.15
217	Scott Erickson	.15
218	Jorge Julio	.15
219	Willis Roberts	.15
220	John Stephens	.15
221	Geronimo Gil	.15
222	Chris Singleton	.15
223	Mike Paradis	.15
224	John Parrish	.15
225	Steve Bechler RC	.50
226	Mike Moriarty RC	.15
227	Luis Garcia	.15
228	Alex Rodriguez	1.50
229	Mark Teixeira	.50
230	Chan Ho Park	.15
231	Todd Van Poppel	.15
232	Mike Young	.15
233	Kenny Rogers	.15
234	Rusty Greer	.15
235	Rafael Palmeiro	.50
236	Francisco Cordero	.15
237	John Rocker	.15
238	Dave Burba	.15
239	Travis Hafner	.15
240	Kevin Mench	.15
241	Carl Everett	.15
242	Ivan Rodriguez	.50
243	Jeff Zimmerman	.15
244	Juan Gonzalez	.50
245	Herbert Perry	.15
246	Rob Bell	.15
247	Doug Davis	.15
248	Frank Catalanotto	.15
249	Jay Powell	.15
250	Gabe Kapler	.15
251	Joaquin Benoit	.15
252	Jovanny Cedeno	.15
253	Hideki Irabu	.15
254	Dan Miceli	.15
255	Danny Kolb	.15
256	Colby Lewis	.15
257	Rich Rodriguez	.15
258	Ismael Valdes	.15
259	Bill Haselman	.15
260	Jason Hart	.15
261	Rudy Seanez	.15
262	Travis Hughes RC	.40
263	Hank Blalock	.50
264	Steve Woodard	.15
265	Nomar Garciaparra	1.50
266	Pedro J. Martinez	.75
267	Frank Castillo	.15
268	Johnny Damon	.15
269	Doug Mirabelli	.15
270	Derek Lowe	.40
271	Shea Hillenbrand	.50
272	Paxton Crawford	.15
273	Tony Clark	.15
274	Dustin Hermanson	.15
275	Trot Nixon	.15
276	John Burkett	.15
277	Rich Garces	.15
278	Josh Hancock RC	.15
279	Michael Coleman	.15
280	Darren Oliver	.15
281	Jason Varitek	.15
282	Jose Offerman	.15
283	Tim Wakefield	.15
284	Rolando Arrojo	.15
285	Rickey Henderson	.50
286	Ugueth Urbina	.15
287	Casey Fossum	.15
288	Manny Ramirez	.50
289	Sun-Woo Kim	.15
290	Juan Diaz	.15
291	Willie Banks	.15
292	Jorge De La Rosa RC	.50
293	Juan Pena	.15
294	Jeff Wallace	.15
295	Calvin Pickering	.15
296	Anastacio Martinez RC	.40
297	Carlos Baerga	.15
298	Rey Sanchez	.15
299	Mike Sweeney	.15
300	Jeff Suppan	.15
301	Brent Mayne	.15
302	Chad Durbin	.15
303	Dan Reichert	.15
304	Raul Ibanez	.15
305	Joe Randa	.15
306	Chris George	.15
307	Michael Tucker	.15
308	Paul Byrd	.15
309	Kris Wilson	.15
310	Luis Alicea	.15
311	Neifi Perez	.15
312	Brian Shouse	.15
313	Chuck Knoblauch	.15
314	Dave McCarty	.15
315	Blake Stein	.15
316	Alexis Gomez	.15
317	Mark Quinn	.15
318	A.J. Hinch	.15
319	Carlos Febles	.15
320	Roberto Hernandez	.15
321	Brandon Berger	.15
322	Jeff Austin RC	.40
323	Corey Bailey	.15
324	Tony Cogan	.15
325	Nate Field RC	.40
326	Jason Grimsley	.15
327	Darrell May	.15
328	Donnie Sadler	.15
329	Carlos Beltran	.15
330	Miguel Asencio RC	.40
331	Jeff Weaver	.15
332	Bobby Higginson	.15
333	Mike Rivera	.15
334	Matt Anderson	.15
335	Craig Paquette	.15
336	Jose Lima	.15
337	Juan Acevedo	.15
338	Danny Patterson	.15
339	Andres Torres	.15
340	Dean Palmer	.15
341	Randall Simon	.15
342	Craig Monroe	.15
343	Damion Easley	.15
344	Robert Fick	.15
345	Steve Sparks	.15
346	Dmitri Young	.15
347	Nate Cornejo	.15
348	Matt Miller	.15
349	Wendell Magee	.15
350	Shane Halter	.15
351	Brian Moehler	.15
352	Mitch Meluskey	.15
353	Jose Macias	.15
354	Mark Redman	.15
355	Jeff Farnsworth	.15
356	Kris Keller	.15
357	Adam Pettyjohn	.15
358	Fernando Rodney	.15
359	Andy Van Hekken	.15
360	Damian Jackson	.15
361	Jose Paniagua	.15
362	Jacob Cruz	.15
363	Doug Mientkiewicz	.15
364	Torii Hunter	.15
365	Brad Radke	.15
366	Denny Hocking	.15
367	Mike Jackson	.15
368	Eddie Guardado	.15
369	Jacque Jones	.15
370	Joe Mays	.15
371	Matt Kinney	.15
372	Kyle Lohse	.15
373	David Ortiz	.15
374	Luis Rivas	.15
375	Jay Canizaro	.15
376	Dustan Mohr	.15
377	LaTroy Hawkins	.15
378	Warren Morris	.15
379	A.J. Pierzynski	.15
380	Eric Milton	.15
381	Bob Wells	.15
382	Cristian Guzman	.15
383	Brian Buchanan	.15
384	Bobby Kielty	.15
385	Corey Koskie	.15
386	J.C. Romero	.15
387	Jack Cressend	.15
388	Mike Duvall	.15
389	Tony Fiore	.15
390	Tom Prince	.15
391	Todd Sears	.15
392	Kevin Frederick RC	.40
393	Frank Thomas	.50
394	Mark Buehrle	.15
395	Jon Garland	.15
396	Jeff Liefer	.15
397	Magglio Ordonez	.50
398	Rocky Biddle	.15
399	Lorenzo Barcelo	.15
400	Ray Durham	.15
401	Bob Howry	.15
402	Aaron Rowand	.15
403	Keith Foulke	.15
404	Paul Konerko	.50
405	Sandy Alomar Jr.	.15
406	Mark Johnson	.15
407	Carlos Lee	.15
408	Jose Valentin	.15
409	Jon Rauch	.15
410	Royce Clayton	.15
411	Kenny Lofton	.40
412	Tony Graffanino	.15
413	Todd Ritchie	.15
414	Antonio Osuna	.15
415	Gary Glover	.15
416	Mike Porzio	.15
417	Danny Wright	.15
418	Kelly Wunsch	.15
419	Miguel Olivo	.15
420	Edwin Almonte RC	.15
421	Kyle Kane RC	.50
422	Mitch Wylie RC	.50
423	Derek Jeter	2.00
424	Jason Giambi	.50
425	Roger Clemens	1.50
426	Enrique Wilson	.15
427	David Wells	.15
428	Mike Mussina	.50
429	Bernie Williams	.50
430	Mike Stanton	.15
431	Sterling Hitchcock	.15
432	Alex Graman	.15
433	Robin Ventura	.15
434	Mariano Rivera	.50
435	Jay Tessmer	.15
436	Andy Pettitte	.15
437	John Vander Wal	.15
438	Adrian Hernandez	.15
439	Alberto Castillo	.15
440	Steve Karsay	.15
441	Alfonso Soriano	.75
442	Rondell White	.15
443	Nick Johnson	.50
444	Jorge Posada	.50
445	Ramiro Mendoza	.15
446	Gerald Williams	.15
447	Orlando Hernandez	.15
448	Randy Choate	.15
449	Randy Keisler	.15
450	Ted Lilly	.15
451	Christian Parker	.15
452	Ron Coomer	.15
453	Marcus Thames	.15
454	Drew Henson	.50
455	Jeff Bagwell	.50
456	Wade Miller	.15
457	Lance Berkman	.50
458	Julio Lugo	.15
459	Roy Oswalt	.40
460	Nelson Cruz	.15
461	Morgan Ensberg	.15
462	Geoff Blum	.15
463	Ryan Jamison RC	.50
464	Billy Wagner	.15
465	Dave Mlicki	.15
466	Brad Ausmus	.15
467	Jose Vizcaino	.15
468	Craig Biggio	.50
469	Shane Reynolds	.15
470	Gregg Zaun	.15
471	Octavio Dotel	.15
472	Carlos Hernandez	.15
473	Richard Hidalgo	.15
474	Daryle Ward	.15
475	Orlando Merced	.15
476	John Buck	.15
477	Adam Everett	.15
478	Doug Brocail	.15
479	Brad Lidge	.15
480	Scott Linebrink	.15
481	T.J. Mathews	.15
482	Greg Miller	.15
483	Hipolito Pichardo	.15
484	Brandon Puffer RC	.15
485	Ricky Stone	.15
486	Jason Lane	.15
487	Brian L. Hunter	.15
488	Rodrigo Rosario RC	.50
489	Tom Shearn RC	.50
490	Gary Sheffield	.40
491	Tom Glavine	.40
492	Mike Remlinger	.15
493	Henry Blanco	.15
494	Vinny Castilla	.15
495	Chris Hammond	.15
496	Kevin Millwood	.50
497	Darren Holmes	.15
498	Cory Aldridge	.15
499	Tim Spooneybarger	.15
500	Rafael Furcal	.50
501	Albie Lopez	.15
502	Javy Lopez	.40
503	Greg Maddux	1.00
504	Andruw Jones	.50
505	Steve Torrealba	.15
506	George Lombard	.15
507	B.J. Surhoff	.15
508	Marcus Giles	.15
509	Derrick Lewis	.15
510	Wes Helms	.15
511	John Smoltz	.50
512	Chipper Jones	.75
513	Jason Marquis	.15
514	Mark DeRosa	.15
515	Jung Bong	.15
516	Kevin Gryboski RC	.15
517	Damian Moss	.15
518	Horacio Ramirez	.15
519	Scott Sobkowiak	.15
520	Billy Sylvester	.15
521	Nick Green	.15
522	Travis Wilson	.15
523	Ryan Langerhans	.15
524	John Ennis RC	.50
525	John Foster RC	.15
526	Keith Lockhart	.15
527	Julio Franco	.15
528	Richie Sexson	.50
529	Jeffrey Hammonds	.15
530	Ben Sheets	.50
531	Mike DeJean	.15
532	Mark Loretta	.15
533	Alex Ochoa	.15
534	Jamey Wright	.15
535	Jose Hernandez	.15
536	Glendon Rusch	.15
537	Geoff Jenkins	.50
538	Luis S. Lopez	.15
539	Curtis Leskanic	.15
540	Chad Fox	.15
541	Tyler Houston	.15
542	Nick Neugebauer	.15
543	Matt Stairs	.15
544	Paul Rigdon	.15
545	Bill Hall	.15
546	Luis Vizcaino	.15
547	Lenny Harris	.15
548	Alex Sanchez	.15
549	Raul Casanova	.15
550	Eric Young	.15
551	Jeff Deardorff RC	.15
552	Nelson Figueroa	.15
553	Ron Belliard	.15
554	Mike Buddie	.15
555	Jose Cabrera	.15
556	J.M. Gold	.15
557	Ray King	.15
558	Jose Mieses	.15
559	Takahito Nomura RC	.50
560	Ruben Quevedo	.15
561	Jackson Melian	.15
562	Cristian Guerrero	.15
563	Paul Bako	.15
564	Luis Martinez RC	.50
565	Brian Mallette RC	.50
566	Matt Morris	.50
567	Tino Martinez	.40
568	Fernando Vina	.15
569	Gene Stechschulte	.15
570	Andy Benes	.15
571	Placido Polanco	.15
572	Luis Garcia	.15
573	Jim Edmonds	.50
574	Bud Smith	.15
575	Mike Matheny	.15
576	Garrett Stephenson	.15
577	Miguel Cairo	.15
578	Darryl Kile	.15
579	Mike Timlin	.15
580	Rick Ankiel	.15
581	Jason Isringhausen	.15
582	Albert Pujols	1.50
583	Eli Marrero	.15
584	Steve Kline	.15
585	J.D. Drew	.50
586	Mike DiFelice	.15
587	Dave Veres	.15
588	Kerry Robinson	.15
589	Edgar Renteria	.15
590	Woody Williams	.15
591	Chance Caple	.15
592	Michael Crudale RC	.15
593	Luther Hackman	.15
594	Josh Pearce	.15
595	Kevin Joseph	.15
596	Jimmy Journell	.15
597	Jeremy Lambert RC	.40
598	Mike Matthews	.15
599	Les Walrond	.15
600	Keith McDonald	.15
601	William Ortega	.15
602	Scotty Layfield RC	.15
603	So Taguchi	1.00
604	Eduardo Perez	.15
605	Sammy Sosa	1.50
606	Kerry Wood	.75
607	Kyle Farnsworth	.15
608	Alex Gonzalez	.15
609	Tom Gordon	.15
610	Carlos Zambrano	.15
611	Roosevelt Brown	.15
612	Bill Mueller	.15
613	Mark Prior	1.50
614	Darren Lewis	.15
615	Joe Girardi	.15
616	Fred McGriff	.50
617	Jon Lieber	.15
618	Robert Machado	.15
619	Corey Patterson	.15
620	Joe Borowski	.15
621	Todd Hundley	.15
622	Jason Bere	.15
623	Moises Alou	.40
624	Jeff Fassero	.15
625	Jesus Sanchez	.15
626	Chris Stynes	.15
627	Delino DeShields	.15
628	Augie Ojeda	.15
629	Juan Cruz	.15
630	Ben Christensen	.15
631	Mike Meyers	.15
632	Will Ohman	.15
633	Steve Smyth	.15
634	Mark Bellhorn	.15
635	Nate Frese	.15
636	David Kelton	.15
637	Francis Beltran RC	.40
638	Antonio Alfonseca	.15
639	Donovan Osborne	.15
640	Shawn Sonnier	.15
641	Matt Clement	.15
642	Luis Gonzalez	.25
643	Brian Anderson	.15
644	Randy Johnson	.75
645	Mark Grace	.50
646	Danny Bautista	.15
647	Junior Spivey	.15
648	Jay Bell	.15
649	Miguel Batista	.15
650	Tony Womack	.15
651	Byung-Hyun Kim	.15
652	Steve Finley	.40
653	Rick Helling	.15
654	Curt Schilling	.50
655	Erubiel Durazo	.15
656	Chris Donnels	.15
657	Greg Colbrunn	.15
658	Mike Morgan	.15
659	Jose Guillen	.15
660	Matt Williams	.50
661	Craig Counsell	.15
662	Greg Swindell	.15
663	Rod Barajas	.15
664	David Dellucci	.15
665	Todd Stottlemyre	.15
666	P.J. Bevis RC	.15
667	Mike Koplove	.15
668	Mike Myers	.15
669	John Patterson	.15
670	Bret Prinz	.15
671	Jeremy Ward RC	.50
672	Danny Klassen	.15
673	Luis Terrero	.15
674	Jose Valverde RC	.50
675	Doug DeVore RC	.50
676	Quinton McCracken	.15
677	Paul LoDuca	.15
678	Mark Grudzielanek	.15
679	Kevin Brown	.15
680	Paul Quantrill	.15
681	Shawn Green	.50
682	Hideo Nomo	.50
683	Eric Gagne	.15
684	Giovanni Carrara	.15
685	Marquis Grissom	.15
686	Hiram Bocachica	.15
687	Guillermo Mota	.15
688	Alex Cora	.15
689	Odalis Perez	.15
690	Brian Jordan	.15
691	Andy Ashby	.15
692	Eric Karros	.40
693	Chad Krueter	.15
694	Dave Roberts	.15
695	Omar Daal	.15
696	Dave Hansen	.15
697	Adrian Beltre	.50
698	Terry Mulholland	.15
699	Cesar Izturis	.15
700	Steve Colyer	.15
701	Carlos Garcia	.15
702	Ricardo Rodriguez	.15
703	Darren Dreifort	.15
704	Jeff Reboulet	.15
705	Victor Alvarez RC	.50
706	Kazuhisa Ishii RC	2.00
707	Jose Vidro	.15
708	Henry Mateo	.15
709	Tony Armas Jr.	.15
710	Carl Pavano	.15
711	Peter Bergeron	.15
712	Bruce Chen	.15
713	Orlando Cabrera	.15
714	Britt Reames	.15
715	Masato Yoshii	.15
716	Fernando Tatis	.15
717	Graeme Lloyd	.15
718	Scott Stewart	.15
719	Lou Collier	.15
720	Michael Barrett	.15
721	Vladimir Guerrero	.75
722	Troy Mattes	.15
723	Brian Schneider	.15
724	Lee Stevens	.15
725	Javier Vazquez	.15
726	Brad Wilkerson	.15
727	Zach Day	.15
728	Ed Vosberg	.15
729	Tomokazu Ohka	.15
730	Mike Mordecai	.15
731	Donnie Bridges	.15
732	Ron Chiavacci	.15
733	T.J. Tucker	.15
734	Scott Hodges	.15
735	Valentino Pascucci	.15
736	Andres Galarraga	.15
737	Scott Downs	.15
738	Eric Good RC	.15
739	Ron Calloway RC	.50
740	Jorge Nunez RC	.15
741	Henry Rodriguez	.15
742	Jeff Kent	.15
743	Russ Ortiz	.15
744	Felix Rodriguez	.15
745	Benito Santiago	.15
746	Tsuyoshi Shinjo	.50
747	Tim Worrell	.15
748	Marvin Benard	.15
749	Kurt Ainsworth	.15
750	Edwards Guzman	.15
751	J.T. Snow	.15
752	Jason Christiansen	.15
753	Robb Nen	.15
754	Barry Bonds	2.00
755	Shawon Dunston	.15
756	Chad Zerbe	.15
757	Ramon E. Martinez	.15
758	Calvin Murray	.15
759	Pedro Feliz	.15
760	Jason Schmidt	.15
761	Damon Minor	.15
762	Reggie Sanders	.15
763	Rich Aurilia	.15
764	Kirk Rueter	.15
765	David Bell	.15
766	Yorvit Torrealba	.15
767	Livan Hernandez	.15
768	Felix Diaz	.15
769	Aaron Fultz	.15
770	Ryan Jensen	.15
771	Arturo McDowell	.15
772	Carlos Valderrama	.15
773	Nelson Castro RC	.50
774	Jay Witasick	.15
775	Deivis Santos	.15
776	Josh Beckett	.15
777	Charles Johnson	.15
778	Derrek Lee	.15
779	A.J. Burnett	.15
780	Vic Darensbourg	.15
781	Cliff Floyd	.50
782	Jose Cueto	.15
783	Nate Teut	.15
784	Alex Gonzalez	.15
785	Brad Penny	.15
786	Kevin Olsen	.15
787	Mike Lowell	.15
788	Mike Redmond	.15
789	Braden Looper	.15
790	Eric Owens	.15
791	Andy Fox	.15
792	Vladimir Nunez	.15
793	Luis Castillo	.15
794	Ryan Dempster	.15
795	Armando Almanza	.15
796	Preston Wilson	.15
797	Pablo Ozuna	.15
798	Gary Knotts	.15
799	Ramon Castro	.15
800	Benito Baez	.15
801	Michael Tejera	.15
802	Claudio Vargas	.15

#	Player	Price
803	Chip Ambres	.15
804	Hansel Izquierdo RC	.50
805	Tim Raines	.15
806	Marty Malloy	.15
807	Julian Tavarez	.15
808	Roberto Alomar	.50
809	Al Leiter	.50
810	Jeromy Burnitz	.15
811	John Franco	.15
812	Edgardo Alfonzo	.15
813	Mike Piazza	1.00
814	Shawn Estes	.15
815	Joe McEwing	.15
816	David Weathers	.15
817	Pedro Astacio	.15
818	Timoniel Perez	.15
819	Grant Roberts	.15
820	Rey Ordonez	.15
821	Steve Trachsel	.15
822	Roger Cedeno	.15
823	Mark Johnson	.15
824	Armando Benitez	.15
825	Vance Wilson	.15
826	Jay Payton	.15
827	Mo Vaughn	.50
828	Scott Strickland	.15
829	Mark Guthrie	.15
830	Jeff D'Amico	.15
831	Mark Corey RC	.50
832	Kane Davis	.15
833	Jae Weong Seo	.15
834	Pat Strange	.15
835	Adam Walker RC	.15
836	Tyler Walker	.15
837	Gary Matthews Jr.	.15
838	Jaime Cerda	.25
839	Satoru Komiyama RC	.50
840	Tyler Yates RC	.50
841	John Valentin	.15
842	Ryan Klesko	.40
843	Wiki Gonzalez	.15
844	Trevor Hoffman	.15
845	Sean Burroughs	.40
846	Alan Embree	.15
847	Dennis Tankersley	.15
848	D'Angelo Jimenez	.15
849	Kevin Jarvis	.15
850	Mark Kotsay	.15
851	Phil Nevin	.25
852	Jeremy Fikac	.15
853	Brett Tomko	.15
854	Brian Lawrence	.15
855	Steve Reed	.15
856	Bubba Trammell	.15
857	Tom Davey	.15
858	Ramon Vazquez	.15
859	Tom Lampkin	.15
860	Bobby Jones	.15
861	Ray Lankford	.15
862	Mark Sweeney	.15
863	Adam Eaton	.15
864	Trenidad Hubbard	.15
865	Jason Boyd	.15
866	Javier Cardona	.15
867	Clifford Bartosh RC	.50
868	Mike Bynum	.15
869	Eric Cyr RC	.50
870	Jose Nunez	.15
871	Ron Gant	.15
872	Deivi Cruz	.15
873	Ben Howard RC	.50
874	Todd Donovan RC	.15
875	Andy Shibilo RC	.15
876	Scott Rolen	.75
877	Jose Mesa	.15
878	Rheal Cormier	.15
879	Travis Lee	.15
880	Mike Lieberthal	.15
881	Brandon Duckworth	.15
882	David Coggin	.15
883	Bobby Abreu	.50
884	Turk Wendell	.15
885	Marlon Byrd	.15
886	Jason Michaels	.15
887	Robert Person	.15
888	Tomas Perez	.15
889	Jimmy Rollins	.50
890	Vicente Padilla	.15
891	Pat Burrell	.50
892	Dave Hollins	.15
893	Randy Wolf	.15
894	Jose Santiago	.15
895	Doug Glanville	.15
896	Cliff Politte	.15
897	Marlon Anderson	.15
898	Ricky Bottalico	.15
899	Terry Adams	.15
900	Brad Baisley	.15
901	Hector Mercado	.15
902	Elio Serrano RC	.15
903	Todd Pratt	.15
904	Peter Zamora RC	.50
905	Nick Punto	.15
906	Ricky Ledee	.15
907	Eric Junge RC	.15
908	Anderson Machado RC	.50
909	Jorge Padilla RC	.50
910	John Mabry	.15
911	Brian Giles	.15
912	Jason Kendall	.40
913	Jack Wilson	.15
914	Kris Benson	.15
915	Aramis Ramirez	.15
916	Mike Fetters	.15
917	Adrian Brown	.15
918	Pokey Reese	.15
919	Dave Williams	.15
920	Mike Benjamin	.15

#	Player	Price
921	Kip Wells	.15
922	Mike Williams	.15
923	Pat Meares	.15
924	Ron Villone	.15
925	Armando Rios	.15
926	Jimmy Anderson	.15
927	Robert Mackowiak	.15
928	Kevin Young	.15
929	Brian Boehringer	.15
930	Joe Beimel	.15
931	Chad Hermansen	.15
932	Scott Sauerbeck	.15
933	Josh Fogg	.15
934	Mike Gonzalez RC	.15
935	Mike Lincoln	.15
936	Sean Lowe	.15
937	Matt Guerrier	.15
938	Ryan Vogelsong	.15
939	J.R. House	.15
940	Craig Wilson	.15
941	Tony Alvarez	.15
942	J.J. Davis	.15
943	Abraham Nunez	.15
944	Adrian Burnside RC	.50
945	Ken Griffey Jr.	1.00
946	Jimmy Haynes	.15
947	Juan Castro	.15
948	Jose Rijo	.15
949	Corky Miller	.15
950	Elmer Dessens	.15
951	Aaron Boone	.15
952	Juan Encarnacion	.15
953	Chris Reitsma	.15
954	Wilton Guerrero	.15
955	Danny Graves	.15
956	Jim Brower	.15
957	Barry Larkin	.50
958	Todd Walker	.15
959	Gabe White	.15
960	Adam Dunn	.50
961	Jason LaRue	.15
962	Reggie Taylor	.15
963	Sean Casey	.40
964	Scott Williamson	.15
965	Austin Kearns	.50
966	Kelly Stinnett	.15
967	Jose Acevedo	.15
968	Gookie Dawkins	.15
969	Brady Clark	.15
970	Scott Sullivan	.15
971	Ricardo Aramboles	.15
972	Lance Davis	.15
973	Seth Etherton	.15
974	Luke Hudson	.15
975	Joey Hamilton	.15
976	Luis Pineda	.15
977	John Riedling	.15
978	Jose Silva	.15
979	Dane Sardinha	.15
980	Ben Broussard	.15
981	David Espinosa	.15
982	Ruben Mateo	.15
983	Larry Walker	.45
984	Juan Uribe	.15
985	Mike Hampton	.15
986	Aaron Cook RC	.15
987	Jose Ortiz	.15
988	Todd Jones	.15
989	Todd Helton	.50
990	Shawn Chacon	.15
991	Jason Jennings	.15
992	Todd Zeile	.15
993	Ben Petrick	.15
994	Denny Neagle	.15
995	Jose Jimenez	.15
996	Juan Pierre	.15
997	Todd Hollandsworth	.15
998	Kent Mercker	.15
999	Greg Norton	.15
1000	Terry Shumpert	.15
1001	Mark Little	.15
1002	Gary Bennett	.15
1003	Dennys Reyes	.15
1004	Justin Speier	.15
1005	John Thomson	.15
1006	Rick White	.15
1007	Colin Young RC	.40
1008	Cam Esslinger RC	.50
1009	Rene Reyes RC	.50
1010	Mike James	.15
1011	Morgan Ensberg	.15
1012	Adam Everett	.15
1013	Rodrigo Rosario	.15
1014	Carlos Pena	.15
1015	Eric Hinske	.15
1016	Orlando Hudson	.15
1017	Reed Johnson	.15
1018	Jung Bong	.15
1019	Bill Hall	.15
1020	Mark Prior	1.50
1021	Francis Beltran	.15
1022	David Kelton	.15
1023	Felix Escalona	.15
1024	Jorge Sosa	.15
1025	Dewon Brazelton	.15
1026	Jose Valverde	.15
1027	Luis Terrero	.15
1028	Kazuhisa Ishii	1.00
1029	Cesar Izturis	.15
1030	Ryan Jensen	.15
1031	Matt Thornton	.15
1032	Hansel Izquierdo	.15
1033	Jaime Cerda	.15
1034	Erik Bedard	.15
1035	Sean Burroughs	.15
1036	Ben Howard	.15
1037	Ramon Vazquez	.15
1038	Marlon Byrd	.15

#	Player	Price
1039	Josh Fogg	.15
1040	Hank Blalock	.50
1041	Mark Teixeira	.50
1042	Kevin Mench	.15
1043	Dane Sardinha	.15
1044	Austin Kearns	.50
1045	Anastacio Martinez	.15
1046	Eric Munson	.15
1047	Jon Rauch	.15
1048	Nick Johnson	.50
1049	Alex Graman	.15
1050	Drew Henson	.50
1051	Darin Erstad	.50
1052	Garret Anderson	.50
1053	Craig Biggio	.50
1054	Lance Berkman	.50
1055	Jeff Bagwell	.50
1056	Shannon Stewart	.15
1057	Chipper Jones	.75
1058	J.D. Drew	.50
1059	Moises Alou	.15
1060	Mark Grace	.50
1061	Jose Vidro Expos	.15
1062	Vladimir Guerrero	.75
1063	Matt Lawton	.15
1064	Ichiro Suzuki	1.50
1065	Edgar Martinez	.15
1066	John Olerud	.15
1067	Jeff Cirillo	.15
1068	Mike Lowell	.15
1069	Mike Piazza	1.00
1070	Roberto Alomar	.50
1071	Bobby Abreu	.15
1072	Jason Kendall	.15
1073	Brian Giles	.15
1074	Rafael Palmeiro	.50
1075	Ivan Rodriguez	.50
1076	Alex Rodriguez	1.50
1077	Juan Gonzalez	.50
1078	Nomar Garciaparra	1.50
1079	Manny Ramirez	.50
1080	Sean Casey	.25
1081	Barry Larkin	.25
1082	Larry Walker	.25
1083	Carlos Beltran	.15
1084	Corey Koskie	.15
1085	Magglio Ordonez	.25
1086	Frank Thomas	.50
1087	Kenny Lofton	.25
1088	Derek Jeter	2.00
1089	Bernie Williams	.50
1090	Jason Giambi	.50
1091	Troy Glaus	.15
1092	Jeff Bagwell	.50
1093	Lance Berkman	.50
1094	David Justice	.25
1095	Eric Chavez	.25
1096	Carlos Delgado	.40
1097	Gary Sheffield	.40
1098	Chipper Jones	.50
1099	Andruw Jones	.50
1100	Richie Sexson	.40
1101	Albert Pujols	1.50
1102	Sammy Sosa	1.50
1103	Fred McGriff	.50
1104	Greg Vaughn	.15
1105	Matt Williams	.15
1106	Luis Gonzalez	.40
1107	Shawn Green	.40
1108	Andres Galarraga	.15
1109	Vladimir Guerrero	.50
1110	Barry Bonds	2.00
1111	Rich Aurilia	.15
1112	Ellis Burks	.15
1113	Jim Thome	.50
1114	Bret Boone	.15
1115	Cliff Floyd	.15
1116	Mike Piazza	1.00
1117	Jeromy Burnitz	.15
1118	Phil Nevin	.15
1119	Brian Giles	.15
1120	Rafael Palmeiro	.50
1121	Juan Gonzalez	.50
1122	Alex Rodriguez	1.50
1123	Manny Ramirez	.50
1124	Ken Griffey Jr.	1.00
1125	Larry Walker	.40
1126	Todd Helton	.50
1127	Mike Sweeney	.15
1128	Frank Thomas	.50
1129	Paul Konerko	.40
1130	Jason Giambi	.50
1131	Aaron Sele	.15
1132	Roy Oswalt	.15
1133	Wade Miller	.15
1134	Tim Hudson	.40
1135	Barry Zito	.40
1136	Mark Mulder	.25
1137	Greg Maddux	1.00
1138	Tom Glavine	.40
1139	Ben Sheets	.40
1140	Darryl Kile	.15
1141	Matt Morris	.15
1142	Kerry Wood	.40
1143	Jon Lieber	.15
1144	Juan Cruz	.15
1145	Randy Johnson	.75
1146	Curt Schilling	.50
1147	Kevin Brown	.15
1148	Javier Vazquez	.15
1149	Russ Ortiz	.15
1150	C.C. Sabathia	.15
1151	Bartolo Colon	.15
1152	Freddy Garcia	.15
1153	Jamie Moyer	.15
1154	Josh Beckett	.50
1155	Brad Penny	.15
1156	Al Leiter	.40

#	Player	Price
1157	Brandon Duckworth	.15
1158	Robert Person	.15
1159	Kris Benson	.15
1160	Chan Ho Park	.15
1161	Pedro J. Martinez	.75
1162	Mike Hampton	.15
1163	Jeff Weaver	.15
1164	Joe Mays	.15
1165	Brad Radke	.15
1166	Eric Milton	.15
1167	Roger Clemens	1.00
1168	Mike Mussina	.50
1169	Andy Pettitte	.15
1170	David Wells	.15
1171	Ken Griffey Jr.	1.00
1172	Ichiro Suzuki	1.00
1173	Jason Giambi	.50
1174	Alex Rodriguez	1.00
1175	Sammy Sosa	.75
1176	Nomar Garciaparra	1.00
1177	Barry Bonds	1.00
1178	Mike Piazza	.75
1179	Derek Jeter	1.50
1180	Randy Johnson	.40
1181	Jeff Bagwell	.40
1182	Albert Pujols	1.00

Lumber Yard

	NM/M
Common Player:	10.00
Inserted 1:168	
LY1 Chipper Jones	15.00
LY2 Joe DiMaggio	40.00
LY3 Albert Pujols	30.00
LY4 Mark McGwire	30.00
LY5 Sammy Sosa	15.00
LY6 Vladimir Guerrero	15.00
LY7 Barry Bonds	25.00
LY8 Mickey Mantle	50.00
LY9 Mike Piazza	15.00
LY10 Alex Rodriguez	15.00
LY11 Nomar Garciaparra	15.00
LY12 Ken Griffey Jr.	20.00
LY13 Frank Thomas	15.00
LY14 Jason Giambi	15.00
LY15 Derek Jeter	25.00
LY16 Luis Gonzalez	10.00
LY17 Jeff Bagwell	10.00
LY18 Todd Helton	10.00

Gargantuan Gear

	NM/M
Common Player:	3.00
Gold:	2X
Production 100 Sets	
G-JB James Baldwin	3.00
G-BC Bruce Chen	3.00
G-JD Jermaine Dye/SP	5.00
G-JG Juan Gonzalez	6.00
G-BG Ben Grieve	3.00
G-KG Ken Griffey Jr.	10.00
G-TH Tim Hudson	6.00
G-AJ Andruw Jones	6.00
G-JK Jeff Kent	3.00
G-ML Mike Lieberthal	3.00
G-TM Tino Martinez	3.00
G-JO John Olerud	3.00
G-MO Magglio Ordonez	5.00
G-MP Mike Piazza	15.00
G-JP Jorge Posada	8.00
G-AP Andy Pettitte	6.00
G-BR Brad Radke	3.00
G-AR Alex Rodriguez	10.00
G-SR Scott Rolen	8.00
G-CS Curt Schilling	8.00
G-AS Aaron Sele	3.00
G-IS Ichiro Suzuki/SP	30.00
G-BW Bernie Williams	8.00
G-DY Dmitri Young	3.00
G-TZ Todd Zeile	3.00

Looming Large Jerseys

	NM/M
Common Player:	8.00
Production 250 Sets	
Gold:	2X
Production 40 Sets	
LBa Jeff Bagwell	10.00
LB Lance Berkman	10.00
JBu John Burkett	10.00
SC Sean Casey	10.00
TC Tony Clark	8.00
RC Roger Clemens	20.00
JC Jeff Cirillo	8.00
JD J.D. Drew	10.00
CE Carl Everett	8.00
CF Chuck Finley	8.00
TF Travis Fryman	8.00
JGi Jason Giambi	10.00
BG Brian Giles	8.00
TG Tom Glavine	10.00
JGo Juan Gonzalez	10.00
KG Ken Griffey Jr.	20.00
TH Todd Helton	15.00
RJ Randy Johnson	15.00
DK Darryl Kile	8.00
AL Al Leiter	8.00
ML Mike Lieberthal	8.00
KL Kenny Lofton	8.00
GM Greg Maddux	15.00
EM Edgar Martinez	10.00
FM Fred McGriff	8.00
MO Magglio Ordonez	8.00
HN Hideo Nomo	50.00
RP Rafael Palmeiro	10.00
JP Jorge Posada	10.00
SR Shane Reynolds	8.00
AR Alex Rodriguez	15.00
JR Jimmy Rollins	8.00
KS Kazuhiro Sasaki	10.00
CS Curt Schilling	10.00
JS J.T. Snow	8.00
SS Sammy Sosa	20.00
FT Frank Thomas	8.00
IV Ismael Valdes	8.00
RV Randy Velarde	8.00
RV Ron Villone	8.00
BZ Barry Zito	10.00

Mark McGwire Flashbacks

Mark McGwire Flashbacks

	NM/M
Complete Set (40):	120.00
Common McGwire:	4.00
Inserted 1:24	
MM1-40 Mark McGwire	4.00

Super Swatches

	NM/M
Common Player:	5.00
Gold:	1-2X
Production 40 Sets	
EA Edgardo Alfonzo	5.00
RA Rich Aurilia	5.00
JB Jeff Bagwell	15.00
SC Sean Casey	8.00
CD Carlos Delgado	8.00
RD Ray Durham	5.00
DE Darin Erstad	8.00
JG Juan Gonzalez	8.00
MG Mark Grace	8.00
SG Shawn Green	8.00
KG Ken Griffey Jr.	20.00
TG Tony Gwynn	15.00
MH Mike Hampton	5.00
TH Trevor Hoffman	5.00
CJ Chipper Jones	10.00
DJ David Justice	8.00
KL Kenny Lofton	5.00
JM Joe Mays	5.00
EM Eric Milton	5.00
MM Matt Morris	5.00
HN Hideo Nomo	50.00
JP Jorge Posada	10.00
MR Manny Ramirez	12.00
MR Mariano Rivera	10.00
AR Alex Rodriguez	15.00
IR Ivan Rodriguez	10.00
KS Kazuhiro Sasaki	5.00
CS Curt Schilling	10.00
BS Ben Sheets	8.00
SS Sammy Sosa	20.00
IS Ichiro Suzuki	40.00
MS Mike Sweeney	5.00
FT Frank Thomas	10.00
GV Greg Vaughn	5.00
JV Jose Vidro	5.00
DW David Wells	5.00
MY Masato Yoshii	5.00

Twizzlers

Specially marked packages of Twizzlers candy contained one of 10 cards in a set comprised of portrait and action cards of each of five athletes. Only a single baseball player was included in the set and listed here. Fronts are bordered in white with vignetted photos. Blue-bordered backs have a few sentences about the player along with Twizzlers and UD logos.

	NM/M
3 Nomar Garciaparra/ Action	2.00
4 Nomar Garciaparra/ Portrait	2.00

2003 Upper Deck

	NM/M
Complete Set (540):	75.00
Common Player:	.15
Common RC (501-529):	.50
Series 1 or 2 Pack (8):	2.50
Series 1 or 2 Box (24):	45.00
1 John Lackey	.15
2 Alex Cintron	.15
3 Jose Leon	.15
4 Bobby Hill	.15
5 Brandon Larson	.15
6 Raul Gonzalez	.15
7 Ben Broussard	.15
8 Earl Snyder	.15
9 Ramon Santiago	.15
10 Jason Lane	.15
11 Keith Ginter	.15
12 Kirk Saarloos	.15
13 Juan Brito	.15
14 Runelvys Hernandez	.15
15 Shawn Sedlacek	.15
16 Jayson Durocher	.15
17 Kevin Frederick	.15
18 Zach Day	.15
19 Marco Scutaro (#96 in error)	.15
20 Marcus Thames	.15
21 Esteban German	.15
22 Brett Myers	.15
23 Oliver Perez	.25
24 Dennis Tankersley	.15
25 Julius Matos	.15
26 Jake Peavy	.15
27 Eric Cyr	.15
28 Mike Crudale	.15
29 Josh Pearce	.15
30 Carl Crawford	.50
31 Tim Salmon	.15
32 Troy Glaus	.50
33 Adam Kennedy	.15
34 David Eckstein	.15
35 Bengie Molina	.15
36 Jarrod Washburn	.15
37 Ramon Ortiz	.15
38 Eric Chavez	.40
39 Miguel Tejada	.50
40 Adam Piatt	.15
41 Jermaine Dye	.15
42 Olmedo Saenz	.15
43 Tim Hudson	.25
44 Barry Zito	.25
45 Billy Koch	.15
46 Shannon Stewart	.15
47 Kelvim Escobar	.15
48 Jose Cruz Jr.	.15
49 Vernon Wells	.15
50 Roy Halladay	.15
51 Esteban Loaiza	.15
52 Eric Hinske	.15
53 Steve Cox	.15
54 Brent Abernathy	.15
55 Ben Grieve	.15
56 Aubrey Huff	.15
57 Jared Sandberg	.15
58 Paul Wilson	.15
59 Tanyon Sturtze	.15
60 Jim Thome	.60
61 Omar Vizquel	.25
62 C.C. Sabathia	.15
63 Chris Magruder	.15
64 Ricky Gutierrez	.15
65 Einar Diaz	.15
66 Danys Baez	.15
67 Ichiro Suzuki	2.00
68 Ruben Sierra	.15
69 Carlos Guillen	.15

#	Player	Price		#	Player	Price		#	Player	Price		#	Player	Price
70	Mark McLemore	.15		188	Cesar Izturis	.15		306	Karim Garcia	.15		424	Miguel Batista	.15
71	Dan Wilson	.15		189	Dave Roberts	.15		307	Cliff Lee	.15		425	Paul LoDuca	.15
72	Jamie Moyer	.15		190	Eric Gagne	.40		308	Jeff Cirillo	.15		426	Kevin Brown	.25
73	Joel Pineiro	.15		191	Kazuhisa Ishii	.15		309	John Olerud	.15		427	Hideo Nomo	.40
74	Edgar Martinez	.25		192	Adrian Beltre	.25		310	Kazuhiro Sasaki	.15		428	Fred McGriff	.15
75	Tony Batista	.15		193	Vladimir Guerrero	.75		311	Freddy Garcia	.15		429	Joe Thurston	.15
76	Jay Gibbons	.15		194	Tony Armas Jr.	.15		312	Bret Boone	.25		430	Odalis Perez	.15
77	Chris Singleton	.15		195	Bartolo Colon	.15		313	Mike Cameron	.15		431	Darren Dreifort	.15
78	Melvin Mora	.15		196	Troy O'Leary	.15		314	Ben Davis	.15		432	Todd Hundley	.15
79	Geronimo Gil	.15		197	Tomokazu Ohka	.15		315	Randy Winn	.15		433	Dave Roberts	.15
80	Rodrigo Lopez	.15		198	Brad Wilkerson	.15		316	Gary Matthews Jr.	.15		434	Jose Vidro	.15
81	Jorge Julio	.15		199	Orlando Cabrera	.15		317	Jeff Conine	.15		435	Javier Vazquez	.15
82	Rafael Palmeiro	.50		200	Barry Bonds	2.00		318	Sidney Ponson	.15		436	Michael Barrett	.15
83	Juan Gonzalez	.50		201	David Bell	.15		319	Jerry Hairston	.15		437	Fernando Tatis	.15
84	Mike Young	.15		202	Tsuyoshi Shinjo	.15		320	David Segui	.15		438	Peter Bergeron	.15
85	Hideki Irabu	.15		203	Benito Santiago	.15		321	Scott Erickson	.15		439	Endy Chavez	.15
86	Chan Ho Park	.15		204	Livan Hernandez	.15		322	Marty Cordova	.15		440	Orlando Hernandez	.15
87	Kevin Mench	.15		205	Jason Schmidt	.40		323	Hank Blalock	.50		441	Marvin Bernard	.15
88	Doug Davis	.15		206	Kirk Reuter	.15		324	Herbert Perry	.15		442	Rich Aurilia	.15
89	Pedro Martinez	.75		207	Ramon E. Martinez	.15		325	Alex Rodriguez	2.00		443	Pedro Feliz	.15
90	Shea Hillenbrand	.15		208	Mike Lowell	.25		326	Carl Everett	.15		444	Robb Nen	.15
91	Derek Lowe	.15		209	Luis Castillo	.15		327	Einar Diaz	.15		445	Ray Durham	.15
92	Jason Varitek	.25		210	Derrek Lee	.25		328	Ugueth Urbina	.15		446	Marquis Grissom	.15
93	Tony Clark	.15		211	Andy Fox	.15		329	Mark Teixeira	.40		447	Damian Moss	.15
94	John Burkett	.15		212	Eric Owens	.15		330	Manny Ramirez	.75		448	Edgardo Alfonzo	.15
95	Frank Castillo	.15		213	Charles Johnson	.15		331	Johnny Damon	.50		449	Juan Pierre	.15
96	Nomar Garciaparra	2.00		214	Brad Penny	.15		332	Trot Nixon	.15		450	Braden Looper	.15
97	Rickey Henderson	.40		215	A.J. Burnett	.15		333	Tim Wakefield	.15		451	Alex Gonzalez	.15
98	Mike Sweeney	.15		216	Edgardo Alfonzo	.15		334	Casey Fossum	.15		452	Justin Wayne	.15
99	Carlos Febles	.15		217	Roberto Alomar	.50		335	Todd Walker	.15		453	Josh Beckett	.25
100	Mark Quinn	.15		218	Rey Ordonez	.15		336	Jeremy Giambi	.15		454	Juan Encarnacion	.15
101	Raul Ibanez	.15		219	Al Leiter	.15		337	Bill Mueller	.15		455	Ivan Rodriguez	.50
102	A.J. Hinch	.15		220	Roger Cedeno	.15		338	Ramiro Mendoza	.15		456	Todd Hollandsworth	.15
103	Paul Byrd	.15		221	Timoniel Perez	.15		339	Carlos Beltran	.50		457	Cliff Floyd	.15
104	Chuck Knoblauch	.15		222	Jeromy Burnitz	.15		340	Jason Grimsley	.15		458	Rey Sanchez	.15
105	Dmitri Young	.15		223	Pedro Astacio	.15		341	Brent Mayne	.15		459	Mike Piazza	1.50
106	Randall Simon	.15		224	Joe McEwing	.15		342	Angel Berroa	.15		460	Mo Vaughn	.15
107	Brandon Inge	.15		225	Ryan Klesko	.15		343	Albie Lopez	.15		461	Armando Benitez	.15
108	Damion Easley	.15		226	Ramon Vazquez	.15		344	Michael Tucker	.15		462	Tsuyoshi Shinjo	.15
109	Carlos Pena	.15		227	Mark Kotsay	.15		345	Bobby Higginson	.15		463	Tom Glavine	.40
110	George Lombard	.15		228	Bubba Trammell	.15		346	Shane Halter	.15		464	David Cone	.15
111	Juan Acevedo	.15		229	Wiki Gonzalez	.15		347	Jeremy Bonderman	2.00		465	Phil Nevin	.15
112	Torii Hunter	.25		230	Trevor Hoffman	.15		348	Eric Munson	.15		466	Sean Burroughs	.15
113	Doug Mientkiewicz	.15		231	Ron Gant	.15		349	Andy Van Hekken	.15		467	Jake Peavy	.15
114	David Ortiz	.50		232	Bobby Abreu	.25		350	Matt Anderson	.15		468	Brian Lawrence	.15
115	Eric Milton	.15		233	Marlon Anderson	.15		351	Jacque Jones	.15		469	Mark Loretta	.15
116	Eddie Guardado	.15		234	Jeremy Giambi	.15		352	A.J. Pierzynski	.15		470	Dennis Tankersley	.15
117	Cristian Guzman	.15		235	Jimmy Rollins	.25		353	Joe Mays	.15		471	Jesse Orosco	.15
118	Corey Koskie	.15		236	Mike Lieberthal	.15		354	Brad Radke	.15		472	Jim Thome	.75
119	Magglio Ordonez	.25		237	Vicente Padilla	.15		355	Dustan Mohr	.15		473	Kevin Millwood	.40
120	Mark Buehrle	.15		238	Randy Wolf	.15		356	Bobby Kielty	.15		474	David Bell	.15
121	Todd Ritchie	.15		239	Pokey Reese	.15		357	Michael Cuddyer	.15		475	Pat Burrell	.40
122	Jose Valentin	.15		240	Brian Giles	.25		358	Luis Rivas	.15		476	Brandon Duckworth	.15
123	Paul Konerko	.25		241	Jack Wilson	.15		359	Frank Thomas	.75		477	Jose Mesa	.15
124	Carlos Lee	.15		242	Mike Williams	.15		360	Joe Borchard	.15		478	Marlon Byrd	.15
125	Jon Garland	.15		243	Kip Wells	.15		361	D'Angelo Jimenez	.15		479	Reggie Sanders	.15
126	Jason Giambi	.40		244	Robert Mackowiak	.15		362	Bartolo Colon	.25		480	Jason Kendall	.25
127	Derek Jeter	2.00		245	Craig Wilson	.15		363	Joe Crede	.15		481	Aramis Ramirez	.40
128	Roger Clemens	1.50		246	Adam Dunn	.60		364	Miguel Olivo	.15		482	Kris Benson	.15
129	Raul Mondesi	.15		247	Sean Casey	.25		365	Billy Koch	.15		483	Matt Stairs	.15
130	Jorge Posada	.25		248	Todd Walker	.15		366	Bernie Williams	.50		484	Kevin Young	.15
131	Rondell White	.15		249	Corky Miller	.15		367	Nick Johnson	.15		485	Kenny Lofton	.25
132	Robin Ventura	.25		250	Ryan Dempster	.15		368	Andy Pettitte	.40		486	Austin Kearns	.40
133	Mike Mussina	.50		251	Reggie Taylor	.15		369	Mariano Rivera	.15		487	Barry Larkin	.25
134	Jeff Bagwell	.50		252	Aaron Boone	.15		370	Alfonso Soriano	.75		488	Jason LaRue	.15
135	Craig Biggio	.25		253	Larry Walker	.30		371	David Wells	.15		489	Ken Griffey Jr.	1.25
136	Morgan Ensberg	.15		254	Jose Ortiz	.15		372	Drew Henson	.15		490	Danny Graves	.15
137	Richard Hidalgo	.15		255	Todd Zeile	.15		373	Juan Rivera	.15		491	Russell Branyan	.15
138	Brad Ausmus	.15		256	Bobby Estalella	.15		374	Steve Karsay	.15		492	Reggie Taylor	.15
139	Roy Oswalt	.25		257	Juan Pierre	.15		375	Jeff Kent	.25		493	Jimmy Haynes	.15
140	Carlos Hernandez	.15		258	Terry Shumpert	.15		376	Lance Berkman	.25		494	Charles Johnson	.15
141	Shane Reynolds	.15		259	Mike Hampton	.15		377	Octavio Dotel	.15		495	Todd Helton	.75
142	Gary Sheffield	.25		260	Denny Stark	.15		378	Julio Lugo	.15		496	Juan Uribe	.15
143	Andruw Jones	.50		261	Shawn Green	.25		379	Jason Lane	.15		497	Preston Wilson	.15
144	Tom Glavine	.40		262	Derek Lowe	.15		380	Wade Miller	.15		498	Chris Stynes	.15
145	Rafael Furcal	.25		263	Barry Bonds	1.00		381	Billy Wagner	.15		499	Jason Jennings	.15
146	Javy Lopez	.25		264	Mike Cameron	.15		382	Brad Ausmus	.15		500	Jay Payton	.15
147	Vinny Castilla	.15		265	Luis Castillo	.15		383	Mike Hampton	.15		501	Hideki Matsui RC	5.00
148	Marcus Giles	.15		266	Vladimir Guerrero	.40		384	Chipper Jones	.75		502	Jose Contreras RC	2.00
149	Kevin Millwood	.15		267	Jason Giambi	.25		385	John Smoltz	.25		503	Brandon Webb RC	.50
150	Jason Marquis	.15		268	Eric Gagne	.25		386	Greg Maddux	1.25		504	Robby Hammock RC	.50
151	Ruben Quevedo	.15		269	Magglio Ordonez	.15		387	Javy Lopez	.25		505	Matt Kata RC	.50
152	Ben Sheets	.25		270	Jim Thome	.40		388	Robert Fick	.15		506	Tim Olson RC	.50
153	Geoff Jenkins	.15		271	Garret Anderson	.40		389	Mark DeRosa	.15		507	Michael Hessman RC	.50
154	Jose Hernandez	.15		272	Tony Percival	.15		390	Russ Ortiz	.15		508	Jon Leicester RC	.50
155	Glendon Rusch	.15		273	Brad Fullmer	.15		391	Julio Franco	.15		509	Todd Wellemeyer RC	.50
156	Jeffrey Hammonds	.15		274	Scott Spezio	.15		392	Richie Sexson	.15		510	David Sanders RC	.50
157	Alex Sanchez	.15		275	Darin Erstad	.40		393	Eric Young	.15		511	Josh Stewart RC	.50
158	Jim Edmonds	.25		276	Francisco Rodriguez	.15		394	Robert Machado	.15		512	Luis Ayala RC	.50
159	Tino Martinez	.25		277	Kevin Appier	.15		395	Mike DeJean	.15		513	Clint Barmes RC	2.00
160	Albert Pujols	1.50		278	Shawn Wooten	.15		396	Todd Ritchie	.15		514	Josh Willingham RC	.50
161	Eli Marrero	.15		279	Eric Owens	.15		397	Royce Clayton	.15		515	Alejandro Machado RC	.50
162	Woody Williams	.15		280	Scott Hatteberg	.15		398	Nick Neugebauer	.15		516	Felix Sanchez RC	.50
163	Fernando Vina	.15		281	Terrence Long	.15		399	J.D. Drew	.25		517	Willie Eyre RC	.50
164	Jason Isringhausen	.15		282	Mark Mulder	.25		400	Edgar Renteria	.25		518	Brent Hoard RC	.50
165	Jason Simontacchi	.15		283	Ramon Hernandez	.15		401	Scott Rolen	.75		519	Lew Ford RC	1.50
166	Kerry Robinson	.15		284	Ted Lilly	.15		402	Matt Morris	.25		520	Terrmel Sledge RC	.50
167	Sammy Sosa	1.25		285	Erubiel Durazo	.15		403	Garrett Stephenson	.15		521	Jeremy Griffiths	.15
168	Juan Cruz	.15		286	Mark Ellis	.15		404	Eduardo Perez	.15		522	Phil Seibel RC	.50
169	Fred McGriff	.25		287	Carlos Delgado	.50		405	Mike Matheny	.15		523	Craig Brazell RC	.50
170	Antonio Alfonseca	.15		288	Orlando Hudson	.15		406	Miguel Cairo	.15		524	Prentice Redman RC	.50
171	Jon Lieber	.15		289	Chris Woodward	.15		407	Brett Tomko	.15		525	Jeff Duncan RC	.50
172	Mark Prior	.50		290	Mark Hendrickson	.15		408	Bobby Hill	.15		526	Shane Bazzell RC	.50
173	Moises Alou	.25		291	Josh Phelps	.15		409	Troy O'Leary	.15		527	Bernie Castro RC	.50
174	Matt Clement	.15		292	Ken Huckaby	.15		410	Corey Patterson	.40		528	Rett Johnson RC	.50
175	Mark Bellhorn	.15		293	Justin Miller	.15		411	Kerry Wood	.75		529	Bobby Madritsch RC	3.00
176	Randy Johnson	.75		294	Travis Lee	.15		412	Eric Karros	.15		530	Rocco Baldelli	.50
177	Luis Gonzalez	.25		295	Jorge Sosa	.15		413	Hee Seop Choi	.15		531	Alex Rodriguez	1.00
178	Tony Womack	.15		296	Joe Kennedy	.15		414	Alex Gonzalez	.15		532	Eric Chavez	.25
179	Mark Grace	.30		297	Carl Crawford	.15		415	Matt Clement	.15		533	Miguel Tejada	.75
180	Junior Spivey	.15		298	Toby Hall	.15		416	Mark Grudzielanek	.15		534	Ichiro Suzuki	.75
181	Byung-Hyun Kim	.15		299	Rey Ordonez	.15		417	Curt Schilling	.50		535	Sammy Sosa	.75
182	Danny Bautista	.15		300	Brandon Phillips	.15		418	Steve Finley	.15		536	Barry Zito	.25
183	Brian Anderson	.15		301	Matt Lawton	.15		419	Craig Counsell	.15		537	Darin Erstad	.15
184	Shawn Green	.25		302	Ellis Burks	.15		420	Matt Williams	.15		538	Alfonso Soriano	.50
185	Brian Jordan	.15		303	Bill Selby	.15		421	Quinton McCracken	.15		539	Troy Glaus	.25
186	Eric Karros	.15		304	Travis Hafner	.15		422	Chad Moeller	.15		540	Nomar Garciaparra	.75
187	Andy Ashby	.15		305	Milton Bradley	.15		423	Lyle Overbay	.15				

Gold

Gold (541-600): 2-3X
One gold set per hobby case.

AL All-Star Swatch

		NM/M
Common Player:		5.00
Inserted 1:144 Retail		
MC	Mike Cameron	5.00
RD	Ray Durham	5.00
CE	Carl Everett	5.00
CF	Chuck Finley	5.00
TF	Travis Fryman	5.00
JG	Juan Gonzalez	8.00
JM	Joe Mays	8.00
MO	Magglio Ordonez	8.00
AP	Andy Pettitte	8.00
JP	Jorge Posada	8.00
MR	Mariano Rivera	10.00
AS	Aaron Sele	5.00
MS	Mike Sweeney	5.00

Big League Breakdown

		NM/M
Complete Set (15):		20.00
Common Player:		.50
Inserted 1:8		
BL1	Troy Glaus	.75
BL2	Miguel Tejada	.75
BL3	Chipper Jones	1.50
BL4	Torii Hunter	.15
BL5	Nomar Garciaparra	3.00
BL6	Sammy Sosa	2.50
BL7	Todd Helton	1.00
BL8	Lance Berkman	.75
BL9	Shawn Green	1.50
BL10	Vladimir Guerrero	1.50
BL11	Jason Giambi	.15
BL12	Derek Jeter	4.00
BL13	Barry Bonds	4.00
BL14	Ichiro Suzuki	3.00
BL15	Alex Rodriguez	4.00

Game Jersey Autograph

		NM/M
Golds:		1.5-2X
Production 25 or 75		
RC	Roger Clemens/350	100.00
JG	Jason Giambi/350	40.00
KG	Ken Griffey Jr./350	110.00
MM	Mark McGwire/150	350.00
CR	Cal Ripken Jr/350	140.00
HM	Hideki Matsui/350	5.00
JC	Jose Contreras RC	2.00
SS	Sammy Sosa/150	140.00

Game Swatches Hobby

		NM/M
Common Player:		5.00
Inserted 1:72		
SB	Sean Burroughs/SP	8.00
CD	Carlos Delgado/SP	8.00
GM	Greg Maddux	15.00
MM	Mike Mussina	10.00
MO	Magglio Ordonez	5.00
CP	Carlos Pena	5.00
MP	Mike Piazza/SP	15.00
AR	Alex Rodriguez	15.00
CC	C.C. Sabathia	10.00
CS	Curt Schilling/100	10.00
SS	Sammy Sosa	10.00
BW	Bernie Williams	10.00

Game Swatches Retail

		NM/M
Common Player:		5.00
Inserted 1:72		
RC	Roger Clemens	15.00
JD	J.D. Drew	5.00

AD	Adam Dunn	8.00
JE	Jim Edmonds	8.00
DE	Darin Erstad	8.00
JG	Jason Giambi	8.00
KG	Ken Griffey Jr.	12.00
TH	Tim Hudson	6.00
RJ	Randy Johnson	6.00
JK	Jeff Kent	5.00
EM	Edgar Martinez	6.00
IR	Ivan Rodriguez	6.00
FT	Frank Thomas	8.00

Leading Swatches

		NM/M
Common Player:		4.00
Inserted 1:24		
Golds:		1-2X
Production 100 Sets		
BA	Bobby Abreu	6.00
GA	Garret Anderson	6.00
JB	Jeff Bagwell	6.00
JB1	Jeff Bagwell	6.00
TB	Tony Batista	4.00
AB	Adrian Beltre	4.00
LB	Lance Berkman	4.00
PB	Pat Burrell	6.00
PB1	Pat Burrell	6.00
EC	Eric Chavez	4.00
RC	Roger Clemens	10.00
RC1	Roger Clemens	10.00
CD	Carlos Delgado	4.00
JD	J.D. Drew	4.00
AD	Adam Dunn	8.00
AD1	Adam Dunn	8.00
JE	Jim Edmonds	4.00
JG	Jason Giambi	6.00
JG1	Jason Giambi	6.00
BG	Brian Giles	4.00
TG	Troy Glaus	4.00
GO	Juan Gonzalez	6.00
LG	Luis Gonzalez	4.00
SG	Shawn Green	4.00
SG1	Shawn Green	4.00
KG	Ken Griffey Jr.	12.00
KG1	Ken Griffey Jr.	12.00
VG	Vladimir Guerrero	8.00
THe	Todd Helton	6.00
THu	Tim Hudson	4.00
TH1	Tim Hudson	4.00
KI	Kazuhisa Ishii	4.00
RJ	Randy Johnson	8.00
RJ1	Randy Johnson	8.00
AJ	Andruw Jones	6.00
AJ1	Andruw Jones	6.00
CJ	Chipper Jones	8.00
KE	Jason Kendall	4.00
JL	Javy Lopez	4.00
GM	Greg Maddux	10.00
GM1	Greg Maddux	10.00
PM	Pedro J. Martinez	8.00
HM	Hideki Matsui	40.00
HM1	Hideki Matsui	50.00
HN	Hideo Nomo	8.00
RO	Roy Oswalt	8.00
RO1	Roy Oswalt	4.00
RP	Rafael Palmeiro	6.00
RP1	Rafael Palmeiro	6.00
CP	Corey Patterson	4.00
JP	Jay Payton	4.00
TP	Troy Percival	4.00
AP	Andy Pettitte	4.00
MP	Mike Piazza	10.00
MP1	Mike Piazza	10.00
MR	Manny Ramirez	8.00
AR	Alex Rodriguez	10.00
AR1	Alex Rodriguez	10.00
IR	Ivan Rodriguez	6.00
SR	Scott Rolen	6.00
KS	Kazuhiro Sasaki	4.00
CS	Curt Schilling	4.00
AS	Aaron Sele	4.00
JS	J.T. Snow	4.00
AS	Alfonso Soriano	8.00
AS1	Alfonso Soriano	8.00
SS	Sammy Sosa	12.00
SS1	Sammy Sosa	12.00
MS	Mike Stanton	4.00
IS	Ichiro Suzuki	25.00
IS1	Ichiro Suzuki	25.00
MS	Mike Sweeney	6.00
MT	Miguel Tejada	6.00
MT1	Miguel Tejada	6.00
JT	Jim Thome	8.00
JT1	Jim Thome	8.00
OV	Omar Vizquel	4.00
LW	Larry Walker	4.00
BW	Bernie Williams	6.00
BW1	Bernie Williams	6.00
KW	Kerry Wood	6.00
BZ	Barry Zito	6.00

Lineup Time Jerseys

	NM/M
Common Player:	6.00

Inserted 1:96
RC	Roger Clemens/SP	20.00
CD	Carlos Delgado	8.00
JD	J.D. Drew	6.00
SG	Shawn Green	8.00
TH	Todd Helton	8.00
RJ	Randy Johnson/SP	15.00
GM	Greg Maddux	10.00
IS	Ichiro Suzuki	40.00
JT	Jim Thome	10.00
BW	Bernie Williams	10.00

Magical Performances

NM/M
Common Player: 8.00
Inserted 1:96
Golds: 1-2X
Production 50 Sets

MP1	Hideki Matsui	20.00
MP2	Ken Griffey Jr.	15.00
MP3	Ichiro Suzuki	15.00
MP4	Ken Griffey Jr.	15.00
MP5	Hideo Nomo	8.00
MP6	Mickey Mantle	40.00
MP7	Ken Griffey Jr.	15.00
MP8	Barry Bonds	20.00
MP9	Mickey Mantle	40.00
MP10	Tom Seaver	8.00
MP11	Mike Piazza	15.00
MP12	Roger Clemens	12.00
MP13	Nolan Ryan	30.00
MP14	Nomar Garciaparra	15.00
MP15	Ernie Banks	15.00
MP16	Stan Musial	25.00
MP17	Mickey Mantle	40.00
MP18	Nolan Ryan	30.00
MP19	Nolan Ryan	30.00
MP20	Mickey Mantle	40.00
MP21	Ichiro Suzuki	15.00
MP22	Nolan Ryan	30.00
MP23	Tom Seaver	8.00
MP24	Ken Griffey Jr.	15.00
MP25	Hideo Nomo	8.00
MP26	Ken Griffey Jr.	15.00
MP27	Mark McGwire	30.00
MP28	Barry Bonds	20.00
MP29	Alex Rodriguez	20.00
MP30	Nolan Ryan	30.00
MP31	Mark McGwire	30.00
MP32	Nolan Ryan	30.00
MP33	Sammy Sosa	15.00
MP34	Ichiro Suzuki	15.00
MP35	Barry Bonds	20.00
MP36	Derek Jeter	20.00
MP37	Roger Clemens	15.00
MP38	Jason Giambi	8.00
MP39	Mickey Mantle	40.00
MP40	Ted Williams	40.00
MP41	Ted Williams	40.00
MP42	Ted Williams	40.00

Mark of Greatness

NM/M
400 Total cards produced

MoG	Mark McGwire	350.00
MoG	Mark McGwire/ Silver/70	400.00

Masters with the Leather

NM/M
Complete Set (12): 20.00
Common Player: .75
Inserted 1:12

L1	Darin Erstad	.75
L2	Andruw Jones	1.50
L3	Greg Maddux	3.00
L4	Nomar Garciaparra	3.00
L5	Torii Hunter	1.00
L6	Roberto Alomar	1.00
L7	Derek Jeter	5.00
L8	Eric Chavez	1.00
L9	Ichiro Suzuki	3.00
L10	Jim Edmonds	1.00
L11	Scott Rolen	1.50
L12	Alex Rodriguez	4.00

Matsui Mania

Complete Set (18):
Common Player:

Mid-Summer Stars

MID-SUMMER STARS SWATCHES

NM/M
Common Player: 5.00
Inserted 1:72

RC	Roger Clemens	12.00
CD	Carlos Delgado	8.00
JE	Jim Edmonds	8.00
DE	Darin Erstad	8.00
FG	Freddy Garcia	5.00
TG	Tom Glavine	8.00
JG	Juan Gonzalez	8.00
SG	Shawn Green/SP	8.00
RJ	Randy Johnson	10.00
AJ	Andruw Jones	6.00
EM	Edgar Martinez	10.00
HN	Hideo Nomo	20.00
MP	Mike Piazza	15.00
MR	Manny Ramirez	8.00
AR	Alex Rodriguez	15.00
KS	Kazuhiro Sasaki	10.00
CS	Curt Schilling	10.00
SS	Sammy Sosa	15.00
IS	Ichiro Suzuki/SP	40.00
FT	Frank Thomas	8.00
RV	Robin Ventura	8.00
DW	David Wells	5.00
BZ	Barry Zito	8.00

National Pride

NM/M
Common Player: 3.00
Inserted 1:24

AA	Abe Alvarez	3.00
MA	Michael Aubrey	15.00
KB	Kyle Bakker	3.00
SB	Sean Burroughs	5.00
CC	Chad Cordero	3.00
SC	Shane Costa	3.00
RF	Robert Fick	3.00
SF	Sam Fuld	3.00
AH	Aaron Hill	8.00
BH	Bobby Hill	3.00
BH1	Bobby Hill	3.00
AJ	A.J. Hinch	3.00
PH	Philip Humber	3.00
CJ	Conor Jackson	3.00
JJe	Jason Jennings	3.00
GJ	Grant Johnson	3.00
JJ	Jacque Jones	8.00
JJ1	Jacque Jones	8.00
MJ	Mark Jurich	3.00
AK	Austin Kearns	12.00
AK1	Austin Kearns	12.00
WL	Wes Littleton	3.00
EM	Eric Milton	5.00
EM1	Eric Milton	5.00
RO	Roy Oswalt	6.00
RO1	Roy Oswalt	6.00
EP	Eric Patterson	3.00
DP	Dustin Pedroia	3.00
LP	Landon Powell	3.00
MP	Mark Prior	15.00
MP1	Mark Prior	15.00
CQ	Carlos Quentin	3.00
KSa	Kirk Saarloos	3.00
KSa1	Kirk Saarloos	3.00
CS	Clint Sammons	5.00
KSl	Kyle Sleeth	5.00
HS	Huston Street	5.00
BS	Brad Sullivan	3.00
BS1	Brad Sullivan	3.00
RW	Rickie Weeks	15.00
RW1	Rickie Weeks	15.00
BZ	Bob Zimmermann	3.00

NL All-Star Swatch

NM/M
Common Player: 5.00
Inserted 1:72

SC	Sean Casey	5.00
CF	Cliff Floyd	5.00
TGl	Tom Glavine	8.00
TGw	Tony Gwynn	12.00
MH	Mike Hampton	5.00
TH	Trevor Hoffman	5.00
RK	Ryan Klesko	5.00
AL	Al Leiter	5.00
FM	Fred McGriff	5.00
MM	Matt Morris	8.00
CS	Curt Schilling	8.00
JV	Jose Vidro	5.00

Patch Logo

NM/M
Quantity produced listed

JB	Jeff Bagwell/41	60.00
KG	Ken Griffey Jr./50	100.00
TH	Todd Helton/41	50.00
KI	Kazuhisa Ishii/54	40.00
RJ	Randy Johnson/50	75.00
CJ	Chipper Jones/52	80.00
GM	Greg Maddux/50	100.00
MP	Mike Piazza/61	120.00
SS	Sammy Sosa/60	100.00
FT	Frank Thomas/52	60.00
BW	Bernie Williams/42	40.00

Patch Number

NM/M
Quantity produced listed

JG	Jason Giambi/68	40.00
KG	Ken Griffey Jr./97	70.00
KI	Kazuhisa Ishii/63	40.00
RJ	Randy Johnson/90	75.00
MG	Mark McGwire/60	180.00
AR	Alex Rodriguez/56	90.00
SS	Sammy Sosa/100	20.00
FT	Frank Thomas/91	60.00
BW	Bernie Williams/66	50.00

Patch Stripes

NM/M
Quantity produced listed

JB	Jeff Bagwell/73	60.00
JG	Jason Giambi/66	40.00
KG	Ken Griffey Jr./63	75.00
KI	Kazuhisa Ishii/58	40.00
RJ	Randy Johnson/58	65.00
CJ	Chipper Jones/58	60.00
MG	Mark McGwire/63	180.00
AR	Alex Rodriguez/63	80.00
SS	Sammy Sosa/63	100.00
IS	Ichiro Suzuki/63	180.00
FT	Frank Thomas/58	60.00
BW	Bernie Williams/58	50.00

Piece of the Action

NM/M
Common Player: 5.00
Inserted 1:288
Cards are not serial numbered.
Print runs provided by Upper Deck.

BA	Bobby Abreu/125	5.00
GA	Garret Anderson/150	5.00
AB	Adrian Beltre/100	10.00
BB	Barry Bonds/125	30.00
KB	Kevin Brown/100	5.00
PB	Pat Burrell/150	8.00
DE	Darin Erstad/125	5.00
FG	Freddy Garcia/100	5.00
BG	Brian Giles/100	5.00
TG	Troy Glaus/150	6.00
JG	Juan Gonzalez/100	5.00
LG	Luis Gonzalez/100	5.00
SG	Shawn Green/175	5.00
VG	Vladimir Guerrero/50	15.00
THe	Todd Helton/100	10.00
THo	Trevor Hoffman/150	5.00
DJ	Derek Jeter/65	40.00
RJ	Randy Johnson/100	10.00
CJ	Chipper Jones/62	15.00
JK	Jason Kendall/100	5.00
KE	Jeff Kent/150	5.00
RK	Ryan Klesko/150	6.00
EM	Edgar Martinez/125	5.00
PM	Pedro Martinez/150	10.00
PN	Phil Nevin/75	5.00
HN	Hideo Nomo/100	20.00
RP	Rafael Palmeiro/150	10.00
Ara	Aramis Ramirez/100	8.00
MP	Mike Piazza/150	15.00
ARo	Alex Rodriguez/100	15.00
KS	Kazuhiro Sasaki/100	5.00
CS	Curt Schilling/100	10.00
RS	Richie Sexson/160	5.00
GS	Gary Sheffield/100	6.00
SS	Sammy Sosa/85	20.00
FT	Frank Thomas/150	8.00
JT	Jim Thome/125	10.00
JV	Jose Vidro/100	5.00
LW	Larry Walker/150	5.00
BW	Bernie Williams/125	6.00

Slammin' Sammy Tribute Jersey

NM/M
384 Total produced

SST	Sammy Sosa	175.00
SST	Sammy Sosa/ Gold/25	290.00
SST	Sammy Sosa/ Silver/66	240.00

Star-Spangled Swatches

STAR SPANGLED

NM/M
Common Player: 4.00
Inserted 1:72

MA	Michael Aubrey	8.00
KB	Kyle Bakker	8.00
CC	Chad Cordero	4.00
SC	Shane Costa	4.00
AH	Aaron Hill	4.00
PH	Philip Humber	6.00
CJ	Conor Jackson	8.00
GJ	Grant Johnson	4.00
EP	Eric Patterson	6.00
DP	Dustin Pedroia	6.00
LP	Landon Powell	6.00
CQ	Carlos Quentin	8.00
KS	Kyle Sleeth	6.00
HS	Huston Street	10.00
BS	Brad Sullivan	4.00
RW	Rickie Weeks	15.00

Superior Sluggers

NM/M
Complete Set (18): 30.00
Common Player: 1.00
Inserted 1:8

S1	Troy Glaus	1.00
S2	Chipper Jones	1.50
S3	Manny Ramirez	1.50
S4	Ken Griffey Jr.	2.50
S5	Jim Thome	1.50
S6	Todd Helton	1.00
S7	Lance Berkman	1.00
S8	Derek Jeter	3.00
S9	Vladimir Guerrero	1.50
S10	Mike Piazza	2.50
S11	Hideki Matsui	3.00
S12	Barry Bonds	4.00
S13	Mickey Mantle	5.00
S14	Alex Rodriguez	3.00
S15	Ted Williams	4.00
S16	Carlos Delgado	1.00
S17	Frank Thomas	1.00
S18	Adam Dunn	1.50

Super Patch Logos

Common Player:
Inserted 1:7,500
No Pricing

Super Patch Numbers

Common Player:
Inserted 1:7,500
No Pricing

Super Patch Stripes

Common Player:
Inserted 1:7,500
No Pricing

Superstar Scrapbooks

No pricing due to scarcity.
Production 24 Sets
Silvers: No Pricing
Production 6 Sets
Golds: No Pricing
Production One Set

Superstar Slam Jerseys

UD Superstar-Slam
THOMAS

NM/M
Common Player: 4.00
Inserted 1:48

JB	Jeff Bagwell	8.00
JG	Jason Giambi	6.00
JGo	Juan Gonzalez	6.00
LG	Luis Gonzalez	4.00
KG	Ken Griffey Jr.	15.00
CJ	Chipper Jones	10.00
MP	Mike Piazza	10.00
AR	Alex Rodriguez	15.00
SS	Sammy Sosa	15.00
FT	Frank Thomas	15.00

The Chase for 755

THE CHASE FOR 755

NM/M
Complete Set (15): 15.00
Common Player: .75
Inserted 1:8

C1	Troy Glaus	.75
C2	Andruw Jones	1.00
C3	Manny Ramirez	1.25
C4	Sammy Sosa	2.50
C5	Ken Griffey Jr.	3.00
C6	Adam Dunn	1.25
C7	Todd Helton	1.00
C8	Lance Berkman	.75
C9	Jeff Bagwell	1.00
C10	Shawn Green	.75
C11	Vladimir Guerrero	1.50
C12	Barry Bonds	4.00
C13	Alex Rodriguez	3.00
C14	Juan Gonzalez	.75
C15	Carlos Delgado	.75

Triple Game Jersey

NM/M
Quantity produced listed
Golds: 1.5-2X
Production 50, 25 or 10

ARZ	Randy Johnson, Curt Schilling, Luis Gonzalez/150	40.00
CIN	Ken Griffey Jr., Sean Casey, Adam Dunn/150	40.00
HOU	Jeff Bagwell, Lance Berkman, Craig Biggio/150	40.00
TEX	Rafael Palmeiro, Alex Rodriguez, Juan Gonzalez/150	40.00
ATL	Chipper Jones, Greg Maddux, Gary Sheffield/75	65.00
CHC	Sammy Sosa, Moises Alou, Kerry Wood/75	50.00
NYM	Mike Piazza, Roberto Alomar, Mo Vaughn/75	40.00
SEA	Ichiro Suzuki, Freddy Garcia, Bret Boone/75	80.00

500 HR Club

NM/M
Production 350 Cards

SS	Sammy Sosa/350	150.00
SS	Sammy Sosa/ Auto./21	2,300

2003 UD Authentics

UD AUTHENTICS — TED WILLIAMS

NM/M
Complete Set (130):
Common Player: .25
Common RK Hype (101-130): 4.00
Production 999
Pack (4): 10.00
Box (10 + Framed Auto.): 170.00

1	Pee Wee Reese	.25
2	Richie Ashburn	.25
3	Derek Jeter	2.50
4	Alex Rodriguez	2.00
5	Jose Vidro	.25
6	Miguel Tejada	.50
7	Nomar Garciaparra	2.00
8	Pat Burrell	.50
9	Albert Pujols	2.00
10	Jeff Bagwell	.75
11	Stan Musial	1.00
12	Mickey Mantle	3.00
13	J.D. Drew	.25
14	Ivan Rodriguez	.75
15	Joe Morgan	.25
16	Ted Williams	2.00
17	Travis Hafner	.25
18	Chipper Jones	1.50
19	Hideo Nomo	.50
20	Gary Sheffield	.50
21	Jacque Jones	.25
22	Alfonso Soriano	1.50
23	Roberto Alomar	.50
24	Jeff Kent	.40
25	Omar Vizquel	.40
26	Ernie Banks	1.00
27	Shawn Green	.50
28	Tim Hudson	.50
29	Jim Edmonds	.50
30	Brandon Larson	.25
31	Doug Mientkiewicz	.25
32	Darin Erstad	.50
33	Bobby Hill	.25
34	Todd Helton	.75
35	Kazuhisa Ishii	.25
36	Lance Berkman	.50
37	Eric Hinske	.25
38	Jason Kendall	.25
39	Bob Feller	.50
40	Luis Gonzalez	.40
41	Sammy Sosa	2.00
42	Mike Piazza	1.50
43	Roger Clemens	2.00
44	Jose Cruz Jr.	.25
45	Mark Prior	1.50
46	Mark Teixeira	.40
47	Phil Nevin	.25
48	Lyle Overbay	.25
49	Manny Ramirez	.75
50	Brian Giles	.40
51	Preston Wilson	.25
52	Jermaine Dye	.25
53	Troy Glaus	.50
54	Frank Thomas	.75
55	Jim Thome	.75
56	Barry Bonds	2.50
57	Carlos Delgado	.75
58	Jason Giambi	1.00
59	Joe Mays	.25
60	Andruw Jones	.75
61	Billy Williams	.25
62	Vladimir Guerrero	.75
63	Scott Rolen	.75
64	Juan Marichal	.25
65	Austin Kearns	.50
66	Kerry Wood	.75
67	Bret Boone	.25
68	Shea Hillenbrand	.25
69	Mike Sweeney	.25
70	Rocco Baldelli	.25
71	Ken Griffey Jr.	1.50
72	Cliff Floyd	.25
73	Greg Maddux	1.50
74	Mike Hampton	.25
75	Larry Walker	.40
76	Nolan Ryan	3.00
77	Rollie Fingers	.25
78	Mike Mussina	.75
79	Matt Morris	.25
80	Robin Roberts	.25
81	Barry Zito	.25
82	Curt Schilling	.50
83	Ken Harvey	.25
84	Troy Percival	.25
85	Tom Seaver	1.00
86	Mariano Rivera	.40
87	Raul Mondesi	.25
88	Adam Dunn	.50
89	Roy Oswalt	.25
90	Pedro J. Martinez	1.00
91	Andy Pettitte	.50
92	Tom Glavine	.50
93	Torii Hunter	.50
94	Joe Thurston	.25
95	Runelvys Hernandez	.25
96	Randy Johnson	1.00
97	Bernie Williams	.75
98	Ichiro Suzuki	1.50
99	C.C. Sabathia	.25
100	Bobby Abreu	.40
101	Jose Contreras RC	.50
102	Hideki Matsui RC	15.00
103	Chris Capuano RC	6.00
104	Willie Eyre RC	4.00
105	Lew Ford RC	6.00
106	Shane Bazzell RC	6.00
107	Guillermo Quiroz RC	6.00
108	Fernando Cabrera RC	4.00
109	Francisco Cruceta RC	4.00
110	Jhonny Peralta RC	4.00
111	Bobby Madritsch RC	8.00
112	Diegomar Markwell RC	4.00
113	Matt Bruback RC	4.00
114	Matt Kata RC	4.00
115	Rob Hammock RC	4.00
116	Brandon Webb RC	10.00
117	Jon Leicester RC	4.00
118	Josh Willingham RC	6.00
119	Prentice Redman RC	4.00
120	Jeff Duncan RC	4.00
121	Craig Brazell RC	6.00
122	Jeremy Griffiths RC	4.00
123	Phil Seibel RC	4.00
124	Luis Ayala RC	4.00
125	Miguel Ojeda RC	6.00
126	Jeremy Wedel RC	4.00
127	Josh Hall RC	6.00
128	Oscar Villarreal RC	4.00
129	Clint Barmes RC	8.00
130	Nook Logan RC	4.00

Rookie Hype Gold

Cards (101-130): 1-2X
Production 50

Cut Signatures

Common Player:

Framed Autograph

NM/M
Common Framed Autograph: 40.00
Inserted 1:Box

Lance Berkman/150	40.00
Lance Berkman/50	60.00
Hank Blalock/325	45.00
Hank Blalock/300	45.00
Hank Blalock/200	45.00
Hank Blalock/175	45.00
Pat Burrell/330	40.00
Pat Burrell/240	40.00
Pat Burrell/150	40.00
Gary Carter/225	50.00
Gary Carter/75	60.00
Jose Contreras/350	50.00
Jose Contreras/120	50.00
Carlton Fisk/250	50.00
Carlton Fisk/125	75.00
Carlton Fisk/70	80.00
Nomar Garciaparra/ 250	100.00
Nomar Garciaparra/ 150	100.00

Nomar Garciaparra/		
75		120.00
Jason Giambi/350		40.00
Jason Giambi/300		40.00
Jason Giambi/200		40.00
Jason Giambi/150		40.00
Jason Giambi/100		40.00
Jason Giambi/75		40.00
Bob Gibson/200		60.00
Bob Gibson/50		120.00
Bob Gibson/45		120.00
Troy Glaus/350		40.00
Troy Glaus/200		40.00
Troy Glaus/100		50.00
Tom Glavine/275		50.00
Tom Glavine/150		50.00
Tom Glavine/47		75.00
Ken Griffey Jr/325		90.00
Ken Griffey Jr./200		90.00
Ken Griffey Jr/75		100.00
Ken Griffey Jr./30		120.00
Vladimir Guerrero/		
150		60.00
Vladimir Guerrero/		
27		125.00
Drew Henson/350		40.00
Drew Henson/300		40.00
Drew Henson/250		40.00
Drew Henson/100		40.00
Chipper Jones/350		70.00
Chipper Jones/200		70.00
Chipper Jones/100		85.00
Austin Kearns/325		40.00
Austin Kearns/300		40.00
Austin Kearns/200		40.00
Austin Kearns/175		40.00
Austin Kearns/28		80.00
Hideki Matsui/75		300.00
Hideki Matsui/55		300.00
Mark Prior/300		60.00
Mark Prior/250		60.00
Mark Prior/175		60.00
Mark Prior/100		60.00
Cal Ripken Jr/125		175.00
Cal Ripken Jr./50		200.00
Phil Rizzuto/350		50.00
Phil Rizzuto/200		60.00
Phil Rizzuto/100		85.00
Scott Rolen/300		50.00
Scott Rolen/100		65.00
Scott Rolen/27		120.00
Nolan Ryan/150		125.00
Nolan Ryan/100		180.00
Nolan Ryan/50		200.00
Nolan Ryan/34		240.00
Tom Seaver/100		75.00
Tom Seaver/50		100.00
Tom Seaver/41		100.00
Ozzie Smith/150		85.00
Ozzie Smith/50		120.00
Duke Snider/150		60.00
Duke Snider/50		100.00
Ichiro Suzuki/75		300.00
Ichiro Suzuki/51		350.00
Mark Teixeira/325		60.00
Mark Teixeira/200		60.00
Mark Teixeira/175		60.00
Mark Teixeira/150		60.00

Star Quality

		NM/M
Common Player:		4.00

Production 350 unless noted.

Golds:		1-2X

Production 50, 25 or 10
No Pricing for #'d to 25 or less.

RA	Roberto Alomar	6.00
JB	Jeff Bagwell	8.00
JO	Josh Beckett	4.00
LB	Lance Berkman	5.00
RC	Roger Clemens	15.00
RC1	Roger Clemens	15.00
CD	Carlos Delgado	5.00
JD	J.D. Drew	4.00
AD	Adam Dunn	6.00
JG	Jason Giambi	6.00
TR	Troy Glaus	5.00
TG	Tom Glavine	4.00
SG	Shawn Green	4.00
KG	Ken Griffey Jr./250	12.00
VG	Vladimir Guerrero	8.00
TH	Todd Helton	6.00
EH	Eric Hinske	4.00
CJ	Chipper Jones	8.00
AK	Austin Kearns	4.00
JK	Jeff Kent	4.00
MM	Mickey Mantle/250	100.00
HM	Hideki Matsui/250	25.00
PM	Paul Molitor/250	8.00
MU	Mike Mussina	4.00
HN	Hideo Nomo	8.00
RO	Roy Oswalt	4.00
RP	Rafael Palmeiro	6.00
MP	Mark Prior	10.00
AP	Albert Pujols	20.00
AP1	Albert Pujols	20.00
CR	Cal Ripken Jr./250	25.00

NR	Nolan Ryan/130	50.00
TS	Tom Seaver	8.00
GS	Gary Sheffield	4.00
AS	Alfonso Soriano	10.00
SS	Sammy Sosa/250	12.00
CS	Casey Stengel	15.00
JT	Jim Thome	8.00
BW	Bernie Williams	4.00
TW	Ted Williams/250	65.00
KW	Kerry Wood	8.00

Threads of Time

		NM/M
Common Player:		4.00

Production 350, unless noted.

Golds:		1-2X

Production 50, 25 or 10
No pricing for #'d to 25 or less.

JB	Johnny Bench	10.00
GC	Gary Carter	4.00
RC	Roger Clemens	15.00
TC	Ty Cobb	100.00
DD	Don Drysdale	15.00
DE	Dennis Eckersley	4.00
RF	Rollie Fingers	4.00
LG	Lou Gehrig/250	140.00
JG	Jason Giambi/250	6.00
JU	Juan Gonzalez	4.00
KG	Ken Griffey Jr./250	12.00
VG	Vladimir Guerrero	6.00
RJ	Randy Johnson	8.00
CJ	Chipper Jones	8.00
HK	Harmon Killebrew	12.00
GM	Greg Maddux	8.00
MM	Mickey Mantle/250	100.00
RM	Roger Maris	40.00
PM	Pedro J. Martinez	8.00
DM	Don Mattingly	20.00
HN	Hideo Nomo	8.00
AP	Andy Pettitte	4.00
MP	Mike Piazza	10.00
AP	Albert Pujols	20.00
CR	Cal Ripken Jr.	25.00
FR	Frank Robinson	8.00
AR	Alex Rodriguez	12.00
IR	Ivan Rodriguez	5.00
NR	Nolan Ryan	30.00
RS	Ryne Sandberg	12.00
TS	Tom Seaver	8.00
OS	Ozzie Smith	10.00
SS	Sammy Sosa/250	12.00
IS	Ichiro Suzuki/250	30.00
FT	Frank Thomas	6.00
JT	Jim Thome	8.00
HW	Honus Wagner	75.00
TW	Ted Williams/250	65.00
MW	Maury Wills	4.00
DW	Dave Winfield/250	6.00

Gary Carter Hawaii Autograph

Participants in the card company's golf outing at the SCD Hawaii Trade Conference received this specially produced card of Gary Carter, long known for his refusal to sign cards except for specific charitable causes. The card has the Hawaii show logo on front, along with a gold-foil notation of his Hall of Fame election. Back has a statement of authenticity.

		NM/M
GC	Gary Carter	25.00

2003 Upper Deck Classic Portraits

		NM/M
Complete Set (232):		
Common Player:		.15
Common SP (101-145):		2.00
Inserted 1:4		
Common SP (145-190):		3.00
Production 2,003		
Common Royalty (191-232):		2.00
Production 1,200		
Pack (5):		3.00
Box (18 + Bust):		75.00
1	Ken Griffey Jr.	1.50
2	Randy Johnson	1.00
3	Rafael Furcal	.25

4	Omar Vizquel	.25
5	Shawn Green	.40
6	Roy Oswalt	.40
7	Hideo Nomo	.40
8	Jason Giambi	.40
9	Barry Bonds	2.50
10	Mike Piazza	1.50
11	Ichiro Suzuki	2.00
12	Carlos Delgado	.40
13	Preston Wilson	.15
14	Lance Berkman	.40
15	Magglio Ordonez	.25
16	Kerry Wood	.75
17	Ivan Rodriguez	.75
18	Chipper Jones	1.00
19	Adam Dunn	.75
20	C.C. Sabathia	.15
21	Mike MacDougal	.15
22	Torii Hunter	.40
23	Jim Thome	.75
24	Hank Blalock	.40
25	Johnny Damon	.50
26	Troy Glaus	.40
27	Manny Ramirez	.75
28	Mark Prior	1.00
29	Brent Mayne	.15
30	Derek Jeter	2.50
31	Tim Hudson	.25
32	Mike Cameron	.15
33	Mark Teixeira	.40
34	Shannon Stewart	.15
35	Tim Salmon	.25
36	Luis Gonzalez	.25
37	Jason Johnson	.15
38	Shea Hillenbrand	.15
39	Bartolo Colon	.25
40	Austin Kearns	.40
41	Vladimir Guerrero	1.00
42	Tom Glavine	.40
43	Andres Galarraga	.25
44	Kazuhiro Sasaki	.15
45	Juan Gonzalez	.75
46	Vernon Wells	.25
47	Jeff Bagwell	.75
48	Mike Sweeney	.15
49	Carlos Beltran	.25
50	Dave Roberts	.15
51	Todd Helton	.75
52	Carlos Pena	.15
53	Darin Erstad	.25
54	Gary Sheffield	.40
55	Lyle Overbay	.15
56	Sammy Sosa	1.50
57	Mike Mussina	.50
58	Matt Morris	.25
59	Roberto Alomar	.50
60	Larry Walker	.25
61	Jacque Jones	.15
62	Josh Beckett	.40
63	Richie Sexson	.25
64	Derek Lowe	.15
65	Pedro J. Martinez	1.00
66	Moises Alou	.25
67	Craig Biggio	.25
68	Curt Schilling	.75
69	Jesse Foppert	.15
70	Nomar Garciaparra	1.50
71	Barry Zito	.40
72	Alfonso Soriano	.75
73	Miguel Tejada	.50
74	Rafael Palmeiro	.50
75	Albert Pujols	2.00
76	Mariano Rivera	.25
77	Bobby Abreu	.25
78	Alex Rodriguez	2.00
79	Andruw Jones	.50
80	Frank Thomas	.75
81	Greg Maddux	1.50
82	Jim Edmonds	.40
83	Bernie Williams	.50
84	Roger Clemens	2.00
85	Eric Chavez	.25
86	Scott Rolen	1.00
87	Jorge Posada	.50
88	Bret Boone	.25
89	Ben Sheets	.25
90	John Olerud	.15
91	J.D. Drew	.25
92	Aaron Boone	.15
93	Corey Koskie	.15
94	Sean Casey	.25
95	Jose Cruz Jr.	.15
96	Pat Burrell	.40
97	Jose Guillen	.15
98	Mark Mulder	.25
99	Garret Anderson	.25
100	Kazuhisa Ishii	.15
101	Dave Matranga **RC**	2.00

102	Colin Porter **RC**	2.00
103	Jason Gilfillan **RC**	2.00
104	Carlos Mendez **RC**	2.00
105	Jason Shiell **RC**	2.00
106	Kevin Tolar **RC**	2.00
107	Terrmel Sledge **RC**	3.00
108	Craig Brazell **RC**	4.00
109	Ramon Castro **RC**	2.00
110	Tim Olson **RC**	3.00
111	Kevin Ohme **RC**	2.00
112	Pedro Liriano **RC**	2.00
113	Joe Borowski **RC**	2.00
114	Edgar Gonzalez **RC**	3.00
115	Joe Thurston **RC**	2.00
116	Bobby Hill	2.00
117	Michel Hernandez **RC**	2.00
118	Arnie Munoz **RC**	2.00
119	David Sanders **RC**	2.00
120	Willie Eyre **RC**	3.00
121	Brent Hoard **RC**	2.00
122	Lew Ford **RC**	4.00
123	Beau Kemp **RC**	2.00
124	Jonathan Pridie **RC**	2.00
125	Mike Ryan **RC**	2.00
126	Richard Fischer **RC**	2.00
127	Luis Ayala **RC**	2.00
128	Mike Neu **RC**	2.00
129	Joe Valentine **RC**	2.00
130	Nate Bland **RC**	2.00
131	Shane Bazzell **RC**	2.00
132	Jason Roach **RC**	2.00
133	Diegomar Markwell **RC**	2.00
134	Francisco Rosario **RC**	2.00
135	Guillermo Quiroz **RC**	4.00
136	Jerome Williams	2.00
137	Fernando Cabrera **RC**	2.00
138	Francisco Cruceta **RC**	2.00
139	Jhonny Peralta **RC**	4.00
140	Rett Johnson **RC**	2.00
141	Aaron Looper **RC**	2.00
142	Bobby Madritsch **RC**	6.00
143	Dan Haren	4.00
144	Jose Castillo	4.00
145	Chris Waters **RC**	3.00
146	Hideki Matsui **RC**	10.00
147	Jose Contreras **RC**	3.00
148	Felix Sanchez **RC**	3.00
149	Jon Leicester **RC**	3.00
150	Todd Wellemeyer **RC**	3.00
151	Matt Bruback **RC**	3.00
152	Chris Capuano **RC**	5.00
153	Oscar Villarreal **RC**	3.00
154	Matt Kata **RC**	3.00
155	Robby Hammock **RC**	3.00
156	Gerald Laird	3.00
157	Brandon Webb **RC**	6.00
158	Tommy Whiteman **RC**	3.00
159	Andrew Brown **RC**	3.00
160	Alfredo Gonzalez **RC**	3.00
161	Carlos Rivera	3.00
162	Rick Roberts	3.00
163	Dontrelle Willis	3.00
164	Josh Willingham **RC**	4.00
165	Prentice Redman **RC**	3.00
166	Jeff Duncan **RC**	3.00
167	Jose Reyes	3.00
168	Jeremy Griffiths	3.00
169	Phil Seibel **RC**	3.00
170	Heath Bell **RC**	3.00
171	Anthony Ferrari **RC**	3.00
172	Mike Nicolas **RC**	3.00
173	Cory Stewart **RC**	3.00
174	Miguel Ojeda **RC**	5.00
175	Rickie Weeks **RC**	10.00
176	Delmon Young **RC**	10.00
177	Tommy Phelps **RC**	3.00
178	Josh Hall **RC**	4.00
179	Ryan Cameron **RC**	3.00
180	Garrett Atkins	3.00
181	Clint Barmes **RC**	6.00
182	Michael Hessman **RC**	3.00
183	Chin-Hui Tsao	3.00
184	Rocco Baldelli	3.00
185	Bo Hart **RC**	3.00
186	Wilfredo Ledezma **RC**	3.00
187	Miguel Cabrera	5.00
188	Ian Ferguson **RC**	3.00
189	Micheal Nakamura **RC**	3.00
190	Alejandro Machado **RC**	3.00
191	Mickey Mantle	12.00
192	Ted Williams	10.00
193	Mark Prior	6.00
194	Stan Musial	6.00
195	Phil Rizzuto	4.00
196	Nolan Ryan	12.00
197	Tom Seaver	4.00
198	Robin Yount	5.00
199	Yogi Berra	3.00
200	Ernie Banks	8.00
201	Willie McCovey	3.00
202	Ralph Kiner	4.00
203	Ken Griffey Jr.	4.00
204	Sammy Sosa	5.00
205	Derek Jeter	8.00
206	Nomar Garciaparra	6.00
207	Alex Rodriguez	6.00
208	Ichiro Suzuki	4.00
209	Mike Piazza	4.00
210	Jackie Robinson	6.00
211	Roberto Clemente	8.00
212	Babe Ruth	12.00
213	Duke Snider	3.00
214	Greg Maddux	4.00
215	Juan Marichal	4.00
216	Joe Morgan	2.00
217	Rollie Fingers	2.00
218	Warren Spahn	4.00
219	Pee Wee Reese	2.00

220	Troy Glaus	2.00
221	Jason Giambi	2.00
222	Roger Clemens	6.00
223	Pedro J. Martinez	3.00
224	Chipper Jones	4.00
225	Randy Johnson	3.00
226	Jim Thome	3.00
227	Barry Bonds	8.00
228	Hideo Nomo	2.00
229	Whitey Ford	3.00
230	Bob Gibson	3.00
231	Alfonso Soriano	4.00
232	Richie Ashburn	3.00

Gold

No pricing due to scarcity.
Production 25 Sets

Bust Signature

		NM/M
Complete Set (17):		
Common Player:		
NG	Nomar Garciaparra	80.00
HM	Hideki Matsui	180.00

Classic Stitches Jersey

		NM/M
Common Player:		4.00

Production 299 Sets

Golds:		No Pricing

Production 25 Sets

JB	Jeff Bagwell	6.00
RB	Rocco Baldelli	4.00
HB	Hank Blalock	6.00
HC	Hee Seop Choi	4.00
RC	Roger Clemens	15.00
JD	J.D. Drew	6.00
AD	Adam Dunn	6.00
JE	Jim Edmonds	6.00
RF	Rafael Furcal	4.00
JG	Jason Giambi	6.00
TG	Troy Glaus	6.00
SG	Shawn Green	4.00
KG	Ken Griffey Jr.	10.00
VG	Vladimir Guerrero	8.00
TH	Torii Hunter	6.00
RJ	Randy Johnson	8.00
AJ	Andruw Jones	6.00
CJ	Chipper Jones	8.00
JK	Jeff Kent	4.00
ML	Mike Lowell	4.00
GM	Greg Maddux	10.00
PM	Pedro J. Martinez	8.00
HM	Hideki Matsui	40.00
MM	Matt Morris	6.00
HN	Hideo Nomo	6.00
MO	Magglio Ordonez	4.00
RO	Roy Oswalt	4.00
CP	Corey Patterson	6.00
AP	Andy Pettitte	6.00
MI	Mike Piazza	8.00
MP	Mark Prior	8.00
AL	Albert Pujols	15.00
AR	Alex Rodriguez	10.00
IR	Ivan Rodriguez	6.00
CS	Curt Schilling	6.00
GS	Gary Sheffield	6.00
AS	Alfonso Soriano	6.00
SS	Sammy Sosa	15.00
IS	Ichiro Suzuki	25.00
JT	Jim Thome	6.00
DW	Dontrelle Willis	8.00
KW	Kerry Wood	8.00

Classic Stitches Patch

Common Player:		15.00

Production 99 Sets

Golds:		No Pricing

Production 10 Sets

JB	Jeff Bagwell	25.00
RB	Rocco Baldelli	15.00
HB	Hank Blalock	25.00
HC	Hee Seop Choi	15.00
RC	Roger Clemens	40.00
JD	J.D. Drew	15.00
AD	Adam Dunn	15.00
JE	Jim Edmonds	15.00
RF	Rafael Furcal	15.00
JG	Jason Giambi	15.00
TG	Troy Glaus	15.00
SG	Shawn Green	15.00
KG	Ken Griffey Jr.	50.00
VG	Vladimir Guerrero	25.00
TH	Torii Hunter	15.00
RJ	Randy Johnson	30.00
AJ	Andruw Jones	15.00
CJ	Chipper Jones	25.00
JK	Jeff Kent	15.00
ML	Mike Lowell	15.00
GM	Greg Maddux	35.00
PM	Pedro J. Martinez	25.00
HM	Hideki Matsui	85.00
MM	Matt Morris	15.00
HN	Hideo Nomo	40.00
MO	Magglio Ordonez	15.00
RO	Roy Oswalt	15.00
CP	Corey Patterson	20.00
AP	Andy Pettitte	20.00
MI	Mike Piazza	40.00
MP	Mark Prior	15.00
AL	Albert Pujols	40.00
AR	Alex Rodriguez	50.00
IR	Ivan Rodriguez	20.00
CS	Curt Schilling	15.00
GS	Gary Sheffield	15.00
AS	Alfonso Soriano	20.00
SS	Sammy Sosa	35.00
IS	Ichiro Suzuki	120.00
JT	Jim Thome	20.00
DW	Dontrelle Willis	20.00
KW	Kerry Wood	25.00

Signs of Success

		NM/M
Common Player:		6.00
MI	Milton Bradley/220	10.00
DB	Dewon Brazelton/299	6.00
JB	John Buck/98	8.00
MB	Mark Buehrle/220	10.00
BR	Brandon Claussen/121	6.00
BC	Brad Cresse/121	6.00
JD	Johnny Damon/297	30.00
BD	Ben Diggins/299	6.00
AG	Alex Graman/215	6.00
KG	Ken Griffey Jr./299	90.00
TG	Tony Gwynn/49	80.00
DH	Drew Henson/246	15.00
BH	Ben Howard/299	8.00
HI	Hansel Izquierdo/299	8.00
JJ	Jimmy Journell/98	8.00
DK	David Kelton/102	8.00
KL	Kenny Lofton/296	15.00
CM	Corwin Malone/103	8.00
BP	Brandon Phillips/131	10.00
SR	Scott Rolen/100	20.00
CC	C.C. Sabathia/106	15.00
MT	Mark Teixeira/280	25.00
TH	Matt Thornton/298	6.00
AH	Andy Van Hekken/299	8.00
JU	Justin Wayne/299	8.00
JW	Jayson Werth/299	8.00
JE	Jerome Williams/103	15.00

Bronze Bust

		NM/M
Common Player:		
YB	Yogi Berra	25.00
RC	Roberto Clemente	60.00
NG	Nomar Garciaparra	40.00
JG	Jason Giambi	25.00
BG	Bob Gibson	25.00
KG	Ken Griffey Jr./300	40.00
MM	Mickey Mantle	70.00
HM	Hideki Matsui	30.00
SM	Stan Musial	25.00
BRS	Babe Ruth/Sox/300	60.00
BRY	Babe Ruth/Yanks	60.00

		NM/M
NRA	Nolan Ryan/Astros	50.00
NRA	Nolan Ryan/Astros/300	50.00
NRM	Nolan Ryan/Mets	50.00
TSM	Tom Seaver/Mets	25.00
TSR	Tom Seaver/Reds/300	25.00
TSR	Tom Seaver/Reds	25.00
DS	Duke Snider	25.00
SS	Sammy Sosa/300	40.00
IS	Ichiro Suzuki/300	40.00
TW	Ted Williams	50.00

Bronze Bust Autograph
NM/M
Some not priced due to scarcity.

YB	Yogi Berra	100.00
NG	Nomar Garciaparra/106	125.00
BG	Bob Gibson	60.00
KG	Ken Griffey Jr.	100.00
HM	Hideki Matsui	250.00
SM	Stan Musial/62	120.00
DS	Duke Snider	90.00
IS	Ichiro Suzuki/62	275.00

Marble Bust
NM/M
Common Player:

YB	Yogi Berra/125	40.00
YB	Yogi Berra/250	25.00
RC	Roberto Clemente/250	70.00
NG	Nomar Garciaparra/250	40.00
JG	Jason Giambi	25.00
BG	Bob Gibson/125	30.00
BG	Bob Gibson/250	25.00
KG	Ken Griffey Jr./250	40.00
MM	Mickey Mantle/80	80.00
MM	Mickey Mantle/125	80.00
HM	Hideki Matsui/250	60.00
SM	Stan Musial/250	50.00
BRS	Babe Ruth Sox/250	60.00
BRY	Babe Ruth/Yanks/125	75.00
BRY	Babe Ruth/Yanks/250	65.00
NRA	Nolan Ryan/Astros/125	60.00
NRA	Nolan Ryan/Astros/250	50.00
NRM	Nolan Ryan/Mets/125	60.00
NRM	Nolan Ryan/Mets/250	50.00
TSM	Tom Seaver/Mets/125	40.00
TSM	Tom Seaver/Mets/250	30.00
TSR	Tom Seaver/Reds/125	40.00
TSR	Tom Seaver/Reds/250	30.00
DS	Duke Snider/100	40.00
DS	Duke Snider/250	40.00
SS	Sammy Sosa/250	40.00
IS	Ichiro Suzuki/250	40.00
TW	Ted Williams/125	65.00
TW	Ted Williams/250	50.00

Marble Autograph
No pricing due to scarcity.

Pewter Bust

NM/M
Common Player:

YB	Yogi Berra/75	40.00
YB	Yogi Berra/100	40.00
RC	Roberto Clemente/100	100.00
NG	Nomar Garciaparra/100	60.00
JG	Jason Giambi/100	40.00
BG	Bob Gibson/75	40.00
BG	Bob Gibson/100	40.00
KG	Ken Griffey Jr./100	70.00
MM	Mickey Mantle/75	125.00
MM	Mickey Mantle/100	125.00
HM	Hideki Matsui/100	50.00
SM	Stan Musial/100	60.00
BRS	Babe Ruth/Sox/100	80.00
BRY	Babe Ruth/Yanks/75	90.00
BRY	Babe Ruth/Yanks/100	90.00
NRA	Nolan Ryan/Astros/75	80.00
NRA	Nolan Ryan/Astros/100	80.00
NRM	Nolan Ryan/Mets/75	80.00
NRM	Nolan Ryan/Mets/100	80.00
TSM	Tom Seaver/Mets/75	40.00
TSM	Tom Seaver/Mets/100	40.00
TSR	Tom Seaver/Reds/100	40.00
TSR	Tom Seaver/Reds/75	40.00
DS	Duke Snider/75	40.00
DS	Duke Snider/100	40.00
SS	Sammy Sosa/100	65.00
IS	Ichiro Suzuki/100	65.00
TW	Ted Williams/75	100.00
TW	Ted Williams/100	100.00

Pewter Autograph Bust
No pricing due to scarcity.

Roger Clemens 300 Wins

To commemorate The Rocket's milestone, fans at Yankee Stadium on August 28 received this cello-wrapped set. Backs repeat the front format and have a line of stats and a career highlight.

NM/M
Complete Set (6): 15.00
Common Card: 3.00

1	Roger Clemens (1999 post-season wins)	3.00
2	Roger Clemens (2000 post-season wins)	3.00
3	Roger Clemens (Sixth Cy Young)	3.00
4	Roger Clemens (4,000 Ks)	3.00
5	Roger Clemens (300th win)	3.00
--	Header Card	3.00

2003 Upper Deck Finite
NM/M
Complete Set (380):
Common Player (1-100): 1.00
Production 1,999
Common (101-150): 1.00
Production 1,599
Common (151-180): 2.00
Production 499
Common (181-200): 2.50
Production 299
Common (201-300): 1.50
Production 1,299
Common (301-330): 3.00
Production 599
Common (331-360): 3.00
Production 299
Common (361-380): 5.00
Production 150
Pack (3): 9.00
Box (10): 80.00

1	Darin Erstad	1.00
2	Garret Anderson	1.50
3	Tim Salmon	1.50
4	Troy Glaus	1.50
5	Luis Gonzalez	1.50
6	Randy Johnson	2.00
7	Curt Schilling	1.50
8	Andruw Jones	1.50
9	Gary Sheffield	1.50
10	Rafael Furcal	1.00
11	Greg Maddux	3.00
12	Chipper Jones	2.50
13	Tony Batista	1.00
14	Jay Gibbons	1.00
15	Johnny Damon	1.00
16	Derek Lowe	1.00
17	Nomar Garciaparra	3.00
18	Pedro J. Martinez	2.00
19	Manny Ramirez	1.50
20	Mark Prior	2.00
21	Kerry Wood	1.50
22	Corey Patterson	1.00
23	Sammy Sosa	3.00
24	Moises Alou	1.00
25	Magglio Ordonez	1.00
26	Frank Thomas	2.00
27	Paul Konerko	1.00
28	Bartolo Colon	1.00
29	Adam Dunn	1.00
30	Austin Kearns	1.00
31	Aaron Boone	1.00
32	Ken Griffey Jr.	2.50
33	Omar Vizquel	1.00
34	C.C. Sabathia	1.00
35	Brandon Phillips	1.00
36	Larry Walker	1.00
37	Preston Wilson	1.00
38	Todd Helton	1.50
39	Eric Munson	1.00
40	Ivan Rodriguez	1.50
41	Josh Beckett	1.50
42	Roy Oswalt	1.00
43	Craig Biggio	1.50
44	Jeff Bagwell	1.50
45	Dontrelle Willis	1.00
46	Carlos Beltran	1.00
47	Brent Mayne	1.00
48	Hideo Nomo	1.00
49	Rickey Henderson	1.00
50	Adrian Beltre	1.00
51	Miguel Cabrera	2.00
52	Kazuhisa Ishii	1.00
53	Richie Sexson	1.00
54	Torii Hunter	1.00
55	Jacque Jones	1.00
56	A.J. Pierzynski	1.00
57	Jose Vidro	1.00
58	Vladimir Guerrero	2.00
59	Tom Glavine	1.00
60	Jose Reyes	1.00
61	Mike Piazza	2.50
62	Jorge Posada	1.50
63	Mike Mussina	1.50
64	Robin Ventura	1.00
65	Mariano Rivera	1.50
66	Roger Clemens	3.00
67	Jason Giambi	2.00
68	Bernie Williams	1.50
69	Alfonso Soriano	2.00
70	Derek Jeter	5.00
71	Miguel Tejada	1.50
72	Eric Chavez	1.00
73	Tim Hudson	1.00
74	Barry Zito	1.50
75	Pat Burrell	1.00
76	Jim Thome	2.00
77	Bobby Abreu	1.00
78	Brian Giles	1.00
79	Reggie Sanders	1.00
80	Ryan Klesko	1.00
81	Edgardo Alfonzo	1.00
82	Rich Aurilia	1.00
83	Barry Bonds	5.00
84	Mike Cameron	1.00
85	Kazuhiro Sasaki	1.00
86	Bret Boone	1.00
87	Ichiro Suzuki	3.00
88	J.D. Drew	1.00
89	Jim Edmonds	1.00
90	Scott Rolen	2.00
91	Matt Morris	1.00
92	Tino Martinez	1.00
93	Albert Pujols	3.00
94	Rocco Baldelli	1.50
95	Hank Blalock	1.50
96	Alex Rodriguez	3.00
97	Rafael Palmeiro	1.50
98	Eric Hinske	1.00
99	Orlando Hudson	1.00
100	Carlos Delgado	1.50
101	Albert Pujols	3.00
102	Alex Rodriguez	3.00
103	Alfonso Soriano	1.50
104	Andruw Jones	1.50
105	Barry Zito	1.50
106	Bernie Williams	1.50
107	Carlos Delgado	1.50
108	Chipper Jones	2.50
109	Curt Schilling	1.50
110	Doug Mientkiewicz	1.00
111	Frank Thomas	1.50
112	Garret Anderson	1.50
113	Gary Sheffield	1.50
114	Greg Maddux	3.00
115	Hank Blalock	1.00
116	Hideki Matsui	4.00
117	Hideo Nomo	1.00
118	Ichiro Suzuki	3.00
119	Ivan Rodriguez	1.50
120	Jason Giambi	2.00
121	Jeff Bagwell	1.50
122	Jeff Kent	1.00
123	Jerome Williams	1.00
124	Jeromy Burnitz	1.00
125	Jim Thome	2.00
126	Jose Cruz Jr.	1.00
127	Ken Griffey Jr.	2.50
128	Kerry Wood	1.50
129	Lance Berkman	1.00
130	Luis Gonzalez	1.50
131	Manny Ramirez	1.50
132	Mark Prior	2.00
133	Miguel Cabrera	1.50
134	Miguel Tejada	1.50
135	Mike Piazza	2.50
136	Pat Burrell	1.00
137	Pedro J. Martinez	1.50
138	Rafael Furcal	1.00
139	Randy Johnson	2.00
140	Rich Harden	1.50
141	Rickey Henderson	1.50
142	Roberto Alomar	1.50
143	Roger Clemens	3.00
144	Sammy Sosa	1.50
145	Shawn Green	1.00
146	Todd Helton	1.50
147	Tom Glavine	1.00
148	Torii Hunter	1.00
149	Troy Glaus	1.50
150	Vladimir Guerrero	2.00
151	Adam Dunn	1.50
152	Albert Pujols	6.00
153	Alex Rodriguez	6.00
154	Alfonso Soriano	3.00
155	Andruw Jones	2.50
156	Barry Bonds	8.00
157	Carlos Delgado	2.50
158	Chipper Jones	3.00
159	Derek Jeter	8.00
160	Gary Sheffield	2.50
161	Hank Blalock	2.50
162	Hideki Matsui	6.00
163	Ichiro Suzuki	6.00
164	J.D. Drew	2.00
165	Jason Giambi	3.00
166	Jeff Bagwell	3.00
167	Jeff Kent	2.00
168	Jim Edmonds	2.00
169	Jim Thome	3.00
170	Ken Griffey Jr.	5.00
171	Luis Gonzalez	2.00
172	Magglio Ordonez	2.00
173	Manny Ramirez	2.50
174	Mike Lowell	2.00
175	Mike Piazza	4.00
176	Nomar Garciaparra	6.00
177	Rafael Palmeiro	2.50
178	Shawn Green	2.00
179	Troy Glaus	2.00
180	Vladimir Guerrero	3.00
181	Albert Pujols	8.00
182	Alex Rodriguez	8.00
183	Alfonso Soriano	4.00
184	Bernie Williams	2.50
185	Chipper Jones	4.00
186	Derek Jeter	10.00
187	Hideki Matsui	8.00
188	Ichiro Suzuki	6.00
189	Jim Thome	3.00
190	Joe DiMaggio	8.00
191	Ken Griffey Jr.	6.00
192	Mickey Mantle	12.00
193	Mike Piazza	5.00
194	Pedro J. Martinez	4.00
195	Randy Johnson	4.00
196	Roger Clemens	6.00
197	Sammy Sosa	6.00
198	Ted Williams	8.00
199	Troy Glaus	2.50
200	Vladimir Guerrero	3.00
201	Aaron Looper RC	2.00
202	Alejandro Machado	1.50
203	Alfredo Gonzalez RC	2.00
204	Andrew Brown RC	2.00
205	Anthony Ferrari	1.50
206	Aquilino Lopez RC	2.00
207	Beau Kemp RC	2.00
208	Bernie Castro	1.50
209	Bobby Madritsch RC	8.00
210	Brandon Villafuerte	1.50
211	Brent Hoard RC	2.00
212	Brian Stokes	1.50
213	Chris Capuano RC	4.00
214	Chris Waters	1.50
215	Clint Barmes RC	5.00
216	Colin Porter RC	1.50
217	Cory Stewart	1.50
218	Craig Brazell RC	3.00
219	Craig Brazell RC	3.00
220	D.J. Carrasco RC	1.50
221	Daniel Cabrera RC	1.50
222	Dave Matranga RC	2.00
223	David Sanders	1.50
224	Diegomar Markwell	1.50
225	Edgar Gonzalez RC	1.50
226	Felix Sanchez	1.50
227	Fernando Cabrera RC	1.50
228	Francisco Cruceta RC	2.00
229	Francisco Rosario RC	1.50
230	Garrett Atkins	1.50
231	Gerald Laird	1.50
232	Guillermo Quiroz RC	4.00
233	Heath Bell RC	2.00
234	Delmon Young RC	10.00
235	Jason Shiell RC	2.00
236	Jeremy Bonderman	10.00
237	Jeremy Griffiths	1.50
238	Jeremy Guthrie	1.50
239	Jeremy Wedel RC	2.00
240	Carlos Rivera	1.50
241	Joe Valentine	1.50
242	Jon Leicester	1.50
243	Jonathan Pridie	1.50
244	Jorge Cordova	1.50
245	Jose Castillo	1.50
246	Josh Hall	2.00
247	Josh Stewart RC	1.50
248	Josh Willingham RC	3.00
249	Julio Manon RC	1.50
250	Kevin Correia RC	1.50
251	Kevin Ohme RC	2.00
252	Kevin Tolar	1.50
253	Luis De Los Santos	1.50
254	Jermaine Clark	1.50
255	Mark Malaska RC	2.00
256	Juan Dominguez	1.50
257	Michael Hessman RC	1.50
258	Micheal Nakamura RC	2.00
259	Miguel Ojeda RC	1.50
260	Mike Gallo	1.50
261	Edwin Jackson RC	6.00
262	Mike Ryan RC	1.50
263	Nate Bland RC	1.50
264	Nate Robertson	3.00
265	Nook Logan RC	2.00
266	Phil Seibel RC	1.50
267	Prentice Redman RC	2.00
268	Rafael Betancourt	1.50
269	Rett Johnson RC	1.50
270	Richard Fischer	1.50
271	Rick Roberts RC	2.00
272	Roger Deago RC	1.50
273	Ryan Cameron RC	1.50
274	Shane Bazzell	1.50
275	Erasmo Ramirez	1.50
276	Terrmel Sledge RC	2.00
277	Tim Olson RC	3.00
278	Tommy Phelps	1.50
279	Tommy Whiteman	1.50
280	Willie Eyre RC	2.00
281	Alex Prieto RC	2.00
282	Michel Hernandez RC	1.50
283	Greg Jones RC	1.50
284	Victor Martinez RC	4.00
285	Tom Gregorio RC	2.00
286	Marcus Thames	1.50
287	Jorge DePaula RC	1.50
288	Aaron Miles RC	3.00
289	Reynaldo Garcia	1.50
290	Brian Sweeney RC	1.50
291	Pete LaForest RC	1.50
292	Pete Zoccolillo RC	1.50
293	Danny Garcia RC	1.50
294	Jonny Gomes	1.50
295	Rosman Garcia RC	1.50
296	Mike Edwards	1.50
297	Marlon Byrd	1.50
298	Khalil Greene	4.00
299	Jose Valverde	1.50
300	Drew Henson	1.50
301	Chris Bootcheck	3.00
302	Matt Belisle	3.00
303	Kevin Gregg	3.00
304	Bobby Jenks	3.00
305	Jason Young	3.00
306	Laynce Nix	3.00
307	Robb Quinlan	3.00
308	Chase Utley	3.00
309	Humberto Quintero RC	4.00
310	Tim Raines Jr.	3.00
311	Stephen Smitherman	3.00
312	Jason Anderson	3.00
313	Joe Dawley	3.00
314	Chad Cordero RC	3.00
315	Victor Alvarez	3.00
316	Jimmy Gobble	3.00
317	Jared Fernandez	3.00
318	Eric Bruntlett	3.00
319	Neal Cotts	3.00
320	Ryan Madson	3.00
321	Rocco Baldelli	3.00
322	Graham Koonce RC	3.00
323	Bobby Crosby	3.00
324	Mike Wood	3.00
325	Jesse Garcia	3.00
326	Noah Lowry	6.00
327	Edwin Almonte	3.00
328	Justin Morneau	3.00
329	Steve Colyer	3.00
330	Vinnie Chulk	3.00
331	Brian Schmack	3.00
332	Stephen Randolph RC	3.00
333	Pedro Feliciano	3.00
334	Koyie Hill	3.00
335	Geoff Geary RC	3.00
336	Jon Switzer	3.00
337	Xavier Nady	3.00
338	Rich Harden	4.00
339	Dontrelle Willis	3.00
340	Angel Berroa	3.00
341	Jerome Williams	3.00
342	Brandon Claussen	3.00
343	Kurt Ainsworth	3.00
344	Horacio Ramirez	3.00
345	Hee Seop Choi	3.00
346	Billy Traber	3.00
347	Brandon Phillips	3.00
348	Jody Gerut	3.00
349	Mark Teixeira	4.00
350	Javier Lopez	3.00
351	Miguel Cabrera	5.00
352	Brad Lidge	3.00
353	Mike MacDougal	3.00
354	Ken Harvey	3.00
355	Chien-Ming Wang RC	40.00
356	Aaron Heilman	3.00
357	Jason Phillips	3.00
358	Jason Bay	5.00
359	Arnie Munoz	3.00
360	Ian Ferguson RC	3.00
361	Ryan Wagner RC	5.00
362	Rickie Weeks RC	40.00
363	Chad Gaudin RC	8.00
364	Jason Gilfillan RC	5.00
365	Jason Roach	5.00
366	Jhonny Peralta	6.00
367	Mike Neu RC	5.00
368	Jose Contreras RC	10.00
369	Wilfredo Ledezma RC	5.00
370	Lew Ford RC	8.00
371	Luis Ayala RC	5.00
372	Bo Hart RC	5.00
373	Brandon Webb RC	15.00
374	Dan Haren RC	8.00
375	Hideki Matsui RC	50.00
376	Jeff Duncan RC	8.00
377	Matt Kata RC	5.00
378	Oscar Villarreal RC	5.00
379	Rob Hammock RC	5.00
380	Todd Wellemeyer RC	5.00

Game Face (193-217):
Common Rookie: 5.00
Production 299

193	Aaron Looper RC	5.00
194	Alex Prieto RC	5.00
195	Bo Hart RC	5.00
196	Chad Gaudin RC	8.00
197	Colin Porter RC	5.00
198	D.J. Carrasco RC	5.00
199	Dan Haren	5.00
200	Delmon Young RC	30.00
201	Dontrelle Willis	5.00
202	Jon Switzer	5.00
203	Edwin Jackson RC	15.00
204	Fernando Cabrera RC	5.00
205	Garrett Atkins	5.00
206	Jeremy Bonderman	12.00
207	Kevin Ohme RC	5.00
208	Khalil Greene	10.00
209	Luis Ayala RC	5.00
210	Matt Kata RC	5.00
211	Noah Lowry	10.00
212	Rich Harden	5.00
213	Rickie Weeks RC	20.00
214	Rosman Garcia RC	5.00
215	Ryan Wagner RC	5.00
216	Tom Gregorio RC	5.00
217	Wilfredo Ledezma RC	5.00

SP Authentic (190-239):
Common SP Authentic Rookie: 4.00
Production 699

190	Aaron Looper	4.00
191	Alex Prieto	4.00
192	Alfredo Gonzalez RC	4.00
193	Andrew Brown RC	4.00
194	Anthony Ferrari	4.00
195	Aquilino Lopez RC	4.00
196	Beau Kemp RC	4.00
197	Bo Hart RC	4.00
198	Chad Gaudin RC	4.00
199	Colin Porter RC	4.00
200	D.J. Carrasco RC	4.00
201	Dan Haren	8.00
202	Danny Garcia RC	4.00
203	Jon Switzer	4.00
204	Edwin Jackson RC	4.00
205	Fernando Cabrera RC	4.00
206	Garrett Atkins	4.00
207	Gerald Laird	4.00
208	Greg Jones RC	4.00
209	Ian Ferguson RC	4.00
210	Jason Roach	4.00
211	Jason Shiell RC	4.00
212	Jeremy Bonderman	15.00
213	Jeremy Wedel RC	4.00
214	Jhonny Peralta	4.00
215	Delmon Young RC	40.00
216	Jorge DePaula RC	4.00
217	Josh Hall RC	4.00
218	Julio Manon RC	4.00
219	Kevin Correia RC	4.00
220	Kevin Ohme RC	4.00
221	Kevin Tolar	4.00
222	Luis Ayala RC	4.00
223	Luis De Los Santos	4.00
224	Chad Cordero RC	4.00
225	Mark Malaska RC	4.00
226	Khalil Greene	10.00
227	Micheal Nakamura RC	4.00
228	Michel Hernandez RC	4.00
229	Miguel Ojeda RC	4.00
230	Mike Neu RC	4.00
231	Nate Bland RC	4.00
232	Pete LaForest RC	4.00
233	Rickie Weeks RC	25.00
234	Rosmari Garcia RC	4.00
235	Ryan Wagner RC	4.00
236	Lance Niekro	4.00
237	Tom Gregorio RC	4.00
238	Tommy Phelps	4.00
239	Wilfredo Ledezma RC	4.00

SPX (179-193, 381-387):

179	Chad Gaudin/150 RC	8.00

180	Chris Capuano/150 RC	25.00
181	Danny Garcia/150 RC	8.00
182	Delmon Young/150 RC	60.00
183	Edwin Jackson/150 RC	20.00
184	Greg Jones/150 RC	8.00
185	Jeremy Bonderman/150	25.00
186	Jorge DePaula/150 RC	8.00
187	Khalil Greene/150	25.00
188	Chad Cordero/150 RC	8.00
189	Miguel Cabrera/150	10.00
190	Rich Harden/150	10.00
191	Rickie Weeks/150 RC	40.00
192	Rosman Garcia/150 RC	8.00
193	Tom Gregorio/150 RC	8.00
381	Andrew Brown/Auto./355 RC	25.00
382	Delmon Young/Jsy/Auto./355 RC	400.00
383	Colin Porter/Jsy/Auto./355 RC	15.00
385	Rickie Weeks/Jsy/Auto./355 RC	200.00
386	Dave Matranga/Jsy/Auto./355 RC	20.00
387	Bo Hart/Jsy/Auto./355 RC	15.00

UD Authentics (131-140):
Common Authentics: 5.00
Production 150

131	Dan Haren	6.00
132	Delmon Young RC	35.00
133	Dontrelle Willis	6.00
134	Edwin Jackson RC	5.00
135	Jeremy Bonderman	15.00
136	Khalil Greene	10.00
137	Rich Harden	6.00
138	Rickie Weeks RC	35.00
139	Rosman Garcia RC	5.00
140	Ryan Wagner RC	5.00

Gold

Gold (1-150): 1-2X
Gold (151-180): 1X
Production 199
Gold (181-200): 1-2X
Production 99

Elements Jersey

NM/M

	Common Player:	4.00
JB	Jeff Bagwell	8.00
RB	Rocco Baldelli	6.00
HB	Hank Blalock	6.00
HC	Hee Seop Choi	4.00
JD	J.D. Drew	4.00
AD	Adam Dunn	6.00
JE	Jim Edmonds	5.00
SG	Shawn Green	4.00
KG	Ken Griffey Jr./SP	15.00
TH	Torii Hunter	6.00
CJ	Chipper Jones	6.00
JK	Jeff Kent	4.00
ML	Mike Lowell	4.00
GM	Greg Maddux	8.00
HM	Hideki Matsui	25.00

ABBREVIATIONS

SP - Short Print

MM	Matt Morris	5.00
RO	Roy Oswalt	5.00
CP	Corey Patterson	5.00
AP	Andy Pettitte	6.00
MI	Mike Piazza	8.00
MP	Mark Prior	10.00
AL	Albert Pujols	15.00
AR	Alex Rodriguez	10.00
AS	Alfonso Soriano	10.00
IS	Ichiro Suzuki	15.00
JT	Jim Thome	10.00
RW	Rickie Weeks/SP	15.00
DW	Dontrelle Willis	6.00
KW	Kerry Wood	10.00
DY	Delmon Young/SP	20.00

Elements Patch

No pricing due to scarcity.
Production 25 Sets
Patch Gold: No Pricing
Production 10 Sets

First Class Jersey

NM/M

	Common Player:	4.00
RC	Roger Clemens	10.00
JD	Joe DiMaggio/SP	80.00
TG	Troy Glaus	5.00
LG	Luis Gonzalez	4.00
KG	Ken Griffey Jr.	12.00
VG	Vladimir Guerrero	8.00
RJ	Randy Johnson	8.00
CJ	Chipper Jones	6.00
MM	Mickey Mantle/SP	100.00
PM	Pedro J. Martinez	8.00
HM	Hideki Matsui	25.00
MP	Mike Piazza	8.00
AP	Albert Pujols	20.00
AR	Alex Rodriguez	10.00
AS	Alfonso Soriano	10.00
SS	Sammy Sosa	10.00
IS	Ichiro Suzuki	15.00
JT	Jim Thome	10.00
BW	Bernie Williams	6.00
TW	Ted Williams/SP	75.00

Signatures

NM/M
Common Auto.: 6.00
Varying quantities produced

EA	Erick Almonte/355	6.00
SZ	Shane Bazzell/250	6.00
MC	Miguel Cabrera/100	50.00
RC	Roger Clemens/50	150.00
WE	Willie Eyre/50	6.00
NG	Nomar Garciaparra/50	120.00
RK	Rob Hammock/200	6.00
RN	Rich Harden/150	25.00
BH	Bo Hart/150	8.00
HM	Hideki Matsui/99	250.00
MP	Mark Prior/75	40.00
JR	Jose Reyes/100	40.00
SR	Scott Rolen/100	40.00
CS	C.C. Sabathia/50	15.00
DS	David Sanders/150	6.00
PS	Phil Seibel/200	6.00
IS	Ichiro Suzuki/25	350.00
MT	Mark Teixeira/200	25.00
BW	Brandon Webb/150	25.00
JW	Jerome Williams/150	15.00
DW	Dontrelle Willis/50	40.00
DY	Delmon Young/50	100.00

SPX Jersey Autograph

NM/M
Production 355

DW	Dontrelle Willis	40.00
KG	Khalil Greene	60.00
RH	Rich Harden	35.00

Stars and Stripes

NM/M
Common Player: 2.00
Production 299 Sets

USA-1	Justin Orenduff	2.00
USA-2	Micah Owings	2.00
USA-3	Steven Register	2.00
USA-4	Huston Street	6.00
USA-5	Justin Verlander	8.00
USA-6	Jered Weaver	8.00
USA-7	Matt Campbell	4.00
USA-8	Stephen Head	2.00
USA-9	Mark Romanczuk	2.00
USA-10	Jeff Clement	10.00
USA-11	Mike Nickeas	2.00
USA-12	Tyler Greene	2.00
USA-13	Paul Janish	2.00
USA-14	Jeff Larish	2.00
USA-15	Eric Patterson	2.00
USA-16	Dustin Pedroia	4.00
USA-17	Michael Griffin	2.00
USA-18	Brent Lillibridge	2.00
USA-19	Danny Putnam	5.00
USA-20	Seth Smith	5.00

Stars and Stripes Jersey

NM/M
Common Player: 4.00

J1	Justin Orenduff	4.00
J2	Micah Owings	4.00
J3	Steven Register	4.00
J4	Huston Street	8.00
J5	Justin Verlander	8.00
J6	Jered Weaver	8.00
J7	Matt Campbell	6.00
J8	Stephen Head	4.00
J9	Mark Romanczuk	4.00
J10	Jeff Clement	10.00
J11	Mike Nickeas	4.00
J12	Tyler Greene	4.00
J13	Paul Janish	4.00
J14	Jeff Larish	4.00
J15	Eric Patterson	4.00
J16	Dustin Pedroia	6.00
J17	Michael Griffin	4.00
J18	Brent Lillibridge	4.00
J19	Danny Putnam	6.00
J20	Seth Smith	6.00

2003 Upper Deck First Pitch

NM/M
Complete Set (300): 50.00
Common Player: .10
Common SP (271-300): 1.00
Inserted 1:4
Pack (5): 1.00
Box (36): 25.00

1	John Lackey	.10
2	Alex Cintron	.10
3	Jose Leon	.10
4	Bobby Hill	.10
5	Brandon Larson	.10
6	Raul Gonzalez	.10
7	Ben Broussard	.10
8	Earl Snyder	.10
9	Ramon Santiago	.10
10	Jason Lane	.10
11	Rob Hammock RC	.50
12	Kirk Saarloos	.10
13	Juan Brito	.10
14	Runelvys Hernandez	.10
15	Shawn Sedlacek	.10
16	Jayson Durocher	.10
17	Kevin Frederick	.10
18	Zach Day	.10
19	Marco Scutaro	.10
20	Marcus Thames	.10
21	Esteban German	.10
22	Brett Myers	.10
23	Oliver Perez	.10
24	Dennis Tankersley	.10
25	Julius Matos	.10
26	Jake Peavy	.10
27	Eric Cyr	.10
28	Mike Crudale	.10
29	Josh Pearce	.10
30	Carl Crawford	.10
31	Tim Salmon	.25
32	Troy Glaus	.50
33	Adam Kennedy	.10
34	David Eckstein	.10
35	Bengie Molina	.10
36	Jarrod Washburn	.10
37	Ramon Ortiz	.10
38	Eric Chavez	.25
39	Miguel Tejada	.25
40	Adam Piatt	.10
41	Jermaine Dye	.10
42	Olmedo Saenz	.10
43	Tim Hudson	.20
44	Barry Zito	.25
45	Billy Koch	.10
46	Shannon Stewart	.10
47	Kelvim Escobar	.10
48	Jose Cruz Jr.	.10
49	Vernon Wells	.10
50	Roy Halladay	.10
51	Esteban Loaiza	.10
52	Eric Hinske	.10
53	Steve Cox	.10
54	Brent Abernathy	.10
55	Ben Grieve	.10
56	Aubrey Huff	.10
57	Jared Sandberg	.10
58	Paul Wilson	.10
59	Tanyon Sturtze	.10
60	Jim Thome	.50
61	Omar Vizquel	.20
62	C.C. Sabathia	.10
63	Chris Magruder	.10
64	Ricky Gutierrez	.10
65	Einar Diaz	.10
66	Danys Baez	.10
67	Ichiro Suzuki	.75
68	Ruben Sierra	.10
69	Carlos Guillen	.10
70	Mark McLemore	.10
71	Dan Wilson	.10
72	Jamie Moyer	.10
73	Joel Pineiro	.10
74	Edgar Martinez	.10
75	Tony Batista	.10
76	Jay Gibbons	.10
77	Chris Singleton	.10
78	Melvin Mora	.10
79	Geronimo Gil	.10
80	Rodrigo Lopez	.10
81	Jorge Julio	.10
82	Rafael Palmeiro	.40
83	Juan Gonzalez	.40
84	Mike Young	.10
85	Hideki Irabu	.10
86	Chan Ho Park	.10
87	Kevin Mench	.10
88	Doug Davis	.10
89	Pedro J. Martinez	.75
90	Shea Hillenbrand	.10
91	Derek Lowe	.10
92	Jason Varitek	.10
93	Tony Clark	.10
94	John Burkett	.10
95	Frank Castillo	.10
96	Nomar Garciaparra	1.00
97	Rickey Henderson	.25
98	Mike Sweeney	.10
99	Carlos Febles	.10
100	Mark Quinn	.10
101	Raul Ibanez	.10
102	A.J. Hinch	.10
103	Paul Byrd	.10
104	Chuck Knoblauch	.10
105	Dmitri Young	.10
106	Randall Simon	.10
107	Brandon Inge	.10
108	Damion Easley	.10
109	Carlos Pena	.10
110	George Lombard	.10
111	Juan Acevedo	.10
112	Torii Hunter	.25
113	Doug Mientkiewicz	.10
114	David Ortiz	.10
115	Eric Milton	.10
116	Eddie Guardado	.10
117	Cristian Guzman	.10
118	Corey Koskie	.10
119	Magglio Ordonez	.20
120	Mark Buehrle	.10
121	Todd Ritchie	.10
122	Jose Valentin	.10
123	Paul Konerko	.10
124	Carlos Lee	.10
125	Jon Garland	.10
126	Jason Giambi	.75
127	Derek Jeter	1.50
128	Roger Clemens	1.00
129	Raul Mondesi	.25
130	Jorge Posada	.25
131	Rondell White	.10
132	Robin Ventura	.20
133	Mike Mussina	.40
134	Jeff Bagwell	.50
135	Craig Biggio	.20
136	Morgan Ensberg	.10
137	Richard Hidalgo	.10
138	Brad Ausmus	.10
139	Roy Oswalt	.20
140	Carlos Hernandez	.10
141	Shane Reynolds	.10
142	Gary Sheffield	.25
143	Andruw Jones	.25
144	Tom Glavine	.25
145	Rafael Furcal	.10
146	Javy Lopez	.10
147	Vinny Castilla	.10
148	Marcus Giles	.10
149	Kevin Millwood	.20
150	Jason Marquis	.10
151	Ruben Quevedo	.10
152	Ben Sheets	.10
153	Geoff Jenkins	.10
154	Jose Hernandez	.10
155	Glendon Rusch	.10
156	Jeffrey Hammonds	.10
157	Alex Sanchez	.10
158	Jim Edmonds	.25
159	Tino Martinez	.10
160	Albert Pujols	.75
161	Eli Marrero	.10
162	Woody Williams	.10
163	Fernando Vina	.10
164	Jason Isringhausen	.10
165	Jason Simontacchi	.10
166	Kerry Robinson	.10
167	Sammy Sosa	.75
168	Juan Cruz	.10
169	Fred McGriff	.20
170	Antonio Alfonseca	.10
171	Jon Lieber	.10
172	Mark Prior	.50
173	Moises Alou	.10
174	Matt Clement	.10
175	Mark Bellhorn	.10
176	Randy Johnson	.50
177	Luis Gonzalez	.10
178	Tony Womack	.10
179	Mark Grace	.25
180	Junior Spivey	.10
181	Byung-Hyun Kim	.10
182	Danny Bautista	.10
183	Brian Anderson	.10
184	Shawn Green	.25
185	Brian Jordan	.10
186	Eric Karros	.10
187	Andy Ashby	.10
188	Cesar Izturis	.10
189	Dave Roberts	.10
190	Eric Gagne	.10
191	Kazuhisa Ishii	.10
192	Adrian Beltre	.10
193	Vladimir Guerrero	.50
194	Tony Armas Jr.	.10
195	Bartolo Colon	.10
196	Troy O'Leary	.10
197	Tomokazu Ohka	.10
198	Brad Wilkerson	.10
199	Orlando Cabrera	.10
200	Barry Bonds	1.50
201	David Bell	.10
202	Tsuyoshi Shinjo	.10
203	Benito Santiago	.10
204	Livan Hernandez	.10
205	Jason Schmidt	.10
206	Kirk Rueter	.10
207	Ramon E. Martinez	.10
208	Mike Lowell	.10
209	Luis Castillo	.10
210	Derek Lee	.10
211	Andy Fox	.10
212	Eric Owens	.10
213	Charles Johnson	.10
214	Brad Penny	.10
215	A.J. Burnett	.10
216	Edgardo Alfonzo	.10
217	Roberto Alomar	.40
218	Rey Ordonez	.10
219	Al Leiter	.10
220	Roger Cedeno	.10
221	Timoniel Perez	.10
222	Jeromy Burnitz	.10
223	Pedro Astacio	.10
224	Joe McEwing	.10
225	Ryan Klesko	.20
226	Ramon Vazquez	.10
227	Mark Kotsay	.10
228	Bubba Trammell	.10
229	Wiki Gonzalez	.10
230	Trevor Hoffman	.10
231	Ron Gant	.10
232	Bobby Abreu	.20
233	Marlon Anderson	.10
234	Jeremy Giambi	.10
235	Jimmy Rollins	.10
236	Mike Lieberthal	.10
237	Vicente Padilla	.10
238	Randy Wolf	.10
239	Pokey Reese	.10
240	Brian Giles	.25
241	Jack Wilson	.10
242	Mike Williams	.10
243	Kip Wells	.10
244	Robert Mackowiak	.10
245	Craig Wilson	.10
246	Adam Dunn	.50
247	Sean Casey	.10
248	Todd Walker	.10
249	Corky Miller	.10
250	Ryan Dempster	.10
251	Reggie Taylor	.10
252	Aaron Boone	.10
253	Larry Walker	.10
254	Jose Ortiz	.10
255	Todd Zeile	.10
256	Bobby Estalella	.10
257	Juan Pierre	.10
258	Terry Shumpert	.10
259	Mike Hampton	.10
260	Denny Stark	.10
261	Shawn Green	.20
262	Derek Lowe	.10
263	Barry Bonds	.50
264	Mike Cameron	.10
265	Luis Castillo	.10
266	Vladimir Guerrero	.40
267	Jason Giambi	.40
268	Eric Gagne	.10
269	Magglio Ordonez	.20
270	Jim Thome	.25
271	Hideki Matsui RC	20.00
272	Jose Contreras RC	4.00
273	Robert Madritsch	1.00
274	Shane Bazzell RC	1.50
275	Felix Sanchez RC	2.00
276	Todd Wellemeyer RC	2.00
277	Lew Ford RC	1.00
278	Jeremy Griffiths	1.00
279	Oscar Villarreal RC	1.00
280	Brandon Webb RC	3.00
281	Delvis Lantigua	3.00
282	Josh Willingham RC	1.00
283	Mike Nicolas RC	1.00
284	Mike Hampton	1.00
285	Jim Thome	2.00
286	Bartolo Colon	1.00
287	Orlando Hernandez	1.00
288	Jeremy Giambi	1.00
289	Jeff Kent	1.50
290	Tom Glavine	1.50
291	Cliff Floyd	1.00
292	Tsuyoshi Shinjo	1.00
293	Jose Cruz Jr.	1.00
294	Edgardo Alfonzo	1.00
295	Andres Galarraga	1.00
296	Troy O'Leary	1.00
297	Eric Karros	1.00
298	Ivan Rodriguez	1.50
299	Fred McGriff	1.50
300	Preston Wilson	1.00

Signature Stars

NM/M
Print Runs Listed:

NM	Nomar Garciaparra/100	100.00
JG	Jason Giambi/100	30.00
KG	Ken Griffey Jr./100	75.00
KGS	Ken Griffey Sr./800	6.00
SS	Sammy Sosa/50	175.00
IS	Ichiro Suzuki/50	375.00

2003 Upper Deck Game Face Promo

This card introduces UD's Game Face brand for '03. Back has a large diagonal "SAMPLE" overprint.

NM/M

30	Ken Griffey Jr.	2.00

2003 Upper Deck Game Face

AUSTIN KEARNS

NM/M
Complete Set (192):
Common Player: .25
Common Base SP: 1.00
Inserted 1:4
Common (121-150): 2.00
Inserted 1:8
Common SP (151-192): 3.00
Inserted 1:16
Pack (4): 4.00
Box (24): 75.00

1 Darin Erstad .50
2 Garret Anderson .50
3 Tim Salmon .50
4 Jarrod Washburn .25
5 Troy Glaus/SP 1.50
6 Luis Gonzalez .50
7 Junior Spivey .25
8 Randy Johnson/SP 2.00
9 Curt Schilling/SP 1.50
10 Andruw Jones .75
11 Gary Sheffield .50
12 Rafael Furcal .25
13 Greg Maddux/SP 3.00
14 Chipper Jones/SP 3.00
15 Tony Batista .25
16 Rodrigo Lopez .25
17 Jay Gibbons .25
18 Shea Hillenbrand .25
19 Johnny Damon .25
20 Derek Lowe .25
21 Nomar Garciaparra 2.50
22 Pedro J. Martinez/SP 2.00
23 Manny Ramirez/SP 1.50
24 Mark Prior .75
25 Kerry Wood .75
26 Corey Patterson .25
27 Sammy Sosa 2.00
28 Magglio Ordonez .50
29 Frank Thomas 1.00
30 Paul Konerko .25
31 Adam Dunn 1.00
32 Austin Kearns 1.00
33 Aaron Boone .25
34 Ken Griffey Jr./SP 3.00
35 Omar Vizquel .40
36 C.C. Sabathia .25
37 Karim Garcia/SP 1.00
38 Larry Walker .40
39 Preston Wilson .25
40 Jay Payton .25
41 Todd Helton/SP 1.50
42 Carlos Pena .25
43 Eric Munson .25
44 Mike Lowell .25
45 Josh Beckett .25
46 A.J. Burnett .25
47 Roy Oswalt .50
48 Craig Biggio .25
49 Jeff Bagwell/SP 1.25
50 Lance Berkman/SP 1.25
51 Mike Sweeney .25
52 Carlos Beltran .25
53 Hideo Nomo .75
54 Odalis Perez .25
55 Adrian Beltre .25
56 Shawn Green/SP 1.00
57 Kazuhisa Ishii/SP 1.00
58 Ben Sheets .50
59 Richie Sexson .50
60 Torii Hunter .50
61 Jacque Jones .25
62 Eric Milton .25
63 Corey Koskie .25
64 A.J. Pierzynski .25
65 Jose Vidro .25
66 Bartolo Colon .25
67 Vladimir Guerrero/SP 1.50
68 Tom Glavine .50
69 Mike Piazza/SP 3.00
70 Roberto Alomar/SP 1.50
71 Jorge Posada .75
72 Mike Mussina .75
73 Robin Ventura .25
74 Raul Mondesi .50
75 Roger Clemens/SP 2.50
76 Jason Giambi/SP 2.00
77 Bernie Williams/SP 1.50
78 Alfonso Soriano/SP 2.00
79 Derek Jeter/SP 6.00
80 Miguel Tejada .75
81 Eric Chavez .50
82 Tim Hudson .50
83 Barry Zito .50
84 Mark Mulder .50
85 Pat Burrell 1.00
86 Jim Thome 1.00
87 Bobby Abreu .50
88 Brian Giles .50
89 Jason Kendall .40
90 Aramis Ramirez .25
91 Ryan Klesko .25
92 Phil Nevin .25
93 Sean Burroughs .25
94 J.T. Snow .25
95 Rich Aurilia .25
96 Benito Santiago .25
97 Barry Bonds/SP 6.00
98 Edgar Martinez .50
99 John Olerud .50
100 Bret Boone .25
101 Ichiro Suzuki/SP 3.00
102 J.D. Drew .50
103 Jim Edmonds .50
104 Scott Rolen 1.00
105 Matt Morris .25
106 Tino Martinez .25
107 Albert Pujols/SP 2.00
108 Aubrey Huff .25
109 Carl Crawford .25
110 Rafael Palmeiro .75
111 Hank Blalock .25
112 Alex Rodriguez/SP 5.00
113 Kevin Mench/SP 1.00
114 Juan Gonzalez/SP 1.50
115 Shannon Stewart .25
116 Vernon Wells .25
117 Josh Phelps .25
118 Eric Hinske .25
119 Orlando Hudson .25
120 Carlos Delgado/SP 1.00
121 David Sanders RC 2.00
122 Rob Hammock RC 2.00
123 Rett Johnson RC 2.00
124 Mike Nicolas RC 2.00
125 Terrmel Sledge RC 3.00
126 Ryan Cameron RC 2.00
127 Prentice Redman RC 2.00
128 Clint Barmes RC 2.00
129 Brent Hoard RC 2.00
130 Willie Eyre RC 2.00
131 Phil Seibel RC 2.00
132 Chris Capuano RC 5.00
133 Bobby Madritsch RC 5.00
134 Shane Bazzell RC 2.00
135 Jeremy Griffiths RC 2.00
136 Jon Leicester RC 3.00
137 Brandon Webb RC 5.00
138 Todd Wellemeyer RC 2.00
139 Jose Contreras RC 5.00
140 Felix Sanchez RC 2.00
141 Arnie Munoz RC 2.00
142 Delvis Lantigua RC 2.00
143 Francisco Cruceta RC 2.00
144 Josh Willingham RC 3.00
145 Oscar Villarreal RC 2.00
146 Ian Ferguson RC 2.00
147 Pedro Liriano RC 2.00
148 Lew Ford RC 5.00
149 Jeff Duncan RC 2.00
150 Richard Fischer RC 2.00
151 Troy Glaus 3.00
152 Randy Johnson 5.00
153 Hideki Matsui RC 15.00
154 Chipper Jones 6.00
155 Nomar Garciaparra 10.00
156 Pedro J. Martinez 8.00
157 Ted Williams 15.00
158 Sammy Sosa 8.00
159 Ken Griffey Jr. 8.00
160 Vladimir Guerrero 8.00
161 Mike Piazza 8.00
162 Mickey Mantle 30.00
163 Alfonso Soriano 6.00
164 Derek Jeter 15.00
165 Roger Clemens 8.00
166 Jason Giambi 4.00
167 Barry Bonds 15.00
168 Ichiro Suzuki 8.00
169 Albert Pujols 8.00
170 Mark McGwire 15.00
171 Alex Rodriguez 10.00
172 Ken Griffey Jr., Roy Oswalt 6.00
173 Barry Zito, Troy Glaus 3.00
174 Tim Hudson, Ichiro Suzuki 8.00
175 Alex Rodriguez, Mark Mulder 10.00
176 Tom Glavine, Vladimir Guerrero 4.00
177 Mike Piazza, Greg Maddux 6.00
178 Mark McGwire, Sammy Sosa 10.00
179 Lance Berkman, Mark Prior 4.00
180 Albert Pujols, Kerry Wood 6.00
181 Randy Johnson, Jeff Bagwell 4.00
182 Derek Jeter, Curt Schilling 10.00
183 Barry Bonds, Hideo Nomo 10.00
184 Todd Helton, Kazuhisa Ishii 4.00
185 Freddy Garcia, Eric Chavez 3.00
186 Al Leiter, Chipper Jones 6.00
187 Ted Williams, Nomar Garciaparra 10.00
188 Pedro J. Martinez, Hideki Matsui 15.00
189 Derek Lowe, Bernie Williams 3.00
190 Roger Clemens, Mike Piazza 10.00
191 Mike Mussina, Manny Ramirez 4.00
192 Jason Giambi, Mickey Mantle 20.00

Autograph

NM/M
Common Player:
Inserted 1:576
Golds: No Pricing
Production 25
LB Lance Berkman/SP 50.00
JG Jason Giambi 40.00
KG Ken Griffey Jr. 125.00
TH Todd Helton/SP 45.00
HM Hideki Matsui/SP 250.00
MM Mark McGwire/SP 350.00
MP Mark Prior/SP 40.00
SS Sammy Sosa 120.00
IS Ichiro Suzuki/SP 300.00
BZ Barry Zito 40.00

Gear

GAME FACE GEAR 44

NM/M
Common Player: 4.00
Inserted 1:8
Patches: 3-5X
Production 100 Sets
BA Bobby Abreu 4.00
EA Edgardo Alfonzo 4.00
JB Jeff Bagwell 4.00
CB Carlos Beltran 6.00
LB Lance Berkman 6.00
AB Aaron Boone/SP 8.00
PB Pat Burrell 6.00
EC Eric Chavez 4.00
RC Roger Clemens 15.00
CD Carlos Delgado 4.00
DR J.D. Drew 4.00
DR2 J.D. Drew 4.00
AD Adam Dunn 8.00
JE Jim Edmonds 6.00
DE Darin Erstad 4.00
DE2 Darin Erstad 4.00
JG Jason Giambi 6.00
BG Brian Giles 4.00
TG Tom Glavine 6.00
GO Juan Gonzalez 4.00
LG Luis Gonzalez 4.00
LG2 Luis Gonzalez 4.00
SG Shawn Green 4.00
TH Todd Helton/SP 8.00
TI Tim Hudson 4.00
HU Torii Hunter 4.00
KI Kazuhisa Ishii 4.00
RJ Randy Johnson 8.00
AJ Andruw Jones 6.00
CJ Chipper Jones 8.00
JJ Jacque Jones 4.00
AK Austin Kearns 4.00
JK Jason Kendall 4.00
KE Jeff Kent 4.00
RK Ryan Klesko 4.00
ML Mike Lowell 4.00
GM Greg Maddux 10.00
GM2 Greg Maddux 10.00
EM Edgar Martinez 4.00
PM Pedro J. Martinez 8.00
MM Mike Mussina 8.00
HN Hideo Nomo 4.00
MO Magglio Ordonez 4.00
RO Roy Oswalt 4.00
RP Rafael Palmeiro 8.00
MiP Mike Piazza 10.00
JP Jorge Posada 8.00
MaP Mark Prior 8.00
MR Manny Ramirez 4.00
AR Alex Rodriguez 10.00
AR2 Alex Rodriguez 10.00
IR Ivan Rodriguez 8.00
SR Scott Rolen 8.00
CS Curt Schilling 8.00
RS Richie Sexson 6.00
AS Alfonso Soriano 6.00
SS Sammy Sosa 10.00
IS Ichiro Suzuki/SP 50.00
MS Mike Sweeney 6.00
MT Miguel Tejada 6.00
FT Frank Thomas 8.00
JT Jim Thome 8.00
JV Jose Vidro 4.00
OV Omar Vizquel 4.00
LW Larry Walker 4.00
BW Bernie Williams 6.00
PW Preston Wilson 4.00
KW Kerry Wood 8.00
BZ Barry Zito 4.00
BZ2 Barry Zito 4.00

Patch

GAME FACE PATCH 055/100

Common Player:
Production 100 Sets

2003 Upper Deck Honor Roll

TIM HUDSON - Athletics
HONOR ROLL

NM/M
Complete Set (161):
Common Player: .20
Common Even # SP (2-60): 1.00
Inserted 1:6
Common SP (131-161): 3.00
Production 2,500
Pack (5): 1.50
Box (24): 30.00
1 Derek Jeter 2.00
2 Derek Jeter/SP 5.00
3 Alex Rodriguez 1.50
4 Alex Rodriguez/SP 5.00
5 Roger Clemens 1.50
6 Roger Clemens/SP 4.00
7 Mike Piazza 1.00
8 Mike Piazza/SP 3.00
9 Jeff Bagwell .50
10 Jeff Bagwell/SP 1.50
11 Vladimir Guerrero .75
12 Vladimir Guerrero/SP 2.00
13 Ken Griffey Jr. 1.00
14 Ken Griffey Jr./SP 3.00
15 Greg Maddux 1.00
16 Greg Maddux/SP 3.00
17 Chipper Jones .75
18 Chipper Jones/SP 2.00
19 Randy Johnson .75
20 Randy Johnson/SP 2.00
21 Miguel Tejada .50
22 Miguel Tejada/SP 1.50
23 Nomar Garciaparra 1.50
24 Nomar Garciaparra/SP 4.00
25 Ichiro Suzuki 1.50
26 Ichiro Suzuki/SP 4.00
27 Sammy Sosa 1.00
28 Sammy Sosa/SP 3.00
29 Albert Pujols 2.00
30 Albert Pujols/SP 5.00
31 Alfonso Soriano .75
32 Alfonso Soriano/SP 2.00
33 Barry Bonds 2.00
34 Barry Bonds/SP 6.00
35 Jeff Kent .30
36 Jeff Kent/SP 1.00
37 Jim Thome .50
38 Jim Thome/SP 1.50
39 Pedro J. Martinez .75
40 Pedro J. Martinez/SP 2.00
41 Todd Helton .50
42 Todd Helton/SP 1.50
43 Troy Glaus .50
44 Troy Glaus/SP 1.50
45 Mark Prior .75
46 Mark Prior/SP 2.00
47 Tom Glavine .40
48 Tom Glavine/SP 1.00
49 Pat Burrell .40
50 Pat Burrell/SP 1.00
51 Barry Zito .40
52 Barry Zito/SP 1.00
53 Bernie Williams .50
54 Bernie Williams/SP 1.50
55 Curt Schilling .50
56 Curt Schilling/SP 1.50
57 Darin Erstad .30
58 Darin Erstad/SP 1.00
59 Carlos Delgado .50
60 Carlos Delgado/SP 1.50
61 Gary Sheffield .40
62 Gary Sheffield .40
63 Frank Thomas .50
64 Frank Thomas .50
65 Lance Berkman .40
66 Lance Berkman .40
67 Shawn Green .40
68 Shawn Green .40
69 Hideo Nomo .40
70 Hideo Nomo .40
71 Torii Hunter .40
72 Torii Hunter .40
73 Roberto Alomar .50
74 Roberto Alomar .50
75 Andruw Jones .50
76 Andruw Jones .50
77 Scott Rolen .75
78 Scott Rolen .75
79 Eric Chavez .40
80 Eric Chavez .40
81 Rafael Palmeiro .50
82 Rafael Palmeiro .50
83 Bobby Abreu .20
84 Bobby Abreu .20
85 Craig Biggio .20
86 Craig Biggio .20
87 Rafael Furcal .20
88 Rafael Furcal .20
89 Jose Vidro .20
90 Jose Vidro .20
91 Luis Gonzalez .20
92 Luis Gonzalez .20
93 Roy Oswalt .20
94 Roy Oswalt .20
95 Cliff Floyd .20
96 Cliff Floyd .20
97 Larry Walker .20
98 Larry Walker .20
99 Jim Edmonds .30
100 Jim Edmonds .30
101 Adam Dunn .40
102 Adam Dunn .40
103 J.D. Drew .20
104 J.D. Drew .20
105 Josh Beckett .20
106 Josh Beckett .20
107 Brian Giles .20
108 Brian Giles .20
109 Magglio Ordonez .40
110 Magglio Ordonez .40
111 Edgardo Alfonzo .20
112 Edgardo Alfonzo .20
113 Bartolo Colon .20
114 Bartolo Colon .20
115 Roy Halladay .20
116 Roy Halladay .20
117 Joe Thurston .20
118 Joe Thurston .20
119 Brandon Phillips .20
120 Brandon Phillips .20
121 Kazuhisa Ishii .20
122 Kazuhisa Ishii .20
123 Mike Mussina .40
124 Mike Mussina .40
125 Tim Hudson .40
126 Tim Hudson .40
127 Mariano Rivera .20
128 Mariano Rivera .20
129 Travis Hafner .20
130 Travis Hafner .20
131 Hideki Matsui RC 20.00
132 Jose Contreras RC 5.00
133 Jason Anderson 3.00
134 Willie Eyre RC 3.00
135 Shane Bazzell RC 3.00
136 Guillermo Quiroz RC 5.00
137 Francisco Cruceta RC 3.00
138 Jhonny Peralta 4.00
139 Aaron Looper RC 3.00
140 Bobby Madritsch RC 6.00
141 Michael Hessman RC 3.00
142 Todd Wellemeyer RC 3.00
143 Matt Bruback RC 3.00
144 Chris Capuano RC 5.00
145 Oscar Villarreal RC 3.00
146 Prentice Redman RC 3.00
147 Jeff Duncan RC 5.00
148 Phil Seibel RC 3.00
149 Arnaldo Munoz 3.00
150 David Sanders RC 3.00
151 Rick Roberts RC 3.00
152 Terrmel Sledge RC 4.00
153 Franklin Perez 3.00
154 Jeremy Wedel RC 3.00
155 Ian Ferguson RC 3.00
156 Josh Hall RC 3.00
157 Rocco Baldelli 3.00
158 Alejandro Machado RC 3.00
159 Jorge Cordova RC 3.00
160 Wilfredo Ledezma RC 3.00
161 Luis Ayala RC 3.00

Silver

Even # SP's (2-60): 1-2X
Non-SP's (1-130): 4-8X
SP's (132-161): .5-1X
Production 150 Sets

Gold

Production 25 Sets:
No pricing due to scarcity.

Dean's List

HONOR ROLL

NM/M
Common Player: 4.00
Inserted 1:24
RC Roger Clemens 10.00
RC1 Roger Clemens 10.00
JG Jason Giambi 4.00
JG1 Jason Giambi 4.00
TG Troy Glaus 4.00
TG1 Troy Glaus 4.00
NG Shawn Green 4.00
NG1 Shawn Green 4.00
VG Vladimir Guerrero 6.00
VG Vladimir Guerrero 6.00
KG Ken Griffey Jr. 10.00
KG1 Ken Griffey Jr. 10.00
CJ Chipper Jones 8.00
CJ1 Chipper Jones 8.00
HM Hideki Matsui 20.00
HM1 Hideki Matsui 20.00
HN Hideo Nomo 10.00
HN1 Hideo Nomo 10.00
MP Mike Piazza 10.00
MP1 Mike Piazza 10.00
MA Mark Prior 8.00
MA1 Mark Prior 8.00
AP Albert Pujols 15.00
AP1 Albert Pujols 15.00
AR Alex Rodriguez 10.00
AR1 Alex Rodriguez 10.00
SS Sammy Sosa 10.00
IS Ichiro Suzuki 20.00
IS1 Ichiro Suzuki 20.00

Grade A Batting Gloves

NM/M
Most not priced due to scarcity.
Inserted 1:960
RA Roberto Alomar/65 20.00
CD Carlos Delgado/65 15.00
TG Troy Glaus/60 15.00
JG Juan Gonzalez/65 15.00
RM Raul Mondesi/65 10.00
RP Rafael Palmeiro/65 20.00
MR Manny Ramirez/69 20.00
AR Alex Rodriguez/67 25.00
IR Ivan Rodriguez/70 20.00
MT Miguel Tejada/70 10.00
FT Frank Thomas/70 20.00

Leather of Distinction

HONOR ROLL - LEATHER OF DISTINCTION

NM/M
Most not priced due to scarcity.
Inserted 1:960
KG Ken Griffey Jr./70 30.00
RP Rafael Palmeiro/70 20.00
MP Mike Piazza/50 40.00
MR Manny Ramirez/70 20.00
AR Alex Rodriguez/70 25.00
IR Ivan Rodriguez/69 20.00
TS Tim Salmon/70 10.00
GS Gary Sheffield/70 10.00
FT Frank Thomas/70 20.00
OV Omar Vizquel/65 10.00

Magazine

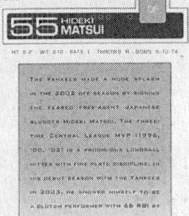

UO2 55 HIDEKI MATSUI

Three baseball players were included in a nine-card sheet inserted into a special-edition collectors' magazine produced by Upper Deck in November, 2003. Cards are in standard 2-1/2" x 3-1/2" format perforated on two, three, or four sides, depending on their placement on the panel. Fronts have game-action photos with player name, position and uniform number. Backs have personal data and a career summary. Only the baseball players are listed here.

NM/M
Complete Magazine: 12.00
Common Player: 1.00
UD2 Hideki Matsui 1.00
UD4 Ichiro 1.50
UD7 Mickey Mantle 3.00

Hideki Matsui Hawaii

The first licensed card of Yankees Japanese import slugger Hideki Matsui was distributed to attendees at the 2003 Hawaii Trade Conference. The card features silver-foil accents on front.

		NM/M
HM	Hideki Matsui	75.00

2003 Upper Deck MVP

		NM/M
Complete Set (220):		20.00
Complete Factory Set (330):		30.00
Common Player:		.10
Pack (8):		1.50
Box (24):		25.00
1	Troy Glaus	.40
2	Darin Erstad	.25
3	Jarrod Washburn	.10
4	Francisco Rodriguez	.10
5	Garret Anderson	.20
6	Tim Salmon	.20
7	Adam Kennedy	.10
8	Randy Johnson	.50
9	Luis Gonzalez	.20
10	Curt Schilling	.50
11	Junior Spivey	.10
12	Craig Counsell	.10
13	Mark Grace	.25
14	Steve Finley	.10
15	Javy Lopez	.10
16	Rafael Furcal	.10
17	John Smoltz	.15
18	Greg Maddux	.75
19	Chipper Jones	.50
20	Gary Sheffield	.20
21	Andruw Jones	.20
22	Tony Batista	.10
23	Geronimo Gil	.10
24	Jay Gibbons	.10
25	Rodrigo Lopez	.10
26	Chris Singleton	.10
27	Melvin Mora	.10
28	Jeff Conine	.10
29	Nomar Garciaparra	1.00
30	Pedro J. Martinez	.50
31	Manny Ramirez	.50
32	Shea Hillenbrand	.10
33	Johnny Damon	.40
34	Jason Varitek	.25
35	Derek Lowe	.10
36	Trot Nixon	.10
37	Sammy Sosa	.75
38	Kerry Wood	.50
39	Mark Prior	.50
40	Moises Alou	.20
41	Corey Patterson	.25
42	Hee Seop Choi	.10
43	Mark Bellhorn	.10
44	Frank Thomas	.40
45	Mark Buehrle	.20
46	Magglio Ordonez	.20
47	Carlos Lee	.20
48	Paul Konerko	.20
49	Joe Borchard	.10
50	Joe Crede	.10
51	Ken Griffey Jr.	.75
52	Adam Dunn	.40
53	Austin Kearns	.40
54	Aaron Boone	.10

55	Sean Casey	.10
56	Danny Graves	.10
57	Russell Branyan	.10
58	Matt Lawton	.10
59	C.C. Sabathia	.10
60	Omar Vizquel	.20
61	Brandon Phillips	.10
62	Karim Garcia	.10
63	Ellis Burks	.10
64	Cliff Lee	.10
65	Todd Helton	.40
66	Larry Walker	.20
67	Jay Payton	.10
68	Brent Butler	.10
69	Juan Uribe	.10
70	Jason Jennings	.10
71	Denny Stark	.10
72	Dmitri Young	.10
73	Carlos Pena	.10
74	Andres Torres	.10
75	Andy Van Hekken	.10
76	George Lombard	.10
77	Eric Munson	.10
78	Bobby Higginson	.10
79	Luis Castillo	.10
80	A.J. Burnett	.10
81	Juan Encarnacion	.10
82	Ivan Rodriguez	.40
83	Mike Lowell	.10
84	Josh Beckett	.25
85	Brad Penny	.10
86	Craig Biggio	.25
87	Jeff Kent	.20
88	Morgan Ensberg	.10
89	Daryle Ward	.10
90	Jeff Bagwell	.40
91	Roy Oswalt	.20
92	Lance Berkman	.25
93	Mike Sweeney	.10
94	Carlos Beltran	.40
95	Raul Ibanez	.10
96	Carlos Febles	.10
97	Joe Randa	.10
98	Shawn Green	.25
99	Kevin Brown	.15
100	Paul LoDuca	.10
101	Adrian Beltre	.25
102	Eric Gagne	.25
103	Kazuhisa Ishii	.10
104	Odalis Perez	.10
105	Brian Jordan	.10
106	Geoff Jenkins	.10
107	Richie Sexson	.25
108	Ben Sheets	.20
109	Alex Sanchez	.10
110	Eric Young	.10
111	Jose Hernandez	.10
112	Torii Hunter	.25
113	Eric Milton	.10
114	Corey Koskie	.10
115	Doug Mientkiewicz	.10
116	A.J. Pierzynski	.10
117	Jacque Jones	.10
118	Cristian Guzman	.10
119	Bartolo Colon	.10
120	Brad Wilkerson	.10
121	Michael Barrett	.10
122	Vladimir Guerrero	.50
123	Jose Vidro	.10
124	Javier Vazquez	.10
125	Endy Chavez	.10
126	Roberto Alomar	.25
127	Mike Piazza	1.00
128	Jeromy Burnitz	.10
129	Mo Vaughn	.15
130	Tom Glavine	.25
131	Al Leiter	.15
132	Armando Benitez	.10
133	Timoniel Perez	.10
134	Roger Clemens	1.00
135	Derek Jeter	1.50
136	Jason Giambi	.25
137	Alfonso Soriano	.50
138	Bernie Williams	.25
139	Mike Mussina	.25
140	Jorge Posada	.20
141	Hideki Matsui RC	4.00
142	Robin Ventura	.10
143	David Wells	.10
144	Nick Johnson	.10
145	Tim Hudson	.20
146	Eric Chavez	.25
147	Barry Zito	.25
148	Miguel Tejada	.40
149	Jermaine Dye	.10
150	Mark Mulder	.20
151	Terrence Long	.10
152	Scott Hatteberg	.10
153	Marlon Byrd	.10
154	Jim Thome	.40
155	Marlon Anderson	.10
156	Vicente Padilla	.10
157	Bobby Abreu	.20
158	Jimmy Rollins	.10
159	Pat Burrell	.40
160	Brian Giles	.20
161	Aramis Ramirez	.20
162	Jason Kendall	.10
163	Josh Fogg	.10
164	Kip Wells	.10
165	Pokey Reese	.10
166	Kris Benson	.10
167	Ryan Klesko	.10
168	Brian Lawrence	.10
169	Mark Kotsay	.10
170	Jake Peavy	.20
171	Phil Nevin	.10
172	Sean Burroughs	.10

173	Trevor Hoffman	.10
174	Jason Schmidt	.20
175	Kirk Rueter	.10
176	Barry Bonds	1.50
177	Pedro Feliz	.10
178	Rich Aurilia	.10
179	Benito Santiago	.10
180	J.T. Snow	.10
181	Robb Nen	.10
182	Ichiro Suzuki	1.00
183	Edgar Martinez	.10
184	Bret Boone	.10
185	Freddy Garcia	.10
186	John Olerud	.20
187	Mike Cameron	.10
188	Joel Pineiro	.10
189	Albert Pujols	1.25
190	Matt Morris	.20
191	J.D. Drew	.20
192	Scott Rolen	.50
193	Tino Martinez	.20
194	Jim Edmonds	.20
195	Edgar Renteria	.10
196	Fernando Vina	.10
197	Jason Isringhausen	.10
198	Ben Grieve	.10
199	Carl Crawford	.10
200	Dewon Brazelton	.10
201	Aubrey Huff	.10
202	Jared Sandberg	.10
203	Steve Cox	.10
204	Carl Everett	.10
205	Kevin Mench	.10
206	Alex Rodriguez	1.00
207	Rafael Palmeiro	.20
208	Michael Young	.10
209	Hank Blalock	.40
210	Juan Gonzalez	.25
211	Carlos Delgado	.20
212	Eric Hinske	.20
213	Josh Phelps	.10
214	Mark Hendrickson	.10
215	Roy Halladay	.10
216	Orlando Hudson	.10
217	Shannon Stewart	.10
218	Vernon Wells	.10
219	Ichiro Suzuki	.40
220	Jason Giambi	.25
221	Scott Spiezio	.10
222	Rich Fischer	.10
223	Bengie Molina	.10
224	David Eckstein	.10
225	Brandon Webb RC	1.50
226	Oscar Villarreal	.10
227	Rob Hammock RC	.40
228	Matt Kata RC	.40
229	Lyle Overbay	.10
230	Chris Capuano RC	.50
231	Horacio Ramirez	.10
232	Shane Reynolds	.10
233	Russ Ortiz	.10
234	Mike Hampton	.10
235	Mike Hessman	.10
236	Byung-Hyun Kim	.10
237	Freddy Sanchez	.10
238	Jason Shiell	.10
239	Ryan Cameron	.10
240	Todd Wellemeyer RC	.40
241	Joe Borowski	.10
242	Alex Gonzalez	.10
243	Jon Leicester	.10
244	David Sanders	.10
245	Roberto Alomar	.25
246	Barry Larkin	.25
247	Jhonny Peralta	.10
248	Zach Sorensen	.10
249	Jason Davis	.10
250	Coco Crisp	.10
251	Greg Vaughn	.10
252	Preston Wilson	.10
253	Denny Neagle	.10
254	Clint Barmes RC	1.00
255	Jeremy Bonderman	1.00
256	Wilfredo Ledezma RC	.10
257	Dontrelle Willis	.25
258	Alex Gonzalez	.10
259	Tommy Phelps	.10
260	Kirk Saarloos	.10
261	Colin Porter RC	.10
262	Nate Bland	.10
263	Jason Gilfillan	.10
264	Mike MacDougal	.10
265	Ken Harvey	.10
266	Brent Mayne	.10
267	Miguel Cabrera	.40
268	Hideo Nomo	.25
269	Dave Roberts	.10
270	Fred McGriff	.20
271	Joe Thurston	.10
272	Royce Clayton	.10
273	Micheal Nakamura	.10
274	Brad Radke	.10
275	Joe Mays	.10
276	Lew Ford RC	1.00
277	Michael Cuddyer	.10
278	Luis Ayala	.10
279	Julio Manon	.10
280	Anthony Ferrari	.10
281	Livan Hernandez	.10
282	Jae Weong Seo	.10
283	Jose Reyes	.40
284	Tony Clark	.10
285	Ty Wigginton	.10
286	Cliff Floyd	.10
287	Jeremy Griffiths	.10
288	Jason Roach	.10
289	Jeff Duncan	.10
290	Phil Seibel	.10

291	Prentice Redman RC	.25
292	Jose Contreras RC	1.00
293	Ruben Sierra	.10
294	Andy Pettitte	.25
295	Aaron Boone	.10
296	Mariano Rivera	.20
297	Michel Hernandez	.10
298	Mike Neu	.10
299	Erubiel Durazo	.10
300	Billy McMillon	.10
301	Rich Harden	.10
302	David Bell	.10
303	Kevin Millwood	.20
304	Mike Lieberthal	.10
305	Jeremy Wedel	.10
306	Kenny Lofton	.20
307	Reggie Sanders	.10
308	Randall Simon	.10
309	Xavier Nady	.10
310	Rod Beck	.10
311	Miguel Ojeda	.10
312	Mark Loretta	.10
313	Edgardo Alfonzo	.10
314	Andres Galarraga	.10
315	Jose Cruz Jr.	.10
316	Jesse Foppert	.10
317	Kurt Ainsworth	.10
318	Dan Wilson	.10
319	Ben Davis	.10
320	Rocco Baldelli	.25
321	Al Martin	.10
322	Runelvys Hernandez	.10
323	Dan Haren	.50
324	Bo Hart RC	.25
325	Einar Diaz	.10
326	Mike Lamb	.10
327	Aquilino Lopez	.10
328	Reed Johnson	.10
329	Diegomar Markwell	.10
330	Hideki Matsui	.75

Gold

		NM/M
Stars (1-220):		6-12X
Production 150 Sets		
Black Stars:		10-20X
Production 50 Sets		
Silver Stars:		1-2X
Inserted 1:2		

Base-to-Base

		NM/M
Inserted 1:488		
CP	Roger Clemens, Mike Piazza	25.00
IG	Ichiro Suzuki, Ken Griffey Jr.	40.00
IJ	Ichiro Suzuki, Derek Jeter	45.00
JW	Derek Jeter, Bernie Williams	25.00
MB	Mark McGwire, Barry Bonds	60.00
RJ	Alex Rodriguez, Derek Jeter	40.00

Covering the Bases

		NM/M
Common Player:		4.00
Inserted 1:125		
BB	Barry Bonds	15.00
CD	Carlos Delgado	4.00
JD	J.D. Drew	4.00
DE	Darin Erstad	6.00
TG	Troy Glaus	6.00
LG	Luis Gonzalez	4.00
SG	Shawn Green	6.00
DJ	Derek Jeter	15.00
MP	Mike Piazza	12.00
AR	Alex Rodriguez	12.00
IR	Ivan Rodriguez	4.00
IS	Ichiro Suzuki	15.00
MT	Miguel Tejada	6.00
FT	Frank Thomas	8.00
JT	Jim Thome	10.00

Covering the Plate Bat

		NM/M
Common Player:		6.00
Inserted 1:160		
RA	Roberto Alomar	15.00
RF	Rafael Furcal	8.00
VG	Vladimir Guerrero	8.00
FM	Fred McGriff	6.00

Dual Aces

		NM/M
Common Card:		8.00
Inserted 1:488		
BS	Kevin Brown, Curt Schilling	10.00
CJ	Roger Clemens, Randy Johnson	20.00
CL	Roger Clemens, Al Leiter	15.00
ML	Matt Morris, Al Leiter	8.00
SJ	Curt Schilling, Randy Johnson	12.00
SM	Curt Schilling, Andy Pettitte	10.00

Express Delivery

		NM/M
Complete Set (15):		10.00
Common Player:		.50
Inserted 1:12		
ED1	Randy Johnson	2.00
ED2	Curt Schilling	1.00
ED3	Pedro J. Martinez	2.00
ED4	Kerry Wood	1.00
ED5	Mark Prior	1.50
ED6	A.J. Burnett	.50
ED7	Josh Beckett	.50
ED8	Roy Oswalt	.75
ED9	Hideo Nomo	.75
ED10	Ben Sheets	.50
ED11	Bartolo Colon	.50
ED12	Roger Clemens	2.50
ED13	Mike Mussina	.75
ED14	Tim Hudson	.75
ED15	Matt Morris	.50

MVP Celebration

		NM/M
Common Player:		1.50
#'d to yr. MVP was won.		
MVP1	Yogi Berra	4.00
MVP2	Mickey Mantle	15.00
MVP3	Mickey Mantle	15.00
MVP4	Mickey Mantle	15.00
MVP5	Roger Clemens	4.00
MVP6	Rickey Henderson	4.00
MVP7	Frank Thomas	4.00
MVP8	Mo Vaughn	1.50
MVP9	Juan Gonzalez	3.00
MVP10	Ken Griffey Jr.	6.00
MVP11	Juan Gonzalez	3.00
MVP12	Ivan Rodriguez	3.00
MVP13	Jason Giambi	4.00
MVP14	Ichiro Suzuki	6.00
MVP15	Miguel Tejada	2.00
MVP16	Barry Bonds	8.00
MVP17	Barry Bonds	8.00
MVP18	Barry Bonds	8.00
MVP19	Jeff Bagwell	4.00
MVP20	Barry Larkin	1.50
MVP21	Larry Walker	1.50
MVP22	Sammy Sosa	6.00
MVP23	Chipper Jones	5.00
MVP24	Jeff Kent	1.50
MVP25	Barry Bonds	8.00
MVP26	Barry Bonds	8.00
MVP27	Ken Griffey Sr.	1.50
MVP28	Roger Clemens	3.00
MVP29	Ken Griffey Jr.	6.00
MVP30	Fred McGriff	1.50
MVP31	Jeff Conine	1.50
MVP32	Mike Piazza	6.00
MVP33	Sandy Alomar Jr.	1.50

MM	Mark McGwire	60.00
JT	Jim Thome	12.00

MVP34	Roberto Alomar	2.50
MVP35	Pedro J. Martinez	4.00
MVP36	Derek Jeter	8.00
MVP37	Rickey Henderson	4.00
MVP38	Roberto Alomar	2.50
MVP39	Bernie Williams	3.00
MVP40	Marquis Grissom	1.50
MVP41	David Wells	1.50
MVP42	Orlando Hernandez	1.50
MVP43	David Justice	1.50
MVP44	Andy Pettitte	2.00
MVP45	Adam Kennedy	1.50
MVP46	John Smoltz	1.50
MVP47	Curt Schilling	2.00
MVP48	Javy Lopez	1.50
MVP49	Livan Hernandez	1.50
MVP50	Sterling Hitchcock	1.50
MVP51	Mike Hampton	1.50
MVP52	Craig Counsell	1.50
MVP53	Benito Santiago	1.50
MVP54	Tom Glavine	2.00
MVP55	Livan Hernandez	1.50
MVP56	Mariano Rivera	1.50
MVP57	Derek Jeter	8.00
MVP58	Randy Johnson	4.00
MVP59	Curt Schilling	2.50
MVP60	Troy Glaus	3.00
MVP61	Yogi Berra	4.00
MVP62	Yogi Berra	4.00
MVP63	Mickey Mantle	15.00
MVP64	Mickey Mantle	15.00
MVP65	Ken Griffey Sr.	1.50
MVP66	Rickey Henderson	4.00
MVP67	Roberto Alomar	2.50
MVP68	Bernie Williams	3.00
MVP69	Livan Hernandez	1.50
MVP70	Sammy Sosa	6.00
MVP71	Sterling Hitchcock	1.50
MVP72	David Wells	1.50
MVP73	Mariano Rivera	1.50
MVP74	Chipper Jones	5.00
MVP75	Ivan Rodriguez	2.00
MVP76	Derek Jeter	8.00
MVP77	Jason Giambi	4.00
MVP78	Jeff Kent	1.50
MVP79	Mike Hampton	1.50
MVP80	Randy Johnson	4.00
MVP81	Curt Schilling	2.50
MVP82	Barry Bonds	8.00
MVP83	Ichiro Suzuki	6.00
MVP84	Ichiro Suzuki	6.00
MVP85	Adam Kennedy	1.50
MVP86	Benito Santiago	1.50
MVP87	Troy Glaus	3.00
MVP88	Troy Glaus	3.00
MVP89	Miguel Tejada	2.00
MVP90	Barry Bonds	8.00

Prosign

Common Autograph:
Production 25 Sets
No Pricing

Pro View

		NM/M
Complete Set (45):		65.00
Common Player:		.75
Inserted 2:Box		
Golds:		2-3X
PV1	Troy Glaus	1.50
PV2	Darin Erstad	1.00
PV3	Randy Johnson	2.00
PV4	Curt Schilling	1.50
PV5	Luis Gonzalez	.75
PV6	Chipper Jones	2.00
PV7	Andruw Jones	1.00
PV8	Greg Maddux	3.00
PV9	Pedro J. Martinez	2.00
PV10	Manny Ramirez	1.50
PV11	Sammy Sosa	3.00
PV12	Mark Prior	1.50
PV13	Magglio Ordonez	1.00
PV14	Frank Thomas	1.50
PV15	Ken Griffey Jr.	3.00
PV16	Adam Dunn	1.50
PV17	Jim Thome	1.50
PV18	Todd Helton	1.00
PV19	Jeff Bagwell	1.50
PV20	Lance Berkman	1.00
PV21	Shawn Green	.75
PV22	Hideo Nomo	1.00
PV23	Vladimir Guerrero	2.00
PV24	Roberto Alomar	1.50
PV25	Mike Piazza	4.00
PV26	Jason Giambi	3.00
PV27	Roger Clemens	3.00
PV28	Alfonso Soriano	2.00
PV29	Derek Jeter	6.00
PV30	Miguel Tejada	1.50
PV31	Eric Chavez	.75
PV32	Barry Zito	.75
PV33	Pat Burrell	1.50
PV34	Brian Giles	.75
PV35	Barry Bonds	6.00
PV36	Ichiro Suzuki	4.00
PV37	Albert Pujols	5.00

PV38	Scott Rolen	1.50
PV39	J.D. Drew	.75
PV40	Mark McGwire	5.00
PV41	Alex Rodriguez	5.00
PV42	Rafael Palmeiro	1.00
PV43	Juan Gonzalez	1.00
PV44	Eric Hinske	.75
PV45	Carlos Delgado	.75

SportsNut Fantasy

	NM/M
Complete Set (90):	45.00
Common Player:	.40
Inserted 1:3	

Prices for unscratched cards.

SN1	Troy Glaus	1.00
SN2	Darin Erstad	.50
SN3	Luis Gonzalez	.50
SN4	Andruw Jones	.75
SN5	Chipper Jones	2.00
SN6	Gary Sheffield	.50
SN7	Jay Gibbons	.40
SN8	Manny Ramirez	1.00
SN9	Shea Hillenbrand	.40
SN10	Johnny Damon	.40
SN11	Nomar Garciaparra	2.50
SN12	Sammy Sosa	2.00
SN13	Magglio Ordonez	.75
SN14	Frank Thomas	.75
SN15	Ken Griffey Jr.	1.50
SN16	Adam Dunn	1.00
SN17	Matt Lawton	.40
SN18	Larry Walker	.40
SN19	Todd Helton	.75
SN20	Carlos Pena	.40
SN21	Mike Lowell	.40
SN22	Jeff Bagwell	1.00
SN23	Lance Berkman	.75
SN24	Mike Sweeney	.50
SN25	Carlos Beltran	.40
SN26	Shawn Green	.75
SN27	Richie Sexson	.50
SN28	Torii Hunter	.50
SN29	Jacque Jones	.40
SN30	Vladimir Guerrero	1.50
SN31	Jose Vidro	.40
SN32	Roberto Alomar	.50
SN33	Mike Piazza	2.00
SN34	Alfonso Soriano	1.50
SN35	Derek Jeter	3.00
SN36	Jason Giambi	2.00
SN37	Bernie Williams	.75
SN38	Eric Chavez	.75
SN39	Miguel Tejada	.75
SN40	Jim Thome	1.00
SN41	Pat Burrell	1.00
SN42	Bobby Abreu	.50
SN43	Brian Giles	.50
SN44	Jason Kendall	.40
SN45	Ryan Klesko	.40
SN46	Phil Nevin	.40
SN47	Barry Bonds	4.00
SN48	Rich Aurilia	.40
SN49	Ichiro Suzuki	2.00
SN50	Bret Boone	.40
SN51	J.D. Drew	.40
SN52	Jim Edmonds	.75
SN53	Albert Pujols	1.50
SN54	Scott Rolen	.75
SN55	Ben Grieve	.40
SN56	Alex Rodriguez	3.00
SN57	Rafael Palmeiro	.50
SN58	Juan Gonzalez	.50
SN59	Carlos Delgado	.40
SN60	Josh Phelps	.40
SN61	Jarrod Washburn	.40
SN62	Randy Johnson	1.00
SN63	Curt Schilling	.75
SN64	Greg Maddux	1.50
SN65	Mike Hampton	.40
SN66	Rodrigo Lopez	.40
SN67	Pedro J. Martinez	1.50
SN68	Derek Lowe	.40
SN69	Mark Prior	1.00
SN70	Kerry Wood	.75
SN71	Mark Buehrle	.40
SN72	Roy Oswalt	.50
SN73	Wade Miller	.40
SN74	Odalis Perez	.40
SN75	Hideo Nomo	.50
SN76	Ben Sheets	.40
SN77	Eric Milton	.40
SN78	Bartolo Colon	.40
SN79	Tom Glavine	.40
SN80	Al Leiter	.40
SN81	Roger Clemens	2.00
SN82	Mike Mussina	.75
SN83	Tim Hudson	.75
SN84	Barry Zito	.50
SN85	Mark Mulder	.50
SN86	Vicente Padilla	.40
SN87	Jason Schmidt	.40
SN88	Freddy Garcia	.40
SN89	Matt Morris	.40
SN90	Roy Halladay	.40

Talk of the Town

	NM/M
Complete Set (15):	20.00
Common Player:	.75
Inserted 1:12	

TT1	Hideki Matsui	3.00
TT2	Chipper Jones	1.00
TT3	Manny Ramirez	1.50
TT4	Sammy Sosa	2.00
TT5	Ken Griffey Jr.	2.00
TT6	Lance Berkman	.75
TT7	Shawn Green	.75
TT8	Vladimir Guerrero	1.50
TT9	Mike Piazza	2.50
TT10	Jason Giambi	1.50
TT11	Alfonso Soriano	1.50
TT12	Ichiro Suzuki	2.50
TT13	Albert Pujols	3.00
TT14	Alex Rodriguez	3.00
TT15	Eric Hinske	.75

Three Bagger

	NM/M
Inserted 1:488	

BMP	Barry Bonds, Mark McGwire, Mike Piazza	80.00
GIB	Ken Griffey Jr., Ichiro Suzuki, Barry Bonds	60.00
GTD	Troy Glaus, Frank Thomas, Carlos Delgado	10.00
IBJ	Ichiro Suzuki, Barry Bonds, Derek Jeter	80.00
JWP	Derek Jeter, Bernie Williams, Jorge Posada	35.00
SCB	Curt Schilling, Roger Clemens, Kevin Brown	20.00

Total Bases

	NM/M
Production 150 Sets	

BB	Barry Bonds	20.00
RC	Roger Clemens	20.00
TG	Troy Glaus	8.00
KG	Ken Griffey Jr.	15.00
DJ	Derek Jeter	20.00
MM	Mark McGwire	25.00
MP	Mike Piazza	15.00
AR	Alex Rodriguez	15.00
IS	Ichiro Suzuki	30.00

2003 Upper Deck Patch Collection Promo

	NM/M
SAMPLEIchiro	6.00

2003 Upper Deck Patch Collection

	NM/M
Complete Set (161):	
Common Player:	.25
Common SP Patch (121-161):	4.00
All-Star & HOF Patches (121-150): Inserted 1:40	
Rookie Patches (151-161): Inserted 1:20	
Pack (5):	4.75
Box (20):	80.00

1	Darin Erstad	.40
2	Troy Glaus	.75
3	Robby Hammock RC	.25
4	Luis Gonzalez	.50
5	Randy Johnson/SP	2.00
6	Curt Schilling/SP	2.50
7	Oscar Villarreal RC	.25
8	Gary Sheffield	.25
9	Mike Hampton	.25
10	Greg Maddux	1.50
11	Chipper Jones	1.50
12	Tony Batista	.25
13	Rodrigo Lopez	.25
14	Jay Gibbons	.25
15	Shea Hillenbrand	.25
16	Johnny Damon	.25
17	Derek Lowe	.25
18	Nomar Garciaparra	2.00
19	Pedro J. Martinez	1.00
20	Manny Ramirez	.75
21	Mark Prior	.75
22	Kerry Wood	.25
23	Corey Patterson	.25
24	Sammy Sosa	1.50
25	Troy O'Leary	.25
26	Frank Thomas	.75
27	Magglio Ordonez	.25
28	Bartolo Colon	.25
29	Austin Kearns	.25
30	Aaron Boone	.25
31	Ken Griffey Jr.	1.50
32	Adam Dunn	.50
33	C.C. Sabathia	.25
34	Karim Garcia	.25
35	Larry Walker	.40
36	Preston Wilson	.25
37	Jason Jennings	.25
38	Todd Helton	.75
39	Carlos Pena	.25
40	Eric Munson	.25
41	Ivan Rodriguez	.50
42	Josh Beckett	.25
43	A.J. Burnett	.25
44	Roy Oswalt	.25
45	Craig Biggio	.40
46	Jeff Bagwell	.50
47	Lance Berkman	.50
48	Jeff Kent	.25
49	Carlos Beltran	.25
50	Mike Sweeney	.25
51	Hideo Nomo	.50
52	Adrian Beltre	.25
53	Shawn Green	.50
54	Kazuhisa Ishii	.25
55	Ben Sheets	.25
56	Richie Sexson	.50
57	Torii Hunter	.50
58	Doug Mientkiewicz	.25
59	Eric Milton	.25
60	Corey Koskie	.25
61	Joe Mays	.25
62	Jose Vidro	.25
63	Vladimir Guerrero	.75
64	Luis Ayala RC	.25
65	Cliff Floyd	.25
66	Tom Glavine	.50
67	Mike Piazza	2.00
68	Roberto Alomar	.50
69	Al Leiter	.25
70	Mike Mussina	.50
71	Mariano Rivera	.50
72	Drew Henson	.25
73	Roger Clemens	1.00
74	Jason Giambi	1.00
75	Bernie Williams	.50
76	Alfonso Soriano	1.50
77	Derek Jeter	3.00
78	Miguel Tejada	.50
79	Jermaine Dye	.25
80	Tim Hudson	.50
81	Barry Zito	.50
82	Mark Mulder	.50
83	Pat Burrell	.50
84	Jim Thome	.75
85	Bobby Abreu	.40
86	Kevin Millwood	.40
87	Jason Kendall	.40
88	Brian Giles	.40
89	Phil Nevin	.25
90	Sean Burroughs	.25
91	Oliver Perez	.25
92	Jose Cruz Jr.	.25
93	Rich Aurilia	.25
94	Edgardo Alfonzo	.25
95	Barry Bonds	3.00
96	J.T. Snow	.25
97	Mike Cameron	.25
98	John Olerud	.50
99	Bret Boone	.25
100	Ichiro Suzuki	1.50
101	J.D. Drew	.40
102	Jim Edmonds	.50
103	Scott Rolen	.75
104	Matt Morris	.40
105	Tino Martinez	.40
106	Albert Pujols	1.50
107	Rocco Baldelli	.25
108	Carl Crawford	.25
109	Mark Teixeira	.50
110	Rafael Palmeiro	.50
111	Hank Blalock	.50
112	Alex Rodriguez	2.50
113	Kevin Mench	.25
114	Juan Gonzalez	.75
115	Shannon Stewart	.25
116	Vernon Wells	.40
117	Josh Phelps	.25
118	Eric Hinske	.25
119	Orlando Hudson	.25
120	Carlos Delgado	.50
121	Alex Rodriguez	10.00
122	Nomar Garciaparra	10.00
123	Miguel Tejada	4.00
124	Jim Thome	8.00
125	Alfonso Soriano	6.00
126	Vladimir Guerrero	6.00
127	Derek Jeter	15.00
128	Mike Piazza	8.00
129	Ichiro Suzuki	12.00
130	Pedro J. Martinez	8.00
131	Luis Gonzalez	4.00
132	Adam Dunn	6.00
133	Shawn Green	4.00
134	Barry Zito	4.00
135	Torii Hunter	5.00
136	Ted Williams	20.00
137	Mickey Mantle	25.00
138	Ernie Banks	10.00
139	Yogi Berra	8.00
140	Rollie Fingers	4.00
141	Jim "Catfish" Hunter	4.00
142	Juan Marichal	8.00
143	Eddie Mathews	10.00
144	Willie McCovey	10.00
145	Joe Morgan	5.00
146	Stan Musial	12.00
147	Pee Wee Reese	10.00
148	Phil Rizzuto	6.00
149	Nolan Ryan	20.00
150	Tom Seaver	8.00
151	Hideki Matsui RC	15.00
152	Jose Contreras RC	5.00
153	Lew Ford RC	5.00
154	Jeremy Griffiths RC	4.00
155	Guillermo Quiroz RC	4.00
156	Ryan Cameron RC	4.00
157	Jon Leicester RC	4.00
158	Josh Willingham RC	4.00
159	Shane Bazzell RC	4.00
160	Willie Eyre RC	4.00
161	Prentice Redman RC	4.00

All-Star Game History Patches

	NM/M
Common Patch:	8.00
Inserted 2:Box	

1	1933 All-Star Game	12.00
2	1934 All-Star Game	15.00
3	1935 All-Star Game	15.00
4	1936 All-Star Game	10.00
5	1937 All-Star Game	15.00
6	1938 All-Star Game	10.00
7	1939 All-Star Game	15.00
8	1940 All-Star Game	15.00
9	1941 All-Star Game	15.00
10	1942 All-Star Game	15.00
11	1943 All-Star Game	12.00
12	1944 All-Star Game	15.00
13	1946 All-Star Game	15.00
14	1947 All-Star Game	15.00
15	1948 All-Star Game	15.00
16	1949 All-Star Game	15.00
17	1950 All-Star Game	12.00
18	1951 All-Star Game	15.00
19	1952 All-Star Game	15.00
20	1953 All-Star Game	12.00
21	1954 All-Star Game	15.00
22	1955 All-Star Game	10.00
23	1956 All-Star Game	12.00
24	1957 All-Star Game	15.00
25	1958 All-Star Game	12.00
26	1959 All-Star Game	15.00
27	1959 All-Star Game	15.00
28	1960 All-Star Game	10.00
29	1960 All-Star Game	15.00
30	1961 All-Star Game	15.00
31	1961 All-Star Game	15.00
32	1962 All-Star Game	8.00
33	1962 All-Star Game	15.00
34	1963 All-Star Game	10.00
35	1964 All-Star Game	10.00
36	1965 All-Star Game	15.00
37	1966 All-Star Game	15.00
38	1967 All-Star Game	12.00
39	1968 All-Star Game	8.00
40	1969 All-Star Game	15.00
41	1970 All-Star Game	15.00
42	1971 All-Star Game	15.00
43	1972 All-Star Game	15.00
44	1973 All-Star Game	10.00
45	1974 All-Star Game	10.00
46	1975 All-Star Game	10.00
47	1976 All-Star Game	15.00
48	1977 All-Star Game	12.00
49	1978 All-Star Game	15.00
50	1979 All-Star Game	8.00
51	1980 All-Star Game	8.00
52	1981 All-Star Game	8.00
53	1982 All-Star Game	8.00
54	1983 All-Star Game	10.00
55	1984 All-Star Game	10.00
56	1985 All-Star Game	10.00
57	1986 All-Star Game	10.00
58	1987 All-Star Game	8.00
59	1988 All-Star Game	8.00
60	1989 All-Star Game	8.00
61	1990 All-Star Game	15.00
62	1991 All-Star Game	8.00
63	1992 All-Star Game	10.00
64	1993 All-Star Game	10.00
65	1994 All-Star Game	8.00
66	1995 All-Star Game	8.00
67	1996 All-Star Game	12.00
68	1997 All-Star Game	10.00
69	1998 All-Star Game	8.00
70	1999 All-Star Game	15.00
71	2000 All-Star Game	10.00
72	2001 All-Star Game	10.00
73	2002 All-Star Game	12.00

MVPs Patches

	NM/M
Common Player:	5.00
Inserted 1:20	

1	Derek Jeter	15.00
2	Randy Johnson	8.00
3	Curt Schilling	6.00
4	Troy Glaus	5.00
5	Ted Williams	15.00
6	Ted Williams	15.00
7	Mickey Mantle	20.00
8	Mickey Mantle	20.00
9	Phil Rizzuto	5.00
10	Roger Clemens	10.00
11	Ken Griffey Jr.	10.00
12	Jason Giambi	10.00
13	Ichiro Suzuki	15.00
14	Roger Clemens	10.00
15	Yogi Berra	6.00
16	Sammy Sosa	15.00
17	Derek Jeter	15.00
18	Mike Piazza	15.00
19	Barry Bonds	15.00
20	Stan Musial	12.00
21	Joe Morgan	5.00

Signature Patches

	NM/M
Common Autograph:	25.00
Inserted 1:320	

JB	Jeff Bagwell	50.00
LB	Lance Berkman	50.00
RC	Roger Clemens	160.00
AD	Adam Dunn	60.00
FG	Freddy Garcia	30.00
JG	Jason Giambi	40.00
LG	Luis Gonzalez	40.00

KG	Ken Griffey Jr.	100.00
DH	Drew Henson	40.00
EH	Eric Hinske	25.00
TP	Troy Percival	.25
SR	Scott Rolen	50.00
CS	Curt Schilling	50.00
GS	Gary Sheffield	50.00
IS	Ichiro Suzuki	300.00
MT	Miguel Tejada	50.00
BZ	Barry Zito	40.00

2003 Upper Deck Play Ball Promos

BARRY ZITO

Each April 2003 newsstand issue of Tuff Stuff magazine included a Play Ball promo card inside its poly bag. The cards differ from the issued version only in the appearance on front of a silver-foil "UD PROMO" notation. It is not known how many different players cards were used in the promotion.

	NM/M
Common Player:	.25
Stars:	1.5-2.5X

2003 Upper Deck Play Ball Sample

MARK McGWIRE

This promo card differs from the issued version in its card number and in the appearance on back of a large overprinted typewriter-style "SAMPLE."

		NM/M
1	Mark McGwire	2.00

2003 Upper Deck Play Ball

ROBIN YOUNT

	NM/M
Complete Set (104):	
Common Player:	.25
Common Summer of '41 (74-88):	4.00
Inserted 1:24	
Common Ted Williams (89-103):	10.00
Inserted 1:24	
Pack (5):	2.50
Box (24):	40.00
1 Troy Glaus	.40

2	Darin Erstad	.25
3	Randy Johnson	.75
4	Luis Gonzalez	.40
5	Curt Schilling	.75
6	Tom Glavine	.40
7	Chipper Jones	.75
8	Greg Maddux	1.00
9	Andruw Jones	.40
10	Pedro J. Martinez	.75
11	Manny Ramirez	.75
12	Nomar Garciaparra	1.00
13	Billy Williams	.25
14	Sammy Sosa	1.00
15	Kerry Wood	.75
16	Mark Prior	.75
17	Ernie Banks	1.00
18	Frank Thomas	.75
19	Joe Morgan	.25
20	Ken Griffey Jr.	1.25
21	Adam Dunn	.50
22	Jim Thome	.75
23	Todd Helton	.50
24	Larry Walker	.40
25	Lance Berkman	.40
26	Roy Oswalt	.40
27	Jeff Bagwell	.50
28	Nolan Ryan	2.00
29	Mike Sweeney	.25
30	Shawn Green	.40
31	Hideo Nomo	.40
32	Kazuhisa Ishii	.25
33	Richie Sexson	.40
34	Robin Yount	.75
35	Harmon Killebrew	.75
36	Torii Hunter	.50
37	Vladimir Guerrero	.75
38	Roberto Alomar	.50
39	Mike Piazza	1.00
40	Tom Seaver	.75
41	Phil Rizzuto	.50
42	Yogi Berra	.75
43	Mike Mussina	.50
44	Roger Clemens	1.50
45	Derek Jeter	2.00
46	Jason Giambi	.25
47	Bernie Williams	.40
48	Alfonso Soriano	.75
49	Jim "Catfish" Hunter	.25
50	Barry Zito	.40
51	Eric Chavez	.40
52	Tim Hudson	.40
53	Rollie Fingers	.25
54	Miguel Tejada	.50
55	Pat Burrell	.40
56	Brian Giles	.40
57	Willie Stargell	.50
58	Phil Nevin	.25
59	Orlando Cepeda	.40
60	Barry Bonds	2.00
61	Jeff Kent	.40
62	Willie McCovey	.25
63	Ichiro Suzuki	1.50
64	Stan Musial	1.50
65	Albert Pujols	2.00
66	J.D. Drew	.40
67	Scott Rolen	.75
68	Mark McGwire	1.00
69	Alex Rodriguez	1.00
70	Juan Gonzalez	.40
71	Ivan Rodriguez	.50
72	Rafael Palmeiro	.50
73	Carlos Delgado	.40
74	Ted Williams	15.00
75	Hank Greenberg	6.00
76	Joe DiMaggio	15.00
77	Lefty Gomez	6.00
78	Tommy Henrich	4.00
79	Pee Wee Reese	5.00
80	Mel Ott	6.00
81	Carl Hubbell	6.00
82	Jimmie Foxx	8.00
83	Joe Cronin	4.00
84	Charlie Gehringer	5.00
85	Frank Hayes	5.00
86	Babe Dahlgren	4.00
87	Dolph Camilli	4.00
88	Johnny Vander Meer	4.00
89	Ted Williams	10.00
90	Ted Williams	10.00
91	Ted Williams	10.00
92	Ted Williams	10.00
93	Ted Williams	10.00
94	Ted Williams	10.00
95	Ted Williams	10.00
96	Ted Williams	10.00
97	Ted Williams	10.00
98	Ted Williams	10.00
99	Ted Williams	10.00
100	Ted Williams	10.00
101	Ted Williams	10.00
102	Ted Williams	10.00
103	Ted Williams	10.00
104	Hideki Matsui RC	5.00

Red Back

	NM/M
Stars (1-73):	1.5-2X
SP's (74-103):	1-1.5X
Matsui Red #104:	10.00
Inserted 1:2	

BuyBacks

No Pricing

Game-Used Memorabilia Tier 1

SAMMY SOSA
Outfield Cubs

	NM/M
Common Player:	5.00
Inserted 1:82	
Golds:	No Pricing
Production 25 Sets	

RC1	Roger Clemens	20.00
CD1	Carlos Delgado	5.00
DR1	J.D. Drew	5.00
AD1	Adam Dunn	10.00
JG1	Jason Giambi	5.00
LG1	Luis Gonzalez	5.00
KG1	Ken Griffey Jr.	15.00
TH1	Tommy Henrich	5.00
KI1	Kazuhisa Ishii	5.00
CJ1	Chipper Jones	10.00
MM1	Mark McGwire	50.00
RP1	Rafael Palmeiro	8.00
MP1	Mike Piazza	10.00
PR1	Mark Prior	8.00
IR1	Ivan Rodriguez	8.00
CS1	Curt Schilling	8.00
AS1	Alfonso Soriano	8.00
SS1	Sammy Sosa	10.00
IS1	Ichiro Suzuki	30.00
MS1	Mike Sweeney	5.00
BW1	Bernie Williams	5.00

Game-Used Memorabilia Tier 2

	NM/M
Common Player:	5.00
Production 150 Sets	

JB2	Jeff Bagwell	10.00
LB2	Lance Berkman	5.00
JD2	Joe DiMaggio	100.00
DE2	Darin Erstad	5.00
JG2	Jason Giambi	5.00
SG2	Shawn Green	5.00
KG2	Ken Griffey Jr.	15.00
RJ2	Randy Johnson	10.00
AJ2	Andruw Jones	8.00
CJ2	Chipper Jones	10.00
GM2	Greg Maddux	15.00
PM2	Pedro J. Martinez	10.00
MM2	Mark McGwire	60.00
MP2	Mike Piazza	10.00
MR2	Manny Ramirez	10.00
AR2	Alex Rodriguez	15.00
CS2	Curt Schilling	10.00
SS2	Sammy Sosa	15.00
IS2	Ichiro Suzuki	50.00
JT2	Jim Thome	10.00
KW2	Kerry Wood	10.00

Game-Used Memorabilia Autograph

MARK McGWIRE

	NM/M
Production 50 except A-Rod.	

JB2	Jeff Bagwell	75.00
LB2	Lance Berkman	75.00
JG2	Jason Giambi	50.00
KG2	Ken Griffey Jr.	125.00
AJ2	Andruw Jones	50.00
MM2	Mark McGwire	350.00
AR2	Alex Rodriguez/285	100.00
CS2	Curt Schilling	75.00
SS2	Sammy Sosa	180.00
IS2	Ichiro Suzuki	375.00
JT2	Jim Thome	75.00
KW2	Kerry Wood	75.00

Mini

RICHIE SEXSON

	NM/M
Complete Set (73):	40.00
Common Player:	.50
Inserted 1:2	

1	Troy Glaus	.50
2	Darin Erstad	.50
3	Randy Johnson	1.00
4	Luis Gonzalez	.50
5	Curt Schilling	.50
6	Tom Glavine	.50
7	Chipper Jones	1.00
8	Greg Maddux	1.50
9	Andruw Jones	.75
10	Pedro J. Martinez	1.00
11	Manny Ramirez	1.00
12	Nomar Garciaparra	2.00
13	Billy Williams	.50
14	Sammy Sosa	1.00
15	Kerry Wood	1.00
16	Mark Prior	1.00
17	Ernie Banks	1.50
18	Frank Thomas	1.00
19	Joe Morgan	.50
20	Ken Griffey Jr.	2.00
21	Adam Dunn	1.00
22	Jim Thome	1.00
23	Todd Helton	.75
24	Larry Walker	.75
25	Lance Berkman	.75
26	Roy Oswalt	.75
27	Jeff Bagwell	1.00
28	Nolan Ryan	3.00
29	Mike Sweeney	.50
30	Shawn Green	.50
31	Hideo Nomo	.75
32	Kazuhisa Ishii	.50
33	Richie Sexson	.50
34	Robin Yount	1.00
35	Harmon Killebrew	1.00
36	Torii Hunter	.75
37	Vladimir Guerrero	1.00
38	Roberto Alomar	.75
39	Mike Piazza	2.00
40	Tom Seaver	1.00
41	Phil Rizzuto	.75
42	Yogi Berra	1.50
43	Mike Mussina	.75
44	Roger Clemens	2.00
45	Derek Jeter	3.00
46	Jason Giambi	.50
47	Bernie Williams	.75
48	Alfonso Soriano	.50
49	Jim "Catfish" Hunter	.50
50	Barry Zito	.50
51	Eric Chavez	.50
52	Tim Hudson	.50
53	Rollie Fingers	.50
54	Miguel Tejada	1.00
55	Pat Burrell	1.00
56	Brian Giles	.50
57	Willie Stargell	.75
58	Phil Nevin	.50
59	Orlando Cepeda	.50
60	Barry Bonds	3.00
61	Jeff Kent	.50
62	Willie McCovey	.50
63	Ichiro Suzuki	2.50
64	Stan Musial	2.00
65	Albert Pujols	3.00
66	J.D. Drew	.50
67	Scott Rolen	1.00
68	Mark McGwire	2.00
69	Alex Rodriguez	2.50
70	Juan Gonzalez	1.00
71	Ivan Rodriguez	1.00
72	Rafael Palmeiro	.75
73	Carlos Delgado	.50

Original Artwork Redemption

89 Total Redemption cards.

Reprint Series Original 1941

	NM/M
Complete Set (25):	15.00
Common Player:	.75
Inserted 1:2	

R1	Ted Williams	2.50
R2	Hank Greenberg	.75
R3	Joe DiMaggio	2.50
R4	Lefty Gomez	.75
R5	Tommy Henrich	.75
R6	Pee Wee Reese	.75
R7	Mel Ott	1.00
R8	Carl Hubbell	.75

RICHIE SEXSON

R9	Jimmie Foxx	1.00
R10	Joe Cronin	.75
R11	Charley Gehringer	.75
R12	Frank Hayes	.75
R13	Babe Dahlgren	.75
R14	Dolph Camilli	.75
R15	Johnny Vander Meer	.75
R16	Bucky Walters	.75
R17	Red Ruffing	.75
R18	Charlie Keller	.75
R19	Bob Johnson	.75
R20	Emil "Dutch" Leonard	.75
R21	Barney McCosky	.75
R22	Soupy Campbell	.75
R23	Roy Weatherly	.75
R24	Bobby Doerr	.75
R25	Bill Dickey	.75

The Yankee Clipper: 1941 Streak

	NM/M
Complete Set (56):	250.00
Common DiMaggio (1-41):	5.00
Inserted 1:12	
Common DiMaggio (42-56):	8.00
Inserted 1:24	
S-1-56 Joe DiMaggio	5.00

Hawaii

JASON GIAMBI

To introduce its retro-styled Play Ball brand, Upper Deck created a special promo set for the SCD Hawaii Trade Conference. Each of the special cards has a whimsical tropical artwork background and the trade show logo on front. Three of the cards, with appropriate authentication on back, were seeded in the promo packs in an autographed version, with the McGwire card reported as much scarcer than the Sosa and Giambi autographs.

	NM/M
Complete Set (10):	30.00
Common Player:	2.00

KY1	"Slammin'" Sammy Sosa	5.00
SS	"Slammin'" Sammy Sosa/Auto.	125.00
KY2	Ken "The Kid" Griffey Jr.	6.00
KY3	Jason Giambi	.12
JG	Jason Giambi/Auto.	35.00
KY4	Ichiro	.50
KY5	Mark "Big Mac" McGwire	7.50
MM	Mark "Big Mac" McGwire/Auto.	250.00
KY6	Troy Glaus	2.00
KY7	Derek Jeter	7.50
KY8	Barry Bonds	6.50

KY9	Alex "A-Rod" Rodriguez	5.00
KY10	Nomar Garciaparra	6.00

2003 Upper Deck Prospect Premieres

DARIN DOWNS
STAR ROOKIE

	NM/M
Complete Set (90):	30.00
Common Player:	.25
Pack (4):	7.00
Box (24):	100.00

1	Bryan Opdyke RC	.25
2	Gabriel Sosa RC	.25
3	Tila Reynolds RC	.25
4	Aaron Hill RC	1.00
5	Aaron Marsden RC	.25
6	Abe Alvarez RC	.25
7	Adam Jones RC	2.50
8	Adam Miller RC	2.50
9	Andre Ethier RC	8.00
10	Tony Gwynn Jr. RC	.75
11	Brad Snyder RC	1.00
12	Brad Sullivan RC	.75
13	Brian Anderson RC	1.50
14	Brian Buscher RC	.25
15	Brian Snyder RC	.25
16	Carlos Quentin RC	3.00
17	Chad Billingsley RC	3.00
18	Fraser Dizard RC	.50
19	Chris Durbin RC	.50
20	Chris Ray RC	.50
21	Conor Jackson RC	2.00
22	Kory Casto RC	.25
23	Craig Whitaker RC	.75
24	Daniel Moore RC	.25
25	Daric Barton RC	2.00
26	Darin Downs RC	.75
27	David Murphy RC	1.00
28	Dustin Majewski RC	.50
29	Edgardo Baez RC	.50
30	Jake Fox RC	.75
31	Jake Stevens RC	.50
32	Jamie D'Antona RC	1.00
33	James Houser RC	.50
34	Jarrod Saltalamacchia RC	.50
35	Jason Hirsh RC	2.00
36	Javi Herrera RC	1.00
37	Jeff Allison RC	.75
38	John Hudgins RC	.50
39	Jo Jo Reyes RC	.50
40	Justin James RC	.50
41	Kurt Isenberg RC	.50
42	Kyle Boyer RC	.50
43	Lastings Milledge RC	5.00
44	Luis Atilano RC	.50
45	Matt Murton RC	1.50
46	Matt Moses RC	1.00
47	Matt Harrison RC	.50
48	Michael Bourn RC	.50
49	Miguel Vega RC	.50
50	Mitch Maier RC	1.00
51	Omar Quintanilla RC	.50
52	Ryan Sweeney RC	1.50
53	Scott Baker RC	.75
54	Sean Rodriguez RC	.75
55	Steve Lerud RC	.25
56	Thomas Pauly RC	.75
57	Tom Gorzelanny RC	.75
58	Tim Moss RC	.50
59	Robbie Wooley RC	.50
60	Trey Webb RC	.25
61	Wes Littleton RC	.50
62	Beau Vaughan RC	.25
63	Willy Jo Ronda RC	.50
64	Chris Lubanski RC	1.50
65	Ian Stewart RC	8.00
66	John Danks RC	1.00
67	Kyle Sleeth RC	.50
68	Michael Aubrey RC	1.50
69	Kevin Kouzmanoff RC	.50
70	Ryan Harvey RC	1.50
71	Tim Stauffer RC	1.00
72	Tony Richie RC	.25
73	Brandon Wood RC	8.00
74	David Aardsma RC	.75
75	David Shinskie RC	.50
76	Dennis Dove RC	.25
77	Eric Sultemeier RC	.25
78	Jay Sborz RC	.25
79	Jimmy Barthmaier RC	.25
80	Josh Whitesell RC	.25
81	Josh Anderson RC	.25
82	Kenny Lewis RC	.50
83	Mateo Miramontes RC	.50

84	Nicholas Markakis RC	8.00
85	Paul Bacot RC	.50
86	Peter Stonard RC	.25
87	Reggie Willits RC	.25
88	Shane Costa RC	.50
89	Billy Sadler RC	.25
90	Delmon Young RC	8.00

Star Rookie Signature

JASON HIRSH / P
STAR ROOKIE

	NM/M
Common Autograph:	5.00
Inserted 1:9	

P1	Bryan Opdyke	10.00
P2	Gabriel Sosa	8.00
P3	Tila Reynolds	5.00
P4	Aaron Hill	15.00
P5	Aaron Marsden	10.00
P6	Abe Alvarez	15.00
P7	Adam Jones	60.00
P8	Adam Miller	75.00
P9	Andre Ethier	90.00
P10	Tony Gwynn Jr.	20.00
P11	Brad Snyder	25.00
P12	Brad Sullivan	15.00
P13	Brian Anderson	40.00
P14	Brian Buscher	8.00
P15	Brian Snyder	15.00
P16	Carlos Quentin	60.00
P17	Chad Billingsley	100.00
P19	Chris Durbin	10.00
P20	Chris Ray	8.00
P21	Conor Jackson	50.00
P22	Kory Casto	8.00
P23	Craig Whitaker	10.00
P24	Daniel Moore	10.00
P25	Daric Barton	60.00
P26	Darin Downs	15.00
P27	David Murphy	15.00
P29	Edgardo Baez	12.00
P30	Jake Fox	12.00
P31	Jake Stevens	20.00
P32	Jamie D'Antona	25.00
P33	James Houser	15.00
P34	Jarrod Saltalamacchia	30.00
P35	Jason Hirsh	35.00
P36	Javi Herrera	15.00
P37	Jeff Allison	25.00
P38	John Hudgins	10.00
P39	Jo Jo Reyes	10.00
P40	Justin James	10.00
P41	Kurt Isenberg	10.00
P42	Kyle Boyer	12.00
P43	Lastings Milledge	80.00
P44	Luis Atilano	8.00
P45	Matt Murton	25.00
P46	Matt Moses	35.00
P48	Michael Bourn	15.00
P49	Miguel Vega	15.00
P50	Mitch Maier	25.00
P51	Omar Quintanilla	15.00
P52	Ryan Sweeney	40.00
P53	Scott Baker	15.00
P55	Steve Lerud	15.00
P56	Thomas Pauly	10.00
P57	Tom Gorzelanny	15.00
P58	Tim Moss	10.00
P60	Trey Webb	10.00
P61	Wes Littleton	15.00
P62	Beau Vaughan	10.00
P63	Willy Jo Ronda	10.00
P64	Chris Lubanski	25.00
P65	Ian Stewart	100.00
P66	John Danks	50.00
P67	Kyle Sleeth	20.00
P68	Michael Aubrey	40.00
P70	Ryan Harvey	30.00
P71	Tim Stauffer	30.00

Star Rookie Jersey

	NM/M
Common Player:	4.00
Inserted 1:18	

P72	Tony Richie	4.00
P73	Brandon Wood	15.00
P74	David Aardsma	5.00
P75	David Shinskie	4.00
P76	Dennis Dove	6.00
P77	Eric Sultemeier	4.00
P78	Jay Sborz	4.00
P79	Jimmy Barthmaier	4.00
P80	Josh Whitesell	4.00
P81	Josh Anderson	8.00
P82	Kenny Lewis	8.00
P83	Mateo Miramontes	8.00

P84	Nicholas Markakis	25.00
P85	Paul Bacot	4.00
P86	Peter Stonard	4.00
P87	Reggie Willits	8.00
P88	Shane Costa	4.00
P89	Billy Sadler	4.00
P91	Kyle Sleeth	8.00
P92	Ian Stewart	25.00
P93	Fraser Dizard	6.00
P94	Abe Alvarez	6.00
P95	Adam Jones	15.00
P96	Brian Anderson	8.00
P97	Chris Durbin	4.00
P98	Craig Whitaker	8.00
P99	Jake Fox	4.00
P100	Kurt Isenberg	4.00
P101	Luis Atilano	4.00
P102	Miguel Vega	4.00
P103	Mitch Maier	8.00
P104	Ryan Sweeney	10.00
P105	Scott Baker	4.00
P106	Sean Rodriguez	8.00
P108	Trey Webb	4.00
P109	Willy Jo Ronda	6.00
P110	John Danks	8.00
P111	Michael Aubrey	4.00
P112	Lastings Milledge	30.00
P113	Chris Lubanski	10.00

Star Rookies

Persons who opened a box of Upper Deck product at the company's booth during the June 27-29 show in Chicago received this cellophane wrapped set of six Star Rookies.

NM/M
Complete Set (6):		6.00
Common Player:		.25
AM	Alejandro Machado	.25
HB	Hank Blalock	.50
HC	Hee Seop Choi	.25
HM	Hideki Matsui	5.00
RB	Rocco Baldelli	1.50
RH	Runelvys Hernandez	.25

2003 Upper Deck Standing O!

NM/M
Complete Set (126):		30.00
Common Player:		.15
Common SP (85-126):		.75
Inserted 1:4		
Pack (4):		1.50
Box (24):		25.00
1	Darin Erstad	.25
2	Troy Glaus	.40
3	Tim Salmon	.25
4	Luis Gonzalez	.25
5	Randy Johnson	.50
6	Curt Schilling	.25
7	Andruw Jones	.25
8	Greg Maddux	.75
9	Chipper Jones	.25
10	Gary Sheffield	.25
11	Rodrigo Lopez	.15
12	Geronimo Gil	.15
13	Nomar Garciaparra	1.00
14	Pedro J. Martinez	.50
15	Manny Ramirez	.40
16	Mark Prior	.50
17	Kerry Wood	.25
18	Sammy Sosa	.75
19	Magglio Ordonez	.25
20	Frank Thomas	.40
21	Adam Dunn	.40
22	Ken Griffey Jr.	.75
23	Sean Casey	.15
24	Omar Vizquel	.15
25	C.C. Sabathia	.15
26	Larry Walker	.25
27	Todd Helton	.40
28	Ivan Rodriguez	.40
29	Josh Beckett	.15
30	Roy Oswalt	.25
31	Jeff Kent	.25
32	Jeff Bagwell	.40
33	Lance Berkman	.25
34	Mike Sweeney	.15
35	Carlos Beltran	.15
36	Hideo Nomo	.40
37	Shawn Green	.25
38	Kazuhisa Ishii	.15
39	Geoff Jenkins	.15
40	Richie Sexson	.25
41	Torii Hunter	.15
42	Jacque Jones	.15
43	Jose Vidro	.15
44	Vladimir Guerrero	.50
45	Cliff Floyd	.15
46	Al Leiter	.15
47	Mike Piazza	1.00
48	Tom Glavine	.25
49	Roberto Alomar	.25
50	Roger Clemens	.75
51	Jason Giambi	.50
52	Bernie Williams	.40
53	Alfonso Soriano	1.00
54	Derek Jeter	1.50
55	Miguel Tejada	.25
56	Eric Chavez	.25
57	Barry Zito	.25
58	Pat Burrell	.25
59	Jim Thome	.25
60	Brian Giles	.25
61	Jason Kendall	.15
62	Ryan Klesko	.15
63	Phil Nevin	.15
64	Sean Burroughs	.15
65	Jason Schmidt	.15
66	Rich Aurilia	.15
67	Barry Bonds	1.50
68	Randy Winn	.15
69	Freddy Garcia	.15
70	Ichiro Suzuki	.75
71	J.D. Drew	.15
72	Jim Edmonds	.25
73	Scott Rolen	.40
74	Matt Morris	.15
75	Albert Pujols	.75
76	Tino Martinez	.15
77	Rey Ordonez	.15
78	Carl Crawford	.15
79	Rafael Palmeiro	.25
80	Kevin Mench	.15
81	Alex Rodriguez	1.25
82	Juan Gonzalez	.40
83	Carlos Delgado	.25
84	Eric Hinske	.15
85	Richard Fischer RC	.25
86	Brandon Webb RC	1.50
87	Rob Hammock RC	.75
88	Matt Kata RC	1.00
89	Tim Olson RC	.75
90	Oscar Villarreal RC	.75
91	Michael Hessman RC	.75
92	Daniel Cabrera RC	.75
93	Jon Leicester RC	.75
94	Todd Wellemeyer RC	1.00
95	Felix Sanchez RC	.75
96	David Sanders RC	.75
97	Josh Stewart RC	.75
98	Arnie Munoz RC	.75
99	Ryan Cameron RC	.75
100	Clint Barmes RC	1.50
101	Josh Willingham RC	.75
102	Willie Eyre RC	.75
104	Brent Hoard RC	.75
105	Terrmel Sledge RC	1.00
106	Phil Seibel RC	.75
107	Craig Brazell RC	2.00
108	Jeff Duncan RC	.75
110	Bernie Castro RC	.75
111	Mike Nicolas RC	.75
112	Rett Johnson RC	.75
113	Bobby Madritsch RC	.75
114	Luis Ayala RC	.75
115	Hideki Matsui RC	10.00
116	Jose Contreras RC	1.50
117	Lew Ford RC	1.50
118	Jeremy Griffiths	.75
119	Guillermo Quiroz RC	.75
120	Alejandro Machado RC	1.00
121	Francisco Cruceta RC	.75
122	Prentice Redman RC	1.00
123	Shane Bazzell RC	1.50
124	Jason Anderson	.75
125	Ian Ferguson RC	.75
126	Nook Logan RC	1.00

O! Die-Cut Disc

Stars (1-84):	1-2X
Inserted 1:1	
SP's (85-126):	1.5-3X
Inserted 1:48	

O! Starring Role Jersey

NM/M
Inserted 1:240
SR-RC	Roger Clemens	20.00
SR-JG	Jason Giambi	10.00
SR-LG	Luis Gonzalez	5.00
SR-SG	Shawn Green	5.00
SR-RJ	Randy Johnson	10.00
SR-MC	Mark McGwire/SP	40.00
SR-AR	Alex Rodriguez	20.00

2003 Upper Deck Sweet Spot

NM/M
Complete Set (232):		
Common Player:		.25
Common SP:		1.00
Inserted 1:4		
Common SP (131-190):		3.00
Production 2,003		
Common SP (191-232):		4.00
Production 1,430 unless noted.		
Pack (4):		9.00
Box (12):		90.00
1	Darin Erstad	.50
2	Garret Anderson	.50
3	Tim Salmon	.50
4	Troy Glaus	.75
5	Luis Gonzalez	.50
6	Randy Johnson	1.00
7	Curt Schilling	.50
8	Lyle Overbay	.25
9	Andruw Jones/SP	2.00
10	Gary Sheffield/SP	1.50
11	Rafael Furcal/SP	1.00
12	Greg Maddux/SP	4.00
13	Chipper Jones/SP	4.00
14	Tony Batista	.25
15	Rodrigo Lopez	.25
16	Jay Gibbons	.25
17	Jason Johnson	.25
18	Byung-Hyun Kim/SP	1.00
19	Johnny Damon/SP	2.50
20	Derek Lowe/SP	1.00
21	Nomar Garciaparra/SP	5.00
22	Pedro Martinez/SP	3.00
23	Manny Ramirez/SP	2.50
24	Mark Prior	1.00
25	Kerry Wood	1.00
26	Corey Patterson	.50
27	Sammy Sosa	2.00
28	Moises Alou	.40
29	Magglio Ordonez	.40
30	Frank Thomas	.75
31	Paul Konerko	.25
32	Roberto Alomar	.50
33	Adam Dunn	.75
34	Austin Kearns	.50
35	Ryan Wagner RC	.25
36	Ken Griffey Jr.	1.50
37	Sean Casey	.25
38	Omar Vizquel	.40
39	C.C. Sabathia	.25
40	Jason Davis	.25
41	Travis Hafner	.25
42	Brandon Phillips	.25
43	Larry Walker	.40
44	Preston Wilson	.25
45	Jay Payton	.25
46	Todd Helton	.75
47	Carlos Pena	.25
48	Eric Munson	.25
49	Ivan Rodriguez	.75
50	Josh Beckett	.50
51	Alex Gonzalez	.25
52	Roy Oswalt	.40
53	Craig Biggio	.40
54	Jeff Bagwell	.75
55	Lance Berkman	.50
56	Mike Sweeney	.25
57	Carlos Beltran	.75
58	Brent Mayne	.25
59	Mike MacDougal	.25
60	Hideo Nomo	.50
61	Dave Roberts	.25
62	Adrian Beltre	.50
63	Shawn Green	.50
64	Kazuhisa Ishii	.25
65	Rickey Henderson	.50
66	Richie Sexson	.50
67	Torii Hunter	.25
68	Jacque Jones	.25
69	Joe Mays	.25
70	Corey Koskie	.25
71	A.J. Pierzynski	.25
72	Jose Vidro	.25
73	Vladimir Guerrero	.75
74	Tom Glavine	.50
75	Mike Piazza	1.50
76	Jose Reyes	.50
77	Jae Weong Seo	.25
78	Jorge Posada/SP	2.00
79	Mike Mussina/SP	2.00
80	Robin Ventura/SP	1.00
81	Mariano Rivera/SP	1.50
82	Roger Clemens/SP	6.00
83	Jason Giambi/SP	1.50
84	Bernie Williams/SP	2.00
85	Alfonso Soriano/SP	3.00
86	Derek Jeter	2.50
87	Miguel Tejada	.75
88	Eric Chavez	.50
89	Tim Hudson	.50
90	Barry Zito	.50
91	Mark Mulder	.50
92	Erubiel Durazo	.25
93	Pat Burrell	.50
94	Jim Thome	.75
95	Bobby Abreu	.50
96	Brian Giles	.40
97	Reggie Sanders	.25
98	Jose Hernandez	.25
99	Ryan Klesko	.25
100	Sean Burroughs	.25
101	Edgardo Alfonzo/SP	1.00
102	Rich Aurilia/SP	1.00
103	Jose Cruz Jr./SP	1.00
104	Barry Bonds/SP	6.00
105	Andres Galarraga/SP	1.00
106	Mike Cameron	.25
107	Kazuhiro Sasaki	.25
108	Bret Boone	.40
109	Ichiro Suzuki	2.00
110	John Olerud	.40
111	J.D. Drew/SP	1.50
112	Jim Edmonds/SP	2.00
113	Scott Rolen/SP	3.00
114	Matt Morris/SP	1.00
115	Tino Martinez/SP	1.00
116	Albert Pujols/SP	6.00
117	Jared Sandberg	.25
118	Carl Crawford	.50
119	Rafael Palmeiro	.50
120	Hank Blalock	.50
121	Alex Rodriguez	2.50
122	Kevin Mench	.25
123	Juan Gonzalez	.75
124	Mark Teixeira	.50
125	Shannon Stewart	.25
126	Vernon Wells	.50
127	Josh Phelps	.25
128	Eric Hinske	.25
129	Orlando Hudson	.25
130	Carlos Delgado	.75
131	Jason Shiell RC	3.00
132	Kevin Tolar RC	3.00
133	Nate Bland RC	3.00
134	Brent Hoard RC	3.00
135	Mike Ryan RC	4.00
136	Jonathan Pridie RC	3.00
137	Francisco Rosario RC	3.00
138	Runelvys Hernandez	3.00
139	Guillermo Quiroz RC	4.00
140	Chin-Hui Tsao	3.00
141	Rett Johnson RC	3.00
142	Colin Porter RC	3.00
143	Jose Castillo	3.00
144	Chris Waters RC	3.00
145	Jeremy Guthrie	3.00
146	Pedro Liriano	3.00
147	Joe Borowski	3.00
148	Felix Sanchez RC	3.00
149	Todd Wellemeyer RC	3.00
150	Gerald Laird	3.00
151	Brandon Webb RC	8.00
152	Tommy Whiteman RC	3.00
153	Carlos Rivera	3.00
154	Rick Roberts RC	3.00
155	Terrmel Sledge RC	3.00
156	Jeff Duncan RC	3.00
157	Craig Brazell RC	3.00
158	Bernie Castro RC	3.00
159	Cory Stewart RC	3.00
160	Brandon Villafuerte RC	3.00
161	Tommy Phelps	3.00
162	Josh Hall RC	3.00
163	Ryan Cameron RC	3.00
164	Garrett Atkins	3.00
165	Brian Stokes RC	3.00
166	Rafael Betancourt RC	3.00
167	Jaime Cerda	3.00
168	Danny Carrasco RC	3.00
169	Ian Ferguson RC	3.00
170	Jorge Cordova RC	3.00
171	Eric Munson	3.00
172	Nook Logan RC	3.00
173	Jeremy Bonderman	10.00
174	Kyle Snyder	3.00
175	Rich Harden	5.00
176	Kevin Ohme RC	3.00
177	Roger Deago RC	3.00
178	Marlon Byrd	5.00
179	Dontrelle Willis	5.00
180	Bobby Hill	3.00
181	Jesse Foppert	3.00
182	Andrew Good	3.00
183	Chase Utley	5.00
184	Bo Hart RC	3.00
185	Dan Haren	3.00
186	Tim Olson RC	3.00
187	Joe Thurston	3.00
188	Jason Anderson	3.00
189	Jason Gilfillan RC	3.00
190	Rickie Weeks RC	12.00
191	Hideki Matsui/500 RC	25.00
192	Jose Contreras RC	8.00
193	Willie Eyre RC	4.00
194	Matt Bruback RC	4.00
195	Heath Bell RC	4.00
196	Lew Ford RC	8.00
197	Jeremy Griffiths	5.00
198	Oscar Villarreal/500 RC	5.00
199	Francisco Cruceta RC	5.00
200	Fernando Cabrera RC	5.00
201	Jhonny Peralta	4.00
202	Shane Bazzell RC	4.00
203	Bobby Madritsch/500 RC	15.00
204	Phil Seibel RC	5.00
205	Josh Willingham RC	6.00
206	Robby Hammock/500 RC	5.00
207	Alejandro Machado RC	5.00
208	David Sanders RC	4.00
209	Mike Neu/500 RC	5.00
210	Andrew Brown RC	4.00
211	Nathan Robertson RC	6.00
212	Miguel Ojeda RC	4.00
213	Beau Kemp RC	4.00
214	Aaron Looper RC	4.00
215	Alfredo Gonzalez RC	4.00
216	Richard Fischer/500 RC	5.00
218	Jeremy Wedel RC	4.00
219	Prentice Redman RC	4.00
220	Michel Hernandez RC	6.00
221	Rocco Baldelli/500	5.00
222	Luis Ayala RC	5.00
223	Arnie Munoz RC	4.00
224	Wilfredo Ledezma RC	4.00
225	Chris Capuano RC	8.00
226	Aquilino Lopez RC	5.00
227	Joe Valentine/500 RC	5.00
228	Matt Kata/1,200 RC	5.00
229	Diegomar Markwell/1,200 RC	4.00
230	Clint Barmes/1,200 RC	15.00
231	Mike Nicolas/500 RC	5.00
232	Jon Leicester/1,200 RC	5.00

Autographs Black Ink

NM/M
Common Player:
Red & Blue Ink variations exist.
Reds not priced due to scarcity.
Mirror Parallel: No Pricing
Production 25
HB	Hank Blalock	30.00
HB	Hank Blalock/Blue/40	40.00
PB	Pat Burrell	30.00
PB	Pat Burrell/Blue/40	40.00
RC	Roger Clemens/73	125.00
RC	Roger Clemens/Blue/40	150.00
JC	Jose Contreras	40.00
JC	Jose Contreras/Blue/40	50.00
AD	Adam Dunn	30.00
AD	Adam Dunn/Blue/40	50.00
NG	Nomar Garciaparra	75.00
NG	Nomar Garciaparra/Blue/40	100.00
JG	Jason Giambi	20.00
JG	Jason Giambi/Blue/40	30.00
TR	Troy Glaus	35.00
TR	Troy Glaus/Blue/40	50.00
GL	Tom Glavine	30.00
GL	Tom Glavine/Blue/40	50.00
KG	Ken Griffey Jr.	75.00
KG	Ken Griffey Jr./Blue/40	100.00
KGs	Ken Griffey Sr.	15.00
KGs	Ken Griffey Sr./Blue/40	20.00
VG	Vladimir Guerrero	50.00
VG	Vladimir Guerrero/Blue/40	65.00
TG	Tony Gwynn	40.00
HA	Travis Hafner	15.00
HA	Travis Hafner/Blue/40	25.00
BH	Bo Hart	10.00
BH	Bo Hart/Blue/40	15.00
TH	Todd Helton/45	75.00
TH	Todd Helton/Blue/40	75.00
DH	Drew Henson	25.00
DH	Drew Henson/Blue/40	40.00
KI	Kazuhisa Ishii	35.00
KI	Kazuhisa Ishii/Blue/40	50.00
HM	Hideki Matsui	300.00
HM	Hideki Matsui/Blue/40	375.00
RO	Roy Oswalt	25.00
RO	Roy Oswalt/Blue/40	35.00
LO	Lyle Overbay	15.00
LO	Lyle Overbay/Blue/40	20.00
BP	Brandon Phillips	10.00
BP	Brandon Phillips/Blue/40	15.00
MP	Mark Prior	30.00
MP	Mark Prior/Blue/40	40.00
JR	Jose Reyes	40.00
JR	Jose Reyes/Blue/40	60.00
CR	Cal Ripken Jr.	165.00
CR	Cal Ripken Jr./Blue/40	220.00
NR	Nolan Ryan	120.00
NR	Nolan Ryan/Blue/40	165.00
TS	Tim Salmon	25.00
TS	Tim Salmon/Blue/40	35.00
CS	Curt Schilling	40.00
CS	Curt Schilling/Blue/40	75.00
GS	Gary Sheffield	30.00
GS	Gary Sheffield/Blue/40	40.00
SS	Sammy Sosa	200.00
IS	Ichiro Suzuki	400.00
IS	Ichiro Suzuki/Red/35	400.00
MT	Mark Teixeira	40.00
MT	Mark Teixeira/Blue/40	50.00
JT	Jim Thome	40.00
JT	Jim Thome/Blue/40	60.00
BW	Brandon Webb	40.00
BW	Brandon Webb/Blue/40	60.00
RW	Rickie Weeks	70.00
JW	Jerome Williams	25.00
JW	Jerome Williams/Blue/40	35.00
DW	Dontrelle Willis	45.00
DW	Dontrelle Willis/Blue/40	75.00

Common Player:
Red & Blue Ink variations exist.
Reds not priced due to scarcity.
Mirror Parallel: No Pricing
Production 25
HB	Hank Blalock	30.00
HB	Hank Blalock/Blue/40	40.00
PB	Pat Burrell	30.00
PB	Pat Burrell/Blue/40	40.00
RC	Roger Clemens/73	125.00
RC	Roger Clemens/Blue/40	150.00
JC	Jose Contreras	40.00
JC	Jose Contreras/Blue/40	50.00
AD	Adam Dunn	30.00
AD	Adam Dunn/Blue/40	50.00
NG	Nomar Garciaparra	75.00
NG	Nomar Garciaparra/Blue/40	100.00
JG	Jason Giambi	20.00
JG	Jason Giambi/Blue/40	30.00
TR	Troy Glaus	35.00
TR	Troy Glaus/Blue/40	50.00
GL	Tom Glavine	30.00
GL	Tom Glavine/Blue/40	50.00
KG	Ken Griffey Jr.	75.00
KG	Ken Griffey Jr./Blue/40	100.00
KGs	Ken Griffey Sr.	15.00
KGs	Ken Griffey Sr./Blue/40	20.00
VG	Vladimir Guerrero	50.00

ABBREVIATIONS

SP - Short Print

Code	Player	Price
VG	Vladimir Guerrero/Blue/40	65.00
TG	Tony Gwynn	40.00
HA	Travis Hafner	15.00
HA	Travis Hafner/Blue/40	25.00
BH	Bo Hart	10.00
BH	Bo Hart/Blue/40	15.00
TH	Todd Helton/45	75.00
TH	Todd Helton/Blue/40	75.00
DH	Drew Henson	25.00
DH	Drew Henson/Blue/40	35.00
KI	Kazuhisa Ishii	35.00
KI	Kazuhisa Ishii/Blue/40	50.00
AK	Austin Kearns	20.00
AK	Austin Kearns/Blue/40	25.00
HM	Hideki Matsui	300.00
HM	Hideki Matsui/Blue/40	375.00
RO	Roy Oswalt	25.00
RO	Roy Oswalt/Blue/40	35.00
LO	Lyle Overbay	15.00
LO	Lyle Overbay/Blue/40	20.00
BP	Brandon Phillips	10.00
BP	Brandon Phillips/Blue/40	15.00
MP	Mark Prior	30.00
MP	Mark Prior/Blue/40	60.00
JR	Jose Reyes	40.00
JR	Jose Reyes/Blue/40	60.00
CR	Cal Ripken Jr.	165.00
CR	Cal Ripken Jr./Blue/40	220.00
NR	Nolan Ryan	120.00
NR	Nolan Ryan/Blue/40	165.00
TS	Tim Salmon	25.00
TS	Tim Salmon/Blue/40	35.00
CS	Curt Schilling	40.00
CS	Curt Schilling/Blue/40	75.00
GS	Gary Sheffield	30.00
GS	Gary Sheffield/Blue/40	40.00
SS	Sammy Sosa/Blue/40	200.00
IS	Ichiro Suzuki/Blue/40	400.00
IS	Ichiro Suzuki/Red/35	400.00
MT	Mark Teixeira	40.00
MT	Mark Teixeira/Blue/40	50.00
JT	Jim Thome	40.00
JT	Jim Thome/Blue/40	60.00
BW	Brandon Webb	40.00
BW	Brandon Webb/Blue/40	60.00
RW	Rickie Weeks	70.00
JW	Jerome Williams	25.00
JW	Jerome Williams/Blue/40	35.00
DW	Dontrelle Willis	45.00
DW	Dontrelle Willis/Blue/40	75.00

Game-Used Barrel

NM/M
Quantity produced listed
No pricing due to scarcity.
| KW-BB | Kerry Wood/2 (2/04 auction) | 1,000 |

Barrel Autographs

NM/M
Quantity produced listed
HB	Hank Blalock/420	35.00
PB	Pat Burrell/345	35.00
RC	Roger Clemens/49	220.00
AD	Adam Dunn/345	40.00
TR	Troy Glaus/345	40.00
TG	Tom Glavine/345	45.00
KG	Ken Griffey Jr./295	125.00
HM	Hideki Matsui/124	400.00
CR	Cal Ripken Jr./149	180.00
NR	Nolan Ryan/445	150.00
JT	Jim Thome/345	65.00

Patch

NM/M
| Common Player: | 4.00 |
Inserted 1:6
Logo Patch Parallel: 1-2X
Production 75 Sets
JB1	Jeff Bagwell	6.00
LB1	Lance Berkman	5.00
BB1	Barry Bonds	15.00
PB1	Pat Burrell	5.00
RC1	Roger Clemens	12.00
CD1	Carlos Delgado	4.00
AD1	Adam Dunn	5.00
JE1	Jim Edmonds	4.00
DE1	Darin Erstad	4.00
NG1	Nomar Garciaparra	10.00
JG1	Jason Giambi	4.00
TG1	Troy Glaus	5.00
TO1	Tom Glavine	5.00
LG1	Luis Gonzalez	4.00
SG1	Shawn Green	5.00
KG1	Ken Griffey Jr.	8.00
VG1	Vladimir Guerrero	6.00
TH1	Torii Hunter	5.00
KI1	Kazuhisa Ishii	4.00
DJ1	Derek Jeter	15.00
RJ1	Randy Johnson	6.00
AJ1	Andruw Jones	5.00
CJ1	Chipper Jones	10.00
JK1	Jeff Kent	4.00
GM1	Greg Maddux	10.00
PM1	Pedro J. Martinez	6.00
HN1	Hideo Nomo	5.00
MO1	Magglio Ordonez	6.00
CP1	Corey Patterson	6.00
MP1	Mike Piazza	10.00
MA1	Mark Prior	8.00
AP1	Albert Pujols	15.00
AR1	Alex Rodriguez	10.00
CS1	Curt Schilling	6.00
GS1	Gary Sheffield	6.00
AS1	Alfonso Soriano	8.00
SS1	Sammy Sosa	10.00
IS1	Ichiro Suzuki	10.00
MT1	Miguel Tejada	4.00
JT1	Jim Thome	6.00
BW1	Bernie Williams	5.00
BZ1	Barry Zito	4.00

Game-Used Patch

Production 25 or 10
No pricing due to scarcity.

Swatches

NM/M
| Common Player: | 4.00 |
Inserted 1:24
Tier 2: 1-2X
Production 75
RA	Roberto Alomar	4.00
PB	Pat Burrell	6.00
RC	Roger Clemens	15.00
NM	Nomar Garciaparra	15.00
NG1	Nomar Garciaparra	4.00
JG	Jason Giambi	8.00
TG	Troy Glaus	4.00
TG1	Troy Glaus	5.00
TO	Tom Glavine	4.00
LG	Luis Gonzalez	4.00
KG	Ken Griffey Jr.	10.00
VG	Vladimir Guerrero	6.00
TH	Torii Hunter	4.00
RJ	Randy Johnson	6.00
AJ	Andruw Jones	4.00
CJ	Chipper Jones	8.00
AK	Austin Kearns	6.00
GM	Greg Maddux	10.00

Classic

NM/M
Complete Set (150):	
Common Player:	.40
Common Ted Williams (91-120):	5.00
Production 1,941
Common Yankee Heritage (121-150):	2.00
Production 1,500
Pack (4):	12.00
Box (12):	120.00
1	Al Hrabosky	.40
2	Al Lopez	.40
3	Andre Dawson	.75
4	Bill Buckner	.40
5	Billy Williams	.50
6	Bob Feller	.75
7	Bob Lemon	.40
8	Bobby Doerr	.40
9	Cecil Cooper	.40
10	Cal Ripken Jr.	2.50
11	Carlton Fisk	.60
12	Jim "Catfish" Hunter	.40
13	Chris Chambliss	.40
14	Dale Murphy	.75
15	Gaylord Perry	.40
16	Dave Kingman	.40
17	Dave Parker	.40
18	Dave Stewart	.40
19	David Cone	.40
20	Dennis Eckersley	.60
21	Don Baylor	.40
22	Don Sutton	.40
23	Duke Snider	1.00
24	Dwight Evans	.40
25	Dwight Gooden	.40
26	Earl Weaver	.40
27	Early Wynn	.40
28	Eddie Mathews	1.50
29	Enos Slaughter	.40
30	Ernie Banks	1.50
31	Fred Lynn	.40
32	Fred Stanley	.40
33	Gary Carter	.75
34	George Foster	.40
35	Hal Newhouser	.40
36	George Kell	.40
37	Harmon Killebrew	1.50
38	Hoyt Wilhelm	.40
39	Jack Morris	.40
40	Jim Bunning	.40
41	Jim Gilliam	.40
42	Jim Leyritz	.40
43	Jimmy Key	.40
44	Joe Carter	.40
45	Joe Morgan	.40
46	John Montefusco	.40
47	Johnny Bench	2.00
48	Johnny Podres	.40
49	Jose Canseco	.75
50	Juan Marichal	.40
51	Keith Hernandez	.40
52	Ken Griffey Sr.	.40
53	Kirby Puckett	1.50
54	Kirk Gibson	.40
55	Larry Doby	.40
56	Lee May	.40
57	Lee Mazzilli	.40
58	Lou Boudreau	.40
59	Mark McGwire	3.00
60	Maury Wills	.40
61	Mike Pagliarulo	.40
62	Monte Irvin	.75
63	Nolan Ryan	3.00
64	Orlando Cepeda	.40
65	Ozzie Smith	1.50
66	Paul O'Neill	.40
67	Pee Wee Reese	.40
68	Phil Niekro	.40
69	Ralph Kiner	.40
70	Red Schoendienst	.40
71	Richie Ashburn	.40
72	Rick Ferrell	.40
73	Robin Roberts	.40
74	Robin Yount	1.50
75	Hideki Matsui 1,999 RC	20.00
75	Hideki Matsui Red/500	25.00
75	Hideki Matsui Blue/250	30.00
75	Hideki Matsui Silver/25	200.00
76	Rollie Fingers	.40
77	Ron Cey	.40
78	Tom Seaver	1.00
79	Sparky Anderson	.40
80	Stan Musial	2.00
81	Steve Garvey	.40
82	Ted Williams	3.00
83	Tommy Lasorda	.40
84	Tony Gwynn	1.00
85	Tony Perez	.40
86	Vida Blue	.40
87	Warren Spahn	.75
88	Bob Gibson	1.00
89	Willie McCovey	.40
90	Willie Stargell	.75
91	Ted Williams	5.00
92	Ted Williams	5.00
93	Ted Williams	5.00
94	Ted Williams	5.00
95	Ted Williams	5.00
96	Ted Williams	5.00
97	Ted Williams	5.00
98	Ted Williams	5.00
99	Ted Williams	5.00
100	Ted Williams	5.00
101	Ted Williams	5.00
102	Ted Williams	5.00
103	Ted Williams	5.00
104	Ted Williams	5.00
105	Ted Williams	5.00
106	Ted Williams	5.00
107	Ted Williams	5.00
108	Ted Williams	5.00
109	Ted Williams	5.00
110	Ted Williams	5.00
111	Ted Williams	5.00
112	Ted Williams	5.00
113	Ted Williams	5.00
114	Ted Williams	5.00
115	Ted Williams	5.00
116	Ted Williams	5.00
117	Ted Williams	5.00
118	Ted Williams	5.00
119	Ted Williams	5.00
120	Ted Williams	5.00
121	Babe Ruth	8.00
122	Bucky Dent	2.00
123	Casey Stengel	3.00
124	Dave Righetti	2.00
125	Dave Winfield	3.00
126	Dick Tidrow	2.00
127	Dock Ellis	2.00
128	Don Mattingly	8.00
129	Hank Bauer	2.00
130	Jim Bouton	2.00
131	Jim Kaat	2.00
132	Joe DiMaggio	6.00
133	Joe Torre	3.00
134	Lou Piniella	2.00
135	Mel Stottlemyre	2.00
136	Mickey Mantle	15.00
137	Mickey Rivers	2.00
138	Phil Rizzuto	4.00
139	Ralph Branca	2.00
140	Ralph Houk	2.00
141	Roger Maris	6.00
142	Ron Guidry	2.00
143	Ruben Amaro Jr.	2.00
144	Sparky Lyle	2.00
145	Thurman Munson	5.00
146	Tommy Henrich	2.00
147	Tommy John	2.00
148	Tony Kubek	2.00
149	Whitey Ford	4.00
150	Yogi Berra	4.00

Classic Game Jersey

Patch

NM/M
MM	Mickey Mantle	120.00
HM	Hideki Matsui	45.00
HM1	Hideki Matsui	4.00
RO	Roy Oswalt	4.00
RO1	Roy Oswalt	4.00
MP	Mike Piazza	10.00
MA	Mark Prior	3.00
AP	Albert Pujols	15.00
AR	Alex Rodriguez	10.00
CS	Curt Schilling	4.00
GS	Gary Sheffield	5.00
AS	Alfonso Soriano	10.00
AS1	Alfonso Soriano	4.00
SS	Sammy Sosa	12.00
IS	Ichiro Suzuki	20.00
MT	Miguel Tejada	4.00
FT	Frank Thomas	6.00
JT	Jim Thome	8.00
BW	Bernie Williams	4.00
TW	Ted Williams	60.00
BZ	Barry Zito	4.00

NM/M
| Common Player: | 5.00 |
Inserted 1:16
EB	Ernie Banks	15.00
JB	Johnny Bench	15.00
JC	Jose Canseco	6.00
GC	Gary Carter	6.00
RC	Ron Cey	5.00
CC	Cecil Cooper	6.00
AD	Andre Dawson	6.00
RF	Rollie Fingers	5.00
CF	Carlton Fisk	8.00
GF	George Foster	5.00
SG	Steve Garvey	5.00
JG	Jim Gilliam	6.00
TG	Tony Gwynn	8.00
HK	Harmon Killebrew	12.00
FL	Fred Lynn	5.00
LM	Lee May	5.00
MM	Mark McGwire	30.00
JM	Joe Morgan	6.00
DM	Dale Murphy	10.00
SM	Stan Musial	25.00
DP	Dave Parker	5.00
JP	Johnny Podres	5.00
KP	Kirby Puckett	12.00
CR	Cal Ripken Jr.	20.00
NR	Nolan Ryan	30.00
OS	Ozzie Smith	10.00
DS	Duke Snider	6.00
WS	Willie Stargell/SP	15.00
TW	Ted Williams/SP	100.00
RY	Robin Yount	10.00

Classic Greats Autograph

NM/M
Common Autograph:
Blue, Black and Red ink variations exist.
Listings without notations are blue ink.
EB	Ernie Banks/Black/73	80.00
DB	Don Baylor	25.00
DB	Don Baylor/Black/50	35.00
JB	Johnny Bench/Black/73	100.00
BB	Bill Buckner	20.00
BB	Bill Buckner/Black/85	25.00
GC	Gary Carter/Black/173	40.00
JC	Joe Carter/Black/173	35.00
OC	Orlando Cepeda	20.00
OC	Orlando Cepeda/Black/34	35.00
AD	Andre Dawson	20.00
AD	Andre Dawson/Black/75	30.00
DEc	Dennis Eckersley	25.00
DE	Dwight Evans	20.00
DE	Dwight Evans/Black/100	30.00
RF	Rollie Fingers/Black/73	30.00
RF	Rollie Fingers/Red/25	90.00
CF	Carlton Fisk	50.00
GF	George Foster/Black/173	35.00
SG	Steve Garvey/Black/174	30.00
GI	Kirk Gibson/Black/173	30.00
KG	Ken Griffey Sr.	20.00
KG	Ken Griffey Sr./Black/100	25.00
TG	Tony Gwynn	45.00
TG	Tony Gwynn/Black/101	60.00
KH	Keith Hernandez/Black/173	40.00
KH	Keith Hernandez/Red/25	110.00
AH	Al Hrabosky	25.00
AH	Al Hrabosky/Black/100	35.00
HK	Harmon Killebrew/Black/73	80.00
MM	Mark McGwire/Black/73	425.00
JoM	Joe Morgan/Black/169	40.00
JMo	Jack Morris/Black/123	40.00
DM	Dale Murphy/Black/169	40.00
PN	Phil Niekro/Black/173	30.00
PN	Phil Niekro/red/25	75.00
DP	Dave Parker/Black/113	30.00
TP	Tony Perez/Black/173	30.00
JP	Johnny Podres/Black/173	30.00
JP	Johnny Podres/Red/25	80.00
KP	Kirby Puckett	45.00
KP	Kirby Puckett/Black/174	60.00

CR	Cal Ripken Jr.	150.00
CR	Cal Ripken Jr/Black/38	250.00
RR	Robin Roberts/Black/173	40.00
TS	Tom Seaver/Black/74	80.00
TS	Tom Seaver/Red/25	135.00
SN	Duke Snider	40.00
SN	Duke Snider/Black/100	50.00
DSt	Dave Stewart	15.00
DSu	Don Sutton/Black/123	30.00
AT	Alan Trammell/Black/173	35.00
BW	Billy Williams/Black/173	35.00
TW	Ted Williams/9	3,650
MW	Maury Wills/Black/173	30.00
RY	Robin Yount/Black/73	100.00
RY	Robin Yount/Red/25	200.00

Classic Patch Logo

NM/M
| Common Player: | 5.00 |
Note: some are actual game-used patches.
EB1	Ernie Banks	12.00
JB1	Johnny Bench	12.00
JB2	Johnny Bench/150	50.00
JB3	Johnny Bench/150	35.00
YB1	Yogi Berra	12.00
YB2	Yogi Berra/350	25.00
YB3	Yogi Berra/150	35.00
JD1	Joe DiMaggio	
JD2	Joe DiMaggio/50	85.00
JD3	Joe DiMaggio/350	30.00
JD4	Joe DiMaggio/150	40.00
CF1	Carlton Fisk	8.00
CF2	Carlton Fisk/150	10.00
GF1	George Foster/350	10.00
GF2	George Foster	5.00
SG1	Steve Garvey	5.00
SG2	Steve Garvey/350	10.00
SG3	Steve Garvey/150	30.00
SG4	Steve Garvey/50	25.00
SG5	Steve Garvey/50	25.00
KG1	Kirk Gibson	5.00
KG2	Kirk Gibson/350	12.00
TG1	Tony Gwynn	8.00
TG2	Tony Gwynn/150	50.00
TG3	Tony Gwynn/25	25.00
CH1	Catfish Hunter/350	10.00
CH2	Catfish Hunter/150	25.00
CH4	Catfish Hunter/50	30.00
FL1	Fred Lynn	5.00
FL2	Fred Lynn/350	10.00
FL3	Fred Lynn/150	15.00
FL4	Fred Lynn/50	20.00
MM1	Mickey Mantle	35.00
MM2	Mickey Mantle/350	85.00
MM3	Mickey Mantle/150	85.00
MM4	Mickey Mantle/150	75.00
RM1	Roger Maris	15.00
RM2	Roger Maris/350	25.00
RM3	Roger Maris/150	40.00
RM4	Roger Maris/50	60.00
HM1	Hideki Matsui	25.00
MC1	Mark McGwire	20.00
MC2	Mark McGwire/350	50.00
JM1	Joe Morgan	6.00
JM2	Joe Morgan/350	8.00
JM3	Joe Morgan/150	15.00
JM4	Joe Morgan/150	30.00
JM5	Joe Morgan/100	15.00
KP1	Kirby Puckett	10.00
KP2	Kirby Puckett/40	100.00
CR1	Cal Ripken Jr.	25.00
CR2	Cal Ripken Jr/75	100.00
CR3	Cal Ripken Jr./150	50.00
BR1	Babe Ruth/350	40.00
BR2	Babe Ruth/30	30.00
BR3	Babe Ruth/50	50.00
NR1	Nolan Ryan	25.00
NR2	Nolan Ryan/350	40.00
NR3	Nolan Ryan/150	60.00
NR4	Nolan Ryan/105	100.00
OS1	Ozzie Smith	10.00
OS2	Ozzie Smith/350	20.00
OS3	Ozzie Smith/150	60.00
OS4	Ozzie Smith/100	40.00
OS5	Ozzie Smith/100	35.00
DS1	Duke Snider	8.00
DS2	Duke Snider/350	25.00
DS3	Duke Snider/350	15.00
DS5	Duke Snider/100	20.00
DS6	Duke Snider/150	15.00
WS1	Willie Stargell	5.00
WS2	Willie Stargell/137	50.00
WS3	Willie Stargell/150	25.00
WS4	Willie Stargell/50	40.00

BW1	Billy Williams	6.00
TW1	Ted Williams	20.00
TW2	Ted Williams/350	40.00
RY1	Robin Yount	8.00
RY2	Robin Yount/150	40.00
RY3	Robin Yount/350	20.00

Classic Pinstripes

		NM/M
Common Player:		5.00
Inserted 1:40		
YB	Yogi Berra	15.00
JB	Jim Bouton	5.00
DE	Bucky Dent	8.00
JD	Joe DiMaggio	100.00
DG	Dwight Gooden	5.00
MM	Mickey Mantle	140.00
DM	Don Mattingly	25.00
TM	Thurman Munson	30.00
DR	Dave Righetti	5.00
PR	Phil Rizzuto	15.00
BR	Babe Ruth	250.00
CS	Casey Stengel	12.00

Classic Yankee Greats Autograph

		NM/M
Common Autograph:		
RA	Ruben Amaro Sr.	25.00
RA	Ruben Amaro Sr./Black/100	30.00
RA	Ruben Amaro Sr./Red/25	60.00
HB	Hank Bauer	30.00
HB	Hank Bauer/Black/75	40.00
YB	Yogi Berra/Black/73	100.00
JB	Jim Bouton	25.00
JB	Jim Bouton/Black/100	30.00
RB	Ralph Branca	25.00
RB	Ralph Branca/Black/100	30.00
JC	Jose Canseco/Black/73	90.00
JC	Jose Canseco/Red/25	150.00
CC	Chris Chambliss	30.00
CC	Chris Chambliss/Black/101	35.00
CC	Chris Chambliss/Red/25	75.00
DC	David Cone/Black/74	75.00
DC	David Cone/Red/25	110.00
BD	Bucky Dent	20.00
JD	Joe DiMaggio/5	2,325
DE	Dock Ellis/Black/174	75.00
DE	Dock Ellis/Red/25	65.00
DG	Dwight Gooden/Black/74	70.00
GU	Ron Guidry	35.00
GU	Ron Guidry/Black/100	45.00
TH	Tommy Henrich	35.00
TH	Tommy Henrich/Black/100	40.00
TH	Tommy Henrich/Red/25	125.00
RH	Ralph Houk	25.00
RH	Ralph Houk/Black/100	30.00
TJ	Tommy John	30.00
TJ	Tommy John/Black/100	35.00
JKa	Jim Kaat	20.00
JKa	Jim Kaat/Black/25	25.00
JKe	Jimmy Key	40.00
JKe	Jimmy Key/Black/100	50.00
DK	Dave Kingman	25.00
DK	Dave Kingman/Black/100	30.00
TK	Tony Kubek/Black/123	15.00
JL	Jim Leyritz	25.00
JL	Jim Leyritz/Black/100	35.00
JL	Jim Leyritz/Red/25	65.00
SL	Sparky Lyle	30.00
SL	Sparky Lyle/Black/100	40.00
MM	Mickey Mantle/Blue/7	2,850
DM	Don Mattingly/Black/74	100.00
DM	Don Mattingly/Red/25	340.00
LM	Lee Mazzilli	30.00

JM	John Montefusco	20.00
JM	John Montefusco/Black/100	25.00
JM	John Montefusco/Red/25	50.00
PO	Paul O'Neill	50.00
PO	Paul O'Neill/Black/100	65.00
PO	Paul O'Neill/Red/25	100.00
MP	Mike Pagliarulo	20.00
MP	Mike Pagliarulo/Black/99	25.00
MP	Mike Pagliarulo/Red/25	60.00
LP	Lou Piniella	40.00
LP	Lou Piniella/Black/100	45.00
DR	Dave Righetti/Black/173	40.00
DR	Dave Righetti/Red/25	85.00
MR	Mickey Rivers/Black/73	40.00
PR	Phil Rizzuto/Black/173	55.00
FS	Fred Stanley	25.00
FS	Fred Stanley/Black/101	25.00
MS	Mel Stottlemyre/Black/73	85.00
DT	Dick Tidrow	20.00
DT	Dick Tidrow/Black/101	25.00
DT	Dick Tidrow/Red/25	70.00
JT	Joe Torre/Black/73	60.00
JT	Joe Torre/Red/25	140.00
DW	Dave Winfield/Black/25	165.00

2003 Upper Deck Ultimate Collection

		NM/M
Complete Set (181):		
Common Player (1-84):		2.00
Production 850		
Common (85-117):		3.00
Production 625		
Common (118-140):		3.00
Production 399		
Common (141-158):		4.00
Production 250		
Common (159-168):		6.00
Production 100		
Common (169-174):		25.00
Common (175-180):		10.00
169-180 Production 250		
Pack (4):		90.00
Box (4):		300.00
1	Ichiro Suzuki	8.00
2	Ken Griffey Jr.	6.00
3	Sammy Sosa	6.00
4	Jason Giambi	4.00
5	Mike Piazza	5.00
6	Derek Jeter	10.00
7	Randy Johnson	4.00
8	Barry Bonds	10.00
9	Carlos Delgado	3.00
10	Mark Prior	3.00
11	Vladimir Guerrero	4.00
12	Alfonso Soriano	4.00
13	Jim Thome	4.00
14	Pedro J. Martinez	4.00
15	Nomar Garciaparra	5.00
16	Chipper Jones	4.00
17	Rocco Baldelli	2.00
18	Dontrelle Willis	2.00
19	Garret Anderson	2.00
20	Jeff Bagwell	3.00
21	Jim Edmonds	2.50
22	Rickey Henderson	3.00
23	Torii Hunter	2.50
24	Tom Glavine	2.50
25	Hideo Nomo	2.50
26	Luis Gonzalez	2.50
27	Alex Rodriguez	8.00
28	Albert Pujols	10.00
29	Manny Ramirez	4.00
30	Rafael Palmeiro	3.00
31	Bernie Williams	3.00
32	Curt Schilling	3.00
33	Roger Clemens	8.00
34	Andruw Jones	3.00
35	J.D. Drew	2.00
36	Kerry Wood	3.00
37	Scott Rolen	3.00
38	Darin Erstad	2.00

39	Joe DiMaggio	8.00
40	Magglio Ordonez	2.00
41	Todd Helton	3.00
42	Barry Zito	2.00
43	Mickey Mantle	10.00
44	Miguel Tejada	3.00
45	Troy Glaus	2.00
46	Kazuhisa Ishii	2.00
47	Adam Dunn	3.00
48	Ted Williams	8.00
49	Mike Mussina	3.00
50	Ivan Rodriguez	3.00
51	Jacque Jones	2.00
52	Stan Musial	6.00
53	Mariano Rivera	2.50
54	Larry Walker	2.00
55	Aaron Boone	2.00
56	Hank Blalock	2.50
57	Rich Harden	2.00
58	Lance Berkman	2.00
59	Eric Chavez	2.00
60	Carlos Beltran	3.00
61	Roy Oswalt	2.00
62	Moises Alou	2.00
63	Nolan Ryan	10.00
64	Jeff Kent	2.00
65	Roberto Alomar	2.00
66	Runelvys Hernandez	2.00
67	Roy Halladay	3.00
68	Tim Hudson	2.50
69	Tom Seaver	4.00
70	Edgardo Alfonzo	2.00
71	Andy Pettitte	2.00
72	Preston Wilson	2.00
73	Frank Thomas	4.00
74	Jerome Williams	2.00
75	Shawn Green	2.50
76	David Wells	2.00
77	John Smoltz	3.00
78	Jorge Posada	3.00
79	Marlon Byrd	2.00
80	Austin Kearns	2.00
81	Bret Boone	2.00
82	Rafael Furcal	2.50
83	Jay Gibbons	2.00
84	Shane Reynolds	2.00
85	Nate Bland RC	3.00
86	Willie Eyre RC	3.00
87	Jeremy Guthrie	3.00
88	Jeremy Wedel RC	3.00
89	Jhonny Peralta	6.00
90	Luis Ayala RC	3.00
91	Michael Hessman RC	3.00
92	Micheal Nakamura RC	3.00
93	Nook Logan RC	3.00
94	Rett Johnson RC	5.00
95	Josh Hall RC	4.00
96	Julio Manon RC	3.00
97	Heath Bell RC	3.00
98	Ian Ferguson RC	3.00
99	Jason Gilfillan RC	3.00
100	Jason Roach RC	3.00
101	Jason Shiell RC	3.00
102	Terrmel Sledge RC	5.00
103	Phil Seibel RC	3.00
104	Jeff Duncan RC	6.00
105	Mike Neu RC	3.00
106	Colin Porter RC	3.00
107	Dave Matranga RC	3.00
108	Aaron Looper RC	3.00
109	Jeremy Bonderman	20.00
110	Miguel Ojeda RC	3.00
111	Chad Cordero RC	3.00
112	Shane Bazell RC	4.00
113	Tim Olson RC	5.00
114	Michel Hernandez RC	3.00
115	Chien-Ming Wang RC	50.00
116	Josh Stewart RC	3.00
117	Clint Barmes RC	10.00
118	Craig Brazell RC	5.00
119	Josh Willingham RC	8.00
120	Brent Hoard RC	3.00
121	Francisco Rosario RC	3.00
122	Rick Roberts RC	3.00
123	Geoff Geary RC	3.00
124	Edgar Gonzalez RC	3.00
125	Kevin Correia RC	3.00
126	Ryan Cameron RC	3.00
127	Beau Kemp RC	3.00
128	Tommy Phelps RC	3.00
129	Mark Malaska RC	3.00
130	Kevin Ohme RC	3.00
131	Humberto Quintero RC	3.00
132	Aquilino Lopez RC	3.00
133	Andrew Brown RC	3.00
134	Wilfredo Ledezma RC	3.00
135	Luis De Los Santos RC	3.00
136	Garrett Atkins RC	3.00
137	Fernando Cabrera RC	3.00
138	D.J. Carrasco RC	3.00
139	Alfredo Gonzalez RC	3.00
140	Alex Prieto RC	3.00
141	Matt Kata RC	5.00
142	Chris Capuano RC	15.00
143	Bobby Madritsch RC	20.00
144	Greg Jones RC	4.00
145	Pete Zoccolillo RC	4.00
146	Chad Gaudin RC	4.00
147	Rosman Garcia RC	4.00
148	Gerald Laird RC	4.00
149	Danny Garcia RC	4.00
150	Stephen Randolph RC	4.00
151	Pete LaForest RC	8.00
152	Brian Sweeney RC	4.00
153	Aaron Miles RC	4.00
154	Jorge DePaula RC	4.00
155	Graham Koonce RC	10.00
156	Tom Gregorio RC	4.00

157	Javier Lopez	4.00
158	Oscar Villarreal RC	4.00
159	Prentice Redman RC	6.00
160	Francisco Cruceta RC	6.00
161	Guillermo Quiroz RC	20.00
162	Jeremy Griffiths	10.00
163	Lew Ford RC	20.00
164	Rob Hammock RC	10.00
165	Todd Wellemeyer RC	10.00
166	Ryan Wagner RC	10.00
167	Edwin Jackson RC	20.00
168	Dan Haren RC	15.00
169	Hideki Matsui/Auto. RC	275.00
170	Jose Contreras/Auto. RC	30.00
171	Delmon Young/Auto. RC	300.00
172	Rickie Weeks/Auto. RC	150.00
173	Brandon Webb/Auto. RC	100.00
174	Bo Hart/Auto. RC	15.00
175	Rocco Baldelli/Auto.	25.00
176	Jose Reyes/Auto.	30.00
177	Dontrelle Willis/Auto.	50.00
178	Bobby Hill/Auto.	25.00
179	Jae Weong Seo/Auto.	25.00
180	Jesse Foppert/Auto.	25.00
CL	Checklist	2.00

Gold

Stars (1-184):		1.5-3X
(85-117):		1-2X
Production 50		
(118-140):		1-2X
Production 35		
(141-158):		1-2X
Production 25		
(159-168):		No Pricing
Production 10		
(169-180):		No Pricing
Production 25		

Buybacks

		NM/M
Production 1-75		
	Hank Blalock/35	40.00
	Hank Blalock	
	03 40M/25	40.00
	Hank Blalock	
	03 GF/25	40.00
	Hank Blalock	
	03 Patch/25	40.00
	Hank Blalock	
	03 SPA/20	40.00
	Hank Blalock	
	03 SPA/25	40.00
	Hank Blalock	
	03 VIN/25	40.00
	Luis Gonzalez	
	03 40M HR/25	40.00
	Luis Gonzalez	
	03 SPA/25	40.00
	Luis Gonzalez	
	03 VIN/25	40.00
	Ken Griffey Jr.	
	02-3 SUP/75	80.00
	Ken Griffey Jr.	
	02-3 SUP Spok/50	80.00
	Ken Griffey Jr.	
	03 40M/50	80.00
	Ken Griffey Jr.	
	03 40M/50	80.00
	Ken Griffey Jr.	
	03 40M/50	80.00
	Ken Griffey Jr.	
	03 40M/50	80.00
	Ken Griffey Jr.	
	03 40M T40/50	80.00
	Ken Griffey Jr.	
	03 GF/50	80.00
	Ken Griffey Jr.	
	03 HON/50	80.00
	Ken Griffey Jr.	
	03 HON SP/30	100.00
	Ken Griffey Jr.	
	03 Patch/75	80.00
	Ken Griffey Jr.	
	03 PB/75	80.00
	Ken Griffey Jr.	
	03 SPA/50	80.00
	Ken Griffey Jr.	
	03 SPA/75	80.00
	Ken Griffey Jr.	
	03 SPx/75	80.00
	Ken Griffey Jr.	
	03 SWS/75	80.00
	Ken Griffey Jr.	
	03 UDA/75	80.00
	Ken Griffey Jr.	
	03 VIN/50	80.00
	Torii Hunter	
	03 Patch/25	40.00
	Torii Hunter	
	03 PB/50	30.00
	Torii Hunter	
	03 VIN/25	40.00
	Austin Kearns	
	03 40M/33	30.00
	Hideki Matsui	
	03 40M/20	250.00
	Hideki Matsui	
	03 40M Flag/20	250.00
	Hideki Matsui	
	03 GF/18	250.00
	Hideki Matsui	
	03 PB/17	250.00

	Hideki Matsui	
	03 UD/25	250.00
	Hideki Matsui	
	03 VIN/25	250.00
	Stan Musial	
	02 SPLC/30	75.00
	Stan Musial	
	02 WSH/25	75.00
	Stan Musial	
	03 PB/50	60.00
	Stan Musial	
	03 SWSC/37	75.00
	Stan Musial	
	03 VIN/50	60.00
	Sammy Sosa	
	02-3 SUP/25	120.00
	Sammy Sosa	
	03 PB/25	120.00
	Sammy Sosa	
	03 SPA/25	120.00
	Sammy Sosa	
	03 VIN/25	120.00
	Mark Teixeira	
	03 40M/50	40.00
	Mark Teixeira	
	03 Patch/50	40.00
	Mark Teixeira	
	03 SPA RA/25	50.00
	Mark Teixeira	
	03 SWS/23	50.00
	Mark Teixeira	
	03 UD/25	50.00
	Mark Teixeira	
	03 VIN/25	50.00

Double Barrel

		NM/M
No pricing due to scarcity.		
DB-AE	Darin Erstad, Garret Anderson/3 (3/04 auction)	645.00
DB-GS	Tom Seaver, Tom Glavine/2 (3/04 auction)	700.00

Game Jersey Tier 1

		NM/M
Common Player:		8.00
Production 99 Sets		
Copper:		No Pricing
Production 10 Sets		
Gold:		.75-2X
No pricing production of 20 or less.		
RB	Rocco Baldelli	8.00
PB	Pat Burrell	8.00
RC	Roger Clemens	20.00
CD	Carlos Delgado	10.00
AD	Adam Dunn	10.00
JE	Jim Edmonds	8.00
RF	Rafael Furcal	8.00
JG	Jason Giambi	8.00
TR	Troy Glaus	8.00
TG	Tom Glavine	10.00
SG	Shawn Green	8.00
KG	Ken Griffey Jr.	20.00
VG	Vladimir Guerrero	10.00
TH	Torii Hunter	8.00
KI	Kazuhisa Ishii	8.00
RJ	Randy Johnson	12.00
AJ	Andruw Jones	10.00
CJ	Chipper Jones	15.00
GM	Greg Maddux	15.00
HM	Hideki Matsui	50.00
MM	Mike Mussina	8.00
HN	Hideo Nomo	15.00
MI	Mike Piazza	15.00
MP	Mark Prior	15.00
AP	Albert Pujols	25.00
MR	Manny Ramirez	12.00
JR	Jose Reyes	10.00
AR	Alex Rodriguez	15.00
CS	Curt Schilling	10.00
GS	Gary Sheffield	8.00
AS	Alfonso Soriano	10.00
SS	Sammy Sosa	25.00
IS	Ichiro Suzuki	50.00
MT	Miguel Tejada	10.00
FT	Frank Thomas	10.00
JT	Jim Thome	10.00
RW	Rickie Weeks	15.00
BW	Bernie Williams	10.00
DW	Dontrelle Willis	10.00
KW	Kerry Wood	10.00
DY	Delmon Young	15.00
BZ	Barry Zito	8.00

Game Jersey Tier 2

Tier 2: 1X Tier 1 Price
Production 75 Sets

Dual Jersey

		NM/M
Common Duo:		10.00
Production 50 Sets		
Gold:		1-1.25X

Production 25 Sets

AH	Alfonso Soriano, Hideki Matsui	40.00
AI	Albert Pujols, Ichiro Suzuki	50.00
BK	Jeff Kent, Jeff Bagwell	15.00
CA	Chipper Jones, Andruw Jones	15.00
CJ	Carlos Delgado, Jason Giambi	15.00
DE	Jim Edmonds, J.D. Drew	10.00
DG	Carlos Delgado, Vladimir Guerrero	15.00
DM	Mickey Mantle, Joe DiMaggio	250.00
DP	Carlos Delgado, Rafael Palmeiro	15.00
DW	Joe DiMaggio, Ted Williams	150.00
GB	Shawn Green, Kevin Brown	10.00
GD	Adam Dunn, Ken Griffey Jr.	25.00
GE	Darin Erstad, Troy Glaus	10.00
GP	Rafael Palmeiro, Ken Griffey Jr.	25.00
GR	Alex Rodriguez, Nomar Garciaparra	25.00
GS	Vladimir Guerrero, Sammy Sosa	25.00
HJ	Torii Hunter, Jacque Jones	10.00
HZ	Roy Halladay, Barry Zito	10.00
IG	Ken Griffey Jr., Ichiro Suzuki	50.00
IN	Ichiro Suzuki, Hideo Nomo	50.00
IS	Sammy Sosa, Ichiro Suzuki	45.00
JF	Andruw Jones, Rafael Furcal	15.00
JM	Mike Piazza, Jorge Posada	20.00
MC	Greg Maddux, Roger Clemens	30.00
MW	Ted Williams, Mickey Mantle	250.00
NI	Hideo Nomo, Kazuhisa Ishii	30.00
NM	Hideki Matsui, Hideo Nomo	60.00
PC	Roger Clemens, Pedro J. Martinez	25.00
PM	Mike Mussina, Andy Pettitte	15.00
PS	Sammy Sosa, Mark Prior	30.00
RM	Pedro J. Martinez, Manny Ramirez	15.00
RP	Rafael Palmeiro, Alex Rodriguez	20.00
SA	Albert Pujols, Scott Rolen	40.00
SB	Alfonso Soriano, Bernie Williams	15.00
SJ	Randy Johnson, Curt Schilling	20.00
SM	Greg Maddux, John Smoltz	25.00
TB	Mark Teixeira, Hank Blalock	15.00
TH	Todd Helton, Jim Thome	15.00
TR	Alex Rodriguez, Miguel Tejada	20.00
WL	Mike Lowell, Dontrelle Willis	15.00
YW	Delmon Young, Rickie Weeks	35.00

Game-Used Patch

		NM/M
Common Player:		15.00
Production 99 Sets		
Copper:		1-1.5X
Production 35 Sets		
Gold:		1-1.5X
Production 25 Sets		
RB	Rocco Baldelli	20.00
PB	Pat Burrell	20.00
RC	Roger Clemens	50.00
CD	Carlos Delgado	15.00

AD Adam Dunn 20.00
JE Jim Edmonds 20.00
RF Rafael Furcal 15.00
JG Jason Giambi 20.00
TR Troy Glaus 25.00
TG Tom Glavine 25.00
SG Shawn Green 15.00
KG Ken Griffey Jr. 45.00
VG Vladimir Guerrero 30.00
RH Roy Halladay 20.00
TH Torii Hunter 20.00
KI Kazuhisa Ishii 20.00
RJ Randy Johnson 25.00
AJ Andruw Jones 25.00
CJ Chipper Jones 30.00
GM Greg Maddux 40.00
HM Hideki Matsui 85.00
MM Mike Mussina 25.00
HN Hideo Nomo 40.00
MI Mike Piazza 35.00
MP Mark Prior 30.00
AP Albert Pujols 50.00
MR Manny Ramirez 30.00
JR Jose Reyes 30.00
AR Alex Rodriguez 50.00
CS Curt Schilling 25.00
AS Alfonso Soriano/42 35.00
SS Sammy Sosa 35.00
IS Ichiro Suzuki 75.00
MT Miguel Tejada 25.00
FT Frank Thomas 25.00
JT Jim Thome 30.00
RW Rickie Weeks 25.00
BW Bernie Williams 20.00
DW Dontrelle Willis 30.00
KW Kerry Wood 40.00
DY Delmon Young 35.00
BZ Barry Zito 20.00

Dual Patch

NM/M
Common Duo: 20.00
Production 99 unless noted.
Gold: .75-1.25X
Production 35
AI Ichiro Suzuki,
  Albert Pujols 100.00
AM Andy Pettitte,
  Mike Mussina 25.00
BK Jeff Bagwell,
  Jeff Kent 25.00
CA Andruw Jones,
  Chipper Jones 30.00
CV Carlos Delgado,
  Vladimir Guerrero 35.00
DE Jim Edmonds,
  J.D. Drew 25.00
DG Carlos Delgado,
  Jason Giambi 25.00
DP Carlos Delgado,
  Rafael Palmeiro/35 40.00
GB Shawn Green,
  Kevin Brown 20.00
GD Adam Dunn,
  Ken Griffey Jr. 45.00
GE Darin Erstad,
  Troy Glaus 30.00
GP Ken Griffey Jr.,
  Rafael Palmeiro/35 50.00
GR Alex Rodriguez,
  Nomar Garciaparra 75.00
GS Vladimir Guerrero,
  Sammy Sosa 40.00
HJ Torii Hunter,
  Jacque Jones/83 20.00
HZ Roy Halladay,
  Barry Zito 35.00
IG Ken Griffey Jr.,
  Ichiro Suzuki 90.00
IN Ichiro Suzuki,
  Hideo Nomo 140.00
IS Sammy Sosa,
  Ichiro Suzuki 90.00
JF Rafael Furcal,
  Andruw Jones 25.00
JG John Smoltz,
  Greg Maddux 40.00
MC Greg Maddux,
  Roger Clemens/75 60.00
NI Hideo Nomo,
  Kazuhisa Ishii/63 65.00
NM Hideki Matsui,
  Hideo Nomo/35 180.00
PM Mike Piazza,
  Jorge Posada/73 35.00
PR Roger Clemens,
  Pedro Martinez/35 60.00
PS Sammy Sosa,
  Mark Prior 40.00
RM Pedro J. Martinez,
  Manny Ramirez 40.00
RP Rafael Palmeiro,
  Alex Rodriguez/35 40.00
SA Albert Pujols,
  Scott Rolen 75.00
SJ Randy Johnson,
  Curt Schilling 40.00

SM Alfonso Soriano,
  Hideki Matsui 80.00
TB Mark Teixeira,
  Hank Blalock 40.00
TH Jim Thome,
  Todd Helton 35.00
TR Alex Rodriguez,
  Miguel Tejada 50.00
WL Mike Lowell,
  Dontrelle Willis/85 35.00
YW Delmon Young,
  Rickie Weeks/28 75.00

Ultimate Signature Tier 1

NM/M
Common Player: 20.00
AP1 Albert Pujols/40 160.00
AP2 Albert Pujols/35 160.00
AR1 Alex Rodriguez/75 Exch 120.00
AR2 Alex Rodriguez/60 Exch 120.00
BG1 Bob Gibson/299 20.00
BG2 Bob Gibson/199 20.00
CD1 Carlos Delgado/150 20.00
CR1 Cal Ripken Jr./85 150.00
CR2 Cal Ripken Jr./85 150.00
CY1 Carl Yastrzemski/199 60.00
DY1 Delmon Young/300 75.00
DY2 Delmon Young/300 75.00
EG1 Eric Gagne/350 40.00
GC1 Gary Carter/199 20.00
GM1 Greg Maddux/250 60.00
GM2 Greg Maddux/140 60.00
HM1 Hideki Matsui/250 250.00
HM2 Hideki Matsui/240 250.00
IS1 Ichiro Suzuki/199 280.00
IS2 Ichiro Suzuki/99 350.00
JG1 Jason Giambi/35 40.00
JG2 Jason Giambi/35 40.00
KG1 Ken Griffey Jr./350 75.00
KG2 Ken Griffey Jr./350 75.00
KW1 Kerry Wood/170 40.00
KW2 Kerry Wood/85 40.00
MP1 Mark Prior/299 40.00
MP2 Mark Prior/225 40.00
NG1 Nomar Garciaparra/125 Exch 90.00
NG2 Nomar Garciaparra/180 90.00
NR1 Nolan Ryan/85 100.00
NR2 Nolan Ryan/75 100.00
OS1 Ozzie Smith/199 100.00
RC1 Roger Clemens/70 125.00
RC2 Roger Clemens/30 150.00
RJ1 Randy Johnson/75 125.00
RJ2 Randy Johnson/50 85.00
RS1 Ryne Sandberg/240 50.00
RS2 Ryne Sandberg/200 50.00
RW1 Rickie Weeks/300 40.00
RW2 Rickie Weeks/300 40.00
TS1 Tom Seaver/75 50.00
TS2 Tom Seaver/60 50.00
VG1 Vladimir Guerrero/75 60.00
VG2 Vladimir Guerrero/50 60.00

Ultimate Signatures Tier 2

NM/M
Production 25 Sets
GC Gary Carter 50.00
RC Roger Clemens 200.00
CD Carlos Delgado 40.00
EG Eric Gagne 75.00
NG Nomar Garciaparra 120.00
JG Jason Giambi 50.00
BG Bob Gibson 60.00
KG Ken Griffey Jr. 120.00
VG Vladimir Guerrero 90.00
RJ Randy Johnson 100.00
GM Greg Maddux 200.00
HM Hideki Matsui 380.00
MP Mark Prior 80.00
AP Albert Pujols 250.00
CR Cal Ripken Jr. 250.00
AR Alex Rodriguez 200.00
NR Nolan Ryan 165.00
RS Ryne Sandberg 120.00
TS Tom Seaver 65.00
OS Ozzie Smith 100.00
IS Ichiro Suzuki 400.00
RW Rickie Weeks 100.00
KW Kerry Wood 75.00
CY Carl Yastrzemski 125.00
DY Delmon Young 125.00

2003 Upper Deck Victory

NM/M
Complete Set (200): 40.00
Common Player (1-100): .10
Common (101-200): .40
Cards (101-128): Inserted 1:4
(129-168): 1:5
(169-188): 1:10
(189-200): 1:20
Pack (6): .75
Box (36): 20.00
1 Troy Glaus .40
2 Garret Anderson .20
3 Tim Salmon .20
4 Darin Erstad .20
5 Luis Gonzalez .20

6 Curt Schilling .25
7 Randy Johnson .50
8 Junior Spivey .10
9 Andruw Jones .25
10 Greg Maddux .75
11 Chipper Jones .75
12 Gary Sheffield .20
13 John Smoltz .20
14 Geronimo Gil .10
15 Tony Batista .10
16 Trot Nixon .10
17 Manny Ramirez .40
18 Pedro J. Martinez .50
19 Nomar Garciaparra 1.00
20 Derek Lowe .10
21 Shea Hillenbrand .10
22 Sammy Sosa .75
23 Kerry Wood .25
24 Mark Prior .40
25 Magglio Ordonez .20
26 Frank Thomas .40
27 Mark Buehrle .10
28 Paul Konerko .10
29 Adam Dunn .40
30 Ken Griffey Jr. .75
31 Austin Kearns .25
32 Matt Lawton .10
33 Larry Walker .20
34 Todd Helton .20
35 Jeff Bagwell .40
36 Roy Oswalt .20
37 Lance Berkman .20
38 Mike Sweeney .10
39 Carlos Beltran .20
40 Kazuhisa Ishii .10
41 Shawn Green .20
42 Hideo Nomo .25
43 Adrian Beltre .25
44 Richie Sexson .25
45 Ben Sheets .25
46 Torii Hunter .25
47 Jacque Jones .10
48 Corey Koskie .10
49 Vladimir Guerrero .50
50 Jose Vidro .10
51 Mo Vaughn .20
52 Mike Piazza 1.00
53 Roberto Alomar .20
54 Derek Jeter 1.50
55 Alfonso Soriano .75
56 Jason Giambi .75
57 Roger Clemens .75
58 Mike Mussina .25
59 Bernie Williams .25
60 Jorge Posada .20
61 Nick Johnson .10
62 Hideki Matsui RC 4.00
63 Eric Chavez .20
64 Barry Zito .20
65 Miguel Tejada .20
66 Tim Hudson .20
67 Pat Burrell .20
68 Bobby Abreu .20
69 Jimmy Rollins .20
70 Brett Myers .10
71 Jim Thome .40
72 Jason Kendall .10
73 Brian Giles .20
74 Aramis Ramirez .10
75 Sean Burroughs .10
76 Ryan Klesko .10
77 Phil Nevin .10
78 Barry Bonds 1.50
79 J.T. Snow .10
80 Rich Aurilia .10
81 Ichiro Suzuki 1.00
82 Edgar Martinez .10
83 Freddy Garcia .10
84 Jim Edmonds .20
85 J.D. Drew .20
86 Scott Rolen .40
87 Albert Pujols .50
88 Mark McGwire 1.25
89 Matt Morris .20
90 Ben Grieve .10
91 Carl Crawford .20
92 Alex Rodriguez 1.25
93 Carl Everett .10
94 Juan Gonzalez .20
95 Rafael Palmeiro .20
96 Hank Blalock .20
97 Carlos Delgado .20
98 Josh Phelps .10
99 Eric Hinske .10
100 Shannon Stewart .10
101 Albert Pujols 1.00
102 Alex Rodriguez 2.50
103 Alfonso Soriano 1.00

104 Barry Bonds 3.00
105 Bernie Williams .50
106 Brian Giles .50
107 Chipper Jones .75
108 Darin Erstad .50
109 Derek Jeter 3.00
110 Eric Chavez .50
111 Miguel Tejada .50
112 Ichiro Suzuki 1.50
113 Rafael Palmeiro .40
114 Jason Giambi 1.50
115 Jeff Bagwell .75
116 Jim Thome .75
117 Ken Griffey Jr. 1.50
118 Lance Berkman .50
119 Luis Gonzalez .40
120 Manny Ramirez .75
121 Mike Piazza 2.00
122 J.D. Drew .40
123 Sammy Sosa 1.50
124 Scott Rolen .75
125 Shawn Green .50
126 Todd Helton .50
127 Troy Glaus .75
128 Vladimir Guerrero 1.00
129 Albert Pujols 1.00
130 Brian Giles .50
131 Carlos Delgado .50
132 Curt Schilling .50
133 Derek Jeter 3.00
134 Frank Thomas .75
135 Greg Maddux 1.50
136 Jeff Bagwell .75
137 Jim Thome .75
138 Jorge Posada .50
139 Kazuhisa Ishii .40
140 Larry Walker .40
141 Luis Gonzalez .40
142 Miguel Tejada .50
143 Pat Burrell .75
144 Pedro J. Martinez 1.00
145 Rafael Palmeiro .50
146 Roger Clemens 1.50
147 Tim Hudson .50
148 Troy Glaus .75
149 Alfonso Soriano 1.00
150 Andruw Jones .50
151 Barry Zito .50
152 Darin Erstad .50
153 Eric Chavez .50
154 Alex Rodriguez 2.50
155 J.D. Drew .40
156 Jason Giambi 1.50
157 Jason Kendall .40
158 Ken Griffey Jr. 1.50
159 Lance Berkman .50
160 Mike Mussina .50
161 Mike Piazza 2.00
162 Nomar Garciaparra 2.00
163 Randy Johnson 1.00
164 Roberto Alomar .50
165 Scott Rolen .75
166 Shawn Green .50
167 Torii Hunter .50
168 Vladimir Guerrero 1.00
169 Alex Rodriguez 2.50
170 Andruw Jones .50
171 Bernie Williams .50
172 Ichiro Suzuki 1.50
173 Miguel Tejada .50
174 Nomar Garciaparra 2.00
175 Pedro J. Martinez 1.00
176 Randy Johnson 1.00
177 Todd Helton .50
178 Vladimir Guerrero 1.00
179 Barry Bonds 3.00
180 Carlos Delgado .50
181 Chipper Jones 1.50
182 Frank Thomas .75
183 Lance Berkman .50
184 Larry Walker .40
185 Manny Ramirez .75
186 Mike Piazza 2.00
187 Sammy Sosa 1.50
188 Shawn Green .50
189 Chipper Jones 1.50
190 Curt Schilling .50
191 Derek Jeter 3.00
192 Ken Griffey Jr. 1.50
193 Sammy Sosa 1.50
194 Vladimir Guerrero 1.00
195 Alex Rodriguez 2.50
196 Barry Bonds 3.00
197 Greg Maddux 1.50
198 Ichiro Suzuki 1.50
199 Jason Giambi 1.50
200 Mike Piazza 2.00

Parallels

Tier 1 Green: 1-2X
Inserted 1:1
Tier 2 Orange: 2-4X
Inserted 1:8
Tier 3 Blue: 3-6X
Production 650
Tier 4 Purple: 10-25X
Production 50 Sets
Tier 5 Red: No Pricing
Production 25 Sets

2003 Upper Deck Vintage

NM/M
Complete Set (280): 40.00
Common Player: .15
Common SP (223-232): 1.50

Inserted 1:7
Common SP (233-247): .50
Inserted 1:5
Common 3D SP (248-277): 6.00
Inserted 1:48
Pack (8): 2.00
Box (24): 45.00
1 Troy Glaus .25
2 Darin Erstad .25
3 Garret Anderson .25
4 Jarrod Washburn .15
5 Nolan Ryan 2.00
6 Tim Salmon .25
7 Troy Percival .15
8 Alex Ochoa/SP 4.00
9 Daryle Ward .15
10 Jeff Bagwell .50
11 Roy Oswalt .25
12 Lance Berkman .40
13 Craig Biggio .25
14 Richard Hidalgo .25
15 Tim Hudson .25
16 Eric Chavez .25
17 Barry Zito .25
18 Miguel Tejada .50
19 Mark Mulder .25
20 Rollie Fingers .15
21 Jim "Catfish" Hunter .25
22 Jermaine Dye .15
23 Ray Durham/SP 4.00
24 Carlos Delgado .25
25 Eric Hinske .15
26 Josh Phelps .15
27 Shannon Stewart .15
28 Vernon Wells .15
29 John Smoltz .25
30 Greg Maddux 1.00
31 Chipper Jones .75
32 Gary Sheffield .25
33 Andruw Jones .40
34 Tom Glavine .25
35 Rafael Furcal .15
36 Phil Niekro .15
37 Eddie Mathews .50
38 Robin Yount .75
39 Richie Sexson .25
40 Ben Sheets .15
41 Geoff Jenkins .15
42 Alex Sanchez .15
43 Jason Isringhausen .15
44 Albert Pujols 1.50
45 Matt Morris .15
46 J.D. Drew .25
47 Jim Edmonds .25
48 Stan Musial 1.00
49 Red Schoendienst .15
50 Edgar Renteria .25
51 Mark McGwire/SP 10.00
52 Scott Rolen/SP 5.00
53 Mark Bellhorn .15
54 Kerry Wood .50
55 Mark Prior .50
56 Moises Alou .25
57 Corey Patterson .25
58 Ernie Banks .75
59 Hee Seop Choi .15
60 Billy Williams .15
61 Sammy Sosa/SP 8.00
62 Ben Grieve .15
63 Jared Sandberg .15
64 Carl Crawford .15
65 Randy Johnson .75
66 Luis Gonzalez .25
67 Steve Finley .15
68 Junior Spivey .15
69 Erubiel Durazo .15
70 Curt Schilling/SP 8.00
71 Al Lopez .15
72 Pee Wee Reese .75
73 Eric Gagne .25
74 Shawn Green .25
75 Kevin Brown .15
76 Paul LoDuca .15
77 Adrian Beltre .25
78 Hideo Nomo .40
79 Eric Karros .15
80 Odalis Perez .15
81 Kazuhisa Ishii/SP 5.00
82 Tommy Lasorda .15
83 Fernando Tatis .15
84 Vladimir Guerrero .25
85 Jose Vidro .15

ABBREVIATIONS
SP - Short Print

86 Javier Vazquez .15
87 Brad Wilkerson .15
88 Bartolo Colon/SP 4.00
89 Monte Irvin .15
90 Robb Nen .15
91 Reggie Sanders .15
92 Jeff Kent .25
93 Rich Aurilia .15
94 Orlando Cepeda .25
95 Juan Marichal .25
96 Willie McCovey .25
97 David Bell .15
98 Barry Bonds/SP 10.00
99 Kenny Lofton/SP 4.00
100 Jim Thome .50
101 C.C. Sabathia .25
102 Omar Vizquel .25
103 Lou Boudreau .15
104 Larry Doby .25
105 Bob Lemon .15
106 John Olerud .25
107 Edgar Martinez .25
108 Bret Boone .15
109 Freddy Garcia .15
110 Mike Cameron .15
111 Kazuhiro Sasaki .15
112 Ichiro Suzuki/SP 8.00
113 Mike Lowell .15
114 Josh Beckett .25
115 A.J. Burnett .15
116 Juan Pierre .15
117 Derrek Lee .15
118 Luis Castillo .15
119 Juan Encarnacion/SP 4.00
120 Roberto Alomar .40
121 Edgardo Alfonzo .15
122 Jeromy Burnitz .15
123 Mo Vaughn .25
124 Tom Seaver .50
125 Al Leiter .15
126 Mike Piazza/SP 8.00
127 Tony Batista .15
128 Geronimo Gil .15
129 Chris Singleton .15
130 Rodrigo Lopez .15
131 Jay Gibbons .15
132 Melvin Mora .15
133 Earl Weaver .15
134 Trevor Hoffman .15
135 Phil Nevin .15
136 Sean Burroughs .15
137 Ryan Klesko .15
138 Mark Kotsay .15
139 Mike Lieberthal .15
140 Bobby Abreu .25
141 Jimmy Rollins .15
142 Pat Burrell .40
143 Vicente Padilla .15
144 Richie Ashburn .15
145 Jeremy Giambi/SP 4.00
146 Josh Fogg .15
147 Brian Giles .25
148 Aramis Ramirez .25
149 Jason Kendall .15
150 Ralph Kiner .15
151 Willie Stargell .25
152 Kevin Mench .15
153 Rafael Palmeiro .25
154 Ivan Rodriguez .40
155 Hank Blalock .25
156 Juan Gonzalez .40
157 Carl Everett .15
158 Alex Rodriguez/SP 10.00
159 Nomar Garciaparra 1.25
160 Derek Lowe .15
161 Manny Ramirez .50
162 Shea Hillenbrand .15
163 Bobby Doerr .15
164 Johnny Damon .40
165 Jason Varitek .25
166 Pedro Martinez/SP 8.00
167 Cliff Floyd/SP 4.00
168 Ken Griffey Jr. 1.25
169 Adam Dunn .50
170 Austin Kearns .25
171 Aaron Boone .15
172 Joe Morgan .25
173 Sean Casey .15
174 Todd Walker .15
175 Ryan Dempster/SP 4.00
176 Shawn Estes/SP 4.00
177 Gabe Kapler/SP 4.00
178 Jason Jennings .15
179 Todd Helton .40
180 Larry Walker .25
181 Preston Wilson .15
182 Jay Payton/SP 4.00
183 Mike Sweeney .15
184 Carlos Beltran .15
185 Paul Byrd .15
186 Raul Ibanez .15
187 Rick Ferrell .15
188 Early Wynn .15
189 Dmitri Young .15
190 Jim Bunning .15
191 George Kell .15
192 Hal Newhouser .15
193 Bobby Higginson .15
194 Carlos Pena/SP 4.00
195 Sparky Anderson .15
196 Torii Hunter .15
197 Eric Milton .15
198 Corey Koskie .15
199 Jacque Jones .15
200 Harmon Killebrew .50
201 Doug Mientkiewicz .15
202 Frank Thomas .50
203 Mark Buehrle .15

204	Magglio Ordonez	.25
205	Paul Konerko	.25
206	Joe Borchard	.15
207	Hoyt Wilhelm	.15
208	Carlos Lee	.15
209	Roger Clemens	1.50
210	Nick Johnson	.15
211	Jason Giambi	.25
212	Alfonso Soriano	.75
213	Bernie Williams	.40
214	Robin Ventura	.15
215	Jorge Posada	.25
216	Mike Mussina	.40
217	Yogi Berra	.75
218	Phil Rizzuto	.40
219	Mariano Rivera	.25
220	Derek Jeter/SP	12.00
221	Jeff Weaver/SP	4.00
222	Raul Mondesi/SP	4.00
223	Freddy Sanchez, Josh Hancock	2.00
224	Joe Borchard, Miguel Olivo	2.00
225	Brandon Phillips, Josh Bard	1.50
226	Andy Van Hekken, Andres Torres	1.50
227	Jason Lane, Jeriome Robertson	1.50
228	Chin-Feng Chen, Joe Thurston	1.50
229	Endy Chavez, Jamey Carroll	1.50
230	Drew Henson, Alex Graman	2.50
231	Dewon Brazelton, Lance Carter	1.50
232	Jayson Werth, Kevin Cash	1.50
233	Randy Johnson, Curt Schilling, Barry Zito	1.50
234	Pedro J. Martinez, Randy Johnson, Derek Lowe	1.00
235	Randy Johnson, Curt Schilling, Pedro J. Martinez	1.00
236	John Smoltz, Eric Gagne, Mike Williams	.50
237	Randy Johnson, Bartolo Colon, A.J. Burnett	1.00
238	Alfonso Soriano, Ichiro Suzuki, Vladimir Guerrero	1.50
239	Alex Rodriguez, Jim Thome, Sammy Sosa	2.00
240	Barry Bonds, Manny Ramirez, Mike Sweeney	2.00
241	Alfonso Soriano, Alex Rodriguez, Derek Jeter	2.00
242	Alex Rodriguez, Magglio Ordonez, Miguel Tejada	2.00
243	Luis Castillo, Juan Pierre, Dave Roberts	.50
244	Nomar Garciaparra, Garret Anderson, Alfonso Soriano	1.00
245	Johnny Damon, Jimmy Rollins, Kenny Lofton	.50
246	Barry Bonds, Jim Thome, Manny Ramirez	2.00
247	Barry Bonds, Brian Giles, Manny Ramirez	2.00
248	Troy Glaus	10.00
249	Luis Gonzalez	6.00
250	Chipper Jones	15.00
251	Nomar Garciaparra	15.00
252	Manny Ramirez	10.00
253	Sammy Sosa	15.00
254	Frank Thomas	10.00
255	Magglio Ordonez	6.00
256	Adam Dunn	10.00
257	Ken Griffey Jr.	15.00
258	Jim Thome	10.00
259	Todd Helton	8.00
260	Larry Walker	6.00
261	Lance Berkman	6.00
262	Jeff Bagwell	10.00
263	Mike Sweeney	6.00
264	Shawn Green	6.00
265	Vladimir Guerrero	12.00
266	Mike Piazza	15.00
267	Jason Giambi	15.00
268	Pat Burrell	20.00
269	Barry Bonds	15.00
270	Mark McGwire	20.00
271	Alex Rodriguez	15.00
272	Carlos Delgado	6.00
273	Richie Sexson	6.00
274	Andruw Jones	8.00
275	Derek Jeter	20.00
276	Juan Gonzalez	8.00
277	Albert Pujols	12.00
278	Jason Giambi/CL	.75
279	Sammy Sosa/CL	.75
280	Ichiro Suzuki/CL	.75

All Caps
NM/M
Common Player: 8.00

Production 250 Sets

JB	Jeff Bagwell	15.00
LB	Lance Berkman	8.00
DE	Darin Erstad	8.00
RF	Rafael Furcal	8.00
JG	Juan Gonzalez	10.00
LG	Luis Gonzalez	8.00
TG	Tony Gwynn	25.00
TH	Tim Hudson	10.00
GM	Greg Maddux	30.00
RP	Rafael Palmeiro	10.00
CP	Chan Ho Park	8.00
MP	Mike Piazza	35.00
KS	Kazuhiro Sasaki	8.00
MV	Mo Vaughn	8.00
RV	Robin Ventura	8.00

Capping the Action

NM/M
Common Player: 10.00
Quantity produced listed

RA	Roberto Alomar/101	20.00
CD	Carlos Delgado/91	10.00
JG	Juan Gonzalez/99	20.00
SG	Shawn Green/125	20.00
KG	Ken Griffey Jr./102	40.00
TH	Todd Helton/99	20.00
PM	Pedro Martinez/125	25.00
MM	Mike Mussina/109	40.00
HM	Hideo Nomo/117	45.00
RP	Rafael Palmeiro/125	40.00
AR	Alex Rodriguez/110	25.00
IR	Ivan Rodriguez/125	15.00
SR	Scott Rolen/109	25.00
AS	Alfonso Soriano/200	20.00
SS	Sammy Sosa/125	40.00

Crackin the Lumber
NM/M
Production 25
Golds: No Pricing
Production 5

JG	Jason Giambi	25.00
IS	Ichiro Suzuki	125.00

Crowning Glory

No pricing due to scarcity.
Production 25 Sets

Dropping the Hammer

NM/M
Common Player: 6.00
Inserted 1:130
Golds: 1.5-2X
Production 100 Sets

BA	Bobby Abreu	8.00
RA	Roberto Alomar	10.00
LB	Lance Berkman	8.00
RF	Rafael Furcal	6.00
JG	Jason Giambi	6.00
SG	Shawn Green	6.00
KG	Ken Griffey Jr.	15.00
TH	Todd Helton	8.00
AJ	Andruw Jones	8.00
DJ	David Justice	8.00
KL	Kenny Lofton	6.00
FM	Fred McGriff	8.00
MO	Magglio Ordonez	6.00
RP	Rafael Palmeiro	6.00
MP	Mike Piazza	15.00
AR	Alex Rodriguez	15.00
SS	Sammy Sosa	20.00
TA	Fernando Tatis	6.00
MT	Miguel Tejada	8.00
FT	Frank Thomas	10.00
JT	Jim Thome	10.00
RV	Robin Ventura	6.00
OV	Omar Vizquel	6.00
LW	Larry Walker	8.00
PW	Preston Wilson	6.00

Men with Hats
NM/M
Common Player: 8.00
Inserted 1:285

VC	Vinny Castilla	8.00
EC	Eric Chavez	10.00
JD	Johnny Damon	15.00
AD	Adam Dunn	15.00
JG	Jason Giambi	8.00
TH	Todd Helton	10.00
HU	Tim Hudson	10.00
AJ	Andruw Jones	10.00
JK	Jason Kendall	8.00
KL	Kenny Lofton	8.00
AR	Alex Rodriguez	20.00
MT	Miguel Tejada	12.00
FT	Frank Thomas	12.00
TW	Todd Walker	8.00
BW	Bernie Williams	10.00

Slugfest
NM/M
Common Player: 8.00
Production 200 Sets
Golds: 1.5-2.5X
Production 50 Sets

CD	Carlos Delgado	8.00
SG	Shawn Green	8.00
AJ	Andruw Jones	8.00
RP	Rafael Palmeiro	8.00
MP	Mike Piazza	20.00
AR	Alex Rodriguez	15.00
FT	Frank Thomas	10.00
JT	Jim Thome	10.00
LW	Larry Walker	10.00
BW	Bernie Williams	10.00

Timeless Teams Bat
NM/M
Common Card: 20.00
Production 175 Sets

BLAR	Pat Burrell, Mike Lieberthal, Bobby Abreu, Jimmy Rollins	25.00
CTDJ	Eric Chavez, Miguel Tejada, Jermaine Dye, David Justice	25.00
DEMR	J.D. Drew, Jim Edmonds, Tino Martinez, Scott Rolen	40.00
DGCL	Adam Dunn, Ken Griffey Jr., Sean Casey, Barry Larkin	40.00
GNBL	Shawn Green, Hideo Nomo, Adrian Beltre, Paul LoDuca	40.00
GPMS	Jason Giambi, Jorge Posada, Raul Mondesi, Alfonso Soriano	30.00
GWVS	Jason Giambi, Bernie Williams, Robin Ventura, Alfonso Soriano	40.00
HWPZ	Todd Helton, Larry Walker, Juan Pierre, Todd Zeile	25.00
IMBC	Ichiro Suzuki, Edgar Martinez, Bret Boone, Mike Cameron	90.00
JGSW	Randy Johnson, Luis Gonzalez, Curt Schilling, Matt Williams	40.00
JJSF	Chipper Jones, Andruw Jones, Gary Sheffield, Rafael Furcal	40.00
KNKB	Ryan Klesko, Phil Nevin, Mark Kotsay, Sean Burroughs	20.00
MGLJ	Greg Maddux, Tom Glavine, Javy Lopez, Chipper Jones	40.00
OTLK	Magglio Ordonez, Frank Thomas, Carlos Lee, Paul Konerko	30.00
PVAA	Mike Piazza, Mo Vaughn, Roberto Alomar, Edgardo Alfonzo	40.00
RGRP	Alex Rodriguez, Juan Gonzalez, Ivan Rodriguez, Rafael Palmeiro	40.00
RMHN	Manny Ramirez, Pedro J. Martinez, Shea Hillenbrand, Trot Nixon	30.00
SMAP	Sammy Sosa, Fred McGriff, Moises Alou, Corey Patterson	40.00

UD Giants

NM/M
Complete Set (42): 45.00
Common Player: .75
Inserted 1:Box

RA	Roberto Alomar	1.00
JB	Jeff Bagwell	1.00
LB	Lance Berkman	1.00
BB	Barry Bonds	4.00
PB	Pat Burrell	1.00
RC	Roger Clemens	4.00
CD	Carlos Delgado	.75
JD	J.D. Drew	.75
AD	Adam Dunn	1.50
NG	Nomar Garciaparra	3.00
JG	Jason Giambi	.75
BG	Brian Giles	.75
GO	Juan Gonzalez	1.00
LG	Luis Gonzalez	.75
SG	Shawn Green	.75
KG	Ken Griffey Jr.	3.00
VG	Vladimir Guerrero	1.50
TH	Todd Helton	1.00
KI	Kazuhisa Ishii	.75
RJ	Randy Johnson	1.50
AJ	Andruw Jones	1.00
CJ	Chipper Jones	2.50
GM	Greg Maddux	2.50
PM	Pedro J. Martinez	1.00
MM	Mike Mussina	1.00
HN	Hideo Nomo	1.00
MO	Magglio Ordonez	.75
RP	Rafael Palmeiro	1.00
MP	Mike Piazza	3.00
PR	Mark Prior	1.00
AP	Albert Pujols	4.00
MR	Manny Ramirez	1.50
AR	Alex Rodriguez	4.00
IR	Ivan Rodriguez	1.50
SR	Scott Rolen	1.50
CS	Curt Schilling	1.50
SS	Sammy Sosa	2.50
IS	Ichiro Suzuki	3.00
FT	Frank Thomas	1.00
JT	Jim Thome	1.50
BW	Bernie Williams	1.00
KW	Kerry Wood	1.50

Vintage Hitmen
NM/M
Production 150 Sets
Golds: No Pricing
Production 10 Sets

JG	Jason Giambi	10.00
KG	Ken Griffey Jr.	30.00
MM	Mark McGwire	60.00
IS	Ichiro Suzuki	60.00

Vintage Hitmen Double Signed
NM/M
Production 75
Gold: No Pricing
Production 5

MS	Mark McGwire, Sammy Sosa	600.00

2003 UD Yankees Signature Series

NM/M
Complete Set (90): 65.00

Common Player: .50
Pack (3): 17.00
Box (10): 140.00

1	Al Downing	.50
2	Allen Gettel	.50
3	Art Ditmar	.50
4	Babe Ruth	6.00
5	Bill Virdon	.50
6	Billy Martin	2.00
7	Bob Cerv	.50
8	Bob Turley	.50
9	Bobby Cox	.75
10	Bobby Richardson	1.00
11	Bobby Shantz	.50
12	Bucky Dent	.75
13	Bud Metheny	.50
14	Casey Stengel	2.00
15	Charlie Hayes	.50
16	Charlie Silvera	.50
17	Chris Chambliss	.50
18	Danny Cater	.50
19	Dave Kingman	.75
20	Dave Righetti	.75
21	Dave Winfield	2.00
22	David Cone	.75
23	Dick Tidrow	.50
24	Doc Medich	.50
25	Dock Ellis	.50
26	Don Gullett	.50
27	Don Mattingly	5.00
28	Dwight Gooden	.75
29	Eddie Robinson	.50
30	Felipe Alou	.50
31	Fred Sanford	.50
32	Fred Stanley	.50
33	Gene Michael	.50
34	Hank Bauer	.50
35	Hector Lopez	.50
36	Horace Clarke	.50
37	Jake Gibbs	.50
38	Jerry Coleman	.50
39	Jerry Lumpe	.50
40	Jim Bouton	.50
41	Jim Kaat	1.00
42	Jim Mason	.50
43	Jimmy Key	.50
44	Joe DiMaggio	5.00
45	Joe Torre	1.00
46	John Montefusco	.50
47	Johnny Blanchard	.50
48	Johnny Callison	.50
49	Lew Burdette	.50
50	Johnny Kucks	.50
51	Steve Balboni	.50
52	Ken Singleton	.50
53	Lee Mazzilli	.50
54	Lou Gehrig	5.00
55	Lou Piniella	1.00
56	Luis Tiant	.50
57	Marius Russo	.50
58	Mel Stottlemyre	.75
59	Mickey Mantle	6.00
60	Mike Pagliarulo	.50
61	Mike Torrez	.50
62	Miller Huggins	.50
63	Norm Siebern	.50
64	Paul O'Neill	.75
65	Phil Niekro	.50
66	Phil Rizzuto	3.00
67	Ralph Branca	.50
68	Ralph Houk	.50
69	Ralph Terry	.50
70	Randy Gumpert	.50
71	Roger Maris	5.00
72	Ron Blomberg	.50
73	Ron Guidry	1.00
74	Ruben Amaro	.50
75	Ryne Duren	.50
76	Sam McDowell	.50
77	Sparky Lyle	.75
78	Thurman Munson	3.00
79	Tom Sturdivant	.50
80	Tom Tresh	.50
81	Tommy Byrne	.50
82	Tommy Henrich	.50
83	Tommy John	.75
84	Tony Kubek	.50
85	Tony Lazzeri	.50
86	Virgil Trucks	.50
87	Wade Boggs	1.00
88	Whitey Ford	3.00
89	Willie Randolph	.50
90	Yogi Berra	3.00

Monumental Cuts

NM/M
30 total cards produced:

MC-LG	Lou Gehrig/1 (6/03 auction)	17,600
MC-MM	Mickey Mantle/1 (1/04 auction)	10,000
MC-BM	Billy Martin/9	825.00
MC-TM	Thurman Munson/1 (1/04 auction)	2,605
MC-BR	Babe Ruth/1 (4/04 auction)	12,600

Pinstripe Excellence Dual
NM/M
Common Dual Autograph: 20.00
Some not priced yet.
Production 125 Sets

AA	Felipe Alou, Ruben Amaro	50.00
BA	Hank Bauer, Felipe Alou	50.00
BP	Wade Boggs, Mike Pagliarulo	60.00
BT	Jim Bouton, Ralph Terry	50.00
CK	Chris Chambliss, Dave Kingman	60.00
DC	Bucky Dent, Chris Chambliss	50.00
DR	Bucky Dent, Willie Randolph	80.00
DS	Ryne Duren, Tom Sturdivant	35.00
FB	Whitey Ford, Yogi Berra	150.00
GB	Jake Gibbs, Johnny Blanchard	40.00
GM	Ron Guidry, John Montefusco	80.00
GR	Ron Guidry, Willie Randolph	80.00
JK	Tommy John, Jim Kaat	60.00
LG	Sparky Lyle, Ron Guidry	75.00
LM	Jerry Lumpe, Jim Mason	25.00
MC	John Montefusco, Chris Chambliss	60.00
MK	Gene Michael, Tony Kubek	60.00
ML	Sam McDowell, Sparky Lyle	50.00
MR	Don Mattingly, Dave Righetti	150.00
NT	Phil Niekro, Luis Tiant	50.00
RB	Bobby Richardson, Hank Bauer	75.00
RC	Bobby Richardson, Jerry Coleman	50.00
SC	Ken Singleton, Jerry Coleman	60.00
ST	Tom Sturdivant, Bob Turley	40.00
TK	Luis Tiant, Jim Kaat	60.00
TM	Mike Torrez, Lee Mazzilli	50.00
BRi	Hank Bauer, Phil Rizzuto	75.00
BRu	Tommy Byrne, Marius Russo	30.00

Pride of New York Autograph

NM/M
Common Autograph: 8.00
Inserted 1:1

JA	Jason Alexander/SP	600.00
FA	Felipe Alou	15.00
RA	Ruben Amaro	8.00
SB	Steve Balboni	8.00
HB	Hank Bauer	10.00
YB	Yogi Berra	85.00
BL	Johnny Blanchard	15.00
RBl	Ron Blomberg	10.00
WB	Wade Boggs	40.00
JB	Jim Bouton	10.00
RBr	Ralph Branca	8.00
LB	Lew Burdette	10.00
TB	Tommy Byrne	10.00
CAS	Johnny Callison	8.00
TC	Tom Carroll	8.00
CAL	Brian Cashman/SP	250.00
DC	Danny Cater	8.00
CE	Bob Cerv	8.00
CC	Chris Chambliss	12.00
HC	Horace Clarke	10.00
JC	Jerry Coleman	10.00
CO	David Cone	25.00
CX	Bobby Cox	12.00
DE	Bucky Dent	10.00
DI	Art Ditmar	10.00
AD	Al Downing	8.00
BD	Brian Doyle	8.00
RD	Ryne Duren	10.00
EL	Dock Ellis	10.00

WF	Whitey Ford	50.00
AG	Allen Gettel	8.00
JG	Jake Gibbs	8.00
GO	Dwight Gooden	15.00
JO	John Goodman	300.00
RaG	Ron Guidry	15.00
DG	Don Gullett	8.00
RoG	Randy Gumpert	8.00
CH	Charlie Hayes	10.00
TH	Tommy Henrich	30.00
RH	Ralph Houk	12.00
TJ	Tommy John	10.00
JK	Jim Kaat	15.00
KE	Jimmy Key	15.00
DK	Dave Kingman	15.00
TK	Tony Kubek	25.00
KU	Johnny Kucks	10.00
HL	Hector Lopez	10.00
JL	Jerry Lumpe	8.00
SL	Sparky Lyle	10.00
JM	Jim Mason	8.00
MA	Don Mattingly	80.00
LM	Lee Mazzilli	8.00
SM	Sam McDowell	8.00
DM	Doc Medich	8.00
GM	Gene Michael	10.00
MO	John Montefusco	8.00
PN	Phil Niekro	15.00
PO	Paul O'Neill/SP	25.00
MP	Mike Pagliarulo	8.00
LP	Lou Piniella/SP	20.00
WR	Willie Randolph/SP	8.00
HR	Hal Reniff	10.00
BR	Bobby Richardson	8.00
DR	Dave Righetti	15.00
PR	Phil Rizzuto	40.00
ER	Eddie Robinson	10.00
MR	Marius Russo	10.00
FS	Fred Sanford	8.00
BS	Bobby Shantz	10.00
NS	Norm Siebern	8.00
CS	Charlie Silvera	8.00
KS	Ken Singleton	8.00
ST	Fred Stanley	8.00
MS	Mel Stottlemyre	15.00
TS	Tom Sturdivant	8.00
RT	Ralph Terry	10.00
LT	Luis Tiant	10.00
DT	Dick Tidrow	10.00
JT	Joe Torre	35.00
MT	Mike Torrez	10.00
TT	Tom Tresh	15.00
VT	Virgil Trucks	10.00
BT	Bob Turley	12.00
BV	Bill Virdon	8.00
DW	Dave Winfield/SP	75.00
JW	Jim Wynn	8.00
DZ	Don Zimmer	40.00

Yankees Forever Triple

NM/M

Common Triple Auto.:
Production 50 Sets

ALB	Felipe Alou, Hector Lopez, Hank Bauer	120.00
AOM	Felipe Alou, Paul O'Neill, Lee Mazzilli	150.00
BSB	Yogi Berra, Bobby Shantz, Hank Bauer	200.00
DFB	Al Downing, Whitey Ford, Yogi Berra	240.00
DRC	Bucky Dent, Willie Randolph, Chris Chambliss	125.00
EMG	Dock Ellis, Doc Medich, Don Gullett	125.00
FKB	Whitey Ford, Johnny Kucks, Jim Bouton	150.00
GCK	Dwight Gooden, David Cone, Jimmy Key	150.00
GRJ	Ron Guidry, Dave Righetti, Tommy John	150.00
HMC	Ralph Houk, Gene Michael, Bobby Cox	120.00
HRB	Tommy Henrich, Phil Rizzuto, Ralph Branca	150.00
JKL	Tommy John, Jim Kaat, Sparky Lyle	120.00
KCC	Dave Kingman, Chris Chambliss, Danny Cater	120.00
KGT	Jim Kaat, Don Gullett, Mike Torrez	120.00
KJB	Jim Kaat, Tommy John, Jim Bouton	120.00
MTT	John Montefusco, Mike Torrez, Dick Tidrow	120.00
OBK	Paul O'Neill, Wade Boggs, Jimmy Key	175.00
PTV	Lou Piniella, Joe Torre, Bill Virdon	150.00
RBC	Phil Rizzuto, Yogi Berra, Jerry Coleman	150.00
RKD	Phil Rizzuto, Tony Kubek, Bucky Dent	150.00
RRC	Bobby Richardson, Willie Randolph, Jerry Coleman	150.00
RSB	Marius Russo, Tom Sturdivant, Tommy Byrne	120.00
SSB	Fred Stanley, Charlie Silvera, Johnny Blanchard	120.00
STE	Mel Stottlemyre, Luis Tiant, Dock Ellis	120.00
TCO	Joe Torre, David Cone, Paul O'Neill	175.00
TLN	Luis Tiant, Sparky Lyle, Phil Niekro	120.00
TMT	Luis Tiant, Sam McDowell, Ralph Terry	120.00
WHM	Dave Winfield, Tommy Henrich, Lee Mazzilli	160.00
WMG	Dave Winfield, Don Mattingly, Ron Guidry	300.00
WPC	Dave Winfield, Lou Piniella, Chris Chambliss	100.00

Yankees 100th Anniversary

NM/M

Complete Set (30):		15.00
Common Player:		.50
1	Babe Ruth	2.00
2	Tony Lazzeri	.50
3	Lou Gehrig	1.50
4	Lou Gehrig	1.50
5	Red Rolfe	.50
6	Lou Gehrig	1.50
7	Bill Dickey	.50
8	Joe DiMaggio	1.50
9	Charlie Keller	.50
10	Frank Crosetti	.50
11	Phil Rizzuto	.50
12	Joe DiMaggio	1.50
13	Joe DiMaggio	1.50
14	Phil Rizzuto	.50
15	Mickey Mantle	2.00
16	Yogi Berra	.75
17	Yogi Berra	.75
18	Mickey Mantle	2.00
19	Whitey Ford	.50
20	Mickey Mantle	2.00
21	Thurman Munson	.75
22	Thurman Munson	.75
23	Bernie Williams	.50
24	Jorge Posada	.50
25	Mariano Rivera	.50
26	Derek Jeter	1.50
27	Hideki Matsui	1.00
28	Hideki Matsui	1.00
29	Roger Clemens	1.50
30	Yankee Stadium	.50

2003 Upper Deck 40-Man Sample

A different front photo and a large black "SAMPLE" on back distinguish the promo card for UD's large set.

NM/M

KG Ken Griffey Jr. 3.00

2003 Upper Deck 40-Man

NM/M

Complete Set (990):		200.00
Common Player:		.25
Common RK (877-960):		.40
Pack (10):		2.00
Box (24):		35.00
1	Troy Glaus	.50
2	Darin Erstad	.40
3	Garret Anderson	.50
4	Aaron Sele	.25
5	Adam Kennedy	.25
6	Scott Spiezio	.25
7	Troy Percival	.25
8	David Eckstein	.25
9	Ramon Ortiz	.25
10	Bengie Molina	.25
11	Tim Salmon	.50
12	John Lackey	.25
13	Brad Fullmer	.25
14	Jarrod Washburn	.25
15	Shawn Wooten	.25
16	Kevin Appier	.25
17	Ben Weber	.25
18	Eric Owens	.25
19	Matt Wise	.25
20	Francisco Rodriguez	.25
21	Scot Shields	.25
22	Jose Molina	.25
23	Scott Schoeneweis	.25
24	Derrick Turnbow	.25
25	Benji Gil	.25
26	Julio Ramirez	.25
27	Mickey Callaway	.25
28	Barry Zito	.50
29	Tim Hudson	.50
30	Mark Mulder	.40
31	Eric Chavez	.40
32	Miguel Tejada	.50
33	Terrence Long	.25
34	Jermaine Dye	.25
35	Erubiel Durazo	.25
36	Scott Hatteberg	.25
37	Chris Singleton	.25
38	Keith Foulke	.25
39	John Halama	.25
40	Mark Ellis	.25
41	Ted Lilly	.25
42	Jim Mecir	.25
43	Adam Piatt	.25
44	Freddie Bynum	.25
45	Adam Morrissey	.25
46	Jeremy Fikac	.25
47	Ricardo Rincon	.25
48	Ramon Hernandez	.25
49	Micah Bowie	.25
50	Chad Bradford	.25
51	Eric Byrnes	.25
52	Ron Gant	.25
53	Jose Flores	.25
54	Mark Johnson	.25
55	Carlos Delgado	.75
56	Orlando Hudson	.25
57	Kelvim Escobar	.25
58	Eric Hinske	.25
59	Doug Creek	.25
60	Josh Phelps	.25
61	Shannon Stewart	.25
62	Roy Halladay	.40
63	Vernon Wells	.40
64	Mark Henrickson	.25
65	Mike Bordick	.25
66	Jayson Werth	.25
67	Chris Woodward	.25
68	Ken Huckaby	.25
69	Frank Catalanotto	.25
70	Jason Kershner	.25
71	Greg Myers	.25
72	Tanyon Sturtze	.25
73	Trever Miller	.25
74	Pete Walker	.25
75	Alexis Rios	.25
76	Tom Wilson	.25
77	Dave Berg	.25
78	Doug Linton	.25
79	Cliff Politte	.25
80	Damian Easley	.25
81	Toby Hall	.25
82	George Lombard	.25
83	Ben Grieve	.25
84	Aubrey Huff	.25
85	Jesus Colome	.25
86	Dewon Brazelton	.25
87	Rey Ordonez	.25
88	Al Martin	.25
89	Carl Crawford	.25
90	Travis Lee	.25
91	Marlon Anderson	.25
92	Javier Valentin	.25
93	Joe Kennedy	.25
94	Jorge Sosa	.25
95	Travis Harper	.25
96	Bobby Seay	.25
97	Seth McClung	.25
98	Delvin James	.25
99	Victor Zambrano	.25
100	Terry Shumpert	.25
101	Josh Hamilton	.50
102	Jared Sandberg	.25
103	Steve Parris	.25
104	C.C. Sabathia	.25
105	Omar Vizquel	.40
106	Milton Bradley	.25
107	Ellis Burks	.25
108	Danys Baez	.25
109	Jason Davis	.25
110	Terry Mulholland	.25
111	Matt Lawton	.25
112	Alex Escobar	.25
113	Mark Wohlers	.25
114	Josh Bard	.25
115	Bill Selby	.25
116	Brandon Phillips	.25
117	Jason Bere	.25
118	Casey Blake	.25
119	Travis Hafner	.25
120	Brian Anderson	.25
121	David Riske	.25
122	Karim Garcia	.25
123	Ricardo Rodriguez	.25
124	Carl Sadler	.25
125	Jose Santiago	.25
126	Tim Laker	.25
127	John McDonald	.25
128	Jake Westbrook	.25
129	Ichiro Suzuki	1.00
130	Freddy Garcia	.25
131	Edgar Martinez	.40
132	Ben Davis	.25
133	Shigetoshi Hasegawa	.25
134	Carlos Guillen	.25
135	Randy Winn	.25
136	John Mabry	.25
137	Matt Thornton	.25
138	Bret Boone	.40
139	Jamie Moyer	.25
140	Giovanni Carrara	.25
141	Kazuhiro Sasaki	.25
142	Jeff Cirillo	.25
143	Mark McLemore	.25
144	Pat Borders	.25
145	Mike Cameron	.25
146	Dan Wilson	.25
147	John Olerud	.40
148	Arthur Rhodes	.25
149	Rafael Soriano	.25
150	Greg Colbrunn	.25
151	Ryan Franklin	.25
152	Joel Pineiro	.25
153	Jeff Nelson	.25
154	Jerry Hairston	.25
155	Rick Helling	.25
156	Gary Matthews Jr.	.25
157	Jeff Conine	.25
158	Sidney Ponson	.25
159	Tony Batista	.25
160	Jay Gibbons	.40
161	Marty Cordova	.25
162	Geronimo Gil	.25
163	Deivi Cruz	.25
164	B.J. Ryan	.25
165	Jason Johnson	.25
166	Buddy Groom	.25
167	Pat Hentgen	.25
168	Omar Daal	.25
169	Willis Roberts	.25
170	Scott Erickson	.25
171	David Segui	.25
172	Brook Fordyce	.25
173	Rodrigo Lopez	.25
174	Jose Leon	.25
175	Jose Morban	.25
176	Melvin Mora	.25
177	B.J. Surhoff	.25
178	Jorge Julio	.25
179	Alex Rodriguez	2.00
180	Mark Teixeira	.40
181	Chan Ho Park	.25
182	Todd Van Poppel	.25
183	Todd Greene	.25
184	Ismael Valdes	.25
185	Rusty Greer	.25
186	Rafael Palmeiro	.50
187	Francisco Cordero	.25
188	Einar Diaz	.25
189	Doug Glanville	.25
190	Michael Young	.25
191	Kevin Mench	.25
192	Carl Everett	.25
193	Herbert Perry	.25
194	Jeff Zimmerman	.25
195	Juan Gonzalez	.50
196	Ugueth Urbina	.25
197	Jermaine Clark	.25
198	John Thomson	.25
199	Hank Blalock	.50
200	Jay Powell	.25
201	Mike Lamb	.25
202	Aaron Fultz	.25
203	Esteban Yan	.25
204	Nomar Garciaparra	2.00
205	Pedro J. Martinez	.75
206	John Burkett	.25
207	Johnny Damon	.40
208	Doug Mirabelli	.25
209	Derek Lowe	.25
210	Shea Hillenbrand	.25
211	Brandon Lyon	.25
212	Trot Nixon	.25
213	Jason Varitek	.25
214	Tim Wakefield	.25
215	Manny Ramirez	.75
216	Todd Walker	.25
217	Jeremy Giambi	.25
218	Ramiro Mendoza	.25
219	Bill Mueller	.25
220	David Ortiz	.25
221	Mike Timlin	.25
222	Alan Embree	.25
223	Bob Howry	.25
224	Chad Fox	.25
225	Damian Jackson	.25
226	Casey Fossum	.25
227	Steve Woodard	.25
228	Freddy Sanchez	.25
229	Mike Sweeney	.25
230	Desi Relaford	.25
231	Brent Mayne	.25
232	Angel Berroa	.25
233	Albie Lopez	.25
234	Raul Ibanez	.25
235	Joe Randa	.25
236	Chris George	.25
237	Michael Tucker	.25
238	Mendy Lopez	.25
239	Kris Wilson	.25
240	Jason Grimsley	.25
241	Carlos Febles	.25
242	Runelvys Hernandez	.25
243	Mike MacDougal	.25
244	Carlos Beltran	.40
245	Brandon Berger	.25
246	Darrell May	.25
247	Miguel Asencio	.25
248	Ryan Bukvich	.25
249	Dee Brown	.25
250	Jeremy Hill	.25
251	Jeremy Affeldt	.25
252	Ken Harvey	.25
253	Bobby Higginson	.25
254	Matt Anderson	.25
255	Dmitri Young	.25
256	Gene Kingsale	.25
257	Craig Paquette	.25
258	Adam Bernero	.25
259	Andres Torres	.25
260	Carlos Pena	.25
261	Dean Palmer	.25
262	Eric Munson	.25
263	Omar Infante	.25
264	Shane Halter	.25
265	Jeremy Bonderman	2.00
266	Steve Sparks	.25
267	Gary Knotts	.25
268	Mike Maroth	.25
269	Nate Cornejo	.25
270	Matt Roney	.25
271	Franklyn German	.25
272	Matt Walbeck	.25
273	Brandon Inge	.25
274	Hiram Bocachica	.25
275	Chris Spurling	.25
276	Craig Monroe	.25
277	Ramon Santiago	.25
278	Doug Mientkiewicz	.25
279	Torii Hunter	.50
280	Brad Radke	.25
281	Denny Hocking	.25
282	Tom Prince	.25
283	Eddie Guardado	.25
284	Jacque Jones	.25
285	Joe Mays	.25
286	Mike Fetters	.25
287	LaTroy Hawkins	.25
288	A.J. Pierzynski	.25
289	Eric Milton	.25
290	Cristian Guzman	.25
291	Bobby Kielty	.25
292	Corey Koskie	.25
293	J.C. Romero	.25
294	Mike Cuddyer	.25
295	Luis Rivas	.25
296	Matt LeCroy	.25
297	Tony Fiore	.25
298	Dustan Mohr	.25
299	Chris Gomez	.25
300	Johan Santana	.25
301	Kyle Lohse	.25
302	Frank Thomas	.75
303	Mark Buehrle	.25
304	Jon Garland	.25
305	Magglio Ordonez	.50
306	Paul Konerko	.25
307	Sandy Alomar Jr.	.25
308	Carlos Lee	.25
309	Jon Rauch	.25
310	Esteban Loaiza	.25
311	Gary Glover	.25
312	Kelly Wunsch	.25
313	Tony Graffanino	.25
314	Aaron Rowand	.25
315	Armando Rios	.25
316	Jose Valentin	.25
317	D'Angelo Jimenez	.25
318	Joe Crede	.25
319	Miguel Olivo	.25
320	Rick White	.25
321	Billy Koch	.25
322	Tom Gordon	.25
323	Bartolo Colon	.40
324	Josh Paul	.25
325	Joe Borchard	.25
326	Damaso Marte	.25
327	Derek Jeter	2.00
328	Jason Giambi	.75
329	Roger Clemens	2.00
330	Enrique Wilson	.25
331	Dave Wells	.25
332	Mike Mussina	.50
333	Bernie Williams	.50
334	Todd Zeile	.25
335	Sterling Hitchcock	.25
336	Juan Acevedo	.25
337	Robin Ventura	.25
338	Mariano Rivera	.25
339	John Flaherty	.25
340	Andy Pettitte	.50
341	Antonio Osuna	.25
342	Erick Almonte	.25
343	Chris Hammond	.25
344	Steve Karsay	.25
345	Alfonso Soriano	1.00
346	Bubba Trammell	.25
347	Nick Johnson	.25
348	Jorge Posada	.50
349	Jeff Weaver	.25
350	Raul Mondesi	.25
351	Randy Choate	.25
352	Drew Henson	.25
353	Jeff Bagwell	.75
354	Wade Miller	.25
355	Lance Berkman	.40
356	Julio Lugo	.25
357	Roy Oswalt	.40
358	Bruce Chen	.25
359	Morgan Ensberg	.25
360	Geoff Blum	.25
361	Brian Moehler	.25
362	Billy Wagner	.40
363	Peter Munro	.25
364	Brad Ausmus	.25
365	Jose Vizcaino	.25
366	Craig Biggio	.40
367	Tim Redding	.25
368	Gregg Zaun	.25
369	Octavio Dotel	.25
370	Carlos Hernandez	.25
371	Richard Hidalgo	.25
372	Jeriome Robertson	.25
373	Orlando Merced	.25
374	John Buck	.25
375	Adam Everett	.25
376	Raul Chavez	.25
377	Brad Lidge	.25
378	Jeff Kent	.40
379	Scott Linebrink	.25
380	Greg Miller	.25
381	Kirk Saarloos	.25
382	Brandon Puffer	.25
383	Ricky Stone	.25
384	Jason Lane	.25
385	Brian L. Hunter	.25
386	Rodrigo Rosario	.25
387	Horacio Ramirez	.25
388	Gary Sheffield	.50
389	Mike Hampton	.25
390	Robert Fick	.25
391	Henry Blanco	.25
392	Vinny Castilla	.25
393	Joe Dawley	.25
394	Jung Bong	.25
395	Rafael Furcal	.40
396	Javy Lopez	.25
397	Greg Maddux	1.25
398	Andruw Jones	.50
399	John Smoltz	.40
400	Chipper Jones	1.00
401	Mark DeRosa	.25
402	Shane Reynolds	.25
403	Kevin Gryboski	.25
404	Russ Ortiz	.25
405	Roberto Hernandez	.25
406	Ray King	.25
407	Matt Franco	.25
408	Marcus Giles	.25
409	Trey Hodges	.25
410	Darren Holmes	.25
411	Julio Franco	.25
412	Darren Bragg	.25
413	Richie Sexson	.50
414	Jeffrey Hammonds	.25
415	Ben Sheets	.25
416	Mike DeJean	.25
417	Royce Clayton	.25
418	Wes Helms	.25
419	Valerio de los Santos	.25
420	Brady Clark	.25
421	Glendon Rusch	.25
422	Geoff Jenkins	.40
423	John Foster	.25
424	Curtis Leskanic	.25
425	Todd Ritchie	.25
426	Enrique Cruz	.25
427	Wayne Franklin	.25
428	Matt Ford	.25
429	Matt Kinney	.25
430	Scott Podsednik	2.00
431	Luis Vizcaino	.25
432	Shane Nance	.25
433	Alex Sanchez	.25
434	John Vander Wal	.25
435	Eric Young	.25
436	Eddie Perez	.25
437	Jason Conti	.25
438	Matt Morris	.25
439	Tino Martinez	.25
440	Fernando Vina	.25
441	Kiko Calero	.25
442	Cal Eldred	.25
443	Jimmy Journell	.25
444	Jim Edmonds	.40
445	Jeff Fassero	.25
446	Mike Matheny	.25
447	Garrett Stephenson	.25
448	Brett Tomko	.25
449	So Taguchi	.25
450	Eduardo Perez	.25
451	Lance Painter	.25
452	Jason Isringhausen	.25
453	Albert Pujols	2.00
454	Eli Marrero	.25
455	Jason Simontacchi	.25
456	J.D. Drew	.25
457	Scott Rolen	.75
458	Orlando Palmeiro	.25
459	Dustin Hermanson	.25
460	Edgar Renteria	.25
461	Woody Williams	.25
462	Chris Carpenter	.25
463	Sammy Sosa	1.50
464	Kerry Wood	.75
465	Kyle Farnsworth	.25
466	Alex Gonzalez	.25
467	Eric Karros	.25
468	Troy O'Leary	.25
469	Mark Grudzielanek	.25
470	Alan Benes	.25
471	Mark Prior	1.50
472	Paul Bako	.25
473	Shawn Estes	.25

#	Player	Price
474	Matt Clement	.25
475	Ramon Martinez	.25
476	Tom Goodwin	.25
477	Corey Patterson	.25
478	Moises Alou	.25
479	Juan Cruz	.25
480	Bobby Hill	.25
481	Mark Bellhorn	.25
482	Mark Guthrie	.25
483	Mike Remlinger	.25
484	Lenny Harris	.25
485	Antonio Alfonseca	.25
486	Dave Veres	.25
487	Hee Seop Choi	.25
488	Luis Gonzalez	.40
489	Lyle Overbay	.25
490	Randy Johnson	.75
491	Mark Grace	.50
492	Danny Bautista	.25
493	Junior Spivey	.25
494	Matt Williams	.25
495	Miguel Batista	.25
496	Tony Womack	.25
497	Byung-Hyun Kim	.25
498	Steve Finley	.25
499	Craig Counsell	.25
500	Curt Schilling	.50
501	Elmer Dessens	.25
502	Rod Barajas	.25
503	David Dellucci	.25
504	Mike Koplove	.25
505	Mike Myers	.25
506	Matt Mantei	.25
507	Stephen Randolph RC	.40
508	Chad Moeller	.25
509	Carlos Baerga	.25
510	Andrew Good	.25
511	Quinton McCracken	.25
512	Jason Romano	.25
513	Jolbert Cabrera	.25
514	Darren Dreifort	.25
515	Kevin Brown	.40
516	Paul Quantrill	.25
517	Shawn Green	.40
518	Hideo Nomo	.40
519	Eric Gagne	.25
520	Troy Brohawn	.25
521	Kazuhisa Ishii	.25
522	Guillermo Mota	.25
523	Alex Cora	.25
524	Odalis Perez	.25
525	Brian Jordan	.25
526	Andy Ashby	.25
527	Fred McGriff	.40
528	Adrian Beltre	.40
529	Daryle Ward	.25
530	Todd Hundley	.25
531	David Ross	.25
532	Paul Shuey	.25
533	Paul LoDuca	.25
534	Dave Roberts	.25
535	Mike Kinkade	.25
536	Cesar Izturis	.25
537	Ron Coomer	.25
538	Jose Vidro	.25
539	Henry Mateo	.25
540	Tony Armas Jr.	.25
541	Joey Eischen	.25
542	Orlando Cabrera	.25
543	Jose Macias	.25
544	Fernando Tatis	.25
545	Jeff Liefer	.25
546	Michael Barrett	.25
547	Vladimir Guerrero	.75
548	Javier Vazquez	.25
549	Brad Wilkerson	.25
550	Zach Day	.25
551	Tomokazu Ohka	.25
552	Livan Hernandez	.25
553	Endy Chavez	.25
554	Dan Smith	.25
555	Scott Stewart	.25
556	T.J. Tucker	.25
557	Jamey Carroll	.25
558	Ron Calloway	.25
559	Brian Schneider	.25
560	Orlando Hernandez	.25
561	Wil Cordero	.25
562	Rocky Biddle	.25
563	Edgardo Alfonzo	.25
564	Andres Galarraga	.25
565	Felix Rodriguez	.25
566	Benito Santiago	.25
567	Jose Cruz	.25
568	Tim Worrell	.25
569	Marvin Benard	.25
570	Kurt Ainsworth	.25
571	Jim Brower	.25
572	J.T. Snow	.25
573	Scott Eyre	.25
574	Robb Nen	.25
575	Barry Bonds	2.50
576	Ray Durham	.25
577	Marquis Grissom	.25
578	Pedro Feliz	.25
579	Jason Schmidt	.25
580	Rich Aurilia	.25
581	Kirk Rueter	.25
582	Chad Zerbe	.25
583	Damian Moss	.25
584	Neifi Perez	.25
585	Joe Nathan	.25
586	Ruben Rivera	.25
587	Yorvit Torrealba	.25
588	Josh Beckett	.50
589	Todd Hollandsworth	.25
590	Derrek Lee	.25
591	A.J. Burnett	.25
592	Juan Pierre	.25
593	Mark Redman	.25
594	Blaine Neal	.25
595	Mike Mordecai	.25
596	Alex Gonzalez	.25
597	Brad Penny	.25
598	Tim Spooneybarger	.25
599	Mike Lowell	.25
600	Mike Redmond	.25
601	Braden Looper	.25
602	Ivan Rodriguez	.50
603	Andy Fox	.25
604	Vladimir Nunez	.25
605	Luis Castillo	.25
606	Juan Encarnacion	.25
607	Armando Almanza	.25
608	Gerald Williams	.25
609	Carl Pavano	.25
610	Michael Tejera	.25
611	Ramon Castro	.25
612	Brian Banks	.25
613	Roberto Alomar	.50
614	Al Leiter	.25
615	Jeromy Burnitz	.25
616	John Franco	.25
617	Tom Glavine	.40
618	Mike Piazza	1.00
619	Cliff Floyd	.25
620	Joe McEwing	.25
621	David Weathers	.25
622	Pedro Astacio	.25
623	Timoniel Perez	.25
624	Jason Phillips	.25
625	Ty Wigginton	.25
626	Steve Trachsel	.25
627	Roger Cedeno	.25
628	Tsuyoshi Shinjo	.25
629	Armando Benitez	.25
630	Vance Wilson	.25
631	Mike Stanton	.25
632	Mo Vaughn	.25
633	Scott Strickland	.25
634	Rey Sanchez	.25
635	Jay Bell	.25
636	David Cone	.25
637	Jae Weong So	.25
638	Ryan Klesko	.40
639	Wiki Gonzalez	.25
640	Trevor Hoffman	.25
641	Sean Burroughs	.25
642	Mike Bynum	.25
643	Clay Condrey	.25
644	Gary Bennett	.25
645	Kevin Jarvis	.25
646	Mark Kotsay	.25
647	Phil Nevin	.25
648	Dave Hansen	.25
649	Keith Lockhart	.25
650	Brian Lawrence	.25
651	Jay Witasick	.25
652	Rondell White	.25
653	Jaret Wright	.25
654	Luther Hackman	.25
655	Jake Peavy	.25
656	Brian Buchanan	.25
657	Mark Loretta	.25
658	Oliver Perez	.25
659	Adam Eaton	.25
660	Xavier Nady	.25
661	Jesse Orosco	.25
662	Ramon Vazquez	.25
663	Jim Thome	.75
664	Jose Mesa	.25
665	Rheal Cormier	.25
666	David Bell	.25
667	Mike Lieberthal	.25
668	Brandon Duckworth	.25
669	David Coggin	.25
670	Bobby Abreu	.40
671	Turk Wendell	.25
672	Marlon Byrd	.25
673	Jason Michaels	.25
674	Kevin Millwood	.25
675	Tomas Perez	.25
676	Jimmy Rollins	.50
677	Vicente Padilla	.25
678	Pat Burrell	.50
679	Tyler Houston	.25
680	Hector Mercado	.25
681	Carlos Silva	.25
682	Nick Punto	.25
683	Ricky Ledee	.25
684	Randy Wolf	.25
685	Todd Pratt	.25
686	Placido Polanco	.25
687	Chase Utley	.25
688	Brian Giles	.25
689	Jason Kendall	.40
690	Matt Stairs	.25
691	Kris Benson	.25
692	Julian Tavarez	.25
693	Reggie Sanders	.25
694	Jeff D'Amico	.25
695	Pokey Reese	.25
696	Kenny Lofton	.25
697	Mike Williams	.25
698	David Williams	.25
699	Kevin Young	.25
700	Brian Boehringer	.25
701	Scott Sauerbeck	.25
702	Josh Fogg	.25
703	Joe Beimel	.25
704	Dennys Reyes	.25
705	Jeff Suppan	.25
706	Solomon Torres	.25
707	Kip Wells	.25
708	Craig Wilson	.25
709	Jack Wilson	.25
710	Robert Mackowiak	.25
711	Abraham Nunez	.25
712	Randall Simon	.25
713	Josias Manzanillo	.25
714	Ken Griffey Jr.	1.00
715	Jimmy Haynes	.25
716	Felipe Lopez	.25
717	Jimmy Anderson	.25
718	Ryan Dempster	.25
719	Russell Branyan	.25
720	Aaron Boone	.25
721	Luke Prokopec	.25
722	Felix Heredia	.25
723	Scott Sullivan	.25
724	Danny Graves	.25
725	Kent Mercker	.25
726	Barry Larkin	.40
727	Jason LaRue	.25
728	Gabe White	.25
729	Adam Dunn	.50
730	Brandon Larson	.25
731	Reggie Taylor	.25
732	Sean Casey	.25
733	Scott Williamson	.25
734	Austin Kearns	.50
735	Kelly Stinnett	.25
736	Ruben Mateo	.25
737	Wily Mo Pena	.25
738	Larry Walker	.40
439	Juan Uribe	.25
740	Denny Neagle	.25
741	Darren Oliver	.25
742	Charles Johnson	.25
743	Todd Jones	.25
744	Todd Helton	.75
745	Shawn Chacon	.25
746	Jason Jennings	.25
747	Preston Wilson	.25
748	Chris Richard	.25
749	Chris Stynes	.25
750	Jose Jimenez	.25
751	Gabe Kapler	.25
752	Jay Payton	.25
753	Aaron Cook	.25
754	Greg Norton	.25
755	Scott Elarton	.25
756	Brian Fuentes	.25
757	Jose Hernandez	.25
758	Nelson Cruz	.25
759	Justin Speier	.25
760	Javier Lopez	.40
761	Garret Anderson	.40
762	Tony Batista	.25
763	Mark Buehrle	.25
764	Johnny Damon	.40
765	Freddy Garcia	.25
766	Nomar Garciaparra	.75
767	Jason Giambi	.50
768	Roy Halladay	.25
769	Shea Hillenbrand	.25
770	Torii Hunter	.40
771	Derek Jeter	1.00
772	Paul Konerko	.25
773	Derek Lowe	.25
774	Pedro J. Martinez	.50
775	A.J. Pierzynski	.25
776	Jorge Posada	.40
777	Manny Ramirez	.40
778	Mariano Rivera	.40
779	Alex Rodriguez	1.00
780	Kazuhiro Sasaki	.25
781	Alfonso Soriano	.50
782	Ichiro Suzuki	.75
783	Mike Sweeney	.25
784	Miguel Tejada	.40
785	Ugueth Urbina	.25
786	Robin Ventura	.25
787	Omar Vizquel	.25
788	Randy Winn	.25
789	Barry Zito	.25
790	Lance Berkman	.25
791	Barry Bonds	1.00
792	Adam Dunn	.40
793	Tom Glavine	.25
794	Luis Gonzalez	.25
795	Shawn Green	.25
796	Vladimir Guerrero	.40
797	Todd Helton	.40
798	Trevor Hoffman	.25
799	Randy Johnson	.50
800	Andruw Jones	.40
801	Byung-Hyun Kim	.25
802	Mike Lowell	.25
803	Eric Gagne	.25
804	Matt Morris	.25
805	Robb Nen	.25
806	Vicente Padilla	.25
807	Odalis Perez	.25
808	Mike Piazza	.50
809	Mike Remlinger	.25
810	Scott Rolen	.40
811	Jimmy Rollins	.50
812	Benito Santiago	.25
813	Curt Schilling	.40
814	Richie Sexson	.40
815	John Smoltz	.25
816	Sammy Sosa	.75
817	Junior Spivey	.25
818	Jose Vidro	.25
819	Mike Williams	.25
820	Luis Castillo	.25
821	Jason Giambi	.40
822	Luis Gonzalez	.25
823	Sammy Sosa	.75
824	Ken Griffey Jr.	.75
825	Ken Griffey Jr.	.75
826	Tino Martinez	.25
827	Barry Bonds	1.00
828	Frank Thomas	.40
829	Ken Griffey Jr.	.75
830	Barry Bonds	1.00
831	Tim Salmon	.25
832	Troy Glaus	.25
833	Robb Nen	.25
834	Jeff Kent	.25
835	Scott Spiezio	.25
836	Darin Erstad	.25
837	Randy Johnson	.50
838	Chipper Jones	.50
839	Greg Maddux	.75
840	Nomar Garciaparra	.75
841	Manny Ramirez	.40
842	Pedro J. Martinez	.50
843	Sammy Sosa	.75
844	Ken Griffey Jr.	.75
845	Jim Thome	.40
846	Vladimir Guerrero	.50
847	Mike Piazza	.50
848	Derek Jeter	1.00
849	Jason Giambi	.40
850	Roger Clemens	1.00
851	Alfonso Soriano	.50
852	Hideki Matsui	4.00
853	Barry Bonds	1.00
854	Ichiro Suzuki	.50
855	Albert Pujols	.75
856	Alex Rodriguez	.75
857	Darin Erstad	.25
858	Troy Glaus	.25
859	Curt Schilling	.25
860	Luis Gonzalez	.25
861	Tom Glavine	.25
862	Andruw Jones	.40
863	Gary Sheffield	.25
864	Frank Thomas	.40
865	Mark Prior	1.00
866	Ivan Rodriguez	.40
867	Jeff Bagwell	.40
868	Lance Berkman	.25
869	Shawn Green	.25
870	Hideo Nomo	.40
871	Torii Hunter	.25
872	Bernie Williams	.25
873	Barry Zito	.25
874	Pat Burrell	.25
875	Carlos Delgado	.25
876	Miguel Tejada	.25
877	Hideki Matsui RC	4.00
878	Jose Contreras RC	2.00
879	Jason Anderson	.40
880	Jason Shiell RC	.40
881	Kevin Tolar RC	.40
882	Michel Hernandez RC	.40
883	Arnie Munoz RC	.40
884	David Sanders RC	.40
885	Willie Eyre RC	.40
886	Brent Hoard RC	.40
887	Lew Ford RC	2.00
888	Beau Kemp RC	.75
889	Jonathan Pridie RC	.40
890	Mike Ryan RC	.40
891	Richard Fischer RC	.40
892	Luis Ayala RC	.40
893	Mike Neu RC	.40
894	Joe Valentine RC	.40
895	Nate Bland RC	.40
896	Shane Bazzell RC	.75
897	Aquilino Lopez RC	.40
898	Diegomar Markwell RC	.40
899	Francisco Rosario RC	.40
900	Guillermo Quiroz RC	.40
901	Luis De Los Santos RC	.40
902	Fernando Cabrera RC	.40
903	Francisco Cruceta RC	.40
904	Jhonny Peralta	.50
905	Rett Johnson RC	.40
906	Aaron Looper RC	.40
907	Bobby Madritsch RC	.40
908	Luis Matos	.40
909	Jose Castillo	.25
910	Chris Waters RC	.40
911	Jeremy Guthrie RC	.25
912	Pedro Liriano RC	.40
913	Joe Borowski	.25
914	Felix Sanchez RC	.40
915	Jon Leicester RC	.40
916	Todd Wellemeyer RC	.75
917	Matt Bruback RC	.25
918	Chris Capuano RC	1.50
919	Oscar Villarreal RC	.25
920	Matt Kata RC	.75
921	Robby Hammock RC	.40
922	Gerald Laird	.25
923	Brandon Webb RC	3.00
924	Tommy Whiteman RC	.40
925	Andrew Brown RC	.40
926	Alfredo Gonzalez RC	.40
927	Carlos Rivera	.25
928	Rick Roberts RC	.40
929	Terrmel Sledge RC	.40
930	Josh Willingham RC	.40
931	Prentice Redman RC	.40
932	Jeff Duncan RC	1.50
933	Craig Brazell RC	1.00
934	Jeremy Griffiths	.25
935	Phil Seibel RC	.40
936	Heath Bell RC	.40
937	Bernie Castro RC	.40
938	Mike Nicolas RC	.40
939	Cory Stewart RC	.40
940	Shane Victorino RC	.40
941	Brandon Villafuerte RC	.40
942	Jeremy Wedel RC	.40
943	Tommy Phelps RC	.25
944	Josh Hall RC	.40
945	Ryan Cameron RC	.40
946	Garrett Atkins	.25
947	Clint Barmes RC	.75
948	Michael Hessman RC	.40
949	Brian Stokes RC	.40
950	Rocco Baldelli	1.00
951	Hector Luna	.25
952	Jaime Cerda	.25
953	D.J. Carrasco RC	.40
954	Ian Ferguson RC	.40
955	Tim Olson RC	.40
956	Alejandro Machado RC	.40
957	Jorge Cordova RC	.40
958	Wilfredo Ledezma RC	.40
959	Nathan Robertson RC	.40
960	Nook Logan RC	.40
961	Anaheim Angels	.25
962	Baltimore Orioles	.25
963	Boston Red Sox	.25
964	Chicago White Sox	.25
965	Cleveland Indians	.25
966	Detroit Tigers	.25
967	Kansas City Royals	.25
968	Minnesota Twins	.25
969	New York Yankees	.25
970	Oakland Athletics	.25
971	Seattle Mariners	.25
972	Tampa Bay Devil Rays	.25
973	Texas Rangers	.25
974	Toronto Blue Jays	.25
975	Arizona Diamondbacks	.25
976	Atlanta Braves	.25
977	Chicago Cubs	.25
978	Cincinnati Reds	.25
979	Colorado Rockies	.25
980	Florida Marlins	.25
981	Houston Astros	.25
982	Los Angeles Dodgers	.25
983	Milwaukee Brewers	.25
984	Montreal Expos	.25
985	New York Mets	.25
986	Philadelphia Phillies	.25
987	Pittsburgh Pirates	.25
988	San Diego Padres	.25
989	San Francisco Giants	.25
990	St. Louis Cardinals	.25
321	Mike MacDougal	.40
322	Sammy Sosa	2.00
323	Mike Hampton	.40
324	Ramiro Mendoza	.40
325	Kevin Millwood	.75
326	Dave Roberts	.40
327	Todd Zeile	.40
328	Reggie Sanders	.40
329	Billy Koch	.40
330	Mike Stanton	.40
331	Orlando Hernandez	.40
332	Tony Clark	.40
333	Chris Hammond	.40
334	Michael Cuddyer	.40
335	Sandy Alomar	.40
336	Jose Cruz Jr.	.40
337	Omar Daal	.40
338	Robert Fick	.40
339	Daryle Ward	.40
340	David Bell	.40
341	Checklist	.40

Rainbow

Stars (1-990):	10-20X
Rookies:	4-8X
Production 40 Sets	

Red, White & Blue

Stars (1-990):	1-3X
Rookies:	1-2X
#'s 1-752 Inserted 1:6	
#'s 877-960 1:36	

Endorsements

NM/M

Inserted 1:500
Some not priced due to scarcity.

RA	Rick Ankiel	20.00
DB	Devon Brazelton/50	15.00
BD	Ben Diggins	15.00
AG	Alex Graman/50	15.00
KGS	Ken Griffey Sr.	15.00
HI	Hansel Izquierdo/50	15.00
JL	Jon Lieber	15.00
CM	Corwin Malone/50	15.00
TO	Tomokazu Ohka	20.00

Vintage Update

NM/M

Complete Set (61): 15.00
Common Player: .40
Inserted 1:Pack

#	Player	Price
281	Tom Glavine	1.00
282	Josh Stewart	.40
283	Aquilino Lopez	.40
284	Horacio Ramirez	.40
285	Brandon Phillips	.40
286	Kirk Saarloos	.40
287	Runelvys Hernandez	.40
288	Hideki Matsui	5.00
289	Jeremy Bonderman	3.00
290	Russ Ortiz	.40
291	Ken Harvey	.40
292	Edgardo Alfonzo	.40
293	Oscar Villarreal	.40
294	Marlon Byrd	.40
295	Josh Bard	.40
296	David Cone	.40
297	Mike Neu	.40
298	Cliff Floyd	.40
299	Travis Lee	.40
300	Jeff Kent	.50
301	Ron Calloway	.40
302	Bartolo Colon	.40
303	Jose Contreras	1.50
304	Mark Teixeira	1.00
305	Ivan Rodriguez	1.00
306	Jim Thome	.50
307	Shane Reynolds	.40
308	Luis Ayala	.40
309	Lyle Overbay	.40
310	Travis Hafner	.40
311	Wilfredo Ledezma	.40
312	Rocco Baldelli	1.50
313	Jason Anderson	.40
314	Kenny Lofton	.75
315	Brandon Larson	.40
316	Ty Wigginton	.40
317	Fred McGriff	.40
318	Antonio Osuna	.40
319	Corey Patterson	.40
320	Erubiel Durazo	.40

Post MVP Action

Half a dozen former MVPs are featured in this cereal-box insert set. Cards have 3-D game-action sequences on front. Backs have another (regular) player photo along with personal data and stats. The cards were issued two per cello pack in special two-box packages of Post cereals.

NM/M

Complete Set (6): 4.00
Common Player: .50

1	Barry Bonds	.75
2	Miguel Tejada	.50
3	Ichiro	1.00
4	Ken Griffey Jr.	.50
5	Jason Giambi	.50
6	Sammy Sosa	.75

Post Redemption

This set of 31 cards was only available via a mail-in redemption offer. Collectors who assembled all six CD-Roms six CD-Roms from Post cereal boxes could find a coded number to order the set. Fronts are white-bordered with an action photo and player name, position and team logo. Backs have a portrait photo, uniform number, personal data, 2002 and career stats, a UD hologram and logos of the sponsors and licensors. Cards are printed on extra-thick stock.

NM/M

Complete Set (31): 15.00
Common Player: .50

1	Troy Percival	.50
2	Curt Schilling	.65
3	John Smoltz	.50
4	Tony Batista	.50
5	Pedro Martinez	.75
6	Sammy Sosa	1.00
7	Paul Konerko	.50
8	Ken Griffey Jr.	.50
9	Jim Thome	.50
10	Larry Walker	.50
11	Bobby Higginson	.50
12	Luis Castillo	.50
13	Craig Biggio	.50
14	Mike Sweeney	.50
15	Shawn Green	.50
16	Richie Sexson	.50
17	Torii Hunter	.60
18	Vladimir Guerrero	.50
19	Mike Piazza	1.50
20	Jason Giambi	.60
21	Miguel Tejada	.60
22	Pat Burrell	.50
23	Brian Giles	.50
24	Trevor Hoffman	.50
25	Barry Bonds	2.00
26	Ichiro	2.00
27	Albert Pujols	2.00
28	Randy Winn	.50
29	Alex Rodriguez	1.00

| 30 | Carlos Delgado | .50 |
| 31 | Troy Glaus | .75 |

SSS Puerto Rico

To commemorate the historic "home" games of the Montreal Expos at San Juan, P.R., the SSS Group health care plan sponsored an uncut sheet featuring Latin players from the Expos and among the five teams which visited the island during the season. Sheets measure 7-1/2" x 10-1/2". Individual cards are UV-coated, silver-foil highlighted and feature color poses or action photos. Back of the sheet has a ghost-image action photo of Jose Vidro overprinted with advertising for the sponsor. Licensor logos also appear.

		NM/M
Uncut Sheet:		10.00
Complete Set (9):		10.00
Common Player:		1.00
(1)	Roberto Alomar	1.00
(2)	Juan Gonzalez	1.50
(3)	Alex Rodriguez	3.00
(4)	Ivan Rodriguez	1.50
(5)	Sammy Sosa	3.00
(6)	Jose Vidro	1.00
(7)	Javier Vazquez	1.00
(8)	Javy Lopez	1.00
(9)	Sponsor's Logo	.10

2004 Upper Deck

DEREK LOWE

		NM/M
Complete Set (540):		75.00
Common Player:		.15
Hobby Pack (8):		2.00
Hobby Box (24):		40.00
1	Dontrelle Willis	.40
2	Edgar Gonzalez	.15
3	Jose Reyes	.50
4	Jae Weong Seo	.15
5	Miguel Cabrera	.25
6	Jesse Foppert	.15
7	Mike Neu	.15
8	Micheal Nakamura	.15
9	Luis Ayala	.15
10	Jared Sandberg	.15
11	Jhonny Peralta	.15
12	Wilfredo Ledezma	.15
13	Jason Roach	.15
14	Kirk Saarloos	.15
15	Cliff Lee	.15
16	Bobby Hill	.15
17	Lyle Overbay	.15
18	Josh Hall	.15
19	Joe Thurston	.15
20	Matt Kata	.15
21	Jeremy Bonderman	.15
22	Julio Manon	.15
23	Rodrigo Rosario	.15
24	Robby Hammock	.15
25	David Sanders	.15
26	Miguel Ojeda	.15
27	Mark Teixeira	.25
28	Franklyn German	.15
29	Ken Harvey	.15
30	Xavier Nady	.15
31	Tim Salmon	.25
32	Troy Glaus	.40
33	Adam Kennedy	.15
34	David Eckstein	.15
35	Bengie Molina	.15
36	Jarrod Washburn	.15
37	Ramon Ortiz	.15
38	Eric Chavez	.25
39	Miguel Tejada	.25
40	Chris Singleton	.15
41	Jermaine Dye	.15
42	John Halama	.15
43	Tim Hudson	.40
44	Barry Zito	.40
45	Ted Lilly	.15
46	Bobby Kielty	.15
47	Kelvim Escobar	.15
48	Josh Phelps	.15
49	Vernon Wells	.25
50	Roy Halladay	.25
51	Orlando Hudson	.15
52	Eric Hinske	.15
53	Brandon Backe	.15
54	Dewon Brazelton	.15
55	Ben Grieve	.15
56	Aubrey Huff	.15
57	Toby Hall	.15
58	Rocco Baldelli	.40
59	Al Martin	.15
60	Brandon Phillips	.15
61	Omar Vizquel	.25
62	C.C. Sabathia	.15
63	Milton Bradley	.15
64	Ricky Gutierrez	.15
65	Matt Lawton	.15
66	Danys Baez	.15
67	Ichiro Suzuki	1.00
68	Randy Winn	.15
69	Carlos Guillen	.15
70	Mark McLemore	.15
71	Dan Wilson	.15
72	Jamie Moyer	.15
73	Joel Pineiro	.15
74	Edgar Martinez	.25
75	Tony Batista	.15
76	Jay Gibbons	.15
77	Jeff Conine	.15
78	Melvin Mora	.15
79	Geronimo Gil	.15
80	Rodrigo Lopez	.15
81	Jorge Julio	.15
82	Rafael Palmeiro	.50
83	Juan Gonzalez	.40
84	Mike Young	.15
85	Alex Rodriguez	1.50
86	Einar Diaz	.15
87	Kevin Mench	.15
88	Hank Blalock	.40
89	Pedro J. Martinez	.75
90	Byung-Hyun Kim	.15
91	Derek Lowe	.25
92	Jason Varitek	.15
93	Manny Ramirez	.50
94	John Burkett	.15
95	Todd Walker	.15
96	Nomar Garciaparra	1.50
97	Trot Nixon	.15
98	Mike Sweeney	.15
99	Carlos Febles	.15
100	Mike MacDougal	.15
101	Raul Ibanez	.15
102	Jason Grimsley	.15
103	Chris George	.15
104	Brent Mayne	.15
105	Dmitri Young	.15
106	Eric Munson	.15
107	A.J. Hinch	.15
108	Andres Torres	.15
109	Bobby Higginson	.15
110	Shane Halter	.15
111	Matt Walbeck	.15
112	Torii Hunter	.40
113	Doug Mientkiewicz	.15
114	Lew Ford	.15
115	Eric Milton	.15
116	Eddie Guardado	.15
117	Cristian Guzman	.15
118	Corey Koskie	.15
119	Magglio Ordonez	.40
120	Mark Buehrle	.15
121	Billy Koch	.15
122	Jose Valentin	.15
123	Paul Konerko	.15
124	Carlos Lee	.15
125	Jon Garland	.15
126	Jason Giambi	.75
127	Derek Jeter	1.50
128	Roger Clemens	1.50
129	Andy Pettitte	.40
130	Jorge Posada	.40
131	David Wells	.15
132	Hideki Matsui	1.50
133	Mike Mussina	.50
134	Jeff Bagwell	.50
135	Craig Biggio	.25
136	Morgan Ensberg	.15
137	Richard Hidalgo	.15
138	Brad Ausmus	.15
139	Roy Oswalt	.25
140	Billy Wagner	.15
141	Octavio Dotel	.15
142	Gary Sheffield	.40
143	Andruw Jones	.40
144	John Smoltz	.25
145	Rafael Furcal	.15
146	Javy Lopez	.25
147	Shane Reynolds	.15
148	Horacio Ramirez	.15
149	Mike Hampton	.15
150	Jung Bong	.15
151	Ruben Quevedo	.15
152	Ben Sheets	.15
153	Geoff Jenkins	.25
154	Royce Clayton	.15
155	Glendon Rusch	.15
156	John Vander Wal	.15
157	Scott Podsednik	.40
158	Jim Edmonds	.40
159	Tino Martinez	.15
160	Albert Pujols	1.50
161	Matt Morris	.15
162	Woody Williams	.15
163	Edgar Renteria	.15
164	Jason Isringhausen	.15
165	Jason Simontacchi	.15
166	Kerry Robinson	.15
167	Sammy Sosa	1.25
168	Joe Borowski	.15
169	Tony Womack	.15
170	Antonio Alfonseca	.15
171	Corey Patterson	.15
172	Mark Prior	1.00
173	Moises Alou	.25
174	Matt Clement	.15
175	Randall Simon	.15
176	Randy Johnson	.75
177	Luis Gonzalez	.25
178	Craig Counsell	.15
179	Miguel Batista	.15
180	Steve Finley	.15
181	Brandon Webb	.15
182	Danny Bautista	.15
183	Oscar Villarreal	.15
184	Shawn Green	.25
185	Brian Jordan	.15
186	Fred McGriff	.25
187	Andy Ashby	.15
188	Rickey Henderson	.50
189	Dave Roberts	.15
190	Eric Gagne	.15
191	Kazuhisa Ishii	.15
192	Adrian Beltre	.15
193	Vladimir Guerrero	.75
194	Livan Hernandez	.15
195	Ron Calloway	.15
196	Sun-Woo Kim	.15
197	Wil Cordero	.15
198	Brad Wilkerson	.15
199	Orlando Cabrera	.15
200	Barry Bonds	2.00
201	Ray Durham	.15
202	Andres Galarraga	.15
203	Benito Santiago	.15
204	Jose Cruz Jr.	.15
205	Jason Schmidt	.15
206	Kirk Rueter	.15
207	Felix Rodriguez	.15
208	Mike Lowell	.15
209	Luis Castillo	.15
210	Derrek Lee	.25
211	Andy Fox	.15
212	Tommy Phelps	.15
213	Todd Hollandsworth	.15
214	Brad Penny	.15
215	Juan Pierre	.15
216	Mike Piazza	1.00
217	Jae Weong Seo	.15
218	Ty Wigginton	.15
219	Al Leiter	.15
220	Roger Cedeno	.15
221	Timoniel Perez	.15
222	Aaron Heilman	.15
223	Pedro Astacio	.15
224	Joe McEwing	.15
225	Ryan Klesko	.15
226	Brian Giles	.25
227	Mark Kotsay	.15
228	Brian Lawrence	.15
229	Rod Beck	.15
230	Trevor Hoffman	.15
231	Sean Burroughs	.15
232	Bobby Abreu	.25
233	Jim Thome	.50
234	David Bell	.15
235	Jimmy Rollins	.25
236	Mike Lieberthal	.15
237	Vicente Padilla	.15
238	Randy Wolf	.15
239	Reggie Sanders	.15
240	Jason Kendall	.15
241	Jack Wilson	.15
242	Jose Hernandez	.15
243	Kip Wells	.15
244	Carlos Rivera	.15
245	Craig Wilson	.15
246	Adam Dunn	.40
247	Sean Casey	.15
248	Danny Graves	.15
249	Ryan Dempster	.15
250	Barry Larkin	.40
251	Reggie Taylor	.15
252	Wily Mo Pena	.15
253	Larry Walker	.25
254	Mark Sweeney	.15
255	Preston Wilson	.15
256	Jason Jennings	.15
257	Charles Johnson	.15
258	Jay Payton	.15
259	Chris Stynes	.15
260	Juan Uribe	.15
261	Hideki Matsui	1.00
262	Barry Bonds	1.00
263	Dontrelle Willis	.25
264	Kevin Millwood	.15
265	Billy Wagner	.15
266	Rocco Baldelli	.25
267	Roger Clemens	.75
268	Rafael Palmeiro	.25
269	Miguel Cabrera	.25
270	Jose Contreras	.15
271	Aaron Sele	.15
272	Bartolo Colon	.25
273	Darin Erstad	.25
274	Francisco Rodriguez	.15
275	Garret Anderson	.40
276	Jose Guillen	.15
277	Troy Percival	.15
278	Alex Cintron	.15
279	Casey Fossum	.15
280	Elmer Dessens	.15
281	Jose Valverde	.15
282	Matt Mantei	.15
283	Richie Sexson	.40
284	Roberto Alomar	.40
285	Shea Hillenbrand	.15
286	Chipper Jones	.75
287	Greg Maddux	1.00
288	J.D. Drew	.15
289	Marcus Giles	.15
290	Mike Hessman	.15
291	John Thomson	.15
292	Russ Ortiz	.15
293	Adam Loewen	.15
294	Jack Cust	.15
295	Jerry Hairston	.15
296	Kurt Ainsworth	.15
297	Luis Matos	.15
298	Marty Cordova	.15
299	Sidney Ponson	.15
300	Bill Mueller	.15
301	Curt Schilling	.15
302	David Ortiz	.50
303	Johnny Damon	.25
304	Keith Foulke	.15
305	Pokey Reese	.15
306	Scott Williamson	.15
307	Tim Wakefield	.15
308	Alex Gonzalez	.15
309	Aramis Ramirez	.40
310	Carlos Zambrano	.40
311	Juan Cruz	.15
312	Kerry Wood	.75
313	Kyle Farnsworth	.15
314	Aaron Rowand	.15
315	Esteban Loaiza	.15
316	Frank Thomas	.50
317	Joe Borchard	.15
318	Joe Crede	.15
319	Miguel Olivo	.15
320	Willie Harris	.15
321	Aaron Harang	.15
322	Austin Kearns	.25
323	Brandon Claussen	.15
324	Brandon Larson	.15
325	Ryan Freel	.15
326	Ken Griffey Jr.	1.00
327	Ryan Wagner	.15
328	Alex Escobar	.15
329	Coco Crisp	.15
330	David Riske	.15
331	Jody Gerut	.15
332	Josh Bard	.15
333	Travis Hafner	.25
334	Chin-Hui Tsao	.15
335	Denny Stark	.15
336	Jeromy Burnitz	.15
337	Shawn Chacon	.15
338	Todd Helton	.50
339	Vinny Castilla	.15
340	Alex Sanchez	.15
341	Carlos Pena	.15
342	Fernando Vina	.15
343	Jason Johnson	.15
344	Matt Anderson	.15
345	Mike Maroth	.15
346	Rondell White	.15
347	A.J. Burnett	.15
348	Alex Gonzalez	.15
349	Armando Benitez	.15
350	Carl Pavano	.15
351	Hee Seop Choi	.15
352	Ivan Rodriguez	.50
353	Josh Beckett	.50
354	Josh Willingham	.15
355	Adam Everett	.15
356	Brandon Duckworth	.15
357	Jason Lane	.15
358	Jeff Kent	.25
359	Jeriome Robertson	.15
360	Lance Berkman	.25
361	Wade Miller	.15
362	Aaron Guiel	.15
363	Angel Berroa	.15
364	Carlos Beltran	.50
365	David DeJesus	.15
366	Desi Relaford	.15
367	Joe Randa	.15
368	Runelvys Hernandez	.15
369	Edwin Jackson	.15
370	Hideo Nomo	.40
371	Jeff Weaver	.15
372	Juan Encarnacion	.15
373	Odalis Perez	.15
374	Paul LoDuca	.15
375	Robin Ventura	.15
376	Bill Hall	.15
377	Chad Moeller	.15
378	Chris Capuano	.15
379	Junior Spivey	.15
380	Rickie Weeks	.15
381	Wes Helms	.15
382	Brad Radke	.15
383	Jacque Jones	.15
384	Joe Mays	.15
385	Joe Nathan	.15
386	Johan Santana	.15
387	Nick Punto	.15
388	Shannon Stewart	.15
389	Carl Everett	.15
390	Claudio Vargas	.15
391	Jose Vidro	.15
392	Nick Johnson	.15
393	Rocky Biddle	.15
394	Tony Armas	.15
395	Braden Looper	.15
396	Cliff Floyd	.15
397	Jason Phillips	.15
398	Mike Cameron	.15
399	Tom Glavine	.40
400	Kenny Lofton	.15
401	Alfonso Soriano	.50
402	Bernie Williams	.40
403	Javier Vazquez	.15
404	Jon Lieber	.15
405	Jose Contreras	.15
406	Kevin Brown	.15
407	Mariano Rivera	.25
408	Arthur Rhodes	.15
409	Eric Byrnes	.15
410	Erubiel Durazo	.15
411	Graham Koonce	.15
412	Marco Scutaro	.15
413	Mark Mulder	.25
414	Mark Redman	.15
415	Rich Harden	.15
416	Brett Myers	.15
417	Chase Utley	.15
418	Kevin Millwood	.25
419	Marlon Byrd	.15
420	Pat Burrell	.25
421	Placido Polanco	.15
422	Tim Worrell	.15
423	Jason Bay	.15
424	Josh Fogg	.15
425	Kris Benson	.15
426	Mike Gonzalez	.15
427	Oliver Perez	.15
428	Tike Redman	.15
429	Adam Eaton	.15
430	Ismael Valdez	.15
431	Jake Peavy	.15
432	Khalil Greene	.15
433	Mark Loretta	.15
434	Phil Nevin	.15
435	Ramon Hernandez	.15
436	A.J. Pierzynski	.15
437	Edgardo Alfonzo	.15
438	J.T. Snow	.15
439	Jerome Williams	.15
440	Marquis Grissom	.15
441	Robb Nen	.15
442	Bret Boone	.25
443	Freddy Garcia	.15
444	Gil Meche	.15
445	John Olerud	.15
446	Rich Aurilia	.15
447	Shigetoshi Hasegawa	.15
448	Bo Hart	.15
449	Dan Haren	.15
450	Jason Marquis	.15
451	Marlon Anderson	.15
452	Scott Rolen	.75
453	So Taguchi	.15
454	Carl Crawford	.25
455	Delmon Young	.25
456	Geoff Blum	.15
457	Jesus Colome	.15
458	Jonny Gomes	.15
459	Lance Carter	.15
460	Robert Fick	.15
461	Chan Ho Park	.15
462	Francisco Cordero	.15
463	Jeff Nelson	.15
464	Jeff Zimmerman	.15
465	Kenny Rogers	.15
466	Aquilino Lopez	.15
467	Carlos Delgado	.50
468	Frank Catalanotto	.15
469	Reed Johnson	.15
470	Pat Hentgen	.15
471	Curt Schilling	.25
472	Gary Sheffield	.25
473	Javier Vazquez	.15
474	Kazuo Matsui	1.00
475	Kevin Brown	.25
476	Rafael Palmeiro	.25
477	Richie Sexson	.25
478	Roger Clemens	.75
479	Vladimir Guerrero	.75
480	Alex Rodriguez	1.00
481	Jake Woods	.25
482	Tim Bittner	.25
483	Brandon Medders	.50
484	Casey Daigle	.15
485	Jerry Gil	.25
486	Mike Gosling	.25
487	Jose Capellan	1.00
488	Onil Joseph	.25
489	Roman Colon	.25
490	David Crouthers	.25
491	Eddy Rodriguez	.25
492	Franklyn Gracesqui	.50
493	Jamie Brown	.25
494	Jerome Gamble	.25
495	Tim Hamulack	.25
496	Carlos Vasquez	.25
497	Renyel Pinto	.50
498	Ronny Cedeno	.25
499	Enemencio Pacheco	.25
500	Ryan Meaux	.25
501	Ryan Wing	.25
502	Shingo Takatsu	1.00
503	William Bergolla	.25
504	Ivan Ochoa	.25
505	Mariano Gomez	.25
506	Justin Hampson	.25
507	Justin Huisman	.25
508	Scott Dohmann	.25
509	Donnie Kelly	.50
510	Chris Aguila	.25
511	Lincoln Holdzkom RC	.25
512	Freddy Guzman	.25
513	Hector Gimenez	.25
514	Jorge Vasquez	.25
515	Jason Frasor	.25
516	Chris Saenz	.50
517	Dennis Sarfate	.25
518	Colby Miller	.25
519	Jason Bartlett	.25
520	Chad Bentz	.25
521	Josh Labandeira	.25
522	Shawn Hill	.25
523	Kazuo Matsui RC	3.00
524	Carlos Hines	.25
525	Michael Vento	2.00
526	Scott Proctor	.50
527	Sean Henn	.50
528	David Aardsma	.25
529	Ian Snell	.50
530	Mike Johnson	.25
531	Akinori Otsuka	.75
532	Rusty Tucker	.25
533	Justin Knoedler	.25
534	Merkin Valdez	1.00
535	Greg Dobbs	.25
536	Justin Leone	.25
537	Shawn Camp	.25
538	Edwin Moreno	.25
539	Angel Chavez	.25
540	Jesse Harper	.25

Reflections Update Set (50): 30.00

341	Shingo Takatsu	3.00
342	Franklyn Gracesqui	.75
343	Angel Chavez	.75
344	Jorge Sequea	.75
345	David Aardsma	.75
346	Ramon Ramirez RC	.75
347	Lino Urdaneta	.75
348	Orlando Rodriguez	.75
349	Jason Szuminski	.75
350	Luis Gonzalez	.75
351	John Gall	1.00
352	Kevin Cave	.75
353	Chris Oxspring	.75
354	Freddy Guzman	.75
355	Jeff Bennett	.75
356	Jorge Vasquez	.75
357	Merkin Valdez	2.00
358	Tim Hamulack	.75
359	Hector Gimenez	.75
360	Jerry Gil	.75
361	Ryan Wing	.75
362	Shawn Hill	.75
363	Jason Bartlett	.75
364	Renyel Pinto	.75
365	Carlos Vasquez	.75
366	Mike Vento	1.50
367	Casey Daigle	.75
368	Chad Bentz	1.00
369	Chris Saenz	.75
370	Shawn Camp	.75
371	Carlos Hines	.75
372	Edwin Moreno	.75
373	Mike Wuertz	.75
374	Aarom Baldiris RC	1.50
375	Ronny Cedeno	.75
376	Akinori Otsuka	1.50
377	Jose Capellan	2.00
378	Justin Germano	.75
379	Justin Knoedler	.75
380	Mariano Gomez	.75
381	Fernando Nieve	1.50
382	Scott Proctor	.75
383	Roman Colon	.75
384	Onil Joseph	.75
385	Eddy Rodriguez	.75
386	Enemencio Pacheco	.75
387	William Bergolla	.75
388	Ivan Ochoa	.75
389	Rusty Tucker	.75
390	Roberto Novoa	.75

SPGU Patch Edition Update Set (50): 85.00

121	Richie Sexson	3.00
122	Javier Vazquez	2.00
123	Alex Rodriguez	8.00
124	Javy Lopez	3.00
125	Miguel Tejada	3.00
126	Bartolo Colon	2.00
127	Ivan Rodriguez	4.00
128	Rafael Palmeiro	3.00
129	Kevin Brown	3.00
130	Gary Sheffield	3.00
131	Greg Maddux	5.00
132	Curt Schilling	4.00
133	Roger Clemens	8.00
134	Alfonso Soriano	3.00
135	Vladimir Guerrero	4.00
136	Carlos Vasquez	2.00
137	Roman Colon	2.00
138	William Bergolla	2.00
139	Jason Bartlett	2.00
140	Casey Daigle	2.00
141	Ryan Wing	2.00
142	Chris Saenz	2.00
143	Edwin Moreno	2.00
144	Shawn Hill	2.00
145	Eddy Rodriguez	2.00
146	Justin Knoedler	2.00
147	Renyel Pinto	2.00
148	Kevin Cave	2.00

149	Carlos Hines	2.00
150	Merkin Valdez RC	4.00
151	Tim Hamulack RC	2.00
152	Hector Gimenez RC	2.00
153	Mike Vento RC	5.00
154	Scott Proctor RC	3.00
155	Rusty Tucker RC	2.00
156	Akinori Otsuka RC	4.00
157	Ronny Cedeno RC	2.00
158	Jose Capellan RC	6.00
159	Justin Germano	2.00
160	Shingo Takatsu RC	5.00
161	Fernando Nieve	2.00
162	Mike Wuertz	2.00
163	Jerry Gil	2.00
164	Jorge Vasquez	2.00
165	Chad Bentz	4.00
166	Luis Gonzalez	2.00
167	Ivan Ochoa	2.00
168	Onil Joseph	2.00
169	Enemencio Pacheco	2.00
170	Kazuo Matsui RC	8.00

Play Ball Update Set (50): 20.00

183	Kazuo Matsui RC	3.00
184	Jerry Gil	.50
185	Jose Capellan RC	2.00
186	Tim Hamulack	.50
187	Renyel Pinto	.50
188	Carlos Vasquez	.50
189	Enemencio Pacheco	.50
190	Ronny Cedeno	.50
191	Mariano Gomez	.50
192	Carlos Hines	.50
193	Michael Vento	.50
194	David Aardsma	.50
195	Hector Gimenez	.50
196	Fernando Nieve	.50
197	Chris Saenz	.50
198	Shawn Hill	.50
199	Angel Chavez	.50
200	Scott Proctor	.50
201	William Bergolla	.50
202	Justin Germano	.50
203	Onil Joseph	.50
204	Rusty Tucker	.50
205	Justin Knoedler	.50
206	Casey Daigle	.50
207	Edwin Moreno	.50
208	Chad Bentz	.50
209	Ryan Wing	.50
210	Shawn Camp	.50
211	Eddy Rodriguez	.50
212	Roman Colon	.50
213	Jason Bartlett	.50
214	Jorge Vasquez	.50
215	Ivan Ochoa	.50
216	Akinori Otsuka	.50
217	Merkin Valdez RC	2.00
218	Shingo Takatsu RC	.50
219	Chris Oxspring	.50
220	Kevin Cave	.50
221	Ramon Ramirez	.50
222	Orlando Rodriguez	.50
223	Lino Urdaneta	.50
224	Franklyn Gracesqui	.50
225	Mike Wuertz	.50
226	Jorge Sequea	.50
227	Luis Gonzalez	.50
228	Jason Szuminski	.50
229	John Gall	.50
230	Freddy Guzman	.50
231	Jeff Bennett	.50
232	Roberto Novoa	.50

Vintage Update Set (50): 10.00

451	Alex Rodriguez	1.50
452	Javy Lopez	.40
453	Alfonso Soriano	.50
454	Vladimir Guerrero	.50
455	Rafael Palmeiro	.50
456	Gary Sheffield	.50
457	Curt Schilling	.50
458	Miguel Tejada	.50
459	Kevin Brown	.40
460	Richie Sexson	.50
461	Roger Clemens	1.50
462	Javier Vazquez	.25
463	Bartolo Colon	.25
464	Ivan Rodriguez	.50
465	Greg Maddux	1.00
466	Jamie Brown	.25
467	David Crouthers	.25
468	Jason Frasor	.25
469	Greg Dobbs	.25
470	Jesse Harper	.25
471	Nick Regilio RC	.25
472	Ryan Wing	.25
473	Akinori Otsuka RC	1.00
474	Shingo Takatsu RC	1.50
475	Kazuo Matsui RC	3.00
476	Michael Vento RC	1.00
477	Mike Gosling	.25
478	Justin Huisman	.25
479	Justin Hampson	.25
480	Dennis Sarfate	.25
481	Ian Snell RC	1.50
482	Tim Bausher RC	.25
483	Donnie Kelly	.25
484	Jerome Gamble	.25
485	Mike Rouse	.50
486	Merkin Valdez RC	.75
487	Lincoln Holdzkom RC	.25
488	Justin Leone RC	.25
489	Sean Henn	.25
490	Brandon Medders RC	.25
491	Mike Johnston RC	.25
492	Tim Bittner	.25
493	Mike Wuertz	.25
494	Chad Bentz	.50
495	Ryan Meaux RC	.25
496	Chris Aguila RC	.25
497	Jake Woods RC	.25
498	Scott Dohmann RC	.25
499	Colby Miller	.25
500	Josh Labandeira	.25

Glossy

Complete Factory Set (590): 85.00
Glossy: 1-2X
Issued only in factory sets.

Authentic Stars Jersey

Mark Teixeira / First Base

NM/M
Common Player: 4.00
Inserted 1:48
Golds: 1-2X
Production 100 Sets

BA	Bobby Abreu	6.00
RO	Roberto Alomar	6.00
JB	Jeff Bagwell	6.00
RB	Rocco Baldelli	10.00
JH	Josh Beckett	5.00
HB	Hank Blalock	5.00
EC	Eric Chavez	4.00
RC	Roger Clemens	15.00
CD	Carlos Delgado	5.00
JD	J.D. Drew	4.00
DE	Darin Erstad	4.00
JG	Jason Giambi	8.00
TG	Troy Glaus	5.00
TL	Tom Glavine	5.00
VG	Vladimir Guerrero	8.00
SG	Shawn Green	5.00
KG	Ken Griffey Jr.	15.00
TH	Todd Helton	8.00
TO	Torii Hunter	5.00
RJ	Randy Johnson	8.00
AJ	Andruw Jones	5.00
CJ	Chipper Jones	8.00
JK	Jeff Kent	5.00
GM	Greg Maddux	10.00
PM	Pedro J. Martinez	8.00
TM	Tino Martinez	4.00
HM	Hideki Matsui	35.00
PN	Phil Nevin	4.00
MI	Mike Piazza	10.00
MP	Mark Prior	10.00
AP	Albert Pujols	15.00
AR	Alex Rodriguez	12.00
IR	Ivan Rodriguez	8.00
CS	Curt Schilling	5.00
AS	Alfonso Soriano	10.00
SS	Sammy Sosa	12.00
IS	Ichiro Suzuki	30.00
MT	Mark Teixeira	8.00
FT	Frank Thomas	8.00
LW	Larry Walker	4.00
BW	Bernie Williams	5.00
BZ	Barry Zito	6.00

Awesome Honors

NM/M
Complete Set (10): 15.00

1	Albert Pujols	5.00
2	Alex Rodriguez	5.00
3	Angel Berroa	5.00
4	Dontrelle Willis	1.00
5	Eric Gagne	1.50
6	Garret Anderson	1.00
7	Ivan Rodriguez	1.50
8	Josh Beckett	1.50
9	Mariano Rivera	1.00
10	Roy Halladay	.75

Awesome Honors Jersey

Jamie Moyer / pitcher

Game Winners

NM/M
Common Player: 5.00
Golds: 1-1.5X
Production 50 Sets

GW-BA	Bobby Abreu	8.00
GW-JB	Jeff Bagwell	8.00
GW-HB	Hank Blalock	8.00
GW-MC	Miguel Cabrera	8.00
GW-JE	Jim Edmonds	5.00
GW-DE	Darin Erstad	5.00
GW-RF	Rafael Furcal (Gold parallel only)	5.00
GW-JG	Jason Giambi	8.00
GW-TG	Troy Glaus	5.00
GW-AG	Alex Gonzalez	5.00
GW-SG	Shawn Green	5.00
GW-VG	Vladimir Guerrero	10.00
GW-TH	Todd Helton	8.00
GW-RH	Ramon Hernandez	5.00
GW-HU	Torii Hunter	5.00
GW-DJ	Derek Jeter	25.00
GW-AJ	Andruw Jones	8.00
GW-CJ	Chipper Jones	8.00
GW-RK	Ryan Klesko	5.00
GW-ML	Mike Lowell	5.00
GW-HM	Hideki Matsui	25.00
GW-TN	Trot Nixon (Gold parallel only)	10.00
GW-MO	Magglio Ordonez	5.00
GW-CP	Corey Patterson	5.00
GW-MP	Mike Piazza	10.00
GW-JP	Jorge Posada	8.00
GW-AP	Albert Pujols	15.00
GW-IR	Ivan Rodriguez	8.00
GW-SR	Scott Rolen	10.00
GW-GS	Gary Sheffield	5.00
GW-AS	Alfonso Soriano	5.00
GW-MT	Mark Teixeira	5.00
GW-TE	Miguel Tejada	5.00
GW-JT	Jim Thome	10.00
GW-BW	Bernie Williams	8.00

Famous Quotes

Ted Williams • Red Sox

NM/M
Complete Set (20): 30.00

Q-1	Al Lopez	.75
Q-2	Bob Feller	1.00
Q-3	Bob Gibson	1.50
Q-4	Brooks Robinson	1.50
Q-5	Cal Ripken Jr.	5.00
Q-6	Carl Yastrzemski	2.00
Q-7	Earl Weaver	.75
Q-8	Eddie Mathews	2.00
Q-9	Ernie Banks	2.00
Q-10	Greg Maddux	3.00
Q-11	Joe DiMaggio	4.00
Q-12	Mickey Mantle	5.00
Q-13	Nolan Ryan	6.00
Q-14	Stan Musial	4.00
Q-15	Ted Williams	5.00
Q-16	Tom Seaver	2.00
Q-17	Tommy Lasorda	.75
Q-18	Warren Spahn	2.00
Q-19	Whitey Ford	1.50
Q-20	Yogi Berra	2.00

Going Deep Bat

NM/M
Common Player: 6.00
Inserted 1:288
Some not priced yet due to scarcity.
Golds: 1-2X
Production 50 Sets

BA	Bobby Abreu/SP/110	6.00
RO	Roberto Alomar	8.00
SC	Sandy Alomar Jr./SP/95	6.00
GA	Garret Anderson	8.00
RA	Rich Aurilia/SP/102	6.00
JB	Jeff Bagwell/SP/92	10.00
RB	Rocco Baldelli/SP	15.00
CB	Craig Biggio/SP/89	6.00
JE	Jim Edmonds/SP	8.00
DE	Darin Erstad	6.00
RF	Rafael Furcal/SP	6.00
TG	Troy Glaus/SP/113	8.00
SG	Shawn Green/SP/100	8.00
KG	Ken Griffey Jr./SP	30.00
RH	Rickey Henderson/SP/77	10.00
TH	Torii Hunter/SP/115	8.00
CJ	Chipper Jones/SP/69	15.00
JL	Javy Lopez/SP/77	8.00
HM	Hideki Matsui/SP/70	45.00
DM	Doug Mientkiewicz/SP/123	8.00
HN	Hideo Nomo	15.00
MO	Magglio Ordonez	6.00
PO	Jay Payton/SP/100	6.00
MP	Mike Piazza	15.00
JP	Jorge Posada	8.00
AP	Albert Pujols	20.00
SR	Scott Rolen/SP/77	10.00
CS	Curt Schilling/SP/57	10.00
AS	Alfonso Soriano/SP/53	10.00
JT	Jim Thome	8.00
OV	Omar Vizquel/SP/115	6.00
BW	Bernie Williams/SP/56	8.00
KW	Kerry Wood/SP/108	10.00

First Pitch

STAR ROOKIES / MIGUEL CABRERA

NM/M
Common Player: 5.00
Inserted 1:72

SP7	LeBron James	20.00
SP8	Mr. Hockey	10.00
SP10	Ernie Banks	10.00
SP11	General Tommy Franks	5.00
SP12	Ben Affleck	10.00
SP13	Halle Berry	5.00
SP14	George H.W. Bush	5.00
SP15	George W. Bush	5.00

Headliners Jersey

NM/M
Common Player: 4.00
Inserted 1:48
Golds: 1-2X
Production 100 Sets

TB	Tony Batista	4.00
JB	Josh Beckett	8.00
LB	Lance Berkman	4.00
MB	Mark Buehrel	4.00
LC	Luis Castillo	4.00

Abbreviations

SP - Short Print

Headliners

Lance Berkman • Houston Astros • Outfield

Magical Performances

NM/M
Common Player: 6.00
Inserted 1:96
Golds: 1-1.5X
Production 50 Sets

MP1	Mickey Mantle	35.00
MP2	Mickey Mantle	35.00
MP3	Joe DiMaggio	25.00
MP4	Joe DiMaggio	25.00
MP5	Derek Jeter	25.00
MP6	Derek Jeter	25.00
MP7	Roger Clemens	20.00
MP8	Roger Clemens	20.00
MP9	Alfonso Soriano	10.00
MP10	Andy Pettitte	8.00
MP11	Hideki Matsui	30.00
MP12	Mike Mussina	10.00
MP13	Jorge Posada	10.00
MP14	Jason Giambi	10.00
MP15	David Wells	6.00
MP16	Mariano Rivera	10.00
MP17	Yogi Berra	15.00
MP18	Phil Rizzuto	10.00
MP19	Whitey Ford	10.00
MP20	Jose Contreras	6.00
MP21	Jim "Catfish" Hunter	6.00
MP22	Mickey Mantle	35.00
MP23	Mickey Mantle	35.00
MP24	Joe DiMaggio	25.00
MP25	Joe DiMaggio	25.00
MP26	Derek Jeter	25.00
MP27	Derek Jeter	25.00
MP28	Roger Clemens	20.00
MP29	Roger Clemens	20.00
MP30	Alfonso Soriano	10.00
MP31	Andy Pettitte	8.00
MP32	Hideki Matsui	30.00
MP33	Mike Mussina	10.00
MP34	Jorge Posada	10.00
MP35	Jason Giambi	10.00
MP36	David Wells	6.00
MP37	Mariano Rivera	10.00
MP38	Yogi Berra	15.00
MP39	Phil Rizzuto	10.00
MP40	Whitey Ford	10.00
MP41	Jose Contreras	10.00
MP42	Jim "Catfish" Hunter	6.00

Matsui Chronicles

NM/M
Complete Set (60): 35.00
Common Matsui: 1.00

HM1-60	Hideki Matsui	1.00

National Pride

JD	Joe DiMaggio/SP/153	90.00
AD	Adam Dunn	6.00
JE	Jim Edmonds	6.00
RF	Robert Fick	4.00
TG	Tom Glavine	6.00
LG	Luis Gonzalez	4.00
SG	Shawn Green	4.00
KG	Ken Griffey Jr.	15.00
VG	Vladimir Guerrero/SP/153	10.00
RH	Roy Halladay	4.00
JH	Jose Hernandez	4.00
TH	Trevor Hoffman	4.00
BK	Byung-Hyun Kim	4.00
RK	Ryan Klesko	4.00
PK	Paul Konerko	4.00
ML	Mike Lowell	4.00
GM	Greg Maddux	12.00
MM	Mickey Mantle/SP/97	125.00
PM	Pedro J. Martinez	8.00
HM	Hideki Matsui	35.00
MY	Matt Morris	4.00
MU	Mike Mussina	4.00
MO	Magglio Ordonez	4.00
RO	Roy Oswalt	4.00
MR	Manny Ramirez	6.00
MA	Mariano Rivera	6.00
JR	Jimmy Rollins	6.00
BS	Benito Santiago	4.00
CS	Curt Schilling	6.00
JS	Junior Spivey	4.00
IS	Ichiro Suzuki/SP/153	30.00
MS	Mike Sweeney	4.00
MT	Miguel Tejada	6.00
JT	Jim Thome	8.00
JV	Jose Vidro	4.00
TW	Ted Williams/SP/153	75.00

NM/M
Complete Set (20): 25.00
Common Player: 1.00
Inserted 1:6

USA1	Justin Orenduff	1.00
USA2	Micah Owings	2.00
USA3	Steven Register	2.00
USA4	Huston Street	1.00
USA5	Justin Verlander	2.00
USA6	Jered Weaver	1.00
USA7	Matt Campbell	1.00
USA8	Stephen Head	1.00
USA9	Mark Romanczuk	1.00
USA10	Jeff Clement	6.00
USA11	Mike Nickeas	2.00
USA12	Tyler Greene	1.00
USA13	Paul Janish	2.00
USA14	Jeff Larish	1.00
USA15	Eric Patterson	1.00
USA16	Dustin Pedroia	1.00
USA17	Michael Griffin	1.00
USA18	Brent Lillibridge	1.00
USA19	Danny Putnam	1.00
USA20	Seth Smith	1.00

National Pride Jersey

NM/M
Common Player: 4.00
Inserted 1:24

USA1	Justin Orenduff	4.00
USA2	Micah Owings	4.00
USA3	Steven Register	4.00
USA4	Huston Street	4.00
USA5	Justin Verlander	10.00
USA6	Jered Weaver	6.00
USA7	Matt Campbell	8.00
USA8	Stephen Head	4.00
USA9	Mark Romanczuk	4.00
USA10	Jeff Clement	15.00
USA11	Mike Nickeas	4.00
USA12	Tyler Greene	4.00
USA13	Paul Janish	4.00
USA14	Jeff Larish	6.00
USA15	Eric Patterson	4.00
USA16	Dustin Pedroia	6.00
USA17	Michael Griffin	4.00
USA18	Brent Lillibridge	4.00
USA19	Danny Putnam	4.00
USA20	Seth Smith	6.00
USA21	Justin Orenduff	4.00
USA22	Micah Owings	4.00
USA23	Steven Register	4.00
USA24	Huston Street	4.00
USA25	Justin Verlander	10.00
USA26	Jered Weaver	4.00
USA27	Matt Campbell	8.00
USA28	Stephen Head	4.00
USA29	Mark Romanczuk	4.00
USA30	Jeff Clement	15.00
USA31	Mike Nickeas	4.00
USA32	Tyler Greene	4.00
USA33	Paul Janish	4.00
USA34	Jeff Larish	6.00
USA35	Eric Patterson	4.00
USA36	Dustin Pedroia	8.00
USA37	Michael Griffin	4.00
USA38	Brent Lillibridge	4.00
USA39	Danny Putnam	4.00
USA40	Seth Smith	6.00
USA41	Delmon Young	35.00
USA42	Rickie Weeks	12.00

Series 2

TB	Thad Bosley	4.00
BB	Brian Bruney	6.00
CB	Chris Burke	9.00
JC	Jesse Crain	8.00
DU	Justin Duchscherer	6.00
JD	J.D. Durbin	6.00
JG	John Grabow	6.00
GG	Gabe Gross	6.00
JH	J.J. Hardy	6.00
GK	Graham Koonce	6.00
GL	Gerald Laird	6.00

ML	Mike Lamb	4.00
JL	Justin Leone	8.00
JM	Joe Mauer	15.00
HR	Horacio Ramirez	8.00
JR	Jeremy Reed	10.00
RR	Royce Ring	6.00
ER	Eddie Rodriguez	5.00
MR	Mike Rouse	8.00
GS	Grady Sizemore	10.00
JS	Jason Stanford	6.00
JB	John Van Benschoten	8.00
TW	Todd Williams	4.00
EY	Ernie Young	4.00

National Pride Pants

NM/M

CB	Chris Burke	9.00
JC	Jesse Crain	4.00
DU	Justin Duchscherer	6.00
GK	Graham Koonce	6.00
JL	Justin Leone	8.00
RM	Ryan Madson	6.00
JM	Joe Mauer	15.00
HR	Horacio Ramirez	8.00
RR	Royce Ring	5.00
ER	Eddie Rodriguez	5.00
MR	Mike Rouse	8.00
GS	Grady Sizemore	10.00
JS	Jason Stanford	6.00
JB	John Van Benschoten	8.00

Peak Performers

NM/M

Golds: 1.5X-2X
Production 165

PP-JB	Jeff Bagwell	8.00
PP-BE	Josh Beckett	6.00
PP-LB	Lance Berkman	5.00
PP-CB	Craig Biggio	5.00
PP-HB	Hank Blalock	8.00
PP-PB	Pat Burrell	6.00
PP-LC	Luis Castillo	6.00
PP-CD	Carlos Delgado	6.00
PP-RF	Rafael Furcal	4.00
PP-EG	Eric Gagne	12.00
PP-SG	Shawn Green	5.00
PP-KG	Ken Griffey Jr.	15.00
PP-VG	Vladimir Guerrero	8.00
PP-TH	Todd Helton	8.00
PP-PL	Paul LoDuca	4.00
PP-PM	Pedro J. Martinez	8.00
PP-HM	Hideki Matsui	25.00
PP-MM	Mike Mussina	8.00
PP-HN	Hideo Nomo	8.00
PP-MO	Magglio Ordonez	5.00
PP-RP	Rafael Palmeiro	5.00
PP-PE	Andy Pettitte	6.00
PP-BP	Brandon Phillips	4.00
PP-MP	Mark Prior	10.00
PP-AP	Albert Pujols	10.00
PP-JR	Jose Reyes	5.00
PP-IR	Ivan Rodriguez	8.00
PP-SR	Scott Rolen	8.00
PP-SA	C.C. Sabathia	4.00
PP-CS	Curt Schilling	8.00
PP-AS	Alfonso Soriano	8.00
PP-IS	Ichiro Suzuki	20.00
PP-MT	Miguel Tejada	5.00
PP-FT	Frank Thomas	8.00
PP-JT	Jim Thome	8.00
PP-DV	Omar Vizquel	4.00
PP-VW	Vernon Wells	4.00
PP-KW	Kerry Wood	10.00

Signature Stars Black Ink

NM/M

Some not priced due to lack of info.
Inserted 1:288

RA	Rich Aurilia/479	8.00
AG	Andres Galarraga/248	10.00
NG	Nomar Garciaparra/69	85.00
VG	Vladimir Guerrero/68	40.00
RH	Rich Harden/163	8.00
AH	Aaron Heilman/49	15.00
TH	Torii Hunter/374	8.00
KI	Kazuhisa Ishii/58	15.00
BK	Billy Koch/429	8.00
HM	Hideki Matsui/25	325.00
MU	Mike Mussina/68	60.00
MO	Magglio Ordonez/377	20.00

JRa	Joe Randa/271	10.00
CR	Cal Ripken Jr./69	200.00
DR	Dave Roberts/278	8.00
NR	Nolan Ryan/69	120.00

Series 2

BB	Bret Boone/43	20.00
DB	Dewon Brazelton/96	8.00
JC	Jose Canseco/160	30.00
EC	Eric Chavez/60	20.00
EG	Eric Gagne/160	40.00
KG	Ken Griffey Jr./450	90.00
RH	Rich Harden/65	15.00
DR	Dave Roberts/450	5.00
NR	Nolan Ryan/95	100.00
DS	Darryl Strawberry/160	10.00
MT	Mark Teixeira/200	25.00
JV	Javier Vazquez/60	20.00
BW	Brandon Webb/60	15.00
RW	Rickie Weeks/65	30.00
DW	Dontrelle Willis/160	20.00

Signature Stars Gold Ink

Gold Ink: 1-2X Black Ink
Production 99 Sets

Signature Stars Blue Ink

NM/M

No Pricing
Production 25 Sets
Matsui #'d to 324.

HM	Hideki Matsui/324	180.00

Signature Stars Red Ink

No Pricing
Production 10 Sets
Series 2

SPGU Patch Edition Update Patch

NM/M

Production 20 unless noted.

BA	Bobby Abreu	40.00
GA	Garret Anderson	40.00
RB	Rocco Baldelli	30.00
LB	Lance Berkman	40.00
HB	Hank Blalock	40.00
BB	Bret Boone	30.00
BC	Bartolo Colon	25.00
JE	Jim Edmonds	35.00
EG	Eric Gagne	75.00
TG	Troy Glaus	35.00
VG	Vladimir Guerrero	50.00
TH	Torii Hunter	25.00
JJ	Jacque Jones	25.00
AK	Austin Kearns	30.00
JK	Jeff Kent	25.00
RK	Ryan Klesko	25.00
EM	Edgar Martinez	25.00
KM	Kevin Millwood	30.00
MM	Mark Mulder	40.00
HN	Hideo Nomo	40.00
RO	Roy Oswalt	35.00
CP	Corey Patterson	40.00
JR	Jose Reyes	30.00
RS	Richie Sexson	40.00
MS	Mike Sweeney	25.00
BW	Brandon Webb	25.00
VW	Vernon Wells/21	25.00
KW	Kerry Wood	50.00

Super Patches Logos

No pricing due to scarcity.
Inserted 1:7,500
Series 2

Super Patches Numbers

No pricing due to scarcity.
Inserted 1:7,500
Series 2

Super Patches Stripes

No pricing due to scarcity.
Inserted 1:7,500
Series 2

Super Sluggers

NM/M

Complete Set (30): 15.00
Common Player: .50
Inserted 1:1 Retail

SL-1	Albert Pujols	2.00
SL-2	Alex Rodriguez	2.00
SL-3	Alfonso Soriano	.75
SL-4	Andruw Jones	.75
SL-5	Bret Boone	.50
SL-6	Carlos Delgado	.50
SL-7	Edgar Renteria	.50
SL-8	Eric Chavez	.50
SL-9	Frank Thomas	.50
SL-10	Garret Anderson	.50
SL-11	Gary Sheffield	.50
SL-12	Jason Giambi	.75
SL-13	Javy Lopez	.50
SL-14	Jeff Bagwell	.75
SL-15	Jim Edmonds	.50
SL-16	Jim Thome	1.00
SL-17	Jorge Posada	.50
SL-18	Lance Berkman	.50
SL-19	Magglio Ordonez	.50
SL-20	Manny Ramirez	.75
SL-21	Mike Lowell	.50
SL-22	Nomar Garciaparra	1.50
SL-23	Preston Wilson	.50
SL-24	Rafael Palmeiro	.75
SL-25	Richie Sexson	.50
SL-26	Sammy Sosa	2.00
SL-27	Shawn Green	.50
SL-28	Todd Helton	.75
SL-29	Vernon Wells	.50
SL-30	Vladimir Guerrero	1.00

Twenty-Five Salute

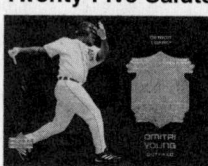

NM/M

Common Player: 6.00
Inserted 1:12

S1	Barry Bonds	3.00
S2	Troy Glaus	.75
S3	Andruw Jones	.75
S4	Jay Gibbons	.75
S5	Jeremy Giambi	.75
S6	Jason Giambi	1.00
S7	Jim Thome	1.00
S8	Rafael Palmeiro	1.00
S9	Carlos Delgado	1.00
S10	Dmitri Young	.75

500 HR Club

NM/M

Production 350

RP	Rafael Palmeiro	180.00

2003 Update

NM/M

Complete Set (60): 18.00
Common Player: .15
One set per hobby box.

541	Bo Hart	1.50
542	Dan Haren	.50
543	Ryan Wagner	1.00
544	Rich Harden	.50
545	Dontrelle Willis	.75
546	Jerome Williams	.25
547	Bobby Crosby	1.00
548	Greg Jones	.25
549	Todd Linden	.25
550	Byung-Hyun Kim	.25
551	Rickie Weeks	4.00
552	Jason Roach	.25
553	Oscar Villarreal	.25
554	Justin Duchscherer	.15
555	Chris Capuano	.15
556	Josh Hall	.50
557	Luis Matos	.15
558	Miguel Ojeda	.15
559	Kevin Ohme	.15
560	Julio Manon	.15
561	Kevin Correia	.15
562	Delmon Young	5.00
563	Aaron Boone	.15
564	Aaron Looper	.15
565	Mike Neu	.15
566	Aquilino Lopez	.15
567	Jhonny Peralta	.15
568	Duaner Sanchez	.15
569	Stephen Randolph	.15
570	Nate Bland	.15
571	Chin-Hui Tsao	.15
572	Michel Hernandez	.15
573	Rocco Baldelli	1.00
574	Robb Quinlan	.15
575	Aaron Heilman	.15
576	Jae Weong Seo	.15
577	Joe Borowski	.15
578	Chris Bootcheck	.15
579	Michael Ryan	.15
580	Mark Malaska	.15
581	Jose Guillen	.15
582	Josh Towers	.15
583	Tom Gregorio	.15
584	Edwin Jackson	.15
585	Jason Anderson	.15
586	Jose Reyes	.50
587	Miguel Cabrera	1.00
588	Nate Bump	.15
589	Jeromy Burnitz	.15
590	David Ross	.15
591	Chase Utley	.15
592	Brandon Webb	1.00
593	Masao Kida	.15
594	Jimmy Journell	.15
595	Eric Young	.15
596	Tony Womack	.15
597	Amaury Telemaco	.15
598	Rickey Henderson	.50
599	Esteban Loaiza	.15
600	Sidney Ponson	.15

2004 Upper Deck Diamond Collection

NM/M

Complete Set (120): 70.00
Common Player: .15
Common (91-120): 2.00
Inserted 1:6
Pack (6): 2.00
Box (24): 40.00

1	Garret Anderson	.25
2	Darin Erstad	.25
3	Troy Glaus	.40
4	Curt Schilling	.50
5	Brandon Webb	.15
6	Randy Johnson	.75
7	Andruw Jones	.50
8	Chipper Jones	.75
9	Gary Sheffield	.40
10	Jay Gibbons	.25
11	Miguel Tejada	.40
12	Tony Batista	.15
13	Nomar Garciaparra	1.25
14	Manny Ramirez	.50
15	Pedro J. Martinez	.75
16	Mark Prior	1.00
17	Kerry Wood	.75
18	Sammy Sosa	1.25
19	Bartolo Colon	.25
20	Magglio Ordonez	.25
21	Frank Thomas	.50
22	Adam Dunn	.40
23	Austin Kearns	.25
24	Ken Griffey Jr.	1.00
25	Brandon Phillips	.15
26	Milton Bradley	.15
27	Jody Gerut	.15
28	Todd Helton	.50
29	Larry Walker	.25
30	Preston Wilson	.25
31	Jeremy Bonderman	.15
32	Carlos Pena	.15
33	Dmitri Young	.15
34	Dontrelle Willis	.40
35	Miguel Cabrera	.50
36	Mike Lowell	.25
37	Jeff Bagwell	.50
38	Roy Oswalt	.25
39	Lance Berkman	.25
40	Carlos Beltran	.40
41	Mike Sweeney	.15
42	Rondell White	.25
43	Hideo Nomo	.40
44	Kevin Brown	.25
45	Shawn Green	.25
46	Ben Sheets	.25
47	Geoff Jenkins	.25
48	Richie Sexson	.40
49	Jacque Jones	.15
50	Johan Santana	.15
51	Torii Hunter	.25
52	Javier Vazquez	.25
53	Jose Vidro	.15
54	Vladimir Guerrero	.75
55	Cliff Floyd	.15
56	Mike Piazza	1.00
57	Jose Reyes	.25
58	Derek Jeter	2.00
59	Jason Giambi	.25
60	Alfonso Soriano	.50
61	Eric Chavez	.25
62	Barry Zito	.25
63	Tim Hudson	.25
64	Bobby Abreu	.25
65	Jim Thome	.75
66	Kevin Millwood	.15
67	Roger Clemens	1.50
68	Jason Kendall	.15
69	Reggie Sanders	.15
70	Phil Nevin	.15
71	Ryan Klesko	.25
72	Brian Giles	.25
73	A.J. Pierzynski	.25
74	Jason Schmidt	.25
75	Sidney Ponson	.15
76	Edgar Martinez	.25
77	Ichiro Suzuki	1.00
78	Bret Boone	.25
79	Albert Pujols	1.50
80	Scott Rolen	.25
81	Jim Edmonds	.25
82	Aubrey Huff	.15
83	Delmon Young	.40
84	Rocco Baldelli	.40
85	Alex Rodriguez	1.50
86	Mark Teixeira	.25
87	Rafael Palmeiro	.25
88	Carlos Delgado	.50
89	Vernon Wells	.25
90	Roy Halladay	.25
91	Brandon Medders RC	2.00
92	Colby Miller RC	2.00
93	David Crouthers RC	2.00
94	Dennis Sarfate RC	3.00
95	Donald Kelly RC	2.00
96	Alec Zumwalt RC	2.00
97	Frank Brooks RC	2.00
98	Greg Dobbs RC	2.00
99	Ian Snell RC	3.00
100	Jake Woods RC	2.00
101	Jamie Brown RC	2.00
102	Jason Frasor RC	2.00
103	Jerome Gamble RC	2.00
104	Jesse Harper RC	2.00
105	Josh Labandeira RC	2.00
106	Justin Hampson RC	2.00
107	Justin Huisman RC	2.00
108	Justin Leone RC	2.00
109	Chris Aguila RC	2.00
110	Lincoln Holdzkom RC	2.00
111	Mike Bumatay RC	2.00
112	Mike Gosling RC	2.00
113	Mike Johnston RC	2.00
114	Mike Rouse RC	2.00
115	Nick Regilio RC	2.00
116	Ryan Meaux RC	2.00
117	Scott Dohmann RC	2.00
118	Sean Henn RC	2.00
119	Tim Bausher RC	2.00
120	Tim Bittner RC	2.00

Silver Honors

Silver (1-90): 2-4X
Silver (91-120): .75-1X
1-90 inserted 1:6
91-120 inserted 1:48

Gold Honors

Gold (1-90): 5-10X
Gold (91-120): 1-2X
Production 50 Sets

All-Star Promo e-Card

NM/M

Common Player: 1.00
Inserted 1:12

CD	Carlos Delgado	1.00
NG	Nomar Garciaparra	2.50
VG	Vladimir Guerrero	1.50
TH	Todd Helton	1.00
AP	Albert Pujols	3.00
AS	Alfonso Soriano	1.00
SS	Sammy Sosa	2.50
IS	Ichiro Suzuki	2.50
AR	Alex Rodriguez	3.00

Class of 2004 Autograph

NM/M

Quantity produced listed

MC	Miguel Cabrera/50	40.00
KG	Ken Griffey Jr./100	75.00
VG	Vladimir Guerrero/100	
RH	Rich Harden/100	15.00
HM	Hideki Matsui/100	250.00
MP	Mark Prior/100	40.00
JR	Jose Reyes/100	30.00
DW	Dontrelle Willis/100	40.00
BZ	Barry Zito/100	25.00

Dean's List Jersey

NM/M

Common Player: 4.00

Inserted 1:72

BA	Jeff Bagwell	8.00
HB	Hank Blalock	6.00
JG	Jason Giambi	6.00
GL	Troy Glaus	6.00
LG	Luis Gonzalez	4.00
SG	Shawn Green	4.00
KG	Ken Griffey Jr.	10.00
VG	Vladimir Guerrero	8.00
GM	Greg Maddux	10.00
HM	Hideki Matsui	20.00
HN	Hideo Nomo	8.00
PI	Mike Piazza	8.00
MP	Mark Prior	8.00
AP	Albert Pujols	15.00
AR	Alex Rodriguez	10.00
AS	Alfonso Soriano	8.00
SS	Sammy Sosa	10.00
IS	Ichiro Suzuki	20.00
JT	Jim Thome	8.00
DW	Dontrelle Willis	6.00

Future Gems Jersey

NM/M

Common Player: 4.00
Inserted 1:72

BA	Josh Bard	4.00
JB	Josh Beckett	8.00
SB	Sean Burroughs	6.00
MC	Mike Cameron	4.00
AE	Adam Eaton	4.00
WE	Willie Eyre	4.00
LF	Lew Ford	4.00
GU	Jeremy Guthrie	4.00
TH	Travis Hafner	6.00
RH	Roy Halladay	4.00
AH	Aaron Heilman	4.00
IS	Kazuhisa Ishii	4.00
JJ	Jason Jennings	4.00
KA	Matt Kata	4.00
MK	Mark Kotsay	4.00
JL	Jon Leicester	4.00
EM	Eric Milton	4.00
JR	Jose Reyes	8.00
RR	Rick Roberts	4.00
PS	Phil Seibel	4.00
BS	Ben Sheets	6.00
MT	Mark Teixeira	4.00
TW	Todd Wellemeyer	6.00
WI	Josh Willingham	4.00

Pick the All-Star MVP

NM/M

Common Player: .50
Inserted 1:1

BA	Bobby Abreu	.50
GA	Garret Anderson	.50
JB	Jeff Bagwell	.50
BE	Josh Beckett	.50
CB	Carlos Beltran	.50
HB	Hank Blalock	.50
BO	Bret Boone	.50
OC	Orlando Cabrera	.50
EC	Eric Chavez	.50
BC	Bartolo Colon	.50
JD	Johnny Damon	.50
CD	Carlos Delgado	.50
AD	Adam Dunn	.50
JE	Jim Edmonds	.50
RF	Rafael Furcal	.50
NG	Nomar Garciaparra	1.50
JG	Jason Giambi	.75
MG	Marcus Giles	.50
TG	Troy Glaus	.50
SG	Shawn Green	.50
KG	Ken Griffey Jr.	1.00
VG	Vladimir Guerrero	.75
RH	Roy Halladay	.50
TH	Todd Helton	.50
HU	Tim Hudson	.50
TH	Torii Hunter	.50
DJ	Derek Jeter	2.50
RJ	Randy Johnson	.75
AJ	Andruw Jones	.50
CJ	Chipper Jones	.75
JJ	Jacque Jones	.50
AK	Austin Kearns	.50
JK	Jeff Kent	.50
JL	Javy Lopez	.50
ML	Mike Lowell	.50
PM	Pedro J. Martinez	.75
HM	Hideki Matsui	1.50
MM	Mark Mulder	.50
MU	Mike Mussina	.75
MO	Magglio Ordonez	.50
RP	Rafael Palmeiro	.50
PI	Mike Piazza	1.00
JP	Jorge Posada	.50
MP	Mark Prior	1.00
AP	Albert Pujols	2.00
MR	Manny Ramirez	.75
ER	Edgar Renteria	.50
AR	Alex Rodriguez	2.00

IR	Ivan Rodriguez	.75
SR	Scott Rolen	.75
CS	Curt Schilling	.75
JS	Jason Schmidt	.50
RS	Richie Sexson	.50
GS	Gary Sheffield	.50
AS	Alfonso Soriano	.75
SS	Sammy Sosa	1.50
IS	Ichiro Suzuki	1.50
MS	Mike Sweeney	.50
MT	Mark Teixeira	.50
TE	Miguel Tejada	.75
FT	Frank Thomas	.75
JT	Jim Thome	.75
JV	Jason Varitek	.50
VI	Jose Vidro	.50
VW	Vernon Wells	.50
DW	Dontrelle Willis	.50
PW	Preston Wilson	.50
KW	Kerry Wood	1.00
BZ	Barry Zito	.50

Premium Stars
Complete Set (15):
Common Player:

Pro Sigs

NM/M

Complete Set (1-240):		
Common Player (1-90):		.15
Common SP (91-150):		2.00
Inserted 1:6		
Common Auto. (151-240):		5.00
Inserted 1:24		
Pack (6):		2.00
Box (24):		40.00
1	Alfonso Soriano	.50
2	Josh Beckett	.50
3	Kerry Wood	.75
4	Brandon Webb	.15
5	Shannon Stewart	.15
6	Larry Walker	.25
7	Tim Hudson	.25
8	Carlos Lee	.25
9	Austin Kearns	.25
10	Vernon Wells	.25
11	Jeff Bagwell	.50
12	Hideo Nomo	.40
13	Jerome Williams	.15
14	Kevin Brown	.25
15	Jose Vidro	.15
16	Rocco Baldelli	.25
17	Frank Thomas	.50
18	Albert Pujols	1.50
19	Bartolo Colon	.25
20	C.C. Sabathia	.15
21	Andruw Jones	.50
22	Reggie Sanders	.15
23	Carlos Beltran	.40
24	Curt Schilling	.50
25	Miguel Tejada	.40
26	Barry Zito	.40
27	Pedro Martinez	.75
28	Sean Burroughs	.15
29	Sammy Sosa	1.50
30	Eric Chavez	.25
31	Roy Halladay	.25
32	Todd Helton	.50
33	Mark Prior	1.00
34	Mike Mussina	.50
35	Alex Rodriguez	2.00
36	Ivan Rodriguez	.50
37	Mike Piazza	1.00
38	Angel Berroa	.15
39	Orlando Cabrera	.25
40	Jim Thome	.75
41	Brian Giles	.25
42	Ichiro Suzuki	1.00
43	Edgar Renteria	.25
44	Eric Gagne	.25
45	Gary Sheffield	.40
46	Torii Hunter	.25
47	Roger Clemens	1.50
48	Scott Rolen	.75
49	Johan Santana	.15
50	Jacque Jones	.15
51	Hank Blalock	.40
52	Rafael Palmeiro	.50
53	Dmitri Young	.15
54	Ryan Klesko	.25
55	Mark Teixeira	.25
56	Nomar Garciaparra	1.50
57	Jose Reyes	.25
58	Vladimir Guerrero	.75
59	Mike Sweeney	.15
60	Jorge Posada	.40
61	Derek Jeter	2.00

62	Milton Bradley	.15
63	Bobby Abreu	.25
64	Greg Maddux	1.00
65	Adam Dunn	.50
66	Troy Glaus	.40
67	Luis Gonzalez	.25
68	Shawn Green	.25
69	Bret Boone	.25
70	Mark Mulder	.25
71	Lance Berkman	.25
72	Preston Wilson	.15
73	Phil Nevin	.15
74	Chipper Jones	.75
75	Garret Anderson	.40
76	Jason Giambi	.75
77	Magglio Ordonez	.25
78	Jeff Kent	.25
79	Richie Sexson	.40
80	Mike Lowell	.25
81	Ben Sheets	.25
82	Randy Johnson	.75
83	Dontrelle Willis	.25
84	Javier Vazquez	.25
85	Geoff Jenkins	.25
86	Manny Ramirez	.50
87	Jim Edmonds	.40
88	Roy Oswalt	.25
89	Edgar Martinez	.25
90	Carlos Delgado	.40
91	Chris Saenz **RC**	5.00
92	Justin Leone **RC**	4.00
93	Shawn Hill **RC**	4.00
94	Chad Bentz **RC**	4.00
95	Jesse Harper **RC**	2.00
96	David Crouthers **RC**	2.00
97	Justin Germano **RC**	2.00
98	Tim Bausher **RC**	2.00
99	Greg Dobbs **RC**	5.00
100	Enemencio Pacheco **RC**	8.00
101	Dennis Sarfate **RC**	2.00
102	Edwin Moreno **RC**	4.00
103	Colby Miller **RC**	2.00
104	Mike Rouse **RC**	2.00
105	Fernando Nieve **RC**	2.00
106	Tim Hamulack **RC**	6.00
107	Jason Frasor **RC**	2.00
108	Jose Capellan **RC**	5.00
109	Jamie Brown **RC**	3.00
110	Mariano Gomez **RC**	2.00
111	Mike Vento **RC**	8.00
112	Josh Labandeira **RC**	3.00
113	Mike Gosling **RC**	2.00
114	Shingo Takatsu **RC**	8.00
115	Justin Hampson **RC**	2.00
116	Tim Bittner **RC**	2.00
117	Jerry Gil **RC**	2.00
118	Carlos Vasquez **RC**	5.00
119	Lincoln Holdzkom **RC**	2.00
120	Mike Johnston **RC**	4.00
121	William Bergolla **RC**	2.00
122	Luis Gonzalez	2.00
123	Ivan Ochoa **RC**	4.00
124	Roman Colon **RC**	2.00
125	Renyel Pinto **RC**	6.00
126	Donnie Kelly **RC**	2.00
127	Chris Oxspring **RC**	2.00
128	Sean Henn **RC**	5.00
129	Ryan Meaux **RC**	2.00
130	Shawn Camp **RC**	2.00
131	Brandon Medders **RC**	2.00
132	Rusty Tucker **RC**	2.00
133	Kazuo Matsui **RC**	10.00
134	Jorge Sequea **RC**	2.00
135	Hector Gimenez **RC**	4.00
136	Casey Daigle **RC**	2.00
137	Ian Snell **RC**	3.00
138	Scott Dohmann **RC**	2.00
139	Ronny Cedeno **RC**	2.00
140	Jorge Vasquez **RC**	4.00
141	David Aardsma	4.00
142	Carlos Hines **RC**	2.00
143	Scott Proctor **RC**	3.00
144	Jerome Gamble **RC**	5.00
145	Jason Bartlett **RC**	6.00
146	Akinori Otsuka **RC**	8.00
147	Merkin Valdez **RC**	2.00
148	Jake Woods **RC**	4.00
149	Chris Aguila **RC**	2.00
150	John Gall **RC**	2.00
151	Aaron Miles	10.00
152	Aquilino Lopez	10.00
153	Bill Hall	10.00
154	Billy Traber	15.00
155	Brad Lidge	12.00
156	Brady Clark	10.00
157	Brandon Duckworth	8.00
158	Brett Tomko	6.00
159	Brian Fuentes	6.00
161	Brooks Kieschnick	8.00
162	Carlos Rivera	6.00
163	Chad Cordero	6.00
164	Chad Tracy	10.00
165	Claudio Vargas	5.00
166	D.J. Carrasco	6.00
167	Damian Rolls	5.00
168	David Sanders	5.00
169	Derrick Turnbow	5.00
170	Desi Relaford	5.00
171	Doug Davis	8.00
172	Dustan Mohr	6.00
173	Frank Catalanotto	8.00
174	Franklyn German	5.00
178	Ron Belliard	5.00
179	Geoff Geary	15.00
180	Greg Colbrunn	5.00
181	Henry Mateo	5.00
183	Brent Mayne	5.00

184	Horacio Ramirez	15.00
185	J.C. Romero	5.00
186	J.J. Putz	8.00
187	Ferdin Tejeda	8.00
188	Jaime Cerda	8.00
189	Jason Michaels	10.00
190	Jason Simontacchi	8.00
191	Jay Witasick	8.00
192	Joe Valentine	8.00
193	Joey Eischen	8.00
194	Johnny Estrada	8.00
195	Jon Garland	5.00
196	Jon Switzer	5.00
197	Jorge Julio	5.00
198	Jorge Sosa	8.00
199	Jose Castillo	5.00
200	Jose Macias	5.00
201	Josh Bard	5.00
202	Juan Cruz	5.00
203	Juan Rivera	5.00
204	Ken Griffey Jr.	150.00
205	Kevin Hooper	5.00
206	Kiko Calero **RC**	15.00
207	Chad Gaudin	5.00
208	Luis Rivas	5.00
209	Mark Corey	5.00
210	Matt Ford	8.00
211	Matt Herges	5.00
212	Miguel Cairo	15.00
213	Fernando Cabrera	5.00
214	Mike MacDougal	5.00
215	Mike Neu	8.00
216	Lew Ford	15.00
217	Mike Wood	5.00
218	Nate Robertson	5.00
219	Nick Punto	5.00
221	Oscar Villarreal	5.00
222	Ramon Vazquez	10.00
223	Randall Simon	5.00
225	Ricky Stone	5.00
229	Ryan Drese	5.00
230	Ryan Ludwick	8.00
231	Scot Shields	5.00
232	Shane Nance	5.00
233	Steve Colyer	5.00
234	Tony Armas	5.00
235	Robby Hammock	5.00
236	Travis Hafner	8.00
237	Victor Martinez	8.00
238	Wilfredo Ledezma	5.00
239	Willie Bloomquist	5.00
240	Yorvit Torrealba	8.00

Pro Sigs Silver

Silver (1-90):		2-3X
Overall odds for parallel 1:6.		

Pro Sigs Gold
Gold (1-90):		3-6X
Overall odds for parallel 1:6.		

Pro Sigs Blue Ink Autograph
No Pricing
Production 25 Sets

Pro Sigs Red Signature
No Pricing
Production 10 Sets

Pro Sigs Hall of Famers
No Pricing

2004 Upper Deck Etchings

NM/M

Complete Set (150):		
Common Player:		.15
Common SP (91-120):		4.00
Production 2,004		
Common SP Black Auto.		
(121-150):		8.00
Production 700		
Blue Auto. (121-150):		.75-1.5X
Production 200		
Red Auto. (121-150):		No Pricing
Production 25		
Pack (5):		12.00
Box (12):		120.00
1	Albert Pujols	1.50
2	Torii Hunter	.40
3	Jim Edmonds	.40

4	Alex Rodriguez	1.50
5	Rafael Palmeiro	.50
6	Ken Griffey Jr.	1.00
7	Adam Dunn	.50
8	Andruw Jones	.50
9	Carlos Lee	.15
10	Mike Piazza	1.00
11	Jeff Bagwell	.50
12	Hideki Matsui	1.50
13	Gary Sheffield	.40
14	Edgar Renteria	.25
15	Shawn Green	.25
16	Kerry Wood	.75
17	Ivan Rodriguez	.25
18	Josh Beckett	.40
19	Scott Rolen	.75
20	Brian Giles	.25
21	Derrek Lee	.25
22	Mike Lowell	.25
23	Mike Mussina	.40
24	Sammy Sosa	1.50
25	Brandon Webb	.15
26	Jacque Jones	.15
27	Randy Johnson	1.00
28	Luis Gonzalez	.25
29	Eric Chavez	.25
30	Carlos Delgado	.40
31	Phil Nevin	.15
32	Ichiro Suzuki	1.50
33	Roy Oswalt	.25
34	Tim Hudson	.25
35	Juan Gonzalez	.50
36	Frank Thomas	.50
37	Mark Mulder	.40
38	Mark Teixeira	.40
39	Miguel Tejada	.40
40	Jeff Kent	.25
41	Andy Pettitte	.25
42	Barry Zito	.25
43	Roy Halladay	.25
44	Rocco Baldelli	.25
45	Derek Jeter	2.00
46	Corey Patterson	.40
47	Javy Lopez	.40
48	A.J. Burnett	.15
49	Chipper Jones	.75
50	Curt Schilling	.50
51	Todd Helton	.50
52	Pedro J. Martinez	.75
53	Hideo Nomo	.40
54	Jose Reyes	.50
55	Vernon Wells	.15
56	Geoff Jenkins	.15
57	Troy Glaus	.25
58	Greg Maddux	1.00
59	Jason Schmidt	.40
60	Preston Wilson	.15
61	Miguel Cabrera	.50
62	Hank Blalock	.50
63	Rafael Furcal	.15
64	Vladimir Guerrero	.75
65	Lance Berkman	.15
66	Javier Vazquez	.15
67	Bret Boone	.15
68	Mark Prior	1.00
69	Magglio Ordonez	.15
70	Dontrelle Willis	.25
71	Richie Sexson	.25
72	Alfonso Soriano	.75
73	Edwin Jackson	.15
74	Jose Vidro	.15
75	Jason Giambi	.25
76	Kevin Brown	.25
77	Orlando Cabrera	.15
78	Nomar Garciaparra	1.00
79	Bobby Abreu	.25
80	Manny Ramirez	.15
81	J.D. Drew	.15
82	Roger Clemens	1.50
83	Pat Burrell	.15
84	Ryan Klesko	.15
85	Garret Anderson	.40
86	Johan Santana	.15
87	Kevin Millwood	.15
88	Austin Kearns	.25
89	Jim Thome	.25
90	Carlos Beltran	.40
91	Kazuo Matsui **RC**	15.00
92	Jamie Brown **RC**	4.00
93	Brandon Medders **RC**	4.00
94	Carlos Vasquez **RC**	4.00
95	Chris Aguila **RC**	4.00
96	David Aardsma **RC**	4.00
97	Justin Leone **RC**	4.00
98	Mike Johnston **RC**	4.00
99	Tim Bittner **RC**	4.00
100	Mike Rouse **RC**	4.00
101	Dennis Sarfate **RC**	4.00

102	Jason Frasor **RC**	4.00
103	Jorge Vasquez **RC**	4.00
104	Mike Gosling **RC**	4.00
105	Jake Woods **RC**	4.00
106	Akinori Otsuka **RC**	8.00
107	Lincoln Holdzkom **RC**	4.00
108	Jesse Harper **RC**	4.00
109	Edwin Moreno **RC**	4.00
110	Shingo Takatsu **RC**	6.00
111	Ryan Meaux **RC**	4.00
112	Donnie Kelly **RC**	4.00
113	Jerome Gamble **RC**	4.00
114	Josh Labandeira **RC**	4.00
115	Ian Snell **RC**	8.00
116	Mike Wuertz **RC**	4.00
117	Greg Dobbs **RC**	4.00
118	Sean Henn **RC**	4.00
119	David Crouthers **RC**	4.00
120	Hector Gimenez **RC**	4.00
121	Renyel Pinto **RC**	10.00
122	Tim Hamulack **RC**	8.00
123	Chris Saenz **RC**	8.00
124	Carlos Hines **RC**	8.00
125	Justin Knoedler **RC**	10.00
126	Onil Joseph **RC**	10.00
127	Ryan Wing	8.00
128	Scott Proctor **RC**	10.00
129	Rusty Tucker **RC**	8.00
130	Fernando Nieve **RC**	8.00
131	Chad Bentz **RC**	10.00
132	Jerry Gil **RC**	8.00
133	Mariano Gomez **RC**	8.00
134	Justin Germano **RC**	10.00
135	Jason Bartlett **RC**	8.00
136	Ronald Belisario **RC**	8.00
137	Enemencio Pacheco **RC**	8.00
138	Justin Hampson **RC**	8.00
139	Michael Vento **RC**	8.00
140	Merkin Valdez **RC**	8.00
141	Casey Daigle **RC**	8.00
142	Eddy Rodriguez	8.00
143	William Bergolla **RC**	25.00
144	Jose Capellan **RC**	8.00
145	Ronny Cedeno **RC**	8.00
146	Franklyn Gracesqui **RC**	8.00
147	Roman Colon **RC**	10.00
148	Roberto Novoa **RC**	8.00
149	Ivan Ochoa **RC**	10.00
150	Shawn Hill **RC**	8.00

Combo Etchings
NM/M

Production 5-115		
Gold Foil:		.75-1.5X
Production 1-50		
Silver Foil:		.75-1X
Production 4-50		
No pricing 15 or less.		
JB	Josh Beckett/25	60.00
MC	Miguel Cabrera/23	50.00
KG	Ken Griffey Jr./100	90.00
KG1	Ken Griffey Jr./90	90.00
KG2	Ken Griffey Jr./90	90.00
VG	Vladimir Guerrero/60	65.00
DJ1	Derek Jeter/25	200.00
MR	Manny Ramirez/60	65.00
MR1	Manny Ramirez/60	65.00
CR	Cal Ripken Jr./15	250.00
CR1	Cal Ripken Jr./15	250.00
AR	Alex Rodriguez/15	200.00
AR1	Alex Rodriguez/15	200.00
AR2	Alex Rodriguez/115	150.00
KW	Kerry Wood/20	65.00
KW1	Kerry Wood/60	65.00
KW2	Kerry Wood/30	50.00

Dual Etchings
NM/M

Production 150 Sets		
RJ	Alex Rodriguez, Derek Jeter	60.00
WP	Kerry Wood, Mark Prior	25.00
RP	Jose Reyes, Mike Piazza	30.00
PG	Albert Pujols, Vladimir Guerrero	30.00
MM	Hideki Matsui, Kazuo Matsui	40.00
MW	Mickey Mantle, Ted Williams	180.00

Master Etchings
No Pricing
Production One Set

Star Etchings
NM/M

Quantity produced listed		
BA	Bobby Abreu/50	20.00
GA	Garret Anderson/50	20.00
JB	Josh Beckett/50	20.00
CB	Carlos Beltran/50	50.00
HB	Hank Blalock/50	25.00
BB	Bret Boone/50	15.00
MC	Miguel Cabrera/50	35.00
EC	Eric Chavez/50	20.00
JD	J.D. Drew/50	20.00
AD	Adam Dunn/50	30.00
NG	Nomar Garciaparra/15	100.00
KG	Ken Griffey Jr./50	85.00
KG1	Ken Griffey Jr./50	85.00
VG	Vladimir Guerrero/15	80.00
RH	Roy Halladay/50	15.00

TH	Tim Hudson/50	30.00
GJ	Geoff Jenkins/50	15.00
DL	Derrek Lee/50	35.00
JL	Javy Lopez/50	20.00
ML	Mike Lowell/50	15.00
MU	Mark Mulder/50	15.00
MO	Magglio Ordonez/50	15.00
RO	Roy Oswalt/50	25.00
PR	Mark Prior/50	40.00
JS	Jason Schmidt/50	40.00
MT	Mark Teixeira/50	40.00
TE	Miguel Tejada/50	25.00
BW	Brandon Webb/50	15.00
VW	Vernon Wells/50	15.00
DW	Dontrelle Willis/50	15.00
KW	Kerry Wood/50	40.00

Triple Etchings
NM/M

Production 50 Sets		
RJM	Alex Rodriguez, Derek Jeter, Hideki Matsui	125.00
PER	Albert Pujols, Jim Edmonds, Scott Rolen	90.00
SRG	Curt Schilling, Manny Ramirez, Nomar Garciaparra	40.00
SBT	Alfonso Soriano, Hank Blalock, Mark Teixeira	40.00
WPS	Kerry Wood, Mark Prior, Sammy Sosa	50.00
DMW	Joe DiMaggio, Mickey Mantle, Ted Williams	400.00

Etched in Time Black Ink
NM/M

Quantity produced listed		
Common Autograph:		6.00
AA	Alfredo Amezaga/375	6.00
SA	Sparky Anderson/375	15.00
TA	Tony Armas/325	6.00
BA	Dusty Baker/150	15.00
JB	Jason Bay/375	15.00
BE	Carlos Beltran/150	30.00
AB	Angel Berroa/1,325	6.00
HB	Hank Blalock/375	15.00
GB	Geoff Blum/375	6.00
BB	Bert Blyleven/375	8.00
CB	Chris Bootcheck/375	8.00
DB	Dewon Brazelton/375	8.00
MB	Marlon Byrd/1,025	8.00
EB	Eric Byrnes/Redemp.	8.00
MC	Miguel Cabrera/1,025	15.00
CA	Chris Capuano/375	8.00
EC	Eric Chavez/375	15.00
AC	Alex Cintron/375	8.00
WC	Will Clark/150	30.00
CL	Brandon Claussen/375	8.00
CC	Chad Cordero/375	8.00
BC	Bobby Crosby/1,325	15.00
AD	Andre Dawson/375	10.00
BD	Brandon Duckworth/375	8.00
ME	Morgan Ensberg/1,325	8.00
DE	Dwight Evans/375	15.00
AE	Adam Everett/325	6.00
WE	Willie Eyre/375	8.00
KF	Kyle Farnsworth/1,325	8.00
PF	Pedro Feliz/325	8.00
RF	Rollie Fingers/375	10.00
JF	Josh Fogg/325	8.00
LF	Lew Ford/375	20.00
NG	Nomar Garciaparra/100	75.00
CG	Chad Gaudin/375	8.00
BG	Brian Giles/375	10.00
MG	Marcus Giles/325	10.00
GO	Jonny Gomes/325	6.00
AG	Adrian Gonzalez/325	6.00
DG	Dwight Gooden/375	10.00
KG	Ken Griffey Jr./1,625	60.00
GR	Ken Griffey Sr./375	10.00
TG	Tony Gwynn/150	40.00
SH	Scott Hairston/375	8.00
RH	Rob Hammock/325	8.00
AH	Aaron Harang/325	12.00
HA	Rich Harden/375	10.00
HE	Ramon Hernandez/325	8.00
RI	Raul Ibanez/325	8.00
EJ	Edwin Jackson/325	8.00
DJ	Derek Jeter	100.00
JJ	Jacque Jones/375	10.00
KA	Al Kaline/375	25.00
MK	Matt Kata/325	8.00
AK	Adam Kennedy/375	6.00
BK	Bobby Kielty/1,325	6.00
HK	Harmon Killebrew/Redemp.	35.00
DK	Dave Kingman/375	8.00
GK	Graham Koonce/375	8.00
LA	Adam LaRoche/1,325	8.00
CS	Carlos Lee/325	8.00
LE	Cliff Lee/1,325	6.00
TL	Ted Lilly/325	6.00
AL	Adam Loewen/375	6.00
ML	Mike Lowell/375	10.00
LM	Luis Matos/325	6.00
DM	Don Mattingly/150	50.00
MA	Joe Mauer/375	30.00

JM Justin Miller/325 8.00
MO Jack Morris/375 10.00
MM Mark Mulder/375 20.00
MU Dale Murphy/375 25.00
MN Mike Neu/325 6.00
LN Laynce Nix/Redemp. 15.00
RO Roy Oswalt/375 12.00
LO Lyle Overbay/1,325 8.00
PA Jim Palmer/375 15.00
CP Corey Patterson/375 20.00
BP Brad Penny/375 8.00
JP Jason Phillips/375 8.00
PO Boog Powell/375 15.00
MP Mark Prior/375 30.00
JR Jose Reyes/325 12.00
JI Jim Rice/375 10.00
CR Cal Ripken Jr./100 120.00
BR Brooks Robinson/375
RS Ryne Sandberg/150 50.00
SO Ron Santo/375 25.00
SS Steve Sax/375 10.00
MS Mike Scioscia/375 12.00
BS Ben Sheets/375 15.00
TS Terrmel Sledge/325 6.00
DS Darryl Strawberry/150 15.00
MT Mark Teixeira/325 20.00
LT Luis Tiant/375 10.00
AT Alan Trammell/375 15.00
CU Chase Utley/375 25.00
RW Ryan Wagner/1,325
WK Rickie Weeks/Redemp. 20.00
JW Jerome Williams/1,325 8.00
WI Josh Willingham/1,325 6.00
RA Randy Winn/375 8.00
KW Kerry Wood/150 35.00
DY Delmon Young/375 8.00
MY Michael Young/1,325 15.00
CZ Carlos Zambrano/375 25.00

Etched in Time Red Ink

No Pricing
Production 25 Sets

Etched in Time Blue Ink

NM/M
Quantity produced listed
Common Autograph: 6.00
AA Alfredo Amezaga/100 8.00
SA Sparky Anderson/250 15.00
TA Tony Armas/150 6.00
JB Jason Bay/250 15.00
AB Angel Berroa/150 8.00
HB Hank Blalock/250 15.00
GB Geoff Blum/250 6.00
BB Bert Blyleven/250 8.00
CB Chris Bootcheck/100 8.00
DB Dewon Brazelton/250 8.00
MB Marlon Byrd/150 8.00
EB Eric Byrnes/Redemp. 8.00
MC Miguel Cabrera/150 25.00
CA Chris Capuano/100 8.00
EC Eric Chavez/150 15.00
AC Alex Cintron/100 10.00
WC Will Clark/50 40.00
CL Brandon Claussen/100 8.00
CC Chad Cordero/100 8.00
BC Bobby Crosby/150 15.00
AD Andre Dawson/100 10.00
BD Brandon Duckworth/100 8.00
ME Morgan Ensberg/150 8.00
DE Dwight Evans/250 15.00
AE Adam Everett/150 8.00
WE Willie Eyre/100 8.00
KF Kyle Farnsworth/150 8.00
PF Pedro Feliz/150 8.00
RF Rollie Fingers/250 10.00
JF Josh Fogg/150 8.00
LF Lew Ford/200 20.00
NG Nomar Garciaparra/50 85.00
CG Chad Gaudin/100 6.00
BG Brian Giles/250 10.00
MG Marcus Giles/150 10.00
GO Jonny Gomes/150 6.00
AG Adrian Gonzalez/150 6.00

DG Dwight Gooden/250 10.00
KG Ken Griffey Jr./150 75.00
GR Ken Griffey Sr./250 12.00
VG Vladimir Guerrero/50 50.00
TG Tony Gwynn/50 50.00
SH Scott Hairston/100 8.00
RH Rob Hammock/150 8.00
AH Aaron Harang/100 8.00
HA Rich Harden/150 15.00
HE Ramon Hernandez/150 8.00
RI Raul Ibanez/150 8.00
EJ Edwin Jackson/100 8.00
DJ Derek Jeter/150 120.00
JJ Jacque Jones/250 8.00
KA Al Kaline/250 25.00
MK Matt Kata/150 8.00
BK Bobby Kielty/150 8.00
DK Dave Kingman/250 8.00
GK Graham Koonce/250 8.00
LA Adam LaRoche/150 10.00
LE Cliff Lee/150 10.00
TL Ted Lilly/150 8.00
ML Mike Lowell/250 8.00
LM Luis Matos/150 8.00
DM Don Mattingly/50 60.00
MA Joe Mauer/250 30.00
JM Justin Miller/150 8.00
MO Jack Morris/250 10.00
MM Mark Mulder/250 8.00
MU Dale Murphy/250 25.00
MN Mike Neu/150 6.00
RO Roy Oswalt/250 12.00
LO Lyle Overbay/150 15.00
PA Jim Palmer/250 15.00
CP Corey Patterson/250 20.00
BP Brad Penny/100 8.00
JP Jason Phillips/250 8.00
LP Lou Piniella/150 8.00
PO Boog Powell/250 15.00
MP Mark Prior/50 40.00
JR Jose Reyes/150 15.00
JI Jim Rice/250 8.00
CR Cal Ripken Jr./50 150.00
BR Brooks Robinson/250
RS Ryne Sandberg/50 25.00
SO Ron Santo/250 25.00
SS Steve Sax/250 8.00
MS Mike Scioscia/250 12.00
BS Ben Sheets/150 15.00
TS Terrmel Sledge/150 6.00
MT Mark Teixeira/150 25.00
LT Luis Tiant/250 15.00
AT Alan Trammell/250 15.00
CU Chase Utley/100 25.00
RW Ryan Wagner/150 10.00
JW Jerome Williams/150 10.00
WI Josh Willingham/150 6.00
RA Randy Winn/100 8.00
KW Kerry Wood/50 50.00
DY Delmon Young/250 20.00
MY Michael Young/150 15.00
CZ Carlos Zambrano/250 25.00

Game Bat Blue

FRANK THOMAS

NM/M
Common Player:
Purple: 1X
Production 250
Red: 1X
Production 150
Green: 1-2X
Production 50
BA Bobby Abreu 6.00
RA Roberto Alomar 6.00
GA Garret Anderson 6.00
CB Carlos Beltran 6.00
AB Adrian Beltre 6.00
LB Lance Berkman 4.00
HB Hank Blalock 6.00
BB Bret Boone 4.00
SC Sean Casey 4.00
EC Eric Chavez 4.00
JC Jose Cruz Jr. 4.00
CD Carlos Delgado 6.00
JD J.D. Drew 4.00
AD Adam Dunn 8.00
JE Jim Edmonds 6.00
CF Cliff Floyd 4.00
RF Rafael Furcal 4.00
NG Nomar Garciaparra 10.00
JG Jason Giambi 6.00
BG Brian Giles 4.00
TG Troy Glaus 6.00

LG Luis Gonzalez 4.00
SG Shawn Green 6.00
KG Ken Griffey Jr. 12.00
VG Vladimir Guerrero 10.00
TH Todd Helton 8.00
HU Torii Hunter 6.00
GJ Geoff Jenkins 4.00
DJ Derek Jeter 20.00
RJ Randy Johnson 8.00
AJ Andruw Jones 8.00
CJ Chipper Jones 8.00
JL Javy Lopez 6.00
ML Mike Lowell 6.00
KM Kazuo Matsui 10.00
MO Magglio Ordonez 4.00
RP Rafael Palmeiro 8.00
JP Jay Payton 4.00
PI Mike Piazza 8.00
AP Albert Pujols 15.00
MR Manny Ramirez 8.00
JR Jose Reyes 6.00
AR Alex Rodriguez 15.00
IR Ivan Rodriguez 8.00
SR Scott Rolen 8.00
TS Tim Salmon 6.00
CS Curt Schilling 6.00
GS Gary Sheffield 6.00
AS Alfonso Soriano 8.00
SS Sammy Sosa 8.00
IS Ichiro Suzuki 15.00
MT Mark Teixeira 6.00
TE Miguel Tejada 8.00
FT Frank Thomas 8.00
JT Jim Thome 8.00
OV Omar Vizquel 4.00
LW Larry Walker 4.00
VW Vernon Wells 4.00
BW Bernie Williams 8.00
KW Kerry Wood 8.00

2004 Upper Deck First Pitch

STAR ROOKIES — MIGUEL CABRERA — MARLINS

NM/M
Complete Set (300): 40.00
Common Player: .10
Common SP (271-300): 1.00
Inserted 1:4
Pack (5): 1.00
Box (36): 25.00
1 Dontrelle Willis .50
2 Edgar Gonzalez .25
3 Jose Reyes .50
4 Jae Weong Seo .25
5 Miguel Cabrera .75
6 Jesse Foppert .25
7 Mike Neu .25
8 Micheal Nakamura .25
9 Luis Ayala .25
10 Jared Sandberg .25
11 Jhonny Peralta .25
12 Wilfredo Ledezma .25
13 Jason Roach .25
14 Kirk Saarloos .25
15 Cliff Lee .25
16 Bobby Hill .25
17 Lyle Overbay .25
18 Josh Hall .25
19 Joe Thurston .25
20 Matt Kata .25
21 Jeremy Bonderman .25
22 Julio Manon .25
23 Rodrigo Rosario .25
24 Robby Hammock .25
25 David Sanders .25
26 Miguel Ojeda .25
27 Mark Teixeira .50
28 Franklyn German .10
29 Ken Harvey .25
30 Xavier Nady .25
31 Tim Salmon .25
32 Troy Glaus .25
33 Adam Kennedy .10
34 David Eckstein .10
35 Bengie Molina .10
36 Jarrod Washburn .10
37 Ramon Ortiz .10
38 Eric Chavez .25
39 Miguel Tejada .25
40 Chris Singleton .10
41 Jermaine Dye .10
42 John Halama .10
43 Tim Hudson .25
44 Barry Zito .25
45 Ted Lilly .25
46 Bobby Kielty .10
47 Kelvim Escobar .10
48 Josh Phelps .10

49 Vernon Wells .20
50 Roy Halladay .20
51 Orlando Hudson .10
52 Eric Hinske .10
53 Brandon Backe .10
54 Dewon Brazelton .10
55 Ben Grieve .10
56 Aubrey Huff .10
57 Toby Hall .10
58 Rocco Baldelli .50
59 Al Martin .10
60 Brandon Phillips .10
61 Omar Vizquel .10
62 C.C. Sabathia .10
63 Ricky Gutierrez .10
64 Milton Bradley .10
65 Matt Lawton .10
66 Danys Baez .10
67 Ichiro Suzuki 1.00
68 Randy Winn .10
69 Carlos Guillen .10
70 Mark McLemore .10
71 Dan Wilson .10
72 Jamie Moyer .10
73 Joel Pineiro .10
74 Edgar Martinez .10
75 Tony Batista .10
76 Jay Gibbons .10
77 Jeff Conine .10
78 Melvin Mora .10
79 Geronimo Gil .10
80 Rodrigo Lopez .10
81 Jorge Julio .10
82 Rafael Palmeiro .40
83 Juan Gonzalez .40
84 Mike Young .10
85 Alex Rodriguez 1.00
86 Einar Diaz .10
87 Kevin Mench .10
88 Hank Blalock .25
89 Pedro J. Martinez .50
90 Byung-Hyun Kim .10
91 Jason Varitek .10
92 Derek Lowe .20
93 Manny Ramirez .40
94 John Burkett .10
95 Todd Walker .10
96 Nomar Garciaparra 1.00
97 Trot Nixon .10
98 Mike Sweeney .10
99 Carlos Febles .10
100 Mike MacDougal .10
101 Raul Ibanez .10
102 Jason Grimsley .10
103 Chris George .10
104 Brent Mayne .10
105 Dmitri Young .10
106 Eric Munson .10
107 A.J. Hinch .10
108 Andres Torres .10
109 Bobby Higginson .10
110 Shane Halter .10
111 Matt Walbeck .10
112 Torii Hunter .25
113 Doug Mientkiewicz .10
114 Lew Ford .10
115 Eric Milton .10
116 Eddie Guardado .10
117 Cristian Guzman .10
118 Corey Koskie .10
119 Magglio Ordonez .25
120 Mark Buehrle .10
121 Billy Koch .10
122 Jose Valentin .10
123 Paul Konerko .10
124 Carlos Lee .10
125 Jon Garland .10
126 Jason Giambi .50
127 Derek Jeter 1.50
128 Roger Clemens 1.00
129 Andy Pettitte .25
130 Jorge Posada .25
131 David Wells .10
132 Hideki Matsui 1.25
133 Mike Mussina .40
134 Jeff Bagwell .40
135 Craig Biggio .20
136 Morgan Ensberg .10
137 Richard Hidalgo .10
138 Brad Ausmus .10
139 Roy Oswalt .25
140 Billy Wagner .20
141 Octavio Dotel .10
142 Gary Sheffield .25
143 Andruw Jones .40
144 John Smoltz .20
145 Rafael Furcal .20
146 Javy Lopez .25
147 Shane Reynolds .10
148 Horacio Ramirez .10
149 Mike Hampton .10
150 Jung Bong .10
151 Ruben Quevedo .10
152 Ben Sheets .10
153 Geoff Jenkins .10
154 Royce Clayton .10
155 Glendon Rusch .10
156 John Vander Wal .10
157 Scott Podsednik .25
158 Jim Edmonds .25
159 Tino Martinez .20
160 Albert Pujols 1.00
161 Matt Morris .10
162 Woody Williams .10
163 Edgar Renteria .10
164 Jason Isringhausen .10
165 Jason Simontacchi .10
166 Kerry Robinson .10

167 Sammy Sosa 1.00
168 Joe Borowski .10
169 Tony Womack .10
170 Antonio Alfonseca .10
171 Corey Patterson .10
172 Mark Prior .75
173 Moises Alou .20
174 Matt Clement .10
175 Randall Simon .10
176 Randy Johnson .20
177 Luis Gonzalez .20
178 Craig Counsell .10
179 Miguel Batista .10
180 Steve Finley .10
181 Brandon Webb .10
182 Danny Bautista .10
183 Oscar Villarreal .10
184 Shawn Green .25
185 Brian Jordan .10
186 Fred McGriff .20
187 Andy Ashby .10
188 Rickey Henderson .25
189 Dave Roberts .10
190 Eric Gagne .20
191 Kazuhisa Ishii .10
192 Adrian Beltre .10
193 Vladimir Guerrero .50
194 Livan Hernandez .10
195 Ron Calloway .10
196 Sun-Woo Kim .10
197 Wil Cordero .10
198 Brad Wilkerson .10
199 Orlando Cabrera .10
200 Sidney Ponson .10
201 Ray Durham .10
202 Andres Galarraga .10
203 Benito Santiago .10
204 Jose Cruz Jr. .10
205 Jason Schmidt .10
206 Kirk Rueter .10
207 Felix Rodriguez .10
208 Mike Lowell .10
209 Luis Castillo .10
210 Derrek Lee .10
211 Andy Fox .10
212 Tommy Phelps .10
213 Todd Hollandsworth .10
214 Brad Penny .10
215 Juan Pierre .10
216 Mike Piazza .75
217 Jae Weong Seo .10
218 Ty Wigginton .10
219 Al Leiter .10
220 Roger Cedeno .10
221 Timoniel Perez .10
222 Aaron Heilman .10
223 Pedro Astacio .10
224 Joe McEwing .10
225 Ryan Klesko .20
226 Brian Giles .20
227 Mark Kotsay .10
228 Brian Lawrence .10
229 Rod Beck .10
230 Trevor Hoffman .10
231 Sean Burroughs .10
232 Bobby Abreu .20
233 Jim Thome .50
234 David Bell .10
235 Jimmy Rollins .20
236 Mike Lieberthal .10
237 Vicente Padilla .10
238 Randy Wolf .10
239 Reggie Sanders .10
240 Jason Kendall .10
241 Jack Wilson .10
242 Jose Hernandez .10
243 Kip Wells .10
244 Carlos Rivera .10
245 Craig Wilson .10
246 Adam Dunn .25
247 Sean Casey .10
248 Danny Graves .10
249 Ryan Dempster .10
250 Barry Larkin .25
251 Reggie Taylor .10
252 Wily Mo Pena .10
253 Larry Walker .10
254 Mark Sweeney .10
255 Preston Wilson .10
256 Jason Jennings .10
257 Charles Johnson .10
258 Jay Payton .10
259 Chris Stynes .10
260 Juan Uribe .10
261 Hideki Matsui/CL .50
262 Josh Beckett/CL .25
263 Dontrelle Willis/CL .25
264 Kevin Millwood/CL .10
265 Billy Wagner/CL .10
266 Rocco Baldelli/CL .25
267 Roger Clemens/CL .50
268 Rafael Palmeiro/CL .20
269 Miguel Cabrera/CL .25
270 Jose Contreras/CL .25
271 Rickie Weeks 3.00
272 Delmon Young 4.00
273 Chien-Ming Wang 1.00
274 Rich Harden 1.00
275 Edwin Jackson 1.50
276 Dan Haren 1.00
277 Todd Wellemeyer 1.00
278 Prentice Redman 1.00
279 Ryan Wagner 1.50
280 Aaron Looper 1.00
281 Rick Roberts 1.00
282 Josh Willingham 1.00
283 David Crouthers 1.00
284 Chris Capuano 1.00

285 Mike Gosling 1.00
286 Brian Sweeney 1.00
287 Donald Kelly RC 1.00
288 Ryan Meaux RC 1.50
289 Colin Porter 1.00
290 Jerome Gamble RC 1.50
291 Colby Miller RC 1.50
292 Ian Ferguson 1.00
293 Tim Bittner RC 1.00
294 Jason Frasor RC 1.00
295 Brandon Medders RC 1.00
296 Mike Johnston RC 1.00
297 Tim Bausher RC 1.00
298 Justin Leone RC 1.00
299 Sean Henn 1.00
300 Michel Hernandez 1.00

First and Foremost

NM/M
Complete Set (14): 40.00
Common Player: 3.00
Inserted 1:Blaster Box
EB Ernie Banks 5.00
GH George H.W. Bush 5.00
GW George W. Bush 5.00
JC Jose Contreras 3.00
WF Whitey Ford 4.00
RH Rich Harden 3.00
DH Dan Haren 3.00
HR Horacio Ramirez 3.00
MS Mike Schmidt 5.00
LT Luis Tiant 3.00
RW Ryan Wagner 3.00
BW Brandon Webb 3.00
JW Jerome Williams 3.00
DW Dontrelle Willis 3.00

Holiday Greeting Card

Continuing its tradition of producing a hobby-related greeting card for its customers, UD in 2004 issued a postcard-sized (6-1/4" x 4-5/8") card featuring a composite black-and-white photo of Yankees greats. The red-and-green design on front includes a replica of the 1939 Baseball Centennial stamp and a Cooperstown postmark.

NM/M
HH04 Babe Ruth, Lou Gehrig, Joe DiMaggio, Mickey Mantle, Derek Jeter 4.00

Japan Series Souvenir Sheet

It was reported that 200,000 of these 7-1/2" x 10-1/2" souvenir sheets were produced to commemorate the 2004 season opening series in Japan between the Yankees and Devil Rays. Sheets were distributed at the exhibition games played between the MLB and Japanese teams. Some were reportedly given to youngsters at the ESPN Zone in New York City as well. Fronts picture three Yankees, three Devil Rays and a pair of Japanese players. On back is a large ghosted image of Hideki Matsui over which is printed in Japanese addresses and phone numbers of UD outlets. The sheets are not perforated.

NM/M
Uncut Sheet: 15.00

2004 UD Legends Timeless Teams

	NM/M
Complete Set (300):	40.00
Common Player:	.15
Pack (5):	5.00
Box (18):	75.00

1 Bob Gibson .50
2 Lou Brock .50
3 Ray Washburn .15
4 Tim McCarver .15
5 Harmon Killebrew 1.00
6 Jim Kaat .25
7 Jim Perry .15
8 Jim "Mudcat" Grant .15
9 Boog Powell .15
10 Brooks Robinson .50
11 Frank Robinson .50
12 Jim Palmer .50
13 Carl Yastrzemski 1.00
14 Jim Lonborg .15
15 George Scott .15
16 Sparky Lyle .15
17 Rico Petrocelli .15
18 Bob Gibson .50
19 Julian Javier .15
20 Lou Brock .50
21 Orlando Cepeda .15
22 Ray Washburn .15
23 Steve Carlton .50
24 Tim McCarver .15
25 Al Kaline .50
26 Bill Freehan .15
27 Denny McLain .15
28 Dick McAuliffe .15
29 Jim Northrup .15
30 John Hiller .15
31 Mickey Lolich .15
32 Mickey Stanley .15
33 Willie Horton .15
34 Bob Gibson .50
35 Julian Javier .15
36 Lou Brock .50
37 Orlando Cepeda .25
38 Steve Carlton .50
39 Boog Powell .15
40 Brooks Robinson .50
41 Davey Johnson .15
42 Merv Rettenmund .15
43 Eddie Watt .15
44 Frank Robinson .50
45 Jim Palmer .25
46 Mike Cuellar .15
47 Paul Blair .15
48 Pete Richert .15
49 Ellie Hendricks .15
50 Billy Williams .25
51 Randy Hundley .15
52 Ernie Banks 1.00
53 Fergie Jenkins .25
54 Jim Hickman .15
55 Ken Holtzman .15
56 Ron Santo .25
57 Ed Kranepool .15
58 Jerry Koosman .15
59 Nolan Ryan 2.00
60 Tom Seaver .50
61 Boog Powell .15
62 Brooks Robinson .50
63 Davey Johnson .15
64 Merv Rettenmund .15
65 Eddie Watt .15
66 Frank Robinson .50
67 Jim Palmer .25
68 Mike Cuellar .15
69 Paul Blair .15
70 Pete Richert .15
71 Ellie Hendricks .15
72 Al Kaline .50
73 Bill Freehan .15
74 Dick McAuliffe .15
75 Jim Northrup .15
76 John Hiller .15
77 Mickey Lolich .15
78 Mickey Stanley .15
79 Willie Horton .15
80 Bert Campaneris .15
81 Blue Moon Odom .15
82 Sal Bando .15
83 Joe Rudi .15
84 Ken Holtzman .15
85 Bill North .15
86 Blue Moon Odom .15
87 Gene Tenace .15

88 Manny Trillo .15
89 Dick Green .15
90 Rollie Fingers .25
91 Sal Bando .15
92 Vida Blue .15
93 Bill Buckner .15
94 Davey Lopes .15
95 Don Sutton .25
96 Al Downing .15
97 Ron Cey .15
98 Steve Garvey .15
99 Tommy John .15
100 Bert Campaneris .15
101 Bill North .15
102 Joe Rudi .15
103 Sal Bando .15
104 Vida Blue .15
105 Carl Yastrzemski .75
106 Carlton Fisk .25
107 Cecil Cooper .15
108 Dwight Evans .15
109 Fred Lynn .15
110 Jim Rice .15
111 Luis Tiant .15
112 Rick Burleson .15
113 Rico Petrocelli .15
114 Pedro Borbon .15
115 Dave Concepcion .15
116 Don Gullett .15
117 George Foster .15
118 Joe Morgan .25
119 Johnny Bench .50
120 Rawly Eastwick .15
121 Sparky Anderson .15
122 Tony Perez .15
123 Billy Williams .25
124 Gene Tenace .15
125 Jim Perry .15
126 Vida Blue .15
127 Pedro Borbon .15
128 Dave Concepcion .15
129 Don Gullett .15
130 George Foster .15
131 Joe Morgan .25
132 Johnny Bench .50
133 Ken Griffey Sr. .15
134 Rawly Eastwick .15
135 Tony Perez .25
136 Bill Russell .15
137 Burt Hooton .15
138 Davey Lopes .15
139 Don Sutton .25
140 Dusty Baker .15
141 Steve Yeager .15
142 Ron Cey .15
143 Steve Garvey .15
144 Tommy John .15
145 Bucky Dent .15
146 Chris Chambliss .15
147 Ed Figueroa .15
148 Graig Nettles .15
149 Lou Piniella .25
150 Roy White .15
151 Don Gullett .15
152 Sparky Lyle .15
153 Brian Doyle .15
154 Bucky Dent .15
155 Chris Chambliss .15
156 Ed Figueroa .15
157 Graig Nettles .15
158 Lou Piniella .25
159 Roy White .15
160 Rich "Goose" Gossage .15
161 Sparky Lyle .15
162 Bobby Grich .15
163 Brian Downing .15
164 Dan Ford .15
165 Nolan Ryan 2.00
166 Dave Concepcion .15
167 George Foster .15
168 Johnny Bench .50
169 Ray Knight .15
170 Tom Seaver .50
171 Bert Blyleven .15
172 Bill Madlock .15
173 Dave Parker .25
174 Phil Garner .15
175 Bill Russell .15
176 Steve Yeager .15
177 Don Sutton .25
178 Dusty Baker .25
179 Jerry Reuss .15
180 Mickey Hatcher .15
181 Pedro Guerrero .15
182 Ron Cey .15
183 Steve Garvey .15
184 Rudy May .15
185 Brian Doyle .15
186 Bucky Dent .15
187 Jim Kaat .15
188 Lou Piniella .15
189 Luis Tiant .15
190 Tommy John .15
191 Bake McBride .15
192 Bob Boone .15
193 Dickie Noles .15
194 Manny Trillo .15
195 Mike Schmidt 1.00
196 Sparky Lyle .15
197 Steve Carlton .50
198 Steve Yeager .15
199 Burt Hooton .15
200 Dusty Baker .15
201 Jerry Reuss .15
202 Mike Scioscia .15
203 Pedro Guerrero .15
204 Ron Cey .15
205 Steve Garvey .15

206 Alejandro Pena .15
207 Steve Sax .15
208 Cecil Cooper .15
209 Gorman Thomas .15
210 Paul Molitor .50
211 Robin Yount 1.00
212 Rollie Fingers .25
213 Don Money .15
214 Rudy May .15
215 Bucky Dent .15
216 Dave Winfield .50
217 Lou Piniella .25
218 Rich "Goose" Gossage .15
219 Tommy John .15
220 Cecil Cooper .15
221 Gorman Thomas .15
222 Paul Molitor .50
223 Robin Yount 1.00
224 Don Money .15
225 Cal Ripken Jr. 2.00
226 Dan Ford .15
227 Jim Palmer .25
228 John Shelby .15
229 Alan Trammell .25
230 Chet Lemon .15
231 Howard Johnson .15
232 Jack Morris .15
233 Kirk Gibson .25
234 Lou Whitaker .15
235 Sparky Anderson .15
236 Dave Winfield .50
237 Don Mattingly 1.00
238 Ken Griffey Sr. .15
239 Phil Niekro .15
240 Yogi Berra .75
241 Bill Buckner .15
242 Bruce Hurst .15
243 Dave Henderson .15
244 Dwight Evans .15
245 Jim Rice .25
246 Tom Seaver .50
247 Wade Boggs .50
248 Bob Boone .15
249 Bobby Grich .15
250 Brian Downing .15
251 Don Sutton .25
252 Terry Forster .15
253 Rick Burleson .15
254 Wally Joyner .15
255 Darryl Strawberry .15
256 Dwight Gooden .15
257 Gary Carter .15
258 Jesse Orosco .15
259 Keith Hernandez .15
260 Lenny Dykstra .15
261 Mookie Wilson .15
262 Ray Knight .15
263 Wally Backman .15
264 Sid Fernandez .15
265 Alan Trammell .25
266 Dan Petry .15
267 Chet Lemon .15
268 Sparky Anderson .15
269 Jack Morris .15
270 Kirk Gibson .15
271 Lou Whitaker .15
272 Bert Blyleven .15
273 Kent Hrbek .15
274 Kirby Puckett .75
275 Alejandro Pena .15
276 Jesse Orosco .15
277 John Shelby .15
278 Kirk Gibson .15
279 Mickey Hatcher .15
280 Mike Scioscia .15
281 Steve Sax .15
282 Darryl Strawberry .15
283 Dwight Gooden .15
284 Gary Carter .15
285 Howard Johnson .15
286 Keith Hernandez .15
287 Lenny Dykstra .15
288 Mookie Wilson .15
289 Wally Backman .15
290 Sid Fernandez .15
291 Jack Morris .15
292 Kent Hrbek .15
293 Kirby Puckett .75
294 Dave Winfield .50
295 Jack Morris .15
296 Joe Carter .15
297 Don Mattingly 1.00
298 Paul O'Neill .15
299 Jack McDowell .15
300 Wade Boggs .50

Teams Gold
No Pricing
Production 5 Sets

Autographs

	NM/M
Common Autograph:	10.00
Golds:	No Pricing
Production 5 Sets	
Platinum:	No Pricing
Production One Set	

2 Lou Brock MM/SP/75 20.00
3 Ray Washburn 10.00
4 Tim McCarver 15.00
5 Harmon Killebrew 40.00
6 Jim Kaat 10.00
7 Jim Perry 12.00
9 Boog Powell 10.00
10 Brooks Robinson 35.00

12 Jim Palmer/SP/50 20.00
13 Carl Yastrzemski/SP/25 80.00
14 Jim Lonborg 10.00
15 George Scott 10.00
16 Sparky Lyle 10.00
17 Rico Petrocelli 10.00
18 Bob Gibson/SP/35 40.00
19 Julian Javier 10.00
20 Lou Brock/SP/60 20.00
21 Orlando Cepeda/SP/50 20.00
23 Ray Washburn 10.00
24 Tim McCarver 12.00
25 Al Kaline 25.00
26 Bill Freehan 10.00
27 Denny McLain 20.00
28 Dick McAuliffe 10.00
29 Jim Northrup 10.00
30 John Hiller 10.00
31 Mickey Lolich 10.00
32 Mickey Stanley 10.00
33 Willie Horton 10.00
35 Julian Javier 10.00
36 Lou Brock/SP/50 20.00
38 Steve Carlton/SP/35 30.00
39 Boog Powell 10.00
40 Brooks Robinson/SP/100 40.00
41 Davey Johnson 10.00
42 Merv Rettenmund 10.00
43 Eddie Watt 10.00
46 Mike Cuellar 10.00
47 Paul Blair 10.00
48 Pete Richert 10.00
49 Ellie Hendricks 10.00
50 Billy Williams/SP/75 25.00
51 Randy Hundley 10.00
53 Fergie Jenkins 15.00
54 Jim Hickman 20.00
55 Ken Holtzman 15.00
56 Ron Santo 25.00
57 Ed Kranepool 10.00
58 Jerry Koosman 15.00
59 Nolan Ryan/SP/50 175.00
60 Tom Seaver/SP/50 50.00
61 Boog Powell 12.00
62 Brooks Robinson/SP/35 50.00
63 Davey Johnson 10.00
64 Merv Rettenmund 10.00
65 Eddie Watt 10.00
66 Frank Robinson/SP/50 30.00
67 Jim Palmer/SP/75 20.00
68 Mike Cuellar 12.00
69 Paul Blair 10.00
70 Pete Richert 10.00
71 Ellie Hendricks 10.00
72 Al Kaline 25.00
73 Bill Freehan 10.00
74 Dick McAuliffe 15.00
75 Jim Northrup 10.00
76 John Hiller 10.00
77 Mickey Lolich 15.00
78 Mickey Stanley 10.00
79 Willie Horton 12.00
80 Bert Campaneris 10.00
81 Blue Moon Odom 15.00
82 Sal Bando Exch 10.00
83 Joe Rudi 10.00
84 Ken Holtzman 10.00
85 Bill North 10.00
86 Blue Moon Odom 15.00
87 Gene Tenace 10.00
88 Manny Trillo 15.00
89 Dick Green 15.00
90 Rollie Fingers 15.00
91 Sal Bando 15.00
92 Vida Blue 15.00
93 Bill Buckner 15.00
94 Davey Lopes 15.00
95 Don Sutton 15.00
96 Al Downing MM 10.00
100 Bert Campaneris 10.00
101 Bill North 10.00
102 Joe Rudi 10.00
103 Sal Bando 10.00
104 Vida Blue/SP/100 15.00
105 Carl Yastrzemski/SP/50 60.00
106 Carlton Fisk/SP/100 30.00

107 Cecil Cooper/SP/75 15.00
108 Dwight Evans/SP/75 10.00
109 Fred Lynn 10.00
110 Jim Rice/SP/100 20.00
111 Luis Tiant/Exch 10.00
112 Rick Burleson 10.00
113 Rico Petrocelli 10.00
114 Pedro Borbon 10.00
115 Dave Concepcion/Exch 10.00
116 Don Gullett 10.00
117 George Foster/SP/50 15.00
119 Johnny Bench/SP/85 50.00
121 Rawly Eastwick 10.00
122 Sparky Anderson 10.00
123 Tony Perez 30.00
124 Billy Williams/SP/50 20.00
125 Gene Tenace 10.00
126 Vida Blue/SP/75 20.00
127 Pedro Borbon 10.00
128 Dave Concepcion/Exch 10.00
129 Don Gullett 15.00
133 Ken Griffey Sr. 10.00
134 Rawly Eastwick 10.00
135 Tony Perez 30.00
137 Bill Russell 10.00
138 Burt Hooton 10.00
139 Davey Lopes 10.00
141 Don Sutton 10.00
144 Tommy John/SP/35 15.00
145 Bucky Dent/SP/75 15.00
147 Ed Figueroa 15.00
148 Graig Nettles 15.00
150 Roy White 15.00
151 Don Gullett 10.00
152 Sparky Lyle 10.00
153 Brian Doyle 10.00
155 Chris Chambliss 10.00
156 Ed Figueroa 15.00
157 Graig Nettles 15.00
160 Rich "Goose" Gossage 15.00
161 Sparky Lyle 15.00
162 Bobby Grich 15.00
163 Brian Downing 10.00
164 Dan Ford 10.00
166 Dave Concepcion/SP/75 Exch 10.00
169 Ray White 10.00
171 Bert Blyleven 15.00
172 Bill Madlock 10.00
173 Dave Parker 12.00
174 Phil Garner 10.00
176 Steve Yeager 15.00
177 Don Sutton/SP/50 20.00
178 Dusty Baker 15.00
179 Jerry Reuss 10.00
180 Mickey Hatcher 10.00
181 Pedro Guerrero 10.00
182 Ron Cey/SP/50 15.00
183 Steve Garvey/SP/50 15.00
184 Rudy May 15.00
185 Brian Doyle 15.00
186 Bucky Dent/SP/60 15.00
187 Jim Kaat 10.00
188 Lou Piniella/SP/50 15.00
189 Luis Tiant 10.00
190 Tommy John/SP/50 15.00
191 Bake McBride 10.00
192 Bob Boone 10.00
193 Dickie Noles 10.00
194 Manny Trillo 15.00
195 Mike Schmidt/SP/50 75.00
196 Sparky Lyle 10.00
197 Steve Carlton/SP/50 20.00
198 Steve Yeager 10.00
199 Burt Hooton 10.00
200 Dusty Baker Exch 15.00
202 Jerry Reuss 10.00
203 Mike Scioscia 10.00
204 Pedro Guerrero 10.00
205 Ron Cey/SP/75 15.00
206 Steve Garvey/SP/75 15.00
207 Alejandro Pena 10.00
208 Steve Sax/SP/100 15.00
209 Cecil Cooper/SP/85 15.00
212 Rollie Fingers 15.00
213 Don Money 10.00
214 Rudy May 10.00
216 Dave Winfield/SP/50 30.00
217 Lou Piniella/SP/75 15.00
218 Rich "Goose" Gossage 15.00
219 Tommy John/SP/75 10.00
220 Cecil Cooper 15.00
221 Gorman Thomas/Exch 10.00
222 Paul Molitor/SP/50 45.00
223 Robin Yount/SP/50 75.00
224 Don Money 10.00
225 Cal Ripken Jr./SP/50 180.00
226 Dan Ford 10.00
228 John Shelby 10.00
229 Alan Trammell 15.00
230 Chet Lemon 10.00
231 Howard Johnson 10.00

232 Jack Morris/SP/35 15.00
233 Kirk Gibson 10.00
234 Lou Whitaker/SP/100 15.00
235 Sparky Anderson 10.00
237 Don Mattingly/SP/50 60.00
238 Ken Griffey Sr. 15.00
239 Phil Niekro 15.00
240 Yogi Berra/SP/47 50.00
241 Bill Buckner 15.00
242 Bruce Hurst 15.00
243 Dave Henderson 10.00
245 Jim Rice/SP/35 Exch
247 Wade Boggs/SP/35 30.00
248 Bob Boone 10.00
249 Bobby Grich 10.00
250 Brian Downing 10.00
251 Don Sutton/SP/75 10.00
252 Terry Forster 10.00
253 Rick Burleson 10.00
254 Wally Joyner 15.00
255 Darryl Strawberry 15.00
256 Dwight Gooden 15.00
257 Gary Carter/SP/75 20.00
258 Jesse Orosco 10.00
259 Keith Hernandez 15.00
260 Lenny Dykstra 10.00
261 Mookie Wilson 10.00
262 Ray Knight 10.00
263 Wally Backman 10.00
264 Sid Fernandez Exch 10.00
265 Alan Trammell 15.00
266 Dan Petry 10.00
267 Chet Lemon 10.00
268 Sparky Anderson 10.00
270 Kirk Gibson 15.00
271 Lou Whitaker/SP/50 20.00
272 Bert Blyleven 10.00
273 Kent Hrbek 15.00
275 Alejandro Pena 10.00
276 Jesse Orosco 10.00
277 John Shelby 10.00
278 Kirk Gibson/SP/50 20.00
279 Mickey Hatcher 10.00
280 Mike Scioscia 10.00
281 Steve Sax 10.00
282 Darryl Strawberry 15.00
283 Dwight Gooden 15.00
284 Gary Carter/SP/50 20.00
285 Howard Johnson 15.00
286 Keith Hernandez 15.00
287 Lenny Dykstra 10.00
288 Mookie Wilson 10.00
289 Wally Backman 10.00
290 Sid Fernandez Exch 10.00
291 Jack Morris/SP/50 15.00
292 Kent Hrbek 15.00
293 Kirby Puckett/SP/50 50.00
294 Dave Winfield/SP/35 35.00
295 Jack Morris/SP/75 15.00
298 Paul O'Neill 40.00
299 Jack McDowell 10.00
300 Wade Boggs/SP/75 25.00

Legendary Combo Signatures
No Pricing

Legendary Combo Cuts
No Pricing

Legendary Signature Dual

	NM/M
Quantity produced listed	

BC Lou Brock, Orlando Cepeda/75 40.00
BJ Lou Brock, Julian Javier/150 25.00
BM Wade Boggs, Don Mattingly/50 140.00
BO Vida Blue, Blue Moon Odom/150 25.00
BW Ernie Banks, Billy Williams/25 100.00
CB Steve Carlton, Bret Boone/150 50.00
CG Ron Cey, Steve Garvey/150 40.00
CH Gary Carter, Keith Hernandez/150 30.00
CM Dave Concepcion, Joe Morgan/75 Exch 35.00
DD Bucky Dent, Brian Doyle/150 25.00
FR Fred Lynn, Jim Rice/150 40.00
GA Kirk Gibson, Sparky Anderson/150 40.00
GB Bob Gibson, Lou Brock/50 75.00
GC Dwight Gooden, Gary Carter/150 30.00
GL Rich "Goose" Gossage, Sparky Lyle/150 Exch 25.00
HJ Ken Holtzman, Fergie Jenkins/150 40.00
HK Keith Hernandez, Ray Knight/150 30.00
JH Fergie Jenkins, Randy Hundley/150 40.00
JS Tommy John, Don Sutton/150

Abbreviations
SP - Short Print

KH	Al Kaline, Willie Horton/150	40.00
KK	Harmon Killebrew, Jim Kaat/150	50.00
LM	Mickey Lolich, Denny McLain/75	60.00
MB	Joe Morgan, Johnny Bench/25	80.00
MF	Denny McLain, Bill Freehan/150	40.00
NC	Graig Nettles, Chris Chambliss/150	30.00
OM	Paul O'Neill, Don Mattingly/75	140.00
PC	Jim Palmer, Mike Cuellar/150	30.00
PF	Tony Perez, George Foster/150	40.00
PH	Kirby Puckett, Kent Hrbek/50	65.00
PN	Lou Piniella, Graig Nettles/150	30.00
PR	Jim Palmer, Merv Rettenmund/150	35.00
RL	Bill Russell, Davey Lopes/150	30.00
RR	Brooks Robinson, Frank Robinson/50	70.00
RS	Nolan Ryan, Tom Seaver/25	250.00
SD	Steve Garvey, Davey Lopes/150	25.00
SG	Darryl Strawberry, Dwight Gooden/150	40.00
SY	Don Sutton, Steve Yeager/150	30.00
TF	Luis Tiant, Carlton Fisk/50	45.00
TM	Gorman Thomas, Paul Molitor/ 150 Exch	35.00
WB	Mookie Wilson, Bill Buckner/150	30.00
WT	Lou Whitaker, Alan Trammell/75	75.00
YM	Robin Yount, Paul Molitor/50	120.00
YP	Carl Yastrzemski, Rico Petrocelli/50	75.00

Legendary Signatrue Triple
NM/M

Quantity produced listed

BCM	Johnny Bench, Dave Concepcion, Joe Morgan/ 25 Exch	100.00
BOM	Wade Boggs, Paul O'Neill, Don Mattingly/50	150.00
BRB	Sal Bando, Joe Rudi, Vida Blue/75	50.00
BSW	Ernie Banks, Ron Santo, Billy Williams/25	140.00
CDK	Gary Carter, Lenny Dykstra, Ray Knight/50	75.00
CND	Chris Chambliss, Graig Nettles, Bucky Dent/50	50.00
ERL	Dwight Evans, Jim Rice, Fred Lynn/50	125.00
GBC	Steve Garvey, Dusty Baker, Ron Cey/50	75.00
GBM	Bob Gibson, Lou Brock, Tim McCarver/25	100.00
GDR	Bobby Grich, Al Downing, Nolan Ryan/25	175.00
GHS	Kirk Gibson, Mickey Hatcher, Mike Scioscia/75	85.00
GMP	Phil Garner, Bill Madlock, Dave Parker/50	75.00
HHS	Jim Hickman, Ken Holtzman, Ron Santo/75	60.00
HSJ	Burt Hooton, Don Sutton, Tommy John/50	50.00
JHH	Fergie Jenkins, Randy Hundley, Ken Holtzman/75	50.00
KKP	Harmon Killebrew, Jim Kaat, Jim Perry/50	65.00
KPG	Jim Kaat, Jim Perry, Jim "Mudcat" Grant/ 75 Exch	40.00
KSR	Jerry Koosman, Tom Seaver, Nolan Ryan/25	250.00
MHP	Jack Morris, Kent Hrbek, Kirby Puckett/50	100.00
MLF	Denny McLain, Mickey Lolich, Bill Freehan/50	60.00
NKH	Jim Northrup, Al Kaline, Willie Horton/75	65.00
PBH	Kirby Puckett, Bert Blyleven, Kent Hrbek/50	90.00
PCR	Jim Palmer, Mike Cuellar, Pete Richert/75	45.00
PPW	Jim Palmer, Boog Powell, Earl Weaver/75	60.00
RPR	Frank Robinson, Boog Powell, Brooks Robinson/50	80.00
RWP	Cal Ripken Jr., Earl Weaver, Jim Palmer/25	250.00
SCB	Mike Schmidt, Steve Carlton, Bob Boone/50	125.00
SGS	Steve Sax, Pedro Guerrero, Mike Scioscia/75	60.00
TWA	Alan Trammell, Lou Whitaker, Sparky Anderson/50	75.00
YCT	Robin Yount, Cecil Cooper, Gorman Thomas/ 50 Exch	120.00
YFT	Carl Yastrzemski, Carlton Fisk, Luis Tiant/25	140.00
YMT	Robin Yount, Paul Molitor, Gorman Thomas/ 75 Exch	140.00

Team Terrific GU Brand Logo
NM/M

Quantity produced listed

BO	Baltimore Orioles/35	90.00
BR	Boston Red Sox/35	80.00
CR	Cincinnati Reds/35	80.00
LD	Los Angeles Dodgers/35	60.00
MB	Milwaukee Brewers/41	50.00
NM	New York Mets/35	50.00
OA	Oakland A's/39	40.00
SC	St. Louis Cardinals/35	75.00

Team Terrific GU Hat Logo
NM/M

Quantity produced listed

BO	Baltimore Orioles/50	90.00
BR	Boston Red Sox/50	80.00
CR	Cincinnati Reds/50	80.00
LD	Los Angeles Dodgers/50	60.00
MB	Milwaukee Brewers/82	40.00
NM	New York Mets/50	50.00
OA	Oakland A's/50	40.00
SC	St. Louis Cardinals/ 50	75.00

Team Terrific GU League
No Pricing
Production 15 Sets

Team Terrific GU Stats
No Pricing
Production 1-5

Team Terrific GU Team Logo
NM/M

Quantity produced listed

BO	Baltimore Orioles/85	60.00
BR	Boston Red Sox/85	50.00
CR	Cincinnati Reds/85	75.00
LD	Los Angeles Dodgers/85	50.00
MB	Milwaukee Brewers/100	30.00
NM	New York Mets/85	50.00
OA	Oakland A's/100	30.00
SC	St. Louis Cardinals/100	50.00

National Trading Card Day

As part of its participation in NTCD on April 3, Upper Deck issued a 15-card foil pack with four baseball player cards, two each football and hockey, three basketball and four golf, plus a header. Only the baseball players are listed here. Fronts have action photos on a ghosted background; backs have recent stats, a photo detail and biographical data. The NTCD logo appears on front in silver foil.

NM/M

Unopened Pack:		4.00
Common Player:		.25
UD-2	Hideki Matsui	.50
UD-3	Ichiro	.50
UD-5	Ken Griffey Jr.	.25
UD-12	Sammy Sosa	.25

National VIP

Persons purchasing a VIP admission package at the 2004 National Sports Collectors Convention in Cleveland received a cello-wrapped pack of five UV-coated cards with silver-foil stamping on front. Only one baseball player was included.

NM/M

Complete Set (5):		12.00
VIP3	Derek Jeter	3.00

2004 Upper Deck Play Ball Promos

Each July 2004 newsstand issue of Tuff Stuff magazine included a Play Ball promo card inside its poly bag. The cards differ from the issued version only in the appearance on front of a silver-foil "UD PROMO" notation. It is not known how many different plauers cards were used in the promotion.

Common Player:	1.5-2.5X
Stars:	

2004 Upper Deck Play Ball

Complete Set (183):	
Common Player:	.15
Common SP (133-162):	3.00
Production 2,004	
Common Classic Combo (163-183):	2.00
Production 1,999	
Pack (5):	3.00

Box (24):		65.00
1	Hideo Nomo	.25
2	Curt Schilling	.50
3	Barry Zito	.40
4	Nomar Garciaparra	1.50
5	Yogi Berra	.50
6	Randy Johnson	.75
7	Jason Giambi	.75
8	Sammy Sosa	1.25
9	David Ortiz	.40
10	Derek Jeter	2.00
11	Warren Spahn	.50
12	Mark Prior	1.00
13	Roger Clemens	1.50
14	Mike Piazza	1.00
15	Nolan Ryan	2.00
16	Joe DiMaggio	1.50
17	Alfonso Soriano	.75
18	Brandon Webb	.25
19	Shawn Green	.25
20	Bob Feller	.25
21	Mike Schmidt	.75
22	Mark Teixeira	.75
23	Pedro J. Martinez	.75
24	Vladimir Guerrero	.75
25	Rafael Furcal	.25
26	Derek Lee	.25
27	Carlos Delgado	.50
28	Mickey Mantle	.25
29	Dontrelle Willis	.25
30	Ted Williams	1.50
31	Vernon Wells	.25
32	Alex Rodriguez	1.50
33	Brooks Robinson	.50
34	Tom Seaver	.50
35	Ernie Banks	.50
36	Bob Gibson	.50
37	Jim Thome	.75
38	Mike Mussina	.50
39	Eric Chavez	.25
40	Roy Halladay	.25
41	Eric Gagne	.40
42	Jose Reyes	.40
43	Jeff Bagwell	.50
44	Rich Harden	.15
45	Jeff Kent	.25
46	Lance Berkman	.25
47	Adam Dunn	.40
48	Richie Sexson	.40
49	Andruw Jones	.50
50	Ichiro Suzuki	1.25
51	Edgar Renteria	.25
52	Rocco Baldelli	.25
53	Jim Edmonds	.25
54	Magglio Ordonez	.25
55	Austin Kearns	.25
56	Garret Anderson	.40
57	Manny Ramirez	.50
58	Roy Oswalt	.25
59	Gary Sheffield	.40
60	Mark Mulder	.25
61	Ben Sheets	.25
62	Scott Rolen	.75
63	Greg Maddux	1.00
64	Jose Contreras	.15
65	Miguel Cabrera	.40
66	Hank Blalock	.40
67	Miguel Tejada	.40
68	Albert Pujols	1.50
69	Hideki Matsui	1.50
70	Mike Lowell	.25
71	Tim Hudson	.25
72	Bret Boone	.25
73	Ivan Rodriguez	.50
74	Josh Beckett	.50
75	Todd Helton	.50
76	Brian Giles	.25
77	Orlando Cabrera	.15
78	Carlos Beltran	.40
79	Jason Schmidt	.25
80	Kerry Wood	.75
81	Preston Wilson	.15
82	Troy Glaus	.40
83	Kevin Brown	.25
84	Rafael Palmeiro	.25
85	Chipper Jones	1.00
86	Reggie Sanders	.15
87	Cliff Floyd	.15
88	Corey Patterson	.25
89	Kevin Millwood	.25
90	Aaron Boone	.15
91	Darin Erstad	.15
92	Richard Hidalgo	.15
93	Dmitri Young	.15
94	Jeremy Bonderman	.15
95	Larry Walker	.25
96	Edgar Martinez	.25
97	Jerome Williams	.15
98	Luis Gonzalez	.25
99	Roberto Alomar	.40
100	Jerry Hairston Jr.	.15
101	Luis Matos	.15
102	Andy Pettitte	.40
103	Frank Thomas	.50
104	Rondell White	.25
105	Jody Gerut	.15
106	Bartolo Colon	.15
107	Johnny Damon	.25
108	Ryan Klesko	.25
109	Geoff Jenkins	.25
110	Jorge Posada	.40
111	Melvin Mora	.15
112	Bernie Williams	.40
113	Shannon Stewart	.15
114	Bobby Abreu	.25
115	Jose Guillen	.25
116	Brandon Phillips	.15
117	Jose Vidro	.15
118	Mike Sweeney	.15
119	Jacque Jones	.15
120	Josh Phelps	.15
121	Milton Bradley	.15
122	Torii Hunter	.25
123	Carl Crawford	.25
124	Javier Vazquez	.25
125	Juan Gonzalez	.50
126	Travis Hafner	.15
127	Ken Griffey Jr.	1.00
128	Phil Nevin	.15
129	Trot Nixon	.15
130	Carlos Lee	.15
131	Javy Lopez	.25
132	Jay Gibbons	.15
133	Brandon Medders RC	3.00
134	Colby Miller RC	3.00
135	David Crouthers RC	3.00
136	Dennis Sarfate RC	5.00
137	Donald Kelly RC	3.00
138	Frank Brooks RC	5.00
139	Chris Aguila RC	3.00
140	Greg Dobbs RC	3.00
141	Ian Snell RC	3.00
142	Jake Woods RC	3.00
143	Jamie Brown RC	3.00
144	Jason Frasor RC	4.00
145	Jerome Gamble RC	4.00
146	Jesse Harper RC	5.00
147	Josh Labandeira RC	4.00
148	Justin Hampson RC	4.00
149	Justin Huisman RC	4.00
150	Justin Leone RC	5.00
151	Lincoln Holdzkom RC	3.00
152	Mike Bumatay RC	3.00
153	Mike Gosling RC	3.00
154	Mike Johnston RC	3.00
155	Mike Rouse RC	3.00
156	Nick Regilio RC	3.00
157	Ryan Meaux RC	3.00
158	Scott Dohmann RC	3.00
159	Sean Henn RC	6.00
160	Tim Bausher RC	3.00
161	Tim Bittner RC	3.00
162	Alec Zumwalt RC	3.00
163	Aaron Boone, Bret Boone, Geoff Jenkins, Mark Prior, Barry Zito	3.00
164	Albert Pujols, Edgar Renteria, Alex Rodriguez	5.00
165	Alfonso Soriano, Sammy Sosa	4.00
166	Bobby Abreu, Jim Thome	2.00
167	Bret Boone, John Olerud, Ichiro Suzuki	4.00
168	Derek Jeter, Alfonso Soriano	6.00
169	Eric Chavez, Miguel Tejada	2.00
170	Garret Anderson, Jim Edmonds, Troy Glaus	2.00
171	Hank Blalock, Alex Rodriguez	5.00
172	Alex Rodriguez, Mark Teixeira, Michael Young, Rafael Palmeiro	5.00
173	Ivan Rodriguez, Dontrelle Willis	2.00
174	Jason Giambi, Derek Jeter	6.00
175	Joe DiMaggio, Mickey Mantle	8.00
176	Joe DiMaggio, Mickey Mantle, Ted Williams	8.00
177	Joe DiMaggio, Ted Williams	6.00
178	Nomar Garciaparra, Alfonso Soriano	6.00
179	Nomar Garciaparra, Jason Giambi	4.00
180	Paul LoDuca, Hideo Nomo	2.00
181	Rafael Palmeiro, Alex Rodriguez, Michael Young	4.00
182	Ralph Kiner, Ted Williams	5.00
183	Aaron Boone, Derek Jeter	6.00

Blue
Blue (1-132):	2-3X
Inserted 1:6	

Die-Cut
Die-Cut (1-132):	3-6X
Production 175	

Green
No Pricing
Production 15 Sets

Purple
No Pricing
Production One Set

Apparel Collection
NM/M
Common Player:	4.00
Inserted 1:24	

APPAREL COLLECTION

JB	Jeff Bagwell	6.00
RB	Rocco Baldelli	8.00
BE	Josh Beckett	6.00
LB	Lance Berkman	4.00
CD	Carlos Delgado	5.00
JD	Joe DiMaggio/ SP/150	75.00
AD	Adam Dunn	6.00
RF	Rafael Furcal	5.00
JG	Jason Giambi	6.00
TG	Troy Glaus	6.00
KG	Ken Griffey Jr.	15.00
HA	Roy Halladay	8.00
RH	Rich Harden/SP	8.00
BH	Bo Hart	4.00
TH	Torii Hunter	4.00
DJ	Derek Jeter	15.00
RJ	Randy Johnson	8.00
CJ	Chipper Jones	8.00
ML	Mike Lowell	5.00
MM	Mickey Mantle/ SP/150	100.00
PM	Pedro J. Martinez	8.00
HM	Hideki Matsui	20.00
MU	Mike Mussina	8.00
HN	Hideo Nomo	8.00
RO	Roy Oswalt	4.00
RP	Rafael Palmeiro	6.00
PI	Mike Piazza	10.00
JP	Jorge Posada	8.00
MP	Mark Prior	8.00
AP	Albert Pujols	10.00
MR	Manny Ramirez	6.00
AR	Alex Rodriguez	8.00
CS	Curt Schilling	6.00
AS	Alfonso Soriano	6.00
SS	Sammy Sosa	10.00
IS	Ichiro Suzuki	15.00
JT	Jim Thome	8.00
BW	Bernie Williams	6.00
TW	Ted Williams/SP/150	70.00
DW	Dontrelle Willis	5.00
KW	Kerry Wood	8.00
BZ	Barry Zito	5.00

Artist's Touch
NM/M
Common Player:		4.00
Production 250		
Parallel:		1-2X
Production 50		
RB	Rocco Baldelli	8.00
JB	Josh Beckett	8.00
LB	Lance Berkman	5.00
CD	Carlos Delgado	6.00
RF	Rafael Furcal	5.00
JG	Jason Giambi	8.00
TG	Troy Glaus	6.00
KG	Ken Griffey Jr.	15.00
HA	Roy Halladay	5.00
BH	Bo Hart	4.00
TH	Torii Hunter	5.00
DJ	Derek Jeter	15.00
RJ	Randy Johnson	8.00
CJ	Chipper Jones	8.00
PM	Pedro J. Martinez	8.00
HM	Hideki Matsui	20.00
MM	Mike Mussina	8.00
HN	Hideo Nomo	8.00
RO	Roy Oswalt	4.00
RP	Rafael Palmeiro	8.00
PI	Mike Piazza	10.00
JP	Jorge Posada	8.00
MP	Mark Prior	10.00
AP	Albert Pujols	10.00
MR	Manny Ramirez/50	10.00
AR	Alex Rodriguez	10.00
AS	Alfonso Soriano	15.00
SS	Sammy Sosa	15.00
IS	Ichiro Suzuki	20.00
JT	Jim Thome	10.00
BW	Bernie Williams	6.00
DW	Dontrelle Willis	5.00
KW	Kerry Wood	8.00
BZ	Barry Zito	6.00

Home Run Heroics

NM/M
Common Player:		2.00
Inserted 1:24		
EB	Ernie Banks	4.00
HB	Hank Blalock	3.00
AB	Aaron Boone	2.00
MC	Miguel Cabrera	4.00
CD	Carlos Delgado	3.00
JD	Joe DiMaggio	8.00

JD1	Joe DiMaggio	8.00
JG	Jason Giambi	3.00
SG	Shawn Green	2.00
KG	Ken Griffey Jr.	6.00
KG1	Ken Griffey Jr.	6.00
RH	Rickey Henderson	2.00
RJ	Randy Johnson	3.00
HK	Harmon Killebrew	4.00
MM	Mickey Mantle	15.00
MM1	Mickey Mantle	15.00
MM2	Mickey Mantle	15.00
EM	Eddie Mathews	4.00
HM	Hideki Matsui	6.00
HM1	Hideki Matsui	6.00
WM	Willie McCovey	2.00
BM	Bill Mueller	2.00
SM	Stan Musial	5.00
RP	Rafael Palmeiro	3.00
CR	Cal Ripken Jr.	10.00
CR1	Cal Ripken Jr.	10.00
AR	Alex Rodriguez	6.00
AR1	Alex Rodriguez	6.00
FR	Frank Robinson	3.00
MS	Mike Schmidt	5.00
RS	Red Schoendienst	2.00
AS	Alfonso Soriano	4.00
SS	Sammy Sosa	6.00
SS1	Sammy Sosa	6.00
SS2	Sammy Sosa	6.00
SS3	Sammy Sosa	6.00
TW	Ted Williams	10.00
TW1	Ted Williams	10.00
TW2	Ted Williams	10.00
TW3	Ted Williams	10.00

Rookie Signature Portfolio

NM/M
Common Player: 5.00
Inserted 1:30

CA	Chris Aguila	6.00
TB	Tim Bausher	8.00
BI	Tim Bittner	8.00
FB	Frank Brooks	8.00
JB	Jamie Brown	8.00
MB	Mike Bumatay	8.00
DC	David Crouthers	8.00
GD	Greg Dobbs	8.00
SD	Scott Dohmann	8.00
JF	Jason Frasor	8.00
JG	Jerome Gamble	8.00
MG	Mike Gosling	8.00
HA	Justin Hampson	6.00
JH	Jesse Harper	8.00
SH	Sean Henn	15.00
LH	Lincoln Holdzkom	5.00
HU	Justin Huisman	5.00
MJ	Mike Johnston	10.00
DK	Donald Kelly	5.00
JL	Josh Labandeira	5.00
LE	Justin Leone	10.00
RM	Ryan Meaux	5.00
BM	Brandon Medders	5.00
CM	Colby Miller	5.00
NR	Nick Regilio	5.00
MR	Mike Rouse	5.00
DS	Dennis Sarfate	8.00
IS	Ian Snell	20.00
JW	Jake Woods	5.00
AZ	Alec Zumwalt	8.00

Signature Portfolio

NM/M
Production 100   No Pricing
Parallel:
Production 25 or 10

KG	Ken Griffey Jr.	100.00
HM	Hideki Matsui	250.00
CR	Cal Ripken Jr.	120.00
TS	Tom Seaver	50.00
CY	Carl Yastrzemski	50.00
BZ	Barry Zito	30.00

Tools of the Stars

NM/M
Common Player: 6.00
Inserted 1:48
Level 1 Parallel: 1-1.5X
Production 250
Level 2 Parallel: No Pricing
Production 25

JB	Josh Beckett	6.00
CD	Carlos Delgado	6.00
KG	Ken Griffey Jr./SP	15.00
DJ	Derek Jeter	15.00

CJ	Chipper Jones	8.00
HM	Hideki Matsui	15.00
HN	Hideo Nomo	6.00
PI	Mike Piazza	10.00
AP	Albert Pujols	15.00
AR	Alex Rodriguez	10.00
AS	Alfonso Soriano	6.00
IS	Ichiro Suzuki	15.00
JT	Jim Thome	6.00
KW	Kerry Wood	8.00

2004 Upper Deck Power Up

KEN GRIFFEY JR. - OF   10

Complete Set (100): 20.00
Common Player: .15
Pack (9): 1.50
Box (24): 25.00

1	Austin Kearns	.25
2	Rafael Furcal	.25
3	Larry Walker	.25
4	Jeremy Bonderman	.15
5	Scott Rolen	.50
6	Nomar Garciaparra	1.00
7	Jody Gerut	.15
8	Troy Glaus	.25
9	Roy Halladay	.25
10	Barry Zito	.40
11	Gary Sheffield	.25
12	Ichiro Suzuki	1.00
13	Juan Gonzalez	.25
14	Jim Edmonds	.25
15	Hank Blalock	.40
16	Roy Oswalt	.25
17	Magglio Ordonez	.25
18	Garret Anderson	.25
19	Mark Teixeira	.25
20	Mike Sweeney	.15
21	Reggie Sanders	.15
22	Rafael Palmeiro	.40
23	Orlando Cabrera	.15
24	Edgar Renteria	.25
25	Ryan Klesko	.25
26	Torii Hunter	.25
27	Bret Boone	.25
28	Roberto Alomar	.25
29	Frank Thomas	.50
30	Chipper Jones	.50
31	Eric Chavez	.25
32	Miguel Tejada	.40
33	Carlos Beltran	.40
34	Geoff Jenkins	.25
35	Hideki Matsui	1.00
36	Jason Kendall	.15
37	Adam Dunn	.40
38	Jay Gibbons	.15
39	Ivan Rodriguez	.50
40	Sidney Ponson	.15
41	Albert Pujols	1.00
42	Bartolo Colon	.25
43	Lance Berkman	.25
44	Brandon Webb	.15
45	Shannon Stewart	.15
46	Josh Beckett	.50
47	Jason Schmidt	.25
48	Luis Gonzalez	.25
49	Jacque Jones	.15
50	Andruw Jones	.40
51	Todd Helton	.50
52	Javier Vazquez	.50
53	Alfonso Soriano	.50
54	Manny Ramirez	.50
55	Bobby Abreu	.25
56	Rocco Baldelli	.25
57	Kerry Wood	.50
58	Derek Jeter	1.50
59	Phil Nevin	.15
60	Jeff Bagwell	.50
61	Sammy Sosa	1.00
62	Tom Glavine	.25
63	Miguel Cabrera	.50
64	Shawn Green	.25
65	Mark Prior	1.00
66	Jose Reyes	.25
67	Curt Schilling	.40
68	Hideo Nomo	.25
69	Mike Lowell	.25
70	Randy Johnson	.50
71	Edgar Martinez	.25
72	Dontrelle Willis	.25
73	Milton Bradley	.15
74	Preston Wilson	.15
75	Mike Piazza	.75
76	Mike Mussina	.40
77	Darin Erstad	.25
78	Greg Maddux	.75
79	Tim Hudson	.25
80	Kevin Millwood	.25
81	Dmitri Young	.15
82	Ben Sheets	.25
83	Alex Rodriguez	1.00
84	Johan Santana	.15
85	Jeff Kent	.25
86	Pedro Martinez	.50
87	Carlos Delgado	.40
88	Jim Thome	.50
89	Aubrey Huff	.15
90	Ken Griffey Jr.	1.00
91	Kevin Brown	.25
92	Tony Batista	.15
93	Richie Sexson	.25
94	Cliff Floyd	.15
95	Jose Vidro	.15
96	Brian Giles	.25
97	Jorge Posada	.40
98	Vernon Wells	.25
99	Vladimir Guerrero	.50
100	Jason Giambi	.50

Rare
Stars: 3-4X
Inserted 1:6

Super Rare
Stars: 5-10X
Inserted 1:96

Ultra Rare
Stars: 4-6X
Inserted 1:24

Mega Rare
No Pricing
Inserted 1:240

Shining Through

DONTRELLE WILLIS - P   50

NM/M

1	Hideo Nomo	.25
2	Mark Prior	1.00
3	Scott Rolen	.75
4	Luis Gonzalez	.25
5	Miguel Tejada	.40
6	Richie Sexson	.40
7	Jim Edmonds	.40
8	Carlos Beltran	.40
9	Manny Ramirez	.50
10	Torii Hunter	.40
11	Garret Anderson	.40
12	Eric Chavez	.40
13	Juan Gonzalez	.40
14	Albert Pujols	1.50
15	Tim Hudson	.40
16	Roy Halladay	.40
17	Roy Oswalt	.25
18	Andruw Jones	.50
19	Gary Sheffield	.40
20	Magglio Ordonez	.40
21	Jason Giambi	.75
22	Brian Giles	.40
23	Barry Zito	.40
24	Todd Helton	.50
25	Randy Johnson	.75
26	Pedro Martinez	.75
27	Vernon Wells	.25
28	Lance Berkman	.40
29	Mike Mussina	.50
30	Carlos Delgado	.40
31	Ivan Rodriguez	.50
32	Kevin Brown	.40
33	Kerry Wood	.75
34	Mark Teixeira	.40
35	Hideki Matsui	1.50
36	Troy Glaus	.40
37	Mike Piazza	1.00
38	Nomar Garciaparra	1.50
39	Vladimir Guerrero	.75
40	Derek Jeter	2.00
41	Jason Schmidt	.40
42	Alex Rodriguez/Yanks	1.50
43	Jeff Bagwell	.50
44	Shawn Green	.40
45	Sammy Sosa	1.50
46	Josh Beckett	.75
47	Bret Boone	.40
48	Ichiro Suzuki	1.00
49	Jeff Kent	.40
50	Rafael Palmeiro	.50
51	Curt Schilling	.40
52	Greg Maddux	1.00
53	Mike Lowell	.40
54	Dontrelle Willis	.40
55	Alfonso Soriano	.50
56	Preston Wilson	.25
57	Jorge Posada	.40
58	Frank Thomas	.50
59	Jim Thome	.75
60	Ken Griffey Jr.	1.00
61	Rocco Baldelli	.40
62	Jose Vidro	.25
63	Austin Kearns	.25
64	Cliff Floyd	.25
65	Phil Nevin	.25
66	Darin Erstad	.25
67	Johan Santana	.25
68	Chipper Jones	.75
69	Brandon Webb	.25
70	Hank Blalock	.40
71	Adam Dunn	.40
72	Javier Vazquez	.25
73	Jacque Jones	.25
74	Bobby Abreu	.40
75	Edgar Renteria	.40
76	Roger Clemens	1.50
77	Rafael Furcal	.40
78	Mike Sweeney	.25
79	Geoff Jenkins	.25
80	Orlando Cabrera	.25
81	Ben Sheets	.40
82	Shannon Stewart	.25
83	Ryan Klesko	.40
84	Edgar Martinez	.40
85	Kevin Millwood	.40
86	Bartolo Colon	.40
87	Larry Walker	.25
88	Tom Glavine	.40
89	Miguel Cabrera	.75
90	Jose Reyes	.40

Stickers

POWER UP YOUR POINTS!
SCRATCH OFF

NM/M

1	Hideo Nomo	.50
2	Mark Prior	2.00
3	Scott Rolen	1.50
4	Luis Gonzalez	.50
5	Miguel Tejada	.75
6	Richie Sexson	.75
7	Jim Edmonds	.75
8	Carlos Beltran	.75
9	Manny Ramirez	1.00
10	Torii Hunter	.75
11	Garret Anderson	.75
12	Eric Chavez	.75
13	Juan Gonzalez	.75
14	Albert Pujols	3.00
15	Tim Hudson	.75
16	Roy Halladay	.75
17	Roy Oswalt	.50
18	Andruw Jones	1.00
19	Gary Sheffield	.75
20	Magglio Ordonez	.75
21	Jason Giambi	1.50
22	Brian Giles	.75
23	Barry Zito	.75
24	Todd Helton	1.00
25	Randy Johnson	1.50
26	Pedro Martinez	1.50
27	Vernon Wells	.50
28	Lance Berkman	.75
29	Mike Mussina	.75
30	Carlos Delgado	.75
31	Ivan Rodriguez	1.00
32	Kevin Brown	.75
33	Kerry Wood	1.50
34	Mark Teixeira	.75
35	Hideki Matsui	2.50
36	Troy Glaus	.75
37	Mike Piazza	2.00
38	Nomar Garciaparra	3.00
39	Vladimir Guerrero	1.50
40	Derek Jeter	4.00
41	Jason Schmidt	.50
42	Alex Rodriguez	3.00
43	Jeff Bagwell	1.00
44	Shawn Green	.75
45	Sammy Sosa	2.50
46	Josh Beckett	1.00
47	Bret Boone	.50
48	Ichiro Suzuki	2.00
49	Jeff Kent	.75
50	Rafael Palmeiro	1.00
51	Curt Schilling	1.00
52	Greg Maddux	2.00
53	Mike Lowell	.75
54	Dontrelle Willis	1.00
55	Alfonso Soriano	1.00
56	Preston Wilson	.50
57	Jorge Posada	.75
58	Frank Thomas	1.00
59	Jim Thome	1.50
60	Ken Griffey Jr.	2.00
61	Rocco Baldelli	.75
62	Jose Vidro	.50
63	Austin Kearns	.50
64	Phil Nevin	.50
65	Darin Erstad	.50
66	Johan Santana	.50
67	Chipper Jones	1.50
68	Brandon Webb	.50
69	Hank Blalock	.75
70	Adam Dunn	.75
71	Javier Vazquez	.75
72	Jacque Jones	.50
73	Bobby Abreu	.75
74	Edgar Renteria	.75
75	Mike Sweeney	.50
76	Geoff Jenkins	.50
77	Shannon Stewart	.50
78	Ryan Klesko	.75
79	Edgar Martinez	.75
80	Kevin Millwood	.75
81	Bartolo Colon	.75
82	Tom Glavine	.75
83	Miguel Cabrera	1.00
84	Jose Reyes	.75
85	Padres/Astros/A's Angels/Cubs/D-Rays	.50
86	Pirates/M's/Expos Twins/Reds/Phils	.50
87	Royals/O's/W.Sox/ Dodgers/Marlins/Yanks	.50
88	Giants/Mets/Cards/ Indians/Braves/Rangers	.50
89	Tigers/R.Sox/Rockies/ D-Backs/Brewers/Jay	.50

2004 Upper Deck R Class

TEXAS   3B   hankBLALOCK

Complete Set (180): 50.00
Common Player: .10
Pack (6): 2.50
Box (24): 50.00

1	Adam Dunn	.50
2	Jose Vidro	.10
3	Vladimir Guerrero	.75
4	Hideo Nomo	.25
5	Eric Chavez	.25
6	Carlos Delgado	.25
7	Javy Lopez	.25
8	Javier Vazquez	.25
9	Miguel Cabrera	.25
10	Manny Ramirez	.50
11	Scott Rolen	.25
12	Rafael Furcal	.10
13	Jim Thome	.25
14	Edgar Renteria	.25
15	Jason Kendall	.10
16	Alfonso Soriano	.25
17	Troy Glaus	.40
18	Vernon Wells	.50
19	Todd Helton	.50
20	Mark Mulder	.25
21	Albert Pujols	2.00
22	Andy Pettitte	.25
23	Kevin Millwood	.10
24	Bret Boone	.10
25	Ken Griffey Jr.	1.00
26	Kevin Brown	.20
27	J.D. Drew	.25
28	Corey Patterson	.25
29	Jason Giambi	.40
30	Jason Schmidt	.25
31	Jose Reyes	.25
32	Torii Hunter	.25
33	Brian Giles	.25
34	Garret Anderson	.25
35	Mark Teixeira	.40
36	Sammy Sosa	1.50
37	Rocco Baldelli	.25
38	Jeff Bagwell	.50
39	Rafael Palmeiro	.25
40	Derek Lee	.25
41	Randy Johnson	.75
42	Roger Clemens	1.50
43	Austin Kearns	.25
44	Dontrelle Willis	.25
45	Lance Berkman	.25
46	Juan Gonzalez	.25
47	Ichiro Suzuki	1.50
48	Pat Burrell	.25
49	Miguel Tejada	.40
50	Mike Piazza	1.00
51	Mark Prior	.75
52	C.C. Sabathia	.25
53	Jacque Jones	.10
54	Carlos Beltran	.75
55	Mike Mussina	.40
56	Mike Lowell	.25
57	Phil Nevin	.10
58	Andruw Jones	.40
59	Barry Zito	.25
60	Magglio Ordonez	.20
61	Carlos Lee	.20
62	Nomar Garciaparra	1.00
63	Kerry Wood	.75
64	Luis Gonzalez	.20
65	Derek Jeter	2.00
66	Preston Wilson	.10
67	Greg Maddux	1.00
68	Pedro J. Martinez	.75
69	Richie Sexson	.50
70	Hank Blalock	.50
71	Chipper Jones	.50
72	Ivan Rodriguez	.50
73	Roy Halladay	.50
74	Tim Hudson	.50
75	Ryan Klesko	.10
76	Hideki Matsui	1.50
77	Josh Beckett	.40
78	Brandon Webb	.10
79	Alex Rodriguez	2.00
80	Jim Edmonds	.40
81	Jeff Kent	.10
82	Bobby Abreu	.25
83	Curt Schilling	.25
84	Roy Oswalt	.25
85	Orlando Cabrera	.25
86	Johan Santana	.50
87	Geoff Jenkins	.10
88	Gary Sheffield	.25
89	Shawn Green	.25
90	Frank Thomas	.25
91	Tim Hamulack RC	.25
92	Shingo Takatsu RC	.25
93	Justin Huisman	.25
94	Sean Henn	.50
95	Jamie Brown	.25
96	Dennis Sarfate RC	.25
97	Lincoln Holdzkom RC	.25
98	Roman Colon RC	.25
99	Scott Dohmann RC	.25
100	Ivan Ochoa	.25
101	Akinori Otsuka RC	.50
102	Fernando Nieve RC	.25
103	Mike Johnston RC	.25
104	Mariano Gomez RC	.25
105	Justin Leone RC	.25
106	Evan Rust RC	.25
107	Mike Rouse	.25
108	Ian Snell RC	.50
109	Jason Bartlett	.25
110	Ryan Wing	.25
111	Nick Regilio RC	.25
112	Merkin Valdez RC	.50
113	Josh Labandeira RC	.25
114	David Aardsma	.75
115	Justin Knoedler RC	.25
116	Shawn Hill RC	.25
117	Casey Daigle RC	.25
118	Donnie Kelly RC	.25
119	Justin Germano RC	.25
120	Eddy Rodriguez	.25
121	Onil Joseph RC	.25
122	Mike Wuertz	.50
123	Roberto Novoa RC	.25
124	Jerome Gamble RC	.50
125	Justin Hampson RC	.25
126	Ronald Belisario RC	.25
127	Tim Bausher RC	.25
128	Chris Saenz RC	.25
129	Hector Gimenez RC	.25
130	Ronny Cedeno RC	.25
131	Jason Frasor RC	.25
132	Kazuo Matsui RC	2.00
133	Mike Gosling	.25
134	Jerry Gil RC	.25
135	Orlando Rodriguez RC	.25
136	Jorge Vasquez RC	.50
137	Chris Aguila RC	.25
138	Justin Lehr RC	.25
139	Jake Woods	.25
140	Enemencio Pacheco	.25
141	David Crouthers	.25
142	Jose Capellan RC	1.00
143	Chad Bentz RC	.25
144	Michael Vento	.75
145	Scott Proctor RC	.50
146	Edwin Moreno RC	.25
147	Brandon Medders RC	.25
148	Renyel Pinto RC	.25
149	Rusty Tucker RC	.25
150	Ryan Meaux RC	.25
151	William Bergolla	.25
152	Angel Chavez	.25
153	Colby Miller RC	.25
154	John Gall RC	.25
155	Carlos Hines RC	.25
156	Carlos Vasquez RC	.50
157	Justin Lehr RC	.25
158	Kevin Cave RC	.25
159	Jeff Bennett RC	.25
160	Greg Dobbs RC	.25
161	Jorge Sequea RC	.25
162	Chris Oxspring RC	.25
163	Franklyn Gracesqui RC	.25
164	Shawn Camp RC	.25
165	Lino Urdaneta RC	.25
166	Luis Gonzalez	.25
167	Ramon Ramirez RC	.25
168	Freddy Guzman RC	.25
169	Chris Shelton RC	.75
170	Andres Blanco	.25
171	Aarom Baldiris RC	.25
172	Kazuhito Tadano RC	.25

173	Brian Dallimore RC	.25
174	Eduardo Villacis RC	.25
175	Frank Francisco RC	.25
176	Edwin Jackson	.25
177	Bobby Crosby	.50
178	Joe Mauer	.50
179	Rickie Weeks	.50
180	Delmon Young	.50

First Class Black Ink Autograph

		NM/M
Inserted 1:2,880		
SA	Sandy Alomar	20.00
PB	Pat Burrell	30.00
MC	Miguel Cabrera	40.00
CD	Carlos Delgado	30.00
EG	Eric Gagne	50.00
KG	Ken Griffey Jr.	80.00
TH	Trevor Hoffman	30.00
BL	Barry Larkin	40.00
PL	Paul LoDuca	30.00
EM	Edgar Martinez	40.00
MP	Mark Prior	40.00
HR	Horacio Ramirez	20.00
DW	Dontrelle Willis	30.00

First Class Blue Ink Autograph

No Pricing
Production Three Sets

Jersey

		NM/M
Common Player:		4.00
Inserted 1:12		
RA	Roberto Alomar	6.00
BA	Jeff Bagwell	8.00
RB	Rocco Baldelli	4.00
JB	Josh Beckett	8.00
HB	Hank Blalock	8.00
BB	Bret Boone	4.00
KB	Kevin Brown	4.00
EC	Eric Chavez	4.00
RC	Roger Clemens	12.00
CD	Carlos Delgado	4.00
JG	Jason Giambi	6.00
GL	Troy Glaus	4.00
TG	Tom Glavine	6.00
KG	Ken Griffey Jr.	12.00
VG	Vladimir Guerrero	8.00
TH	Todd Helton	8.00
HU	Torii Hunter	4.00
DJ	Derek Jeter	15.00
RJ	Randy Johnson	8.00
AJ	Andruw Jones	6.00
CJ	Chipper Jones	8.00
EM	Edgar Martinez	8.00
PM	Pedro J. Martinez	8.00
HM	Hideki Matsui	20.00
KM	Kazuo Matsui	10.00
HN	Hideo Nomo	8.00
PI	Mike Piazza	10.00
MP	Mark Prior	6.00
AP	Albert Pujols	15.00
MR	Manny Ramirez	8.00
RI	Mariano Rivera	8.00
IR	Ivan Rodriguez	8.00
SR	Scott Rolen	8.00
CS	Curt Schilling	8.00
GS	Gary Sheffield	6.00
AS	Alfonso Soriano	8.00
SS	Sammy Sosa	10.00
IS	Ichiro Suzuki	25.00
MT	Miguel Tejada	6.00
BW	Bernie Williams	8.00
DW	Dontrelle Willis	6.00
KW	Kerry Wood	8.00

Taking Over!

		NM/M
Common Player:		3.00
1-20 production 650		
21-30 production 150		
TO-1	Richie Sexson, Lyle Overbay	3.00
TO-2	Jason Phillips, Mike Piazza	6.00
TO-3	Barry Larkin, William Bergolla	4.00
TO-4	Jason Dubois, Moises Alou	3.00
TO-5	Nook Logan, Alex Sanchez	3.00
TO-6	Merkin Valdez, Robb Nen	4.00
TO-7	Troy Percival, Francisco Rodriguez	3.00
TO-8	Carlos Beltran, David DeJesus	4.00
TO-9	Alex Rodriguez, Michael Young	6.00
TO-10	Alexis Rios, Vernon Wells	3.00
TO-11	Matt Lawton, Grady Sizemore	3.00
TO-12	Danny Graves, Ryan Wagner	3.00
TO-13	Miguel Cabrera, Jeff Conine	3.00
TO-14	Josh Willingham, Ramon Castro	3.00
TO-15	Junior Spivey, Rickie Weeks	3.00
TO-16	Guillermo Quiroz, Greg Myers	3.00
TO-17	Scott Hatteberg, Graham Koonce	3.00
TO-18	Rene Reyes, Larry Walker	4.00
TO-19	Khalil Greene, Ramon Vazquez	4.00
TO-20	Billy Wagner, Octavio Dotel	3.00
TO-21	Joe Mauer, A.J. Pierzynski	8.00
TO-22	Javier Vazquez, Roger Clemens	10.00
TO-23	Curt Schilling, Brandon Webb	3.00
TO-24	Delmon Young, Cirilo Cruz Jr.	8.00
TO-25	Vladimir Guerrero, Tim Salmon	8.00
TO-26	Gary Sheffield, J.D. Drew	3.00
TO-27	Miguel Tejada, Bobby Crosby	8.00
TO-28	Edwin Jackson, Kevin Brown	3.00
TO-29	Kazuo Matsui, Jose Reyes	10.00
TO-30	Wily Mo Pena, Ken Griffey Jr.	10.00

2004 Upper Deck Reflections Sample

		NM/M
S38	Ichiro	3.00

2004 Upper Deck Reflections

		NM/M
Complete Set (340)		
Common (1-100)		.50
Common SP (101-130)		4.00
Production 1,250		
Common Jersey (131-214)		4.00
Common Jersey (215-298)		5.00
Production 100 (215-298)		
Common Auto. (299-340)		15.00
Production 35		
Pack (4):		10.00
Box (8):		70.00
1	Adam Dunn	1.00
2	Albert Pujols	3.00
3	Alex Rodriguez	3.00
4	Alfonso Soriano	1.00
5	Andruw Jones	1.00
6	Austin Kearns	.50
7	Rafael Furcal	.50
8	Barry Zito	.75
9	Bartolo Colon	.50
10	Ben Sheets	.50
11	Bernie Williams	.75
12	Bobby Abreu	.75
13	Brandon Webb	.50
14	Bret Boone	.50
15	Brian Giles	.50
16	Carlos Beltran	.75
17	Carlos Delgado	.75
18	Carlos Lee	.50
19	Chipper Jones	1.50
20	Corey Patterson	.50
21	Curt Schilling	.75
22	Delmon Young	.50
23	Derek Jeter	4.00
24	Dmitri Young	.50
25	Dontrelle Willis	.50
26	Edgar Martinez	.50
27	Edgar Renteria	.50
28	Eric Chavez	.50
29	Eric Gagne	.75
30	Frank Thomas	1.50
31	Garret Anderson	.50
32	Gary Sheffield	.50
33	Geoff Jenkins	.50
34	Greg Maddux	2.00
35	Hank Blalock	.75
36	Hideki Matsui	3.00
37	Hideo Nomo	.75
38	Ichiro Suzuki	2.50
39	Ivan Rodriguez	1.00
40	Jacque Jones	.50
41	Jason Giambi	1.50
42	Jason Schmidt	.75
43	Javy Lopez	.75
44	Jay Gibbons	.50
45	Jeff Bagwell	1.00
46	Jeff Kent	.50
47	Jeremy Bonderman	.75
48	Jim Edmonds	.75
49	Jim Thome	.75
50	Johnny Damon	.50
51	Jorge Posada	.75
52	Jose Contreras	.50
53	Jose Reyes	.75
54	Jose Vidro	.50
55	Josh Beckett	1.00
56	Juan Gonzalez	.75
57	Ken Griffey Jr.	2.50
58	Kerry Wood	1.50
59	Kevin Brown	.50
60	Kevin Millwood	.50
61	Lance Berkman	.50
62	Larry Walker	.50
63	Luis Gonzalez	.50
64	Magglio Ordonez	.50
65	Manny Ramirez	1.00
66	Mark Mulder	.50
67	Mark Prior	2.00
68	Mark Teixeira	1.50
69	Miguel Cabrera	1.50
70	Miguel Tejada	.75
71	Mike Lowell	.75
72	Mike Mussina	.75
73	Mike Piazza	2.00
74	Mike Sweeney	.50
75	Milton Bradley	.50
76	Nomar Garciaparra	2.00
77	Orlando Cabrera	.50
78	Pedro Martinez	1.50
79	Phil Nevin	.50
80	Preston Wilson	.50
81	Rafael Palmeiro	.50
82	Randy Johnson	1.50
83	Rich Harden	.50
84	Richie Sexson	.50
85	Rickie Weeks	.50
86	Rocco Baldelli	.50
87	Roy Halladay	.75
88	Roy Oswalt	.75
89	Ryan Klesko	.50
90	Sammy Sosa	2.50
91	Scott Rolen	1.50
92	Shannon Stewart	.50
93	Shawn Green	.50
94	Tim Hudson	.75
95	Todd Helton	1.00
96	Torii Hunter	.50
97	Trot Nixon	.50
98	Troy Glaus	.50
99	Vernon Wells	.50
100	Vladimir Guerrero	1.50
101	Brandon Medders RC	4.00
102	Colby Miller RC	4.00
103	David Crouthers RC	4.00
104	Dennis Sarfate RC	4.00
105	Donnie Kelly RC	4.00
106	Alec Zumwalt RC	4.00
107	Chris Aguila RC	4.00
108	Greg Dobbs RC	4.00
109	Ian Snell RC	8.00
110	Jake Woods RC	4.00
111	Jamie Brown RC	4.00
112	Jason Frasor RC	4.00
113	Jerome Gamble RC	4.00
114	Jesse Harper RC	4.00
115	Josh Labandeira RC	5.00
116	Justin Hampson RC	4.00
117	Justin Huisman RC	4.00
118	Justin Leone RC	4.00
119	Kazuo Matsui RC	15.00
120	Lincoln Holdzkom RC	4.00
121	Mike Bumatay RC	4.00
122	Mike Gosling	4.00
123	Mike Johnston RC	4.00
124	Mike Rouse	4.00
125	Nick Regilio RC	4.00
126	Ryan Meaux RC	4.00
127	Scott Dohmann RC	4.00
128	Sean Henn RC	6.00
129	Tim Bausher RC	4.00
130	Tim Bittner RC	4.00
131	Adam Dunn	6.00
132	Andruw Jones	6.00
133	Austin Kearns	5.00
134	Bartolo Colon	5.00
135	Ben Sheets	5.00
136	Bernie Williams	5.00
137	Bobby Abreu	4.00
138	Brian Giles	4.00
139	Carlos Lee	4.00
140	Chipper Jones	8.00
141	Corey Patterson	5.00
142	Darin Erstad	4.00
143	Edgar Martinez	5.00
144	Vladimir Guerrero	8.00
145	Eric Gagne	8.00
146	Frank Thomas	5.00
147	Garret Anderson	5.00
148	Roger Clemens	12.00
149	Greg Maddux	8.00
150	Jacque Jones	4.00
151	Randy Johnson	8.00
152	Javy Lopez	6.00
153	Mike Piazza	8.00
154	Albert Pujols	12.00
155	Jim Edmonds	5.00
156	Eric Milton	5.00
157	Jorge Posada	6.00
158	J.D. Drew	5.00
159	Jose Vidro	4.00
160	Kevin Millwood	5.00
161	Larry Walker	4.00
162	Luis Gonzalez	5.00
163	Mike Sweeney	5.00
164	Kerry Wood	10.00
165	Mike Cameron	5.00
166	Phil Nevin	5.00
167	Rocco Baldelli	6.00
168	Ryan Klesko	6.00
169	Shannon Stewart	4.00
170	Torii Hunter	6.00
171	Trot Nixon	6.00
172	Vernon Wells	6.00
173	Alfonso Soriano	6.00
174	Andruw Jones	6.00
175	Barry Zito	6.00
176	Brandon Webb	4.00
177	Bret Boone	4.00
178	Scott Rolen	10.00
179	Carlos Delgado	6.00
180	Curt Schilling	8.00
181	Dontrelle Willis	8.00
182	Eric Chavez	5.00
183	Frank Thomas	8.00
184	Gary Sheffield	8.00
185	Greg Maddux	8.00
186	Hank Blalock	8.00
187	Hideki Matsui	15.00
188	Hideo Nomo	8.00
189	Ichiro Suzuki	15.00
190	Ivan Rodriguez	8.00
191	Jason Giambi	6.00
192	Rafael Furcal	5.00
193	Jeff Bagwell	8.00
194	Jeff Kent	4.00
195	Jim Thome	8.00
196	Jose Reyes	4.00
197	Josh Beckett	6.00
198	Juan Gonzalez	6.00
199	Ken Griffey Jr.	15.00
200	Kevin Brown	5.00
201	Lance Berkman	6.00
202	Magglio Ordonez	6.00
203	Mark Mulder	4.00
204	Mark Teixeira	6.00
205	Miguel Tejada	6.00
206	Mike Mussina	6.00
207	Preston Wilson	4.00
208	Rafael Palmeiro	6.00
209	Alex Rodriguez	15.00
210	Richie Sexson	5.00
211	Roy Halladay	5.00
212	Roy Oswalt	5.00
213	Tim Hudson	5.00
214	Troy Glaus	5.00
215	Adam Dunn	8.00
216	Austin Kearns	6.00
217	Bartolo Colon	6.00
218	Ben Sheets	6.00
219	Bernie Williams	6.00
220	Bobby Abreu	5.00
221	Bret Boone	5.00
222	Todd Helton	8.00
223	Chipper Jones	8.00
224	Corey Patterson	6.00
225	Darin Erstad	5.00
226	Dontrelle Willis	6.00
227	Edgar Martinez	6.00
228	Eric Gagne	10.00
229	Garret Anderson	6.00
230	Roger Clemens	20.00
231	Hank Blalock	6.00
232	Jacque Jones	5.00
233	Jeff Bagwell	10.00
234	Jeff Kent	5.00
235	Jeremy Bonderman	6.00
236	Jim Edmonds	8.00
237	Jorge Posada	8.00
238	J.D. Drew	8.00
239	Jose Reyes	5.00
240	Jose Vidro	5.00
241	Kevin Millwood	6.00
242	Luis Gonzalez	5.00
243	Mike Sweeney	5.00
244	Jason Giambi	6.00
245	Manny Ramirez	10.00
246	Phil Nevin	5.00
247	Preston Wilson	5.00
248	Alex Rodriguez	20.00
249	Richie Sexson	6.00
250	Rocco Baldelli	5.00
251	Ryan Klesko	6.00
252	Sammy Sosa	20.00
253	Torii Hunter	6.00
254	Mike Lowell	8.00
255	Troy Glaus	6.00
256	Vernon Wells	6.00
257	Albert Pujols	25.00
258	Alex Rodriguez	20.00
259	Alfonso Soriano	8.00
260	Roger Clemens	20.00
261	Barry Zito	6.00
262	Brandon Webb	6.00
263	Carlos Delgado	8.00
264	Curt Schilling	10.00
265	Derek Jeter	30.00
266	Eric Chavez	8.00
267	Gary Sheffield	8.00
268	Hideki Matsui	25.00
269	Hideo Nomo	8.00
270	Ichiro Suzuki	25.00
271	Ivan Rodriguez	10.00
272	Jason Giambi	8.00
273	Jim Thome	10.00
274	Josh Beckett	10.00
275	Juan Gonzalez	8.00
276	Ken Griffey Jr.	20.00
277	Kerry Wood	15.00
278	Kevin Brown	5.00
279	Lance Berkman	8.00
280	Magglio Ordonez	8.00
281	Manny Ramirez	10.00
282	Mark Mulder	8.00
283	Mark Prior	10.00
284	Mark Teixeira	8.00
285	Miguel Tejada	8.00
286	Mike Mussina	8.00
287	Mike Piazza	15.00
288	Pedro Martinez	15.00
289	Rafael Palmeiro	8.00
290	Randy Johnson	12.00
291	Roy Halladay	6.00
292	Roy Oswalt	6.00
293	Sammy Sosa	20.00
294	Scott Rolen	12.00
295	Shawn Green	6.00
296	Tim Hudson	6.00
297	Todd Helton	8.00
298	Vladimir Guerrero	10.00
299	Bret Boone	35.00
300	Alex Rodriguez	200.00
301	Dontrelle Willis	30.00
302	Barry Larkin	35.00
303	Barry Zito	35.00
304	Eric Chavez	35.00
305	Bernie Williams	85.00
306	Brandon Webb	30.00
307	Cal Ripken Jr.	175.00
308	Carl Yastrzemski	65.00
309	Carlos Delgado	30.00
310	Shawn Green	25.00
311	Eric Gagne	15.00
312	Frank Thomas	40.00
313	Carlos Lee	20.00
314	Garret Anderson	20.00
315	Hideki Matsui	300.00
316	Jim Edmonds	40.00
317	Jeff Bagwell	40.00
318	Luis Gonzalez	25.00
319	Mike Mussina	40.00
320	John Smoltz	60.00
321	Jose Reyes	40.00
322	Josh Beckett	40.00
323	Juan Gonzalez	35.00
324	Ken Griffey Jr.	140.00
325	Rich Harden	20.00
326	Pat Burrell	30.00
327	Mark Teixeira	25.00
328	Roy Oswalt	30.00
329	Miguel Tejada	40.00
330	Mike Hampton	25.00
331	Mike Piazza	175.00
332	Nolan Ryan	120.00
333	Orlando Hernandez	40.00
334	Paul Lo Duca	30.00
335	Roberto Alomar	45.00
336	Rocco Baldelli	40.00
337	Trevor Hoffman	40.00
338	Tom Glavine	50.00
339	Tom Seaver	100.00
340	Mark Prior	40.00

Gold

Gold (1-100):	5-10X
Production 15	
Gold Auto. (101-130):	2X
Production 250	
Gold Auto. Parallel (101-130):	2X
Production 125	
Gold Jersey (131-172):	1.5-3X
Production 15	
Gold Jersey (257-298):	No Pricing
Production 5	
Gold Jsy Auto. (299-340):	1X
Production 15	

Red

Red (1-100):	4-6X
Production 50	
Red Jersey (131-214):	1.5-2X
Production 50	
Red Jersey (215-256):	1-1.5X
Production 50	

2004 Upper Deck Rivals: Yankees vs. Red Sox

		NM/M
Complete Sealed Set (32):		25.00
Common Player (1-30):		.50
1	Alex Rodriguez	2.00
2	Bobby Doerr	.75
3	Don Mattingly	1.50
4	Dwight Evans	.50
5	Fred Lynn	.50
6	Jason Giambi	.50
7	Jim Rice	.50
8	Lou Gehrig	2.00
9	Luis Tiant	.50
10	Manny Ramirez	1.00
11	Mike Mussina	.75
12	Pedro Martinez	1.00
13	Phil Rizzuto	.75
14	Whitey Ford	.75
15	Yogi Berra	1.00
16	Tim Wakefield	.50
17	Billy Martin	.75
18	Mike Torrez, Bucky Dent	.50
19	Nomar Garciaparra, Derek Jeter	2.00
20	Gary Sheffield, Curt Schilling	1.00
21	Joe DiMaggio, Dick Newsome	1.50
22	Joe DiMaggio, Lefty Grove	1.50
23	Joe DiMaggio, Ted Williams	1.50
24	Jorge Posada, Jason Varitek	.50
25	Mickey Mantle, Carl Yastrzemski	2.00
26	Tracy Stallard, Roger Maris	1.00
27	Carlton Fisk, Thurman Munson	1.00
28	Babe Ruth	2.00
29	Roger Clemens	1.50
30	Wade Boggs	.50

Black

Black (1-100):	No Pricing
Production One Set	
Black Auto. (101-130):	No Pricing
Production One Set	
Black Jersey (173-214):	No Pricing
Production One Set	
Black Jersey (257-298):	No Pricing
Production One Set	
Black Jsy Auto. (299-340):	No Pricing
Production One Set	

Blue

Blue (1-100):	2-4X
Blue (215-256):	1-2X
Production 15	

Commemorative

	NM/M
Complete Set (5):	10.00

One oversized card per set.

Babe Ruth	4.00
Ted Williams	3.00
Derek Jeter	3.00
Nomar Garciaparra	2.00
Mickey Mantle	5.00

"What If"

NM/M
Common Player: 4.00
Production 2,150 Sets

1	Aaron Boone	4.00
2	Alex Rodriguez	10.00
3	Babe Ruth	10.00
4	Babe Ruth	10.00
5	Billy Martin	4.00
6	Bucky Dent	4.00
7	Carl Yastrzemski	8.00
8	Carlton Fisk	4.00
9	Derek Jeter	10.00
10	Hideki Matsui	8.00
11	Joe DiMaggio	8.00
12	Joe Torre	4.00
13	Mickey Mantle	15.00
14	Pedro Martinez	6.00
15	Pee Wee Reese	4.00
16	Roger Clemens	8.00
17	Roger Maris	8.00
18	Ted Williams	8.00
19	Ted Williams	8.00
20	Carl Yastrzemski	8.00

What If Autograph
No Pricing

SportsNut
Complete Set (90):
Common Player:

2004 Upper Deck Sweet Spot

NM/M
Complete Set (262):
Common Player: .25
Common (91-170): 3.00
Production 799
Common SP (171-230): 1.50
Production 399
Common SP (231-250): 1.50
Production 299
Common SP (251-260): 3.00
Production 199
Pack (4): 10.00
Box (12): 100.00

1	Albert Pujols	3.00
2	Alex Rodriguez	3.00
3	Alfonso Soriano	1.00
4	Andruw Jones	.50
5	Andy Pettitte	.50
6	Aubrey Huff	.25
7	Austin Kearns	.50
8	Barry Zito	.50
9	Bobby Abreu	.50
10	Brandon Webb	.25
11	Bret Boone	.25
12	Brian Giles	.25
13	C.C. Sabathia	.25
14	Carlos Beltran	1.00
15	Carlos Delgado	.50
16	Chipper Jones	1.00
17	Cliff Floyd	.25
18	Curt Schilling	1.00
19	Delmon Young	.25
20	Derek Jeter	3.00
21	Dontrelle Willis	.25
22	Edgar Martinez	.50
23	Edgar Renteria	.50
24	Eric Chavez	.50
25	Eric Gagne	.50
26	Frank Thomas	.75
27	Garret Anderson	.50
28	Gary Sheffield	.75
29	Geoff Jenkins	.25
30	Greg Maddux	1.50
31	Hank Blalock	.75
32	Hideo Nomo	.50
33	Ichiro Suzuki	2.00
34	Ivan Rodriguez	.75
35	Jacque Jones	.25
36	Jason Giambi	.50
37	Jason Schmidt	.50
38	Javier Vazquez	.25
39	Javy Lopez	.50
40	Jeff Bagwell	.75
41	Jim Edmonds	.50
42	Jim Thome	.75
43	Joe Mauer	.50
44	John Smoltz	.50
45	Jose Cruz Jr.	.25
46	Jose Reyes	.50
47	Jose Vidro	.25
48	Josh Beckett	.50
49	Ken Griffey Jr.	1.50
50	Kerry Wood	1.00
51	Kevin Brown	.25
52	Larry Walker	.50
53	Magglio Ordonez	.25
54	Manny Ramirez	.75
55	Mark Mulder	.50
56	Mark Prior	1.00
57	Mark Teixeira	.50
58	Miguel Cabrera	1.00
59	Miguel Tejada	.50
60	Mike Lowell	.40
61	Mike Mussina	.75
62	Mike Piazza	1.50
63	Nomar Garciaparra	1.50
64	Orlando Cabrera	.40
65	Pat Burrell	.25
66	Pedro J. Martinez	1.00
67	Phil Nevin	.25
68	Preston Wilson	.25
69	Rafael Furcal	.25
70	Rafael Palmeiro	.75
71	Randy Johnson	1.00
72	Craig Wilson	.25
73	Rich Harden	.25
74	Richie Sexson	.50
75	Rickie Weeks	.50
76	Rocco Baldelli	.50
77	Roger Clemens	2.50
78	Roy Halladay	.25
79	Roy Oswalt	.25
80	Ryan Klesko	.25
81	Sammy Sosa	2.00
82	Scott Podsednik	.25
83	Scott Rolen	1.00
84	Shawn Green	.40
85	Tim Hudson	.40
86	Todd Helton	.75
87	Torii Hunter	.40
88	Troy Glaus	.25
89	Vernon Wells	.25
90	Vladimir Guerrero	1.00
91	Aarom Baldiris **RC**	3.00
92	Akinori Otsuka **RC**	8.00
93	Andres Blanco **RC**	5.00
94	Angel Chavez **RC**	3.00
95	Brian Dallimore **RC**	8.00
96	Carlos Hines **RC**	5.00
97	Carlos Vasquez **RC**	5.00
98	Casey Daigle **RC**	3.00
99	Chad Bentz **RC**	3.00
100	Chris Aguila **RC**	3.00
101	Chris Oxspring **RC**	5.00
102	Chris Saenz **RC**	3.00
103	Chris Shelton **RC**	10.00
104	Colby Miller **RC**	5.00
105	David Crouthers **RC**	5.00
106	David Aardsma **RC**	5.00
107	Dennis Sarfate **RC**	3.00
108	Donnie Kelly **RC**	3.00
109	Eddy Rodriguez **RC**	3.00
110	Eduardo Villacis **RC**	3.00
111	Edwin Moreno **RC**	5.00
112	Enemencio Pacheco **RC**	5.00
113	Fernando Nieve **RC**	5.00
114	Franklyn Gracesqui **RC**	3.00
115	Freddy Guzman **RC**	3.00
116	Greg Dobbs **RC**	3.00
117	Hector Gimenez **RC**	3.00
118	Ian Snell **RC**	5.00
119	Ivan Ochoa **RC**	3.00
120	Jake Woods **RC**	3.00
121	Jamie Brown **RC**	3.00
122	Jason Bartlett **RC**	5.00
123	Jason Frasor **RC**	3.00
124	Jeff Bennett **RC**	3.00
125	Jerome Gamble **RC**	3.00
126	Jerry Gil **RC**	3.00
127	Brandon Medders **RC**	3.00
128	Ryan Meaux **RC**	3.00
129	John Gall **RC**	3.00
130	Jorge Sequea **RC**	3.00
131	Jorge Vasquez **RC**	5.00
132	Jose Capellan **RC**	8.00
133	Josh Labandeira **RC**	3.00
134	Justin Germano **RC**	8.00
135	Justin Hampson **RC**	5.00
136	Justin Huisman **RC**	5.00
137	Justin Knoedler **RC**	5.00
138	Justin Leone **RC**	5.00
139	Kazuhito Tadano **RC**	5.00
140	Kazuo Matsui **RC**	10.00
141	Kevin Cave **RC**	5.00
142	Lincoln Holdzkom **RC**	5.00
143	Lino Urdaneta **RC**	3.00
144	Luis A. Gonzalez **RC**	5.00
145	Mariano Gomez **RC**	3.00
146	Merkin Valdez **RC**	5.00
147	Michael Vento **RC**	8.00
148	Mike Wuertz **RC**	5.00
149	Mike Gosling **RC**	5.00
150	Mike Johnston **RC**	3.00
151	Mike Rouse **RC**	3.00
152	Nick Regilio **RC**	5.00
153	Onil Joseph **RC**	3.00
154	Orlando Rodriguez **RC**	5.00
155	Ramon Ramirez **RC**	5.00
156	Renyel Pinto **RC**	5.00
157	Roberto Novoa **RC**	5.00
158	Roman Colon **RC**	3.00
159	Ronald Belisario **RC**	5.00
160	Ronny Cedeno **RC**	8.00
161	Rusty Tucker **RC**	5.00
162	Ryan Wing **RC**	3.00
163	Scott Dohmann **RC**	5.00
164	Scott Proctor **RC**	5.00
165	Sean Henn **RC**	5.00
166	Shawn Camp **RC**	5.00
167	Shawn Hill **RC**	3.00
168	Shingo Takatsu **RC**	8.00
169	Tim Hamulack **RC**	5.00
170	William Bergolla **RC**	3.00
171	Adam Dunn	2.00
172	Albert Pujols	8.00
173	Alex Rodriguez	8.00
174	Alfonso Soriano	3.00
175	Andruw Jones	2.00
176	Bret Boone	1.50
177	Brian Giles	1.50
178	Carlos Delgado	2.00
179	Derek Lee	2.00
180	Eric Chavez	1.50
181	Frank Thomas	2.00
182	Garret Anderson	1.50
183	Gary Sheffield	2.00
184	Hank Blalock	2.00
185	Jason Giambi	1.50
186	Javy Lopez	1.50
187	Jeff Bagwell	2.00
188	Jim Edmonds	2.00
189	Jim Thome	2.00
190	Ken Griffey Jr.	4.00
191	Lance Berkman	1.50
192	Magglio Ordonez	1.50
193	Manny Ramirez	3.00
194	Mike Lowell	1.50
195	Mike Piazza	5.00
196	Preston Wilson	1.50
197	Rafael Palmeiro	2.00
198	Richie Sexson	1.50
199	Sammy Sosa	5.00
200	Scott Rolen	4.00
201	Shawn Green	1.50
202	Todd Helton	2.00
203	Troy Glaus	1.50
204	Vernon Wells	1.50
205	Vladimir Guerrero	3.00
206	Garret Anderson, Vladimir Guerrero	2.00
207	Luis Gonzalez, Richie Sexson	2.00
208	Andruw Jones, Chipper Jones	3.00
209	Javy Lopez, Miguel Tejada	2.00
210	Manny Ramirez, David Ortiz	5.00
211	Derek Lee, Sammy Sosa	5.00
212	Frank Thomas, Magglio Ordonez	2.00
213	Austin Kearns, Ken Griffey Jr.	4.00
214	Preston Wilson, Todd Helton	2.00
215	Delmon Young, Ivan Rodriguez	2.00
216	Miguel Cabrera, Mike Lowell	3.00
217	Jeff Bagwell, Lance Berkman	2.00
218	Lyle Overbay, Geoff Jenkins	1.50
219	Adrian Beltre, Shawn Green	2.00
220	Jacque Jones, Torii Hunter	1.50
221	Jose Vidro, N. Johnson	1.50
222	Kazuo Matsui, Mike Piazza	5.00
223	Alex Rodriguez, Jason Giambi	6.00
224	Eric Chavez, Jermaine Dye	1.50
225	Jim Thome, Pat Burrell	2.50
226	Brian Giles, Phil Nevin	1.50
227	Bret Boone, Ichiro Suzuki	6.00
228	Albert Pujols, Scott Rolen	8.00
229	Hank Blalock, Mark Teixeira	3.00
230	Carlos Delgado, Vernon Wells	2.00
231	Albert Pujols	8.00
232	Alex Rodriguez	8.00
233	Chipper Jones	3.00
234	Craig Biggio	1.50
235	Curt Schilling	3.00
236	Derek Jeter	8.00
237	Ivan Rodriguez	2.00
238	Jeff Bagwell	2.00
239	Jim Edmonds	2.00
240	Jim Thome	2.00
241	Josh Beckett	2.00
242	Kerry Wood	3.00
243	Kevin Brown	1.50
244	Mark Prior	2.00
245	Miguel Tejada	2.00
246	Mike Mussina	3.00
247	Nomar Garciaparra	4.00
248	Pedro J. Martinez	3.00
249	Randy Johnson	3.00
250	Roger Clemens	6.00
251	Alex Rodriguez, Derek Jeter	12.00
252	Alfonso Soriano, Hank Blalock	4.00
253	Bobby Abreu, Pat Burrell	3.00
254	Edgar Renteria, Scott Rolen	4.00
255	Garret Anderson, Vladimir Guerrero	4.00
256	Jeff Bagwell, Jeff Kent	3.00
257	Jose Reyes, Kazuo Matsui	3.00
258	K. Greene, S. Burroughs	4.00
259	Marcus Giles, Rafael Furcal	3.00
260	Manny Ramirez, Johnny Damon	6.00
261	Tim Bausher **RC**	3.00
262	Tim Bittner **RC**	5.00

Limited
No Pricing
Production 10 Sets

Sweet Impressions Plates
No Pricing
Production One Set

Wood
Stars (1-90): 3-6X
SP's (91-262): .75-1.5X
Production 99 Sets

Diamond Champs Jersey
NM/M
Common Player: 5.00
Production 150 Sets

GA	Garret Anderson	5.00
JB	Josh Beckett	8.00
RC	Roger Clemens	12.00
EG	Eric Gagne	8.00
KG	Ken Griffey Jr.	12.00
RH	Roy Halladay	5.00
DJ	Derek Jeter	20.00
RJ	Randy Johnson	10.00
CJ	Chipper Jones	8.00
GM	Greg Maddux	10.00
PM	Pedro J. Martinez	8.00
PE	Andy Pettitte	5.00
MP	Mike Piazza	10.00
AP	Albert Pujols	20.00
AR	Alex Rodriguez/Yanks	15.00
IR	Ivan Rodriguez	8.00
CS	Curt Schilling	8.00
IS	Ichiro Suzuki	30.00
MT	Miguel Tejada	6.00
BZ	Barry Zito	5.00

Home Run Heroes Jersey
NM/M
Common Player: 5.00
Production 199 Sets

GA	Garret Anderson	5.00
JB	Jeff Bagwell	8.00
CB	Carlos Beltran	8.00
AB	Adrian Beltre	5.00
LB	Lance Berkman	5.00
HB	Hank Blalock	5.00
BB	Bret Boone	5.00
PB	Pat Burrell	5.00
MC	Miguel Cabrera	10.00
EC	Eric Chavez	5.00
CD	Carlos Delgado	5.00
JD	J.D. Drew	5.00
AD	Adam Dunn	8.00
JE	Jim Edmonds	5.00
JG	Jason Giambi	5.00
BG	Brian Giles	5.00
TG	Troy Glaus	5.00
LG	Luis Gonzalez	5.00
SG	Shawn Green	5.00

KG	Ken Griffey Jr. Bat Up	12.00
KG1	Ken Griffey Jr. Swing	12.00
VG	Vladimir Guerrero	10.00
HA	Travis Hafner	5.00
TH	Todd Helton	8.00
DJ	Derek Jeter	20.00
AJ	Andruw Jones	6.00
CJ	Chipper Jones	8.00
JK	Jeff Kent	5.00
DL	Derek Lee	5.00
ML	Mike Lowell	5.00
HM	Hideki Matsui	25.00
JM	Joe Mauer	8.00
FM	Fred McGriff	5.00
MO	Magglio Ordonez	5.00
DO	David Ortiz	15.00
RP	Rafael Palmeiro	8.00
MP	Mike Piazza	10.00
JP	Jorge Posada	5.00
AP	Albert Pujols	20.00
MR	Manny Ramirez	8.00
AR	Alex Rodriguez/Yanks Bat Up	15.00
AR1	Alex Rodriguez/Yanks Swing	15.00
IR	Ivan Rodriguez	8.00
SR	Scott Rolen	10.00
RS	Richie Sexson	5.00
GS	Gary Sheffield	8.00
AS	Alfonso Soriano	8.00
SS	Sammy Sosa	12.00
MT	Mark Teixeira	6.00
TE	Miguel Tejada	6.00
JT	Jim Thome	10.00
VW	Vernon Wells	5.00
BW	Bernie Williams	8.00
PW	Preston Wilson	5.00

Marquee Attractions Jersey
NM/M
Common Player: 5.00
Production 199 Sets

HB	Hank Blalock	8.00
MC	Miguel Cabrera	10.00
EC	Eric Chavez	5.00
RC	Roger Clemens	12.00
CD	Carlos Delgado	5.00
EG	Eric Gagne	8.00
BG	Brian Giles	5.00
KG	Ken Griffey Jr.	12.00
VG	Vladimir Guerrero	10.00
TH	Todd Helton	8.00
HU	Torii Hunter	5.00
DJ	Derek Jeter	20.00
RJ	Randy Johnson	10.00
AJ	Andruw Jones	5.00
PI	Mike Piazza	10.00
MP	Mark Prior	8.00
AP	Albert Pujols	20.00
AR	Alex Rodriguez	15.00
IR	Ivan Rodriguez	8.00
CS	Curt Schilling	10.00
JS	Jason Schmidt	8.00
IS	Ichiro Suzuki	30.00
MS	Mike Sweeney	5.00
MT	Miguel Tejada	8.00
FT	Frank Thomas	8.00
JT	Jim Thome	10.00

Signatures

NM/M
Common Player: 10.00
Black Stitch: No Pricing
Production One Set

GA	Garret Anderson	20.00
RB	Rocco Baldelli	30.00
BE	Josh Beckett	25.00
CB	Carlos Beltran	30.00
AB	Angel Berroa	10.00
HB	Hank Blalock	25.00
BB	Bret Boone	15.00
PB	Pat Burrell	25.00
SB	Sean Burroughs	15.00
MC	Miguel Cabrera	40.00
EC	Eric Chavez	20.00
WC	Will Clark	30.00
RC	Roger Clemens	150.00
JD	J.D. Drew	40.00
AD	Adam Dunn	30.00
NG	Nomar Garciaparra	80.00
BG	Brian Giles	12.00
MG	Marcus Giles	15.00
GL	Tom Glavine	40.00
JG	Juan Gonzalez	35.00
LG	Luis Gonzalez	20.00
KG	Ken Griffey Jr.	75.00
VG	Vladimir Guerrero	75.00
TG	Tony Gwynn	40.00
HA	Roy Halladay	20.00
RH	Rich Harden	10.00
TH	Todd Helton	50.00
HI	Richard Hidalgo	10.00
HO	Trevor Hoffman	20.00
TI	Tim Hudson	30.00
HU	Torii Hunter	20.00
GJ	Geoff Jenkins	15.00
DJ	Derek Jeter	160.00
JJ	Jacque Jones	15.00
AK	Austin Kearns	20.00
RK	Ryan Klesko	15.00
CL	Carlos Lee	15.00
DL	Derek Lee	25.00
ML	Mike Lieberthal	10.00
EL	Esteban Loaiza	10.00
LO	Mike Lowell	20.00
MA	Mike Marshall/SP/34	120.00
EM	Edgar Martinez	50.00
DM	Don Mattingly	65.00
JM	Joe Mauer	25.00
MU	Mark Mulder	20.00
MM	Mike Mussina	40.00
RO	Roy Oswalt	25.00
CP	Corey Patterson	35.00
OP	Odalis Perez	20.00
PI	Mike Piazza	150.00
SP	Scott Podsednik	15.00
MP	Mark Prior	40.00
AP	Albert Pujols	220.00
MR	Manny Ramirez	80.00
JR	Jose Reyes	30.00
CR	Cal Ripken Jr.	180.00
IR	Ivan Rodriguez	60.00
SR	Scott Rolen	40.00
NR	Nolan Ryan	150.00
RS	Ryne Sandberg	75.00
SA	Johan Santana	50.00
JS	Jason Schmidt	25.00
TS	Tom Seaver	50.00
BS	Ben Sheets	20.00
GS	Gary Sheffield	35.00
SM	John Smoltz	50.00
IS	Ichiro Suzuki	250.00
MT	Mark Teixeira	30.00
TE	Miguel Tejada	50.00
FT	Frank Thomas	50.00
JV	Javier Vazquez	20.00
WA	Billy Wagner	15.00
BW	Brandon Webb	15.00
WE	Rickie Weeks	20.00
VW	Vernon Wells/30	25.00
DW	Dontrelle Willis	25.00
RW	Randy Wolf	15.00
KW	Kerry Wood	20.00
DY	Delmon Young	15.00
CZ	Carlos Zambrano	40.00

Signatures Red-Blue Stitch
NM/M
Quantity produced listed

GA	Garret Anderson/45	25.00
RB	Rocco Baldelli/35	40.00
BE	Josh Beckett/45	30.00
CB	Carlos Beltran/45	40.00
AB	Angel Berroa/45	20.00
HB	Hank Blalock/45	25.00
BB	Bret Boone/45	20.00
PB	Pat Burrell/35	40.00
SB	Sean Burroughs/45	15.00
MC	Miguel Cabrera/45	40.00
EC	Eric Chavez/45	35.00
WC	Will Clark/45	35.00
RC	Roger Clemens/30	175.00
JD	J.D. Drew/40	50.00
AD	Adam Dunn/45	40.00
NG	Nomar Garciaparra/45	85.00
BG	Brian Giles/45	15.00
MG	Marcus Giles/45	15.00
GL	Tom Glavine/45	60.00
JG	Juan Gonzalez/45	30.00
LG	Luis Gonzalez/45	25.00
KG	Ken Griffey Jr./.44	150.00
VG	Vladimir Guerrero/45	85.00
TG	Tony Gwynn/45	65.00
HA	Roy Halladay/35	25.00
RH	Rich Harden/45	25.00
TH	Todd Helton/45	30.00
HI	Richard Hidalgo/45	15.00
HO	Trevor Hoffman/45	30.00
TI	Tim Hudson/45	30.00
HU	Torii Hunter/45	30.00
EJ	Edwin Jackson/45	15.00
GJ	Geoff Jenkins/45	15.00
DJ	Derek Jeter/35	275.00
JJ	Jacque Jones/45	15.00
AK	Austin Kearns/45	25.00
RK	Ryan Klesko/45	15.00
CL	Carlos Lee/45	20.00
DL	Derek Lee/45	35.00
ML	Mike Lieberthal/45	15.00
EL	Esteban Loaiza/45	15.00
LO	Mike Lowell/35	30.00
EM	Edgar Martinez/30	70.00
DM	Don Mattingly/45	85.00
JM	Joe Mauer/45	35.00
MU	Mark Mulder/45	25.00
RO	Roy Oswalt/45	25.00
CP	Corey Patterson/45	20.00
OP	Odalis Perez/45	20.00
SP	Scott Podsednik/45	20.00
MP	Mark Prior/45	60.00
AP	Albert Pujols/45	250.00
MR	Manny Ramirez/40	85.00
JR	Jose Reyes/45	40.00
CR	Cal Ripken Jr./35	250.00
IR	Ivan Rodriguez/45	75.00
NR	Nolan Ryan/40	170.00
RS	Ryne Sandberg/40	80.00

SA Johan Santana/45 65.00
JS Jason Schmidt/45 75.00
TS Tom Seaver/35 75.00
BS Ben Sheets/55 25.00
GS Gary Sheffield/45 50.00
SM John Smoltz/40 80.00
IS Ichiro Suzuki/25 500.00
MT Mark Teixeira/45 60.00
TE Miguel Tejada/45 60.00
FT Frank Thomas/25 75.00
JV Javier Vazquez/45 20.00
WA Billy Wagner/45 20.00
BW Brandon Webb/45 20.00
WE Rickie Weeks/45 30.00
VW Vernon Wells/29 35.00
DW Dontrelle Willis/45 40.00
RW Randy Wolf/45 40.00
KW Kerry Wood/45 50.00
DY Delmon Young/45 40.00
CZ Carlos Zambrano/30 50.00

Signatures Barrel
NM/M
Cards not serial numbered, quantity produced provided by Upper Deck.
GA Garret Anderson/74 40.00
RB Rocco Baldelli/19 50.00
BE Josh Beckett/65 35.00
CB Carlos Beltran/55 40.00
AB Angel Berroa/64 25.00
HB Hank Blalock/74 40.00
BB Bret Boone/64 35.00
SB Sean Burroughs/64 20.00
MC Miguel Cabrera/64 40.00
EC Eric Chavez/74 35.00
AD Adam Dunn/74 40.00
NG Nomar Garciaparra/38 100.00
BG Brian Giles/64 25.00
MG Marcus Giles/64 30.00
GL Tom Glavine/64 40.00
KG Ken Griffey Jr./64 125.00
VG Vladimir Guerrero/38 70.00
HA Roy Halladay/64 30.00
RH Rich Harden/64 30.00
TH Todd Helton/38 65.00
HI Richard Hidalgo/64 25.00
HO Trevor Hoffman/68 30.00
TI Tim Hudson/64 40.00
HU Torii Hunter/64 30.00
EJ Edwin Jackson/64 Exch
GJ Geoff Jenkins/64 30.00
DJ Derek Jeter/53 275.00
JJ Jacque Jones/64 25.00
AK Austin Kearns/64 25.00
RK Ryan Klesko/64 25.00
CL Carlos Lee/64 35.00
DL Derrek Lee/64 40.00
ML Mike Lieberthal/64 30.00
EL Esteban Loaiza/64 25.00
LO Mike Lowell/64 35.00
EM Edgar Martinez/64 60.00
DM Don Mattingly/64 125.00
JM Joe Mauer/72 50.00
MU Mark Mulder/64 40.00
MM Mike Mussina/64 50.00
RO Roy Oswalt/64 40.00
CP Corey Patterson/74 Exch 25.00
OP Odalis Perez/64 25.00
PI Mike Piazza/38 150.00
SP Scott Podsednik/64 35.00
MP Mark Prior/64 75.00
AP Albert Pujols/64 250.00
MR Manny Ramirez/63 85.00
JR Jose Reyes/49 50.00
CR Cal Ripken Jr./38 220.00
AR Alex Rodriguez/28 300.00
IR Ivan Rodriguez/64 65.00
NR Nolan Ryan/38 180.00
SA Johan Santana/64 100.00
JS Jason Schmidt/64 35.00
TS Tom Seaver/38 75.00
BS Ben Sheets/64 35.00
GS Gary Sheffield/38 65.00
IS Ichiro Suzuki/64 500.00
MT Mark Teixeira/64 50.00
TE Miguel Tejada/64 50.00
JV Javier Vazquez/64 35.00
WA Billy Wagner/64 30.00
BW Brandon Webb/64 35.00
WE Rickie Weeks/64 35.00
VW Vernon Wells/33 30.00
DW Dontrelle Willis/64 40.00
RW Randy Wolf/64 25.00
KW Kerry Wood/64 40.00
DY Delmon Young/74 50.00
CZ Carlos Zambrano/38 40.00

Signatures Dual
No Pricing
Production 10 Sets

Signatures Glove
NM/M
Production 5-25
GA Garret Anderson/25 50.00
RB Rocco Baldelli/25 50.00
BE Josh Beckett/25 60.00
CB Carlos Beltran/25 50.00
AB Angel Berroa/25 40.00
HB Hank Blalock/25 60.00
BB Bret Boone/25 60.00
PB Pat Burrell/15 65.00
SB Sean Burroughs/25 40.00

MC Miguel Cabrera/25 100.00
EC Eric Chavez/25 50.00
WC Will Clark/25 120.00
AD Adam Dunn/25 80.00
NG Nomar Garciaparra/25 140.00
BG Brian Giles/25 35.00
MG Marcus Giles/25 40.00
GL Tom Glavine/25 65.00
JG Juan Gonzalez/25 50.00
LG Luis Gonzalez/25 50.00
KG Ken Griffey Jr./25 200.00
VG Vladimir Guerrero/25
TG Tony Gwynn/25 100.00
HA Roy Halladay/24 50.00
RH Rich Harden/25 40.00
TH Todd Helton/25 80.00
HI Richard Hidalgo/15 40.00
HO Trevor Hoffman/15 60.00
TI Tim Hudson/15 65.00
HU Torii Hunter/25 40.00
EJ Edwin Jackson/25 35.00
GJ Geoff Jenkins/25 20.00
JJ Jacque Jones/25 20.00
AK Austin Kearns/25 50.00
CL Carlos Lee/25 50.00
DL Derrek Lee/25 65.00
ML Mike Lieberthal/25 40.00
EL Esteban Loaiza/25 40.00
MA Mike Marshall/25 75.00
EM Edgar Martinez/25 85.00
DM Don Mattingly/25 180.00
JM Joe Mauer/25 75.00
MU Mark Mulder/25 40.00
MM Mike Mussina/25 100.00
RO Roy Oswalt/25 65.00
CP Corey Patterson/25 40.00
OP Odalis Perez/25 40.00
SP Scott Podsednik/25 40.00
MP Mark Prior/25 50.00
AP Albert Pujols/25 300.00
MR Manny Ramirez/25 120.00
JR Jose Reyes/25 65.00
CR Cal Ripken Jr./25 275.00
IR Ivan Rodriguez/25 90.00
NR Nolan Ryan/25 250.00
RS Ryne Sandberg/20 125.00
SA Johan Santana/25 85.00
JS Jason Schmidt/25 50.00
BS Ben Sheets/25 50.00
GS Gary Sheffield/20 75.00
MT Mark Teixeira/25 100.00
TE Miguel Tejada/25 75.00
JV Javier Vazquez/25 45.00
WA Billy Wagner/25 65.00
BW Brandon Webb/25 40.00
WE Rickie Weeks/25 35.00
DW Dontrelle Willis/25 70.00
KW Kerry Wood/25 60.00
DY Delmon Young/25 60.00

Signatures Historical Ball
No Pricing
Production One Set

Sweet Sticks

Common Player: 4.00
Production 199 Sets
BA Bobby Abreu 6.00
MA Moises Alou 6.00
GA Garret Anderson 4.00
JB Jeff Bagwell 8.00
BE Carlos Beltran 8.00
AB Adrian Beltre 4.00
LB Lance Berkman 4.00
CB Craig Biggio 4.00
HB Hank Blalock 8.00
BB Bret Boone 4.00
PB Pat Burrell 4.00
MC Miguel Cabrera 8.00
EC Eric Chavez 6.00
RC Roger Clemens 15.00
CD Carlos Delgado 6.00
JD J.D. Drew 6.00
AD Adam Dunn 8.00
JE Jim Edmonds 6.00
RF Rafael Furcal 4.00
NG Nomar Garciaparra 12.00
JG Jason Giambi 6.00
BG Brian Giles 4.00
MG Marcus Giles 4.00
TG Troy Glaus 4.00
GL Tom Glavine 6.00

LG Luis Gonzalez 4.00
SG Shawn Green 4.00
KG Ken Griffey Jr. 15.00
VG Vladimir Guerrero 8.00
TH Todd Helton 8.00
DJ Derek Jeter 25.00
RJ Randy Johnson 8.00
CJ Chipper Jones 10.00
AJ Andruw Jones 6.00
JK Jeff Kent 4.00
DL Derrek Lee 4.00
ML Mike Lowell 4.00
GM Greg Maddux 10.00
HM Hideki Matsui 35.00
KM Kazuo Matsui 15.00
MO Magglio Ordonez 4.00
RP Rafael Palmeiro 8.00
MP Mike Piazza 10.00
PR Mark Prior 6.00
AP Albert Pujols 20.00
MR Manny Ramirez 8.00
ER Edgar Renteria 6.00
JR Jose Reyes 6.00
CR Cal Ripken Jr. 30.00
AR Alex Rodriguez 15.00
IR Ivan Rodriguez 8.00
SR Scott Rolen 10.00
CS Curt Schilling 6.00
RS Richie Sexson 6.00
GS Gary Sheffield 8.00
AS Alfonso Soriano 6.00
SS Sammy Sosa 10.00
IS Ichiro Suzuki 40.00
MT Mark Teixeira 6.00
TE Miguel Tejada 6.00
FT Frank Thomas 8.00
JT Jim Thome 6.00
LW Larry Walker 4.00
TW Ted Williams 60.00
PW Preston Wilson 4.00

Sweet Sticks Dual
NM/M
Common Duo: 10.00
Production 100 Sets
BT Hank Blalock, Mark Teixeira 10.00
CL Miguel Cabrera, Mike Lowell 10.00
JC Randy Johnson, Roger Clemens 25.00
JG Derek Jeter, Nomar Garciaparra 25.00
JM Jose Reyes, Kazuo Matsui 25.00
MM Hideki Matsui, Kazuo Matsui 40.00
PR Albert Pujols, Scott Rolen 40.00
RG Manny Ramirez, Nomar Garciaparra 15.00
RJ Alex Rodriguez, Derek Jeter 50.00
RP Ivan Rodriguez, Mike Piazza 15.00
TB Jim Thome, Pat Burrell 20.00
WP Kerry Wood, Mark Prior 12.00

Sweet Sticks Triple
NM/M
Production 50 Sets
GPS Ken Griffey Jr., Rafael Palmeiro, Sammy Sosa 40.00
JJD Andruw Jones, Chipper Jones, J.D. Drew 25.00
JSG Derek Jeter, Ichiro Suzuki, Ken Griffey Jr. 120.00
MWP Greg Maddux, Kerry Wood, Mark Prior 35.00
RJG Alex Rodriguez, Derek Jeter, Jason Giambi 65.00

Sweet Sticks Quad
NM/M
Production 25 Sets
PRSG Albert Pujols, Alex Rodriguez, Ichiro Suzuki, Ken Griffey Jr. 125.00
RGDM Babe Ruth, Lou Gehrig, Joe DiMaggio, Mickey Mantle 1,200

Sweet Threads
NM/M
Common Player: 4.00
Patch: 1.5-2.5X
Production 85 Sets
JB Jeff Bagwell 8.00
CB Carlos Beltran 4.00
LB Lance Berkman 4.00
HB Hank Blalock 8.00
BB Bret Boone 4.00
MC Miguel Cabrera 8.00
EC Eric Chavez 4.00
BC Bartolo Colon 4.00
CD Carlos Delgado 4.00
JG Jason Giambi 6.00
BG Brian Giles 4.00
TG Troy Glaus 4.00

SWEET THREADS — ROY OSWALT — PITCHER

SG Shawn Green 4.00
VG Vladimir Guerrero 8.00
RH Rich Harden 4.00
TH Todd Helton 8.00
TH Tim Hudson 4.00
ML Mike Lowell 4.00
EM Edgar Martinez 4.00
KM Kazuo Matsui/SP 15.00
JM Joe Mauer 8.00
MM Mark Mulder 4.00
HM Hideo Nomo 8.00
MO Magglio Ordonez 4.00
RO Roy Oswalt 4.00
MP Mark Prior 6.00
MR Manny Ramirez 8.00
JR Jose Reyes 8.00
SS Sammy Sosa 10.00
JS Jason Schmidt 6.00
RS Richie Sexson 4.00
GS Gary Sheffield 6.00
AS Alfonso Soriano 8.00
MT Mark Teixeira 6.00
FT Frank Thomas 8.00
JT Jim Thome 6.00
RW Rickie Weeks 4.00
VW Vernon Wells 4.00
DW Dontrelle Willis 4.00
PW Preston Wilson 4.00
KW Kerry Wood 8.00
DY Delmon Young 4.00

Sweet Threads Dual
NM/M
Common Duo: 5.00
Production 150 Sets
Patch: 1.5-2X
Production 60 Sets
BP Angel Berroa, Scott Podsednik 4.00
BT Hank Blalock, Mark Teixeira 10.00
CK Curt Schilling, Kevin Brown 10.00
CS Roger Clemens, Sammy Sosa 20.00
DT Carlos Delgado, Jim Thome 8.00
GH Eric Gagne, Roy Halladay 8.00
HG Tim Hudson, Vladimir Guerrero 10.00
JC Randy Johnson, Roger Clemens 25.00
JH Andruw Jones, Torii Hunter 8.00
JJ Andruw Jones, Chipper Jones 5.00
MM Hideki Matsui, Kazuo Matsui 50.00
MP Joe Mauer, Mark Prior 10.00
PC Andy Pettitte, Roger Clemens 20.00
PP Jorge Posada, Mike Piazza 15.00
PS Albert Pujols, Ichiro Suzuki 50.00
PW Albert Pujols, Kerry Wood 15.00
RJ Alex Rodriguez, Derek Jeter 50.00
RM Jose Reyes, Kazuo Matsui 15.00
SB Alfonso Soriano, Bret Boone 8.00
SM Gary Sheffield, Pedro J. Martinez 12.00
WP Kerry Wood, Mark Prior 10.00
YW Delmon Young, Rickie Weeks 10.00

Sweet Threads Triple

SWEET THREADS

NM/M
Common Trio: 10.00
Production 99 Sets
Triple Patch: 2X
No pricing 15 or less.
AGG Garret Anderson, Troy Glaus, Vladimir Guerrero 20.00
BKE Jeff Bagwell, Jeff Kent, Morgan Ensberg 15.00
BLR Adrian Beltre, Mike Lowell, Scott Rolen 20.00
BMS Bret Boone, Edgar Martinez, Ichiro Suzuki 50.00
BWC Josh Beckett, Kerry Wood, Roger Clemens 20.00
CMM Bobby Crosby, Joe Mauer, Kazuo Matsui 30.00
DHW Carlos Delgado, Roy Halladay, Vernon Wells 15.00
DKG Adam Dunn, Austin Kearns, Ken Griffey Jr. 20.00
DMJ Joe DiMaggio, Mickey Mantle, Derek Jeter 220.00
DMW Joe DiMaggio, Mickey Mantle, Ted Williams 250.00
DRN Johnny Damon, Manny Ramirez, Trot Nixon 40.00
FRP Keith Foulke, Mariano Rivera, Troy Percival 25.00
GPS Ken Griffey Jr., Rafael Palmeiro, Sammy Sosa 35.00
JJD Andruw Jones, Chipper Jones, J.D. Drew 20.00
JTG Derek Jeter, Miguel Tejada, Nomar Garciaparra 40.00
JWH Edwin Jackson, Jerome Williams, Rich Harden 35.00
KVG Jeff Kent, Jose Vidro, Marcus Giles 10.00
LTO Carlos Lee, Frank Thomas, Magglio Ordonez 20.00
LTP Javy Lopez, Miguel Tejada, Rafael Palmeiro 20.00
MCF Kazuo Matsui, Miguel Cabrera, Rafael Furcal 20.00
MMH Mike Mussina, Pedro J. Martinez, Tim Hudson 25.00
MSH Joe Mauer, Johan Santana, Torii Hunter 35.00
MWP Greg Maddux, Kerry Wood, Mark Prior 25.00
PAS Corey Patterson, Moises Alou, Sammy Sosa 30.00
PCO Andy Pettitte, Roger Clemens, Roy Oswalt 25.00
PRR Albert Pujols, Edgar Renteria, Scott Rolen 40.00
PTH Albert Pujols, Jim Thome, Todd Helton 30.00
RCB Alex Rodriguez, Eric Chavez, Hank Blalock 30.00
RGJ Alex Rodriguez, Ken Griffey Jr., Randy Johnson 35.00
RGW Jose Reyes, Khalil Greene, Rickie Weeks 30.00
RJG Alex Rodriguez, Derek Jeter, Jason Giambi 60.00
RMP Jose Reyes, Kazuo Matsui, Mike Piazza 25.00
SBK Alfonso Soriano, Bret Boone, Jeff Kent 20.00
SBP Jason Schmidt, Josh Beckett, Mark Prior 15.00
SBT Alfonso Soriano, Hank Blalock, Mark Teixeira 20.00
SLM Curt Schilling, Derek Lowe, Pedro J. Martinez 40.00
VBM Javier Vazquez, Kevin Brown, Mike Mussina 20.00
WBP Brandon Webb, Josh Beckett, Mark Prior 15.00
WGS Billy Wagner, Eric Gagne, John Smoltz 20.00
WRC Kerry Wood, Nolan Ryan, Roger Clemens 20.00
YCW Delmon Young, Miguel Cabrera, Rickie Weeks 60.00
ZMH Barry Zito, Mark Mulder, Tim Hudson 10.00

Sweet Threads Quad
NM/M
Common Quad: 20.00

Production 99 Sets
Quad Patch: No Pricing
Production 1-15
BADH Carlos Beltran, Garret Anderson, Johnny Damon, Torii Hunter 30.00
BBGS Angel Berroa, Carlos Beltran, Alex Gonzalez, Mike Sweeney 20.00
BPJC Josh Beckett, Mark Prior, Randy Johnson, Roger Clemens 30.00
BWRC Josh Beckett, Kerry Wood, Nolan Ryan, Roger Clemens 50.00
CAGG Bartolo Colon, Garret Anderson, Troy Glaus, Vladimir Guerrero 25.00
DHHW Carlos Delgado, Eric Hinske, Roy Halladay, Vernon Wells 20.00
DOGP Carlos Delgado, David Ortiz, Jason Giambi, Rafael Palmeiro 25.00
GNKB Brian Giles, Phil Nevin, Ryan Klesko, Sean Burroughs 25.00
GNLG Eric Gagne, Hideo Nomo, Paul LoDuca, Shawn Green 30.00
JBGB Chipper Jones, Lance Berkman, Luis Gonzalez, Pat Burrell 25.00
JEGW Andruw Jones, Jim Edmonds, Ken Griffey Jr., Preston Wilson 35.00
JJDF Andruw Jones, Chipper Jones, J.D. Drew, Rafael Furcal 25.00
JMSH Jacque Jones, Joe Mauer, Shannon Stewart, Torii Hunter 35.00
JRMT Derek Jeter, Edgar Renteria, Kazuo Matsui, Miguel Tejada 40.00
KGCS Austin Kearns, Brian Giles, Miguel Cabrera, Sammy Sosa 25.00
LMRS Carlos Lee, Hideki Matsui, Manny Ramirez, Shannon Stewart 75.00
LTOK Carlos Lee, Frank Thomas, Magglio Ordonez, Paul Konerko 25.00
LTPP Javy Lopez, Miguel Tejada, Raffy, Sidney Ponson 25.00
MMMH Mark Mulder, Mike Mussina, Pedro J. Martinez, Roy Halladay 25.00
MTTS Edgar Martinez, Jim Thome, Mark Teixeira, Mike Sweeney 20.00
NSGH Phil Nevin, Richie Sexson, Shawn Green, Todd Helton 20.00
PBBC Andy Pettitte, Craig Biggio, Jeff Bagwell, Roger Clemens 40.00
PLBT Albert Pujols, Lee, Jeff Bagwell, Jim Thome 40.00
PRER Albert Pujols, Edgar Renteria, Jim Edmonds, Scott Rolen 70.00
PWPS Corey Patterson, Kerry Wood, Mark Prior, Sammy Sosa 40.00
RCBG Alex Rodriguez, Eric Chavez, Hank Blalock, Troy Glaus 30.00
RJDM Alex Rodriguez, Derek Jeter, Joe DiMaggio, Mickey Mantle 275.00
RLPM Ivan Rodriguez, Javy Lopez, Jorge Posada, Joe Mauer 40.00
RMPG Jose Reyes, Kazuo Matsui, Mike Piazza, Tom Glavine 30.00
SBKV Alfonso Soriano, Bret Boone, Jeff Kent, Jose Vidro 20.00
SBMM Curt Schilling, Kevin Brown, Mike Mussina, Pedro J. Martinez 40.00
SDRM Curt Schilling, Johnny Damon, Manny Ramirez, Pedro J. Martinez 60.00
SSOG Gary Sheffield, Ichiro Suzuki, Magglio Ordonez, Vladimir Guerrero 50.00
VCBM Javier Vazquez, Jose Contreras, Kevin Brown, Mike Mussina 25.00

WATM Billy Wagner, Bobby Abreu, Jim Thome, Kevin Millwood 30.00
WBCL Dontrelle Willis, Josh Beckett, Miguel Cabrera, Mike Lowell 20.00
WGJS Brandon Webb, Luis Gonzalez, Randy Johnson, Richie Sexson 25.00
ZMHH Barry Zito, Mark Mulder, Rich Harden, Tim Hudson 35.00

2004 Upper Deck Sweet Spot Classic

NM/M

Complete Set (161):		
Common Player (1-90):		.40
Common (91-161):		2.00
Production 1,910-1,999		
Pack (4):		15.00
Box (12):		150.00
1	Al Kaline	1.00
2	Andre Dawson	.40
3	Bert Blyleven	.40
4	Bill Dickey	.40
5	Bill Mazeroski	.40
6	Billy Martin	.40
7	Bob Feller	.50
8	Bob Gibson	.40
9	Bob Lemon	.40
10	George Kell	.40
11	Bobby Doerr	.40
12	Brooks Robinson	1.00
13	Cal Ripken Jr.	4.00
14	Carl Hubbell	.40
15	Carl Yastrzemski	1.50
16	Charlie Keller	.40
17	Chuck Dressen	.40
18	Cy Young	1.00
19	Dave Winfield	.75
20	Dizzy Dean	.75
21	Don Drysdale	.75
22	Don Larsen	.75
23	Don Mattingly	2.50
24	Don Newcombe	.40
25	Duke Snider	.75
26	Early Wynn	.40
27	Eddie Mathews	1.00
28	Elston Howard	.40
29	Frank Robinson	.75
30	Gary Carter	.40
31	Gil Hodges	.40
32	Gil McDougald	.40
33	Hank Greenberg	.75
34	Harmon Killebrew	1.50
35	Harry Caray	.40
36	Honus Wagner	1.00
37	Hoyt Wilhelm	.40
38	Jackie Robinson	2.00
39	Jim Bunning	.40
40	Jim Palmer	.75
41	Jimmie Foxx	1.00
42	Jimmy Wynn	.40
43	Joe DiMaggio	3.00
44	Joe Torre	.40
45	Johnny Mize	.40
46	Juan Marichal	.75
47	Larry Doby	.40
48	Lefty Gomez	.40
49	Lefty Grove	.40
50	Leo Durocher	.40
51	Lou Boudreau	.40
52	Lou Brock	.50
53	Lou Gehrig	3.00
54	Luis Aparicio	.40
55	Maury Wills	.40
56	Mel Allen	.40
57	Mel Ott	.40
58	Mickey Cochrane	.40
59	Mickey Mantle	4.00
60	Mike Schmidt	2.00
61	Monte Irvin	.40
62	Nolan Ryan	4.00
63	Pee Wee Reese	.40
64	Phil Rizzuto	.50
65	Ralph Kiner	.40
66	Richie Ashburn	.40
67	Rick Ferrell	.40
68	Roberto Clemente	2.50
69	Robin Roberts	.40
70	Robin Yount	1.00
71	Rogers Hornsby	.75
72	Rollie Fingers	.40
73	Roy Campanella	.75
74	Ryne Sandberg	1.50
75	Tony Gwynn	1.00
76	Satchel Paige	.75
77	Shoeless Joe Jackson	2.00
78	Stan Musial	2.00
79	Ted Williams	3.00
80	Thurman Munson	.75
81	Tom Seaver	1.50
82	Tommy Henrich	.40
83	Tony Perez	.40
84	Tris Speaker	.40
85	Vida Blue	.40
86	Wade Boggs	.50
87	Walter Johnson	.75
88	Warren Spahn	1.00
89	Whitey Ford	.75
90	Willie McCovey	.40
91	Andre Dawson	2.50
92	Andre Dawson	2.50
93	Ernie Banks	4.00
94	Bob Lemon	2.00
95	Cal Ripken Jr.	8.00
96	Cal Ripken Jr.	8.00
97	Carl Yastrzemski	3.00
98	Carlton Fisk	2.50
99	Cy Young	4.00
100	Don Larsen	2.50
101	Don Newcombe	2.00
102	Don Newcombe	2.00
103	Dwight Evans	2.00
104	Elston Howard	2.50
105	Frank Robinson	3.00
106	Frank Robinson	3.00
107	Frank Robinson	3.00
108	Gil McDougald	2.00
109	Hank Greenberg	4.00
110	Harmon Killebrew	4.00
111	Hoyt Wilhelm	2.00
112	Hoyt Wilhelm	2.00
113	Jackie Robinson	5.00
114	Jackie Robinson	5.00
115	Jackie Robinson	5.00
116	Jackie Robinson	5.00
117	Jim Bunning	2.00
118	Joe DiMaggio	6.00
119	Joe Morgan	2.00
120	Johnny Mize	2.50
121	Johnny Mize	2.50
122	Juan Marichal	3.00
123	Ken Griffey Sr.	2.00
124	Larry Doby	2.50
125	Lefty Gomez	2.00
126	Lou Boudreau	2.00
127	Lou Gehrig	6.00
128	Lou Gehrig	6.00
129	Mark McGwire	6.00
130	Mark McGwire	6.00
131	Maury Wills	2.00
132	Mel Ott	3.00
133	Mike Schmidt	5.00
134	Nolan Ryan	8.00
135	Nolan Ryan	8.00
136	Pee Wee Reese	2.00
137	Nolan Ryan	8.00
138	Richie Ashburn	2.50
139	Roberto Clemente	8.00
140	Roberto Clemente	8.00
141	Robin Roberts	2.00
142	Robin Yount	3.00
143	Roger Clemens	2.00
144	Rollie Fingers	2.00
145	Rollie Fingers	2.00
146	Roy Campanella	3.00
147	Ryne Sandberg	4.00
148	Satchel Paige	4.00
149	Satchel Paige	4.00
150	Stan Musial	5.00
151	Stan Musial	5.00
152	Stan Musial	5.00
153	Ted Williams	6.00
154	Ted Williams	6.00
155	Tom Seaver	3.00
156	Tom Seaver	3.00
157	Wade Boggs	2.50
158	Warren Spahn	3.00
159	Warren Spahn	3.00
160	Joe DiMaggio	6.00
161	Yogi Berra	4.00

Game-Used Patch
NM/M
Some not priced due to scarcity.
Holofoil: No Pricing
Production 10

BB	Bert Blyleven/113	25.00
WB	Wade Boggs/90	30.00
AD	Andre Dawson/100	20.00
TG	Tony Gwynn/100	35.00
CK	Charlie Keller/55	30.00
ML	Mickey Lolich/115	15.00
DM	Don Mattingly/176	40.00
GM	Gil McDougald/31	25.00
TM	Thurman Munson/100	
FR	Frank Robinson/50	30.00
NR	Nolan Ryan/96	65.00
TS	Tom Seaver/94	30.00
MW	Maury Wills/78	25.00
CY	Carl Yastrzemski/20	65.00
RY	Robin Yount/100	30.00

Jersey

NM/M
Common Player: 5.00
Production 275 Sets
Holofoils: 1.5-2X
Production 50

SA	Sparky Anderson	6.00
SB	Sal Bando	5.00
RB	Ron Blomberg	5.00
BB	Bert Blyleven	5.00
WB	Wade Boggs	8.00
WB1	Wade Boggs	8.00
JB	Jim Bunning	5.00
GC	Gary Carter	6.00
RC	Roberto Clemente	65.00
AD	Andre Dawson	5.00
AD1	Andre Dawson	5.00
JD	Joe DiMaggio	70.00
CD	Chuck Dressen	5.00
KG	Ken Griffey Sr.	5.00
TG	Tony Gwynn	10.00
EH	Elston Howard	8.00
CK	Charlie Keller	15.00
ML	Mickey Lolich	6.00
MM	Mickey Mantle	125.00
JM	Juan Marichal	6.00
RM	Roger Maris	45.00
BM	Billy Martin	5.00
EM	Eddie Mathews	10.00
DM	Don Mattingly	20.00
GM	Gil McDougald	8.00
JO	Johnny Mize	10.00
TM	Thurman Munson	20.00
SM	Stan Musial	25.00
JP	Jim Palmer	5.00
CR	Cal Ripken Jr.	20.00
PR	Phil Rizzuto	15.00
FR	Frank Robinson	8.00
JR	Jackie Robinson	40.00
NR	Nolan Ryan	25.00
TS	Tom Seaver	15.00
OS	Ozzie Smith	10.00
JT	Joe Torre	8.00
TW	Ted Williams	70.00
MW	Maury Wills	5.00
CY	Carl Yastrzemski	15.00
RY	Robin Yount	10.00

Logo Patch

NM/M
Common Level 1: 5.00
Production 300
Level 2: 1X
Production 230
Level 3: 1X
Production 200
Level 4: 1-1.5X
Production 150
Level 5: 1-1.5X
Production 125
Level 6: 1-2X
Production 75
Level 7: 1.5-2.5X
Production 50
Level 8: No Pricing
Production 25

AL	Mel Allen	5.00
LA	Luis Aparicio	5.00
RA	Richie Ashburn	6.00
WB	Wade Boggs	8.00
LB	Lou Boudreau	5.00
BR	Lou Brock	8.00
JB	Jim Bunning	5.00
CA	Roy Campanella	8.00
GC	Gary Carter	5.00
HC	Harry Caray	10.00
RC	Roberto Clemente	25.00
TC	Ty Cobb	12.00
CO	Mickey Cochrane	5.00
AD	Andre Dawson	8.00
DD	Dizzy Dean	8.00
BD	Bill Dickey	5.00
JD	Joe DiMaggio	15.00
LD	Larry Doby	6.00
DO	Bobby Doerr	6.00
DR	Don Drysdale	5.00
DU	Leo Durocher	5.00
BF	Bob Feller	8.00
RF	Rick Ferrell	5.00
FI	Rollie Fingers	5.00
WF	Whitey Ford	6.00
JF	Jimmie Foxx	8.00
FF	Frankie Frisch	5.00
GE	Lou Gehrig	15.00
CG	Charlie Gehringer	8.00
BG	Bob Gibson	8.00
LG	Lefty Gomez	5.00
HG	Hank Greenberg	10.00
GR	Lefty Grove	6.00
TH	Tommy Henrich	5.00
GH	Gil Hodges	8.00
RH	Rogers Hornsby	8.00
CH	Carl Hubbell	5.00
IR	Monte Irvin	5.00
JJ	Shoeless Joe Jackson	20.00
FJ	Ferguson Jenkins	6.00
WJ	Walter Johnson	8.00
AK	Al Kaline	15.00
HK	Harmon Killebrew	15.00
RK	Ralph Kiner	8.00
DL	Don Larsen	5.00
TL	Tommy Lasorda	5.00
BL	Bob Lemon	5.00
ML	Mickey Lolich	5.00
MI	Mickey Mantle	40.00
MA	Juan Marichal	6.00
BM	Billy Martin	8.00
EM	Eddie Mathews	8.00
CM	Christy Mathewson	10.00
DM	Don Mattingly	20.00
WM	Willie McCovey	8.00
JM	Johnny Mize	6.00
TM	Thurman Munson	10.00
SM	Stan Musial	10.00
DN	Don Newcombe	5.00
MO	Mel Ott	5.00
SP	Satchel Paige	10.00
JP	Jim Palmer	8.00
TP	Tony Perez	5.00
GP	Gaylord Perry	5.00
PR	Pee Wee Reese	6.00
CR	Cal Ripken Jr.	30.00
RI	Phil Rizzuto	8.00
RR	Robin Roberts	6.00
RO	Brooks Robinson	12.00
RF	Frank Robinson	8.00
JR	Jackie Robinson	12.00
RU	Babe Ruth	20.00
NR	Nolan Ryan	25.00
RS	Ryne Sandberg	20.00
MS	Mike Schmidt	15.00
TS	Tom Seaver	5.00
SK	Bill "Moose" Skowron	5.00
ES	Enos Slaughter	5.00
DS	Duke Snider	8.00
WS	Warren Spahn	10.00
TR	Tris Speaker	8.00
JT	Joe Torre	5.00
HW	Honus Wagner	10.00
WI	Hoyt Wilhelm	5.00
TW	Ted Williams	20.00
MW	Maury Wills	5.00
DW	Dave Winfield	5.00
EW	Early Wynn	5.00
YA	Carl Yastrzemski	12.00
CY	Cy Young	10.00

Signature Black Ink
NM/M
Common Autograph: 15.00

3	Preacher Roe/225	25.00
4	Bob Feller/65	45.00
5	Bob Gibson/50	50.00
6	Harry Kalas/100	45.00
7	Bobby Doerr/100	25.00
8	Cal Ripken Jr./50	165.00
9	Carl Yastrzemski/35	110.00
10	Carlton Fisk/100	45.00
11	Chuck Tanner/150	15.00
12	Cito Gaston/150	15.00
13	Danny Ozark/150	15.00
14	Dave Winfield/80	50.00
15	Davey Johnson/175	15.00
16	Ernie Harwell/100	50.00
17	Dick Williams/150	15.00
18	Don Mattingly/40	100.00
19	Don Newcombe/40	35.00
20	Duke Snider/35	60.00
21	Steve Carlton/150	35.00
22	Felipe Alou/175	20.00
23	Frank Robinson/65	40.00
24	Gary Carter/100	35.00
25	Gene Mauch/225	15.00
26	George Bamberger/225	15.00
28	Gus Suhr/50	30.00
29	Harmon Killebrew/50	70.00
30	Jack McKeon/225	15.00
31	Jim Bunning/100	25.00
32	Jimmy Piersall/212	20.00
35	Johnny Bench/50	75.00
36	Juan Marichal/50	40.00
37	Lou Brock/50	50.00
38	George Kell/40	50.00
41	Maury Wills/40	30.00
42	Mike Schmidt/40	100.00
43	Nolan Ryan/50	135.00
44	Eddie Mayo/140	15.00
45	Phil Rizzuto/50	50.00
46	Ralph Kiner/40	45.00
47	Lonny Frey/114	15.00
48	Bill Mazeroski/50	40.00
49	Robin Roberts/40	40.00
51	Robin Yount/40	75.00
52	Roger Craig/175	15.00
53	Tony Perez/40	70.00
56	Sparky Anderson/175	20.00
57	Stan Musial/40	100.00
58	Ted Radcliffe/225	15.00
60	Tom Seaver/25	70.00
61	Tony Gwynn/65	75.00
62	Tony LaRussa/275	15.00
63	Tony Oliva/150	20.00
64	Tony Pena/50	15.00
66	Whitey Ford/45	65.00
67	Yogi Berra/65	75.00

Signature Blue Ink
NM/M
Common Autograph: 15.00
Some not priced due to scarcity.

2	Preacher Roe/150	25.00
4	Bob Feller/150	45.00
5	Bob Gibson/25	60.00
6	Harry Kalas/50	50.00
7	Bobby Doerr/50	30.00
8	Cal Ripken Jr./25	200.00
10	Carlton Fisk/50	50.00
11	Chuck Tanner/125	15.00
12	Cito Gaston/125	15.00
13	Danny Ozark/125	15.00
14	Dave Winfield/35	60.00
15	Davey Johnson/150	15.00
16	Ernie Harwell/50	15.00
17	Dick Williams/125	15.00
21	Steve Carlton/100	35.00
22	Felipe Alou/150	20.00
23	Frank Robinson/50	40.00
24	Gary Carter/75	35.00
25	Gene Mauch/150	15.00
26	George Bamberger/150	15.00
29	Gus Suhr/85	30.00
31	Jack McKeon/150	25.00
32	Jim Bunning/65	60.00
33	Jimmy Piersall/150	25.00
35	Johnny Bench/20	90.00
38	George Kell/25	50.00
39	Maury Wills/25	40.00
42	Nolan Ryan/25	175.00
43	Ozzie Smith/50	75.00
44	Eddie Mayo/50	20.00
45	Phil Rizzuto/25	60.00
47	Lonny Frey/75	15.00
48	Bill Mazeroski/25	40.00
49	Robin Roberts/25	40.00
50	Robin Yount/25	75.00
52	Roger Craig/150	15.00
56	Sparky Anderson/150	25.00
57	Stan Musial/25	120.00
58	Ted Radcliffe/150	50.00
62	Tony LaRussa/50	15.00
63	Tony Oliva/25	25.00
64	Tony Pena/115	15.00
67	Yogi Berra/50	70.00

Signature Holofoil
NM/M
Many not priced due to scarcity.

SSA-4	Bob Feller/25	70.00
SSA-5	Bob Gibson/25	60.00
SSA-11	Chuck Tanner/100	15.00
SSA-12	Cito Gaston/100	15.00
SSA-13	Danny Ozark/100	15.00
SSA-15	Davey Johnson/70	15.00
SSA-17	Dick Williams/100	15.00
SSA-22	Felipe Alou/50	30.00
SSA-24	Gary Carter/50	45.00
SSA-45	Phil Rizzuto/25	60.00
SSA-49	Robin Roberts/25	40.00
SSA-50	Robin Yount/25	75.00
SSA-52	Roger Craig/50	20.00
SSA-56	Sparky Anderson/50	30.00
SSA-57	Stan Musial/25	120.00
SSA-62	Tony LaRussa/50	15.00
SSA-63	Tony Oliva/25	25.00
SSA-64	Tony Pena/100	15.00

Signature Red Ink
NM/M
Many not priced due to scarcity.

SSA-14	Dave Winfield/25	65.00
SSA-25	Gene Mauch/25	25.00
SSA-26	George Bamberger/25	30.00

Wood Barrel Autograph
NM/M
Varying quantities produced
Some not priced due to scarcity.

HB	Harold Baines/200	35.00
JB	Johnny Bench/50	120.00
WB	Wade Boggs/200	60.00
SM	Stan Musial/25	185.00
CR	Cal Ripken Jr./25	300.00
NR	Nolan Ryan/25	200.00
RS	Ron Santo/203	45.00
TS	Tom Seaver/25	140.00
BW	Billy Williams/200	35.00

2004 Upper Deck Ultimate Collection

NM/M

Complete Set (222):		
Common Player (1-126):		2.00
Production 675		
Common (127-168):		4.00
Production 525		
Common (169-194):		6.00
Production 299		
Common (195-209, 222):		8.00
Production 199		
Common (210-221):		15.00
Production 75		
Pack (4):		80.00
Box (4):		275.00
1	Al Kaline	4.00
2	Billy Williams	2.00
3	Bob Feller	2.00
4	Bob Gibson	4.00
5	Bob Lemon	2.00
6	Bobby Doerr	2.00
7	Brooks Robinson	3.00
8	Cal Ripken Jr.	10.00
9	Jim "Catfish" Hunter	2.00
10	Eddie Mathews	4.00
11	Enos Slaughter	2.00
12	Ernie Banks	4.00
13	Fergie Jenkins	2.00
14	Gaylord Perry	2.00
15	Harmon Killebrew	4.00
16	Jim Bunning	2.00
17	Joe DiMaggio	6.00
18	Joe Morgan	2.00
19	Juan Marichal	2.00
20	Lou Brock	2.00
21	Luis Aparicio	2.00
22	Mickey Mantle	12.00
23	Mike Schmidt	6.00
24	Monte Irvin	2.00
25	Nolan Ryan	8.00
26	Pee Wee Reese	2.00
27	Phil Niekro	2.00
28	Phil Rizzuto	2.00
29	Ralph Kiner	3.00
30	Richie Ashburn	2.00
31	Robin Roberts	3.00
32	Robin Yount	5.00
33	Rod Carew	2.00
34	Rollie Fingers	2.00
35	Stan Musial	6.00
36	Ted Williams	8.00
37	Tom Seaver	4.00
38	Warren Spahn	4.00
39	Whitey Ford	3.00
40	Willie McCovey	2.00
41	Willie Stargell	3.00
42	Yogi Berra	4.00
43	Adrian Beltre	2.00
44	Albert Pujols	8.00
45	Alex Rodriguez	3.00
46	Alfonso Soriano	3.00
47	Andruw Jones	2.00
48	Andy Pettitte	2.00
49	Aubrey Huff	2.00
50	Barry Larkin	2.00
51	Ben Sheets	2.00
52	Bernie Williams	2.00
53	Bobby Abreu	2.00
54	Brad Penny	2.00
55	Bret Boone	2.00
56	Brian Giles	2.00
57	Carlos Beltran	3.00
58	Carlos Delgado	2.00
59	Carlos Guillen	2.00
60	Carlos Lee	2.00
61	Carlos Zambrano	2.00
62	Chipper Jones	4.00
63	Craig Biggio	2.00
64	Craig Wilson	2.00
65	Curt Schilling	3.00
66	David Ortiz	4.00
67	Derek Jeter	10.00
68	Eric Chavez	2.00
69	Eric Gagne	3.00
70	Frank Thomas	3.00
71	Garret Anderson	2.00

No.	Player	Price
72	Gary Sheffield	3.00
73	Greg Maddux	5.00
74	Hank Blalock	3.00
75	Hideki Matsui	6.00
76	Ichiro Suzuki	6.00
77	Ivan Rodriguez	3.00
78	J.D. Drew	2.00
79	Jake Peavy	2.00
80	Jason Schmidt	2.00
81	Jeff Bagwell	3.00
82	Jeff Kent	2.00
83	Jim Thome	4.00
84	Joe Mauer	2.00
85	Johan Santana	3.00
86	Jose Reyes	2.00
87	Jose Vidro	2.00
88	Ken Griffey Jr.	5.00
89	Kerry Wood	2.00
90	Larry Walker	2.00
91	Luis Gonzalez	2.00
92	Lyle Overbay	2.00
93	Magglio Ordonez	4.00
94	Manny Ramirez	4.00
95	Mark Mulder	2.00
96	Mark Prior	3.00
97	Mark Teixeira	2.00
98	Melvin Mora	2.00
99	Michael Young	2.00
100	Miguel Cabrera	4.00
101	Miguel Tejada	3.00
102	Mike Lowell	2.00
103	Mike Piazza	6.00
104	Mike Sweeney	2.00
105	Nomar Garciaparra	6.00
106	Oliver Perez	2.00
107	Pedro J. Martinez	4.00
108	Preston Wilson	2.00
109	Rafael Palmeiro	4.00
110	Randy Johnson	4.00
111	Roger Clemens	10.00
112	Roy Halladay	2.00
113	Roy Oswalt	2.00
114	Sammy Sosa	6.00
115	Scott Podsednik	2.00
116	Scott Rolen	2.00
117	Shawn Green	2.00
118	Tim Hudson	2.00
119	Todd Helton	3.00
120	Tom Glavine	3.00
121	Torii Hunter	2.00
122	Travis Hafner	2.00
123	Troy Glaus	2.00
124	Vernon Wells	2.00
125	Victor Martinez	2.00
126	Vladimir Guerrero	4.00
127	Aarom Baldiris RC	8.00
128	Alfredo Simon RC	4.00
129	Andres Blanco RC	4.00
130	Jeff Bajenaru RC	4.00
131	Bartolome Fortunato RC	4.00
132	Brandon Medders RC	4.00
133	Brian Dallimore RC	4.00
134	Carlos Hines RC	4.00
135	Carlos Vasquez RC	8.00
136	Casey Daigle RC	4.00
137	Chad Bentz RC	4.00
138	Chris Aguila RC	4.00
139	Chris Saenz RC	4.00
140	Chris Shelton RC	10.00
141	Colby Miller RC	4.00
142	David Crouthers RC	4.00
143	David Aardsma RC	4.00
144	Dennis Sarfate RC	4.00
145	Donnie Kelly RC	4.00
146	Eddy Rodriguez RC	8.00
147	Eduardo Villacis RC	4.00
148	Edwardo Sierra RC	4.00
149	Edwin Moreno RC	6.00
150	Kyle Denney RC	4.00
151	Evan Rust RC	4.00
152	Fernando Nieve RC	4.00
153	Frank Francisco RC	4.00
154	Franklyn Gracesqui RC	4.00
155	Freddy Guzman RC	4.00
156	Greg Dobbs RC	4.00
157	Hector Gimenez RC	4.00
158	Jason Alfaro RC	4.00
159	Jake Woods RC	4.00
160	Andy Green RC	4.00
161	Jason Bartlett RC	8.00
162	Jason Frasor RC	4.00
163	Jeff Bennett RC	4.00
164	Jerome Gamble RC	4.00
165	Jerry Gil RC	4.00
166	Joe Hietpas RC	4.00
167	Jorge Sequea RC	4.00
168	Jorge Vasquez RC	6.00
169	Josh Labandeira RC	6.00
170	Justin Germano RC	6.00
171	Justin Hampson RC	6.00
172	Chris Young RC	30.00
173	Justin Knoedler RC	6.00
174	Justin Lehr RC	6.00
175	Justin Leone RC	10.00
176	Kazuhito Tadano RC	6.00
177	Kevin Cave RC	6.00
178	Lincoln Holdzkom RC	6.00
179	Mike Rose RC	6.00
180	Luis Gonzalez RC	6.00
181	Mariano Gomez RC	6.00
182	Rene Rivera RC	6.00
183	Mike Wuertz RC	8.00
184	Mike Gosling RC	6.00
185	Mike Johnston RC	6.00
186	Mike Rouse RC	6.00
187	Nick Regilio RC	6.00
188	Onil Joseph RC	6.00
189	Orlando Rodriguez RC	6.00
190	Phil Stockman RC	6.00
191	Renyel Pinto RC	10.00
192	Roberto Novoa RC	12.00
193	Roman Colon RC	6.00
194	Ronald Belisario RC	6.00
195	Ronny Cedeno RC	8.00
196	Ryan Meaux RC	8.00
197	Ryan Wing RC	8.00
198	Scott Dohmann RC	8.00
199	Joey Gathright RC	10.00
200	Shawn Camp RC	8.00
201	Shawn Hill RC	8.00
202	Steve Andrade RC	8.00
203	Tim Bausher RC	8.00
204	Tim Bittner RC	8.00
205	Brad Halsey RC	10.00
206	William Bergolla RC	8.00
207	Kameron Loe RC	8.00
208	Jesse Crain RC	10.00
209	Scott Kazmir	25.00
210	Akinori Otsuka/ Auto. RC	60.00
211	Chris Oxspring/ Auto. RC	15.00
212	Ian Snell/Auto. RC	30.00
213	John Gall/Auto. RC	20.00
214	Jose Capellan/ Auto. RC	50.00
215	Yadier Molina/ Auto. RC	40.00
216	Merkin Valdez/ Auto. RC	25.00
217	Ramon Ramirez/ Auto. RC	15.00
218	Rusty Tucker/ Auto. RC	20.00
219	Scott Proctor/ Auto. RC	25.00
220	Sean Henn/Auto.	15.00
221	Shingo Takatsu/ Auto. RC	75.00
222	Kazuo Matsui RC	30.00

Gold

Gold (1-194): 1-2X
Gold (195-222): No Pricing
Production 25
Gold 210-221 Production 15

Platinum

Platinum (1-126): No Pricing
Production 10
Platinum (210-221): No Pricing
Production One

Rainbow

Rainbows: No Pricing
Production One Set

Achievement Materials

NM/M

Common Player:

	Player	Price
EB	Ernie Banks/58	25.00
JB	Johnny Bench/68	15.00
YB	Yogi Berra/51	20.00
GB	George Brett/80	25.00
CA	Roy Campanella/51	25.00
RO	Rod Carew/77	15.00
SC	Steve Carlton/72	10.00
OC	Orlando Cepeda/58	10.00
CL	Roger Clemens/86	25.00
RC	Roberto Clemente/ 66	100.00
JD	Joe DiMaggio/39	100.00
DD	Don Drysdale/62	15.00
BG	Bob Gibson/68	15.00
KG	Ken Griffey Jr./97	25.00
DJ	Derek Jeter/96	40.00
RJ	Randy Johnson/99	15.00
HK	Harmon Killebrew/69	15.00
GM	Greg Maddux/92	20.00
MA	Mickey Mantle/56	200.00
RM	Roger Maris/61	60.00
PM	Pedro J. Martinez/99	15.00
DM	Don Mattingly/85	20.00
MC	Willie McCovey/59	15.00
TM	Thurman Munson/70	15.00
EM	Eddie Murray/77	15.00
JP	Jim Palmer/73	10.00
MP	Mike Piazza/93	20.00
CR	Cal Ripken Jr./82	15.00
BR	Brooks Robinson/64	15.00
FR	Frank Robinson/66	15.00
JR	Jackie Robinson/47	65.00
RS	Ryne Sandberg/84	40.00
MS	Mike Schmidt/80	25.00
TS	Tom Seaver/19	15.00
SS	Sammy Sosa/98	20.00
TW	Ted Williams/42	100.00
CY	Carl Yastrzemski/67	25.00
RY	Robin Yount/82	15.00

All-Stars Signatures

NM/M

Most not priced.

	Player	Price
RC	Rod Carew/18	40.00
SM	Stan Musial/24	75.00
BR	Brooks Robinson/15	60.00
CY	Carl Yastrzemski/18	80.00

Bat Barrel Signatures

No Pricing
Production 1-5

Dual Legendary Materials

NM/M

Common Player:
Production 50 Sets

	Players	Price
BM	Willie McCovey, Ernie Banks	40.00
BR	Roger Maris, Babe Ruth	300.00
CB	Yogi Berra, Roy Campanella	35.00
CM	Roberto Clemente, Thurman Munson	100.00
CS	Duke Snider, Roy Campanella	40.00
DM	Mickey Mantle, Joe DiMaggio	200.00
DW	Joe DiMaggio, Ted Williams	150.00
FD	Don Drysdale, Bob Feller	25.00
MB	Yogi Berra, Thurman Munson	50.00
MC	Mickey Mantle, Roberto Clemente	180.00
MM	Mickey Mantle, Roger Maris	220.00
MW	Mickey Mantle, Ted Williams	200.00
RB	Ernie Banks, Jackie Robinson	75.00
RC	Jackie Robinson, Roy Campanella	75.00
RD	Joe DiMaggio, Babe Ruth	275.00
RM	Babe Ruth, Mickey Mantle	400.00
RP	Jackie Robinson, Satchel Paige	100.00
RW	Roberto Clemente, Willie McCovey	100.00
WM	Eddie Mathews, Ted Williams	125.00

Dual Materials

NM/M

Common Player:
Production 60 Sets

	Players	Price
BC	Brooks Robinson, Cal Ripken Jr.	50.00
BM	Yogi Berra, Thurman Munson	40.00
BP	Johnny Bench, Mike Piazza	25.00
BS	Mike Schmidt, George Brett	40.00
CK	Harmon Killebrew, Rod Carew	30.00
CM	Willie McCovey, Will Clark	30.00
ER	Ryne Sandberg, Ernie Banks	60.00
GS	Sammy Sosa, Ken Griffey Jr.	40.00
JC	Randy Johnson, Roger Clemens	40.00
JM	Derek Jeter, Don Mattingly	60.00
MB	Johnny Bench, Thurman Munson	40.00
MC	Don Mattingly, Will Clark	40.00
MP	Mark Prior, Joe Mauer	25.00
MR	Bill Mazeroski, Jackie Robinson	60.00
MT	Kazuo Matsui, Shingo Takatsu	30.00
MY	Robin Yount, Paul Molitor	40.00
PR	Manny Ramirez, Albert Pujols	50.00
RC	Nolan Ryan, Roger Clemens	60.00
RP	Mike Piazza, Ivan Rodriguez	20.00
RR	Brooks Robinson, Frank Robinson	25.00
RT	Thurman Munson, Roy Campanella	30.00
SG	Ken Griffey Jr., Ichiro Suzuki	60.00
SP	Mark Prior, Ben Sheets	10.00
SR	Duke Snider, Pee Wee Reese	30.00
SS	Sammy Sosa, Ryne Sandberg	50.00
TS	Jim Thome, Mike Schmidt	35.00
WM	Don Mattingly, Dave Winfield	40.00
WP	Mark Prior, Kerry Wood	20.00
WR	Kerry Wood, Nolan Ryan	50.00
YR	Manny Ramirez, Carl Yastrzemski	35.00

Dual Materials Signature

NM/M

Production 25 Sets

	Players	Price
AB	Luis Aparicio, Ernie Banks	100.00
BB	Wade Boggs, Hank Blalock	80.00
BC	Brooks Robinson, Cal Ripken Jr.	250.00
BF	Carlton Fisk, Johnny Bench	100.00
BG	Carlos Beltran, Ken Griffey Jr.	150.00
BJ	Derek Jeter, Yogi Berra	200.00
BM	Brian Giles, Marcus Giles	35.00
BP	Johnny Bench, Mike Piazza	160.00
BR	Jim Bunning, Robin Roberts	40.00
BT	Hank Blalock, Mark Teixeira	60.00
CB	Hank Blalock, Eric Chavez	50.00
CC	Steve Carlton, Roger Clemens	150.00
CJ	Roger Clemens, Randy Johnson	300.00
CK	Harmon Killebrew, Rod Carew	80.00
CL	Miguel Cabrera, Mike Lowell	75.00
CM	Miguel Cabrera, Carlos Beltran	125.00
DD	Derek Jeter, Don Mattingly	300.00
DG	Gaylord Perry, Don Sutton	50.00
DJ	Jim Rice, Dave Parker	80.00
DS	Ryne Sandberg, Andre Dawson	125.00
DW	Andre Dawson, Billy Williams	50.00
ER	Ryne Sandberg, Ernie Banks	160.00
FC	Bob Feller, Rocky Colavito	75.00
FR	Bob Feller, Nolan Ryan	180.00
GB	Brooks Robinson, George Brett	140.00
GC	Ron Guidry, Steve Carlton	50.00
GG	Ken Griffey Sr., Ken Griffey Jr.	150.00
GM	Mike Schmidt, George Brett	150.00
GP	Rafael Palmeiro, Ken Griffey Jr.	150.00
GR	Greg Maddux, Roger Clemens	300.00
GS	John Smoltz, Eric Gagne	75.00
IV	Ivan Rodriguez, Victor Martinez	65.00
JB	Ernie Banks, Fergie Jenkins	100.00
JC	Randy Johnson, Steve Carlton	125.00
JD	Johnny Podres, Don Sutton	50.00
JG	Randy Johnson, Ken Griffey Jr.	200.00
JM	Chipper Jones, Dale Murphy	150.00
JP	Jim Palmer, Fergie Jenkins	50.00
JR	Cal Ripken Jr., Derek Jeter	500.00
KG	Ken Griffey Jr., Harmon Killebrew	150.00
KN	Kerry Wood, Nolan Ryan	175.00
KT	Scott Kazmir, Shingo Takatsu	75.00
LB	Yogi Berra, Don Larsen	180.00
MB	Johnny Bench, Joe Morgan	80.00
MC	Don Mattingly, Will Clark	125.00
MH	Mark Mulder, Tim Hudson	50.00
MP	Mark Prior, Joe Mauer	80.00
MS	Bill Mazeroski, Ryne Sandberg	150.00
MW	Will Clark, Mark Grace	75.00
MY	Robin Yount, Paul Molitor	150.00
NR	Roger Clemens, Nolan Ryan	300.00
OR	Manny Ramirez, David Ortiz	200.00
OS	Stan Musial, Ozzie Smith	150.00
PC	Will Clark, Rafael Palmeiro	100.00
PN	Phil Niekro, Gaylord Perry	50.00
PS	Johnny Podres, Duke Snider	60.00
RB	Rod Carew, Bill Mazeroski	75.00
RC	Eric Chavez, Brooks Robinson	60.00
RM	Eddie Murray, Cal Ripken Jr.	275.00
RP	Brooks Robinson, Jim Palmer	65.00
RR	Brooks Robinson, Frank Robinson	75.00
RS	Robin Roberts, Steve Carlton	60.00
RT	Miguel Tejada, Cal Ripken Jr.	200.00
SC	Mike Schmidt, Steve Carlton	150.00
SF	Ben Sheets, Bob Feller	50.00
SG	Eric Gagne, Bruce Sutter	75.00
SO	Ben Sheets, Roy Oswalt	50.00
SP	Mark Prior, Ben Sheets	80.00
SR	Brooks Robinson, Mike Schmidt	150.00
SS	Tom Seaver, Ben Sheets	75.00
TB	Tony Gwynn, Brian Giles	75.00
TC	Mark Teixeira, Miguel Cabrera	75.00
WM	Dave Winfield, Don Mattingly	150.00
WO	Orlando Cepeda, Willie McCovey	75.00
WW	Will Clark, Willie McCovey	75.00
YR	Carl Yastrzemski, Manny Ramirez	160.00

Game Materials

NM/M

Common Player: 8.00
Production 99 Sets

	Player	Price
EB	Ernie Banks	15.00
JB	Johnny Bench	10.00
WB	Wade Boggs	8.00
GB	George Brett	20.00
LB	Lou Brock	8.00
RC	Rod Carew	8.00
SC	Steve Carlton	8.00
WC	Will Clark	8.00
CL	Roger Clemens	20.00
TC	Ty Cobb	100.00
DD	Don Drysdale	8.00
BF	Bob Feller	8.00
CF	Carlton Fisk	10.00
BG	Bob Gibson	10.00
KG	Ken Griffey Jr.	20.00
TG	Tony Gwynn	8.00
DJ	Derek Jeter	30.00
RJ	Randy Johnson	15.00
AK	Al Kaline	15.00
HK	Harmon Killebrew	10.00
MA	Juan Marichal	8.00
RM	Roger Maris	50.00
ED	Eddie Mathews	15.00
DM	Don Mattingly	25.00
BM	Bill Mazeroski	8.00
WM	Willie McCovey	8.00
PM	Paul Molitor	10.00
TM	Thurman Munson	15.00
EM	Eddie Murray	15.00
SM	Stan Musial	25.00
JP	Jim Palmer	8.00
PI	Mike Piazza	15.00
MP	Mark Prior	10.00
AP	Albert Pujols	25.00
CR	Cal Ripken Jr.	40.00
BR	Brooks Robinson	8.00
FR	Frank Robinson	8.00
JR	Jackie Robinson	40.00
RS	Ryne Sandberg	25.00
MS	Mike Schmidt	15.00
TS	Tom Seaver	10.00
OS	Ozzie Smith	8.00
DS	Duke Snider	15.00
WS	Warren Spahn	15.00
WSt	Willie Stargell	8.00
IS	Ichiro Suzuki	60.00
DW	Dave Winfield	8.00
KW	Kerry Wood	10.00
CY	Carl Yastrzemski	20.00
RY	Robin Yount	10.00

Game Patch

NM/M

Common Player:
Production 75 unless noted.
5 Color +: 1.5X

	Player	Price
BA	Jeff Bagwell	25.00
BE	Josh Beckett	15.00
CB	Carlos Beltran	25.00
JB	Johnny Bench	15.00
YB	Yogi Berra	50.00
HB	Hank Blalock	15.00
WB	Wade Boggs	20.00
GB	George Brett	50.00
LB	Lou Brock	40.00
BU	Jim Bunning/66	30.00
CA	Miguel Cabrera	30.00
RC	Rod Carew	30.00
RO	Rod Carew	30.00
GC	Gary Carter	30.00
EC	Eric Chavez	15.00
WC	Will Clark	30.00
WC1	Will Clark	30.00
RC	Roger Clemens	40.00
RB	Roberto Clemente	200.00
CO1	Rocky Colavito	80.00
JD	Joe DiMaggio	180.00
BF	Bob Feller	40.00
NF	Nellie Fox/55	125.00
GL	Troy Glaus	20.00
KG	Ken Griffey Jr.	50.00
VG	Vladimir Guerrero	30.00
RG	Ron Guidry	30.00
TG	Tony Gwynn	30.00
TH	Todd Helton	30.00
CH	Jim "Catfish" Hunter	30.00
DJ	Derek Jeter	40.00
RJ	Randy Johnson	25.00
RJ1	Randy Johnson	25.00
CJ	Chipper Jones	25.00
HK	Harmon Killebrew	40.00
GM	Greg Maddux	35.00
GM1	Greg Maddux	35.00
MA	Joe Mauer	20.00
PE	Pedro J. Martinez	25.00
HM	Hideki Matsui/44	100.00
KM	Kazuo Matsui	40.00
DM	Don Mattingly	40.00
JM	Joe Mauer	25.00
BM	Bill Mazeroski/55	60.00
WM	Willie McCovey	35.00
PM	Paul Molitor	30.00
MO	Joe Morgan	20.00
TM	Thurman Munson	40.00
MU	Eddie Murray	40.00
SM	Stan Musial	75.00
RP	Rafael Palmeiro	25.00
JP	Jim Palmer	25.00
PI	Mike Piazza	30.00
PO	Johnny Podres	25.00
MP	Mark Prior	20.00
AP	Albert Pujols	50.00
MR	Manny Ramirez	25.00
CR	Cal Ripken Jr.	60.00
BR	Brooks Robinson	25.00
IR	Ivan Rodriguez	25.00
SR	Scott Rolen	25.00
NR	Nolan Ryan/51	50.00
NR1	Nolan Ryan	50.00
NR2	Nolan Ryan	50.00
RS	Ryne Sandberg	50.00
CS	Curt Schilling	25.00
MS	Mike Schmidt	40.00
TS	Tom Seaver	20.00
BS	Ben Sheets	25.00
GS	Gary Sheffield	20.00
OS	Ozzie Smith	40.00
AS	Alfonso Soriano	25.00
SS	Sammy Sosa	25.00
SP	Warren Spahn/62	60.00
WS	Willie Stargell	30.00
IS	Ichiro Suzuki	120.00
MT	Mark Teixeira	15.00
TE	Miguel Tejada	25.00
JT	Jim Thome	35.00
BW	Bernie Williams	20.00
WI	Billy Williams	20.00
DW	Dave Winfield	35.00
KW	Kerry Wood	25.00
CY	Carl Yastrzemski	50.00
RY	Robin Yount	40.00

Dual Game Patch

NM/M

Production 25 Sets

	Players	Price
BB	Carlos Beltran, Jeff Bagwell	40.00
BC	Josh Beckett, Miguel Cabrera	40.00
BG	Lou Brock, Tony Gwynn	75.00
BS	Mike Schmidt, George Brett	100.00
BT	Hank Blalock, Mark Teixeira	40.00
CG	Rod Carew, Tony Gwynn	50.00
CP	Mike Piazza, Gary Carter	50.00
CR	Eric Chavez, Scott Rolen	50.00
FB	Johnny Bench, Carlton Fisk	50.00
FR	Nolan Ryan, Bob Feller	100.00
GC	Will Clark, Mark Grace	40.00
GG	Ken Griffey Sr., Ken Griffey Jr.	75.00
GM	Stan Musial, Bob Gibson	60.00
GS	Mark Grace, Ryne Sandberg	100.00
HF	Rollie Fingers, Jim "Catfish" Hunter	30.00
JC	Roger Clemens, Randy Johnson	75.00
JJ	Chipper Jones, Andruw Jones	40.00
JM	Derek Jeter, Hideki Matsui	125.00
KC	Rod Carew, Harmon Killebrew	50.00
KM	Willie McCovey, Harmon Killebrew	50.00
KS	Sammy Sosa, Ken Griffey Jr.	75.00
LS	Fred Lynn, Ichiro Suzuki	100.00

MG	Greg Maddux, Tom Glavine	50.00
MJ	Chipper Jones, Eddie Mathews	75.00
MM	Kazuo Matsui, Hideki Matsui	120.00
MY	Robin Yount, Paul Molitor	60.00
PC	Will Clark, Rafael Palmeiro	40.00
PR	Scott Rolen, Albert Pujols	100.00
RC	Nolan Ryan, Roger Clemens	100.00
RM	Cal Ripken Jr., Eddie Murray	150.00
RP	Cal Ripken Jr., Jim Palmer	125.00
RR	Jackie Robinson, Pee Wee Reese	150.00
RS	Nolan Ryan, Tom Seaver	100.00
RT	Cal Ripken Jr., Miguel Tejada	75.00
SB	Jim Bunning, Mike Schmidt	75.00
SM	Pedro J. Martinez, Curt Schilling	60.00
ST	Mike Schmidt, Jim Thome	75.00
WM	Don Mattingly, Dave Winfield	75.00
WP	Mark Prior, Kerry Wood	50.00
WS	Billy Williams, Sammy Sosa	60.00
YR	Carl Yastrzemski, Jim Rice	75.00

Game Patch Signatures
NM/M
Common Player:
Production 30 Sets

EB	Ernie Banks	75.00
CB	Carlos Beltran	65.00
JB	Johnny Bench	65.00
HB	Hank Blalock	50.00
WB	Wade Boggs	65.00
GB	George Brett	100.00
MC	Miguel Cabrera	65.00
RC	Rod Carew	50.00
EC	Eric Chavez	40.00
WC	Will Clark	60.00
AD	Andre Dawson	40.00
BG	Bob Gibson	50.00
KG	Ken Griffey Jr.	125.00
TG	Tony Gwynn	65.00
DJ	Derek Jeter	200.00
RJ	Randy Johnson	125.00
AK	Al Kaline	50.00
HK	Harmon Killebrew	75.00
GM	Greg Maddux	150.00
MA	Juan Marichal	50.00
DM	Don Mattingly	100.00
JM	Joe Mauer	60.00
WM	Willie McCovey	50.00
PM	Paul Molitor	60.00
MU	Mark Mulder	40.00
EM	Eddie Murray	80.00
SM	Stan Musial	120.00
RO	Roy Oswalt	50.00
JP	Jim Palmer	50.00
PI	Mike Piazza	125.00
MP	Mark Prior	60.00
JR	Jim Rice	50.00
CR	Cal Ripken Jr.	200.00
BR	Brooks Robinson	60.00
FR	Frank Robinson	50.00
NR	Nolan Ryan	150.00
RS	Ryne Sandberg	150.00
MS	Mike Schmidt	125.00
SC	Red Schoendienst	40.00
TS	Tom Seaver	75.00
BS	Ben Sheets	50.00
OS	Ozzie Smith	75.00
MT	Mark Teixeira	50.00
KW	Kerry Wood	75.00
CY	Carl Yastrzemski	100.00
RY	Robin Yount	80.00

Stat Patch
NM/M
Quantity produced listed
5+ Color Patch: 1.5X

JB	Jeff Bagwell/47	25.00
CB	Carlos Beltran/29	35.00
CB1	Carlos Beltran/41	30.00
BE	Johnny Bench/45	50.00
HB	Hank Blalock/29	20.00
GB	George Brett/20	80.00
GB1	George Brett/30	75.00
WC	Will Clark/35	50.00
CL1	Roger Clemens/24	50.00
DD	Don Drysdale/25	50.00
EG	Eric Gagne/55	25.00
VG	Vladimir Guerrero/44	25.00
VG1	Vladimir Guerrero/40	25.00
TG	Tony Gwynn/45	50.00
TG1	Tony Gwynn/25	50.00
DJ	Derek Jeter/32	60.00
DJ1	Derek Jeter/24	60.00
RJ	Randy Johnson/20	40.00
CJ	Chipper Jones/45	25.00
HK	Harmon Killebrew/49	50.00
GM1	Greg Maddux/20	40.00
GM2	Greg Maddux/17	40.00
JM	Juan Marichal/26	30.00
MA	Pedro Martinez/23	35.00
HM	Hideki Matsui/31	120.00
DM	Don Mattingly/35	75.00
PM	Paul Molitor/39	40.00
TM	Thurman Munson/20	75.00
PN	Phil Niekro/23	30.00
PN1	Phil Niekro/23	30.00
RP	Rafael Palmeiro/47	25.00
JP1	Jim Palmer/23	30.00
PI	Mike Piazza/40	40.00
AP	Albert Pujols/43	60.00
AP1	Albert Pujols/51	50.00
MR	Manny Ramirez/45	25.00
JR1	Jim Rice/46	25.00
CR	Cal Ripken Jr./34	75.00
CR1	Cal Ripken Jr./47	75.00
IR	Ivan Rodriguez/35	30.00
IR1	Ivan Rodriguez/25	30.00
SR	Scott Rolen/31	35.00
RS	Ryne Sandberg/40	65.00
RS1	Ryne Sandberg/19	100.00
MS	Mike Schmidt/48	65.00
TS	Tom Seaver/25	30.00
JS	John Smoltz/24	30.00
JS1	John Smoltz/55	25.00
AS	Alfonso Soriano/39	20.00
AS1	Alfonso Soriano/43	20.00
SS1	Sammy Sosa/66	30.00
WS	Willie Stargell/48	50.00
IS	Ichiro Suzuki/56	120.00
MT	Miguel Tejada/34	25.00
JT	Jim Thome/52	25.00
CY	Carl Yastrzemski/44	50.00
RY	Robin Yount/43	50.00
DW	Dave Winfield/37	25.00

Super Patch
No Pricing
Production 4-20

Gold Glove Signature Materials
No Pricing
Production 1-16

Legendary Materials
NM/M
Common Player: 10.00
Production 50 Sets

EB	Ernie Banks	20.00
YB	Yogi Berra	20.00
CA	Roy Campanella	15.00
RC	Roberto Clemente	100.00
TC	Ty Cobb	100.00
JD	Joe DiMaggio	100.00
DD	Don Drysdale	15.00
BF	Bob Feller	10.00
MM	Mickey Mantle	200.00
RM	Roger Maris	60.00
EM	Eddie Mathews	20.00
WM	Willie McCovey	15.00
TM	Thurman Munson	25.00
SM	Stan Musial	40.00
SP	Satchel Paige	60.00
JR	Jackie Robinson	60.00
BR	Babe Ruth	250.00
DS	Duke Snider	15.00
TW	Ted Williams	80.00

Logo Patch Signatures
No Pricing
Production One Set

Loyalty Game Jersey Signature
NM/M
Quantity produced listed

EB	Ernie Banks/19	85.00
GB	George Brett/21	100.00
TG	Tony Gwynn/20	70.00
HK	Harmon Killebrew/21	75.00
CR	Cal Ripken Jr./21	200.00
BR	Brooks Robinson/23	50.00
MS	Mike Schmidt/18	100.00
CY	Carl Yastrzemski/23	85.00
RY	Robin Yount/20	85.00

Materials Signatures
NM/M
Production 50 Sets

BA	Bobby Abreu	25.00
JE	Jeff Bagwell	75.00
EB	Ernie Banks	75.00
BE	Josh Beckett	50.00
CB	Carlos Beltran	60.00
JB	Johnny Bench	75.00
HB	Hank Blalock	30.00
WB	Wade Boggs	50.00
WB1	Wade Boggs	50.00
GB	George Brett	80.00
LB	Lou Brock	40.00
JB	Jim Bunning	30.00
CA	Miguel Cabrera	60.00
RC	Rod Carew	40.00
RC1	Rod Carew	40.00
SC	Steve Carlton	35.00
SC1	Steve Carlton	35.00
GC	Gary Carter	30.00
GC1	Gary Carter	30.00
JC	Joe Carter	30.00
OC	Orlando Cepeda	35.00
OC1	Orlando Cepeda	35.00
EC	Eric Chavez	30.00
WC	Will Clark	40.00
WC1	Will Clark	40.00
WC2	Will Clark	40.00
WC3	Will Clark	40.00
CL	Roger Clemens	125.00
CL1	Roger Clemens	125.00
CL2	Roger Clemens	125.00
CO	Rocky Colavito	75.00
CO1	Rocky Colavito	75.00
AD	Andre Dawson	30.00
AD1	Andre Dawson	30.00
DE	Dennis Eckersley	30.00
DE1	Dennis Eckersley	30.00
BF	Bob Feller	30.00
RF	Rollie Fingers	30.00
RF1	Rollie Fingers	30.00
CF	Carlton Fisk	40.00
CF1	Carlton Fisk	40.00
EG	Eric Gagne	50.00
NG	Nomar Garciaparra	125.00
NG1	Nomar Garciaparra	125.00
BG	Bob Gibson	75.00
MG	Mark Grace	40.00
KG	Ken Griffey Jr.	100.00
KG1	Ken Griffey Jr.	100.00
VG	Vladimir Guerrero	65.00
RG	Ron Guidry	40.00
TG	Tony Gwynn	50.00
HE	Todd Helton	40.00
TH	Tim Hudson	30.00
FJ	Fergie Jenkins	30.00
DJ	Derek Jeter	150.00
RJ	Randy Johnson	100.00
RJ1	Randy Johnson	100.00
CJ	Chipper Jones	50.00
AK	Al Kaline	50.00
HK	Harmon Killebrew	60.00
DL	Don Larsen	40.00
ML	Mike Lowell	20.00
GM	Greg Maddux	100.00
GM1	Greg Maddux	100.00
JU	Juan Marichal	30.00
DO	Don Mattingly	80.00
JM	Joe Mauer	40.00
JM1	Joe Mauer	40.00
BM	Bill Mazeroski	40.00
MC	Willie McCovey	50.00
PM	Paul Molitor	50.00
PM1	Paul Molitor	50.00
PM2	Paul Molitor	50.00
MO	Joe Morgan	30.00
MU	Mark Mulder	40.00
DM	Dale Murphy	40.00
EM	Eddie Murray	80.00
EM1	Eddie Murray	80.00
RO	Roy Oswalt	25.00
RP	Rafael Palmeiro	50.00
JP	Jim Palmer	50.00
TP	Tony Perez	25.00
GP	Gaylord Perry	25.00
GP1	Gaylord Perry	25.00
PI	Mike Piazza	100.00
PI1	Mike Piazza	100.00
PO	Johnny Podres	30.00
MP	Mark Prior	60.00
MP1	Mark Prior	60.00
MR	Manny Ramirez	75.00
JR	Jim Rice	30.00
CR	Cal Ripken Jr.	180.00
RR	Robin Roberts	30.00
BR	Brooks Robinson	50.00
FR	Frank Robinson	35.00
FR1	Frank Robinson	35.00
IR	Ivan Rodriguez	50.00
SR	Scott Rolen	50.00
NR	Nolan Ryan	120.00
NR1	Nolan Ryan	120.00
NR2	Nolan Ryan	120.00
NR3	Nolan Ryan	120.00
SA	Ryne Sandberg	100.00
MS	Mike Schmidt	75.00
RS	Red Schoendienst	25.00
TS	Tom Seaver	50.00
TS1	Tom Seaver	50.00
BS	Ben Sheets	30.00
BS1	Ben Sheets	30.00
OS	Ozzie Smith	60.00
JS	John Smoltz	50.00
SN	Duke Snider	40.00
SN1	Duke Snider	40.00
AS	Alfonso Soriano	30.00
DS	Don Sutton	30.00
MT	Mark Teixeira	40.00
TE	Miguel Tejada	40.00
TE1	Miguel Tejada/34	40.00
FT	Frank Thomas	60.00
RW	Rickie Weeks	30.00
RW1	Rickie Weeks	30.00
BW	Billy Williams	40.00
DW	Dave Winfield	40.00
DW1	Dave Winfield	40.00
KW	Kerry Wood	50.00
CY	Carl Yastrzemski	75.00
DY	Delmon Young	40.00
DY1	Delmon Young	40.00
RY	Robin Yount	60.00

Quadruple Materials
No Pricing
Production 15 Sets

Signature Numbers Patch
NM/M
Quantity produced listed

WB	Wade Boggs/26	65.00
LB	Lou Brock/20	50.00
MC	Miguel Cabrera/24	60.00
BF	Bob Feller/19	50.00
EG	Eric Gagne/38	50.00
KG	Ken Griffey Jr./30	120.00
VG	Vladimir Guerrero/27	80.00
DM	Don Mattingly/23	100.00
WM	Willie McCovey/44	60.00
RO	Roy Oswalt/44	30.00
PI	Mike Piazza/31	60.00
MP	Mark Prior/22	60.00
RS	Ryne Sandberg/23	125.00
MS	Mike Schmidt/20	100.00
MT	Mark Teixeira/23	40.00
BW	Billy Williams/26	50.00
DW	Dave Winfield/31	50.00
RY	Robin Yount/19	100.00

Signatures
NM/M
Common Player: 20.00
Production 25 unless noted.
Gold: 1-1.5X
Production 10-25
No pricing 20 or less.
Platinum: No Pricing
Production One Set

LA1	Luis Aparicio	20.00
BE	Johnny Bench	50.00
YB	Yogi Berra	50.00
WB	Wade Boggs	50.00
MC1	Miguel Cabrera	50.00
CW	Rod Carew	40.00
CA1	Steve Carlton	30.00
CL	Roger Clemens	125.00
BF1	Bob Feller	35.00
RF1	Rollie Fingers	25.00
WF	Whitey Ford	50.00
NG	Nomar Garciaparra	100.00
GI	Bob Gibson	40.00
VG	Vladimir Guerrero	50.00
RJ	Randy Johnson	100.00
AK1	Al Kaline	50.00
HK1	Harmon Killebrew	60.00
RK1	Ralph Kiner	40.00
GM	Greg Maddux	80.00
WI	Willie McCovey	40.00
MO	Joe Morgan	25.00
EM	Eddie Murray	40.00
MU	Stan Musial	75.00
JP1	Jim Palmer	30.00
PI	Mike Piazza	100.00
MP	Mark Prior	40.00
KP	Kirby Puckett	65.00
CR	Cal Ripken Jr.	160.00
RR1	Robin Roberts	30.00
BR1	Brooks Robinson	50.00
RY	Ryne Sandberg	75.00
TS	Tom Seaver	50.00
OS	Ozzie Smith	60.00
SN	Duke Snider	40.00
DW	Dave Winfield	35.00
CY	Carl Yastrzemski	75.00

Signatures Tier B
NM/M
Common Player:

BA	Bobby Abreu/25	30.00
LA	Luis Aparicio/25	25.00
CB	Carlos Beltran/25	50.00
BI	Craig Biggio/25	40.00
HB	Hank Blalock/25	35.00
BL	Bert Blyleven/99	20.00
JB	Jim Bunning/99	20.00
MC	Miguel Cabrera/99	30.00
SC	Sean Casey/99	20.00
OC	Orlando Cepeda/25	25.00
EC	Eric Chavez/25	30.00
WC	Will Clark/25	40.00
RC	Rocky Colavito/99	20.00
DC	David Cone/99	20.00
CC	Carl Crawford/99	10.00
AD	Andre Dawson/25	25.00
BD	Bobby Doerr/99	20.00
DE	Dennis Eckersley/25	35.00
BF	Bob Feller/25	30.00
RF	Rollie Fingers/25	30.00
GF	George Foster/25	20.00
EG	Eric Gagne/25	50.00
BG	Brian Giles/99	10.00
MG	Marcus Giles/99	10.00
DG	Dwight Gooden/99	20.00
GG	Rich "Goose" Gossage/99	10.00
KG	Ken Griffey Sr./69	15.00
RG	Ron Guidry/25	40.00
TH	Travis Hafner/99	20.00
KH	Keith Hernandez/99	15.00
FH	Frank Howard/99	20.00
MI	Monte Irvin/25	25.00
JK	Jim Kaat/99	20.00
AK	Al Kaline/25	60.00
GK	George Kell/99	20.00
HK	Harmon Killebrew/25	60.00
RK	Ralph Kiner/25	40.00
ML	Mike Lowell/99	10.00
SL	Sparky Lyle/99	10.00
FL	Fred Lynn/25	20.00
VM	Victor Martinez/99	20.00
JM	Joe Mauer/99	25.00
BM	Bill Mazeroski/25	50.00
MM	Mark Mulder/99	20.00
DM	Dale Murphy/99	15.00
GN	Graig Nettles/99	15.00
DN	Don Newcombe/25	25.00
RO	Roy Oswalt/99	20.00
AO	Akinori Otsuka/99	40.00
JP	Jim Palmer/99	20.00
DP	Dave Parker/25	25.00
CP	Corey Patterson/99	20.00
TP	Tony Perez/25	35.00
GP	Gaylord Perry/25	20.00
PO	Johnny Podres/25	25.00
RR	Robin Roberts/25	30.00
BR	Brooks Robinson/25	50.00
AR	Al Rosen/99	20.00
SA	Ron Santo/99	25.00
JS	Jason Schmidt/99	25.00
RS	Red Schoendienst/25	30.00
BS	Ben Sheets/99	25.00
SM	John Smoltz/25	50.00
SU	Bruce Sutter/99	25.00
ST	Shingo Takatsu/99	40.00
MT	Mark Teixeira/25	40.00
LT	Luis Tiant/99	10.00
RW	Rickie Weeks/99	20.00
BW	Billy Williams/25	30.00
MW	Maury Wills/25	20.00
DY	Delmon Young/99	25.00

Signatures Duals
NM/M
Production 25 Sets

BB	Wade Boggs, Hank Blalock	80.00
BC	Miguel Cabrera, Carlos Beltran	120.00
BG	Carlos Beltran, Ken Griffey Jr.	175.00
BR	Jim Bunning, Robin Roberts	75.00
BS	George Brett, Mike Schmidt	150.00
BT	Hank Blalock, Mark Teixeira	70.00
CB	Hank Blalock, Eric Chavez	50.00
CJ	Roger Clemens, Randy Johnson	300.00
CL	Mike Lowell, Miguel Cabrera	50.00
CR	Eric Chavez, Brooks Robinson	65.00
DW	Billy Williams, Andre Dawson	40.00
EF	Rollie Fingers, Dennis Eckersley	50.00
FR	Bob Feller, Nolan Ryan	160.00
GC	Will Clark, Mark Grace	65.00
GG	Marcus Giles, Brian Giles	40.00
GK	Ken Griffey Jr., Harmon Killebrew	150.00
GS	John Smoltz, Eric Gagne	85.00
IC	Monte Irvin, Orlando Cepeda	50.00
JC	Steve Carlton, Randy Johnson	125.00
JM	Derek Jeter, Don Mattingly	300.00
JP	Jim Palmer, Fergie Jenkins	50.00
JT	Fergie Jenkins, Luis Tiant	50.00
KG	Ken Griffey Sr., Ken Griffey Jr.	175.00
KK	Al Kaline, Harmon Killebrew	80.00
MC	Don Mattingly, Will Clark	125.00
MH	Mark Mulder, Tim Hudson	40.00
MP	Joe Mauer, Mark Prior	60.00
NR	Roger Clemens, Nolan Ryan	400.00
NS	Don Sutton, Don Newcombe	25.00
PC	Rafael Palmeiro, Will Clark	120.00
PN	Phil Niekro, Gaylord Perry	40.00
PR	Jim Rice, Dave Parker	60.00
PS	Ben Sheets, Mark Prior	60.00
RC	Steve Carlton, Robin Roberts	50.00
RJ	Derek Jeter, Cal Ripken Jr.	500.00
RP	Brooks Robinson, Jim Palmer	75.00
SF	Ben Sheets, Bob Feller	40.00
SG	Eric Gagne, Bruce Sutter	60.00
SO	Ben Sheets, Roy Oswalt	
SP	Don Sutton, Gaylord Perry	40.00
TC	Mark Teixeira, Miguel Cabrera	80.00
VM	Miguel Cabrera, Vladimir Guerrero	100.00
WS	Billy Williams, Ron Santo	60.00

Signatures Triple
No Pricing
Production 20 Sets

Signatures Quadruple
No Pricing
Production 10 Sets

Signatures Six
No Pricing
Production 5 Sets

Signatures Eight
No Pricing
Production One Set

2004 Upper Deck USA
NM/M
Complete Factory Set (204): 50.00
Complete Set (200): 25.00
Common Player: .15

1	Jim Abbott	.25
2	Brent Abernathy	.15
3	Kurt Ainsworth	.15
4	Abe Alvarez	.15
5	Matt Anderson	.15
6	Jeff Austin	.15
7	Justin Wayne	.15
8	Scott Bankhead	.15
9	Josh Bard	.15
10	Michael Barrett	.25
11	Mark Bellhorn	.25
12	Buddy Bell	.15
13	Andy Benes	.25
14	Kris Benson	.15
15	Peter Bergeron	.15
16	Rocky Biddle	.15
17	Casey Blake	.15
18	Willie Bloomquist	.25
19	Jeremy Bonderman	.25
20	Jeff Weaver	.25
21	Joe Borchard	.25
22	Rickie Weeks	.50
23	Rob Bowen	.15
24	Milton Bradley	.25
25	Dan Wheeler	.15
26	Ben Broussard	.15
27	Brian Bruney	.15
28	Mark Budzinski	.15
29	Kirk Bullinger	.15
30	Chris Burke	.25
31	Sean Burnett	.15
32	Jeromy Burnitz	.25
33	Pat Burrell	.50
34	Sean Burroughs	.50
35	Paul Byrd	.25
36	Chris Capuano	.15
37	Scott Cassidy	.15
38	Will Clark	.15
39	Chad Cordero	.25
40	Carl Crawford	.75
41	Bobby Crosby	.25
42	Brad Wilkerson	.15
43	Michael Cuddyer	.25
44	Ben Davis	.15
45	Gookie Dawkins	.15
46	Rod Dedeaux	.15
47	R.A. Dickey	.15
48	Ben Diggins	.15
49	Lenny DiNardo	.15
50	Ryan Drese	.15
51	Tim Drew	.15
52	Todd Williams	.15
53	Justin Duchscherer	.15
54	J.D. Durbin	.15
55	Scott Elarton	.15
56	Adam Everett	.15
57	Dan Wilson	.25
58	Steve Finley	.25
59	Casey Fossum	.15
60	Terry Francona	.15
61	Ryan Franklin	.15
62	Ryan Freel	.15
63	John Van Benschoten	.15
64	Nomar Garciaparra	1.00
65	Chris George	.15
66	Jody Gerut	.15
67	Jason Giambi	.40
68	Matt Ginter	.15
69	Troy Glaus	.50
70	Tom Goodwin	.15
71	Mike Gosling	.15
72	Danny Graves	.15
73	Shawn Green	.50
74	Khalil Greene	.50
75	Todd Greene	.15
76	Seth Greisinger	.15
77	Gabe Gross	.15
78	Jeffrey Hammonds	.15
79	Aaron Heilman	.15
80	Paul Wilson	.15
81	Todd Helton	.75
82	Dustin Hermanson	.15
83	Bobby Hill	.15

#	Player	Price
84	Koyie Hill	.15
85	A.J. Hinch	.15
86	Matt Holliday	.15
87	Ted Wood	.15
88	Ken Huckaby	.15
89	Orlando Hudson	.15
90	Ernie Young	.15
91	Jason Jennings	.25
92	Charles Johnson	.25
93	Jacque Jones	.15
94	Matt Kata	.15
95	Austin Kearns	.25
96	Adam Kennedy	.25
97	Brooks Kieschnick	.25
98	Jesse Crain	.15
99	Scott Kazmir	1.50
100	Billy Koch	.25
101	Paul Konerko	.25
102	Graham Koonce	.15
103	Casey Kotchman	.50
104	Chris Snyder	.15
105	Nick Swisher	.50
106	Gerald Laird	.15
107	Barry Larkin	.50
108	Mike Lamb	.15
109	Tommy Lasorda	.25
110	Matt LeCroy	.15
111	Travis Lee	.25
112	Justin Leone	.15
113	John Vander Wal	.15
114	Braden Looper	.15
115	Shane Loux	.15
116	Ryan Ludwick	.40
117	Jason Varitek	.40
118	Ryan Madson	.15
119	Dave Magadan	.15
120	Tino Martinez	.25
121	Joe Mauer	.50
122	David McCarty	.15
123	Robin Ventura	.25
124	Jack McDowell	.15
125	Todd Walker	.15
126	Mark McGwire	1.50
127	Gil Meche	.15
128	Doug Mientkiewicz	.25
129	Matt Morris	.15
130	Warren Morris	.15
131	Mark Mulder	.50
132	Calvin Murray	.15
133	Eric Munson	.15
134	Mike Mussina	.50
135	Xavier Nady	.15
136	Shane Nance	.15
137	Mike Neill	.15
138	Augie Ojeda	.15
139	John Olerud	.25
140	Gregg Olson	.15
141	Roy Oswalt	.50
142	Jim Parque	.15
143	John Patterson	.15
144	Brad Penny	.15
145	Jay Powell	.15
146	Mark Prior	.75
147	Horacio Ramirez	.15
148	Jon Rauch	.15
149	Jeremy Reed	.25
150	Bob Watson	.15
151	Matt Riley	.15
152	Brian Roberts	.15
153	Dave Roberts	.15
154	Frank Robinson	.15
155	J.C. Romero	.15
156	David Ross	.15
157	Cory Vance	.15
158	Kirk Saarloos	.15
159	Anthony Sanders	.15
160	Dane Sardinha	.15
161	Bobby Seay	.15
162	Phil Seibel	.15
163	Aaron Sele	.15
164	Ben Sheets	.50
165	Paul Shuey	.15
166	Grady Sizemore	.15
167	Reggie Smith	.15
168	John Smoltz	.50
169	Zach Sorensen	.15
170	Scott Spezio	.25
171	Ed Sprague	.15
172	Jason Stanford	.15
173	Dave Stewart	.15
174	Scott Stewart	.15
175	B.J. Surhoff	.15
176	Bill Swift	.15
177	Mike Tonis	.15
178	Jason Tyner	.15
179	Michael Tucker	.15
180	B.J. Upton	.75
181	Eric Valent	.15
182	Ron Villone	.15
183	2000: Team USA Shocks Cuba	.15
184	1984: Abbott halts Japan	.15
185	1996: Berman's Boys Take Third	.15
186	1984: Team USA Takes Second	.15
187	2000: Home Run Heroics	.15
188	1999: Neill's Hit Boosts Team USA	.15
189	1996: High Five for Team USA	.15
190	1992: Garciaparra Makes the Mark	.50
191	2003: USA Rolls to Record	.15
192	1995: Juniors Are Golden In Boston	.15
193	1999: The Streak Goes On	.15
194	1998: Perfect Finish in St. Louis	.15
195	1999: McGwire's Number Retired	1.00
196	2000: Filled with Firsts	.15
197	Red, White and Blue Cardinal	.15
198	2000: Quick Start for Neill	.15
199	1999: Jensen Goes Deep vs. Cuba	.15
200	2000: Mauer on the Mark	.25

Team USA Jersey

		NM/M
	Common Player:	4.00
	Inserted 1:Factory Set	
KA	Kurt Ainsworth	4.00
BB	Brian Bruney	4.00
CB	Chris Burke	4.00
SB	Sean Burroughs	4.00
JD	Justin Duchscherer	4.00
AE	Adam Everett	4.00
JG	Jason Giambi	6.00
GG	Gabe Gross	4.00
DH	Dustin Hermanson	4.00
MH	Matt Holliday	4.00
GK	Graham Koonce	4.00
GL	Gerald Laird	4.00
JL	Justin Leone	6.00
JM	Joe Mauer	10.00
DM	Doug Mientkiewicz	4.00
EM	Eric Munson	8.00
XN	Xavier Nady	4.00
RO	Roy Oswalt	6.00
MP	Mark Prior	4.00
HR	Horacio Ramirez	4.00
JR	Jon Rauch	4.00
RE	Jeremy Reed	5.00
FR	Frank Robinson	8.00
MR	Mike Rouse	4.00
BS	Ben Sheets	8.00
GS	Grady Sizemore	10.00
DS	Dave Stewart	6.00
JV	John Van Benschoten	4.00
JW	Jeff Weaver	4.00
BW	Brad Wilkerson	4.00

Team USA Signature Black Ink

		NM/M
	Common Autograph:	5.00
	Signatures Inserted 3:Factory Set	
ABB	Jim Abbott/180	20.00
ABE	Brent Abernathy/360	5.00
AIN	Kurt Ainsworth/360	8.00
ALV	Abe Alvarez/360	10.00
AND	Matt Anderson/360	5.00
AUS	Jeff Austin/360	5.00
BANK	Scott Bankhead/360	5.00
BARD	Josh Bard/350	5.00
BARR	Michael Barrett/360	8.00
BELL	Buddy Bell/81	25.00
BEN	Andy Benes/350	5.00
BENS	Kris Benson/180	15.00
BERG	Peter Bergeron/360	5.00
BLA	Casey Blake/360	10.00
BLO	Willie Bloomquist/175	15.00
BON	Jeremy Bonderman/150	15.00
BOR	Joe Borchard/350	10.00
BRAD	Milton Bradley/360	15.00
BRO	Ben Broussard/210	8.00
BRU	Brian Bruney/160	5.00
BUD	Mark Budzinski/360	5.00
BULL	Kirk Bullinger/360	5.00
BURK	Chris Burke/360	8.00
BU	Sean Burnett/180	5.00
BURN	Jeromy Burnitz/360	15.00
BUR	Pat Burrell/360	5.00
BURR	Sean Burroughs/360	10.00
BYRD	Paul Byrd/360	5.00
CAP	Chris Capuano/150	8.00
CASS	Scott Cassidy/360	5.00
CLA	Will Clark/60	75.00
COR	Chad Cordero/360	5.00
CR	Jesse Crain/180	5.00
CRA	Carl Crawford/60	35.00
CUD	Michael Cuddyer/370	5.00
DAV	Ben Davis/344	5.00
DED	Rod Dedeaux/29	40.00
DIC	R.A. Dickey/180	5.00
DIG	Ben Diggins/180	8.00
DIN	Lenny DiNardo/150	5.00
DRE	Ryan Drese/180	5.00
DREW	Tim Drew/360	5.00
DUCH	Justin Duchscherer/210	8.00
DUR	J.D. Durbin/180	8.00
ELAR	Scott Elarton/180	5.00
EVER	Adam Everett/120	8.00
FIN	Steve Finley/360	10.00
FOSS	Casey Fossum/360	5.00
FRAN	Terry Francona/150	40.00
FRA	Ryan Franklin/360	5.00
FRE	Ryan Freel/360	5.00
GEO	Chris George/360	5.00
GER	Jody Gerut/350	5.00
GIAM	Jason Giambi/60	50.00

GIN	Matt Ginter/179	8.00
GLA	Troy Glaus/120	35.00
GOS	Mike Gosling/150	8.00
DRA	Danny Graves/360	8.00
GR	Shawn Green/150	40.00
GRE	Khalil Greene/180	40.00
GREE	Todd Greene/120	10.00
GREI	Seth Greisinger/360	5.00
GRO	Gabe Gross/150	5.00
HAM	Jeffrey Hammonds/150	10.00
HEIL	Aaron Heilman/350	5.00
HELT	Todd Helton/71	50.00
HERM	Dustin Hermanson/150	10.00
HI	Bobby Hill/360	5.00
HILL	Koyie Hill/150	8.00
HIN	A.J. Hinch/360	5.00
HUCK	Ken Huckaby/360	5.00
HUD	Orlando Hudson/360	10.00
JENN	Jason Jennings/350	8.00
JON	Jacque Jones/150	8.00
KATA	Matt Kata/350	5.00
KAZ	Scott Kazmir/360	30.00
KENN	Adam Kennedy/150	8.00
KIES	Brooks Kieschnick/360	8.00
KOCH	Billy Koch/71	20.00
KON	Paul Konerko/179	15.00
KOO	Graham Koonce/360	5.00
KOTC	Casey Kotchman/150	20.00
LAMB	Mike Lamb/360	5.00
LAR	Barry Larkin/60	75.00
LEC	Matt LeCroy/360	5.00
LEE	Travis Lee/360	5.00
LEO	Justin Leone/150	10.00
LOO	Braden Looper/360	5.00
LOUX	Shane Loux/360	5.00
MAD	Ryan Madson/360	8.00
MAG	Dave Magadan/360	5.00
MART	Tino Martinez/360	20.00
MAU	Joe Mauer/360	35.00
MCC	David McCarty/360	5.00
MCDO	Jack McDowell/60	20.00
MEC	Gil Meche/360	5.00
MIE	Doug Mientkiewicz/300	5.00
MOR	Matt Morris/150	10.00
MORR	Warren Morris/360	5.00
MUL	Mark Mulder/180	8.00
MUN	Eric Munson/360	8.00
MURR	Calvin Murray/360	8.00
MUSS	Mike Mussina/360	50.00
NADY	Xavier Nady/360	5.00
NAN	Shane Nance/150	5.00
NEI	Mike Neill/360	5.00
OJE	Augie Ojeda/360	5.00
OLE	John Olerud/360	20.00
OLS	Gregg Olson/180	5.00
OSW	Roy Oswalt/350	15.00
PARQ	Jim Parque/360	5.00
PATT	John Patterson/210	5.00
PEN	Brad Penny/360	8.00
POW	Jay Powell/180	5.00
PRI	Mark Prior/350	40.00
RAM	Horacio Ramirez/150	10.00
RAU	Jon Rauch/359	5.00
REED	Jeremy Reed/180	10.00
RIL	Matt Riley/60	15.00
ROB	Brian Roberts/60	20.00
ROBE	Dave Roberts/360	10.00
ROM	J.C. Romero/360	5.00
ROSS	David Ross/360	5.00
SAAR	Kirk Saarloos/360	5.00
SAND	Anthony Sanders/360	5.00
SAR	Dane Sardinha/360	5.00
SEAY	Bobby Seay/360	5.00
SEI	Phil Seibel/150	8.00
SELE	Aaron Sele/360	5.00
SHE	Ben Sheets/143	25.00
SHU	Paul Shuey/360	5.00
SIZE	Grady Sizemore/160	35.00
SMI	Reggie Smith/360	5.00
SMO	John Smoltz/360	35.00
SNY	Chris Snyder/360	5.00
SPI	Scott Spiezio/360	5.00
SPR	Ed Sprague/360	5.00
STE	Dave Stewart/180	5.00
STEW	Scott Stewart/360	5.00
SUR	B.J. Surhoff/360	30.00
SWIF	Bill Swift/360	5.00
SWI	Nick Swisher/360	5.00
TON	Mike Tonis/350	5.00
TUCK	Michael Tucker/150	10.00
TYN	Jason Tyner/360	8.00
VAL	Eric Valent/360	5.00
VANB	John Van Benschoten/180	10.00
VAN	Cory Vance/360	5.00
VAND	John Vander Wal/360	10.00
VAR	Jason Varitek/360	15.00
VENT	Robin Ventura/360	15.00
VILL	Ron Villone/359	5.00
WALK	Todd Walker/360	20.00
WAT	Bob Watson/150	8.00
WAY	Justin Wayne/360	5.00
WEA	Jeff Weaver/360	5.00
WEEK	Rickie Weeks/360	5.00
WHEE	Dan Wheeler/360	5.00
WILL	Todd Williams/360	5.00
WI	Paul Wilson/360	5.00
WOOD	Ted Wood/330	5.00
YOUN	Ernie Young/350	5.00

Team USA Signature Blue Ink

		NM/M
	Common Autograph:	8.00
ABB	Jim Abbott/60	30.00
ABE	Brent Abernathy/120	8.00
AIN	Kurt Ainsworth/120	8.00
ALV	Abe Alvarez/120	10.00
AND	Matt Anderson/110	8.00
AUS	Jeff Austin/120	8.00
BANK	Scott Bankhead/120	8.00
BARD	Josh Bard/100	8.00
BARR	Michael Barrett/120	8.00
BELL	Buddy Bell/29	25.00
BEN	Andy Benes/100	10.00
BENS	Kris Benson/60	25.00
BERG	Peter Bergeron/120	8.00
BLA	Casey Blake/60	20.00
BLO	Willie Bloomquist/51	20.00
BON	Jeremy Bonderman/90	10.00
BOR	Joe Borchard/100	8.00
BOW	Rob Bowen/510	8.00
BRAD	Milton Bradley/120	15.00
BRO	Ben Broussard/150	8.00
BRU	Brian Bruney/60	8.00
BUD	Mark Budzinski/120	8.00
BULL	Kirk Bullinger/120	8.00
BURK	Chris Burke/110	8.00
BU	Sean Burnett/60	8.00
BURN	Jeromy Burnitz/120	15.00
BUR	Pat Burrell/80	8.00
BURR	Sean Burroughs/142	8.00
BYRD	Paul Byrd/120	8.00
CAP	Chris Capuano/90	8.00
CASS	Scott Cassidy/120	8.00
CLA	Will Clark/30	80.00
COR	Chad Cordero/120	8.00
CR	Jesse Crain/60	8.00
CUD	Michael Cuddyer/89	8.00
DAV	Ben Davis/100	8.00
DED	Rod Dedeaux/25	30.00
DIC	R.A. Dickey/120	10.00
DIG	Ben Diggins/30	15.00
DIN	Lenny DiNardo/60	10.00
DRE	Ryan Drese/60	10.00
DREW	Tim Drew/120	8.00
DUCH	Justin Duchscherer/110	8.00
DUR	J.D. Durbin/60	10.00
ELAR	Scott Elarton/60	10.00
EVER	Adam Everett/120	8.00
FIN	Steve Finley/120	15.00
FOSS	Casey Fossum/100	8.00
FRAN	Terry Francona/40	40.00
FRA	Ryan Franklin/120	8.00
FRE	Ryan Freel/110	8.00
GAR	Nomar Garciaparra/60	100.00
GEO	Chris George/120	8.00
GER	Jody Gerut/100	8.00
GIAM	Jason Giambi/50	50.00
GIN	Matt Ginter/42	8.00
GLA	Troy Glaus/60	30.00
GOS	Mike Gosling/60	8.00
DRA	Danny Graves/120	8.00
GR	Shawn Green/90	30.00
GRE	Khalil Greene/60	50.00
GREE	Todd Greene/60	10.00
GREI	Seth Greisinger/120	8.00
GRO	Gabe Gross/90	8.00
HAM	Jeffrey Hammonds/90	10.00
HEIL	Aaron Heilman/100	8.00
HELT	Todd Helton/20	65.00
HERM	Dustin Hermanson/90	10.00
HI	Bobby Hill/120	8.00
HILL	Koyie Hill/90	8.00
HIN	A.J. Hinch/120	8.00
HUCK	Ken Huckaby/120	8.00
HUD	Orlando Hudson/110	15.00
JENN	Jason Jennings/60	8.00
JON	Jacque Jones/60	20.00
KATA	Matt Kata/100	8.00
KAZ	Scott Kazmir/110	35.00
KEAR	Austin Kearns/110	8.00
KENN	Adam Kennedy/90	8.00
KIES	Brooks Kieschnick/120	8.00
KOCH	Billy Koch/18	25.00
KON	Paul Konerko/52	20.00
KOO	Graham Koonce/120	8.00
KOTC	Casey Kotchman/60	30.00
LAMB	Mike Lamb/120	8.00
LAR	Barry Larkin/20	80.00
LAS	Tommy Lasorda/60	60.00
LEC	Matt LeCroy/120	8.00
LEE	Travis Lee/120	8.00
LEO	Justin Leone/60	15.00
LOO	Braden Looper/120	8.00
LOUX	Shane Loux/110	8.00
LUD	Ryan Ludwick/450	8.00
MAD	Ryan Madson/110	8.00
MAG	Dave Magadan/120	8.00
MART	Tino Martinez/120	20.00
MAU	Joe Mauer/120	35.00
MCC	David McCarty/120	8.00
MCDO	Jack McDowell/30	20.00
MEC	Gil Meche/30	8.00
MIE	Doug Mientkiewicz/120	8.00
MOR	Matt Morris/90	15.00
MORR	Warren Morris/120	8.00
MUL	Mark Mulder/110	15.00
MURR	Calvin Murray/120	8.00
MUSS	Mike Mussina/30	50.00
NADY	Xavier Nady/120	8.00
NAN	Shane Nance/60	10.00
NEI	Mike Neill/110	8.00
OJE	Augie Ojeda/119	8.00
OLE	John Olerud/120	20.00
OLS	Gregg Olson/60	10.00
OSW	Roy Oswalt/100	15.00
PARQ	Jim Parque/120	8.00
PATT	John Patterson/120	8.00
PEN	Brad Penny/110	8.00
POW	Jay Powell/110	8.00
PRI	Mark Prior/108	40.00
RAM	Horacio Ramirez/90	8.00
RAU	Jon Rauch/120	8.00
REED	Jeremy Reed/45	20.00
ROBE	Dave Roberts/120	10.00
ROBI	Frank Robinson/90	90.00
ROM	J.C. Romero/120	8.00
ROSS	David Ross/120	8.00
SAAR	Kirk Saarloos/120	8.00
SAND	Anthony Sanders/120	8.00
SAR	Dane Sardinha/110	8.00
SEAY	Bobby Seay/120	8.00
SEI	Phil Seibel/90	8.00
SELE	Aaron Sele/120	10.00
SHU	Paul Shuey/120	8.00
SIZE	Grady Sizemore/60	35.00
SMI	Reggie Smith/120	8.00
SMO	John Smoltz/120	40.00
SNY	Chris Snyder/120	8.00
SOR	Zach Sorensen/450	8.00
SPI	Scott Spiezio/120	8.00
SPR	Ed Sprague/120	8.00
STAN	Jason Stanford/450	8.00
STE	Dave Stewart/90	10.00
STEW	Scott Stewart/119	8.00
SWIF	Bill Swift/120	8.00
SWI	Nick Swisher/110	20.00
TON	Mike Tonis/120	8.00
TUCK	Michael Tucker/90	8.00
TYN	Jason Tyner/120	8.00
UPT	B.J. Upton/120	30.00
VAL	Eric Valent/120	8.00
VANB	John Van Benschoten/60	20.00
VAN	Cory Vance/120	8.00
VAND	John Vander Wal/120	8.00
VAR	Jason Varitek/40	40.00
VENT	Robin Ventura/120	15.00
VILL	Ron Villone/120	8.00
WAT	Bob Watson/60	10.00
WAY	Justin Wayne/90	8.00
WEA	Jeff Weaver/120	10.00
WEEK	Rickie Weeks/120	15.00
WILL	Todd Williams/90	8.00
WIL	Dan Wilson/120	8.00
WI	Paul Wilson/110	8.00
WOOD	Ted Wood/120	8.00
YOUN	Ernie Young/130	8.00

Team USA Signature Red Ink

		NM/M
	Common Autograph:	10.00
	Some not priced due to scarcity.	
ABE	Brent Abernathy/20	15.00
AIN	Kurt Ainsworth/30	15.00
AND	Matt Anderson/30	15.00
AUS	Jeff Austin/20	15.00
BARD	Josh Bard/50	10.00
BARR	Michael Barrett/20	20.00
BEN	Andy Benes/20	15.00
BLO	Willie Bloomquist/25	25.00
BOR	Joe Borchard/20	15.00
BRAD	Milton Bradley/20	25.00
BRO	Ben Broussard/40	15.00
BRU	Brian Bruney/20	15.00
BURK	Chris Burke/50	10.00
BUR	Pat Burrell/29	25.00
BYRD	Paul Byrd/20	15.00
CRO	Bobby Crosby/60	50.00
CUD	Michael Cuddyer/40	10.00
DAV	Ben Davis/40	15.00
DIN	Lenny DiNardo/40	10.00
EVER	Adam Everett/30	15.00
FIN	Steve Finley/20	25.00
FOSS	Casey Fossum/42	10.00
FRE	Ryan Freel/30	15.00
GAR	Nomar Garciaparra/30	125.00
GER	Jody Gerut/50	15.00
GLA	Troy Glaus/20	60.00
GOS	Mike Gosling/40	15.00
HEIL	Aaron Heilman/50	10.00
HIN	A.J. Hinch/20	15.00
HUD	Orlando Hudson/25	25.00
JENN	Jason Jennings/50	15.00
JON	Jacque Jones/40	20.00
KATA	Matt Kata/50	15.00
KAZ	Scott Kazmir/30	75.00
KEAR	Austin Kearns/30	15.00
KON	Paul Konerko/23	25.00
KOO	Graham Koonce/20	15.00
KOTC	Casey Kotchman/40	35.00
LEC	Matt LeCroy/20	15.00
LEE	Travis Lee/20	15.00
LEO	Justin Leone/40	20.00
LOUX	Shane Loux/30	15.00
LUD	Ryan Ludwick/50	10.00
MAD	Ryan Madson/30	15.00
MART	Tino Martinez/20	40.00
MAU	Joe Mauer/65	40.00
MCC	David McCarty/20	25.00

MURR	Calvin Murray/120	8.00
MUSS	Mike Mussina/30	50.00
NADY	Xavier Nady/20	15.00
NAN	Shane Nance/40	15.00
NEI	Mike Neill/30	15.00
OJE	John Olerud/120	20.00
OLS	Gregg Olson/60	10.00
OSW	Roy Oswalt/50	20.00
PARQ	Jim Parque/20	15.00
PATT	John Patterson/20	15.00
PEN	Brad Penny/30	15.00
PRI	Mark Prior/48	60.00
RAU	Jon Rauch/53	10.00
REED	Jeremy Reed/25	25.00
ROM	J.C. Romero/20	15.00
SAR	Dane Sardinha/30	15.00
SIZE	Grady Sizemore/30	40.00
SMO	John Smoltz/20	65.00
SOR	Zach Sorensen/50	10.00
SPR	Ed Sprague/20	15.00
STAN	Jason Stanford/50	10.00
STE	Dave Stewart/20	25.00
SWI	Nick Swisher/30	40.00
TON	Mike Tonis/50	10.00
UPT	B.J. Upton/40	40.00
VAR	Jason Varitek/30	70.00
VENT	Robin Ventura/20	25.00
WAT	Bob Watson/30	15.00
WAY	Justin Wayne/40	10.00
WEA	Jeff Weaver/20	25.00
WEEK	Rickie Weeks/20	25.00
WILL	Todd Williams/50	10.00
WIL	Paul Wilson/30	15.00
WOOD	Ted Wood/30	15.00
YOUN	Ernie Young/50	10.00

Team USA Signature Green Ink

No Pricing
Production 1-3

2004 Upper Deck Vintage

ROGER CLEMENS
HOUSTON ASTROS — PITCHER

	NM/M
Complete Set (450):	
Common Player:	.15
Common SP (301-315):	.50
Inserted 1:5	
Common SP (316-325):	.40
Inserted 1:7	
Common SP (326-350):	.40
Inserted 1:5	
Common SP (351-440) SP:	2.00
Inserted 1:12	
Old Judge (441-450) found in bonus packs.	
Pack (8):	2.50
Box (24 + 1 bonus pack):	50.00
1	Albert Pujols	1.50
2	Carlos Delgado	.50
3	Todd Helton	.50
4	Nomar Garciaparra	1.50
5	Vladimir Guerrero	.75
6	Alfonso Soriano	.75
7	Alex Rodriguez	1.50
8	Jason Giambi	.75
9	Derek Jeter	2.00
10	Pedro J. Martinez	.75
11	Ivan Rodriguez	.50
12	Mark Prior	1.00
13	Marquis Grissom	.15
14	Barry Zito	.25
15	Alex Cintron	.15
16	Wade Miller	.15
17	Eric Chavez	.25
18	Matt Clement	.15
19	Orlando Cabrera	.15
20	Odalis Perez	.15
21	Lance Berkman	.25
22	Keith Foulke	.15
23	Shawn Green	.25
24	Byung-Hyun Kim	.15
25	Geoff Jenkins	.15
26	Torii Hunter	.40
27	Richard Hidalgo	.15
28	Edgar Martinez	.25
29	Placido Polanco	.15
30	Brad Lidge	.15
31	Alex Escobar	.15
32	Garret Anderson	.25
33	Larry Walker	.25
34	Ken Griffey Jr.	1.00
35	Junior Spivey	.15
36	Carlos Beltran	.25
37	Bartolo Colon	.25
38	Ichiro Suzuki	1.00

#	Player	Price
39	Ramon Ortiz	.15
40	Roy Oswalt	.25
41	Mike Piazza	1.00
42	Benito Santiago	.15
43	Mike Mussina	.50
44	Jeff Kent	.25
45	Curt Schilling	.50
46	Adam Dunn	.40
47	Mike Sweeney	.15
48	Chipper Jones	1.00
49	Frank Thomas	.50
50	Kerry Wood	.50
51	Rod Beck	.15
52	Brian Giles	.25
53	Hank Blalock	.25
54	Andruw Jones	.50
55	Dmitri Young	.15
56	Juan Pierre	.15
57	Jacque Jones	.15
58	Phil Nevin	.15
59	Rocco Baldelli	.25
60	Greg Maddux	1.00
61	Eric Gagne	.15
62	Tim Hudson	.25
63	Brian Lawrence	.15
64	Sammy Sosa	1.00
65	Corey Koskie	.15
66	Bobby Abreu	.25
67	Preston Wilson	.15
68	Jay Gibbons	.15
69	Dontrelle Willis	.25
70	Richie Sexson	.40
71	Kevin Millwood	.25
72	Randy Johnson	.75
73	Jack Cust	.15
74	Randy Wolf	.15
75	Johan Santana	.25
76	Magglio Ordonez	.25
77	Sean Casey	.15
78	Billy Wagner	.25
79	Javier Vazquez	.15
80	Jorge Posada	.40
81	Jason Schmidt	.15
82	Bret Boone	.25
83	Jeff Bagwell	.50
84	Rickie Weeks	.25
85	Troy Percival	.15
86	Jose Vidro	.15
87	Freddy Garcia	.15
88	Manny Ramirez	.50
89	John Smoltz	.25
90	Moises Alou	.25
91	Ugueth Urbina	.15
92	Bobby Hill	.15
93	Marcus Giles	.15
94	Aramis Ramirez	.25
95	Brad Wilkerson	.15
96	Ray Durham	.15
97	David Wells	.15
98	Paul LoDuca	.15
99	Danny Graves	.15
100	Jason Kendall	.25
101	Carlos Lee	.25
102	Rafael Furcal	.25
103	Mike Lowell	.15
104	Kevin Brown	.15
105	Vicente Padilla	.15
106	Miguel Tejada	.40
107	Bernie Williams	.40
108	Octavio Dotel	.15
109	Steve Finley	.15
110	Lyle Overbay	.15
111	Delmon Young	.25
112	Bo Hart	.15
113	Jason Lane	.15
114	Matt Roney	.15
115	Brian Roberts	.15
116	Tom Glavine	.25
117	Rich Aurilia	.15
118	Adam Kennedy	.15
119	Hee Seop Choi	.15
120	Trot Nixon	.15
121	Gary Sheffield	.40
122	Jay Payton	.15
123	Brad Penny	.15
124	Garrett Atkins	.15
125	Aubrey Huff	.15
126	Juan Gonzalez	.40
127	Jason Jennings	.15
128	Luis Gonzalez	.25
129	Vinny Castilla	.15
130	Esteban Loaiza	.15
131	Erubiel Durazo	.15
132	Eric Hinske	.15
133	Scott Rolen	.75
134	Craig Biggio	.25
135	Tim Wakefield	.25
136	Darin Erstad	.25
137	Denny Stark	.15
138	Ben Sheets	.25
139	Hideo Nomo	.40
140	Derrek Lee	.25
141	Matt Mantei	.15
142	Reggie Sanders	.15
143	Jose Guillen	.15
144	Joe Mays	.15
145	Jimmy Rollins	.25
146	Juan Encarnacion	.15
147	Joe Crede	.15
148	Aaron Guiel	.15
149	Mark Mulder	.25
150	Travis Lee	.15
151	Josh Phelps	.15
152	Michael Young	.15
153	Paul Konerko	.15
154	John Lackey	.15
155	Damian Moss	.15
156	Javy Lopez	.25

#	Player	Price
157	Joe Borowski	.15
158	Jose Cruz Jr.	.15
159	Ramon Hernandez	.15
160	Raul Ibanez	.15
161	Adrian Beltre	.15
162	Bobby Higginson	.15
163	Jorge Julio	.15
164	Miguel Batista	.15
165	Luis Castillo	.15
166	Aaron Harang	.15
167	Ken Harvey	.15
168	Rocky Biddle	.15
169	Mariano Rivera	.25
170	Matt Morris	.15
171	Laynce Nix	.15
172	Mike Maroth	.15
173	Francisco Rodriguez	.15
174	Livan Hernandez	.15
175	Aaron Heilman	.15
176	Nick Johnson	.15
177	Woody Williams	.15
178	Joe Kennedy	.15
179	Jesse Foppert	.15
180	Ryan Franklin	.15
181	Endy Chavez	.15
182	Chin-Hui Tsao	.15
183	Todd Walker	.15
184	Edgardo Alfonzo	.15
185	Edgar Renteria	.15
186	Matt LeCroy	.15
187	Carl Everett	.15
188	Jeff Conine	.15
189	Jason Varitek	.25
190	Russ Ortiz	.15
191	Melvin Mora	.15
192	Mark Buehrle	.15
193	Bill Mueller	.15
194	Miguel Cabrera	.25
195	Carlos Zambrano	.15
196	Jose Valverde	.15
197	Danys Baez	.15
198	Mike MacDougal	.15
199	Zach Day	.15
200	Roy Halladay	.25
201	Jerome Williams	.15
202	Josh Fogg	.15
203	Mark Kotsay	.15
204	Pat Burrell	.40
205	A.J. Pierzynski	.15
206	Fred McGriff	.25
207	Brandon Larson	.15
208	Robb Quinlan	.15
209	David Ortiz	.15
210	A.J. Burnett	.15
211	John Vander Wal	.15
212	Jim Thome	.75
213	Matt Kata	.15
214	Kip Wells	.15
215	Scott Podsednik	.40
216	Rickey Henderson	.25
217	Travis Hafner	.15
218	Tony Batista	.15
219	Robert Fick	.15
220	Derek Lowe	.25
221	Ryan Klesko	.25
222	Joe Beimel	.15
223	Doug Mientkiewicz	.15
224	Angel Berroa	.15
225	Adam Eaton	.15
226	C.C. Sabathia	.15
227	Wilfredo Ledezma	.15
228	Jason Johnson	.15
229	Ryan Wagner	.15
230	Al Leiter	.15
231	Joel Pineiro	.15
232	Jason Isringhausen	.15
233	John Olerud	.25
234	Ron Calloway	.15
235	Jose Reyes	.40
236	J.D. Drew	.15
237	Jared Sandberg	.15
238	Gil Meche	.15
239	Jose Contreras	.15
240	Eric Milton	.15
241	Jason L. Phillips	.15
242	Luis Ayala	.15
243	Bobby Kielty	.15
244	Jose Lima	.15
245	Brooks Kieschnick	.15
246	Xavier Nady	.15
247	Dan Haren	.15
248	Victor Zambrano	.15
249	Kelvim Escobar	.15
250	Oliver Perez	.15
251	Jamie Moyer	.15
252	Orlando Hudson	.15
253	Danny Kolb	.15
254	Jake Peavy	.15
255	Kris Benson	.15
256	Roger Clemens	1.50
257	Jim Edmonds	.40
258	Rafael Palmeiro	.50
259	Jae Weong Seo	.15
260	Chase Utley	.15
261	Rich Harden	.15
262	Mark Teixeira	.25
263	Johnny Damon	.25
264	Luis Matos	.15
265	Shigetoshi Hasegawa	.15
266	Alfredo Amezaga	.15
267	Tim Worrell	.15
268	Kazuhisa Ishii	.15
269	Miguel Ojeda	.15
270	Kazuhiro Sasaki	.15
271	Hideki Matsui	2.00
272	Troy Glaus	.40
273	Michael Tucker	.15
274	Lew Ford	.15

#	Player	Price
275	Brian Jordan	.15
276	David Eckstein	.15
277	Robby Hammock	.15
278	Corey Patterson	.25
279	Wes Helms	.15
280	Jermaine Dye	.15
281	Cliff Floyd	.15
282	Dustan Mohr	.15
283	Kevin Mench	.15
284	Ellis Burks	.15
285	Jerry Hairston Jr.	.15
286	Tim Salmon	.25
287	Omar Vizquel	.25
288	Andy Pettitte	.40
289	Guillermo Mota	.15
290	Tino Martinez	.15
291	Lance Carter	.15
292	Francisco Cordero	.15
293	Robb Nen	.15
294	Mike Cameron	.15
295	Jhonny Peralta	.15
296	Braden Looper	.15
297	Jarrod Washburn	.15
298	Mark Prior	.50
299	Alfonso Soriano	.25
300	Rocco Baldelli	.25
301	Pedro J. Martinez	1.50
302	Mark Prior	2.00
303	Barry Zito	.75
304	Roger Clemens	2.50
305	Randy Johnson	1.50
306	Roy Halladay	.50
307	Hideo Nomo	.75
308	Roy Oswalt	.50
309	Kerry Wood	1.00
310	Dontrelle Willis	.75
311	Mark Mulder	.50
312	Brandon Webb	.35
313	Mike Mussina	.75
314	Curt Schilling	.75
315	Tim Hudson	.75
316	Dontrelle Willis	.75
317	Juan Pierre	.35
318	Hideki Matsui	4.00
319	Andy Pettitte	.75
320	Mike Mussina	.75
321	Roger Clemens	2.50
322	Alex Gonzalez	.40
323	Brad Penny	.40
324	Ivan Rodriguez	.75
325	Josh Beckett	1.00
326	Aaron Boone	.40
327	Jeff Suppan	.40
328	Shea Hillenbrand	.40
329	Jeromy Burnitz	.40
330	Sidney Ponson	.40
331	Rondell White	.50
332	Shannon Stewart	.40
333	Armando Benitez	.40
334	Roberto Alomar	1.00
335	Raul Mondesi	.50
336	Morgan Ensberg	.40
337	Milton Bradley	.40
338	Brandon Webb	.50
339	Marlon Byrd	.40
340	Carlos Pena	.40
341	Brandon Phillips	.40
342	Josh Beckett	1.00
343	Eric Munson	.40
344	Brett Myers	.40
345	Austin Kearns	1.00
346	Jody Gerut	.40
347	Vernon Wells	.40
348	Jeff Duncan	.40
349	Sean Burroughs	.40
350	Jeremy Bonderman	.40
351	Hideki Matsui	15.00
352	Jason Giambi	8.00
353	Alfonso Soriano	6.00
354	Derek Jeter	15.00
355	Aaron Boone	3.00
356	Jorge Posada	5.00
357	Bernie Williams	5.00
358	Manny Ramirez	5.00
359	Nomar Garciaparra	12.00
360	Johnny Damon	3.00
361	Jason Varitek	2.50
362	Carlos Delgado	5.00
363	Vernon Wells	4.00
364	Jay Gibbons	4.00
365	Tony Batista	2.00
366	Rocco Baldelli	5.00
367	Aubrey Huff	2.00
368	Carlos Beltran	4.00
369	Mike Sweeney	3.00
370	Magglio Ordonez	4.00
371	Frank Thomas	6.00
372	Carlos Lee	2.00
373	Roberto Alomar	4.00
374	Jacque Jones	2.00
375	Torii Hunter	4.00
376	Milton Bradley	2.00
377	Travis Hafner	2.00
378	Jody Gerut	2.00
379	Dmitri Young	2.00
380	Carlos Pena	2.00
381	Ichiro Suzuki	10.00
382	Bret Boone	3.00
383	Edgar Martinez	3.00
384	Eric Chavez	3.00
385	Miguel Tejada	3.00
386	Erubiel Durazo	2.00
387	Jose Guillen	2.00
388	Garret Anderson	3.00
389	Troy Glaus	4.00
390	Alex Rodriguez	10.00
391	Rafael Palmeiro	5.00
392	Hank Blalock	4.00

#	Player	Price
393	Mark Teixeira	4.00
394	Gary Sheffield	4.00
395	Andruw Jones	5.00
396	Chipper Jones	8.00
397	Javy Lopez	3.00
398	Marcus Giles	2.00
399	Rafael Furcal	3.00
400	Jim Thome	5.00
401	Bobby Abreu	3.00
402	Pat Burrell	4.00
403	Mike Lowell	3.00
404	Ivan Rodriguez	5.00
405	Derrek Lee	3.00
406	Miguel Cabrera	5.00
407	Vladimir Guerrero	6.00
408	Orlando Cabrera	2.00
409	Jose Vidro	2.00
410	Mike Piazza	8.00
411	Cliff Floyd	3.00
412	Albert Pujols	15.00
413	Scott Rolen	6.00
414	Jim Edmonds	4.00
415	Edgar Renteria	3.00
416	Lance Berkman	3.00
417	Jeff Bagwell	5.00
418	Jeff Kent	3.00
419	Richard Hidalgo	2.00
420	Morgan Ensberg	2.00
421	Sammy Sosa	10.00
422	Moises Alou	3.00
423	Ken Griffey Jr.	10.00
424	Adam Dunn	4.00
425	Austin Kearns	4.00
426	Richie Sexson	4.00
427	Geoff Jenkins	3.00
428	Brian Giles	3.00
429	Reggie Sanders	2.00
430	Rich Aurilia	2.00
431	Jose Cruz Jr.	2.00
432	Shawn Green	3.00
433	Jeromy Burnitz	2.00
434	Luis Gonzalez	3.00
435	Todd Helton	5.00
436	Preston Wilson	2.00
437	Larry Walker	3.00
438	Ryan Klesko	3.00
439	Phil Nevin	2.00
440	Sean Burroughs	2.00
441	Sammy Sosa	3.00
442	Albert Pujols	8.00
443	Magglio Ordonez	.50
444	Vladimir Guerrero	1.50
445	Todd Helton	1.50
446	Jason Giambi	1.50
447	Ichiro Suzuki	3.00
448	Alex Rodriguez	3.00
449	Carlos Delgado	.75
450	Manny Ramirez	1.00

Black & White

Cards (1-300):		1-2X
Inserted 1:6		
SP's (301-325):		1-2X
Inserted 1:24		
SP's (326-350):		1-2X
Inserted 1:20		
B/W Color Variations:		6-10X
Inserted 1:48		

Old Judge

HIDEKI MATSUI, OF
THE UPPER DECK COMPANY, LLC

	NM/M
Complete Set (20):	15.00
Common Player:	.40
Inserted 3:bonus pack.	
Blue Back:	1-2X
Inserted 1:4 bonus packs.	
Red Back:	2-3X
Inserted 1:12 bonus packs.	
11	Randy Johnson	1.50
12	Pedro J. Martinez	1.50
13	Mark Prior	2.00
14	Barry Zito	.75
15	Roy Oswalt	.40
16	Roy Halladay	.50
17	Curt Schilling	.75
18	Mike Mussina	.75
19	Kevin Brown	.40
20	Roger Clemens	2.50
21	Eric Gagne	.50
22	Mariano Rivera	.75
23	Mike Piazza	2.00
24	Jorge Posada	.50
25	Jeff Kent	.50
26	Alfonso Soriano	1.00
27	Scott Rolen	1.00
28	Eric Chavez	.50
29	Edgar Renteria	.40

30	Hideki Matsui	4.00

Stellar Signatures

NM/M

Inserted 1:600

HM	Hideki Matsui	300.00
MP	Mike Piazza	150.00
AR	Alex Rodriguez	100.00
TS	Tom Seaver	50.00
IS	Ichiro Suzuki	200.00
CY	C. Yastrzemski/125	75.00
BZ	Barry Zito	40.00

Stellar Stat Men

	NM/M
Common Player:	4.00
Inserted 1:24	
1	Jose Reyes	6.00
2	Bo Hart	8.00
3	Hideki Matsui	30.00
4	Dontrelle Willis	6.00
5	Rocco Baldelli	6.00
6	Ichiro Suzuki	20.00
7	Mike Lowell	6.00
8	Derek Jeter	20.00
9	Ken Griffey Jr.	15.00
10	Sammy Sosa	12.00
11	Kerry Wood	10.00
12	Chipper Jones	8.00
13	Alfonso Soriano	8.00
14	Khalil Greene	6.00
15	Jim Thome	8.00
16	Rafael Furcal	5.00
17	Andrew Brown	4.00
18	Mark Prior	10.00
19	Barry Zito	5.00
20	Al Leiter	4.00
21	Carlos Delgado	6.00
22	Pedro J. Martinez	8.00
23	Alex Rodriguez	10.00
24	Lance Berkman	6.00
25	Jeff Bagwell	6.00
26	Bernie Williams	6.00
27	Hideo Nomo	6.00
28	Randy Johnson	8.00
29	Curt Schilling	8.00
30	Mike Piazza	10.00
31	Albert Pujols	12.00
32	Joe DiMaggio	100.00
33	Ted Williams	60.00
34	Mickey Mantle	100.00
35	Mike Mussina	8.00
36	Rich Harden	5.00
37	Roy Oswalt	4.00
38	Torii Hunter	8.00
39	Jorge Posada	6.00
40	Troy Glaus	6.00
41	Manny Ramirez	6.00
42	Roy Halladay	5.00

Timeless Teams

NM/M

Common Quad:	15.00
Inserted 1:400	
Production 175 Sets	

1	Derek Jeter, Jason Giambi, Alfonso Soriano, Hideki Matsui	90.00
2	Randy Johnson, Luis Gonzalez, Steve Finley, Curt Schilling	20.00
4	Johnny Damon, Manny Ramirez, Nomar Garciaparra, Trot Nixon	35.00
5	Alex Rodriguez, Rafael Palmeiro, Mark Teixeira, Hank Blalock	35.00
6	Roberto Alomar, Frank Thomas, Magglio Ordonez, Carl Everett	20.00
7	Shannon Stewart, Torii Hunter, Jacque Jones, Doug Mientkiewicz	15.00
8	Jim Edmonds, Scott Rolen, J.D. Drew, Albert Pujols	40.00
9	Bret Boone, John Olerud, Mike Cameron, Ichiro Suzuki	45.00
10	Jeff Bagwell, Craig Biggio, Jeff Kent, Lance Berkman	20.00
11	Tim Salmon, Garret Anderson, Darin Erstad, Troy Glaus	15.00
12	Bernie Williams, Alfonso Soriano, Jorge Posada, Hideki Matsui	85.00

13	Carlos Beltran, Michael Tucker, Mike Sweeney, Brent Mayne	15.00
14	Jim Thome, Mike Lieberthal, Bobby Abreu, Marlon Byrd	30.00
15	Ivan Rodriguez, Juan Encarnacion, Mike Lowell, Miguel Cabrera	25.00
16	Sammy Sosa, Kerry Wood, Moises Alou, Corey Patterson	50.00
17	Andres Galarraga, Edgardo Alfonzo, Jose Cruz Jr., Rich Aurilia	15.00
18	Derek Jeter, Bernie Williams, Alfonso Soriano, Hideki Matsui	90.00

2004 Upper Deck Yankees Classics Promos

Each of the cards in Yankees Classics was issued in a foil-overprinted version with "UD PROMO" across the front. Cards were inserted into specially marked card shop and newsstand issues of Tuff Stuff magazine.

	NM/M
Common Player:	.50
Stars:	1.5X

2004 Upper Deck Yankees Classics

	NM/M
Complete Set (90):	20.00
Common Player:	.25
Pack (5):	6.00
Box (24):	120.00
1	Bill "Moose" Skowron	.50
2	Bob Cerv	.25
3	Bobby Murcer	.50
4	Bobby Richardson	.25
5	Brian Doyle	.25
6	Bucky Dent	.25
7	Chris Chambliss	.25
8	Clete Boyer	.25
9	Dave Kingman	.25
10	Dave Righetti	.25
11	Dave Winfield	.50
12	David Cone	.25
13	Red Ruffing	.25
14	Dock Ellis	.25
15	Don Baylor	.25
16	Don Larsen	.75
17	Don Mattingly	1.50
18	Dwight Gooden	.40
19	Ed Figueroa	.25
20	Joe Torre	.50
21	Darryl Strawberry	.25
22	Horace Clarke	.25
23	Gaylord Perry	.25
24	Phil Linz	.25
25	Gil McDougald	.25
26	Rich "Goose" Gossage	.25
27	Graig Nettles	.25
28	Hank Bauer	.25

29	Jack Clark	.25
30	Don Gullett	.25
31	Jim Abbott	.25
32	Jim Bouton	.25
33	Jim Kaat	.40
34	Jim Leyritz	.25
35	Jim Wynn	.25
36	Jimmy Key	.25
37	Joe Niekro	.25
38	Joe Pepitone	.25
39	John Wetteland	.25
40	Ken Griffey Sr.	.25
41	Felipe Alou	.25
42	Kevin Maas	.25
43	Lindy McDaniel	.25
44	Lou Piniella	.50
45	Luis Tiant	.25
46	Mel Stottlemyre	.25
47	Mickey Rivers	.25
48	Oscar Gamble	.25
49	Pat Dobson	.25
50	Paul O'Neill	.50
51	Phil Niekro	.25
52	Phil Rizzuto	.75
53	Doc Medich	.25
54	Rick Cerone	.25
55	Ron Blomberg	.25
56	Ron Guidry	.50
57	Roy White	.25
58	Rudy May	.25
59	Sam McDowell	.25
60	Sparky Lyle	.25
61	Steve Balboni	.25
62	Steve Sax	.25
63	Jerry Coleman	.25
64	Tom Tresh	.25
65	Tommy John	.25
66	Tony Kubek	.50
67	Wade Boggs	.50
68	Whitey Ford	.75
69	Willie Randolph	.25
70	Yogi Berra	1.00
71	Babe Ruth	3.00
72	Bill Dickey	.50
73	Billy Martin	.50
74	Bob Meusel	.25
75	Casey Stengel	.50
76	Elston Howard	.50
77	Jim "Catfish" Hunter	.50
78	Joe DiMaggio	2.00
79	Lefty Gomez	.50
80	Lou Gehrig	2.00
81	Mickey Mantle	3.00
82	Miller Huggins	.50
83	Roger Maris	1.50
84	Thurman Munson	.75
85	Tony Lazzeri	.50
86	Yankee Stadium	.75
87	Times Square	.50
88	Central Park	.50
89	Empire State Building	.50
90	Statue of Liberty	.50

Bronze
Bronze: 4-8X
Production 99 Sets

Silver
Silver: No Pricing

Gold
Gold: 8-15X
Production 30 Sets

Classic Cuts
No Pricing
Production One Set

Classic Scripts Single Autograph

		NM/M
Common Autograph:		10.00
Inserted 1:8		
AU-1	Bill "Moose" Skowron	15.00
AU-2	Bob Cerv	10.00
AU-3	Bobby Murcer/SP	60.00
AU-4	Bobby Richardson	15.00
AU-5	Brian Doyle	10.00
AU-6	Bucky Dent	10.00
AU-7	Chris Chambliss	12.00
AU-8	Clete Boyer	15.00
AU-9	Dave Kingman	10.00
AU-10	Dave Righetti	10.00
AU-11	Dave Winfield/SP	60.00
AU-12	David Cone	10.00
AU-14	Dock Ellis	10.00
AU-15	Don Baylor/SP	25.00
AU-16	Don Larsen/SP	40.00
AU-17	Don Mattingly/SP	85.00
AU-18	Dwight Gooden	15.00
AU-19	Ed Figueroa	10.00
AU-20	Joe Torre/SP	125.00
AU-21	Darryl Strawberry	20.00
AU-23	Gaylord Perry	20.00
AU-24	Phil Linz	10.00
AU-25	Gil McDougald	15.00
AU-26	Rich "Goose" Gossage	20.00
AU-27	Graig Nettles	15.00
AU-28	Hank Bauer	15.00
AU-29	Jack Clark	15.00
AU-31	Jim Abbott	15.00
AU-32	Jim Bouton	15.00
AU-33	Jim Kaat	15.00
AU-34	Jim Leyritz/SP	25.00
AU-35	Jim Wynn	10.00
AU-36	Jimmy Key	10.00
AU-37	Joe Niekro	15.00
AU-38	Joe Pepitone	15.00
AU-39	John Wetteland/SP	20.00
AU-40	Ken Griffey Sr.	12.00
AU-42	Kevin Maas	10.00
AU-43	Lindy McDaniel	10.00
AU-44	Lou Piniella/SP	35.00
AU-45	Luis Tiant	20.00
AU-46	Mel Stottlemyre	15.00
AU-47	Mickey Rivers	15.00
AU-48	Oscar Gamble	15.00
AU-49	Pat Dobson	15.00
AU-50	Paul O'Neill/SP	40.00
AU-51	Phil Niekro	15.00
AU-52	Phil Rizzuto/SP	75.00
AU-53	Doc Medich	10.00
AU-54	Rick Cerone	15.00
AU-55	Ron Blomberg	10.00
AU-56	Ron Guidry	25.00
AU-57	Roy White	12.00
AU-58	Rudy May	10.00
AU-59	Sam McDowell	10.00
AU-60	Sparky Lyle	12.00
AU-61	Steve Balboni	10.00
AU-62	Steve Sax	15.00
AU-63	Jerry Coleman	15.00
AU-64	Tom Tresh	15.00
AU-65	Tommy John	15.00
AU-66	Tony Kubek/SP	400.00
AU-67	Wade Boggs/SP	60.00
AU-68	Whitey Ford/SP	60.00
AU-69	Willie Randolph/SP	25.00
AU-70	Yogi Berra/SP	75.00

Classic Scripts Dual Autograph

Production 100 Sets		NM/M
SC	Bill "Moose" Skowron, Bob Cerv	50.00
MP	Bobby Murcer, Lou Piniella	65.00
CB	Chris Chambliss, Ron Blomberg	50.00
BN	Clete Boyer, Graig Nettles	50.00
RC	Dave Righetti, Rick Cerone	60.00
ED	Dock Ellis, Pat Dobson	70.00
BG	Don Baylor, Ken Griffey Sr.	65.00
MW	Don Mattingly, Dave Winfield	150.00
FG	Ed Figueroa, Ron Guidry	60.00
MB	Bobby Murcer, Hank Bauer	75.00
GL	Rich "Goose" Gossage, Sparky Lyle	50.00
NB	Graig Nettles, Wade Boggs	80.00
KJ	Jim Kaat, Tommy John	60.00
KA	Jimmy Key, Jim Abbott	50.00
PS	Joe Pepitone, Bill "Moose" Skowron	50.00
MM	Kevin Maas, Don Mattingly	100.00
RW	Mickey Rivers, Roy White	50.00
OL	Paul O'Neil, Jim Leyritz	75.00
RM	Phil Rizzuto, Gil McDougald	100.00
SD	Steve Sax, Brian Doyle	40.00
KR	Tony Kubek, Bobby Richardson	100.00
FL	Whitey Ford, Don Larsen	125.00
BL	Yogi Berra, Don Larsen	150.00
BH	Yogi Berra, Joe Torre	100.00
BF	Yogi Berra, Whitey Ford	150.00
WM	Bobby Murcer, Roy White	75.00
DN	Bucky Dent, Graig Nettles	50.00
CN	Chris Chambliss, Graig Nettles	50.00
CL	David Cone, Don Larsen	100.00
MC	Don Mattingly, Jack Clark	85.00
BM	Don Mattingly, Wade Boggs	150.00
SG	Darryl Strawberry, Dwight Gooden	75.00
CG	David Cone, Dwight Gooden	70.00

Classic Scripts Triple Autograph
No Pricing
Production 20 Sets

Classic Scripts Single Autograph

		NM/M
Common Autograph:		10.00
Inserted 1:8		
AU-1	Bill "Moose" Skowron	15.00
AU-2	Bob Cerv	10.00
AU-3	Bobby Murcer/SP	60.00
AU-4	Bobby Richardson	15.00
AU-5	Brian Doyle	10.00
AU-6	Bucky Dent	10.00
AU-7	Chris Chambliss	12.00
AU-8	Clete Boyer	15.00
AU-9	Dave Kingman	10.00
AU-10	Dave Righetti	10.00
AU-11	Dave Winfield/SP	60.00
AU-12	David Cone	10.00
AU-14	Dock Ellis	10.00
AU-15	Don Baylor/SP	25.00
AU-16	Don Larsen/SP	40.00
AU-17	Don Mattingly/SP	85.00
AU-18	Dwight Gooden	15.00
AU-19	Ed Figueroa	10.00
AU-20	Joe Torre/SP	125.00
AU-21	Darryl Strawberry	20.00
AU-23	Gaylord Perry	20.00
AU-24	Phil Linz	10.00
AU-25	Gil McDougald	15.00
AU-26	Rich "Goose" Gossage	20.00
AU-27	Graig Nettles	15.00
AU-28	Hank Bauer	15.00
AU-29	Jack Clark	15.00
AU-31	Jim Abbott	15.00
AU-32	Jim Bouton	15.00
AU-33	Jim Kaat	15.00
AU-34	Jim Leyritz/SP	25.00
AU-35	Jim Wynn	10.00
AU-36	Jimmy Key	10.00
AU-37	Joe Niekro	10.00
AU-38	Joe Pepitone	15.00
AU-39	John Wetteland/SP	20.00
AU-40	Ken Griffey Sr.	12.00
AU-42	Kevin Maas	10.00
AU-43	Lindy McDaniel	10.00
AU-44	Lou Piniella/SP	35.00
AU-45	Luis Tiant	20.00
AU-46	Mel Stottlemyre	15.00
AU-47	Mickey Rivers	15.00
AU-48	Oscar Gamble	15.00
AU-49	Pat Dobson	15.00
AU-50	Paul O'Neill/SP	40.00
AU-51	Phil Niekro	15.00
AU-52	Phil Rizzuto/SP	75.00
AU-53	Doc Medich	15.00
AU-54	Rick Cerone	15.00
AU-55	Ron Blomberg	10.00
AU-56	Ron Guidry	25.00
AU-57	Roy White	12.00
AU-58	Rudy May	10.00
AU-59	Sam McDowell	10.00
AU-60	Sparky Lyle	12.00
AU-61	Steve Balboni	10.00
AU-62	Steve Sax	10.00
AU-63	Jerry Coleman	15.00
AU-64	Tom Tresh	15.00
AU-65	Tommy John	15.00
AU-66	Tony Kubek/SP	400.00
AU-67	Wade Boggs/SP	60.00
AU-68	Whitey Ford/SP	60.00
AU-69	Willie Randolph/SP	25.00
AU-70	Yogi Berra/SP	75.00

Classic Scripts Dual Autograph

Production 100 Sets		NM/M
SC	Bill "Moose" Skowron, Bob Cerv	50.00
MP	Bobby Murcer, Lou Piniella	65.00
CB	Chris Chambliss, Ron Blomberg	50.00
BN	Clete Boyer, Graig Nettles	50.00
RC	Dave Righetti, Rick Cerone	60.00
ED	Dock Ellis, Pat Dobson	70.00
BG	Don Baylor, Ken Griffey Sr.	65.00
MW	Don Mattingly, Dave Winfield	150.00
FG	Ed Figueroa, Ron Guidry	60.00
MB	Bobby Murcer, Hank Bauer	75.00
GL	Rich "Goose" Gossage, Sparky Lyle	50.00
NB	Graig Nettles, Wade Boggs	80.00
KJ	Jim Kaat, Tommy John	60.00
KA	Jimmy Key, Jim Abbott	50.00
PS	Joe Pepitone, Bill "Moose" Skowron	50.00
MM	Kevin Maas, Don Mattingly	100.00
RW	Mickey Rivers, Roy White	50.00
OL	Paul O'Neil, Jim Leyritz	75.00
RM	Phil Rizzuto, Gil McDougald	100.00
SD	Steve Sax, Brian Doyle	40.00
KR	Tony Kubek, Bobby Richardson	100.00
FL	Whitey Ford, Don Larsen	125.00
BL	Yogi Berra, Don Larsen	150.00
BH	Yogi Berra, Joe Torre	100.00
BF	Yogi Berra, Whitey Ford	150.00
WM	Bobby Murcer, Roy White	75.00
DN	Bucky Dent, Graig Nettles	50.00
CN	Chris Chambliss, Graig Nettles	50.00
CL	David Cone, Don Larsen	100.00
MC	Don Mattingly, Jack Clark	85.00
BM	Don Mattingly, Wade Boggs	150.00
SG	Darryl Strawberry, Dwight Gooden	75.00
CG	David Cone, Dwight Gooden	70.00

Classic Scripts Triple Autograph
No Pricing
Production 20 Sets

Classic Scripts Quad Autograph
No Pricing
Production 10 Sets

Mitchell & Ness Pennant

		NM/M
Inserted 1:Box		
Cards:		.3X
P2	1927 World Series/96	25.00
P3	1928 World Series/96	25.00
P4	1932 World Series/96	25.00
P6	1937 World Series/96	25.00
P8	1939 World Series/96	25.00
P10	1943 World Series/97	25.00
P11	1947 World Series/97	25.00
P13	1950 World Series/97	25.00
P15	1952 World Series/97	25.00
P17	1956 World Series/97	25.00
P18	1958 World Series/97	25.00
P23	1996 World Series/99	25.00
P24	1998 World Series/99	25.00
P25	1999 World Series/99	25.00
P26	2000 World Series/100	25.00
MM57	Mickey Mantle - 1957 MVP/97	30.00
MM62	Mickey Mantle - 1962 MVP/98	30.00

Mitchell & Ness Pennant Card

		NM/M
Inserted 1:Box		
P2	1927 World Series/1927	5.00
P3	1928 World Series/1928	5.00
P4	1932 World Series/1932	5.00
P5	1936 World Series/36	10.00
P6	1937 World Series/1937	5.00
P7	1938 World Series/38	5.00
P8	1939 World Series/1939	5.00
P9	1941 World Series/41	10.00
P10	1943 World Series/1943	5.00
P11	1947 World Series/1947	5.00
P12	1949 World Series/49	10.00
P13	1950 World Series/1950	5.00
P14	1951 World Series/51	10.00
P15	1952 World Series/1952	5.00
P16	1953 World Series/53	10.00
P17	1956 World Series/1956	5.00
P18	1958 World Series/1958	5.00
P19	1961 World Series/61	10.00
P20	1962 World Series/62	10.00
P21	1977 World Series/77	5.00
P22	1978 World Series/78	5.00
P23	1996 World Series/1996	5.00
P24	1998 World Series/1998	5.00
P25	1999 World Series/1999	5.00
P26	2000 World Series/2,000	5.00
MM57	Mickey Mantle - 1957 MVP/1,957	8.00
MM62	Mickey Mantle - 1962 MVP/1,962	8.00

Mitchell & Ness Jersey Redemption

		NM/M
Inserted 1:384		
Production 40-99		
MNJ1	Babe Ruth/40	350.00
MNJ2	Bill Dickey/75	150.00
MNJ3	Billy Martin/99	150.00
MNJ4	Bobby Murcer/99	100.00
MNJ5	Bucky Dent/92	100.00
MNJ6	Casey Stengel/65	120.00
MNJ7	"Catfish" Hunter/92	120.00
MNJ8	Chris Chambliss/99	80.00
MNJ9	Don Larsen/75	120.00
MNJ10	Don Mattingly/92	150.00
MNJ11	Elston Howard/88	100.00
MNJ12	Rich "Goose" Gossage/92	100.00
MNJ13	Graig Nettles/99	100.00
MNJ14	Joe DiMaggio/55	200.00
MNJ15	Lefty Gomez/81	120.00
MNJ16	Lou Gehrig/40	200.00
MNJ17	Lou Piniella/99	100.00
MNJ18	Mickey Mantle/50	275.00
MNJ19	Bill "Moose" Skowron/85	125.00
MNJ20	Phil Rizzuto/40	150.00
MNJ21	Roy White/50	100.00
MNJ22	Roger Maris/92	200.00
MNJ23	Ron Guidry/99	100.00
MNJ24	Sparky Lyle/99	100.00
MNJ25	Thurman Munson/91	200.00
MNJ26	Tony Kubek/75	150.00
MNJ27	Tony Lazzeri/79	120.00
MNJ28	Whitey Ford/43	180.00
MNJ29	Willie Randolph/92	100.00
MNJ30	Yogi Berra/50	200.00

Gravity Games Cleveland Indians

In conjunction with the Gravity Games held September 15-19 in Cleveland, Upper Deck created this team set. Cards were distributed in team-logoed foil packs containing four player cards and a header card. Fronts are bordered in red with game action photos. Backs have a close-up from the front photo, personal data, career highlights, 2003 and lifetime stats.

		NM/M
Complete Set (12):		7.50
Common Player:		.50
1	C.C. Sabathia	.65
2	Travis Hafner	.75
3	Casey Blake	.75
4	Matt Lawton	.50
5	Jason Davis	.50
6	Ben Broussard	.50
7	Omar Vizquel	.50
8	Cliff Lee	.50
9	Ronnie Belliard	.50
10	Jody Gerut	.75
11	Victor Martinez	1.00
12	Coco Crisp	1.00
---	Header Card	.05

Sunkist

Photos of six former major leaguers in their Little League days are featured on this set. Five million of the cards were inserted into bags of oranges to help promote the fruit company's sponsorship of the youth program.

		NM/M
Complete Set (6):		6.00
Common Player:		.50
1	Rollie Fingers	1.00

2 Gary Carter 2.00
3 Mark McGwire 3.00
4 Mickey Morandini .50
5 Paul O'Neill .50
6 Dave Steib .50

2005 Upper Deck

NM/M
Complete Set (500): 75.00
Common Player: .15
Common (211-250): .50
Hobby Pack (8): 3.00
Hobby Box (24): 65.00
1 Casey Kotchman .15
2 Chone Figgins .15
3 David Eckstein .15
4 Jarrod Washburn .15
5 Robb Quinlan .15
6 Troy Glaus .25
7 Vladimir Guerrero .75
8 Brandon Webb .15
9 Danny Bautista .15
10 Luis Gonzalez .15
11 Matt Kata .15
12 Randy Johnson .75
13 Robby Hammock .15
14 Shea Hillenbrand .15
15 Adam LaRoche .15
16 Andruw Jones .25
17 Horacio Ramirez .15
18 John Smoltz .25
19 Johnny Estrada .15
20 Mike Hampton .15
21 Rafael Furcal .15
22 Brian Roberts .15
23 Javy Lopez .25
24 Jay Gibbons .15
25 Jorge Julio .15
26 Melvin Mora .15
27 Miguel Tejada .25
28 Rafael Palmeiro .50
29 Derek Lowe .25
30 Jason Varitek .25
31 Kevin Youkilis .15
32 Manny Ramirez .75
33 Curt Schilling .75
34 Pedro Martinez .75
35 Trot Nixon .15
36 Corey Patterson .25
37 Derrek Lee .25
38 LaTroy Hawkins .15
39 Mark Prior .75
40 Matt Clement .15
41 Moises Alou .15
42 Sammy Sosa 1.50
43 Aaron Rowand .15
44 Carlos Lee .15
45 Jose Valentin .15
46 Juan Uribe .15
47 Magglio Ordonez .25
48 Mark Buehrle .15
49 Paul Konerko .25
50 Adam Dunn .50
51 Barry Larkin .25
52 D'Angelo Jimenez .15
53 Danny Graves .15
54 Paul Wilson .15
55 Sean Casey .25
56 Wily Mo Pena .25
57 Ben Broussard .15
58 C.C. Sabathia .15
59 Casey Blake .15
60 Cliff Lee .15
61 Matt Lawton .15
62 Omar Vizquel .15
63 Victor Martinez .15
64 Charles Johnson .15
65 Joe Kennedy .15
66 Jeromy Burnitz .15
67 Matt Holliday .15
68 Preston Wilson .15
69 Royce Clayton .15
70 Shawn Estes .15
71 Bobby Higginson .15
72 Brandon Inge .15
73 Carlos Guillen .15
74 Dmitri Young .15
75 Eric Munson .15
76 Jeremy Bonderman .15
77 Ugueth Urbina .15
78 Josh Beckett .40
79 Dontrelle Willis .75
80 Jeff Conine .15
81 Juan Pierre .15
82 Luis Castillo .15
83 Miguel Cabrera .75
84 Mike Lowell .25

85 Andy Pettitte .25
86 Brad Lidge .15
87 Carlos Beltran .50
88 Craig Biggio .25
89 Jeff Bagwell .50
90 Roger Clemens 1.50
91 Roy Oswalt .25
92 Benito Santiago .15
93 Jeremy Affeldt .15
94 Juan Gonzalez .25
95 Ken Harvey .15
96 Mike MacDougal .15
97 Mike Sweeney .15
98 Zack Greinke .15
99 Adrian Beltre .40
100 Alex Cora .15
101 Cesar Izturis .15
102 Eric Gagne .40
103 Kazuhisa Ishii .15
104 Milton Bradley .15
105 Shawn Green .25
106 Danny Kolb .15
107 Ben Sheets .25
108 Brooks Kieschnick .15
109 Craig Counsell .15
110 Geoff Jenkins .15
111 Lyle Overbay .15
112 Scott Podsednik .15
113 Corey Koskie .15
114 Johan Santana .40
115 Joe Mauer .25
116 Justin Morneau .25
117 Lew Ford .15
118 Matt LeCroy .15
119 Torii Hunter .25
120 Brad Wilkerson .15
121 Chad Cordero .15
122 Livan Hernandez .15
123 Jose Vidro .15
124 Terrmel Sledge .15
125 Tony Batista .15
126 Zach Day .15
127 Al Leiter .25
128 Jae Weong Seo .15
129 Jose Reyes .40
130 Kazuo Matsui .15
131 Mike Piazza 1.00
132 Todd Zeile .15
133 Cliff Floyd .15
134 Alex Rodriguez 2.00
135 Derek Jeter 2.00
136 Gary Sheffield .40
137 Hideki Matsui 1.50
138 Jason Giambi .25
139 Jorge Posada .25
140 Mike Mussina .40
141 Barry Zito .25
142 Bobby Crosby .25
143 Octavio Dotel .15
144 Eric Chavez .25
145 Jermaine Dye .15
146 Mark Kotsay .15
147 Tim Hudson .25
148 Billy Wagner .15
149 Bobby Abreu .25
150 David Bell .15
151 Jim Thome .50
152 Jimmy Rollins .25
153 Mike Lieberthal .15
154 Randy Wolf .15
155 Craig Wilson .15
156 Daryle Ward .15
157 Jack Wilson .15
158 Jason Kendall .15
159 Kip Wells .15
160 Oliver Perez .15
161 Robert Mackowiak .15
162 Brian Giles .25
163 Brian Lawrence .15
164 David Wells .15
165 Jay Payton .15
166 Ryan Klesko .15
167 Sean Burroughs .15
168 Trevor Hoffman .15
169 Brett Tomko .15
170 J.T. Snow .15
171 Jason Schmidt .25
172 Kirk Rueter .15
173 A.J. Pierzynski .15
174 Pedro Feliz .15
175 Ray Durham .15
176 Eddie Guardado .15
177 Edgar Martinez .15
178 Ichiro Suzuki 1.50
179 Jamie Moyer .15
180 Joel Pineiro .15
181 Randy Winn .15
182 Raul Ibanez .15
183 Albert Pujols 2.00
184 Edgar Renteria .25
185 Jason Isringhausen .15
186 Jim Edmonds .40
187 Matt Morris .15
188 Reggie Sanders .15
189 Tony Womack .15
190 Aubrey Huff .15
191 Danys Baez .15
192 Carl Crawford .25
193 Jose Cruz Jr. .15
194 Rocco Baldelli .15
195 Tino Martinez .15
196 Dewon Brazelton .15
197 Alfonso Soriano .75
198 Brad Fullmer .15
199 Gerald Laird .15
200 Hank Blalock .50
201 Laynce Nix .15
202 Mark Teixeira .25

203 Mike Young .15
204 Alexis Rios .15
205 Eric Hinske .15
206 Miguel Batista .15
207 Orlando Hudson .15
208 Roy Halladay .15
209 Ted Lilly .15
210 Vernon Wells .15
211 Aarom Baldiris .50
212 B.J. Upton 1.00
213 Dallas McPherson .50
214 Brian Dallimore .50
215 Chris Oxspring .50
216 Chris Shelton .50
217 David Wright 1.50
218 Edwardo Sierra .50
219 Fernando Nieve .50
220 Frank Francisco .50
221 Jeff Bennett .50
222 Justin Lehr .50
223 John Gall .50
224 Jorge Sequea .50
225 Justin Germano .50
226 Kazuhito Tadano .50
227 Kevin Cave .50
228 Joe Blanton .50
229 Luis Gonzalez .50
230 Mike Wuertz .50
231 Mike Rouse .50
232 Nick Regilio .50
233 Orlando Rodriguez .50
234 Phil Stockman .50
235 Ramon Ramirez .50
236 Roberto Novoa .50
237 Dioner Navarro .50
238 Tim Bausher .50
239 Logan Kensing .50
240 Andy Green .50
241 Brad Halsey .50
242 Charles Thomas .50
243 George Sherrill .50
244 Jesse Crain .50
245 Jimmy Serrano .50
246 Joe Horgan .50
247 Chris Young RC 1.50
248 Joey Gathright .50
249 Gavin Floyd .50
250 Ryan Howard 1.00
251 Lance Cormier .15
252 Matt Treanor .15
253 Jeff Francis .15
254 Nick Swisher .15
255 Scott Atchison .15
256 Travis Blackley .15
257 Travis Smith .15
258 Yadier Molina .15
259 Jeff Keppinger .15
260 Scott Kazmir 1.00
261 Garret Anderson, Vladimir Guerrero .40
262 Luis Gonzalez, Randy Johnson .40
263 Andruw Jones, Chipper Jones .40
264 Miguel Tejada, Rafael Palmeiro .40
265 Curt Schilling, Manny Ramirez .50
266 Mark Prior, Sammy Sosa .75
267 Frank Thomas, Magglio Ordonez .25
268 Barry Larkin, Ken Griffey Jr. .75
269 C.C. Sabathia, Victor Martinez .15
270 Jeromy Burnitz, Todd Helton .25
271 Dmitri Young, Ivan Rodriguez .40
272 Josh Beckett, Miguel Cabrera .25
273 Jeff Bagwell, Roger Clemens .75
274 Ken Harvey, Mike Sweeney .15
275 Adrian Beltre, Eric Gagne .25
276 Ben Sheets, Geoff Jenkins .15
277 Joe Mauer, Torii Hunter .15
278 Jose Vidro, Livan Hernandez .15
279 Kazuo Matsui, Mike Piazza .50
280 Alex Rodriguez, Derek Jeter 1.00
281 Eric Chavez, Tim Hudson .15
282 Bobby Abreu, Jim Thome .40
283 Craig Wilson, Jason Kendall .15
284 Brian Giles, Phil Nevin .15
285 A.J. Pierzynski, Jason Schmidt .15
286 Bret Boone, Ichiro Suzuki .75
287 Albert Pujols, Scott Rolen .75
288 Aubrey Huff, Tino Martinez .15
289 Hank Blalock, Mark Teixeira .15
290 Carlos Delgado, Roy Halladay .15
291 Vladimir Guerrero .40
292 Curt Schilling .25

293 Mark Prior .40
294 Josh Beckett .15
295 Roger Clemens .75
296 Derek Jeter .75
297 Eric Chavez .15
298 Jim Thome .25
299 Albert Pujols .75
300 Hank Blalock .25
301 Bartolo Colon .25
302 Darin Erstad .15
303 Garret Anderson .25
304 Orlando Cabrera .15
305 Steve Finley .15
306 Javier Vazquez .15
307 Russ Ortiz .15
308 Chipper Jones .75
309 Marcus Giles .15
310 Raul Mondesi .15
311 B.J. Ryan .15
312 Luis Matos .15
313 Sidney Ponson .15
314 Bill Mueller .15
315 David Ortiz .75
316 Johnny Damon .75
317 Keith Foulke .15
318 Mark Bellhorn .15
319 Wade Miller .15
320 Aramis Ramirez .40
321 Carlos Zambrano .15
322 Greg Maddux 1.25
323 Kerry Wood .15
324 Nomar Garciaparra 1.00
325 Todd Walker .15
326 Frank Thomas .50
327 Freddy Garcia .15
328 Joe Crede .15
329 Jose Contreras .15
330 Orlando Hernandez .15
331 Shingo Takatsu .15
332 Austin Kearns .15
333 Eric Milton .15
334 Ken Griffey Jr. 1.00
335 Aaron Boone .15
336 David Riske .15
337 Jake Westbrook .15
338 Kevin Millwood .15
339 Travis Hafner .25
340 Aaron Miles .15
341 Jeff Baker .15
342 Todd Helton .50
343 Garrett Atkins .15
344 Carlos Pena .15
345 Ivan Rodriguez .50
346 Rondell White .15
347 Troy Percival .15
348 A.J. Burnett .25
349 Carlos Delgado .40
350 Guillermo Mota .15
351 Paul LoDuca .15
352 Jason Lane .15
353 Lance Berkman .25
354 Angel Berroa .15
355 David DeJesus .15
356 Ruben Gotay .15
357 Jose Lima .15
358 Brad Penny .15
359 J.D. Drew .25
360 Jayson Werth .15
361 Jeff Kent .25
362 Odalis Perez .15
363 Brady Clark .15
364 Junior Spivey .15
365 Rickie Weeks .15
366 Jacque Jones .15
367 Joe Nathan .15
368 Nick Punto .15
369 Shannon Stewart .15
370 Doug Mientkiewicz .15
371 Kris Benson .15
372 Tom Glavine .25
373 Victor Zambrano .15
374 Bernie Williams .40
375 Carl Pavano .15
376 Jaret Wright .15
377 Kevin Brown .15
378 Mariano Rivera .25
379 Dan Haren .15
380 Eric Byrnes .15
381 Erubiel Durazo .15
382 Rich Harden .15
383 Brett Myers .15
384 Chase Utley .25
385 Marlon Byrd .15
386 Pat Burrell .15
387 Placido Polanco .15
388 Freddy Sanchez .15
389 Jason Bay .25
390 Josh Fogg .15
391 Adam Eaton .15
392 Jake Peavy .40
393 Khalil Greene .15
394 Mark Loretta .15
395 Phil Nevin .15
396 Ramon Hernandez .15
397 Woody Williams .15
398 Armando Benitez .15
399 Edgardo Alfonzo .15
400 Marquis Grissom .15
401 Mike Matheny .15
402 Richie Sexson .40
403 Bret Boone .15
404 Gil Meche .15
405 Chris Carpenter .40
406 Jeff Suppan .15
407 Larry Walker .40
408 Mark Grudzielanek .15
409 Mark Mulder .25
410 Scott Rolen .75

411 Josh Phelps .15
412 Jonny Gomes .15
413 Francisco Cordero .15
414 Kenny Rogers .15
415 Richard Hidalgo .15
416 David Bush .15
417 Frank Catalanotto .15
418 Gabe Gross .15
419 Guillermo Quiroz .15
420 Reed Johnson .15
421 Cristian Guzman .15
422 Esteban Loaiza .15
423 Jose Guillen .25
424 Nick Johnson .25
425 Vinny Castilla .15
426 Peter Orr RC .50
427 Tadahito Iguchi RC 4.00
428 Jeff Baker .15
429 Marcos Carvajal RC .15
430 Justin Verlander RC 3.00
431 Luke Scott RC 1.00
432 Willy Taveras .15
433 Ambiorix Burgos RC .50
434 Andy Sisco .15
435 Denny Bautista .15
436 Mark Teahen .15
437 Ervin Santana .15
438 Dennis Houlton RC .50
439 Philip Humber RC 1.00
440 Steve Schmoll RC .15
441 J.J. Hardy .15
442 Ambiorix Concepcion RC .50
443 Dae-Sung Koo RC .15
444 Andy Phillips .15
445 Dan Meyer .15
446 Huston Street .15
447 Keiichi Yabu RC .15
448 Jeff Niemann RC 1.00
449 Jeremy Reed .15
450 Tony Blanco .15
451 Albert Pujols .75
452 Alex Rodriguez .75
453 Curt Schilling .40
454 Derek Jeter .75
455 Greg Maddux .50
456 Ichiro Suzuki .50
457 Ivan Rodriguez .25
458 Jeff Bagwell .25
459 Jim Thome .25
460 Ken Griffey Jr. .50
461 Manny Ramirez .40
462 Mike Mussina .15
463 Mike Piazza .40
464 Pedro Martinez .40
465 Rafael Palmeiro .25
466 Randy Johnson .40
467 Roger Clemens .75
468 Sammy Sosa .50
469 Todd Helton .25
470 Vladimir Guerrero .40
471 Vladimir Guerrero .25
472 Shawn Green .15
473 John Smoltz .15
474 Miguel Tejada .25
475 Curt Schilling .25
476 Mark Prior .40
477 Frank Thomas .25
478 Ken Griffey Jr. .50
479 C.C. Sabathia .15
480 Todd Helton .25
481 Ivan Rodriguez .25
482 Miguel Cabrera .40
483 Roger Clemens .50
484 Mike Sweeney .15
485 Eric Gagne .15
486 Ben Sheets .15
487 Johan Santana .25
488 Mike Piazza .40
489 Derek Jeter .50
490 Eric Chavez .15
491 Jim Thome .15
492 Craig Wilson .15
493 Jake Peavy .15
494 Jason Schmidt .15
495 Ichiro Suzuki .50
496 Albert Pujols .50
497 Carl Crawford .15
498 Mark Teixeira .25
499 Vernon Wells .15
500 Jose Vidro .15

Emerald
Stars (301-500): 10-20X
Production 25 Sets
Exclusive to Series 2

Blue
Stars (301-500): 4-6X
Production 150 Sets
Exclusive to Series 2

Gold
Stars (301-500): 4-8X
Production 99 Sets
Exclusive to Series 2

Platinum
No Pricing
Production 5 Sets
Exclusive to Series 2

American Flag
No Pricing
Production 15 Sets

Retro
Retro: 2-3X
One retro box per hobby case.

Lasting Impressions
No Pricing
Production One Set
One press plate per color.

Plates
No Pricing
Production one set per color.

Diamond Images - Wingfield Collection

NM/M
Complete Set (20): 45.00
Common Player: 2.00
Inserted 1:9
DI-1 Eddie Mathews 3.00
DI-2 Ernie Banks 4.00
DI-3 Joe DiMaggio 6.00
DI-4 Mickey Mantle 8.00
DI-5 Pee Wee Reese 2.00
DI-6 Phil Rizzuto 2.00
DI-7 Stan Musial 4.00
DI-8 Ted Williams 6.00
DI-9 Bob Feller 2.00
DI-10 Whitey Ford 2.00
DI-11 Willie Stargell 2.00
DI-12 Yogi Berra 2.00
DI-13 Roy Campanella 2.00
DI-14 Franklin D. Roosevelt 2.00
DI-15 Harry S. Truman 2.00
DI-16 Dwight D. Eisenhower 2.00
DI-17 John F. Kennedy 2.00
DI-18 Lyndon B. Johnson 2.00
DI-19 Richard Nixon 2.00
DI-20 Thurman Munson 3.00

Hall of Fame Plaques

NM/M
Complete Set (10): 40.00
Common Player: 3.00
Inserted 1:36
SP-16 Ernie Banks 4.00
SP-17 Yogi Berra 4.00
SP-18 Whitey Ford 3.00
SP-19 Bob Gibson 3.00
SP-20 Willie McCovey 3.00
SP-21 Stan Musial 5.00
SP-22 Nolan Ryan 12.00
SP-23 Mike Schmidt 8.00
SP-24 Tom Seaver 4.00
SP-25 Robin Yount 4.00

Game Jersey
NM/M
Common Jersey: 5.00
Inserted 1:8
JB Jeff Bagwell/SP 8.00
CB Carlos Beltran/SP 8.00
AB Adrian Beltre 5.00
LB Lance Berkman 5.00
HB Hank Blalock 5.00
MC Miguel Cabrera 8.00
EC Eric Chavez 5.00
EG Eric Gagne 5.00
TG Troy Glaus 5.00
KG Ken Griffey Jr./SP 15.00

VG	Vladimir Guerrero	8.00
HE	Todd Helton	8.00
TH	Tim Hudson	5.00
HU	Torii Hunter	5.00
DJ	Derek Jeter	25.00
RJ	Randy Johnson/SP	10.00
CJ	Chipper Jones	8.00
JK	Jeff Kent	5.00
GM	Greg Maddux/SP	10.00
PM	Pedro Martinez	8.00
MM	Mark Mulder	5.00
DO	David Ortiz/SP	10.00
PI	Mike Piazza	8.00
MP	Mark Prior	8.00
AP	Albert Pujols	20.00
MR	Manny Ramirez/SP	10.00
IR	Ivan Rodriguez	8.00
SR	Scott Rolen	8.00
JS	Johan Santana/SP	10.00
CS	Curt Schilling	8.00
SM	John Smoltz	8.00
AS	Alfonso Soriano	8.00
SS	Sammy Sosa	10.00
MT	Mark Teixeira/SP	8.00
TE	Miguel Tejada	8.00
FT	Frank Thomas	8.00
JT	Jim Thome/SP	8.00
KW	Kerry Wood	8.00
DW	David Wright	10.00

Game Patch

NM/M

Inserted 1:288

DJ	Derek Jeter	75.00
CR	Cal Ripken Jr.	75.00

Marquee Attractions

NM/M

Common Player: 4.00

Inserted 1:12

GA	Garret Anderson	4.00
JB	Jeff Bagwell	8.00
BE	Josh Beckett	4.00
KB	Kevin Brown	4.00
MC	Miguel Cabrera	8.00
RC	Roger Clemens	15.00
CD	Carlos Delgado	4.00
AD	Adam Dunn	8.00
EG	Eric Gagne	6.00
JG	Jason Giambi	4.00
BG	Brian Giles	4.00
SG	Shawn Green	4.00
KG	Ken Griffey Jr.	12.00
VG	Vladimir Guerrero	8.00
TH	Todd Helton	8.00
HO	Trevor Hoffman	4.00
DJ	Derek Jeter	20.00
RJ	Randy Johnson	8.00
AJ	Andruw Jones	6.00
CJ	Chipper Jones	8.00
GM	Greg Maddux	10.00
PM	Pedro Martinez	8.00
HM	Hideki Matsui	30.00
KM	Kazuo Matsui	8.00
JM	Joe Mauer	8.00
HN	Hideo Nomo	10.00
RO	Roy Oswalt	4.00
PE	Andy Pettitte	6.00
PI	Mike Piazza	8.00
MP	Mark Prior	6.00
AP	Albert Pujols	15.00
IR	Ivan Rodriguez	8.00
CS	Curt Schilling	8.00
JS	Jason Schmidt	6.00
SS	Sammy Sosa	12.00
IS	Ichiro Suzuki	25.00
MT	Miguel Tejada	6.00
JT	Jim Thome	8.00
BW	Billy Wagner	4.00
DW	Dontrelle Willis	4.00
PW	Preston Wilson	4.00
KW	Kerry Wood	8.00

Matinee Idols

NM/M

Common Player: 4.00

Inserted 1:12 Hobby

JB	Jeff Bagwell	8.00
RB	Rocco Baldelli	4.00
BE	Josh Beckett	6.00
HB	Hank Blalock	8.00
BB	Bret Boone/SP	6.00
PB	Pat Burrell	6.00
SB	Sean Burroughs	4.00
EC	Eric Chavez	6.00
RC	Roger Clemens	15.00
CD	Carlos Delgado	4.00
JE	Jim Edmonds	6.00
JG	Jason Giambi	4.00
TG	Troy Glaus	8.00
KG	Ken Griffey Jr.	12.00
VG	Vladimir Guerrero	8.00
RH	Roy Halladay	4.00
TH	Todd Helton	8.00
HU	Torii Hunter	8.00
DJ	Derek Jeter	20.00
RJ	Randy Johnson	8.00
CJ	Chipper Jones	8.00
ML	Mike Lowell	4.00
MM	Mike Mussina	6.00
PI	Mike Piazza	10.00
MP	Mark Prior	6.00
CR	Cal Ripken Jr.	25.00
SR	Scott Rolen	8.00
NR	Nolan Ryan	25.00
CS	Curt Schilling	8.00
TS	Tom Seaver	8.00
GS	Gary Sheffield	6.00
SS	Sammy Sosa	12.00
MT	Mark Teixeira	6.00
JT	Jim Thome	8.00
BW	Billy Wagner	4.00
RW	Rickie Weeks	4.00
VW	Vernon Wells	4.00
DW	Dontrelle Willis	4.00
KW	Kerry Wood	8.00
BZ	Barry Zito	4.00

Milestone Materials

NM/M

Common Jersey: 5.00

BA	Jeff Bagwell	8.00
JB	Jason Bay	5.00
CB	Carlos Beltran	8.00
BC	Bobby Crosby	5.00
EG	Eric Gagne	5.00
KG	Ken Griffey Jr.	15.00
VG	Vladimir Guerrero	8.00
RJ	Randy Johnson	8.00
GM	Greg Maddux	10.00
DO	David Ortiz	8.00
RP	Rafael Palmeiro	8.00
JP	Jake Peavy	5.00
AP	Albert Pujols	20.00
MR	Manny Ramirez	8.00
JS	Johan Santana	8.00
CS	Curt Schilling	8.00
MT	Miguel Tejada	5.00
JT	Jim Thome	8.00

Origins

NM/M

Common Player: 4.00

Inserted 1:12 Hobby

Inserted 1:24 Retail

GA	Garret Anderson	4.00
CB	Carlos Beltran	10.00
AB	Adrian Beltre	6.00
LB	Lance Berkman	4.00
MC	Miguel Cabrera	8.00
RF	Rafael Furcal	4.00
EG	Eric Gagne	4.00
BG	Brian Giles	4.00
JG	Juan Gonzalez	8.00
LG	Luis Gonzalez	4.00
VG	Vladimir Guerrero	8.00
TH	Tim Hudson	4.00
AJ	Andruw Jones	6.00
JK	Jeff Kent	4.00
JL	Javy Lopez	4.00
GM	Greg Maddux	10.00
PM	Pedro Martinez	10.00
HM	Hideki Matsui	30.00
KM	Kazuo Matsui	8.00
MM	Mark Mulder	4.00
HN	Hideo Nomo	10.00
MO	Magglio Ordonez	4.00
RP	Rafael Palmeiro	8.00
PE	Jake Peavy	4.00
JP	Jorge Posada	4.00
AP	Albert Pujols	15.00
MR	Manny Ramirez	8.00
JR	Jose Reyes	4.00
IR	Ivan Rodriguez	8.00
JS	Jason Schmidt	8.00
RS	Richie Sexson	4.00
AS	Alfonso Soriano	8.00
SS	Sammy Sosa	12.00
IS	Ichiro Suzuki	25.00
MT	Miguel Tejada	6.00
BU	B.J. Upton	8.00
JV	Javier Vazquez	4.00
PW	Preston Wilson	4.00

Rewind to 1997 Jersey

NM/M

Common Jersey:

Inserted 1:288

JB	Jeff Bagwell	25.00
WC	Will Clark	20.00
KG	Ken Griffey Jr.	40.00
VG	Vladimir Guerrero	25.00
TG	Tony Gwynn	30.00
DJ	Derek Jeter	40.00
RJ	Randy Johnson	25.00
AJ	Andruw Jones	25.00
CJ	Chipper Jones	30.00
GM	Greg Maddux	40.00
PM	Pedro Martinez	25.00
MP	Mike Piazza	30.00
MR	Manny Ramirez	30.00
CR	Cal Ripken Jr.	40.00
IR	Ivan Rodriguez	20.00
SR	Scott Rolen	25.00
CS	Curt Schilling	20.00
JS	John Smoltz	25.00
FT	Frank Thomas	25.00
JT	Jim Thome	25.00

Signature Sensations

No Pricing

Production 15 Sets

Die-Cut No Pricing

Production 10 Sets

Signature Stars

NM/M

Common Player:

Inserted 1:288 Hobby

CB	Carlos Beltran/SP	40.00
HB	Hank Blalock	25.00
MC	Miguel Cabrera	35.00
BC	Bobby Crosby	30.00
LF	Lew Ford	10.00
KG	Ken Griffey Jr.	80.00
JL	Javy Lopez	15.00
JM	Joe Mauer	20.00
OP	Odalis Perez	20.00
CR	Cal Ripken Jr./SP	180.00
BS	Ben Sheets	15.00
DW	Dontrelle Willis	20.00
KW	Kerry Wood	25.00
DY	Delmon Young	25.00

Signature Stars Retail

Inserted 1:480 Retail

Super Patch - Names

No Pricing

Cards are not serial numbered

Super Patch - Numbers

No Pricing

Cards are not serial numbered.

Super Patch - Logos

No Pricing

Cards are not serial numbered.

World Series Heroes

NM/M

Complete Set (45): 20.00

Common Player: .25

Inserted 1:1 Retail

WS-1	Garret Anderson	.50
WS-2	Troy Glaus	.50
WS-3	Vladimir Guerrero	1.00
WS-4	Andruw Jones	.50
WS-5	Chipper Jones	1.00
WS-6	Curt Schilling	1.00
WS-7	Keith Foulke	.25
WS-8	Manny Ramirez	.75
WS-9	Nomar Garciaparra	1.00
WS-10	Pedro Martinez	1.00
WS-11	Kerry Wood	1.00
WS-12	Mark Prior	1.00
WS-13	Sammy Sosa	2.00
WS-14	Frank Thomas	.75
WS-15	Magglio Ordonez	.25
WS-16	Dontrelle Willis	.25
WS-17	Josh Beckett	.50
WS-18	Miguel Cabrera	.75
WS-19	Jeff Bagwell	.75
WS-20	Lance Berkman	.25
WS-21	Roger Clemens	2.00
WS-22	Eric Gagne	.50
WS-23	Torii Hunter	.50
WS-24	Mike Piazza	1.50
WS-25	Alex Rodriguez	2.00
WS-26	Derek Jeter	2.00
WS-27	Gary Sheffield	.75
WS-28	Hideki Matsui	1.50
WS-29	Jason Giambi	.50
WS-30	Jorge Posada	.50
WS-31	Kevin Brown	.25
WS-32	Mariano Rivera	.75
WS-33	Mike Mussina	.50
WS-34	Eric Chavez	.25
WS-35	Mark Mulder	.25
WS-36	Tim Hudson	.25
WS-37	Billy Wagner	.25
WS-38	Jim Thome	.75
WS-39	Brian Giles	.25
WS-40	Jason Schmidt	.25
WS-41	Albert Pujols	2.00
WS-42	Scott Rolen	.75
WS-43	Alfonso Soriano	.75
WS-44	Hank Blalock	.75
WS-45	Mark Teixeira	.50

2004 Update Set

NM/M

Complete Set (50): 10.00

Common Player: .15

Inserted 1:Hobby Box

541	Alex Rodriguez	1.50
542	Roger Clemens	1.50
543	Andy Pettitte	.25
544	Vladimir Guerrero	.75
545	David Wells	.15
546	Derek Lee	.15
547	Carlos Beltran	.50
548	Orlando Cabrera	.15
549	Paul LoDuca	.15
550	Dave Roberts	.15
551	Guillermo Mota	.15
552	Steve Finley	.15
553	Juan Encarnacion	.15
554	Larry Walker	.50
555	Ty Wigginton	.15
556	Doug Mientkiewicz	.15
557	Roberto Alomar	.40
558	B.J. Upton	.15
559	Brad Penny	.15
560	Hee Seop Choi	.15
561	David Wright	1.00
562	Nomar Garciaparra	1.00
563	Felix Rodriguez	.15
564	Victor Zambrano	.15
565	Kris Benson	.15
566	Aarom Baldiris	.15
567	Joey Gathright	.15
568	Charles Thomas	.15
569	Brian Dallimore	.15
570	Chris Oxspring	.15
571	Chris Shelton	.15
572	Dioner Navarro	.25
573	Edwardo Sierra	.15
574	Fernando Nieve	.15
575	Frank Francisco	.15
576	Jeff Bennett	.15
577	Justin Lehr	.15
578	John Gall	.15
579	Jorge Sequea	.15
580	Justin Germano	.15
581	Kazuhito Tadano	.15
582	Kevin Cave	.15
583	Jesse Crain	.15
584	Luis Gonzalez	.15
585	Mike Wuertz	.15
586	Orlando Rodriguez	.15
587	Phil Stockman	.15
588	Ramon Ramirez	.15
589	Roberto Novoa	.15
590	Scott Kazmir	1.50

2004 Update - Authentic Stars

NM/M

Common Player: 8.00

1:12 '04 Update Sets

Production 75 Sets

CB	Carlos Beltran	15.00
LB	Lance Berkman	8.00
JE	Jim Edmonds	8.00
RF	Rafael Furcal	8.00
HA	Roy Halladay	8.00
RH	Rich Harden	8.00
HU	Tim Hudson	8.00
DJ	Derek Jeter	35.00
AK	Austin Kearns	8.00
HN	Hideo Nomo	20.00
MO	Magglio Ordonez	8.00
OS	Roy Oswalt	8.00
RP	Rafael Palmeiro	12.00
MR	Manny Ramirez	15.00
JR	Jose Reyes	8.00
SR	Scott Rolen	15.00
TE	Miguel Tejada	8.00
JT	Jim Thome	12.00
WE	Brandon Webb	8.00
VW	Vernon Wells	8.00
PW	Preston Wilson	8.00
KW	Kerry Wood	8.00

2004 Update - Awesome Honors

NM/M

Common Player: 8.00

1:12 '04 Update Set

Production 75 Sets

BE	Adrian Beltre	10.00
AB	Angel Berroa	8.00
KB	Kevin Brown	8.00
MC	Miguel Cabrera	15.00
RC	Roger Clemens	20.00
EG	Eric Gagne	12.00
BG	Brian Giles	8.00
DL	Derek Lee	8.00
KM	Kazuo Matsui	20.00
JM	Joe Mauer	10.00
PE	Andy Pettitte	10.00
SP	Scott Podsednik	8.00
AP	Albert Pujols	25.00
IR	Ivan Rodriguez	12.00
SC	Curt Schilling	12.00
RS	Richie Sexson	8.00
GS	Gary Sheffield	8.00
AS	Alfonso Soriano	15.00
VA	Javier Vazquez	8.00

4,000 Strikeout Autographs

Production 50 Sets

Quad Signature No Pricing

Production 10

4,000-Strikeout Commemorative

NM/M

Production 4,000

Steve Carlton, Nolan Ryan, Roger Clemens, Randy Johnson 12.00

2005 UD All-Star Classics

NM/M

Complete Set (100): 25.00

Common Player: .15

Pack (8): 3.00

Box (24):		60.00
1	Albert Pujols	2.00
2	Alex Rodriguez	1.50
3	Alfonso Soriano	.75
4	Barry Zito	.25
5	Bobby Abreu	.40
6	Carlos Beltran	.50
7	Carlos Delgado	.40
8	Chipper Jones	.75
9	Curt Schilling	.75
10	David Ortiz	.75
11	Derek Jeter	2.00
12	Edgar Renteria	.25
13	Eric Gagne	.25
14	Frank Thomas	.50
15	Gary Sheffield	.40
16	Greg Maddux	1.00
17	Hank Blalock	.40
18	Hideki Matsui	1.50
19	Ichiro Suzuki	1.50
20	Ivan Rodriguez	.50
21	Jason Schmidt	.25
22	Jason Varitek	.25
23	Jeff Kent	.25
24	Jim Thome	.75
25	Jorge Posada	.25
26	Ken Griffey Jr.	1.00
27	Kerry Wood	.25
28	Lance Berkman	.25
29	Manny Ramirez	.75
30	Mariano Rivera	.40
31	Mark Mulder	.25
32	Mark Prior	.75
33	Miguel Cabrera	.50
34	Miguel Tejada	.50
35	Mike Piazza	.75
36	Nomar Garciaparra	1.00
37	Pedro Martinez	.75
38	Randy Johnson	.75
39	Richie Sexson	.25
40	Roger Clemens	2.00
41	Roy Halladay	.25
42	Sammy Sosa	1.50
43	Scott Rolen	.75
44	Sean Casey	.25
45	Tim Hudson	.25
46	Todd Helton	.50
47	Tom Glavine	.40
48	Torii Hunter	.40
49	Troy Glaus	.25
50	Vladimir Guerrero	.75
51	Adrian Beltre	.25
52	Alexis Rios	.15
53	Aubrey Huff	.15
54	Brandon Webb	.25
55	Dallas McPherson	.25
56	David Wright	.75
57	Edwin Jackson	.15
58	Grady Sizemore	.25
59	Tadahito Iguchi RC	3.00
60	Jake Peavy	.40
61	Jake Westbrook	.15
62	Jason Bay	.25
63	Jeff Francis	.15
64	Jeremy Reed	.15
65	Joe Mauer	.40
66	Johan Santana	.40
67	Jose Capellan	.15
68	Jose Reyes	.25
69	Justin Morneau	.40
70	Mark Teixeira	.40
71	Oliver Perez	.25
72	Rich Harden	.25
73	Rickie Weeks	.25
74	Ryan Howard	.75
75	Scott Kazmir	.75
76	Al Kaline	.75
77	Bill Mazeroski	.25
78	Bob Feller	.50
79	Bob Gibson	.50
80	Brooks Robinson	.50
81	Cal Ripken Jr.	3.00
82	Carlton Fisk	.50
83	Eddie Murray	.50
84	Gaylord Perry	.25
85	Harmon Killebrew	.75
86	Jim Palmer	.50
87	Joe DiMaggio	1.50
88	Joe Morgan	.25
89	Johnny Bench	.75
90	Juan Marichal	.25
91	Lou Brock	.25
92	Mike Schmidt	1.00
93	Nolan Ryan	2.00
94	Ozzie Smith	.75
95	Phil Niekro	.25
96	Robin Yount	.50
97	Rollie Fingers	.25
98	Tom Seaver	.50
99	Willie McCovey	.50
100	Yogi Berra	.75

Gold

Stars (1-100): 4-8X

Production 499 Sets

Box Scores

NM/M
Complete Set (20): 50.00
Common Player: 1.50
Inserted 1:24

1 Juan Marichal 2.00
2 Brooks Robinson 3.00
3 Tony Perez 1.50
4 Willie McCovey 2.00
5 Harmon Killebrew 3.00
6 Johnny Bench 3.00
7 Joe Morgan 1.50
8 Lou Brock 1.50
9 Jim Palmer 1.50
10 Mike Schmidt 5.00
11 Ozzie Smith 4.00
12 Roger Clemens 6.00
13 Cal Ripken Jr. 8.00
14 Ken Griffey Jr. 4.00
15 Greg Maddux 4.00
16 Alex Rodriguez 5.00
17 Derek Jeter 6.00
18 Johnny Damon 3.00
19 Garret Anderson 1.50
20 Alfonso Soriano 2.00

Matchups

NM/M
Complete Set (20): 40.00
Common Player: 1.50
Inserted 1:24

1 Hank Blalock 2.00
2 Curt Schilling 3.00
3 Manny Ramirez 3.00
4 Ken Griffey Jr. 4.00
5 Brooks Robinson 3.00
6 Harmon Killebrew 3.00
7 Carl Yastrzemski 4.00
8 Cal Ripken Jr. 8.00
9 Trevor Hoffman 1.50
10 Eric Gagne 2.00
11 Alfonso Soriano 2.00
12 David Ortiz 3.00
13 Andruw Jones 1.50
14 Garret Anderson 1.50
15 Magglio Ordonez 1.50
16 Derek Jeter 6.00
17 Chipper Jones 3.00
18 Roberto Alomar 2.00
19 Mike Piazza 3.00
20 Alex Rodriguez 5.00

Midsummer Classics

NM/M
Complete Set (20): 40.00
Common Player: 1.50
Inserted 1:24

1 Derek Jeter 6.00
2 Pedro Martinez 2.00
3 Mike Piazza 3.00
4 Randy Johnson 3.00
5 Gary Sheffield 2.00
6 Albert Pujols 6.00
7 David Ortiz 3.00
8 Manny Ramirez 3.00
9 Garret Anderson 1.50
10 Andruw Jones 1.50
11 Todd Helton 2.00
12 Paul Konerko 1.50
13 Alfonso Soriano 2.00
14 Magglio Ordonez 1.50
15 Cal Ripken Jr. 8.00
16 Ken Griffey Jr. 3.00
17 Harmon Killebrew 3.00
18 Mike Schmidt 5.00
19 Frank Thomas 2.00
20 Alex Rodriguez 5.00

Midsummer Swatches

PAUL LO DUCA • C

NM/M
Common Player: 4.00
Inserted 1:12
Patches: No Pricing
Production 25 Sets

MA Moises Alou/Jsy 6.00
JB Jeff Bagwell/Jsy 6.00
CB Carlos Beltran/Jsy 6.00
CI Craig Biggio/Jsy 6.00
BB Bret Boone/Jsy 4.00
CD Carlos Delgado/Jsy 6.00
JE Jim Edmonds/Jsy 6.00
KF Keith Foulke/Jsy 6.00
RF Rafael Furcal/Jsy 4.00
EG Eric Gagne/Jsy 4.00
SG Shawn Green/Jsy 4.00
KG Ken Griffey Jr./Jsy 25.00
TH Todd Helton/Jsy 8.00
TI Torii Hunter/Jsy 6.00
AJ Andruw Jones/Pants 8.00
CJ Chipper Jones/Jsy 8.00
JK Jeff Kent/Jsy 4.00
RK Ryan Klesko 4.00
ML Matt Lawton/Jsy 4.00
PL Paul LoDuca/Jsy 4.00
JL Javy Lopez/Jsy 4.00
PM Pedro Martinez/Jsy 4.00
VM Victor Martinez/Jsy 4.00
DO David Ortiz/Pants 4.00
RP Rafael Palmeiro/Jsy 8.00
MP Mike Piazza/Jsy 15.00
ER Edgar Renteria/Jsy 4.00
CR Cal Ripken Jr./Pants 35.00
CC C.C. Sabathia/Jsy 4.00
SC Jason Schmidt/Jsy 4.00
BS Ben Sheets/Jsy 4.00
GS Gary Sheffield/Jsy 8.00
JS John Smoltz/Jsy 10.00
SS Sammy Sosa/Jsy 10.00
IS Ichiro Suzuki/Jsy 30.00
MS Mike Sweeney/Jsy 4.00
MT Miguel Tejada/Jsy 8.00
FT Frank Thomas/Jsy 8.00
JT Jim Thome/Jsy 8.00
OM Omar Vizquel/Jsy 6.00
WE David Wells/Jsy 4.00
DW Dontrelle Willis/Jsy 8.00

MVP's

NM/M
Complete Set (20): 45.00
Common Player: 1.00
Inserted 1:24

1 Alfonso Soriano 2.00
2 Ken Griffey Sr. 4.00
3 Brooks Robinson 3.00
4 Cal Ripken Jr. 8.00
5 Cal Ripken Jr. 8.00
6 Derek Jeter 6.00
7 Carl Yastrzemski 4.00
8 Garret Anderson 1.50
9 Jeff Conine 1.00
10 Joe Morgan 1.50
11 Juan Marichal 2.00
12 Julio Franco 1.00
13 Ken Griffey Jr. 4.00
14 Mike Piazza 3.00
15 Pedro Martinez 3.00
16 Roberto Alomar 2.00
17 Roger Clemens 6.00
18 Sandy Alomar Jr. 1.00
19 Tony Perez 1.50
20 Willie McCovey 2.00

Perennial All-Stars

2005 Upper Deck Artifacts Promos

NM/M
Complete Set (20): 40.00
Common Player: 2.00
Inserted 1:24

1 Albert Pujols 6.00
2 Alex Rodriguez 5.00
3 Alfonso Soriano 2.00
4 Curt Schilling 3.00
5 Derek Jeter 6.00
6 Eric Gagne 2.00
7 Greg Maddux 4.00
8 Ichiro Suzuki 5.00
9 Ivan Rodriguez 2.00
10 Jim Thome 2.00
11 Ken Griffey Jr. 2.00
12 Mariano Rivera 2.00
13 Miguel Tejada 2.00
14 Mike Piazza 3.00
15 Randy Johnson 2.00
16 Roger Clemens 6.00
17 Sammy Sosa 4.00
18 Scott Rolen 3.00
19 Todd Helton 2.00
20 Vladimir Guerrero 2.00

Each of the first 100 cards in Upper Deck Artifacts was issued in a foil-overprinted version with "UD PROMO" across the front. Cards were inserted into specially marked card shop and newsstand issues of Tuff Stuff magazine.

NM/M
Common Player: .50
Stars: 1.5X

2005 Upper Deck Artifacts

NM/M
Complete Set (200):
Common Player (1-100): .25
Common (101-150): 2.00
Production 1,350
Common (151-200): 2.00
Production 1,999
Pack (4): 10.00
Box (10): 90.00

1 Adam Dunn .75
2 Adrian Beltre .75
3 Albert Pujols 3.00
4 Alex Rodriguez 2.50
5 Alfonso Soriano 1.00
6 Andruw Jones .50
7 Andy Pettitte .50
8 Aramis Ramirez .50
9 Aubrey Huff .25
10 Barry Larkin .50
11 Ben Sheets .50
12 Bernie Williams .50
13 Bobby Abreu .50
14 Brad Penny .25
15 Bret Boone .25
16 Brian Giles .25
17 Carl Crawford .25
18 Carl Pavano .50
19 Carlos Beltran .75
20 Carlos Delgado .75
21 Carlos Guillen .25
22 Carlos Lee .50
23 Carlos Zambrano .25
24 Chipper Jones 1.00
25 Craig Biggio .50
26 Craig Wilson .25
27 Curt Schilling 1.00
28 David Ortiz 1.00
29 Derek Jeter 3.00
30 Eric Chavez .50
31 Eric Gagne .50
32 Frank Thomas .75
33 Garret Anderson .50
34 Gary Sheffield .50
35 Greg Maddux 1.50
36 Hank Blalock .75
37 Hideki Matsui 2.00
38 Ichiro Suzuki 2.50
39 Ivan Rodriguez .75
40 J.D. Drew .50
41 Jake Peavy .50
42 Jason Kendall .25
43 Jason Schmidt .50
44 Jeff Bagwell .50
45 Jeff Kent .50
46 Jim Edmonds .50
47 Jim Thome 1.00
48 Joe Mauer .75
49 Johan Santana .75
50 John Smoltz .50
51 Jose Reyes .25
52 Jose Vidro .25
53 Josh Beckett .50
54 Ken Griffey Jr. 1.50
55 Kerry Wood 1.00
56 Kevin Brown .25
57 Lance Berkman .50
58 Larry Walker .25
59 Livan Hernandez .25
60 Luis Gonzalez .25
61 Lyle Overbay .25
62 Magglio Ordonez .25
63 Manny Ramirez 1.00
64 Mark Mulder .50
65 Mark Prior 1.00
66 Mark Teixeira .50
67 Melvin Mora .25
68 Michael Young .25
69 Miguel Cabrera 1.00
70 Miguel Tejada .75
71 Mike Lowell .25
72 Mike Mussina .50
73 Mike Piazza 1.50
74 Mike Sweeney .25
75 Nomar Garciaparra 2.00
76 Oliver Perez .25
77 Paul Konerko .25
78 Pedro Martinez 1.00
79 Preston Wilson .25
80 Rafael Furcal .25
81 Rafael Palmeiro .75
82 Randy Johnson 1.00
83 Richie Sexson .50
84 Roger Clemens 3.00
85 Roy Halladay .50
86 Roy Oswalt .50
87 Sammy Sosa 2.00
88 Scott Podsednik .25
89 Scott Rolen 1.00
90 Shawn Green .25
91 Steve Finley .25
92 Tim Hudson .50
93 Todd Helton .75
94 Tom Glavine .50
95 Torii Hunter .25
96 Travis Hafner .50
97 Troy Glaus .50
98 Vernon Wells .25
99 Victor Martinez .50
100 Vladimir Guerrero 1.00
101 Aaron Rowand 2.00
102 Adam LaRoche 2.00
103 Adrian Gonzalez 2.00
104 Alexis Rios 2.00
105 Angel Guzman 2.00
106 B.J. Upton 3.00
107 Bobby Crosby 2.00
108 Bobby Madritsch 2.00
109 Brandon Claussen 2.00
110 Bucky Jacobsen 2.00
111 Casey Kotchman 2.00
112 Chad Cordero 2.00
113 Chase Utley 2.00
114 Chris Burke 2.00
115 Dallas McPherson 4.00
116 Daniel Cabrera 2.00
117 David DeJesus 2.00
118 David Wright 6.00
119 Eddy Rodriguez 2.00
120 Edwin Jackson 2.00
121 Gabe Gross 2.00
122 Garrett Atkins 2.00
123 Gavin Floyd 2.00
124 Gerald Laird 2.00
125 Guillermo Quiroz 2.00
126 J.D. Closser 2.00
127 Jason Bay 4.00
128 Jason Dubois 2.00
129 Jason Lane 2.00
130 Jayson Werth 2.00
131 Jeff Francis 2.00
132 Jesse Crain 2.00
133 Joe Blanton 2.00
134 Joe Mauer 2.00
135 Jose Capellan 2.00
136 Kevin Youkilis 2.00
137 Khalil Greene 3.00
138 Laynce Nix 2.00
139 Nick Swisher 3.00
140 Oliver Perez 2.00
141 Rickie Weeks 2.00
142 Robb Quinlan 2.00
143 Roman Colon 2.00
144 Ryan Howard 4.00
145 Ryan Wagner 2.00
146 Scott Kazmir 4.00
147 Scott Proctor 2.00
148 Wily Mo Pena 2.00
149 Yhency Brazoban 2.00
150 Zack Greinke 4.00
151 Al Kaline 5.00
152 Babe Ruth 8.00
153 Billy Williams 2.00
154 Bob Feller 3.00
155 Bob Gibson 4.00
156 Bob Lemon 2.00
157 Bobby Doerr 2.00
158 Brooks Robinson 4.00
159 Cal Ripken Jr. 10.00
160 Christy Mathewson 4.00
161 Cy Young 5.00
162 Dizzy Dean 2.00
163 Don Drysdale 2.00
164 Eddie Mathews 2.00
165 Enos Slaughter 2.00
166 Ernie Banks 5.00
167 Fergie Jenkins 2.00
168 George Sisler 2.00
169 Harmon Killebrew 4.00
170 Honus Wagner 5.00
171 Jackie Robinson 5.00
172 Jimmie Foxx 4.00
173 Joe DiMaggio 6.00
174 Joe Morgan 2.00
175 Juan Marichal 2.00
176 Lou Brock 2.00
177 Lou Gehrig 6.00
178 Luis Aparicio 2.00
179 Mel Ott 4.00
180 Mickey Cochrane 2.00
181 Mickey Mantle 10.00
182 Mike Schmidt 6.00
183 Nolan Ryan 8.00
184 Pee Wee Reese 2.00
185 Phil Rizzuto 2.00
186 Ralph Kiner 2.00
187 Rogers Hornsby 3.00
188 Roy Campanella 3.00
189 Satchel Paige 4.00
190 Stan Musial 5.00
191 Rick Ferrell 2.00
192 Thurman Munson 5.00
193 Tom Seaver 4.00
194 Ty Cobb 6.00
195 Walter Johnson 5.00
196 Warren Spahn 4.00
197 Whitey Ford 4.00
198 Willie McCovey 3.00
199 Willie Stargell 4.00
200 Yogi Berra 4.00

Rainbow Blue
Blue (1-100): 3-5X
Blue (101-200): 1-2X
Production 100 Sets

Rainbow Gold
Gold (1-100): 6-10X
Gold (101-200): 2-3X
Production 25 Sets

Rainbow Platinum
No Pricing
Production One Set

Rainbow Red
Red (1-100): 4-8X
Red (101-200): 1.5-3X
Production 50 Sets

AL/NL Artifacts

NM/M
Common Player: 4.00
Production 325 unless noted.
Rainbow: .75-1.5X
Production 99 Sets

BA Bobby Abreu/Jsy 6.00
JB Jason Bay/Jsy 6.00
CB Carlos Beltran/Jsy 8.00
AB Adrian Beltre/Jsy 6.00
BE Johnny Bench/Jsy 10.00
YB Yogi Berra/Pants 15.00
HB Hank Blalock/Jsy 8.00
GB George Brett/Jsy 15.00
MC Miguel Cabrera/Jsy 10.00
RCA Rod Carew/Jsy 8.00
CA Steve Carlton/Jsy 6.00
SC Sean Casey/Jsy 4.00
OC Orlando Cepeda/Jsy/185 8.00
EC Eric Chavez/Jsy 4.00
WC Will Clark/Jsy/100 10.00
CN Roger Clemens/Jsy 15.00
BC Bobby Crosby/Jsy 6.00
AD Andre Dawson/Jsy 6.00
BD Bobby Doerr/Bat 6.00
BF Bob Feller/Pants 10.00
EG Eric Gagne/Jsy 8.00
BG Bob Gibson/Pants 10.00
GI Brian Giles/Jsy 4.00
MG Marcus Giles/Jsy 4.00
DG Dwight Gooden/Jsy 4.00
MK Mark Grace/Jsy/175 8.00
KG Ken Griffey Jr./Jsy 15.00
GR Ken Griffey Sr./Jsy 4.00
TG Tony Gwynn/Jsy 10.00
TH Travis Hafner/Jsy 4.00
RH Rich Harden/Jsy 8.00
KHN Keith Hernandez/Bat 4.00
KHA Kent Hrbek/Jsy 4.00
AH Aubrey Huff/Jsy 4.00
DJ Derek Jeter/Jsy 20.00
RJ Randy Johnson/Jsy 10.00
JK Jim Kaat/Jsy 6.00
AK Al Kaline/Jsy 10.00
GK George Kell/Bat 6.00
HK Harmon Killebrew/Jsy 10.00
RK Ralph Kiner/Bat 6.00
DK Dave Kingman/Bat 4.00
CK Casey Kotchman/Jsy 4.00
DL Derrek Lee/Jsy 6.00
ML Mike Lowell/Jsy 4.00
SL Sparky Lyle/Pants 4.00
FL Fred Lynn/Bat 4.00
GM Greg Maddux/Jsy/275 12.00
VM Victor Martinez/Jsy 6.00
MA Don Mattingly/Jsy 20.00
JM Joe Mauer/Jsy 10.00
WM Willie McCovey/Jsy 8.00
DMA Dallas McPherson/Jsy 8.00
PM Paul Molitor/Jsy 6.00
MM Mark Mulder/Jsy 6.00
DMN Dale Murphy/Jsy/150 8.00
GN Graig Nettles/Jsy 4.00
PN Phil Niekro/Jsy 4.00
LN Laynce Nix/Jsy 4.00
DO David Ortiz/Jsy 10.00
RO Roy Oswalt/Jsy 4.00
AO Akinori Otsuka/Jsy 4.00
JPA Jim Palmer/Jsy 8.00
CP Corey Patterson/Jsy 6.00
JPN Jake Peavy/Jsy 8.00
BPN Brad Penny/Jsy 4.00
RP Rico Petrocelli/Pants 8.00
SP Scott Podsednik/Jsy 8.00
BPA Boog Powell/Jsy 6.00
MP Mark Prior/Jsy 8.00
AP Albert Pujols/Jsy 25.00
JRN Jose Reyes/Jsy/250 8.00
JRA Jim Rice/Jsy 8.00
CR Cal Ripken Jr./Jsy 25.00
BR Brooks Robinson/Jsy 8.00
FR Frank Robinson/Jsy 8.00
SR Scott Rolen/Jsy 10.00
NR Nolan Ryan/Jsy 25.00
JSA Johan Santana/Jsy 10.00
JSN Jason Schmidt/Jsy 6.00
MS Mike Schmidt/Jsy 15.00
TS Tom Seaver/Jsy 8.00
BS Ben Sheets/Jsy 6.00
SM John Smoltz/Jsy 8.00
SU Bruce Sutter/Jsy 6.00
ST Shingo Takatsu/Jsy 6.00
MT Mark Teixeira/Jsy 8.00
BU B.J. Upton/Jsy 6.00
RW Rickie Weeks/Jsy 6.00
MW Maury Wills/Jsy 6.00
KW Kerry Wood/Jsy 8.00
DW David Wright/Jsy 10.00
CY Carl Yastrzemski/Jsy 15.00
MY Michael Young/Jsy 6.00
RY Robin Yount/Jsy 15.00
CZ Carlos Zambrano/Jsy 6.00

AL/NL Artifacts Signatures

NM/M
Production 30 Sets
Rare Artifacts: No Pricing
Production One Set

BA Bobby Abreu/Jsy/Redemp. 20.00
JB Jason Bay/Jsy 30.00
CB Carlos Beltran/Jsy/Redemp. 25.00
AB Adrian Beltre/Jsy 30.00
BE Johnny Bench/Jsy 65.00
YB Yogi Berra/Pants 60.00
HB Hank Blalock/Jsy 25.00
BB Bert Blyleven/Jsy 30.00
WB Wade Boggs/Jsy 50.00
GB George Brett/Jsy 120.00
MC Miguel Cabrera/Jsy 40.00
RCA Rod Carew/Jsy 40.00
SC Sean Casey/Jsy 30.00
CA Steve Carlton/Jsy 40.00
OC Orlando Cepeda/Jsy 35.00
EC Eric Chavez/Jsy 30.00
WC Will Clark/Jsy 50.00
RCN Roger Clemens/Jsy/Redemp. 100.00
BC Bobby Crosby/Jsy/Redemp. 20.00
AD Andre Dawson/Jsy 30.00
BD Bobby Doerr/Bat 35.00
BF Bob Feller/Pants 40.00
EG Eric Gagne/Jsy 50.00
BG Bob Gibson/Pants 50.00
GI Brian Giles/Jsy 20.00

Code	Player	Price
MG	Marcus Giles/Jsy	20.00
DG	Dwight Gooden/Pants	30.00
MK	Mark Grace/Jsy	50.00
KL	Khalil Greene/Jsy	50.00
KG	Ken Griffey Jr./Jsy	120.00
GR	Ken Griffey Sr./Jsy	25.00
TG	Tony Gwynn/Jsy	90.00
TH	Travis Hafner/Jsy	20.00
RH	Rich Harden/Jsy	40.00
KHN	Keith Hernandez/Bat	20.00
KHA	Kent Hrbek/Jsy	50.00
AH	Aubrey Huff/Jsy	25.00
DJ	Derek Jeter/Jsy	200.00
JK	Jim Kaat/Jsy	25.00
AK	Al Kaline/Jsy	50.00
GK	George Kell/Bat	30.00
HK	Harmon Killebrew/Jsy	60.00
RK	Ralph Kiner/Bat	50.00
DK	Dave Kingman/Bat	25.00
CK	Casey Kotchman/Jsy	25.00
DL	Derrek Lee/Jsy	40.00
ML	Mike Lowell/Jsy	20.00
SL	Sparky Lyle/Pants	20.00
FL	Fred Lynn/Bat	25.00
GM	Greg Maddux/Jsy/Redemp.	150.00
VM	Victor Martinez/Jsy	30.00
MA	Don Mattingly/Jsy	100.00
JM	Joe Mauer/Jsy/Redemp.	35.00
BM	Bill Mazeroski/Jsy/Redemp.	30.00
WM	Willie McCovey/Jsy	50.00
DMA	Dallas McPherson/Jsy/Redemp.	30.00
PM	Paul Molitor/Jsy	40.00
MM	Mark Mulder/Jsy	25.00
DMN	Dale Murphy/Jsy	35.00
GN	Graig Nettles/Jsy	35.00
PN	Phil Niekro/Jsy	25.00
LN	Laynce Nix/Jsy	20.00
DO	David Ortiz/Jsy	50.00
RO	Roy Oswalt/Jsy	25.00
AO	Akinori Otsuka/Jsy	40.00
JPA	Jim Palmer/Jsy	40.00
CP	Corey Patterson/Jsy/Redemp.	30.00
JPN	Jake Peavy/Jsy	50.00
BPN	Brad Penny/Jsy	50.00
RP	Rico Petrocelli/Pants	25.00
SP	Scott Podsednik/Jsy	25.00
MP	Mark Prior/Jsy	50.00
AP	Albert Pujols/Jsy/Redemp.	220.00
JRN	Jose Reyes/Jsy/Redemp.	40.00
JRA	Jim Rice/Jsy	40.00
CR	Cal Ripken Jr./Jsy	200.00
BR	Brooks Robinson/Jsy	50.00
FR	Frank Robinson/Jsy	40.00
SR	Scott Rolen/Jsy/Redemp.	75.00
NR	Nolan Ryan/Jsy	125.00
JSA	Johan Santana/Jsy/Redemp.	65.00
JSN	Jason Schmidt/Jsy	50.00
MS	Mike Schmidt/Jsy	60.00
TS	Tom Seaver/Jsy	50.00
BS	Ben Sheets/Jsy/Redemp.	30.00
SM	John Smoltz/Jsy/Redemp.	75.00
SU	Bruce Sutter/Jsy	20.00
ST	Shingo Takatsu/Jsy	50.00
MT	Mark Teixeira/Jsy	45.00
BU	B.J. Upton/Jsy	50.00
RW	Rickie Weeks/Jsy	25.00
MW	Maury Wills/Jsy	25.00
KW	Kerry Wood/Jsy	50.00
DW	David Wright/Jsy	65.00
CY	Carl Yastrzemski/Jsy	85.00
MY	Michael Young/Jsy/Redemp.	25.00
RY	Robin Yount/Jsy	75.00
CZ	Carlos Zambrano/Jsy	35.00

Autofacts

NM/M

Production 15-699
Rainbow: No Pricing
Production One Set

Code	Player	Price
JB	Jason Bay/599	15.00
AB	Adrian Beltre/75 Redemp.	25.00
BE	Johnny Bench/15	75.00
HB	Hank Blalock/25	35.00
GB	George Brett/15	140.00
MI	Miguel Cabrera/25	40.00
OC	Orlando Cepeda/25	35.00
EC	Eric Chavez/25	30.00
RC	Rocky Colavito/75	75.00
BC	Bobby Crosby/350 Redemp.	15.00
AD	Andre Dawson/25	30.00
BF	Bob Feller/25	40.00
SF	Sid Fernandez/599	10.00
LD1	Lenny Dykstra/Mets/599	10.00
LD2	Lenny Dykstra/Phils/599	10.00
FR	Bill Freehan/599 Redeem.	10.00
GI	Marcus Giles/350	12.00
DG1	Dwight Gooden/Mets/350	15.00
DG2	Dwight Gooden/Yanks/350	15.00
GR	Khalil Greene/599	15.00
JR	Ken Griffey Jr./699	75.00
KG1	Ken Griffey Sr./Reds/699	10.00
KG2	Ken Griffey Sr./Yanks/699	10.00
TH	Travis Hafner/599	12.00
RH	Rich Harden/599	20.00
KH1	Keith Hernandez/Mets/350	15.00
KH2	Keith Hernandez/Cards/350	15.00
HO	Ken Holtzman/599	10.00
BH	Burt Hooton/599	8.00
HR	Kent Hrbek/599	15.00
AH	Aubrey Huff/350	8.00
DJ	Derek Jeter/350	150.00
JK1	Jim Kaat Cards/458	15.00
JK2	Jim Kaat Twins/458	15.00
AK	Al Kaline/15	80.00
DK	Dave Kingman/75	25.00
CK	Casey Kotchman/599	10.00
EK	Ed Kranepool	12.00
JL	Jim Lonborg/599	15.00
ML	Mike Lowell/75	15.00
SL1	Sparky Lyle/Sox/599	8.00
SL2	Sparky Lyle/Yanks/599	8.00
FL	Fred Lynn/25	25.00
VM	Victor Martinez/599	15.00
JM	Joe Mauer/25 Redemp.	30.00
MC	Dallas McPherson/599 Redemp.	20.00
DM	Dale Murphy/599	25.00
GN	Graig Nettles/75	25.00
PN1	Phil Niekro/Braves/75	20.00
PN2	Phil Niekro/Yanks/75	20.00
LN	Laynce Nix/599	10.00
RO	Roy Oswalt/350	15.00
AO	Akinori Otsuka/599	25.00
JP	Jim Palmer/25	35.00
CP	Corey Patterson/75 Redemp.	25.00
JA	Jake Peavy/75	30.00
BP	Brad Penny/75	15.00
OP	Oliver Perez/350	20.00
PE	Jim Perry/599	10.00
RP	Rico Petrocelli/599	15.00
SP	Scott Podsednik/75	15.00
PO	Boog Powell/350	15.00
MP	Mark Prior/50	50.00
CR	Cal Ripken Jr./15	200.00
BR	Brooks Robinson/25	50.00
NR	Nolan Ryan/15	175.00
JS	Johan Santana/350 Redemp.	40.00
BS	Ben Sheets/75 Redemp.	20.00
SU	Bruce Sutter/350	12.00
ST	Shingo Takatsu/599	20.00
MT	Mark Teixeira/25	40.00
LT	Luis Tiant/75	15.00
BU	B.J. Upton/599	15.00
RW	Rickie Weeks/599	15.00
KW	Kerry Wood/15	50.00
DW	David Wright/599	50.00
MY	Michael Young/599 Redemp.	12.00

Dual Artifacts

NM/M

Production 99 Sets
Rainbow: 1-2X
Production 25 Sets

Code	Players	Price
AB	Bobby Abreu/Jsy, Carlos Beltran/Jsy	15.00
AD	Adrian Beltre/Jsy, Dallas McPherson/Jsy	15.00
AG	Bobby Abreu/Jsy, Ken Griffey Jr./Jsy	15.00
BB	George Brett/Jsy, Wade Boggs/Jsy	20.00
BC	Adrian Beltre/Jsy, Eric Chavez/Jsy	8.00
BD	Bob Gibson/Pants, Dwight Gooden/Pants	8.00
BE	Bobby Crosby/Jsy, Eric Chavez/Jsy	10.00
BJ	Brooks Robinson/Jsy, Jim Palmer/Jsy	20.00
BK	Jason Bay/Jsy, Ralph Kiner/Bat	10.00
BM	Brian Giles/Jsy, Marcus Giles/Jsy	8.00
BN	Hank Blalock/Jsy, Laynce Nix/Jsy	8.00
BP	Carlos Beltran/Jsy, Corey Patterson/Jsy	12.00
BR	Ernie Banks/Pants, Frank Robinson/Jsy	20.00
BS	Ben Sheets/Jsy, Scott Podsednik/Jsy	8.00
BY	Hank Blalock/Jsy, Michael Young/Jsy	8.00
CB	Jason Bay/Jsy, Bobby Crosby/Jsy	8.00
CC	Miguel Cabrera/Jsy, Orlando Cepeda/Jsy	12.00
CG	Dwight Gooden/Pants, Gary Carter/Jsy	10.00
CH	Sean Casey/Jsy, Travis Hafner/Jsy	8.00
CK	Harmon Killebrew/Jsy, Rod Carew/Jsy	25.00
CL	Miguel Cabrera/Jsy, Mike Lowell/Jsy	10.00
CM	Will Clark/Jsy, Willie McCovey/Jsy/56	25.00
CN	Eric Chavez/Jsy, Graig Nettles/Jsy	8.00
CO	Roger Clemens/Jsy, Roy Oswalt/Jsy	15.00
CR	Bobby Crosby/Jsy, Cal Ripken Jr./Jsy	40.00
DC	Andre Dawson/Jsy, Orlando Cepeda/Jsy	10.00
DK	Bobby Doerr/Bat, George Kell/Bat	10.00
FB	Carlton Fisk/Jsy, Johnny Bench/Jsy	20.00
FW	Bob Feller/Pants, Kerry Wood/Jsy	15.00
GB	Brian Giles/Jsy, Jason Bay/Jsy	8.00
GC	Ken Griffey Jr./Jsy, Sean Casey/Jsy	15.00
GG	Ken Griffey Sr./Jsy, Ken Griffey Jr./Jsy	15.00
GK	Ken Griffey Jr./Jsy, Ralph Kiner/Bat	20.00
GL	Eric Gagne/Jsy, Sparky Lyle/Pants	10.00
GS	Dwight Gooden/Pants, Tom Seaver/Jsy	15.00
HC	Bobby Crosby/Jsy, Rich Harden/Jsy	8.00
HG	Keith Hernandez/Bat, Mark Grace/Jsy	10.00
HH	Aubrey Huff/Jsy, Travis Hafner/Jsy	8.00
HM	Travis Hafner/Jsy, Victor Martinez/Jsy	8.00
HU	Aubrey Huff/Jsy, B.J. Upton/Jsy	10.00
HW	Harmon Killebrew/Jsy, Willie McCovey/Jsy/44	25.00
JG	Derek Jeter/Jsy, Khalil Greene/Jsy	35.00
JJ	Joe Mauer/Jsy, Johan Santana/Jsy	15.00
JR	Jim Rice/Jsy, Rico Petrocelli/Pants	8.00
JW	Derek Jeter/Jsy, Maury Wills/Jsy	35.00
JY	Johnny Bench/Jsy, Yogi Berra/Pants	25.00
KB	Jim Kaat/Jsy, Bert Blyleven/Jsy	10.00
KC	Jim Kaat/Jsy, Steve Carlton/Jsy	10.00
KD	Keith Hernandez/Bat, Don Mattingly/Jsy	20.00
KK	Al Kaline/Jsy, Ralph Kiner/Bat	15.00
KM	Al Kaline/Jsy, Dale Murphy/Jsy	15.00
KN	Jim Kaat/Jsy, Phil Niekro/Jsy	10.00
LC	Derrek Lee/Jsy, Sean Casey/Jsy	10.00
LG	Derrek Lee/Jsy, Mark Grace/Jsy	10.00
LP	Fred Lynn/Bat, Rico Petrocelli/Pants	10.00
LR	Fred Lynn/Bat, Jim Rice/Jsy	10.00
MC	Don Mattingly/Jsy, Will Clark/Jsy	20.00
MD	Bill Mazeroski/Jsy, Bobby Doerr/Bat	10.00
MH	Mark Mulder/Jsy, Rich Harden/Jsy	10.00
MK	Bill Mazeroski/Jsy, Ralph Kiner/Bat	20.00
MM	Joe Mauer/Jsy, Victor Martinez/Jsy	8.00
MS	Dale Murphy/Jsy, Mike Schmidt/Jsy	20.00
MW	Paul Molitor/Jsy, Rickie Weeks/Jsy	15.00
NL	Graig Nettles/Jsy, Sparky Lyle/Pants	15.00
NT	Laynce Nix/Jsy, Mark Teixeira/Jsy	10.00
NY	Laynce Nix/Jsy, Michael Young/Jsy	10.00
OF	David Ortiz/Jsy, Carlton Fisk/Jsy	15.00
OG	Akinori Otsuka/Jsy, Khalil Greene/Jsy	15.00
OP	Akinori Otsuka/Jsy, Jake Peavy/Jsy	15.00
OT	Akinori Otsuka/Jsy, Shingo Takatsu/Jsy	20.00
PD	Andre Dawson/Jsy, Corey Patterson/Jsy	15.00
PG	Brad Penny/Jsy, Eric Gagne/Jsy	10.00
PH	Jake Peavy/Jsy, Rich Harden/Jsy	12.00
PP	Boog Powell/Jsy, Jim Palmer/Jsy	15.00
PR	Boog Powell/Jsy, Brooks Robinson/Jsy	20.00
PS	Brad Penny/Jsy, Jason Schmidt/Jsy	8.00
RB	Ernie Banks/Pants, Cal Ripken Jr./Jsy	40.00
RC	Nolan Ryan/Jsy, Steve Carlton/Jsy	30.00
RJ	Jose Reyes/Jsy, Rickie Weeks/Jsy	10.00
RP	Frank Robinson/Jsy, Boog Powell/Jsy	25.00
RR	Frank Robinson/Jsy, Brooks Robinson/Jsy	25.00
RW	David Wright/Jsy, Scott Rolen/Jsy	15.00
SB	Bert Blyleven/Jsy, Johan Santana/Jsy	15.00
SC	Johan Santana/Jsy, Roger Clemens/Jsy	20.00
SF	Ben Sheets/Jsy, Bob Feller/Pants	15.00
SG	Bruce Sutter/Jsy, Eric Gagne/Jsy	15.00
SM	Jason Schmidt/Jsy, Mark Mulder/Jsy	10.00
SO	Ben Sheets/Jsy, Roy Oswalt/Jsy	10.00
SP	Ben Sheets/Jsy, Brad Penny/Jsy	10.00
TH	Mark Teixeira/Jsy, Travis Hafner/Jsy	10.00
TL	Shingo Takatsu/Jsy, Sparky Lyle/Pants	10.00
TY	Mark Teixeira/Jsy, Michael Young/Jsy	10.00
UJ	B.J. Upton/Jsy, Derek Jeter/Jsy	30.00
WL	David Wright/Jsy, Mike Lowell/Jsy	10.00
WR	David Wright/Jsy, Jose Reyes/Jsy	10.00
YM	Robin Yount/Jsy, Paul Molitor/Jsy	25.00
YP	Carl Yastrzemski/Jsy, Rico Petrocelli/Pants	15.00
ZM	Carlos Zambrano/Jsy, Greg Maddux/Jsy	15.00
ZP	Carlos Zambrano/Jsy, Mark Prior/Jsy	10.00
ZW	Carlos Zambrano/Jsy, Kerry Wood/Jsy	20.00

Dual Artifacts Bat

NM/M

Production 25 Sets

Code	Players	Price
BC	Josh Beckett, Miguel Cabrera	20.00
BW	Josh Beckett, Kerry Wood	20.00
DR	Carlos Delgado, Manny Ramirez	20.00
GC	Ken Griffey Jr., Miguel Cabrera	30.00
GS	Ken Griffey Sr., Ichiro Suzuki	80.00
JP	Derek Jeter, Mike Piazza	50.00
JR	Derek Jeter, Manny Ramirez	50.00
RG	Manny Ramirez, Vladimir Guerrero	20.00
RJ	Cal Ripken Jr., Derek Jeter	100.00
RT	Cal Ripken Jr., Miguel Tejada	60.00
SG	Ichiro Suzuki, Vladimir Guerrero	60.00
WP	Kerry Wood, Mark Prior	25.00

Dual Artifacts Signatures

No Pricing
Production 10 Sets

MLB Apparel

NM/M

Production 325 unless noted.
Rainbow: 1-2X

Production 99 Sets

Code	Player	Price
BA	Bobby Abreu/Jsy	6.00
GA	Garret Anderson/Jsy	6.00
JB	Jason Bay/Jsy	6.00
CB	Carlos Beltran/Jsy	8.00
AB	Adrian Beltre/Jsy	6.00
BE	Johnny Bench/Jsy	10.00
YB	Yogi Berra/Jsy	15.00
BB	Bert Blyleven/Jsy/150	8.00
WB	Wade Boggs/Jsy	8.00
BO	Bret Boone/Jsy	4.00
GB	George Brett/Jsy	15.00
MI	Miguel Cabrera/Jsy	8.00
RC	Rod Carew/Jsy	8.00
CA	Steve Carlton/Jsy	8.00
GC	Gary Carter/Jsy	8.00
SC	Sean Casey/Jsy	4.00
OC	Orlando Cepeda/Jsy	8.00
EC	Eric Chavez/Jsy	4.00
CL	Roger Clemens/Jsy	15.00
BC	Bobby Crosby/Jsy	6.00
AD	Andre Dawson/Jsy	6.00
CF	Carlton Fisk/R. Sox/175	10.00
CF1	Carlton Fisk/W. Sox/175	10.00
EG	Eric Gagne/Jsy	8.00
BG	Bob Gibson/Pants	10.00
GI	Brian Giles/Jsy	4.00
GS	Marcus Giles/Jsy	4.00
DG	Dwight Gooden/Pants	4.00
MK	Mark Grace/Jsy/175	8.00
KL	Khalil Greene/Jsy	4.00
KG	Ken Griffey Jr./Jsy	15.00
GR	Ken Griffey Sr./Jsy	4.00
TG	Tony Gwynn/Jsy	8.00
TH	Travis Hafner/Jsy	4.00
RH	Rich Harden/Jsy	4.00
KH	Kent Hrbek/Jsy	4.00
HU	Tim Hudson/Jsy	6.00
AH	Aubrey Huff/Jsy	4.00
TO	Torii Hunter/Jsy	4.00
DJ	Derek Jeter/Jsy	20.00
JJ	Jacque Jones/Jsy	4.00
JK	Jim Kaat/Jsy	6.00
AK	Al Kaline/Jsy	10.00
HK	Harmon Killebrew/Jsy	10.00
CK	Casey Kotchman/Jsy	4.00
DL	Derrek Lee/Jsy	6.00
ML	Mike Lowell/Jsy	4.00
SL	Sparky Lyle/Pants	4.00
VM	Victor Martinez/Jsy	6.00
MA	Don Mattingly/Jsy	20.00
JM	Joe Mauer/Jsy	10.00
BM	Bill Mazeroski/Jsy/100	12.00
WM	Willie McCovey/Jsy	8.00
MC	Dallas McPherson/Jsy	8.00
PM	Paul Molitor/Jsy	8.00
MM	Mark Mulder/Jsy	6.00
DM	Dale Murphy/Jsy/150	8.00
GN	Graig Nettles/Jsy	4.00
PN	Phil Niekro/Jsy	4.00
LN	Laynce Nix/Jsy	4.00
DO	David Ortiz/Jsy	10.00
RO	Roy Oswalt/Jsy	4.00
AO	Akinori Otsuka/Jsy	4.00
PA	Jim Palmer/Jsy	6.00
CP	Corey Patterson/Jsy	6.00
JP	Jake Peavy/Jsy	6.00
PE	Brad Penny/Jsy	4.00
RP	Rico Petrocelli/Pants	8.00
SP	Scott Podsednik/Jsy	6.00
BP	Boog Powell/Jsy	6.00
MP	Mark Prior/Jsy	6.00
RE	Jose Reyes/Jsy	8.00
JR	Jim Rice/Jsy	6.00
CR	Cal Ripken Jr./Jsy	25.00
BR	Brooks Robinson/Jsy	8.00
FR	Frank Robinson/Jsy	8.00
SR	Scott Rolen/Jsy	10.00
NR	Nolan Ryan/Jsy	25.00
SA	Johan Santana/Jsy	10.00
JS	Jason Schmidt/Jsy	8.00
MS	Mike Schmidt/Jsy	15.00
TS	Tom Seaver/Jsy/300	8.00
BS	Ben Sheets/Jsy	6.00
SM	John Smoltz/Jsy	8.00
SU	Bruce Sutter/Jsy	6.00
ST	Shingo Takatsu/Jsy	6.00
MT	Mark Teixeira/Jsy	6.00
BU	B.J. Upton/Jsy	6.00
JV	Jose Vidro/Jsy	6.00
RW	Rickie Weeks/Jsy	6.00
MW	Maury Wills/Jsy	6.00
DW	David Wright/Jsy	10.00
CY	Carl Yastrzemski/Jsy/175	15.00
RY	Robin Yount/Jsy	15.00
MY	Michael Young/Jsy	6.00
CZ	Carlos Zambrano/Jsy	6.00

MLB Apparel Autographs

NM/M

Production 30 Sets
Rare: No Pricing
Production One Set

Code	Player	Price
BA	Bobby Abreu/Jsy/Redemp.	25.00
GA	Garret Anderson/Jsy	20.00
JB	Jason Bay/Jsy	30.00
CB	Carlos Beltran/Jsy/Redemp.	25.00
AB	Adrian Beltre/Jsy	25.00
BE	Johnny Bench/Jsy	65.00
YB	Yogi Berra/Pants	60.00
HB	Hank Blalock/Jsy	30.00
BB	Bert Blyleven/Jsy	50.00
WB	Wade Boggs/Jsy	50.00
BO	Bret Boone/Jsy	25.00
GB	George Brett/Jsy	100.00
MI	Miguel Cabrera/Jsy	40.00
RC	Rod Carew/Jsy	40.00
CA	Steve Carlton/Jsy	30.00
GC	Gary Carter/Jsy	30.00
SC	Sean Casey/Jsy	35.00
OC	Orlando Cepeda/Jsy	35.00
EC	Eric Chavez/Jsy/Redemp.	30.00
WC	Will Clark/Jsy	50.00
CL	Roger Clemens/Jsy/Redemp.	120.00
BC	Bobby Crosby/Jsy/Redemp.	20.00
AD	Andre Dawson/Jsy	30.00
BF	Bob Feller/Pants	40.00
CF	Carlton Fisk/R. Sox/Jsy	40.00
CF1	Carlton Fisk/W. Sox/Jsy	40.00
EG	Eric Gagne/Jsy	30.00
BG	Bob Gibson/Pants	50.00
GI	Brian Giles/Jsy	25.00
GS	Marcus Giles/Jsy	20.00
DG	Dwight Gooden/Pants	30.00
MK	Mark Grace/Jsy	40.00
KL	Khalil Greene/Jsy	25.00
KG	Ken Griffey Jr./Jsy	120.00
GR	Ken Griffey Sr./Jsy	30.00
TG	Tony Gwynn/Jsy	80.00
TH	Travis Hafner/Jsy	25.00
RH	Rich Harden/Jsy	25.00
KH	Kent Hrbek/Jsy	50.00
HU	Tim Hudson/Jsy	25.00
AH	Aubrey Huff/Jsy	25.00
TO	Torii Hunter/Jsy	25.00
DJ	Derek Jeter/Jsy	200.00
JJ	Jacque Jones/Jsy	20.00
JK	Jim Kaat/Jsy	25.00
AK	Al Kaline/Jsy	50.00
HK	Harmon Killebrew/Jsy	60.00
CK	Casey Kotchman/Jsy	25.00
DL	Derrek Lee/Jsy	25.00
ML	Mike Lowell/Jsy	20.00
SL	Sparky Lyle/Pants	25.00
VM	Victor Martinez/Jsy	25.00
MA	Don Mattingly/Jsy	100.00
JM	Joe Mauer/Jsy/Redemp.	35.00
BM	Bill Mazeroski/Jsy	25.00
WM	Willie McCovey/Jsy	50.00
MC	Dallas McPherson/Jsy/Redemp.	20.00
PM	Paul Molitor/Jsy	40.00
MM	Mark Mulder/Jsy	20.00
DM	Dale Murphy/Jsy	35.00
GN	Graig Nettles/Jsy	35.00
PN	Phil Niekro/Jsy	25.00
LN	Laynce Nix/Jsy	20.00
DO	David Ortiz/Jsy	50.00
RO	Roy Oswalt/Jsy	25.00
AO	Akinori Otsuka/Jsy	25.00
PA	Jim Palmer/Jsy	40.00
CP	Corey Patterson/Jsy/Redemp.	30.00
JP	Jake Peavy/Jsy	40.00
PE	Brad Penny/Jsy	20.00
RP	Rico Petrocelli/Pants	25.00
SP	Scott Podsednik/Jsy	25.00
BP	Boog Powell/Jsy	25.00
MP	Mark Prior/Jsy	35.00
RE	Jose Reyes/Jsy/Redemp.	40.00
JR	Jim Rice/Jsy	30.00
CR	Cal Ripken Jr./Jsy	200.00
BR	Brooks Robinson/Jsy	50.00
FR	Frank Robinson/Jsy	40.00
SR	Scott Rolen/Jsy/Redemp.	75.00
NR	Nolan Ryan/Jsy	125.00
SA	Johan Santana/Jsy/Redemp.	50.00
JS	Jason Schmidt/Jsy	30.00
MS	Mike Schmidt/Jsy	60.00
TS	Tom Seaver/Jsy	50.00
BS	Ben Sheets/Jsy/Redemp.	25.00
SM	John Smoltz/Jsy/Redemp.	75.00
SU	Bruce Sutter/Jsy	20.00
ST	Shingo Takatsu/Jsy	25.00
MT	Mark Teixeira/Jsy	40.00
BU	B.J. Upton/Jsy	25.00
JV	Jose Vidro/Jsy	20.00
RW	Rickie Weeks/Jsy	25.00
MW	Maury Wills/Jsy	25.00
KW	Kerry Wood/Jsy	30.00
DW	David Wright/Jsy	80.00
CY	Carl Yastrzemski/Jsy	85.00
MY	Michael Young/Jsy	25.00
RY	Robin Yount/Jsy	75.00
CZ	Carlos Zambrano/Jsy	35.00

Patches

Production 50 unless noted.

Code	Player	NM/M
BA	Bobby Abreu	15.00
GA	Garret Anderson	15.00
JB	Jason Bay	20.00
CB	Carlos Beltran	20.00
AB	Adrian Beltre	20.00
BE	Johnny Bench	25.00
HB	Hank Blalock	20.00
BB	Bert Blyleven	20.00
WB	Wade Boggs	20.00
BO	Bret Boone	12.00
GB	George Brett	40.00
MI	Miguel Cabrera	25.00
RC	Rod Carew	20.00
CA	Steve Carlton/30	25.00
GC	Gary Carter	30.00
SC	Sean Casey	12.00
EC	Eric Chavez	15.00
WC	Will Clark/20	50.00
CL	Roger Clemens	30.00
BC	Bobby Crosby	20.00
AD	Andre Dawson	20.00
EG	Eric Gagne	20.00
GI	Brian Giles	12.00
GS	Marcus Giles	12.00
DG	Dwight Gooden	20.00
MK	Mark Grace	35.00
KL	Khalil Greene	25.00
KG	Ken Griffey Jr.	40.00
GR	Ken Griffey Sr.	12.00
TG	Tony Gwynn	25.00
TH	Travis Hafner	15.00
RH	Rich Harden	20.00
KH	Kent Hrbek	35.00
HU	Tim Hudson	20.00
AH	Aubrey Huff	12.00
TO	Torii Hunter	15.00
DJ	Derek Jeter	65.00
RJ	Randy Johnson	25.00
JJ	Jacque Jones	15.00
JK	Jim Kaat	20.00
HK	Harmon Killebrew	40.00
CK	Casey Kotchman	20.00
DL	Derrek Lee	15.00
ML	Mike Lowell	12.00
GM	Greg Maddux	35.00
VM	Victor Martinez	15.00
MA	Don Mattingly	40.00
JM	Joe Mauer	30.00
WM	Willie McCovey	25.00
MC	Dallas McPherson	20.00
MM	Mark Mulder	20.00
DM	Dale Murphy	25.00
GN	Graig Nettles	20.00
PN	Phil Niekro	20.00
LN	Laynce Nix	12.00
DO	David Ortiz	25.00
RO	Roy Oswalt	15.00
AO	Akinori Otsuka	25.00
PA	Jim Palmer	20.00
CP	Corey Patterson	25.00
JP	Jake Peavy	20.00
PE	Brad Penny	12.00
SP	Scott Podsednik	12.00
BP	Boog Powell	20.00
MP	Mark Prior	20.00
RE	Jose Reyes	20.00
CR	Cal Ripken Jr.	60.00
BR	Brooks Robinson/35	25.00
FR	Frank Robinson	20.00
SR	Scott Rolen	25.00
NR	Nolan Ryan	50.00
SA	Johan Santana	25.00
JS	Jason Schmidt	25.00
MS	Mike Schmidt	30.00
BS	Ben Sheets	20.00
SM	John Smoltz	30.00
SU	Bruce Sutter	15.00
ST	Shingo Takatsu	20.00
MT	Mark Teixeira	20.00
BU	B.J. Upton	20.00
JV	Jose Vidro	12.00
RW	Rickie Weeks	20.00
MW	Maury Wills/20	20.00
KW	Kerry Wood	25.00
DW	David Wright	35.00
CY	Carl Yastrzemski	40.00
MY	Michael Young	15.00
RY	Robin Yount	30.00
CZ	Carlos Zambrano	25.00

Signature Patches

No Pricing
Production 10 unless noted.

2005 Upper Deck Baseball Heroes

NM/M

Complete Set (200):
Common (1-100): 2.00
Common (101-200): 2.00
Production 575
Tin (8): 50.00

#	Player	Price
1	Bob Feller	3.00
2	Bob Feller	3.00
3	Bob Feller	3.00
4	Bob Feller	3.00
5	Bob Feller	3.00
6	Brooks Robinson	3.00
7	Brooks Robinson	3.00
8	Brooks Robinson	3.00
9	Brooks Robinson	3.00
10	Brooks Robinson	3.00
11	Cal Ripken Jr.	8.00
12	Cal Ripken Jr.	8.00
13	Cal Ripken Jr.	8.00
14	Cal Ripken Jr.	8.00
15	Cal Ripken Jr.	8.00
16	Carl Yastrzemski	5.00
17	Carl Yastrzemski	5.00
18	Carl Yastrzemski	5.00
19	Carl Yastrzemski	5.00
20	Carl Yastrzemski	5.00
21	Don Mattingly	6.00
22	Don Mattingly	6.00
23	Don Mattingly	6.00
24	Don Mattingly	6.00
25	Don Mattingly	6.00
26	Tom Seaver	3.00
27	Tom Seaver	3.00
28	Tom Seaver	3.00
29	Tom Seaver	3.00
30	Tom Seaver	3.00
31	Harmon Killebrew	3.00
32	Harmon Killebrew	3.00
33	Harmon Killebrew	3.00
34	Harmon Killebrew	3.00
35	Harmon Killebrew	3.00
36	Jim Palmer	2.00
37	Jim Palmer	2.00
38	Jim Palmer	2.00
39	Jim Palmer	2.00
40	Jim Palmer	2.00
41	Mike Schmidt	6.00
42	Mike Schmidt	6.00
43	Mike Schmidt	6.00
44	Mike Schmidt	6.00
45	Mike Schmidt	6.00
46	Ozzie Smith	4.00
47	Ozzie Smith	4.00
48	Ozzie Smith	4.00
49	Ozzie Smith	4.00
50	Ozzie Smith	4.00
51	Paul Molitor	3.00
52	Paul Molitor	3.00
53	Paul Molitor	3.00
54	Paul Molitor	3.00
55	Paul Molitor	3.00
56	Al Kaline	3.00
57	Al Kaline	3.00
58	Al Kaline	3.00
59	Al Kaline	3.00
60	Al Kaline	3.00
61	Robin Yount	4.00
62	Robin Yount	4.00
63	Robin Yount	4.00
64	Robin Yount	4.00
65	Robin Yount	4.00
66	Ryne Sandberg	4.00
67	Ryne Sandberg	4.00
68	Ryne Sandberg	4.00
69	Ryne Sandberg	4.00
70	Ryne Sandberg	4.00
71	Stan Musial	5.00
72	Stan Musial	5.00
73	Stan Musial	5.00
74	Stan Musial	5.00
75	Stan Musial	5.00
76	Steve Carlton	2.00
77	Steve Carlton	2.00
78	Steve Carlton	2.00
79	Steve Carlton	2.00
80	Steve Carlton	2.00
81	Tony Gwynn	3.00
82	Tony Gwynn	3.00
83	Tony Gwynn	3.00
84	Tony Gwynn	3.00
85	Tony Gwynn	3.00
86	Wade Boggs	3.00
87	Wade Boggs	3.00
88	Wade Boggs	3.00
89	Wade Boggs	3.00
90	Wade Boggs	3.00
91	Will Clark	3.00
92	Will Clark	3.00
93	Will Clark	3.00
94	Will Clark	3.00
95	Will Clark	3.00
96	Yogi Berra	4.00
97	Yogi Berra	4.00
98	Yogi Berra	4.00
99	Yogi Berra	4.00
100	Yogi Berra	4.00
101	Babe Ruth	8.00
102	Babe Ruth	8.00
103	Babe Ruth	8.00
104	Babe Ruth	8.00
105	Babe Ruth	8.00
106	Roger Maris	6.00
107	Roger Maris	6.00
108	Roger Maris	6.00
109	Roger Maris	6.00
110	Roger Maris	6.00
111	Don Drysdale	2.00
112	Don Drysdale	2.00
113	Don Drysdale	2.00
114	Don Drysdale	2.00
115	Don Drysdale	2.00
116	Eddie Mathews	4.00
117	Eddie Mathews	4.00
118	Eddie Mathews	4.00
119	Eddie Mathews	4.00
120	Eddie Mathews	4.00
121	Honus Wagner	6.00
122	Honus Wagner	6.00
123	Honus Wagner	6.00
124	Honus Wagner	6.00
125	Honus Wagner	6.00
126	Jackie Robinson	5.00
127	Jackie Robinson	5.00
128	Jackie Robinson	5.00
129	Jackie Robinson	5.00
130	Jackie Robinson	5.00
131	Jimmie Foxx	5.00
132	Jimmie Foxx	5.00
133	Jimmie Foxx	5.00
134	Jimmie Foxx	5.00
135	Jimmie Foxx	5.00
136	Joe DiMaggio	6.00
137	Joe DiMaggio	6.00
138	Joe DiMaggio	6.00
139	Joe DiMaggio	6.00
140	Joe DiMaggio	6.00
141	Johnny Mize	4.00
142	Johnny Mize	4.00
143	Johnny Mize	4.00
144	Johnny Mize	4.00
145	Johnny Mize	4.00
146	Lefty Grove	3.00
147	Lefty Grove	3.00
148	Lefty Grove	3.00
149	Lefty Grove	3.00
150	Lefty Grove	3.00
151	Lou Gehrig	6.00
152	Lou Gehrig	6.00
153	Lou Gehrig	6.00
154	Lou Gehrig	6.00
155	Lou Gehrig	6.00
156	Mel Ott	4.00
157	Mel Ott	4.00
158	Mel Ott	4.00
159	Mel Ott	4.00
160	Mel Ott	4.00
161	Mickey Mantle	12.00
162	Mickey Mantle	12.00
163	Mickey Mantle	12.00
164	Mickey Mantle	12.00
165	Mickey Mantle	12.00
166	Roberto Clemente	8.00
167	Roberto Clemente	8.00
168	Roberto Clemente	8.00
169	Roberto Clemente	8.00
170	Roberto Clemente	8.00
171	Rogers Hornsby	6.00
172	Rogers Hornsby	6.00
173	Rogers Hornsby	6.00
174	Rogers Hornsby	6.00
175	Rogers Hornsby	6.00
176	Roy Campanella	3.00
177	Roy Campanella	3.00
178	Roy Campanella	3.00
179	Roy Campanella	3.00
180	Roy Campanella	3.00
181	Satchel Paige	6.00
182	Satchel Paige	6.00
183	Satchel Paige	6.00
184	Satchel Paige	6.00
185	Satchel Paige	6.00
186	Ted Williams	8.00
187	Ted Williams	8.00
188	Ted Williams	8.00
189	Ted Williams	8.00
190	Ted Williams	8.00
191	Thurman Munson	5.00
192	Thurman Munson	5.00
193	Thurman Munson	5.00
194	Thurman Munson	5.00
195	Thurman Munson	5.00
196	Ty Cobb	5.00
197	Ty Cobb	5.00
198	Ty Cobb	5.00
199	Ty Cobb	5.00
200	Ty Cobb	5.00

Emerald

Emerald (1-100): 1-1.5X
Emerald (101-200): 1-1.5X
Production 199 Sets

Red

Red (1-200): 1-2X
Production 75 Sets

Blue

No Pricing
Production 10 Sets

Gold

No Pricing
Production One Set

Jeter Jersey

Common Jeter:
Production 75 Sets

Jeter

NM/M

Complete Set (9): 25.00
Common Jeter: 3.00
Inserted 1:6

#	Player	Price
91	Derek Jeter	3.00
92	Derek Jeter	3.00
93	Derek Jeter	3.00
94	Derek Jeter	3.00
95	Derek Jeter	3.00
96	Derek Jeter	3.00
97	Derek Jeter	3.00
98	Derek Jeter	3.00
99	Derek Jeter	3.00
	Derek Jeter	3.00

Jeter Jersey

Common Jeter:
Production 75 Sets

Jeter Signature

No Pricing
Production 2 Sets

Memorabilia

No Pricing
Production 10 Sets

Memorabilia Emerald

NM/M

Blue: 1X
Production 99 Sets
Bronze: 1-1.5X
Production 50 Sets
Gold: No Pricing
Production One Set
Red: 1X
Production 99 Sets
Silver: No Pricing
Production 15 Sets

Signature Cuts

No Pricing
Production 1-10

Signature Emerald

NM/M

Production 99 Sets
Blue: 1-1.5X
Production 20 Sets
Red: 1X
Production 49 Sets
Gold: No Pricing
Production One Set
Patches: No Pricing
Production 5 Sets

#	Player	Price
1	Bob Feller	10.00
2	Bob Feller	10.00
3	Bob Feller	10.00
4	Bob Feller	10.00
5	Bob Feller	10.00
6	Brooks Robinson	10.00
7	Brooks Robinson	10.00
8	Brooks Robinson	10.00
9	Brooks Robinson	10.00
10	Brooks Robinson	10.00
11	Cal Ripken Jr.	25.00
12	Cal Ripken Jr.	25.00
13	Cal Ripken Jr.	25.00
14	Cal Ripken Jr.	25.00
15	Cal Ripken Jr.	25.00
16	Carl Yastrzemski	15.00
17	Carl Yastrzemski	15.00
18	Carl Yastrzemski	15.00
19	Carl Yastrzemski	15.00
20	Carl Yastrzemski	15.00
21	Don Mattingly	20.00
22	Don Mattingly	20.00
23	Don Mattingly	20.00
24	Don Mattingly	20.00
25	Don Mattingly	20.00
26	Tom Seaver	10.00
27	Tom Seaver	10.00
28	Tom Seaver	10.00
29	Tom Seaver	10.00
30	Tom Seaver	10.00
31	Harmon Killebrew	10.00
32	Harmon Killebrew	10.00
33	Harmon Killebrew	10.00
34	Harmon Killebrew	10.00
35	Harmon Killebrew	10.00
36	Jim Palmer	8.00
37	Jim Palmer	8.00
38	Jim Palmer	8.00
39	Jim Palmer	8.00
40	Jim Palmer	8.00
41	Mike Schmidt	20.00
42	Mike Schmidt	20.00
43	Mike Schmidt	20.00
44	Mike Schmidt	20.00
45	Mike Schmidt	20.00
46	Ozzie Smith	20.00
47	Ozzie Smith	20.00
48	Ozzie Smith	20.00
49	Ozzie Smith	20.00
50	Ozzie Smith	20.00
51	Paul Molitor	10.00
52	Paul Molitor	10.00
53	Paul Molitor	10.00
54	Paul Molitor	10.00
55	Paul Molitor	10.00
56	Al Kaline	12.00
57	Al Kaline	12.00
58	Al Kaline	12.00
59	Al Kaline	12.00
60	Al Kaline	12.00
61	Robin Yount	15.00
62	Robin Yount	15.00
63	Robin Yount	15.00
64	Robin Yount	15.00
65	Robin Yount	15.00
66	Ryne Sandberg	15.00
67	Ryne Sandberg	15.00
68	Ryne Sandberg	15.00
69	Ryne Sandberg	15.00
70	Ryne Sandberg	15.00
71	Stan Musial	20.00
72	Stan Musial	20.00
73	Stan Musial	20.00
74	Stan Musial	20.00
75	Stan Musial	20.00
76	Steve Carlton	10.00
77	Steve Carlton	10.00
78	Steve Carlton	10.00
79	Steve Carlton	10.00
80	Steve Carlton	10.00
81	Tony Gwynn	20.00
82	Tony Gwynn	20.00
83	Tony Gwynn	20.00
84	Tony Gwynn	20.00
85	Tony Gwynn	20.00
86	Wade Boggs	10.00
87	Wade Boggs	10.00
88	Wade Boggs	10.00
89	Wade Boggs	10.00
90	Wade Boggs	10.00
91	Will Clark	10.00
92	Will Clark	10.00
93	Will Clark	10.00
94	Will Clark	10.00
95	Will Clark	10.00
96	Yogi Berra	15.00
97	Yogi Berra	15.00
98	Yogi Berra	15.00
99	Yogi Berra	15.00
100	Yogi Berra	15.00

Signature Memorabilia

No Pricing
Production 15 Sets

#	Player	Price
1	Bob Feller	35.00
2	Bob Feller	35.00
3	Bob Feller	35.00
4	Bob Feller	35.00
5	Bob Feller	35.00
6	Brooks Robinson	35.00
7	Brooks Robinson	35.00
8	Brooks Robinson	35.00
9	Brooks Robinson	35.00
10	Brooks Robinson	35.00
11	Cal Ripken Jr.	125.00
12	Cal Ripken Jr.	125.00
13	Cal Ripken Jr.	125.00
14	Cal Ripken Jr.	125.00
15	Cal Ripken Jr.	125.00
16	Carl Yastrzemski	65.00
17	Carl Yastrzemski	65.00
18	Carl Yastrzemski	65.00
19	Carl Yastrzemski	65.00
20	Carl Yastrzemski	65.00
21	Don Mattingly	60.00
22	Don Mattingly	60.00
23	Don Mattingly	60.00
24	Don Mattingly	60.00
25	Don Mattingly	60.00
26	Tom Seaver	50.00
27	Tom Seaver	50.00
28	Tom Seaver	50.00
29	Tom Seaver	50.00
30	Tom Seaver	50.00
31	Harmon Killebrew	40.00
32	Harmon Killebrew	40.00
33	Harmon Killebrew	40.00
34	Harmon Killebrew	40.00
35	Harmon Killebrew	40.00
36	Jim Palmer	25.00
37	Jim Palmer	25.00
38	Jim Palmer	25.00
39	Jim Palmer	25.00
40	Jim Palmer	25.00
41	Mike Schmidt	50.00
42	Mike Schmidt	50.00
43	Mike Schmidt	50.00
44	Mike Schmidt	50.00
45	Mike Schmidt	50.00
46	Ozzie Smith	50.00
47	Ozzie Smith	50.00
48	Ozzie Smith	50.00
49	Ozzie Smith	50.00
50	Ozzie Smith	50.00
51	Paul Molitor	30.00
52	Paul Molitor	30.00
53	Paul Molitor	30.00
54	Paul Molitor	30.00
55	Paul Molitor	30.00
56	Al Kaline	40.00
57	Al Kaline	40.00
58	Al Kaline	40.00
59	Al Kaline	40.00
60	Al Kaline	40.00
61	Robin Yount	40.00
62	Robin Yount	40.00
63	Robin Yount	40.00
64	Robin Yount	40.00
65	Robin Yount	40.00
66	Ryne Sandberg	50.00
67	Ryne Sandberg	50.00
68	Ryne Sandberg	50.00
69	Ryne Sandberg	50.00
70	Ryne Sandberg	50.00
71	Stan Musial	75.00
72	Stan Musial	75.00
73	Stan Musial	75.00
74	Stan Musial	75.00
75	Stan Musial	75.00
76	Steve Carlton	25.00
77	Steve Carlton	25.00
78	Steve Carlton	25.00
79	Steve Carlton	25.00
80	Steve Carlton	25.00
81	Tony Gwynn	40.00
82	Tony Gwynn	40.00
83	Tony Gwynn	40.00
84	Tony Gwynn	40.00
85	Tony Gwynn	40.00
86	Wade Boggs	35.00
87	Wade Boggs	35.00
88	Wade Boggs	35.00
89	Wade Boggs	35.00
90	Wade Boggs	35.00
91	Will Clark	30.00
92	Will Clark	30.00
93	Will Clark	30.00
94	Will Clark	30.00
95	Will Clark	30.00
96	Yogi Berra	60.00
97	Yogi Berra	60.00
98	Yogi Berra	60.00
99	Yogi Berra	60.00
100	Yogi Berra	60.00

2005 Upper Deck Classics Promos

BILL MAZEROSKI

Each of the first 100 cards in Upper Deck Classics was issued in a silver foil-overprinted version with "UD PROMO" across the front. Cards were inserted into specially marked card shop and newsstand issues of Tuff Stuff magazine.

Common Player:
Stars: 1.5X

2005 Upper Deck Classics

WARREN SPAHN

NM/M

Complete Set (130): 50.00
Common Player: .15
Common SP (101-130): 1.00
Inserted 1:4
Pack (8): 3.00
Hobby Box (28): 60.00

#	Player	Price
1	Al Kaline	.50
2	Al Lopez	.15
3	Allie Reynolds	.15

#	Player	
4	Babe Herman	.15
5	Bill Mazeroski	.15
6	Bill Russell	.15
7	Billy Herman	.15
8	Billy Williams	.25
9	Bob Feller	.50
10	Bob Gibson	.75
11	Bob Lemon	.15
12	Bobby Doerr	.15
13	Boog Powell	.15
14	Ken Hubbs	.15
15	Brooks Robinson	.75
16	Buck Leonard	.15
17	Cal Ripken Jr.	2.00
18	Carl Hubbell	.15
19	Jim "Catfish" Hunter	.25
20	Johnny Hopp	.15
21	Charlie Gehringer	.15
22	Curt Flood	.15
23	Jimmie Foxx	.75
24	Dave McNally	.15
25	Davey Lopes	.15
26	Don Drysdale	.50
27	Don Sutton	.50
28	Earl Weaver	.15
29	Early Wynn	.15
30	Edd Roush	.15
31	Eddie Mathews	.75
32	Enos Slaughter	.15
33	Fergie Jenkins	.50
34	Frank Howard	.15
35	Leon Wagner	.15
36	Frank Crosetti	.15
37	Gaylord Perry	.15
38	George Bell	.15
39	George Kell	.15
40	Graig Nettles	.15
41	Hal Newhouser	.15
42	Harmon Killebrew	.75
43	Harvey Kuenn	.15
44	Howard Johnson	.15
45	Hoyt Wilhelm	.15
46	Jack Clark	.15
47	Jack Morris	.15
48	Jim Bunning	.15
49	Jim Palmer	.50
50	Joe Adcock	.15
51	Joe Carter	.15
52	Casey Stengel	.50
53	Joe Morgan	.50
54	Joe Sewell	.15
55	"Smoky" Joe Wood	.15
56	Johnny Bench	.75
57	Johnny Mize	.15
58	Jose Canseco	.50
59	Juan Marichal	.50
60	Keith Hernandez	.15
61	Ken Griffey Sr.	.15
62	Kent Hrbek	.15
63	Kevin Mitchell	.15
64	Kirk Gibson	.25
65	Larry Doby	.15
66	Lou Boudreau	.15
67	Lou Brock	.50
68	Luis Aparicio	.15
69	Luke Appling	.15
70	Monte Irvin	.50
71	Nellie Fox	.15
72	Norm Cash	.15
73	Orlando Cepeda	.25
74	Pedro Guerrero	.15
75	Pee Wee Reese	.15
76	Phil Niekro	.15
77	Phil Rizzuto	.50
78	Ralph Kiner	.15
79	Ray Dandridge	.15
80	Red Schoendienst	.15
81	Richie Ashburn	.15
82	Rick Ferrell	.15
83	Robin Roberts	.50
84	Rollie Fingers	.15
85	Ron Cey	.15
86	Sparky Anderson	.15
87	Stan Coveleski	.15
88	Ted Kluszewski	.15
89	Ted Lyons	.15
90	Tom Seaver	.50
91	Tommie Agee	.15
92	Tommy Lasorda	.15
93	Tony Perez	.25
94	Vada Pinson	.15
95	Waite Hoyt	.15
96	Warren Spahn	.75
97	Willie McCovey	.50
98	Lyman Bostock	.15
99	Willie Stargell	.50
100	Yogi Berra	.75
101	Andre Dawson	1.00
102	Andy Van Slyke	1.00
103	Bret Saberhagen	1.00
104	Carl Yastrzemski	2.50
105	Carlton Fisk	1.50
106	Dale Murphy	1.50
107	Darryl Strawberry	1.50
108	David Cone	1.00
109	Dennis Eckersley	1.00
110	Don Mattingly	2.50
111	Dwight Gooden	1.00
112	Eddie Murray	1.50
113	Eric Davis	1.00
114	Fred Lynn	1.00
115	George Brett	3.00
116	Jim Rice	1.00
117	John Kruk	1.50
118	Lenny Dykstra	1.00
119	Mickey Mantle	4.00
120	Mike Schmidt	3.00
121	Nolan Ryan	3.00
122	Ozzie Smith	2.00
123	Paul Molitor	2.00
124	Robin Yount	2.00
125	Ryne Sandberg	2.00
126	Steve Carlton	1.50
127	Ted Williams	3.00
128	Tony Gwynn	2.00
129	Wade Boggs	2.00
130	Will Clark	2.00

Silver
Silver (1-100): 2-3X
Silver (101-130): 1-2X
Production 399 Sets

Gold
Gold (1-100): 2-4X
Gold (101-130): 1-2X
Production 199 Sets

Platinum
Platinum (1-100): 5-10X
Platinum (101-130): 3-5X
Production 25 Sets

Classic Counterparts

NM/M
Common Duo: 2.00
Production 1,999 Sets
CC Will Clark, Jack Clark 2.00
CG David Cone, Dwight Gooden 2.00
DS Darryl Strawberry, Lenny Dykstra 2.00
GB Wade Boggs, Tony Gwynn 4.00
GP Ken Griffey Sr., Tony Perez 2.00
KD John Kruk, Lenny Dykstra 2.00
KH John Kruk, Kent Hrbek 2.00
LR Jim Rice, Fred Lynn 2.00
MC Kevin Mitchell, Will Clark 2.00
MH Don Mattingly, Keith Hernandez 6.00
MY Robin Yount, Paul Molitor 5.00
NC Ron Cey, Graig Nettles 2.00
PH Boog Powell, Frank Howard 2.00
RC Steve Carlton, Nolan Ryan 8.00
RL Bill Russell, Davey Lopes 2.00
RS Tom Seaver, Nolan Ryan 8.00
SD Darryl Strawberry, Eric Davis
SG Dwight Gooden, Darryl Strawberry 2.00
SR Cal Ripken Jr., Mike Schmidt 10.00
VC Andy Van Slyke, Jack Clark 2.00

Classic Counterparts Materials
NM/M
CC Jack Clark, Will Clark 8.00
CG David Cone, Dwight Gooden 8.00
DS Darryl Strawberry, Lenny Dykstra 8.00
GB Wade Boggs, Tony Gwynn 20.00
GP Ken Griffey Sr., Tony Perez 8.00
KD John Kruk, Lenny Dykstra 15.00
KH John Kruk, Kent Hrbek 8.00
LR Jim Rice, Fred Lynn 8.00
MC Kevin Mitchell, Will Clark 8.00
MH Don Mattingly, Keith Hernandez 15.00
MY Robin Yount, Paul Molitor 15.00
NC Graig Nettles, Ron Cey 8.00
PH Boog Powell, Frank Howard 10.00
RC Steve Carlton, Nolan Ryan 40.00
RL Bill Russell, Davey Lopes 8.00
RS Tom Seaver, Nolan Ryan 50.00
SD Darryl Strawberry, Eric Davis 10.00
SG Dwight Gooden, Darryl Strawberry 8.00
SR Cal Ripken Jr., Mike Schmidt 50.00
VC Andy Van Slyke, Jack Clark 10.00

Classic Counterparts Signature
NM/M
DS Darryl Strawberry, Lenny Dykstra 20.00
GP Ken Griffey Sr., Tony Perez 30.00
KD John Kruk, Lenny Dykstra 40.00
KH John Kruk, Kent Hrbek 40.00
LR Jim Rice, Fred Lynn 40.00
NC Graig Nettles, Ron Cey 35.00
RL Bill Russell, Davey Lopes 25.00

Classic Cuts
NM/M
Quantity produced listed
FC Frankie Crosetti/84 100.00
BH Babe Herman/50 150.00
CH Carl Hubbell/25 150.00
TL Ted Lyons/83 120.00

Classic Fantasy Team
No Pricing
Inserted 1:448

Classic Materials

BILL RUSSELL
NM/M
Common Player: 5.00
WB Wade Boggs 10.00
GB George Brett 10.00
CA Jose Canseco 10.00
JO Joe Carter 5.00
RC Ron Cey 5.00
JC Jack Clark 5.00
WC Will Clark 8.00
DC David Cone 8.00
ED Eric Davis 10.00
AD Andre Dawson 8.00
AD1 Andre Dawson 8.00
LD Lenny Dykstra 5.00
DE Dennis Eckersley 8.00
FI Carlton Fisk 8.00
GI Kirk Gibson 5.00
DG Dwight Gooden 5.00
GG Rich "Goose" Gossage 5.00
KG Ken Griffey Jr. 5.00
PG Pedro Guerrero 5.00
TG Tony Gwynn 10.00
KH Keith Hernandez 5.00
FH Frank Howard 8.00
HR Kent Hrbek 5.00
DL Davey Lopes 5.00
FL Fred Lynn 5.00
MA Don Mattingly 15.00
PM Paul Molitor 10.00
PM1 Paul Molitor/SP 10.00
JM Jack Morris 5.00
DM Dale Murphy 8.00
GN Graig Nettles 10.00
BP Boog Powell/SP 8.00
JR Jim Rice 5.00
CR Cal Ripken Jr. 25.00
BR Bill Russell 5.00
NR Nolan Ryan 20.00
RS Ryne Sandberg 15.00
MS Mike Schmidt 15.00
DS Darryl Strawberry 5.00
AV Andy Van Slyke 20.00
CY Carl Yastrzemski 20.00
RY Robin Yount 10.00

Classic Moments

CAL RIPKEN JR.
NM/M
Common Player: 2.00
Production 1,999 Sets
WB Wade Boggs 4.00
SC Steve Carlton 2.00
CA Joe Carter 2.00
JC Jack Clark 2.00
LD Lenny Dykstra 2.00
FI Carlton Fisk 3.00
KG Kirk Gibson 2.00
TG Tony Gwynn 4.00
WJ Wally Joyner 2.00
KM Kevin Mitchell 2.00
PM Paul Molitor 4.00
JM Jack Morris 2.00
GP Gaylord Perry 2.00
CR Cal Ripken Jr. 10.00
NR Nolan Ryan 8.00
BS Bret Saberhagen 2.00
RS Ryne Sandberg 5.00
MS Mike Schmidt 6.00
DS Don Sutton 2.00
RY Robin Yount 5.00

Classic Moments Materials
NM/M
Common Player: 5.00
WB Wade Boggs 10.00
SC Steve Carlton 8.00
CA Joe Carter 5.00
JC Jack Clark 5.00
LD Lenny Dykstra 5.00
FI Carlton Fisk 8.00
KG Kirk Gibson 5.00
TG Tony Gwynn 10.00
WJ Wally Joyner 5.00
KM Kevin Mitchell 5.00
PM Paul Molitor 10.00
JM Jack Morris 5.00
GP Gaylord Perry 5.00
CR Cal Ripken Jr. 25.00
NR Nolan Ryan 20.00
RS Ryne Sandberg 15.00
MS Mike Schmidt 15.00
DS Don Sutton 5.00
RY Robin Yount 12.00

Classic Moments Signatures
NM/M
Common Autograph: 10.00
SC Steve Carlton 20.00
JC Jack Clark 15.00
LD Lenny Dykstra 15.00
FI Carlton Fisk 40.00
KG Kirk Gibson 25.00
TG Tony Gwynn 40.00
WJ Wally Joyner 10.00
PM Paul Molitor 25.00
JM Jack Morris 20.00
GP Gaylord Perry 15.00
BS Bret Saberhagen 15.00
MS Mike Schmidt 60.00
DS Don Sutton 15.00
RY Robin Yount 40.00

Classic Seasons

ANDRE DAWSON
NM/M
Common Player: 2.00
Production 1,999 Sets
BE George Bell 2.00
JC Jose Canseco 3.00
CL Jack Clark 2.00
WC Will Clark 3.00
DC David Cone 2.00
ED Eric Davis 2.00
AD Andre Dawson 2.00
KG Kirk Gibson 2.00
DG Dwight Gooden 2.00
FL Fred Lynn 2.00
MA Don Mattingly 6.00
KM Kevin Mitchell 2.00
DM Dale Murphy 3.00
JR Jim Rice 2.00
CR Cal Ripken Jr. 10.00
NR Nolan Ryan 8.00
BS Bret Saberhagen 2.00
RS Ryne Sandberg 5.00
MS Mike Schmidt 4.00
CY Carl Yastrzemski 6.00

Classic Seasons Materials
NM/M
Common Player: 5.00
BE George Bell 5.00
JC Jose Canseco 10.00
CL Jack Clark 5.00
WC Will Clark 8.00
DC David Cone 5.00
ED Eric Davis/SP 8.00
AD Andre Dawson 5.00
KG Kirk Gibson 5.00
DG Dwight Gooden 5.00
FL Fred Lynn 5.00
MA Don Mattingly 15.00
KM Kevin Mitchell 5.00
DM Dale Murphy 8.00
JR Jim Rice 5.00
CR Cal Ripken Jr. 25.00
NR Nolan Ryan 20.00
RS Ryne Sandberg 15.00
MS Mike Schmidt 15.00
CY Carl Yastrzemski 20.00

Classic Seasons Signatures
NM/M
Common Auto.: 10.00
BE George Bell 15.00
JC Jose Canseco 40.00
CL Jack Clark 15.00
WC Will Clark 40.00
DC David Cone 15.00
ED Eric Davis 20.00
AD Andre Dawson 20.00
KG Kirk Gibson 25.00
DG Dwight Gooden 12.00
FL Fred Lynn 15.00
MA Don Mattingly 60.00
KM Kevin Mitchell 10.00
DM Dale Murphy 20.00
BS Bret Saberhagen 15.00
MS Mike Schmidt 60.00

League Leaders

Frank Howard
NM/M
Common Player: 2.00
Production 999 Sets
GB George Bell 2.00
WB Wade Boggs 4.00
JC Jack Clark 2.00
WC Will Clark 3.00
AD Andre Dawson 3.00
LD Lenny Dykstra 2.00
DE Dennis Eckersley 3.00
DG Dwight Gooden 2.00
GG Rich "Goose" Gossage 2.00
PG Pedro Guerrero 2.00
TG Tony Gwynn 4.00
KH Keith Hernandez 2.00
FH Frank Howard 2.00
HJ Howard Johnson 2.00
MA Don Mattingly 8.00
KM Kevin Mitchell 2.00
PM Paul Molitor 4.00
DM Dale Murphy 3.00
JR Jim Rice 2.00
AV Andy Van Slyke 2.00

League Leaders Materials
NM/M
Common Player: 5.00
GB George Bell 5.00
WB Wade Boggs 10.00
JC Jack Clark 5.00
WC Will Clark 8.00
AD Andre Dawson 5.00
LD Lenny Dykstra 5.00
DE Dennis Eckersley 8.00
DG Dwight Gooden 5.00
GG Rich "Goose" Gossage 5.00
PG Pedro Guerrero 5.00
TG Tony Gwynn/SP 10.00
KH Keith Hernandez 5.00
FH Frank Howard 8.00
HJ Howard Johnson 5.00
MA Don Mattingly 15.00
KM Kevin Mitchell 5.00
PM Paul Molitor 10.00
DM Dale Murphy 5.00
JR Jim Rice 5.00
AV Andy Van Slyke 20.00

League Leaders Signatures
NM/M
Common Auto.: 10.00
GB George Bell 10.00
JC Jack Clark 15.00
WC Will Clark 40.00
AD Andre Dawson 20.00
LD Lenny Dykstra 15.00
DE Dennis Eckersley 15.00
DG Dwight Gooden 15.00
GG Rich "Goose" Gossage 15.00
PG Pedro Guerrero 10.00
KH Keith Hernandez 15.00
FH Frank Howard 15.00
HJ Howard Johnson 15.00
MA Don Mattingly 60.00
KM Kevin Mitchell 10.00
PM Paul Molitor 25.00
DM Dale Murphy 20.00
JR Jim Rice 15.00

Post Season Performers

Pedro Guerrero
NM/M
Common Player: 2.00
Production 999 Sets
JO Jose Canseco 3.00
CA Joe Carter 2.00
JC Jack Clark 2.00
WC Will Clark 3.00
DC David Cone 2.00
ED Eric Davis 2.00
LD Lenny Dykstra 2.00
CF Carlton Fisk 3.00
DG Dwight Gooden 2.00
PG Pedro Guerrero 2.00
KH Kent Hrbek 2.00
JK John Kruk 3.00
KM Kevin Mitchell 2.00
PM Paul Molitor 4.00
JM Jack Morris 2.00
CR Cal Ripken Jr. 10.00
BR Brooks Robinson 4.00
BS Bret Saberhagen 2.00
MS Mike Schmidt 6.00
DS Darryl Strawberry 2.00

Post Season Performers Materials
NM/M
Common Player: 5.00
JO Jose Canseco 10.00
CA Joe Carter 5.00
JC Jack Clark/SP 5.00
WC Will Clark 8.00
DC David Cone 8.00
ED Eric Davis/SP 10.00
LD Lenny Dykstra/SP 8.00
CF Carlton Fisk 8.00
DG Dwight Gooden 5.00
PG Pedro Guerrero 5.00
KH Kent Hrbek 5.00
JK John Kruk/SP 15.00
KM Kevin Mitchell 5.00
PM Paul Molitor/SP 10.00
JM Jack Morris 5.00
CR Cal Ripken Jr./SP 25.00
BR Brooks Robinson 10.00
MS Mike Schmidt 15.00
DS Darryl Strawberry 5.00

Post Season Performers Signatures

		NM/M
	Common Auto.:	10.00
JO	Jose Canseco	40.00
JC	Jack Clark	15.00
WC	Will Clark	40.00
DC	David Cone	15.00
ED	Eric Davis	20.00
LD	Lenny Dykstra	15.00
CF	Carlton Fisk	40.00
DG	Dwight Gooden	12.00
PG	Pedro Guerrero	10.00
KH	Kent Hrbek	20.00
JK	John Kruk	30.00
KM	Kevin Mitchell	10.00
PM	Paul Molitor	25.00
JM	Jack Morris	20.00
BR	Brooks Robinson	25.00
BS	Bret Saberhagen	15.00
MS	Mike Schmidt	60.00
SS	Darryl Strawberry	20.00

Pirates All-Stars

An All-Star Game logo was added to UD Classics cards of seven Pirates All-Stars and the cards were given away at PNC Park one per game between September 19-22 and September 30-October 2.

		NM/M
	Complete Set (7):	20.00
	Common Player:	2.00
PP1	Ralph Kiner	4.00
PP2	Bill Mazeroski	5.00
PP3	Roberto Clemente	7.50
PP4	Willie Stargell	4.00
PP5	Tony Pena	2.00
PP6	Andy Van Slyke	2.00
PP7	Jason Bay	2.00

2005 Upper Deck ESPN

		NM/M
	Complete Set (90):	20.00
	Common Player:	.15
	Pack (9):	3.00
	Box (24):	60.00
1	Garret Anderson	.25
2	Troy Glaus	.25
3	Vladimir Guerrero	.75
4	Luis Gonzalez	.25
5	Randy Johnson	.75
6	Andruw Jones	.40
7	Chipper Jones	.75
8	J.D. Drew	.25
9	John Smoltz	.25
10	Miguel Tejada	.50
11	Rafael Palmeiro	.50
12	Curt Schilling	.75
13	David Ortiz	.75
14	Manny Ramirez	.75
15	Pedro J. Martinez	.75
16	Carlos Zambrano	.25
17	Greg Maddux	1.00
18	Kerry Wood	.75
19	Mark Prior	.75
20	Nomar Garciaparra	1.50
21	Sammy Sosa	1.50
22	Carlos Lee	.25
23	Frank Thomas	.50
24	Magglio Ordonez	.25
25	Paul Konerko	.25
26	Adam Dunn	.50
27	Ken Griffey Jr.	1.00
28	Travis Hafner	.15
29	Victor Martinez	.25
30	Todd Helton	.50
31	Ivan Rodriguez	.50
32	Carl Pavano	.15
33	Josh Beckett	.25
34	Miguel Cabrera	.75
35	Mike Lowell	.15
36	Carlos Beltran	.50
37	Craig Biggio	.25
38	Jeff Bagwell	.50
39	Lance Berkman	.25
40	Roger Clemens	2.00
41	Roy Oswalt	.25
42	Mike Sweeney	.15
43	Adrian Beltre	.25
44	Brad Penny	.15
45	Eric Gagne	.40
46	Shawn Green	.25
47	Steve Finley	.15
48	Ben Sheets	.25
49	Scott Podsednik	.25
50	Joe Mauer	.25
51	Johan Santana	.50
52	Torii Hunter	.25
53	Jose Vidro	.15
54	Livan Hernandez	.15
55	Jose Reyes	.25
56	Mike Piazza	1.00
57	Tom Glavine	.25
58	Alex Rodriguez	1.50
59	Bernie Williams	.25
60	Derek Jeter	2.00
61	Gary Sheffield	.50
62	Hideki Matsui	1.50
63	Kevin Brown	.15
64	Mike Mussina	.25
65	Eric Chavez	.25
66	Mark Mulder	.25
67	Tim Hudson	.25
68	Bobby Abreu	.25
69	Jim Thome	.75
70	Craig Wilson	.15
71	Jason Kendall	.15
72	Oliver Perez	.15
73	Brian Giles	.15
74	Jake Peavy	.15
75	Jason Schmidt	.25
76	Bret Boone	.15
77	Ichiro Suzuki	1.50
78	Albert Pujols	2.00
79	Jim Edmonds	.25
80	Larry Walker	.40
81	Scott Rolen	.75
82	Aubrey Huff	.15
83	Carl Crawford	.15
84	Alfonso Soriano	.75
85	Hank Blalock	.50
86	Mark Teixeira	.50
87	Michael Young	.25
88	Carlos Delgado	.40
89	Roy Halladay	.25
90	Vernon Wells	.25

Award Winners

		NM/M
	25th Anniv.:	4X-8X
	Production 25 Sets	
AW-1	Gary Sheffield	1.00
AW-2	Greg Maddux	2.00
AW-3	Mike Piazza	2.00
AW-4	Jeff Bagwell	1.00
AW-5	Kenny Rogers	.50
AW-6	Cal Ripken Jr.	4.00
AW-7	Greg Maddux	2.00
AW-8	Hideo Nomo	.75
AW-9	Javier Lopez	.50
AW-10	Jim Edmonds	.75
AW-11	Ken Griffey Jr.	2.00
AW-12	Larry Walker	.75
AW-13	Nomar Garciaparra	2.50
AW-14	Roger Clemens	4.00
AW-15	David Wells	.50
AW-16	Sammy Sosa	2.50
AW-17	Pedro J. Martinez	1.50
AW-18	Andres Galarraga	.50
AW-19	Derek Jeter	4.00
AW-20	Alfonso Soriano	1.50

Ink
Inserted 1:480

Sports Center Swatches

		NM/M
	Common Player:	4.00
	Inserted 1:12	
GA	Garret Anderson	4.00
RB	Rocco Baldelli	4.00
CB	Carlos Beltran	8.00

AB	Adrian Beltre	8.00
LB	Lance Berkman	4.00
BI	Craig Biggio	4.00
HB	Hank Blalock	8.00
BB	Bret Boone	4.00
MG	Miguel Cabrera	8.00
EC	Eric Chavez	4.00
BC	Bartolo Colon	4.00
CC	Carl Crawford	4.00
JD	J.D. Drew	4.00
AD	Adam Dunn	8.00
JE	Jim Edmonds	4.00
EG	Eric Gagne	6.00
TG	Troy Glaus	4.00
KG	Ken Griffey Jr.	15.00
TH	Tim Hudson	4.00
AH	Aubrey Huff	4.00
DJ	Derek Jeter	20.00
JK	Jeff Kent	4.00
PK	Paul Konerko	4.00
DL	Derek Lee	4.00
LO	Derek Lowe	4.00
MM	Mark Mulder	4.00
CP	Corey Patterson	6.00
AP	Albert Pujols	20.00
IR	Ivan Rodriguez	8.00
SA	Johan Santana	8.00
JS	Jason Schmidt	4.00
BS	Ben Sheets	4.00
AS	Alfonso Soriano	4.00
IS	Ichiro Suzuki	25.00
MS	Mike Sweeney	4.00
MT	Mark Teixeira	6.00
JT	Jim Thome	10.00
BU	B.J. Upton	6.00
VW	Vernon Wells	4.00
DW	David Wright/SP	15.00
MY	Mike Young/SP	10.00

Sports Century

		NM/M
	Inserted 1:5	
	25th Anniv.:	4-8X
	Production 25 Sets	
SC-1	Babe Ruth	4.00
SC-2	Jackie Robinson	2.00
SC-4	Ty Cobb	2.00
SC-5	Joe DiMaggio	3.00
SC-6	Lou Gehrig	3.00
SC-7	Mickey Mantle	5.00
SC-8	Walter Johnson	1.00
SC-9	Stan Musial	2.00
SC-10	Satchel Paige	1.00
SC-11	Bob Gibson	1.00
SC-12	Roberto Clemente	3.00
SC-13	Cy Young	1.00
SC-14	Honus Wagner	2.00
SC-15	Rogers Hornsby	1.00

Sports Century Signatures
Inserted 1:480

The Magazine Covers

		NM/M
	Inserted 1:5	
	25th Anniv.:	4-8X
	Production 25 Sets	
MC-1	Roger Clemens	4.00
MC-2	Derek Jeter	4.00
MC-3	Randy Johnson, Pedro J. Martinez	1.50
MC-4	Nomar Garciaparra	2.50
MC-5	Manny Ramirez	1.50

MC-6	Ken Griffey Jr.	2.00
MC-7	Mike Piazza	2.00
MC-8	Ichiro Suzuki	3.00
MC-9	Vladimir Guerrero	1.50
MC-10	Randy Johnson	1.50
MC-11	A.J. Pierzynski, Doug Mientkiewicz, Jacque Jones, Torii Hunter	.50
MC-12	Jason Giambi	.50
MC-13	Jeff Kent	.50
MC-14	Albert Pujols	4.00
MC-15	Kazuo Matsui	.50
MC-16	Miguel Cabrera	1.50
MC-17	Alex Rodriguez	3.00
MC-18	Ivan Rodriguez	1.00
MC-19	Eric Gagne	1.00
MC-20	Jim Edmonds, Albert Pujols, Scott Rolen	.75

This Day in Baseball History

		NM/M
	Inserted 1:5	
	25th Anniv.:	4-8X
	Production 25 Sets	
BH-1	Cal Ripken Jr.	4.00
BH-2	Nolan Ryan	4.00
BH-3	Nolan Ryan	4.00
BH-4	Roger Clemens	4.00
BH-5	Thurman Munson	2.00
BH-6	Mickey Mantle	5.00
BH-7	Ernie Banks	2.00
BH-8	Roy Campanella	1.00
BH-9	Yogi Berra	2.00
BH-10	Mickey Mantle	5.00
BH-11	Jackie Robinson	3.00
BH-12	Joe DiMaggio	3.00
BH-13	Bob Feller	1.00
BH-14	Lou Gehrig	3.00
BH-15	Ty Cobb	2.00
BH-16	Babe Ruth	4.00
BH-17	Walter Johnson	1.00
BH-18	Rogers Hornsby	1.00
BH-19	George Sisler	1.00
BH-20	Cy Young	1.00

Web Gems

		NM/M
	Inserted 1:5	
	25th Anniv.:	4-8X
	Production 25 Sets	
WG-1	Adrian Beltre	.75
WG-2	Alex Rodriguez	3.00
WG-3	Andruw Jones	.75
WG-4	Bernie Williams	.75
WG-5	Bret Boone	.50
WG-6	Cesar Izturis	.50
WG-7	Darin Erstad	.50
WG-8	Derek Jeter	4.00
WG-9	Derek Lee	.75
WG-10	Eric Chavez	.75
WG-11	Greg Maddux	2.00
WG-12	Ichiro Suzuki	3.00
WG-13	Ivan Rodriguez	.50

WG-14	Jim Edmonds	.75
WG-15	Ken Griffey Jr.	2.00
WG-16	Larry Walker	.75
WG-17	Miguel Tejada	.75
WG-18	Mike Mussina	.75
WG-19	Nomar Garciaparra	2.50
WG-20	Scott Rolen	1.50
WG-21	Steve Finley	.50
WG-22	Todd Helton	1.00
WG-23	Torii Hunter	.50
WG-24	Vernon Wells	.50
WG-25	Vladimir Guerrero	1.50

2005 Upper Deck First Pitch

		NM/M
	Complete Set (330):	
	Common (1-330):	.10
	Common (301-330):	1.00
	Inserted 1:4	
	Common (321-330):	2.00
	Inserted 1:36	
	Pack (5):	1.00
	Box (36):	30.00
1	Casey Kotchman	.10
2	Chone Figgins	.10
3	David Eckstein	.10
4	Jarrod Washburn	.10
5	Robb Quinlan	.10
6	Troy Glaus	.25
7	Vladimir Guerrero	.50
8	Brandon Webb	.25
9	Danny Bautista	.10
10	Luis Gonzalez	.25
11	Matt Kata	.10
12	Randy Johnson	.50
13	Robby Hammock	.10
14	Shea Hillenbrand	.10
15	Adam LaRoche	.10
16	Andruw Jones	.40
17	Horacio Ramirez	.10
18	John Smoltz	.25
19	Johnny Estrada	.10
20	Mike Hampton	.10
21	Rafael Furcal	.10
22	Brian Roberts	.10
23	Javy Lopez	.10
24	Jay Gibbons	.10
25	Jorge Julio	.10
26	Melvin Mora	.10
27	Miguel Tejada	.40
28	Rafael Palmeiro	.40
29	Derek Lowe	.10
30	Jason Varitek	.25
31	Kevin Youkilis	.10
32	Manny Ramirez	.50
33	Curt Schilling	.50
34	Pedro J. Martinez	.50
35	Trot Nixon	.10
36	Corey Patterson	.25
37	Derrek Lee	.25
38	LaTroy Hawkins	.10
39	Mark Prior	.50
40	Matt Clement	.10
41	Moises Alou	.25
42	Sammy Sosa	1.00
43	Aaron Rowand	.10
44	Carlos Lee	.10
45	Jose Valentin	.10
46	Juan Uribe	.10
47	Magglio Ordonez	.10
48	Mark Buehrle	.10
49	Paul Konerko	.10
50	Adam Dunn	.40
51	Barry Larkin	.25
52	D'Angelo Jimenez	.10
53	Danny Graves	.10
54	Paul Wilson	.10
55	Sean Casey	.10
56	Wily Mo Pena	.10
57	Ben Broussard	.10
58	C.C. Sabathia	.10
59	Casey Blake	.10
60	Cliff Lee	.10
61	Matt Lawton	.10
62	Omar Vizquel	.10
63	Victor Martinez	.25
64	Charles Johnson	.10
65	Joe Kennedy	.10
66	Jeromy Burnitz	.10
67	Matt Holliday	.10
68	Preston Wilson	.10
69	Royce Clayton	.10
70	Shawn Estes	.10
71	Bobby Higginson	.10
72	Brandon Inge	.10
73	Carlos Guillen	.10
74	Dmitri Young	.10
75	Eric Munson	.10
76	Jeremy Bonderman	.10
77	Ugueth Urbina	.10
78	Josh Beckett	.25
79	Dontrelle Willis	.25
80	Jeff Conine	.10
81	Juan Pierre	.10
82	Luis Castillo	.10
83	Miguel Cabrera	.50
84	Mike Lowell	.10
85	Andy Pettitte	.25
86	Brad Lidge	.10
87	Carlos Beltran	.40
88	Craig Biggio	.25
89	Jeff Bagwell	.40
90	Roger Clemens	1.50
91	Roy Oswalt	.10
92	Benito Santiago	.10
93	Jeremy Affeldt	.10
94	Juan Gonzalez	.25
95	Ken Harvey	.10
96	Mike MacDougal	.10
97	Mike Sweeney	.10
98	Zack Greinke	.10
99	Adrian Beltre	.25
100	Alex Cora	.10
101	Cesar Izturis	.10
102	Eric Gagne	.10
103	Kazuhisa Ishii	.10
104	Milton Bradley	.10
105	Shawn Green	.25
106	Danny Kolb	.10
107	Ben Sheets	.25
108	Brooks Kieschnick	.10
109	Craig Counsell	.10
110	Geoff Jenkins	.10
111	Lyle Overbay	.10
112	Scott Podsednik	.10
113	Corey Koskie	.10
114	Johan Santana	.50
115	Joe Mauer	.25
116	Justin Morneau	.10
117	Lew Ford	.10
118	Matt LeCroy	.10
119	Torii Hunter	.25
120	Brad Wilkerson	.10
121	Chad Cordero	.10
122	Livan Hernandez	.10
123	Jose Vidro	.10
124	Terrmel Sledge	.10
125	Tony Batista	.10
126	Zach Day	.10
127	Al Leiter	.10
128	Jae Weong Seo	.10
129	Jose Reyes	.25
130	Kazuo Matsui	.10
131	Mike Piazza	.75
132	Todd Zeile	.10
133	Cliff Floyd	.10
134	Alex Rodriguez	1.50
135	Derek Jeter	1.50
136	Gary Sheffield	.40
137	Hideki Matsui	1.00
138	Jason Giambi	.25
139	Jorge Posada	.25
140	Mike Mussina	.25
141	Barry Zito	.25
142	Bobby Crosby	.25
143	Octavio Dotel	.10
144	Eric Chavez	.10
145	Jermaine Dye	.10
146	Mark Kotsay	.10
147	Tim Hudson	.25
148	Billy Wagner	.10
149	Bobby Abreu	.25
150	David Bell	.10
151	Jim Thome	.50
152	Jimmy Rollins	.20
153	Mike Lieberthal	.10
154	Randy Wolf	.10
155	Craig Wilson	.10
156	Daryle Ward	.10
157	Jack Wilson	.10
158	Jason Kendall	.10
159	Kip Wells	.10
160	Oliver Perez	.25
161	Robert Mackowiak	.10
162	Brian Giles	.10
163	Brian Lawrence	.10
164	David Wells	.10
165	Jay Payton	.10
166	Ryan Klesko	.10
167	Sean Burroughs	.10
168	Trevor Hoffman	.10
169	Brett Tomko	.10
170	J.T. Snow	.10
171	Jason Schmidt	.25
172	Kirk Rueter	.10
173	A.J. Pierzynski	.10
174	Pedro Feliz	.10
175	Ray Durham	.10
176	Eddie Guardado	.10
177	Edgar Martinez	.10
178	Ichiro Suzuki	1.00
179	Jamie Moyer	.10
180	Joel Pineiro	.10
181	Randy Winn	.10
182	Raul Ibanez	.10
183	Albert Pujols	1.50
184	Edgar Renteria	.10
185	Jason Isringhausen	.10
186	Jim Edmonds	.25
187	Matt Morris	.10
188	Reggie Sanders	.10
189	Tony Womack	.10
190	Aubrey Huff	.10
191	Danys Baez	.10

#	Player	Price
192	Carl Crawford	.10
193	Jose Cruz Jr.	.10
194	Rocco Baldelli	.10
195	Tino Martinez	.10
196	Dewon Brazelton	.10
197	Alfonso Soriano	.50
198	Brad Fullmer	.10
199	Gerald Laird	.10
200	Hank Blalock	.50
201	Laynce Nix	.10
202	Mark Teixeira	.40
203	Mike Young	.25
204	Alexis Rios	.10
205	Eric Hinske	.10
206	Miguel Batista	.10
207	Orlando Hudson	.10
208	Roy Halladay	.10
209	Ted Lilly	.10
210	Vernon Wells	.10
211	Aarom Baldiris	.10
212	B.J. Upton	.25
213	Dallas McPherson	.25
214	Brian Dallimore	.10
215	Chris Oxspring	.10
216	Chris Shelton	.10
217	David Wright	.75
218	Edwardo Sierra	.10
219	Fernando Nieve	.10
220	Frank Francisco	.10
221	Jeff Bennett	.10
222	Justin Lehr	.10
223	John Gall	.10
224	Jorge Sequea	.10
225	Justin Germano	.10
226	Kazuhito Tadano	.10
227	Kevin Cave	.10
228	Joe Blanton	.10
229	Luis Gonzalez	.10
230	Mike Wuertz	.10
231	Mike Rouse	.10
232	Nick Regilio	.10
233	Orlando Rodriguez	.10
235	Ramon Ramirez	.10
236	Roberto Novoa	.10
237	Dioner Navarro	.10
238	Tim Bausher	.10
239	Logan Kensing	.10
240	Andy Green	.10
241	Brad Halsey	.10
242	Charles Thomas	.10
243	George Sherrill	.10
244	Jesse Crain	.10
245	Jimmy Serrano	.10
246	Joe Horgan	.10
247	Chris Young	.10
248	Joey Gathright	.10
249	Gavin Floyd	.10
250	Ryan Howard	.50
251	Lance Cormier	.10
252	Matt Treanor	.10
253	Jeff Francis	.10
254	Nick Swisher	.10
255	Scott Atchison	.10
256	Travis Blackley	.10
257	Travis Smith	.10
258	Yadier Molina	.10
259	Jeff Keppinger	.10
260	Scott Kazmir	.50
261	Garret Anderson, Vladimir Guerrero	.25
262	Luis Gonzalez, Randy Johnson	.25
263	Chipper Jones, Andruw Jones	.25
264	Miguel Tejada, Rafael Palmeiro	.25
265	Manny Ramirez, Curt Schilling	.25
266	Mark Prior, Sammy Sosa	.25
267	Frank Thomas, Magglio Ordonez	.25
268	Barry Larkin, Ken Griffey Jr.	.50
269	C.C. Sabathia, Victor Martinez	.10
270	Jeromy Burnitz, Todd Helton	.25
271	Ivan Rodriguez, Dmitri Young	.25
272	Josh Beckett, Miguel Cabrera	.25
273	Jeff Bagwell, Roger Clemens	.50
274	Mike Sweeney, Ken Harvey	.10
275	Eric Gagne, Adrian Beltre	.25
276	Ben Sheets, Geoff Jenkins	.10
277	Torii Hunter, Joe Mauer	.10
278	Jose Vidro, Livan Hernandez	.10
279	Mike Piazza, Kazuo Matsui	.25
280	Alex Rodriguez, Derek Jeter	.75
281	Eric Chavez, Tim Hudson	.10
282	Bobby Abreu, Jim Thome	.25
283	Jason Kendall, Craig Wilson	.10
284	Phil Nevin, Brian Giles	.10
285	Jason Schmidt, A.J. Pierzynski	.10
286	Bret Boone, Ichiro Suzuki	.50
287	Albert Pujols, Scott Rolen	.75
288	Aubrey Huff, Tino Martinez	.10
289	Hank Blalock, Mark Teixeira	.25
290	Roy Halladay, Carlos Delgado	.10
291	Vladimir Guerrero	.50
292	Curt Schilling	.50
293	Mark Prior	.50
294	Josh Beckett	.25
295	Roger Clemens	1.00
296	Derek Jeter	1.00
297	Eric Chavez	.10
298	Jim Thome	.50
299	Albert Pujols	1.00
300	Hank Blalock	.25
301	Guillermo Quiroz	1.00
302	Jeff Bajenaru	1.00
303	Bartolome Fortunato	1.00
304	Jason Alfaro	1.00
305	Mike Rose	1.00
306	Joe Hietpas	1.00
307	Kyle Denney	1.00
308	Rene Rivera	1.00
309	Kameron Loe	1.00
310	Rickie Weeks	1.50
311	Gustavo Chacin	1.00
312	Chris Burke	1.00
313	Yhency Brazoban	1.00
314	Brandon League	1.00
315	Jose Capellan	1.00
316	Russ Adams	1.00
317	Adrian Gonzalez	1.00
318	Jason Dubois	1.00
319	Abe Alvarez	1.00
320	Eric Crozier	1.00
321	Bengie Molina, Bartolo Colon	2.00
322	C.C. Sabathia, Victor Martinez	2.00
323	Jake Peavy, Ramon Hernandez	2.00
324	A.J. Pierzynski, Jason Schmidt	3.00
325	Joe Mauer, Johan Santana	3.00
326	Mark Prior, Michael Barrett	3.00
327	Jorge Posada, Mike Mussina	3.00
328	Roger Clemens, Brad Ausmus	4.00
329	Roy Halladay, Guillermo Quiroz	2.00
330	Mike Piazza, Tom Glavine	3.00

Fabric

NM/M

Common Player: Inserted 1:180

	Player	Price
JB	Jeff Bagwell	8.00
BE	Josh Beckett	5.00
BB	Bret Boone	5.00
EC	Eric Chavez	5.00
JE	Jim Edmonds	5.00
EG	Eric Gagne	8.00
TG	Troy Glaus	5.00
KG	Ken Griffey Jr./SP	20.00
TH	Torii Hunter	5.00
DJ	Derek Jeter	20.00
AJ	Andruw Jones	5.00
CJ	Chipper Jones	8.00
MM	Mark Mulder	5.00
MO	Magglio Ordonez	8.00
SR	Scott Rolen	8.00
CS	Curt Schilling	8.00
GS	Gary Sheffield/SP	8.00
AS	Alfonso Soriano	5.00
SS	Sammy Sosa	10.00
IS	Ichiro Suzuki/SP	25.00

Jumbos

NM/M

Common Player: 1.00

	Player	Price
FP-1	Shingo Takatsu	1.00
FP-2	Jeff Francis	1.00
FP-3	Jesse Crain	1.00
FP-4	Jose Capellan	1.00
FP-5	Zack Greinke	1.00
FP-6	Scott Proctor	1.00
FP-7	Scott Kazmir	3.00
FP-8	Gavin Floyd	1.00
FP-9	Joe Blanton	1.00
FP-10	Akinori Otsuka	1.00

Signature Stars

Inserted 1:720

2005 UD Hall of Fame

NM/M

Complete Set (100):
Common Player: 3.00
Production 550 Sets
Tin (4): 125.00

#	Player	Price
1	Al Kaline	4.00
2	Al Lopez	3.00
3	Bill Mazeroski	3.00
4	Billy Williams	4.00
5	Bob Feller	4.00
6	Bob Gibson	4.00
7	Bob Lemon	3.00

JACKIE ROBINSON — 2B • Brooklyn Dodgers — 042/550 — INDUCTED 1962

#	Player	Price
8	Bobby Doerr	3.00
9	Brooks Robinson	5.00
10	Buck Leonard	3.00
11	Carl Yastrzemski	5.00
12	Carlton Fisk	4.00
13	Casey Stengel	3.00
14	Jim "Catfish" Hunter	3.00
15	Dave Winfield	4.00
16	Dennis Eckersley	3.00
17	Dizzy Dean	4.00
18	Don Drysdale	4.00
19	Don Sutton	3.00
20	Duke Snider	4.00
21	Early Wynn	3.00
22	Eddie Mathews	5.00
23	Eddie Murray	4.00
24	Enos Slaughter	3.00
25	Ernie Banks	5.00
26	Fergie Jenkins	3.00
27	Frank Robinson	6.00
28	Gary Carter	3.00
29	Gaylord Perry	5.00
30	George Brett	8.00
31	George Kell	3.00
32	George Sisler	3.00
33	Hal Newhouser	3.00
34	Harmon Killebrew	5.00
35	Hoyt Wilhelm	3.00
36	Jackie Robinson	5.00
37	Jim Bunning	3.00
38	Jim Palmer	4.00
39	Jimmie Foxx	5.00
40	Joe Morgan	3.00
41	Johnny Bench	5.00
42	Johnny Mize	3.00
43	Juan Marichal	3.00
44	Kirby Puckett	4.00
45	Larry Doby	3.00
46	Lefty Grove	3.00
47	Lou Boudreau	3.00
48	Lou Brock	4.00
49	Luis Aparicio	3.00
50	Mel Ott	4.00
51	Mickey Cochrane	4.00
52	Monte Irvin	3.00
53	Orlando Cepeda	3.00
54	Ozzie Smith	5.00
55	Paul Molitor	4.00
56	Pee Wee Reese	3.00
57	Phil Niekro	3.00
58	Phil Rizzuto	3.00
59	Pie Traynor	3.00
60	Ralph Kiner	3.00
61	Red Schoendienst	3.00
62	Richie Ashburn	3.00
63	Rick Ferrell	3.00
64	Robin Roberts	4.00
65	Robin Yount	5.00
66	Rod Carew	4.00
67	Rogers Hornsby	4.00
68	Rollie Fingers	3.00
69	Roy Campanella	4.00
70	Steve Carlton	4.00
71	Tony Perez	3.00
72	Warren Spahn	5.00
73	Whitey Ford	4.00
74	Willie McCovey	4.00
75	Willie Stargell	4.00
76	Yogi Berra	5.00
77	Babe Ruth	8.00
78	Honus Wagner	5.00
79	Lou Gehrig	6.00
80	Mickey Mantle	15.00
81	Ty Cobb	6.00
82	Ryne Sandberg	5.00
83	Satchel Paige	5.00
84	Wade Boggs	4.00
85	Reggie Jackson	5.00
86	Babe Ruth	8.00
87	Christy Mathewson	4.00
88	Cy Young	4.00
89	Honus Wagner	5.00
90	Joe DiMaggio	6.00
91	Lou Gehrig	6.00
92	Mickey Mantle	15.00
93	Mike Schmidt	6.00
94	Nolan Ryan	8.00
95	Satchel Paige	5.00
96	Stan Musial	5.00
97	Ted Williams	6.00
98	Tom Seaver	4.00
99	Ty Cobb	6.00
100	Walter Johnson	4.00

Green

Green (1-100): 1X
Production 200 Sets

Silver

Silver (1-100): 1-1.5X
Production 99 Sets

Gold

Gold (1-100): 1.5-2X
Production 25 Sets

Rainbow

No Pricing
Production One Set

Class of Cooperstown

NM/M

Production 50 Sets
Gold: No Pricing
Production 5 Sets
Silver: No Pricing
Production 15 Sets
Rainbow: No Pricing
Production One Set

	Player	Price
LA1	Luis Aparicio	4.00
LA2	Luis Aparicio	4.00
EB1	Ernie Banks	6.00
EB2	Ernie Banks	6.00
BE1	Johnny Bench	6.00
BE2	Johnny Bench	6.00
YB1	Yogi Berra	5.00
YB2	Yogi Berra	5.00
GB1	George Brett	10.00
GB2	George Brett	10.00
GB3	George Brett	10.00
LB1	Lou Brock	4.00
JB1	Jim Bunning	4.00
JB2	Jim Bunning	4.00
RC1	Rod Carew	4.00
RC2	Rod Carew	4.00
SC1	Steve Carlton	4.00
SC2	Steve Carlton	4.00
SC3	Steve Carlton	4.00
SC4	Steve Carlton	4.00
GC1	Gary Carter	4.00
GC2	Gary Carter	4.00
OC1	Orlando Cepeda	4.00
BD1	Bobby Doerr	4.00
BD2	Bobby Doerr	4.00
DE1	Dennis Eckersley	4.00
BF1	Bob Feller	4.00
BF2	Bob Feller	4.00
RF1	Rollie Fingers	4.00
CF1	Carlton Fisk	4.00
CF2	Carlton Fisk	4.00
WF1	Whitey Ford	5.00
WF2	Whitey Ford	5.00
BG1	Bob Gibson	5.00
BG2	Bob Gibson	5.00
MI1	Monte Irvin	4.00
MI2	Monte Irvin	4.00
RJ1	Reggie Jackson	5.00
RJ2	Reggie Jackson	5.00
RJ3	Reggie Jackson	5.00
FJ1	Fergie Jenkins	4.00
AK1	Al Kaline	6.00
AK2	Al Kaline	6.00
AK3	Al Kaline	6.00
GK1	George Kell	4.00
HK1	Harmon Killebrew	6.00
HK2	Harmon Killebrew	6.00
HK3	Harmon Killebrew	6.00
HK4	Harmon Killebrew	6.00
RK1	Ralph Kiner	5.00
RK2	Ralph Kiner	5.00
MA1	Juan Marichal	5.00
MA2	Juan Marichal	5.00
BM1	Bill Mazeroski	4.00
WM1	Willie McCovey	5.00
WM2	Willie McCovey	5.00
PM1	Paul Molitor	5.00
PM2	Paul Molitor	5.00
JM1	Joe Morgan	4.00
JM2	Joe Morgan	4.00
JM3	Joe Morgan	4.00
EM1	Eddie Murray	4.00
SM1	Stan Musial	6.00
SM2	Stan Musial	6.00
PN1	Phil Niekro	4.00
JP1	Jim Palmer	4.00
JP2	Jim Palmer	4.00
TP1	Tony Perez	4.00
GP1	Gaylord Perry	4.00
GP2	Gaylord Perry	4.00
KP1	Kirby Puckett	5.00
RR1	Robin Roberts	4.00
BR1	Brooks Robinson	5.00
BR2	Brooks Robinson	5.00
BR3	Brooks Robinson	5.00
FR1	Frank Robinson	5.00
FR2	Frank Robinson	5.00
NR1	Nolan Ryan	10.00
NR2	Nolan Ryan	10.00
NR3	Nolan Ryan	10.00
NR4	Nolan Ryan	10.00
MS1	Mike Schmidt	6.00
MS2	Mike Schmidt	6.00
MS3	Mike Schmidt	6.00
RS1	Red Schoendienst	4.00
TS1	Tom Seaver	5.00
TS2	Tom Seaver	5.00
OS1	Ozzie Smith	6.00
OS2	Ozzie Smith	6.00
SN1	Duke Snider	5.00
DS1	Don Sutton	4.00
BW1	Billy Williams	4.00
BW2	Billy Williams	4.00
BW3	Billy Williams	4.00
DW1	Dave Winfield	4.00
DW2	Dave Winfield	4.00
CY1	Carl Yastrzemski	6.00
CY2	Carl Yastrzemski	6.00
RY1	Robin Yount	6.00
RY2	Robin Yount	6.00

Class of Cooperstown Autograph

NM/M

Production 25 Sets
Gold: No Pricing
Production 5 Sets
Silver: No Pricing
Production 15 Sets
Rainbow: No Pricing
Material Gold: No Pricing
Production 5 Sets
Material Silver: No Pricing
Production 15 Sets
Patch Gold: No Pricing
Production 5 Sets
Patch Silver: No Pricing
Production 10 Sets

	Player	Price
LA1	Luis Aparicio	20.00
LA2	Luis Aparicio	20.00
EB1	Ernie Banks	50.00
EB2	Ernie Banks	50.00
BE1	Johnny Bench	40.00
BE2	Johnny Bench	40.00
YB1	Yogi Berra	60.00
YB2	Yogi Berra	60.00
GB1	George Brett	60.00
GB2	George Brett	60.00
GB3	George Brett	60.00
LB1	Lou Brock	35.00
JB1	Jim Bunning	25.00
JB2	Jim Bunning	25.00
RC1	Rod Carew	30.00
RC2	Rod Carew	30.00
SC1	Steve Carlton	20.00
SC2	Steve Carlton	20.00
SC3	Steve Carlton	20.00
SC4	Steve Carlton	20.00
GC1	Gary Carter	25.00
GC2	Gary Carter	25.00
OC1	Orlando Cepeda	25.00
BD1	Bobby Doerr	15.00
BD2	Bobby Doerr	15.00
DE1	Dennis Eckersley	20.00
BF1	Bob Feller	30.00
BF2	Bob Feller	30.00
RF1	Rollie Fingers	20.00
CF1	Carlton Fisk	30.00
CF2	Carlton Fisk	30.00
WF1	Whitey Ford	50.00
WF2	Whitey Ford	50.00
BG1	Bob Gibson	35.00
BG2	Bob Gibson	35.00
MI1	Monte Irvin	25.00
MI2	Monte Irvin	25.00
RJ1	Reggie Jackson	40.00
RJ2	Reggie Jackson	40.00
RJ3	Reggie Jackson	40.00
FJ1	Fergie Jenkins	20.00
AK1	Al Kaline	40.00
AK2	Al Kaline	40.00
AK3	Al Kaline	40.00
GK1	George Kell	20.00
HK1	Harmon Killebrew	40.00
HK2	Harmon Killebrew	40.00
HK3	Harmon Killebrew	40.00
HK4	Harmon Killebrew	40.00
RK1	Ralph Kiner	40.00
RK2	Ralph Kiner	40.00
MA1	Juan Marichal	25.00
MA2	Juan Marichal	25.00
BM1	Bill Mazeroski	40.00
WM1	Willie McCovey	40.00
WM2	Willie McCovey	40.00
PM1	Paul Molitor	30.00
PM2	Paul Molitor	30.00
PM3	Paul Molitor	30.00
JM1	Joe Morgan	25.00
JM2	Joe Morgan	25.00
EM1	Eddie Murray	50.00
SM1	Stan Musial	60.00
SM2	Stan Musial	60.00
PN1	Phil Niekro	20.00
JP1	Jim Palmer	20.00
JP2	Jim Palmer	20.00
TP1	Tony Perez	20.00
GP1	Gaylord Perry	20.00
GP2	Gaylord Perry	20.00
KP1	Kirby Puckett	40.00
RR1	Robin Roberts	25.00
BR1	Brooks Robinson	30.00
BR2	Brooks Robinson	30.00
BR3	Brooks Robinson	30.00
FR1	Frank Robinson	20.00
FR2	Frank Robinson	20.00
NR1	Nolan Ryan	90.00
NR2	Nolan Ryan	90.00
NR3	Nolan Ryan	90.00
NR4	Nolan Ryan	90.00
MS1	Mike Schmidt	50.00
MS2	Mike Schmidt	50.00
MS3	Mike Schmidt	50.00
RS1	Red Schoendienst	35.00
TS1	Tom Seaver	40.00
TS2	Tom Seaver	40.00
OS1	Ozzie Smith	40.00
OS2	Ozzie Smith	40.00
SN1	Duke Snider	40.00
DS1	Don Sutton	20.00
BW1	Billy Williams	20.00
BW2	Billy Williams	20.00
BW3	Billy Williams	20.00
DW1	Dave Winfield	30.00
DW2	Dave Winfield	30.00
CY1	Carl Yastrzemski	50.00
CY2	Carl Yastrzemski	50.00
RY1	Robin Yount	40.00
RY2	Robin Yount	40.00

Class of Cooperstown Calling

NM/M

Production 50 Sets
Gold: No Pricing
Production 5 Sets
Green: .75-1.5X
Production 25 Sets
Silver: No Pricing
Production 15 Sets
Rainbow: No Pricing
Production One Set

	Player	Price
LA1	Luis Aparicio	4.00
LA2	Luis Aparicio	4.00
EB1	Ernie Banks	6.00
BE1	Johnny Bench	6.00
YB1	Yogi Berra	5.00
WB1	Wade Boggs	5.00
WB2	Wade Boggs	5.00
WB3	Wade Boggs	5.00
GB1	George Brett	10.00
GB2	George Brett	10.00
LB1	Lou Brock	4.00
LB2	Lou Brock	4.00
JB1	Jim Bunning	4.00
RC1	Rod Carew	4.00
RC2	Rod Carew	4.00
SC1	Steve Carlton	4.00
SC2	Steve Carlton	4.00
GC1	Gary Carter	4.00
GC2	Gary Carter	4.00
GC3	Gary Carter	4.00
OC1	Orlando Cepeda	4.00
OC2	Orlando Cepeda	4.00
BD1	Bobby Doerr	4.00
BD2	Bobby Doerr	4.00
DE1	Dennis Eckersley	4.00
DE2	Dennis Eckersley	4.00
BF1	Bob Feller	4.00
BF2	Bob Feller	4.00
RF1	Rollie Fingers	4.00
RF2	Rollie Fingers	4.00
CF1	Carlton Fisk	4.00
CF2	Carlton Fisk	4.00
WF1	Whitey Ford	5.00
BG1	Bob Gibson	5.00
MI1	Monte Irvin	4.00
RJ1	Reggie Jackson	5.00
RJ2	Reggie Jackson	5.00
RJ3	Reggie Jackson	5.00
FJ1	Fergie Jenkins	4.00
FJ2	Fergie Jenkins	4.00
AK1	Al Kaline	6.00
AK2	Al Kaline	6.00
GK1	George Kell	4.00
HK1	Harmon Killebrew	6.00
HK2	Harmon Killebrew	6.00
RK1	Ralph Kiner	4.00
JM1	Juan Marichal	4.00
WM1	Willie McCovey	5.00
PM1	Paul Molitor	5.00
PM2	Paul Molitor	5.00
PM3	Paul Molitor	5.00
MO1	Joe Morgan	4.00
MO2	Joe Morgan	4.00
EM1	Eddie Murray	4.00
EM2	Eddie Murray	4.00
SM1	Stan Musial	6.00
SM2	Stan Musial	6.00
PN1	Phil Niekro	4.00
PN2	Phil Niekro	4.00
JP1	Jim Palmer	4.00
JP2	Jim Palmer	4.00
TP1	Tony Perez	4.00
TP2	Tony Perez	4.00
GP1	Gaylord Perry	4.00
GP2	Gaylord Perry	4.00
KP1	Kirby Puckett	5.00
KP2	Kirby Puckett	5.00
RR1	Robin Roberts	4.00
BR1	Brooks Robinson	5.00
BR2	Brooks Robinson	5.00
BR3	Brooks Robinson	5.00

FR1 Frank Robinson 5.00
NR1 Nolan Ryan 10.00
NR2 Nolan Ryan 10.00
NR3 Nolan Ryan 10.00
NR4 Nolan Ryan 10.00
SA1 Ryne Sandberg 6.00
SA2 Ryne Sandberg 6.00
SA3 Ryne Sandberg 6.00
MS1 Mike Schmidt 6.00
MS2 Mike Schmidt 6.00
MS3 Mike Schmidt 6.00
RS1 Red Schoendienst 4.00
TS1 Tom Seaver 5.00
OS1 Ozzie Smith 6.00
OS2 Ozzie Smith 6.00
OS3 Ozzie Smith 6.00
SN1 Duke Snider 5.00
DS1 Don Sutton 4.00
DS2 Don Sutton 4.00
DS3 Don Sutton 4.00
BW1 Billy Williams 4.00
BW2 Billy Williams 4.00
DW1 Dave Winfield 4.00
CY1 Carl Yastrzemski 6.00
CY2 Carl Yastrzemski 6.00
RY1 Robin Yount 6.00
RY2 Robin Yount 6.00
RY3 Robin Yount 6.00

Class of Cooperstown Calling Autograph
NM/M
Production 25 Sets
Gold: No Pricing
Production 5 Sets
Silver: No Pricing
Production 15 Sets
Rainbow: No Pricing
Production One Set
Material Gold: No Pricing
Production 5 Sets
Material Silver: No Pricing
Production 15 Sets
Patch Gold: No Pricing
Production 2 Sets
Patch Silver: No Pricing
Production 10 Sets
LA1 Luis Aparicio 20.00
LA2 Luis Aparicio 20.00
EB1 Ernie Banks 50.00
BE1 Johnny Bench 40.00
YB1 Yogi Berra 60.00
WB1 Wade Boggs 35.00
WB2 Wade Boggs 35.00
WB3 Wade Boggs 35.00
GB1 George Brett 60.00
GB2 George Brett 60.00
LB1 Lou Brock 35.00
LB2 Lou Brock 35.00
JB1 Jim Bunning 25.00
RC1 Rod Carew 30.00
RC2 Rod Carew 30.00
SC1 Steve Carlton 20.00
SC2 Steve Carlton 20.00
GC1 Gary Carter 25.00
GC2 Gary Carter 25.00
GC3 Gary Carter 25.00
OC1 Orlando Cepeda 25.00
OC2 Orlando Cepeda 25.00
BD1 Bobby Doerr 15.00
BD2 Bobby Doerr 15.00
DE1 Dennis Eckersley 20.00
DE2 Dennis Eckersley 20.00
BF1 Bob Feller 30.00
BF2 Bob Feller 30.00
RF1 Rollie Fingers 20.00
RF2 Rollie Fingers 20.00
CF1 Carlton Fisk 30.00
CF2 Carlton Fisk 30.00
WF1 Whitey Ford 50.00
BG1 Bob Gibson 35.00
MI1 Monte Irvin 25.00
RJ1 Reggie Jackson 40.00
RJ2 Reggie Jackson 40.00
RJ3 Reggie Jackson 40.00
FJ1 Fergie Jenkins 20.00
FJ2 Fergie Jenkins 20.00
AK1 Al Kaline 40.00
AK2 Al Kaline 40.00
GK1 George Kell 20.00
HK1 Harmon Killebrew 40.00
HK2 Harmon Killebrew 40.00
RK1 Ralph Kiner 40.00
JM1 Juan Marichal 25.00
BM1 Bill Mazeroski 40.00
WM1 Willie McCovey 40.00
PM1 Paul Molitor 30.00
PM2 Paul Molitor 30.00
PM3 Paul Molitor 30.00
MO1 Joe Morgan 25.00
MO2 Joe Morgan 25.00
EM1 Eddie Murray 50.00
EM2 Eddie Murray 50.00
SM1 Stan Musial 60.00
SM2 Stan Musial 60.00
PN1 Phil Niekro 20.00
PN2 Phil Niekro 20.00
JP1 Jim Palmer 20.00
JP2 Jim Palmer 20.00
TP1 Tony Perez 20.00
TP2 Tony Perez 20.00
GP1 Gaylord Perry 20.00
GP2 Gaylord Perry 20.00
KP1 Kirby Puckett 40.00
KP2 Kirby Puckett 40.00

RR1 Robin Roberts 40.00
BR1 Brooks Robinson 30.00
BR2 Brooks Robinson 30.00
BR3 Brooks Robinson 30.00
FR1 Frank Robinson 20.00
NR1 Nolan Ryan 90.00
NR2 Nolan Ryan 90.00
NR3 Nolan Ryan 90.00
NR4 Nolan Ryan 90.00
SA1 Ryne Sandberg 60.00
SA2 Ryne Sandberg 60.00
SA3 Ryne Sandberg 60.00
MS1 Mike Schmidt 50.00
MS2 Mike Schmidt 50.00
MS3 Mike Schmidt 50.00
RS1 Red Schoendienst 35.00
TS1 Tom Seaver 40.00
OS1 Ozzie Smith 40.00
OS2 Ozzie Smith 40.00
OS3 Ozzie Smith 40.00
SN1 Duke Snider 40.00
DS1 Don Sutton 20.00
DS2 Don Sutton 20.00
DS3 Don Sutton 20.00
BW1 Billy Williams 20.00
BW2 Billy Williams 20.00
DW1 Dave Winfield 20.00
CY1 Carl Yastrzemski 50.00
CY2 Carl Yastrzemski 50.00
RY1 Robin Yount 40.00
RY2 Robin Yount 40.00
RY3 Robin Yount 40.00

Cooperstown Cuts
NM/M
Production 1-20
JM Johnny Mize/20 180.00

Cooperstown Cuts Memorabilia
No Pricing
Production 1-20

Essential Enshrinement
NM/M
Production 50 Sets
Gold: No Pricing
Production 5 Sets
Silver: No Pricing
Production 15 Sets
Rainbow: No Pricing
Production One Set
LA1 Luis Aparicio 4.00
EB1 Ernie Banks 6.00
BE1 Johnny Bench 6.00
BE2 Johnny Bench 6.00
YB1 Yogi Berra 5.00
YB2 Yogi Berra 5.00
WB1 Wade Boggs 5.00
WB2 Wade Boggs 5.00
WB3 Wade Boggs 5.00
GB1 George Brett 10.00
GB2 George Brett 10.00
GB3 George Brett 10.00
LB1 Lou Brock 4.00
LB2 Lou Brock 4.00
JB1 Jim Bunning 4.00
RC1 Rod Carew 4.00
RC2 Rod Carew 4.00
SC1 Steve Carlton 4.00
SC2 Steve Carlton 4.00
GC1 Gary Carter 4.00
GC2 Gary Carter 4.00
OC1 Orlando Cepeda 4.00
BD1 Bobby Doerr 4.00
BD2 Bobby Doerr 4.00
DE1 Dennis Eckersley 4.00
BF1 Bob Feller 4.00
BF2 Bob Feller 4.00
RF1 Rollie Fingers 4.00
CF1 Carlton Fisk 4.00
CF2 Carlton Fisk 4.00
WF1 Whitey Ford 5.00
WF2 Whitey Ford 5.00
BG1 Bob Gibson 5.00
BG2 Bob Gibson 5.00
MI1 Monte Irvin 4.00
RJ1 Reggie Jackson 5.00
RJ2 Reggie Jackson 5.00
RJ3 Reggie Jackson 5.00
FJ1 Fergie Jenkins 4.00
FJ2 Fergie Jenkins 4.00
AK1 Al Kaline 6.00
AK2 Al Kaline 6.00
GK1 George Kell 4.00
HK1 Harmon Killebrew 6.00
HK2 Harmon Killebrew 6.00
RK1 Ralph Kiner 4.00
JM1 Juan Marichal 4.00
BM1 Bill Mazeroski 4.00
WM1 Willie McCovey 4.00
PM1 Paul Molitor 5.00
PM2 Paul Molitor 5.00
PM3 Paul Molitor 5.00

MO1 Joe Morgan 4.00
MO2 Joe Morgan 4.00
MO3 Joe Morgan 4.00
EM1 Eddie Murray 4.00
EM2 Eddie Murray 4.00
SM1 Stan Musial 6.00
SM2 Stan Musial 6.00
PN1 Phil Niekro 4.00
PN2 Phil Niekro 4.00
JP1 Jim Palmer 4.00
JP2 Jim Palmer 4.00
TP1 Tony Perez 4.00
GP1 Gaylord Perry 4.00
GP2 Gaylord Perry 4.00
KP1 Kirby Puckett 5.00
KP2 Kirby Puckett 5.00
RR1 Robin Roberts 5.00
BR1 Brooks Robinson 5.00
BR2 Brooks Robinson 5.00
BR3 Brooks Robinson 5.00
FR1 Frank Robinson 5.00
FR2 Frank Robinson 5.00
NR1 Nolan Ryan 10.00
NR2 Nolan Ryan 10.00
NR3 Nolan Ryan 10.00
NR4 Nolan Ryan 10.00
SA1 Ryne Sandberg 6.00
SA2 Ryne Sandberg 6.00
SA3 Ryne Sandberg 6.00
MS1 Mike Schmidt 6.00
MS2 Mike Schmidt 6.00
RS1 Red Schoendienst 4.00
TS1 Tom Seaver 5.00
OS1 Ozzie Smith 6.00
OS2 Ozzie Smith 6.00
SN1 Duke Snider 5.00
SN2 Duke Snider 5.00
DS1 Don Sutton 4.00
DS2 Don Sutton 4.00
BW1 Billy Williams 4.00
BW2 Billy Williams 4.00
DW1 Dave Winfield 4.00
CY1 Carl Yastrzemski 6.00
CY2 Carl Yastrzemski 6.00
CY3 Carl Yastrzemski 6.00
RY1 Robin Yount 6.00
RY2 Robin Yount 6.00
RY3 Robin Yount 6.00

Essential Enshrinement Autograph
NM/M
Production 25 Sets
Gold: No Pricing
Production 5 Sets
Silver: No Pricing
Production 15 Sets
Rainbow: No Pricing
Production One Set
Material Gold: No Pricing
Production 5 Sets
Material Silver: No Pricing
Production 15 Sets
Patch Gold: No Pricing
Production 5 Sets
Patch Silver: No Pricing
Production 10 Sets
LA1 Luis Aparicio 20.00
EB1 Ernie Banks 50.00
BE1 Johnny Bench 40.00
BE2 Johnny Bench 40.00
YB1 Yogi Berra 60.00
YB2 Yogi Berra 60.00
WB1 Wade Boggs 35.00
WB2 Wade Boggs 35.00
WB3 Wade Boggs 35.00
GB1 George Brett 60.00
GB2 George Brett 60.00
GB3 George Brett 60.00
LB1 Lou Brock 35.00
LB2 Lou Brock 35.00
JB1 Jim Bunning 25.00
RC1 Rod Carew 30.00
RC2 Rod Carew 30.00
SC1 Steve Carlton 20.00
SC2 Steve Carlton 20.00
GC1 Gary Carter 25.00
GC2 Gary Carter 25.00
OC1 Orlando Cepeda 25.00
BD1 Bobby Doerr 15.00
BD2 Bobby Doerr 15.00
DE1 Dennis Eckersley 20.00
BF1 Bob Feller 30.00
BF2 Bob Feller 30.00
RF1 Rollie Fingers 20.00
CF1 Carlton Fisk 30.00
CF2 Carlton Fisk 30.00
WF1 Whitey Ford 50.00
WF2 Whitey Ford 50.00
BG1 Bob Gibson 35.00
BG2 Bob Gibson 35.00
MI1 Monte Irvin 25.00
RJ1 Reggie Jackson 40.00
RJ2 Reggie Jackson 40.00
RJ3 Reggie Jackson 40.00
FJ1 Fergie Jenkins 20.00
FJ2 Fergie Jenkins 20.00
AK1 Al Kaline 40.00
AK2 Al Kaline 40.00
GK1 George Kell 20.00
HK1 Harmon Killebrew 40.00
HK2 Harmon Killebrew 40.00
RK1 Ralph Kiner 40.00
JM1 Juan Marichal 25.00
BM1 Bill Mazeroski 40.00

WM1 Willie McCovey 40.00
PM1 Paul Molitor 30.00
PM2 Paul Molitor 30.00
PM3 Paul Molitor 30.00
MO1 Joe Morgan 25.00
MO2 Joe Morgan 25.00
MO3 Joe Morgan 25.00
EM1 Eddie Murray 50.00
EM2 Eddie Murray 50.00
SM1 Stan Musial 60.00
SM2 Stan Musial 60.00
PN1 Phil Niekro 20.00
PN2 Phil Niekro 20.00
JP1 Jim Palmer 20.00
JP2 Jim Palmer 20.00
TP1 Tony Perez 20.00
GP1 Gaylord Perry 20.00
GP2 Gaylord Perry 20.00
KP1 Kirby Puckett 40.00
KP2 Kirby Puckett 40.00
RR1 Robin Roberts 25.00
BR1 Brooks Robinson 30.00
BR2 Brooks Robinson 30.00
BR3 Brooks Robinson 30.00
FR1 Frank Robinson 20.00
FR2 Frank Robinson 20.00
NR1 Nolan Ryan 90.00
NR2 Nolan Ryan 90.00
NR3 Nolan Ryan 90.00
NR4 Nolan Ryan 90.00
SA1 Ryne Sandberg 60.00
SA2 Ryne Sandberg 60.00
SA3 Ryne Sandberg 60.00
MS1 Mike Schmidt 50.00
MS2 Mike Schmidt 50.00
RS1 Red Schoendienst 35.00
TS1 Tom Seaver 40.00
OS1 Ozzie Smith 40.00
OS2 Ozzie Smith 40.00
SN1 Duke Snider 40.00
SN2 Duke Snider 40.00
DS1 Don Sutton 20.00
DS2 Don Sutton 20.00
BW1 Billy Williams 20.00
BW2 Billy Williams 20.00
DW1 Dave Winfield 30.00
CY1 Carl Yastrzemski 50.00
CY2 Carl Yastrzemski 50.00
CY3 Carl Yastrzemski 50.00
RY1 Robin Yount 40.00
RY2 Robin Yount 40.00
RY3 Robin Yount 40.00

Hall of Fame Materials
NM/M
Production 25 Sets
Gold: No Pricing
Production 5 Sets
Silver: No Pricing
Production 15 Sets
Rainbow: No Pricing
Production One Set
Green: No Pricing
Production 10 Sets
RC1 Roberto Clemente 120.00
RC2 Roberto Clemente 120.00
RC3 Roberto Clemente 120.00
TC1 Ty Cobb 100.00
TC2 Ty Cobb 100.00
TC3 Ty Cobb 100.00
MC1 Mickey Cochrane 40.00
DD1 Dizzy Dean 80.00
DD2 Dizzy Dean 80.00
JD1 Joe DiMaggio 90.00
JD2 Joe DiMaggio 90.00
JD3 Joe DiMaggio 90.00
JF1 Jimmie Foxx 60.00
JF2 Jimmie Foxx 60.00
LG1 Lou Gehrig 180.00
LG2 Lou Gehrig 180.00
LG3 Lou Gehrig 180.00
RH1 Rogers Hornsby 80.00
MM1 Mickey Mantle 250.00
MM2 Mickey Mantle 250.00
MM3 Mickey Mantle 250.00
JM1 Johnny Mize 30.00
JM2 Johnny Mize 30.00
JM3 Johnny Mize 30.00
MO1 Mel Ott 40.00
MO2 Mel Ott 40.00
SP1 Satchel Paige 50.00
SP2 Satchel Paige 50.00
SP3 Satchel Paige 50.00
JR1 Jackie Robinson 60.00
JR2 Jackie Robinson 60.00
JR3 Jackie Robinson 60.00
BR1 Babe Ruth 250.00
BR2 Babe Ruth 250.00
BR3 Babe Ruth 250.00
GS1 George Sisler 40.00
GS2 George Sisler 40.00
TW1 Ted Williams 85.00
TW2 Ted Williams 85.00
TW3 Ted Williams 85.00

Hall of Fame Seasons
NM/M
Production 50 Sets
Gold: No Pricing
Production 5 Sets
Silver: No Pricing
Production 15 Sets
Rainbow: No Pricing
Production One Set

WM1 Willie McCovey 40.00
PM1 Paul Molitor 30.00
PM2 Paul Molitor 30.00
PM3 Paul Molitor 30.00
MO1 Joe Morgan 25.00
MO2 Joe Morgan 25.00
EM1 Eddie Murray 50.00
EM2 Eddie Murray 50.00
SM1 Stan Musial 60.00
SM2 Stan Musial 60.00
PN1 Phil Niekro 20.00
PN2 Phil Niekro 20.00
JP1 Jim Palmer 20.00
JP2 Jim Palmer 20.00
JP3 Jim Palmer 20.00
TP1 Tony Perez 20.00
GP1 Gaylord Perry 20.00
GP2 Gaylord Perry 20.00
KP1 Kirby Puckett 40.00
KP2 Kirby Puckett 40.00
RR1 Robin Roberts 25.00
BR1 Brooks Robinson 30.00
BR2 Brooks Robinson 30.00
BR3 Brooks Robinson 30.00
FR1 Frank Robinson 20.00
FR2 Frank Robinson 20.00
NR1 Nolan Ryan 90.00
NR2 Nolan Ryan 90.00
NR3 Nolan Ryan 90.00
NR4 Nolan Ryan 90.00
SA1 Ryne Sandberg 60.00
SA2 Ryne Sandberg 60.00
MS1 Mike Schmidt 50.00
MS2 Mike Schmidt 50.00
MS3 Mike Schmidt 50.00
RS1 Red Schoendienst 35.00
TS1 Tom Seaver 40.00
TS2 Tom Seaver 40.00
OS1 Ozzie Smith 40.00
OS2 Ozzie Smith 40.00
SN1 Duke Snider 40.00
DS1 Don Sutton 20.00
DS2 Don Sutton 20.00
BW1 Billy Williams 20.00
BW2 Billy Williams 20.00
DW1 Dave Winfield 30.00
CY1 Carl Yastrzemski 50.00
CY2 Carl Yastrzemski 50.00
RY1 Robin Yount 40.00
RY2 Robin Yount 40.00

Hall of Fame Seasons Autograph
NM/M
Production 25 Sets
Gold: No Pricing
Production 5 Sets
Silver: No Pricing
Production 15 Sets
Rainbow: No Pricing
Production One Set
Material Gold: No Pricing
Production 5 Sets
Material Silver: No Pricing
Production 15 Sets

Patch Gold: No Pricing
Production 5 Sets
Patch Silver: No Pricing
Production 10 Sets
LA1 Luis Aparicio 20.00
EB1 Ernie Banks 50.00
BE1 Johnny Bench 40.00
BE2 Johnny Bench 40.00
YB1 Yogi Berra 60.00
YB2 Yogi Berra 60.00
WB1 Wade Boggs 35.00
WB2 Wade Boggs 35.00
WB3 Wade Boggs 35.00
GB1 George Brett 60.00
GB2 George Brett 60.00
LB1 Lou Brock 35.00
LB2 Lou Brock 35.00
JB1 Jim Bunning 25.00
RC1 Rod Carew 30.00
RC2 Rod Carew 30.00
GC1 Gary Carter 25.00
SC1 Steve Carlton 20.00
SC2 Steve Carlton 20.00
SC3 Steve Carlton 20.00
OC1 Orlando Cepeda 25.00
BD1 Bobby Doerr 15.00
DE1 Dennis Eckersley 20.00
DE2 Dennis Eckersley 20.00
DE3 Dennis Eckersley 20.00
BF1 Bob Feller 30.00
BF2 Bob Feller 30.00
RF1 Rollie Fingers 20.00
CF1 Carlton Fisk 30.00
CF2 Carlton Fisk 30.00
WF1 Whitey Ford 50.00
WF2 Whitey Ford 50.00
BG1 Bob Gibson 35.00
BG2 Bob Gibson 35.00
MI1 Monte Irvin 25.00
RJ1 Reggie Jackson 40.00
RJ2 Reggie Jackson 40.00
RJ3 Reggie Jackson 40.00
FJ1 Fergie Jenkins 20.00
FJ2 Fergie Jenkins 20.00
AK1 Al Kaline 40.00
AK2 Al Kaline 40.00
AK3 Al Kaline 40.00
GK1 George Kell 20.00
HK1 Harmon Killebrew 40.00
HK2 Harmon Killebrew 40.00
HK3 Harmon Killebrew 40.00
RK1 Ralph Kiner 40.00
JM1 Juan Marichal 25.00
BM1 Bill Mazeroski 40.00
WM1 Willie McCovey 40.00
PM1 Paul Molitor 30.00
PM2 Paul Molitor 30.00
PM3 Paul Molitor 30.00
MO1 Joe Morgan 25.00
MO2 Joe Morgan 25.00
EM1 Eddie Murray 50.00
EM2 Eddie Murray 50.00
SM1 Stan Musial 60.00
SM2 Stan Musial 60.00
PN1 Phil Niekro 20.00
PN2 Phil Niekro 20.00
JP1 Jim Palmer 20.00
JP2 Jim Palmer 20.00
JP3 Jim Palmer 20.00
TP1 Tony Perez 20.00
GP1 Gaylord Perry 20.00
GP2 Gaylord Perry 20.00
KP1 Kirby Puckett 40.00
KP2 Kirby Puckett 40.00
RR1 Robin Roberts 25.00
BR1 Brooks Robinson 30.00
BR2 Brooks Robinson 30.00
BR3 Brooks Robinson 30.00
FR1 Frank Robinson 20.00
FR2 Frank Robinson 20.00
NR1 Nolan Ryan 90.00
NR2 Nolan Ryan 90.00
NR3 Nolan Ryan 90.00
NR4 Nolan Ryan 90.00
SA1 Ryne Sandberg 60.00
SA2 Ryne Sandberg 60.00
MS1 Mike Schmidt 50.00
MS2 Mike Schmidt 50.00
MS3 Mike Schmidt 50.00
RS1 Red Schoendienst 35.00
TS1 Tom Seaver 40.00
TS2 Tom Seaver 40.00
OS1 Ozzie Smith 40.00
OS2 Ozzie Smith 40.00
SN1 Duke Snider 40.00
DS1 Don Sutton 20.00
DS2 Don Sutton 20.00
BW1 Billy Williams 20.00
BW2 Billy Williams 20.00
DW1 Dave Winfield 30.00
CY1 Carl Yastrzemski 50.00
CY2 Carl Yastrzemski 50.00
RY1 Robin Yount 40.00
RY2 Robin Yount 40.00

Hall Worthy
NM/M
Production 50 Sets
Gold: No Pricing
Production 5 Sets
Silver: No Pricing
Production 15 Sets
Rainbow: No Pricing
Production One Set
LA1 Luis Aparicio 4.00
EB1 Ernie Banks 6.00
BE1 Johnny Bench 6.00

Signs of Cooperstown / Signs of Cooperstown Autograph (singles)

Code	Player	Base	Autograph
EB1	Ernie Banks		50.00
BE1	Johnny Bench		40.00
BE2	Johnny Bench	6.00	40.00
YB1	Yogi Berra	5.00	60.00
WB1	Wade Boggs	5.00	35.00
WB2	Wade Boggs	5.00	35.00
WB3	Wade Boggs	5.00	35.00
GB1	George Brett	10.00	60.00
GB2	George Brett	10.00	60.00
GB3	George Brett	10.00	60.00
LB1	Lou Brock	4.00	35.00
LB2	Lou Brock	4.00	35.00
JB1	Jim Bunning	4.00	25.00
RC1	Rod Carew	4.00	30.00
RC2	Rod Carew	4.00	30.00
SC1	Steve Carlton	4.00	20.00
SC2	Steve Carlton	4.00	20.00
GC1	Gary Carter	4.00	25.00
GC2	Gary Carter	4.00	25.00
OC1	Orlando Cepeda	4.00	25.00
OC2	Orlando Cepeda	4.00	25.00
BD1	Bobby Doerr	4.00	15.00
DE1	Dennis Eckersley	4.00	20.00
DE2	Dennis Eckersley	4.00	20.00
DE3	Dennis Eckersley	4.00	20.00
DE4	Dennis Eckersley	4.00	20.00
BF1	Bob Feller	4.00	30.00
BF2	Bob Feller	4.00	30.00
RF1	Rollie Fingers	4.00	20.00
RF2	Rollie Fingers	4.00	20.00
CF1	Carlton Fisk	4.00	30.00
CF2	Carlton Fisk	4.00	30.00
WF1	Whitey Ford	5.00	50.00
BG1	Bob Gibson	5.00	35.00
MI1	Monte Irvin	4.00	25.00
RJ1	Reggie Jackson	5.00	40.00
RJ2	Reggie Jackson	5.00	40.00
RJ3	Reggie Jackson	5.00	40.00
RJ4	Reggie Jackson	5.00	40.00
FJ1	Fergie Jenkins	4.00	20.00
FJ2	Fergie Jenkins	4.00	20.00
FJ3	Fergie Jenkins	4.00	20.00
AK1	Al Kaline	4.00	40.00
AK2	Al Kaline	4.00	40.00
GK1	George Kell	4.00	20.00
HK1	Harmon Killebrew	6.00	40.00
HK2	Harmon Killebrew	6.00	40.00
RK1	Ralph Kiner	4.00	40.00
JM1	Juan Marichal	4.00	25.00
BM1	Bill Mazeroski	4.00	40.00
WM1	Willie McCovey	5.00	40.00
PM1	Paul Molitor	4.00	30.00
PM2	Paul Molitor	5.00	30.00
MO1	Joe Morgan	4.00	25.00
MO2	Joe Morgan	4.00	25.00
EM1	Eddie Murray	4.00	50.00
EM2	Eddie Murray	4.00	50.00
EM3	Eddie Murray	4.00	50.00
SM1	Stan Musial	6.00	60.00
PN1	Phil Niekro	4.00	20.00
PN2	Phil Niekro	4.00	20.00
JP1	Jim Palmer	4.00	20.00
JP2	Jim Palmer	4.00	20.00
TP1	Tony Perez	4.00	20.00
TP2	Tony Perez	4.00	20.00
GP1	Gaylord Perry	4.00	20.00
GP2	Gaylord Perry	4.00	20.00
KP1	Kirby Puckett	5.00	40.00
RR1	Robin Roberts	4.00	25.00
BR1	Brooks Robinson	5.00	30.00
BR2	Brooks Robinson	5.00	30.00
FR1	Frank Robinson	5.00	20.00
FR2	Frank Robinson	5.00	20.00
NR1	Nolan Ryan	10.00	90.00
NR2	Nolan Ryan	10.00	90.00
NR3	Nolan Ryan	10.00	90.00
NR4	Nolan Ryan	10.00	90.00
SA1	Ryne Sandberg	6.00	60.00
SA2	Ryne Sandberg	6.00	60.00
SA3	Ryne Sandberg	6.00	60.00
MS1	Mike Schmidt	6.00	50.00
MS2	Mike Schmidt	6.00	50.00
MS3	Mike Schmidt	6.00	50.00
RS1	Red Schoendienst	4.00	35.00
TS1	Tom Seaver	5.00	40.00
TS2	Tom Seaver	5.00	40.00
OS1	Ozzie Smith	6.00	40.00
OS2	Ozzie Smith	6.00	40.00
SN1	Duke Snider	5.00	40.00
SN2	Duke Snider	5.00	40.00
DS1	Don Sutton	4.00	20.00
DS2	Don Sutton	4.00	20.00
DS3	Don Sutton	4.00	20.00
BW1	Billy Williams	4.00	30.00
DW1	Dave Winfield	4.00	30.00
CY1	Carl Yastrzemski	6.00	50.00
CY2	Carl Yastrzemski	6.00	50.00
RY1	Robin Yount	6.00	40.00
RY2	Robin Yount	6.00	40.00

Hall Worthy Autograph

NM/M

Production 25 Sets
Gold: No Pricing
Production 5 Sets
Silver: No Pricing
Production 15 Sets
Rainbow: No Pricing
Production One Set
Material Gold: No Pricing
Production 5 Sets
Material Silver: No Pricing
Production 15 Sets
Patch Gold: No Pricing
Production 5 Sets
Patch Silver: No Pricing
Production 10 Sets

Code	Player	Price
LA1	Luis Aparicio	20.00

Signs of Cooperstown Duals / Signs of Cooperstown Duals Autograph

NM/M

Production 50 Sets
Gold: No Pricing
Production 5 Sets
Silver: No Pricing
Production 15 Sets
Rainbow: No Pricing
Production One Set

(Duals Autograph — Production 20 Sets / Gold: No Pricing / Production 5 Sets / Silver: No Pricing / Production 10 Sets / Rainbow: No Pricing / Production One Set)

Code	Players	Dual	Dual Autograph
AB	Ernie Banks, Luis Aparicio	6.00	80.00
AS	Luis Aparicio, Ozzie Smith	8.00	60.00
BC	Steve Carlton, Jim Bunning	4.00	35.00
BF	Frank Robinson, Brooks Robinson	5.00	60.00
BG	George Brett, Brooks Robinson	10.00	90.00
BM	Lou Brock, Stan Musial	8.00	100.00
BR	Jim Bunning, Robin Roberts	4.00	60.00
BS	Ernie Banks, Ryne Sandberg	10.00	120.00
CM	Orlando Cepeda, Willie McCovey	4.00	50.00
CS	Tom Seaver, Gary Carter	4.00	80.00
DB	Wade Boggs, Bobby Doerr	4.00	50.00
EF	Dennis Eckersley, Rollie Fingers	4.00	35.00
FB	Johnny Bench, Carlton Fisk	6.00	75.00
FC	Bob Feller, Steve Carlton	4.00	40.00
FP	Bob Feller, Gaylord Perry	4.00	40.00
GC	Bob Gibson, Steve Carlton	5.00	60.00
GF	Bob Gibson, Whitey Ford	5.00	75.00
IM	Monte Irvin, Willie McCovey	5.00	60.00
JJ	Joe Morgan, Johnny Bench	6.00	80.00
JM	Reggie Jackson, Willie McCovey	5.00	100.00
JW	Reggie Jackson, Dave Winfield	5.00	80.00
JY	Yogi Berra, Johnny Bench	6.00	150.00
KK	Al Kaline, George Kell	6.00	85.00
KP	Kirby Puckett, Harmon Killebrew	6.00	80.00
LO	Lou Brock, Ozzie Smith	8.00	65.00
MK	Bill Mazeroski, Ralph Kiner	5.00	75.00
MP	Joe Morgan, Tony Perez	4.00	50.00
MY	Robin Yount, Paul Molitor	5.00	85.00
NS	Steve Carlton, Nolan Ryan	10.00	150.00
PM	Gaylord Perry, Juan Marichal	4.00	40.00
PN	Gaylord Perry, Phil Niekro	4.00	40.00
PR	Rod Carew, Paul Molitor	5.00	50.00
RC	Rod Carew, Nolan Ryan	10.00	150.00
RP	Jim Palmer, Brooks Robinson	5.00	50.00
RS	Tom Seaver, Nolan Ryan	10.00	180.00
RW	Ryne Sandberg, Wade Boggs	10.00	100.00
SB	George Brett, Mike Schmidt	10.00	140.00
SC	Mike Schmidt, Steve Carlton	10.00	85.00
SK	Ralph Kiner, Duke Snider	5.00	65.00
SM	Ozzie Smith, Stan Musial	8.00	120.00
SP	Gaylord Perry, Don Sutton	4.00	40.00
SR	Mike Schmidt, Brooks Robinson	10.00	75.00
SS	Red Schoendienst, Ozzie Smith	6.00	65.00
SW	Billy Williams, Ryne Sandberg	10.00	90.00
WB	Billy Williams, Ernie Banks	6.00	90.00
WJ	Billy Williams, Fergie Jenkins	4.00	50.00
WS	Ozzie Smith, Dave Winfield	6.00	75.00
WY	Yogi Berra, Whitey Ford	6.00	100.00
YF	Carlton Fisk, Carl Yastrzemski	6.00	100.00
YJ	Reggie Jackson, Carl Yastrzemski	6.00	100.00

Signs of Cooperstown Triples / Signs of Cooperstown Triple Autograph

NM/M

Triples: Production 50 Sets / Gold: No Pricing / Production 5 Sets / Silver: No Pricing / Production 15 Sets / Rainbow: No Pricing / Production One Set

Triple Autograph: Production 20 Sets 75.00 / Gold: No Pricing / Production 5 Sets / Silver: No Pricing / Production 10 Sets / Rainbow: No Pricing / Production One Set

Code	Players	Triple	Triple Autograph
ASY	Robin Yount, Luis Aparicio, Ozzie Smith	8.00	140.00
BFJ	Jim Palmer, Frank Robinson, Brooks Robinson	5.00	80.00
BSB	George Brett, Mike Schmidt, Wade Boggs	10.00	185.00
BSY	Ernie Banks, Robin Yount, Ozzie Smith	8.00	150.00
CMI	Monte Irvin, Orlando Cepeda, Willie McCovey	5.00	75.00
DFY	Carlton Fisk, Carl Yastrzemski, Bobby Doerr	8.00	125.00
DYB	Carl Yastrzemski, Wade Boggs, Bobby Doerr	8.00	125.00
FPE	Bob Feller, Dennis Eckersley, Gaylord Perry	4.00	
FRC	Bob Feller, Steve Carlton, Nolan Ryan	10.00	200.00
FSE	Dennis Eckersley, Rollie Fingers, Don Sutton	4.00	
GCE	Bob Gibson, Dennis Eckersley, Steve Carlton	4.00	
GSM	Bob Gibson, Stan Musial, Ozzie Smith	8.00	185.00
JFB	Yogi Berra, Reggie Jackson, Whitey Ford	8.00	185.00
JPR	Nolan Ryan, Gaylord Perry, Fergie Jenkins	10.00	150.00
KKB	Al Kaline, George Kell, Jim Bunning	6.00	
KPC	Rod Carew, Kirby Puckett, Harmon Killebrew	6.00	120.00
KSR	Ralph Kiner, Duke Snider, Frank Robinson	5.00	120.00
KWR	Al Kaline, Frank Robinson, Dave Winfield	6.00	
MBP	Johnny Bench, Tony Perez, Joe Morgan	6.00	160.00
MCM	Orlando Cepeda, Willie McCovey, Juan Marichal	5.00	100.00
MMS	Joe Morgan, Red Schoendienst, Bill Mazeroski	4.00	
MRJ	Eddie Murray, Reggie Jackson, Frank Robinson	5.00	
MSC	Rod Carew, Joe Morgan, Ryne Sandberg		125.00
MYF	Robin Yount, Paul Molitor, Rollie Fingers	6.00	125.00
PMC	Rod Carew, Kirby Puckett, Paul Molitor	6.00	100.00
RAP	Jim Palmer, Luis Aparicio, Brooks Robinson	5.00	80.00
RBC	Steve Carlton, Jim Bunning, Robin Roberts		85.00
RBS	George Brett, Mike Schmidt, Brooks Robinson		200.00
SRC	Mike Schmidt, Steve Carlton, Robin Roberts		150.00
WBI	Billy Williams, Monte Irvin, Lou Brock	4.00	
WBJ	Billy Williams, Ernie Banks, Fergie Jenkins	6.00	
WJB	Reggie Jackson, Wade Boggs, Dave Winfield	6.00	120.00
WSP	Dave Winfield, Ozzie Smith, Gaylord Perry	6.00	120.00
YKM	Ralph Kiner, Carl Yastrzemski, Stan Musial		140.00

Signs of Cooperstown Quads

NM/M

Production 50 Sets
Gold: No Pricing
Production 5 Sets
Silver: No Pricing
Production 15 Sets
Rainbow: No Pricing
Production One Set

Code	Players	Price
BMYC	George Brett, Rod Carew, Robin Yount, Paul Molitor	10.00
BSAY	Ernie Banks, Robin Yount, Luis Aparicio, Ozzie Smith	8.00
FCBB	Yogi Berra, Johnny Bench, Carlton Fisk, Gary Carter	6.00
FGRC	Bob Feller, Bob Gibson, Steve Carlton, Nolan Ryan	10.00
KCPM	Tony Perez, Orlando Cepeda, Harmon Killebrew, Willie McCovey	6.00
KYBM	Al Kaline, Lou Brock, Carl Yastrzemski, Stan Musial	8.00
MBKM	Ernie Banks, Eddie Murray, Harmon Killebrew, Willie McCovey	8.00
MDMC	Bill Mazeroski, Rod Carew, Joe Morgan, Bobby Doerr	5.00
MRKS	Eddie Murray, Mike Schmidt, Frank Robinson, Harmon Killebrew	10.00
RBKS	George Brett, Mike Schmidt, Brooks Robinson, George Kell	
SPNS	Tom Seaver, Phil Niekro, Don Sutton, Gaylord Perry	
SPSF	Tom Seaver, Jim Palmer, Whitey Ford, Don Sutton	6.00
SRCS	Tom Seaver, Steve Carlton, Don Sutton, Nolan Ryan	10.00
WYKM	Billy Williams, Ralph Kiner, Carl Yastrzemski, Stan Musial	8.00
YWMM	Eddie Murray, Carl Yastrzemski, Stan Musial, Dave Winfield	8.00

Signs of Cooperstown Quads Autograph

No Pricing
Production 10 Sets
Gold: No Pricing
Production 5 Sets

Rainbow: No Pricing
Production One Set

2005 UD Mini Jersey Collection

DAVID ORTIZ

		NM/M
Complete Set (100):		15.00
Common Player:		.15
Pack (3 + Mini Jersey):		6.00
Box (18):		90.00
1	Garret Anderson	.25
2	Vladimir Guerrero	.75
3	Luis Gonzalez	.15
4	Shawn Green	.25
5	Troy Glaus	.25
6	Andruw Jones	.50
7	Chipper Jones	.75
8	John Smoltz	.40
9	Tim Hudson	.40
10	Miguel Tejada	.50
11	Sammy Sosa	1.00
12	Curt Schilling	.75
13	David Ortiz	.75
14	Johnny Damon	.75
15	Manny Ramirez	.75
16	Greg Maddux	1.00
17	Kerry Wood	.50
18	Mark Prior	.75
19	Nomar Garciaparra	1.00
20	Frank Thomas	.50
21	Adam Dunn	.50
22	Ken Griffey Jr.	1.50
23	Travis Hafner	.25
24	Victor Martinez	.15
25	Todd Helton	.50
26	Ivan Rodriguez	.50
27	Magglio Ordonez	.15
28	Carlos Delgado	.40
29	Miguel Cabrera	.75
30	Jeff Bagwell	.25
31	Lance Berkman	.25
32	Roger Clemens	2.00
33	Roy Oswalt	.25
34	Mike Sweeney	.15
35	Eric Gagne	.15
36	J.D. Drew	.15
37	Ben Sheets	.40
38	Johan Santana	.50
39	Torii Hunter	.15
40	Carlos Beltran	.50
41	Mike Piazza	1.00
42	Pedro Martinez	.75
43	Alex Rodriguez	1.50
44	Derek Jeter	2.00
45	Hideki Matsui	1.50
46	Mike Mussina	.40
47	Randy Johnson	.75
48	Bobby Crosby	.40
49	Eric Chavez	.40
50	Bobby Abreu	.40
51	Jim Thome	.15
52	Jason Bay	.15
53	Oliver Perez	.15
54	Jake Peavy	.40
55	Khalil Greene	.40
56	Jason Schmidt	.15
57	Moises Alou	.40
58	Adrian Beltre	.15
59	Ichiro Suzuki	1.50
60	Albert Pujols	2.00
61	Jim Edmonds	.40
62	Mark Mulder	.40
63	Scott Rolen	.75
64	Aubrey Huff	.15
65	Alfonso Soriano	.50
66	Hank Blalock	.40
67	Mark Teixeira	.50
68	Roy Halladay	.40
69	Jose Vidro	.15
70	Livan Hernandez	.15
71	Atlanta Braves	.15
72	Chicago Cubs	.15
73	Chicago White Sox	.15
74	Cincinnati Reds	.15
75	Cleveland Indians	.15
76	Houston Astros	.15
77	L.A. Angels of Anaheim	.15
78	Los Angeles Dodgers	.15
79	New York Yankees	.15
80	Oakland Athletics	.15
81	Philadelphia Phillies	.15
82	Pittsburgh Pirates	.15
83	San Diego Padres	.15
84	San Francisco Giants	.15
85	Texas Rangers	.15
86	Cal Ripken Jr.	2.00
87	Derek Jeter	2.00
88	Hank Blalock	.40
89	Hideo Nomo	.40
90	Joe DiMaggio	1.00
91	Joe Morgan	.50
92	Ken Griffey Jr.	1.50
93	Larry Doby	.50
94	Pedro J. Martinez	.75
95	Randy Johnson	.75
96	Rick Ferrell	.15
97	Roger Clemens	2.00
98	Stan Musial	1.00
99	Ted Williams	1.50
100	Torii Hunter	.15

Mini Jerseys

		NM/M
1	Vladimir Guerrero	5.00
2	Chipper Jones	5.00
3	Curt Schilling	5.00
4	Johnny Damon	5.00
5	Manny Ramirez	5.00
6	Kerry Wood	5.00
7	Nomar Garciaparra	5.00
8	Ken Griffey Jr.	5.00
9	Miguel Cabrera	5.00
10	Roger Clemens	10.00
11	Eric Gagne	5.00
12	Johan Santana	5.00
13	Carlos Beltran	5.00
14	Mike Piazza	5.00
15	Pedro Martinez	5.00
16	Alex Rodriguez	5.00
17	Derek Jeter	15.00
18	Hideki Matsui	8.00
19	Randy Johnson	5.00
20	Jim Thome	5.00
21	Ichiro Suzuki	8.00
22	Albert Pujols	10.00

Mini Jersey Autograph

		NM/M
Inserted 1:480		
1	Ken Griffey Jr.	150.00
3	David Wright	50.00
5	Adrian Beltre	50.00

Mini Replica Flannel Jerseys

		NM/M
Inserted 1:18		
1	Ted Williams	20.00
2	Jackie Robinson	15.00
3	Satchel Paige	15.00
4	Ty Cobb	15.00
5	Babe Ruth	30.00
6	Joe DiMaggio	20.00
7	Lou Gehrig	25.00
8	Mickey Mantle	30.00
9	Roberto Clemente	20.00

2005 Upper Deck MVP

		NM/M
Complete Set (90):		20.00
Common Player:		.10
Pack (6):		1.50
Box (24):		30.00
1	Adam Dunn	.40
2	Adrian Beltre	.40
3	Albert Pujols	1.50
4	Alex Rodriguez	1.50
5	Alfonso Soriano	.40
6	Andruw Jones	.40
7	Aubrey Huff	.10
8	Barry Zito	.25
9	Ben Sheets	.25
10	Bobby Abreu	.25
11	Bobby Crosby	.25
12	Bret Boone	.10
13	Brian Giles	.10
14	Carlos Beltran	.40
15	Carlos Delgado	.25
16	Carlos Lee	.25
17	Chipper Jones	.50
18	Craig Biggio	.25
19	Curt Schilling	.50
20	Dallas McPherson	.10
21	David Ortiz	.50
22	David Wright	1.50
23	Derek Jeter	1.50
24	Derek Lowe	.10
25	Eric Chavez	.25
26	Eric Gagne	.25
27	Frank Thomas	.40
28	Garret Anderson	.25
29	Gary Sheffield	.25
30	Greg Maddux	1.00
31	Hank Blalock	.25
32	Hideki Matsui	1.00
33	Ichiro Suzuki	1.00
34	Ivan Rodriguez	.25
35	J.D. Drew	.10
36	Jake Peavy	.25
37	Jason Bay	.25
38	Jason Giambi	.25
39	Jason Schmidt	.10
40	Jeff Bagwell	.40
41	Jeff Kent	.25
42	Jim Edmonds	.25
43	Jim Thome	.40
44	Joe Mauer	.50
45	Johan Santana	.50
46	John Smoltz	.25
47	Johnny Damon	.25
48	Jorge Posada	.25
49	Jose Vidro	.10
50	Josh Beckett	.25
51	Kazuo Matsui	.10
52	Ken Griffey Jr.	1.00
53	Kerry Wood	.25
54	Khalil Greene	.25
55	Lance Berkman	.25
56	Livan Hernandez	.10
57	Luis Gonzalez	.10
58	Magglio Ordonez	.10
59	Manny Ramirez	.25
60	Mark Mulder	.25
61	Mark Prior	.50
62	Mark Teixeira	.40
63	Miguel Cabrera	.50
64	Miguel Tejada	.50
65	Mike Mussina	.25
66	Mike Piazza	1.00
67	Mike Sweeney	.10
68	Moises Alou	.25
69	Nomar Garciaparra	.75
70	Oliver Perez	.10
71	Paul Konerko	.25
72	Pedro Martinez	.50
73	Rafael Palmeiro	.25
74	Randy Johnson	.50
75	Richie Sexson	.25
76	Roger Clemens	1.50
77	Roy Halladay	.25
78	Roy Oswalt	.25
79	Sammy Sosa	.75
80	Scott Rolen	.50
81	Shawn Green	.10
82	Steve Finley	.10
83	Tim Hudson	.25
84	Todd Helton	.40
85	Tom Glavine	.25
86	Torii Hunter	.25
87	Travis Hafner	.10
88	Troy Glaus	.25
89	Victor Martinez	.25
90	Vladimir Guerrero	.50

All-Star Signatures

NM/M
No Pricing
Inserted 1:480

Batter Up!

		NM/M
Common Player:		.25
Inserted 1:1		
BU-1	Al Kaline	.50
BU-2	Bill Mazeroski	.25
BU-3	Billy Williams	.25
BU-4	Bob Feller	.50
BU-5	Bob Gibson	.50
BU-6	Bob Lemon	.25
BU-7	Brooks Robinson	.50
BU-8	Carlton Fisk	.25
BU-9	Jim "Catfish" Hunter	.25
BU-10	Dennis Eckersley	.25
BU-11	Eddie Mathews	.75
BU-12	Eddie Murray	.50
BU-13	Fergie Jenkins	.25
BU-14	Gaylord Perry	.75
BU-15	Harmon Killebrew	.25
BU-16	Jim Bunning	.25
BU-17	Jim Palmer	.75
BU-18	Joe DiMaggio	1.50
BU-19	Joe Morgan	.25
BU-20	Johnny Bench	.75
BU-21	Juan Marichal	.25
BU-22	Lou Brock	.50
BU-23	Luis Aparicio	.25
BU-24	Mike Schmidt	1.50
BU-25	Monte Irvin	.25
BU-26	Nolan Ryan	2.00
BU-27	Orlando Cepeda	.25
BU-28	Ozzie Smith	.75
BU-29	Pee Wee Reese	.25
BU-30	Phil Niekro	.25
BU-31	Phil Rizzuto	.50
BU-32	Ralph Kiner	.25
BU-33	Richie Ashburn	.25
BU-34	Robin Roberts	.25
BU-35	Robin Yount	.75
BU-36	Rollie Fingers	.25
BU-37	Tom Seaver	.75
BU-38	Tony Perez	.25
BU-39	Warren Spahn	.75
BU-40	Willie McCovey	.50
BU-41	Willie Stargell	.50
BU-42	Yogi Berra	.75

Jersey

		NM/M
Common Jersey:		4.00
Inserted 1:24		
CB	Carlos Beltran	6.00
AB	Adrian Beltre	4.00
HB	Hank Blalock	4.00
SB	Sean Burroughs	4.00
MC	Miguel Cabrera	6.00
EC	Eric Chavez	4.00
EG	Eric Gagne	4.00
KG	Ken Griffey Jr.	10.00
VG	Vladimir Guerrero	6.00
TH	Todd Helton	6.00
DJ	Derek Jeter	15.00
RJ	Randy Johnson	6.00
CJ	Chipper Jones	6.00
GM	Greg Maddux	8.00
PI	Mike Piazza	8.00
MP	Mark Prior	6.00
AP	Albert Pujols	15.00
MR	Manny Ramirez	6.00
IR	Ivan Rodriguez	6.00
SR	Scott Rolen	6.00
JS	Johan Santana	6.00
CS	Curt Schilling	6.00
AS	Alfonso Soriano	6.00
SS	Sammy Sosa	8.00
MT	Mark Teixeira	6.00
TE	Miguel Tejada	6.00
JT	Jim Thome	6.00
KW	Kerry Wood	4.00

2005 UD Origins Promos

DAVID DeJESUS

Each of the cards in UD Origins was issued in a foil-overprinted version with "UD PROMO" across the front. Cards were inserted into specially marked card shop and newsstand issues of Tuff Stuff magazine.

	NM/M
Common Player:	.50
Stars:	1.5X

2005 UD Origins

BOB GIBSON

		NM/M
Complete Set (200):		
Common Player:		.50
Tin (20):		50.00
1	Jim Edmonds	.75
2	Jason Schmidt	.75
3	J.D. Drew	.75
4	Luis Gonzalez	.50
5	Nomar Garciaparra	2.00
6	Jake Peavy	.75
7	Rafael Furcal	.50
8	Craig Biggio	.75
9	Ken Griffey Jr.	3.00
10	Mike Piazza	2.00
11	Jose Vidro	.50
12	Ivan Rodriguez	1.00
13	Carl Crawford	.50
14	Roger Clemens	4.00
15	Kerry Wood	.50
16	Vernon Wells	.50
17	Carlos Guillen	.50
18	Tim Hudson	.75
19	Carl Pavano	.50
20	Carlos Beltran	1.00
21	Pedro Martinez	1.50
22	Hideki Matsui	3.00
23	Frank Thomas	1.00
24	Curt Schilling	1.50
25	Manny Ramirez	1.50
26	Alex Rodriguez	4.00
27	Aubrey Huff	.50
28	David Ortiz	1.50
29	Mark Prior	1.00
30	Albert Pujols	4.00
31	Miguel Cabrera	1.00
32	Brad Penny	.50
33	Carlos Delgado	.75
34	Aramis Ramirez	1.00
35	Josh Beckett	.75
36	Rafael Palmeiro	1.00
37	Bret Boone	.50
38	Lance Berkman	.75
39	Carlos Zambrano	.75
40	Adam Dunn	1.00
41	Livan Hernandez	.50
42	Mike Mussina	.75
43	Ben Sheets	.75
44	Derek Jeter	4.00
45	Kazuo Matsui	.50
46	Bobby Abreu	.75
47	Jeff Bagwell	1.00
48	Travis Hafner	.50
49	Torii Hunter	.75
50	Kevin Brown	.50
51	Alfonso Soriano	1.50
52	Jim Thome	.75
53	John Smoltz	.75
54	Mike Sweeney	.50
55	Andy Pettitte	.75
56	Chipper Jones	1.50
57	Randy Johnson	1.50
58	Steve Finley	.50
59	Larry Walker	.75
60	Troy Glaus	.75
61	Greg Maddux	2.50
62	Shawn Green	.50
63	Roy Halladay	.75
64	Jeff Kent	.50
65	Scott Podsednik	.50
66	Miguel Tejada	1.00
67	Lyle Overbay	.50
68	Bernie Williams	.75
69	Todd Helton	1.00
70	Melvin Mora	.50
71	Magglio Ordonez	.50
72	Carlos Lee	.75
73	Roy Oswalt	.75
74	Victor Martinez	.50
75	Scott Rolen	1.50
76	Eric Chavez	.75
77	Paul Konerko	.75
78	Jose Reyes	.50
79	Barry Larkin	.75
80	Johnny Damon	1.00
81	Eric Gagne	.75
82	Andruw Jones	1.00
83	Gary Sheffield	1.00
84	Richie Sexson	.75
85	Sammy Sosa	2.50
86	Mark Teixeira	1.00
87	Vladimir Guerrero	1.50
88	Michael Young	1.00
89	Johan Santana	1.00
90	Adrian Beltre	.75
91	Tom Glavine	.75
92	Hank Blalock	.75
93	Preston Wilson	.50
94	Jason Kendall	.50
95	Mike Lowell	.50
96	Craig Wilson	.50
97	Ichiro Suzuki	3.00
98	Mark Mulder	.75
99	Garret Anderson	.75
100	Brian Giles	.50
101	Robin Yount	3.00
102	Ernie Banks	3.00
103	Mike Schmidt	5.00
104	Enos Slaughter	1.00
105	Red Schoendienst	1.00
106	Hoyt Wilhelm	1.00
107	Lou Brock	2.00
108	Rollie Fingers	1.00
109	Gaylord Perry	1.00
110	Bobby Doerr	1.00
111	Larry Doby	1.00
112	Al Lopez	1.00
113	Joe Morgan	1.50
114	Luis Aparicio	1.00
115	Willie McCovey	1.00
116	Bob Lemon	1.00
117	Early Wynn	1.00
118	Bob Feller	2.00
119	Cal Ripken Jr.	8.00
120	George Kell	1.00
121	Juan Marichal	1.50
122	Monte Irvin	1.50
123	Harmon Killebrew	3.00
124	Lou Boudreau	1.00
125	Mickey Mantle	8.00
126	Richie Ashburn	1.00
127	Pee Wee Reese	1.50
128	Whitey Ford	2.00
129	Tom Seaver	2.00
130	Phil Rizzuto	2.00
131	Yogi Berra	3.00
132	Warren Spahn	2.00
133	Billy Williams	1.50
134	Jim Bunning	1.00
135	Ralph Kiner	1.00
136	Ted Williams	6.00
137	Rick Ferrell	1.00
138	Robin Roberts	1.00
139	Brooks Robinson	3.00
140	Hal Newhouser	1.00
141	Jim "Catfish" Hunter	1.00
142	Phil Niekro	1.00
143	Fergie Jenkins	1.00
144	Al Kaline	3.00
145	Stan Musial	4.00
146	Joe DiMaggio	6.00
147	Willie Stargell	2.00
148	Nolan Ryan	6.00
149	Babe Ruth	6.00
150	Bob Gibson	2.00
151	David DeJesus	.50
152	Chris Burke	.50
153	Chad Cordero	.50
154	Kevin Youkilis	.50
155	Bucky Jacobsen	.50
156	B.J. Upton	.50
157	Aaron Rowand	.50
158	Jose Capellan	.50
159	David Wright	2.00
160	Jason Bay	.50
161	Edwin Jackson	.50
162	Scott Kazmir	.50
163	J.D. Closser	.50
164	Chase Utley	1.00
165	Nick Swisher	.50
166	Casey Kotchman	.50
167	Bobby Crosby	.50
168	Zack Greinke	.50
169	Gavin Floyd	.50
170	Jeff Francis	.50
171	Dallas McPherson	.50
172	Gabe Gross	.50
173	Brandon Claussen	.50
174	Wily Mo Pena	.50
175	Robb Quinlan	.50
176	Oliver Perez	.50
177	Guillermo Quiroz	.50
178	Ryan Howard	1.00
179	Gerald Laird	.50
180	Jayson Werth	.50
181	Bobby Madritsch	.50
182	Laynce Nix	.50
183	Eddy Rodriguez	.50
184	Rickie Weeks	1.00
185	Scott Proctor	.50
186	Adam LaRoche	.50
187	Yhency Brazoban	.50
188	Adrian Gonzalez	.50
189	Jason Lane	.50
190	Ryan Wagner	.50
191	Roman Colon	.50
192	Alexis Rios	.50
193	Joe Mauer	1.00
194	Garrett Atkins	.50
195	Daniel Cabrera	.50
196	Khalil Greene	2.00
197	Joe Blanton	.50
198	Jason Dubois	.50
199	Angel Guzman	.50
200	Jesse Crain	.50

Black

No Pricing
Production One Set

Blue

Stars (1-200):	2-4X
Production 50 Sets	

Gold

No Pricing
Production 20 Sets

Red

Stars (1-200):	2-3X
Production 99 Sets	

Origins Materials Jersey

MIGUEL CABRERA

		NM/M
Inserted 2:Tin		
Old Judge:		1X
JB	Jeff Bagwell	8.00
CB	Carlos Beltran	8.00
AB	Adrian Beltre	5.00
LB	Lance Berkman	5.00
HB	Hank Blalock	5.00
MC	Miguel Cabrera	8.00
EC	Eric Chavez	5.00
JD	J.D. Drew	5.00
GL	Troy Glaus	5.00
KG	Ken Griffey Jr.	10.00
VG	Vladimir Guerrero	8.00
TG	Tony Gwynn/SP	10.00
HE	Todd Helton	5.00

TH	Tim Hudson	5.00
HU	Torii Hunter	5.00
DJ	Derek Jeter	15.00
RJ	Randy Johnson	8.00
AJ	Andruw Jones	5.00
CJ	Chipper Jones	8.00
GM	Greg Maddux	10.00
HM	Hideki Matsui	15.00
KM	Hideki Matsui	5.00
DO	David Ortiz	8.00
PI	Mike Piazza	8.00
MP	Mark Prior	8.00
AP	Albert Pujols	15.00
MR	Manny Ramirez	8.00
CR	Cal Ripken Jr./SP	25.00
IR	Ivan Rodriguez	8.00
SR	Scott Rolen	8.00
NR	Nolan Ryan/SP	30.00
CS	Curt Schilling	8.00
BS	Ben Sheets	5.00
GS	Gary Sheffield	5.00
AS	Alfonso Soriano	5.00
SS	Sammy Sosa	8.00
IS	Ichiro Suzuki	20.00
MT	Mark Teixeira	8.00
TE	Miguel Tejada	8.00
FT	Frank Thomas	8.00
JT	Jim Thome	8.00
KW	Kerry Wood	8.00

Origins Nostalgic Signs

NM/M
One sign per tin.

CB	Carlos Beltran	8.00
AB	Adrian Beltre	5.00
HB	Hank Blalock	5.00
MC	Miguel Cabrera	5.00
EC	Eric Chavez	5.00
RC	Roger Clemens	15.00
TC	Ty Cobb	20.00
JD	Joe DiMaggio	20.00
LG	Lou Gehrig	15.00
KG	Ken Griffey Jr.	12.00
VG	Vladimir Guerrero	8.00
TH	Todd Helton	8.00
DJ	Derek Jeter	15.00
RJ	Randy Johnson	8.00
WJ	Walter Johnson	15.00
CJ	Chipper Jones	8.00
PM	Pedro Martinez	8.00
HM	Hideki Matsui	20.00
DO	David Ortiz	8.00
SP	Satchel Paige	12.00
MP	Mike Piazza	10.00
MPR	Mark Prior	8.00
AP	Albert Pujols	20.00
MR	Manny Ramirez	8.00
CR	Cal Ripken Jr.	25.00
JR	Jackie Robinson	8.00
AR	Alex Rodriguez	12.00
IR	Ivan Rodriguez	8.00
SR	Scott Rolen	8.00
BR	Babe Ruth	20.00
NR	Nolan Ryan	20.00
JS	Johan Santana	8.00
CS	Curt Schilling	10.00
AS	Alfonso Soriano	8.00
SS	Sammy Sosa	8.00
IS	Ichiro Suzuki	12.00
MT	Miguel Tejada	8.00
FT	Frank Thomas	8.00
JT	Jim Thome	8.00
HW	Honus Wagner	10.00
TW	Ted Williams	25.00

Origins Old Judge

NM/M
Common Player: .50
Blue: 2-3X
Red: 1-2X
Gold: No Pricing

1	Jake Peavy	.50
2	Derek Jeter	1.00
3	Adrian Beltre	1.00
4	Hank Blalock	1.00
5	Preston Wilson	.50
6	Randy Johnson	2.00
7	Pedro Martinez	2.00
8	Michael Young	1.00
9	Steve Finley	.50
10	Shawn Green	.75
11	Carlos Beltran	1.50
12	Bernie Williams	1.00
13	Brian Giles	.50
14	Kevin Brown	.50
15	Barry Larkin	1.00
16	Troy Glaus	1.00
17	Bret Boone	.50
18	Jason Kendall	.50
19	Johnny Damon	1.50
20	Josh Beckett	1.00
21	Carl Pavano	.50
22	Chipper Jones	2.00
23	Ivan Rodriguez	1.50
24	Kerry Wood	1.50
25	Ken Griffey Jr.	3.00
26	Greg Maddux	3.00
27	Kazuo Matsui	.50
28	Albert Pujols	3.00
29	Victor Martinez	.50
30	Johan Santana	1.50
31	Bobby Abreu	.75
32	Paul Konerko	.75
33	Gary Sheffield	1.00
34	Jose Vidro	.50
35	Alex Rodriguez	4.00
36	Alfonso Soriano	1.50
37	Mark Teixeira	1.50
38	Nomar Garciaparra	2.50
39	Sammy Sosa	3.00
40	Garret Anderson	1.00
41	Eric Chavez	1.00
42	Magglio Ordonez	.50
43	Larry Walker	1.00
44	Brad Penny	.50
45	Jeff Bagwell	1.50
46	Craig Biggio	.75
47	Torii Hunter	.75
48	Mike Lowell	.50
49	Ben Sheets	1.00
50	Miguel Tejada	1.50
51	Jim Edmonds	1.00
52	Mark Mulder	1.00
53	Curt Schilling	1.50
54	Roger Clemens	5.00
55	Jason Schmidt	.50
56	Rafael Furcal	.50
57	Scott Rolen	2.00
58	Carlos Zambrano	.75
59	Mike Sweeney	.50
60	Vladimir Guerrero	2.00
61	Miguel Cabrera	2.00
62	Lance Berkman	.50
63	Lyle Overbay	.50
64	Livan Hernandez	.50
65	Aramis Ramirez	1.00
66	Ichiro Suzuki	4.00
67	Roy Oswalt	.50
68	Carl Crawford	.50
69	Craig Wilson	.50
70	Carlos Lee	.75
71	J.D. Drew	.50
72	Rafael Palmeiro	1.50
73	Jeff Kent	.50
74	Adam Dunn	1.50
75	Andy Pettitte	1.00
76	Luis Gonzalez	.50
77	Frank Thomas	1.50
78	John Smoltz	1.00
79	Hideki Matsui	3.00
80	Tom Glavine	.50
81	Jose Reyes	.50
82	Jim Thome	1.50
83	Mark Prior	2.00
84	Roy Halladay	.75
85	Carlos Delgado	1.00
86	Melvin Mora	.50
87	David Ortiz	2.00
88	Travis Hafner	.50
89	Carlos Guillen	.50
90	Tim Hudson	.50
91	Vernon Wells	.50
92	Andruw Jones	1.50
93	Mike Mussina	1.50
94	Mike Piazza	3.00
95	Richie Sexson	1.00
96	Aubrey Huff	.50
97	Scott Podsednik	.50
98	Eric Gagne	.50
99	Manny Ramirez	2.00
100	Todd Helton	1.50
101	Joe Morgan	.50
102	Billy Williams	1.00
103	Pee Wee Reese	1.00
104	Lou Boudreau	1.00
105	Richie Ashburn	1.00
106	Jim Bunning	1.00
107	Hal Newhouser	1.00
108	Rick Ferrell	1.00
109	Ted Williams	5.00
110	Ralph Kiner	1.00
111	Warren Spahn	2.50
112	George Kell	.50
113	Willie Stargell	2.00
114	Jim "Catfish" Hunter	.50
115	Tom Seaver	1.00
116	Cal Ripken Jr.	8.00
117	Al Lopez	.50
118	Ernie Banks	3.00
119	Lou Brock	3.00
120	Robin Yount	3.00
121	Nolan Ryan	6.00
122	Larry Doby	1.00
123	Al Kaline	2.00
124	Willie McCovey	1.00
125	Stan Musial	3.00
126	Phil Niekro	1.00
127	Babe Ruth	6.00
128	Rollie Fingers	1.00
129	Juan Marichal	1.00
130	Early Wynn	1.00
131	Luis Aparicio	1.00
132	Brooks Robinson	3.00
133	Mike Schmidt	3.00
134	Gaylord Perry	1.00
135	Bob Lemon	1.00
136	Monte Irvin	1.00
137	Mickey Mantle	8.00
138	Phil Rizzuto	1.50
139	Robin Roberts	1.50
140	Bobby Doerr	1.50
141	Bob Gibson	2.00
142	Enos Slaughter	1.00
143	Yogi Berra	3.00
144	Whitey Ford	2.00
145	Red Schoendienst	1.00
146	Joe DiMaggio	5.00
147	Harmon Killebrew	2.00
148	Hoyt Wilhelm	1.00
149	Fergie Jenkins	1.00
150	Bob Feller	1.50
151	Scott Proctor	.50
152	Adam LaRoche	.50
153	Ryan Howard	1.00
154	Laynce Nix	.50
155	Garrett Atkins	.50
156	Chris Burke	.50
157	Oliver Perez	.50
158	Wily Mo Pena	.50
159	B.J. Upton	.50
160	Gavin Floyd	.50
161	Jesse Crain	.50
162	Khalil Greene	3.00
163	Eddy Rodriguez	.50
164	Edwin Jackson	.50
165	Scott Kazmir	.50
166	Ryan Wagner	.50
167	Nick Swisher	.50
168	Joe Blanton	.50
169	Alexis Rios	.50
170	Chad Cordero	.50
171	Jason Dubois	.50
172	Chase Utley	1.00
173	David DeJesus	.50
174	Zack Greinke	.50
175	Bobby Crosby	1.00
176	Angel Guzman	.50
177	Adrian Gonzalez	.50
178	Guillermo Quiroz	.50
179	Gerald Laird	.50
180	Rickie Weeks	1.00
181	Jayson Werth	.50
182	Buck Jacobsen	.50
183	J.D. Closser	.50
184	Jason Bay	.50
185	Roman Colon	.50
186	Casey Kotchman	.50
187	Yhency Brazoban	.50
188	Bobby Madritsch	.50
189	Gabe Gross	.50
190	Brandon Claussen	.50
191	Aaron Rowand	.50
192	Jeff Francis	.50
193	David Wright	2.00
194	Jose Capellan	.50
195	Jason Lane	.50
196	Daniel Cabrera	.50
197	Joe Mauer	1.00
198	Kevin Youkilis	.50
199	Dallas McPherson	.50
200	Robb Quinlan	.50

Origins Old Judge Autographs

NM/M
Common Auto.: 12.00
Bronze: No Pricing

JB	Jason Bay	15.00
AB	Adrian Beltre	12.00
MC	Miguel Cabrera	25.00
CC	Carl Crawford/Exch	12.00
BC	Bobby Crosby/Exch	15.00
BD	Bobby Doerr	15.00
BF	Bob Feller	25.00
MG	Marcus Giles/Exch	15.00
DG	Dwight Gooden	15.00
GR	Khalil Greene	20.00
KG	Ken Griffey Jr.	75.00
RG	Ron Guidry	15.00
TG	Tony Gwynn	50.00
TH	Travis Hafner	15.00
RH	Rich Harden	15.00
KH	Keith Hernandez	15.00
FH	Frank Howard	20.00
HO	Ryan Howard	75.00
AH	Aubrey Huff	8.00
DJ	Derek Jeter	150.00
SK	Scott Kazmir	20.00
DK	Dave Kingman	15.00
CK	Casey Kotchman	15.00
SL	Sparky Lyle	12.00
VM	Victor Martinez	15.00
MA	Don Mattingly	65.00
DM	Dallas McPherson	12.00
PM	Paul Molitor	40.00
OS	Roy Oswalt	15.00
AO	Akinori Otsuka	15.00
JP	Jim Palmer	15.00
PE	Jake Peavy	25.00
OP	Oliver Perez	15.00
CR	Cal Ripken Jr./25	180.00
BR	Brooks Robinson	30.00
RO	Al Rosen	15.00
JS	Johan Santana/Exch	35.00
RS	Ron Santo	25.00
MS	Mike Schmidt	15.00
BS	Ben Sheets	12.00
ST	Shingo Takatsu	15.00
MT	Mark Teixeira	15.00
BU	B.J. Upton	15.00
CU	Chase Utley	25.00
RW	Rickie Weeks	15.00
DW	David Wright	60.00
RY	Robin Yount	50.00
CZ	Carlos Zambrano	20.00

Origins Old Judge Materials Jersey

NM/M
Common Jersey: 5.00

JB	Jeff Bagwell	8.00
CB	Carlos Beltran	8.00
AB	Adrian Beltre	5.00
LB	Lance Berkman	5.00
HB	Hank Blalock	5.00
MC	Miguel Cabrera	8.00
EC	Eric Chavez	5.00
JD	J.D. Drew	5.00
GL	Troy Glaus	5.00
KG	Ken Griffey Jr.	10.00
VG	Vladimir Guerrero	8.00
TG	Tony Gwynn/SP	10.00
HE	Todd Helton	5.00
TH	Tim Hudson	5.00
HU	Torii Hunter	5.00
DJ	Derek Jeter	15.00
RJ	Randy Johnson	8.00
AJ	Andruw Jones	5.00
CJ	Chipper Jones	8.00
GM	Greg Maddux	10.00
HM	Hideki Matsui	15.00
KM	Kazuo Matsui	5.00
DO	David Ortiz	8.00
PI	Mike Piazza	8.00
MP	Mark Prior	8.00
AP	Albert Pujols	15.00
MR	Manny Ramirez	8.00
CR	Cal Ripken Jr./SP	25.00
SR	Scott Rolen	8.00
NR	Nolan Ryan/SP	30.00
CS	Curt Schilling	8.00
BS	Ben Sheets	5.00
GS	Gary Sheffield	5.00
AS	Alfonso Soriano	8.00
SS	Sammy Sosa	8.00
IS	Ichiro Suzuki	20.00
MT	Mark Teixeira	5.00
TE	Miguel Tejada	8.00
FT	Frank Thomas	8.00
JT	Jim Thome	8.00
KW	Kerry Wood	8.00

Origins Signatures

NM/M
Common Auto.: 12.00
Bronze: No Pricing
Production 5 Sets

JB1	Jason Bay	15.00
AB1	Adrian Beltre	12.00
MC1	Miguel Cabrera	25.00
CC1	Carl Crawford/Exch	12.00
BC1	Bobby Crosby/Exch	15.00
BD1	Bobby Doerr	15.00
BF1	Bob Feller	25.00
MG1	Marcus Giles	15.00
DG1	Dwight Gooden	15.00
GR1	Khalil Greene	20.00
KG1	Ken Griffey Jr.	75.00
RG1	Ron Guidry	15.00
TG1	Tony Gwynn	50.00
TH1	Travis Hafner	15.00
RH1	Rich Harden	15.00
KH1	Keith Hernandez	15.00
FH1	Frank Howard	20.00
HO1	Ryan Howard	75.00
AH1	Aubrey Huff	8.00
DJ1	Derek Jeter	150.00
SK1	Scott Kazmir	20.00
DK1	Dave Kingman	15.00
CK1	Casey Kotchman	15.00
SL1	Sparky Lyle	12.00
VM1	Victor Martinez	15.00
MA1	Don Mattingly	65.00
DM1	Dallas McPherson	12.00
PM1	Paul Molitor	40.00
OS1	Roy Oswalt	15.00
AO1	Akinori Otsuka	15.00
JP1	Jim Palmer	15.00
PE1	Jake Peavy	25.00
OP1	Oliver Perez	15.00
CR1	Cal Ripken Jr./25	180.00
BR1	Brooks Robinson	30.00
RO1	Al Rosen	15.00
JS1	Johan Santana/Exch	35.00
RS1	Ron Santo	25.00
MS1	Mike Schmidt	75.00
BS1	Ben Sheets	12.00
ST1	Shingo Takatsu	15.00
MT1	Mark Teixeira	25.00
BU1	B.J. Upton	15.00
CU1	Chase Utley	25.00
RW1	Rickie Weeks	15.00
DW1	David Wright	60.00
RY1	Robin Yount	50.00
CZ1	Carlos Zambrano	20.00

Origins Tins

NM/M
Common Tin: 5.00

TC	Ty Cobb	5.00
DJ	Derek Jeter	10.00
WJ	Walter Johnson	5.00
HW	Honus Wagner	5.00

2005 UD Past Time Pennants

NM/M
Complete Set (90): 20.00
Common Player: .20
Pack (5): 4.00
Box (20): 70.00

1	Al Kaline	.50
2	Al Rosen	.20
3	Bert Blyleven	.20
4	Bill Mazeroski	.20
5	Billy Williams	.20
6	Bob Feller	.50
7	Bob Gibson	.75
8	Bob Lemon	.20
9	Bobby Doerr	.40
10	Brooks Robinson	.40
11	Bruce Sutter	.30
12	Bucky Dent	.20
13	Cal Ripken Jr.	2.00
14	Carl Yastrzemski	.75
15	Carlton Fisk	.40
16	Jim "Catfish" Hunter	.20
17	Dale Murphy	.40
18	Dave Parker	.20
19	Don Larsen	.20
20	Don Mattingly	1.00
21	Don Newcombe	.20
22	Duke Snider	.50
23	Early Wynn	.20
24	Eddie Mathews	.50
25	Eddie Murray	.50
26	Enos Slaughter	.20
27	Ernie Banks	.75
28	Fergie Jenkins	.20
29	Frank Howard	.20
30	Frank Robinson	.50
31	Fred Lynn	.20
32	Gary Carter	.20
33	Gaylord Perry	.20
34	George Brett	1.50
35	George Kell	.20
36	Rich "Goose" Gossage	.20
37	Graig Nettles	.20
38	Harmon Killebrew	.75
39	Jack Morris	.20
40	Jim Bunning	.20
41	Felipe Alou	.20
42	Jim Palmer	.40
43	Jim Rice	.20
44	Joe DiMaggio	1.50
45	Joe Morgan	.20
46	Johnny Bench	.75
47	Johnny Podres	.20
48	Juan Marichal	.20
49	Keith Hernandez	.20
50	Kirby Puckett	.75
51	Larry Doby	.20
52	Lou Brock	.40
53	Luis Aparicio	.20
54	Luis Tiant	.20
55	Maury 4illis	.20
56	Mickey Mantle	2.00
57	Mike Schmidt	1.50
58	Monte Irvin	.20
59	Nolan Ryan	1.50
60	Orlando Cepeda	.20
61	Ozzie Smith	.50
62	Paul Molitor	.50
63	Pee Wee Reese	.20
64	Phil Niekro	.20
65	Phil Rizzuto	.50
66	Ralph Kiner	.20
67	Richie Ashburn	.20
68	Rico Petrocelli	.20
69	Robin Roberts	.20
70	Robin Yount	.75
71	Rocky Colavito	.20
72	Rod Carew	.40
73	Rollie Fingers	.20
74	Ron Guidry	.20
75	Ron Santo	.20
76	Tony Gwynn	.75
77	Sparky Lyle	.20
78	Stan Musial	1.00
79	Steve Carlton	.40
80	Rick Ferrell	.20
81	Tom Seaver	.75
82	Tommy John	.20
83	Tony Perez	.20
84	Wade Boggs	.50
85	Warren Spahn	.40
86	Whitey Ford	.40
87	Will Clark	.50
88	Willie McCovey	.50
89	Willie Stargell	.40
90	Yogi Berra	.75

Silver
Gold: 3-5X
Production 100 Sets

Gold
Gold: 4-8X
Production 50 Sets

Mitchell & Ness Jersey Redem
Total Production
Per Player 36-37

Mitchell & Ness Pennants

NM/M
Common Pennant: 15.00
Inserted 1:Hobby Box

1903	1903 Boston Americans/100	20.00
1905	1095 New York Giants/100	20.00
1906	1906 Chicago White Sox/100	20.00
1907	1907 Detroit Tigers/100	20.00
1908	1908 Chicago Cubs/105	25.00
1909	1909 Pittsburgh Pirates/125	20.00
1910	1910 Philadelphia A's/125	20.00
1912	1912 Boston Red Sox/125	20.00
1914	1914 Boston Braves/125	20.00
1915	1915 Phileldphia Phillies/125	20.00
1916	1916 Brooklyn Robins/200	20.00
1917	1917 New York Giants/200	20.00
1918	1918 Boston Red Sox/200	20.00
1919	1919 Chicago White Sox/200	20.00
1920	1920 Cleveland Indians/200	15.00
1921	1921 New York Yankees/200	25.00
1922	1922 New York Giants/200	20.00
1924	1924 Washington Senators/200	20.00
1925	1925 Pittsburgh Pirates/200	15.00
1926	1926 Saint Louis Cardinals/200	20.00
1927	1927 New York Yankees/500	25.00
1928	1928 New York Yankees/500	25.00
1929	1929 Chicago Cubs/337	20.00
1930	1930 Philadelphia A's/337	15.00
1931	1931 Saint Louis Cardinals/337	20.00
1932	1932 Chicago Cubs/337	20.00
1934	1934 Detroit Tigers/337	15.00
1935	1935 Chicago Cubs/337	20.00
1936	1936 New York Yankees/337	25.00
1937	1937 New York Giants/337	20.00
1938	1938 New York Yankees/337	25.00
1939	1939 Cincinnati Reds/337	15.00
1940	1940 Cincinnati Reds/337	15.00
1941	1941 Brooklyn Dodgers/337	25.00
1942	1942 Saint Louis Cardinals/337	20.00
1943	1943 New York Yankees/500	25.00
1944	1944 Saint Louis Browns/337	20.00
1945	1945 Chicago Cubs/337	20.00
1946	1946 Boston Red Sox/337	20.00
1947	1947 Brooklyn Dodgers/337	25.00
1948	1948 Boston Braves/337	15.00
1949	1949 New York Yankees/337	25.00
1950	1950 Philadelphia Phillies/337	15.00
1951	1951 New York Giants/337	15.00
1952	1952 Brooklyn Dodgers/500	20.00
1953	1953 New York Yankees/337	25.00
1954	1954 Cleveland Indians/337	15.00
1955	1955 Brooklyn Dodgers/337	25.00

Year	Team	Price
1956	1956 Brooklyn Dodgers/500	25.00
1957	1957 Milwaukee Braves/337	20.00
1958	1958 New York Yankees/500	25.00
1959	1959 Los Angeles Dodgers/337	20.00
1960	1960 Pittsburgh Pirates/337	15.00
1961	1961 Cincinnati Reds/337	15.00
1962	1962 San Francisco Giants/337	20.00
1963	1963 Los Angeles Dodgers/337	20.00
1964	1964 Saint Louis Cardinals/337	20.00
1965	1965 Minnesota Twins/337	15.00
1966	1966 Baltimore Orioles/337	20.00
1967	1967 Boston Red Sox/337	20.00
1968	1968 Detroit Tigers/337	15.00
1969	1969 New York Mets/337	20.00
1970	1970 Baltimore Orioles/337	20.00
1971	1971 Pittsburgh Pirates/337	15.00
1972	1972 Oakland A's/337	20.00
1973	1973 Oakland A's/337	20.00
1974	1974 Los Angeles Dodgers/337	20.00
1977	1977 New York Yankees/337	25.00
1978	1978 Los Angeles Dodgers/337	20.00
1979	1979 Pittsburgh Pirates/337	15.00
1980	1980 Philadelphia Phillies/337	20.00
1981	1981 Los Angeles Dodgers/337	20.00
1982	1982 Milwaukee Brewers/337	20.00
1983	1983 Baltimore Orioles/337	20.00
1984	1984 San Diego Padres/337	15.00
1985	1985 Kansas City Royals/337	15.00
1986	1986 Boston Red Sox/337	25.00
1988	1988 Los Angeles Dodgers/337	20.00
1975B	1975 Boston Red Sox/337	25.00
1975C	1975 Cincinnati Reds/337	20.00

Mitchell & Ness Penn Autograph
NM/M

Production 86-87

JB	Johnny Bench/87	80.00
SC	Steve Carlton/87	60.00
RF	Rollie Fingers/87	40.00
CF	Carlton Fisk/87	60.00
SG	Steve Garvey/40	40.00
AK	Al Kaline/87	75.00
PM	Paul Molitor/87	75.00
GN	Graig Nettles/87	50.00
DN	Don Newcombe/87	40.00
BR	Brooks Robinson/87	75.00
TS	Tom Seaver/87	80.00
CY	Carl Yastrzemski/86	80.00

Signatures Bronze
NM/M

SP's Production 3-25

FA	Felipe Alou	15.00
RB	Rick Burleson	10.00
DC	David Cone	15.00
LD	Lenny Dykstra	12.00
SF	Sid Fernandez	10.00
BF	Bill Freehan	10.00
DG	Dwight Gooden	15.00
KG	Ken Griffey Sr.	10.00
GU	Don Gullett	8.00
PG	Pedro Guerrero	10.00
HO	Ken Holtzman	10.00
BH	Burt Hooton	10.00
WH	Willie Horton/Exch	12.00
FH	Frank Howard	15.00
HR	Kent Hrbek	15.00
RH	Randy Hundley	10.00
TJ	Tommy John	15.00
WJ	Wally Joyner	15.00
DK	Dave Kingman	10.00
KN	Ray Knight	10.00
SL	Sparky Lyle	15.00
BM	Bill Madlock	10.00
BO	Bobby Murcer	15.00
RP	Rico Petrocelli	12.00
BP	Boog Powell	25.00
AR	Al Rosen	15.00
SS	Steve Sax	10.00
SC	Mike Scioscia/Exch	15.00
WI	Mookie Wilson	15.00

Signatures Silver
NM/M

FA	Felipe Alou	10.00
LA	Luis Aparicio	20.00
BB	Bert Blyleven	15.00
BR	Lou Brock	30.00
JB	Jim Bunning/Exch	15.00
RB	Rick Burleson	10.00
ST	Steve Carlton	35.00
GC	Gary Carter	20.00
OC	Orlando Cepeda	20.00
CC	Chris Chambliss	15.00
WC	Will Clark	40.00
RC	Rocky Colavito	65.00
DC	David Cone	15.00
DE	Bucky Dent	12.00
BD	Bobby Doerr	15.00
LD	Lenny Dykstra	15.00
CE	Carl Erskine/Exch	12.00
EV	Dwight Evans	30.00
FE	Bob Feller	30.00
SF	Sid Fernandez	10.00
RF	Rollie Fingers	20.00
BF	Bill Freehan	10.00
DG	Dwight Gooden	15.00
GG	Rich "Goose" Gossage	15.00
KG	Ken Griffey Sr.	15.00
GU	Don Gullett	8.00
PG	Pedro Guerrero	10.00
KH	Keith Hernandez	15.00
HO	Ken Holtzman	10.00
BH	Burt Hooton	10.00
WH	Willie Horton/Exch	10.00
FH	Frank Howard	15.00
HR	Kent Hrbek	15.00
RH	Randy Hundley	10.00
MI	Monte Irvin	25.00
FJ	Fergie Jenkins	20.00
TJ	Tommy Jones	15.00
WJ	Wally Joyner	15.00
AK	Al Kaline	50.00
GK	George Kell	15.00
HK	Harmon Killebrew	50.00
RK	Ralph Kiner	40.00
DK	Dave Kingman	10.00
KN	Ray Knight	10.00
DL	Don Larsen/Exch	30.00
SL	Sparky Lyle	15.00
FL	Fred Lynn	15.00
BM	Bill Madlock	10.00
JU	Juan Marichal/Exch	30.00
MA	Bill Mazeroski	30.00
PM	Paul Molitor	40.00
MO	Joe Morgan	20.00
JM	Jack Morris	20.00
BO	Bobby Murcer	20.00
MU	Dale Murphy	25.00
GN	Graig Nettles	15.00
DN	Don Newcombe	15.00
JP	Jim Palmer	30.00
DP	Dave Parker	15.00
TP	Tony Perez/Exch	40.00
GP	Gaylord Perry	15.00
RP	Rico Petrocelli	15.00
PO	Johnny Podres	25.00
BP	Boog Powell	20.00
JR	Jim Rice	25.00
RO	Brooks Robinson	60.00
AR	Al Rosen	15.00
RS	Ron Santo	25.00
SS	Steve Sax	10.00
SC	Mike Scioscia/Exch	20.00
BS	Bill "Moose" Skowron	15.00
SU	Bruce Sutter	15.00
LT	Luis Tiant	15.00
BW	Billy Williams/Exch	15.00
MW	Maury Wills	15.00

Signatures Gold
NM/M

Many not priced due to scarcity.

FA	Felipe Alou	20.00
RB	Rick Burleson	15.00
LD	Lenny Dykstra	20.00
SF	Sid Fernandez	15.00
BF	Bill Freehan	15.00
KG	Ken Griffey Sr.	15.00
PG	Pedro Guerrero	15.00
GU	Don Gullett	10.00
HO	Ken Holtzman	15.00
BH	Burt Hooton	15.00
WH	Willie Horton/Exch	15.00
HR	Kent Hrbek	20.00
RH	Randy Hundley	10.00
DK	Dave Kingman	15.00
KN	Ray Knight	15.00
SL	Sparky Lyle	15.00
BM	Bill Madlock	15.00
BO	Bobby Murcer	15.00
RP	Rico Petrocelli	15.00

Signatures Dual
Production 15-24

2005 Upper Deck Portraits
NM/M

Complete Set (100):		25.00
Common Player:		.25
Box (7 Cards + 8x10):		100.00
1	Dallas McPherson	.25
2	Steve Finley	.25
3	Vladimir Guerrero	.75
4	Troy Glaus	.25
5	Andruw Jones	.50
6	Chipper Jones	.75
7	John Smoltz	.50
8	Marcus Giles	.25
9	Tim Hudson	.50
10	Cal Ripken Jr.	3.00
11	Miguel Tejada	.50
12	Curt Schilling	.75
13	David Ortiz	.75
14	Edgar Renteria	.25
15	Jason Varitek	.50
16	Jim Rice	.50
17	Johnny Damon	.75
18	Matt Clement	.25
19	Wade Boggs	.75
20	Aramis Ramirez	.50
21	Carlos Zambrano	.50
22	Corey Patterson	.25
23	Fergie Jenkins	.25
24	Greg Maddux	1.50
25	Kerry Wood	.50
26	Mark Prior	.75
27	Nomar Garciaparra	.75
28	Ryne Sandberg	1.50
29	Frank Thomas	.50
30	Adam Dunn	.50
31	Barry Larkin	.50
32	Ken Griffey Jr.	1.50
33	Sean Casey	.25
34	Travis Hafner	.25
35	Victor Martinez	.25
36	Todd Helton	.50
37	Ivan Rodriguez	.50
38	Magglio Ordonez	.25
39	Josh Beckett	.25
40	Miguel Cabrera	.75
41	Mike Lowell	.25
42	Craig Biggio	.50
43	Jeff Bagwell	.50
44	Roger Clemens	2.00
45	Roy Oswalt	.25
46	Bo Jackson	.50
47	Prince Fielder	5.00
48	Eric Gagne	.25
49	J.D. Drew	.25
50	Ben Sheets	.50
51	Robin Yount	.75
52	Jacque Jones	.25
53	Joe Mauer	.50
54	Johan Santana	.75
55	Justin Morneau	.25
56	Torii Hunter	.25
57	Dontrelle Willis	.50
58	David Wright	1.00
59	Gary Carter	.25
60	Jose Reyes	.40
61	Keith Hernandez	.25
62	Mike Piazza	1.00
63	Pedro Martinez	.75
64	Tom Glavine	.50
65	Carl Pavano	.25
66	Derek Jeter	2.00
67	Don Mattingly	1.00
68	Mike Mussina	.50
69	Randy Johnson	.75
70	Bobby Crosby	.25
71	Eric Chavez	.25
72	Rich Harden	.25
73	Bobby Abreu	.50
74	Mike Schmidt	1.00
75	Jason Bay	.25
76	Oliver Perez	.25
77	Brian Giles	.25
78	Jake Peavy	.25
79	Khalil Greene	.25
80	Tony Gwynn	.75
81	Jason Schmidt	.25
82	Will Clark	.50
83	Adrian Beltre	.25
84	Justin Verlander	2.00
85	Albert Pujols	2.00
86	Jim Edmonds	.50
87	Mark Mulder	.25
88	Scott Rolen	.75
89	Aubrey Huff	.25
90	B.J. Upton	.25
91	Carl Crawford	.25
92	Tadahito Iguchi	4.00
93	Scott Kazmir	.25
94	Alfonso Soriano	.75
95	Hank Blalock	.25
96	Mark Teixeira	.50
97	Michael Young	.25
98	Nolan Ryan	2.00
99	Roy Halladay	.50
100	Jose Vidro	.25

Emerald Jersey
NM/M

Common Player:		4.00
Production 99 Sets		
Blue:		1-1.5X
Production 25 Sets		
Gold:		1-2X
Production 15 Sets		
1	Dallas McPherson	4.00
2	Steve Finley	4.00
3	Vladimir Guerrero	8.00
4	Troy Glaus	4.00
5	Andruw Jones	6.00
6	Chipper Jones	8.00
7	John Smoltz	6.00
8	Marcus Giles	4.00
9	Tim Hudson	6.00
10	Cal Ripken Jr.	25.00
11	Miguel Tejada	6.00
12	Curt Schilling	8.00
13	David Ortiz	8.00
14	Edgar Renteria	4.00
15	Jason Varitek	8.00
16	Jim Rice	8.00
17	Johnny Damon	8.00
18	Matt Clement	4.00
19	Wade Boggs	8.00
20	Aramis Ramirez	6.00
21	Carlos Zambrano	6.00
22	Corey Patterson	4.00
23	Fergie Jenkins	6.00
24	Greg Maddux	10.00
25	Kerry Wood	6.00
26	Mark Prior	8.00
27	Nomar Garciaparra	8.00
28	Ryne Sandberg	12.00
29	Frank Thomas	6.00
30	Adam Dunn	6.00
31	Barry Larkin	6.00
32	Ken Griffey Jr.	15.00
33	Sean Casey	4.00
34	Travis Hafner	4.00
35	Victor Martinez	4.00
36	Todd Helton	6.00
37	Ivan Rodriguez	6.00
38	Magglio Ordonez	4.00
39	Josh Beckett	4.00
40	Miguel Cabrera	8.00
41	Mike Lowell	4.00
42	Craig Biggio	6.00
43	Jeff Bagwell	8.00
44	Roger Clemens	15.00
45	Roy Oswalt	4.00
46	Bo Jackson	10.00
47	Eric Gagne	6.00
48	J.D. Drew	4.00
49	Ben Sheets	4.00
50	Robin Yount	15.00
51	Jacque Jones	4.00
52	Joe Mauer	6.00
53	Johan Santana	6.00
54	Justin Morneau	4.00
55	Torii Hunter	4.00
56	Dontrelle Willis	6.00
57	David Wright	10.00
58	Gary Carter	6.00
59	Jose Reyes	6.00
60	Keith Hernandez	6.00
61	Mike Piazza	8.00
62	Pedro Martinez	6.00
63	Tom Glavine	6.00
64	Carl Pavano	4.00
65	Derek Jeter	15.00
66	Don Mattingly	15.00
67	Mike Mussina	6.00
68	Randy Johnson	8.00
69	Bobby Crosby	4.00
70	Eric Chavez	4.00
71	Rich Harden	4.00
72	Bobby Abreu	6.00
73	Mike Schmidt	10.00
74	Jason Bay	4.00
75	Oliver Perez	4.00
76	Brian Giles	4.00
77	Jake Peavy	4.00
78	Khalil Greene	4.00
79	Tony Gwynn	8.00
80	Jason Schmidt	4.00
81	Will Clark	8.00
82	Adrian Beltre	4.00
83	Albert Pujols	15.00
84	Jim Edmonds	6.00
85	Mark Mulder	6.00
86	Scott Rolen	6.00
87	Aubrey Huff	4.00
88	B.J. Upton	4.00
89	Carl Crawford	4.00
90	Tadahito Iguchi	15.00
91	Scott Kazmir	4.00
92	Alfonso Soriano	6.00
93	Hank Blalock	4.00
94	Mark Teixeira	6.00
95	Michael Young	4.00
96	Nolan Ryan	15.00
97	Roy Halladay	6.00

Jersey Autograph Platinum
No Pricing
Production 10 Sets

Scrapbook Materials
NM/M

Complete Set (59):

Common Player:		4.00
BA	Bobby Abreu	4.00
JB	Jeff Bagwell	6.00
BE	Josh Beckett	4.00
AB	Adrian Beltre	4.00
BI	Craig Biggio	6.00
CA	Miguel Cabrera	8.00
WC	Will Clark	6.00
CL	Matt Clement	4.00
BC	Bobby Crosby	4.00
JE	Jim Edmonds	6.00
SF	Steve Finley	4.00
BG	Brian Giles	4.00
GR	Khalil Greene	4.00
KG	Ken Griffey Jr.	15.00
TG	Tony Gwynn	8.00
RH	Roy Halladay	6.00
TH	Todd Helton	6.00
KH	Keith Hernandez	4.00
HU	Torii Hunter	4.00
BJ	Bo Jackson	10.00
DJ	Derek Jeter	20.00
AJ	Andruw Jones	4.00
CJ	Chipper Jones	8.00
JJ	Jacque Jones	4.00
SK	Scott Kazmir	4.00
BL	Barry Larkin	6.00
ML	Mike Lowell	4.00
VM	Victor Martinez	4.00
MA	Don Mattingly	15.00
JM	Joe Mauer	6.00
MC	Dallas McPherson	4.00
MO	Justin Morneau	4.00
DM	Dale Murphy	4.00
MM	Mike Mussina	6.00
OR	Magglio Ordonez	4.00
DO	David Ortiz	4.00
PA	Corey Patterson	4.00
CP	Carl Pavano	4.00
JP	Jake Peavy	6.00
OP	Oliver Perez	4.00
MP	Mark Prior	6.00
AP	Albert Pujols	15.00
JR	Jim Rice	6.00
CR	Cal Ripken Jr.	20.00
NR	Nolan Ryan	15.00
RS	Ryne Sandberg	10.00
SA	Johan Santana	6.00
JS	Jason Schmidt	4.00
MS	Mike Schmidt	10.00
SM	John Smoltz	6.00
MT	Mark Teixeira	6.00
FT	Frank Thomas	6.00
BU	B.J. Upton	4.00
JV	Jose Vidro	4.00
WI	Dontrelle Willis	6.00
DW	David Wright	10.00
CZ	Carlos Zambrano	6.00

BG	Brian Giles	1.00
GR	Khalil Greene	1.50
KG	Ken Griffey Jr.	4.00
TG	Tony Gwynn	2.00
RH	Roy Halladay	1.00
TH	Todd Helton	1.50
KH	Keith Hernandez	1.00
HU	Torii Hunter	1.00
BJ	Bo Jackson	2.00
DJ	Derek Jeter	6.00
AJ	Andruw Jones	1.50
CJ	Chipper Jones	2.00
JJ	Jacque Jones	1.00
SK	Scott Kazmir	1.00
BL	Barry Larkin	1.50
ML	Mike Lowell	1.00
VM	Victor Martinez	1.00
MA	Don Mattingly	4.00
JM	Joe Mauer	1.50
MC	Dallas McPherson	1.00
MO	Justin Morneau	1.00
DM	Dale Murphy	1.50
MM	Mike Mussina	2.00
OR	Magglio Ordonez	1.00
DO	David Ortiz	2.00
PA	Corey Patterson	1.00
CP	Carl Pavano	1.00
JP	Jake Peavy	1.50
OP	Oliver Perez	1.00
MP	Mark Prior	2.00
AP	Albert Pujols	6.00
JR	Jim Rice	1.50
CR	Cal Ripken Jr.	8.00
NR	Nolan Ryan	6.00
RS	Ryne Sandberg	4.00
SA	Johan Santana	2.00
JS	Jason Schmidt	1.00
MS	Mike Schmidt	4.00
SM	John Smoltz	1.50
MT	Mark Teixeira	1.50
FT	Frank Thomas	1.50
BU	B.J. Upton	1.00
VE	Justin Verlander	2.00
JV	Jose Vidro	1.00
WI	Dontrelle Willis	1.50
DW	David Wright	3.00
CZ	Carlos Zambrano	1.50

Scrapbook Signatures
No Pricing
Production 20 Sets

Signature Portraits 8x10
NM/M

Common Player:		
DB	Dusty Baker/100	25.00
JB	Jason Bay	25.00
HB	Hank Blalock	25.00
WB	Wade Boggs/40	50.00
CA	Miguel Cabrera	40.00
JD	Johnny Damon/99	50.00
GR	Khalil Greene	35.00
VG	Vladimir Guerrero/40	75.00
KH	Keith Hernandez	20.00
DJ	Derek Jeter/150	200.00
SK	Scott Kazmir	25.00
VM	Victor Martinez	25.00
MA	Don Mattingly	65.00
JM	Joe Mauer	30.00
DM	Dale Murphy	30.00
SM	Stan Musial/40	80.00
JN	Jeff Niemann	25.00
RO	Roy Oswalt	30.00
PI	Mike Piazza/35	125.00
MP	Mark Prior/50	40.00
CR	Cal Ripken Jr./50	160.00
BR	Brooks Robinson	50.00
NR	Nolan Ryan/25	140.00
RS	Ryne Sandberg/99	100.00
MS	Mike Schmidt	50.00
BS	Ben Sheets	25.00
OS	Ozzie Smith	50.00
DS	Duke Snider/150	60.00
MT	Mark Teixeira	35.00
BU	B.J. Upton	20.00
VE	Justin Verlander	40.00
DW	David Wright	80.00

Signature Portraits Cuts 8x10 Card
No Pricing
Production 1-25

Signature Portraits Dual 8x10
NM/M

Production 25-99

BT	Mark Teixeira, Hank Blalock/99	50.00
HS	Rich Harden, Ben Sheets/99	40.00
NV	Justin Verlander, Jeff Niemann/99	75.00
SH	Tim Hudson, John Smoltz/75	75.00
WP	Kerry Wood, Mark Prior/99	85.00
WR	David Wright, Jose Reyes/99	140.00

Scrapbook Moments

Signature Portraits Dual Cuts 8x10

No Pricing
Production 1-2

Signature Portraits Triple 8x10

No Pricing
Production 15 Sets

Signature Portraits Quad 8x10

No Pricing
Production 5 Sets

2005 Upper Deck Pros & Prospects

		NM/M
Complete Set (200):		
Common Player (1-100):		.15
Common SP (101-150):		3.00
Production 999		
Common SP (151-175):		4.00
Production 499		
Common SP (176-200):		5.00
Production 199		
Pack (6):		2.75
Box (24):		60.00
1	Adam Dunn	.40
2	Aramis Ramirez	.40
3	Bobby Abreu	.25
4	Mike Lowell	.15
5	Josh Beckett	.25
6	Derek Jeter	1.50
7	Alex Rodriguez	1.25
8	Andruw Jones	.25
9	Brian Giles	.15
10	Ivan Rodriguez	.40
11	Aubrey Huff	.15
12	Jake Peavy	.25
13	Hank Blalock	.25
14	Curt Schilling	.50
15	Carlos Zambrano	.40
16	Mike Mussina	.40
17	Travis Hafner	.15
18	Scott Rolen	.50
19	Luis Gonzalez	.25
20	Torii Hunter	.25
21	Greg Maddux	1.00
22	J.D. Drew	.25
23	Kevin Brown	.15
24	Carl Pavano	.15
25	David Ortiz	.50
26	Jose Reyes	.40
27	Johan Santana	.50
28	Todd Helton	.25
29	Jason Kendall	.15
30	Pedro Martinez	.50
31	Chipper Jones	.50
32	Ben Sheets	.25
33	Garret Anderson	.25
34	Carl Crawford	.15
35	Jason Schmidt	.25
36	Johnny Damon	.50
37	Richie Sexson	.15
38	Brad Penny	.15
39	Carlos Delgado	.40
40	Gary Sheffield	.40
41	John Smoltz	.25
42	Eric Chavez	.25
43	Carlos Guillen	.15
44	Jeff Kent	.25
45	Miguel Tejada	.40
46	Shawn Green	.25
47	Vernon Wells	.15
48	Albert Pujols	1.50
49	Alfonso Soriano	.50
50	Eric Gagne	.25
51	Mark Prior	.50
52	Rafael Furcal	.15
53	Preston Wilson	.15
54	Barry Larkin	.25
55	Randy Johnson	.50
56	Craig Wilson	.15
57	Victor Martinez	.25
58	Jim Thome	.50
59	Paul Konerko	.15
60	Jeff Bagwell	.25
61	Lyle Overbay	.15
62	Miguel Cabrera	.50
63	Melvin Mora	.15
64	Scott Podsednik	.25
65	Mark Mulder	.25
66	Mark Teixeira	.40

67	Tom Glavine	.25
68	Frank Thomas	.40
69	Livan Hernandez	.15
70	Kazuo Matsui	.15
71	Jose Vidro	.15
72	Ichiro Suzuki	1.25
73	Roger Clemens	1.50
74	Manny Ramirez	.50
75	Michael Young	.15
76	Rafael Palmeiro	.40
77	Steve Finley	.15
78	Andy Pettitte	.25
79	Lance Berkman	.25
80	Adrian Beltre	.25
81	Carlos Lee	.25
82	Bret Boone	.15
83	Magglio Ordonez	.15
84	Sammy Sosa	1.00
85	Tim Hudson	.25
86	Vladimir Guerrero	.50
87	Carlos Beltran	.40
88	Kerry Wood	.50
89	Jim Edmonds	.25
90	Mike Sweeney	.15
91	Nomar Garciaparra	1.00
92	Mike Piazza	1.00
93	Roy Halladay	.25
94	Troy Glaus	.25
95	Bernie Williams	.25
96	Larry Walker	.25
97	Craig Biggio	.25
98	Roy Oswalt	.25
99	Ken Griffey Jr.	1.00
100	Hideki Matsui	1.00
101	Bucky Jacobsen	3.00
102	J.D. Closser	3.00
103	Antonio Perez	3.00
104	Chris Shelton	3.00
105	David Aardsma	3.00
106	Jake Woods	3.00
107	Jung Bong	3.00
108	Kazuhito Tadano	3.00
109	John Van Benschoten	3.00
110	Jesse Foppert	3.00
111	Joe Borchard	3.00
112	Brandon Phillips	3.00
113	J.D. Durbin	3.00
114	Brandon Claussen	3.00
115	Robb Quinlan	3.00
116	Aaron Harang	3.00
117	Chris Burke	3.00
118	Sergio Mitre	3.00
119	David DeJesus	3.00
120	Gustavo Chacin	3.00
121	Xavier Nady	3.00
122	Garrett Atkins	3.00
123	Jimmy Gobble	3.00
124	Yhency Brazoban	3.00
125	David Kelton	3.00
126	Dewon Brazelton	3.00
127	Koyie Hill	3.00
128	Roman Colon	3.00
129	Daniel Cabrera	3.00
130	Chris Bootcheck	3.00
131	Brad Halsey	3.00
132	Bobby Madritsch	3.00
133	Grady Sizemore	3.00
134	Akinori Otsuka	3.00
135	Wilfredo Ledezma	3.00
136	Russ Adams	3.00
137	Joe Crede	3.00
138	Chad Cordero	3.00
139	Willie Harris	3.00
140	Joey Gathright	3.00
141	Logan Kensing	3.00
142	Jon Leicester	3.00
143	Freddy Guzman	3.00
144	Jonny Gomes	3.00
145	Jeff Bajenaru	3.00
146	Andres Blanco	3.00
147	Jhonny Peralta	3.00
148	Jayson Werth	3.00
149	Bill Hall	3.00
150	Jason Davis	3.00
151	Gabe Gross	4.00
152	Abe Alvarez	4.00
153	Josh Willingham	4.00
154	Merkin Valdez	4.00
155	Jeff Niemann **RC**	8.00
156	Yadier Molina	4.00
157	Guillermo Quiroz	4.00
158	Ian Snell	4.00
159	Dan Meyer	4.00
160	Jason Lane	4.00
161	Adrian Gonzalez	4.00
162	Eddy Rodriguez	4.00
163	Jason Dubois	4.00
164	Juan Rincon	4.00
165	Ryan Wagner	4.00
166	Nick Swisher	4.00
167	Chad Tracy	4.00
168	Dioner Navarro	4.00
169	Gerald Laird	4.00
170	Alexis Rios	4.00
171	Aaron Rowand	4.00
172	Adam LaRoche	4.00
173	Kevin Youkilis	4.00
174	Philip Humber **RC**	6.00
175	Chin-Hui Tsao	4.00
176	Jeff Francis	5.00
177	Chase Utley	5.00
178	Gavin Floyd	5.00
179	David Wright	10.00
180	B.J. Upton	5.00
181	Laynce Nix	5.00
182	Joe Mauer	8.00
183	Justin Morneau	5.00
184	Zack Greinke	5.00

185	Jose Capellan	5.00
186	Khalil Greene	5.00
187	Oliver Perez	5.00
188	Joe Blanton	5.00
189	Wily Mo Pena	5.00
190	Dallas McPherson	6.00
191	Edwin Jackson	5.00
192	Casey Kotchman	5.00
193	Jesse Crain	5.00
194	Ryan Howard	6.00
195	Bobby Crosby	5.00
196	Jason Bay	5.00
197	Rickie Weeks	5.00
198	Scott Proctor	5.00
199	Dan Haren	5.00
200	Scott Kazmir	5.00

Gold

Gold (1-100):		4-8X
Production 125		
Gold (101-150):		1X
Production 150		
Gold (151-175):		1X
Production 99		
Gold (176-200):		No Pricing
Production 25		

Future Fabrics

		NM/M
Common Player:		4.00
Gold:		1-2X
Production 75 Sets		
MC	Miguel Cabrera	8.00
BC	Bobby Crosby	6.00
KG	Khalil Greene	6.00
RH	Rich Harden	4.00
EH	Eric Hinske	4.00
JJ	Jacque Jones	4.00
KE	Austin Kearns	4.00
AK	Adam Kennedy	4.00
CK	Casey Kotchman	4.00
VM	Victor Martinez	4.00
KM	Kazuo Matsui	4.00
JM	Joe Mauer	8.00
DM	Dallas McPherson	6.00
TN	Trot Nixon	4.00
SP	Sidney Ponson	4.00
JR	Jose Reyes	4.00
CS	C.C. Sabathia	4.00
SS	Shannon Stewart	4.00
BU	B.J. Upton	4.00
JW	Jayson Werth	4.00
DW	David Wright	15.00

Pro Material

		NM/M
Common Player:		6.00
Gold:		1-2X
Production 50 Sets		
JB	Jeff Bagwell	6.00
CB	Carlos Beltran	8.00
AB	Adrian Beltre	6.00
HB	Hank Blalock	6.00
EC	Eric Chavez	6.00
KG	Ken Griffey Jr.	10.00
VG	Vladimir Guerrero	8.00
TH	Todd Helton	8.00
DJ	Derek Jeter	20.00
RJ	Randy Johnson	8.00
CJ	Chipper Jones	8.00
PI	Mike Piazza	8.00
MP	Mark Prior	8.00
AP	Albert Pujols	15.00
MR	Manny Ramirez	8.00
SR	Scott Rolen	8.00
CS	Curt Schilling	8.00
SS	Sammy Sosa	8.00
IS	Ichiro Suzuki	25.00
MT	Miguel Tejada	8.00
JT	Jim Thome	8.00

Signs of Stardom

		NM/M
Common Autograph:		8.00
RB	Rocco Baldelli	8.00
JB	Josh Beckett	15.00
AB	Angel Berroa	8.00
HB	Hank Blalock	20.00
SB	Sean Burroughs	8.00
MC	Miguel Cabrera	30.00
CC	Chad Cordero	8.00
BC	Bobby Crosby	8.00
AE	Adam Eaton	12.00
FF	Frank Francisco	8.00
JF	Jason Frasor	8.00

GA	John Gall	8.00
MG	Marcus Giles	15.00
GR	Khalil Greene	25.00
RH	Rich Harden	20.00
MJ	Mike Johnston	8.00
SK	Scott Kazmir	20.00
JK	Jeff Keppinger	8.00
CK	Casey Kotchman	15.00
CL	Cliff Lee	8.00
JL	Justin Leone	8.00
MA	Joe Mauer	25.00
AO	Akinori Otsuka	20.00
LO	Lyle Overbay	10.00
CP	Corey Patterson	15.00
PE	Jake Peavy	30.00
OP	Oliver Perez	20.00
SP	Scott Podsednik	15.00
HR	Horacio Ramirez	8.00
JR	Jose Reyes	30.00
MR	Mike Rouse	8.00
BS	Ben Sheets	15.00
TS	Terrmel Sledge	10.00
KT	Kazuhito Tadano	20.00
ST	Shingo Takatsu	25.00
MT	Mark Teixeira	30.00
WA	Ryan Wagner	10.00
WE	Brandon Webb	10.00
RW	Rickie Weeks	15.00
JW	Jerome Williams	8.00
DW	Dontrelle Willis	25.00

Stardom Signatures

		NM/M
EB	Ernie Banks/240	50.00
BE	Josh Beckett/50	20.00
BL	Hank Blalock/50	20.00
JG	Jason Giambi/100	15.00
KG	Ken Griffey Jr./198	75.00
AK	Al Kaline/99	50.00
JM	Joe Morgan/194	25.00
KP	Kirby Puckett/156	50.00

2005 Upper Deck Pro Sigs

MANNY RAMIREZ

		NM/M
Complete Set (132):		25.00
Common Player:		.10
Common Rookie (91-132):		.25
Inserted 1:1		
Pack (6):		2.00
Box (24):		40.00
1	Dallas McPherson	.25
2	Garret Anderson	.25
3	Steve Finley	.10
4	Vladimir Guerrero	.50
5	Luis Gonzalez	.10
6	Shawn Green	.10
7	Troy Glaus	.25
8	Andruw Jones	.25
9	Chipper Jones	.50
10	John Smoltz	.25
11	Tim Hudson	.40
12	Miguel Tejada	.40
13	Rafael Palmeiro	.40
14	Sammy Sosa	.75
15	Curt Schilling	.50
16	David Ortiz	.50
17	Johnny Damon	.50
18	Manny Ramirez	.50
19	Greg Maddux	1.00
20	Kerry Wood	.50
21	Mark Prior	.50
22	Nomar Garciaparra	.50
23	Frank Thomas	.40
24	Paul Konerko	.25
25	Adam Dunn	.40
26	Ken Griffey Jr.	1.00
27	Travis Hafner	.10
28	Victor Martinez	.25
29	Todd Helton	.50
30	Ivan Rodriguez	.40
31	Magglio Ordonez	.25
32	Carlos Delgado	.25
33	Josh Beckett	.25
34	Miguel Cabrera	.50
35	Craig Biggio	.25
36	Jeff Bagwell	.25
37	Lance Berkman	.25
38	Roger Clemens	1.50

Silver

Silver:		1-3X
Inserted 1:5		

Gold

Gold:		2-4X
Production 350 Sets		

Signature Sensations

39	Roy Oswalt	.25
40	Mike Sweeney	.10
41	Derek Lowe	.10
42	Eric Gagne	.25
43	J.D. Drew	.10
44	Jeff Kent	.10
45	Ben Sheets	.25
46	Carlos Lee	.25
47	Joe Mauer	.25
48	Johan Santana	.50
49	Torii Hunter	.25
50	Carlos Beltran	.40
51	David Wright	1.00
52	Kazuo Matsui	.10
53	Mike Piazza	.75
54	Pedro Martinez	.25
55	Tom Glavine	.25
56	Alex Rodriguez	1.50
57	Derek Jeter	1.50
58	Gary Sheffield	.40
59	Hideki Matsui	1.00
60	Jason Giambi	.25
61	Jorge Posada	.25
62	Mike Mussina	.25
63	Randy Johnson	.25
64	Barry Zito	.25
65	Bobby Crosby	.25
66	Eric Chavez	.25
67	Bobby Abreu	.25
68	Jim Thome	.40
69	Jason Bay	.25
70	Oliver Perez	.25
71	Brian Giles	.10
72	Jake Peavy	.25
73	Khalil Greene	.25
74	Jason Schmidt	.10
75	Moises Alou	.25
76	Adrian Beltre	.25
77	Bret Boone	.25
78	Ichiro Suzuki	1.00
79	Richie Sexson	.25
80	Albert Pujols	1.50
81	Jim Edmonds	.25
82	Mark Mulder	.25
83	Scott Rolen	.50
84	Aubrey Huff	.25
85	Alfonso Soriano	.50
86	Hank Blalock	.25
87	Mark Teixeira	.25
88	Roy Halladay	.25
89	Jose Vidro	.10
90	Livan Hernandez	.10
91	Tony Pena **RC**	.25
92	Luis Hernandez **RC**	.25
93	Peter Orr **RC**	.25
94	Anibal Sanchez **RC**	.75
95	Luis Mendoza **RC**	.25
96	Stephen Drew **RC**	6.00
97	Russel Rohlicek **RC**	.25
98	Casey Rogowski **RC**	.25
99	Pedro Lopez **RC**	.25
100	Tadahito Iguchi **RC**	2.00
101	Daylan Childress **RC**	.25
102	Juan Morillo **RC**	.50
103	Marcos Carvajal **RC**	.25
104	Ubaldo Jimenez **RC**	.25
105	Justin Verlander **RC**	2.00
106	Chris Resop **RC**	.25
107	Yorman Bazardo **RC**	.25
108	Jared Gothreaux **RC**	.25
109	Luke Scott **RC**	1.00
110	Ambiorix Burgos **RC**	.50
111	Prince Fielder **RC**	4.00
112	Dennis Houlton **RC**	.25
113	Franquelis Osoria **RC**	.25
114	Norihiro Nakamura **RC**	1.00
115	Oscar Robles **RC**	.25
116	Steve Schmoll **RC**	.25
117	Luis Pena **RC**	.25
118	David Gassner **RC**	.25
119	Ambiorix Concepcion **RC**	.50
120	Dae-Sung Koo **RC**	.25
121	Matt Lindstrom **RC**	.25
122	Colter Bean **RC**	.25
123	Keiichi Yabu **RC**	.25
124	Philip Humber **RC**	1.00
125	Wladimir Balentien **RC**	1.00
126	Tony Giarratano **RC**	1.00
127	Shane Costa **RC**	.25
128	Jeff Niemann **RC**	1.00
129	Nick Masset **RC**	.25
130	Ismael Ramirez **RC**	.25
131	John Hattig Jr. **RC**	.25
132	Brandon McCarthy **RC**	1.50

		NM/M
Inserted 1:24		
Silver:		1-2X
Production 50 Sets		
Gold:		No Pricing
Production 5 Sets		
AA	Abe Alvarez	10.00
BA	Bronson Arroyo	25.00
GA	Garrett Atkins	5.00
DB	Denny Bautista	5.00
RB	Russell Branyan	5.00
MC	Miguel Cabrera	35.00
KC	Kiko Calero	5.00
CC	Chad Cordero	10.00
JC	Juan Cruz	5.00
BD	Brandon Duckworth	5.00
JE	Johnny Estrada	8.00
LF	Lew Ford/SP	10.00
TH	Travis Hafner	15.00
KH	Keith Hernandez/SP	20.00
OH	Orlando Hernandez	75.00
OI	Omar Infante	5.00
DJ	Derek Jeter/SP	150.00
JJ	Jorge Julio	5.00
AM	Aaron Miles	5.00
YM	Yadier Molina	15.00
RN	Roberto Novoa	5.00
NP	Nick Punto	5.00
HR	Horacio Ramirez/SP	5.00
AR	Aaron Rowand	25.00
CS	Cory Sullivan	8.00
JS	Jeff Suppan	10.00
BT	Brett Tomko	5.00
MV	Merkin Valdez	5.00
DW	David Wright	70.00

2005 Upper Deck Reflections Promos

Each of the first 100 cards in Upper Deck Reflections was issued in a foil-overprinted version with "UD PROMO" across the front. Cards were inserted into specially marked card shop and newsstand issues of Tuff Stuff magazine.

		NM/M
Common Player:		.50
Stars:		1.5X

2005 Upper Deck Reflections

		NM/M
Complete Set (200):		
Common (1-100):		.50
Common SP (101-150):		1.00
Inserted 1:2		
Common SP (151-200):		2.00
Inserted 1:2		
Pack (4):		12.00
Box (12):		120.00
1	Corey Patterson	.50
2	Curt Schilling	1.00
3	Todd Helton	.75
4	Johnny Damon	.75
5	Alex Rodriguez	2.50
6	Vladimir Guerrero	1.00
7	John Smoltz	.50
8	Ivan Rodriguez	.75
9	Roy Halladay	.50
10	Carlos Beltran	.75
11	Ichiro Suzuki	2.00
12	Jim Edmonds	.50

ABBREVIATIONS

SP - Short Print

13	Andruw Jones	.50
14	Scott Podsednik	.50
15	Troy Glaus	.50
16	Miguel Cabrera	1.00
17	Adrian Beltre	.50
18	Ben Sheets	.50
19	Alfonso Soriano	1.00
20	Brian Giles	.50
21	Carl Crawford	.50
22	Frank Thomas	.75
23	Jeff Kent	.50
24	Eric Gagne	.50
25	Shawn Green	.50
26	Sammy Sosa	2.00
27	Carlos Lee	.50
28	Ken Griffey Jr.	2.00
29	Mike Lowell	.50
30	Magglio Ordonez	.50
31	Aubrey Huff	.50
32	Travis Hafner	.50
33	Albert Pujols	3.00
34	Vernon Wells	.50
35	Roy Oswalt	.50
36	Jose Guillen	.50
37	Jim Thome	.75
38	Bobby Abreu	.50
39	Bret Boone	.50
40	Mark Teixeira	.50
41	Garret Anderson	.50
42	Jose Reyes	.75
43	Bernie Williams	.50
44	Greg Maddux	1.50
45	Gary Sheffield	.50
46	Josh Beckett	.50
47	Chipper Jones	1.00
48	Hank Blalock	.50
49	C.C. Sabathia	.50
50	Manny Ramirez	1.00
51	Pedro Martinez	1.00
52	Michael Young	.50
53	Jacque Jones	.50
54	Marcus Giles	.50
55	Steve Finley	.50
56	Miguel Tejada	.75
57	Mike Sweeney	.50
58	Lance Berkman	.50
59	J.D. Drew	.50
60	Jeromy Burnitz	.50
61	Johan Santana	.75
62	Victor Martinez	.50
63	Carl Pavano	.50
64	Roger Clemens	3.00
65	Richie Sexson	.50
66	Tim Hudson	.50
67	Melvin Mora	.50
68	Angel Berroa	.50
69	Rafael Palmeiro	.50
70	Randy Johnson	1.00
71	Torii Hunter	.50
72	Luis Gonzalez	.50
73	Kazuo Matsui	.50
74	Hideki Matsui	2.00
75	Mark Prior	1.00
76	Jeff Bagwell	.75
77	Eric Chavez	.50
78	Mark Loretta	.50
79	Adam Dunn	.75
80	Kerry Wood	1.00
81	Jose Vidro	.50
82	Jason Schmidt	.50
83	Carlos Delgado	.50
84	Scott Rolen	1.00
85	David Ortiz	1.00
86	Edgar Renteria	1.00
87	Nomar Garciaparra	1.50
88	Mike Piazza	1.50
89	Mark Mulder	.50
90	Tom Glavine	.50
91	Paul Konerko	.50
92	Larry Walker	.50
93	Derek Jeter	3.00
94	Jake Peavy	.50
95	Carlos Zambrano	.50
96	Russ Ortiz	.50
97	Barry Zito	.50
98	Austin Kearns	.50
99	Pedro Feliz	.50
100	Rich Harden	.50
101	Adam LaRoche	1.00
102	Brandon Claussen	1.00
103	Gavin Floyd	1.00
104	Daniel Cabrera	1.00
105	Joe Mauer	2.00
106	Khalil Greene	2.00
107	David Wright	3.00
108	Rickie Weeks	1.00
109	Robb Quinlan	1.00
110	Bucky Jacobsen	1.00
111	Ryan Howard	2.00
112	Jeff Francis	1.00
113	Jason Lane	1.00
114	Alexis Rios	1.00
115	Bobby Madritsch	1.00
116	Jesse Crain	1.00
117	Oliver Perez	1.00
118	Garrett Atkins	1.00
119	Casey Kotchman	1.00
120	B.J. Upton	1.00
121	Laynce Nix	1.00
122	Adrian Gonzalez	1.00
123	Joe Blanton	1.00
124	Gabe Gross	1.00
125	Scott Kazmir	2.00
126	Zack Greinke	1.00
127	Edwin Jackson	1.00
128	Jason Bay	1.00
129	J.D. Closser	1.00
130	Jason Dubois	1.00
131	Dallas McPherson	2.00
132	Chad Cordero	1.00
133	Angel Guzman	1.00
134	Jayson Werth	1.00
135	Ryan Wagner	1.00
136	Guillermo Quiroz	1.00
137	Scott Proctor	1.00
138	Chris Burke	1.00
139	Nick Swisher	1.00
140	David DeJesus	1.00
141	Yhency Brazoban	1.00
142	Bobby Crosby	1.00
143	Chase Utley	1.00
144	Wily Mo Pena	1.00
145	Roman Colon	1.00
146	Eddy Rodriguez	1.00
147	Gerald Laird	1.00
148	Jose Capellan	1.00
149	Aaron Rowand	1.00
150	Kevin Youkilis	1.00
151	Bob Feller	2.00
152	Robin Yount	4.00
153	Willie Stargell	2.00
154	Cal Ripken Jr.	8.00
155	Monte Irvin	2.00
156	Nolan Ryan	6.00
157	Bob Lemon	2.00
158	Richie Ashburn	2.00
159	Billy Williams	2.00
160	Luis Aparicio	2.00
161	Phil Niekro	2.00
162	Bobby Doerr	2.00
163	Mike Schmidt	6.00
164	Stan Musial	4.00
165	George Kell	2.00
166	Joe Morgan	2.00
167	Whitey Ford	3.00
168	Rick Ferrell	2.00
169	Jim "Catfish" Hunter	2.00
170	Red Schoendienst	2.00
171	Tom Seaver	4.00
172	Pee Wee Reese	2.00
173	Lou Boudreau	2.00
174	Hal Newhouser	2.00
175	Harmon Killebrew	3.00
176	Jim Bunning	2.00
177	Willie McCovey	3.00
178	Bob Gibson	3.00
179	Juan Marichal	2.00
180	Robin Roberts	2.00
181	Gaylord Perry	2.00
182	Brooks Robinson	4.00
183	Al Lopez	2.00
184	Joe DiMaggio	6.00
185	Al Kaline	3.00
186	Rollie Fingers	2.00
187	Mickey Mantle	10.00
188	Enos Slaughter	2.00
189	Ernie Banks	4.00
190	Eddie Mathews	2.00
191	Tommy Lasorda	2.00
192	Fergie Jenkins	2.00
193	Lou Brock	2.00
194	Larry Doby	2.00
195	Phil Rizzuto	3.00
196	Warren Spahn	4.00
197	Ralph Kiner	2.00
198	Hoyt Wilhelm	2.00
199	Early Wynn	2.00
200	Yogi Berra	4.00

Blue
Blue (1-100):	2-4X
Blue (101-200):	1-2.5X
Production 75 Sets	

Emerald
Emerald (1-100):	4-8X
Emerald (101-200):	3-5X
Production 25 Sets	

Platinum
| Platinum (1-200): | No Pricing |
| Production One Set | |

Purple
Purple (1-100):	2-4X
Purple (101-200):	1-2.5X
Production 99 Sets	

Red
Red (1-100):	2-4X
Red (101-200):	1-2.5X
Production 99 Sets	

Turquoise
Turquoise (1-100):	3-5X
Turquoise (101-200):	1.5-3X
Production 50 Sets	

Cut From the Same Cloth
NM/M
Common Duo:	8.00
Production 225 Sets	
Red:	1-1.5X
Production 99 Sets	
Blue:	1-2X
Production 50 Sets	
Platinum:	No Pricing
Production One Set	

AA	Albert Pujols, Adrian Beltre	20.00
AB	Carlos Beltran, Bobby Abreu	10.00
AG	Garret Anderson, Vladimir Guerrero	10.00
AH	Alfonso Soriano, Hank Blalock	10.00
AJ	Albert Pujols, Jim Thome	20.00
AM	Adrian Beltre, Miguel Cabrera	10.00
AT	Jim Thome, Bobby Abreu	10.00
AW	Albert Pujols, Will Clark	20.00
BB	Jeff Bagwell, Craig Biggio	10.00
BG	Carlos Beltran, Ken Griffey Jr.	15.00
BM	Paul Molitor, George Brett	20.00
BO	Josh Beckett, Roy Oswalt	8.00
BP	Johnny Bench, Mike Piazza	15.00
BS	Adrian Beltre, Scott Rolen	10.00
BT	George Brett, Mike Schmidt	25.00
BW	Mark Teixeira, Hank Blalock	10.00
	Hank Blalock, David Wright	15.00
CB	Bobby Crosby, Jason Bay	8.00
CC	Bobby Crosby, Eric Chavez	8.00
CG	Bobby Crosby, Khalil Greene	8.00
CL	Miguel Cabrera, Mike Lowell	10.00
CP	Carl Crawford, Scott Podsednik	8.00
CR	Scott Rolen, Eric Chavez	10.00
CT	Miguel Tejada, Bobby Crosby	10.00
DM	Mike Schmidt, Dale Murphy	15.00
DR	Manny Ramirez, Johnny Damon	15.00
GI	Brian Giles, Marcus Giles	8.00
GS	Sammy Sosa, Ken Griffey Jr.	20.00
GV	Jose Guillen, Jose Vidro	8.00
HH	Tim Hudson, Rich Harden	8.00
HK	Kent Hrbek, Harmon Killebrew	20.00
JD	J.D. Drew, Chipper Jones	10.00
JH	Torii Hunter, Jacque Jones	8.00
JJ	Chipper Jones, Andruw Jones	10.00
JM	Don Mattingly, Derek Jeter	30.00
JR	Randy Johnson, Nolan Ryan	30.00
JS	Steve Carlton, Johan Santana	10.00
JT	Miguel Tejada, Derek Jeter	25.00
KH	Jason Kendall, Tim Hudson	8.00
KM	Dallas McPherson, Casey Kotchman	10.00
MB	Wade Boggs, Don Mattingly	20.00
MC	Don Mattingly, Will Clark	20.00
MH	Mark Mulder, Tim Hudson	8.00
MJ	Dale Murphy, Chipper Jones	15.00
MK	Harmon Killebrew, Justin Morneau	15.00
MM	Kazuo Matsui, Hideki Matsui	30.00
MS	Johan Santana, Joe Mauer	12.00
MW	Dallas McPherson, David Wright	20.00
MY	Robin Yount, Paul Molitor	20.00
OD	Johnny Damon, David Ortiz	15.00
OT	Shingo Takatsu, Akinori Otsuka	15.00
PB	Jim Bunning, Jim Palmer	10.00
PC	Miguel Cabrera, Albert Pujols	20.00
PG	Albert Pujols, Vladimir Guerrero	25.00
PP	Mike Piazza, Jorge Posada	15.00
PR	Albert Pujols, Scott Rolen	25.00
PS	Tom Seaver, Mark Prior	10.00
PT	Mark Teixeira, Albert Pujols	20.00
RJ	Cal Ripken Jr., Derek Jeter	40.00
RM	Ivan Rodriguez, Victor Martinez	8.00
RO	Manny Ramirez, David Ortiz	20.00
RP	Ivan Rodriguez, Mike Piazza	15.00
RR	Cal Ripken Jr., Brooks Robinson	35.00
RT	Miguel Tejada, Cal Ripken Jr.	30.00
RW	Scott Rolen, David Wright	15.00
SB	Ryne Sandberg, Wade Boggs	25.00
SM	Pedro J. Martinez, Curt Schilling	15.00
SO	Curt Schilling, David Ortiz	15.00
SP	Ben Sheets, Mark Prior	10.00
SR	Scott Rolen, Mike Schmidt	15.00
ST	Alfonso Soriano, Mark Teixeira	15.00
TC	Mark Teixeira, Miguel Cabrera	15.00
TH	Todd Helton, Jim Thome	10.00
TP	Rafael Palmeiro, Miguel Tejada	10.00
TR	Manny Ramirez, Jim Thome	12.00
TS	Jim Thome, Mike Schmidt	15.00
UJ	Derek Jeter, B.J. Upton	25.00
UK	B.J. Upton, Scott Kazmir	8.00
UW	B.J. Upton, David Wright	15.00
VJ	Jose Vidro, Nick Johnson	8.00
WB	Bernie Williams, Carlos Beltran	10.00
WJ	Bernie Williams, Derek Jeter	25.00
WM	Bernie Williams, Hideki Matsui	30.00
WP	Mark Prior, Kerry Wood	10.00
WR	Kerry Wood, Nolan Ryan	30.00
YR	Manny Ramirez, Carl Yastrzemski	20.00
ZM	Mark Mulder, Barry Zito	8.00
BD1	Carlos Beltran, Johnny Damon	10.00
BD2	Johnny Damon, Carlos Beltran	10.00
GG1	Ken Griffey Jr., Ken Griffey Sr.	15.00
GG2	Ken Griffey Sr., Ken Griffey Jr.	15.00

Cut From Same Cloth Patch
NM/M
Production 99 Sets
AM	Adrian Beltre, Miguel Cabrera	25.00
BR	Adrian Beltre, Scott Rolen	25.00
BS	George Brett, Mike Schmidt	40.00
BT	Mark Teixeira, Hank Blalock	20.00
CB	Jason Bay, Bobby Crosby	20.00
CG	Bobby Crosby, Khalil Greene	20.00
CP	Gary Carter, Mike Piazza	35.00
CR	Eric Chavez, Scott Rolen	25.00
DG	Ken Griffey Jr., Adam Dunn	40.00
GC	Miguel Cabrera, Ken Griffey Jr.	40.00
GI	Brian Giles, Marcus Giles	15.00
JM	Derek Jeter, Don Mattingly	60.00
JR	Cal Ripken Jr., Derek Jeter	80.00
KM	Dallas McPherson, Casey Kotchman	25.00
MJ	Chipper Jones, Dale Murphy	30.00
MP	Mike Piazza, Joe Mauer	30.00
MW	Dallas McPherson, David Wright	30.00
MY	Robin Yount, Paul Molitor	40.00
OB	Wade Boggs, David Ortiz	30.00
OT	Shingo Takatsu, Akinori Otsuka	30.00
PB	Albert Pujols, Adrian Beltre	40.00
PC	Albert Pujols, Miguel Cabrera	40.00
PR	Albert Pujols, Scott Rolen	40.00
RJ	Randy Johnson, Nolan Ryan	40.00
RP	Ivan Rodriguez, Mike Piazza	30.00
RR	Cal Ripken Jr., Brooks Robinson	50.00
RW	Nolan Ryan, Kerry Wood	40.00
SB	Ryne Sandberg, Wade Boggs	50.00
SP	Ben Sheets, Mark Prior	20.00
TC	Mark Teixeira, Miguel Cabrera	30.00
TO	Mark Teixeira, David Ortiz	25.00
UJ	Derek Jeter, B.J. Upton	40.00
UW	B.J. Upton, David Wright	25.00
WB	David Wright, Hank Blalock	30.00
WP	Mark Prior, Kerry Wood	30.00
WR	David Wright, Scott Rolen	30.00
YO	David Ortiz, Carl Yastrzemski	50.00
GG1	Ken Griffey Sr., Ken Griffey Jr.	40.00
GG2	Ken Griffey Jr., Ken Griffey Sr.	40.00

Cut From the Same Cloth Autograph Patch
NM/M
Production 25 Sets
BT	Mark Teixeira, Hank Blalock	120.00
DG	Ken Griffey Jr., Adam Dunn	240.00
GC	Miguel Cabrera, Ken Griffey Jr.	240.00
JR	Derek Jeter, Cal Ripken Jr.	500.00
MJ	Chipper Jones, Dale Murphy	140.00
PC	Albert Pujols, Miguel Cabrera	350.00
RP	Mike Piazza, Ivan Rodriguez	140.00
SB	Ryne Sandberg, Wade Boggs	160.00
TO	Mark Teixeira, David Ortiz	100.00
WB	David Wright, Hank Blalock	100.00
WR	David Wright, Scott Rolen	100.00

Dual Signature
NM/M
Red:	1-1.5X
Production 99 Sets	
Blue:	1.5-2X
Production 35 Sets	
Platinum:	No Pricing
Production One Set	

ABAR	Al Rosen, Adrian Beltre	30.00
ABDM	Adrian Beltre, Dallas McPherson	30.00
ABDW	David Wright, Adrian Beltre	40.00
ABEC	Adrian Beltre, Eric Chavez	30.00
ABJL	Adrian Beltre, Justin Leone	30.00
ABSR	Adrian Beltre, Scott Rolen	30.00
AHBU	Aubrey Huff, B.J. Upton	25.00
AHCC	Carl Crawford, Aubrey Huff	25.00
AKDM	Al Kaline, Dale Murphy	50.00
AOST	Akinori Otsuka, Shingo Takatsu	40.00
ARCC	Alexis Rios, Carl Crawford	20.00
ARKG	Alexis Rios, Ken Griffey Jr.	65.00
ARTH	Al Rosen, Travis Hafner	25.00
BAKY	Kevin Youkilis, Bronson Arroyo	50.00
BCCR	Bobby Crosby, Cal Ripken Jr.	160.00
BCDJ	Derek Jeter, Bobby Crosby	125.00
BCEC	Bobby Crosby, Eric Chavez	25.00
BCJB	Bobby Crosby, Jason Bay	35.00
BCKG	Khalil Greene, Bobby Crosby	35.00
BDWB	Bobby Doerr, Wade Boggs	50.00
BGMG	Brian Giles, Marcus Giles	25.00
BPFH	Frank Howard, Boog Powell	30.00
BRRS	Brooks Robinson, Ron Santo	40.00
BSJC	Ben Sheets, Jose Capellan	20.00
BSRW	Ben Sheets, Rickie Weeks	35.00
BSSK	Ben Sheets, Scott Kazmir	20.00
BUDJ	B.J. Upton, Derek Jeter	125.00
BURW	B.J. Upton, Rickie Weeks	30.00
BUSK	B.J. Upton, Scott Kazmir	25.00
BWKG	Billy Williams, Ken Griffey Jr.	80.00
CCNJ	Nick Johnson, Chad Cordero	25.00
CKDM	Casey Kotchman, Dallas McPherson	35.00
CKKH	Keith Hernandez, Casey Kotchman	20.00
CKMT	Casey Kotchman, Mark Teixeira	35.00
CTDM	Charles Thomas, Dale Murphy	30.00
CTJC	Charles Thomas, Jose Capellan	15.00
CTRH	Charles Thomas, Ryan Howard	50.00
CZJS	Johan Santana, Carlos Zambrano	60.00
CZLT	Carlos Zambrano, Luis Tiant	20.00
DGDB	Dwight Gooden, Dewon Brazelton	20.00
DGJB	Jim Bouton, Dwight Gooden	20.00
DGJS	Dwight Gooden, Johan Santana	50.00
DJDM	Derek Jeter, Don Mattingly	200.00
DJKG	Derek Jeter, Khalil Greene	140.00
DKFH	Frank Howard, Dave Kingman	25.00
DMDW	David Wright, Dallas McPherson	50.00
DMJB	Dale Murphy, Jason Bay	40.00
DMJL	Justin Leone, Dallas McPherson	20.00
DMKY	Dallas McPherson, Kevin Youkilis	20.00
DMMS	Dallas McPherson, Mike Schmidt	75.00
DMRH	Dallas McPherson, Ryan Howard	50.00
DOKY	David Ortiz, Kevin Youkilis	60.00
DWJL	Justin Leone, David Wright	40.00
DWKH	David Wright, Keith Hernandez	65.00
DWKY	David Wright, Kevin Youkilis	40.00
DWMS	David Wright, Mike Schmidt	100.00
DWSR	David Wright, Scott Rolen	65.00
ECSR	Scott Rolen, Eric Chavez	50.00
FHMT	Mark Teixeira, Frank Howard	40.00
FHNJ	Frank Howard, Nick Johnson	25.00
GPJP	Gaylord Perry, Jake Peavy	30.00
ISJC	Jose Capellan, Ian Snell	15.00
ISMV	Ian Snell, Merkin Valdez	15.00
ISSK	Ian Snell, Scott Kazmir	20.00
JBIS	Ian Snell, Joe Blanton	20.00
JBJP	Jim Bunning, Jim Palmer	30.00
JBMV	Merkin Valdez, Joe Blanton	15.00
JBRH	Joe Blanton, Rich Harden	20.00
JBSK	Scott Kazmir, Joe Blanton	20.00
JCMV	Merkin Valdez, Jose Capellan	15.00
JLRH	Justin Leone, Ryan Howard	50.00
JPJB	Jake Peavy, Joe Blanton	25.00
JPKG	Jake Peavy, Khalil Greene	50.00
JPRH	Jake Peavy, Rich Harden	40.00
JPSK	Jake Peavy, Scott Kazmir	30.00
JRDW	Jose Reyes, David Wright	75.00
JSMP	Johan Santana, Mark Prior	100.00
JSSC	Johan Santana, Steve Carlton	50.00
JSSK	Johan Santana, Scott Kazmir	40.00
JVMG	Marcus Giles, Jose Vidro	
KGKG	Ken Griffey Sr., Ken Griffey Jr.	100.00
KGMC	Ken Griffey Jr., Miguel Cabrera	100.00
KYWB	Kevin Youkilis, Wade Boggs	50.00
MCRH	Ryan Howard, Miguel Cabrera	80.00
MGRW	Rickie Weeks, Marcus Giles	35.00

		NM/M
MTHB	Hank Blalock, Mark Teixeira	50.00
MTMC	Miguel Cabrera, Mark Teixeira	60.00
MTRH	Mark Teixeira, Ryan Howard	80.00
MVRH	Merkin Valdez, Rich Harden	20.00
PBKG	Pat Burrell, Ken Griffey Jr.	85.00
PBMC	Pat Burrell, Miguel Cabrera	40.00
RHDO	Ryan Howard, David Ortiz	80.00
RHRO	Roy Oswalt, Rich Harden	30.00
RHSK	Rich Harden, Scott Kazmir	25.00
THVM	Victor Martinez, Travis Hafner	20.00
TOKH	Kent Hrbek, Tony Oliva	30.00
VMYM	Victor Martinez, Yadier Molina	20.00

Fabric Jersey

Common Player: Inserted 1:12 — NM/M

CB	Carlos Beltran	8.00
AB	Adrian Beltre	6.00
HB	Hank Blalock	6.00
WB	Wade Boggs/SP	10.00
GB	George Brett/SP	15.00
MC	Miguel Cabrera	8.00
EC	Eric Chavez	4.00
WC	Will Clark/SP	10.00
JD	Johnny Damon	10.00
KG	Ken Griffey Jr.	15.00
VG	Vladimir Guerrero	8.00
TH	Todd Helton	6.00
DJ	Derek Jeter/SP	20.00
RJ	Randy Johnson	8.00
CJ	Chipper Jones	8.00
GM	Greg Maddux	10.00
HM	Hideki Matsui	20.00
DM	Don Mattingly/SP	20.00
PM	Paul Molitor/SP	8.00
DO	David Ortiz	8.00
PI	Mike Piazza	10.00
MP	Mark Prior	6.00
AP	Albert Pujols	15.00
MR	Manny Ramirez	8.00
CR	Cal Ripken Jr./SP	25.00
IR	Ivan Rodriguez	8.00
SR	Scott Rolen	8.00
NR	Nolan Ryan/SP	25.00
JS	Johan Santana	8.00
CS	Curt Schilling	8.00
MS	Mike Schmidt/SP	15.00
AS	Alfonso Soriano	8.00
MT	Mark Teixeira	6.00
TE	Miguel Tejada	8.00
JT	Jim Thome	8.00
BW	Bernie Williams	6.00
KW	Kerry Wood	8.00
DW	David Wright	15.00
CY	Carl Yastrzemski/SP	25.00
RY	Robin Yount/SP	10.00

Fabric Reflections Patch

Production 99 Sets — NM/M

JB	Jason Bay	15.00
AB	Adrian Beltre	10.00
HB	Hank Blalock	15.00
WB	Wade Boggs	20.00
GB	George Brett	50.00
PB	Pat Burrell	15.00
CA	Miguel Cabrera	20.00
EC	Eric Chavez	10.00
BC	Bobby Crosby	10.00
MG	Marcus Giles	10.00
DG	Dwight Gooden	15.00
GR	Khalil Greene	10.00
KG	Ken Griffey Jr.	40.00
RH	Rich Harden	15.00
DJ	Derek Jeter	50.00
RJ	Randy Johnson	20.00
AJ	Andruw Jones	15.00
SK	Scott Kazmir	10.00
MA	Don Mattingly	30.00
MC	Dallas McPherson	10.00
PM	Paul Molitor	20.00
DM	Dale Murphy	15.00
DO	David Ortiz	20.00
RO	Roy Oswalt	10.00
JP	Jake Peavy	15.00
GP	Gaylord Perry	15.00
PI	Mike Piazza	20.00
MP	Mark Prior	15.00
AP	Albert Pujols	50.00
CR	Cal Ripken Jr.	60.00
SR	Scott Rolen	10.00
NR	Nolan Ryan	40.00
JS	Johan Santana	20.00
MS	Mike Schmidt	25.00
BS	Ben Sheets	15.00
ST	Shingo Takatsu	15.00
MT	Mark Teixeira	15.00
BU	B.J. Upton	15.00
DW	David Wright	20.00
RY	Robin Yount	30.00
CZ	Carlos Zambrano	15.00

Fabric Reflections Autograph Patch

Production 50 Sets — NM/M

JB	Jason Bay	50.00
AB	Adrian Beltre	30.00
HB	Hank Blalock	40.00
WB	Wade Boggs	60.00
PB	Pat Burrell	35.00
CA	Miguel Cabrera	40.00
EC	Eric Chavez	30.00
BC	Bobby Crosby	30.00
DG	Dwight Gooden	40.00
GR	Khalil Greene	50.00
KG	Ken Griffey Jr.	125.00
RH	Rich Harden	35.00
DJ	Derek Jeter	275.00
RJ	Randy Johnson	100.00
AJ	Andruw Jones	75.00
SK	Scott Kazmir	40.00
MA	Don Mattingly	125.00
MC	Dallas McPherson	30.00
PM	Paul Molitor	50.00
DM	Dale Murphy	40.00
DO	David Ortiz	75.00
RO	Roy Oswalt	50.00
JP	Jake Peavy	40.00
GP	Gaylord Perry	30.00
PI	Mike Piazza	120.00
MP	Mark Prior	50.00
AP	Albert Pujols	300.00
CR	Cal Ripken Jr.	225.00
SR	Scott Rolen	50.00
NR	Nolan Ryan	150.00
JS	Johan Santana	50.00
MS	Mike Schmidt	100.00
BS	Ben Sheets	30.00
ST	Shingo Takatsu	40.00
MT	Mark Teixeira	50.00
BU	B.J. Upton	50.00
DW	David Wright	100.00
RY	Robin Yount	75.00
CZ	Carlos Zambrano	40.00

Super Swatch

NM/M
Production 50 Sets
Red: 1-1.5X
Production 25 Sets
Blue: No Pricing
Production 10 Sets

BO	Bobby Abreu	15.00
RA	Roberto Alomar	15.00
MA	Moises Alou	10.00
GA	Garret Anderson	10.00
BA	Jeff Bagwell	15.00
RB	Rocco Baldelli	10.00
JB	Jason Bay	15.00
BE	Josh Beckett	10.00
CB	Carlos Beltran	15.00
AB	Adrian Beltre	8.00
LB	Lance Berkman	10.00
BI	Craig Biggio	10.00
HB	Hank Blalock	10.00
BB	Bret Boone	8.00
KB	Kevin Brown	8.00
MC	Miguel Cabrera	15.00
EC	Eric Chavez	10.00
CC	Carl Crawford	10.00
BC	Bobby Crosby	10.00
DA	Johnny Damon	20.00
CD	Carlos Delgado	15.00
JD	J.D. Drew	10.00
AD	Adam Dunn	15.00
JE	Jim Edmonds	15.00
KF	Keith Foulke	10.00
EG	Eric Gagne	10.00
JG	Jason Giambi	10.00
BG	Brian Giles	8.00
MG	Marcus Giles	8.00
TG	Tom Glavine	10.00
LG	Luis Gonzalez	10.00
SG	Shawn Green	10.00
GR	Khalil Greene	12.00
KG	Ken Griffey Jr.	40.00
VG	Vladimir Guerrero	15.00
HA	Roy Halladay	10.00
RH	Rich Harden	10.00
HE	Todd Helton	10.00
HO	Trevor Hoffman	10.00
TH	Tim Hudson	12.00
AH	Aubrey Huff	8.00
HU	Torii Hunter	10.00
DJ	Derek Jeter	40.00
RJ	Randy Johnson	15.00
AJ	Andruw Jones	15.00
CJ	Chipper Jones	15.00
JJ	Jacque Jones	8.00
SK	Scott Kazmir	8.00
JK	Jason Kendall	8.00
ML	Mike Lowell	8.00
GM	Greg Maddux	30.00
PM	Pedro Martinez	15.00
VM	Victor Martinez	10.00
HM	Hideki Matsui	50.00
KM	Kazuo Matsui	15.00
DM	Dallas McPherson	12.00
JM	Justin Morneau	20.00
MM	Mark Mulder	10.00
MU	Mike Mussina	15.00
HN	Hideo Nomo	40.00
MO	Magglio Ordonez	8.00
DO	David Ortiz	15.00
RO	Roy Oswalt	10.00
AO	Akinori Otsuka	15.00
RP	Rafael Palmeiro	15.00

CP	Corey Patterson	10.00
PI	Mike Piazza	20.00
SP	Scott Podsednik	10.00
JP	Jorge Posada	15.00
MP	Mark Prior	15.00
AP	Albert Pujols	40.00
MR	Manny Ramirez	20.00
ER	Edgar Renteria	10.00
JR	Jose Reyes	12.00
IR	Ivan Rodriguez	12.00
SR	Scott Rolen	15.00
CS	C.C. Sabathia	8.00
SA	Johan Santana	15.00
SC	Curt Schilling	15.00
JS	Jason Schmidt	12.00
RS	Richie Sexson	10.00
BS	Ben Sheets	15.00
GS	Gary Sheffield	15.00
AS	Alfonso Soriano	15.00
SS	Sammy Sosa	20.00
MS	Mike Sweeney	8.00
ST	Shingo Takatsu	15.00
MT	Mark Teixeira	15.00
TE	Miguel Tejada	15.00
JT	Jim Thome	15.00
JV	Jose Vidro	8.00
WA	Billy Wagner	10.00
VW	Vernon Wells	8.00
BW	Bernie Williams	15.00
KW	Kerry Wood	15.00
DW	David Wright	25.00
BZ	Barry Zito	10.00

San Diego Padres

This cello-wrapped team set was a stadium giveaway at a promotional game.

		NM/M
Complete Set (33):		7.00
Common Player:		.25
1	Rod Beck	.25
2	Adam Eaton	.25
3	Trevor Hoffman	.40
4	Brian Lawrence	.25
5	Scott Linebrink	.25
6	Blaine Neal	.25
7	Akinori Otsuka	.50
8	Jake Peavy	.25
9	Ricky Stone	.25
10	David Wells	.25
11	Jay Witasick	.25
12	Ramon Hernandez	.25
13	Miguel Ojeda	.25
14	Rich Aurilia	.25
15	Sean Burroughs	.35
16	Brian Buchanan	.25
17	Khalil Greene	.40
18	Dave Hansen	.25
19	Mark Loretta	.25
20	Phil Nevin	.25
21	Brian Giles	.35
22	Ryan Klesko	.25
23	Terrence Long	.25
24	Xavier Nady	.25
25	Jay Payton	.25
26	Sterling Hitchcock	.25
27	Bruce Bochy	.25
28	Rob Picciolo	.25
29	Swinging Friar/Mascot	.25
30	Davey Lopes	.25
31	Dave Magadan	.25
32	Tony Muser	.25
33	Darren Balsley	.25

SportsFest Redemption

Six-card cello packs with individual cards serially numbered on front from an edition of 750 were available to persons redeeming wrappers from Upper Deck products purchased at SportsFest 2005 in Chicago.

		NM/M
Complete Set (6):		5.00
Common Player:		.50
MLB1	Ken Griffey Jr.	1.50
MLB2	Mark Prior	.75
MLB3	Derek Jeter	2.00
MLB4	Carlos Beltran	1.00
MLB5	Albert Pujols	1.50
MLB6	Curt Schilling	.50

2005 Upper Deck Sweet Spot

		NM/M
Complete Set (90):		20.00
Common Player:		.25
Pack (5):		12.00
Box (12):		120.00
1	Magglio Ordonez	.25
2	Craig Biggio	.50
3	Hank Blalock	.40
4	Nomar Garciaparra	.75
5	Ken Griffey Jr.	1.50
6	Khalil Greene	.40
7	Andruw Jones	.50
8	Ichiro Suzuki	1.50
9	Philip Humber RC	1.50
10	Vladimir Guerrero	1.00
11	Carlos Delgado	.40
12	Jeff Niemann RC	1.50
13	Chipper Jones	.75
14	Jose Vidro	.25
15	Miguel Cabrera	.75
16	Albert Pujols	2.00
17	Tadahito Iguchi RC	2.50
18	Norihiro Nakamura RC	1.50
19	Jeff Bagwell	.75
20	Troy Glaus	.40
21	Scott Rolen	.75
22	Derek Lowe	.25
23	Mark Prior	.75
24	Bobby Abreu	.40
25	David Wright	1.00
26	Barry Zito	.40
27	Livan Hernandez	.25
28	Mark Teixeira	.50
29	Manny Ramirez	.75
30	Paul Konerko	.40
31	Victor Martinez	.25
32	Greg Maddux	1.50
33	Jim Thome	.50
34	Miguel Tejada	.50
35	Ivan Rodriguez	.50
36	Carlos Beltran	.50
37	Steve Finley	.25
38	Torii Hunter	.40
39	Bobby Crosby	.25
40	Jorge Posada	.40
41	Ben Sheets	.40
42	Mike Piazza	1.00
43	Luis Gonzalez	.25
44	Joe Mauer	.50
45	Shawn Green	.25
46	Eric Gagne	.40
47	Kerry Wood	.40
48	Derek Jeter	2.00
49	Josh Beckett	.25
50	Alex Rodriguez	1.50
51	Aubrey Huff	.25
52	Eric Chavez	.40
53	Sammy Sosa	1.00
54	Roger Clemens	2.00
55	Mike Mussina	.50
56	Mike Sweeney	.25
57	Oliver Perez	.25
58	Tim Hudson	.40
59	Justin Verlander RC	2.00
60	Johan Santana	.40
61	Hideki Matsui	1.50
62	Mark Mulder	.40
63	Jake Peavy	.40
64	Adam Dunn	.50
65	Dallas McPherson	.40
66	Jeff Kent	.25
67	Pedro Martinez	.75
68	J.D. Drew	.25
69	Frank Thomas	.50
70	Kazuo Matsui	.25

71	Travis Hafner	.40
72	John Smoltz	.40
73	Jason Schmidt	.25
74	Carlos Lee	.25
75	Todd Helton	.50
76	David Ortiz	.75
77	Roy Oswalt	.25
78	Brian Giles	.25
79	Gary Sheffield	.50
80	Jason Bay	.40
81	Alfonso Soriano	.75
82	Randy Johnson	.75
83	Tom Glavine	.40
84	Richie Sexson	.40
85	Curt Schilling	.75
86	Adrian Beltre	.40
87	Jim Edmonds	.40
88	Roy Halladay	.40
89	Johnny Damon	.75
90	Lance Berkman	.40

Gold

Gold (1-90): 1-2X
Production 599 Sets

Platinum

Platinum (1-90): 2-4X
Production 99 Sets

Plutonium

No Pricing
Production One Set

Majestic Materials

		NM/M
Common Player:		
Gold:		1-1.5X
Production 75 Sets		
Platinum:		No Pricing
Production 10 Sets		
Plutonium:		No Pricing
Production One Set		
Patch:		2-3X
Production 35 Sets		
BA	Bobby Abreu	4.00
MA	Moises Alou	6.00
JB	Jason Bay	4.00
BE	Josh Beckett	4.00
LB	Lance Berkman	4.00
CB	Craig Biggio	6.00
BB	Bret Boone	4.00
BC	Bobby Crosby	4.00
CD	Carlos Delgado	4.00
JD	J.D. Drew	4.00
AD	Adam Dunn	4.00
JE	Jim Edmonds	6.00
JG	Jason Giambi	4.00
BG	Brian Giles	4.00
TG	Troy Glaus	4.00
LG	Luis Gonzalez	4.00
SG	Shawn Green	4.00
KG	Khalil Greene	6.00
HA	Travis Hafner	4.00
RH	Roy Halladay	4.00
TH	Tim Hudson	4.00
HU	Torii Hunter	4.00
TI	Tadahito Iguchi	5.00
AJ	Andruw Jones	6.00
SK	Scott Kazmir	4.00
JK	Jeff Kent	4.00
VM	Victor Martinez	4.00
KM	Kazuo Matsui	4.00
JM	Joe Mauer	6.00
DM	Dallas McPherson	4.00
MM	Mark Mulder	4.00
MU	Mike Mussina	6.00
MO	Magglio Ordonez	4.00
RO	Roy Oswalt	4.00
JP	Jake Peavy	4.00
OP	Oliver Perez	4.00
AP	Andy Pettitte	6.00
PO	Jorge Posada	6.00
ER	Edgar Renteria	4.00
JR	Jose Reyes	4.00
JS	Jason Schmidt	4.00
RS	Richie Sexson	4.00
BS	Ben Sheets	4.00
GS	Gary Sheffield	4.00
ST	Shingo Takatsu	4.00
BU	B.J. Upton	4.00
JV	Jose Vidro	4.00
VW	Vernon Wells	4.00
DW	David Wright	10.00
BZ	Barry Zito	4.00

Majestic Materials Dual

NM/M
Production 25 Sets
Gold: No Pricing
Production 5 Sets
Plutonium: No Pricing
Production One Set
Patch: No Pricing
Production 5 Sets

BB	Craig Biggio, Jeff Bagwell	15.00
BP	Jason Bay, Oliver Perez	10.00
BS	Adrian Beltre, Richie Sexson	10.00
BT	Hank Blalock, Mark Teixeira	12.00
CC	Bobby Crosby, Eric Chavez	10.00
DG	Adam Dunn, Ken Griffey Jr.	25.00
DK	J.D. Drew, Jeff Kent	10.00
DR	Johnny Damon, Manny Ramirez	15.00
GG	Shawn Green, Troy Glaus	10.00
GR	Eric Gagne, Mariano Rivera	15.00
HM	Travis Hafner, Victor Martinez	10.00
JJ	Andruw Jones, Chipper Jones	15.00
MC	Don Mattingly, Will Clark	25.00
MW	Dallas McPherson, David Wright	15.00
PC	Albert Pujols, Miguel Cabrera	25.00
PG	Jake Peavy, Khalil Greene	12.00
PL	Albert Pujols, Derrek Lee	25.00
RM	Jose Reyes, Kazuo Matsui	10.00
RO	Ivan Rodriguez, Magglio Ordonez	10.00
RT	Brian Roberts, Miguel Tejada	15.00
SH	John Smoltz, Tim Hudson	12.00
SM	Joe Mauer, Johan Santana	15.00
TI	Shingo Takatsu, Tadahito Iguchi	20.00
UK	B.J. Upton, Scott Kazmir	10.00
WC	David Wright, Miguel Cabrera	15.00

Majestic Materials Triple

NM/M
Production 25 Sets
Gold: No Pricing
Production 5 Sets
Plutonium: No Pricing
Production One Set
Patch: No Pricing
Production 5 Sets

BPO	Josh Beckett, Mark Prior, Roy Oswalt	15.00
BSB	George Brett, Mike Schmidt, Wade Boggs	30.00
BTH	Jeff Bagwell, Jim Thome, Todd Helton	20.00
HRG	Torii Hunter, Manny Ramirez, Vladimir Guerrero	20.00
JCG	Andruw Jones, Miguel Cabrera, Vladimir Guerrero	15.00
JRT	Derek Jeter, Edgar Renteria, Miguel Tejada	25.00
MMP	Greg Maddux, Pedro Martinez, Jake Peavy	25.00
MSG	Greg Maddux, John Smoltz, Tom Glavine	40.00
OGP	David Ortiz, Jason Giambi, Rafael Palmeiro	20.00
PBC	Albert Pujols, Carlos Beltran, Miguel Cabrera	40.00
RBW	Nolan Ryan, Josh Beckett, Kerry Wood	40.00
RGB	Cal Ripken Jr., Tony Gwynn, Wade Boggs	50.00
SSJ	Curt Schilling, Johan Santana, Randy Johnson	25.00
VPP	Jason Varitek, Jorge Posada, Mike Piazza	20.00
WRG	David Wright, Scott Rolen, Troy Glaus	25.00

Majestic Materials Quad

NM/M
Production 25 Sets

Gold: No Pricing
Production 5 Sets
Plutonium: No Pricing
Production One Set
Patch: No Pricing
Production 5 Sets
JJSH Andruw Jones,
Chipper Jones,
John Smoltz,
Tim Hudson 25.00
JSJP Derek Jeter,
Gary Sheffield,
Randy Johnson,
Jorge Posada 60.00
OVDR David Ortiz, Jason Varitek,
Johnny Damon,
Manny Ramirez 40.00
PEWR Albert Pujols,
Jim Edmonds,
Larry Walker,
Scott Rolen 50.00
ZMWP Carlos Zambrano,
Greg Maddux,
Kerry Wood,
Mark Prior 30.00

Signatures Game-Used Ball
No Pricing
Production One Set

Signature Black Stitch Black Ink
No Pricing
Production One Set
Blue Ink: No Pricing
Production One Set
Red Ink: No Pricing
Production One Set

Signature Red Stitch Black Ink
NM/M
Production 58-350
JB	Jason Bay/350	20.00
HB	Hank Blalock/175	20.00
WB	Wade Boggs/175	40.00
CA	Miguel Cabrera/175	40.00
SC	Steve Carlton/58	25.00
SE	Sean Casey/350	15.00
WC	Will Clark/175	25.00
RC	Roger Clemens/175	120.00
CC	Carl Crawford/350	15.00
BC	Bobby Crosby/350	15.00
DA	Andre Dawson/175	20.00
AD	Adam Dunn/175	25.00
GF	Gavin Floyd/350	15.00
NG	Nomar Garciaparra/175	60.00
MG	Marcus Giles/350	15.00
GL	Khalil Greene/350	15.00
KG	Ken Griffey Jr./175	75.00
RH	Rich Harden/350	15.00
KH	Keith Hernandez/350	15.00
HO	Ryan Howard/350	75.00
AH	Aubrey Huff/350	15.00
PH	Philip Humber/350	15.00
BJ	Bo Jackson/350	70.00
DJ	Derek Jeter/175	150.00
RJ	Randy Johnson/175	75.00
AJ	Andruw Jones/175	40.00
SK	Scott Kazmir/350	15.00
BL	Barry Larkin/175	25.00
EM	Edgar Martinez/175	30.00
MA	Don Mattingly/175	60.00
PM	Paul Molitor/175	25.00
MO	Justin Morneau/350	25.00
MM	Mark Mulder/350	20.00
JN	Jeff Niemann/350	15.00
RO	Roy Oswalt/350	25.00
LO	Lyle Overbay/350	12.00
JP	Jake Peavy/350	20.00
PI	Mike Piazza/175	80.00
MP	Mark Prior/175	40.00
AP	Albert Pujols/175	160.00
AR	Aramis Ramirez/350	25.00
RE	Jose Reyes/350	35.00
CR	Cal Ripken Jr./175	120.00
NR	Nolan Ryan/175	80.00
RS	Ryne Sandberg/175	65.00
MS	Mike Schmidt/175	50.00
MT	Mark Teixeira/175	40.00
BU	B.J. Upton/350	15.00
JV	Justin Verlander/350	35.00
DW	David Wright/350	60.00
RY	Robin Yount/175	50.00
CZ	Carlos Zambrano/350	20.00

Signature Red Stitch Blue Ink
NM/M
Production 75-135
JB	Jason Bay	25.00
HB	Hank Blalock/75	20.00
WB	Wade Boggs/75	40.00
CA	Miguel Cabrera/75	40.00
SE	Sean Casey/135	15.00
WC	Will Clark/75	25.00
RC	Roger Clemens/75	120.00
CC	Carl Crawford/135	15.00
BC	Bobby Crosby/135	20.00
DA	Andre Dawson/75	20.00
AD	Adam Dunn/75	30.00
GF	Gavin Floyd/135	15.00

NG	Nomar Garciaparra/75	65.00
MG	Marcus Giles/135	15.00
GL	Tom Glavine/135	25.00
GR	Khalil Greene/135	25.00
KG	Ken Griffey Jr./75	80.00
HA	Travis Hafner/135	15.00
RH	Rich Harden/135	15.00
KH	Keith Hernandez/135	15.00
HO	Ryan Howard/135	75.00
AH	Aubrey Huff/135	15.00
PH	Philip Humber/135	15.00
BJ	Bo Jackson/75	75.00
DJ	Derek Jeter/75	150.00
RJ	Randy Johnson/75	85.00
AJ	Andruw Jones/75	40.00
SK	Scott Kazmir/135	15.00
BL	Barry Larkin/75	25.00
EM	Edgar Martinez/75	35.00
MA	Don Mattingly/75	70.00
PM	Paul Molitor/75	25.00
MO	Justin Morneau/135	30.00
MM	Mark Mulder/135	15.00
JN	Jeff Niemann/135	15.00
RO	Roy Oswalt/135	25.00
LO	Lyle Overbay/135	12.00
CP	Corey Patterson/135	15.00
JP	Jake Peavy/135	25.00
PI	Mike Piazza/75	80.00
MP	Mark Prior/75	50.00
AP	Albert Pujols/75	160.00
AR	Aramis Ramirez/135	25.00
RE	Jose Reyes/135	35.00
CR	Cal Ripken Jr./75	120.00
NR	Nolan Ryan/75	80.00
RS	Ryne Sandberg/75	65.00
MS	Mike Schmidt/75	50.00
MT	Mark Teixeira/75	40.00
BU	B.J. Upton/75	15.00
JV	Justin Verlander/135	35.00
DW	David Wright/135	60.00
RY	Robin Yount/75	50.00
CZ	Carlos Zambrano/135	20.00

Signature Red Stitch Red Ink
NM/M
Production 15-35
JB	Jason Bay/35	25.00
SE	Sean Casey/35	25.00
CC	Carl Crawford/35	20.00
BC	Bobby Crosby	35.00
AD	Adam Dunn/15	60.00
GF	Gavin Floyd/35	25.00
MG	Marcus Giles/35	15.00
GL	Tom Glavine/35	40.00
GR	Khalil Greene/35	40.00
HA	Travis Hafner/35	30.00
RH	Rich Harden/35	30.00
KH	Keith Hernandez/35	25.00
HO	Ryan Howard/35	90.00
AH	Aubrey Huff/35	20.00
PH	Philip Humber/35	25.00
SK	Scott Kazmir/35	20.00
MO	Justin Morneau/35	30.00
MM	Mark Mulder/35	30.00
JN	Jeff Niemann/35	25.00
RO	Roy Oswalt/35	40.00
LO	Lyle Overbay/35	15.00
CP	Corey Patterson/35	20.00
JP	Jake Peavy/35	30.00
AP	Albert Pujols/15	250.00
AR	Aramis Ramirez/35	40.00
RE	Jose Reyes/35	40.00
BU	B.J. Upton/35	25.00
JV	Justin Verlander/35	50.00
DW	David Wright/35	100.00
CZ	Carlos Zambrano/35	35.00

Signatures Dual Red Stitch
NM/M
Production 25 Sets
BJ	Bobby Crosby, Jason Bay	40.00
BW	Adrian Beltre, David Wright	90.00
CG	Bobby Crosby, Khalil Greene	50.00
DC	Adam Dunn, Sean Casey	50.00
FH	Gavin Floyd, Ryan Howard	120.00
GC	Ken Griffey Jr., Miguel Cabrera	120.00
GL	Khalil Greene, Mark Loretta	60.00
JC	Randy Johnson, Roger Clemens	240.00
JG	Andruw Jones, Ken Griffey Jr.	150.00
JM	Derek Jeter, Don Mattingly	300.00
LG	Barry Larkin, Ken Griffey Jr.	120.00
LR	Barry Larkin, Cal Ripken Jr.	160.00
MG	Greg Maddux, Tom Glavine	150.00
MJ	Pedro Martinez, Randy Johnson	125.00
NH	Jeff Niemann, Philip Humber	50.00
PB	Jason Bay, Oliver Perez	40.00

PC	Albert Pujols, Miguel Cabrera	300.00
PO	Jake Peavy, Roy Oswalt	75.00
RJ	Cal Ripken Jr., Derek Jeter	300.00
SB	Ryne Sandberg, Wade Boggs	125.00
SG	Nomar Garciaparra, Ryne Sandberg	150.00
SP	Ben Sheets, Jake Peavy	50.00
WC	David Wright, Miguel Cabrera	120.00
WR	David Wright, Jose Reyes	180.00

Signature Red-Blue Stitch Black Ink
NM/M
Production 25-50
JB	Jason Bay/50	25.00
HB	Hank Blalock/25	25.00
WB	Wade Boggs/25	50.00
CA	Miguel Cabrera/25	65.00
SC	Steve Carlton/25	25.00
SE	Sean Casey/50	20.00
WC	Will Clark/25	35.00
RC	Roger Clemens/25	160.00
CC	Carl Crawford/25	15.00
BC	Bobby Crosby/50	35.00
DA	Andre Dawson/25	40.00
AD	Adam Dunn/25	40.00
GF	Gavin Floyd/50	15.00
NG	Nomar Garciaparra/25	65.00
MG	Marcus Giles/50	15.00
GR	Khalil Greene/50	30.00
KG	Ken Griffey Jr./25	120.00
RH	Rich Harden/50	20.00
KG	Keith Hernandez/50	20.00
HO	Ryan Howard/50	85.00
AH	Aubrey Huff/50	20.00
PH	Philip Humber/50	20.00
BJ	Bo Jackson/25	90.00
DJ	Derek Jeter/25	250.00
RJ	Randy Johnson/25	120.00
AJ	Andruw Jones/25	50.00
SK	Scott Kazmir/25	20.00
BL	Barry Larkin/25	40.00
EM	Edgar Martinez/25	40.00
MA	Don Mattingly/25	90.00
PM	Paul Molitor/25	40.00
MO	Justin Morneau/50	25.00
MM	Mark Mulder/50	25.00
JN	Jeff Niemann/50	20.00
RO	Roy Oswalt/50	35.00
LO	Lyle Overbay/50	12.00
JP	Jake Peavy/50	25.00
PI	Mike Piazza/25	100.00
MP	Mark Prior/25	60.00
AP	Albert Pujols/25	220.00
AR	Aramis Ramirez/25	30.00
CR	Cal Ripken Jr./25	180.00
NR	Nolan Ryan/25	100.00
RS	Ryne Sandberg/25	75.00
MS	Mike Schmidt/25	75.00
MT	Mark Teixeira/25	40.00
BU	B.J. Upton/25	25.00
JV	Justin Verlander/50	40.00
DW	David Wright/50	100.00
RY	Robin Yount/25	90.00
CZ	Carlos Zambrano/50	

Signatures Barrel Blue Ink
NM/M
Production 15-30
JB	Jason Bay/30	25.00
SE	Sean Casey/30	25.00
CC	Carl Crawford/30	20.00
BC	Bobby Crosby/30	35.00
AD	Adam Dunn/15	60.00
GF	Gavin Floyd/30	25.00
MG	Marcus Giles/30	15.00
GL	Tom Glavine/30	40.00
GR	Khalil Greene/30	40.00
HA	Travis Hafner/30	30.00
RH	Rich Harden/30	25.00
KH	Keith Hernandez/30	25.00
HO	Ryan Howard/30	90.00
AH	Aubrey Huff/30	20.00
PH	Philip Humber/30	30.00
SK	Scott Kazmir/30	30.00
MO	Justin Morneau/30	30.00
MM	Mark Mulder/30	25.00
JN	Jeff Niemann/30	25.00
RO	Roy Oswalt/30	40.00
LO	Lyle Overbay/30	15.00
CP	Corey Patterson/30	20.00
JP	Jake Peavy/30	30.00
AP	Albert Pujols/15	250.00
AR	Aramis Ramirez/30	40.00
BU	B.J. Upton/30	25.00
JV	Justin Verlander/30	50.00
DW	David Wright/30	100.00
CZ	Carlos Zambrano/30	35.00

Signatures Barrel Red Ink
No Pricing
Production 5-10

Signatures Dual Barrel
No Pricing
Production 15 Sets

Signatures Game-Used Glove
No Pricing
Production 9-10

Signatures Glove Black Ink
NM/M
Production 15-30
JB	Jason Bay/30	40.00
SE	Sean Casey/30	35.00

Signatures Barrel Black Ink
NM/M
Production 25-50
JB	Jason Bay/50	20.00
HB	Hank Blalock/25	25.00
CA	Miguel Cabrera/25	70.00
SC	Steve Carlton/25	20.00
SE	Sean Casey/50	20.00
WC	Will Clark/25	25.00
CC	Carl Crawford/50	15.00
BC	Bobby Crosby/50	35.00
DA	Andre Dawson/25	25.00
AD	Adam Dunn/25	40.00
GF	Gavin Floyd/50	20.00
NG	Nomar Garciaparra/25	80.00
MG	Marcus Giles/50	15.00
GL	Tom Glavine/50	30.00
GR	Khalil Greene/50	35.00
KG	Ken Griffey Jr./25	85.00
HA	Travis Hafner/50	20.00
RH	Rich Harden/50	20.00
KH	Keith Hernandez/50	20.00
HO	Ryan Howard/50	90.00
AH	Aubrey Huff/50	15.00
PH	Philip Humber/50	25.00
BJ	Bo Jackson/25	75.00
DJ	Derek Jeter/25	250.00
RJ	Randy Johnson/25	125.00
AJ	Andruw Jones/25	50.00
SK	Scott Kazmir/25	20.00
BL	Barry Larkin/25	40.00
EM	Edgar Martinez/25	40.00
MA	Don Mattingly/25	85.00
PM	Paul Molitor/25	25.00
MO	Justin Morneau/50	25.00
MM	Mark Mulder/50	25.00
JN	Jeff Niemann/50	20.00
RO	Roy Oswalt/50	35.00
LO	Lyle Overbay/50	15.00
JP	Jake Peavy/50	25.00
PI	Mike Piazza/50	100.00
MP	Mark Prior/25	50.00
AP	Albert Pujols/25	220.00
AR	Aramis Ramirez/50	30.00
CR	Cal Ripken Jr./25	180.00
NR	Nolan Ryan/25	100.00
RS	Ryne Sandberg/25	75.00
MS	Mike Schmidt/25	75.00
MT	Mark Teixeira/25	40.00
BU	B.J. Upton/25	25.00
JV	Justin Verlander/50	40.00
DW	David Wright/50	100.00
RY	Robin Yount/25	90.00
CZ	Carlos Zambrano/50	

Signatures Glove Blue Ink
No Pricing
Production 5-10
Red Ink: No Pricing
Production 2-5

Signatures Dual Glove
No Pricing
Production 10 Sets

Sweet Threads

NM/M
Common Player:	4.00
Gold:	1-1.5X

Production 75 Sets
Platinum: No Pricing
Production 10 Sets
Plutonium: No Pricing
Production One Set
Patch: 2-4X
Production 35 Sets
JB	Jeff Bagwell	6.00
CB	Carlos Beltran	6.00
AB	Adrian Beltre	6.00
HB	Hank Blalock	6.00
WB	Wade Boggs	8.00
GB	George Brett	10.00
MC	Miguel Cabrera	8.00
EC	Eric Chavez	6.00
WC	Will Clark	6.00
BC	Bartolo Colon	6.00
JD	Johnny Damon	6.00
EG	Eric Gagne	4.00
TG	Tom Glavine	6.00
KG	Ken Griffey Jr.	12.00
VG	Vladimir Guerrero	8.00
GW	Tony Gwynn	8.00
TH	Todd Helton	8.00
HO	Trevor Hoffman	4.00
BJ	Bo Jackson	8.00
DJ	Derek Jeter	20.00
RJ	Randy Johnson	8.00
CJ	Chipper Jones	8.00
CL	Carlos Lee	4.00
GM	Greg Maddux	10.00
PM	Pedro Martinez	8.00
DM	Don Mattingly	10.00
DO	David Ortiz	8.00
RP	Rafael Palmeiro	6.00
PI	Mike Piazza	8.00
MP	Mark Prior	6.00
AP	Albert Pujols	15.00
MR	Manny Ramirez	8.00
CR	Cal Ripken Jr.	20.00
IR	Ivan Rodriguez	6.00
SR	Scott Rolen	6.00
NR	Nolan Ryan	12.00
RS	Ryne Sandberg	8.00
JS	Johan Santana	6.00
CS	Curt Schilling	6.00
MS	Mike Schmidt	10.00
SM	John Smoltz	6.00
AS	Alfonso Soriano	6.00
SS	Sammy Sosa	8.00
MT	Mark Teixeira	6.00
TE	Miguel Tejada	6.00
FT	Frank Thomas	6.00
JT	Jim Thome	6.00

CC	Carl Crawford/30	30.00
BC	Bobby Crosby/30	40.00
GF	Gavin Floyd/30	30.00
MG	Marcus Giles/30	30.00
GL	Tom Glavine/30	50.00
GR	Khalil Greene/30	40.00
HA	Travis Hafner/30	40.00
RH	Rich Harden/30	35.00
KH	Keith Hernandez/30	40.00
HO	Ryan Howard/30	100.00
AH	Aubrey Huff/30	30.00
PH	Philip Humber/30	40.00
SK	Scott Kazmir/30	30.00
MO	Justin Morneau/30	40.00
MM	Mark Mulder/30	30.00
JN	Jeff Niemann/30	30.00
RO	Roy Oswalt/30	50.00
LO	Lyle Overbay/30	30.00
CP	Corey Patterson/30	25.00
JP	Jake Peavy/30	40.00
AR	Aramis Ramirez/30	50.00
BU	B.J. Upton/30	35.00
JV	Justin Verlander/30	50.00
DW	David Wright/30	100.00
CZ	Carlos Zambrano/30	40.00
JV	Jason Varitek	10.00
BW	Bernie Williams	6.00
KW	Kerry Wood	4.00

Sweet Threads Dual
NM/M
Production 25 Sets
Gold: No Pricing
Production 5 Sets
Patch: No Pricing
Production 5 Sets
Plutonium: No Pricing
Production One Set
BG	Carlos Beltran, Ken Griffey Jr.	25.00
BM	Carlos Beltran, Pedro Martinez	15.00
DC	Carlos Delgado, Miguel Cabrera	15.00
GC	Ken Griffey Jr., Miguel Cabrera	25.00
GM	Dallas McPherson, Vladimir Guerrero	15.00
JB	Bo Jackson, George Brett	25.00
JJ	Randy Johnson, Derek Jeter	40.00
JM	Derek Jeter, Don Mattingly	50.00
JS	Jim Thome, Mike Schmidt	30.00
MG	Greg Maddux, Tom Glavine	25.00
MJ	Mike Mussina, Randy Johnson	20.00
MP	Greg Maddux, Mark Prior	25.00
OR	David Ortiz, Manny Ramirez	20.00
PO	Andy Pettitte, Roy Oswalt	10.00
PR	Pedro Martinez, Randy Johnson	20.00
PS	Rafael Palmeiro, Sammy Sosa	20.00
PW	David Wright, Mike Piazza	30.00
RJ	Cal Ripken Jr., Derek Jeter	70.00
RP	Albert Pujols, Scott Rolen	30.00
RT	Cal Ripken Jr., Miguel Tejada	40.00
SB	Ryne Sandberg, Wade Boggs	30.00
SJ	Curt Schilling, Randy Johnson	20.00
SV	Curt Schilling, Jason Varitek	20.00
WP	Kerry Wood, Mark Prior	15.00

Sweet Threads Triple
NM/M
Production 25 Sets
Gold: No Pricing
Production 5 Sets
Plutonium: No Pricing
Production One Set
Patch: No Pricing
Production 5 Sets
BBB	Craig Biggio, Jeff Bagwell, Lance Berkman	20.00
BWP	Carlos Beltran, David Wright, Mike Piazza	25.00
GGG	Luis Gonzalez, Shawn Green, Troy Glaus	10.00
JMB	Randy Johnson, Mike Mussina, Kevin Brown	25.00
JWS	Derek Jeter, Bernie Williams, Gary Sheffield	50.00
KGD	Austin Kearns, Ken Griffey Jr., Adam Dunn	30.00
LOP	Brad Lidge, Roy Oswalt, Andy Pettitte	15.00
ODR	David Ortiz, Johnny Damon, Manny Ramirez	25.00
PER	Albert Pujols, Jim Edmonds, Scott Rolen	40.00
PWM	Mark Prior, Kerry Wood, Greg Maddux	30.00
RDN	Manny Ramirez, Johnny Damon, Trot Nixon	30.00
SBT	Alfonso Soriano, Hank Blalock, Mark Teixeira	20.00
SMJ	Curt Schilling, Pedro Martinez, Randy Johnson	20.00
TPS	Miguel Tejada, Rafael Palmeiro, Sammy Sosa	20.00

Signature Red-Blue Stitch Blue Ink
NM/M
Production 15-30
Red Ink: No Pricing
Production 5-10
JB	Jason Bay/30	25.00
SE	Sean Casey/30	25.00
CC	Carl Crawford/30	20.00
BC	Bobby Crosby/30	35.00
GF	Gavin Floyd/30	25.00
MG	Marcus Giles/30	15.00
GL	Tom Glavine/30	40.00
GR	Khalil Greene/30	40.00
HA	Travis Hafner/30	30.00
RH	Rich Harden/30	30.00
KH	Keith Hernandez/30	25.00
HO	Ryan Howard/30	90.00
PH	Philip Humber/30	30.00
SK	Scott Kazmir/30	30.00
MO	Justin Morneau/30	30.00
MM	Mark Mulder/30	25.00
JN	Jeff Niemann/30	25.00
RO	Roy Oswalt/30	40.00
LO	Lyle Overbay/30	15.00
CP	Corey Patterson/30	20.00
JP	Jake Peavy/30	30.00
AP	Albert Pujols/15	250.00
AR	Aramis Ramirez/30	40.00
RE	Jose Reyes/30	45.00
BU	B.J. Upton/30	25.00
JV	Justin Verlander/30	50.00
DW	David Wright/30	100.00
CZ	Carlos Zambrano/30	35.00

Signature Game-Used Barrel
No Pricing
Production 1-10

Sweet Threads Quad

NM/M
Production 25 Sets
Gold: No Pricing
Production 5 Sets
Plutonium: No Pricing
Production One Set
Patch: No Pricing
Production 5 Sets

BMCB	Adrian Beltre, Dallas McPherson, Eric Chavez, Hank Blalock	25.00
BRGG	Carlos Beltran, Manny Ramirez, Ken Griffey Jr., Vladimir Guerrero	40.00
POTH	Albert Pujols, David Ortiz, Jim Thome, Todd Helton	40.00
RBGB	Cal Ripken Jr., Brett George, Tony Gwynn, Wade Boggs	90.00
RVMP	Ivan Rodriguez, Jason Varitek, Joe Mauer, Jorge Posada	30.00

2005 Upper Deck Sweet Spot Classic

Silver
Cards (1-100): 2-4X
Production 100 Sets

Gold

Cards (1-100): 4-8X
Production 50 Sets

		NM/M
	Complete Set (100):	30.00
	Common Player:	.40
	Pack (4):	12.00
	Box (12):	120.00
1	Al Kaline	1.00
2	Al Rosen	.40
3	Babe Ruth	4.00
4	Bill Mazeroski	.40
5	Billy Williams	.40
6	Bob Feller	.75
7	Bob Gibson	1.00
8	Bobby Doerr	.40
9	Brooks Robinson	1.00
10	Cal Ripken Jr.	4.00
11	Carl Yastrzemski	2.00
12	Carlton Fisk	.40
13	Casey Stengel	.40
14	Christy Mathewson	2.00
15	Cy Young	1.50
16	Dale Murphy	.75
17	Dave Winfield	.75
18	Dennis Eckersley	.40
19	Dizzy Dean	1.00
20	Don Drysdale	.75
21	Don Mattingly	3.00
22	Don Newcombe	.40
23	Don Sutton	.40
24	Duke Snider	1.00
25	Dwight Evans	.40
26	Eddie Mathews	1.50
27	Eddie Murray	1.00
28	Enos Slaughter	.40
29	Ernie Banks	2.00
30	Frank Howard	.40
31	Frank Robinson	.75
32	Gary Carter	.40
33	Gaylord Perry	.40
34	George Brett	3.00
35	George Kell	.40
36	George Sisler	.40
37	Larry Doby	.40
38	Harmon Killebrew	1.50
39	Honus Wagner	4.00
40	Jackie Robinson	2.00
41	Jim Bunning	.40
42	Jim Palmer	.75
43	Jim Rice	.40
44	Jimmie Foxx	.40
45	Joe DiMaggio	3.00
46	Joe Morgan	.40
47	Johnny Bench	2.00
48	Johnny Mize	.40
49	Johnny Podres	.40
50	Juan Marichal	.40
51	Keith Hernandez	.40
52	Kirby Puckett	1.00
53	Lefty Grove	.40
54	Lou Brock	.75
55	Lou Gehrig	4.00
56	Luis Aparicio	.40
57	Fergie Jenkins	.40
58	Maury Wills	.40
59	Mel Ott	1.50
60	Mickey Cochrane	1.00
61	Mickey Mantle	4.00
62	Mike Schmidt	3.00
63	Monte Irvin	.75
64	Nolan Ryan	4.00
65	Orlando Cepeda	.40
66	Ozzie Smith	1.50
67	Paul Molitor	1.00
68	Pee Wee Reese	.40
69	Phil Niekro	.40
70	Phil Rizzuto	1.00
71	Ralph Kiner	.40
72	Richie Ashburn	.40
73	Roberto Clemente	4.00
74	Robin Roberts	.40
75	Robin Yount	2.00
76	Rocky Colavito	1.00
77	Rod Carew	.75
78	Rogers Hornsby	1.00
79	Rollie Fingers	1.00
80	Roy Campanella	1.00
81	Bob Lemon	.40
82	Red Schoendienst	.40
83	Satchel Paige	2.00
84	Stan Musial	2.50
85	Steve Carlton	.75
86	Ted Williams	3.00
87	Thurman Munson	1.50
88	Tom Seaver	1.00
89	Tony Gwynn	1.50
90	Tony Perez	.40
91	Ty Cobb	2.00
92	Wade Boggs	1.00
93	Walter Johnson	1.50
94	Warren Spahn	1.50
95	Whitey Ford	1.00
96	Will Clark	.75
97	Jim "Catfish" Hunter	.40
98	Willie McCovey	.75
99	Willie Stargell	1.00
100	Yogi Berra	1.50

Classic Materials

		NM/M
	Common Player:	6.00
BE	Johnny Bench	15.00
YB	Yogi Berra	20.00
WB	Wade Boggs	10.00
GB	George Brett	10.00
GB1	George Brett	10.00
LB	Lou Brock	8.00
JB	Jim Bunning	10.00
CP	Roy Campanella	12.00
CA	Rod Carew	8.00
SC	Steve Carlton	8.00
GC	Gary Carter	8.00
OC	Orlando Cepeda	8.00
WC	Will Clark	10.00
WC1	Will Clark	10.00
RC	Roberto Clemente	60.00
TC	Ty Cobb/SP	100.00
CO	Rocky Colavito	25.00
DC	David Cone	8.00
AD	Andre Dawson	6.00
JD	Joe DiMaggio	80.00
DD	Don Drysdale	10.00
BF	Bob Feller	12.00
CF	Carlton Fisk	8.00
LG	Lou Gehrig/SP	160.00
BG	Bob Gibson	10.00
MG	Mark Grace	8.00
RG	Ron Guidry	8.00
TG	Tony Gwynn	12.00
CH	Jim "Catfish" Hunter	8.00
FJ	Fergie Jenkins	8.00
AK	Al Kaline	10.00
HK	Harmon Killebrew	12.00
MM	Mickey Mantle/SP	120.00
MA	Juan Marichal	8.00
EM	Eddie Mathews	10.00
DM	Dale Murphy	15.00
DM1	Don Mattingly	15.00
BM	Bill Mazeroski	10.00
WI	Willie McCovey	10.00
PM	Paul Molitor	10.00
JM	Joe Morgan	6.00
JM1	Joe Morgan	6.00
TM	Thurman Munson/SP	25.00
MU	Dale Murphy	10.00
ED	Eddie Murray	8.00
ED1	Eddie Murray	8.00
SM	Stan Musial/SP	20.00
PN	Phil Niekro	6.00
SP	Satchel Paige/SP	50.00
JP	Jim Palmer	8.00
TP	Tony Perez	8.00
GP	Gaylord Perry	6.00
RE	Pee Wee Reese/SP	15.00
RI	Jim Rice	8.00
CR	Cal Ripken Jr.	20.00
CR1	Cal Ripken Jr.	20.00
PR	Phil Rizzuto	15.00
RR	Robin Roberts	10.00
RO	Brooks Robinson	10.00
FR	Frank Robinson	8.00
JR	Jackie Robinson	50.00
BR	Babe Ruth/SP	275.00
NR	Nolan Ryan	25.00
NR1	Nolan Ryan	25.00
MS	Mike Schmidt	15.00
MS1	Mike Schmidt	15.00
SD	Red Schoendienst	8.00
TS	Tom Seaver	10.00
OS	Ozzie Smith/SP	15.00
SN	Duke Snider	10.00
WS	Warren/SPahn	15.00
DS	Don Sutton	6.00
DS1	Don Sutton	6.00
FV	Fernando Valenzuela	6.00
TW	Ted Williams/SP	75.00
MW	Maury Wills	6.00
MW1	Maury Wills	6.00
DW	Dave Winfield	6.00
DW1	Dave Winfield	6.00
EW	Early Wynn	10.00
CY	Carl Yastrzemski	15.00
RY	Robin Yount	12.00

Dual Signatures
No Pricing
Production 15 Sets

Patch

NM/M
Some not priced due to scarcity.

		NM/M
LA	Luis Aparicio/19	150.00
BE	Johnny Bench/32	100.00
WB	Wade Boggs/25	60.00
WB1	Wade Boggs/34	60.00
GB	George Brett/38	80.00
GB1	George Brett/50	80.00
LB	Lou Brock/34	90.00
SC	Steve Carlton/50	60.00
GC	Gary Carter/47	50.00
GC1	Gary Carter/34	50.00
OC	Orlando Cepeda/40	50.00
DC	David Cone/39	50.00
JD	Joe DiMaggio/38	250.00
CF1	Carlton Fisk/50	75.00
RG	Ron Guidry/30	40.00
TG	Tony Gwynn/34	80.00
TG1	Tony Gwynn/30	80.00
FH	Frank Howard/34	85.00
FJ	Fergie Jenkins/34	60.00
WI	Willie McCovey/50	60.00
JM	Joe Morgan/34	80.00
MU	Dale Murphy/34	80.00
ED	Eddie Murray/34	70.00
ED1	Eddie Murray/50	70.00
PN	Phil Niekro/44	50.00
TP	Tony Perez/34	75.00
GP	Gaylord Perry/34	50.00
PO	Johnny Podres/50	50.00
RI	Jim Rice/34	50.00
CR	Cal Ripken Jr./34	150.00
CR1	Cal Ripken Jr./34	150.00
RO	Brooks Robinson/85	85.00
RO1	Brooks Robinson/43	85.00
FR	Frank Robinson/34	80.00
JR	Jackie Robinson/12	250.00
SD	Red Schoendienst/42	60.00
TS	Tom Seaver/50	50.00
TS1	Tom Seaver/50	50.00
OS	Ozzie Smith/34	100.00
ST	Willie Stargell/50	65.00
BS	Bruce Sutter/50	50.00
DS	Don Sutton/34	40.00
DS1	Don Sutton/34	50.00
MW	Maury Wills/50	60.00
MW1	Maury Wills/47	50.00
DW1	Dave Winfield/50	75.00
CY	Carl Yastrzemski/35	100.00
RY	Robin Yount/SP	75.00

Sweet Leather Signatures
No Pricing
Production 25 Sets

Sweet Spot Signatures

NM/M
Common Autograph: 20.00
Inserted 1:12
Blue/Red Stitch: 1.5-2X
Production 40 Sets
Black Stitch: No Pricing
Production One Set

LA	Luis Aparicio	25.00
HB	Harold Baines	20.00
EB	Ernie Banks	75.00
BE	Johnny Bench	60.00
YB	Yogi Berra/SP	60.00
WB	Wade Boggs	50.00
GB	George Brett	85.00
JB	Jim Bunning	20.00
JC	Jose Canseco	40.00
CA	Rod Carew	50.00
SC	Steve Carlton	40.00
GC	Gary Carter	25.00
OC	Orlando Cepeda	25.00
WC	Will Clark	30.00
RC	Rocky Colavito/SP	85.00
DC	David Cone	20.00
AD	Andre Dawson	20.00
BD	Bobby Doerr	25.00
DE	Dennis Eckersley	25.00
EV	Dwight Evans	20.00
BF	Bob Feller	40.00
RF	Rollie Fingers	20.00
CF	Carlton Fisk	40.00
WF	Whitey Ford	60.00
BG	Bob Gibson	40.00
MG	Mark Grace	40.00
TG	Tony Gwynn	50.00
EH	Ernie Harwell/SP	40.00
KH	Keith Hernandez	20.00
FH	Frank Howard	25.00
MI	Monte Irvin	25.00
BJ	Bo Jackson	75.00
DJ	David Justice	20.00
HK	Harry Kalas	25.00
AK	Al Kaline	40.00
GK	George Kell	25.00
HK	Harmon Killebrew	50.00
RK	Ralph Kiner/SP	50.00
MA	Juan Marichal	25.00
DM	Don Mattingly	80.00
BM	Bill Mazeroski	40.00
MC	Willie McCovey/SP	60.00
PM	Paul Molitor	40.00
JM	Joe Morgan/SP	35.00
MU	Dale Murphy	20.00
SM	Stan Musial	100.00
DN	Don Newcombe	25.00
PN	Phil Niekro	25.00
JP	Jim Palmer	25.00
TP	Tony Perez	25.00
PO	Gaylord Perry	25.00
KP	Kirby Puckett/SP	50.00
JR	Jim Rice	25.00
CR	Cal Ripken Jr.	160.00
PR	Phil Rizzuto	50.00
RR	Robin Roberts	30.00
BR	Brooks Robinson	40.00
FR	Frank Robinson	40.00
AR	Al Rosen	20.00
NR	Nolan Ryan	125.00
RS	Ron Santo	35.00
MS	Mike Schmidt	80.00
RE	Red Schoendienst	30.00
TS	Tom Seaver	60.00
OS	Ozzie Smith	60.00
SN	Duke Snider	40.00
ST	Rusty Staub	20.00
SU	Bruce Sutter	20.00
DS	Don Sutton	20.00
LT	Luis Tiant	20.00
FV	Fernando Valenzuela	30.00
BW	Billy Williams	25.00
MW	Matt Williams	20.00
WI	Maury Wills	25.00
CY	Carl Yastrzemski	100.00
RY	Robin Yount/SP	85.00

Sweet Sticks Signatures

NM/M
Production 35 Sets

LA	Luis Aparicio	50.00
HB	Harold Baines	40.00
EB	Ernie Banks	125.00
BE	Johnny Bench	75.00
YB	Yogi Berra	80.00
WB	Wade Boggs	75.00
GB	George Brett	140.00
JB	Jim Bunning	40.00
JC	Jose Canseco	75.00
CA	Rod Carew	75.00
SC	Steve Carlton	50.00
GC	Gary Carter	40.00
OC	Orlando Cepeda	50.00
WC	Will Clark	65.00
RC	Rocky Colavito	120.00
DC	David Cone	50.00
AD	Andre Dawson	50.00
BD	Bobby Doerr	50.00
DE	Dennis Eckersley	50.00
EV	Dwight Evans	60.00
BF	Bob Feller	75.00
RF	Rollie Fingers	45.00
CF	Carlton Fisk	75.00
WF	Whitey Ford	85.00
BG	Bob Gibson	65.00
MG	Mark Grace	75.00
TG	Tony Gwynn	85.00
EH	Ernie Harwell	50.00
KH	Keith Hernandez	40.00
FH	Frank Howard	40.00
MI	Monte Irvin	50.00
BJ	Bo Jackson	140.00
DJ	David Justice	40.00
AK	Al Kaline	80.00
GK	George Kell	40.00
HK	Harmon Killebrew	80.00
RK	Ralph Kiner	75.00
MA	Juan Marichal	50.00
DM	Don Mattingly	125.00
BM	Bill Mazeroski	90.00
MC	Willie McCovey	85.00
PM	Paul Molitor	60.00
JM	Joe Morgan	50.00
MU	Dale Murphy	50.00
SM	Stan Musial	140.00
DN	Don Newcombe	40.00
PN	Phil Niekro	40.00
JP	Jim Palmer	50.00
TP	Tony Perez	50.00
GP	Gaylord Perry	40.00
PO	Johnny Podres	40.00
KP	Kirby Puckett	100.00
JR	Jim Rice	50.00
CR	Cal Ripken Jr.	240.00
PR	Phil Rizzuto	75.00
RR	Robin Roberts	75.00
BR	Brooks Robinson	65.00
FR	Frank Robinson	60.00
AR	Al Rosen	40.00
NR	Nolan Ryan	150.00
RS	Ron Santo	65.00
MS	Mike Schmidt	125.00
RE	Red Schoendienst	50.00
TS	Tom Seaver	85.00
OS	Ozzie Smith	90.00
SN	Duke Snider	75.00
ST	Rusty Staub	40.00
SU	Bruce Sutter	30.00
DS	Don Sutton	40.00
LT	Luis Tiant	40.00
BW	Billy Williams	50.00
MW	Matt Williams	50.00
WI	Maury Wills	40.00
CY	Carl Yastrzemski	120.00
RY	Robin Yount	100.00

Wingfield Classic Collection

NM/M
Common Player: 4.00
Inserted 1:Box

1	Al Kaline	4.00
2	Pee Wee Reese	4.00
3	Stan Musial, Ted Williams	6.00
4	Bill Dickey	4.00
5	Frank Robinson	5.00
6	Billy Martin	4.00
7	Casey Stengel, Joe DiMaggio	6.00
8	Bob Feller, Dwight D. Eisenhower	4.00
9	Duke Snider	5.00
10	Carl Yastrzemski	8.00
11	Honus Wagner	4.00
12	Dwight D. Eisenhower, Clark Griffith	4.00
13	Mickey Mantle, Joe DiMaggio	15.00
14	Don Drysdale	4.00
15	Ted Williams	8.00
16	Al Kaline, Mickey Mantle	15.00
17	Ernie Banks	6.00
18	Lou Boudreau	4.00
19	George Sisler, Harmon Killebrew	6.00
20	Gil Hodges	4.00
21	Rogers Hornsby	6.00
22	Luis Aparicio	4.00
23	Jackie Robinson	10.00
24	Joe Morgan	4.00
25	Enos Slaughter	4.00
26	Joe DiMaggio	8.00
27	Mickey Mantle, Ted Kluszewski	15.00
28	John F. Kennedy	4.00
29	Johnny Bench	8.00
30	Juan Marichal	4.00
31	Larry Doby	4.00
32	Don Newcombe, Elston Howard	4.00
33	Harmon Killebrew, Dwight D. Eisenhower	6.00
34	Roger Maris, Mickey Mantle	20.00
35	Mickey Mantle, Stan Musial	15.00
36	Ted Williams, Mickey Mantle, Yogi Berra	15.00
37	Nellie Fox	6.00
38	Richie Asburn	4.00
39	Roberto Clemente	15.00
40	Stan Musial, Robin Roberts	8.00
41	Tommy Heinrich, Joe DiMaggio	8.00
42	Roy Campanella	6.00
43	Rocky Colavito, Harmon Killebrew	6.00
44	Steve Carlton	4.00
45	Thurman Munson	6.00
46	Luis Aparicio, rnie Banks	6.00
47	Gil Hodges, Yogi Berra, Dwight D. Eisenhower	6.00
48	Whitey Ford	6.00
49	Mickey Mantle, Yogi Berra, Joe DiMaggio	15.00
50	Yogi Berra	8.00

The National Chicago Legends

These gold-foil enhanced cards were only available as an Upper Deck wrapper redemption on July 31 during the National Sports Collectors Convention in Chicago. On front cards have a serial number from within an edition of 750 each. Two of the six cards in the set were former Cubs.

		NM/M
CL1	Ernie Banks	3.00
CL2	Ryne Sandberg	3.00

The National Cubs/White Sox

These gold-foil enhanced cards were only available as an Upper Deck wrapper redemption on July 30 during the National Sports Collectors Convention in Chicago. On front cards have a serial number from within an edition of 750 each. Special autographed versions of each card, serially numbered to five each, were randomly distributed.

		NM/M
	Complete Set (6):	12.50
	Common Player:	2.00
MLB1	Mark Prior	3.00
MLB2	Greg Maddux	4.00
MLB3	Derrek Lee	4.00
MLB4	Kerry Wood	3.00
MLB5	Tadahito Iguchi	2.00
MLB6	Paul Konerko	2.00

2005 UD Ultimate Collection

NM/M
Common (1-100): 1.50

#	Player	Price
	Production 475	
	Common (101-237):	3.00
	Production 275	
	Common (238-242):	50.00
	Production 99	
	Pack (4):	85.00
	Box (4):	300.00
1	A.J. Burnett	1.50
2	Adam Dunn	2.00
3	Adrian Beltre	2.00
4	Albert Pujols	8.00
5	Alex Rodriguez	8.00
6	Alfonso Soriano	3.00
7	Andruw Jones	3.00
8	Andy Pettitte	2.00
9	Aramis Ramirez	2.00
10	Aubrey Huff	1.50
11	Ben Sheets	2.00
12	Bobby Abreu	2.00
13	Bobby Crosby	1.50
14	Chris Carpenter	2.00
15	Brian Giles	1.50
16	Brian Roberts	2.00
17	Carl Crawford	2.00
18	Carlos Beltran	3.00
19	Carlos Delgado	2.00
20	Carlos Zambrano	2.00
21	Chipper Jones	3.00
22	Corey Patterson	1.50
23	Craig Biggio	3.00
24	Curt Schilling	3.00
25	Dallas McPherson	1.50
26	David Ortiz	3.00
27	David Wright	5.00
28	Delmon Young	4.00
29	Derek Jeter	8.00
30	Derrek Lee	2.00
31	Dontrelle Willis	2.00
32	Eric Chavez	2.00
33	Eric Gagne	2.00
34	Francisco Rodriguez	1.50
35	Gary Sheffield	2.00
36	Greg Maddux	5.00
37	Hank Blalock	2.00
38	Hideki Matsui	5.00
39	Ichiro Suzuki	8.00
40	Ivan Rodriguez	3.00
41	J.D. Drew	1.50
42	Jake Peavy	2.00
43	Jason Bay	2.00
44	Jason Schmidt	2.00
45	Jeff Bagwell	2.00
46	Jeff Kent	2.00
47	Jeremy Bonderman	2.00
48	Jim Edmonds	2.00
49	Jim Thome	2.00
50	Joe Mauer	2.00
51	Johan Santana	2.00
52	John Smoltz	2.00
53	Johnny Damon	3.00
54	Jose Reyes	2.00
55	Jose Vidro	1.50
56	Josh Beckett	1.50
57	Justin Morneau	2.00
58	Ken Griffey Jr.	8.00
59	Kerry Wood	2.00
60	Khalil Greene	1.50
61	Lance Berkman	2.00
62	Larry Walker	2.00
63	Luis Gonzalez	1.50
64	Manny Ramirez	3.00
65	Mark Buehrle	2.00
66	Mark Mulder	2.00
67	Mark Prior	3.00
68	Mark Teixeira	2.00
69	Michael Young	2.00
70	Miguel Cabrera	3.00
71	Miguel Tejada	3.00
72	Mike Mussina	3.00
73	Mike Piazza	4.00
74	Moises Alou	2.00
75	Nomar Garciaparra	4.00
76	Oliver Perez	1.50
77	Pat Burrell	2.00
78	Paul Konerko	2.00
79	Pedro Feliz	1.50
80	Pedro Martinez	3.00
81	Randy Johnson	3.00
82	Richie Sexson	2.00
83	Rickie Weeks	2.00
84	Roger Clemens	8.00
85	Roy Halladay	2.00
86	Roy Oswalt	2.00
87	Sammy Sosa	3.00
88	Scott Kazmir	1.50
89	Scott Rolen	2.00
90	Shawn Green	2.00
91	Tim Hudson	2.00
92	Todd Helton	2.00
93	Tom Glavine	2.00
94	Torii Hunter	2.00
95	Travis Hafner	2.00
96	Troy Glaus	2.00
97	Vernon Wells	1.50
98	Victor Martinez	1.50
99	Vladimir Guerrero	3.00
100	Zack Greinke	1.50
101	Al Kaline	4.00
102	Babe Ruth	10.00
103	Bo Jackson	5.00
104	Bob Gibson	5.00
105	Brooks Robinson	4.00
106	Cal Ripken Jr.	12.00
107	Carl Yastrzemski	5.00
108	Carlton Fisk	3.00
109	Jim "Catfish" Hunter	5.00
110	Christy Mathewson	5.00
111	Cy Young	5.00
112	Don Mattingly	6.00
113	Eddie Mathews	5.00
114	Eddie Murray	4.00
115	Gary Carter	3.00
116	Harmon Killebrew	4.00
117	Jim Palmer	3.00
118	Jimmie Foxx	4.00
119	Joe DiMaggio	8.00
120	Johnny Bench	4.00
121	Lefty Grove	3.00
122	Lou Gehrig	8.00
123	Mel Ott	3.00
124	Reggie Jackson	4.00
125	Mike Schmidt	5.00
126	Nolan Ryan	8.00
127	Ozzie Smith	4.00
128	Paul Molitor	4.00
129	Pee Wee Reese	3.00
130	Robin Yount	6.00
131	Ryne Sandberg	6.00
132	Ted Williams	8.00
133	Thurman Munson	4.00
134	Tom Seaver	4.00
135	Tony Gwynn	4.00
136	Wade Boggs	3.00
137	Walter Johnson	4.00
138	Warren Spahn	4.00
139	Will Clark	3.00
140	Willie McCovey	3.00
141	Willie Stargell	4.00
142	Yogi Berra	4.00
143	Ambiorix Burgos RC	4.00
144	Ambiorix Concepcion RC	4.00
145	Anibal Sanchez RC	15.00
146	Bill McCarthy RC	4.00
147	Brian Burres RC	4.00
148	Carlos Ruiz RC	4.00
149	Casey Rogowski RC	6.00
150	Chris Resop RC	4.00
151	Chris Roberson RC	4.00
152	Chris Seddon RC	4.00
153	Colter Bean RC	4.00
154	Dae-Sung Koo RC	4.00
155	Danny Rueckel RC	4.00
156	David Gassner RC	4.00
157	Ryan Howard RC	8.00
158	D.J. Houlton RC	4.00
159	Derek Wathan RC	4.00
160	Devon Lowery RC	4.00
161	Enrique Gonzalez RC	4.00
162	Erick Threets RC	4.00
163	Eude Brito RC	4.00
164	Francisco Butto RC	4.00
165	Franquelis Osoria RC	4.00
166	Garrett Jones RC	4.00
167	Geovany Soto RC	4.00
168	Ismael Ramirez RC	4.00
169	Jared Gothreaux RC	4.00
170	Jason Hammel RC	4.00
171	Jeff Housman RC	4.00
172	Jeff Miller RC	4.00
173	Jeff Francoeur RC	10.00
174	John Hattig Jr. RC	4.00
175	Jorge Campillo RC	4.00
176	Juan Morillo RC	4.00
177	Justin Wechsler RC	4.00
178	Keiichi Yabu RC	4.00
179	Kendry Morales RC	15.00
180	Luis Hernandez RC	4.00
181	Luis Mendoza RC	4.00
182	Luis Pena RC	4.00
183	Luis Rodriguez RC	4.00
184	Luke Scott RC	10.00
185	Marcos Carvajal RC	4.00
186	Mark Woodyard RC	4.00
187	Matt Smith RC	4.00
188	Matt Lindstrom RC	4.00
189	Miguel Negron RC	6.00
190	Mike Morse RC	4.00
191	Nate McLouth RC	4.00
192	Nick Masset RC	4.00
193	Paulino Reynoso RC	4.00
194	Pedro Lopez RC	4.00
195	Peter Orr RC	4.00
196	Randy Messenger RC	4.00
197	Randy Williams RC	4.00
198	Raul Tablado RC	4.00
199	Ronny Paulino RC	8.00
200	Russel Rohlicek RC	4.00
201	Russell Martin RC	15.00
202	Scott Baker RC	6.00
203	Scott Munter RC	4.00
204	Sean Thompson RC	4.00
205	Sean Tracey RC	4.00
206	Steve Schmoll RC	4.00
207	Tony Pena RC	4.00
208	Travis Bowyer RC	4.00
209	Ubaldo Jimenez RC	4.00
210	Wladimir Balentien RC	10.00
211	Yorman Bazardo RC	4.00
212	Yuniesky Betancourt RC	8.00
213	Adam Shabala RC	4.00
214	Brandon McCarthy RC	10.00
215	Chad Orvella RC	4.00
216	Jermaine Van Buren RC	4.00
217	Anthony Reyes RC	30.00
218	Dana Eveland RC	4.00
219	Brian Anderson RC	10.00
220	Hayden Penn RC	8.00
221	Chris Denorfia RC	4.00
222	Joel Peralta RC	4.00
223	Ryan Garko RC	10.00
224	Felix Hernandez RC	15.00
225	Mark McLemore RC	4.00
226	Melky Cabrera RC	15.00
227	Nelson Cruz RC	8.00
228	Norihiro Nakamura RC	8.00
229	Oscar Robles RC	4.00
230	Rick Short RC	4.00
231	Ryan Zimmerman RC	35.00
232	Ryan Speier RC	4.00
233	Ryan Spilborghs RC	6.00
234	Shane Costa RC	6.00
235	Zachary Duke RC	6.00
236	Tony Giarratano RC	4.00
237	Jeff Niemann RC	10.00
238	Stephen Drew/ Auto. RC	250.00
239	Justin Verlander/ Auto. RC	250.00
240	Prince Fielder/Auto.	400.00
241	Philip Humber/ Auto. RC	85.00
242	Tadahito Iguchi/ Auto.	100.00

Silver

Silver (101-237):		1X-2X
Production 50 Sets		

2005 UD Ultimate Signature Edition

#	Player	Price
	Complete Set (110):	
	Common (1-100):	2.00
	Production 825	
	Common (101-110):	8.00
	Production 225	
	Tin (3):	85.00
1	Al Kaline	4.00
2	Babe Ruth	10.00
3	Billy Williams	2.00
4	Bob Feller	2.00
5	Bob Gibson	3.00
6	Brooks Robinson	3.00
7	Carlton Fisk	2.00
8	Cy Young	3.00
9	Dizzy Dean	3.00
10	Don Drysdale	3.00
11	Eddie Mathews	4.00
12	Enos Slaughter	3.00
13	Ernie Banks	5.00
14	Fergie Jenkins	2.00
15	Eddie Murray	3.00
16	Harmon Killebrew	3.00
17	Honus Wagner	5.00
18	Jackie Robinson	5.00
19	Jimmie Foxx	3.00
20	Joe DiMaggio	6.00
21	Joe Morgan	2.00
22	Juan Marichal	2.00
23	Larry Doby	2.00
24	Jim Palmer	2.00
25	Johnny Bench	4.00
26	Lou Brock	2.00
27	Lou Gehrig	6.00
28	Mel Ott	3.00
29	Mickey Cochrane	2.00
30	Mickey Mantle	12.00
31	Mike Schmidt	5.00
32	Nolan Ryan	8.00
33	Pee Wee Reese	4.00
34	Phil Rizzuto	4.00
35	Ralph Kiner	2.00
36	Robin Yount	4.00
37	Ozzie Smith	4.00
38	Roy Campanella	4.00
39	Satchel Paige	4.00
40	Stan Musial	5.00
41	Ted Williams	8.00
42	Thurman Munson	4.00
43	Tom Seaver	4.00
44	Ty Cobb	4.00
45	Walter Johnson	4.00
46	Warren Spahn	4.00
47	Whitey Ford	3.00
48	Willie McCovey	3.00
49	Willie Stargell	4.00
50	Yogi Berra	4.00
51	Adrian Beltre	2.00
52	Albert Pujols	6.00
53	Alex Rodriguez	6.00
54	Alfonso Soriano	2.00
55	Andruw Jones	2.00
56	B.J. Upton	2.00
57	Ben Sheets	2.00
58	Bret Boone	2.00
59	Brian Giles	2.00
60	Carlos Beltran	3.00
61	Carlos Delgado	2.00
62	Chipper Jones	4.00
63	Curt Schilling	4.00
64	David Ortiz	4.00
65	Derek Jeter	8.00
66	Eric Chavez	2.00
67	Frank Thomas	3.00
68	Gary Sheffield	2.00
69	Greg Maddux	5.00
70	Hank Blalock	2.00
71	Hideki Matsui	6.00
72	Ichiro Suzuki	6.00
73	Ivan Rodriguez	3.00
74	Jason Schmidt	2.00
75	Jeff Bagwell	2.00
76	Jim Thome	3.00
77	Johnny Damon	2.00
78	Jose Vidro	2.00
79	Ken Griffey Jr.	6.00
80	Kerry Wood	3.00
81	Manny Ramirez	4.00
82	Mark Prior	4.00
83	Mark Teixeira	2.00
84	Miguel Cabrera	3.00
85	Miguel Tejada	3.00
86	Mike Mussina	3.00
87	Mike Piazza	4.00
88	Mike Sweeney	2.00
89	Oliver Perez	2.00
90	Pedro Martinez	4.00
91	Rafael Palmeiro	4.00
92	Randy Johnson	4.00
93	Roger Clemens	5.00
94	Sammy Sosa	4.00
95	Scott Rolen	3.00
96	Tim Hudson	2.00
97	Todd Helton	2.00
98	Torii Hunter	2.00
99	Victor Martinez	2.00
100	Vladimir Guerrero	4.00
101	Adrian Gonzalez	8.00
102	Ambiorix Burgos RC	25.00
103	Ambiorix Concepcion RC	20.00
104	Dan Meyer	15.00
105	Ervin Santana	25.00
106	Gavin Floyd	20.00
107	Joe Blanton	20.00
108	Eric Crozier	10.00
109	Mark Teahen	25.00
110	Ryan Howard	50.00

Platinum

Cards (101-110):
Production One Set

Immortal Inscriptions

NM/M

Production 10-99
Platinum: No Pricing
Production One Set

WB	Wade Boggs/75	80.00
JB	Jim Bunning/99	60.00
SC	Steve Carlton/99	40.00
WC	Will Clark/99	60.00
EG	Eric Gagne/99	80.00
KG	Ken Griffey Jr./99	200.00
TG	Tony Gwynn/50	140.00
DM	Don Mattingly/75	150.00
BR	Brooks Robinson/99	50.00
TS	Tom Seaver/25	90.00
OS	Ozzie Smith/75	80.00
FT	Frank Thomas/50	100.00

Signature Cuts

Production One Set

Signature Cy Young

NM/M

Production 1-250

CM	David Cone, Greg Maddux/35	150.00
EG	Eric Gagne, Dennis Eckersley/200	50.00
ES	Dennis Eckersley, Bruce Sutter/250	30.00
GF	Ron Guidry, Whitey Ford/250	65.00
GM	Bob Gibson, Denny McLain/175	40.00
LC	Sparky Lyle, Steve Carlton/250	30.00
MS	Tom Seaver, Denny McLain	50.00
NF	Don Newcombe, Whitey Ford	60.00
PC	Gaylord Perry, Steve Carlton/250	40.00
PS	Jim Palmer, Tom Seaver/100	75.00

Signature Decades

NM/M

Some not priced due to scarcity.

	Platinum:	No Pricing
	Production One Set	
LA	Luis Aparicio	20.00
LA1	Luis Aparicio	20.00
CB	Carlos Beltran/99	35.00
YB	Yogi Berra	80.00
WB	Wade Boggs/25	65.00
WB1	Wade Boggs/25	65.00
LB	Lou Brock/50	35.00
JB	Jim Bunning	20.00
MC	Miguel Cabrera	30.00
JC	Jose Canseco/99	40.00
SC	Steve Carlton	20.00
SC1	Steve Carlton	20.00
GC	Gary Carter/50	25.00
OC	Orlando Cepeda	15.00
WC	Will Clark/99	40.00
RC	Rocky Colavito	50.00
RC1	Rocky Colavito	50.00
AD	Andre Dawson	15.00
BD	Bobby Doerr	15.00
DE	Dennis Eckersley	25.00
BF	Bob Feller	25.00
RF	Rollie Fingers	15.00
KG	Ken Griffey Jr.	65.00
RG	Ron Guidry	25.00
KH	Keith Hernandez	10.00
KH1	Keith Hernandez	10.00
MI	Monte Irvin	20.00
BJ	Bo Jackson/50	60.00
FJ	Fergie Jenkins/50	20.00
DJ	Derek Jeter/99	160.00
AK	Al Kaline/99	30.00
GK	George Kell	15.00
HK	Harmon Killebrew/99	40.00
RK	Ralph Kiner/99	30.00
DL	Don Larsen/99	25.00
FL	Fred Lynn	15.00
JM	Juan Marichal/99	25.00
DM	Don Mattingly/25	85.00
BM	Bill Mazeroski/99	40.00
PM	Paul Molitor/99	25.00
MO	Joe Morgan/50	25.00
MU	Dale Murphy	25.00
DN	Don Newcombe/99	20.00
PN	Phil Niekro	20.00
DO	David Ortiz	40.00
RO	Roy Oswalt	15.00
JP	Jim Palmer	25.00
TP	Tony Perez	25.00
GP	Gaylord Perry	15.00
GP1	Gaylord Perry	15.00
JR	Jim Rice	25.00
BR	Brooks Robinson	30.00
FR	Frank Robinson/25	40.00
AR	Al Rosen	15.00
JS	Johan Santana	40.00
RS	Ron Santo	25.00
BS	Ben Sheets	15.00
SU	Don Sutton	15.00
MT	Mark Teixeira	25.00
LT	Luis Tiant	15.00
LT1	Luis Tiant	15.00
BU	B.J. Upton	15.00
RW	Rickie Weeks	15.00
BW	Billy Williams	20.00
MW	Maury Wills	15.00
RY	Robin Yount/25	70.00

Signature Hits

NM/M

Production 1-125

BM	Stan Musial, Lou Brock/35	125.00
MY	Robin Yount, Paul Molitor/125	75.00
WG	Dave Winfield, Tony Gwynn/35	90.00
YB	Wade Boggs, Carl Yastrzemski/35	

Signature HRs

NM/M

Production 1-250

BS	Mike Schmidt, Ernie Banks/25	180.00
GM	Ken Griffey Jr., Willie McCovey/250	100.00
KM	Willie McCovey, Harmon Killebrew/35	75.00
RG	Frank Robinson, Ken Griffey Jr./250	85.00

Signature MVPs

NM/M

Production 1-250

BM	Don Mattingly, Yogi Berra/175	100.00
BS	Ernie Banks, Ryne Sandberg/25	200.00
CM	Stan Musial, Orlando Cepeda/75	
DS	Ryne Sandberg, Andre Dawson/175	80.00
EF	Dennis Eckersley, Rollie Fingers/250	30.00
FC	George Foster, Rod Carew/125	40.00
GM	Joe Morgan, Ken Griffey Jr./250	75.00
HY	Robin Yount, Keith Hernandez/200	50.00
JR	Ivan Rodriguez, Chipper Jones/35	125.00
KC	Harmon Killebrew, Rod Carew/100	80.00
KM	Harmon Killebrew, Willie McCovey/35	80.00
LM	Fred Lynn, Joe Morgan/200	30.00
LW	Maury Wills, Barry Larkin/250	35.00
MB	Joe Morgan, Johnny Bench/100	40.00
MG	Denny McLain, Bob Gibson/175	40.00
MY	Robin Yount, Dale Murphy/175	60.00
PR	Dave Parker, Jim Rice/250	40.00
SF	Mike Schmidt, Rollie Fingers/175	60.00
SS	Mike Schmidt, Ryne Sandberg/75	140.00
TB	Frank Thomas, Jeff Bagwell/50	90.00
YC	Orlando Cepeda, Carl Yastrzemski/100	65.00
YS	Carl Yastrzemski, Jim Rice/100	75.00

Signature No-Hitters

NM/M

Production 1-250

BG	Bob Gibson, Jim Bunning/125	60.00
CL	Don Larsen, David Cone/250	40.00
FR	Nolan Ryan, Bob Feller/25	150.00
GP	Bob Gibson, Jim Palmer/125	50.00

Signature Numbers

NM/M

Production 1-49
Platinum: No Pricing
Production One Set

WB	Wade Boggs/26	40.00
MC	Miguel Cabrera/24	50.00
JC	Jose Canseco/33	50.00
CA	Rod Carew/29	35.00
SC	Steve Carlton/32	25.00
OC	Orlando Cepeda/30	25.00
WC	Will Clark/22	60.00
CL	Roger Clemens/22	200.00
RF	Rollie Fingers/34	20.00
CF	Carlton Fisk/27	40.00
EG	Eric Gagne/38	40.00
BG	Bob Gibson/45	25.00
GL	Tom Glavine/47	40.00
KG	Ken Griffey Jr./30	125.00
VG	Vladimir Guerrero/27	50.00
RG	Ron Guidry/49	60.00
TG	Tony Gwynn/19	50.00
MI	Monte Irvin/20	30.00
FJ	Fergie Jenkins/31	20.00
RJ	Randy Johnson/41	75.00
MA	Juan Marichal/27	40.00
DM	Don Mattingly/23	125.00
WM	Willie McCovey/44	40.00
EM	Eddie Murray/33	120.00
DO	David Ortiz/34	50.00
RO	Roy Oswalt/44	25.00
JP	Jim Palmer/22	30.00
PI	Mike Piazza/31	100.00
MP	Mark Prior/22	60.00
KP	Kirby Puckett/34	85.00
FR	Frank Robinson/20	50.00
SR	Scott Rolen/27	40.00
NR	Nolan Ryan/34	120.00
TS	Tom Seaver/41	75.00
JS	John Smoltz/29	60.00
FT	Frank Thomas/35	80.00
BW	Billy Williams/26	30.00
DW	Dave Winfield/31	35.00
KW	Kerry Wood/34	40.00
RY	Robin Yount/19	75.00

Signature ROYs

NM/M

Production 1-250

CM	Willie McCovey, Orlando Cepeda/75	65.00
CS	Rod Carew, Tom Seaver/25	100.00
DM	Andre Dawson, Eddie Murray/25	70.00
FB	Carlton Fisk, Johnny Bench/35	80.00
FL	Fred Lynn/125, Carlton Fisk/125	60.00
GR	Nomar Garciaparra, Scott Rolen/200	85.00
GS	Dwight Gooden, Tom Seaver/100	60.00
JG	Derek Jeter, Nomar Garciaparra/75	185.00
RA	Frank Robinson, Luis Aparicio/125	50.00
RJ	Derek Jeter, Cal Ripken Jr./75	300.00
SG	Dwight Gooden, Darryl Strawberry/250	40.00
WD	Andre Dawson, Billy Williams/250	30.00

Signature Supremacy

		NM/M
Production 15-99		
LA	Luis Aparicio/50	40.00
JB	Jeff Bagwell	75.00
CB	Carlos Beltran/50	30.00
BE	Johnny Bench/25	60.00
YB	Yogi Berra/25	60.00
HB	Hank Blalock/50	25.00
WB	Wade Boggs/25	60.00
LB	Lou Brock/25	40.00
BU	Jim Bunning/99	25.00
MC	Miguel Cabrera/99	40.00
JC	Jose Canseco/25	60.00
CA	Rod Carew/25	35.00
SC	Steve Carlton/99	25.00
OC	Orlando Cepeda/99	20.00
EC	Eric Chavez/99	15.00
WC	Will Clark/50	40.00
AD	Andre Dawson/99	20.00
BD	Bobby Doerr/99	25.00
BF	Bob Feller/99	25.00
RF	Rollie Fingers/99	15.00
CF	Carlton Fisk/25	40.00
EG	Eric Gagne/50	25.00
KG	Ken Griffey Jr./99	80.00
RG	Ron Guidry/99	20.00
TH	Tim Hudson/50	25.00
MI	Monte Irvin/50	20.00
DJ	Derek Jeter/50	200.00
AK	Al Kaline/50	60.00
GK	George Kell/99	25.00
HK	Harmon Killebrew/50	40.00
RK	Ralph Kiner/25	40.00
JU	Juan Marichal/25	50.00
MA	Don Mattingly/99	80.00
BM	Bill Mazeroski/50	40.00
PM	Paul Molitor/50	40.00
JM	Joe Morgan/25	30.00
MM	Mark Mulder/99	15.00
DM	Dale Murphy/99	25.00
MU	Stan Musial/25	125.00
DN	Don Newcombe/99	20.00
DO	David Ortiz/99	25.00
RO	Roy Oswalt/99	15.00
JP	Jim Palmer/99	25.00
TP	Tony Perez/25	25.00
MP	Mark Prior/25	60.00
JR	Jim Rice/99	15.00
RR	Robin Roberts/99	30.00
BR	Brooks Robinson/99	30.00
FR	Frank Robinson/25	40.00
SR	Scott Rolen/25	25.00
AR	Al Rosen/99	15.00
SA	Ryne Sandberg/25	85.00
JS	Johan Santana/99	15.00
RS	Ron Santo	25.00
MS	Mike Schmidt/25	100.00
TS	Tom Seaver/25	50.00
BS	Ben Sheets/99	20.00
OS	Ozzie Smith/25	50.00
SM	John Smoltz/25	50.00
AS	Alfonso Soriano/25	25.00
MT	Mark Teixeira/99	25.00
FT	Frank Thomas/25	80.00
BW	Billy Williams/99	25.00
DW	Dave Winfield/25	50.00
CY	Carl Yastrzemski/25	100.00
RY	Robin Yount/25	75.00

Signs of October

		NM/M
Production 1-250		
BW	Mookie Wilson, Bill Buckner/250	40.00
CS	John Smoltz, Joe Carter/250	50.00
EG	Kirk Gibson, Dennis Eckersley/200	40.00
FM	Carlton Fisk, Joe Morgan/100	50.00
GB	Bob Gibson, Lou Brock/100	70.00
GG	Ron Guidry, Steve Garvey/250	30.00
GL	Mickey Lolich, Bob Gibson/100	40.00
JG	Derek Jeter, Tony Gwynn/250	185.00
LB	Yogi Berra, Don Larsen/250	85.00
MP	Jack Morris, Kirby Puckett/100	85.00
PS	Ozzie Smith, Kirby Puckett/35	125.00
RR	Frank Robinson, Brooks Robinson/250	65.00
SB	George Brett, Ozzie Smith	150.00
SY	Ozzie Smith, Robin Yount/100	85.00
TG	Kirk Gibson, Alan Trammell/250	40.00

2005 Upper Deck Trilogy

		NM/M
Complete Set (100):		40.00
Common Player:		.50
Pack (5):		20.00
Box (9):		170.00
1	A.J. Burnett	.50
2	Adam Dunn	1.00
3	Adrian Beltre	.50
4	Albert Pujols	4.00
5	Alex Rodriguez	3.00
6	Alfonso Soriano	1.00
7	Andruw Jones	1.00
8	Aramis Ramirez	.50
9	Ben Sheets	.75
10	Bobby Abreu	.50
11	Bobby Crosby	.50
12	Ryan Zimmerman RC	15.00
13	Brian Giles	.50
14	Brian Roberts	.50
15	Carl Crawford	.50
16	Carlos Beltran	1.00
17	Carlos Delgado	.75
18	Carlos Zambrano	.75
19	Chipper Jones	1.00
20	Corey Patterson	.50
21	Craig Biggio	.50
22	Curt Schilling	1.50
23	Dallas McPherson	.50
24	David Ortiz	1.50
25	David Wright	1.50
26	Delmon Young	1.00
27	Derek Jeter	4.00
28	Derrek Lee	1.00
29	Dontrelle Willis	1.00
30	Eric Chavez	.50
31	Eric Gagne	.50
32	Francisco Rodriguez	.50
33	Gary Sheffield	1.00
34	Greg Maddux	2.00
35	Hank Blalock	.50
36	Hideki Matsui	2.50
37	Ichiro Suzuki	3.00
38	Ivan Rodriguez	1.00
39	J.D. Drew	.50
40	Jake Peavy	.75
41	Jason Bay	.50
42	Jason Schmidt	.50
43	Jeff Bagwell	1.00
44	Jeff Kent	.50
45	Jeff Niemann RC	2.00
46	Jeremy Bonderman	.50
47	Jim Edmonds	.75
48	Jim Thome	1.00
49	Joe Mauer	.75
50	Johan Santana	1.00
51	John Smoltz	.75
52	Johnny Damon	1.00
53	Jose Reyes	.75
54	Jose Vidro	.50
55	Josh Beckett	.75
56	Justin Morneau	.50
57	Justin Verlander RC	4.00
58	Ken Griffey Jr.	3.00
59	Kendry Morales RC	6.00
60	Kerry Wood	.75
61	Khalil Greene	.75
62	Lance Berkman	.75
63	Luis Gonzalez	.50
64	Manny Ramirez	1.50
65	Mark Buehrle	.75
66	Mark Mulder	.50
67	Mark Prior	1.00
68	Mark Teixeira	1.00
69	Michael Young	.50
70	Miguel Cabrera	1.50
71	Miguel Tejada	1.00
72	Mike Mussina	1.00
73	Mike Piazza	1.50
74	Nomar Garciaparra	1.00
75	Pat Burrell	.50
76	Paul Konerko	.75
77	Pedro Martinez	1.50
78	Philip Humber RC	2.00
79	Prince Fielder	8.00
80	Randy Johnson	1.50
81	Richie Sexson	.75
82	Rickie Weeks	.75
83	Roger Clemens	4.00
84	Roy Halladay	.75
85	Roy Oswalt	.75
86	Sammy Sosa	1.50
87	Scott Kazmir	.50
88	Scott Rolen	1.00
89	Stephen Drew RC	8.00
90	Tadahito Iguchi RC	4.00
91	Tim Hudson	.50
92	Todd Helton	1.00
93	Tom Glavine	.75
94	Torii Hunter	.75
95	Travis Hafner	.75
96	Troy Glaus	.75
97	Vernon Wells	.50
98	Victor Martinez	.50
99	Vladimir Guerrero	1.50
100	Zack Greinke	.50

Generations

Complete Set (6):	
Common Player:	

Generation Future Lumber Silver

		NM/M
Production 100 Sets		
Gold:		1X
Production 60 Sets		
RC	Robinson Cano	20.00
CA	Jorge Cantu	6.00
GF	Gavin Floyd	4.00
BH	Brad Halsey	4.00
JJ	J.J. Hardy	4.00
RH	Ryan Howard	50.00
LN	Laynce Nix	4.00
JP	Jhonny Peralta	6.00
JR	Jeremy Reed	4.00
AR	Alexis Rios	6.00
RI	Juan Rivera	4.00
BJ	B.J. Upton	6.00
JW	Jayson Werth	4.00
YO	Kevin Youkilis	6.00

Generation Future Materials Silver

		NM/M
Common Player:		4.00
Production 120 Sets		
Gold:		1X
Production 75 Sets		
BA	Bronson Arroyo	6.00
GA	Garrett Atkins	4.00
JB	Jeff Baker	4.00
CL	Clint Barmes	6.00
JB	Jason Bartlett	4.00
BL	Joe Blanton	4.00
DB	Dewon Brazelton	4.00
YB	Yhency Brazoban	4.00
CB	Chris Burke	6.00
DC	Daniel Cabrera	4.00
RC	Robinson Cano	20.00
CA	Jorge Cantu	6.00
GC	Gustavo Chacin	4.00
JC	J.D. Closser	4.00
DD	David DeJesus	4.00
DU	Jason Dubois	4.00
GF	Gavin Floyd	4.00
JF	Jeff Francis	4.00
AG	Adrian Gonzalez	4.00
BH	Brad Halsey	4.00
JJ	J.J. Hardy	4.00
DH	Danny Haren	4.00
AH	Aaron Hill	4.00
HO	Dennis Houlton	4.00
RH	Ryan Howard	20.00
TI	Tadahito Iguchi	15.00
EJ	Edwin Jackson	4.00
DK	Dae-Sung Koo	4.00
KO	Casey Kotchman	4.00
JL	Jason Lane	4.00
DM	Dallas McPherson	4.00
AM	Aaron Miles	4.00
YM	Yadier Molina	4.00
MY	Brett Myers	4.00
XN	Xavier Nady	4.00
LN	Laynce Nix	4.00
JP	Jhonny Peralta	6.00
RQ	Robb Quinlan	4.00
JR	Jeremy Reed	4.00
AR	Alexis Rios	6.00
RI	Juan Rivera	4.00
ES	Ervin Santana	6.00
SS	Steve Schmoll	4.00
LS	Luke Scott	4.00
SI	Grady Sizemore	10.00
HS	Huston Street	10.00
NS	Nick Swisher	8.00
WT	Willy Taveras	8.00
MT	Mark Teahen	4.00
CT	Charles Thomas	4.00
CT	Chad Tracy	4.00
BJ	B.J. Upton	6.00
CU	Chase Utley	10.00
WA	Ryan Wagner	4.00
RW	Rickie Weeks	8.00
JW	Jayson Werth	4.00
KY	Keiichi Yabu	4.00
YO	Kevin Youkilis	6.00

Generations Future Signature Silver

	NM/M
Common Player:	8.00

Generations

		NM/M
Production 50-199		
Bronze:		1-1.5X
Production 35 Sets		
Gold:		No Pricing
Production 15 Sets		
GA	Garrett Atkins/199	10.00
JB	Jason Bartlett/199	8.00
BE	Colter Bean/199	8.00
BL	Joe Blanton/99	10.00
YB	Yhency Brazoban/199	10.00
AB	Ambiorix Burgos/199	8.00
CB	Chris Burke/199	15.00
DC	Daniel Cabrera/199	12.00
JO	Jose Capellan/199	10.00
JB	J.D. Closser/99	10.00
AC	Ambiorix Concepcion/199	8.00
DD	David DeJesus/99	12.00
SD	Stephen Drew/75	125.00
DU	Jason Dubois/99	10.00
PF	Prince Fielder/99	90.00
GF	Gavin Floyd/99	10.00
JF	Jeff Francis/99	12.00
AG	Adrian Gonzalez/99	10.00
JG	Jared Gothreaux/199	8.00
GG	Gabe Gross/99	10.00
JJ	J.J. Hardy/199	15.00
JH	John Hattig Jr./199	10.00
FH	Felix Hernandez/60	80.00
HO	Dennis Houlton/199	10.00
RH	Ryan Howard/99	40.00
PH	Philip Humber/75	20.00
TI	Tadahito Iguchi/75	175.00
EJ	Edwin Jackson/99	10.00
KO	Casey Kotchman/99	10.00
JL	Jason Lane/99	10.00
ML	Matt Lindstrom/199	8.00
PL	Pedro Lopez/189	10.00
RM	Russell Martin/199	15.00
KM	Kendry Morales/199	10.00
JN	Jeff Niemann/75	40.00
PO	Peter Orr/199	15.00
TP	Tony Pena/199	8.00
RQ	Robb Quinlan/199	8.00
AR	Alexis Rios/199	15.00
CR	Casey Rogowski/199	10.00
RR	Russel Rohlicek/199	8.00
SS	Steve Schmoll/199	8.00
LS	Luke Scott/199	10.00
TS	Tim Stauffer/199	8.00
NS	Nick Swisher/99	15.00
MT	Mark Teahen/199	12.00
TH	Charles Thomas/199	12.00
BJ	B.J. Upton/50	20.00
CU	Chase Utley/50	15.00
JV	Justin Verlander/75	50.00
RW	Rickie Weeks/50	25.00
JW	Jayson Werth/99	15.00
KY	Keiichi Yabu/199	25.00
YO	Kevin Youkilis/99	20.00
DY	Delmon Young/50	40.00
RZ	Ryan Zimmerman/150	125.00

Generations of Lumber Triple

		NM/M
Production 85 Sets		10.00
ARU	B.J. Upton, Jimmy Rollins, Luis Aparicio	15.00
BCU	Wade Boggs, B.J. Upton, Carl Crawford	15.00
BHH	Travis Hafner, Ryan Howard, Harold Baines	15.00
BMY	Bill Mueller, Wade Boggs, Kevin Youkilis	15.00
CCC	Will Clark, Jack Clark, Orlando Cepeda	12.00
DAR	Bobby Abreu, Eric Davis, Alex Rios	10.00
EDY	Kevin Youkilis, Dwight Evans, Johnny Damon	20.00
GDP	Ken Griffey Jr., Wily Mo Pena, Adam Dunn	25.00
GGC	Miguel Cabrera, Ken Griffey Jr., Tony Gwynn	25.00
HDH	Ryan Howard, Adam Dunn, Frank Howard	15.00
HOH	Frank Howard, Ryan Howard, David Ortiz	20.00
JGU	Bo Jackson, Ken Griffey Jr., B.J. Upton	25.00
JHR	Alex Rios, Bo Jackson, Torii Hunter	25.00
JSP	Bo Jackson, Gary Sheffield, Wily Mo Pena	15.00
KBH	Pat Burrell, John Kruk, Ryan Howard	15.00
LJU	Barry Larkin, Derek Jeter, B.J. Upton	30.00
LYU	B.J. Upton, Barry Larkin, Michael Young	12.00
MDW	Jayson Werth, Dale Murphy, Adam Dunn	15.00
MMJ	Don Mattingly, Derek Jeter, Bobby Murcer	50.00
MOH	Ryan Howard, David Ortiz, Eddie Murray	20.00

Generations of Materials Triple

		NM/M
Common Trio:		10.00
Production 50 Sets		
AAD	Aramis Ramirez, Al Rosen, Dallas McPherson	15.00
AFB	Luis Aparicio, Rafael Furcal, Jason Bartlett	15.00
API	Tadahito Iguchi, Scott Podsednik, Luis Aparicio	25.00
ARU	Jimmy Rollins, Luis Aparicio, B.J. Upton	15.00
BCU	B.J. Upton, Carl Crawford, Wade Boggs	15.00
BHH	Ryan Howard, Harold Baines, Travis Hafner	15.00
BLS	Craig Biggio, Jason Lane, Luke Scott	15.00
BMY	Kevin Youkilis, Wade Boggs, Bill Mueller	15.00
CCC	Will Clark, Jack Clark, Orlando Cepeda	15.00
CCK	Sean Casey, Will Clark, Casey Kotchman	15.00
CMG	Justin Morneau, Adrian Gonzalez, Will Clark	15.00
CTG	Will Clark, Adrian Gonzalez, Mark Teixeira	15.00
DAR	Alex Rios, Eric Davis, Bobby Abreu	15.00
DBS	Lenny Dykstra, Jason Bay, Nick Swisher	15.00
DGL	Jason Lane, Ken Griffey Jr., Andre Dawson	25.00
DHL	Lenny Dykstra, Torii Hunter, Jason Lane	10.00
DPD	Jason Dubois, Corey Patterson, Andre Dawson	10.00
DPT	Lenny Dykstra, Scott Podsednik, Willy Taveras	15.00
EDY	Kevin Youkilis, Johnny Damon, Dwight Evans	20.00
GAS	Bobby Abreu, Tony Gwynn, Nick Swisher	25.00
GDP	Wily Mo Pena, Adam Dunn, Ken Griffey Jr.	25.00
GGC	Ken Griffey Jr., Tony Gwynn, Miguel Cabrera	25.00
GMY	Kevin Youkilis, Mike Greenwell, Bill Mueller	15.00
GWJ	Dwight Gooden, Dontrelle Willis, Edwin Jackson	15.00
HDH	Frank Howard, Adam Dunn, Ryan Howard	15.00
HOH	Ryan Howard, David Ortiz, Frank Howard	20.00
JGU	B.J. Upton, Bo Jackson, Ken Griffey Jr.	25.00
JHR	Bo Jackson, Torii Hunter, Alex Rios	20.00
JMK	Casey Kotchman, Wally Joyner, Dallas McPherson	10.00
JSP	Bo Jackson, Gary Sheffield, Wily Mo Pena	15.00
KBH	Pat Burrell, John Kruk, Ryan Howard	15.00
KBU	John Kruk, Pat Burrell, Chase Utley	15.00
LJU	B.J. Upton, Barry Larkin, Derek Jeter	35.00
LYU	Barry Larkin, Michael Young, B.J. Upton	35.00
MBS	Nick Swisher, Pat Burrell, Dale Murphy	20.00
MCG	Don Mattingly, Sean Casey, Adrian Gonzalez	30.00
MDW	Adam Dunn, Jayson Werth, Dale Murphy	20.00
MMJ	Don Mattingly, Derek Jeter, Bobby Murcer	60.00
MOH	David Ortiz, Ryan Howard, Eddie Murray	20.00
NBW	Adrian Beltre, David Wright, Graig Nettles	20.00
OAR	Bobby Abreu, Tony Oliva, Alex Rios	20.00
PDP	Wily Mo Pena, Eric Davis, Tony Perez	20.00
PGD	Tony Perez, Brian Giles, Jason Dubois	10.00
PGP	Wily Mo Pena, Ken Griffey Jr., Tony Perez	30.00
RBT	Brooks Robinson, Adrian Beltre, Mark Teahen	20.00
RCD	Carl Crawford, David DeJesus, Tim Raines	10.00
RJC	Derek Jeter, Cal Ripken Jr., Bobby Crosby	50.00
ROY	Jim Rice, David Ortiz, Kevin Youkilis	25.00
RRM	Brooks Robinson, Cal Ripken Jr., Melvin Mora	50.00
RRT	Miguel Tejada, Cal Ripken Jr., Brooks Robinson	50.00
SBM	Dallas McPherson, Adrian Beltre, Mike Schmidt	20.00
SBW	Mike Schmidt, Adrian Beltre, David Wright	20.00
SDW	Duke Snider, Jayson Werth, J.D. Drew	20.00
SGU	Ryne Sandberg, Chase Utley, Marcus Giles	35.00
SRU	Chase Utley, Mike Schmidt, Jimmy Rollins	40.00
SRW	Ryne Sandberg, Brian Roberts, Rickie Weeks	25.00
VGB	Jason Bay, Brian Giles, Andy Van Slyke	10.00
VPD	Andy Van Slyke, Corey Patterson, David DeJesus	10.00
WBI	Tadahito Iguchi, Frank White, Craig Biggio	20.00
WCT	Willie Wilson, Willy Taveras, Carl Crawford	15.00

Generations of Signatures

		NM/M
Production 35 Sets		
AYU	B.J. Upton, Luis Aparicio, Michael Young	40.00
BPN	Jake Peavy, Jeff Niemann, Jim Bunning	
CTG	Will Clark, Mark Teixeira, Adrian Gonzalez	60.00
DBU	Chase Utley, Craig Biggio, Bobby Doerr	50.00
DGL	Ken Griffey Jr., Andre Dawson, Jason Lane	100.00
DGU	Marcus Giles, Chase Utley, Bobby Doerr	50.00
DLB	Bobby Doerr, Mark Loretta, Chris Burke	30.00
FPH	Rich Harden, Mark Prior, Bob Feller	50.00
GDP	Ken Griffey Jr., Adam Dunn, Wily Mo Pena	100.00
HDG	Adam Dunn, Frank Howard, Gabe Gross	40.00
JHR	Torii Hunter, Bo Jackson, Alex Rios	85.00

JKM Casey Kotchman, Kendry Morales, Wally Joyner 50.00
LJU Barry Larkin, Derek Jeter, B.J. Upton 250.00
MBV Justin Verlander, Jack Morris, Jeremy Bonderman 90.00
MMJ Derek Jeter, Don Mattingly, Bobby Murcer 260.00
NBW David Wright, Graig Nettles, Adrian Beltre 75.00
OHM Tony Oliva, Kent Hrbek, Justin Morneau 50.00
PBF Gaylord Perry, Jeremy Bonderman, Gavin Floyd 35.00
PGP Tony Perez, Ken Griffey Jr., Wily Mo Pena 100.00
PPH Philip Humber, Jim Palmer, Jake Peavy
PPS Jake Peavy, Tim Stauffer, Gaylord Perry 40.00
RCD Tim Raines, David DeJesus, Carl Crawford 40.00
RJC Bobby Crosby, Cal Ripken Jr., Derek Jeter 400.00
RRM Cal Ripken Jr., Melvin Mora, Brooks Robinson 180.00
RSH Nolan Ryan, John Smoltz, Philip Humber 165.00
SBT Mark Teahen, Adrian Beltre, Ron Santo 50.00
SBW Adrian Beltre, Mike Schmidt, David Wright 100.00
SGH J.J. Hardy, Ozzie Smith, Khalil Greene 70.00
SMR Ron Santo, Bill Madlock, Aramis Ramirez 50.00
SRW Brian Roberts, Ryne Sandberg, Rickie Weeks 85.00
VGB Jason Bay, Brian Giles, Andy Van Slyke 65.00

Generations Past Lumber
NM/M
Common Player: 4.00
Production 115 unless noted.
Gold: 1-1.5X
Production 25-75
LA Luis Aparicio 8.00
HB Harold Baines 4.00
DB Dusty Baker 6.00
JB Johnny Bench 10.00
WB Wade Boggs 8.00
BB Bill Buckner 6.00
CA Rod Carew 8.00
SC Steve Carlton 6.00
GC Gary Carter 6.00
OC Orlando Cepeda 6.00
CY Ron Cey 4.00
JC Jack Clark 4.00
WC Will Clark 8.00
TC Ty Cobb/99 100.00
MC Mickey Cochrane/99 25.00
ED Eric Davis 8.00
AD Andre Dawson 6.00
JD Joe DiMaggio/99 65.00
BD Bobby Doerr 8.00
LD Lenny Dykstra 4.00
DE Dwight Evans 6.00
CF Carlton Fisk 6.00
GF George Foster 4.00
JF Jimmie Foxx/99 50.00
FR Bill Freehan 4.00
LG Lou Gehrig/99 140.00
DG Dwight Gooden 4.00
GR Lefty Grove/99 40.00
TG Tony Gwynn 10.00
KH Keith Hernandez 4.00
RH Rogers Hornsby/99 40.00
FH Frank Howard 6.00
BJ Bo Jackson 10.00
RJ Reggie Jackson 10.00
JO Wally Joyner 4.00
GK George Kell 8.00
JK John Kruk 4.00
BL Barry Larkin 6.00
DL Davey Lopes 4.00
BM Bill Madlock 4.00
MA Don Mattingly 25.00
FM Fred McGriff 4.00
JM Johnny Mize 4.00
TM Thurman Munson 20.00
MU Bobby Murcer 4.00
DM Dale Murphy 8.00
MY Eddie Murray 8.00
SM Stan Musial 20.00
GN Graig Nettles 6.00
TO Tony Oliva 6.00
MO Mel Ott 25.00
TP Tony Perez 6.00
GP Gaylord Perry 6.00
RP Rico Petrocelli 6.00
BP Boog Powell 4.00
TR Tim Raines 6.00
RI Jim Rice 6.00
CR Cal Ripken Jr. 25.00
RO Brooks Robinson 8.00

JR Jackie Robinson 4.00
AR Al Rosen 10.00
BR Babe Ruth/99 140.00
NR Nolan Ryan 25.00
SA Ryne Sandberg 15.00
RS Ron Santo 10.00
MS Mike Schmidt 15.00
SI George Sisler 6.00
SK Bill "Moose" Skowron 4.00
OS Ozzie Smith 20.00
SN Duke Snider 10.00
DS Darryl Strawberry 6.00
AT Alan Trammell 6.00
AV Andy Van Slyke 8.00
FW Frank White 4.00
WW Willie Wilson 4.00
YA Carl Yastrzemski 25.00

Generation Past Material Silver
NM/M
Common Player: 4.00
Production 99 unless noted.
Gold: 1-1.5X
Production 25 Sets
LA Luis Aparicio 8.00
HB Harold Baines 4.00
DB Dusty Baker 6.00
JB Johnny Bench 10.00
WB Wade Boggs 8.00
BU Jim Bunning 6.00
RC Roy Campanella 20.00
CA Rod Carew 8.00
SC Steve Carlton 6.00
GC Gary Carter 6.00
OC Orlando Cepeda 6.00
CY Ron Cey 4.00
JC Jack Clark 4.00
WC Will Clark 8.00
DC David Cone 6.00
ED Eric Davis 8.00
AD Andre Dawson 6.00
DD Dizzy Dean/75 40.00
JD Joe DiMaggio/75 85.00
DR Don Drysdale 10.00
LD Lenny Dykstra 4.00
BF Bob Feller 10.00
CF Carlton Fisk 8.00
LG Lou Gehrig/75 150.00
DG Dwight Gooden 4.00
RG Ron Guidry 4.00
TG Tony Gwynn 10.00
KH Keith Hernandez 4.00
RH Rogers Hornsby/75 65.00
FH Frank Howard 6.00
HR Kent Hrbek 8.00
BJ Bo Jackson 10.00
RJ Reggie Jackson 10.00
JO Wally Joyner 6.00
JK John Kruk 8.00
BL Barry Larkin 4.00
DL Davey Lopes 4.00
BM Bill Madlock 6.00
EM Eddie Mathews/75 20.00
CM Christy Mathewson/75 80.00
MA Don Mattingly 25.00
JM Johnny Mize 15.00
JA Jack Morris 4.00
TM Thurman Munson 20.00
MU Bobby Murcer 8.00
DM Dale Murphy 8.00
MY Eddie Murray 8.00
SM Stan Musial 20.00
GN Graig Nettles 6.00
TO Tony Oliva 6.00
MO Mel Ott/75 75.00
SP Satchel Paige/75 50.00
JP Jim Palmer 6.00
TP Tony Perez 6.00
GP Gaylord Perry 6.00
RP Rico Petrocelli 4.00
BP Boog Powell 4.00
TR Tim Raines 6.00
RI Jim Rice 6.00
CR Cal Ripken Jr. 25.00
RO Brooks Robinson 10.00
AR Al Rosen 10.00
NR Nolan Ryan 25.00
SA Ryne Sandberg 15.00
MS Mike Schmidt 15.00
AV Andy Van Slyke 15.00
OS Ozzie Smith 15.00
SN Duke Snider 10.00
DS Darryl Strawberry 6.00
FW Frank White 4.00
WW Willie Wilson 4.00
YA Carl Yastrzemski 15.00

Generations Past Autograph Silver
NM/M
Common Player: 10.00
Production 24-99.
Bronze: 1-1.5X
Production 10 or 35.
No pricing for prod. of 10.
Gold: No Pricing
Production 5-15
LA Luis Aparicio/50 20.00
HB Harold Baines/199 15.00
DB Dusty Baker/25 20.00
WB Wade Boggs/35 35.00
BB Bill Buckner/50 15.00
BU Jim Bunning/99 20.00
CA Rod Carew/25 35.00

SC Steve Carlton/25 20.00
CY Ron Cey/199 15.00
JC Jack Clark/199 10.00
WC Will Clark/25 40.00
DC David Cone/99 15.00
ED Eric Davis/199 15.00
AD Andre Dawson/99 20.00
BD Bobby Doerr/199 15.00
LD Lenny Dykstra/199 15.00
DE Dwight Evans/50 20.00
BF Bob Feller/99 25.00
GF George Foster/199 10.00
FR Bill Freehan/199 15.00
RG Ron Guidry/199 15.00
KH Keith Hernandez/199 15.00
FH Frank Howard/199 15.00
HR Kent Hrbek/199 15.00
BJ Bo Jackson/50 50.00
RJ Reggie Jackson/25 50.00
JO Wally Joyner/199 15.00
GK George Kell/199 15.00
JK John Kruk/199 20.00
BL Barry Larkin/99 25.00
DL Davey Lopes/199 10.00
BM Bill Madlock/199 10.00
MA Don Mattingly/25 75.00
FM Fred McGriff/199 15.00
JA Jack Morris/199 15.00
MU Bobby Murcer/199 25.00
DM Dale Murphy/199 25.00
SM Stan Musial/25 80.00
GN Graig Nettles/199 15.00
TO Tony Oliva/199 15.00
JP Jim Palmer/50 20.00
TP Tony Perez/25 30.00
GP Gaylord Perry/199 15.00
BP Boog Powell/199 15.00
TR Tim Raines/199 15.00
RI Jim Rice/99 15.00
RO Brooks Robinson/50 30.00
AR Al Rosen/199 15.00
NR Nolan Ryan/25 100.00
SA Ryne Sandberg/50 60.00
RS Ron Santo/199 30.00
MS Mike Schmidt/25 15.00
SK Bill Skowron/25 15.00
OS Ozzie Smith/25 50.00
DS Darryl Strawberry/99 15.00
AT Alan Trammell/50 20.00
AV Andy Van Slyke/199 20.00
FW Frank White/199 15.00
WW Willie Wilson/199 15.00

Generation Present Lumber Silver
NM/M
Common Player: 4.00
Production 115 Sets
Gold: 1X
Production 75 Sets
BA Bobby Abreu 4.00
GA Garret Anderson 4.00
JE Jeff Bagwell 4.00
CB Carlos Beltran 6.00
AB Adrian Beltre 4.00
LB Lance Berkman 4.00
BI Craig Biggio 6.00
HB Hank Blalock 4.00
BO Jeremy Bonderman 4.00
PB Pat Burrell 4.00
AJ A.J. Burnett 4.00
MC Miguel Cabrera 8.00
SC Sean Casey 4.00
EC Eric Chavez 4.00
RC Roger Clemens 12.00
CC Carl Crawford 4.00
BC Bobby Crosby 4.00
DA Johnny Damon 8.00
CD Carlos Delgado 4.00
JD J.D. Drew 4.00
AD Adam Dunn 6.00
RF Rafael Furcal 4.00
JG Jason Giambi 6.00
BG Brian Giles 4.00
MG Marcus Giles 4.00
TG Troy Glaus 4.00
GR Khalil Greene 6.00
KG1 Ken Griffey Jr. 20.00
KG2 Ken Griffey Jr. 20.00
KG3 Ken Griffey Jr. 20.00
VG Vladimir Guerrero 8.00
HA Travis Hafner 4.00
RH Rich Harden 4.00
TH Todd Helton 6.00
AH Aubrey Huff 6.00
HU Torii Hunter 4.00
DJ Derek Jeter 20.00
RJ Randy Johnson 8.00
JO Andruw Jones 6.00
CJ Chipper Jones 8.00
JK Jeff Kent 4.00
DL Derek Lee 8.00
ML Mark Loretta 4.00
GM Greg Maddux 15.00
PM Pedro Martinez 8.00
VM Victor Martinez 6.00
JM Joe Mauer 6.00
ME Melvin Mora 4.00
MO Justin Morneau 8.00
BM Bill Mueller 4.00
MM Mark Mulder 4.00
DO David Ortiz 8.00
RO Roy Oswalt 4.00
PA Corey Patterson 4.00
JP Jake Peavy 4.00
WM Wily Mo Pena 4.00
PI Mike Piazza 8.00
SP Scott Podsednik 6.00
MP Mark Prior 6.00
AP Albert Pujols 20.00
AR Aramis Ramirez 4.00
MR Manny Ramirez 8.00
RE Jose Reyes 4.00
BR Brian Roberts 4.00
IR Ivan Rodriguez 6.00
SR Scott Rolen 6.00
JR Jimmy Rollins 4.00
CS Curt Schilling 8.00
GS Gary Sheffield 6.00
SM John Smoltz 6.00
AS Alfonso Soriano 6.00
SS Sammy Sosa 6.00
MT Mark Teixeira 8.00
TE Miguel Tejada 6.00
FT Frank Thomas 6.00
JT Jim Thome 6.00
JV Jason Varitek 8.00
VI Jose Vidro 4.00
BW Bernie Williams 6.00
WI Dontrelle Willis 6.00
KW Kerry Wood 4.00
DW David Wright 20.00
MY Michael Young 4.00
CZ Carlos Zambrano 4.00

Generations Present Materials Silver
NM/M
Common Player: 4.00
Production 99 Sets
Gold: 1-1.5X
Production 25 Sets
BA Bobby Abreu 4.00
GA Garret Anderson 4.00
JE Jeff Bagwell 6.00
JB Jason Bay 4.00
CB Carlos Beltran 6.00
AB Adrian Beltre 4.00
BI Craig Biggio 6.00
HB Hank Blalock 4.00
BO Jeremy Bonderman 4.00
PB Pat Burrell 4.00
AJ A.J. Burnett 4.00
MC Miguel Cabrera 8.00
SC Sean Casey 4.00
EC Eric Chavez 4.00
RC Roger Clemens 12.00
CC Carl Crawford 4.00
BC Bobby Crosby 4.00
DA Johnny Damon 8.00
CD Carlos Delgado 4.00
JD J.D. Drew 4.00
AD Adam Dunn 6.00
RF Rafael Furcal 4.00
JG Jason Giambi 6.00
BG Brian Giles 4.00
MG Marcus Giles 4.00
TG Troy Glaus 4.00
GR Khalil Greene 4.00
ZG Zack Greinke 4.00
KG1 Ken Griffey Jr. 20.00
KG2 Ken Griffey Jr. 20.00
KG3 Ken Griffey Jr. 20.00
VG Vladimir Guerrero 8.00
HA Travis Hafner 4.00
RH Rich Harden 4.00
TH Todd Helton 6.00
AH Aubrey Huff 4.00
HU Torii Hunter 4.00
DJ Derek Jeter 20.00
RJ Randy Johnson 8.00
JO Andruw Jones 6.00
CJ Chipper Jones 6.00
SK Scott Kazmir 4.00
JK Jeff Kent 4.00
DL Derek Lee 8.00
BL Brad Lidge 4.00
ML Mark Loretta 4.00
GM Greg Maddux 15.00
PM Pedro Martinez 8.00
VM Victor Martinez 4.00
JM Joe Mauer 6.00
ME Melvin Mora 4.00
MO Justin Morneau 8.00
BM Bill Mueller 4.00
MM Mark Mulder 4.00
DO David Ortiz 8.00
RO Roy Oswalt 4.00
PA Corey Patterson 4.00
JP Jake Peavy 4.00
WM Wily Mo Pena 4.00
PI Mike Piazza 8.00
SP Scott Podsednik 6.00
MP Mark Prior 6.00
AP Albert Pujols 20.00
AR Aramis Ramirez 4.00
MR Manny Ramirez 8.00
RE Jose Reyes 4.00
BR Brian Roberts 4.00
IR Ivan Rodriguez 6.00
SR Scott Rolen 6.00
JR Jimmy Rollins 4.00
JS Johan Santana 6.00
CS Curt Schilling 8.00
BS Ben Sheets 4.00
GS Gary Sheffield 6.00
SM John Smoltz 6.00
AS Alfonso Soriano 6.00
SS Sammy Sosa 6.00
MT Mark Teixeira 8.00
TE Miguel Tejada 6.00
FT Frank Thomas 6.00
JT Jim Thome 6.00
JV Jason Varitek 8.00
VI Jose Vidro 4.00
BW Bernie Williams 6.00
WI Dontrelle Willis 6.00
KW Kerry Wood 4.00
DW David Wright 20.00
MY Michael Young 4.00
CZ Carlos Zambrano 4.00

Generations Present Signatures
NM/M
Common Player: 10.00
Production 25-199.
Bronze: 1-1.5X
Production 10 or 35.
No pricing for prod. of 10.
Gold: No Pricing
Production 5-15.
GA Garret Anderson/25 20.00
JB Jason Bay/199 15.00
BI Craig Biggio/99 35.00
BO Jeremy Bonderman/199 15.00
MC Miguel Cabrera/25 40.00
SC Sean Casey/50 15.00
CC Carl Crawford/99 15.00
BC Bobby Crosby/99 15.00
AD Adam Dunn/95 25.00
RF Rafael Furcal/99 15.00
BG Brian Giles/99 12.00
MG Marcus Giles/199 10.00
GR Khalil Greene/135 25.00
ZG Zack Greinke/99 15.00
KG1 Ken Griffey Jr./199 75.00
KG2 Ken Griffey Jr./199 75.00
KG3 Ken Griffey Jr./199 75.00
HA Travis Hafner/99 15.00
RH Rich Harden/199 15.00
AH Aubrey Huff/199 15.00
HU Torii Hunter/25 25.00
DJ Derek Jeter/99 150.00
DL Derek Lee/25 40.00
BL Brad Lidge/25 15.00
ML Mark Loretta/99 15.00
VM Victor Martinez/99 15.00
JM Joe Mauer/25 25.00
ME Melvin Mora/199 10.00
MO Justin Morneau/99 15.00
MM Mark Mulder/99 15.00
DO David Ortiz/25 50.00
RO Roy Oswalt/25 30.00
JP Jake Peavy/99 15.00
WM Wily Mo Pena/199 15.00
SP Scott Podsednik/99 20.00
MP Mark Prior/40 40.00
AR Aramis Ramirez/99 15.00
BR Brian Roberts/99 15.00
BS Ben Sheets/99 15.00
GS Gary Sheffield/25 35.00
SM John Smoltz/25 50.00
MT Mark Teixeira/25 50.00
TE Miguel Tejada/25 40.00
FT Frank Thomas/25 50.00
VI Jose Vidro/99 10.00
WI Dontrelle Willis/25 30.00
DW David Wright/135 50.00
MY Michael Young/199 15.00

Signature Dual Material
NM/M
Common Player: 20.00
Production 75 Sets
HB Harold Baines 25.00
AB Adrian Beltre 25.00
BI Craig Biggio 40.00
WB Wade Boggs 50.00
MC Miguel Cabrera 50.00
SC Sean Casey 25.00
OC Orlando Cepeda 40.00
CL Jack Clark 20.00
WC Will Clark 50.00
CC Carl Crawford 20.00
BC Bobby Crosby 20.00
ED Eric Davis 35.00
AD Andre Dawson 30.00
DU Adam Dunn 40.00
LD Lenny Dykstra 20.00
BG Brian Giles 20.00
GI Marcus Giles 20.00
KG Ken Griffey Jr. 150.00
TG Tony Gwynn 60.00
TH Travis Hafner 30.00
FH Frank Howard 20.00
RH Ryan Howard 75.00
AH Aubrey Huff 20.00
HU Torii Hunter 30.00
DJ Derek Jeter 300.00
WJ Wally Joyner 20.00
BL Barry Larkin 40.00
MA Bill Madlock 40.00
VM Victor Martinez 25.00
DM Don Mattingly 90.00
BM Bobby Murcer 35.00
GN Graig Nettles 30.00
TO Tony Oliva 20.00
DO David Ortiz 75.00
CP Corey Patterson 20.00
WM Wily Mo Pena 25.00
TP Tony Perez 40.00
SP Scott Podsednik 50.00
AP Albert Pujols 125.00
TR Tim Raines 30.00
RA Aramis Ramirez 35.00
RE Jose Reyes 40.00

RI Jim Rice 35.00
CR Cal Ripken Jr. 150.00
RO Brooks Robinson 50.00
RS Ryne Sandberg 80.00
MS Mike Schmidt 75.00
MT Mark Teixeira 60.00
MI Miguel Tejada 50.00
BU B.J. Upton 25.00
AV Andy Van Slyke 30.00
JV Jose Vidro 20.00
JW Jayson Werth 20.00
DW David Wright 80.00
KY Kevin Youkilis 20.00

2005 Upper Deck Update
NM/M
Complete Update Set (186):
Common Player (1-100): .15
Common Rookie (101-177): 3.00
Production 599
Common RK Auto.
(178-186): 10.00
Production 75
Pack (5): 5.00
Box (24): 110.00
1 A.J. Burnett .15
2 Adam Dunn .50
3 Adrian Beltre .25
4 Albert Pujols 2.00
5 Alex Rodriguez 2.00
6 Alfonso Soriano .50
7 Andruw Jones .50
8 Aramis Ramirez .25
9 Barry Zito .25
10 Bartolo Colon .15
11 Ben Sheets .25
12 Bobby Abreu .25
13 Bobby Crosby .25
14 Michael Cuddyer .15
15 Brian Giles .15
16 Brian Roberts .15
17 Carl Crawford .25
18 Carlos Beltran .25
19 Carlos Delgado .40
20 Carlos Lee .15
21 Carlos Zambrano .25
22 Chase Utley .25
23 Chipper Jones .75
24 Chris Carpenter .25
25 Craig Biggio .25
26 Curt Schilling .75
27 David Ortiz .75
28 David Wright 1.00
29 Derek Jeter 2.00
30 Derek Lee .50
31 Dontrelle Willis .25
32 Eric Chavez .25
33 Eric Gagne .25
34 Francisco Rodriguez .15
35 Gary Sheffield .40
36 Greg Maddux 1.00
37 Hank Blalock .25
38 Hideki Matsui 1.50
39 Ichiro Suzuki 1.50
40 Ivan Rodriguez .50
41 J.D. Drew .15
42 Jake Peavy .25
43 Jason Bay .25
44 Jason Schmidt .15
45 Jeff Bagwell .40
46 Jeff Kent .25
47 Jeremy Bonderman .15
48 Jim Edmonds .40
49 Jim Thome .50
50 Joe Mauer .50
51 Johan Santana .50
52 John Smoltz .25
53 Johnny Damon .25
54 Jose Reyes .25
55 Jose Vidro .15
56 Josh Beckett .25
57 Justin Morneau .15
58 Ken Griffey Jr. 1.50
59 Kenny Rogers .15
60 Kerry Wood .25
61 Khalil Greene .25
62 Lance Berkman .25
63 Livan Hernandez .15
64 Luis Gonzalez .25
65 Manny Ramirez .75
66 Mark Buehrle .15
67 Mark Mulder .25
68 Mark Prior .50
69 Mark Teixeira .25
70 Michael Young .25
71 Miguel Cabrera .75
72 Miguel Tejada .50
73 Mike Mussina .40
74 Mike Piazza .75
75 Moises Alou .25
76 Morgan Ensberg .25
77 Nomar Garciaparra .50
78 Pat Burrell .25
79 Paul Konerko .25
80 Pedro Martinez .75
81 Randy Johnson .75
82 Rich Harden .25
83 Richie Sexson .25
84 Rickie Weeks .25
85 Robinson Cano .75
86 Roger Clemens 2.00
87 Roy Halladay .25
88 Roy Oswalt .25
89 Sammy Sosa .75
90 Scott Kazmir .25
91 Scott Rolen .75

92	Shawn Green	.25
93	Tim Hudson	.25
94	Todd Helton	.50
95	Tom Glavine	.25
96	Torii Hunter	.25
.25	Travis Hafner	.15
.25	Troy Glaus	.15
99	Vernon Wells	.15
100	Vladimir Guerrero	.75
101	Adam Shabala RC	3.00
102	Ambiorix Burgos RC	3.00
103	Anibal Sanchez RC	10.00
104	Bill McCarthy RC	3.00
105	Brandon McCarthy RC	6.00
106	Brian Burres RC	3.00
107	Carlos Ruiz RC	4.00
108	Casey Rogowski RC	3.00
109	Chad Orvella RC	3.00
110	Chris Resop RC	5.00
111	Chris Roberson RC	3.00
112	Chris Seddon RC	3.00
113	Colter Bean RC	3.00
114	Dae-Sung Koo RC	3.00
115	David Gassner RC	3.00
116	Brian Anderson RC	3.00
117	D.J. Houlton RC	3.00
118	Derek Wathan RC	3.00
119	Devon Lowery RC	3.00
120	Enrique Gonzalez RC	3.00
121	Eude Brito RC	3.00
122	Francisco Butto RC	3.00
123	Franquelis Osoria RC	5.00
124	Garrett Jones RC	3.00
125	Geovany Soto RC	3.00
126	Hayden Penn RC	5.00
127	Ismael Ramirez RC	3.00
128	Jared Gothreaux RC	3.00
129	Jason Hammel RC	3.00
130	Jeff Miller RC	3.00
131	Joel Peralta RC	3.00
132	John Hattig Jr. RC	3.00
133	Jorge Campillo RC	3.00
134	Juan Morillo RC	3.00
135	Ryan Garko RC	6.00
136	Keiichi Yabu RC	6.00
137	Luis Hernandez RC	3.00
138	Luis Pena RC	3.00
139	Luis Rodriguez RC	3.00
140	Luke Scott RC	5.00
141	Marcos Carvajal RC	3.00
142	Mark Woodyard RC	3.00
143	Matt Smith RC	3.00
144	Matt Lindstrom RC	3.00
145	Miguel Negron RC	3.00
146	Mike Morse RC	3.00
147	Nate McLouth RC	3.00
148	Nelson Cruz RC	5.00
149	Nick Masset RC	3.00
150	Oscar Robles RC	3.00
151	Paulino Reynoso RC	3.00
152	Pedro Lopez RC	3.00
153	Peter Orr RC	3.00
154	Randy Messenger RC	3.00
155	Randy Williams RC	3.00
156	Raul Tablado RC	3.00
157	Ronny Paulino RC	4.00
158	Russel Rohlicek RC	3.00
159	Russell Martin RC	5.00
160	Scott Baker RC	4.00
161	Scott Munter RC	4.00
162	Sean Thompson RC	4.00
163	Sean Tracey RC	3.00
164	Shane Costa RC	3.00
165	Steve Schmoll RC	3.00
166	Tony Giarratano RC	5.00
167	Tony Pena RC	5.00
168	Travis Bowyer RC	5.00
169	Ubaldo Jimenez RC	3.00
170	Wladimir Balentien RC	5.00
171	Yorman Bazardo RC	3.00
172	Yuniesky Betancourt RC	5.00
173	Chris Denorfia RC	5.00
174	Dana Eveland RC	5.00
175	Jermaine Van Buren RC	3.00
176	Mark McLemore RC	3.00
177	Ryan Spilborghs RC	3.00
178	Ambiorix Concepcion RC	10.00
179	Jeff Niemann RC	25.00
180	Justin Verlander RC	70.00
181	Kendry Morales RC	50.00
182	Philip Humber RC	25.00
183	Prince Fielder RC	120.00
184	Stephen Drew RC	150.00
185	Tadahito Iguchi RC	8.00
186	Ryan Zimmerman RC	160.00

Common Artifacts RC (201-285): 3.00
Production 799

201	Adam Shabala RC	3.00
202	Ambiorix Burgos RC	3.00
203	Ambiorix Concepcion RC	3.00
204	Anibal Sanchez RC	10.00
205	Bill McCarthy RC	3.00
206	Brandon McCarthy RC	5.00
207	Brian Burres RC	3.00
208	Carlos Ruiz RC	4.00
209	Casey Rogowski RC	3.00
210	Chad Orvella RC	3.00
211	Chris Resop RC	3.00
212	Chris Roberson RC	3.00
213	Chris Seddon RC	3.00
214	Colter Bean RC	3.00
215	Dae-Sung Koo RC	3.00

216	David Gassner RC	3.00
217	Brian Anderson RC	4.00
218	D.J. Houlton RC	3.00
219	Derek Wathan RC	3.00
220	Devon Lowery RC	3.00
221	Enrique Gonzalez RC	3.00
222	Eude Brito RC	3.00
223	Francisco Butto RC	3.00
224	Franquelis Osoria RC	5.00
225	Garrett Jones RC	3.00
226	Geovany Soto RC	3.00
227	Hayden Penn RC	3.00
228	Ismael Ramirez RC	3.00
229	Jared Gothreaux RC	3.00
230	Jason Hammel RC	3.00
231	Jeff Miller RC	3.00
232	Jeff Niemann RC	5.00
233	Joel Peralta RC	3.00
234	John Hattig Jr. RC	3.00
235	Jorge Campillo RC	3.00
236	Juan Morillo RC	3.00
237	Justin Verlander RC	15.00
238	Ryan Garko RC	5.00
239	Keiichi Yabu RC	5.00
240	Kendry Morales RC	5.00
241	Luis Hernandez RC	3.00
242	Luis Pena RC	3.00
243	Luis Rodriguez RC	3.00
244	Luke Scott RC	5.00
245	Marcos Carvajal RC	3.00
246	Mark Woodyard RC	3.00
247	Matt Smith RC	3.00
248	Matt Lindstrom RC	3.00
249	Miguel Negron RC	3.00
250	Mike Morse RC	3.00
251	Nate McLouth RC	4.00
252	Nelson Cruz RC	5.00
253	Nick Masset RC	3.00
254	Oscar Robles RC	3.00
255	Paulino Reynoso RC	3.00
256	Pedro Lopez RC	3.00
257	Peter Orr RC	3.00
258	Philip Humber RC	3.00
259	Prince Fielder RC	10.00
260	Randy Messenger RC	3.00
261	Randy Williams RC	3.00
262	Raul Tablado RC	3.00
263	Ronny Paulino RC	4.00
264	Russel Rohlicek RC	3.00
265	Russell Martin RC	5.00
266	Scott Baker RC	5.00
267	Scott Munter RC	3.00
268	Sean Thompson RC	3.00
269	Sean Tracey RC	3.00
270	Shane Costa RC	3.00
271	Stephen Drew RC	10.00
272	Steve Schmoll RC	3.00
273	Tadahito Iguchi RC	6.00
274	Tony Giarratano RC	4.00
275	Tony Pena RC	3.00
276	Travis Bowyer RC	5.00
277	Ubaldo Jimenez RC	3.00
278	Wladimir Balentien RC	5.00
279	Yorman Bazardo RC	4.00
280	Yuniesky Betancourt RC	5.00
281	Ryan Zimmerman RC	15.00
282	Chris Denorfia RC	5.00
283	Dana Eveland RC	5.00
284	Jermaine Van Buren RC	3.00
285	Mark McLemore RC	3.00

Common Reflections RC (201-286): 1.00

201	Adam Shabala RC	1.00
202	Ambiorix Burgos RC	1.00
203	Ambiorix Concepcion RC	1.00
204	Anibal Sanchez RC	3.00
205	Bill McCarthy RC	1.00
206	Brandon McCarthy RC	2.00
207	Brian Burres RC	1.00
208	Carlos Ruiz RC	1.00
209	Casey Rogowski RC	1.00
210	Chad Orvella RC	1.00
211	Chris Resop RC	1.50
212	Chris Roberson RC	1.00
213	Chris Seddon RC	1.00
214	Colter Bean RC	1.00
215	Dae-Sung Koo RC	1.00
216	Yuniesky Betancourt RC	2.00
217	David Gassner RC	1.00
218	Brian Anderson RC	1.50
219	Dennis Houlton RC	1.00
220	Derek Wathan RC	1.00
221	Devon Lowery RC	1.00
222	Enrique Gonzalez RC	1.00
223	Ryan Zimmerman RC	8.00
224	Eude Brito RC	1.00
225	Francisco Butto RC	1.00
226	Franquelis Osoria RC	1.00
227	Garrett Jones RC	1.00
228	Geovany Soto RC	1.00
229	Hayden Penn RC	1.00
230	Ismael Ramirez RC	1.00
231	Jared Gothreaux RC	1.00
232	Jason Hammel RC	1.00
233	Chris Denorfia RC	1.50
234	Jeff Miller RC	1.00
235	Jeff Niemann RC	1.50
236	Dana Eveland RC	2.00
237	Joel Peralta RC	1.00
238	John Hattig Jr. RC	1.00
239	Jorge Campillo RC	1.00
240	Juan Morillo RC	1.00
241	Justin Verlander RC	5.00
242	Ryan Garko RC	2.50
243	Keiichi Yabu RC	1.00

244	Kendry Morales RC	2.00
245	Luis Hernandez RC	1.00
246	Jermaine Van Buren RC	1.00
247	Luis Pena RC	1.00
248	Luis Rodriguez RC	1.00
249	Luke Scott RC	1.50
250	Marcos Carvajal RC	1.00
251	Mark Woodyard RC	1.00
252	Matt Smith RC	1.00
253	Matt Lindstrom RC	1.00
254	Miguel Negron RC	1.00
255	Mike Morse RC	1.00
256	Nate McLouth RC	1.00
257	Nelson Cruz RC	2.00
258	Nick Masset RC	1.00
259	Mark McLemore RC	1.00
260	Oscar Robles RC	1.00
261	Paulino Reynoso RC	1.00
262	Pedro Lopez RC	1.00
263	Peter Orr RC	1.00
264	Philip Humber RC	2.00
265	Prince Fielder	5.00
266	Randy Messenger RC	1.00
267	Randy Williams RC	1.00
268	Raul Tablado RC	1.00
269	Ronny Paulino RC	1.50
270	Russel Rohlicek RC	1.00
271	Russell Martin RC	2.00
272	Scott Baker RC	1.00
273	Scott Munter RC	1.00
274	Sean Thompson RC	1.00
275	Sean Tracey RC	1.00
276	Shane Costa RC	1.00
277	Stephen Drew RC	5.00
278	Steve Schmoll RC	1.00
279	Ryan Spilborghs RC	1.50
280	Tadahito Iguchi RC	2.00
281	Tony Giarratano RC	1.00
282	Tony Pena RC	1.00
283	Travis Bowyer RC	1.50
284	Ubaldo Jimenez RC	1.00
285	Wladimir Balentien RC	2.50
286	Yorman Bazardo RC	1.00

Common Origins RC (201-286): .75

201	Adam Shabala RC	.75
202	Ambiorix Burgos RC	.75
203	Ambiorix Concepcion RC	.75
204	Anibal Sanchez RC	2.00
205	Bill McCarthy RC	.75
206	Brandon McCarthy RC	2.00
207	Brian Burres RC	.75
208	Carlos Ruiz RC	1.00
209	Casey Rogowski RC	1.00
210	Chad Orvella RC	1.00
211	Chris Resop RC	1.00
212	Chris Roberson RC	.75
213	Chris Seddon RC	.75
214	Colter Bean RC	.75
215	Dae-Sung Koo RC	.75
216	Yuniesky Betancourt RC	1.50
217	David Gassner RC	.75
218	Brian Anderson RC	1.00
219	Dennis Houlton RC	.75
220	Derek Wathan RC	.75
221	Devon Lowery RC	.75
222	Enrique Gonzalez RC	.75
223	Ryan Zimmerman RC	5.00
224	Eude Brito RC	.75
225	Francisco Butto RC	.75
226	Franquelis Osoria RC	.75
227	Garrett Jones RC	.75
228	Geovany Soto RC	.75
229	Hayden Penn RC	.75
230	Ismael Ramirez RC	.75
231	Jared Gothreaux RC	.75
232	Jason Hammel RC	.75
233	Chris Denorfia RC	1.00
234	Jeff Miller RC	.75
235	Jeff Niemann RC	1.50
236	Dana Eveland RC	1.00
237	Joel Peralta RC	.75
238	John Hattig Jr. RC	1.00
239	Jorge Campillo RC	1.00
240	Juan Morillo RC	1.00
241	Justin Verlander RC	5.00
242	Ryan Garko RC	2.00
243	Keiichi Yabu RC	1.00
244	Kendry Morales RC	2.00
245	Luis Hernandez RC	.75
246	Jermaine Van Buren RC	.75
247	Luis Pena RC	.75
248	Luis Rodriguez RC	.75
249	Luke Scott RC	1.50
250	Marcos Carvajal RC	1.00
251	Mark Woodyard RC	1.00
252	Matt Smith RC	1.00
253	Matt Lindstrom RC	1.00
254	Miguel Negron RC	1.50
255	Mike Morse RC	1.50
256	Nate McLouth RC	1.00
257	Nelson Cruz RC	1.50
258	Nick Masset RC	1.00
259	Mark McLemore RC	1.00
260	Oscar Robles RC	1.00
261	Paulino Reynoso RC	.75
262	Pedro Lopez RC	1.00
263	Peter Orr RC	1.00
264	Philip Humber RC	1.50
265	Prince Fielder	5.00
266	Randy Messenger RC	.75
267	Randy Williams RC	1.00
268	Raul Tablado RC	.75
269	Ronny Paulino RC	1.50
270	Russel Rohlicek RC	.75

271	Russell Martin RC	1.50
272	Scott Baker RC	1.50
273	Ryan Spilborghs RC	1.00
274	Scott Munter RC	.75
275	Sean Thompson RC	1.00
276	Sean Tracey RC	1.00
277	Shane Costa RC	1.00
278	Stephen Drew RC	4.00
279	Steve Schmoll RC	1.00
280	Tadahito Iguchi RC	2.00
281	Tony Giarratano RC	.75
282	Tony Pena RC	.75
283	Travis Bowyer RC	1.00
284	Ubaldo Jimenez RC	1.00
285	Wladimir Balentien RC	2.00
286	Yorman Bazardo RC	1.00

Common SP Authentic Auto. (101-186): 8.00
Production 185

101	Adam Shabala RC	10.00
102	Ambiorix Burgos RC	10.00
103	Ambiorix Concepcion RC	10.00
104	Anibal Sanchez RC	75.00
106	Brandon McCarthy	35.00
107	Brian Burres RC	10.00
108	Carlos Ruiz RC	15.00
109	Casey Rogowski RC	10.00
110	Chad Orvella RC	10.00
111	Chris Resop RC	12.00
112	Chris Roberson RC	10.00
113	Chris Seddon RC	10.00
114	Colter Bean RC	15.00
116	David Gassner RC	10.00
117	Brian Anderson RC	30.00
120	Devon Lowery RC	10.00
121	Enrique Gonzalez RC	10.00
122	Eude Brito RC	8.00
123	Francisco Butto RC	10.00
124	Franquelis Osoria RC	15.00
125	Garrett Jones RC	10.00
126	Geovany Soto RC	10.00
127	Hayden Penn RC	15.00
128	Ismael Ramirez RC	10.00
129	Jared Gothreaux RC	10.00
130	Jason Hammel RC	10.00
131	Jeff Miller RC	8.00
132	Jeff Niemann RC	40.00
133	Joel Peralta RC	10.00
134	John Hattig Jr. RC	15.00
135	Jorge Campillo RC	10.00
136	Juan Morillo RC	10.00
137	Justin Verlander RC	185.00
139	Ryan Garko RC	50.00
139	Keiichi Yabu RC	15.00
140	Kendry Morales RC	80.00
143	Luis Hernandez RC	10.00
143	Luis Rodriguez RC	10.00
145	Luke Scott RC	40.00
146	Marcos Carvajal RC	10.00
146	Mark Woodyard RC	10.00
147	Matt Smith RC	8.00
148	Matt Lindstrom RC	10.00
149	Miguel Negron RC	15.00
150	Mike Morse RC	20.00
152	Nate McLouth RC	15.00
152	Nelson Cruz RC	40.00
153	Nick Masset RC	8.00
155	Paulino Reynoso RC	10.00
156	Pedro Lopez RC	15.00
157	Peter Orr RC	10.00
158	Philip Humber RC	20.00
159	Prince Fielder	160.00
160	Randy Messenger RC	8.00
162	Raul Tablado RC	10.00
163	Ronny Paulino RC	20.00
164	Russel Rohlicek RC	10.00
166	Russell Martin RC	50.00
166	Scott Baker RC	20.00
167	Scott Munter RC	10.00
168	Sean Thompson RC	10.00
169	Sean Tracey RC	15.00
170	Shane Costa RC	10.00
171	Stephen Drew RC	140.00
173	Steve Schmoll RC	10.00
173	Tadahito Iguchi RC	75.00
174	Tony Giarratano RC	15.00
175	Tony Pena RC	8.00
176	Travis Bowyer RC	10.00
177	Ubaldo Jimenez RC	15.00
178	Wladimir Balentien RC	25.00
179	Yorman Bazardo RC	15.00
181	Ryan Zimmerman RC	225.00
182	Chris Denorfia RC	30.00
184	Jermaine Van Buren RC	15.00
185	Mark McLemore RC	10.00

Common SPx Auto. (101-179): 8.00
Production 185

101	Adam Shabala RC	10.00
102	Ambiorix Burgos RC	10.00
103	Ambiorix Concepcion RC	10.00
104	Anibal Sanchez RC	50.00
106	Brandon McCarthy	30.00
107	Brian Burres RC	10.00
108	Carlos Ruiz RC	15.00
109	Casey Rogowski RC	15.00
110	Chad Orvella RC	10.00
111	Chris Resop RC	15.00
112	Chris Roberson RC	15.00
113	Chris Seddon RC	10.00
114	Colter Bean RC	15.00

115	David Gassner RC	10.00
116	Brian Anderson RC	30.00
119	Enrique Gonzalez RC	10.00
120	Eude Brito RC	8.00
121	Francisco Butto RC	10.00
122	Franquelis Osoria RC	10.00
123	Garrett Jones RC	10.00
124	Geovany Soto RC	10.00
125	Hayden Penn RC	15.00
126	Ismael Ramirez RC	10.00
127	Jared Gothreaux RC	10.00
128	Jason Hammel RC	10.00
129	Jeff Miller RC	8.00
130	Jeff Niemann RC	40.00
131	Joel Peralta RC	10.00
132	Philip Humber RC	20.00
133	Prince Fielder	140.00
135	Jorge Campillo RC	10.00
136	Ryan Garko RC	40.00
137	Kendry Morales RC	80.00
138	Luis Hernandez RC	10.00
140	Luis Rodriguez RC	10.00
141	Mark Woodyard RC	10.00
142	Matt Smith RC	8.00
143	Matt Lindstrom RC	10.00
144	Miguel Negron RC	15.00
145	Mike Morse RC	20.00
146	Nate McLouth RC	15.00
147	Nelson Cruz RC	30.00
148	Nick Masset RC	10.00
150	Paulino Reynoso RC	10.00
151	Pedro Lopez RC	15.00
152	Philip Humber RC	20.00
153	Prince Fielder	140.00
154	Randy Messenger RC	8.00
156	Raul Tablado RC	10.00
157	Ronny Paulino RC	15.00
158	Russel Rohlicek RC	15.00
159	Russell Martin RC	40.00
160	Scott Baker RC	20.00
161	Scott Munter RC	10.00
162	Sean Thompson RC	10.00
163	Sean Tracey RC	10.00
164	Shane Costa RC	10.00
165	Stephen Drew RC	125.00
166	Tony Giarratano RC	15.00
167	Tony Pena RC	8.00
168	Travis Bowyer RC	8.00
169	Ubaldo Jimenez RC	15.00
170	Wladimir Balentien RC	25.00
171	Yorman Bazardo RC	10.00
173	Ryan Zimmerman RC	160.00
174	Chris Denorfia RC	15.00
176	Jermaine Van Buren RC	1.00
177	Mark McLemore RC	8.00
179	Ryan Speier RC	10.00

Common Sweet Spot RC (91-174): .75

91	Adam Shabala RC	.75
92	Ambiorix Burgos RC	.75
93	Ambiorix Concepcion RC	1.00
94	Anibal Sanchez RC	2.00
95	Bill McCarthy RC	1.00
96	Brandon McCarthy RC	2.00
97	Brian Burres RC	.75
99	Carlos Ruiz RC	1.00
100	Casey Rogowski RC	.75
101	Chad Orvella RC	.75
102	Chris Resop RC	.75
103	Chris Roberson RC	.75
104	Chris Seddon RC	.75
105	Dae-Sung Koo RC	.75
106	Ryan Zimmerman RC	6.00
107	David Gassner RC	.75
108	Brian Anderson RC	1.50
109	D.J. Houlton RC	.75
110	Derek Wathan RC	.75
111	Devon Lowery RC	.75
112	Enrique Gonzalez RC	.75
113	Chris Denorfia RC	.75
114	Eude Brito RC	.75
115	Francisco Butto RC	1.00
116	Franquelis Osoria RC	.75
117	Garrett Jones RC	.75
118	Geovany Soto RC	.75
119	Hayden Penn RC	.75
120	Ismael Ramirez RC	.75
121	Jared Gothreaux RC	.75
122	Jason Hammel RC	.75
123	Dana Eveland RC	1.50
124	Jeff Miller RC	.75
125	Jermaine Van Buren RC	1.00
126	Joel Peralta RC	.75
127	John Hattig Jr. RC	.75
128	Jorge Campillo RC	.75
129	Juan Morillo RC	.75
130	Ryan Garko RC	2.00
131	Keiichi Yabu RC	.75
132	Kendry Morales RC	2.00
133	Luis Hernandez RC	.75
134	Mark McLemore RC	.75
135	Luis Pena RC	.75
136	Luis Rodriguez RC	.75
137	Luke Scott RC	1.50
138	Marcos Carvajal RC	.75
139	Mark Woodyard RC	1.00
140	Matt Smith RC	.75
141	Matt Lindstrom RC	.75
142	Miguel Negron RC	1.00
143	Mike Morse RC	1.00

144	Nate McLouth RC	1.00
145	Nelson Cruz RC	1.50
146	Nick Masset RC	.75
147	Ryan Spilborghs RC	.75
148	Oscar Robles RC	.75
149	Paulino Reynoso RC	1.00
150	Pedro Lopez RC	1.00
151	Peter Orr RC	.75
152	Prince Fielder	5.00
153	Randy Messenger RC	.75
154	Randy Williams RC	1.00
155	Raul Tablado RC	.75
156	Ronny Paulino RC	1.50
157	Russel Rohlicek RC	.75
158	Russell Martin RC	1.50
159	Scott Baker RC	1.50
160	Scott Munter RC	.75
161	Sean Thompson RC	.75
162	Sean Tracey RC	.75
163	Shane Costa RC	.75
164	Stephen Drew RC	4.00
165	Steve Schmoll RC	.75
166	Ryan Speier RC	.75
167	Tadahito Iguchi RC	2.00
168	Tony Giarratano RC	1.00
169	Tony Pena RC	.75
170	Travis Bowyer RC	.75
171	Ubaldo Jimenez RC	1.00
172	Wladimir Balentien RC	1.50
173	Yorman Bazardo RC	.75
174	Yuniesky Betancourt RC	1.50

Common Ultimate Signature Ed. (111-193): 8.00
Production 125

111	Adam Shabala RC	10.00
112	Anibal Sanchez RC	50.00
114	Brandon McCarthy	30.00
115	Brian Burres RC	10.00
116	Carlos Ruiz RC	12.00
117	Casey Rogowski RC	12.00
118	Chad Orvella RC	10.00
119	Chris Resop RC	12.00
120	Chris Roberson RC	12.00
121	Chris Seddon RC	12.00
122	Colter Bean RC	15.00
124	David Gassner RC	10.00
125	Brian Anderson RC	30.00
128	Devon Lowery RC	10.00
129	Enrique Gonzalez RC	15.00
130	Eude Brito RC	8.00
131	Francisco Butto RC	10.00
132	Franquelis Osoria RC	10.00
133	Garrett Jones RC	10.00
134	Geovany Soto RC	10.00
135	Hayden Penn RC	10.00
136	Ismael Ramirez RC	8.00
137	Jared Gothreaux RC	10.00
138	Jason Hammel RC	10.00
139	Jeff Miller RC	10.00
140	Jeff Niemann RC	30.00
141	Joel Peralta RC	10.00
142	John Hattig Jr. RC	15.00
143	Jorge Campillo RC	10.00
144	Juan Morillo RC	10.00
145	Justin Verlander RC	150.00
146	Ryan Garko RC	30.00
147	Keiichi Yabu RC	15.00
148	Kendry Morales RC	60.00
149	Luis Hernandez RC	10.00
151	Luis Rodriguez RC	10.00
152	Luke Scott RC	30.00
153	Marcos Carvajal RC	10.00
154	Mark Woodyard RC	10.00
155	Matt Smith RC	10.00
156	Matt Lindstrom RC	10.00
157	Miguel Negron RC	15.00
158	Mike Morse RC	15.00
159	Nate McLouth RC	15.00
160	Nelson Cruz RC	25.00
161	Nick Masset RC	8.00
162	Mark McLemore RC	10.00
163	Paulino Reynoso RC	10.00
164	Pedro Lopez RC	10.00
165	Peter Orr RC	10.00
166	Philip Humber RC	20.00
168	Prince Fielder	120.00
169	Randy Messenger RC	10.00
171	Raul Tablado RC	10.00
172	Ronny Paulino RC	15.00
173	Russel Rohlicek RC	8.00
174	Russell Martin RC	50.00
175	Scott Baker RC	20.00
176	Scott Munter RC	10.00
177	Sean Thompson RC	10.00
178	Sean Tracey RC	10.00
179	Shane Costa RC	10.00
180	Stephen Drew RC	120.00
181	Steve Schmoll RC	10.00
182	Tadahito Iguchi RC	60.00
183	Tony Giarratano RC	10.00
184	Tony Pena RC	10.00
185	Travis Bowyer RC	10.00
186	Ubaldo Jimenez RC	15.00
187	Wladimir Balentien RC	20.00
188	Yorman Bazardo RC	10.00
190	Ryan Zimmerman RC	140.00
191	Chris Denorfia RC	15.00
192	Ryan Speier RC	10.00
193	Jermaine Van Buren RC	10.00

Silver

Silver (101-177): 1X

Production 450
Silver (178-186): No Pricing
Production 25 Sets

Gold
Gold (101-177): 1-1.5X
Production 150
Gold (178-186): No Pricing
Production 10 Sets

Platinum
Platinum (101-177): No Pricing
Production 25
Platinum (178-186): No Pricing
Production One Set

Artifacts Blue
Blue (201-285): 1-1.5X
Production 100

Artifacts Gold
Gold (201-285): No Pricing
Production 25 Sets

Artifacts Red
Red (201-285): 1-2X
Production 50

Artifacts Platinum
No Pricing
Production One Set

Draft Generations Triple Signatures
No Pricing
Production 10 Sets

Link to Future Dual Autographs

		NM/M
	Common Duo:	15.00
	Production 35 Sets	
BR	Wladimir Balentien, Jeremy Reed	20.00
BW	Dontrelle Willis, Yorman Bazardo	40.00
CD	David DeJesus, Shane Costa	15.00
DD	J.D. Drew, Stephen Drew	125.00
DJ	Stephen Drew, Derek Jeter	275.00
FO	Prince Fielder, Lyle Overbay	75.00
FT	Prince Fielder, Mark Teixeira	100.00
FW	Prince Fielder, Rickie Weeks	100.00
GO	Roy Oswalt, Jared Gothreaux	25.00
HF	Luis Hernandez, Rafael Furcal	20.00
HG	Tom Glavine, Philip Humber	50.00
MB	Jason Bay, Nate McLouth	30.00
MK	Casey Kotchman, Kendry Morales	40.00
NK	Scott Kazmir, Jeff Niemann	40.00
NW	Vernon Wells, Miguel Negron	25.00
OB	Yhency Brazoban, Franquelis Osoria	20.00
OG	Peter Orr, Marcus Giles	25.00
PV	Javier Vazquez, Tony Pena	15.00
RH	Roy Halladay, Ismael Ramirez	30.00
SK	Chris Seddon, Scott Kazmir	30.00
SL	Jason Lane, Luke Scott	40.00
VB	Justin Verlander, Jeremy Bonderman	100.00
VC	Roger Clemens, Justin Verlander	175.00
ZC	Ryan Zimmerman, Chad Cordero	100.00

Link to the Past Dual Autographs

		NM/M
	Common Duo:	20.00
	Production 25 Sets	
BC	Steve Carlton, Eude Brito	30.00
BM	Juan Marichal, Brian Burres	30.00
CS	Darryl Strawberry, Ambiorix Concepcion	25.00
GT	Alan Trammell, Tony Giarratano	30.00
HG	Dwight Gooden, Philip Humber	40.00
HS	Philip Humber, Tom Seaver	50.00
IA	Luis Aparicio, Tadahito Iguchi	125.00
IC	Tadahito Iguchi, Rod Carew	125.00
JH	Kent Hrbek, Garrett Jones	40.00
JJ	Jack Morris, Justin Verlander	75.00
MC	Rod Carew, Kendry Morales	40.00
MJ	Kendry Morales, Wally Joyner	40.00
MV	Andy Van Slyke, Nate McLouth	40.00
NB	Miguel Negron, George Bell	40.00
NR	Nolan Ryan, Jeff Niemann	150.00
PP	Jim Palmer, Hayden Penn	40.00
RD	Lenny Dykstra, Chris Roberson	30.00
TP	Gaylord Perry, Sean Thompson	20.00
VM	Justin Verlander, Denny McLain	75.00

Origins Blue
Blue (201-286): 2-4X
Production 50 Sets

Origins Gold
Gold (201-286): No Pricing
Production 20 Sets

Origins Black
No Pricing
Production One Set

Origins Red
Red (201-286): 2-3X
Production 99 Sets

Origins Old Judge
Old Judge (201-286): 1X
Inserted 1:2
Blue: 2-3X
Production 50 Sets
Red: 1-2X
Production 99 Sets
Gold: No Pricing
Production 20 Sets
Black: No Pricing
Production One Set

Quad Signatures
No Pricing
Production 5 Sets

Reflections Blue
Blue (201-286): 2-4X
Production 75 Sets

Reflections Emerald
Emerald (201-286): 3-6X
Production 25 Sets

Reflections Purple
Purple (201-286): 1.5-3X
Production 99 Sets

Reflections Platinum
No Pricing
Production One Set

Reflections Red
Red (201-286): 1.5-3X
Production 99 Sets

Reflections Turquoise
Turquoise (201-286): 2-4X
Production 50 Sets

SP Authentic Gold
Gold (101-186): No Pricing
Production 10

SPx Silver
Silver (101-179): No Pricing
Production 10

Sweet Spot Gold
Gold (91-174): 1.5-2X
Production 399

Sweet Spot Platinum
Platinum (91-174): 2-3X
Production 99

Sweet Spot Plutonium
No Pricing
Production One Set

Ultimate Signature Edition Platinum

No Pricing
Production One Set

2006 Upper Deck

		NM/M
	Complete Series 1 (500):	150.00
	Complete Series 2 (500):	100.00
	Complete Update (250):	
	Common Player:	.15
	Common Update SP:	4.00
	Inserted 1:2 Update	
	Series 1 Pack (8):	3.50
	Series 1 Box (24):	70.00
	Series 2 Pack (6):	3.50
	Series 2 Box (24):	75.00
	Update Pack (8):	3.00
	Update Box (24):	60.00

#	Player	Price
1	Adam Kennedy	.15
2	Bartolo Colon	.25
3	Bengie Molina	.15
4	Casey Kotchman	.15
5	Chone Figgins	.15
6	Dallas McPherson	.15
7	Darin Erstad	.25
8	Ervin Santana	.25
9	Francisco Rodriguez	.15
10	Garret Anderson	.15
11	Jarrod Washburn	.15
12	John Lackey	.15
13	Juan Rivera	.15
14	Orlando Cabrera	.15
15	Paul Byrd	.15
16	Steve Finley	.15
17	Vladimir Guerrero	.75
18	Alex Cintron	.15
19	Brandon Lyon	.15
20	Brandon Webb	.15
21	Chad Tracy	.15
22	Chris Snyder	.15
23	Claudio Vargas	.15
24	Conor Jackson (RC)	.15
25	Craig Counsell	.15
26	Javier Vazquez	.15
27	Jose Valverde	.15
28	Luis Gonzalez	.15
29	Royce Clayton	.15
30	Russ Ortiz	.15
31	Shawn Green	.15
32	Dustin Nippert (RC)	.15
33	Tony Clark	.15
34	Troy Glaus	.15
35	Adam LaRoche	.15
36	Andruw Jones	.50
37	Craig Hansen RC	3.00
38	Chipper Jones	.75
39	Horacio Ramirez	.15
40	Jeff Francoeur	.25
41	John Smoltz	.15
42	Joey Devine RC	.50
43	Johnny Estrada	.15
44	Anthony Lerew (RC)	.15
45	Julio Franco	.15
46	Kyle Farnsworth	.15
47	Marcus Giles	.15
48	Mike Hampton	.15
49	Rafael Furcal	.25
50	Chuck James (RC)	.25
51	Tim Hudson	.40
52	B.J. Ryan	.15
53	Bernie Castro	.15
54	Brian Roberts	.25
55	Walter Young	.15
56	Daniel Cabrera	.15
57	Eric Byrnes	.15
58	Alejandro Freire RC	.50
59	Erik Bedard	.15
60	Javy Lopez	.25
61	Jay Gibbons	.15
62	Jorge Julio	.15
63	Luis Matos	.15
64	Melvin Mora	.15
65	Miguel Tejada	.40
66	Rafael Palmeiro	.25
67	Rodrigo Lopez	.15
68	Sammy Sosa	.15
69	Alejandro Machado	.15
70	Bill Mueller	.15
71	Bronson Arroyo	.15
72	Curt Schilling	.75
73	David Ortiz	.75
74	David Wells	.15
75	Edgar Renteria	.15
76	Ryan Jorgensen RC	.25
77	Jason Varitek	.50
78	Johnny Damon	.75
79	Keith Foulke	.15
80	Kevin Youkilis	.15
81	Manny Ramirez	.75
82	Matt Clement	.15
83	Hanley Ramirez (RC)	.25
84	Tim Wakefield	.15
85	Trot Nixon	.15
86	Wade Miller	.15
87	Aramis Ramirez	.40
88	Carlos Zambrano	.25
89	Corey Patterson	.15
90	Derrek Lee	.50
91	Geovany Soto (RC)	.15
92	Greg Maddux	1.00
93	Jeromy Burnitz	.15
94	Jerry Hairston	.15
95	Kerry Wood	.25
96	Mark Prior	.15
97	Matt Murton	.15
98	Michael Barrett	.15
99	Neifi Perez	.15
100	Nomar Garciaparra	.50
101	Rich Hill	.15
102	Ryan Dempster	.15
103	Todd Walker	.15
104	A.J. Pierzynski	.15
105	Aaron Rowand	.15
106	Bobby Jenks	.15
107	Carl Everett	.15
108	Dustin Hermanson	.15
109	Frank Thomas	.40
110	Freddy Garcia	.15
111	Jermaine Dye	.15
112	Joe Crede	.15
113	Jon Garland	.15
114	Jose Contreras	.25
115	Juan Uribe	.15
116	Mark Buehrle	.25
117	Orlando Hernandez	.15
118	Paul Konerko	.40
119	Scott Podsednik	.15
120	Tadahito Iguchi	.25
121	Aaron Harang	.15
122	Adam Dunn	.50
123	Austin Kearns	.25
124	Brandon Claussen	.15
125	Chris Denorfia (RC)	.15
126	Edwin Encarnacion	.15
127	Miguel Perez (RC)	.15
128	Felipe Lopez	.15
129	Jason LaRue	.15
130	Ken Griffey Jr.	1.50
131	Chris Booker	.15
132	Luke Hudson	.15
133	Jason Bergmann RC	.50
134	Ryan Freel	.15
135	Sean Casey	.15
136	Wily Mo Pena	.15
137	Aaron Boone	.15
138	Ben Broussard	.15
139	Ryan Garko (RC)	.15
140	C.C. Sabathia	.15
141	Casey Blake	.15
142	Cliff Lee	.15
143	Coco Crisp	.15
144	David Riske	.15
145	Grady Sizemore	.40
146	Jake Westbrook	.15
147	Jhonny Peralta	.15
148	Josh Bard	.15
149	Kevin Millwood	.25
150	Ronnie Belliard	.15
151	Scott Elarton	.15
152	Travis Hafner	.40
153	Victor Martinez	.25
154	Aaron Cook	.15
155	Aaron Miles	.15
156	Brad Hawpe	.15
157	Mike Esposito	.15
158	Chin-Hui Tsao	.15
159	Clint Barmes	.15
160	Cory Sullivan	.15
161	Garrett Atkins	.15
162	J.D. Closser	.15
163	Jason Jennings	.15
164	Jeff Baker	.15
165	Jeff Francis	.15
166	Luis Gonzalez	.15
167	Matt Holliday	.15
168	Todd Helton	.50
169	Brandon Inge	.15
170	Carlos Guillen	.15
171	Carlos Pena	.15
172	Chris Shelton	.15
173	Craig Monroe	.15
174	Curtis Granderson	.15
175	Dmitri Young	.15
176	Ivan Rodriguez	.40
177	Jason Johnson	.15
178	Jeremy Bonderman	.15
179	Magglio Ordonez	.25
180	Mark Woodyard (RC)	.15
181	Nook Logan	.15
182	Omar Infante	.15
183	Placido Polanco	.15
184	Chris Heintz RC	.50
185	A.J. Burnett	.15
186	Alex Gonzalez	.15
187	Josh Johnson (RC)	.15
188	Carlos Delgado	.40
189	Dontrelle Willis	.25
190	Josh Wilson (RC)	.15
191	Jason Vargas	.15
192	Jeff Conine	.15
193	Jeremy Hermida (RC)	.15
194	Josh Beckett	.25
195	Juan Encarnacion	.15
196	Juan Pierre	.15
197	Luis Castillo	.15
198	Miguel Cabrera	.15
199	Mike Lowell	.15
200	Paul LoDuca	.15
201	Todd Jones	.15
202	Adam Everett	.15
203	Andy Pettitte	.40
204	Brad Ausmus	.15
205	Brad Lidge	.15
206	Brandon Backe	.15
207	Charlton Jimerson	.15
208	Chris Burke	.15
209	Craig Biggio	.25
210	Daniel Wheeler	.15
211	Jason Lane	.15
212	Jeff Bagwell	.50
213	Lance Berkman	.40
214	Luke Scott	.15
215	Morgan Ensberg	.15
216	Roger Clemens	2.00
217	Roy Oswalt	.25
218	Willy Taveras	.15
219	Andres Blanco	.15
220	Angel Berroa	.15
221	Ruben Gotay	.15
222	David DeJesus	.15
223	Emil Brown	.15
224	J.P. Howell	.15
225	Jeremy Affeldt	.15
226	Jimmy Gobble	.15
227	John Buck	.15
228	Jose Lima	.15
229	Mark Teahen	.15
230	Matt Stairs	.15
231	Mike MacDougal	.15
232	Mike Sweeney	.15
233	Runelvys Hernandez	.15
234	Terrence Long	.15
235	Zack Greinke	.15
236	Ron Flores RC	.50
237	Brad Penny	.15
238	Cesar Izturis	.15
239	D.J. Houlton	.15
240	Derek Lowe	.15
241	Eric Gagne	.25
242	Hee Seop Choi	.15
243	J.D. Drew	.15
244	Jason Phillips	.15
245	Jason Repko	.15
246	Jayson Werth	.15
247	Jeff Kent	.25
248	Jeff Weaver	.15
249	Milton Bradley	.15
250	Odalis Perez	.15
251	Hong-Chih Kuo	.15
252	Oscar Robles	.15
253	Ben Sheets	.25
254	Bill Hall	.15
255	Brady Clark	.15
256	Carlos Lee	.25
257	Chris Capuano	.15
258	Nelson Cruz (RC)	.15
259	Derrick Turnbow	.15
260	Doug Davis	.15
261	Geoff Jenkins	.15
262	J.J. Hardy	.15
263	Lyle Overbay	.15
264	Prince Fielder (RC)	.50
265	Rickie Weeks	.25
266	Russell Branyan	.15
267	Tomokazu Ohka	.15
268	Jonah Bayliss RC	.75
269	Brad Radke	.15
270	Carlos Silva	.15
271	Francisco Liriano (RC)	.50
272	Jacque Jones	.15
273	Joe Mauer	.25
274	Travis Bower	.15
275	Joe Nathan	.15
276	Johan Santana	.50
277	Justin Morneau	.15
278	Kyle Lohse	.15
279	Lew Ford	.15
280	Matthew LeCroy	.15
281	Michael Cuddyer	.15
282	Nick Punto	.15
283	Scott Baker	.15
284	Shannon Stewart	.15
285	Torii Hunter	.25
286	Braden Looper	.15
287	Carlos Beltran	.50
288	Cliff Floyd	.15
289	David Wright	.75
290	Doug Mientkiewicz	.15
291	Anderson Hernandez (RC)	.15
292	Jose Reyes	.50
293	Kazuo Matsui	.15
294	Kris Benson	.15
295	Miguel Cairo	.15
296	Mike Cameron	.15
297	Robert Andino RC	.50
298	Mike Piazza	.75
299	Pedro Martinez	.75
300	Tom Glavine	.25
301	Victor Diaz	.15
302	Tim Hamulack	.15
303	Alex Rodriguez	2.00
304	Bernie Williams	.25
305	Carl Pavano	.15
306	Chien-Ming Wang	.40
307	Derek Jeter	2.00
308	Gary Sheffield	.40
309	Hideki Matsui	1.00
310	Jason Giambi	.40
311	Jorge Posada	.25
312	Kevin Brown	.15
313	Mariano Rivera	.25
314	Matt Lawton	.15
315	Mike Mussina	.25
316	Randy Johnson	.75
317	Robinson Cano	.15
318	Michael Vento	.15
319	Tino Martinez	.25
320	Tony Womack	.15
321	Barry Zito	.15
322	Bobby Crosby	.15
323	Bobby Kielty	.15
324	Dan Johnson	.15
325	Danny Haren	.15
326	Eric Chavez	.25
327	Erubiel Durazo	.15
328	Huston Street	.25
329	Jason Kendall	.15
330	Jay Payton	.15
331	Joe Blanton	.15
332	Joe Kennedy	.15
333	Kirk Saarloos	.15
334	Mark Kotsay	.15
335	Nick Swisher	.25
336	Rich Harden	.25
337	Scott Hatteberg	.15
338	Billy Wagner	.15
339	Bobby Abreu	.50
340	Brett Myers	.15
341	Chase Utley	.40
342	Danny Sandoval RC	.15
343	David Bell	.15
344	Gavin Floyd	.15
345	Jim Thome	.50
346	Jimmy Rollins	.40
347	Jon Lieber	.15
348	Kenny Lofton	.15
349	Mike Lieberthal	.15
350	Pat Burrell	.25
351	Randy Wolf	.15
352	Ryan Howard	.75
353	Vicente Padilla	.15
354	Bryan Bullington	.15
355	J.J. Furmaniak (RC)	.15
356	Craig Wilson	.15
357	Matt Capps (RC)	.15
358	Tom Gorzelanny (RC)	.15
359	Jack Wilson	.15
360	Jason Bay	.25
361	Jose Mesa	.15
362	Josh Fogg	.15
363	Kip Wells	.15
364	Steve Stemle RC	.50
365	Oliver Perez	.15
366	Robert Mackowiak	.15
367	Ronny Paulino (RC)	.15
368	Tike Redman	.15
369	Zachary Duke	.15
370	Adam Eaton	.15
371	Scott Feldman RC	.50
372	Brian Giles	.15
373	Brian Lawrence	.15
374	Damian Jackson	.15
375	Dave Roberts	.15
376	Jake Peavy	.25
377	Joe Randa	.15
378	Khalil Greene	.15
379	Mark Loretta	.15
380	Ramon Hernandez	.15
381	Robert Fick	.15
382	Ryan Klesko	.15
383	Trevor Hoffman	.15
384	Woody Williams	.15
385	Xavier Nady	.15
386	Armando Benitez	.15
387	Brad Hennessey	.15
388	Brian Myrow RC	.15
389	Edgardo Alfonzo	.15
390	J.T. Snow	.15
391	Jeremy Accardo RC	.15
392	Jason Schmidt	.25
393	Lance Niekro	.15
394	Matt Cain (RC)	.25
395	Daniel Ortmeier (RC)	.15
396	Moises Alou	.15
397	Doug Clark	.15
398	Omar Vizquel	.15
399	Pedro Feliz	.15
400	Randy Winn	.15
401	Ray Durham	.15
402	Adrian Beltre	.15
403	Eddie Guardado	.15
404	Felix Hernandez	.50
405	Gil Meche	.15
406	Ichiro Suzuki	1.50
407	Jamie Moyer	.15
408	Jeff Nelson	.15
409	Jeremy Reed	.15
410	Joel Pineiro	.15

No.	Player	Price
411	Jaime Bubela (RC)	.15
412	Raul Ibanez	.15
413	Richie Sexson	.40
414	Ryan Franklin	.15
415	Willie Bloomquist	.15
416	Yorvit Torrealba	.15
417	Yuniesky Betancourt	.15
418	Jeff Harris RC	.25
419	Albert Pujols	2.00
420	Chris Carpenter	.25
421	David Eckstein	.15
422	Jason Isringhausen	.15
423	Jason Marquis	.15
424	Adam Wainwright (RC)	.25
425	Jim Edmonds	.25
426	Ryan Theriot (RC)	1.00
427	Chris Duncan	.15
428	Mark Grudzielanek	.15
429	Mark Mulder	.15
430	Matt Morris	.25
431	Reggie Sanders	.15
432	Scott Rolen	.50
433	Tyler Johnson (RC)	.15
434	Yadier Molina	.15
435	Alex Gonzalez	.15
436	Aubrey Huff	.15
437	Tim Corcoran RC	.40
438	Carl Crawford	.15
439	Casey Fossum	.15
440	Danys Baez	.15
441	Edwin Jackson	.15
442	Joey Gathright	.15
443	Jonny Gomes	.25
444	Jorge Cantu	.15
445	Julio Lugo	.15
446	Nick Green	.15
447	Rocco Baldelli	.15
448	Scott Kazmir	.15
449	Seth McClung	.15
450	Toby Hall	.15
451	Travis Lee	.15
452	Craig Breslow RC	.25
453	Alfonso Soriano	.50
454	Chris Young	.15
455	David Dellucci	.15
456	Francisco Cordero	.15
457	Gary Matthews	.15
458	Hank Blalock	.25
459	Juan Dominguez	.15
460	Josh Rupe	.15
461	Kenny Rogers	.15
462	Kevin Mench	.15
463	Laynce Nix	.15
464	Mark Teixeira	.50
465	Michael Young	.25
466	Richard Hidalgo	.15
467	Jason Botts (RC)	.15
468	Aaron Hill	.15
469	Alex Rios	.15
470	Corey Koskie	.15
471	Chris Demaria RC	.50
472	Eric Hinske	.15
473	Frank Catalanotto	.15
474	John-Ford Griffin (RC)	.15
475	Gustavo Chacin	.15
476	Josh Towers	.15
477	Miguel Batista	.15
478	Orlando Hudson	.15
479	Reed Johnson	.15
480	Roy Halladay	.40
481	Shaun Marcum (RC)	.15
482	Shea Hillenbrand	.15
483	Ted Lilly	.15
484	Vernon Wells	.25
485	Brad Wilkerson	.15
486	Darrell Rasner (RC)	.15
487	Chad Cordero	.15
488	Cristian Guzman	.15
489	Esteban Loaiza	.15
490	John Patterson	.15
491	Jose Guillen	.15
492	Jose Vidro	.15
493	Livan Hernandez	.15
494	Marlon Byrd	.15
495	Nick Johnson	.15
496	Preston Wilson	.15
497	Ryan Church	.15
498	Ryan Zimmerman (RC)	.50
499	Tony Armas	.15
500	Vinny Castilla	.15
501	Andy Green	.15
502	Damion Easley	.15
503	Eric Byrnes	.15
504	Jason Grimsley	.15
505	Jeff DaVanon	.15
506	Johnny Estrada	.15
507	Luis Vizcaino	.15
508	Miguel Batista	.15
509	Orlando Hernandez	.15
510	Orlando Hudson	.15
511	Terry Mulholland	.15
512	Chris Reitsma	.15
513	Edgar Renteria	.25
514	John Thomson	.15
515	Jorge Sosa	.15
516	Oscar Villarreal	.15
517	Peter Orr	.15
518	Ryan Langerhans	.15
519	Todd Pratt	.15
520	Wilson Betemit	.15
521	Brian Jordan	.15
522	Lance Cormier	.15
523	Matt Diaz	.15
524	Mike Remlinger	.15
525	Bruce Chen	.15
526	Chris Gomez	.15
527	Chris Ray	.15
528	Corey Patterson	.15
529	David Newhan	.15
530	Ed Rogers (RC)	.25
531	John Halama	.15
532	Kris Benson	.15
533	LaTroy Hawkins	.15
534	Raul Chavez	.15
535	Alex Cora	.15
536	Alex Gonzalez	.15
537	Coco Crisp	.15
538	David Riske	.15
539	Doug Mirabelli	.15
540	Josh Beckett	.25
541	J.T. Snow	.15
542	Mike Timlin	.15
543	Julian Tavarez	.15
544	Rudy Seanez	.15
545	Wily Mo Pena	.15
546	Bob Howry	.15
547	Glendon Rusch	.15
548	Henry Blanco	.15
549	Jacque Jones	.15
550	Jerome Williams	.15
551	John Mabry	.15
552	Juan Pierre	.25
553	Scott Eyre	.15
554	Scott Williamson	.15
555	Wade Miller	.15
556	Will Ohman	.15
557	Alex Cintron	.15
558	Robert Mackowiak	.15
559	Brandon McCarthy	.15
560	Chris Widger	.15
561	Cliff Politte	.15
562	Javier Vazquez	.15
563	Jim Thome	.75
564	Matt Thornton	.15
565	Neal Cotts	.15
566	Pablo Ozuna	.15
567	Ross Gload	.15
568	Brandon Phillips	.15
569	Bronson Arroyo	.15
570	Dave Williams	.15
571	David Ross	.15
572	David Weathers	.15
573	Eric Milton	.15
574	Javier Valentin	.15
575	Kent Mercker	.15
576	Matt Belisle	.15
577	Paul Wilson	.15
578	Rich Aurilia	.15
579	Rick White	.15
580	Scott Hatteberg	.15
581	Todd Coffey (RC)	.15
582	Bob Wickman	.15
583	Danny Graves	.15
584	Eduardo Perez	.15
585	Guillermo Mota	.15
586	Jason Davis	.15
587	Jason Johnson	.15
588	Jason Michaels	.15
589	Rafael Betancourt	.15
590	Ramon Vazquez	.15
591	Scott Sauerbeck	.15
592	Todd Hollandsworth	.15
593	Brian Fuentes	.15
594	Danny Ardoin	.15
595	David Cortes	.15
596	Eli Marrero	.15
597	Jamey Carroll	.15
598	Jason Smith	.15
599	Josh Fogg	.15
600	Miguel Ojeda	.15
601	Mike DeJean	.15
602	Ray King	.15
603	Omar Quintanilla (RC)	.25
604	Zach Day	.15
605	Fernando Rodney	.15
606	Kenny Rogers	.15
607	Mike Maroth	.15
608	Nate Robertson	.15
609	Todd Jones	.15
610	Vance Wilson	.15
611	Bobby Seay	.15
612	Chris Spurling	.15
613	Raul Colon	.15
614	Jason Grilli	.15
615	Marcus Thames	.15
616	Ramon Santiago	.15
617	Alfredo Amezaga	.15
618	Brian Moehler	.15
619	Chris Aguila	.15
620	Franklyn German	.15
621	Joe Borowski	.15
622	Logan Kensing (RC)	.25
623	Matt Treanor	.15
624	Miguel Olivo	.15
625	Sergio Mitre	.15
626	Todd Wellemeyer	.15
627	Wes Helms	.15
628	Chad Qualls	.15
629	Eric Bruntlett	.15
630	Mike Gallo	.15
631	Mike Lamb	.15
632	Orlando Palmeiro	.15
633	Russ Springer	.15
634	Dan Wheeler	.15
635	Eric Munson	.15
637	Trever Miller	.15
638	Ambiorix Burgos	.15
639	Andrew Sisco	.15
640	Denny Bautista	.15
641	Doug Mientkiewicz	.15
642	Elmer Dessens	.15
643	Esteban German	.15
644	Joe Nelson (RC)	.15
645	Mark Grudzielanek	.15
646	Mark Redman	.15
647	Mike Wood	.15
648	Paul Bako	.15
649	Reggie Sanders	.15
650	Scott Elarton	.15
651	Shane Costa	.15
652	Tony Graffanino	.15
653	Jason Bulger (RC)	.25
654	Chris Bootcheck (RC)	.25
655	Esteban Yan	.15
656	Hector Carrasco	.15
657	J.C. Romero	.15
658	Jeff Weaver	.15
659	Jose Molina	.15
660	Kelvim Escobar	.15
661	Maicer Izturis	.15
662	Robb Quinlan	.15
663	Scot Shields	.15
664	Tim Salmon	.15
665	Bill Mueller	.15
666	Brett Tomko	.15
667	Dioner Navarro	.15
668	Jae Weong Seo	.15
669	Jose Cruz	.15
670	Kenny Lofton	.15
671	Lance Carter	.15
672	Nomar Garciaparra	.75
673	Olmedo Saenz	.15
674	Rafael Furcal	.15
675	Ramon Martinez	.15
676	Ricky Ledee	.15
677	Sandy Alomar	.15
678	Yhency Brazoban	.15
679	Corey Koskie	.15
680	Dan Kolb	.15
681	Gabe Gross	.15
682	Jeff Cirillo	.15
683	Matt Wise	.15
684	Rick Helling	.15
685	Chad Moeller	.15
686	David Bush	.15
687	Jorge De La Rosa	.15
688	Justin Lehr	.15
689	Jason Bartlett	.15
690	Jesse Crain	.15
691	Juan Rincon	.15
692	Luis Castillo	.15
693	Mike Redmond	.15
694	Rondell White	.15
695	Tony Batista	.15
696	Juan Castro	.15
697	Luis Rodriguez	.15
698	Matt Guerrier	.15
699	Willie Eyre (RC)	.15
700	Aaron Heilman	.15
701	Billy Wagner	.25
702	Carlos Delgado	.50
703	Chad Bradford	.15
704	Chris Woodward	.15
705	Darren Oliver	.15
706	Duaner Sanchez	.15
707	Endy Chavez	.15
708	Jorge Julio	.15
709	Jose Valentin	.15
710	Julio Franco	.15
711	Paul LoDuca	.15
712	Ramon Castro	.15
713	Steve Trachsel	.15
714	Victor Zambrano	.15
715	Xavier Nady	.15
716	Andy Phillips	.15
717	Bubba Crosby	.15
718	Jaret Wright	.15
719	Kelly Stinnett	.15
720	Kyle Farnsworth	.15
721	Mike Meyers	.15
722	Octavio Dotel	.15
723	Ron Villone	.15
724	Scott Proctor	.15
725	Shawn Chacon	.15
726	Tanyon Sturtze	.15
727	Adam Melhuse	.15
728	Brad Halsey	.15
729	Esteban Loaiza	.15
730	Frank Thomas	.50
731	Jay Witasick	.15
732	Justin Duchscherer	.15
733	Kiko Calero	.15
734	Marco Scutaro	.15
735	Mark Ellis	.15
736	Milton Bradley	.15
737	Aaron Fultz	.15
738	Aaron Rowand	.15
739	Geoff Geary	.15
740	Arthur Rhodes	.15
741	Chris Coste RC	.40
742	Rheal Cormier	.15
743	Ryan Franklin	.15
744	Ryan Madson	.15
745	Sal Fasano	.15
746	Tom Gordon	.15
747	Abraham Nunez	.15
748	David Dellucci	.15
749	Julio Santana	.15
750	Shane Victorino	.15
751	Damaso Marte	.15
752	Freddy Sanchez	.15
753	Humberto Cota	.15
754	Jeromy Burnitz	.15
755	Joe Randa	.15
756	Jose Castillo	.15
757	Mike Gonzalez	.15
758	Ryan Doumit	.15
759	Sean Burnett	.15
760	Sean Casey	.15
761	Ian Snell	.15
762	John Grabow	.15
763	Jose Hernandez	.15
764	Roberto Hernandez	.15
765	Ryan Vogelsong	.15
766	Victor Sanchez	.15
767	Adrian Gonzalez	.15
768	Alan Embree	.15
769	Brian Sweeney (RC)	.25
770	Chan Ho Park	.15
771	Clay Hensley	.15
772	Dewon Brazelton	.15
773	Doug Brocail	.15
774	Eric Young	.15
775	Geoff Blum	.15
776	Josh Bard	.15
777	Mark Bellhorn	.15
778	Mike Cameron	.15
779	Mike Piazza	.75
780	Rob Bowen	.15
781	Scott Cassidy	.15
782	Scott Linebrink	.15
783	Shawn Estes	.15
784	Termmel Sledge	.15
785	Vinny Castilla	.15
786	Jeff Fassero	.15
787	Jose Vizcaino	.15
788	Mark Sweeney	.15
789	Matt Morris	.15
790	Steve Finley	.15
791	Tim Worrell	.15
792	Jamey Wright	.15
793	Jason Ellison	.15
794	Noah Lowry	.15
795	Steve Kline	.15
796	Todd Greene	.15
797	Carl Everett	.15
798	George Sherrill	.15
799	J.J. Putz	.15
800	Jake Woods	.15
801	Jose Lopez	.15
802	Julio Mateo	.15
803	Mike Morse	.15
804	Rafael Soriano	.15
805	Roberto Petagine	.15
806	Aaron Miles	.15
807	Braden Looper	.15
808	Gary Bennett	.15
809	Hector Luna	.15
810	Jeff Suppan	.15
811	John Rodriguez	.15
812	Josh Hancock	.15
813	Juan Encarnacion	.15
814	Larry Bigbie	.15
815	Scott Spiezio	.15
816	Sidney Ponson	.15
817	So Taguchi	.15
818	Brian Meadows	.15
819	Damon Hollins	.15
820	Dan Miceli	.15
821	Doug Waechter	.15
822	Jason Childers	.25
823	Josh Paul	.15
824	Julio Lugo	.15
825	Mark Hendrickson	.15
826	Sean Burroughs	.15
827	Shawn Camp	.15
828	Travis Harper	.15
829	Ty Wigginton	.15
830	Adam Eaton	.15
831	Adrian Brown	.15
832	Akinori Otsuka	.15
833	Antonio Alfonseca	.15
834	Brad Wilkerson	.15
835	D'Angelo Jimenez	.15
836	Gerald Laird	.15
837	Joaquin Benoit	.15
838	Kameron Loe	.15
839	Kevin Millwood	.15
840	Mark DeRosa	.15
841	Phil Nevin	.15
842	Rod Barajas	.15
843	Vicente Padilla	.15
844	A.J. Burnett	.15
845	Bengie Molina	.15
846	Gregg Zaun	.15
847	John McDonald	.15
848	Lyle Overbay	.15
849	Russ Adams	.15
850	Troy Glaus	.15
851	Vinnie Chulk	.15
852	B.J. Ryan	.15
853	Justin Speier	.15
854	Pete Walker	.15
855	Scott Downs	.15
856	Scott Schoeneweis	.15
857	Alfonso Soriano	.75
858	Brian Schneider	.15
859	Daryle Ward	.15
860	Felix Rodriguez	.15
861	Gary Majewski	.15
862	Joey Eischen	.15
863	Jon Rauch	.15
864	Marlon Anderson	.15
865	Matthew LeCroy	.15
866	Mike Stanton	.15
867	Ramon Ortiz	.15
868	Robert Fick	.15
869	Royce Clayton	.15
870	Ryan Drese	.15
871	Vladimir Guerrero	.40
872	Craig Biggio	.15
873	Barry Zito	.15
874	Vernon Wells	.15
875	Chipper Jones	.40
876	Prince Fielder	.50
877	Albert Pujols	1.00
878	Greg Maddux	.75
879	Carl Crawford	.15
880	Brandon Webb	.15
881	J.D. Drew	.15
882	Jason Schmidt	.15
883	Victor Martinez	.15
884	Ichiro Suzuki	.75
885	Miguel Cabrera	.40
886	David Wright	.75
887	Alfonso Soriano	.40
888	Miguel Tejada	.40
889	Khalil Greene	.15
890	Ryan Howard	1.00
891	Jason Bay	.25
892	Mark Teixeira	.25
893	Manny Ramirez	.40
894	Ken Griffey Jr.	.75
895	Todd Helton	.25
896	Angel Berroa	.15
897	Ivan Rodriguez	.25
898	Johan Santana	.25
899	Paul Konerko	.15
900	Derek Jeter	1.00
901	Macay McBride (RC)	.15
902	Tony Pena (RC)	.25
903	Peter Moylan RC	.50
904	Aaron Rakers (RC)	.15
905	Chris Britton RC	.50
906	Nicholas Markakis (RC)	.50
907	Sendy Rleal RC	.50
908	Val Majewski (RC)	.25
909	Jermaine Van Buren (RC)	.25
910	Jonathan Papelbon (RC)	4.00
911	Angel Pagan (RC)	.50
912	David Aardsma (RC)	.25
913	Sean Marshall (RC)	.25
914	Brian Anderson (RC)	.25
915	Freddie Bynum (RC)	.15
916	Fausto Carmona (RC)	.25
917	Kelly Stoppach (RC)	.15
918	Choo Freeman (RC)	.15
919	Ryan Shealy (RC)	.25
920	Joel Zumaya (RC)	6.00
921	Jordan Tata RC	1.00
922	Justin Verlander (RC)	1.00
923	Carlos Martinez (RC)	.25
924	Chris Resop (RC)	.25
925	Dan Uggla (RC)	.50
926	Eric Reed (RC)	.15
927	Hanley Ramirez (RC)	.50
928	Yusmeiro Petit (RC)	.25
929	Josh Willingham (RC)	.25
930	Mike Jacobs (RC)	.25
931	Reggie Abercrombie (RC)	.25
932	Ricky Nolasco (RC)	.25
933	Scott Olsen (RC)	.25
934	Fernando Nieve (RC)	.25
935	Taylor Buchholz (RC)	.25
936	Cody Ross (RC)	.25
937	James Loney (RC)	.25
938	Takashi Saito RC	2.00
939	Chris Demaria RC	.50
940	Jose Capellan (RC)	.25
941	David Gassner (RC)	.15
942	Jason Kubel (RC)	.25
943	Brian Bannister (RC)	.25
944	Mike Thompson RC	.50
945	Cole Hamels RC	5.00
946	John Van Benschoten (RC)	.25
947	Paul Maholm (RC)	.25
948	John Van Benschoten (RC)	.25
949	Nate McLouth (RC)	.25
950	Ben Johnson (RC)	.15
951	Josh Barfield (RC)	.25
952	Travis Ishikawa (RC)	.25
953	Jack Taschner (RC)	.25
954	Kenji Johjima RC	5.00
955	Skip Schumaker (RC)	.25
956	Ruddy Lugo (RC)	.25
957	Jason Hammel (RC)	.25
958	Chris Roberson (RC)	.25
959	Fabio Castro RC	.50
960	Ian Kinsler (RC)	.50
961	John Koronka (RC)	.25
962	Brandon Watson (RC)	.25
963	Jon Lester RC	5.00
964	Ben Hendrickson (RC)	.25
965	Martin Prado (RC)	.25
966	Erick Aybar (RC)	.25
967	Bobby Livingston (RC)	.25
968	Ryan Spilborghs (RC)	.25
969	Tommy Murphy (RC)	.25
970	Howie Kendrick (RC)	5.00
971	Casey Janssen (RC)	1.00
972	Michael O'Connor RC	.50
973	Conor Jackson (RC)	.25
974	Jeremy Hermida (RC)	.25
975	Renyel Pinto (RC)	.25
976	Prince Fielder (RC)	1.50
977	Kevin Frandsen (RC)	.25
978	Ty Taubenheim RC	.50
979	Rich Hill (RC)	.25
980	Jonathan Broxton (RC)	.25
981	Jamie Shields RC	.50
982	Carlos Villanueva RC	.50
983	Boone Logan RC	1.00
984	Brian Wilson RC	.50
985	Andre Ethier (RC)	3.00
986	Michael Napoli RC	1.50
987	Agustin Montero (RC)	.15
988	Jack Hannahan (RC)	.50
989	Boof Bonser (RC)	.25
990	Carlos Ruiz (RC)	.25
991	Jason Botts (RC)	.25
992	Kendry Morales (RC)	.50
993	Alay Soler RC	3.00
994	Santiago Ramirez (RC)	.25
995	Saul Rivera (RC)	.25
996	Anthony Reyes (RC)	.25
997	Matthew Kemp (RC)	.50
998	Jae-Kuk Ryu RC	.50
999	Lastings Milledge (RC)	1.00
1000	Jered Weaver (RC)	4.00
1001	Stephen Drew (RC)	1.00
1002	Carlos Quentin (RC)	.50
1003	Chris Young (RC)	.50
1004	Livan Hernandez	.15
1005	Alberto Callaspo/SP (RC)	6.00
1006	Enrique Gonzalez (RC)	.25
1007	Tony Pena (RC)	.25
1008	Bob Melvin	.15
1009	Fernando Tatis	.15
1010	Willy Aybar (RC)	.25
1011	Ken Ray (RC)	.25
1012	Scott Thorman (RC)	.50
1013	Eric Hinske/SP	4.00
1014	Kevin Barry (RC)	.50
1015	Bobby Cox	.25
1016	Phil Stockman (RC)	.25
1017	Brayan Pena (RC)	.25
1018	Adam Loewen (RC)	.25
1019	Brandon Fahey RC	.50
1020	Jim Hoey RC	.50
1021	Kurt Birkins/SP RC	8.00
1022	Jim Johnson RC	.75
1023	Sam Perlozzo	.15
1024	Cory Morris RC	.50
1025	Hayden Penn (RC)	.25
1026	Javy Lopez	.15
1027	Dustin Pedroia (RC)	.50
1028	Kason Gabbard (RC)	.25
1029	David Pauley (RC)	.25
1030	Kyle Snyder	.15
1031	Terry Francona	.15
1032	Craig Breslow (RC)	.50
1033	Bryan Corey (RC)	.25
1034	Manny Delcarmen (RC)	1.00
1035	Carlos Marmol RC	.25
1036	Buck Coats (RC)	.25
1037	Ryan O'Malley/SP RC	10.00
1038	Angel Guzman (RC)	.25
1039	Ronny Cedeno	.15
1040	Juan Mateo RC	.50
1041	Cesar Izturis	.15
1042	Les Walrond (RC)	.25
1043	Geovany Soto (RC)	.50
1044	Sean Tracey (RC)	.25
1045	Ozzie Guillen/SP	6.00
1046	Royce Clayton	.15
1047	Norris Hopper RC	.25
1048	Bill Bray (RC)	.25
1049	Jerry Narron	.15
1050	Brendan Harris (RC)	.25
1051	Brian Shackelford	.15
1052	Jeremy Sowers (RC)	.50
1053	Joe Inglett RC	1.50
1054	Brian Slocum (RC)	.25
1055	Andrew Brown (RC)	.25
1056	Rafael Perez RC	.50
1057	Edward Mujica RC	.25
1058	Andy Marte (RC)	.25
1059	Shin-Soo Choo (RC)	.50
1060	Jeremy Guthrie (RC)	.25
1061	Franklin Gutierrez/SP (RC)	6.00
1062	Kazuo Matsui	.15
1063	Chris Iannetta (RC)	.50
1064	Manny Corpas RC	.25
1065	Clint Hurdle	.15
1066	Ramon Ramirez (RC)	.25
1067	Sean Casey	.15
1068	Zach Miner (RC)	.25
1069	Brent Clevlen/SP (RC)	8.00
1070	Bob Wickman	.15
1071	Jim Leyland	.15
1072	Alexis Gomez	.25
1073	Anibal Sanchez (RC)	.50
1074	Taylor Tankersley (RC)	.25
1075	Eric Wedge	.15
1076	Jonah Bayliss RC	.25
1077	Paul Hoover/SP (RC)	8.00
1078	Eddie Guardado	.15
1079	Cody Ross	.25
1080	Aubrey Huff	.15
1081	Jason Hirsh (RC)	.25
1082	Brandon League	.15
1083	Matt Albers (RC)	.25
1084	Chris Sampson RC	1.50
1085	Phil Garner	.15
1086	J.R. House (RC)	.25
1087	Ryan Shealy (RC)	.25
1088	Stephen Andrade (RC)	.25
1089	Bob Keppel (RC)	.25
1090	Buddy Bell	.15
1091	Justin Huber (RC)	.25
1092	Paul Phillips (RC)	.15
1093	Greg Jones/SP (RC)	8.00
1094	Jeff Mathis (RC)	.50
1095	Dustin Moseley (RC)	.25
1096	Joe Saunders (RC)	.25
1097	Reggie Willits RC	.25
1098	Mike Scioscia	.15
1099	Greg Maddux	1.50
1100	Wilson Betemit	.15
1101	Chad Billingsley/SP (RC)	8.00
1102	Russell Martin (RC)	.25
1103	Grady Little	.15
1104	David Bell	.15
1105	Kevin Brown	.15
1106	Laynce Nix	.15
1107	Chris Barnwell RC	.25
1108	Tony Gwynn Jr. (RC)	.25
1109	Corey Hart (RC)	.25
1110	Zach Jackson (RC)	.25

1111	Francisco Cordero	.15
1112	Joe Winklesas **(RC)**	.25
1113	Ned Yost	.15
1114	Matt Garza **(RC)**	.50
1115	Chris Heintz	.15
1116	Pat Neshek **RC**	.25
1117	Josh Rabe/SP **RC**	15.00
1118	Mike Rivera	.15
1119	Ron Gardenhire	.15
1120	Shawn Green	.15
1121	Oliver Perez	.15
1122	Heath Bell	.15
1123	Bartolome Fortunato **(RC)**	.25
1124	Anderson Garcia **RC**	.75
1125	John Maine **RC** **(RC)**	10.00
1126	Henry Owens **RC**	.50
1127	Mike Pelfrey **RC**	3.00
1128	Royce Ring **(RC)**	.50
1129	Willie Randolph	.15
1130	Bobby Abreu	.50
1131	Craig Wilson	.15
1132	T.J. Beam **(RC)**	.25
1133	Colter Bean/SP **(RC)**	8.00
1134	Melky Cabrera **(RC)**	.50
1135	Mitch Jones **(RC)**	.50
1136	Jeffrey Karstens **RC**	1.00
1137	Wilbert Nieves **(RC)**	.25
1138	Kevin Reese **(RC)**	.50
1139	Kevin Thompson **(RC)**	.50
1140	Jose Veras **RC**	.15
1141	Joe Torre	.50
1142	Jeremy Brown **(RC)**	.25
1143	Santiago Casilla **(RC)**	.25
1144	Shane Komine **(RC)**	1.00
1145	Mike Rouse **(RC)**	.25
1146	Jason Windsor **(RC)**	.75
1147	Ken Macha	.15
1148	Jamie Moyer	.15
1149	Phil Nevin/SP	8.00
1150	Eude Brito **(RC)**	.50
1151	Fabio Castro	.15
1152	Jeff Conine	.15
1153	Scott Mathieson **(RC)**	.25
1154	Brian Sanches **(RC)**	.25
1155	Matt Smith **RC**	.50
1156	Joe Thurston **(RC)**	.25
1157	Marlon Anderson/SP	8.00
1158	Xavier Nady	.15
1159	Shawn Chacon	.15
1160	Rajai Davis **(RC)**	.25
1161	Yurendell de Caster **(RC)**	.50
1162	Marty McLeary **(RC)**	.25
1163	Chris Duffy	.15
1164	Joshua Sharpless **RC**	1.00
1165	Jim Tracy	.15
1166	David Wells	.15
1167	Russell Branyan	.15
1168	Todd Walker	.15
1169	Paul McAnulty **(RC)**	.25
1170	Bruce Bochy	.15
1171	Shea Hillenbrand	.15
1172	Eliezer Alfonzo **RC**	.50
1173	Justin Knoedler/SP **(RC)**	8.00
1174	Jonathan Sanchez **(RC)**	.25
1175	Travis Smith **(RC)**	.25
1176	Cha Sueng Baek	.15
1177	T.J. Bohn **(RC)**	.25
1178	Emiliano Fruto **RC**	.50
1179	Sean Green **RC**	.50
1180	Jon Huber **RC**	.50
1181	Adam Jones/SP **RC**	8.00
1182	Mark Lowe **(RC)**	.25
1183	Eric O'Flaherty **RC**	.50
1184	Preston Wilson	.15
1185	Mike Hargrove	.15
1186	Jeff Weaver	.15
1187	Ronnie Belliard	.15
1188	John Gall **(RC)**	.25
1189	Josh Kinney/SP **RC**	10.00
1190	Tony LaRussa	.15
1191	Scott Dunn **(RC)**	.25
1192	B.J. Upton	.15
1193	Jon Switzer **(RC)**	.25
1194	Benjamin Zobrist **(RC)**	.50
1195	Joe Maddon	.15
1196	Carlos Lee	.15
1197	Matt Stairs	.15
1198	Nick Massett **(RC)**	.25
1199	Nelson Cruz **(RC)**	.50
1200	Francisco Rosario **(RC)**	.25
1201	Wes Littleton **(RC)**	.25
1202	Drew Meyer **(RC)**	.25
1203	John Rheinecker **(RC)**	.15
1204	Robinson Tejeda	.15
1205	Jeremy Accardo/SP	8.00
1206	Luis Figueroa **RC**	.50
1207	John Hattig Jr. **(RC)**	.25
1208	Dustin McGowan **(RC)**	.25
1209	Ryan Roberts **RC**	.50
1210	Davis Romero **(RC)**	.25
1211	Ty Taubenheim	.15
1212	John Gibbons	.15
1213	Shawn Hill/SP **(RC)**	8.00
1214	Brandon Harper **RC**	.25
1215	Travis Hughes **(RC)**	.25
1216	Chris Schroder **RC**	.15
1217	Austin Kearns	.15
1218	Felipe Lopez	.15
1219	Roy Corcoran **RC**	.25
1220	Melvin Dorta **RC**	.25
1221	Brandon Webb/SP	4.00
1222	Andruw Jones/SP	6.00
1223	Miguel Tejada/SP	8.00
1224	David Ortiz/SP	8.00
1225	Derrek Lee/SP	6.00
1226	Jim Thome/SP	6.00
1227	Ken Griffey Jr./SP	8.00
1228	Travis Hafner/SP	6.00
1229	Todd Helton/SP	6.00
1230	Magglio Ordonez/SP	4.00
1231	Miguel Cabrera/SP	8.00
1232	Lance Berkman/SP	4.00
1233	Mike Sweeney/SP	4.00
1234	Vladimir Guerrero/SP	8.00
1235	Nomar Garciaparra/SP	8.00
1236	Prince Fielder/SP	8.00
1237	Johan Santana/SP	8.00
1238	Pedro Martinez/SP	6.00
1239	Derek Jeter/SP	10.00
1240	Barry Zito/SP	6.00
1241	Ryan Howard/SP	10.00
1242	Jason Bay/SP	6.00
1243	Trevor Hoffman/SP	4.00
1244	Jason Schmidt/SP	4.00
1245	Ichiro Suzuki/SP	8.00
1246	Albert Pujols/SP	10.00
1247	Carl Crawford/SP	4.00
1248	Mark Teixeira/SP	6.00
1249	Vernon Wells/SP	6.00
1250	Alfonso Soriano/SP	8.00

Blue
Blue: 2-4X
Production 299 Sets

Gold

Gold: 2-4X
Production 299 Sets

Amazing Greats

NM/M
Complete Set: 25.00
Common Player: .50

BA	Bobby Abreu	.75
JB	Jeff Bagwell	.75
CB	Carlos Beltran	1.00
AB	Adrian Beltre	.50
MC	Miguel Cabrera	1.00
RC	Roger Clemens	3.00
CC	Carl Crawford	.50
JD	Johnny Damon	1.00
JE	Jim Edmonds	.50
RF	Rafael Furcal	.50
EG	Eric Gagne	.50
JG	Jason Giambi	.75
TG	Tom Glavine	.50
KG	Ken Griffey Jr.	2.00
HE	Todd Helton	.75
TH	Tim Hudson	.50
DJ	Derek Jeter	3.00
RJ	Randy Johnson	1.00
AJ	Andruw Jones	1.00
CJ	Chipper Jones	1.00
JJ	Jacque Jones	.50
PK	Paul Konerko	.75
CL	Carlos Lee	.50
JL	Javy Lopez	.50
GM	Greg Maddux	2.00
PM	Pedro Martinez	1.00
DO	David Ortiz	1.00
RO	Roy Oswalt	1.00
RP	Rafael Palmeiro	.75
CP	Corey Patterson	.50
MP	Mike Piazza	1.00
PR	Mark Prior	.75
AP	Albert Pujols	3.00
MR	Manny Ramirez	1.00
JR	Jose Reyes	.75
IR	Ivan Rodriguez	.75
SR	Scott Rolen	.50
JS	Johan Santana	1.00
CS	Curt Schilling	1.00
GS	Gary Sheffield	.75
SM	John Smoltz	.50
AS	Alfonso Soriano	.75
SS	Sammy Sosa	1.00
MT	Mark Teixeira	.75
TE	Miguel Tejada	.75
FT	Frank Thomas	.75
JT	Jim Thome	.75
DW	Dontrelle Willis	.50
KW	Kerry Wood	.50
WR	David Wright	1.50

Amazing Greats Materials

NM/M
Common Player:

BA	Bobby Abreu	6.00
JB	Jeff Bagwell	6.00
CB	Carlos Beltran	6.00
AB	Adrian Beltre	4.00
MC	Miguel Cabrera	8.00
RC	Roger Clemens	15.00
CC	Carl Crawford	6.00
JD	Johnny Damon	10.00
JE	Jim Edmonds	6.00
RF	Rafael Furcal	4.00
EG	Eric Gagne	4.00
JG	Jason Giambi	6.00
TG	Tom Glavine	6.00
KG	Ken Griffey Jr.	20.00
HE	Todd Helton	6.00
TH	Tim Hudson	4.00
DJ	Derek Jeter	20.00
RJ	Randy Johnson	8.00
AJ	Andruw Jones	8.00
CJ	Chipper Jones	8.00
JJ	Jacque Jones	4.00
PK	Paul Konerko	6.00
CL	Carlos Lee	4.00
JL	Javy Lopez	4.00
GM	Greg Maddux	12.00
PM	Pedro Martinez	8.00
DO	David Ortiz	8.00
RO	Roy Oswalt	6.00
RP	Rafael Palmeiro	6.00
CP	Corey Patterson	4.00
MP	Mike Piazza	10.00
PR	Mark Prior	6.00
AP	Albert Pujols	20.00
MR	Manny Ramirez	8.00
JR	Jose Reyes	8.00
IR	Ivan Rodriguez	6.00
SR	Scott Rolen	8.00
JS	Johan Santana	8.00
CS	Curt Schilling	6.00
GS	Gary Sheffield	6.00
SM	John Smoltz	6.00
AS	Alfonso Soriano	6.00
SS	Sammy Sosa	10.00
MT	Mark Teixeira	8.00
TE	Miguel Tejada	10.00
FT	Frank Thomas	8.00
JT	Jim Thome	8.00
DW	Dontrelle Willis	6.00
KW	Kerry Wood	4.00
WR	David Wright	15.00

Diamond Collection Materials
NM/M
Common Player: 4.00

AL	Moises Alou	4.00
JB	Jeff Bagwell	6.00
RB	Rocco Baldelli	4.00
OC	Orlando Cabrera	4.00
MC	Mike Cameron	4.00
EC	Eric Chavez	4.00
CO	Jose Contreras	4.00
JC	Jesse Crain	4.00
BC	Bobby Crosby	4.00
JD	Johnny Damon	10.00
AE	Adam Eaton	4.00
JE	Jim Edmonds	6.00
SF	Steve Finley	4.00
FG	Freddy Garcia	4.00
GO	Juan Gonzalez	4.00
KG	Ken Griffey Jr.	20.00
JG	Jose Guillen	4.00
MH	Mike Hampton	4.00
AH	Aubrey Huff	4.00
EJ	Edwin Jackson	4.00
DJ	Derek Jeter	20.00
NJ	Nick Johnson	4.00
RJ	Randy Johnson	8.00
JJ	Jacque Jones	4.00
SK	Scott Kazmir	4.00
KE	Austin Kearns	4.00
JK	Jason Kendall	4.00
AK	Adam Kennedy	4.00
CK	Casey Kotchman	4.00
LA	Matt Lawton	4.00
ML	Mike Lieberthal	4.00
PL	Paul LoDuca	4.00
KL	Kenny Lofton	4.00
LO	Mike Lowell	4.00
GM	Greg Maddux	12.00
MA	Kazuo Matsui	4.00
KM	Kevin Millwood	4.00
DO	David Ortiz	8.00
AO	Akinori Otsuka	4.00
CP	Carl Pavano	4.00
JP	Jorge Posada	6.00
BR	Brad Radke	4.00
IR	Ivan Rodriguez	6.00
CC	C.C. Sabathia	4.00
CS	Chris Shelton	10.00
JS	John Smoltz	8.00
SS	Shannon Stewart	4.00
JT	Jim Thome	8.00
JW	Jayson Werth	4.00
PW	Preston Wilson	4.00

Diamond Debut
NM/M
Common Player: 1.00
#'s 1-40 found in Series 1 packs.
#'s 41-82 found in Series 2 packs.
Inserted 1:4 Walmart packs.
Series 2 Common Player: .50

1	Tadahito Iguchi	1.00
2	Huston Street	.50
3	Norihiro Nakamura	.50
4	Chien-Ming Wang	1.00
5	Pedro Lopez	.50
6	Robinson Cano	2.00
7	Tim Stauffer	.50
8	Ervin Santana	.50
9	Brandon McCarthy	.50
10	Hayden Penn	.50
11	Mike Morse	.50
12	Chad Orvella	.50
13	Prince Fielder	3.00
14	Edwin Encarnacion	.50
15	Scott Olsen	.50
16	Chris Resop	.50
17	Justin Verlander	2.00
18	Melky Cabrera	.50
19	Jeff Francoeur	.50
20	Yuniesky Betancourt	.50
21	Conor Jackson	.50
22	Felix Hernandez	1.00
23	Anthony Reyes	.50
24	John-Ford Griffin	.50
25	Adam Wainwright	.50
26	Ryan Garko	.50
27	Chuck James	.50
28	Tom Seaver	2.00
29	Johnny Bench	2.00
30	Reggie Jackson	2.00
31	Rod Carew	2.00
32	Nolan Ryan	4.00
33	Richie Ashburn	.50
34	Yogi Berra	2.00
35	Lou Brock	1.50
36	Carlton Fisk	1.50
37	Joe Morgan	.50
38	Bob Gibson	2.00
39	Willie McCovey	2.00
40	Harmon Killebrew	2.00
41	Takashi Saito	1.00
42	Kenji Johjima	5.00
43	Joel Zumaya	1.50
44	Dan Uggla	1.00
45	Taylor Buchholz	1.00
46	Josh Barfield	1.00
47	Brian Bannister	1.00
48	Nicholas Markakis	1.00
49	Carlos Martinez	1.00
50	Macay McBride	1.00
51	Brian Anderson	1.00
52	Freddie Bynum	1.00
53	Kelly Stoppach	1.00
54	Choo Freeman	1.00
55	Ryan Shealy	1.00
56	Chris Resop	1.00
57	Hanley Ramirez	1.50
58	Mike Jacobs	1.00
59	Cody Ross	1.00
60	Jose Capellan	1.00
61	David Gassner	1.00
62	Jason Kubel	1.00
63	Jered Weaver	4.00
64	Paul Maholm	1.00
65	Nate McLouth	1.00
66	Ben Johnson	1.00
67	Jack Taschner	1.00
68	Skip Schumaker	1.00
69	Brandon Watson	1.00
70	David Wright	3.00
71	David Ortiz	2.50
72	Alex Rodriguez	4.00
73	Johan Santana	2.00
74	Greg Maddux	2.00
75	Ichiro Suzuki	3.00
76	Albert Pujols	4.00
77	Hideki Matsui	3.00
78	Vladimir Guerrero	2.00
79	Pedro Martinez	2.00
80	Mike Schmidt	2.00
81	Al Kaline	2.00
82	Robin Yount	2.00

Promo

First Class Cuts
No Pricing
Production One Set

First Class Legends

NM/M
Gold: 1-2X
Production 699 Sets
Platinum: 2-3X
Production 99 Sets
Spectrum: No Pricing
Production One Set

1	Babe Ruth	3.00
2	Babe Ruth	3.00
3	Babe Ruth	3.00
4	Babe Ruth	3.00
5	Babe Ruth	3.00
6	Babe Ruth	3.00
7	Babe Ruth	3.00
8	Babe Ruth	3.00
9	Babe Ruth	3.00
10	Babe Ruth	3.00
11	Babe Ruth	3.00
12	Babe Ruth	3.00
13	Babe Ruth	3.00
14	Babe Ruth	3.00
15	Babe Ruth	3.00
16	Babe Ruth	3.00
17	Babe Ruth	3.00
18	Babe Ruth	3.00
19	Babe Ruth	3.00
20	Babe Ruth	3.00
21	Ty Cobb	2.00
22	Ty Cobb	2.00
23	Ty Cobb	2.00
24	Ty Cobb	2.00
25	Ty Cobb	2.00
26	Ty Cobb	2.00
27	Ty Cobb	2.00
28	Ty Cobb	2.00
29	Ty Cobb	2.00
30	Ty Cobb	2.00
31	Ty Cobb	2.00
32	Ty Cobb	2.00
33	Ty Cobb	2.00
34	Ty Cobb	2.00
35	Ty Cobb	2.00
36	Ty Cobb	2.00
37	Ty Cobb	2.00
38	Ty Cobb	2.00
39	Ty Cobb	2.00
40	Ty Cobb	2.00
41	Honus Wagner	2.00
42	Honus Wagner	2.00
43	Honus Wagner	2.00
44	Honus Wagner	2.00
45	Honus Wagner	2.00
46	Honus Wagner	2.00
47	Honus Wagner	2.00
48	Honus Wagner	2.00
49	Honus Wagner	2.00
50	Honus Wagner	2.00
51	Honus Wagner	2.00
52	Honus Wagner	2.00
53	Honus Wagner	2.00
54	Honus Wagner	2.00
55	Honus Wagner	2.00
56	Honus Wagner	2.00
57	Honus Wagner	2.00
58	Honus Wagner	2.00
59	Honus Wagner	2.00
60	Honus Wagner	2.00
61	Christy Mathewson	1.00
62	Christy Mathewson	1.00
63	Christy Mathewson	1.00
64	Christy Mathewson	1.00
65	Christy Mathewson	1.00
66	Christy Mathewson	1.00
67	Christy Mathewson	1.00
68	Christy Mathewson	1.00
69	Christy Mathewson	1.00
70	Christy Mathewson	1.00
71	Christy Mathewson	1.00
72	Christy Mathewson	1.00
73	Christy Mathewson	1.00
74	Christy Mathewson	1.00
75	Christy Mathewson	1.00
76	Christy Mathewson	1.00
77	Christy Mathewson	1.00
78	Christy Mathewson	1.00
79	Christy Mathewson	1.00
80	Christy Mathewson	1.00
81	Walter Johnson	1.00
82	Walter Johnson	1.00
83	Walter Johnson	1.00
84	Walter Johnson	1.00
85	Walter Johnson	1.00
86	Walter Johnson	1.00
87	Walter Johnson	1.00
88	Walter Johnson	1.00
89	Walter Johnson	1.00
90	Walter Johnson	1.00
91	Walter Johnson	1.00
92	Walter Johnson	1.00
93	Walter Johnson	1.00
94	Walter Johnson	1.00
95	Walter Johnson	1.00
96	Walter Johnson	1.00
97	Walter Johnson	1.00
98	Walter Johnson	1.00
99	Walter Johnson	1.00
100	Walter Johnson	1.00

Signature Sensations
NM/M
Inserted 1:288 Hobby

BA	Bronson Arroyo	20.00
GA	Garrett Atkins	10.00
SB	Scott Baker	15.00
KC	Kiko Calero	5.00
JE	Johnny Estrada	8.00
KG	Ken Griffey Jr.	100.00
TR	Travis Hafner	25.00
BH	Bobby Hill	5.00
JJ	Josh Johnson	10.00
AL	Al Leiter	15.00
AM	Aaron Miles	15.00
YM	Yadier Molina	20.00
NP	Nick Punto	8.00
AR	Aaron Rowand	15.00
CS	Cory Sullivan	10.00
JS	Jeff Suppan	15.00
JV	Joe Valentine	10.00
DY	Delmon Young	25.00

Star Attractions

NM/M
Gold: 1X-2X
Production 699 Sets

BA	Bobby Abreu	.75
GA	Garret Anderson	.50
JB	Josh Beckett	.50
CB	Carlos Beltran	.75
AB	Adrian Beltre	.50
LB	Lance Berkman	.50
JC	Jose Contreras	.50
JD	Johnny Damon	1.00
CD	Carlos Delgado	.75
JE	Jim Edmonds	.75
EG	Eric Gagne	.50
JG	Jason Giambi	.75
SG	Shawn Green	.50
GK	Khalil Greene	.50
KG	Ken Griffey Jr.	2.00
GU	Joe Guillen	.50
RH	Rich Harden	.50
AH	Aubrey Huff	.50
TH	Torii Hunter	.50
TI	Tadahito Iguchi	.50
DJ	Derek Jeter	3.00
AJ	Andruw Jones	.50
CJ	Chipper Jones	1.00
JJ	Jacque Jones	.50
CL	Carlos Lee	.50
DL	Derrek Lee	1.00
JL	Javy Lopez	.50
GM	Greg Maddux	2.00
PM	Pedro Martinez	1.00
JM	Joe Mauer	.50
MM	Mark Mulder	.50
MO	Magglio Ordonez	.50
DO	David Ortiz	1.00
AP	Andy Pettitte	.50
JP	Jorge Posada	.75
MP	Mark Prior	.75
PU	Albert Pujols	3.00
MR	Manny Ramirez	1.00
JR	Jose Reyes	.75
CS	Curt Schilling	1.00
JS	Jason Schmidt	.75
GS	Gary Sheffield	.75
SM	John Smoltz	.75
AS	Alfonso Soriano	.75
MT	Mark Teixeira	.75
FT	Frank Thomas	.75
DW	Dontrelle Willis	.50
KW	Kerry Wood	.50
WR	David Wright	1.50
BZ	Barry Zito	.50

Star Attractions Swatches
NM/M
Common Player: 4.00

BA	Bobby Abreu	6.00
GA	Garret Anderson	

JB	Josh Beckett	4.00
CB	Carlos Beltran	6.00
AB	Adrian Beltre	4.00
LB	Lance Berkman	6.00
JC	Jose Contreras	4.00
JD	Johnny Damon	10.00
CD	Carlos Delgado	6.00
JE	Jim Edmonds	6.00
EG	Eric Gagne	4.00
JG	Jason Giambi	4.00
SG	Shawn Green	4.00
GR	Khalil Greene	4.00
KG	Ken Griffey Jr.	20.00
GU	Jose Guillen	4.00
RH	Rich Harden	6.00
AH	Aubrey Huff	4.00
TH	Torii Hunter	4.00
TI	Tadahito Iguchi	10.00
DJ	Derek Jeter	20.00
AJ	Andruw Jones	8.00
CJ	Chipper Jones	8.00
JJ	Jacque Jones	4.00
CL	Carlos Lee	4.00
DL	Derrek Lee	8.00
JL	Javy Lopez	4.00
GM	Greg Maddux	12.00
PM	Pedro Martinez	6.00
JM	Joe Mauer	4.00
MM	Mark Mulder	4.00
MO	Magglio Ordonez	4.00
DO	David Ortiz	8.00
AP	Andy Pettitte	6.00
JP	Jorge Posada	6.00
PU	Albert Pujols	20.00
MR	Manny Ramirez	8.00
JR	Jose Reyes	8.00
CS	Curt Schilling	6.00
JS	Jason Schmidt	4.00
GS	Gary Sheffield	6.00
SM	John Smoltz	6.00
AS	Alfonso Soriano	6.00
MT	Mark Teixeira	6.00
FT	Frank Thomas	6.00
DW	Dontrelle Willis	6.00
KW	Kerry Wood	4.00
WR	David Wright	15.00
BZ	Barry Zito	4.00

Team Pride

NM/M
Gold: 1X-2X
Production 699 Sets

BA	Bobby Abreu	.75
GA	Garret Anderson	.50
JB	Jeff Bagwell	.75
RB	Rocco Baldelli	.50
SC	Sean Casey	.50
LC	Luis Castillo	.50
EC	Eric Chavez	.50
JD	Johnny Damon	1.00
CD	Carlos Delgado	.75
JE	Jim Edmonds	.75
ME	Morgan Ensberg	.50
KF	Keith Foulke	.50
EG	Eric Gagne	.50
LG	Luis Gonzalez	.50
GR	Khalil Greene	.50
KG	Ken Griffey Jr.	2.00
RH	Rich Harden	.50
TH	Trevor Hoffman	.50
AH	Aubrey Huff	.50
DJ	Derek Jeter	.50
NJ	Nick Johnson	.50
AJ	Andruw Jones	.50
CJ	Chipper Jones	1.00
RK	Ryan Klesko	.50
CK	Casey Kotchman	.50
ML	Mike Lieberthal	.50
LO	Mike Lowell	.50
GM	Greg Maddux	2.00
MA	Joe Mauer	.50
JM	Jamie Moyer	.50
DO	David Ortiz	1.00
PE	Andy Pettitte	.50
JP	Jorge Posada	.50
MP	Mark Prior	.50
AP	Albert Pujols	3.00
JR	Jose Reyes	.50
IR	Ivan Rodriguez	.75
CC	C.C. Sabathia	.50
CS	Curt Schilling	1.00
JS	John Smoltz	.75
MS	Mike Sweeney	.75
FT	Frank Thomas	.75
JT	Jim Thome	.75
VA	Jason Varitek	.75
JV	Jose Vidro	.50
BW	Bernie Williams	.50
DW	Dontrelle Willis	.50
KW	Kerry Wood	.50
MY	Michael Young	.50

Diamond Collection

NM/M
Gold: 1-2X

Production 699 Sets

AL	Moises Alou	.50
JB	Jeff Bagwell	.75
RB	Rocco Baldelli	.50
OC	Orlando Cabrera	.50
MC	Mike Cameron	.50
EC	Eric Chavez	.50
CO	Jose Contreras	.50
JC	Jesse Crain	.50
BC	Bobby Crosby	.50
JD	Johnny Damon	1.00
AE	Adam Eaton	.50
JE	Jim Edmonds	.50
SF	Steve Finley	.50
FG	Freddy Garcia	.50
GO	Juan Gonzalez	.50
KG	Ken Griffey Jr.	2.00
JG	Jose Guillen	.50
MH	Mike Hampton	.50
AH	Aubrey Huff	.50
EJ	Edwin Jackson	.50
DJ	Derek Jeter	3.00
NJ	Nick Johnson	.50
RJ	Randy Johnson	1.00
JJ	Jacque Jones	.50
SK	Scott Kazmir	.50
KE	Austin Kearns	.50
JK	Jason Kendall	.50
AK	Adam Kennedy	.50
CK	Casey Kotchman	.50
LA	Matt Lawton	.50
ML	Mike Lieberthal	.50
PL	Paul LoDuca	.50
KL	Kenny Lofton	.50
LO	Mike Lowell	.50
GM	Greg Maddux	2.00
MA	Kazuo Matsui	.50
KM	Kevin Millwood	.50
DO	David Ortiz	1.00
AO	Akinori Otsuka	.50
CP	Carl Pavano	.50
JP	Jorge Posada	.50
BR	Brad Radke	.50
IR	Ivan Rodriguez	.75
CC	C.C. Sabathia	.50
CS	Chris Shelton	.50
JS	John Smoltz	.75
SS	Shannon Stewart	.50
JT	Jim Thome	.50
JW	Jayson Werth	.50
PW	Preston Wilson	.50

Game Jersey

NM/M

	Common Player:	4.00
JB	Jeff Bagwell	6.00
MC	Miguel Cabrera	8.00
EC	Eric Chavez	4.00
RC	Roger Clemens	15.00
JD	Johnny Damon	10.00
JE	Jim Edmonds	6.00
RF	Rafael Furcal	4.00
EG	Eric Gagne	4.00
JG	Jason Giambi	6.00
KG	Ken Griffey Jr.	8.00
VG	Vladimir Guerrero	8.00
RH	Roy Halladay	4.00
DJ	Derek Jeter	20.00
RJ	Randy Johnson	8.00
AJ	Andruw Jones	8.00
CJ	Chipper Jones	8.00
JJ	Jacque Jones	8.00
DL	Derrek Lee	8.00
GM	Greg Maddux	12.00
PM	Pedro Martinez	8.00
DO	David Ortiz	8.00
RP	Rafael Palmeiro	8.00
CP	Corey Patterson	4.00
JP	Jake Peavy	6.00
PO	Jorge Posada	6.00
PR	Mark Prior	6.00
AP	Albert Pujols	20.00
MR	Manny Ramirez	8.00
BR	Brian Roberts	8.00
IR	Ivan Rodriguez	6.00
SR	Scott Rolen	8.00
JS	Johan Santana	8.00
CS	Curt Schilling	8.00
SM	John Smoltz	8.00
AS	Alfonso Soriano	8.00
MT	Mark Teixeira	8.00
TE	Miguel Tejada	8.00
FT	Frank Thomas	8.00
JT	Jim Thome	8.00
DW	Dontrelle Willis	6.00

WR	David Wright	15.00

Series 2

BA	Bobby Abreu	6.00
GA	Garrett Atkins	4.00
JB	Josh Beckett	4.00
CB	Carlos Beltran	8.00
AB	Adrian Beltre	4.00
BI	Craig Biggio	6.00
HB	Hank Blalock	4.00
SC	Sean Casey	4.00
JD	Johnny Damon	10.00
CD	Carlos Delgado	6.00
AD	Adam Dunn	6.00
PF	Prince Fielder	10.00
TG	Tom Glavine	6.00
GR	Khalil Greene	4.00
KG	Ken Griffey Jr.	20.00
HA	Travis Hafner	6.00
TH	Todd Helton	6.00
RH	Ryan Howard	20.00
TI	Tadahito Iguchi	10.00
DJ	Derek Jeter	20.00
PK	Paul Konerko	6.00
CL	Carlos Lee	6.00
JL	Javy Lopez	4.00
VM	Victor Martinez	6.00
JM	Joe Mauer	8.00
MM	Mike Mussina	6.00
MO	Magglio Ordonez	4.00
RO	Roy Oswalt	6.00
AP	Andy Pettitte	6.00
MP	Mike Piazza	8.00
JR	Jose Reyes	8.00
GS	Gary Sheffield	6.00
SI	Grady Sizemore	10.00
JV	Jason Varitek	6.00
CW	Chien-Ming Wang	15.00
RW	Rickie Weeks	6.00
KW	Kerry Wood	4.00
MY	Michael Young	4.00
RZ	Ryan Zimmerman	15.00
BZ	Barry Zito	6.00

Team Pride Materials

NM/M

	Common Player:	4.00
BA	Bobby Abreu	4.00
GA	Garret Anderson	4.00
JB	Jeff Bagwell	6.00
RB	Rocco Baldelli	4.00
SC	Sean Casey	4.00
LC	Luis Castillo	4.00
EC	Eric Chavez	4.00
JD	Johnny Damon	10.00
CD	Carlos Delgado	6.00
JE	Jim Edmonds	6.00
ME	Morgan Ensberg	4.00
KF	Keith Foulke	4.00
EG	Eric Gagne	4.00
LG	Luis Gonzalez	4.00
GR	Khalil Greene	4.00
KG	Ken Griffey Jr.	20.00
RH	Rich Harden	4.00
TH	Trevor Hoffman	4.00
AH	Aubrey Huff	4.00
DJ	Derek Jeter	20.00
NJ	Nick Johnson	4.00
AJ	Andruw Jones	8.00
CJ	Chipper Jones	8.00
RK	Ryan Klesko	4.00
CK	Casey Kotchman	4.00
ML	Mike Lieberthal	4.00
LO	Mike Lowell	4.00
GM	Greg Maddux	12.00
MA	Joe Mauer	4.00
JM	Jamie Moyer	4.00
DO	David Ortiz	6.00
PE	Andy Pettitte	4.00
JP	Jorge Posada	6.00
MP	Mark Prior	6.00
AP	Albert Pujols	20.00
JR	Jose Reyes	6.00
IR	Ivan Rodriguez	4.00
CC	C.C. Sabathia	4.00
CS	Curt Schilling	8.00
JS	John Smoltz	8.00
MS	Mike Sweeney	4.00
FT	Frank Thomas	8.00
JT	Jim Thome	8.00
VA	Jason Varitek	6.00
JV	Jose Vidro	4.00
BW	Bernie Williams	6.00
DW	Dontrelle Willis	6.00
KW	Kerry Wood	4.00
MY	Michael Young	4.00
BZ	Barry Zito	4.00

Game Patch

NM/M
Inserted 1:288

JB	Jeff Bagwell	20.00
MC	Miguel Cabrera	25.00
RC	Roger Clemens	30.00
JD	Johnny Damon	25.00
JE	Jim Edmonds	20.00
RF	Rafael Furcal	15.00
KG	Ken Griffey Jr.	40.00
VG	Vladimir Guerrero	25.00
RH	Roy Halladay	15.00
DJ	Derek Jeter	50.00
RJ	Randy Johnson	25.00
AJ	Andruw Jones	20.00
DL	Derrek Lee	20.00
GM	Greg Maddux	25.00
PM	Pedro Martinez	25.00
RP	Rafael Palmeiro	15.00
JP	Jake Peavy	20.00
MP	Mike Piazza	20.00
PR	Mark Prior	20.00
AP	Albert Pujols	50.00
MR	Manny Ramirez	25.00
BR	Brian Roberts	15.00
SR	Scott Rolen	20.00
JS	Johan Santana	20.00
SM	John Smoltz	25.00
TE	Miguel Tejada	20.00
FT	Frank Thomas	20.00
JT	Jim Thome	20.00
DW	Dontrelle Willis	20.00
WR	David Wright	40.00

Series 2: No Pricing

Silver Spectrum

No Pricing
Production 25 Sets

Printing Plates

No Pricing
Production one set per color.

Rookie Foil Gold

Gold: 4X-8X
Production 99 Sets
Platinum: No Pricing
Production 15 Sets

Rookie Foil Silver

NM/M
Silver: 2X-4X
Production 399 Sets

Inaugural Images

NM/M

	Common Player:	.50
II-1	Sung-Heon Hong	.50
II-2	Yulieski Gourriel	.50
II-3	Tsuyoshi Nishioka	1.00
II-4	Miguel Cabrera	1.50
II-5	Yung-Chi Chen	.50
II-6	Omari Romero	.50
II-7	Ken Griffey Jr.	2.00
II-8	Bernie Williams	.75
II-9	Daniel Cabrera	.50
II-10	David Ortiz	1.50
II-11	Alex Rodriguez	3.00
II-12	Frederich Cepeda	.50
II-13	Derek Jeter	3.00
II-14	Jorge Cantu	1.00
II-15	Alexi Ramirez	.50
II-16	Yoandy Garlobo	.50
II-17	Koji Uehara	.50
II-18	Nobuhiko Matsunaka	.50
II-19	Tomoya Satozaki	.50
II-20	Seung-Yeop Lee	.50
II-21	Yulieski Gourriel	.50
II-22	Adrian Beltre	.50
II-23	Ken Griffey Jr.	2.00
II-24	Jong Beom Lee	.50
II-25	Ichiro Suzuki	.50
II-26	Yoandy Garlobo	.50
II-27	Daisuke Matsuzaka	.50
II-28	Yadel Marti	.50
II-29	Chan Ho Park	.50
II-30	Daisuke Matsuzaka	.50

INKredible

NM/M
Inserted 1:288

JB	Joe Blanton	10.00
CA	Miguel Cabrera	40.00
CO	Chad Cordero	20.00
JC	Jesse Crain	15.00
CC	Carl Crawford	20.00
NG	Nomar Garciaparra	60.00
KG	Ken Griffey Jr.	120.00
TH	Travis Hafner	30.00
JH	J.J. Hardy	20.00
TI	Tadahito Iguchi/ SP 91	50.00
DJ	Derek Jeter	200.00
SK	Scott Kazmir	30.00
CK	Casey Kotchman	10.00
VM	Victor Martinez	20.00
JM	Joe Mauer/SP 91	40.00
MO	Justin Morneau	25.00
BM	Brett Myers/SP 72	15.00
LO	Lyle Overbay/SP 91	25.00
JR	Jeremy Reed	15.00
RE	Jose Reyes/SP 91	35.00
AR	Alexis Rios	25.00
BR	Brian Roberts	20.00
MT	Mark Teixeira	25.00
JV	Justin Verlander/ SP 91	40.00
WI	Dontrelle Willis	20.00
DW	David Wright/SP 91	60.00
KY	Kevin Youkilis	30.00
RZ	Ryan Zimmerman/ SP 91	50.00

Player Highlights

NM/M

	Common Player:	.50
PH-1	Andruw Jones	1.00
PH-2	Manny Ramirez	1.00
PH-3	Travis Hafner	1.00
PH-4	Johnny Damon	1.00
PH-5	Miguel Cabrera	1.00
PH-6	Chris Carpenter	.75
PH-7	Derrek Lee	1.00
PH-8	Jason Bay	.75
PH-9	Jason Varitek	1.00
PH-10	Ryan Howard	2.00
PH-11	Mark Teixeira	.75
PH-12	Carlos Delgado	.75
PH-13	Bartolo Colon	.50
PH-14	David Wright	2.00
PH-15	Miguel Tejada	.75
PH-16	Mike Piazza	2.00
PH-17	Paul Konerko	.75
PH-18	Jermaine Dye	.75
PH-19	Ichiro Suzuki	2.00
PH-20	Brad Wilkerson	.50
PH-21	Hideki Matsui	2.00
PH-22	Albert Pujols	3.00
PH-23	Chris Burke	.50
PH-24	Derek Jeter	2.00
PH-25	Brian Roberts	.75
PH-26	David Ortiz	1.50
PH-27	Alex Rodriguez	3.00
PH-28	Ken Griffey Jr.	2.00
PH-29	Prince Fielder	2.00
PH-30	Bobby Abreu	.75
PH-31	Vladimir Guerrero	1.00
PH-32	Tadahito Iguchi	1.00
PH-33	Jose Reyes	1.00
PH-34	Scott Podsednik	.75
PH-35	Gary Sheffield	.75

Run Producers

NM/M

	Common Player:	.50
RP-1	Ty Cobb	2.00
RP-2	Derrek Lee	1.00
RP-3	Andruw Jones	1.00
RP-4	David Ortiz	1.50
RP-5	Lou Gehrig	3.00
RP-6	Ken Griffey Jr.	2.00
RP-7	Albert Pujols	3.00

run producers
DEREK JETER

RP-8	Derek Jeter	3.00
RP-9	Manny Ramirez	1.00
RP-10	Alex Rodriguez	3.00
RP-11	Gary Sheffield	.75
RP-12	Miguel Cabrera	1.00
RP-13	Hideki Matsui	2.00
RP-14	Vladimir Guerrero	1.00
RP-15	David Wright	2.00
RP-16	Mike Schmidt	2.00
RP-17	Mark Teixeira	.75
RP-18	Babe Ruth	4.00
RP-19	Jimmie Foxx	2.00
RP-20	Honus Wagner	2.00

Speed to Burn

NM/M

	Common Player:	.50
SB-3	Lou Brock	1.00
SB-4	Alfonso Soriano	1.50
SB-5	Carl Crawford	.75
SB-6	Chone Figgins	.50
SB-7	Ichiro Suzuki	2.00
SB-8	Jose Reyes	1.00
SB-9	Juan Pierre	.50
SB-11	Scott Podsednik	.75
SB-12	Alex Rodriguez	3.00
SB-13	David Wright	2.00
SB-14	Bobby Abreu	.75
SB-15	Brian Roberts	.75

All-Time Legends

NM/M

	Common Player:	1.00
AT-1	Ty Cobb	3.00
AT-2	Lou Gehrig	4.00
AT-3	Babe Ruth	5.00
AT-4	Jimmie Foxx	3.00
AT-5	Honus Wagner	3.00
AT-6	Lou Brock	2.00
AT-8	Christy Mathewson	2.00
AT-9	Walter Johnson	2.00
AT-10	Mike Schmidt	2.00
AT-11	Al Kaline	2.00
AT-12	Robin Yount	2.00
AT-13	Johnny Bench	2.00
AT-14	Yogi Berra	2.00
AT-15	Rod Carew	1.00
AT-16	Bob Feller	1.00
AT-17	Carlton Fisk	2.00
AT-18	Bob Gibson	2.00
AT-19	Cy Young	2.00
AT-21	Jackie Robinson	3.00
AT-22	Harmon Killebrew	2.00
AT-23	Mickey Cochrane	1.00
AT-24	Eddie Mathews	2.00
AT-25	Bill Mazeroski	1.00
AT-26	Willie McCovey	1.00
AT-27	Eddie Murray	2.00
AT-28	Lefty Grove	1.00
AT-29	Jim Palmer	1.00
AT-30	Pee Wee Reese	1.00
AT-31	Phil Rizzuto	2.00
AT-32	Brooks Robinson	2.00
AT-33	Nolan Ryan	4.00
AT-34	Tom Seaver	2.00
AT-35	Ozzie Smith	2.00
AT-36	Roy Campanella	2.00
AT-37	Thurman Munson	3.00
AT-38	Mel Ott	2.00
AT-39	Satchel Paige	2.00
AT-40	Rogers Hornsby	2.00

World Baseball Classic Jersey

NM/M
Inserted 1:24
Patch: No Pricing
Production 8 Sets

JB	Jason Bay	10.00
EB	Erik Bedard	4.00
CB	Carlos Beltran	15.00
MC	Miguel Cabrera	15.00
VC	Vinny Castilla	4.00
FC	Frederich Cepeda	15.00
TC	Tai-San Chang	200.00

RC	Roger Clemens	30.00
JD	Johnny Damon	15.00
CD	Carlos Delgado	10.00
ME	Michel Enriquez	20.00
MF	Maikel Folch	20.00
JF	Jeff Francis	4.00
FR	Jeff Francoeur	15.00
FG	Freddy Garcia	4.00
YG	Yulieski Gourriel	25.00
KG	Ken Griffey Jr.	25.00
JG	Jason Grilli	4.00
HS	Chia-Hsien Hseih	125.00
CH	Chin-Lung Hu	75.00
JH	Justin Huber	4.00
AI	Akinori Iwamura	50.00
AJ	Andruw Jones	15.00
MK	Munenori Kawasaki	50.00
PL	Pedro Lazo	20.00
CL	Carlos Lee	4.00
DL	Derrek Lee	10.00
JL	Jong Beom Lee	8.00
WL	Wei-Chu Lin	180.00
GL	Guangbiao Liu	60.00
VM	Victor Martinez	10.00
NM	Nobuhiko Matsunaka	60.00
DM	Daisuke Matsuzaka	350.00
YM	Yunieski Maya	15.00
JM	Justin Morneau	10.00
TN	Tsuyoshi Nishioka	60.00
MO	Michihiro Ogasawara	60.00
DO	David Ortiz	20.00
WP	Wei-Lun Pan	80.00
EP	Eduardo Paret	20.00
JP	Jin Man Park	15.00
OP	Oliver Perez	4.00
PE	Ariel Pestano	20.00
MP	Mike Piazza	25.00
AP	Albert Pujols	30.00
AR	Alex Rodriguez	25.00
IR	Ivan Rodriguez	10.00
JS	Johan Santana	15.00
MS	Min Han Son	10.00
AS	Alfonso Soriano	15.00
I	Ichiro Suzuki	220.00
HT	Hitoshi Tamura	50.00
MT	Mark Teixeira	10.00
TE	Miguel Tejada	15.00
KU	Koji Uehara	100.00
JV	Jason Varitek	20.00
TW	Tsuyoshi Wada	60.00
WW	Wei Wang	60.00
SW	Shunsuke Watanabe	50.00
GY	Guogang Yang	10.00

Update Gold

Gold (1001-1250): 4-8X
Gold SP's: .5-1X
Production 99 sets

Update Inkredible

NM/M

Inserted 1:24 Retail

BA	Brandon Backe	10.00
CB	Colter Bean	10.00
YB	Yuniesky Betancourt	10.00
GC	Gustavo Chacin	8.00
CA	Carl Crawford	15.00
CC	Coco Crisp	15.00
CD	Chris Duffy	10.00
JD	Jermaine Dye	15.00
GF	Gavin Floyd	5.00
RF	Ryan Freel	15.00
RG	Ryan Garko	15.00
KG	Ken Griffey Jr./SP	125.00
AH	Aaron Harang	10.00
JH	John Hattig Jr.	5.00
MH	Matt Holliday	10.00
TI	Tadahito Iguchi/SP	5.00
CI	Cesar Izturis	3.00
AJ	Adam Jones	25.00
CK	Casey Kotchman	10.00
CL	Cliff Lee	8.00
NL	Noah Lowry	8.00
BM	Brandon McCarthy/SP	15.00
ZM	Zach Miner	15.00
MM	Matt Murton	15.00
LN	Leo Nunez	5.00
AP	Angel Pagan	10.00
PA	John Patterson	5.00
RP	Ronny Paulino	10.00
JP	Jhonny Peralta	12.00
PE	Joel Pineiro	8.00
PI	Joel Pineiro	8.00
KR	Ken Ray	5.00
BR	Brian Roberts	15.00
NS	Nick Swisher	10.00

MT	Mark Teahen	15.00
MV	Michael Vento	5.00
BW	Brian Wilson	8.00
CW	C.J. Wilson	5.00
KY	Kevin Youkilis	15.00

Update Star Attractions

NM/M

Inserted 1:2 Retail
Silver: 2-3X
Production 99 Sets

BR	Brian Anderson	.50
EA	Erick Aybar	.50
WA	Willy Aybar	.50
JO	Josh Barfield	.50
BI	Chad Billingsley	.75
MC	Matt Cain	.75
RC	Ronny Cedeno	.50
SD	Stephen Drew	1.50
AE	Andre Ethier	1.00
PF	Prince Fielder	1.50
TG	Tony Gwynn Jr.	.50
CH	Cole Hamels	1.00
HI	Jason Hirsh	.50
HU	Justin Huber	.50
CO	Conor Jackson	.50
JA	Chuck James	.50
KJ	Kenji Johjima	1.50
JJ	Josh Johnson	.50
AJ	Adam Jones	.50
MK	Matthew Kemp	.50
HK	Howie Kendrick	1.00
JK	Jason Kubel	.50
LE	Jon Lester	1.50
FL	Francisco Liriano	1.00
AL	Adam Loewen	.50
NM	Nicholas Markakis	.75
AM	Andy Marte	.50
RM	Russell Martin	.50
MA	Jeff Mathis	.50
DM	Dustin McGowan	.50
LM	Lastings Milledge	1.00
KM	Kendry Morales	.50
SO	Scott Olsen	.50
PA	Jonathan Papelbon	1.00
DP	Dustin Pedroia	.50
PE	Mike Pelfrey	1.50
HP	Hayden Penn	.50
CQ	Carlos Quentin	.75
HR	Hanley Ramirez	1.00
AR	Anthony Reyes	.50
AN	Anibal Sanchez	.50
SW	Jeremy Sowers	.50
DU	Dan Uggla	.50
JV	Justin Verlander	2.00
CY	Chris Young	.50
AW	Adam Wainwright	1.00
JW	Jered Weaver	1.00
RZ	Ryan Zimmerman	1.50
JZ	Joel Zumaya	1.00

World Baseball Classic

NM/M

Complete Set (50): 20.00
Common Player: .25

1	Derek Jeter	1.50
2	Ken Griffey Jr.	1.00
3	Derrek Lee	.50
4	Dontrelle Willis	.25
5	Alex Rodriguez	1.50
6	Jeff Francoeur	.50
7	Roger Clemens	1.50
8	Johnny Damon	.50
9	Chipper Jones	.50
10	Mark Teixeira	.50
11	Chase Utley	.50
12	Jake Peavy	.50
13	Michael Collins	.25
14	Justin Huber	.25
15	Jason Bay	.50
16	Jeff Francis	.25
17	Justin Morneau	.50
18	Guogang Yang	.25
19	Wei Wang	.25
20	Chia-Hsien Hseih	.25
21	Chin-Lung Hu	.25
22	Wei-Lun Pan	.25
23	Yung-Chi Chen	.25
24	Mike Piazza	.50
25	Albert Pujols	1.50
26	David Ortiz	.50
27	Jose Reyes	.50
28	Miguel Tejada	.50
29	Ichiro Suzuki	1.00
30	Nobuhiko Matsunaka	.25
31	Toshiaki Imae	.25
32	Kazuhiro Wada	.25
33	Shunsuke Watanabe	.25
34	Jung Bong	.25
35	Jong Beom Lee	.25
36	Seung-Yeop Lee	.25
37	Vinny Castilla	.25
38	Oliver Perez	.50
39	Jorge Cantu	.50
40	Andruw Jones	.50
41	Carlos Lee	.50
42	Carlos Beltran	.50
43	Carlos Delgado	.50
44	Ivan Rodriguez	.50
45	Bernie Williams	.50
46	Bobby Abreu	.50
47	Miguel Cabrera	.75
48	Johan Santana	.50
49	Victor Martinez	.50
50	Omar Vizquel	.25

2006 Upper Deck Artifacts

NM/M

Complete Set (100):
Common Player: .25
Pack (4): 10.00
Box (10): 90.00

1	Luis Gonzalez	.25
2	Conor Jackson (RC)	.25
3	Joey Devine RC	1.00
4	Andruw Jones	.75
5	Chipper Jones	1.00
6	John Smoltz	.50
7	Jeff Francoeur	.50
8	Brian Roberts	.25
9	Miguel Tejada	.75
10	Nicholas Markakis (RC)	.25
11	Curt Schilling	1.00
12	David Ortiz	1.00
13	Johnny Damon	1.00
14	Manny Ramirez	1.00
15	Jonathan Papelbon (RC)	6.00
16	Aramis Ramirez	.50
17	Carlos Zambrano	.50
18	Derrek Lee	.75
19	Greg Maddux	2.00
20	Mark Prior	.75
21	Mark Buehrle	.50
22	Paul Konerko	.50
23	Adam Dunn	.75
24	Ken Griffey Jr.	2.00
25	Travis Hafner	.50
26	Victor Martinez	.75
27	Todd Helton	.75
28	Ivan Rodriguez	.75
29	Jeremy Bonderman	.25
30	Jeremy Hermida (RC)	.25
31	Carlos Delgado	.50
32	Dontrelle Willis	.50
33	Josh Beckett	.50
34	Miguel Cabrera	1.00
35	Craig Biggio	.50
36	Lance Berkman	.50
37	Roger Clemens	3.00
38	Roy Oswalt	.50
39	Josh Willingham (RC)	.25
40	Hanley Ramirez (RC)	1.00
41	Prince Fielder (RC)	2.00
42	Zack Greinke	.25
43	Francisco Rodriguez	.25
44	Vladimir Guerrero	1.00
45	Tim Hamulack (RC)	.25
46	Jeff Kent	.50
47	Ben Sheets	.50
48	Rickie Weeks	.50
49	Francisco Liriano (RC)	4.00
50	Joe Mauer	1.00
51	Johan Santana	.75
52	Justin Morneau	.50
53	Torii Hunter	.50
54	Carlos Beltran	.75
55	David Wright	2.00
56	Jose Reyes	.75
57	Mike Piazza	1.00
58	Pedro Martinez	.75
59	Alex Rodriguez	3.00
60	Derek Jeter	3.00
61	Hideki Matsui	.75
62	Randy Johnson	1.00
63	Justin Verlander (RC)	1.00
64	Bobby Crosby	.50
65	Eric Chavez	.50
66	Brian Anderson (RC)	.25
67	Bobby Abreu	.50
68	Pat Burrell	.50
69	Jason Bay	.50
70	Oliver Perez	.50
71	Chuck James (RC)	.25
72	Brian Giles	.25
73	Jake Peavy	.25
74	Khalil Greene	.25
75	Jason Schmidt	.25
76	Kenji Johjima RC	4.00
77	Jeremy Accardo RC	.50
78	Adrian Beltre	.50
79	Ichiro Suzuki	2.00
80	Jeff Harris RC	.25
81	Felix Hernandez	.75
82	Albert Pujols	3.00
83	Chris Carpenter	.75
84	Jim Edmonds	.50
85	Scott Rolen	.75
86	Mike Jacobs (RC)	.25
87	Carl Crawford	.50

88	Anderson Hernandez (RC)	.25
89	Scott Kazmir	.50
90	Josh Rupe (RC)	.25
91	Scott Feldman RC	.50
92	Alfonso Soriano	.75
93	Hank Blalock	.50
94	Mark Teixeira	.75
95	Michael Young	.50
96	Roy Halladay	.50
97	Vernon Wells	.50
98	Jason Bergmann RC	.50
99	Ryan Zimmerman (RC)	4.00
100	Jose Vidro	.25

AL/NL Artifacts

NM/M

Common Player: 4.00
Production 325 Sets
Red: .75-1.5X
Production 100-250
Green: .75-1.5X
Production 150 Sets

GA	Garrett Atkins	4.00
JB	Jeff Bagwell	8.00
SB	Scott Baker	4.00
RB	Rocco Baldelli	4.00
CL	Clint Barmes	4.00
JA	Jason Bay	8.00
HB	Hank Blalock	4.00
BL	Joe Blanton	4.00
JB	Jeremy Bonderman	6.00
BB	Ben Broussard	4.00
MB	Mark Buehrle	6.00
CB	Chris Burke	4.00
MC	Miguel Cabrera	8.00
MA	Matt Cain	6.00
JC	Jorge Cantu	4.00
CA	Chris Capuano	4.00
CC	Chris Carpenter	10.00
GC	Gustavo Chacin	4.00
EC	Eric Chavez	4.00
RC	Ryan Church	4.00
CH	Chad Cordero	4.00
CC	Carl Crawford	6.00
CR	Joe Crede	4.00
CO	Coco Crisp	6.00
ZD	Zachary Duke	4.00
AD	Adam Dunn/250	8.00
JE	Jim Edmonds	6.00
ME	Morgan Ensberg	4.00
PF	Prince Fielder	15.00
JF	Jeff Francoeur	6.00
EG	Eric Gagne	4.00
GA	Jon Garland	4.00
MG	Marcus Giles	4.00
JG	Jonny Gomes	6.00
KG	Ken Griffey Jr.	15.00
VG	Vladimir Guerrero	8.00
TH	Travis Hafner	4.00
BH	Bill Hall/235	4.00
AH	Aaron Harang	4.00
DH	Danny Haren	4.00
TH	Todd Helton	6.00
FH	Felix Hernandez	6.00
RH	Ramon Hernandez	4.00
MH	Matt Holliday	4.00
RY	Ryan Howard	15.00
TI	Tadahito Iguchi	8.00
CO	Conor Jackson	4.00
DJ	Derek Jeter	25.00
DA	Dan Johnson	4.00
NJ	Nick Johnson	4.00
RJ	Randy Johnson/235	8.00
CJ	Chipper Jones	8.00
SK	Scott Kazmir	6.00
LE	Carlos Lee	4.00
CL	Cliff Lee	4.00
DL	Derrek Lee	6.00
BL	Brad Lidge	4.00
FL	Felipe Lopez	4.00
ML	Mark Loretta	4.00
NL	Noah Lowry	4.00
PM	Pedro Martinez	8.00
VM	Victor Martinez	4.00
JM	Joe Mauer	10.00
BM	Brian McCann	8.00
BM	Brandon McCarthy	4.00
YM	Yadier Molina	4.00
JU	Justin Morneau	6.00
JN	Joe Nathan	4.00
DO	David Ortiz	10.00
RO	Roy Oswalt	4.00
JP	Jake Peavy	6.00
PE	Jhonny Peralta	4.00

JP	Joel Pineiro	4.00
SP	Scott Podsednik	6.00
MP	Mark Prior	6.00
AP	Albert Pujols/250	20.00
MR	Manny Ramirez	8.00
JR	Jose Reyes	8.00
IR	Ivan Rodriguez	6.00
ES	Ervin Santana	4.00
CS	Chris Shelton	4.00
GS	Grady Sizemore	10.00
JS	John Smoltz/250	250.00
AS	Alfonso Soriano	8.00
HS	Huston Street	4.00
NS	Nick Swisher	4.00
MT	Miguel Tejada	6.00
CU	Chase Utley	10.00
JV	Jason Varitek	8.00
RW	Rickie Weeks	6.00
JW	Jake Westbrook	4.00
DW	Dontrelle Willis	8.00
JW	Jack Wilson/200	4.00
WR	David Wright	20.00
DY	Dmitri Young	4.00
MY	Michael Young	4.00
RZ	Ryan Zimmerman	15.00

Awesome Artifacts

NM/M

Common Player: 10.00
Production 45 unless noted.

BA	Jeff Bagwell	12.00
HB	Harold Baines	10.00
SB	Scott Baker	10.00
RB	Rocco Baldelli	10.00
CB	Clint Barmes	10.00
JB	Jason Bay	12.00
HA	Hank Blalock	10.00
BL	Joe Blanton	10.00
MB	Mark Buehrle	10.00
BU	Chris Burke	10.00
MC	Miguel Cabrera	15.00
CA	Matt Cain	10.00
CH	Chris Carpenter	15.00
CH	Gustavo Chacin	10.00
EC	Eric Chavez	10.00
WC	Will Clark	12.00
CC	Carl Crawford	15.00
DD	Don Drysdale/25	25.00
ZD	Zachary Duke	10.00
AD	Adam Dunn	15.00
JE	Jim Edmonds	12.00
ME	Morgan Ensberg	10.00
PF	Prince Fielder	20.00
CF	Carlton Fisk	15.00
FG	Gavin Floyd	10.00
JF	Jeff Francoeur	12.00
EG	Eric Gagne	10.00
GA	Jon Garland	10.00
SG	Steve Garvey	10.00
JG	Jonny Gomes	10.00
KG	Ken Griffey Jr.	30.00
VG	Vladimir Guerrero	15.00
BH	Bill Hall	10.00
AH	Aaron Harang	10.00
DH	Danny Haren	10.00
TH	Todd Helton	15.00
FH	Felix Hernandez	15.00
TR	Trevor Hoffman	10.00
RH	Rogers Hornsby/25	25.00
RY	Ryan Howard	100.00
BO	Bo Jackson	15.00
CO	Conor Jackson	10.00
DJ	Derek Jeter	40.00
DA	Dan Johnson	10.00
NJ	Nick Johnson	10.00
RA	Randy Johnson	10.00
CJ	Chipper Jones	15.00
JL	Jason Lane	10.00
DL	Don Larsen/25	25.00
CL	Cliff Lee	10.00
DE	Derrek Lee	10.00
NL	Noah Lowry	10.00
PM	Pedro Martinez	15.00
EM	Eddie Mathews	15.00
BR	Brian McCann	15.00
BM	Brandon McCarthy	10.00
JM	Johnny Mize/25	20.00
YM	Yadier Molina	10.00
JU	Justin Morneau	12.00
DO	David Ortiz	25.00
RO	Roy Oswalt	10.00
SP	Satchel Paige	100.00
DP	Dave Parker	10.00
JP	Jake Peavy	10.00
PE	Jhonny Peralta	10.00
GP	Gaylord Perry	10.00
JO	Joel Pineiro	10.00
MP	Mark Prior	10.00
AP	Albert Pujols	40.00
MR	Manny Ramirez	15.00
CR	Cal Ripken Jr.	40.00
IR	Ivan Rodriguez	10.00
AR	Aaron Rowand	10.00
ES	Ervin Santana	10.00
RS	Ron Santo	10.00
CS	Chris Shelton	10.00
GS	Grady Sizemore	15.00
JS	John Smoltz	15.00
AS	Alfonso Soriano	15.00
HS	Huston Street	10.00
NS	Nick Swisher	10.00
MI	Miguel Tejada	10.00
FT	Frank Thomas	15.00
CU	Chase Utley	20.00
AV	Andy Van Slyke	10.00

JV	Jason Varitek	20.00
RW	Rickie Weeks	10.00
DW	David Wells	10.00
WE	Jake Westbrook	10.00
WI	Dontrelle Willis	12.00
JW	Jack Wilson	10.00
WR	David Wright	30.00
CY	Carl Yastrzemski/25	40.00
RZ	Ryan Zimmerman	25.00

Apparel

NM/M

Common Player:
Production 325 Sets
Gold: .75-1.5X
Production 150 Sets
Silver: 1X
Production 250 Sets
Rare Apparel: No Pricing
Production One Set

AT	Garrett Atkins	4.00
HB	Harold Baines	4.00
SB	Scott Baker	6.00
RB	Rocco Baldelli	4.00
BA	Clint Barmes	4.00
BY	Jason Bay	8.00
YB	Yuniesky Betancourt	4.00
JO	Joe Blanton	4.00
JE	Jeremy Bonderman	4.00
BB	Ben Broussard	4.00
CB	Chris Burke	4.00
MC	Miguel Cabrera	8.00
MA	Matt Cain	4.00
CU	Jorge Cantu	6.00
CS	Chris Capuano	4.00
CH	Chris Carpenter	10.00
GC	Gustavo Chacin	4.00
RC	Ryan Church	4.00
WC	Will Clark	8.00
CD	Chad Cordero	4.00
CA	Carl Crawford	6.00
CO	Coco Crisp	6.00
PF	Prince Fielder	15.00
CF	Carlton Fisk	8.00
GF	Gavin Floyd	4.00
GA	Jon Garland	4.00
SG	Steve Garvey	4.00
MG	Marcus Giles	4.00
GO	Jonny Gomes	4.00
GO	Adrian Gonzalez	4.00
RG	Rich "Goose" Gossage	4.00
KG	Ken Griffey Jr.	15.00
AH	Aaron Harang	4.00
DH	Danny Haren	4.00
JH	Jeremy Hermida	4.00
FH	Felix Hernandez	8.00
RH	Ramon Hernandez	4.00
MH	Matt Holliday	4.00
HO	Ryan Howard	15.00
TI	Tadahito Iguchi	10.00
BO	Bo Jackson	10.00
CJ	Conor Jackson	4.00
DJ	Derek Jeter	25.00
DA	Dan Johnson	4.00
SK	Scott Kazmir	4.00
KE	Jason Kendall	4.00
CK	Casey Kotchman	4.00
JK	John Kruk	4.00
JL	Jason Lane	4.00
DO	Don Larsen	15.00
LE	Carlos Lee	6.00
CL	Cliff Lee	4.00
DL	Derrek Lee	8.00
BL	Brad Lidge	4.00
FL	Felipe Lopez	4.00
ML	Mark Loretta	4.00
NL	Noah Lowry	4.00
BI	Bill Madlock	4.00
JM	Joe Mauer	10.00
BC	Brian McCann	8.00
BM	Brandon McCarthy	4.00
FM	Fred McGriff	7.00
YM	Yadier Molina	4.00
MO	Justin Morneau	8.00
JN	Joe Nathan	4.00
GN	Graig Nettles	4.00
OR	Magglio Ordonez	4.00
RO	Roy Oswalt	4.00
PE	Jake Peavy	6.00
JP	Jhonny Peralta	4.00
GP	Gaylord Perry	6.00
PI	Joel Pineiro	4.00
SP	Scott Podsednik	4.00
BP	Boog Powell	4.00
JY	Jeremy Reed	4.00
HR	Jose Reyes	8.00
CR	Cal Ripken Jr.	20.00
BR	Brian Roberts	4.00
AR	Aaron Rowand	4.00
ES	Ervin Santana	4.00
RS	Ron Santo	15.00
MS	Mike Schmidt	10.00
SH	Chris Shelton	4.00
GS	Grady Sizemore	10.00
HS	Huston Street	4.00
NS	Nick Swisher	4.00

ST So Taguchi 6.00
CU Chase Utley 10.00
AV Andy Van Slyke 4.00
RW Rickie Weeks 6.00
JW Jake Westbrook 4.00
DW Dontrelle Willis 6.00
WR David Wright 20.00
CY Carl Yastrzemski 15.00
DY Dmitri Young 4.00
MY Michael Young 4.00
RZ Ryan Zimmerman 15.00

Apparel Autographs
NM/M
Production 30 Sets
Patch Auto.: No Pricing
Production 10 Sets
AT Garrett Atkins 20.00
HB Harold Baines 20.00
SB Scott Baker 15.00
BA Clint Barmes 20.00
BY Jason Bay 30.00
YB Yuniesky Betancourt 25.00
JO Joe Blanton 20.00
JE Jeremy Bonderman 30.00
BB Ben Broussard 15.00
CB Chris Burke 15.00
MC Miguel Cabrera 40.00
MA Matt Cain 40.00
CS Chris Capuano 20.00
CH Chris Carpenter 50.00
GC Gustavo Chacin 15.00
RC Ryan Church 20.00
WC Will Clark 40.00
CD Chad Cordero 20.00
CA Carl Crawford 25.00
CO Coco Crisp 40.00
JD Jermaine Dye 20.00
PF Prince Fielder 60.00
CF Carlton Fisk 40.00
SG Steve Garvey 25.00
MG Marcus Giles 25.00
JG Jonny Gomes 30.00
GO Adrian Gonzalez 20.00
GG Rich "Goose" Gossage 35.00
KG Ken Griffey Jr. 100.00
AH Aaron Harang 15.00
DH Danny Haren 20.00
JH Jeremy Hermida 30.00
FH Felix Hernandez 50.00
RH Ramon Hernandez 15.00
HO Ryan Howard/23 85.00
TI Tadahito Iguchi 50.00
BO Bo Jackson 100.00
CJ Conor Jackson 40.00
DJ Derek Jeter 175.00
DA Dan Johnson 20.00
SK Scott Kazmir 40.00
CK Casey Kotchman 25.00
JK John Kruk 30.00
DO Don Larsen 25.00
LE Carlos Lee 25.00
CL Carlos Lee 15.00
DL Derrek Lee 40.00
BL Brad Lidge 20.00
FL Felipe Lopez 30.00
NL Noah Lowry 40.00
BI Bill Madlock 15.00
JM Joe Mauer 50.00
BM Brandon McCarthy 20.00
YM Yadier Molina 40.00
MO Justin Morneau 30.00
JN Joe Nathan 25.00
GN Graig Nettles 30.00
OR Magglio Ordonez 35.00
RO Roy Oswalt 25.00
PE Jake Peavy 35.00
JP Jhonny Peralta 15.00
GP Gaylord Perry 25.00
PI Joel Pineiro 25.00
SP Scott Podsednik 30.00
BP Boog Powell 25.00
JR Jose Reyes 40.00
CR Cal Ripken Jr. 180.00
AR Aaron Rowand 20.00
RS Ron Santo 75.00
MS Mike Schmidt 60.00
SH Chris Shelton 15.00
HS Huston Street 20.00
NS Nick Swisher 25.00
CU Chase Utley 75.00
AV Andy Van Slyke 25.00
RW Rickie Weeks 25.00
JW Jake Westbrook 20.00
DW Dontrelle Willis 35.00
WR David Wright 85.00
CY Carl Yastrzemski 65.00
DY Dmitri Young 15.00
MY Michael Young 25.00
RZ Ryan Zimmerman 75.00

Autofacts

NM/M
Production 5-800

JA Jeremy Accardo/800 15.00
LA Luis Aparicio/250 15.00
GA Garrett Atkins/800 15.00
CB Clint Barmes/800 15.00
JB Jason Bay/200 20.00
GB George Bell/715 20.00
BE Jason Bergmann/800 10.00
BY Clete Boyer/485 15.00
MC Miguel Cabrera/250 30.00
MA Matt Cain/700 20.00
CP Jose Capellan/800 12.00
CA Chris Capuano/800 15.00
CH Chris Carpenter/51 50.00
JC Joe Carter/400 15.00
GC Gustavo Chacin/800 12.00
CC Chris Chambliss/400 15.00
RC Ryan Church/800 15.00
CK Jack Clark/800 10.00
CO Coco Crisp/800 30.00
ED Eric Davis/487 20.00
AD Andre Dawson/300 25.00
CD Chris Demaria/800 10.00
DA Chris Denorfia/659 15.00
DE Joey Devine/150 15.00
JD Jermaine Dye/652 20.00
LD Lenny Dykstra/412 15.00
SF Scott Feldman/800 15.00
PF Prince Fielder/200 45.00
GF George Foster/300 12.00
SG Steve Garvey/300 25.00
MG Marcus Giles/350 20.00
GO Jonny Gomes/700 15.00
GG Rich "Goose" Gossage/300 20.00
KG Ken Griffey Jr./800 70.00
TH Travis Hafner/400 20.00
TM Tim Hamulack/742 10.00
AH Aaron Harang/800 12.00
DH Danny Haren/800 15.00
JE Jeff Harris/800 10.00
FH Felix Hernandez/300 30.00
KH Kent Hrbek/239 20.00
TI Tadahito Iguchi/700 35.00
BO Bo Jackson/250 50.00
CJ Conor Jackson/800 15.00
RJ Reggie Jackson/200 50.00
DJ Derek Jeter/100 140.00
AJ Andruw Jones/150 30.00
IK Ian Kinsler/800 25.00
JK Jason Kubel/400 12.00
JL Jason Lane/800 12.00
BL Barry Larkin/300 35.00
CL Cliff Lee/600 10.00
DL Derrek Lee/300 40.00
BI Bill Madlock/300 15.00
PM Pedro Martinez/100 60.00
JM Joe Mauer/400 35.00
AM Aaron Miles/494 15.00
YM Yadier Molina/800 20.00
JN Joe Nathan/800 15.00
GN Graig Nettles/800 25.00
TO Tony Oliva/300 15.00
MO Magglio Ordonez/437 25.00
JP Jhonny Peralta/700 15.00
TP Tony Perez/251 15.00
HR Hanley Ramirez/500 15.00
RE Chris Resop/800 15.00
JR Jim Rice/200 20.00
CR Cal Ripken Jr./100 100.00
BR Brian Roberts/200 15.00
AR Aaron Rowand/520 15.00
JS Johan Santana/150 50.00
CS Chris Shelton/350 15.00
HS Huston Street/500 15.00
NS Nick Swisher/200 15.00
WT Willy Taveras/500 10.00
CU Chase Utley/800 50.00
JV Justin Verlander/700 40.00
RW Rickie Weeks/91 25.00
JW Jake Westbrook/800 12.00
WI Dontrelle Willis/50 75.00
MW Maury Wills/150 20.00
DW David Wright/700 65.00
CY Chris Young/700 20.00
DY Dmitri Young/300 15.00
MY Michael Young/600 20.00
CZ Carlos Zambrano/200 25.00
RZ Ryan Zimmerman/800 50.00

Cardinals World Series
NM/M
Complete Set (25): 25.00
Complete Factory Set: 40.00
Common Player: .50
1 Ronnie Belliard .50
2 Gary Bennett .50
3 Chris Carpenter 3.00
4 Chris Duncan 1.00
5 David Eckstein 3.00
6 Jim Edmonds 3.00
7 Juan Encarnacion 1.00
8 Randy Flores .50
9 Josh Hancock .50
10 Tyler Johnson .50
11 Josh Kinney .50
12 Braden Looper .50
13 Aaron Miles .50
14 Yadier Molina 1.00
15 Albert Pujols 5.00
16 Anthony Reyes 1.50
17 John Rodriguez .50
18 Scott Rolen 3.00
19 Jeff Suppan 1.00
20 Scott Spiezio .50
21 So Taguchi .50
22 Brad Thompson .50
23 Adam Wainwright 2.00
24 Jeff Weaver .50
25 Preston Wilson .50

Cardinals World Series Jumbo
NM/M
Jumbo Team Photo: 2.00

Cardinals World Series Memorable Moment
NM/M
Complete Set (9): 5.00
1 Albert Pujols 2.00
2 Juan Encarnacion .50
3 So Taguchi .50
4 Jeff Suppan .50
5 Albert Pujols 2.00
6 Yadier Molina .50
7 Anthony Reyes .50
8 David Eckstein 1.00
9 Jeff Weaver .50

Cardinals World Series Season Highlight
NM/M
Complete Set (15): 5.00
1 Scott Rolen 1.00
2 Mark Mulder 1.00
3 Albert Pujols 2.00
4 Albert Pujols 2.00
5 Chris Carpenter 1.00
6 Juan Encarnacion .50
7 Adam Wainwright .50
8 Yadier Molina .50
9 So Taguchi .50
10 Jeff Suppan .50
11 Jim Edmonds 1.00
12 Chris Duncan .50
13 Scott Spiezio .50
14 Scott Rolen 1.00
15 Ronnie Belliard .50

2006 Upper Deck Epic
NM/M
Complete Set (300):
Common Player: 2.00
Production 450 Sets
Pack (3): 35.00
Box (5): 150.00
1 Conor Jackson (RC) 2.00
2 Brandon Webb 3.00
3 Craig Counsell 2.00
4 Luis Gonzalez 2.00
5 Miguel Batista 2.00
6 Orlando Hudson 2.00
7 Russ Ortiz 2.00
8 Shawn Green 2.00
9 Andruw Jones 2.00
10 Chipper Jones 5.00
11 Edgar Renteria 3.00
12 Jeff Francoeur 3.00
13 John Smoltz 3.00
14 Marcus Giles 2.00
15 Mike Hampton 2.00
16 Tim Hudson 2.00
17 Erik Bedard 2.00
18 Brian Roberts 2.00
19 Javy Lopez 2.00
20 Jay Gibbons 2.00
21 Jeff Conine 2.00
22 Melvin Mora 2.00
23 Miguel Tejada 4.00
24 Daniel Cabrera 2.00
25 Rodrigo Lopez 2.00
26 Ramon Hernandez 2.00
27 Bronson Arroyo 2.00
28 Curt Schilling 5.00
29 David Ortiz 5.00
30 David Wells 2.00
31 Jason Varitek 4.00
32 Josh Beckett 3.00
33 Kevin Youkilis 3.00
34 Manny Ramirez 5.00
35 Matt Clement 2.00
36 Mike Lowell 2.00
37 Tim Wakefield 2.00
38 Trot Nixon 2.00
39 Aramis Ramirez 3.00
40 Carlos Zambrano 3.00
41 Derrek Lee 3.00
42 Greg Maddux 10.00
43 Juan Pierre 3.00
44 Kerry Wood 3.00
45 Mark Prior 4.00
46 Michael Barrett 2.00
47 Ryan Dempster 2.00
48 Todd Walker 2.00
49 Wade Miller 2.00
50 A.J. Pierzynski 2.00
51 Brian Anderson (RC) 2.00
52 Frank Thomas 4.00
53 Javier Vazquez 2.00
54 Jim Thome 4.00
55 Joe Crede 2.00
56 Jon Garland 2.00
57 Juan Uribe 2.00
58 Mark Buehrle 3.00
59 Paul Konerko 3.00
60 Scott Podsednik 2.00
61 Tadahito Iguchi 3.00
62 Aaron Harang 2.00
63 Adam Dunn 4.00
64 Austin Kearns 3.00
65 Edwin Encarnacion 2.00
66 Eric Milton 2.00
67 Felipe Lopez 2.00
68 Jason LaRue 2.00
69 Ken Griffey Jr. 10.00
70 Wily Mo Pena 2.00
71 Aaron Boone 2.00
72 Ben Broussard 2.00
73 C.C. Sabathia 2.00
74 Casey Blake 2.00
75 Cliff Lee 2.00
76 Grady Sizemore 3.00
77 Jake Westbrook 3.00
78 Josh Bard 2.00
79 Travis Hafner 4.00
80 Victor Martinez 2.00
81 Chin-Hui Tsao 2.00
82 Clint Barmes 2.00
83 Garrett Atkins 2.00
84 Josh Wilson (RC) 2.00
85 Luis Gonzalez 2.00
86 Matt Holliday 2.00
87 Todd Helton 4.00
88 Brandon Inge 2.00
89 Carlos Guillen 2.00
90 Chris Shelton 2.00
91 Craig Monroe 2.00
92 Dmitri Young 2.00
93 Ivan Rodriguez 4.00
94 Jeremy Bonderman 3.00
95 Magglio Ordonez 2.00
96 Alberto Gonzalez 2.00
97 Brian Moehler 2.00
98 Dontrelle Willis 3.00
99 Jeremy Hermida (RC) 3.00
100 Jason Vargas 2.00
101 Miguel Cabrera 5.00
102 Adam Everett 2.00
103 Andy Pettitte 3.00
104 Brad Ausmus 2.00
105 Brad Lidge 2.00
106 Craig Biggio 3.00
107 Dan Wheeler 2.00
108 Jeff Bagwell 4.00
109 Lance Berkman 2.00
110 Morgan Ensberg 2.00
111 Preston Wilson 2.00
112 Roger Clemens 10.00
113 Roy Oswalt 3.00
114 David Gassner (RC) 2.00
115 Angel Berroa 2.00
116 Doug Mientkiewicz 2.00
117 Joe Mays 2.00
118 Mark Grudzielanek 2.00
119 Mike Sweeney 2.00
120 Reggie Sanders 2.00
121 Runelvys Hernandez 2.00
122 Scott Elarton 2.00
123 Brandon Watson (RC) 2.00
124 Zack Greinke 2.00
125 Brad Penny 2.00
126 Derek Lowe 2.00
127 Eric Gagne 2.00
128 J.D. Drew 2.00
129 Jayson Werth 2.00
130 Jeff Kent 3.00
131 Nomar Garciaparra 4.00
132 Olmedo Saenz 2.00
133 Rafael Furcal 3.00
134 Ben Sheets 3.00
135 Bill Hall 2.00
136 Carlos Lee 3.00
137 Geoff Jenkins 2.00
138 Prince Fielder (RC) 10.00
139 Rickie Weeks 3.00
140 Jose Capellan (RC) 2.00
141 Brad Radke 2.00
142 Joe Mauer 6.00
143 Joe Nathan 2.00
144 Johan Santana 4.00
145 Justin Morneau 3.00
146 Kyle Lohse 2.00
147 Lew Ford 2.00
148 Luis Castillo 2.00
149 Matthew LeCroy 2.00
150 Michael Cuddyer 2.00
151 Shannon Stewart 2.00
152 Torii Hunter 3.00
153 Billy Wagner 2.00
154 Carlos Beltran 4.00
155 Carlos Delgado 4.00
156 Cliff Floyd 2.00
157 David Wright 10.00
158 Jose Reyes 5.00
159 Kazuo Matsui 2.00
160 Mike Piazza 5.00
161 Paul LoDuca 2.00
162 Pedro Martinez 5.00
163 Tom Glavine 3.00
164 Victor Diaz 2.00
165 Alex Rodriguez 15.00
166 Bernie Williams 3.00
167 Carl Pavano 2.00
168 Chien-Ming Wang 3.00
169 Derek Jeter 15.00
170 Gary Sheffield 4.00
171 Hideki Matsui 8.00
172 Jason Giambi 4.00
173 Johnny Damon 5.00
174 Jorge Posada 3.00
175 Robinson Cano 4.00
176 Mariano Rivera 4.00
177 Mike Mussina 4.00
178 Randy Johnson 5.00
179 Miguel Cairo 2.00
180 Barry Zito 3.00
181 Bobby Crosby 2.00
182 Bobby Kielty 2.00
183 Eric Chavez 2.00
184 Josh Barfield (RC) 2.00
185 Esteban Loaiza 2.00
186 Huston Street 2.00
187 Jason Kendall 2.00
188 Nick Swisher 3.00
189 Aaron Rowand 2.00
190 Bobby Abreu 2.00
191 Chase Utley 4.00
192 Gavin Floyd 2.00
193 Jimmy Rollins 3.00
194 Mike Lieberthal 2.00
195 Pat Burrell 3.00
196 Ryan Howard 6.00
197 Craig Wilson 2.00
198 Jack Wilson 2.00
199 Jason Bay 4.00
200 Joe Randa 2.00
201 Josh Fogg 2.00
202 Kip Wells 2.00
203 Sean Casey 2.00
204 Zachary Duke 2.00
205 Brian Giles 3.00
206 Dave Roberts 2.00
207 Jake Peavy 3.00
208 Khalil Greene 2.00
209 Mike Cameron 2.00
210 Ryan Klesko 2.00
211 Trevor Hoffman 3.00
212 Vinny Castilla 2.00
213 Armando Benitez 2.00
214 Jason Schmidt 2.00
215 Matt Morris 2.00
216 Moises Alou 3.00
217 Omar Vizquel 2.00
218 Ray Durham 2.00
219 Adrian Beltre 2.00
220 Carl Everett 2.00
221 Kenji Johjima RC 15.00
222 Felix Hernandez 4.00
223 Ichiro Suzuki 10.00
224 Jamie Moyer 2.00
225 Jeremy Reed 2.00
226 Joel Pineiro 2.00
227 Raul Ibanez 2.00
228 Rickie Sexson 3.00
229 Albert Pujols 15.00
230 Chris Carpenter 4.00
231 David Eckstein 2.00
232 Jason Marquis 2.00
233 Jeff Suppan 2.00
234 Jim Edmonds 3.00
235 Yadier Molina 2.00
236 Mark Mulder 3.00
237 Scott Rolen 5.00
238 Alex Gonzalez 2.00
239 Aubrey Huff 2.00
240 Carl Crawford 3.00
241 Casey Fossum 2.00
242 Joey Gathright 2.00
243 Scott Kazmir 3.00
244 Toby Hall 2.00
245 Travis Lee 2.00
246 Adam Eaton 2.00
247 Francisco Cordero 2.00
248 Hank Blalock 2.00
249 Kevin Mench 2.00
250 Kevin Millwood 2.00
251 Laynce Nix 2.00
252 Mark Teixeira 4.00
253 Michael Young 2.00
254 A.J. Burnett 2.00
255 Alex Rios 2.00
256 B.J. Ryan 2.00
257 Corey Koskie 2.00
258 Josh Towers 2.00
259 Lyle Overbay 2.00
260 Reed Johnson 2.00
261 Roy Halladay 3.00
262 Russ Adams 2.00
263 Troy Glaus 2.00
264 Vernon Wells 3.00
265 Alfonso Soriano 4.00
266 John Patterson 2.00
267 Damian Jackson 2.00
268 Jose Guillen 2.00
269 Jose Vidro 2.00
270 Livan Hernandez 2.00
271 Adam Kennedy 2.00
272 Bartolo Colon 2.00
273 Bengie Molina 2.00
274 Casey Kotchman 2.00
275 Chone Figgins 2.00
276 Matt Cain (RC) 2.00
277 Darin Erstad 2.00
278 Edgardo Alfonzo 2.00
279 Francisco Rodriguez 2.00
280 Garret Anderson 2.00
281 Vladimir Guerrero 5.00
282 Chris Denorfia (RC) 2.00
283 Joey Devine RC 4.00
284 Justin Verlander (RC) 10.00
285 Scott Feldman RC 8.00
286 Jason Bergmann RC 4.00
287 Jeremy Accardo RC 4.00
288 Adam Wainwright (RC) 8.00
289 Hanley Ramirez (RC) 4.00
290 Josh Johnson (RC) 3.00
291 Ryan Zimmerman (RC) 20.00
292 Anderson Hernandez (RC) 4.00
293 Francisco Liriano (RC) 25.00
294 Josh Willingham (RC) 3.00
295 Hong-Chih Kuo (RC) 4.00
296 Steve Stemle RC 4.00
297 Jeff Harris RC 4.00
298 John Van Benschoten (RC) 4.00
299 Jonathan Papelbon (RC) 30.00
300 Jason Kubel (RC) 4.00

Awesome 8 Materials
Production 1-10

Epic Endorsements
NM/M
Production 10-45
JB Jason Bay/45 30.00
CB Craig Biggio/30 60.00
WB Wade Boggs/30 100.00
LB Lou Brock/30 75.00
JI Jim Bunning/30 30.00
MC1 Miguel Cabrera/30 40.00
MC2 Miguel Cabrera/30 50.00
RC Rod Carew/30 50.00
SC1 Steve Carlton/27 35.00
SC2 Steve Carlton/30 40.00
EC Eric Chavez/30 40.00
WC Will Clark/23 50.00
AD Adam Dunn/30 40.00
BF1 Bob Feller/45 40.00
BF2 Bob Feller/45 40.00
PF Prince Fielder/45 75.00
CF Carlton Fisk/30 50.00
SG Steve Garvey/45 40.00
BG Bob Gibson/30 50.00
KG1 Ken Griffey Jr./30 150.00
KG2 Ken Griffey Jr./30 150.00
KG3 Ken Griffey Jr./30 150.00
TG Tony Gwynn/30 50.00
JH1 Jeremy Hermida/45 30.00
JH2 Jeremy Hermida/45 30.00
FH1 Felix Hernandez/30 50.00
FH2 Felix Hernandez/30 50.00
RH Ryan Howard/45 100.00
BO Bo Jackson/30 85.00
DJ1 Derek Jeter/30 200.00
DJ2 Derek Jeter/30 200.00
DJ3 Derek Jeter/30 200.00
AJ Andruw Jones/30 40.00
LA Don Larsen/30 75.00
FL Fred Lynn/45 25.00
BM Bill Mazeroski/30 80.00
PM1 Paul Molitor/30 40.00
PM2 Paul Molitor/30 40.00
TO Tony Oliva/45 40.00
DO David Ortiz/30 80.00
RO1 Roy Oswalt/45 40.00
RO2 Roy Oswalt/45 40.00
JP1 Jim Palmer/30 40.00
JP2 Jim Palmer/30 40.00
JA Jake Peavy/45 25.00
TP Tony Perez/30 40.00
AP Albert Pujols/15 400.00
CR Cal Ripken Jr./15 280.00
BN Brian Roberts/45 30.00
BR1 Brooks Robinson/30 75.00
BR2 Brooks Robinson/30 75.00
FR Frank Robinson/30 40.00
RS1 Ryne Sandberg/45 100.00
CS Curt Schilling/15 75.00
TS Tom Seaver/30 75.00
OS Ozzie Smith/30 75.00
SM John Smoltz/30 150.00
AS Alfonso Soriano/30 40.00
DS Don Sutton/30 30.00
CU Chase Utley/45 50.00
BW Billy Williams/45 25.00
DW1 Dontrelle Willis/30 40.00
DW2 Dontrelle Willis/30 40.00
MW Maury Wills/30 25.00
WR David Wright/25 100.00
RZ1 Ryan Zimmerman/30 100.00
RZ2 Ryan Zimmerman/30 100.00

Epic Events
NM/M
Common Player: 2.00
Production 675 Sets
EE1 Ryan Howard 4.00
EE2 Tadahito Iguchi 2.00
EE3 Paul Konerko 2.00
EE4 Craig Biggio 2.00
EE5 Alex Rodriguez 6.00
EE6 Ichiro Suzuki 4.00
EE7 David Ortiz 4.00
EE8 Miguel Cabrera 3.00
EE9 Dontrelle Willis 3.00
EE10 Mark Teixeira 3.00
EE11 Hideki Matsui 5.00
EE12 Albert Pujols 8.00
EE13 Albert Pujols 8.00
EE14 Greg Maddux 5.00
EE15 Greg Maddux 5.00
EE16 Manny Ramirez 3.00
EE17 Mark Teixeira 3.00

EE18	Alex Rodriguez	6.00
EE19	Manny Ramirez	3.00
EE20	Randy Johnson	3.00
EE21	Jason Varitek	3.00
EE22	Vladimir Guerrero	3.00
EE23	Roger Clemens	8.00
EE24	Manny Ramirez	3.00
EE25	Curt Schilling	3.00
EE26	Johnny Damon	3.00
EE27	David Ortiz	4.00
EE28	David Wright	6.00
EE29	Ichiro Suzuki	5.00
EE30	Ichiro Suzuki	5.00
EE31	Adam Dunn	2.00
EE32	Adrian Beltre	2.00
EE33	Javy Lopez	2.00
EE34	Greg Maddux	5.00
EE35	Randy Johnson	3.00
EE36	Jim Thome	3.00
EE37	Adam Dunn	2.00
EE38	Bobby Abreu	2.00
EE39	Felix Hernandez	3.00
EE40	Greg Maddux	5.00
EE41	Ken Griffey Jr.	6.00
EE42	Randy Johnson	3.00
EE43	Johan Santana	3.00
EE44	Magglio Ordonez	2.00
EE45	Josh Beckett	3.00
EE46	Ivan Rodriguez	3.00
EE47	Alfonso Soriano	3.00
EE48	Eric Gagne	2.00
EE49	Hank Blalock	2.00
EE50	Roger Clemens	8.00
EE51	Derek Jeter	8.00
EE52	Derek Jeter	8.00
EE53	Barry Zito	2.00
EE54	Alex Rodriguez	6.00
EE55	Nomar Garciaparra	3.00
EE56	Torii Hunter	2.00
EE57	Ichiro Suzuki	5.00
EE58	Randy Johnson	3.00
EE59	Ichiro Suzuki	5.00
EE60	Albert Pujols	8.00
EE61	Albert Pujols	8.00
EE62	Ichiro Suzuki	5.00
EE63	Derek Jeter	8.00
EE64	Pedro Martinez	3.00
EE65	Chris Shelton	2.00
EE66	Ivan Rodriguez	3.00
EE67	Chipper Jones	3.00
EE68	Pedro Martinez	3.00
EE69	Ken Griffey Jr.	6.00
EE70	Jeff Bagwell	3.00
EE71	Nomar Garciaparra	3.00
EE72	Mark Prior	3.00
EE73	Kerry Wood	2.00
EE74	Andruw Jones	3.00
EE75	Derek Jeter	8.00
EE76	Cal Ripken Jr.	10.00
EE77	Ken Griffey Jr.	6.00
EE78	Ken Griffey Jr.	6.00
EE79	Mike Piazza	4.00
EE80	Nolan Ryan	6.00
EE81	Greg Maddux	5.00
EE82	Greg Maddux	5.00
EE83	Roger Clemens	8.00
EE84	Ozzie Smith	4.00
EE85	Tom Seaver	4.00
EE86	Thurman Munson	4.00
EE87	Reggie Jackson	3.00
EE88	Johnny Bench	4.00
EE89	Mike Schmidt	4.00
EE90	Carlton Fisk	2.00
EE91	Eddie Mathews	3.00
EE92	Roy Campanella	4.00
EE93	Jackie Robinson	6.00
EE94	Joe DiMaggio	8.00
EE95	Jimmie Foxx	5.00
EE96	Lou Gehrig	8.00
EE97	Babe Ruth	10.00
EE98	Ty Cobb	6.00
EE99	Honus Wagner	5.00
EE100	Cy Young	5.00

Four Barrel
No Pricing
Production One Set

Foursome Fabrics
NM/M
Production 5-50

CMBF	Carlton Fisk, Thurman Munson, Johnny Bench, Gary Carter/25	70.00
GRSM	Tom Seaver, Nolan Ryan, Juan Marichal, Bob Gibson/50	60.00
MBSP	Albert Pujols, Lou Brock, Stan Musial, Ozzie Smith/30	100.00
PJGG	Ken Griffey Jr., Derek Jeter, Vladimir Guerrero, Albert Pujols/50	100.00
RCJP	Mark Prior, Nolan Ryan, Roger Clemens, Randy Johnson/50	50.00
WRRJ	Pee Wee Reese, Honus Wagner, Cal Ripken Jr., Derek Jeter/20	300.00
WYBS	Ted Williams, Wade Boggs, Curt Schilling, Carl Yastrzemski/50	85.00

2006 Upper Deck Epic Materials
NM/M

Production 10-185
No pricing production 15 or less.

Orange:		.75-1.5X
Production 5-185		
Red:		.75-1.5X
Production 10-185		
Light Purple:		.75-1.5X
Production 4-185		
Dark Purple:		.75-1.5X
Production 3-185		
Blue:		.75-1.5X
Production 3-99		
Teal:		.75-1.5X
Production 5-99		
Green:		1-1.5X
Production 3-75		
Dark Green:		1-2X
Production 3-50		
Grey:		1-2X
Production 3-40		
Gold:		1-1.25X
Production 1-25		

EB	Ernie Banks/155	15.00
JB1	Johnny Bench/155	10.00
JB2	Johnny Bench/155	10.00
WB1	Wade Boggs/185	10.00
WB2	Wade Boggs/185	10.00
LB1	Lou Brock/48	10.00
LB2	Lou Brock/48	10.00
RC1	Roger Clemens/155	20.00
RC2	Roger Clemens/155	20.00
RC3	Roger Clemens/155	20.00
CL1	Roberto Clemente/50	75.00
JD1	Joe DiMaggio/185	65.00
JD2	Joe DiMaggio/173	65.00
JD3	Joe DiMaggio/99	75.00
CF	Carlton Fisk/169	10.00
CF2	Carlton Fisk/185	10.00
WF	Whitey Ford/155	15.00
LG1	Lou Gehrig/15	165.00
LG2	Lou Gehrig/15	165.00
LG3	Lou Gehrig/15	165.00
BG	Bob Gibson/155	15.00
BG2	Bob Gibson/155	15.00
HG	Hank Greenberg/50	40.00
KG1	Ken Griffey Jr./175	15.00
KG2	Ken Griffey Jr./175	15.00
KG3	Ken Griffey Jr./175	15.00
VG	Vladimir Guerrero/145	8.00
VG2	Vladimir Guerrero/145	8.00
GH	Gil Hodges/39	15.00
RH	Rogers Hornsby/50	75.00
RE1	Reggie Jackson/52	12.00
RE2	Reggie Jackson/52	12.00
RE3	Reggie Jackson/52	12.00
DJ1	Derek Jeter/185	25.00
DJ2	Derek Jeter/185	25.00
DJ3	Derek Jeter/185	25.00
RJ1	Randy Johnson/145	10.00
RJ2	Randy Johnson/145	10.00
HK	Harmon Killebrew/155	15.00
JM	Juan Marichal/155	8.00
ED	Eddie Mathews/75	10.00
DM1	Don Mattingly/185	15.00
DM2	Don Mattingly/185	15.00
WM	Willie McCovey/155	15.00
WM2	Willie McCovey/155	15.00
WM3	Willie McCovey/155	15.00
PM1	Paul Molitor/155	10.00
PM2	Paul Molitor/155	10.00
JO	Joe Morgan/145	8.00
JO2	Joe Morgan/155	8.00
TH1	Thurman Munson/35	30.00
TH2	Thurman Munson/35	30.00
EM1	Eddie Murray/185	8.00
EM2	Eddie Murray/165	8.00
EM3	Eddie Murray/155	8.00
SM1	Stan Musial/50	25.00
SM2	Stan Musial/75	25.00
MP1	Mike Piazza/145	12.00
MP2	Mike Piazza/145	12.00
MA	Mark Prior/185	8.00
MA2	Mark Prior/185	8.00
KP1	Kirby Puckett/155	15.00
KP2	Kirby Puckett/155	15.00
AP1	Albert Pujols/185	20.00
AP2	Albert Pujols/185	20.00
AP3	Albert Pujols/185	20.00
PR1	Pee Wee Reese/145	15.00
PR2	Pee Wee Reese/145	15.00
CR1	Cal Ripken Jr./185	25.00
CR2	Cal Ripken Jr./177	25.00
CR3	Cal Ripken Jr./155	25.00
RO	Brooks Robinson/49	15.00
RO2	Brooks Robinson/99	15.00
FR1	Frank Robinson/130	15.00
FR2	Frank Robinson/130	15.00
BR1	Babe Ruth/15	250.00
BR2	Babe Ruth/15	250.00
NR1	Nolan Ryan/155	20.00
NR2	Nolan Ryan/155	20.00
NR3	Nolan Ryan/155	20.00
RS1	Ryne Sandberg/155	15.00
RS2	Ryne Sandberg/155	15.00
RS3	Ryne Sandberg/155	15.00
MS1	Mike Schmidt/185	15.00
MS2	Mike Schmidt/185	15.00
MS3	Mike Schmidt/185	15.00
TS	Tom Seaver/155	15.00
TS2	Tom Seaver/155	15.00
OS1	Ozzie Smith/155	15.00
OS2	Ozzie Smith/185	15.00

Signatures
No Pricing
Production Five Sets

Epic Swatch
NM/M

Common Player: 10.00
Production 50 Sets

JB	Jason Bay	15.00
EC	Eric Chavez	15.00
RC	Roger Clemens	30.00
CF	Carlton Fisk	15.00
KG1	Ken Griffey Jr.	30.00
KG2	Ken Griffey Jr.	30.00
VG	Vladimir Guerrero	15.00
TG	Tony Gwynn	25.00
DJ1	Derek Jeter	50.00
DJ2	Derek Jeter	50.00
RJ	Randy Johnson	20.00
PM	Pedro J. Martinez	15.00
JM	Joe Morgan	10.00
DO	David Ortiz	25.00
RO	Roy Oswalt	10.00
JP	Jake Peavy	10.00
MP	Mark Prior	10.00
AP	Albert Pujols	40.00
MR	Manny Ramirez	15.00
JR	Jose Reyes	15.00
CR	Cal Ripken Jr.	40.00
IR	Ivan Rodriguez	12.00
SR	Scott Rolen	20.00
JS	Johan Santana	15.00
CS	Curt Schilling	15.00
MT	Mark Teixeira	12.00
MI	Miguel Tejada	10.00
DW	Dontrelle Willis	10.00
CY	Carl Yastrzemski	20.00
RZ	Ryan Zimmerman	30.00

Epic Triple Materials
NM/M

Production 3-99

BER	Eddie Murray, Brooks Robinson, Johnny Bench/60	35.00
BMR	Brooks Robinson, Wade Boggs, Paul Molitor/99	30.00
BSP	Ryne Sandberg, Ernie Banks, Mark Prior/99	40.00
CDG	Ken Griffey Jr., Ty Cobb, Joe DiMaggio/15	300.00
FJJ	Whitey Ford, Reggie Jackson, Derek Jeter/99	60.00
FMJ	Don Mattingly, Reggie Jackson, Whitey Ford/51	40.00
GJC	Randy Johnson, Roger Clemens, Bob Gibson/99	40.00
GMG	Eddie Murray, Hank Greenberg, Lou Gehrig/25	150.00
GPS	Tom Seaver, Bob Gibson, Mark Prior/99	30.00
GRM	Ken Griffey Jr., Willie McCovey, Frank Robinson/99	40.00
JGK	Vladimir Guerrero, Reggie Jackson, Harmon Killebrew/99	40.00
JKR	Harmon Killebrew, Frank Robinson, Reggie Jackson/99	40.00
JMM	Derek Jeter, Don Mattingly, Thurman Munson/25	125.00
JPG	Albert Pujols, Ken Griffey Jr., Derek Jeter/99	100.00
MBF	Carlton Fisk, Thurman Munson, Johnny Bench/99	40.00
MBG	Johnny Bench, Joe Morgan, Ken Griffey Jr./99	50.00
MBP	Albert Pujols, Lou Brock, Stan Musial/24	90.00
MFM	Carlton Fisk, Eddie Murray, Thurman Munson/99	30.00
MMG	Steve Garvey, Eddie Murray, Don Mattingly/49	40.00
MPS	Tom Seaver, Mike Piazza, Eddie Murray/30	
MSY	Ozzie Smith, Paul Molitor, Robin Yount/49	40.00
RBS	Cal Ripken Jr., Wade Boggs, Mike Schmidt/99	50.00
RCJ	Nolan Ryan, Roger Clemens, Randy Johnson/75	50.00
RJD	Reggie Jackson, Joe DiMaggio, Babe Ruth/99	300.00
RRM	Jackie Robinson, Frank Robinson, Willie McCovey/50	50.00
SMH	Ryne Sandberg, Rogers Hornsby, Joe Morgan/25	80.00
WSR	Honus Wagner, Pee Wee Reese, Ozzie Smith/99	100.00
YRJ	Cal Ripken Jr., Derek Jeter, Robin Yount/99	60.00
YWB	Ted Williams, Wade Boggs, Carl Yastrzemski/25	140.00

Epic Pairings
NM/M

Production 5-99

BB	Wade Boggs, Brooks Robinson/99	25.00
BM	Johnny Bench, Joe Morgan/99	20.00
BR	Bob Gibson, Nolan Ryan/99	30.00
BS	Lou Brock, Ozzie Smith/99	30.00
BS2	Wade Boggs, Ryne Sandberg/99	25.00
CJ	Roger Clemens, Randy Johnson/99	25.00
CR	Roger Clemens, Nolan Ryan/99	40.00
DG	Joe DiMaggio, Lou Gehrig/25	220.00
FB	Carlton Fisk, Johnny Bench/99	20.00
FP	Carlton Fisk, Mike Piazza/99	20.00
GB	Bob Gibson, Lou Brock/99	25.00
GC	Hank Greenberg, Ty Cobb/25	150.00
GG	Ken Griffey Jr., Vladimir Guerrero/99	40.00
GP	Ken Griffey Jr., Kirby Puckett/99	35.00
GR	Lou Gehrig, Cal Ripken Jr./45	180.00
JD	Derek Jeter, Joe DiMaggio/99	125.00
JG	Derek Jeter, Ken Griffey Jr./99	75.00
JJ	Reggie Jackson, Derek Jeter/99	40.00
JK	Reggie Jackson, Harmon Killebrew/99	30.00
JM	Derek Jeter, Don Mattingly/99	80.00
JS	Reggie Jackson, Mike Schmidt/99	30.00
KP	Harmon Killebrew, Kirby Puckett/99	30.00
MB	Thurman Munson, Johnny Bench/30	40.00
MM	Juan Marichal, Willie McCovey/99	25.00
MM2	Don Mattingly, Thurman Munson/30	75.00
MR	Eddie Mathews, Brooks Robinson/50	50.00
MS	Eddie Mathews, Mike Schmidt/50	40.00
MY	Paul Molitor, Robin Yount/99	25.00
PH	Albert Pujols, Rogers Hornsby/99	75.00
PM	Albert Pujols, Stan Musial/99	60.00
RJ	Pee Wee Reese, Derek Jeter/99	35.00
RM	Cal Ripken Jr., Eddie Murray/99	35.00
RR2	Brooks Robinson, Frank Robinson/99	25.00
RY	Frank Robinson, Carl Yastrzemski/99	40.00
SB	Ryne Sandberg, Ernie Banks/99	40.00
SM	Ryne Sandberg, Joe Morgan/99	30.00
SR	Tom Seaver, Nolan Ryan/99	40.00
SS	Ryne Sandberg, Ozzie Smith/99	35.00
WC	Honus Wagner, Roberto Clemente/25	225.00
WD	Ted Williams, Joe DiMaggio/45	200.00
WM	Ted Williams, Stan Musial/45	75.00
YW	Carl Yastrzemski, Ted Williams/50	100.00

2006 Upper Deck First Pitch
NM/M

Complete Set (220): 35.00
Common Player: .10
Pack (5): 1.50
Box (36): 40.00

1	Chad Tracy	.10
2	Conor Jackson (RC)	.10
3	Craig Counsell	.10
4	Javier Vazquez	.10
5	Luis Gonzalez	.10
6	Shawn Green	.25
7	Troy Glaus	.25
8	Joey Devine RC	1.00
9	Andruw Jones	.40
10	Chipper Jones	.50
11	John Smoltz	.25
12	Marcus Giles	.10
13	Jeff Francoeur	.25
14	Tim Hudson	.25
15	Brian Roberts	.10
16	Erik Bedard	.10
17	Javy Lopez	.10
18	Melvin Mora	.10
19	Miguel Tejada	.40
20	Alejandro Freire RC	.10
21	Sammy Sosa	.75
22	Craig Hansen RC	3.00
23	Curt Schilling	.50
24	David Ortiz	.50
25	Edgar Renteria	.25
26	Johnny Damon	.50
27	Manny Ramirez	.50
28	Matt Clement	.10
29	Trot Nixon	.10
30	Aramis Ramirez	.25
31	Carlos Zambrano	.25
32	Derrek Lee	.50
33	Greg Maddux	1.00
34	Jeromy Burnitz	.10
35	Kerry Wood	.25
36	Mark Prior	.40
37	Nomar Garciaparra	.40
38	Aaron Rowand	.10
39	Chris Demaria RC	.10
40	Jon Garland	.10
41	Mark Buehrle	.25
42	Paul Konerko	.25
43	Scott Podsednik	.25
44	Tadahito Iguchi	.25
45	Adam Dunn	.40
46	Austin Kearns	.10
47	Felipe Lopez	.10
48	Ken Griffey Jr.	1.00
49	Ryan Freel	.10
50	Sean Casey	.10
51	Wily Mo Pena	.10
52	C.C. Sabathia	.10
53	Cliff Lee	.10
54	Coco Crisp	.10
55	Grady Sizemore	.25
56	Jake Westbrook	.10
57	Travis Hafner	.25
58	Victor Martinez	.25
59	Aaron Miles	.10
60	Clint Barmes	.10
61	Garrett Atkins	.10
62	Jeff Baker	.10
63	Jeff Francis	.10
64	Matt Holliday	.10
65	Todd Helton	.40
66	Carlos Guillen	.10
67	Chris Shelton	.10
68	Dmitri Young	.10
69	Ivan Rodriguez	.40
70	Jeremy Bonderman	.10
71	Magglio Ordonez	.25
72	Placido Polanco	.10
73	A.J. Burnett	.10
74	Carlos Delgado	.25
75	Dontrelle Willis	.25
76	Josh Beckett	.25
77	Juan Pierre	.10
78	Ryan Jorgensen RC	.50
79	Miguel Cabrera	.50
80	Robert Andino RC	.50
81	Andy Pettitte	.10
82	Brad Lidge	.25
83	Craig Biggio	.25
84	Jeff Bagwell	.40
85	Lance Berkman	.25
86	Morgan Ensberg	.25
87	Roger Clemens	1.50
88	Roy Oswalt	.25
89	Angel Berroa	.10
90	David DeJesus	.10
91	Steve Stemle RC	1.00
92	Jonah Bayliss RC	2.00
93	Mike Sweeney	.25
94	Ryan Theriot (RC)	1.00
95	Zack Greinke	.25
96	Brad Penny	.10
97	Cesar Izturis	.10
98	Brian Myrow RC	1.00
99	Eric Gagne	.25
100	J.D. Drew	.25
101	Jeff Kent	.25
102	Milton Bradley	.10
103	Odalis Perez	.10
104	Ben Sheets	.25
105	Brady Clark	.10
106	Carlos Lee	.25
107	Geoff Jenkins	.10
108	Lyle Overbay	.10
109	Prince Fielder (RC)	.50
110	Rickie Weeks	.25
111	Jacque Jones	.10
112	Joe Mauer	.25
113	Joe Nathan	.10
114	Johan Santana	.50
115	Justin Morneau	.20
116	Chris Heintz RC	1.00
117	Torii Hunter	.25
118	Carlos Beltran	.25
119	Cliff Floyd	.10
120	David Wright	.75
121	Jose Reyes	.40
122	Mike Cameron	.10
123	Mike Piazza	.50
124	Pedro Martinez	.50
125	Tom Glavine	.25
126	Alex Rodriguez	1.50
127	Derek Jeter	.50
128	Gary Sheffield	.40
129	Hideki Matsui	.75
130	Jason Giambi	.25
131	Jorge Posada	.25
132	Mariano Rivera	.25
133	Mike Mussina	.25
134	Randy Johnson	.50
135	Barry Zito	.25
136	Bobby Crosby	.10
137	Danny Haren	.10
138	Eric Chavez	.25
139	Huston Street	.50
140	Ron Flores RC	.50
141	Nick Swisher	.25
142	Rich Harden	.25
143	Bobby Abreu	.25
144	Danny Sandoval RC	.50
145	Chase Utley	.25
146	Jim Thome	.40
147	Jimmy Rollins	.25
148	Pat Burrell	.25
149	Ryan Howard	.50
150	Craig Wilson	.10
151	Jack Wilson	.10
152	Jason Bay	.25
153	Matt Lawton	.10
154	Oliver Perez	.10
155	Robert Mackowiak	.10
156	Zachary Duke	.50
157	Brian Giles	.25
158	Jake Peavy	.25
159	Craig Breslow RC	1.00
160	Khalil Greene	.10
161	Mark Loretta	.10
162	Ryan Klesko	.10
163	Trevor Hoffman	.25
164	J.T. Snow	.10
165	Jason Schmidt	.25
166	Marquis Grissom	.10
167	Moises Alou	.10
168	Omar Vizquel	.10
169	Pedro Feliz	.10
170	Jeremy Accardo RC	.50
171	Adrian Beltre	.25
172	Ichiro Suzuki	1.00
173	Felix Hernandez	.50
174	Jeff Harris RC	.50
175	Randy Winn	.10
176	Raul Ibanez	.10
177	Richie Sexson	.25
178	Albert Pujols	1.50
179	Chris Carpenter	.10
180	David Eckstein	.10
181	Jim Edmonds	.25
182	Larry Walker	.25
183	Matt Morris	.10
184	Reggie Sanders	.10
185	Scott Rolen	.40
186	Aubrey Huff	.10
187	Jonny Gomes	.10
188	Carl Crawford	.25
189	Tim Corcoran RC	1.00
190	Julio Lugo	.10
191	Rocco Baldelli	.10
192	Scott Kazmir	.25
193	Alfonso Soriano	.40
194	Hank Blalock	.25
195	Kenny Rogers	.10
196	Scott Feldman	1.00
197	Laynce Nix	.10
198	Mark Teixeira	.50
199	Michael Young	.25
200	Aaron Hill	.10
201	Alex Rios	.25
202	Eric Hinske	.10
203	Gustavo Chacin	.10
204	Roy Halladay	.25
205	Shea Hillenbrand	.25
206	Vernon Wells	.25
207	Brad Wilkerson	.10
208	Chad Cordero	.10
209	Jose Guillen	.10
210	Jose Vidro	.10
211	Livan Hernandez	.10
212	Preston Wilson	.10
213	Jason Bergmann RC	1.00
214	Bartolo Colon	.25
215	Chone Figgins	.10
216	Darin Erstad	.10
217	Francisco Rodriguez	.25
218	Garret Anderson	.25
219	Steve Finley	.10
220	Vladimir Guerrero	.50

Diamond Stars
NM/M

Complete Set (35): 30.00
Common Player: .50
Inserted 1:3

1	Luis Gonzalez	.50
2	Andruw Jones	.75
3	John Smoltz	.75
4	Miguel Tejada	1.00
5	Johnny Damon	1.50
6	Manny Ramirez	1.50
7	Derrek Lee	1.50
8	Mark Prior	1.00
9	Mark Buehrle	.50
10	Ken Griffey Jr.	3.00
11	Travis Hafner	.75
12	Todd Helton	1.00

13	Ivan Rodriguez	.75
14	Miguel Cabrera	1.50
15	Roger Clemens	4.00
16	Mike Sweeney	.50
17	Jeff Kent	.75
18	Carlos Lee	.50
19	Johan Santana	1.50
20	Torii Hunter	.50
21	Pedro Martinez	1.50
22	Alex Rodriguez	4.00
23	Derek Jeter	4.00
24	Eric Chavez	.75
25	Bobby Abreu	.75
26	Jason Bay	.75
27	Jake Peavy	.75
28	Moises Alou	.50
29	Ichiro Suzuki	3.00
30	Albert Pujols	4.00
31	Carl Crawford	.75
32	Mark Teixeira	1.50
33	Roy Halladay	.50
34	Jose Guillen	.50
35	Vladimir Guerrero	1.50

Goin' Deep

NM/M
Complete Set (35): 20.00
Common Player: .50
Inserted 1:3

1	Adam Dunn	1.00
2	Albert Pujols	4.00
3	Alex Rodriguez	4.00
4	Alfonso Soriano	1.00
5	Andruw Jones	1.00
6	Aramis Ramirez	.75
7	Bobby Abreu	.75
8	Brian Giles	.50
9	Carlos Delgado	.75
10	Carlos Lee	.50
11	Chipper Jones	1.50
12	David Ortiz	1.50
13	David Wright	2.00
14	Derek Lee	1.00
15	Eric Chavez	.50
16	Gary Sheffield	.75
17	Hideki Matsui	2.50
18	Jeff Kent	.75
19	Jim Edmonds	.75
20	Ken Griffey Jr.	3.00
21	Luis Gonzalez	.50
22	Manny Ramirez	1.50
23	Mark Teixeira	1.00
24	Miguel Cabrera	1.00
25	Miguel Tejada	1.00
26	Moises Alou	.50
27	Pat Burrell	.75
28	Paul Konerko	.75
29	Rafael Palmeiro	.75
30	Richie Sexson	.75
31	Todd Helton	1.00
32	Torii Hunter	.50
33	Travis Hafner	.50
34	Vernon Wells	.50
35	Vladimir Guerrero	1.50

Hot Stove Headlines

NM/M
Complete Set (20): 15.00
Common Player: .50
Inserted 1:3

1	Alex Rodriguez	3.00
2	Carlos Beltran	.75
3	Carlos Delgado	.50
4	Curt Schilling	1.00
5	Derek Lee	.75
6	Greg Maddux	2.00
7	Hideki Matsui	2.00
8	Ichiro Suzuki	2.00
9	Ivan Rodriguez	.50
10	Jim Thome	.50
11	Johnny Damon	1.00
12	Ken Griffey Jr.	2.00
13	Manny Ramirez	1.00
14	Miguel Tejada	.75
15	Nomar Garciaparra	.75
16	Pedro Martinez	.75
17	Randy Johnson	1.00
18	Roger Clemens	3.00
19	Scott Rolen	.75
20	Vladimir Guerrero	1.00

Signature Stars

NM/M
Common Player:

DR	J.D. Drew	25.00
JE	Johnny Estrada	10.00
RH	Rich Harden	15.00
PL	Paul LoDuca	15.00
VM	Victor Martinez	15.00
YM	Yadier Molina	10.00
GQ	Guillermo Quiroz	10.00
RI	Juan Rivera	15.00
IS	Ian Snell	10.00
RW	Ryan Wagner	10.00

2006 Upper Deck Future Stars

SIZEMORE

NM/M
Complete Set (159):
Common Player (1-75): .25
Common Autograph (76-159): 5.00
Some SP Autos. not priced yet
Pack (4): 5.00
Box (24): 100.00

1	Miguel Tejada	.75
2	Brian Roberts	.25
3	Brandon Webb	.25
4	Luis Gonzalez	.25
5	Andruw Jones	.75
6	Chipper Jones	1.00
7	John Smoltz	.25
8	Curt Schilling	1.00
9	Josh Beckett	.25
10	David Ortiz	1.00
11	Manny Ramirez	1.00
12	Jim Thome	.75
13	Paul Konerko	.75
14	Jermaine Dye	.25
15	Derek Lee	.75
16	Greg Maddux	2.00
17	Ken Griffey Jr.	2.00
18	Adam Dunn	.75
19	Felipe Lopez	.25
20	Travis Hafner	.25
21	Victor Martinez	.25
22	Grady Sizemore	.75
23	Todd Helton	.75
24	Matt Holliday	.75
25	Jeremy Bonderman	.75
26	Ivan Rodriguez	.75
27	Miguel Cabrera	1.00
28	Dontrelle Willis	.75
29	Roger Clemens	2.00
30	Roy Oswalt	.25
31	Lance Berkman	.75
32	Reggie Sanders	.25
33	Vladimir Guerrero	1.00
34	Chone Figgins	.25
35	Jeff Kent	.25
36	Eric Gagne	.25
37	Carlos Lee	.25
38	Rickie Weeks	.25
39	Johan Santana	1.00
40	Torii Hunter	.25
41	Alex Rodriguez	2.00
42	Derek Jeter	2.50
43	Randy Johnson	1.00
44	Hideki Matsui	1.50
45	Johnny Damon	1.00
46	Pedro Martinez	1.00
47	David Wright	2.00
48	Carlos Beltran	.75
49	Rich Harden	.25
50	Eric Chavez	.75
51	Huston Street	.25
52	Ryan Howard	2.00
53	Bobby Abreu	.75
54	Chase Utley	.75
55	Jason Bay	.75
56	Jake Peavy	.25
57	Brian Giles	.25
58	Trevor Hoffman	.25
59	Jason Schmidt	.25
60	Randy Winn	.25
61	Kenji Johjima	.75
62	Ichiro Suzuki	1.50
63	Felix Hernandez	.75
64	Albert Pujols	2.50
65	Chris Carpenter	.75
66	Jim Edmonds	.25
67	Carl Crawford	.25
68	Scott Kazmir	.25
69	Jonny Gomes	.25
70	Mark Teixeira	.75
71	Michael Young	.25
72	Vernon Wells	.75
73	Roy Halladay	.25
74	Nick Johnson	.25
75	Alfonso Soriano	.75
76	Adam Wainwright (RC)	20.00
77	Anderson Hernandez (RC)	5.00
78	Andre Ethier (RC)	40.00
79	Colter Bean (RC)	8.00
80	Ben Johnson (RC)	5.00
81	Boof Bonser (RC)	20.00
82	Boone Logan (RC)	5.00
83	Brian Anderson (RC)	5.00
84	Brian Bannister (RC)	8.00
85	Chris Denorfia (RC)	8.00
86	Chad Billingsley/ SP (RC)	25.00
87	Cody Ross (RC)	5.00
88	Cole Hamels (RC)	50.00
91	Dave Gassner (RC)	5.00
92	Jordan Tata RC	15.00
93	Eric Reed (RC)	8.00
94	Fausto Carmona (RC)	5.00
96	Francisco Liriano (RC)	35.00
97	Freddie Bynum (RC)	5.00
98	Hanley Ramirez/ SP (RC)	40.00
99	Hong-Chih Kuo (RC)	50.00
100	Ian Kinsler (RC)	20.00
101	Nelson Cruz/SP (RC)	15.00
102	Ruddy Lugo (RC)	5.00
103	Jason Kubel (RC)	35.00
104	Jeff Harris (RC)	5.00
105	Santiago Ramirez (RC)	5.00
107	Jeremy Accardo RC	10.00
108	Jeremy Hermida (RC)	15.00
109	Joel Zumaya/ SP (RC)	50.00
110	Joey Devine (RC)	8.00
111	John Koronka (RC)	5.00
112	Jonathan Papelbon (RC)	35.00
113	Jose Capellan (RC)	5.00
114	Josh Johnson (RC)	15.00
115	Josh Rupe (RC)	10.00
116	Josh Willingham (RC)	15.00
117	Josh Wilson (RC)	8.00
119	Kelly Shoppach (RC)	8.00
120	Kendry Morales (RC)	15.00
121	Sean Tracey (RC)	8.00
122	Macay McBride (RC)	8.00
123	Matt Cain (RC)	20.00
125	Russell Martin (RC)	15.00
126	Tim Hamulack (RC)	8.00
127	Mike Jacobs (RC)	8.00
128	Ben Hendrickson (RC)	5.00
129	Jack Taschner (RC)	5.00
130	Nate McLouth (RC)	10.00
131	Jeremy Sowers/ SP (RC)	20.00
132	Paul Maholm (RC)	5.00
134	Jason Bergmann RC	8.00
135	Rich Hill (RC)	20.00
137	Scott Dunn (RC)	5.00
138	Ryan Zimmerman (RC)	40.00
139	Anibal Sanchez (RC)	20.00
140	Sean Marshall (RC)	15.00
141	Takashi Saito RC	40.00
142	Taylor Buchholz (RC)	8.00
143	Carlos Quentin (RC)	15.00
144	Matt Garza (RC)	20.00
145	Wilbert Nieves (RC)	8.00
147	Jamie Shields (RC)	10.00
149	Aaron Rakers (RC)	5.00
150	Bobby Livingston (RC)	8.00
151	Brendan Harris (RC)	5.00
153	Chris Britton RC	10.00
154	Howie Kendrick (RC)	60.00
155	Jermaine Van Buren (RC)	8.00
157	Matt Capps (RC)	10.00
158	Peter Moylan (RC)	5.00
159	Ty Taubenheim RC	20.00

Black
Black (1-75): 8-15X
Production 50 Sets

Blue
Blue (1-75): 4-8X
Production 99 Sets

Gold
Gold (1-75): 15-25X
Production 25 Sets

Green
Green (1-75): 2-4X
Production 499 Sets

Purple
Purple (1-75): 1-2X
Production 1,799 Sets

Red
Red (1-75): 3-5X
Production 299 Sets

Rookie Signatures Red Ink
Red Ink (76-159): 1.5-2X
Production 35 Sets

Future Stars
NM/M
Common Player: 1.00
Black: 8-15X
Production 50 Sets
Blue: 4-8X
Production 99 Sets
Gold: 15-25X
Production 25 Sets
Green: 2-4X
Production 499 Sets
Purple: 1-2X
Production 1,799 Sets
Red: 3-5X
Production 299 Sets

1	Adam Loewen	1.00
2	Nan Wang	2.00
3	Yi Feng	1.50
4	Chien-Ming Chang	2.00
5	Yung-Chi Chen	2.00
6	Chin-Lung Hu	1.50
7	Yadel Marti	1.00
8	Frederich Cepeda	1.00
9	Pedro Luis Lazo	1.00
10	Osmany Urrutia	1.00
11	Yoandy Garlobo	1.00
12	Nobuhiko Matsunaka	2.00
13	Daisuke Matsuzaka	5.00
14	Tsuyoshi Nishioka	2.00
15	Tomoya Satozaki	1.00
16	Koji Uehara	1.00
17	Shunsuke Watanabe	2.00
18	Jong Beom Lee	1.00
19	Sidney de Jong	1.00
21	Shairon Martis	1.00
22	Dicky Gonzalez	1.00
23	Nicholas Dempsey	1.00
24	Jason Kubel	1.00
25	Chase Utley	2.00

Clear Patch to History Triple Signature

NM/M

BSJ	Andruw Jones, Alfonso Soriano, Jason Bay	40.00
CUK	Carl Crawford, Scott Kazmir, B.J. Upton	50.00
DRR	Jose Reyes, Stephen Drew, Hanley Ramirez	75.00
GEH	Andre Ethier, Jeremy Hermida, Tony Gwynn Jr.	40.00
MML	Justin Morneau, Joe Mauer, Francisco Liriano	75.00
MOH	Travis Hafner, Justin Morneau, Lyle Overbay	60.00
NHP	Trevor Hoffman, Joe Nathan, Jonathan Papelbon	60.00
PSO	Ben Sheets, Roy Oswalt, Jake Peavy	50.00
PVW	Justin Verlander, Jonathan Papelbon, Jered Weaver	100.00
SBH	Chad Billingsley, Alay Soler, Cole Hamels	40.00
SHL	Francisco Liriano, Jeremy Sowers, Cole Hamels	60.00
TZU	Ryan Zimmerman, B.J. Upton, Troy Tulowitzki	60.00
VBZ	Jeremy Bonderman, Justin Verlander, Joel Zumaya	100.00

2006 Upper Deck Ovation

NM/M
Complete Set (126):
Common (1-84): .25
Common SP (85-126): 5.00
Production 999
Pack (5): 5.00
Box (18): 75.00

1	Vladimir Guerrero	.75
2	Bartolo Colon	.25
3	Chone Figgins	.25
4	Lance Berkman	.40
5	Roy Oswalt	.40
6	Craig Biggio	.40
7	Rich Harden	.25
8	Eric Chavez	.40
9	Huston Street	.25
10	Vernon Wells	.40
11	Roy Halladay	.50
12	Troy Glaus	.40
13	Andruw Jones	.50
14	Chipper Jones	.75
15	John Smoltz	.40
16	Carlos Lee	.40
17	Rickie Weeks	.25
18	J.J. Hardy	.25
19	Albert Pujols	2.00
20	Chris Carpenter	.50
21	Scott Rolen	.75
22	Derek Lee	.50
23	Mark Prior	.40
24	Aramis Ramirez	.40
25	Carl Crawford	.40
26	Scott Kazmir	.40
27	Luis Gonzalez	.25
28	Brandon Webb	.25
29	Chad Tracy	.25
30	Jeff Kent	.40
31	J.D. Drew	.40
32	Jason Schmidt	.40
33	Randy Winn	.25
34	Travis Hafner	.50
35	Victor Martinez	.40
36	Grady Sizemore	.40
37	Ichiro Suzuki	.40
38	Felix Hernandez	.40
39	Adrian Beltre	.25
40	Miguel Cabrera	.75
41	Dontrelle Willis	.40
42	David Wright	1.50
43	Jose Reyes	.50
44	Pedro Martinez	.75
45	Carlos Beltran	.50
46	Alfonso Soriano	.75
47	Livan Hernandez	.25
48	Jose Guillen	.25
49	Miguel Tejada	.50
50	Brian Roberts	.25
51	Melvin Mora	.25
52	Jake Peavy	.40
53	Brian Giles	.25
54	Khalil Greene	.25
55	Bobby Abreu	.40
56	Ryan Howard	1.00
57	Chase Utley	.50
58	Jason Bay	.40
59	Sean Casey	.25
60	Mark Teixeira	.50
61	Michael Young	.40
62	Hank Blalock	.40
63	Manny Ramirez	.75
64	David Ortiz	.75
65	Josh Beckett	.40
66	Jason Varitek	.25
67	Ken Griffey Jr.	1.50
68	Adam Dunn	.50
69	Todd Helton	.50
70	Garrett Atkins	.25
71	Reggie Sanders	.25
72	Mike Sweeney	.25
73	Chris Shelton	.25
74	Ivan Rodriguez	.50
75	Johan Santana	.75
76	Torii Hunter	.40
77	Justin Morneau	.40
78	Jim Thome	.50
79	Paul Konerko	.40
80	Scott Podsednik	.40
81	Derek Jeter	2.00
82	Hideki Matsui	1.50
83	Johnny Damon	.75
84	Alex Rodriguez	2.00
85	Conor Jackson (RC)	8.00
86	Joey Devine RC	5.00
87	Jonathan Papelbon (RC)	25.00
88	Freddie Bynum (RC)	5.00
89	Chris Denorfia (RC)	8.00
90	Ryan Shealy (RC)	5.00
91	Josh Wilson (RC)	5.00
92	Brian Anderson (RC)	5.00
93	Justin Verlander (RC)	15.00
94	Jeremy Hermida (RC)	5.00
95	Mike Jacobs (RC)	5.00
96	Josh Johnson (RC)	8.00
97	Hanley Ramirez (RC)	8.00
98	Josh Willingham (RC)	5.00
99	Cole Hamels (RC)	10.00
100	Hong-Chih Kuo (RC)	20.00
101	Cody Ross (RC)	8.00
102	Jose Capellan (RC)	5.00
103	Prince Fielder (RC)	15.00
104	Dave Gassner (RC)	8.00
105	Jason Kubel (RC)	8.00
106	Francisco Liriano (RC)	10.00
107	Anderson Hernandez (RC)	5.00
108	Boof Bonser (RC)	8.00
109	Jered Weaver (RC)	10.00
110	Ben Johnson (RC)	5.00
111	Jeff Harris RC	8.00
112	Stephen Drew (RC)	10.00
114	Matt Cain (RC)	8.00
115	Skip Schumaker (RC)	8.00
116	Adam Wainwright (RC)	15.00
117	Jeremy Sowers (RC)	5.00
118	Jason Bergmann RC	5.00
119	Chad Billingsley (RC)	10.00
119	Ryan Zimmerman (RC)	20.00
120	Macay McBride (RC)	8.00
121	Aaron Rakers (RC)	8.00
122	Alay Soler RC	8.00
123	Melky Cabrera (RC)	20.00
124	Tim Hamulack (RC)	10.00
125	Andre Ethier (RC)	15.00
126	Kenji Johjima RC	15.00

Gold
Gold (1-84): 4-8X
Production 499 Sets

Gold Autographs

NM/M
Production 99 Sets

85	Conor Jackson	25.00
86	Joey Devine	15.00
87	Jonathan Papelbon	75.00
88	Freddie Bynum	10.00
89	Chris Denorfia	10.00
90	Ryan Shealy	20.00
92	Brian Anderson	10.00
93	Justin Verlander	50.00
94	Jeremy Hermida	20.00
95	Mike Jacobs	10.00
96	Josh Johnson	20.00
97	Hanley Ramirez	25.00
98	Josh Willingham	25.00
99	Cole Hamels	60.00
101	Cody Ross	20.00
102	Jose Capellan	15.00
105	Jason Kubel	15.00
106	Francisco Liriano	50.00
107	Anderson Hernandez	10.00
108	Boof Bonser	15.00
109	Jered Weaver	40.00
110	Ben Johnson	15.00
111	Jeff Harris	15.00
113	Matt Cain	25.00
114	Skip Schumaker	15.00
115	Adam Wainwright	25.00
116	Jeremy Sowers	15.00
117	Jason Bergmann	10.00
118	Chad Billingsley	25.00
119	Ryan Zimmerman	90.00
120	Macay McBride	10.00
121	Aaron Rakers	10.00
122	Alay Soler	15.00
123	Melky Cabrera	50.00
124	Tim Hamulack	20.00
125	Andre Ethier	70.00

Apparel

NM/M
Common Player: 4.00

BA	Jason Bay	8.00
LB	Lance Berkman	8.00
JB	Jeremy Bonderman	8.00
AB	A.J. Burnett	6.00
EC	Eric Chavez	6.00
CC	Carl Crawford	6.00
JE	Jim Edmonds	8.00
PF	Prince Fielder	10.00
CF	Chone Figgins	6.00
JF	Jeff Francoeur	10.00
JG	Jonny Gomes	6.00
KG	Khalil Greene	8.00
GR	Ken Griffey Jr.	20.00
VG	Vladimir Guerrero	8.00
HA	Travis Hafner	6.00
JH	J.J. Hardy	4.00
HE	Todd Helton	8.00
FH	Felix Hernandez	8.00
TH	Trevor Hoffman	8.00
RH	Ryan Howard	20.00
HU	Torii Hunter	6.00
DJ	Derek Jeter	25.00
JK	Jeff Kent	6.00
RK	Ryan Klesko	4.00
CL	Carlos Lee	6.00
VM	Victor Martinez	8.00
JM	Joe Mauer	8.00
TN	Trot Nixon	6.00
DO	David Ortiz	15.00
RO	Roy Oswalt	8.00
AO	Akinori Otsuka	6.00
MP	Mark Prior	6.00
AP	Albert Pujols	25.00
MR	Manny Ramirez	10.00
SR	Scott Rolen	8.00
CS	Chris Shelton	4.00
GS	Grady Sizemore	8.00
HS	Huston Street	6.00
MT	Mark Teixeira	8.00
VW	Vernon Wells	8.00
DW	David Wright	15.00
RZ	Ryan Zimmerman/SP	25.00

Center Stage

NM/M
Common Player: 1.00

JB	Josh Beckett	1.00
DC	Miguel Cabrera	1.00
CA	Miguel Cabrera	3.00
JC	Jose Contreras	1.00
AC	Aaron Cook	1.00
BC	Bobby Crosby	1.00
MC	Michael Cuddyer	1.00
DD	David DeJesus	1.00
SD	Stephen Drew	2.00
JF	Jason Frasor	1.00
KG	Ken Griffey Jr.	5.00
VG	Vladimir Guerrero	3.00
FH	Felix Hernandez	2.00
RH	Runelvys Hernandez	1.00
DJ	Derek Jeter	8.00
DL	Derek Lee	2.00
YM	Yadier Molina	1.00
MP	Mark Prior	2.00
AP	Albert Pujols	8.00
FS	Freddy Sanchez	1.00
CS	Chris Shelton	1.00

The election of players to the Hall of Fame does not always have an immediate upward effect on card values. The hobby market generally has done a good job of predicting those inductions and adjusting values over the course of several years.

Abbreviations
SP - Short Print

IS	Ian Snell	1.00
MT	Mark Teixeira	2.00
CW	Chien-Ming Wang	10.00
DW	David Wright	4.00

Center Stage Signatures

No Pricing
Production 25 Sets

Curtain Calls

		NM/M
	Common Player:	1.00
DC	Daniel Cabrera	1.00
EC	Eric Chavez	1.00
JC	Jose Contreras	1.00
BC	Bobby Crosby	1.00
DD	David DeJesus	1.00
KG1	Ken Griffey Jr.	4.00
KG2	Ken Griffey Jr.	4.00
RH	Rich Harden	1.00
HE	Runelvys Hernandez	1.00
YM	Yadier Molina	1.00
TO	Tomokazu Ohka	1.00
MP	Mark Prior	2.00
HR	Horacio Ramirez	1.00
FS	Freddy Sanchez	1.00
CS	Chris Shelton	1.00
MT	Miguel Tejada	2.00
CW	Chien-Ming Wang	10.00
JE	Jered Weaver	2.00
JW	Josh Willingham	1.00
MY	Michael Young	1.00

Curtain Calls Signatures

No Pricing
Production 25 Sets

Ovation Nation

		NM/M
	Common Player:	2.00
JB	Jason Bay	3.00
DC	Daniel Cabrera	2.00
MC	Miguel Cabrera	4.00
FC	Frederich Cepeda	2.00
YG	Yoandy Garlobo	2.00
KG	Ken Griffey Jr.	8.00
DJ	Derek Jeter	8.00
AJ	Andruw Jones	3.00
SL	Seung-Yeop Lee	4.00
DM	Daisuke Matsuzaka	15.00
NM	Nobuhiko Matsunaka	4.00
AP	Albert Pujols	8.00
JS	Johan Santana	3.00
JA	Jae Weong Seo	2.00
MT	Miguel Tejada	3.00

Ovation Nation Signatures

No Pricing
Production 25 Sets

Spotlight Signatures

		NM/M
	Common Autograph:	10.00
JB	Josh Beckett/SP	40.00
DC	Daniel Cabrera	15.00
CA	Miguel Cabrera	25.00
SC	Shawn Camp	10.00
EC	Eric Chavez/SP	15.00
JC	Jose Contreras	30.00
AC	Aaron Cook	6.00
LC	Lance Cormier	10.00
BC	Bobby Crosby	10.00
MC	Michael Cuddyer/SP	15.00
DD	David DeJesus	15.00
JD	Jorge De La Rosa	15.00
JF	Jason Frasor	15.00
FG	Franklyn German	10.00
MG	Mike Gonzalez	10.00
AG	Andy Green	6.00
KG1	Ken Griffey Jr.	85.00
KG2	Ken Griffey Jr.	85.00
HA	Rich Harden/SP	15.00
RH	Runelvys Hernandez	10.00
EJ	Edwin Jackson	10.00
YM	Yadier Molina	25.00
FN	Fernando Nieve	10.00
TO	Tomokazu Ohka	30.00
MP	Mark Prior	25.00
HR	Horacio Ramirez/SP	10.00
DR	David Ross	20.00
KS	Kirk Saarloos	10.00
FS	Freddy Sanchez	25.00
CS1	Chris Shelton	10.00
CS2	Chris Shelton	10.00
TE	Miguel Tejada/SP	25.00
MT	Matt Thornton	10.00
TR	Matt Treanor	20.00
RW	Ryan Wagner	10.00
CW	Chien-Ming Wang	200.00
JW	Josh Willingham/SP	15.00
MW	Mike Wuertz	15.00
MY	Michael Young	15.00

Superstar Theatre

		NM/M
	Common Player:	1.00
BA	Jason Bay	2.00
JB	Josh Beckett	1.00
DC	Daniel Cabrera	1.00
MC	Miguel Cabrera	3.00
CC	Chris Carpenter	2.00
JC	Jose Contreras	1.00
BC	Bobby Crosby	1.00
DD	David DeJesus	1.00
KG1	Ken Griffey Jr.	6.00
KG2	Ken Griffey Jr.	6.00
TH	Travis Hafner	2.00
RH	Rich Harden	1.00
DJ	Derek Jeter	8.00
AJ	Andruw Jones	2.00
DL	Derek Lee	3.00
PM	Pedro Martinez	3.00
HM	Hideki Matsui	4.00
YM	Yadier Molina	1.00
TO	Tomokazu Ohka	1.00
DO	David Ortiz	3.00
MP	Mark Prior	2.00
AP	Albert Pujols	8.00
MR	Manny Ramirez	3.00
AR	Alex Rodriguez	6.00
CS	Chris Shelton	1.00
IS	Ichiro Suzuki	6.00
TE	Mark Teixeira	2.00
MT	Miguel Tejada	2.00
CW	Chien-Ming Wang	10.00
MY	Michael Young	2.00

Superstar Theatre Signatures

No Pricing
Production 25 Sets

2006 Upper Deck Special FX

		NM/M
	Complete Set (1025):	
	Common Player:	.25
	Common RC (901-1025):	.25
	Pack (4):	5.00
	Box (16):	75.00
1	Adam Kennedy	.25
2	Bartolo Colon	.25
3	Bengie Molina	.25
4	Casey Kotchman	.25
5	Chone Figgins	.25
6	Dallas McPherson	.25
7	Darin Erstad	.25
8	Ervin Santana	.50
9	Francisco Rodriguez	.25
10	Garret Anderson	.25
11	Jarrod Washburn	.25
12	John Lackey	.25
13	Juan Rivera	.25
14	Orlando Cabrera	.25
15	Paul Byrd	.25
16	Steve Finley	.25
17	Vladimir Guerrero	1.00
18	Alex Cintron	.25
19	Brandon Lyon	.25
20	Brandon Webb	.50
21	Chad Tracy	.25
22	Chris Snyder	.25
23	Claudio Vargas	.25
24	Conor Jackson	.50
25	Craig Counsell	.25
26	Javier Vazquez	.25
27	Jose Valverde	.25
28	Luis Gonzalez	.25
29	Royce Clayton	.25
30	Russ Ortiz	.25
31	Shawn Green	.25
32	Dustin Nippert	.25
33	Tony Clark	.25
34	Troy Glaus	.50
35	Adam LaRoche	.25
36	Andruw Jones	1.00
37	Craig Hansen	.25
38	Chipper Jones	1.00
39	Horacio Ramirez	.25
40	Jeff Francoeur	.50
41	John Smoltz	.50
42	Joey Devine	.25
43	Johnny Estrada	.25
44	Anthony Lerew	.25
45	Julio Franco	.25
46	Kyle Farnsworth	.25
47	Marcus Giles	.25
48	Mike Hampton	.25
49	Rafael Furcal	.50
50	Chuck James	.25
51	Tim Hudson	.50
52	B.J. Ryan	.25
53	Bernie Castro	.25
54	Brian Roberts	.25
55	Walter Young	.25
56	Daniel Cabrera	.25
57	Eric Byrnes	.25
58	Alejandro Freire	.25
59	Erik Bedard	.50
60	Javy Lopez	.25
61	Jay Gibbons	.25
62	Jorge Julio	.25
63	Luis Matos	.25
64	Melvin Mora	.25
65	Miguel Tejada	.75
66	Rafael Palmeiro	.75
67	Rodrigo Lopez	.25
68	Sammy Sosa	1.00
69	Alejandro Machado	.25
70	Bill Mueller	.25
71	Bronson Arroyo	.25
72	Curt Schilling	.50
73	David Ortiz	1.00
74	David Wells	.25
75	Edgar Renteria	.25
76	Ryan Jorgensen	.25
77	Jason Varitek	.75
78	Johnny Damon	1.00
79	Keith Foulke	.25
80	Kevin Youkilis	.50
81	Manny Ramirez	1.00
82	Matt Clement	.25
83	Hanley Ramirez	.50
84	Tim Wakefield	.25
85	Trot Nixon	.25
86	Wade Miller	.25
87	Aramis Ramirez	.50
88	Carlos Zambrano	.50
89	Corey Patterson	.25
90	Derrek Lee	.75
91	Geovany Soto	.25
92	Greg Maddux	2.00
93	Jeromy Burnitz	.25
94	Jerry Hairston Jr.	.25
95	Kerry Wood	.50
96	Mark Prior	.25
97	Matt Murton	.25
98	Michael Barrett	.25
99	Neifi Perez	.25
100	Nomar Garciaparra	1.00
101	Rich Hill	.25
102	Ryan Dempster	.25
103	Todd Walker	.25
104	A.J. Pierzynski	.25
105	Aaron Rowand	.25
106	Bobby Jenks	.25
107	Carl Everett	.25
108	Dustin Hermanson	.25
109	Frank Thomas	1.00
110	Freddy Garcia	.25
111	Jermaine Dye	.25
112	Joe Crede	.50
113	Jon Garland	.25
114	Jose Contreras	.25
115	Juan Uribe	.25
116	Mark Buehrle	.25
117	Orlando Hernandez	.25
118	Paul Konerko	.75
119	Scott Podsednik	.25
120	Tadahito Iguchi	.25
121	Aaron Harang	.25
122	Adam Dunn	.75
123	Austin Kearns	.25
124	Brandon Claussen	.25
125	Chris Denorfia	.25
126	Edwin Encarnacion	.25
127	Miguel Perez	.25
128	Felipe Lopez	.25
129	Jason LaRue	.25
130	Ken Griffey Jr.	2.00
131	Chris Booker	.25
132	Luke Hudson	.25
133	Jason Bergmann	.25
134	Ryan Freel	.25
135	Sean Casey	.25
136	Wily Mo Pena	.25
137	Aaron Boone	.25
138	Ben Broussard	.25
139	Ryan Garko	.25
140	C.C. Sabathia	.25
141	Casey Blake	.25
142	Cliff Lee	.25
143	Coco Crisp	.25
144	David Riske	.25
145	Grady Sizemore	.50
146	Jake Westbrook	.25
147	Jhonny Peralta	.25
148	Josh Bard	.25
149	Kevin Millwood	.25
150	Ronnie Belliard	.25
151	Scott Elarton	.25
152	Travis Hafner	.50
153	Victor Martinez	.25
154	Aaron Cook	.25
155	Aaron Miles	.25
156	Brad Hawpe	.25
157	Mike Esposito	.25
158	Chin-Hui Tsao	.25
159	Clint Barmes	.25
160	Cory Sullivan	.25
161	Garrett Atkins	.25
162	J.D. Closser	.25
163	Jason Jennings	.25
164	Jeff Baker	.25
165	Jeff Francis	.25
166	Luis Gonzalez	.25
167	Matt Holliday	.50
168	Todd Helton	.75
169	Brandon Inge	.25
170	Carlos Guillen	.25
171	Carlos Pena	.25
172	Chris Shelton	.25
173	Craig Monroe	.25
174	Curtis Granderson	.25
175	Dmitri Young	.25
176	Ivan Rodriguez	.75
177	Jason Johnson	.25
178	Jeremy Bonderman	.50
179	Magglio Ordonez	.25
180	Mark Woodyard	.25
181	Nook Logan	.25
182	Omar Infante	.25
183	Placido Polanco	.25
184	Chris Heintz	.25
185	A.J. Burnett	.25
186	Alex Gonzalez	.25
187	Josh Johnson	.25
188	Carlos Delgado	.75
189	Dontrelle Willis	.25
190	Josh Wilson	.25
191	Jason Vargas	.25
192	Jeff Conine	.25
193	Jeremy Hermida	.50
194	Josh Beckett	.50
195	Juan Encarnacion	.25
196	Juan Pierre	.25
197	Luis Castillo	.25
198	Miguel Cabrera	1.00
199	Mike Lowell	.25
200	Paul LoDuca	.25
201	Todd Jones	.25
202	Adam Everett	.25
203	Andy Pettitte	.25
204	Brad Ausmus	.25
205	Brad Lidge	.25
206	Brandon Backe	.25
207	Charlton Jimerson	.25
208	Chris Burke	.25
209	Craig Biggio	.50
210	Dan Wheeler	.25
211	Jason Lane	.25
212	Jeff Bagwell	.50
213	Lance Berkman	.50
214	Luke Scott	.25
215	Morgan Ensberg	.25
216	Roger Clemens	2.50
217	Roy Oswalt	.50
218	Willy Taveras	.25
219	Andres Blanco	.25
220	Angel Berroa	.25
221	Ruben Gotay	.25
222	David DeJesus	.25
223	Emil Brown	.25
224	J.P. Howell	.25
225	Jeremy Affeldt	.25
226	Jimmy Gobble	.25
227	John Buck	.25
228	Jose Lima	.25
229	Mark Teahen	.25
230	Matt Stairs	.25
231	Mike MacDougal	.25
232	Mike Sweeney	.25
233	Runelvys Hernandez	.25
234	Terrence Long	.25
235	Zack Greinke	.25
236	Ron Flores	.25
237	Brad Penny	.25
238	Cesar Izturis	.25
239	D.J. Houlton	.25
240	Derek Lowe	.25
241	Eric Gagne	.25
242	Hee Seop Choi	.25
243	J.D. Drew	.25
244	Jason Phillips	.25
245	Jason Repko	.25
246	Jayson Werth	.25
247	Jeff Kent	.50
248	Jeff Weaver	.25
249	Milton Bradley	.25
250	Odalis Perez	.25
251	Hong-Chih Kuo	.25
252	Oscar Robles	.25
253	Ben Sheets	.50
254	Bill Hall	.25
255	Brady Clark	.25
256	Carlos Lee	.50
257	Chris Capuano	.25
258	Nelson Cruz	.25
259	Derrick Turnbow	.25
260	Doug Davis	.25
261	Geoff Jenkins	.25
262	J.J. Hardy	.25
263	Lyle Overbay	.25
264	Prince Fielder	.50
265	Rickie Weeks	.25
266	Russell Branyan	.25
267	Tomokazu Ohka	.25
268	Jonah Bayliss	.25
269	Brad Radke	.25
270	Carlos Silva	.25
271	Francisco Liriano	.50
272	Jacque Jones	.25
273	Joe Mauer	.50
274	Travis Bowyer	.25
275	Joe Nathan	.25
276	Johan Santana	1.00
277	Justin Morneau	.75
278	Kyle Lohse	.25
279	Lew Ford	.25
280	Matthew LeCroy	.25
281	Michael Cuddyer	.25
282	Nick Punto	.25
283	Scott Baker	.25
284	Shannon Stewart	.25
285	Torii Hunter	.50
286	Braden Looper	.25
287	Carlos Beltran	.75
288	Cliff Floyd	.25
289	David Wright	1.50
290	Doug Mientkiewicz	.25
291	Anderson Hernandez	.25
292	Jose Reyes	1.00
293	Kazuo Matsui	.25
294	Kris Benson	.25
295	Miguel Cairo	.25
296	Mike Cameron	.25
297	Robert Andino	.25
298	Mike Piazza	1.00
299	Pedro Martinez	1.00
300	Tom Glavine	.50
301	Victor Diaz	.25
302	Tim Hamulack	.25
303	Alex Rodriguez	2.50
304	Bernie Williams	.50
305	Carl Pavano	.25
306	Chien-Ming Wang	1.00
307	Derek Jeter	2.50
308	Gary Sheffield	.50
309	Hideki Matsui	1.50
310	Jason Giambi	.75
311	Jorge Posada	.50
312	Kevin Brown	.25
313	Mariano Rivera	.50
314	Matt Lawton	.25
315	Mike Mussina	.50
316	Randy Johnson	1.00
317	Robinson Cano	.50
318	Michael Vento	.25
319	Tino Martinez	.25
320	Tony Womack	.25
321	Barry Zito	.50
322	Bobby Crosby	.25
323	Bobby Kielty	.25
324	Dan Johnson	.25
325	Danny Haren	.25
326	Eric Chavez	.50
327	Erubiel Durazo	.25
328	Huston Street	.25
329	Jason Kendall	.25
330	Jay Payton	.25
331	Joe Blanton	.25
332	Joe Kennedy	.25
333	Kirk Saarloos	.25
334	Mark Kotsay	.25
335	Nick Swisher	.50
336	Rich Harden	.25
337	Scott Hatteberg	.25
338	Billy Wagner	.25
339	Bobby Abreu	.50
340	Brett Myers	.25
341	Chase Utley	1.00
342	Danny Sandoval	.25
343	David Bell	.25
344	Gavin Floyd	.25
345	Jim Thome	.75
346	Jimmy Rollins	.50
347	Jon Lieber	.25
348	Kenny Lofton	.25
349	Mike Lieberthal	.25
350	Pat Burrell	.50
351	Randy Wolf	.25
352	Ryan Howard	1.50
353	Vicente Padilla	.25
354	Bryan Bullington	.25
355	J.J. Furmaniak	.25
356	Craig Wilson	.25
357	Matt Capps	.25
358	Tom Gorzelanny	.25
359	Jack Wilson	.25
360	Jason Bay	.50
361	Jose Mesa	.25
362	Josh Fogg	.25
363	Kip Wells	.25
364	Steve Stemle	.25
365	Oliver Perez	.25
366	Robert Mackowiak	.25
367	Ronny Paulino	.25
368	Tike Redman	.25
369	Zachary Duke	.25
370	Adam Eaton	.25
371	Scott Feldman	.25
372	Brian Giles	.25
373	Brian Lawrence	.25
374	Damian Jackson	.25
375	Dave Roberts	.25
376	Jake Peavy	.50
377	Joe Randa	.25
378	Khalil Greene	.25
379	Mark Loretta	.25
380	Ramon Hernandez	.25
381	Robert Fick	.25
382	Ryan Klesko	.25
383	Trevor Hoffman	.25
384	Woody Williams	.25
385	Xavier Nady	.25
386	Armando Benitez	.25
387	Brad Hennessey	.25
388	Brian Myrow	.25
389	Edgardo Alfonzo	.25
390	J.T. Snow	.25
391	Jeremy Accardo	.25
392	Jason Schmidt	.50
393	Lance Niekro	.25
394	Matt Cain	.25
395	Daniel Ortmeier	.25
396	Moises Alou	.50
397	Doug Clark	.25
398	Omar Vizquel	.25
399	Pedro Feliz	.25
400	Randy Winn	.25
401	Ray Durham	.25
402	Adrian Beltre	.50
403	Eddie Guardado	.25
404	Felix Hernandez	.50
405	Gil Meche	.25
406	Ichiro Suzuki	1.50
407	Jamie Moyer	.25
408	Jeff Nelson	.25
409	Jeremy Reed	.25
410	Joel Pineiro	.25
411	Jaime Bubela	.25
412	Raul Ibanez	.25
413	Richie Sexson	.50
414	Ryan Franklin	.25
415	Willie Bloomquist	.25
416	Yorvit Torrealba	.25
417	Yuniesky Betancourt	.25
418	Jeff Harris	.25
419	Albert Pujols	2.50
420	Chris Carpenter	.75
421	David Eckstein	.25
422	Jason Isringhausen	.25
423	Jason Marquis	.25
424	Adam Wainwright	.25
425	Jim Edmonds	.50
426	Ryan Theriot	.25
427	Tim Duncan	.25
428	Mark Grudzielanek	.25
429	Mark Mulder	.50
430	Matt Morris	.25
431	Reggie Sanders	.25
432	Scott Rolen	1.00
433	Tyler Johnson	.25
434	Yadier Molina	.25
435	Alex Gonzalez	.25
436	Aubrey Huff	.25
437	Tim Corcoran	.25
438	Carl Crawford	.50
439	Casey Fossum	.25
440	Danys Baez	.25
441	Edwin Jackson	.25
442	Joey Gathright	.25
443	Jonny Gomes	.25
444	Jorge Cantu	.25
445	Julio Lugo	.25
446	Nick Green	.25
447	Rocco Baldelli	.25
448	Scott Kazmir	.50
449	Seth McClung	.25
450	Toby Hall	.25
451	Travis Lee	.25
452	Craig Breslow	.25
453	Alfonso Soriano	1.00
454	Chris Young	.25
455	David Dellucci	.25
457	Francisco Cordero	.25
457	Gary Matthews	.25
458	Hank Blalock	.50
459	Juan Dominguez	.25
460	Josh Rupe	.25
461	Kenny Rogers	.25
462	Kevin Mench	.25
463	Laynce Nix	.25
464	Mark Teixeira	.75
465	Michael Young	.25
466	Richard Hidalgo	.25
467	Jason Botts	.25
468	Aaron Hill	.25
469	Alex Rios	.25
470	Corey Koskie	.25
471	Chris Demaria	.25
472	Eric Hinske	.25
473	Frank Catalanotto	.25
474	John-Ford Griffin	.25
475	Gustavo Chacin	.25
476	Josh Towers	.25
477	Miguel Batista	.25
478	Orlando Hudson	.25
479	Reed Johnson	.25
480	Roy Halladay	.50
481	Shaun Marcum	.25
482	Shea Hillenbrand	.25
483	Ted Lilly	.25
484	Vernon Wells	.50
485	Brad Wilkerson	.25
486	Darrell Rasner	.25
487	Chad Cordero	.25
488	Cristian Guzman	.25
489	Esteban Loaiza	.25
490	John Patterson	.25
491	Jose Guillen	.25
492	Jose Vidro	.25
493	Livan Hernandez	.25
494	Marlon Byrd	.25
495	Nick Johnson	.25
496	Preston Wilson	.25
497	Ryan Church	.25
498	Ryan Zimmerman	.50
499	Tony Armas	.25
500	Vinny Castilla	.25
501	Andy Green	.25
502	Damion Easley	.25
503	Eric Byrnes	.25
504	Jason Grimsley	.25
505	Jeff DaVanon	.25
506	Johnny Estrada	.25
507	Luis Vizcaino	.25
508	Miguel Batista	.25
509	Orlando Hernandez	.25
510	Orlando Hudson	.25
511	Terry Mulholland	.25
512	Chris Reitsma	.25
513	Edgar Renteria	.25
514	John Thomson	.25
515	Jorge Sosa	.25
516	Oscar Villarreal	.25
517	Peter Orr	.25
518	Ryan Langerhans	.25
519	Todd Pratt	.25
520	Wilson Betemit	.25
521	Brian Jordan	.25
522	Lance Cormier	.25
523	Matt Diaz	.25
524	Mike Remlinger	.25
525	Bruce Chen	.25
526	Chris Gomez	.25
527	Chris Ray	.25
528	Corey Patterson	.25
529	David Newhan	.25
530	Ed Rogers	.25
531	John Halama	.25
532	Kris Benson	.25
533	LaTroy Hawkins	.25
534	Raul Chavez	.25
535	Alex Cora	.25
536	Alex Gonzalez	.25
537	Coco Crisp	.25
538	David Riske	.25
539	Doug Mirabelli	.25
540	Josh Beckett	.50
541	J.T. Snow	.25
542	Mike Timlin	.25
543	Julian Tavarez	.25
544	Rudy Seanez	.25
545	Wily Mo Pena	.25
546	Bob Howry	.25
547	Glendon Rusch	.25

No.	Player	Price
548	Henry Blanco	.25
549	Jacque Jones	.25
550	Jerome Williams	.25
551	John Mabry	.25
552	Juan Pierre	.25
553	Scott Eyre	.25
554	Scott Williamson	.25
555	Wade Miller	.25
556	Will Ohman	.25
557	Alex Cintron	.25
558	Robert Mackowiak	.25
559	Brandon McCarthy	.25
560	Chris Widger	.25
561	Cliff Politte	.25
562	Javier Vazquez	.25
563	Jim Thome	.75
564	Matt Thornton	.25
565	Neal Cotts	.25
566	Pablo Ozuna	.25
567	Ross Gload	.25
568	Brandon Phillips	.25
569	Bronson Arroyo	.25
570	Dave Williams	.25
571	David Ross	.25
572	David Weathers	.25
573	Eric Milton	.25
574	Javier Valentin	.25
575	Kent Mercker	.25
576	Matt Belisle	.25
577	Paul Wilson	.25
578	Rich Aurilia	.25
579	Rick White	.25
580	Scott Hatteberg	.25
581	Todd Coffey	.25
582	Bob Wickman	.25
583	Danny Graves	.25
584	Eduardo Perez	.25
585	Guillermo Mota	.25
586	Jason Davis	.25
587	Jason Johnson	.25
588	Jason Michaels	.25
589	Rafael Betancourt	.25
590	Ramon Vazquez	.25
591	Scott Sauerbeck	.25
592	Todd Hollandsworth	.25
593	Brian Fuentes	.25
594	Danny Ardoin	.25
595	David Cortes	.25
596	Eli Marrero	.25
597	Jamey Carroll	.25
598	Jason Smith	.25
599	Josh Fogg	.25
600	Miguel Ojeda	.25
601	Mike DeJean	.25
602	Ray King	.25
603	Omar Quintanilla	.25
604	Zach Day	.25
605	Fernando Rodney	.25
606	Kenny Rogers	.25
607	Mike Maroth	.25
608	Nate Robertson	.25
609	Todd Jones	.25
610	Vance Wilson	.25
611	Bobby Seay	.25
612	Chris Spurling	.25
613	Ramon Colon	.25
614	Jason Grilli	.25
615	Marcus Thames	.25
616	Ramon Santiago	.25
617	Alfredo Amezaga	.25
618	Brian Moehler	.25
619	Chris Aguila	.25
620	Franklyn German	.25
621	Joe Borowski	.25
622	Logan Kensing	.25
623	Matt Treanor	.25
624	Miguel Olivo	.25
625	Sergio Mitre	.25
626	Todd Wellemeyer	.25
627	Wes Helms	.25
628	Chad Qualls	.25
629	Eric Bruntlett	.25
630	Mike Gallo	.25
631	Mike Lamb	.25
632	Orlando Palmeiro	.25
633	Russ Springer	.25
634	Dan Wheeler	.25
635	Eric Munson	.25
636	Preston Wilson	.25
637	Trever Miller	.25
638	Ambiorix Burgos	.25
639	Andrew Sisco	.25
640	Denny Bautista	.25
641	Doug Mientkiewicz	.25
642	Elmer Dessens	.25
643	Esteban German	.25
644	Joe Nelson	.25
645	Mark Grudzielanek	.25
646	Mark Redman	.25
647	Mike Wood	.25
648	Paul Bako	.25
649	Reggie Sanders	.25
650	Scott Elarton	.25
651	Shane Costa	.25
652	Tony Graffanino	.25
653	Jason Bulger	.25
654	Chris Bootcheck	.25
655	Esteban Yan	.25
656	Hector Carrasco	.25
657	J.C. Romero	.25
658	Jeff Weaver	.25
659	Jose Molina	.25
660	Kelvim Escobar	.25
661	Maicer Izturis	.25
662	Robb Quinlan	.25
663	Scot Shields	.25
664	Tim Salmon	.25
665	Bill Mueller	.25
666	Brett Tomko	.25
667	Dioner Navarro	.25
668	Jae Weong Seo	.25
669	Jose Cruz	.25
670	Kenny Lofton	.25
671	Lance Carter	.25
672	Nomar Garciaparra	1.00
673	Olmedo Saenz	.25
674	Rafael Furcal	.25
675	Ramon Martinez	.25
676	Ricky Ledee	.25
677	Sandy Alomar	.25
678	Yhency Brazoban	.25
679	Corey Koskie	.25
680	Danny Kolb	.25
681	Gabe Gross	.25
682	Jeff Cirillo	.25
683	Matt Wise	.25
684	Rick Helling	.25
685	Chad Moeller	.25
686	David Bush	.25
687	Jorge De La Rosa	.25
688	Justin Lehr	.25
689	Jason Bartlett	.25
690	Jesse Crain	.25
691	Juan Rincon	.25
692	Luis Castillo	.25
693	Mike Redmond	.25
694	Rondell White	.25
695	Tony Batista	.25
696	Juan Castro	.25
697	Luis Rodriguez	.25
698	Matt Guerrier	.25
699	Willie Eyre	.25
700	Aaron Heilman	.25
701	Billy Wagner	.25
702	Carlos Delgado	.75
703	Chad Bradford	.25
704	Chris Woodward	.25
705	Darren Oliver	.25
706	Duaner Sanchez	.25
707	Endy Chavez	.25
708	Jorge Julio	.25
709	Jose Valentin	.25
710	Julio Franco	.25
711	Paul LoDuca	.25
712	Ramon Castro	.25
713	Steve Trachsel	.25
714	Victor Zambrano	.25
715	Xavier Nady	.25
716	Andy Phillips	.25
717	Bubba Crosby	.25
718	Jaret Wright	.25
719	Kelly Stinnett	.25
720	Kyle Farnsworth	.25
721	Mike Myers	.25
722	Octavio Dotel	.25
723	Ron Villone	.25
724	Scott Proctor	.25
725	Shawn Chacon	.25
726	Tanyon Sturtze	.25
727	Adam Melhuse	.25
728	Brad Halsey	.25
729	Esteban Loaiza	.25
730	Frank Thomas	1.00
731	Jay Witasick	.25
732	Justin Duchscherer	.25
733	Kiko Calero	.25
734	Marco Scutaro	.25
735	Mark Ellis	.25
736	Milton Bradley	.25
737	Aaron Fultz	.25
738	Aaron Rowand	.25
739	Geoff Geary	.25
740	Arthur Rhodes	.25
741	Chris Coste	.25
742	Rheal Cormier	.25
743	Ryan Franklin	.25
744	Ryan Madson	.25
745	Sal Fasano	.25
746	Tom Gordon	.25
747	Abraham Nunez	.25
748	David Dellucci	.25
749	Julio Santana	.25
750	Shane Victorino	.25
751	Damaso Marte	.25
752	Freddy Sanchez	.25
753	Humberto Cota	.25
754	Jeromy Burnitz	.25
755	Joe Randa	.25
756	Jose Castillo	.25
757	Mike Gonzalez	.25
758	Ryan Doumit	.25
759	Sean Burnett	.25
760	Sean Casey	.25
761	Ian Snell	.25
762	John Grabow	.25
763	Jose Hernandez	.25
764	Roberto Hernandez	.25
765	Ryan Vogelsong	.25
766	Victor Sanchez	.25
767	Adrian Gonzalez	.25
768	Alan Embree	.25
769	Brian Sweeney	.25
770	Chan Ho Park	.25
771	Clay Hensley	.25
772	Dewon Brazelton	.25
773	Doug Brocail	.25
774	Eric Young	.25
775	Geoff Blum	.25
776	Josh Bard	.25
777	Mark Bellhorn	.25
778	Mike Cameron	.25
779	Mike Piazza	1.00
780	Rob Bowen	.25
781	Scott Cassidy	.25
782	Scott Linebrink	.25
783	Shawn Estes	.25
784	Terrmel Sledge	.25
785	Vinny Castilla	.25
786	Jeff Fassero	.25
787	Jose Vizcaino	.25
788	Mark Sweeney	.25
789	Matt Morris	.25
790	Steve Finley	.25
791	Tim Worrell	.25
792	Jamey Wright	.25
793	Jason Ellison	.25
794	Noah Lowry	.25
795	Steve Kline	.25
796	Todd Greene	.25
797	Carl Everett	.25
798	George Sherrill	.25
799	J.J. Putz	.25
800	Jake Woods	.25
801	Jose Lopez	.25
802	Julio Mateo	.25
803	Mike Morse	.25
804	Rafael Soriano	.25
805	Roberto Petagine	.25
806	Aaron Miles	.25
807	Braden Looper	.25
808	Gary Bennett	.25
809	Hector Luna	.25
810	Jeff Suppan	.25
811	John Rodriguez	.25
812	Josh Hancock	.25
813	Juan Encarnacion	.25
814	Larry Bigbie	.25
815	Scott Spiezio	.25
816	Sidney Ponson	.25
817	So Taguchi	.25
818	Brian Meadows	.25
819	Damon Hollins	.25
820	Dan Miceli	.25
821	Doug Waechter	.25
822	Jason Childers	.25
823	Josh Paul	.25
824	Julio Lugo	.25
825	Mark Hendrickson	.25
826	Sean Burroughs	.25
827	Shawn Camp	.25
828	Travis Harper	.25
829	Ty Wigginton	.25
830	Adam Eaton	.25
831	Adrian Brown	.25
832	Akinori Otsuka	.25
833	Antonio Alfonseca	.25
834	Brad Wilkerson	.25
835	D'Angelo Jimenez	.25
836	Gerald Laird	.25
837	Joaquin Benoit	.25
838	Kameron Loe	.25
839	Kevin Millwood	.25
840	Mark DeRosa	.25
841	Phil Nevin	.25
842	Rod Barajas	.25
843	Vicente Padilla	.25
844	A.J. Burnett	.25
845	Bengie Molina	.25
846	Gregg Zaun	.25
847	John McDonald	.25
848	Lyle Overbay	.25
849	Russ Adams	.25
850	Troy Glaus	.25
851	Vinnie Chulk	.25
852	B.J. Ryan	.25
853	Justin Speier	.25
854	Pete Walker	.25
855	Scott Downs	.25
856	Scott Schoeneweis	.25
857	Alfonso Soriano	1.00
858	Brian Schneider	.25
859	Daryle Ward	.25
860	Felix Rodriguez	.25
861	Gary Majewski	.25
862	Joey Eischen	.25
863	Jon Rauch	.25
864	Marlon Anderson	.25
865	Matthew LeCroy	.25
866	Mike Stanton	.25
867	Ramon Ortiz	.25
868	Robert Fick	.25
869	Royce Clayton	.25
870	Ryan Drese	.25
871	Vladimir Guerrero	.50
872	Craig Biggio	.50
873	Barry Zito	.50
874	Vernon Wells	.50
875	Chipper Jones	.50
876	Prince Fielder	.50
877	Albert Pujols	1.50
878	Greg Maddux	1.00
879	Carl Crawford	.50
880	Brandon Webb	.50
881	J.D. Drew	.25
882	Jason Schmidt	.25
883	Victor Martinez	.25
884	Ichiro Suzuki	.75
885	Miguel Cabrera	.50
886	David Wright	.75
887	Alfonso Soriano	.50
888	Miguel Tejada	.50
889	Khalil Greene	.25
890	Ryan Howard	1.00
891	Jason Bay	.50
892	Mark Teixeira	.50
893	Manny Ramirez	.50
894	Ken Griffey Jr.	1.00
895	Todd Helton	.50
896	Angel Berroa	.25
897	Ivan Rodriguez	.50
898	Johan Santana	.50
899	Paul Konerko	.50
900	Derek Jeter	1.50
901	Macay McBride (RC)	.50
902	Tony Pena	.50
903	Peter Moylan RC	.75
904	Aaron Rakers RC	.50
905	Chris Britton RC	.75
906	Nicholas Markakis (RC)	1.00
907	Sendy Rleal RC	.50
908	Val Majewski (RC)	.50
909	Jermaine Van Buren (RC)	.50
910	Jonathan Papelbon (RC)	3.00
911	Angel Pagan (RC)	.50
912	David Aardsma (RC)	.50
913	Sean Marshall (RC)	.50
914	Brian Anderson (RC)	.50
915	Freddie Bynum (RC)	.50
916	Fausto Carmona (RC)	.50
917	Kelly Shoppach (RC)	.50
918	Choo Freeman (RC)	.50
919	Ryan Shealy (RC)	.50
920	Joel Zumaya (RC)	2.00
921	Jordan Tata RC	1.00
922	Justin Verlander (RC)	2.00
923	Carlos Martinez (RC)	.50
924	Chris Resop (RC)	.50
925	Dan Uggla (RC)	.50
926	Eric Reed (RC)	.50
927	Hanley Ramirez (RC)	1.00
928	Yusmeiro Petit (RC)	.50
929	Josh Willingham (RC)	.50
930	Mike Jacobs (RC)	.50
931	Reggie Abercrombie (RC)	.50
932	Ricky Nolasco (RC)	.50
933	Scott Olsen (RC)	.50
934	Fernando Nieve (RC)	.50
935	Taylor Buchholz (RC)	.50
936	Cody Ross (RC)	.50
937	James Loney (RC)	.50
938	Takashi Saito RC	1.00
939	Tim Hamulack (RC)	.50
940	Chris Demaria RC	.50
941	Jose Capellan (RC)	.50
942	Dave Gassner (RC)	.50
943	Jason Kubel (RC)	.50
944	Brian Bannister (RC)	.50
945	Mike Thompson RC	.50
946	Cole Hamels (RC)	2.00
947	Paul Maholm (RC)	.50
948	John Van Benschoten (RC)	.50
949	Nate McLouth (RC)	.50
950	Ben Johnson (RC)	.50
951	Josh Barfield (RC)	.50
952	Travis Ishikawa (RC)	.50
953	Jack Taschner (RC)	.50
954	Kenji Johjima RC	3.00
955	Skip Schumaker (RC)	.50
956	Ruddy Lugo (RC)	.50
957	Jason Hammel (RC)	.50
958	Chris Roberson (RC)	.50
959	Fabio Castro RC	.50
960	Ian Kinsler (RC)	.50
961	John Koronka (RC)	.50
962	Brandon Watson (RC)	.50
963	Jon Lester RC	3.00
964	Ben Hendrickson (RC)	.50
965	Martin Prado (RC)	.50
966	Erick Aybar (RC)	.50
967	Bobby Livingston (RC)	.50
968	Ryan Spilborghs (RC)	.50
969	Tommy Murphy (RC)	.50
970	Howie Kendrick (RC)	1.50
971	Casey Janssen (RC)	.50
972	Michael O'Connor RC	.50
973	Conor Jackson (RC)	1.00
974	Jeremy Hermida (RC)	.50
975	Renyel Pinto (RC)	.50
976	Prince Fielder (RC)	2.00
977	Kevin Frandsen (RC)	.50
978	Ty Taubenheim RC	.50
979	Rich Hill (RC)	.50
980	Jonathan Broxton (RC)	.50
981	Jamie Shields RC	.50
982	Carlos Villanueva RC	1.00
983	Boone Logan RC	.50
984	Brian Wilson RC	.50
985	Andre Ethier (RC)	2.00
986	Michael Napoli RC	1.00
987	Agustin Montero (RC)	.50
988	Jack Hannahan RC	.50
989	Boof Bonser (RC)	.50
990	Carlos Ruiz (RC)	.75
991	Jason Botts (RC)	.50
992	Kendry Morales (RC)	.50
993	Alay Soler (RC)	.50
994	Santiago Ramirez (RC)	.50
995	Saul Rivera (RC)	.50
996	Anthony Reyes (RC)	1.00
997	Matthew Kemp (RC)	1.00
998	Jae-Kuk Ryu (RC)	1.50
999	Lastings Milledge (RC)	1.00
1000	Jered Weaver (RC)	2.00
1001	Jeremy Sowers (RC)	1.00
1002	Chad Billingsley (RC)	1.00
1003	Stephen Drew (RC)	1.00
1004	Tony Gwynn (RC)	.50
1005	Melky Cabrera (RC)	.50
1006	Eliezer Alfonzo RC	.50
1007	Dana Eveland (RC)	.50
1008	Luis Figueroa RC	.50
1009	Emiliano Fruto RC	.50
1010	Clay Hensley (RC)	.50
1011	Zach Jackson (RC)	.50
1012	Bobby Keppel (RC)	.50
1013	Carlos Marmol RC	1.00
1014	Russell Martin (RC)	1.00
1015	Leo Nunez (RC)	.50
1016	Ken Ray (RC)	.50
1017	Mike Rouse (RC)	.50
1018	Kevin Thompson (RC)	.50
1019	C.J. Wilson (RC)	.50
1020	Steve Andrade (RC)	.50
1021	Ed Rogers (RC)	.50
1022	Joe Nelson (RC)	.50
1023	Omar Quintanilla (RC)	.50
1024	Chris Bootcheck (RC)	.50
1025	Jason Childers RC	.50

Blue

Blue (1-900):	1-1.5X
Blue RC:	1X
Inserted 1:4	

Green

Green (1-900):	2-3X
Green RC:	1-2X
Production 99 Sets	

Purple

Purple (1-900):	2-3X
Purple RC:	1-2X
Production 150 Sets	

Red

Red (1-900):	3-4X
Red RC:	2-3X
Production 50 Sets	

Materials

Code	Player	NM/M
	Common Player:	5.00
JB	Jason Bay	8.00
LB	Lance Berkman	5.00
MC	Miguel Cabrera	10.00
MA	Matt Cain	5.00
CA	Chris Carpenter	8.00
CC	Carl Crawford	5.00
CR	Coco Crisp	5.00
AD	Adam Dunn	8.00
PF	Prince Fielder	10.00
RF	Rafael Furcal	5.00
JG	Jason Giambi	5.00
TG	Troy Glaus	5.00
KG	Ken Griffey Jr.	15.00
VG	Vladimir Guerrero	8.00
HA	Roy Halladay	8.00
CH	Cole Hamels	15.00
JH	Jeremy Hermida	5.00
FH	Felix Hernandez	10.00
RH	Ryan Howard	20.00
DJ	Derek Jeter	20.00
KJ	Kenji Johjima	15.00
AJ	Andruw Jones	8.00
SK	Scott Kazmir	5.00
IK	Ian Kinsler	5.00
DL	Derek Lee	10.00
FL	Francisco Liriano	10.00
PM	Pedro Martinez	8.00
VM	Victor Martinez	5.00
JM	Joe Mauer	10.00
LM	Lastings Milledge	10.00
KM	Kendry Morales	5.00
DO	David Ortiz	15.00
JP	Jonathan Papelbon	10.00
AP	Albert Pujols	20.00
HR	Hanley Ramirez	5.00
JR	Jose Reyes	5.00
JS	Johan Santana	10.00
GS	Grady Sizemore	10.00
AS	Alfonso Soriano	8.00
MT	Mark Teixeira	8.00
TE	Miguel Tejada	8.00
JT	Jim Thome	10.00
CU	Chase Utley	8.00
JV	Justin Verlander	15.00
WE	Jered Weaver	10.00
RW	Rickie Weeks	8.00
JW	Josh Willingham	8.00
RZ	Ryan Zimmerman	15.00

Player Highlights

No.	Player	NM/M
	Common Player:	.50
1	Andruw Jones	1.00
2	Manny Ramirez	1.00
3	Travis Hafner	.75
4	Johnny Damon	.50
5	Miguel Cabrera	1.00
6	Chris Carpenter	.50
7	Derek Lee	1.00
8	Jason Bay	.75
9	Jason Varitek	1.00
10	Ryan Howard	3.00
11	Mark Teixeira	1.00
12	Carlos Delgado	.75
13	Bartolo Colon	.50
14	David Wright	2.00
15	Miguel Cabrera	.75
16	Mike Piazza	1.50
17	Paul Konerko	.75
18	Jermaine Dye	.50
19	Ichiro Suzuki	2.00
20	Brad Wilkerson	.50
21	Hideki Matsui	2.00
22	Albert Pujols	3.00
23	Chris Burke	.50
24	Derek Jeter	3.00
25	Brian Roberts	.50
26	David Ortiz	1.00
27	Alex Rodriguez	2.00
28	Ken Griffey Jr.	2.00
29	Prince Fielder	.75
30	Bobby Abreu	.75
31	Vladimir Guerrero	1.00
32	Tadahito Iguchi	.50
33	Jose Reyes	.75
34	Scott Podsednik	.50
35	Gary Sheffield	.75

Run Producers

No.	Player	NM/M
	Common Player:	1.00
1	Ty Cobb	3.00
2	Derrek Lee	1.50
3	Andruw Jones	1.50
4	David Ortiz	1.50
5	Lou Gehrig	4.00
6	Ken Griffey Jr.	4.00
7	Albert Pujols	5.00
8	Derek Jeter	5.00
9	Manny Ramirez	1.50
10	Alex Rodriguez	5.00
11	Gary Sheffield	1.00
12	Miguel Cabrera	1.50
13	Hideki Matsui	3.00
14	Vladimir Guerrero	1.50
15	David Wright	3.00
16	Mike Schmidt	1.50
17	Mark Teixeira	1.00
18	Babe Ruth	5.00
19	Jimmie Foxx	3.00
20	Honus Wagner	3.00

Special Endorsements

Code	Player	NM/M
	Common Player:	5.00
	Inserted 1:16	
RA	Reggie Abercrombie	5.00
AC	Jeremy Accardo	5.00
BA	Brian Anderson	5.00
AN	Robert Andino	5.00
BR	Brian Bannister	10.00
JB	Jason Bay	20.00
BW	Craig Breslow	8.00
CB	Chris Britton	5.00
TB	Taylor Buchholz	10.00
FB	Freddie Bynum	8.00
MI	Miguel Cabrera	25.00
MC	Matt Cain	20.00
JC	Jose Capellan/SP	8.00
MS	Matt Capps	5.00
FC	Fausto Carmona	5.00
TC	Tim Corcoran	5.00
DE	Chris Denorfia	5.00
JD	Joey Devine	8.00
JO	Andre Ethier	10.00
EV	Dana Eveland	10.00
RF	Ron Flores	5.00
KF	Kevin Frandsen /	8.00
DG	Dave Gassner	8.00
DG	Ken Griffey Jr.	60.00
TH	Travis Hafner	15.00
CH	Cole Hamels	30.00
BH	Brendan Harris	5.00
HA	Jeff Harris	5.00
HG	Keith Hattig	8.00
HE	Jeremy Hermida	15.00
AH	Anderson Hernandez/SP	5.00
JU	Justin Huber	8.00
JA	Conor Jackson	15.00
MJ	Mike Jacobs	8.00
DJ	Derek Jeter	200.00
BJ	Ben Johnson	8.00
JJ	Josh Johnson	10.00
KE	Howie Kendrick	20.00
IK	Ian Kinsler	15.00
KO	John Koronka	8.00
JK	Jason Kubel	8.00
HK	Hong-Chih Kuo	50.00
FL	Francisco Liriano	20.00
BL	Boone Logan	5.00
RL	Ruddy Lugo	5.00
PM	Paul Maholm	8.00
SM	Sean Marshall	10.00
NI	Nick Massett	8.00
MM	Macay McBride	8.00
NM	Nate McLouth	8.00
KM	Kendry Morales	10.00
PE	Peter Moylan	8.00
FN	Fernando Nieve	5.00
WN	Wilbert Nieves	8.00
JP	Jonathan Papelbon	30.00
AA	Aaron Rakers	5.00
HR	Hanley Ramirez	20.00
RE	Chris Resop	5.00
RB	Chris Roberson	10.00
CR	Cody Ross	8.00
RC	Carlos Ruiz	10.00
RU	Josh Rupe	8.00
TS	Takashi Saito	30.00
RS	Ryan Shealy	15.00
JS	Jamie Shields	10.00
KS	Kelly Shoppach	8.00
MS	Matt Smith	8.00
GS	Geovany Soto	8.00
DU	Dan Uggla	5.00
CU	Chase Utley	40.00
JV	John Van Benschoten	5.00
VE	Justin Verlander/SP	20.00
AW	Adam Wainwright	20.00
RW	Rickie Weeks	8.00
WI	Josh Willingham	15.00
DW	Dontrelle Willis	20.00
JO	Josh Wilson	8.00

RZ	Ryan Zimmerman/SP	40.00
JZ	Joel Zumaya	25.00

Star Attractions

NM/M

Common Player: .50
Inserted 1:8

BA	Bobby Abreu	.75
JB	Josh Beckett	.50
CB	Carlos Beltran	1.00
LB	Lance Berkman	.75
JC	Jose Contreras	.50
CD	Carlos Delgado	.75
JE	Jim Edmonds	.75
JG	Jason Giambi	1.00
KG	Ken Griffey Jr.	3.00
RH	Rich Harden	.50
DJ	Derek Jeter	4.00
AJ	Andruw Jones	1.00
CJ	Chipper Jones	1.50
DL	Derek Lee	1.50
GM	Greg Maddux	3.00
PM	Pedro Martinez	1.50
JM	Joe Mauer	1.00
MO	Magglio Ordonez	1.50
DO	David Ortiz	1.50
PU	Albert Pujols	4.00
MR	Manny Ramirez	1.50
JR	Jose Reyes	1.50
CS	Curt Schilling	1.50
JS	Jason Schmidt	.50
SM	John Smoltz	.50
AS	Alfonso Soriano	1.50
MT	Mark Teixeira	1.00
DW	Dontrelle Willis	.50
WR	David Wright	2.50

WBC Counterparts

NM/M

Common Duo: 1.00
Inserted 1:6

1	Yulieski Gourriel, Daisuke Matsuzaka	5.00
2	Ken Griffey Jr., Yoandy Garlobo	3.00
3	Ken Griffey Jr., Ichiro Suzuki	3.00
4	Derek Jeter, Chin-Lung Hu	4.00
5	Frederich Cepeda, Jong Beom Lee	
6	Nobuhiko Matsunaka, Seung-Yeop Lee	2.00
7	Tsuyoshi Nishioka, Guangbiao Liu	1.00
8	Ichiro Suzuki, Osmany Urrutia	2.50
9	Daisuke Matsuzaka, Roger Clemens	8.00
10	Yadel Marti, Chan Ho Park	1.00
11	Koji Uehara, Jae Weong Seo	1.00
12	Shunsuke Watanabe, Bartolo Colon	2.00
13	Daisuke Matsuzaka, Johan Santana	5.00
14	Pedro Luis Lazo, Freddy Garcia	1.00
15	Koji Uehara, Roger Clemens	3.00

2006 Upper Deck Sweet Spot

NM/M

Complete Set (184):
Common Player: .25
Common Auto. (101-184): 15.00
Production 45-275

Pack (5): 10.00
Box (12): 110.00

1	Bartolo Colon	.25
2	Garret Anderson	.25
3	Francisco Rodriguez	.25
4	Dallas McPherson	.25
5	Andy Pettitte	.40
6	Lance Berkman	.50
7	Willy Taveras	.25
8	Bobby Crosby	.25
9	Danny Haren	.25
10	Nick Swisher	.25
11	Vernon Wells	.50
12	Orlando Hudson	.25
13	Roy Halladay	.50
14	Andruw Jones	.75
15	Chipper Jones	.75
16	Jeff Francoeur	.40
17	John Smoltz	.50
18	Carlos Lee	.40
19	Rickie Weeks	.25
20	Bill Hall	.25
21	Jim Edmonds	.40
22	David Eckstein	.25
23	Mark Mulder	.40

24	Aramis Ramirez	.50
25	Greg Maddux	1.50
26	Nomar Garciaparra	.75
27	Carlos Zambrano	.40
28	Scott Kazmir	.40
29	Jorge Cantu	.25
30	Carl Crawford	.40
31	Luis Gonzalez	.25
32	Troy Glaus	.25
33	Shawn Green	.25
34	Jeff Kent	.40
35	Milton Bradley	.25
36	Cesar Izturis	.25
37	Omar Vizquel	.25
38	Moises Alou	.40
39	Randy Winn	.25
40	Jason Schmidt	.40
41	Coco Crisp	.25
42	C.C. Sabathia	.40
43	Cliff Lee	.25
44	Ichiro Suzuki	1.50
45	Richie Sexson	.50
46	Jeremy Reed	.25
47	Carlos Delgado	.50
48	Miguel Cabrera	.75
49	Luis Castillo	.25
50	Carlos Beltran	.50
51	Tom Glavine	.50
52	David Wright	1.50
53	Cliff Floyd	.25
54	Chad Cordero	.25
55	Jose Vidro	.25
56	Jose Guillen	.25
57	Nick Johnson	.25
58	Miguel Tejada	.50
59	Melvin Mora	.25
60	Javy Lopez	.25
61	Khalil Greene	.25
62	Brian Giles	.25
63	Trevor Hoffman	.25
64	Bobby Abreu	.40
65	Jimmy Rollins	.25
66	Pat Burrell	.40
67	Billy Wagner	.25
68	Jack Wilson	.25
69	Zachary Duke	.25
70	Craig Wilson	.25
71	Mark Teixeira	.40
72	Hank Blalock	.40
73	David Dellucci	.25
74	Manny Ramirez	.75
75	Johnny Damon	.75
76	Jason Varitek	.50
77	Trot Nixon	.25
78	Adam Dunn	.50
79	Felipe Lopez	.25
80	Brandon Claussen	.25
81	Sean Casey	.25
82	Todd Helton	.50
83	Clint Barmes	.25
84	Matt Holliday	.25
85	Mike Sweeney	.25
86	Zack Greinke	.25
87	David DeJesus	.25
88	Ivan Rodriguez	.50
89	Jeremy Bonderman	.25
90	Magglio Ordonez	.40
91	Torii Hunter	.40
92	Joe Nathan	.25
93	Michael Cuddyer	.25
94	Paul Konerko	.50
95	Jermaine Dye	.25
96	Jon Garland	.25
97	Alex Rodriguez	2.00
98	Hideki Matsui	1.50
99	Jason Giambi	.50
100	Mariano Rivera	.40
101	Adrian Beltre/99	25.00
102	Matt Cain/275 (RC)	30.00
103	Craig Biggio/99	35.00
104	Eric Chavez/99	25.00
105	J.D. Drew/99	25.00
106	Eric Gagne/99	50.00
107	Tim Hudson/275	40.00
108	Tom Glavine/275	40.00
109	David Ortiz/99	85.00
110	Scott Rolen/275	25.00
111	Johan Santana/99	50.00
112	Curt Schilling/96	75.00
113	John Smoltz/99	50.00
114	Alfonso Soriano/99	75.00
115	Kerry Wood/99	25.00
116	Edwin Jackson/99	20.00
117	Felix Hernandez/125	50.00
118	Prince Fielder/99 (RC)	100.00
119	Vladimir Guerrero/86	75.00
120	Roger Clemens/99	140.00
121	Albert Pujols/85	250.00
122	Chris Carpenter/99	25.00
123	Derek Lee/99	40.00
124	Dontrelle Willis/99	30.00
125	Roy Oswalt/99	35.00
126	Ryan Garko/275 (RC)	25.00
127	Tadahito Iguchi/275	60.00
128	Mark Loretta/275	25.00
129	Joe Mauer/275	40.00
130	Victor Martinez/275	20.00
131	Wily Mo Pena/275	30.00
132	Oliver Perez/274	15.00
133	Corey Patterson/275	25.00
134	Ben Sheets/275	20.00
135	Michael Young/275	25.00
136	Jonny Gomes/275	25.00
137	Derek Jeter/99	175.00
138	Ken Griffey Jr./275	100.00
139	Ryan Zimmerman/275 (RC)	60.00

140	Scott Baker/275 (RC)	20.00
141	Huston Street/275	30.00
142	Jason Bay/275	30.00
143	Ryan Howard/275	75.00
145	Travis Hafner/275	35.00
146	Brian Myrow/275 (RC)	20.00
147	Scott Podsednik/275	35.00
148	Brian Roberts/275	20.00
149	Grady Sizemore/135	45.00
150	Chris Demaria/275 (RC)	15.00
151	Jonah Bayliss/275 (RC)	20.00
152	Geovany Soto/275 (RC)	20.00
153	Lyle Overbay/275	20.00
154	Joey Devine/275 (RC)	20.00
155	Alejandro Freire/275 (RC)	15.00
156	Conor Jackson/275 (RC)	35.00
157	Danny Sandoval/275 (RC)	15.00
158	Chase Utley/275	50.00
159	Jeff Harris/275 (RC)	20.00
160	Ron Flores/275 (RC)	20.00
161	Scott Feldman/275 (RC)	20.00
162	Yadier Molina/275	30.00
163	Tim Corcoran/275 (RC)	20.00
164	Craig Hansen/275 (RC)	40.00
165	Jason Bergmann/275 (RC)	25.00
166	Craig Breslow/275 (RC)	25.00
167	Jhonny Peralta/275	30.00
168	Jeremy Hermida/275 (RC)	30.00
169	Scott Kazmir/275	25.00
170	Bobby Crosby/99	25.00
171	Rich Harden/275	25.00
172	Casey Kotchman/275	15.00
173	Tim Hamulack/275 (RC)	15.00
174	Justin Morneau/275	30.00
175	Jake Peavy/275	30.00
176	Yuniesky Betancourt/275	30.00
177	Jeremy Accardo/275 (RC)	25.00
178	Jorge Cantu/200	25.00
179	Marlon Byrd/275	20.00
180	Ryan Jorgensen/275 (RC)	20.00
181	Chris Denorfia/275 (RC)	20.00
182	Steve Stemle/275	15.00
183	Robert Andino/275 (RC)	20.00
184	Chris Heintz/275 RC	15.00

Signature Bat Barrel Black Ink

NM/M

Production 13-25

107	Tim Hudson/25	50.00
110	Scott Rolen/25	50.00
111	Johan Santana/25	60.00
115	Kerry Wood/25	30.00
117	Felix Hernandez/25	40.00
118	Prince Fielder/25	100.00
119	Vladimir Guerrero/25	75.00
121	Albert Pujols/25	275.00
125	Roy Oswalt/25	40.00
127	Tadahito Iguchi/25	90.00
131	Wily Mo Pena/25	40.00
139	Ryan Zimmerman/25	100.00
143	Ryan Howard/25	90.00
151	Jonah Bayliss/25	30.00
153	Lyle Overbay/25	30.00
154	Joey Devine/25	30.00
160	Ron Flores/25	30.00
167	Jhonny Peralta/25	40.00
174	Justin Morneau/25	40.00
178	Jorge Cantu/25	40.00
182	Steve Stemle/25	25.00

Signature Bat Barrel Blue Ink

No Pricing
Production 3-5 Sets

Signature Black Stitch Black Ink

No Pricing
Production One Set
Blue Ink: No Pricing
Production One Set

Signature Glove Leather Black Ink

No Pricing
Production 5-15
Blue Ink: No Pricing
Production 5-15

Signnature Red Stitch Blue Ink

NM/M

Production 15-150

101	Adrian Beltre/25	35.00

102	Matt Cain/150	40.00
103	Craig Biggio/25	50.00
106	Eric Gagne/25	60.00
107	Tim Hudson/25	40.00
109	David Ortiz/25	120.00
110	Scott Rolen/25	40.00
111	Johan Santana/25	60.00
112	Curt Schilling/25	100.00
113	John Smoltz/25	50.00
116	Edwin Jackson/25	20.00
118	Prince Fielder/25	100.00
119	Vladimir Guerrero/25	80.00
122	Chris Carpenter/25	50.00
123	Derrek Lee/25	60.00
124	Dontrelle Willis/25	40.00
125	Roy Oswalt/25	40.00
126	Ryan Garko/150	25.00
127	Tadahito Iguchi/150	75.00
128	Mark Loretta/114	35.00
129	Joe Mauer/150	40.00
130	Victor Martinez/150	35.00
131	Wily Mo Pena/150	40.00
132	Oliver Perez/135	15.00
133	Corey Patterson/150	30.00
134	Ben Sheets/150	20.00
135	Michael Young/150	30.00
136	Jonny Gomes/150	40.00
137	Derek Jeter/25	200.00
138	Ken Griffey Jr./150	100.00
139	Ryan Zimmerman/150	60.00
140	Scott Baker/150	20.00
141	Huston Street/150	40.00
142	Jason Bay/150	40.00
143	Ryan Howard/150	75.00
144	Mike Piazza/100	100.00
145	Travis Hafner/150	40.00
146	Brian Myrow/150	20.00
147	Scott Podsednik/150	40.00
148	Brian Roberts/150	20.00
149	Grady Sizemore/75	50.00
150	Chris Demaria/150	20.00
151	Jonah Bayliss/150	20.00
152	Geovany Soto/150	20.00
153	Lyle Overbay/150	20.00
154	Joey Devine/150	20.00
155	Alejandro Freire/150	20.00
156	Conor Jackson/150	40.00
157	Danny Sandoval/150	20.00
158	Chase Utley/150	50.00
159	Jeff Harris/150	20.00
160	Ron Flores/150	20.00
161	Scott Feldman/150	20.00
162	Yadier Molina/135	30.00
163	Tim Corcoran/150	20.00
164	Craig Hansen/150	40.00
165	Jason Bergmann/150	20.00
166	Craig Breslow/150	20.00
167	Jhonny Peralta/120	30.00
168	Jeremy Hermida/150	20.00
169	Scott Kazmir/150	35.00
170	Bobby Crosby/25	35.00
171	Rich Harden/150	25.00
172	Casey Kotchman/150	20.00
173	Tim Hamulack/150	20.00
174	Justin Morneau/150	35.00
175	Jake Peavy/150	40.00
176	Yuniesky Betancourt/150	30.00
177	Jeremy Accardo/150	20.00
178	Jorge Cantu/25	40.00
179	Marlon Byrd/40	20.00
180	Ryan Jorgensen/150	20.00
181	Chris Denorfia/150	20.00
182	Steve Stemle/150	15.00
183	Robert Andino/150	25.00
184	Chris Heintz/150	20.00

Signature Red-Blue Stitch Black Ink

NM/M

Production 25-99

101	Adrian Beltre/50	30.00
102	Matt Cain/99	40.00
103	Craig Biggio/50	50.00
105	J.D. Drew/50	30.00
106	Eric Gagne/50	50.00
107	Tim Hudson/50	40.00
108	Tom Glavine/99	50.00
109	David Ortiz/50	85.00
110	Scott Rolen/40	40.00
111	Johan Santana/50	60.00
112	Curt Schilling/45	80.00
113	John Smoltz/50	50.00
114	Alfonso Soriano/50	80.00
115	Kerry Wood/49	30.00
116	Edwin Jackson/50	20.00
117	Felix Hernandez/60	65.00
118	Prince Fielder/50	100.00
119	Vladimir Guerrero/50	50.00
120	Roger Clemens/50	150.00
121	Albert Pujols/50	250.00
122	Chris Carpenter/50	50.00
123	Derek Lee/50	40.00
124	Dontrelle Willis/50	30.00
125	Roy Oswalt/50	40.00
126	Ryan Garko/99	30.00
127	Tadahito Iguchi/99	75.00
128	Mark Loretta/99	35.00
129	Joe Mauer/99	50.00
130	Victor Martinez/99	35.00
131	Wily Mo Pena/99	40.00
132	Oliver Perez/99	15.00
133	Corey Patterson/99	30.00
134	Ben Sheets/99	25.00

135	Michael Young/99	30.00
136	Jonny Gomes/99	40.00
137	Derek Jeter/25	175.00
138	Ken Griffey Jr./99	100.00
139	Ryan Zimmerman/99	75.00
140	Scott Baker/99	20.00
141	Huston Street/99	35.00
142	Jason Bay/99	35.00
143	Ryan Howard/99	75.00
145	Travis Hafner/99	40.00
146	Brian Myrow/99	20.00
147	Scott Podsednik/99	40.00
148	Brian Roberts/99	25.00
149	Grady Sizemore/50	50.00
150	Chris Demaria/99	20.00
151	Jonah Bayliss/99	20.00
152	Geovany Soto/99	20.00
153	Lyle Overbay/99	20.00
154	Joey Devine/99	20.00
155	Alejandro Freire/99	20.00
156	Conor Jackson/99	40.00
157	Danny Sandoval/99	20.00
158	Chase Utley/99	50.00
159	Jeff Harris/99	20.00
160	Ron Flores/99	20.00
161	Scott Feldman/99	20.00
162	Yadier Molina/99	30.00
163	Tim Corcoran/99	20.00
164	Craig Hansen/99	40.00
165	Jason Bergmann/99	20.00
166	Craig Breslow/99	25.00
167	Jhonny Peralta/99	35.00
168	Jeremy Hermida/99	35.00
169	Scott Kazmir/99	35.00
170	Bobby Crosby/50	35.00
171	Rich Harden/99	25.00
172	Casey Kotchman/99	20.00
173	Tim Hamulack/99	20.00
174	Justin Morneau/99	35.00
175	Jake Peavy/99	30.00
176	Yuniesky Betancourt/99	30.00
177	Jeremy Accardo/99	25.00
178	Jorge Cantu/50	30.00
179	Marlon Byrd/99	25.00
180	Ryan Jorgensen/99	20.00
181	Chris Denorfia/99	25.00
182	Steve Stemle/99	15.00
183	Robert Andino/91	20.00
184	Chris Heintz/99	20.00

Signature Red-Blue Stitch Blue Ink

NM/M

Production 10-50

102	Matt Cain/40	40.00
110	Scott Rolen/50	40.00
116	Edwin Jackson/50	20.00
127	Tadahito Iguchi/50	75.00
128	Mark Loretta/50	40.00
129	Joe Mauer/50	40.00
130	Victor Martinez/50	35.00
131	Wily Mo Pena/50	35.00
132	Oliver Perez/30	20.00
133	Corey Patterson/50	30.00
134	Ben Sheets/50	25.00
136	Jonny Gomes/50	30.00
138	Ken Griffey Jr./50	125.00
139	Ryan Zimmerman/50	75.00
140	Scott Baker/50	20.00
141	Huston Street/50	40.00
142	Jason Bay/50	40.00
143	Ryan Howard/50	75.00
144	Mike Piazza/50	140.00
145	Travis Hafner/50	50.00
146	Brian Myrow/50	20.00
147	Scott Podsednik/50	40.00
148	Brian Roberts/50	25.00
149	Grady Sizemore/25	60.00
150	Chris Demaria/50	20.00
151	Jonah Bayliss/50	20.00
152	Geovany Soto/50	20.00
153	Lyle Overbay/50	20.00
154	Joey Devine/50	20.00
155	Alejandro Freire/50	20.00
156	Conor Jackson/50	40.00
157	Danny Sandoval/50	20.00
158	Chase Utley/50	60.00
159	Jeff Harris/50	20.00
160	Ron Flores/50	20.00
161	Scott Feldman/50	20.00
162	Yadier Molina/30	40.00
163	Tim Corcoran/50	20.00
164	Craig Hansen/50	50.00
165	Jason Bergmann/50	20.00
166	Craig Breslow/50	25.00
167	Jhonny Peralta/50	35.00
168	Jeremy Hermida/50	40.00
170	Bobby Crosby/50	25.00
171	Rich Harden/50	25.00
172	Casey Kotchman/50	20.00
173	Tim Hamulack/50	20.00
174	Justin Morneau/50	35.00
175	Jake Peavy/49	30.00
180	Ryan Jorgensen/50	20.00
181	Chris Denorfia/50	20.00
182	Steve Stemle/50	15.00
183	Robert Andino/50	20.00
184	Chris Heintz/50	20.00

Super Sweet Swatch

NM/M

Production 299 Sets

	Gold:	1-2X
	Production 75 Sets	
	Platinum:	1.5-3X
	Production 45 Sets	
BA	Bobby Abreu	8.00
GA	Garret Anderson	5.00
AT	Garrett Atkins	5.00
JB	Jeff Bagwell	10.00
RB	Rocco Baldelli	8.00
JB	Jason Bay	10.00
BE	Josh Beckett	8.00
LB	Lance Berkman	10.00
CB	Craig Biggio	6.00
HB	Hank Blalock	6.00
MI	Miguel Cabrera	12.00
MA	Matt Cain	8.00
EC	Eric Chavez	5.00
BC	Brandon Claussen	5.00
MC	Matt Clement	5.00
CR	Bobby Crosby/136	5.00
CD	Carlos Delgado	8.00
ZD	Zachary Duke	5.00
AD	Adam Dunn	8.00
DY	Jermaine Dye	5.00
AE	Adam Eaton	5.00
ED	Jim Edmonds	8.00
JE	Johnny Estrada	5.00
PF	Prince Fielder	20.00
FR	Jeff Francoeur	10.00
EG	Eric Gagne	6.00
FG	Freddy Garcia	5.00
JG	Jason Giambi	10.00
BG	Brian Giles	5.00
MG	Marcus Giles	5.00
TG	Troy Glaus/160	8.00
GL	Tom Glavine	8.00
KG	Ken Griffey Jr.	30.00
VG	Vladimir Guerrero	12.00
HA	Travis Hafner	10.00
HY	Roy Halladay	8.00
TO	Todd Helton/232	10.00
FH	Felix Hernandez	5.00
HE	Ramon Hernandez	5.00
HO	Trevor Hoffman	5.00
RH	Ryan Howard	20.00
TH	Tim Hudson	8.00
HU	Torii Hunter	6.00
DJ	Derek Jeter	30.00
NJ	Nick Johnson	5.00
AJ	Andruw Jones	10.00
CJ	Chipper Jones	10.00
JJ	Jacque Jones	5.00
SK	Scott Kazmir	8.00
RK	Ryan Klesko	5.00
KO	Paul Konerko	10.00
DL	Derek Lee	8.00
ML	Mark Loretta	6.00
NL	Noah Lowry	5.00
PM	Pedro Martinez	15.00
VM	Victor Martinez	5.00
JM	Joe Mauer	12.00
JU	Justin Morneau	8.00
MM	Mark Mulder	5.00
TN	Trot Nixon	8.00
DO	David Ortiz	12.00
RO	Roy Oswalt	5.00
JA	Jay Payton	5.00
PE	Jake Peavy	5.00
AN	Andy Pettitte	5.00
PI	Mike Piazza	15.00
JP	Jorge Posada	12.00
MP	Mark Prior	5.00
AP	Albert Pujols	30.00
MR	Manny Ramirez	12.00
JR	Jose Reyes	8.00
IR	Ivan Rodriguez/193	10.00
SR	Scott Rolen	5.00
SA	Johan Santana	10.00
CS	Curt Schilling	10.00
JS	Jason Schmidt	5.00
RS	Richie Sexson	10.00
BS	Ben Sheets	8.00
GS	Gary Sheffield	12.00
GR	Grady Sizemore	20.00
JO	John Smoltz	10.00
ST	Huston Street	8.00
MS	Mike Sweeney	5.00
NS	Nick Swisher	10.00
TX	Mark Teixeira	10.00
MT	Miguel Tejada	10.00
FT	Frank Thomas	20.00
JV	Jason Varitek	15.00
RW	Rickie Weeks	10.00
WE	David Wells	5.00
VW	Vernon Wells	10.00
BW	Bernie Williams	10.00
DW	Dontrelle Willis	8.00
JW	Jack Wilson	5.00
KW	Kerry Wood	8.00
RZ	Ryan Zimmerman	15.00
BZ	Barry Zito	6.00

2006 UD Sweet Spot Update

NM/M

Complete Set (182):
Common Player (1-100): .25
Common Auto. (101-184): 10.00
Production 98-499

Pack (5): 10.00
Box (12): 110.00

1	Luis Gonzalez	.25
2	Chad Tracy	.25
3	Brandon Webb	.50
4	Andruw Jones	1.00
5	Chipper Jones	1.00

#	Player	Price
6	John Smoltz	.50
7	Tim Hudson	.50
8	Miguel Tejada	.50
9	Brian Roberts	.25
10	Ramon Hernandez	.25
11	Curt Schilling	.75
12	David Ortiz	1.00
13	Manny Ramirez	1.00
14	Jason Varitek	1.00
15	Josh Beckett	.50
16	Greg Maddux	2.00
17	Derrek Lee	.75
18	Mark Prior	.75
19	Aramis Ramirez	.50
20	Jim Thome	.75
21	Paul Konerko	.75
22	Scott Podsednik	.50
23	Jose Contreras	.25
24	Ken Griffey Jr.	2.00
25	Adam Dunn	.75
26	Felipe Lopez	.25
27	Travis Hafner	.50
28	Victor Martinez	.25
29	Grady Sizemore	.75
30	Jhonny Peralta	.25
31	Todd Helton	.75
32	Garrett Atkins	.25
33	Clint Barmes	.25
34	Ivan Rodriguez	.75
35	Chris Shelton	.25
36	Jeremy Bonderman	.50
37	Miguel Cabrera	1.00
38	Dontrelle Willis	.50
39	Lance Berkman	.50
40	Morgan Ensberg	.25
41	Roy Oswalt	.50
42	Reggie Sanders	.25
43	Mike Sweeney	.25
44	Vladimir Guerrero	1.00
45	Bartolo Colon	.50
46	Chone Figgins	.25
47	Nomar Garciaparra	1.00
48	Jeff Kent	.50
49	J.D. Drew	.50
50	Carlos Lee	.50
51	Ben Sheets	.50
52	Rickie Weeks	.50
53	Johan Santana	1.00
54	Torii Hunter	.50
55	Joe Mauer	.75
56	Pedro Martinez	1.00
57	David Wright	2.00
58	Carlos Beltran	.75
59	Carlos Delgado	.75
60	Jose Reyes	.75
61	Derek Jeter	3.00
62	Alex Rodriguez	2.50
63	Randy Johnson	1.00
64	Hideki Matsui	2.00
65	Gary Sheffield	.75
66	Rich Harden	.50
67	Eric Chavez	.50
68	Huston Street	.25
69	Bobby Crosby	.25
70	Bobby Abreu	.50
71	Ryan Howard	2.00
72	Chase Utley	1.00
73	Pat Burrell	.50
74	Jason Bay	.50
75	Sean Casey	.50
76	Mike Piazza	1.50
77	Jake Peavy	.50
78	Brian Giles	.25
79	Milton Bradley	.25
80	Omar Vizquel	.50
81	Jason Schmidt	.50
82	Ichiro Suzuki	2.00
83	Felix Hernandez	.50
84	Kenji Johjima	.50
85	Albert Pujols	3.00
86	Chris Carpenter	.75
87	Scott Rolen	1.00
88	Jim Edmonds	.50
89	Carl Crawford	.50
90	Jonny Gomes	.25
91	Scott Kazmir	.50
92	Mark Teixeira	.75
93	Michael Young	.50
94	Phil Nevin	.25
95	Vernon Wells	.50
96	Roy Halladay	.50
97	Troy Glaus	.50
98	Alfonso Soriano	1.00
99	Nick Johnson	.25
100	Jose Vidro	.25
101	Adam Wainwright/100 (RC)	40.00

#	Player	Price
102	Anderson Hernandez/100 (RC)	15.00
103	Andre Ethier/150 (RC)	35.00
104	Jason Botts/100 (RC)	15.00
105	Ben Johnson/400 (RC)	10.00
106	Boof Bonser/100 (RC)	20.00
107	Boone Logan/200 RC	10.00
108	Brian Anderson/200 (RC)	10.00
109	Brian Bannister/100 (RC)	15.00
110	Chris Denorfia/100 (RC)	10.00
111	Agustin Montero/100 (RC)	15.00
112	Cody Ross/100 (RC)	10.00
113	Cole Hamels/399 (RC)	35.00
114	Conor Jackson/400 (RC)	10.00
115	Dan Uglay/125 (RC)	25.00
116	Dave Gassner/100 (RC)	10.00
117	C.J. Wilson/150 (RC)	10.00
118	Eric Reed/150 (RC)	10.00
119	Fausto Carmona/99 (RC)	10.00
120	Fernando Nieve/100 (RC)	10.00
121	Francisco Liriano/499 (RC)	25.00
122	Freddie Bynum/100 (RC)	10.00
123	Hanley Ramirez/100 (RC)	30.00
124	Hong-Chih Kuo/100 (RC)	125.00
125	Ian Kinsler/100 (RC)	40.00
126	Carlos Marmol/100 RC	15.00
127	Bobby Keppel/200 (RC)	10.00
128	Jason Kubel/100 (RC)	15.00
129	Jeff Harris/100 RC	15.00
130	Alay Soler/100 RC	15.00
131	Jered Weaver/100 (RC)	30.00
132	Carlos Quentin/100 (RC)	30.00
133	Jeremy Hermida/100 (RC)	20.00
134	Joel Zumaya/100 (RC)	50.00
135	Joey Devine/100 RC	15.00
136	John Koronka/98 (RC)	10.00
137	Jonathan Papelbon/399 (RC)	40.00
138	Jose Capellan/240 (RC)	10.00
139	Josh Johnson/100 (RC)	20.00
140	Josh Rupe/100 (RC)	10.00
141	Josh Willingham/100 (RC)	20.00
143	Justin Verlander/100 (RC)	40.00
144	Kelly Shoppach/100 (RC)	10.00
145	Kendry Morales/100 (RC)	20.00
146	Kevin Thompson/100 (RC)	10.00
147	Macay McBride/100 (RC)	15.00
148	Martin Prado/100 (RC)	10.00
149	Matt Cain/150 (RC)	25.00
150	Clay Hensley/100 (RC)	10.00
151	Ty Taubenheim/100 RC	30.00
152	Mike Jacobs/200 (RC)	15.00
153	Saul Rivera/100 (RC)	15.00
154	Mike Thompson/100 (RC)	15.00
155	Nate McLouth/100 (RC)	15.00
156	Michael Vento/100 (RC)	15.00
157	Paul Maholm/100 (RC)	10.00
159	Reggie Abercrombie/100 (RC)	15.00
160	Mike Rouse/100 (RC)	10.00
161	Ken Ray/100 (RC)	15.00
162	Ron Flores/100 RC	15.00
163	Ryan Zimmerman/100 (RC)	50.00
164	Erick Aybar/100 (RC)	20.00
165	Sean Marshall/150 (RC)	20.00
166	Takashi Saito/100 RC	40.00
167	Taylor Buchholz/100 (RC)	15.00
168	Matt Murton/100 (RC)	30.00
169	Luis Figueroa/100 RC	15.00
170	Wilbert Nieves/100 (RC)	15.00
171	James Shields/100 RC	20.00
172	Jon Lester/399 (RC)	30.00

#	Player	Price
173	Craig Hansen/100 RC	30.00
174	Aaron Rakers/100 (RC)	10.00
175	Bobby Livingston/100 (RC)	15.00
176	Brendan Harris/100 (RC)	10.00
177	Zach Jackson/100 (RC)	15.00
178	Chris Britton/100 RC	10.00
179	Howie Kendrick/399 (RC)	25.00
180	Zach Miner/100 (RC)	15.00
181	Kevin Frandsen/100 (RC)	15.00
182	Matt Capps/100 (RC)	10.00
183	Peter Moylan/100 RC	15.00
184	Melky Cabrera/100 (RC)	50.00

Signature Red/Blue Stitch Red Ink
NM/M

Production 40-225

#	Player	Price
101	Adam Wainwright/50	40.00
103	Andre Ethier/50	40.00
105	Ben Johnson/100	10.00
106	Boof Bonser/50	20.00
107	Boone Logan/50	15.00
108	Brian Anderson/100	10.00
109	Brian Bannister/100	15.00
110	Chris Denorfia/50	10.00
112	Cody Ross/50	10.00
113	Cole Hamels/225	40.00
114	Conor Jackson/100	10.00
115	Dan Uggla/50	30.00
116	Dave Gassner/50	10.00
117	C.J. Wilson/50	10.00
118	Eric Reed/100	10.00
119	Fausto Carmona/50	10.00
120	Fernando Nieve/50	10.00
121	Francisco Liriano/175	30.00
122	Freddie Bynum/50	10.00
123	Hanley Ramirez/50	30.00
124	Hong-Chih Kuo/50	200.00
125	Ian Kinsler/45	50.00
126	Carlos Marmol/50	20.00
127	Bobby Keppel/100	10.00
128	Jason Kubel/50	20.00
130	Alay Soler/50	20.00
131	Jered Weaver/40	40.00
132	Carlos Quentin/50	30.00
133	Jeremy Hermida/50	20.00
134	Joel Zumaya/50	50.00
135	Joey Devine/50	20.00
136	John Koronka/50	10.00
137	Jonathan Papelbon/175	50.00
138	Jose Capellan/100	20.00
139	Josh Johnson/100	20.00
140	Josh Rupe/50	10.00
141	Josh Willingham/50	20.00
143	Justin Verlander/50	50.00
144	Kelly Shoppach/50	15.00
146	Kevin Thompson/50	15.00
147	Macay McBride/50	15.00
150	Clay Hensley/49	10.00
151	Ty Taubenheim/50	35.00
152	Mike Jacobs/100	15.00
153	Saul Rivera/50	10.00
154	Mike Thompson/50	15.00
155	Nate McLouth/50	15.00
156	Michael Vento/50	15.00
159	Reggie Abercrombie/50	15.00
160	Mike Rouse/50	10.00
161	Ken Ray/50	15.00
162	Ron Flores/50	10.00
163	Ryan Zimmerman/50	60.00
164	Erick Aybar/50	20.00
165	Sean Marshall/50	30.00
167	Taylor Buchholz/50	15.00
168	Matt Murton/50	40.00
169	Luis Figueroa/50	20.00
170	Wilbert Nieves/50	20.00
171	James Shields/50	20.00
172	Jon Lester/175	40.00
174	Aaron Rakers/50	10.00
175	Bobby Livingston/50	20.00
176	Brendan Harris/50	10.00
177	Zach Jackson/50	20.00
178	Chris Britton/50	10.00
179	Howie Kendrick/175	30.00
181	Kevin Frandsen/50	10.00
182	Matt Capps/50	10.00
183	Peter Moylan/50	10.00

Veteran Red Stitch Blue Ink
NM/M

Production 30-525

#	Player	Price
AG	Tony Gwynn Jr./425	20.00
AH	Aaron Harang/425	20.00
AP	Albert Pujols/50	250.00
AZ	Aramis Ramirez/225	25.00
BJ	B.J. Upton/193	15.00
BR	Brian Roberts/300	15.00
CC	Carl Crawford/425	15.00
CU	Chase Utley/425	40.00
DJ	Derek Jeter/75	200.00
DW	Dontrelle Willis/125	25.00
HS	Huston Street/200	15.00
JB	Jason Bay/425	20.00
JM	Joe Mauer/57	70.00

#	Player	Price
JN	Joe Nathan/200	20.00
JS	Jeremy Sowers/425	20.00
JT	Jim Thome/75	35.00
KG	Ken Griffey Jr./359	80.00
KG2	Ken Griffey Jr./358	80.00
KY	Kevin Youkilis/425	25.00
LO	Lyle Overbay/525	15.00
MC	Miguel Cabrera/525	40.00
MO	Justin Morneau/425	25.00
RC	Roger Clemens/35	150.00
SD	Stephen Drew/525	25.00
SK	Scott Kazmir/522	25.00
SM	John Smoltz/507	20.00
SP	Scott Podsednik/247	15.00
SS	Mark Mulder/300	15.00
TH	Travis Hafner/525	25.00
TI	Tadahito Iguchi/425	30.00
VM	Victor Martinez/71	20.00

Veteran Red/Blue Stitch Red Ink
NM/M

Production 10-299

#	Player	Price
AG	Tony Gwynn Jr./299	25.00
AH	Aaron Harang/299	20.00
AZ	Aramis Ramirez/99	30.00
BJ	B.J. Upton/100	25.00
BR	Brian Roberts/100	20.00
CC	Carl Crawford/299	20.00
CU	Chase Utley/299	40.00
DW	Dontrelle Willis/35	35.00
HS	Huston Street/100	20.00
JB	Jason Bay/299	20.00
JN	Joe Nathan/100	20.00
JS	Jeremy Sowers/299	20.00
KG	Ken Griffey Jr./38	120.00
KG2	Ken Griffey Jr./37	120.00
KY	Kevin Youkilis/299	30.00
LO	Lyle Overbay/299	15.00
MC	Miguel Cabrera/299	30.00
MO	Justin Morneau/299	30.00
SD	Stephen Drew/299	20.00
SK	Scott Kazmir/296	25.00
SP	Scott Podsednik/199	15.00
SS	Mark Mulder/298	15.00
TH	Travis Hafner/299	25.00
TI	Tadahito Iguchi/299	40.00
VM	Victor Martinez/61	20.00

Signatures Black Stitch/Ink

No Pricing
Production One Set

Sweet Beginnings Swatches
NM/M

Common Player: 5.00

#	Player	Price
AB	Adrian Beltre	5.00
AI	Akinori Iwamura	40.00
AJ	Andruw Jones	10.00
AP	Ariel Pestano	5.00
AR	Alex Rios	8.00
AS	Alfonso Soriano	10.00
BA	Bobby Abreu	5.00
BB	Brian Bannister	5.00
BI	Chad Billingsley	10.00
BW	Bernie Williams	10.00
CA	Miguel Cabrera	10.00
CB	Carlos Beltran	10.00
CD	Carlos Delgado	8.00
CH	Chin-Lung Hu	50.00
CJ	Conor Jackson	5.00
CL	Carlos Lee	5.00
CM	Matt Cain	10.00
CU	Chris Duncan	10.00
CZ	Carlos Zambrano	8.00
DL	Derrek Lee	8.00
DO	David Ortiz	10.00
EB	Erik Bedard	10.00
EP	Eduardo Paret	8.00
FA	Fausto Carmona	8.00
FC	Frederich Cepeda	8.00
FL	Francisco Liriano/SP	35.00
GY	Guogang Yang	8.00
HA	Cole Hamels	15.00
HC	Hee Seop Choi	5.00
HT	Hitoshi Tamura	30.00
IK	Ian Kinsler	8.00
IR	Ivan Rodriguez	10.00
IS	Ichiro Suzuki	150.00
JB	Jason Bay	10.00
JD	Johnny Damon	8.00
JF	Jeff Francis	5.00
JH	Jeremy Hermida	8.00
JL	Jong Beom Lee	8.00
JM	Justin Morneau	15.00
JP	Jin Man Park	8.00
JS	Johan Santana	15.00
JV	Jason Varitek	5.00
JZ	Joel Zumaya	15.00
KE	Matthew Kemp	10.00
KG	Ken Griffey Jr.	20.00
KJ	Kenji Johjima/SP	35.00
KU	Koji Uehara	30.00
LO	Javy Lopez	5.00
MA	Moises Alou	8.00
MC	Michael Collins	8.00
ME	Michel Enriquez	8.00
MF	Maikel Folch	8.00
MJ	Mike Jacobs	8.00
MK	Munenori Kawasaki	40.00
MN	Michael Napoli	8.00
MO	Michihiro Ogasawara	30.00
MP	Mike Piazza	15.00

#	Player	Price
MS	Min Han Son	10.00
MT	Miguel Tejada	8.00
NM	Nobuhiko Matsunaka	25.00
NS	Naoyuki Shimizu	25.00
OU	Osmany Urrutia	10.00
PF	Prince Fielder/SP	25.00
PL	Pedro Luis Lazo	5.00
PU	Albert Pujols	25.00
RO	Alex Rodriguez	20.00
SH	Jamie Shields	10.00
SW	Shunsuke Watanabe	30.00
TN	Tsuyoshi Nishioka	30.00
TW	Tsuyoshi Wada	30.00
VE	Justin Verlander	20.00
VM	Victor Martinez	10.00
VO	Vicyohandry Odelin	5.00
WI	Josh Willingham	8.00
WL	Wei-Chu Lin	50.00
YG	Yulieski Gourriel	10.00
YM	Yuneiski Maya	10.00

Dual Signatures
NM/M

Production 1-55

#	Player	Price
BN	Taylor Buchholz, Fernando Nieve/55	30.00
CK	Scott Kazmir, Carl Crawford/55	40.00
CU	Carl Crawford, B.J. Upton/45	40.00
CW	Chris Carpenter, Dontrelle Willis/35	50.00
CZ	Miguel Cabrera, Ryan Zimmerman/35	75.00
EG	Andre Ethier, Tony Gwynn Jr./35	40.00
GG	Vladimir Guerrero, Ken Griffey Jr./35	150.00
GT	Ken Griffey Jr., Jim Thome/35	150.00
HD	Dan Uggla, Howie Kendrick/55	40.00
HK	Jeremy Hermida, Jason Kubel/55	30.00
HW	Jeremy Hermida, Josh Willingham/55	30.00
KR	Brian Roberts, Howie Kendrick/35	40.00
KU	B.J. Upton, Scott Kazmir/55	35.00
KW	Scott Kazmir, Dontrelle Willis/35	35.00
LN	Francisco Liriano, Joe Nathan/35	50.00
MM	Joe Mauer, Justin Morneau/35	60.00
MO	Justin Morneau, Lyle Overbay/35	40.00
PO	Jake Peavy, Roy Oswalt/35	40.00
PZ	Jonathan Papelbon, Joel Zumaya/35	90.00
RO	Alex Rios, Lyle Overbay/35	30.00
RR	Jose Reyes, Hanley Ramirez/35	60.00
SN	Huston Street, Joe Nathan/35	30.00
TI	Jim Thome, Tadahito Iguchi/35	100.00
TJ	Jeremy Sowers, Travis Hafner/35	40.00
UD	Stephen Drew, B.J. Upton/35	75.00
UH	Cole Hamels, Chase Utley/35	90.00
UU	Chase Utley, Dan Uggla/35	50.00
UW	Dan Uggla, Josh Willingham/55	30.00
ZU	Ryan Zimmerman, B.J. Upton/35	60.00

Spokesmen Signatures
No Pricing
Production 5 Sets

Sweet Beginnings Patch
NM/M

Common Player:

#	Player	Price
AB	Adrian Beltre	30.00
AE	Andre Ethier	50.00
AJ	Andruw Jones	40.00
AP	Ariel Pestano	40.00
AS	Alfonso Soriano	75.00
BA	Bobby Abreu	60.00
BB	Brian Bannister	40.00
BI	Chad Billingsley	40.00
BW	Bernie Williams	80.00
CA	Miguel Cabrera	60.00
CB	Carlos Beltran	60.00
CD	Carlos Delgado	50.00
CJ	Conor Jackson	40.00
CL	Carlos Lee	40.00
CM	Matt Cain	75.00
CU	Chris Duncan	50.00
CZ	Carlos Zambrano	40.00
DL	Derrek Lee	60.00
DO	David Ortiz	75.00
DU	Dan Uggla	40.00
EB	Erik Bedard	40.00
EP	Eduardo Paret	30.00
FA	Fausto Carmona	40.00

#	Player	Price
FC	Frederich Cepeda	40.00
FL	Francisco Liriano	50.00
HA	Cole Hamels	50.00
HK	Hong-Chih Kuo	200.00
JB	Jason Bay	50.00
JD	Johnny Damon	40.00
JF	Jeff Francis	40.00
JH	Jeremy Hermida	40.00
JJ	Josh Johnson	40.00
JO	Josh Barfield	40.00
JS	Johan Santana	80.00
JV	Jason Varitek	50.00
JZ	Joel Zumaya	50.00
KE	Matthew Kemp	50.00
KJ	Kenji Johjima	150.00
KU	Koji Uehara	200.00
LE	Jon Lester	50.00
LO	Javy Lopez	50.00
MC	Michael Collins	40.00
ME	Michel Enriquez	40.00
MF	Maikel Folch	40.00
MJ	Mike Jacobs	40.00
MK	Munenori Kawasaki	250.00
MN	Michael Napoli	40.00
MO	Michihiro Ogasawara	200.00
MP	Mike Piazza	85.00
MS	Min Han Son/SP	140.00
NI	Nicholas Markakis	60.00
NM	Nobuhiko Matsunaka	75.00
NS	Naoyuki Shimizu	120.00
OU	Osmany Urrutia	85.00
PA	Jonathan Papelbon	85.00
PE	Mike Pelfrey	75.00
PL	Pedro Luis Lazo	40.00
PU	Albert Pujols	150.00
RN	Ricky Nolasco	40.00
RZ	Ryan Zimmerman	60.00
TW	Tsuyoshi Wada	250.00
VE	Justin Verlander	60.00
VM	Victor Martinez	50.00
VO	Vicyohandry Odelin	30.00
WE	Jered Weaver	50.00
WI	Josh Willingham	40.00
YG	Yulieski Gourriel	75.00
YM	Yuneiski Maya	35.00
RM	Russell Martin	60.00

Signatures Barrels Black Ink
NM/M

Production 34-70
Blue Ink: No Pricing
Production 9-20
Silver Ink: No Pricing
Production One Set

#	Player	Price
101	Adam Wainwright/35	50.00
103	Andre Ethier/35	50.00
105	Ben Johnson/35	25.00
106	Boof Bonser/35	25.00
107	Boone Logan/35	20.00
108	Brian Anderson/35	20.00
109	Brian Bannister/35	25.00
110	Chris Denorfia/35	20.00
112	Cody Ross/35	20.00
113	Cole Hamels/70	50.00
114	Conor Jackson/35	20.00
115	Dan Uggla/35	35.00
116	Dave Gassner/35	20.00
117	C.J. Wilson/35	15.00
118	Eric Reed/35	15.00
119	Fausto Carmona/35	20.00
120	Fernando Nieve/35	15.00
121	Francisco Liriano/70	40.00
122	Freddie Bynum/35	15.00
123	Hanley Ramirez/35	50.00
124	Hong-Chih Kuo/35	200.00
125	Ian Kinsler/35	60.00
126	Carlos Marmol/35	20.00
127	Bobby Keppel/35	15.00
128	Jason Kubel/35	20.00
130	Alay Soler/35	15.00
132	Carlos Quentin/35	30.00
133	Jeremy Hermida/35	25.00
134	Joel Zumaya/35	65.00
135	Joey Devine/35	20.00
136	John Koronka/35	15.00
137	Jonathan Papelbon/70	60.00
138	Jose Capellan/35	20.00
139	Josh Johnson/35	20.00
141	Josh Willingham/35	20.00
143	Justin Verlander/35	50.00
144	Kelly Shoppach/35	20.00
146	Kevin Thompson/35	20.00
147	Macay McBride/35	15.00
149	Matt Cain/35	40.00
150	Clay Hensley/35	15.00
151	Ty Taubenheim/35	35.00
152	Mike Jacobs/35	25.00
153	Saul Rivera/35	15.00
154	Mike Thompson/35	20.00
155	Nate McLouth/35	20.00
156	Michael Vento/35	20.00
157	Paul Maholm/35	25.00
159	Reggie Abercrombie/35	20.00
160	Mike Rouse/35	15.00
161	Ken Ray/35	15.00
162	Ron Flores/35	15.00
163	Ryan Zimmerman/35	65.00
164	Erick Aybar/35	25.00
165	Sean Marshall/35	25.00
167	Taylor Buchholz/35	25.00
168	Matt Murton/35	50.00
169	Luis Figueroa/34	20.00
170	Wilbert Nieves/30	25.00

171	Jamie Shields/35	35.00
172	Jon Lester/70	50.00
174	Aaron Rakers/35	15.00
175	Bobby Livingston/35	20.00
176	Brendan Harris/35	15.00
177	Zach Jackson/35	20.00
178	Chris Britton/35	20.00
179	Howie Kendrick/70	40.00
181	Kevin Frandsen/35	15.00
182	Matt Capps/35	15.00
183	Peter Moylan/35	20.00

Signatures Leather Black Ink

NM/M

Production 20-40
Blue Ink: No Pricing
Production 5-10
Silver Ink: No Pricing
Production One Set

113	Cole Hamels/40	60.00
121	Francisco Liriano/40	60.00
137	Jonathan Papelbon/40	75.00
172	Jon Lester/40	60.00
179	Howie Kendrick/40	50.00

Signature - Veterans Barrels Black Ink

NM/M

Production 10-35
Blue Ink: No Pricing
Production 1-20
Silver Ink: No Pricing
Production One Set

AG	Tony Gwynn Jr./35	35.00
AH	Aaron Harang/35	35.00
AZ	Aramis Ramirez/35	30.00
BJ	B.J. Upton/35	35.00
BR	Brian Roberts/35	25.00
CC	Carl Crawford/35	35.00
CU	Chase Utley/35	70.00
HS	Huston Street/35	30.00
JB	Jason Bay/35	30.00
JN	Joe Nathan/35	30.00
JS	Jeremy Sowers/35	35.00
KG	Ken Griffey Jr./28	100.00
KG2	Ken Griffey Jr./27	100.00
KY	Kevin Youkilis/35	40.00
LO	Lyle Overbay/35	25.00
MC	Miguel Cabrera/35	50.00
MO	Justin Morneau/35	35.00
SD	Stephen Drew/35	60.00
SK	Scott Kazmir/33	50.00
SM	John Smoltz/35	50.00
SO	Scott Podsednik/35	25.00
SS	Mark Mulder/35	25.00
TH	Travis Hafner/35	40.00
TI	Tadahito Iguchi/35	60.00
VM	Victor Martinez/35	30.00

Signature - Veteran Leather Black Ink

Production 5-20
Blue Ink: No Pricing
Production 1-5
Silver Ink: No Pricing
Production One Set

2006 UD Ultimate Collection

NM/M

Complete Set (290):
Common Player (1-100): 1.50
Common RC Auto.
(101-175): 10.00
Production 180 unless noted
Common (191-290): 2.00
Production 799
Pack (4): 80.00
Box (4): 300.00

1	Babe Ruth	8.00
2	Chad Tracy	1.50
3	Brandon Webb	1.50
4	Andruw Jones	3.00
5	Chipper Jones	4.00
6	John Smoltz	4.00
7	Eddie Mathews	4.00
8	Miguel Tejada	4.00
9	Brian Roberts	1.50
10	Mickey Cochrane	2.00
11	Curt Schilling	3.00
12	David Ortiz	4.00
13	Manny Ramirez	4.00
14	Johnny Bench	4.00
15	Cy Young	4.00
16	Greg Maddux	5.00
17	Derrek Lee	2.00
18	Yogi Berra	4.00
19	Walter Johnson	2.00
20	Jim Thome	3.00
21	Paul Konerko	2.00
22	Lou Gehrig	6.00
23	Jose Contreras	1.50
24	Ken Griffey Jr.	5.00
25	Adam Dunn	3.00
26	Reggie Jackson	3.00
27	Travis Hafner	2.00
28	Victor Martinez	1.50
29	Grady Sizemore	4.00
30	Casey Stengel	3.00
31	Todd Helton	3.00
32	Nolan Ryan	8.00
33	Clint Barmes	1.50
34	Ivan Rodriguez	3.00
35	Chris Shelton	1.50
36	Ty Cobb	5.00
37	Miguel Cabrera	4.00
38	Dontrelle Willis	2.00
39	Lance Berkman	2.00
40	Tom Seaver	4.00
41	Roy Oswalt	2.00
42	Christy Mathewson	3.00
43	Luis Aparicio	1.50
44	Vladimir Guerrero	4.00
45	Bartolo Colon	1.50
46	Roy Campanella	2.00
47	George Sisler	1.50
48	Jeff Kent	1.50
49	J.D. Drew	1.50
50	Carlos Lee	1.50
51	Willie Stargell	3.00
52	Rickie Weeks	1.50
53	Johan Santana	4.00
54	Torii Hunter	1.50
55	Joe Mauer	2.00
56	Pedro Martinez	4.00
57	David Wright	5.00
58	Carlos Beltran	3.00
59	Jimmie Foxx	3.00
60	Jose Reyes	3.00
61	Derek Jeter	8.00
62	Alex Rodriguez	6.00
63	Randy Johnson	3.00
64	Hideki Matsui	5.00
65	Thurman Munson	4.00
66	Rich Harden	1.50
67	Eric Chavez	2.00
68	Don Drysdale	3.00
69	Bobby Crosby	1.50
70	Pee Wee Reese	1.50
71	Ryan Howard	6.00
72	Chase Utley	4.00
73	Jackie Robinson	6.00
74	Jason Bay	3.00
75	Honus Wagner	3.00
76	Lefty Grove	3.00
77	Jake Peavy	1.50
78	Brian Giles	1.50
79	Eddie Murray	3.00
80	Omar Vizquel	1.50
81	Jason Schmidt	2.00
82	Ichiro Suzuki	8.00
83	Felix Hernandez	3.00
84	Kenji Johjima	1.50
85	Albert Pujols	8.00
86	Chris Carpenter	3.00
87	Brooks Robinson	3.00
88	Dizzy Dean	3.00
89	Carl Crawford	3.00
90	Rogers Hornsby	3.00
91	Scott Kazmir	3.00
92	Mark Teixeira	3.00
93	Michael Young	2.00
94	Johnny Mize	1.50
95	Vernon Wells	3.00
96	Roy Halladay	3.00
97	Mel Ott	1.50
98	Alfonso Soriano	4.00
99	Joe Morgan	3.00
100	Satchel Paige	4.00
101	Adam Wainwright (RC)	30.00
102	Anderson Hernandez (RC)	10.00
103	Andre Ethier (RC)	35.00
104	Ben Johnson (RC)	15.00
105	Boof Bonser (RC)	20.00
106	Boone Logan RC	10.00
107	Brian Anderson (RC)	15.00
108	Brian Bannister (RC)	15.00
109	Chris Demaria (RC)	10.00
110	Chris Denorfia (RC)	10.00
111	Cody Ross (RC)	10.00
112	Cole Hamels (RC)	50.00
113	Conor Jackson (RC)	10.00
114	Dan Uggla (RC)	25.00
115	Dave Gassner (RC)	10.00
116	Eric Reed (RC)	10.00
117	Fausto Carmona (RC)	10.00
118	Fernando Nieve (RC)	10.00
119	Francisco Liriano (RC)	50.00
120	Freddie Bynum (RC)	10.00
121	Hanley Ramirez (RC)	25.00
122	Hong-Chih Kuo (RC)	85.00
123	Ian Kinsler (RC)	15.00
124	Jason Hammel (RC)	10.00
125	Jason Kubel (RC)	10.00
126	Jeff Harris RC	10.00
127	Jered Weaver/ 150	60.00
128	Jeremy Accardo (RC)	10.00
129	Jeremy Hermida (RC)	20.00
130	Joel Zumaya (RC)	40.00
131	Joey Devine RC	10.00
132	John Koronka (RC)	15.00
133	John Van Benschoten (RC)	10.00
134	Jonathan Papelbon (RC)	50.00
135	Jose Capellan (RC)	10.00
136	Josh Johnson (RC)	10.00
137	Josh Rupe (RC)	10.00
138	Josh Willingham (RC)	15.00
139	Josh Wilson (RC)	10.00
140	Justin Verlander (RC)	60.00
141	Kelly Shoppach (RC)	10.00
142	Kendry Morales (RC)	15.00
143	Macay McBride (RC)	10.00
144	Martin Prado (RC)	10.00
145	Matt Cain (RC)	30.00
146	Mike Jacobs (RC)	10.00
147	Mike Thompson RC	10.00
148	Nate McLouth (RC)	10.00
149	Paul Maholm (RC)	10.00
150	Prince Fielder (RC)	50.00
151	Reggie Abercrombie (RC)	10.00
152	Rich Hill (RC)	75.00
153	Ron Flores RC	15.00
154	Ruddy Lugo (RC)	10.00
155	Ryan Zimmerman (RC)	60.00
156	Sean Marshall (RC)	20.00
157	Takashi Saito (RC)	30.00
158	Taylor Buchholz (RC)	15.00
159	Tony Pena (RC)	10.00
160	Wilbert Nieves (RC)	10.00
161	Jamie Shields RC	20.00
162	Jon Lester (RC)	40.00
163	Craig Hansen RC	10.00
164	Aaron Rakers (RC)	10.00
165	Yusmeiro Petit (RC)	10.00
166	Bobby Livingston (RC)	10.00
167	Brendan Harris (RC)	10.00
168	Carlos Ruiz (RC)	15.00
170	Chris Britton RC	10.00
171	Howie Kendrick (RC)	40.00
172	Jermaine Van Buren (RC)	10.00
173	Kevin Frandsen (RC)	20.00
174	Matt Capps (RC)	10.00
175	Peter Moylan RC	10.00
191	Richie Ashburn/799	3.00
192	Lou Brock	4.00
193	Lou Boudreau	2.00
194	Orlando Cepeda	4.00
195	Bobby Doerr	2.00
196	Dennis Eckersley	2.00
197	Bob Feller	3.00
198	Rollie Fingers	2.00
199	Carlton Fisk	4.00
200	Bob Gibson	4.00
201	Jim "Catfish" Hunter	3.00
202	Fergie Jenkins	2.00
203	Al Kaline	5.00
204	Harmon Killebrew	3.00
205	Ralph Kiner	3.00
206	Buck Leonard	3.00
207	Juan Marichal	2.00
208	Bill Mazeroski	4.00
209	Willie McCovey	2.00
210	Jim Palmer	2.00
211	Tony Perez	2.00
212	Gaylord Perry	2.00
213	Phil Rizzuto	4.00
214	Robin Roberts	2.00
215	Mike Schmidt	6.00
216	Enos Slaughter	2.00
217	Ozzie Smith	5.00
218	Billy Williams	2.00
219	Robin Yount	5.00
220	Carlos Quentin (RC)	4.00
221	Jeff Francoeur	2.00
222	Brian McCann	2.00
223	Nicholas Markakis (RC)	6.00
224	Josh Beckett	4.00
225	Jason Varitek	4.00
226	Mark Prior	4.00
227	Aramis Ramirez	3.00
228	Jermaine Dye	2.00
229	Tadahito Iguchi	2.00
230	Bobby Jenks	2.00
231	C.C. Sabathia	2.00
232	Jeff Francis	2.00
233	Matt Holliday	2.00
234	Magglio Ordonez	2.00
235	Kenny Rogers	2.00
236	Roger Clemens	8.00
237	Andy Pettitte	3.00
238	Craig Biggio	3.00
239	Chone Figgins	2.00
240	John Lackey	2.00
241	Nomar Garciaparra	4.00
242	Prince Fielder (RC)	6.00
243	Ben Sheets	3.00
244	Bill Hall	2.00
245	Justin Morneau	4.00
246	Joe Nathan	2.00
247	Carlos Delgado	2.00
248	Shawn Green	2.00
249	Billy Wagner	2.00
250	Jason Giambi	4.00
251	Mike Mussina	4.00
252	Mariano Rivera	4.00
253	Robinson Cano	4.00
254	Bobby Abreu	2.00
255	Huston Street	2.00
256	Frank Thomas	4.00
257	Danny Haren	2.00
258	Jason Kendall	2.00
259	Nick Swisher	3.00
260	Pat Burrell	3.00
261	Tom Gordon	2.00
262	Freddy Sanchez	2.00
263	Trevor Hoffman	2.00
264	Khalil Greene	2.00
265	Adrian Gonzalez	2.00
266	Moises Alou	2.00
267	Matt Morris	2.00
268	Pedro Feliz	2.00
269	Richie Sexson	2.00
270	Hoyt Wilhelm	2.00
271	Adrian Beltre	2.00
272	Jim Edmonds	3.00
273	Scott Rolen	4.00
274	Jason Isringhausen	2.00
275	Jorge Cantu	2.00
276	Hank Blalock	2.00
277	Kevin Millwood	2.00
278	Alex Rios	2.00
279	Troy Glaus	3.00
280	B.J. Ryan	2.00
281	Nick Johnson	2.00
282	Chad Cordero	2.00
283	Austin Kearns	2.00
284	Ricky Nolasco (RC)	2.00
285	Travis Ishikawa (RC)	2.00
286	Lastings Milledge (RC)	4.00
287	James Loney (RC)	4.00
288	Red Schoendienst	3.00
289	Warren Spahn	4.00
290	Early Wynn (RC)	2.00

Printing Plates

No Pricing
Production one set per color

Ensemble Materials 3

Production 25 Sets
Patch: No Pricing
Production 20 Sets

Ensemble Materials 4

Production 20 Sets
Patch: No Pricing
Production 15 Sets

Ensemble Signature 3

NM/M

Production 50 Sets
Triple 15: No Pricing
Production 15 Sets
Triple 1 of 1: No Pricing

AHW	Josh Willingham, Reggie Abercrombie, Jeremy Hermida	40.00
BBB	Jeff Bagwell, Craig Biggio, Lance Berkman	100.00
BBW	Taylor Buchholz, Adam Wainwright, Brian Bannister	50.00
BDD	George Bell, Eric Davis, Andre Dawson	50.00
BHR	Roy Halladay, A.J. Burnett, Alex Rios	50.00
BKM	Ralph Kiner, Bill Mazeroski, Jason Bay	85.00
BNO	Taylor Buchholz, Roy Oswalt, Fernando Nieve	30.00
BSH	A.J. Burnett, Rich Harden, Ben Sheets	40.00
BUK	Craig Biggio, Chase Utley, Ian Kinsler	75.00
BWC	Matt Cain, Brian Bannister, Adam Wainwright	40.00
BWV	Justin Verlander, Boof Bonser, Jered Weaver	85.00
CBP	Oliver Perez, Jason Bay, Sean Casey	30.00
CBS	Ron Cey, Dusty Baker, Don Sutton	50.00
CBZ	Boof Bonser, Joel Zumaya, Matt Cain	50.00
CDV	Jack Clark, Eric Davis, Andy Van Slyke	50.00
CHK	Jason Kubel, Melky Cabrera, Jeremy Hermida	50.00
CHO	Chris Carpenter, Roy Oswalt, Rich Harden	60.00
CKH	Rich Harden, Bobby Crosby, Jason Kendall	40.00
CKS	Carl Crawford, Scott Kazmir, Jamie Shields	50.00
CLH	Cole Hamels, Fausto Carmona, Francisco Liriano	80.00
CMH	Victor Martinez, Travis Hafner, Fausto Carmona	60.00
CNS	Graig Nettles, Ron Cey, Ron Santo	50.00
CPC	Carl Crawford, Coco Crisp, Scott Podsednik	40.00
CSS	John Smoltz, Roger Clemens, Curt Schilling	200.00
CWW	Josh Willingham, Dontrelle Willis, Miguel Cabrera	50.00
CZC	Miguel Cabrera, Eric Chavez, Ryan Zimmerman	80.00
DJH	Hanley Ramirez, Derek Jeter, Jose Reyes	200.00
DPA	Scott Podsednik, Jermaine Dye, Brian Anderson	40.00
DPI	Jermaine Dye, Scott Podsednik, Tadahito Iguchi	60.00
FGC	David Cone, Dwight Gooden, Sid Fernandez	75.00
FJM	Prince Fielder, Conor Jackson, Kendry Morales	50.00
FWL	Rickie Weeks, Prince Fielder, Carlos Lee	60.00
GCN	Graig Nettles, Rich "Goose" Gossage, Chris Chambliss	50.00
GCS	Bret Saberhagen, Dwight Gooden, David Cone	30.00
GJB	Derek Jeter, Ken Griffey Jr., Jason Bay	250.00
GJP	Derek Jeter, Albert Pujols, Ken Griffey Jr.	500.00
GLK	Dave Gassner, Jason Kubel, Francisco Liriano	50.00
GPN	Joe Nathan, Eric Gagne, Jonathan Papelbon	50.00
GRS	Alex Rios, Alfonso Soriano, Vladimir Guerrero	50.00
HBS	Rich Harden, Nick Swisher, Joe Blanton	50.00
HKP	Boog Powell, John Kruk, Kent Hrbek	40.00
HMK	Mark Mulder, Scott Kazmir, Cole Hamels	60.00
HNP	Jonathan Papelbon, Trevor Hoffman, Joe Nathan	75.00
HOT	David Ortiz, Travis Hafner, Mark Teixeira	100.00
HWU	Jeremy Hermida, Josh Willingham, Dan Uggla	30.00
IKU	Dan Uggla, Ian Kinsler, Tadahito Iguchi	85.00
JCN	Melky Cabrera, Wilbert Nieves, Derek Jeter	150.00
JGS	Ken Griffey Jr., Andruw Jones, Alfonso Soriano	120.00
JRR	Derek Jeter, Jose Reyes, Hanley Ramirez	200.00
JWV	Jered Weaver, Justin Verlander, Josh Johnson	75.00
KGJ	John Kruk, Mark Grace, Wally Joyner	80.00
KLB	Francisco Liriano, Boof Bonser, Jason Kubel	50.00
KUU	Ian Kinsler, Dan Uggla, Chase Utley	65.00
KWM	Josh Willingham, Victor Martinez, Jason Kendall	30.00
LGB	Francisco Liriano, Boof Bonser, Dave Gassner	40.00
LHC	Felix Hernandez, Fausto Carmona, Francisco Liriano	85.00
LPO	Derrek Lee, David Ortiz, Albert Pujols	250.00
MCN	Ron Cey, Graig Nettles, Bill Madlock	50.00
MMK	Jason Kendall, Joe Mauer, Victor Martinez	40.00
MNL	Joe Mauer, Francisco Liriano, Joe Nathan	50.00
MWC	Chris Carpenter, Mark Mulder, Adam Wainwright	75.00
MWP	Josh Willingham, Russell Martin, Ronny Paulino	30.00
NLP	Jonathan Papelbon, Brad Lidge, Joe Nathan	50.00
OBL	Brad Lidge, Roy Oswalt, Taylor Buchholz	40.00
PCL	Oliver Perez, Francisco Liriano, Fausto Carmona	50.00
PHL	Cole Hamels, Francisco Liriano, Oliver Perez	65.00
PSO	Roy Oswalt, Jake Peavy, Ben Sheets	40.00
PVW	Justin Verlander, Jered Weaver, Jonathan Papelbon	90.00
RHW	Jeremy Hermida, Josh Willingham, Cody Ross	30.00
RMM	Victor Martinez, Joe Mauer, Ivan Rodriguez	65.00
RRB	Jose Reyes, Yuniesky Betancourt, Hanley Ramirez	60.00
SGM	Greg Maddux, John Smoltz, Tom Glavine	180.00
SJF	Prince Fielder, Mike Jacobs, Chris Shelton	40.00
SKM	Russell Martin, Takashi Saito, Hong-Chih Kuo	200.00
SWB	Taylor Buchholz, Jamie Shields, Jered Weaver	60.00
TGB	Frank Thomas, Ken Griffey Jr., Jeff Bagwell	150.00
TKY	Michael Young, Mark Teixeira, Ian Kinsler	75.00
UHC	Jeremy Hermida, Dan Uggla, Miguel Cabrera	75.00
URC	Miguel Cabrera, Dan Uggla, Hanley Ramirez	40.00
URW	Hanley Ramirez, Dan Uggla, Josh Willingham	35.00
VBZ	Justin Verlander, Jeremy Bonderman, Joel Zumaya	120.00
VWL	Jered Weaver, Francisco Liriano, Justin Verlander	120.00
WJC	Josh Johnson, Jered Weaver, Matt Cain	70.00
WJO	Scott Olsen, Josh Johnson, Dontrelle Willis	40.00
WSV	Justin Verlander, Jered Weaver, Jamie Shields	65.00
ZBC	Joel Zumaya, Matt Cain, Boof Bonser	60.00
ZHZ	Carlos Zambrano, Felix Hernandez, Joel Zumaya	60.00

Ensemble Signatures 4

No Pricing
Production 25 Sets

Ensemble Signatures 5

No Pricing
Production 15 Sets

Ensemble Signatures 6

No Pricing
Production 10 Sets

Ensemble Signatures 8

Production One Set

Game Materials

NM/M

Common Player: 8.00
Production 50 Sets

AB	A.J. Burnett	8.00
AD	Adam Dunn	10.00
AJ	Andruw Jones	12.00
AP	Albert Pujols	30.00
AR	Alex Rios	8.00
AS	Alfonso Soriano	10.00
BA	Brian Bannister	8.00
BG	Brian Giles	8.00
BM	Bill Mazeroski	15.00
BO	Jeremy Bonderman	10.00
BR	Brian Roberts	8.00
CA	Melky Cabrera	15.00
CC	Carl Crawford	15.00
CH	Chris Carpenter	15.00
CJ	Conor Jackson	10.00
CL	Carlos Lee	10.00
CR	Coco Crisp	10.00
CS	Chris Shelton	8.00
CU	Chase Utley	20.00
CZ	Carlos Zambrano	10.00
DJ	Derek Jeter	30.00
DJ2	Derek Jeter	30.00
DL	Derrek Lee	30.00
DU	Dan Uggla	10.00
DW	Dontrelle Willis	10.00
FH	Felix Hernandez	12.00
FL	Francisco Liriano	15.00
GA	Garrett Atkins	8.00
GP	Gaylord Perry	10.00
HA	Cole Hamels	15.00
HB	Hank Blalock	10.00
HC	Craig Hansen	15.00
HO	Trevor Hoffman	10.00
HR	Hanley Ramirez	15.00
HT	Tim Hudson	10.00
HU	Torii Hunter	10.00
HY	Roy Halladay	10.00
IK	Ian Kinsler	10.00
IR	Ivan Rodriguez	10.00
JB	Jason Bay	12.00
JD	Jermaine Dye	8.00
JH	Jeremy Hermida	8.00
JJ	Josh Johnson	10.00
JK	Jason Kendall	8.00
JM	Joe Mauer	10.00
JN	Joe Nathan	10.00
JP	Jake Peavy	10.00
JR	Jose Reyes	15.00
JS	Johan Santana	12.00
JV	Justin Verlander	15.00
JW	Jered Weaver	15.00

Code	Player	Price
JZ	Joel Zumaya	15.00
KG	Ken Griffey Jr.	25.00
KG2	Ken Griffey Jr.	25.00
KH	Khalil Greene	8.00
KJ	Kenji Johjima	20.00
KM	Kendry Morales	8.00
KU	Jason Kubel	8.00
KY	Kevin Youkilis	10.00
LA	Luis Aparicio	10.00
LM	Lastings Milledge	8.00
LY	Fred Lynn	8.00
MA	Matt Cain	15.00
MC	Miguel Cabrera	15.00
MG	Marcus Giles	8.00
MH	Matt Holliday	12.00
ML	Mark Loretta	8.00
MM	Melvin Mora	8.00
MO	Justin Morneau	12.00
MS	Mike Schmidt	20.00
MT	Mark Teixeira	12.00
MU	Mark Mulder	10.00
MY	Michael Young	10.00
NS	Nick Swisher	10.00
PA	Jonathan Papelbon	10.00
PF	Prince Fielder	12.00
PM	Paul Molitor	15.00
RC	Cal Ripken Jr.	40.00
RH	Rich Harden	10.00
RI	Jim Rice	15.00
RO	Roy Oswalt	10.00
RW	Rickie Weeks	10.00
RZ	Ryan Zimmerman	20.00
SK	Scott Kazmir	10.00
SP	Scott Podsednik	10.00
TE	Miguel Tejada	12.00
TG	Tony Gwynn	15.00
TH	Travis Hafner	10.00
TI	Tadahito Iguchi	10.00
TP	Tony Perez	10.00
VM	Victor Martinez	10.00
WC	Will Clark	15.00
WI	Josh Willingham	8.00
YB	Yuniesky Betancourt	8.00

Legendary Materials
NM/M

Production 5-55

Code	Player	Price
AR	Al Rosen/55	15.00
BD	Bill Dickey/55	30.00
BD2	Bill Dickey/55	30.00
BG	Bob Gibson/25	20.00
BM	Bill Mazeroski/25	20.00
BO	Bo Jackson/55	20.00
BO2	Bo Jackson/55	20.00
CF	Carlton Fisk/55	10.00
CF2	Carlton Fisk/55	10.00
CW	Rod Carew/55	10.00
CW2	Rod Carew/55	10.00
CY	Carl Yastrzemski/25	20.00
CY2	Carl Yastrzemski/25	20.00
GP	Gaylord Perry/55	10.00
GP2	Gaylord Perry/55	10.00
JB	Johnny Bench/55	20.00
JO	Joe Morgan/55	10.00
JO2	Joe Morgan/55	10.00
JU	Juan Marichal/55	10.00
KI	Kirk Gibson/55	10.00
KP	Kirby Puckett/55	20.00
KP2	Kirby Puckett/55	20.00
MA	Don Mattingly/55	25.00
MA2	Don Mattingly/55	25.00
MW	Maury Wills/41	10.00
NR	Nolan Ryan/55	35.00
NR2	Nolan Ryan/25	40.00
NR3	Nolan Ryan/25	40.00
OS	Ozzie Smith/55	20.00
OS2	Ozzie Smith/55	20.00
PM	Paul Molitor/55	10.00
PM2	Paul Molitor/55	10.00
PN	Phil Niekro/55	10.00
PN2	Phil Niekro/55	10.00
RJ	Reggie Jackson/25	20.00
RJ2	Reggie Jackson/35	20.00
RK	Ralph Kiner/25	20.00
RO	Brooks Robinson/35	15.00
RO2	Brooks Robinson/35	15.00
RS	Ryne Sandberg/35	25.00
RY	Robin Yount/25	15.00
RY2	Robin Yount/25	15.00
SC	Steve Carlton/55	10.00
SC2	Steve Carlton/47	10.00
SU	Don Sutton/55	10.00
SU2	Don Sutton/55	10.00
TG	Tony Gwynn/55	20.00
TG2	Tony Gwynn/55	20.00
TP	Tony Perez/55	15.00
TP2	Tony Perez/55	15.00
WB	Wade Boggs/55	15.00
WB2	Wade Boggs/55	15.00
WC	Will Clark/45	15.00
WC2	Will Clark/45	15.00

Legendary Ensemble Signatures
No Pricing

Production 25 Sets

Maximum Materials
Production 25 Sets

Patch: No Pricing

Production 15 Sets

Numbers Materials
NM/M

Production 35 Sets

Code	Player	Price
AB	A.J. Burnett	10.00
AD	Adam Dunn	12.00
AJ	Andruw Jones	15.00
AP	Albert Pujols	40.00
AR	Alex Rios	10.00
AS	Alfonso Soriano	10.00
BA	Brian Bannister	10.00
BG	Brian Giles	10.00
BM	Bill Mazeroski	15.00
BO	Jeremy Bonderman	15.00
BR	Brian Roberts	15.00
CA	Melky Cabrera	15.00
CC	Carl Crawford	15.00
CH	Chris Carpenter	15.00
CJ	Conor Jackson	15.00
CL	Carlos Lee	10.00
CR	Coco Crisp	15.00
CS	Chris Shelton	10.00
CU	Chase Utley	20.00
CZ	Carlos Zambrano	15.00
DJ	Derek Jeter	40.00
DJ2	Derek Jeter	40.00
DL	Derrek Lee	15.00
DU	Dan Uggla	15.00
DW	Dontrelle Willis	15.00
FH	Felix Hernandez	15.00
FL	Francisco Liriano	20.00
GA	Garrett Atkins	15.00
GP	Gaylord Perry	15.00
HA	Cole Hamels	25.00
HB	Hank Blalock	10.00
HC	Craig Hansen	10.00
HO	Trevor Hoffman	10.00
HR	Hanley Ramirez	10.00
HT	Tim Hudson	10.00
HU	Torii Hunter	10.00
HY	Roy Halladay	10.00
IK	Ian Kinsler	10.00
IR	Ivan Rodriguez	15.00
JB	Jason Bay	15.00
JD	Jermaine Dye	10.00
JH	Jeremy Hermida	10.00
JJ	Josh Johnson	12.00
JK	Jason Kendall	10.00
JM	Joe Mauer	15.00
JN	Joe Nathan	10.00
JP	Jake Peavy	10.00
JR	Jose Reyes	20.00
JS	Johan Santana	20.00
JV	Justin Verlander	20.00
JW	Jered Weaver	20.00
JZ	Joel Zumaya	10.00
KG	Ken Griffey Jr.	35.00
KG2	Ken Griffey Jr.	35.00
KH	Khalil Greene	10.00
KJ	Kenji Johjima	30.00
KM	Kendry Morales	10.00
KU	Jason Kubel	10.00
KY	Kevin Youkilis	15.00
LA	Luis Aparicio	10.00
LM	Lastings Milledge	15.00
LY	Fred Lynn	10.00
MA	Matt Cain	15.00
MC	Miguel Cabrera	15.00
MG	Marcus Giles	10.00
MH	Matt Holliday	10.00
ML	Mark Loretta	10.00
MM	Melvin Mora	10.00
MO	Justin Morneau	10.00
MS	Mike Schmidt	25.00
MT	Mark Teixeira	15.00
MU	Mark Mulder	10.00
MY	Michael Young	10.00
NS	Nick Swisher	10.00
PA	Jonathan Papelbon	25.00
PF	Prince Fielder	20.00
PM	Paul Molitor	15.00
RC	Cal Ripken Jr.	75.00
RH	Rich Harden	10.00
RI	Jim Rice	15.00
RO	Roy Oswalt	25.00
RW	Rickie Weeks	10.00
RZ	Ryan Zimmerman	50.00
SK	Scott Kazmir	10.00
SP	Scott Podsednik	15.00
TE	Miguel Tejada	20.00
TG	Tony Gwynn	30.00
TH	Travis Hafner	10.00
TI	Tadahito Iguchi	30.00
VM	Victor Martinez	10.00
WC	Will Clark	15.00
WI	Josh Willingham	15.00
YB	Yuniesky Betancourt	15.00

Ultimate Patch
NM/M

Production 50 unless noted

Patch Signature: No Pricing

Production 10 Sets

Code	Player	Price
AB	A.J. Burnett	15.00
AD	Adam Dunn	20.00
AJ	Andruw Jones	20.00
AP	Albert Pujols	60.00
AR	Alex Rios	15.00
AS	Alfonso Soriano	25.00
BA	Brian Bannister	15.00
BG	Brian Giles	15.00
BO	Jeremy Bonderman	25.00
BR	Brian Roberts	25.00
CA	Melky Cabrera	25.00
CC	Carl Crawford	15.00
CH	Chris Carpenter	20.00
CJ	Conor Jackson	15.00
CL	Carlos Lee	15.00
CR	Coco Crisp	20.00
CS	Chris Shelton	15.00
CU	Chase Utley	35.00
CZ	Carlos Zambrano	20.00
DJ	Derek Jeter	50.00
DJ2	Derek Jeter	50.00
DL	Derrek Lee	20.00
DU	Dan Uggla	20.00
DW	Dontrelle Willis	15.00
FH	Felix Hernandez	15.00
FL	Francisco Liriano	25.00
GA	Garrett Atkins	15.00
GP	Gaylord Perry/27	15.00
HA	Cole Hamels	25.00
HB	Hank Blalock	10.00
HO	Trevor Hoffman	15.00
HR	Hanley Ramirez	25.00
HT	Tim Hudson	15.00
HU	Torii Hunter	15.00
HY	Roy Halladay	15.00
IR	Ivan Rodriguez	20.00
JB	Jason Bay	15.00
JD	Jermaine Dye	15.00
JH	Jeremy Hermida	20.00
JJ	Josh Johnson	15.00
JK	Jason Kendall	15.00
JM	Joe Mauer	15.00
JN	Joe Nathan	15.00
JP	Jake Peavy	15.00
JR	Jose Reyes	30.00
JS	Johan Santana	30.00
JV	Justin Verlander	40.00
JW	Jered Weaver	25.00
JZ	Joel Zumaya/47	30.00
KG	Ken Griffey Jr.	50.00
KG2	Ken Griffey Jr.	50.00
KH	Khalil Greene	15.00
KJ	Kenji Johjima	35.00
KM	Kendry Morales	15.00
KU	Jason Kubel	15.00
LA	Luis Aparicio	15.00
LM	Lastings Milledge	30.00
LY	Fred Lynn	15.00
MA	Matt Cain	15.00
MC	Miguel Cabrera	25.00
MG	Marcus Giles	10.00
MH	Matt Holliday	20.00
ML	Mark Loretta/40	15.00
MM	Melvin Mora	15.00
MO	Justin Morneau	30.00
MS	Mike Schmidt	40.00
MT	Mark Teixeira	25.00
MU	Mark Mulder	15.00
MY	Michael Young	20.00
NS	Nick Swisher	20.00
PF	Prince Fielder	20.00
PM	Paul Molitor	15.00
RC	Cal Ripken Jr.	75.00
RH	Rich Harden	20.00
RI	Jim Rice/31	15.00
RO	Roy Oswalt	25.00
RW	Rickie Weeks	10.00
RZ	Ryan Zimmerman	50.00
SK	Scott Kazmir	15.00
SP	Scott Podsednik	15.00
TE	Miguel Tejada	20.00
TG	Tony Gwynn	30.00
TH	Travis Hafner	15.00
TI	Tadahito Iguchi	30.00
VM	Victor Martinez	20.00
WC	Will Clark	15.00
WI	Josh Willingham	15.00
YB	Yuniesky Betancourt	15.00

Tandem Materials
NM/M

Production 25 Sets

Signature: No Pricing

Production 15 Sets

Signature Patch: No Pricing

Production 5 Sets

Signature Logo: No Pricing

Production One Set

Code	Players	Price
AA	Alfonso Soriano, Alex Rios	20.00
AH	Garrett Atkins, Matt Holliday	10.00
BH	Felix Hernandez, Yuniesky Betancourt	20.00
BM	Brian Bannister, Lastings Milledge	20.00
BR	Yuniesky Betancourt, Hanley Ramirez	25.00
BV	Justin Verlander, Jeremy Bonderman	40.00
CL	Coco Crisp, Mark Loretta	20.00
CP	Carl Crawford, Scott Podsednik	15.00
CS	Cole Hamels, Scott Kazmir	25.00
CW	Dontrelle Willis, Chris Carpenter	15.00
CZ	Miguel Cabrera, Ryan Zimmerman	25.00
FP	Tony Perez, Prince Fielder	
FW	Prince Fielder, Rickie Weeks	
GP	Ken Griffey Jr., Albert Pujols	50.00
HB	Matt Holliday, Jason Bay	15.00
HF	Prince Fielder, Travis Hafner	20.00
HG	Trevor Hoffman, Brian Giles	10.00
HJ	Andruw Jones, Torii Hunter	15.00
HK	Jeremy Hermida, Jason Kubel	10.00
HM	Travis Hafner, Victor Martinez	10.00
HN	Trevor Hoffman, Joe Nathan	15.00
HO	Roy Oswalt, Rich Harden	15.00
HP	Trevor Hoffman, Jonathan Papelbon	25.00
HR	Hanley Ramirez, Jeremy Hermida	15.00
HW	Jeremy Hermida, Josh Willingham	10.00
ID	Jermaine Dye, Tadahito Iguchi	15.00
JB	Bill Mazeroski, Jason Bay	20.00
JG	Derek Jeter, Ken Griffey Jr.	40.00
JR	Derek Jeter, Cal Ripken Jr.	60.00
KB	Brian Giles, Khalil Greene	10.00
KM	Joe Mauer, Jason Kendall	15.00
KU	Ian Kinsler, Dan Uggla	10.00
KY	Ian Kinsler, Michael Young	10.00
LF	Prince Fielder, Carlos Lee	20.00
MH	Livan Hernandez, Kendry Morales	10.00
MM	Joe Mauer, Victor Martinez	10.00
MP	Tony Perez, Kendry Morales	15.00
MR	Melvin Mora, Brian Roberts	10.00
MW	Rickie Weeks, Paul Molitor	20.00
NJ	Joe Mauer, Joe Nathan	20.00
NM	Joe Mauer, Joe Nathan	15.00
PO	Roy Oswalt, Jake Peavy	15.00
PP	Jake Peavy, Gaylord Perry	15.00
SH	Rich Harden, Nick Swisher	15.00
TY	Michael Young, Mark Teixeira	15.00
VM	Justin Verlander, Jack Morris	20.00
WM	Josh Willingham, Joe Mauer	20.00
YL	Kevin Youkilis, Mark Loretta	15.00
ZJ	Josh Johnson, Joel Zumaya	20.00
ZZ	Joel Zumaya, Carlos Zambrano	20.00

Tri-Marks Signatures
No Pricing

Production 15 Sets

Game Materials Signatures
NM/M

Production 35 Sets

Code	Player	Price
AB	A.J. Burnett	25.00
AD	Adam Dunn	25.00
AJ	Andruw Jones	50.00
AP	Albert Pujols	250.00
AR	Alex Rios	25.00
AS	Alfonso Soriano	60.00
BA	Brian Bannister	25.00
BG	Brian Giles	25.00
BM	Bill Mazeroski	40.00
BO	Jeremy Bonderman	50.00
BR	Brian Roberts	25.00
CA	Melky Cabrera	40.00
CC	Carl Crawford	25.00
CH	Chris Carpenter	30.00
CJ	Conor Jackson	35.00
CL	Carlos Lee	25.00
CR	Coco Crisp	25.00
CS	Chris Shelton	25.00
CU	Chase Utley	60.00
CZ	Carlos Zambrano	40.00
DJ	Derek Jeter	250.00
DJ2	Derek Jeter	250.00
DL	Derrek Lee	35.00
DU	Dan Uggla	30.00
DW	Dontrelle Willis	30.00
FH	Felix Hernandez	40.00
FL	Francisco Liriano	50.00
GA	Garrett Atkins	25.00
GP	Gaylord Perry	25.00
HA	Cole Hamels	60.00
HB	Hank Blalock	25.00
HC	Craig Hansen	25.00
HO	Trevor Hoffman	40.00
HR	Hanley Ramirez	60.00
HT	Tim Hudson	30.00
HU	Torii Hunter	25.00
HY	Roy Halladay	25.00
IK	Ian Kinsler	30.00
IR	Ivan Rodriguez	35.00
JB	Jason Bay	30.00
JD	Jermaine Dye	25.00
JH	Jeremy Hermida	25.00
JJ	Josh Johnson	35.00
JK	Jason Kendall	25.00
JM	Joe Mauer	40.00
JN	Joe Nathan	25.00
JP	Jake Peavy	30.00
JR	Jose Reyes	50.00
JS	Johan Santana	50.00
JV	Justin Verlander	60.00
JW	Jered Weaver	40.00
JZ	Joel Zumaya	60.00
KG	Ken Griffey Jr.	120.00
KG2	Ken Griffey Jr.	120.00
KH	Khalil Greene	35.00
KM	Kendry Morales	30.00
KU	Jason Kubel	25.00
KY	Kevin Youkilis	25.00
LA	Luis Aparicio	25.00
LY	Fred Lynn	25.00
MA	Matt Cain	40.00
MC	Miguel Cabrera	50.00
MG	Marcus Giles	25.00
MH	Matt Holliday	30.00
ML	Mark Loretta	25.00
MM	Melvin Mora	25.00
MO	Justin Morneau	50.00
MS	Mike Schmidt	50.00
MU	Mark Mulder	25.00
MY	Michael Young	25.00
NS	Nick Swisher	25.00
PA	Jonathan Papelbon	60.00
PM	Paul Molitor	35.00
RC	Cal Ripken Jr.	150.00
RH	Rich Harden	30.00
RI	Jim Rice	30.00
RO	Roy Oswalt	25.00
RW	Rickie Weeks	25.00
RZ	Ryan Zimmerman	65.00
SK	Scott Kazmir	30.00
SP	Scott Podsednik	25.00
TE	Miguel Tejada	25.00
TG	Tony Gwynn	60.00
TH	Travis Hafner	30.00
TI	Tadahito Iguchi	40.00
TP	Tony Perez	30.00
VM	Victor Martinez	30.00
WC	Will Clark	35.00
WI	Josh Willingham	25.00
YB	Yuniesky Betancourt	25.00

Numbers Patch
NM/M

Production 35 unless noted

Code	Player	Price
AB	A.J. Burnett	20.00
AD	Adam Dunn	25.00
AJ	Andruw Jones	25.00
AP	Albert Pujols	80.00
AR	Alex Rios	25.00
AS	Alfonso Soriano	25.00
BA	Brian Bannister	15.00
BG	Brian Giles	20.00
BO	Jeremy Bonderman	25.00
BR	Brian Roberts	20.00
CC	Carl Crawford	20.00
CH	Chris Carpenter	25.00
CJ	Conor Jackson	20.00
CL	Carlos Lee	20.00
CR	Coco Crisp	20.00
CS	Chris Shelton	15.00
CU	Chase Utley	40.00
CZ	Carlos Zambrano	25.00
DJ	Derek Jeter	65.00
DJ2	Derek Jeter	65.00
DL	Derrek Lee	20.00
DU	Dan Uggla	20.00
DW	Dontrelle Willis	25.00
FH	Felix Hernandez	25.00
FL	Francisco Liriano	30.00
GA	Garrett Atkins	20.00
HA	Cole Hamels	40.00
HB	Hank Blalock	20.00
HO	Trevor Hoffman	20.00
HR	Hanley Ramirez	30.00
HT	Tim Hudson	20.00
HU	Torii Hunter	20.00
HY	Roy Halladay	20.00
IK	Ian Kinsler	20.00
IR	Ivan Rodriguez	20.00
JB	Jason Bay	20.00
JD	Jermaine Dye	20.00
JH	Jeremy Hermida	20.00
JJ	Josh Johnson	20.00
JK	Jason Kendall	20.00
JM	Joe Mauer	40.00
JP	Jake Peavy	20.00
JR	Jose Reyes	25.00
JS	Johan Santana	30.00
JV	Justin Verlander	40.00
JW	Jered Weaver	40.00
JZ	Joel Zumaya	35.00
KG	Ken Griffey Jr.	50.00
KG2	Ken Griffey Jr.	50.00
KH	Khalil Greene	20.00
KJ	Kenji Johjima	20.00
KU	Jason Kubel	20.00
KY	Kevin Youkilis	20.00
LA	Luis Aparicio	20.00
LM	Lastings Milledge	20.00
LY	Fred Lynn	20.00
MA	Matt Cain	30.00
MC	Miguel Cabrera	25.00
MG	Marcus Giles	20.00
MH	Matt Holliday	20.00
ML	Mark Loretta	20.00
MM	Melvin Mora	20.00
MO	Justin Morneau	25.00
MS	Mike Schmidt	50.00
MT	Mark Teixeira	25.00
MU	Mark Mulder	20.00
MY	Michael Young	20.00
NS	Nick Swisher	20.00
PF	Prince Fielder	30.00
PM	Paul Molitor	30.00
RC	Cal Ripken Jr.	100.00
RH	Rich Harden	20.00
RI	Jim Rice	25.00
RO	Roy Oswalt	20.00
RW	Rickie Weeks	20.00
RZ	Ryan Zimmerman	35.00
SK	Scott Kazmir	20.00
SP	Scott Podsednik	20.00
TE	Miguel Tejada	25.00
TG	Tony Gwynn	30.00
TH	Travis Hafner	25.00
TI	Tadahito Iguchi	25.00
VM	Victor Martinez	20.00
WC	Will Clark	25.00
WI	Josh Willingham	20.00
YB	Yuniesky Betancourt	15.00

Signature Patch
No Pricing

Production 10 Sets

Tandem Patch
NM/M

Production 35 Sets

Code	Players	Price
AA	Alfonso Soriano, Alex Rios	15.00
AH	Garrett Atkins, Matt Holliday	
AJ	Luis Aparicio, Derek Jeter	40.00
BH	Felix Hernandez, Yuniesky Betancourt	20.00
BM	Brian Bannister, Lastings Milledge	15.00
BR	Yuniesky Betancourt, Hanley Ramirez	20.00
BV	Justin Verlander, Jeremy Bonderman	40.00
CH	Melky Cabrera, Jeremy Hermida	
CL	Coco Crisp, Mark Loretta	15.00
CM	Lastings Milledge, Melky Cabrera	25.00
CO	Roy Oswalt, Roger Clemens	50.00
CP	Carl Crawford, Scott Podsednik	15.00
CR	Miguel Cabrera, Hanley Ramirez	20.00
CS	Cole Hamels, Scott Kazmir	50.00
CV	Justin Verlander, Matt Cain	40.00
CW	Dontrelle Willis, Chris Carpenter	30.00
CZ	Miguel Cabrera, Ryan Zimmerman	30.00
DH	Hanley Ramirez, Derek Jeter	60.00
FW	Prince Fielder, Rickie Weeks	30.00
GD	Adam Dunn, Ken Griffey Jr.	40.00
GG	Tony Gwynn, Brian Giles	30.00
GP	Ken Griffey Jr., Albert Pujols	80.00
GR	Ken Griffey Jr., Alex Rios	
GT	Ken Griffey Jr., Frank Thomas	50.00
HB	Matt Holliday, Jason Bay	20.00
HF	Prince Fielder, Travis Hafner	30.00
HG	Trevor Hoffman, Brian Giles	15.00
HJ	Andruw Jones, Torii Hunter	25.00
HK	Jeremy Hermida, Jason Kubel	15.00
HM	Travis Hafner, Victor Martinez	15.00
HN	Trevor Hoffman, Joe Nathan	15.00
HO	Roy Oswalt, Rich Harden	
HP	Trevor Hoffman, Jonathan Papelbon	30.00
HR	Hanley Ramirez, Jeremy Hermida	25.00
HW	Jeremy Hermida, Josh Willingham	15.00
ID	Jermaine Dye, Tadahito Iguchi	
JC	Derek Jeter, Melky Cabrera	65.00
JG	Derek Jeter, Ken Griffey Jr.	80.00
JJ	Derek Jeter, Reggie Jackson	60.00
JK	Kendry Morales, Jered Weaver	30.00
JM	Kenji Johjima, Victor Martinez	30.00

Code	Players	Price
JR	Derek Jeter, Cal Ripken Jr.	100.00
KB	Brian Giles, Khalil Greene	20.00
KC	Scott Kazmir, Carl Crawford	15.00
KM	Joe Mauer, Jason Kendall	25.00
KU	Ian Kinsler, Dan Uggla	20.00
KY	Ian Kinsler, Michael Young	15.00
LC	Fred Lynn, Coco Crisp	20.00
LF	Prince Fielder, Carlos Lee	20.00
LH	Francisco Liriano, Cole Hamels	40.00
MF	Kendry Morales, Prince Fielder	25.00
MH	Livan Hernandez, Kendry Morales	15.00
ML	Francisco Liriano, Joe Mauer	35.00
MM	Joe Mauer, Victor Martinez	25.00
MR	Melvin Mora, Brian Roberts	15.00
MW	Rickie Weeks, Paul Molitor	20.00
NJ	Joe Mauer, Joe Nathan	20.00
NL	Joe Nathan, Francisco Liriano	30.00
NM	Joe Mauer, Joe Nathan	30.00
NP	Joe Nathan, Jonathan Papelbon	30.00
PC	Matt Cain, Gaylord Perry	30.00
PH	Jonathan Papelbon, Craig Hansen	50.00
PO	Roy Oswalt, Jake Peavy	20.00
PP	Jake Peavy, Gaylord Perry	15.00
RC	Coco Crisp, Alex Rios	15.00
RM	Lastings Milledge, Jose Reyes	30.00
RR	Jose Reyes, Hanley Ramirez	40.00
RS	Mike Schmidt, Cal Ripken Jr.	75.00
RU	Hanley Ramirez, Dan Uggla	25.00
RV	Ivan Rodriguez, Justin Verlander	35.00
SH	Rich Harden, Nick Swisher	15.00
SJ	Conor Jackson, Chris Shelton	25.00
SZ	Ryan Zimmerman, Mike Schmidt	40.00
TY	Michael Young, Mark Teixeira	20.00
UK	Chase Utley, Ian Kinsler	40.00
UM	Chase Utley, Joe Morgan	40.00
UR	Brian Roberts, Dan Uggla	15.00
VM	Justin Verlander, Jack Morris	40.00
VZ	Justin Verlander, Joel Zumaya	40.00
WM	Josh Willingham, Joe Mauer	25.00
WR	Hanley Ramirez, Josh Willingham	25.00
WV	Justin Verlander, Jered Weaver	40.00
YL	Kevin Youkilis, Mark Loretta	20.00
ZA	Garrett Atkins, Ryan Zimmerman	40.00
ZC	Ryan Zimmerman, Miguel Cabrera	40.00
ZJ	Josh Johnson, Joel Zumaya	20.00
ZZ	Joel Zumaya, Carlos Zambrano	30.00

2007 Upper Deck

NM/M

Complete Set (500): —
Common Player: .15
Rookie Redemption: 75.00
Hobby Pack (15): 5.00
Hobby Box (16): 70.00

#	Player	Price
1	Doug Slaten RC	.25
2	Miguel Montero (RC)	.25
3	Brian Burres (RC)	.25
4	Devern Hansack RC	2.00
5	David Murphy (RC)	.25
6	Jose Reyes RC	.25
7	Scott Moore (RC)	.25
8	Josh Fields (RC)	.50
9	Chris Stewart (RC)	.50
10	Jerry Owens (RC)	.25
11	Ryan Sweeney (RC)	.25
12	Kevin Kouzmanoff (RC)	.50
13	Jeff Baker (RC)	.25
14	Justin Hampson (RC)	.25
15	Jeff Salazar (RC)	.25
16	Alvin Colina RC	.50
17	Troy Tulowitzki (RC)	.50
18	Andrew Miller RC	4.00
19	Mike Rabelo RC	.50
20	Jose Diaz (RC)	.25
21	Angel Sanchez RC	.25
22	Ryan Braun RC	.50
23	Delwyn Young (RC)	.25
24	Drew Anderson (RC)	.25
25	Dennis Sarfate (RC)	.25
26	Vinny Rottino (RC)	.25
27	Glen Perkins (RC)	.25
28	Alexi Casilla RC	1.00
29	Philip Humber (RC)	.50
30	Andy Cannizaro (RC)	.25
31	Jeremy Brown	.25
32	Sean Henn (RC)	.25
33	Brian Rogers	.15
34	Carlos Maldonado (RC)	.25
35	Juan Morillo (RC)	.25
36	Fred Lewis (RC)	.25
37	Patrick Misch (RC)	.25
38	Billy Sadler (RC)	.25
39	Ryan Feierabend (RC)	.25
40	Cesar Jimenez RC	.75
41	Oswaldo Navarro (RC)	.50
42	Travis Chick (RC)	.25
43	Delmon Young (RC)	1.00
44	Shawn Riggans (RC)	.25
45	Brian Stokes (RC)	.25
46	Juan Salas (RC)	.25
47	Joaquin Arias (RC)	.25
48	Adam Lind (RC)	.50
49	Beltran Perez (RC)	.25
50	Brett Campbell RC	.50
51	Brian Roberts	.15
52	Miguel Tejada	.50
53	Brandon Fahey	.15
54	Jay Gibbons	.15
55	Corey Patterson	.15
56	Nicholas Markakis	.25
57	Ramon Hernandez	.15
58	Kris Benson	.15
59	Adam Loewen	.15
60	Erik Bedard	.25
61	Chris Ray	.15
62	Chris Britton	.15
63	Daniel Cabrera	.15
64	Sendy Rleal	.15
65	Manny Ramirez	.75
66	David Ortiz	.75
67	Gabe Kapler	.15
68	Alex Cora	.15
69	Dustin Pedroia	.25
70	Trot Nixon	.15
71	Doug Mirabelli	.15
72	Mark Loretta	.15
73	Curt Schilling	.75
74	Jonathan Papelbon	.50
75	Tim Wakefield	.25
76	Jon Lester	.25
77	Craig Hansen	.15
78	Keith Foulke	.15
79	Jermaine Dye	.25
80	Jim Thome	.50
81	Tadahito Iguchi	.15
82	Robert Mackowiak	.15
83	Brian Anderson	.15
84	Juan Uribe	.15
85	A.J. Pierzynski	.15
86	Alex Cintron	.15
87	Jon Garland	.15
88	Jose Contreras	.15
89	Neal Cotts	.15
90	Bobby Jenks	.15
91	Mike MacDougal	.15
92	Javier Vazquez	.15
93	Travis Hafner	.40
94	Jhonny Peralta	.25
95	Ryan Garko	.15
96	Victor Martinez	.25
97	Hector Luna	.15
98	Casey Blake	.15
99	Jason Michaels	.15
100	Shin-Soo Choo	.15
101	C.C. Sabathia	.25
102	Paul Byrd	.15
103	Jeremy Sowers	.15
104	Cliff Lee	.15
105	Rafael Betancourt	.15
106	Francisco Cruceta	.15
107	Sean Casey	.15
108	Brandon Inge	.15
109	Placido Polanco	.15
110	Omar Infante	.15
111	Ivan Rodriguez	.50
112	Magglio Ordonez	.25
113	Craig Monroe	.15
114	Marcus Thames	.15
115	Justin Verlander	.50
116	Todd Jones	.15
117	Kenny Rogers	.15
118	Joel Zumaya	.25
119	Jeremy Bonderman	.25
120	Nate Robertson	.15
121	Mark Teahen	.25
122	Ryan Shealy	.15
123	Mitch Maier (RC)	.25
124	Doug Mientkiewicz	.15
125	Mark Grudzielanek	.15
126	Shane Costa	.15
127	John Buck	.15
128	Reggie Sanders	.15
129	Mike Sweeney	.15
130	Mark Redman	.15
131	Todd Wellemeyer	.15
132	Scott Elarton	.15
133	Ambiorix Burgos	.15
134	Joe Nelson	.15
135	Howie Kendrick	.40
136	Chone Figgins	.15
137	Orlando Cabrera	.25
138	Maicer Izturis	.15
139	Jose Molina	.15
140	Vladimir Guerrero	.75
141	Darin Erstad	.15
142	Juan Rivera	.15
143	Jered Weaver	.40
144	John Lackey	.25
145	Joe Saunders	.15
146	Bartolo Colon	.15
147	Scot Shields	.15
148	Francisco Rodriguez	.25
149	Justin Morneau	.50
150	Jason Bartlett	.15
151	Luis Castillo	.15
152	Nick Punto	.15
153	Shannon Stewart	.15
154	Michael Cuddyer	.15
155	Jason Kubel	.15
156	Joe Mauer	.50
157	Francisco Liriano	.25
158	Joe Nathan	.15
159	Dennys Reyes	.15
160	Brad Radke	.15
161	Boof Bonser	.15
162	Juan Rincon	.15
163	Derek Jeter	2.00
164	Jason Giambi	.50
165	Robinson Cano	.50
166	Andy Phillips	.15
167	Bobby Abreu	.40
168	Gary Sheffield	.50
169	Bernie Williams	.50
170	Melky Cabrera	.25
171	Mike Mussina	.50
172	Chien-Ming Wang	.50
173	Mariano Rivera	.50
174	Scott Proctor	.15
175	Jaret Wright	.15
176	Kyle Farnsworth	.15
177	Eric Chavez	.25
178	Bobby Crosby	.15
179	Frank Thomas	.40
180	Dan Johnson	.15
181	Marco Scutaro	.15
182	Nick Swisher	.40
183	Milton Bradley	.15
184	Jay Payton	.15
185	Joe Blanton	.15
186	Barry Zito	.40
187	Rich Harden	.25
188	Esteban Loaiza	.15
189	Huston Street	.25
190	Chad Gaudin	.15
191	Richie Sexson	.40
192	Yuniesky Betancourt	.15
193	Willie Bloomquist	.15
194	Ben Broussard	.15
195	Kenji Johjima	.25
196	Ichiro Suzuki	1.00
197	Raul Ibanez	.15
198	Chris Snelling/SP	.15
199	Felix Hernandez	.50
200	Cha Seung Baek	.15
201	Joel Pineiro	.15
202	Julio Mateo	.15
203	J.J. Putz	.15
204	Rafael Soriano	.15
205	Jorge Cantu	.15
206	B.J. Upton	.25
207	Ty Wigginton	.15
208	Greg Norton	.15
209	Dioner Navarro	.15
210	Carl Crawford	.40
211	Jonny Gomes	.15
212	Damon Hollins	.15
213	Scott Kazmir	.25
214	Casey Fossum	.15
215	Ruddy Lugo	.15
216	James Shields	.15
217	Tyler Walker	.15
218	Shawn Camp	.15
219	Mark Teixeira	.50
220	Hank Blalock	.25
221	Ian Kinsler	.25
222	Jerry Hairston Jr.	.15
223	Gerald Laird	.15
224	Carlos Lee	.40
225	Gary Matthews	.15
226	Mark DeRosa	.15
227	Kip Wells	.15
228	Akinori Otsuka	.15
229	Vicente Padilla	.15
230	John Koronka	.15
231	Kevin Millwood	.25
232	Wes Littleton	.15
233	Troy Glaus	.40
234	Lyle Overbay	.25
235	Aaron Hill	.25
236	John McDonald	.15
237	Bengie Molina	.15
238	Vernon Wells	.25
239	Reed Johnson	.15
240	Frank Catalanotto	.15
241	Roy Halladay	.40
242	B.J. Ryan	.15
243	Gustavo Chacin	.15
244	Scott Downs	.15
245	Casey Janssen	.15
246	Justin Speier	.15
247	Stephen Drew	.40
248	Conor Jackson	.15
249	Orlando Hudson	.15
250	Chad Tracy	.15
251	Johnny Estrada	.15
252	Luis Gonzalez	.15
253	Eric Byrnes	.15
254	Carlos Quentin	.15
255	Brandon Webb	.25
256	Claudio Vargas	.15
257	Juan Cruz	.15
258	Jorge Julio	.15
259	Luis Vizcaino	.15
260	Livan Hernandez	.15
261	Chipper Jones	.75
262	Edgar Renteria	.25
263	Adam LaRoche	.25
264	Willy Aybar	.15
265	Brian McCann	.40
266	Ryan Langerhans	.15
267	Jeff Francoeur	.40
268	Matt Diaz	.15
269	Tim Hudson	.25
270	John Smoltz	.40
271	Oscar Villarreal	.15
272	Horacio Ramirez	.15
273	Bob Wickman	.15
274	Chad Paronto	.15
275	Derek Lee	.15
276	Ryan Theriot	.15
277	Cesar Izturis	.15
278	Ronny Cedeno	.15
279	Michael Barrett	.15
280	Juan Pierre	.25
281	Jacque Jones	.15
282	Matt Murton	.25
283	Carlos Zambrano	.25
284	Mark Prior	.25
285	Rich Hill	.40
286	Sean Marshall	.15
287	Ryan Dempster	.15
288	Ryan O'Malley	.15
289	Scott Hatteberg	.15
290	Brandon Phillips	.25
291	Edwin Encarnacion	.15
292	Rich Aurilia	.15
293	David Ross	.15
294	Ken Griffey Jr.	1.00
295	Ryan Freel	.15
296	Chris Denorfia	.15
297	Bronson Arroyo	.15
298	Aaron Harang	.15
299	Brandon Claussen	.15
300	Todd Coffey	.15
301	David Weathers	.15
302	Eric Milton	.15
303	Todd Helton	.50
304	Clint Barmes	.15
305	Kazuo Matsui	.15
306	Jamey Carroll	.15
307	Yorvit Torrealba	.15
308	Matt Holliday	.25
309	Choo Freeman	.15
310	Brad Hawpe	.25
311	Jason Jennings	.15
312	Jeff Francis	.15
313	Josh Fogg	.15
314	Aaron Cook	.15
315	Ubaldo Jimenez	.15
316	Manny Corpas	.15
317	Miguel Cabrera	.75
318	Dan Uggla	.25
319	Hanley Ramirez	.50
320	Wes Helms	.15
321	Miguel Olivo	.15
322	Jeremy Hermida	.15
323	Cody Ross	.15
324	Josh Willingham	.15
325	Dontrelle Willis	.25
326	Anibal Sanchez	.15
327	Josh Johnson	.15
328	Jose Garcia	.15
329	Joe Borowski	.15
330	Taylor Tankersley	.15
331	Lance Berkman	.50
332	Craig Biggio	.40
333	Aubrey Huff	.15
334	Adam Everett	.15
335	Brad Ausmus	.15
336	Willy Taveras	.15
337	Luke Scott	.15
338	Chris Burke	.15
339	Roger Clemens	1.50
340	Andy Pettitte	.40
341	Brandon Backe	.15
342	Hector Gimenez	.15
343	Brad Lidge	.15
344	Dan Wheeler	.15
345	Nomar Garciaparra	.75
346	Rafael Furcal	.25
347	Wilson Betemit	.15
348	Julio Lugo	.15
349	Russell Martin	.25
350	Andre Ethier	.25
351	Matthew Kemp	.25
352	Kenny Lofton	.15
353	Brad Penny	.15
354	Derek Lowe	.15
355	Chad Billingsley	.25
356	Greg Maddux	1.00
357	Takashi Saito	.15
358	Jonathan Broxton	.15
359	Prince Fielder	.50
360	Rickie Weeks	.40
361	Bill Hall	.15
362	J.J. Hardy	.15
363	Jeff Cirillo	.15
364	Tony Gwynn Jr.	.15
365	Corey Hart	.15
366	Laynce Nix	.15
367	Doug Davis	.15
368	Ben Sheets	.40
369	Chris Capuano	.15
370	David Bush	.15
371	Derrick Turnbow	.15
372	Francisco Cordero	.15
373	Jose Reyes	1.00
374	Carlos Delgado	.50
375	Julio Franco	.15
376	Jose Valentin	.15
377	Paul LoDuca	.15
378	Carlos Beltran	.50
379	Shawn Green	.15
380	Lastings Milledge	.25
381	Endy Chavez	.15
382	Pedro Martinez	.75
383	John Maine	.15
384	Orlando Hernandez	.15
385	Steve Trachsel	.15
386	Billy Wagner	.15
387	Ryan Howard	1.50
388	Chase Utley	.75
389	Jimmy Rollins	.50
390	Chris Coste	.15
391	Jeff Conine	.15
392	Aaron Rowand	.15
393	Shane Victorino	.15
394	David Dellucci	.15
395	Cole Hamels	.40
396	Jamie Moyer	.15
397	Ryan Madson	.15
398	Brett Myers	.25
399	Tom Gordon	.15
400	Geoff Geary	.15
401	Freddy Sanchez	.15
402	Xavier Nady	.15
403	Jose Castillo	.15
404	Joe Randa	.15
405	Jason Bay	.40
406	Chris Duffy	.15
407	Jose Bautista	.15
408	Ronny Paulino	.15
409	Ian Snell	.25
410	Zachary Duke	.15
411	Tom Gorzelanny	.15
412	Shane Youman	.15
413	Mike Gonzalez	.15
414	Matt Capps	.15
415	Adrian Gonzalez	.25
416	Josh Barfield	.15
417	Todd Walker	.15
418	Khalil Greene	.15
419	Mike Piazza	.75
420	Dave Roberts	.15
421	Mike Cameron	.15
422	Geoff Blum	.15
423	Jake Peavy	.40
424	Chris Young	.25
425	Woody Williams	.15
426	Clay Hensley	.15
427	Cla Meredith	.15
428	Trevor Hoffman	.25
429	Shea Hillenbrand	.15
430	Pedro Feliz	.15
431	Ray Durham	.15
432	Mark Sweeney	.15
433	Eliezer Alfonzo	.15
434	Moises Alou	.25
435	Steve Finley	.15
436	Todd Linden	.15
437	Jason Schmidt	.25
438	Matt Cain	.25
439	Noah Lowry	.15
440	Brad Hennessey	.15
441	Armando Benitez	.15
442	Jonathan Sanchez	.15
443	Albert Pujols	2.00
444	Ronnie Belliard	.15
445	David Eckstein	.15
446	Aaron Miles	.15
447	Yadier Molina	.15
448	Jim Edmonds	.25
449	Chris Duncan	.15
450	Juan Encarnacion	.15
451	Chris Carpenter	.50
452	Jeff Suppan	.15
453	Jason Marquis	.15
454	Jeff Weaver	.15
455	Jason Isringhausen	.15
456	Braden Looper	.15
457	Ryan Zimmerman	.40
458	Nick Johnson	.15
459	Felipe Lopez	.25
460	Brian Schneider	.15
461	Alfonso Soriano	.75
462	Austin Kearns	.15
463	Ryan Church	.15
464	Alex Escobar	.15
465	Ramon Ortiz	.15
466	Tony Armas	.15
467	Michael O'Connor	.15
468	Chad Cordero	.15
469	Jon Rauch	.15
470	Pedro Astacio	.15
471	Miguel Tejada	.25
472	David Ortiz	.50
473	Jermaine Dye	.25
474	Travis Hafner	.25
475	Magglio Ordonez	.25
476	Mark Teahen	.15
477	Vladimir Guerrero	.50
478	Justin Morneau	.50
479	Derek Jeter	1.00
480	Nick Swisher	.25
481	Ichiro Suzuki	.50
482	Scott Kazmir	.25
483	Mark Teixeira	.25
484	Vernon Wells	.25
485	Brandon Webb	.25
486	Andruw Jones	.40
487	Carlos Zambrano	.25
488	Adam Dunn	.25
489	Matt Holliday	.25
490	Miguel Cabrera	.50
491	Lance Berkman	.25
492	Nomar Garciaparra	.25
493	Prince Fielder	.50
494	Carlos Beltran	.40
495	Ryan Howard	1.00
496	Jason Bay	.25
497	Adrian Gonzalez	.25
498	Matt Cain	.25
499	Albert Pujols	1.00
500	Ryan Zimmerman	.25

Gold

Gold: 8-15X
Production 75 Sets

Printing Plates

No Pricing
Production one set per color.

First Edition

NM/M

Complete Set (300): 35.00
Common Player: .10
Pack (10): 1.00
Box (36): 30.00

#	Player	Price
1	Doug Slaten RC	.25
2	Miguel Montero (RC)	.25
3	Brian Burres (RC)	.25
4	Devern Hansack RC	1.00
5	David Murphy (RC)	.25
6	Jose Reyes RC	.25
7	Scott Moore (RC)	.25
8	Josh Fields (RC)	.25
9	Chris Stewart (RC)	.25
10	Jerry Owens (RC)	.25
11	Ryan Sweeney (RC)	.25
12	Kevin Kouzmanoff (RC)	.40
13	Jeff Baker (RC)	.25
14	Justin Hampson (RC)	.25
15	Jeff Salazar (RC)	.25
16	Alvin Colina RC	.25
17	Troy Tulowitzki (RC)	.50
18	Andrew Miller RC	3.00
19	Mike Rabelo RC	.25
20	Jose Diaz (RC)	.25
21	Angel Sanchez RC	.25
22	Ryan Braun RC	.25
23	Delwyn Young (RC)	.25
24	Drew Anderson (RC)	.25
25	Dennis Sarfate (RC)	.25
26	Vinny Rottino (RC)	.25
27	Glen Perkins (RC)	.25
28	Alexi Casilla RC	.25
29	Philip Humber (RC)	.25
30	Andy Cannizaro RC	.25
31	Jeremy Brown	.10
32	Sean Henn (RC)	.25
33	Brian Rogers (RC)	.25
34	Carlos Maldonado (RC)	.25
35	Juan Morillo (RC)	.25
36	Fred Lewis (RC)	.25
37	Patrick Misch (RC)	.25
38	Billy Sadler (RC)	.25
39	Ryan Feierabend (RC)	.25
40	Cesar Jimenez RC	.25
41	Oswaldo Navarro RC	.25
42	Travis Chick (RC)	.25
43	Delmon Young (RC)	.50
44	Shawn Riggans (RC)	.25
45	Brian Stokes (RC)	.25
46	Juan Salas (RC)	.25
47	Joaquin Arias (RC)	.25
48	Adam Lind (RC)	.50
49	Beltran Perez (RC)	.25
50	Brett Campbell RC	.25
51	Miguel Tejada	.40
52	Brandon Fahey	.10
53	Jay Gibbons	.10
54	Nicholas Markakis	.10
55	Kris Benson	.10
56	Erik Bedard	.10
57	Chris Ray	.10
58	Chris Britton	.10
59	Manny Ramirez	.50
60	David Ortiz	.50
61	Alex Cora	.10
62	Trot Nixon	.10
63	Doug Mirabelli	.10
64	Curt Schilling	.50
65	Jonathan Papelbon	.50
66	Craig Hansen	.15
67	Jermaine Dye	.25
68	Jim Thome	.50
69	Robert Mackowiak	.10
70	Brian Anderson	.10
71	A.J. Pierzynski	.10
72	Alex Cintron	.10
73	Jose Contreras	.10
74	Bobby Jenks	.10
75	Mike MacDougal	.10
76	Travis Hafner	.40
77	Ryan Garko	.10
78	Victor Martinez	.25
79	Casey Blake	.10
80	Shin-Soo Choo	.10
81	Paul Byrd	.10
82	Jeremy Sowers	.15
83	Cliff Lee	.10
84	Sean Casey	.10
85	Brandon Inge	.10
86	Omar Infante	.10
87	Magglio Ordonez	.25
88	Marcus Thames	.10
89	Justin Verlander	.50
90	Todd Jones	.10

91	Joel Zumaya	.25
92	Nate Robertson	.10
93	Mark Teahen	.25
94	Ryan Shealy	.10
95	Mark Grudzielanek	.10
96	Shane Costa	.10
97	Reggie Sanders	.10
98	Mark Redman	.10
99	Todd Wellemeyer	.10
100	Ambiorix Burgos	.10
101	Joe Nelson	.10
102	Orlando Cabrera	.25
103	Maicer Izturis	.10
104	Vladimir Guerrero	.50
105	Juan Rivera	.10
106	Jered Weaver	.40
107	Joe Saunders	.10
108	Bartolo Colon	.10
109	Francisco Rodriguez	.25
110	Justin Morneau	.50
111	Luis Castillo	.10
112	Michael Cuddyer	.10
113	Joe Mauer	.40
114	Francisco Liriano	.25
115	Joe Nathan	.25
116	Brad Radke	.10
117	Juan Rincon	.10
118	Derek Jeter	1.50
119	Jason Giambi	.25
120	Bobby Abreu	.40
121	Gary Sheffield	.25
122	Melky Cabrera	.25
123	Chien-Ming Wang	.50
124	Mariano Rivera	.40
125	Jaret Wright	.10
126	Kyle Farnsworth	.10
127	Frank Thomas	.50
128	Dan Johnson	.10
129	Marco Scutaro	.10
130	Jay Payton	.10
131	Joe Blanton	.10
132	Rich Harden	.25
133	Esteban Loaiza	.10
134	Chad Gaudin	.10
135	Yuniesky Betancourt	.10
136	Willie Bloomquist	.10
137	Ichiro Suzuki	1.00
138	Raul Ibanez	.10
139	Chris Snelling	.10
140	Cha Sueng Baek	.10
141	Julio Mateo	.10
142	Rafael Soriano	.10
143	Jorge Cantu	.10
144	B.J. Upton	.10
145	Dioner Navarro	.10
146	Carl Crawford	.40
147	Damon Hollins	.10
148	Casey Fossum	.10
149	Ruddy Lugo	.10
150	Tyler Walker	.10
151	Shawn Camp	.10
152	Ian Kinsler	.25
153	Jerry Hairston Jr.	.10
154	Gerald Laird	.10
155	Mark DeRosa	.10
156	Kip Wells	.10
157	Vicente Padilla	.10
158	John Koronka	.10
159	Wes Littleton	.10
160	Lyle Overbay	.10
161	Aaron Hill	.10
162	John McDonald	.10
163	Vernon Wells	.10
164	Frank Catalanotto	.10
165	Roy Halladay	.25
166	B.J. Ryan	.10
167	Casey Janssen	.10
168	Stephen Drew	.50
169	Conor Jackson	.10
170	Chad Tracy	.10
171	Johnny Estrada	.10
172	Eric Byrnes	.10
173	Carlos Quentin	.25
174	Brandon Webb	.25
175	Jorge Julio	.10
176	Luis Vizcaino	.10
177	Chipper Jones	.50
178	Adam LaRoche	.25
179	Brian McCann	.25
180	Ryan Langerhans	.10
181	Matt Diaz	.10
182	John Smoltz	.25
183	Oscar Villarreal	.10
184	Chad Paronto	.10
185	Derrek Lee	.40
186	Ryan Theriot	.10
187	Ronny Cedeno	.10
188	Juan Pierre	.10
189	Matt Murton	.10
190	Carlos Zambrano	.25
191	Mark Prior	.25
192	Ryan Dempster	.10
193	Ryan O'Malley	.10
194	Brandon Phillips	.10
195	Rich Aurilia	.10
196	Ken Griffey Jr.	1.00
197	Ryan Freel	.10
198	Aaron Harang	.10
199	Brandon Claussen	.10
200	David Weathers	.10
201	Eric Milton	.10
202	Kazuo Matsui	.10
203	Jamey Carroll	.10
204	Matt Holliday	.25
205	Brad Hawpe	.10
206	Jason Jennings	.10
207	Josh Fogg	.10
208	Aaron Cook	.10

209	Miguel Cabrera	.50
210	Dan Uggla	.10
211	Hanley Ramirez	.40
212	Jeremy Hermida	.10
213	Cody Ross	.10
214	Josh Willingham	.10
215	Anibal Sanchez	.10
216	Jose Garcia	.10
217	Taylor Tankersley	.10
218	Lance Berkman	.40
219	Craig Biggio	.25
220	Brad Ausmus	.10
221	Willy Taveras	.10
222	Chris Burke	.10
223	Roger Clemens	1.00
224	Brandon Backe	.10
225	Brad Lidge	.10
226	Dan Wheeler	.10
227	Wilson Betemit	.10
228	Julio Lugo	.10
229	Russell Martin	.25
230	Kenny Lofton	.10
231	Brad Penny	.10
232	Chad Billingsley	.10
233	Greg Maddux	1.00
234	Jonathan Broxton	.10
235	Rickie Weeks	.25
236	Bill Hall	.10
237	Tony Gwynn Jr.	.10
238	Corey Hart	.10
239	Laynce Nix	.10
240	Ben Sheets	.25
241	David Bush	.10
242	Francisco Cordero	.10
243	Jose Reyes	.50
244	Carlos Delgado	.40
245	Paul LoDuca	.10
246	Carlos Beltran	.40
247	Lastings Milledge	.25
248	Pedro Martinez	.50
249	John Maine	.10
250	Steve Trachsel	.10
251	Ryan Howard	1.00
252	Jimmy Rollins	.25
253	Chris Coste	.10
254	Jeff Conine	.10
255	David Dellucci	.10
256	Cole Hamels	.25
257	Ryan Madson	.10
258	Brett Myers	.25
259	Freddy Sanchez	.10
260	Xavier Nady	.10
261	Jose Castillo	.10
262	Jason Bay	.25
263	Jose Bautista	.10
264	Ronny Paulino	.10
265	Zachary Duke	.10
266	Shane Youman	.10
267	Matt Capps	.10
268	Adrian Gonzalez	.25
269	Josh Barfield	.10
270	Mike Piazza	.75
271	Dave Roberts	.10
272	Geoff Blum	.10
273	Chris Young	.10
274	Woody Williams	.10
275	Cla Meredith	.10
276	Trevor Hoffman	.25
277	Ray Durham	.10
278	Mark Sweeney	.10
279	Eliezer Alfonzo	.10
280	Todd Linden	.10
281	Jason Schmidt	.25
282	Noah Lowry	.10
283	Brad Hennessey	.10
284	Jonathan Sanchez	.10
285	Albert Pujols	1.50
286	David Eckstein	.10
287	Jim Edmonds	.25
288	Chris Duncan	.10
289	Juan Encarnacion	.10
290	Jeff Suppan	.10
291	Jeff Weaver	.10
292	Braden Looper	.10
293	Ryan Zimmerman	.25
294	Nick Johnson	.10
295	Alfonso Soriano	.50
296	Austin Kearns	.10
297	Alex Escobar	.10
298	Tony Armas	.10
299	Chad Cordero	.10
300	Jon Rauch	.10

First Edition Printing Plates

No Pricing
Production one set per color.

1993 USA Rice

To promote rice consumption and raise money for the pictured athletes' favorite charities, the USA Rice Council issued this multi-sport card set and made it available by mail for a $2 donation. All players are pictured in civilian clothes with either a blue or red border around. Backs of most cards have rice recipes and indicate the charity to which the athlete

STEVE SAX

is donating their portion of the proceeds. Cards are standard 2-1/2" x 3-1/2".

		NM/M
Complete Set (10):		10.00
Common Card:		.50
1	Steve Sax/Cooking	1.00
2	Troy Aikman/Football	3.00
3	Roger Clemens	7.50
4	Zina Garrison/Tennis	.50
5	Warren Moon/Football	2.00
6	Summer Sanders/ Swimming	.50
7	Steve Sax/ Lifting Weights	1.00
8	Brian Shimer/ Bobsledder	.50
9	Food Guide Pyramid	.25
10	Healthy Eating Tips	.25

1999 U.S. Cellular Milwaukee Brewers

The four Milwaukee Brewers who have had their uniform numbers retired by the team, plus Jackie Robinson, whose #42 was retired by MLB edict, are honored on this foldout promotion given to fans October 2 at County Stadium. Five 4" x 6" cards make up the panel, which is perforated between the cards for ease of separation. Cards have player action photos on front (color except for Robinson) on a muted blue-green stadium photo background. At lower-right is a gold-foil seal with the player's name and number. At top is a sponsor logo and part of the legend "COMMEMORATING GREATNESS" which runs contiguously across the panel. Backs have a black-and-white photo, career data and highlights.

		NM/M
Complete Set, Panel:		12.00
Complete Set, Singles (5):		8.00
Common Player:		1.00
4	Paul Molitor	4.00
19	Robin Yount	4.00
34	Rollie Fingers	1.00
42	Jackie Robinson	3.00
44	Hank Aaron	5.00

1993 U.S. Department of Transportation Safety Set

This six-card set (issued in three-card panels) was sponsored by the U.S. Department of Transportation and distributed

MO VAUGHN

at the Little League World Series. Standard size cards have red and blue borders on front, along with the Little League logo. Backs are printed in red and blue and include a highway safety message and sponsors/licensors logos.

		NM/M
Complete Set (6):		11.00
Common Player:		1.50
Panel 1		4.00
1	Orel Hershiser	.50
2	Don Mattingly	3.00
3	Mike Mussina	1.00
Panel 2		6.00
(4)	Mike Piazza	2.50
(5)	Cal Ripken Jr.	4.00
(6)	Mo Vaughn	.50

1987 U.S. Forestry Service Smokey Bear's Team

The U.S. Forestry Service and Major League Baseball united in an effort to promote National Smokey the Bear Day. Two perforated sheets of baseball cards, one each for the American and National Leagues, were produced. The sheet of American Leaguers measures 18" x 24" and contains 16 full-color cards. The National League sheet measures 20" x 18" and contains 15 cards. Each individual card is 4" x 6" and contains a fire prevention tip on the back. An average number of 25,000 sets was sent to all teams.

		NM/M
Complete Set (31):		12.00
Complete A.L. Sheet:		7.00
Complete N.L. Sheet:		7.00
Common Player:		.25
1A	Jose Canseco	.75
1N	Steve Sax	.25
2A	Dennis "Oil Can" Boyd	.25
2Na	Dale Murphy (Shirttail out.)	5.00
2Nb	Dale Murphy (Shirttail in.)	.90
3A	John Candelaria	.25
3Na	Jody Davis/Standing	3.00
3Nb	Jody Davis/Kneeling	.25
4A	Harold Baines	.25
4N	Bill Gullickson	.25
5A	Joe Carter	.25
5N	Mike Scott	.25
6A	Jack Morris	.25
6N	Roger McDowell	.25
7A	Buddy Biancalana	.25
7N	Steve Bedrosian	.25
8A	Kirby Puckett	3.00
8N	Johnny Ray	.25
9A	Mike Pagliarulo	.25
9N	Ozzie Smith	3.00
10A	Larry Sheets	.25
10N	Steve Garvey	.50

11A	Mike Moore	.25
11N	Smokey Bear Logo Card	.05
12A	Charlie Hough	.25
12N	Mike Krukow	.25
13A	Smokey Bear Logo Card	.05
13N	Smokey Bear	.05
14A	Tom Henke	.25
14N	Mike Fitzgerald	.25
15A	Jim Gantner	.25
15N	National League Logo Card	.05
16A	American League Logo Card	.05

1990 U.S. Playing Card All-Stars

KEN GRIFFEY JR. OUTFIELD

Sold as a boxed set, these cards are the standard 2-1/2 x 3-1/2" format but feature rounded corners. Each card features a color player photo with the upper-left and lower-right corners inset to provide for playing card designations. A team logo appears in the lower-left corner. On American League players' cards (Clubs and Spades) the player's name and position appear in white in a blue box beneath the photo. On National Leaguers' cards (Hearts and Diamonds) the box is red and the printing black. Card backs are identical, with blue borders and a multi-colored "1990 Baseball Major League All-Stars" logo on a pinstriped white center panel. A premium version with the cards' edges silvered was also issued. These cards have a small diagonal "nip" at each rounded corner.

		NM/M
Complete Set (56):		5.00
Common Player:		.05
HEARTS		
J	Bobby Bonilla	.05
Q	Kevin Mitchell	.05
K	Darryl Strawberry	.05
A	Ramon Martinez	.05
2	Mike Scioscia	.05
3	Jeff Brantley	.05
4	Ryne Sandberg	.75
5	Chris Sabo	.05
6	Ozzie Smith	.75
7	John Franco	.05
8	Matt Williams	.05
9	Andre Dawson	.25
10	Benito Santiago	.05
CLUBS		
J	Wade Boggs	.75
Q	George Bell	.05
K	Rickey Henderson	.50
A	Bob Welch	.05
2	Lance Parrish	.05
3	Bret Saberhagen	.05
4	Gregg Olson	.05
5	Brook Jacoby	.05
6	Ozzie Guillen	.05
7	Ellis Burks	.05
8	Dennis Eckersley	.40
9	Bobby Thigpen	.05
10	Dave Stieb	.05
DIAMONDS		
J	Tony Gwynn	.75
Q	Will Clark	.25
K	Barry Bonds	1.50
A	Frank Viola	.05
2	Greg Olson	.05
3	Dennis Martinez	.05
4	Roberto Alomar	.20
5	Tim Wallach	.05
6	Barry Larkin	.05
7	Neal Heaton	.05
8	Dave Smith	.05
9	Lenny Dykstra	.05
10	Shawon Dunston	.05
SPADES		
J	Ken Griffey Jr.	1.00
Q	Dave Parker	.05

K	Cecil Fielder	.05
A	Roger Clemens	.85
2	Sandy Alomar	.05
3	Randy Johnson	.50
4	Steve Sax	.05
5	Kelly Gruber	.05
6	Chuck Finley	.05
7	Doug Jones	.05
8	Kirby Puckett	.75
9	Cal Ripken, Jr.	1.50
10	Alan Trammell	.05
WILD CARDS/JOKERS		
J	Jack Armstrong (Joker)	.05
---	Julio Franco (Joker)	.05
---	Rob Dibble, Randy Myers (Wild Card)	.05
---	Mark McGwire, Jose Canseco (Wild Card)	1.00

1991 U.S. Playing Card All-Stars

PAUL MOLITOR • CF

In standard 2-1/2" x 3-1/2" format, though with rounded corners, this 56-card set was produced by the country's leading maker of playing cards and sold as a boxed set. Fronts have a color player photo with the top-left and bottom-right corners inset to include playing card designations. A team logo appears in the upper-right corner. On American Leaguers' cards (Hearts and Diamonds), the player's name and position appear in white in a green stripe beneath the photo. National League players (Clubs and Spades) have a yellow stripe with black printing. Backs are red-bordered with a colorful "1991 Baseball Major League All-Stars" logo on a pinstriped white center panel. A silver-edged premium version was also issued. These cards have a diagonal "nip" at each rounded corner. A Canadian version, with the imprint of International Playing Card, also exists.

		NM/M
Complete Set (56):		4.00
Common Player:		.05
HEARTS		
J	Rickey Henderson	.50
Q	Roberto Alomar	.20
K	Dave Henderson	.05
A	Jack Morris	.05
2	Ozzie Guillen	.05
3	Jack McDowell	.05
4	Joe Carter	.05
5	Mark Langston	.05
6	Julio Franco	.05
7	Rick Aguilera	.05
8	Paul Molitor	.50
9	Ruben Sierra	.05
10	Roger Clemens	.85
CLUBS		
J	Andre Dawson	.25
Q	Chris Sabo	.05
K	Ivan Calderon	.05
A	Tony Gwynn	.75
2	Paul O'Neill	.05
3	John Smiley	.05
4	Howard Johnson	.05
5	Mike Morgan	.05
6	Barry Larkin	.05
7	Frank Viola	.05
8	Juan Samuel	.05
9	Craig Biggio	.05
10	Lee Smith	.05
DIAMONDS		
J	Sandy Alomar	.05
Q	Cecil Fielder	.05
K	Cal Ripken Jr.	1.50
A	Ken Griffey Jr.	1.00
2	Carlton Fisk	.50
3	Scott Sanderson	.05
4	Kirby Puckett	.75
5	Jeff Reardon	.05
6	Rafael Palmeiro	.40

7	Bryan Harvey	.05
8	Jimmy Key	.05
9	Harold Baines	.05
10	Dennis Eckersley	.40

SPADES

J	Benito Santiago	.05
Q	Ryne Sandberg	.75
K	Ozzie Smith	.75
A	Tom Glavine	.10
2	Eddie Murray	.60
3	Pete Harnisch	.05
4	John Kruk	.05
5	Tom Browning	.05
6	George Bell	.05
7	Dennis Martinez	.05
8	Brett Butler	.05
9	Terry Pendleton	.05
10	Rob Dibble	.05

WILD CARDS/JOKERS

---	Bobby Bonilla (Joker)	.05
---	Danny Tartabull	.05
---	Wade Boggs (Wild Card)	.75
---	Will Clark (Wild Card)	.05

1992 U.S. Playing Card Aces

This 56-card boxed set features 13 top players in each of four major statistical categories, ranked by performance. Hearts feature RBI leaders, Clubs depict home run hitters, batting average leaders are featured on Diamonds and Spades have pitchers with lowest ERAs. Card fronts feature full-bleed color photos, with the playing card suit and rank overprinted in opposing corners. A team logo is in the lower-left, along with a black box containing the player's name and position in gold. Backs have a red, white and gold "Major League Baseball 1992 Aces" against a black background. The 2-1/2" x 3-1/2" cards have rounded corners.

		NM/M
Complete Set (56):		4.00
Common Player:		.05

HEARTS

J	Will Clark	.05
Q	Howard Johnson	.05
K	Jose Canseco	.35
A	Cecil Fielder	.05
2	Juan Gonzalez	.25
3	Andre Dawson	.25
4	Ron Gant	.05
5	Fred McGriff	.05
6	Joe Carter	.05
7	Frank Thomas	.50
8	Cal Ripkin (Ripken)	1.50
9	Ruben Sierra	1.50
10	Barry Bonds	1.50

CLUBS

J	Cal Ripkin (Ripken)	1.50
Q	Howard Johnson	.05
K	Cecil Fielder	.05
A	Jose Canseco	.40
2	Chili Davis	.05
3	Mickey Tettleton	.05
4	Danny Tartabull	.05
5	Fred McGriff	.05
6	Andre Dawson	.25
7	Frank Thomas	.75
8	Ron Gant	.05
9	Cal Ripkin (Ripken)	1.50
10	Matt Williams	.05

DIAMONDS

J	Ken Griffey Jr.	1.00
Q	Willie Randolph	.05
K	Wade Boggs	.75
A	Julio Franco	.05
2	Danny Tartabull	.05
3	Tony Gwynn	.75
4	Frank Thomas	.60
5	Hal Morris	.05
6	Kirby Puckett	.75
7	Terry Pendleton	.05
8	Rafael Palmeiro	.50
9	Cal Ripkin (Ripken)	1.50
10	Paul Molitor	.60

SPADES

J	Tim Belcher	.05
Q	Tom Glavine	.15
K	Jose Rijo	.05
A	Dennis Martinez	.05
2	Mike Moore	.05
3	Nolan Ryan	1.50
4	Jim Abbott	.05
5	Bill Wegman	.05
6	Mike Morgan	.05
7	Jose DeLeon	.05
8	Pete Harnisch	.05
9	Tom Candiotti	.05
10	Roger Clemens	.85

JOKERS

---	Roger Clemens (Joker)	.85
---	Tom Glavine (Joker)	.15
---	Home Run Rummy Game Instructions	.05
---	Header Card	.05

All-Stars

IVAN RODRIGUEZ ★ C

Players from the 1992 All-Star Game are featured in this set of 56 playing cards. In playing card format of 2-1/2" x 3-1/2" with rounded corners, the cards have a photo on front with a team logo in the upper-right corner. Traditional playing card suits and values are in the upper-left and lower-right corners. Player names are in a yellow (American League) or red (National League) box beneath the photo. Backs have a large product logo on a white background with a dark blue-green border. Appropriate licensor and manufacturer logos appear at bottom. The set was sold in a box featuring miniature representations of some of the cards.

		NM/M
Complete Set (56):		5.00
Common Player:		.05

HEARTS

AC	Roberto Alomar	.20
2C	Joe Carter	.05
3C	Juan Guzman	.05
4C	Charles Nagy	.05
5C	Robin Ventura	.05
6C	Chuck Knoblauch	.05
7C	Ruben Sierra	.05
8C	Paul Molitor	.60
9C	Carlos Baerga	.05
10C	Edgar Martinez	.05
JC	Sandy Alomar Jr.	.05
QC	Mark McGwire	1.25
KC	Wade Boggs	.75
AS	Ken Griffey Jr.	1.00
2S	Ivan Rodriguez	.50
3S	Roberto Kelly	.05
4S	Brady Anderson	.05
5S	Travis Fryman	.05
6S	Jeff Montgomery	.05
7S	Jack McDowell	.05
8S	Rick Aguilera	.05
9S	Kevin Brown	.05
10S	Roger Clemens	.85
JS	Jose Canseco	.35
QS	Cal Ripken Jr.	1.50
KS	Kirby Puckett	.75
AH	Andy Van Slyke	.05
2H	Greg Maddux	.75
3H	Larry Walker	.05
4H	Tom Pagnozzi	.05
5H	David Cone	.05
6H	Tony Fernandez	.05
7H	Will Clark	.05
8H	Gary Sheffield	.30
9H	Mike Sharperson	.05
10H	John Kruk	.05
JH	Ryne Sandberg	.75
QH	Ozzie Smith	.75
KH	Fred McGriff	.05
AD	Tony Gwynn	.75
2D	Bob Tewksbury	.05
3D	Ron Gant	.05
4D	Doug Jones	.05
5D	Craig Biggio	.05
6D	Bip Roberts	.05
7D	Norm Charlton	.05
8D	John Smoltz	.05

9D	Lee Smith	.05
10D	Tom Glavine	.25
JD	Benito Santiago	.05
QD	Terry Pendleton	.05
KD	Barry Bonds	1.50
Wild	Dennis Eckersley	.50
Joker	Mike Mussina, Mark Langston	.15
Joker	Darren Daulton, Dennis Martinez	.05
---	Advertising card	.05

Team Sets

Besides two All-Star sets, the U.S. Playing Card Co. in 1992 issued playing card team sets for five teams. All were issued as 56-card boxed sets in a similar format. Cards are 2-1/2" x 3-1/2" with rounded corners. Fronts feature player photos with insets at the upper-left and lower-right corners displaying card suit designations and rankings. The player's name and position appear in a colored strip beneath the photo. Backs feature a large color team logo set on a gray background with either dark blue or red pinstriping and heavy vertical side bars. A silver-edged World Series premium version of the Braves and Twins sets were also issued; on these cards each rounded corner has a diagonal "nip."

Atlanta Braves

STEVE AVERY ★ P

		NM/M
Complete Set (56):		5.00
Common Player:		.10

HEARTS

J	Dave Justice	.10
Q	Juan Berenguer	.10
K	Ron Gant	.10
A	Otis Nixon	.10
2	Deion Sanders	.20
3	Mike Stanton	.10
4	Sid Bream	.10
5	Armando Reynoso	.10
6	Brian Hunter	.10
7	Kent Mercker	.10
8	Lonnie Smith	.10
9	Jeff Treadway	.10
10	Tom Glavine	.35

CLUBS

J	Pete Smith	.10
Q	Jeff Blauser	.10
K	Charlie Leibrandt	.10
A	Terry Pendleton	.10
2	Mark Lemke	.10
3	Armando Reynoso	.10
4	Kent Mercker	.10
5	Marvin Freeman	.10
6	Rico Rossy	.10
7	Dave Justice	.10
8	Juan Berenguer	.10
9	Ron Gant	.10
10	Otis Nixon	.10

DIAMONDS

J	Brian Hunter	.10
Q	Rafael Belliard	.10
K	Greg Olson	.10
A	Steve Avery	.10
2	Marvin Freeman	.10
3	Pete Smith	.10
4	Mike Heath	.10
5	Jeff Blauser	.10
6	Jim Clancy	.10
7	Rico Rossy	.10
8	John Smoltz	.10
9	Charlie Leibrandt	.10
10	Terry Pendleton	.10

SPADES

J	John Smoltz	.10
Q	Lonnie Smith	.10
K	Jeff Treadway	.10
A	Tom Glavine	.35
2	Jim Clancy	.10
3	Deion Sanders	.20
4	Mark Lemke	.10
5	Mike Heath	.10
6	Mike Stanton	.10

7	Sid Bream	.10
8	Rafael Belliard	.10
9	Greg Olson	.10
10	Steve Avery	.10

JOKERS

---	N.L. logo (Joker)	.05
---	N.L. logo (Joker)	.05
---	'92 Braves Home Schedule	.05
---	Atlanta Braves History	.05

World Series - Braves

		NM/M
Complete Set (56):		5.00
Common Player:		.05

AC	Charlie Leibrandt	.10
2C	Vinny Castilla	.10
3C	Alejandro Pena	.10
4C	Mark Lemke	.10
5C	Marvin Freeman	.10
6C	Dave Justice	.10
7C	Mike Stanton	.10
8C	Terry Pendleton	.10
9C	Jeff Treadway	.10
10C	Brian Hunter	.10
JC	Steve Avery	.10
QC	Jeff Blauser	.10
KC	Ron Gant	.10
AS	Terry Pendleton	.10
2S	Ryan Klesko	.10
3S	Jeff Treadway	.10
4S	Pete Smith	.10
5S	Ron Gant	.10
6S	Sid Bream	.10
7S	Deion Sanders	.15
8S	Tom Glavine	.35
9S	Kent Mercker	.10
10S	Lonnie Smith	.10
JS	Damon Berryhill	.10
QS	Marvin Freeman	.10
KS	John Smoltz	.10
AH	Dave Justice	.10
2H	Kent Mercker	.10
3H	Lonnie Smith	.10
4H	Greg Olson	.10
5H	Jeff Reardon	.10
6H	Steve Avery	.10
7H	Otis Nixon	.10
8H	Juan Berenguer	.10
9H	Greg Olson	.10
10H	Mike Bielecki	.10
JH	Mike Stanton	.10
QH	Deion Sanders	.15
KH	Pete Smith	.10
AD	Otis Nixon	.10
2D	Juan Berenguer	.10
3D	Francisco Cabrera	.10
4D	Damon Berryhill	.10
5D	Brian Hunter	.10
6D	Charlie Leibrandt	.10
7D	Jeff Blauser	.10
8D	John Smoltz	.10
9D	Alejandro Pena	.10
10D	Mark Lemke	.10
JD	Jeff Reardon	.10
QD	Sid Bream	.10
KD	Tom Glavine	.35
Wild	Mike Bielecki	.10
Wild	David Nied	.10
Wild	Mark Wohlers	.10
Joker	Checklist	.05

Boston Red Sox

		NM/M
Complete Set (56):		5.00
Common Player:		.10

HEARTS

J	Jack Clark	.10
Q	Jeff Gray	.10
K	Greg Harris	.10
A	Roger Clemens	1.00
2	Matt Young	.10
3	John Marzano	.10
4	Dennis Lamp	.10
5	Danny Darwin	.10
6	Jeff Reardon	.10
7	Phil Plantier	.10
8	Tony Fossas	.10
9	Carlos Quintana	.10
10	Wade Boggs	.75

CLUBS

J	Luis Rivera	.10
Q	John Marzano	.10
K	Jody Reed	.10
A	Mike Greenwell	.10
2	Danny Darwin	.10
3	Dan Petry	.10
4	Dana Kiecker	.10
5	Greg Harris	.10
6	Tony Pena	.10
7	Dan Petry	.10
8	Jeff Gray	.10
9	Jack Clark	.10
10	Roger Clemens	1.00

DIAMONDS

J	Tom Brunansky	.10
Q	Mo Vaughn	.25
K	Ellis Burks	.10
A	Joe Hesketh	.10
2	Steve Lyons	.10
3	Dana Kiecker	.10
4	Tony Fossas	.10
5	Matt Young	.10
6	Luis Rivera	.10
7	Tom Bolton	.10

8	Kevin Morton	.10
9	Jody Reed	.10
10	Mike Greenwell	.10

SPADES

J	Tony Pena	.10
Q	Phil Plantier	.10
K	Carlos Quintana	.10
A	Wade Boggs	.75
2	Tom Bolton	.10
3	Mo Vaughn	.25
4	Kevin Morton	.10
5	Steve Lyons	.10
6	Tom Brunansky	.10
7	Dennis Lamp	.10
8	Joe Hesketh	.10
9	Ellis Burks	.10
10	Jeff Reardon	.10

JOKERS

---	A.L. Logo (Joker)	.10
---	A.L. Logo (Joker) (Joker)	.10
---	'92 Red Sox Home Schedule	.10
---	Boston Red Sox Team History	.10

Chicago Cubs

GREG MADDUX ★ P

		NM/M
Complete Set (56):		5.00
Common Player:		.10

HEARTS

J	Jerome Walton	.10
Q	Chico Walker	.10
K	Chuck McElroy	.10
A	Andre Dawson	.30
2	Dwight Smith	.10
3	Rick Wilkins	.10
4	Doug Dascenzo	.10
5	Bob Scanlan	.10
6	Chico Walker	.10
7	Paul Assenmacher	.10
8	Mark Grace	.25
9	Ryne Sandberg	1.00
10	Danny Jackson	.10

CLUBS

J	Hector Villanueva	.10
Q	Doug Dascenzo	.10
K	Shawon Dunston	.10
A	George Bell	.10
2	Greg Scott	.10
3	Jose Vizcaino	.10
4	Heathcliff Slocumb	.10
5	Danny Jackson	.10
6	Shawn Boskie	.10
7	Luis Salazar	.10
8	Chuck McElroy	.10
9	Andre Dawson	.30
10	Dave Smith	.10

DIAMONDS

J	Frank Castillo	.10
Q	Les Lancaster	.10
K	Paul Assenmacher	.10
A	Greg Maddux	1.00
2	Shawn Boskie	.10
3	Ced Landrum	.10
4	Gary Scott	.10
5	Ced Landrum	.10
6	Jose Vizcaino	.10
7	Mike Harkey	.10
8	Jerome Walton	.10
9	George Bell	.10
10	Frank Castillo	.10

SPADES

J	Bob Scanlan	.10
Q	Luis Salazar	.10
K	Mark Grace	.25
A	Ryne Sandberg	1.00
2	Frank Castillo	.10
3	Mike Harkey	.10
4	Dave Smith	.10
5	Les Lancaster	.10
6	Hector Villanueva	.10
7	Shawon Dunston	.10
8	Heathcliff Slocumb	.10
9	Greg Maddux	1.00
10	Dwight Smith	.10

JOKERS

---	N.L. logo (Joker)	.10
---	N.L. logo (Joker)	.10
---	'92 Cubs Home Schedule	.10
---	Chicago Cubs Team History	.10

Detroit Tigers

		NM/M
Complete Set (56):		5.00

Common Player:		.10

HEARTS

J	Lloyd Moseby	.10
Q	Walt Terrell	.10
K	Mickey Tettleton	.10
A	Cecil Fielder	.10
2	Andy Allanson	.10
3	Dave Bergman	.10
4	Steve Searcy	.10
5	Dan Galeker	.10
6	Jerry Don Gleaton	.10
7	Paul Gibson	.10
8	Alan Trammell	.25
9	Frank Tanana	.10
10	John Cerutti	.10

CLUBS

J	Rob Deer	.10
Q	Skeeter Barnes	.10
K	Pete Incaviglia	.10
A	Tony Phillips	.10
2	Dan Galeker	.10
3	Walt Terrell	.10
4	David Haas	.10
5	Pete Incaviglia	.10
6	Travis Fryman	.10
7	Scott Aldred	.10
8	Skeeter Barnes	.10
9	Mickey Tettleton	.10
10	Cecil Fielder	.10

DIAMONDS

J	Milt Cuyler	.10
Q	Travis Fryman	.10
K	Lou Whitaker	.10
A	Bill Gullickson	.10
2	John Cerutti	.10
3	Steve Searcy	.10
4	David Haas	.10
5	Lloyd Moseby	.10
6	Scott Livingstone	.10
7	John Shelby	.10
8	Mike Henneman	.10
9	Dave Bergman	.10
10	Tony Phillips	.10

SPADES

J	Alan Trammell	.25
Q	Jerry Don Gleaton	.10
K	Mike Henneman	.10
A	Frank Tanana	.10
2	Scott Aldred	.10
3	Scott Livingstone	.10
4	John Shelby	.10
5	Rob Deer	.10
6	Milt Cuyler	.10
7	Andy Allanson	.10
8	Paul Gibson	.10
9	Lou Whitaker	.10
10	Bill Gullickson	.10

JOKERS

---	A.L. Logo (Joker)	.10
---	A.L. Logo (Joker)	.10
---	'92 Tigers Home Schedule	.10
---	Detroit Tigers team history	.10

Minnesota Twins

		NM/M
Complete Set (56):		5.00
Common Player:		.10

HEARTS

J	Scott Leius	.10
Q	Rick Aguilera	.10
K	Jack Morris	.10
A	Kirby Puckett	.75
2	Junior Ortiz	.10
3	Paul Abbott	.10
4	Steve Bedrosian	.10
5	Pedro Munoz	.10
6	Mike Pagliarulo	.10
7	Greg Gagne	.10
8	Chuck Knoblauch	.10
9	Kevin Tapani	.10
10	Scott Erickson	.10

CLUBS

J	Carl Willis	.10
Q	Dan Gladden	.10
K	Kent Hrbek	.10
A	Shane Mack	.10
2	Allan Anderson	.10
3	Al Newman	.10
4	Junior Ortiz	.10
5	Mike Pagliarulo	.10
6	Terry Leach	.10
7	Scott Leius	.10
8	Rick Aguilera	.10
9	Jack Morris	.10
10	Kirby Puckett	.75

DIAMONDS

J	Gene Larkin	.10
Q	Randy Bush	.10
K	Chili Davis	.10
A	Brian Harper	.10
2	Al Newman	.10
3	Allan Anderson	.10
4	David West	.10
5	Terry Leach	.10
6	Mark Guthrie	.10
7	Carl Willis	.10
8	Dan Gladden	.10
9	Kent Hrbek	.10
10	Shane Mack	.10

SPADES

J	Greg Gagne	.10
Q	Chuck Knoblauch	.10
K	Kevin Tapani	.10
A	Scott Erickson	.10
2	Paul Abbott	.10

3	David West	.10
4	Steve Bedrosian	.10
5	Mark Guthrie	.10
6	Pedro Munoz	.10
7	Gene Larkin	.10
8	Randy Bush	.10
9	Chili Davis	.10
10	Brian Harper	.10
JOKERS		
---	A.L. Logo (Joker)	.10
---	A.L. Logo (Joker)	.10
---	'92 Twins Home Schedule	.10
----	Minnesota Twins team history	.10

1993 U.S. Playing Card Aces

Major league superstars with the top 1992 statistical performance in four major categories are featured in this set of playing cards. Spades feature the 13 lowest ERAs; Hearts depict the baker's dozen stolen base leaders; the 13 players with highest home run totals and batting average are featured on clubs and diamonds, respectively. The 2-1/2" x 3-1/2" cards have rounded corners and traditional trading card suits and values in the upper-left and lower-right corners. Borderless color player photos are featured on front, with color team logos at lower-left. Player names and positions are printed in a black box at bottom. Backs have a red background with a large product logo and smaller licensor and manufacturer logos at bottom. The box in which the cards were sold is enhanced with gold foil and features miniature representations of some of the cards.

		NM/M
Complete Set (56):		4.00
Common Player:		.05
AC	Juan Gonzalez	.15
2C	Dave Hollins	.05
3C	Darren Daulton	.05
4C	Ken Griffey Jr.	.75
5C	Rob Deer	.05
6C	Mickey Tettleton	.05
7C	Gary Sheffield	.25
8C	Joe Carter	.05
9C	Albert Belle	.05
10C	Barry Bonds	1.50
JC	Fred McGriff	.05
QC	Cecil Fielder	.05
KC	Mark McGwire	1.00
AS	Bill Swift	.05
2S	Tom Glavine	.35
3S	Sid Fernandez	.05
4S	Greg Swindell	.05
5S	Juan Guzman	.05
6S	Jose Rijo	.05
7S	Mike Morgan	.05
8S	Mike Mussina	.35
9S	Dennis Martinez	.05
10S	Kevin Appier	.05
JS	Roger Clemens	.65
QS	Curt Schilling	.35
KS	Greg Maddux	.60
AH	Marquis Grissom	.05
2H	Chad Curtis	.05
3H	Ozzie Smith	.60
4H	Bip Roberts	.05
5H	Steve Finley	.05
6H	Tim Raines	.05
7H	Delino DeShields	.05
8H	Rickey Henderson	.50
9H	Roberto Alomar	.05
10H	Luis Polonia	.05
JH	Brady Anderson	.05
QH	Pat Listach	.05
KH	Kenny Lofton	.05
AD	Edgar Martinez	.05
2D	Roberto Alomar	.10
3D	Terry Pendleton	.05
4D	Carlos Baerga	.05
5D	Shane Mack	.05
6D	Tony Gwynn	.60
7D	Paul Molitor	.50
8D	Frank Thomas	.50
9D	Bip Roberts	.05
10D	John Kruk	.05
JD	Andy Van Slyke	.05
QD	Kirby Puckett	.60
KD	Gary Sheffield	.25
Wild	Cal Ripken Jr.	1.50
Joker	National League Logo	.05
Joker	American League Logo	.05
---	Advertising Card	.10

1992 Rookies

Top rookies of the 1992 season are featured in full-color on the fronts of these playing cards. Player name and position are printed in white in a green stripe beneath the photo. A team logo is in the upper-right corner. Backs are printed in dark green with gold pinstripes and a large gold, red and purple logo.

		NM/M
Complete Boxed Set (56):		4.00
Common Player:		.10
AC	Kenny Lofton	.10
2C	Eric Fox	.10
3C	Mark Wohlers	.10
4C	John Patterson	.10
5C	Eric Young	.10
6C	Arthur Rhodes	.10
7C	Jeff Frye	.10
8C	Scott Servais	.10
9C	Ruben Amaro Jr.	.10
10C	Reggie Sanders	.10
JC	Alan Mills	.10
QC	Bob Zupcic	.10
KC	Cal Eldred	.10
AS	Eric Karros	.10
2S	Butch Henry	.10
3S	Wil Cordero	.10
4S	Pedro Astacio	.10
5S	Derek Bell	.10
6S	David Nied	.10
7S	Jeff Kent	.35
8S	David Haas	.10
9S	Ed Taubensee	.10
10S	Royce Clayton	.10
JS	Moises Alou	.10
QS	Rusty Meacham	.10
KS	Chad Curtis	.10
AH	Pat Listach	.10
2H	Pat Mahomes	.10
3H	Greg Colbrunn	.10
4H	Dan Walters	.10
5H	John Vander Wal	.10
6H	Jeff Branson	.10
7H	Monty Fariss	.10
8H	Rey Sanchez	.10
9H	Robert Wickman	.10
10H	Derrick May	.10
JH	Donovan Osborne	.10
QH	Scott Livingstone	.10
KH	Gary DiSarcina	.10
AD	Dave Fleming	.10
2D	Reggie Jefferson	.10
3D	Anthony Young	.10
4D	Kevin Koslofski	.10
5D	Brian Williams	.10
6D	Brian Jordan	.10
7D	John Doherty	.10
8D	Lenny Webster	.10
9D	Roberto Hernandez	.10
10D	Frank Seminara	.10
JD	Scott Cooper	.10
QD	Andy Stankiewicz	.10
KD	Tim Wakefield	.10
Joker	Eric Karros (N.L. ROY)	.10
Joker	Pat Listach (A.L. ROY)	.10
---	Rookie qualification rules	.10
---	Checklist	.10

Team Sets

For a second year the leading U.S. manufacturer of playing cards produced several team sets depicting ballplayers. Each was sold as a 56-card set in standard 2-1/2" x 3-1/2" round-corner playing card format in a colorful flip-top box. Backs of each team set carry a team logo. Fronts have portrait or action photo and playing card suits and values. Most players are represented twice in each team set in different photos.

Cincinnati Reds

		NM/M
Complete Set (56):		4.00
Common Player:		.10
AC	Tim Belcher	.10
2C	Jacob Brumfield	.10
3C	Rob Dibble	.10
4C	Jose Rijo	.10
5C	Dan Wilson	.10
6C	Cecil Espy	.10
7C	Tom Browning	.10
8C	Steve Foster	.10
9C	Jacob Brumfield	.10
10C	Jeff Branson	.10
JC	Greg Cadaret	.10
QC	Hal Morris	.10
KC	Joe Oliver	.10
AS	Bip Roberts	.10
2S	Cesar Hernandez	.10
3S	Chris Hammond	.10
4S	Scott Ruskin	.10
5S	John Smiley	.10
6S	Roberto Kelly	.10
7S	Barry Larkin	.25
8S	Gary Varsho	.10
9S	Hal Morris	.10
10S	Dwayne Henry	.10
JS	Tommy Gregg	.10
QS	Kevin Mitchell	.10
KS	Rob Dibble	.10
AH	Barry Larkin	.25
2H	Willie Greene	.10
3H	Steve Foster	.10
4H	Greg Cadaret	.10
5H	Chris Sabo	.10
6H	Joe Oliver	.10
7H	Milton Hill	.10
8H	Tim Belcher	.10
9H	Scott Ruskin	.10
10H	Cecil Espy	.10
JH	Roberto Kelly	.10
QH	Tom Browning	.10
KH	Reggie Sanders	.10
AD	Jose Rijo	.10
2D	Dwayne Henry	.10
3D	Jeff Branson	.10
4D	Milton Hill	.10
5D	Tim Costo	.10
6D	Bip Roberts	.10
7D	Kevin Mitchell	.10
8D	Tim Pugh	.10
9D	Reggie Sanders	.10
10D	Chris Hammond	.10
JD	Gary Varsho	.10
QD	John Smiley	.10
KD	Chris Sabo	.10
Wild	Tony Perez	.50
Joker	Riverfront Stadium	.10
---	Reds schedule	.10
---	Checklist	.10

Colorado Rockies

		NM/M
Complete Set (56):		4.00
Common Player:		.10
AC	Jim Tatum	.10
2C	Charlie Hayes	.10
3C	Dale Murphy	.50
4C	Scott Aldred	.10
5C	Braulio Castillo	.10
6C	Danny Sheaffer	.10
7C	Jerald Clark	.10
8C	Willie Blair	.10
9C	Daryl Boston	.10
10C	Andy Ashby	.10
JC	Butch Henry	.10
QC	Alex Cole	.10
KC	Vinny Castilla	.10
AS	David Nied	.10
2S	Andres Galarraga	.10
3S	Gary Wayne	.10
4S	Freddie Benavides	.10
5S	Butch Henry	.10
6S	Gerald Young	.10
7S	Jeff Parrett	.10
8S	Braulio Castillo	.10
9S	Darren Holmes	.10
10S	Dale Murphy	.50
JS	Eric Young	.10
QS	Bruce Ruffin	.10
KS	Joe Girardi	.10
AH	Charlie Hayes	.10
2H	Jim Tatum	.10
3H	Andy Ashby	.10
4H	Vinny Castilla	.10
5H	Steve Reed	.10
6H	Daryl Boston	.10
7H	Alex Cole	.10
8H	Bryn Smith	.10
9H	Danny Sheaffer	.10
10H	Willie Blair	.10
JH	Dante Bichette	.10
QH	Jerald Clark	.10
DH	Scott Aldred	.10
AD	Andres Galarraga	.10
2D	David Nied	.10
3D	Dante Bichette	.10
4D	Joe Girardi	.10
5D	Bryn Smith	.10
6D	Darren Holmes	.10
7D	Bruce Ruffin	.10
8D	Eric Young	.10
9D	Gerald Young	.10
10D	Gary Wayne	.10
JD	Steve Reed	.10
QD	Jeff Parrett	.10
KD	Freddie Benavides	.10

Florida Marlins

		NM/M
Complete Set (56):		4.00
Common Player:		.10
AC	Walt Weiss	.10
2C	Dave Magadan	.10
3C	Chris Carpenter	.10
4C	Dave Magadan	.10
5C	Bob McClure	.10
6C	Junior Felix	.10
7C	Walt Weiss	.10
8C	Steve Decker	.10
9C	Jeff Conine	.15
10C	Bryan Harvey	.10
JC	Orestes Destrade	.10
QC	Chris Hammond	.10
KC	Monty Fariss	.10
AS	Alex Arias	.10
2S	Benito Santiago	.10
3S	Ryan Bowen	.10
4S	Steve Decker	.10
5S	Jeff Conine	.15
6S	Bret Barberie	.10
7S	Orestes Destrade	.10
8S	Greg Briley	.10
9S	Charlie Hough	.10
10S	Bob Natal	.10
JS	Jack Armstrong	.10
QS	Junior Felix	.10
KS	Richie Lewis	.10
AH	Benito Santiago	.10
2H	Walt Weiss	.10
3H	Monty Fariss	.10
4H	Chris Hammond	.10
5H	Joe Klink	.10
6H	Chuck Carr	.10
7H	Alex Arias	.10
8H	Charlie Hough	.10
9H	Junior Felix	.10
10H	Jim Corsi	.10
JH	Jeff Conine	.15
QH	Trevor Hoffman	.10
KH	Rich Renteria	.10
AD	Dave Magadan	.10
2D	Jack Armstrong	.10
3D	Bryan Harvey	.10
4D	Richie Lewis	.10
5D	Scott Pose	.10
6D	Rich Renteria	.10
7D	Trevor Hoffman	.10
8D	Jim Corsi	.10
9D	Ryan Bowen	.10
10D	Orestes Destrade	.10
JD	Bret Barberie	.10
QD	Chuck Carr	.10
KD	Chris Carpenter	.10
Joker	N.L. logo	.10
Joker	N.L. logo	.10
---	Opening Day roster	.10
---	Marlins schedule	.10

1994 U.S. Playing Card Aces

Statistical leaders from the 1993 season are featured in this deck of playing cards. Pitchers with the lowest ERAs are shown on the spades; stolen base leaders are featured on the hearts; home run hitters are depicted on the clubs, and diamonds host the batting average leaders. Cards are 2-1/2" x 3-1/2" with rounded corners. Fronts have full-bleed photos with the suit and value of the playing card in the upper-left and lower-right corners. The player's name, position and team logo are at lower-left. Backs are printed in dark blue with vertical silver stripes at each side and a red, white and blue "Baseball Aces" logo at top. Licensing logos appear at the bottom. Besides the 52 player cards in the boxed set, there is a checklist card, A.L. and N.L. logo cards and a U.S. Playing Card Co. advertising card.

ANDRES GALARRAGA FIRST BASE

		NM/M
Complete Set (56):		6.00
Common Player:		.10
AC	Barry Bonds	1.50
2C	Phil Plantier	.10
3C	Bobby Bonilla	.10
4C	Mike Piazza	1.00
5C	Ron Gant	.10
6C	Rafael Palmeiro	.50
7C	Fred McGriff	.10
8C	Matt Williams	.10
9C	Albert Belle	.10
10C	Dave Justice	.10
JC	Frank Thomas	.60
QC	Ken Griffey Jr.	1.00
KC	Juan Gonzalez	.30
AS	Greg Maddux	.75
2S	Tom Candiotti	.10
3S	Jimmy Key	.10
4S	Jack McDowell	.10
5S	John Burkett	.10
6S	Tom Glavine	.25
7S	Pete Harnisch	.10
8S	Wilson Alvarez	.10
9S	Steve Avery	.10
10S	Bill Swift	.10
JS	Mark Portugal	.10
QS	Kevin Appier	.10
KS	Jose Rijo	.10
AH	Kenny Lofton	.10
2H	Brett Butler	.10
3H	Eric Young	.10
4H	Delino DeShields	.10
5H	Darren Lewis	.10
6H	Gregg Jefferies	.10
7H	Otis Nixon	.10
8H	Chad Curtis	.10
9H	Rickey Henderson	.60
10H	Marquis Grissom	.10
JH	Luis Polonia	.10
QH	Roberto Alomar	.20
KH	Chuck Carr	.10
AD	Andres Galarraga	.10
2D	John Kruk	.10
3D	Frank Thomas	.60
4D	Mike Piazza	1.00
5D	Jeff Bagwell	.60
6D	Carlos Baerga	.10
7D	Mark Grace	.10
8D	Kenny Lofton	.10
9D	Roberto Alomar	.20
10D	Paul Molitor	.60
JD	Barry Bonds	1.50
QD	Gregg Jefferies	.10
KD	John Olerud	.10
Joker	National League Logo	.10
Joker	American League Logo	.05
---	Checklist	.05
---	Advertising Card	.10

Atlanta Braves

The most popular Braves are pictured on up to three of the cards in this deck. In 2-1/2" x 3-1/2" round-cornered format, the large color photos on the card fronts have their upper-left and lower-right corners clipped to display traditional playing card suits and values. The player name and position are printed in black in a gold strip below the photo. Backs have the Braves logo on a dark blue background with red stripes on the left and right edges. Brand and licensor logos are at bottom. The cards were sold in a colorful box.

MIKE KELLY • OF

		NM/M
Complete Set (56):		4.00
Common Player:		.10
AC	Ron Gant	.10
2C	Chipper Jones	1.00
3C	Terry Pendleton	.10
4C	Mark Wohlers	.10
5C	Pedro Borbon	.10
6C	Steve Avery	.10
7C	Deion Sanders	.15
8C	Dave Justice	.10
9C	Dave Gallagher	.10
10C	Rafael Belliard	.10
JC	Greg McMichael	.10
QC	John Smoltz	.10
KC	Fred McGriff	.10
AS	Jeff Blauser	.10
2S	Mike Stanton	.10
3S	Ryan Klesko	.10
4S	Mike Potts	.10
5S	Charlie O'Brien	.10
6S	Steve Bedrosian	.10
7S	Javier Lopez	.10
8S	Greg Maddux	.75
9S	Deion Sanders	.15
10S	Ramon Caraballo	.10
JS	Kent Mercker	.10
QS	Mark Wohlers	.10
KS	Tom Glavine	.25
AH	Dave Justice	.10
2H	Mark Lemke	.10
3H	Javier Lopez	.10
4H	Rafael Belliard	.10
5H	Bill Pecota	.10
6H	Tom Glavine	.25
7H	Milt Hill	.10
8H	Jeff Blauser	.10
9H	Ryan Klesko	.10
10H	Terry Pendleton	.10
JH	Mike Stanton	.10
QH	Steve Avery	.10
KH	Deion Sanders	.15
AD	Greg Maddux	.75
2D	Ron Gant	.10
3D	Kent Mercker	.10
4D	Greg McMichael	.10
5D	Tony Tarasco	.10
6D	John Smoltz	.10
7D	Fred McGriff	.10
8D	Ron Gant	.10
9D	Mike Kelly	.10
10D	Steve Bedrosian	.10
QD	Bill Pecota	.10
QD	Mark Lemke	.10
KD	Terry Pendleton	.10
Joker	Atlanta Braves logo	.10
Joker	National League logo	.10
---	Checklist	.10
---	'94 Braves Home Schedule	.10

Baltimore Orioles

MIKE MUSSINA P

The 1994 Baltimore Orioles are featured in this deck of playing cards. Color photos of the players have clipped corners to display traditional playing card suits and values in the upper-left and lower-right corners. Beneath the photo is an orange strip with the player's name and position in white. Backs have a large Orioles logo on a pinstriped background. Company and licensor logos are at the bottom. Cards measure 2-1/2" x 3-1/2" with rounded corners. The set was sold in a colorful cardboard box.

		NM/M
Complete Set (56):		4.00
Common Player:		.10
AC	Chris Hoiles	.10
2C	Mike Cook	.10
3C	Paul Carey	.10
4C	Jeff Tackett	.10
5C	Arthur Rhodes	.10
6C	Damon Buford	.10
7C	David Segui	.10
8C	Ben McDonald	.10
9C	Cal Ripken Jr.	1.00
10C	Brad Pennington	.10
JC	Jack Voigt	.10
QC	Jeffrey Hammonds	.10
KC	Rafael Palmeiro	.60
AS	Mark McLemore	.10
2S	Manny Alexander	.10
3S	Kevin McGehee	.10
4S	Jim Poole	.10
5S	Leo Gomez	.10
6S	Tim Hulett	.10
7S	Mike Devereaux	.10
8S	Brady Anderson	.10
9S	Mike Mussina	.40
10S	Sherman Obando	.10
JS	Alan Mills	.10
QS	Jamie Moyer	.10
KS	Harold Baines	.10
AH	Cal Ripken Jr.	1.00
2H	Harold Baines	.10
3H	John O'Donoghue	.10
4H	Sid Fernandez	.10
5H	Alan Mills	.10
6H	Jamie Moyer	.10
7H	Harold Baines	.10
8H	Mark McLemore	.10
9H	Jeff Tackett	.10
10H	Arthur Rhodes	.10
JH	Damon Buford	.10
QH	David Segui	.10
KH	Ben McDonald	.10
AD	Mike Mussina	.40
2D	Mike Oquist	.10
3D	Brad Pennington	.10
4D	Jeffrey Hammonds	.10
5D	Jack Voigt	.10
6D	Chris Sabo	.10
7D	Rafael Palmeiro	.60
8D	Chris Hoiles	.10
9D	Jim Poole	.10
10D	Leo Gomez	.10
JD	Tim Hulett	.10
QD	Mike Devereaux	.10
KD	Brady Anderson	.10
Joker	Baltimore Orioles Logo	.10
Joker	American League Logo	.10
---	Checklist	.10
---	'94 Orioles Home Schedule	.10

Philadelphia Phillies

JOHN KRUK • 1B

Veterans and rookies on the roster of the '94 Phils are featured in this deck of playing cards; the most popular players appear on up to three cards each. In standard 2-1/2" x 3-1/2" round-cornered format, the large color photos have their top-left and bottom-right corners clipped to display traditional playing card suits and values. The player's name and position are printed in black on a red strip beneath the photo. Backs have a large Phillies logo on a gray pinstriped background. Company and licensor logos are at bottom. The cards were sold in a decorative box.

		NM/M
Complete Set (56):		4.00
Common Player:		.10
AC	Pete Incaviglia	.10
2C	Lenny Dykstra	.10
3C	Milt Thompson	.10
4C	Mickey Morandini	.10
5C	Kevin Stocker	.10
6C	Terry Mulholland	.10
7C	Curt Schilling	.35
8C	Darren Daulton	.10
9C	Terry Mulholland	.10
10C	Roger Mason	.10
JC	Mariano Duncan	.10
QC	Ben Rivera	.10
KC	John Kruk	.10
AS	Dave Hollins	.10
2S	Danny Jackson	.10
3S	Todd Pratt	.10
4S	David West	.10
5S	Lenny Dykstra	.10
6S	Wes Chamberlain	.10
7S	Tommy Greene	.10
8S	Tony Longmire	.10
9S	Brad Brink	.10
10S	Ricky Jordan	.10
JS	Kim Batiste	.10
QS	Tyler Green	.10
KS	Jim Eisenreich	.10
AH	Lenny Dykstra	.10
2H	Tony Longmire	.10
3H	Kim Batiste	.10
4H	Pete Incaviglia	.10
5H	Ben Rivera	.10
6H	Ricky Jordan	.10
7H	Dave Hollins	.10
8H	Kevin Foster	.10
9H	Kevin Stocker	.10
10H	Mike Williams	.10
JH	Milt Thompson	.10
QH	Curt Schilling	.10
KH	Darren Daulton	.10
AD	Terry Mulholland	.10
2D	Brad Brink	.10
3D	Roger Mason	.10
4D	Mariano Duncan	.10
5D	Danny Jackson	.10
6D	Jim Eisenreich	.10
7D	John Kruk	.10
8D	David West	.10
9D	Todd Pratt	.10
10D	Wes Chamberlain	.10
JD	Jim Eisenreich	.10
QD	Mickey Morandini	.10
KD	Tommy Greene	.10
Joker	Phillies logo	.10
Joker	National League Logo	.10
---	Checklist	.10
---	'94 Phillies Home Schedule	.10

1993 Rookies

CHUCK CARR-CF

The top rookies from the 1993 season are featured on this deck of playing cards; several players appear on more than one card in the deck. Fronts have color player photos at center, with traditional playing card suits and values in the upper-left and lower-right borders. A team logo is at upper-right. The player's name and position appear in white in a purple strip at lower-left. Backs are purple with a large product logo at top-center and licensor/licensee logos at bottom. Cards measure 2-1/2" x 3-1/2" with rounded corners and were sold in a specially decorated cardboard box.

		NM/M
Complete Set (56):		4.00
Common Player:		.10
AC	Mike Piazza	1.00
2C	Vinny Castilla	.10
3C	Wil Cordero	.10
4C	Ryan Thompson	.10
5C	Craig Paquette	.10
6C	Carlos Garcia	.10
7C	Jeff Conine	.10
8C	Bret Boone	.10
9C	Jeromy Burnitz	.10
10C	J.T. Snow	.10
JC	Al Martin	.10
QC	Troy Neel	.10
AS	Greg McMichael	.10
2S	Paul Quantrill	.10
3S	Steve Reed	.10
5C	Mike Jackson	.10
6C	Kirt Manwaring	.10
7C	Royce Clayton	.10
8C	Robby Thompson	.10
9C	Luis Mercedes	.10
10C	Mike Benjamin	.10
JC	Mark Carreon	.10
QC	Dave Burba	.10
KC	John Burkett	.10
AS	Barry Bonds	1.00
2S	Salomon Torres	.10
3S	Kevin Rogers	.10
4S	Todd Benzinger	.10
5S	Dave Martinez	.10
6S	Darren Lewis	.10
7S	Willie McGee	.10
8S	Bill Swift	.10
9S	Paul Faries	.10
10S	Trevor Wilson	.10
JS	Steve Scarsone	.10
QS	Bryan Hickerson	.10
KS	Rod Beck	.10
AH	Robby Thompson	.10
2H	Paul Faries	.10
3H	Trevor Wilson	.10
4H	Steve Scarsone	.10
5H	Bryan Hickerson	.10
6H	Rod Beck	.10
7H	Barry Bonds	1.00
8H	John Patterson	.10
9H	J.R. Phillips	.10
10H	Jeff Reed	.10
JH	Mike Jackson	.10
QH	Kirt Manwaring	.10
KH	Royce Clayton	.10
AD	Bill Swift	.10
2D	Luis Mercedes	.10
3D	Mike Benjamin	.10
4D	Mark Carreon	.10
5D	Dave Burba	.10
6D	John Burkett	.10
7D	Matt Williams	.10
8D	Salomon Torres	.10
9D	Kevin Rogers	.10
10D	Todd Benzinger	.10
JD	Dave Martinez	.10
QD	Darren Lewis	.10
KD	Willie McGee	.10
Joker	Giants Home Schedule	.10
Joker	Checklist	.10
---	N.L. Logo	.10
---	Giants Logo	.10

S.F. Giants

Veterans and rookies on the roster of the '94 Giants are featured in this deck of playing cards; the most popular players appear on up to three cards each. In standard 2-1/2" x 3-1/2" round-cornered format, the large color photos have their top-left and bottom-right corners clipped to display traditional playing card suits and values. The player's name and position are printed in white on an orange strip beneath the photo. Backs have a large Giants logo on a gray pinstriped background. Company and licensor logos are at bottom. The cards were sold in a decorative box.

		NM/M
Complete Set (56):		4.00
Common Player:		.10
AC	Matt Williams	.10
2C	John Patterson	.10
3C	Steve Hosey	.10
4C	Jeff Reed	.10
4S	Trevor Hoffman	.10
5S	Tim Pugh	.10
6S	Angel Miranda	.10
7S	Steve Cooke	.10
8S	Aaron Sele	.10
9S	Kirk Rueter	.10
10S	Rene Arocha	.10
JS	Pedro Martinez	.75
QS	Armando Reynoso	.10
KS	Jason Bere	.10
AH	Kevin Stocker	.10
2H	Alex Arias	.10
3H	Carlos Garcia	.10
4H	Erik Pappas	.10
5H	Al Martin	.10
6H	Tim Salmon	.10
7H	Mike Lansing	.10
8H	Rich Amaral	.10
9H	Brent Gates	.10
10H	David Hulse	.10
JH	Troy Neel	.10
QH	Jeff Conine	.10
KH	Mike Piazza	1.00
AD	Chuck Carr	.10
2D	Jeff McNeeley	.10
3D	Joe Kmak	.10
4D	Phil Hiatt	.10
5D	Brent Gates	.10
6D	Wil Cordero	.10
7D	Al Martin	.10
8D	Wayne Kirby	.10
9D	Lou Frazier	.10
10D	Carlos Garcia	.10
JD	Rich Amaral	.10
QD	Mike Lansing	.10
KD	David Hulse	.10
Joker	Tim Salmon (Rookie of the Year)	.10
Joker	Mike Piazza (Rookie of the Year)	.75
--	Checklist	.10
--	Rookie Qualification Rules	.10

1995 U.S. Playing Card Aces

WADE BOGGS THIRD BASE

Baseball's 1994 statistical leaders in home runs (clubs), ERA (spades), stolen bases (hearts) and batting average (diamonds) are featured in this deck of playing cards. Measuring a standard 2-1/2" x 3-1/2" with rounded corners, cards have borderless action photos on front with traditional playing card suits and denominations in the upper-left and lower-right corners. The player's color team logo, name and position appear in the lower-left corner. Backs are silver with black side stripes and a red-and-black Aces logo at center. Sets were sold in a colorful cardboard box.

		NM/M
Complete Set (56):		5.00
Common Player:		.10
AC	Matt Williams	.10
2C	Joe Carter	.10
3C	Dante Bichette	.10
4C	Cecil Fielder	.10
5C	Kevin Mitchell	.10
6C	Andres Galarraga	.10
7C	Jose Canseco	.35
8C	Fred McGriff	.10
9C	Albert Belle	.10
QC	Barry Bonds	1.00
JC	Frank Thomas	.50
KC	Jeff Bagwell	.50
KC	Ken Griffey Jr.	.75
AS	Greg Maddux	.60
3S	Steve Trachsel	.10
3S	Randy Johnson	.50
4S	Bobby Jones	.10
5S	Jose Rijo	.10
6S	Mike Mussina	.30
7S	Shane Reynolds	.10
8S	Jeff Fassero	.10
9S	David Cone	.10
10S	Roger Clemens	.65
JS	Doug Drabek	.10
QS	Bret Saberhagen	.10
KS	Steve Ontiveros	.10
AH	Kenny Lofton	.10
2H	Brian McRae	.10
3H	Alex Cole	.10
4H	Barry Bonds	1.00
5H	Darren Lewis	.10
6H	Brady Anderson	.10
7H	Chuck Carr	.10
8H	Chuck Knoblauch	.10
9H	Marquis Grissom	.10
10H	Deion Sanders	.15
JH	Craig Biggio	.10
QH	Otis Nixon	.10
KH	Vince Coleman	.10
AD	Tony Gwynn	.60
2D	Gregg Jefferies	.10
3D	Kevin Mitchell	.10
4D	Will Clark	.10
5D	Hal Morris	.10
6D	Moises Alou	.10
7D	Paul Molitor	.50
8D	Wade Boggs	.60
9D	Kenny Lofton	.10
10D	Frank Thomas	.50
JD	Albert Belle	.10
QD	Paul O'Neill	.10
KD	Jeff Bagwell	.50
Joker	American League Logo	.05
Joker	National League Logo	.05
---	Checklist	.05
---	MicroMini Team Card	
---	Order Form	.05

2000 U.S. Playing Card All Century Baseball Team

Robert Feller

Fifty-two members of baseball's All Century team are featured on this deck of playing cards. On round-cornered playing card stock in 2-1/2" x 3-1/2" format, cards have black-and-white photos vignetted on front with the player name at bottom. In opposite corners are a color baseball with the card's value at center and the suit printed in red or black below. Backs are predominantly blue with gold borders and pinstriping. The cards were issued with four All Century team logos in a cardboard box within an embossed lithographed steel case.

		NM/M
Complete Boxed Set (56):		6.00
Common Player:		.10
AC	"Wee" Willie Keeler	.10
2C	Bob Feller	.10
3C	Luke Appling	.10
4C	Jerome "Dizzy" Dean	.15
5C	Johnny Bench	.25
6C	Lou Brock	.10
7C	Joe Cronin	.10
8C	Mickey Cochrane	.10
9C	Rod Carew	.10
10C	Bill Dickey	.10
JC	Josh Gibson	.10
QC	Lou Gehrig	.75
KC	Jackie Robinson	.75
AS	Babe Ruth	1.00
2S	Leroy "Satchel" Paige	.40
3S	Willie McCovey	.10
4S	Joe Morgan	.10
5S	Mel Ott	.10
6S	Jim Palmer	.10
7S	Frank Robinson	.10
8S	Mike Schmidt	.40
9S	George Sisler	.10
10S	Al Simmons	.10
JS	Denton "Cy" Young	.10
QS	Ozzie Smith	.25
KS	Tris Speaker	.10
AH	Bob Gibson	.10
2H	Whitey Ford	.10
3H	Christy Mathewson	.15
4H	Ralph Kiner	.10
5H	Juan Marichal	.10
6H	Bob "Lefty" Grove	.10
7H	Carl Hubbell	.10
8H	Al Kaline	.15
9H	Rogers Hornsby	.10
10H	Harmon Killebrew	.10
JH	Walter Johnson	.10
QH	Jimmie Foxx	.10
KH	Carlton Fisk	.10
AD	Eddie Collins	.10
2D	Robin Roberts	.10
3D	Honus Wagner	.20
4D	Warren Spahn	.10
5D	Mickey Mantle	1.50
6D	Brooks Robinson	.10
7D	Hank Aaron	.75
8D	Rollie Fingers	.10
9D	Dennis Eckersley	.10
10D	Ty Cobb	.75
JD	Joe Medwick	.10
QD	Ernie Banks	.15
KD	Grover Cleveland Alexander	.10

1989 U.S. Postal Service Legends

Roberto Clemente — USA 20c

In 1989 the U.S. Postal Service offered to collectors a Legends set for $7.95. The set consists of a heavily illustrated 24-page "Baseball Scrapbook and Stamp Album," a set of the four U.S. postage stamps which had been issued to that time honoring individual players, and a set of cards matching the stamps. The 2-1/2" x 3-1/2" cards have color reproductions of the stamps on front, bordered in white with red and blue striping. Backs are in red, black and orange and feature player data and major league stats.

		NM/M
Complete Set, album, stamps, cards:		24.00
Card Set (4):		15.00
3	Babe Ruth	4.00
4	Lou Gehrig	3.00
21	Roberto Clemente	5.00
42	Jackie Robinson	3.00

2000 U.S. Postal Service Legends of Baseball Stamps

Legends of Baseball

Twenty of the players nominated to baseball's All-Century team are featured on this souvenir sheet of 33-cent stamps issued by the USPS during ceremonies in Atlanta for the 2000 All-Star Game. The players chosen to appear were all Hall of Famers and, as per post office rules, had been deceased at least 10 years prior to the stamps' issue. Many of the pastel paintings by Joseph Saffold are familiar to card collectors because the illustrations are based on earlier photos which have been seen on vintage cards. A total of 225 million of the self-adhesive 1-1/4" x 1-9/16" stamps was produced, with the 7-1/8" x 7-

13/16" souvenir panel originally retailing at face value - $6.60. It was reported that 11,250,000 sheets were printed.

		NM/M
Complete Sheet:		8.00
Common Player:		.35
(1)	Roberto Clemente	.60
(2)	Ty Cobb	.45
(3)	Mickey Cochrane	.35
(4)	Eddie Collins	.35
(5)	Dizzy Dean	.35
(6)	Jimmie Foxx	.35
(7)	Lou Gehrig	.50
(8)	Josh Gibson	.35
(9)	Lefty Grove	.35
(10)	Rogers Hornsby	.35
(11)	Walter Johnson	.35
(12)	Christy Mathewson	.35
(13)	Satchel Paige	.45
(14)	Jackie Robinson	.60
(15)	Babe Ruth	.60
(16)	George Sisler	.35
(17)	Tris Speaker	.35
(18)	Pie Traynor	.35
(19)	Honus Wagner	.35
(20)	Cy Young	.35

Post Cards

CHRISTY MATHEWSON

In conjunction with the issue of a souvenir sheet of 33-cent stamps, the USPS also issued a boxed set of "Legends of Baseball" post cards. The 5" x 7" cards have a large reproduction of each stamp on front against a beige background. Postcard-style backs have color logos of the USPS and MLB's All-Century Team, along with address lines and a stamp box. At upper-left is a summary of the player's career. The cards were issued in a colorful folder with an All-Century Team hologram. The boxed sets sold for $5.95. Production was reported as 62,500 sets.

		NM/M
Complete Boxed Set (20):		9.00
Common Player:		.75
(1)	Roberto Clemente	1.50
(2)	Ty Cobb	1.25
(3)	Mickey Cochrane	.75
(4)	Eddie Collins	.75
(5)	Dizzy Dean	.75
(6)	Jimmie Foxx	.75
(7)	Lou Gehrig	1.25
(8)	Josh Gibson	.75
(9)	Lefty Grove	.75
(10)	Rogers Hornsby	.75
(11)	Walter Johnson	.75
(12)	Christy Mathewson	.75
(13)	Satchel Paige	1.25
(14)	Jackie Robinson	1.50
(15)	Babe Ruth	1.50
(16)	George Sisler	.75
(17)	Tris Speaker	.75
(18)	Pie Traynor	.75
(19)	Honus Wagner	.75
(20)	Cy Young	.75

Postal Card Booklet

In conjunction with the issue of a souvenir sheet of 33-cent stamps, the USPS also issued a bound booklet of "Legends of Baseball" postal cards. By definition, postal cards have the "stamp" pre-printed. The 4-1/4" x 6-1/16" cards have borderless color artwork on front, pastel paintings which reproduce the stamps' artwork. On the divided back a 20-cent "stamp" version of the player picture is printed at top-right. There is a short biography at top-left.

The cards were perforated with an 11/16" stub attaching it to the bound book. With a $4 face value, the booklets were originally sold for $8.95 at the post office. Production was reported as 105,000 sets.

		NM/M
Complete Booklet (20):		12.50
Common Player:		.75
(1)	Roberto Clemente	1.50
(2)	Ty Cobb	1.25
(3)	Mickey Cochrane	.75
(4)	Eddie Collins	.75
(5)	Dizzy Dean	.75
(6)	Jimmie Foxx	.75
(7)	Lou Gehrig	1.25
(8)	Josh Gibson	.75
(9)	Lefty Grove	.75
(10)	Rogers Hornsby	.75
(11)	Walter Johnson	.75
(12)	Christy Mathewson	.75
(13)	Satchel Paige	1.25
(14)	Jackie Robinson	1.50
(15)	Babe Ruth	1.50
(16)	George Sisler	.75
(17)	Tris Speaker	.75
(18)	Pie Traynor	.75
(19)	Honus Wagner	.75
(20)	Cy Young	.75

2000 Verizon Tampa Bay Devil Rays

This team set was a stadium giveaway at a promotional date. Fronts of the 2-1/2" x 3-1/2" cards have game-action photos on which a silver dollar-size portion remains in natural color while the balance of the picture is a purple duo-tone. Backs are in gray with a purple box for complete pro stats, capped by a dime-size color player portrait. The set is listed here according to uniform numbers which appear on back.

		NM/M
Complete Set (28):		7.50
Common Player:		.25
1	Miguel Cairo	.25
2	Randy Winn	.25
4	Gerald Williams	.25
6	John Flaherty	.25
8	Mike DiFelice	.25
9	Vinny Castilla	.25
10	Russ Johnson	.25
11	Larry Rothschild	.25
13	Ozzie Guillen	.25
16	Felix Martinez	.25
21	Bubba Trammell	.25
23	Greg Vaughn	.25
28	Steve Cox	.25
29	Fred McGriff	.50
30	Jose Guillen	.25
32	Albie Lopez	.25
33	Jose Canseco	2.50
35	Bryan Rekar	.25
39	Roberto Hernandez	.25
40	Wilson Alvarez	.25
43	Esteban Yan	.25
46	Steve Trachsel	.25
51	Rick White	.25
57	Juan Guzman	.25
---	Coaches (Orlando Gomez, Billy Hatcher, Bill Russell, Jose Cardenal, Bill Fischer, Leon Roberts)	.25
00	Raymond/Mascot	.25
---	Wade Boggs (Literacy Champion)	3.50
---	A's for the Rays	.10

1989 Very Fine Pirates

PITTSBURGH PIRATES

BILL LANDRUM 43

Veryfine
Fruit Juices and Drinks

This 30-card set Pirates set was sponsored by Veryfine fruit juices and issued in the form of two uncut, perforated panels, each containing 15 standard-size cards. A third panel featured color action photographs. The panels were distributed in a promotion to fans attending the April 23 game at Three Rivers Stadium. The cards display the Pirates' traditional black and gold color scheme. The backs include player data and complete stats.

		NM/M
Complete 3-Panel Set:		15.00
Complete Singles Set (30):		13.50
Common Player:		.25
0	Junior Ortiz	.25
2	Gary Redus	.25
3	Jay Bell	.25
5	Sid Bream	.25
6	Rafael Belliard	.25
10	Jim Leyland	.25
11	Glenn Wilson	.25
12	Mike La Valliere	.25
13	Jose Lind	.25
14	Ken Oberkfell	.25
15	Doug Drabek	.25
16	Bob Kipper	.25
17	Bob Walk	.25
18	Andy Van Slyke	.25
23	R.J. Reynolds	.25
24	Barry Bonds	12.00
25	Bobby Bonilla	.25
26	Neal Heaton	.25
30	Benny Distefano	.25
35	Jim Gott	.25
41	Mike Dunne	.25
43	Bill Landrum	.25
44	John Cangelosi	.25
49	Jeff Robinson	.25
52	Dorn Taylor	.25
54	Brian Fisher	.25
57	John Smiley	.25
31/37	Ray Miller, Tommy Sandt	.25
32/36	Bruce Kimm, Gene Lamont	.25
39/45	Milt May, Rich Donnelly	.25
---	Rich Donnelly (39-45)	.25

2002 Viagra Rafael Palmeiro

TEXAS
RAFAEL PALMEIRO

Spokesman Rafael Palmeiro is featured on five of the nine cards in this set issued to promote the drug Viagra. (Models are pictured on the other four cards.) Sets were issued in a cello-wrapped pack with a detailed information sheet on the drug. Evidently distributed to medical professionals, the exact manner and range of the cards' distribution is unknown. In standard 2-1/2" x 3-1/2" for-

mat, cards are printed on rather thin stock which is UV coated on each side. Except for one card which has a Palmeiro portrait photo on back along with personal data and stats, the backs have information on the drug.

		NM/M
Complete Set (9):		4.50
Common Card:		.05
(1)	Rafael Palmeiro (Game-action photo.)	1.25
(2)	Rafael Palmeiro (Bat at ready pose.)	1.25
(3)	Rafael Palmeiro (batting follow-through.)	1.25
(4)	Rafael Palmeiro (Jersey close-up.)	1.25
(5)	Rafael Palmeiro/ Portrait	1.25
(6)	Communication	.05
(7)	Diabetes	.05
(8)	Hyperlipidemia	.05
(9)	Hypertension	.05

1991 Vine Line Chicago Cubs

VINE LINE

23 Ryne Sandberg IF

This set was produced in conjunction with the official fan magazine of the Chicago Cubs, "Vine Line." Issued in nine-card panels for insertion into issues of the magazine, the panels were apparently also offered as a complete set via a mail-in offer. Cards measure the standard 2-1/2" x 3-1/2" and will be perforated on two, three or four sides, depending on their placement on the panel. Fronts are bordered in black with white typography that has the player name, position and uniform number. The player photo is in color with the background in stippled black-and-white. Backs have a black-and-white player portrait, biographical data, career highlights, 1990 and career stats and a brown and green background. The cards are listed here by uniform number.

		NM/M
Complete Singles Set (36):		6.00
Complete Panel Set (4):		7.50
Common Card:		.25
3	Jose Martinez	.25
4	Don Zimmer	.25
5	Chuck Cottier	.25
7	Joe Altobelli	.25
8	Andre Dawson	.45
9	Damon Berryhill	.25
10	Luis Salazar	.25
11	George Bell	.25
12	Shawon Dunston	.25
16	Jose Vizcaino	.25
17	Mark Grace	.50
18	Dwight Smith	.25
19	Hector Villanueva	.25
20	Jerome Walton	.25
22	Mike Harkey	.25
23	Ryne Sandberg	2.00
24	Chico Walker	.25
25	Gary Scott	.25
29	Doug Dascenzo	.25
31	Greg Maddux	2.00
34	Danny Jackson	.25
35	Dick Pole	.25
36	Chuck McElroy	.25
37	Mike Bielecki	.25
37	Erik Pappas	.25
42	Rick Sutcliffe	.25
43	Dave Smith	.25
44	Steve Wilson	.25
45	Paul Assenmacher	.25
47	Shawn Boskie	.25
48	Phil Roof	.25
50	Les Lancaster	.25
51	Heathcliff Slocumb	.25
31	Fergie Jenkins (Hall of Fame)	.50
---	Most Valuable Players (Ryne Sandberg, Andre Dawson, George Bell)	.40

1994 Vine Line Chicago Cubs Postcards

Chicago Cubs Vine Line, the team's official monthly paper, produced this set of promotional postcards. The 4" x 5-1/2" cards have black-and-white or color pictures with maroon borders. Backs are in color with a description of the front photo. The unnumbered cards are checklisted here in chronological order.

		NM/M
Complete Set (10):		10.00
Common Card:		1.00
(1)	Wrigley Field 1914-1994 (1935)	1.00
(2)	Wrigley Field 1914-1994 (1988)	1.00
(3)	Harry Caray 50 Seasons (7th inning stretch)	1.00
(4)	Harry Caray 50 Seasons (1989 w/Stan Musial)	1.00
(5)	1969 (Team composite.)	2.50
(6)	1969 Ken Holtzman (No-hitter.)	1.50
(7)	1984 (Clinching NL East)	1.00
(8)	1969 (Final game celebration.)	1.00
(9)	1989 (Boys of Zimmer)	1.00
(10)	1989 (Clinching NL East)	1.00

1998 Virginia Lottery Baseball Legends Cards

BASEBALL LEGENDS

PHIL NIEKRO
HALL OF FAME: 1997

This set of cards was one of several consolation prizes available in the commonwealth's scratch-off lottery game featuring Hall of Famers who had played in Virginia. The 2-1/2" x 3-1/2" cards have larger versions of the player photos found on the tickets. Borders are in red, white, blue, and black. Black-and-white backs have career highlights and stats. Cards can be found in either signed or autographed versions.

		NM/M
Complete Set (4):		4.00
Autographed Set (4):		25.00
Common Player:		1.00
Common Autograph:		8.00
(1)	Yogi Berra	2.00
(1)	Yogi Berra/Auto.	15.00
(2)	Willie McCovey	1.00
(2)	Willie McCovey/Auto.	10.00
(3)	Phil Niekro	1.00
(3)	Phil Niekro/Auto.	8.00
(4)	Duke Snider	1.50
(4)	Duke Snider/Auto.	12.00

1986 Wallich Enterprises Padres Sports Cards

This set of artwork postcards was designed to be the first in a series which never materialized. The cards feature color artwork on front with a wide border and player name beneath.

		NM/M
Complete Set (15):		35.00
Common Player:		3.00
(1)	Kurt Bevacqua	3.00
(2)	Dave Dravecky	4.00
(3)	Tim Flannery, Jerry Royster	3.00
(4)	Steve Garvey	6.00
(5)	Rich Gossage	4.00
(6)	Tony Gwynn	9.00
(7)	Andy Hawkins	3.00
(8)	LaMarr Hoyt	3.00
(9)	Terry Kennedy	3.00
(10)	Carmelo Martinez	3.00
(11)	Kevin McReynolds	4.00
(12)	Graig Nettles	4.00
(13)	Eric Show	3.00
(14)	Garry Templeton	4.00
(15)	Player composite	3.00

1998 Washington Senators 1969 Reunion

SENATORS

Frank Howard   OF/1st BASE

In conjunction with a card-show reunion of the '69 Nats, this set of cards was issued in uncut sheet form at the reunion breakfast. Featuring original artwork portraits atop cartoon bodies in the style of 1938 Goudey Heads-Up cards, the 2-1/2" x 2-7/8" cards have a reunion logo in an upper-corner. Backs have a team logo, player personal data, 1969 and career stats, and a quote about the player by Washington sports talk radio personality Phil Wood. Cards are listed here alphabetically.

		NM/M
Complete Set, Uncut Sheet:		15.00
Complete Set, Singles (28):		12.00
Common Player:		.25
(1)	Bernie Allen	.25
(2)	Hank Allen	.25
(3)	Frank Bertaina	.25
(4)	Dick Billings	.25
(5)	Dick Bosman	.25
(6)	Ed Brinkman	.25
(7)	Joe Camacho	.25
(8)	Casey Cox	.25
(9)	Tim Cullen	.25
(10)	Mike Epstein	.40
(11)	Jim French	.25
(12)	Jim Hannan	.25
(13)	Dennis Higgins	.25
(14)	Johnny Holliday/ Announcer	.25
(15)	Frank Howard	.50
(16)	Sid Hudson	.25
(17)	Bob Humphreys	.25
(18)	Frank Kreutzer	.25
(19)	Lee Maye	.25
(20)	Ken McMullen	.25

(21)	Ron Menchine/	
	Announcer	.25
(22)	Ed Stroud	.25
(23)	Wayne Terwilliger	.25
(24)	Del Unser	.25
(25)	Fred Valentine	.25
(26)	Shelby Whitfield/	
	Announcer	.25
(27)	Ted Williams	6.00
(28)	Checklist	.25

1988 Weis Winners Super Stars Discs

1985 Wendy's Tigers

This set contains 22 cards measuring 2-1/2" x 3-1/2", which carry both Wendy's Hamburgers and Coca-Cola logos and were produced by Topps. The cards feature a color photo with the player's identification underneath the picture. Backs are identical to 1985 Topps cards except they have different card numbers and are done in a red and black color scheme. Cards were distributed three to a pack along with a "Header" checklist in a cellophane package at selected Wendy's outlets in Michigan only.

		NM/M
Complete Set (22):		5.00
Common Player:		.25
1	Sparky Anderson	.50
2	Doug Bair	.25
3	Juan Berenguer	.25
4	Dave Bergman	.25
5	Tom Brookens	.25
6	Marty Castillo	.25
7	Darrell Evans	.40
8	Barbaro Garbey	.25
9	Kirk Gibson	.65
10	Johnny Grubb	.25
11	Willie Hernandez	.25
12	Larry Herndon	.25
13	Rusty Kuntz	.25
14	Chet Lemon	.25
15	Aurelio Lopez	.25
16	Jack Morris	.35
17	Lance Parrish	.65
18	Dan Petry	.25
19	Bill Scherrer	.25
20	Alan Trammell	1.00
21	Lou Whitaker	.50
22	Milt Wilcox	.25

1994 Wendy's Roberto Clemente Hologram

This single-card set was issued by the restaurant chain in a stated edition of 90,000.

The front has a black-bordered hologram picturing Clemente at bat, with the number 3,000 in a box at upper-right. The back has a couple of color photos of the Pirates' star along with biographical data and a career summary.

		NM/M
(1)	Roberto Clemente	6.00

1993 Whataburger Nolan Ryan

Issued in two-card cello packs at Whataburger restaurants, this set honors the career of Nolan Ryan. Cards have action photos set against colorized backgrounds and overlayed with ribbed plastic to create a 3-D effect. A card title is printed in white in the lower-left corner, with the logo of Triad (the card's maker) in the lower-right. In the upper-left corner is a red "Nolan Ryan's Recollections" logo. Backs have color logos of the hamburger chain, Triad, Coca-Cola and Major League Baseball, along with a quote from Ryan about the career highlight and a facsimile autograph. The cards are unnumbered.

		NM/M
Complete Set (10):		6.00
Common Card:		1.00
(1)	Nolan Ryan (1st No-hitter)	1.00
(2)	Nolan Ryan (2nd No-Hitter)	1.00
(3)	Nolan Ryan (3rd No-hitter)	1.00
(4)	Nolan Ryan (4th No-hitter)	1.00
(5)	Nolan Ryan (5th No-hitter)	1.00
(6)	Nolan Ryan (6th No-hitter)	1.00
(7)	Nolan Ryan (7th No-hitter)	1.00
(8)	Nolan Ryan (5,000th Strikeout)	1.00
(9)	Nolan Ryan (300th Win)	1.00
(10)	Nolan Ryan (on horse)	1.00

1982 Wheaties Indians

These 2-13/16" x 4-1/8" cards were given out ten at a time during three special promotional games; later the complete set was placed on sale at the Indians' gift shop. The cards represented the first time in 30 years that Wheaties had been

---

associated with a baseball card set. Fronts feature color photos surrounded by a wide white border with the player's name and position below the picture. The Indians logo is in the lower-left corner while the Wheaties logo is in the lower-right. Card backs have a Wheaties ad.

		NM/M
Complete Set (30):		7.50
Common Player:		.25
(1)	Chris Bando	.25
(2)	Alan Bannister	.25
(3)	Len Barker	.25
(4)	Bert Blyleven	.75
(5)	Tom Brennan	.25
(6)	Joe Charboneau	1.00
(7)	Rodney Craig	.25
(8)	John Denny	.25
(9)	Miguel Dilone	.25
(10)	Jerry Dybzinski	.25
(11)	Mike Fischlin	.25
(12)	Dave Garcia	.25
(13)	Johnny Goryl	.25
(14)	Mike Hargrove	.50
(15)	Toby Harrah	.50
(16)	Ron Hassey	.25
(17)	Von Hayes	.25
(18)	Dennis Lewallyn	.25
(19)	Rick Manning	.25
(20)	Bake McBride	.25
(21)	Tommy McCraw	.25
(22)	Jack Perconte	.25
(23)	Mel Queen	.25
(24)	Dennis Sommers	.25
(25)	Lary Sorensen	.25
(26)	Dan Spillner	.25
(27)	Rick Sutcliffe	.75
(28)	Andre Thornton	.50
(29)	Rick Waits	.25
(30)	Eddie Whitson	.25

1983 Wheaties Indians

A 32-card set marked the second year of Wheaties involvement with the Indians. Distribution of the 2-13/16" x 4-1/8" cards changed slightly in that the entire set was given away on the day of the special promotional game. As happened in 1982, the set was then placed on sale at the team's gift shop. The set includes 27 players, four coaches and the manager. The format of the cards remained basically the same on the front although the backs of player cards were changed to include complete major and minor league statistics.

		NM/M
Complete Set (32):		5.00
Common Player:		.25
(1)	Bud Anderson	.25
(2)	Jay Baller	.25
(3)	Chris Bando	.25
(4)	Alan Bannister	.25
(5)	Len Barker	.25
(6)	Bert Blyleven	.50
(7)	Wil Culmer	.25
(8)	Miguel Dilone	.25
(9)	Juan Eichelberger	.25
(10)	Jim Essian	.25
(11)	Mike Ferraro	.25
(12)	Mike Fischlin	.25
(13)	Julio Franco	.35
(14)	Ed Glynn	.25
(15)	Johnny Goryl	.25
(16)	Mike Hargrove	.35
(17)	Toby Harrah	.35
(18)	Ron Hassey	.25
(19)	Neal Heaton	.25
(20)	Rick Manning	.25
(21)	Bake McBride	.25
(22)	Don McMahon	.25
(23)	Ed Napoleon	.25
(24)	Broderick Perkins	.25

---

(25)	Dennis Sommers	.25
(26)	Lary Sorensen	.25
(27)	Dan Spillner	.25
(28)	Rick Sutcliffe	.35
(29)	Andre Thornton	.35
(30)	Manny Trillo	.25
(31)	George Vukovich	.25
(32)	Rick Waits	.25

1984 Wheaties Indians

The 2-13/16" x 4-1/8" cards again were given out at Municipal Stadium as part of a promotion involving Wheaties and the Indians on July 22. The set was down from 32 cards in 1983 to 29. There are 26 players as well as cards for the manager, coaches and team mascot. Design of the cards is virtually identical to prior years. The 1984 set is numbered by uniform number. A total of 15,000 sets were printed and any left over from the promotion were placed on sale in the team's gift shop.

		NM/M
Complete Set (29):		9.00
Common Player:		.50
2	Brett Butler	.75
4	Tony Bernazard	.50
8	Carmelo Castillo	.50
10	Pat Tabler	.50
13	Ernie Camacho	.50
14	Julio Franco	.75
15	Broderick Perkins	.50
16	Jerry Willard	.50
18	Pat Corrales	.50
21	Mike Hargrove	.75
22	Mike Fischlin	.50
23	Chris Bando	.50
24	George Vukovich	.50
26	Brook Jacoby	.50
27	Steve Farr	.50
28	Bert Blyleven	1.00
29	Andre Thornton	.75
30	Joe Carter	1.50
31	Steve Comer	.50
33	Roy Smith	.50
34	Mel Hall	.50
36	Jamie Easterly	.50
37	Don Schulze	.50
38	Luis Aponte	.50
44	Neal Heaton	.50
46	Mike Jeffcoat	.50
54	Tom Waddell	.50
---	Coaching Staff (Bobby Bonds, John Goryl, Don McMahon, Ed Napoleon, Dennis Sommers)	.50
---	Tom-E-Hawk/Mascot	.50

1997 Wheaties All-Stars

Forty-five years after it last printed baseball cards on its cereal boxes, Wheaties issued a cross-brand set of 30 cards in 1997. Top players are generally grouped by positions in groups of six on the box backs. Boxes also feature three player photos on front and an ad for obtaining a player photoball. The three series of cards found on 18 oz. boxes of Wheaties carry a Topps logo in upper-right cor-

---

ner. The top of the cards' fronts have action photos. A blue box below the photo has the player name and career highlights in white. A green, blue or orange border surrounds the card, which is separated from the rest of the box back by a black dotted line. Backs, printed inside the box, have limited personal data and full major league stats. Perfectly cut cards from these boxes measure about 2-1/2" x 3-13/16". Somewhat smaller at 2-1/16" x 3-3/8", though identical in format, are the cards found on the backs of Honey Frosted Wheaties and Crispy Wheaties 'n Raisins. Cards on the former carry a Pinnacle logo; the latter an Upper Deck. Both have orange borders surrounding the cards.

		NM/M
Complete Set, Boxes (5):		12.00
Complete Set, Singles (30):		15.00
Common Player:		.25
	All-Star Players	
	Complete Box:	3.50
(1)	Ken Griffey Jr.	.75
(2)	Greg Maddux	.65
(3)	Paul Molitor	.50
(4)	Cal Ripken Jr.	1.50
(5)	Frank Thomas	.50
(6)	Mo Vaughn	.25
	All-Star Players	
	Complete Box:	3.00
(7)	Barry Bonds	1.50
(8)	Ken Caminiti	.25
(9)	Ken Griffey Jr.	.75
(10)	Chipper Jones	.65
(11)	Chuck Knoblauch	.25
(12)	Alex Rodriguez	1.00
	All-Star Infielders	
	Complete Box:	2.50
(13)	Jeff Bagwell	.50
(14)	Mark McGwire	1.00
(15)	Mike Piazza	.75
(16)	Cal Ripken Jr.	1.50
(17)	Ryne Sandberg	.65
(18)	Frank Thomas	.50
	All-Star Outfielders	
	Complete Box:	2.50
(19)	Barry Bonds	1.50
(20)	Ellis Burks	.25
(21)	Juan Gonzalez	.35
(22)	Ken Griffey Jr.	.75
(23)	Tony Gwynn	.65
(24)	Bernie Williams	.25
	All-Star Pitchers	
	Complete Box:	2.00
(25)	Andy Benes	.25
(26)	David Cone	.25
(27)	Greg Maddux	.65
(28)	Mike Mussina	.35
(29)	Hideo Nomo	.35
(30)	John Smoltz	.25

1995 Wienerschnitzel L.A. Dodgers POGs

The Dodger Stadium hot dog concessionaire sponsored this promotion which was given away to youngsters attending a May 13 Dodgers game. The issue consists of 14 POGs die cut from an 8-1/2" x 10-3/4" cardboard sheet. The POGs picture the team's winners of the Rookie of the Year Award from Jackie Robinson in 1947 through Raul Mondesi in 1994. The individual POGs measure 1-5/8" in diameter. Fronts have a sepia or color player portrait at center, with a blue border of lighter blue stars. Backs are printed in red and blue on white and have a

---

bit of player information plus the logos of the team, sponsor and World POG Federation.

		NM/M
Complete Set, Panel:		8.00
Complete Set, Singles (14):		7.00
Common Player:		.25
1	Jackie Robinson	3.00
2	Don Newcombe	.50
3	Joe Black	.50
4	Jim Gilliam	.35
5	Frank Howard	.35
6	Jim Lefebvre	.25
7	Ted Sizemore	.25
8	Rick Sutcliffe	.25
9	Steve Howe	.25
10	Fernando Valenzuela	.35
11	Steve Sax	.25
12	Eric Karros	.25
13	Mike Piazza	2.00
14	Raul Mondesi	.25

1993 Ted Williams Co. Promos

Though they are unmarked as sample cards, the promos issued for the debut Ted Williams Card Co. are easily distinguished from the regularly issued versions. The #1 Williams card has different front photos and his name in green, rather than orange, and the Paige and Gonzalez cards have text backs in the promo version, rather than checklists.

		NM/M
Complete Set (3):		10.00
Common Player:		2.00
1	Ted Williams	5.00
115	Satchel Paige	3.00
160	Juan Gonzalez	2.00

1993 Ted Williams Card Co.

Without a license from the players' union, the premiere issue of the Ted Williams Card Co. relied on innovative subsets to create interest in its "old-timers" set. The first 96 cards in the set comprise the base issue. Those cards feature a black-and-white or color action photo set against a background of a second ghost-image photo. The player's name is at bottom with the card company logo conspicuous at top. Backs have some biographical detail, a career summary, the player's five best seasons' and career stats. Subsets numbered contiguously with the base set include a 19-card Negro Leagues series highlighted with green-foil; five cards featuring the All-American Girls Professional Baseball League; a 10-card "Ted's Greatest Hitters" series; 10 "Barrier Breakers" cards featuring Negro Leagues veterans who later played in the majors; a 10-card "Goin' North" subset featuring minor league stars of the 1940s-1970s in minor league photos, and, a pair of five-card "Dawning of a Legacy" series featuring Juan Gonzalez and Jeff Bagwell. There were also several insert card series which are listed separately. The cards were packaged with a pair of die-cut player or team logo POGs.

	NM/M
Complete Set (160):	12.00
Common Player:	.05
Wax Pack (12):	.75
Wax Box (36):	20.00
1 Ted Williams	3.00
2 Rick Ferrell	.05
3 Jim Lonborg	.05
4 Mel Parnell	.05
5 Jim Piersall	.05
6 Luis Tiant	.05
7 Carl Yastrzemski	.50
8 Ralph Branca	.05
9 Roy Campanella	.50
10 Ron Cey	.05
11 Tommy Davis	.05
12 Don Drysdale	.35
13 Carl Erskine	.10
14 Steve Garvey	.10
15 Don Newcombe	.10
16 Duke Snider	.50
17 Maury Wills	.05
18 Jim Fregosi	.05
19 Bobby Grich	.05
20 Bill Buckner	.05
21 Billy Herman	.05
22 Ferguson Jenkins	.10
23 Ron Santo	.15
24 Billy Williams	.10
25 Luis Aparicio	.10
26 Luke Appling	.10
27 Minnie Minoso	.15
28 Johnny Bench	.50
29 George Foster	.05
30 Joe Morgan	.15
31 Buddy Bell	.05
32 Lou Boudreau	.10
33 Rocky Colavito	.25
34 Jim "Mudcat" Grant	.05
35 Tris Speaker	.10
36 Ray Boone	.05
37 Darrell Evans	.05
38 Al Kaline	.35
39 George Kell	.05
40 Mickey Lolich	.05
41 Cesar Cedeno	.05
42 Sal Bando	.05
43 Vida Blue	.05
44 Bert Campaneris	.05
45 Ken Holtzman	.05
46 Lew Burdette	.05
47 Bob Horner	.05
48 Warren Spahn	.10
49 Cecil Cooper	.05
50 Tony Oliva	.10
51 Bobby Bonds	.10
52 Alvin Dark	.05
53 Dave Dravecky	.05
54 Monte Irvin	.10
55 Willie Mays	1.00
56 Bud Harrelson	.05
57 Dave Kingman	.10
58 Yogi Berra	.50
59 Don Baylor	.05
60 Jim Bouton	.05
61 Bobby Brown	.05
62 Whitey Ford	.40
63 Lou Gehrig	1.50
64 Charlie Keller	.05
65 Eddie Lopat	.05
66 Johnny Mize	.10
67 Bobby Murcer	.05
68 Graig Nettles	.05
69 Bobby Shantz	.05
70 Richie Ashburn	.10
71 Larry Bowa	.05
72 Steve Carlton	.40
73 Robin Roberts	.10
74 Matty Alou	.05
75 Harvey Haddix	.05
76 Ralph Kiner	.10
77 Bill Madlock	.05
78 Bill Mazeroski	.35
79 Al Oliver	.05
80 Manny Sanguillen	.05
81 Willie Stargell	.10
82 Al Brumbry	.05
83 Davey Johnson	.10
84 Boog Powell	.10
85 Earl Weaver	.10
86 Lou Brock	.10
87 Orlando Cepeda	.10
88 Curt Flood	.05
89 Joe Garagiola	.35
90 Bob Gibson	.10
91 Rogers Hornsby	.20
92 Enos Slaughter	.10
93 Joe Torre	.20
94 Gaylord Perry	.10
95 Checklist 1-49	.05
96 Checklist 50-96	.05
97 Cool Papa Bell	.10
98 Garnett Blair	.05
99 Gene Benson	.05
100 Lyman Bostock, Sr.	.05
101 Marlin Carter	.05
102 Oscar Charleston	.10
103 Ray Dandridge	.10
104 Mahlon Duckett	.05
105 Josh Gibson	.20
106 Cowan Hyde	.05
107 "Judy" Johnson	.10
108 Buck Leonard	.10
109 Pop Lloyd	.10
110 Lester Lockett	.05
111 Max Manning	.05
112 Satchel Paige	.50

113 Armando Vazquez	.05
114 Smokey Joe Williams	.10
115 Negro Leagues Checklist	
(Satchel Paige)	.05
116 Alice Hohlmeyer	.05
117 Dotty Kamenshek	.05
118 Pepper Davis	.05
119 Marge Wenzell	.05
120 AAGPBA Checklist	.05
121 The Babe (Babe Ruth)	1.50
122 The Iron Horse	
(Lou Gehrig)	.75
123 Double X	
(Jimmie Foxx)	.20
124 Rajah	
(Rogers Hornsby)	.10
125 The Georgia Peach	
(Ty Cobb)	.75
126 The Say Hey Kid	
(Willie Mays)	.50
127 Ralph (Ralph Kiner)	.10
128 The Grey Eagle	
(Tris Speaker)	.10
129 The Big Cat	
(Johnny Mize)	.10
130 Ted's Greatest Hitters	
Checklist	.05
131 Satchel Paige	.25
132 Joe Black	.10
133 Roy Campanella	.25
134 Larry Doby	.10
135 Jim Gilliam	.05
136 Monte Irvin	.10
137 Sam Jethroe	.05
138 Willie Mays	.50
139 Don Newcombe	.05
140 Barrier Breakers	
Checklist	.05
141 Roy Campanella	.25
142 Bob Gibson	.10
143 Boog Powell	.10
144 Willie Mays	.50
145 Johnny Mize	.10
146 Monte Irvin	.10
147 Earl Weaver	.10
148 Ted Williams	1.50
149 Jim Gilliam	.05
150 Goin' North Checklist	.05
151 Juan Gonzalez (Footsteps	
to Greatness)	.25
151a Juan Gonzalez/Auto.	
(Edition of 43.)	60.00
152 Juan Gonzalez	
(Sign 'em Up.)	.25
152a Juan Gonzalez/Auto.	
(Edition of 43.)	60.00
153 Juan Gonzalez	
(The Road to Success.)	.25
153a Juan Gonzalez/Auto.	
(Edition of 43.)	60.00
154 Juan Gonzalez	
(Looking Ahead.)	.25
154a Juan Gonzalez/Auto.	
(Edition of 43.)	60.00
155 "Dawning of a Legacy"	
Checklist	.05
156 Jeff Bagwell (Born with Red	
Sox Blood.)	.05
157 Jeff Bagwell	
(Movin' Up, Then Out.)	.50
158 Jeff Bagwell (Year 1)	.50
159 Jeff Bagwell (Year 2)	.50
160 "Dawning of a Legacy"	
Checklist	
(Juan Gonzalez)	.05

Etched in Stone

This 10-card insert set documents the career of Roberto Clemente, using sepiatoned and color photographs on the card front, highlighted by a gold-foil embossed "Tribute '93" logo in the lower-left corner and an "Etched in Stone" logo at upper-right. Backs have a detailed biography. Cards are numbered ES1 through ES10.

	NM/M
Complete Set (10):	12.00
Common Player:	2.00
1 Youth	
(Roberto Clemente)	2.00

2 Sign Up	
(Roberto Clemente)	2.00
3 Try-Out	
(Roberto Clemente)	2.00
4 Playing Mad	
(Roberto Clemente)	2.00
5 Minor Leagues	
(Roberto Clemente)	2.00
6 1955-1959	
(Roberto Clemente)	2.00
7 1960	
(Roberto Clemente)	2.00
8 1963	
(Roberto Clemente)	2.00
9 1970	
(Roberto Clemente)	2.00
10 Etched in Stone	
Checklist	2.00

Locklear Collection

The paintings of former major leaguer Gene Locklear are featured in this 10-card insert set. The central image of the player is set against a background of multiple player images in orange, red and purple tones. The player's name is in dark blue on the left edge and a "Gene Locklear Collection" logo is in lower-right. On back is a commentary on the player, a card number with an "LC" suffix and, at bottom center, a serial number. The cards of Ted Williams can be found in an autographed insert version numbered on back from within an edition of 406.

	NM/M
Complete Set (10):	12.00
Common Player:	.75
Ted Williams Autographed:	500.00
1 Yogi Berra	1.00
2 Lou Brock	.75
3 Willie Mays	2.00
4 Johnny Mize	.75
5 Satchel Paige	1.50
6 Babe Ruth	3.00
7 Enos Slaughter	.75
8 Carl Yastrzemski	1.00
9 Ted Williams	2.50
10 Locklear Collection	
Checklist	.10

Memories

Four historical World Series of the 1950s-1970s are featured in five-card runs within the "Memories" insert set. Fronts have black-and-white or color player photos. In the lower-left corner is a vintage press camera with "Memories" and the year emanating from the flashbulb. The Ted Williams Card Co. logo is at upper-right. The player's name is in white at bottom-center. Cards are

numbered with an "M" prefix on back and feature a headline announcing the team's World Series victory and a summary of the featured player's performance in that Fall Classic.

	NM/M
Complete Set (20):	45.00
Common Player:	1.00
1955 BROOKLYN DODGERS	
1 Roy Campanella	3.50
2 Jim Gilliam	2.00
3 Gil Hodges	3.50
4 Duke Snider	3.50
5 1955 Dodgers Checklist	.60
1963 L.A. DODGERS	
6 Don Drysdale	3.50
7 Tommy Davis	2.25
8 Johnny Podres	2.25
9 Maury Wills	3.50
10 1963 Dodgers Checklist	.60
1971 PITTSBURGH PIRATES	
11 Roberto Clemente	9.00
12 Al Oliver	1.00
13 Manny Sanguillen	1.00
14 Willie Stargell	2.00
15 1971 Pirates Checklist	.60
1975 CINCINNATI REDS	
16 Johnny Bench	4.50
17 George Foster	1.25
18 Joe Morgan	3.00
19 Tony Perez	2.00
20 1975 Red Checklist	.60

POGs

These 26 cards featuring two die-cut POGs on each were issued as inserts in 1993 Ted Williams packs. Fronts of the extra-thick cardboard cards have a black background with the logos of the card company and the Cooperstown Collection. Two 1-5/8" diameter POGs appear on each card, picturing either players or team logos. Backs are blank. The unnumbered POG cards are listed here alphabetically, with player POGs listed first.

	NM/M
Complete Set (26):	4.00
Common Player:	.25
(1) Yogi Berra,	
Roy Campanella	1.00
(2) Brooklyn Dodgers	
(Roy Campanella)	.50
(3) Tommy Davis,	
George Foster	.25
(4) Lou Gehrig,	
Ted Williams	2.00
(5) New York Yankees	
(Lou Gehrig)	1.50
(6) Ted Williams, #9 patch	.75
(7) 1993 World Series	
Patch	.25
(8) Baltimore Elite Giants	.25
(9) New York Mets	.25
(10) New York Cuban Stars	.25
(11) Minnesota Twins	.25
(12) St. Louis Browns	.25
(13) Detroit Tigers	.25
(14) Kansas City Royals	.25
(15) Detroit Stars	.25
(16) Kansas City Athletics	.25
(17) Florida Marlins	.25
(18) New York Black	
Yankees	.25
(19) New York Yankees	.25
(20) New York Harlem Stars	.25
(21) Philadelphia Stars	.25
(22) New York Giants	.25
(23) San Diego Padres	.25
(24) Negro Leagues Classic	
Teams	.25
(25) #21 (Clemente) patch	.25
(26) St. Louis Cardinals	.25

Brooks Robinson

This 10-card insert set, numbered BR1 through BR10, traces the baseball career of Hall of Fame Orioles third baseman Brooks Robinson. Card fronts feature sepia-toned or color photos highlighted by the player's name in gold foil down the left side and a "Brooks Robinson Collection" diamond logo at lower-right. Backs include a career summary or batting or fielding stats. Autographed versions were a random retail packaging insert.

	NM/M
Complete Set (10):	7.50
Common Player:	1.00
Autographed:	20.00
1BR Salad Days	
(Brooks Robinson)	1.00
2BR Career Batting Stats	
(Brooks Robinson)	1.00
3BR '66 World Series	
(Brooks Robinson)	1.00
4BR Career Fielding Stats	
(Brooks Robinson)	1.00
5BR '70 Series #2	
(Brooks Robinson)	1.00
6BR '70 Series #1	
(Brooks Robinson)	1.00
7BR Comin' Up	
(Brooks Robinson)	1.00
8BR All-Star Games	
(Brooks Robinson)	1.00
9BR 1964	
(Brooks Robinson)	1.00
10BR Brooks Robinson	
Collection Checklist	1.00

1994 Ted Williams Card Co.

Lack of a players' association license again limited the company to using two major leaguers in its second annual card set, but it spiced up its 1994 edition with hot prospects in the minor leagues, more high-tech production values and innovative subsets and chase cards. The base set for 1994 includes 162 cards. The first 92 feature retired or deceased players. Those cards feature a color or colorized photo set against a background of a second ghost-image photo or the actual photo background. Vertically at right is a stone image on which the player's name is printed in extremely difficult to read gold letters. The edge of the stone and the card company logo are embossed. Backs have biographical and career details, and stats for the player's five top sea-

sons. Subsets numbered consecutively with the base cards include a seven-card "Women of Baseball" series; 18 Negro Leaguers, 18 current minor leaguers in a series titled "The Campaign;" 10 "Goin' North" cards of former superstars as minor leaguers; nine "Swingin'" for the Fences" cards of home run hitters, and, a nine-card "Dawning of a Legacy" series featuring Cliff Floyd and Tim Salmon. The several insert card series are listed separately. Autographed cards of Leon Day were random pack inserts.

	NM/M
Complete Set (162):	15.00
Common Player:	.10
Wax Pack (12):	1.00
Wax Box (36):	30.00
Jumbo Pack(20):	2.00
Jumbo Box (24):	35.00
1 Ted Williams	4.00
P1 Ted Williams/PC	2.50
2 Bernie Carbo	.10
3 Bobby Doerr	.10
4 Fred Lynn	.10
5 Johnny Pesky	.10
6 Rico Petrocelli	.10
7 Cy Young	.25
8 Paul Blair	.10
9 Andy Etchebarren	.10
10 Brooks Robinson	.20
11 Gil Hodges	.20
12 Tommy John	.15
13 Rick Monday	.10
14 Dean Chance	.10
15 Doug DeCinces	.10
16 Gabby Hartnett	.10
17 Don Kessinger	.10
18 Bruce Sutter	.10
19 Eddie Collins	.10
20 Nellie Fox	.20
21 Carlos May	.10
22 Ted Kluszewski	.25
23 Vada Pinson	.10
24 Johnny Vander Meer	.10
25 Bob Feller	.10
26 Mike Garcia	.10
27 Sam McDowell	.10
28 Al Rosen	.10
29 Norm Cash	.15
30 Ty Cobb	1.50
31 Mark Fidrych	.20
32 Hank Greenberg	.25
33 Denny McLain	.10
34 Virgil Trucks	.10
35 Enos Cabell	.10
36 Mike Scott	.10
37 Bob Watson	.10
38 Amos Otis	.10
39 Frank White	.10
40 Joe Adcock	.10
41 Rico Carty	.10
42 Ralph Garr	.10
43 Eddie Mathews	.25
44 Ben Oglivie	.10
45 Gorman Thomas	.10
46 Earl Battey	.10
47 Rod Carew	.20
48 Jim Kaat	.10
49 Harmon Killebrew	.20
50 Gary Carter	.25
51 Steve Rogers	.10
52 Rusty Staub	.10
53 Sal Maglie	.10
54 Juan Marichal	.20
55 Mel Ott	.25
56 Bobby Thomson	.10
57 Tommie Agee	.10
58 Tug McGraw	.10
59 Elston Howard	.15
60 Sparky Lyle	.10
61 Billy Martin	.15
62 Thurman Munson	.25
63 Bobby Richardson	.15
64 Bill Skowron	.10
65 Mickey Cochrane	.25
66 Rollie Fingers	.10
67 Lefty Grove	.10
68 Catfish Hunter	.10
69 Connie Mack	.10
70 Al Simmons	.10
71 Dick Allen	.15
72 Bob Boone	.10
73 Del Ennis	.10
74 Chuck Klein	.10
75 Mike Schmidt	.50
76 Dock Ellis	.10
77 Elroy Face	.10
78 Phil Garner	.10
79 Bill Mazeroski	.20
80 Pie Traynor	.10
81 Honus Wagner	.25
82 Dizzy Dean	.25
83 Red Schoendienst	.10
84 Randy Jones	.10
85 Nate Colbert	.10
86 Jeff Burroughs	.10
87 Jim Sundberg	.10
88 Frank Howard	.10
89 Walter Johnson	.20

90	Eddie Yost	.10
91	Checklist 1-46	.10
92	Checklist 47-92	.10
93	Faye Dancer	.10
94	Snookie Doyle	.10
95	Maddy English	.10
96	Nickie Fox	.10
97	Sophie Kurys	.10
98	Alma Ziegler	.10
99	Women of Baseball Checklist	.10
100	Newton Allen	.10
101	Willard Brown	.10
102	Larry Brown	.10
103	Leon Day	.10
103a	Leon Day (autographed)	20.00
104	John Donaldson	.10
105	Rube Foster	.10
106	Bud Fowler	.10
107	Vic Harris	.10
108	Webster McDonald	.10
109	John "Buck" O'Neil	.10
110	Ted "Double Duty" Radcliffe	.10
111	Wilber "Bullet" Rogan	.10
112	Toni Stone	.10
113	Jim Taylor	.10
114	Moses "Fleetwood" Walker	.15
115	George Wilson	.10
116	Judson Wilson	.10
117	Negro Leagues Checklist	.10
118	Howard Battle	.10
119	John Burke	.10
120	Brian Dubose	.10
121	Alex Gonzalez	.15
122	Jose Herrera	.10
123	Jason Giambi	1.00
124	Derek Jeter	4.50
125	Charles Johnson	.25
126	Daron Kirkreit	.10
127	Jason Moler	.10
128	Vince Moore	.10
129	Chad Mottola	.10
130	Jose Silva	.10
131	Makato Suzuki (Makoto)	.10
132	Brien Taylor	.10
133	Michael Tucker	.10
134	Billy Wagner	.25
135	The Campaign Checklist	.10
136	Gary Carter	.10
137	Tony Conigliaro	.10
138	Sparky Lyle	.10
139	Roger Maris	.45
140	Vada Pinson	.10
141	Mike Schmidt	.50
142	Frank White	.10
143	Ted Williams	2.50
144	Goin' North Checklist	.10
145	Joe Adcock	.10
146	Rocky Colavito	.25
147	Lou Gehrig	2.00
148	Gil Hodges	.25
149	Bob Horner	.10
150	Willie Mays	1.50
151	Mike Schmidt	.50
152	Pat Seery	.10
153	Swingin' for the Fences Checklist	.10
154	Cliff Floyd (The Honors Begin)	.15
155	Cliff Floyd (The Top Polecat)	.15
156	Cliff Floyd (Minor League Team of the Year)	.15
157	Cliff Floyd (Major League Debut)	.15
158	Tim Salmon (Award Winner)	.15
159	Tim Salmon (Early Professional Career)	.15
160	Tim Salmon (An MVP Season)	.15
161	Tim Salmon (Rookie of the Year)	.15
162	Dawning of a Legacy Checklist	.10

Etched in Stone

A metallized effect highlights the front design of this insert series commemorating the career of Roger Maris. Color (or colorized) photos appear to have been revealed by chiseling away a rock face which forms much of the front border. Backs have career write-ups overprinted on a design which forms a large "Etched in Stone" design when the cards are laid together in order. Cards have an "ES" prefix to the card number. Cards can be found with either brown or red "rock" borders. The red version is valued at double the brown.

		NM/M
Complete Set (9):		7.50
Common Player:		1.00
1	Roger Maris (Scouting Report)	1.00
2	Roger Maris (Traded)	1.00
3	Roger Maris (Career Year)	1.00
4	Roger Maris/1961	1.00
5	Roger Maris (Silent Accomplishments)	1.00
6	Roger Maris (Team Player)	1.00
7	Roger Maris (Reborn)	1.00
8	Roger Maris (Hero's Welcome)	1.00
9	Checklist (Roger Maris)	.20

Dan Gardiner

Sports artist Dan Gardiner was commissioned to produce a series of nine insert cards depicting hot minor league prospects for this insert set. Players are depicted in posed portraits on front and in action paintings on the back. Cards carry a "DG" prefix to the card number and each card is serially numbered in the upper-left corner.

		NM/M
Complete Set (9):		6.00
Common Player:		.25
1	Michael Jordan	2.50
2	Michael Tucker	.25
3	Derek Jeter	3.50
4	Charles Johnson	.25
5	Howard Battle	.25
6	Quivio Vergas (Veras)	.25
7	Brian Hunter	.25
8	Brien Taylor	.25
9	Checklist	.05

Locklear Collection

Paintings of eight Hall of Famers plus a checklist are featured in this insert set. The art is the work of former major leaguer Gene Locklear. The cards are numbered with an "LC" suffix.

		NM/M
Complete Set (9):		7.50
Common Player:		1.00
11	Ty Cobb	2.00
12	Bob Feller	1.00
13	Lou Gehrig	2.00
14	Josh Gibson	1.00
15	Walter Johnson	1.00
16	Casey Stengel	1.00
17	Honus Wagner	1.00
18	Cy Young	1.00
19	Checklist	.05

LP Cards

Two premium insert cards in the 1994 Ted Williams Co. set carry an "LP" card number prefix. One depicts basketball superstar Larry Bird playing baseball during his college days at Indiana State University. The other card depicts Ted Williams speaking at the opening of the Ted Williams Museum. Fronts use a metallized technology. Backs describe the action. A few genuinely autographed Bird cards are known, featuring an embossed seal of authenticity.

		NM/M
Complete Set (2):		8.00
1	Larry Bird	5.00
1a	Larry Bird/Auto.	200.00
2	Ted Williams	5.00

Memories

Continuing the card numbers from the 1993 Memories insert set, the 1994 version features highlights of the 1954, 1961, 1968 and 1975 World Series. Card fronts feature metallized images in a snapshot format. The year is noted in large pink numbers at lower-left. Backs describe each player's participation in that particular World Series and are numbered with an "M" prefix.

		NM/M
Complete Set (20):		11.00
Common Player:		.50
21	Monte Irvin	.50
22	Sal Maglie	.50
23	Dusty Rhodes	.50
24	Hank Thompson	.50
25	Yogi Berra	1.25
26	Elston Howard	.75
27	Roger Maris	1.50
28	Bobby Richardson	.75
29	Norm Cash	.75
30	Al Kaline	1.00
31	Mickey Lolich	.50
32	Denny McLain	.50
33	Bernie Carbo	.50
34	Fred Lynn	.50
35	Rico Petrocelli	.50
36	Luis Tiant	.50
37	Checklist	.05

Mike Schmidt Collection

This nine-card insert set honors the career of Hall of Fame Phillies third baseman

Mike Schmidt. Fronts feature full-bleed metallized color photos. Backs have a Phillies flag design with a career biography. Cards are numbered with an "MS" prefix.

		NM/M
Complete Set (9):		7.50
Common Player:		1.00
1	Mike Schmidt (Mike)	1.00
2	Mike Schmidt (The White House)	1.00
3	Mike Schmidt (Soaping Up)	1.00
4	Mike Schmidt (The Promised Land)	1.00
5	Mike Schmidt (Who's Who)	1.00
6	Mike Schmidt (The Call)	1.00
7	Mike Schmidt (Leading the Way)	1.00
8	Mike Schmidt (Award Winner)	1.00
9	Checklist	.35

The 500 Club

Major leaguers with 500 or more career home runs are featured in this nine-card insert set. Fronts have full-bleed metallized photos, some in color and some which have been colorized. A logo picturing a hanging "The 500 Club" sign appears at lower-left, with the player's name in gold. Backs have a basic design that looks for all the world like a toilet seat, in which the player's home run prowess is recalled. Cards are numbered with a "5C" prefix. Two versions of each card exist, one has brown graphic highlights on front, one has red. The red highlighted cards are worth about 25 percent more than the brown.

		NM/M
Complete Set (9):		7.50
Common Player:		.75
1	Hank Aaron	1.50
2	Reggie Jackson	1.25
3	Harmon Killebrew	.75
4	Mickey Mantle	2.25
5	Jimmie Foxx	.75
6	Babe Ruth	2.00
7	Mike Schmidt	1.25
8	Ted Williams	1.50
9	Checklist	.05

Trade for Babe

This nine-card set was available to persons who found a randomly packaged "Trade for Babe" redemption card in packs of Ted Williams Co. cards. A $4.50 postage/handling fee was necessary for redemption and a re-

ported 9,999 trade sets were available. Card fronts feature colorized photos of Ruth while backs have text concerning the front theme. Cards are numbered with a "TB" prefix.

		NM/M
Complete Set (9):		15.00
Common Player:		2.00
----	Babe Ruth (Redemption card, expired Nov. 30, 1994.)	2.00
1	Babe Ruth (George Herman Ruth)	2.00
2	Babe Ruth (King of the Hill)	2.00
3	Babe Ruth (On to New York)	2.00
4	Babe Ruth (Called Shot?)	2.00
5	Babe Ruth (The Bambino and the Iron Horse)	2.00
6	Babe Ruth (Larger Than Life)	2.00
7	Babe Ruth (Always a Yankee)	2.00
8	Babe Ruth (The Babe)	2.00
9	Babe Ruth (Checklist)	2.00

1990 Windwalker Discs

The origins of this disc set, even its name, are not recorded. The set is comprised on nine dual-headed 3-7/8" discs. Each disc features two players from the 1990 American League All-Star team. No similar issue is known for the National League. Each side has a color action photo and a facsimile autograph. The un-numbered discs are checklisted here alphabetically.

		NM/M
Complete Set (9):		15.00
Common Disc:		.70
(1)	Sandy Alomar Jr., Dave Parker	.75
(2)	George Bell, Julio Franco	.75
(3)	Wade Boggs, Kirby Puckett	3.00
(4)	Jose Canseco, Rickey Henderson	2.50
(5)	Roger Clemens, Bob Welch	3.50
(6)	Cecil Fielder, Bret Saberhagen	.75
(7)	Chuck Finley, Kelly Gruber	.75
(8)	Ken Griffey Jr., Steve Sax	4.00
(9)	Ozzie Guillen, Cal Ripken Jr.	5.00

1991 Wiz Mets

This 450-card issue was one of several sponsored by the East Coast WIZ home entertainment stores in the early 1990s. Virtually every player in Mets history is included in the set. Each of three series of 15-card perforated sheets was co-sponsored by a large electronics

manufacturer: AT&T, Fisher or Maxell. Sheets measure 10"x9", with individual cards measuring 2" x 3". Card fronts have a black-and-white photo at center with the player's name at left and position at right. A color Mets logo is above and a WIZ logo below. Blue corner decorations complete the front design. Backs are printed in black-and-white, have Mets and sponsors' logos, years the player appeared with the Mets and his Mets career stats. Single cards from this set are seldom available.

		NM/M
Complete Set (450):		45.00
Common Player:		.10
1	Don Aase	.10
2	Tommie Agee	.30
3	Rick Aguilera	.20
4	Jack Aker	.10
5	Neil Allen	.10
6	Bill Almon	.10
7	Sandy Alomar	.10
8	Jesus Alou	.10
9	George Altman	.10
10	Luis Alvarado	.10
11	Craig Anderson	.10
12	Rick Anderson	.10
13	Bob Apodaca	.10
14	Gerry Arrigo	.10
15	Richie Ashburn	6.00
16	Tucker Ashford	.10
17	Bob Aspromonte	.10
18	Benny Ayala	.10
19	Wally Backman	.10
20	Kevin Baez	.10
21	Bob Bailor	.10
22	Rick Baldwin	.10
23	Billy Baldwin	.10
24	Lute Barnes	.10
25	Ed Bauta	.10
26	Billy Beane	.10
27	Larry Bearnarth	.10
28	Blaine Beatty	.10
29	Jim Beauchamp	.10
30	Gus Bell	.30
31	Dennis Bennett	.10
32	Butch Benton	.10
33	Juan Berenguer	.10
34	Bruce Berenyi	.10
35	Dwight Bernard	.10
36	Yogi Berra	6.00
37	Jim Bethke	.10
38	Mike Bishop	.10
39	Terry Blocker	.10
40	Bruce Bochy	.10
41	Bruce Boisclair	.10
42	Dan Boitano	.10
43	Mark Bombard	.10
44	Don Bosch	.10
45	Daryl Boston	.10
46	Ken Boswell	.10
47	Ed Bouchee	.10
48	Larry Bowa	.20
49	Ken Boyer	.50
50	Mark Bradley	.10
51	Eddie Bressoud	.10
52	Hubie Brooks	.30
53	Kevin Brown	.10
54	Leon Brown	.10
55	Mike Bruhert	.10
56	Jerry Buchek	.10
57	Larry Burright	.10
58	Ray Burris	.10
59	John Candelaria	.10
60	Chris Cannizzaro	.10
61	Buzz Capra	.10
62	Jose Cardenal	.10
63	Don Cardwell	.10
64	Duke Carmel	.10
65	Chuck Carr	.10
66	Mark Carreon	.10
67	Gary Carter	4.00
68	Elio Chacon	.10
69	Dean Chance	.10
70	Kelvin Chapman	.10
71	Ed Charles	.40
72	Rich Chiles	.10
73	Harry Chiti	.10
74	John Christensen	.10

No.	Name	Price
75	Joe Christopher	.10
76	Galen Cisco	.10
77	Donn Clendenon	.40
78	Gene Clines	.10
79	Choo Choo Coleman	.40
80	Kevin Collins	.10
81	David Cone	.75
82	Bill Connors	.10
83	Cliff Cook	.10
84	Tim Corcoran	.10
85	Mardie Cornejo	.10
86	Billy Cowan	.10
87	Roger Craig	.10
88	Jerry Cram	.10
89	Mike Cubbage	.10
90	Ron Darling	.20
91	Ray Daviault	.10
92	Tommie Davis	.10
93	John DeMerit	.10
94	Bill Denehy	.10
95	Jack DiLauro	.10
96	Carlos Diaz	.10
97	Mario Diaz	.10
98	Steve Dillon	.10
99	Sammy Drake	.10
100	Jim Dwyer	.10
101	Duffy Dyer	.10
102	Len Dykstra	.50
103	Tom Edens	.10
104	Dave Eilers	.10
105	Larry Elliot	.10
106	Dock Ellis	.10
107	Kevin Elster	.20
108	Nino Espinosa	.10
109	Chuck Estrada	.10
110	Francisco Estrada	.10
111	Pete Falcone	.10
112	Sid Fernandez	.20
113	Chico Fernandez	.10
114	Sergio Ferrer	.10
115	Jack Fisher	.10
116	Mike Fitzgerald	.10
117	Shaun Fitzmaurice	.10
118	Gil Flores	.10
119	Doug Flynn	.10
120	Tim Foli	.10
121	Rich Folkers	.10
122	Larry Foss	.10
123	George Foster	.30
124	Leo Foster	.10
125	Joe Foy	.10
126	John Franco	.30
127	Jim Fregosi	.20
128	Bob Friend	.10
129	Danny Frisella	.10
130	Brent Gaff	.10
131	Bob Gallagher	.10
132	Ron Gardenhire	.10
133	Rob Gardner	.10
134	Wes Gardner	.10
135	Wayne Garrett	.10
136	Rod Gaspar	.10
137	Gary Gentry	.10
138	Jim Gibbons	.10
139	Bob Gibson	.10
140	Brian Giles	.10
141	Joe Ginsberg	.10
142	Ed Glynn	.10
143	Jesse Gonder	.30
144	Dwight Gooden	1.00
145	Greg Goossen	.10
146	Tom Gorman	.10
147	Jim Gosger	.10
148	Bill Graham	.10
149	Wayne Graham	.10
150	Dallas Green	.30
151	Pumpsie Green	.10
152	Tom Grieve	.10
153	Jerry Grote	.20
154	Joe Grzenda	.10
155	Don Hahn	.10
156	Tom Hall	.10
157	Jack Hamilton	.10
158	Ike Hampton	.10
159	Tim Harkness	.10
160	Bud Harrelson	.40
161	Greg Harris	.10
162	Greg Harts	.10
163	Andy Hassler	.10
164	Tom Hausman	.10
165	Ed Hearn	.10
166	Richie Hebner	.30
167	Danny Heep	.10
168	Jack Heidemann	.10
169	Bob Heise	.10
170	Ken Henderson	.10
171	Steve Henderson	.10
172	Bob Hendley	.10
173	Phil Hennigan	.10
174	Bill Hepler	.10
175	Ron Herbel	.10
176	Manny Hernandez	.10
177	Keith Hernandez	.50
178	Tommy Herr	.10
179	Rick Herrscher	.10
180	Jim Hickman	.10
181	Joe Hicks	.10
182	Chuck Hiller	.10
183	Dave Hillman	.10
184	Jerry Hinsley	.10
185	Gil Hodges	2.00
186	Ron Hodges	.10
187	Scott Holman	.10
188	Jay Hook	.10
189	Mike Howard	.10
190	Jesse Hudson	.10
191	Keith Hughes	.10
192	Todd Hundley	.30
193	Ron Hunt	.10
194	Willard Hunter	.10
195	Clint Hurdle	.10
196	Jeff Innis	.10
197	Al Jackson	.10
198	Roy Lee Jackson	.10
199	Gregg Jefferies	1.00
200	Stan Jefferson	.10
201	Chris Jelic	.10
202	Bob Johnson	.10
203	Howard Johnson	.75
204	Bob W. Johnson	.10
205	Randy Jones	.10
206	Sherman Jones	.10
207	Cleon Jones	.30
208	Ross Jones	.10
209	Mike Jorgensen	.10
210	Rod Kanehl	.10
211	Bobby Klaus	.10
212	Bobby Klaus	.10
213	Jay Kleven	.10
214	Lou Klimchock	.10
215	Ray Knight	.30
216	Kevin Kobel	.10
217	Gary Kolb	.10
218	Cal Koonce	.10
219	Jerry Koosman	.30
220	Ed Kranepool	.30
221	Gary Kroll	.10
222	Clem Labine	.30
223	Jack Lamabe	.10
224	Hobie Landrith	.10
225	Frank Lary	.10
226	Bill Latham	.10
227	Terry Leach	.10
228	Tim Leary	.10
229	John Lewis	.10
230	David Liddell	.10
231	Phil Linz	.10
232	Ron Locke	.10
233	Skip Lockwood	.10
234	Mickey Lolich	.30
235	Phil Lombardi	.10
236	Al Luplow	.10
237	Ed Lynch	.10
238	Barry Lyons	.10
239	Ken MacKenzie	.10
240	Julio Machado	.10
241	Elliot Maddox	.10
242	Dave Magadan	.10
243	Phil Mankowski	.10
244	Felix Mantilla	.10
245	Mike Marshall	.10
246	Dave Marshall	.10
247	Jim Marshall	.10
248	Mike A. Marshall	.10
249	J.C. Martin	.10
250	Jerry Martin	.10
251	Teddy Martinez	.10
252	Jon Matlack	.20
253	Jon Matlack	.20
254	Jerry May	.10
255	Willie Mays	15.00
256	Lee Mazzilli	.20
257	Jim McAndrew	.10
258	Bob McClure	.10
259	Roger McDowell	.30
260	Tug McGraw	.40
261	Jeff McKnight	.10
262	Roy McMillan	.10
263	Kevin McReynolds	.30
264	George Medich	.10
265	Orlando Mercado	.10
266	Butch Metzger	.10
267	Felix Millan	.10
268	Bob G. Miller	.10
269	Bob L. Miller	.10
270	Dyar Miller	.10
271	Larry Miller	.10
272	Keith Miller	.10
273	Randy Milligan	.10
274	John Milner	.10
275	John Mitchell	.10
276	Kevin Mitchell	.30
277	Wilmer Mizell	.10
278	Herb Moford	.10
279	Willie Montanez	.10
280	Joe Moock	.10
281	Tommy Moore	.10
282	Bob Moorhead	.10
283	Jerry Morales	.10
284	Al Moran	.10
285	Jose Moreno	.10
286	Bill Murphy	.10
287	Dale Murray	.10
288	Dennis Musgraves	.10
289	Jeff Musselman	.10
290	Randy Myers	.30
291	Bob Myrick	.10
292	Danny Napoleon	.10
293	Charlie Neal	.10
294	Randy Niemann	.10
295	Joe Nolan	.10
296	Dan Norman	.10
297	Ed Nunez	.10
298	Charlie O'Brien	.10
299	Tom O'Malley	.10
300	Bob Ojeda	.30
301	Jose Oquendo	.10
302	Jesse Orosco	.10
303	Junior Ortiz	.10
304	Brian Ostrosser	.10
305	Amos Otis	.30
306	Rick Ownbey	.10
307	John Pacella	.10
308	Tom Paciorek	.10
309	Harry Parker	.10
310	Tom Parsons	.10
311	Al Pedrique	.10
312	Brock Pemberton	.10
313	Alejandro Pena	.10
314	Bobby Pfeil	.10
315	Mike Phillips	.10
316	Jim Piersall	.30
317	Joe Pignatano	.10
318	Grover Powell	.10
319	Rich Puig	.10
320	Charlie Puleo	.10
321	Gary Rajsich	.10
322	Mario Ramirez	.10
323	Lenny Randle	.10
324	Bob Rauch	.10
325	Jeff Reardon	.30
326	Darren Reed	.10
327	Hal Reniff	.10
328	Ronn Reynolds	.10
329	Tom Reynolds	.10
330	Dennis Ribant	.10
331	Gordie Richardson	.10
332	Dave Roberts	.10
333	Les Rohr	.10
334	Luis Rosado	.10
335	Don Rose	.10
336	Don Rowe	.10
337	Dick Rusteck	.10
338	Nolan Ryan	15.00
339	Ray Sadecki	.10
340	Joe Sambito	.10
341	Amado Samuel	.10
342	Juan Samuel	.10
343	Ken Sanders	.10
344	Rafael Santana	.10
345	Mackey Sasser	.10
346	Mac Scarce	.10
347	Jim Schaffer	.10
348	Dan Schatzeder	.10
349	Calvin Schiraldi	.10
350	Al Schmelz	.10
351	Dave Schneck	.10
352	Ted Schreiber	.10
353	Don Schulze	.10
354	Mike Scott	.30
355	Ray Searage	.10
356	Tom Seaver	10.00
357	Dick Selma	.10
358	Art Shamsky	.30
359	Bob Shaw	.10
360	Don Shaw	.10
361	Norm Sherry	.10
362	Craig Shipley	.10
363	Bart Shirley	.10
364	Bill Short	.10
365	Paul Siebert	.10
366	Ken Singleton	.30
367	Doug Sisk	.10
368	Bobby Gene Smith	.10
369	Charley Smith	.10
370	Dick Smith	.10
371	Duke Snider	10.00
372	Warren Spahn	4.00
373	Larry Stahl	.10
374	Roy Staiger	.10
375	Tracy Stallard	.10
376	Leroy Stanton	.10
377	Rusty Staub	1.00
378	John Stearns	.10
379	John Stephenson	.10
380	Randy Sterling	.10
381	George Stone	.10
382	Darryl Strawberry	1.00
383	John Strohmayer	.10
384	Brent Strom	.10
385	Dick Stuart	.30
386	Tom Sturdivant	.10
387	Bill Sudakis	.10
388	John Sullivan	.10
389	Darrell Sutherland	.10
390	Ron Swoboda	.30
391	Craig Swan	.10
392	Rick Sweet	.10
393	Pat Tabler	.10
394	Kevin Tapani	.10
395	Randy Tate	.10
396	Frank Taveras	.10
397	Chuck Taylor	.10
398	Ron Taylor	.10
399	Bob Taylor	.10
400	Sammy Taylor	.10
401	Walt Terrell	.10
402	Ralph Terry	.10
403	Tim Teufel	.30
404	George Theodore	.10
405	Frank Thomas	.10
406	Lou Thornton	.10
407	Marv Throneberry	.50
408	Dick Tidrow	.10
409	Rusty Tillman	.10
410	Jackson Todd	.10
411	Joe Torre	1.50
412	Mike Torrez	.10
413	Kelvin Torve	.10
414	Alex Trevino	.10
415	Wayne Twitchell	.10
416	Del Unser	.10
417	Mike Vail	.10
418	Bobby Valentine	.40
419	Ellis Valentine	.10
420	Julio Valera	.10
421	Tom Veryzer	.10
422	Frank Viola	.30
423	Bill Wakefield	.10
424	Gene Walter	.10
425	Claudell Washington	.10
426	Hank Webb	.10
427	Al Weis	.20
428	Dave West	.10
429	Wally Whitehurst	.10
430	Carl Willey	.10
431	Nick Willhite	.10
432	Charlie Williams	.10
433	Mookie Wilson	.60
434	Herm Winningham	.10
435	Gene Woodling	.30
436	Billy Wynne	.10
437	Joel Youngblood	.10
438	Pat Zachry	.10
439	Don Zimmer	.30
(440)	Checklist 1-40	.10
(441)	Checklist 41-80	.10
(442)	Checklist 81-120	.10
(443)	Checklist 121-160	.10
(444)	Checklist 161-200	.10
(445)	Checklist 201-240	.10
(446)	Checklist 241-280	.10
(447)	Checklist 281-320	.10
(448)	Checklist 321-360	.10
(449)	Checklist 361-400	.10
(450)	Checklist 401-439	.10

1991 Wiz Yankees of the '50's

Yankees players from the 1950s dynasty are featured in this set distributed in several series at various promotional games. The cards were produced in a perforated sheet format, the 2" x 3" individual cards can be separated with ease. Fronts feature blue-and-white duo-tone photos with the familiar Yankee Stadium facade in blue at top and the player name in black below. Backs are printed in blue on white. The series name is printed beneath the top name bar, along with a line indicating the player's years with the Yankees and a few career stats. At bottom of all cards are Wiz Home Entertainment Centers and AT&T logos, along with a Yankees Classics logo. The unnumbered cards are checklisted here alphabetically.

		NM/M
Complete Set, Panels (9):		20.00
Complete Set, Singles (125):		20.00
Common Player:		.25
(1)	Loren Babe	.25
(2)	Hank Bauer	.40
(3)	Zeke Bella	.25
(4)	Lou Berberet	.25
(5)	Yogi Berra	2.00
(6)	Ewell Blackwell	.35
(7)	Johnny Blanchard	.35
(8)	Gary Blaylock	.25
(9)	Don Bollweg	.25
(10)	Clete Boyer	.35
(11)	Ralph Branca	.25
(12)	Fritzie Brickell	.25
(13)	Jim Brideweser	.25
(14)	Jim Bronstad	.50
(15)	Bobby Brown	.35
(16)	Lew Burdette	.35
(17)	Harry Byrd	.25
(18)	Tommy Byrne	.25
(19)	Andy Carey	.25
(20)	Tommy Carroll	.25
(21)	Bob Cerv	.35
(22)	Al Cicotte	.25
(23)	Jim Coates	.25
(24)	Jerry Coleman	.25
(25)	Rip Coleman	.25
(26)	Joe Collins	.25
(27)	Clint Courtney	.25
(28)	Bobby Del Greco	.25
(29)	Jim Delsing	.25
(30)	Murry Dickson	.25
(31)	Joe DiMaggio	6.00
(32)	Art Ditmar	.25
(33)	Sonny Dixon	.25
(34)	Ryne Duren	.35
(35)	Tom Ferrick	.25
(36)	Whitey Ford	2.00
(37)	Mark Freeman	.25
(38)	Tom Gorman	.25
(39)	Ted Gray	.25
(40)	Eli Grba	.25
(41)	Bob Grim	.25
(42)	Woodie Held	.25
(43)	Tommy Henrich	.35
(44)	Johnny Hopp	.25
(45)	Ralph Houk	.35
(46)	Elston Howard	.35
(47)	Ken Hunt	.25
(48)	Billy Hunter	.25
(49)	Johnny James	.25
(50)	Jackie Jensen	.45
(51)	Billy Johnson	.25
(52)	Darrell Johnson	.25
(53)	Charlie Keller	.35
(54)	Jim Konstanty	.25
(55)	Steve Kraly	.25
(56)	Jack Kramer	.25
(57)	Tony Kubek	.50
(58)	Johnny Kucks	.25
(59)	Bob Kuzava	.25
(60)	Don Larsen	1.00
(61)	Frank Leja	.25
(62)	Johnny Lindell	.25
(63)	Ed Lopat	.40
(64)	Hector Lopez	.25
(65)	Jerry Lumpe	.25
(66)	Duke Maas	.25
(67)	Dave Madison	.25
(68)	Sal Maglie	.35
(69)	Mickey Mantle	12.00
(70)	Cliff Mapes	.25
(71)	Billy Martin	1.50
(72)	Mickey McDermott	.25
(73)	Jim McDonald	.25
(74)	Gil McDougald	.45
(75)	Bill Miller	.25
(76)	Willie Miranda	.25
(77)	Johnny Mize	.75
(78)	Zack Monroe	.25
(79)	Tom Morgan	.25
(80)	Bob Muncrief	.25
(81)	Ernie Nevel	.50
(82)	Irv Noren	.25
(83)	Joe Ostrowski	.25
(84)	Stubby Overmire	.25
(85)	Joe Page	.25
(86)	Duane Pillette	.25
(87)	Jim Pisoni	.25
(88)	Bob Porterfield	.25
(89)	Bill Renna	.25
(90)	Vic Raschi	.50
(91)	Allie Reynolds	.50
(92)	Bobby Richardson	.75
(93)	Phil Rizzuto	2.00
(94)	Eddie Robinson	.25
(95)	Johnny Sain	.50
(96)	Fred Sanford	.25
(97)	Ray Scarborough	.25
(98)	Harry Schaeffer	.25
(99)	Art Schallok (Schallock)	.50
(100)	Johnny Schmitz	.25
(101)	Art Schults	.50
(102)	Kal Segrist	.25
(103)	Bobby Shantz	.35
(104)	Spec Shea	.25
(105)	Norm Siebern	.25
(106)	Charlie Silvera	.25
(107)	Harry Simpson	.35
(108)	Lou Skizas	.25
(109)	Bill Skowron	.75
(110)	Enos Slaughter	1.00
(111)	Gerry Staley	.25
(112)	Snuffy Stirnweiss	.25
(113)	Marlin Stuart	.25
(114)	Tom Sturdivant	.25
(115)	Bill Terry	.25
(116)	Dick Tettelbach	.50
(117)	Marv Throneberry	.35
(118)	Gus Triandos	.35
(119)	Virgil Trucks	.25
(120)	Bob Turley	.35
(121)	Frank Verdi	.25
(122)	Dick Wakefield	.25
(123)	Bob Wiesler	.25
(124)	Archie Wilson	.25
(125)	George Wilson	.25

1992 Wiz Yankees Classics

TUCKER ASHFORD

More than 600 different Yankees players from the turn of the century through the 1980s are featured in this set. Produced and distributed in five series at various promotional games, the cards share a common design and theme. Originally in a 10" x 9" perforated sheet format, the 2" x 3" individual cards can be separated with ease. Fronts feature blue-and-white duo-tone photos with the familiar Yankee Stadium facade in blue at top and the player name in black below. Backs are printed in blue on white. The series name is printed beneath the top name bar, along with a line indicating the player's years with the Yankees and a few career stats. At bottom of all cards are the Yankees Classics and Wiz Home Entertainment Centers logos, along with the logo of the co-sponsor. The Yankees of the '60s and All-Star series were co-sponsored by American Express; the '70s series by Fisher; the '80s by Minolta and the Hall of Famers by Aiwa. The unnumbered cards are checklisted alphabetically within series.

		NM/M
Complete Set (638):		95.00
Common Player:		.20
Complete series, Yankees of the '60s:		25.00
(1)	Jack Aker	.20
(2)	Ruben Amaro	.20
(3)	Luis Arroyo	.20
(4)	Stan Bahnsen	.20
(5)	Steve Barber	.20
(6)	Ray Barker	.20
(7)	Rich Beck	.20
(8)	Yogi Berra	2.00
(9)	Johnny Blanchard	.50
(10)	Gil Blanco	.20
(11)	Ron Blomberg	.20
(12)	Len Boehmer	.20
(13)	Jim Bouton	.50
(14)	Clete Boyer	.50
(15)	Jim Brenneman	.20
(16)	Marshall Bridges	.20
(17)	Harry Bright	.20
(18)	Hal Brown	.20
(19)	Billy Bryan	.20
(20)	Bill Burbach	.20
(21)	Andy Carey	.20
(22)	Duke Carmel	.20
(23)	Bob Cerv	.20
(24)	Horace Clarke	.20
(25)	Tex Clevenger	.20
(26)	Lu Clinton	.20
(27)	Jim Coates	.20
(28)	Rocky Colavito	1.50
(29)	Billy Cowan	.20
(30)	Bobby Cox	.50
(31)	Jack Cullen	.20
(32)	John Cumberland	.20
(33)	Bud Daley	.20
(34)	Joe DeMaestri	.20
(35)	Art Ditmar	.20
(36)	Al Downing	.30
(37)	Ryne Duren	.30
(38)	Doc Edwards	.20
(39)	John Ellis	.20
(40)	Frank Fernandez	.20
(41)	Mike Ferraro	.20
(42)	Whitey Ford	2.00
(43)	Bob Friend	.20
(44)	John Gabler	.20
(45)	Billy Gardner	.20
(46)	Jake Gibbs	.20
(47)	Jesse Gonder	.20
(48)	Pedro Gonzalez	.20
(49)	Eli Grba	.20
(50)	Kent Hadley	.20
(51)	Bob Hale	.20
(52)	Jimmie Hall	.20
(53)	Steve Hamilton	.20
(54)	Mike Hegan	.30
(55)	Bill Henry	.20
(56)	Elston Howard	.90
(57)	Dick Howser	.50
(58)	Ken Hunt	.20
(59)	Johnny James	.20
(60)	Elvio Jiminez	.20
(61)	Deron Johnson	.30
(62)	Ken Johnson	.20
(63)	Mike Jurewicz	.20
(64)	Mike Kekich	.20
(65)	John Kennedy	.20
(66)	Jerry Kenney	.20
(67)	Fred Kipp	.20
(68)	Ron Klimkowski	.20
(69)	Andy Kosco	.20
(70)	Tony Kubek	.75
(71)	Bill Kunkel	.20
(72)	Phil Linz	.20
(73)	Dale Long	.20
(74)	Art Lopez	.20
(75)	Hector Lopez	.20
(76)	Jim Lyttle	.20
(77)	Duke Maas	.20
(78)	Mickey Mantle	10.00
(79)	Roger Maris	4.00
(80)	Lindy McDaniel	.20
(81)	Danny McDevitt	.20
(82)	Dave McDonald	.20
(83)	Gil McDougald	.50
(84)	Tom Metcalf	.20
(85)	Bob Meyer	.20
(86)	Gene Michael	.30
(87)	Pete Mikkelsen	.20
(88)	John Miller	.20
(89)	Bill Monbouquette	.20
(90)	Archie Moore	.20
(91)	Ross Moschitto	.20
(92)	Thurman Munson	2.00
(93)	Bobby Murcer	.75
(94)	Don Nottebart	.20
(95)	Nate Oliver	.20
(96)	Joe Pepitone	.50
(97)	Cecil Perkins	.20
(98)	Fritz Peterson	.20
(99)	Jim Pisoni	.20

(100) Pedro Ramos .20
(101) Jack Reed .20
(102) Hal Reniff .20
(103) Roger Repoz .20
(104) Bobby Richardson .90
(105) Dale Roberts .50
(106) Bill Robinson .20
(107) Ellie Rodriguez .20
(108) Charlie Sands .20
(109) Bob Schmidt .20
(110) Dick Schofield .30
(111) Billy Shantz .20
(112) Bobby Shantz .30
(113) Rollie Sheldon .20
(114) Tom Shopay .20
(115) Bill Short .20
(116) Dick Simpson .20
(117) Bill Skowron .50
(118) Charley Smith .20
(119) Tony Solaita .20
(120) Bill Stafford .20
(121) Mel Stottlemyre .30
(122) Hal Stowe .20
(123) Fred Talbot .20
(124) Frank Tepedino .20
(125) Ralph Terry .20
(126) Lee Thomas .20
(127) Bobby Tiefenauer .20
(128) Bob Tillman .20
(129) Thad Tillotson .20
(130) Earl Torgeson .20
(131) Tom Tresh .50
(132) Bob Turley .40
(133) Elmer Valo .20
(134) Joe Verbanic .20
(135) Steve Whitaker .20
(136) Roy White .40
(137) Stan Williams .20
(138) Dooley Womack .20
(139) Ron Woods .20
(140) John Wyatt .20
Complete series, Yankees of the '70s 16.00
(1) Jack Aker .20
(2) Doyle Alexander .20
(3) Bernie Allen .20
(4) Sandy Alomar .20
(5) Felipe Alou .25
(6) Matty Alou .20
(7) Dell Alston .20
(8) Rick Anderson .20
(9) Stan Bahnsen .20
(10) Frank Baker .20
(11) Jim Beattie .20
(12) Fred Beene .20
(13) Juan Beniquez .20
(14) Dave Bergman .20
(15) Juan Bernhardt .20
(16) Rick Bladt .20
(17) Paul Blair .20
(18) Wade Blasingame .20
(19) Steve Blateric .20
(20) Curt Blefary .20
(21) Ron Blomberg .20
(22) Len Boehmer .20
(23) Bobby Bonds .30
(24) Ken Brett .20
(25) Ed Brinkman .20
(26) Bobby Brown .20
(27) Bill Burbach .20
(28) Ray Burris .20
(29) Tom Buskey .20
(30) Johnny Callison .20
(31) Danny Cater .20
(32) Chris Chambliss .30
(33) Horace Clarke .20
(34) Ken Clay .20
(35) Al Closter .20
(36) Rich Coggins .20
(37) Loyd Colson .20
(38) Casey Cox .20
(39) John Cumberland .20
(40) Ron Davis .20
(41) Jim Deidel .20
(42) Rick Dempsey .30
(43) Bucky Dent .40
(44) Kerry Dineen .20
(45) Pat Dobson .20
(46) Brian Doyle .20
(47) Rawly Eastwick .20
(48) Dock Ellis .20
(49) John Ellis .20
(50) Ed Figueroa .20
(51) Oscar Gamble .40
(52) Damaso Garcia .20
(53) Rob Gardner .20
(54) Jake Gibbs .20
(55) Fernando Gonzalez .20
(56) Rich Gossage .40
(57) Larry Gowell .20
(58) Wayne Granger .20
(59) Mike Griffin .20
(60) Ron Guidry .75
(61) Brad Gulden .20
(62) Don Gullett .20
(63) Larry Gura .20
(64) Roger Hambright .20
(65) Steve Hamilton .20
(66) Ron Hansen .20
(67) Jim Hardin .20
(68) Jim Ray Hart .20
(69) Fran Healy .20
(70) Mike Heath .20
(71) Mike Hegan .30
(72) Elrod Hendricks .20
(73) Ed Herrmann .20
(74) Rich Hinton .20
(75) Ken Holtzman .20

(76) Don Hood .20
(77) Catfish Hunter 1.00
(78) Grant Jackson .20
(79) Reggie Jackson 2.00
(80) Tommy John .90
(81) Alex Johnson .20
(82) Cliff Johnson .20
(83) Jay Johnstone .30
(84) Darryl Jones .20
(85) Gary Jones .20
(86) Jim Kaat .40
(87) Bob Kammeyer .20
(88) Mike Kekich .20
(89) Jerry Kenney .20
(90) Dave Kingman .50
(91) Ron Klimkowski .20
(92) Steve Kline .20
(93) Mickey Klutts .20
(94) Hal Lanier .20
(95) Eddie Leon .20
(96) Terry Ley .20
(97) Paul Lindblad .20
(98) Gene Locklear .20
(99) Sparky Lyle .40
(100) Jim Lyttle .20
(101) Elliott Maddox .20
(102) Jim Magnuson .20
(103) Tippy Martinez .20
(104) Jim Mason .20
(105) Carlos May .20
(106) Rudy May .20
(107) Larry McCall .20
(108) Mike McCormick .20
(109) Lindy McDaniel .20
(110) Sam McDowell .30
(111) Rich McKinney .20
(112) George Medich .20
(113) Andy Messersmith .30
(114) Gene Michael .20
(115) Paul Mirabella .20
(116) Bobby Mitchell .20
(117) Gerry Moses .20
(118) Thurman Munson 2.00
(119) Bobby Murcer .75
(120) Larry Murray .20
(121) Jerry Narron .20
(122) Graig Nettles .40
(123) Bob Oliver .20
(124) Dave Pagan .20
(125) Gil Patterson .20
(126) Marty Perez .20
(127) Fritz Peterson .20
(128) Lou Piniella .50
(129) Dave Rajsich .20
(130) Domingo Ramos .20
(131) Lenny Randle .20
(132) Willie Randolph .50
(133) Dave Righetti .30
(134) Mickey Rivers .30
(135) Bruce Robinson .20
(136) Jim Roland .20
(137) Celerino Sanchez .20
(138) Rick Sawyer .20
(139) George Scott .30
(140) Duke Sims .20
(141) Roger Slagle .20
(142) Jim Spencer .20
(143) Charlie Spikes .20
(144) Roy Staiger .20
(145) Fred Stanley .30
(146) Bill Sudakis .20
(147) Ron Swoboda .20
(148) Frank Tepedino .20
(149) Stan Thomas .20
(150) Gary Thomasson .20
(151) Luis Tiant .40
(152) Dick Tidrow .20
(153) Rusty Torres .20
(154) Mike Torrez .20
(155) Cesar Tovar .20
(156) Cecil Upshaw .20
(157) Otto Velez .20
(158) Joe Verbanic .20
(159) Mike Wallace .20
(160) Danny Walton .20
(161) Pete Ward .20
(162) Gary Waslewski .20
(163) Dennis Werth .20
(164) Roy White .30
(165) Terry Whitfield .20
(166) Walt Williams .20
(167) Ron Woods .20
(168) Dick Woodson .20
(169) Ken Wright .20
(170) Jimmy Wynn .20
(171) Jim York .20
(172) George Zeber .20
Complete series, Yankees of the '80s 17.50
(1) Luis Aguayo .20
(2) Doyle Alexander .20
(3) Neil Allen .20
(4) Mike Armstrong .20
(5) Brad Arnsberg .20
(6) Tucker Ashford .20
(7) Steve Balboni .20
(8) Jesse Barfield .30
(9) Don Baylor .40
(10) Dale Berra .20
(11) Doug Bird .20
(12) Paul Blair .20
(13) Mike Blowers .20
(14) Juan Bonilla .20
(15) Rich Bordi .20
(16) Scott Bradley .20
(17) Marshall Brant .20
(18) Tom Brookens .20
(19) Bob Brower .20

(20) Bobby Brown .20
(21) Curt Brown .20
(22) Jay Buhner .50
(23) Marty Bystrom .20
(24) Greg Cadaret .20
(25) Bert Campaneris .30
(26) John Candelaria .20
(27) Chuck Cary .50
(28) Bill Castro .20
(29) Rick Cerone .20
(30) Chris Chambliss .30
(31) Clay Christiansen .20
(32) Jack Clark .30
(33) Pat Clements .20
(34) Dave Collins .25
(35) Don Cooper .20
(36) Henry Cotto .20
(37) Joe Cowley .20
(38) Jose Cruz .20
(39) Bobby Davidson .20
(40) Ron Davis .20
(41) Brian Dayett .20
(42) Ivan DeJesus .20
(43) Bucky Dent .50
(44) Jim Deshaies .20
(45) Orestes Destrade .20
(46) Brian Dorsett .20
(47) Rich Dotson .20
(48) Brian Doyle .20
(49) Doug Drabek .30
(50) Mike Easler .20
(51) Dave Eiland .20
(52) Roger Erickson .20
(53) Juan Espino .20
(54) Alvaro Espinoza .20
(55) Barry Evans .20
(56) Ed Figueroa .20
(57) Pete Filson .20
(58) Mike Fischlin .20
(59) Brian Fisher .20
(60) Tim Foli .20
(61) Ray Fontenot .20
(62) Barry Foote .20
(63) George Frazier .20
(64) Bill Fulton .20
(65) Oscar Gamble .20
(66) Bob Geren .20
(67) Rich Gossage .40
(68) Mike Griffin .20
(69) Ken Griffey .30
(70) Cecilio Guante .20
(71) Lee Guetterman .20
(72) Ron Guidry .50
(73) Brad Gulden .20
(74) Don Gullett .20
(75) Bill Gullickson .20
(76) Mel Hall .20
(77) Toby Harrah .25
(78) Ron Hassey .20
(79) Andy Hawkins .20
(80) Rickey Henderson 1.50
(81) Leo Hernandez .20
(82) Butch Hobson .20
(83) Al Holland .20
(84) Roger Holt .20
(85) Jay Howell .25
(86) Rex Hudler .20
(87) Charles Hudson .20
(88) Keith Hughes .20
(89) Reggie Jackson 2.00
(90) Stan Javier .20
(91) Stan Jefferson .20
(92) Tommy John .50
(93) Jimmy Jones .20
(94) Ruppert Jones .20
(95) Jim Kaat .30
(96) Curt Kaufman .20
(97) Roberto Kelly .30
(98) Steve Kemp .25
(99) Matt Keough .20
(100) Steve Kiefer .20
(101) Ron Kittle .20
(102) Dave LaPoint .20
(103) Marcus Lawton .20
(104) Joe Lefebvre .20
(105) Al Leiter .20
(106) Jim Lewis .20
(107) Bryan Little .20
(108) Tim Lollar .20
(109) Phil Lombardi .20
(110) Vic Mata .20
(111) Don Mattingly 4.00
(112) Rudy May .20
(113) John Mayberry .20
(114) Lee Mazzilli .25
(115) Lance McCullers .20
(116) Andy McGaffigan .20
(117) Lynn McGlothen .20
(118) Bobby Meacham .20
(119) Hensley Meulens .30
(120) Larry Milbourne .20
(121) Kevin Mmahat .20
(122) Dale Mohorcic .20
(123) John Montefusco .20
(124) Omar Moreno .20
(125) Mike Morgan .20
(126) Jeff Moronko .20
(127) Hal Morris .25
(128) Jerry Mumphrey .20
(129) Bobby Murcer .35
(130) Dale Murray .20
(131) Gene Nelson .20
(132) Joe Niekro .20
(133) Phil Niekro .90
(134) Scott Nielsen .20
(135) Otis Nixon .20
(136) Johnny Oates .20
(137) Mike O'Berry .20

(138) Rowland Office .20
(139) John Pacella .20
(140) Mike Pagliarulo .20
(141) Clay Parker .20
(142) Dan Pasqua .20
(143) Mike Patterson .20
(144) Hipolito Pena .20
(145) Gaylord Perry .50
(146) Ken Phelps .20
(147) Lou Piniella .40
(148) Eric Plunk .20
(149) Luis Polonia .30
(150) Alfonso Pulido .20
(151) Jamie Quirk .20
(152) Bobby Ramos .20
(153) Willie Randolph .40
(154) Dennis Rasmussen .20
(155) Shane Rawley .20
(156) Rick Reuschel .20
(157) Dave Revering .20
(158) Rick Rhoden .20
(159) Dave Righetti .30
(160) Jose Rijo .20
(161) Andre Robertson .20
(162) Bruce Robinson .20
(163) Aurelio Rodriguez .20
(164) Edwin Rodriguez .20
(165) Gary Roenicke .20
(166) Jerry Royster .20
(167) Lenn Sakata .20
(168) Mark Salas .20
(169) Billy Sample .20
(170) Deion Sanders 1.00
(171) Rafael Santana .20
(172) Steve Sax .30
(173) Don Schulze .20
(174) Rodney Scott .20
(175) Rod Scurry .20
(176) Dennis Sherrill .20
(177) Steve Shields .20
(178) Bob Shirley .20
(179) Joel Skinner .20
(180) Don Slaught .20
(181) Roy Smalley .20
(182) Keith Smith .20
(183) Eric Soderholm .20
(184) Jim Spencer .20
(185) Fred Stanley .20
(186) Dave Stegman .20
(187) Tim Stoddard .20
(188) Walt Terrell .20
(189) Bob Tewksbury .25
(190) Luis Tiant .40
(191) Wayne Tolleson .20
(192) Steve Trout .20
(193) Tom Underwood .20
(194) Randy Velarde .30
(195) Gary Ward .20
(196) Claudell Washington .30
(197) Bob Watson .20
(198) Dave Wehrmeister .20
(199) Dennis Werth .20
(200) Stefan Wever .20
(201) Ed Whitson .20
(202) Ted Wilborn .20
(203) Dave Winfield 1.00
(204) Butch Wynegar .20
(205) Paul Zuvella .20
Complete series, Yankees All-Stars 17.50
(1) Luis Arroyo .20
(2) Hank Bauer .35
(3) Yogi Berra 2.00
(4) Bobby Bonds .30
(5) Ernie Bonham .20
(6) Hank Borowy .20
(7) Jim Bouton .30
(8) Tommy Byrne .20
(9) Chris Chambliss .20
(10) Spud Chandler .20
(11) Ben Chapman .20
(12) Jim Coates .20
(13) Jerry Coleman .20
(14) Frank Crosetti .20
(15) Ron Davis .20
(16) Bucky Dent .30
(17) Bill Dickey .50
(18) Joe DiMaggio 6.00
(19) Al Downing .20
(20) Ryne Duren .20
(21) Whitey Ford 2.00
(22) Lou Gehrig 6.00
(23) Lefty Gomez .40
(24) Joe Gordon .20
(25) Rich Gossage .30
(26) Bob Grim .20
(27) Ron Guidry .30
(28) Rollie Hemsley .20
(29) Rickey Henderson 1.50
(30) Tommy Henrich .20
(31) Elston Howard .35
(32) Catfish Hunter .30
(33) Reggie Jackson 2.00
(34) Tommy John .30
(35) Billy Johnson .20
(36) Charlie Keller .20
(37) Tony Kubek .35
(38) Johnny Kucks .20
(39) Tony Lazzeri .30
(40) Johnny Lindell .20
(41) Ed Lopat .30
(42) Sparky Lyle .20
(43) Mickey Mantle 10.00
(44) Roger Maris 4.00
(45) Billy Martin .75
(46) Don Mattingly 4.00
(47) Gil McDougald .30
(48) George McQuinn .20

(49) Johnny Mize .40
(50) Thurman Munson 2.00
(51) Bobby Murcer .30
(52) Johnny Murphy .20
(53) Graig Nettles .25
(54) Phil Niekro .80
(55) Irv Noren .25
(56) Joe Page .20
(57) Monte Pearson .20
(58) Joe Pepitone .30
(59) Fritz Peterson .20
(60) Willie Randolph .30
(61) Vic Raschi .20
(62) Allie Reynolds .30
(63) Bobby Richardson .35
(64) Dave Righetti .20
(65) Mickey Rivers .20
(66) Phil Rizzuto 2.00
(67) Aaron Robinson .20
(68) Red Rolfe .20
(69) Buddy Rosar .20
(70) Red Ruffing .20
(71) Marius Russo .20
(72) Babe Ruth 7.50
(73) Johnny Sain .40
(74) Scott Sanderson .20
(75) Steve Sax .20
(76) George Selkirk .20
(77) Bobby Shantz .20
(78) Spec Shea .20
(79) Bill Skowron .35
(80) Snuffy Stirnweiss .20
(81) Mel Stottlemyre .20
(82) Ralph Terry .20
(83) Tom Tresh .20
(84) Bob Turley .20
(85) Roy White .30
(86) Dave Winfield 1.00
Complete series, Yankees Hall of Famers 15.00
(1) Home Run Baker .50
(2) Ed Barrow .20
(3) Yogi Berra 2.00
(4) Frank Chance .50
(5) Jack Chesbro .20
(6) Earle Combs .20
(7) Stan Coveleski .20
(8) Bill Dickey .50
(9) Joe DiMaggio 6.00
(10) Whitey Ford 2.00
(11) Lou Gehrig 6.00
(12) Lefty Gomez .50
(13) Clark C. Griffith .20
(14) Burleigh Grimes .20
(15) Bucky Harris .20
(16) Waite Hoyt .20
(17) Miller Huggins .20
(18) Catfish Hunter .30
(19) Willie Keeler .20
(20) Tony Lazzeri .20
(21) Larry MacPhail .20
(22) Mickey Mantle 10.00
(23) Joe McCarthy .20
(24) Johnny Mize .35
(25) Herb Pennock .20
(26) Gaylord Perry .20
(27) Branch Rickey .20
(28) Red Ruffing .20
(29) Babe Ruth 7.50
(30) Joe Sewell .20
(31) Enos Slaughter .30
(32) Casey Stengel .30
(33) Dazzy Vance .20
(34) Paul Waner .20
(35) George M. Weiss .20

1990 Wonder Stars

The cards were found in specially marked loaves of Wonder Bread, in a special plastic pocket to protect them from product stains (and vice versa). Uncut sheets could also be obtained for $3 and proofs of purchase. Produced by Mike Schechter Associates, the photos at the center of the cards have team logos airbrushed away for lack of a license from MLB; the cards are licensed by the players' union. A red border surrounds the photo on front. Backs are printed in red and blue on white and have up to five years' worth of stats, a few lines of career highlights and a facsimile autograph.

	NM/M
Complete Set (20):	9.00
Common Player:	.25
Uncut Sheet:	12.50
1 Bo Jackson	.30
2 Roger Clemens	1.00
3 Jim Abbott	.25
4 Orel Hershiser	.25
5 Ozzie Smith	.75
6 Don Mattingly	1.00
7 Kevin Mitchell	.25
8 Jerome Walton	.25
9 Kirby Puckett	.75
10 Darryl Strawberry	.60
11 Robin Yount	.60
12 Tony Gwynn	.75
13 Alan Trammell	.25
14 Jose Canseco	.50
15 Greg Swindell	.25
16 Nolan Ryan	2.00
17 Howard Johnson	.25
18 Ken Griffey Jr.	2.00
19 Will Clark	.25
20 Ryne Sandberg	.60

1985 Woolworth

This 44-card boxed set was produced by Topps for the Woolworth's chain stores, though "Woolworth's" does not appear anywhere on the individual cards. Featuring a combination of black-and-white and color photos of baseball record holders from all eras, the set is in the standard 2-1/2" x 3-1/2" format. Backs, printed in blue and orange, give career details and personal data. Because it combined old-timers with current players, the set did not achieve a great deal of collector popularity. The set was reissued in 1987 in a different box at the Boardwalk and Baseball theme park in Florida.

	NM/M
Complete Set (44):	7.50
Common Player:	.15
1 Hank Aaron	.60
2 Grover Alexander	.15
3 Ernie Banks	.30
4 Yogi Berra	.30
5 Lou Brock	.10
6 Steve Carlton	.10
7 Jack Chesbro	.10
8 Ty Cobb	.60
9 Sam Crawford	.10
10 Rollie Fingers	.10
11 Whitey Ford	.30
12 Johnny Frederick	.10
13 Frankie Frisch	.10
14 Lou Gehrig	.75
15 Jim Gentile	.10
16 Dwight Gooden	.10
17 Rickey Henderson	.40
18 Rogers Hornsby	.10
19 Frank Howard	.10
20 Cliff Johnson	.10
21 Walter Johnson	.25
22 Hub Leonard	.10
23 Mickey Mantle	2.00
24 Roger Maris	.50
25 Christy Mathewson	.25
26 Willie Mays	.60
27 Stan Musial	.20
28 Dan Quisenberry	.10
29 Frank Robinson	.10
30 Pete Rose	1.00
31 Babe Ruth	1.50
32 Nolan Ryan	1.50
33 George Sisler	.10
34 Tris Speaker	.10
35 Ed Walsh	.10
36 Lloyd Waner	.10
37 Earl Webb	.10
38 Ted Williams	.75
39 Maury Wills	.10

		NM/M
40	Hack Wilson	.10
41	Owen Wilson	.10
42	Willie Wilson	.10
43	Rudy York	.10
44	Cy Young	.25

1986 Woolworth

Labeled "Topps' Collector Series" in a red band at the top of the front, this set marked the second year of Topps' production of a special boxed set for the Woolworth chain of stores, though Woolworth's name does not appear anywhere on the card. The 2-1/2 x 3-1/2 cards feature a color photo with its lower-right corner rolled up to reveal the words "Super Star" on a bright yellow border. The player's name appears in the lower-left corner.

		NM/M
Complete Set (33):		6.00
Common Player:		.10
1	Tony Armas	.10
2	Don Baylor	.10
3	Wade Boggs	.75
4	George Brett	1.00
5	Bill Buckner	.10
6	Rod Carew	.75
7	Gary Carter	.75
8	Cecil Cooper	.10
9	Darrell Evans	.10
10	Dwight Evans	.10
11	George Foster	.10
12	Bobby Grich	.10
13	Tony Gwynn	.75
14	Keith Hernandez	.10
15	Reggie Jackson	.75
16	Dave Kingman	.10
17	Carney Lansford	.10
18	Fred Lynn	.10
19	Bill Madlock	.10
20	Don Mattingly	1.50
21	Willie McGee	.10
22	Hal McRae	.10
23	Dale Murphy	.35
24	Eddie Murray	.75
25	Ben Oglivie	.10
26	Al Oliver	.10
27	Dave Parker	.10
28	Jim Rice	.35
29	Pete Rose	1.50
30	Mike Schmidt	1.00
31	Gorman Thomas	.10
32	Willie Wilson	.10
33	Dave Winfield	.75

1987 Woolworth

The "Baseball Highlights" boxed set of 33 cards was prepared by Topps for distribution at stores in the Woolworth's chain, although the retailer's name does not appear on the cards. Each card measures 2-1/2 x 3-1/2 in size and features a memorable baseball event that occurred during the 1986 season. The glossy set sold for $1.99.

		NM/M
Complete Set (33):		2.00
Common Player:		.05
1	Steve Carlton	.20
2	Cecil Cooper	.05
3	Rickey Henderson	.20
4	Reggie Jackson	.35
5	Jim Rice	.15
6	Don Sutton	.15
7	Roger Clemens	.40
8	Mike Schmidt	.40
9	Jesse Barfield	.05
10	Wade Boggs	.35
11	Tim Raines	.05
12	Jose Canseco	.25
13	Todd Worrell	.05
14	Dave Righetti	.05
15	Don Mattingly	.40
16	Tony Gwynn	.25
17	Marty Barrett	.05
18	Mike Scott	.05
19	World Series Game #1 (Bruce Hurst)	.05
20	World Series Game #1 (Calvin Schiraldi)	.05
21	World Series Game #2 (Dwight Evans)	.05
22	World Series Game #2 (Dave Henderson)	.05
23	World Series Game #3 (Len Dykstra)	.05
24	World Series Game #3 (Bob Ojeda)	.05
25	World Series Game #4 (Gary Carter)	.05
26	World Series Game #4 (Ron Darling)	.05
27	Jim Rice	.15
28	Bruce Hurst	.05
29	World Series Game #6 (Darryl Strawberry)	.05
30	World Series Game #6 (Ray Knight)	.05
31	World Series Game #6 (Keith Hernandez)	.05
32	World Series Game #7 (Mets Celebrate)	.05
33	Ray Knight	.05

1988 Woolworth

This 33-card boxed set was produced by Topps for exclusive distribution at Woolworth stores. The set includes 18 individual player cards and 15 World Series game-action photo cards. World Series cards include two for each game of the Series, plus a card of 1987 Series MVP Frank Viola. A white-lettered caption beneath the photo consists of either the player's name or a World Series game notation. Card backs are red, white and blue and contain a brief description of the photo on the front.

		NM/M
Complete Set (33):		2.00
Common Player:		.05
1	Don Baylor	.05
2	Vince Coleman	.05
3	Darrell Evans	.05
4	Don Mattingly	.60
5	Eddie Murray	.35
6	Nolan Ryan	.75
7	Mike Schmidt	.60
8	Andre Dawson	.20
9	George Bell	.05
10	Steve Bedrosian	.05
11	Roger Clemens	.60
12	Tony Gwynn	.50
13	Wade Boggs	.50
14	Benny Santiago	.05
15	Mark McGwire	.65
16	Dave Righetti	.05
17	Jeffrey Leonard	.05
18	Gary Gaetti	.05
19	World Series Game #1 (Frank Viola)	.05
20	World Series Game #1 (Dan Gladden)	.05
21	World Series Game #2 (Bert Blyleven)	.05
22	World Series Game #2 (Gary Gaetti)	.05
23	World Series Game #3 (John Tudor)	.05
24	World Series Game #3 (Todd Worrell)	.05
25	World Series Game #4 (Tom Lawless)	.05
26	World Series Game #4 (Willie McGee)	.05
27	World Series Game #5 (Danny Cox)	.05
28	World Series Game #5 (Curt Ford)	.05
29	World Series Game #6 (Don Baylor)	.05
30	World Series Game #6 (Kent Hrbek)	.05
31	World Series Game #7 (Kirby Puckett)	.35
32	World Series Game #7 (Greg Gagne)	.05
33	World Series MVP (Frank Viola)	.05

1989 Woolworth

This 33-card set was produced by Topps for the Woolworth store chain and was sold in a special box with a checklist on the back. The glossy-coated cards commemorate the most memorable moments in baseball from the 1988 season. The backs include a description of the various highlights.

		NM/M
Complete Set (33):		4.00
Common Player:		.05
1	Jose Canseco	.30
2	Kirk Gibson	.05
3	Frank Viola	.05
4	Orel Hershiser	.05
5	Walt Weiss	.05
6	Chris Sabo	.05
7	George Bell	.05
8	Wade Boggs	.65
9	Tom Browning	.05
10	Gary Carter	.50
11	Andre Dawson	.20
12	John Franco	.05
13	Randy Johnson	.50
14	Doug Jones	.05
15	Kevin McReynolds	.05
16	Gene Nelson	.05
17	Jeff Reardon	.05
18	Pat Tabler	.05
19	Tim Belcher	.05
20	Dennis Eckersley	.35
21	Orel Hershiser	.05
22	Gregg Jefferies	.05
23	Jose Canseco	.30
24	Kirk Gibson	.05
25	Orel Hershiser	.05
26	Mike Marshall	.05
27	Mark McGwire	1.00
28	Rick Honeycutt	.05
29	Tim Belcher	.05
30	Jay Howell	.05
31	Mickey Hatcher	.05
32	Mike Davis	.05
33	Orel Hershiser	.05

1990 Woolworth

This 33-card boxed set recalls baseball highlights of 1989. The cards are styled like past Woolworth sets, with game-action or posed photos framed in green. Backs are in blue, white and black with a headline and explanation of the commemoration. The set features award winners and regular and post-season highlights.

		NM/M
Complete Set (33):		2.50
Common Player:		.05
1	Robin Yount	.30
2	Kevin Mitchell	.05
3	Bret Saberhagen	.05
4	Mark Davis	.05
5	Gregg Olson	.05
6	Jerome Walton	.05
7	Bert Blyleven	.05
8	Wade Boggs	.45
9	George Brett	.50
10	Vince Coleman	.05
11	Andre Dawson	.20
12	Dwight Evans	.05
13	Carlton Fisk	.30
14	Rickey Henderson	.30
15	Dale Murphy	.15
16	Eddie Murray	.30
17	Jeff Reardon	.05
18	Rick Reuschel	.05
19	Cal Ripken, Jr.	.75
20	Nolan Ryan	.75
21	Ryne Sandberg	.45
22	Robin Yount	.30
23	Rickey Henderson	.30
24	Will Clark	.05
25	Dave Stewart	.05
26	Walt Weiss	.05
27	Mike Moore	.05
28	Terry Steinbach	.05
29	Dave Henderson	.05
30	Matt Williams	.05
31	Rickey Henderson	.30
32	Kevin Mitchell	.05
33	Dave Stewart	.05

1991 Woolworth

This 33-card boxed set was produced by Topps for distribution at Woolworth stores. Yellow borders are featured on the fronts of the glossy cards. The backs feature baseball highlights from the previous season. Award winners, regular season and World Series highlights are showcased.

		NM/M
Complete Set (33):		3.00
Common Player:		.05
1	Barry Bonds	.75
2	Rickey Henderson	.45
3	Doug Drabek	.05
4	Bob Welch	.05
5	Dave Justice	.10
6	Sandy Alomar, Jr.	.05
7	Bert Blyleven	.05
8	George Brett	.60
9	Andre Dawson	.25
10	Dwight Evans	.05
11	Alex Fernandez	.05
12	Carlton Fisk	.45
13	Kevin Maas	.05
14	Dale Murphy	.20
15	Eddie Murray	.45
16	Dave Parker	.05
17	Jeff Reardon	.05
18	Cal Ripken, Jr.	.75
19	Nolan Ryan	.75
20	Ryne Sandberg	.50
21	Bobby Thigpen	.05
22	Robin Yount	.45
23	Nasty Boys (Rob Dibble, Randy Myers)	.05
24	Dave Stewart	.05
25	Eric Davis	.05
26	Rickey Henderson	.45
27	Billy Hatcher	.05
28	Joe Oliver	.05
29	Chris Sabo	.05
30	Barry Larkin	.05
31	Jose Rijo	.05
32	Reds Celebrate	.05
33	Jose Rijo (World Series MVP)	.05

1986-88 World Wide Sports Conlon Collection

Marketed as complete series through World Wide Sports, five sets of black-and-white cards featuring the game's great players of the 1905-1935 era were made utilizing the photos of Charles Martin Conlon. The 2-1/2 x 3-1/2 cards carry the copyright of "The Sporting News," owner of the Conlon photos. The 60 cards of Series one each feature a Babe Ruth logo in the lower-left corner, the only graphic on the borderless card front. Series two has no front logo. Series 3-5 have a sliding Ty Cobb logo. Backs feature a line of career stats, a few bits of biographical data and a paragraph of highlights written by TSN historian Paul MacFarlane. The first two series were produced in an edition of 12,000 sets each; production of the other series was not announced. Cards in Series 3-5 are not numbered and are checklisted here alphabetically. Series designations are in small print at back-bottom.

		NM/M
Complete Set (211):		100.00
Common Player:		.25
Series 1 - 1986:		**18.00**
1	Lou Gehrig	1.50
2	Ty Cobb	1.00
3	Grover C. Alexander	.35
4	Walter Johnson	.50
5	Bill Klem	.25
6	Ty Cobb	1.00
7	Gordon S. Cochrane	.25
8	Paul Waner	.25
9	Joe Cronin	.25
10	Jay Hannah Dean	.25
11	Leo Durocher	.25
12	Jimmie Foxx	.25
13	Babe Ruth	2.00
14	Mike Gonzalez, Frank Frisch, Clyde Wares	.25
15	Carl Hubbell	.25
16	Miller Huggins	.25
17	Lou Gehrig	1.50
18	Connie Mack	.25
19	Heinie Manush	.25
20	Babe Ruth	2.00
21	Al Simmons	.25
22	Pepper Martin	.25
23	Christy Mathewson	.50
24	Ty Cobb	1.00
25	Stanley Harris	.25
26	Waite Hoyt	.25
27	Rube Marquard	.25
28	Joe McCarthy	.25
29	John McGraw	.25
30	Tris Speaker	.25
31	Bill Terry	.25
32	Christy Mathewson	.50
33	Casey Stengel	.25
34	Robert W. Meusel	.25
35	George Edward Waddell	.25
36	Mel Ott	.25
37	Roger Peckinpaugh	.25
38	Pie Traynor	.25
39	Chief Bender	.25
40	John W. Coombs	.25
41	Ty Cobb	1.00
42	Harry Heilmann	.25
43	Charlie Gehringer	.25
44	Rogers Hornsby	.25
45	Vernon Gomez	.25
46	Christy Mathewson	.50
47	Robert M. Grove	.25
48	Babe Ruth	2.00
49	Fred Merkle	.25
50	Babe Ruth	2.00
51	Herb Pennock	.25
52	Lou Gehrig	1.50
53	Fred Clarke	.25
54	Babe Ruth	2.00
55	John P. Wagner	.50
56	Hack Wilson	.25
57	Lou Gehrig	1.50
58	Lloyd Waner	.25
59	Charles Martin Conlon	.25
60	Charles & Margie Conlon	.25
---	Header Card	.25
Series 2 - 1987:		**15.00**
1	Lou Gehrig	1.50
2	Vernon Gomez	.25
3	Christy Mathewson	.50
4	Grover Alexander	.50
5	Ty Cobb	1.00
6	Walter Johnson	.50
7	Charles (Babe) Adams	.25
8	Nick Altrock	.25
9	Al Schacht	.25
10	Hugh Critz	.25
11	Henry Cullop	.25
12	Jake Daubert	.25
13	Bill Donovan	.25
14	Chick Hafey	.25
15	Bill Hallahan	.25
16	Fred Haney	.25
17	Charles Hartnett	.25
18	Walter Henline	.25
19	Ed Rommel	.25
20	Ralph "Babe" Pinelli	.25
21	Bob Meusel	.25
22	Emil Meusel	.25
23	Smead Jolley	.25
24	Ike Boone	.25
25	Earl Webb	.25
26	Charles Comiskey	.25
27	Edward Collins	.25
28	Geroge (Buck) Weaver	.50
29	Eddie Cicotte	.50
30	Sam Crawford	.25
31	Chuck Dressen	.25
32	Arthur Fletcher	.25
33	Hugh Duffy	.25
34	Ira Flagstead	.25
35	Harry Hooper	.25
36	George E. Lewis	.25
37	James Dykes	.25
38	Leon Goslin	.25
39	Henry Gowdy	.25
40	Charles Grimm	.25
41	Mark Koenig	.25
42	James Hogan	.25
43	William Jacobson	.25
44	Fielder Jones	.25
45	George Kelly	.25
46	Adolfo Luque	.40
47	Walter Maranville	.25
48	Carl Mays	.25
49	Eddie Plank	.25
50	Hubert Pruett	.25
51	John (Picus) Quinn	.25
52	Charles (Flint) Rhem	.25
53	Amos Rusie	.25
54	Edd Roush	.25
55	Ray Schalk	.25
56	Ernie Shore	.25
57	Joe Wood	.25
58	George Sisler	.25
59	James Thorpe	3.00
60	Earl Whitehill	.25
Series 3 - 1988:		**35.00**
(1)	Ace Adams	1.00
(2)	Grover C. Alexander	2.00
(3)	Eldon Auker	1.00
(4)	Jack Barry	1.00
(5)	Wally Berger	1.00
(6)	Ben Chapman	1.00
(7)	Mickey Cochrane	1.00
(8)	Frank Crosetti	1.00
(9)	Paul Dean	1.00
(10)	Leo Durocher	1.00
(11)	Wes Ferrell	1.00
(12)	Hank Gowdy	1.00
(13)	Andy High	1.00
(14)	Rogers Hornsby	2.00
(15)	Carl Hubbell	1.00
(16)	Joe Judge	1.00
(17)	Tony Lazzeri	1.00
(18)	Pepper Martin	1.00
(19)	Lee Meadows	1.00
(20)	Jimmy Murphy	1.00
(21)	Steve O'Neill	1.00
(22)	Ed Plank	1.00
(23)	John P. Quinn	1.00
(24)	Charlie Root	1.00
(25)	Babe Ruth	6.00
(26)	Fred Snodgrass	1.00
(27)	Tris Speaker	2.00
(28)	Bill Terry	1.00
(29)	Jeff Tesreau	1.00
(30)	George Torporcer	1.00
Series 4 - 1988:		**30.00**
(1)	Dale Alexander	1.00
(2)	Morris "Red" Badgro	1.00
(3)	Dick Bartell	1.00
(4)	Max Bishop	1.00
(5)	Hal Chase	1.50
(6)	Ty Cobb	2.00
(7)	Nick Cullop	1.00
(8)	Dizzy Dean	2.50
(9)	Chuck Dressen	1.00

(10)	Jimmy Dykes	1.00
(11)	Art Fletcher	1.00
(12)	Charlie Grimm	1.00
(13)	Lefty Grove	1.00
(14)	Baby Doll Jacobson	1.00
(15)	Bill Klem	1.00
(16)	Mark Koenig	1.00
(17)	Duffy Lewis	1.00
(18)	Carl Mays	1.00
(19)	Fred Merkle	1.00
(20)	Greasy Neale	1.50
(21)	Mel Ott	1.00
(22)	"Babe" Pinelli	1.00
(23)	Flint Rhem	1.00
(24)	Slim Sallee	1.00
(25)	Al Simmons	1.00
(26)	George Sisler	1.00
(27)	Riggs Stephenson	1.00
(28)	Jim Thorpe	4.00
(29)	Bill Wambsganss	1.00
(30)	Cy Young	2.50

Series 5 - 1988: 30.00

(1)	Nick Altrock	1.00
(2)	Del Baker	1.00
(3)	Moe Berg	4.50
(4)	Zeke Bonura	1.00
(5)	Eddie Collins	1.00
(6)	Hugh Critz	1.00
(7)	George Dauss	1.00
(8)	Joe Dugan	1.00
(9)	Howard Ehmke	1.00
(10)	Jimmie Foxx	2.50
(11)	Frank Frisch	1.00
(12)	Lou Gehrig	6.00
(13)	Charlie Gehringer	1.00
(14)	Kid Gleason	1.00
(15)	Lefty Gomez	1.00
(16)	Babe Herman	1.00
(17)	Bill James	1.00
(18)	Joe Kuhel	1.00
(19)	Dolf Luque	1.50
(20)	John McGraw	1.00
(21)	Stuffy McInnis	1.00
(22)	Bob Meusel	1.00
(23)	Lefty O'Doul	1.00
(24)	Hub Pruett	1.00
(25)	Paul Richards	1.00
(26)	Bob Shawkey	1.00
(27)	Gabby Street	1.00
(28)	Johnny Tobin	1.00
(29)	Rube Waddell	1.00
(30)	Billy Werber	1.00

1988 World Wide Sports 1933 All-Stars

The photos of Charles M. Conlon in The Sporting News' archive are the basis for this collectors' issue depicting the players of the original All-Star Game of 1933. Fronts have sepia photo of the players on a 2-1/2" x 3-1/2" format. The only graphics added to the front are in the upper-right corner designating the league which the player represented. Backs have 1933 and career stats, along with a career summary. The unnumbered cards are checklisted here in alphabetical order within league.

		NM/M
Complete Set (48):		12.00
Common Player:		.25
	American League	6.00
(1)	Luke Appling	.25
(2)	Earl Averill	.25
(3)	Tommy Bridges	.25
(4)	Ben Chapman	.25
(5)	Mickey Cochrane	.25
(6)	Joe Cronin	.25
(7)	Alvin Crowder	.25
(8)	Bill Dickey	.35
(9)	Jimmie Foxx	.45
(10)	Lou Gehrig	1.00
(11)	Charlie Gehringer	.35
(12)	Lefty Gomez	.25
(13)	Lefty Grove	.25
(14)	Mel Harder	.25
(15)	Pinky Higgins	.25
(16)	Urban Hodapp	.25

(17)	Roy Johnson	.25
(18)	Joe Kuhel	.25
(19)	Tony Lazzeri	.25
(20)	Heinie Manush	.25
(21)	Babe Ruth	1.50
(22)	Al Simmons	.25
(23)	Evar Swanson	.25
(24)	Earl Whitehill	.25
	National League	6.00
(1)	Wally Berger	.25
(2)	Guy Bush	.25
(3)	Ripper Collins	.25
(4)	Spud Davis	.25
(5)	Dizzy Dean	.45
(6)	Johnny Frederick	.25
(7)	Larry French	.25
(8)	Frank Frisch	.25
(9)	Chick Fullis	.25
(10)	Chick Hafey	.25
(11)	Carl Hubbell	.25
(12)	Chuck Klein	.25
(13)	Freddie Lindstrom	.25
(14)	Pepper Martin	.25
(15)	Ducky Medwick	.25
(16)	Tony Piet	.25
(17)	Wes Schulmerich	.25
(18)	Hal Schumacher	.25
(19)	Riggs Stephenson	.25
(20)	Bill Terry	.25
(21)	Paul Traynor	.25
(22)	Arky Vaughan	.25
(23)	Paul Waner	.25
(24)	Lon Warneke	.25

1988 World Wide Sports 1933 Negro All-Stars

The photos of Charles M. Conlon in The Sporting News' archive are the basis for this collectors' issue depicting "1933 Negro All-Stars. Fronts have borderless sepia photos of the players on a 2-1/2" x 3-1/2" format. The only graphics added to the front are in the upper-right corner designating the All-Star status. Backs have a few personal data along with a career summary. The unnumbered cards are checklisted here in alphabetical order.

		NM/M
Complete Set (12):		7.50
Common Player:		1.00
(1)	Cool Papa Bell	1.00
(2)	Oscar Charleston	1.00
(3)	Martin Dihigo	1.00
(4)	Andrew "Rube" Foster	1.00
(5)	Josh Gibson	2.00
(6)	Judy Johnson	1.00
(7)	Buck Leonard	1.00
(8)	Pop Lloyd	1.00
(9)	Dave Malarcher	1.00
(10)	Satchel Paige	2.50
(11)	Willie Wells	1.00
(12)	Joe Williams	1.00

1989 W/R Associates Mark Grace

This set of 5-1/2" x 7-1/2" cards was issued by WWOR-TV in New York City, which carried the Mets telecasts in 1991. The cards were evident-

This collectors' issue traces the career of Mark Grace on a nine-card panel which includes eight standard 2-1/2" x 3-1/2" cards and a 5" x 7" card on a sheet with overall dimensions of 10-5/8"x14". Because the issue was licensed only by the player, and not Major League Baseball, all Cubs uniform logos have been removed from the photos. Cards are numbered on front and back with a year identifying the photo. Backs are printed in red, white and blue and include biographical data and career summary. The large-format card offers complete major and minor league stats on back. The cards on the sheet are not perforated and individual cards are rarely encountered. Sheets were offered in either autographed or unautographed form with production limited to 15,000 sheets.

		NM/M
Complete Sheet:		7.50
Complete Sheet, Autographed:		25.00
Complete Set, Cut (9):		7.50
Common Player:		.50
73	Mark Grace (boyhood photo)	.50
83	Mark Grace (San Diego State)	.50
86	Mark Grace (minor league)	.50
87	Mark Grace/Throwing	.50
88a	Mark Grace/Fielding	.50
88b	Mark Grace/Wedding	.50
89a	Mark Grace/Btg,	.50
89b	Mark Grace/Btg	.50
----	Mark Grace (batting)	.50
----	Mark Grace (5" x 7" portrait, autographed)	25.00
----	Mark Grace (5" x 7" portrait, unsigned)	4.00

1985 WTBS Atlanta Braves

This set of large-format (8-1/4" x 10-3/4") cards was issued by the Braves' TV broadcaster, WTBS. The sets were given to potential sponsors as part of a "kit" inviting them to Florida to attend a spring training game. It was reported that only 600 sets were printed and 150 of them were destroyed. Fronts feature player portraits on brightly colored backgrounds. There is a facsimile autograph and a large star-boxed "AMERICA'S TEAM." Backs are in red and black and have some vital data and stats for the 1982-84 seasons. Cards are numbered according to uniform number.

		NM/M
Complete Set (4):		50.00
Common Player:		7.50
3	Dale Murphy	35.00
7	Brad Komminsk	7.50
15	Claudell Washington	7.50
42	Bruce Sutter	15.00

1991 WWOR N.Y. Mets

ly intended for use as a sales promotion, as the backs detail Neilsen ratings for the games. Fronts have game action photos with green borders in a design not unlike 1991 Donruss.

		NM/M
Complete Set (12):		15.00
Common Player:		2.00
(1)	Darryl Boston	2.00
(2)	Vince Coleman	2.00
(3)	David Cone	2.00
(4)	Kevin Elster	2.00
(5)	Sid Fernandez	2.00
(6)	John Franco	2.00
(7)	Dwight Gooden	2.00
(8)	Jeff Innis	2.00
(9)	Howard Johnson	2.00
(10)	Dave Magadan	2.00
(11)	Mackey Sasser	2.00
(12)	Wally Whitehurst	2.00

Y

1993 Yoo-Hoo

The Yoo-Hoo beverage company, which had a promotional affiliation with Yogi Berra as far back as the 1950's, made Berra the #1 card in a 1993 set of 20 baseball legends that was released in two series. All of the players included in the set are retired, and all but five are Hall of Famers (at this printing). The unnumbered cards feature a yellow border with a color photo on the front; the backs have the player's statistics and biographical information.

		NM/M
Complete Set (20):		7.00
Common Player:		.25
Series 1		
(1)	Yogi Berra	.50
(2)	Joe Morgan	.35
(3)	Duke Snider	.50
(4)	Steve Garvey	.30
(5)	Jim Rice	.35
(6)	Bob Feller	.35
(7)	Pete Rose	1.00
(8)	Rod Carew	.35
(9)	Gaylord Perry	.25
(10)	Graig Nettles	.25
Series 2		
(1)	Johnny Bench	.40
(2)	Lou Brock	.35
(3)	Stan Musial	1.00
(4)	Willie McCovey	.35
(5)	Whitey Ford	.50
(6)	Phil Rizzuto	.50
(7)	Tom Seaver	.50
(8)	Willie Stargell	.35
(9)	Brooks Robinson	.35
(10)	Al Kaline	.45

1994 Yoo-Hoo

Issued in conjunction with Rawling's, sponsor of the Gold Glove Award, this set features past winners. Cards have color photos on which team logos have been airbrushed away. Borders are bright yellow. Backs have career stats and highlights. A limited number of Yaz autographed cards were randomly inserted into the packs in which the cards were distributed.

		NM/M
Complete Set (20):		6.00

		NM/M
Common Player:		.25
Yastrzemski Autograph:		30.00
1	Luis Aparicio	.25
2	Bobby Bonds	.25
3	Bob Boone	.25
4	Steve Carlton	.35
5	Roberto Clemente	2.00
6	Bob Gibson	.25
7	Keith Hernandez	.25
8	Jim Kaat	.25
9	Roger Maris	.60
10	Don Mattingly	1.00
11	Thurman Munson	.60
12	Phil Rizzuto	.50
13	Brooks Robinson	.40
14	Ryne Sandberg	.75
15	Mike Schmidt	1.00
16	Carl Yastrzemski	.60
17	Fact Card	.05
18	Fact Card	.05
19	Fact Card	.05
20	Fact Card	.05

Z

1982 Zellers Expos

Issued by Zellers department stores in Canada, this 60-card set was produced in the form of 20 three-card panels. The cards feature a round photo of the player on a yellow background. A red "Zellers" is above the photo and on either side of it are the words "Baseball Pro Tips" in English on the left and in French on the right. The player's name and the title of the playing tip are under the photo. Backs have the playing tip in both languages. Single cards measure 2-1/2" x 3-1/2" while the whole panel is 7-1/2" x 3-1/2". Although a number of stars are depicted, this set is not terribly popular as collectors do not generally like the playing tips idea. Total panels are worth more than separated cards.

		NM/M
Complete Set (20):		6.00
Common Player:		.25
1	Gary Carter/ Catching Position	1.50
2	Steve Rogers/ Pitching Stance	.25
3	Tim Raines/Sliding	.50
4	Andre Dawson/ Batting Stance	.60
5	Terry Francona/ Contact Hitting	.25
6	Gary Carter/ Fielding Pop Fouls	.25
7	Warren Cromartie/ Fielding at First Base	.25
8	Chris Speier/ Fielding at Shortstop	.25
9	Billy DeMars/Signals	.25
10	Andre Dawson/ Batting Stroke	.60
11	Terry Francona/ Outfield Throws	.25
12	Woodie Fryman/Holding the Runner-Left Handed	.25
13	Gary Carter/ Fielding Low Balls	1.50
14	Andre Dawson/ Playing Centerfield	.60
15	Bill Gullickson/ The Slurve	.25
16	Gary Carter/ Catching Stance	1.50
17	Scott Sanderson/ Fielding as a Pitcher	.25
18	Warren Cromartie/ Handling Bad Throws	.25
19	Gary Carter/ Hitting Stride	1.50
20	Ray Burris/Holding the Runner-Right Handed	.25

1995 Zenith Samples

As Pinnacle extended its top-of-the-line brand name into baseball, this nine-card cello-wrapped samples set was sent to dealers to familiarize them with the product. Using the same state of the art all-foil metalized printing on extra heavy 24-point cardboard stock, the samples are virtually identical to the issued version, except for a white "SAMPLE" printed diagonally across front and back.

		NM/M
Complete Set (9):		10.00
Common Player:		.75
12	Cal Ripken Jr.	3.00
20	Dante Bichette	.75
51	Jim Thome	1.00
70	Mark Grace	1.00
97	Ryan Klesko	.75
111	Chipper Jones (Rookie)	2.00
113	Curtis Goodwin (Rookie)	.75
7	Hideo Nomo (Rookie Roll Call)	2.00
---	Header Card	.05

1995 Zenith

At the top of the pyramid of Pinnacle's baseball card lines for 1995 was Zenith, a super-premium brand utilizing all-foil metalized printing technology on double-thick 24-point cardboard stock to emphasize the quality look and feel. Six-card packs carried a retail price of $3.99. Two styles comprise the 150-card base set. The 110 veteran player cards are curiously arranged in alphabetical order according to the player's first names (with the exception of card #48, a special Japanese-language card of Hideo Nomo). These cards have a color player action photo on a black and gold background that is a view of a pyramid from its pinnacle. One the horizontal back, a portrait photo of the player in a partly-cloudy blue sky overlooks a playing field which offers his hit location preferences versus righty and lefty pitching. A scoreboard has his 1994 and career stats. The Pinnacle anti-counterfeiting optical-variable bar is in the lower-right corner. The rookie cards which comprise the final 40 cards in the set have a color photo at center with a gold-tone version of the same picture in the background. A large gold "ROOKIE" is vertically at right. Backs are similar to those on the verterans' cards except they have a scouting report in place of the hit-location chart.

		NM/M
Complete Set (150):		15.00
Common Player:		.10
Pack (6):		1.50
Wax Box (24):		17.50
1	Albert Belle	.10
2	Alex Fernandez	.10
3	Andy Benes	.10
4	Barry Larkin	.10
5	Barry Bonds	2.50
6	Ben McDonald	.10
7	Bernard Gilkey	.10
8	Billy Ashley	.10
9	Bobby Bonilla	.10
10	Bret Saberhagen	.10
11	Brian Jordan	.10
12	Cal Ripken Jr.	2.50
13	Carlos Baerga	.10
14	Carlos Delgado	.35
15	Cecil Fielder	.10
16	Chili Davis	.10
17	Chuck Knoblauch	.10
18	Craig Biggio	.10
19	Danny Tartabull	.10
20	Dante Bichette	.10
21	Darren Daulton	.10
22	Dave Justice	.10
23	Dave Winfield	.75
24	David Cone	.10
25	Dean Palmer	.10
26	Deion Sanders	.20
27	Dennis Eckersley	.65
28	Derek Bell	.10
29	Don Mattingly	1.50
30	Edgar Martinez	.10
31	Eric Karros	.10
32	Erik Hanson	.10
33	Frank Thomas	.75
34	Fred McGriff	.10
35	Gary Sheffield	.45
36	Gary Gaetti	.10
37	Greg Maddux	1.25
38	Gregg Jefferies	.10
39	Ivan Rodriguez	.65
40	Kenny Rogers	.10
41	J.T. Snow	.10
42	Hal Morris	.10
43	Eddie Murray (3,000 hit)	.50
44	Javier Lopez	.10
45	Jay Bell	.10
46	Jeff Conine	.10
47	Jeff Bagwell	.75
48	Hideo Nomo RC	2.00
49	Jeff Kent	.10
50	Jeff King	.10
51	Jim Thome	.65
52	Jimmy Key	.10
53	Joe Carter	.10
54	John Valentin	.10
55	John Olerud	.10
56	Jose Canseco	.45
57	Jose Rijo	.10
58	Jose Offerman	.10
59	Juan Gonzalez	.45
60	Ken Caminiti	.10
61	Ken Griffey Jr.	1.75
62	Kenny Lofton	.10
63	Kevin Appier	.10
64	Kevin Seitzer	.10
65	Kirby Puckett	1.25
66	Kirk Gibson	.10
67	Larry Walker	.10
68	Lenny Dykstra	.10
69	Manny Ramirez	.75
70	Mark Grace	.10
71	Mark McGwire	2.00
72	Marquis Grissom	.10
73	Jim Edmonds	.10
74	Matt Williams	.10
75	Mike Mussina	.45
76	Mike Piazza	1.75
77	Mo Vaughn	.10
78	Moises Alou	.10
79	Ozzie Smith	1.25
80	Paul O'Neill	.10
81	Paul Molitor	.75
82	Rafael Palmeiro	.65
83	Randy Johnson	.75
84	Raul Mondesi	.10
85	Ray Lankford	.10
86	Reggie Sanders	.10
87	Rickey Henderson	.75
88	Rico Brogna	.10
89	Roberto Alomar	.25
90	Robin Ventura	.10
91	Roger Clemens	1.50
92	Ron Gant	.10
93	Rondell White	.10
94	Royce Clayton	.10
95	Ruben Sierra	.10
96	Rusty Greer	.10
97	Ryan Klesko	.10
98	Sammy Sosa	1.25
99	Shawon Dunston	.10
100	Steve Ontiveros	.10
101	Tim Naehring	.10
102	Tim Salmon	.10
103	Tino Martinez	.10
104	Tony Gwynn	1.25
105	Travis Fryman	.10
106	Vinny Castilla	.10
107	Wade Boggs	1.25
108	Wally Joyner	.10
109	Wil Cordero	.10
110	Will Clark	.10
111	Chipper Jones	1.25
112	C.J. Nitkowski	.10
113	Curtis Goodwin	.10
114	Tim Unroe	.10
115	Vaughn Eshelman	.10
116	Marty Cordova	.10
117	Dustin Hermanson	.10
118	Rich Becker	.10
119	Ray Durham	.10
120	Shane Andrews	.10
121	Scott Ruffcorn	.10
122	Mark Grudzielanek RC	.25
123	James Baldwin	.10
124	Carlos Perez RC	.10
125	Julian Tavarez	.10
126	Joe Vitiello	.10
127	Jason Bates	.10
128	Edgardo Alfonzo	.10
129	Juan Acevedo	.10
130	Bill Pulsipher	.10
131	Bob Higginson RC	.25
132	Russ Davis	.10
133	Charles Johnson	.10
134	Derek Jeter	2.50
135	Phil Nevin	.10
136	LaTroy Hawkins	.10
137	Brian Hunter	.10
138	Roberto Petagine	.10
139	Jim Pittsley	.10
140	Garret Anderson	.10
141	Ugueth Urbina	.10
142	Antonio Osuna	.10
143	Michael Tucker	.10
144	Benji Gil	.10
145	Jon Nunnally	.10
146	Alex Rodriguez	2.00
147	Todd Hollandworth	.10
148	Alex Gonzalez	.10
149	Hideo Nomo RC	2.00
150	Shawn Green	.30
---	Numeric checklist	.10
---	Chase program checklist	.10

All-Star Salute

The most common of the Zenith inserts is a series of 18 All-Star Salute cards. Fronts have action photos printed on foil. Backs have the 1995 All-Star Game logo and a large photo of the player taken at the game, with a few words about his All-Star history. The Salute cards are seeded at the rate of one per six packs, on average.

		NM/M
Complete Set (19):		16.00
Common Player:		.50
1	Cal Ripken Jr.	3.00
2	Frank Thomas	1.00
3	Mike Piazza	2.00
4	Kirby Puckett	1.50
5	Manny Ramirez	1.00
6	Tony Gwynn	1.50
7	Hideo Nomo	.75
8	Matt Williams	.50
9	Randy Johnson	1.00
10	Raul Mondesi	.50
11	Albert Belle	.50

Rookie Roll Call

Dufex foil printing technology on both front and back is featured on this insert set. Fronts have a large and a small player photo on a green background dominated by a large star. Backs have another photo on a green and gold background. A prestigious black and gold box at left in the horizontally formatted design has a few good words about the prospect. Stated odds of finding a Rookie Roll Call card are one per 24 packs, on average.

		NM/M
Complete Set (18):		17.50
Common Player:		.60
1	Alex Rodriguez	6.00
2	Derek Jeter	7.50
3	Chipper Jones	5.00
4	Shawn Green	1.50
5	Todd Hollandsworth	.60
6	Bill Pulsipher	.60
7	Hideo Nomo	1.50
8	Ray Durham	.60
9	Curtis Goodwin	.60
10	Brian Hunter	.60
11	Julian Tavarez	.60
12	Marty Cordova	.60
13	Michael Tucker	.60
14	Edgardo Alfonzo	.60
15	LaTroy Hawkins	.60
16	Carlos Perez	.60
17	Charles Johnson	.60
18	Benji Gil	.60

Z-Team

The scarcest of the Zenith insert cards are those of 18 "living legends" profiled in the Z-Team series. Found at an average rate of only one per 72 packs, the cards are printed in technology Pinnacle calls 3-D Dufex.

		NM/M
Complete Set (18):		85.00
Common Player:		2.00
1	Cal Ripken Jr.	15.00
2	Ken Griffey Jr.	10.00
3	Frank Thomas	6.00
4	Matt Williams	2.00
5	Mike Piazza	10.00
6	Barry Bonds	15.00
7	Raul Mondesi	2.00
8	Greg Maddux	7.50
9	Jeff Bagwell	6.00
10	Manny Ramirez	6.00
11	Larry Walker	2.00
12	Tony Gwynn	7.50
13	Will Clark	2.00
14	Albert Belle	2.00
15	Kenny Lofton	2.00
16	Rafael Palmeiro	4.50
17	Don Mattingly	9.00
18	Carlos Baerga	2.00

1996 Zenith

Pinnacle's 1996 Zenith set has 150 cards in the regular set, including 30 Rookies, 20 Honor roll and two checklist cards. Each card in the set has a parallel Artist's Proof version (seeded one per every 35 packs). Insert sets include Z-Team, Mozaics, and two versions of Diamond Club. Normal Dufex versions of Diamond Club appear one per every 24 packs; parallel versions, which have an actual diamond chip incorporated into the card design, were seeded one per every 350 packs.

		NM/M
Complete Set (150):		15.00
Common Player:		.10
Common Artist's Proofs:		2.00
Star Artist's Proofs:		12X
Pack (6):		1.50
Wax Box (24):		25.00
1	Ken Griffey Jr.	2.00
2	Ozzie Smith	1.50
3	Greg Maddux	1.50
4	Rondell White	.10
5	Mark McGwire	2.50
6	Jim Thome	.75
7	Ivan Rodriguez	.75
8	Marc Newfield	.10
9	Travis Fryman	.10
10	Fred McGriff	.10
11	Shawn Green	.25
12	Mike Piazza	2.00
13	Dante Bichette	.10
14	Tino Martinez	.10
15	Sterling Hitchcock	.10
16	Ryne Sandberg	1.50
17	Rico Brogna	.10
18	Roberto Alomar	.25
19	Barry Larkin	.10
20	Bernie Williams	.10
21	Gary Sheffield	.50
22	Frank Thomas	1.00
23	Gregg Jefferies	.10
24	Jeff Bagwell	1.00
25	Marty Cordova	.10
26	Jim Edmonds	.10
27	Jay Bell	.10
28	Ben McDonald	.10
29	Barry Bonds	3.00
30	Mo Vaughn	.10
31	Johnny Damon	.35
32	Dean Palmer	.10
33	Ismael Valdes	.10
34	Manny Ramirez	1.00
35	Edgar Martinez	.10
36	Cecil Fielder	.10
37	Ryan Klesko	.10
38	Ray Lankford	.10
39	Tim Salmon	.10
40	Joe Carter	.10
41	Jason Isringhausen	.10
42	Rickey Henderson	1.00
43	Lenny Dykstra	.10
44	Andre Dawson	.25
45	Paul O'Neill	.10
46	Ray Durham	.10
47	Raul Mondesi	.10
48	Jay Buhner	.10
49	Eddie Murray	1.00
50	Henry Rodriguez	.10
51	Hal Morris	.10
52	Mike Mussina	.50
53	Wally Joyner	.10
54	Will Clark	.10
55	Chipper Jones	1.50
56	Brian Jordan	.10
57	Larry Walker	.10
58	Wade Boggs	1.50
59	Melvin Nieves	.10
60	Charles Johnson	.10
61	Juan Gonzalez	.50
62	Carlos Delgado	.35
63	Reggie Sanders	.10
64	Brian Hunter	.10
65	Edgardo Alfonzo	.10
66	Kenny Lofton	.10
67	Paul Molitor	.10
68	Mike Bordick	.10
69	Garret Anderson	.10
70	Orlando Merced	.10
71	Craig Biggio	.10
72	Chuck Knoblauch	.10
73	Mark Grace	.10
74	Jack McDowell	.10
75	Randy Johnson	1.00
76	Cal Ripken Jr.	3.00
77	Matt Williams	.10
78	Benji Gil	.10
79	Moises Alou	.10
80	Robin Ventura	.10
81	Greg Vaughn	.10
82	Carlos Baerga	.10
83	Roger Clemens	1.75
84	Hideo Nomo	.50
85	Pedro Martinez	1.00
86	John Valentin	.10
87	Andres Galarraga	.10
88	Andy Pettitte	.30
89	Derek Bell	.10
90	Kirby Puckett	1.50
91	Tony Gwynn	1.50
92	Brady Anderson	.10
93	Derek Jeter	3.00
94	Michael Tucker	.10
95	Albert Belle	.10
96	David Cone	.10
97	J.T. Snow	.10
98	Tom Glavine	.35
99	Alex Rodriguez	2.50
100	Sammy Sosa	.50
101	Karim Garcia	.15
102	Alan Benes	.10
103	Chad Mottola	.10
104	Robin Jennings RC	.10
105	Bob Abreu	.10
106	Tony Clark	.10
107	George Arias	.10
108	Jermaine Dye	.10
109	Jeff Suppan	.10
110	Ralph Milliard RC	.10
111	Ruben Rivera	.10
112	Billy Wagner	.10
113	Jason Kendall	.10
114	Mike Grace RC	.10
115	Edgar Renteria	.10
116	Jason Schmidt	.10
117	Paul Wilson	.10
118	Rey Ordonez	.10
119	Rocky Coppinger RC	.10
120	Wilton Guerrero RC	.10
121	Brooks Kieschnick	.10
122	Raul Casanova	.10
123	Alex Ochoa	.10
124	Chan Ho Park	.10
125	John Wasdin	.10
126	Eric Owens	.10
127	Justin Thompson	.10
128	Chris Snopek	.10
129	Terrell Wade	.10
130	Darin Erstad RC	1.50
131	Albert Belle (Honor Roll)	.10
132	Cal Ripken Jr. (Honor Roll)	1.50
133	Frank Thomas (Honor Roll)	.60
134	Greg Maddux (Honor Roll)	.75
135	Ken Griffey Jr. (Honor Roll)	1.00
136	Mo Vaughn (Honor Roll)	.10
137	Chipper Jones (Honor Roll)	.75
138	Mike Piazza (Honor Roll)	1.00
139	Ryan Klesko (Honor Roll)	.10
140	Hideo Nomo (Honor Roll)	.20
141	Roberto Alomar (Honor Roll)	.10
142	Manny Ramirez (Honor Roll)	.60
143	Gary Sheffield (Honor Roll)	.10
144	Barry Bonds (Honor Roll)	1.50
145	Matt Williams (Honor Roll)	.10
146	Jim Edmonds (Honor Roll)	.10
147	Derek Jeter (Honor Roll)	1.50
148	Sammy Sosa (Honor Roll)	.75
149	Kirby Puckett (Honor Roll)	.75
150	Tony Gwynn (Honor Roll)	.75

Artist's Proofs

Each card in the '96 Zenith base set can also be found in a specially marked Artist's Proof version. The AP cards were found on average of once per 35 packs.

	NM/M
Common Player:	2.00
Stars:	12X

Diamond Club

Twenty different players are featured on these two 1996 Pinnacle Zenith insert cards. Normal Dufex versions are inserted one per every 24 packs. Parallel versions of these cards, containing an actual diamond chip incorporated into the design, were seeded one per every 350 packs.

		NM/M
Complete Set (20):		17.50
Common Player:		.45
Diamond Versions:		12X
1	Albert Belle	.45
2	Mo Vaughn	.45
3	Ken Griffey Jr.	1.50
4	Mike Piazza	1.50
5	Cal Ripken Jr.	2.50
6	Jermaine Dye	.45
7	Jeff Bagwell	1.00
8	Frank Thomas	1.00
9	Alex Rodriguez	2.00
10	Ryan Klesko	.45
11	Roberto Alomar	.60
12	Sammy Sosa	1.25
13	Matt Williams	.45
14	Gary Sheffield	.75
15	Ruben Rivera	.45
16	Darin Erstad	.60
17	Randy Johnson	1.00
18	Greg Maddux	1.25
19	Karim Garcia	.60
20	Chipper Jones	1.25

Mozaics

Each of these 1996 Pinnacle Zenith cards contains multiple player images for the team represented on the card. The cards were inserted one per every 10 packs.

		NM/M
Complete Set (25):		30.00
Common Card:		.45
1	Greg Maddux, Chipper Jones, Ryan Klesko	3.00

2	Juan Gonzalez, Will Clark,	
	Ivan Rodriguez	1.00
3	Frank Thomas,	
	Robin Ventura,	
	Ray Durham	1.00
4	Matt Williams,	
	Barry Bonds,	
	Osvaldo Fernandez	5.00
5	Ken Griffey Jr.,	
	Randy Johnson,	
	Alex Rodriguez	4.00
6	Sammy Sosa,	
	Ryne Sandberg,	
	Mark Grace	4.00
7	Jim Edmonds,	
	Tim Salmon,	
	Garret Anderson	.45
8	Cal Ripken Jr.,	
	Roberto Alomar,	
	Mike Mussina	5.00
9	Mo Vaughn,	
	Roger Clemens,	
	John Valentin	3.50
10	Barry Larkin,	
	Reggie Sanders,	
	Hal Morris	.45
11	Ray Lankford,	
	Brian Jordan,	
	Ozzie Smith	1.50
12	Dante Bichette,	
	Larry Walker,	
	Andres Galarraga	.45
13	Mike Piazza, Hideo Nomo,	
	Raul Mondesi	4.00
14	Ben McDonald,	
	Greg Vaughn,	
	Kevin Seitzer	.45
15	Joe Carter, Carlos Delgado,	
	Alex Gonzalez	.60
16	Gary Sheffield,	
	Charles Johnson,	
	Jeff Conine	.45
17	Rondell White,	
	Moises Alou,	
	Henry Rodriguez	.45
18	Albert Belle,	
	Manny Ramirez,	
	Carlos Baerga	1.00
19	Kirby Puckett, Paul Molitor,	
	Chuck Knoblauch	1.50
20	Tony Gwynn,	
	Rickey Henderson,	
	Wally Joyner	2.00
21	Mark McGwire,	
	Mike Bordick,	
	Scott Brosius	4.00
22	Paul O'Neill,	
	Bernie Williams,	
	Wade Boggs	1.50
23	Jay Bell, Orlando Merced,	
	Jason Kendall	.45
24	Rico Brogna, Paul Wilson,	
	Jason Isringhausen	.45
25	Jeff Bagwell, Craig Biggio,	
	Derek Bell	1.00

Z-Team Samples

Each of the first nine micro-etched plastic-printed Z-Team insert cards can also be found in an edition which is overprinted "SAMPLE" on the front. These cards were distributed to hobby dealers.

		NM/M
Complete Set (9):		35.00
Common Player:		3.00
1	Ken Griffey Jr.	4.50
2	Albert Belle	3.00
3	Cal Ripken Jr.	7.50
4	Frank Thomas	3.50
5	Greg Maddux	4.00
6	Mo Vaughn	3.00
7	Chipper Jones	4.00
8	Mike Piazza	4.50
9	Ryan Klesko	3.00

Z-Team

Pinnacle's 1996 Zenith baseball continues the Z-Team insert concept with a new clear plastic treatment that is micro-etched for a see-through design that allows light to shine

through etched highlights and a green baseball field background. The 18 cards were seeded one per every 72 packs.

		NM/M
Complete Set (18):		100.00
Common Player:		3.00
1	Ken Griffey Jr.	12.50
2	Albert Belle	3.00
3	Cal Ripken Jr.	20.00
4	Frank Thomas	7.50
5	Greg Maddux	10.00
6	Mo Vaughn	3.00
7	Chipper Jones	10.00
8	Mike Piazza	12.50
9	Ryan Klesko	3.00
10	Hideo Nomo	4.50
11	Roberto Alomar	3.00
12	Manny Ramirez	6.00
13	Gary Sheffield	3.50
14	Barry Bonds	20.00
15	Matt Williams	3.00
16	Jim Edmonds	3.00
17	Kirby Puckett	10.00
18	Sammy Sosa	10.00

1997 Zenith Samples

The extent of the sample-marked version of the standard-size '97 Zenith cards is unknown.

		NM/M
Common Player:		1.50
S1	Ken Griffey Jr.	5.00
S6	Kenny Lofton	1.50

1997 Zenith

This set combines standard size trading cards with cards in an 8" x 10" format. The standard size set consists of 60 cards. Card fronts feature full-bleed photos and the word "Zenith," but no reference to the player's name or team is found on the fronts. Backs have another player photo, a hit location chart and 1996/career stats. There are four inserts in the set, all of which are printed on the larger size for-

mat - 8" x 10", 8" x 10" Dufex, 8" x 10" V-2, and Z-Team. Each sale unit contained one pack of five standard-size cards and two larger size cards for a suggested retail price of $9.99.

		NM/M
Complete Set (50):		15.00
Common Player:		.10
Pack (5 cards, 2 8x10)		2.00
Wax Box (12):		25.00
1	Frank Thomas	.75
2	Tony Gwynn	1.00
3	Jeff Bagwell	.75
4	Paul Molitor	.75
5	Roberto Alomar	.20
6	Mike Piazza	1.25
7	Albert Belle	.10
8	Greg Maddux	1.00
9	Barry Larkin	.10
10	Tony Clark	.10
11	Larry Walker	.10
12	Chipper Jones	1.00
13	Juan Gonzalez	.40
14	Barry Bonds	2.00
15	Ivan Rodriguez	.65
16	Sammy Sosa	1.00
17	Derek Jeter	2.00
18	Hideo Nomo	.40
19	Roger Clemens	1.00
20	Ken Griffey Jr.	1.25
21	Andy Pettitte	.25
22	Alex Rodriguez	1.50
23	Tino Martinez	.10
24	Bernie Williams	.10
25	Ken Caminiti	.10
26	John Smoltz	.10
27	Javier Lopez	.10
28	Mark McGwire	1.50
29	Gary Sheffield	.50
30	David Justice	.10
31	Randy Johnson	.75
32	Chuck Knoblauch	.10
33	Mike Mussina	.40
34	Deion Sanders	.20
35	Cal Ripken Jr.	2.00
36	Darin Erstad	.30
37	Kenny Lofton	.10
38	Jay Buhner	.10
39	Brady Anderson	.10
40	Edgar Martinez	.10
41	Mo Vaughn	.10
42	Ryne Sandberg	1.00
43	Andruw Jones	.75
44	Nomar Garciaparra	1.00
45	Hideki Irabu RC	.25
46	Wilton Guerrero	.10
47	Jose Cruz Jr. RC	.45
48	Vladimir Guerrero	.75
49	Scott Rolen	.65
50	Jose Guillen	.10

V-2

This eight-card die-cut insert utilizes motion technology as well as foil printing to create a very high-tech 8" x 10" card. Cards were inserted 1:47 packs.

		NM/M
Complete Set (8):		45.00
Common Player:		5.00
1	Ken Griffey Jr.	7.50
2	Andruw Jones	5.00
3	Frank Thomas	5.00
4	Mike Piazza	7.50
5	Alex Rodriguez	10.00
6	Cal Ripken Jr.	12.00
7	Derek Jeter	12.00
8	Vladimir Guerrero	5.00

Z-Team

This nine-card 8" x 10" insert is printed on a mirror gold mylar foil stock with each card sequentially numbered to 1,000.

		NM/M
Complete Set (9):		60.00
Common Player:		3.00
1	Ken Griffey Jr.	9.00
2	Larry Walker	3.00
3	Frank Thomas	6.00
4	Alex Rodriguez	10.00
5	Mike Piazza	9.00
6	Cal Ripken Jr.	12.50
7	Derek Jeter	12.50
8	Andruw Jones	6.00
9	Roger Clemens	7.50

8x10 and 8x10 Dufex

This 24-card insert takes select cards from the standard set and blows them up to an 8" x 10" format. Cards were inserted one per pack. A Dufex version of each 8" x 10" insert card was also available at a rate of one per pack (except in packs which contained either a Z-Team or V-2 card).

		NM/M
Complete Set (24):		20.00
Common Player:		.50
Dufex versions:		1X
Samples:		1X
1	Frank Thomas	1.00
2	Tony Gwynn	1.50
3	Jeff Bagwell	1.00
4	Ken Griffey Jr.	2.00
5	Mike Piazza	2.00
6	Greg Maddux	1.50
7	Ken Caminiti	.50
8	Albert Belle	.50
9	Ivan Rodriguez	.75
10	Sammy Sosa	1.50
11	Mark McGwire	2.50
12	Roger Clemens	1.75
13	Alex Rodriguez	2.50
14	Chipper Jones	1.50
15	Juan Gonzalez	.60
16	Barry Bonds	3.00
17	Derek Jeter	3.00
18	Hideo Nomo	.60
19	Cal Ripken Jr.	3.00
20	Hideki Irabu	.50
21	Andruw Jones	1.00
22	Nomar Garciaparra	1.50
23	Vladimir Guerrero	1.00
24	Scott Rolen	.75

1998 Zenith Samples

To introduce its "Dare to Tear" concept, Zenith's promo cards for 1998 included a specially-marked standard-size (2-1/2" x 3-1/2") sample card within a 5" x 7" card. All cards are marked "SAMPLE" on back, but are otherwise identical to the issued versions.

		NM/M
Complete Set, Large (9):		17.50
Common Player, Large:		1.00
Complete Set, Small (6):		12.00
Common Player, Small:		1.00
Z1	Nomar Garciaparra	2.00
Z3	Greg Maddux	2.00
Z4	Frank Thomas	1.50
Z9	Andruw Jones	1.50
Z15	Derek Jeter	4.00
Z21	Mike Piazza	2.50
Z22	Tony Gwynn	2.50
Z35	Ivan Rodriguez	1.00
Z40	Ken Griffey Jr.	2.50
2	Ken Griffey Jr.	2.50
12	Greg Maddux	2.00
14	Mike Piazza	2.50
17	Derek Jeter	4.00
18	Nomar Garciaparra	2.00
19	Ivan Rodriguez	1.00

1998 Zenith

Zenith was part of Pinnacle's "Dare to Tear" program. Sold in three-card packs, the set consists of 5" x 7" cards, each with a standard-size card packaged inside. Collectors had to decide whether to keep the large cards or tear them open to get the smaller card inside. Eighty 5" x 7" cards and 100 regular cards comprise the set. The regular, or Z2, cards were paralleled twice - Z-Silver (1:7) and Z-Gold (numbered to 100). The large cards also had two parallels - Impulse (1:7) and Gold Impulse (numbered to 100).

		NM/M
Complete Set (100):		25.00
Common Player:		.10
Silvers:		2X
Inserted 1:7		
Pack (3):		2.50
Wax Box (18):		35.00
1	Larry Walker	.10
2	Ken Griffey Jr.	1.75
3	Cal Ripken Jr.	2.50
4	Sammy Sosa	1.50
5	Andruw Jones	1.00
6	Frank Thomas	1.00
7	Tony Gwynn	1.50
8	Rafael Palmeiro	.75
9	Tim Salmon	.10
10	Randy Johnson	1.00
11	Juan Gonzalez	.50
12	Greg Maddux	1.50
13	Vladimir Guerrero	1.00
14	Mike Piazza	1.75
15	Andres Galarraga	.10
16	Alex Rodriguez	2.00
17	Derek Jeter	2.50
18	Nomar Garciaparra	1.50
19	Ivan Rodriguez	.75
20	Chipper Jones	1.50
21	Barry Larkin	.10
22	Mo Vaughn	.10
23	Albert Belle	.10
24	Scott Rolen	.65
25	Sandy Alomar Jr.	.10
26	Roberto Alomar	.30
27	Andy Pettitte	.30
28	Chuck Knoblauch	.10
29	Jeff Bagwell	1.00
30	Mike Mussina	.30
31	Fred McGriff	.10
32	Roger Clemens	1.50
33	Rusty Greer	.10
34	Edgar Martinez	.10
35	Paul Molitor	1.00
36	Mark Grace	.10
37	Darin Erstad	.30
38	Kenny Lofton	.10
39	Tom Glavine	.35
40	Javier Lopez	.10
41	Will Clark	.10
42	Tino Martinez	.10
43	Raul Mondesi	.10
44	Brady Anderson	.10
45	Chan Ho Park	.10
46	Jason Giambi	.75
47	Manny Ramirez	1.00
48	Jay Buhner	.10
49	Dante Bichette	.10
50	Jose Cruz Jr.	.10
51	Charles Johnson	.10
52	Bernard Gilkey	.10
53	Johnny Damon	.35
54	David Justice	.10
55	Justin Thompson	.10
56	Bobby Higginson	.10
57	Todd Hundley	.10
58	Gary Sheffield	.50
59	Barry Bonds	2.50
60	Mark McGwire	2.00
61	John Smoltz	.10
62	Tony Clark	.10
63	Brian Jordan	.10
64	Jason Kendall	.10
65	Mariano Rivera	.20
66	Pedro Martinez	1.00
67	Jim Thome	.75

68	Neifi Perez	.10
69	Kevin Brown	.10
70	Hideo Nomo	.50
71	Craig Biggio	.10
72	Bernie Williams	.10
73	Jose Guillen	.10
74	Ken Caminiti	.10
75	Livan Hernandez	.10
76	Ray Lankford	.10
77	Jim Edmonds	.10
78	Matt Williams	.10
79	Mark Kotsay	.10
80	Moises Alou	.10
81	Antone Williamson	.10
82	Jaret Wright	.10
83	Jacob Cruz	.10
84	Abraham Nunez	.10
85	Raul Ibanez	.10
86	Miguel Tejada	.50
87	Derek Lee	.10
88	Juan Encarnacion	.10
89	Todd Helton	.75
90	Travis Lee	.50
91	Ben Grieve	.50
92	Ryan McGuire	.10
93	Richard Hidalgo	.10
94	Paul Konerko	.15
95	Shannon Stewart	.10
96	Homer Bush	.10
97	Lou Collier	.10
98	Jeff Abbott	.10
99	Brett Tomko	.10
100	Fernando Tatis	.10

Z-Silver

This parallel set reprinted all 100 standard sized cards in Zenith on silver foilboard, with a "Z-Silver" logo across the bottom center. Z-Silvers were inserted one per seven packs.

		NM/M
Common Player:		1.00
Stars/RC's:		2X
Inserted 1:7		

Z-Gold

		NM/M
Common Player:		3.00
Stars/Rookies:		12X
Production 100 Sets		

Epix

Epix is a cross-brand insert. The set honors Plays, Games, Seasons and Moments in the careers of top baseball players. Epix consisted of 24 cards in Zenith, inserted 1:11. The cards have orange, purple and emerald versions.

		NM/M
Complete Set (24):		95.00
Common (Orange) Card:		1.50
Purples:		1X
Emeralds:		2X
1	Ken Griffey Jr./S	7.50
2	Juan Gonzalez/S	2.50
3	Jeff Bagwell/S	4.50
4	Ivan Rodriguez/S	4.00
5	Nomar Garciaparra/S	6.00
6	Ryne Sandberg/S	6.00
7	Frank Thomas/M	4.50
8	Derek Jeter/M	12.00
9	Tony Gwynn/M	6.00
10	Albert Belle/M	1.50
11	Scott Rolen/M	3.50
12	Barry Larkin/M	1.50
13	Alex Rodriguez/P	9.00
14	Cal Ripken Jr./P	12.00
15	Chipper Jones/P	6.00
16	Roger Clemens/P	6.50
17	Mo Vaughn/P	1.50
18	Mark McGwire/P	9.00
19	Mike Piazza/G	7.50
20	Andruw Jones/G	4.50
21	Greg Maddux/G	6.00
22	Barry Bonds/G	12.00
23	Paul Molitor/G	4.50
24	Eddie Murray/G	4.50

Raising the Bar

Raising the Bar is a 15-card insert seeded 1:25. The set features players who have set high standards for other players to follow.

		NM/M
Complete Set (15):		25.00
Common Player:		1.25
Inserted 1:25		
1	Ken Griffey Jr.	3.00
2	Frank Thomas	1.50
3	Alex Rodriguez	3.50
4	Tony Gwynn	2.50
5	Mike Piazza	3.00
6	Ivan Rodriguez	1.25
7	Cal Ripken Jr.	4.50
8	Greg Maddux	2.50
9	Hideo Nomo	1.25
10	Mark McGwire	3.50
11	Juan Gonzalez	1.25
12	Andruw Jones	1.50
13	Jeff Bagwell	1.50
14	Chipper Jones	2.50
15	Nomar Garciaparra	2.50

Rookie Thrills

Rookie Thrills is a 15-card insert set seeded 1:25. The set features many of the top rookies of 1998 in action photos printed on a silver-foil background. Backs have a few words about the player's career to that point.

		NM/M
Complete Set (15):		20.00
Common Player:		1.50
Inserted 1:25		
1	Travis Lee	1.50
2	Juan Encarnacion	1.50
3	Derrek Lee	1.50
4	Raul Ibanez	1.50
5	Ryan McGuire	1.50
6	Todd Helton	3.00
7	Jacob Cruz	1.50
8	Abraham Nunez	1.50
9	Paul Konerko	2.00
10	Ben Grieve	1.50
11	Jeff Abbott	1.50
12	Richard Hidalgo	1.50
13	Jaret Wright	1.50
14	Lou Collier	1.50
15	Miguel Tejada	2.00

Z-Team

The Z Team insert was created in 5" x 7" and standard-

size versions, each inserted at a 1:35 pack rate. The nine Rookie Z Team cards were seeded 1:58 and gold versions of both were found 1:175.

		NM/M
Complete Set (18):		35.00
Common Player:		1.25
Golds:		2X
Inserted 1:175		
1	Frank Thomas	2.50
2	Ken Griffey Jr.	3.50
3	Mike Piazza	3.50
4	Cal Ripken Jr.	6.00
5	Alex Rodriguez	5.00
6	Greg Maddux	3.00
7	Derek Jeter	6.00
8	Chipper Jones	3.00
9	Roger Clemens	3.25
10	Ben Grieve	1.25
11	Derrek Lee	1.75
12	Jose Cruz Jr.	1.25
13	Nomar Garciaparra	3.00
14	Travis Lee	1.50
15	Todd Helton	2.00
16	Paul Konerko	1.75
17	Miguel Tejada	1.25
18	Scott Rolen	2.00

Z-Team 5x7

The 5" x 7" Z-Team insert is a nine-card set seeded one per 35 packs.

		NM/M
Complete Set (9):		40.00
Common Player:		3.00
Inserted 1:35		
1	Frank Thomas	3.00
2	Ken Griffey Jr.	5.00
3	Mike Piazza	5.00
4	Cal Ripken Jr.	7.50
5	Alex Rodriguez	6.00
6	Greg Maddux	4.00
7	Derek Jeter	7.50
8	Chipper Jones	4.00
9	Roger Clemens	4.50

5x7

The 80 Zenith 5" x 7" cards all contained a regular-size card. Collectors could tear open the 5" x 7" to get at the smaller card inside. The set has two parallels: 5" x 7" Impulse (1:7) and 5" x 7" Gold Impulse (1:43).

		NM/M
Complete Set (80):		30.00
Common Player:		.25
Impulse Silvers:		1.5X
Inserted 1:7		
1	Nomar Garciaparra	2.00
2	Andres Galarraga	.25
3	Greg Maddux	2.00
4	Frank Thomas	1.00
5	Mark McGwire	3.00
6	Rafael Palmeiro	.75
7	John Smoltz	.25
8	Jeff Bagwell	1.00
9	Andruw Jones	1.00
10	Rusty Greer	.25
11	Paul Molitor	1.00
12	Bernie Williams	.25
13	Kenny Lofton	.25
14	Alex Rodriguez	3.00
15	Derek Jeter	4.00
15s	Derek Jeter/OPS	4.00
16	Scott Rolen	.65
17	Albert Belle	.25
18	Mo Vaughn	.25
19	Chipper Jones	2.00
20	Chuck Knoblauch	.25
21	Mike Piazza	3.00
22	Tony Gwynn	2.00
22s	Tony Gwynn/OPS	2.00
23	Juan Gonzalez	.50
24	Andy Pettitte	.35
25	Tim Salmon	.25
26	Brady Anderson	.25
27	Mike Mussina	.40
28	Edgar Martinez	.25
29	Jose Guillen	.25
30	Hideo Nomo	.50
31	Jim Thome	.65
32	Mark Grace	.25
33	Darin Erstad	.50
34	Bobby Higginson	.25
35	Ivan Rodriguez	.75
36	Todd Hundley	.25
37	Sandy Alomar Jr.	.25
38	Gary Sheffield	.40
39	David Justice	.25
40	Ken Griffey Jr.	2.50
40s	Ken Griffey Jr./OPS	2.50
41	Vladimir Guerrero	1.00
42	Larry Walker	.25
43	Barry Bonds	4.00
44	Randy Johnson	1.00
45	Roger Clemens	2.25
46	Raul Mondesi	.25
47	Tino Martinez	.25
48	Jason Giambi	.50
49	Matt Williams	.25
50	Cal Ripken Jr.	4.00
51	Barry Larkin	.25
52	Jim Edmonds	.25
53	Ken Caminiti	.25
54	Sammy Sosa	2.00
55	Tony Clark	.25
56	Manny Ramirez	1.00
57	Bernard Gilkey	.25
58	Jose Cruz Jr.	.25
59	Brian Jordan	.25
60	Kevin Brown	.25
61	Craig Biggio	.25
62	Javier Lopez	.25
63	Jay Buhner	.25
64	Roberto Alomar	.40
65	Justin Thompson	.25
66	Todd Helton	.75
67	Travis Lee	.25
68	Paul Konerko	.35
69	Jaret Wright	.25
70	Ben Grieve	.25
71	Juan Encarnacion	.25
72	Ryan McGuire	.25
73	Derrek Lee	.60
74	Abraham Nunez	.25
75	Richard Hidalgo	.25
76	Miguel Tejada	.25
77	Jacob Cruz	.25
78	Homer Bush	.25
79	Jeff Abbott	.25
80	Lou Collier	.25
	Checklist	.10

5x7 Impulse Silver

These silver parallels reprinted each of the 80 cards in the 5" x 7" set. Cards were called Impulse and carried that logo on the front and were inserted one per seven packs. Since these cards contained other cards inside them, they are condition sensitive and only worth full price if left in mint condition and not cut open.

	NM/M
Common Player:	2.00
Stars/RC's:	1.5X
Inserted 1:7	

ABBREVIATIONS

OPS - Overprinted "Promotional Sample"

5x7 Impulse Gold

These gold parallels reprint each of the 80 cards in the 5" x 7" set. Cards carry a Gold Impulse logo on front and are serially numbered from within an edition of 100 each on back. Silver or Gold Impulse parallels were inserted one per seven packs. Since these cards contained other cards inside them, they are condition sensitive and only worth full price if left in mint condition and not cut open.

	NM/M
Common Player:	5.00
Stars/RC's:	20X
Inserted 1:7	

1992 Ziploc

Dow Brands produced an 11-card set of All-Stars in 1992 that featured mostly Hall of Famers, with the exception only of Nellie Fox. The cards were included in specially-marked Ziploc packages, and also could be purchased by mail.

		NM/M
Complete Set (11):		4.00
Common Player:		.45
1	Warren Spahn	.50
2	Bob Gibson	.50
3	Rollie Fingers	.50
4	Carl Yastrzemski	1.00
5	Brooks Robinson	.50
6	Pee Wee Reese	.75
7	Willie McCovey	.50
8	Willie Mays	2.00
9	Nellie Fox	.50
10	Yogi Berra	.75
11	Hank Aaron	2.00

MINOR LEAGUE (1867-1969)

Prior to 1970 virtually all minor league baseball cards were issued as single cards rather than the complete sets. Like contemporary major league cards they were usually intended as premiums given away with the purchase of goos and services.

The listings which follow offer individual card prices in three grades of preservation to allow accurate valuations of superstar and other special interest cards, along with cards that were short-printed or otherwise are scarce.

1959 APCO Meat Packing Co. San Antonio Missions

The extent of this issue, as well as its distribution are not known. The 3-1/2" x 4-1/2" black-and-white cards may have been packaged with meat products and/or given away at the ballpark. The team was Class AA affiliate of the Chicago Cubs.

		NM	EX	VG
Common Player:		50.00	25.00	15.00
(1)	Russell Gragg	50.00	25.00	15.00
(2)	Mike Lutz	50.00	25.00	15.00
	(In Corpus Chriti uniform.)			

1960 Armour Meats Denver Bears

Ten cards from this Class AA farm team of the Detroit Tigers have been checklisted, with others possibly to be discovered. The black-and-white blank-backed cards measure 2-1/2" x 3-1/4" and were issued with a coupon attached to the right side. The unnumbered cards are checklisted here alphabetically.

		NM	EX	VG
Complete Set (10):		650.00	325.00	195.00
Common Player:		75.00	37.00	22.00
(1)	George Alusik	75.00	37.00	22.00
(2)	Tony Bartirome	75.00	37.00	22.00
(3)	Edward J. Donnelly	75.00	37.00	22.00
(4)	James R. McDaniel	75.00	37.00	22.00
(5)	Charlie Metro	75.00	37.00	22.00
(6)	Harry Perkowski	75.00	37.00	22.00
(7)	Vernon E. Rapp	75.00	37.00	22.00
(8)	James Stump	75.00	37.00	22.00
(9)	Ozzie Virgil	75.00	37.00	22.00
(10)	Robert Walz	75.00	37.00	22.00

1940 Associated Stations San Francisco Seals

This album and sticker set was created as a premium by a Northern California gas company. Individual stickers were given away each week at participating service stations. The blank-backed, 1-3/4" x 2-5/8" stickers have the player's name in a black strip at the bottom. Pages in the accompanying 3-1/2" x 6" album have space for an autograph and a few career highlights for each player. The checklist is presented in page order of the album.

		NM	EX	VG
Complete Set (26):		500.00	250.00	125.00
Common Player:		20.00	10.00	6.00
Album:		100.00	50.00	30.00
(1)	"Lefty" O'Doul	40.00	20.00	12.00
(2)	Sam Gibson	20.00	10.00	6.00
(3)	Brooks Holder	20.00	10.00	6.00
(4)	Ted Norbert	20.00	10.00	6.00
(5)	Win Ballou	20.00	10.00	6.00
(6)	Al Wright	20.00	10.00	6.00
(7)	Al Epperly	20.00	10.00	6.00
(8)	Orville Jorgens	20.00	10.00	6.00
(9)	Larry Powell	20.00	10.00	6.00
(10)	Joe Sprinz	20.00	10.00	6.00
(11)	Harvey Storey	20.00	10.00	6.00
(12)	Jack Burns	20.00	10.00	6.00
(13)	Bob Price	20.00	10.00	6.00
(14)	Larry Guay	20.00	10.00	6.00
(15)	Frank Dasso	20.00	10.00	6.00
(16)	Eddie Stutz	20.00	10.00	6.00
(17)	John Barrett	20.00	10.00	6.00
(18)	Eddie Botelho	20.00	10.00	6.00
(19)	Ferris Fain	30.00	15.00	9.00
(20)	Larry Woodall	20.00	10.00	6.00
(21)	Ted Jennings	20.00	10.00	6.00
(22)	Jack Warner	20.00	10.00	6.00
(23)	Wil Leonard	20.00	10.00	6.00
(24)	Gene Kiley	20.00	10.00	6.00
(25)	Bob Jensen	20.00	10.00	6.00
(26)	Wilfrid Le Febvre	20.00	10.00	6.00

1952 Atlanta Crackers Souvenir Pictures Album

Rather than a set of individual baseball cards, the Class AA Southern Association farm club of the Boston Braves issued this souvenir picture album depicting players (including future major leaguers like Chuck Tanner, Art Fowler and Carl Wiley), staff and media. About 8-1/8" x 7-1/2", the album has embossed metallic light blue covers and dark blue graphics. Inside are eight black-and-white pages with three card-like images per page. The pictures are in about the same size and format as Globe Printing's contemporary minor league baseball card team sets.

	NM	EX	VG
Complete Souvenir Book:	400.00	200.00	120.00
1952 Atlanta Crackers			

1910 A.W.H./A.W.A. Caramels Virginia League (E222)

This rare set of cards picturing players from the Virginia League was issued by the A.W.H. (or A.W.A.) Caramel Company in 1910. The cards measure 1-1/2" x 2-3/4" and feature player portraits in either red, black, brown, or blue duotones. Examples of 12 different cards have been found. The front of the card displays the player's last name and team below his photo. The back states "A.W.H. (or A.W.A.) Brand Caramels" in large letters with "Base Ball Series/Va. State League" below. At least four variations in back typography and borders are known.

		NM	EX	VG
Complete Set (12):		100,000	40,000	25,000
Common Player:		9,000	3,600	2,250
(1)	Tom Guiheen	9,000	3,600	2,250
(2)	Hooker	9,000	3,600	2,250
(3)	Ison	9,000	3,600	2,250
(4)	Lipe	9,000	3,600	2,250
(5)	McCauley	9,000	3,600	2,250
(6)	Otey	9,000	3,600	2,250
(7)	Revelle	9,000	3,600	2,250
(8)	Ryan	9,000	3,600	2,250
(9)	Shaugnessy	9,000	3,600	2,250
(10)	Sieber	9,000	3,600	2,250
(11)	Smith	9,000	3,600	2,250
(12)	Titman	9,000	3,600	2,250

B

1910 Baltimore News Orioles

The Eastern League Baltimore Orioles are featured in this set of schedule cards issued by a local newspaper. Cards measure 2-3/4" x 3-1/2" and feature player photographs on front, with a wide border. Player name, position, team and league are printed at the bottom of the photo. Backs have both the "Home" and "Abroad" schedule for the team, along with ads at top and bottom for the newspaper. All printing on front is in red-and-white; backs are in black-and-white. The checklist here is likely incomplete.

		NM	EX	VG
Common Player:		1,200	600.00	350.00
(1)	Byers	1,200	600.00	350.00
(2)	Jim Egan	1,200	600.00	350.00
(3)	Maisel	1,200	600.00	350.00
(4)	Malloy	1,200	600.00	350.00
(5)	Jimmy Murray	1,200	600.00	350.00

1914 Baltimore News Orioles

The International League Baltimore Orioles are one of two teams featured (along with the city's Federal League team) in this set of newspaper promotional cards. The 2-5/8" x 3-5/8" cards are monochrome printed in either blue or red with wide borders on front framing full-length action poses on which the background has been erased in favor of artificial shadows. Player name, position and league are printed on front. Backs have a "HOME" and "ABROAD" schedule with an ad for the paper at top and a line at bottom that reads, "This Card is Given to," with space for a signature. At least one card, a Babe Ruth, has been seen with "Compliments Baltimore International League" replacing the newspaper ad at top. Only the minor league Orioles players are listed here, the Terrapins cards are listed in the major league section of this catalog. This checklist is almost certainly incomplete.

		NM	EX	VG
	Common Player:	3,000	1,500	900.00
(1)	Neal Ball	3,000	1,500	900.00
(2)	Ensign Cottrell	3,000	1,500	900.00
(3)	Birdie Cree	3,000	1,500	900.00
(4)	Bert Daniels	3,000	1,500	900.00
(5)	Davidson	3,000	1,500	900.00
(6)	Jack Dunn	4,500	2,250	1,350
(8)	Gleichmann	3,000	1,500	900.00
(9)	Allen Russell (Allan)	3,000	1,500	900.00
(10)	Babe Ruth (Blue PSA 4 (VG-EX) card sold in 5/05 auction for $244,000. Red PSA 1 (Poor-Fair) sold in 4/06 auction for $150,800.)			
(11)	Ernie Shore	3,000	1,500	900.00
(12)	George Twombley (Twombly)	3,000	1,500	900.00

1952 Baltimore Orioles Team Issue

ROY WEATHERLY

While most of the company's issues were for minor league teams in the lower classifications, Globe Printing of San Jose, Calif., also produced a set for the International League Baltimore Orioles. Similar to the company's other issues, the black-and-white cards measure about 2-1/4" x 3-3/8". Reliable reports indicates that individual cards were given away with ice cream purchases at the ballpark. The checklist here is obviously incomplete. In 1952 the O's were the top farm club of the Philadelphia Phillies.

		NM	EX	VG
	Common Player:	75.00	37.50	22.50
(1)	Al Cihocki	75.00	37.50	22.50
(2)	Blix Donnelly	75.00	37.50	22.50
(3)	Bob Greenwood	75.00	37.50	22.50
(4)	Don Heffner	75.00	37.50	22.50
(5)	Russ Kerns	75.00	37.50	22.50
(6)	Howie Moss	75.00	37.50	22.50
(7)	Dee Phillips	75.00	37.50	22.50
(8)	Jerry Scala	75.00	37.50	22.50
(9)	Danny Schell	75.00	37.50	22.50
(10)	Paul Stuffel	75.00	37.50	22.50
(11)	Roy Weatherly	75.00	37.50	22.50

1923 Baltimore Shirt Co. Kansas City Blues

LENA BLACKBURNE

This unusual souvenir of the American Association Champion K.C. Blues is in the form of a 48" x 3-5/8" accordian-fold packet. Individual 1-7/8" x 3-1/4" black-and-white photos of the players are glued onto the black backing paper. Because the photos are rather easily removed, they may be encountered as singles. The players are checklisted here as they originally appeared, from left to right, on the foldout. There is no advertising on the individual pictures, just on the outer covers.

		NM	EX	VG
	Complete Foldout:	1,000	500.00	300.00
	Complete Set, Singles:	750.00	375.00	225.00
	Common Player:	50.00	25.00	15.00
(1)	Wilbur Good	50.00	25.00	15.00
(2)	Bill Skiff	50.00	25.00	15.00
(3)	Lew McCarty	50.00	25.00	15.00
(4)	Dudley Branom	50.00	25.00	15.00
(5)	Lena Blackburne	55.00	27.50	16.50
(6)	Walter Hammond	50.00	25.00	15.00
(7)	Glen Wright (Glenn)	60.00	30.00	18.00
(8)	Geo. Armstrong	50.00	25.00	15.00
(9)	Beals Becker	50.00	25.00	15.00
(10)	"Dutch" Zwilling	50.00	25.00	15.00
(11)	Pete Scott	50.00	25.00	15.00
(12)	"Bunny" Brief	50.00	25.00	15.00
(13)	Jimmie Zinn	50.00	25.00	15.00
(14)	Ferd Schupp	50.00	25.00	15.00
(15)	Roy Wilkinson	50.00	25.00	15.00
(16)	Ray Caldwell	50.00	25.00	15.00
(17)	Joe Dawson	50.00	25.00	15.00
(18)	John Saladna	50.00	25.00	15.00
(19)	Herb Thormahlen	50.00	25.00	15.00
(20)	"Nick" Carter	50.00	25.00	15.00
(21)	George Muehlebach/President	50.00	25.00	15.00

1909 Bastian Gum Pin

It is unknown whether other members of the championship 1909 Rochester Bronchos of the Eastern League were honored on these black-and-white pinback celluloid buttons or only their manager. The pin measures about 1-1/4" in diameter and as originally issued had a paper insert in back crediting it to Bastian Bros. Gum.

	NM	EX	VG
John H. Ganzel	150.00	75.00	45.00

1961 Bee Hive Starch Toronto Maple Leafs

BEE HIVE PLAYER PHOTO
DAVE POPE, outfielder - 1961

This 24-card set features players of the Toronto Maple Leafs, an independent team in the International League which featured future Hall of Fame Manager Sparky Anderson as its second baseman. The black-and-white cards are printed on thin, blank-backed stock and measure approximately 2-1/2" x 3-1/4". As the cards are not numbered, the checklist below is presented alphabetically.

		NM	EX	VG
	Complete Set (24):	2,400	1,200	725.00
	Common Player:	90.00	45.00	25.00
(1)	George Anderson	450.00	225.00	135.00
(2)	Fritzie Brickell	90.00	45.00	25.00
(3)	Ellis Burton	90.00	45.00	25.00
(4)	Bob Chakales	90.00	45.00	25.00
(5)	Rip Coleman	90.00	45.00	25.00
(6)	Steve Demeter	90.00	45.00	25.00
(7)	Joe Hannah	90.00	45.00	25.00
(8)	Earl Hersh	90.00	45.00	25.00
(9)	Lou Jackson	90.00	45.00	25.00
(10)	Ken Johnson	90.00	45.00	25.00
(11)	Lou Johnson	90.00	45.00	25.00
(12)	John Lipon	90.00	45.00	25.00
(13)	Carl Mathias	90.00	45.00	25.00
(14)	Bill Moran	90.00	45.00	25.00
(15)	Ron Negray	90.00	45.00	25.00
(16)	Herb Plews	90.00	45.00	25.00
(17)	Dave Pope	90.00	45.00	25.00
(18)	Steve Ridzik	90.00	45.00	25.00
(19)	Raul Sanchez	90.00	45.00	25.00
(20)	Pat Scantlebury	90.00	45.00	25.00
(21)	Bill Smith	90.00	45.00	25.00
(22)	Bob Smith	90.00	45.00	25.00
(23)	Chuck Tanner	125.00	65.00	35.00
(24)	Tim Thompson	90.00	45.00	25.00

1911 Big Eater Sacramento Solons

BYRAM SAC'TO HE EATS "BIG EATER"

This very rare set was issued circa 1911 and includes only members of the Pacific Coast League Sacramento Solons. The black-and-white cards measure 2-1/8" x 4" and feature action photos. The lower part of the card contains a three-line caption that includes the player's last name, team designation (abbreviated to "Sac'to"), and the promotional line: "He Eats 'Big Eater'." Although the exact origin is undetermined, it is believed that "Big Eaters" were a candy novelty.

		NM	EX	VG
	Complete Set (20):	50,000	20,000	12,000
	Common Player:	2,750	1,100	700.00
(1)	Frank Arellanes	2,750	1,100	700.00
(2)	Spider Baum	2,750	1,100	700.00
(3)	Herb Byram	2,750	1,100	700.00
(4)	Babe Danzig	2,750	1,100	700.00
(5)	Jack Fitzgerald	2,750	1,100	700.00
(6)	George Gaddy	2,750	1,100	700.00
(7)	Al Heister	2,750	1,100	700.00
(8)	Ben Hunt	2,750	1,100	700.00
(9)	Butch Kerns	2,750	1,100	700.00
(10)	Mickey LaLonge	2,750	1,100	700.00
(11)	Dutch Lerchen	2,750	1,100	700.00
(12)	Jimmy Lewis	2,750	1,100	700.00
(13)	Chris Mahoney	2,750	1,100	700.00
(14)	Dick Nebinger	2,750	1,100	700.00
(15)	Patsy O'Rourke	2,750	1,100	700.00
(16)	Jimmy Shinn	2,750	1,100	700.00
(17)	Chester Thomas	2,750	1,100	700.00
(18)	Fuller Thompson	2,750	1,100	700.00
(19)	Frank Thornton	2,750	1,100	700.00
(20)	Deacon Van Buren	2,750	1,100	700.00

1950 Big League Stars (V362)

Chuck Connors
MONTREAL ROYALS
Infielder
Born at Brooklyn, N.Y., on April 10, 1921. Bats left. Throws left. 6'5". 210 lbs. Hit .319, 20 homers and batted in 108 runs with Royals in 1949.
Champ intérieur
Né à Brooklyn, N.Y., le 10 avril 1921. Frappe de la gauche, lance de la gauche. 6'5", 210 livres. Frappa .319, 20 coups de circuit et participa à 108 buts avec les Royaux en 1949.

BIG LEAGUE STARS — No. 2

International League players are featured in this 48-card set. Measuring 3-1/4" x 2-5/8", the blank-backed cards are printed in blue-on-white with English and French stats and biographical data.

	NM	EX	VG
Complete Set (48):	4,500	2,750	1,200

Common Player:	90.00	40.00	25.00
1 Rocky Bridges	100.00	50.00	30.00
2 Chuck Connors	650.00	325.00	200.00
3 Jake Wade	90.00	40.00	25.00
4 Al Cihocki	90.00	40.00	25.00
5 John Simmons	90.00	40.00	25.00
6 Frank Trechock	90.00	40.00	25.00
7 Steve Lembo	90.00	40.00	25.00
8 Johnny Welaj	90.00	40.00	25.00
9 Seymour Block	90.00	40.00	25.00
10 Pat McGlothlin	90.00	40.00	25.00
11 Bryan Stephens	90.00	40.00	25.00
12 Clarence Podbielan	90.00	40.00	25.00
13 Clem Hausmann	90.00	40.00	25.00
14 Turk Lown	90.00	40.00	25.00
15 Joe Payne	90.00	40.00	25.00
16 Coacker Triplett (Coaker)	90.00	40.00	25.00
17 Nick Strincevich	90.00	40.00	25.00
18 Charlie Thompson	90.00	40.00	25.00
19 Erick Silverman	90.00	40.00	25.00
20 George Schmees	90.00	40.00	25.00
21 George Binks	90.00	40.00	25.00
22 Gino Cimoli	100.00	50.00	30.00
23 Marty Tabacheck	90.00	40.00	25.00
24 Al Gionfriddo	100.00	50.00	30.00
25 Ronnie Lee	90.00	40.00	25.00
26 Clyde King	90.00	40.00	25.00
27 Harry Heslet	90.00	40.00	25.00
28 Jerry Scala	90.00	40.00	25.00
29 Boris Woyt	90.00	40.00	25.00
30 Jack Collum	90.00	40.00	25.00
31 Chet Laabs	90.00	40.00	25.00
32 Carden Gillwater	90.00	40.00	25.00
33 Irving Medlinger	90.00	40.00	25.00
34 Toby Atwell	90.00	40.00	25.00
35 Charlie Marshall	90.00	40.00	25.00
36 Johnny Mayo	90.00	40.00	25.00
37 Gene Markland	90.00	40.00	25.00
38 Russ Kerns	90.00	40.00	25.00
39 Jim Prendergast	90.00	40.00	25.00
40 Lou Welaj	90.00	40.00	25.00
41 Clyde Kluttz	90.00	40.00	25.00
42 Bill Glynn	90.00	40.00	25.00
43 Don Richmond	90.00	40.00	25.00
44 Hank Biasatti	90.00	40.00	25.00
45 Tom Lasorda	600.00	300.00	180.00
46 Al Roberge	90.00	40.00	25.00
47 George Byam	90.00	40.00	25.00
48 Dutch Mele	90.00	40.00	25.00

1910 Bishop & Co. P.C.L. Teams (E221)

A very rare issue, this series of team pictures of clubs in the Pacific Coast League was distributed by Bishop & Co. of Los Angeles in 1910. The team photos were printed on a thin, newsprint-type paper that measures an elongated 10" x 2-3/4". Although there were six teams in the PCL at the time, only five clubs have been found - the sixth team, Sacramento, was apparently never issued. The cards indicate that they were issued with five-cent packages of Bishop's Milk Chocolate and that the photos were taken by the Los Angeles Examiner. The black-and-white team photos are found with red, blue, yellow, purple or green background.

	NM	EX	VG
Complete Set (5):	32,000	13,000	8,000
Common Team:	6,000	2,700	1,700
(1) Los Angeles	6,000	2,700	1,700
(2) Oakland	6,000	2,700	1,700
(3) Portland	6,000	2,700	1,700
(4) San Francisco	6,000	2,700	1,700
(5) Vernon	6,000	2,700	1,700

1910 Bishop & Co. P.C.L. (E99)

 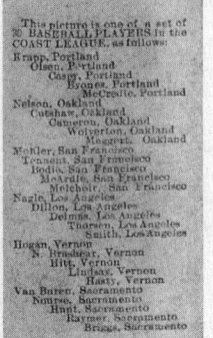

Hap. Hogan, c. Vernon

The first of two obscure sets produced by the Los Angeles candy maker Bishop & Co., this 30-card set was issued in 1910 and depicts players from the Pacific Coast League, showing five players from each of the six teams. The cards measure approxi-

mately 1-1/2" x 2-3/4" and feature black-and-white player photos with colored backgrounds (green, blue, purple, yellow, or rarely, black). The player's last name, position and team appear along the bottom. The backs of the cards contain the complete checklist in groups of five, according to team, with each name indented slightly more than the name above. Cards in the 1910 set do not contain the name "Bishop & Company, California" along the bottom on the back.

	NM	EX	VG
Complete Set (30):	50,000	21,000	13,000
Common Player:	1,750	700.00	435.00
(1) Bodie	2,000	800.00	500.00
(2) N. Brashear	1,750	700.00	435.00
(3) Briggs	1,750	700.00	435.00
(4) Byones (Byrnes)	1,750	700.00	435.00
(5) Cameron	1,750	700.00	435.00
(6) Casey	1,750	700.00	435.00
(7) Cutshaw	1,750	700.00	435.00
(8) Delmas	1,750	700.00	435.00
(9) Dillon	1,750	700.00	435.00
(10) Hasty	1,750	700.00	435.00
(11) Hitt	1,750	700.00	435.00
(12) Hap. Hogan	1,750	700.00	435.00
(13) Hunt	1,750	700.00	435.00
(14) Krapp	1,750	700.00	435.00
(15) John Lindsay	1,750	700.00	435.00
(16) Maggert	1,750	700.00	435.00
(17) McArdle	1,750	700.00	435.00
(18) McCredie (McCreedie)	1,750	700.00	435.00
(19) Melchior	1,750	700.00	435.00
(20) Mohler	1,750	700.00	435.00
(21) Nagle	1,750	700.00	435.00
(22) Nelson	1,750	700.00	435.00
(23) Nourse	1,750	700.00	435.00
(24) Olsen	1,750	700.00	435.00
(25) Raymer	1,750	700.00	435.00
(26) Smith	1,750	700.00	435.00
(27) Tennent (Tennant)	1,750	700.00	435.00
(28) Thorsen	1,750	700.00	435.00
(29) Van Buren	1,750	700.00	435.00
(30) Wolverton	1,750	700.00	435.00

1911 Bishop & Co. P.C.L. Type I (E100)

This set was issued by the confectioner Bishop & Co. of Los Angeles, which had produced a similar set a year earlier. Both sets showcased star players from the Pacific Coast League. The cards measure approximately 1-1/2" x 2-3/4" and feature black-and-white photos with a background of green, blue, yellow, purple or red. The backs contain the complete checklist of the set, listing the players in groups of five by team, with one line indented slightly more than the previous one. In addition to the checklist, the 1911 set can be differentiated from the previous year because the line "Bishop & Company, California" appears along the bottom.

	NM	EX	VG
Complete Set (30):	55,000	22,000	13,500
Common Player:	1,700	675.00	425.00
(1) Spider Baum	1,700	675.00	425.00
(2) Burrell	1,700	675.00	425.00
(3) Carlisle	1,700	675.00	425.00
(4) Cutshaw	1,700	675.00	425.00
(5) Pete Daley	1,700	675.00	425.00
(6) Danzig	1,700	675.00	425.00
(7) Delhi	1,700	675.00	425.00
(8) Delmas	1,700	675.00	425.00
(9) Hitt	1,700	675.00	425.00
(10) Hap Hogan (Actually Walter Bray.)	1,700	675.00	425.00
(11) Lerchen	1,700	675.00	425.00
(12) McCreddie (McCreedie)	1,700	675.00	425.00
(13) Mohler	1,700	675.00	425.00
(14) Moore	1,700	675.00	425.00
(15) Slim Nelson	1,700	675.00	425.00
(16) P. O'Rourke	1,700	675.00	425.00
(17) Patterson	1,700	675.00	425.00
(18) Bunny Pearce	1,700	675.00	425.00
(19) Peckinpaugh	1,700	675.00	425.00
(20) Monte Pfyle (Pfyl)	1,700	675.00	425.00
(21) Powell	1,700	675.00	425.00
(22) Rapps	1,700	675.00	425.00
(23) Seaton	1,700	675.00	425.00
(24) Steen	1,700	675.00	425.00
(25) Suter	1,700	675.00	425.00
(26) Tennant	1,700	675.00	425.00
(27) Thomas	1,700	675.00	425.00
(28) Tozer	1,700	675.00	425.00
(29) Clyde Wares	1,700	675.00	425.00
(30) Weaver	6,500	2,600	1,625

1911 Bishop & Co. P.C.L. Type II (E100)

Currently little over half of the checklist of Bishop & Co. (E100) has been found in a second version. These cards have thus far been seen only with green and orange backgrounds, are blank-backed, have larger, reversed negatives, cropping of the photos and have caption differences.

	NM	EX	VG
Common Player:	1,850	750.00	450.00
(1) Burrell	1,850	750.00	450.00
(2) Danzig	1,850	750.00	450.00
(3) Delhi	1,850	750.00	450.00
(4) Hitt	1,850	750.00	450.00
(5) Lerchen	1,850	750.00	450.00
(6) McCreddie (McCreedie)	1,850	750.00	450.00
(7) Slim Nelson	1,850	750.00	450.00
(8) P. O'Rourke	1,850	750.00	450.00
(9) Patterson	1,850	750.00	450.00
(10) Bunny Pearce	1,850	750.00	450.00
(11) Monte Pfyle	1,850	750.00	450.00
(12) Rapps	1,850	750.00	450.00
(13) Seaton	1,850	750.00	450.00
(14) Steen	1,850	750.00	450.00
(15) Suter	1,850	750.00	450.00
(16) Tennant	1,850	750.00	450.00
(17) Weaver	6,500	2,600	1,625

1954 Blossom Dairy Charleston Senators

JOE TORPEY
Compliments of
Blossom Dairy Company

The Class AAA farm team of the Chicago White Sox is featured in this team set sponsored by a Charleston, W. Va., dairy. The 2-1/4" x 3-3/16" black-and-white cards are either a late issue by Globe Printing (which issued many minor league sets from 1951-52) or were patterned after the Globe issues, right down to the issue of an album to house the cards. A white box is superimposed over the posed action photos and contains the player and sponsor identification. Cards are blank-backed.

	NM	EX	VG
Complete Set (22):	2,200	1,100	650.00
Common Player:	100.00	50.00	30.00
Album:	150.00	75.00	45.00
(1) Al Baro	100.00	50.00	30.00
(2) Joe Becker	100.00	50.00	30.00
(3) Joe Carroll	100.00	50.00	30.00
(4) Gerald "Red" Fahr	100.00	50.00	30.00
(5) Dick Fowler	100.00	50.00	30.00
(6) Alex Garbowski	100.00	50.00	30.00
(7) Gordon Goldsberry	100.00	50.00	30.00
(8) Ross Grimsley	100.00	50.00	30.00
(9) Sam Hairston	125.00	65.00	35.00
(10) Phil Haugstad	100.00	50.00	30.00
(11) Tom Hurd	100.00	50.00	30.00
(12) Bill Killinger	100.00	50.00	30.00
(13) John Kropf	100.00	50.00	30.00
(14) Bob Masser	100.00	50.00	30.00
(15) Danny Menendez	100.00	50.00	30.00
(16) Bill Paolisso	100.00	50.00	30.00
(17) Bill Pope	100.00	50.00	30.00
(18) Lou Sleater	100.00	50.00	30.00
(19) Dick Strahs	100.00	50.00	30.00
(20) Joe Torpey	100.00	50.00	30.00
(21) Bill Voiselle	100.00	50.00	30.00
(22) Al Ware	100.00	50.00	30.00

Right column top table:

(5) Lerchen	1,850	750.00	450.00
(6) McCreddie (McCreedie)	1,850	750.00	450.00
(7) Slim Nelson	1,850	750.00	450.00
(8) P. O'Rourke	1,850	750.00	450.00
(9) Patterson	1,850	750.00	450.00
(10) Bunny Pearce	1,850	750.00	450.00
(11) Monte Pfyle	1,850	750.00	450.00
(12) Rapps	1,850	750.00	450.00
(13) Seaton	1,850	750.00	450.00
(14) Steen	1,850	750.00	450.00
(15) Suter	1,850	750.00	450.00
(16) Tennant	1,850	750.00	450.00
(17) Weaver	6,500	2,600	1,625

1958 Bond Bread Buffalo Bisons

LUKE EASTER, First Base

EASTER, LUSCIOUS "LUKE" First Baseman

WATCH "CASEY JONES" CHANNEL 2 — THURSDAY 7 P.M.

Bond Bread & Pastry

Nine members of the International League affiliate of the Kansas City Athletics are featured in this set. The 2-1/2" x 3-1/2" cards are printed on very thin cardboard. Fronts have a black-and-white player photo, the player's name and position, and an ad for a TV Western. Card backs are printed in red and blue and include a few biographical details and a career summary, along with an illustrated ad.

	NM	EX	VG
Complete Set (9):	350.00	175.00	100.00
Common Player:	40.00	20.00	12.00

(1)	Al Aber	40.00	20.00	12.00
(2)	Joe Caffie	40.00	20.00	12.00
(3)	Phil Cavaretta	40.00	20.00	12.00
(4)	Rip Coleman	40.00	20.00	12.00
(5)	Luke Easter	60.00	30.00	18.00
(6)	Ken Johnson	40.00	20.00	12.00
(7)	Lou Ortiz	40.00	20.00	12.00
(8)	Jack Phillips	40.00	20.00	12.00
(9)	Jim Small	40.00	20.00	12.00

1949 Bowman Pacific Coast League

One of the scarcest issues of the post-war period, the 1949 Bowman PCL set was issued only on the West Coast. Like the 1949 Bowman regular issue, the cards contain black-and-white photos overprinted with various pastel colors. Thirty-six cards, which measure 2-1/16" x 2-1/2", make up the set. It is believed that the cards may have been issued only in sheets and not sold in gum packs. Consequently, many cards are found which display evidence of having been cut with a scissors.

		NM	EX	VG
Complete Set (36):		15,000	7,500	4,500
Common Player:		500.00	240.00	145.00
1	Lee Anthony	500.00	240.00	145.00
2	George Metkovich	500.00	240.00	145.00
3	Ralph Hodgin	500.00	240.00	145.00
4	George Woods	500.00	240.00	145.00
5	Xavier Rescigno	500.00	240.00	145.00
6	Mickey Grasso	500.00	240.00	145.00
7	Johnny Rucker	500.00	240.00	145.00
8	Jack Brewer	500.00	240.00	145.00
9	Dom D'Allessandro	500.00	240.00	145.00
10	Charlie Gassaway	500.00	240.00	145.00
11	Tony Freitas	500.00	240.00	145.00
12	Gordon Maltzberger	500.00	240.00	145.00
13	John Jensen	500.00	240.00	145.00
14	Joyner White	500.00	240.00	145.00
15	Harvey Storey	500.00	240.00	145.00
16	Dick Lajeski	500.00	240.00	145.00
17	Albie Glossop	500.00	240.00	145.00
18	Bill Raimondi	500.00	240.00	145.00
19	Ken Holcombe	500.00	240.00	145.00
20	Don Ross	500.00	240.00	145.00
21	Pete Coscarart	500.00	240.00	145.00
22	Tony York	500.00	240.00	145.00
23	Jake Mooty	500.00	240.00	145.00
24	Charles Adams	500.00	240.00	145.00
25	Les Scarsella	500.00	240.00	145.00
26	Joe Marty	500.00	240.00	145.00
27	Frank Kelleher	500.00	240.00	145.00
28	Lee Handley	500.00	240.00	145.00
29	Herman Besse	500.00	240.00	145.00
30	John Lazor	500.00	240.00	145.00
31	Eddie Malone	500.00	240.00	145.00
32	Maurice Van Robays	500.00	240.00	145.00
33	Jim Tabor	500.00	240.00	145.00
34	Gene Handley	500.00	240.00	145.00
35	Tom Seats	500.00	240.00	145.00
36	Ora Burnett	500.00	240.00	145.00

1933 Buffalo Bisons Jigsaw Puzzles

Produced as a stadium promotional giveaway, this set consists of 19 player puzzles and one for Hall of Fame Manager Ray Schalk. Each of the 11" x 14", 200-piece, black-and-white puzzles was produced in an edition of 10,000. Puzzles carried a red serial number, and certain numbers could be redeemed for tickets and other prizes. The known puzzles are checklisted below in alphabetical order.

		NM	EX	VG
Complete Set (15):		5,000	2,500	1,500
Common Player:		335.00	165.00	100.00
(1)	Joe Bartulis	335.00	165.00	100.00
(2)	Joe Bloomer	335.00	165.00	100.00
(3)	Ollie Carnegie	335.00	165.00	100.00
(4)	Clyde "Buck" Crouse	335.00	165.00	100.00
(5)	Harry Danning	335.00	165.00	100.00
(6)	Gilbert English	335.00	165.00	100.00
(7)	Fred Fussell	335.00	165.00	100.00
(8)	Bob Gould	335.00	165.00	100.00
(9)	Len Koenecke	335.00	165.00	100.00
(10)	Ray Lucas	335.00	165.00	100.00
(11)	Clarence Mueller	335.00	165.00	100.00
(12)	Ray Schalk	500.00	250.00	150.00
(13)	Jack Smith	335.00	165.00	100.00
(14)	Roy Tarr	335.00	165.00	100.00
(15)	Johnny Wilson	335.00	165.00	100.00

1934 Buffalo Bisons Team Issue

Apparently a team issue, these 4" x 7-1/16" black-and-white blank-backed cards feature posed action photos with white borders and a facsimile autograph. The player's full name and position are printed in the bottom border, along with a career summary. This checklist is probably incomplete though the exact scope of the issue is unknown.

		NM	EX	VG
Common Player:		200.00	100.00	60.00
(1)	Kenneth L. Ash	200.00	100.00	60.00
(2)	Harold "Ace" Elliott	200.00	100.00	60.00
(3)	Gregory T. Mulleavy	200.00	100.00	60.00
(4)	Irving M. Plummer	200.00	100.00	60.00

1940 Buffalo Bisons Team Issue

FRED HUTCHINSON
Pitcher

One of the brightest pitching prospects in baseball, owned by Detroit . . . Was in headlines in every paper in country when purchased from Seattle by Tigers for $75,000 at close of 1938 season . . . In '38, his first year in baseball, "Hutch" won 25, lost only 7, hurled 29 complete games, five shutouts . . . . Also fine batter . . Throws right, bats left . . . . Born Aug. 12, 1919, in Seattle.

FRED HUTCHINSON, Pitcher

Many former and future big leaguers are included in this set of black-and-white, 2" x 3" cards. Fronts picture the players in poses at old Offerman Stadium. The player's name and position are printed in the white border at bottom. Backs have a career summary and highlights. The unnumbered cards are checklisted here alphabetically.

		NM	EX	VG
Complete Set (24):		4,500	2,250	1,350
Common Player:		200.00	100.00	60.00
(1)	Ollie Carnegie	200.00	100.00	60.00
(2)	Dan Carnevale	200.00	100.00	60.00
(3)	Earl Cook	200.00	100.00	60.00
(4)	Les Fleming	200.00	100.00	60.00
(5)	Floyd Giebel	200.00	100.00	60.00
(6)	Jimmy Hutch	200.00	100.00	60.00
(7)	Fred Hutchinson	200.00	100.00	60.00
(8)	Art Jacobs	200.00	100.00	60.00
(9)	John Kroner	200.00	100.00	60.00
(10)	Sal Maglie	300.00	150.00	90.00
(11)	Joe Martin	200.00	100.00	60.00
(12)	Clyde McCullough	200.00	100.00	60.00
(13)	Greg Mulleavy	200.00	100.00	60.00
(14)	Pat Mullin	200.00	100.00	60.00
(15)	Hank Nowak	200.00	100.00	60.00
(16)	Steve O'Neil	200.00	100.00	60.00
(17)	Jimmy Outlaw	200.00	100.00	60.00
(18)	Joe Rogalski	200.00	100.00	60.00
(19)	Les Scarsella	200.00	100.00	60.00
(20)	Mayo Smith	200.00	100.00	60.00
(21)	Floyd Stromme	200.00	100.00	60.00
(22)	Jim Trexler	200.00	100.00	60.00
(23)	Hal White	200.00	100.00	60.00
(24)	Frank Zubik	200.00	100.00	60.00

1947 Buffalo Bisons Team Issue

Despite some anomalies among the players checklisted thus far, this appears to have been a 1947 team-issued set of 8" a 10" black-and-white player photographs. Fronts include player identification in the form of a facsimile autograph. Backs are blank.

Values shown are a national average. Some teams and players enjoy regional popularity that may affect market prices.

		NM	EX	VG
Common Player:		30.00	15.00	9.00
(1)	Johnny Bero	30.00	15.00	9.00
(2)	Hank Biasatti	30.00	15.00	9.00
(3)	Eddie Boland	30.00	15.00	9.00
(4)	Ray Coleman	30.00	15.00	9.00
(5)	Zeb "Red" Eaton	30.00	15.00	9.00
(6)	Lonny Frey	30.00	15.00	9.00
(8)	Freddie Hancock	30.00	15.00	9.00
(9)	Gabby Hartnett	65.00	32.00	19.50
(10)	Clem Hausman	30.00	15.00	9.00
(11)	Manuel Hidalgo	30.00	15.00	9.00
(12)	Chet Laabs	30.00	15.00	9.00
(14)	Johnny McHale	30.00	15.00	9.00
(15)	Edward Mierkowicz	30.00	15.00	9.00
(16)	Eddie Mordarski	30.00	15.00	9.00
(17)	Hank Perry	30.00	15.00	9.00
(18)	Billy Pierce, Ted Gray	45.00	22.00	13.50
(19)	Bill Radulovich	30.00	15.00	9.00
(21)	Earl Rapp, Clint Conatser, Anse Moore, Coaker Triplett	30.00	15.00	9.00
(22)	Vic Wertz	40.00	20.00	12.00

1950 Bush & Hancock/ Oak Hall Roanoke Red Sox

These blank-back, black-and-white cards have a portrait photo on front surrounded by a white border. Beneath the photo is a credit line and space for an autograph. Cards exist in 3-1/2" x 5" size with sponsor's credit reading "Compliments of Bush & Hancock", and in 4" x 6" format with sponsor's credit reading, "Compliments of Oak Hall." It is not known whether the checklist presented here is complete. Roanoke was a Class B Piedmont League farm club.

		NM	EX	VG
Common Player:		50.00	25.00	15.00
(1)	Tom Casey	50.00	25.00	15.00
(2)	George Contratto	50.00	25.00	15.00
(3)	Ike Delock	65.00	32.50	20.00
(4)	Red Marion	50.00	25.00	15.00
(5)	Rod Morgan	50.00	25.00	15.00
(6)	Julio Ondani	50.00	25.00	15.00
(7)	Joe Reedy	50.00	25.00	15.00
(8)	Johnny Sehrt	50.00	25.00	15.00
(9)	Sammy White	65.00	32.50	20.00
(10)	Bob Wilson	50.00	25.00	15.00

1943 Centennial Flour Seattle Rainiers

The 25 cards in this 4" x 5" black-and-white set feature players of the Pacific Coast League Seattle Rainiers. Identical in format to the set issued in 1944, the '43s can be identified by the lines of type at the bottom of the card back reading, "Compliments of/CENTENNIAL FLOURING MILLS."

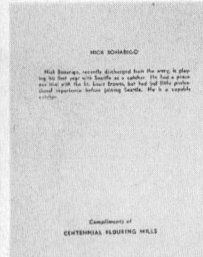

		NM	EX	VG
Complete Set (25):		1,100	550.00	325.00
Common Player:		60.00	30.00	18.00
(1)	John Babich	60.00	30.00	18.00
(2)	Nick Bonarigo (Buonarigo)	60.00	30.00	18.00
(3)	Eddie Carnett	60.00	30.00	18.00
(4)	Lloyd Christopher	60.00	30.00	18.00
(5)	Joe Demoran	60.00	30.00	18.00
(6)	Joe Dobbins	60.00	30.00	18.00
(7)	Glenn Elliott	60.00	30.00	18.00
(8)	Carl Fischer	60.00	30.00	18.00
(9)	Leonard Gabrielson	60.00	30.00	18.00
(10)	Stanley Gray	60.00	30.00	18.00
(11)	Dick Gyselman	60.00	30.00	18.00
(12)	Jim Jewell	60.00	30.00	18.00
(13)	Syl Johnson	60.00	30.00	18.00
(14)	Pete Jonas	60.00	30.00	18.00
(15)	Bill Kats	60.00	30.00	18.00
(16)	Lynn King	60.00	30.00	18.00
(17)	Bill Lawrence	60.00	30.00	18.00
(18)	Clarence Marshall	60.00	30.00	18.00
(19)	Bill Matheson	60.00	30.00	18.00
(20)	Ford Mullen	60.00	30.00	18.00
(21)	Bill Skiff	60.00	30.00	18.00
(22)	Byron Speece	60.00	30.00	18.00
(23)	Hal Sueme	60.00	30.00	18.00
(24)	Hal Turpin	60.00	30.00	18.00
(25)	John Yelovic	60.00	30.00	18.00

1944 Centennial Flour Seattle Rainiers

Identical in format to the previous year's issue, the 25 black-and-white 4" x 5" cards issued in 1944 can be differentiated from the 1943 set by the two lines of type at the bottom of each card's back. In the 1944 set, it reads, "Compliments of/CENTENNIAL HOTCAKE AND WAFFLE FLOUR."

		NM	EX	VG
Complete Set (25):		1,350	675.00	400.00
Common Player:		60.00	30.00	18.00
(1)	John Babich	60.00	30.00	18.00
(2)	Paul Carpenter	60.00	30.00	18.00
(3)	Lloyd Christopher	60.00	30.00	18.00
(4)	Joe Demoran	60.00	30.00	18.00
(5)	Joe Dobbins	60.00	30.00	18.00
(6)	Glenn Elliott	60.00	30.00	18.00
(7)	Carl Fischer	60.00	30.00	18.00
(8)	Bob Garbould (Gorbould)	60.00	30.00	18.00
(9)	Stanley Gray	60.00	30.00	18.00
(10)	Dick Gyselman	60.00	30.00	18.00
(11)	Gene Holt	60.00	30.00	18.00
(12)	Roy Johnson	60.00	30.00	18.00
(13)	Syl Johnson	60.00	30.00	18.00
(14)	Al Libke	60.00	30.00	18.00
(15)	Bill Lyman	60.00	30.00	18.00
(16)	Bill Matheson	60.00	30.00	18.00
(17)	Jack McClure	60.00	30.00	18.00
(18)	Jimmy Ripple	60.00	30.00	18.00
(19)	Bill Skiff	60.00	30.00	18.00
(20)	Byron Speece	60.00	30.00	18.00
(21)	Hal Sueme	60.00	30.00	18.00
(22)	Frank Tincup	60.00	30.00	18.00
(23)	Jack Treece	60.00	30.00	18.00
(24)	Hal Turpin	60.00	30.00	18.00
(25)	Sicks Stadium	65.00	32.50	20.00

1945 Centennial Flour Seattle Rainiers

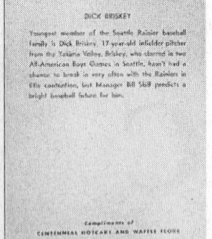

The 27 blue-and-white cards in the third consecutive issue for this Pacific Coast League team are distinguished from the two previous issues by the borderless photo on the front and the fact that the name and team are printed in a black bar at the bottom. The set can be distinguished from the 1947 issue by virtue of the fact that the player biography on back is not surrounded by a frame. The cards measure slightly narrower but longer than the 1943-44 issues, at 3-7/8" x 5-1/8".

		NM	EX	VG
Complete Set (27):		1,500	750.00	450.00
Common Player:		60.00	30.00	18.00
(1)	Charley Aleno	60.00	30.00	18.00
(2)	Dick Briskey	60.00	30.00	18.00
(3)	John Carpenter	60.00	30.00	18.00
(4)	Joe Demoran	60.00	30.00	18.00
(5)	Joe Dobbins	60.00	30.00	18.00
(6)	Glenn Elliott	60.00	30.00	18.00
(7)	Bob Finley	60.00	30.00	18.00
(8)	Carl Fischer	60.00	30.00	18.00
(9)	Keith Frazier	60.00	30.00	18.00
(10)	Johnny Gill	60.00	30.00	18.00
(11)	Bob Gorbould	60.00	30.00	18.00
(12)	Chet Johnson	60.00	30.00	18.00
(13)	Syl Johnson	60.00	30.00	18.00
(14)	Bill Kats	60.00	30.00	18.00
(15)	Billy Lyman	60.00	30.00	18.00
(16)	Bill Matheson	60.00	30.00	18.00
(17)	George McDonald	60.00	30.00	18.00
(18)	Ted Norbert	60.00	30.00	18.00
(19)	Alex Palica	60.00	30.00	18.00
(20)	Joe Passero	60.00	30.00	18.00
(21)	Hal Patchett	60.00	30.00	18.00
(22)	Bill Skiff	60.00	30.00	18.00
(23)	Byron Speece	60.00	30.00	18.00
(24)	Hal Sueme	60.00	30.00	18.00
(25)	Eddie Taylor	60.00	30.00	18.00
(26)	Hal Turpin	60.00	30.00	18.00
(27)	Jack Whipple	60.00	30.00	18.00

1947 Centennial Flour Seattle Rainiers

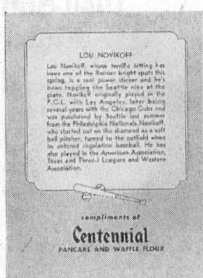

After a lapse of one year, Centennial Flour returned to issue a final black-and-white 32-card set for 1947. Identical in size (3-7/8" x 5-1/8") and front format to the 1945 issue, the '47s can be identified by the white framed box on back containing the player's biography.

		NM	EX	VG
Complete Set (32):		1,100	550.00	325.00
Common Player:		50.00	25.00	15.00
(1)	Dick Barrett	50.00	25.00	15.00
(2)	Joe Buzas	50.00	25.00	15.00
(3)	Paul Carpenter	50.00	25.00	15.00
(4)	Rex Cecil	50.00	25.00	15.00
(5)	Tony Criscola	50.00	25.00	15.00
(6)	Walter Dubiel	50.00	25.00	15.00
(7)	Doug Ford	50.00	25.00	15.00
(8)	Rollie Hemsley	50.00	25.00	15.00
(9)	Jim Hill	50.00	25.00	15.00
(10)	Jim Hopper	50.00	25.00	15.00
(11)	Sigmund Jakucki	50.00	25.00	15.00
(12)	Bob Johnson	60.00	30.00	18.00
(13)	Pete Jonas	50.00	25.00	15.00
(14)	Joe Kaney	50.00	25.00	15.00
(15)	Hillis Layne	50.00	25.00	15.00
(16)	Lou Novikoff	50.00	25.00	15.00
(17)	Johnny O'Neil	50.00	25.00	15.00
(18)	John Orphal	50.00	25.00	15.00
(19)	Ike Pearson	50.00	25.00	15.00
(20)	Bill Posedel	50.00	25.00	15.00
(21)	Don Pulford	50.00	25.00	15.00
(22)	Tom Reis	50.00	25.00	15.00
(23)	Charley Ripple	50.00	25.00	15.00
(24)	Mickey Rocco	50.00	25.00	15.00
(25)	Johnny Rucker	50.00	25.00	15.00
(26)	Earl Sheely	50.00	25.00	15.00
(27)	Bob Stagg	50.00	25.00	15.00
(28)	Hal Sueme	50.00	25.00	15.00
(29)	Eddie Taylor	50.00	25.00	15.00
(30)	Ed Vanni	50.00	25.00	15.00
(31)	JoJo White	50.00	25.00	15.00
(32)	Tony York	50.00	25.00	15.00

1957-58 Chattanooga Lookouts Team Issue

Based on the known and certainly incomplete checklist seen thus far, this issue of 8" x 10" black-and-white, blank-back player photos can only be generally attributed to year of issue. With a credit line to Moss Photo Service of New York City, the pictures feature action poses of the players taken in historic Engel Stadium. Facsimile autographs are pre-printed on the front. During the late 1950s the Lookouts were the top farm club of the Washington Senators.

		NM	EX	VG
Common Player:		30.00	15.00	9.00
(1)	Bobby Brown	30.00	15.00	9.00
(2)	Hal Griggs	30.00	15.00	9.00
(2)	Harmon Killebrew	200.00	100.00	60.00
(3)	Jesse Levan	30.00	15.00	9.00
(3)	Ernie Oravetz	30.00	15.00	9.00
(4)	Stan Roseboro	30.00	15.00	9.00
(5)	Bunky Stewart	30.00	15.00	9.00

1967 Chevron/Uniroyal Vancouver Mounties

ROBERTO RODRIGUEZ
PITCHER

These 2" x 3" black-and-white cards were distributed by local gas stations and picture members of the top farm club of the Kansas City A's. Backs are printed in red and black on white.

		NM	EX	VG
Complete Set (27):		4,500	2,250	1,300
Common Player:		200.00	100.00	60.00
(1)	Sal Bando	350.00	175.00	105.00
(2)	Frank Bastrire/Trainer	200.00	100.00	60.00
(3)	Ossie Chavarria	200.00	100.00	60.00
(4)	Jim Dickson	200.00	100.00	60.00
(5)	John Donaldson	200.00	100.00	60.00
(6)	Jim Driscoll	200.00	100.00	60.00
(7)	Bob Duliba	200.00	100.00	60.00
(8)	Bill Edgerton	200.00	100.00	60.00
(9)	Larry Elliot	200.00	100.00	60.00
(10)	Ernie Foli	200.00	100.00	60.00
(11)	Joe Gaines	200.00	100.00	60.00
(12)	Vern Handrahan	200.00	100.00	60.00
(13)	Jim Hughes	200.00	100.00	60.00
(14)	Woody Huyke	200.00	100.00	60.00
(15)	Rene Lachemann	225.00	110.00	67.00
(16)	Bob Meyer	200.00	100.00	60.00
(17)	Wayne Norton	200.00	100.00	60.00
(18)	Gerry Reimer	200.00	100.00	60.00
(19)	Roberto Rodriguez	200.00	100.00	60.00
(20)	Ken Sanders	200.00	100.00	60.00
(21)	Randy Schwartz	200.00	100.00	60.00
(22)	Diego Segui	275.00	135.00	82.00
(23)	Paul Seitz	200.00	100.00	60.00
(24)	Ron Tompkins	200.00	100.00	60.00
(25)	Mickey Vernon	350.00	175.00	105.00
(26)	Jim Ward	200.00	100.00	60.00
(27)	Don Yingling	200.00	100.00	60.00

1909 Clement Bros. Bread (D380-1)

Holly, s. s. Rochester.

This set features only players of the Rochester team in the Eastern League. According to the bakery ad on back, the cards were distributed one per loaf of bread. The 1-1/2" x 2-3/4" cards feature a player photo on front in an oval frame against a white background. The player's last name, position and "Rochester" are printed beneath.

		NM	EX	VG
Complete Set (8):		25,000	12,500	7,500
Common Player:		4,500	2,000	1,300
(1)	Anderson	4,500	2,000	1,300
(2)	Heinie Batch	4,500	2,000	1,300
(3)	Butler	4,500	2,000	1,300
(4)	Ed Holly	4,500	2,000	1,300
(5)	Holmes	4,500	2,000	1,300
(6)	McConnell	4,500	2,000	1,300
(7)	Osborn	4,500	2,000	1,300
(8)	Partee	4,500	2,000	1,300

1910 Clement Bros. Bread (D380)

For the second of two annual issues, the bakery added an unknown number of major league players' cards to those of six of the hometeam Rochester club of the Eastern League. While the backs remained identical to the previous issue, featuring advertising for the bakery's bread and pies, the fronts adopted the standard format of the era, black-and-white player photos surrounded by a white border, with the player's last name, position and city printed at bottom. Size remained 1-1/2" x 2-3/4".

		NM	EX	VG
Common Player:		5,750	2,850	1,700
(1)	Whitey Alperman	5,750	2,850	1,700
(2)	Bailey	5,750	2,850	1,700
(3)	Blair	5,750	2,850	1,700
(4)	Ty Cobb	40,000	20,000	12,000
(5)	Eddie Collins	6,500	3,250	1,950
(6)	Roy Hartzell	5,750	2,850	1,700
(7)	Harry Howell	5,750	2,850	1,700
(8)	Addie Joss	10,000	6,000	3,000
(9)	McConnell	5,750	2,850	1,700
(10)	Osborn	5,750	2,850	1,700
(11)	Pattee	5,750	2,850	1,700
(12)	Don Carlos Ragan	5,750	2,850	1,700
(13)	Oscar Stanage	5,750	2,850	1,700
(14)	George Stone	5,750	2,850	1,700
(15)	Ed Summers	5,750	2,850	1,700
(16)	Joe Tinker	10,000	6,000	3,000
(17)	Bert Tooley	5,750	2,850	1,700
(18)	Heinie Zimmerman	5,750	2,850	1,700

1953 Coca-Cola Galveston White Caps

This set may have been an issue of the Globe Printing Co., which produced many lower-minors team sets in the years preceding, or it may just share the format. The 2-1/4" x 3-3/8" cards have borderless black-and-white photos on front and blank backs. In a white box near the bottom of the picture is the player name and "Compliments of / Coca-Cola Bottling Co." Galveston was champion of the 1953 Class B Gulf Coast League and not affiliated with any major league team.

		NM	EX	VG
Complete Set (16):		1,000	500.00	300.00
Common Player:		75.00	37.50	22.00
(1)	Ed Bohnslav	75.00	37.50	22.00
(2)	Mike Conovan	75.00	37.50	22.00
(3)	Pop Faucett	75.00	37.50	22.00
(4)	Bobby Flis	75.00	37.50	22.00
(5)	Stan Goletz	75.00	37.50	22.00
(6)	Jerry Kleinsmith	75.00	37.50	22.00
(7)	Charlie Lehrmann	75.00	37.50	22.00
(8)	Jim Logan	75.00	37.50	22.00
(9)	Bob Miller	75.00	37.50	22.00
(10)	Tom Moore	75.00	37.50	22.00
(11)	Bob Pugatch	75.00	37.50	22.00
(12)	Bob Ramsey	75.00	37.50	22.00
(13)	Hank Robinson	75.00	37.50	22.00
(14)	Charlie Schmidt	75.00	37.50	22.00
(15)	Barnie White	75.00	37.50	22.00
(16)	Hank Yzquierdo (Izquierdo)	75.00	37.50	22.00

1952 Colorado Springs Sky Sox Team Issue

From the Class A Western League runners-up, this is one of many minor league sets issued in the early 1950s by the Globe Printing Co., of San Jose, Calif. The '52 Sky Sox were a farm team of the Chicago White Sox. Players included former Negro Leaguers and future major leaguers Connie Johnson and Sam Hairston, plus bonus-baby bust Gus Keriazakos. Cards are about 2-1/4" x 3-1/4", printed in black-and-white with blank backs. An album with die-cut pages to allow the corners of the cards to be slipped in was also available. Cards were likely given away one or two at a time at home games.

		NM	EX	VG
Complete Set (19):		1,200	600.00	360.00
Common Player:		60.00	30.00	18.00
Album:		100.00	50.00	30.00
(1)	Jerry Crosby	60.00	30.00	18.00
(2)	Vic Fucci	60.00	30.00	18.00
(3)	Don Gutteridge	60.00	30.00	18.00
(4)	Sam Hairston	90.00	45.00	27.00
(5)	Al Jacinto	60.00	30.00	18.00
(6)	Connie Johnson	75.00	37.50	22.00
(7)	Bob Kellogg	60.00	30.00	18.00
(8)	Gus Keriazakos	60.00	30.00	18.00
(9)	Ken Landenberger	60.00	30.00	18.00
(10)	George Noga	60.00	30.00	18.00
(11)	Floyd Penfold	60.00	30.00	18.00
(12)	Bill Pope	60.00	30.00	18.00
(13)	J.W. Porter	60.00	30.00	18.00
(14)	Bill (Red) Rose	60.00	30.00	18.00
(15)	Don Rudolph	60.00	30.00	18.00
(16)	Andy Skurski	60.00	30.00	18.00
(17)	Dick Strahs	60.00	30.00	18.00
(18)	Bill Wells	60.00	30.00	18.00
(19)	Dick Welteroth	60.00	30.00	18.00

1952 Columbus Cardinals Team Issue

This set of cards was a product of the Globe Printing company of San Jose, Calif. The cards were given away at Golden Park during the 1952 season. The cards measure 2-1/8" x 3-3/8" and have black-and-white photos of players with the player's name in a white box in the bottom-left corner of the photograph. The backs are blank. The cards are unnumbered and listed in alphabetical order, although this checklist may not be complete. The team was a Class A South Atlantic League affiliate of the St. Louis Cardinals.

		NM	EX	VG
Complete Set (17):		1,000	500.00	300.00
Common Player:		60.00	30.00	18.00
(1)	Chief Bender	60.00	30.00	18.00
(2)	Bob Betancourt	60.00	30.00	18.00
(3)	Tom Burgess	60.00	30.00	18.00
(4)	Jack Byers	60.00	30.00	18.00

		NM	EX	VG
(5)	Mike Curnan	60.00	30.00	18.00
(6)	Gil Daley	60.00	30.00	18.00
(7)	Bill Harris	60.00	30.00	18.00
(8)	Ev Joyner	60.00	30.00	18.00
(9)	Bob Kerce	60.00	30.00	18.00
(10)	Ted Lewandowski	60.00	30.00	18.00
(11)	John Mackey	60.00	30.00	18.00
(12)	Bill Paolisso	60.00	30.00	18.00
(13)	Dennis Reeder	60.00	30.00	18.00
(14)	Whit Ulrich	60.00	30.00	18.00
(15)	Norman Shope	60.00	30.00	18.00
(16)	Don Swartz	60.00	30.00	18.00
(17)	Len Wile	60.00	30.00	18.00

1955 Columbus Jets Photos

A top farm club of the Kansas City A's in 1955 the Columbus (Ohio) Jets issued these black-and-white glossy photocards. In 3-5/8" x 5-5/8" format, the cards have a facsimile autograph on front. It is possible that the checklist presented here in alphabetical order of the unnumbered cards may be incomplete.

		NM	EX	VG
Complete Set (21):		900.00	450.00	275.00
Common Player:		45.00	22.50	13.50
(1)	Hal Bevan	45.00	22.50	13.50
(2)	Paul Burris	45.00	22.50	13.50
(3)	Ted Del Guercio	45.00	22.50	13.50
(4)	Carl Duser	45.00	22.50	13.50
(5)	Charlie Haag	45.00	22.50	13.50
(6)	Forrest "Spook" Jacobs	60.00	30.00	18.00
(7)	Dick Kryhoski	45.00	22.50	13.50
(8)	Mike Kume	45.00	22.50	13.50
(9)	Al Lakeman	45.00	22.50	13.50
(10)	Jackie Mayo	45.00	22.50	13.50
(11)	Jim Miller	45.00	22.50	13.50
(12)	Al Pinkston	50.00	25.00	15.00
(13)	Al Romberger	45.00	22.50	13.50
(14)	Bill Stewart	45.00	22.50	13.50
(15)	Russ Sullivan	45.00	22.50	13.50
(16)	"Jake" Thies	45.00	22.50	13.50
(17)	Bob Trice	45.00	22.50	13.50
(18)	Ozzie VanBrabant	45.00	22.50	13.50
(19)	Frank Verdi	45.00	22.50	13.50
(20)	Leroy Wheat	45.00	22.50	13.50
(21)	Spider Wilhelm	45.00	22.50	13.50

1957 Columbus Jets Postcards

In 1957, the Columbus (Ohio) Jets began a long association as a top farm team of the Pittsburgh Pirates. That year, the team issued this set of postcards. The black-and-white glossy cards measure 3-9/16" x 5-1/2" and have the player name and position overprinted in black block letters near the bottom of the photo. Backs have postcard indicia and a notice of printing by the Howard Photo Service of New York City. The unnumbered cards are presented here alphabetically but it is unknown whether this checklist is complete at 20.

		NM	EX	VG
Complete Set (20):		900.00	450.00	275.00
Common Player:		45.00	22.50	13.50
(1)	Dick Barone	45.00	22.50	13.50
(2)	Ron Blackburn	45.00	22.50	13.50
(3)	Jackie Brown	45.00	22.50	13.50
(4)	Ed Burtschy	45.00	22.50	13.50
(5)	Whammy Douglas	50.00	25.00	15.00
(6)	Howie Goss	45.00	22.50	13.50
(7)	Al Grunwald	45.00	22.50	13.50

		NM	EX	VG
(8)	Gail Henley	45.00	22.50	13.50
(9)	Don Kildoo	45.00	22.50	13.50
(10)	Danny Kravitz	45.00	22.50	13.50
(11)	Bob Kuzava	45.00	22.50	13.50
(12)	Johnny Lipon	45.00	22.50	13.50
(13)	Cholly Naranjo	45.00	22.50	13.50
(14)	Eddie O'Brien	60.00	30.00	18.00
(15)	Frank Oceak	45.00	22.50	13.50
(16)	Harding Peterson	60.00	30.00	18.00
(17)	John Powers	45.00	22.50	13.50
(18)	James Rice	45.00	22.50	13.50
(19)	Russ Sullivan	45.00	22.50	13.50
(20)	Ken Toothman	45.00	22.50	13.50

1958 Columbus Jets Photos

In format similar to the postcard issue of the previous year, and sharing some of the same pictures, this set of photocards is smaller, at 4" x 5", and is blank-backed. It is unknown whether the alphabetical checklist of the unnumbered cards presented here is complete.

		NM	EX	VG
Complete Set (17):		650.00	325.00	200.00
Common Player:		40.00	20.00	12.00
(1)	Gair Allie	40.00	20.00	12.00
(2)	Luis Arroyo	40.00	20.00	12.00
(3)	Tony Bartirome	45.00	22.50	13.50
(4)	Jim Baumer	40.00	20.00	12.00
(5)	Bill Causion	40.00	20.00	12.00
(6)	Whammy Douglas	40.00	20.00	12.00
(7)	Joe Gibbon	40.00	20.00	12.00
(8)	Howie Goss	40.00	20.00	12.00
(9)	Spook Jacobs	50.00	25.00	15.00
(10)	Clyde King	40.00	20.00	12.00
(11)	Cholly Naranjo	40.00	20.00	12.00
(12)	George O'Donnell	40.00	20.00	12.00
(13)	Laurin Pepper	40.00	20.00	12.00
(14)	Dick Rand	40.00	20.00	12.00
(15)	Leo Rodriguez	40.00	20.00	12.00
(16)	Don Rowe	40.00	20.00	12.00
(17)	Art Swanson	40.00	20.00	12.00

1910 Contentnea First Series (T209)

The 1910 Contentnea minor league set actually consists of two distinctively different series, both featuring players from the Virginia League, Carolina Association and Eastern Carolina League. The cards were distributed in packages of Contentnea cigarettes. The first series, featuring color photographs, consists of just 16 cards, each measuring 1-9/16" x 2-11/16". The front of the card has the player's last name and team printed at the bottom, while the back identifies the card as "First Series" and carries an advertisement for Contentnea cigarettes. The second series, believed to have been issued later in 1910, is a massive 221-card set consisting of black-and-white player photos. The cards in this series are slightly larger, measuring 1-5/8" x 2-3/4". They carry the words "Photo Series" on the back, along with the cigarette advertisement. Only a handful of the players in the Contentnea set ever advanced to the major leagues and the set contains no major stars. Subsequently, it generally holds interest only to collectors who specialize in the old southern minor leagues.

	NM	EX	VG
Complete Set (16):	12,500	6,250	3,725
Common Player:	850.00	400.00	250.00
(1) Armstrong	850.00	400.00	250.00
(2) Booles	850.00	400.00	250.00
(3) Bourquise (Bourquoise)	850.00	400.00	250.00
(4) Cooper	850.00	400.00	250.00
(5) Cowell	850.00	400.00	250.00
(6) Crockett	850.00	400.00	250.00
(7) Fullenwider	850.00	400.00	250.00
(8) Gilmore	850.00	400.00	250.00
(9) Hoffman	850.00	400.00	250.00
(10) Lane	850.00	400.00	250.00
(11) Martin	850.00	400.00	250.00
(12) McGeehan	850.00	400.00	250.00
(13) Pope	850.00	400.00	250.00
(14) Sisson	850.00	400.00	250.00
(15) Stubbe	850.00	400.00	250.00
(16) Walsh	850.00	400.00	250.00

1910 Contentnea Photo Series (T209)

PHOTO SERIES OF Virginia Carolina Association Eastern Carolina Leagues. PACKED WITH CONTENTNEA CIGARETTES. Factory No. 12, 4th Dist., N.C.

WOOLUMS, LYNCHBURG

	NM	EX	VG
Common Player:	450.00	200.00	125.00
(1) Abercrombie	450.00	200.00	125.00
(2) Andrada	450.00	200.00	125.00
(3) Armstrong	450.00	200.00	125.00
(4) Averett	450.00	200.00	125.00
(5) Baker	450.00	200.00	125.00
(6) Banner (Bonner)	450.00	200.00	125.00
(7) Bausewein (Bansewein)	450.00	200.00	125.00
(8) Beatty	450.00	200.00	125.00
(9) Bentley	450.00	200.00	125.00
(10) Beusse	450.00	200.00	125.00
(11) Biel	450.00	200.00	125.00
(12) Bigbie (Raleigh)	450.00	200.00	125.00
(13) Bigbie (Richmond)	450.00	200.00	125.00
(14) Blackstone	450.00	200.00	125.00
(15) Bonner	450.00	200.00	125.00
(16) Bourquin	450.00	200.00	125.00
(17) Bowen	450.00	200.00	125.00
(18) Boyle	450.00	200.00	125.00
(19) Brandon	450.00	200.00	125.00
(20) Brazelle (Brazell)	450.00	200.00	125.00
(21) Brent	450.00	200.00	125.00
(22) Brown	450.00	200.00	125.00
(23) Busch	450.00	200.00	125.00
(24) Bussey	450.00	200.00	125.00
(25) Byrd	450.00	200.00	125.00
(26) Cafalu (Cefalu)	450.00	200.00	125.00
(27) Callahan	450.00	200.00	125.00
(28) Chandler	450.00	200.00	125.00
(29) Clapp	450.00	200.00	125.00
(30) Clark (Clarke)	450.00	200.00	125.00
(31) Clemens	450.00	200.00	125.00
(32) Clunk	450.00	200.00	125.00
(33) Cooper	450.00	200.00	125.00
(34) Corbett	450.00	200.00	125.00
(35) Cote	450.00	200.00	125.00
(36) Coutts	450.00	200.00	125.00
(37) Cowan (Cowen)	450.00	200.00	125.00
(38) Cowells (Cowell)	450.00	200.00	125.00
(39) Creagan (Cregan)	450.00	200.00	125.00
(40) Crockett	450.00	200.00	125.00
(41) Lave Cross	450.00	200.00	125.00
(42) Dailey	450.00	200.00	125.00
(43) C. Derrck (Derrick)	450.00	200.00	125.00
(44) F. Derrick	450.00	200.00	125.00
(45) Doak (Greensboro)	450.00	200.00	125.00
(46) Doak (Wilmington)	450.00	200.00	125.00
(47) Dobard	450.00	200.00	125.00
(48) Dobson	450.00	200.00	125.00
(49) Doyle	450.00	200.00	125.00
(50) Drumm	450.00	200.00	125.00
(51) Duvie	450.00	200.00	125.00
(52) Ebinger	450.00	200.00	125.00
(53) Eldridge	450.00	200.00	125.00
(54) Evans	450.00	200.00	125.00
(55) Fairbanks	450.00	200.00	125.00
(56) Farmer	450.00	200.00	125.00
(57) Ferrell	450.00	200.00	125.00
(58) Fisher	450.00	200.00	125.00
(59) Flowers	450.00	200.00	125.00
(60) Fogarty	450.00	200.00	125.00
(61) Foltz	450.00	200.00	125.00
(62) Foreman	450.00	200.00	125.00
(63) Forque	450.00	200.00	125.00
(64) Francis	450.00	200.00	125.00
(65) Fulton	450.00	200.00	125.00
(66) Galvin	450.00	200.00	125.00
(67) Gardin	450.00	200.00	125.00
(68) Garman	450.00	200.00	125.00
(69) Gastmeyer	450.00	200.00	125.00
(70) Gaston	450.00	200.00	125.00
(71) Gates	450.00	200.00	125.00
(72) Gehring	450.00	200.00	125.00
(73) Gillespie	450.00	200.00	125.00
(74) Gorham	450.00	200.00	125.00
(75) Griffin (Danville)	450.00	200.00	125.00
(76) Griffin (Lynchburg)	450.00	200.00	125.00
(77) Guiheen	450.00	200.00	125.00
(78) Gunderson	450.00	200.00	125.00
(79) Hale	450.00	200.00	125.00
(80) Halland (Holland)	450.00	200.00	125.00
(81) Hamilton	450.00	200.00	125.00
(82) Hammersley	450.00	200.00	125.00
(83) Handiboe	450.00	200.00	125.00
(84) Hannifen (Hannifan)	450.00	200.00	125.00
(85) Hargrave	450.00	200.00	125.00
(86) Harrington	450.00	200.00	125.00
(87) Harris	450.00	200.00	125.00
(88) Hart	450.00	200.00	125.00
(89) Hartley	450.00	200.00	125.00
(90) Hawkins	450.00	200.00	125.00
(91) Hearne (Hearn)	450.00	200.00	125.00
(92) Hicks	450.00	200.00	125.00
(93) Hobbs	450.00	200.00	125.00
(94) Hoffman	450.00	200.00	125.00
(95) Hooker	450.00	200.00	125.00
(96) Howard	450.00	200.00	125.00
(97) Howedel (Howedell)	450.00	200.00	125.00
(98) Hudson	450.00	200.00	125.00
(99) Humphrey	450.00	200.00	125.00
(100) Hyames	450.00	200.00	125.00
(101) Irvine	450.00	200.00	125.00
(102) Irving	450.00	200.00	125.00
(103) Jackson (Greensboro)	450.00	200.00	125.00
(104) Jackson (Spartanburg)	450.00	200.00	125.00
(105) Jenkins (Greenville)	450.00	200.00	125.00
(106) Jenkins (Roanoke)	450.00	200.00	125.00
(107) Jobson	450.00	200.00	125.00
(108) Johnson	450.00	200.00	125.00
(109) Keating	450.00	200.00	125.00
(110) Kelley	450.00	200.00	125.00
(111) Kelly (Anderson)	450.00	200.00	125.00
(112) Kelly (Goldsboro)	450.00	200.00	125.00
(113) "King" Kelly	450.00	200.00	125.00
(114) King	450.00	200.00	125.00
(115) Kite	450.00	200.00	125.00
(116) Kunkle	450.00	200.00	125.00
(117) Landgraff	450.00	200.00	125.00
(118) Lane	450.00	200.00	125.00
(119) Lathrop	450.00	200.00	125.00
(120) Lavoia	450.00	200.00	125.00
(121) Levy	450.00	200.00	125.00
(122) Lloyd	450.00	200.00	125.00
(123) Loval	450.00	200.00	125.00
(124) Lucia	450.00	200.00	125.00
(125) Luyster	450.00	200.00	125.00
(126) MacConachie	450.00	200.00	125.00
(127) Malcolm	450.00	200.00	125.00
(128) Martin	450.00	200.00	125.00
(129) Mayberry	450.00	200.00	125.00
(130) A. McCarthy	450.00	200.00	125.00
(131) J. McCarthy	450.00	200.00	125.00
(132) McCormick	450.00	200.00	125.00
(133) McFarland	450.00	200.00	125.00
(134) McFarlin	450.00	200.00	125.00
(135) C. McGeehan	450.00	200.00	125.00
(136) Dan McGeehan	450.00	200.00	125.00
(137) McHugh	450.00	200.00	125.00
(138) McKeavitt (McKevitt)	450.00	200.00	125.00
(139) Merchant	450.00	200.00	125.00
(140) Midkiff	450.00	200.00	125.00
(141) Miller	450.00	200.00	125.00
(142) Missitt	450.00	200.00	125.00
(143) Morgan	450.00	200.00	125.00
(144) Morrissey (Morrisey)	450.00	200.00	125.00
(145) Mullany (Mullaney)	450.00	200.00	125.00
(146) Mullinix	450.00	200.00	125.00
(147) Mundell	450.00	200.00	125.00
(148) Munsen (Munson)	450.00	200.00	125.00
(149) Murdock (Murdoch)	450.00	200.00	125.00
(150) Newton	450.00	200.00	125.00
(151) Noojin	450.00	200.00	125.00
(152) Novak	450.00	200.00	125.00
(153) Ochs	450.00	200.00	125.00
(154) Painter	450.00	200.00	125.00
(155) Peloguin	450.00	200.00	125.00
(156) Phealean (Phelan)	450.00	200.00	125.00
(157) Phoenix	450.00	200.00	125.00
(158) Powell	450.00	200.00	125.00
(159) Presley (Pressley), Pritchard	450.00	200.00	125.00
(160) Priest	450.00	200.00	125.00
(161) Prim	450.00	200.00	125.00
(162) Pritchard	450.00	200.00	125.00
(163) Rawe (Rowe)	450.00	200.00	125.00
(164) Redfern (Redfearn)	450.00	200.00	125.00
(165) Reggy	450.00	200.00	125.00
(166) Richardson	450.00	200.00	125.00
(167) Rickard	450.00	200.00	125.00
(168) Rickert	450.00	200.00	125.00
(169) Ridgeway (Ridgway)	450.00	200.00	125.00
(170) Roth	450.00	200.00	125.00
(171) Salve	450.00	200.00	125.00
(172) Schmidt	450.00	200.00	125.00
(173) Schrader	450.00	200.00	125.00
(174) Schumaker	450.00	200.00	125.00
(175) Sexton	450.00	200.00	125.00
(176) Shanghnessy (Shaughnessy)	450.00	200.00	125.00
(177) Sharp	450.00	200.00	125.00
(178) Shaw	450.00	200.00	125.00
(179) Simmons	450.00	200.00	125.00
(180) A. Smith	450.00	200.00	125.00
(181) D. Smith	450.00	200.00	125.00
(182) Smith (Portsmouth)	450.00	200.00	125.00

		NM	EX	VG
(183)	Spratt	450.00	200.00	125.00
(184)	Springs	450.00	200.00	125.00
(185)	Stewart	450.00	200.00	125.00
(186)	Stoehr	450.00	200.00	125.00
(187)	Stouch	450.00	200.00	125.00
(188)	Sullivan	450.00	200.00	125.00
(189)	Swindell	450.00	200.00	125.00
(190)	Taxis	450.00	200.00	125.00
(191)	Templin	450.00	200.00	125.00
(192)	Thompson	450.00	200.00	125.00
(193)	B.E. Thompson	1,100	500.00	325.00
	(Dressed as Uncle Sam.)			
(194)	Tiedeman	450.00	200.00	125.00
(195)	Titman	450.00	200.00	125.00
(196)	Toner	450.00	200.00	125.00
(197)	Turner	450.00	200.00	125.00
(198)	Tydeman	450.00	200.00	125.00
(199)	Vail	450.00	200.00	125.00
(200)	Verbout	450.00	200.00	125.00
(201)	Vickery	450.00	200.00	125.00
(202)	Walker (Norfolk)	450.00	200.00	125.00
(203)	Walker (Spartanburg)	450.00	200.00	125.00
(204)	Wallace	450.00	200.00	125.00
(205)	Walsh	450.00	200.00	125.00
(206)	Walters	450.00	200.00	125.00
(207)	Waters	450.00	200.00	125.00
(208)	Waymack	450.00	200.00	125.00
(209)	Webb	450.00	200.00	125.00
(210)	Wehrell	450.00	200.00	125.00
(211)	Weldon	450.00	200.00	125.00
(212)	Welsher	450.00	200.00	125.00
(213)	Westlake	450.00	200.00	125.00
(214)	Williams	450.00	200.00	125.00
(215)	Willis	450.00	200.00	125.00
(216)	Wingo	450.00	200.00	125.00
(217)	Wolf	450.00	200.00	125.00
(218)	Wood	450.00	200.00	125.00
(219)	Woolums	450.00	200.00	125.00
(220)	Workman	450.00	200.00	125.00
(221)	Wright	450.00	200.00	125.00
(222)	Wynne	450.00	200.00	125.00

1924 Crescent Ice Cream Hanbury

 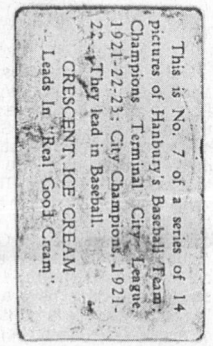

7—Art. Morse
Short Stop

Rather than a professional minor league team, this Canadian set features members of an amateur or semi-pro team sponsored by the Hanbury Sawmill in the Vancouver, B.C., Terminal Amateur League. The 2-1/4" x 1-5/8" black-and-white cards have a player portrait photo in an oval on front, with identification and card number below. On back is an identically worded summation of the team's recent seasons' championships, the card number, and an ad for the sponsor.

		NM	EX	VG
Complete Set (14):		4,000	1,350	800.00
Common Player:		300.00	150.00	90.00
1	Jack Lester/ Mascot	300.00	150.00	90.00
2	Frank Coyle	300.00	150.00	90.00
3	Fred Inch	300.00	150.00	90.00
4	Robt. Mills	300.00	150.00	90.00
5	John Daniels (Capt.)	300.00	150.00	90.00
6	Doug. May	300.00	150.00	90.00
7	Art Morse	300.00	150.00	90.00
8	Chas. Stevenson	300.00	150.00	90.00
9	Tom Raftery	300.00	150.00	90.00
10	Frank Williams	300.00	150.00	90.00
11	Unknown	300.00	150.00	90.00
12	Don Stewart	300.00	150.00	90.00
13	Roy Goodall	300.00	150.00	90.00
14	Cecil Kimberley	300.00	150.00	90.00

1940 Crowley's Milk Binghamton Triplets

Members of the Binghamton, N.Y., Eastern League team are known in this set of 3" x 5" cards. Some have been seen with stamped postcard backs. Blue-and-white player photos are framed by a red rendition of a ballpark scene on the front of the unnumbered cards. Each card has a facsimile autograph ostensibly written by the pictured player. It is unknown whether the checklist below is complete. Several of the players later appeared with the N.Y. Yankees and other teams.

		NM	EX	VG
Complete Set (18):		6,000	3,000	1,800
Common Player:		400.00	200.00	120.00
(1)	Jimmy Adlam	400.00	200.00	120.00
(2)	Russ Bergman	400.00	200.00	120.00
(3)	Bruno Betzel	400.00	200.00	120.00
(4)	Bill Bevens	400.00	200.00	120.00
(5)	Johnny Bianco	400.00	200.00	120.00
(6)	Fred Collins	400.00	200.00	120.00
(7)	Vince DeBiassi	400.00	200.00	120.00
(8)	Jack Graham	400.00	200.00	120.00
(9)	Randy Gumpert	400.00	200.00	120.00
(10)	Al Gurske	400.00	200.00	120.00
(11)	Mike Milosevich	400.00	200.00	120.00
(12)	Billie O'Donnell/Trainer	200.00	100.00	60.00
(13)	Earl Reid	400.00	200.00	120.00
(14)	Aaron Robinson	400.00	200.00	120.00
(15)	Frankie Silvanic	400.00	200.00	120.00
(16)	Pete Suder	400.00	200.00	120.00
(17)	Ray Volps	400.00	200.00	120.00
(18)	Herb White	400.00	200.00	120.00

D

1952 Dallas Eagles Team Issue

A Class AA Texas League farm team of the Cleveland Indians, the Eagles were one of the higher minor league teams chronicled by Globe Printing in its series of 2-1/4" x 3-3/8" blank-back, black-and-white cards sets of the early 1950s. The checklist here is not complete.

		NM	EX	VG
Common Player:		60.00	30.00	18.00
(1)	Dick Aylward	60.00	30.00	18.00
(2)	Jodie Beeler	60.00	30.00	18.00
(3)	Bob Bundy	60.00	30.00	18.00
(4)	Hal Erickson	60.00	30.00	18.00
(5)	Dave Hoskins	60.00	30.00	18.00
(6)	Edward Knoblauch	60.00	30.00	18.00
(7)	Joe Kotrany	60.00	30.00	18.00
(8)	Joe Macko	60.00	30.00	18.00
(9)	Peter Mazar	60.00	30.00	18.00
(10)	Harry Sullivan	60.00	30.00	18.00
(11)	Edward Varhely	60.00	30.00	18.00

1959 Darigold Farms Spokane Indians

TOM DAVIS, Center Field
Compliments of DARIGOLD FARMS

The unnumbered cards in this set were glued to milk cartons by a folded tab at the top of each card. The basic card measures 2-1/2" x 2-3/8", with a 2-1/2" x 2-1/8" tab. Black-and-white player photos are set against colored backgrounds of yellow (1-8), red (9-16) and blue (17-22). Player biographical details and stats are printed in black on the back. Values shown are for cards without the superfluous tabs.

		NM	EX	VG
Complete Set (22):		4,500	2,250	1,350
Common Player:		200.00	100.00	60.00
(1)	Facundo Barragan	200.00	100.00	60.00
(2)	Steve Bilko	225.00	110.00	65.00
(3)	Bobby Bragan	225.00	110.00	65.00
(4)	Chuck Churn	200.00	100.00	60.00
(5)	Tom Davis	450.00	225.00	135.00
(6)	Dom Domenichelli	200.00	100.00	60.00
(7)	Bob Giallombardo	200.00	100.00	60.00
(8)	Connie Grob	200.00	100.00	60.00

		NM	EX	VG
(9)	Fred Hatfield	200.00	100.00	60.00
(10)	Bob Lillis	225.00	110.00	65.00
(11)	Lloyd Merritt	200.00	100.00	60.00
(12)	Larry Miller	200.00	100.00	60.00
(13)	Chris Nicolosi	200.00	100.00	60.00
(14)	Allen Norris	200.00	100.00	60.00
(15)	Phil Ortega	200.00	100.00	60.00
(16)	Phillips Paine	200.00	100.00	60.00
(17)	Bill Parsons	200.00	100.00	60.00
(18)	Hisel Patrick	200.00	100.00	60.00
(19)	Tony Roig	200.00	100.00	60.00
(20)	Tom Saffell	200.00	100.00	60.00
(21)	Norm Sherry	250.00	125.00	75.00
(22)	Ben Wade	200.00	100.00	60.00

1960 Darigold Farms Spokane Indians

For its second annual baseball card set, the dairy added two cards and numbered the issue on the back. Card fronts were black-and-white photos against colored backgrounds of yellow (1-8), green (9-16) and red (17-24). A facsimile autograph appears on the front, as well. The basic card measures 2-3/8" x 2-11/16", with a folded 2-3/8" x 2-1/16" tab at the top, by which the card was glued to a milk carton. Backs are black-and-white. Values shwn are for cards without the superfluous tab.

		NM	EX	VG
Complete Set (24):		4,500	2,250	1,350
Common Player:		145.00	75.00	40.00
1	Chris Nicolosi	145.00	75.00	40.00
2	Jim Pagliaroni	145.00	75.00	40.00
3	Roy Smalley	145.00	75.00	40.00
4	Bill Bethel	145.00	75.00	40.00
5	Joe Liscio	145.00	75.00	40.00
6	Curt Roberts	145.00	75.00	40.00
7	Ed Palmquist	145.00	75.00	40.00
8	Willie Davis	300.00	150.00	90.00
9	Bob Giallombardo	145.00	75.00	40.00
10	Pedro Gomez	145.00	75.00	40.00
11	Mel Nelson	145.00	75.00	40.00
12	Charley Smith	145.00	75.00	40.00
13	Clarence Churn	145.00	75.00	40.00
14	Ramon Conde	145.00	75.00	40.00
15	George O'Donnell	145.00	75.00	40.00
16	Tony Roig	145.00	75.00	40.00
17	Frank Howard	450.00	225.00	135.00
18	Billy Harris	145.00	75.00	40.00
19	Mike Brumley	145.00	75.00	40.00
20	Earl Robinson	145.00	75.00	40.00
21	Ron Fairly	400.00	200.00	120.00
22	Joe Frazier	145.00	75.00	40.00
23	Allen Norris	145.00	75.00	40.00
24	Ford Young	145.00	75.00	40.00

E

1928 Pacific Coast League Exhibits

This regional series of 32 cards pictures players from the six California teams in the Pacific Coast League. Like the 1928 major league Exhibits, the

PCL cards have a blue tint and are not numbered. They are blank-backed and measure 3-3/8" x 5-3/8". The set includes several misspellings. Cards are occasionally found with a corner clipped, the card corner to be used as a coupon with redemption value.

		NM	EX	VG
	Complete Set (32):	17,500	8,750	5,250
	Common Player:	500.00	250.00	150.00
1	Buzz Arlett	800.00	400.00	240.00
2	Earl Averill	1,750	875.00	525.00
3	Carl Berger (Walter)	800.00	400.00	240.00
4	"Ping" Bodie	700.00	350.00	210.00
5	Carl Dittmar	500.00	250.00	150.00
6	Jack Fenton	500.00	250.00	150.00
7	Neal "Mickey" Finn (Cornelius)	500.00	250.00	150.00
8	Ray French	500.00	250.00	150.00
9	Tony Governor	500.00	250.00	150.00
10	"Truck" Hannah	500.00	250.00	150.00
11	Mickey Heath	500.00	250.00	150.00
12	Wally Hood	500.00	250.00	150.00
13	"Fuzzy" Hufft	500.00	250.00	150.00
14	Snead Jolly (Smead Jolley)	600.00	300.00	180.00
15	Bobby "Ducky" Jones	500.00	250.00	150.00
16	Rudy Kallio	500.00	250.00	150.00
17	Ray Keating	500.00	250.00	150.00
18	Johnny Kerr	500.00	250.00	150.00
19	Harry Krause	500.00	250.00	150.00
20	Lynford H. Larry (Lary)	500.00	250.00	150.00
21	Dudley Lee	500.00	250.00	150.00
22	Walter "Duster" Mails	500.00	250.00	150.00
23	Jimmy Reese	650.00	325.00	200.00
24	"Dusty" Rhodes	500.00	250.00	150.00
25	Hal Rhyne	500.00	250.00	150.00
26	Hank Severied (Severeid)	500.00	250.00	150.00
27	Earl Sheely	500.00	250.00	150.00
28	Frank Shellenback	500.00	250.00	150.00
29	Gordon Slade	500.00	250.00	150.00
30	Hollis Thurston	500.00	250.00	150.00
31	"Babe" Twombly	500.00	250.00	150.00
32	Earl "Tex" Weathersby	500.00	250.00	150.00

1953 Montreal Royals Exhibits

Twenty-four Montreal Royals, including many future Brooklyn and L.A. Dodgers and Hall of Fame managers Walt Alston and Tommy Lasorda, were included in a 64-card Canadian issue by Exhibit Supply Co., of Chicago. The cards are slightly smaller, at 3-1/4" x 5-1/4", than standard Exhibits and printed - blank-backed - on gray stock. Numbered on front, cards of the Montreal players can be found in either blue or reddish-brown tint. Only the Royals players from the issue are checklisted here.

		NM	EX	VG
	Complete Set (24):	450.00	225.00	135.00
	Common Player:	15.00	7.50	4.50
33	Don Hoak	25.00	12.50	7.50
34	Bob Alexander	15.00	7.50	4.50
35	John Simmons	15.00	7.50	4.50
36	Steve Lembo	15.00	7.50	4.50
37	Norm Larker	20.00	10.00	6.00
38	Bob Ludwick	15.00	7.50	4.50
39	Walt Moryn	20.00	10.00	6.00
40	Charlie Thompson	15.00	7.50	4.50
41	Ed Roebuck	20.00	10.00	6.00
42	Russell Rose	15.00	7.50	4.50
43	Edmundo (Sandy) Amoros	25.00	12.50	7.50
44	Bob Milliken	15.00	7.50	4.50
45	Art Fabbro	15.00	7.50	4.50
46	Spook Jacobs	15.00	7.50	4.50
47	Carmen Mauro	15.00	7.50	4.50
48	Walter Fiala	15.00	7.50	4.50
49	Rocky Nelson	15.00	7.50	4.50
50	Tom La Sorda (Lasorda)	60.00	30.00	18.00
51	Ronnie Lee	15.00	7.50	4.50
52	Hampton Coleman	15.00	7.50	4.50
53	Frank Marchio	15.00	7.50	4.50
54	William Sampson	15.00	7.50	4.50
55	Gil Mills	15.00	7.50	4.50
56	Al Ronning	15.00	7.50	4.50
61	Walt Alston	40.00	20.00	12.00

F

1953 Fargo-Moorhead Twins Team Issue

This set of team-issued cards includes the first of future home-run king Roger Maris (spelled Maras in the traditional family manner). The cards are about 3-1/4" x 5-5/16" with a white border surrounding a black-and-white posed photo. Player identification is in three lines of white type at lower-left. Backs are blank, except some cards which bear a rubber-stamped promotional message from the "Red River Scenes" newspaper. The unnumbered cards are checklisted here in alphabetical order. Three of the players are known in two or more poses.

		NM	EX	VG
	Complete Set (21):	3,500	1,750	1,000
	Common Player:	60.00	30.00	18.00
(1)	Zeke Bonura	60.00	30.00	18.00
(2)	Bob Borovicka	60.00	30.00	18.00
(3)	Ken Braeseke	60.00	30.00	18.00
(4)	Joe Camacho	60.00	30.00	18.00
(5)	Galen Fiss	60.00	30.00	18.00
(6)	Frank Gravino (Batting follow-through.)	60.00	30.00	18.00
(7)	Frank Gravino (Hands on hips.)	60.00	30.00	18.00
(8)	Frank Gravino (Hands on knees.)	60.00	30.00	18.00
(9)	Santo Luberto/Fielding	60.00	30.00	18.00
(10)	Roger Maras/Fielding	1,250	625.00	375.00
(11)	Roger Maras/Btg	1,250	625.00	375.00
(12)	Jerry Mehlish (Mehlisch)	60.00	30.00	18.00
(13)	Bob Melton	60.00	30.00	18.00
(14)	Ray Mendoza (Stretching at 1B, ball in glove.)	60.00	30.00	18.00
(15)	Ray Mendoza (Stretching at 1B, no ball.)	60.00	30.00	18.00
(16)	John Morse	60.00	30.00	18.00
(17)	Don Nance	60.00	30.00	18.00
(18)	Ray Seif	60.00	30.00	18.00
(19)	Will Sirois	60.00	30.00	18.00
(20)	Dick Wegner	60.00	30.00	18.00
(21)	Don Wolf	60.00	30.00	18.00

1966 Foremost Milk St. Petersburg Cardinals

This 20-card black-and-white set includes players and the manager, Sparky Anderson, of the Florida State League farm club of the St. Louis Cardinals. The unnumbered, blank-backed cards measure 3-1/2" x 5-1/2".

		NM	EX	VG
	Complete Set (20):	50.00	25.00	15.00
	Common Player:	2.50	1.25	.75
(1)	George "Sparky" Anderson	17.50	8.75	5.25
(2)	Dave Bakenhaster	2.50	1.25	.75
(3)	Leonard Boyer	4.00	2.00	1.25
(4)	Ron Braddock	2.50	1.25	.75
(5)	Thomas "Chip" Coulter	2.50	1.25	.75
(6)	Ernest "Sweet Pea" Davis	2.50	1.25	.75
(7)	Phil Knuckles	2.50	1.25	.75
(8)	Doug Lukens	2.50	1.25	.75
(9)	Terry Milani	2.50	1.25	.75
(10)	Tim Morgan	2.50	1.25	.75
(11)	Harry Parker	2.50	1.25	.75
(12)	Jerry Robertson	2.50	1.25	.75
(13)	Francisco Rodriguez	2.50	1.25	.75
(14)	John "Sonny" Ruberto	2.50	1.25	.75
(15)	Charlie Stewart	2.50	1.25	.75
(16)	Gary L. Stone	2.50	1.25	.75
(17)	Charles "Tim" Thompson	2.50	1.25	.75
(18)	Jose Villar	2.50	1.25	.75
(19)	Archie L. Wade	2.50	1.25	.75
(20)	Jim Williamson	2.50	1.25	.75

1921 Frederick Foto Service

This issue comprises a mix of Pacific Coast League and Major League players. Because Frederick Foto was located in Sacramento, a preponderance of the minor leaguers are Sacramento Senators. The method of the cards' distribution is unknkown. The cards are black-and-white glossy photographs glued to a cardboard backing. The photos are bordered in white with top and bottom borders considerably wider than those on the sides. About 1-3/16" x 2-5/8", the cards have blank backs. On front is the player's last name and city, printed in a hand-lettered style. Most cards have a "Freredick / Foto." credit in the same style. Other cards have a banner-and-circle "Foto / Frederick / Service logo." It is likely this checklist is not complete. Gaps have been left in the assigned numbering for future additions.

		NM	EX	VG
	Common Player:	300.00	150.00	90.00
(1)	Alexander	300.00	150.00	90.00
(2)	Ike Caveny (Caveney)	300.00	150.00	90.00
(3)	Pete Compton	300.00	150.00	90.00
(4)	Les Cook/Btg	300.00	150.00	90.00
(5)	Les Cook/Fielding	300.00	150.00	90.00
(7)	Carroll Canfield	300.00	150.00	90.00
(8)	Brick Eldred	300.00	150.00	90.00
(9)	Rowdy Elliott	300.00	150.00	90.00
(11)	Tony Faeth	300.00	150.00	90.00
(12)	Paul Fittery	300.00	150.00	90.00
(14)	Griffith	300.00	150.00	90.00
(15)	Charlie Hollocher	300.00	150.00	90.00
(16)	Willie Kamm	300.00	150.00	90.00
(18)	Manny Kopp	300.00	150.00	90.00
(19)	Earl Kuntz (Kunz)	300.00	150.00	90.00
(21)	Duster Mails (Arms at sides.)	300.00	150.00	90.00
(22)	Duster Mails (Hands at chest.)	300.00	150.00	90.00
(23)	Duster Mails (Follow-thru.)	300.00	150.00	90.00
(24)	Duster Mails (Wind-up.)	300.00	150.00	90.00
(26)	Patsy McGaffigan	300.00	150.00	90.00
(27)	Roxie Middleton	300.00	150.00	90.00
(28)	Hack Miller	350.00	175.00	105.00
(31)	Dick Niehaus	300.00	150.00	90.00
(32)	Billy Orr/Btg	300.00	150.00	90.00
(32)	Billy Orr (Hands on knees.)	300.00	150.00	90.00
(33)	Dode Paskert	300.00	150.00	90.00
(34)	Ken Penner (Right foot off ground.)	300.00	150.00	90.00
(35)	Ken Penner (Right foot on ground.)	300.00	150.00	90.00
(36)	Charlie Pick	300.00	150.00	90.00
(37)	Babe Pinelli	400.00	200.00	120.00
(39)	Bill Prough	300.00	150.00	90.00
(41)	Addison Read	300.00	150.00	90.00
(43)	Bill Rodgers	300.00	150.00	90.00
(44)	Pete Rose	300.00	150.00	90.00
(45)	Babe Ruth	20,000	10,000	6,000
(46)	Buddy Ryan (Holding bat, 3/4 length.)	300.00	150.00	90.00
(47)	Buddy Ryan (Holding bat, full-length.)	300.00	150.00	90.00
(48)	Buddy Ryan (Swinging bat.)	300.00	150.00	90.00
(50)	Bobby Schang	300.00	150.00	90.00
(52)	Les Sheehan	300.00	150.00	90.00
(60)	Kettle Wirts (Chicago)	300.00	150.00	90.00

		NM	EX	VG
(61)	Kettle Wirts (Dallas)	300.00	150.00	90.00
(62)	Archie Yelle	300.00	150.00	90.00
		300.00	150.00	90.00
	Unidentified player, arms folded.	300.00	150.00	90.00
	Unidentified player, batting follow-thru.	300.00	150.00	90.00

1951 Fresno Cardinals Team Issue

These 2-1/4" x 3-3/8" black-and-white, unnumbered, blank-backed cards were one of many minor league team sets issued by Globe Printing of San Jose, Calif., in the early 1950s. Cards were usually given away at the ballpark on a one-per-week or one-per-homestand basis, accounting for the rarity of surviving sets. The team was a California League (Class C) affiliate of the St. Louis Cardinals.

		NM	EX	VG
	Complete Set (17):	1,000	500.00	300.00
	Common Player:	60.00	30.00	18.00
(1)	Hal Atkinson	60.00	30.00	18.00
(2)	Larry Barton	60.00	30.00	18.00
(3)	Charlie Brooks	60.00	30.00	18.00
(4)	Bill Burton	60.00	30.00	18.00
(5)	Ray Herrera	60.00	30.00	18.00
(6)	Earl Jones	60.00	30.00	18.00
(7)	Jim King	60.00	30.00	18.00
(8)	Whitey Lageman	60.00	30.00	18.00
(9)	Wally Lamers	60.00	30.00	18.00
(10)	John McNamara	75.00	37.00	22.00
(11)	Gerry Mertz	60.00	30.00	18.00
(12)	Frank Olasin	60.00	30.00	18.00
(13)	Howie Phillips	60.00	30.00	18.00
(14)	Jack Ramsey	60.00	30.00	18.00
(15)	Tony Stathos	60.00	30.00	18.00
(16)	Whit Ulrich	60.00	30.00	18.00
(17)	Pete Younie	60.00	30.00	18.00

1952 Frostade

(See 1952 Parkhurst)

1954 Fruiterie Saint Louis Tommy Lasorda

The date of issue attributed is only a best guess. It is also unknown how many other Montreal Royals players may be found in this issue. Printed in black-and-white on fairly thick 5-1/2" x 7" cardboard, this card features a portrait photo of the Royals' pitcher and future Hall of Fame manager along with a facsimile autograph on the borderless front. Rubber-stamped at top of the otherwise blank back is: "Fruiterie / Saint Louis De Franos / 515 RUE ROY PL. 1729," presumably identification of a Montreal business which distributed the card.

	NM	EX	VG
Tommy Lasorda	100.00	50.00	30.00

G

1911 Gilmartin Printing Co. S.F. Seals

These extremely scarce cards were issued as a premium by the Gilmartin Printing Co. of San Fran-

cisco and feature only members of the city's PCL Seals team. The 5" x 7" cards have full-length posed portraits of the players at center, printed in a blue-green tone and surrounded by a wide white border. The player's name, position team and year are scripted in the lower-left corner of the photo. Backs are blank. This checklist is known to be incomplete. Some cards have the sponsor's imprint below the photo.

		NM	EX	VG
	Common Player:	3,000	1,500	900.00
(1)	Claude Berry	3,000	1,500	900.00
(2)	Frank Browning	3,000	1,500	900.00
(6)	Willard Meikle	3,000	1,500	900.00
(7)	Frank Miller	3,000	1,500	900.00
(9)	Harry Sutor	3,000	1,500	900.00
(10)	Tom Tennant	3,000	1,500	900.00
(12)	Geo. Weaver	9,000	4,500	2,700

1956-57 Gil's Drive-Ins Seattle Rainiers

(See 1956-57 Seattle Popcorn for checklist and values.)

1951-1954 Globe Printing

The team-issue card sets and souvenir picture albums listed in previous editions under the heading of Globe Printing are now found alphabetically by team name as per this list:

1951 Fresno Cardinals
1951 San Jose Red Sox
1952 Atlanta Crackers
1952 Baltimore Orioles
1952 Colorado Springs Sky Sox
1952 Columbus Cardinals
1952 Dallas Eagles
1952 Ft. Worth Cats
1952 Great Falls Electrics
1952 Jamestown Falcons
1952 Miami Beach Flamingos
1952 Ogden Reds
1952 Oshkosh Giants
1952 San Diego Padres
1952 Shawnee Hawks
1952-1953 Sioux City Soos
1952 Syracuse Chiefs
1952 Ventura Braves
1954 Sioux City Soos

1943 Golden Quality Ice Cream Wilkes-Barre Barons

This rare war-time minor league issue depicts the Hall of Fame manager, Tony Lazzeri, and players on the Class A Eastern League Barons. The 4" x 5" black-and-white cards have facsimile player autographs. Printed in the bottom border at left are the team and year; at right is "Compliments of Golden Quality Ice Cream Co."

		NM	EX	VG
	Complete Set (6):	600.00	300.00	180.00
	Common Player:	75.00	37.50	22.50
(1)	Alex Damalitron	75.00	37.50	22.50
(2)	Tony Lazzeri (Bat on shoulder.)	175.00	90.00	55.00
(3)	Tony Lazzeri (Hands on knees.)	175.00	90.00	55.00
(4)	Jim McDonnell	75.00	37.50	22.50
(5)	Joe Pennington	75.00	37.50	22.50
(6)	Ned Tryon	75.00	37.50	22.50

1957 Golden State Dairy S.F. Seals Stickers

There are 23 stickers known in this set, featuring the last minor league team in San Francisco. Virtually every player who appeared in more than 10 games for the Seals that season is included in the set. The stickers measure approximately 2" x 2-1/2", are printed in black-and-white, and blank-backed. A 3-1/2" x 6" album to house the stickers was also issued, with biographical data and space for an autograph on each player's page. The stickers are checklisted here alphabetically, as the stickers are unnumbered.

		NM	EX	VG
	Complete Set (23):	550.00	275.00	165.00
	Common Player:	25.00	12.50	7.50
	Album:	150.00	75.00	45.00
(1)	William "Bill" Abernathie	25.00	12.50	7.50
(2)	Kenneth "Chip" Aspromonte	25.00	12.50	7.50
(3)	Harry "Fritz" Dorish	25.00	12.50	7.50
(4)	Joe "Flash" Gordon	25.00	12.50	7.50
(5)	Grady Hatton Jr.	25.00	12.50	7.50
(6)	Thomas "Tommy" Hurd	25.00	12.50	7.50
(7)	Frank Kellert	25.00	12.50	7.50
(8)	Richard "Marty" Keough	25.00	12.50	7.50
(9)	Leo "Black Cat" Kiely	25.00	12.50	7.50
(10)	Harry William Malmberg	25.00	12.50	7.50
(11)	John McCall	25.00	12.50	7.50
(12)	Albert "Albie" Pearson	40.00	20.00	12.00
(13)	Jack Phillips	25.00	12.50	7.50
(14)	William "Bill" Renna	25.00	12.50	7.50
(15)	Edward "Ed" Sadowski	25.00	12.50	7.50
(16)	Robert W. Smith	25.00	12.50	7.50
(17)	Jack Spring	25.00	12.50	7.50
(18)	Jospeh H. Tanner	25.00	12.50	7.50
(19)	Salvador "Sal" Taormina	25.00	12.50	7.50
(20)	Maynard "Bert" Thiel	25.00	12.50	7.50
(21)	Anthony "Nini" Tornay	25.00	12.50	7.50
(22)	Thomas "Tommy" Umphlett	25.00	12.50	7.50
(23)	Glenn "Cap" Wright	25.00	12.50	7.50

1943 Grand Studio Milwaukee Brewers

It's unknown how these blank-backed, black-and-white, 3-1/2" x 5-1/2" pictures were distributed. The only identification is "PHOTO BY GRAND STUDIO" in the lower-right corner. It's likely the pictures were sold as a set at Borchert Field.

		NM	EX	VG
Complete Set (22):		1,000	500.00	300.00
Common Player:		60.00	30.00	20.00
(1)	Joe Berry	60.00	30.00	20.00
(2)	Bob Bowman	60.00	30.00	20.00
(3)	Earl Caldwell	60.00	30.00	20.00
(4)	Grey Clarke	60.00	30.00	20.00
(5)	Merv Conner	60.00	30.00	20.00
(6)	Paul Erickson	60.00	30.00	20.00
(7)	Charlie Grimm	80.00	40.00	25.00
(8)	Hank Helf	60.00	30.00	20.00
(9)	Don Johnson	60.00	30.00	20.00
(10)	Wes Livengood	60.00	30.00	20.00
(11)	Hershell Martin	60.00	30.00	20.00
(12)	Tommy Nelson	60.00	30.00	20.00
(13)	Ted Norbert	60.00	30.00	20.00
(14)	Bill Norman	60.00	30.00	20.00
(15)	Henry Oana	125.00	65.00	40.00
(16)	Jimmy Pruett	60.00	30.00	20.00
(17)	Bill Sahlin	60.00	30.00	20.00
(18)	Frank Secroy	60.00	30.00	20.00
(19)	Red Smith	60.00	30.00	20.00
(20)	Charles Sproull	60.00	30.00	20.00
(21)	Hugh Todd	60.00	30.00	20.00
(22)	Tony York	60.00	30.00	20.00

1944 Grand Studio Milwaukee Brewers

Future Hall of Fame manager Casey Stengel is featured in the second of three annual team-issued photocard sets. The 3-1/2" x 5-1/2" cards have black-and-white portrait photos with facsimile autographs, bordered in white. Backs are blank.

		NM	EX	VG
Complete Set (26):		900.00	450.00	275.00
Common Player:		50.00	25.00	15.00
(1)	Julio Acosta	50.00	25.00	15.00
(2)	Heinz Becker	50.00	25.00	15.00
(3)	George Binks	50.00	25.00	15.00
(4)	Bob Bowman	50.00	25.00	15.00
(5)	Earl Caldwell	50.00	25.00	15.00
(6)	Dick Culler	50.00	25.00	15.00
(7)	Roy Easterwood	50.00	25.00	15.00
(8)	Jack Farmer	50.00	25.00	15.00
(9)	Charles Gassaway	50.00	25.00	15.00
(10)	Dick Hearn	50.00	25.00	15.00
(11)	Don Hendrickson	50.00	25.00	15.00
(12)	Ed Levy	50.00	25.00	15.00
(13)	Hershel Martin	50.00	25.00	15.00
(14)	Bill Nagel	50.00	25.00	15.00
(15)	Tommy Nelson	50.00	25.00	15.00
(16)	Bill Norman	50.00	25.00	15.00
(17)	Hal Peck	50.00	25.00	15.00
(18)	Jimmy Pruett	50.00	25.00	15.00
(19)	Ken Raddant	50.00	25.00	15.00
(20)	Owen Scheetz	50.00	25.00	15.00
(21)	Eddie Scheive	50.00	25.00	15.00
(22)	Frank Secory	50.00	25.00	15.00
(23)	Red Smith	50.00	25.00	15.00
(24)	Floyd Speer	50.00	25.00	15.00
(25)	Charlie Sproull	50.00	25.00	15.00
(26)	Casey Stengel	300.00	150.00	90.00

1945 Grand Studio Milwaukee Brewers

The format remained unchanged for the last of three annual team-issued photocard sets. The 3-1/2" x 5-1/2" cards have black-and-white portrait photos with facsimile autographs, bordered in white. Backs are blank.

		NM	EX	VG
Complete Set (16):		625.00	300.00	175.00
Common Player:		50.00	25.00	15.00
(1)	Julio Acosta	50.00	25.00	15.00
(2)	Arky Biggs	50.00	25.00	15.00
(3)	Bill Burgo	50.00	25.00	15.00
(4)	Nick Cullop	50.00	25.00	15.00
(5)	Wendell "Peaches" Davis	50.00	25.00	15.00
(6)	Otto Denning	50.00	25.00	15.00
(7)	Lew Flick	50.00	25.00	15.00
(8)	Don Hendrickson	50.00	25.00	15.00
(9)	Ed Kobersky	50.00	25.00	15.00
(10)	Carl Lindquist	50.00	25.00	15.00
(11)	Jack McGillen	50.00	25.00	15.00
(12)	Gene Nance	50.00	25.00	15.00
(13)	Bill Norman	50.00	25.00	15.00
(14)	Joe Rullo	50.00	25.00	15.00
(15)	Owen Scheetz	50.00	25.00	15.00
(16)	Floyd Speer	50.00	25.00	15.00

1952 Great Falls Electrics Team Issue

Formatted like the other known minor league issues from Globe Printing of San Jose, Calif., in the early 1950s, this set chronicles the 1952 version of the Class C (Pioneer League) Great Falls (Montana) Electrics, a farm club of the Brooklyn Dodgers. The blank-backed cards are black-and-white and measure about 2-1/4" x 3-3/8". An album was issued with the cards.

		NM	EX	VG
Complete Set (16):		800.00	400.00	240.00
Common Player:		60.00	30.00	18.00
(1)	Don Bricker	60.00	30.00	18.00
(2)	Larry Hampshire	60.00	30.00	18.00
(3)	Ernie Jordan	60.00	30.00	18.00
(4)	Lou Landini	60.00	30.00	18.00
(5)	Danny Lastres	60.00	30.00	18.00
(6)	Joe Oliffe	60.00	30.00	18.00
(7)	Len Payne	60.00	30.00	18.00
(8)	Lou Rochelli	60.00	30.00	18.00
(9)	Earl Silverthorn	60.00	30.00	18.00
(10)	Eddie Serrano	60.00	30.00	18.00
(11)	Rick Small	60.00	30.00	18.00
(12)	Dick Smith	60.00	30.00	18.00
(13)	Hal Snyder	60.00	30.00	18.00
(14)	Armando Suarez	60.00	30.00	18.00
(15)	Emy Unzicker	60.00	30.00	18.00
Album:		100.00	50.00	30.00

1888 Gypsy Queen California League

Until further specimens are reported, the attributed date of issue is speculative between about 1887-89. Undiscovered until 1998 was the fact that Gypsy Queen, a cigarette manufactured by Goodwin & Co. (Old Judge, etc.) had issued minor league cards, presumably of the relatively new California League. Like some contemporary issues, the card is a stiff piece of cardboard with a sepia-toned player photo glued to it. Size is about 1-1/2" x 2-1/2". As of November, 2001, only one card was known from this issue. In Fair to Good condition it was sold at auction for $80,273, then a record price for any 19th Century card.

(1)   Jas McDonald

1949 Hage's Dairy

Hage's Dairy of California began a three-year run of regional baseball cards featuring Pacific Coast League players in 1949. The cards were distributed inside popcorn boxes at the concession stand in Lane Field Park, home of the P.C.L. San Diego Padres. The 1949 set, like the following two years, was printed on thin stock measuring on average 2-5/8" x 3-1/8". The checklist includes several different poses for some of the players. Cards were continually being added or withdrawn to reflect roster changes on the minor league clubs. The Hage's sets were dominated by San Diego players, but also included representatives from the seven other P.C.L. teams. The 1949 cards can be found in four different tints - sepia, green, blue, and black-and-white. The unnumbered cards have blank backs or advertising messages on back. The player's name and team appear inside a box on the front of the card, and the 1949 cards can be dated by the large (quarter-inch) type used for the team names, which are sometimes referred to by city and other times by nickname.

		NM	EX	VG
Complete Set (106):		40,000	20,000	10,000
Common Player:		400.00	200.00	100.00
(1)	"Buster" Adams	400.00	200.00	100.00
(2)	"Red" Adams	400.00	200.00	100.00
(3)	Lee Anthony	400.00	200.00	100.00
(4)	Rinaldo Ardizoia	400.00	200.00	100.00
(5)	Del Baker	400.00	200.00	100.00
(6)	Ed Basinski	400.00	200.00	100.00
(7)	Jim Baxes	400.00	200.00	100.00
(8)	H. Becker	400.00	200.00	100.00
(9)	Herman Besse	400.00	200.00	100.00
(10)	Tom Bridges	400.00	200.00	100.00
(11)	Gene Brocker	400.00	200.00	100.00
(12)	Ralph Buxton	400.00	200.00	100.00
(13)	Mickey Burnett	400.00	200.00	100.00
(14)	Dain Clay/Pose	400.00	200.00	100.00
(15)	Dain Clay/Btg	400.00	200.00	100.00
(16)	Dain Corriden, Jim Reese	475.00	235.00	120.00
(17)	Pete Coscarart	400.00	200.00	100.00
(18)	Dom Dallessandro	400.00	200.00	100.00
(19)	Con Dempsey	400.00	200.00	100.00
(20)	Vince DiBiasi	400.00	200.00	100.00
(21)	Luke Easter (Batting stance.)	600.00	300.00	150.00
(22)	Luke Easter (Batting follow thru.)	600.00	300.00	150.00
(23)	Ed Fernandez	400.00	200.00	100.00
(24)	Les Fleming	400.00	200.00	100.00
(25)	Jess Flores	400.00	200.00	100.00
(26)	Cecil Garriott	400.00	200.00	100.00
(27)	Charles Gassaway	400.00	200.00	100.00
(28)	Mickey Grasso	400.00	200.00	100.00
(29)	Will Hafey/Pitching	400.00	200.00	100.00
(30)	Will Hafey/Pose	400.00	200.00	100.00
(31)	"Jeep" Handley	400.00	200.00	100.00
(32)	"Bucky" Harris/Pose	600.00	300.00	150.00
(33)	"Bucky" Harris/Shouting	600.00	300.00	150.00
(34)	Roy Helser	400.00	200.00	100.00
(35)	Lloyd Hittle	400.00	200.00	100.00
(36)	Ralph Hodgin	400.00	200.00	100.00
(37)	Leroy Jarvis	400.00	200.00	100.00
(38)	John Jensen	400.00	200.00	100.00
(39)	Al Jurisich	400.00	200.00	100.00
(40)	Herb Karpel	600.00	300.00	150.00
(41)	Frank Kelleher	400.00	200.00	100.00
(42)	Bill Kelly	400.00	200.00	100.00
(43)	Bob Kelly	400.00	200.00	100.00
(44)	Frank Kerr	400.00	200.00	100.00

		NM	EX	VG
(45)	Thomas Kipp	400.00	200.00	100.00
(46)	Al Lien	400.00	200.00	100.00
(47)	Lyman Linde/Pose	400.00	200.00	100.00
(48)	Lyman Linde/Pitching	400.00	200.00	100.00
(49)	Dennis Luby	400.00	200.00	100.00
(50)	"Red" Lynn	400.00	200.00	100.00
(51)	Pat Malone	400.00	200.00	100.00
(52)	Billy Martin	1,250	625.00	375.00
(53)	Joe Marty	400.00	200.00	100.00
(54)	Cliff Melton	400.00	200.00	100.00
(55)	Steve Mesner	400.00	200.00	100.00
(56)	Leon Mohr	400.00	200.00	100.00
(57)	"Butch" Moran	400.00	200.00	100.00
(58)	Glen Moulder	400.00	200.00	100.00
(59)	Steve Nagy	400.00	200.00	100.00
(60)	Roy Nicely	400.00	200.00	100.00
(61)	Walt Nothe	400.00	200.00	100.00
(62)	John O'Neill	400.00	200.00	100.00
(63)	"Pluto" Oliver	400.00	200.00	100.00
(64)	Al Olsen/Pose	400.00	200.00	100.00
(65)	Al Olsen/Throwing	400.00	200.00	100.00
(66)	John Ostrowski	400.00	200.00	100.00
(67)	Roy Partee	400.00	200.00	100.00
(68)	Bill Raimondi	400.00	200.00	100.00
(69)	Bill Ramsey	400.00	200.00	100.00
(70)	Len Ratto	400.00	200.00	100.00
(71)	Xavier Rescigno	400.00	200.00	100.00
(72)	John Ritchey/Btg	400.00	200.00	100.00
(73)	John Ritchey/Catching	400.00	200.00	100.00
(74)	Mickey Rocco	400.00	200.00	100.00
(75)	John Rucker	400.00	200.00	100.00
(76)	Clarence Russell	400.00	200.00	100.00
(77)	Jack Salverson	400.00	200.00	100.00
(78)	Charlie Schanz	400.00	200.00	125.00
(79)	Bill Schuster	400.00	200.00	100.00
(80)	Tom Seats	400.00	200.00	100.00
(81)	Neil Sheridan	400.00	200.00	100.00
(82)	Vince Shupe	400.00	200.00	100.00
(83)	Joe Sprinz	400.00	200.00	100.00
(84)	Chuck Stevens	400.00	200.00	100.00
(85)	Harvey Storey	400.00	200.00	100.00
(86)	Jim Tabor (Sacramento)	400.00	200.00	100.00
(87)	Jim Tabor (Seattle)	400.00	200.00	100.00
(88)	"Junior" Thompson	400.00	200.00	100.00
(89)	Arky Vaughn	625.00	310.00	175.00
(90)	Jackie Warner	400.00	200.00	100.00
(91)	Jim Warner	400.00	200.00	100.00
(92)	Dick Wenner	400.00	200.00	100.00
(93)	Max West/Pose	400.00	200.00	100.00
(94)	Max West (Batting swing.)	400.00	200.00	100.00
(95)	Max West (Batting follow-thru.)	400.00	200.00	100.00
(96)	Hank Weyse	400.00	200.00	100.00
(97)	"Fuzzy" White	400.00	200.00	100.00
(98)	Jo Jo White	400.00	200.00	100.00
(99)	Artie Wilson	400.00	200.00	100.00
(100)	Bill Wilson	400.00	200.00	100.00
(101)	Bobbie Wilson/Pose	400.00	200.00	100.00
(102)	Bobbie Wilson/Pitching	400.00	200.00	100.00
(103)	"Pinky" Woods	400.00	200.00	100.00
(104)	Tony York	400.00	200.00	100.00
(105)	Del Young	400.00	200.00	100.00
(106)	Frank Zak	400.00	200.00	100.00

1950 Hage's Dairy

Orestes Minoso
SAN DIEGO

Your FAVORITE Brand

Hage's ICE CREAM

ORESTES MINOSO... The Padres...

The 1950 P.C.L. set from Hage's Dairy was similar in design and size (about 2-5/8" x 3-1/8") to the previous year and was again distributed in popcorn boxes at San Diego's Lane Field. The 1950 cards are in black-and-white with a back containing an advertisement for Hage's Milk, Ice Cream or Ice Cream Bars. The advertising backs also contain the player's name and either brief 1949 statistics or career highlights at bottom. Many players were issued in more than one pose. Again, Padres dominate the unnumbered set with lesser representation from the other P.C.L. clubs. For the 1950 edition all team names are referred to by city (no nicknames) and the typeface is smaller. Gaps have been left in the assigned numbering to accommodate future additions to the checklist.

		NM	EX	VG
Complete Set (128):		45,000	22,500	13,500
Common Player:		375.00	185.00	110.00
(1)	"Buster" Adams/Kneeling	375.00	185.00	110.00
(2a)	"Buster" Adams (Batting follow-thru, with inscription.)	375.00	185.00	110.00
(2b)	"Buster" Adams (Batting follow-thru, no inscription.)	375.00	185.00	110.00
(2c)	"Buster" Adams (Batting follow-thru, body to left.)	375.00	185.00	110.00
(3a)	"Buster" Adams (Batting stance, caption box touching waist.)	375.00	185.00	110.00
(3b)	"Buster" Adams (Batting stance, caption box not touching waist.)	375.00	185.00	110.00
(4)	"Red" Adams	375.00	185.00	110.00

		NM	EX	VG
(5)	Dewey Adkins (Photo actually Albie Glossop.)	375.00	185.00	110.00
(6)	Rinaldo Ardizoia	375.00	185.00	110.00
(7)	Jose Bache	375.00	185.00	110.00
(8a)	Del Baker, Jim Reese (Bat visible at lower right.)	375.00	185.00	110.00
(8b)	Del Baker, Jim Reese (No bat visible.)	375.00	185.00	110.00
(9)	George Bamberger	375.00	185.00	110.00
(10)	Richard Barrett	375.00	185.00	110.00
(11)	Frank Baumholtz	375.00	185.00	110.00
(12)	Henry Behrman	375.00	185.00	110.00
(13)	Bill Bevens	375.00	185.00	110.00
(14)	Ernie Bickhaus	375.00	185.00	110.00
(15)	Bill Burgher/Pose	375.00	185.00	110.00
(16)	Bill Burgher/Catching	375.00	185.00	110.00
(17)	Mark Christman	375.00	185.00	110.00
(18)	Clint Conatser	375.00	185.00	110.00
(19)	Herb Conyers/Fielding	375.00	185.00	110.00
(20)	Herb Conyers/Btg	375.00	185.00	110.00
(21)	Jim Davis	375.00	185.00	110.00
(22)	Ted Del Guercio	375.00	185.00	110.00
(23)	Vince DiBiasi	375.00	185.00	110.00
(24)	Jess Dobernic	375.00	185.00	110.00
(25)	"Red" Embree/Pose	375.00	185.00	110.00
(26)	"Red" Embree/Pitching	375.00	185.00	110.00
(27)	Elbie Fletcher	375.00	185.00	110.00
(28)	Guy Fletcher	375.00	185.00	110.00
(30)	Tony Freitas	375.00	185.00	110.00
(31)	Denny Galehouse	375.00	185.00	110.00
(32)	Jack Graham/Pose (Looking to left.)	375.00	185.00	110.00
(33)	Jack Graham/Pose (Looking straight ahead.)	375.00	185.00	110.00
(34)	Jack Graham (Batting swing.)	375.00	185.00	110.00
(35)	Jack Graham (Batting stance.)	375.00	185.00	110.00
(36)	Orval Grove	375.00	185.00	110.00
(37)	Lee Handley	375.00	185.00	110.00
(38)	Ralph Hodgin	375.00	185.00	110.00
(39)	Don Johnson	375.00	185.00	110.00
(40)	Al Jurisich/Pose	375.00	185.00	110.00
(41)	Al Jurisich (Pitching wind-up.)	375.00	185.00	110.00
(42)	Al Jurisich (Pitching follow-thru.)	375.00	185.00	110.00
(43)	Bill Kelly	375.00	185.00	110.00
(44)	Frank Kerr	375.00	185.00	110.00
(45)	Tom Kipp/Pose	375.00	185.00	110.00
(46)	Tom Kipp/Pitching	375.00	185.00	110.00
(47)	Mel Knezovich	375.00	185.00	110.00
(48)	Red Kress	375.00	185.00	110.00
(49)	Dario Lodigiani	375.00	185.00	110.00
(50)	Dennis Luby/Pose	375.00	185.00	110.00
(51)	Dennis Luby/Throwing	375.00	185.00	110.00
(52)	Al Lyons	375.00	185.00	110.00
(53)	Clarence Maddern	375.00	185.00	110.00
(54)	Joe Marty	375.00	185.00	110.00
(55)	Bob McCall	375.00	185.00	110.00
(56)	Cal McIrvin	375.00	185.00	110.00
(57)	Orestes Minoso (Batting follow-thru.)	850.00	425.00	250.00
(58)	Orestes Minoso/Bunting	850.00	425.00	250.00
(59)	Leon Mohr	375.00	185.00	110.00
(60)	Dee Moore/Btg	375.00	185.00	110.00
(61)	Dee Moore/Catching	375.00	185.00	110.00
(62)	Jim Moran	375.00	185.00	110.00
(63)	Glen Moulder	375.00	185.00	110.00
(64)	Milt Neilsen/Pose	375.00	185.00	110.00
(65)	Milt Neilsen/Btg	375.00	185.00	110.00
(66)	Milt Neilsen/Throwing	375.00	185.00	110.00
(67)	Rube Novotney	375.00	185.00	110.00
(68)	Al Olsen	375.00	185.00	110.00
(69)	Manny Perez	375.00	185.00	110.00
(70)	Bill Raemondi (Raimondi)	375.00	185.00	110.00
(71)	Len Ratto	375.00	185.00	110.00
(72)	Mickey Rocco	375.00	185.00	110.00
(73)	Marv Rotblatt	375.00	185.00	110.00
(74)	Lynwood Rowe/Pose	400.00	200.00	120.00
(75)	Lynwood Rowe/Pitching	400.00	200.00	120.00
(76)	Clarence Russell	375.00	185.00	110.00
(77)	Hal Saltzman (Pitching follow-thru.)	375.00	185.00	110.00
(78)	Hal Saltzman (Pitching wind-up.)	375.00	185.00	110.00
(79)	Hal Saltzman (Pitching, leg in air.)	375.00	185.00	110.00
(81)	Mike Sandlock	375.00	185.00	110.00
(82)	Bob Savage/Pose	375.00	185.00	110.00
(83)	Bob Savage/Pitching	375.00	185.00	110.00
(84)	Charlie Schanz	375.00	185.00	110.00
(85)	Bill Schuster	375.00	185.00	110.00
(86)	Neill Sheridan	375.00	185.00	110.00
(87)	Harry Simpson (Batting swing.)	525.00	260.00	150.00
(88)	Harry Simpson (Batting stance.)	525.00	260.00	150.00
(89)	Harry Simpson (Batting stance, close up.)	525.00	260.00	150.00
(90)	Harry Simpson (Batting follow-thru.)	525.00	260.00	150.00
(91)	Elmer Singleton	375.00	185.00	110.00
(92)	Al Smith/Pose	375.00	185.00	110.00
(93)	Al Smith (Batting stance.)	375.00	185.00	110.00
(94)	Al Smith/Fielding	375.00	185.00	110.00
(95)	Alphonse Smith (Glove above knee.)	375.00	185.00	110.00
(96)	Alphonse Smith (Glove below knee.)	375.00	185.00	110.00
(97)	Steve Souchock	375.00	185.00	110.00
(98)	Jim Steiner	375.00	185.00	110.00
(99)	Harvey Storey (Batting stance.)	375.00	185.00	110.00
(100)	Harvey Storey (Swinging bat.)	375.00	185.00	110.00
(101)	Harvey Storey/Throwing	375.00	185.00	110.00
(102)	Harvey Storey/Fielding (Ball in glove.)	375.00	185.00	110.00
(103)	Max Surkont	375.00	185.00	110.00

		NM	EX	VG
(104)	Jim Tabor	375.00	185.00	110.00
(105)	Forrest Thompson	375.00	185.00	110.00
(106)	Mike Tresh/Pose	375.00	185.00	110.00
(107)	Mike Tresh/Catching	375.00	185.00	110.00
(108)	Ben Wade	375.00	185.00	110.00
(109)	Kenny Washington	375.00	185.00	110.00
(110)	Bill Waters/Pose	375.00	185.00	110.00
(111)	Bill Waters/Pitching	375.00	185.00	110.00
(112)	Roy Welmaker/Pose	375.00	185.00	110.00
(113)	Roy Welmaker/Pitching	375.00	185.00	110.00
(114)	Max West/Pose	375.00	185.00	110.00
(115)	Max West (Batting stance.)	375.00	185.00	110.00
(116)	Max West/Kneeling	375.00	185.00	110.00
(117)	Max West (Batting follow-thru.)	375.00	185.00	110.00
(118)	Al White	375.00	185.00	110.00
(119)	"Whitey" Wietelmann/Pose	375.00	185.00	110.00
(120)	"Whitey" Wietelmann/Bunting	375.00	185.00	110.00
(121)	"Whitey" Wietelmann (Batting stance.)	375.00	185.00	110.00
(122)	"Whitey" Wietelmann/Throwing	375.00	185.00	110.00
(123)	Bobbie Wilson	375.00	185.00	110.00
(124)	Bobby Wilson	375.00	185.00	110.00
(125)	Roy Zimmerman	375.00	185.00	110.00
(126)	George Zuverink	375.00	185.00	110.00

1951 Hage's Dairy

Harry Malmberg
SAN DIEGO

The final year of the Hage's P.C.L. issues saw the set reduced to 53 different unnumbered cards, all but 12 of them Padres. Among them are seven cards of Cleveland Indians players, which were issued during an exhibition series with the major league club, and six cards picturing members of the Hollywood Stars. No other P.C.L. teams are represented. The cards maintained the same size and style of the previous two years but were printed in more color tints, including blue, green, burgundy, gold, gray and sepia (but not black-and-white). The 1951 cards have blank backs and were again distributed in popcorn boxes at the San Diego stadium. The 1951 cards are the most common of the three sets issued by Hage's Dairy. The Indians and Stars players were issued in lesser quantities than the Padres, however, and command a higher value.

		NM	EX	VG
Complete Set (53):		18,000	9,000	5,500
Common Player:		300.00	150.00	90.00
(1)	"Buster" Adams	300.00	150.00	90.00
(2)	Del Baker	300.00	150.00	90.00
(3)	Ray Boone	850.00	425.00	250.00
(4)	Russ Christopher	300.00	150.00	90.00
(5)	Allie Clark	850.00	425.00	250.00
(6)	Herb Conyers	300.00	150.00	90.00
(7)	Luke Easter	450.00	225.00	135.00
(8)	"Red" Embree/Pitching (Foot in air.)	300.00	150.00	90.00
(9)	"Red" Embree/Pitching (Hands up.)	300.00	150.00	90.00
(10)	Jess Flores	850.00	425.00	250.00
(11)	Murray Franklin	300.00	150.00	90.00
(12)	Jack Graham/Portrait	300.00	150.00	90.00
(13)	Jack Graham/Btg	300.00	150.00	90.00
(14)	Gene Handley	300.00	150.00	90.00
(15)	Charles Harris	300.00	150.00	90.00
(16)	Sam Jones/Pitching (Hands back.)	300.00	150.00	90.00
(17)	Sam Jones/Pitching (Hands up.)	300.00	150.00	90.00
(18)	Sam Jones/Pitching (Leg in air.)	300.00	150.00	90.00
(19)	Al Jurisich	300.00	150.00	90.00
(20)	Frank Kerr/Btg	300.00	150.00	90.00
(21)	Frank Kerr/Catching	300.00	150.00	90.00
(22)	Dick Kinaman	300.00	150.00	90.00
(23)	Clarence Maddern/Btg	300.00	150.00	90.00
(24)	Clarence Maddern/Fielding	300.00	150.00	90.00
(25)	Harry Malmberg/Bunting	300.00	150.00	90.00
(26)	Harry Malmberg (Batting follow-thru.)	300.00	150.00	90.00
(27)	Harry Malmberg/Fielding	300.00	150.00	90.00
(28)	Gordon Maltzberger	300.00	150.00	90.00
(29)	Al Olsen (Cleveland)	850.00	425.00	250.00
(30)	Al Olsen (San Diego)	300.00	150.00	90.00
(31)	Jimmy Reese/Clapping	350.00	175.00	100.00
(32)	Jimmy Reese (Hands on knees.)	350.00	175.00	100.00
(33)	Al Rosen	900.00	450.00	270.00
(34)	Joe Rowell	300.00	150.00	90.00
(35)	Mike Sandlock	300.00	150.00	90.00
(36)	George Schmees	300.00	150.00	90.00
(37)	Charlie Sipple	300.00	150.00	90.00
(38)	Harvey Storey (Batting follow-thru.)	300.00	150.00	90.00

(39)	Harvey Storey (Batting stance.)	300.00	150.00	90.00
(40)	Harvey Storey/Fielding	300.00	150.00	90.00
(41)	Jack Tobin	300.00	150.00	90.00
(42)	Frank Tornay	300.00	150.00	90.00
(43)	Thurman Tucker	300.00	150.00	90.00
(44)	Ben Wade	300.00	150.00	90.00
(45)	Roy Welmaker	300.00	150.00	90.00
(46)	Leroy Wheat	300.00	150.00	90.00
(47)	Don White	300.00	150.00	90.00
(48)	"Whitey" Wietelman/Btg	300.00	150.00	90.00
(49)	"Whitey" Wietelman/Fielding	300.00	150.00	90.00
(50)	Bobby Wilson/Btg	300.00	150.00	90.00
(51)	Bobby Wilson/Fielding	300.00	150.00	90.00
(52)	Tony York	300.00	150.00	90.00
(53)	George Zuverink	850.00	425.00	250.00

1886 Hancock's Syracuse Stars

Currently representing the earliest known minor league baseball cards is this issue by a Syracuse department store's menswear department. The 1-5/8" x 3-3/16" cards feature sepia photos glued to a stiff black cardboard backing with a gilt edge. The photos show the players in suits, presumably from the sponsor's racks. Backs have the player name and position printed at top. At center is an ad for Hancock's. At bottom is a credit line to "Goodwin" as photographer. Each card is currently known in only a single example. It is possible other players of the International League Stars may yet be discovered.

Values undetermined.
(1)	Richard D. Buckley			
(2)	Douglas Crothers (SGC-graded Ex., 2005 auction, $18,304.)			
(3)	Philip H. Tomney			

1960 Henry House Wieners Seattle Rainiers

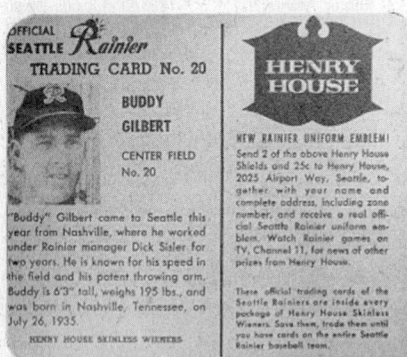

Eighteen different cards are known in this hot dog set; most players played major league baseball prior to their appearance with the Pacific Coast League Seattle Rainiers in 1960. Printed in red, the 4-1/2" x 3-3/4" cards are skip-numbered by player uniform number.

		NM	EX	VG
Complete Set (18):		5,500	2,750	1,600
Common Player:		300.00	150.00	90.00
2	Harry Malmberg	300.00	150.00	90.00
3	Francisco Obregon	300.00	150.00	90.00
4	Johnny O'Brien	375.00	185.00	110.00
5	Gordon Coleman	300.00	150.00	90.00
6	Bill Hain	300.00	150.00	90.00
8	Dick Sisler	300.00	150.00	90.00
9	Jerry Zimmerman	300.00	150.00	90.00
10	Hal Bevan	300.00	150.00	90.00
14	Rudy Regaldo	300.00	150.00	90.00
15	Paul Pettit	300.00	150.00	90.00
20	Buddy Gilbert	300.00	150.00	90.00
21	Erv Palica	300.00	150.00	90.00

22	Joe Taylor	300.00	150.00	90.00
25	Bill Kennedy	300.00	150.00	90.00
26	Dave Stenhouse	300.00	150.00	90.00
28	Ray Ripplemeyer	300.00	150.00	90.00
30	Charlie Beamon	300.00	150.00	90.00
33	Don Rudolph	300.00	150.00	90.00

1888 S.F. Hess California League (N321)

One of several tobacco card sets produced by S.F. Hess & Co. of Rochester, this rare 40-card issue features players from the California League. The cards measure 2-7/8" x 1-1/2" and feature color drawings of players. The player's name and team are printed along the top margin of the card, while the words "S.F. Hess and Co.'s/Creole Cigarettes" appear at the bottom. "California League" is also printed in large capital letters above the player drawing, while the 1888 copyright date appears below. There are 35 players (including one umpire) in the set, and five players are pictured on two cards each, resulting in 40 different cards. One example each of 30 of the cards have been discovered printed on thin paper stock, though the exact nature of that version is undetermined; currently values are about equal to the regular-issue version.

		NM	EX	VG
Common Player:		4,500	2,500	1,500
(1)	Bennett	4,500	2,500	1,500
(2)	Borchers	4,500	2,500	1,500
(3)	Buckley	4,500	2,500	1,500
(4)	Burke/Btg	4,500	2,500	1,500
(5)	Burke (Ready to pitch.)	4,500	2,500	1,500
(6)	Burnett	4,500	2,500	1,500
(7)	Carroll	4,500	2,500	1,500
(8)	Donohue	4,500	2,500	1,500
(9)	Donovan	4,500	2,500	1,500
(10)	Finn	4,500	2,500	1,500
(11)	Gagus	4,500	2,500	1,500
(12)	Hanley	4,500	2,500	1,500
(13)	Hardie (C., wearing mask.)	4,500	2,500	1,500
(14)	Hardie (C.F., with bat.)	4,500	2,500	1,500
(15)	Hayes	4,500	2,500	1,500
(16)	Lawton	4,500	2,500	1,500
(17)	Levy	4,500	2,500	1,500
(18)	Long	4,500	2,500	1,500
(19)	McCord	4,500	2,500	1,500
(20)	Meegan	4,500	2,500	1,500
(21)	Moore	4,500	2,500	1,500
(22)	Mullee	4,500	2,500	1,500
(23)	Newhert	4,500	2,500	1,500
(24)	Noonan	4,500	2,500	1,500
(25)	O'Day	4,500	2,500	1,500
(26)	Perrier	4,500	2,500	1,500
(27)	Powers/Catching (1st B.)	4,500	2,500	1,500
(28)	Powers (1st B. & Capt., with bat.)	4,500	2,500	1,500
(29)	Ryan	4,500	2,500	1,500
(30)	Selna	4,500	2,500	1,500
(31)	Shea	4,500	2,500	1,500
(32)	J. Sheridan/Umpire	4,500	2,500	1,500
(33)	"Big" Smith	4,500	2,500	1,500
(34)	H. Smith	4,500	2,500	1,500
(35)	J. Smith	4,500	2,500	1,500
(36)	Smett	4,500	2,500	1,500
(37)	Stockwell/Throwing	4,500	2,500	1,500
(38)	Stockwell (With bat.)	4,500	2,500	1,500
(39)	Sweeney	4,500	2,500	1,500
(40)	Whitehead	4,500	2,500	1,500

1888 S.F. Hess California League (N338-1)

This tobacco card set picturing players from the California League is one of the rarest of all 19th century issues. Issued in the late 1880s by S.F. Hess & Co. of Rochester, these 2-7/8" x 1-1/2" cards are so rare that only several examples are known to exist. Some of the photos in the N338-1 set are identical to the drawings in the N321 set, issued by S.F. Hess in 1888. The N338-1 cards are found with the words "California League" printed in an arc either above or below the player photo.

The player's name appears below the photo. At the bottom of the card the words "S.F. Hess & Co.'s Creole Cigarettes" are printed in a rolling style.

		NM	EX	VG
Common Player:		12,000	6,000	3,500
(1)	Borsher	12,000	6,000	3,500
(2)	Buckley	12,000	6,000	3,500
(3)	Carroll	12,000	6,000	3,500
(4)	Ebright	12,000	6,000	3,500
(5)	Gagur (Gagus)	12,000	6,000	3,500
(6)	Incell	12,000	6,000	3,500
(7)	Lawton	12,000	6,000	3,500
(8)	Levy/Throwing	12,000	6,000	3,500
(9)	Levy (With bat.)	12,000	6,000	3,500
(10)	McDonald	12,000	6,000	3,500
(11)	McGinty	13,500	6,750	4,050
(12)	Meegan	12,000	6,000	3,500
(13)	Newhert	12,000	6,000	3,500
(14)	Noonan	12,000	6,000	3,500
(15)	Perrier	12,000	6,000	3,500
(16)	Perrier, H. Smith	12,000	6,000	3,500
(17)	Ryan	12,000	6,000	3,500
(18)	J. Smith, N. Smith	12,000	6,000	3,500
(19)	Sweeney	12,000	6,000	3,500

1888 S.F. Hess Newsboys League (N333)

Although not picturing professional baseball players, these cards issued by S.F. Hess and Co. have a baseball theme. Cards measure 1-1/2" x 2-7/8" and feature pictures of "newsies" from papers in eight different cities (Rochester, Cleveland, Philadelphia, Boston, Albany, Detroit, New York and Syracuse). The boys are pictured in a photographs wearing baseball uniforms, often bearing the name of their newspaper. The boy's name, position and newspaper are printed below, while the words "Newsboys League" appears in capital letters at the top of the card. No identification is provided for the four Philadelphia newsboys, so a photo description is provided in the checklist that follows. Gaps have been left in the assigned numbering for future additions.

		NM	EX	VG
Common Player:		2,400	1,200	725.00
(1)	R.J. Bell	2,400	1,200	725.00
(2)	Bibby (Boston Globe)	2,400	1,200	725.00
(3)	Binden	2,400	1,200	725.00
(4)	Bowen	2,400	1,200	725.00
(5)	Boyle	2,400	1,200	725.00
(6)	Britcher	2,400	1,200	725.00
(7)	Caine	2,400	1,200	725.00
(8)	I. Cohen	2,400	1,200	725.00
(9)	R. Cohen	2,400	1,200	725.00

(10)	Collins (Boston Globe)	2,400	1,200	725.00
(11)	Cross	2,400	1,200	725.00
(12)	F. Cuddy	2,400	1,200	725.00
(13)	E. Daisey	2,400	1,200	725.00
(14)	Davis	2,400	1,200	725.00
(15)	B. Dinsmore	2,400	1,200	725.00
(16)	Donovan	2,400	1,200	725.00
(17)	A. Downer	2,400	1,200	725.00
(18)	Fanelly	2,400	1,200	725.00
(19)	J. Flood	2,400	1,200	725.00
(21)	C. Gallagher	2,400	1,200	725.00
(22)	M.H. Gallagher	2,400	1,200	725.00
(23)	D. Galligher	2,400	1,200	725.00
(24)	J. Galligher	2,400	1,200	725.00
(25)	Haskins	2,400	1,200	725.00
(26)	Herze	2,400	1,200	725.00
(27)	Holmes (Press & Knickerbocker)	2,400	1,200	725.00
(28)	F. Horan	2,400	1,200	725.00
(29)	Hosler	2,400	1,200	725.00
(30)	Hyde	2,400	1,200	725.00
(31)	Keilty	2,400	1,200	725.00
(32)	C. Kellogg	2,400	1,200	725.00
(33)	Mahoney (Rochester Post-Express)	2,400	1,200	725.00
(34)	Mayer	2,400	1,200	725.00
(35)	McCourt (Boston Globe)	2,400	1,200	725.00
(36)	I. McDonald	2,400	1,200	725.00
(37)	McDowell (Rochester)	2,400	1,200	725.00
(38)	McGrady	2,400	1,200	725.00
(39)	O'Brien	2,400	1,200	725.00
(41)	E.C. Murphy	2,400	1,200	725.00
(42)	Sabin	2,400	1,200	725.00
(43)	Shedd	2,400	1,200	725.00
(44)	R. Sheehan	2,400	1,200	725.00
(45)	Smith	2,400	1,200	725.00
(46)	Talbot	2,400	1,200	725.00
(47)	Walsh	2,400	1,200	725.00
(48)	Whitman	2,400	1,200	725.00
(49)	Yeomans	2,400	1,200	725.00
(50)	Cleveland newsboy (In cap, facing right.)	2,400	1,200	725.00
(51)	Philadelphia newsboy (Hair parted on right side.)	2,400	1,200	725.00
(52)	Philadelphia newsboy (Hair parted on left side.)	2,400	1,200	725.00
(53)	Philadelphia newsboy (No part in hair.)	2,400	1,200	725.00
(54)	Philadelphia newsboy (Head shaved.)	2,400	1,200	725.00

1949 Hollywood Stars Team Issue

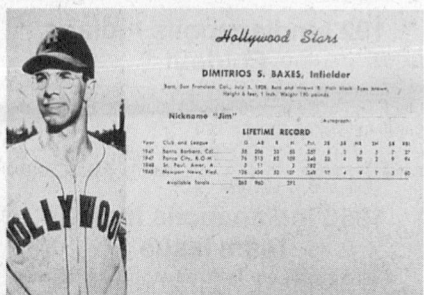

A team issue probably related to similar 1948-49 cards produced by Pacific Coast League cross-town rivals the L.A. Angels, these cards were likely produced by the publisher of the teams' yearbooks and sold at stadium souvenir stands. The cards are blank-backed, printed in black-and-white on thin semi-gloss cardboard, measuring 7-1/16" x 4-7/8". Portrait or posed action photos appear at left with complete major and minor league stats at right. A space for an autograph appears beneath the player's biographical data. The unnumbered cards are checklisted here in alphabetical order.

		NM	EX	VG
Complete Set (24):		500.00	250.00	150.00
Common Player:		25.00	12.50	7.50
(1)	Jim Baxes	25.00	12.50	7.50
(2)	George Fallon	25.00	12.50	7.50
(3)	John Fitzpatrick	25.00	12.50	7.50
(4)	George Genovese	25.00	12.50	7.50
(5)	Herb Gorman	75.00	37.50	22.50
(6)	Gene Handley	25.00	12.50	7.50
(7)	Fred Haney	25.00	12.50	7.50
(8)	Jim Hughes	25.00	12.50	7.50
(9)	Frank Kelleher	25.00	12.50	7.50
(10)	Gordy Maltzberger	25.00	12.50	7.50
(11)	Glen Moulder	25.00	12.50	7.50
(12)	Irv Noren	25.00	12.50	7.50
(13)	Ed Oliver	25.00	12.50	7.50
(14)	Karl Olsen	25.00	12.50	7.50
(15)	John O'Neil	25.00	12.50	7.50
(16)	Jack Paepke	25.00	12.50	7.50
(17)	Willard Ramsdell	25.00	12.50	7.50
(18)	Jack Salveson	25.00	12.50	7.50
(19)	Mike Sandlock	25.00	12.50	7.50
(20)	Art Shallock	25.00	12.50	7.50
(21)	Andy Skurski	25.00	12.50	7.50
(22)	Chuck Stevens	25.00	12.50	7.50
(23)	Al Unser	25.00	12.50	7.50
(24)	George Woods	25.00	12.50	7.50

1950 Hollywood Stars Team Issue

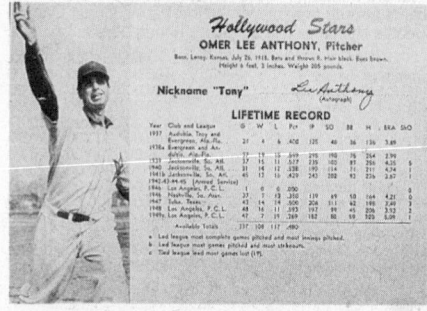

Virtually identical in format to the previous year's issue, the 1950 set differs principally in the inclusion of a facsimile autograph on front. In 1950 the Hollywood Stars were the PCL affiliate of the Brooklyn Dodgers. Both sets were listed in "The American Card Catalog" as W720.

		NM	EX	VG
Complete Set (32):		850.00	425.00	250.00
Common Player:		25.00	12.50	7.50
(1)	Lee Anthony	25.00	12.50	7.50
(2)	Bill Antonello	25.00	12.50	7.50
(3)	Dick Barrett	25.00	12.50	7.50
(4)	Jim Baxes	25.00	12.50	7.50
(5)	Clint Conatser	25.00	12.50	7.50
(6)	Cliff Dapper	25.00	12.50	7.50
(7)	George Fallon	25.00	12.50	7.50
(8)	John Fitzpatrick	25.00	12.50	7.50
(9)	Murray Franklin	25.00	12.50	7.50
(10)	Herb Gorman	75.00	37.50	22.50
(11)	Gene Handley	25.00	12.50	7.50
(12)	Fred Haney	25.00	12.50	7.50
(13)	Clarence Hicks	25.00	12.50	7.50
(14)	Herb Karpel	200.00	100.00	60.00
(15)	Frank Kelleher	25.00	12.50	7.50
(16)	Ken Lehman	25.00	12.50	7.50
(17)	Johnny Lindell	25.00	12.50	7.50
(18)	Gordy Maltzberger	25.00	12.50	7.50
(19)	Dan Menendez	25.00	12.50	7.50
(20)	Pershing Mondroff	25.00	12.50	7.50
(21)	Glen Moulder	25.00	12.50	7.50
(22)	John O'Neil	25.00	12.50	7.50
(23)	Jack Paepke	25.00	12.50	7.50
(24)	Jean Roy	25.00	12.50	7.50
(25)	Jack Salveson	25.00	12.50	7.50
(26)	Mike Sandlock	25.00	12.50	7.50
(27)	Ed Saver	25.00	12.50	7.50
(28)	George Schmees	25.00	12.50	7.50
(29)	Art Shallock	25.00	12.50	7.50
(30)	Chuck Stevens	25.00	12.50	7.50
(31)	Ben Wade	25.00	12.50	7.50
(32)	George Woods	25.00	12.50	7.50

1957 Hollywood Stars Team Issue

Presumably issued by the team, which had a working relationship with the Pittsburgh Pirates, this 23-card set features black-and-white blank-backed photos in a 4-1/8" x 6-3/16" format. Each picture has a facsimile autograph printed in black across the front. The unnumbered cards are checklisted here alphabetically.

		NM	EX	VG
Complete Set (23):		900.00	450.00	275.00
Common Player:		40.00	20.00	12.00
(1)	Jim Baumer	40.00	20.00	12.00
(2)	Carlos Bernier	40.00	20.00	12.00
(3)	Bill Causion	40.00	20.00	12.00
(4)	Chuck Churn	40.00	20.00	12.00
(5)	Bennie Daniels	40.00	20.00	12.00
(6)	Joe Duhem	40.00	20.00	12.00
(7)	John Fitzpatrick	40.00	20.00	12.00
(8)	Bob Garber	40.00	20.00	12.00
(9)	Bill Hall	40.00	20.00	12.00
(10)	Forrest "Spook" Jacobs	50.00	25.00	15.00
(11)	Clyde King	40.00	20.00	12.00
(12)	Nick Koback	40.00	20.00	12.00
(13)	Pete Naton	40.00	20.00	12.00
(14)	George O'Donnell	40.00	20.00	12.00
(15)	Paul Pettit	40.00	20.00	12.00
(16)	Curt Raydon	40.00	20.00	12.00
(17)	Leo Rodriguez	40.00	20.00	12.00
(18)	Don Rowe	40.00	20.00	12.00
(19)	Dick Smith	40.00	20.00	12.00
(20)	R.C. Stevens	40.00	20.00	12.00
(21)	Ben Wade	40.00	20.00	12.00
(22)	Fred Waters	40.00	20.00	12.00
(23)	George Witt	40.00	20.00	12.00

1912 Home Run Kisses (E136)

This 90-card set of Pacific Coast League players was produced in 1912 by the San Francisco candy company of Collins-McCarthy. Each card measures about 2-1/4" x 4-3/16" and features sepia-toned player photos surrounded by an ornate frame. The front of the card has the words "Home Run Kisses" above the player's name. Most cards found are blank-backed, but others exist with a back that advises "Save Home Run Kisses Pictures for Valuable Premiums" along with other details of the Collins-McCarthy promotion. A third type of back exists with an advertising logo for "BARDELL / SEPIA/ SAN FRANCISCO". Redeemed cards were punch-cancelled, often with a heart-shaped hole.

		NM	EX	VG
Complete Set (90):		70,000	28,000	16,000
Common Player:		750.00	300.00	185.00
(1)	Ables	750.00	300.00	185.00
(2)	Agnew	750.00	300.00	185.00
(3)	Altman	750.00	300.00	185.00
(4)	Frank Arrelanes (Arellanes)	750.00	300.00	185.00
(5)	Auer	750.00	300.00	185.00
(6)	Bancroft	3,500	1,400	875.00
(7)	Bayless	750.00	300.00	185.00
(8)	Berry	750.00	300.00	185.00
(9)	Boles	750.00	300.00	185.00
(10)	Brashear	750.00	300.00	185.00
(11)	Brooks (Los Angeles)	750.00	300.00	185.00
(12)	Brooks (Oakland)	750.00	300.00	185.00
(13)	Brown	750.00	300.00	185.00
(14)	Burrell	750.00	300.00	185.00
(15)	Butler	750.00	300.00	185.00
(16)	Carlisle	750.00	300.00	185.00
(17)	Carson	750.00	300.00	185.00
(18)	Castleton	750.00	300.00	185.00
(19)	Chadbourne	750.00	300.00	185.00
(20)	Check	750.00	300.00	185.00
(21)	Core	750.00	300.00	185.00
(22)	Corhan	750.00	300.00	185.00
(23)	Coy	750.00	300.00	185.00
(24)	Daley	750.00	300.00	185.00
(25)	Dillon	750.00	300.00	185.00
(26)	Doane	750.00	300.00	185.00
(27)	Driscoll	750.00	300.00	185.00
(28)	Fisher	750.00	300.00	185.00
(29)	Flater	750.00	300.00	185.00
(30)	Gaddy	750.00	300.00	185.00
(31)	Gregg	750.00	300.00	185.00
(32)	Gregory	750.00	300.00	185.00
(33)	Harkness	750.00	300.00	185.00
(34)	Heitmuller	750.00	300.00	185.00
(35)	Henley	750.00	300.00	185.00
(36)	Hiester	750.00	300.00	185.00
(37)	Hoffman	750.00	300.00	185.00
(38)	Hogan	750.00	300.00	185.00
(39)	Hosp	750.00	300.00	185.00
(40)	Howley	750.00	300.00	185.00
(41)	Ireland	750.00	300.00	185.00
(42)	Johnson	750.00	300.00	185.00
(43)	Kane	750.00	300.00	185.00
(44)	Klawitter	750.00	300.00	185.00
(45)	Kreitz	750.00	300.00	185.00
(46)	Krueger	750.00	300.00	185.00
(47)	Leard	750.00	300.00	185.00
(48)	Leverencz	750.00	300.00	185.00
(49)	Lewis	750.00	300.00	185.00
(50)	Bill Lindsay	750.00	300.00	185.00
(51)	Litschi	750.00	300.00	185.00
(52)	Lober	750.00	300.00	185.00
(53)	Malarkey	750.00	300.00	185.00
(54)	Martinoni	750.00	300.00	185.00
(55)	McArdle	750.00	300.00	185.00
(56)	McCorry	750.00	300.00	185.00

(57)	McDowell	750.00	300.00	185.00
(58)	McIver	750.00	300.00	185.00
(59)	Metzger	750.00	300.00	185.00
(60)	Miller	750.00	300.00	185.00
(61)	Mundorf	750.00	300.00	185.00
(62)	Nagle	750.00	300.00	185.00
(63)	Noyes	750.00	300.00	185.00
(64)	Olmstead	750.00	300.00	185.00
(65)	O'Rourke	750.00	300.00	185.00
(66)	Page	750.00	300.00	185.00
(67)	Parkins	750.00	300.00	185.00
(68)	Patterson (Oakland)	750.00	300.00	185.00
(69)	Patterson (Vernon)	750.00	300.00	185.00
(70)	Pernoll	750.00	300.00	185.00
(71)	Powell	750.00	300.00	185.00
(72)	Price	750.00	300.00	185.00
(73)	Raftery	750.00	300.00	185.00
(74)	Raleigh	750.00	300.00	185.00
(75)	Rogers	750.00	300.00	185.00
(76)	Schmidt	750.00	300.00	185.00
(77)	Schwenk	750.00	300.00	185.00
(78)	Sheehan	750.00	300.00	185.00
(79)	Shinn	750.00	300.00	185.00
(80)	Slagle	750.00	300.00	185.00
(81)	Smith	750.00	300.00	185.00
(82)	Stone	750.00	300.00	185.00
(83)	Swain	750.00	300.00	185.00
(84)	Taylor	750.00	300.00	185.00
(85)	Tiedeman	750.00	300.00	185.00
(86)	Toner	750.00	300.00	185.00
(87)	Tozer	750.00	300.00	185.00
(88)	Van Buren	750.00	300.00	185.00
(89)	Williams	750.00	300.00	185.00
(90)	Zacher	750.00	300.00	185.00

1940 Hughes Frozen Confections Sacramento Solons

Courtesy of HUGHES FROZEN CONFECTIONS West Sacramento

These borderless 2" x 3" black-and-white cards of the Sacramento Solons can be found in two versions, either blank-backed or with the 1940 Solons Pacific Coast League schedule printed on back. Fronts featured action poses with a facsimile autograph.

		NM	EX	VG
Complete Set (20):		7,500	3,750	2,250
Common Player:		400.00	200.00	125.00
(1)	Mel Almada	400.00	200.00	125.00
(2)	Frank Asbell	400.00	200.00	125.00
(3)	Larry Barton	400.00	200.00	125.00
(4)	Robert Blattner	400.00	200.00	125.00
(5)	Bennie Borgmann	400.00	200.00	125.00
(6)	Tony Freitas	400.00	200.00	125.00
(7)	Art Garibaldi	400.00	200.00	125.00
(8)	Jim Grilk	400.00	200.00	125.00
(9)	Gene Handley	400.00	200.00	125.00
(10)	Oscar Judd	400.00	200.00	125.00
(11)	Lynn King	400.00	200.00	125.00
(12)	Norbert Kleinke	400.00	200.00	125.00
(13)	Max Marshall	400.00	200.00	125.00
(14)	William McLaughlin	400.00	200.00	125.00
(15)	Bruce Ogrodowski	400.00	200.00	125.00
(16)	Franich Riel	400.00	200.00	125.00
(17)	Bill Schmidt	400.00	200.00	125.00
(18)	Melvin Wasley	400.00	200.00	125.00
(19)	Chet Wieczorek	400.00	200.00	125.00
(20)	Deb Williams	400.00	200.00	125.00

1957 Hygrade Meats Seattle Rainiers

While the front of the cards mentions a complete set of 22 cards, only a dozen have been checklisted to date. The round-cornered cards measure 4-1/2 x 3-3/4" and are printed in red on white. Backs are blank. The cards feature only players of the Pacific Coast League Seattle Rainiers. The cards are unnumbered.

		NM	EX	VG
Common Player:		400.00	200.00	120.00
(1)	Dick Aylward	400.00	200.00	120.00
(2)	Bob Balcena	400.00	200.00	120.00
(3)	Jim Dyck	400.00	200.00	120.00
(4)	Marion Fricano	400.00	200.00	120.00
(5)	Bill Glynn	400.00	200.00	120.00
(6)	Larry Jansen	400.00	200.00	120.00
(7)	Bill Kennedy	400.00	200.00	120.00
(8)	Jack Lohrke	400.00	200.00	120.00
(9)	Frank O'Doul	800.00	400.00	240.00
(10)	Ray Orteig	400.00	200.00	120.00
(11)	Joe Taylor	400.00	200.00	120.00
(12)	Morrie (Maury) Wills	800.00	400.00	240.00

I

1912 Imperial Tobacco (C46)

JOSEPH KELLEY

Joseph Kelley, manager Toronto Base Ball Club, of the International League, is one of the best known base ball men in the country. He has been in the game for many years. He was with the Baltimore club when they were three times winners of the National League Championship, playing left field. He was also with Brooklyn when they were pennant winners. He was playing manager of the Boston Club of the National League and also played with Cincinnatti.

BASEBALL SERIES. NO. 27

This minor league set, issued in 1912 by the Imperial Tobacco Company, is the only tobacco baseball set issued in Canada. Designated as C46 in the American Card Catalog, each sepia-toned card measures 1-1/2" x 2-5/8" and features a distinctive card design that pictures the player inside an oval surrounded by a simulated woodgrain background featuring a bat, ball and glove in the borders. The player's last name appears in capital letters in a panel beneath the oval. (An exception is the card of James Murray, whose caption includes both first and last names.) The backs include the player's name and team at the top, followed by a brief biography. The 90 subjects in the set are members of the eight teams in the Eastern League (Rochester, Toronto, Buffalo, Newark, Providence, Baltimore, Montreal and Jersey City), even though the card backs refer to it as the International League. The set contains many players with major league experience, including Hall of Famers Joe Kelley and Joe "Iron Man" McGinnity.

		NM	EX	VG
Complete Set (90):		13,000	6,500	4,000
Common Player:		150.00	75.00	40.00
1	William O'Hara	180.00	90.00	55.00
2	James McGinley	160.00	80.00	50.00
3	"Frenchy" LeClaire	150.00	75.00	40.00
4	John White	150.00	75.00	40.00
5	James Murray	150.00	75.00	40.00
6	Joe Ward	150.00	75.00	40.00
7	Whitey Alperman	150.00	75.00	40.00
8	"Natty" Nattress	150.00	75.00	40.00
9	Fred Sline	150.00	75.00	40.00
10	Royal Rock	150.00	75.00	40.00
11	Ray Demmitt	150.00	75.00	40.00
12	"Butcher Boy" Schmidt	150.00	75.00	40.00
13	Samuel Frock	150.00	75.00	40.00
14	Fred Burchell	150.00	75.00	40.00
15	Jack Kelley	150.00	75.00	40.00
16	Frank Barberich	150.00	75.00	40.00
17	Frank Corridon	150.00	75.00	40.00
18	"Doc" Adkins	150.00	75.00	40.00
19	Jack Dunn	150.00	75.00	40.00
20	James Walsh	150.00	75.00	40.00
21	Charles Hanford	150.00	75.00	40.00
22	Dick Rudolph	150.00	75.00	40.00
23	Curt Elston	150.00	75.00	40.00
24	Silton	150.00	75.00	40.00
25	Charlie French	150.00	75.00	40.00
26	John Ganzel	150.00	75.00	40.00
27	Joe Kelley	750.00	375.00	230.00
28	Benny Meyers	150.00	75.00	40.00
29	George Schirm	150.00	75.00	40.00
30	William Purtell	150.00	75.00	40.00
31	Bayard Sharpe	150.00	75.00	40.00
32	Tony Smith	150.00	75.00	40.00
33	John Lush	150.00	75.00	40.00
34	William Collins	150.00	75.00	40.00
35	Art Phelan	150.00	75.00	40.00
36	Edward Phelps	150.00	75.00	40.00
37	"Rube" Vickers	150.00	75.00	40.00
38	Cy Seymour	150.00	75.00	40.00
39	"Shadow" Carroll	150.00	75.00	40.00
40	Jake Gettman	150.00	75.00	40.00
41	Luther Taylor	300.00	150.00	95.00
42	Walter Justis	150.00	75.00	40.00
43	Robert Fisher	150.00	75.00	40.00
44	Fred Parent	150.00	75.00	40.00
45	James Dygert	150.00	75.00	40.00
46	Johnnie Butler	150.00	75.00	40.00
47	Fred Mitchell	150.00	75.00	40.00
48	Heinie Batch	150.00	75.00	40.00
49	Michael Corcoran	150.00	75.00	40.00
50	Edward Doescher	150.00	75.00	40.00
51	Wheeler	150.00	75.00	40.00
52	Elijah Jones	150.00	75.00	40.00
53	Fred Truesdale	150.00	75.00	40.00
54	Fred Beebe	150.00	75.00	40.00
55	Louis Brockett	150.00	75.00	40.00
56	Wells	150.00	75.00	40.00
57	"Lew" McAllister	150.00	75.00	40.00
58	Ralph Stroud	150.00	75.00	40.00
59	Manser	150.00	75.00	40.00
60	"Ducky" Holmes	150.00	75.00	40.00
61	Rube Dessau	150.00	75.00	40.00
62	Fred Jacklitsch	150.00	75.00	40.00
63	Graham	150.00	75.00	40.00
64	Noah Henline	150.00	75.00	40.00
65	"Chick" Gandil	775.00	385.00	240.00
66	Tom Hughes	150.00	75.00	40.00
67	Joseph Delehanty	150.00	75.00	40.00
68	Pierce	150.00	75.00	40.00
69	Gaunt	150.00	75.00	40.00
70	Edward Fitzpatrick	150.00	75.00	40.00
71	Wyatt Lee	150.00	75.00	40.00
72	John Kissinger	150.00	75.00	40.00
73	William Malarkey	150.00	75.00	40.00
74	William Byers	150.00	75.00	40.00
75	George Simmons	150.00	75.00	40.00
76	Daniel Moeller	150.00	75.00	40.00
77	Joseph McGinnity	750.00	375.00	230.00
78	Alex Hardy	150.00	75.00	40.00
79	Bob Holmes	150.00	75.00	40.00
80	William Baxter	150.00	75.00	40.00
81	Edward Spencer	150.00	75.00	40.00
82	Bradley Kocher	150.00	75.00	40.00
83	Robert Shaw	150.00	75.00	40.00
84	Joseph Yeager	150.00	75.00	40.00
85	Carlo	150.00	75.00	40.00
86	William Abstein	150.00	75.00	40.00
87	Tim Jordan	150.00	75.00	40.00
88	Dick Breen	150.00	75.00	40.00
89	Tom McCarty	150.00	75.00	46.00
90	Ed Curtis	160.00	80.00	50.00

1923 Indianapolis Indians Foldout

Twenty-one players and staff are featured in this black-and-white accordian-fold souvenir. Each of the cards measures about 2" x 3".

	NM	EX	VG
Complete Foldout:	650.00	325.00	195.00
(Checklist not available.)			

1950 Indianapolis Indians Team Issue

Action poses are featured in this set of team-issue 8" x 10" black-and-white glossy photos. Players are identified by a facsimile autograph on front. It is unknown whether the checklist is complete. The Indians were the Class AAA American Association affiliate of the Pittsburgh Pirates in 1950.

		NM	EX	VG
Common Player:		30.00	15.00	9.00
(1)	Monty Basgall	30.00	15.00	9.00
(2)	Ted Beard	30.00	15.00	9.00
(3)	Gus Bell	40.00	20.00	12.00
(4)	Eddie Bockman	30.00	15.00	9.00
(5)	Dale Coogan	30.00	15.00	9.00
(6)	"Del" Dallessandro	30.00	15.00	9.00
(7)	Nanny Fernandez	30.00	15.00	9.00
(8)	Eddy Fitz Gerald	30.00	15.00	9.00
(9)	Al Grunwald	30.00	15.00	9.00
(10)	Frank Kalin	30.00	15.00	9.00
(11)	Paul LaPalme	30.00	15.00	9.00
(12)	Royce Lint	30.00	15.00	9.00
(13)	Al Lopez	45.00	22.00	13.50
(14)	Forrest Main	30.00	15.00	9.00
(15)	Danny O'Connell	30.00	15.00	9.00
(16)	Frank Papish	30.00	15.00	9.00
(17)	Eddie Stevens	30.00	15.00	9.00
(18)	Leo Wells	30.00	15.00	9.00

J

1952 Jamestown Falcons Team Issue

This Class D farm club of the Detroit Tigers won the 1952 Pony (Pennsylvania-Ontario-New York) League playoffs. Like other issues of Globe Printing,

CHARLEY LAU

the roughly 2-1/4" x 3-3/8" cards are black-and-white with blank backs and the player name in a white strip at bottom-front. A light green album slotted to hold the cards is known for this issue.

		NM	EX	VG
Complete Set (18):		800.00	400.00	240.00
Common Player:		60.00	30.00	18.00
Album:		100.00	50.00	30.00
(1)	Dick Barr	60.00	30.00	18.00
(2)	Jerry Davie	60.00	30.00	18.00
(3)	John Fickinger	60.00	30.00	18.00
(4)	Paul Franks	60.00	30.00	18.00
(5)	Red Gookin	60.00	30.00	18.00
(6)	Bill Harbour	60.00	30.00	18.00
(7)	Dick Hatfield	60.00	30.00	18.00
(8)	Charley Lau	90.00	45.00	30.00
(9)	Dick Lisiecki	60.00	30.00	18.00
(10)	Tony Lupien	60.00	30.00	18.00
(11)	Joe Melago	60.00	30.00	18.00
(12)	Claude Mitschele	60.00	30.00	18.00
(13)	Bob Neebling	60.00	30.00	18.00
(14)	Fran Oneto	60.00	30.00	18.00
(15)	George Risley	60.00	30.00	18.00
(16)	Bob Szabo	60.00	30.00	18.00
(17)	Ken Walters	60.00	30.00	18.00
(18)	Gabby Witucki	60.00	30.00	18.00

1909 Walter Johnson "Weiser Wonder" Postcards

This issue-date(s) on these postcards are conjectural. Two distinct styles are known using versions of the same full-length portrait of Johnson in a studio standing on an ornate rug in front of a curtain depicting drapes, urn, etc. Johnson is wearing the uniform of the Weiser (Idaho) semi-pro team for whom he pitched prior to beginning his Hall of Fame career with the Washington Senators in 1907. The earlier of the cards utilizes the undivided-back postcard format which was current only until 1908. It is printed in sepia tones and identifies Johnson as the "Weiser Wonder" in a line of white type at the bottom. A later version, on a post-1908 divided-back postcard, is printed in bluetone. The card identifies him in a white strip at bottom. It is likely one or both of these cards continued to be produced or at least available after Johnson became a major league star. Both cards are in standard 3-1/2" x 5-1/2" format.

	NM	EX	VG
Walter Johnson (Bluetone)	2,500	1,250	750.00
Walter Johnson (Sepia)	2,500	1,250	750.00

1967 Jones Dairy Buffalo Bison All-Stars

Apparently printed as part of a milk carton, only a single player is known for this issue. Printed in red and yellow, the piece includes a 1967 team home schedule, a player drawing and career highlights in a 2-3/4" x 3-1/8" format. Other players may yet surface.

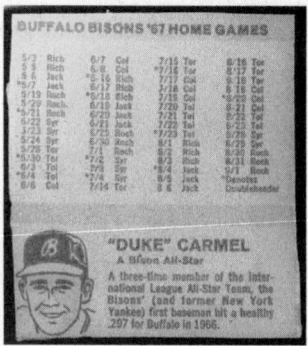

		NM	EX	VG
(1)	"Duke" Carmel	80.00	40.00	25.00

K

1962 Kahn's Wieners Atlanta Crackers

 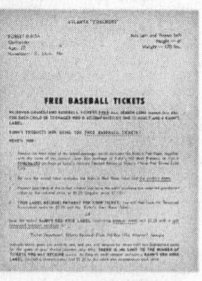

Kahn's made a single foray into the minor league market in 1962 with a separate 24-card set of Atlanta Crackers. The cards feature the same basic format, 3-1/4" x 4", borderless black-and-white photos with a Kahn's ad message in a white panel below the picture, as the major league issue. The backs are slightly different, having a free ticket offer in place of the player stats. Atlanta was the top farm club of the St. Louis Cardinals in 1962. The most famous alumnus in the set is Tim McCarver.

		NM	EX	VG
Complete Set (24):		850.00	425.00	250.00
Common Player:		35.00	17.50	10.00
(1)	James (Jimmy) Edward Beauchamp	35.00	17.50	10.00
(2)	Gerald Peter Buchek	35.00	17.50	10.00
(3)	Robert Burda	35.00	17.50	10.00
(4)	Hal Deitz	35.00	17.50	10.00
(5)	Robert John Duliba	35.00	17.50	10.00
(6)	Harry Michael Fanok	35.00	17.50	10.00
(7)	Phil Gagliano	35.00	17.50	10.00
(8)	John Glenn	35.00	17.50	10.00
(9)	Leroy Gregory	35.00	17.50	10.00
(10)	Richard (Dick) Henry Hughes	35.00	17.50	10.00
(11)	John Charles Kucks, Jr.	35.00	17.50	10.00
(12)	Johnny Joe Lewis	35.00	17.50	10.00
(13)	James (Mac - Timmie) Timothy McCarver	75.00	37.50	22.00
(14)	Robert F. Milliken	35.00	17.50	10.00
(15)	Joe Morgan	35.00	17.50	10.00
(16)	Ronald Charles Plaza	35.00	17.50	10.00
(17)	Bob Sadowski	35.00	17.50	10.00
(18)	Jim Saul	35.00	17.50	10.00
(19)	Willard Schmidt	35.00	17.50	10.00
(20)	Joe Schultz	35.00	17.50	10.00
(21)	Thomas Michael (Mike) Shannon	50.00	25.00	15.00
(22)	Paul Louis Toth	35.00	17.50	10.00
(23)	Andrew Lou Vickery	35.00	17.50	10.00
(24)	Fred Dwight Whitfield	35.00	17.50	10.00

1939 Kimball Automobile Trois-Rivieres Photocards

This set of 18 postcards and an accompanying envelope features the player of the Trois-Rivieres (Three Rivers) club of the Quebec Provincial League. Until 1940, the six-team QPL was not a part of organized baseball's minor league system. Several of the players were either former or future minor leaguers within OB. Paul "Pepper" Martin in the set is not the Pepper Martin of the contemporary, Gas House Gang St. Louis Cardinals. The black-and-white cards are about postcard-size and blank-backed, printed on sturdy card stock.

	NM	EX	VG
Complete Set (18):	1,350	675.00	400.00

		NM	EX	VG
Common Player:		90.00	45.00	25.00
(1)	George Andrews	90.00	45.00	25.00
(2)	Norm Bell	90.00	45.00	25.00
(3)	Henry Block	90.00	45.00	25.00
(4)	Addie Copple	90.00	45.00	25.00
(5)	Phil Corrigan	90.00	45.00	25.00
(6)	Joe Dickinson	90.00	45.00	25.00
(7)	Bill Hoffner	90.00	45.00	25.00
(8)	Jack Leroy	90.00	45.00	25.00
(9)	Leo Maloney	90.00	45.00	25.00
(10)	Martin	90.00	45.00	25.00
(11)	McGurk	90.00	45.00	25.00
(12)	Connie O'Leary	90.00	45.00	25.00
(13)	James Pickens	90.00	45.00	25.00
(14)	Dutch Prather	90.00	45.00	25.00
(15)	Jamie Skelton	90.00	45.00	25.00
(16)	Byron Speece	90.00	45.00	25.00
(17)	Gene Sullivan	90.00	45.00	25.00
(18)	Grover Wearshing	90.00	45.00	25.00

1952 Knowles Service Stations Stockton Ports

FIBBER HIRAYAMA

Contemporary, and sharing a format with the many Globe minor league issues of the early '50s, this set of Stockton Ports (Class C California League) cards carries the advertising of Knowles Service Stations. The blank-backed, black-and-white cards measure 2-1/4" x 3-1/2" and are unnumbered. Among the players is a Japanese national whose card is in strong demand.

		NM	EX	VG
Complete Set (11):		1,000	500.00	300.00
Common Player:		90.00	45.00	25.00
Album:		150.00	75.00	45.00
(1)	Wayne Clary	90.00	45.00	25.00
(2)	Harry Clements	90.00	45.00	25.00
(3)	John Crocco	90.00	45.00	25.00
(4)	Tony Freitas	90.00	45.00	25.00
(5)	Fibber Hirayama	250.00	125.00	75.00
(6)	Dave Mann	90.00	45.00	25.00
(7)	Larry Mann	90.00	45.00	25.00
(8)	Hank Moreno	90.00	45.00	25.00
(9)	Frank Romero	90.00	45.00	25.00
(10)	Chuck Thomas	90.00	45.00	25.00
(11)	Bud Watkins	90.00	45.00	25.00

1922-23 Kolb's Mothers' Bread Pins (PB4)

GILHOOLEY-F.

Over a two-year period, Kolb's bakery sponsored a series of pins featuring members of the Reading (Pa.) Aces of the International League. The pins are 7/8" in diameter with black-and-white portraits on a white background. The player name (last name only, usually) and position are indicated beneath the photo. Above the photo, in red, is the sponsor's identification. The pins issued in 1922 have 'MOTHERS' in all capital letters; the 1923 pins have 'Mothers' in upper and lower case.

		NM	EX	VG
Complete Set (32):		675.00	350.00	200.00
Common Player:		50.00	25.00	15.00
(1)	Spencer Abbott	50.00	25.00	15.00
(2)	Charlie Babington	50.00	25.00	15.00
(3)	Bill Barrett	50.00	25.00	15.00
(4)	R. Bates	50.00	25.00	15.00
(5)	Chief Bender	75.00	37.50	22.50

		NM	EX	VG
(6)	Myrl Brown	50.00	25.00	15.00
(7)	Fred Carts	50.00	25.00	15.00
(8)	Nig Clarke	50.00	25.00	15.00
(9)	Tom Connelly	50.00	25.00	15.00
(10)	Gus Getz	50.00	25.00	15.00
(11)	Frank Gilhooley	50.00	25.00	15.00
(12)	Ray Gordonier	50.00	25.00	15.00
(13)	Hinkey Haines	60.00	30.00	18.00
(14)	Francis Karpp	50.00	25.00	15.00
(15)	Joseph Kelley	50.00	25.00	15.00
(16)	Andrew Kotch	50.00	25.00	15.00
(17)	William Lightner	50.00	25.00	15.00
(18)	Byrd Lynn	50.00	25.00	15.00
(19)	Al Mamaux	50.00	25.00	15.00
(20)	Martin	50.00	25.00	15.00
(21)	Ralph Miller	50.00	25.00	15.00
(22)	Otto Pahlman	50.00	25.00	15.00
(23)	Sam Post	50.00	25.00	15.00
(24)	Al Schact	62.00	31.00	18.50
(25)	John Scott	50.00	25.00	15.00
(26)	Walt Smallwood	50.00	25.00	15.00
(27)	Ross Swartz	50.00	25.00	15.00
(28)	Fred Thomas	50.00	25.00	15.00
(29)	Myles Thomas	50.00	25.00	15.00
(30)	Walt Tragesser	50.00	25.00	15.00
(31)	Washburn	50.00	25.00	15.00
(32)	Walter Wolfe	50.00	25.00	15.00

L

1952 La Patrie Album Sportif

Ballplayers from Montreal of the International League and several of the teams from the Class C Provincial (Quebec) League were featured in a series of colorized photos printed in the Sunday rotogravure section of "La Patrie" newspaper. The photos are approximately 11" x 15-3/8" with red left and bottom trim and a vertical blue stripe at far left. Player information is printed in black and is in French. A number of the players went on to stardom with the Brooklyn and/or Los Angeles Dodgers.

		NM	EX	VG
Complete Set (20):		700.00	350.00	210.00
Common Player:		25.00	12.50	7.50
(1)	Bob Alexander	25.00	12.50	7.50
(2)	Herbie Bush	25.00	12.50	7.50
(3)	Georges Carpentier	25.00	12.50	7.50
(4)	Hampton Coleman	25.00	12.50	7.50
(5)	Walter Fiala	25.00	12.50	7.50
(6)	Jim Gilliams (Gilliam)	45.00	22.50	13.50
(7)	Tom Hackett	25.00	12.50	7.50
(8)	Don Hoak	35.00	17.50	10.00
(9)	Herbie Lash	25.00	12.50	7.50
(10)	Tommy Lasorda	150.00	75.00	45.00
(11)	Mal Mallette	25.00	12.50	7.50
(12)	Georges Maranda (Aug. 17)	25.00	12.50	7.50
(13)	Carmen Mauro	25.00	12.50	7.50
(14)	Solly Mohn	25.00	12.50	7.50
(15)	Jacques Monette	25.00	12.50	7.50
(16)	Johnny Podres	75.00	37.50	22.50
(17)	Ed Roebuck	25.00	12.50	7.50
(18)	Charlie Thompson	25.00	12.50	7.50
(19)	Don Thompson	25.00	12.50	7.50
(20)	John Wingo	25.00	12.50	7.50

1928-1932 La Presse Baseball Rotos

Players from Montreal's team in the International League (and occasionally other major and minor league teams' stars) were featured in a series of photos between 1928-32 in the Saturday rotogravure section of Montreal's "La Presse" newspaper. The format remained fairly consistent over the years. Large hand-tinted player photos were featured on the approximately 11" x 17-3/4" pages, with writeup in French below. On back was whatever features and ads happened to appear on the following page. The known baseball player list is presented here in chronological order. Other athletes were also featured in the issue, but are not listed here. Gaps have been left in the numbering to better accommodate future additions to this list.

		NM	EX	VG
Common Player:		60.00	30.00	20.00
1928				
(2)	Aldrick Gaudette (May 19)	60.00	30.00	20.00
(4)	Robert Shawkey (June 2)	80.00	40.00	24.00
(5)	Lachine team photo, portraits of starting nine (June 9)	60.00	30.00	20.00
(6)	Roy Buckalew, Frank Dunagan, Chester Fowler, Thomas Gulley, Peter Radwan, Richard Smith (June 16)	60.00	30.00	20.00
(7)	Seymour Edward Bailey (June 23)	60.00	30.00	20.00
(8)	Wilson F. Fewster (June 30)	60.00	30.00	20.00
(10)	Tom Daly (July 14)	60.00	30.00	20.00
(14)	Red Holt (Aug. 11)	60.00	30.00	20.00
(17)	George Herman Ruth (Oct. 13)	750.00	375.00	225.00
(20)	Johnny Prud'homme (Nov. 3)	60.00	30.00	20.00
1929				
(2)	Walter Paul Gautreau (April 13)	60.00	30.00	20.00
(4)	Herb Thormahlen (April 27)	60.00	30.00	20.00
(9)	Elon Hogsett (July 13)	60.00	30.00	20.00
(12)	Robert M. "Lefty" Grove (Oct. 19)	200.00	100.00	60.00
(15)	Philadelphia A's Stars (Mickey Cochrane, Jimmie Foxx, Connie Mack, Al Simmons, Rube Walberg, Bing Miller) (Nov. 16)	90.00	45.00	27.00
1930				
(3)	Martin Griffin, John Pomorski, Arthur Smith, Herb Thormahlen (May 31)	60.00	30.00	20.00
(4)	James Calleran, Edward Conley, Lee Head, Jimmy Ripple (June 7)	60.00	30.00	20.00
(7)	Del Bissonette (June 28)	60.00	30.00	20.00
(9)	Joe Hauser (July 12)	75.00	37.00	22.00
(14)	Gowell Sylvester Claset (Sept. 13)	60.00	30.00	20.00
(17)	Hack Wilson (Oct. 11)	200.00	100.00	60.00
1931				
(2)	Chuck Klein (May 30)	175.00	87.00	52.00
(3)	Jocko Conlan (June 6)	100.00	50.00	30.00
(5)	Lee Head (June 20)	60.00	30.00	20.00
(7)	Jimmy Ripple (July 4)	60.00	30.00	20.00
(9)	Sol Mishkin (July 18)	60.00	30.00	20.00
(11)	Walter Brown (Aug. 15)	60.00	30.00	20.00
(15)	Johnny Allen, Frank Barnes, Guy Cantrell, Ken Strong (Nov. 14)	60.00	30.00	20.00
(16)	John Pepper Martin (Nov. 21)	80.00	40.00	24.00
1932				
(2)	Johnny Grabowski (May 28)	60.00	30.00	20.00
(3)	Charles Sullivan (June 4)	60.00	30.00	20.00
(5)	Walter "Doc" Gautreau (June 18)	60.00	30.00	20.00
(6)	John Clancy (June 25)	60.00	30.00	20.00
(7)	Buck Walters (July 2)	75.00	37.00	22.00
(8)	Bill McAfee (July 9)	60.00	30.00	20.00
(9)	George Puccinelli (July 16)	60.00	30.00	20.00
(11)	Buck Crouse (Aug. 6)	60.00	30.00	20.00
(12)	Ollie Carnegie (Aug. 13)	60.00	30.00	20.00
(13)	Leo Mangum (Aug. 20)	60.00	30.00	20.00
(17)	Roy Parmelee (Nov. 19) (Dates of issue not confirmed)	60.00	30.00	20.00
	Dan Howley	60.00	30.00	20.00

1952 Laval Dairy Provincial League

This scarce Canadian minor league issue includes only players from the Class C Provincial League, centered in Quebec. The black-and-white cards are blank-backed and measure 1-3/4" x 2-1/2". The player name, position, date and place of birth and card number is in French. Teams represented in the set are Quebec (Braves), St. Jean (Pirates), Three Rivers (independent), Drummondville (Senators), Granby (Phillies) and Ste. Hyacinthe (Philadelphia A's).

		NM	EX	VG
Complete Set (114):		4,000	2,000	1,200
Common Player:		35.00	17.50	10.00
1	Georges McQuinn	35.00	17.50	10.00
2	Cliff Statham	35.00	17.50	10.00
3	Frank Wilson	35.00	17.50	10.00
4	Frank Neri	35.00	17.50	10.00
5	Georges Maranda	35.00	17.50	10.00
6	Richard "Dick" Cordeiro	35.00	17.50	10.00
7	Roger McCardell	35.00	17.50	10.00
8	Joseph Janiak	35.00	17.50	10.00
9	Herbert Shankman	35.00	17.50	10.00
10	Joe Subbiondo	35.00	17.50	10.00
11	Jack Brenner	35.00	17.50	10.00
12	Donald Buchanan	35.00	17.50	10.00
13	Robert Smith	35.00	17.50	10.00
14	Raymond Lague	35.00	17.50	10.00
15	Mike Fandozzi	35.00	17.50	10.00
16	Dick Moler	35.00	17.50	10.00
17	Edward Bazydio	35.00	17.50	10.00
18	Danny Mazurek	35.00	17.50	10.00
19	Edwin Charles	35.00	17.50	10.00
20	Jack Nullaney	35.00	17.50	10.00
21	Bob Bolan	35.00	17.50	10.00
22	Bob Long	35.00	17.50	10.00
23	Cleo Lewright	35.00	17.50	10.00
24	Herb Taylor	35.00	17.50	10.00
25	Frankie Gaeta	35.00	17.50	10.00
26	Bill Truitt	35.00	17.50	10.00
27	Jean Prats	35.00	17.50	10.00
28	Tex Taylor	35.00	17.50	10.00
29	Ron Delbianco	35.00	17.50	10.00
30	Joe DiLorenzo	35.00	17.50	10.00
31	Johnny Paszek	35.00	17.50	10.00
32	Ken Suess	35.00	17.50	10.00
33	Harry Sims	35.00	17.50	10.00
34	William Jackson	35.00	17.50	10.00
35	Jerry Mayers	35.00	17.50	10.00
36	Gordon Maltzberger	35.00	17.50	10.00
37	Gerry Cabana	35.00	17.50	10.00
38	Gary Rutkey	35.00	17.50	10.00
39	Ken Hatcher	35.00	17.50	10.00
40	Vincent Cosenza	35.00	17.50	10.00
41	Edward Yaeger	35.00	17.50	10.00
42	Jimmy Orr	35.00	17.50	10.00
43	Johnny Di Matino	35.00	17.50	10.00
44	Lenny Wisneski	35.00	17.50	10.00
45	Pete Caniglia	35.00	17.50	10.00
46	Guy Coleman	35.00	17.50	10.00
47	Herb Fleischer	35.00	17.50	10.00
48	Charles Yahrling	35.00	17.50	10.00
49	Roger Bedard	35.00	17.50	10.00
50	Al Barillari	35.00	17.50	10.00
51	Hugh Mulcahy	50.00	25.00	15.00
52	Vincent Canepa	35.00	17.50	10.00
53	Bob Loranger	35.00	17.50	10.00
54	Georges Carpentier	35.00	17.50	10.00
55	Bill Hamilton	35.00	17.50	10.00
56	Hector Lopez	65.00	32.00	19.50
57	Joel Taylor	35.00	17.50	10.00
58	Alonzo Brathwaite	100.00	50.00	30.00
59	Carl McQuillen	35.00	17.50	10.00
60	Robert Trice	35.00	17.50	10.00
61	John Dworak	35.00	17.50	10.00
62	Al Pinkston	50.00	25.00	15.00
63	William Shannon	35.00	17.50	10.00
64	Stanley Wotychowisz	35.00	17.50	10.00
65	Roger Herbert	35.00	17.50	10.00
66	Troy Spencer	35.00	17.50	10.00
67	Johnny Rohan	35.00	17.50	10.00
68	John Sosh	35.00	17.50	10.00
69	Ramon Mason	35.00	17.50	10.00
70	Tom Smith	35.00	17.50	10.00
71	Douglas McBean	35.00	17.50	10.00
72	Bill Babik	35.00	17.50	10.00
73	Dante Cozzi	35.00	17.50	10.00
74	Melville Doxtater	35.00	17.50	10.00
75	William Gilray	35.00	17.50	10.00
76	Armando Diaz	35.00	17.50	10.00
77	Ackroyd Smith	35.00	17.50	10.00
78	Germain Pizarro	35.00	17.50	10.00
79	Jim Heap	35.00	17.50	10.00
80	Herbert Crompton	35.00	17.50	10.00
81	Howard Bodell	35.00	17.50	10.00
82	Andre Schreiser	35.00	17.50	10.00
83	John Wingo	35.00	17.50	10.00
84	Salvatore Arduini	35.00	17.50	10.00
85	Fred Pallito	35.00	17.50	10.00
86	Aaron Osofsky	35.00	17.50	10.00
87	Jack DiGrace	35.00	17.50	10.00
88	Alphonso Chico Girard (Gerrard)	35.00	17.50	10.00
89	Manuel Trabous	35.00	17.50	10.00
90	Tom Barnes	35.00	17.50	10.00
91	Humberto Robinson	35.00	17.50	10.00

		NM	EX	VG
92	Jack Bukowatz	35.00	17.50	10.00
93	Marco Mainini	35.00	17.50	10.00
94	Claude St. Vincent	35.00	17.50	10.00
95	Fernand Brosseau	35.00	17.50	10.00
96	John Malangone	35.00	17.50	10.00
97	Pierre Nantel	35.00	17.50	10.00
98	Donald Stevens	35.00	17.50	10.00
99	Jim Prappas	35.00	17.50	10.00
100	Richard Fitzgerald	35.00	17.50	10.00
101	Yves Aubin	35.00	17.50	10.00
102	Frank Novosel	35.00	17.50	10.00
103	Tony Campos	35.00	17.50	10.00
104	Gelso Oviedo	35.00	17.50	10.00
105	Guly Becker	35.00	17.50	10.00
106	Aurelio Ala	35.00	17.50	10.00
107	Orlando Andux	35.00	17.50	10.00
108	Tom Hackett	35.00	17.50	10.00
109	Guillame Vargas	35.00	17.50	10.00
110	Fransisco Salfran	35.00	17.50	10.00
111	Jean-Marc Blais	35.00	17.50	10.00
112	Vince Pizzitola	35.00	17.50	10.00
113	John Olsen	35.00	17.50	10.00
114	Jacques Monette	35.00	17.50	10.00

1948 Los Angeles Angels Team Issue

A team-issued set sold in a paper envelope for $1 at the ballpark, these cards were produced by the same firm which published the team's yearbook, Pacific Coast Sports Publishing Co., of Los Angeles. The blank-backed cards measure 6-3/4" x 4-3/4" and are printed in black-and-white on thin cardboard with a semi-gloss front surface. Cards feature a facsimile player autograph on front, along with a posed action or portrait photo and complete major and minor league stats. The cards are listed in the American Card Catalog, along with the subsequent year's issue, as W725. Many of the players on this Pacific Coast League team were former or future Chicago Cubs. The unnumbered cards are checklisted here alphabetically.

		NM	EX	VG
Complete Set (26):		650.00	325.00	200.00
Common Player:		30.00	15.00	9.00
(1)	Cliff Aberson	30.00	15.00	9.00
(2)	Red Adams	30.00	15.00	9.00
(3)	John Adkins	30.00	15.00	9.00
(4)	Lee Anthony	30.00	15.00	9.00
(5)	Russ Bauers	30.00	15.00	9.00
(6)	Ora Burnett	30.00	15.00	9.00
(7)	Donald Carlsen	30.00	15.00	9.00
(8)	Dom Dallessandro	30.00	15.00	9.00
(9)	Cecil Garriott	30.00	15.00	9.00
(10)	Paul Gillespie	30.00	15.00	9.00
(11)	Al Glossop	30.00	15.00	9.00
(12)	Tom Hafey	30.00	15.00	9.00
(13)	Don Johnson	30.00	15.00	9.00
(14)	Bill Kelly	30.00	15.00	9.00
(15)	Hal Kleine	30.00	15.00	9.00
(16)	Walt Lanfranconi	30.00	15.00	9.00
(17)	Ed Lukon	30.00	15.00	9.00
(18)	Red Lynn	30.00	15.00	9.00
(19)	Eddie Malone	30.00	15.00	9.00
(20)	Len Merullo	30.00	15.00	9.00
(21)	Ralph Novotney	30.00	15.00	9.00
(22)	John Ostrowski	30.00	15.00	9.00
(23)	John Sanford	30.00	15.00	9.00
(24)	Ed Sauer	30.00	15.00	9.00
(25)	Bill Schuster	30.00	15.00	9.00
(26)	John Warner	30.00	15.00	9.00

1949 Los Angeles Angels Team Issue

Little changed in the second year of this team issue. Cards remained at 6-3/4" x 4-3/4" in format, printed black-and-white on semi-gloss cardboard with a blank back. Many of the players (and even some of the photos) were repeated from the previous year. The unnumbered cards are checklisted here in alphabetical order.

		NM	EX	VG
Complete Set (39):		1,000	500.00	300.00
Common Player:		30.00	15.00	9.00
(1)	Cliff Aberson	30.00	15.00	9.00
(2)	Donald Alfano	30.00	15.00	9.00
(3)	Quentin Altizer	30.00	15.00	9.00
(4)	Lee Anthony	30.00	15.00	9.00
(5)	Nels Burbrink	30.00	15.00	9.00
(6)	Smoky Burgess	75.00	37.50	22.00
(7)	Don Carlsen	30.00	15.00	9.00
(8)	Joe Damato	30.00	15.00	9.00
(9)	Bill Emmerich	30.00	15.00	9.00
(10)	Ken Gables	30.00	15.00	9.00
(11)	Cecil Garriott	30.00	15.00	9.00
(12)	Al Glossop	30.00	15.00	9.00
(13)	Gordon Goldsberry	30.00	15.00	9.00
(14)	Frank Gustine	30.00	15.00	9.00
(15)	Lee Handley	30.00	15.00	9.00
(16)	Alan Ihde	30.00	15.00	9.00
(17)	Bob Kelley/Announcer	30.00	15.00	9.00
(18)	Bill Kelly	30.00	15.00	9.00
(19)	Bob Kelly	30.00	15.00	9.00
(20)	Walt Lanfranconi	30.00	15.00	9.00
(21)	Red Lynn	30.00	15.00	9.00
(22)	Clarence Maddern	30.00	15.00	9.00
(23)	Eddie Malone	30.00	15.00	9.00
(24)	Carmen Mauro	30.00	15.00	9.00
(25)	Booker McDaniels	75.00	37.50	22.00
(26)	Cal McLish	50.00	25.00	15.00
(27)	Butch Moran	30.00	15.00	9.00
(28)	Ralph Novotney	30.00	15.00	9.00
(29)	John Ostrowski	30.00	15.00	9.00
(30)	Bobby Rhawn	30.00	15.00	9.00
(31)	Bill Schuster	30.00	15.00	9.00
(32)	Pat Seerey	30.00	15.00	9.00
(33)	Bryan Stephens	30.00	15.00	9.00
(34)	Bob Sturgeon	30.00	15.00	9.00
(35)	Wayne Terwilliger	45.00	22.00	13.50
(36)	Gordon Van Dyke	30.00	15.00	9.00
(37)	John Warner	30.00	15.00	9.00
(38)	Don Watkins	30.00	15.00	9.00
(39)	Trainers, bat boys (Dickie Evans, Joe Liscio, Dave Flores, Billy Lund)	30.00	15.00	9.00

1930-31 Lucke Badge & Button Baltimore Orioles Pins

These 7/8" diameter celluloid pinback buttons were produced by the Baltimore novelty firm of Lucke Badge & Button Co. Issued to honor fan favorites on their "Day," the buttons have black-and-white portrait photos at center, surrounded by a white rim. At top is the player name, at bottom is the team name and year. A paper label inside the back of the button identifies the maker and includes a union label.

	NM	EX	VG
Joe Hauser/1930	300.00	150.00	90.00
Don Heffner/1931	200.00	100.00	60.00

M

1910 Mascot Gum Pins

Only players from the Eastern League champion Rochester Bronchos are known on these 7/8" diameter pinback buttons. Fronts have a black-and-white player photo on a blue background with the player's last name at left and "ROCHESTER" at right. A paper insert on the reverse advertises "Ball Player's Buttons Free With Mascot Gum." This checklist may not be complete.

		NM	EX	VG
Common Player:		250.00	125.00	80.00
(1)	Anderson	250.00	125.00	80.00
(2)	Heinie Batch	250.00	125.00	80.00
(3)	Blair	250.00	125.00	80.00
(4)	Holmes	250.00	125.00	80.00
(5)	Lafitte	250.00	125.00	80.00
(6)	Manning	250.00	125.00	80.00
(7)	McConnell	250.00	125.00	80.00
(8)	Moeller	250.00	125.00	80.00
(9)	Moran	250.00	125.00	80.00
(10)	Osborn	250.00	125.00	80.00
(11)	Don Carlos Ragan	250.00	125.00	80.00
(12)	Savidge	250.00	125.00	80.00
(13)	Simmons	250.00	125.00	80.00
(14)	Spencer	250.00	125.00	80.00
(15)	Tooley	250.00	125.00	80.00

1952 May Co. Chuck Stevens Premium

The date given is speculative, about midway through the player's term with the Hollywood Stars of the Pacific Coast League. The 4-1/2" x 6" blank-backed black-and-white card features a portrait of what the caption at bottom calls the "popular first baseman." The caption also calls the piece a "MAY CO. 'Back To School' Party Souvenir Photo." The cards are often found bearing the player's autograph, presumably obtained at the event.

	NM	EX	VG
Chuck Stevens	75.00	40.00	25.00

1960s-70s J.D. McCarthy Postcards

For details of J.D. McCarthy's prolific body of black-and-white player postcards, see the introductory material in the vintage major league section.

Common Player: $1-3

SPOKANE INDIANS
(1) Roy Hartsfield
TOLEDO MUD HENS
(1) Loren Babe
(2) Stan Bahnsen
(3) Bill Bethea
(4) Joe Cherry
(5) Horace Clark
(6) Wayne Comer
(7) Jack Cullen (2)
(8) Jack Curtis (2)
(9) Gil Downs
(10) Joe Faraci
(11) Frank Fernandez
(12) Mike Ferraro
(13) Mickey Harrington
(14) Mike Hegan
(15) Jim Horsford (2)
(16) Dick Hughes
(17) Elvio Jiminez (2)
(18) Robert Lasko
(19) Artie Lopez
(20) Roy Majtyka
(21) Tom Martz
(22) Ed Merritt (2)
(23) Archie Moore (2)
(24) Al Moran
(25) Bobby Murcer
(26) Tony Przybycien
(27) Bill Roman
(28) Bob Schmidt (2)
(29) Tom Shafer
(30) Billy Shantz
(31) Shantz-Senger-Babe
(32) Bob Tiefenauer
(33) Paul Toth (2)
(34) Andrew Vickery
(35) Jerry Walker
(36) Don Wallace
(37) Dooley Womack

1954 MD Super Service Sacramento Solons

HANK SCHENZ
M D Super Service
16th and T Streets

This issue features only players of the Pacific Coast League Sacramento Solons. The unnumbered cards are printed in black-and-white and carry an ad for a local gas station. The borderless, blank-backed cards measure 2-1/8" x 3-3/8".

		NM	EX	VG
Complete Set (6):		850.00	425.00	250.00
Common Player:		150.00	75.00	45.00
(1)	Joe Brovia	150.00	75.00	45.00
(2)	Al Cicotte	150.00	75.00	45.00
(3)	Nippy Jones	150.00	75.00	45.00
(4)	Richie Meyers	150.00	75.00	45.00
(5)	Hank Schenz	150.00	75.00	45.00
(6)	Bud Sheeley	150.00	75.00	45.00

1952 Miami Beach Flamingos Team Issue

GEORGE HANDY

These 2-1/4" x 3-3/8" black-and-white, unnumbered, blank-backed cards were one of many minor league team sets issued by Globe Printing of San Jose, Calif., in the early 1950s. Cards were usually given away at the ballpark on a one-per-week or one-per-homestand basis, accounting for the rarity of surviving sets. An embossed album slotted to accommodate the cards was also issued. The Flamingos were an unaffiliated team in the Class B Florida International League.

		NM	EX	VG
Complete Set (25):		1,000	500.00	300.00
Common Player:		60.00	30.00	18.00
Album:		100.00	50.00	30.00
(1)	Billy Barrett	60.00	30.00	18.00
(2)	Art Bosch	60.00	30.00	18.00
(3)	Jack Caro	60.00	30.00	18.00
(4)	Chuck Ehlman	60.00	30.00	18.00
(5)	Oscar Garmendia	60.00	30.00	18.00
(6)	George Handy	60.00	30.00	18.00
(7)	Clark Henry	60.00	30.00	18.00
(8)	Dario Jiminez	60.00	30.00	18.00
(9)	Jesse Levan	60.00	30.00	18.00
(10)	Bobby Lyons	60.00	30.00	18.00
(11)	Pepper Martin	125.00	62.00	37.00
(12)	Dick McMillin	60.00	30.00	18.00
(13)	Pete Morant	60.00	30.00	18.00
(14)	Chico Morilla	60.00	30.00	18.00
(15)	Ken Munroe	60.00	30.00	18.00
(16)	Walt Nothe	60.00	30.00	18.00
(17)	Marshall O'Coine	60.00	30.00	18.00
(18)	Whitey Platt	60.00	30.00	18.00
(19)	Johnny Podgajny	60.00	30.00	18.00
(20)	Knobby Rosa	60.00	30.00	18.00
(21)	Harry Raulerson	60.00	30.00	18.00
(22)	Mort Smith	60.00	30.00	18.00
(23)	Tommy Venn	60.00	30.00	18.00
(24)	George Wehmeyer	60.00	30.00	18.00
(25)	Ray Williams	60.00	30.00	18.00

1963 Milwaukee Sausage Seattle Rainiers

Inserted into meat packages by a Seattle sausage company, the 11 cards known in this set are all Seattle Rainiers players, several of whom had big league experience. Cards measure approximately 4-1/4"-square and are printed in blue, red and yellow. The unnumbered cards are checklisted in alphabetical order.

		NM	EX	VG
Complete Set (11):		6,000	3,000	1,800
Common Player:		600.00	300.00	180.00
(1)	Dave Hall	600.00	300.00	180.00
(2)	Bill Harrell	600.00	300.00	180.00
(3)	Pete Jernigan	600.00	300.00	180.00
(4)	Bill McLeod	600.00	300.00	180.00
(5)	Mel Parnell	650.00	325.00	200.00
(6)	Elmer Singleton	600.00	300.00	180.00
(7)	Archie Skeen	600.00	300.00	180.00
(8)	Paul Smith	600.00	300.00	180.00
(9)	Pete Smith	600.00	300.00	180.00
(10)	Bill Spanswick	600.00	300.00	180.00
(11)	George Spencer	600.00	300.00	180.00

1909 Minneapolis Tribune/ St. Paul Pioneer Press Mirrors

From the few players known, it is apparent these mirrors were issued in 1909 by two of the Twin Cities' daily newspapers. Each mirror is 2-1/8" diameter with a celluloid back. At center is a black-and-white player photo. All typography is in b/w, as well. A pair of concentric circles around the photo contain the player's name and a short description of his prowess. Olmstead's reads, "Unhittable in the Pinches"; Carisch's reads, "Nails 'em to the Cross Every Time". The outer circle contains an ad for the newspaper. This checklist is probably incomplete.

		NM	EX	VG
Common Player:		200.00	100.00	60.00
(1)	Fred Carisch	200.00	100.00	60.00
(2)	Michael Kelly	200.00	100.00	60.00
(3)	Fred Olmstead	200.00	100.00	60.00

1911 Mono Cigarettes (T217)

As was common with many tobacco issues of the period, the T217 set - distributed on the West Coast by Mono Cigarettes - feature both baseball players and "Leading Actresses." The 23 baseball players in the Mono set are all from the Pacific Coast League. Two of the players (Delhi and Hughie Smith) are shown in two poses, resulting in a total of 25 different cards. The players are pictured in black-and-white photos on a card

that measures approximately 1-1/2" x 2-5/8", the standard size of a tobacco card. The player's name and team appear at the bottom, while the back of the card carries an advertisement for Mono Cigarettes. The Mono set, which can be dated to the 1909-1911 period, is among the rarest of all tobacco cards.

		NM	EX	VG
Complete Set (25):		100,000	50,000	30,000
Common Player:		4,250	2,000	1,100
(1)	Aiken	4,250	2,000	1,100
(2)	Curtis Bernard	4,250	2,000	1,100
(3)	L. Burrell	4,250	2,000	1,100
(4)	Chadbourn	4,250	2,000	1,100
(5)	R. Couchman	4,250	2,000	1,100
(6)	Elmer Criger	4,250	2,000	1,100
(7)	Pete Daley	4,250	2,000	1,100
(8)	W. Delhi (Glove at chest level.)	4,250	2,000	1,100
(9)	W. Delhi (Glove at shoulder level.)	4,250	2,000	1,100
(10)	Bert Delmas	4,250	2,000	1,100
(11)	Ivan Howard	4,250	2,000	1,100
(12)	Kitty Knight	4,250	2,000	1,100
(13)	Gene Knapp (Krapp)	4,250	2,000	1,100
(14)	Metzger	4,250	2,000	1,100
(15)	Carl Mitze	4,250	2,000	1,100
(16)	J. O'Rourke	4,250	2,000	1,100
(17)	R. Peckinpaugh	4,250	2,000	1,100
(18)	Walter Schmidt	4,250	2,000	1,100
(19)	Hughie Smith/Btg	4,250	2,000	1,100
(20)	Hughie Smith/Fielding	4,250	2,000	1,100
(21)	Wm. Stein	4,250	2,000	1,100
(22)	Elmer Thorsen	4,250	2,000	1,100
(23)	Oscar Vitt	4,250	2,000	1,100
(24)	Clyde Wares	4,250	2,000	1,100
(25)	Geo. Wheeler	4,250	2,000	1,100

1961 Jeffrey W. Morey Postcards

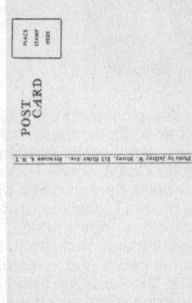

This set of 3-1/2" x 5-1/2", black-and-white postcards was produced to accomodate fan mail requests by two players each from the Columbus Clippers and Syracuse Chiefs. Fronts have a facsimile autograph. Divided-postcard backs have a credit line to the photographer and standard postcard markings.

		NM	EX	VG
Complete Set (4):		125.00	65.00	37.50
Common Player:		35.00	17.50	10.50
(1)	Larry Elliot	35.00	17.50	10.50
(2)	Don Rowe	35.00	17.50	10.50
(3)	Ted Sadowski	35.00	17.50	10.50
(4)	Ron Stillwell	35.00	17.50	10.50

1947 Morley Studios Team Cards

Besides issuing individual player cards of the Tacoma team, Morley Studios also issued postcard-size pictures of the teams in the Class B Western International League of 1947. The 3-1/2" x 5-1/2" cards are blank-backed and carry a "Morley Studios / 1947" imprint on front.

		NM	EX	VG
Complete Set (8):		600.00	300.00	180.00
Common Player:		75.00	37.50	22.50
(1)	Bremerton Bluejackets	75.00	37.50	22.50
(2)	Salem Senators	75.00	37.50	22.50
(3)	Spokane Indians	75.00	37.50	22.50
(4)	Tacoma Tigers	75.00	37.50	22.50
(5)	Vancouver Capilanos	75.00	37.50	22.50
(6)	Victoria Athletics	75.00	37.50	22.50
(7)	Yakima Stars	75.00	37.50	22.50
(8)	Wenatchee Chiefs	75.00	37.50	22.50

1947 Morley Studios Tacoma Tigers

This set of Tacoma Tigers (Western International League) features borderless black-and-white posed action photos with a facsimile autograph. A "Morley Sports Photos" or "Morley Studios" credit line appears at the bottom. Backs of the first seven cards are blank, while the others feature player biographies credited to "Jordan's (bread sponsor) Broadcaster" Clay Huntington and a Series A through F designation (though some cards lack the letter code). The unnumbered cards measure 2-1/2" x 3-1/2".

A *Morley* SPORTGRAFIC

Stanley "Gilly" Gilson is a pitcher recommended by Jackie Warner, Los Angeles Coach, who scouted him pitching for L. A. Cherubs. Born Philadelphia, Pa., May 27, 1926, he now makes Los Angeles his home. Has brown hair, hazel eyes, 5' 10" and weighs 165. He hits and throws right. Attended the U.C.L.A. but did not participate in sports. Played baseball in high school. His first year in professional ball but played for Donny High School, Los Angeles Cherubs and Dick Bartell's Treasure Island service team. Has ambitions to be a Major leaguer. His dog is his pet and his hobby is photography. His greatest thrill in baseball was playing with big-leaguers at Treasure Island. He is a bachelor. Served both in the Army and Navy from 1943 to 1946. Was overseas six months in Battles at Leyte and Saipan.

Clay Huntington
Jordan's Broadcaster

		NM	EX	VG
Complete Set (28):		3,500	1,750	1,000
Common Player:		125.00	65.00	40.00
	Blank-backed			
(1)	Hank Bartolomei	125.00	65.00	40.00
(2)	Rod Belcher/Broadcaster	125.00	65.00	40.00
(3)	Tip Berg/Trainer	125.00	65.00	40.00
(4)	Gene Clough	125.00	65.00	40.00
(5)	Clay Huntington/Broadcaster	125.00	65.00	40.00
(6)	Donald Mooney (Bat boy.)	125.00	65.00	40.00
(7)	Buck Tinsley	125.00	65.00	40.00
	Series A			
(8)	Richard A. Greco	125.00	65.00	40.00
(9)	Cy Greenlaw	125.00	65.00	40.00
(10)	Bob Joratz	125.00	65.00	40.00
(11)	Earl Kuper	125.00	65.00	40.00
	Series B			
(12)	Neil Clifford	125.00	65.00	40.00
(13)	Red Harvel	125.00	65.00	40.00
(14)	Julian Morgan	125.00	65.00	40.00
(15)	Pete Tedeschi	125.00	65.00	40.00
	Series C			
(16)	Stanley Gilson	125.00	65.00	40.00
(17)	Harry Nygard	125.00	65.00	40.00
(18)	Cleve Ramsey	125.00	65.00	40.00
(19)	Pete Sabutis	125.00	65.00	40.00
	Series D			
(20)	Mitch Chetkovich	125.00	65.00	40.00
(21)	Leroy Paton	125.00	65.00	40.00
(22)	Carl Shaply	125.00	65.00	40.00
(23)	Glenn Stetter	125.00	65.00	40.00
	Series E			
(24)	Bob Hedington	125.00	65.00	40.00
(25)	Ed Keehan	125.00	65.00	40.00
(26)	Gordon Walden	125.00	65.00	40.00
	Series F			
(27)	Maury Donovan	125.00	65.00	40.00
(28)	Guy Miller	125.00	65.00	40.00

1952 Mother's Cookies

This is one of the most popular regional minor league sets ever issued. Cards of Pacific Coast League players were included in packages of cookies. Distribution was limited to the West Coast. The 64 cards feature full color photos on a colored background, with player name and team. The cards measure 2-13/16" x 3-1/2", though the cards' rounded corners cause some variation in listed size. Card backs feature a very brief player statistic, card numbers and an offer for purchasing postage stamps. Five cards (11, 16, 29, 37 and 43) are considered scarce, while card #4 (Chuck Connors) is the most popular.

		NM	EX	VG
Complete Set (64):		4,500	2,100	1,250
Common Player:		60.00	30.00	20.00
1a	Johnny Lindell (Regular back.)	80.00	40.00	25.00
1b	Johnny Lindell ('52 Hollywood schedule on back.)	80.00	40.00	25.00
2	Jim Davis	60.00	30.00	20.00
3	Al Gettle (Gettel)	60.00	30.00	20.00
4	Chuck Connors	600.00	300.00	200.00
5	Joe Grace	60.00	30.00	20.00
6	Eddie Basinski	60.00	30.00	20.00
7a	Gene Handley (Regular back.)	60.00	30.00	20.00
7b	Gene Handley (Schedule back.)	60.00	30.00	20.00
8	Walt Judnich	60.00	30.00	20.00
9	Jim Marshall	60.00	30.00	20.00
10	Max West	60.00	30.00	20.00
11	Bill MacCawley	120.00	60.00	35.00
12	Moreno Peiretti	60.00	30.00	20.00
13a	Fred Haney (Regular back.)	75.00	37.50	22.50
13b	Fred Haney ('52 Hollywood schedule on back.)	75.00	37.50	22.50
14	Earl Johnson	60.00	30.00	20.00
15	Dave Dahle	60.00	30.00	20.00
16	Bob Talbot	120.00	60.00	35.00
17	Smokey Singleton	60.00	30.00	20.00
18	Frank Austin	60.00	30.00	20.00
19	Joe Gordon	90.00	45.00	27.50
20	Joe Marty	60.00	30.00	20.00
21	Bob Gillespie	60.00	30.00	20.00
22	Red Embree	60.00	30.00	20.00
23a	Lefty Olsen (Brown belt.)	60.00	30.00	20.00
23b	Lefty Olsen (Black belt.)	90.00	45.00	27.50
24a	Whitey Wietelmann (Large photo, much of bat missing.)	60.00	30.00	20.00
24b	Whitey Wietelmann (Small photo, more bat shows.)	60.00	30.00	20.00
25	Frank O'Doul	100.00	50.00	30.00
26	Memo Luna	60.00	30.00	20.00
27	John Davis	60.00	30.00	20.00
28	Dick Faber	60.00	30.00	20.00
29	Buddy Peterson	225.00	110.00	67.00
30	Hank Schenz	60.00	30.00	20.00
31	Tookie Gilbert	60.00	30.00	20.00
32	Mel Ott	200.00	100.00	60.00
33	Sam Chapman	60.00	30.00	20.00
34a	John Ragni/Outfielder	60.00	30.00	20.00
34b	John Ragni/Pitcher	100.00	50.00	30.00
35	Dick Cole	60.00	30.00	20.00
36	Tom Saffell	60.00	30.00	20.00
37	Roy Welmaker	120.00	60.00	35.00
38	Lou Stringer	60.00	30.00	20.00
39a	Chuck Stevens (Team on back Hollywood.)	60.00	30.00	20.00
39b	Chuck Stevens (Team on back Seattle.)	60.00	30.00	20.00
39c	Chuck Stevens (No team on back.)	60.00	30.00	20.00
40	Artie Wilson	90.00	45.00	30.00
41	Charlie Schanz	60.00	30.00	20.00
42	Al Lyons	60.00	30.00	20.00
43	Joe Erautt	300.00	150.00	90.00
44	Clarence Maddern	60.00	30.00	20.00
45	Gene Baker	60.00	30.00	20.00
46	Tom Heath	60.00	30.00	20.00
47	Al Lien	60.00	30.00	20.00
48	Bill Reeder	60.00	30.00	20.00
49	Bob Thurman	60.00	30.00	20.00
50	Ray Orteig	60.00	30.00	20.00
51	Joe Brovia	60.00	30.00	20.00
52	Jim Russell	60.00	30.00	20.00
53	Fred Sanford	60.00	30.00	20.00
54	Jim Gladd	60.00	30.00	20.00
55	Clay Hopper	60.00	30.00	20.00
56	Bill Glynn	60.00	30.00	20.00
57	Mike McCormick	60.00	30.00	20.00
58	Richie Myers	60.00	30.00	20.00
59	Vinnie Smith	60.00	30.00	20.00
60a	Stan Hack (Brown belt.)	80.00	40.00	25.00
60b	Stan Hack (Black belt.)	80.00	40.00	25.00
61	Bob Spicer	60.00	30.00	20.00
62	Jack Hollis	60.00	30.00	20.00
63	Ed Chandler	60.00	30.00	20.00
64	Bill Moisan	85.00	45.00	25.00

1953 Mother's Cookies

The 1953 Mother's Cookies cards are again 2-3/16" x 3-1/2", with rounded corners. There are 63 players from Pacific Coast League teams included. The full-color fronts have facsimile autographs rather than printed player names, and card backs offer a trading card album. Cards are generally more plentiful than in the 1952 set, with 11 of the cards apparently double printed.

		NM	EX	VG
Complete Set (63):		1,725	850.00	525.00
Common Player:		30.00	15.00	9.00
Album:		125.00	65.00	40.00
1	Lee Winter	35.00	17.50	10.00
2	Joe Ostrowski	30.00	15.00	9.00
3	Will Ramsdell	30.00	15.00	9.00
4	Bobby Bragan	40.00	20.00	12.00
5	Fletcher Robbe	30.00	15.00	9.00
6	Aaron Robinson	30.00	15.00	9.00
7	Augie Galan	30.00	15.00	9.00
8	Buddy Peterson	30.00	15.00	9.00
9	Frank Lefty O'Doul	65.00	32.50	20.00
10	Walt Pocekay	30.00	15.00	9.00
11	Nini Tornay	30.00	15.00	9.00
12	Jim Moran	30.00	15.00	9.00
13	George Schmees	30.00	15.00	9.00
14	Al Widmar	30.00	15.00	9.00
15	Ritchie Myers	30.00	15.00	9.00
16	Bill Howerton	30.00	15.00	9.00
17	Chuck Stevens	30.00	15.00	9.00
18	Joe Brovia	30.00	15.00	9.00
19	Max West	30.00	15.00	9.00
20	Eddie Malone	30.00	15.00	9.00
21	Gene Handley	30.00	15.00	9.00
22	William D. McCawley	30.00	15.00	9.00
23	Bill Sweeney	30.00	15.00	9.00
24	Tom Alston	30.00	15.00	9.00
25	George Vico	30.00	15.00	9.00
26	Hank Arft	30.00	15.00	9.00
27	Al Benton	30.00	15.00	9.00
28	"Pete" Milne	30.00	15.00	9.00
29	Jim Gladd	30.00	15.00	9.00
30	Earl Rapp	35.00	17.50	10.00
31	Ray Orteig	30.00	15.00	9.00
32	Eddie Basinski	30.00	15.00	9.00
33	Reno Cheso	30.00	15.00	9.00
34	Clarence Maddern	30.00	15.00	9.00
35	Marino Pieretti	30.00	15.00	9.00
36	Bill Raimondi	30.00	15.00	9.00
37	Frank Kelleher	30.00	15.00	9.00
38	George Bamberger	35.00	17.50	10.00
39	Dick Smith	30.00	15.00	9.00
40	Charley Schanz	30.00	15.00	9.00
41	John Van Cuyk	30.00	15.00	9.00
42	Lloyd Hittle	30.00	15.00	9.00
43	Tommy Heath	30.00	15.00	9.00
44	Frank Kalin	30.00	15.00	9.00
45	Jack Tobin	30.00	15.00	9.00
46	Jim Davis	30.00	15.00	9.00
47	Claude Christie	30.00	15.00	9.00
48	Elvin Tappe	30.00	15.00	9.00
49	Stan Hack	60.00	30.00	18.00
50	Fred Richards	30.00	15.00	9.00
51	Clay Hopper	30.00	15.00	9.00
52	Roy Welmaker	30.00	15.00	9.00
53	Red Adams	30.00	15.00	9.00
54	Piper Davis	60.00	30.00	18.00
55	Spider Jorgensen	30.00	15.00	9.00
56	Lee Walls	30.00	15.00	9.00
57	Jack Phillips	30.00	15.00	9.00
58	Red Lynn	30.00	15.00	9.00
59	Eddie Beckman	30.00	15.00	9.00
60	Gene Desautels	30.00	15.00	9.00
61	Bob Dillinger	30.00	15.00	9.00
62	Al Federoff	55.00	27.50	16.50
63	Bill Boemler	30.00	15.00	9.00

1920 Mrs. Sherlock's Bread Pins

Members of the Toledo Mud Hens of the American Association are featured on this set of pins sponsored by Mrs. Sherlock's Bread. The 7/8" celluloid pins have a player portrait in black-and-white at center, with his name and position indicated below. At top, in either red or black type is, "Mrs. Sherlock's Home Made Bread." Backs credit manufacture to Bastian Bros. of Rochester, N.Y., "Mfr's of ribbon metal and celluloid novelties." The unnumbered pins are checklisted here alphabetically.

		NM	EX	VG
Complete Set (19):		850.00	425.00	250.00
Common Player:		60.00	30.00	18.00
(1)	Brady	60.00	30.00	18.00
(2)	Roger Bresnahan	90.00	45.00	27.00
(3)	Jean Dubuc	60.00	30.00	18.00
(4)	Dyer	60.00	30.00	18.00
(5)	Fox	60.00	30.00	18.00
(6)	Ham Hyatt	60.00	30.00	18.00
(7)	Jones	60.00	30.00	18.00
(8)	Joe Kelly	60.00	30.00	18.00
(9)	M. Kelly	60.00	30.00	18.00
(10)	Art Kores	60.00	30.00	18.00
(11)	McColl	60.00	30.00	18.00
(12)	Norm McNeill (McNeil)	60.00	30.00	18.00
(13)	Middleton	60.00	30.00	18.00
(14)	Murphy	60.00	30.00	18.00
(15)	Nelson	60.00	30.00	18.00
(16)	Dutch Stryker	60.00	30.00	18.00
(17)	Thompson	60.00	30.00	18.00
(18)	Al Wickland	60.00	30.00	18.00
(19)	Joe Wilhoit	60.00	30.00	18.00

1922 Mrs. Sherlock's Bread Pins (PB5)

Members of the Toledo Mud Hens of the American Association are featured on this set of pins sponsored by Mrs. Sherlock's Bread. The 5/8" celluloid pins have a player portrait in brown or green at center, with his name and position indicated below. At top, in either brown or green type is, "Eat Mrs. Sherlock's Bread." The pins are numbered at lower-left.

		NM	EX	VG
Complete Set (21):		900.00	450.00	275.00
Common Player:		60.00	30.00	18.00
1	Roger Bresnahan	90.00	45.00	27.00
2	Brad Kocher	60.00	30.00	18.00
3	Hill	60.00	30.00	18.00
4	Huber	60.00	30.00	18.00
5	Doc Ayers	60.00	30.00	18.00
6	Parks	60.00	30.00	18.00
7	Giard	60.00	30.00	18.00
8	Grimes	60.00	30.00	18.00
9	McCullough	60.00	30.00	18.00
10	Shoup	60.00	30.00	18.00
11	Al Wickland	60.00	30.00	18.00
12	Baker	60.00	30.00	18.00
13	Schauffle	60.00	30.00	18.00
14	Wright	60.00	30.00	18.00
15	Lamar	60.00	30.00	18.00
16	Sallee	60.00	30.00	18.00
17	Fred Luderus	60.00	30.00	18.00
18	Walgomat	60.00	30.00	18.00
19	Ed Konetchy	60.00	30.00	18.00
20	O'Neill	60.00	30.00	18.00
21	Hugh Bedient	60.00	30.00	18.00

1933 Mrs. Sherlock's Bread Pins

Members of the Toledo Mud Hens of the American Association are featured on this set of pins sponsored by Mrs. Sherlock's Bread. The 7/8" celluloid pins have a player portrait in black-and-white at center, with his name and position indicated below. At top, in red type, is "Mrs. Sherlock's Home Made Bread" in two lines. The unnumbered pins are checklisted here alphabetically.

		NM	EX	VG
Complete Set (18):		800.00	400.00	240.00
Common Player:		50.00	25.00	15.00
(1)	LeRoy Bachman	50.00	25.00	15.00
(2)	George Detore	50.00	25.00	15.00
(3)	Frank Doljack	50.00	25.00	15.00
(4)	Milt Galatzer	50.00	25.00	15.00
(5)	Walter Henline	50.00	25.00	15.00
(6)	Roxie Lawson	50.00	25.00	15.00
(7)	Thornton Lee	50.00	25.00	15.00
(8)	Ed Montague	50.00	25.00	15.00
(9)	Steve O'Neill	50.00	25.00	15.00
(10)	Monte Pearson	50.00	25.00	15.00
(11)	Bob Reis	50.00	25.00	15.00
(12)	Scott	50.00	25.00	15.00
(13)	Bill Sweeney	50.00	25.00	15.00
(14)	Hal Trosky	50.00	25.00	15.00
(15)	Pete Turgeon	50.00	25.00	15.00
(16)	Forrest Twogood	50.00	25.00	15.00
(17)	Max West	50.00	25.00	15.00
(18)	Ralph Winegarner	50.00	25.00	15.00

1956 Mutual Savings Dick Stuart

Possibly issued in conjunction with an autograph appearance at the bank, Dick Stuart is pictured on this black-and-white postcard-sized photocard as an outfielder for the Western League Lincoln Chiefs in 1956, the season in which he hit 66 home runs.

	NM	EX	VG
Dick Stuart	100.00	50.00	30.00

N

1960 National Bank of Washington Tacoma Giants

These 3" x 5" unnumbered cards have color photos on front and are usually found with black-and-white backs with the bank's advertising. Uncut sheets of the cards were sold at Cheney Stadium in Tacoma either blank-backed or with a message from the Tacoma Athletic Commission. Only members of the Pacific Coast League Tacoma Giants are included in the set. The set contains the first card issued of Hall of Fame pitcher Juan Marichal. Unfortunately, fellow Hall of Famer Willie McCovey who played in 17 games for Tacoma in 1960 is not included in the set.

		NM	EX	VG
Complete Set (21):		1,000.	500.00	300.00
Common Player:		30.00	15.00	9.00
(1)	Matty Alou	75.00	37.00	22.00
(2)	Ossie Alvarez	30.00	15.00	9.00
(3)	Don Choate	30.00	15.00	9.00
(4)	Red Davis	30.00	15.00	9.00
(5)	Bob Farley	30.00	15.00	9.00
(6)	Eddie Fisher	30.00	15.00	9.00
(7)	Tom Haller	30.00	15.00	9.00
(8)	Sherman Jones	30.00	15.00	9.00
(9)	Juan Marichal	400.00	200.00	120.00
(10)	Ray Monzant	30.00	15.00	9.00
(11)	Danny O'Connell	30.00	15.00	9.00
(12)	Jose Pagan	30.00	15.00	9.00
(13)	Bob Perry	30.00	15.00	9.00
(14)	Dick Phillips	30.00	15.00	9.00
(15)	Bobby Prescott	30.00	15.00	9.00
(16)	Marshall Renfroe	30.00	15.00	9.00
(17)	Frank Reveira	30.00	15.00	9.00
(18)	Dusty Rhodes	35.00	17.50	10.00
(19)	Sal Taormina	30.00	15.00	9.00
(20)	Verle Tiefenthaler	30.00	15.00	9.00
(21)	Dom Zanni	30.00	15.00	9.00

1961 National Bank of Washington Tacoma Giants

 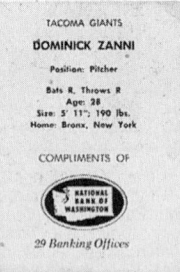

These 3" x 4" cards feature borderless sepia photos on the front. Backs have a sponsor's ad and a few player stats printed in dark blue. The unnumbered cards are checklisted here in alphabetical order.

		NM	EX	VG
Complete Set (21):		800.00	400.00	240.00
Common Player:		30.00	15.00	10.00
(1)	Rafael Alomar	40.00	20.00	12.00
(2)	Ernie Bowman	30.00	15.00	10.00
(3)	Bud Byerly	30.00	15.00	10.00
(4)	Ray Daviault	30.00	15.00	10.00
(5)	Red Davis	30.00	15.00	10.00
(6)	Bob Farley	30.00	15.00	10.00
(7)	Gil Garrido	30.00	15.00	10.00
(8)	John Goetz	30.00	15.00	10.00
(9)	Bill Hain	30.00	15.00	10.00
(10)	Ronald Herbel	30.00	15.00	10.00
(11)	Lynn Lovenguth	30.00	15.00	10.00
(12)	Georges H. Maranda	30.00	15.00	10.00
(13)	Manuel Mota	100.00	50.00	30.00
(14)	John Orsino	30.00	15.00	10.00
(15)	Bob Perry	30.00	15.00	10.00
(16)	Gaylord Perry	175.00	90.00	55.00
(17)	Dick Phillips	30.00	15.00	10.00
(18)	Frank Reveira	30.00	15.00	10.00
(19)	Dusty Rhodes	40.00	20.00	12.00
(20)	Verle Tiefenthaler	30.00	15.00	10.00
(21)	Dom Zanni	30.00	15.00	10.00

1907 Newark Evening World Supplements

The Newark Sailors of the Class A Eastern League are featured in this set of supplements from a local newspaper. The 7-1/2" x 10-15/16" pieces are printed in either sepia or black-and-white. An ornate border surrounds a player pose on a plain background. In a box beneath is player identification. Backs are blank. The unnumbered supplements are checklisted here in alphabetical order, though the list may not yet be complete.

		NM	EX	VG
Common Player:		400.00	200.00	120.00
(1)	William Carrick	400.00	200.00	120.00
(2)	James Cockman	400.00	200.00	120.00
(3)	Clyde Engle	400.00	200.00	120.00
(4)	James Jones	400.00	200.00	120.00
(5)	Paul Krichell	400.00	200.00	120.00
(6)	Henry LaBelle	400.00	200.00	120.00
(7)	William Mahling	400.00	200.00	120.00
(8)	Chas. McCafferty	400.00	200.00	120.00
(9)	Thomas McCarthy	400.00	200.00	120.00
(10)	James Mullen (Mullin)	400.00	200.00	120.00
(11)	Al Pardee	400.00	200.00	120.00
(12)	Bayard Sharpe	400.00	200.00	120.00
(13)	John E. Shea	400.00	200.00	120.00
(14)	Oscar Stanage	400.00	200.00	120.00
(15)	Elmer Zacher	400.00	200.00	120.00

O

1950 Oak Hall Roanoke Red Sox

(See 1950 Bush & Hancock Roanoke Red Sox.)

1913 Oakland Oaks Team Issue

Stylistically similar to contemporary Zeenuts cards, little is known about this series. The blank-back, approximately 2" x 3-5/8" black-and-white cards have full-length player poses on a white background. The player's last name and city are printed in all caps in two lines at bottom. It is unknown whether the cards on this list comprise a complete set. Their manner of distribution is likewise unknown, they may have been a strip card issue or a candy insert.

		NM	EX	VG
	Common Player:	2,000	1,000	600.00
(1)	Ody Abbott	2,000	1,000	600.00
(2)	Harry Ables	2,000	1,000	600.00
(3)	Jesse Becker	2,000	1,000	600.00
(4)	W.W. Cook	2,000	1,000	600.00
(5)	Bert Coy	2,000	1,000	600.00
(6)	Rube Gardner	2,000	1,000	600.00
(7)	Howard Gregory	2,000	1,000	600.00
(8)	Gus Hetling	2,000	1,000	600.00
(9)	Jack Killilay	2,000	1,000	600.00
(10)	Bill Leard	2,000	1,000	600.00
(11)	John Malarkey	2,000	1,000	600.00
(12)	Carl Mitze	2,000	1,000	600.00
(13)	John Ness	2,000	1,000	600.00
(14)	Henry Olmstead	2,000	1,000	600.00
(15)	Cy Parkin	2,000	1,000	600.00
(16)	W.J. Pearce	2,000	1,000	600.00
(17)	Heine Pernoll	2,000	1,000	600.00
(18)	Ashley Pope	2,000	1,000	600.00
(19)	George Schirm	2,000	1,000	600.00
(20)	Elmer Zacher	2,000	1,000	600.00

1909 Obak (T212)

OLSON, Portland

Produced annually from 1909 to 1911, the Obak cards were actually three separate and distinct sets, but they were all grouped together under a single T212 designation in the American Card Catalog. The Obak sets are closely related in style to the more popular T206 "White Border" set issued over the same three-year period, and, in fact, were produced by the California branch of the same American Tobacco Company conglomerate. The Obaks are the standard tobacco card size, about 1-1/2" x 2-5/8", and feature a colored lithograph, along with the player's name and team, on the front of the card. The year of issue can easily be determined by examining the back. The 1909 issue has blue printing with the name "Obak" appearing in an "Old English" type style. For 1910 the type face was changed to straight block letters; and in 1911 the backs were printed in red and include a brief biography and player statistics. The 1909 edition featured only teams from the Pacific Coast League. Cards can be found with backs that have or do not have a border around the text, though neither version appears to be scarcer than the other. Many 1909 Obaks with the "no-frame" back design show evidence of having been cut by hand from sheets, rather than machine-cut.

		NM	EX	VG
	Complete Set (76):	45,000	27,500	11,000
	Common Player:	600.00	300.00	140.00
(1)	Baum	600.00	300.00	140.00
(2)	Beall	600.00	300.00	140.00
(3)	Bernard	600.00	300.00	140.00
(4)	Berry	600.00	300.00	140.00
(5)	Bodie	600.00	300.00	140.00
(6)	Boyce	600.00	300.00	140.00
(7)	Brackenridge	600.00	300.00	140.00
(8)	N. Brashear	600.00	300.00	140.00
(9)	Breen	600.00	300.00	140.00
(10)	Brown	600.00	300.00	140.00
(11)	D. Brown	600.00	300.00	140.00
(12)	Browning	600.00	300.00	140.00
(13)	Byrnes	600.00	300.00	140.00
(14)	Cameron	600.00	300.00	140.00
(15)	Carroll	600.00	300.00	140.00
(16)	Carson	600.00	300.00	140.00
(17)	Christian	600.00	300.00	140.00
(18)	Coy	600.00	300.00	140.00
(19)	Delmas	600.00	300.00	140.00
(20)	Dillon	600.00	300.00	140.00
(21)	Eagan	600.00	300.00	140.00
(22)	Easterly (Eastley)	600.00	300.00	140.00
(23)	Ehman	600.00	300.00	140.00
(24)	Fisher	600.00	300.00	140.00
(25)	Fitzgerald	600.00	300.00	140.00
(26)	Flannagan	600.00	300.00	140.00
(27)	Gandil	4,000	1,800	1,200
(28)	Garrett	600.00	300.00	140.00
(29)	Graham	600.00	300.00	140.00
(30)	Graney	600.00	300.00	140.00
(31)	Griffin	600.00	300.00	140.00

(32)	Guyn	600.00	300.00	140.00
(33)	Haley	600.00	300.00	140.00
(34)	Harkins	600.00	300.00	140.00
(35)	Henley	600.00	300.00	140.00
(36)	Hitt	600.00	300.00	140.00
(37)	Hogan	600.00	300.00	140.00
(38)	W. Hogan	600.00	300.00	140.00
(39)	Howard	600.00	300.00	140.00
(40)	Howse	600.00	300.00	140.00
(41)	Jansing	600.00	300.00	140.00
(42)	LaLonge	600.00	300.00	140.00
(43)	C. Lewis	600.00	300.00	140.00
(44)	D. Lewis	600.00	300.00	140.00
(45)	J. Lewis	600.00	300.00	140.00
(46)	Martinke	600.00	300.00	140.00
(47)	McArdle	600.00	300.00	140.00
(48)	McCredie	600.00	300.00	140.00
(49)	McKune	600.00	300.00	140.00
(50)	Melchior	600.00	300.00	140.00
(51)	Mohler	600.00	300.00	140.00
(52)	Mott	600.00	300.00	140.00
(53)	Mundorff	600.00	300.00	140.00
(54)	Murphy	600.00	300.00	140.00
(55)	Nagle	600.00	300.00	140.00
(56)	Nelson	600.00	300.00	140.00
(57)	Olson	600.00	300.00	140.00
(58)	Ornsdorff	600.00	300.00	140.00
(59)	Ort	600.00	300.00	140.00
(60)	Ragan	600.00	300.00	140.00
(61)	Raymer	600.00	300.00	140.00
(62)	Reidy	600.00	300.00	140.00
(63)	Ryan	600.00	300.00	140.00
(64)	Shinn	600.00	300.00	140.00
(65)	Smith	600.00	300.00	140.00
(66)	Speas	600.00	300.00	140.00
(67)	Stoval (Stovall)	600.00	300.00	140.00
(68)	Tennant	600.00	300.00	140.00
(69)	Whalen	600.00	300.00	140.00
(70)	Wheeler	600.00	300.00	140.00
(71)	Wiggs	600.00	300.00	140.00
(72)	Willett	600.00	300.00	140.00
(73)	J. Williams	600.00	300.00	140.00
(74)	R. Williams	600.00	300.00	140.00
(75)	Willis	600.00	300.00	140.00
(76)	Zeider	600.00	300.00	140.00

1910 Obak 150 Subjects (T212)

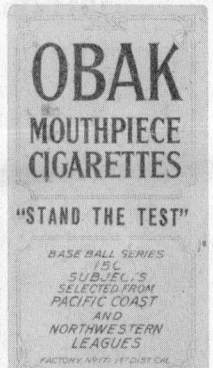

CRIGER, Los Angeles, P.C.L.

The most common, yet most complex, of the three annual T212 baseball card issues from Obak Cigarettes is the 1910 edition. Besides players from the six Pacific Coast League teams, cards were also issued for the four-team Northwestern League. This change caused the addition of a league abbreviation, along with the player's last name and city on front. Backs are again printed in blue, but utilize a less ornate typography than the 1909 cards. The 1910 Obak set is formatted similar to the more popular T206 "White Border" set issued at the same time "back East," and, in fact, was produced by the California branch of the same American Tobacco Company conglomerate. Obaks are the standard tobacco-card size, about 1-1/2" x 2-5/8", featuring a color lithograph on front. The 1910 issue comprises two major types, one which mentions "150 SUBJECTS," on back, the other specifying "175 SUBJECTS." Forty player cards, all from the PCL, are known to exist in both 150- and 175-subject versions, the former being much scarcer. Many of the 150-subject cards can be found with significant picture variations, such as missing team names on jerseys, plain versus striped caps, different background colors or different picture cropping. Unique to the 1910 Obaks is a selection of 35 different advertising slogans which are found on back between the boxed text elements. How many of the slogans can be found on each player's cards is unknown; some are seen on only a handful of different players' cards while others are found on dozens.

		NM	EX	VG
	Complete Set (40):	30,000	16,000	7,000
	Common Player:	750.00	400.00	175.00
(1)	Charlie Armbuster (Armbruster)	750.00	400.00	175.00
(2)	Claude Berry	750.00	400.00	175.00
(3)	John Brackenridge	750.00	400.00	175.00

(4)	N. Brashear (Norman)	750.00	400.00	175.00
(5)	Hap Briggs	750.00	400.00	175.00
(6)	Don Cameron	750.00	400.00	175.00
(7)	Bert Coy	750.00	400.00	175.00
(8)	Elmer Criger	750.00	400.00	175.00
(9)	Babe Danzig	750.00	400.00	175.00
(10)	Cap Dillon	750.00	400.00	175.00
(11)	Bill Fisher	750.00	400.00	175.00
(12)	Ed Griffin	750.00	400.00	175.00
(13)	Cack Henley	750.00	400.00	175.00
(14)	Al Hiester	750.00	400.00	175.00
(15)	Happy Hogan	750.00	400.00	175.00
(16)	Ivan Howard	750.00	400.00	175.00
(17)	Gene Krapp	750.00	400.00	175.00
(18)	Mickey LaLonge	750.00	400.00	175.00
(19)	George Manush	750.00	400.00	175.00
(20)	Roy McArdle	750.00	400.00	175.00
(21)	Walt McCredie	750.00	400.00	175.00
(22)	Henry Melchoir	750.00	400.00	175.00
(23)	Kid Mohler	750.00	400.00	175.00
(24)	Walter Moser	750.00	400.00	175.00
(25)	Howard Mundorf	750.00	400.00	175.00
(26)	Howard Murphy	750.00	400.00	175.00
(27)	George Ort	750.00	400.00	175.00
(28)	Hank Perry	750.00	400.00	175.00
(29)	Bill Rapps	750.00	400.00	175.00
(30)	H. Smith (Hugh)	750.00	400.00	175.00
(31)	J. Smith (Jud)	750.00	400.00	175.00
(32)	Bill Steen	750.00	400.00	175.00
(33)	Harry Stewart	750.00	400.00	175.00
(34)	Pinky Swander	750.00	400.00	175.00
(35)	Lefty Tonnesen (Tonneson)	750.00	400.00	175.00
(36)	Jimmy Whalen	750.00	400.00	175.00
(37)	Roy Willett	750.00	400.00	175.00
(38)	Jimmy Williams	750.00	400.00	175.00
(39)	Ralph Willis	750.00	400.00	175.00
(40)	Harry Wolverton	750.00	400.00	175.00

1910 Obak 175 Subjects (T212)

STOVELL, Vernon. P.C.L.

The most common, yet most complex, of the three annual T212 baseball card issues from Obak Cigarettes is the 1910 edition. Besides players from the six Pacific Coast League teams, cards were also issued for the four-team Northwestern League. This change caused the addition of a league abbreviation, along with the player's last name and city on front. Backs are again printed in blue, but utilize a less ornate typography than the 1909 cards. The 1910 Obak set is formatted similar to the more popular T206 "White Border" set issued at the same time "back East," and, in fact, was produced by the California branch of the same American Tobacco Company conglomerate. Obaks are the standard tobacco-card size, about 1-1/2" x 2-5/8", featuring a color lithograph on front. The 1910 issue comprises two major types, one which mentions "150 SUBJECTS," on back, the other specifying "175 SUBJECTS." Forty player cards, all from the PCL, are known to exist in both 150- and 175-subject versions, the former being much scarcer. Many of the 150-subject cards can be found with significant picture variations, such as missing team names on jerseys, plain versus striped caps, different background colors or different picture cropping. Unique to the 1910 Obaks is a selection of 35 different advertising slogans which are found on back between the boxed text elements. How many of the slogans can be found on each player's cards is unknown; some are seen on only a handful of different players' cards while others are found on dozens.

		NM	EX	VG
	Complete Set (175):	40,000	22,500	10,000
	Common Player:	250.00	130.00	60.00
(1)	Agnew	250.00	130.00	60.00
(2)	Akin	250.00	130.00	60.00
(3)	Ames	250.00	130.00	60.00
(4)	Annis	250.00	130.00	60.00
(5)	Armbuster (Armbruster)	250.00	130.00	60.00
(6)	Baker	250.00	130.00	60.00
(7)	Bassey	250.00	130.00	60.00
(8)	Baum	250.00	130.00	60.00
	Beall			
	(Now believed not to exist.)			
(9)	Bennett	250.00	130.00	60.00
(10)	Bernard	250.00	130.00	60.00

		NM	EX	VG
(11)	Berry	250.00	130.00	60.00
(12)	Blankenship	250.00	130.00	60.00
(13)	Boardman	250.00	130.00	60.00
(14)	Bodie	250.00	130.00	60.00
(15)	Bonner	250.00	130.00	60.00
(16)	Brackenridge	250.00	130.00	60.00
(17)	N. Brashear	250.00	130.00	60.00
(18)	R. Brashear	250.00	130.00	60.00
(19)	Breen	250.00	130.00	60.00
(20)	Briggs	250.00	130.00	60.00
(21)	Brinker	250.00	130.00	60.00
(22)	Briswalter	250.00	130.00	60.00
(23)	Brooks	250.00	130.00	60.00
(24)	Brown (Sacramento)	250.00	130.00	60.00
(25)	Brown (Vernon)	250.00	130.00	60.00
(26)	D. Brown	250.00	130.00	60.00
(27)	Browning	250.00	130.00	60.00
(28)	Burrell	250.00	130.00	60.00
(29)	Byrd	250.00	130.00	60.00
(30)	Byrnes	250.00	130.00	60.00
(31)	Cameron	250.00	130.00	60.00
(32)	Capron	250.00	130.00	60.00
(33)	Carlisle	250.00	130.00	60.00
(34)	Carroll	250.00	130.00	60.00
(35)	Cartwright	250.00	130.00	60.00
(36)	Casey	250.00	130.00	60.00
(37)	Caslleton (Castleton)	350.00	185.00	90.00
(38)	Chenault	250.00	130.00	60.00
(39)	Christian	250.00	130.00	60.00
(40)	Coleman	250.00	130.00	60.00
(41)	Cooney	250.00	130.00	60.00
(42)	Coy	250.00	130.00	60.00
(43)	Criger	250.00	130.00	60.00
(44)	Custer	250.00	130.00	60.00
(45)	Cutshaw	250.00	130.00	60.00
(46)	Daley	250.00	130.00	60.00
(47)	Danzig	250.00	130.00	60.00
(48)	Daringer	250.00	130.00	60.00
(49)	Davis	250.00	130.00	60.00
(50)	Delhi	250.00	130.00	60.00
(51)	Delmas	250.00	130.00	60.00
(52)	Dillon	250.00	130.00	60.00
(53)	Dretchko	250.00	130.00	60.00
(54)	Eastley	250.00	130.00	60.00
(55)	Erickson	250.00	130.00	60.00
(56)	Flannagan	250.00	130.00	60.00
(57)	Fisher (Portland)	250.00	130.00	60.00
(58)	Fisher (Vernon)	250.00	130.00	60.00
(59)	Fitzgerald	250.00	130.00	60.00
(60)	Flood	250.00	130.00	60.00
(61)	Fournier	250.00	130.00	60.00
(62)	Frisk	250.00	130.00	60.00
(63)	Gaddy	250.00	130.00	60.00
(64)	Gardner	250.00	130.00	60.00
(65)	Garrett	250.00	130.00	60.00
(66)	Greggs (Gregg)	250.00	130.00	60.00
(67)	Griffin	250.00	130.00	60.00
(68)	Gurney	250.00	130.00	60.00
(69)	Hall (Seattle)	250.00	130.00	60.00
(70)	Hall (Tacoma)	250.00	130.00	60.00
(71)	Harkins	250.00	130.00	60.00
(72)	Hartman	250.00	130.00	60.00
(73)	Hendrix	250.00	130.00	60.00
(74)	Henley	250.00	130.00	60.00
(75)	Hensling	250.00	130.00	60.00
(76)	Hetling	250.00	130.00	60.00
(77)	Hickey	250.00	130.00	60.00
(78)	Hiester	250.00	130.00	60.00
(79)	Hitt	250.00	130.00	60.00
(80)	Hogan (Oakland)	250.00	130.00	60.00
(81)	Hogan (Vernon)	250.00	130.00	60.00
(82)	Hollis	250.00	130.00	60.00
(83)	Holm	250.00	130.00	60.00
(84)	Howard	250.00	130.00	60.00
(85)	Hunt	250.00	130.00	60.00
(86)	James	250.00	130.00	60.00
(87)	Jansing	250.00	130.00	60.00
(88)	Jensen	250.00	130.00	60.00
(89)	Johnston	250.00	130.00	60.00
(90)	Keener	250.00	130.00	60.00
(91)	Killilay	250.00	130.00	60.00
(92)	Kippert	250.00	130.00	60.00
(93)	Klein	250.00	130.00	60.00
(94)	Krapp	250.00	130.00	60.00
(95)	Kusel	250.00	130.00	60.00
(96)	LaLonge	250.00	130.00	60.00
(97)	Lewis	250.00	130.00	60.00
(98)	J. Lewis	250.00	130.00	60.00
(99)	John Lindsay	250.00	130.00	60.00
(100)	Lively	250.00	130.00	60.00
(101)	Lynch	250.00	130.00	60.00
(102)	Manush	250.00	130.00	60.00
(103)	Martinke	250.00	130.00	60.00
(104)	McArdle	250.00	130.00	60.00
(105)	McCredie	250.00	130.00	60.00
(106)	Melchior	250.00	130.00	60.00
(107)	Miller (San Francisco)	250.00	130.00	60.00
(108)	Miller (Seattle)	250.00	130.00	60.00
(109)	Mitze	250.00	130.00	60.00
(110)	Mohler	250.00	130.00	60.00
(111)	Moser	250.00	130.00	60.00
(112)	Mott	250.00	130.00	60.00
(113)	Mundorff (Mundorf)	250.00	130.00	60.00
(114)	Murphy	250.00	130.00	60.00
(115)	Nagle	250.00	130.00	60.00
(116)	Nelson	250.00	130.00	60.00
(117)	Netzel	250.00	130.00	60.00
(118)	Nourse	250.00	130.00	60.00
(119)	Nordyke	250.00	130.00	60.00
(120)	Olson	250.00	130.00	60.00
(121)	Orendorff (Orsnsdorff)	250.00	130.00	60.00
(122)	Ort	250.00	130.00	60.00
(123)	Ostdiek	250.00	130.00	60.00
(124)	Pennington	250.00	130.00	60.00
(125)	Perrine	250.00	130.00	60.00
(126)	Perry	250.00	130.00	60.00
(127)	Persons	250.00	130.00	60.00
(128)	Rapps	250.00	130.00	60.00

		NM	EX	VG
(129)	Raymer	250.00	130.00	60.00
(130)	Raymond	250.00	130.00	60.00
(131)	Rockenfield	250.00	130.00	60.00
(132)	Roth	250.00	130.00	60.00
(133)	D. Ryan	250.00	130.00	60.00
(134)	J. Ryan	250.00	130.00	60.00
(135)	Scharnweber	250.00	130.00	60.00
(136)	Schmutz	250.00	130.00	60.00
(137)	Seaton (Portland)	250.00	130.00	60.00
(138)	Seaton (Seattle)	250.00	130.00	60.00
(139)	Shafer	250.00	130.00	60.00
(140)	Shaw	250.00	130.00	60.00
(141)	Shea	250.00	130.00	60.00
(142)	Shinn	250.00	130.00	60.00
(143)	Smith	250.00	130.00	60.00
(144)	H. Smith	250.00	130.00	60.00
(145)	J. Smith	250.00	130.00	60.00
(146)	Speas	250.00	130.00	60.00
(147)	Spiesman	250.00	130.00	60.00
(148)	Starkell	250.00	130.00	60.00
(149)	Steen	250.00	130.00	60.00
(150)	Stevens	250.00	130.00	60.00
(151)	Stewart	250.00	130.00	60.00
(152)	Stovell (Stovall)	250.00	130.00	60.00
(153)	Streib	250.00	130.00	60.00
(154)	Sugden	250.00	130.00	60.00
(155)	Sutor	250.00	130.00	60.00
(156)	Swain	250.00	130.00	60.00
(157)	Swander	250.00	130.00	60.00
(158)	Tennant	250.00	130.00	60.00
(159)	Thomas	250.00	130.00	60.00
(160)	Thompson	250.00	130.00	60.00
(161)	Thorsen	250.00	130.00	60.00
(162)	Tonnesen (Tonneson)	250.00	130.00	60.00
(163)	Tozer	250.00	130.00	60.00
(164)	Van Buren	250.00	130.00	60.00
(165)	Vitt	250.00	130.00	60.00
(166)	Wares	250.00	130.00	60.00
(167)	Waring	250.00	130.00	60.00
(168)	Warren	250.00	130.00	60.00
(169)	Weed	250.00	130.00	60.00
(170)	Whalen	250.00	130.00	60.00
(171)	Willett	250.00	130.00	60.00
(172)	Williams	250.00	130.00	60.00
(173)	Willis	250.00	130.00	60.00
(174)	Wolverton	250.00	130.00	60.00
(175)	Zackert	250.00	130.00	60.00

1911 Obak (T212)

WEAVER, SAN FRANCISCO, P.C.L.

OBAK SPEAKS QUALITY IN ANY COMPANY

The last of the three annual T212 baseball card issues from Obak Cigarettes is the 1911 edition, again featuring players from the six Pacific Coast League teams and the four-team Northwestern League. Often using the same chromolithographic picture on front as the 1910 cards, the 1911s are easily distinguished by the use of red, rather than blue, printing on back. Also new to the 1911s was the addition of a sentence or two about the player and, on most cards, recent years' statistics, an innovation also seen on the contemporary T205 cards "back East." In fact the Obaks were produced by the California branch of the same American Tobacco Company conglomerate. Obaks are the standard tobacco card size, about 1-1/2" x 2-5/8".

		NM	EX	VG
Complete Set (175):		60,000	30,000	12,000
Common Player:		325.00	160.00	65.00
(1)	Abbott	325.00	160.00	65.00
(2)	Ables	325.00	160.00	65.00
(3)	Adams	325.00	160.00	65.00
(4)	Agnew	325.00	160.00	65.00
(5)	Akin	325.00	160.00	65.00
(6)	Annis	325.00	160.00	65.00
(7)	Arrelanes (Arellanes)	325.00	160.00	65.00
(8)	Barry	325.00	160.00	65.00
(9)	Bassey	325.00	160.00	65.00
(10)	Baum	325.00	160.00	65.00
(11)	Bennett	325.00	160.00	65.00
(12)	Bernard	325.00	160.00	65.00
(13)	Berry	325.00	160.00	65.00
(14)	Bloomfield	325.00	160.00	65.00
(15)	Bonner	325.00	160.00	65.00
(16)	Brackenridge	325.00	160.00	65.00
(17)	Brashear	325.00	160.00	65.00
(18)	R. Brashear	325.00	160.00	65.00
(19)	Brinker	325.00	160.00	65.00
(20)	Brown	325.00	160.00	65.00
(21)	Browning	325.00	160.00	65.00

		NM	EX	VG
(22)	Bues	325.00	160.00	65.00
(23)	Burrell	325.00	160.00	65.00
(24)	Burns	325.00	160.00	65.00
(25)	Butler	325.00	160.00	65.00
(26)	Byram	325.00	160.00	65.00
(27)	Carlisle	325.00	160.00	65.00
(28)	Carson	325.00	160.00	65.00
(29)	Cartwright	325.00	160.00	65.00
(30)	Casey	325.00	160.00	65.00
(31)	Castleton	500.00	240.00	160.00
(32)	Chadbourne	325.00	160.00	65.00
(33)	Christian	325.00	160.00	65.00
(34)	Coleman	325.00	160.00	65.00
(35)	Cooney	325.00	160.00	65.00
(36)	Coy	325.00	160.00	65.00
(37)	Criger	325.00	160.00	65.00
(38)	Crukshank	325.00	160.00	65.00
(39)	Cutshaw	325.00	160.00	65.00
(40)	Daley	325.00	160.00	65.00
(41)	Danzig	325.00	160.00	65.00
(42)	Dashwood	325.00	160.00	65.00
(43)	Davis	325.00	160.00	65.00
(44)	Delhi	325.00	160.00	65.00
(45)	Delmas	325.00	160.00	65.00
(46)	Dillon	325.00	160.00	65.00
(47)	Engel	325.00	160.00	65.00
(48)	Erickson	325.00	160.00	65.00
(49)	Fitzgerald	325.00	160.00	65.00
(50)	Flater	325.00	160.00	65.00
(51)	Frisk	325.00	160.00	65.00
(52)	Fullerton	325.00	160.00	65.00
(53)	Garrett	325.00	160.00	65.00
(54)	Goodman	325.00	160.00	65.00
(55)	Gordon	325.00	160.00	65.00
(56)	Grindle	325.00	160.00	65.00
(57)	Hall	325.00	160.00	65.00
(58)	Harris	325.00	160.00	65.00
(59)	Hasty	325.00	160.00	65.00
(60)	Henderson	325.00	160.00	65.00
(61)	Henley	325.00	160.00	65.00
(62)	Hetling	325.00	160.00	65.00
(63)	Hiester	325.00	160.00	65.00
(64)	Higgins	325.00	160.00	65.00
(65)	Hitt	325.00	160.00	65.00
(66)	Hoffman	325.00	160.00	65.00
(67)	Hogan	325.00	160.00	65.00
(68)	Holm	325.00	160.00	65.00
(69)	Householder	325.00	160.00	65.00
(70)	Hosp	325.00	160.00	65.00
(71)	Howard	325.00	160.00	65.00
(72)	Hunt	325.00	160.00	65.00
(73)	James	325.00	160.00	65.00
(74)	Jensen	325.00	160.00	65.00
(75)	Kading	325.00	160.00	65.00
(76)	Kane	325.00	160.00	65.00
(77)	Kippert	325.00	160.00	65.00
(78)	Knight	325.00	160.00	65.00
(79)	Koestner	325.00	160.00	65.00
(80)	Krueger	325.00	160.00	65.00
(81)	Kuhn	325.00	160.00	65.00
(82)	LaLonge	325.00	160.00	65.00
(83)	Lamline	325.00	160.00	65.00
(84)	Leard	325.00	160.00	65.00
(85)	Lerchen	325.00	160.00	65.00
(86)	Lewis	325.00	160.00	65.00
(87)	Madden	325.00	160.00	65.00
(88)	Maggert	325.00	160.00	65.00
(89)	Mahoney	325.00	160.00	65.00
(90)	McArdle	325.00	160.00	65.00
(91)	McCredie	325.00	160.00	65.00
(92)	McDonnell	325.00	160.00	65.00
(93)	Meikle	325.00	160.00	65.00
(94)	Melchior	325.00	160.00	65.00
(95)	Mensor	650.00	310.00	210.00
(96)	Metzger	325.00	160.00	65.00
(97)	Miller (Oakland)	325.00	160.00	65.00
(98)	Miller (San Francisco)	325.00	160.00	65.00
(99)	Ten Million	1,800	1,100	500.00
(100)	Mitze	325.00	160.00	65.00
(101)	Mohler	325.00	160.00	65.00
(102)	Moore	325.00	160.00	65.00
(103)	Morse	325.00	160.00	65.00
(104)	Moskiman	325.00	160.00	65.00
(105)	Mundorff	325.00	160.00	65.00
(106)	Murray	325.00	160.00	65.00
(107)	Netzel	325.00	160.00	65.00
(108)	Nordyke	325.00	160.00	65.00
(109)	Nourse	325.00	160.00	65.00
(110)	O'Rourke	325.00	160.00	65.00
(111)	Ostdiek	325.00	160.00	65.00
(112)	Patterson	325.00	160.00	65.00
(113)	Pearce	325.00	160.00	65.00
(114)	Peckinpaugh	250.00	125.00	80.00
(115)	Pernoll	325.00	160.00	65.00
(116)	Pfyl	325.00	160.00	65.00
(117)	Powell	325.00	160.00	65.00
(118)	Raleigh	325.00	160.00	65.00
(119)	Rapps	325.00	160.00	65.00
(120)	Raymer	325.00	160.00	65.00
(121)	Raymond	325.00	160.00	65.00
(122)	Reddick	325.00	160.00	65.00
(123)	Roche	325.00	160.00	65.00
(124)	Rockenfield	325.00	160.00	65.00
(125)	Rogers	325.00	160.00	65.00
(126)	Ross	325.00	160.00	65.00
(127)	Ryan	325.00	160.00	65.00
(128)	J. Ryan	325.00	160.00	65.00
(129)	Scharnweber	325.00	160.00	65.00
(130)	Schmidt	325.00	160.00	65.00
(131)	Schmutz	325.00	160.00	65.00
(132)	Seaton (Portland)	325.00	160.00	65.00
(133)	Seaton (Seattle)	325.00	160.00	65.00
(134)	Shaw	325.00	160.00	65.00
(135)	Shea	325.00	160.00	65.00
(136)	Sheehan (Portland)	325.00	160.00	65.00
(137)	Sheehan (Vernon)	325.00	160.00	65.00
(138)	Shinn	325.00	160.00	65.00
(139)	Skeels	325.00	160.00	65.00

(140)	H. Smith	325.00	160.00	65.00
(141)	Speas	325.00	160.00	65.00
(142)	Spencer	325.00	160.00	65.00
(143)	Spiesman	325.00	160.00	65.00
(144)	Starkel	325.00	160.00	65.00
(145)	Steen	325.00	160.00	65.00
(146)	Stewart	325.00	160.00	65.00
(147)	Stinson	325.00	160.00	65.00
(148)	Stovall	325.00	160.00	65.00
(149)	Strand	325.00	160.00	65.00
(150)	Sutor	325.00	160.00	65.00
(151)	Swain	325.00	160.00	65.00
(152)	Tennant	325.00	160.00	65.00
(153)	Thomas (Sacramento)	325.00	160.00	65.00
(154)	Thomas (Victoria)	325.00	160.00	65.00
(155)	Thompson	325.00	160.00	65.00
(156)	Thornton	325.00	160.00	65.00
(157)	Thorsen	325.00	160.00	65.00
(158)	Tiedeman	325.00	160.00	65.00
(159)	Tozer	325.00	160.00	65.00
(160)	Van Buren	325.00	160.00	65.00
(161)	Vitt	325.00	160.00	65.00
(162)	Ward	325.00	160.00	65.00
(163)	Wares	325.00	160.00	65.00
(164)	Warren	325.00	160.00	65.00
(165)	Weaver	4,500	2,000	1,250
(166)	Weed	325.00	160.00	65.00
(167)	Wheeler	325.00	160.00	65.00
(168)	Wiggs	325.00	160.00	65.00
(169)	Willett	325.00	160.00	65.00
(170)	Williams	325.00	160.00	65.00
(171)	Wolverton	325.00	160.00	65.00
(172)	Zacher	325.00	160.00	65.00
(173)	Zackert	325.00	160.00	65.00
(174)	Zamlock	325.00	160.00	65.00
(175)	Zimmerman	325.00	160.00	65.00

1911 Obak Cabinets (T4)

Among the scarcest of all the 20th Century tobacco issues, the T4 Obak Premiums are cabinet-sized cards distributed in conjunction with the better-known Obak T212 card set of players from the Northwestern and Pacific Coast Leagues. The Obak Premiums measure about 5" x 7" and are printed on a cardboard-like paper. The cards featured a black-and-white player photo inside a 3-1/2" x 5" oval. There is no printing on the front of the card to identify the player or indicate the manufacturer. The backs are blank. In most cases the photos used for the premiums are identical to the T212 pictures, except for some cropping differences. Under the Obak mail-in promotion, 50 coupons from cigarette packages were required to obtain just one premium card, which explains their extreme scarcity today. All 175 players pictured in the T212 set were theoretically available as premium cards, but to date many remain undiscovered. Only those cards that have been confirmed to survive are listed with a value here. Most of the Obak premiums that exist in original condition contain a number, written in pencil on the back of the card, that corresponds to the checklist printed on the coupon. A large group of the cabinets, most of which had been cut down to just the oval portrait, was offered in a September 2002 auction.

		NM	EX	VG
Common Player:		6,750	3,500	2,200
LOS ANGELES				
1	H. Smith	5,750	2,875	1,725
2	Tozer	5,750	2,875	1,725
3	Howard	5,750	2,875	1,725
4	Daley	5,750	2,875	1,725
5	Bernard			
6	Dillon	5,750	2,875	1,725
7	Delmas			
8	Delhi	5,750	2,875	1,725
9	Criger			
10	Thorsen	5,750	2,875	1,725
11	Agnew			
12	Akin			
13	Metzger			
14	Abbott			
15	Wheeler	5,750	2,875	1,725
16	Moore			
17	Grindle			
OAKLAND				
18	Wolverton			
19	Mitze	5,750	2,875	1,725
20	Wares	5,750	2,875	1,725
21	Cutshaw	5,750	2,875	1,725

22	Christian	5,750	2,875	1,725
23	Wiggs			
24	Maggert	5,750	2,875	1,725
25	Pfyl			
26	Pearce			
27	Hetling			
28	Hoffman			
29	Pernoll			
30	Coy			
31	Tiedeman	5,750	2,875	1,725
32	Knight			
33	Flater	5,750	2,875	1,725
34	Zacher	5,750	2,875	1,725
35	Ables	5,750	2,875	1,725
36	Miller			
PORTLAND (PCL)				
37	Ryan	5,750	2,875	1,725
38	Rapps	5,750	2,875	1,725
39	McCredie			
40	Seaton			
41	Steen			
42	Chadbourne	5,750	2,875	1,725
43	Krueger			
44	Sheehan			
45	Roger Peckinpaugh	5,750	2,875	1,725
46	Bill Rodgers	5,750	2,875	1,725
47	Murray			
48	Fullerton			
49	Kuhn	5,750	2,875	1,725
50	Koestner			
51	Henderson			
52	Barry			
SACRAMENTO				
53	LaLonge			
54	Heister			
55	Hunt			
56	Van Buren			
57	Fitzgerald	5,750	2,875	1,725
58	Danzig	5,750	2,875	1,725
59	Baum	5,750	2,875	1,725
60	Shinn	5,750	2,875	1,725
61	Nourse			
62	O'Rourke			
63	Lerchen			
64	Thornton			
65	Thomas	5,750	2,875	1,725
66	Thompson			
67	Byram			
68	Frank Arrelanes (Arellanes)			
69	Mahoney			
SAN FRANCISCO				
70	McArdle			
71	Melchior	5,750	2,875	1,725
72	Vitt	5,750	2,875	1,725
73	Henley			
74	Berry	5,750	2,875	1,725
75	Miller	5,750	2,875	1,725
76	Tennant	5,750	2,875	1,725
77	Mohler	5,750	2,875	1,725
78	Shaw			
79	Sutor	5,750	2,875	1,725
80	Browning	5,750	2,875	1,725
81	Ryan	5,750	2,875	1,725
82	Powell	5,750	2,875	1,725
83	Schmidt	5,750	2,875	1,725
84	Meikle	5,750	2,875	1,725
85	Madden	5,750	2,875	1,725
86	Buck Weaver			
(VG-EX example auctioned in 2005 for $26,435.)				
87	Moskiman	5,750	2,875	1,725
88	Zamlock	5,750	2,875	1,725
VERNON				
89	Brown			
90	Hogan			
91	Brashear			
92	Carlisle	5,750	2,875	1,725
93	Burrell	5,750	2,875	1,725
94	Brackenridge	5,750	2,875	1,725
95	Hitt			
96	Willett	5,750	2,875	1,725
97	Stewart	5,750	2,875	1,725
98	Carson	5,750	2,875	1,725
99	Raleigh	5,750	2,875	1,725
100	Ham Patterson	5,750	2,875	1,725
101	Hosp			
102	Sheehan			
103	Castleton			
104	Ross			
105	Stinson	5,750	2,875	1,725
106	McDonnell	5,750	2,875	1,725
107	Kane	5,750	2,875	1,725
PORTLAND (NWL)				
108	Harris			
109	Garrett			
110	Stovall			
111	Mundorff	5,750	2,875	1,725
112	Lamline			
113	Bloomfield			
114	Williams			
115	Mensor			
116	Casey			
117	Speas			
SPOKANE				
118	Netzel			
119	Strand			
120	Hasty			
121	Zimmerman			
122	Cooney			
123	Frisk			
124	Nordyke			
125	Kippert			
126	Bonner			
127	Ostdiek			
128	Cartwright			
129	Holm			
TACOMA				
130	Higgins			
131	Warren			

132	Morse			
133	Burns			
134	Gordon			
135	Bassey			
136	Rockenfield			
137	Coleman			
138	Schmutz			
139	Hall			
140	Annis	5,750	2,875	1,725
VANCOUVER				
141	Engel			
142	Brashear			
143	Adams			
144	Spiesman			
145	Brinker			
146	Bennett			
147	James			
148	Lewis			
149	Scharnweber			
150	Swain			
151	Jensen			
152	Erickson			
VICTORIA				
153	Roche			
154	Davis			
155	Goodman			
156	Ward			
157	Reddick			
158	Householder	5,750	2,875	1,725
159	Dashwood	5,750	2,875	1,725
160	Starkel			
161	Thomas			
162	Ten Million			
163	Raymer			
SEATTLE				
164	Bues			
165	Crukshank			
166	Kading			
167	Spencer	5,750	2,875	1,725
168	Leard			
169	Seaton			
170	Shea			
171	Butler			
172	Skeels			
173	Weed			
174	Raymond	5,750	2,875	1,725
175	Zackert			

1911 Obak Coupon

 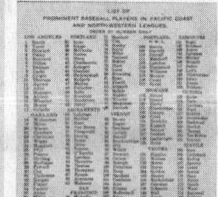

About 3" x 3", this coupon was found in each box of Obak cigarettes. Printed in green on white, the coupon has a list of the cabinet cards which could be obtained by redeeming 50 of the coupons.

	NM	EX	VG
Obak Coupon	100.00	50.00	30.00

1908 Offerman Buffalo Bisons Postcards

Virtually identical in format to the Major League player postcards issued by American League Publishing Co., Cleveland, these cards carry the imprint of F.J. Offerman and depict Buffalo Bisons players of the Eastern League. The 3-1/2" x 4-1/2" black-and-white cards have a large posed action photo on a white background with a vignetted oval portrait at top. Player information and stats are printed below. The back has typical postcard markings. It is unknown whether this checklist is complete.

		NM	EX	VG
Common Player:		600.00	300.00	180.00
(1)	James Archer	600.00	300.00	180.00
(2)	Larry Hesterfer	600.00	300.00	180.00

		NM	EX	VG
(3)	William H. Keister	600.00	300.00	180.00
(4)	Charles Kisinger	600.00	300.00	180.00
(5)	Lewis Knapp	600.00	300.00	180.00
(6)	George McConnell	600.00	300.00	180.00
(7)	William J. Milligan	600.00	300.00	180.00
(8)	William Nattress	600.00	300.00	180.00
(9)	John B. Ryan	600.00	300.00	180.00
(10)	George Schirm	600.00	300.00	180.00
(11)	George Smith	600.00	300.00	180.00
(12)	John White	600.00	300.00	180.00
(13)	Merton Whitney	600.00	300.00	180.00

1952 Ogden Reds Team Issue

These 2-1/4" x 3-3/8" black-and-white, unnumbered, blank-backed cards were one of many minor league team sets issued by Globe Printing of San Jose, Calif., in the early 1950s. Cards were usually given away at the ballpark on a one-per-week or one-per-homestand basis, accounting for the rarity of surviving sets. The O-Reds were a Class C Pioneer League farm club of the Cincinnati Reds.

		NM	EX	VG
Complete Set (18):		800.00	400.00	240.00
Common Player:		60.00	30.00	18.00
Album:		100.00	50.00	30.00
(1)	Ralph Birkofer	60.00	30.00	18.00
(2)	William A. Bowman	60.00	30.00	18.00
(3)	David Bristol	60.00	30.00	18.00
(4)	Vincent E. Capece	60.00	30.00	18.00
(5)	Gerald Davis	60.00	30.00	18.00
(6)	Ralph Dollinger	60.00	30.00	18.00
(7)	Robert E. Durnbaugh	60.00	30.00	18.00
(8)	Raymond Estes	60.00	30.00	18.00
(9)	Robert J. Flowers	60.00	30.00	18.00
(10)	Nunzio Izzo	60.00	30.00	18.00
(11)	Howard E. Leister	60.00	30.00	18.00
(12)	Steve Mesner	60.00	30.00	18.00
(13)	Dee C. Moore	60.00	30.00	18.00
(14)	Augie Navarro/Announcer	60.00	30.00	18.00
(15)	John Omerza	60.00	30.00	18.00
(16)	James W. St. Claire	60.00	30.00	18.00
(17)	Grady N. Watts	60.00	30.00	18.00
(18)	Carl M. Wells	60.00	30.00	18.00

1955 Old Homestead Franks Des Moines Bruins

A very rare minor league issue, this set features players of the Class A Western League farm team of the Chicago Cubs. Many of the players were future major leaguers. Cards measure about 2-1/2" x 3-3/4" and have black-and-white portrait photos of the players with a facsimile autograph across the jersey. A black strip at the bottom of the card has the player and team name, and the position. Backs have an ad for the issuing hot dog company.

		NM	EX	VG
Complete Set (21):		5,000	2,500	1,500
Common Player:		250.00	125.00	75.00
(1)	Bob Andersoon	250.00	125.00	75.00
(2)	Ray Bellino	250.00	125.00	75.00
(3)	Don Biebel	250.00	125.00	75.00
(4)	Bobby Cooke	250.00	125.00	75.00
(5)	Dave Cunningham	250.00	125.00	75.00
(6)	Bert Flammini	250.00	125.00	75.00
(7)	Gene Fodge	250.00	125.00	75.00
(8)	Eddie Haas	250.00	125.00	75.00
(9)	Paul Hoffmeister	250.00	125.00	75.00
(10)	Pepper Martin	350.00	175.00	100.00
(11)	Jim McDaniel	250.00	125.00	75.00
(12)	Bob McKee	250.00	125.00	75.00
(13)	Paul Menking	250.00	125.00	75.00
(14)	Vern Morgan	250.00	125.00	75.00
(15)	Joe Pearson	250.00	125.00	75.00
(16)	John Pramesa	250.00	125.00	75.00
(17)	Joe Stanka	250.00	125.00	75.00
(18)	Jim Stoddard	250.00	125.00	75.00
(19)	Bob Thorpe	250.00	125.00	75.00
(20)	Burdy Thurlby	250.00	125.00	75.00
(21)	Don Watkins	250.00	125.00	75.00

1959 O'Keefe Ale Montreal Royals

This set of large (3" x 4") player stamps was issued in conjunction with an album as a promotion by O'Keefe Ale in Quebec. The pictures are black-and-white with player identification in the bottom border. Backs are blank and the edges are perforated.

TOM LASORDA
Lanceur gaucher — L. H. Pitcher

Many former Brooklyn Dodgers are included in the issue. The unnumbered stamps are listed here in alphabetical order.

		NM	EX	VG
Complete Set (24):		900.00	450.00	275.00
Common Player:		30.00	15.00	9.00
Album:		200.00	100.00	60.00
(1)	Edmundo Amoros	45.00	22.50	13.50
(2)	Bob Aspromonte	35.00	17.50	10.00
(3)	Batters Records	12.50	6.25	3.75
(4)	Babe Birrer	30.00	15.00	9.00
(5)	Clay Bryant	30.00	15.00	9.00
(6)	Mike Brumley	30.00	15.00	9.00
(7)	Yvon Dunn/Trainer	20.00	10.00	6.00
(8)	Bill George	30.00	15.00	9.00
(9)	Mike Goliat	30.00	15.00	9.00
(10)	John Gray	30.00	15.00	9.00
(11)	Billy Harris	30.00	15.00	9.00
(12)	Jim Koranda	30.00	15.00	9.00
(13)	Paul LaPalme	30.00	15.00	9.00
(14)	Tom Lasorda	200.00	100.00	60.00
(15)	Bob Lennon	30.00	15.00	9.00
(16)	Clyde Parris	30.00	15.00	9.00
(17)	Pitchers Records	12.50	6.25	3.75
(18)	Ed Rakow	30.00	15.00	9.00
(19)	Curt Roberts	30.00	15.00	9.00
(20)	Freddy Rodriguez	30.00	15.00	9.00
(21)	Harry Schwegman	30.00	15.00	9.00
(22)	Angel Scull	30.00	15.00	9.00
(23)	Dick Teed	30.00	15.00	9.00
(24)	Rene Valdes (Valdez)	30.00	15.00	9.00

1910 Old Mill Cigarettes Series 1 (S. Atlantic League)

Because of their distinctive red borders, this 1910 minor league tobacco issue is often called the Red Border set by collectors. It's ACC designation is T210. A massive set, it consists of some 640 cards, each measuring 1-1/2" x 2-5/8". Fronts feature a glossy black-and-white photo, while the backs carry an ad for Old Mill Cigarettes. Each of the eight series is devoted to a different minor league. Series 1 features players from the South Atlantic League; Series 2 pictures players from the Virginia League; Series 3 is devoted to the Texas League; Series 4 features the Virginia Valley League; Series 5 pictures players from the Carolina Associations; Series 6 spotlights the Blue Grass League; Series 7 is devoted to the Eastern Carolina League; and Series 8 show players from the Southern Association. The various series are identified by a number along the top on the back of the cards. Collectors generally agree that Series 8 cards, which are often found irregularly sized due to hand-cutting from original sheets, are the scarcest of the series. The relative scarcity of the various series is reflected in the prices listed. Collectors should be aware that some Series 3 cards (Texas League) can be found with orange, rather than red, borders - apparently because not enough red ink was used during part of the print run.

		NM	EX	VG
Common Player:		350.00	150.00	90.00
(1)	Bagwell	350.00	150.00	90.00
(2)	Balenti	350.00	150.00	90.00
(3)	Becker	350.00	150.00	90.00
(4)	Bensen	350.00	150.00	90.00
(5)	Benton	350.00	150.00	90.00
(6)	Bierkortte	350.00	150.00	90.00
(7)	Bierman	350.00	150.00	90.00
(8)	Breitenstein	350.00	150.00	90.00
(9)	Bremmerhof	350.00	150.00	90.00
(10)	Carter	350.00	150.00	90.00
(11)	Cavender	350.00	150.00	90.00
(12)	Collins	350.00	150.00	90.00
(13)	DeFraites	350.00	150.00	90.00
(14)	Dudley	350.00	150.00	90.00
(15)	Dwyer	350.00	150.00	90.00
(16)	Edwards	350.00	150.00	90.00
(17)	Enbanks	350.00	150.00	90.00
(18)	Eubank	350.00	150.00	90.00
(19)	Fox	350.00	150.00	90.00
(20)	Hannifan	350.00	150.00	90.00
(21)	Hartley	350.00	150.00	90.00
(22)	Hauser	350.00	150.00	90.00
(23)	Hille	350.00	150.00	90.00
(24)	Howard	350.00	150.00	90.00
(25)	Hoyt	350.00	150.00	90.00
(26)	Huber	350.00	150.00	90.00
(27)	Ison	350.00	150.00	90.00
(28)	Jones	350.00	150.00	90.00
(29)	Kalkhoff	350.00	150.00	90.00
(30)	Krebs	350.00	150.00	90.00
(31)	Lawrence	350.00	150.00	90.00
(32)	Lee (Jacksonville)	350.00	150.00	90.00
(33)	Lee (Macon)	350.00	150.00	90.00
(34)	Lewis (Columbia)	350.00	150.00	90.00
(35)	Lewis (Columbus)	350.00	150.00	90.00
(36)	Lipe (batting)	350.00	150.00	90.00
(37)	Lipe (portrait)	350.00	150.00	90.00
(38)	Long	350.00	150.00	90.00
(39)	Magoon	350.00	150.00	90.00
(40)	Manion	350.00	150.00	90.00
(41)	Marshall	350.00	150.00	90.00
(42)	Martin	350.00	150.00	90.00
(43)	Martina	350.00	150.00	90.00
(44)	Massing	350.00	150.00	90.00
(45)	McLeod	350.00	150.00	90.00
(46)	McMahon	350.00	150.00	90.00
(47)	Morse	350.00	150.00	90.00
(48)	Mullane	350.00	150.00	90.00
(49)	Mulldowney	350.00	150.00	90.00
(50)	Murch	350.00	150.00	90.00
(51)	Norcum	350.00	150.00	90.00
(52)	Pelkey	350.00	150.00	90.00
(53)	Petit	350.00	150.00	90.00
(54)	Pierce	350.00	150.00	90.00
(55)	Pope	350.00	150.00	90.00
(56)	Radebaugh	350.00	150.00	90.00
(57)	Raynolds	350.00	150.00	90.00
(58)	Reagan	350.00	150.00	90.00
(59)	Redfern (Redfearn)	350.00	150.00	90.00
(60)	Reynolds	350.00	150.00	90.00
(61)	Schulz	350.00	150.00	90.00
(62)	Schulze	350.00	150.00	90.00
(63)	Schwietzka	350.00	150.00	90.00
(64)	Shields	350.00	150.00	90.00
(65)	Sisson	350.00	150.00	90.00
(66)	Smith	350.00	150.00	90.00
(67)	Sweeney	350.00	150.00	90.00
(68)	Taffee	350.00	150.00	90.00
(69)	Toren	350.00	150.00	90.00
(70)	Viola	350.00	150.00	90.00
(71)	Wagner	350.00	150.00	90.00
(72)	Wahl	350.00	150.00	90.00
(73)	Weems	350.00	150.00	90.00
(74)	Wells	350.00	150.00	90.00
(75)	Wohlleben	350.00	150.00	90.00

1910 Old Mill Cigarettes Series 2 (Virginia League)

		NM	EX	VG
Common Player:		275.00	135.00	80.00
(1)	Andrada	275.00	135.00	80.00
(2)	Archer	275.00	135.00	80.00
(3)	Baker	275.00	135.00	80.00
(4)	Beham	275.00	135.00	80.00
(5)	Bonner	275.00	135.00	80.00
(6)	Bowen	275.00	135.00	80.00
(7)	Brandon	275.00	135.00	80.00
(8)	Breivogel	275.00	135.00	80.00
(9)	Brooks	275.00	135.00	80.00
(10)	Brown	275.00	135.00	80.00
(11)	Busch	275.00	135.00	80.00
(12)	Bussey	275.00	135.00	80.00
(13)	Cefalu	275.00	135.00	80.00
(14)	Chandler	275.00	135.00	80.00
(15)	Clarke	275.00	135.00	80.00
(16)	Clunk	275.00	135.00	80.00
(17)	Cote	275.00	135.00	80.00
(18)	Cowan	275.00	135.00	80.00
(19)	Decker	275.00	135.00	80.00
(20)	Doyle	275.00	135.00	80.00
(21)	Eddowes	275.00	135.00	80.00
(22)	Fisher	275.00	135.00	80.00
(23)	Fox	275.00	135.00	80.00
(24)	Foxen	275.00	135.00	80.00
(25)	Gaston	275.00	135.00	80.00
(26)	Gehring	275.00	135.00	80.00
(27)	Griffin (Danville)	275.00	135.00	80.00
(28)	Griffin (Lynchburg)	275.00	135.00	80.00
(29)	Hale	275.00	135.00	80.00
(30)	Hamilton	275.00	135.00	80.00
(31)	Hanks	275.00	135.00	80.00
(32)	Hannafin	275.00	135.00	80.00
(33)	Hoffman	275.00	135.00	80.00
(34)	Holland	275.00	135.00	80.00
(35)	Hooker	275.00	135.00	80.00
(36)	Irving	275.00	135.00	80.00

		NM	EX	VG
(37)	Jackson (Lynchburg)	275.00	135.00	80.00
(38)	Jackson (Norfolk)	275.00	135.00	80.00
(39)	Jackson (Portsmouth)	275.00	135.00	80.00
(40)	Jackson (Richmond)	275.00	135.00	80.00
(41)	Jenkins	275.00	135.00	80.00
(42)	Keifel	275.00	135.00	80.00
(43)	Kirkpatrick	275.00	135.00	80.00
(44)	Kunkel	275.00	135.00	80.00
(45)	Landgraff	275.00	135.00	80.00
(46)	Larkins	275.00	135.00	80.00
(47)	Laughlin	275.00	135.00	80.00
(48)	Lawlor	275.00	135.00	80.00
(49)	Levy	275.00	135.00	80.00
(50)	Lloyd	275.00	135.00	80.00
(51)	Loos	275.00	135.00	80.00
(52)	Lovell	275.00	135.00	80.00
(53)	Lucia	275.00	135.00	80.00
(54)	MacConachie	275.00	135.00	80.00
(55)	Mayberry	275.00	135.00	80.00
(56)	McFarland	275.00	135.00	80.00
(57)	Messitt	275.00	135.00	80.00
(58)	Michel	275.00	135.00	80.00
(59)	Mullaney	275.00	135.00	80.00
(60)	Munson	275.00	135.00	80.00
(61)	Neuton	275.00	135.00	80.00
(62)	Nimmo	275.00	135.00	80.00
(63)	Norris	275.00	135.00	80.00
(64)	Peterson	275.00	135.00	80.00
(65)	Powell	275.00	135.00	80.00
(66)	Pressly (Pressley)	275.00	135.00	80.00
(67)	Pritchard	275.00	135.00	80.00
(68)	Revelle	275.00	135.00	80.00
(69)	Rowe	275.00	135.00	80.00
(70)	Schmidt	275.00	135.00	80.00
(71)	Schrader	275.00	135.00	80.00
(72)	Sharp	275.00	135.00	80.00
(73)	Shaw	275.00	135.00	80.00
(74)	Smith/Btg (Lynchburg)	275.00	135.00	80.00
(75)	Smith/Catching (Lynchburg)	275.00	135.00	80.00
(76)	Smith (Portsmouth)	275.00	135.00	80.00
(77)	Spicer	275.00	135.00	80.00
(78)	Tittman	275.00	135.00	80.00
(79)	Toner	275.00	135.00	80.00
(80)	Tydeman	275.00	135.00	80.00
(81)	Vail	275.00	135.00	80.00
(82)	Verbout	275.00	135.00	80.00
(83)	Walker	275.00	135.00	80.00
(84)	Wallace	275.00	135.00	80.00
(85)	Waymack	275.00	135.00	80.00
(86)	Woolums	275.00	135.00	80.00
(87)	Zimmerman	275.00	135.00	80.00

1910 Old Mill Cigarettes Series 3 (Texas League)

		NM	EX	VG
Common Player:		275.00	125.00	80.00
(1)	Alexander	275.00	125.00	80.00
(2)	Ash	275.00	125.00	80.00
(3)	Bandy	275.00	125.00	80.00
(4)	Barenkemp	275.00	125.00	80.00
(5)	Belew	275.00	125.00	80.00
(6)	Bell	275.00	125.00	80.00
(7)	Bennett	275.00	125.00	80.00
(8)	Berlck	275.00	125.00	80.00
(9)	Billiard	275.00	125.00	80.00
(10)	Blanding	275.00	125.00	80.00
(11)	Blue	275.00	125.00	80.00
(12)	Burch	275.00	125.00	80.00
(13)	Burk	275.00	125.00	80.00
(14)	Carlin	275.00	125.00	80.00
(15)	Conaway	275.00	125.00	80.00
(16)	Corkhill	275.00	125.00	80.00
(17)	Cowan	275.00	125.00	80.00
(18)	Coyle	275.00	125.00	80.00
(19)	Crable	275.00	125.00	80.00
(20)	Curry	275.00	125.00	80.00
(21)	Dale	275.00	125.00	80.00
(22)	Davis	275.00	125.00	80.00
(23)	Deardorff	275.00	125.00	80.00
(24)	Donnelley	275.00	125.00	80.00
(25)	Doyle	275.00	125.00	80.00
(26)	Druke	275.00	125.00	80.00
(27)	Dugey	275.00	125.00	80.00
(28)	Ens	275.00	125.00	80.00
(29)	Evans	275.00	125.00	80.00
(30)	Fillman	275.00	125.00	80.00
(31)	Firestine	275.00	125.00	80.00
(32)	Francis	275.00	125.00	80.00
(33)	Galloway	275.00	125.00	80.00
(34)	Gardner	275.00	125.00	80.00

		NM	EX	VG
(35)	Gear	275.00	125.00	80.00
(36)	Glawe	275.00	125.00	80.00
(37)	Gordon	275.00	125.00	80.00
(38)	Gowdy	275.00	125.00	80.00
(39)	Harbison	275.00	125.00	80.00
(40)	Harper	275.00	125.00	80.00
(41)	Hicks	275.00	125.00	80.00
(42)	Hill	275.00	125.00	80.00
(43)	Hinninger	275.00	125.00	80.00
(44)	Hirsch	275.00	125.00	80.00
(45)	Hise	275.00	125.00	80.00
(46)	Hooks	275.00	125.00	80.00
(47)	Hornsby	275.00	125.00	80.00
(48)	Howell	275.00	125.00	80.00
(49)	Johnston	275.00	125.00	80.00
(50)	Jolley	275.00	125.00	80.00
(51)	Jones	275.00	125.00	80.00
(52)	Kaphan	275.00	125.00	80.00
(53)	Kipp	275.00	125.00	80.00
(54)	Leidy	275.00	125.00	80.00
(55)	Malloy	275.00	125.00	80.00
(56)	Maloney	275.00	125.00	80.00
(57)	Meagher	275.00	125.00	80.00
(58)	Merritt	275.00	125.00	80.00
(59)	McKay	275.00	125.00	80.00
(60)	Mills	275.00	125.00	80.00
(61)	Morris	275.00	125.00	80.00
(62)	Mullen	275.00	125.00	80.00
(63)	Munsell	275.00	125.00	80.00
(64)	Nagel	275.00	125.00	80.00
(65)	Northen	275.00	125.00	80.00
(66)	Ogle	275.00	125.00	80.00
(67)	Onslow	275.00	125.00	80.00
(68)	Pendleton	275.00	125.00	80.00
(69)	Powell	275.00	125.00	80.00
(70)	Riley	275.00	125.00	80.00
(71)	Robertson	275.00	125.00	80.00
(72)	Rose	275.00	125.00	80.00
(73)	Salazor	275.00	125.00	80.00
(74)	Shindel	275.00	125.00	80.00
(75)	Shontz	275.00	125.00	80.00
(76)	Slaven	275.00	125.00	80.00
(77)	Smith (bat over shoulder)	275.00	125.00	80.00
(78)	Smith (bat at hip level)	275.00	125.00	80.00
(79)	Spangler	275.00	125.00	80.00
(80)	Stadeli	275.00	125.00	80.00
(81)	Stinson	275.00	125.00	80.00
(82)	Storch	275.00	125.00	80.00
(83)	Stringer	275.00	125.00	80.00
(84)	Tesreau	275.00	125.00	80.00
(85)	Thebo	275.00	125.00	80.00
(86)	Tullas	275.00	125.00	80.00
(87)	Walsh	275.00	125.00	80.00
(88)	Watson	275.00	125.00	80.00
(89)	Weber	275.00	125.00	80.00
(90)	Weeks	275.00	125.00	80.00
(91)	Wertherford	275.00	125.00	80.00
(92)	Wickenhofer	275.00	125.00	80.00
(93)	Williams	275.00	125.00	80.00
(94)	Woodburn	275.00	125.00	80.00
(95)	Yantz	275.00	125.00	80.00

1910 Old Mill Cigarettes Series 4 (Va. Valley League)

		NM	EX	VG
Common Player:		400.00	175.00	100.00
(1)	Aylor	400.00	175.00	100.00
(2)	Benney	400.00	175.00	100.00
(3)	Best	400.00	175.00	100.00
(4)	Bonno	400.00	175.00	100.00
(5)	Brown	400.00	175.00	100.00
(6)	Brumfield	400.00	175.00	100.00
(7)	Campbell	400.00	175.00	100.00
(8)	Canepa	400.00	175.00	100.00
(9)	Carney	400.00	175.00	100.00
(10)	Carter	400.00	175.00	100.00
(11)	Cochrane	400.00	175.00	100.00
(12)	Coller	400.00	175.00	100.00
(13)	Connolly	400.00	175.00	100.00
(14)	Davis	400.00	175.00	100.00
(15)	Connell	400.00	175.00	100.00
(16)	Doshmer	400.00	175.00	100.00
(17)	Dougherty	400.00	175.00	100.00
(18)	Erlewein	400.00	175.00	100.00
(19)	Farrell	400.00	175.00	100.00
(20)	Geary	400.00	175.00	100.00
(21)	Halterman	400.00	175.00	100.00
(22)	Headly	400.00	175.00	100.00
(23)	Hollis	400.00	175.00	100.00
(24)	Hunter	400.00	175.00	100.00
(25)	Johnson	400.00	175.00	100.00
(26)	Kane	400.00	175.00	100.00
(27)	Kuehn	400.00	175.00	100.00
(28)	Leonard	400.00	175.00	100.00
(29)	Lux	400.00	175.00	100.00
(30)	McClain	400.00	175.00	100.00
(31)	Mollenkamp	400.00	175.00	100.00
(32)	Moore	400.00	175.00	100.00
(33)	Moye	400.00	175.00	100.00
(34)	O'Connor	400.00	175.00	100.00
(35)	Orcutt	400.00	175.00	100.00
(36)	Pick	400.00	175.00	100.00
(37)	Pickels	400.00	175.00	100.00
(38)	Schafer	400.00	175.00	100.00
(39)	Seaman	400.00	175.00	100.00
(40)	Spicer	400.00	175.00	100.00
(41)	Stanley	400.00	175.00	100.00
(42)	Stockum	400.00	175.00	100.00
(43)	Titlow	400.00	175.00	100.00
(44)	Waldron	400.00	175.00	100.00
(45)	Wills	400.00	175.00	100.00
(46)	Witter	400.00	175.00	100.00
(47)	Womach	400.00	175.00	100.00
(48)	Young	400.00	175.00	100.00
(49)	Zurlage	400.00	175.00	100.00

1910 Old Mill Cigarettes Series 5 (Carolina Assn.)

		NM	EX	VG
Common Player:		400.00	175.00	100.00
(1)	Abercrombie	400.00	175.00	100.00
(2)	Averett	400.00	175.00	100.00
(3)	Bansewein	400.00	175.00	100.00
(4)	Bentley	400.00	175.00	100.00
(5)	C.G. Beusse	400.00	175.00	100.00
(6)	Fred Beusse	400.00	175.00	100.00
(7)	Bigbie	400.00	175.00	100.00
(8)	Bivens	400.00	175.00	100.00
(9)	Blackstone	400.00	175.00	100.00
(10)	Brannon	400.00	175.00	100.00
(11)	Brazell	400.00	175.00	100.00
(12)	Brent	400.00	175.00	100.00
(13)	Bullock	400.00	175.00	100.00
(14)	Cashion	400.00	175.00	100.00
(15)	Corbett (3/4 length view.)	400.00	175.00	100.00
(16)	Corbett (Full length view.)	400.00	175.00	100.00
(17)	Coutts	400.00	175.00	100.00
(18)	Lave Cross	400.00	175.00	100.00
(19)	Crouch	400.00	175.00	100.00
(20)	C.L. Derrick	400.00	175.00	100.00
(21)	F.B. Derrick	400.00	175.00	100.00
(22)	Dobard	400.00	175.00	100.00
(23)	Drumm	400.00	175.00	100.00
(24)	Duvie	400.00	175.00	100.00
(25)	Ehrhardt	400.00	175.00	100.00
(26)	Eldridge	400.00	175.00	100.00
(27)	Fairbanks	400.00	175.00	100.00
(28)	Farmer	400.00	175.00	100.00
(29)	Ferrell	400.00	175.00	100.00
(30)	Finn	400.00	175.00	100.00
(31)	Flowers	400.00	175.00	100.00
(32)	Fogarty	400.00	175.00	100.00
(33)	Francisco	400.00	175.00	100.00
(34)	Gardin	400.00	175.00	100.00
(35)	Gilmore	400.00	175.00	100.00
(36)	Gorham	400.00	175.00	100.00
(37)	Gorman	400.00	175.00	100.00
(38)	Guss	400.00	175.00	100.00
(39)	Hammersley	400.00	175.00	100.00
(40)	Hargrave	400.00	175.00	100.00
(41)	Harrington	400.00	175.00	100.00
(42)	Harris	400.00	175.00	100.00
(43)	Hartley	400.00	175.00	100.00
(44)	Hayes	400.00	175.00	100.00
(45)	Hicks	400.00	175.00	100.00
(46)	Humphrey	400.00	175.00	100.00
(47)	Jackson	400.00	175.00	100.00
(48)	James	400.00	175.00	100.00
(49)	Jenkins	400.00	175.00	100.00
(50)	Johnston	400.00	175.00	100.00
(51)	Kelly	400.00	175.00	100.00
(52)	Laval	400.00	175.00	100.00
(53)	Lothrop	400.00	175.00	100.00
(54)	MacConachie	400.00	175.00	100.00
(55)	Mangum	400.00	175.00	100.00
(56)	A. McCarthy	400.00	175.00	100.00
(57)	J. McCarthy	400.00	175.00	100.00
(58)	McEnroe	400.00	175.00	100.00
(59)	McFarlin	400.00	175.00	100.00
(60)	McHugh	400.00	175.00	100.00
(61)	McKevitt	400.00	175.00	100.00
(62)	Midkiff	400.00	175.00	100.00
(63)	Moore	400.00	175.00	100.00
(64)	Noojin	400.00	175.00	100.00
(65)	Ochs	400.00	175.00	100.00
(66)	Painter	400.00	175.00	100.00
(67)	Redfern (Redfearn)	400.00	175.00	100.00
(68)	Reis	400.00	175.00	100.00
(69)	Rickard	400.00	175.00	100.00
(70)	Roth/Btg	400.00	175.00	100.00
(71)	Roth/Fielding	400.00	175.00	100.00
(72)	Smith	400.00	175.00	100.00
(73)	Springs	400.00	175.00	100.00
(74)	Stouch	400.00	175.00	100.00
(75)	Taxis	400.00	175.00	100.00
(76)	Templin	400.00	175.00	100.00
(77)	Thrasher	400.00	175.00	100.00
(78)	Trammell	400.00	175.00	100.00
(79)	Walker	400.00	175.00	100.00
(80)	Walters	400.00	175.00	100.00
(81)	Wehrell	400.00	175.00	100.00
(82)	Weldon	400.00	175.00	100.00
(83)	Williams	400.00	175.00	100.00
(84)	Wingo	400.00	175.00	100.00
(85)	Workman	400.00	175.00	100.00
(86)	Wynne	400.00	175.00	100.00
(87)	Wysong	400.00	175.00	100.00

1910 Old Mill Cigarettes Series 6 (Blue Grass League)

		NM	EX	VG
	Common Player:	600.00	250.00	150.00
(1)	Angermeier/Fielding	600.00	250.00	150.00
(2)	Angermeir/Portrait	600.00	250.00	150.00
(3)	Atwell	600.00	250.00	150.00
(4)	Badger	600.00	250.00	150.00
(5)	Barnett	600.00	250.00	150.00
(6)	Barney	600.00	250.00	150.00
(7)	Beard	600.00	250.00	150.00
(8)	Bohannon	600.00	250.00	150.00
(9)	Callahan	600.00	250.00	150.00
(10)	Chapman	600.00	250.00	150.00
(11)	Chase	600.00	250.00	150.00
(12)	Coleman	600.00	250.00	150.00
(13)	Cornell (Frankfort)	600.00	250.00	150.00
(14)	Cornell (Winchester)	600.00	250.00	150.00
(15)	Creager	600.00	250.00	150.00
(16)	Dailey	600.00	250.00	150.00
(17)	Edington	600.00	250.00	150.00
(18)	Elgin	600.00	250.00	150.00
(19)	Ellis	600.00	250.00	150.00
(20)	Everden	600.00	250.00	150.00
(21)	Gisler	600.00	250.00	150.00
(22)	Goodman	600.00	250.00	150.00
(23)	Goostree (Hands behind back.)	600.00	250.00	150.00
(24)	Goostree (Leaning on bat.)	600.00	250.00	150.00
(25)	Haines	600.00	250.00	150.00
(26)	Harold	600.00	250.00	150.00
(27)	Heveron	600.00	250.00	150.00
(28)	Hicks	600.00	250.00	150.00
(29)	Hoffmann	600.00	250.00	150.00
(30)	Horn	600.00	250.00	150.00
(31)	Kaiser	600.00	250.00	150.00
(32)	Keifel	600.00	250.00	150.00
(33)	Kimbrough	600.00	250.00	150.00
(34)	Kircher (Shelbyville)	600.00	250.00	150.00
(35)	Kircher (Winchester)	600.00	250.00	150.00
(36)	Kuhlman (3/4 length)	600.00	250.00	150.00
(37)	Kuhlmann (portrait)	600.00	250.00	150.00
(38)	L'Heureux	600.00	250.00	150.00
(39)	McIlvain	600.00	250.00	150.00
(40)	McKernan	600.00	250.00	150.00
(41)	Meyers	600.00	250.00	150.00
(42)	Moloney	600.00	250.00	150.00
(43)	Mullin	600.00	250.00	150.00
(44)	Olson	600.00	250.00	150.00
(45)	Oyler	600.00	250.00	150.00
(46)	Reed	600.00	250.00	150.00
(47)	Ross	600.00	250.00	150.00
(48)	Scheneberg/Fielding	600.00	250.00	150.00
(49)	Scheneberg/Portrait	600.00	250.00	150.00
(50)	Schultz	600.00	250.00	150.00
(51)	Scott	600.00	250.00	150.00
(52)	Sinex	600.00	250.00	150.00
(53)	Stengel (SGC-graded EX sold for $35,009 in 2005. PSA-graded VG sold for $20,880 in 2006.)			
(54)	Thoss	600.00	250.00	150.00
(55)	Tilford	600.00	250.00	150.00
(56)	Toney	600.00	250.00	150.00
(57)	Van Landingham (Valladingham) (Lexington)	600.00	250.00	150.00
(58)	Van Landingham (Valladingham) (Shelbyville)	600.00	250.00	150.00
(59)	Viox	600.00	250.00	150.00
(60)	Walden	600.00	250.00	150.00
(61)	Whitaker	600.00	250.00	150.00
(62)	Wills	600.00	250.00	150.00
(63)	Womble	600.00	250.00	150.00
(64)	Wright	600.00	250.00	150.00
(65)	Yaeger	600.00	250.00	150.00
(66)	Yancey	600.00	250.00	150.00

1910 Old Mill Cigarettes Series 7 (E. Carolina League)

		NM	EX	VG
	Common Player:	450.00	200.00	125.00
(1)	Armstrong	450.00	200.00	125.00
(2)	Beatty	450.00	200.00	125.00
(3)	Biel	450.00	200.00	125.00
(4)	Bonner	450.00	200.00	125.00
(5)	Brandt	450.00	200.00	125.00
(6)	Brown	450.00	200.00	125.00
(7)	Cantwell	450.00	200.00	125.00
(8)	Carrol	450.00	200.00	125.00
(9)	Cooney	450.00	200.00	125.00
(10)	Cooper	450.00	200.00	125.00
(11)	Cowell	450.00	200.00	125.00
(12)	Creager (Cregan)	450.00	200.00	125.00
(13)	Crockett	450.00	200.00	125.00
(14)	Dailey	450.00	200.00	125.00
(15)	Dobbs	450.00	200.00	125.00
(16)	Dussault	450.00	200.00	125.00
(17)	Dwyer	450.00	200.00	125.00
(18)	Evans	450.00	200.00	125.00
(19)	Forgue	450.00	200.00	125.00
(20)	Fulton	450.00	200.00	125.00
(21)	Galvin	450.00	200.00	125.00
(22)	Gastmeyer/Btg	450.00	200.00	125.00
(23)	Gastmeyer/Fielding	450.00	200.00	125.00
(24)	Gates	450.00	200.00	125.00
(25)	Gillespie	450.00	200.00	125.00
(26)	Griffin	450.00	200.00	125.00
(27)	Gunderson	450.00	200.00	125.00
(28)	Ham	450.00	200.00	125.00
(29)	Handibe (Handiboe)	450.00	200.00	125.00
(30)	Hart	450.00	200.00	125.00
(31)	Hartley	450.00	200.00	125.00
(32)	Hobbs	450.00	200.00	125.00
(33)	Hyames	450.00	200.00	125.00
(34)	Irving	450.00	200.00	125.00
(35)	Kaiser	450.00	200.00	125.00
(36)	Kelley	450.00	200.00	125.00
(37)	Kelly	450.00	200.00	125.00
(38)	Kelly/Mascot (Goldsboro)	450.00	200.00	125.00

(39)	Luyster	450.00	200.00	125.00
(40)	MacDonald	450.00	200.00	125.00
(41)	Malcolm	450.00	200.00	125.00
(42)	J. Erskine Mayer	450.00	200.00	125.00
(43)	McCormac (McCormick)	450.00	200.00	125.00
(44)	McGeeham (McGeehan)	450.00	200.00	125.00
(45)	Merchant	450.00	200.00	125.00
(46)	Mills	450.00	200.00	125.00
(47)	Morgan	450.00	200.00	125.00
(48)	Morris	450.00	200.00	125.00
(49)	Munson	450.00	200.00	125.00
(50)	Newman	450.00	200.00	125.00
(51)	Noval (Novak)	450.00	200.00	125.00
(52)	O'Halloran	450.00	200.00	125.00
(53)	Phelan	450.00	200.00	125.00
(54)	Prim	450.00	200.00	125.00
(55)	Reeves	450.00	200.00	125.00
(56)	Richardson	450.00	200.00	125.00
(57)	Schumaker	450.00	200.00	125.00
(58)	Sharp	450.00	200.00	125.00
(59)	Sherrill	450.00	200.00	125.00
(60)	Simmons	450.00	200.00	125.00
(61)	Steinbach	450.00	200.00	125.00
(62)	Stoehr	450.00	200.00	125.00
(63)	Taylor	450.00	200.00	125.00
(64)	Webb	450.00	200.00	125.00
(65)	Whelan	450.00	200.00	125.00
(66)	Wolf	450.00	200.00	125.00
(67)	Wright	450.00	200.00	125.00

1910 Old Mill Cigarettes Series 8 (Southern Assn.)

		NM	EX	VG
	Common Player:	700.00	325.00	200.00
(1)	Allen (Memphis)	700.00	325.00	200.00
(2)	Allen (Mobile)	700.00	325.00	200.00
(3)	Anderson	700.00	325.00	200.00
(4)	Babb	700.00	325.00	200.00
(5)	Bartley	700.00	325.00	200.00
(6)	Bauer	700.00	325.00	200.00
(7)	Bay	700.00	325.00	200.00
(8)	Bayliss	700.00	325.00	200.00
(9)	Berger	700.00	325.00	200.00
(10)	Bernhard	700.00	325.00	200.00
(11)	Bitroth	700.00	325.00	200.00
(12)	Breitenstein	700.00	325.00	200.00
(13)	Bronkie	700.00	325.00	200.00
(14)	Brooks	700.00	325.00	200.00
(15)	Burnett	700.00	325.00	200.00
(16)	Cafalu	700.00	325.00	200.00
(17)	Carson	700.00	325.00	200.00
(18)	Case	700.00	325.00	200.00
(19)	Chappelle	700.00	325.00	200.00
(20)	Cohen	700.00	325.00	200.00
(21)	Collins	700.00	325.00	200.00
(22)	Crandall	700.00	325.00	200.00
(23)	Cross	700.00	325.00	200.00
(24)	Jud. Daly	700.00	325.00	200.00
(25)	Davis	700.00	325.00	200.00
(26)	Demaree	700.00	325.00	200.00
(27)	DeMontreville	700.00	325.00	200.00
(28)	E. DeMontreville	700.00	325.00	200.00
(29)	Dick	700.00	325.00	200.00
(30)	Dobbs	700.00	325.00	200.00
(31)	Dudley	700.00	325.00	200.00
(32)	Dunn	700.00	325.00	200.00
(33)	Elliot	700.00	325.00	200.00
(34)	Emery	700.00	325.00	200.00
(35)	Erloff	700.00	325.00	200.00
(36)	Farrell	700.00	325.00	200.00
(37)	Fisher	700.00	325.00	200.00
(38)	Fleharty	700.00	325.00	200.00
(39)	Flood	700.00	325.00	200.00
(40)	Foster	700.00	325.00	200.00
(41)	Fritz	700.00	325.00	200.00
(42)	Greminger	700.00	325.00	200.00
(43)	Gribbon	700.00	325.00	200.00
(44)	Griffin	700.00	325.00	200.00
(45)	Gygli	700.00	325.00	200.00
(46)	Hanks	700.00	325.00	200.00
(47)	Hart	700.00	325.00	200.00
(48)	Hess	700.00	325.00	200.00
(49)	Hickman	700.00	325.00	200.00
(50)	Hohnhorst	700.00	325.00	200.00
(51)	Huelsman	700.00	325.00	200.00
(52)	Jackson			115,000
(53)	Jordan	700.00	325.00	200.00

(54)	Kane	700.00	325.00	200.00
(55)	Kelly	700.00	325.00	200.00
(56)	Kerwin	700.00	325.00	200.00
(57)	Keupper	700.00	325.00	200.00
(58)	LaFitte	700.00	325.00	200.00
(59)	Larsen	700.00	325.00	200.00
(60)	Bill Lindsay	700.00	325.00	200.00
(61)	Lynch	700.00	325.00	200.00
(62)	Manuel	700.00	325.00	200.00
(63)	Manush	700.00	325.00	200.00
(64)	Marcan	700.00	325.00	200.00
(65)	Maxwell	700.00	325.00	200.00
(66)	McBride	700.00	325.00	200.00
(67)	McCreery	700.00	325.00	200.00
(68)	McGilvray	700.00	325.00	200.00
(69)	McLaurin	700.00	325.00	200.00
(70)	McTigue	700.00	325.00	200.00
(71)	Miller (Chattanooga)	700.00	325.00	200.00
(72)	Miller (Montgomery)	700.00	325.00	200.00
(73)	Molesworth	700.00	325.00	200.00
(74)	Moran	700.00	325.00	200.00
(75)	Newton	700.00	325.00	200.00
(76)	Nolley	700.00	325.00	200.00
(77)	Osteen	700.00	325.00	200.00
(78)	Owen	700.00	325.00	200.00
(79)	Paige	700.00	325.00	200.00
(80)	Patterson	700.00	325.00	200.00
(81)	Pepe	700.00	325.00	200.00
(82)	Perdue	700.00	325.00	200.00
(83)	Peters	700.00	325.00	200.00
(84)	Phillips	700.00	325.00	200.00
(85)	Pratt	700.00	325.00	200.00
(86)	Rementer	700.00	325.00	200.00
(87)	Rhodes	700.00	325.00	200.00
(88)	Rhoton	700.00	325.00	200.00
(89)	Robertson	700.00	325.00	200.00
(90)	Rogers	700.00	325.00	200.00
(91)	Rohe	700.00	325.00	200.00
(92)	Seabough (Seabaugh)	700.00	325.00	200.00
(93)	Seitz	700.00	325.00	200.00
(94)	Schlitzer	700.00	325.00	200.00
(95)	Schopp	700.00	325.00	200.00
(96)	Siegle	700.00	325.00	200.00
(97)	Smith	700.00	325.00	200.00
(98)	Sid. Smith	700.00	325.00	200.00
(99)	Steele	700.00	325.00	200.00
(100)	Swacina	700.00	325.00	200.00
(101)	Sweeney	700.00	325.00	200.00
(102)	Thomas/Fielding	700.00	325.00	200.00
(103)	Thomas/Portrait	700.00	325.00	200.00
(104)	Vinson	700.00	325.00	200.00
(105)	Wagner (Birmingham)	700.00	325.00	200.00
(106)	Wagner (Mobile)	700.00	325.00	200.00
(107)	Walker	700.00	325.00	200.00
(108)	Wanner	700.00	325.00	200.00
(109)	Welf	700.00	325.00	200.00
(110)	Whiteman	700.00	325.00	200.00
(111)	Whitney	700.00	325.00	200.00
(112)	Wilder	700.00	325.00	200.00
(113)	Wiseman	700.00	325.00	200.00
(114)	Yerkes	700.00	325.00	200.00

1910 Old Mill Cabinets (H801-7)

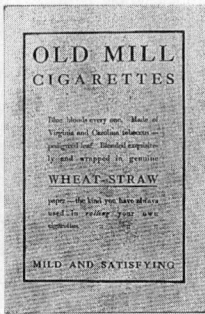

Similar in size and style to the more popular T3 Turkey Red cabinet cards of the same period, the Old Mill cabinets are much scarcer and picture fewer players. Issued in 1910 as a premium by Old Mill Cigarettes, these minor league cards measure approximately 5-3/8" x 7-5/8". Unlike the Turkey Reds, which feature full-color lithographs, the Old Mill cabinet cards picture the players in black-and-white photos surrounded by a wide tan border. The player's last name is printed in black in the lower-left corner, while his team designation appears in the lower-right. Backs carry an advertisement for Old Mill. There are currently 34 known subjects in the set. The Old Mill cabinet cards carry the ACC designation H801-7. Gaps have been left in the numbering to accomodate future additions to this checklist.

		NM	EX	VG
	Common Player:	7,500	3,750	2,250
(1)	Armstrong	7,500	3,750	2,250
(2)	Bentley	7,500	3,750	2,250
(3)	Bonner	7,500	3,750	2,250
(4)	Bowen	7,500	3,750	2,250
(5)	Brazille (Brazell)	7,500	3,750	2,250
(6)	Bush (Busch)	7,500	3,750	2,250
(7)	Bussey	7,500	3,750	2,250
(8)	Cross	7,500	3,750	2,250
(9)	Derrick	7,500	3,750	2,250
(10)	Doane	7,500	3,750	2,250
(11)	Doyle	7,500	3,750	2,250

(12)	Fox	7,500	3,750	2,250
(13)	Galvin	7,500	3,750	2,250
(14)	Griffin	7,500	3,750	2,250
(15)	Hearn	7,500	3,750	2,250
(16)	Hobbs	7,500	3,750	2,250
(17)	Hooker	7,500	3,750	2,250
(18)	Kirkpatrick	7,500	3,750	2,250
(19)	Laughlin	7,500	3,750	2,250
(20)	McKevitt	7,500	3,750	2,250
(21)	Munson	7,500	3,750	2,250
(22)	Noojn (Noojin)	7,500	3,750	2,250
(23)	O'Halloran	7,500	3,750	2,250
(24)	Pressly	7,500	3,750	2,250
(25)	Revelle	7,500	3,750	2,250
(26)	Richardson	7,500	3,750	2,250
(27)	Rickard	7,500	3,750	2,250
(28)	Simmons	7,500	3,750	2,250
(29)	A. Smith	7,500	3,750	2,250
(30)	Spratt	7,500	3,750	2,250
(32)	Titman	7,500	3,750	2,250
(33)	Walters	7,500	3,750	2,250
(34)	Wallace	7,500	3,750	2,250
(35)	Weherell (Wehrell)	7,500	3,750	2,250
(36)	Ivey Wingo	7,500	3,750	2,250
(37)	Woolums	7,500	3,750	2,250

1949 Omaha Cardinals Player Picture Book

JIM BARKLEY, Outfield

While not baseball cards, this team booklet served the same purpose - providing fans with pictures of the local Western League (Class A) affiliate of the St. Louis Cardinals. It's also possible that individual player pages of the book have made their way into card collections over the years. The booklet is 5" x 3-1/4" in size, with 20 pages of photos and semi-gloss front and back covers, stapled together at the spine. The front has printed in red: "OMAHA CARDINALS / BASEBALL TEAM / 1949." Each inside page has back-to-back black-and-white photos with identification beneath. The pairings are checklisted here in the order in which they appear in the booklet.

		NM	EX	VG
Complete Booklet:		350.00	175.00	100.00
(1-2)	Ced Durst, Russ Kerns			
(3-4)	Nick Adzick, Bob Rausch			
(5-6)	Ed Nietopski, Fran Haus			
(7-8)	Fritz Marolewski, Bernie Creger			
(9-10)	Vaughn Hazen, Sid Langston			
(11-12)	Bob Reash, Jim Barkley			
(13-14)	Marty Garlock, Hank Williams			
(15-16)	Lou Ciola, Joe Presko			
(17-18)	Dave Thomas, Bob Mahoney			
(19-20)	Stadium Photo (Dick Bokelmann)			

1956 Omaha Cardinals Picture-Pak

Evidently a concession stand souvenir, this "Picture-Pak" is a comb-bound set of 3-1/2" x 4-3/8" black-and-white player portraits. Each picture is printed on semi-gloss cardboard with a white facsimile autograph.

Complete Book:		300.00	150.00	90.00
(1)	Tom Alston			
(2)	Alberto Baro			
(3)	Nels Burbrink			
(4)	Tom Cheney			
(5)	Ray Coleman			
(6)	Jim Command			

(7)	Chuck Harmon
(8)	Walt Jamison (?)
(9)	Stan Jok
(10)	Gordon Jones
(11)	Johnny Keane
(12)	Marty Kutyna
(13)	Ed Mayer
(14)	Herb Moford
(15)	Mo Mozzali
(16)	Jim Pearce
(17)	Charlie Peete
(18)	Danny Schell
(19)	Dick Schofield
(20)	Barney Schultz
(21)	Wally Shannon
(22)	Glen Stabelfeld

1957 Omaha Cardinals Picture-Pak

These 3-3/8" x 4-3/8" black-and-white, blank-back photos were sold in a team picture pack. Fronts have a facsimile autograph. The unnumbered cards are checklisted here in alphabetical order.

		NM	EX	VG
Complete Set (25):		800.00	400.00	240.00
Common Player:		35.00	17.50	10.00
(1)	Frank Barnes	35.00	17.50	10.00
(2)	Bill Bergesch	35.00	17.50	10.00
(3)	Dick Brown	35.00	17.50	10.00
(4)	Tom Cheney	35.00	17.50	10.00
(5)	Nels Chittum	35.00	17.50	10.00
(6)	Jim Command	35.00	17.50	10.00
(7)	Chuck Diering	35.00	17.50	10.00
(8)	Sherry Dixon	35.00	17.50	10.00
(9)	Bob Durnbaugh	35.00	17.50	10.00
(10)	Glen Gorbous	35.00	17.50	10.00
(11)	Johnny Keane	35.00	17.50	10.00
(12)	Jim King	35.00	17.50	10.00
(13)	Paul Kippels	35.00	17.50	10.00
(14)	Don Lassetter	35.00	17.50	10.00
(15)	Don Liddle	35.00	17.50	10.00
(16)	Lou Limmer	35.00	17.50	10.00
(17)	Boyd Linker	35.00	17.50	10.00
(18)	Bob Mabe	35.00	17.50	10.00
(19)	Herb Moford	35.00	17.50	10.00
(20)	Rance Pless	35.00	17.50	10.00
(21)	Kelton Russell	35.00	17.50	10.00
(22)	Barney Schultz	35.00	17.50	10.00
(23)	Milt Smith	35.00	17.50	10.00
(24)	Glen Stabelfeld	35.00	17.50	10.00
(25)	Header card	35.00	17.50	10.00

1958 Omaha Cardinals Picture-Pak

This rare late-1950s minor league issue contains the first card of Hall of Fame pitcher Bob Gibson. Probably sold as a complete set in format similar to major league picture packs of the era, there are 23 player cards and a header card. Cards measure 3-3/8" x 4-3/8", have a black-and-white player picture and facsimile autograph. They are blank-backed. The checklist of the unnumbered cards is printed here in alphabetical order.

		NM	EX	VG
Complete Set (24):		1,500	750.00	450.00
Common Player:		40.00	20.00	12.00
(1)	Tony Alomar	60.00	30.00	18.00
(2)	Dave Benedict	40.00	20.00	12.00
(3)	Bill Bergesch	40.00	20.00	12.00

(4)	Bob Blaylock	40.00	20.00	12.00
(5)	Prentice "Pidge" Browne	40.00	20.00	12.00
(6)	Chris Cannizzaro	40.00	20.00	12.00
(7)	Nels Chittum	40.00	20.00	12.00
(8)	Don Choate	40.00	20.00	12.00
(9)	Phil Clark	40.00	20.00	12.00
(10)	Jim Frey	75.00	37.50	22.50
(11)	Bob Gibson	500.00	250.00	150.00
(12)	Ev Joyner	40.00	20.00	12.00
(13)	Johnny Keane	40.00	20.00	12.00
(14)	Paul Kippels	40.00	20.00	12.00
(15)	Boyd Linker	40.00	20.00	12.00
(16)	Bob Mabe	40.00	20.00	12.00
(17)	Bernard Mateosky	40.00	20.00	12.00
(18)	Ronnie Plaza	40.00	20.00	12.00
(19)	Bill Queen	40.00	20.00	12.00
(20)	Bill Smith	40.00	20.00	12.00
(21)	Bobby G. Smith	40.00	20.00	12.00
(22)	Lee Tate	40.00	20.00	12.00
(23)	Benny Valenzuela	40.00	20.00	12.00
(24)	Header card	40.00	20.00	12.00

1962 Omaha Dodgers

This unnumbered black-and-white set measures 3-3/8" x 4-1/4" and is blank-backed. It was produced by photographer/collector Mel Bailey in an edition of 1,000 sets, sold for 50 cents by mail and at the stadium concession stand. Cards bear a facsimile autograph.

		NM	EX	VG
Complete Set (22):		175.00	90.00	50.00
Common Player:		12.50	6.25	3.75
(1)	Joe Altobelli	12.50	6.25	3.75
(2)	Jim Barbieri	12.50	6.25	3.75
(3)	Scott Breeden	12.50	6.25	3.75
(4)	Mike Brumley	12.50	6.25	3.75
(5)	Jose Cesar	12.50	6.25	3.75
(6)	Bill Hunter	12.50	6.25	3.75
(7)	Don LeJohn	12.50	6.25	3.75
(8)	Jack Lutz	12.50	6.25	3.75
(9)	Ken McMullen	12.50	6.25	3.75
(10)	Danny Ozark	12.50	6.25	3.75
(11)	Curt Roberts	12.50	6.25	3.75
(12)	Ernie Rodriguez	12.50	6.25	3.75
(13)	Dick Scarbrough	12.50	6.25	3.75
(14)	Bart Shirley	12.50	6.25	3.75
(15)	Dick Smith	12.50	6.25	3.75
(16)	Jack Smith	12.50	6.25	3.75
(17)	Nate Smith	12.50	6.25	3.75
(18)	Gene Snyder	12.50	6.25	3.75
(19)	Burbon Wheeler	12.50	6.25	3.75
(20)	Nick Wilhite (Willhite)	12.50	6.25	3.75
(21)	Jim Williams	12.50	6.25	3.75
(22)	Larry Williams	12.50	6.25	3.75

1952 Oshkosh Giants Team Issue

GORDON WINDHORN

These 2-1/4" x 3-3/8" black-and-white, unnumbered, blank-backed cards were one of many minor league team sets issued by Globe Printing of San Jose, Calif., in the early 1950s. Cards were usually given away at the ballpark on a one-per-week or one-per-homestand basis, accounting for the rarity of surviving sets. The O-Giants were the Wisconsin State League affiliate of the N.Y. Giants. For a Class D team, a surprising number of the Oshkosh players graduated to the major leagues.

	NM	EX	VG

Complete Set (19):		1,000	500.00	300.00
Common Player:		60.00	30.00	18.00
Album:		100.00	50.00	30.00
(1)	Dan Banaszak	60.00	30.00	18.00
(2)	Paul Bentley	60.00	30.00	18.00
(3)	Joe Berke	60.00	30.00	18.00
(4)	Joe DeBellis	60.00	30.00	18.00
(5)	Ron Edwards	60.00	30.00	18.00
(6)	Dave Garcia	60.00	30.00	18.00
(7)	Weldon Grimesley	60.00	30.00	18.00
(8)	Cam Lewis	60.00	30.00	18.00
(9)	Paul McAuley	60.00	30.00	18.00
(10)	Don Mills	60.00	30.00	18.00
(11)	Ed Opich	60.00	30.00	18.00
(12)	John Practico	60.00	30.00	18.00
(13)	Rob R. Schmidt	60.00	30.00	18.00
(14)	Rob W. Schmidt	60.00	30.00	18.00
(15)	Frank Szekula	60.00	30.00	18.00
(16)	Victor Vick	60.00	30.00	18.00
(17)	Donald Wall	60.00	30.00	18.00
(18)	Ken Whitehead	60.00	30.00	18.00
(19)	Gordon Windhorn	60.00	30.00	18.00

P

1911 Pacific Coast Biscuit (D310)

A dozen players each from six Pacific Coast League teams are represented in this set. Cards are about 2-1/2" x 4-1/4" with either black-and-white or sepia pictures on front. Backs have a checklist arranged by team.

		NM	EX	VG
Complete Set (72):		45,000	27,500	13,500
Common Player:		575.00	300.00	175.00
(1)	Ables	575.00	300.00	175.00
(2)	Agnew	575.00	300.00	175.00
(3)	Akin	575.00	300.00	175.00
(4)	Frank Arrelanes (Arellanes)	575.00	300.00	175.00
(5)	Baum	575.00	300.00	175.00
(6)	Bernard	575.00	300.00	175.00
(7)	Berry	575.00	300.00	175.00
(8)	Brashear	575.00	300.00	175.00
(9)	Browning	575.00	300.00	175.00
(10)	Burrell	575.00	300.00	175.00
(11)	Byram	575.00	300.00	175.00
(12)	Carlisle	575.00	300.00	175.00
(13)	Chadbourne	575.00	300.00	175.00
(14)	Christian	575.00	300.00	175.00
(15)	Cutshaw	575.00	300.00	175.00
(16)	Daley	575.00	300.00	175.00
(17)	Danzig	575.00	300.00	175.00
(18)	Delhi	575.00	300.00	175.00
(19)	Delmas	575.00	300.00	175.00
(20)	Dillon	575.00	300.00	175.00
(21)	Fitzgerald	575.00	300.00	175.00
(22)	Gipe	575.00	300.00	175.00
(23)	Heister	575.00	300.00	175.00
(24)	Henderson	575.00	300.00	175.00
(25)	Henley	575.00	300.00	175.00
(26)	Hitt	575.00	300.00	175.00
(27)	Hoffman	575.00	300.00	175.00
(28)	Hogan	575.00	300.00	175.00
(29)	Holland	575.00	300.00	175.00
(30)	Hosp	575.00	300.00	175.00
(31)	Howard	575.00	300.00	175.00
(32)	Kostner	575.00	300.00	175.00
(33)	Kuhn	575.00	300.00	175.00
(34)	LaLonge	575.00	300.00	175.00
(35)	Lewis	575.00	300.00	175.00
(36)	Maddern	575.00	300.00	175.00
(37)	Maggert	575.00	300.00	175.00
(38)	McArdle	575.00	300.00	175.00
(39)	McCredie	575.00	300.00	175.00
(40)	McDonnell	575.00	300.00	175.00
(41)	Metzger	575.00	300.00	175.00
(42)	Mitze	575.00	300.00	175.00
(43)	Mohler	575.00	300.00	175.00
(44)	Moore	575.00	300.00	175.00
(45)	Murray	575.00	300.00	175.00
(46)	Nourse	575.00	300.00	175.00
(47)	O'Rourke	575.00	300.00	175.00
(48)	Patterson	575.00	300.00	175.00
(49)	Peckinpaugh	600.00	300.00	180.00
(50)	Pernoll	575.00	300.00	175.00
(51)	Pfyl	575.00	300.00	175.00
(52)	Raleigh	575.00	300.00	175.00
(53)	Rapps	575.00	300.00	175.00
(54)	Ross	575.00	300.00	175.00
(55)	Ryan	575.00	300.00	175.00
(56)	Seaton	575.00	300.00	175.00
(57)	Sheehan	575.00	300.00	175.00
(58)	A. Smith	575.00	300.00	175.00
(59)	H. Smith	575.00	300.00	175.00
(60)	Steen	575.00	300.00	175.00
(61)	Stinson	575.00	300.00	175.00
(62)	Sutor	575.00	300.00	175.00
(63)	Tennant	575.00	300.00	175.00
(64)	Thompson	575.00	300.00	175.00
(65)	Tiedeman	575.00	300.00	175.00
(66)	Tozer	575.00	300.00	175.00
(67)	Van Buren	575.00	300.00	175.00
(68)	Witt	575.00	300.00	175.00
(69)	Wares	575.00	300.00	175.00
(70)	Weaver	6,000	3,000	1,800
(71)	Wolverton	575.00	300.00	175.00
(72)	Zacher	575.00	300.00	175.00

1911 Pacific Coast Biscuit (D311)

A dozen players each from six Pacific Coast League teams are represented in this set. Cards are about 1-1/2" x 2-5/8" with pastel colored pictures on front. Backs have a checklist arranged by team.

		NM	EX	VG
Complete Set (72):		40,000	20,000	12,000
Common Player:		575.00	300.00	175.00
(1)	Agnew	575.00	300.00	175.00
(2)	Akin	575.00	300.00	175.00
(3)	Frank Arrelanes (Arellanes)	575.00	300.00	175.00
(4)	Baum	575.00	300.00	175.00
(5)	Bernard	575.00	300.00	175.00
(6)	Berry	575.00	300.00	175.00
(7)	Brashear	575.00	300.00	175.00
(8)	Brown	575.00	300.00	175.00
(9)	Browning	575.00	300.00	175.00
(10)	Burrell	575.00	300.00	175.00
(11)	Byram	575.00	300.00	175.00
(12)	Castleton	575.00	300.00	175.00
(13)	Chadbourne	575.00	300.00	175.00
(14)	Christian	575.00	300.00	175.00
(15)	Cutshaw	575.00	300.00	175.00
(16)	Daley	575.00	300.00	175.00
(17)	Danzig	575.00	300.00	175.00
(18)	Delhi	575.00	300.00	175.00
(19)	Delmas	575.00	300.00	175.00
(20)	Dillon	575.00	300.00	175.00
(21)	Fitzgerald	575.00	300.00	175.00
(22)	Gipe	575.00	300.00	175.00
(23)	Gregory	575.00	300.00	175.00
(24)	Harkness	575.00	300.00	175.00
(25)	Heister	575.00	300.00	175.00
(26)	Henderson	575.00	300.00	175.00
(27)	Hoffman	575.00	300.00	175.00
(28)	Hogan	575.00	300.00	175.00
(29)	Holland	575.00	300.00	175.00
(30)	Hosp	575.00	300.00	175.00
(31)	Howard	575.00	300.00	175.00
(32)	Kuhn	575.00	300.00	175.00
(33)	LaLonge	575.00	300.00	175.00
(34)	Lewis	575.00	300.00	175.00
(35)	Maggert	575.00	300.00	175.00
(36)	McArdle	575.00	300.00	175.00
(37)	McCredie	575.00	300.00	175.00
(38)	McDonnell	575.00	300.00	175.00
(39)	Meikle	575.00	300.00	175.00
(40)	Melchior	575.00	300.00	175.00
(41)	Metzger	575.00	300.00	175.00
(42)	Mitze	575.00	300.00	175.00
(43)	Mohler	575.00	300.00	175.00
(44)	Moore	575.00	300.00	175.00
(45)	Murray	575.00	300.00	175.00
(46)	Nourse	575.00	300.00	175.00
(47)	O'Rourke	575.00	300.00	175.00
(48)	Patterson	575.00	300.00	175.00
(49)	Pearce	575.00	300.00	175.00
(50)	Peckinpaugh	600.00	300.00	180.00
(51)	Pernoll	575.00	300.00	175.00
(52)	Pfyl	575.00	300.00	175.00
(53)	Raleigh	575.00	300.00	175.00
(54)	Rapps	575.00	300.00	175.00
(55)	Ryan	575.00	300.00	175.00
(56)	Schmidt	575.00	300.00	175.00
(57)	Seaton	575.00	300.00	175.00
(58)	Sheehan	575.00	300.00	175.00
(59)	A. Smith	575.00	300.00	175.00
(60)	H. Smith	575.00	300.00	175.00
(61)	Stamfield	575.00	300.00	175.00
(62)	Steen	575.00	300.00	175.00
(63)	Stinson	575.00	300.00	175.00
(64)	Sutor	575.00	300.00	175.00
(65)	Tennant	575.00	300.00	175.00
(66)	Thompson	575.00	300.00	175.00
(67)	Tiedeman	575.00	300.00	175.00
(68)	Tozer	575.00	300.00	175.00
(69)	Van Buren	575.00	300.00	175.00
(70)	Vitt	575.00	300.00	175.00
(71)	Wares	575.00	300.00	175.00
(72)	Wolverton	575.00	300.00	175.00

1943-47 Parade Sportive

Over a period of years in the mid-1940s, Montreal sports radio personality Paul Stuart's Parade Sportive program issued a series of baseball player pic-

Jackie Robinson

tures of Montreal Royals and, occasionally, other International League stars. The pictures were issued in 5" x 9-1/2" and 7" x 10" black-and-white, blank-back format. Each picture carries the name of the radio station on which Stuart's program was broadcast, along with an ad at the bottom for one of his sponsors. The unnumbered pictures are listed here alphabetically; it is unknown whether this list constitutes the complete issue.

		NM	EX	VG
Common Player:		30.00	15.00	9.00
(1)	Jack Banta	30.00	15.00	9.00
(2)	Stan Briard	30.00	15.00	9.00
(3)	Les Burge	30.00	15.00	9.00
(4)	Paul Calvert	30.00	15.00	9.00
(5)	Al Campanis	45.00	22.50	13.50
(6)	Red Durrett	30.00	15.00	9.00
(7)	Herman Franks	30.00	15.00	9.00
(8)	John Gabbard	30.00	15.00	9.00
(9)	Roland Gladu	30.00	15.00	9.00
(10)	Ray Hathaway	30.00	15.00	9.00
(11)	Clay Hopper	30.00	15.00	9.00
(12)	John Jorgensen	30.00	15.00	9.00
(13)	Paul "Pepper" Martin	30.00	15.00	9.00
(14)	Steve Nagy	30.00	15.00	9.00
(15)	Roy Portlow (Partlow)	40.00	20.00	12.00
(16)	Marv Rackley	30.00	15.00	9.00
(17)	Jackie Robinson	300.00	150.00	90.00
(18)	Jean-Pierre Roy	30.00	15.00	9.00
(19)	1944 Montreal Royals Team Photo	50.00	25.00	15.00
(20)	1945 Montreal Royals Team Photo (CLUB MONTREAL (ROYAUX) 1945)	60.00	30.00	18.00
(21)	1945 Montreal Royals Team Photo (Les "Royaux" 1945)	60.00	30.00	18.00
(22)	1946 Montreal Royals Team Photo	200.00	100.00	60.00
(23)	Stan Briard, Roland Gladu, Jean-Pierre Roy	30.00	15.00	9.00
(24)	Checklist (Paul Stuart)	30.00	15.00	9.00

1952 Parkhurst

Produced by a Canadian competitor to Kool-Aid, this 100-card set features players from three International League teams, the Toronto Maple Leafs, Montreal Royals and Ottawa Athletics, along with cards featuring baseball playing tips and quizzes. Measuring 2" x 2-1/2", the cards feature black-and-white player photos on front. Backs are printed in red and have a few biographical details, 1951 stats and an ad for Frostade.

		NM	EX	VG
Complete Set (100):		2,400	1,200	725.00
Common Player (1-25, 49-100):		25.00	12.50	7.50
Common Card (26-48):		10.00	5.00	3.00
1	Joe Becker	80.00	35.00	9.00
2	Aaron Silverman	75.00	37.50	22.50
3	Bobby Rhawn	25.00	12.50	7.50
4	Russ Bauers	25.00	12.50	7.50
5	Bill Jennings	25.00	12.50	7.50
6	Grover Bowers	25.00	12.50	7.50
7	Vic Lombardi	25.00	12.50	7.50
8	Billy DeMars	25.00	12.50	7.50
9	Frank Colman	25.00	12.50	7.50
10	Charley Grant	25.00	12.50	7.50
11	Irving Medlinger	25.00	12.50	7.50
12	Burke McLaughlin	25.00	12.50	7.50
13	Lew Morton	25.00	12.50	7.50
14	Red Barrett	25.00	12.50	7.50

15	Leon Foulk	25.00	12.50	7.50
16	Neil Sheridan	25.00	12.50	7.50
17	Ferrell Anderson	25.00	12.50	7.50
18	Roy Shore	25.00	12.50	7.50
19	Duke Markell	75.00	37.50	22.50
20	Bobby Balcena	25.00	12.50	7.50
21	Wilmer Fields	25.00	12.50	7.50
22	Charlie White	25.00	12.50	7.50
23	Red Fahr	25.00	12.50	7.50
24	Jose Bracho	25.00	12.50	7.50
25	Ed Stevens	25.00	12.50	7.50
26	Maple Leaf Stadium	25.00	12.50	7.50
27	Throwing Home	15.00	7.50	4.50
28	Regulation Baseball Diamond	15.00	7.50	4.50
29	Gripping the Bat	15.00	7.50	4.50
30	Hiding the Pitch	15.00	7.50	4.50
31	Catcher's Stance	15.00	7.50	4.50
32	Quiz: "How long does..."	15.00	7.50	4.50
33	Finger and Arm Exercises	15.00	7.50	4.50
34	First Baseman	15.00	7.50	4.50
35	Pitcher's Stance	15.00	7.50	4.50
36	Swinging Bats	15.00	7.50	4.50
37	Quiz: "Can a player advance..."	15.00	7.50	4.50
38	Watch the Ball	15.00	7.50	4.50
39	Quiz: "Can a team..."	15.00	7.50	4.50
40	Quiz: "Can a player put ..."	15.00	7.50	4.50
41	How to Bunt	15.00	7.50	4.50
42	Wrist Snap	15.00	7.50	4.50
43	Pitching Practice	15.00	7.50	4.50
44	Stealing Bases	15.00	7.50	4.50
45	Pitching 1	15.00	7.50	4.50
46	Pitching 2	15.00	7.50	4.50
47	Signals	15.00	7.50	4.50
48	Regulation baseballs	15.00	7.50	4.50
49	Al Ronning	25.00	12.50	7.50
50	Bill Lane	25.00	12.50	7.50
51	Will Sampson	25.00	12.50	7.50
52	Charlie Thompson	25.00	12.50	7.50
53	Ezra McGlothin	25.00	12.50	7.50
54	Spook Jacobs	30.00	15.00	9.00
55	Art Fabbro	25.00	12.50	7.50
56	Jim Hughes	25.00	12.50	7.50
57	Don Hoak	30.00	15.00	9.00
58	Tommy Lasorda	100.00	50.00	30.00
59	Gil Mills	25.00	12.50	7.50
60	Malcolm Mallette	25.00	12.50	7.50
61	Rocky Nelson	25.00	12.50	7.50
62	John Simmons	25.00	12.50	7.50
63	Bob Alexander	25.00	12.50	7.50
64	Dan Bankhead	35.00	17.50	10.00
65	Solomon Coleman	25.00	12.50	7.50
66	Walt Alston	100.00	50.00	30.00
67	Walt Fiala	25.00	12.50	7.50
68	Jim Gilliam	40.00	20.00	12.00
69	Jim Pendleton	25.00	12.50	7.50
70	Gino Cimoli	30.00	15.00	9.00
71	Carmen Mauro	25.00	12.50	7.50
72	Walt Moryn	25.00	12.50	7.50
73	Jim Romano	25.00	12.50	7.50
74	Joe Lutz	25.00	12.50	7.50
75	Ed Roebuck	25.00	12.50	7.50
76	Johnny Podres	40.00	20.00	12.00
77	Walter Novik	25.00	12.50	7.50
78	Lefty Gohl	25.00	12.50	7.50
79	Tom Kirk	25.00	12.50	7.50
80	Bob Betz	25.00	12.50	7.50
81	Bill Hockenbury	25.00	12.50	7.50
82	Al Rubeling	25.00	12.50	7.50
83	Julius Watlington	25.00	12.50	7.50
84	Frank Fanovich	25.00	12.50	7.50
85	Hank Foiles	25.00	12.50	7.50
86	Lou Limmer	25.00	12.50	7.50
87	Ed Hrabcsak	25.00	12.50	7.50
88	Bob Gardner	25.00	12.50	7.50
89	John Metkovich	25.00	12.50	7.50
90	Jean-Pierre Roy	25.00	12.50	7.50
91	Frank Skaff	25.00	12.50	7.50
92	Harry Desert	25.00	12.50	7.50
93	Stan Jok	25.00	12.50	7.50
94	Russ Swingle	25.00	12.50	7.50
95	Bob Wellman	25.00	12.50	7.50
96	John Conway	25.00	12.50	7.50
97	George Maskovich	25.00	12.50	7.50
98	Charlie Bishop	25.00	12.50	7.50
99	Joe Murray	25.00	12.50	7.50
100	Mike Kume	25.00	12.50	7.50

1935 Pebble Beach Clothiers

This series of black-and-white postcards includes only members of the three Bay area Pacific Coast League teams - the Oakland Oaks, Mission Reds and San Francisco Seals. The 3-1/2" x 5-3/8" cards have player identification at left in the bottom white border. The logotype of the clothier which sponsored the issued is at lower-right. The cards - each authentically autographed - were distributed by an area radio station. Backs have typical postcard indicia. This checklist may not be complete.

		NM	EX	VG
	Common Player:	750.00	375.00	225.00
(1)	Leroy Anton	750.00	375.00	225.00
(2)	Joe DiMaggio	7,500	3,750	2,250
(3)	Wee Ludolph	750.00	375.00	225.00
(4)	Walter "The Great" Mails	750.00	375.00	225.00
(5)	Lefty O'Doul	3,650	1,825	1,100
(6)	Gabby Street	1,200	600.00	360.00
(7)	Oscar Vitt	900.00	450.00	270.00

1962 Pepsi-Cola Tulsa Oilers

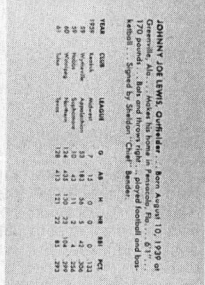

The Texas League farm club of the St. Louis Cardinals is featured in this issue of sepia-colored 2-1/2" x 3-1/2" cards issued regionally by Pepsi. The unnumbered cards are checklisted here alphabetically.

		NM	EX	VG
Complete Set (24):		275.00	135.00	80.00
	Common Player:	12.00	6.00	3.50
(1)	Bob Blaylock	12.00	6.00	3.50
(2)	Bud Bloomfield	12.00	6.00	3.50
(3)	Dick Hughes	12.00	6.00	3.50
(4)	Gary Kolb	12.00	6.00	3.50
(5)	Chris Krug	12.00	6.00	3.50
(6)	Hank Kuhlmann	12.00	6.00	3.50
(7)	Whitey Kurowski	12.00	6.00	3.50
(8)	Johnny Joe Lewis	12.00	6.00	3.50
(9)	Elmer Lindsey	12.00	6.00	3.50
(10)	Jeoff Long	12.00	6.00	3.50
(11)	Pepper Martin	15.00	7.50	4.50
(12)	Jerry Marx	12.00	6.00	3.50
(13)	Weldon Maudin	12.00	6.00	3.50
(14)	Dal Maxvill	15.00	7.50	4.50
(15)	Bill McNamee	12.00	6.00	3.50
(16)	Joe Patterson	12.00	6.00	3.50
(17)	Gordon Richardson	12.00	6.00	3.50
(18)	Daryl Robertson	12.00	6.00	3.50
(19)	Tom Schwaner	12.00	6.00	3.50
(20)	Joe Shipley	12.00	6.00	3.50
(21)	Jon Smith	12.00	6.00	3.50
(22)	Clint Stark	12.00	6.00	3.50
(23)	Terry Tucker	12.00	6.00	3.50
(24)	Bill Wakefield	12.00	6.00	3.50

1963 Pepsi-Cola Tulsa Oilers

These 2-1/2" x 3-1/2", unnumbered, cards were issued in two-card panels with a holed top panel to hang on bottles. Each player's name could also be found under the cork liner of the bottle caps and when all 24 cards and caps were collected, a $24 prize could be collected. It must be assumed that some player caps were short-printed.

		NM	EX	VG
Complete Set, Singles (24):		75.00	37.50	22.50
Complete Set, Panels (12):		90.00	45.00	27.50
	Common Player:	4.00	2.00	1.25
(1)	Dennis Aust	4.00	2.00	1.25
(2)	Jimmy Beauchamp	4.00	2.00	1.25
(3)	"Bud" Bloomfield	4.00	2.00	1.25
(4)	Felix de Leon	4.00	2.00	1.25
(5)	Don Dennis	4.00	2.00	1.25
(6)	Lamar Drummonds	4.00	2.00	1.25
(7)	Tom Hilgendorf	4.00	2.00	1.25
(8)	Gary Kolb	4.00	2.00	1.25
(9)	Chris Krug	4.00	2.00	1.25
(10)	"Bee" Lindsey	4.00	2.00	1.25
(11)	Roy Majtyka	4.00	2.00	1.25
(12)	Pepper Martin	7.50	3.75	2.25
(13)	Jerry Marx	4.00	2.00	1.25
(14)	"Hunkey" Mauldin	4.00	2.00	1.25
(15)	Joe Patterson	4.00	2.00	1.25
(16)	Grover Resinger	4.00	2.00	1.25
(17)	Gordon Richardson	4.00	2.00	1.25
(18)	Jon Smith	4.00	2.00	1.25
(19)	Chuck Taylor	4.00	2.00	1.25
(20)	Terry Tucker (Batboy)	4.00	2.00	1.25
(21)	Lou Vickery	4.00	2.00	1.25
(22)	Bill Wakefield	4.00	2.00	1.25
(23)	Harry Watts	4.00	2.00	1.25
(24)	Jerry Wild	4.00	2.00	1.25

1964 Pepsi-Cola Tulsa Oiler Autograph Cards

These unusual baseball cards - they don't have pictures! - were one of several 1960s issues by Pepsi in conjunction with the Tulsa Oilers. Apparently carton stuffers (they measure 2-3/16" x 9"), the cards provided free children's admission on special Pepsi-Oiler nights. The cards are printed in red, white and blue and have short player biographies under the baseball containing the facsimile autograph. The unnumbered cards are listed here in alphabetical order.

		NM	EX	VG
Complete Set (8):		30.00	15.00	9.00
	Common Player:	5.00	2.50	1.50
(1)	Bob Blaylock	5.00	2.50	1.50
(2)	Nelson Briles	5.00	2.50	1.50
(3)	Bobby Dews	5.00	2.50	1.50
(4)	Roy Majtyka	5.00	2.50	1.50
(5)	Otto Meischner	5.00	2.50	1.50
(6)	Rogers Robinson	5.00	2.50	1.50
(7)	Jerry Wild	5.00	2.50	1.50
(8)	Lou Vickery	5.00	2.50	1.50

1966 Pepsi-Cola Tulsa Oilers

These 2-1/2" x 3-1/2" unnumbered cards were issued in two-card panels. Four cards were double-printed, each appearing on two different panels. Each player's name could also be found under the cork liner of the bottle caps and when all 24 cards and caps were collected, a $24 prize could be collected. It must be assumed that some player cards or caps were short-printed.

		NM	EX	VG
Complete Set (24):		175.00	90.00	55.00
Complete Panel Set (16):		225.00	115.00	70.00
Common Player:		10.00	5.00	3.00
Common Panel:		15.00	7.50	4.50
(1)	Florian Ackley	10.00	5.00	3.00
(2)	Dennis Aust	10.00	5.00	3.00
(3)	Elio Chacon/DP	10.00	5.00	3.00
(4)	James Cosman	10.00	5.00	3.00
(5)	Mack Creager	10.00	5.00	3.00
(6)	Robert Dews/DP	10.00	5.00	3.00
(7)	Harold Gilson	10.00	5.00	3.00
(8)	Larry Jaster	10.00	5.00	3.00
(9)	Alex Johnson	10.00	5.00	3.00
(10)	George Kernek/DP	10.00	5.00	3.00
(11)	Jose Laboy	10.00	5.00	3.00
(12)	Richard LeMay	10.00	5.00	3.00
(13)	Charles Metro	10.00	5.00	3.00
(14)	David Pavlesic	10.00	5.00	3.00
(15)	Robert Pfeil	10.00	5.00	3.00
(16)	Ronald Piche	10.00	5.00	3.00
(17)	Robert Radovich	10.00	5.00	3.00
(18)	David Ricketts/DP	10.00	5.00	3.00
(19)	Theodore Savage	10.00	5.00	3.00
(20)	George Schultz	10.00	5.00	3.00
(21)	Edward Spiezio	10.00	5.00	3.00
(22)	Clint Stark	10.00	5.00	3.00
(23)	Robert Tolan	10.00	5.00	3.00
(24)	Walter Williams	10.00	5.00	3.00

1956 Portland Beaver All-Star Pins

Stars of the Pacific Coast League Portland Beavers, all former and/or future major leaguers, are featured on these 1" black-and-white celluloid pins.

		NM	EX	VG
Complete Set (8):		1,300	650.00	375.00
Common Player:		175.00	90.00	55.00
(1)	Jim Baxes	175.00	90.00	55.00
(2)	Bob Borkowski	175.00	90.00	55.00
(3)	Sam Calderone	175.00	90.00	55.00
(4)	Jack Littrell	175.00	90.00	55.00
(5)	Luis Marquez	175.00	90.00	55.00
(6)	Ed Mickelson	175.00	90.00	55.00
(7)	Tom Saffell	175.00	90.00	55.00
(8)	Rene Valdez	175.00	90.00	55.00

1958 Ralph's Thriftway Seattle Rainiers

(See 1958 Seattle Popcorn for checklist and values.)

1968 Red Barn Memphis Blues

A regional issue from a Memphis chain of fast-food restaurants, these 2-1/2" x 3-3/4" cards feature members of the New York Mets' Class AA farm team. Cards have a blue-tinted player photo within an orange barn design. Player information is printed below. Backs are blank. The cards are checklisted here by uniform number.

		NM	EX	VG
Complete Set (8):		600.00	300.00	180.00
Common Player:		75.00	37.50	22.50
3	Mike "Spider" Jorgensen	75.00	37.50	22.50
6	Joe Moock	75.00	37.50	22.50
9	Rod Gaspar	75.00	37.50	22.50
16	Barry "Chief" Raziano	75.00	37.50	22.50

17	Curtis "Bubba" Brown	75.00	37.50	22.50
18	Roger Stevens	75.00	37.50	22.50
19	Ron Paul	75.00	37.50	22.50
24	Steve "Teddy" Christopher	75.00	37.50	22.50

1910 Red Sun (T211)

The 1910 minor league tobacco set issued by Red Sun Cigarettes features 75 players from the Southern Association. The Red Sun issue is similar in size and and style to the massive 640-card Old Mill set (T210) issued the same year. Cards in both sets measure 1-1/2" x 2-5/8" and feature glossy black-and-white player photos. Unlike the Old Mill set, however, the Red Sun cards have a green border surrounding the photograph and a bright red and white advertisement for Red Sun cigarettes on the back. A line at the bottom promotes the cards as "First Series 1 to 75." implying that additional sets would follow, but apparently none ever did. Each of the 75 subjects in the Red Sun set was also pictured in Series Eight of the Old Mill set. Because of the "Glossy" nature of the photographs, cards in both the Old Mill and Red Sun sets are susceptible to cracking, making condition and proper grading of these cards especially important to collectors.

		NM	EX	VG
Complete Set (75):		65,000	35,000	20,000
Common Player:		1,300	500.00	300.00
(1)	Allen	1,300	500.00	300.00
(2)	Anderson	1,300	500.00	300.00
(3)	Babb	1,300	500.00	300.00
(4)	Bartley	1,300	500.00	300.00
(5)	Bay	1,300	500.00	300.00
(6)	Bayliss	1,300	500.00	300.00
(7)	Berger	1,300	500.00	300.00
(8)	Bernard	1,300	500.00	300.00
(9)	Bitroff	1,300	500.00	300.00
(10)	Breitenstein	1,300	500.00	300.00
(11)	Bronkie	1,300	500.00	300.00
(12)	Brooks	1,300	500.00	300.00
(13)	Cafalu	1,300	500.00	300.00
(14)	Case	1,300	500.00	300.00
(15)	Chappelle	1,300	500.00	300.00
(16)	Cohen	1,300	500.00	300.00
(17)	Cross	1,300	500.00	300.00
(18)	Jud. Daly	1,300	500.00	300.00
(19)	Davis	1,300	500.00	300.00
(20)	DeMontreville	1,300	500.00	300.00
(21)	E. DeMontreville	1,300	500.00	300.00
(22)	Dick	1,300	500.00	300.00
(23)	Dunn	1,300	500.00	300.00
(24)	Erloff	1,300	500.00	300.00
(25)	Fisher	1,300	500.00	300.00
(26)	Flood	1,300	500.00	300.00
(27)	Foster	1,300	500.00	300.00
(28)	Fritz	1,300	500.00	300.00
(29)	Greminger	1,300	500.00	300.00
(30)	Gribbon	1,300	500.00	300.00
(31)	Griffin	1,300	500.00	300.00
(32)	Gygli	1,300	500.00	300.00
(33)	Hanks	1,300	500.00	300.00
(34)	Hart	1,300	500.00	300.00
(35)	Hess	1,300	500.00	300.00
(36)	Hickman	1,300	500.00	300.00
(37)	Hohnhorst	1,300	500.00	300.00
(38)	Huelsman	1,300	500.00	300.00
(39)	Jordan	1,300	500.00	300.00
(40)	Kane	1,300	500.00	300.00
(41)	Kelly	1,300	500.00	300.00
(42)	Kerwin	1,300	500.00	300.00
(43)	Keupper	1,300	500.00	300.00
(44)	LaFitte	1,300	500.00	300.00
(45)	Bill Lindsay	1,300	500.00	300.00
(46)	Lynch	1,300	500.00	300.00
(47)	Manush	1,300	500.00	300.00
(48)	McCreery	1,300	500.00	300.00

(49)	Miller	1,300	500.00	300.00
(50)	Molesworth	1,300	500.00	300.00
(51)	Moran	1,300	500.00	300.00
(52)	Nolley	1,300	500.00	300.00
(53)	Paige	1,300	500.00	300.00
(54)	Pepe	1,300	500.00	300.00
(55)	Perdue	1,300	500.00	300.00
(56)	Pratt	1,300	500.00	300.00
(57)	Rhoton	1,300	500.00	300.00
(58)	Robertson	1,300	500.00	300.00
(59)	Rogers	1,300	500.00	300.00
(60)	Rohe	1,300	500.00	300.00
(61)	Seabaugh	1,300	500.00	300.00
(62)	Seitz	1,300	500.00	300.00
(63)	Siegle	1,300	500.00	300.00
(64)	Smith	1,300	500.00	300.00
(65)	Sid. Smith	1,300	500.00	300.00
(66)	Steele	1,300	500.00	300.00
(67)	Swacina	1,300	500.00	300.00
(68)	Sweeney	1,300	500.00	300.00
(69)	Thomas	1,300	500.00	300.00
(70)	Vinson	1,300	500.00	300.00
(71)	Wagner	1,300	500.00	300.00
(72)	Walker	1,300	500.00	300.00
(73)	Welf	1,300	500.00	300.00
(74)	Wilder	1,300	500.00	300.00
(75)	Wiseman	1,300	500.00	300.00

1945 Remar Bread Oakland Oaks

This 4-7/8" x 3-5/8" card features on front a black-and-white team photo, borderless at the top and sides. In the white strip at bottom, the players are identified. The back is printed in black with red highlights and presents the season stats for batting average and pitchers' won-lost percentage. At right is a picture of a loaf of the sponsor's bread. At present, only two examples of this card are known to exist.

	NM	EX	VG
Oakland Oaks Team Photo	2,500	1,250	750.00

1946 Remar Bread Oakland Oaks

CHARLES (Casey) STENGEL
Oaks Manager 10

REMAR BREAD

Remar Baking Co. issued several baseball card sets in the northern California area from 1946-1950, all picturing members of the Oakland Oaks of the Pacific Coast League. The 1946 set consists of 23 cards (five unnumbered, 18 numbered). Measuring 2" x 3", the cards were printed on heavy paper and feature black and white photos with the player's name, team and position at the bottom. The backs contain a brief write-up plus an ad for Remar Bread printed in red. The cards were distributed one per week. The first five cards were unnumbered. The rest of the set is numbered on the front, but begins with number "5," rather than "6."

		NM	EX	VG
Complete Set (23):		600.00	300.00	180.00
Common Player:		25.00	12.50	7.50
5	Hershell Martin (Herschel)	25.00	12.50	7.50
6	Bill Hart	25.00	12.50	7.50

		NM	EX	VG
7	Charlie Gassaway	25.00	12.50	7.50
8	Wally Westlake	25.00	12.50	7.50
9	Mickey Burnett	25.00	12.50	7.50
10	Charles (Casey) Stengel	110.00	55.00	35.00
11	Charlie Metro	25.00	12.50	7.50
12	Tom Hafey	25.00	12.50	7.50
13	Tony Sabol	25.00	12.50	7.50
14	Ed Kearse	25.00	12.50	7.50
15	Bud Foster/Announcer	25.00	12.50	7.50
16	Johnny Price	25.00	12.50	7.50
17	Gene Bearden	25.00	12.50	7.50
18	Floyd Speer	25.00	12.50	7.50
19	Bryan Stephens	25.00	12.50	7.50
20	Rinaldo (Rugger) Ardizoia	25.00	12.50	7.50
21	Ralph Buxton	25.00	12.50	7.50
22	Ambrose (Bo) Palica	25.00	12.50	7.50
----	Brooks Holder	25.00	12.50	7.50
----	Henry (Cotton) Pippen	25.00	12.50	7.50
----	Billy Raimondi	90.00	45.00	27.50
----	Les Scarsella	25.00	12.50	7.50
----	Glen (Gabby) Stewart	25.00	12.50	7.50

1947 Remar Bread Oakland Oaks

BILLY RAIMONDI
Oaks Catcher

BILLY RAIMONDI, 33, has been with the Oaks for 16 years. Managed Acorns part of '45. Believes it's bad luck to cross bats or walk between umpire and catcher. Learned baseball on San Francisco sandlots. Boyhood idol: Baby Ruth; present-day favorite: Joe Di Maggio. Hobby is photography.

"Let's Be Friends"

Listen to baseball play by play with "Bud Foster" KROW, 960

REMAR BAKING CO.

Remar's second set consisted of 25 numbered cards, again measuring 2" x 3". The cards are nearly identical to the previous year's set, except the loaf of bread on the back is printed in blue, rather than red.

		NM	EX	VG
Complete Set (25):		600.00	300.00	180.00
Common Player:		25.00	12.50	7.50
1	Billy Raimondi	25.00	12.50	7.50
2	Les Scarsella	25.00	12.50	7.50
3	Brooks Holder	25.00	12.50	7.50
4	Charlie Gassaway	25.00	12.50	7.50
5	Mickey Burnett	25.00	12.50	7.50
6	Ralph Buxton	25.00	12.50	7.50
7	Ed Kearse	25.00	12.50	7.50
8	Charles (Casey) Stengel	75.00	37.50	22.50
9	Bud Foster/Announcer	25.00	12.50	7.50
10	Ambrose (Bo) Palica	25.00	12.50	7.50
11	Tom Hafey	25.00	12.50	7.50
12	Hershel Martin (Herschel)	25.00	12.50	7.50
13	Henry (Cotton) Pippen	25.00	12.50	7.50
14	Floyd Speer	25.00	12.50	7.50
15	Tony Sabol	25.00	12.50	7.50
16	Will Hafey	25.00	12.50	7.50
17	Ray Hamrick	25.00	12.50	7.50
18	Maurice Van Robays	25.00	12.50	7.50
19	Dario Lodigiani	25.00	12.50	7.50
20	Mel (Dizz) Duezabou	25.00	12.50	7.50
21	Damon Hayes	25.00	12.50	7.50
22	Gene Lillard	25.00	12.50	7.50
23	Aldon Wilkie	25.00	12.50	7.50
24	Dewey Soriano	25.00	12.50	7.50
25	Glen Crawford	25.00	12.50	7.50

1948 Remar/Sunbeam Bread Oakland Oaks

1948 Oakland OAKS

Let's Be Friends... REACH FOR SUNBEAM BREAD

One of the great minor league rarities, only two examples of this 3-1/4" x 5-1/2" black-and-white team photo card are known.

BILLY MARTIN
Oaks Infielder

Vital Statistics on Billy Martin

Age 20		1948 Club Oakland, P.C.L.	
B R	T R	Wt. 165	Ht. 5:10½	G 129
AB 400	R 59	H 111	2B 27	3B
HR 3	SB 7	BB 15	RBI 41	PCT .278

"Let's Be Friends"

Listen to baseball play by play with Bud Foster KLX, 910 on your dial

REMAR BAKING CO.

1949 Remar Bread Oakland Oaks

	NM	EX	VG
1948 Oakland Oaks Team Photo	2,500	1,250	750.00

The 1949 Remar Bread issue was increased to 32 cards, again measuring 2" x 3". Unlike the two earlier sets, photos in the 1949 Remar set are surrounded by a thin, white border and are unnumbered. The player's name, team and position appear below the black and white photo. The backs are printed in blue and include the player's 1948 statistics and the distinctive loaf of bread.

		NM	EX	VG
Complete Set (32):		700.00	350.00	210.00
Common Player:		20.00	10.00	6.00
(1)	Ralph Buxton	20.00	10.00	6.00
(2)	Milo Candini	20.00	10.00	6.00
(3)	Rex Cecil	20.00	10.00	6.00
(4)	Loyd Christopher (Lloyd)	20.00	10.00	6.00
(5)	Charles Dressen	20.00	10.00	6.00
(6)	Mel Duezabou	20.00	10.00	6.00
(7)	Bud Foster/Sportscaster	20.00	10.00	6.00
(8)	Charlie Gassaway	20.00	10.00	6.00
(9)	Ray Hamrick	20.00	10.00	6.00
(10)	Jack Jensen	25.00	12.50	7.50
(11)	Earl Jones	20.00	10.00	6.00
(12)	George Kelly	60.00	30.00	18.00
(13)	Frank Kerr	20.00	10.00	6.00
(14)	Richard Kryhoski	20.00	10.00	6.00
(15)	Harry Lavagetto	20.00	10.00	6.00
(16)	Dario Lodigiani	20.00	10.00	6.00
(17)	Billy Martin	75.00	37.50	22.50
(18)	George Metkovich	20.00	10.00	6.00
(19)	Frank Nelson	20.00	10.00	6.00
(20)	Don Padgett	20.00	10.00	6.00
(21)	Alonzo Perry	40.00	20.00	12.00
(22)	Bill Raimondi	20.00	10.00	6.00
(23)	Earl Rapp	20.00	10.00	6.00
(24)	Eddie Samcoff	20.00	10.00	6.00
(25)	Les Scarsella	20.00	10.00	6.00
(26)	Forest Thompson (Forrest)	20.00	10.00	6.00
(27)	Earl Toolson	20.00	10.00	6.00
(28)	Lou Tost	20.00	10.00	6.00
(29)	Maurice Van Robays	20.00	10.00	6.00
(30)	Jim Wallace	20.00	10.00	6.00
(31)	Arthur Lee Wilson	40.00	20.00	12.00
(32)	Parnell Woods	20.00	10.00	6.00

1950 Remar Bread Oakland Oaks

RAFAEL (RAY) NOBLE
Oaks Catcher

Vital Statistics on Rafael (Ray) Noble

Age 28		1949 Club Jersey City, I.L.	
B: R		AB: 189	HR: 7
T: R		R: 33	SB: 1
Wt: 210		H: 49	BB: —
Ht: 5:11		2B: 2	RBI: 29
G: 67		3B: 1	PCT: .259

"Let's Be Friends"

Listen to baseball play by play with Bud Foster KLX-AM and KGO-TV

REMAR BAKING CO.

The most common of the Remar Bread issues, the 1950 set contains 27 unnumbered cards, again measuring 2" x 3" and featuring members of the Oakland Oaks. The cards are nearly identical to the previous year's set but can be differentiated by the 1949 statistics on the back.

		NM	EX	VG
Complete Set (27):		500.00	250.00	150.00
Common Player:		20.00	10.00	6.00
(1)	George Bamberger	20.00	10.00	6.00
(2)	Hank Behrman	20.00	10.00	6.00
(3)	Loyd Christopher (Lloyd)	20.00	10.00	6.00
(4)	Chuck Dressen	20.00	10.00	6.00
(5)	Mel Duezabou	20.00	10.00	6.00
(6)	Augie Galan	20.00	10.00	6.00
(7)	Charlie Gassaway	20.00	10.00	6.00
(8)	Allen Gettel	20.00	10.00	6.00
(9)	Ernie W. Groth	20.00	10.00	6.00
(10)	Ray Hamrick	20.00	10.00	6.00
(11)	Earl Harrist	20.00	10.00	6.00
(12)	Billy Herman	60.00	30.00	18.00
(13)	Bob Hofman	20.00	10.00	6.00
(14)	George Kelly	60.00	30.00	18.00
(15)	Harry Lavagetto	20.00	10.00	6.00
(16)	Eddie Malone	20.00	10.00	6.00
(17)	George Metkovich	20.00	10.00	6.00
(18)	Frank Nelson	20.00	10.00	6.00
(19)	Rafael (Ray) Noble	20.00	10.00	6.00
(20)	Don Padgett	20.00	10.00	6.00
(21)	Earl Rapp	20.00	10.00	6.00
(22)	Clyde Shoun	20.00	10.00	6.00
(23)	Forrest Thompson	20.00	10.00	6.00
(24)	Louis Tost	20.00	10.00	6.00
(25)	Dick Wakefield	20.00	10.00	6.00
(26)	Artie Wilson	40.00	20.00	12.00
(27)	Roy Zimmerman	20.00	10.00	6.00

1958 Richmond Virginians Team Issue

This set of black-and-white cards features members of the N.Y. Yankees' top farm club in posed action photos with a stadium background. Issued on a pair of 8-1/2" x 10" sheets, single cards measure about 2-1/8" x 3" including the white borders around the picture. The player name is in a white strip within the photo. Backs have only the player name and a two-line credit at bottom to Galeski Photo Finishing.

		NM	EX	VG
Complete Set (21):		1,200	600.00	360.00
Common Player:		60.00	30.00	18.00
(1)	Billy Bethel	60.00	30.00	18.00
(2)	Cletis Boyer	90.00	45.00	27.50
(3)	Wade Browning	60.00	30.00	18.00
(4)	Bob Chakales	60.00	30.00	18.00
(5)	Jim Coates	60.00	30.00	18.00
(6)	Jim Command	60.00	30.00	18.00
(7)	Bobby Deakin	60.00	30.00	18.00
(8)	Bob Del Greco	60.00	30.00	18.00
(9)	John Jaciuk	60.00	30.00	18.00
(10)	John James	60.00	30.00	18.00
(11)	Deron Johnson	75.00	37.50	22.50
(12)	Len Johnston	60.00	30.00	18.00
(13)	Bob Kline	60.00	30.00	18.00
(14)	Ed Lopat	80.00	40.00	24.00
(15)	Bob Oldis	60.00	30.00	18.00
(16)	Wilson Parsons	60.00	30.00	18.00
(17)	Rance Pless	60.00	30.00	18.00
(18)	Jim Post	60.00	30.00	18.00
(19)	Danny Schell	60.00	30.00	18.00
(20)	Gerry Thomas	60.00	30.00	18.00
(21)	Bob Weisler	60.00	30.00	18.00

1959 Richmond Virginians

Photos of half a dozen local favorites of the International League Richmond Virginians were featured on ticket stubs during the 1959 season. The black-and-white player portions of the stub measure 2" x 3" and are blank-backed. The unnumbered cards are listed here alphabetically. Richmond was a farm club of the N.Y. Yankees.

		NM	EX	VG
Complete Set (6):		1,200	625.00	375.00
Common Player:		90.00	45.00	25.00
(1)	Clete Boyer	300.00	150.00	90.00
(2)	Jim Coates	200.00	100.00	60.00
(3)	Eli Grba	200.00	100.00	60.00
(4)	John James	200.00	100.00	60.00
(5)	Dick Sanders	200.00	100.00	60.00
(6)	Bill Short	200.00	100.00	60.00

The Mint-Mint examples of vintage cards carry a significant premium over the Near Mint values shown here. This premium reflects limited availability of the highest-grade cards as well as demand for particular cards or sets in the best possible condition.

1960 Richmond Virginians

Jerry Thomas
MADISON HEIGHTS, VA.

In 1960 the Richmond Virginians of the International League continued the practice of using player photos on their game tickets. Black-and-white with a blank-back, the player portions of the tickets can be found in two sizes. Unnumbered cards are checklisted here alphabetically. The Richmond team was a farm club of the N.Y. Yankees.

	NM	EX	VG
Complete Set (6):	1,750	875.00	525.00
Common Player:	300.00	150.00	90.00
SMALL SIZE (2" x 2-3/4")			
(1) Bob Martyn	300.00	150.00	90.00
(2) Jack Reed	300.00	150.00	90.00
LARGE SIZE (2-3/8" x 2-7/8")			
(1) Tony Asaro	300.00	150.00	90.00
(2) Bill Shantz	300.00	150.00	90.00
(3) Jerry Thomas	300.00	150.00	90.00
(4) Bob Weisler	300.00	150.00	90.00

1966 Royal Crown Cola Columbus Yankees

This set of 20 cards was distributed in eight packs of Royal Crown Cola, then based in Columbus, Ga. They were part of a strip measuring 2-1/4" wide. The first 3" of the 9-1/2" strip has a black-and-white photo of the player with his name, position and other biographical data, along with an RC logo in blue and red. The bottom of the strip has a promotion sponsored by the ball club and RC, offering a case of cola for turning in a complete set in an album provided for the cards. Those who turned in the cards were also eligible to win baseball equipment or picnic coolers in a giveaway at a July 31 game that year. Most cards have the advertisement removed. Strips that include the advertisement should be valued at 1.5X of values shown. The cards are unnumbered and listed in alphabetical order.

	NM	EX	VG
Complete Set (20):	800.00	400.00	240.00
Common Player:	40.00	20.00	12.00

		NM	EX	VG
Album:		800.00	400.00	240.00
(1)	Gil Blanco	40.00	20.00	12.00
(2)	Ronnie Boyer	50.00	25.00	15.00
(3)	Jim Brenneman	40.00	20.00	12.00
(4)	Butch Cretara	40.00	20.00	12.00
(5)	Bill Henry	40.00	20.00	12.00
(6)	Joe Jeran	40.00	20.00	12.00
(7)	Jerry Kenney	40.00	20.00	12.00
(8)	Ronnie Kirk	40.00	20.00	12.00
(9)	Tom Kowalski	40.00	20.00	12.00
(10)	Jim Marrujo	40.00	20.00	12.00
(11)	Dave McDonald	40.00	20.00	12.00
(12)	Ed Merritt	40.00	20.00	12.00
(13)	Jim Palma	40.00	20.00	12.00
(14)	Cecil Perkins	40.00	20.00	12.00
(15)	Jack Reed	40.00	20.00	12.00
(16)	Ellie Rodriguez	60.00	30.00	18.00
(17)	John Schroeppel	40.00	20.00	12.00
(18)	Dave Truelock	40.00	20.00	12.00
(19)	Steve Whitaker	40.00	20.00	12.00
(20)	Earl Willoughby	40.00	20.00	12.00

S

1952 San Diego Padres Team Issue

LONNIE SUMMERS

The Padres were one of the highest classification minor league teams for which Globe Printing produced baseball cards in the early 1950s. Like other sets from the San Jose, Calif., printer, the 2-1/8" x 3-3/8" cards are black-and-white, blank-backed and feature the player's name on a white strip on front. Because the Padres are quite often found as a team set, it's likely they were not distributed a card at a time as seems to have been the case with other sets. In 1952, the team was in the Open Classification Pacific Coast League.

		NM	EX	VG
Complete Set (18):		1,000	500.00	300.00
Common Player:		60.00	30.00	18.00
(1)	Al Benton	60.00	30.00	18.00
(2)	Dain Clay	60.00	30.00	18.00
(3)	John Davis	125.00	62.00	37.00
(4)	Dick Faber	60.00	30.00	18.00
(5)	Ben Flowers	60.00	30.00	18.00
(6)	Murray Franklin	60.00	30.00	18.00
(7)	Herb Gorman	90.00	45.00	27.50
(8)	Jack Graham	60.00	30.00	18.00
(9)	Memo Luna	60.00	30.00	18.00
(10)	Lefty O'Doul (Seated, light background.)	125.00	62.00	37.00
(11)	Lefty O'Doul (Standing, dark background.)	125.00	62.00	37.00
(12)	Al Olsen	60.00	30.00	18.00
(13)	Jimmie Reese	100.00	50.00	30.00
(14)	Al Richter	60.00	30.00	18.00
(15)	Jack Salveson	60.00	30.00	18.00
(16)	Lou Stringer	60.00	30.00	18.00
(17)	Lonnie Summers	60.00	30.00	18.00
(18)	Jack Tobin	60.00	30.00	18.00

1950 San Francisco Seals Popcorn

These 3-1/4" x 4-1/2" black-and-white cards were issued with the purchase of caramel corn at Sicks Stadium.

	NM	EX	VG
Complete Set (13):	700.00	350.00	210.00
Common Player:	60.00	30.00	17.50

(1)	Dick Briskey	60.00	30.00	17.50
(2)	Ralph Buxton	60.00	30.00	17.50
(3)	Harry Feldman	60.00	30.00	17.50
(4)	Chet Johnson	60.00	30.00	17.50
(5)	Al Lien	60.00	30.00	17.50
(6)	Dario Lodigiani	60.00	30.00	17.50
(7)	Cliff Melton	60.00	30.00	17.50
(8)	Roy Nicely	60.00	30.00	17.50
(9)	Roy Partee	60.00	30.00	17.50
(10)	Manny Perez	60.00	30.00	17.50
(11)	Neill Sheridan	60.00	30.00	17.50
(12)	Elmer Singleton	60.00	30.00	17.50
(13)	Jack Tobin	60.00	30.00	17.50

1953 San Francisco Seals Team Issue

This set of 25 cards was sold at Seals Stadium and by mail for 25 cents. Fronts of the 4" x 5" black-and-white cards contain a player photo with facsimile autograph. The player's name, team and position are printed in the white bottom border. Backs of the unnumbered cards are blank. Melton is a rare short-print which has been reprinted.

		NM	EX	VG
Complete Set (25):		600.00	300.00	180.00
Common Player:		30.00	15.00	9.00
(1)	Bill Boemler	30.00	15.00	9.00
(2)	Bill Bradford	30.00	15.00	9.00
(3)	Reno Cheso	30.00	15.00	9.00
(4)	Harlond Clift	30.00	15.00	9.00
(5)	Walt Clough	30.00	15.00	9.00
(6)	Cliff Coggin	30.00	15.00	9.00
(7)	Tommy Heath	30.00	15.00	9.00
(8)	Leo Hughes/Trainer	30.00	15.00	9.00
(9)	Frank Kalin	30.00	15.00	9.00
(10)	Al Lien	30.00	15.00	9.00
(11)	Al Lyons	30.00	15.00	9.00
(12)	John McCall	30.00	15.00	9.00
(13)	Bill McCawley	30.00	15.00	9.00
(14)	Dave Melton/SP	200.00	100.00	60.00
(15)	Jim Moran	30.00	15.00	9.00
(16)	Bob Muncrief	30.00	15.00	9.00
(17)	Leo Righetti	30.00	15.00	9.00
(18)	Ted Shandor	30.00	15.00	9.00
(19)	Elmer Singleton	30.00	15.00	9.00
(20)	Lou Stringer	30.00	15.00	9.00
(21)	Sal Taormina	30.00	15.00	9.00
(22)	Will Tiesiera	30.00	15.00	9.00
(23)	Nini Tornay	30.00	15.00	9.00
(24)	George Vico	30.00	15.00	9.00
(25)	Jerry Zuvela	30.00	15.00	9.00

1951 San Jose Red Sox Team Issue

MARVIN OWEN

These 2-1/4" x 3-3/8" black-and-white, unnumbered, blank-backed cards were one of many minor league team sets issued by Globe Printing of San Jose, Calif., in the early 1950s. Cards were usually given away at the ballpark on a one-per-week or one-per-homestand basis, accounting for the rarity of surviving sets. The team was a Class C farm club for the Boston Red Sox in the California League. An album exists for the set, but curiously, it is dated 1952.

	NM	EX	VG
Complete Set (18):	1,000	500.00	300.00
Common Player:	60.00	30.00	18.00
(1) Ken Aspromonte	75.00	37.00	22.00
(2) Joe Buck	60.00	30.00	18.00
(3) Harold Buckwalter	60.00	30.00	18.00
(4) Al Curtis	60.00	30.00	18.00
(5) Marvin Eyre	60.00	30.00	18.00
(6) Jack Heinen	60.00	30.00	18.00
(7) John Kinney	60.00	30.00	18.00
(8) Walt Lucas	60.00	30.00	18.00
(9) Syl McNinch	60.00	30.00	18.00
(10) Stan McWilliams	60.00	30.00	18.00
(11) Marvin Owen	60.00	30.00	18.00
(12) Dick Piedrotti	60.00	30.00	18.00
(13) Al Schroll	60.00	30.00	18.00
(14) Ed Sobczak	60.00	30.00	18.00
(15) Joe Stephenson	60.00	30.00	18.00
(16) George Storti	60.00	30.00	18.00
(17) Allan Van Alstyne	60.00	30.00	18.00
(18) Floyd Warr	60.00	30.00	18.00

1963 Scheible Press Rochester Red Wings

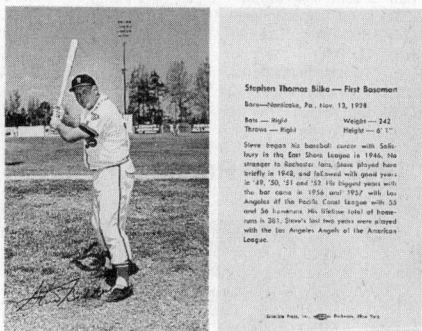

Apparently sold as a stadium concession stand item in a paper and cellophane envelope, the full-color 3-13/16" x 5-7/8" cards are found printed on either a heavy paper stock or thin cardboard stock, each with identical black-and-white back. Two blank-backed cards in slightly larger (4" x 5-7/8") format are checklisted here, although their relationship to the other photos is unknown. The '63 Red Wings were the International League affiliate of the Baltimore Orioles.

	NM	EX	VG
Complete Set (11):	250.00	125.00	75.00
Common Player:	20.00	10.00	6.00
(1) Joe Altobelli	25.00	12.50	7.50
(2) Steve Bilko	20.00	10.00	6.00
(3) Sam E. Bowens	20.00	10.00	6.00
(4) Don Brummer	20.00	10.00	6.00
(5) Nelson Chittum (Cardboard only.)	20.00	10.00	6.00
(6a) Luke Easter (Small format.)	40.00	20.00	12.00
(6b) Luke Easter (Large format.)	75.00	40.00	25.00
(7) Darrell Johnson, Chris Krug (Paper only.)	25.00	12.50	7.50
(8) Ron Kabbes (Large format.)	20.00	10.00	6.00
(9) Fred Valentine	20.00	10.00	6.00
(10) Ozzie Virgil	20.00	10.00	6.00
(11) Ray Youngdahl	20.00	10.00	6.00

1954-1968 Seattle Rainiers/Angels Popcorn

One of the longest-running minor league baseball card promotions was the 1954-68 Seattle popcorn cards. The principal sponsor was Centennial Mills, which had issued cards in the 1940s. Similar in format throughout their period of issue, the cards are 2" x 3" in size, black-and-white, usually featuring portrait photos on the front with the player's name or name and position below. In some years the cards were printed on semi-glossy stock. Some years' card backs are blank, in other years, backs feature ads for various local businesses; in a few years, cards could be found with both blank and printed backs. Many photo and spelling variations are known throughout the series; most are noted in the appropriate checklists. The unnumbered cards are checklisted alphabetically. It is possible a few stragglers will be added to these checklists in the future. In most years a group of 20 cards was released early in the year, supplemented later in the season as roster changes dictated. The cards were given

away with the purchase of a box of popcorn sold at Seattle's Sicks stadium. During the card-issuing era, Seattle was an independent team in the Pacific Coast League in 1954-55. From 1956-60 they were a top farm team in the Reds system. They were a Red Sox affiliate from 1961-64, before tying up with the California Angels in 1965.

(Consult checklists for attribution of blank-back cards.)

1954 Seattle Rainiers Popcorn

BOB HALL
Pitcher

(Blank-back. Most players photographed in dark cap with light "S.")

	NM	EX	VG
Complete Set (26):	2,500	1,250	750.00
Common Player:	110.00	55.00	35.00
(1) Gene Bearden	110.00	55.00	35.00
(2) Al Brightman	110.00	55.00	35.00
(3) Jack Burkowatz	110.00	55.00	35.00
(4) Tommy Byrne (Photo reversed, backwards "S" on cap.)	110.00	55.00	35.00
(5) Joe Erautt	110.00	55.00	35.00
(6) Bill Evans	110.00	55.00	35.00
(7) Van Fletcher	110.00	55.00	35.00
(8) Bob Hall	110.00	55.00	35.00
(9) Pete Hernandez	110.00	55.00	35.00
(10) Lloyd Jenney	110.00	55.00	35.00
(11) Joe Joshua	110.00	55.00	35.00
(12) Vern Kindsfather	110.00	55.00	35.00
(13) Tom Lovrich	110.00	55.00	35.00
(14) Clarence Maddern	110.00	55.00	35.00
(15) Don Mallott	110.00	55.00	35.00
(16) Loren Meyers	110.00	55.00	35.00
(17) Steve Nagy	110.00	55.00	35.00
(18) Ray Orteig	110.00	55.00	35.00
(19) Gerry Priddy	110.00	55.00	35.00
(20) George Schmees	110.00	55.00	35.00
(21) Bill Schuster	110.00	55.00	35.00
(22) Leo Thomas	110.00	55.00	35.00
(23) Jack Tobin	110.00	55.00	35.00
(24) Al Widmer	110.00	55.00	35.00
(25) Artie Wilson	175.00	85.00	50.00
(26) Al Zarilla	110.00	55.00	35.00

1955 Seattle Rainiers Popcorn

(Blank-back. All players wearing light caps with "R" logo.)

	NM	EX	VG
Complete Set (22):	2,000	1,000	600.00
Common Player:	110.00	55.00	35.00
(1) Bob Balcena	110.00	55.00	35.00
(2) Monty Basgall	110.00	55.00	35.00
(3) Ewell Blackwell	135.00	65.00	40.00
(4) Bill Brenner	110.00	55.00	35.00
(5) Jack Burkowatz	110.00	55.00	35.00
(6) Van Fletcher	110.00	55.00	35.00
(7) Joe Ginsberg	110.00	55.00	35.00
(8) Jehosie Heard	110.00	55.00	35.00
(9) Fred Hutchinson	110.00	55.00	35.00
(10) Larry Jansen	110.00	55.00	35.00
(11) Bob Kelly	110.00	55.00	35.00
(12) Bill Kennedy	110.00	55.00	35.00
(13) Lou Kretlow	110.00	55.00	35.00
(14) Rocco Krsnich	110.00	55.00	35.00
(15) Carmen Mauro	110.00	55.00	35.00
(16) John Oldham	110.00	55.00	35.00
(17) George Schmees	110.00	55.00	35.00
(18) Elmer Singleton	110.00	55.00	35.00
(19) Alan Strange	110.00	55.00	35.00
(20) Gene Verble	110.00	55.00	35.00
(21) Marv Williams	110.00	55.00	35.00
(22) Harvey Zernia	110.00	55.00	35.00

1956 Seattle Rainiers Popcorn

JOE TAYLOR
Outfielder

(Blank-back or Gil's Drive-Ins (two locations) ad on back. Players wearing light cap with white "R.")

	NM	EX	VG
Complete Set (27):	2,500	1,250	750.00
Common Player:	110.00	55.00	35.00
(1) Fred Baczewski	110.00	55.00	35.00
(2) Bob Balcena	110.00	55.00	35.00
(3) Bill Brenner	110.00	55.00	35.00
(4) Sherry Dixon	110.00	55.00	35.00
(5) Don Fracchia	110.00	55.00	35.00
(6) Bill Glynn	110.00	55.00	35.00
(7) Larry Jansen	110.00	55.00	35.00
(8) Howie Judson	110.00	55.00	35.00
(9) Bill Kennedy	110.00	55.00	35.00
(10) Jack Lohrke	110.00	55.00	35.00
(11) Vic Lombardi	110.00	55.00	35.00
(12) Carmen Mauro	110.00	55.00	35.00
(13) Ray Orteig	110.00	55.00	35.00
(14) Bud Podbielan	110.00	55.00	35.00
(15) Leo Righetti	110.00	55.00	35.00
(16) Jim Robertson	110.00	55.00	35.00
(17) Art Shallock (Schallock)	110.00	55.00	35.00
(18) Art Schult	110.00	55.00	35.00
(19) Luke Sewell	135.00	65.00	40.00
(20) Elmer Singleton	110.00	55.00	35.00
(21a) Milt Smith/Action	110.00	55.00	35.00
(21b) Milt Smith/Portrait	110.00	55.00	35.00
(22) Vern Stephens	110.00	55.00	35.00
(23) Alan Strange	110.00	55.00	35.00
(24) Joe Taylor	110.00	55.00	35.00
(25) Artie Wilson	175.00	85.00	50.00
(26) Harvey Zernia	110.00	55.00	35.00

1957 Seattle Rainiers Popcorn

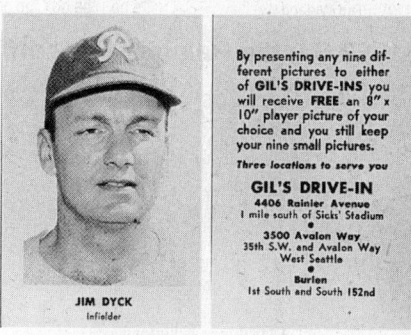

JIM DYCK
Infielder

By presenting any nine different pictures to either of GIL'S DRIVE-INS you will receive FREE an 8" x 10" player picture of your choice and you still keep your nine small pictures.

Three locations to serve you

GIL'S DRIVE-IN
4406 Rainier Avenue
1 mile south of Sicks' Stadium
*
3500 Avalon Way
35th S.W. and Avalon Way
West Seattle
*
Burien
1st South and South 152nd

(Blank-back or Gil's Drive-Ins (three locations) ad on back. Players wearing lighter caps with white "R." No base on letter "T" on outfielders or pitchers cards.)

	NM	EX	VG
Complete Set (24):	2,000	1,000	600.00
Common Player:	100.00	50.00	30.00
(1) Dick Aylward	100.00	50.00	30.00
(2) Bob Balcena	100.00	50.00	30.00
(3) Eddie Basinki	100.00	50.00	30.00
(4) Hal Bevan	100.00	50.00	30.00
(5) Joe Black	125.00	65.00	35.00
(6) Juan Delis	100.00	50.00	30.00
(7) Jim Dyck	100.00	50.00	30.00
(8) Marion Fricano	100.00	50.00	30.00
(9) Bill Glynn	100.00	50.00	30.00
(10) Larry Jansen	100.00	50.00	30.00
(11) Howie Judson	100.00	50.00	30.00
(12) Bill Kennedy	100.00	50.00	30.00
(13) Jack Lohrke	100.00	50.00	30.00
(14) Carmen Mauro	100.00	50.00	30.00

(15)	George Munger	100.00	50.00	30.00
(16)	Lefty O'Doul	150.00	75.00	45.00
(17)	Ray Orteig	100.00	50.00	30.00
(18)	Duane Pillette	100.00	50.00	30.00
(19)	Bud Podbielan	100.00	50.00	30.00
(20)	Charley Rabe	100.00	50.00	30.00
(21)	Leo Righetti	100.00	50.00	30.00
(22)	Joe Taylor	100.00	50.00	30.00
(23)	Edo Vanni	100.00	50.00	30.00
(24)	Morrie Wills (Maury)	250.00	125.00	75.00

1958 Seattle Rainiers Popcorn

TED WIEAND
Pitcher

(All cards have Ralph's Thriftway Market ad on back.)

		NM	EX	VG
Complete Set (19):		1,250	625.00	375.00
Common Player:		75.00	35.00	20.00
(1)	Bob Balcena	75.00	35.00	20.00
(2)	Ed Basinki	75.00	35.00	20.00
(3)	Hal Bevan	75.00	35.00	20.00
(4)	Jack Bloomfield	75.00	35.00	20.00
(5)	Juan Delis	75.00	35.00	20.00
(6)	Dutch Dotterer	75.00	35.00	20.00
(7)	Jim Dyck	75.00	35.00	20.00
(8)	Al Federoff	90.00	45.00	27.50
(9)	Art Fowler	75.00	35.00	20.00
(10)	Bill Kennedy	75.00	35.00	20.00
(11)	Marty Kutyna	75.00	35.00	20.00
(12)	Ray Orteig	75.00	35.00	20.00
(13)	Duane Pillette	75.00	35.00	20.00
(14)	Vada Pinson	225.00	110.00	70.00
(15)	Connie Ryan	75.00	35.00	20.00
(16)	Phil Shartzer	75.00	35.00	20.00
(17)	Max Surkont	75.00	35.00	20.00
(18)	Gale Wade	75.00	35.00	20.00
(19)	Ted Wieand	75.00	35.00	20.00

1959 Seattle Rainiers Popcorn

DON RUDOLPH
Pitcher

(Blank-back. First printing cards have players in lighter cap with white "R." Second printing cards have darker caps with shadow around "R.")

		NM	EX	VG
Complete Set (37):		2,500	1,250	750.00
Common Player:		75.00	35.00	20.00
(1)	Bobby Adams	75.00	35.00	20.00
(2)	Frank Amaya	75.00	35.00	20.00
(3)	Hal Bevan	75.00	35.00	20.00
(4)	Jack Bloomfield	75.00	35.00	20.00
(5)	Clarence Churn	75.00	35.00	20.00
(6)	Jack Dittmer	75.00	35.00	20.00
(7)	Jim Dyck	75.00	35.00	20.00
(8)	Dee Fondy	75.00	35.00	20.00
(9)	Mark Freeman	75.00	35.00	20.00
(10)	Dick Hanlon	75.00	35.00	20.00
(11)	Carroll Hardy	75.00	35.00	20.00
(12)	Bobby Henrich	75.00	35.00	20.00
(13)	Jay Hook	75.00	35.00	20.00
(14)	Fred Hutchinson	75.00	35.00	20.00
(15)	Jake Jenkins	75.00	35.00	20.00
(16)	Eddie Kazak	75.00	35.00	20.00
(17)	Bill Kennedy	75.00	35.00	20.00
(18)	Harry Lowrey	75.00	35.00	20.00
(19a)	Harry Malmbeg (Malmberg)	75.00	35.00	20.00
(19b)	Harry Malmberg	75.00	35.00	20.00
(20)	Bob Mape (Mabe)	75.00	35.00	20.00
(21)	Darrell Martin	75.00	35.00	20.00
(22)	John McCall	75.00	35.00	20.00
(23)	Claude Osteen	75.00	35.00	20.00
(24)	Paul Pettit	75.00	35.00	20.00
(25)	Charley Rabe	75.00	35.00	20.00
(26)	Rudy Regalado	75.00	35.00	20.00
(27)	Eric Rodin	75.00	35.00	20.00
(28)	Don Rudolph	75.00	35.00	20.00
(29)	Lou Skizas	75.00	35.00	20.00
(30)	Dave Stenhouse	75.00	35.00	20.00
(31)	Alan Strange	75.00	35.00	20.00
(32)	Max Surkont	75.00	35.00	20.00
(33)	Ted Tappe	75.00	35.00	20.00
(34)	Elmer Valo	75.00	35.00	20.00
(35)	Gale Wade	75.00	35.00	20.00
(36)	Bill Wight	75.00	35.00	20.00
(37)	Ed Winceniak	75.00	35.00	20.00

1960 Seattle Rainiers Popcorn

JOHNNY O'BRIEN
Infielder

(Blank-back. All players posed against outfield fence wearing dark caps with shadowed "R.")

		NM	EX	VG
Complete Set (18):		1,200	600.00	350.00
Common Player:		75.00	35.00	20.00
(1)	Charlie Beamon	75.00	35.00	20.00
(2)	Hal Bevan	75.00	35.00	20.00
(3)	Whammy Douglas	75.00	35.00	20.00
(4)	Buddy Gilbert	75.00	35.00	20.00
(5)	Hal Jeffcoat	75.00	35.00	20.00
(6)	Leigh Lawrence	75.00	35.00	20.00
(7)	Darrell Martin	75.00	35.00	20.00
(8)	Francisco Obregon	75.00	35.00	20.00
(9)	Johnny O'Brien	90.00	45.00	27.50
(10)	Paul Pettit	75.00	35.00	20.00
(11)	Ray Rippelmeyer (Ripplemeyer)	75.00	35.00	20.00
(12)	Don Rudolph	75.00	35.00	20.00
(13)	Willard Schmidt	75.00	35.00	20.00
(14)	Dick Sisler	75.00	35.00	20.00
(15)	Lou Skizas	75.00	35.00	20.00
(16)	Joe Taylor	75.00	35.00	20.00
(17)	Bob Thurman	75.00	35.00	20.00
(18)	Gerald Zimmerman	75.00	35.00	20.00

1961 Seattle Rainiers Popcorn

JOHN TILLMAN
Infielder

(Blank-back. New uniforms: dark cap with stylized "S," "Rainiers" on chest. Many players have both portrait and action poses. Tough to distinguish from 1962 set; names on '61s are more compact, bold than on '62 which has taller, lighter names.)

		NM	EX	VG
Complete Set (29):		2,000	1,000	600.00
Common Player:		75.00	35.00	20.00
(1)	Galen Cisco	75.00	35.00	20.00
(2)	Marlan Coughtry/Btg	75.00	35.00	20.00
(3)	Marlin Coughtry/Portrait	75.00	35.00	20.00
(4)	Pete Cronin	75.00	35.00	20.00
(5)	Arnold Earley	75.00	35.00	20.00
(6)	Bob Heffner/Pitching	75.00	35.00	20.00
(7)	Bob Heffner/Portrait	75.00	35.00	20.00
(8)	Curt Jensen/Action	75.00	35.00	20.00
(9)	Curt Jensen/Portrait	75.00	35.00	20.00
(10)	Harry Malmberg/Coach	75.00	35.00	20.00
(11)	Harry Malmberg (Player-coach.)	75.00	35.00	20.00
(12)	Dave Mann	75.00	35.00	20.00
(13)	Darrell Martin	75.00	35.00	20.00
(14)	Erv Palica/Pitching	75.00	35.00	20.00
(15)	Ervin Palica/Portrait	75.00	35.00	20.00
(16)	Johnny Pesky/Action	90.00	45.00	27.50
(17)	Johnny Pesky/Portrait	90.00	45.00	27.50
(18)	Dick Radatz	100.00	50.00	30.00
(19)	Ted Schreiber/Btg	75.00	35.00	20.00
(20)	Ted Shreiber/Portrait	75.00	35.00	20.00
(21)	Paul Smith/Action	75.00	35.00	20.00
(22)	Paul Smith/Portrait	75.00	35.00	20.00
(23)	John Tillman/Infielder	75.00	35.00	20.00
(24)	Bob Tillman/Catcher	75.00	35.00	20.00
(25)	Bo Toft	75.00	35.00	20.00
(26)	Tom Umphlett/Action	75.00	35.00	20.00
(27)	Tom Umphlett/Portrait	75.00	35.00	20.00
(28)	Earl Wilson	75.00	35.00	20.00
(29)	Ken Wolfe	75.00	35.00	20.00

1962 Seattle Rainiers Popcorn

BILLY HARRELL

(Blank-back. Nearly identical to '61s except for player name. On 1961 cards, name is compact and bold; on '62s the name is taller, lighter. Some photos repeated from 1961.)

		NM	EX	VG
Complete Set (19):		1,250	625.00	375.00
Common Player:		75.00	35.00	20.00
(1)	Dave Hall	75.00	35.00	20.00
(2)	Billy Harrell	75.00	35.00	20.00
(3)	Curt Jensen (Jenson)	75.00	35.00	20.00
(4)	Stew MacDonald	75.00	35.00	20.00
(5)	Bill MacLeod	75.00	35.00	20.00
(6)	Dave Mann/Action	75.00	35.00	20.00
(7)	Dave Mann/Portrait	75.00	35.00	20.00
(8)	Dave Morehead	75.00	35.00	20.00
(9)	John Pesky	90.00	45.00	27.50
(10)	Ted Schreiber (Second baseman.)	75.00	35.00	20.00
(11)	Ted Schreiber/Infielder	75.00	35.00	20.00
(12)	Elmer Singleton	75.00	35.00	20.00
(13)	Archie Skeen	75.00	35.00	20.00
(14)	Pete Smith	75.00	35.00	20.00
(15)	George Spencer	75.00	35.00	20.00
(16)	Bo Toft (1961 photo.)	75.00	35.00	20.00
(17)	Bo Toft (new photo.)	75.00	35.00	20.00
(18)	Tom Umphlett	75.00	35.00	20.00
(19)	Ken Wolfe	75.00	35.00	20.00

The Mint-Mint examples of vintage cards carry a significant premium over the Near Mint values shown here. This premium reflects limited availability of the highest-grade cards as well as demand for particular cards or sets in the best possible condition.

1963 Seattle Rainiers Popcorn

WILBUR WOOD

(Blank-back. No positions stated on cards except for manager and coach. Impossible to differentiate 1963 issue from 1964 except by player selection.)

		NM	EX	VG
Complete Set (15):		800.00	400.00	240.00
Common Player:		60.00	30.00	17.50
(1)	Don Gile	60.00	30.00	17.50
(2)	Dave Hall	60.00	30.00	17.50
(3)	Billy Harrell	60.00	30.00	17.50
(4)	Pete Jernigan	60.00	30.00	17.50
(5)	Stan Johnson	60.00	30.00	17.50
(6)	Dalton Jones	60.00	30.00	17.50
(7)	Mel Parnell	60.00	30.00	17.50
(8)	Joe Pedrazzini	60.00	30.00	17.50
(9)	Elmer Singleton	60.00	30.00	17.50
(10)	Archie Skeen	60.00	30.00	17.50
(11)	Rac Slider	60.00	30.00	17.50
(12)	Pete Smith	60.00	30.00	17.50
(13)	Bill Spanswick	60.00	30.00	17.50
(14)	George Spencer	60.00	30.00	17.50
(15)	Wilbur Wood	90.00	45.00	27.50

1964 Seattle Rainiers Popcorn

EARL AVERILL

(Blank-back. Impossible to differentiate between 1963 and 1964 issues except by player selection.)

		NM	EX	VG
Complete Set (18):		1,000	500.00	300.00
Common Player:		60.00	30.00	17.50
(1)	Earl Averill	60.00	30.00	17.50
(2)	Billy Gardner	60.00	30.00	17.50
(3)	Russ Gibson	60.00	30.00	17.50
(4)	Guido Grilli	60.00	30.00	17.50
(5)	Bob Guindon	60.00	30.00	17.50
(6)	Billy Harrell	60.00	30.00	17.50
(7)	Fred Holmes	60.00	30.00	17.50
(8)	Stan Johnson	60.00	30.00	17.50
(9)	Hal Kolstad	60.00	30.00	17.50
(10)	Felix Maldonado	60.00	30.00	17.50
(11)	Gary Modrell	60.00	30.00	17.50
(12)	Merlin Nippert	60.00	30.00	17.50
(13)	Rico Petrocelli	100.00	50.00	30.00
(14)	Jay Ritchie	60.00	30.00	17.50
(15)	Barry Shetrone	60.00	30.00	17.50
(16)	Pete Smith	60.00	30.00	17.50
(17)	Bill Tuttle	60.00	30.00	17.50
(18)	Edo Vanni	60.00	30.00	17.50

1965 Seattle Angels Popcorn

(Back has cartoon angel batting. Several cards, issued prior to the season, have blank-backs.)

		NM	EX	VG
Complete Set (22):		600.00	300.00	180.00
Common Player:		30.00	15.00	9.00
(1)	Earl Averill	30.00	15.00	9.00
(2)	Tom Burgmeier	30.00	15.00	9.00
(3)	Bob Guindon	30.00	15.00	9.00

(4)	Jack Hernandez	30.00	15.00	9.00
(5)	Fred Holmes	30.00	15.00	9.00
(6)	Ed Kirkpatrick	30.00	15.00	9.00
(7)	Hal Kolstad	30.00	15.00	9.00
(8)	Joe Koppe	30.00	15.00	9.00
(9)	Les Kuhnz	30.00	15.00	9.00
(10)	Bob Lemon	60.00	30.00	17.50
(11)	Bobby Locke	30.00	15.00	9.00
(12)	Jim McGlothlin	30.00	15.00	9.00
(13a)	Bob Radovich (Blank-back.)	30.00	15.00	9.00
(13b)	Bob Radovich (Ad-back.)	30.00	15.00	9.00
(14)	Merritt Ranew	30.00	15.00	9.00
(15)	Jimmie Reese (Blank-back.)	45.00	22.50	13.50
(16a)	Rick Reichardt (Blank-back.)	30.00	15.00	9.00
(16b)	Rick Reichardt (Ad-back.)	30.00	15.00	9.00
(17)	Tom Satriano	30.00	15.00	9.00
(18)	Dick Simpson	30.00	15.00	9.00
(19)	Jack Spring (Blank-back.)	30.00	15.00	9.00
(20)	Ed Sukla	30.00	15.00	9.00
(21)	Jackie Warner	30.00	15.00	9.00
(22)	Stan Williams	30.00	15.00	9.00

1966 Seattle Angels Popcorn

(Cartoon angel pitching on back, first "Presented by" advertiser at bottom is Chevron Dealers.)

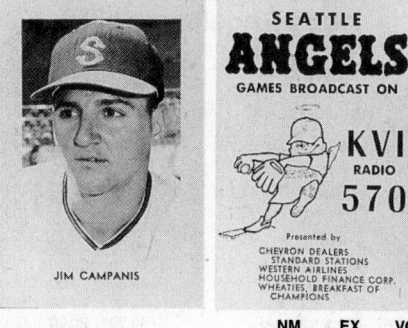

JIM CAMPANIS

SEATTLE ANGELS
GAMES BROADCAST ON
KVI RADIO 570

Presented by
CHEVRON DEALERS
STANDARD STATIONS
WESTERN AIRLINES
HOUSEHOLD FINANCE CORP.
WHEATIES, BREAKFAST OF
CHAMPIONS

		NM	EX	VG
Complete Set (29):		900.00	450.00	275.00
Common Player:		30.00	15.00	9.00
(1)	Del Bates	30.00	15.00	9.00
(2)	Tom Burgmeier	30.00	15.00	9.00
(3)	Jim Campanis	40.00	20.00	12.00
(4)	Jim Coates	30.00	15.00	9.00
(5)	Tony Cortopassi	30.00	15.00	9.00
(6)	Chuck Estrada	30.00	15.00	9.00
(7)	Ray Hernandez	30.00	15.00	9.00
(8)	Jay Johnstone	50.00	25.00	15.00
(9)	Bill Kelso	30.00	15.00	9.00
(10)	Vic LaRose	30.00	15.00	9.00
(11)	Bobby Locke	30.00	15.00	9.00
(12)	Rudy May	30.00	15.00	9.00
(13)	Andy Messersmith	50.00	25.00	15.00
(14)	Bubba Morton	30.00	15.00	9.00
(15)	Cotton Nash	30.00	15.00	9.00
(16)	John Olerud	50.00	25.00	15.00
(17)	Marty Pattin	30.00	15.00	9.00
(18)	Merritt Ranew	30.00	15.00	9.00
(19)	Minnie Rojas	30.00	15.00	9.00
(20)	George Rubio	30.00	15.00	9.00
(21)	Al Spangler	30.00	15.00	9.00
(22)	Ed Sukla	30.00	15.00	9.00
(23)	Felix Torres	30.00	15.00	9.00
(24)	Hector Torres	30.00	15.00	9.00
(25)	Ken Turner	30.00	15.00	9.00
(26)	Chuck Vinson	30.00	15.00	9.00
(27)	Don Wallace	30.00	15.00	9.00
(28)	Jack D. Warner	30.00	15.00	9.00
(29)	Mike White	30.00	15.00	9.00

1967 Seattle Angels Popcorn

(Cartoon angel pitching on back, first "Presented by" advertiser is Western Airlines.)

		NM	EX	VG
Complete Set (19):		500.00	250.00	150.00
Common Player:		30.00	15.00	9.00
(1)	George Banks	30.00	15.00	9.00
(2)	Tom Burgmeier	30.00	15.00	9.00
(3)	Jim Coates	30.00	15.00	9.00
(4)	Chuck Cottier	30.00	15.00	9.00
(5)	Tony Curry	30.00	15.00	9.00
(6)	Vern Geishert	30.00	15.00	9.00
(7)	Jesse Hickman	30.00	15.00	9.00
(8)	Bill Kelso	30.00	15.00	9.00
(9)	Ed Kirkpatrick	30.00	15.00	9.00
(10)	Chris Krug	30.00	15.00	9.00
(11)	Bobby Locke	30.00	15.00	9.00
(12)	Bill Murphy	30.00	15.00	9.00
(13)	Marty Pattin	30.00	15.00	9.00

(14)	Merritt Ranew	30.00	15.00	9.00
(15)	Bob Sadowski	30.00	15.00	9.00
(16)	Ed Sukla	30.00	15.00	9.00
(17)	Hector Torres	30.00	15.00	9.00
(18)	Chuck Vinson	30.00	15.00	9.00
(19)	Don Wallace	30.00	15.00	9.00

1968 Seattle Angels Popcorn

JARVIS TATUM

(Blank-back.)

		NM	EX	VG
Complete Set (18):		500.00	250.00	150.00
Common Player:		30.00	15.00	9.00
(1)	Ethan Blackaby	30.00	15.00	9.00
(2)	Jim Coates	30.00	15.00	9.00
(3)	Tom Egan	30.00	15.00	9.00
(4)	Larry Elliott (Elliot)	30.00	15.00	9.00
(5)	Jim Engelhardt	30.00	15.00	9.00
(6)	Gus Gil	30.00	15.00	9.00
(7)	Bill Harrelson	30.00	15.00	9.00
(8)	Steve Hovley	30.00	15.00	9.00
(9)	Jim Mahoney	30.00	15.00	9.00
(10)	Mickey McGuire	30.00	15.00	9.00
(11)	Joe Overton	30.00	15.00	9.00
(12)	Marty Pattin	30.00	15.00	9.00
(13)	Larry Sherry	30.00	15.00	9.00
(14)	Marv Staehle	30.00	15.00	9.00
(15)	Ed Sukla	30.00	15.00	9.00
(16)	Jarvis Tatum	30.00	15.00	9.00
(17)	Hawk Taylor	30.00	15.00	9.00
(18)	Chuck Vinson	30.00	15.00	9.00

1952 Shawnee Hawks Team Issue

LOYD McPHERSON

Formatted like the other known minor league issues from Globe Printing of San Jose, Calif., this set chronicles the 1952 version of the Class D (Sooner State League) Shawnee (Okla.) Hawks. The blank-backed cards are black-and-white and measure about 2-1/4" x 3-3/8". The checklist here is incomplete, the set probably having been originally issued with about 18 cards.

		NM	EX	VG
Common Player:		60.00	30.00	18.00
(1)	Russell Bland (Blanco)	60.00	30.00	18.00
(2)	Perry Haddock	60.00	30.00	18.00
(3)	Jim Kenaga	60.00	30.00	18.00
(4)	Hal Long	60.00	30.00	18.00
(5)	Loyd McPherson	60.00	30.00	18.00
(6)	Rolando Olmo	60.00	30.00	18.00
(7)	Dave Rolette	60.00	30.00	18.00
(8)	Hank Salazar	60.00	30.00	18.00

1960 Shopsy's Frankfurters Toronto Maple Leafs

SHOPSY'S PLAYER PHOTO

ARCHIE WILSON - 1960

Only the Toronto Maple Leafs of the International League - including many former and future major leaguers - are included in this set. The cards are about 2-1/4" x 3-1/4", blank-back and printed in black-and-white. The unnumbered cards are check-listed here alphabetically.

		NM	EX	VG
	Complete Set (23):	2,000	1,000	600.00
	Common Player:	90.00	45.00	30.00
	Album:	100.00	50.00	30.00
(1)	George Anderson (Sparky)	150.00	75.00	45.00
(2)	Bob Chakales	90.00	45.00	30.00
(3)	Al Cicotte	90.00	45.00	30.00
(4)	Rip Coleman	90.00	45.00	30.00
(5)	Steve Demeter	90.00	45.00	30.00
(6)	Don Dillard	90.00	45.00	30.00
(7)	Frank Funk	90.00	45.00	30.00
(8)	Russ Heman	90.00	45.00	30.00
(9)	Earl Hersh	90.00	45.00	30.00
(10)	Allen Jones	90.00	45.00	30.00
(11)	Jim King	90.00	45.00	30.00
(12)	Jack Kubiszyn	90.00	45.00	30.00
(13)	Mel McGaha	90.00	45.00	30.00
(14)	Bill Moran	90.00	45.00	30.00
(15)	Ron Negray	90.00	45.00	30.00
(16)	Herb Plews	90.00	45.00	30.00
(17)	Steve Ridzik	90.00	45.00	30.00
(18)	Pat Scantlebury	90.00	45.00	30.00
(19)	Bill Smith/Trainer	90.00	45.00	30.00
(20)	Bob Smith	90.00	45.00	30.00
(21)	Tim Thompson	90.00	45.00	30.00
(22)	Jack Waters	90.00	45.00	30.00
(23)	Archie Wilson	90.00	45.00	30.00

1947 Signal Gasoline Pacific Coast League

Five of the eight PCL teams participated in this baseball card promotion, giving away cards of home-team players. Because of vagaries of local distribution, some teams, notably Sacramento and Seattle, are scarcer than others, and there are specific player rarities among other teams. The black-and-white cards are 5-9/16" x 3-1/2" and feature on the front a drawing of the player and several personal or career highlights in cartoon form. The artwork was done by former N.Y. Giants pitcher Al Demaree. On the backs are player biographical details, an ad for Signal Gas and an ad for the co-sponsoring radio station in each locale. Cards are unnumbered.

	NM	EX	VG
Complete Set (89):	6,000	3,000	1,800
(Team sets listed below.)			

1947 Signal Gasoline Hollywood Stars

		NM	EX	VG
	Complete Set (20):	1,200	600.00	350.00
	Common Player:	50.00	25.00	15.00
(1)	Ed Albosta	50.00	25.00	15.00
(2)	Carl Cox	50.00	25.00	15.00
(3)	Frank Dasso	50.00	25.00	15.00
(4)	Tod Davis	50.00	25.00	15.00
(5)	Jim Delsing	50.00	25.00	15.00
(6)	Jimmy Dykes	50.00	25.00	15.00
(7)	Paul Gregory	50.00	25.00	15.00
(8)	Fred Haney	50.00	25.00	15.00
(9)	Frank Kelleher	50.00	25.00	15.00
(10)	Joe Krakauskas	50.00	25.00	15.00
(11)	Al Libke	50.00	25.00	15.00
(12)	Tony Lupien	50.00	25.00	15.00
(13)	Xaiver Rescigno	50.00	25.00	15.00
(14)	Jack Sherman	50.00	25.00	15.00
(15)	Andy Skurski	50.00	25.00	15.00
(16)	Glen (Glenn) Stewart	50.00	25.00	15.00
(17)	Al Unser	50.00	25.00	15.00
(18)	Fred Vaughn	50.00	25.00	15.00
(19)	Woody Williams	250.00	125.00	75.00
(20)	Dutch (Gus) Zernial	75.00	37.00	22.00

1947 Signal Gasoline Los Angeles Angels

		NM	EX	VG
	Complete Set (18):	700.00	350.00	210.00
	Common Player:	40.00	20.00	12.00
(1)	Red Adams	40.00	20.00	12.00
(2)	Larry Barton	40.00	20.00	12.00
(3)	Cliff Chambers	40.00	20.00	12.00
(4)	Lloyd Christopher	40.00	20.00	12.00
(5)	Cece Garriott	40.00	20.00	12.00
(6)	Al Glossop	40.00	20.00	12.00
(7)	Bill Kelly	40.00	20.00	12.00
(8)	Red Lynn	40.00	20.00	12.00
(9)	Eddie Malone	40.00	20.00	12.00
(10)	Dutch McCall	40.00	20.00	12.00
(11)	Don Osborne	40.00	20.00	12.00
(12)	John Ostrowski	40.00	20.00	12.00
(13)	Reggie Otero	40.00	20.00	12.00
(14)	Ray Prim	40.00	20.00	12.00
(15)	Ed Sauer	40.00	20.00	12.00
(16)	Bill Schuster	40.00	20.00	12.00
(17)	Tuck Stainback	40.00	20.00	12.00
(18)	Lou Stringer	40.00	20.00	12.00

1947 Signal Gasoline Oakland Oaks

		NM	EX	VG
	Complete Set (19):	800.00	400.00	240.00
	Common Player:	40.00	20.00	12.00
(1)	Vic Buccola	40.00	20.00	12.00
(2)	Mickey Burnett	40.00	20.00	12.00
(3)	Ralph Buxton	40.00	20.00	12.00
(4)	Vince DiMaggio	95.00	47.00	28.00
(5)	Dizz Duezabou	40.00	20.00	12.00
(6)	Bud Foster	40.00	20.00	12.00
(7)	Sherriff Gassaway	40.00	20.00	12.00
(8)	Tom Hafey	40.00	20.00	12.00
(9)	Brooks Holder	40.00	20.00	12.00
(10)	Gene Lillard	40.00	20.00	12.00
(11)	Dario Lodigiani	40.00	20.00	12.00
(12)	Hershel Martin	40.00	20.00	12.00
(13)	Cotton Pippen	40.00	20.00	12.00
(14)	Billy Raimondi	40.00	20.00	12.00
(15)	Tony Sabol	40.00	20.00	12.00
(16)	Les Scarsella	40.00	20.00	12.00
(17)	Floyd Speer	40.00	20.00	12.00
(18)	Casey Stengel	100.00	50.00	30.00
(19)	Maurice Van Robays	40.00	20.00	12.00

1947 Signal Gasoline Sacramento Solons

		NM	EX	VG
	Complete Set (16):	2,000	1,000	600.00
	Common Player:	60.00	30.00	18.00
(1)	Bud Beasley	60.00	30.00	18.00
(2)	Frank Dasso	60.00	30.00	18.00
(3)	Ed Fitzgerald (Fitz Gerald)	60.00	30.00	18.00
(4)	Guy Fletcher	60.00	30.00	18.00
(5)	Tony Freitas	60.00	30.00	18.00
(6)	Red Mann	60.00	30.00	18.00
(7)	Joe Marty	60.00	30.00	18.00
(8)	Steve Mesner	60.00	30.00	18.00
(9)	Bill Ramsey	60.00	30.00	18.00
(10)	Charley Ripple	250.00	125.00	75.00
(11)	John Rizzo	250.00	125.00	75.00
(12)	Al Smith	250.00	125.00	75.00

		NM	EX	VG
(13)	Ronnie Smith	250.00	125.00	75.00
(14)	Tommy Thompson	250.00	125.00	75.00
(15)	Jim Warner	115.00	55.00	35.00
(16)	Ed Zipay	115.00	55.00	35.00

1947 Signal Gasoline Seattle Rainiers

		NM	EX	VG
	Complete Set (16):	1,750	875.00	525.00
	Common Player:	75.00	37.00	22.00
(1)	Kewpie Barrett	100.00	50.00	30.00
(2)	Herman Besse	100.00	50.00	30.00
(3)	Guy Fletcher	100.00	50.00	30.00
(4)	Jack Jakucki	100.00	50.00	30.00
(5)	Bob Johnson	100.00	50.00	30.00
(6)	Pete Jonas	275.00	135.00	82.00
(7)	Hillis Layne	100.00	50.00	30.00
(8)	Red Mann	100.00	50.00	30.00
(9)	Lou Novikoff	100.00	50.00	30.00
(10)	John O'Neill	100.00	50.00	30.00
(11)	Bill Ramsey	100.00	50.00	30.00
(12)	Mickey Rocco	100.00	50.00	30.00
(13)	George Scharein	100.00	50.00	30.00
(14)	Hal Sueme	100.00	50.00	30.00
(15)	Jo Jo White	100.00	50.00	30.00
(16)	Tony York	100.00	50.00	30.00

1948 Signal Gasoline Oakland Oaks

Issued by Signal Oil in the Oakland area in 1948, this 24-card set features members of the Oakland Oaks of the Pacific Coast League. The unnumbered cards, measuring 2-3/8" x 3-1/2", were given away at gas stations. The front consists of a color photo, while the backs (printed in either blue or black) contain a brief player write-up along with a Signal Oil ad and logo.

		NM	EX	VG
	Complete Set (24):	900.00	450.00	275.00
	Common Player:	40.00	20.00	12.00
(1)	John C. Babich	40.00	20.00	12.00
(2)	Ralph Buxton	40.00	20.00	12.00
(3)	Loyd E. Christopher (Lloyd)	40.00	20.00	12.00
(4)	Merrill Russell Combs	40.00	20.00	12.00
(5)	Melvin E. Deuzabou	40.00	20.00	12.00
(6)	Nicholas ("Nick") Etten	40.00	20.00	12.00
(7)	Bud Foster/Announcer	40.00	20.00	12.00
(8)	Charles Gassaway	40.00	20.00	12.00
(9)	Will Hafey	40.00	20.00	12.00
(10)	Ray Hamrick	40.00	20.00	12.00
(11)	Brooks Richard Holder	40.00	20.00	12.00
(12)	Earl Jones	40.00	20.00	12.00
(13)	Harry "Cookie" Lavagetto	40.00	20.00	12.00
(14)	Robert E. Lillard	40.00	20.00	12.00
(15)	Dario Lodigiani	40.00	20.00	12.00
(16)	Ernie Lombardi	75.00	37.50	22.50
(17a)	Alfred Manuel Martin (Born 1921.)	65.00	32.50	20.00
(17b)	Alfred Manuel Martin (Born 1928.)	75.00	37.50	22.50
(18)	George Michael Metkovich	40.00	20.00	12.00
(19)	William L. Raimondi	40.00	20.00	12.00
(20)	Les George Scarsella	40.00	20.00	12.00
(21)	Floyd Vernie Speer	40.00	20.00	12.00
(22)	Charles "Casey" Stengel	115.00	57.00	34.00

		NM	EX	VG
(23)	Maurice Van Robays	40.00	20.00	12.00
(24)	Aldon Jay Wilkie	40.00	20.00	12.00

1951 Sioux City Soos Postcards

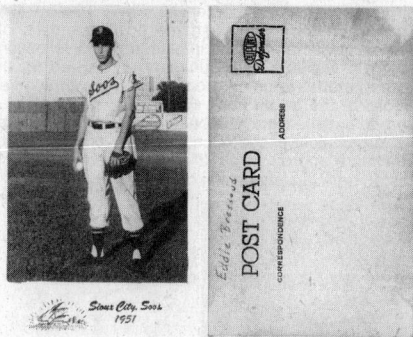

These black-and-white team-issued postcards feature on their fronts posed full-length photos of members of the Class A Western League farm team of the New York Giants. In standard 3-1/2" x 5-1/2" size, the cards have a wide border at bottom which has the team name, the year and a logo featuring an ear of corn. Backs have typical postcard indicia. Players are not identified anywhere on the cards. It is presumed this checklist is incomplete.

		NM	EX	VG
Common Player:		60.00	30.00	18.00
(1)	Ray Berns	60.00	30.00	18.00
(2)	Ed Bressoud	60.00	30.00	18.00
(3)	Mario Picone	60.00	30.00	18.00
(4)	Bob Reid	60.00	30.00	18.00

1952-1953 Sioux City Soos Team Issue

From the Class A Western League, this is one of many minor league team sets issued in the early 1950s by Globe Printing of San Jose, Calif. The early Fifties' Soos were a farm team of the New York Giants. Cards are about 2-1/4" x 3-3/8", printed in black-and-white with blank backs. It appears as if the Soos were the only team to have issued cards in both 1952 and 1953, since some cards are known with players unique to each season as well as cards of players who were with Sioux City in both 1952 and 1953.

		NM	EX	VG
Complete Set (29):		1,500	750.00	450.00
Common Player:		60.00	30.00	18.00
Album:		100.00	50.00	30.00
1952				
(1)	Ray Berns	60.00	30.00	18.00
(2)	Eddie Bressoud	60.00	30.00	18.00
(3)	Irv Burton	60.00	30.00	18.00
(4)	Bob Easterbrook	60.00	30.00	18.00
(5)	George Erath	60.00	30.00	18.00
(6)	Don Fracchia	60.00	30.00	18.00
(7)	Dick Hamlin	60.00	30.00	18.00
(8)	Gail Harris	60.00	30.00	18.00
(9)	Chico Ibanez	60.00	30.00	18.00
(10)	Bob Lee	60.00	30.00	18.00
(11)	Bill McMillan	60.00	30.00	18.00
(12)	Dick Messner	60.00	30.00	18.00
(13)	Roy Pardue	60.00	30.00	18.00
(14)	Mario Picone	60.00	30.00	18.00
(15)	Jim Singleton	60.00	30.00	18.00
(16)	John Uber	60.00	30.00	18.00
(17)	Ernie Yelen	60.00	30.00	18.00
1952/1953				
(18)	Bob Giddings	60.00	30.00	18.00

		NM	EX	VG
(19)	Ray Johnson	60.00	30.00	18.00
(20)	Denny Landry (Bat boy.)	60.00	30.00	18.00
(21)	Vince LaSala	60.00	30.00	18.00
(22)	Ray Mueller	60.00	30.00	18.00
1953				
(23)	Dick Getter	60.00	30.00	18.00
(24)	Dick Hamlin	60.00	30.00	18.00
(25)	Jake Jenkins	60.00	30.00	18.00
(26)	Jim Jones	60.00	30.00	18.00
(27)	Bob Myers	60.00	30.00	18.00
(28)	Clyde Stevens	60.00	30.00	18.00
(29)	Joe Stupak	60.00	30.00	18.00

1954 Sioux City Soos Souvenir Pictures Album

Rather than a set of individual baseball cards, the Class A Western League farm club of the New York Giants issued this souvenir picture album depicting players (including future major league star and N.L. president Bill White), staff and media. About 8-1/8" x 7-1/2", the album has embossed metallic gold covers and orange graphics. Inside are eight black-and-white pages with three card-like images per page. The pictures are in about the same size and format as Globe Printing's contemporary minor league baseball card team sets.

	NM	EX	VG
Complete Souvenir Book: 1954 Sioux City Soos	300.00	150.00	90.00

1947 Smith's Oakland Oaks

CHARLES (Casey) STENGEL
Oaks Manager 1

This regional set of Oakland Oaks (Pacific Coast League) cards was issued in 1947 by Smith's Clothing stores and is numbered in the lower right corner. The card fronts include a black and white photo with the player's name, team and position below. The backs carry a brief player write-up and an advertisement for Smith's Clothing. The cards measure 2" x 3". The Max Marshall card was apparently short-printed and is much scarcer than the rest of the set.

		NM	EX	VG
Complete Set (25):		800.00	400.00	240.00
Common Player:		25.00	12.50	7.50
1	Charles (Casey) Stengel	125.00	65.00	35.00
2	Billy Raimondi	25.00	12.50	7.50
3	Les Scarsella	25.00	12.50	7.50
4	Brooks Holder	25.00	12.50	7.50
5	Ray Hamrick	25.00	12.50	7.50
6	Gene Lillard	25.00	12.50	7.50
7	Maurice Van Robays	25.00	12.50	7.50
8	Charlie (Sheriff) Gassaway	25.00	12.50	7.50
9	Henry (Cotton) Pippen	25.00	12.50	7.50
10	James Arnold	25.00	12.50	7.50
11	Ralph (Buck) Buxton	25.00	12.50	7.50
12	Ambrose (Bo) Palica	25.00	12.50	7.50
13	Tony Sabol	25.00	12.50	7.50
14	Ed Kearse	25.00	12.50	7.50
15	Bill Hart	25.00	12.50	7.50
16	Donald (Snuffy) Smith	25.00	12.50	7.50
17	Oral (Mickey) Burnett	25.00	12.50	7.50
18	Tom Hafey	25.00	12.50	7.50
19	Will Hafey	25.00	12.50	7.50
20	Paul Gillespie	25.00	12.50	7.50
21	Damon Hayes	25.00	12.50	7.50
22	Max Marshall	350.00	175.00	100.00
23	Mel (Dizz) Duezabou	25.00	12.50	7.50
24	Mel Reeves	25.00	12.50	7.50
25	Joe Faria	25.00	12.50	7.50

1948 Smith's Oakland Oaks

BILLY MARTIN
Oaks Third Baseman 17

The 1948 Smith's Clothing issue was another 25-card regional set featuring members of the Oakland Oaks of the Pacific Coast League. Almost identical to the 1947 Smith's issue, the black and white cards again measure 2" x 3" but were printed on heavier, glossy stock. The player's name, team and position appear below the photo with the card number in the lower right corner. The back has a brief player write-up and an ad for Smith's clothing.

		NM	EX	VG
Complete Set (25):		700.00	350.00	210.00
Common Player:		25.00	12.50	7.50
1	Billy Raimondi	25.00	12.50	7.50
2	Brooks Holder	25.00	12.50	7.50
3	Will Hafey	25.00	12.50	7.50
4	Nick Etten	25.00	12.50	7.50
5	Lloyd Christopher	25.00	12.50	7.50
6	Les Scarsella	25.00	12.50	7.50
7	Ray Hamrick	25.00	12.50	7.50
8	Gene Lillard	25.00	12.50	7.50
9	Maurice Van Robays	25.00	12.50	7.50
10	Charlie Gassaway	25.00	12.50	7.50
11	Ralph (Buck) Buxton	25.00	12.50	7.50
12	Tom Hafey	25.00	12.50	7.50
13	Damon Hayes	25.00	12.50	7.50
14	Mel (Dizz) Duezabou	25.00	12.50	7.50
15	Dario Lodigiani	25.00	12.50	7.50
16	Vic Buccola	25.00	12.50	7.50
17	Billy Martin	90.00	45.00	27.00
18	Floyd Speer	25.00	12.50	7.50
19	Eddie Samcoff	25.00	12.50	7.50
20	Charles (Casey) Stengel	90.00	45.00	27.00
21	Lloyd Hittle	25.00	12.50	7.50
22	Johnny Babich	25.00	12.50	7.50
23	Merrill Combs	25.00	12.50	7.50
24	Eddie Murphy	25.00	12.50	7.50
25	Bob Klinger	25.00	12.50	7.50

1948 Sommer & Kaufmann San Francisco Seals

WILFRED "BILL" LEONARD
Seals Catcher 20

One of the more common of the many Pacific Coast League issues of the late 1940s, this emission from the San Francisco boys' clothier features 30 black-and-white 2" x 3" cards. Fronts have a player photo, name, position and card number. Backs have a few biographical details and stats, along with an ad. The 1948 issue can be differentiated from the 1949 issue by the words "BOYS SHOP" above the company logo on back.

		NM	EX	VG
Complete Set (30):		1,500	750.00	450.00
Common Player:		60.00	30.00	18.50
1	Lefty O'Doul	100.00	50.00	30.00

		NM	EX	VG
2	Jack Brewer	60.00	30.00	18.50
3	Con Dempsey	60.00	30.00	18.50
4	Tommy Fine	60.00	30.00	18.50
5	Kenneth Gables	60.00	30.00	18.50
6	Robert Joyce	60.00	30.00	18.50
7	Al Lien	60.00	30.00	18.50
8	Cliff Melton	60.00	30.00	18.50
9	Frank Shofner	60.00	30.00	18.50
10	Don Trower	60.00	30.00	18.50
11	Joe Brovia	60.00	30.00	18.50
12	Dino Paul Restelli	60.00	30.00	18.50
13	Gene Woodling	75.00	37.00	22.00
14	Ben Guintini	60.00	30.00	18.50
15	Felix Mackiewicz	60.00	30.00	18.50
16	John Patrick Tobin	60.00	30.00	18.50
17	Manuel Perez	60.00	30.00	18.50
18	Bill Werle	60.00	30.00	18.50
19	Homer Howell	60.00	30.00	18.50
20	Wilfred Leonard	60.00	30.00	18.50
21	Bruce Ogrodowski	60.00	30.00	18.50
22	Dick Lajeskie	60.00	30.00	18.50
23	Hugh Luby	60.00	30.00	18.50
24	Roy Nicely	60.00	30.00	18.50
25	Ray Orteig	60.00	30.00	18.50
26	Michael Rocco	60.00	30.00	18.50
27	Del Young	60.00	30.00	18.50
28	Joe Sprinz	60.00	30.00	18.50
29	Doc Hughes	60.00	30.00	18.50
30	Batboys (Don Rode, Albert Boro, Charlie Barnes)	60.00	30.00	18.50

1949 Sommer & Kaufmann San Francisco Seals

JACK NICHOLAS BACCIOCCO, outfielder, Born, San Francisco, Feb. 10, 1925. Height 6', weight 185. Throws and bats right. Italian-Swedish descent. With Salt Lake and Reno in 1947. With Salt Lake in 1948. Hit .277.

JACK NICHOLAS BACCIOCCO
Seals Outfielder   19

Sommer & Kaufmann
838 MARKET ST.   2600 OCEAN AVE.
SAN FRANCISCO
35 FOURTH AVE., SAN MATEO
Famous for Boys' "Hot Rod" Shoes

Twenty-eight black-and-white cards numbered 1-29 (#24 unknown) make up the second and final card issue of the "Frisco area clothier". Measuring 2" x 3", the cards are nearly identical to the '48 issue. The '49s can be identified by the mention of "Hot Rod" shoes on the back. Fronts feature a borderless player photo with a panel at the bottom giving name, position and card number. Backs have the ad for the boy's shop and a brief biographical player sketch.

		NM	EX	VG
	Complete Set (29):	2,000	1,000	600.00
	Common Player:	75.00	37.00	22.00
1	Lefty O'Doul	100.00	50.00	30.00
2	Jack Brewer	75.00	37.00	22.00
3	Kenneth Gables	75.00	37.00	22.00
4	Con Dempsey	75.00	37.00	22.00
5	Al Lien	75.00	37.00	22.00
6	Cliff Melton	75.00	37.00	22.00
7	Steve Nagy	75.00	37.00	22.00
8	Manny Perez	75.00	37.00	22.00
9	Roy Jarvis	75.00	37.00	22.00
10	Roy Partee	75.00	37.00	22.00
11	Reno Cheso	75.00	37.00	22.00
12	Dick Lajeskie	75.00	37.00	22.00
13	Roy Nicely	75.00	37.00	22.00
14	Mickey Rocco	75.00	37.00	22.00
15	Frank Shofner	75.00	37.00	22.00
16	Richard Holder	75.00	37.00	22.00
17	Dino Restelli	75.00	37.00	22.00
18	Floyd J. "Arky" Vaughan	150.00	75.00	45.00
19	Jackie Baccioccu	75.00	37.00	22.00
20	Bob Drilling	75.00	37.00	22.00
21	Del Young	75.00	37.00	22.00
22	Joe Sprinz	75.00	37.00	22.00
23	Doc Hughes	75.00	37.00	22.00
24	Unknown	75.00	37.00	22.00
25	Bert Singleton	75.00	37.00	22.00
26	John Brocker	75.00	37.00	22.00
27	Jack Tobin	75.00	37.00	22.00
28	Walt Judnich	75.00	37.00	22.00
29	Hal Feldman	75.00	37.00	22.00

1909 Spargo Hartford Senators Postcards

Members on the Connecticut League (Class B) champion Hartford Senators are pictured on these black-and-white postcards. Player portraits are featured in an oval on front with identication below. A photo credit to "Oliver" is provided. The typically formatted back has a credit line for the publisher, A.W. Spargo. It is likely other members of the team exist on cards yet to be reported.

C. P. ARBOGAST.

		NM	EX	VG
	Common Player:	700.00	350.00	200.00
(1)	C.P. Arbogast	700.00	350.00	200.00
(2)	Tom J. Connery	700.00	350.00	200.00
(3)	Ray L. Fisher	700.00	350.00	200.00
(4)	C.A. Wadleigh	700.00	350.00	200.00

1867 Sterey Photographers Troy Haymakers

Pre-dating the use of baseball cards as promotional premiums for other products, this issue comprises cartes de visites of members of the Troy Haymakers, one of the powerhouse "amateur" teams in the days prior to the 1871 formation of the National Association, the first professional baseball league. The approximately 2-1/2" x 4" cards have black-and-white player portrait photos glued to a heavy cardboard backing which on its reverse carries in blue the advertising of E.S. Sterey & Co., Photographers, of Lansingburgh, N.Y. The players are not identified on the cards except for the names and, sometimes, positions pencilled on back. While many CDVs of individual players of the era, along with team poses and composites, are known, this issue is important because it represents one of the first efforts to create a "team set". It is likely cards of other Troy players were issued and may surface someday.

		NM	EX	VG
	Common Player:	3,000	1,500	900.00
(1)	Abrams	3,000	1,500	900.00
(2)	Bill Craver	4,000	2,000	1,200
(3)	Steve King	4,500	2,250	1,350
(4)	Bub McAtee	4,500	2,250	1,350
(5)	Peter McKeon	3,000	1,500	900.00
(6)	McQuide	3,000	1,500	900.00

1933 St. Paul Daily News

(See 1933 Worch Cigar American Association.)

1946 Sunbeam Bread Sacramento Solons

The 21 unnumbered cards in this Pacific Coast League team set are printed with black-and-white fronts containing a borderless player photo with a panel beneath containing name, position and a photo credit. Backs are printed in blue, red and yellow and contain a brief career summary and an ad for the bread brand. Each card can be found with two versions of the ad on back. One has a smaller loaf of bread and the word "Sunbeam" in blue, the other has a larger picture and "Sunbeam" in red. The cards measure approximately 2" x 3". Players are checklisted here in alphabetical order.

STEVE "LITTLE GOLIATH" MESNER, 28, born Los Angeles, Calif.; second season with Solons. Greatest baseball thrill: hitting three home runs in one game. Played in majors with Chicago White Sox, St. Louis Cards, Cincinnati Reds. Hobby: collecting all articles pertaining to baseball.

Listen to Baseball Play by Play With "Tony" Koester KFBK

Sunbeam BREAD
BREAD That Broadcasts BASEBALL

STEVE MESNER
1946 Solons Third Baseman
Photo by Joe Benetti

		NM	EX	VG
	Complete Set (21):	900.00	450.00	240.00
	Common Player:	75.00	35.00	20.00
(1)	Bud Beasley	75.00	35.00	20.00
(2)	Jack Calvey	75.00	35.00	20.00
(3)	Gene Corbett	75.00	35.00	20.00
(4)	Bill Conroy	75.00	35.00	20.00
(5)	Guy Fletcher	75.00	35.00	20.00
(6)	Tony Freitas	75.00	35.00	20.00
(7)	Ted Greenhalgh	75.00	35.00	20.00
(8)	Al Jarlett	75.00	35.00	20.00
(9)	Jesse Landrum	75.00	35.00	20.00
(10)	Gene Lillard	75.00	35.00	20.00
(11)	Garth Mann	75.00	35.00	20.00
(12)	Lilo Marcucci	75.00	35.00	20.00
(13)	Joe Marty/SP	225.00	110.00	65.00
(14)	Steve Mesner	75.00	35.00	20.00
(15)	Herm Pillette	75.00	35.00	20.00
(16)	Earl Sheely	75.00	35.00	20.00
(17)	Al Smith	75.00	35.00	20.00
(18)	Gerald Staley	75.00	35.00	20.00
(19)	Averett Thompson	75.00	35.00	20.00
(20)	Jo Jo White	75.00	35.00	20.00
(21)	Bud Zipay	75.00	35.00	20.00

1947 Sunbeam Bread Sacramento Solons

THE BREAD THAT BROADCASTS BASEBALL

Sunbeam

TOMMY THOMPSON
1947 Solons Outfielder
Photo by Joe Benetti

Similar in format to the 1946 issue, the 26 cards in the '47 set again featured black-and-white player photos on front, with a panel beneath giving player name, position and photo credit. Backs of the 2" x 3" cards had a color depiction of a loaf of the sponsoring company's bread. The unnumbered cards are alphabetically checklisted here.

		NM	EX	VG
	Complete Set (26):	1,250	625.00	375.00
	Common Player:	50.00	25.00	15.00
(1)	Gene Babbit	50.00	25.00	15.00
(2)	Bob Barthelson	50.00	25.00	15.00
(3)	Bud Beasley	50.00	25.00	15.00
(4)	Chuck Cronin	50.00	25.00	15.00
(5)	Eddie Fernandes	50.00	25.00	15.00
(6)	Ed Fitz Gerald	50.00	25.00	15.00
(7)	Guy Fletcher	50.00	25.00	15.00
(8)	Tony Freitas	50.00	25.00	15.00
(9)	Garth Mann	50.00	25.00	15.00
(10)	Joe Marty	50.00	25.00	15.00

		NM	EX	VG
(11)	Lou McCollum	50.00	25.00	15.00
(12)	Steve Mesner	50.00	25.00	15.00
(13)	Frank Nelson	50.00	25.00	15.00
(14)	Tommy Nelson	50.00	25.00	15.00
(15)	Joe Orengo	50.00	25.00	15.00
(16)	Hugh Orphan	50.00	25.00	15.00
(17)	Nick Pesut	50.00	25.00	15.00
(18)	Bill Ramsey	50.00	25.00	15.00
(19)	Johnny Rizzo	50.00	25.00	15.00
(20)	Mike Schemer	250.00	125.00	75.00
(21)	Al Smith	50.00	25.00	15.00
(22)	Tommy Thompson	50.00	25.00	15.00
(23)	Jim Warner	50.00	25.00	15.00
(24)	Mel Wasley	50.00	25.00	15.00
(25)	Leo Wells	50.00	25.00	15.00
(26)	Eddie Zipay	50.00	25.00	15.00

1949 Sunbeam/Pureta Sacramento Solons

Players of the Pacific Coast League's Sacramento Solons were featured in this postcard-size (3-1/4" x 5-1/2") set. Fronts featured black-and-white player photos and the logo of the team's radio broadcaster. Backs feature ads for Sunbeam Bread and Pureta meats.

		NM	EX	VG
Complete Set (12):		2,000	1,000	600.00
Common Player:		250.00	125.00	80.00
(1)	Del Baker	250.00	125.00	80.00
(2)	Frankie Dasso	250.00	125.00	80.00
(3)	Walt Dropo	325.00	160.00	100.00
(4)	Bob Gillespie	250.00	125.00	80.00
(5)	Joe Grace	250.00	125.00	80.00
(6)	Ralph Hodgin	250.00	125.00	80.00
(7)	Freddie Marsh	250.00	125.00	80.00
(8)	Joe Marty	250.00	125.00	80.00
(9)	Len Ratto	250.00	125.00	80.00
(10)	Jim Tabor	250.00	125.00	80.00
(11)	Al White	250.00	125.00	80.00
(12)	Bill Wilson	250.00	125.00	80.00

1949 Sunbeam Bread Stockton Ports

These 2" x 3" unnumbered cards can be found printed in either black-and-white or blue tinted. The Ports were the Class C California League farm club of the Chicago White Sox.

		NM	EX	VG
Complete Set (12):		3,000	1,500	900.00
Common Player:		275.00	135.00	85.00
(1)	Nino Bongiovanni	275.00	135.00	85.00
(2)	Lou Bronzan	275.00	135.00	85.00
(3)	Jimmie Brown	275.00	135.00	85.00
(4)	Rocco Cardinale	275.00	135.00	85.00
(5)	Harry Clements	275.00	135.00	85.00
(6)	Norm Grabar	275.00	135.00	85.00
(7)	Bud Guldborg	275.00	135.00	85.00
(8)	Carl Hoberg	275.00	135.00	85.00

		NM	EX	VG
(9)	Eddie Murphy	275.00	135.00	85.00
(10)	Sandy Sandel	275.00	135.00	85.00
(11)	Dick Stone	275.00	135.00	85.00
(12)	Matt Zidich	275.00	135.00	85.00

1950 Sunbeam Bread Stockton Ports

These 2" x 3" unnumbered cards are printed in black-and-white. The Ports were an unaffiliated team in the Class C California League.

		NM	EX	VG
Complete Set (13):		1,800	900.00	550.00
Common Player:		150.00	75.00	45.00
(1)	Richard L. Adams	150.00	75.00	45.00
(2)	James Edward Brown	150.00	75.00	45.00
(3)	Harry Clements	150.00	75.00	45.00
(4)	John Burton Goldborg	150.00	75.00	45.00
(5)	Gerald Lee Haines	150.00	75.00	45.00
(6)	Alfred Michael Heist	150.00	75.00	45.00
(7)	Don Masterson	150.00	75.00	45.00
(8)	Lauren Hugh Monroe	150.00	75.00	45.00
(9)	Frank E. Murray	150.00	75.00	45.00
(10)	Lauren Keith Simon Jr.	150.00	75.00	45.00
(11)	George Anthony Stanich	150.00	75.00	45.00
(12)	Robert Louis Stevens	150.00	75.00	45.00
(13)	Harold Lee Zurcher	150.00	75.00	45.00

1962 Supertest Toronto Maple Leafs

The extent of the checklist for this issue is unknown. It is assumed the cards were given away with gasoline purchases. Printed on thick, porous paper in a 5-1/2" x 8-1/2" format, the cards have a black-and-white photo, facsimile autograph and sponsor's logo on front. Backs are blank.

		NM	EX	VG
Common Player:		60.00	30.00	18.00
(1)	Chuck Dressen	75.00	37.50	22.50
(2)	Russ Heman	60.00	30.00	18.00

1952 Syracuse Chiefs Team Issue

Like the other contemporary issues of Globe Printing, the cards of the '52 Chiefs (International League, unaffiliated) share a blank-back, black-and-white format. Player names are in black in a white strip on front. Cards measure about 2-1/4" x 3-3/8". The checklist here is incomplete.

		NM	EX	VG
Common Player:		60.00	30.00	18.00
(1)	Bruno Betzel	60.00	30.00	18.00
(2)	Johnny Blatnick	60.00	30.00	18.00
(3)	Charles Eisenmann	60.00	30.00	18.00
(4)	Myron Hayworth	60.00	30.00	18.00
(5)	John Welaj	60.00	30.00	18.00

T

1966 Toledo Mud Hens Team Issue

(3-1/4" x 5-1/2") (Unnumbered)

		NM	EX	VG
Complete Set (25):		1,000	500.00	300.00
Common Player:		40.00	20.00	12.00
(1)	Loren Babe	40.00	20.00	12.00
(2)	Stan Bahnsen	40.00	20.00	12.00
(3)	Bill Bethea	40.00	20.00	12.00
(4)	Wayne Comer	40.00	20.00	12.00
(5)	Jack Cullen	40.00	20.00	12.00
(6)	Jack Curtis	40.00	20.00	12.00
(7)	Gil Downs	40.00	20.00	12.00
(8)	Joe Faroci	40.00	20.00	12.00
(9)	Frank Fernandez	40.00	20.00	12.00
(10)	Mike Ferraro	40.00	20.00	12.00
(11)	Doc Foley	40.00	20.00	12.00
(12)	Mike Hegan	40.00	20.00	12.00
(13)	Jim Horsford	40.00	20.00	12.00
(14)	Dick Hughes	40.00	20.00	12.00
(15)	Elvio Jiminez	40.00	20.00	12.00
(16)	Bob Lasko	40.00	20.00	12.00
(17)	Jim Merritt	40.00	20.00	12.00
(18)	Archie Moore	40.00	20.00	12.00
(19)	Bobby Murcer	90.00	45.00	27.00
(20)	Tony Preybycian	40.00	20.00	12.00
(21)	Bob Schmidt	40.00	20.00	12.00
(22)	Charlie Senger, Loren Babe, Bill Shantz	40.00	20.00	12.00
(23)	Bill Shantz	40.00	20.00	12.00
(24)	Paul Toth	40.00	20.00	12.00
(25)	Jerry Walker	40.00	20.00	12.00

1964 True Ade/ WGR Buffalo Bisons

Members of the International League Buffalo Bisons, Class AAA farm club of the N.Y. Mets are featured in this set of contest cards. Persons who assembled a complete nine-player set could redeem the cards for ballgame tickets. The cards were found in cartons of Tru Ade beverage. The blank-back cards are printed in red and about 1-1/4" x 6-1/2" overall. At bottom is a player photo with his name and position above, and team below, separated by a dotted line from the upper portion of the card which has contest details and logos of the sponsoring beverage company and WGR radio. The player portion of the card measures about 1-1/4" x 1-1/4". It is evident that at least nine players were issued in the set, possibly with some short-printed; this checklist is, therefore, incomplete. The unnumbered cards are listed here in alphabetical order.

		NM	EX	VG
Common Player:		150.00	75.00	45.00
(1)	Ed Bauta	150.00	75.00	45.00
(2)	Choo Choo Coleman	200.00	100.00	60.00
(3)	Pumpsie Green	300.00	150.00	90.00
(4)	Cleon Jones	200.00	100.00	60.00

1960 Tulsa Oilers Team Issue

This team-issue by the St. Louis Cardinals' farm club consists of a dozen black-and-white player photos. Players are identifed by a facsimile autograph on front. Backs of the approximately 4-1/8" x 5" photos are blank.

		NM	EX	VG
Complete Set (18):		350.00	175.00	100.00
Common Player:		20.00	10.00	6.00
(1)	Jim Beauchamp	15.00	7.50	4.50
(2)	Bob Blaylock	20.00	10.00	6.00
(3)	Artie Burnett	20.00	10.00	6.00
(4)	Bill Carpenter	20.00	10.00	6.00
(5)	Julio Gotay	20.00	10.00	6.00
(6)	Jim Hickman	20.00	10.00	6.00
(7)	Ray Katt	20.00	10.00	6.00
(8)	Harry Keister	20.00	10.00	6.00
(9)	Fred Koenig	20.00	10.00	6.00
(10)	Gordon Richardson	20.00	10.00	6.00
(11)	Rich Rogers	20.00	10.00	6.00
(12)	Lynn Rube	20.00	10.00	6.00
(13)	Jim Schaffer	20.00	10.00	6.00
(14)	Clint Stark	20.00	10.00	6.00
(15)	Ted Thiem	20.00	10.00	6.00
(16)	Dixie Walker	20.00	10.00	6.00
(17)	Harry Watts	20.00	10.00	6.00
(18)	Fred Whitfield	20.00	10.00	6.00

U

1888 Uhlman St. Paul Cabinets

While this cabinet-card issue utilizes the same format (about 4-1/4" x 6-1/2") and the same Goodwin & Co. copyright photos found on contemporary Old Judge cards, they are, according to advertising on the bottom, the product of Uhlman (presumably a studio) in St. Joseph, Mo. All cards known to date depict members of the St. Paul Apostles of the newly formed Western Association.

		NM	EX	VG
Common Player:		900.00	525.00	275.00
(1)	Cal Broughton	900.00	525.00	275.00
(2)	George Treadway	900.00	525.00	275.00
(3)	A.M. Tuckerman	900.00	525.00	275.00

1958 Union Oil Sacramento Solons

Ten members of the independent Pacific Coast League team were included in a black-and-white card set distributed at Union 76 gas stations in that locale. Fronts feature borderless player photos with a wide white strip at the bottom on which is printed the player, team name and the position. Backs have brief stats, a "76 Sports Club" pennant and information about a specific game for which the card can be exchanged for admission by a child. Cards measure approximately 2-1/2" x 3-1/4".

		NM	EX	VG
Complete Set (10):		500.00	250.00	150.00
Common Player:		50.00	25.00	15.00
(1)	Marshall Bridges	65.00	32.00	19.50

(2)	Dick Cole	50.00	25.00	15.00
(3)	Jim Greengrass	50.00	25.00	15.00
(4)	Al Heist	50.00	25.00	15.00
(5)	Nippy Jones	50.00	25.00	15.00
(6)	Carlos Paula	50.00	25.00	15.00
(7)	Kal Segrist	50.00	25.00	15.00
(8)	Sibbi Sisti	50.00	25.00	15.00
(9)	Joe Stanka	80.00	40.00	24.00
(10)	Bud Watkins	50.00	25.00	15.00

1960 Union Oil Seattle Rainiers

Given away at Union 76 gas stations in the Seattle area, this set of nine full-color cards measure approximately 3-1/8" x 4". Backs have brief biographical data, a career summary and a large Union 76 logo. The cards are skip-numbered.

		NM	EX	VG
Complete Set (9):		200.00	100.00	60.00
Common Player:		12.00	6.00	3.50
4	Francisco Obregon	20.00	10.00	6.00
6	Drew Gilbert	12.00	6.00	3.50
7	Bill Hain	12.00	6.00	3.50
10	Ray Ripplemeyer	100.00	50.00	30.00
13	Joe Taylor	12.00	6.00	3.50
15	Lou Skizas	12.00	6.00	3.50
17	Don Rudolph	12.00	6.00	3.50
19	Gordy Coleman	15.00	7.50	4.50
22	Hal Beven	12.00	6.00	3.50

1961 Union Oil Pacific Coast League

The last of three Union Oil PCL issues, the 67 cards in this set feature sepia-toned borderless photos on front in a 3" to 3-1/8" x 4" format. Backs are printed in blue and feature biographical data, a career summary, and ads by the issuing oil company and participating radio station co-sponsors. Six of the eight teams in the '61 PCL are featured, with Salt Lake City and Vancouver not participating in the promotion. Presumably because of smaller print runs, the cards distributed in Hawaii and Spokane bring a premium price. Hall of Fame pitcher Gaylord Perry is featured on his first baseball card in this set. Only the Tacoma cards are numbered and they are skip-numbered.

(Team sets listed below.)

1961 Union Oil Hawaii Islanders

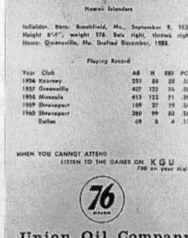

		NM	EX	VG
Complete Set (10):		375.00	185.00	110.00
Common Player:		40.00	20.00	12.00
(1)	Ray Jablonski	40.00	20.00	12.00
(2)	Jim McManus	40.00	20.00	12.00
(3)	George Prescott	75.00	37.50	22.50
(4)	Diego Segui	45.00	22.50	13.50
(5)	Rachel Slider	40.00	20.00	12.00
(6)	Jim Small	40.00	20.00	12.00
(7)	Milt Smith	40.00	20.00	12.00
(8)	Dave Thies	40.00	20.00	12.00
(9)	Jay Ward	40.00	20.00	12.00
(10)	Bill Werle	40.00	20.00	12.00

1961 Union Oil Portland Beavers

		NM	EX	VG
Complete Set (13):		150.00	75.00	45.00
Common Player:		12.00	6.00	3.50
(1)	Ed Bauta	12.00	6.00	3.50
(2)	Vern Benson	12.00	6.00	3.50
(3)	Jerry Buchek	12.00	6.00	3.50
(4)	Bob Burda	12.00	6.00	3.50
(5)	Duke Carmel	12.00	6.00	3.50
(6)	Don Choate	12.00	6.00	3.50
(7)	Phil Gagliano	12.00	6.00	3.50
(8)	Jim Hickman	12.00	6.00	3.50
(9)	Ray Katt	12.00	6.00	3.50
(10)	Mel Nelson	12.00	6.00	3.50
(11)	Jim Shaffer	12.00	6.00	3.50
(12)	Mike Shannon	17.50	8.75	5.25
(13)	Clint Stark	12.00	6.00	3.50

1961 Union Oil San Diego Padres

		NM	EX	VG
Complete Set (12):		175.00	90.00	45.00
Common Player:		12.00	6.00	3.50
(1)	Dick Barone	12.00	6.00	3.50
(2)	Jim Bolger	12.00	6.00	3.50
(3)	Kent Hadley	12.00	6.00	3.50
(4)	Mike Hershberger	15.00	7.50	4.50
(5)	Stan Johnson	12.00	6.00	3.50
(6)	Dick Lines	12.00	6.00	3.50
(7)	Jim Napier	12.00	6.00	3.50
(8)	Tony Roig	12.00	6.00	3.50
(9)	Herb Score	40.00	20.00	12.00
(10)	Harry Simpson	20.00	10.00	6.00
(11)	Joe Taylor	12.00	6.00	3.50
(12)	Ben Wade	12.00	6.00	3.50

1961 Union Oil Seattle Rainiers

		NM	EX	VG
Complete Set (11):		100.00	50.00	30.00
Common Player:		10.00	5.00	3.00
(1)	Galen Cisco	10.00	5.00	3.00
(2)	Lou Clinton	10.00	5.00	3.00
(3)	Marlan Coughtry	10.00	5.00	3.00
(4)	Harry Malmberg	10.00	5.00	3.00
(5)	Dave Mann	10.00	5.00	3.00
(6)	Derrell Martin	10.00	5.00	3.00
(7)	Erv Palica	10.00	5.00	3.00
(8)	John Pesky	15.00	7.50	4.50
(9)	Bob Tillman	10.00	5.00	3.00
(10)	Marv Toft	10.00	5.00	3.00
(11)	Tom Umphlett	10.00	5.00	3.00

1961 Union Oil Spokane Indians

		NM	EX	VG
Complete Set (11):		450.00	225.00	135.00
Common Player:		35.00	17.50	10.00
(1)	Doug Camilli	35.00	17.50	10.00
(2)	Ramon Conde	35.00	17.50	10.00
(3)	Bob Giallombardo	35.00	17.50	10.00
(4)	Mike Goliat	35.00	17.50	10.00

		NM	EX	VG
(5)	Preston Gomez/SP	135.00	67.00	40.00
(6)	Rod Graber	35.00	17.50	10.00
(7)	Tim Harkness	35.00	17.50	10.00
(8)	Jim Harwell	35.00	17.50	10.00
(9)	Howie Reed	35.00	17.50	10.00
(10)	Curt Roberts	35.00	17.50	10.00
(11)	Rene Valdes (Valdez)	35.00	17.50	10.00

1961 Union Oil Tacoma Giants

		NM	EX	VG
Complete Set (10):		200.00	100.00	60.00
Common Player:		15.00	7.50	4.50
10	Red Davis	15.00	7.50	4.50
12	Dick Phillips	15.00	7.50	4.50
17	Gil Garrido	15.00	7.50	4.50
20	Georges Maranda	15.00	7.50	4.50
25	John Orsino	15.00	7.50	4.50
26	Dusty Rhodes	20.00	10.00	6.00
28	Ron Herbel	15.00	7.50	4.50
29	Gaylord Perry	60.00	30.00	18.00
30	Rafael Alomar	20.00	10.00	6.00
34	Bob Farley	15.00	7.50	4.50

1961 Union Oil Taiyo Whales

This three-card set was produced in conjunction with an exhibition series played in October, 1961, between the Taiyo Whales of Japan's Central League, and the Hawaii Islanders, a Class AAA Pacific Coast League farm club of the K.C. Athletics. The player cards measure just over 3" x 4", while the team photo card is 5" x 3-3/4". Cards are black-and-white and have some player biography and ads for Union Oil Co., and the English - and Japanese - language radio stations that carried the games.

		NM	EX	VG
Complete Set (3):		175.00	87.00	52.00
(1)	Akihito Kondo	50.00	25.00	15.00
(2)	Gentaro Shimada	50.00	25.00	15.00
(3)	Taiyo Whales Team	90.00	45.00	27.00

1951 Vancouver Capilanos Popcorn Issue

 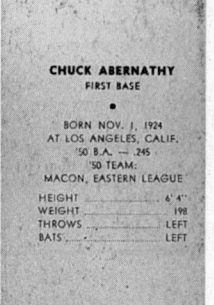

These cards measure 1-7/8" x 2-7/8", are printed in black-and-white and have 1950 stats on back. Names may appear in slightly different form than checklisted here. The Caps played in the Class B Western International League and were not affiliated with any major league club.

	NM	EX	VG
Complete Set (24):	4,000	2,000	1,200
Common Player:	200.00	100.00	60.00

		NM	EX	VG
(1)	Chuck Abernathy	200.00	100.00	60.00
(2)	Jerry Barta	200.00	100.00	60.00
(3)	Bud Beasley	200.00	100.00	60.00
(4)	Gordy Brunswick	200.00	100.00	60.00
(5)	Reno Cheso	200.00	100.00	60.00
(6)	Ken Chorlton	200.00	100.00	60.00
(7)	Carl Gunnarson	200.00	100.00	60.00
(8)	Pete Hernandez	200.00	100.00	60.00
(9)	Vern Kindsfather	200.00	100.00	60.00
(10)	Bobby McGuire	200.00	100.00	60.00
(11)	Bob McLean	200.00	100.00	60.00
(12)	Charlie Mead	200.00	100.00	60.00
(13)	Jimmy Moore	200.00	100.00	60.00
(14)	George Nicholas	200.00	100.00	60.00
(15)	John Ritchey	200.00	100.00	60.00
(16)	Sandy Robertson	200.00	100.00	60.00
(17)	Bill Schuster	200.00	100.00	60.00
(18)	Dick Sinovic	200.00	100.00	60.00
(19)	Ron Smith	200.00	100.00	60.00
(20)	Bob Snyder	200.00	100.00	60.00
(21)	Don Tisnerat	200.00	100.00	60.00
(22)	Ray Tran	200.00	100.00	60.00
(23)	Reg Wallis/Trainer	200.00	100.00	60.00
(24)	Bill Whyte	200.00	100.00	60.00

1952 Vancouver Capilanos Popcorn Issue

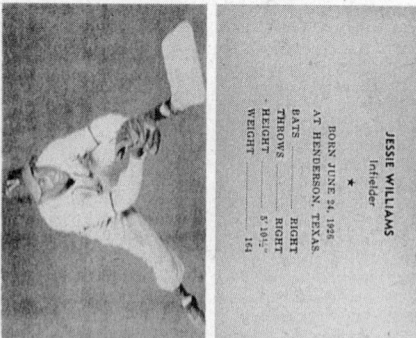

These cards measure 2" x 3-1/8", are printed in black-and-white and have 1951 stats on back. Names may appear in slightly different form than checklisted here. The Caps played in the Class A Western International League and were not affiliated with any major league club.

		NM	EX	VG
Complete Set (20):		3,500	1,750	1,000
Common Player:		200.00	100.00	60.00
(1)	Gordie Brunswick	200.00	100.00	60.00
(2)	Bob Duretto	200.00	100.00	60.00
(3)	Van Fletcher	200.00	100.00	60.00
(4)	John Guldborg	200.00	100.00	60.00
(5)	Paul Jones	200.00	100.00	60.00
(6)	Eddie Locke	200.00	100.00	60.00
(7)	Tom Lovrich	200.00	100.00	60.00
(8)	Jimmy Moore	200.00	100.00	60.00
(9)	George Nicholas	200.00	100.00	60.00
(10a)	John Ritchey	200.00	100.00	60.00
(10b)	Johnny Ritchie	200.00	100.00	60.00
(11)	Bill Schuster	200.00	100.00	60.00
(12)	Bob Snyder	200.00	100.00	60.00
(13)	Len Tran	200.00	100.00	60.00
(14)	Ray Tran	200.00	100.00	60.00
(15)	Edo Vanni	200.00	100.00	60.00
(16)	Jim Wert	200.00	100.00	60.00
(17)	Bill Whyte	200.00	100.00	60.00
(18)	Jessie Williams/Btg	200.00	100.00	60.00
(19)	Jesse Williams/Fielding	200.00	100.00	60.00

1953 Vancouver Capilanos Popcorn Issue

These cards measure 2-3/16" x 3-3/16", are printed in black-and-white and have 1952 stats on back. Names may appear in slightly different form than checklisted here. The Caps played in the Class A Western International League and were not affiliated with any major league club.

		NM	EX	VG
Complete Set (18):		3,000	1,500	900.00
Common Player:		200.00	100.00	60.00
(1)	Dick Briskey	200.00	100.00	60.00
(2)	Jack Bukowatz	200.00	100.00	60.00
(3)	Ken Chorlton	200.00	100.00	60.00
(4)	Van Fletcher	200.00	100.00	60.00
(5)	John Guldborg	200.00	100.00	60.00
(6)	Carl Gunnerson	200.00	100.00	60.00
(7)	Jim Hedgecock	200.00	100.00	60.00
(8)	Gordon Hernandez	200.00	100.00	60.00
(9)	Pete Hernandez	200.00	100.00	60.00
(10)	Jim Leavitt	200.00	100.00	60.00
(11)	Rod MacKay	200.00	100.00	60.00
(12)	Frank Mascaro	200.00	100.00	60.00
(13)	Lonnie Myers	200.00	100.00	60.00
(14)	Rod Owen	200.00	100.00	60.00
(15)	Harvey Storey	200.00	100.00	60.00
(16)	Bob Stuart	200.00	100.00	60.00
(17)	Dale Thomason	200.00	100.00	60.00
(18)	Jim Wert	200.00	100.00	60.00

1954 Vancouver Capilanos Popcorn Issue

These cards measure 2-3/16" x 3-5/16" and are printed in black-and-white. Names may appear in slightly different form than checklisted here. The Caps were the 1954 champs of the Class A Western International League and were not affiliated with any major league club.

		NM	EX	VG
Complete Set (15):		2,500	1,250	750.00
Common Player:		200.00	100.00	60.00
(1)	Bill Brenner	200.00	100.00	60.00
(2)	Ken Chorlton	200.00	100.00	60.00
(3)	Jim Clarke (Clark)	200.00	100.00	60.00
(4)	John Cordell	200.00	100.00	60.00
(5)	Bob Duretto	200.00	100.00	60.00
(6)	Dick Greco	200.00	100.00	60.00
(7)	Arnie Hallgren	200.00	100.00	60.00
(8)	Danny Holden	200.00	100.00	60.00
(9)	Rod McKay	200.00	100.00	60.00
(10)	George Nicholas	200.00	100.00	60.00
(11)	Nick Pesut	200.00	100.00	60.00
(12)	Ken Richardson	200.00	100.00	60.00
(13)	Bob Roberts	200.00	100.00	60.00
(14)	Bob Wellman	200.00	100.00	60.00
(15)	Marvin Williams	200.00	100.00	60.00

The Mint-Mint examples of vintage cards carry a significant premium over the Near Mint values shown here. This premium reflects limited availability of the highest-grade cards as well as demand for particular cards or sets in the best possible condition.

1954 Veltex Lewiston Broncs

It is evident from the format of the card and of the accompanying album that this is a product of Globe Printing, which produced many minor league sets in the early 1950s. What makes this set of the 1954 Class A (Western International League) affiliate of the Baltimore Orioles unusual among Globe issues is the mention of a sponsor. The blank-back, black-and-white cards measure 2-3/16" x 3-3/8". The checklist below is obviously incomplete.

	NM	EX	VG
Common player:	60.00	30.00	18.00
Album:	150.00	75.00	45.00
(1) Larry Barton	60.00	30.00	18.00

1952 Ventura Braves Team Issue

These 2-1/4" x 3-3/8" black-and-white, unnumbered, blank-backed cards were one of many minor league team sets issued by Globe Printing of San Jose, Calif., in the early 1950s. Cards were usually given away at the ballpark on a one-per-week or one-per-homestand basis, accounting for the rarity of surviving complete sets. It is known that 18 V-Braves were issued in this set, though only 14 have been checklisted to date. The team was a Class C California League farm club of the Boston Braves.

	NM	EX	VG
Common Player:	60.00	30.00	18.00
Album:	100.00	50.00	30.00
(1) Al Aguilar	60.00	30.00	18.00
(2) Bud Belardi	60.00	30.00	18.00
(3) Frank Followell	60.00	30.00	18.00
(4) Glenn Hittner	60.00	30.00	18.00
(5) Lee Kast	60.00	30.00	18.00
(6) Richie Morse	60.00	30.00	18.00
(7) Frank Nubin	60.00	30.00	18.00
(8) George Owen	60.00	30.00	18.00
(9) Manny Perez	60.00	30.00	18.00
(10) Jose Perez	60.00	30.00	18.00
(11) Harley Resh	60.00	30.00	18.00
(12) Jack Schlarb	60.00	30.00	18.00
(13) Bob Sturgeon	60.00	30.00	18.00
(14) Billy Wells	60.00	30.00	18.00

1911 Western Playground Association

 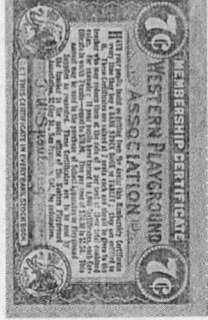

Stars from around the Pacific Coast League are featured on this rare and unusual issue. The 2-1/4" x 3-1/2" cards have a front design similar to contemporary Zee Nuts cards: A dark brown border surrounding a sepia posed action picture (which appears to be a heavily retouched photo). Printed in white at left or right are "WESTERN PLAYGROUND ASSOCIATION / P.C. (or sometimes "P.S.") LEAGUE" and the player's last name. Backs are a "Membership Certificate" indicating the cards could be redeemed for 5 percent of their seven-cent "face value" toward the purchase of school playground apparatus or supplies. The cards were received with the purchase of "Bank Stock" brand composition books.

	NM	EX	VG
Common Player:	6,000	3,000	1,800
(1) Claude Berry	6,000	3,000	1,800
(2) Roy Brashear	6,000	3,000	1,800
(3) Herb Byram	6,000	3,000	1,800
(4) Walt Carlisle	6,000	3,000	1,800
(5) Roy Cassleton (Castleton)	6,000	3,000	1,800
(6) Chet Chadborne (Chadbourne)	6,000	3,000	1,800
(7) Tyler Christian	6,000	3,000	1,800
(8) Bert Coy	6,000	3,000	1,800
(9) Pete Daley	6,000	3,000	1,800
(10) Pop Dillon	6,000	3,000	1,800
(11) Joe French	6,000	3,000	1,800
(12) Howie Gregory	6,000	3,000	1,800
(13) Spec Harkness	6,000	3,000	1,800
(14) Heinie Heitmuller	6,000	3,000	1,800
(15) Ben Henderson	6,000	3,000	1,800
(16) Cack Henley	6,000	3,000	1,800
(17) Izzy Hoffman	6,000	3,000	1,800
(18) Happy Hogan	6,000	3,000	1,800
(19) Johnny Kane	6,000	3,000	1,800
(20) Jimmy Lewis	6,000	3,000	1,800
(21) Tom Madden	6,000	3,000	1,800
(22) Chris Mahoney	6,000	3,000	1,800
(23) George Metzger	6,000	3,000	1,800
(24) Fred Miller	6,000	3,000	1,800
(25) Kid Mohler	6,000	3,000	1,800
(26) Walter Nagle	6,000	3,000	1,800
(27) Patsy O'Rourke	6,000	3,000	1,800
(28) Ham Patterson	6,000	3,000	1,800
(29) Roger Peckinpaugh	6,000	3,000	1,800
(30) Bill Rapps	6,000	3,000	1,800
(31) Bill Rogers (Rodgers)	6,000	3,000	1,800
(32) Buddy Ryan	6,000	3,000	1,800
(33) Walter Schmitt (Schmidt)	6,000	3,000	1,800
(34) Tom Seaton	6,000	3,000	1,800
(35) Jerry Sheehan	6,000	3,000	1,800
(36) Harry Stewart	6,000	3,000	1,800
(37) George Stinson	6,000	3,000	1,800
(38) Harry Suter (Sutor)	6,000	3,000	1,800
(39) Harry Wolverton	6,000	3,000	1,800
(40) Elmer Zacher	6,000	3,000	1,800

1932 Wheaties Minneapolis Millers

Because of their similarity to the 1933 issue which carried Wheaties advertising on the back, these postcard-size photos of the 1932 Millers are believed to also have been issued by the Minneapolis-based cereal company. The 3-7/16" x 5-7/16" cards have black-and-white portraits or posed action photos on front, along with a facsimile autograph. Backs are blank.

	NM	EX	VG
Complete Set (24):	900.00	450.00	275.00
Common Player:	40.00	20.00	12.00
(1) J.C. "Rube" Benton	40.00	20.00	12.00
(2) Donie Bush	40.00	20.00	12.00
(3) Andy Cohen	45.00	22.00	13.50
(4) "Pea Ridge" Day	40.00	20.00	12.00
(5) Ray Fitzgerald	40.00	20.00	12.00
(6) F.P. "Babe" Ganzel	40.00	20.00	12.00
(7) Wes Griffin	40.00	20.00	12.00
(8) Spencer Harris	40.00	20.00	12.00
(9) Joe Hauser	75.00	37.00	22.00
(10) Frank J. "Dutch" Henry	40.00	20.00	12.00
(11) Phil Hensick	40.00	20.00	12.00
(12) Bunker Hill	40.00	20.00	12.00
(13) Joe Mowry	40.00	20.00	12.00
(14) Jess Petty	40.00	20.00	12.00
(15) Paul Richards	45.00	22.00	13.50
(16) Bill Rodda	40.00	20.00	12.00
(17) Harry Rose	40.00	20.00	12.00
(18) Art Ruble	40.00	20.00	12.00
(19) "Rosy" Ryan	40.00	20.00	12.00
(20) Al Sheehan	40.00	20.00	12.00
(21) Ed Sicking	40.00	20.00	12.00
(22) Ernie Smith	40.00	20.00	12.00
(23) Hy Van Denberg	40.00	20.00	12.00
(24) E.R. Vangilder	40.00	20.00	12.00

1933 Wheaties Minneapolis Millers

Prior to printing their first major league baseball cards on the backs of cereal boxes in 1935, Wheaties sponsored a minor league set for the hometown Minneapolis Millers in 1933. The 4" x 5-3/4" cards have a sepia-toned posed action photo on front, along with a facsimile autograph. The player's name, position, team and year are printed in the bottom border. The postcard back, printed in black-and-white, has a drawing of a Wheaties box and an ad for the cereal. All unmailed examples seen to date have a purple rubber-stamped "VOID" in the postage box at top. The unnumbered cards are checklisted here alphabetically.

	NM	EX	VG
Complete Set (24):	2,250	1,125	650.00
Common Player:	90.00	45.00	27.00
(1) Dave Bancroft	150.00	75.00	45.00
(2) Rube Benton	90.00	45.00	27.00
(3) Andy Cohen	150.00	75.00	45.00
(4) Bob Fothergill	90.00	45.00	27.00
(5) "Babe" Ganzel	90.00	45.00	27.00
(6) Joe Glenn	90.00	45.00	27.00
(7) Wes Griffin	90.00	45.00	27.00
(8) Jack Hallet	90.00	45.00	27.00
(9) Jerry Harrington/Announcer	90.00	45.00	27.00
(10) Spencer Harris	100.00	50.00	30.00
(11) Joe Hauser	200.00	100.00	60.00
(12) Butch Henline	90.00	45.00	27.00
(13) Walter Hilcher	90.00	45.00	27.00
(14) Dutch Holland	90.00	45.00	27.00
(15) Harry Holsclaw	90.00	45.00	27.00
(16) Wes Kingdon	90.00	45.00	27.00
(17) George Murray	90.00	45.00	27.00
(18) Leo Norris	90.00	45.00	27.00
(19) Jess Petty	90.00	45.00	27.00
(20) Art Ruble	90.00	45.00	27.00
(21) Al Sheehan/Announcer	90.00	45.00	27.00
(22) Ernie Smith	90.00	45.00	27.00
(23) Wally Tauscher	90.00	45.00	27.00
(24) Hy VanDenberg	90.00	45.00	27.00

The Mint-Mint examples of vintage cards carry a significant premium over the Near Mint values shown here. This premium reflects limited availability of the highest-grade cards as well as demand for particular cards or sets in the best possible condition.

1933 Wheaties Seattle Indians

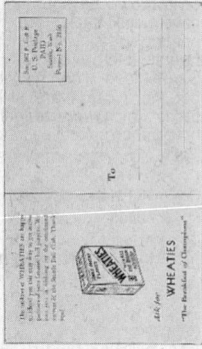

Prior to printing their first major league baseball cards on the backs of cereal boxes in 1935, Wheaties sponsored a minor league set for the Seattle Indians in 1933. The 4-1/8" x 7" cards have a sepia-toned posed portrait or action photo on front, along with a facsimile autograph. The player's name, position, team and year are printed in the bottom border. The postcard back, printed in black-and-white, has a drawing of a Wheaties box and an ad for the cereal. The unnumbered cards are checklisted here alphabetically; it is likely this list is incomplete.

		NM	EX	VG
Common Player:		450.00	225.00	135.00
(1)	George Burns	600.00	300.00	180.00
(2)	Joe Coscarart	450.00	225.00	135.00
(3)	Bill Radonits	450.00	225.00	135.00
(4)	"Junk" Walters	450.00	225.00	135.00

1912 Whitehead & Hoag P.C.L. Pins

A paper insert originally in the back of these pins identifies the maker as Whitehead & Hoag of San Francisco. The 7/8" diameter celluloid pins are printed in either black or blue on a white background. A player portrait photo is at center, with his last name below. Above is the city of his team and the Pacific Coast League initials. Listed in the "American Card Catalog" as PM5, the unnumbered pins are checklisted here alphabetically; it's possible additional pins in the issue remain to be reported. All pins seen are Oakland players except McCredie (Portland) and Berry (San Francisco).

		NM	EX	VG
Complete Set (26):		5,000	2,500	1,500
Common Player:		275.00	135.00	85.00
(1)	Harry Ables	275.00	135.00	85.00
(2)	Claude Berry	275.00	135.00	85.00
(3)	Tyler Christian	275.00	135.00	85.00
(4)	Cook	275.00	135.00	85.00
(5)	Bert Coy	275.00	135.00	85.00
(6)	Jack Flater	275.00	135.00	85.00
(7)	Gregory	275.00	135.00	85.00
(8)	Hamilton	275.00	135.00	85.00
(9)	Gus Hetling	275.00	135.00	85.00
(10a)	Hille	275.00	135.00	85.00
(10b)	Mgr. Hille	275.00	135.00	85.00
(11)	Izzy Hoffman	275.00	135.00	85.00
(12)	Bill Leard	275.00	135.00	85.00
(13)	Malarkey	275.00	135.00	85.00
(14)	Martinoni	275.00	135.00	85.00
(15)	Walter McCredie	275.00	135.00	85.00
(16)	Honus Mitze	275.00	135.00	85.00
(17)	Parkins	275.00	135.00	85.00
(18)	Pope	275.00	135.00	85.00
(19)	Bill Rapp (Rapps)	275.00	135.00	85.00
(20)	Tom Seaton	275.00	135.00	85.00
(21a)	Sharpe	275.00	135.00	85.00
(21b)	Mgr. Sharpe	275.00	135.00	85.00
(22)	Tommy Sheehan	275.00	135.00	85.00
(23)	Smith	275.00	135.00	85.00
(24)	John Tiedeman (Tiedemann)	275.00	135.00	85.00
(25)	Wilkinson	275.00	135.00	85.00
(26)	Elmer Zacher	275.00	135.00	85.00

1919 Winkelman's Quaker Bread Pins

This issue of 1-1/4" diameter celluloid pinback buttons features members of the Memphis Chickasaws in black-and-white portraits on a pale yellow background, surrounded by an orange border with the sponsor's advertising. A large turtle is pictured at bottom. Currently only three players are known, though it is likely more were issued.

		NM	EX	VG
Common Player:		1,300	650.00	400.00
(1)	Baerwald	1,300	650.00	400.00
(2)	Carey	1,300	650.00	400.00
(3)	Bob Coulson	1,300	650.00	400.00

1933-34 Worch Cigar American Association

Though the issuer is not identified anywhere on these blank-backed, 3-7/16" x 5-7/16" black-and-white cards (though some are found with a box on front crediting the photo to the St. Paul Daily News), the individual player photos were available as premiums for redemption of cigar bands by the Worch Cigar Co., of St. Paul, Minn. The issue is similar in format to the major league cards of the same era, and indeed the cards were offered together. Most collectors prefer to chase either the major leaguers or the minor leaguers independently, so they are cataloged in that fashion. The set encompasses players from the 1932-35 Minneapolis Millers, the 1933 St. Paul Saints and a handful from the Columbus Redbirds, Kansas City Blues and a few other teams. The unnumbered cards are checklisted below alphabetically. Player identification is presented in several different styles and may include just the last name or also the first name. Several players are known in more than one pose. The checklist here is likely incomplete.

		NM	EX	VG
Common Player:		45.00	22.50	13.50
(1)	Dave Bancroft	100.00	50.00	30.00
(2)	Clyde Beck	45.00	22.50	13.50
(3)	Rube Benton	45.00	22.50	13.50
(4)	W. Berger	45.00	22.50	13.50
(5)	Brannon	45.00	22.50	13.50
(6)	Spurgeon Chandler	45.00	22.50	13.50
(7)	Tiny Chaplin	45.00	22.50	13.50
(8)	Andy Cohen	45.00	22.50	13.50
(9)	Nick Cullop	45.00	22.50	13.50
(10)	Bob Fenner	45.00	22.50	13.50
(11)	Fischall	45.00	22.50	13.50
(12)	Gaffke	45.00	22.50	13.50
(13a)	Foster Ganzel	45.00	22.50	13.50
(13b)	Foster Ganzel	45.00	22.50	13.50
(14)	Louis Garland	45.00	22.50	13.50
(15)	Joe Glenn	45.00	22.50	13.50
(16)	Angelo Guiliani	45.00	22.50	13.50
(17)	Pinky Hargrave	45.00	22.50	13.50
(18)	Slim Harriss	45.00	22.50	13.50
(19)	Spencer Harris	45.00	22.50	'13.50
(20)	Joe Hauser	75.00	37.50	22.50
(21)	Walter Henline	45.00	22.50	13.50
(22)	Phil Hensick	45.00	22.50	13.50
(23)	Walter Hilcher	45.00	22.50	13.50
(24)	Jesse Hill	45.00	22.50	13.50
(25)	Bob Holand	45.00	22.50	13.50
(26)	Harry Holsclaw	45.00	22.50	13.50
(27)	Meredith Hopkins	45.00	22.50	13.50
(28)	Irvine Jeffries	45.00	22.50	13.50
(29)	Monk Joyner	45.00	22.50	13.50
(30)	Fred Koster	45.00	22.50	13.50
(31)	Walter Mails	45.00	22.50	13.50
(32)	Chuck Marrow	45.00	22.50	13.50
(33)	Emmett McCann	45.00	22.50	13.50
(34)	Joe Mowry	45.00	22.50	13.50
(35)	Les Munns	45.00	22.50	13.50
(36)	George Murray	45.00	22.50	13.50
(37)	Floyd Newkirk	45.00	22.50	13.50
(38)	Leo Norris	45.00	22.50	13.50
(39)	Frank Packard	45.00	22.50	13.50
(40)	Ben Paschal	45.00	22.50	13.50
(41a)	Jess Petty/Throwing (Right foot off ground.)	45.00	22.50	13.50
(41b)	Jess Petty	45.00	22.50	13.50
(42)	Ray Radcliff	45.00	22.50	13.50
(43)	Larry Rosenthal	45.00	22.50	13.50
(44a)	Art Ruble	45.00	22.50	13.50
(44b)	Art Ruble	45.00	22.50	13.50
(45)	Art Shires	45.00	22.50	13.50
(46a)	Ernest Smith	45.00	22.50	13.50
(46b)	Ernest Smith	45.00	22.50	13.50
(47)	Ray Starr	45.00	22.50	13.50
(48)	Walter Tauscher	45.00	22.50	13.50
(49)	Myles Thomas	45.00	22.50	13.50
(50)	Phil Todt	45.00	22.50	13.50
(51)	Gene Trow	45.00	22.50	13.50
(52)	Hy Van Denburg	45.00	22.50	13.50
(53)	Elam Van Gilder	45.00	22.50	13.50
(54)	Charles Wilson	45.00	22.50	13.50
(55)	Ab. Wright	45.00	22.50	13.50
(56)	Emil Yde	45.00	22.50	13.50
(57)	Russ Young	45.00	22.50	13.50

Z

1911 Zeenut Pacific Coast League

Produced annually for 28 years, these Pacific Coast League cards were the longest-running and most popular baseball issues ever to appear on the West Coast. Issued by the Collins-McCarthy Candy Co. (later known as the Collins-Hencke Candy Co. and then simply the Collins Candy Co.) of San Francisco, Zeenut cards were inserted in boxes of the company's products: Zeenuts, Ruf-Neks and Home Run Kisses. All Zeenut cards issued from 1913 through 1937 had an approximately half-inch coupon at the bottom that could be redeemed for various prizes. Since most of these coupons were removed (and many not too carefully) Zeenuts are difficult to find in top condition today, and only a very small percentage survived with the coupon intact. (The sizes listed in the following descriptions are for cards without coupons.) Over the 28-year span, it is estimated that nearly 3,700 different cards were issued as part of the Zeenuts series, but new discoveries are still being made, and the checklist continues to grow. It is sometimes difficult to differentiate one year from another after 1930. Because it is so rare to find Zeenuts cards with the coupon still attached, values listed are for cards without the coupon. Cards with the coupon still intact will generally command a significant premium. The first Zeenut cards measure about 2-1/8" x 4" and feature a sepia-toned photo on a brown background surrounded by an off-white border. The backs of the cards are blank. Although the 1911 cards did not include the coupon bottom, some cards have been found with punch holes, indicating they may have also been used for redemptions. A total of 122 different players have been found.

		NM	EX	VG
Common Player:		200.00	85.00	50.00
(1)	Abbott	200.00	85.00	50.00
(2)	Ables	200.00	85.00	50.00
(3a)	Agnew (Large pose.)	200.00	85.00	50.00
(3b)	Agnew (Small pose.)	200.00	85.00	50.00
(4a)	Akin (Large pose.)	200.00	85.00	50.00
(4b)	Akin (Small pose.)	200.00	85.00	50.00
(5)	Frank Arellanes	200.00	85.00	50.00
(6a)	Arlett (Large pose.)	200.00	85.00	50.00
(6b)	Arlett (Middle size pose.)	200.00	85.00	50.00
(6c)	Arlett (Small pose.)	200.00	85.00	50.00
(7)	Barry	200.00	85.00	50.00
(8)	Baum	200.00	85.00	50.00
(9)	Bernard	200.00	85.00	50.00
(10)	Berry	200.00	85.00	50.00
(11)	Bohen	4,500	1,900	1,250
(12)	Brackenridge	200.00	85.00	50.00
(13)	Brashear	200.00	85.00	50.00
(14a)	Brown (Large pose.)	200.00	85.00	50.00
(14b)	Brown (Small pose.)	200.00	85.00	50.00
(15)	Browning	200.00	85.00	50.00
(16a)	Burrell (Large pose.)	200.00	85.00	50.00
(16b)	Burrell (Small pose.)	200.00	85.00	50.00
(17)	Byram	200.00	85.00	50.00
(18)	Carlisle	200.00	85.00	50.00
(19)	Carman	200.00	85.00	50.00
(20a)	Carson (Large pose.)	200.00	85.00	50.00
(20b)	Carson (Middle size pose.)	200.00	85.00	50.00
(20c)	Carson (Small pose.)	200.00	85.00	50.00
(21)	Castleton	200.00	85.00	50.00
(22)	Chadbourne	200.00	85.00	50.00
(23)	Christian	200.00	85.00	50.00
(24)	Couchman	200.00	85.00	50.00
(25)	Coy	200.00	85.00	50.00
(26)	Criger	200.00	85.00	50.00
(27)	Cutshaw	200.00	85.00	50.00
(28)	Daley	200.00	85.00	50.00
(29)	Danzig	200.00	85.00	50.00
(30)	Delhi	200.00	85.00	50.00
(31a)	Delmas (Large pose.)	200.00	85.00	50.00
(31b)	Delmas (Small pose.)	200.00	85.00	50.00
(32)	Dillon	200.00	85.00	50.00
(33a)	Discoll (Name incorrect.)	200.00	85.00	50.00
(33b)	Driscoll (Name correct.)	200.00	85.00	50.00
(34)	Dulin	200.00	85.00	50.00
(35)	Fanning	200.00	85.00	50.00
(36)	Fitzgerald	200.00	85.00	50.00
(37)	Flater	200.00	85.00	50.00
(38)	French	200.00	85.00	50.00
(39)	Fullerton	200.00	85.00	50.00
(40)	Gleason	200.00	85.00	50.00
(41)	Gregory	200.00	85.00	50.00
(42)	Halla	200.00	85.00	50.00
(43)	Harkness	200.00	85.00	50.00
(44a)	Heitmuller (Large pose.)	200.00	85.00	50.00
(44b)	Heitmuller (Small pose)	200.00	85.00	50.00
(45)	Henley	200.00	85.00	50.00
(46)	Hetling	200.00	85.00	50.00
(47)	Hiester	200.00	85.00	50.00
(48a)	Hitt (Large pose.)	200.00	85.00	50.00
(48b)	Hitt (Small pose.)	200.00	85.00	50.00
(50)	Hoffman	200.00	85.00	50.00
(51)	Hogan	200.00	85.00	50.00
(52a)	Holland (Large pose.)	200.00	85.00	50.00
(52b)	Holland (Small pose.)	200.00	85.00	50.00
(53)	Hosp	200.00	85.00	50.00
(54a)	Howard (Large pose.)	200.00	85.00	50.00
(54b)	Howard (Small pose.)	200.00	85.00	50.00
(55)	Kane	200.00	85.00	50.00
(56)	Kerns	200.00	85.00	50.00
(57)	Kilroy	200.00	85.00	50.00
(58)	Knight	200.00	85.00	50.00
(59)	Koestner	200.00	85.00	50.00
(60)	Krueger	200.00	85.00	50.00
(61)	Kuhn	200.00	85.00	50.00
(62)	LaLonge	200.00	85.00	50.00
(63)	Lerchen	200.00	85.00	50.00
(64)	Leverenz	200.00	85.00	50.00
(65)	Lewis	200.00	85.00	50.00
(66)	Bill Lindsay	200.00	85.00	50.00
(67)	Lober	200.00	85.00	50.00
(68)	Madden	200.00	85.00	50.00
(69)	Maggert	200.00	85.00	50.00
(70)	Mahoney	200.00	85.00	50.00
(71)	Martinoni	200.00	85.00	50.00
(72)	McArdle	200.00	85.00	50.00
(73)	McCredie	200.00	85.00	50.00
(74)	McDonnell	200.00	85.00	50.00
(75a)	McKune (Large pose.)	200.00	85.00	50.00
(75b)	McKune (Middle size pose.)	200.00	85.00	50.00
(75c)	McKune (Small pose.)	200.00	85.00	50.00
(76)	Meikle	200.00	85.00	50.00
(77)	Melchior	200.00	85.00	50.00
(78)	Metzger	200.00	85.00	50.00
(79)	Miller	200.00	85.00	50.00
(80)	Mitze	200.00	85.00	50.00
(81)	Mohler	200.00	85.00	50.00
(82a)	Moore (Large pose.)	200.00	85.00	50.00
(82b)	Moore (Small pose.)	200.00	85.00	50.00
(83a)	Moskiman (Lettering size large.)	200.00	85.00	50.00
(83b)	Moskiman (Lettering size small.)	200.00	85.00	50.00
(84)	Murray	200.00	85.00	50.00
(85)	Naylor	200.00	85.00	50.00
(86)	Nebinger	200.00	85.00	50.00
(87)	Nourse	200.00	85.00	50.00
(88a)	Noyes (Large pose.)	200.00	85.00	50.00
(88b)	Noyes (Small pose.)	200.00	85.00	50.00
(89)	O'Rourke	200.00	85.00	50.00
(90)	Patterson (Oakland)	200.00	85.00	50.00
(91)	Patterson (Vernon)	200.00	85.00	50.00
(92)	Pearce	200.00	85.00	50.00
(93)	Peckinpaugh	250.00	100.00	60.00
(94)	Pernoll	200.00	85.00	50.00
(95)	Pfyl	200.00	85.00	50.00
(96)	Powell	200.00	85.00	50.00
(97a)	Raleigh (Large pose.)	200.00	85.00	50.00
(97b)	Raleigh (Small pose.)	200.00	85.00	50.00
(98)	Rapps	200.00	85.00	50.00
(99)	Rodgers	200.00	85.00	50.00
(100a)	Ryan (Portland, box around name and team.)	300.00	125.00	75.00
(100b)	Ryan (Portland, no box around name and team.)	200.00	85.00	50.00
(101)	Ryan (San Francisco)	200.00	85.00	50.00
(102)	Seaton	200.00	85.00	50.00
(103)	Shaw	200.00	85.00	50.00
(104)	Sheehan	200.00	85.00	50.00
(105)	Shinn	200.00	85.00	50.00
106a	Smith (Los Angeles, large pose.)	200.00	85.00	50.00
(106b)	Smith (Los Angeles, small pose.)	200.00	85.00	50.00
(107a)	Smith (San Francisco, large pose.)	200.00	85.00	50.00
(107b)	Smith (San Francisco, small pose.)	200.00	85.00	50.00
(108)	Steen	200.00	85.00	50.00
(109)	Stewart	200.00	85.00	50.00
(110a)	Stinson (Large pose.)	200.00	85.00	50.00
(110b)	Stinson (Small pose.)	200.00	85.00	50.00
(111)	Sutor	200.00	85.00	50.00
(112)	Tennant	200.00	85.00	50.00
(113)	Thomas	200.00	85.00	50.00
(114)	Thompson	200.00	85.00	50.00
(115)	Thornton	200.00	85.00	50.00
(116)	Tiedeman	200.00	85.00	50.00
(117)	Van Buren	200.00	85.00	50.00
(118)	Vitt	200.00	85.00	50.00
(119)	Wares	200.00	85.00	50.00
(120)	Buck Weaver	14,000	5,500	3,500
(121)	Wolverton	200.00	85.00	50.00
(122)	Zacher	200.00	85.00	50.00
(123)	Zamloch	200.00	85.00	50.00

1912 Zeenut Pacific Coast League

The second series of Zeenut cards measure about 2-1/8" x 4-1/16" and featured sepia-toned photographs on a brown background with no border. Most cards have blank backs, but some have been found with printing advising collectors to "Save Zeenut pictures for valuable premiums," or with one of two sizes of a Bardell logo. The checklist consists of 158 subjects, but more cards are still being discovered. Zeenut cards which were redeemed for prizes will exhibit a hole-punch cancellation, often heart-shaped.

		NM	EX	VG
Common Player:		100.00	45.00	25.00
(1)	Abbott	100.00	45.00	25.00
(2)	Ables	100.00	45.00	25.00
(3)	Agnew	100.00	45.00	25.00
(4)	Altman	100.00	45.00	25.00
(5)	Frank Arellanes	100.00	45.00	25.00
(6)	Auer	100.00	45.00	25.00
(7)	Baker (Horizontal pose.)	100.00	45.00	25.00
(8)	Baker (Vertical pose.)	100.00	45.00	25.00
(9)	Bancroft	1,200	550.00	300.00
(10)	Baum	100.00	45.00	25.00
(11)	Bayless	100.00	45.00	25.00
(12)	Berger	100.00	45.00	25.00
(13)	Berry	100.00	45.00	25.00
(14)	Bohen	100.00	45.00	25.00
(15)	Boles	100.00	45.00	25.00
(16)	Bonner	100.00	45.00	25.00
(17)	Boone	100.00	45.00	25.00
(18)	Brackenridge	100.00	45.00	25.00
(19)	Brashear	100.00	45.00	25.00
(20)	Breen	100.00	45.00	25.00
(21)	Brooks (Los Angeles)	100.00	45.00	25.00
(22)	Brooks (Oakland)	100.00	45.00	25.00
(23)	Brown	100.00	45.00	25.00
(24)	Burch	100.00	45.00	25.00
(25)	Burrell	100.00	45.00	25.00
(26)	Butcher	100.00	45.00	25.00
(27)	Butler	100.00	45.00	25.00
(28)	Byram	100.00	45.00	25.00
(29)	Carlisle	100.00	45.00	25.00
(30)	Carson	100.00	45.00	25.00
(31)	Castleton	100.00	45.00	25.00
(32)	Chadbourne	100.00	45.00	25.00
(33)	Chech	100.00	45.00	25.00
(34)	Cheek	100.00	45.00	25.00
(35)	Christian	100.00	45.00	25.00
(36)	Cook	100.00	45.00	25.00
(37)	Core	100.00	45.00	25.00
(38)	Corhan	100.00	45.00	25.00
(39)	Coy	100.00	45.00	25.00
(40)	Daley	100.00	45.00	25.00
(41)	Delhi	100.00	45.00	25.00
(42)	Dillon	100.00	45.00	25.00
(43)	Doane	100.00	45.00	25.00
(44)	Driscoll	100.00	45.00	25.00
(45)	Durbin	100.00	45.00	25.00
(46)	Fanning	100.00	45.00	25.00
(47)	Felts	100.00	45.00	25.00
(48)	Fisher	100.00	45.00	25.00
(49)	Fitzgerald	100.00	45.00	25.00
(50)	Flater	100.00	45.00	25.00
(51)	Frick	100.00	45.00	25.00
(52)	Gaddy	100.00	45.00	25.00
(53)	Gedeon	100.00	45.00	25.00
(54)	Gilligan	100.00	45.00	25.00
(55)	Girot	100.00	45.00	25.00
(56)	Gray	100.00	45.00	25.00
(57)	Gregg	100.00	45.00	25.00
(58)	Gregory	100.00	45.00	25.00
(59)	Halla	100.00	45.00	25.00
(60)	Hamilton (Oakland)	100.00	45.00	25.00
(61)	Hamilton (San Francisco)	100.00	45.00	25.00
(62)	Harkness	100.00	45.00	25.00
(63)	Hartley	100.00	45.00	25.00
(64)	Heitmuller	100.00	45.00	25.00
(65)	Henley	100.00	45.00	25.00
(66)	Hetling (Glove open.)	100.00	45.00	25.00
(67)	Hetling (Glove closed.)	100.00	45.00	25.00
(68)	Hiester	100.00	45.00	25.00
(69)	Higginbottom	100.00	45.00	25.00
(70)	Hitt	100.00	45.00	25.00
(71)	Hoffman	100.00	45.00	25.00
(72)	Hogan	100.00	45.00	25.00
(73)	Hosp	100.00	45.00	25.00

		NM	EX	VG
(74)	Howard	100.00	45.00	25.00
(75)	Howley	100.00	45.00	25.00
(76)	Ireland	100.00	45.00	25.00
(77)	Jackson	100.00	45.00	25.00
(78)	Johnson	100.00	45.00	25.00
(79)	Kane	100.00	45.00	25.00
(80)	Killilay	100.00	45.00	25.00
(81)	Klawitter	100.00	45.00	25.00
(82)	Knight	100.00	45.00	25.00
(83)	Koestner ("P" visible.)	100.00	45.00	25.00
(84)	Koestner (No "P" visible.)	100.00	45.00	25.00
(85)	Kreitz	100.00	45.00	25.00
(86)	Krueger	100.00	45.00	25.00
(87)	LaLonge	100.00	45.00	25.00
(88)	Leard	100.00	45.00	25.00
(89)	Leverenz	100.00	45.00	25.00
(90)	Lewis	100.00	45.00	25.00
(91)	Bill Lindsay	100.00	45.00	25.00
(92)	Litschi	100.00	45.00	25.00
(93)	Lober	100.00	45.00	25.00
(94)	Madden	100.00	45.00	25.00
(95)	Mahoney	100.00	45.00	25.00
(96)	Malarkey	100.00	45.00	25.00
(97)	Martinoni	100.00	45.00	25.00
(98)	McArdle	100.00	45.00	25.00
(99)	McAvoy	100.00	45.00	25.00
(100)	McCorrey	100.00	45.00	25.00
(101)	McCredie	100.00	45.00	25.00
(102)	McDonald	100.00	45.00	25.00
(103)	McDowell	100.00	45.00	25.00
(104)	McIver	100.00	45.00	25.00
(105)	Meikle	100.00	45.00	25.00
(106)	Metzger	100.00	45.00	25.00
(107)	Miller (Sacramento)	100.00	45.00	25.00
(108)	Miller (San Francisco)	100.00	45.00	25.00
(109)	Mitze	100.00	45.00	25.00
(110)	Mohler	100.00	45.00	25.00
(111)	Moore	100.00	45.00	25.00
(112)	Mundorf/Btg	100.00	45.00	25.00
(113)	Mundorf/Fielding	100.00	45.00	25.00
(114)	Nagle	100.00	45.00	25.00
(115)	Noyes	100.00	45.00	25.00
(116)	O'Rourke	100.00	45.00	25.00
(117)	Olmstead	100.00	45.00	25.00
(118)	Orr	100.00	45.00	25.00
(119)	Page	100.00	45.00	25.00
(120)	Parkins	100.00	45.00	25.00
(121)	Patterson (Oakland)	100.00	45.00	25.00
(122)	Patterson (Vernon)	100.00	45.00	25.00
(123)	Pernol	100.00	45.00	25.00
(124)	Pope	100.00	45.00	25.00
(125)	Powell	100.00	45.00	25.00
(126)	Price	100.00	45.00	25.00
(127)	Raftery	100.00	45.00	25.00
(128)	Raleigh	100.00	45.00	25.00
(129)	Rapps ("P" visible.)	100.00	45.00	25.00
(130)	Rapps (No "P" visible.)	100.00	45.00	25.00
(131)	Reidy	100.00	45.00	25.00
(132)	Rodgers	100.00	45.00	25.00
(133)	Rohrer	100.00	45.00	25.00
(134)	Schmidt	100.00	45.00	25.00
(135)	Schwenk	100.00	45.00	25.00
(136)	Sharpe	100.00	45.00	25.00
(137)	Sheehan	100.00	45.00	25.00
(138)	Shinn	100.00	45.00	25.00
(139)	Slagle	100.00	45.00	25.00
(140)	Smith	100.00	45.00	25.00
(141)	Stewart	100.00	45.00	25.00
(142)	Stinson	100.00	45.00	25.00
(143)	Stone	100.00	45.00	25.00
(144)	Sullivan	100.00	45.00	25.00
(145)	Swain	100.00	45.00	25.00
(146)	Taylor	100.00	45.00	25.00
(147)	Temple	100.00	45.00	25.00
(148)	Tiedeman	100.00	45.00	25.00
(149)	Toner	100.00	45.00	25.00
(150)	Tozer	100.00	45.00	25.00
(151)	Van Buren	100.00	45.00	25.00
(152)	Wagner	100.00	45.00	25.00
(153)	Whalen	100.00	45.00	25.00
(154)	Williams (Sacramento)	100.00	45.00	25.00
(155)	Williams (San Francisco)	100.00	45.00	25.00
(156)	Joe Williams	100.00	45.00	25.00
(157)	Wuffli	100.00	45.00	25.00
(158)	Zacher	100.00	45.00	25.00
(159)	Zimmerman	100.00	45.00	25.00

1913 Zeenut Pacific Coast League

The 1913 Zeenut cards measure about 2" x 3-3/4" without the coupon, and feature black-and-white photos on a white, borderless background. To date, 146 different poses have been found. The backs are blank.

		NM	EX	VG
	Common Player:	100.00	45.00	25.00
(1)	Abbott	100.00	45.00	25.00
(2)	Ables	100.00	45.00	25.00
(3)	Frank Arelanes (Arellanes)	100.00	45.00	25.00
(4)	Arlett	100.00	45.00	25.00
(5)	Baker	100.00	45.00	25.00
(6)	Baum	100.00	45.00	25.00
(7)	Bayless	100.00	45.00	25.00
(8)	Becker	100.00	45.00	25.00
(9)	Berry	100.00	45.00	25.00
(10)	Bliss	100.00	45.00	25.00
(11)	Boles	100.00	45.00	25.00
(12)	Brackenridge	100.00	45.00	25.00
(13)	Brashear	100.00	45.00	25.00
(14)	Brooks	100.00	45.00	25.00
(15)	Byrnes	100.00	45.00	25.00
(16)	Cadreau	100.00	45.00	25.00
(17)	Carlisle	100.00	45.00	25.00
(18)	Carson	100.00	45.00	25.00
(19)	Cartwright	100.00	45.00	25.00
(20)	Chadbourne	100.00	45.00	25.00
(21)	Charles	100.00	45.00	25.00
(22)	Cheek	100.00	45.00	25.00
(23)	Christian	100.00	45.00	25.00
(24)	Clarke	100.00	45.00	25.00
(25)	Clemons	100.00	45.00	25.00
(26)	Cook	100.00	45.00	25.00
(27)	Corhan	100.00	45.00	25.00
(28)	Coy	100.00	45.00	25.00
(29)	Crabb	100.00	45.00	25.00
(30)	Crisp	100.00	45.00	25.00
(31)	Derrick	100.00	45.00	25.00
(32)	DeCanniere	100.00	45.00	25.00
(33)	Dillon	100.00	45.00	25.00
(34)	Doane	100.00	45.00	25.00
(35)	Douglass	100.00	45.00	25.00
(36)	Downs	100.00	45.00	25.00
(37)	Driscoll	100.00	45.00	25.00
(38)	Drucke	100.00	45.00	25.00
(39)	Elliott	100.00	45.00	25.00
(40)	Ellis	100.00	45.00	25.00
(41)	Fanning	100.00	45.00	25.00
(42)	Fisher	100.00	45.00	25.00
(43)	Fitzgerald	100.00	45.00	25.00
(44)	Gardner	100.00	45.00	25.00
(45)	Gill	100.00	45.00	25.00
(46)	Goodwin	100.00	45.00	25.00
(47a)	Gregory (Large pose.)	100.00	45.00	25.00
(47b)	Gregory (Small pose.)	100.00	45.00	25.00
(48)	Grey	100.00	45.00	25.00
(49)	Guest	100.00	45.00	25.00
(50)	Hagerman	100.00	45.00	25.00
(51)	Halla	100.00	45.00	25.00
(52)	Hallinan	100.00	45.00	25.00
(53)	Harry Heilmann	1,200	550.00	300.00
(54)	Henley	100.00	45.00	25.00
(55)	Hetling	100.00	45.00	25.00
(56)	Higginbotham	100.00	45.00	25.00
(57)	Hitt	100.00	45.00	25.00
(58)	Hoffman	100.00	45.00	25.00
(59)	Hogan (San Francisco)	100.00	45.00	25.00
(60)	Hogan (Vernon)	100.00	45.00	25.00
(61)	Hosp	100.00	45.00	25.00
(62)	Howard (Los Angeles)	100.00	45.00	25.00
(63)	Howard (San Francisco)	100.00	45.00	25.00
(64)	Hughes	100.00	45.00	25.00
(65)	Jackson	100.00	45.00	25.00
(66)	James	100.00	45.00	25.00
(67)	Johnson	100.00	45.00	25.00
(68)	Johnston	100.00	45.00	25.00
(69)	Kane	100.00	45.00	25.00
(70)	Kaylor	100.00	45.00	25.00
(71)	Kenworthy	100.00	45.00	25.00
(72)	Killilay	100.00	45.00	25.00
(73)	Klawitter	100.00	45.00	25.00
(74)	Koestner	100.00	45.00	25.00
(75)	Kores	100.00	45.00	25.00
(76)	Krapp	100.00	45.00	25.00
(77)	Kreitz	100.00	45.00	25.00
(78)	Krause	100.00	45.00	25.00
(79)	Krueger	100.00	45.00	25.00
(80)	Leard	100.00	45.00	25.00
(81)	Leifield	100.00	45.00	25.00
(82)	Lewis	100.00	45.00	25.00
(83)	Bill Lindsay	100.00	45.00	25.00
(84)	Litschi	100.00	45.00	25.00
(85)	Lively	100.00	45.00	25.00
(86)	Lober	100.00	45.00	25.00
(87)	Lohman	100.00	45.00	25.00
(88)	Maggart	100.00	45.00	25.00
(89)	Malarky	100.00	45.00	25.00
(90)	McArdle	100.00	45.00	25.00
(91)	McCarl	100.00	45.00	25.00
(92)	McCormick	100.00	45.00	25.00
(93)	McCorry	100.00	45.00	25.00
(94)	McCredie	100.00	45.00	25.00
(95)	McDonnell	100.00	45.00	25.00
(96)	Meloan	100.00	45.00	25.00
(97)	Metzger	100.00	45.00	25.00
(98)	Miller	100.00	45.00	25.00
(99)	Mitze	100.00	45.00	25.00
(100)	Moore	100.00	45.00	25.00
(101)	Moran	100.00	45.00	25.00
(102)	Mundorf	100.00	45.00	25.00
(103)	Munsell	100.00	45.00	25.00
(104)	Ness	100.00	45.00	25.00
(105)	O'Rourke	100.00	45.00	25.00
(106)	Overall	100.00	45.00	25.00
(107)	Page	100.00	45.00	25.00
(108)	Parkin	100.00	45.00	25.00
(109)	Patterson	100.00	45.00	25.00
(110)	Pearce	100.00	45.00	25.00
(111)	Pernoll	100.00	45.00	25.00
(112)	Perritt	100.00	45.00	25.00
(113)	Pope	100.00	45.00	25.00
(114)	Pruitt	100.00	45.00	25.00
(115)	Raleigh	100.00	45.00	25.00
(116)	Reitmyer	100.00	45.00	25.00
(117)	Riordan	100.00	45.00	25.00
(118)	Rodgers	100.00	45.00	25.00
(119)	Rogers	100.00	45.00	25.00
(120)	Rohrer	100.00	45.00	25.00
(121)	Ryan	100.00	45.00	25.00
(122)	Schaller	100.00	45.00	25.00
(123)	Schirm	100.00	45.00	25.00
(124)	Schmidt	100.00	45.00	25.00
(125)	Schulz	100.00	45.00	25.00
(126)	Sepulveda	100.00	45.00	25.00
(127)	Shinn	100.00	45.00	25.00
(128)	Spenger	100.00	45.00	25.00
(129)	Stanley	100.00	45.00	25.00
(130)	Stanridge	100.00	45.00	25.00
(131)	Stark	100.00	45.00	25.00
(132)	Sterritt	100.00	45.00	25.00
(133)	Stroud	100.00	45.00	25.00
(134)	Tennant	100.00	45.00	25.00
(135)	Thomas	100.00	45.00	25.00
(136)	Todd	100.00	45.00	25.00
(137)	Tonneman	100.00	45.00	25.00
(138)	Tozer	100.00	45.00	25.00
(139)	Van Buren	100.00	45.00	25.00
(140)	Wagner	100.00	45.00	25.00
(141)	West	100.00	45.00	25.00
(142)	Williams	100.00	45.00	25.00
(143)	Wolverton	100.00	45.00	25.00
(144)	Wotell	100.00	45.00	25.00
(145)	Wuffli	100.00	45.00	25.00
(146)	Young	100.00	45.00	25.00
(147)	Zacher	100.00	45.00	25.00
(148)	Zimmerman	100.00	45.00	25.00

The Mint-Mint examples of vintage cards carry a significant premium over the Near Mint values shown here. This premium reflects limited availability of the highest-grade cards as well as demand for particular cards or sets in the best possible condition.

1914 Zeenut Pacific Coast League

The 1914 Zeenut cards measure about 2" x 4-1/16" without the coupon, and feature black-and-white photos on a gray, borderless background. To date, 146 different poses have been found. The backs are blank.

		NM	EX	VG
	Common Player:	75.00	35.00	17.00
(1)	Ables	75.00	35.00	17.00
(2)	Abstein	75.00	35.00	17.00
(3)	Alexander	75.00	35.00	17.00
(4)	Arbogast	75.00	35.00	17.00
(5)	Arlett	75.00	35.00	17.00
(6)	Frank Arrelanes (Arellanes)	75.00	35.00	17.00
(7)	Bancroft	450.00	210.00	100.00
(8)	Barham	75.00	35.00	17.00
(9)	Barrenkamp	75.00	35.00	17.00
(10)	Barton	75.00	35.00	17.00
(11)	Baum	75.00	35.00	17.00
(12)	Bayless	75.00	35.00	17.00
(13a)	Bliss (Large pose.)	75.00	35.00	17.00
(13b)	Bliss (Small pose.)	75.00	35.00	17.00
(14)	Boles	75.00	35.00	17.00
(15)	Borton	75.00	35.00	17.00
(16)	Brashear	75.00	35.00	17.00
(17)	Brenegan	75.00	35.00	17.00
(18)	Brooks	75.00	35.00	17.00
(19)	Brown	75.00	35.00	17.00
(20)	Butler	75.00	35.00	17.00
(21)	Jacinto Calvo	350.00	165.00	80.00
(22)	Carlisle	75.00	35.00	17.00
(23)	Cartwright	75.00	35.00	17.00
(24)	Charles	75.00	35.00	17.00
(25)	Chech	75.00	35.00	17.00
(26)	Christian	75.00	35.00	17.00
(27)	Clarke	75.00	35.00	17.00
(28)	Colligan	75.00	35.00	17.00
(29)	Cook	75.00	35.00	17.00
(31)	Coy	75.00	35.00	17.00
(32)	Crabb	75.00	35.00	17.00
(33)	Davis	75.00	35.00	17.00
(34)	Derrick	75.00	35.00	17.00
(35)	Devlin	75.00	35.00	17.00
(36)	DeCannier	75.00	35.00	17.00
(37)	Dillon	75.00	35.00	17.00
(38)	Doane	75.00	35.00	17.00
(39)	Downs	75.00	35.00	17.00
(40)	Ehmke	75.00	35.00	17.00
(41)	Ellis	75.00	35.00	17.00
(42)	Evans	75.00	35.00	17.00
(43)	Fanning	75.00	35.00	17.00
(44)	Fisher	75.00	35.00	17.00
(45)	Fitzgerald	75.00	35.00	17.00
(46)	Fleharty	75.00	35.00	17.00
(47)	Frambach	75.00	35.00	17.00
(48)	Gardner	75.00	35.00	17.00
(49)	Gedeon	75.00	35.00	17.00
(50)	Geyer	75.00	35.00	17.00
(51)	Gianini	75.00	35.00	17.00
(52)	Gregory	75.00	35.00	17.00
(53)	Guest	75.00	35.00	17.00
(54)	Hallinan	75.00	35.00	17.00
(55)	Hannah	75.00	35.00	17.00
(56)	Harkness/Btg	75.00	35.00	17.00
(57)	Haworth/Btg	75.00	35.00	17.00
(58)	Haworth/Catching	75.00	35.00	17.00
(59)	Henderson	75.00	35.00	17.00
(60)	Henley	75.00	35.00	17.00
(61)	Hern	75.00	35.00	17.00

(62)	Hettling	75.00	35.00	17.00
(63)	Higginbotham	75.00	35.00	17.00
(64)	Hitt	75.00	35.00	17.00
(65)	Hogan	75.00	35.00	17.00
(66a)	Hosp (Large pose.)	75.00	35.00	17.00
(66b)	Hosp (Small pose.)	75.00	35.00	17.00
(67)	Howard	75.00	35.00	17.00
(68)	Hughes (Los Angeles)	75.00	35.00	17.00
(69)	Hughes (San Francisco)	75.00	35.00	17.00
(70)	Johnson	75.00	35.00	17.00
(71)	Kane	75.00	35.00	17.00
(72)	Kaylor	75.00	35.00	17.00
(73)	Killilay	75.00	35.00	17.00
(74)	Klawitter	75.00	35.00	17.00
(75)	Klepfler	75.00	35.00	17.00
(76)	Kores	75.00	35.00	17.00
(77)	Kramer	75.00	35.00	17.00
(78)	Krause	75.00	35.00	17.00
(79a)	Leard (Large pose.)	75.00	35.00	17.00
(79b)	Leard (Small pose.)	75.00	35.00	17.00
(80)	Liefeld	75.00	35.00	17.00
(81)	Litschi	75.00	35.00	17.00
(82)	Lober	75.00	35.00	17.00
(83)	Loomis	75.00	35.00	17.00
(84)	Love	75.00	35.00	17.00
(85)	Lynn	75.00	35.00	17.00
(86)	Maggart	75.00	35.00	17.00
(87)	Malarkey	75.00	35.00	17.00
(88)	Martinoni	75.00	35.00	17.00
(89)	McArdle	75.00	35.00	17.00
(90)	McCredie	75.00	35.00	17.00
(91)	McDonald	75.00	35.00	17.00
(92)	Meek	75.00	35.00	17.00
(93)	Meloan	75.00	35.00	17.00
(94)	Menges	75.00	35.00	17.00
(95)	Metzger	75.00	35.00	17.00
(96)	Middleton	75.00	35.00	17.00
(97)	Mitze	75.00	35.00	17.00
(98)	Mohler	75.00	35.00	17.00
(99)	Moore	75.00	35.00	17.00
(100)	Moran	75.00	35.00	17.00
(101)	Mundorf	75.00	35.00	17.00
(102)	Murphy	75.00	35.00	17.00
(103)	Musser	75.00	35.00	17.00
(104)	Ness	75.00	35.00	17.00
(105)	O'Leary	75.00	35.00	17.00
(106)	Orr	75.00	35.00	17.00
(107)	Page	75.00	35.00	17.00
(108)	Pape	75.00	35.00	17.00
(109)	Parkin	75.00	35.00	17.00
(110a)	Peet (Large pose.)	75.00	35.00	17.00
(110b)	Peet (Small pose.)	75.00	35.00	17.00
(111)	Perkins	75.00	35.00	17.00
(112)	Pernoll	75.00	35.00	17.00
(113)	Perritt	75.00	35.00	17.00
(114)	Powell	75.00	35.00	17.00
(115)	Prough	75.00	35.00	17.00
(116)	Pruiett	75.00	35.00	17.00
(117)	Quinlan	75.00	35.00	17.00
(118a)	Raney (Incorrect spelling.)	75.00	35.00	17.00
(118b)	Ramey (Correct spelling.)	75.00	35.00	17.00
(119)	Rieger	75.00	35.00	17.00
(120)	Rodgers	75.00	35.00	17.00
(121)	Rogers	75.00	35.00	17.00
(122)	Rohrer	75.00	35.00	17.00
(123)	Ryan	75.00	35.00	17.00
(124)	Ryan	75.00	35.00	17.00
(125)	Sawyer	75.00	35.00	17.00
(126)	Schaller	75.00	35.00	17.00
(127)	Schmidt	75.00	35.00	17.00
(128)	Sepulveda	75.00	35.00	17.00
(129)	Shinn	75.00	35.00	17.00
(130)	Slagle	75.00	35.00	17.00
(131)	Speas	75.00	35.00	17.00
(132)	Stanridge	75.00	35.00	17.00
(133)	Stroud	75.00	35.00	17.00
(134)	Tennant	75.00	35.00	17.00
(135)	Tobin	75.00	35.00	17.00
(136)	Tozer	75.00	35.00	17.00
(137)	Van Buren	75.00	35.00	17.00
(138)	West	75.00	35.00	17.00
(139)	White	75.00	35.00	17.00
(140)	Wolter	75.00	35.00	17.00
(141)	Wolverton	75.00	35.00	17.00
(142)	Yantz	75.00	35.00	17.00
(143)	Young	75.00	35.00	17.00
(144)	Zacher	75.00	35.00	17.00
(145)	Zumwalt	75.00	35.00	17.00

1915 Zeenut Pacific Coast League

The 1915 Zeenut cards are dated on the front, making identification very easy. They measure about 2" x 3-3/4" without the coupon and feature a black-and-white photo on a light background. To date 141 different cards are known to exist. This year is among the toughest of all Zeenuts to find.

		NM	EX	VG
	Common Player:	100.00	45.00	25.00
	With Coupon:	900.00	400.00	240.00
(1)	Ables	100.00	45.00	25.00
(2)	Abstein	100.00	45.00	25.00
(3)	Alcock	100.00	45.00	25.00
(4)	Arbogast	100.00	45.00	25.00
(5)	Baerwald	100.00	45.00	25.00
(6)	Barbour	100.00	45.00	25.00
(7)	Bates	100.00	45.00	25.00
(8)	Baum	100.00	45.00	25.00
(9)	Bayless	100.00	45.00	25.00
(10)	Beatty	100.00	45.00	25.00
(11)	Beer	100.00	45.00	25.00
(12)	Benham	100.00	45.00	25.00
(13)	Berger	100.00	45.00	25.00
(14)	Beumiller	100.00	45.00	25.00
(15)	Blankenship	100.00	45.00	25.00
(16)	Block	100.00	45.00	25.00
(17)	Bodie	100.00	45.00	25.00
(18)	Boles	100.00	45.00	25.00
(19)	Boyd	100.00	45.00	25.00
(20)	Bromley	100.00	45.00	25.00
(21)	Brown	100.00	45.00	25.00
(22)	Burns	300.00	135.00	75.00
(23)	Carlisle	100.00	45.00	25.00
(24)	Carrisch	100.00	45.00	25.00
(25)	Charles	100.00	45.00	25.00
(26)	Chech	100.00	45.00	25.00
(27)	Christian	100.00	45.00	25.00
(28)	Clarke	100.00	45.00	25.00
(29)	Couch	100.00	45.00	25.00
(30)	Stan Covaleski (Coveleski)	1,200	550.00	300.00
(31)	Daniels	100.00	45.00	25.00
(32)	Davis	100.00	45.00	25.00
(33)	DeCanniere	100.00	45.00	25.00
(34)	Dent	100.00	45.00	25.00
(35)	Derrick	100.00	45.00	25.00
(36)	Dillon	100.00	45.00	25.00
(37)	Doane	100.00	45.00	25.00
(38)	Downs	100.00	45.00	25.00
(39)	Elliott	100.00	45.00	25.00
(40)	F. Elliott	100.00	45.00	25.00
(41)	Ellis	100.00	45.00	25.00
(42)	Evans	100.00	45.00	25.00
(43)	Fanning	100.00	45.00	25.00
(44)	Faye	100.00	45.00	25.00
(45)	Fisher	100.00	45.00	25.00
(46)	Fittery	100.00	45.00	25.00
(47)	Fitzgerald	100.00	45.00	25.00
(48)	Fromme	100.00	45.00	25.00
(49)	Gardiner	100.00	45.00	25.00
(50)	Gedeon	100.00	45.00	25.00
(51)	Gleischmann	100.00	45.00	25.00
(52)	Gregory	100.00	45.00	25.00
(53)	Guest	100.00	45.00	25.00
(54)	Hall	100.00	45.00	25.00
(55)	Halla	100.00	45.00	25.00
(56)	Hallinan	100.00	45.00	25.00
(57)	Hannah	100.00	45.00	25.00
(58)	Harper	100.00	45.00	25.00
(59)	Harry Heilmann	750.00	335.00	185.00
(60)	Henley	100.00	45.00	25.00
(61)	Hetling	100.00	45.00	25.00
(62)	Higginbotham	100.00	45.00	25.00
(63)	Hilliard	100.00	45.00	25.00
(64)	Hitt (Winding up.)	100.00	45.00	25.00
(65)	Hitt/Throwing	100.00	45.00	25.00
(66)	Hogan	100.00	45.00	25.00
(67)	Hosp	100.00	45.00	25.00
(68)	Howard	100.00	45.00	25.00
(69)	Hughes	100.00	45.00	25.00
(70)	Johnson	100.00	45.00	25.00
(71)	Jones	100.00	45.00	25.00
(72)	Kahler	100.00	45.00	25.00
(73)	Kane	100.00	45.00	25.00

(74)	Karr	100.00	45.00	25.00
(75)	Killilay	100.00	45.00	25.00
(76)	Klawitter	100.00	45.00	25.00
(77)	Koerner	100.00	45.00	25.00
(78)	Krause	100.00	45.00	25.00
(79)	Kuhn	100.00	45.00	25.00
(80)	LaRoy	100.00	45.00	25.00
(81)	Leard	100.00	45.00	25.00
(82)	Bill Lindsay	100.00	45.00	25.00
(83)	Litschi	100.00	45.00	25.00
(84)	Lober	100.00	45.00	25.00
(85)	Love	100.00	45.00	25.00
(86)	Lush	100.00	45.00	25.00
(87)	Maggart	100.00	45.00	25.00
(88)	Malarkey	100.00	45.00	25.00
(89)	Manda	100.00	45.00	25.00
(90)	Marcan	100.00	45.00	25.00
(91)	Martinoni	100.00	45.00	25.00
(92)	McAvoy	100.00	45.00	25.00
(93)	McCredie	100.00	45.00	25.00
(94)	McDonell	100.00	45.00	25.00
(95)	Fred McMullen (McMullin)	7,500	3,500	2,000
(96)	Meek	100.00	45.00	25.00
(97)	Meloan	100.00	45.00	25.00
(98)	Metzger	100.00	45.00	25.00
(99)	Middleton	100.00	45.00	25.00
(100)	Mitchell	100.00	45.00	25.00
(101)	Mitze	100.00	45.00	25.00
(102)	Morgan	100.00	45.00	25.00
(103)	Mundorff	100.00	45.00	25.00
(104)	Murphy	100.00	45.00	25.00
(105)	Ness	100.00	45.00	25.00
(106)	Nutt	100.00	45.00	25.00
(107)	Orr	100.00	45.00	25.00
(108)	Pernoll	100.00	45.00	25.00
(109)	Perritt	100.00	45.00	25.00
(110)	Piercey	100.00	45.00	25.00
(111)	Price	100.00	45.00	25.00
(112)	Prough	100.00	45.00	25.00
(113)	Prueitt	100.00	45.00	25.00
(114)	Purtell	100.00	45.00	25.00
(115)	Reed	100.00	45.00	25.00
(116)	Reisigl	100.00	45.00	25.00
(117)	Remneas	100.00	45.00	25.00
(118)	Swede Risberg	5,500	2,500	1,500
(119)	Rohrer	100.00	45.00	25.00
(120)	Russell	100.00	45.00	25.00
(121)	Ryan (Los Angeles)	100.00	45.00	25.00
(122)	Ryan	100.00	45.00	25.00
(123)	Schaller	100.00	45.00	25.00
(124)	Schmidt	100.00	45.00	25.00
(125)	Scoggins	100.00	45.00	25.00
(126)	Sepulveda	100.00	45.00	25.00
(127)	Shinn	100.00	45.00	25.00
(128)	Smith	100.00	45.00	25.00
(129)	Speas	100.00	45.00	25.00
(130)	Spencer	100.00	45.00	25.00
(132)	Tennant	100.00	45.00	25.00
(133)	Terry	100.00	45.00	25.00
(134)	Tobin	100.00	45.00	25.00
(135)	West	100.00	45.00	25.00
(136)	White	100.00	45.00	25.00
(137)	Claude Williams	5,500	2,500	1,500
(138)	Johnny Williams	250.00	110.00	65.00
(139)	Wolter	100.00	45.00	25.00
(140)	Wolverton	100.00	45.00	25.00
(141)	Zacher	100.00	45.00	25.00

1916 Zeenut Pacific Coast League

The 1916 Zeenuts measure about 2" x 3-3/4" without the coupon and are dated on the front (some cards were misdated 1915 however). The card fronts feature black-and-white photos on a blue background. There are 144 known subjects. The 1916 series is among the more difficult.

		NM	EX	VG
Common Player:		75.00	30.00	17.50
(1)	Autrey	75.00	30.00	17.50
(2)	Barbeau	75.00	30.00	17.50
(3)	Barry	75.00	30.00	17.50
(4)	Bassler	75.00	30.00	17.50
(5)	Bates	75.00	30.00	17.50
(6)	Baum	75.00	30.00	17.50
(7)	Bayless	75.00	30.00	17.50
(8)	Beer	75.00	30.00	17.50
(9)	Berg	75.00	30.00	17.50
(10)	Berger	75.00	30.00	17.50
(11)	Blankenship	75.00	30.00	17.50
(12)	Block	75.00	30.00	17.50
(13)	Bodie	75.00	30.00	17.50
(14)	Bohne	250.00	125.00	75.00
(15)	Boles	75.00	30.00	17.50
(16)	Boyd	75.00	30.00	17.50
(17)	Brief	75.00	30.00	17.50
(18)	Brooks	75.00	30.00	17.50
(19)	Brown	75.00	30.00	17.50
(20)	Butler	75.00	30.00	17.50
(21)	Callahan	75.00	30.00	17.50
(22)	Carrisch	75.00	30.00	17.50
(23)	Frank Chance	750.00	375.00	225.00
(24)	Jimmy Claxton	15,000	9,500	7,000
(25)	Coffey	75.00	30.00	17.50
(26)	Cook	75.00	30.00	17.50
(27)	Corbett	75.00	30.00	17.50
(28)	Couch	75.00	30.00	17.50
(29)	Crandall	75.00	30.00	17.50
(30)	Dalton	75.00	30.00	17.50
(31)	Davis	75.00	30.00	17.50
(32)	Derrick	75.00	30.00	17.50
(33)	Doane	75.00	30.00	17.50
(34)	Downs	75.00	30.00	17.50
(35)	Dugan	75.00	30.00	17.50
(36)	Eldred	75.00	30.00	17.50
(37)	F. Elliott	75.00	30.00	17.50
(38)	H. Elliott	75.00	30.00	17.50
(39)	Ellis	75.00	30.00	17.50
(40)	Erickson	75.00	30.00	17.50
(41)	Fanning	75.00	30.00	17.50
(42)	Fisher	75.00	30.00	17.50
(43)	Fittery	75.00	30.00	17.50
(44)	Fitzgerald	75.00	30.00	17.50
(45)	Fromme	75.00	30.00	17.50
(46)	Galloway	75.00	30.00	17.50
(47)	Gardner	75.00	30.00	17.50
(48)	Gay	75.00	30.00	17.50
(49)	Gleischmann	75.00	30.00	17.50
(50)	Griffith	75.00	30.00	17.50
(51)	Griggs	75.00	30.00	17.50
(52)	Guisto	75.00	30.00	17.50
(53)	Hagerman	75.00	30.00	17.50
(54)	Hall	75.00	30.00	17.50
(55)	Hallinan	75.00	30.00	17.50
(56)	Hannah	75.00	30.00	17.50
(57)	Harstadt	75.00	30.00	17.50
(58)	Haworth	75.00	30.00	17.50
(59)	Hess	75.00	30.00	17.50
(60)	Higginbotham	75.00	30.00	17.50
(61)	Hitt	75.00	30.00	17.50
(62)	Hogg	75.00	30.00	17.50
(63)	Hollocher	75.00	30.00	17.50
(64)	Horstman	75.00	30.00	17.50
(65)	Houck	75.00	30.00	17.50
(66)	Howard	75.00	30.00	17.50
(67)	Hughes	75.00	30.00	17.50
(68)	E. Johnston	75.00	30.00	17.50
(69)	G. Johnston	75.00	30.00	17.50
(70)	Jones	75.00	30.00	17.50
(71)	Kahler	75.00	30.00	17.50
(72)	Kane	75.00	30.00	17.50
(73)	Kelly	75.00	30.00	17.50
(74)	Kenworthy	75.00	30.00	17.50
(75)	Klawitter	75.00	30.00	17.50
(76)	Klein	75.00	30.00	17.50
(77)	Koerner	75.00	30.00	17.50
(78)	Krause	75.00	30.00	17.50
(79)	Kuhn	75.00	30.00	17.50
(80)	Lane	75.00	30.00	17.50
(81)	Larsen	75.00	30.00	17.50
(82)	Lush	75.00	30.00	17.50
(83)	Machold	75.00	30.00	17.50
(84)	Maggert	75.00	30.00	17.50
(85)	Manser	75.00	30.00	17.50
(86)	Martin	75.00	30.00	17.50
(87)	Mattick	75.00	30.00	17.50
(88)	McCredie	75.00	30.00	17.50
(89)	McGaffigan	75.00	30.00	17.50
(90)	McLarry	75.00	30.00	17.50
(91)	Menges	75.00	30.00	17.50
(92)	Middleton	75.00	30.00	17.50
(93)	Mitchell	75.00	30.00	17.50
(94)	Mitze	75.00	30.00	17.50
(95)	Munsell	75.00	30.00	17.50
(96)	Murphy	75.00	30.00	17.50
(97)	Nixon	75.00	30.00	17.50
(98)	Noyes	75.00	30.00	17.50
(99)	Nutt	75.00	30.00	17.50
(100)	O'Brien	75.00	30.00	17.50
(101)	Oldham	75.00	30.00	17.50
(102)	Orr	75.00	30.00	17.50
(103)	Patterson	75.00	30.00	17.50
(104)	Perritt	75.00	30.00	17.50
(105)	Prough	75.00	30.00	17.50
(106)	Prueitt	75.00	30.00	17.50
(107)	Quinlan	75.00	30.00	17.50
(108)	Quinn (Portland)	75.00	30.00	17.50
(109)	Quinn (Vernon)	75.00	30.00	17.50
(110)	Rader	75.00	30.00	17.50
(111)	Randall	75.00	30.00	17.50
(112)	Rath	75.00	30.00	17.50
(113)	Reisegl	75.00	30.00	17.50
(114)	Reuther (Ruether)	75.00	30.00	17.50
(115)	Swede Risberg	5,000	2,000	1,250
(116)	Roche	75.00	30.00	17.50
(117)	Ryan	75.00	30.00	17.50
(118)	Ryan	75.00	30.00	17.50
(119)	Scoggins	75.00	30.00	17.50
(120)	Sepulveda	75.00	30.00	17.50
(121)	Schaller	75.00	30.00	17.50
(122)	Sheehan	75.00	30.00	17.50
(123)	Shinn	75.00	30.00	17.50
(124)	Smith	75.00	30.00	17.50
(125)	Sothoron	75.00	30.00	17.50
(126)	Southworth	75.00	30.00	17.50
(127)	Speas	75.00	30.00	17.50
(128)	Spencer	75.00	30.00	17.50
(129)	Standridge	75.00	30.00	17.50
(130)	Steen	75.00	30.00	17.50
(131)	Stumpf	75.00	30.00	17.50
(132)	Vann	75.00	30.00	17.50
(133)	Vaughn	75.00	30.00	17.50
(134)	Ward	75.00	30.00	17.50
(135)	Whalling	75.00	30.00	17.50
(136)	Wilie	75.00	30.00	17.50
(137)	Williams	75.00	30.00	17.50
(138)	Wolverton	75.00	30.00	17.50
(139)	Wuffli	75.00	30.00	17.50
(140)	Zabel	75.00	30.00	17.50
(141)	Zacher	75.00	30.00	17.50
(142)	Zimmerman	75.00	30.00	17.50

1917 Zeenut Pacific Coast League

The 1917 Zeenuts measure about 1-3/4" x 3-3/4" and feature black-and-white photos on a light background. They are dated on the front and have blank backs. An advertising poster has been found listing 119 players (two pose variations brings the total to 121), but to date, six players on the list have not been found.

		NM	EX	VG
Common Player:		70.00	35.00	20.00
(1)	Arlett	70.00	35.00	20.00
(2)	Frank Arrelanes (Arellanes)	70.00	35.00	20.00
(3)	Baker/Catching	70.00	35.00	20.00
(4)	Baker/Throwing	70.00	35.00	20.00
(5)	Baldwin	70.00	35.00	20.00
(6)	Bassler	70.00	35.00	20.00
(7)	Baum	70.00	35.00	20.00
(8)	Beer	70.00	35.00	20.00
(9)	Bernhard	70.00	35.00	20.00
(10)	Bliss	70.00	35.00	20.00
(11)	Boles	70.00	35.00	20.00
(12)	Brenton	70.00	35.00	20.00
(13)	Brief	70.00	35.00	20.00
(14)	Brown	70.00	35.00	20.00
(15)	Burns	70.00	35.00	20.00
(16)	Callahan	70.00	35.00	20.00
(17)	Callan	70.00	35.00	20.00
(18)	Jacinto Calvo	375.00	185.00	110.00

		NM	EX	VG
(19)	Chadbourne	70.00	35.00	20.00
(20)	Frank Chance	750.00	375.00	225.00
(21)	Coltrin	70.00	35.00	20.00
(22)	Connifer	70.00	35.00	20.00
(23)	Corhan	70.00	35.00	20.00
(24)	Crandall (Los Angeles)	70.00	35.00	20.00
(25)	Crandall (Salt Lake)	70.00	35.00	20.00
(26)	Cress	70.00	35.00	20.00
(27)	Davis	70.00	35.00	20.00
(28)	DeCanniere	70.00	35.00	20.00
(29)	Doane	70.00	35.00	20.00
(30)	Dougan	70.00	35.00	20.00
(31)	Dougherty	70.00	35.00	20.00
(32)	Downs	70.00	35.00	20.00
(33)	Dubuc	70.00	35.00	20.00
(34)	Ellis	70.00	35.00	20.00
(35)	Erickson	70.00	35.00	20.00
(36)	Evans	70.00	35.00	20.00
(37)	Farmer	70.00	35.00	20.00
(38)	Fincher	70.00	35.00	20.00
(39)	Fisher	70.00	35.00	20.00
(40)	Fitzgerald	70.00	35.00	20.00
(41)	Fournier	70.00	35.00	20.00
(42)	Fromme	70.00	35.00	20.00
(43)	Galloway	70.00	35.00	20.00
(44)	Gislason	70.00	35.00	20.00
(45)	Goodbred	70.00	35.00	20.00
(46)	Griggs	70.00	35.00	20.00
(47)	Groehling	70.00	35.00	20.00
(48)	Hall (Los Angeles)	70.00	35.00	20.00
(49)	Hall (San Francisco)	70.00	35.00	20.00
(50)	Hannah	70.00	35.00	20.00
(51)	Harstad	70.00	35.00	20.00
(52)	Helfrich	70.00	35.00	20.00
(53)	Hess	70.00	35.00	20.00
(54)	Hitt	70.00	35.00	20.00
(55)	Hoff	70.00	35.00	20.00
(56)	Hollacher	70.00	35.00	20.00
(57)	Hollywood	70.00	35.00	20.00
(58)	Houck	70.00	35.00	20.00
(59)	Howard	70.00	35.00	20.00
(60)	Hughes	70.00	35.00	20.00
(61)	Johnson	70.00	35.00	20.00
(62)	Kilhullen	70.00	35.00	20.00
(63)	Killiffer (Killefer)	70.00	35.00	20.00
(64)	Koerner	70.00	35.00	20.00
(65)	Krause	70.00	35.00	20.00
(66)	Lane	70.00	35.00	20.00
(67)	Lapan	70.00	35.00	20.00
(68)	Leake	70.00	35.00	20.00
(69)	Lee	70.00	35.00	20.00
(70)	Leverenz	70.00	35.00	20.00
(71)	Maggert	70.00	35.00	20.00
(72)	Maisel	70.00	35.00	20.00
(73)	Mattick	70.00	35.00	20.00
(74)	McCreedie	70.00	35.00	20.00
(75)	McLarry	70.00	35.00	20.00
(76)	Mensor	650.00	325.00	200.00
(77)	Emil "Irish" Meusel	350.00	175.00	100.00
(78)	Middleton	70.00	35.00	20.00
(79)	Miller/Btg	70.00	35.00	20.00
(80)	Miller/Throwing	70.00	35.00	20.00
(81)	Mitchell	70.00	35.00	20.00
(82)	Mitze	70.00	35.00	20.00
(83)	Murphy	70.00	35.00	20.00
(84)	Murray	70.00	35.00	20.00
(85)	O'Brien	70.00	35.00	20.00
(86)	O'Mara	70.00	35.00	20.00
(87)	Oldham	70.00	35.00	20.00
(88)	Orr	70.00	35.00	20.00
(89)	Penelli	70.00	35.00	20.00
(90)	Penner	70.00	35.00	20.00
(91)	Pick	70.00	35.00	20.00
(92)	Prough	70.00	35.00	20.00
(93)	Pruiett	70.00	35.00	20.00
(94)	Quinlan	70.00	35.00	20.00
(95)	Quinn	70.00	35.00	20.00
(96)	Rath	70.00	35.00	20.00
(97)	Roche	70.00	35.00	20.00
(98)	Ryan (Los Angeles)	70.00	35.00	20.00
(99)	Ryan (Salt Lake)	70.00	35.00	20.00
(100)	Schaller	70.00	35.00	20.00
(101)	Schinkle	70.00	35.00	20.00
(102)	Schultz	70.00	35.00	20.00
(103)	Sheehan	70.00	35.00	20.00
(104)	Sheeley	70.00	35.00	20.00
(105)	Shinn	70.00	35.00	20.00
(106)	Siglin	70.00	35.00	20.00
(107)	Simon	70.00	35.00	20.00
(108)	Smith	70.00	35.00	20.00
(109)	Snyder	70.00	35.00	20.00
(110)	Stanridge	70.00	35.00	20.00
(111)	Steen	70.00	35.00	20.00
(112)	Stovall	70.00	35.00	20.00
(113)	Stumpf	70.00	35.00	20.00
(114)	Sullivan	70.00	35.00	20.00
(115)	Terry	70.00	35.00	20.00
(116)	Tobin	70.00	35.00	20.00
(117)	Valencia	70.00	35.00	20.00
(118)	Vaughn	70.00	35.00	20.00
(119)	Whalling	70.00	35.00	20.00
(120)	Wilie	70.00	35.00	20.00
(121)	Wolverton	70.00	35.00	20.00

1918 Zeenut Pacific Coast League

The 1918 Zeenuts are among the most distinctive because of the red borders surrounding the photos. They measure about 1-13/16" x 3-5/8" and are among the more difficult years to find.

		NM	EX	VG
Common Player:		75.00	35.00	20.00
With Coupon:		800.00	400.00	240.00
(1)	Alcock	75.00	35.00	20.00
(2)	Arkenburg	75.00	35.00	20.00
(3)	A. Arlett	75.00	35.00	20.00
(4)	Baum	75.00	35.00	20.00
(5)	Boles	75.00	35.00	20.00
(6)	Borton	75.00	35.00	20.00
(7)	Brenton	75.00	35.00	20.00
(8)	Bromley	75.00	35.00	20.00
(9)	Brooks	75.00	35.00	20.00
(10)	Brown	75.00	35.00	20.00
(11)	Caldera	75.00	35.00	20.00
(12)	Camm (Kamm)	75.00	35.00	20.00
(13)	Chadbourne	75.00	35.00	20.00
(14)	Chappell	75.00	35.00	20.00
(15)	Codington	75.00	35.00	20.00
(16)	Conwright	75.00	35.00	20.00
(17)	Cooper	75.00	35.00	20.00
(18)	Cox	75.00	35.00	20.00
(19)	Crandall (Los Angeles)	75.00	35.00	20.00
(20)	Crandall (Salt Lake)	75.00	35.00	20.00
(21)	Crawford	900.00	450.00	275.00
(22)	Croll	75.00	35.00	20.00
(23)	Davis	75.00	35.00	20.00
(24)	DeVormer	75.00	35.00	20.00
(25)	Dobbs	75.00	35.00	20.00
(26)	Downs	75.00	35.00	20.00
(27)	Dubuc	75.00	35.00	20.00
(28)	Dunn	75.00	35.00	20.00
(29)	Easterly	75.00	35.00	20.00
(30)	Eldred	75.00	35.00	20.00
(31)	Elliot	75.00	35.00	20.00
(32)	Ellis	75.00	35.00	20.00
(33)	Essick	75.00	35.00	20.00
(34)	Farmer	75.00	35.00	20.00
(35)	Fisher	75.00	35.00	20.00
(36)	Fittery	75.00	35.00	20.00
(37)	Forsythe	75.00	35.00	20.00
(38)	Fournier	75.00	35.00	20.00
(39)	Fromme	75.00	35.00	20.00
(40)	Gardner (Oakland)	75.00	35.00	20.00
(41)	Gardner (Sacramento)	75.00	35.00	20.00
(42)	Goldie	75.00	35.00	20.00
(43)	Griggs	75.00	35.00	20.00
(44)	Hawkes	75.00	35.00	20.00
(45)	Hollander	75.00	35.00	20.00
(46)	Hosp	75.00	35.00	20.00
(47)	Howard	75.00	35.00	20.00
(48)	Hummel	75.00	35.00	20.00
(49)	Hunter	75.00	35.00	20.00
(50)	Johnson	75.00	35.00	20.00
(51)	G. Johnson	75.00	35.00	20.00
(52)	Kantlehner	75.00	35.00	20.00
(53)	Killefer	75.00	35.00	20.00
(54)	Koerner	75.00	35.00	20.00
(55)	Konnick	75.00	35.00	20.00
(56)	Kremer	75.00	35.00	20.00
(57)	Lapan	75.00	35.00	20.00
(58)	Leake	75.00	35.00	20.00
(59)	Leathers	75.00	35.00	20.00
(60)	Leifer	75.00	35.00	20.00

		NM	EX	VG
(61)	Leverenz	75.00	35.00	20.00
(62)	Llewlyn	75.00	35.00	20.00
(63)	Martin	75.00	35.00	20.00
(64)	McCabe	75.00	35.00	20.00
(65)	McCredie	75.00	35.00	20.00
(66)	McKee	75.00	35.00	20.00
(67)	McNulty	75.00	35.00	20.00
(68)	Mensor	500.00	250.00	150.00
(69)	Middleton	75.00	35.00	20.00
(70)	Miller (Oakland)	75.00	35.00	20.00
(71)	Miller (Salt Lake)	75.00	35.00	20.00
(72)	J. Mitchell	75.00	35.00	20.00
(73)	R. Mitchell	75.00	35.00	20.00
(74)	Mitze	75.00	35.00	20.00
(75)	Moore	75.00	35.00	20.00
(76)	Morton	75.00	35.00	20.00
(77)	Murray	75.00	35.00	20.00
(78)	O'Doul	450.00	225.00	135.00
(79)	Orr	75.00	35.00	20.00
(80)	Pepe	75.00	35.00	20.00
(81)	Pertica	75.00	35.00	20.00
(82)	Phillips	75.00	35.00	20.00
(83)	Pick	75.00	35.00	20.00
(84)	Pinelli	75.00	35.00	20.00
(85)	Prentice	75.00	35.00	20.00
(86)	Prough	75.00	35.00	20.00
(87)	Quinlan	75.00	35.00	20.00
(88)	Ritchie	75.00	35.00	20.00
(89)	Rogers	75.00	35.00	20.00
(90)	Ryan	75.00	35.00	20.00
(91)	Sand	75.00	35.00	20.00
(92)	Shader	75.00	35.00	20.00
(93)	Sheely	75.00	35.00	20.00
(94)	Siglin	75.00	35.00	20.00
(95)	Smale	75.00	35.00	20.00
(96)	Smith (Salt Lake City)	75.00	35.00	20.00
(97)	Smith (San Francisco)	200.00	100.00	60.00
(98)	Stanbridge	75.00	35.00	20.00
(99)	Terry	75.00	35.00	20.00
(100)	Valencia	75.00	35.00	20.00
(101)	West	75.00	35.00	20.00
(102)	Wilie	75.00	35.00	20.00
(103)	Williams	75.00	35.00	20.00
(104)	Wisterzill	75.00	35.00	20.00

1919 Zeenut Pacific Coast League

The 1919 Zeenuts cards are dated on the front and measure about 1-3/4" x 3-5/8". They featured borderless, sepia-toned photos. To date, 144 subjects exist in the series.

		NM	EX	VG
Common Player:		80.00	35.00	20.00
(1)	Ally	80.00	35.00	20.00
(2)	Fatty Arbuckle	5,500	2,750	1,650
(3)	A. Arlett	80.00	35.00	20.00
(4)	R. Arlett	80.00	35.00	20.00
(5)	Baker	80.00	35.00	20.00
(6)	Baldwin	80.00	35.00	20.00
(7)	Baum	80.00	35.00	20.00
(8)	Beck	80.00	35.00	20.00
(9)	Bigbee	80.00	35.00	20.00
(10)	Blue	80.00	35.00	20.00
(11)	Bohne	200.00	100.00	60.00
(12)	Boles	80.00	35.00	20.00
(13)	Borton	80.00	35.00	20.00
(14)	Bowman	80.00	35.00	20.00
(15)	Brooks	80.00	35.00	20.00
(16)	Brown	80.00	35.00	20.00
(17)	Byler	80.00	35.00	20.00
(18)	Caldera	80.00	35.00	20.00
(19)	Cavaney	80.00	35.00	20.00
(20)	Chadbourne	80.00	35.00	20.00
(21)	Chech	80.00	35.00	20.00
(22)	Church	80.00	35.00	20.00
(23)	Clymer	80.00	35.00	20.00
(24)	Coleman	80.00	35.00	20.00

		NM	EX	VG
(25)	Compton	80.00	35.00	20.00
(26)	Conkwright	80.00	35.00	20.00
(27)	Connolly	80.00	35.00	20.00
(28)	Cook	80.00	35.00	20.00
(29)	Cooper (Los Angeles)	80.00	35.00	20.00
(30)	Cooper (Oakland)	80.00	35.00	20.00
(31)	Cooper (Portland)	80.00	35.00	20.00
(32)	Corhan	80.00	35.00	20.00
(33)	Couch	80.00	35.00	20.00
(34)	Cox	80.00	35.00	20.00
(35)	Crandall (Los Angeles)	80.00	35.00	20.00
(36)	Crandall (San Francisco)	80.00	35.00	20.00
(37)	Crespi	80.00	35.00	20.00
(38)	Croll	80.00	35.00	20.00
(39)	Cunningham	80.00	35.00	20.00
(40)	Dawson	80.00	35.00	20.00
(41)	Dell	80.00	35.00	20.00
(42)	DeVormer	80.00	35.00	20.00
(43)	Driscoll	80.00	35.00	20.00
(44)	Eastley	80.00	35.00	20.00
(45)	Edington	80.00	35.00	20.00
(46)	Eldred	80.00	35.00	20.00
(47)	Elliott	80.00	35.00	20.00
(48)	Ellis	80.00	35.00	20.00
(49)	Essick	80.00	35.00	20.00
(50)	Fabrique	80.00	35.00	20.00
(51)	Falkenberg	80.00	35.00	20.00
(52)	Fallentine	80.00	35.00	20.00
(53)	Finneran	80.00	35.00	20.00
(54)	Fisher (Sacramento)	80.00	35.00	20.00
(55)	Fisher (Vernon)	80.00	35.00	20.00
(56)	Fitzgerald	80.00	35.00	20.00
(57)	Flannigan	80.00	35.00	20.00
(58)	Fournier	80.00	35.00	20.00
(59)	French	80.00	35.00	20.00
(60)	Fromme	80.00	35.00	20.00
(61)	Gibson	80.00	35.00	20.00
(62)	Griggs	80.00	35.00	20.00
(63)	Haney	80.00	35.00	20.00
(64)	Harper	80.00	35.00	20.00
(65)	Henkle	80.00	35.00	20.00
(66)	Herr	80.00	35.00	20.00
(67)	Hickey	80.00	35.00	20.00
(68)	High	80.00	35.00	20.00
(69)	Holling	80.00	35.00	20.00
(70)	Hosp	80.00	35.00	20.00
(71)	Houck	80.00	35.00	20.00
(72)	Howard	80.00	35.00	20.00
(73)	Kamm	80.00	35.00	20.00
(74)	Kenworthy	80.00	35.00	20.00
(75)	Killefer	80.00	35.00	20.00
(76)	King	80.00	35.00	20.00
(77)	Koehler	80.00	35.00	20.00
(78)	Koerner	80.00	35.00	20.00
(79)	Kramer (Oakland)	80.00	35.00	20.00
(80)	Kramer (San Francisco)	80.00	35.00	20.00
(81)	Land	80.00	35.00	20.00
(82)	Lane	80.00	35.00	20.00
(83)	Lapan	80.00	35.00	20.00
(84)	Larkin	80.00	35.00	20.00
(85)	Lee	80.00	35.00	20.00
(86)	Long	80.00	35.00	20.00
(87)	Mails	80.00	35.00	20.00
(88)	Mains	80.00	35.00	20.00
(89)	Maisel	80.00	35.00	20.00
(90)	Mathes	80.00	35.00	20.00
(91)	McCredie	80.00	35.00	20.00
(92)	McGaffigan	80.00	35.00	20.00
(93)	McHenry	80.00	35.00	20.00
(94)	McNulty	80.00	35.00	20.00
(95)	Meusel	80.00	35.00	20.00
(96)	Middleton	80.00	35.00	20.00
(97)	Mitchell	80.00	35.00	20.00
(98)	Mitze	80.00	35.00	20.00
(99)	Mulory	80.00	35.00	20.00
(100)	Murphy	80.00	35.00	20.00
(101)	Murray	80.00	35.00	20.00
(102)	Niehoff (Los Angeles)	80.00	35.00	20.00
(103)	Niehoff (Seattle)	80.00	35.00	20.00
(104)	Norse	80.00	35.00	20.00
(105)	Oldham	80.00	35.00	20.00
(106)	Orr	80.00	35.00	20.00
(107)	Penner	80.00	35.00	20.00
(108)	Pennington	80.00	35.00	20.00
(109)	Piercy	80.00	35.00	20.00
(110)	Pinelli	150.00	75.00	45.00
(111)	C. Prough	80.00	35.00	20.00
(112)	Rader	80.00	35.00	20.00
(113)	Reiger	80.00	35.00	20.00
(114)	Ritchie	80.00	35.00	20.00
(115)	Roach	80.00	35.00	20.00
(116)	Rodgers	80.00	35.00	20.00
(117)	Rumler	80.00	35.00	20.00
(118)	Sands	80.00	35.00	20.00
(119)	Schick	80.00	35.00	20.00
(120)	Schultz	80.00	35.00	20.00
(121)	Scott	80.00	35.00	20.00
(122)	Seaton	80.00	35.00	20.00
(123)	Sheely	80.00	35.00	20.00
(124)	Siglin	80.00	35.00	20.00
(125)	Smith	80.00	35.00	20.00
(126)	Bill Smith	80.00	35.00	20.00
(127)	Snell	80.00	35.00	20.00
(128)	Spangler	80.00	35.00	20.00
(129)	Speas	80.00	35.00	20.00
(130)	Spencer	80.00	35.00	20.00
(131)	Starasenich	80.00	35.00	20.00
(132)	Stumpf	80.00	35.00	20.00
(133)	Sutherland	80.00	35.00	20.00
(134)	Dazzy Vance	600.00	300.00	180.00
(135)	Walker	80.00	35.00	20.00
(136)	Walsh	80.00	35.00	20.00
(137)	Ware	80.00	35.00	20.00
(138)	Weaver	80.00	35.00	20.00
(139)	Westerzil	80.00	35.00	20.00
(140)	Wilhoit	80.00	35.00	20.00
(141)	Wilie	80.00	35.00	20.00
(142)	Willets	80.00	35.00	20.00
(143)	Zamloch	80.00	35.00	20.00
(144)	Zweifel	80.00	35.00	20.00

1920 Zeenut Pacific Coast League

The 1920 Zeenuts cards were dated on the front and measure about 1-3/4" x 3-5/8". They featured borderless, sepia-toned photos. To date, 151 have been found for 1920.

		NM	EX	VG
Common Player:		80.00	35.00	20.00
(1)	Adams	80.00	35.00	20.00
(2)	Agnew	80.00	35.00	20.00
(3)	Alcock	80.00	35.00	20.00
(4)	Aldrige	80.00	35.00	20.00
(5)	Andrews	80.00	35.00	20.00
(6)	Anfinson	80.00	35.00	20.00
(7)	A. Arlett	80.00	35.00	20.00
(8)	R. Arlett	80.00	35.00	20.00
(9)	Baker	80.00	35.00	20.00
(10)	Baldwin	80.00	35.00	20.00
(11)	Bassler	80.00	35.00	20.00
(12)	Baum	80.00	35.00	20.00
(13)	Blue	80.00	35.00	20.00
(14)	Bohne	200.00	100.00	60.00
(15)	Brenton	80.00	35.00	20.00
(16)	Bromley (Dark hat.)	80.00	35.00	20.00
(17)	Bromley (Light hat.)	80.00	35.00	20.00
(18)	Brown	80.00	35.00	20.00
(19)	Butler	80.00	35.00	20.00
(20)	Caveney	80.00	35.00	20.00
(21)	Chadbourne	80.00	35.00	20.00
(22)	Compton	80.00	35.00	20.00
(23)	Connolly	80.00	35.00	20.00
(24)	Cook	80.00	35.00	20.00
(25)	Corhan	80.00	35.00	20.00
(26)	Cox	80.00	35.00	20.00
(27)	K. Crandall	80.00	35.00	20.00
(28)	O. Crandall	80.00	35.00	20.00
(29)	Crawford	450.00	225.00	135.00
(30)	Cullop	80.00	35.00	20.00
(31)	Cunningham	80.00	35.00	20.00
(32)	DeVitalis	80.00	35.00	20.00
(33)	DeVormer	80.00	35.00	20.00
(34)	Dooley	80.00	35.00	20.00
(35)	Dorman	80.00	35.00	20.00
(36)	Dumovich	80.00	35.00	20.00
(37)	Dylar	80.00	35.00	20.00
(38)	Edington	80.00	35.00	20.00
(39)	Eldred	80.00	35.00	20.00
(40)	Ellis	80.00	35.00	20.00
(41)	Essick	80.00	35.00	20.00
(42)	Fisher	80.00	35.00	20.00
(43)	Fitzgerald	80.00	35.00	20.00
(44)	Fromme	80.00	35.00	20.00
(45)	Gardner	80.00	35.00	20.00
(46)	Ginglardi	80.00	35.00	20.00
(47)	Gough	80.00	35.00	20.00
(48)	Griggs	80.00	35.00	20.00
(49)	Guisto	80.00	35.00	20.00
(50)	Hamilton	80.00	35.00	20.00
(51)	Hanicy	80.00	35.00	20.00
(52)	Hartford	80.00	35.00	20.00
(53)	High	80.00	35.00	20.00
(54)	Hill	80.00	35.00	20.00
(55)	Hodges	80.00	35.00	20.00
(56)	Howard	80.00	35.00	20.00
(57)	James	80.00	35.00	20.00
(58)	Jenkins	80.00	35.00	20.00
(59)	Johnson (Portland)	80.00	35.00	20.00
(60)	Johnson (Salt Lake)	80.00	35.00	20.00
(61)	Jones	80.00	35.00	20.00
(62)	Juney	80.00	35.00	20.00
(63)	Kallio	80.00	35.00	20.00
(64)	Kamm	80.00	35.00	20.00
(65)	Keating	80.00	35.00	20.00
(66)	Kenworthy	80.00	35.00	20.00
(67)	Killeen	80.00	35.00	20.00
(68)	Killefer	80.00	35.00	20.00
(69)	Kingdon	80.00	35.00	20.00
(70)	Knight	80.00	35.00	20.00
(71)	Koehler	80.00	35.00	20.00
(72)	Koerner	80.00	35.00	20.00
(73)	Kopp	80.00	35.00	20.00
(74)	Kremer	80.00	35.00	20.00
(75)	Krug	80.00	35.00	20.00
(76)	Kunz	80.00	35.00	20.00
(77)	Lambert	80.00	35.00	20.00
(78)	Lane	80.00	35.00	20.00
(79)	Larkin	80.00	35.00	20.00
(80)	Leverenz	80.00	35.00	20.00
(81)	Long	80.00	35.00	20.00
(82)	Love	80.00	35.00	20.00
(83)	Maggart	80.00	35.00	20.00
(84)	Mails	80.00	35.00	20.00
(85)	Maisel	80.00	35.00	20.00
(86)	Matterson	80.00	35.00	20.00
(87)	Matteson	80.00	35.00	20.00
(88)	McAuley	80.00	35.00	20.00
(89)	McCredie	80.00	35.00	20.00
(90)	McGaffigan	80.00	35.00	20.00
(91)	McHenry	80.00	35.00	20.00
(92)	McQuaid	80.00	35.00	20.00
(93)	Miller	80.00	35.00	20.00
(94)	Mitchell	80.00	35.00	20.00
(95)	J. Mitchell	80.00	35.00	20.00
(96)	Mitchell	80.00	35.00	20.00
(97)	Mitze	80.00	35.00	20.00
(98)	Moffitt	80.00	35.00	20.00
(99)	Mollwitz	80.00	35.00	20.00
(100)	Morse	80.00	35.00	20.00
(101)	Mulligan	80.00	35.00	20.00
(102)	Murphy	80.00	35.00	20.00
(103)	Niehoff	80.00	35.00	20.00
(104)	Nixon	80.00	35.00	20.00
(105)	O'Shaughnessy	80.00	35.00	20.00
(106)	Orr	80.00	35.00	20.00
(107)	Paull	80.00	35.00	20.00
(108)	Penner	80.00	35.00	20.00
(109)	Pertica	80.00	35.00	20.00
(110)	Peterson	80.00	35.00	20.00
(111)	Polson	80.00	35.00	20.00
(112)	Prough	80.00	35.00	20.00
(113)	Reagan	80.00	35.00	20.00
(114)	Reiger	80.00	35.00	20.00
(115)	Reilly	80.00	35.00	20.00
(116)	Rheinhart	80.00	35.00	20.00
(117)	Rodgers	80.00	35.00	20.00
(118)	Ross	80.00	35.00	20.00
(119)	Rumler	80.00	35.00	20.00
(120)	Russell	80.00	35.00	20.00
(121)	Sands	80.00	35.00	20.00
(122)	Schaller	80.00	35.00	20.00
(123)	Schang	80.00	35.00	20.00
(124)	Schellenback	80.00	35.00	20.00
(125)	Schick	80.00	35.00	20.00
(126)	Schorr	80.00	35.00	20.00
(127)	Schroeder	80.00	35.00	20.00
(128)	Scott	80.00	35.00	20.00
(129)	Seaton	80.00	35.00	20.00
(130)	Sheely	80.00	35.00	20.00
(131)	Siebold	80.00	35.00	20.00
(132)	Siglin	80.00	35.00	20.00
(133)	Smith	80.00	35.00	20.00
(134)	G. Smith	80.00	35.00	20.00
(135)	Spellman	80.00	35.00	20.00
(136)	Spranger	80.00	35.00	20.00
(137)	Stroud	80.00	35.00	20.00
(138)	Stumpf	80.00	35.00	20.00
(139)	Sullivan	80.00	35.00	20.00
(140)	Sutherland	80.00	35.00	20.00
(141)	Thurston (Dark hat.)	80.00	35.00	20.00
(142)	Thurston (Light hat.)	80.00	35.00	20.00

		NM	EX	VG
(143)	Walsh	80.00	35.00	20.00
(144)	Wares	80.00	35.00	20.00
(145)	Weaver	80.00	35.00	20.00
(146)	Willie	80.00	35.00	20.00
(147)	Winn	80.00	35.00	20.00
(148)	Wisterzill	80.00	35.00	20.00
(149)	Worth	80.00	35.00	20.00
(150)	Yelle	80.00	35.00	20.00
(151)	Zamlock	80.00	35.00	20.00
(152)	Zeider	80.00	35.00	20.00

1921 Zeenut Pacific Coast League

The 1921 Zeenuts cards were dated on the front and measure about 1-3/4" x 3-11/16". They featured borderless, sepia-toned photos. To date, 168 different subjects have been discovered for 1921 (even though a promotional flier indicates 180 players).

		NM	EX	VG
Common Player:		60.00	25.00	15.00
With Coupon:		1,200	500.00	300.00
(1)	Adams	60.00	25.00	15.00
(2)	Alcock	60.00	25.00	15.00
(3)	Aldridge	60.00	25.00	15.00
(4)	Alton	60.00	25.00	15.00
(5)	Anfinson	60.00	25.00	15.00
(6)	Arlett	60.00	11.00	6.50
(7)	Baker	60.00	25.00	15.00
(8)	Baldwin	60.00	25.00	15.00
(9)	Bates	60.00	25.00	15.00
(10)	Berry	60.00	25.00	15.00
(11)	Blacholder	60.00	25.00	15.00
(12)	Blossom	60.00	25.00	15.00
(13)	Bourg	60.00	25.00	15.00
(14)	Brinley	60.00	25.00	15.00
(15)	Bromley	60.00	25.00	15.00
(16)	Brown	60.00	25.00	15.00
(17)	Brubaker	60.00	25.00	15.00
(18)	Butler	60.00	25.00	15.00
(19)	Byler	60.00	25.00	15.00
(20)	Carroll	60.00	25.00	15.00
(21)	Casey	60.00	25.00	15.00
(22)	Cather	60.00	25.00	15.00
(23)	Caveney	60.00	25.00	15.00
(24)	Chadbourne	60.00	25.00	15.00
(25)	Compton	60.00	25.00	15.00
(26)	Connel	60.00	25.00	15.00
(27)	Cook	60.00	25.00	15.00
(28)	Cooper	60.00	25.00	15.00
(29)	Couch	60.00	25.00	15.00
(30)	Cox	60.00	25.00	15.00
(31)	Crandall	60.00	25.00	15.00
(32)	Cravath	60.00	25.00	15.00
(33)	Crawford	450.00	225.00	135.00
(34)	Crumpler	60.00	25.00	15.00
(35)	Cunningham	60.00	25.00	15.00
(36)	Daley	60.00	25.00	15.00
(37)	Dell	60.00	25.00	15.00
(38)	Demaree	60.00	25.00	15.00
(39)	Douglas	60.00	25.00	15.00
(40)	Dumovich	60.00	25.00	15.00
(41)	Elliott	60.00	25.00	15.00
(42)	Ellis	60.00	25.00	15.00
(43)	Ellison	60.00	25.00	15.00
(44)	Essick	60.00	25.00	15.00
(45)	Faeth	60.00	25.00	15.00
(46)	Fisher	60.00	25.00	15.00
(47)	Fittery	60.00	25.00	15.00
(48)	Fitzgerald	60.00	25.00	15.00
(49)	Flaherty	60.00	25.00	15.00
(50)	Francis	60.00	25.00	15.00
(51)	French	60.00	25.00	15.00
(52)	Fromme	60.00	25.00	15.00
(53)	Gardner	60.00	25.00	15.00
(54)	Geary	60.00	25.00	15.00
(55)	Gennin	60.00	25.00	15.00
(56)	Gorman	60.00	25.00	15.00
(57)	Gould	60.00	25.00	15.00
(58)	Griggs	60.00	25.00	15.00
(59)	Hale	60.00	25.00	15.00
(60)	Hannah	60.00	25.00	15.00
(61)	Hansen	60.00	25.00	15.00
(62)	Hesse	60.00	25.00	15.00
(63)	High	60.00	25.00	15.00
(64)	Hughes	60.00	25.00	15.00
(65)	Hyatt	60.00	25.00	15.00
(66)	Jackson	60.00	25.00	15.00
(67)	Jacobs	60.00	25.00	15.00
(68)	Jacobs	60.00	25.00	15.00
(69)	Jenkins	60.00	25.00	15.00
(70)	Johnson	60.00	25.00	15.00
(71)	Jones	60.00	25.00	15.00
(72)	Jourden	60.00	25.00	15.00
(73)	Kallio	60.00	25.00	15.00
(74)	Kamm	60.00	25.00	15.00
(75)	Kearns	60.00	25.00	15.00
(76)	Kelly	60.00	25.00	15.00
(77)	Kersten	60.00	25.00	15.00
(78)	Kifer	60.00	25.00	15.00
(79)	Killefer	60.00	25.00	15.00
(80)	King	60.00	25.00	15.00
(81)	Kingdon	60.00	25.00	15.00
(82)	Knight	60.00	25.00	15.00
(83)	Koehler	60.00	25.00	15.00
(84)	Kopp	60.00	25.00	15.00
(85)	Krause	60.00	25.00	15.00
(86)	Kremer	60.00	25.00	15.00
(87)	Krug	60.00	25.00	15.00
(88)	Kunz	60.00	25.00	15.00
(89)	Lane	60.00	25.00	15.00
(90)	Leverenz	60.00	25.00	15.00
(91)	Lewis	60.00	25.00	15.00
(92)	Lindimore	60.00	25.00	15.00
(93)	Love	60.00	25.00	15.00
(94)	Ludolph	60.00	25.00	15.00
(95)	Lynn	60.00	25.00	15.00
(96)	Lyons	60.00	25.00	15.00
(97)	McAuley	60.00	25.00	15.00
(98)	McCredie	60.00	25.00	15.00
(99)	McGaffigan	60.00	25.00	15.00
(100)	McGraw	60.00	25.00	15.00
(101)	McQuaid	60.00	25.00	15.00
(102)	Merritt	60.00	25.00	15.00
(103)	Middleton	60.00	25.00	15.00
(104)	Miller	60.00	25.00	15.00
(105)	Mitchell	60.00	25.00	15.00
(106)	Mitze	60.00	25.00	15.00
(107)	Mollwitz	60.00	25.00	15.00
(108)	Morse	60.00	25.00	15.00
(109)	Murphy (Seattle)	60.00	25.00	15.00
(110)	Murphy (Vernon)	60.00	25.00	15.00
(111)	Mustain	60.00	25.00	15.00
(112)	Nickels	60.00	25.00	15.00
(113)	Niehaus	60.00	25.00	15.00
(114)	Niehoff	60.00	25.00	15.00
(115)	Nofziger	60.00	25.00	15.00
(116)	O'Connell	60.00	25.00	15.00
(117)	O'Doul	350.00	175.00	100.00
(118)	O'Malia	60.00	25.00	15.00
(119)	Oldring	60.00	25.00	15.00
(120)	Oliver	60.00	25.00	15.00
(121)	Orr	60.00	25.00	15.00
(122)	Paton	60.00	25.00	15.00
(123)	Penner	60.00	25.00	15.00
(124)	Pick	60.00	25.00	15.00
(125)	Pillette	60.00	25.00	15.00
(126)	Pinelli	60.00	25.00	15.00
(127)	Polson	60.00	25.00	15.00
(128)	Poole	60.00	25.00	15.00
(129)	Prough	60.00	25.00	15.00
(130)	Rath	60.00	25.00	15.00
(131)	Read	60.00	25.00	15.00
(132)	Reinhardt	60.00	25.00	15.00
(133)	Rieger	60.00	25.00	15.00
(134)	Rogers	60.00	25.00	15.00
(135)	Rose (Sacramento)	60.00	25.00	15.00
(136)	Rose (Salt Lake)	60.00	25.00	15.00
(137)	Ross (Portland)	60.00	25.00	15.00
(138)	Ross (Sacramento)	60.00	25.00	15.00
(139)	Ryan	60.00	25.00	15.00
(140)	Sand	60.00	25.00	15.00
(141)	Schick	60.00	25.00	15.00
(142)	Schneider	60.00	25.00	15.00
(143)	Scott	60.00	25.00	15.00
(144)	Shang	60.00	25.00	15.00
(145)	Sheehan	60.00	25.00	15.00
(146)	Shore	60.00	25.00	15.00
(147)	Shorr	60.00	25.00	15.00
(148)	Shultis	60.00	25.00	15.00
(149)	Siebold	60.00	25.00	15.00
(150)	Siglin	60.00	25.00	15.00
(151)	Smallwood	60.00	25.00	15.00
(152)	Smith	60.00	25.00	15.00
(153)	Spencer	60.00	25.00	15.00
(154)	Stanage	60.00	25.00	15.00
(155)	Statz	60.00	25.00	15.00
(156)	Stumph	60.00	25.00	15.00
(157)	Thomas	60.00	25.00	15.00
(158)	Thurston	60.00	25.00	15.00
(159)	Tyrrell	60.00	25.00	15.00
(160)	Van Osdoll	60.00	25.00	15.00
(161)	Walsh	60.00	25.00	15.00
(162)	White	60.00	25.00	15.00
(163)	Wilhoit	60.00	25.00	15.00
(164)	Wilie	60.00	25.00	15.00
(165)	Winn	60.00	25.00	15.00
(166)	Wolfer	60.00	25.00	15.00
(167)	Yelle	60.00	25.00	15.00
(168)	Young	60.00	25.00	15.00
(169)	Zeider	60.00	25.00	15.00

1922 Zeenut Pacific Coast League

The 1922 Zeenuts are dated on the front, measure about 1-13/16" x 3-9/16" and feature black-and-white photos with sepia highlights. There are 162 subjects, and four of them (Koehler, Williams, Gregg and Schneider) have been found with variations in color tones.

		NM	EX	VG
Common Player:		60.00	25.00	15.00
(1)	J. Adams	60.00	25.00	15.00
(2)	S. Adams	60.00	25.00	15.00
(3)	Agnew	60.00	25.00	15.00
(4)	Anfinson	60.00	25.00	15.00
(5)	Arlett	60.00	25.00	15.00
(6)	Baldwin	60.00	25.00	15.00
(7)	Barney	60.00	25.00	15.00
(8)	Bell	60.00	25.00	15.00
(9)	Blaeholder	60.00	25.00	15.00
(10)	Bodie	60.00	25.00	15.00
(11)	Brenton	60.00	25.00	15.00
(12)	Bromley	60.00	25.00	15.00
(13)	Brovold	60.00	25.00	15.00
(14)	Brown	60.00	25.00	15.00
(15)	Brubaker	60.00	25.00	15.00
(16)	Burger	60.00	25.00	15.00
(17)	Byler	60.00	25.00	15.00
(18)	Canfield	60.00	25.00	15.00
(19)	Carroll	60.00	25.00	15.00
(20)	Cartwright	60.00	25.00	15.00
(21)	Chadbourne	60.00	25.00	15.00
(22)	Compton	60.00	25.00	15.00
(23)	Connolly	60.00	25.00	15.00
(24)	Cook	60.00	25.00	15.00
(25)	Cooper	60.00	25.00	15.00
(26)	Coumbe	60.00	25.00	15.00
(27)	Cox	60.00	25.00	15.00
(28)	Crandall	60.00	25.00	15.00
(29)	Crumpler	60.00	25.00	15.00
(30)	Cueto	100.00	50.00	30.00
(31)	Dailey	60.00	25.00	15.00
(32)	Daly	60.00	25.00	15.00
(33)	Deal	60.00	25.00	15.00
(34)	Dell	60.00	25.00	15.00
(35)	Doyle	60.00	25.00	15.00
(36)	Dumovich	60.00	25.00	15.00
(37)	Eldred	60.00	25.00	15.00
(38)	Eller	60.00	25.00	15.00
(39)	Elliott	60.00	25.00	15.00
(40)	Ellison	60.00	25.00	15.00
(41)	Essick	60.00	25.00	15.00
(42)	Finneran	60.00	25.00	15.00
(43)	Fittery	60.00	25.00	15.00
(44)	Fitzgerald	60.00	25.00	15.00
(45)	Freeman	60.00	25.00	15.00

		NM	EX	VG
(46)	French	60.00	25.00	15.00
(47)	Gardner	60.00	25.00	15.00
(48)	Geary	60.00	25.00	15.00
(49)	Gibson	60.00	25.00	15.00
(50)	Gilder	60.00	25.00	15.00
(51)	Gould	60.00	25.00	15.00
(52)	Gregg	60.00	25.00	15.00
(53)	Gressett	60.00	25.00	15.00
(54)	Griggs	60.00	25.00	15.00
(55)	Hampton	60.00	25.00	15.00
(56)	Hannah	60.00	25.00	15.00
(57)	Hawks	60.00	25.00	15.00
(58)	Henke	60.00	25.00	15.00
(59)	High (Portland)	60.00	25.00	15.00
(60)	High (Vernon)	60.00	25.00	15.00
(61)	Houck	60.00	25.00	15.00
(62)	Howard	60.00	25.00	15.00
(63)	Hughes	60.00	25.00	15.00
(64)	Hyatt	60.00	25.00	15.00
(65)	Jacobs	60.00	25.00	15.00
(66)	James	60.00	25.00	15.00
(67)	Jenkins	60.00	25.00	15.00
(68)	Jones	60.00	25.00	15.00
(69)	Kallio	60.00	25.00	15.00
(70)	Kamm	60.00	25.00	15.00
(71)	Keiser	60.00	25.00	15.00
(72)	Kelly	60.00	25.00	15.00
(73)	Kenworthy	60.00	25.00	15.00
(74)	Kilduff	60.00	25.00	15.00
(75)	Killefer	60.00	25.00	15.00
(76)	Killhullen	60.00	25.00	15.00
(77)	King	60.00	25.00	15.00
(78)	Knight	60.00	25.00	15.00
(79)	Koehler	60.00	25.00	15.00
(80)	Kremer	60.00	25.00	15.00
(81)	Kunz	60.00	25.00	15.00
(82)	Lafayette	60.00	25.00	15.00
(83)	Lane	60.00	25.00	15.00
(84)	Tony Lazzeri	1,200	600.00	360.00
(85)	Lefevre	60.00	25.00	15.00
(86)	D. Lewis	60.00	25.00	15.00
(87)	S. Lewis	60.00	25.00	15.00
(88)	Lindimore	60.00	25.00	15.00
(89)	Locker	60.00	25.00	15.00
(90)	Lyons	60.00	25.00	15.00
(91)	Mack	60.00	25.00	15.00
(92)	Marriott	60.00	25.00	15.00
(93)	May	60.00	25.00	15.00
(94)	McAuley	60.00	25.00	15.00
(95)	McCabe	60.00	25.00	15.00
(96)	McCann	60.00	25.00	15.00
(97)	McCredie	60.00	25.00	15.00
(98)	McNeely	60.00	25.00	15.00
(99)	McQuaid	60.00	25.00	15.00
(100)	Miller	60.00	25.00	15.00
(101)	Mitchell	60.00	25.00	15.00
(102)	Mitze	60.00	25.00	15.00
(103)	Mollwitz	60.00	25.00	15.00
(104)	Monahan	60.00	25.00	15.00
(105)	Murphy (Seattle)	60.00	25.00	15.00
(106)	Murphy (Vernon)	60.00	25.00	15.00
(107)	Niehaus	60.00	25.00	15.00
(108)	O'Connell	60.00	25.00	15.00
(109)	Orr	60.00	25.00	15.00
(110)	Owen	60.00	25.00	15.00
(111)	Pearce	60.00	25.00	15.00
(112)	Pick	60.00	25.00	15.00
(113)	Ponder	60.00	25.00	15.00
(114)	Poole	60.00	25.00	15.00
(115)	Prough	60.00	25.00	15.00
(116)	Read	60.00	25.00	15.00
(117)	Richardson	60.00	25.00	15.00
(118)	Rieger	60.00	25.00	15.00
(119)	Ritchie	60.00	25.00	15.00
(120)	Ross	60.00	25.00	15.00
(121)	Ryan	60.00	25.00	15.00
(122)	Sand	60.00	25.00	15.00
(123)	Sargent	60.00	25.00	15.00
(124)	Sawyer	60.00	25.00	15.00
(125)	Schang	60.00	25.00	15.00
(126)	Schick	60.00	25.00	15.00
(127)	Schneider	60.00	25.00	15.00
(128)	Schorr	60.00	25.00	15.00
(129)	Schulte (Oakland)	60.00	25.00	15.00
(130)	Schulte (Seattle)	60.00	25.00	15.00
(131)	Scott	60.00	25.00	15.00
(132)	See	60.00	25.00	15.00
(133)	Shea	60.00	25.00	15.00
(134)	Sheehan	60.00	25.00	15.00
(135)	Siglin	60.00	25.00	15.00
(136)	Smith	60.00	25.00	15.00
(137)	Soria	60.00	25.00	15.00
(138)	Spencer	60.00	25.00	15.00
(139)	Stanage	60.00	25.00	15.00
(140)	Strand	60.00	25.00	15.00
(141)	Stumpf	60.00	25.00	15.00
(142)	Sullivan	60.00	25.00	15.00
(143)	Sutherland	60.00	25.00	15.00
(144)	Thomas	60.00	25.00	15.00
(145)	Jim Thorpe	15,000	7,500	4,500
(146)	Thurston	60.00	25.00	15.00
(147)	Tobin	60.00	25.00	15.00
(148)	Turner	60.00	25.00	15.00
(149)	Twombly	60.00	25.00	15.00
(150)	Valla	60.00	25.00	15.00
(151)	Vargas	60.00	25.00	15.00
(152)	Viveros	60.00	25.00	15.00
(153)	Wallace	60.00	25.00	15.00
(154)	Walsh	60.00	25.00	15.00
(155)	Wells	60.00	25.00	15.00
(156)	Westersil	60.00	25.00	15.00
(157)	Wheat	60.00	25.00	15.00
(158)	Wilhoit	60.00	25.00	15.00
(159)	Wilie	60.00	25.00	15.00
(160)	Williams	60.00	25.00	15.00
(161)	Yelle	60.00	25.00	15.00
(162)	Zeider	60.00	25.00	15.00

1923 Zeenut Pacific Coast League

This is the only year that Zeenuts cards were issued in two different sizes. Cards in the "regular" series measure about 1-7/8" x 3-1/2", feature black-and-white photos and are dated 1923. A second series, containing just 24 cards (all San Francisco and Oakland players), are sepia-toned re-issues of the 1922 series with a "1923" date and measure about 1/16" longer. The re-issued cards have coupons with an expiration date of April 1, 1923. The dated cards have coupons with an expiration date of April 1, 1924.

		NM	EX	VG
Common Player:		60.00	25.00	15.00
With Coupon:		1,000	500.00	300.00
(1)	Agnew (1923 photo.)	60.00	25.00	15.00
(2)	Agnew (1922 photo re-dated.)	60.00	25.00	15.00
(3)	Alten	60.00	25.00	15.00
(4)	Anderson	60.00	25.00	15.00
(5)	Anfinson	60.00	25.00	15.00
(6)	Arlett	60.00	25.00	15.00
(7)	Baker	60.00	25.00	15.00
(8)	Baldwin	60.00	25.00	15.00
(9)	Barney	60.00	25.00	15.00
(10)	Blake	60.00	25.00	15.00
(11)	Bodie	60.00	25.00	15.00
(12)	Brazil	60.00	25.00	15.00
(13)	Brenton	60.00	25.00	15.00
(14)	Brown (Oakland)	60.00	25.00	15.00
(15)	Brown (Sacramento)	60.00	25.00	15.00
(16)	Brubaker	60.00	25.00	15.00
(17)	Buckley	60.00	25.00	15.00
(18)	Canfield	60.00	25.00	15.00
(19)	Carroll	60.00	25.00	15.00
(20)	Cather	60.00	25.00	15.00
(21)	Chadbourne	60.00	25.00	15.00
(22)	Charvez	60.00	25.00	15.00
(23)	Cochrane	60.00	25.00	15.00
(24)	Colwell	60.00	25.00	15.00
(25)	Compton	60.00	25.00	15.00
(26)	Cook	60.00	25.00	15.00
(27)	Cooper (1923 photo.)	60.00	25.00	15.00
(28)	Cooper (1922 photo re-date.)	60.00	25.00	15.00
(29)	Coumbe	60.00	25.00	15.00
(30)	Courtney	60.00	25.00	15.00
(31)	Crandall	60.00	25.00	15.00
(32)	Crane	60.00	25.00	15.00
(33)	Crowder	60.00	25.00	15.00
(34)	Crumpler	60.00	25.00	15.00
(35)	Daly (Los Angeles)	60.00	25.00	15.00
(36)	Daly (Portland)	60.00	25.00	15.00
(37)	Deal	60.00	25.00	15.00
(38)	Doyle	60.00	25.00	15.00
(39)	Duchalsky	60.00	25.00	15.00
(40)	Eckert	60.00	25.00	15.00
(41)	Eldred	60.00	25.00	15.00
(42)	Eley	60.00	25.00	15.00
(43)	Eller	60.00	25.00	15.00
(44)	Ellison (1923 photo.)	60.00	25.00	15.00
(45)	Ellison (1922 photo re-dated.)	60.00	25.00	15.00
(46)	Essick	60.00	25.00	15.00
(47)	Fittery	60.00	25.00	15.00
(48)	Flashkamper	60.00	25.00	15.00
(49)	Frederick	60.00	25.00	15.00
(50)	French	60.00	25.00	15.00
(51)	Geary (1923 photo.)	60.00	25.00	15.00
(52)	Geary (1922 photo re-dated.)	60.00	25.00	15.00
(53)	Gilder	60.00	25.00	15.00
(54)	Golvin	60.00	25.00	15.00
(55)	Gorman	60.00	25.00	15.00
(56)	Gould	60.00	25.00	15.00
(57)	Gressett	60.00	25.00	15.00
(58)	Griggs	60.00	25.00	15.00
(59)	Hannah (Los Angeles)	60.00	25.00	15.00
(60)	Hannah (Vernon)	60.00	25.00	15.00
(61)	Hemingway	60.00	25.00	15.00
(62)	Hendryx	60.00	25.00	15.00
(63)	High	60.00	25.00	15.00
(64)	H. High	60.00	25.00	15.00
(65)	Hodge	60.00	25.00	15.00
(66)	Hood	60.00	25.00	15.00
(67)	Houghs	60.00	25.00	15.00
(68)	Howard (1923 photo.)	60.00	25.00	15.00
(69)	Howard (1922 photo re-date.)	60.00	25.00	15.00
(70)	Del Howard	60.00	25.00	15.00
(71)	Jacobs	60.00	25.00	15.00
(72)	James	60.00	25.00	15.00
(73)	Johnson	60.00	25.00	15.00
(74)	Johnston	60.00	25.00	15.00
(75)	Jolly (Jolley)	60.00	25.00	15.00
(76)	Jones (Los Angeles)	60.00	25.00	15.00
(77)	Jones (Oakland)	60.00	25.00	15.00
(78)	Jones (Portland)	60.00	25.00	15.00
(79)	Kallio	60.00	25.00	15.00
(80)	Kearns	60.00	25.00	15.00
(81)	Keiser	60.00	25.00	15.00
(82)	Keller	60.00	25.00	15.00
(83)	Kelly (San Francisco)	60.00	25.00	15.00
(84)	Kelly (Seattle)	60.00	25.00	15.00
(85)	Kenna	60.00	25.00	15.00
(86)	Kilduff	60.00	25.00	15.00
(87)	Killifer	60.00	25.00	15.00
(88)	King	60.00	25.00	15.00
(89)	Knight (1923 photo.)	60.00	25.00	15.00
(90)	Knight (1922 photo re-dated.)	60.00	25.00	15.00
(91)	Koehler	60.00	25.00	15.00
(92)	Kopp	60.00	25.00	15.00
(93)	Krause	60.00	25.00	15.00
(94)	Kremer	60.00	25.00	15.00
(95)	Krug	60.00	25.00	15.00
(96)	Lafayette (1923 photo.)	60.00	25.00	15.00
(97)	Lafayette (1922 photo re-dated.)	60.00	25.00	15.00
(98)	Lane	60.00	25.00	15.00
(99)	Lefevre	60.00	25.00	15.00
(100)	Leslie	60.00	25.00	15.00
(101)	Levere	60.00	25.00	15.00
(102)	Leverenz	60.00	25.00	15.00
(103)	Lewis	60.00	25.00	15.00
(104)	Lindimore	60.00	25.00	15.00
(105)	Locker	60.00	25.00	15.00
(106)	Lyons	60.00	25.00	15.00
(107)	Maderas	60.00	25.00	15.00
(108)	Mails	60.00	25.00	15.00
(109)	Marriott	60.00	25.00	15.00
(110)	Matzen	60.00	25.00	15.00
(111)	McAuley	60.00	25.00	15.00
(112)	McAuliffe	60.00	25.00	15.00
(113)	McCabe (Los Angeles)	60.00	25.00	15.00
(114)	McCabe (Salt Lake)	60.00	25.00	15.00
(115)	McCann	60.00	25.00	15.00
(116)	McGaffigan	60.00	25.00	15.00
(117)	McGinnis	60.00	25.00	15.00
(118)	McNeilly	60.00	25.00	15.00
(119)	McWeeney	60.00	25.00	15.00
(120)	Middleton	60.00	25.00	15.00
(121)	Miller	60.00	25.00	15.00
(122)	Mitchell (1923 photo.)	60.00	25.00	15.00
(123)	Mitchell (1922 photo re-date.)	60.00	25.00	15.00
(124)	Mitze	60.00	25.00	15.00
(125)	Mulligan	60.00	25.00	15.00
(126)	Murchio	60.00	25.00	15.00
(127)	D. Murphy	60.00	25.00	15.00
(128)	R. Murphy	60.00	25.00	15.00
(129)	Noack	60.00	25.00	15.00
(130)	O'Brien	60.00	25.00	15.00
(131)	Onslow	60.00	25.00	15.00
(132)	Orr	60.00	25.00	15.00
(133)	Pearce	60.00	25.00	15.00
(134)	Penner	60.00	25.00	15.00
(135)	Peters	60.00	25.00	15.00

		NM	EX	VG
(136)	Pick	60.00	25.00	15.00
(137)	Pigg	60.00	25.00	15.00
(138)	Plummer	60.00	25.00	15.00
(139)	Ponder	60.00	25.00	15.00
(140)	Poole	60.00	25.00	15.00
(141)	Ramage	60.00	25.00	15.00
(142)	Read (1923 photo.)	60.00	25.00	15.00
(143)	Read (1922 photo re-dated.)	60.00	25.00	15.00
(144)	Rhyne	60.00	25.00	15.00
(145)	Ritchie	60.00	25.00	15.00
(146)	Robertson	60.00	25.00	15.00
(147)	Rohwer (Sacramento)	60.00	25.00	15.00
(148)	Rohwer (Seattle)	60.00	25.00	15.00
(149)	Ryan	60.00	25.00	15.00
(150)	Sawyer	60.00	25.00	15.00
(151)	Schang	60.00	25.00	15.00
(152)	Schneider	60.00	25.00	15.00
(153)	Schroeder	60.00	25.00	15.00
(154)	Scott	60.00	25.00	15.00
(155)	See	60.00	25.00	15.00
(156)	Shea	60.00	25.00	15.00
(157)	M. Shea	60.00	25.00	15.00
(158)	Spec Shea	60.00	25.00	15.00
(159)	Sheehan	60.00	25.00	15.00
(160)	Shellenback	60.00	25.00	15.00
(161)	Siglin	60.00	25.00	15.00
(162)	Singleton	60.00	25.00	15.00
(163)	Smith	60.00	25.00	15.00
(164)	M.H. Smith	60.00	25.00	15.00
(165)	Stanton	60.00	25.00	15.00
(166)	Strand	60.00	25.00	15.00
(167)	Stumpf	60.00	25.00	15.00
(168)	Sutherland	60.00	25.00	15.00
(169)	Tesar	60.00	25.00	15.00
(170)	Thomas (Los Angeles)	60.00	25.00	15.00
(171)	Thomas (Oakland)	60.00	25.00	15.00
(172)	Tobin	60.00	25.00	15.00
(173)	Twombly	60.00	25.00	15.00
(174)	Valla	60.00	25.00	15.00
(175)	Vargas	60.00	25.00	15.00
(176)	Vitt	60.00	25.00	15.00
(177)	Wallace	60.00	25.00	15.00
(178)	Walsh (San Francisco)	60.00	25.00	15.00
(179)	Walsh (Seattle)	60.00	25.00	15.00
(180)	Paul Waner	1,500	750.00	450.00
(181)	Wells (Oakland)	60.00	25.00	15.00
(182)	Wells (San Francisco)	60.00	25.00	15.00
(183)	Welsh	60.00	25.00	15.00
(184)	Wilhoit	60.00	25.00	15.00
(185)	Wilie (1923 photo.)	60.00	25.00	15.00
(186)	Wilie (1922 photo re-dated.)	60.00	25.00	15.00
(187)	Williams	60.00	25.00	15.00
(188)	Witzel	60.00	25.00	15.00
(189)	Wolfer	60.00	25.00	15.00
(190)	Wolverton	60.00	25.00	15.00
(191)	Yarrison	60.00	25.00	15.00
(192)	Yaryan	60.00	25.00	15.00
(193)	Yelle (1923 photo.)	60.00	25.00	15.00
(194)	Yelle (1922 photo re-dated.)	60.00	25.00	15.00
(195)	Moses Yellowhorse	600.00	300.00	180.00
(196)	Zeider	60.00	25.00	15.00

1924 Zeenut Pacific Coast League

Zeenut cards in 1924 measure about 1-3/4" x 3-7/16" and display the date on the front. The cards include a full photographic background. There are 144 subjects known.

		NM	EX	VG
Common Player:		60.00	25.00	15.00
(1)	Adams	125.00	65.00	40.00
(2)	Agnew	60.00	25.00	15.00
(3)	Arlett	60.00	25.00	15.00
(4)	Baker	60.00	25.00	15.00
(5)	E. Baldwin	60.00	25.00	15.00

		NM	EX	VG
(6)	T. Baldwin	60.00	25.00	15.00
(7)	Beck	60.00	25.00	15.00
(8)	Benton	60.00	25.00	15.00
(9)	Bernard	60.00	25.00	15.00
(10)	Bigbee	60.00	25.00	15.00
(11)	Billings	60.00	25.00	15.00
(12)	Blakesly	60.00	25.00	15.00
(13)	Brady	60.00	25.00	15.00
(14)	Brazil	60.00	25.00	15.00
(15)	Brown	60.00	25.00	15.00
(16)	Brubaker	60.00	25.00	15.00
(17)	Buckley	60.00	25.00	15.00
(18)	Burger	60.00	25.00	15.00
(19)	Byler	60.00	25.00	15.00
(20)	Cadore	60.00	25.00	15.00
(21)	Cather	60.00	25.00	15.00
(22)	Chadbourne	60.00	25.00	15.00
(23)	Christian	60.00	25.00	15.00
(24)	Mickey Cochrane (Portland)	1,200	600.00	360.00
(25)	Cochrane (Sacramento)	60.00	25.00	15.00
(26)	Cooper	60.00	25.00	15.00
(27)	Coumbe	60.00	25.00	15.00
(28)	Cox	60.00	25.00	15.00
(29)	Crandall	60.00	25.00	15.00
(30)	Daly	60.00	25.00	15.00
(31)	Deal	60.00	25.00	15.00
(32)	Distel	60.00	25.00	15.00
(33)	Durst	60.00	25.00	15.00
(34)	Eckert	60.00	25.00	15.00
(35)	Eldred	60.00	25.00	15.00
(36)	Ellison	60.00	25.00	15.00
(37)	Essick	60.00	25.00	15.00
(38)	Flashkamper	60.00	25.00	15.00
(39)	Foster	60.00	25.00	15.00
(40)	Fredericks	60.00	25.00	15.00
(41)	Geary	60.00	25.00	15.00
(42)	Goebel	60.00	25.00	15.00
(43)	Golvin	60.00	25.00	15.00
(44)	Gorman	60.00	25.00	15.00
(45)	Gould	60.00	25.00	15.00
(46)	Gressett	60.00	25.00	15.00
(47)	Griffin (San Francisco)	60.00	25.00	15.00
(48)	Griffin (Vernon)	60.00	25.00	15.00
(49)	Guisto	60.00	25.00	15.00
(50)	Gunther	60.00	25.00	15.00
(51)	Hall	60.00	25.00	15.00
(52)	Hannah	60.00	25.00	15.00
(53)	Hendryx	60.00	25.00	15.00
(54)	High	60.00	25.00	15.00
(55)	Hodge	60.00	25.00	15.00
(56)	Hood	60.00	25.00	15.00
(57)	Ivan Howard	60.00	25.00	15.00
(58)	Hughes (Los Angeles)	60.00	25.00	15.00
(59)	Hughes (Sacramento)	60.00	25.00	15.00
(60)	Jacobs	60.00	25.00	15.00
(61)	James	60.00	25.00	15.00
(62)	Jenkins	60.00	25.00	15.00
(63)	Johnson	60.00	25.00	15.00
(64)	Jones	60.00	25.00	15.00
(65)	Keck	60.00	25.00	15.00
(66)	Kelley	60.00	25.00	15.00
(67)	Kenworthy	60.00	25.00	15.00
(68)	Kilduff	60.00	25.00	15.00
(69)	Killifer	60.00	25.00	15.00
(70)	Kimmick	60.00	25.00	15.00
(71)	Kopp	60.00	25.00	15.00
(72)	Krause	60.00	25.00	15.00
(73)	Krug	60.00	25.00	15.00
(74)	Kunz	60.00	25.00	15.00
(75)	Lafayette	60.00	25.00	15.00
(76)	Lennon	60.00	25.00	15.00
(77)	Leptich	60.00	25.00	15.00
(78)	Leslie	60.00	25.00	15.00
(79)	Leverenz	60.00	25.00	15.00
(80)	Lewis	60.00	25.00	15.00
(81)	Maderas	60.00	25.00	15.00
(82)	Mails	60.00	25.00	15.00
(83)	McAuley	60.00	25.00	15.00
(84)	McCann	60.00	25.00	15.00
(85)	McDowell	60.00	25.00	15.00
(86)	McNeely	60.00	25.00	15.00
(87)	Menosky	60.00	25.00	15.00
(88)	Meyers	60.00	25.00	15.00
(89)	Miller	60.00	25.00	15.00
(90)	Mitchell	60.00	25.00	15.00
(91)	Mulligan	60.00	25.00	15.00
(92)	D. Murphy	60.00	25.00	15.00
(93)	R. Murphy	60.00	25.00	15.00
(94)	Osborne	60.00	25.00	15.00
(95)	Paynter	60.00	25.00	15.00
(96)	Penner	60.00	25.00	15.00
(97)	Peters (Sacramento)	60.00	25.00	15.00
(98)	Peters (Salt Lake)	60.00	25.00	15.00
(99)	Pick	60.00	25.00	15.00
(100)	Pillette	60.00	25.00	15.00
(101)	Poole	60.00	25.00	15.00
(102)	Prough	60.00	25.00	15.00

		NM	EX	VG
(103)	Querry	60.00	25.00	15.00
(104)	Read	60.00	25.00	15.00
(105)	Rhyne	60.00	25.00	15.00
(106)	Ritchie	60.00	25.00	15.00
(107)	Root	60.00	25.00	15.00
(108)	Rowher	60.00	25.00	15.00
(109)	Schang	60.00	25.00	15.00
(110)	Schneider	60.00	25.00	15.00
(111)	Schorr	60.00	25.00	15.00
(112)	Schroeder	60.00	25.00	15.00
(113)	Scott	60.00	25.00	15.00
(114)	Sellers	60.00	25.00	15.00
(115)	"Speck" Shay	60.00	25.00	15.00
(116)	Shea (Sacramento)	60.00	25.00	15.00
(117)	Shea (San Francisco)	60.00	25.00	15.00
(118)	Shellenback	60.00	25.00	15.00
(119)	Siebold	60.00	25.00	15.00
(120)	Siglin	60.00	25.00	15.00
(121)	Slade	60.00	25.00	15.00
(122)	Smith (Sacramento)	60.00	25.00	15.00
(123)	Smith (San Francisco)	60.00	25.00	15.00
(124)	Stanton	60.00	25.00	15.00
(125)	Tanner	60.00	25.00	15.00
(126)	Twomley	60.00	25.00	15.00
(127)	Valla	60.00	25.00	15.00
(128)	Vargas	60.00	25.00	15.00
(129)	Vines	60.00	25.00	15.00
(130)	Vitt	60.00	25.00	15.00
(131)	Wallace	60.00	25.00	15.00
(132)	Walsh	60.00	25.00	15.00
(133)	Paul Waner	750.00	375.00	225.00
(134)	Warner/Fielding	60.00	25.00	15.00
(135)	Warner/Throwing	60.00	25.00	15.00
(136)	Welsh	60.00	25.00	15.00
(137)	Wetzel	60.00	25.00	15.00
(138)	Whalen	60.00	25.00	15.00
(139)	Wilhoit	60.00	25.00	15.00
(140)	Williams (San Francisco)	60.00	25.00	15.00
(141)	Williams (Seattle)	60.00	25.00	15.00
(142)	Wolfer	60.00	25.00	15.00
(143)	Yelle	60.00	25.00	15.00
(144)	Moses Yellowhorse	350.00	175.00	100.00

1925 Zeenut Pacific Coast League

Zeenut cards in 1925 measure about 1-3/4" x 3-7/16" and display the date on the front. The cards include a full photographic background. There are 162 subjects known for 1925.

		NM	EX	VG
Common Player:		60.00	25.00	15.00
With Coupon:		300.00	150.00	90.00
(1)	Adeylatte	60.00	25.00	15.00
(2)	Agnew	60.00	25.00	15.00
(3)	Arlett	60.00	25.00	15.00
(4)	Bagby	60.00	25.00	15.00
(5)	Bahr	60.00	25.00	15.00
(6)	Baker	60.00	25.00	15.00
(7)	E. Baldwin	60.00	25.00	15.00
(8)	Barfoot	60.00	25.00	15.00
(9)	Beck	60.00	25.00	15.00
(10)	Becker	60.00	25.00	15.00
(11)	Blakesley	60.00	25.00	15.00
(12)	Boehler	60.00	25.00	15.00
(13)	Brady	60.00	25.00	15.00
(14)	Brandt	60.00	25.00	15.00
(15)	Bratcher	60.00	25.00	15.00
(16)	Brazil	60.00	25.00	15.00
(17)	Brower	60.00	25.00	15.00
(18)	Brown	60.00	25.00	15.00
(19)	Brubaker	60.00	25.00	15.00
(20)	Bryan	60.00	25.00	15.00
(21)	Canfield	60.00	25.00	15.00
(22)	W. Canfield	60.00	25.00	15.00
(23)	Cather	60.00	25.00	15.00
(24)	Chavez	60.00	25.00	15.00
(25)	Christain	60.00	25.00	15.00

		NM	EX	VG
(26)	Cochrane	60.00	25.00	15.00
(27)	Connolly	60.00	25.00	15.00
(28)	Cook	60.00	25.00	15.00
(29)	Cooper	60.00	25.00	15.00
(30)	Coumbe	60.00	25.00	15.00
(31)	Crandall	60.00	25.00	15.00
(32)	Crane	60.00	25.00	15.00
(33)	Crockett	60.00	25.00	15.00
(34)	Crosby	60.00	25.00	15.00
(35)	Cutshaw	60.00	25.00	15.00
(36)	Daly	60.00	25.00	15.00
(37)	Davis	60.00	25.00	15.00
(38)	Deal	60.00	25.00	15.00
(39)	Delaney	60.00	25.00	15.00
(40)	Dempsey	60.00	25.00	15.00
(41)	Dumovich	60.00	25.00	15.00
(42)	Eckert	60.00	25.00	15.00
(43)	Eldred	60.00	25.00	15.00
(44)	Elliott	60.00	25.00	15.00
(45)	Ellison	60.00	25.00	15.00
(46)	Emmer	60.00	25.00	15.00
(47)	Ennis	60.00	25.00	15.00
(48)	Essick	60.00	25.00	15.00
(49)	Finn	60.00	25.00	15.00
(50)	Flowers	60.00	25.00	15.00
(51)	Frederick	60.00	25.00	15.00
(52)	Fussell	60.00	25.00	15.00
(53)	Geary	60.00	25.00	15.00
(54)	Gorman	60.00	25.00	15.00
(55)	Griffin (San Francisco)	60.00	25.00	15.00
(56)	Griffin (Vernon)	60.00	25.00	15.00
(57)	Grimes	60.00	25.00	15.00
(58)	Guisto	60.00	25.00	15.00
(59)	Hannah	60.00	25.00	15.00
(60)	Haughy	60.00	25.00	15.00
(61)	Hemingway	60.00	25.00	15.00
(62)	Hendryx	60.00	25.00	15.00
(63)	Herman	400.00	200.00	120.00
(64)	High	60.00	25.00	15.00
(65)	Hoffman	60.00	25.00	15.00
(66)	Hood	60.00	25.00	15.00
(67)	Horan	60.00	25.00	15.00
(68)	Horton	60.00	25.00	15.00
(69)	Howard	60.00	25.00	15.00
(70)	Hughes	60.00	25.00	15.00
(71)	Hulvey	60.00	25.00	15.00
(72)	Hunnefield	60.00	25.00	15.00
(73)	Jacobs	60.00	25.00	15.00
(74)	James	60.00	25.00	15.00
(75)	Keating	60.00	25.00	15.00
(76)	Keefe	60.00	25.00	15.00
(77)	Kelly	60.00	25.00	15.00
(78)	Kilduff	60.00	25.00	15.00
(79)	Kohler	60.00	25.00	15.00
(80)	Kopp	60.00	25.00	15.00
(81)	Krause	60.00	25.00	15.00
(82)	Krug	60.00	25.00	15.00
(83)	Kunz	60.00	25.00	15.00
(84)	Lafayette	60.00	25.00	15.00
(85)	Tony Lazzeri	450.00	225.00	135.00
(86)	Leslie	60.00	25.00	15.00
(87)	Leverenz	60.00	25.00	15.00
(88)	Duffy Lewis	60.00	30.00	20.00
(89)	Lindemore	60.00	25.00	15.00
(90)	Ludolph	60.00	25.00	15.00
(91)	Makin	60.00	25.00	15.00
(92)	Martin (Sacramento)	60.00	25.00	15.00
(93)	Martin (Portland)	60.00	25.00	15.00
(94)	McCabe	60.00	25.00	15.00
(95)	McCann	60.00	25.00	15.00
(96)	McCarren	60.00	25.00	15.00
(97)	McDonald	60.00	25.00	15.00
(98)	McGinnis (Portland)	60.00	25.00	15.00
(99)	McGinnis (Sacramento)	60.00	25.00	15.00
(100)	McLaughlin	60.00	25.00	15.00
(101)	Milstead	60.00	25.00	15.00
(102)	Mitchell	60.00	25.00	15.00
(103)	Moudy	60.00	25.00	15.00
(104)	Mulcahy	60.00	25.00	15.00
(105)	Mulligan	60.00	25.00	15.00
(106)	Lefty O'Doul	250.00	125.00	75.00
(107)	O'Neil	60.00	25.00	15.00
(108)	Ortman	60.00	25.00	15.00
(109)	Pailey	60.00	25.00	15.00
(110)	Paynter	60.00	25.00	15.00
(111)	Peery	60.00	25.00	15.00
(112)	Penner	60.00	25.00	15.00
(113)	Pfeffer	60.00	25.00	15.00
(114)	Phillips	60.00	25.00	15.00
(115)	Pickering	60.00	25.00	15.00
(116)	Piercy	60.00	25.00	15.00
(117)	Pillette	60.00	25.00	15.00
(118)	Plummer	60.00	25.00	15.00
(119)	Ponder	60.00	25.00	15.00
(120)	Pruett	60.00	25.00	15.00
(121)	Rawlings	60.00	25.00	15.00
(122)	Read	60.00	25.00	15.00
(123)	Jimmy Reese	300.00	150.00	90.00
(124)	Rhyne	60.00	25.00	15.00
(125)	Riconda	60.00	25.00	15.00
(126)	Ritchie	60.00	25.00	15.00
(127)	Rohwer	60.00	25.00	15.00
(128)	Rowland	60.00	25.00	15.00
(129)	Ryan	60.00	25.00	15.00
(130)	Sandberg	60.00	25.00	15.00
(131)	Schang	60.00	25.00	15.00
(132)	Shea	60.00	25.00	15.00
(133)	M. Shea	60.00	25.00	15.00
(134)	Shellenbach	60.00	25.00	15.00
(135)	Sherling	60.00	25.00	15.00
(136)	Siglin	60.00	25.00	15.00
(137)	Slade	60.00	25.00	15.00
(138)	Spencer	60.00	25.00	15.00
(139)	Steward	60.00	25.00	15.00
(140)	Stivers	60.00	25.00	15.00
(141)	Suhr	60.00	25.00	15.00
(142)	Sutherland	60.00	25.00	15.00
(143)	Thomas (Portland)	60.00	25.00	15.00
(144)	Thomas (Vernon)	60.00	25.00	15.00
(145)	Thompson	60.00	25.00	15.00
(146)	Tobin	60.00	25.00	15.00
(147)	Twombly	60.00	25.00	15.00
(148)	Valla	60.00	25.00	15.00
(149)	Vinci	60.00	25.00	15.00
(150)	O. Vitt	60.00	25.00	15.00
(151)	Wachenfeld	60.00	25.00	15.00
(152)	Paul Waner	750.00	375.00	225.00
(153)	Lloyd Waner	1,200	600.00	360.00
(154)	Warner	60.00	25.00	15.00
(155)	Watson	60.00	25.00	15.00
(156)	Weinert	60.00	25.00	15.00
(157)	Whaley	60.00	25.00	15.00
(158)	Whitney	60.00	25.00	15.00
(159)	Williams	60.00	25.00	15.00
(160)	Winters	60.00	25.00	15.00
(161)	Wolfer	60.00	25.00	15.00
(162)	Woodring	60.00	25.00	15.00
(163)	Yeargin	60.00	25.00	15.00
(164)	Yelle	60.00	25.00	15.00

1926 Zeenut Pacific Coast League

Except for their slightly smaller size (1-3/4" x 3-7/16"), the 1926 Zeenut cards are nearly identical to the previous two years. Considered more difficult than other Zeenuts series of this era, the 1926 set consists of more than 170 known subjects.

		NM	EX	VG
Common Player:		40.00	20.00	12.00
(1)	Agnew	40.00	20.00	12.00
(2)	Allen	40.00	20.00	12.00
(3)	Alley	40.00	20.00	12.00
(4)	Averill	400.00	200.00	120.00
(5)	Bagwell	40.00	20.00	12.00
(6)	Baker	40.00	20.00	12.00
(7)	T. Baldwin	40.00	20.00	12.00
(8)	Berry	40.00	20.00	12.00
(9)	Bool	40.00	20.00	12.00
(10)	Boone	40.00	20.00	12.00
(11)	Boyd	40.00	20.00	12.00
(12)	Brady	40.00	20.00	12.00
(13)	Brazil	40.00	20.00	12.00
(14)	Brower	40.00	20.00	12.00
(15)	Brubaker	40.00	20.00	12.00
(16)	Bryan	40.00	20.00	12.00
(17)	Burns	40.00	20.00	12.00
(18)	C. Canfield	40.00	20.00	12.00
(19)	W. Canfield	40.00	20.00	12.00
(20)	Carson	40.00	20.00	12.00
(21)	Christian	40.00	20.00	12.00
(22)	Cole	40.00	20.00	12.00
(23)	Connolly	40.00	20.00	12.00
(24)	Cook	40.00	20.00	12.00
(25)	Couch	40.00	20.00	12.00
(26)	Coumbe	40.00	20.00	12.00
(27)	Crockett	40.00	20.00	12.00
(28)	Cunningham	40.00	20.00	12.00
(29)	Cutshaw	40.00	20.00	12.00
(30)	Daglia	40.00	20.00	12.00
(31)	Danning	40.00	20.00	12.00
(32)	Davis	40.00	20.00	12.00
(33)	Delaney	40.00	20.00	12.00
(34)	Eckert	40.00	20.00	12.00
(35)	Eldred	40.00	20.00	12.00
(36)	Elliott	40.00	20.00	12.00
(37)	Ellison	40.00	20.00	12.00
(38)	Ellsworth	40.00	20.00	12.00
(39)	Elsh	40.00	20.00	12.00
(40)	Fenton	40.00	20.00	12.00
(41)	Finn	40.00	20.00	12.00
(42)	Flashkamper	40.00	20.00	12.00
(43)	Fowler	40.00	20.00	12.00
(44)	Frederick	40.00	20.00	12.00
(45)	Freeman	40.00	20.00	12.00
(46)	French	40.00	20.00	12.00
(47)	Garrison	40.00	20.00	12.00
(48)	Geary	40.00	20.00	12.00
(49)	Gillespie	40.00	20.00	12.00
(50)	Glazner	40.00	20.00	12.00
(51)	Gould	40.00	20.00	12.00
(52)	Governor	40.00	20.00	12.00
(53)	Griffin (Missions)	40.00	20.00	12.00
(54)	Griffin (San Francisco)	40.00	20.00	12.00
(55)	Guisto	40.00	20.00	12.00
(56)	Hamilton	40.00	20.00	12.00
(57)	Hannah	40.00	20.00	12.00
(58)	Hansen	40.00	20.00	12.00
(59)	Hasty	40.00	20.00	12.00
(60)	Hemingway	40.00	20.00	12.00
(61)	Hendryx	40.00	20.00	12.00
(62)	Hickok	40.00	20.00	12.00
(63)	Hillis	40.00	20.00	12.00
(64)	Hoffman	40.00	20.00	12.00
(65)	Hollerson	40.00	20.00	12.00
(66)	Holmes	40.00	20.00	12.00
(67)	Hood	40.00	20.00	12.00
(68)	Howard	40.00	20.00	12.00
(69)	Hufft	40.00	20.00	12.00
(70)	Hughes	40.00	20.00	12.00
(71)	Hulvey	40.00	20.00	12.00
(72)	Hurst	40.00	20.00	12.00
(73)	R. Jacobs	40.00	20.00	12.00
(74)	Jahn	40.00	20.00	12.00
(75)	Jenkins	40.00	20.00	12.00
(76)	Johnson	40.00	20.00	12.00
(77)	Jolly (Jolley)	65.00	32.50	20.00
(78)	Jones	40.00	20.00	12.00
(79)	Kallio	40.00	20.00	12.00
(80)	Keating	40.00	20.00	12.00
(81)	Kerr (Hollywood)	40.00	20.00	12.00
(82)	Kerr (San Francisco)	40.00	20.00	12.00
(83)	Kilduff	40.00	20.00	12.00
(84)	Killifer	40.00	20.00	12.00
(85)	Knight	40.00	20.00	12.00
(86)	Koehler	40.00	20.00	12.00
(87)	Kopp	40.00	20.00	12.00
(88)	Krause	40.00	20.00	12.00
(89)	Krug	40.00	20.00	12.00
(90)	Kunz	40.00	20.00	12.00
(91)	Lafayette	40.00	20.00	12.00
(92)	Lane	40.00	20.00	12.00
(93)	Lang	40.00	20.00	12.00
(94)	Lary	40.00	20.00	12.00
(95)	Leslie	40.00	20.00	12.00
(96)	Lindemore	40.00	20.00	12.00
(97)	Ludolph	40.00	20.00	12.00
(98)	Makin	40.00	20.00	12.00
(99)	Mangum	40.00	20.00	12.00
(100)	Martin	40.00	20.00	12.00
(101)	McCredie	40.00	20.00	12.00
(102)	McDowell	40.00	20.00	12.00
(103)	McKenry	40.00	20.00	12.00
(104)	McLoughlin	40.00	20.00	12.00
(105)	McNally	40.00	20.00	12.00
(106)	McPhee	40.00	20.00	12.00
(107)	Meeker	40.00	20.00	12.00
(108)	Metz	40.00	20.00	12.00
(109)	Miller	40.00	20.00	12.00
(110)	Mitchell (Los Angeles)	40.00	20.00	12.00
(111)	Mitchell (San Francisco)	40.00	20.00	12.00
(112)	Monroe	40.00	20.00	12.00
(113)	Moudy	40.00	20.00	12.00
(114)	Mulcahy	40.00	20.00	12.00
(115)	Mulligan	40.00	20.00	12.00
(116)	Murphy	40.00	20.00	12.00
(117)	Lefty O'Doul	100.00	50.00	30.00
(118)	O'Neill	40.00	20.00	12.00
(119)	Oeschger	40.00	20.00	12.00
(120)	Oliver	40.00	20.00	12.00
(121)	Ortman	40.00	20.00	12.00
(122)	Osborn	40.00	20.00	12.00
(123)	Paynter	40.00	20.00	12.00
(124)	Peters	40.00	20.00	12.00

		NM	EX	VG
(125)	Pfahler	40.00	20.00	12.00
(126)	Pillette	40.00	20.00	12.00
(127)	Plummer	40.00	20.00	12.00
(128)	Prothro	40.00	20.00	12.00
(129)	Pruett	40.00	20.00	12.00
(130)	Rachac	40.00	20.00	12.00
(131)	Ramsey	40.00	20.00	12.00
(132)	Rathjen	40.00	20.00	12.00
(133)	Read	40.00	20.00	12.00
(134)	Redman	40.00	20.00	12.00
(135)	Jimmy Reese	40.00	20.00	12.00
(136)	Rodda	40.00	20.00	12.00
(137)	Rohwer	40.00	20.00	12.00
(138)	Ryan	40.00	20.00	12.00
(139)	Sandberg	40.00	20.00	12.00
(140)	Sanders	40.00	20.00	12.00
(141)	E. Shea	40.00	20.00	12.00
(142)	M. Shea	40.00	20.00	12.00
(143)	Sheehan	40.00	20.00	12.00
(144)	Shellenbach	40.00	20.00	12.00
(145)	Sherlock	40.00	20.00	12.00
(146)	Siglin	40.00	20.00	12.00
(147)	Slade	40.00	20.00	12.00
(148)	E. Smith	40.00	20.00	12.00
(149)	M. Smith	40.00	20.00	12.00
(150)	Staley	40.00	20.00	12.00
(151)	Statz	75.00	37.50	22.50
(152)	Stroud	40.00	20.00	12.00
(153)	Stuart	40.00	20.00	12.00
(154)	Suhr	40.00	20.00	12.00
(155)	Swanson	40.00	20.00	12.00
(156)	Sweeney	40.00	20.00	12.00
(157)	Tadevich	40.00	20.00	12.00
(158)	Thomas	40.00	20.00	12.00
(159)	Thompson	40.00	20.00	12.00
(160)	Tobin	40.00	20.00	12.00
(161)	Valla	40.00	20.00	12.00
(162)	Vargas	40.00	20.00	12.00
(163)	Vinci	40.00	20.00	12.00
(164)	Walters	40.00	20.00	12.00
(165)	Lloyd Waner	450.00	225.00	135.00
(166)	Weis	40.00	20.00	12.00
(167)	Whitney	40.00	20.00	12.00
(168)	Williams	40.00	20.00	12.00
(169)	Wright	40.00	20.00	12.00
(170)	Yelle	40.00	20.00	12.00
(171)	Zaeffel	40.00	20.00	12.00
(172)	Zoellers	40.00	20.00	12.00

1927 Zeenut Pacific Coast League

The 1927 Zeenuts are about the same size (1-3/4" x 3-3/8") and color as the 1926 issue, except the year is expressed in just two digits (27), a practice that continued through 1930. There are 144 subjects known.

		NM	EX	VG
Common Player:		40.00	20.00	12.00
With Coupon:		275.00	135.00	85.00
(1)	Agnew	40.00	20.00	12.00
(2)	Arlett	40.00	20.00	12.00
(3)	Averill	600.00	300.00	180.00
(4)	Backer	40.00	20.00	12.00
(5)	Bagwell	40.00	20.00	12.00
(6)	Baker	40.00	20.00	12.00
(7)	D. Baker	40.00	20.00	12.00
(8)	Ballenger	40.00	20.00	12.00
(9)	Baumgartner	40.00	20.00	12.00
(10)	Bigbee	40.00	20.00	12.00
(11)	Boehler	40.00	20.00	12.00
(12)	Bool	40.00	20.00	12.00
(13)	Borreani	40.00	20.00	12.00
(14)	Brady	40.00	20.00	12.00
(15)	Bratcher	40.00	20.00	12.00
(16)	Brett	40.00	20.00	12.00
(17)	Brown	40.00	20.00	12.00
(18)	Brubaker	40.00	20.00	12.00
(19)	Bryan	40.00	20.00	12.00

		NM	EX	VG
(20)	Callaghan	40.00	20.00	12.00
(21)	Caveney	40.00	20.00	12.00
(22)	Christian	40.00	20.00	12.00
(23)	Cissell	40.00	20.00	12.00
(24)	Cook	40.00	20.00	12.00
(25)	Cooper (Oakland)	40.00	20.00	12.00
(26)	Cooper (Sacramento)	40.00	20.00	12.00
(27)	Cox	40.00	20.00	12.00
(28)	Cunningham	40.00	20.00	12.00
(29)	Daglia	40.00	20.00	12.00
(30)	Dickerman	40.00	20.00	12.00
(31)	Dumovitch	40.00	20.00	12.00
(32)	Eckert	40.00	20.00	12.00
(33)	Eldred	40.00	20.00	12.00
(34)	Ellison	40.00	20.00	12.00
(35)	Fenton	40.00	20.00	12.00
(36)	Finn	40.00	20.00	12.00
(37)	Fischer	40.00	20.00	12.00
(38)	Frederick	40.00	20.00	12.00
(39)	French	40.00	20.00	12.00
(40)	Fullerton	40.00	20.00	12.00
(41)	Geary	40.00	20.00	12.00
(42)	Gillespie	40.00	20.00	12.00
(43)	Gooch	40.00	20.00	12.00
(44)	Gould	40.00	20.00	12.00
(45)	Governor	40.00	20.00	12.00
(46)	Guisto	40.00	20.00	12.00
(47)	Hannah	40.00	20.00	12.00
(48)	Hasty	40.00	20.00	12.00
(49)	Hemingway	40.00	20.00	12.00
(50)	Hoffman	40.00	20.00	12.00
(51)	Hood	40.00	20.00	12.00
(52)	Hooper	450.00	225.00	135.00
(53)	Hudgens	40.00	20.00	12.00
(54)	Hufft	40.00	20.00	12.00
(55)	Hughes	40.00	20.00	12.00
(56)	Jahn	40.00	20.00	12.00
(57)	Johnson (Portland)	40.00	20.00	12.00
(58)	Johnson (Seals)	40.00	20.00	12.00
(59)	Jolly (Jolley)	60.00	30.00	18.00
(60)	Jones	40.00	20.00	12.00
(61)	Kallio	40.00	20.00	12.00
(62)	Keating	40.00	20.00	12.00
(63)	Keefe	40.00	20.00	12.00
(64)	Killifer	40.00	20.00	12.00
(65)	Kimmick	40.00	20.00	12.00
(66)	Kinney	40.00	20.00	12.00
(67)	Knight	40.00	20.00	12.00
(68)	Koehler	40.00	20.00	12.00
(69)	Kopp	40.00	20.00	12.00
(70)	Krause	40.00	20.00	12.00
(71)	Krug	40.00	20.00	12.00
(72)	Kunz	40.00	20.00	12.00
(73)	Lary	40.00	20.00	12.00
(74)	Leard	40.00	20.00	12.00
(75)	Lingrel	40.00	20.00	12.00
(76)	Ludolph	40.00	20.00	12.00
(77)	Mails	40.00	20.00	12.00
(78)	Makin	40.00	20.00	12.00
(79)	Martin	40.00	20.00	12.00
(80)	May	40.00	20.00	12.00
(81)	McCabe	40.00	20.00	12.00
(82)	McCurdy	40.00	20.00	12.00
(83)	McDaniel	40.00	20.00	12.00
(84)	McGee	40.00	20.00	12.00
(85)	McLaughlin	40.00	20.00	12.00
(86)	McMurtry	40.00	20.00	12.00
(87)	Metz	40.00	20.00	12.00
(88)	Miljus	40.00	20.00	12.00
(89)	Mitchell	40.00	20.00	12.00
(90)	Monroe	40.00	20.00	12.00
(91)	Moudy	40.00	20.00	12.00
(92)	Mulligan	40.00	20.00	12.00
(93)	Murphy	40.00	20.00	12.00
(94)	O'Brien	40.00	20.00	12.00
(95)	Lefty O'Doul	250.00	125.00	75.00
(96)	Oliver	40.00	20.00	12.00
(97)	Osborn	40.00	20.00	12.00
(98)	Parker/Btg (Missions)	40.00	20.00	12.00
(99)	Parker/Throwing (Missions)	40.00	20.00	12.00
(100)	Parker (Portland)	40.00	20.00	12.00
(101)	Peters	40.00	20.00	12.00
(102)	Pillette	40.00	20.00	12.00
(103)	Ponder	40.00	20.00	12.00
(104)	Prothro	40.00	20.00	12.00
(105)	Rachac	40.00	20.00	12.00
(106)	Ramsey	40.00	20.00	12.00
(107)	Read	40.00	20.00	12.00
(108)	Jimmy Reese	250.00	125.00	75.00
(109)	Rodda	40.00	20.00	12.00
(110)	Rohwer	40.00	20.00	12.00
(111)	Rose	40.00	20.00	12.00
(112)	Ryan	40.00	20.00	12.00
(113)	Sandberg	40.00	20.00	12.00
(114)	Sanders	40.00	20.00	12.00
(115)	Severeid	40.00	20.00	12.00
(116)	Shea	40.00	20.00	12.00
(117)	Sheehan (Hollywood)	40.00	20.00	12.00

		NM	EX	VG
(118)	Sheehan (Seals)	40.00	20.00	12.00
(119)	Sherlock	40.00	20.00	12.00
(120a)	Shinners (Date is "1927.")	40.00	20.00	12.00
(120b)	Shinners (Date is "27.")	40.00	20.00	12.00
(121)	Singleton	40.00	20.00	12.00
(122)	Slade	40.00	20.00	12.00
(123)	E. Smith	40.00	20.00	12.00
(124)	Sparks	40.00	20.00	12.00
(125)	Stokes	40.00	20.00	12.00
(126)	J. Storti	40.00	20.00	12.00
(127)	L. Storti	40.00	20.00	12.00
(128)	Strand	40.00	20.00	12.00
(129)	Suhr	40.00	20.00	12.00
(130)	Sunseri	40.00	20.00	12.00
(131)	Swanson	40.00	20.00	12.00
(132)	Tierney	40.00	20.00	12.00
(133)	Valla	40.00	20.00	12.00
(134)	Vargas	40.00	20.00	12.00
(135)	Vitt	40.00	20.00	12.00
(136)	Weinert	40.00	20.00	12.00
(137)	Weis	40.00	20.00	12.00
(138)	Wendell	40.00	20.00	12.00
(139)	Whitney	40.00	20.00	12.00
(140)	Williams	40.00	20.00	12.00
(141)	Guy Williams	40.00	20.00	12.00
(142)	Woodson	40.00	20.00	12.00
(143)	Wright	40.00	20.00	12.00
(144)	Yelle	40.00	20.00	12.00

1928 Zeenut Pacific Coast League

Zeenut cards from 1928 through 1930 maintain the same format as the 1927 series. Measuring about 1-3/4" x 3-3/8", the 1928 series consists of 168 known subjects.

		NM	EX	VG
Common Player:		40.00	20.00	12.00
(1)	Agnew	40.00	20.00	12.00
(2)	Earl Averill	300.00	150.00	90.00
(3)	Backer	40.00	20.00	12.00
(4)	Baker	40.00	20.00	12.00
(5)	Baldwin	40.00	20.00	12.00
(6)	Barfoot	40.00	20.00	12.00
(7)	Bassler	40.00	20.00	12.00
(8)	Berger	40.00	20.00	12.00
(9)	Bigbee (Los Angeles)	40.00	20.00	12.00
(10)	Bigbee (Portland)	40.00	20.00	12.00
(11)	Bodie	40.00	20.00	12.00
(12)	Boehler	40.00	20.00	12.00
(13)	Bool	40.00	20.00	12.00
(14)	Boone	40.00	20.00	12.00
(15)	Borreani	40.00	20.00	12.00
(16)	Bratcher	40.00	20.00	12.00
(17)	Brenzel	40.00	20.00	12.00
(18)	Brubaker	40.00	20.00	12.00
(19)	Bryan	40.00	20.00	12.00
(20)	Burkett	40.00	20.00	12.00
(21)	Camilli	40.00	20.00	12.00
(22)	W. Canfield	40.00	20.00	12.00
(23)	Caveney	40.00	20.00	12.00
(24)	Cohen	40.00	20.00	12.00
(25)	Cook	40.00	20.00	12.00
(26)	Cooper	40.00	20.00	12.00
(27)	Craghead	40.00	20.00	12.00
(28)	Crosetti	200.00	100.00	60.00
(29)	Cunningham	40.00	20.00	12.00
(30)	Daglia	40.00	20.00	12.00
(31)	Davis	40.00	20.00	12.00
(32)	Dean	40.00	20.00	12.00
(33)	Dittmar	40.00	20.00	12.00
(34)	Donovan	40.00	20.00	12.00
(35)	Downs	40.00	20.00	12.00
(36)	Duff	40.00	20.00	12.00
(37)	Eckert	40.00	20.00	12.00
(38)	Eldred	40.00	20.00	12.00
(39)	Ellsworth	40.00	20.00	12.00
(40)	Fenton	40.00	20.00	12.00

(41)	Finn	40.00	20.00	12.00
(42)	Fitterer	40.00	20.00	12.00
(43)	Flynn	40.00	20.00	12.00
(44)	Frazier	40.00	20.00	12.00
(45)	French (Portland)	40.00	20.00	12.00
(46)	French (Sacramento)	40.00	20.00	12.00
(47)	Fullerton	40.00	20.00	12.00
(48)	Gabler	40.00	20.00	12.00
(49)	Gomes	40.00	20.00	12.00
(50)	Gooch	40.00	20.00	12.00
(51)	Gould	40.00	20.00	12.00
(52)	Governor	40.00	20.00	12.00
(53)	Graham ("S" on uniform.)	40.00	20.00	12.00
(54)	Graham (No "S" on uniform.)	40.00	20.00	12.00
(55)	Guisto	40.00	20.00	12.00
(56)	Hannah	40.00	20.00	12.00
(57)	Hansen	40.00	20.00	12.00
(58)	Harris	40.00	20.00	12.00
(59)	Hasty	40.00	20.00	12.00
(60)	Heath	40.00	20.00	12.00
(61)	Hoffman	40.00	20.00	12.00
(62)	Holling	40.00	20.00	12.00
(63)	Hood	40.00	20.00	12.00
(64)	House	40.00	20.00	12.00
(65)	Howard	40.00	20.00	12.00
(66)	Hudgens	40.00	20.00	12.00
(67)	Hufft	40.00	20.00	12.00
(68)	Hughes	40.00	20.00	12.00
(69)	Hulvey	40.00	20.00	12.00
(70)	Jacobs	40.00	20.00	12.00
(71)	Johnson (Portland)	40.00	20.00	12.00
(72)	Johnson (San Francisco)	40.00	20.00	12.00
(73)	Jolley	60.00	30.00	18.00
(74)	Jones/Btg	40.00	20.00	12.00
(75)	Jones/Throwing	40.00	20.00	12.00
(76)	Kallio	40.00	20.00	12.00
(77)	Keating	40.00	20.00	12.00
(78)	Keefe	40.00	20.00	12.00
(79)	Keesey	40.00	20.00	12.00
(80)	Kerr	40.00	20.00	12.00
(81)	Killifer	40.00	20.00	12.00
(82)	Kinney	40.00	20.00	12.00
(83)	Knight	40.00	20.00	12.00
(84)	Knothe	40.00	20.00	12.00
(85)	Koehler	40.00	20.00	12.00
(86)	Kopp	40.00	20.00	12.00
(87)	Krause	40.00	20.00	12.00
(88)	Krug	40.00	20.00	12.00
(89)	Lary	40.00	20.00	12.00
(90)	LeBourveau	40.00	20.00	12.00
(91)	Lee	40.00	20.00	12.00
(92)	Ernie Lombardi	900.00	450.00	275.00
(93)	Mails	40.00	20.00	12.00
(94)	Martin (Missions)	40.00	20.00	12.00
(95)	Martin (Seattle)	40.00	20.00	12.00
(96)	May	40.00	20.00	12.00
(97)	McCabe	40.00	20.00	12.00
(98)	McCrea	40.00	20.00	12.00
(99)	McDaniel	40.00	20.00	12.00
(100)	McLaughlin	40.00	20.00	12.00
(101)	McNulty	40.00	20.00	12.00
(102)	Mellano	40.00	20.00	12.00
(103)	Irish Muesel (Meusel)	40.00	20.00	12.00
(104)	Middleton	40.00	20.00	12.00
(105)	Mishkin	40.00	20.00	12.00
(106)	Mitchell	40.00	20.00	12.00
(107)	Monroe	40.00	20.00	12.00
(108)	Moudy	40.00	20.00	12.00
(109)	Mulcahy	40.00	20.00	12.00
(110)	Muller	40.00	20.00	12.00
(111)	Mulligan	40.00	20.00	12.00
(112)	W. Murphy	40.00	20.00	12.00
(113)	Nance	40.00	20.00	12.00
(114)	Nelson	40.00	20.00	12.00
(115)	Osborn	40.00	20.00	12.00
(116)	Osborne	40.00	20.00	12.00
(117)	Parker	40.00	20.00	12.00
(118)	Peters	40.00	20.00	12.00
(119)	Pillette	40.00	20.00	12.00
(120)	Pinelli	40.00	20.00	12.00
(121)	Plitt	40.00	20.00	12.00
(122)	Ponder	40.00	20.00	12.00
(123)	Rachac	40.00	20.00	12.00
(124)	Read	40.00	20.00	12.00
(125)	Reed	40.00	20.00	12.00
(126)	Jimmy Reese	150.00	75.00	45.00
(127)	Rego	40.00	20.00	12.00
(128)	Rhodes	40.00	20.00	12.00
(129)	Rhyne	40.00	20.00	12.00
(130)	Rodda	40.00	20.00	12.00
(131)	Rohwer	40.00	20.00	12.00
(132)	Rose	40.00	20.00	12.00
(133)	Roth	40.00	20.00	12.00
(134)	Ruble	40.00	20.00	12.00
(135)	Ryan	40.00	20.00	12.00
(136)	Sandberg	40.00	20.00	12.00
(137)	Schulmerich	40.00	20.00	12.00
(138)	Severeid	40.00	20.00	12.00

(139)	Shea	40.00	20.00	12.00
(140)	Sheely	40.00	20.00	12.00
(141)	Shellenback	40.00	20.00	12.00
(142)	Sherlock	40.00	20.00	12.00
(143)	Sigafoos	40.00	20.00	12.00
(144)	Singleton	40.00	20.00	12.00
(145)	Slade	40.00	20.00	12.00
(146)	Smith	40.00	20.00	12.00
(147)	Sprinz	40.00	20.00	12.00
(148)	Staley	40.00	20.00	12.00
(149)	Suhr	40.00	20.00	12.00
(150)	Sunseri	40.00	20.00	12.00
(151)	Swanson	40.00	20.00	12.00
(152)	Sweeney	40.00	20.00	12.00
(153)	Teachout	40.00	20.00	12.00
(154)	Twombly	40.00	20.00	12.00
(155)	Vargas	40.00	20.00	12.00
(156)	Vinci	40.00	20.00	12.00
(157)	Vitt	40.00	20.00	12.00
(158)	Warhop	40.00	20.00	12.00
(159)	Weathersby	40.00	20.00	12.00
(160)	Weiss	40.00	20.00	12.00
(161)	Welch	40.00	20.00	12.00
(162)	Wera	40.00	20.00	12.00
(163)	Wetzel	40.00	20.00	12.00
(164)	Whitney	40.00	20.00	12.00
(165)	Williams	40.00	20.00	12.00
(166)	Wilson	40.00	20.00	12.00
(167)	Wolfer	40.00	20.00	12.00
(168)	Yerkes	40.00	20.00	12.00

1929 Zeenut Pacific Coast League

Zeenut cards from 1928 through 1930 maintain the same format as the 1927 series. Measuring about 1-3/4" x 3-1/2", the 1929 series consists of 168 known subjects.

		NM	EX	VG
Common Player:		40.00	20.00	12.00
With Coupon:		400.00	200.00	120.00
(1)	Albert	40.00	20.00	12.00
(2)	Almada	100.00	50.00	30.00
(3)	Anderson	40.00	20.00	12.00
(4)	Anton	40.00	20.00	12.00
(5)	Backer	40.00	20.00	12.00
(6)	Baker	40.00	20.00	12.00
(7)	Baldwin	40.00	20.00	12.00
(8)	Barbee	40.00	20.00	12.00
(9)	Barfoot	40.00	20.00	12.00
(10)	Bassler	40.00	20.00	12.00
(11)	Bates	40.00	20.00	12.00
(12)	Berger	40.00	20.00	12.00
(13)	Boehler	40.00	20.00	12.00
(14)	Boone	40.00	20.00	12.00
(15)	Borreani	40.00	20.00	12.00
(16)	Brenzel	40.00	20.00	12.00
(17)	Brooks	40.00	20.00	12.00
(18)	Brubaker	40.00	20.00	12.00
(19)	Bryan	40.00	20.00	12.00
(20)	Burke	40.00	20.00	12.00
(21)	Burkett	40.00	20.00	12.00
(22)	Burns	40.00	20.00	12.00
(23)	Bush	40.00	20.00	12.00
(24)	Butler	40.00	20.00	12.00
(25)	Camilli	40.00	20.00	12.00
(26)	Carlyle (Hollywood)	40.00	20.00	12.00
(27)	Carlyle	40.00	20.00	12.00
(28)	Cascarella	40.00	20.00	12.00
(29)	Caveney	40.00	20.00	12.00
(30)	Childs	40.00	20.00	12.00
(31)	Christensen	40.00	20.00	12.00
(32)	Cole	40.00	20.00	12.00
(33)	Collard	40.00	20.00	12.00
(34)	Cooper	40.00	20.00	12.00
(35)	Couch	40.00	20.00	12.00
(36)	Cox	40.00	20.00	12.00
(37)	Craghead	40.00	20.00	12.00

(38)	Crandall	40.00	20.00	12.00
(39)	Cronin	40.00	20.00	12.00
(40)	Crosetti	100.00	50.00	30.00
(41)	Daglia	40.00	20.00	12.00
(42)	Davis	40.00	20.00	12.00
(43)	Dean	40.00	20.00	12.00
(44)	Dittmar	40.00	20.00	12.00
(45)	Donovan	40.00	20.00	12.00
(46)	Dumovich	40.00	20.00	12.00
(47)	Eckardt	40.00	20.00	12.00
(48)	Ellsworth	40.00	20.00	12.00
(49)	Fenton	40.00	20.00	12.00
(50)	Finn	40.00	20.00	12.00
(51)	Fisch	40.00	20.00	12.00
(52)	Flynn	40.00	20.00	12.00
(53)	Frazier	40.00	20.00	12.00
(54)	Freitas	40.00	20.00	12.00
(55)	French	40.00	20.00	12.00
(56)	Gabler	40.00	20.00	12.00
(57)	Glynn	40.00	20.00	12.00
(58)	Lefty Gomez	1,200	600.00	360.00
(59)	Gould	40.00	20.00	12.00
(60)	Governor	40.00	20.00	12.00
(61)	Graham	40.00	20.00	12.00
(62)	Hand	40.00	20.00	12.00
(63)	Hannah	40.00	20.00	12.00
(64)	Harris	40.00	20.00	12.00
(65)	Heath	40.00	20.00	12.00
(66)	Heatherly	40.00	20.00	12.00
(67)	Hepting	40.00	20.00	12.00
(68)	Hillis	40.00	20.00	12.00
(69)	Hoffman	40.00	20.00	12.00
(70)	Holling	40.00	20.00	12.00
(71)	Hood	40.00	20.00	12.00
(72)	House	40.00	20.00	12.00
(73)	Howard	40.00	20.00	12.00
(74)	Hubbell	40.00	20.00	12.00
(75)	Hufft	40.00	20.00	12.00
(76)	Hurst	40.00	20.00	12.00
(77)	Jacobs (Los Angeles)	40.00	20.00	12.00
(78)	Jacobs (San Francisco)	40.00	20.00	12.00
(79)	Jahn	40.00	20.00	12.00
(80)	Jeffcoat	40.00	20.00	12.00
(81)	Johnson	40.00	20.00	12.00
(82)	Jolley	60.00	30.00	18.00
(83)	Jones	40.00	20.00	12.00
(84)	Jones	40.00	20.00	12.00
(85)	Kallio	40.00	20.00	12.00
(86)	Kasich	40.00	20.00	12.00
(87)	Keane	40.00	20.00	12.00
(88)	Keating	40.00	20.00	12.00
(89)	Keesey	40.00	20.00	12.00
(90)	Killifer	40.00	20.00	12.00
(91)	Knight	40.00	20.00	12.00
(92)	Knothe	40.00	20.00	12.00
(93)	Knott	40.00	20.00	12.00
(94)	Koehler	40.00	20.00	12.00
(95)	Krasovich	40.00	20.00	12.00
(96)	Krause	40.00	20.00	12.00
(97)	Krug (Hollywood)	40.00	20.00	12.00
(98)	Krug (Los Angeles)	40.00	20.00	12.00
(99)	Kunz	40.00	20.00	12.00
(100)	Langford	40.00	20.00	12.00
(101)	Lee	40.00	20.00	12.00
(102)	Ernie Lombardi	450.00	225.00	135.00
(103)	Mahaffey	40.00	20.00	12.00
(104)	Mails	40.00	20.00	12.00
(105)	Maloney	40.00	20.00	12.00
(106)	McCabe	40.00	20.00	12.00
(107)	McDaniel	40.00	20.00	12.00
(108)	McEvoy	40.00	20.00	12.00
(109)	McIssacs	40.00	20.00	12.00
(110)	McQuaid	40.00	20.00	12.00
(111)	Miller	40.00	20.00	12.00
(112)	Monroe	40.00	20.00	12.00
(113)	Muller	40.00	20.00	12.00
(114)	Mulligan	40.00	20.00	12.00
(115)	Nance	40.00	20.00	12.00
(116)	Nelson	40.00	20.00	12.00
(117)	Nevers	40.00	20.00	12.00
(118)	Oana	450.00	225.00	135.00
(119)	Olney	40.00	20.00	12.00
(120)	Ortman	40.00	20.00	12.00
(121)	Osborne	40.00	20.00	12.00
(122)	Ostenberg	40.00	20.00	12.00
(123)	Peters	40.00	20.00	12.00
(124)	Pillette	40.00	20.00	12.00
(125)	Pinelli	40.00	20.00	12.00
(126)	Pipgras	40.00	20.00	12.00
(127)	Plitt	40.00	20.00	12.00
(128)	Polvogt	40.00	20.00	12.00
(129)	Rachac	40.00	20.00	12.00
(130)	Read	40.00	20.00	12.00
(131)	Reed	40.00	20.00	12.00
(132)	Jimmy Reese	100.00	50.00	30.00
(133)	Rego	40.00	20.00	12.00
(134)	Ritter	40.00	20.00	12.00
(135)	Roberts	40.00	20.00	12.00

	NM	EX	VG
(136) Rodda	40.00	20.00	12.00
(137) Rodgers	40.00	20.00	12.00
(138) Rohwer	40.00	20.00	12.00
(139) Rollings	40.00	20.00	12.00
(140) Rumler	40.00	20.00	12.00
(141) Ryan	40.00	20.00	12.00
(142) Sandberg	40.00	20.00	12.00
(143) Schino	40.00	20.00	12.00
(144) Schmidt	40.00	20.00	12.00
(145) Schulmerich	40.00	20.00	12.00
(146) Scott	40.00	20.00	12.00
(147) Severeid	40.00	20.00	12.00
(148) Shanklin	40.00	20.00	12.00
(149) Sherlock	40.00	20.00	12.00
(150) Slade	40.00	20.00	12.00
(151) Staley	40.00	20.00	12.00
(152) Statz	60.00	30.00	18.00
(153) Steinecke	40.00	20.00	12.00
(154) Suhr	40.00	20.00	12.00
(155) Taylor	40.00	20.00	12.00
(156) Thurston	40.00	20.00	12.00
(157) Tierney	40.00	20.00	12.00
(158) Tolson	40.00	20.00	12.00
(159) Tomlin	40.00	20.00	12.00
(160) Vergez	40.00	20.00	12.00
(161) Vinci	40.00	20.00	12.00
(162) Volkman	40.00	20.00	12.00
(163) Walsh	40.00	20.00	12.00
(164) Warren	40.00	20.00	12.00
(165) Webb	40.00	20.00	12.00
(166) Weustling	40.00	20.00	12.00
(167) Williams	40.00	20.00	12.00
(168) Wingo	40.00	20.00	12.00

1930 Zeenut Pacific Coast Leag.

Zeenut cards from 1928 through 1930 maintain the same format as the 1927 series. Measuring about 1-13/16" x 3-1/2", the 1930 series consists of 186 known subjects. There are some lettering variations in the series. Most coupons carry an expiration date of April 1, 1931, but some coupons have no expiration date stated.

	NM	EX	VG
Common Player:	40.00	20.00	12.00
(1) Allington	40.00	20.00	12.00
(2) Almada	50.00	25.00	15.00
(3) Andrews	40.00	20.00	12.00
(4) Anton	40.00	20.00	12.00
(5) Arlett	40.00	20.00	12.00
(6) Backer	40.00	20.00	12.00
(7) Baecht	40.00	20.00	12.00
(8) Baker	40.00	20.00	12.00
(9) Baldwin	40.00	20.00	12.00
(10) Ballou	40.00	20.00	12.00
(11) Barbee	40.00	20.00	12.00
(12) Barfoot	40.00	20.00	12.00
(13) Bassler	40.00	20.00	12.00
(14) Bates	40.00	20.00	12.00
(15) Beck	40.00	20.00	12.00
(16) Boone	40.00	20.00	12.00
(17) Bowman	40.00	20.00	12.00
(18) Brannon	40.00	20.00	12.00
(19) Brenzel	40.00	20.00	12.00
(20) Brown	40.00	20.00	12.00
(21) Brubaker	40.00	20.00	12.00
(22) Brucker	40.00	20.00	12.00
(23) Bryan	40.00	20.00	12.00
(24) Burkett	40.00	20.00	12.00
(25) Burns	40.00	20.00	12.00
(26) Butler	40.00	20.00	12.00
(27) Camilli	40.00	20.00	12.00
(28) Carlyle	40.00	20.00	12.00
(29) Caster	40.00	20.00	12.00
(30) Caveney	40.00	20.00	12.00
(31) Chamberlain	40.00	20.00	12.00
(32) Chatham	40.00	20.00	12.00
(33) Childs	40.00	20.00	12.00
(34) Christensen	40.00	20.00	12.00
(35) Church	40.00	20.00	12.00
(36) Cole	40.00	20.00	12.00
(37) Coleman	40.00	20.00	12.00
(38) Collins	40.00	20.00	12.00
(39) Coscarart	40.00	20.00	12.00
(40) Cox	40.00	20.00	12.00
(41) Coyle	40.00	20.00	12.00
(42) Craghead	40.00	20.00	12.00
(43) Cronin	40.00	20.00	12.00
(44) Crosetti	100.00	50.00	30.00
(45) Daglia	40.00	20.00	12.00
(46) Davis	40.00	20.00	12.00
(47) Dean	40.00	20.00	12.00
(48) DeViveiros	40.00	20.00	12.00
(49) Dittmar	40.00	20.00	12.00
(50) Donovan	40.00	20.00	12.00
(51) Douglas	40.00	20.00	12.00
(52) Dumovich	40.00	20.00	12.00
(53) Edwards	40.00	20.00	12.00
(54) Ellsworth	40.00	20.00	12.00
(55) Falk	40.00	20.00	12.00
(56) Fisch	40.00	20.00	12.00
(57) Flynn	40.00	20.00	12.00
(58) Freitas	40.00	20.00	12.00
(59) French (Portland)	40.00	20.00	12.00
(60) French (Sacramento)	40.00	20.00	12.00
(61) Gabler	40.00	20.00	12.00
(62) Gaston	40.00	20.00	12.00
(63) Gazella	40.00	20.00	12.00
(64) Gould	40.00	20.00	12.00
(65) Governor	40.00	20.00	12.00
(66) Green	40.00	20.00	12.00
(67) Griffin	40.00	20.00	12.00
(68) Haney	40.00	20.00	12.00
(69) Hannah	40.00	20.00	12.00
(70) Harper	40.00	20.00	12.00
(71) Heath	40.00	20.00	12.00
(72) Hillis	40.00	20.00	12.00
(73) Hoag	40.00	20.00	12.00
(74) Hoffman	40.00	20.00	12.00
(75) Holland	40.00	20.00	12.00
(76) Hollerson	40.00	20.00	12.00
(77) Holling	40.00	20.00	12.00
(78) Hood	40.00	20.00	12.00
(79) Horn	40.00	20.00	12.00
(80) House	40.00	20.00	12.00
(81) Hubbell	40.00	20.00	12.00
(82) Hufft	40.00	20.00	12.00
(83) Hurst	40.00	20.00	12.00
(84) Jacobs (Los Angeles)	40.00	20.00	12.00
(85) Jacobs (Oakland)	40.00	20.00	12.00
(86) Jacobs	40.00	20.00	12.00
(87) Jahn	40.00	20.00	12.00
(88) Jeffcoat	40.00	20.00	12.00
(89) Johns	40.00	20.00	12.00
(90) Johnson (Portland)	40.00	20.00	12.00
(91) Johnson (Seattle)	40.00	20.00	12.00
(92) Joiner	40.00	20.00	12.00
(93) Kallio	40.00	20.00	12.00
(94) Kasich	40.00	20.00	12.00
(95) Keating	40.00	20.00	12.00
(96) Kelly	40.00	20.00	12.00
(97) Killifer	40.00	20.00	12.00
(98) Knight	40.00	20.00	12.00
(99) Knothe	40.00	20.00	12.00
(100) Koehler	40.00	20.00	12.00
(101) Kunz	40.00	20.00	12.00
(102) Lamanski	40.00	20.00	12.00
(103) Lawrence	40.00	20.00	12.00
(104) Lee	40.00	20.00	12.00
(105) Leishman	40.00	20.00	12.00
(106) Lelivelt	40.00	20.00	12.00
(107) Lieber	40.00	20.00	12.00
(108) Ernie Lombardi	450.00	225.00	135.00
(109) Mails	40.00	20.00	12.00
(110) Maloney	40.00	20.00	12.00
(111) Martin	40.00	20.00	12.00
(112) McDougal	40.00	20.00	12.00
(113) McLaughlin	40.00	20.00	12.00
(114) McQuaide	40.00	20.00	12.00
(115) Mellana	40.00	20.00	12.00
(116) Miljus ("S" on uniform)	40.00	20.00	12.00
(117) Miljus ("Seals" on uniform)	40.00	20.00	12.00
(118) Monroe	40.00	20.00	12.00
(119) Montgomery	40.00	20.00	12.00
(120) Moore	40.00	20.00	12.00
(121) Mulana	40.00	20.00	12.00
(122) Muller	40.00	20.00	12.00
(123) Mulligan	40.00	20.00	12.00
(124) Nelson	40.00	20.00	12.00
(125) Nevers	750.00	375.00	225.00
(126) Odell	40.00	20.00	12.00
(127) Olney	40.00	20.00	12.00
(128) Osborne	40.00	20.00	12.00
(129) Page	40.00	20.00	12.00
(130) Palmisano	40.00	20.00	12.00
(131) Parker	40.00	20.00	12.00
(132) Pasedel	40.00	20.00	12.00
(133) Pearson	40.00	20.00	12.00
(134) Penebskey	40.00	20.00	12.00
(135) Perry	40.00	20.00	12.00
(136) Peters	40.00	20.00	12.00
(137) Petterson	40.00	20.00	12.00
(138) H. Pillette	40.00	20.00	12.00
(139) T. Pillette	40.00	20.00	12.00
(140) Pinelli	40.00	20.00	12.00
(141) Pipgrass	40.00	20.00	12.00
(142) Porter	40.00	20.00	12.00
(143) Powles	40.00	20.00	12.00
(144) Read	40.00	20.00	12.00
(145) Reed	40.00	20.00	12.00
(146) Rehg	40.00	20.00	12.00
(147) Ricci	40.00	20.00	12.00
(148) Roberts	40.00	20.00	12.00
(149) Rodda	40.00	20.00	12.00
(150) Rohwer	40.00	20.00	12.00
(151) Rosenberg	2,500	1,250	750.00
(152) Rumler	40.00	20.00	12.00
(153) Ryan	40.00	20.00	12.00
(154) Schino	40.00	20.00	12.00
(155) Severeid	40.00	20.00	12.00
(156) Shanklin	40.00	20.00	12.00
(157) Sheely	40.00	20.00	12.00
(158) Sigafoos	40.00	20.00	12.00
(159) Statz	60.00	30.00	18.00
(160) Steinbacker	40.00	20.00	12.00
(161) Stevenson	40.00	20.00	12.00
(162) Sulik	40.00	20.00	12.00
(163) Taylor	40.00	20.00	12.00
(164) Thomas (Sacramento)	40.00	20.00	12.00
(165) Thomas (San Francisco)	40.00	20.00	12.00
(166) Trembly	40.00	20.00	12.00
(167) Turner	40.00	20.00	12.00
(168) Turpin	40.00	20.00	12.00
(169) Uhalt	40.00	20.00	12.00
(170) Vergez	40.00	20.00	12.00
(171) Vinci	40.00	20.00	12.00
(172) Vitt	40.00	20.00	12.00
(173) Wallgren	40.00	20.00	12.00
(174) Walsh	40.00	20.00	12.00
(175) Ward	40.00	20.00	12.00
(176) Warren	40.00	20.00	12.00
(177) Webb	40.00	20.00	12.00
(178) Wetzell	40.00	20.00	12.00
(179) F. Wetzel	40.00	20.00	12.00
(180) Williams	40.00	20.00	12.00
(181) Wilson	40.00	20.00	12.00
(182) Wingo	40.00	20.00	12.00
(183) Wirts	40.00	20.00	12.00
(184) Woodall	40.00	20.00	12.00
(185) Zamlack	40.00	20.00	12.00
(186) Zinn	40.00	20.00	12.00

1931 Zeenut Pacific Coast Leag.

CUT **COUPON** HERE
GOOD FOR VALUABLE PREMIUMS
ASK YOUR DEALER FOR LIST
This offer expires April 1st, 1932

Beginning in 1931, Zeenuts cards were no longer dated on the front, and cards without the coupon are very difficult to date. The words "Zeenuts Series" were also dropped from the front and replaced with the words "Coast League." Zeenut cards in 1931 measure 1-3/4" x 3-1/2".

	NM	EX	VG
Common Player:	40.00	20.00	12.00
With Coupon:	800.00	400.00	240.00
(1) Abbott	40.00	20.00	12.00
(2) Andrews	40.00	20.00	12.00
(3) Anton	40.00	20.00	12.00
(4) Backer	40.00	20.00	12.00
(5) Baker	40.00	20.00	12.00
(6) Baldwin	40.00	20.00	12.00
(7) Barbee	40.00	20.00	12.00
(8) Barton	40.00	20.00	12.00
(9) Bassler	40.00	20.00	12.00
(10) Berger (Missions)	40.00	20.00	12.00
(11) Berger (Portland)	40.00	20.00	12.00
(12) Biggs	40.00	20.00	12.00
(13) Bowman	40.00	20.00	12.00
(14) Brenzel	40.00	20.00	12.00
(15) Bryan	40.00	20.00	12.00
(16) Burns	40.00	20.00	12.00
(17) Camilli	40.00	20.00	12.00
(18) Campbell	40.00	20.00	12.00
(19) Carlyle	40.00	20.00	12.00
(20) Caveney	40.00	20.00	12.00
(21) Chesterfield	40.00	20.00	12.00
(22) Cole	40.00	20.00	12.00
(23) Coleman	40.00	20.00	12.00
(24) Coscarart	40.00	20.00	12.00
(25) Crosetti	200.00	100.00	60.00
(26) Davis	40.00	20.00	12.00
(27) DeBerry	40.00	20.00	12.00
(28) Demaree	40.00	20.00	12.00
(29) Dean	40.00	20.00	12.00
(30) Delaney	40.00	20.00	12.00
(31) Dondero	40.00	20.00	12.00
(32) Donovan	40.00	20.00	12.00
(33) Douglas	40.00	20.00	12.00
(34) Ellsworth	40.00	20.00	12.00
(35) Farrell	40.00	20.00	12.00
(36) Fenton	40.00	20.00	12.00
(37) Fitzpatrick	40.00	20.00	12.00
(38) Flagstead	40.00	20.00	12.00
(39) Flynn	40.00	20.00	12.00
(40) Frazier	40.00	20.00	12.00
(41) Freitas	40.00	20.00	12.00
(42) French	40.00	20.00	12.00
(43) Fullerton	40.00	20.00	12.00
(44) Gabler	40.00	20.00	12.00
(45) Gazella	40.00	20.00	12.00
(46) Hale	40.00	20.00	12.00
(47) Hamilton	40.00	20.00	12.00
(48) Haney	40.00	20.00	12.00
(49) Hannah	40.00	20.00	12.00
(50) Harper	40.00	20.00	12.00
(51) Henderson	40.00	20.00	12.00
(52) Herrmann	40.00	20.00	12.00
(53) Hoffman	40.00	20.00	12.00

		NM	EX	VG
(54)	Holland	40.00	20.00	12.00
(55)	Holling	40.00	20.00	12.00
(56)	Hubbell	40.00	20.00	12.00
(57)	Hufft	40.00	20.00	12.00
(58)	Hurst	40.00	20.00	12.00
(59)	Jacobs	40.00	20.00	12.00
(60)	Kallio	40.00	20.00	12.00
(61)	Keating	40.00	20.00	12.00
(62)	Keesey	40.00	20.00	12.00
(63)	Knothe	40.00	20.00	12.00
(64)	Knott	40.00	20.00	12.00
(65)	Kohler	40.00	20.00	12.00
(66)	Lamanski	40.00	20.00	12.00
(67)	Lee	40.00	20.00	12.00
(68)	Lelivelt	40.00	20.00	12.00
(69)	Lieber	40.00	20.00	12.00
(70)	Lipanovic	40.00	20.00	12.00
(71)	McDonald	40.00	20.00	12.00
(72)	McDougall	40.00	20.00	12.00
(73)	McLaughlin	40.00	20.00	12.00
(74)	Monroe	40.00	20.00	12.00
(75)	Moss	40.00	20.00	12.00
(76)	Mulligan	40.00	20.00	12.00
(77)	Ortman	40.00	20.00	12.00
(78)	Orwoll	40.00	20.00	12.00
(79)	Parker	40.00	20.00	12.00
(80)	Penebskey	40.00	20.00	12.00
(81)	H. Pillette	40.00	20.00	12.00
(82)	T. Pillette	40.00	20.00	12.00
(83)	Pinelli	40.00	20.00	12.00
(84)	Pool	40.00	20.00	12.00
(85)	Posedel	40.00	20.00	12.00
(86)	Powers	40.00	20.00	12.00
(87)	Read	40.00	20.00	12.00
(88)	Andy Reese	40.00	20.00	12.00
(89)	Rhiel	40.00	20.00	12.00
(90)	Ricci	40.00	20.00	12.00
(91)	Rohwer	40.00	20.00	12.00
(92)	Ryan	40.00	20.00	12.00
(93)	Schino	40.00	20.00	12.00
(94)	Schulte	40.00	20.00	12.00
(95)	Severeid	40.00	20.00	12.00
(96)	Sharpe	40.00	20.00	12.00
(97)	Shellenback	40.00	20.00	12.00
(98)	Simas	40.00	20.00	12.00
(99)	Steinbacker	40.00	20.00	12.00
(100)	Summa	40.00	20.00	12.00
(101)	Tubbs	40.00	20.00	12.00
(102)	Turner	40.00	20.00	12.00
(103)	Turpin	40.00	20.00	12.00
(104)	Uhalt	40.00	20.00	12.00
(105)	Vinci	40.00	20.00	12.00
(106)	Vitt	40.00	20.00	12.00
(107)	Wade	40.00	20.00	12.00
(108)	Walsh	40.00	20.00	12.00
(109)	Walters	40.00	20.00	12.00
(110)	Wera	40.00	20.00	12.00
(111)	Wetzel	40.00	20.00	12.00
(112)	Williams (Portland)	40.00	20.00	12.00
(113)	Williams (San Francisco)	40.00	20.00	12.00
(114)	Wingo	40.00	20.00	12.00
(115)	Wirts	40.00	20.00	12.00
(116)	Wise	40.00	20.00	12.00
(117)	Woodall	40.00	20.00	12.00
(118)	Yerkes	40.00	20.00	12.00
(119)	Zamlock	40.00	20.00	12.00
(120)	Zinn	40.00	20.00	12.00

1932 Zeenut Pacific Coast Leag.

Beginning in 1931, Zeenuts cards were no longer dated on the front, and cards without the coupon are very difficult to date. The words "Zeenuts Series" were dropped from the front and replaced with "Coast League." Zeenut cards in 1932 measure 1-3/4" x 3-1/2".

		NM	EX	VG
Common Player:		40.00	20.00	12.00
With Coupon:		600.00	300.00	180.00
(1)	Abbott	40.00	20.00	12.00
(2)	Almada	50.00	25.00	15.00
(3)	Anton	40.00	20.00	12.00
(4)	Babich	40.00	20.00	12.00
(5)	Backer	40.00	20.00	12.00
(6)	Baker	40.00	20.00	12.00
(7)	Ballou	40.00	20.00	12.00
(8)	Bassler	40.00	20.00	12.00
(9)	Berger	40.00	20.00	12.00
(10)	Blackerby	40.00	20.00	12.00
(11)	Bordagaray	40.00	20.00	12.00
(12)	Brannon	40.00	20.00	12.00
(13)	Briggs	40.00	20.00	12.00
(14)	Brubaker	40.00	20.00	12.00
(15)	Callaghan	40.00	20.00	12.00
(16)	Camilli	40.00	20.00	12.00

		NM	EX	VG
(17)	Campbell	40.00	20.00	12.00
(18)	Carlyle	40.00	20.00	12.00
(19)	Caster	40.00	20.00	12.00
(20)	Caveney	40.00	20.00	12.00
(21)	Chamberlain	40.00	20.00	12.00
(22)	Cole	40.00	20.00	12.00
(23)	Collard	40.00	20.00	12.00
(24)	Cook	40.00	20.00	12.00
(25)	Coscarart	40.00	20.00	12.00
(26)	Cox	40.00	20.00	12.00
(27)	Cronin	40.00	20.00	12.00
(28)	Daglia	40.00	20.00	12.00
(29)	Dahlgren	45.00	22.00	13.50
(30)	Davis	40.00	20.00	12.00
(31)	Dean	40.00	20.00	12.00
(32)	Delaney	40.00	20.00	12.00
(33)	Demaree	40.00	20.00	12.00
(34)	Devine	40.00	20.00	12.00
(35)	DeViveiros	40.00	20.00	12.00
(36)	Dittmar	40.00	20.00	12.00
(37)	Donovan	40.00	20.00	12.00
(38)	Ellsworth	40.00	20.00	12.00
(39)	Fitzpatrick	40.00	20.00	12.00
(40)	Frazier	40.00	20.00	12.00
(41)	Freitas	40.00	20.00	12.00
(42)	Garibaldi	40.00	20.00	12.00
(43)	Gaston	40.00	20.00	12.00
(44)	Gazella	40.00	20.00	12.00
(45)	Gillick	40.00	20.00	12.00
(46)	Hafey	40.00	20.00	12.00
(47)	Haney	40.00	20.00	12.00
(48)	Hannah	40.00	20.00	12.00
(49)	Henderson	40.00	20.00	12.00
(50)	Herrmann	40.00	20.00	12.00
(51)	Hipps	40.00	20.00	12.00
(52)	Hofman	40.00	20.00	12.00
(53)	Holland	40.00	20.00	12.00
(54)	House	40.00	20.00	12.00
(55)	Hufft	40.00	20.00	12.00
(56)	Hunt	40.00	20.00	12.00
(57)	Hurst	40.00	20.00	12.00
(58)	Jacobs	40.00	20.00	12.00
(59)	Johns	40.00	20.00	12.00
(60)	Johnson (Missions)	40.00	20.00	12.00
(61)	Johnson (Portland)	40.00	20.00	12.00
(62)	Johnson (Seattle)	40.00	20.00	12.00
(63)	Joiner	40.00	20.00	12.00
(64)	Kallio	40.00	20.00	12.00
(65)	Kasich	40.00	20.00	12.00
(66)	Keesey	40.00	20.00	12.00
(67)	Kelly	40.00	20.00	12.00
(68)	Koehler	40.00	20.00	12.00
(69)	Lee	40.00	20.00	12.00
(70)	Lieber	40.00	20.00	12.00
(71)	Mailho	40.00	20.00	12.00
(72)	Martin (Oakland)	40.00	20.00	12.00
(73)	Martin (San Francisco)	40.00	20.00	12.00
(74)	McNeely	40.00	20.00	12.00
(75)	Miljus	40.00	20.00	12.00
(76)	Monroe	40.00	20.00	12.00
(77)	Mosolf	40.00	20.00	12.00
(78)	Moss	40.00	20.00	12.00
(79)	Muller	40.00	20.00	12.00
(80)	Mulligan	40.00	20.00	12.00
(81)	Oana	300.00	150.00	90.00
(82)	Osborn	40.00	20.00	12.00
(83)	Page	40.00	20.00	12.00
(84)	Penebsky	40.00	20.00	12.00
(85)	H. Pillette	40.00	20.00	12.00
(86)	Pinelli	50.00	25.00	15.00
(87)	Poole	40.00	20.00	12.00
(88)	Quellich	40.00	20.00	12.00
(89)	Read	40.00	20.00	12.00
(90)	Ricci	40.00	20.00	12.00
(91)	Salvo	40.00	20.00	12.00
(92)	Sankey	40.00	20.00	12.00
(93)	Sheehan	40.00	20.00	12.00
(94)	Shellenback	40.00	20.00	12.00
(95)	Sherlock (Hollywood)	40.00	20.00	12.00
(96)	Sherlock (Missions)	40.00	20.00	12.00
(97)	Shores	40.00	20.00	12.00
(98)	Simas	40.00	20.00	12.00
(99)	Statz	60.00	30.00	18.00
(100)	Steinbacker	40.00	20.00	12.00
(101)	Sulik	40.00	20.00	12.00
(102)	Summa	40.00	20.00	12.00
(103)	Thomas	40.00	20.00	12.00
(104)	Uhalt	40.00	20.00	12.00
(105)	Vinci	40.00	20.00	12.00
(106)	Vitt	40.00	20.00	12.00
(107)	Walsh (Missions)	40.00	20.00	12.00
(108)	Walsh (Oakland)	40.00	20.00	12.00
(109)	Walters	40.00	20.00	12.00
(110)	Ward	40.00	20.00	12.00
(111)	Welsh	40.00	20.00	12.00
(112)	Wera	40.00	20.00	12.00
(113)	Williams	40.00	20.00	12.00
(114)	Willoughby	40.00	20.00	12.00
(115)	Wirts	40.00	20.00	12.00
(116)	Wise	40.00	20.00	12.00
(117)	Woodall	40.00	20.00	12.00
(118)	Yde	40.00	20.00	12.00
(119)	Zahniser	40.00	20.00	12.00
(120)	Zamloch	40.00	20.00	12.00

1933 Zeenut Pacific Coast League (Sepia)

This is the most confusing era for Zeenut cards. The cards of 1933-36 are nearly identical, displaying the words, "Coast League" in a small rectangle with rounded corners, along with the player's name and team. The photos are black-and-white (except 1933 Zeenuts have also been found with sepia photos). Because no date appears on the photos, cards from these years are impossible to tell apart without the coupon bottom that lists an expiration date. To date over 161 subjects have been found, with some known to exist in all four years. There are cases where the exact same photo was used from one year to the next (sometimes with minor cropping differences). All cards of Joe and Vince DiMaggio have their last name misspelled "DeMaggio." Cards of all years measure about 1-3/4" x 3-1/2" with coupon.

		NM	EX	VG
Common Player:		40.00	20.00	12.00
With Coupon:		400.00	200.00	120.00
(1)	L. Almada	50.00	25.00	15.00
(2)	Anton	40.00	20.00	12.00
(3)	Bassler	40.00	20.00	12.00
(4)	Bonnelly	40.00	20.00	12.00
(5)	Bordagary	40.00	20.00	12.00
(6)	Bottarini	40.00	20.00	12.00
(7)	Brannan	40.00	20.00	12.00
(8)	Brubaker	40.00	20.00	12.00
(9)	Bryan	40.00	20.00	12.00
(10)	Burns	40.00	20.00	12.00
(11)	Camilli	40.00	20.00	12.00
(12)	Chozen	40.00	20.00	12.00
(13)	Cole	40.00	20.00	12.00
(14)	Cronin	40.00	20.00	12.00
(15)	Dahlgren	40.00	20.00	12.00
(16)	Donovan	40.00	20.00	12.00
(17)	Douglas	40.00	20.00	12.00
(18)	Flynn	40.00	20.00	12.00
(19)	French	40.00	20.00	12.00
(20)	Frietas	40.00	20.00	12.00
(21)	Galan	40.00	20.00	12.00
(22)	Hofmann	40.00	20.00	12.00
(23)	Kelman	40.00	20.00	12.00
(24)	Lelivelt	40.00	20.00	12.00
(25)	Ludolph	40.00	20.00	12.00
(26)	McDonald	40.00	20.00	12.00
(27)	McNeely	40.00	20.00	12.00
(28)	McQuaid	40.00	20.00	12.00
(29)	Moncrief	40.00	20.00	12.00
(30)	Nelson	40.00	20.00	12.00
(31)	Osborne	40.00	20.00	12.00
(32)	Petersen	40.00	20.00	12.00
(33)	Reeves	40.00	20.00	12.00
(34)	Scott	40.00	20.00	12.00
(35)	Shellenback	40.00	20.00	12.00
(36)	J. Sherlock	40.00	20.00	12.00
(37)	V. Sherlock	40.00	20.00	12.00
(38)	Steinbacker	40.00	20.00	12.00
(39)	Stine	40.00	20.00	12.00
(40)	Strange	40.00	20.00	12.00
(41)	Sulik	40.00	20.00	12.00
(42)	Sweetland	40.00	20.00	12.00
(43)	Uhalt	40.00	20.00	12.00
(44)	Vinci	40.00	20.00	12.00
(45)	Vitt	40.00	20.00	12.00
(46)	Wetzel	40.00	20.00	12.00
(47)	Woodall	40.00	20.00	12.00
(48)	Zinn	40.00	20.00	12.00

1933-36 Zeenut Pacific Coast League (Black-and-White)

		NM	EX	VG
Common Player:		40.00	20.00	12.00
With Coupon:		400.00	200.00	120.00
(1a)	Almada (Large pose.)	50.00	25.00	15.00
(1b)	Almada (Small pose.)	50.00	25.00	15.00
(2a)	Anton (Large pose.)	40.00	20.00	12.00

(2b)	Anton (Small pose.)	40.00	20.00	12.00
(3)	Babich	40.00	20.00	12.00
(4)	Backer	40.00	20.00	12.00
(5)	Ballou (Black stockings.)	40.00	20.00	12.00
(6a)	Ballou (Stockings with band, large pose.)	40.00	20.00	12.00
(6b)	Ballou (Stockings with band, small pose.)	40.00	20.00	12.00
(7)	Barath	40.00	20.00	12.00
(8)	Beck	40.00	20.00	12.00
(9)	C. Beck	40.00	20.00	12.00
(10)	W. Beck	40.00	20.00	12.00
(11)	Becker	40.00	20.00	12.00
(12)	Biongovanni	40.00	20.00	12.00
(13)	Blackerby	40.00	20.00	12.00
(14)	Blakely	40.00	20.00	12.00
(15)	Borja (Sacramento)	40.00	20.00	12.00
(16)	Borja (Seals)	40.00	20.00	12.00
(17)	Brundin	40.00	20.00	12.00
(18)	Carlyle	40.00	20.00	12.00
(19a)	Caveney (Name incorrect.)	40.00	20.00	12.00
(19b)	Cavaney (Name correct.)	40.00	20.00	12.00
(20)	Chelini	40.00	20.00	12.00
(21)	Cole (With glove.)	40.00	20.00	12.00
(22)	Cole (No glove.)	40.00	20.00	12.00
(23)	Connors	40.00	20.00	12.00
(24)	Coscarart (Missions)	40.00	20.00	12.00
(25)	Coscarart (Seattle)	40.00	20.00	12.00
(26)	Cox	40.00	20.00	12.00
(27)	Davis	40.00	20.00	12.00
(28)	J. DeMaggio/Btg (DiMaggio)	15,000	5,500	3,750
(29)	J. DeMaggio/Throwing (DiMaggio)	15,000	5,500	3,750
(30)	V. DeMaggio (DiMaggio)	1,200	600.00	360.00
(31)	DeViveiros	40.00	20.00	12.00
(32)	Densmore	40.00	20.00	12.00
(33)	Dittmar	40.00	20.00	12.00
(34)	Donovan	40.00	20.00	12.00
(35)	Douglas (Oakland)	40.00	20.00	12.00
(36)	Douglas (Seals)	40.00	20.00	12.00
(37a)	Duggan (Large pose.)	40.00	20.00	12.00
(37b)	Duggan (Small pose.)	40.00	20.00	12.00
(38)	Durst	40.00	20.00	12.00
(39a)	Eckhardt (Large pose.)	40.00	20.00	12.00
(39b)	Eckhardt (Small pose.)	40.00	20.00	12.00
(40)	Ellsworth	40.00	20.00	12.00
(41)	Fenton	40.00	20.00	12.00
(42)	Fitzpatrick	40.00	20.00	12.00
(43)	Francovich	40.00	20.00	12.00
(44)	Funk	40.00	20.00	12.00
(45a)	Garibaldi (Large pose.)	40.00	20.00	12.00
(45b)	Garibaldi (Small pose.)	40.00	20.00	12.00
(46)	Gibson (Black sleeves.)	40.00	20.00	12.00
(47)	Gibson (White sleeves.)	40.00	20.00	12.00
(48)	Gira	40.00	20.00	12.00
(49)	Glaister	40.00	20.00	12.00
(50)	Graves	40.00	20.00	12.00
(51a)	Hafey (Missions, large pose.)	40.00	20.00	12.00
(51b)	Hafey (Missions, middle-size pose.)	40.00	20.00	12.00
(51c)	Hafey (Missions, small pose.)	40.00	20.00	12.00
(52)	Hafey (Sacramento)	40.00	20.00	12.00
(53)	Haid (Missions)	40.00	20.00	12.00
(54)	Haid (Seattle)	40.00	20.00	12.00
(55)	Haney	40.00	20.00	12.00
(56a)	Hartwig (Sacramento, large pose.)	40.00	20.00	12.00
(56b)	Hartwig (Sacramento, small pose.)	40.00	20.00	12.00
(57)	Hartwig (Seals)	40.00	20.00	12.00
(58)	Henderson	40.00	20.00	12.00
(59)	Herrmann	40.00	20.00	12.00
(60)	B. Holder	40.00	20.00	12.00
(61)	Holland	40.00	20.00	12.00
(62)	Horne	40.00	20.00	12.00
(63)	House	40.00	20.00	12.00
(64)	Hunt	40.00	20.00	12.00
(65)	A.E. Jacobs	40.00	20.00	12.00
(66)	Johns	40.00	20.00	12.00
(67)	D. Johnson	40.00	20.00	12.00
(68)	L. Johnson	40.00	20.00	12.00
(69)	Joiner	40.00	20.00	12.00
(70)	Jolley	60.00	30.00	18.00
(71)	Joost	40.00	20.00	12.00
(72)	Jorgensen	40.00	20.00	12.00
(73)	Kallio	40.00	20.00	12.00
(74)	Kamm	40.00	20.00	12.00
(75)	Kampouris	40.00	20.00	12.00
(76)	E. Kelly (Oakland)	40.00	20.00	12.00
(77)	E. Kelly (Seattle)	40.00	20.00	12.00
(78)	Kenna	40.00	20.00	12.00
(79)	Kintana	40.00	20.00	12.00
(80)	Lahman	40.00	20.00	12.00
(81)	Lieber	40.00	20.00	12.00
(82)	Ludolph	40.00	20.00	12.00
(83)	Mailho	40.00	20.00	12.00
(84a)	Mails (Large pose.)	40.00	20.00	12.00
(84b)	Mails (Small pose.)	40.00	20.00	12.00
(85)	Marty (Black sleeves.)	40.00	20.00	12.00
(86)	Marty (White sleeves.)	40.00	20.00	12.00
(87)	Massuci (Batting follow-through.)	40.00	20.00	12.00
(88)	Masucci (Different pose.)	40.00	20.00	12.00
(89a)	McEvoy (Large pose.)	40.00	20.00	12.00
(89b)	McEvoy (Small pose.)	40.00	20.00	12.00
(90)	McIsaacs	40.00	20.00	12.00
(91)	McMullen (Oakland)	40.00	20.00	12.00
(92)	McMullen (Seals)	40.00	20.00	12.00
(93)	Mitchell	40.00	20.00	12.00
(94a)	Monzo (Large pose.)	40.00	20.00	12.00
(94b)	Monzo (Small pose.)	40.00	20.00	12.00
(95)	Mort/Throwing	40.00	20.00	12.00
(96)	Mort/Btg	40.00	20.00	12.00
(97a)	Muller (Oakland, large pose)	40.00	20.00	12.00
(97b)	Muller (Oakland, small pose)	40.00	20.00	12.00
(98)	Muller (Seattle)	40.00	20.00	12.00
(99)	Mulligan (Hands showing.)	40.00	20.00	12.00

(100)	Mulligan (Hands not showing.)	40.00	20.00	12.00
(101)	Newkirk	40.00	20.00	12.00
(102)	Nicholas	40.00	20.00	12.00
(103)	Nitcholas	40.00	20.00	12.00
(103a)	Norbert (Large pose.)	40.00	20.00	12.00
(103b)	Norbert (Small pose.)	40.00	20.00	12.00
(105)	O'Doul (Black sleeves.)	125.00	65.00	35.00
(106)	O'Doul (White sleeves.)	125.00	65.00	35.00
(107)	Oglesby	40.00	20.00	12.00
(108)	Ostenberg	40.00	20.00	12.00
(109)	Outen/Throwing	40.00	20.00	12.00
(110)	Outen/Btg	40.00	20.00	12.00
(111)	Page (Hollywood)	40.00	20.00	12.00
(112)	Page (Seattle)	40.00	20.00	12.00
(113)	Palmisano	40.00	20.00	12.00
(114)	Parker	40.00	20.00	12.00
(115)	Phebus	40.00	20.00	12.00
(116)	T. Pillette	40.00	20.00	12.00
(117)	Pool	40.00	20.00	12.00
(118)	Powers	40.00	20.00	12.00
(119)	Quellich	40.00	20.00	12.00
(120)	Radonitz	40.00	20.00	12.00
(121a)	Raimondi (Large pose.)	40.00	20.00	12.00
(121b)	Raimondi (Small pose.)	40.00	20.00	12.00
(122a)	Jimmy Reese (Large pose.)	100.00	50.00	30.00
(122b)	Jimmy Reese (Small pose.)	100.00	50.00	30.00
(123)	Rego	40.00	20.00	12.00
(124)	Rhyne (Front)	40.00	20.00	12.00
(125)	Rosenberg	40.00	20.00	12.00
(126)	Salinsen	40.00	20.00	12.00
(127)	Salkeld	40.00	20.00	12.00
(128)	Salvo	40.00	20.00	12.00
(129)	Sever	40.00	20.00	12.00
(130)	Sheehan (Black sleeves.)	40.00	20.00	12.00
(131)	Sheehan (White sleeves.)	40.00	20.00	12.00
(132a)	Sheely (Large pose.)	40.00	20.00	12.00
(132b)	Sheely (Small pose.)	40.00	20.00	12.00
(134)	Sprinz	40.00	20.00	12.00
(135)	Starritt	40.00	20.00	12.00
(136)	Statz	60.00	30.00	18.00
(137a)	Steinbacker (Large pose.)	40.00	20.00	12.00
(137b)	Steinbacker (Small pose.)	40.00	20.00	12.00
(138)	Stewart	40.00	20.00	12.00
(139)	Stitzel (Los Angeles)	40.00	20.00	12.00
(140)	Stitzel (Missions)	40.00	20.00	12.00
(141)	Stitzel (Seals)	40.00	20.00	12.00
(142)	Stoneham	40.00	20.00	12.00
(143)	Street	40.00	20.00	12.00
(144)	Stroner	40.00	20.00	12.00
(145)	Stutz	40.00	20.00	12.00
(146)	Sulik	40.00	20.00	12.00
(147a)	Thurston (Mission)	40.00	20.00	12.00
(147b)	Thurston (Missions)	40.00	20.00	12.00
(148)	Vitt (Hollywood)	40.00	20.00	12.00
(149)	Vitt (Oakland)	40.00	20.00	12.00
(150)	Wallgren	40.00	20.00	12.00
(151)	Walsh	40.00	20.00	12.00
(152)	Walters	40.00	20.00	12.00
(153)	West	40.00	20.00	12.00
(154a)	Wirts (Large pose.)	40.00	20.00	12.00
(154b)	Wirts (Small pose.)	40.00	20.00	12.00
(155)	Woodall/Btg	40.00	20.00	12.00
(156)	Woodall/Throwing	40.00	20.00	12.00
(157)	Wright (Facing to front.)	40.00	20.00	12.00
(158)	Wright (Facing to left.)	40.00	20.00	12.00
(159)	Zinn	40.00	20.00	12.00

1937-38 Zeenut Pacific Coast League

The 1937 and 1938 Zeenuts are similar to the 1933-1936 issues, except the black rectangle containing the player's name and team has square (rather than rounded) corners. Again, it is difficult to distinguish between the two years. In 1938, Zeenuts eliminated the coupon bottom and began including a separate coupon in the candy package along with the baseball card. The final two years of the Zeenuts issues, the 1937 and 1938 cards, are among the more difficult to find. With coupon, the 1937 cards measure about 1-5/8" x 3-7/16". The coupon-less 1938 cards measure about 1-3/4" x 2-13/16".

		NM	EX	VG
Common Player:		60.00	25.00	15.00
With Coupon:		400.00	200.00	120.00
(1)	Annunzio	60.00	25.00	15.00
(2)	Baker	60.00	25.00	15.00
(3)	Ballou	60.00	25.00	15.00
(4)	C. Beck	60.00	25.00	15.00

(5)	W. Beck	60.00	25.00	15.00
(6)	Bolin	60.00	25.00	15.00
(7)	Bongiavanni	60.00	25.00	15.00
(8)	Boss	60.00	25.00	15.00
(9)	Carson	60.00	25.00	15.00
(10)	Clabaugh	60.00	25.00	15.00
(11)	Clifford	60.00	25.00	15.00
(12)	B. Cole	60.00	25.00	15.00
(13)	Coscarart	60.00	25.00	15.00
(14)	Cronin	60.00	25.00	15.00
(15)	Cullop	60.00	25.00	15.00
(16)	Daglia	60.00	25.00	15.00
(17)	D. DeMaggio (DiMaggio)	1,200	600.00	360.00
(18)	Douglas	60.00	25.00	15.00
(19)	Frankovich	60.00	25.00	15.00
(20)	Frazier	60.00	25.00	15.00
(21)	Fredericks	60.00	25.00	15.00
(22)	Freitas	60.00	25.00	15.00
(23)	Gabrielson (Oakland)	60.00	25.00	15.00
(24)	Gabrielson (Seattle)	60.00	25.00	15.00
(25)	Garibaldi	60.00	25.00	15.00
(26)	Gibson	60.00	25.00	15.00
(27)	Gill	60.00	25.00	15.00
(28)	Graves	60.00	25.00	15.00
(29)	Guay	60.00	25.00	15.00
(30)	Gudat	60.00	25.00	15.00
(31)	Haid	60.00	25.00	15.00
(32)	Hannah	60.00	25.00	15.00
(33)	Hawkins	60.00	25.00	15.00
(34)	Herrmann	60.00	25.00	15.00
(35)	Holder	60.00	25.00	15.00
(36)	Jennings	60.00	25.00	15.00
(37)	Judnich	60.00	25.00	15.00
(38)	Klinger	60.00	25.00	15.00
(39)	Koenig	60.00	25.00	15.00
(40)	Koupal	60.00	25.00	15.00
(41)	Koy	60.00	25.00	15.00
(42)	Lamanski	60.00	25.00	15.00
(43)	Leishman (Oakland)	60.00	25.00	15.00
(44)	Leishman (Seattle)	60.00	25.00	15.00
(45)	G. Lillard	60.00	25.00	15.00
(46)	Mann	60.00	25.00	15.00
(47)	Marble (Hollywood)	60.00	25.00	15.00
(49)	Miller	60.00	25.00	15.00
(50)	Mills	60.00	25.00	15.00
(51)	Monzo	60.00	25.00	15.00
(52)	B. Mort (Hollywood)	60.00	25.00	15.00
(53)	B. Mort (Missions)	60.00	25.00	15.00
(54)	Muller	60.00	25.00	15.00
(55)	Murray	60.00	25.00	15.00
(56)	Newsome	60.00	25.00	15.00
(57)	Nitcholas	60.00	25.00	15.00
(58)	Olds	60.00	25.00	15.00
(59)	Orengo	60.00	25.00	15.00
(60)	Osborne	60.00	25.00	15.00
(61)	Outen	60.00	25.00	15.00
(62)	C. Outen (Hollywood)	60.00	25.00	15.00
(63)	C. Outen (Missions)	60.00	25.00	15.00
(64)	Pippin	60.00	25.00	15.00
(65)	Powell	60.00	25.00	15.00
(66)	Radonitz	60.00	25.00	15.00
(67)	Raimondi (Oakland)	60.00	25.00	15.00
(68)	Raimondi (San Francisco)	60.00	25.00	15.00
(69)	A. Raimondi	60.00	25.00	15.00
(70)	W. Raimondi	60.00	25.00	15.00
(71)	Rhyne	60.00	25.00	15.00
(72)	Rosenberg (Missions)	1,200	600.00	360.00
(73)	Rosenberg (Portland)	1,200	600.00	360.00
(74)	Sawyer	60.00	25.00	15.00
(75)	Seats	60.00	25.00	15.00
(76)	Sheehan (Oakland)	60.00	25.00	15.00
(77)	Sheehan (San Francisco)	60.00	25.00	15.00
(78)	Shores	60.00	25.00	15.00
(79)	Slade (Hollywood)	60.00	25.00	15.00
(80)	Slade (Missions)	60.00	25.00	15.00
(81)	Sprinz (Missions)	60.00	25.00	15.00
(82)	Sprinz (San Francisco)	60.00	25.00	15.00
(83)	Statz	75.00	37.50	22.50
(84)	Storey	60.00	25.00	15.00
(85)	Stringfellow	60.00	25.00	15.00
(86)	Stutz	60.00	25.00	15.00
(87)	Sweeney	60.00	25.00	15.00
(88)	Thomson	60.00	25.00	15.00
(89)	Tost (Hollywood)	60.00	25.00	15.00
(90)	Tost (Missions)	60.00	25.00	15.00
(91)	Ulrich	60.00	25.00	15.00
(92)	Vergez	60.00	25.00	15.00
(93)	Vezelich	60.00	25.00	15.00
(94)	Vitter (Hollywood)	60.00	25.00	15.00
(95)	Vitter (San Francisco)	60.00	25.00	15.00
(96)	West	60.00	25.00	15.00
(97)	Wilson	60.00	25.00	15.00
(98)	Woodall	60.00	25.00	15.00
(99)	Wright	60.00	25.00	15.00

The Mint-Mint examples of vintage cards carry a significant premium over the Near Mint values shown here. This premium reflects limited availability of the highest-grade cards as well as demand for particular cards or sets in the best possible condition.

Chronological Index

1860s

1870s

1880s

1890s

1900s

1910s

Ed Herrmann | CATCHER

LARRY DOBY

Paul Erickson

BILL GLYNN — Infielder

1920s

1930s

1940s

1950s

JULIO
FRANCO
Infield
WHEATIES

WALLY   WALLY JOYNER
CHECKLIST

1960s

Geo.H."Babe" Ruth
OUTFIELDER, NEW YORK, AM.L.

1970s

GRADY SIZEMORE

JimEdmonds
st. louis cardinals®

1980s

LIFE GRAND SLAM

DALE MURPHY
OUTFIELD

Francisco Rodriguez

ROY HALLADAY
TORONTO BLUE JAYS

1990s

JOHN BENCH

Ryne Sandberg
CUBS · 2B

KEN ASPROMONTE / Manager

skybox® Autograph ics

NEW YORK METS® OF

CARLOS BELTRAN 15

Randy Winn

TOPPS 1964 ALL-STAR ROOKIE

RED SOX
OUTFIELD
TONY CONIGLIARO

2000s

Souvenir photo of BABE RUTH courtesy of R.K.O. THEATRES

ANDRUW JONES
OUTFIELD • ATLANTA BRAVES
2 0 0 1

FRANK THOMAS
1B-DH • CHICAGO WHITE SOX®
2 0 0 1